The Wordsworth
English–Spanish
Spanish–English
Dictionary

The Wordsworth

ENGLISH–SPANISH
SPANISH–ENGLISH

Dictionary

Wordsworth Reference

1

Readers who are interested in other titles from
Wordsworth Editions are invited to visit our website at
www.wordsworth-editions.com

For our latest list and a full mail-order service, contact
Bibliophile Books, 5 Thomas Road, London E14 7BN
TEL: +44 (0)20 7515 9222   FAX: +44 (0)20 7538 4115
E-MAIL: orders@bibliophilebooks.com

This edition published in 2006 by Wordsworth Editions Limited
8B East Street, Ware, Hertfordshire SG12 9HJ

ISBN 1 84022 496 7

Typeset in Great Britain by Antony Gray
Printed and bound by Clays Ltd, St Ives plc

Abbreviations and symbols used in this dictionary

abbr	abbreviations	def	definite
adj phrase	adjective	defect	defective
adj	phrase	dem	demonstrative
Admin	administration	Dent	dentistry
adv	adverb	dimin	diminutive
adv phrase	adverbial phrase	Draughts	draughts
Agr	agriculture	Ecol	ecology
also	also	Econ	economics
Am	Latin America in general	Educ	education
Anat	anatomy	eg	for example
approx	approximately	Elec	electricity
arch	archaic	Ent	entomology
Archeol	archaeology	Equit	horse riding
Archit	architecture	esp	especially
Art	art	etc	etcetera
art	article	euph	euphemism
Astrol	astrology	exclam	exclamatory
Astron	astronomy	f	feminine
Astronaut	space travel	fam	familiar, colloquial
Athlet	athletics	Fenc	fencing
Austral	Australia	fig	figurative use
Aut	motoring, road traffic	Fin	finance
aux	auxiliary	Fishing	fishing
Av	aviation	fml	formal use
Baseb	baseball	fpl	feminine plural
Bill	billiards	Ftb	football
Biol	biology	Furn	furniture
Bot	botany	fut	future
Bowling	bowling	GB	British, Great Britain
Box	boxing	gen	general
Bridge	bridge	Geog	geography
CAm	Central America	Geol	geology
Canada	Canada	Geom	geometry
Cards	cards	ger	gerund
Carib	Caribbean	Golf	golf
Carp	carpentry	Gymn	gymnastics
Cat	Catalonia	Hairdr	hairdressing
Chem	chemistry	Herald	heraldry
Chess	chess	Hist	history
Chi	Chile	Hond	Honduras
Cin	cinema, films	Hortic	horticulture
C of E	Church of England	hum	Humorous
Com	commerce	Hunt	hunting
comp	comparative	imperat	imperative
Comput	computers, data processing	impers	impersonal
cond	conditional	Ind	industry
conj	conjunction	indef	indefinite
Constr	building industry	indic	indicative
Crick	cricket	infin	infinitive
Culin	cookery	Ins	insurance
Cycl	cycling, bicycles	interj	interjection

Abbreviations and symbols used in this dictionary

interr	interrogative	prov	proverb
inv	invariable	Psych	psychology, psychiatry
Ir	Ireland	pt	past tense
iron	ironic	®	registered trademark
irreg	irregular	Rad	radio
Jur	law, legal	Rail	railways
Knit	knitting	RC	Roman Catholic Church
Ling	linguistic	Rel	religion
Lit	literature	rel	relative
lit	literary	Rugby	rugby
m	masculine	SAm	South American
Math	mathematics	sb	somebody, someone
Med	medicine	Sch	school
Metal	metallurgy	Scot	Scotland
Meteor	meteorology, weather	see	see
Mil	military	Sew	sewing
Min	mining, mineralogy	sing	singular
Mount	mountaineering	Ski	skiing
mpl	masculine plural	sl	slang
Mus	music	Span	Spanish, Spain
Myth	mythology	Sport	sport
n	noun	sth	something
Naut	navigation, naval	subj	subjunctive
neg	negative	suff	suffix
neut	neuter	superl	superlative
Numis	coin collecting, coins	Swimming	swimming
offens	offensive	Tech	technical
Opt	optics	Tel	telephones
Orn	ornithology	Telec	telecommunications
Parl	Parliament	Ten	tennis
pass	passive voice	Tex	textiles
pej	pejorative	Theat	theatre
pers	personal	TV	television
Petrol	petroleum industry	Typ	typography
Pharm	pharmacy	Univ	university
Philat	philately	US	United States
Philos	philosophy	usu	usually
phot	photography	v	verb
phr	phrase	v aux	auxiliary verb
Phys	physics	v impers	impersonal verb
Physiol	physiology	Vet	veterinary medicine
pl	plural	vi	intransitive verb
Pol	politics	vr	reflexive verb
poss	possessive	vtr	transitive verb
pp	past participle	vulg	vulgar
pref	prefix	W	Wales
prep	preposition	Wrest	wrestling
pres	present	Zool	zoology
pres p	present participle		
Press	press	■	fixed noun combinations
Print	printing	◆	phrasal verbs or adverbs of manner
pron	pronoun		as sub-headwords

Fonética

En este diccionario la transcripción fonética de las palabras inglesas se basa en el sistema de la Asociación Fonética International (AFI) con algunas modificaciones. Cada entrada viene seguida de su correspondiente transcripción fonética entre corchetes ([ ]). El acento primario se indica mediante un ' delante de la sílaba acentuada.

Las consonantes

[p]	–	pen [pen], capital ['kæpitəl], rip [rɪp]
[b]	–	bill [bil], rubber ['rʌbəʳ], rib [rɪb]
[t]	–	tent [tent], writer['raɪtəʳ], writ [rɪt]
[d]	–	desk [desk], rider ['raɪdəʳ], rid [rɪd]
[k]	–	car [kɑːʳ], baker['beɪkəʳ],lock [lɒk]
[g]	–	goal [gəʊl], bigger ['bɪgəʳ], dog [dɒg]
[tʃ]	–	church[tʃɜːtʃ], teacher ['tiːtʃəʳ], watch [wɒtʃ]
[dʒ]	–	jam [dʒæm], suggest [sə'dʒest], age [eɪdʒ]
[f]	–	fish [fɪʃ], offer ['ɒfəʳ], roof [ruːf]
[v]	–	voice [vɔɪs], ever ['evəʳ], have [hæv]
[θ]	–	throw [θrəʊ], method ['meθəd], earth [ɜːθ]
[ð]	–	then [ðen], mother ['mʌðəʳ], with [wɪð]
[s]	–	sat [sæt], pencil ['pensəl], ice [aɪs]
[z]	–	zero['zɪərəʊ], easy ['iːzɪ], is[ɪz]
[ʃ]	–	shoe [ʃuː], machine [mə'ʃiːn], wash [wɒʃ]
[ʒ]	–	gigolo ['ʒɪgələʊ], measure['meʒəʳ], prestige [pre'stiːʒ]
[h]	–	how [haʊ], hat [hæt], behind [bɪ'haɪnd]
[m]	–	milk [mɪlk], lemon ['lemən], game [geɪm]
[n]	–	name [neɪm], dinner ['dɪnəʳ], gone [gon]
[ŋ]	–	finger ['fɪŋgəʳ], think [θɪŋk], sing [sɪŋ]
[l]	–	light [laɪt], ugly ['ʌglɪ], will [wɪl]
[r]	–	read [riːd], very ['verɪ]
[j]	–	yoghurt ['jɒgət], university [juːnɪ'vɜːsɪtɪ], huge [hjuːdʒ]
[w]	–	watch [wɒtʃ], squash [skwɒʃ], language ['læŋgwɪdʒ]
[x]	–	loch [lɒx]
[']	–	se llama '*linking r*' y se encuentra únicamente a final de palabra. Se pronuncia sólo cuando la palabra siguiente empieza por una vocal: mother ['mʌðəʳ]

Las vocales y los diptongos

[iː]	–	sheep [ʃhːp], be [biː], leaf [liːf], field [fiːld]
[ɪ]	–	ship [ʃɪp], city ['sɪtɪ], houses ['haʊzɪz], ladies ['leɪdɪz], village ['vɪlɪdʒ]
[e]	–	bed [bed], head [hed], many ['menɪ], bury ['berɪ], friend [frend]
[ae]	–	cat [cæt], hand [hænd], plait [plæt]
[aː]	–	father ['fɑːðəʳ], car [kɑːʳ], heart [hɑːt], clerk [klɑːk], calm [kɑːm], aunt [aːnt]
[ɒ]	–	dog [dɒg], was [wɒz], cough [kɒf], because [bɪ'kɒz]
[ɔː]	–	horse [hɔːs], saw [sɔː], bought [bɔːt], cause [kɔːz], all [aːl], oar [aːʳ], floor [flɔːʳ]
[ʊ]	–	foot [fʊt], full [fʊl], woman ['wʊmən], could [kʊd]
[uː]	–	food [fuːd], do [duː], group [gruːp], rude [ruːd], blue [bluː], shoe [ʃuː], chew [tʃuː]
[ʌ]	–	cup [kʌp], son [sʌn], young [jʌŋ], flood [flʌd], does [dʌz]
[ɜː]	–	bird [bɜːd], her [hɜːʳ], earth [ɜːθ], turn [tɜːn], word [wɜːd], journey ['dʒɜːnɪ]
[ə]	–	doctor ['dɒktəʳ], colour ['kʌləʳ], about [ə'baʊt]
[ə]	–	opcional. En algunos casos se pronuncia y en otros se omite: trifle ['traɪfəl]
[eɪ]	–	table ['teɪbəl], day [deɪ], rain [reɪn], eight [eɪt], they [ðeɪ], great [greɪt]
[əʊ]	–	go [gəʊ], road [rəʊd], toe [təʊ], though [ðəʊ], know [nəʊ]
[aɪ]	–	time [taɪm], high [haɪ], height [haɪt], die [daɪ], dye [daɪ], aisle [aɪl], either ['aɪðəʳ]
[aʊ]	–	house [haʊs], cow [kaʊ]
[ɔɪ]	–	boy [bɔɪ], boil [bɔɪl]
[ɪə]	–	ear [ɪəʳ], here [hɪəʳ], deer [dɪəʳ], idea [aɪ'dɪə], museum [mjuː'zɪəm], weird [wɪəd], fierce [fɪəs]
[eə]	–	care [keəʳ], air [eəʳ], bear [beəʳ]
[ʊə]	–	sure [ʃʊəʳ], during ['djʊərɪŋ], tourist ['tʊərɪst]

English–Spanish
Dictionary

A

A, a [eɪ] n 1 *(the letter)* A, a *f*; **a for ace,** a de as; *fig* **from A to Z,** de principio a fin. 2 *Mus* la *m*.

A *abbr of* **ampère,** amperio *m*, **A.**

a [eɪ, *unstressed* ə] *indef art (before vowel or silent h an)* 1 un, una; **a man/a woman,** un hombre/una mujer; **an idea,** una idea; **a woman has to be strong,** las mujeres tienen que ser fuertes; **I didn't understand a word,** no entendí ni jota; **he has a big nose,** tiene la nariz grande. 2 *(omitted in Span)* **half a litre/an hour,** medio litro/media hora; **Bangor, a city in Wales,** Bangor, ciudad de Gales; **let's have a drink/a snack,** vamos a beber/comer algo; **he's a doctor,** es médico; **many a time,** muchas veces; **she got in without an invitation,** entró sin invitación; **what a coincidence!,** ¡qué casualidad!; **what a day!,** ¡vaya día!; **what a pity,** qué pena *or* lástima. 3 *(each)* **60 pence a kilo,** 60 peniques el kilo; **to eat grapes two at a time,** comer las uvas de dos en dos; **three times a week,** tres veces a la *or* por semana. 4 *(a certain)* un *or* una tal; **a Mr Rees phoned,** llamó un tal Sr. Rees; **in a sense,** hasta cierto punto.

AA [eɪˈeɪ] 1 *abbr of* **Alcoholics Anonymous,** Alcohólicos *mpl* Anónimos, AA. 2 *abbr of* **Automobile Association,** ≈ Automóvil Club *m*, AC.

AAA [eɪeɪˈeɪ] 1 *GB abbr of* **Amateur Athletic Association,** Asociatión *f* Atlética Amateur, AAA. 2 *US abbr of* **Automobile Association of America,** ≈ Automóvil Club *m*, AC.

AB [eɪˈbiː] 1 *GB abbr of* **able-bodied (seaman),** marinero *m* de primera. 2 *US abbr see* **BA.**

aback [əˈbæk] *adv* **to be taken a.,** sorprenderse; *fam* quedarse de una pieza (**by,** por).

abacus [ˈæbəkəs] n *(pl* **abacuses** *or* **abaci** [ˈæbəsaɪ]) ábaco *m*.

abandon [əˈbændən] **I** n desenfreno *m*; **with reckless a.,** desenfrenadamente. **II** *vtr (child, family)* abandonar; *(job)* dejar; *(project)* renunciar a; **the match was abandoned because of rain,** se suspendió el partido a causa de la lluvia; **to a. ship,** abandonar el barco.

abase [əˈbeɪs] *vtr* humillar, degradar; **to a. oneself,** humillarse, degradarse.

abashed [əˈbæʃt] *adj* desconcertado,-a, confuso,-a.

abate [əˈbeɪt] *vi (anger)* apaciguarse; *(flood)* decrecer; *(storm, wind)* amainar.

abatement [əˈbeɪtmənt] n reducción *f*, supresión *f*; **noise a. campaign,** campaña *f* contra el ruido (en el medio ambiente).

abattoir [ˈæbætwɑːr] n matadero *m*.

abbess [ˈæbɪs] n abadesa *f*.

abbey [ˈæbɪ] n abadía *f*.

abbot [ˈæbət] n abad *m*.

abbreviate [əˈbriːvɪeɪt] *vtr* abreviar.

abbreviation [əbriːvɪˈeɪʃən] n abreviatura *f*.

ABC¹ [eɪbiːˈsiː] n abecé *m*, abecedario *m*, alfabeto *m*; **an ABC of hotels,** una guía completa de hoteles.

ABC² [eɪbiːˈsiː] 1 *abbr of* **American Broadcasting Company,** compañía *f* americana de radiodifusión, ABC. 2 *abbr of* **Australian Broadcasting Commission,** Comisión *f* australiana de radiodifusión, ABC.

abdicate [ˈæbdɪkeɪt] **I** *vtr (throne)* abdicar; *(right, responsibility)* renunciar; **he abdicated in favour of his son,** abdicó en su hijo. **II** *vi (monarch)* abdicar.

abdication [æbdɪˈkeɪʃen] n *(of throne by monarch)* abdicación *f*; *(of right, responsibility)* renunciación *f*.

abdomen [ˈæbdəmən] n abdomen *m*, vientre *m*.

abdominal [æbˈdɒmɪnəl] *adj* abdominal, de vientre, ventral.

abduct [æbˈdʌkt] *vtr* raptar, secuestrar.

abduction [æbˈdʌkʃən] n rapto *m*, secuestro *m*.

abductor [æbˈdʌktər] n secuestrador,-a *m,f*.

aberrant [æˈberənt] *adj (behaviour)* anormal; *(example, specimen)* aberrante.

aberration [æbəˈreɪʃən] n aberración *f*, defecto *m*; **mental a.,** desvarío *m*.

abet [əˈbet] *vtr Jur* **to aid and a. sb,** ser cómplice de algn.

abeyance [əˈbeɪəns] n desuso *m*; **to be in/fall into a.,** estar en/caer en desuso.

abhor [əbˈhɔːr] *vtr (pt & pp* **abhorred)** aborrecer, detestar.

abhorrence [əbˈhɒrəns] n aborrecimiento *m*; **to have an a. of sth,** aborrecer algo.

abhorrent [əbˈhɒrənt] *adj* aborrecible, odioso,-a; **it is a. to me,** lo aborrezco.

abide [əˈbaɪd] *vtr (pt & pp* **abode** *or* **abided)** *(tolerate)* tolerar, aguantar; **I can't a. him,** no le puedo ver, me cae muy mal; **I can't a. it,** no lo aguanto. ◆ **abide by** *vtr (promise)* cumplir con; *(rules)* atenerse a.

ability [əˈbɪlɪtɪ] n *(capability)* capacidad *f*, aptitud *f*; *(talent)* talento *m*, dotes *fpl*; **a pupil of great a.,** un alumno de grandes dotes; **she did it to the best of her a.,** lo hizo lo mejor que pudo; **to have a. to do sth,** tener capacidad para hacer algo.

abject [ˈæbdʒekt] *adj (state)* miserable; *(apology)* rastrero,-a; **a. poverty,** miseria *f*.

ablaze [əˈbleɪz] *adj & adv* en llamas, ardiendo; **to be a.,** arder; *fig* **a. with light,** resplandeciente de luz.

able [ˈeɪbəl] *adj (person) (capable)* capaz; *(piece of work) (satisfactory)* bien hecho,-a; **is he a. to swim ten miles?,** ¿es capaz de nadar diez millas?; **will you be a. to come on Tuesday?,** ¿podrás venir el martes?

able-bodied [eɪbəlˈbɒdɪd] *adj* sano,-a, robusto,-a. **a.-b. seaman,** marinero *m* de primera.

ablutions [əˈbluːʃənz] *npl fml hum* **to perform one's a.,** lavarse.

ABM [eɪbiːˈem] *abbr of* **anti-ballistic missile,** misil *m* antibalístico, **ABM.**

abnormal [æbˈnɔːməl] *adj* anormal. ◆ **abnormally** *adv* anormalmente; *(large etc)* de modo anormal, extraordinariamente.

abnormality [æbnɔːˈmælɪtɪ] n anormalidad *f*; *Biol* anomalía *f*; *Med* deformidad *f*.

aboard [əˈbɔːd] **I** *adv* a bordo; **to go a.,** *(ship)* embarcarse, subir a bordo; *(train)* subir; **all aboard!,** *(ship)* ¡pasajeros a bordo!; *(train)* ¡viajeros al tren! **II** *prep* a bordo de; **a. ship,** a bordo del barco, en barco; **a. the train,** en el tren.

abode [əˈbəud] *pt & pp see* **abide. II** n *Jur* **of no fixed a.,** sin domicilio fijo.

abolish [əˈbɒlɪʃ] *vtr* abolir, suprimir; *(law)* derogar.

abolition [æbəˈlɪʃən] n abolición *f*, supresión *f*; *(of law)* derogación *f*.

abominable [əˈbɒmɪnəbəl] *adj* abominable; *(dreadful)* terrible; **the A. Snowman,** el Abominable Hombre de las Nieves, el Yeti. ◆ **abominably** *adv* abominablemente; **a. rude,** terriblemente grosero,-a (**towards,** hacia).

abomination [əbɒmɪˈneɪʃən] n abominación *f*; **it's an a.,** es un escándalo.

aboriginal [æbəˈrɪdʒɪnəl] *adj* aborigen.

aborigine [æbəˈrɪdʒɪnɪ] n aborigen *mf* australiano,-a.

abort [ə'bɔːt] **I** vtr Med (foetus) hacer abortar; fig (plan etc) archivar, cancelar. **II** vi Med abortar.

abortion [ə'bɔːʃən] n Med aborto m; **a. law**, ley f del aborto; **to have an a.**, abortar.

abortionist [ə'bɔːʃənɪst] n abortista mf.

abortive [ə'bɔːtɪv] adj fig (attempt, plan, etc) fracasado,-a.

abound [ə'baʊnd] vi **to a. in** or **with**, abundar en.

about [ə'baʊt] adv & prep **1** (concerning) acerca de, sobre; **a book a. Keats**, un libro sobre Keats; **I've come a. the washing machine**, vengo por lo de la lavadora; **to be worried a. sth**, estar preocupado,-a por algo; **to enquire a. sth**, preguntar por algo; **to speak a. sth**, hablar de algo; **tell me all a. it**, cuéntamelo todo; **what's it all a.?**, (what's happening?) ¿qué pasa?; (what does it mean?) ¿qué quiere decir?; (story, play, etc), ¿de qué se trata?; **what a. it?**, (what do you think?) ¿qué te parece?; (so what?) ¿y qué?; **you know all a. it**, ya estás muy enterado,-a; fam **how a. a game of tennis?**, ¿qué te parece un partido de tenis?; fam **how a. a cup of coffee?**, ¿te apetece un café? **2** (around) por todas partes, de un lado para otro; **don't leave things lying a.**, no dejes las cosas por ahí; **he's somewhere a.**, está aquí por algún lado; **there are a lot of crazy people a.**, anda mucha gente loca suelta; **there's a lot of violence a.**, hoy en día hay mucha violencia; **there's nobody a.**, no hay nadie; **to be up and a.**, estar levantado,-a; (after illness) hacer vida normal; **to look a.**, mirar a su alrededor; **to rush a.**, correr de un lado para otro; **we went for a walk a. the town**, dimos una vuelta por el pueblo; fam **bring me a cup of tea while you're a. it**, y tráeme un té, de paso. **3** (approximately) más o menos, casi, a eso de; **it's a. 3 o'clock**, son más o menos las 3; **it's a. time you got up**, ya es hora de que te levantes; **it's just a. finished**, está casi terminado; **on or a. the 5th of May**, hacia el día 5 de mayo; **she's a. 40**, tendrá unos 40 años; iron **a. time too!**, ¡a buenas horas! **4** Mil **a turn!**, ¡media vuelta! **5** (just ready) **I'm a. to do it now**, lo voy a hacer ahora; **it's a. to start**, está a punto de empezar; **they'll be just a. arriving**, estarán al llegar. **6 to go a.** (doing) sth, hacer algo; **how do you go a. opening a bank account?**, ¿qué hay que hacer para abrir una cuenta bancaria?

about-turn [əbaʊt'tɜːn], US **about-face** [əbaʊt'feɪs] **I** n media vuelta f; **to do an a.-t.**, hacer media vuelta; fig cambiar de idea por completo. **II** vi dar media vuelta; fig cambiar de idea por completo.

above [ə'bʌv] adv & prep **1** (higher, higher than) encima de, sobre, arriba; **a voice from a.**, una voz desde lo alto; **his voice was heard a. the noise**, se oyó su voz por encima del ruido or a pesar de tanto ruido; **100 metres a. sea level**, 100 metros sobre el nivel del mar; **it's a. the door**, está encima de la puerta; **the flat a.**, el piso de arriba; **the River Miño a. Orense**, el río Miño antes de pasar por Orense; **the shelf a. the sink**, el estante de encima del fregadero; **the town seen from a.**, el pueblo visto desde arriba or a vista de pájaro. **2** (greater, greater than) superior (a); **amounts a. £10**, cantidades superiores a las 10 libras; **tickets numbered 200 and a.**, entradas a partir del número 200; **to be a. sb in rank/status**, estar por encima de algn en rango/jerarquía; fig **a policy imposed from a.**, una política impuesta desde arriba. **3** fig (beyond) **a. all**, sobre todo, encima de todo; **a. reproach**, intachable; **he's not a. stealing**, es capaz incluso de robar; **she's a. all that**, está muy encima de todo esto; **it's a. me**, está por encima de mis posibilidades, es demasiado difícil para mí. **4** (in book etc) más arriba; **see paragraph 6 a.**, véase el párrafo 6 más arriba.

above-board [ə'bʌvbɔːd] adj (scheme) legítimo,-a; (person) honesto,-a.

above-mentioned [ə'bʌvmenʃənd] adj arriba citado,-a, susodicho,-a.

Abp abbr of **Archbishop**, Arzobispo m, Arz., Arzpo.

abrasion [ə'breɪʒən] n abrasión f.

abrasive [ə'breɪsɪv] **I** adj (substance) abrasivo,-a; fig (voice, wit, etc) cáustico,-a. **II** n abrasivo m.

abreast [ə'brest] adv **to walk 3 abreast**, ir de 3 en fondo; fig **to keep a. of things**, mantenerse al día, estar al tanto de las cosas.

abridged [ə'brɪdʒd] adj (book) abreviado,-a, resumido,-a.

abroad [ə'brɔːd] adv **1** (foreign places) en el or al extranjero; **to be a.**, estar en el extranjero; **to go a.**, irse al extranjero; **to live a.**, vivir en el extranjero. **2** (extensively) **the news spread a.**, la noticia se divulgó rápidamente; **there's a rumour a. that ...**, corre el rumor que ... .

abrupt [ə'brʌpt] adj (manner) brusco,-a; (tone, voice) áspero,-a; (change, stop) repentino,-a, súbito,-a. ◆ **abruptly** adv (act) bruscamente; (speak) con aspereza; (change, stop) repentinamente.

abscess ['æbses] n absceso m; (on gum) flemón m.

abscond [əb'skɒnd] vi huir, fugarse; **he absconded with the money**, se fugó con el dinero.

absence ['æbsəns] n (of person) ausencia f; (of thing) falta f; Jur **she was sentenced in her a.**, fue juzgada en rebeldía; **in the a. of any details ...**, a falta de datos ...; fig **a. of mind**, distracción f.

absent ['æbsənt] **I** adj ausente; Mil **a. without leave**, ausente sin permiso; **to be a. from school**, faltar a clase; fig **an a. look**, una mirada distraída. **II** [æb'sent] vtr **to a. oneself**, ausentarse. ◆ **absently** adv (distractedly) distraídamente.

absentee [æbsən'tiː] n ausente mf. ■ **a. landlord**, absentista m.

absenteeism [æbsən'tiːɪzəm] n absentismo m.

absent-minded [æbsənt'maɪndɪd] adj distraído,-a, despistado,-a.

absolute ['æbsəluːt] adj (majority, power) absoluto,-a; (certain) completo,-a; (confidence, failure) total; (truth) puro,-a; (proof) incontrovertible; **it's an a. disgrace**, es una auténtica vergüenza. ◆ **absolutely I** adv (completely) completamente, totalmente; **a. wrong**, totalmente equivocado,-a; **a. not**, en absoluto; **you're a. right**, tienes toda la razón. **II** interj **a.!**, ¡desde luego!, ¡claro!, ¡por supuesto!

absolution [æbsə'luːʃən] n Rel absolución f.

absolve [əb'zɒlv] vtr absolver (**from**, de).

absorb [əb'zɔːb] vtr (liquid, costs) absorber; (heat, sound, blow) amortiguar; (energy, time) ocupar; fig **to be absorbed in sth**, estar absorto,-a en algo.

absorbing [əb'zɔːbɪŋ] adj (book, work) absorbente; **It's an a. hobby**, es un pasatiempo que distrae mucho.

abstain [əb'steɪn] vi abstenerse (**from**, de).

abstainer [əb'steɪnə'] n abstemio,-a m,f.

abstemious [əb'stiːmɪəs] adj abstemio,-a, sobrio,-a.

abstention [əb'stenʃən] n abstención f.

abstinence ['æbstɪnəns] n abstinencia f.

abstract ['æbstrækt] **I** adj abstracto,-a; **an a. painting**, una pintura de estilo abstracto. **II** n (of thesis etc) resumen m; (painting) abstracto m; **to talk in the a.**, hablar en términos abstractos. **III** [æb'strækt] vtr (summarize) abstraer; euph (steal) sustraer.

abstruse [əb'struːs] adj abstruso,-a, embrollado,-a.

absurd [əb'sɜːd] adj absurdo,-a; **it's a.!**, ¡qué disparate!; **don't be a.!**, ¡no seas ridículo,-a!

absurdity [əb'sɜːdɪtɪ] n disparate m, locura f.

ABTA ['æbtə] abbr of **Association of British Travel Agents**, Asociación f de agentes de viaje británicos.

abundance [ə'bʌndəns] n abundancia f; **in a.**, en abundancia, abundantemente.

abundant [ə'bʌndənt] adj abundante, rico,-a (**in**, en). ◆ **abundantly** adv abundantemente, en abundancia; **it's a. clear**, está clarísimo, es evidente; **she made it a. clear to me that she was offended**, me constató claramente que se sentía ofendida.

abuse [ə'bju:s] **I** *n* **1** *(ill-treatment)* malos tratos *mpl*; *(misuse) (of power, confidence)* abuso *m*. **2** *(insults)* insultos *mpl*, improperios *mpl*, injurias *fpl*; **to shower a. on sb,** colmar a algn de insultos *or* injurias. **II** [ə'bju:z] *vtr* **1** *(ill-treat)* maltratar; *(misuse)* abusar de. **2** *(insult)* insultar, injuriar.

abusive [əb'ju:sɪv] *adj (insulting)* insultante, grosero,-a, ofensivo,-a; **to use a. language,** decir groserías *or* injurias.

abysmal [ə'bɪzməl] *adj (poverty, conditions)* extremo,-a; *fam (very bad) (weather, film, food, etc)* fatal, pésimo,-a.

abyss [ə'bɪs] *n* abismo *m*, sima *f*; *fig* extremo *m*.

Abyssinia [æbɪ'sɪnɪə] *n* Abisinia.

Abyssinian [æbɪ'sɪnɪən] *adj & n* abisinio,-a *(m,f)*.

AC ['eɪsi:] *Elec abbr of* **alternating current,** corriente *f* alterna, CA.

a/c *Fin abbr of* **account,** cuenta *f*, cta.

acacia [ə'keɪʃə] *n Bot* acacia *f*. ▪ **false a.,** acacia *f* falsa, robinia *f*.

academic [ækə'demɪk] **I** *adj* **1** *Educ* académico,-a, escolar; *(career)* universitario,-a; *(question, discussion)* teórico,-a; **a. year,** año escolar. **II** *n* académico,-a *m, f*, profesor,-a *m,f* de universidad.

academy [ə'kædəmɪ] *n (society)* academia *f*; *Scot Educ* instituto *m* de enseñanza media; **Royal A. (of Arts),** Real Academia (de Bellas Artes). ▪ **military a.,** escuela *f* militar; **a. of music,** conservatorio *m*.

ACAS ['eɪkæs] *GB abbr of* **Advisory Conciliation and Arbitration Service,** organismo que arbitra en cuestiones laborales.

accede [æk'si:d] *vi (throne)* acceder **(to,** a); *(petition, request)* consentir **(to,** en), acceder **(to,** a).

accelerate [æk'seləreɪt] **I** *vtr (engine)* acelerar; *(step)* apretar, apresurar. **II** *vi (car, engine)* acelerar.

acceleration [æksələ'reɪʃən] *n Aut* aceleración *f*.

accelerator [æk'seləreɪtəʳ] *n Aut* acelerador *m*.

accent ['æksənt] *n* acento *m*; **he has a Scottish a.,** tiene acento escocés; *fig* **fashion with the a. on comfort,** la moda con especial atención al confort.

accentuate [æk'sentʃʊeɪt] *vtr (word)* acentuar; *(difference etc)* subrayar.

accept [ək'sept] *vtr & vi (cheque, gift, invitation)* aceptar; *(theory)* admitir, aprobar; *(person)* aceptar, acoger; **do you a. that ...?,** ¿estás de acuerdo en que ...?; **it's the accepted thing,** es la norma, es lo normal; **to a. defeat,** admitir la derrota.

acceptable [ək'septəbəl] *adj (satisfactory)* aceptable; *(tolerable)* admisible; *(welcome)* grato,-a; **that isn't (socially) a.,** eso no se hace *or* no se admite (entre gente educada).

acceptance [ək'septəns] *n (act of accepting)* aceptación *f*, admisión *f*; *(good reception)* aprobación *f*, acogida *f*.

access ['ækses] *n* acceso *m*; **a. road,** carretera *f or* camino *m* de acceso; **to have/gain a. to sth,** tener/conseguir libre acceso a algo.

accessibility [əksesə'bɪlɪtɪ] *n* accesibilidad *f*.

accessible [ək'sesəbəl] *adj (place, position)* accesible; *(person)* asequible.

accession [ək'seʃən] *n* **1** *(of monarch)* subida *f* (al trono). **2** *(acquisition) (in library etc)* adquisición *f*.

accesory [ək'sesərɪ] *n* **1** *Jur* cómplice *mf*; **a. before/after the fact,** cómplice instigador/encubridor. **2** **accessories,** accessorios *mpl*; *(for outfit)* complementos *mpl*.

accident ['æksɪdənt] *n* **1** *(misadventure)* accidente *m*; **to have an a.,** tener *or* sufrir un accidente; **it was an a. on my part,** lo hice sin querer. ▪ **car** *or* **road a.,** accidente *m* de carretera; **industrial a.,** accidente laboral. **2** *(coincidence)* casualidad *f*; **by a.,** por casualidad; **it was quite by a.,** fue una pura casualidad.

accidental [æksɪ'dentəl] *adj (by chance)* fortuito,-a; *(unexpected)* imprevisto,-a. ◆ **accidentally** *adv (by chance)* por casualidad; **he did it a.,** *(unintentionally)* lo hizo sin querer.

accident-prone ['æksɪdəntprəʊn] *adj* propenso,-a a los accidentes.

acclaim [ə'kleɪm] **I** *n* aclamación *f*. **II** *vtr* aclamar.

acclamation [æklə'meɪʃən] *n* aclamación *f*, alabanza *f*.

acclimate [ə'klaɪmət] *vtr US see* **acclimatize.**

acclimated ['æklɪmeɪtɪd] *adj US see* **acclimatized.**

acclimation [æklɪ'meɪʃən] *n US see* **acclimatization.**

acclimatization [æklaɪmətaɪ'zeɪʃən] *n* aclimatación *f*.

acclimatize [ə'klaɪmətaɪz] *vtr* aclimatar; **to a. oneself,** aclimatarse.

acclimatized [ə'klaɪmətaɪzd] *adj* aclimatado,-a; **to become a.,** aclimatarse.

accolade ['ækəleɪd] *n* elogio *m*.

accommodate [ə'kɒmədeɪt] *vtr* **1** *(guests etc)* alojar, hospedar; **the hotel can a. 100 guests,** el hotel tiene capacidad para cien huéspedes. **2** *(satisfy, provide for)* **to a. sb's wishes,** complacer a algn; **whatever you need, we try to a. you,** procuramos facilitarle cualquier cosa que necesite. **3** *(adapt)* **to a. oneself to a new situation,** amoldarse *or* adaptarse a una nueva situación.

accommodating [ə'kɒmədeɪtɪŋ] *adj (obliging)* complaciente; *(understanding)* comprensivo,-a.

accommodation [əkɒmə'deɪʃən] *n* **1** *(US also* **accommodations***) (lodgings)* alojamiento *m*; *(space)* sitio *m*; **do you have any a. for tonight?,** ¿tiene *or* quedan habitaciones libres para esta noche?; **overnight a.,** camas *fpl*; **we don't have the a. for so many people,** no tenemos sitio para tanta gente. **2** *(agreement)* acuerdo *m*; **to reach an a. over sth,** llegar a un acuerdo sobre algo.

accompaniment [ə'kʌmpənɪmənt] *n* acompañamiento *m*.

accompanist [ə'kʌmpənɪst] *n Mus* acompañante *mf*.

accompany [ə'kʌmpənɪ] *vtr* acompañar; **to be accompanied by sb,** ir acompañado de algn; *Mus* **to a. sb on the piano,** acompañar a algn al piano.

accomplice [ə'kʌmplɪs] *n* cómplice *mf*.

accomplish [ə'kʌmplɪʃ] *vtr (aim)* conseguir, lograr, realizar; *(task, mission)* llevar a cabo; **what have you accomplished?,** ¿qué has conseguido?

accomplished [ə'kʌmplɪʃt] *adj (musician)* dotado,-a, experto,-a.

accomplishment [ə'kʌmplɪʃmənt] *n* **1** *(fulfilment) (of task)* realización *f*; *(of duty)* cumplimiento *m*. **2** **accomplishments,** *(talents)* talentos *mpl*, dotes *fpl*.

accord [ə'kɔ:d] **I** *n (agreement)* acuerdo *m*; **of her** *or* **his own a.,** espontáneamente, voluntariamente; **with one a.,** de común acuerdo, de una voz. **II** *vtr (honour, permission)* conceder. **III** *vi (agree)* concordar **(with,** con).

accordance [ə'kɔ:dəns] *n* **in a. with,** de acuerdo con, conforme a.

according [ə'kɔ:dɪŋ] *prep* **a. to,** según; **a. to instructions,** con arreglo a las instrucciones; **a. to them,** según ellos; **everything went a. to plan,** todo salió conforme a los planes; **lined up a. to age,** alienados por edades.

accordingly [ə'kɔ:dɪŋlɪ] *adv* **1** *(appropriately)* en consecuencia; **to act a.,** obrar según y conforme. **2** *(therefore)* así pues, por consiguiente; **a. I rang her,** así pues, la llamé.

accordion [ə'kɔ:dɪən] *n Mus* acordeón *m*.

account [ə'kaʊnt] *n* **1** *(report)* informe *m*; **by all accounts,** al decir de todos; **to bring** *or* **call sb to a.,** pedirle cuentas a algn; **to give sb an a. of sth,** informar a algn de algo. **2** *(importance)* importancia *f*; *(consideration)* consideración *f*; *(advantage)* provecho *m*; **I was fearful on her a.,** sufría por ella; **it's of no a.,** no tiene importancia; **on a. of,** a causa de; **on no a.,** bajo ningún concepto; **to take a. of sth, take sth into a.,** tener algo en cuenta; **to turn sth to good a.,** sacar proyecho de *or* aprovechar algo. **3** *Com* cuenta *f*; **to keep the accounts,** llevar las cuentas *or* la contabilidad; **to open/ close an a.,** abrir/cancelar una cuenta; *fig* **to settle accounts with sb,** ajustar cuentas con algn. ■ **bank a.,** cuenta *f* bancaria; **current/deposit a.,** cuenta *f* corriente/ de ahorros; **joint a.,** cuenta *f* indistinta; **charge a.,** cuenta *f* abierta. ◆ **account for** *vtr (explain)* explicar, dar cuentas de; **everyone has been accounted for,** no falta nadie; **I can't a. for it,** no me lo explico; **there's no accounting for tastes,** sobre gustos no hay nada escrito.

accountable [ə'kaʊntəbəl] *adj* **a. to sb for sth,** ser responsible ante algn de algo; **I'm not a. to them,** no tengo por qué darles explicaciones a ellos.

accountancy [ə'kaʊntənsɪ] *n* contabilidad *f*; **to study a.,** estudiar para contable.

accountant [ə'kaʊntənt] *n* contable *mf*; **chartered a.,** perito,-a *m,f* contable.

accredited [ə'kredɪtɪd] *adj* acreditado,-a, autorizado,-a.

accrue [ə'kruː] *vi (interest)* acumularse; **interest will a. at a rate of 10 per cent,** le corresponderá un interés del 10 por ciento.

acct. *Fin abbr of* **account,** cuenta *f*, cta.

accumulate [ə'kjuːmjʊleɪt] **I** *vtr* acumular, amontonar; *(fortune)* amasar. **II** *vi* acumularse, amontonarse.

accumulation [əkjuːmjʊ'leɪʃən] *n* acumulación *f*, amontonamiento *m*; **an a. of things,** un montón de cosas.

accuracy ['ækjʊrəsɪ] *n (of figure, number, instrument)* exactitud *f*, precisión *f*; *(of shot, criticism)* certeza *f*; *(of translation)* fidelidad *f*.

accurate ['ækjʊrɪt] *adj (figure, number)* exacto,-a, preciso,-a; *(shot, criticism)* certero,-a; *(answer)* correcto,-a; *(comment, observation)* acertado,-a; *(instrument, watch)* de precisión; *(translation)* fiel. ◆ **accurately** *adv* exactamente; *(translate)* fielmente.

accusation [ækjʊ'zeɪʃən] *n* acusación *f*.

accuse [ə'kjuːz] *vtr* acusar; **they accused Peter of stealing the money,** acusaron a Peter de robar el dinero.

accused [ə'kjuːzd] *n Jur* **the a.,** *(man)* el acusado; *(woman)* la acusada.

accusing [ə'kjuːzɪŋ] *adj (look, tone)* acusador,-a. ◆ **accusingly** *adv* acusatoriamente, en un tono acusador.

accustom [ə'kʌstəm] *vtr* acostumbrar; **to a. sb to (doing) sth,** acostumbrar a algn a (hacer) algo; **to be accustomed to doing sth,** acostumbrado,-a a hacer algo; **to get accustomed to sth,** acostumbrarse a algo.

ace [eɪs] *n* **1** *Cards* as *m*; **a. of clubs/spades,** as de tréboles/ picas; **to play one's a.,** jugar su mejor baza; *fig* **to have an a. up one's sleeve,** guardar un as en la manga. **2** *fig* **as** *m*; **he's an a. driver,** es un as del volante. **3** *Tennis (service)* ace *m*.

acerbic [ə'sɜːbɪk] *adj (wit)* acerbo,-a, mordaz.

acerbity [ə'sɜːbɪtɪ] *n (of wit)* acerbidad *f*.

acetate ['æsɪteɪt] *n* acetato *m*.

acetone ['æsɪtəʊn] *n* acetona *f*.

ache [eɪk] **I** *n (pain)* dolor *m*; **aches and pains,** achaques *mpl*. **II** *vi (hurt)* doler; **it makes my head a.,** me da dolor de cabeza; **my back aches,** me duele la espalda; *fig* **I was aching to tell them,** ansiaba decírselo.

achieve [ə'tʃiːv] *vtr (attain)* conseguir, lograr, alcanzar; *(complete, accomplish)* llevar a cabo, realizar.

achievement [ə'tʃiːvmənt] *n (attainment, success)* logro *m*; *(completion)* realización *f*; *(feat)* hazaña *f*; éxito *m*; **what an a.!,** ¡vaya hazaña!

acid ['æsɪd] **I** *adj Chem* ácido,-a; *(taste)* agrio,-a; *fig (remark, wit)* mordaz. **II** *n* **1** *Chem* ácido *m*. ■ *fig* **a. test,** prueba *f* decisiva. **2** *(drugs)* ácido *m*.

acidity [ə'sɪdɪtɪ] *n* acidez *f*; *fig (of remark, wit)* mordacidad *f*.

acknowledge [ək'nɒlɪdʒ] *vtr* **1** *(recognize) (person, truth)* reconocer; *(claim, defeat)* admitir; *(present)* agradecer, dar las gracias por; *(letter, invoice)* acusar recibo de. **2** *(greet)* saludar.

acknowledgement [ək'nɒlɪdʒmənt] *n* **1** *(recognition)* reconocimiento *m*; *(admission)* admisión *f*; *(of letter, invoice)* acuse *m* de recibo. **2** **acknowledgements,** *(in preface)* menciones *fpl*.

acme ['ækmɪ] *n* colmo *m*, punto *m* culminante, apogeo *m*.

acne ['æknɪ] *n* acné *m*.

acolyte ['ækəlaɪt] *n Rel* acólito *m*; *fig* seguidor,-a *m,f*.

acorn ['eɪkɔːn] *n* bellota *f*.

acoustic [ə'kuːstɪk] **I** *adj* acústico,-a. **II acoustics** *npl* acústica *f sing*.

acquaint [ə'kweɪnt] *vtr* **1** *(facts)* dar a conocer; **to a. sb with the facts,** informar a algn de *or* sobre los detalles; **to a. oneself with sth,** familiarizarse con algo; **to be acquainted with the procedure,** estar al corriente de como se procede. **2** *(person)* **to be acquainted with sb,** conocer a algn; **they are acquainted,** se conocen; **they're getting acquainted,** se van conociendo.

acquaintance [ə'kweɪntəns] *n* **1** *(familiarity) (with facts etc)* conocimiento *m*; *(with person)* conocimiento *m*, relación *f*; **to make sb's a.,** conocer a algn. **2** *(person)* conocido,-a *m,f*; **he's an a. of ours,** le conocemos.

acquiesce [ækwɪ'es] *vi* consentir **(in,** en), conformarse **(in,** con).

acquiescence [ækwɪ'esəns] *n* consentimiento *m*, conformidad *f*.

acquiescent [ækwɪ'esənt] *adj* conforme.

acquire [ə'kwaɪə'] *vtr (get)* obtener, adquirir; *(possessions, property)* adquirir; *(territories)* tomar posesión de; *(habit, reputation)* adquirir, contraer; **to a. a taste for sth,** tomarle gusto a algo; **it's an acquired taste,** es un gusto que hay que aprender a apreciar.

acquisition [ækwɪ'zɪʃən] *n* adquisición *f*.

acquisitive [ə'kwɪzɪtɪv] *adj* codicioso,-a, acaparador,-a.

acquit [ə'kwɪt] *vtr (pt & pp acquitted)* **1** *Jur* **to a. sb of sth,** absolver a algn de algo. **2 to a. oneself well,** comportarse *or* defenderse bien.

acquittal [ə'kwɪtəl] *n Jur* absolución *f*.

acre ['eɪkə'] *n* acre *m* (= 40, 47 áreas).

acrid ['ækrɪd] *adj (smell, taste)* acre; *fig (remark, manner)* cáustico,-a, mordaz.

acrimonious [ækrɪ'məʊnɪəs] *adj (remark, manner)* cáustico,-a, mordaz; *(dispute)* enconado,-a, amargo,-a.

acrimony ['ækrɪmənɪ] *n* acritud *f*, aspereza *f*.

acrobat ['ækrəbæt] *n* acróbata *mf*.

acrobatics [ækrə'bætɪks] *npl* acrobacia *f sing*.

across [ə'krɒs] **I** *adv* **1** *a or* de través; **the river is 30 metres a.,** el río mide 30 metros de ancho; **to go** *or* **come a.,** atravesar; **to lay sth a.,** poner algo transversalmente *or* de través; **to run/jump a.,** atravesar corriendo/de un salto; *fig* **to put one's point of view a. to sb,** exponer su punto de vista a algn; *fig* **we couldn't get it a. to him,** no logramos hacerle comprender. **2** *(in crossword)* horizontalmente. **II** *prep* **1** a través de; **they live a. the road.** viven enfrente; **to go a. the bridge/the street,** cruzar *or* atravesar el puente/la calle. **2** *(at the other side of)* al otro lado; **our house is a. the park,** nuestra casa se encuentra al otro lado del parque.

across-the-board [əkrɒsðə'bɔːd] *adj* generalizado,-a, indiscriminado,-a.

acrylic [ə'krɪlɪk] *adj* acrílico,-a.

act [ækt] **I** *n* **1** *(action)* acto *m*, acción *f*; **an a. of aggression/ violence,** una agresión/violencia; **an a. of folly,** una tontería, una locura; **an a. of kindness,** un gesto de amabilidad; **to catch sb in the a.,** sorprender a algn en flagrante; *fam* pillar a algn con las manos en la masa. ■ **a. of God,** caso *m* de fuerza mayor. **2** *Parl* ley *f*, decreto *m*. **3**

Theat (part of play) acto *m*; *(turn in circus, show)* número *m*; *fig* **to put on an a.**, fingir, disimular; *fig* **to get in on the a.**, meterse en el asunto. II *vtr Theat (part)* hacer el papel de, interpretar; *(character)* representar; *fig* **to a. the fool**, hacer el tonto, hacer tonterías; *fig* **to a. big**, presumir. III *vi* **1** *Theat* hacer teatro, ser actor *or* actriz; *Cin* hacer cine, ser estrella de cine; *fig (pretend)* fingir, disimular; **to a. dumb**, hacerse el sueco. **2** *(behave)* comportarse; *(react)* reaccionar; **why did she a. like that?**, ¿por qué se comportó así? **3** *(take action)* actuar, obrar, tomar medidas; **to a. for** *or* **on behalf of sb**, representar a algn, obrar en nombre de algn; **to a. on sb's advice**, seguir el consejo de algn; **to a. with the best of intentions**, obrar con las mejores intenciones. **4** *(work)* funcionar; *(drug, medicine, etc)* actuar; **to a. as a brake**, servir de freno; **to a. as an incentive/a deterrent**, servir de incentivo/disuasivo. **5 to a. as director/secretary**, hacer de director/de secretaria. ◆ **act out** *vtr (feelings)* exteriorizar. ◆ **act up** *vi fam (machine)* funcionar mal; *(child)* dar guerra; *(injury, wound, etc)* doler.

acting ['æktɪŋ] I *adj* interino,-a, en funciones. II *n* **1** *(profession)* profesión *f* de actor, teatro *m*; **he's done some a.**, ha hecho algo de teatro; **she wants to do a.**, quiere hacer teatro *or* ser actriz. **2** *(performance)* actuación *f*, interpretación *f*, representación *f*; *fig* **it's only a.**, es pura comedia.

action ['ækʃən] *n* **1** *(functioning)* funcionamiento *m*, marcha *f*; *(deed)* acción *f*, hecho *m*; *Theat Cin* acción, historia *f*; *Mil* acción de combate; *Mil* **killed in a.**, muerto en batalla; **the a. takes place in Africa**, la acción transcurre en Africa; **to be out of a.**, *(machine)* estar estropeado,-a *or* averiado,-a; *(person)* estar fuera de servicio; **to put sth into a.**, poner algo en marcha; **to take a.**, tomar medidas; *prov* **actions speak louder than words**, hechos son amores y no buenas razones. **2** *Jur* demanda *f*, proceso *m*; **to bring an a. against sb**, entablar una demanda contra algn. **3** *TV Sport* **a. replay**, repetición *f* (de la jugada).

activate ['æktɪveɪt] *vtr* activar.

active ['æktɪv] *adj* activo,-a; *(energetic)* vigoroso,-a, enérgico,-a; *(interest)* vivo,-a; *(volcano)* en erupción; *(law)* vigente; *(life)* ajetreado,-a; *Ling* **a. voice**, voz *f* activa; *Mil* **to be on a. service**, estar en servicio activo; **to take an a. part in sth**, tomar parte activa en algo. ◆ **actively** *adv* activamente; **to be a. involved in sth**, estar metido,-a en algo.

activist ['æktɪvɪst] *n* activista *mf*.

activity [æk'tɪvɪtɪ] *n (movement) (of person)* actividad *f*; *(of street, office, etc)* movimiento *m*, bullicio *m*; **outdoor activities**, actividades al aire libre; **social activities**, vida *f* social.

actor ['æktə'] *n* actor *m*.

actress ['æktrɪs] *n* actriz *f*.

actual ['æktʃʊəl] *adj* real, verdadero,-a; **his a. address**, su dirección verdadera; **in a. fact**, en realidad; **let's look at an a. case**, veamos un caso concreto.

actually ['æktʃʊəlɪ] *adv (really)* en efecto, realmente; *(even)* incluso, hasta; *(well, in fact)* pues, de hecho; **he a. paid for our meal!**, ¡y hasta nos pagó la comida!; **well a. I'm not hungry**, pues no tengo hambre; **what a. happened?**, ¿qué pasó realmente?

actuary ['æktʃʊərɪ] *n* actuario *m*.

actuate ['æktʃʊeɪt] *vtr* mover, motivar; **to be actuated by**, ser movido,-a *or* motivado,-a por.

acumen ['ækjʊmən] *n* perspicacia *f*.

acupuncture ['ækjʊpʌŋktʃə'] *n* acupuntura *f*.

acute [ə'kjuːt] *adj (illness)* agudo,-a; *(pain)* intenso,-a; *(hearing, smell)* muy fino,-a; *(danger, situation, shortage)* grave, crítico,-a; *(person, mind)* perspicaz, sagaz; *(angle)* agudo,-a; *Ling* **a. accent**, acento agudo. ◆ **acutely** *adv (suffer)* intensamente; **to be a. aware of sth**, ser perfectamente consciente de algo.

AD [eɪ'diː] *abbr of* **Anno Domini** (in the year of our Lord), después de Cristo, d.d.C.

ad [æd] *n fam* anuncio *m*.

Adam ['ædəm] *n* Adán *m*; *Anat* **A.'s apple**, nuez *f* de la garganta; *fam* **I don't know him from A.**, no le conozco ni por asomo.

adamant ['ædəmənt] *adj* firme, inflexible; **to be a. about sth**, mantenerse firme en algo.

adapt [ə'dæpt] I *vtr* adaptar, ajustar, acomodar **(to,** a); **a play adapted from a novel**, una obra adaptada de una novela; **to a. oneself to sth**, adaptarse *or* amoldarse a algo. II *vi* adaptarse, acomodarse, amoldarse; **to a. to a situation**, adaptarse a una situación.

adaptability [ədæptə'bɪlɪt] *n* capacidad *f* de adaptación.

adaptable [ə'dæptəbəl] *adj (instrument, tool)* ajustable; *(person)* adaptable; **he's very a.**, se amolda fácilmente a las circunstancias.

adaptation [ædəp'teɪʃən] *n* adaptación *f*; *(of play, text)* versión *f*.

adapter *n*, **adaptor** [ə'dæptə'] *n Elec* ladrón *m*.

ADC [eɪdiː'siː] *Mil abbr of* **aide-de-camp**, edecán *m*.

add [æd] I *vtr (numbers)* sumar; *(one thing to another)* añadir, agregar. II *vi (count)* sumar. ◆ **add to** *vtr* ampliar, aumentar. ◆ **add up** I *vtr (numbers)* sumar. II *vi (numbers)* sumar; *fig (make sense)* tener sentido; **it doesn't a. up**, no tiene sentido, no lo entiendo; **it doesn't a. up to much**, no es gran cosa.

added ['ædɪd] *adj* adicional.

adder ['ædə'] *n* víbora *f*.

addict ['ædɪkt] *n* adicto,-a, *m*,*f*; **drug a.**, drogadicto,-a *m*, *f*, toxicómano,-a *m*,*f*; **heroin a.**, heroinómano,-a *m*,*f*; *fam* **football a.**, hincha *mf*; *fam* **television a.**, fanático,-a *m*,*f* de la televisión.

addicted [ə'dɪktɪd] *adj* adicto,-a; **to become a. to sth**, enviciarse con algo.

addiction [ə'dɪkʃən] *n (to gambling etc)* vicio *m*; *(to drugs)* adicción *f*.

addictive [ə'dɪktɪv] *adj* que crea dependencia, que causa adición; **smoking is a.**, el fumar crea hábito.

addition [ə'dɪʃən] *n (adding)* el añadir; *Math* adición *f*, suma *f*; *(increase)* aumento *m*, adición *f*; **an a. to the family**, un nuevo miembro de la familia; **additions to the staff**, aumento *m* del personal; **in a. to**, además de.

additional [ə'dɪʃənəl] *adj* adicional, suplementario,-a, supletorio,-a; **that's an a. reason for going**, eso es una razón de más para ir.

additive ['ædɪtɪv] *n* aditivo *m*.

address [ə'dres] I *n* **1** *(on letter)* dirección *f*, señas *fpl*; **a. book**, libreta *f* de direcciones. **2** *(speech)* discurso *m*, conferencia *f*; **election a.**, discurso electoral. **3 form of a.**, tratamiento *m*. II *vtr* **1** *(send) (letter)* dirigir, poner la dirección en; **the letter was incorrectly addressed**, la carta llevaba la dirección incorrecta. **2** *(speak to)* dirigirse **(to,** a); **to a. an assembly**, pronunciar un discurso ante una asamblea; *Pol Parl* **to a. the floor**, tomar la palabra. **3** *(use form of address)* tratar de; **they addressed me as sister**, me trataron de *or* me llamaron hermana.

addressee [ædre'siː] *n* destinatario,-a *m*,*f*.

Adelaide ['ædɪleɪd] *n* Adelaida.

Aden ['eɪdən] *n* Adén.

adenoidal [ædɪ'nɔɪdəl] *adj* gangoso,-a.

adenoids ['ædɪnɔɪdz] *npl Med* vegetaciones *fpl* (adenoideas).

adept [ə'dept] I *adj* experto,-a, ducho,-a **(at,** en); **to be a. at doing sth**, ser experto,-a en hacer algo. II *n* experto,-a; **to be a. in sth**, ser experto,-a en algo.

adequate ['ædɪkwɪt] *adj (enough)* bastante, suficiente; *(satisfactory)* apropiado,-a, adecuado,-a, idóneo,-a; *(person)* **to feel/prove a. to a task**, sentirse/mostrarse competente para hacer una tarea. ◆ **adequately** *adv* suficientemente; *(satisfactorily)* apropiadamente.

adhere [əd'hɪər] *vi (stick)* pegarse **(to,** a). ◆ **adhere to** *vtr (cause, policy)* adherirse a; *(contract, promise)* cumplir con; *(regulations)* observar; *(belief)* aferrarse a.

adherence [əd'hɪərəns] *n (to cause etc)* adhesión *f*; *(to beliefs)* fidelidad *f*.

adherent [əd'hɪərənt] *n (supporter)* partidario,-a *m, f*; *(to religious beliefs)* adepto,-a *m, f*.

adhesive [əd'hiːsɪv] **I** *adj* adhesivo,-a, adherente; *(sticky)* pegajoso,-a. ■ **a. tape,** cinta *f* adhesiva, celo *m*. **II** *n* adhesivo *m*, pegamento *m*.

ad hoc [æd'hɒk] *adj* a propósito; **an ad h. committee,** un comité especial.

ad infinitum [ædɪnfɪ'naɪtəm] *adv* a lo infinito, sin fin; **it goes on ad i.,** no tiene fin.

adjacent [ə'dʒeɪsənt] *adj (building)* contiguo,-a; *(land)* colindante; *(country)* limítrofe; *Geom* **a. angle,** ángulo *m* adyacente; **a. to,** contiguo,-a a.

adjective ['ædʒektɪv] *n* adjetivo *m*.

adjoin [ə'dʒɔɪn] **I** *vtr (building)* ser contiguo,-a a; *(land)* lindar con. **II** *vi (building)* estar contiguo,-a; *(land)* colindar.

adjoining [ə'dʒɔɪnɪŋ] *adj (buildings)* contiguo,-a; *(land)* colindante; **the a. room,** la habitación de al lado.

adjourn [ə'dʒɜːn] **I** *vtr (postpone)* aplazar, suspender; *(court, session, etc)* levantar; **the meeting was adjourned,** se levantó la sesión; **the trial is adjourned until after lunch,** se aplaza el juicio hasta después de comer. **II** *vi (meeting etc)* aplazarse **(until,** hasta), suspenderse; *(parliament)* disolverse; **fam let's a. to the sitting room,** pasemos *or* vamos al salón.

adjournment [ə'dʒɜːnmənt] *n (of trial, meeting, etc)* aplazamiento *m*, suspensión *f*.

adjudicate [ə'dʒuːdɪkeɪt] *vtr (contest etc)* juzgar, actuar de juez *or* de árbitro.

adjudication [ədʒuːdɪ'keɪʃən] *n (of contest)* fallo *m*.

adjudicator [ə'dʒuːdɪkeɪtə'] *n* juez *mf*, árbitro,-a *m, f*.

adjunct ['ædʒʌŋkt] *n* adjunto *m*, accesorio *m*, añadidura *f*.

adjust [ə'dʒʌst] **I** *vtr (machine, piece of furniture)* ajustar; *(engine)* arreglar; *fig (methods)* variar; **to a. oneself to sth,** adaptarse a algo. **II** *vi (person)* adaptarse **(to,** a), amoldarse **(to,** a).

adjustable [ə'dʒʌstəbəl] *adj* ajustable.

adjusted [ə'dʒʌstɪd] *adj* equilibrado,-a.

adjustment [ə'dʒʌstmənt] *n* **1** *(act of adjusting)* *(machine etc)* ajuste *m*; *(person)* adaptación *f*; **period of a.,** período *m* de adaptación. **2** *(change)* cambio *m*, modificación *f*.

ad lib [æd'lɪb] **I** *adv (speak)* sin preparación; *(continue)* a voluntad. **II** *adj (speech, performance)* improvisado,-a. **III ad-lib** *vtr (pt & pp ad-libbed)* improvisar. **IV ad-lib** *vi (pt & pp ad-libbed)* improvisar; *(actor)* meter morcillas.

Adm 1 *abbr of* **Admiral,** Almirante *m*, Almte. **2** *abbr of* **Admiralty,** Almirantazgo *m*.

adman ['ædmæn] *n (pl admen* ['ædmen]*)* agente *m* publicitario.

administer [əd'mɪnɪstə'] *vtr (country)* gobernar; *(goods, company)* administrar; *(justice, laws)* aplicar; **to a. an oath to sb,** tomar juramento a algn.

administration [ədmɪnɪ'streɪʃən] *n* **1** *(act of administering)* *(of country)* gobierno *m*; *(of goods, company)* administración *f*; *(of justice, laws)* aplicación *f*. **2** *(governing body)* dirección *f*; administración *f*, gobierno *m*.

administrative [əd'mɪnɪstrətɪv] *adj* administrativo,-a.

administrator [əd'mɪnɪstreɪtə'] *n* administrador,-a *m, f*.

admirable [æd'mərəbəl] *adj* admirable, digno,-a de admiración.

admiral ['ædmərəl] *n* almirante *m*.

admiration [ædmə'reɪʃən] *n* admiración *f*.

admire [əd'maɪə'] *vtr* admirar; **to a. oneself,** contemplarse con satisfacción.

admirer [əd'maɪərə'] *n* admirador,-a *m, f*; *(wooer)* pretendiente *mf*.

admiring [əd'maɪərɪŋ] *adj (look)* lleno,-a de admiración. ◆ **admiringly** *adv (look)* con admiración.

admissible [əd'mɪsəbəl] *adj* admisible, aceptable.

admission [əd'mɪʃən] *n* **1** *(to school, hospital)* ingreso *m*; *(price)* entrada *f*; **'free a.',** 'entrada libre *or* gratis'. **2** *(acknowledgement)* reconocimiento *m*; *(confession)* confesión *f*; **that's an a. of failure,** eso es reconocer el fracaso.

admit [əd'mɪt] *vtr (pt & pp admitted)* **1** *(allow to enter)* *(person)* dejar entrar, admitir; *(to hospital)* admitir; **an invitation which admits two people,** una entrada para dos personas; **'dogs are not admitted',** 'no se admiten perros'; **to be admitted to hospital,** ser ingresado,-a en el hospital. **2** *(acknowledge)* reconocer, admitir; *(crime, guilt)* confesar; **I must a. it's difficult,** debo reconocer que es difícil.

admittance [əd'mɪtəns] *n (entry)* entrada *f*; **'no admittance',** 'se prohíbe la entrada', 'prohibida la entrada'; **to gain a.,** lograr entrar.

admittedly [əd'mɪtɪdlɪ] *adv* la verdad es que, lo cierto es que; **a., it was dark when I saw him,** reconozco que era de noche cuando le vi.

admonish [əd'mɒnɪʃ] *vtr (scold)* amonestar, reprender; **to a. sb for (doing) sth,** amonestar *or* reprender a algn por (hacer) algo.

ad nauseam [æd'nɔːzɪæm] *adv* hasta la saciedad.

ado [ə'duː] *n without further a.,* sin más; *prov* **much a. about nothing,** mucho ruido y pocas nueces.

adolescence [ædə'lesəns] *n* adolescencia *f*.

adolescent [ædə'lesənt] *n* adolescente *mf*.

adopt [ə'dɒpt] *vtr (child, method, tone of voice)* adoptar; *(suggestion)* aceptar.

adopted [ə'dɒptɪd] *adj* adoptado,-a; **a. child,** hijo,-a *m, f* adoptivo,-a.

adoption [ə'dɒpʃən] *n* adopción *f*; **country of a.,** país *m* adoptivo.

adorable [ə'dɔːrəbəl] *adj* adorable; *fam* encantador,-a; **what an a. little dog!,** ¡qué perrito más lindo!

adoration [ædə'reɪʃən] *n* adoración *f*.

adore [ə'dɔː'] *vtr (worship)* adorar; *fam (love) (person)* querer muchísimo a; **I a. your new hairstyle,** me encanta tu nuevo peinado; **we a. eating out,** nos encanta comer fuera.

adorn [ə'dɔːn] *vtr* adornar, embellecer.

adornment [ə'dɔːnmənt] *n* adorno *m*.

adrenaline [ə'drenəlɪn] *n* adrenalina *f*.

Adriatic [eɪdrɪ'ætɪk] *adj* adriático,-a; **the A. (Sea),** el (Mar) Adriático.

adrift [ə'drɪft] *adv* **to come a.,** *(boat)* irse a la deriva; *(rope)* soltarse, desatarse; *fig (plans)* **to go a.,** ir a la deriva.

adroit [ə'drɔɪt] *adj* hábil, mañoso,-a, diestro,-a. ◆ **adroitly** *adv* hábilmente.

adulation [ædjʊ'leɪʃən] *n* adulación *f*.

adult ['ædʌlt] **I** *adj (person)* adulto,-a, mayor; *(film, education)* para adultos. **II** *n* adulto,-a *m, f*, persona *f* mayor.

adulterate [ə'dʌltəreɪt] *vtr* adulterar.

adulteration [ə'dʌltə'reɪʃən] *n* adulteración *f*.

adulterer [ə'dʌltərə'] *n* adúltero *m*.

adulteress [ə'dʌltrɪs] *n* adúltera *f*.

adulterous [ə'dʌltərəs] *adj* adúltero,-a.

adultery [ə'dʌltərɪ] *n* adulterio *m*.

advance [əd'vɑːns] **I** *n* **1** *(movement)* avance *m*; *fig (progress)* adelanto *m*, progreso *m*; **the latest advances in medicine,** los últimos adelantos en medicina; **to arrive**

half an hour in a., llegar media hora antes; **to book tickets in a.,** reservar entradas con anticipación; **to have sth ready in a.,** tener algo preparado de antemano; **to make advances,** *(move forward)* avanzar; *fig (to a person)* insinuarse **(to,** a); **to pay in a.,** pagar por adelantado. 2 *(loan)* adelanto *m*, anticipo *m*. **II** *adj (before time)* adelantado,-a, anticipado,-a; *Mil* **a. party** *or* **guard,** avanzadilla *f*; *Cin Theat* **a. bookings,** reservas *fpl* por adelantado; *Print* **a. copy,** ejemplar *m* de anticipo; **a. notice,** previo aviso *m*. **III** *vtr* 1 *(move forward) (troops)* avanzar; *(time, date)* adelantar; *fig (promote) (arts, sciences)* fomentar, promover; *(interest)* promover; *(cause)* favorecer. 2 *(propose) (idea)* proponer; *(suggestion)* hacer; *(opinion)* dar. 3 *Fin (salary)* adelantar, anticipar; *(loan)* prestar. **IV** *vi (move forward)* avanzar, adelantarse; *(troops)* avanzar; *fig (make progress) (person)* hacer progresos; *(technology etc)* progresar, adelantarse; *(gain promotion)* ascender.

advanced [əd'vɑːnst] *adj (developed) (civilization)* avanzado,-a; *(child, student)* adelantado,-a; *(course)* superior; **to be a. in years,** estar entrado,-a en años; *Educ* **A. level,** examen *m* superior de segunda enseñanza, ≈ COU *m* (Curso *m* de Orientación Universitaria).

advancement [əd'vɑːnsmənt] *n (progress)* adelanto *m*, progreso *m*; *(promotion)* ascenso *m*.

advantage [əd'vɑːntɪdʒ] *n* ventaja *f*; *Tennis* **a.** Velasco, ventaja para Velasco; **he has the a.** of being tall, tiene la ventaja de ser alto; **it would be to your a. if you went,** saldrías ganando si te fueras; **to show sth off to a.,** hacer lucir algo; **to take a. of sb/sth,** abusar de algo/aprovechar algo; **to turn sth to a.,** sacar partido de algo.

advantageous [ædvən'teɪdʒəs] *adj* ventajoso,-a, conveniente **(to,** para).

advent ['ædvent] *n (arrival)* llegada *f*; *(coming) (of Christ)* advenimiento *m*; **A.,** Adviento *m*. ■ **A. calendar,** calendario *m* de Adviento.

adventure [əd'ventʃəʳ] *n* aventura *f*; **a. story,** historia *f or* novela *f* de aventuras.

adventurous [əd'ventʃərəs] *adj (person)* aventurero,-a; *(plan, decision)* aventurado,-a, arriesgado,-a.

adverb ['ædvɜːb] *n* adverbio *m*.

adversary ['ædvəsərɪ] *n* adversario,-a *m*,*f*, contrario,-a *m*,*f*.

adverse ['ædvɜːs] *adj (effect)* desfavorable; *(conditions, decision)* adverso,-a; *(winds)* contrario,-a. ◆ **adversely** *adv* desfavorablemente.

adversity [əd'vɜːsɪtɪ] *n* adversidad *f*.

advert ['ædvɜːt] *n fam* anuncio *m*.

advertise ['ædvətaɪz] **I** *vtr* anunciar; **to a. sth in the newspaper,** anunciar algo en el periódico. **II** *vi* hacer publicidad; *(in newspaper)* poner un anuncio; **to a. for sth/sb,** buscar algo/a algn mediante un anuncio.

advertisement [əd'vɜːtɪsmənt] *n (on television)* anuncio *m*, spot *m* publicitario; *(in newspaper)* anuncio *m*; **advertisements,** publicidad *f sing*, anuncios *mpl*.

advertiser ['ædvətaɪzəʳ] *n* anunciante *mf*.

advertising ['ædvətaɪzɪŋ] **I** *n* publicidad *f*, propaganda *f*; *(in newspaper)* anuncios *mpl*. **II** *adj* publicitario,-a. ■ **a. agency,** agencia *f* de publicidad; **a. campaign,** campaña *f* publicitaria.

advice [əd'vaɪs] *n* consejos *mpl*; **a piece of a.,** un consejo; **to ask for sb's a.,** pedir consejos a algn; **to take legal a. on a matter,** consultar el caso con un abogado; **to take sb's a.,** seguir los consejos de algn.

advisable [əd'vaɪzəbəl] *adj* aconsejable, conveniente; **it's a. for us to start again,** mejor si volvemos a empezar.

advise [əd'vaɪz] *vtr (give advice)* aconsejar, recomendar; *(on business, financial matters)* asesorar; **I a. you to do it,** te aconsejo que lo hagas; **we don't a. it,** no lo recomendamos *or* aconsejamos.

adviser [əd'vaɪzəʳ] *n* consejero,-a *m*, *f*; *(in business, financial matters)* asesor,-a *m*,*f*.

advisory [əd'vaɪzərɪ] *adj (in business etc)* consultivo,-a, asesor,-a.

advocate ['ædvəkɪt] **I** *n* *Scot Jur* abogado,-a *m*, *f* defensor,-a; *fig (supporter)* defensor,-a *m*, *f*. **II** ['ædvəkeɪt] *vtr (reform)* abogar por; *(plan)* apoyar.

aegis ['iːdʒɪs] *n* **under the a. of,** bajo el patrocinio de.

aeon ['iːən] *n* eón *m*, eternidad *f*.

aerate ['eəreɪt] *vtr (liquid)* airear, gasificar; *(blood)* oxigenar.

aerial ['eərɪəl] **I** *adj* aéreo,-a; **a. photograph,** aerofoto *f*. **II** *n (for radio, television)* antena *f*.

aero- ['eərəʊ] *pref* aero-.

aerobatics [eərəʊ'bætɪks] *n sing & pl* acrobacia *f* aérea.

aerobics [eə'rəʊbɪks] *n* aerobic *m*.

aerodrome ['eərədrəʊm] *n GB* aeródromo *m*.

aerodynamics [eərəʊdaɪ'næmɪks] *n* 1 *(science)* aerodinámica *f*. 2 *pl (qualities)* aerodinámica *f sing*.

aerogram(me) ['eərəʊgræm] *n* aerograma *m*.

aeronautics [eərə'nɔːtɪks] *n* aeronáutica *f*.

aeroplane ['eərəpleɪn] *n* avión *m*.

aerosol ['eərəsɒl] *n* aerosol *m*, atomizador *m*.

aerospace ['eərəʊspeɪs] **I** *n* aire *m* y espacio *m* extraterrestre. **II** *adj* **a. industry,** industria *f* aeroespacial.

aesthetic [iːs'θetɪk] *adj* estético,-a.

aesthetics [iːs'θetɪks] *n* estética *f*.

afar [ə'fɑːʳ] *adv* lejos; **from a.,** desde lejos.

affable ['æfəbəl] *adj* afable, amable.

affair [ə'feəʳ] *n (matter)* asunto *m*; *(event)* acontecimiento *m*; **to put one's affairs in order,** arreglar sus asuntos personales; **the wedding was a big a.,** la boda fue todo un acontecimiento; **that's my a.,** eso es asunto mío. ■ **business affairs,** negocios *mpl*; **foreign affairs,** asuntos *mpl* exteriores; **love a.,** aventura *f* amorosa.

affect [ə'fekt] *vtr* 1 *(influence) (person, health)* afectar; *(prices, decision, future, etc)* influir en; *Med (attack) (organ, people)* afectar *or* atacar a; **countries affected by cholera,** países afectados *or* atacados por el cólera; **it affects us all,** nos afecta a todos; **will the delay a. the price?,** ¿influirá el retraso en el precio? 2 *(touch emotionally)* afectar, conmover, emocionar; **to be affected by sth,** conmoverse *or* emocionarse por algo; **we were greatly affected by her death,** su muerte nos afectó mucho.

affectation [æfek'teɪʃən] *n (false behaviour)* afectación *f*; amaneramiento *m*.

affected [ə'fektɪd] *adj* 1 *(unnatural)* afectado,-a, amanerado,-a. 2 *(influenced)* afectado,-a, influido,-a; *Med* atacado,-a **(by,** por). 3 *(touched emotionally)* afectado,-a, conmovido,-a, emocionado,-a **(by,** por). 4 *(pretended)* fingido,-a.

affection [ə'fekʃən] *n* afecto *m*, cariño *m*.

affectionate [ə'fekʃənɪt] *adj* afectuoso,-a, cariñoso,-a. ◆ **affectionately** *adv* afectuosamente, cariñosamente, con cariño.

affidavit [æfɪ'deɪvɪt] *n Jur* declaración *f* escrita y jurada.

affiliated [ə'fɪlieɪtɪd] *adj* afiliado,-a, asociado,-a; **to be** *or* **become a.,** afiliarse **(to, with,** a), asociarse **(to, with,** a); **a. company,** filial *f*.

affiliation [əfɪlɪ'eɪʃən] *n* afiliación *f*.

affinity [ə'fɪnɪtɪ] *n (connexion)* afinidad *f*, punto *m* de contacto; *(liking)* simpatía *f*; **there's a great a. between them,** les une una gran simpatía.

affirm [ə'fɜːm] *vtr* afirmar, sostener.

affirmation [æfə'meɪʃən] *n* afirmación *f*.

affirmative [ə'fɜːmətɪv] **I** *adj* afirmativo,-a. **II** *n* afirmativa *f*; **he answered in the a.,** contestó que sí.

affix [ə'fɪks] *vtr (stamp)* poner, pegar.

afflict [ə'flɪkt] *vtr* afligir; **to be afflicted with,** sufrir *or* padecer de.

affliction [ə'flɪkʃən] *n (suffering)* aflicción *f; (grief)* pena *f; (illness)* mal *m*.

affluence ['æfluəns] *n* opulencia *f*.

affluent ['æfluənt] *adj* opulento,-a, rico,-a; **the a. society,** la sociedad del consumo.

afford [ə'fɔːd] *vtr* **1** *(be able to buy)* darse *or* permitirse el lujo de; **I can't a. a new car,** no puedo pagar un coche nuevo; **she can a. it,** se lo puede permitir. **2** *(be able to do)* permitirse; **I can a. to leave it for a few days,** no pasa nada si lo dejo unos días; **you can't a. to miss the opportunity,** no puedes perderte la ocasión.

affray [ə'freɪ] *n* refriega *f*, reyerta *f*.

affront [ə'frʌnt] **I** *n* afrenta *f*, ofensa *f*. **II** *vtr* afrentar, ofender; **to be affronted,** ofenderse.

afield [ə'fiːld] *adv* **far a.,** muy lejos.

AFL-CIO [eɪefelsiːaɪ'əʊ] *US abbr of* **American Fed—eration of Labor and Congress of Industrial Organizations.**

afloat [ə'fləʊt] *adv* a flote; **to keep a.,** mantenerse a flote.

afoot [ə'fʊt] *adv* **there's a plan a.,** hay un proyecto en marcha; **there's something strange a.,** se está tramando algo.

aforementioned [ə'fɔːmenʃənd] *adj*, **aforesaid** [ə'fɔːsed] *adj* susodicho,-a, arriba citado,-a.

afraid [ə'freɪd] *adj* **1** *(frightened)* **to be a.,** tener miedo **(of sb,** a algn; **of sth,** de algo); **I'm a. of it,** me da miedo; **we were a. to go in,** nos daba miedo entrar. **2** *(sorry)* **I'm a. he's out,** lo siento pero no está; **I'm a. not,** me temo que no; **I'm a. so,** me temo que sí, eso me temo; **I'm a. you're wrong,** me temo que estás equivocado,-a.

afresh [ə'freʃ] *adv* de nuevo, otra vez; **to start a.,** volver a empezar.

Africa ['æfrɪkə] *n* Africa. ■ **South A.,** Sudáfrica.

African ['æfrɪkən] *adj & n* africano,-a *(m, f)*.

Afro ['æfrəʊ] *n & adj fam (hairstyle)* afro *(m)*.

Afro-American [æfrəʊə'merɪkən] *adj & n* afro-americano,-a *(m, f)*.

aft [ɑːft] *adv Naut* en popa; **to go a.,** ir en popa.

after ['ɑːftə'] **I** *adv* después; **soon a.,** poco después; **the day/week a.,** el día/la semana siguiente; **to come a.,** seguir; **to run a.,** perseguir. **II** *prep* **I** *(later)* después de, al cabo de; **a. a few weeks,** al cabo de unas semanas; **come a. lunch,** ven después de comer; *US* **it's half a. five,** son las cinco y media; **soon a. arriving,** al poco rato de llegar; **the day a. tomorrow,** pasado mañana. **2** *(behind)* detrás de, tras; **a. you!,** ¡usted primero!, ¡pase usted!; **it comes a. 'M' in the alphabet,** sigue a la 'M' en el alfabeto; **she came day a. day,** vino día tras día; **they went in one a. the other,** entraron uno tras otro; *fam* **the police are a. them,** la policía anda tras ellos. **3** *(about, concerning)* por; **I see what you're a.,** ya veo lo que buscas; **they asked a. you,** preguntaron por ti; **what's he a.?,** ¿qué pretende? **4** *(like)* **he takes a. his uncle,** se parece a su tío; **she was named a. her grandmother,** la llamaron como su abuela. **III** *conj* después de, después que; **I came a. you left,** vine después de que te marchases.

afterbirth ['ɑːftəbɜːθ] *n* placenta *f*.

aftercare ['ɑːftəkeə'] *n (after hospital)* convalecencia *f; (after prison)* vigilancia *f*.

after-effect ['ɑːftərɪfekt] *n* efecto *m* secundario.

afterlife ['ɑːftəlaɪf] *n* vida *f* después de la muerte.

aftermath ['ɑːftəmæθ] *n* secuelas *fpl*, consecuencias *fpl*, repercusiones *fpl*.

afternoon [ɑːftə'nuːn] *n* tarde *f*; **good a.!,** ¡buenas tardes!; **in the a.,** por la tarde.

afters ['ɑːftəz] *npl fam (dessert)* postre *m*; **what's for a.?,** ¿qué hay de postre?

after-sales service [ɑːftəseɪlz'sɜːvɪs] *n Com* servicio *m* posventa.

aftershave (lotion) ['ɑːftəʃeɪv ('ləʊʃən)] *n* loción *f* para después del afeitado.

aftertaste ['ɑːftəteɪst] *n* regusto *m*.

afterthought ['ɑːftəθɔːt] *n* ocurrencia *f* tardía.

afterwards ['ɑːftəwədz] *adv* después, más, tarde.

again [ə'gen] *adv* **1** *(another time)* otra vez, de nuevo; **don't do it a.,** no lo vuelves a hacer; **I'm well a.,** ya estoy bien; **I tried a. and a.,** lo intenté repetidas veces; **to begin a.,** volver a empezar; **to do sth a.,** volver a hacer algo; **never a.!,** ¡nunca más!; **now and a.,** de vez en cuando; **once a.,** otra vez; **come a.?,** ¿cómo? **2** *(besides)* además; **then a.,** por otra parte.

against [ə'genst] *prep* **1** *(touching)* contra; **put the ladder a. the wall,** coloca la escalera en la pared; **to lean a. sth,** apoyarse contra algo. **2** *(opposing)* contra, en contra (de); **a. the grain,** a contrapelo; *fig* **it goes a. the grain,** esto va contra mis principios; **his height is a. him,** su estatura no le ayuda nada; **it's a. the law,** es ilegal, va en contra de la ley; **my father is a. it,** mi padre se opone: **6 votes in favour, 4 a.,** 6 votos a favor, 4 en contra; **to fight a. sth,** luchar contra algo; **to work a. the clock,** trabajar contra reloj. **3 as a.,** en contraste con, comparado con; **she had two, as a. my one,** ella tenía dos, y yo solamente uno.

agape [ə'geɪp] *adj (open-mouthed)* boquiabierto,-a.

age [eɪdʒ] **I** *n* **1** *(of person)* edad *f*; **he doesn't look his a.,** no representa la edad que tiene; **she's 18 years of a.,** tiene 18 años; **the 20-30 a. group,** las personas de edades comprendidas entre los 20 y 30 años; **to be under a.,** ser menor de edad; **to come of a.,** llegar a la mayoría de edad; **what a. are you?,** ¿qué edad tienes? ■ **a. of consent,** edad *f* núbil; **a. limit,** límite *m* de edad; **old a.,** vejez *f*. **2** *(period)* edad *f*, época *f*, era *f*; **the Middle Ages,** la Edad Media; **the Golden A.,** el Siglo de Oro; **the Iron A.,** la Edad de Hierro. **3** *fam (very long time)* eternidad *f*; **it's ages since I last saw her,** hace siglos que no la veo; **I've been waiting ages for you,** hace una eternidad que te estoy esperando. **II** *vtr & vi* envejecer.

aged¹ [eɪdʒd] *adj de or* a la edad de; **Anne, a. 26,** Anne, de 26 años; **he died a. 80,** murió a la edad de 80 años.

aged² ['eɪdʒɪd] **I** *adj (very old)* anciano,-a. **II the a.** *npl* los ancianos, la gente *sing* muy mayor.

ageing ['eɪdʒɪŋ] **I** *adj (person)* envejecido,-a, viejo,-a; *(thing)* viejo,-a. **II** *n (process)* envejecimiento *m*.

ageless ['eɪdʒlɪs] *adj (person)* siempre joven; *(beauty etc)* eterno,-a.

agency ['eɪdʒənsɪ] *n* **1** *Com* agencia *f; US (delegation)* representación *f*, delegación *f*; **advertising/employment/travel a.,** agencia de publicidad/de trabajo/de viajes. **2 by the a. of,** por medio de.

agenda [ə'dʒendə] *n* programa *m*, orden *m* del día; **what's on the a. today?,** ¿qué programa tenemos para hoy?

agent ['eɪdʒənt] *n* **1** *(person)* agente *mf; (representative)* representante *mf*, delegado,-a *m, f*; **estate/insurance a.,** agente inmobiliario/de seguros; **to be a free a.,** actuar *or* trabajar por cuenta propia *or* por libre. **2** *(instrument)* agente *m*. causa *f*.

age-old ['eɪdʒəʊld] *adj (custom etc)* viejo,-a, antiquísimo,-a, milenario,-a.

agglomeration [əglɒmə'reɪʃən] *n* aglomeración *f*, concentración *f*.

aggravate ['ægrəveɪt] *vtr (worsen)* agravar, empeorar; *fam (annoy)* molestar.

aggravating ['ægrəveɪtɪŋ] *adj* **1** agravador,-a. **2** *fam (annoying)* molesto,-a.

aggravation [ægrə'veɪʃən] *n* **1** agravamiento *m*, empeoramiento *m; fam (problems)* líos *mpl*, camorra *f*.

aggregate ['ægrɪgɪt] *n* **1** *(total)* conjunto *m*, total *m*; **on a.,** en conjunto, en total. **2** *(stones)* conglomerado *m*.

aggression [əˈgreʃən] n agresión f.

aggressive [əˈgresɪv] adj (violent) agresivo,-a, violento,-a; (dynamic) dinámico,-a. ◆ **aggressively** adv (violently) agresivamente; (dynamically) dinámicamente.

aggressor [əˈgresər] n agresor,-a m,f.

aggrieved [əˈgriːvd] adj apenado,-a; **to be a. about sth**, estar herido,-a por algo.

aggro [ˈægrəʊ] n fam see **aggravation 2.**

aghast [əˈgɑːst] adj (shocked) espantado,-a, horrorizado,-a; **to be a. at the thought of sth**, quedarse horrorizado,-a or pasmado,-a de pensar en algo.

agile [ˈædʒaɪl] adj ágil.

agility [əˈdʒɪlɪtɪ] n agilidad f.

agitate [ˈædʒɪteɪt] I vtr (shake) agitar; fig (disturb, worry) inquietar, perturbar; **to be agitated about sth**, estar inquieto,-a or nervioso,-a por algo. II vi Pol **to a. about/against sth**, hacer campaña a favor de/en contra de algo.

agitated [ˈædʒɪteɪtɪd] adj (person) inquieto,-a, perturbado,-a, nervioso,-a.

agitation [ædʒɪˈteɪʃən] n 1 (anxiety) inquietud f, perturbación f, nerviosismo m. 2 Pol agitación f.

agitator [ˈædʒɪteɪtər] n Pol agitador,-a m,f, alborotador,-a m,f.

aglow [əˈgləʊ] adj (glowing) resplandeciente, brillante; **to be a.**, resplandecer, brillar.

AGM [eɪdʒiːˈem] abbr of **annual general meeting**, junta f general anual.

agnostic [ægˈnɒstɪk] n agnóstico,-a m,f.

agnosticism [ægˈnɒstɪsɪzəm] n agnosticismo m.

ago [əˈgəʊ] adv hace; **a long time a.**, hace mucho tiempo; **a short while a.**, hace un ratito; **as long a as 1910**, ya en 1910; **a week a.**, hace una semana; **how long a. was it that you last saw him?**, ¿cuánto tiempo hace que no le ves?

agog [əˈgɒg] adj (expectant) ansioso,-a, curioso,-a; **the whole town was a.**, en todo el pueblo había una gran expectación.

agonize [ˈægənaɪz] vi angustiarse, atormentarse (**over**, por).

agonizing [ˈægənaɪzɪŋ] adj (pain) atroz, horroroso,-a; (decision) angustioso,-a.

agony [ˈægənɪ] n (great pain) dolor m muy fuerte; (anguish) angustia f; **he was in a. with his back**, tenía un dolor insoportable de espalda; **it was a. having to wait**, fue horroroso tener que esperar. ■ **a. column**, consultorio m del corazón.

agoraphobia [ægərəˈfəʊbɪə] n agorafobia f.

agoraphobic [ægərəˈfəʊbɪk] adj & n agorafóbico,-a (m,f).

agree [əˈgriː] I vi 1 (be in agreement) estar de acuerdo; (reach agreement) ponerse or quedar de acuerdo; (consent) consentir; **don't you a.?**, ¿no te parece?; **I agreed to see him on Monday**, quedé en verle el lunes; **to a. about or on (doing) sth**, ponerse de acuerdo en (hacer) algo; **to a. to do sth**, consentir en hacer algo; **to a. with sb**, estar de acuerdo con algn; **we agreed to differ**, acordamos conservar cada uno sus propias opiniones. 2 (harmonize) (things, adjectives) concordar; (people) congeniar; (food) sentar bien; climate) convenir; **raw onion doesn't a. with me**, la cebolla cruda no me sienta bien. II vtr convenir, acordar; **I a. that she should come**, estoy de acuerdo en que venga; **it was agreed that he would pay**, se acordó que pagaría; **to a. a price/the terms of a contract**, convenir un precio/los términos de un contrato.

agreeable [əˈgriːəbəl] adj (pleasant) agradable; (person) simpático,-a; (in agreement) de acuerdo, conforme; **to be a. to (doing) sth**, consentir en (hacer) algo.

agreement [əˈgriːmənt] n (arrangement) acuerdo m, arreglo m; Pol (treaty) pacto m; Com contrato m, trato m; **by mutual a.**, de común acuerdo; **to be in a. with sb**,

estar de acuerdo con algn; **to come to or reach an a. with sb**, llegar a un acuerdo or ponerse de acuerdo con algn.

agricultural [ægrɪˈkʌltʃərəl] adj agrícolo,-a; (college) de agricultura.

agriculturalist [ægrɪˈkʌltʃərəlɪst] n ingeniero,-a m,f agrónomo,-a.

agriculture [ˈægrɪkʌltʃər] n agricultura f.

agronomy [əˈgrɒnəmɪ] n agronomía f.

aground [əˈgraʊnd] adv Naut encallado,-a, varado,-a; **to run a.**, encallar, varar.

ahead [əˈhed] adv (in front) adelante, delante; (early) antes, con antelación; Naut **full speed a.!**, ¡avante toda!; **go a.!**, ¡adelante!; **to be a.**, ir en cabeza; fig llevar la ventaja; **to go a.**, adelantar, ir adelante; fig **to go a. with sth**, llevar algo adelante; fig **to get a.**, triunfar, tener éxito; fig **to look a.**, pensar en el futuro; **to plan a.**, planear el futuro; (anticipate) anticipar.

ahoy [əˈhɔɪ] interj Naut **ship a.!**, ¡barco a la vista!

AI [eɪˈaɪ] 1 abbr of **artificial intelligence**, inteligencia f artificial. 2 abbr of **artificial insemination**, inseminación f artificial.

aid [eɪd] I n (help) ayuda f; (rescue) auxilio m, socorro m; **in a. of**, a beneficio de, en pro de; **to come to the a. of sb**, acudir en ayuda or en auxilio de algn; fam **what's all this in a. of?**, ¿a qué viene todo esto? ■ Educ **audiovisual a.**, ayuda f audiovisual; **hearing a.**, audífono m. II vtr ayudar; Jur **to a. and abet sb**, ser cómplice de algn.

aide [eɪd] n Pol ayudante mf, consejero,-a m,f.

aide-de-camp [eɪddəˈkɒŋ] n (pl **aides-de-camp**) Mil edecán m.

AIDS [eɪdz] n (abbr of **Acquired Immune Deficiency Syndrome**), SIDA m (Síndrome m de Inmunodeficiencia Adquirida).

ailment [ˈeɪlmənt] n enfermedad f (leve), achaque m.

ailing [ˈeɪlɪŋ] adj enfermizo,-a, achacoso,-a.

aim [eɪm] I n (with weapon) puntería f; fig (target) propósito m, objetivo m; **he has no a. in life**, no tiene objetivos en la vida; **to miss one's a.**, errar el tiro; **to take a.**, apuntar; **what's her a.?**, ¿qué se propone? II vtr (gun) apuntar (**at**, a, hacia); (stone) lanzar (**at**, a, hacia); fig (attack, action) dirigir (**at**, a, hacia). ◆ **aim at** vtr (target) tirar para; fig **to a. at doing sth**, querer or tener pensado hacer algo. ◆ **aim to** vtr **to a. to do sth**, tener la intención de or pensar or proponer hacer algo.

aimless [ˈeɪmlɪs] adj sin objeto, sin propósito ◆ **aimlessly** adv (wander) sin rumbo fijo

air [eər] I n 1 aire m, **fresh a.**, aire fresco, **in the open a.**, al aire libre, **to go out for a breath of a.**, salir a tomar el aire, **to send a letter by a.**, mandar una carta por avión, **to travel by a.**, viajar en avión, **to throw sth up in the a.**, arrojar or lanzar algo al aire; fig **it's still in the a. at the moment**, todavía queda por resolver, fig **there's something in the a.**, se está tramando algo, fig **to be walking on a.**, estar en la gloria, fig **to vanish into thin a.**, esfumarse ■ **a. base**, base f aérea, **a. bed**, colchón m hinchable or neumático, **a. brake**, freno m neumático, **a. conditioner**, acondicionador m de aire, **a. conditioning**, aire m acondicionado, **A. Force**, Fuerzas fpl Aéreas, **a. freight**, transporte m aéreo, **a. gun**, pistola f de aire comprimido, **a. hostess**, azafata f (de vuelo), **a. lane**, ruta f aérea, **a. letter**, carta f aérea, **a. pocket**, bache m, **a. pressure**, presión f atmosférica, **a. raid**, ataque m aéreo, **a. shuttle**, puente m aéreo, **a. terminal**, terminal f aérea, **a. traffic control**, control m de tráfico aéreo; **a. traffic controller**, controlador,-a m,f aéreo,-a 2 Rad TV **to be on the a.**, (programme) estar emitiendo, (person) estar transmitiendo, **to go off the a.**, (programme) cerrar la emisión, (person) dejar de transmitir 3 Mus aire m, tonada f 4 (appearance, feeling) aire m, aspecto m, **there was an a. of expectancy about the meeting**, había cierta expectación entre los asistentes a la reunión, **to put on**

airs (and graces), darse tono, presumir **II** *vtr (bed, clothes)* airear, *(room, cupboard)* ventilar, *fig (grievance)* airear, *(knowledge)* hacer alarde de

airborne ['eəbɔːn] *adj (aircraft)* en vuelo, en el aire; *Mil (troops)* aerotransportado,-a; **soon we were a.,** pronto estuvimos volando.

air-conditioned ['eəkɒndɪʃənd] *adj* climatizado,-a, con aire acondicionado

aircraft ['eəkrɑːft] *n inv* avión *m* ■ **a. carrier,** portaviones *m inv*

aircrew ['eəkruː] *n* tripulación *f* del avión.

airdrome ['eədrəʊm] *n US* aeródromo *m*

airfield ['eəfiːld] *n* campo *m* de aviación

airing ['eərɪŋ] *n* **to give a room/clothes an a.,** ventilar un cuarto/airear la ropa; *fig* **the subject needs a good a.,** hace falta someter el tema a una buena discusión ■ **a. cupboard,** armario *m* caliente para secar la ropa

airless ['eəlɪs] *adj (room)* mal ventilado,-a, *(atmosphere)* cargado,-a

airlift ['eəlɪft] **I** *n* puente *m* aéreo. **II** *vtr* transportar por avión

airline ['eəlaɪn] *n* línea *f* aérea

airlock ['eəlɒk] *n (in pipe)* bolsa *f* de aire, *(in spacecraft)* esclusa *f* de aire

airmail ['eəmeɪl] *n* correo *m* aéreo, **by a.,** por avión.

airplane ['eəpleɪn] *n US* avión *m*

airport ['eəpɔːt] *n* aeropuerto *m*

airship ['eəʃɪp] *n* aeronave *f*

airsick ['eəsɪk] *adj* mareado,-a, **to be a.,** marearse en avión

airsickness ['eəsɪknɪs] *n* mareos *mpl* (en avión)

airspace ['eəspeɪs] *n* espacio *m* aéreo

airspeed ['eəspiːd] *n* velocidad *f* relativa *or* aerodinámica

airstrip ['eəstrɪp] *n* pista *f* de aterrizaje.

airtight ['eətaɪt] *adj* hermético,-a

airworthy ['eəwɜːðɪ] *adj (airworthier, airworthiest)* en condiciones de vuelo

airy ['eərɪ] *adj (airier, airiest) (well-ventilated)* bien ventilado,-a, *(vague, carefree)* ligero,-a, despreocupado,-a

airy-fairy [eərɪ'feərɪ] *adj (impractical)* poco realista

aisle [aɪl] *n (in church)* nave *f* lateral; *(in theatre, bus)* pasillo *m, fam* **they were rolling in the aisles,** se troncharon de risa.

ajar [ə'dʒɑː'] *adj & adv* entreabierto,-a

akimbo [ə'kɪmbəʊ] *adj & adv* en jarras; **with armas a.,** con los brazos en jarras

akin [ə'kɪn] *adj* parecido,-a a, semejante a; **my lifestyle is a. to yours,** mi forma de vivir se parece a la tuya

alabaster ['æləbɑːstə'] *n* alabastro *m*.

alacrity [ə'lækrɪtɪ] *n* **with a.,** con presteza.

Alan ['ælən] *adj & n Hist* alano,-a *(m, f)*

alarm [ə'lɑːm] **I** *n* **1** *(warning signal)* alarma *f*, alerta *m*, **to give** *or* **raise the a.,** dar la alarma. ■ **a. clock,** despertador *m*; **burglar a.,** alarma *f* antirrobo; **false a.,** falsa alarma *f* **2** *(fear)* temor *m*, inquietud *f*, alarma *f*, **to cause a.,** provocar temor **II** *vtr* alarmar, asustar, **to be alarmed at sth,** asustarse por *or* de algo

alarming [ə'lɑːmɪŋ] *adj* alarmante.

alarmist [ə'lɑːmɪst] *n* alarmista *mf*.

alas [ə'læs] *interj* ¡ay!, ¡ay de mí!

albatross ['ælbətrɒs] *n* albatros *m*

albeit [ɔːl'biːɪt] *conj* aunque, no obstante, **things are changing, a. slowly,** las cosas están cambiando, aunque lentamente

albino [æl'biːnəʊ] *adj & n* albino,-a *(m, f)*.

album ['ælbəm] *n* álbum *m*.

albumen ['ælbjʊmɪn] *n* albúmina *f*.

alcohol ['ælkəhɒl] *n* alcohol *m*, alcool *m*, **he doesn't drink a.,** no bebe alcohol, es abstemio

alcoholic [ælkə'hɒlɪk] *adj & n* alcohólico,-a *(m, f)*

alcoholism ['ælkəhɒlɪzəm] *n* alcoholismo *m*

alcove ['ælkəʊv] *n* nicho *m*, hueco *m*

alder [ɔːldə'] *n Bot* aliso *m*.

ale [eɪl] *n* cerveza *f*; **brown/pale a.,** cerveza negra/rubia

alert [ə'lɜːt] **I** *adj (person) (quick to act)* alerta, vigilante; *(lively)* despierto,-a, despabilado,-a, *(mind)* vivo,-a **II** *n* alerta *m*, **to be on the a.,** estar alerta. **III** *vtr* **to a. sb to sth,** alertar *or* avisar a algn de algo

Aleutian [ə'luːʃən] *adj & n* aleutiano,-a *(m, f)* ■ **A. Islands,** Islas *fpl* Aleutianas.

A-level ['eɪlevəl] *GB Educ abbr of* **Advanced level,** ≈ Curso *m* de Orientación Universitaria, COU *m*.

Alexandria [ælɪg'zændrɪə] *n* Alejandría.

alfalfa [æl'fælfə] *n* alfalfa *f*

alfresco [æl'freskəʊ] *adj & adv* al aire libre.

algae ['ældʒiː] *npl Bot* algas *fpl*

algebra ['ældʒɪbrə] *n* álgebra *f*.

Algeria [æl'dʒɪərɪə] *n* Argelia

Algerian [æl'dʒɪərɪən] *adj & n* argelino,-a *(m, f)*.

Algiers [æl'dʒɪəz] *n* Argel.

alias ['eɪlɪəs] **I** *n* alias *m*, apodo *m* **II** *adv* ahas, apodado,-a

alibi ['ælɪbaɪ] *n (pl alibis)* coartada *f*

alien ['eɪlɪən] **I** *adj (foreign)* extranjero,-a, *(from space)* extraterrestre, *(stranger)* ajeno,-a; **such behaviour is a. to him,** semejante comportamiento es ajeno a él. **II** *n (foreigner)* extranjero,-a *m, f*; *(from space)* extraterrestre *mf*; *(stranger)* ajeno,-a *m, f*.

alienate ['eɪlɪəneɪt] *vtr* **1 to a. sb,** ofender a algn, ganarse la antipatía de algn; **to a. oneself from sb,** alejarse de algn. **2** *Jur* enajenar.

alienation [eɪlɪə'neɪʃən] *n (feeling of not belonging)* alienación *f*; *(separation)* alejamiento *m*.

alight¹ [ə'laɪt] *adj (on fire)* ardiendo,-a, encendido,-a; **to be a.,** *(fire)* estar ardiendo; *(light)* estar encendido,-a; **to catch a.,** incendiarse; **to set sth a.,** prender fuego a algo.

alight² [ə'laɪt] *vi (get off)* apearse, bajar *(from,* de*)*; *(bird)* posarse *(on,* en*)*.

align [ə'laɪn] *vtr* alinear; **to a. oneself with sb,** alinearse con algn.

alignment [ə'laɪnmənt] *n* alineación *f*; **out of a. with,** mal alineado,-a con.

alike [ə'laɪk] **I** *adj (similar)* parecidos,-as, semejantes; *(the same)* iguales; **they're all a.!,** ¡son todos iguales! **II** *adv (in the same way)* de la misma manera, igualmente; **dressed a.,** vestidos,-as iguales; **summer and winter a.,** tanto en verano como en invierno.

alimentary [ælɪ'mentərɪ] *adj* alimenticio,-a; *Anat* **a. canal,** tubo *m* digestivo.

alimony ['ælɪmənɪ] *n Jur* pensión *f* alimenticia, alimentos *mpl*.

alive [ə'laɪv] *adj (living)* vivo,-a, con vida; *(lively)* vivaz, vivaracho,-a, activo,-a; *fig (teeming)* lleno,-a (**with,** de); *(aware)* consciente (**to,** de); **look a.!,** ¡anímate!, ¡despabílate!; **to be a.,** estar vivo,-a *or* con vida; *fig* **to come a.,** *(party etc)* animarse; *(person)* despabilarse; **she's a. to the risks,** es consciente de los riesgos; **to keep the conversation a.,** mantener (viva) la conversación.

alkali ['ælkəlaɪ] *n (pl alkalis or alkalies)* álcali *m*.

alkaline ['ælkəlaɪn] *adj* alcalino,-a.

all [ɔːl] **I** *adj* todo,-a, todos,-as; **a. along the valley,** a lo largo del valle; **a. children,** todos los niños; **a. the town,** todo el pueblo, el pueblo entero; **a. year,** (durante) todo el año; **a. kinds of things,** todo tipo de cosas; **at a.**

hours, a todas horas; **at a. times,** siempre; **by a. accounts,** según se dice; **in a. honesty,** con toda franqueza, francamente; **John of a. people,** John entre todos; **of a. the cheek!,** ¡qué carota!, ¡qué jeta!; **on a. fours,** a gatas; **she works a. the time,** siempre está trabajando; *fam* **to be a. in,** estar agotado,-a. ■ *Rel* **A. Saints' Day,** Día *m* de Todos los Santos; **A. Souls' Day,** Día *m* de los Santos Difuntos. **II** *pron* todo,-a, todos,-as; **after a.,** al fin y al cabo, después de todo; **a. but Paul are here,** todos menos Paul están aquí; **a. of his work,** toda su obra; **a. of us,** todos,-as nosotros,-as; **a. who saw it,** todos los que lo vieron; **a. you can do is wait,** lo único que puedes hacer es esperar; **it costs £50 in a.,** cuesta 50 libras en total; **I don't like it at a.,** no me gusta en absoluto; **is that a.?,** ¿eso es todo?; **it wasn't a. that good,** no era nada del otro mundo; **most of** *or* **above a.,** sobre todo; **not at a.,** en absoluto; **once and for a.,** de una vez para siempre; **thanks —not at a.,** gracias —de nada; **that's a.,** ya está; **that's a. there is,** se acabó; **the score was one a.,** empataron a uno; **they watched a, a of it,** lo miraron en su totalidad; **they will arrive late, if they come at a.,** llegarán tarde, si es que vienen; **we ate a. of it,** nos lo comimos todo. **III** *adv* todo, completamente; **a. alone,** completamente solo,-a; **a. at once,** *(suddenly)* de repente; *(altogether)* de una vez; **a. over the place,** por todas partes; **a. the better,** tanto mejor; **a. the same,** de todos modos; **he knew a. along,** lo sabía desde el principio; **I'd like to go a. the same,** a pesar de todo, me gustaría ir; **if it's a. the same to you,** si no te importa; **I'm a. for it,** me parece estupendo; **I'm not a. that tired,** no estoy tan cansado,-a como eso; **it's a. but impossible,** es casi imposible; **it's a. the same to me,** me da igual; **I've a. but finished,** me falta poco para terminar; **painted a. in red,** pintago,-a todo,-a de rojo; **there were ten a. told,** había diez en total; *fam* **she's not a. there,** es un poco tonta. **IV** *n* todo *m*; **to give one's a.,** darse por completo.

Allah [ˈælə] *n* Alá *m*.

allay [əˈleɪ] *vtr (fears, doubts)* clamar, apaciguar.

allegation [ælɪˈgeɪʃən] *n* alegato *m*.

allege [əˈledʒ] *vtr* alegar, pretender **(that,** que); **the alleged criminal,** el presunto criminal.

allegedly [əˈledʒɪdlɪ] *adv* supuestamente.

allegiance [əˈliːdʒəns] *n* lealtad *f*; **to swear a. to the crown,** rendir homenaje a la corona.

allegorical [ælɪˈgɒrɪkəl] *adj* alegórico,-a.

allegory [ˈælɪgərɪ] *n* alegoría *f*.

allergic [əˈlɜːdʒɪk] *adj* alérgico,-a **(to,** a).

allergy [ˈælədʒɪ] *n* alergia *f*.

alleviate [əˈliːvɪeɪt] *vtr (pain)* aliaviar, mitigar.

alleviation [əliːvɪˈeɪʃən] *n* alivio *m*.

alley [ˈælɪ] *n* callejón *m*, callejuela *f*; **blind a.,** callejón sin salida.

alliance [əˈlaɪəns] *n* alianza *f*; **to enter into an a. with sb,** aliarse con algn.

allied [ˈælaɪd] *adj Pol* aliado,-a; *(connected)* relacionado,-a, asociado,-a **(with, to,** con).

alligator [ˈælɪgeɪtəʳ] *n* caimán *m*.

all-important [ɔːlɪmˈpɔːtənt] *adj* transcendental, de suma importancia.

all-in [ˈɔːlɪn] *adj (price)* todo incluido, global. ■ *Sport* **a.-in wrestling,** lucha *f* libre.

alliteration [əlɪtəˈreɪʃən] *n* aliteración *f*.

all-night [ˈɔːlnaɪt] *adj (café, cinema, etc)* abierto,-a toda la noche; *(vigil)* que dura toda la noche.

allocate [ˈæləkeɪt] *vtr (time, accommodation)* asignar; *(money)* destinar **(to,** para).

allocation [æləˈkeɪʃən] *n* **1** *(distribution) (of time, accommodation)* asignación *f*; *(of money)* distribución *f*. **2** *(amount allocated)* cuota *f*.

allot [əˈlɒt] *vtr (pt & pp allotted) (time)* asignar; *(money)* destinar, distribuir.

allotment [əˈlɒtmənt] *n* **1** *(distribution) (of time)* asignación *f*; *(of money)* distribución *f*. **2** *(land)* parcela *f*, huerta *f*.

all-out [ˈɔːlaʊt] **I** *adj (effort)* supremo,-a; *(attack)* concentrado,-a; *(strike)* total. **II all out** *adv* **to go a.-o. to do sth,** emplearse a fondo para hacer algo.

allow [əˈlaʊ] *vtr* **1** *(permit)* permitir, dejar; *(a request)* acceder a; **a. me!,** ¡permítame!; **are we allowed to smoke here?,** ¿se puede fumar aquí?; **to a. sb to do sth,** permitir *or* dejar que algn haga algo; **you are not allowed to go in,** está prohibido *or* se prohíbe entrar. **2** *(allot) (time)* dejar, conceder; *(money)* destinar; **to a. a week to finish the job,** dejar una semana para terminar el trabajo; **to a. sb time to pay,** conceder a algn tiempo para pagar. ◆ **allow for** *vi* tener en cuenta, tomar en consideración; **allowing for delays,** teniendo en cuenta los retrasos.

allowable [əˈlaʊəbəl] *adj (expense)* deducible.

allowance [əˈlaʊəns] *n (payment)* pensión *f*, subvención *f*; *(of food)* ración *f*; *(discount)* descuento *m*, rebaja *f*; **to make allowances for sb/sth,** disculpar a algn/tener algo en cuenta. ■ **family a.,** subsidio *m* familiar; **tax a.,** desgravación *f* fiscal; **travel a.,** dietas *fpl* de viaje.

alloy [ˈælɔɪ] *n* aleación *f*.

all-powerful [ɔːlˈpaʊəfʊl] *adj* todopoderoso,-a.

all-purpose [ˈɔːlpɜːpəs] *adj* para todos los usos.

all-right [ɔːlˈraɪt] **I** *adj (okay)* bien; **it's a. r., but it's nothing special,** está bien, pero no es nada especial; **don't worry, you'll soon be a. r.,** no te preocupes, pronto te encontrarás bien; **thank you very much —that's a. r.,** muchas gracias —de nada; *fam* **she's a bit of a. r.,** está buenísima. **II** *adv* **1** *(well)* bien; **is the car going a. r.?,** ¿va bien el coche? **2** *(definitely)* ciertamente, sin duda; **he's dead a. r.,** está muerto y bien muerto. **3** *(agreement)* de acuerdo, vale; **I'll give you a ring tomorrow —a. r.,** te llamaré mañana —vale.

all-round [ɔːlˈraʊnd] *adj (artist, athlete, picture, etc)* completo,-a, polifacético,-a.

all-rounder [ɔːlˈraʊndəʳ] *n* polifacético,-a *m,f*, persona *f* que hace de todo.

allspice *n* [ˈɔːlspaɪs] pimienta *f* inglesa.

all-star [ˈɔːlstɑːʳ] *adj Theat Cin* **a.-s. cast,** reparto *m* estelar.

all-time [ˈɔːltaɪm] *adj* **an a.-t. low,** una baja sin antecedente; *Theat Cin* **the a.-t. greats,** los grandes de siempre.

allude [əˈluːd] *vi* aludir, hacer alusión *or* referencia **(to,** a).

allure [əˈljʊəʳ] *n* atractivo *m*, encanto *m*.

alluring [əˈljʊərɪŋ] *adj (person)* atractivo,-a; *(thing)* tentador,-a.

allusion [əˈluːʒən] *n* alusión *f*, referencia *f*.

alluvial [əˈluːvɪəl] *adj* aluvial.

ally [ˈælaɪ] **I** *n* aliado,-a *m, f*. **II** *vtr (pt & pp allied)* **to a. oneself to/with sb,** aliarse a/con algn.

almanac [ˈɔːlmənæk] *n* almanaque *m*.

almighty [ɔːlˈmaɪtɪ] *adj (all-powerful)* todopoderoso,-a, omnipotente; *fam (great, terrible)* **an a. din,** un ruido de mil demonios. **II the A.** *n* El Todopoderoso.

Almohade [ˈælməheɪd] *n Hist* almohade *m*.

almond [ˈɑːmənd] *n (nut)* almendra *f*. ■ **a. tree,** almendro *m*.

almost [ˈɔːlməʊst] *adv* casi, por poco; **it's a. noon,** es casi mediodía; **he a. cried,** por poco llora.

alms [ɑːmz] *npl* limosna *f* sing.

aloft [əˈlɒft] *adv* arriba, en lo alto; *Naut* en la arboladura.

alone [əˈləʊn] **I** *adj* solo,-a; **can I speak to you a.?,** ¿puedo hablar contigo a solas?; **I can't afford a bicycle, let a car,** no me puedo pagar una bicicleta, y muchos menos un coche; **I did it a.,** lo hice yo solo; **leave it a.!,** ¡no lo toques!; **leave me a.,** déjame en paz, déjame tranquilo; **to be a.,** estar solo,-a; **you're not a. in thinking like that,** no eres el único que piensa así. **II** *adv* solamente, sólo; **they a. know,** sólo ellos lo saben.

along [ə'lɒŋ] I adv (forward, on) come a.!, ¡anda, ven!; he'll be a. in 10 minutes, llegará dentro de 10 min.; move a. please!, ¡circulen, por favor!; she came a. with us, vino con nosotros, nos acompañó; the whole family was there, a. with the dog, estaba allí toda la familia, junto con el perro; to go or move a., avanzar. II prep (the length of) a lo largo de, por; he walked a. the street, anduvo por la calle; their house is a. here, su casa está por aquí; there are trees a. the path, hay árboles a lo largo del camino.

alongside [ə'lɒŋsaɪd] I adv Naut de costado; to come a., atracar. II prep (beside) al costado de; to come a. the quay, atracar en el muelle.

aloof [ə'lu:f] I adj (person) distante, reservado,-a. II adv a distancia; to keep oneself a., mantenerse a distancia (from, de).

aloofness [ə'lu:fnɪs] n distanciamiento m, reserva f.

aloud [ə'laʊd] adv en voz alta.

alphabet ['ælfəbet] n alfabeto m.

alphabetical [ælfə'betɪkəl] adj alfabético,-a. ◆ alphabetically adv por orden alfabético.

alpine ['ælpaɪn] adj (club, hotel) alpino,-a; (scenery) alpestre.

Alps ['ælps] npl the A., los Alpes.

already [ɔːl'redɪ] adv ya; have you finished a.?, ¿ya has terminado?

alright [ɔːl'raɪt] adj & adv see **all right**.

Alsatian [æl'seɪʃən] n (dog) pastor m alemán.

also ['ɔːlsəʊ] adv también, además; not only milk but a. butter, no solamente leche sino también mantequilla.

also-ran ['ɔːlsəʊræn] n (horse) caballo m no clasificado; fam (person) nulidad f.

alt abbr of **altitude**, altitud f, alt.

altar ['ɔːltəʳ] n altar m.

alter ['ɔːltəʳ] I vtr (change) (plan) cambiar, retocar; (project) modificar; (opinion) cambiar de; (clothing) arreglar, retocar; (timetable) revisar. II vi cambiar, cambiarse; we found it greatly altered, lo encontramos muy cambiado.

alteration [ɔːltə'reɪʃən] n (to plan) cambio m; (to project) modificación f; (to clothing) arreglo m, retoque m; (to timetable) revisión f; Archit **alterations**, reformas fpl, obras fpl.

altercation [ɔːltə'keɪʃən] n altercado m, disputa f.

alternate [ɔːl'tɜːnɪt] I adj alterno,-a; on a. days, cada dos días, un día sí y otro no. II ['ɔːltəneɪt] vtr alternar. III vi to a. with sb/sth, alternar con algn/algo; Elec **alternating current**, corriente f alterna. ◆ alternately adv alternativamente; a. hot and cold, ahora caliente, ahora frío.

alternative [ɔːl'tɜːnətɪv] I adj (possibilities, routes, etc) alternativo,-a; (medicine, theatre, etc) an a. proposal, una contrapropuesta. II n alternativa f, opción f; I have no a. but to accept, no tengo más remedio que aceptar; let's look at the alternatives, miremos las alternativas. ◆ alternatively adv por otra parte, o bien; a. you could walk, o bien podrías ir andando.

alternator ['ɔːltəneɪtəʳ] n Aut Elec alternador m.

although [ɔːl'ðəʊ] conj aunque; a. it's late, aunque es tarde.

altitude ['æltɪtjuːd] n altitud f.

alto ['æltəʊ] adj & n (pl altos) Mus (male singer, instrument) alto m; (female singer) contralto (f).

altogether [ɔːltə'geðəʳ] adv (in total) en conjunto, en total; (completely) enteramente, completamente, del todo; we weren't a. happy with the result, no quedamos del todo satisfechos con el resultado; fam in the a., (naked) en cueros.

altruism ['æltruːɪzəm] n altruismo m.

altruist ['æltruːɪst] n altruista mf.

aluminium [æljʊ'mɪnɪəm] n, US **aluminum** [ə'luːmɪnəm] n aluminio m.

always ['ɔːlweɪz] adv 1 siempre; he's a. working, siempre está trabajando, I will a. love you, te quiero para siempre. 2 (as a last resort) como último recurso, you can a. take the train, como último recurso puedes ir en tren

AM [eɪ'em] 1 Rad abbr of **amplitude modulation**, modulación f de amplitud, AM 2 US see **MA**.

am [æm] 1st person sing pres see **be**.

a.m. [eɪ'em] abbr of ante meridiem (before noon), de la mañana

amalgam [ə'mælgəm] n amalgama f

amalgamate [ə'mælgəmeɪt] I vtr (metals) amalgamar; (companies) fusionar II vt (metals) amalgamarse; (companies) fusionarse

amalgamation [əmælgə'meɪʃən] n fusión f, unión f

amass [ə'mæs] vtr (fortune) amasar, (money) amontonar, (information) acumular

amateur ['æmətəʳ] I n amateur mf, aficionado,-a m,f, pej chapucero,-a m,f II adj (painter etc) aficionado,-a, (work etc) de aficionado,-a, pej chapucero,-a, poco profesional

amateurish ['æmətərɪʃ] adj chapucero,-a, inexperto,-a

amaze [ə'meɪz] vtr asombrar, pasmar, to be amazed at sth, quedarse pasmado,-a de algo

amazement [ə'meɪzmənt] n asombro m, sorpresa f, they watched in a., miraron asombrados, to my a., they arrived, para gran sorpresa mía, llegaron

amazing [ə'meɪzɪŋ] adj asombroso,-a, extraordinario,-a, increíble

ambassador [æm'bæsədəʳ] n embajador,-a m,f

amber ['æmbəʳ] I n ámbar m II adj ambarino,-a; (traffic light) amarillo,-a

ambidextrous [æmbɪ'dekstrəs] adj ambidextro,-a, ambidiestro,-a.

ambiguity [æmbɪ'gjuːɪtɪ] n ambigüedad f, doble sentido m

ambiguous [æm'bɪgjʊəs] adj ambiguo,-a

ambition [æm'bɪʃən] n ambición f, her a. is to be famous, ambiciona ser famosa, to have a., tener ambición

ambitious [æm'bɪʃəs] adj (person) ambicioso,-a, (plan) grandioso,-a

ambivalent [æm'bɪvələnt] adj ambivalente.

amble ['æmbəl] vt (horse) amblar, (person) deambular, andar a paso lento

ambulance ['æmbjʊləns] n ambulancia f ■ a. man, ambulanciero m

ambush ['æmbʊʃ] I n emboscada f II vtr tender una emboscada a, fig atacar por sorpresa

ameba [ə'miːbə] n (pl amebas or amebi [ə'miːbiː]) US amiba f

amen [ɑː'men] interj amén.

amenable [ə'miːnəbəl] adj susceptible, sumiso,-a, a. to reason, razonable, he isn't a. to reason, no se deja convencer

amend [ə'mend] I vtr (text, law) enmendar, (error) subsangar, corregir. II vt (text, law) enmendarse, (error) subsanarse, corregirse

amendment [ə'mendmənt] n enmienda f

amends [ə'mendz] npl to make a. to sb for sth, compensar a algn por algo

amenities [ə'miːnɪtɪz] npl (of house etc) comodidades fpl, (of district etc) facilidades fpl

America [ə'merɪkə] n (continent) América, (USA) (los) Estados Unidos ■ Central A., América Central, Centroamérica, North A., América del Norte, Norteamérica, South A., América del Sur, Sudamérica, (the) United States of A., (los) Estados Unidos

American [ə'merɪkən] adj & n (gen) americano,-a (m,f), (of USA) norteamericano,-a (m, f), estadounidense (mf), Central A., centroamericano,-a (m, f), North A., norteamericano,-a (m,f), South A., sudamericano,-a (m,f)

Americanism [ə'merɪkənɪzəm] *n* americanismo *m*

amethyst ['æmɪθɪst] *n* amatista *f*

amiable [eɪmɪəbəl] *adj* amable, afable, simpático,-a **(to, towards,** con)

amicable ['æmɪkəbəl] *adj (relationship, agreement, etc)* amistoso,-a, amigable

amid(st) ['əmɪd(st)] *prep* entre, en medio de

amiss [ə'mɪs] *adj & adv* mal, **there's sth a.,** algo anda mal, **to take sth a.,** tomar algo a mal

ammonia [ə'məʊnɪə] *n* amoníaco *m*

ammunition [æmju'nɪʃən] *n* municiones *fpl*, *fig (in argument etc)* argumentos *mpl*

amnesia [æm'niːʒə] *n* amnesia *f*

amnesty ['æmnɪstɪ] *n* amnistía *f*

amoeba [ə'miːbə] *n (pl amoebas or amoebae* [ə'miːbiː]) amiba *f*

amok [ə'mɒk] *adv* **to run a.,** *(person)* volverse loco,-a, destruirlo todo a su paso, *fig (inflation etc)* desbocarse

among(st) [ə'mʌŋ(st)] *prep* entre, **he was a. those chosen,** se encontraba entre los elegidos, **sort it out a. yourselves,** arregláoslo entre vosotros, **the money was divided a. them,** se repartieron el dinero entre sí

amoral [eɪ'mɒrəl] *adj* amoral

amorous ['æmərəs] *adj* cariñoso,-a, tierno,-a

amorphous [ə'mɔːfəs] *adj* amorfo,-a

amount [ə'maʊnt] *n (quantity)* cantidad *f*, *(of money)* suma *f*, *(of bill)* importe *m*, **don't worry, you'll have any a. of time,** no te preocupes, tendrás muchísimo tiempo, **the work requires a certain a. of patience,** el trabajo exige mucha paciencia. ◆ **amount to** *vtr* ascender or subir a, *fig* equivaler a, significar, **her debts a. to £500,** sus deudas ascienden a 500 libras esterlinas, *fig* **it amounts to a go-ahead,** equivale a una autorización, *fig* **it amounts to the same thing,** esco viene a ser lo mismo, *fig* **it doesn't a. to much,** no llega a ser gran cosa

amp ['æmp] *n fam*, **ampère** ['æmpeə'] *n Elec* amperio *m*, **13 a. plug,** enchufe de 13 amperios

ampersand ['æmpəsænd] *n Typ* signo *m* '&' que significa **and**

amphetamine [æm'fetəmiːn] *n* amfetamina *f*

amphibian [æm'fɪbɪən] *adj & n* anfibio,-a *(m)*

amphibious [æm'fɪbɪəs] *adj* anfibio,-a

amphitheatre, *US* **amphitheater** ['æmfɪθɪətə'] *n* anfiteatro *m*

ample ['æmpəl] *adj (enough)* bastante, *(more than enough)* abundante, *(large)* amplio,-a, **a. resources,** grandes recursos, **a. time,** mucho tiempo ◆ **amply** *adv (sufficiently)* bastante, suficientemente, *(abundantly)* abundantemente, *(greatly)* ampliamente, **we were a. rewarded,** nos recompensaron plenamente

amplifier ['æmplɪfaɪə'] *n* amplificador *m*

amplify ['æmplɪfaɪ] *vtr (pt & pp **amplified**) (sound)* amplificar; *(statement etc)* ampliar.

amputate ['æmpjʊteɪt] *vtr* amputar.

amputation [æmpjʊ'teɪʃən] *n* amputación *f*.

Amsterdam ['æmstədæm] *n* Amsterdam.

amuck [ə'mʌk] *adv see* **amok.**

amuse [ə'mjuːz] *vtr* divertir, entretener, distraer; **to a. oneself (by) doing sth,** entretenerse haciendo algo; **to be amused by sth,** encontrar a log divertido; **to keep sb amused,** entretener a algn.

amusement [ə'mjuːzmənt] *n (enjoyment)* diversión *f*, distracción *f*; *(laughter)* risa *f*; *(pastime)* pasatiempo *m*; **much to our a.,** para gran regocijo nuestro. ■ **a. arcade,** salón *m* de juegos; **a. park,** parque *m* de atracciones.

amusing [ə'mjuːzɪŋ] *adj (fun)* divertido,-a, entretenido,-a; *(funny)* gracioso,-a; **I found it very a.,** me reí mucho; **the a. thing is ...,** lo gracioso del caso es ... .

an [æn, *unstressed* ən] *indef art see* **a.**

anabolic steroid [ænəbɒlɪk'stɪərɔɪd] *n* esteroide *m* anabolizante.

anachronism [ə'nækrənɪzəm] *n* anacronismo *m*.

anaemia [ə'niːmɪə] *n* anemia *f*.

anaemic [ə'niːmɪk] *adj* anémico,-a; *fig (weak)* débil.

anaesthesia [ænɪs'θiːzɪə] *n* anestesia *f*.

anaesthetic [ænɪs'θetɪk] *n* anestesia *f*; **local/ general a.,** anestesia local/general *or* total.

anaesthetist [ə'niːsθətɪst] *n* anestesista *mf*.

anaesthetize [ə'niːsθətaɪz] *vtr* anestesiar.

anagram ['ænəgræm] *n* anagrama *m*.

anal ['eɪnəl] *adj* anal.

analgesic [ænəl'dʒiːsɪk] *adj & n* analgésico,-a *(m)*.

analog ['ænəlɒg] *n US see* **analogue.**

analogous [ə'næləgəs] *adj* **a. to** *or* **with,** análogo,-a *or* semejante a.

analogue ['ænəlɒg] *n* análogo *m*. ■ **a. computer,** ordenador *m* analógico; **a. watch,** reloj *m* de agujas.

analogy [ə'nælədʒɪ] *n* analogía *f*, semejanza *f*; **to draw an a. with sth/between two things,** señalar una semejanza con algo/entre dos cosas.

analyse ['ænəlaɪz] *vtr* analizar; *(psychoanalyse)* sicoanalizar.

analysis [ə'nælɪsɪs] *n (pl analyses* [ə'nælɪsiːz]) análisis *m inv*; *(psychoanalysis)* sicoanálisis *m*; **in the final a.,** a fin de cuentas.

analyst ['ænəlɪst] *n* analista *mf*; *(psychoanalyst)* sicoanalista *mf*.

analyze ['ænəlaɪz] *vtr US see* **analyse.**

analytic(al) [ænə'lɪtɪk(əl)] *adj* analítico,-a.

anarchist ['ænəkɪst] *n* anarquist *mf*.

anarchy ['ænəkɪ] *n* anarquía *f*.

anathema [ə'næθəmə] *n Rel* anatema *m*; *fig (curse)* maldición *f*; **the very idea was a. to him,** le repugnaba sólo de pensarlo.

anatomical [ænə'tɒmɪkəl] *adj* anatómico,-a.

anatomy [ə'nætəmɪ] *n* anatomía *f*.

ancestor ['ænsestə'] *n* antepasado *m*.

ancestral [æn'sestrəl] *adj* ancestral; **a. home,** casa *f* solariega.

ancestry ['ænsestrɪ] *n (ancestors)* ascendencia *f*; *(line)* solera *f*, abolengo *m*; **of noble a.,** de rancio abolengo.

anchor ['æŋkə'] **I** *n Naut* ancla *f*; *fig* ancora *f*, seguridad *f*; **to drop a.,** echar el ancla; **to weigh a.,** levar anclas, zarpar. **II** *vtr Naut* anclar; *fig (fix securely)* sujetar. **III** *vi Naut* anclar, echar el ancla.

anchovy ['æntʃəvɪ] *n (pl anchovy or anchovies) (salted)* anchoa *f*; *(fresh)* boquerón *m*.

ancient ['eɪnʃənt] *adj (gen)* antiguo,-a; *(monument)* histórico,-a; *fam (very old)* viejísimo,-a; **the a. world,** el mundo antiguo; **the ancients,** los antiguos.

ancillary [æn'sɪlərɪ] *adj* **a** auxiliar *(mf)*; **a. staff,** *(in hospital)* personal *m* auxiliar.

and [ænd, *unstressed* ənd, ən] *conj* y; *(before i-, hi-)* e; **a hundred a. one,** ciento uno; **a. so on,** etcétera; **Bill a. Pat,** Bill y Pat; **Chinese a. Indian,** chino e indio; **come a. see us,** ven a vernos; **four a. a half,** cuatro y medio; **she cried a. cried,** no paró de llorar; **try a. help me,** trata de ayudarme; **wait a. see,** espera a ver; **worse a. worse,** cada vez peor.

Andalusia [ændə'luːzɪə] *n* Andalucía.

Andalusian [ændə'luːzɪən] *adj & n* andaluz,-a.

Andean [æn'diːən, 'ændɪən] *adj* andino,-a.

Andes ['ændiːz] *npl* **the A.,** los Andes.

Andorra [æn'dɔːrə] *n* Andorra.

Andorran [æn'dɔːrən] *adj & n* andorrano,-a *(m, f)*.

androgynous [ənˈdrɒdʒɪnəs] *adj* andrógino,-a.

anecdote [ˈænɪkdəʊt] *n* anécdota *f*.

anemia [əˈniːmɪə] *n US see* **anaemia.**

anemic [əˈniːmɪk] *adj US see* **anaemic.**

anemone [əˈnemənɪ] *n Bot* anémona *f*. ■ **sea a.,** anémona *f* de mar.

aneroid [ˈænərɔɪd] *adj* aneroide.

anesthesia [ænɪsˈθiːzɪə] *n US see* **anaesthesia.**

anesthesiologist [ænɪsθiːzɪˈɒlədʒɪst] *n US see* **anaesthetist.**

anesthetic [ænɪsˈθetɪk] *n US see* **anaesthetic.**

anesthetize [əˈniːsθətaɪz] *vtr US see* **anaesthetize.**

angel [ˈeɪndʒəl] *n* ángel *m*; *fam (nice person)* encanto *m*, cielo *m*, sol *m*; **be an a.,** sé amable; **you're an a.!,** ¡eres un cielo! ■ **guardian a.,** ángel *m* custodio *or* de la guarda.

angelic [ænˈdʒelɪk] *adj (face)* angelical; *(smile, expression)* angélico,-a.

angelica [ænˈdʒelɪkə] *n Culin* angélica *f*.

anger [ˈæŋɡəʳ] **I** *n* cólera *f*, ira *f*; **fit of a.,** ataque *m* de cólera; **to act/speak in a.,** obrar llevado,-a por la cólera/ hablar con indignación. **II** *vtr* ecolerizar, enojar.

angina (pectoris) [ænˈdʒaɪnə (ˈpektərɪs)] *n Med* angina *f* (del pecho).

Angle [ˈæŋɡəl] *n Hist* anglo,-a *m,f*.

angle¹ [ˈæŋɡəl] *n Math* ángulo *m*; *fig* punto *m* de vista, perspectiva *f*; **a new a. to the story,** una nueva perspective de la historia; **at an a. of 45°,** en ángulo de 45 grados. ■ **right a.,** ángulo *m* recto.

angle² [ˈæŋɡəl] *vi (fish)* pescar con caña; *fig* **to a. for an invitation,** intentar hacerse con una invitación.

angler [ˈæŋɡləʳ] *n* pescador,-a *m,f* de caña. ■ **a. fish,** rape *m*.

Anglican [ˈæŋɡlɪkən] *adj & n* anglicano,-a *(m,f)*.

Anglicism [ˈæŋɡlɪsɪzəm] *n* anglicismo *m*.

anglicize [ˈæŋɡlɪsaɪz] *vtr* anglicanizar.

Anglophile [ˈæŋɡləʊfaɪl] *n* anglófilo,-a *m,f*.

Anglo-Saxon [æŋɡləʊˈsæksən] *adj & n* anglosajón,-ona *(m,f)*.

Angola [æŋˈɡəʊlə] *n* Angola.

Angolan [æŋˈɡəʊlən] *adj & n* angoleño,-a *(m,f)*.

angora [æˈŋɡɔːrə] *n Tex* angora *f*. ■ **a. goat/rabbit,** cabra *f*/conejo *m* de angora.

angry [ˈæŋɡrɪ] *adj (angrier, angriest) (person, letter, etc)* enfadado,-a, ofendido,-a; *(wound)* inflamado,-a; *(sky)* tormentoso,-a; *(voice)* airado,-a; **to be a.,** ofenderse; **to get a. with sth about sth,** enfadarse con algn por algo. ◆ **angrily** *adv* con enfado, furiosamente.

anguish [ˈæŋɡwɪʃ] *n* angustia *f*.

anguished [ˈæŋɡwɪʃt] *adj* angustiado,-a.

angular [ˈæŋɡjuləʳ] *adj (shape)* angular; *(face, features)* anguloso,-a.

animal [ˈænɪməl] **I** *adj* animal. **II** *n* animal *m*; *fig* bestia *f*.

animate [ˈænɪmɪt] **I** *adj* vivo,-a, animado,-a. **II** [ˈænɪmeɪt] *vtr* animar; *fig* estimular.

animated [ˈænɪmeɪtɪd] *adj (lively)* animado,-a, vivo,-a; **a. cartons,** dibujos *mpl* animados; **to become a.,** animarse.

animation [ænɪˈmeɪʃən] *n (liveliness)* animación *f*, vivacidad *f*.

animator [ˈænɪmeɪtəʳ] *n* animador,-a *m,f*.

animosity [ænɪˈmɒsɪtɪ] *n* animosidad *f*.

aniseed [ˈænɪsiːd] *n* anís *m*.

Ankara [ˈæŋkərə] *n* Ankara.

ankle [ˈæŋkəl] *n* tobillo *m*. ■ **a. boots,** botines *mpl*; **a. socks,** calcetines *mpl* cortos.

anklebone [ˈæŋkəlbəʊn] *n* hueso *m* del tobillo.

annals [ˈænəlz] *npl* anales *mpl*.

annex [æˈneks] *vtr (territory)* anexar.

annexe, *US* **annex** [ˈæneks] *n (building)* (edifice *m*) anexo *m*.

annihilate [əˈnaɪəleɪt] *vtr* aniquilar.

annihilation [ənaɪəˈleɪʃən] *n* aniquilación *f*.

anniversary [ænɪˈvɜːsərɪ] *n* aniversario *m*. ■ **wedding a.,** aniversario *m* de bodas.

annotate [ˈænəteɪt] *vtr (book etc)* hacer anotaciones en, comentar; **an annotated edition,** una edición crítica.

annotation [ænəˈteɪʃən] *n* anotación *f*; **annotations,** notas *fpl*.

announce [əˈnaʊns] *vtr (arrival, wedding)* anunciar; *(news)* comunicar, participar; *(fact, statement)* hacer saber, declarar; **she announced that she was going home,** declaró que se iba a casa; *(in competition etc)* **to a. the winner,** proclamar *or* anunciar el ganador.

announcement [əˈnaʊnsmənt] *n (of arrival, wedding)* anuncio *m*; *(news)* comunicación *f*, participación *f*; *(statement)* declaración *f*; *(in newspaper)* **announcements,** anuncios *mpl*; **to make an a. about sth,** anunciar *or* comunicar *or* participar algo.

announcer [əˈnaʊnsəʳ] *n TV Rad* locutor,-a *m,f*.

annoy [əˈnɔɪ] *vtr (irritate)* molestar, contrariar, fastidiar; *(anger)* enfadar; **he only does it to a.,** lo hace sólo para fastidiar; **to be annoyed with sb about** *or* **because of sth,** enfadarse *or* molestarse con algn por algo; **to get annoyed,** enfadarse, molestarse.

annoyance [əˈnɔɪəns] *n (feeling)* enfado *m*, enojo *m*; *(annoying thing)* molestia *f*, fastidio *m*.

annoying [əˈnɔɪɪŋ] *adj* molesto,-a, fastidioso,-a, enojoso,-a; **how a.!,** ¡qué fastidio!

annual [ˈænjʊəl] **I** *adj* annual. **II** *n (book)* anuario *m*; *(plant)* annual *m*, planta *f* anual. ◆ **annually** *adv* anualmente, cada año.

annuity [əˈnjuːɪtɪ] *n (pension)* renta *f* vitalicia.

annul [əˈnʌl] *vtr (pt & pp annulled) (contract, marriage)* anular.

annulment [əˈnʌlmənt] *n (of contract, marriage)* anulación *f*.

anode [ˈænəʊd] *n Elec* ánodo *m*.

anodyne [ˈænədaɪn] **I** *adj (bland)* anodino,-a, neutro,-a. **II** *n (comforter)* calmante *m*.

anoint [əˈnɔɪnt] *vtr* ungir, untar **(with,** con).

anomaly [əˈnɒməlɪ] *n* anomalía *f*.

anomalous [əˈnɒmələs] *adj* anómalo,-a.

anon¹ [əˈnɒn] *adv lit & hum (soon)* dentro de poco, ahora.

anon² [əˈnɒn] *abbr of* **anonymous,** anónimo,-a.

anonymity [ænəˈnɪmɪtɪ] *n* anonimato *m*.

anonymous [əˈnɒnɪməs] *adj* anónimo,-a; **a. letter,** anónimo *m*; **to remain a.,** conserver el anonimato. ◆ **anonymously** *adv* anónimamente.

anorak [ˈænəræk] *n* anorak *m*.

anorexia [ænəˈreksɪə] *n Med* anorexia *f*. ■ **a. nervosa,** anorexia *f* nerviosa.

another [əˈnʌðəʳ] **I** *adj (additional)* otro,-a; *(different)* (otro,-a) distinto,-a; **a. one,** otro,-a; **a. orange,** otra naranja; **in a. few days,** dentro de unos pocos días; **in a. 10 years,** en otros 10 años; **one way or a.,** de una forma o de otra; **that's a. matter,** eso es harina de otro costal; **they say he's a. Picasso,** según dicen, él es otro Picasso; **we'll do it a. time,** lo haremos en otra ocasión; **without a. word,** sin más. **II** *pron* otro,-a; have a., toma otro,-a; **to love one a.,** quererse el uno al otro *or* los unos a los otros; **we help one a.,** nos ayudamos mutuamente.

answer [ˈɑːnsəʳ] **I** *n (to letter, telephone call)* contestación *f*; *(to question)* respuesta *f*; *(to problem)* solución *f*, arreglo *m*; *(to criticism)* explicación *f*, justificación *f*; **in a. to your letter,** contestando a sucarta; **in a. to your question,** en respuesta a su pregunta; **the only a. is to**

spend less, la única solución es gastar menos; **there's no a.,** *(on telephone)* no contestan; *(at door)* no abren. **II** *vtr (letter)* contestar a; *(person, question)* contestar *or* responder a; *(criticism)* explicar, justificar; **to a. the door to sb,** abrir la puerta a algn; **to a. the telephone,** contestar el teléfono. **III** *vi* contestar, responder. ◆ **answer back** *vi* replicar; **don't a. back!,** ¡no repliques!, ¡no seas respondón! ◆ **answer for** *vtr* responder de; **to a. to sb for sth,** ser responsable ante algn de algo; **he's got a lot to a. for,** es responsible de muchas cosas. ◆ **answer to** *vtr (name)* responder a; *(description)* corresponder a; **it answers to the name of Shandy,** atiende por Shandy.

answerable ['ɑːnsərəbəl] *adj (responsible)* responsible; *(question)* que tiene solución; **he's a. to no one,** no tiene que dar cuentas a nadie; **to be a. to sb for sth,** ser responsable ante algn de algo.

answering machine ['ɑːnsərɪŋməʃiːn] *n* contestador *m* automático.

ant [ænt] *n* hormiga *f.* ■ **a. hill,** hormiguero *m.*

antacid [ænt'æsɪd] *n* antiácido *m.*

antagonism [æn'tægənɪzəm] *n* antagonismo *m,* rivalidad *f* **(between,** entre), hostilidad *f* **(towards,** hacia).

antagonist [æn'tægənɪst] *n* antagonista *mf,* adversario,-a *m,f.*

antagonistic [æntægə'nɪstɪk] *adj* hostil, agresivo,-a **(to, towards,** con).

antagonize [æn'tægənaɪz] *vtr* enemistarse con, provocar la enemistad de.

Antartic [ænt'ɑːktɪk] **I** *adj* antártico,-a. ■ **A. Ocean,** océano *m* Antártico. **II the A.** *n (polar region)* la zona antártica.

Antarctica [ænt'ɑːktɪkə] *n* Antártida.

ante- ['æntɪ] *pref* ante-.

anteater ['æntiːtəʳ] *n* oso *m* hormiguero.

antecedent ['æntɪsiːdənt] *n* antecedente *m;* **antecedents,** *(past family)* antepasados *mpl; (past events)* antecedentes *mpl.*

antedate ['æntɪdeɪt] *vtr (document, cheque)* antedatar, poner fecha anterior a; *(building, invention, etc)* anteceder, ser anterior a; **this building antedates that one by 50 years,** este edificio es cincuenta años más antiguo a aquél.

antelope ['æntɪləʊp] *n (pl* **antelope** *or* **antelopes)** antílope *m.*

antenatal [æntɪ'neɪtəl] *adj* antenatal; *(clinic)* prenatal.

antenna [æn'tenə] *n* **1** *(pl* **antennae** [æn'teniː])* *(of animal, insect)* antena *f.* **2** *(pl* **antennas)** TV Rad antena *f.*

anteroom ['æntɪruːm] *n* antesala *f; (waiting room)* sala *f* de espera.

anthem ['ænθəm] *n Mus Rel* motete *m.* ■ **national a.,** himno *m* nacional.

anthology [æn'θɒlədʒɪ] *n* antología *f.*

anthracite ['ænθrəsaɪt] *n* antracita *f.*

anthropologist [ænθrə'pɒlədʒɪst] *n* antropólogo,-a *m,f.*

anthropology [ænθrə'pɒlədʒɪ] *n* antropología *f.*

anti- ['æntɪ] **I** *pref* anti-, contra-. **II** *prep* en contra de. **III** *adj fam* en contra; **she's very a.,** está muy en contra.

anti-aircraft [æntɪ'eəkrɑːft] *adj* antiaéreo,-a.

antibiotic [æntɪbaɪ'ɒtɪk] *n* antibiótico *m.*

antibody [æntɪbɒdɪ] *n* anticuerpo *m.*

anticipate [æn'tɪsɪpeɪt] *vtr* **1** *(expect)* esperar; **do you a. any problems?,** ¿crees que surgirá algún problema?; **it was better than I anticipated,** era mejor de lo que esperaba. **2** *(predict)* prever; *(problems)* anticipar; *(get ahead of)* anticiparse a, adelantarse a.

anticipation [æntɪsɪ'peɪʃən] *n (expectation)* esperanza *f; (expectancy)* ilusión *f;* **in a. of good weather,** esperando el buen tiempo; **we waited in eager a.,** esperamos con gran ilusión.

anticlimax [æntɪ'klaɪmæks] *n* gen anticlímax *m; (disappointment)* decepción *f.*

anticlockwise [æntɪ'klɒkwaɪs] *adv* en sentido contrario a las agujas del reloj.

antics ['æntɪks] *npl (foolish behaviour)* payasadas *fpl; (naughtiness)* travesuras *fpl.*

anticyclone [æntɪ'saɪkləʊn] *n* anticiclón *m.*

antidote ['æntɪdəʊt] *n Med* antídoto *m; fig* remedio *m,* solución *f.*

antifreeze ['æntɪfriːz] *n* anticongelante *m.*

Antigua [æn'tiːgə] *n* Antigua.

antihistamine [æntɪ'hɪstəmɪn] *n* antihistamínico *m.*

Antilles [æn'tɪliːz] *npl* Antillas. ■ **Greater A.,** Grandes Antillas; **Lesser A.,** Pequeñas Antillas.

antinuclear [æntɪ'njuːklɪəʳ] *adj* antinuclear.

antipathy [æn'tɪpəθɪ] *n* antipatía *f,* ojeriza *f* **(to, towards, a,** hacia).

antipodes [æn'tɪpədiːz] *npl (point)* antípoda *m* sing; *(people)* antípodas *mpl;* **the A.,** Australia y Nueva Zelanda.

antiquarian [æntɪ'kweərɪən] **I** *adj* **a. bookseller,** librero *m* de viejo. **II** *n* anticuario,-a *m,f.*

antiquated [æntɪkweɪtɪd] *adj* anticuado,-a.

antique [æn'tiːk] **I** *adj (furniture etc)* antiguo,-a, de época. **II** *n* antigüedad *f.* ■ **a. dealer,** anticuario,-a *m,f;* **a. shop,** tienda *f* de antigüedades.

antiquity [æn'tɪkwɪtɪ] *n (ancient times)* antigüedad *f; (ancient monument)* monumento *m* antiguo *or* histórico; **of great a.,** muy antiguo,-a.

anti-Semitic [æntɪsɪ'mɪtɪk] *adj* antisemita, antisemítico,-a.

anti-Semitism [æntɪ'semɪtɪzəm] *n* antisemitismo *m.*

antiseptic [æntɪ'septɪk] *adj & n* antiséptico,-a *(m).*

antisocial [æntɪ'səʊʃəl] *adj (delinquent) (behaviour)* antisocial; *(unsociable) (person)* insociable.

antitheft [æntɪ'θeft] *adj (device etc)* antirrobo *inv.*

antithesis [æn'tɪθɪsɪs] *n (pl* **antitheses** [æn'tɪθɪsiːz])* antítesis *f.*

antler ['æntləʳ] *n* cuerna *f;* **antlers,** cornamenta *f.*

antonym ['æntənɪm] *n* antónimo *m.*

Antwerp ['æntwɜːp] *n* Amberes.

anus ['eɪnəs] *n* ano *m.*

anvil ['ænvɪl] *n* yunque *m.*

anxiety [æŋ'zaɪɪtɪ] *n (concern)* inquietud *f,* desasosiego *m; (worry)* preocupación *f; (fear)* ansiedad *f,* angustia *f; (eagerness)* ansia *f,* ansias *fpl;* **it's a great a. to us,** nos preocupa muchísimo.

anxious ['æŋkʃəs] *adj (concerned)* inquieto,-a; *(worried)* preocupado,-a; *(fearful)* angustiado,-a; *(eager)* ansioso,-a, deseoso,-a; **an a. moment,** un momento de angustia; **a. to please,** deseoso,-a de complacer; **to be a. about sth,** estar preocupado,-a or algo. ◆ **anxiously** *adv (worriedly)* con inquietud *or* preocupación; *(eagerly)* ansiosamente.

any ['enɪ] **I** *adj (in questions)* algún-una; *(in negative clauses)* ningún,-una; *(no matter which)* cualquier,-a; *(every)* todo,-a; **a. doctor will tell you the same thing,** cualquier médico te dirá lo mismo; **are there a. seats left on the express?,** ¿quedan plazas en el expreso?; **at a. moment,** en cualquier momento; **have you a. apples?,** ¿tienes manzanas?; **have you a. money?,** ¿tienes (algo de) dinero?; **have you a. time,** no tengo tiempo; **in a. case,** en todo caso, de todas formas; **she did it without a. difficulty,** lo hizo sin ninguna dificultad. **II** *prep (in questions)* alguno,-a; *(in negative clauses)* ninguno,-a; *(no matter which)* cualquiera; **have they got a.?,** ¿tienen alguno?; **I don't want a.,** no quiero ninguno,-a; **I need some paper, have you a.?,** necesito papel, ¿tienes?; **we can have a. (one),** coge el *or* la que quieras. **III** *adv* **we**

don't go **a. longer,** ya no vamos más; **is there a. more?,** ¿hay más?; **I used to like it but not a. more,** antes me gustaba pero ya no; **is it a. good?,** ¿sirve para algo?

anybody ['enɪbɒdɪ] *pron (in questions)* alguien, alguno,-a; *(in negative clauses)* nadie, ninguno,-a; *(no matter who)* caulquiera, cualquier persona; **a. but me,** caulquiera menos yo; **a. will tell you so,** cualquiera te lo dirá; **a. would think he was poor,** cualquiera diría que es pobre; **bring a. you like,** trae a quien quieras; **do you see a. over there?,** ¿ves a alguien allí?; **I can't find a.,** no encuentro a nadie; **it's a.'s guess,** quién sabrá; **we don't know a. else,** no conocemos a nadie más.

anyhow ['enɪhaʊ] *adv* **1** *(in spite of that)* en todo caso, de todas formas; *(changing the subject)* bueno, pues; **a., I said to him ...,** bueno, pues le dije ...; **a., they arrived eventually,** de todas formas al final llegaron. **2** *(carelessly)* desordenadamente, de cualquier modo *or* forma; **don't just leave it a.,** no lo dejes de cualquier forma.

anyone ['enɪwʌn] *pron see* **anybody.**

anyplace ['enɪpleɪs] *adv US Canada see* **anywhere.**

anything ['enɪθɪŋ] **I** *pron* **1** *(in questions)* algo, alguna cosa; *(in negative clauses)* nada; *(no matter what)* cualquier cosa; **a. but that,** cualquier cosa menos eso; **a. else?,** ¿algo más?; **can I do a. for you?,** ¿puedo ayudarte en algo?; **don't think a. of it,** no tiene importancia; **hardly a.,** casi nada; **he's a. but shy,** tímido no lo es; **if a., I'd buy the big one,** de comprar uno compraría el grande. **II** *adv fam* **as easy/hard as a.,** de lo más fácil/difícil; **is this a. like what you wanted?,** ¿viene a ser éste lo que te querías?; **to run/work like a.,** correr/trabajar a más no poder.

anyway ['enɪweɪ] *adv see* **anyhow.**

anywhere ['enɪweəʳ] *adv* **1** *(in questions) (situation)* en algún sitio, en alguna parte; *(movement)* a algún sitio *or* alguna parte; **could it be a. else?,** ¿podría estar en otro sitio?; **did you go a. yesterday?,** ¿fuiste a alguna parte ayer? **2** *(in negative clauses) (situation)* en ningún sitio *or* ninguna parte; *(movement)* a ningún sitio *or* ninguna parte; *(no matter where)* dondequiera, donde sea, a *or* en caulquier parte; **go a. you like,** ve a donde quieras; **she isn't a. near as clever as her sister,** no es ni con mucho tan inteligente como su hermana; **she'll look for a job a. she can,** buscará un trabajo donde sea; **we aren't a. near finished,** no hemos terminado ni mucho menos; **we couldn't find a shop open a.,** no encontramos una tienda abierta en ningún sitio.

aorta [eɪˈɔːtə] *n (pl* **aortas** *or* **aortae** [eɪˈɔːtiː]) aorta *f*.

apart [əˈpɑːt] *adv* **1** *(in pieces)* aparte; **to come** *or* **fall a.,** deshacerse; *(unstuck)* despegarse; **to take sth a.,** desmontar algo. **2** *(distant)* alejado,-a; *(separate)* aparte, separado,-a; **the chairs are too far a.,** las sillas están demasiado separadas; **they live a.,** viven separados; **to be poles a.,** ser polos opuestos; **you can't tell the twins a.,** no se puede distinguir los mellizos el uno del otro. **3** *(except for)* aparte de; **joking a.,** bromas aparte; **a. from a few scratches he was unhurt,** aparte de algunos rasguños salió ileso; **a. from the fact that it was late,** dejando aparte el hecho de que era tarde.

apartheid [əˈpɑːtheɪt] *n* apartheid *m*.

apartment [əˈpɑːtmənt] *n (large room)* salón *m*; *US (flat)* apartamento *m*, piso *m*. ■ **a. block,** bloque *m* de pisos.

apathetic [æpəˈθetɪk] *adj* apático,-a.

apathy ['æpəθɪ] *n* apatía *f*.

ape [eɪp] **I** *n (anthropoid)* antropomorfo *m*, antropoideo *m*; *(loosely)* mono *m*, simio *m*. **II** *vtr* imitar, copiar.

Apennines ['æpənaɪnz] *npl* **the A.,** los Apeninos

apéritif [əˈperɪtiːf] *n* aperitivo *m*.

aperture ['æpətʃəʳ] *n (hole, crack)* resquicio *m*, rendija *f*; *Phot* abertura *f*.

APEX ['eɪpeks] *Av abbr of* **Advance Purchase Excursion,** APEX.

apex ['eɪpeks] *n (pl* **apexes** *or* **apices** ['eɪpɪsiːz]) *(top)* ápice *m*; *(of triangle)* vértice *m*; *fig* cumbre *f*.

aphid ['eɪfɪd] *n* afidio *m*.

aphorism ['æfərɪzəm] *n* aforismo *m*.

aphrodisiac [æfrəˈdɪzɪæk] **I** *adj* afrodisíaco,-a. **II** *n* afrodisíaco *m*.

apiece [əˈpiːs] *adv* cada uno,-a; **they cost 100 pesetas a.,** cuestan 100 pesetas la unidad; **we were given two a.,** nos dieron dos para cada uno.

aplomb [əˈplɒm] *n* aplomo *m*, sangre *f* fría.

apocalypse [əˈpɒkəlɪps] *n* apocalipsis *m inv*.

apocalyptic [əpɒkəˈlɪptɪk] *adj* apocalíptico,-a.

Apocrypha [əˈpɒkrɪfə] *npl* libros *mpl* apócrifos de la Biblia.

apocryphal [əˈpɒkrɪfəl] *adj* apócrifo,-a.

apogee ['æpədʒiː] *n* apogeo *m*.

apolitical [eɪpəˈlɪtɪkəl] *adj* apolítico,-a.

apologetic [əpɒləˈdʒetɪk] *adj (remorseful)* compungido,-a; **he was very a.,** pidió mil perdones; **to be a. towards sb about sth,** pedirle a algn perdón por algo. ◆ **apologetically** *adv* disculpándose, pidiendo perdón.

apologize [əˈpɒlədʒaɪz] *vi (say sorry)* disculparse, pedir perdón; *(for absence)* presentar sus excusas; **they apologized to us for the delay,** nos pidieron perdón por el retraso, se disculparon con nosotros por el retraso.

apology [əˈpɒlədʒɪ] *n* disculpa *f*, excusa *f*; **I owe you an a.,** tengo que pedirte perdón; **please accept our apologies,** le rogamos nos disculpe; **to offer one's apologies,** presentar sus excusas, disculparse; *fam* **what an a. for a meal!,** ¡vaya birria de comida!

apoplectic [æpəˈplektɪk] *adj Med* apopléctico,-a; *fam* **to be a. with rage,** ponerse furioso,-a.

apoplexy ['æpəpleksɪ] *n Med* apoplegía *f*.

apostasy [əˈpɒstəsɪ] *n* apostasía *f*.

apostle [əˈpɒsəl] *n* apóstol *m*.

apostolic [æpəˈstɒlɪk] *adj* apostólico,-a.

apostrophe [əˈpɒstrəfɪ] *n* apóstrofo *m*.

apotheosis [əpɒθɪˈəʊsɪs] *n (pl* **apotheoses** [əpɒθɪˈəʊsiːz]) apoteosis *f inv*.

appal, *US* **appall** [əˈpɔːl] *vtr (pt & pp* **appalled)** horrorizar; **to be appalled by sth,** quedar horrorizado,-a por algo.

Appalachians [æpəˈleɪtʃɪənz] *npl* los (montes) Appalaches.

appalling [əˈpɔːlɪŋ] *adj (horrifying)* horroroso,-a; *fam (very bad)* pésimo,-a, fatal.

apparatus [æpəˈreɪtəs] *n (pl* **apparatuses** *or* **apparatus)** *(instrument)* aparato *m*; *(equipment)* equipo *m*; *(in gymnasium)* aparatos de gimnasia; **a piece of a.,** un aparato. ■ **breathing a.,** aparato *m* respiratorio; **scientific a.,** utensilios *mpl* de laboratorio.

apparent [əˈpærənt] *adj (obvious)* evidente, manifiesto,-a; *(seeming)* aparente; **it's a. that he's wrong,** está claro *or* es evidente que está equivocado; **her a. indifference,** su aire de indiferencia; **to become a.,** ponerse de manifiesto, quedar claro. ◆ **apparently** *adv (obviously)* evidentemente; *(seemingly)* aparentemente, por lo visto.

apparition [æpəˈrɪʃən] *n (appearance)* aparición *f*; *(spirit)* aparición *f*, fantasma *m*, espectro *m*.

appeal [əˈpiːl] **I** *n* **1** *(request)* ruego *m*, solicitud *f*; *(plea)* súplica *f*; **an a. for help/money,** una solicitud de ayuda/dinero; **to make an a. for sth,** pedir *or* solicitar algo. **2** *(attraction)* atractivo *m*, encanto *m*; *(interest)* interés *m*; **that type of music has lost its a.,** esa clase de música ha perdido su encanto. ■ **sex a.,** atractivo *m* sexual. **3** *Jur* apelación *f*, recurso *m*; **to lodge an a.,** presentar una apelación, interponer un recurso. ■ **right of a.,** derecho *m* de apelación. **II** *vi* **1** *(plead)* rogar, suplicar **(to,** a); **to a. for help,** pedir *or* solicitar ayuda; **to a. to sb's better nature,** apelar a los sentimientos humanitarios de algn. **2** *(attract)* atraer; *(interest)* interesar; **it doesn't a. to me,** no me atrae. **3** *Jur* apelar; **to a. against a decision,** apelar contra un fallo. **4** *Sport* apelar; **to a. to the referee,** apelar al árbitro.

appealing [ə'pi:lɪŋ] *adj (moving)* conmovedor,-a; *(attractive)* atractivo,-a, bonito,-a; *(tempting)* atrayente, tentador,-a.

appear [ə'pɪəʳ] *vi (become visible)* aparecer; *(publicly)* presentarse; *(on stage)* actuar; **she appeared round the corner,** apareció por la esquina; **to a. before a court/a committee,** comparecer ante un tribunal/un comité; **to a. in the shops,** salir a la venta; **to a. on behalf of sb,** aparecer en nombre de algn; **to a. on television,** salir en la televisión. **2** *(seem)* parecer; **he appears relaxed,** parece relajado; **she appears to be right,** parece qué tiene razón; **so it appears,** según parece; **there appears to have been a mistake,** parece que ha habido un error.

appearance [ə'pɪərəns] *n* **1** *(becoming visible)* aparición *f*; *(publicly)* presentación *f*; *(on stage)* actuación *f*; *(before court, committee)* comparecencia *f*; *(of book etc)* publicación *f*; *(in shops)* salida *f* a la venta; **to make one's first a.,** debutar; **to put in an a.,** hacer acto de presencia. **2** *(look)* apariencia *f*, aspecto *m*; **by** *or* **to all appearances,** al parecer, a todas luces; **don't judge by appearances,** no juzgues según las apariencias; **smart in a.,** de aspecto elegante; **to keep up apperances,** guardar las apariencias.

appease [ə'pi:z] *vtr (anger)* apaciguar, aplacar; *(curiosity, hunger)* satisfacer.

appeasement [ə'pi:zmənt] *n Pol* **policy of a.,** política *f* de pacificación.

append [ə'pend] *vtr* añadir **(to,** a).

appendage [ə'pendɪdʒ] *n* apéndice *m*, añadidura *f*.

appendicitis [əpendɪ'saɪtɪs] *n Med* apendicitis *f*.

appendix [ə'pendɪks] *n (pl* **appendixes** *or* **appendices** [ə'pendɪsɪːz]) apéndice *m*; **to have one's a. taken out,** operarse de apendicitis.

appetite ['æpɪtaɪt] *n* apetito *m* **(for,** para); *fig* deseo *m*, ganas *fpl* **(for,** de); **it will spoil your a.,** te quitará el apetito; **to have a good** *or* **healthy a.,** tener buen apetito; **to whet one's a.,** abrirse el apetito.

appetizer ['æpɪtaɪzəʳ] *n (drink)* aperitivo *m*; *(snack)* aperitivo *m*, tapa *f*, pincho *m*.

appetizing ['æpɪtaɪzɪŋ] *adj* apetitoso,-a.

applaud [ə'plɔːd] **I** *vtr* aplaudir; *fig (actions, decision)* aprobar. **II** *vi* aplaudir, palmotear.

applause [ə'plɔːz] *n* aplausos *mpl.*

apple ['æpəl] *n (fruit)* manzana *f*; **she's the a. of his eye,** la cuida sí fuera la niña de los ojos. ■ **a. core,** corazón *m* de la manzana; **a. pie,** tarta *f* de manzana; **a. tree,** manzano *m*; **cooking a.,** manzana *f* para compota.

apple-pie ['æpəlpaɪ] *adj fam* **in a.-p. order,** arregladito,-a, ordenadito,-a.

appliance [ə'plaɪəns] *n* aparato *m*, dispositivo *m*; **electrical appliances,** electrodomésticos *mpl.*

applicable [ə'plɪkəbəl] *adj* aplicable; **it's a. only to students,** se aplica *or* se refiere *or* se extiende sólo a estudiantes; **this rule is a. only after 6 o'clock,** estanorma sólo es aplicable a partir de las 6.

applicant ['æplɪkənt] *n (for post)* candidato,-a *m, f*; *(to court, for tickets)* solicitante *mf.*

application [æplɪ'keɪʃən] *n* **1** *(of cream, ointment)* aplicación *f*; **for external a. only,** para uso externo. **2** *(request) (for post, tickets, to court, etc)* solicitud *f*, petición *f*; *Com* **samples on a.,** pídanos muestras. ■ **a. form,** solicitud *f*; **job a.,** solicitud *f* de empleo. **3** *(effort)* aplicación *f*; **she lacks a.,** no se aplica.

applied [ə'plaɪd] *adj* aplicado,-a; **a. mathematics,** matemática *f* aplicada.

appliqué [æ'pli:keɪ] *n Sew* aplicación *f.*

apply [ə'plaɪ] *(pt & pp* **applied)** **I** *vtr (cream, ointment, paint)* aplicar; *(brake)* echar; *(law)* aplicar; *(force)* usar; *(discoveries, knowledge)* aplicar; **to a. oneself to a task,** dedicarse a una tarea; **to a. one's mind to sth,** concentrarse en algo. **II** *vi* **1** *(refer)* aplicarse,

referirse **(to,** a); **does it a. in this case?,** ¿se aplica en este caso?; **this rule does not a. to children,** esta norma no se aplica a los niños. **2** *(ask) (for job)* presentar una solicitud; *(for information, to court)* presentar una petición. ◆ **apply for** *vtr (post)* solicitar; *(information, tickets)* pedir.

appoint [ə'pɔɪnt] *vtr* **1** *(choose) (person)* nombrar; *(committee)* elegir; **he was appointed Treasurer,** le nombraron Tesorero. **2** *(fix) (time, place, etc)* fijar, señalar; **at the appointed time,** a la hora señalada.

appointment [ə'pɔɪntmənt] *n* **1** *(to post)* nombramiento *m*; *(post)* cargo *m*, puesto *m*; **to make an a.,** nombrar a algn. **2** *(meeting)* cita *f*, compromiso *m*; **to make an a. with sb,** tener una cita/citarse con algn; *(at doctor's)* tener/pedir hora; **to keep an a.,** acudir a una cita.

apportion [ə'pɔːʃən] *vtr (food, money)* distribuir, repartir; *fig (blame)* asignar, echar **(between, among,** a).

appraisal [ə'preɪzəl] *n* evaluación *f*, valoración *f*; **to make an a. of sth,** evaluar algo.

appraise [ə'preɪz] *vtr* evaluar, valorar.

appreciable [ə'priːʃəbəl] *adj (difference)* appreciable; *(loss)* sensible; *(sum)* importante. ◆ **appreciably** *adv* sensiblemente.

appreciate [ə'priːʃɪeɪt] **I** *vtr* **1** *(be thankful for) (help, advice, etc)* apreciar, agradecer; **I would a. it if you didn't do that,** te agradecería que no hicieras eso. **2** *(understand) (difficulty, difference)* entender, reconocer; **I a. the problem,** entiendo el problema; **do you a. the danger involved?,** ¿te das cuenta del peligro que representa? **3** *(value)* apreciar, valorar; **to a. classical music/fine wine,** saber apreciar la música clásica/el buen vino. **II** *vi (increase in value)* cobrar valor, aumentarse en valor.

appreciation [əpriːʃɪ'eɪʃən] *n* **1** *(of help, advice)* aprecio *m*, agradecimiento *m*, gratitud *f*; *(of difficulty, difference)* comprensión *f*; *(of music, wine, etc)* aprecio *m*; *(appraisal) (of play)* evaluación *f*, comentario *m*; *(of situation)* evaluación *f*; **as a token of our a.,** en señal de nuestra gratitud; **to show one's a.,** mostrar su aprecio. **2** *(increase in value)* aumento *m* en valor.

appreciative [ə'priːʃɪətɪv] *adj (thankful)* agradecido,-a; *(responsive)* apreciativo,-a, sensible; *(audience)* atento,-a; **to be a. of sb's efforts,** agradecerle los esfuerzos a algn.

apprehend [æprɪ'hend] *vtr* **1** *(arrest)* detener, apresar. **2** *(old use) (understand)* comprender.

apprehension [æprɪ'henʃən] *n* **1** *(arrest)* detención *f*. **2** *(fear)* aprensión *f*, temor *m*, recelo *m*; **he did it with a certain amount of a.,** lo hizo con cierto recelo.

apprehensive [æprɪ'hensɪv] *adj (fearful)* aprensivo,-a, receloso,-a; **to be a. about sth,** temer por algo. ◆ **apprehensively** *adv* con aprensión, con recelo.

apprentice [ə'prentɪs] **I** *n* aprendiz,-a *m, f.* **II** *vtr* **to a. sb to a firm,** colocar *or* poner a algn de aprendiz en una empresa; **to be apprenticed to a firm,** estar de aprendiz en una empresa.

apprenticeship [ə'prentɪsʃɪp] *n* aprendizaje *m.*

appro ['æprəʊ] *n (abbr of* **approval)** *fam* **to get sth on a.,** adquirir algo sin compromiso de compra.

approach [ə'prəʊtʃ] **I** *n* **1** *(coming near)* acercamiento *m*; *(of season)* llegada *f*; *(to town etc)* acceso *m*, entrada *f*; **the approaches to the city,** los alrededores de la ciudad; *fig* **to make approaches to sb about sth,** abordar *or* dirigirse a algn sobre algo. ■ **a. road,** vía *f* de acceso. **2** *(to problem etc)* enfoque *m*, planteamiento *m*; **his a. to the problem was different,** su manera de enfocar el problema era distinta. **II** *vtr (come near to)* acercarse a; *(city)* entrar en; *(be similar to)* aproximarse a; *fig (tackle) (problem etc)* abordar, enfocar; *(person)* abordar a, dirigirse a; **his ideas are approaching fanaticism,** sus ideas se aproximan al fanatismo; **she's approaching forty,** tiene casi cuarenta años; **temperatures approaching 40 °C,** temperaturas llegando a los 40 grados centígrados; **to a. sb about sth,** dirigirse a algn sobre algo; **we approached the house,** nos acercamos a la casa. **III** *vi* acercarse.

approachable [ə'prəʊtʃəbəl] *adj (person)* abordable, afable.

approaching [ə'prəʊtʃɪŋ] *adj (event)* próximo,-a; *(traffic)* en dirección opuesta; **the a. car,** el coche que viene de frente.

approbation [æprə'beɪʃən] *n* aprobación *f*; **a look of a.,** una mirada aprobatoria.

appropriate¹ [ə'prəʊprɪɪt] *adj (suitable) (clothing, style, etc)* apropiado,-a, adecuado,-a, apto,-a; *(convenient) (moment, comment, etc)* oportuno,-a; **you must contact the a. authority,** tendrás que dirigirte a la autoridad competente. ◆ **appropriately** *adv (suitably)* de una forma apropiada *or* adecuada; *(conveniently)* convenientemente.

appropriate² [ə'prəʊprɪeɪt] *vtr (allocate) (money etc)* asignar, destinar; *(steal)* apropiarse de.

appropriation [əprəʊprɪ'eɪʃən] *n (allocation)* asignación *f*; *(seizure)* apropiación *f*.

approval [ə'pruːvəl] *n (approbation)* aprobación *f*, visto bueno *m*; **to give one's a. to sth,** dar el visto bueno a algo; *Com* **to get sth on a.,** adquirir algo sin compromiso de compra.

approve [ə'pruːv] *vtr (plans etc)* aprobar, sancionar, dar el visto bueno a; **approved school,** reformatorio *m*. ◆ **approve of** *vtr* aprobar, estar de acuerdo con, consentir en; **I don't a. of his friends,** no me agradan sus amigos.

approving [ə'pruːvɪŋ] *adj (look etc)* aprobatorio,-a, de aprobación. ◆ **approvingly** *adv* en aprobación; **she smiled a.,** hizo una sonrisa de aprobación.

approx [ə'prɒks] **1** *abbr of* **approximate,** aproximado,-a. **2** *abbr of* **approximately,** aproximadamente, aprox.

approximate [ə'prɒksɪmɪt] **I** *adj* aproximado,-a. **II** [ə'prɒksɪmeɪt] *vtr* aproximarse a, acercarse a. ◆ **approximately** *adv* aproximadamente; **it's a. 10 miles away,** está a 10 millas más o menos de distancia.

approximation [əprɒksɪ'meɪʃən] *n* aproximación *f*; **a rough a. of the cost,** una estimación aproximadadel coste.

Apr *abbr of* **April,** abril *m*, abr.

apricot ['eɪprɪkɒt] *n (fruit)* albaricoque *m*. ■ **a. tree,** albaricoquero *m*.

April ['eɪprəl] *n* abril *m*; **to play an A. Fool on sb,** hacerle una inocentada a algn; **A. Fool!,** ¡inocente! ■ **A. Fool's Day,** día *m* uno de abril, ≈ día *m* de los Inocentes (28 de diciembre); *see also* **May.**

apron ['eɪprən] *n (for cook, cleaner)* delantal *m*; *(for workman)* mandil *m*; *Av* pista *f* de servicio; *fam* **he's tied to his wife's/mother's a. strings,** está pegado a las faldas de su mujer/de su madre. ■ *Theat* **a. stage,** proscenio *m*.

apropos [æprə'pəʊ] **I** *adj (suitable)* oportuno,-a, acertado,-a. **II** *adv* **a. of her new job,** y hablando de su nuevo trabajo.

apse [æps] *n* ábside *m*.

APT [eɪpiː'tiː] *GB abbr of* **Advanced Passenger Train,** ≈ Tren *m* de Alta Velocidad, TAV.

apt [æpt] *adj* **1** *(suitable)* apropiado,-a, conveniente; *(remark, reply)* acertado,-a, oportuno,-a; *(word, name)* justo,-a; *(description)* exacto,-a; *(student)* dotado,-a, inteligente. **2** *(inclined)* **to be a. to do sth,** ser propenso,-a a *or* tender a hacer algo; **he's a. to forget,** tiende a *or* suele olvidar. ◆ **aptly** *adv* acertadamente.

apt. *abbr of* **apartment,** apartamento *m*, piso *m*.

aptitude ['æptɪtjuːd] *n (ability)* capacidad *f*. ■ **a. test,** prueba *f* de aptitud.

aptness ['æptnɪs] *n (of remarks etc)* lo acertado, lo oportuno.

aqualung ['ækwəlʌŋ] *n* botella *f* de oxígeno.

aquamarine [ækwəmə'riːn] **I** *n* *Min* aguamarina *f*; *(colour)* color *m* de aguamarina. **II** *adj* de color de aguamarina.

aquaplane ['ækwəpleɪn] **I** *n* esquí *m* acuático. **II** *vi Sport* hacer esquí acuático; *Aut* patinar.

aquarium [ə'kweərɪəm] *n* acuario *m*.

Aquarius [ə'kweərɪəs] *n Astrol Astron* Acuario *m*.

aquatic [ə'kwætɪk] *adj* acuático,-a.

aqueduct ['ækwɪdʌkt] *n* acueducto *m*.

aquiline ['ækwɪlaɪn] *adj* aguileño,-a.

Arab ['ærəb] *adj & n* árabe *(mf)*.

arabesque [ærə'besk] *n* arabesco *m*.

Arabian [ə'reɪbɪən] *adj* árabe, arábigo,-a; **the A. Gulf,** el golfo Arábigo.

Arabic ['ærəbɪk] **I** *adj* árabe, arábigo,-a; **A. literature/ numerals,** literatura *f*/numeración *f* arábiga. **II** *n (language)* árabe *m*.

arable ['ærəbəl] *adj (land)* cultivable, de cultivo.

Aragon ['ærəgən] *n* Aragón *m*.

Aragonese [ærəgə'niːz] *adj & n* aragonés,-esa *(m,f)*.

arbiter ['ɑːbɪtəʳ] *n (referee)* árbitro *m*.

arbitrary ['ɑːbɪtrərɪ] *adj (choice, decision)* arbitrario,-a.

arbitrate ['ɑːbɪtreɪt] *vtr & vi* arbitrar (**between,** entre).

arbitration [ɑːbɪ'treɪʃən] *n* arbitraje *m*; **they agreed to submit the dispute to a.,** acordaron someter la cuestión a arbitraje.

arbitrator ['ɑːbɪtreɪtəʳ] *n* árbitro *m*.

arc [ɑːk] *n* arco *m*. ■ **a. lamp, a. light,** arco *m* voltaico; **a. welding,** soldadura *f* por arco.

arcade [ɑː'keɪd] *n Archit (arches)* arcos *mpl*; *(passageway)* pasaje *m*. ■ **amusement a.,** salón *m* de juegos; **shopping a.,** galerías *fpl* (comerciales).

arch [ɑːtʃ] **I** *n* **1** *Archit* arco *m*; *(vault)* bóveda *f*. **2** *Anat* empeine *m*; **fallen arches,** pies *mpl* planos. **II** *vtr (back)* arquear, doblar; **to a. one's back,** arquear la espalda.

arch- ['ɑːtʃ] *pref* archi-.

archaeological [ɑːkɪə'lɒdʒɪkəl] *adj* arqueológico,-a.

archaeologist [ɑːkɪ'ɒlədʒɪst] *n* arqueólogo,-a *m,f*.

archaeology [ɑːkɪ'ɒlədʒɪ] *n* arqueología *f*.

archaic [ɑː'keɪɪk] *adj* arcaico,-a.

archaism ['ɑːkeɪɪzəm] *n* arcaísmo *m*.

archangel ['ɑːkeɪndʒəl] *n* arcángel *m*.

archbishop [ɑːtʃ'bɪʃəp] *n* arzobispo *m*; **the A. of York,** el Arzobispo de York.

arched [æːtʃt] *adj Archit* arqueado,-a; *(vaulted)*, abovedado,-a.

archeological [aːkɪə'lɒdʒɪkəl] *adj US see* **archaeological.**

archeologist [aːkɪ'ɒlədʒɪst] *n US see* **archaeologist.**

archeology [aːkɪ'ɒlədʒɪ] *n US see* **archaeology.**

archer ['ɑːtʃəʳ] *n* arquero,-a *m,f*.

archery ['ɑːtʃərɪ] *n* tiro *m* al arco.

archetypal ['ɑːkɪtaɪpəl] *adj* arquetípico,-a.

archetype [ɑːkɪ'taɪp] *n (original)* arquetipo *m*; *(example)* modelo *m*.

archipelago [ɑːkɪ'pelɪgəʊ] *n (pl* **archipelagos** *or* **archipelagoes)** archipiélago *m*.

architect ['ɑːkɪtekt] *n* arquitecto,-a *m,f*.

architectural ['ɑːkɪtektʃərəl] *adj* arquitectónico,-a.

architecture ['ɑːkɪtektʃəʳ] *n* arquitectura *f*.

archives ['ɑːkaɪvz] *npl* archivos *mpl*.

archway ['ɑːtʃweɪ] *n (arch)* arco *m*; *(vault)* bóveda *f*; *(in church)* atrio *m*; *(passage)* pasaje *m*.

arctic ['ɑːktɪk] **I** *adj (conditions, weather)* ártico,-a; *fam (very cold)* glacial. **II the A.** *n* el Ártico. ■ **A. Cricle,** círculo *m* ploar Ártico; **A. Ocean,** océano *m* Ártico.

ardent ['ɑːdənt] *adj (admirer, supporter, lover)* apasionado,-a; *(desire)* ardiente.

ardour, US **ardor** ['ɑːdəʳ] n (passion) pasión f, ardor m; (zeal) fervor m.

arduous ['ɑːdjʊəs] adj (climb, journey) arduo,-a, penoso,-a; (task, work) difícil.

are [ɑːʳ] 2nd person sing pres, 1st, 2nd, 3rd person pl pres see **be**.

area ['eərɪə] n (surface) area f, superficie f; (space) espacio m, extensión f; (región) región f; (of town, city) zona f; fig (field) (of knowledge etc) campo m, terreno m; **an a. of 10 square metres**, una superficie de 10 metros cuadrados; **disaster a.**, zona del desastre; fig **his personal life is a disaster a.**, tiene una vida personal desastrosa; **it's a grey a.**, es un campo poco trabajado. ■ US Tel **a. code**, prefijo m local; Com **a. sales manager**, representante mf regional; Sport **penalty a.**, área f de castigo; **postal a.**, distrito m postal; Educ **subject a.**, especialidad f.

arena [ə'riːnə] n (stadium) estadio m; (bullring) plaza f; (circus) pista f; fig (stage) palestra f, campo m de batalla.

Argentina [ɑːdʒən'tiːnə] n Argentina.

Argentinian [ɑːdʒən'tɪnɪən] adj & n argentino,-a (m, f).

arguable [ɑːgjʊəbəl] adj discutible (that, whether, que). ◆ **arguably** adv it's a. the best, hay quienes dicen que es el mejor.

argue ['ɑːgjuː] I vtr (reason) (case etc) discutir, debatir; (point of view, position) mantener; **she argued that it wouldn't be practical**, sostenía que no sería factible. II vi (quarrel) discutir, reñir; (reason) argumentar, razonar; **don't a. just do it**, hazlo y no discutas; **to a. for**, abogar por; **to a. against sth**, ponerse en contra de algo; **to a. about sth with sb**, discutir algo con algn, reñir con algn por algo.

argument ['ɑːgjʊmənt] n (reason) argumento m, razonamiento m (for, en pro de, a favor de; against, en contra de); (quarrel) discusión f, disputa f, riña f; **let's say £50 for the sake of a.**, ponagmos 50 libras (esterlinas) por decir algo; **to follow sb's (line of) a.**, seguir el razonamiento de algn; **to have an a. with sb**, discutir or reñir con algn.

argumentative [ɑːgjʊ'mentətɪv] adj discutidor,-a.

aria ['ɑːrɪə] n Mus aria f.

arid ['ærɪd] adj árido,-a.

aridity [ə'rɪdɪtɪ] n aridez f.

Aries ['eəriːz] n Astrol Astron Aries m.

arise [ə'raɪz] vi (pt arose; pp arisen [ə'rɪzən]) (old use) (get up) levantarse; (happen) surgir, presentarse; **problems have arisen**, han surgido problemas; **difficulties which arise from lack of time**, dificultades que provienen de la falta de tiempo; **should the occasion/need a.**, si se presenta la ocasión/si hace falta.

aristocracy [ærɪ'stɒkrəsɪ] n aristocracia f.

aristocrat ['ærɪstəkræt] n aristócrata mf.

aristocratic [ærɪstə'krætɪk] adj aristocrático,-a.

arithmetic [ə'rɪθmətɪk] n aritmética f. ■ **mental a.**, cálculo m mental.

arithmetical [ærɪθ'metɪkəl] adj aritmético,-a.

ark [ɑːk] n arca f; Noah's A., el arca de Noé.

arm [ɑːm] I n 1 Anat brazo m; (of garment) manga f; (of chair) brazo; **he took my a.**, me agarró del brazo; **to walk a. in a.**, ir cogidos,-as del brazo; fig **to keep sb al a.'s length**, mantener a algn a distancia; fig **to welcome sb with open arms**, recibir a algn con los brazos abiertos. 2 Mil **arms**, armas fpl; fig **to be up in a. about sth**, protestar por or rebelar contra algo. ■ **a. race**, carrera f armamentística; Herald **coat of a.**, escudo m, blasón m. II vtr (person, country) armar; **to a. oneself against sth**, armarse contra algo.

armaments ['ɑːməmənts] npl (weapons) armamentos mpl, material m sing bélico.

armband ['ɑːmbænd] n Mil etc brazalete m; (for swimming) flotador m.

armchair ['ɑːmtʃeəʳ] n sillón m.

armed ['ɑːmd] adj armado,-a. ■ **a. forces**, fuerzas fpl armadas. **a. robbery**, robo m a mano armada.

armful ['ɑːmfʊl] n brazada f.

armhole ['ɑːmhəʊl] n (of garment) sisa f.

armistice ['ɑːmɪstɪs] n armisticio m.

armour, US **armor** ['ɑːməʳ] n Mil (suit of) a., armadura f; (on vehicle) blindaje m.

armoured car, US **armored car** [ɑːməd'kɑːʳ] n coche m blindado.

armour-plated, US **armor-plated** ['ɑːməpleɪtɪd] adj acorazado,-a.

armoury, US **armory** ['ɑːmərɪ] n armería f, arsenal m.

armpit ['ɑːmpɪt] n axila f, sobaco m.

army ['ɑːmɪ] n ejército m; **to join the a.**, alistarse, hacerse militar; **to be in the a.**, ser militar; fig **an a. of workers**, un ejército de trabajadores.

aroma [ə'rəʊmə] n aroma m, olor m.

aromatic [ærə'mætɪk] adj aromático,-a.

arose [ə'rəʊz] pt see **arise**.

around [ə'raʊnd] I adv (in the vicinity) alrededor; **all a.**, por todos los lados; **are the children a.?**, ¿están los niños por aquí?; **computers have been a. for some time**, hace bastante tiempo que la gente tiene ordenadores; **he looked a.**, miró (a su) alrededor; **let me show you a.**, ven que te enseñe (la casa, etc); **to fool a.**, hacer el tonto or el indio; **to rush a.**, correr de un lado para otro; **to turn a.**, darse media vuelta; fam **he's been a.**, ha corrido mucho mundo. II prep 1 (in the vicinity of) alrededor de; **a. the corner**, a la vuelta de la esquina; **a. the world**, por todo el mundo; **is there a bank a. here?**, ¿hay un banco por aquí? 2 (approximately) aproximadamente, a eso de; **it's a. 10 o'clock**, son a eso de las 10.

arouse [ə'raʊz] vtr (wake up) (person) despertar; fig (desire) despertar; (suspicion) levantar; (person) (incite) estimular; (sexually) excitar.

arr 1 abbr of **arrival**, llegada f. 2 abbr of **arrives**, llega. 3 abbr of **arriving**, llega. 4 abbr of **arrived**, llegó.

arrange [ə'reɪndʒ] I vtr 1 (put into order) (books, furniture) ordenar, colocar; (hair, flowers) arreglar; Mus adaptar. 2 (plan) (visit, outing) organizar, planear; (agree on) quedar en; **to a. a time**, fijar una hora; **it was arranged that ...**, se acordó que ...; **we arranged to meet in the hotel**, quedamos en vernos en el hotel; **arranged marriage**, boda f arreglada. II vi (make plans) hacer preparativos or planes, arreglarlo; **he's arranged for a taxi to come**, ha avisado a un taxi para que venga; **I shall a. for him to be there**, lo arreglará para que puede asistir; **we arranged for flowers to be bought**, mandamos comprar flores.

arrangement [ə'reɪndʒmənt] n 1 (display) colocación f; Mus adaptación f. ■ **flower a.**, adorno m floral. 2 (agreement) acuerdo m, arreglo m; **appointments by a.**, visitas fpl a horas convenidas; **I'm pleased with the a.**, me gusta el arreglo; **to come to an a. with sb about sth/to do sth**, llegar a un acuerdo con algn sobre algo/para hacer algo. 3 **arrangements**, (plans) planes mpl; (preparations) preparativos mpl; (projects) proyectos mpl; **to make a. to do sth**, hacer planes or preparativos or proyectos para hacer algo; **what are your holiday a.?**, ¿qué proyectos de vacaciones tienes?

arrant ['ærənt] adj total, absoluto,-a.

array [ə'reɪ] n (collection) colección f; **a great a. of goods**, un gran surtido de productos.

arrears [ə'rɪəz] npl (money, work) atrasos mpl; **to be in a. with the rent**, estar atrasado,-a con el alquiler; **to be paid in a.**, cobrar con retraso.

arrest [ə'rest] I n 1 (of criminal) detención f; **to be under a.**, quedar detenido,-a. 2 (of machine) paro m. ■ Med **cardiac a.**, paro m cardíaco. II vtr (criminal) detener; fig (development, progress) frenar, detener.

arresting [ə'restɪŋ] *adj* llamativo,-a, que llama la atención.

arrival [ə'raɪvəl] *n* llegada *f*; **a new a.,** un,-a recién llegado,-a; *(in class etc)* un nuevo miembro; *(in family)* un,-a recién nacido,-a; **I'll phone on a.,** llamaré al llegar.

arrive [ə'raɪv] *vi* llegar (**at, in,** a); *fig (succeed)* triunfar; **to a. unexpectedly,** llegar de improviso. ◆ **arrive at** *vtr (reach) (decision, agreement)* llegar a; *(price)* fijar.

arrogance ['ærəgəns] *n* arrogancia *f*.

arrogant ['ærəgənt] *adj* arrogante, altanero,-a. ◆ **arrogantly** *adv* con arrogancia.

arrow ['ærəʊ] *n* flecha *f*.

arse ['ɑːs] *n vulg* culo *m*.

arsenal ['ɑːsənəl] *n* arsenal *m*.

arsenic ['ɑːsənɪk] *n* arsénico *m*.

arson ['ɑːsən] *n* incendio *m* provocado.

arsonist ['ɑːsənɪst] *n* pirómano,-a *m,f*, incendiario,-a *m,f*.

art [ɑːt] *n* **1** *(painting, drama, etc)* arte *m*; *(drawing)* dibujo *m*; **the arts,** las bellas artes; **arts and crafts,** artes *fpl* y oficios *mpl*; **a. exhibition,** exposición *f* de arte; **a. school,** escuela *f* de bellas artes. ■ **a. gallery,** galería *f* (de arte); **a. nouveau,** art *m* nouveau; **fine a.,** arte *f*; **work of a.,** obra *f* de arte. **2** *(skill)* habilidad *f*, arte *m*; **there's an a. to driving in thick snow,** conducir en mucha nieve requiere su técnica; **the a. of conversation,** saber conversar. **3 arts,** *(branch of knowledge)* letras *fpl*; **a. and science,** ciencias y letras. ■ *Univ* **Faculty of A.,** Facultad *f* de Filosofía y Letras.

artefact ['ɑːtɪfækt] *n* artefacto *m*.

arterial [ɑː'tɪərɪəl] *adj Anat* arterial; *(road)* principal.

arteriosclerosis [ɑːtɪərɪəʊsklɪ'rəʊsɪs] *n* (*pl* **arterioscleroses** [ɑːtɪərɪəʊsklɪ'rəʊsiːz]) arterioesclerosis *f inv*.

artery ['ɑːtərɪ] *n Anat* arteria *f*; *(road)* vía *f* principal; *(railway)* línea *f* principal.

artesian well [ɑːtiːzɪən'wel] *n* pozo *m* artesiano.

artful ['ɑːtfʊl] *adj (cunning)* mañoso,-a, ladino,-a, astuto,-a.

arthritic [ɑː'θrɪtɪk] *adj* artrítico,-a.

arthritis [ɑː'θraɪtɪs] *n* artritis *f*.

artichoke ['ɑːtɪtʃəʊk] *n* alcachofa *f*. ■ **globe a.,** alcachofa *f*; **Jerusalem a.,** aguaturma *f*.

article ['ɑːtɪkəl] *n* **1** *(thing)* artículo *m*, cosa *f*; *Press* artículo *m*; *Jur* artículo, cláusula *f*. ■ **a. of clothing,** prenda *f* de vestir; *Ling* **definite/indefinite a.,** artículo *m* definido/ indefinido; *Press* **leading a.,** editorial *m*. **2 articles,** contrato *m sing* de aprendizaje. **II** *vtr* **to be articled to** *or* **with a firm of solicitors,** ser abogado,-a en aprendizaje con un gabinete de abogados.

articulate[1] [ɑː'tɪkjʊlɪt] *adj (speech)* claro,-a; *(person)* que se expresa bien *or* con facilidad.

articulate[2] [ɑː'tɪkjʊleɪt] *vtr & vi* articular; *(words)* pronunciar. ■ **articulated lorry,** camión *m* articulado.

articulation [ɑːtɪkjʊ'leɪʃən] *n* articulación *f*.

artifact ['ɑːtɪfækt] *n see* **artefact.**

artifice ['ɑːtɪfɪs] *n (cunning)* astucia *f*, ingenio *m*; *(clever trick)* artificio *m*, estratagema *f*.

artificial [ɑːtɪ'fɪʃəl] *adj (light, flowers, flavouring)* artificial; *(hair, limb)* postizo,-a; *(smile)* falso,-a. ■ **a. insemination,** inseminación *f* artificial; **a. intelligence,** inteligenicia *f* artificial; **a. respiration,** respiración *f* artificial. ◆ **artificially** *adv* de un modo artificial.

artillery [ɑː'tɪlərɪ] *n Mil* artillería *f*.

artisan ['ɑːtɪzæn] *n* artesano,-a *m, f*.

artist ['ɑːtɪst] *n* artista *mf*; *(painter)* pintor,-a *m, f*.

artistic [ɑː'tɪstɪk] *adj* artístico,-a; **he's a.,** tiene talento artístico.

artistry ['ɑːtɪstrɪ] *n* arte *m*, talento *m* artístico.

artless ['ɑːtlɪs] *adj (simple)* sencillo,-a, simple.

arty ['ɑːtɪ] *adj (artier, artiest) fam (person)* que se las da de artista.

as [æz, *unstressed* əz] **I** *adj & conj* **1** *(comparison)* **as ... as ...,** tan ... como ...; *(distance)* **as far as,** hasta; *fig* **as far as I'm concerned,** por lo que a mi respecta; **as many as,** tantos,-as como; **as much as,** tanto,-a; **as tall as me,** tan alto,-a como yo; **as opposed to,** a diferencia de; **at the same time as us,** a la (misma) vez que nosotros; **from as little as £18 a week,** desde tan sólo dieciocho libras por semana; **I did as much as I could,** hice todo que pude; **I'll stay as long as I can,** me quedo tanto como puedo; **just as big,** igual de grande; **there were as many as 500,** hubo hasta 500; **the same as,** igual que, el mismo que **we now pay £100, as against last year's £80,** ahora nos cuesta 100 libras, comparado con las 80 del año pasado. **2** *(manner)* como; **as a motorist, I can't agree,** como conductor, no estoy de acuerdo; **as a rule,** por regla general; **as you know, it isn't true,** como ya sabéis, no es verdad; **as you like,** como quieras; **do as I say, not as I do,** haz lo que yo te digo, no lo que yo hago; **he's working as a doctor,** está trabajando de médico; **I thought as much,** ya me lo suponía; **it serves as a table,** sirve de mesa; **leave it as it is,** déjalo tal como está; **she was dressed as a gypsy,** iba vestida de gitana; *Theat* **with Núria Espert as Phaedra,** con Núria Espert en el papel de Fedra. **3** *(while, when)* mientras (que); **as a child, she was very bright,** de niña era muy espabilada; **as I was eating,** mientras comía; **as we were leaving we saw Pat,** al salir vimos a Pat. **4** *(though)* ya que, aunque; **be that as it may,** por mucho que así sea; **much as I like it I can't afford to buy it,** por mucho que me guste, no me lo puedo comprar; **young as he is,** aunque es joven. **5** *(because)* como, puesto que, ya que; **as he was out, we left a message,** como no estaba, dejamos un recado; **I'll come early as I want to see your mother,** vendré temprano porque quiero ver a tu madre. **6** *(and so)* como, igual que; **as well,** también; **I like fish, as does my wife,** me gusta el pescado y a mi mujer también. **7** *(purpose)* para; **so as to do sth,** para hacer algo; **they left early so as to avoid the traffic,** salieron temprano para evitar el tráfico. **8** *(concerning)* en cuanto a; **as for my brother,** en cuanto a mi hermano, en lo que se refiere a mi hermano. **9 as from, as of,** a partir de; **as of tomorrow,** a partir de mañana, empezando mañana. **10 as if, as though,** que; **he did it as if his life depended on it,** lo hizo como si su vida dependiera de ello; **it looks as if the concert is off,** parece ser que no habrá concierto; **she spoke as though (she was) tired,** habló como si estuviera atontada; *fam* **as if I cared!,** ¿y a mí qué? **11 as it is,** *(in fact)* de por si; **as it is we won't finish till tomorrow,** tal como van las cosas no terminaremos hasta mañana; **it's late enough as it is, without stopping for a meal,** ya es muy tarde, no hay tiempo para parar a comer; **as it were,** por así decirlo, como si dijéramos. **12 as long as,** *(only if)* siempre que, con tal de que; **I'll come as long as it isn't for long,** vendré siempre que no sea por mucho rato; **I'll go as long as you come too,** yo iré con tal de que vayas tú también **13 as regards,** en cuanto a, por lo que se refiere a; **as usual,** como siempre; **as yet,** aún, todavía; **there's no news as yet,** no hay noticias todavía. **II** *rel pron* **such as,** como por ejemplo, tal como; **fruits such as apples and pears,** frutas tales como manzanas y peras.

ASA [eɪes'eɪ] *GB abbr of* **Advertising Standards Authority,** organismo *m* regulador de la publicidad.

asbestos [æz'bestəs] *n* amianto *m*, asbesto *m*.

asbestosis [æzbes'təʊsɪs] *n Med* amiantosis *f*.

ascend [ə'send] **I** *vtr (mountain)* subir a, ascender; *(throne)* subir *or* acceder a. **II** *vi* subir, ascender.

ascendancy [ə'sendənsɪ] *n* ascendiente *m*, dominio *m*.

ascendant [ə'sendənt] *n* ascendiente *m*; **to be in the a.,** estar en auge, predominar.

ascension [ə'senʃən] *n Rel* ascensión *f*. ■ **A. Day,** Día *m* de la Ascensión.

ascent [ə'sent] *n (slope)* subida *f*, cuesta *f*; *(act of going up)* subida *f*, ascenso *m*.

ascertain [æsə'teɪn] *vtr* averiguar, enterarse de.

ascetic [ə'setɪk] I *adj* ascético,-a. II *n* asceta *mf*.

asceticism [ə'setɪsɪzəm] *n* ascetismo *m*.

ascribe [ə'skraɪb] *vtr* **to a. sth to sb/sth**, atribuir *or* imputar algo a algn/algo.

aseptic [eɪ'septɪk] *adj* aséptico,-a.

asexual [eɪ'seksjʊəl] *adj* asexual.

ASH [æʃ] *GB abbr of* **Action on Smoking and Health**, organización *f* anti-tabaco.

ash¹ [æʃ] *n Bot* fresno *m*. ▪ **mountain a.**, serbal *m* silvestre.

ash² [æʃ] *n* ceniza *f*. ▪ **a. bin**, *US* **a. can**, cubo *m* de la basura; *Rel* **A. Wednesday**, miércoles *m inv* de ceniza.

ashamed [ə'ʃeɪmd] *adj* avergonzado,-a; **he was too a. to answer**, le daba vergüenza contestar; **I'm a. of you**, esperaba otra cosa de ti; **it's nothing to be a. of**, no es motivo para avergonzarte; **she was a. of her behaviour**, estaba avergonzada de su comportamiento; **you ought to be a. of yourself!**, ¡se te debería caer la cara de vergüenza!, ¡no te da vergüenza!

ashen ['æʃən] *adj (face)* pálido,-a, lívido,-a.

ashore [ə'ʃɔːʳ] *adv Naut* en tierra; **to go a.**, desembarcar.

ashtray ['æʃtreɪ] *n* cenicero *m*.

Asia ['eɪʃə] *n* Asia. ▪ **A. Minor**, Asia Menor.

Asian ['eɪʃən] *adj & n* asiático,-a *(m, f)*.

aside [ə'saɪd] I *adv* al lado, aparte; **to cast a.**, echar a un lado; **to put** *or* **set sth a.**, apartar *or* reservar algo; **to stand a.**, hacerse a un lado, apartarse; **to take sb a.**, llevarle a algn a un lado. II *prep US* **a. from**, *(apart from)* aparte de; *(as well as)* además de. III *n Theat* aparte *m*; **to say in an a.**, decir un aparte.

asinine ['æsɪnaɪn] *adj* estúpido,-a, imbécil.

ask [ɑːsk] I *vtr* **1** *(inquire)* preguntar; **to a. sb a question**, hacer una pregunta a algn; **to a. sb the time**, preguntar la hora a algn; **don't a. me!**, ¡yo que sé!, ¡ni idea!; **I only asked!**, ¡sólo era por saber! **2** *(request)* pedir, solicitar; **I asked them to go**, les pedí que se fueran; **I asked permission to leave**, pedí permiso para marcharme; **she asked me to post it**, me pidió que le echara al buzón; **she asked to see the manager**, dijo que quería hablar con el encargado; **that's asking a lot**, eso es mucho pedir. **3** *(invite)* invitar; **we didn't go to the party because we weren't asked**, no fuimos a la fiesta porque no nos invitaron. II *vi (inquire)* preguntar; *(request)* pedir. ◆ **ask after** *vtr* **a. after sb**, preguntar por algn. ◆ **ask back** *vtr* **to a. sb back**, devolver la invitación a algn. ◆ **ask for** *vtr (help, advice)* pedir, solicitar; *(person)* preguntar por, buscar; *(price)* pedir por; **he asked for a grant**, solicitó una beca; **how much are they asking for the car?**, ¿cuánto piden por el coche?; **it's someone asking for Clare**, preguntan por Clare; **that's asking for trouble**, eso es buscarse problemas; **you asked for it**, ¡te lo buscaste! ◆ **ask out** *vtr* **to a. sb out**, invitar a algn a salir. ◆ **ask round** *vtr* **to a. sb round (to one's home)**, invitar a algn a casa.

askance [ə'skæns] *adv* **to look a. at sth/sb**, mirar algo/algn con recelo.

askew [ə'skjuː] I *adj* ladeado,-a. II *adv* de lado, de través.

asleep [ə'sliːp] *adj (person)* dormido,-a; *(limb)* adormecido,-a; **to be fast** *or* **sound a.**, estar profundamente dormido,-a; **to fall a.**, quedarse dormido,-a; **my foot is a.**, se me ha dormido el pie.

asp [æsp] *n* áspid *m*.

asparagus [ə'spærəgəs] *n inv (plant)* espárrago *m*; *(shoots)* espárragos *mpl*.

aspect ['æspekt] *n* **1** *(of question, situation)* aspecto *m*; **to examine all the aspects of a problem**, estudiar un problema bajo todos los aspectos. **2** *(of building)* orientación *f*; **a house with a south-facing a.**, una casa orientada al sur.

aspen ['æspən] *n Bot* álamo *m* temblón.

asperity [æ'sperɪtɪ] *n* aspereza *f*.

aspersions [ə'spɜːʃənz] *npl* **to cast a. on sb**, difamar a algn.

asphalt ['æsfælt] *n* asfalto *m*. ▪ **a. road**, carretera *f* asfaltada.

asphyxia [æs'fɪksɪə] *n* asfixia *f*.

asphyxiate [æs'fɪksɪeɪt] I *vtr* asfixiar; **to be asphyxiated**, morir asfixiado,-a. II *vi* asfixiarse, morir asfixiado,-a.

asphyxiation [æsfɪksɪ'eɪʃən] *n* asfixia *f*.

aspic ['æspɪk] *n Culin* gelatina *f*; **chicken in a.**, poll *m* en gelatina.

aspidistra [æspɪ'dɪstrə] *n Bot* aspidistra *f*.

aspirant [ə'spaɪərənt] *n* aspirante *mf*.

aspirate¹ ['æspɪreɪt] *vtr & vi Ling* aspirar.

aspirate² ['æspɪrɪt] *n Ling* aspirado *m*.

aspiration [æspə'reɪʃən] *n* **1** *(ambition)* aspiración *f*, ambición *f*. **2** *Ling* aspiración *f*.

aspire [ə'spaɪəʳ] *vi* **to a. to do sth**, aspirar a hacer algo.

aspirin® ['æsprɪn] *n (pl* **aspirin** *or* **aspirins)** aspirina® *f*.

ass¹ [æs] *n Zool* asno,-a *m,f*, burro,-a *m,f*, *fam fig (stupid person)* burro,-a *m,f*; **to make an a. of oneself**, hacer el ridículo.

ass² [æs] *n US vulg* culo *m*.

assail [ə'seɪl] *vtr (attack)* atacar **(with**, con); *fig* asaltar; **assailed by doubts**, asaltado,-a por las dudas.

assailant [ə'seɪlənt] *n (attacker)* agresor,-a *m,f*, atacante *mf*.

assassin [ə'sæsɪn] *n* asesino,-a *m,f*.

assassinate [ə'sæsɪneɪt] *vtr* asesinar.

assassination [əsæsɪneɪ'ʃən] *n* asesinato *m*.

assault [ə'sɔːlt] I *n* **1** *Mil* ataque *m* **(on**, a, contra), asalto *m* **(on**, sobre); *Jur* agresión *f*, violencia *f*. ▪ **a. and battery**, lesiones *fpl*; *Mil* **a. course**, pista *f* de entrenamiento; **indecent a.**, ofensa *f* al pudor. II *vtr Mil* asaltar, atacar; *Jur* agredir; *(sexually)* violar; **to be assaulted**, ser agredido,-a.

assemble [ə'sembəl] I *vtr (people)* reunir, juntar; *(furniture)* montar. II *vi (people)* reunirse, juntarse.

assembly [ə'semblɪ] *n (meeting)* reunión *f*, asamblea *f*; *Tech* montaje *m*. ▪ *Comput* **a. language**, lenguaje *m* ensamblador; *Ind* **a. line**, cadena *f* de montaje; *Educ* **morning a.**, servicio *m* matinal; **right of a.**, derecho *m* de reunión.

assent [ə'sent] I *n (agreement)* asentimiento *m*; *(consent)* consentimiento *m*; *(approval)* aprobación *f*. II *vi (agree)* asentir **(to**, a); *(consent)* consentir **(to**, en).

assert [ə'sɜːt] *vtr (declare)* afirmar, mantener; **he asserted that ...**, mantuvo que ...; **to a. oneself**, imponerse; **to a. one's rights**, hacer valer sus derechos.

assertion [ə'sɜːʃən] *n (declaration)* afirmación *f*, declaración *f*; *(of a right)* reivindicación *f*.

assertive [ə'sɜːtɪv] *adj* enérgico,-a, dinámico,-a.

assess [ə'ses] *vtr (estimate, value)* valorar, tasar; *(calculate) (damages, price)* calcular, fijar; *(tax)* gravar; *fig (evaluate) (effect etc)* evaluar, juzgar.

assessment [ə'sesmənt] *n (of value)* valoración *f*, tasación *f*; *(of damages, price)* cálculo *m*; *(of taxes)* gravamen *m*; *fig (evaluation)* evaluación *f*, juicio *m*.

assessor [ə'sesəʳ] *n* asesor,-a *m,f*. ▪ **tax a.**, tasador,-a *m,f*.

asset ['æset] *n* **1** *(valuable quality)* calidad *f* positiva, ventaja *f*; **her greatest a. is her sense of humour**, lo mejor que tiene es su sentido del humor; **he's an a. to the firm**, es una valiosa aportación a la empresa. **2** *Fin* **assets**, bienes *mpl*. ▪ **current a.**, activo *m* disponible; **fixed a.**, bienes *mpl* raíces.

asset-stripping ['æsetstrɪpɪŋ] *n Fin* acaparamiento *m* de activos de una empresa en crisis para su posterior reventa.

assiduous [ə'sɪdjʊəs] *adj* asiduo,-a. ◆ **assiduously** *adv* asiduamente.

assign [ə'saɪn] *vtr (allot) (task, duty)* asignar, señalar; *(give) (property etc)* ceder; **to a. sb to a job,** asignar *or* designar a algn para un trabajo.

assignation [æsɪg'neɪʃən] *n (secret meeting)* cita *f* a escondidas.

assignment [ə'saɪnmənt] *n (allocation)* asignación *f*; *(task)* tarea *f*; *(mission)* misión *f*; *(appointment)* cita *f*.

assimilate [ə'sɪmɪleɪt] *vtr (food, facts)* asimilar; **to be assimilated into,** asimilarse *or* incorporarse a.

assimilation [əsɪmɪ'leɪʃən] *n* asimilación *f*.

assist [ə'sɪst] **I** *vtr (help)* ayudar; **to a. sb in doing** *or* **to do sth,** ayudar a algn a *or* en hacer algo; *Jur* **he's assisting the police with their inquiries,** le está interrogando la policía. **II** *vi* ayudar; **to a. in sth/in doing sth,** ayudar en algo/en hacer algo.

assistance [ə'sɪstəns] *n (help)* ayuda *f*, auxilio *m*; **can I be of any a.?,** ¿puedo ayudarle?; *(in shop)* ¿qué quería?; **to come to sb's a.,** acudir en ayuda *or* en auxilio de algn.

assistant [ə'sɪstənt] *n* ayudante *mf*. ■ **a. manager,** subdirector,-a *m, f*; *(in school)* **a. master/mistress** profesor,-a *m, f* (de instituto); **laboratory a.,** ayudante *mf* de laboratorio; **shop a.,** dependiente,-a *m, f*.

assizes [ə'saɪzɪz] *npl Jur* sesión *f* sing de un tribunal.

assoc 1 *abbr of* **association,** asociación *f*. **2** *abbr of* **associated,** asociado,-a.

associate¹ [ə'səʊʃɪeɪt] **I** *vtr (connect) (ideas)* relacionar, asociar; *(companies)* asociar; **to be associated with sth,** estar relacionado,-a con algo, estar involucrado,-a en algo. **II** *vi (person)* relacionarse, tratar **(with,** con).

associate² [ə'səʊʃɪɪt] **I** *adj (company, etc)* associado,-a; *(member)* correspondiente. **II** *n (colleague)* colega *mf*; *(partner)* socia,-a *m, f*; *(accomplice)* cómplice *mf*; *(member)* socio,-a *m, f*.

association [əsəʊsɪ'eɪʃən] *n (partnership)* asociación *f*; *(company, organization)* sociedad *f*; *(connection)* asociación *f*, conexión *f*; **to set up an a.,** formar una sociedad; **in a. with,** asociado,-a con; **a. of ideas,** asociación de ideas; **it has pleasant associations for me,** me trae buenos recuerdos. ■ **a. football,** fútbol *m*.

assorted [ə'sɔːtɪd] *adj* surtido,-a, variado,-a.

assortment [ə'sɔːtmənt] *n* surtido *m*, variedad *f*.

asst. *abbr of* **assistant,** ayudante *mf*, ayte.

assuage [ə'sweɪdʒ] *vtr (pain)* aliviar; *(thirst)* saciar, apagar.

assume [ə'sjuːm] *vtr* **1** *(power, authority)* asumir; *(attitude, name)* adoptar; **to a. power,** tomar el poder; **an assumed name,** un nombre falso. **2** *(suppose)* suponer, dar por sentado,-a; **we can a. that the store is true,** es de suponer que la historia es de verdad; **assuming that they arrive on time,** suponiendo que lleguen a la hora.

assumption [ə'sʌmpʃən] *n* **1** *(of power, authority)* toma *f*; **a. of office,** toma de posesión, entrada *f* en funciones. **2** *(supposition)* suposición *f*, supuesto *m*; **on the a. that we succeed,** suponiendo que tengamos éxito. **3** *Rel* **the A.,** la Asunción.

assurance [ə'ʃʊərəns] *n* **1** *(guarantee)* garantía *f*; **to give one's a. that ...,** asegurar *or* prometer que ... . **2** *(confidence)* confianza *f*, aplomo *m*. **3** *(insurance)* seguro *m*. ■ **life a.,** seguro *m* de vida.

assure [ə'ʃʊə'] *vtr* asegurar; **I can a. you of that,** se lo puedo asegurar; **she will do it, I a. you,** te aseguro que lo hará.

assured [ə'ʃʊəd] *adj* seguro,-a, asegurado,-a; **you can rest a. that ...,** puede estar totalmente seguro,-a de que ... .

Assyria [ə'sɪrɪə] *n Hist* Asiria.

Assyrian [ə'sɪrɪən] *adj & n Hist* asirio,-a *(m, f)*.

aster ['æstə'] *n Bot* áster *f*.

asterisk ['æstərɪsk] *n* asterisco *m*.

astern [ə'stɜːn] *adv* a popa.

asteroid ['æstərɔɪd] *n* asteroide *m*.

asthma ['æsmə] *n* asma *f*.

asthmatic [æs'mætɪk] *adj & n* asmático,-a *(m, f)*.

astigmatism [ə'stɪgmətɪzəm] *n* astigmatismo *m*.

astonish [ə'stɒnɪʃ] *vtr* asombrar, pasmar; **he looked astonished,** pareció asombrado; **I was astonished,** me quedé pasmado,-a; **you a. me!,** ¡no me digas!, ¡fíjate tú!

astonishing [ə'stɒnɪʃɪŋ] *adj* asombroso,-a, pasmoso,-a; **I find it a. that ...,** me asombra que ... . ◆ **astonishingly** *adv* asombrosamente.

astonishment [ə'stɒnɪʃmənt] *n* asombro *m*; **a look of a.,** una expresión de desconcierto; **to my a.,** para gran sorpresa mía.

astound [ə'staʊnd] *vtr* asombrar, pasmar; **we were astounded,** nos quedamos pasmados; **you a. me,** me dejas de piedra.

astounding [ə'staʊndɪŋ] *adj* asombroso,-a, pasmosa,-a.

astral ['æstrəl] *adj* estelar.

astray [ə'streɪ] *adv* **to go a.,** *(be lost)* extraviarse; *fig (make a mistake)* equivocarse; *(decline morally)* ir por mal camino; **to lead sb a.,** llevar a algn por mal camino.

astride [ə'straɪd] *prep* a horcajadas sobre; **to sit a. a chair,** sentarse a caballo *or* a horcajadas sobre una silla.

astringent [ə'strɪndʒənt] *adj & n* astringente *(m)*.

astrologer [ə'strɒlədʒə'] *n* astrólogo,-a *m, f*.

astrology [ə'strɒlədʒɪ] *n* astrología *f*.

astronaut ['æstrənɔːt] *n* astronauta *mf*.

astronomer [ə'strɒnəmə'] *n* astrónomo,-a *m, f*.

astronomical [æstrə'nɒmɪkəl] *adj* astronómico,-a.

astronomy [ə'strɒnəmɪ] *n* astronomía *f*.

astrophysics [æstrəʊ'fɪzɪks] *n* astrofísica *f*.

astute [ə'stjuːt] *adj* astuto,-a. ◆ **astutely** *adv* astutamente.

asylum [ə'saɪləm] *n* **1** *(protection)* asilo *m*; **to seek political a.** pedir asilo político. **2 mental a.,** manicomio *m*.

asymmetrical [æsɪ'metrɪkəl] *adj* asimétrico,-a.

at [æt] *prep* **1** *(place) (position)* a, en; **at home,** en casa; **at school,** en el colegio *or* la escuela; **at the door/window,** a la puerta/la ventana; **at the top,** en lo alto; **at work,** en el trabajo; **he's at work,** está trabajando; **to knock at the door,** llamar a la puerta. **2** *(direction)* a; **to be angry at sth,** enfadarse con algn/por algo; **to be surprised at sth,** sorprenderse por algo; **to laugh at sb,** reírse de algn; **to look at sth/sb,** mirar algo/a algn; **to shoot at sb,** disparar contra algn; **to shout at sb,** gritarle a algn. **3** *(time)* a; **at Christmas,** por Navidades, en Navidad; **at Easter,** en Semana Santa; **at 4 o'clock,** a las 4; **at first,** al principio; **at last,** por fin; **at once,** en seguida; **at that time,** en aquel momento, entonces; **at the moment,** ahora. **4** *(manner)* a, en; **at all events,** en cualquier caso; **at best/worst,** lo mejor/peor de los casos; **at hand,** a mano; **at least,** por lo menos; **at peace,** en paz; **not at all,** *(absolutely not)* en absoluto; *(don't mention it)* de nada; **to be at a loss for words,** no saber qué decir; **to be good at sth,** ser fuerte en algo. **5** *(cause)* **to be angry at sb,** enfadarse con algn; **to be surprised at sth,** sorprenderse por algo. **6** *(rate)* a; **they retail at 100 pesetas each,** se venden a 100 pesetas la unidad; **two at a time,** de dos en dos; *fam* **it isn't a very good one at that,** ni siquiera es bueno. **7 while you're at it, could you make a cup of tea?,** ¿y de paso, podrías hacer un té?; **she's at it again,** ya empieza con la misma canción; *(working hard)* **they've been hard at it all morning,** han estado dándole que te pego toda la mañana.

ate [et, eɪt] *pt see* **eat.**

atheism ['eɪθɪɪzəm] *n* ateísmo *m*.

atheist ['eɪθɪɪst] *n* ateo,-a *m, f*.

Athenian [ə'θiːnɪən] *adj & n* ateniense *(mf)*.

Athens ['æθɪnz] *n* Atenas.

athlete ['æθliːt] *n* atleta *mf*. ▪ *Med* **a.'s foot**, pie *m* de atleta.

athletic [æθ'letɪk] **I** *adj* atlético,-a; *(sporty)* deportista. **II** **athletics** *npl* atletismo *m sing*.

Atlantic [ət'læntɪk] *adj* **the A. (Ocean)**, el (océano) Atlántico.

atlas ['ætləs] *n* atlas *m*; **world a.**, atlas del mundo.

ATM [eɪtiː'em] *abbr of* **automated telling machine**, cajero *m* automático.

atmosphere ['ætməsfɪər] *n (air)* atmósfera *f*; *fig (ambience)* ambiente *m*; **a tense a.**, un ambiente de tensión; **the earth's a.**, la atmósfera terrestre.

atmospheric [ætməs'ferɪk] **I** *adj (pressure etc)* atmosférico,-a. **II atmospherics** *npl Rad* perturbaciones *fpl* atmosféricas, parásitos *mpl*.

ATOL ['ætɒl] *GB abbr of* **Air Tour Operating Licence**, permiso *m* para organizar vuelos chárter.

atom ['ætəm] *n* átomo *m*; *fig* pizca *f*. ▪ **a. bomb**, bomba *f* atómica.

atomic [ə'tɒmɪk] *adj* atómico,-a. ▪ **a. energy**, energía *f* atómica; **a. warfare**, guerra *f* atómica.

atone [ə'təʊn] *vi (crime, sin)* expiar **(for,** -); *(mistake)* reparar **(for,** -).

atonement [ə'təʊnmənt] *n (for crime, sin)* expiación *f*; *(for mistake)* reparación *f*.

atrocious [ə'trəʊʃəs] *adj (wicked, cruel)* atroz; *fam (very bad)* fatal, malísimo,-a.

atrocity [ə'trɒsɪti] *n* atrocidad *f*.

atrophy ['ætrəfɪ] **I** *n Med* atrofia f. **II** *vi* atrofiarse.

attach [ə'tætʃ] *vtr (tie) (stick)* pegar; *(fasten)* sujetar; *(document)* adjuntar; **she's attached to the embassy**, está agregada a la embajada; **the attached letter**, la carta adjunta; **to a. importance to sth**, conceder *or* dar importancia a algo; **to a. oneself to a group**, unirse *or* pegarse a un grupo; *fig (be fond of)* **to be attached to sb/sth**, encariñarse a algn/algo; *fig* **Tom's very attached to that old pullover**, Tom le tiene mucho cariño a ese viejo jersey.

attaché [ə'tæʃeɪ] *n Pol* agregado,-a *m, f*. ▪ **a. case**, maletín *m*; **cultural a.**, agregado,-a *m, f* cultural.

attachment [ə'tætʃmənt] *n* **1** *Tech (piece)* accesorio *m*, dispositivo *m*; *(action)* acoplamiento *m*. **2** *(fondness)* cariño *m*, apego *m* **(to**, por).

attack [ə'tæk] **I** *n* **1** *(assault)* ataque *m*, asalto *m*; *fig (criticism)* ataque *m*; **an a. on sb's life**, un atentado contra la vida de algn; **to come under a.**, ser agredido,-a; **to lauch an a. on sb**, lanzar un ataque sobre algn. **2** *Med* ataque *m*; *(of fever)* acceso *m*; *(of nerves)* crisis *f*. ▪ **heart a.**, infarto *m*. **II** *vtr (assault)* atacar, asaltar; *fig (problem)* abordar, enfrentar; *(job)* emprender; *fig (criticize)* atacar, criticar; *fig (theory)* impugnar.

attacker [ə'tækər] *n* asaltante *mf*, agresor,-a *m, f*.

attain [ə'teɪn] *vtr (ambition, aim)* lograr; *(rank, age)* llegar a.

attainment [ə'teɪnmənt] *n (achievement)* logro *m*; *(skill)* talento *m*; **the a. of his goals**, la realización de sus metas.

attempt [ə'tempt] **I** *n (trip)* intento *m*, tentativa *f*; **at the second/third a.**, a la segunda/tercera; **to make an a. to do sth**, procurar *or* intentar hacer algo; **at least make an a. to smile**, por lo menos procura sonreír; **an a. on sb's life**, un atentado contra la vida de algn. **II** *vtr (task, problem, etc)* intentar; **to a. to do sth**, tratar de *or* intentar hacer algo; *Jur* **attempted murder/rape**, intento *m* de asesinato/violación.

attend [ə'tend] **I** *vtr (be present at) (meeting, school, etc)* asistir a; *(care for) (patient)* atender, cuidar; *(wait on)* servir; *(bride)* acompañar. **II** *vi (be present)* asistir; *(pay attention)* atender, prestar atención; **he'll a. if he's free**, irá

attend to *vtr (business, job, etc)* atender a, ocuparse de; *(in shop)* **to a. to a customer**, servir a un cliente.

attendance [ə'tendəns] *n (being, present)* asistencia *f*; *(those present)* asistentes *mpl*; **regular a.**, asiduidad *f*; **there was a good a.**, asistió mucha gente.

attendant [ə'tendənt] *n (in cinema, theatre)* acomodador,-a *m, f*; *(in museum)* guía *mf*; *(in car park)* vigilante,-a *m, f*; *(at wedding)* acompañante *mf*; *(bridesmaid)* dama *f* de honor.

attention [ə'tenʃən] *n* **1** atención *f*; **for the a. of Miss Jones**, a la atención de la Srta. Jones; **pay a.!**, ¡atiende!; **to attract sb's a.**, llamar la atención de algn; **to pay a. to sb/sth**, atender *or* prestar atención a algn/algo. **2** *Mil* **a.!**, ¡firmes!; **to stand to a.**, cuadrarse, ponerse firmes, cuadrarse.

attentive [ə'tentɪv] *adj (listener, class)* atento,-a; *(helpful)* solícito,-a; **to be a. to** *or* **towards sb**, ser solícito,-a con algn.

attest [ə'test] **I** *vtr (verify)* atestiguar; *Jur (document, signature)* legalizar. **II** *vi (bear witness to)* **to a. to**, dar testimonio a.

attic ['ætɪk] *n* desván *m*.

attire [ə'taɪər] *n fml* traje *m*; **formal a.**, traje de ceremonia.

attitude ['ætɪtjuːd] *n (opinion, way of behaving)* actitud *f*; *(position of body)* postura *f*; **an a. of mind**, un estado de ánimo; **don't take that a.**, no te pongas así.

attn *Com abbr of* **(for the) attention of**, a la atención de.

attorney [ə'tɜːnɪ] *n* **1** *US (lawyer)* abogado,-a *m, f*. ▪ **A. General**, ≈ Ministro,-a *m*, *f* de Justicia; **district a.**, fiscal *mf*. **2** *Jur* **power of a.**, poderes *mpl*.

attract [ə'trækt] *vtr* atraer; **to a. attention**, llamar la atención; **to a. a waiter's attention**, llamar a un camarero; **to be attracted to sb/sth**, sentirse atraído,-a por algn/algo.

attraction [ə'trækʃən] *n* **1** *(power)* atracción *f*; **to feel a. towards sb**, sentirse atraído,-a por algn; **what's the a.?**, ¿porqué te atrae? **2** *(attractive thing)* atractivo *m*; *(charm)* encanto *m*; *(incentive)* aliciente *m*; **the job has many attractions**, el trabajo tiene muchos alicientes; **the main a.**, el número fuerte.

attractive [ə'træktɪv] *adj (person)* atractivo,-a, guapo,-a; *(idea, proposition)* interesante, atrayente. ◆ **attractively** *adv* atractivamente, de modo atrayente.

attribute¹ ['ætrɪbjuːt] *n (quality)* atributo *m*.

attribute² [ə'trɪbjuːt] *vtr* atribuir; **the poem is attributed to Keats**, el poema se atribuye a Keats.

attributable [ə'trɪbjʊtəbəl] *adj* atribuible, imputable **(to**, a).

attributive [ə'trɪbjʊtɪv] *adj Ling* atributivo,-a.

attrition [ə'trɪʃən] *n* **war of a.**, guerra *f* de agotamiento *or* de desgaste.

attuned [ə'tjuːnd] *adj* **to be a. to sb's way of thinking**, entender la forma de pensar de algn.

atypical [eɪ'tɪpɪkəl] *adj* atípico,-a, anormal.

aubergine ['əʊbəʒiːn] *n Bot* berenjena *f*.

auburn ['ɔːbən] *adj (hair)* castaño rojizo *inv*.

auction ['ɔːkʃən] **I** *n* subasta *f*; **to put sth up for a.**, poner algo a subasta. ▪ **a. room**, sala *f* de subastas; **a. sale**, subasta *f*. **II** *vtr* subastar.

auctioneer [ɔːkʃə'nɪər] *n* subastador,-a *m, f*.

audacious [ɔː'deɪʃəs] *adj (daring)* audaz, intrépido,-a; *(bold)* atrevido,-a; *(impudent)* descarado,-a.

audacity [ɔː'dæsɪtɪ] *n (daring)* audacia *f*, intrepidez *f*; *(boldness)* atrevimiento *m*; *(impudence)* descaro *m*.

audible ['ɔːdɪbəl] *adj* audible, perceptible al oído; **it was barely** *or* **scarcely a.**, apenas se le oía. ◆ **audibly** *adv* audiblemente; *(clearly)* claramente.

audience ['ɔːdɪəns] *n* **1** *(spectators etc)* público *m*, espectadores *mpl*; *(at concert, conference)* auditorio *m*; *(television)* telespectadores *mpl*. ▪ **a. participation**, participación f del público. 2 *(meeting)* audiencia f; **to be granted an a. with sb,** ser recibido,-a en audiencia por algn.

audio-visual [ɔːdɪəʊ'vɪzjʊəl] *adj* audiovisual. ■ **a. aids,** ayudas fpl or medios mpl audiovisuales.

audit ['ɔːdɪt] **I** *n* revisión f de cuentas, intervención f. **II** *vtr* revisar, intervenir.

audition [ɔː'dɪʃən] **I** *n Theat Cin* prueba f; **to hold auditions for a part,** probar gente para un papel. **II** *vtr* **to a. sb for a part,** probar a algn para un papel. **III** *vi* **to a. for a part,** presentarse a una prueba para un papel.

auditor ['ɔːdɪtə'] *n Com* revisor,-a m, f de cuentas, interventor,-a m,f.

auditorium [ɔːdɪ'tɔːrɪəm] *n (pl auditoriums or auditoria* [ɔːdɪ'tɔːrɪə]*)* auditorio m, sala f.

Aug *abbr of* **August,** agosto m, ago.

augment [ɔːg'ment] *vtr* aumentar.

augur ['ɔːgə'] *vi* **to a. well/ill for sth,** ser buen/mal agüero para algo.

August ['ɔːgəst] *n* agosto m; *see also* **May.**

aunt [ɑːnt] *n (also fam* **auntie, aunty** ['ɑːntɪ]*)* tía f; **her a. and uncle,** sus tíos. ■ **A. Sally,** objeto m de burla.

au pair [əʊ'peə'] *n* **au p. (girl),** (chica f) au pair f.

aura ['ɔːrə] *n (pl auras or aurae* ['ɔːriː]*) (of person)* aura f; *Rel* aureola f; *(of place)* sensación f.

aural ['ɔːrəl] *adj* auditivo,-a, del oído.

auricle ['ɔːrɪkəl] *n Anat* aurícula f.

auspices ['ɔːspɪsɪz] *npl* **under the a. of,** bajo los auspicios de, patrocinado,-a por.

auspicious [ɔː'spɪʃəs] *adj* propicio,-a, de buen augurio; **an a. start,** un feliz comienzo. ◆ **auspiciously** *adv* felizmente.

Aussie ['ɒzɪ] *adj & n fam* australiano,-a (m,f).

austere [ɒ'stɪə'] *adj* austero,-a, sobrio,-a.

austerity [ɒ'sterɪtɪ] *n* austeridad f; *Pol* **economic a.,** restricciones fpl.

Australia [ɒ'streɪlɪə] *n* Australia.

Australian [ɒ'streɪlɪən] *adj & n* australiano,-a (m,f).

Austria ['ɒstrɪə] *n* Austria.

Austrian ['ɒstrɪən] *adj & n* austríaco,-a (m,f).

authentic [ɔː'θentɪk] *adj* auténtico,-a. ◆ **authentically** *adv* auténticamente.

authenticate [ɔː'θentɪkeɪt] *vtr (document etc)* probar la autenticidad de.

authenticity [ɔːθen'tɪsɪtɪ] *n* autenticidad f.

author ['ɔːθə'] *n* autor,-a m, f.

authoritarian [ɔːθɒrɪ'teərɪən] *adj* autoritario,-a.

authoritative [ɔː'θɒrɪtətɪv] *adj (reliable)* autorizado,-a, digno,-a de crédito, fidedigno,-a; *(authoritarian)* autoritario,-a.

authority [ɔː'θɒrɪtɪ] *n (power, right)* autoridad f; *(governing body)* autoridad; *(expert)* autoridad, experto,-a m,f; **the authorities,** las autoridades; **to be an a. on sth,** ser experto,-a *or* una autoridad en algo; **to be in** *or* **have a. over sb,** tener autoridad sobre algn; **I have it on good a. that ...,** sé de buena fuente que ...; **who is in a. here?,** ¿quién manda aquí? ■ *Pol* **local a.,** ayuntamiento m.

authorization [ɔːθəraɪ'zeɪʃən] *n* autorización f.

authorize ['ɔːθəraɪz] *vtr (person)* autorizar; *(payment etc)* aprobar; **to a. sb to do sth,** autorizar a algn a *or* para hacer algo.

autistic [ɔː'tɪstɪk] *adj* autístico,-a, autista.

auto- ['ɔːtəʊ] *n US Canada fam* coche m, auto m.

auto- ['ɔːtəʊ] *pref* auto-.

autobiographical [ɔːtəbaɪə'græfɪkəl] *adj* autobiográfico,-a.

autobiography [ɔːtəʊbaɪ'ɒgrəfɪ] *n* autobiografía f.

autocratic [ɔːtə'krætɪk] *adj* autocrático,-a.

autograph ['ɔːtəgrɑːf] **I** *n (signature)* autógrafo m. **II** *vtr (sign)* firmar; *(book, photo)* dedicar.

automat ['ɔːtəmæt] *n US* restaurante m de autoservicio.

automatic [ɔːtə'mætɪk] **I** *adj (washing machine, car, gun, etc)* automático,-a. ■ **a. pilot,** piloto m automático. **II** *n (car)* coche m automático; *(gun)* pistola f automática. ◆ **automatically** *adv* automáticamente.

automation [ɔːtə'meɪʃən] *n* automatización f.

automaton [ɔː'tɒmətɒn] *n (pl automatons or automata* [ɔː'tɒməte]*) (robot)* autómata m; *fig (person)* autómata mf.

automobile ['ɔːtəməbiːl] *n US* coche m, automóvil m, auto m.

autonomous [ɔː'tɒnəməs] *adj* autónomo,-a.

autonomy [ɔː'tɒnəmɪ] *n* autonomía f.

autopsy ['ɔːtəpsɪ] *n* autopsía f.

autumn ['ɔːtəm] *n* otoño m.

autumnal [ɔː'tʌmnəl] *adj* otoñal, de otoño.

auxiliary [ɔːg'zɪljərɪ] **I** *adj* auxiliar. **II** *n* 1 *(helper)* auxiliar mf, ayudante mf; *Mil* **auxiliaries,** tropas fpl auxiliares. 2 *Ling (verb)* auxiliar m.

a-v, A-V, AV [eɪ'viː] *abbr of* **audio-visual,** audiovisual.

av *abbr of* **average,** promedio.

Av., av. *abbr of* **Avenue,** avenida f, Av., Avda.

avail [ə'veɪl] **I** *n* **to no a.,** en vano. **II** *vtr* **to a. oneself of sth,** aprovecharse de algo.

available [ə'veɪləbəl] *adj (thing)* disponible; *(person)* libre; **is Mr Marshall a.?,** ¿está libre el Sr. Marshall?; **it's a. in green and blue,** lo hay en verde y en azul; **there are no tickets a.,** están agotadas las localidades; **to make sth a. to sb,** poner algo a la disposición de algn.

availability [əveɪlə'bɪlɪt] *n* disponibilidad f.

avalanche ['ævəlɑːnʃ] *n* avalancha f.

avarice ['ævərɪs] *n* avaricia f.

avaricious [ævə'rɪʃəs] *adj* avaro,-a.

Ave *abbr of* **Avenue,** Avenida f, Av., Avda.

avenge [ə'vendʒ] *vtr* vengar; **to a. oneself on sb,** vengarse en algn.

avenue ['ævɪnjuː] *n (road)* avenida f, paseo m; *fig* vía f, posibilidad f.

average ['ævərɪdʒ] **I** *n* promedio m, media f; **above/below a.,** por encima de/debajo de la media; **on a.,** por término medio. **II** *adj* medio,-a, mediano,-a; *(result, conditions)* regular. **III** *vtr* sacar la media de; **he averages 8 hours' work a day,** hace un promedio de 8 horas de trabajo al día. ◆ **average out at** *vtr* salir en un promedio de.

averse [ə'vɜːs] *adj* opuesto,-a, reacio,-a; **to be a. to sth,** ser reacio,-a a algo; **he's not a. to an occasional glass of wine,** no rechaza una copa de vino de vez en cuando.

aversion [ə'vɜːʃən] *n (feeling)* aversión f; *(thing)* bestia f negra; **it's my pet a.,** es lo que más odio; **to have an a. to sth,** odiar algo, sentir repugnancia hacia algo.

avert [ə'vɜːt] *vtr (turn away) (eyes, thoughts)* apartar *(from,* de); *(prevent) (accident)* impedir; *(danger)* evitar.

aviary ['eɪvjərɪ] *n* pajarera f.

aviation [eɪvɪ'eɪʃən] *n* aviación f.

avid ['ævɪd] *adj (reader)* voraz; **to be a. for sth,** ser ávido,-a por algo. ◆ **avidly** *adv* vorazmente, con voracidad.

avocado [ævə'kɑːdəʊ] *n (pl avocados) (also avocado pear)* aguacate m.

avocet ['ævəset] *n Orn* avoceta f.

avoid [ə'vɔɪd] *vtr (object)* evitar; *(person)* esquivar; *(question)* eludir; *(answer)* evadir; *(argument, danger)* evitar; **to a. doing sth,** evitar hacer algo, procurar no hacer algo.

avoidable [ə'vɔɪdəbəl] *adj* evitable.

avow [ə'vaʊ] *vtr* reconocer, confesar, declarar.

avowal [ə'vaʊəl] *n* confesión *f*, declaración *f*.

avowed [ə'vaʊd] *adj* confesado,-a, declarado,-a.

await [ə'weɪt] *vtr* esperar, aguardar; **a warm welcome awaited her,** le esperaba una calurosa acogida; **parcels awaiting delivery,** paquetes *mpl* para repartir.

awake [ə'weɪk] *adj* despierto,-a; **coffee keeps me a.,** el café me desvela; **to be a.,** estar despierto,-a; **to lie a.,** desvelar; **wide a.,** totalmente despierto,-a. II *vtr (pt awoke, awaked; pp awoken, awaked)* despertar; *fig (memories etc)* despertar, traer. III *vi fig* **to a. to the dangers/consequences of sth,** darse cuenta del peligro/de las consecuencias de algo.

awaken [ə'weɪkən] *vtr & vi (pt awakened; pp awoken) see* **awake** II & III.

awakening [ə'weɪkənɪŋ] *n* despertar *m*; *fig* **a rude a.,** un brusco despertar.

award [ə'wɔːd] I *n (prize)* premio *m*; *(medal)* condecoración *f*; *(trophy)* trofeo *m*; *Jur (grant)* beca *f*; *Educ (grant)* beca *f.* II *vtr (prize)* conceder, otorgar; *(medal)* dar, conferir; *Jur (damages)* adjudicar.

aware [ə'weə'] *adj (knowledgeable)* enterado,-a, informado,-a; **not that I'm a. of,** que yo sepa no; **politically a.,** políticamente consciente; **to be a. of sth,** ser consciente de algo; **to become a. of sth,** darse cuenta de algo.

awareness [ə'weənɪs] *n* conciencia *f* **(of,** de).

awash [ə'wɒʃ] *adj* inundado,-a **(with,** de).

away [ə'weɪ] *adv* **a long way a.,** lejos; **far a.,** lejos; **go a.!,** ¡fuera de aquí!; *(familiar form)* ¡vete!; ¡lárgate!; *(polite form)* ¡váyase!; está a 3 millas de distancia; **keep a. from the fire!,** ¡no te acerques al fuego!; *(at once)* **right a.,** en seguida, ahora mismo; **to be a.,** *(absent)* estar ausente; *(out)* estar fuera; *(travelling)* estar de viaje; **to die a.,** *(sound)* desvanecerse; **to give sth a.,** *(thing)* regalar algo; *(secret)* revelar algo; **to go a.,** irse, largarse; *Sport* **to play a.,** jugar fuera; **to put sth a.,** guardar algo; **to sign one's rights a.,** ceder sus derechos; **to stand a. from sth,** mantenerse a distancia de algo; **to turn a.,**

volver la cara; *(continue working)* **to work a.,** seguir trabajando.

awe [ɔː] *n (fear)* temor *m*; *(amazement)* asombro *m*; **to be or stand in a. of sb,** ser intimidado,-a por algn.

awe-inspiring ['ɔːɪnspaɪərɪŋ] *adj* impresionante, imponente; **an a. sight,** un espectáculo grandioso.

awesome ['ɔːsəm] *adj* impresionante.

awful ['ɔːfʊl] *adj fam* espantoso,-a, horroroso,-a; **an a. noise,** un escándalo, un ruido de mil demonios; **an a. lot of work,** muchísimo trabajo; **how a.!,** ¡qué horror!; **what a. weather!,** ¡qué tiempo tan horrible! ◆ **awfully** *adv fam* terriblemente; **I'm a. sorry,** lo siento muchísimo; **it's a. funny,** es graciosísimo, es de lo más divertido.

awhile [ə'waɪl] *adv* **wait a.,** espera un poco.

awkward ['ɔːkwəd] *adj (person) (clumsy)* torpe; *(difficult)* difícil, pesado,-a; *(object)* incómodo,-a; *(moment, time)* inoportuno,-a; *(situation)* embarazoso,-a; *(problem)* difícil; **an a. silence,** un silencio embarazoso; **a. to handle,** difícil de manejar; **he's being a.,** está poniendo reparos.

awl [ɔːl] *n* lezna *f.*

awning ['ɔːnɪŋ] *n (on ship)* toldo *m*, toldilla *f*; *(on shop etc)* marquesina *f.*

awoke [ə'wəʊk] *pt see* **awake.**

awoken [ə'wəʊkən] *pp see* **awake.**

axe, *US* **ax** [æks] I *n* hacha *f*; *fig* **to have an a. to grind,** tener un interés creado *or* personal. II *vtr fig (jobs, costs)* reducir; *(plan)* cancelar; *(person)* despedir.

axiom ['æksɪəm] *n* axioma *m.*

axiomatic [æksɪə'mætɪk] *adj* axiomático,-a; **it's a.,** está claro.

axis ['æksɪs] *n (pl axes* ['æksiːz]*) Geom etc* eje *m.*

axle ['æksəl] *n* eje *m*, árbol *m.* ■ *Aut* **rear a.,** eje *m* trasero; **a. shaft,** palier *m.*

ayatollah [aɪə'tɒlə] *n Rel* ayatolá *m.*

azalea [ə'zeɪljə] *n Bot* azalea *f.*

Aztec ['æztek] *adj & n* azteca *(mf).*

azure ['eɪʒə'] *adj & n* azul *(m)* celeste.

B

B, b [biː] *n* **1** *(the letter)* B, b *f.* ■ **B movie,** película *f* de serie B; *Aut* **B road,** carretera *f* secundaria. **2** *Mus* si *m.* ■ **B flat,** si *m* bemol.

b *abbr of* **born,** nacido,-a, n.

BA [biː'eɪ] *abbr of* **Bachelor of Arts,** Licenciado,-a *m,f* en Filosofía y Letras, Lic en Fil y Let.

baa [bɑː] I *n* balido *m.* II *vi* balar.

babble ['bæbəl] I *n* **1** *(of baby)* balbuceo *m*; *(of adult)* barboteo *m*, parloteo *m.* **2** *(of brook)* murmullo *m.* II *vi* **1** *(baby)* balbucear; *(adult)* barbotear, farfullar, parlotear. **2** *(brook)* murmurar.

babbling ['bæblɪŋ] I *n see* **babble** I. II *adj* **1** *(baby)* balbuceante; *(adult)* farfullador,-a. **2** *(brook)* murmurador,-a.

babe [beɪb] *n* **1** *(baby)* bebé *m*, rorro *m*; **b. in arms,** niño *m* de pecho. **2** *US fam (young woman)* chica *f*; **hi, b.!,** ¡hola, nena!; ¡hola, guapa!

baboon [bə'buːn] *n Zool* zambo *m*, babuino *m*, papión *m.*

baby ['beɪbɪ] *n* **1** *(infant)* bebé *m*; *(young child)* niño,-a *m, f*; **the b. of the family,** el benjamín; **to have a b.,** tener un bebé; *fam* **that's your b.,** eso es cosa tuya; *fam* **to be left holding the b.,** cargar con el muerto, pagar el pato. ■ **b. buggy,** *US* **b. carriage,** cochecito *m* de niño; **b. face,** cara *f* de niño; **b. sling,** canguro *m*; **b. tooth,** diente *m* de leche.

2 *(animal)* cría *f.* **3** *fam (darling)* querido,-a *m,f.* **4** *Mus* **b. grand,** piano *m* de media cola.

baby-battering ['beɪbɪbæt ərɪŋ] *n* malos tratos *mpl* a los niños.

babyhood ['beɪbɪhʊd] *n* infancia *f.*

babyish ['beɪbɪʃ] *adj* infantil.

Babylonian [bæbɪ'ləʊnɪən] *adj & n* babilonio,-a *(m,f).*

baby-scales ['beɪbɪskeɪlz] *n* pesabebés *m inv.*

baby-sit ['beɪbɪsɪt] *vi (pt & pp baby-sat)* cuidar a niños, hacer de canguro.

baby-sitter ['beɪbɪsɪtə'] *n* canguro *mf.*

baby-sitting ['beɪbɪsɪtɪŋ] *n* hacer *m* de canguro.

baby-walker ['beɪbɪwɔːkə'] *n* tacataca *m*, tacatá *m*, andador *m.*

bachelor ['bætʃələ'] *n* **1** soltero *m*; **old b.,** solterón *m.* ■ **b. girl,** soltera *f*; *fam* **b. pad,** piso *m* de soltero. **2** *Univ* licenciado,-a *m, f.* ■ **B. of Arts,** licenciado,-a *m, f* en Filosofía y Letras; **B. of Science** licenciado,-a *m, f* en Ciencias.

bacillus [bə'sɪləs] *n (pl bacilli* [bə'sɪlaɪ]*) Biol* bacilo *m.*

back [bæk] I *n* **1** *(of person)* espalda *f*; *(of animal)* lomo *m*; **b. to b.,** espalda con espalda; **b. to front,** al revés; **to fall on one's b.,** caer(se) de espaldas; *fig* **to be glad to see the**

b. of sb, alegrarse de que algn se vaya; *fig* **to break the b. of a job**, hacer la parte más difícil de un trabajo; *fig* **to do sth behind sb's b.**, hacer algo a espaldas de algn; *fig* **to get sb's b. up**, fastidiar a algn, poner negro a algn; *fig* **to have one's b. to the wall**, estar en un aprieto; *fig* **to put one's b. into sth**, deslomarse en hacer algo; *fam* **get off my b.!**, ¡deja de fastidiarme! **2** *(of book)* lomo *m; (of chair)* respaldo *m; (of coin)* dorso *m; (of coin)* reverso *m; (of hand)* dorso *m,* revés *m; (of head)* parte *f* posterior; *(of house, car)* parte *f* de atrás; **at the b. of**, *US* **in b. of**, detrás de; **the dress fastens at the b.**, el vestido se abrocha por detrás; *fig* **he knows Leeds like the b. of his hand**, conoce Leeds como la palma de la mano; *fig* **who is at the b. of all this?**, ¿quién está detrás de todo esto? **3** *(of garden, stage, cupboard)* fondo *m; fam* **to live at the b. of beyond**, vivir en el quinto pino. **4** *Ftb (position)* defensa *f; (player)* defensa *mf.* **II** *adj* **1** trasero,-a, posterior, de atrás. ■ *Aut* **b. axle**, eje *m* trasero; **b. door**, *(house)* puerta *f* de atrás; *(tradesman's entrance)* puerta *f* de servicio; **to get in by the b. door**, conseguir algo por enchufe; **b. room**, cuarto *m* trasero; **b. seat**, asiento *m* de detrás; *fig* **to take a b. seat**, pasar al segundo plano; *Aut* **b. wheel**, rueda *f* trasera; **the b. streets**, las callejuelas. **2** *(in arrears)* atrasado,-a. ■ **b. rent**, alquiler *m* atrasado; **b. pay**, atrasos *mpl; Press* **b. number**, número *m* atrasado. **III** *adv* **1** *(to the rear)* atrás, detrás; *(towards the rear)* hacia atrás; **b. and forth**, de acá para allá; **stand b.!**, ¡atrás! **2** *(in return)* **to hit b.**, devolver el golpe; *fig* contestar a una denuncia *or* acusación; **he hit b. at his critics**, replicó a sus detractores. **3** *(to starting point)* **as soon as you get b.**, tan pronto como vuelvas; **to be b.**, estar de vuelta; **to call sb b.**, hacer volver a algn; *Tel* volver a llamar a algn; **to come b.**, volver; **to put sth b.**, *(replace)* devolver algo a su sitio; *(delay)* aplazar algo; **to put the clock b.**, retrasar el reloj. **4** *(in time)* **as far b. as 1950**, ya en 1950; **some years b.**, hace unos años. **IV** *vtr* **1** *(support)* apoyar, respaldar. **3** *(bet)* apostar por. **4** *(car, bus, lorry)* dar marcha atrás a, hacer marcha atrás con; **he tried to b. the car into the garage**, intentó meter el coche en el garaje marcha atrás. **V** *vi* **1** *(move backwards)* retroceder. **2** *Aut (car, bus)* ir marcha atrás, dar marcha atrás, **she backed into a tree**, chocó por detrás con un árbol. ◆ **back away** *vi* retirarse. ◆ **back down** *vi* echarse atrás, claudicar. ◆ **back off** *vi* echarse atrás, desistir. ◆ **back on to** *vtr* dar a. ◆ **back out** *vi* **1** *Aut* salir marcha atrás. **2** *(withdraw)* retractarse, volverse atrás. ◆ **back up 1** *vtr* apoyar. **II** *vi Aut* ir marcha atrás.

backache ['bækeɪk] *n* dolor *m* de espalda, dolor *m* de riñones.

backbencher ['bækbentʃəʳ] *n Parl* diputado,-a *m, f* que no es ministro.

backbite ['bækbaɪt] *vi (pt backbit* ['bækbɪt]*; pp backbitten* ['bækbɪtən]*, US backbit)* murmurar, hablar mal de.

backbiter ['bækbaɪtəʳ] *n* murmurador,-a *m,f.*

backbiting ['bækbaɪtɪŋ] *n* murmuración *f,* maledicencia *f.*

backbone ['bækbəʊn] *n Anat* columna *f, fig* **he's got no b.**, le faltan agallas.

backbreaking ['bækbreɪkɪŋ] *adj* agotador,-a, matador,-a.

backchat ['bæktʃæt] *n fam* impertinencias *fpl;* **I don't want any more b. from you**, ¡deja de contestarme!, ¡no seas respondón!

backcloth ['bækklɒθ] *n Theat* telón *m* de fondo.

backcomb ['bækkəʊm] *vtr* cardar.

backdate [bæk'deɪt] *vtr* antedatar.

backdated [bæk'deɪtɪd] *adj* con efecto retroactivo; **b. pay rise**, aumento *m* de sueldo con efecto retroactivo.

backdrop ['bækdrɒp] *n Theat* telón *m* de fondo.

backer ['bækəʳ] *n* **1** *Fin* promotor,-a *m,f.* **2** *Pol* partidario,-a *m,f.* **3** *(person who bets)* apostante *mf.*

backfire [bæk'faɪəʳ] **I** *vi* **1** *Aut* petardear. **2** *fig* salir rana, fallar; **our plan backfired**, nos salió el tiro por la culata. **II** *n Aut* petardeo *m.*

backgammon ['bækgæmən] *n* backgammon *m.*

background ['bækgraʊnd] *n* **1** fondo *m; Art Phot* fondo *m,* ultimo término *m;* **on a yellow b.**, sobre un fondo amarillo; **to stay in the b.**, quedarse en segundo plano. ■ **b. music**, música *f* de fondo. **2** *(origin)* origen *m; (past)* pasado *m; (education)* formación *f;* **from a working-class b.**, de clase obrera. **3** *(circumstances)* antecedentes *mpl.* **4** *(atmosphere)* ambiente *m;* **against a b. of political unrest**, en un ambiente de malestar político.

backhand ['bækhænd] *n* **1** *sport* revés *m.* ■ **b. volley**, volea *f* de revés. **2** *(handwriting)* letra *f* inclinada hacia la izquierda.

backhanded ['bækhændɪd] *adj* equívoca,-a, ambiguo,-a; **a b. compliment**, un cumplido ambiguo.

backhander ['bækhændəʳ] *n* **1** *(blow with hand)* revés *m.* **2** *sl (bribe)* soborno *m.*

backing ['bækɪŋ] *n* **1** *(support)* apoyo *m; Com Fin* respaldo *m* financiero. **2** *(of picture)* soporte *m.* **3** *Mus* acompañamiento *m.*

backlash ['bæklæʃ] *n* reacción *f* violenta y repentina.

backlog ['bæklɒg] *n* acumulación *f* (de cosas); **to have a b. of work**, tener un montón de trabajo atrasado.

backpack ['bækpæk] *n* mochila *f.*

backpacker ['bækpækəʳ] *n* mochilero,-a *m, f; (hiker)* excursionista *mf.*

backpacking ['bækpækɪŋ] *n* **to go b.**, viajar con mochila; *(hiking)* ir de excursión.

backpedal ['bækpedəl] *vi (pt & pp backpedalled) fam* dar marcha atrás.

back-seat ['bæksiːt] *adj Aut* **b.-s. driver**, pasajero *m* que da consejos innecesarios al conductor.

backside [bæk'saɪd] *n fam* trasero *m,* culo *m.*

backslide ['bækslaɪd] *vi* reincidir.

backsliding ['bækslaɪdɪŋ] *n* reincidencia *f.*

backstage [bæk'steɪdʒ] *adv Theat* entre bastidores.

backstairs ['bæksteəz] *n* escalera *f* de servicio. ■ **b. gossip**, comadreo *m;* **b. influence**, enchufe *m.*

backstroke ['bækstrəʊk] *n Swimming* espalda *f.*

backtrack ['bæktræk] *vi* volver hacia atrás; *fig* volverse *or* retractarse.

backup ['bækʌp] *n* apoyo *m,* respaldo *m.*

backward ['bækwəd] **I** *adj* **1** *(movement)* hacia atrás. **2** *(country)* subdesarrollado,-a; *(child)* atrasado,-a. **II** *adv esp US* atrás, hacia atrás.

backwardness ['bækwədnɪs] *n (of country)* subdesarrollo *m; (of child)* atraso *m,* retraso *m.*

backwards ['bækwəds] *adv* hacia atrás, al revés; **to walk b.**, andar de espaldas; **to walk b. and forwards**, andar de acá para allá.

backwash ['bækwɒʃ] *n* **1** remolinos *mpl* de agua. **2** *fig (of event, situation)* repercusión *f.*

backyard [bæk'jɑːd] *n* patio *m* trasero; *US* jardín *m* trasero.

bacon ['beɪkən] *n* tocino *m,* bacon *m;* **streaky b.**, tocino entreverado; *fam* **to bring home the b.**, *(provide)* ganarse los garbanzos *or* el pan; *(be successful)* llevarse la palma; *fam* **to save sb's b.**, salvarle el pellejo a algn.

bacteria [bæk'tɪərɪə] *npl (sing bacterium)* bacterias *fpl.*

bacterial [bæk'tɪərɪəl] *adj* bacteriano,-a.

bactericide [bæk'tɪərɪsaɪd] *n* bactericida *m.*

bacteriological [bæktɪərɪə'lɒdʒɪkəl] *adj* bacteriológico,-a.

bacteriologist [bæktɪərɪ'ɒlədʒɪst] *n* bacteriólogo,-a *m,f.*

bacteriology [bæktɪərɪ'ɒlədʒɪ] *n* bacteriología *f.*

bacterium [bæk'tɪərɪəm] *n (pl bacteria)* bacteria *f.*

bad [bæd] **I** *adj (worse, worst)* **1** *(poor, inferior)* malo,-a; **a b. translation**, una mala traducción; **he's a b. driver**, conduce muy mal; **she's b. at mathematics**, se le dan mal las matemáticas; **to go from b. to worse,** ir de mal en peor. **2** (*decayed*) podrido,-a; **to go b.,** echarse a perder, estropearse. **3** (*unfortunate*) **he'll come to a b. end,** acabará mal; **it's too b. that ...,** qué lástima que ...; **that's too b.!,** ¡qué pena!; **to be in a b. way,** estar en un mal paso. **4** (*wicked*) malo,-a; (*naughty*) travieso,-a; **a b. word,** un taco; **to use b. language,** ser mal hablado,-a; *fam* **she's a b. lot,** es un elemento de mucho cuidado. **5** (*unpleasant*) **b. joke,** broma de mal gusto; **b. news,** malas noticias; **b. smell,** mal olor; **they had a b. time,** lo pasaron muy mal; **to be in a b. mood,** estar de mal humor; **to be on b. terms with sb,** estar a malas con algn. **6** (*serious*) (*accident, mistake*) grave; (*headache*) fuerte; **to have a b. cold,** estar muy acatarrado,-a. **7** (*harmful*) nocivo,-a; **to be b. for one's health,** ser perjudicial para la salud. **8** (*ill*) enfermo,-a, malo,-a; **she's very b. today,** hoy está muy mal; **to have a b. leg,** tener problemas con la pierna, dolerle la pierna a uno. **9 b. coin,** moneda falsa; **b. debt,** deuda incobrable. **II** *n* lo malo; **to take the b. with the good,** aceptar lo bueno y lo malo; **I'm a thousand pounds to the b.,** he perdido mil libras. ◆ **badly** *adv* **1** mal; **he did b. in the exam,** le salió mal el examen; **to be b. off,** andar mal de dinero. **2** (*seriously*) gravemente; **b. injured,** gravemente herido,-a, herido,-a de gravedad. **3** (*very much*) mucho; **to miss sb b.,** echar mucho de menos a algn; **we need it b.,** nos hace mucha falta.

baddie *n*, **baddy** ['bædɪ] *n Cin fam* malo *m*.

bade [beɪd] *pt see* **bid.**

badge [bædʒ] *n* **1** (*emblem*) insignia *f*; (*metal disc*) chapa *f*. **2** *fig* símbolo *m*, señal *f*.

badger ['bædʒə'] **I** *n Zool* tejón *m*. **II** *vtr* acosar, importunar, fastidiar; **to b. sb with questions,** acosar a algn con preguntas.

bad-looking [bæd'lʊkɪŋ] *adj* **he's not b,-l.,** no está nada mal.

badminton ['bædmɪntən] *n Sport* bádminton *m*.

badness ['bædnɪs] *n* **1** (*of person*) maldad *f*. **2** (*of road*) mal estado *m*.

bad-tempered [bæd'tempəd] *adj* gruñón,-ona; **to be b.-t.,** (*temperament*) tener mal genio; (*temporarily*) estar de mal humor.

baffle ['bæfəl] **I** *vtr* desconcertar, confundir. **II** *n* baffle *m*, pantalla *f* acústica.

baffling ['bæflɪŋ] *adj* incomprensible, enigmático,-a.

BAFTA ['bæftə] *abbr of* **British Academy of Film and Television Arts,** Academia *f* Británica de Cine y Televisión.

bag [bæg] **I** *n* **1** (*gen*) bolsa *f*; (*handbag*) bolso *m*; **to pack one's bags and go,** liar el petate; *fig* **to be a b. of bones,** estar en los huesos; *fam* **bags of,** montones de; *fam* **I've got bags of them,** tengo la tira; *fam* **they've got bags of time,** tienen tiempo de sobra. ■ **diplomatic b.,** valija *f* diplomática; **shopping b.,** bolsa *f* de la compra; **sleeping b.,** saco *m* de dormir; **travel b.,** bolsa *f* de viaje. **2** (*hunting*) caza *f*; *fam* **it's in the b.,** está en el bote, es cosa hecha. **3** *pej* (*woman*) old **b.,** arpía *f*, bruja *f*. **4 bags,** (*under eyes*) ojeras *fpl*. **5** *fam* **bags,** pantalones *mpl*. **II** *vtr* (*pt & pp* **bagged**) **1** (*put into sacks*) ensacar, meter en sacos. **2** (*hunting*) cazar. **3** *fam* coger; **he always bags the best seat,** siempre coge el mejor sitio.

bagatelle [bægə'tel] *n* **1** (*trifle*) bagatela *f*, fruslería *f*. **2** (*pinball*) millón *m*.

bagful ['bægfʊl] *n* bolsa *f*, saco *m*.

baggage ['bægɪdʒ] *n* **1** equipaje *m*. ■ *US Rail* **b. car,** furgón *m* de equipajes. **2** *Mil* bagaje *m*.

baggy ['bægɪ] *adj* (**baggier, baggiest**) holgado,-a; **b. trousers,** pantalones anchos; **my trousers have gone b. at the knees,** mis pantalones han dado de sí por las rodillas.

Baghdad [bæg'dæd] *n* Bagdad.

bagpiper ['bægpaɪpə'] *n* gaitero,-a *m,f*.

bagpipes ['bægpaɪps] *npl* gaita *f sing*; **to play the b.,** tocar la gaita.

Bahamas [bə'hɑːməz] *npl* **the B.,** las Bahamas.

Bahamian [bə'heɪmɪən] *adj & n* bahameño,-a (*m,f*).

Bahrain [bɑː'reɪn] *n* Bahrein.

bail¹ [beɪl] *n Jur* fianza *f*; **on b.,** bajo fianza; **to jump b.,** huir estando bajo fianza; **to release sb on b.,** poner en libertad bajo fianza; **to stand b. for sb,** salir fiador por algn. ◆ **bail out** *vtr* **1** *Jur* conseguir la libertad de algn bajo fianza; *fig* (*person*) sacar de un apuro; *fam* echar un cable a. **2** *Av* saltar en paracaídas de un avión.

bail² [beɪl] *vi Naut* achicar (**out, -**).

bail³ [beɪl] *n Crick* travesaño *m*.

bailiff ['beɪlɪf] *n* **1** *Jur* alguacil *m*. **2** (*steward*) administrador *m*.

bain-marie [bænmə'riː] *n Culin* baño *m* maría.

bairn [beən] *n Scot* niño,-a *m,f*.

bait [beɪt] **I** *n* **1** *Fishing* cebo *m*, carnada *f*. **2** *fig* cebo *m*, señuelo *m*; *Fishing & fig* **to swallow the b., rise to the b.,** tragar el anzuelo, picar. **II** *vtr* **1** *Fish* (*hook*) cebar. **2** (*torment*) hostigar.

baize [beɪz] *n* bayeta *f*; (*on games tables*) **green b.,** tapete *m* verde.

bake [beɪk] **I** *vtr* **1** (*cake etc*) cocer al horno. **2** (*harden*) endurecer. **II** *vi fam* hacer mucho calor; **it's baking in here!,** ¡hace un calor terrible aquí dentro!

baked ['beɪkt] *adj* al horno; **freshly b. bread,** pan recién hecho. ■ **b. potato,** patata *f* al horno.

baker ['beɪkə'] *n* panadero,-a *m*, *f*; (*pastrycook*) pastelero,-a *m,f*. ■ **b.'s (shop),** panadería *f*; **b.'s dozen,** docena *f* de fraile.

bakery ['beɪkərɪ] *n* panadería *f*.

baking ['beɪkɪŋ] *n* cocción *f*. ■ **b. dish,** fuente *f* para horno; **b. powder,** levadura *f* en polvo; **b. tin,** molde *m*.

balaclava [bælə'klɑːvə] *n* **b. (helmet),** pasamontañas *m inv*.

balance ['bæləns] **I** *n* **1** (*scales*) balanza *f*; *fig* **to hang in the b.,** estar en juego, estar en la balanza. **2** (*equilibrium*) equilibrio *m*; *Pol* **b. of power,** equilibrio *m* de fuerzas; **to lose one's b.,** perder el equilibrio; *fig* trastornarse; *fig* **to throw sb off his b.,** hacerle perder el equilibrio a algn; *fig* desconcertar a algn. **3** *Fin* saldo *m* de una cuenta. ■ **b. due,** saldo *m* deudor; **b. in hand,** saldo *m* disponible; **b. of payments,** balanza *f* de pagos; **b. sheet,** balance *m*; **credit b.,** saldo *m* acreedor. **4** (*remainder*) resto *m*. **5** (*of clock*) volante *m*. **II** *vtr* **1** poner en equilibrio (**on,** en). **2** *Fin* (*budget*) equilibrar; (*account*) saldar; **to b. the books,** hacer el balance. **3** (*weigh up*) sopesar, comparar. **III** *vi* **1** guardar el equilibrio, mantenerse en equilibrio. **2** *Fin* (*tally*) cuadrar. ◆ **balance out** *vi* compensarse.

balanced ['bælənst] *adj* equilibrado,-a; **a b. diet,** una alimentación equilibrada.

balcony ['bælkənɪ] *n* **1** *Archit* balcón *m*. **2** *Theat* anfiteatro *m*.

bald [bɔːld] *adj* **1** (*person*) calvo,-a; **b. patch,** calva *f*; **to go b.,** quedarse calvo; *fam* **to be as b. as a coot,** estar más calvo que una bola de billar. **2** (*tyre*) desgastado,-a. **3** (*style*) escueto,-a, sencillo,-a; **b. statement,** simple exposición de los hechos. ◆ **baldly** *adv* francamente.

balderdash ['bɔːldədæʃ] *n fam* tonterías *fpl*, disparates *mpl*.

bald-headed [bɔːld'hedɪd] *adj* calvo,-a.

baldness ['bɔːldnɪs] *n* **1** (*of person*) calvicie *f*. **2** (*of tyre*) desnudez *m*. **3** (*of style*) sencillez *f*.

bale¹ [beɪl] **I** *n* **1** *Com* (*of goods*) bala *f*, fardo *m*; (*of cotton*) bala *f*, paca *f*. **II** *vtr* embalar, empacar.

bale² [beɪl] *vtr see* **bail².** ◆ **bale out I** *vi* **1** *Naut* achicar. **2** *Av* saltar en paracaídas de un avión. **II** *vtr fig* (*person*) sacar de apuro; *fam* echar un cable a.

Balearic [bælɪ'ærɪk] *adj* balear, baleárico,-a; **the B. Islands,** las Islas Baleares.

baleful ['beɪlfʊl] *adj* funesto,-a, siniestro,-a.

balk [bɔːk] **I** vtr poner obstáculos a; (project, plan) frustrar. **II** vi (horse) plantarse (**at**, en); (person) **to b. at doing sth**, negarse or resistirse a hacer algo.

Balkan ['bɔːlkən] adj balcánico,-a; **the B. States, the Balkans**, los Balcanes.

ball[^1] [bɔːl] **I** n **1** Crick Ten Baseb pelota f; Ftb balón m; Bill Golf bola f; **to play b.**, jugar a la pelota; fig **the b. is in your court**, ahora te toca a ti; fig **to keep the b. rolling**, mantener; fig **to play b. with sb**, cooperar con algn; fig **to start the b. rolling**, poner las cosas en marcha; fam **to be on the b.**, ser un espabilado. ▪ Tech **b. bearing**, rodamiento m de bolas, cojinete m de bolas; Ten **b. boy, b. girl**, recogepelotas mf inv. **2** (of paper) bola f; (of wool) ovillo m. **3** Anat **b. of the foot**, metatarso m. **4** US béisbol m. ▪ **b. game**, partido m de béisbol; fig **it's a whole new b. game**, es otra historia; **b. park**, campo m de béisbol; fam **a b. park figure**, una cifra aproximativa. **5** vulg offens **balls**, cojones mpl, huevos mpl; **b.!**, ¡y una mierda!; **he's got a lot of b.**, tiene huevos, tiene mucha cara. **II** vtr US vulg follar. ◆ **ball(s) up** vtr US vulg (task, activity) cagar, pifiar, joder.

ball[^2] [bɔːl] n baile m de etiqueta; fam **to have a b.**, pasarlo en grande.

ballad ['bæləd] n **1** Lit balada f. **2** Mus balada f, copla f.

ball-and-socket joint [bɔːlənd'sɒkɪtdʒɔɪnt] n Tech articulación f de rótula.

ballast ['bæləst] n **1** Naut lastre m. **2** Rail balasto m.

ballcock ['bɔːlkɒk] n Tech llave f de bola, llave f de flotador.

ballerina [bælə'riːnər] n bailarina f.

ballet ['bæleɪ] n ballet m, baile m clásico. ▪ **b. dancer**, bailarín,-ina m,f; **b. shoe**, zapatilla f de ballet.

ballistic [bə'lɪstɪk] adj balístico,-a; **b. missile**, misil balístico.

ballistics [bə'lɪstɪks] n balística f.

balloon [bə'luːn] **I** n **1** (gen) globo m; Av **hot-air b.**, globo aerostático; **to go up in a b.**, montar en un globo; **to go down like a lead b.**, ser un fracaso total. **2** (in cartoon) bocadillo m. **II** vi hincharse (**out, up, -**); fig aumentar rápidamente.

ballooning [bə'luːnɪŋ] n aerostación f.

balloonist [bə'luːnɪst] n aeróstata mf.

ballot ['bælət] **I** n **1** (vote) votación f; **to take a b. on sth**, someter algo a votación. ▪ **b. box**, urna f; **b. paper**, papeleta f; **postal b.**, votación f por correo; **secret b.**, votación f secreta. **2** (paper) papeleta f. **II** vi votar (**for**, por). **III** vtr someter a votación, hacer votar; **the union has balloted its members on the issue**, el sindicato ha sometido el asunto a la votación de sus miembros.

ballpen ['bɔːlpen] n fam boli m.

ballpoint (pen) ['bɔːlpɔɪnt ('pen)] n bolígrafo m.

ballroom ['bɔːlruːm] n salón m de baile.

balls-up ['bɔːlzʌp] n vulg cagada f; **he's made a real b.-up of the project!**, en este proyecto, la ha cagado.

ballyhoo [bælɪ'huː] n fam **1** (fuss) jaleo m. **2** (noisy publicity) propaganda f sensacionalista.

balm [bɑːm] n bálsamo m.

balmy ['bɑːmɪ] adj (**balmier, balmiest**) (like balm) balsámico,-a; (fragrant) fragante; (weather) suave.

baloney [bə'ləʊnɪ] n fam tonterías fpl.

balsa ['bɔːlsə] n balsa f.

balsam ['bɔːlsəm] n bálsamo m.

Baltic ['bɔːltɪk] adj báltico,-a; **the B. (Sea)**, el (Mar) Báltico.

balustrade [bæləstreɪd] n balaustrada f, barandilla f.

bamboo [bæm'buː] n Bot bambú m; **b. shoots**, brotes mpl de bambú.

bamboozle [bæm'buːzəl] vtr fam **1** (puzzle) dejar perplejo a. **2** (trick) burlar, embaucar.

ban [bæn] **I** n prohibición f. **II** vtr (pt & pp **banned**) **1** (prohibit) prohibir. **2** (exclude) excluir. **3** (driving) suspender; **he was banned from driving for six months**, le retiraron el carnet durante seis meses.

banal [bə'nɑːl] adj banal, trivial. ◆ **banally** adv trivialmente.

banality [bə'nælɪtɪ] n banalidad f, trivialidad f.

banana [bə'nɑːnə] n **1** (fruit) plátano m, banana f; fam **to be bananas**, estar chiflado,-a; fam **to go bananas**, volverse loco,-a. ▪ Pol **b. republic**, república f bananera; Culin **b. split**, postre m de plátano, helado y jarabe. **2** (tree) plátano m, banano m.

band [bænd] **I** n **1** (strip of material) tira f, faja f; (ribbon) cinta f. ▪ **elastic b.**, goma f elástica. **2** (stripe) raya f, franja f. **3** Rad banda f. ▪ **frequency b.**, banda f de frecuencia. **4** (group) grupo m; (of youths) pandilla f; (of thieves) banda f. **5** Mus banda f. ▪ **jazz b.**, orquesta f de jazz; **military b.**, banda f militar; **pop b.**, conjunto m. **II** vi **to b. together**, unirse, juntarse.

bandage ['bændɪdʒ] Med **I** n venda f. **II** vtr vendar.

Band-Aid® ['bændeɪd] n US tirita® f.

B & B [biːən'biː] n abbr of **bed and breakfast**, cama f y desayuno m.

bandit ['bændɪt] n bandido m. ▪ **one-armed b.**, máquina f tragaperras.

bandmaster ['bændmɑːstər] n director m de una banda.

bandsman ['bændzmən] n (pl **bandsmen**) músico m de banda.

bandstand ['bændstænd] n quiosco m de música.

bandwagon ['bændwægən] n fig **to jump on the b.**, subirse al tren.

bandy ['bændɪ] **I** vtr (pt & pp **bandied**) (words, ideas) intercambiar. **II** adj (**bandier, bandiest**) torcido,-a hacia fuera; **with b. legs**, patizambo,-a. ◆ **bandy about** vtr (rumours, ideas) propagar, difundir.

bandy-legged ['bændɪleg(ɪ)d] adj patizambo,-a.

bane [beɪn] n perdición f, ruina f; **it's the b. of my life**, me está amargando la vida.

bang [bæŋ] **I** n **1** (blow) golpe m. **2** (noise) ruido m; (explosion) estallido m; (of gun) estampido m, detonación f; **supersonic b.**, estampido supersónico; **to go off with a b.**, estallar; fam fig ser un exitazo; **to shut the door with a b.**, dar un portazo. **II** vtr **1** golpear, dar golpes en; **to b. one's head**, darse un golpe en la cabeza; **to b. sth shut**, cerrar algo de golpe; fam **to b. one's head against a brick wall**, hacer esfuerzos en vano. **2** vulg (have sex with) follar. **III** vi golpear, dar golpes; **to b. at the door**, dar golpes en la puerta; **to b. shut**, cerrarse de golpe. **IV** interj (blow) ¡zas!; (crash) ¡cataplum!; (of gun) **b., b.!**, ¡pum, pum! **V** adv fam justo; **b. in the middle**, justo en medio; **b. on time**, justo a tiempo. ◆ **bang about, bang around** vi fam hacer mucho ruido.

banger ['bæŋər] n **1** (firework) petardo m. **2** fam (sausage) salchicha f. **3** Aut fam (car) **old b.**, cacharro m.

Bangladesh [bæŋglə'deʃ] n Bangladesh.

Bangladeshi [bæŋglə'deʃɪ] **I** adj de Bangladesh. **II** n habitante mf de Bangladesh.

bangle ['bæŋgəl] n ajorca f, brazalete m.

banish ['bænɪʃ] vtr desterrar.

banishment ['bænɪʃmənt] n destierro m.

banister ['bænɪstər] n barandilla f, pasamanos m inv.

banjo ['bændʒəʊ] n (pl **banjos** or **banjoes**) Mus banjo m.

bank[^1] [bæŋk] n **1** Com Fin banco m. ▪ **b. account**, cuenta f bancaria; **b. bill**, letra f de cambio; US billete m de banco; **b. clerk**, empleado,-a m, f de banca; **b. credit**, crédito m bancario; **b. draft**, letra f bancaria; **b. holiday**, fiesta f nacional; **b. rate**, tipo m de interés bancario; **b. statement**, extracto m de cuenta; **merchant b.**, banco m mercantil; **savings b.**, caja f de ahorros; **World B.**, Banco m Mundial. **2** (in gambling) banca f; **to break the b.**, hacer saltar la banca. **3** (store) banco m. ■ Med **blood b.**, banco m de sangre; Comput **data b.**, banco m de datos. **II** vtr Com Fin depositar, ingresar. **III** vi Com Fin **to b. with**, tener una cuenta en. ◆ **bank on** vtr contar con.

bank² [bæŋk] **I** n **1** (mound) loma f; (embankment) terraplén m; (slope) pendiente f; **b. of snow**, montón m de nieve. **2** (of river) ribera f; (edge) orilla f; **on the banks of the Thames**, a orillas del Támesis. **II** vtr (heap up) amontonar. **III** vtr & vi Av ladear, ladearse. ◆ **bank up** vtr (fire) avivar.

bank³ [bæŋk] n hilera f, fila f; Elec **b. of lights**, batería f de luces.

bankbook ['bæŋkbʊk] n libreta f or cartilla f de ahorros.

banker ['bæŋkə'] n banquero,-a m,f.

banking ['bæŋkɪŋ] n banca f; **to be in b.**, ser banquero,-a. ■ **b. house**, banco m.

banknote ['bæŋknəʊt] n billete m de banco.

bankroll ['bæŋkrəʊl] US **I** n fondos mpl. **II** vtr fam financiar.

bankrupt ['bæŋkrʌpt] **I** adj quebrado,-a, en quiebra, insolvente; **to go b.**, quebrar. **II** n quebrado m. **III** vtr hacer quebrar, llevar a la bancarrota.

bankruptcy ['bæŋkrʌptsɪ] n Com quiebra f, bancarrota f.

banner ['bænə'] n (in demonstration, festival) pancarta f; (flag) bandera f, fig **under the b. of socialism**, en nombre del socialismo. ■ Press **b. headlines**, grandes titulares mpl.

bannister ['bænɪstə'] n see **banister**.

banns [bænz] npl amonestaciones fpl; **to publish the b.**, correr las amonestaciones.

banquet ['bæŋkwɪt] **I** n banquete m. **II** vi banquetear.

banshee [bæn'ʃiː] n Ir hada f que anuncia la muerte.

bantam ['bæntəm] n (cock) gallo m; (hen) gallina f bantam.

bantamweight ['bæntəmweɪt] n Box peso m gallo.

banter ['bæntə'] **I** n bromas fpl, chanzas fpl. **II** vi bromear.

bap [bæp] n Culin bollo m, panecillo m.

baptise [bæp'taɪz] vtr see **baptize**.

baptism ['bæptɪzəm] n **1** (sacrament) bautismo m. **2** (christening) bautizo m.

baptistry ['bæptɪstrɪ] n bautisterio m.

baptize [bæp'taɪz] vtr bautizar.

bar [baː'] **I** n **1** (of iron, gold) barra f; (of chocolate) tableta f; (of soap) pastilla f. **2** (of cage, prison) barrote m; fam **to be behind bars**, estar a la sombra. **3** (sand, mud) barra f, bajío m, medano m. **4** (obstacle) obstáculo m; (barrier) barrera f. ■ **colour b.**, segregación f racial. **5** Jur (dock) banquillo m; (court) tribunal m; **the prisoner at the b.**, el acusado, la acusada. **6** Jur **the B.**, (profession) abogacía f; (body of lawyers) colegio m de abogados; **to be called to the B.**, entrar en el colegio de abogados. **7** (room in pub etc) bar m; (counter) barra f, mostrador m. ■ **singles b.**, bar m de solteros. **8** Gymn barra f; **horizontal b.**, barra fija. **9** Mus compás m. **II** vtr (pt & pp **barred**) **1** (door) atrancar; Aut (road) cortar; (window) poner barrotes a. **2** (exclude) excluir (**from**, de). **3** (prohibit) prohibir; **no holds barred**, todo vale; **she was barred from the club**, le prohibieron la entrada en el club. **III** prep salvo, a excepción de; **b. none**, sin excepción.

barb [baːb] **I** n **1** (point) lengüeta f. **2** (gibe) observación f mordaz. **II** vtr poner lengüetas en un dardo.

Barbados [baː'beɪdɒs] n Barbados.

barbarian [baː'beərɪən] adj & n bárbaro,-a (m,f).

barbaric [baː'bærɪk] adj bárbaro,-a; **the hunting of foxes is b.**, la caza de zorros es una barbaridad.

barbarity [baː'bærɪtɪ] n barbaridad f.

barbarous ['baːbərəs] adj bárbaro,-a.

Barbary ['baːbərɪ] n Hist Berbería f. ■ Zool **B. ape**, mona f de Berbería or de Gibraltar.

barbecue ['baːbɪkjuː] **I** n barbacoa f. **II** vtr asar a la parrilla.

barbed [baːbd] adj **1** (arrow) con lengüeta; **b. wire**, alambre m de púas. **2** fig (remark) mordaz.

barbel ['baːbəl] n (fish) barbo m.

barber ['baːbə'] n barbero,-a m,f, peluquero,-a m,f; **b.'s (shop)**, barbería f, peluquería f.

barbershop ['baːbəʃɒp] n US **1** barbería f. **2 b. quartet**, cuarteto m de voces.

barbiturate [baː'bɪtjʊrɪt] n Med barbitúrico m.

Barcelona [baːsɪ'ləʊnə] n Barcelona.

bard [baːd] n Lit bardo m.

bare [beə'] **I** adj **1** (naked) desnudo,-a; (head) descubierto,-a; (foot) descalzo,-a; (room) sin muebles; (landscape) raso,-a; (style) escueto,-a; Elec **b. wire**, cable descubierto; **to lay b.**, poner al descubierto; **with his b. hands**, sólo con las manos. **2** (basic) mero,-a; **the b. minimum**, lo mínimo; **to earn a b. living**, ganar lo justo para vivir. **II** vtr (make naked) desnudar; (uncover) descubrir; **to b. one's head**, descubrirse; fig **to b. one's soul**, desnudar el alma.

bareback(ed) ['beəbæk(t)] adj & adv **to ride b.**, montar un caballo a pelo.

barefaced ['beəfeɪst] adj desvergonzado,-a; **b. lie**, mentira descarada.

barefoot ['beəfʊt] adj & adv descalzo,-a; **to go b.**, ir descalzo.

bareheaded [beə'hedɪd] adj descubierto,-a, sin sombrero.

barely ['beəlɪ] adv apenas; **I b. know you**, apenas te conozco.

bareness ['beənɪs] n desnudez f; (of style) sencillez f, claridad f.

bargain ['baːgɪn] **I** n **1** (agreement) trato m; pacto m; (deal) negocio m; **into the b.**, por añadidura, además; **it's a b.!**, ¡trato hecho!; **to drive a hard b.**, imponer condiciones duras; **to make or strike a b.**, cerrar un trato. **2** (cheap purchase) ganga f, oportunidad f; **it's a real b.**, es una verdadera ganga. ■ **b. basement**, sección f de oportunidades; **b. offer**, oferta f; **b. price**, precio m de oferta. **II** vi **1** negociar; **the union bargained with the management for more pay**, el sindicato negoció el aumento de salario con la patronal. **2** (haggle) regatear; **to b. over the price of sth**, regatear el precio de algo. ◆ **bargain for** vtr esperar, contar con; **I didn't b. for that**, no contaba con eso.

bargaining ['baːgɪnɪŋ] n **1** (negotiation) negociación f. ■ Ind **collective b.**, negociación f sobre el convenio colectivo. **2** (about price) regateo m.

barge [baːdʒ] **I** n gabarra f. ■ **b. pole**, bichero m; fam **I wouldn't touch it with a b. pole**, no lo quiero ni regalado, no lo cogería ni con pinzas. **II** vtr fam **to b. into**, (room) irrumpir en; (person) tropezar con. ◆ **barge in** vi fam **1** (go in) entrar sin permiso. **2** (interfere) entrometerse.

bargee [baː'dʒiː] n gabarrero m.

baritone ['bærɪtəʊn] adj & n Mus barítono (m).

barium ['beərɪəm] n Chem bario m. ■ Med **b. meal**, sulfato m de bario.

bark¹ [baːk] **I** n ladrido m; **his b. is worse than his bite**, perro ladrador poco mordedor. **II** vi (dog) ladrar; fam **to b. up the wrong tree**, ir descaminado,-a. **III** vtr gritar; **to b. (out) an order**, gritar una orden.

bark² [baːk] **I** n Bot corteza f. **II** vtr rasguñar; **she barked her shins on the desk**, se hizo un rasguño en la espinilla con el borde de la mesa.

bark³ [baːk] n US Naut barco m de vela; Lit barco m.

barking ['baːkɪŋ] n ladridos mpl.

barley ['baːlɪ] n cebada f. ■ Culin **pearl b.**, cebada f perlada; **b. sugar**, azúcar m cande.

barmaid ['bɑ:meɪd] *n* camarera *f*.

barman ['bɑ:mən] *n (pl barmen)* camarero *m*, barman *m*.

barmy ['bɑ:mɪ] *adj (barmier, barmiest) fam* chalado,-a, chiflado,-a.

barn [bɑ:n] *n* 1 *Agr* granero *m*. ■ **b. dance**, baile *m* popular. 2 *pej (large house)* caserón *m*.

barnacle ['bɑ:nəkəl] *n Zool* percebe *m*.

barnstorm ['bɑ:nstɔ:m] *vi US* hacer campaña electoral por los pueblos.

barnyard ['bɑ:njɑ:d] *n* corral *m*.

barometer [bə'rɒmɪtə'] *n* barómetro *m*.

barometric [bærə'metrɪc] *adj* barométrico,-a.

baron ['bærən] *n* 1 *(nobleman)* barón *m*. 2 *(powerful businessman)* barón *m*, magnate *m*. ■ **oil b.**, magnate *m* del petróleo; **the press barons**, los barones de la prensa.

baroness ['bærənɪs] *n* baronesa *f*.

baronet ['bærənɪt] *n* baronet *m*.

baronial [bə'rəʊnɪəl] *adj* de barón.

baroque [bə'rɒk] *adj* barroco,-a.

barque [bɑ:k] *n Naut* barco *m* de vela; *Lit* barco *m*.

barrack¹ ['bærək] 1 *n (usu pl) Mil* cuartel *m sing*; **confined to barracks**, bajo arresto en el cuartel. II *vtr Mil* acuartelar.

barrack² ['bærək] *vtr* abuchear.

barrack-room ['bærəkru:m] *n Mil* dormitorio *m* de cuartel. ■ **b.-r. language**, lenguaje *m* de cuartel.

barrage ['bærɑ:dʒ] *n* 1 *(dam)* presa *f*. 2 *Mil* barrera *f* de fuego. 3 *fig (of questions)* bombardeo *m*, lluvia *f*.

barrel ['bærəl] *n* 1 *(of wine)* tonel *m*, cuba *f*; *(of beer, oil)* barril *m*; *fig* **to scrape the bottom of the b.**, tocar fondo, estar a las últimas; *fam* **to have sb over a b.**, tener contra las cuerdas a algn. ■ **biscuit b.**, caja *f* de galletas. 2 *(firearm)* cañón *m*. 3 *Mus* **b. organ**, organillo *m*.

barren ['bærən] *adj* estéril.

barrenness ['bærənɪs] *n* esterilidad *f*.

barricade [bærɪ'keɪd] I *n* barricada *f*. II *vtr* levantar *or* montar barricadas; **to b. oneself in**, parapetarse.

barrier ['bærɪə'] *n* 1 barrera *f*, valla *f*. ■ **b. method**, método *m* de barrera; **b. reef**, banco *m* de coral, barrera *f* de coral; **sound b.**, barrera *f* del sonido. 2 *fig (hindrance)* barrera *f*, obstáculo *m*; **a b. to progress**, un obstáculo para el progreso.

barrister ['bærɪstə'] *n GB* abogado,-a *m, f* capacitado,-a para ejercer ante tribunales superiores.

barrow ['bærəʊ] *n* 1 *(wheelbarrow)* carretilla *f*. 2 *(handcart)* carretilla *f*, carrito *m*. ■ **b. boy**, vendedor *m* ambulante de fruta. 3 *(burial mound)* túmulo *m*.

barstool ['bɑ:stu:l] *n* taburete *m* de bar.

Bart [bɑ:t] *abbr see* **Bt.**

bartender ['bɑ:tendə'] *n US* camarero *m*, barman *m*.

barter ['bɑ:tə'] I *n* trueque *m*, permuta *f*. II *vtr* trocar **(for, por)**.

base [beɪs] I *n (gen)* base *f*; *(foot)* pie *m*; *Archit (of column)* basa *f*. ■ **air/naval/submarine b.**, base *f* aérea/naval/submarina; **b. camp**, campo *m* base, campamento *m* permanente. II *vtr* basar, fundar **(on, en)**. 2 *Mil (troops)* estacionar. III *adj* 1 *(low, despicable)* bajo,-a, vil, despreciable; **b. motives**, móviles despreciables. 2 *(metals)* común.

baseball ['beɪsbɔ:l] *n Sport* béisbol *m*.

baseboard ['beɪsbɔ:d] *n US Archit* zócalo *m*.

Basel ['bɑ:zəl] *n* Basilea.

baseless ['beɪslɪs] *adj* infundado,-a, que carece de fundamento.

baseline ['beɪslaɪn] *n Ten* línea *f* de saque.

basement ['beɪsmənt] *n* sótano *m*.

baseness ['beɪsnɪs] *n* bajeza *f*, vileza *f*.

bash [bæʃ] I *n* 1 *(heavy blow)* golpetazo *m*. 2 *(dent)* bollo *m*; **his car has had a b.**, tiene el coche abollado. 3 *fam (attempt)* intento *m*; **to have a b. at sth**, intentar hacer algo. II *vtr (hit)* golpear, aporrear; **she bashed her head against the wall**, se dio con la cabeza contra la pared; *fam* **to b. sb's head in**, romperle la crisma a algn. ◆ **bash up** *vtr fam* dar una paliza a.

bashful ['bæʃfʊl] *adj* tímido,-a.

bashfulness ['bæʃfʊlnɪs] *n* timidez *f*.

basic ['beɪsɪc] I *adj* básico,-a, fundamental; **b. pay**, sueldo *m* base; **b. vocabulary**, vocabulario elemental. II **basics** *npl* lo fundamental, lo esencial, la base. ◆ **basically** *adv* fundamentalmente, esencialmente.

basil ['bæzəl] *n Bot* albahaca *f*.

basilica [bə'zɪlɪkə] *n* basílica *f*.

basilisk ['bæzɪlɪsk] *n* basilisco *m*.

basin ['beɪsən] *n* 1 *(washbowl)* palangana *f*, jofaina *f*; *(for washing up)* barreño *m*; *(in bathroom)* lavabo *m*; *Culin (dish)* cuenco *m*, taza *f*, fuente *f*. 2 *Geog (of river)* cuenca *f*.

basis ['beɪsɪs] *n (pl bases* ['beɪsi:z]) base *f*; **on the b. of**, en base a.

bask [bɑ:sk] *vi* tostarse; **to b. in the sun**, tomar el sol, estar tumbado al sol; *fig* **to b. in sb's favour**, gozar del favor de algn.

basket ['bɑ:skɪt] *n* cesta *f*, cesto *m*. ■ **b. chair**, sillón *m* de mimbre; **b. maker**, cestero,-a *m, f*; **shopping b.**, cesta *f* de la compra; **wastepaper b.**, papelera *f*.

basketball ['bɑ:skɪtbɔ:l] *n Sport* baloncesto *m*. ■ **b. player**, baloncestista *mf*.

basketwork ['bɑ:skɪtwɜ:k] *n* cestería *f*.

Basque [bæsk, bɑ:sk] I *adj* vasco,-a. ■ **B. Country**, País Vasco, Vascongadas, Euskadi. II *n* 1 *(person)* vasco,-a *m, f*. 2 *(language)* vasco *m*, vascuence *m*, euskera *m*.

bas-relief ['bæsrɪli:f] *n* bajorrelieve *m*.

bass¹ [bæs] *n inv (fish) (seawater)* lubina *f*, róbalo *m*; *(freshwater)* perca *f*.

bass² [beɪs] I *n* 1 *(singer)* bajo *m*. 2 *(notes)* graves *mpl*; **turn up the b. a little**, sube los graves un poco. ■ **b. clef**, clave *f* de fa; **b. drum**, bombo *m*; **b. guitar**, guitarra *f* baja; **double b.**, violón *m*, contrabajo *m*. II *adj* bajo,-a.

basset ['bæsɪt] *n Zool* basset *m*; **b. (hound)**, perro *m* basset.

bassoon [bə'su:n] *n Mus* fagot *m*.

bassoonist [bə'su:nɪst] *n* fagotista *mf*.

bastard ['bɑ:stəd, 'bæstəd] *n* 1 bastardo,-a *m, f*. 2 *fam* **the poor b.'s broken his leg**, el pobre desgraciado se ha roto la pierna; **this car's a b. to start**, este coche es la hostia de difícil de arrancar; **you lucky b.!** ¡qué suerte tienes, cabrón! 3 *offens* cabrón *m*, hijo *m* de puta; **he's a real b.!**, ¡es un hijo de puta! II *adj* bastardo,-a.

bastardize ['bɑ:stədaɪz, 'bæstədaɪz] *vtr* corromper.

baste¹ [beɪst] *vtr Culin* pringar, untar.

baste² [beɪst] *vtr Sew* hilvanar.

bastion ['bæstɪən] *n* baluarte *m*, bastión *m*.

bat¹ [bæt] I *n Baseb Crick* bate *m*; *(table tennis)* pala *f*, paleta *f*; *fig* **to do sth off one's own b.**, hacer algo por cuenta propia. II *vi (pt & pp batted) Baseb Crick* batear.

bat² [bæt] *n Zool* murciélago *m*; *fam* **to have bats in the belfry**, estar mal de la azotea.

bat³ [bæt] *vtr (pt & pp batted)* pestañear; *fam* **without batting an eyelid**, sin inmutarse, sin pestañear.

batch [bætʃ] *n (bread)* hornada *f*; *(goods)* lote *m*, serie *f*, remesa *f*; *Mil (recruits)* partida *f*, grupo *m*. ■ *Comput* **b. processing**, procesamiento *m* por lotes.

bated ['beɪtɪd] *adj* **with b. breath**, sin respirar.

bath [bɑ:θ] I *n* 1 baño *m*; **to give sb a b.**, bañar a algn; **to have** *or* **take a b.**, bañarse; **to run a b.**, llenar una bañera de agua. ■ **b. mat**, alfombra *f* de baño; **b. salts**, sales *fpl* de baño; **b. towel**, toalla *f* de baño; **swimming b.**, piscina *f* municipal 2 *(tub)* bañera *f*. **3** *Phot Ind* baño *m*. **4 baths**, piscina *f* municipal; **I go to the b. once a week**, voy a la piscina una vez por semana. **II** *vi (baby)* bañar. **III** *vi* bañarse.

bathe [beɪð] **I** *vi* **1** *(swim)* bañarse. **2** *US (wash)* bañarse, tomar un baño. **II** *vtr* **1** *Med (wound)* lavar. **2** *(cover)* empapar; **he was bathed in sweat**, estaba empapado de sudor; *fig* **the room was bathed in sunlight**, el sol bañaba la habitación. **III** *n (in the sea, river)* baño *m*; **let's go for a b.**, vamos a bañarnos.

bather ['beɪðəʳ] *n* bañista *mf*.

bathing ['beɪðɪŋ] *n* baño *m*; **no b!**, ¡prohibido bañarse! ■ **b. cap**, gorro *m* de baño; **b. costume**, traje *m* de baño, bañador *m* de mujer; **b. trunks**, bañador *m* de hombre.

bathos ['beɪθɒs] *n Lit* paso *m* de lo sublime a lo común.

bathrobe ['bɑːθrəʊb] *n* albornoz *m*.

bathroom ['bɑːθruːm] *n* cuarto *m* de baño.

bathtub ['bɑːθtʌb] *n* bañera *f*.

batman ['bætmən] *n (pl batmen)* Mil ordenanza *m*.

baton ['bætən, 'bætɒn] *n* **1** *Mus* batuta *f*. **2** *(truncheon)* porra *f*. ■ **b. charge**, carga *f* con la porra. **3** *Athlet (in relay race)* testigo *m*.

batsman ['bætsmən] *n (pl batsmen)* Crick bateador *m*.

batswoman ['bætswʊmən] *n (pl batswomen* ['bætswɪmɪn]) *Crick* bateadora *f*.

battalion [bə'tæljən] *n Mil* batallón *m*.

batten¹ ['bætən] **I** *n Naut* listón *m*. **II** *vtr* listonar. ◆ **batten down** *vtr* **to b. down the hatches**, sujetar las escotillas con listones.

batten² ['bætən] *vi* cebarse, enriquecerse **(on**, de, a costa de).

batter¹ ['bætəʳ] *vtr* aporrear, apalear; **to b. down a door**, derribar una puerta a golpes; **to b. sb to death**, matar a algn a palos.

batter² ['bætəʳ] *n Baseb Crick* bateador-a, *m, f*.

batter³ ['bætəʳ] *Culin* **I** *n* pasta *f* (para rebozar); **fish in b.**, pescado rebozado. **II** *vtr* rebozar.

battered ['bætəd] *adj (car)* abollado,-a, desvencijado,-a; *(hat)* estropeado,-a; *(person)* maltratado,-a; **b. baby**, niño maltratado; **b. wives**, mujeres maltratadas *or* apaleadas.

battering ['bætərɪŋ] *n* paliza *f*; **to take a b.**, recibir golpes *or* una paliza. ■ **b. ram**, ariete *m*.

battery ['bætərɪ] *n* **1** *Elec (for torch, radio)* pila *f*; *Aut* batería *f*; **the b. has gone flat**, se ha descargado la batería. ■ **storage b.**, acumulador *m*. **2** *Mil* batería *f*. **3** *Agr (for hens)* batería *f*. ■ **b. hens**, gallinas *fpl* de batería. **4** *Jur* **assault and b.**, lesiones *fpl*, agresión *f*.

battle ['bætəl] **I** *n* batalla *f*, combate *m*; *fig* lucha *f* (**for**, por); **that's half the b.**, ya llevamos medio camino andado; **the B. of Hastings**, la batalla de Hastings; **to do b.**, **fight a b.**, librar batalla; **to fight a losing b.**, luchar por una causa perdida. ■ **b. cry**, *Mil* grito *m* de guerra; *fig* lema *m*; **b. dress**, uniforme *m* de campaña; **b. royal** *or* **pitched b.**, batalla *f* campal. **II** *vi* luchar (**for**, por; **against**, contra).

battle-axe ['bætəlæks] *n* **1** *Mil* hacha *f* de guerra. **2** *fam (woman)* arpía *f*, bruja *f*.

battlefield ['bætəlfiːld] *n* campo *m* de batalla.

battlements ['bætəlmənts] *npl* almenas *fpl*.

battleship ['bætəlʃɪp] *n* acorazado *m*.

batty ['bætɪ] *adj fam (crazy)* loco,-a; *(eccentric)* excéntrico,-a.

bauble ['bɔːbəl] *n* chuchería *f*.

baulk [bɔːlk] *vtr & vi see* **balk**.

Bavaria [bə'veərɪə] *n* Baviera *f*.

Bavarian [bə'veərɪən] *adj & n* bávaro,-a *(m, f)*.

bawdy ['bɔːdɪ] *adj* obsceno,-a; **a b. joke**, un chiste verde.

bawl [bɔːl] *vi* gritar, chillar. ◆ **bawl out** *vtr* gritar, vociferar; *US fam* **to b. sb out**, echar una bronca a algn.

bay¹ [beɪ] *n Geog* bahía *f*; *(large)* golfo *m*; **B. of Biscay**, golfo *m* de Vizcaya; **B. of Bengal**, golfo *m* de Bengala.

bay² [beɪ] *n* **1** *Archit (recess)* hueco *m*. ■ **b. window**, ventana *f* salediza. **2** *Arch (building)* crujía *f*; *(factory)* nave *f*. ■ *Naut* **cargo b.**, bodega *f* de carga; *Com* **loading b.**, cargadero *m*; *Aut* **parking b.**, lugar *m* de aparcamiento.

bay³ [beɪ] *n Bot* laurel *m*. ■ *Culin* **b. leaf**, hoja *f* de laurel.

bay⁴ [beɪ] *n Zool* caballo *m* bayo.

bay⁵ [beɪ] **I** *vi (dog)* ladrar, aullar. **II** *n* ladrido *m*; *fig* **at b.**, acorralado,-a; *fig* **to keep sb at b.**, mantener a algn a raya.

bayonet ['beɪənɪt] *n Mil* bayoneta *f*.

bazaar [bə'zɑːʳ] *n* **1** *(market)* bazar *m* oriental. **2** *(charity sale)* **(Church) b.**, venta *f* benéfica, rastrillo *m* benéfico.

bazooka [bə'zuːkə] *n Mil* bazuca *f*.

BBC [biːbiː'siː] *abbr of* **British Broadcasting Corporation**, Compañía *f* británica de radiofusión, BBC *f*.

BC [biː'siː] **1** *abbr of* **before Christ**, antes de Cristo, a.d.C; antes de Jesucristo, a.d.J.C. **2** *abbr of* **British Council**, consejo *m* británico (para la promoción de la cultura británica en el extranjero).

be [biː, *unstressed* bɪ] **I** *vi (pres 1st person sing* **am***; 3rd person sing* **is***; 2nd person sing & all persons pl* **are***; pt 1st & 3rd persons sing* **was***; 2nd person sing & all persons pl* **were***; pp* **been***)* **1** *(permanent characteristic, essential quality)* ser; **he is very tall**, es muy alto; **Madrid is the capital**, Madrid es la capital; **sugar is sweet**, el azúcar es dulce; **they are intelligent**, son inteligentes; *Math* **three and two are five**, tres y dos son cinco; **to be or not to be**, ser o no ser. **2** *(nationality, religion, occupation)* ser; **he's Italian**, es italiano; **she's a Catholic**, es católica; **they are both doctors**, ambos son médicos. **3** *(origin, ownership, authorship)* ser; *(price) (established)* costar, valer; *(variable)* estar a, valer; *(total)* ser; **a return ticket is £24**, un billete de ida y vuelta cuesta £24; **how much is a kilo of cod?**, ¿a cuánto está el kilo de bacalao?, ¿cuánto vale el kilo de bacalao?; **how much is a single room?**, ¿cuánto cuesta una habitación individual?; **how much is it?**, ¿cuánto es?; **it's £5 for adults and £2 for children, so that's £14**, son £5 para (los) adultos y £2 para (los) niños, así que son £14; **peaches are 25 pence each**, los melocotones están *or* valen 25 peniques la unidad; **I am from Boston**, soy de Boston; **the car is Domingo's**, el coche es de Domingo; **this painting is by Goya**, este cuadro es de Goya. **4** *(temporary state)* estar; **how are you? —I'm very well, thank you**, ¿cómo estás? —estoy muy bien, gracias; **she's tired**, está cansada; **this soup is cold**, esta sopa está fría; **to be cold/afraid/hungry**, tener frío/miedo/hambre; **to be in danger**, estar en peligro; **to be in a fix**, estar en un apuro; **to be very lucky**, tener mucha suerte. **5** *(location)* estar; **Aberdeen is in Scotland**, Aberdeen está en Escocia; **the ashtray is on the table**, el cenicero está encima de la mesa. **6** *(age)* tener; **how old are you?**, ¿cuántos años tienes?; **she is thirty (years old)**, tiene treinta años. **II** *v aux* **1** *(with pres p)* estar; **he is writing a letter**, está escribiendo una carta; **she was singing**, cantaba; **they are always laughing at us**, siempre se ríen de nosotros; **they are leaving tomorrow**, se van mañana; **we have been waiting for a long time**, hace mucho que esperamos. **2** *(passive)* ser; **he was murdered**, fue asesinado; **it was invented by an Australian**, lo inventó un australiano; **she is allowed to smoke**, se le permite fumar; **what's to be done?**, ¿qué se puede hacer? **3** *(expectation, intention, obligation)* **I am to see him this afternoon**, debo verle esta tarde; **you are not to smoke here**, no se puede fumar aquí. **III** *v impers* **1** *(with there)* haber; **there is, there are**, hay; **there was, there were**, había; **there will be**, habrá; **there would be**, habría; **there have been a lot of complaints**, ha habido muchas quejas; **there is lots to see**, hay mucho que ver; **there weren't any potatoes**, no había patatas; **there were ten of us**, éramos diez. **2** *(with it)* **it is essential that we go**, es imprescindible que vayamos; **it's late,** es tarde, se hace tarde; **it is said/thought that,** se dice/piensa que; **it was easy to learn,** era fácil de aprender; **who is it?** —**it's me,** ¿quién es? —soy yo; **what is it?,** ¿qué hay?, ¿qué pasa? **3** *(weather)* **it's foggy/misty,** hay niebla/neblina; **it's cold/cool/hot,** hace frío/fresco/calor; **it's sunny/windy,** hace sol/viento. **4** *(time)* ser; **it's one o'clock/half past one,** es la una/la una y media; **it's four o'clock/twenty to four,** son las cuatro/cuatro menos veinte. **5** *(date)* **it's the 11th/Tuesday today,** hoy es el día 11/martes, hoy estamos a 11/a martes. **6** *(tag questions)* ¿verdad?, ¿no?; **it's lovely, isn't it?,** ¿es mono, no?, ¿verdad que es mono?; **you're happy, aren't you?,** ¿estás contento, verdad? **7** *(unreal conditions)* **if I was/were you ...,** yo en tu lugar ...; **if you were a millionaire ...,** si fueras millionaire ... . **8** *pres & past perfect (visit, go)* estar, ir; **I've been to Paris,** he estado en París.

beach [biːtʃ] **I** *n* playa *f*; **on the b.,** en la playa. **II** *vtr* varar.

beachcomber ['biːtʃkəʊməʳ] *n* **1** *(person)* raquero,-a *m, f*. **2** *(wave)* ola *f*.

beachhead ['biːtʃhed] *n* Mil cabeza *f* de playa.

beachwear ['biːtʃweəʳ] *n* ropa *f* de playa.

beacon ['biːkən] *n* **1** *(fire)* almenara *f*. **2** *Av Naut* baliza *f*. **3** *(lighthouse)* faro *m*.

bead [biːd] *n* **1** *(of rosary, necklace, etc)* cuenta *f*; **glass b.,** abalorio *m*; **string of beads,** collar *m*. **2** *(drop of liquid)* gota *f*; **beads of sweat,** gotas de sudor. **3** **beads,** *(rosary)* rosario *m* sing; **to say** *or* **tell one's b.,** rezar el rosario.

beading ['biːdɪŋ] *n* Archit astrágaio *m*.

beady ['biːdɪ] *adj* *(beadier, beadiest) (eyes)* pequeños y brillantes.

beagle ['biːgəl] *n* Zool beagle *m*.

beak [biːk] *n* **1** *(of bird)* pico *m*. **2** *fam (nose)* nariz *f* ganchuda.

beaker ['biːkəʳ] *n* **1** *(cup, tumbler)* taza *f* alta, jarra *f*. **2** *Chem* vaso *m* de precipitación.

be-all ['biːɔːl] *n* *fam* **the be-a. and end-all,** lo único importante, la razón de vivir.

beam [biːm] **I** *n* **1** Archit viga *f*. **2** *(of light)* rayo *m*; *Phys* haz *m*; *Rad (signal)* onda *f* dirigida; *fam* **to be off the b.,** estar equivocado. **3** *Gymn* barra *f* fija, barra *f* de equilibrio. **4** *(smile)* sonrisa *f* radiante. **5** *Naut (width of ship)* manga *f*; *fam* **broad in the b.,** ancho de caderas. **II** *vi* **1** *(sun)* brillar. **2** *(smile)* sonreír. **III** *vtr* **1** *(broadcast)* difundir, emitir. **2** *(transmit)* transmitir.

beaming ['biːmɪŋ] *adj* *(smiling)* radiante.

bean [biːn] *n* **1** *Bot* alubia *f*, judía *f*, fríjol *m*; *fam* **not to have a b.,** no tener un duro; *fam* **to be full of beans,** rebosar vitalidad; *fam* **to spill the beans,** descubrir el pastel. ◼ *Culin* **baked beans,** alubias *fpl* cocidas en salsa de tomate; **broad b.,** haba *f*; **butter b.,** judía *f*; **coffee b.,** grano *m* de café; **French** *or* **green b.,** judía *f* verde; **haricot b.,** alubia *f*; **kidney b.,** fríjol *m*; **runner** *or* **string b.,** judía *f* verde. **2** *GB fam (chap)* hombre *m*; **thank you, old b.!,** ¡gracias, hombre!

beanfeast ['biːnfiːst] *n fam* comilona *f*.

beanpole ['biːnpəʊl] *n* **1** *(stick)* palo *m*, estaca *f*. **2** *fam (person)* larguirucho,-a *m, f*.

beansprout ['biːnspraʊt] *n* brote *m* de soja.

bear¹ [beəʳ] **I** *vtr (pt* **bore;** *pp* **borne) 1** *(carry) (inscription, signature)* llevar. **2** *(support) (weight)* soportar, aguantar, sostener. **3** *(endure)* soportar, aguantar; **I can't b. him,** no lo soporto; **I couldn't b. it any longer,** ya no aguantaba más. **4** *(produce) (fruit)* dar; *Fin (interest)* devengar. **5** *(show) (scar etc)* llevar; **to b. a resemblance to,** parecerse a. **6** *(hold)* **to b. a grudge against sb,** guardar rencor a algn; **to b. in mind,** tener presente, tener en cuenta. **7** *(render, supply)* **to b. witness,** atestiguar, dar testimonio. **8** *(pp* **born** *passive only, not followed by* **by)** *(give birth to) (child)* dar a luz; **he was born in Wakefield,** nació en Wakefield. **II** *vi (turn) (car, road)* girar, torcer; **to b. left,** girar a la izquierda; *(ship)* **to b. north,** dirigirse hacia el

norte. ◆ **bear down** *vi (press)* apoyarse (**on,** en); *Naut (approach)* correr (**on,** sobre). ◆ **bear out** *vtr (confirm)* confirmar. ◆ **bear up** *vi (endure)* resistir; **b. up!,** ¡ánimo! ◆ **bear with** *vtr* tener paciencia con; **b. with me,** ten paciencia conmigo.

bear² [beəʳ] *n* **1** *Zool* oso *m*. ◼ **b. cub,** osezno *m*; *Astr* **Great B.,** Osa *f* Mayor; **Little B.,** Osa *f* Menor; **polar b.,** oso *m* polar; **teddy b.,** osito *m* de peluche. **2** *Fin* bajista *mf*.

bearable ['beərəbəl] *adj* soportable.

beard [bɪəd] *n* barba *f*; **to have a b.,** llevar barba.

bearded ['bɪədɪd] *adj* barbudo,-a.

beardless ['bɪədlɪs] *adj (youth)* imberbe; *(man)* barbilampiño.

bearer ['beərəʳ] *n* **1** *(porter)* portador,-a *m, f*; **b. of sad news,** portador,-a de malas noticias. **2** *(of cheque)* portador,-a *m, f*; *(of passport)* titular *mf*; *(of office)* poseedor,-a *m, f*.

bearing ['beərɪŋ] *n* **1** *(posture)* porte *m*; **of noble b.,** de noble porte. **2** *(relevance)* relación *f*, conexión *f*; **to have a b. on,** estar relacionado,-a con. **3** *Tech* cojinete *m*, soporte *m*. **4** *Naut* **bearings,** posición *f*, orientación *f*; **to get one's b.,** orientarse; **to lose one's b.,** desorientarse.

bearish ['beərɪʃ] *adj* Fin de tendencia bajista.

beast [biːst] *n* **1** *(animal)* bestia *f*; **wild b.,** fiera *f*. ◼ **b. of burden,** bestia *f* de carga; **b. of prey,** depredador *m*. **2** *fig* bestia *f*, bruto *m*. **3 beasts,** *(cattle)* reses *fpl*, ganado *m* sing.

beastly ['biːstlɪ] *adj (beastlier, beastliest)* fam asqueroso,-a, abominable; **what b. weather!,** ¡qué tiempo más feo!

beat [biːt] **I** *vtr (pt* **beat;** *pp* **beaten** ['biːtən]) **1** *(hit) (person)* pegar, azotar, golpear; *(clothes)* sacudir; *(metal)* martillear; **it's off the beaten track,** está en un lugar muy apartado; **to b. a drum,** tocar un tambor; *fam* **to b. sb's brains (out),** estrujarse el cerebro; *sl* **b. it!,** ¡lárgate!; *sl* **to b. sb's brains out,** matar a algn a palizas. **2** *Culin* batir; **add the eggs and b. well,** añada los huevos y bata bien. **3** *(defeat)* batir, vencer; **we b. them 5-2,** les ganamos 5 a 2; *fig* **that beats everything!,** ¡eso ya es el colmo!; *fam* **to b. sb hollow, b. the pants off sb,** aplastar a algn. **4** *(hunting) (game)* batir. **5** *Mil* **to b. a retreat,** batirse en retirada. **6** *Mus (indicate) (time)* marcar, llevar. **7** *(anticipate)* llegar antes que; **he left early to b. the heavy traffic,** se marchó temprano para evitar los embotellamientos de tráfico; *fam* **I b. you to it,** te gané. **8** *sl (puzzle)* extrañar; **it beats me how she stands him,** es que no entiendo como la aguanta; **it beats me that they refused to come,** me extraña cantidad que se negaran a venir. **II** *vi* **1** *(heart)* latir. **2** *(strike, pound)* dar golpes; **someone's beating at the door,** alguien da golpes en la puerta; *fig* **to b. about the bush,** andarse por las ramas. **III** *n* **1** *(of heart)* latido *m*. **2** *Mus* ritmo *m*, compás *m*. **3** *(of policeman)* ronda *f*; **to walk one's b.,** hacer la ronda. **IV** *adj fam (exhausted)* agotado,-a, rendido,-a; **I'm dead b.,** estoy rendido,-a. ◆ **beat back** *vtr* rechazar; **to b. back the tears,** reprimir las lágrimas. ◆ **beat down** *vi (rain)* azotar; *(sun)* caer a plomo. **II** *vtr (price)* regatear. ◆ **beat off** *vtr (attack)* rechazar. ◆ **beat up** *vtr fam* dar una paliza a.

beater ['biːtəʳ] *n* **1** *Culin* batidora *f*. **2** *(hunting)* batidor *m*, ojeador *m*.

beatification [bɪætɪfɪ'keɪʃən] *n Rel* beatificación *f*.

beatify [bɪ'ætɪfaɪ] *vtr (pt & pp* **beatified)** *Rel* beatificar.

beating ['biːtɪŋ] *n* **1** *(thrashing)* paliza *f*. **2** *(defeat)* derrota *f*; **to take a b.,** sufrir una derrota; *fam* **that idea takes some b.,** esa idea es inmejorable. **3** *(of drum)* toque *m*. **4** *(of heart)* latido *m*. **5** *(of wings)* aleteo *m*.

beatitude [bɪ'ætɪtjuːd] *n Rel* beatitud *f*; **the Beatitudes,** las Bienaventuranzas.

beatnik ['biːtnɪk] *n* hippy *mf*, pasota *mf*.

beautician [bjuː'tɪʃən] *n* esteticista *mf*, esteticienne *f*.

beautiful ['bjuːtɪfʊl] *adj (lovely)* hermoso,-a, bello,-a, precioso,-a; *(delicious) (meal, dish)* delicioso,-a; **what a b. woman!,** ¡qué mujer más bonita! ◼ **b. people,** gente *f* guapa. ◆ **beautifully** *adv* hermosamente; *fam (very)* **she did b. well in her exams,** le fueron estupendamente los exámenes.

beautify ['bjuːtɪfaɪ] *vtr (pt & pp **beautified**)* embellecer, adornar.

beauty ['bjuːtɪ] *n* belleza *f*, hermosura *f*. ■ **b. contest**, concurso *m* de belleza; **b. parlour** *or* **salon**, salón *m* de belleza; **b. spot**, *(on face)* lunar *m*; *(place)* lugar *m* pintoresco.

beaver ['biːvə'] I *n Zool* castor *m; fig* **to work like a b.**, trabajar como un negro. ■ *fam* **eager b.**, lanzado,-a *m,f.* II *vi* **to b. away at sth**, meterse de lleno en algo.

became [bɪ'keɪm] *pt see* **become**.

because [bɪ'kɒz] I *conj* porque; **I'm hot b. I've been playing tennis**, tengo calor porque he estado jugando al tenis. II *prep* **b. of**, a causa de, debido a; **he lost his job b. of his wife**, perdió el empleo por culpa de su mujer.

beckon ['bekən] *vtr & vi* llamar (con la mano); **to b. to sb**, hacer señas a algn.

become [bɪ'kʌm] I *vtr (pt* **became**; *pp* **become**) 1 *(come to be) (doctor, priest, etc)* hacerse; *(mayor, officer)* llegar a ser; *(angry, sad)* volverse, ponerse; **the palace became a hotel**, el palacio se convirtió en hotel; **to b. accustomed to**, acostumbrarse a. 2 *(fall to)* acontecer; **what has b. of them?**, ¿qué ha sido de ellos? II *vtr* 1 *(suit)* sentar bien a, favorecer; **that hat really becomes you**, ese sombrero te sienta muy bien. 2 *(be appropriate)* ser propio de; **it doesn't b. you to say that**, no te conviene decir eso.

becoming [bɪ'kʌmɪŋ] *adj* 1 *(dress)* favorecedor,-a, que sienta bien. 2 *(behaviour)* conveniente, apropiado,-a.

bed [bed] I *n* 1 cama *f.* **double b.**, cama de matrimonio; **single b.**, cama individual; **to get into b.**, meterse en la cama; **to get out of b.**, levantarse de la cama; **to go to b.**, acostarse; **to make the b.**, hacer la cama; **to put to b.**, acostar; *Press (magazine etc)* cerrar; **to take to one's b.**, guardar cama; *fam* **to get out of b. on the wrong side**, levantarse con el pie izquierdo. ■ *GB* **b. and breakfast**, *(service)* cama *f* y desayuno *m; (sign)* 'pensión'; **b. linen**, ropa *f* de cama; **bunk b.**, litera *f*; **spare b.**, cama *f* adicional *or* supletoria. 2 *(of river)* lecho *m*, cauce *m; (of sea)* fondo *m.* 3 *Geol* capa *f*, yacimiento *m.* 4 *(flower) b.*, macizo *m*, cuadro *m*, arriate *m; fam* **a b. of roses**, un lecho de rosas. II *vtr (pt & pp **bedded**) sl* acostarse con. ◆ **bed down** *vi* acostarse.

bedbug ['bedbʌg] *n (insect)* chinche *mf.*

bedclothes ['bedkləʊðz] *npl*, **bedding** ['bedɪŋ] *n* ropa *f* de cama.

bedfellow ['bedfeləʊ] *n* compañero,-a *m*,*f* de cama.

bedlam ['bedləm] *n (uproar)* algarabía *f*, alboroto *m*, jaleo *m.*

Bedouin ['beduɪn] *adj & n* beduino,-a *(m,f).*

bedpan ['bedpæn] *n* orinal *m* (de cama).

bedraggled [bɪ'drægəld] *adj (wet)* mojado,-a; *(dirty)* ensuciado,-a.

bedridden ['bedrɪdən] *adj* postrado,-a en cama.

bedrock ['bedrɒk] *n* 1 *Geol* roca *f* de fondo. 2 *fig* fondo *m*; **to get down to b.**, ir al grano.

bedroom ['bedruːm] *n* dormitorio *m*, habitación *f*, cuarto *m* de dormir, alcoba *f*, *Am* recámara *f*; **master b.**, dormitorio principal.

bedside ['bedsaɪd] *n* cabecera *f*; **at sb's b.**, junto a la cama. ■ *Med* **b. manner**, comportamiento *m* para con los enfermos; **b. table**, mesilla *f* de noche.

bedsit ['bedsɪt] *n fam*, **bedsitter** [bed'sɪtə'] *n* cuarto *m* con cama y cocina, estudio *m.*

bedspread ['bedspred] *n* cubrecama *f*, colcha *f.*

bedtime ['bedtaɪm] *n* hora *f* de acostarse.

bed-wetting ['bedwetɪŋ] *n Med* enuresis *f.*

bee [biː] *n* abeja *f*; *fam* **the b.'s knees**, lo ideal; *fam* **to have a b. in one's bonnet**, tener una idea fija *or* una obsesión. ■ **queen b.**, abeja *f* reina *or* maestra; **worker b.**, abeja *f* neutra *or* obrera.

Beeb [biːb] *n fam* **the B.**, la BBC.

beech [biːtʃ] *n Bot* haya *f.* ■ **copper b.**, haya *f* cobriza.

beechnut ['biːtʃnʌt] *n* hayuco *m.*

bee-eater ['biːiːtə'] *n Orn* abejaruco *m común.*

beef [biːf] I *n Culin* carne *f* de vaca, *Am* carne *f* de res. ■ **b. tea**, caldo *m* de carne de vaca; *Agr* **b. cattle**, ganado *m* vacuno; **roast b.**, rosbif *m.* II *vi fam* quejarse (**about**, de). ◆ **beef up** *vtr fam* reforzar.

beefburger ['biːfbɜːgə'] *n* hamburguesa *f.*

beefeater ['biːfiːtə'] *n* alabardero *m* de la Torre de Londres.

beefsteak ['biːfsteɪk] *n Culin* bistec *m*, *Arg* bife *m.*

beefy ['biːfɪ] *adj (beefier, beefiest) fam (muscular)* robusto,-a, corpulento,-a.

beehive ['biːhaɪv] *n* colmena *f.*

beekeeper ['biːkiːpə'] *n* apicultor,-a *m*,*f.*

beeline ['biːlaɪn] *n fam* atajo *m*; **to make a b. for sth**, ir directo hacia algo.

been [biːn, bɪn] *pp see* **be**.

beep [biːp] *n (noise) (of apparatus)* pitido *m; (of horn)* pito *m.*

beer [bɪə'] *n* cerveza *f*; **a glass of b.**, una caña; **draught b.**, cerveza de barril.

beery ['bɪərɪ] *adj (beerier, beeriest)* que huele *or* sabe a cerveza.

beeswax ['biːzwæks] *n* cera *f* de abejas.

beet [biːt] *n* remolacha *f.* ■ *US* **red b.**, remolacha *f*; **sugar b.**, remolacha *f* azucarera.

beetle ['biːtəl] *n Zool* escarabajo *m.* ◆ **beetle off** *vi fam* escabullirse.

beetroot ['biːtruːt] *n* remolacha *f.*

befall [bɪ'fɔːl] I *vtr (pt* **befell** [bɪ'fel]; *pp* **befallen** [bɪ'fɔːlən])* acontecer a. II *vi* acontecer, ocurrir.

befit [bɪ'fɪt] *vtr (pt & pp **befitted**)* convenir a, corresponder a.

befitting [bɪ'fɪtɪŋ] *adj* conveniente, propio,-a.

before [bɪ'fɔː'] I *conj* 1 *(earlier than)* antes de que (+ *subj)*, antes de (+ *infin)*; **b. leaving**, antes de salir; **I'll see her b. she goes**, la veré antes de que se vaya. II *prep* 1 *(place)* delante de; *(in the presence of)* ante; **b. God**, ante Dios; **to appear b. court**, comparecer ante el juez. 2 *(order, time)* antes de; **b. Christ**, antes de Jesucristo; **b. long**, dentro de poco; **b. 1950**, antes de 1950; **b. tax**, antes de deducir los impuestos; **I saw it b. you**, lo vi antes que tú; **ladies b. gentlemen**, las señoras primero; **that was b. my time**, eso fue antes de que yo naciera. 3 *(preference)* **death b. defeat**, antes morir que entregarse. III *adv* 1 *(time)* antes; **I have met him b.**, ya lo conozco; **not long b.**, poco antes; **the night b.**, la noche anterior. 2 *(place)* delante, por delante.

beforehand [bɪ'fɔːhænd] *adv* 1 *(earlier)* antes; **tell me b.**, déjame saberlo antes; **they left 10 minutes b.**, se fueron diez minutos antes. 2 *(in advance)* de antemano, con anticipación; **to pay b.**, pagar por adelantado.

befriend [bɪ'frend] *vtr* trabar amistad con; **he befriended her**, le ofreció su amistad.

befuddled [bɪ'fʌdəld] *adj* 1 *(confused)* perplejo,-a. 2 *(by alcohol)* atontado,-a.

beg [beg] I *vtr (pt & pp **begged**)* 1 *(ask for) (money etc)* pedir. 2 *(beseech)* rogar, suplicar; **he begged her to help him**, le rogó que le ayudara; **I b. to differ**, no estoy de acuerdo, no estoy conforme; **I b. to inform you that**, tengo el honor de informarles que; **I b. you!**, ¡se lo suplico!; **I b. your pardon!**, ¡perdone usted!, ¡perdón!; **b. your pardon?**, ¿cómo ha dicho usted?; **to b. the question**, hacer una petición de principio. II *vi* 1 *(solicit)* mendigar; **to b. for money**, pedir limosna; *(dog)* pedir; *fam* **it's going begging**, no lo quiere nadie. 2 *(beseech)* **to b. for help/mercy**, implorar ayuda/compasión.

began [bɪ'gæn] *pt see* **begin**.

beget [bɪ'get] *vtr* (*pt* **begot**; *pp* **begotten**) (*children*) engendrar.

beggar ['begəʳ] **I** *n* 1 (*mendicant*) mendigo,-a *m, f*, pordiosero,-a *m, f; prov* **beggars can't be choosers**, los pobres no escogen. 2 *fam euph* (*chap*) tío *m*, tipo *m*; **he's a lucky b.!**, ¡qué suerte tiene el tío!; **poor b.!**, ¡pobre diablo!; **what a silly b.!**, ¡qué tío más tonto! **II** *vtr* 1 (*impoverish*) arruinar, empobrecer. 2 (*defy*) sobrepasar; **it beggars description**, es imposible describirlo.

beggarly ['begəlɪ] *adj* miserable; mezquino,-a; **a b. wage**, un sueldo irrisorio.

begin [bɪ'gɪn] *vtr & vi* (*pt* **began**; *pp* **begun**) empezar, comenzar; **classes b. at nine**, las clases empiezan a las nueve; **he began a letter to his mother**, empezó una carta a su madre; **I cannot b. to thank you**, no encuentro palabras para agradecerle; **she can't b. to level up to the rest**, no puede ni mucho menos compararse con los demás; **they began a campaign against him**, iniciaron una campaña en contra suya; **to b. again**, volver a empezar; **to b. a new life**, comenzar una nueva vida; **to b. at the beginning**, empezar por el principio; **to b. doing** *or* **to do sth**, empezar a hacer algo; **to b. on sth**, emprender algo; (*initially*) **to b. with ...**, para empezar ..., en primer lugar ...; **to b. with sth**, empezar con algo.

beginner [bɪ'gɪnəʳ] *n* principiante *mf*; **English for beginners**, inglés para principiantes.

beginning [bɪ'gɪnɪŋ] *n* 1 (*start*) principio *m*, comienzo *m*; **at the b. of May**, a principios de mayo; **at the b. of the month**, a principios de mes; **from b. to end**, desde el principio hasta el final; **from the b.**, desde el principio; **in the b.**, al principio; **the b. of the civil war**, el comienzo de la guerra civil; **the b. of the end**, el principio del fin; **to make a b.**, empezar. 2 (*origin, cause*) origen *m*, causa *f*; **the b. of the incident**, el origen del incidente; **the beginnings of the cold war**, los orígenes de la guerra fría.

begone [bɪ'gɒn] *interj arch* ¡fuera de aquí!, ¡vade retro!

begonia [bɪ'gəʊnjə] *n Bot* begonia *f*.

begot [bɪ'gɒt] *pt see* **beget**.

begotten [bɪ'gɒtən] *pp see* **beget**.

begrudge [bɪ'grʌdʒ] *vtr* 1 (*give unwillingly*) dar de mala gana; regatear, escatimar; **she begrudges spending money on clothes**, le duele gastar dinero en ropa. 2 (*envy*) envidiar; **to b. sb sth**, envidiarle algo a algn.

beguile [bɪ'gaɪl] *vtr* 1 (*deceive*) engañar; **he beguiled me out of my money**, me timó. 2 (*charm, seduce*) seducir.

beguiling [bɪ'gaɪlɪŋ] *adj* 1 (*deceiving*) engañoso,-a, tramposo,-a. 2 (*seducing*) seductor,-a.

begun [bɪ'gʌn] *pp see* **begin**.

behalf [bɪ'hɑːf] *n* nombre *m*; **on b. of**, *US* **in b. of**, en nombre de; **a collection on b. of orphans**, una colecta en favor de los huérfanos; **don't worry on my b.**, no te preocupes por mí; **I thanked them on her b.**, les di las gracias de su parte; **on b. of everyone**, en nombre de todos; **to plead on sb's b.**, abogar por algn.

behave [bɪ'heɪv] *vi* 1 (*person*) portarse, comportarse; **b. yourself!**, ¡pórtate bien!; **she behaved herself all afternoon**, se portó bien toda la tarde; **to b. well/badly**, portarse bien/mal. 2 (*machine*) funcionar.

behaviour, *US* **behavior** [bɪ'heɪvjəʳ] *n* 1 (*of person*) comportamiento *m*, conducta *f*; **to be on one's best b.**, portarse lo mejor posible. 2 (*of machine*) funcionamiento *m*.

behavioural, *US* **behavioral** [bɪ'heɪvjərəl] *adj* conductista, behaviorístico,-a. ■ **b. science**, ciencia *f* de la conducta.

behaviourism, *US* **behaviorism** [bɪ'heɪvjərɪzəm] *n* conductismo *m*, behaviorismo *m*.

behaviourist, *US* **behaviorist** [bɪ'heɪvjərɪst] *adj* conductista, behaviorístico,-a.

behead [bɪ'hed] *vtr* decapitar, descabezar.

beheld [bɪ'held] *pt & pp see* **behold**.

behest [bɪ'hest] *n* instancia *f*; **at the b. of**, a petición de, a instancia de.

behind [bɪ'haɪnd] **I** *prep* 1 (*at the back of*) detrás de; **b. sb's back**, a espaldas de algn; **b. the house**, detrás de la casa; **b. the scenes**, entre bastidores; **she left a bitter memory b. her**, dejó tras ella un recuerdo amargo; **to be b. sb**, apoyar a algn; **we're solidly b. you**, te apoyamos de todo corazón; **what is b. all this?**, ¿qué hay detrás de todo esto?; **what is there b. that smile?**, ¿qué hay tras esa sonrisa?; **what motive was there b. the crime?**, ¿qué motivo había para el crimen?; *fig* **to put sth b. one**, olvidarse de algo, dejar algo atrás. 2 (*less advanced than*) **b. the times**, anticuado,-a; **Paul is b. the rest of the class in maths**, Paul está por debajo del resto de la clase en matemáticas; **that country is b. Japan in the data-processing field**, ese país es inferior al Japón en el campo de la informática; **to be b. schedule**, (*work*) ir atrasado,-a; (*plane, train*) llevar retraso. **II** *adv* 1 (*in the rear*) detrás, atrás; **I've left my umbrella b.**, se me ha olvidado el paraguas; **to approach sb from b.**, acercarse a algn por detrás; **to attack sb from b.**, atacar a algn por la espalda; **to fall** *or* **lag b.**, quedarse atrás; **to leave sb behind**, dejar atrás a algn; **to stay b.**, quedarse. 2 (*late*) **to be b. with one's payments**, estar atrasado,-a en los pagos; **to be b. with one's work**, tener trabajo atrasado. **III** *n fam* trasero *m*, culo *m*.

behindhand [bɪ'haɪndhænd] **I** *adj* retrasado,-a, atrasado,-a. **II** *adv* en retraso.

behind-the-scenes [bɪ'haɪndðəsiːnz] *adj* de entre bastidores; **b.-t.-s. talks**, negociaciones de entre bastidores.

behold [bɪ'həʊld] *vtr* (*pt & pp* **beheld**) *arch* (*see*) percibir; (*observe*) contemplar; **b.!**, ¡mirad!, ¡he aquí!

beholden [bɪ'həʊldən] *adj* agradec do,-a (**to**, a); **he is b. to nobody for anything**, no le debe nada a nadie.

beholder [bɪ'həʊldəʳ] *n prov* **beauty is in the eye of the b.**, el amor depende del color del cristal con que se mire.

beige [beɪʒ] *adj & n* beige (*m*).

being ['biːɪŋ] *n* 1 (*living thing*) ser *m*. ■ **human b.**, ser *m* humano. 2 (*existence*) existencia *f*; **to come into b.**, nacer.

bel [bel] *n Phys* bel *m*, belio *m*.

belated [bɪ'leɪtɪd] *adj* tardío,-a.

belay [bɪ'leɪ] *vtr* 1 *Naut* (*line*) amarrar. 2 (*mountaineering*) (*climber*) asegurar.

belch [beltʃ] **I** *vi* (*person*) eructar. **II** *vtr* (*chimney etc*) (*smoke, flames*) vomitar, arrojar. **III** *n* eructo *m*, regüeldo *m*.

beleaguered [bɪ'liːgəd] *adj* (*city*) sitiado,-a, asediado,-a; (*person*) acosado,-a, asediado,-a.

belfry ['belfrɪ] *n* campanario *m*.

Belgian ['beldʒən] *adj & n* belga (*mf*).

Belgium ['beldʒəm] *n* Bélgica.

Belgrade [bel'greɪd] *n* Belgrado.

belie [bɪ'laɪ] *vtr* 1 (*contradict*) desmentir, contradecir. 2 (*disguise*) falsear. 3 (*disappoint*) defraudar.

belief [bɪ'liːf] *n* 1 (*gen*) creencia *f*; **beyond b.**, increíble; **religious/political beliefs**, creencias religiosas/políticas. 2 (*opinion*) opinión *f*; **it is my b. that ...**, estoy convencido de que ...; **to the best of my b.**, que yo sepa, a mi entender. 3 *Rel* (*faith*) fe *f*. 4 (*confidence*) confianza *f* (**in**, en).

believable [bɪ'liːvəbəl] *adj* creíble, verosímil.

believe [bɪ'liːv] **I** *vi* 1 (*have faith in*) creer; **1 b. in God**, creo en Dios. 2 (*be in favour of*) ser partidario,-a de; **she believes in having a good breakfast**, es de las que cree que un buen desayuno es importante. 3 (*think, suppose*) creer; **I b. so**, creo que sí. **II** *vtr* creer; **b. me!**, ¡créeme!; **don't you b. it!**, ¡no te lo creas!; **I can't b. it of her**, me parece imposible que ella hiciera tal cosa; **she is believed to be in Brazil**, se supone que está en Brasil.

believer [bɪ'liːvəʳ] *n* 1 *Rel* creyente *mf*; **I'm no b. in miracles**, yo no creo en los milagros. 2 partidario,-a *m, f* (**in**, de), entusiasta *mf* (**in**, de); **he's a great b. in telling the truth**, es partidario de decir la verdad.

belittle [bɪ'lɪtəl] *vtr* despreciar; **to b. oneself,** rebajarse, quitarse importancia.

Belize [be'liːz] *n* Belice.

Belizean [be'liːzɪən] *adj* & *n* belicense *(mf)*, beliceño,-a *(m,f)*.

bell [bel] *n (of church, school)* campana *f*; *(handbell)* campanilla *f*; *(decorative)* cascabel *m*; *(on animal)* cencerro *m*; *(of door, bicycle, device)* timbre *m*; **to ring the b.,** tocar el timbre; *fig* **that rings a b.,** eso me suena. ■ **b. jar** *or* **glass,** campana *f*, fanal *m*; **b. tower,** campanario *m*.

belladonna [belə'dɒnə] *n Bot* belladona *f*.

bell-bottoms ['belbɒtəmz] *npl* pantalones *mpl* acampanados.

bellboy ['belbɔɪ] *n* botones *m inv*.

belle [bel] *n (beautiful woman)* belleza *f*.

belles-lettres [bel'letrə] *npl* bellas *or* buenas letras *fpl*.

bellhop ['belhɒp] *n US* botones *m inv*.

bellicose ['belɪkəʊs] *adj* belicoso,-a, pendenciero,-a.

belligerence [bɪ'lɪdʒərəns] *n* agresividad *f*.

belligerent [bɪ'lɪdʒərənt] *adj* agresivo,-a.

bellow ['beləʊ] **I** *vi (bull)* bramar; *(person)* bramar, rugir. **II** *n (bull)* bramido *m*; *(person)* bramido *m*, rugido *m*.

bellows ['beləʊz] *npl* **(pair of) b.,** fuelle *m sing*.

bell-ringer ['belrɪŋə'] *n* campanero,-a *m,f*.

belly ['belɪ] *n* **1** *(of person)* vientre *m*, barriga *f*; *fam* tripa *f*. ■ **b. dance,** danza *f* del vientre; *Swimming* **b. flop,** panzada *f*; *fam* **b. laugh,** carcajada *f*. **2** *(of animal, plane)* panza *f*. ■ *Av* **b. landing,** aterrizaje *m* sobre la panza.

bellyache ['belɪeɪk] **I** *n fam* dolor *m* de vientre *or* barriga. **II** *vi sl* refunfuñar.

bellybutton ['belɪbʌtən] *n fam* ombligo *m*.

bellyful ['belɪfʊl] *n* panzada *f*, hartazgo *m*; *sl* **to have had a b.,** estar harto,-a, estar hasta las narices **(of,** de).

belong [bɪ'lɒŋ] *vi* **1** *(be the property of)* pertenecer **(to,** a); **this book belongs to him,** este libro le pertenece, este libro es suyo. **2** *(be a member)* ser socio,-a **(to,** de); **to b. to a club,** ser socio de un club; *Pol* **to b. to a party,** ser miembro de un partido. **3** *(have a proper place)* corresponder; **put it back where it belongs,** ponlo en su sitio; **she felt she didn't b.,** no se sentía cómoda; **this chair belongs in the other room,** esta silla va en la otra habitación; **this record doesn't b. in this cover,** este disco no corresponde a este disco.

belongings [bɪ'lɒŋɪŋz] *npl* efectos *mpl* personales, pertenencias *fpl*.

beloved [bɪ'lʌvɪd, bɪ'lʌvd] **I** *adj* amado,-a, querido,-a; **b. by all,** querido,-a de todos. **II** *n* amado,-a *m,f*.

below [bɪ'ləʊ] **I** *prep* debajo de; **b. sea level,** por debajo del nivel del mar; **b. (the) average,** por debajo de la media; *(skirt)* **b. the knee,** por debajo de la rodilla; **he lives b. us,** vive debajo de nosotros; **temperatures b. normal,** temperaturas inferiores a las normales; **ten degrees b. zero,** diez grados bajo cero. **II** *adv* abajo; **above and b.,** arriba y abajo; **here b.,** aquí abajo; *(on document etc)* **see b.,** véase más abajo; **the shops b.,** las tiendas de abajo.

belt [belt] **I** *n* **1** cinturón *m*; **blow below the b.,** golpe *m* bajo; *fig* **to tighten one's b.,** apretarse el cinturón. ■ *Sport* **black b.,** cinturón *m* negro; *Aut Av* **safety b., seat b.,** cinturón *m* de seguridad; **please fasten your seat belts,** abróchense los cinturones de seguridad, por favor. **2** *Tech* correa *f*, cinta *f*. ■ **conveyor b.,** cinta *f* transportadora; *Aut* **fan b.,** correa *f* del ventilador. **3** *(area)* zona *f*. ■ *US* **cotton b.,** zona *f* algodonera; **green b.,** franja *f* de protección, zona *f* rural no urbanizable. **II** *vtr sl* pegar una paliza. ◆ **belt along** *vi fam* ir a todo gas. ◆ **belt out** *vtr fam (song)* cantar a voz en grito. ◆ **belt up** *vi fam* callarse; **b. up!,** ¡cierra el pico!, ¡cállate la boca!

bemoan [bɪ'məʊn] *vtr (loss, fate)* lamentar, llorar.

bemused [bɪ'mjuːzd] *adj* perplejo,-a.

bench [bentʃ] *n* **1** *(seat)* banco *m*; **to sit on a b.,** sentarse en un banco. **2** *(work table)* banco *m*. **3** *Parl* escaño *m*. **4** *Jur* **the b.,** *(judges)* la magistratura; **to be on the b.,** ser juez *or* magistrado. **5** *Sport* banquillo *m*. **6** *Geol* banco *m*. ■ **b. mark,** cota *f* de referencia; *fig* punto *m* de referencia.

bend [bend] **I** *vtr (pt & pp* **bent)** *(metal)* curvar, doblar; *(envelope)* doblar; *(back)* encorvar; *(head)* inclinar; *(knee, elbow)* doblar; **'do not b.',** 'no doblar'; **on bended knee,** de rodillas; *fam* **to b. the rules,** hacer una excepción. **II** *vi* **1** *(metal)* curvarse, doblarse; *(road)* torcerse, desviarse. **2 to b. (over),** *(person) (stoop down)* inclinarse, agacharse; *fam* **he bends over backwards to please her,** hace lo imposible por complacerla. **III** *n* **1** *(in river, road)* curva *f*; *(in pipe)* recoda *m*, ángulo *m*; *GB sl* **round the b.,** loco,-a perdido,-a. ■ **hairpin b.,** curva *f* cerrada. **2** *Med* **the bends,** aeroembolismo *m sing*, enfermedad *f* sing de los buzos. ◆ **bend back** *vi* inclinarse hacia atrás. ◆ **bend down** *vi* inclinarse. ◆ **bend forward** *vi* inclinarse hacia adelante.

bender ['bendə'] *n fam* **to go on a b.,** irse de borrachera.

beneath [bɪ'niːθ] **I** *prep (below)* bajo, debajo de; **b. the bushes,** entre los arbustos; **to marry b. oneself,** casarse con algn de clase inferior; *fig* **it's b. him,** es indigno de él. **II** *adv* debajo.

Benedictine [benɪ'dɪktɪn] **I** *n* **1** *Rel (monk)* benedictino,-a *m,f*. **2** [benɪ'dɪktiːn] *(liqueur)* benedictino *m*. **II** *adj Rel* benedictino,-a.

benediction [benɪ'dɪkʃən] *n Rel* bendición *f*.

benefactor ['benɪfæktə'] *n* benefactor *m*, bienhechor *m*.

benefactress ['benɪfæktrɪs] *n* benefactora *f*, bienhechora *f*.

benefice ['benɪfɪs] *n Rel* beneficio *m*.

beneficent [bɪ'nefɪsənt] *adj (person)* benefactor,-a; *(thing)* benéfico,-a.

beneficial [benɪ'fɪʃəl] *adj* **1** *(doing good)* benéfico,-a; **b. climate,** clima benéfico. **2** *(advantageous)* beneficioso,-a, provechoso,-a.

beneficiary [benɪ'fɪʃərɪ] *n* beneficiario,-a *m,f*.

benefit ['benɪfɪt] **I** *vtr (US pt & pp* **benefitted)** beneficiar. **II** *vi* beneficiarse, aprovecharse, sacar provecho **(from** *or* **by,** de). **III** *n* **1** *(advantage)* beneficio *m*, ventaja *f*, provecho *m*; **for the b. of,** en beneficio de. **2** *Com (gain)* beneficio *m*, ganancia *f*. **3** *(good)* bien *m*; **I did it for your b.,** lo hice por tu bien. **4** *(allowance)* subsidio *m*; **unemployment b.,** subsidio *m or* seguro *m* de desempleo. ■ **fringe b.,** extra *m*. **5** *(event)* función *f* benéfica. ■ *Sport* **b. match,** partido *m* benéfico.

benevolence [bɪ'nevələns] *n (kindness)* benevolencia *f*, bondad *f*; *(generosity)* caridad *f*.

benevolent [bɪ'nevələnt] *adj* **1** *(kindly)* benévolo,-a. **2** *(charitable)* caritativo,-a; **b. society,** sociedad de beneficiencia.

Bengal [beŋ'gɔːl] *n* Bengala. ■ **B. light,** bengala *f*, luz *f* de Bengala.

Bengali [beŋ'gɔːlɪ] *adj* & *n* bengalí *(mf)*.

benign [bɪ'naɪn] *adj* benigno,-a; *Med* **b. tumour,** tumor benigno.

Benin [be'niːn] *n* Benín.

Beninese [benɪ'niːz] *adj* & *n* benimeño,-a *(m, f)*.

bent [bent] **I** *pt & pp see* **bend. II** *adj* **1** *(curved)* curvado,-a, doblado,-a, torcido,-a. **2** *(determined)* empeñado,-a; **to be b. on doing sth,** estar empeñado,-a en hacer algo. **3** *sl (corrupt)* deshonesto,-a. **4** *sl (homosexual)* gay, de la acera de enfrente. **III** *n* **1** *(inclination)* inclinación *f* **(towards,** hacia); **to follow one's b.,** hacer lo que le apetezca. **2** *(aptitude)* facilidad *f* **(for,** para).

Benzedrine® ['benzədriːn] *n Med* Bencedrina® *f*.

benzene ['benziːn] *n Chem* benceno *m*.

benzine ['benziːn] *n Chem* bencina *f*.

bequeath [bɪ'kwiːð] *vtr Jur* legar.

bequest [bɪ'kwest] *n Jur* legado *m*.

berate [bɪˈreɪt] *vtr (scold)* regañar.

Berber [ˈbɜːbəˈ] *adj & n* bereber *(mf)*, berebere *(mf)*.

bereaved [bɪˈriːvd] I *adj* desconsolado,-a. II **the b.** *npl* su desconsolada familia.

bereavement [bɪˈriːvmənt] *n* **1** *(loss)* pérdida *f*. **2** *(mourning)* duelo *m*, luto *m*.

bereft [bɪˈreft] *adj* **b. of**, privado,-a de.

beret [ˈbereɪ] *n* boina *f*.

bergamot [ˈbɜːgəmɒt] *n Bot* **1** *(fruit)* bergamota *f*. **2** *(tree)* bergamoto *m*.

beriberi [berɪˈberɪ] *n Med* beriberi *m*.

Berlin [bɜːˈlɪn] *n* Berlín. ■ **East B.**, Berlín Este; **West B.**, Berlín Oeste.

Berliner [bɜːˈlɪnəˈ] *n* berlinés,-esa *m, f*.

Bermuda [bəˈmjuːdə] *n* las (Islas) Bermudas; **B. shorts**, bermudas *mpl*.

Bern [bɜːn] *n* Berna.

berry [ˈberɪ] *n Bot* baya *f*.

berserk [bəˈsɜːk, bəˈzɜːk] *adj* enloquecido,-a; **he'll drive me b.**, me volverá loco,-a; **to go b.**, volverse loco,-a.

berth [bɜːθ] *Naut* I *n* **1** *(mooring place)* atracadero *m*, amarradero *m*; *fig* **to give sb a wide b.**, evitar a algn. **2** *(on train, ship) (bed)* litera *f*. II *vtr (dock) (ship)* poner en dique. III *vi* atracar.

beryl [ˈberɪl] *n Min* berilo *m*.

beseech [bɪˈsiːtʃ] *vtr (pt & pp beseeched or besought)* suplicar, implorar; **to b. sb to do sth**, suplicar a algn que haga algo.

beset [bɪˈset] *vtr (pt & pp beset)* acosar; **it is b. with dangers**, está plagado de peligros; **to be b. by temptations**, estar acosado por las tentaciones.

beside [bɪˈsaɪd] *prep* **1** *(next to)* al lado a; *(near)* cerca de. **2** *(compared with)* comparado con, al lado de. **3** *(away from)* **he was b. himself with joy**, estaba loco de alegría; **that's b. the point**, eso no viene al caso; **to be b. oneself**, ester fuera de sí.

besides [bɪˈsaɪdz] I *prep* **1** *(in addition to)* además de; **who is coming b. Alan?**, ¿quién viene además de Alan? **2** *(except)* excepto, menos; **no one b. me**, nadie más que yo. II *adv* además; **it's late and b., I'm tired**, es tarde, y además estoy cansado.

besiege [bɪˈsiːdʒ] *vtr* **1** *Mil (city)* sitiar, asediar. **2** *fig (person)* asediar, acosar.

besom [ˈbiːzəm] *n* escoba *f*.

besotted [bɪˈsɒtɪd] *adj* **1** *(infatuated)* locamente enamorado,-a **(with**, de). **2** *(intoxicated)* atontado,-a; **b. with drink**, aturdido,-a por la bebida.

besought [bɪˈsɔːt] *pt & pp see* **beseech**.

bespatter [bɪˈspætəˈ] *vtr* salpicar **(with**, de).

bespectacled [bɪˈspektəkəld] *adj* con gafas, que lleva gafas.

bespoke [bɪˈspəʊk] *adj esp GB* **1** *(suit)* hecho,-a a la medida. **2** *(tailor)* que confecciona ropa a la medida.

best [best] I *adj (superl of good)* mejor; **b. man**, ≈ padrino *m* de boda; **her b. friend**, su mejor amiga; **it's the b. film of the year**, es la mejor película del año; **he's the b. (pupil) in the class**, es el mejor (alumno) de la clase; **the b. thing would be to phone them**, lo mejor sería llamarles; **we had to wait the b. part of a year**, tuvimos que esperar casi un año; *(in letter)* **with b. wishes from Mary**, con mis mejores deseos, Mary. II *adv (superl of well)* mejor; **as b. I can**, lo mejor que pueda; **I like this one b.**, éste es el que más me gusta; **I sleep b. in winter**, en invierno duermo mejor; **the world's b. dressed man**, el hombre mejor vestido del mundo; **to come off b.**, salir ganando; **we had b. go**, es mejor que nos vayamos. III *n* lo mejor; **all the b.!**, ¡que te vaye bien!; **at b.**, a lo mas; **it's all for the b.**, más vale que sea así; **one has to make the b. of it**, hay que conformarse; **she wants the b. of both worlds**, quiere tenerlo todo; **the b. of it is that ...**, lo mejor del caso es

que ...; **to be at one's b.**, estar en plena forma, estar como nunca; **to do one's b.**, hacer todo lo posible; **to do sth to the b. of one's ability**, hacer algo lo mejor posible; **to get the b. out of sth**, aprovechar algo al máximo; **to look one's b.**, tener muy buen aspecto; **to make the b. of a bad job**, poner al mal tiempo buena cara; **to make the b. of sth**, sacar el mejor partido de algo; **to the b. of my knowledge**, que yo sepa; **with the b. of them**, como el que más.

bestial [ˈbestɪəl] *adj* bestial.

bestiality [bestɪˈælɪtɪ] *n* bestialidad *f*.

bestow [bɪˈstəʊ] *vtr (favour etc)* conceder; *(honours, power)* otorgar **(on**, a); *(title etc)* conferir **(on**, a).

best-seller [bestˈseləˈ] *n* superventas *m inv*, best-seller *m*.

best-selling [bestˈselɪŋ] *adj* **a b.-s. author**, un autor de superventas *or* éxito.

bet [bet] I *n* apuesta *f*; **to make *or* place a b.**, hacer una apuesta; **to make a b. on sth**, apostar a algo. II *vtr (pt & pp bet or betted)* apostar; **I b. you five pounds that ...**, te apuesto cinco libras a que ... . III *vi* apostar **(on**, a); *fam* **you b.!**, ¡y tanto!

beta [ˈbiːtə] *n (Greek letter)* beta *f*. ■ *Phys* **b. particle**, partícula *f* beta; **b. ray**, rayo *m* beta.

betel [ˈbiːtəl] *n Bot* betel *m*.

bête noire [betˈnwɑːˈ] *n (pl bêtes noires)* bestia *f* negra.

Bethlehem [ˈbeθlɪhem] *n* Belén.

betide [bɪˈtaɪd] *vtr & vi* woe b. you if ...!, ¡ay de ti si ...!

betray [bɪˈtreɪ] *vtr* **1** traicionar. **2** *(be unfaithful to)* engañar. **3** *(reveal)* revelar; **to b. one's ignorance**, demostrar *or* dejar ver la ignorancia.

betrayal [bɪˈtreɪəl] *n* **1** traición *f*; **b. of trust**, abuso *m* de confianza. **2** *(unfaithfulness)* engaño *m*.

betrayer [bɪˈtreɪəˈ] *n* traidor,-a *m, f*.

betrothal [bɪˈtrəʊðəl] *n Lit* desposorios *mpl*, esponsales *mpl*.

betrothed [bɪˈtrəʊðd] I *adj* prometido,-a. II **the b.** *npl* los prometidos.

betted [ˈbetɪd] *pt & pp see* **bet**.

better¹ [ˈbetəˈ] I *adj* **1** *(comp of good)* mejor; **a b. class of hotel**, un hotel de más categoría; **Suzanne's a b. athlete than me**, Suzanne es mejor atleta que yo; **that's b.!**, ¡eso es!, ¡eso está mejor!; **the weather is b. that last week**, hace mejor tiempo que la semana pasada; **to be no b. than ...**, no ser más que ...; **to get b.**, mejorar; *fam (spouse)* **b. half**, media naranja *f*, costilla *f*. **2** *(healthier)* mejor (de salud); **she was ill, but she's b. now**, estuvo enferma, pero ahora está mejor. **3 b. off**, *(better)* mejor; *(richer)* mejor situado,-a; **you'd be b. off going home**, mejor es que te vayas a casa; **they are b. off than we are**, tienen más dinero que nosotros. **4** *(larger)* mayor; **the b. part of the day**, la mayor parte del día. II *adv (comp of well)* **1** *(gen)* mejor; **all the b., so much the b.**, tanto mejor; *(healthier)* **are you b.?**, ¿te encuentras mejor?, ¿estás mejor?; **b. and b.**, cada vez mejor; **he knows b. than to make such a silly mistake**, un error así no es propio de él; **he swims b. than me**, nada mejor que yo; **the sooner the b.**, cuanto antes mejor; *prov* **b. late than never**, más vale tarde que nunca. **2 had b.**, más vale que (+ *subj*); **we had b. leave**, más vale que nos vayamos. **3** *to think b. of*, *(plan, idea)* cambiar de; *(person)* tener en más consideración. III *n* **1** mejor; **a change for the b.**, una mejora; **for b. (or) for worse**, *(marriage)* en lo bueno y en lo malo; *(come what may)* pase lo que pase; **this one is the b. of the two**, éste es el mejor de los dos; **to get the b. of sb**, vencer a algn. **2 betters**, superiores *mpl*; **to respect one's b.**, respetar a los superiores. IV *vtr* **1** *(improve)* mejorar; **he must b. himself**, debe mejorar su situación. **2** *Com (surpass)* superar.

better², US bettor [ˈbetəˈ] *n* apostante *mf*; *(committed)* apostador,-a *m, f*.

betterment [ˈbetəmənt] *n* mejoría *f*.

betting [ˈbetɪŋ] *n* apuestas *fpl*. ■ *GB* **b. shop**, quiosco *m* de apuestas; **b. slip**, resguardo *m* de una apuesta.

between [bɪ'twiːn] I *prep* entre; **b. now and October,** de ahora a octubre; **b. the door and the window,** entre la puerta y la ventana; **b. you and me,** entre nosotros; **the supermarket is closed b. 1 and 2,** el supermercado está cerrado de 1 a 2. II *adv* en *or* por medio; **in b.,** *(position)* en medio; *(time)* entretanto, mientras (tanto).

betwixt [bɪ'twɪkst] *adv arch* entre; **b. and between,** entre las dos cosas, ni una cosa ni la otra.

bevel ['bevəl] I n bisel *m*. II *vtr (pt & pp bevelled)* biselar.

beverage ['bevərɪdʒ] *n* bebida *f*; **non-alcoholic b.,** bebida sin alcohol.

bevvy ['bevɪ] *n sl* cacharro *m*.

bevy ['bevɪ] *n* bandada *f*.

beware [bɪ'weəʳ] *vi* tener cuidado (**of,** con); **b.!,** ¡cuidado!, ¡ojo!; *Com* '**b. of imitations**', 'desconfíe de las imitaciones'; *(sign)* '**b. of the dog**', 'cuidado con el perro'.

bewilder [bɪ'wɪldəʳ] *vtr* desconcertar, confundir.

bewildered [bɪ'wɪldəd] *adj* desconcertado,-a, perplejo,-a.

bewilderment [bɪ'wɪldərmənt] *n* desconcierto *m*.

bewitch [bɪ'wɪtʃ] *vtr* **1** *(cast a spell over)* hechizar. **2** *(enchant)* fascinar, encantar.

bewitching [bɪ'wɪtʃɪŋ] *adj* fascinante.

beyond [bɪ'jɒnd] I *prep* **1** *(on the other side of)* más allá de; **b. the mountains,** más allá de las montañas; **b. the seas,** allende los mares, acullá de los mares. **2** *(outside the scope of)* más allá de; **b. belief,** increíble; **b. doubt,** sin lugar a dudas, indudablemente; **b. my reach,** fuera de mi alcance; **it's b. me why ...,** no comprendo por qué ...; **it's b. a joke,** ya no tiene gracia; **she is b. caring,** ya no le importa; **this task is b. me,** no puedo con esta tarea; **to live b. one's means,** vivir por encima de las posibilidades de uno. II *adv* más allá, más lejos; **he owns the palace and the gardens b.,** es dueño del palacio y de los jardines de más allá. III **the b.** *n* el más allá.

Bhutan [buː'tɑːn] *n* Bhutan.

bias ['baɪəs] *n* **1** *(tendency)* tendencia *f*, inclinación *f* (**towards,** hacia). **2** *(prejudice)* prejuicio *m*. **3** *Sew* sesgo *m*; **cut on the b.,** cortado al sesgo.

bias(s)ed ['baɪəst] *adj* parcial; **to be b. against sth/sb,** tener prejuicio en contra de algo/algn.

bib [bɪb] *n* **1** *(for baby)* babero *m*. **2** *(of apron, dungarees)* peto *m*. **3** *(fish)* faneca *f*.

Bible ['baɪbəl] *n* Biblia *f*; **the Holy B.,** la Santa Biblia. ■ *sl* **B. basher, B. thumper,** evangelista *mf*, proselitista *mf*; *US* **B. Belt,** zona *f* habitada por los integristas protestantes; **B. paper,** papel *m* biblia.

biblical ['bɪblɪkəl] *adj* bíblico,-a.

bibliographer [bɪblɪ'ɒgrəfəʳ] *n* bibliógrafo,-a *m,f*.

bibliographic(al) [bɪblɪəʊ'græfɪk(əl)] *adj* bibliográfico,-a.

bibliography [bɪblɪ'ɒgrəfɪ] *n* bibliografía *f*.

bibliophile ['bɪblɪəʊfaɪl] *n* bibliófilo,-a *m,f*.

bicameral [baɪ'kæmərəl] *adj Parl* bicameral.

bicameralism [baɪ'kæmərəlɪzəm] *n Parl* bicameralismo *m*.

bicarbonate [baɪ'kɑːbənɪt] *n Chem* bicarbonato *m*. ■ **b. of soda,** bicarbonato *m* sódico *or* de sosa.

bicentenary [baɪsen'tiːnərɪ] *US* **bicentennial** [baɪsen'tenɪəl] I *adj* bicentenario,-a. II *n* bicentenario *m*.

biceps ['baɪseps] *n Anat* bíceps *m*.

bicker ['bɪkəʳ] *vi* discutir, reñir.

bickering ['bɪkərɪŋ] *n* discusiones *fpl*, riñas *fpl*.

bicycle ['baɪsɪkəl] I n bicicleta *f*; **b. pump,** bomba *f* de aire; **to go by b.,** ir en bicicleta; **to ride a b.,** montar en bicicleta. II *vi* ir en bicicleta.

bid [bɪd] I *vtr (pt bid or bade; pp bid or bidden* ['bɪdən]*)* I *(say)* decir; **to b. sb farewell,** despedirse de algn; **to b. sb welcome,** dar la bienvenida a algn. **2** *(command)* mandar, ordenar; **she bade him be quiet,** le mandó que se callase. **3** *(invite)* invitar; **he bade me sit down,** me invitó a

sentarme. **4** *(seem)* parecer; **to b. fair,** parecer probable. **5** *(at auction) (pt & pp bid)* pujar, ofrecer, **6** *Bridge (pt & pp bid)* subastar, cantar. II *vi* **1** *(at auction)* pujar, hacer una oferta (**for,** por). **2** *Bridge* declarar. III *n* **1** *(offer)* oferta *f*. **2** *(at auction)* puja *f*, postura *f*. **3** *Bridge* subasta *f*. **4** *(attempt)* intento *m*, tentativa *f*; **a b. for power,** un intento por conseguir el poder.

bidder ['bɪdəʳ] *n (at auction)* postor,-a *m,f*; **the highest b.,** el mejor postor.

bidding ['bɪdɪŋ] *n* **1** *(at auction)* puja *f*, licitación *f*. **2** *Bridge* subasta *f*. **3** *(order)* orden *f*; **to do sb's b.,** cumplir la orden de algn.

biddy ['bɪdɪ] *n fam (gossip)* **old b.,** vieja *f* chismosa.

bide [baɪd] *vtr (pt bided or bode; pp bided)* esperar; **to b. one's time,** esperar el momento oportuno.

bidet ['biːdeɪ] *n* bidé *m*.

biennial [baɪ'enɪəl] I *adj* bienal. II *n* **1** *(plant)* planta *f* bienal. **2** *(event)* bienal *f*.

bier [bɪəʳ] *n (stand)* féretro *m*, andas *fpl*.

biff [bɪf] *fam* I *n* puñetazo *m*. II *vtr* dar un puñetazo a.

bifocal [baɪ'fəʊkəl] I *adj* bifocal. II **bifocals** *npl* lentes *fpl* bifocales.

big [bɪg] I *adj (bigger, biggest)* grande (gran *before sing noun*); **a b. clock,** un reloj grande; **a b. surprise,** una gran sorpresa; **he's too b. for his boots** *or US* **for his breeches,** es muy fanfarrón; **my b. brother,** mi hermano mayor; **she's bigger than me,** es más alta que yo; **to get b.,** *(gen)* hacerse grande; *(child)* crecer, hacerse mayor; **to have b. ideas,** tener las cosas en grande; *fam* **what's the b. idea?,** ¿qué pretendes?; *fam iron* **that's b. of you,** ¡qué amable eres conmigo!; *fam iron* **b. deal!,** ¿y qué? ■ **B. Brother,** el Gran Hermano; *US fam* **b. bucks,** muchas pelas *fpl*; **b. business,** los grandes negocios; *(at fairground)* **b. dipper,** montaña *f* rusa; *Astron US* **B. Dipper,** Osa *f* Mayor; *Aut GB* **b. end,** cabeza *f* de biela; **b. game,** caza *f* mayor; **b. toe,** dedo *m* gordo del pie; *Pol* **the B. Five,** las Cinco Potencias *or* Superpotencias; *fam* **b. gun, b. noise, b. shot,** pez *m* gordo; *fam* **b. time,** éxito *m* profesional; **to make the b. time,** tener éxito; *fam* **b. top,** tienda *f* mayor del circo. II *adv* **1** *(on a grand scale)* a gran escala; **to think b.,** planear a lo grande; *fam* **to talk b.,** fanfarronear. **2** *(well)* de manera excepcional; **his plans went over b. with the committee,** sus planes tuvieron mucho éxito entre los miembros del comité.

bigamist ['bɪgəmɪst] *n* bígamo,-a *m,f*.

bigamous ['bɪgəməs] *adj* bígamo,-a.

bigamy ['bɪgəmɪ] *n* bigamia *f*.

big-boned [bɪg'bəʊnd] *adj* corpulento,-a.

big-eared [bɪg'ɪəd] *adj* orejudo,-a.

bighead ['bɪghed] *n fam* creído,-a *m,f*, engreído,-a *m,f*.

bigheaded [bɪg'hedɪd] *adj* creído,-a engreído,-a.

big-hearted [bɪg'hɑːtɪd] *adj* generoso,-a.

bighorn ['bɪghɔːn] *n Zool* carnero *m* de cuernos grandes (oriundo de las Montañas Rocosas).

bight [baɪt] *n* bahía *f*. ■ **Great Australian B.,** Gran Bahía *f* Australiana.

bigmouth ['bɪgmaʊθ] *n fam* bocazas *mf inv*.

bigot ['bɪgət] *n* fanático,-a *m, f*, intolerante *mf*.

bigoted ['bɪgətɪd] *adj* fanático,-a, intolerante.

bigotry ['bɪgətrɪ] *n* fanatismo *m*, intolerancia *f*.

big-sounding [bɪg'saʊndɪŋ] *adj* altisonante.

bigwig ['bɪgwɪg] *n fam* pez *m* gordo.

bike [baɪk] *fam (abbr of bicycle or motorbike)* I *n* **1** *(bicycle)* bici *f*; **b. lane,** carril-bici *m*; *sl* **on your b.!,** ¡vete de aquí!, ¡lárgate de aquí! **2** *(motorcycle)* moto *f*. II *vi* **1** *(bicycle)* ir en bici. **2** *(motorcycle)* ir en moto.

bikini [bɪ'kiːnɪ] *n* bikini *m*.

bilabial [baɪ'leɪbɪəl] *adj Ling* bilabial.

bilateral [baɪ'lætərəl] *adj (agreement etc)* bilateral.

bilberry ['bɪlbərɪ] *n Bot* arándano *m.*

bile [baɪl] *n* **1** *Med* bilis *f,* hiel *f;* **b. stone,** cálculo *m* biliar. **2** *fig (irritability)* bilis *f,* hiel *f,* mal genio *m.*

bilge [bɪldʒ] *n* **1** *Naut (bottom)* pantoque *m.* ■ **b. keel,** quilla *f.* **2** *Naut (also pl) (cavity)* sentina *f.* ■ **b.water,** agua *f* de sentina. **3** *fam (rubbish)* tonterías *fpl,* idioteces *fpl.*

bilingual [baɪ'lɪŋgwəl] *adj* bilingüe.

bilingualism [baɪ'lɪŋgwəlɪzəm] *n* bilingüismo *m.*

bilious ['bɪlɪəs] *adj* **1** *Med* bilioso,-a; **b. attack,** cólico bilioso. **2** *fam (colour etc)* asqueroso,-a. **3** *fig (irritable)* bilioso,-a, colérico,-a.

Bill [bɪl] *n dimin of* **William;** *GB sl* **the Old B.,** *(police)* la poli.

bill¹ [bɪl] **I** *n* **1** *(for electricity, services, etc)* factura *f;* **the gas b.,** la factura del gas. **2** *esp GB (in restaurant, hotel)* cuenta *f;* **the b., please,** la cuenta, por favor; *fam* **to foot the b.,** pagar la cuenta. **3** *Parl* proyecto *m* de ley; **to pass a b.,** aprobar un proyecto de ley. **4** *US (banknote)* billete *m* de banco; **a ten-dollar b.,** un billete de diez dólares. **5** *(poster)* cartel *m;* **on the b.,** en cartel; **'post no bills'**, 'prohibido fijar carteles'; *Theat* **to top the b.,** encabezar el reparto; *fam* **to fit the b.,** cumplir. **6** *(document)* documento *m.* ■ **b. of exchange,** letra *f* de cambio; **b. of fare,** menú *m; Naut* **b. of health,** patente *f* de sanidad; *fam* **the doctor gave him a clean b. of health,** el médico certificó su buen estado de salud; **b. of lading,** conocimiento *m* de embarque; *Pol* **B. of Rights,** declaración *f* de derechos; *Jur* **b. of sale,** contrato *m* or escritura *f* de venta. **II** *vtr* **1** *(send bill to)* facturar, extender una factura. **2** *Theat (schedule)* programar; **she is billed to appear as Joan of Arc,** figura en el cartel en el papel de Juana de Arco; **the play is billed for next Monday,** la obra se representará el lunes que viene.

bill² [bɪl] *n (of bird)* pico *m.*

billabong ['bɪləbɒŋ] *n Austral* rebalsa *f,* embalse *m.*

billboard ['bɪlbɔːd] *n US (hoarding)* cartelera *f.*

billet ['bɪlɪt] *Mil* **I** *n* alojamiento *m,* acantonamiento *m.* **II** *vtr (troops)* alojar, acantonar.

billet-doux [bɪlɪ'duː] *n (pl* **billets-doux)** *arch* carta *f* de amor.

billfold ['bɪlfəʊld] *n US* cartera *f,* billetero *m,* billetera *f.*

billhook ['bɪlhʊk] *n Agr* podadera *f.*

billiard ['bɪljəd] *n* billar *m.* ■ **b. ball,** bola *f* de billar; **b. cue,** taco *m* de billar; **b. room,** sala *f* de billar.

billiards ['bɪljədz] *n* billar *m.*

billing ['bɪlɪŋ] *n Theat* **to get top b.,** estar a la cabeza del reparto.

billion ['bɪljən] *n (pl* **billion** *or* **billions) 1** *GB* billón *m.* **2** *US* mil millones *mpl.*

billionaire [bɪljə'neəʳ] *n* multimillonario,-a *m, f.*

billow ['bɪləʊ] **I** *n* **1** *(of water)* ola *f.* **2** *(of smoke)* nube *f.* **II** *vi* **1** *(sea)* ondear. **2** *(sail)* hincharse, in flarse; **clouds of black smoke billowed from the burning building,** grandes nubes de humo negro surgían del edificio en llamas.

billowy ['bɪləʊɪ] *adj (sea)* ondoso,-a; *(sail)* hinchado,-a.

billposter ['bɪlpəʊstəʳ] *n,* **billsticker** ['bɪlstɪkəʳ] *n* cartelero,-a *m,f.*

billycan ['bɪlɪkæn] *n* cazo *m.*

billy goat ['bɪlɪgəʊt] *n* macho *m* cabrío.

billy-(h)o ['bɪlɪəʊ] *adj GB fam* **like b.-(h)o,** a más no poder, a toda pastilla.

bin [bɪn] *n* **1** *(for storage)* cajón *m,* arca *f.* ■ **bread b.,** caja *f* del pan; *GB* **wine b.,** botellero *m; sl* **loony b.,** manicomio *m.* **2** *(for rubbish)* **(rubbish) b.,** cubo *m* de la basura; **waste-paper b.,** papelera *f.*

binary ['baɪnərɪ] *adj* binario,-a; *Math* **b. number,** número binario.

bind [baɪnd] **I** *vtr (pt & pp* **bound) 1** *(tie up) (hands, package, etc)* atar; *Agr (cereal)* agavillar. **2** *Med (bandage)* vendar. **3** *Print (book)* encuadernar. **4** *(require)*

obligar; **the contract binds him to pay interest,** el contrato le obliga a pagar intereses. **5** *(cohere) (glue etc)* unir. **II** *vi (agreement)* tener fuerza obligatoria. **III** *n fam* aprieto *m;* **to be in a b.,** estar en un aprieto. ◆ **bind over** *vtr Jur* obligar legalmente.

binder ['baɪndəʳ] *n* **1** *Agr* agavilladora *f.* **2** *Print (person)* encuadernador,-a *m,f.* **3** *(file)* carpeta *f.*

binding ['baɪndɪŋ] **I** *adj* **1** *(promise)* comprometedor,-a; *(decision)* obligatorio,-a. **2** *Med (constipating)* que estriñe, astringente. **II** *n* **1** *Print* encuadernación *f.* **2** *Sew* ribete *m.* **3** *Ski* fijación *f.*

bindweed ['baɪndwiːd] *n Bot* enredadera *f.*

binge [bɪndʒ] *n fam* borrachera *f;* **to go on a b.,** irse de juerga, irse de parranda.

bingo ['bɪŋgəʊ] *n* bingo *m;* **to play b.,** jugar al bingo. ■ **b. hall,** (sala *f* de) bingo *m.*

binoculars [bɪ'nɒkjʊləz] *npl* prismáticos *mpl,* gemelos *mpl.*

biochemical [baɪəʊ'kemɪkəl] *adj* bioquímico,-a.

biochemist [baɪəʊ'kemɪst] *n* bioquímico,-a *m,f.*

biochemistry [baɪəʊ'kemɪstrɪ] *n* bioquímica *f.*

biodegradable [baɪəʊdɪ'greɪdəbəl] *adj* biodegradable.

biofeedback [baɪəʊ'fiːdbæk] *n* bioretracción *f.*

biographer [baɪ'ɒgrəfəʳ] *n* biógrafo,-a *m,f.*

biographical [baɪə'græfɪkəl] *adj* biográfico,-a.

biography [baɪ'ɒgrəfɪ] *n* biografía *f.*

biological [baɪə'lɒdʒɪkəl] *adj* biológico,-a; **b. warfare,** guerra biológica.

biologist [baɪ'ɒlədʒɪst] *n* biólogo,-a *m,f.*

biology [baɪ'ɒlədʒɪ] *n* biología *f.*

bionic [baɪ'ɒnɪk] *adj* biónico,-a.

bionics [baɪ'ɒnɪks] *n* biónica *f.*

biophysical [baɪəʊ'fɪzɪkəl] *adj* biofísico,-a.

biophysicist [baɪəʊ'fɪzɪsɪst] *n* biofísico,-a *m,f.*

biophysics [baɪəʊ'fɪzɪks] *n* biofísica *f.*

biopsy ['baɪɒpsɪ] *n Med* biopsia *f.*

biorhythm ['baɪəʊrɪðəm] *n* biorritmo *m.*

biosphere ['baɪəsfɪəʳ] *n* biosfera *f.*

bipartisan [baɪ'pɑːtɪzæn] *adj* bipartito,-a.

bipartite [baɪ'pɑːtaɪt] *adj* **1** *(with two parts)* bipartido,-a, bipartito,-a. **2** *(shared by two parties)* bipartito,-a, bilateral; **b. agreement,** acuerdo bipartito.

biped ['baɪped] **I** *n Zool* bípedo *m.* **II** *adj* bípedo,-a.

biplane ['baɪpleɪn] *n Av* biplano *m.*

birch [bɜːtʃ] **I** *n* **1** *Bot* abedul *m.* **2** *(rod)* vara *f* (de abedul). **II** *vtr* azotar.

bird [bɜːd] *n* **1** *Orn (small)* pájaro *m; (large)* ave *f; fig Theat* **to give sb the b.,** abuchear a algn; *fig* **to kill two birds with one stone,** matar dos pájaros de un tiro; *sl* **to do b.,** estar en el talego; *prov* **a b. in the hand is worth two in the bush,** más vale pájaro en mano que ciento volando; *prov* **birds of a feather flock together,** Dios los cría y ellos se juntan; **they're birds of a feather,** son tal para cual; *prov* **the early b. catches the worm,** a quien madruga Dios le ayuda. ■ **b. of paradise,** ave *f* del Paraíso; **b. of passage,** ave *f* de paso; **b. of prey,** ave *f* de rapiña; **night b.,** ave *f* nocturna. **2** *GB sl (girl)* tía *f,* chica *f.*

birdbath ['bɜːdbɑːθ] *n* pila *f* para pájaros.

birdcage ['bɜːdkeɪdʒ] *n* jaula *f.*

birdie ['bɜːdɪ] *n* **1** *fam (bird)* pajarito *m.* **2** *Golf* birdie *m.*

birdseed ['bɜːdsiːd] *n* alpiste *m.*

bird's-eye view [bɜːdzaɪ'vjuː] *n* vista *f* panorámica *or* de pájaro.

bird-watcher ['bɜːdwɒtʃəʳ] *n* ornitólogo,-a *m, f,* observador,-a *m,f* de pájaros.

bird-watching ['bɜːdwɒtʃɪŋ] *n* ornitología *f,* observación *f* de pájaros.

biretta [bɪˈretə] *n Rel* birrete *m*, birreta *f*.

Biro® [ˈbaɪrəʊ] *n fam* boli *m*.

birth [bɜ:θ] *n* **1** *(of baby etc)* nacimiento *m*; *Med (childbirth)* parto *m*; **Spanish by b.**, español de nacimiento; **to give b. to a child**, dar a luz a un niño. ■ **b. certificate**, partida *f* de nacimiento; **b. control**, *(family planning)* control *m* de la natalidad; *(contraception)* métodos *mpl* anticonceptivos; **b. rate**, índice *m* de natalidad. **2** *(descent, parentage)* linaje *m*, origen *m*; **of noble b.**, de noble linaje.

birthday [ˈbɜ:θdeɪ] *n* cumpleaños *m inv*; **happy b.!**, ¡feliz cumpleaños!; *fam* **to be in one's b. suit**, estar como Dios le trajo al mundo, estar en cueros. ■ **b. party**, fiesta *f* de cumpleaños.

birthmark [ˈbɜ:θmɑ:k] *n* antojo *m*, marca *f* de nacimiento.

birthplace [ˈbɜ:θpleɪs] *n* lugar *m* de nacimiento.

birthright [ˈbɜ:θraɪt] *n (individual)* derechos *mpl* de nacimiento, derechos *mpl* de primogenitura; *(heritage)* patrimonio *m*.

birthstone [ˈbɜ:θstəʊn] *n* piedra *f* preciosa que corresponde al mes de nacimiento y que trae suerte al portador.

Biscay [ˈbɪskeɪ] *n* Vizcaya; **the Bay of B.**, el golfo de Vizcaya.

biscuit [ˈbɪskɪt] *n* **1** *Culin* galleta *f*; *fam* **that really takes the b.!**, ¡eso ya es el colmo!; ¡eso realmente se lleva la palma! **2** *(muffin)* bollo *m*, bizcocho *m*. **3** *(colour)* beige *m*.

bisect [baɪˈsekt] *vtr* bisegmentar; *Geom* bisecar.

bisexual [baɪˈseksjʊəl] *adj* bisexual.

bishop [ˈbɪʃəp] *n* **1** *Rel* obispo *m*. **2** *Chess* alfil *m*.

bishopric [ˈbɪʃəprɪk] *n Rel* obispado *m*.

bismuth [ˈbɪzməθ] *n Chem* bismuto *m*.

bison [ˈbaɪsən] *n inv Zool* bisonte *m*.

bistro [ˈbi:strəʊ] *n* restaurante *m* pequeño.

bit¹ [bɪt] *n* **1** *(small piece)* trozo *m*, pedazo *m*; **a b. of cake**, un trozo de pastel; **the table has come to bits**, la mesa se ha roto; **to smash sth to bits**, hacer añicos algo; **to take sth to bits**, desmontar algo; *fig* **he went to bits**, se puso histérico; *fig* **I'm every b. as keen as you**, estoy tan entusiasmado,-a como tú; *fig* **thrilled to bits**, muy emocionado,-a, entusiasmado,-a; *fig* **to do one's b.**, hacer or poner de su parte; *fam* **b. of all right**, *(woman)* tía *f* buena; *(man)* tío *m* bueno. ■ *Theat* **b. part**, papel *m* secundario. **2** *(small quantity)* poco *m*; **a b. of sugar**, un poco de azúcar; **a b. of advice**, un consejo; **a b. of news**, una noticia; **bits and pieces**, trastos *mpl*; **he's a b. of a philosopher**, es un poco filósofo; **she's got a b. of money put aside**, tiene algo de dinero ahorrado; *fig* **b. by b.**, poco a poco; *fig* **not a b. of it!**, ¡ni hablar!; **are you angry?** —**not a b.!**, ¿estás enfadado? —¡en absoluto! **3** *(slightly, quite)* **a b.**, un poco; **a b. longer**, un ratito más; **a b. worried**, un poco preocupado; **a good b.**, bastante. **4** *(coin)* moneda *f*. ■ *Hist* **threepenny b.**, moneda *f* de tres peniques.

bit² [bɪt] *n (of bridle)* bocado *m*; *fig* **to take the b. between one's teeth**, desbocarse.

bit³ [bɪt] *n (of tool)* broca *f*, filo *m*; *(of drill)* broca *f*, taladro *m*, barrena *f*.

bit⁴ [bɪt] *n Comput* bit *m*.

bit⁵ [bɪt] *pt see* **bite**.

bitch [bɪtʃ] **I** *n* **1** *Zool (female)* hembra *f*; *(dog)* perra *f*. **2** *fam (spiteful woman)* bruja *f*, arpía *f*; *(prostitute)* zorra *f*; *sl offens* **son of a b.**, hijo *m* de puta or perra. **II** *vi fam* **to b. (about)**, *(complain)* quejarse (de); *(criticize)* criticar, despellejar; **he's always bitching about his workmates**, *(criticizing)* siempre habla mal de sus compañeros de trabajo.

bitchy [ˈbɪtʃɪ] *adj fam (spiteful)* maldiciente; *(resentful)* rencoroso,-a; *(malicious)* malicioso,-a; *(malevolent)* malévolo,-a, malintencionado,-a.

bite [baɪt] **I** *n* **1** *(act)* mordisco *m*. **2** *(wound)* mordedura *f*; **(insect) b.**, picadura *f* (de insecto). **3** *(mouthful)* bocado *m*; **a b. of chocolate**, un bocado de chocolate. **4** *fam (snack)* bocado *m*, piscolabis *m*; **she hasn't had a b. to eat all day**, no ha probado bocado en todo el día. **5** *fig* mordacidad *f*, garra *f*. **II** *vtr (pt bit; pp bitten)* morder; *(insect)* picar; **to b. one's nails**, morderse las uñas; *fig* **to b. the dust**, morder el polvo; *fam* **don't b. off more than you can chew**, quien mucho abarca, poco aprieta; *fam* **to b. sb's head off**, echarle una bronca a algn; *fam* **what's biting you?**, ¿qué mosca te ha picado?; *prov* **once bitten twice shy**, gato escaldado del agua fría huye. **III** *vi* **1** morder; *(insect)* picar. **2** *fig (take effect)* surtir efecto; **the economic measures are beginning to b.**, las medidas económicas están empezando a tener efecto. **3** *Fishing* picar, morder el anzuelo.

biting [ˈbaɪtɪŋ] *adj (wind)* cortante; *fig (criticism)* mordaz, cáustico,-a.

bitten [ˈbɪtən] *pp see* **bite**.

bitter [ˈbɪtə] **I** *adj* **1** amargo,-a; **b. lemon**, limonada *f* amarga. **2** *(weather)* glacial; *(wind)* cortante. **3** *(memory)* amargo,-a; *(person)* amargado,-a; **the experience has made him feel b.**, la experiencia le ha amargado. **4** *(struggle)* enconado,-a; *(hatred)* implacable; **to the b. end**, hasta el final. **II** *n* **1** *(beer)* cerveza *f* amarga. **2 bitters**, bíter *m*. ◆ **bitterly** *adv* **1** amargamente, con amargura; **she was b. disappointed**, sufrió una terrible decepción. **2** *(weather)* **it's b. cold**, hace un frío glacial.

bittern [ˈbɪtən] *n Orn* avetoro *m* común. ■ **little b.**, avetorillo *m* común.

bitterness [ˈbɪtənɪs] *n* **1** *(gen)* amargura *f*. **2** *(weather)* crudeza *f*, severidad *f*. **3** *(person)* amargura *f*, rencor *m*. **4** *(of struggle)* encono *m*.

bittersweet [ˈbɪtəˈswi:t] *adj* agridulce.

bitty [ˈbɪtɪ] *adj (bitter, bittiest)* fragmentario,-a, incoherente.

bitumen [ˈbɪtjumɪn] *n* betún *m*.

bituminous [bɪˈtju:mɪnəs] *adj* bituminoso,-a.

bivouac [ˈbɪvuæk, ˈbɪvwæk] *Mil* **I** *n* vivaque *m*, vivac *m*. **II** *vi (pt & pp bivouacked)* vivaquear.

biweekly [baɪˈwi:klɪ] **I** *adj* **1** *(every two weeks)* quincenal. **2** *(twice a week)* bisemanal. **II** *adv* **1** *(every two weeks)* quincenalmente, cada quincena. **2** *(twice a week)* dos veces por semana. **III** *n* publicación *f* quincenal or bisemanal.

bizarre [bɪˈzɑ:] *adj* **1** *(odd)* extraño,-a, raro,-a. **2** *(eccentric)* estrafalario,-a, extravagante.

blab [blæb] *vi (pt & pp blabbed)* **1** *fam* parlotear; *(chatter)* **he's always blabbing**, nunca para de hablar. **2** *(let out a secret)* descubrir el pastel, chivarse.

black [blæk] **I** *adj* **1** *(colour)* negro,-a; **a b. and white television**, un televisor en blanco y negro; **as b. as coal**, negro como el carbón; *fig* **b. and blue**, amoratado,-a, lleno,-a de cardenales; *fig* **to be in sb's b. books**, estar en la lista negra de algn; *fam* **to put sth down in b. and white**, poner algo por escrito. ■ *Av* **b. box**, caja *f* negra; **b. coffee**, café *m* solo; **b. eye**, ojo *m* morado or a la funerala; *Astron* **b. hole**, agujero *m* negro; **b. humour**, humor *m* negro; **b. magic**, magia *f* negra; *GB* **B. Maria**, coche *m* celular, furgón *m* policial; **b. mark**, mala nota *f*; **b. market**, mercado *m* negro; **b. market goods**, artículos *mpl* de estraperlo; **b. marketeer**, estraperlista *mf*; *US* **B. Power**, movimiento *m* a favor de los derechos de los negros; **b. pudding**, morcilla *f*; **B. Sea**, Mar *m* Negro; *Aut* **b. spot**, punto *m* negro; *GB* **the B. Country**, la región de los Midlands; *Hist* **the B. Death**, la peste negra; **the b. economy**, la economía negra; *fig* **b. sheep**, oveja *f* negra. **2** *(gloomy)* negro,-a; **it was a b. day for the army**, fue un día aciago para el ejército; **the outlook is b.**, la perspectiva es negra. **II** *n* **1** *(colour)* negro *m*. **2** *(person)* negro,-a *m,f*. **3** *(mourning)* luto *m*; **he was in b.**, iba de luto. **III** *vtr* **1** *(make black)* ennegrecer; *fig* **to b. sb's eye**, ponerle a algn un ojo a la funerala. **2** *(polish)* limpiar, lustrar. **3** *(boycott)* boicotear. ◆ **black out I** *vtr* **1**

(extinguish lights) apagar las luces de; **the city was blacked out during the air raids,** durante los bombardeos se apagaron todas las luces de la ciudad. **2** *Rad TV (censor)* censurar. **II** *vi (faint)* perder el conocimiento, desmayarse.

blackball ['blækbɔːl] **I** *n (veto)* veto *m*; *(negative vote)* voto *m* negativo *or* en contra. **II** *vtr* votar en contra de algn.

blackberry ['blækbərɪ] *n Bot* zarzamora *f*, mora *f*; **to go blackberrying,** ir a recoger moras.

blackbird ['blækbɜːd] *n Orn* mirlo *m*.

blackboard ['blækbɔːd] *n* pizarra *f*, encerado *m*.

blackcap ['blækkæp] *n Orn* curruca *f* capirotada.

blackcurrant [blæk'kʌrənt] *n Bot* grosella *f* negra.

blacken ['blækən] *vtr* **1** *(make black)* ennegrecer, tiznar. **2** *fig (defame)* manchar.

blackguard ['blægɑːd] *n* sinvergüenza *mf*.

blackhead ['blækhed] *n Med* espinilla *f*.

blackish ['blækɪʃ] *adj* negruzco,-a.

blackjack ['blækdʒæk] *n* **1** *US (truncheon)* porra *f*, cachiporra *f*. **2** *Cards* veintiuna *f*.

blackleg ['blækleg] *n* esquirol *m*.

blacklist ['blæklɪst] **I** *n* lista *f* negra. **II** *vtr* poner en la lista negra.

blackmail ['blækmeɪl] **I** *n* chantaje *m*. **II** *vtr* hacer chantaje, chantajear.

blackmailer ['blækmeɪlə'] *n* chantajista *mf*.

blackness ['blæknɪs] *n (colouring)* negrura *f*; *(darkness)* oscuridad *f*.

blackout ['blækaʊt] *n* **1** *(of lights)* apagón *m*. **2** *Rad TV (censorship)* censura *f*. **3** *(fainting)* pérdida *f* de conocimiento.

Blackshirt ['blækʃɜːt] *n Hist* camisa negra *m*, fascista *mf*.

blacksmith ['blæksmɪθ] *n* herrero *m*.

blackthorn ['blækθɔːn] *n* **1** *Bot* endrino *m*. **2** *(stick)* bastón *m*.

black-tie ['blæktaɪ] *adj* de etiqueta. ■ **b.-t. dinner,** cena *f* de etiqueta.

bladder ['blædə'] *n Anat* vejiga *f*. ■ **gall b.,** vesícula *f* biliar.

blade [bleɪd] *n* **1** *(of grass)* brizna *f*. **2** *(of knife, sword, razor)* hoja *f*; *(of ice skate)* cuchilla *f*. ■ **razor b.,** hoja *f* de afeitar. **3** *(of propeller)* pala *f*, paleta *f*; *(of oar)* pala *f*.

blame [bleɪm] **I** *n* culpa *f*; **to put the b. for sth on sb,** echar la culpa de algo a algn; **to take the b. for sth,** asumir la responsabilidad de algo. **II** *vtr* culpar, echar la culpa a; **he is to be-,** él tiene la culpa; **I don't b. Tom,** la culpa no es de Tom; **I've only myself to b.,** la culpa es sólo mía; **to be to b.,** ser el culpable *or* el responsable, tener la culpa.

blameless ['bleɪmlɪs] *adj (person)* inocente; *(conduct)* intachable.

blameworthy ['bleɪmwɜːðɪ] *adj* culpable, censurable.

blanch [blɑːntʃ] **I** *vtr Culin (boil)* escaldar. **II** *vi (go pale)* palidecer.

blancmange [blə'mɒnʒ] *n Culin* tipo de budín *m* dulce.

bland [blænd] *adj* **1** *(climate)* suave, templado,-a. **2** *(person)* agradable, amable. **3** *(food)* soso,-a.

blandishments ['blændɪʃmənts] *npl* halagos *mpl*, lisonjas *fpl*.

blank [blæŋk] **I** *adj* **1** *(without writing)* en blanco; **leave a b. space,** deja un espacio en blanco. **2** *(empty)* vacío,-a; **a. b. look,** una mirada vacía; **my mind went b.,** me quedé en blanco. ■ *Mil* **b. cartridge,** cartucho *m* de fogueo; *Fin* **b. cheque,** cheque *m* en blanco; *Lit* **b. verse,** verso *m* blanco *or* suelto. **3** *(absolute)* tajante, categórico,-a; **a b. refusal,** una negativa rotunda. **II** *n* **1** *(space)* espacio *m* en blanco, blanco *m*, hueco *m*; **fill in the blanks,** rellene los espacios en blanco; **his mind was a b.,** se quedó en blanco; **to draw a b.,** no tener éxito. **2** *Mil* cartucho *m* de fogueo. **3**

US (form) impreso *m*, formulario *m*. ◆ **blankly** *adv* **1** *(expressionless)* con la mirada vacía. **2** *(without understanding)* sin comprender.

blanket ['blæŋkɪt] **I** *n* **1** manta *f*, frazada *f*; **electric b.,** manta eléctrica. ■ *fam* **wet b.,** aguafiestas *mf inv*. **2** *fig* capa *f*, manto *m*; **a b. of snow,** una capa de nieve. **II** *adj* general, comprensivo,-a; **a b. agreement,** un acuerdo general.

blare [bleə'] **I** *n* **1** *(loud noise)* estruendo *m*. **2** *(of trumpet)* trompetazo *m*. **II** *vi (trumpet)* sonar, resonar. ◆ **blare out** *vtr (announce)* pregonar.

blarney ['blɑːnɪ] *n fam* coba *f*, labia *f*.

blasé ['blɑːzeɪ] *adj* hastiado,-a, de vuelta de todo.

blaspheme [blæs'fiːm] *vtr & vi* blasfemar **(against,** contra).

blasphemer [blæs'fiːmə'] *n* blasfemador,-a *m*, *f*, blasfemo,-a *m*, *f*.

blasphemous ['blæsfɪməs] *adj* blasfemo,-a.

blasphemy ['blæsfɪmɪ] *n* blasfemia *f*.

blast [blɑːst] **I** *n* **1** *(of wind)* ráfaga *f*; *(of sand, water, compressed air)* chorro *m*. **2** *Mus (of horn etc)* toque *m*; **at full b.,** a toda marcha; **the radio was on full b.,** la radio sonaba a todo volumen; **trumpet b.,** trompetazo *m*. **3** *(explosion)* explosión *f*. ■ **b. furnace,** alto horno *m*. **4** *(shock wave)* onda *f* expansiva, onda *f* de choque. **II** *vtr* **1** *(blow up)* volar, hacer volar; *fam* **b. (it)!,** ¡maldito sea! **2** *fig (destroy)* acabar con, arruinar. **3** *fig (criticize)* criticar. ◆ **blast off** *vi Astronaut* despegar.

blasted ['blɑːstɪd] *adj* maldito,-a, condenado,-a; *sl (drugs)* **to get b.,** ponerse ciego,-a.

blasting ['blɑːstɪŋ] *n Min* voladura *f*. ■ **b. charge,** carga *f* explosiva.

blast-off ['blɑːstɒf] *n Astronaut* despegue *m*.

blatant ['bleɪtənt] *adj (very obvious)* evidente, patente; *(shameless)* descarado,-a; **a b. lie,** una mentira patente.

blather ['blæðə'] *vi esp US* decir disparates.

blaze¹ [bleɪz] **I** *n* **1** *(burst of flame)* llamarada *f*. **2** *(fierce fire)* incendio *m*. **3** *(of sun, light)* resplandor *m*. **4** *(outburst)* ataque *m*, arranque *m*; *fig* **in a b. of anger,** en un arranque de cólera. **5** *fam* **blazes,** *(hell)* **go to b.!,** ¡vete a la porra!; **to run like b.,** correr como un descosido; **to work like b.,** trabajar como un demonio; **what the b. are you doing here?,** ¿qué demonios haces tú aquí? **II** *vi* **1** *(fire)* arder; *fig* **to b. with anger,** echar chispas. **2** *(sun, light, jewels)* resplandecer, brillar; **the sun was blazing down,** el sol pegaba con fuerza.

blaze² [bleɪz] **I** *n Zool* estrella *f*, mancha *f* blanca. **II** *vtr* **to b. a trail,** abrir un camino.

blazer ['bleɪzə'] *n* chaqueta *f* sport, blazer *m*.

blazing ['bleɪzɪŋ] *adj* **1** *(building)* en llamas. **2** *(sun)* abrasador,-a; *(light)* brillante. **3** *(rowdy)* violento,-a; **a b. row,** una discusión muy violenta.

blazon ['bleɪzən] **I** *n Herald* blasón *m*. **II** *vtr Herald* blasonar; *fig* proclamar.

bleach [bliːtʃ] **I** *n (household)* lejía *f*; *Chem* decolorante *m*. **II** *vtr* **1** *(whiten)* blanquear; *(fade)* descolorir; **the sun has bleached the dress,** el sol ha descolorido el vestido. **2** *Hairdr* decolorar, aclarar con agua oxigenada.

bleachers ['bliːtʃəz] *npl US sport (seats)* gradas *fpl*, graderío *m*.

bleak¹ [bliːk] *adj* **1** *(countryside)* desolado,-a. **2** *(weather)* frío,-a, desapacible. **3** *(future)* poco prometedor,-a.

bleak² [bliːk] *n (fish)* alburno *m*.

bleary ['blɪərɪ] *adj (blearier, bleariest) (eyes) (due to tears)* nublado,-a; *(due to tiredness)* legañoso,-a.

bleary-eyed [blɪərɪ'aɪd] *adj* con los ojos nublados *or* legañosos.

bleat [bliːt] **I** *n* balido *m*. **II** *vi* **1** *(animal)* balar. **2** *fam (person)* quejarse.

bled [bled] *pt & pp see* **bleede.**

bleed [bli:d] **I** *vi (pt & pp bled) Med* sangrar; **his nose is bleeding,** le sangra la nariz; **to b. to death,** morir desangrado,-a; *iron* **my heart bleeds for you,** ¡qué pena me das! **II** *vtr Med* sangrar; *fam* **to b. sb white** *or* **dry,** sacarle a algn hasta el último céntimo.

bleeder ['bli:dǝ'] *n* **1** *fam Med* hemofílico,-a *m, f.* **2** *sl offens* hijo *m* de tal; **you lucky b.!,** ¡menuda suerte tienes, macho!

bleeding ['bli:dɪŋ] **I** *n Med (blood-letting)* sangría *f; (loss of blood)* pérdida *f* de sangre, hemorragia *f.* **II** *adj* **1** *Med* sangrante, que sangra. **2** *sl offens* puñetero,-a, jodido,-a.

bleed-valve ['bli:dvælv] *n Tech* válvula *f* de desahogo.

bleep [bli:p] **I** *n* bip *m*, pitido *m*. **II** *vi* hacer bip, pitar. **III** *vtr fam* **to b. sb,** localizar a algn con un busca.

bleeper ['bli:pǝ'] *n fam* busca *m*, buscapersonas *m inv.*

blemish ['blemɪʃ] *n* **I** *(defect, flaw)* defecto *m*, imperfección *f; (on fruit)* maca *f; fig* mancha *f, fig* **without b.,** sin tacha. **2** *(on skin)* mancha *f.*

blench[1] [blentʃ] *vi (flinch)* echarse atrás; **without blenching,** sin pestañear.

blench[2] [blentʃ] *vi (turn pale)* palidecer.

blend [blend] **I** *n (mixture)* mezcla *f*, combinación *f.* **II** *vtr (mix)* mezclar, combinar; *(match)* casar, armonizar. **III** *vi (mix)* mezclarse, combinarse; *(colours)* casar, armonizar.

blender ['blendǝ'] *n Culin* licuadora *f.* ■ **hand b.,** batidora *f.*

bless [bles] *vtr (pt & pp blessed or blest)* **1** bendecir; *fam* **b. my soul!,** ¡caramba!; *fam (after a sneeze)* **b. you!,** ¡Jesús!; *fam* **God b. you!,** ¡Dios te bendiga! **2** dotar; **blessed with good eyesight,** dotado,-a de buena vista; **they were blessed with five children,** Dios les bendijo con cinco hijos.

blessed ['blesɪd] *adj* **1** *Rel* bendito,-a; **b. be Thy Name,** bendito sea Tu Nombre; **the B. Sacrament,** el Santísimo Sacramento; **the B. Virgin,** la Santa Virgen. **2** *(happy)* bienaventurado,-a, feliz. **3** *fam (damned)* maldito,-a, dichoso,-a; **I don't know a b. thing about it,** no tengo ni la más remota idea; **the whole b. day,** todo el santo día; **where's that b. book?,** ¿dónde estará ese maldito libro?

blessing ['blesɪŋ] *n* **1** *Rel* bendición *f*; **to give the b.,** dar la bendición; *fig* **the government gave its b. to the project,** el gobierno aprobó el proyecto. **2** *(advantage)* ventaja *f*; **a mixed b.,** una ventaja relativa; **it's a b. in disguise,** no hay mal que por bien no venga; **one must count one's blessings,** se debe apreciar lo que uno tiene; **the blessings of civilization,** las ventajas de la civilización.

blest [blest] *pt & pp see* **bless.**

blew [blu:] *pt see* **blow.**

blight [blaɪt] **1** *n Agr* añublo *m; fig* plaga *f.* **II** *vtr* **1** *Agr* tener añublo, atizonar. **2** *fig (spoil)* arruinar, destrozar; *(frustrate)* frustrar.

blighter ['blaɪtǝ'] *n fam* **1** *(fellow)* tío *m*, tipo *m*; **you lucky b.!,** ¡qué suerte tienes, tío! **2** *(annoying person)* cabrón,-ona *m, f.*

Blighty ['blaɪtɪ] *n fam* Inglaterra.

blimey ['blaɪmɪ] *interj fam* ¡caramba!, ¡caray!

blimp [blɪmp] *n Av* dirigible *m*.

blind [blaɪnd] **I** *adj* **1** *(medical condition)* ciego,-a; **a b. man,** un ciego; **a b. woman,** una ciega; **b. in one eye,** tuerto,-a; **b. man's buff,** *(game)* la gallinita ciega; **to go b.,** quedarse ciego; *fig* **b. faith,** fe ciega; *fig* **b. obedience,** obediencia ciega; *fig* **to b. to sth,** no ver algo; **he is b. to the consequences,** no ve las consecuencias; *fig* **to turn a b. eye,** hacer la vista gorda; *fam* **to be as b. as a bat,** no ver tres en un burro. **2** *(bad visibility)* ciego,-a. ■ **b. alley,** callejón *m* sin salida; *Aut* **b. corner,** curva *f* sin visibilidad; *Sport* **b. side,** lado *m* estrecho; **b. spot,** ángulo *m* muerto; *fam* **b. date,** cita *f* a ciegas. **II** *adv* a ciegas; *Av* **to fly b.,** volar sin visibilidad; *fam* **to get b. drunk,** agarrar una curda; *Cards* **to go b.,** apostar a ciegas. **III** *n* **1** *(on window)* persiana *f.* **2** *pl* **the b.,** los ciegos; *fig* **it's the b. leading the b.,** es como un ciego conduciendo a otro ciego. **IV** *vtr* **1** *(deprive of sight)* cegar, dejar ciego; **blinded by ambition,** cegado por la ambición. **2** *(dazzle)* deslumbrar.

blinder ['blaɪndǝ'] *n fam* borrachera *f*; **to go on a b.,** irse de juerga; *GB Sport* **to have** *or* **play a b.,** jugar muy bien.

blinders ['blaɪndǝz] *npl US* anteojeras *fpl.*

blindfold ['blaɪndfǝʊld] **I** *n* venda *f.* **II** *vtr* vendar los ojos.

blindfolded ['blaɪndfǝʊldɪd] *adj & adv* con los ojos vendados.

blinding ['blaɪndɪŋ] *adj* cegador,-a, deslumbrante.

blindly ['blaɪndlɪ] *adv* a ciegas, ciegamente.

blindness ['blaɪndnɪs] *n Med* ceguera *f; fig* ceguera *f*, obcecación *f.*

blink [blɪŋk] **I** *n (of eyes)* parpadeo *m; fam* **to be on the b.,** estar averiado,-a. **II** *vi* **1** *(eyes)* pestañear, parpadear. **2** *(lights)* parpadear.

blinkered ['blɪŋkǝd] *adj (horse)* con anteojeras; *fig (attitude)* de miras estrechas.

blinkers ['blɪŋkǝz] *npl* **1** *(on horse)* anteojeras *fpl.* **2** *Aut* intermitentes *mpl.* **3** *fam (eyes)* ojos *mpl.*

blinking ['blɪŋkɪŋ] *adj fam (damned)* maldito,-a, condenado,-a.

blip [blɪp] *n Rad* pip *m.*

bliss [blɪs] *n* felicidad *f*, dicha *f*; **it was b.!,** ¡fue maravilloso!, ¡fue estupendo!

blissful ['blɪsfʊl] *adj (happy)* feliz, dichoso,-a; *(marvellous)* maravilloso,-a. ◆ **blissfully** *adv* **b. happy,** verdaderamente feliz.

blister ['blɪstǝ'] **I** *n* **1** *Med (on skin)* ampolla *f.* **2** *(on paint)* burbuja *f.* **II** *vtr Med* ampollar, provocar ampollas. **III** *vi Med* ampollarse.

blithe [blaɪð] *adj* alegre. ◆ **blithely** *adv* alegremente.

blithering ['blɪðǝrɪŋ] *adj fam* **he's a b. idiot,** es tonto perdido.

blitz [blɪts] **I** *n* bombardeo *m* aéreo; *fig* **to have a b. on sth,** atacar algo. **II** *vtr* bombardear.

blitzkrieg ['blɪtskri:g] *n* guerra *f* relámpago.

blizzard ['blɪzǝd] *n* ventisca *f.*

bloated ['blǝʊtɪd] *adj* hinchado,-a, inflado,-a; *fig* **b. with pride,** henchido de orgullo.

bloater ['blǝʊtǝ'] *n Culin* arenque *m* ahumado.

blob [blɒb] *n (of liquid)* gota *f; (of colour)* mancha *f.*

bloc [blɒk] *n Pol* bloque *m*; **the Eastern B. countries,** los países del bloque del Este.

block [blɒk] **I** *n* **1** bloque *m; (of wood)* taco *m; (butcher's)* tajo *m; (toy)* **building b.,** cubo *m* de madera; **in b. capitals,** en mayúsculas. ■ **b. diagram,** diagrama *m* de bloques. **2** *(building)* edificio *m*, bloque *m*; **a b. of flats,** un bloque de pisos *or* de viviendas. **3** *(group of buildings)* manzana *f*; **to run round the b.,** dar la vuelta a la manzana. **4** *(obstruction)* bloqueo *m*, obstrucción *f*; **a mental b.,** un bloqueo mental. **5** *(group, series)* bloque *m; Theat* **a b. of seats,** un grupo de asientos; *Fin* **a b. of shares,** una serie de acciones. ■ **b. vote,** voto *m* por delegación. **6** *Tech* **b. and tackle,** aparejo *m* de poleas. **7** *fam (head)* coco *m*; **to knock sb's b. off,** romperle la crisma a algn. **II** *vtr* **1** *(obstruct)* bloquear, obstruir; *Aut* **'road blocked',** 'carretera cortada'; **to b. the way,** cerrar el paso; **to b. (up) a pipe,** obstruir una tubería. **2** *Sport (player)* obstaculizar; *(ball)* bloquear. **3** *Fin Parl* bloquear. **III** *vi* **1** obstruirse. **2** *Theat* poner en escena. ◆ **block up** *vtr* bloquear, obstruir; *(pipe)* **to get blocked up,** obstruirse.

blockade [blɒ'keɪd] *n* bloqueo *m*; **to run a b.,** romper *or* burlar un bloqueo.

blockage ['blɒkɪdʒ] *n* **1** bloqueo *m*, obstrucción *f.* **2** *Aut (traffic jam)* atasco *m*, embotellamiento *f.*

blockbuster ['blɒkbʌstəʳ] *n fam* **1** *Mil* bomba *f* de gran potencia. **2** *(success)* exitazo *m*; *Cin TV* gran éxito *m* de taquilla; *(book)* éxito *m* de ventas.

blockhead ['blɒkhed] *n* tarugo,-a *m,f*, zoquete *mf*.

blockhouse ['blɒkhaʊs] *n Mil* blocao *m*, fortín *m*.

blocking ['blɒkɪŋ] *n Theat* puesta *f* en escena, dirección *f* escénica.

bloke [bləʊk] *n fam* tío *m*, tipo *m*, individuo *m*.

blond [blɒnd] *adj & n* rubio *(m)*.

blonde [blɒnd] *adj & n* rubia *(f)*. ■ *Cin* **dumb b.,** rubia *f* tonta.

blood [blʌd] *n* **1** *Biol* sangre *f*; *fig* **in cold b.,** a sangre fría; *fig* **to make sb's b. run cold,** helarle la sangre a algn; *fig* **to sweat b.,** sudar sangre; *fam* **it makes my b. boil,** me hierve la sangre; *fam* **it's like trying to get b. from a stone,** es como querer sacar agua del desierto. ■ **b. bank,** banco *m* de sangre; **b. cell,** glóbulo *m*; **b. count,** recuento *m* de glóbulos sanguíneos; **b. donor,** donante *mf* de sangre; **b. group,** grupo *m* sanguíneo; **b. orange,** naranja *f* sanguina; **b. poisoning,** envenenamiento *m* de la sangre; **b. pressure,** tensión *f* arterial; **b. sports,** deportes *mpl* cruentos; **b. test,** análisis *m* de sangre; **b. transfusion,** transfusión *f* de sangre; **b. vessel,** vaso *m* sanguíneo; **blue b.,** sangre *f* azul; **high/low b. pressure,** hipertensión *fl* hipotensión *f*; **to have high/low b. pressure,** tener la tensión alta/baja. **2** *(race)* sangre *f*, raza *f*; **of Scottish b.,** de descendencia escocesa; *fig* **new b.,** sangre *f* nueva; *fam* **b. is thicker than water,** son muy fuertes los lazos de parentesco. ■ **b. brother,** hermano *m* carnal; **b. relation,** pariente *m* consanguíneo, parienta *f* consanguínea.

blood-and-thunder [blʌdən'θʌndəʳ] *adj Cin Theat* emocionante, melodramático,-a.

bloodbath ['blʌdbɑːθ] *n fig* baño *m* de sangre, carnicería *f*.

bloodcurdling ['blʌdkɜːdlɪŋ] *adj* espeluznante, horripilante.

bloodhound ['blʌdhaʊnd] *n Zool* sabueso *m*.

bloodless ['blʌdlɪs] *adj* **1** *(anaemic)* anémico,-a. **2** *(without bloodshed)* sin derramamiento de sangre, incruento,-a.

bloodletting ['blʌdletɪŋ] *n Med* sangría *f*; *fig* carnicería *f*.

blood-red ['blʌdred] *adj* de color rojo sangre.

bloodshed ['blʌdʃed] *n* derramamiento *m* de sangre.

bloodshot ['blʌdʃɒt] *adj (eyes)* inyectado,-a de sangre.

bloodstain ['blʌdsteɪn] *n* mancha *f* de sangre.

bloodstained ['blʌdsteɪnd] *adj* manchado,-a de sangre.

bloodstream ['blʌdstriːm] *n* corriente *f* sanguínea.

bloodsucker ['blʌdsʌkəʳ] *n Zool* sanguijuela *f*.

bloodthirsty ['blʌdθɜːstɪ] *adj* sanguinario,-a.

bloody ['blʌdɪ] **I** *adj (bloodier, bloodiest)* **1** *(battle)* sangriento,-a. **2** *(bloodstained)* manchado,-a de sangre. **3** *sl (damned)* condenado,-a, puñetero,-a; **they took no b. notice of me,** no me hicieron ni puñetero caso; **where's that b. book?,** ¿dónde está ese condenado libro? **II** *adv sl* **it's b. difficult,** ¡joder, qué difícil!; **not b. likely!,** ¡ni de coña!; **not b. once,** ¡ni una puñetera vez.

bloody-minded [blʌdɪ'maɪndɪd] *adj fam* terco,-a, tozudo,-a.

bloody-mindedness [blʌdɪ'maɪndɪdnɪs] *n fam* terquedad *f*.

bloom [bluːm] *n* **1** *(flower)* flor *f*; **in full b.,** en flor, florecido,-a; *fig* **in the b. of youth,** en la flor de la juventud. **2** *(on fruit)* vello *m*, pelusa *f*. **II** *vi* **1** *(blossom)* florecer; *fig* prosperar, florecer. **2** *(look radiant)* resplandecer; **blooming with health,** rebosante de salud.

bloomer¹ ['bluːməʳ] *n Culin* pan *m* casero.

bloomer² ['bluːməʳ] *n fam* metedura *f* de pata, plancha *f*.

bloomers ['bluːməz] *npl* pololos *mpl*, bombachos *mpl*.

blooming ['bluːmɪŋ] *adj* **1** *(blossoming)* floreciente. **2** *(glowing)* resplandeciente, radiante. **3** *fam euph (damned)* maldito,-a, condenado,-a.

blooper ['bluːpəʳ] *n US fam* metedura *f* de pata, plancha *f*.

blossom ['blɒsəm] **I** *n (flower)* flor *f*; **in b.,** en flor. ■ **orange b.,** flor *f* de azahar. **II** *vi* florecer; *fig* **to b. out,** alcanzar la plenitud.

blot [blɒt] **I** *n (of ink)* borrón *m*, mancha *f*; *fig* mancha *f*, *fig* **to be a b. on the landscape,** afear el paisaje. **II** *vtr (pt & pp **blotted**)* **1** *(with ink)* emborronar; *fam* **to blot one's copybook,** manchar su reputación. **2** *(dry with blotting paper)* secar. **III** *vi (ink)* correrse. ◆ **blot out** *vtr (memories)* borrar; *(view)* ocultar.

blotch [blɒtʃ] **I** *n (on skin)* mancha *f*, rojez *f*. **II** *vi* enrojecer.

blotchy ['blɒtʃɪ] *adj (skin, face, etc)* enrojecido,-a; *(paint etc)* cubierto,-a de manchas.

blotter ['blɒtəʳ] *n* **1** *(blotting paper)* papel *m* secante. **2** *US (record book)* registro *m*.

blotting-paper ['blɒtɪŋpeɪpəʳ] *n* papel *m* secante.

blotto ['blɒtəʊ] *adj sl* **to be b.,** estar trompa *or* como una cuba.

blouse [blaʊz] *n* blusa *f*.

blow¹ [bləʊ] *n* **1** golpe *m*; **b. with a hammer,** martillazo *m*; **b. with the fist,** puñetazo *m*; **to exchange blows,** pegarse; **to come to blows,** llegar a las manos; *fig* **a b. by b. account,** un relato minucioso; *fig* **to strike sb a b.,** asestar un golpe a algn. **2** *(shock)* golpe *m*; **it was a terrible b. for her,** fue un golpe duro para ella.

blow² [bləʊ] **I** *vi (pt blew; pp blown)* **1** *(wind)* soplar; **it blew out of the window,** voló por la ventana; **it's blowing hard,** hace mucho viento; **to b. on one's fingers,** soplarse los dedos; **to b. open/shut,** abrirse/cerrarse de golpe; *fig* **to b. hot and cold,** jugar con dos barajas. **2** *(whistle)* sonar. **3** *Elec (fuse)* fundirse. **4** *Aut (tyre)* reventar. **II** *vtr* **1** *(kiss)* mandar, enviar. **2** *Mus (trumpet etc)* tocar; *(horn)* tocar; *(whistle)* pitar; *fig* **to b. one's own trumpet,** darse bombo. **3** *(glass)* soplar. **4** *(one's nose)* sonarse. **5** *Elec (fuse)* fundir. **6** *fam (waste)* despilfarrar; **to b. all one's savings on a new car,** ventilarse todos sus ahorros en un coche nuevo; *fam* **b. the expense!,** ¡no importa el gasto! **7** *fam euph (damn)* **b. you!,** ¡vete a hacer puñetas!; **well, I'm blowed!,** ¡caray! **8** *fam (lose)* pifiar; **he blew his chances of getting the job,** perdió cualquier posibilidad de conseguir el empleo. **9** *(explode)* volar, hacer explotar; **to blow the bank sky-high,** hizo volar el banco por los aires; *fig* **to b. sb's cover,** descubrir la tapadera de algn; *fam* **to b. the gaff,** descubrir el pastel; *fam* **to b. one's top,** salirse de sus casillas. ◆ **blow away** *vtr (wind)* arrastrarse, llevarse. ◆ **blow down** *vtr* derribar. ◆ **blow in** *vtr* derribar. ◆ **blow off** *vtr (remove)* quitar; *fam (in anger)* **to b. sb's head off,** volarle la cabeza a algn. **II** *vi (hat)* salir volando. ◆ **blow out I** *vtr (extinguish)* apagar. **II** *vi* **1** *(become extinguished)* apagarse. **2** *Aut (tyre)* reventar. ◆ **blow over** *vtr* derribar. **II** *vi* **1** *(storm)* calmarse. **2** *fig (scandal)* olvidarse. ◆ **blow up I** *vtr* **1** *(building)* volar. **2** *(inflate)* inflar. **3** *Phot* ampliar. **II** *vi* **1** *(explode)* explotar. **2** *fam (lose one's temper)* salirse de sus casillas.

blower ['bləʊəʳ] *n* **1** *glass* **b.,** soplador,-a *m, f* de vidrio. **2** *fam (telephone)* teléfono *m*; **to get on the b. to sb,** llamar a algn por teléfono.

blowfly ['bləʊflaɪ] *n Ent* moscarda *f*, mosca *f* azul.

blowhole ['bləʊhəʊl] *n* **1** *(in tunnel)* ventilador *m*. **2** *(in ice)* respiradero *m*. **3** *(of whale)* orificio *m* nasal.

blowlamp ['bləʊlæmp] *n* soplete *m*.

blown [bləʊn] *pp see* **blow**.

blowout ['bləʊaʊt] *n* **1** *Aut* reventón *m*. **2** *sl* comilona *f*.

blowsy ['blaʊzɪ] *adj (blowsier, blowsiest) fam* desaliñado,-a.

blowtorch ['bləʊtɔːtʃ] *n US* soplete *m*.

blow-up ['bləʊʌp] *n Phot* ampliación *f*.

blowy ['bləʊɪ] *adj (blowier, blowiest)* ventoso,-a.

blub [blʌb] *vi fam (pt & pp **blubbed**)* lloriquear.

blubber ['blʌbə'] **I** *n Zool* grasa *f* de ballena. **II** *vi fam* lloriquear, llorar a moco tendido.

bludgeon ['blʌdʒən] **I** *n* maza *f*, cachiporra *f*. **II** *vtr* aporrear; *fig* **to b. sb into doing sth,** forzar a algn a hacer algo.

blue [bluː] **I** *adj* **1** *(colour)* azul; **b. with cold,** amoratado de frío; *fig* **once in a b. moon,** de Pascuas a Ramos, de higos a brevas; *fig* **you can complain till you're b. in the face,** te puedes quejar hasta desgañitarte; *fam* **to be in a b. funk,** tener canguelo; *fam* **to scream b. murder,** gritar como un loco. ■ *Med* **b. baby,** niño *m* azul; **b. cheese,** queso *m* azul; **b. jeans,** vaqueros *mpl*, tejanos *mpl*; **b. whale,** ballena *f* azul. **2** *(sad)* triste, melancólico,-a; *(depressed)* deprimido,-a; **to feel b.,** sentirse deprimido. **3** *(obscene)* verde; **b. joke,** chiste *m* verde; **b. film,** película *f* pornográfica. **II** *n* **1** *(colour)* azul *m*. ■ **navy b.,** azul marino; **sky b.,** azul *m* celeste; *fam* **the boys in b.,** los maderos, la bofia, la policía. **2** *(in laundering)* añil *m*, azulete *m*. **3** *Pol* conservador,-a *m*, *f*. **4** *GB Univ Sport* jugador,-a *m*, *f* que representa la universidad. **5 the b.,** *(sea)* el mar; *(sky)* el cielo; **out of the b.,** *(suddenly)* de repente; *(unexpectedly)* como llovido del cielo.

bluebell ['bluːbel] *n Bot* campanilla *f*.

blueberry ['bluːbərɪ] *n Bot* arándano *m*.

bluebird ['bluːbɜːd] *n Orn* azulejo *m*.

bluebottle ['bluːbɒtəl] *n Ent* moscarda *f*, mosca *f* azul.

blue-collar ['bluːkɒlə'] *adj* **b.-c. worker,** obrero,-a *m*, *f*.

blue-eyed ['bluːaɪd] *adj* de ojos azules; *GB fam* **he's mummy's b.-e. boy,** es el niño mimado de mamá.

blueprint ['bluːprɪnt] *n Archit* cianotipo *m*; *fig* anteproyecto *m*.

blues [bluːz] *n* **1** *Mus* **the b.,** el blues. **2** *fam (sadness)* tristeza *f*, melancolía *f*; **to have the b.,** sentirse deprimido.

bluestocking ['bluːstɒkɪŋ] *n* sabionda *f*, marisabidilla *f*.

bluetit ['bluːtɪt] *n Orn* herrerillo *m* común.

bluff [blʌf] **I** *n* **1** *(trick)* bluff *m*, farol *m*, fanfarronada *f*; **to call sb's b.,** hacer que algn ponga sus cartas encima de la mesa. **2** *Geog (cliff)* acantilado *m*. **II** *adj* **1** *(down-to-earth)* campechano,-a; *(abrupt)* brusco,-a; *(forthright)* francote,-a. **2** *Geog (cliff)* escarpado,-a. **III** *vi* tirarse un farol, fanfarronear; **to b. one's way through sth,** hacer colar algo.

bluffer ['blʌfə'] *n* farolero,-a *m*, *f*, fanfarrón,-ona *m*, *f*.

bluish ['bluːɪʃ] *adj* azulado,-a.

blunder ['blʌndə'] **I** *n* metedura *f* de pata; *fam* plancha *f*. **II** *vi* meter la pata *or* una plancha, cometer un planchazo; **to b. into sth,** tropezar con algo.

blunderbuss ['blʌndəbʌs] *n* trabuco *m*.

blunderer ['blʌndərə'] *n* torpe *mf*, metepatas *mf inv*.

blunt [blʌnt] **I** *adj* **1** *(knife)* embotado,-a, desafilado,-a; *(pencil)* despuntado,-a, romo,-a; **b. instrument,** instrumento contundente. **2** *(direct, frank)* directo,-a, franco,-a; *(statement, answer)* tajante, terminante, categórico,-a. **II** *vtr* **1** embotar, desafilar; *(knife)* despuntar. **2** *fig (emotions, feelings)* embotar. ◆ **bluntly** *adv* francamente, sin rodeos.

bluntness ['blʌntnɪs] *n fig* franqueza *f*.

blur [blɜː'] **I** *n* aspecto *m* borroso; **everything was just a b.,** veía todo borroso. **II** *vtr (pt & pp* **blurred)** *(windows)* empañar; *(shape)* desdibujar; *(vision, memory)* enturbiar; **his memory was blurred,** no se acordaba de nada.

blurb [blɜːb] *n (bumph)* propaganda *f*; *(book)* resumen *m*, reseña *f*.

blurred [blɜːd] *adj Phot TV* borroso,-a.

blurt [blɜːt] *vtr* **to b. out,** dejar escapar, soltar.

blush [blʌʃ] **I** *n* rubor *m*, sonrojo *m*. **II** *vi* ruborizarse, ponerse colorado.

blusher ['blʌʃə'] *n* colorete *m*.

blushing ['blʌʃɪŋ] *adj* ruborizado,-a.

bluster ['blʌstə'] **I** *n fig* fanfarronadas *fpl*, bravatas *fpl*. **II** *vi* **1** *(sea, wind)* bramar. **2** *fig (person)* fanfarronear, echar bravatas.

blustery ['blʌstərɪ] *adj* borrascoso,-a; **a b. day,** un día ventoso.

boa ['bəʊə] *n* **1** *Zool (snake)* boa *f*. ■ **b. constrictor,** boa *f* constrictor. **2** *(of fur, feathers)* boa *m*.

boar [bɔː'] *n Zool* verraco *m*. ■ **wild b.,** jabalí *m*.

board [bɔːd] **I** *n* **1** *(plank)* tabla *f*; *Theat* **to tread the boards,** pisar las tablas. **2** *(work surface)* tabla *f*, mesa *f*; *(blackboard)* pizarra *f*, encerado *m*; *(for games)* tablero *m*. ■ **chess b.,** tablero *m* de ajedrez; **drawing b.,** tablero *m* de dibujo; **it's back to the drawing b.!,** ¡volvamos a empezar!; **ironing b.,** tabla *f* de planchar; **notice b.,** *US* **bulletin b.,** tablón *m* de anuncios. **3** *Print* **in boards,** en cartoné. **4** *(meals)* pensión *f*; **full b.,** pensión completa; **b. and lodging,** casa *f* y comida. **5** *(committee, council)* junta *f*, consejo *m*; **b. of directors,** junta directiva, consejo de administración; *Com* **B. of Trade,** Ministerio *m* de Comercio. ■ **b.room,** sala *f* del consejo. **6** *Naut* **on b.,** a bordo; **to go on b.,** subir a bordo. **7** *fig* **above b.,** en regla; **across-the-b.,** general; **an across-the-b. pay increase,** un aumento lineal del sueldo; **is it all above b.?,** ¿es legal?; **to let sth go by the b.,** abandonar algo. **II** *vtr* **1** *(lodge)* alojar. **2** *(ship, plane, etc)* embarcar, embarcarse en, subir. **III** *vi* **1** *(lodge)* alojarse; **he boarded with my sister,** se alojó en casa de mi hermana. **2** *(at school)* estar interno,-a. ◆ **board up** *vtr* tapar.

boarder ['bɔːdə'] *n* **1** *(in boarding house)* huésped *mf*. **2** *(at school)* interno,-a *m*, *f*, pensionista *mf*.

boardgame ['bɔːdgeɪm] *n* juego *m* de mesa.

boarding ['bɔːdɪŋ] **1** *(floor)* entablado *m*. **2** *(embarkation)* embarque *m*. ■ **b. card, b. pass,** tarjeta *f* de embarque. **3** *(lodging)* alojamiento *m*, pensión *f*. ■ **b. house,** casa *f* de huéspedes, pensión *f*; **b. school,** internado *m*.

boardsailing ['bɔːdseɪlɪŋ] *n US* windsurf *m*, windsurfing *m*.

boardwalk ['bɔːdwɔːk] *n US* paseo *m* marítimo construido sobre tablas.

boast [bəʊst] **I** *n* jactancia *f*, alarde *m*. **II** *vi* jactarse, alardear *(about,* de). **III** *vtr* presumir de, alardear de; **the town boasts an Olympic swimming pool,** la ciudad disfruta de una piscina olímpica.

boaster ['bəʊstə'] *n* jactancioso,-a *m*, *f*.

boastful ['bəʊstfʊl] *adj* jactancioso,-a.

boasting ['bəʊstɪŋ] *n* jactancia *f*.

boat [bəʊt] *n* **1** *Naut* barco *m*; *(small)* barca *f*, bote *m*; *(launch)* lancha *f*; *(large)* buque *m*; **to go by b.,** ir en barco; *fig* **to burn one's boats,** quemar las naves; *fig* **to miss the b.,** perder el tren; *fig* **we're all in the same b.,** todos estamos en el mismo barco. ■ **fishing b.,** barco *m* de pesca; **rowing b.,** bote *m* de remos; **sailing b.,** barco *m* de vela, velero *m*. **2** *Culin* **gravy b.,** salsera *f*.

boatbuilder ['bəʊtbɪldə'] *n* constructor,-a *m*, *f* de barcos.

boater ['bəʊtə'] *n* canotié *m*, canotier *m*.

boathouse ['bəʊthaʊs] *n* cobertizo *m* (para barcas).

boating ['bəʊtɪŋ] *n* paseo *m* en barco; **to go boating,** dar un paseo en barco. ■ **b. club,** club *m* náutico.

boatload ['bəʊtləʊd] *n* barcada *f*; *fam* montón *m*.

boatman ['bəʊtmən] *n (pl* **boatmen)** barquero *m*.

boatswain ['bəʊsən] *n* contramaestre *m*.

boatwoman ['bəʊtwʊmən] *n (pl* **boatwomen** ['bəʊtwɪmɪn]) barquera *f*.

boatyard ['bəʊtjɑːd] *n* astillero *m*.

Bob [bɒb] *n dimin* of **Robert**; *fam* **you just add a little water, and B.'s your uncle!,** ¡le añades un poco de agua y listo!

bob [bɒb] **I** *n* **1** *(haircut)* pelo *m* a lo chico. **2** *fam inv (shilling)* chelín *m*; **five b.,** cinco chelines. **3** *(curtsey)* reverencia *f*. **4** *Sport* trineo *m*. **II** *vi (pt & pp* **bobbed)** **to b.**

up and down, balancearse, subir y bajar. **III** *vtr (hair)* cortar; **she's had her hair bobbed,** le han cortado el pelo a lo chico.

bobbin ['bɒbɪn] *n (of spinning machine)* bobina *f*; *(of sewing machine)* canilla *f*; *(for lace-making)* bolillo *m*.

bobby ['bɒbɪ] *n* **1** *fam (policeman)* poli *m*. **2** *US Hairdr* **b. pin,** pasador *m*. **3** *US* **b. socks, b. sox,** calcetines *mpl*.

bobby-soxer ['bɒbɪsɒksəʳ] *n US* adolescente *f*, quinceañera *f*.

bobsled ['bɒbsled] *n Sport see* **bobsleigh.**

bobsleigh ['bɒbsleɪ] *n Sport* bobsleigh *m*, trineo *m*.

bobtail ['bɒbteɪl] *adj* **1** *(tail)* cortada. **2** *(horse)* rabicorto,-a.

bod [bɒd] *n fam* tío *m*.

bode¹ [bəʊd] *pt see* **bide.**

bode² [bəʊd] *vtr & vi* presagiar; **to b. well/ill,** ser de buen/mal agüero.

bodice ['bɒdɪs] *n* **1** *(sleeveless undergarment)* corpiño *m*. **2** *(of dresss)* cuerpo *m*.

bodily ['bɒdɪlɪ] **I** *adj* físico,-a; **b. harm,** daños *mpl* corporales; **b. needs,** necesidades *fpl* físicas. **II** *adv* **to carry sb b.,** llevar a algn en brazos.

body ['bɒdɪ] *n* **1** *Anat* cuerpo *m*; *fig* **to earn enough to keep b. and soul together,** ganar lo justo para vivir. **b. language,** expresión *f* corporal; **b. odour,** olor *m* corporal. **2** *(corpse)* cadáver *m*; *fam* **over my dead b.!,** ¡tendrás *etc* que pasar por encima de mi cadáver! ■ **b. snatcher,** ladrón *m* de cadáveres. **3** *Chem Phys* cuerpo *m*. ■ *Astron* **heavenly b.,** cuerpo *m* celeste. **4** *(main part)* parte *f* principal, parte *f* central. **5** *Aut* carrocería *f*; *Av* fuselaje *m*; *Naut* casco *m*. **6** *(organization)* organismo *m*; *(profession)* cuerpo *m*; **legislative b.,** cuerpo *m* órgano *m* legislativo; **the b. politic,** el estado. **7** *(group of people)* conjunto *m*, grupo *m*; **a large b. of students,** un gran número de estudiantes. **8** *(wine)* cuerpo *m*.

body-blow ['bɒdɪbləʊ] *n fig* golpe *m* duro.

body-builder ['bɒdɪbɪldəʳ] *n* culturista *mf*.

body-building ['bɒdɪbɪldɪŋ] *n* culturismo *m*.

bodyguard ['bɒdɪgɑːd] *n* guardaespaldas *mf inv*.

bodystocking ['bɒdɪstɒkɪŋ] *n* body *m*.

bodywave ['bɒdɪweɪv] *n Hairdr* moldeado *m*.

bodywork ['bɒdɪwɜːk] *n Aut* carrocería *f*.

Boer ['bəʊəʳ] *adj & n* bóer *(mf)*; **the B. War,** la guerra del Transvaal.

boffin ['bɒfɪn] *n fam* científico,-a *m,f*, investigador,-a *m,f*.

bog [bɒg] *n* **I** ciénaga *f*, pantano *m*; *Ir* *(peat)* **b.,** turbera *f*. **2** *sl (lavatory)* meódromo *m*. ◆ **bog down** *vtr fig* atascar; **to get bogged down,** atascarse.

bogey ['bəʊgɪ] *n* **1** *(spectre)* espectro *m*, fantasma *m*. **2** *(bugbear)* pesadilla *f*. **3** *Golf* bogey *m*. **4** *sl (mucus)* moco *m*.

bogeyman ['bəʊgɪmən] *n (pl bogeymen)* *fam* **the b.,** el hombre del saco, el coco.

boggle ['bɒgəl] *vi* sobresaltarse; *fam* **the mind boggles,** ¡es alucinante!

boggy ['bɒgɪ] *adj (boggier, boggiest)* pantanoso,-a.

bogie ['bəʊgɪ] *n Rail* carretón *m*, bogie *m*.

bogus ['bəʊgəs] *adj* falso,-a; **b. company,** compañía *f* fantasma; **b. policemen,** policía *f* ful.

bogy ['bəʊgɪ] *n see* **bogey.**

Bohemia [bəʊ'hiːmɪə] *n* Bohemia.

Bohemian [bəʊ'hiːmɪən] *adj & n* bohemo,-a *(m, f)*, bohemio,-a *(m,f)*.

boil¹ [bɔɪl] **I** *n Culin* **to be on the b.,** hervir, estar hirviendo; **to come to the b.,** empezar a hervir. **II** *vtr Culin (water)* hervir; *(food)* hervir, cocer; *(egg)* cocer, pasar por agua. **III** *vi Culin* hervir, cocer; *fig* **to b. with rage,** estar furioso. ◆ **boil down** *vi* reducirse (**to**, a); *fig* **it boils down to money,** en el fondo es una cuestión de dinero; *fig* **it all boils down to this,** todo se reduce a esto. ◆ **boil over** *vi (milk)* salirse.

boil² [bɔɪl] *n Med* furúnculo *m*.

boiled [bɔɪld] *adj* hervido,-a; **b. egg,** huevo *m* pasado por agua.

boiler ['bɔɪləʳ] *n* caldera *f*; **b. room,** sala *f* de calderas. ■ **b. suit,** mono *m*.

boilermaker ['bɔɪləmeɪkəʳ] *n* calderero,-a *m,f*.

boiling ['bɔɪlɪŋ] *adj (water)* hirviente; **it's b. hot,** *(food)* quema, está quemando; *(weather)* hace un calor agobiante. ■ **b. point,** punto *m* de ebullición.

boisterous ['bɔɪstərəs] *adj* **1** *(person, party)* alborotador,-a, bullicioso,-a. **2** *(weather)* borrascoso,-a, tempestuoso,-a.

bold [bəʊld] *adj* **1** *(brave)* valiente, intrépido,-a. **2** *(daring)* audaz, atrevido,-a. **3** *(marked)* marcado,-a, pronunciado,- a; **b. features,** rasgos marcados. ■ *Typ* **b. type,** negrita *f*. **4** *Lit (style)* vigoroso,-a. **5** *(impudent)* descarado,-a; **to b as be. as brass,** tener mucha cara.

bold-faced [bəʊld'feɪst] *adj* descarado,-a.

boldness ['bəʊldnɪs] *n* **1** *(courage)* valor *m*. **2** *(daring)* audacia *f*, osadía *f*. **3** *(impudence)* descaro *m*.

bolero¹ [bə'leərəʊ] *n Mus* bolero *m*.

bolero² ['bɒlərəʊ] *n (jacket)* chaleco *m*.

Bolivia [bə'lɪvɪə] *n* Bolivia.

Bolivian [bə'lɪvɪən] *adj & n* boliviano,-a *(m,f)*.

bollard ['bɒlɑːd] *n* **1** *Naut* bolardo *m*, noray *m*. **2** *Aut* baliza *f*.

bollocking ['bɒlɒkɪŋ] *n GB vulg* bronca *f*.

bollocks ['bɒlɒks] *npl vulg* cojones *mpl*, huevos *mpl*; **b.!,** *(anger)* ¡cojones!; *(disagreement)* ¡y un huevo!, ¡y una mierda!

boloney [bə'ləʊnɪ] *n fam* disparates *mpl*, tonterías *fpl*.

Bolshevik ['bɒlʃəvɪk] *adj & n* bolchevique *(mf)*.

Bolshevism ['bɒlʃɪvɪzəm] *n* bolchevismo *m*, bolcheviquismo *m*.

Bolshevist ['bɒlʃəvɪst] *adj & n* bolchevique *(mf)*.

bolshie ['bɒlʃɪ] *adj GB fam* **1** *Pol* rojo,-a. **2** *(rebellious)* rebelde.

bolster ['bəʊlstəʳ] **I** *n (pillow)* cabezal *m*, travesaño *m*. **II** *vtr (strengthen)* reforzar; *(support)* sostener, apoyar.

bolt [bəʊlt] *n* **1** *(on door, window) (large)* cerrojo *m*; *(small)* pestillo *m*. **2** *Tech* perno *m*, tornillo *m*. **3** *(of lightning)* rayo *m*. **4** *(crossbow)* flecha *f*; *fig* **a b. from the blue,** un acontecimiento inesperado. **5** *(dash)* huida *f*, fuga *f*; **to make a b. for it,** huir, escaparse. **II** *vtr* **1** *(lock)* cerrar con cerrojo *or* pestillo, echar el cerrojo. **2** *Tech* sujetar con pernos *or* tornillos. **3** *fam (food)* engullir. **III** *vi (person)* largarse, escaparse; *(horse)* desbocarse. **IV** *adv* **b. upright,** derecho; **to sit b. upright in bed,** sentarse muy derecho en la cama.

bomb [bɒm] **I** *n* bomba *f*; **to burst like a b.,** caer como una bomba; **to plant a b.,** poner una bomba; *GB fam* **to go like a b.,** *(vehicle etc)* andar como un rayo; *(party etc)* ser todo un éxito; *GB sl* **to cost a b.,** costar un ojo de la cara. ■ **atomic b.,** bomba *f* atómica; **b. disposal squad,** brigada *f* de artificieros; **b. scare,** amenaza *f* de bomba; **b. shelter,** refugio *m* antiaéreo; **b. site,** sitio *m* bombardeado; **car b.,** coche-bomba *m*; **hydrogen b.,** bomba *f* de hidrógeno; **letter b.,** carta-bomba *f*; **smoke b.,** bomba *f* de humo; **stink b.,** bomba *f* fétida. **II** *vtr (city etc)* bombardear; *(terrorists)* volar, colocar una bomba en. **III** *vi fam* **to b. (along),** *(car)* ir a toda pastilla *or* mecha.

bombard [bɒm'bɑːd] *vtr* **1** *Mil (bomb)* bombardear. **2** *fig (attack)* bombardear; **she was bombarded with questions,** la bombardearon a preguntas.

bombardment [bɒm'bɑːdmənt] *n* bombardeo *m*.

bombast ['bɒmbæst] *n* rimbombancia *f*, ampulosidad *f*.

bombastic [bɒm'bæstɪk] *adj (language)* rimbombante, altisonante, pomposo,-a.

bomber ['bɒməʳ] *n* **1** *Av* bombardero *m*. ■ **b. jacket,** cazadora *f* de piel *or* de piloto. **2** terrorista *mf* que coloca bombas.

bombing ['bɒmɪŋ] *n* bombardeo *m*.

bomb-proof ['bɒmpru:f] *adj* a prueba de bombas.

bombshell ['bɒmʃel] *n* **1** *Mil* obús *m*. **2** *fig* (*surprise*) bomba *f*; **to fall like a b.**, caer como una bomba. **3** *fam* (*attractive woman*) mujer *f* explosiva; **a blonde b.**, una rubia explosiva.

bona fide [bəʊnə'faɪdɪ] *adj* **1** (*genuine*) auténtico,-a; **a b. f. document**, un documento auténtico. **2** (*in good faith*) de buena fe; **a b. f. offer**, una oferta seria.

bonanza [bə'nænzə] *n* **1** (*luck*) bonanza *f*. **2** *fig* mina *f* de oro.

bonbon ['bɒnbɒn] *n* (*sweet*) caramelo *m*.

bonce [bɒns] *n* *GB sl* (*head*) coco *m*, mollera *f*.

bond [bɒnd] **I** *n* **1** (*link, tie*) lazo *m*, vínculo *m*; **the bonds of friendship**, los lazos de la amistad. **2** *Fin* bono *m*, obligación *f*; **Treasury bonds**, bonos *mpl* del Tesoro; **b. issue**, emisión *f* de bonos. **3** *Jur* (*bail*) fianza *f*. **4** (*binding agreement*) acuerdo *m*, contrato *m*. **5** *Com* (*warehouse*) depósito *m*; **to be in b.**, estar en depósito. **6** *US* (*guarantee*) garantía *f*. **7** *Constr* (*of bricks*) aparejo *m*. **8** **bonds**, (*shackles*) cadenas *fpl*; **to be in b.**, estar en cautiverio. **II** *vtr* **1** (*join, unite*) ligar. **2** *Com* (*merchandise*) poner en depósito. **3** (*guarantee*) (*employee etc*) garantizar. **4** *Constr* (*bricks*) aparejar.

bondage ['bɒndɪdʒ] *n* (*slavery*) esclavitud *f*; (*servitude*) servilismo *m*.

bonded ['bɒndɪd] *adj* **1** *Fin* (*debt*) garantizado,-a. **2** *Com* (*goods*) depositado,-a, en depósito. ■ **b. warehouse**, almacén *m* de depósito.

bondholder ['bɒndhəʊldə'] *n* *Fin* obligacionista *mf*.

bone [bəʊn] **I** *n* **1** *Anat* (*gen*) hueso *m*; (*in corset*) ballena *f*; (*in fish*) espina *f*; *fig* **b. of contention**, manzana *f* de la discordia; *fig* **to feel sth in one's bones**, tener un presentimiento de algo; *fig* **to have a b.** to pick with sb, tener que ajustar cuentas a algn; *fig* **to make no bones about sth**, no andarse con rodeos en un asunto; *fam* **funny b.**, hueso de la alegría. ■ **b. china**, porcelana *f* fina; **b. meal**, harina *f* de huesos. **2** **bones**, (*remains*) huesos *mpl*, restos *mpl*; (*essentials*) **the bare b.**, el meollo *sing*, lo esencial. **II** *vtr* *Culin* (*meat, chicken*) deshuesar; (*fish*) quitar las espinas a. ◆ **bone up** *vi fam* empollar; **to b. up on a subject**, empollar una asignatura.

bone-dry [bəʊn'draɪ] *adj* completamente seco,-a.

bonehead ['bəʊnhed] *n sl* majadero,-a *m,f*, imbécil *mf*.

bone-idle [bəʊn'aɪdəl] *adj* muy vago,-a, gandul,-a.

boner ['bəʊnə'] *n sl* metedura *f* de pata, plancha *f*, planchazo *m*, patinazo *m*.

bonesetter ['bəʊnsetə'] *n* ensalmador,-a *m,f*, curandero,-a *m,f*.

boneshaker ['bəʊnʃeɪkə'] *n sl* (*car*) cacharro *m*, cafetera *f*.

bonfire ['bɒnfaɪə'] *n* hoguera *f*, fogata *f*; **B. Night**, noche *f* del cinco de noviembre.

bongo ['bɒŋgəʊ] *n* (*pl bongos or bongoes*) *Mus* **b. (drum)**, bongó *m*, bongo *m*.

bonhomie ['bɒnɒmi:] *n* afabilidad *f*.

bonkers ['bɒŋkəz] *adj GB sl* chalado,-a; **to drive sb b.**, volver tarumba a algn.

Bonn [bɒn] *n* Bonn.

bonnet ['bɒnɪt] *n* **1** (*child's*) gorra *f*, gorro *m*; *Hist* (*woman's*) toca *f*. **2** *Aut* capó *m*.

bonny ['bɒnɪ] *adj* (*bonnier, bonniest*) *Scot* (*gen*) precioso,-a *f*; (*of person*) majo,-a, mono,-a.

bonus ['bəʊnəs] *n* **1** (*on wages, salary*) prima *f*; **b. scheme**, sistema *m* de primas; **Christmas b.**, prima de Navidad; **cost-of-living b.**, plus *m* de carestía de vida. **2** *Fin* (*on shares*) dividendo *m* extraordinario. **3** *GB Ins* (*on policy*) beneficio *m*.

bony ['bəʊnɪ] *adj* (*bonier, boniest*) (*person*) huesudo,-a; (*fish*) lleno,-a de espinas.

boo [bu:] **I** *interj* ¡bu!; **not to say b.**, no decir ni pío; **she wouldn't say b. to a goose**, es incapaz de matar una mosca. **II** *n* abucheo *m*, pateo *m*. **III** *vtr* abuchear, patear.

boob [bu:b] *sl* **I** *n* **1** *GB* (*silly mistake*) plancha *f*, planchazo *m*, metedura *f* de pata. **2** **boobs**, (*breasts*) tetas *fpl*. **II** *vi GB* tirarse una plancha, meter la pata.

booby ['bu:bɪ] *n* (*fool*) bobo,-a *m,f*. ■ **b. prize**, premio *m* de consolación; **b. trap**, trampa *f*; *Mil* trampa *f* explosiva.

booby-trap ['bu:bɪtræp] *vtr* (*pt & pp booby-trapped*) *Mil* poner una trampa explosiva en; **booby-trapped car**, coche *m* cebo.

boogie ['bu:gɪ] *vi fam* bailar.

boogie-woogie ['bu:gɪ'wu:gɪ] *n* *Mus* bugui-bugui *m*.

boohoo [bu:'hu:] *vi* berrear.

book [bʊk] **I** *n* **1** (*gen*) libro *m*; **a b. on do-it-yourself**, un libro sobre bricolaje; **economics is a closed b. to me**, no sé nada de economía; **in my b.**, según mi punto de vista; *fig* **by the b.**, según las reglas; *fig* **to be in sb's bad books**, estar en la lista negra de algn; *fig* **to be in sb's good books**, estar en buenos términos con algn; *fig* **to take a leaf out of sb's b.**, tomar ejemplo de algn. ■ **address b.**, agenda *f*, libro *m* de direcciones; **b. review**, reseña *f* de libros; **b. club**, círculo *m* de lectores; **b. end**, sujetalibros *m inv*; *GB* **b. token**, vale *m* para comprar libros; **b. trade**, sector *m* editorial; **complaints b.**, libro *m* de reclamaciones; **exercise b.**, cuaderno *m*; **reference b.**, libro *m* de consulta; **savings b.**, libreta *f* de ahorros; **telephone b.**, guía *f* telefónica, listín *m* (telefónico). **2** (*of stamps*) carpeta *f*; (*of tickets*) taco *m*; (*of matches*) cajetilla *f*. **3** *Com* **books**, libros *mpl*, cuentas *fpl*; **to keep the b.**, llevar las cuentas. **II** *vtr* **1** (*reserve*) (*room, passage*) reservar; **the hotel is fully booked up**, el hotel está completo. **2** (*engage*) (*performer etc*) contratar. **3** (*police*) poner una multa; **he was booked for speeding**, le multaron por exceso de velocidad. **4** *Ftb* (*player*) amonestar. ◆ **book into** *vtr* (*hotel*) reservar una habitación en. ◆ **book out** *vi* (*of hotel*) marcharse. ◆ **book up** *vtr* reservar; *Av* **the flight is booked up**, el vuelo está completo.

bookable ['bʊkəbəl] *adj* que se puede(n) reservar; *Theat* 'seats b. in advance', 'las localidades se pueden reservar con antelación'.

bookbinder ['bʊkbaɪndə'] *n* encuadernador,-a *m,f*.

bookbinding ['bʊkbaɪndɪŋ] *n* encuadernación *f*.

bookie ['bʊkɪ] *n fam see* **bookmaker**.

booking ['bʊkɪŋ] *n* **1** *esp GB* (*reservation*) reserva *f*. ■ *Theat Rail* **b. office**, taquilla *f*. **2** *Theat* (*hiring*) (*of performer etc*) contratación *f*.

bookish ['bʊkɪʃ] *adj* **1** (*fond of reading*) aficionado,-a a la lectura. **2** (*academic*) (*view etc*) académico,-a. **3** *Lit* (*style*) libresco,-a.

bookmaker ['bʊkmeɪkə'] *n* corredor,-a *m,f* de apuestas.

bookmobile ['bʊkməbi:l] *n* *US* bibliobús *m*, biblioteca *f* ambulante.

bookplate ['bʊkpleɪt] *n* ex libris *m inv*.

bookrest ['bʊkrest] *n* atril *m*.

bookseller ['bʊkselə'] *n* librero,-a *m,f*.

bookshelf ['bʊkʃelf] *n* (*pl bookshelves* ['bʊkʃelvz]) estante *m*; **bookshelves**, estantería *f sing*.

bookshop ['bʊkʃɒp] *n* librería *f*.

bookstall ['bʊkstɔ:l] *n*, **bookstand** ['bʊkstænd] *n* quiosco *m*.

bookstore ['bʊkstɔ:'] *n* *US* librería *f*.

bookworm ['bʊkwɜ:m] *n fam* ratón *m* de biblioteca.

boom[1] [bu:m] **I** *n* **1** (*noise*) estampido *m*, trueno *m*. **2** (*sudden prosperity*) boom *m*, auge *m*. ■ **b. town**, ciudad *f* en pleno desarrollo. **II** *vi* **1** (*thunder*) retumbar, tronar; (*cannon*) tronar. **2** (*prosper*) estar en auge.

boom[2] [bu:m] *n* **1** *Naut* (*mast*) botalón *m*. **2** *Cin Rad* (*of microphone*) jirafa *f*. ■ **b. operator**, jirafista *mf*. **3** (*barrier across harbour*) barrera *f*.

boomerang | both

boomerang ['bu:məræŋ] *n* bumerang *m*, bumeran *m*.

booming ['bu:mɪŋ] *adj* **1** *(resonant) (cannon)* que truena; *(voice, thunder)* que retumba. **2** *(prosperous) (industry etc)* en auge.

boon [bu:n] *n (blessing)* bendición *f*; **the new computer is a real b.**, el nuevo ordenador es una verdadera bendición.

boor [buə‿ʳ] *n* patán *m*, paleto,-a *m*,*f*, palurdo,-a *m*,*f*.

boorish ['buərɪʃ] *adj* tosco,-a, paleto,-a.

boost [bu:st] **I** *n* **1** *(push)* empujón *m*. **2** *fig (encouragement)* estímulo *m*, empujón *m*. **II** *vtr* **1** *(increase) (sales)* aumentar, incrementar **2** *(improve) (morale)* levantar; **to b. sb's confidence**, subirle la moral a algn. **3** *(promote) (product)* promover; *(business)* fomentar. **4** *Elec (voltage)* elevar.

booster ['bu:stə‿ʳ] *n* **1** *Elec* elevador *m* de voltaje. **2** *Astronaut* **b. rocket**, cohete *m* acelerador. **3** *Rad TV (amplifier)* amplificador *m*. **4** *Med* **b. (shot)**, revacunación *f*.

boot¹ [bu:t] **I** *n* **1** bota *f*; *(short)* botín *m*; *fig* **he's too big for his boots**, es muy creído; *fig* **the b. is on the other foot**, se ha dado la vuelta a la tortilla; *fig* **to die with one's boots on**, morir con las botas puestas; *fig* **to lick sb's boots**, hacer la pelota a algn; *fam* **to put the b. in**, pisotear; *fam* **she got the b.**, la echaron (del trabajo). ■ **b. polish**, betún *m*. **2** *GB Aut* maletero *m*. **II** *vtr fam* **1** *Ftb (kick) (ball)* chutar. **2** **to b. (out)**, *(expel)* echar a patadas. **3** *(dismiss from employment)* dar la patada a, echar, despedir.

boot² [bu:t] *n* **to b.**, además; **he's handsome, and rich to b.**, es guapo, y además, rico.

bootblack ['bu:tblæk] *n esp US* limpiabotas *mf inv*, *Am* lustrabotas *mf inv*.

bootee [bu:ti:, bu:'ti:] *n* **1** *(baby's)* peúco *m*, botita *f* de lana. **2** *(woman's)* botín *m*.

booth [bu:ð, bu:θ] *n* **1** *(in language lab etc)* cabina *f*. ■ **telephone b.**, cabina *f* telefónica. **2** *(in market, fair)* puesto *m*.

bootleg ['bu:tleg] *adj (liquor etc)* de contrabando.

bootlegger ['bu:tlegə‿ʳ] *n* contrabandista *m*.

bootlicker ['bu:tlɪkə‿ʳ] *n fam* pelota *mf*.

booty ['bu:tɪ] *n* botín *m*.

booze [bu:z] *fam* **I** *n* alpiste *m*; **to go on the b.**, irse de juerga *or* de borrachera. **II** *vi* mamar, soplar, mamarse.

boozer ['bu:zə‿ʳ] *n fam* **1** *(person)* borracho,-a *m*,*f*. **2** *GB (pub)* tasca *f*.

booze-up ['bu:zʌp] *n fam* borrachera *f*.

bop¹ [bɒp] **I** *n* **1** *Mus* be-bop *m*. **2** *fam (dance)* baile *m*. **II** *vi fam (pt & pp bopped) (dance)* bailar, menear el esqueleto.

bop² [bɒp] *vtr (pt & pp bopped) fam (hit)* golpear.

boracic [bə'ræsɪk] *adj Chem* bórico,-a.

borage ['bɒrɪdʒ] *n Bot* borraja *f*.

borax ['bɔ:ræks] *n (pl boraxes or boraces* ['bɔ:rəsi:z]*) Chem* bórax *m*.

Bordeaux [bɔ:'dəu] *n* **1** *(city)* Burdeos. **2** *(wine)* burdeos *m*.

border ['bɔ:də‿ʳ] **I** *n* **1** *(edge)* borde *m*, margen *m*. **2** *Sew* ribete *m*. **3** *(frontier)* frontera *f*; **to cross the b.**, cruzar la frontera; **to escape over the b.**, pasar la frontera. ■ **b. incident**, incidente *m* fronterizo; **b. town**, pueblo *m* fronterizo. **4** *(flower bed)* arriate *m*. **III** *vtr Sew (edge)* ribetear. ◆ **border on** *vi* **1** *Geog* lindar con. **2** *fig* rayar en, bordear; **this borders on the ridiculous**, esto raya en lo ridículo.

bordering ['bɔ:dərɪŋ] *adj* limítrofe; **Spain and France are b. countries**, España y Francia son países limítrofes.

borderland ['bɔ:dələænd] *n* zona *f* fronteriza.

borderline ['bɔ:dəlaɪn] **I** *n* **1** *(border)* frontera *f*. **2** *(dividing line)* línea *f* divisoria. **II** *adj* **1** *(on the border)* fronterizo,-a. **2** *fig (case etc)* dudoso,-a.

bore¹ [bɔ:ʳ] **I** *vtr Tech* taladrar, barrenar, perforar. **II** *n* **1** *Tech (hole)* taladro *m*. **2** *Mil (inside of gun barrel)* ánima *f*, alma *f*; *(calibre)* calibre *m*; **a 12-b. shotgun**, una escopeta de calibre 12.

bore² [bɔ:ʳ] **I** *vtr* aburrir; **the film bored me to tears**, la película fue aburridísima. **II** *n (person)* pesado,-a *m*,*f*, pelma *mf*, pelmazo,-a *m*,*f*; *(thing)* lata *f*, rollo *m*; **what a b.!**, ¡qué rollo!

bore³ [bɔ:ʳ] *pt see* **bear¹**.

bored [bɔ:d] *adj* aburrido,-a; **to be b. stiff** *or* **to tears**, aburrirse como una ostra; **to be b. with sth**, estar harto,-a de algo.

boredom ['bɔ:dəm] *n* aburrimiento *m*.

borer ['bɔ:rə‿ʳ] *n Tech (machine)* taladradora *f*; *(hand tool)* taladro *m*.

boric ['bɔ:rɪk] *adj Chem* bórico,-a.

boring ['bɔ:rɪŋ] *adj (uninteresting)* aburrido,-a; *(tedious)* pesado,-a, latoso,-a; **a b. film**, una película aburrida.

born [bɔ:n] **I** *pp see* **bear¹**; **to be b.**, nacer; **I wasn't b. yesterday**, no nací ayer; **she was b. in 1900**, nació en 1900; **to be b. again**, volver a nacer; *fam* **in all my b. days**, en toda mi vida. **II** *adj (having natural ability)* nato,-a; **b. poet**, poeta nato; **she's a b. leader**, nació para mandar; *fig* **b. fool**, tonto,-a de remate.

born-again ['bɔ:nəgen] *adj* converso,-a, renacido,-a.

borne [bɔ:n] *pp see* **bear¹**.

borough ['bʌrə] *n* **1** *(town)* ciudad *f*, villa *f*; *US (municipality)* municipio *m*. **2** *(local district)* barrio *m*, distrito *m*; **2** *esp GB (constituency)* distrito *m* electoral.

borrow ['bɒrəu] **I** *vtr* **1** pedir *or* tomar prestado; **can I b. your pen?**, ¿me dejas tu bolígrafo?; **to be living on borrowed time**, estar a dos pasos de la muerte. **2** *(appropriate) (ideas etc)* apropiarse. **II** *vi* pedir *or* tomar prestado.

borrower ['bɒrəuə‿ʳ] *n (of money)* prestatario,-a *m*,*f*.

borstal ['bɔ:stəl] *n GB fam* reformatorio *m*.

bosh [bɒʃ] *n fam* tonterías *fpl*; **that's a load of b.**, no son más que tonterías.

bosom ['buzəm] *n* **1** *(breast)* pecho *m*; *(breasts)* pechos *mpl*. ■ **b. friend**, amigo,-a *m*,*f* íntimo,-a, amigo,-a *m*,*f* del alma. **2** *fig (centre)* seno *m*; **the b. of the family**, el seno de la familia.

bosomy ['buzəmɪ] *adj fam (woman)* pechugona.

Bosphorus ['bɒsfərəs] *n (strait)* **the B.**, el Bósforo.

boss [bɒs] **I** *n* **1** *(head)* jefe,-a *m*,*f*; *(factory owner etc)* patrón,-ona *m*,*f*, amo *m*. **2** *esp US Pol* jefe *m*; *pej* cacique *m*. **II** *vtr* **to b. sb about** *or* **around**, mangonear a algn.

boss-eyed ['bɒsaɪd] *adj GB sl* bizco,-a.

Bostonian [bɒ'stəunɪən] *adj & n* bostoniano,-a *(m*,*f*).

bosun ['bəusən] *n Naut* contramaestre *m*.

botanic(al) [bə'tænɪk(əl)] *adj* botánico,-a. ■ **b. garden**, jardín *m* botánico.

botanist ['bɒtənɪst] *n* botánico,-a *m*, *f*, botanista *mf*.

botany ['bɒtənɪ] *n* botánica *f*.

botch [bɒtʃ] **I** *vtr* chapucear; **a botched job**, una chapuza. **II** *n* chapucería *f*, chapuza *f*; **to make a b. of sth**, chapucear algo.

botcher ['bɒtʃə‿ʳ] *n (person)* chapucero,-a *m*,*f*.

both [bəuθ] **I** *adj* ambos,-as, los dos, las dos; **b. men are teachers**, ambos (hombres) son profesores; **hold it with b. hands**, sujétalo con las dos manos; **she wants to have it b. ways**, quiere tenerlo todo; **there were mistakes on b. sides**, hubo errores por ambas partes. **II** *pron* **b.** *(of them)*, ambos,-as, los dos, las dos; **b. of you**, vosotros dos. **III** *conj* a la vez; **b. England and Spain are in Europe**, tanto Inglaterra como España están en Europa; **it is b. sad and depressing**, es triste y deprimente a la vez.

bother ['bɒðəʳ] **I** vtr **1** (disturb) molestar; (be a nuisance to) dar la lata a; **don't b. me!,** ¡déjame en paz! **2** (worry) preocupar; **his behaviour bothered me,** me extrañó su comportamiento; fam **I can't be bothered,** no tengo ganas. **II** vi molestarse; **don't b. about me,** no te preocupes por mí; **don't b. to write,** no se moleste en escribir; **he didn't b. shaving,** no se molestó en afeitarse. **III** n **1** (disturbance) molestia f; (nuisance) lata f; **to give sb a lot of b.,** dar mucha lata a algn. **2** (trouble) problemas mpl; **I had a spot of b. with the police,** tuve un pequeño roce con la policía. **IV** interj GB ¡maldito sea!

bothersome ['bɒðəsəm] adj molesto,-a, fastidioso,-a.

Botswana [bɒt'ʃwɑːnə] n Botsuana

Botswanan [bɒt'ʃwɑːnən] adj & n botsuano,-a (m,f).

bottle ['bɒtəl] **I** n **1** (gen) (of drink) botella f; (of perfume, ink) frasco m; fam **to take to** or **hit the b.,** darse a la bebida. ■ **baby's b.,** biberón m; **b. opener,** abrebotellas m inv; **b. party,** fiesta f en la que cada invitado lleva una botella de vino o de licor; **b. rack,** botellero m; **hot-water b.,** bolsa f de agua caliente. **2** sl (nerve) agallas fpl; **to have a lot of b.,** tener muchas agallas. **II** vtr (wine) embotellar; (fruit etc) enfrascar, envasar. ◆ **bottle out** vi GB sl (lose one's nerve) encogerse, achantarse. ◆ **bottle up** vtr (restrain) (emotion etc) reprimir, sofocar.

bottle-bank ['bɒtəlbæŋk] n contenedor m de vidrio (para reciclar).

bottlebrush ['bɒtəlbrʌʃ] n escobilla f.

bottled ['bɒtəld] adj (beer, wine) en botella, embotellado,-a; (fruit) envasado,-a.

bottle-feed ['bɒtəlfiːd] vtr (pt & pp **bottle-fed** ['bɒtəlfed]) (baby) criar con biberón.

bottle-green ['bɒtəlgriːn] adj verde botella; **a b.-g. car,** un coche verde botella.

bottleneck ['bɒtəlnek] n Aut embotellamiento m, atasco m.

bottler ['bɒtələʳ] n embotellador,-a m,f.

bottling ['bɒtəlɪŋ] n (of wine etc) embotellado m.

bottom ['bɒtəm] **I** adj **1** (lowest) más bajo,-a; **b. price,** precio más bajo. ■ GB **b. drawer,** ajuar m; Aut **b. gear,** primera f. **2** (last) último,-a; **to bet one's b. dollar,** jugarse hasta la camisa. ■ **b. line,** Fin saldo m final; fig resultado m final. **3** (at the end) del fondo; **the b. room,** la habitación del fondo. ■ Aut GB **b. end,** cabeza f de biela. **II** n **1** (gen) parte f inferior; (of river, sea, garden, street, corridor, bag, box) fondo m; (of bottle) culo m; (of page, hill) pie m; (of dress) bajo m; (of trousers) bajos mpl; (of suitcase) **false b.,** doble fondo; Fin **the b. has fallen out of the market,** los precios han caído en vertical; Educ **to be (at) the b. of the class,** ser el último de la clase; **to sink to the b.,** irse a pique; **to touch b.,** tocar fondo; fig **to scrape the b. of the barrel,** estar en las últimas; fam **bottoms up!,** ¡salud! **2** (cause) origen m, causa f; **to get to the b. of a matter,** llegar al meollo de una cuestión; **who is at the b. of all this?,** ¿quién está detrás de todo esto? **3** (buttocks) trasero m. ◆ **bottom out** vi Fin tocar fondo; **the recession is bottoming out,** la recesión se está estabilizando.

bottomless ['bɒtəmlɪs] adj **1** (pit) sin fondo; (mystery) insondable. **2** (supply) inagotable.

bottommost ['bɒtəmməʊst] adj (lowest) del fondo; (last) último,-a.

botulism ['bɒtjulɪzəm] n Med botulismo m.

boudoir ['buːdwɑːʳ] n boudoir m, tocador m.

bougainvillea [buːgən'vɪlɪə] n Bot buganvilla f.

bough [baʊ] n Bot rama f.

bought [bɔːt] pt & pp see **buy.**

bouillabaisse ['buːjəbes] n Culin (sopa f) bullabesa f.

bouillon ['buːjɒn] n Culin caldo m. ■ **b. cube,** pastilla f de caldo.

boulder ['bəʊldəʳ] n canto m rodado.

boulevard ['buːlvɑːʳ] n bulevar m.

bounce [baʊns] **I** vi **1** (ball) botar, rebotar. **2** (jump) (person) saltar; **he bounced into the room,** irrumpió en la habitación; **stop bouncing on the bed!,** ¡para de saltar encima de la cama! **3** sl (cheque) ser rechazado (por el banco): **she gave him a cheque which bounced,** le dio un cheque sin fondos. **II** vtr (ball) hacer botar. **II** n (of ball) bote m. **2** (jump) salto m, brinco m. **3** (life, energy) (of person, hair) vitalidad f; **she's full of b.,** es muy dinámica. ◆ **bounce back** vi (recover health) recuperarse, recobrarse.

bouncer ['baʊnsəʳ] n sl gorila m.

bouncing ['baʊnsɪŋ] adj (of baby) robusto,-a, con nervio.

bouncy ['baʊnsɪ] adj (**bouncier, bounciest**) **1** (ball) elástico,-a. **2** (person) dinámico,-a, vital.

bound¹ [baʊnd] **I** pt & pp see **bind** **II** adj **1** (tied up) atado,-a; **b. hand and foot,** atado de pies y manos. **2** Print (book) encuadernado,-a; **b. in leather,** encuadernado en piel. **3** (obliged) obligado,-a; **you're b. by the contract,** estás obligado por el contrato. **4 b. (up), (linked)** vinculado,-a, ligado,-a (**with,** a); **it is b. up with government policy,** está estrechamente vinculado a la política del gobierno. **5** to be **b. to** (+ infin), (certain) ser seguro que (+ fut); **he is b. to arrive on time,** seguro que llegará a tiempo; **it's b. to happen,** sucederá con toda seguridad; **it was b. to fail,** estaba destinado al fracaso.

bound² [baʊnd] **I** vi **1** (jump) saltar, moverse dando saltos. **2** (bounce) (ball) botar. **II** n **1** (jump) salto m. **2** (bounce) (of ball) bote m, rebote m.

bound³ [baʊnd] adj (destined) **b. for,** con destino a, rumbo a; **to be b. for,** dirigirse a; **this train is b. for London,** este tren se dirige a Londres.

boundary ['baʊndərɪ] n (border) límite m, frontera f.

bounder ['baʊndəʳ] n GB sl sinvergüenza mf.

boundless ['baʊndlɪs] adj ilimitado,-a, sin límites; (universe) infinito,-a.

bounds [baʊndz] npl (limits) límites mpl; **beyond the b. of reality,** más allá de la realidad; **her ambition knows no b.,** su ambición no conoce límites; **the river is out of b.,** está prohibido bajar al río.

bounteous ['baʊntɪəs] adj, **bountiful** ['baʊntɪful] adj **1** (generous) generoso,-a. **2** (abundant) abundante.

bounty ['baʊntɪ] n **1** (generosity) generosidad f. **2** (gift) regalo m, presente m. **3** (reward) prima f, gratificación f.

bouquet [buː'keɪ, bəʊ'keɪ] n **1** (of flowers) ramo m de flores, ramillete m. **2** [buː'keɪ] (of wine) aroma m, bouquet m, buqué m.

bourbon ['bɜːbən] n whisky m americano, bourbon m.

Bourbon ['bʊəbən] **I** n Borbón m. **II** adj Borbón, borbónico,-a.

bourgeois ['bʊəʒwɑː] adj & n burgués,-esa (m,f).

bourgeoisie [bʊəʒwɑː'ziː] n burguesía f.

bout [baʊt] n **1** (of time) rato m; (of work) turno m, tanda f; (of illness) ataque m; **drinking b.,** juerga f, borrachera f. **2** Box encuentro m, combate m.

boutique [buː'tiːk] n boutique f, tienda f.

bovine ['bəʊvaɪn] **I** adj bovino,-a. **II** n bovino m.

bovver ['bɒvəʳ] n GB sl (rowdiness) camorra f; **b. boys,** camorristas mpl, delincuentes mpl.

bow¹ [baʊ] **I** vi **1** hacer una reverencia, inclinarse; **to b. and scrape,** hacer zalemas or zalamerías. **2** (give in) ceder; **to b. to the inevitable,** someterse a lo inevitable. **II** n **1** (with head, body) reverencia f; Theat **to take a b.,** salir a saludar. ◆ **bow out** vi retirarse (**of,** de).

bow² [bəʊ] **I** n **1** Sport arco m. **2** Mus (of violin) arco m; fig **to have more than one string to one's b.,** ser una persona de recursos. **3** (knot) lazo m. ■ **b. tie,** pajarita f. **4** Archit bóveda f. ■ **b. window,** mirador m. **II** vi (wall) arquearse, combarse.

bow³ [baʊ] n esp Naut proa f.

bowdlerize ['baʊdləraɪz] vtr (book etc) expurgar.

bowed [baʊd] *adj* **1** *(head, body)* inclinado,-a. **2 b. down**, cargado,-a (**by** *or* **with**, de); **b. down by sorrow**, apenado,-a.

bowel ['baʊəl] *n* **1** *(intestine)* intestino *m*. ■ **b. movement**, evacuación *f* intestinal. **2 bowels**, entrañas *fpl*; *fig* **the b. of the earth**, las entrañas de la tierra.

bower ['baʊəʳ] *n (arbour)* emparrado *m*, enramada *f*.

bowl¹ ['bəʊl] *n* **1** *(dish)* cuenco *m*; *(for soup)* tazón *m*, plato *m* hondo; *(for washing hands)* jofaina *f*, palangana *f*; *(for washing clothes, dishes)* barreño *m*; *(of toilet)* taza *f*; *(of pipe)* cazoleta *f*; **sugar b.**, azucarero *m*. **2** *Geol* cuenca *f*.

bowl² [bəʊl] *Sport* **I** *n (ball)* bola. **II** *vtr Crick (ball)* lanzar, tirar. **III** *vi* **1** *(play bowls)* jugar a los bolos. **2** *Crick* lanzar la pelota. ◆ **bowl along** *vi fam (of car)* deslizarse rápidamente. ◆ **bowl out** *vtr Crick* eliminar, poner fuera de juego. ◆ **bowl over** *vtr* **1** *(knock down)* derribar. **2** *fig (astonish)* desconcertar; **he was bowled over by the news**, quedó pasmado ante la noticia.

bow-legged ['baʊleg(ɪ)d] *adj* patizambo,-a.

bowler¹ ['bəʊlə'] *n Crick* lanzador,-a *m,f*.

bowler² ['bəʊlə'] *n (hat)* bombín *m*, sombrero *m* hongo.

bowling ['bəʊlɪŋ] *n* **1** *(game)* bolos *mpl*. ■ **b. alley**, bolera *f*; **b. green**, campo *m* de bolos. **2** *Crick* lanzamiento *m* de la pelota.

bowls [bəʊlz] *npl* Sport bolos *mpl*, bochas *fpl*.

bowser ['baʊzə'] *n Av Naut* camión *m* cisterna.

bowsprit ['bəʊsprɪt] *n Naut* bauprés *m*.

bow-wow ['baʊwaʊ] *n (baby talk)* guau-guau *m*.

box¹ [bɒks] **I** *n* **1** *(gen)* caja *f*; *(large)* cajón *m*; *(of chocolates)* caja *f*; *(of matches)* cajetilla *f*; *Av* **black b.**, caja *f* negra; **jewellery b.**, joyero *m*. ■ *Phot* **b. camera**, cámara *f* de cajón; *Theat* **b. office**, taquilla *f*; **b. office success**, éxito *m* taquillero *or* de taquilla; *(tools)* **b. spanner**, llave *f* de tubo; **Christmas b.**, aguinaldo *m*; **letter b.**, buzón *m*; **post-office b.**, apartado *m* de correos. **2** *Press* recuadro *m*. **3** *Jur (witness)* **b.**, barra *f* de los testigos. **4** *Theat* palco *m*; **b. seat**, asiento *m* de palco. **5** *Equit (in stable)* box *m*; *(vehicle)* furgón *m* para el transporte de caballos. **6** *GB fam (television)* caja *f* tonta. **II** *vtr* **1** *(pack)* embalar. **2** *Naut* **to b. the compass**, cuartear la aguja.

box² [bɒks] *Sport* **I** *vi* boxear. **II** *vtr* **1** boxear con. **2** *fam (hit)* pegar; **to b. sb's ears**, dar un cachete a algn, abofetear a algn. **III** *n (punch on the ears)* cachete *m*, bofetada *f*.

box³ [bɒks] *n Bot* boj *m*.

boxer ['bɒksə'] *n* **1** *Box* boxeador *m*. **2** *Zool (dog)* bóxer *m*.

boxing ['bɒksɪŋ] *n Sport* boxeo *m*. ■ **b. glove**, guante *m* de boxeo; **b. match**, encuentro *m* de boxeo; **b. ring**, cuadrilátero *m*.

Boxing Day ['bɒksɪŋdeɪ] *n GB* el día de San Esteban (26 de diciembre).

boxroom ['bɒksruːm] *n* trastero *m*.

boy [bɔɪ] *n* **I** *(child)* niño *m*, chico *m*, muchacho *m*; *(youth)* joven *m*; **old b.**, *(former pupil)* antiguo alumno *m*; *(old man)* viejo *m*; *(old friend)* amigo *m*; **listen, old b.**, escúchame, amigo; *fam* **the boys**, los amigotes; *fam* **oh b.!**, ¡vaya!; *prov* **boys will be boys**, así son los chicos. ■ **b. scout**, explorador *m*. **2** *(son)* hijo *m*.

boycott ['bɔɪkɒt] **I** *n* boicot *m*, boicoteo *m*. **II** *vtr* boicotear.

boyfriend ['bɔɪfrend] *n (gen)* novio *m*; *(live-in)* compañero *m*.

boyhood ['bɔɪhʊd] *n* niñez *f*, juventud *f*.

boyish ['bɔɪɪʃ] *adj* juvenil, de muchacho.

bra [brɑː] *n abbr of* **brassiere**.

brace [breɪs] **I** *n* **1** *(clamp)* abrazadera *f*; *Tech (of drill)* beibiquí *m*; *(for straightening teeth)* aparato *m*. ■ **b. and bit**, berbiquí y barrena *f*. **2** *Constr (gen)* riostra *f*; *(of wood)* puntal *m*. **3** *Naut (rope)* braza *f*. **4** *Typ* llave *f*, corchete *m*. **5** *Mus (accolade)* corchete *m*. **6** *(pair)* par *m*;

a b. of pheasants, un par de faisanes. **7** *GB* **braces**, tirantes *mpl*. **II** *vtr* **1** *(prop) (wall)* apuntalar. **2** *(strengthen) (building)* reforzar. **3** *(steady)* **to b. oneself**, prepararse (**for**, para), ◆ **brace up** *vi* cobrar ánimo, animarse.

bracelet ['breɪslɪt] *n* pulsera *f*.

bracing ['breɪsɪŋ] *adj (of wind, climate) (cool)* fresco,-a; *(stimulating)* tonificante.

bracken ['brækən] *n Bot* helecho *m*.

bracket ['brækɪt] **I** *n* **1** *(support)* soporte *m*; *(for lamp)* brazo *m*; *(for balcony)* ménsula *f*; *(shelf)* repisa *f*. **2** *Typ (round)* paréntesis *m*; *(square)* corchete *m*; *(brace)* llave *f*; **in brackets**, entre paréntesis. **3** *(group)* grupo *m*, sector *m*; **the middle-income b.**, el sector de ingresos medios. **II** *vtr* **1** *Ling (phrase etc)* poner entre paréntesis. **2** *(group together)* agrupar, juntar.

brackish ['brækɪʃ] *adj (water)* salobre.

bradawl ['brædɔːl] *n* lezna *f*, punzón *m*.

brag [bræg] **I** *vi (pt & pp bragged)* jactarse (**about**, de); **stop bragging!**, ¡deja de fanfarronear! **II** *n* **1** *(bragging)* jactancia *f*, fanfarronería *f*. **2** *(braggart)* fanfarrón,-ona *m,f*.

braggart ['brægət] *n* fanfarrón,-ona *m,f*.

Brahman ['brɑːmən] *n (pl Brahmans)*, **Brahmin** ['brɑːmɪn] *n (pl Brahmin or Brahmins)* brahmán *m*, brahmín *m*.

braid [breɪd] **I** *vtr (hair, thread)* trenzar. **II** *n* **1** *Sew* galón *m*; **gold b.**, galón de oro. **2** *esp US* trenza *f*.

Braille [breɪl] *n* Braille *m*; **books in B.**, libros en Braille.

brain [breɪn] **I** *n* **1** *Anat* cerebro *m*; **he was the brains behind the job**, fue el cerebro del trabajo; **she's got cars on the b.**, está obsesionada por los coches; **to blow one's brains out**, saltarse *or* volarse la tapa de los sesos; **to pick sb's brains**, aprovechar los conocimientos de algn; **to rack one's brains**, devanarse los sesos; *fam* **use your b.!**, ¡usa la cabeza! ■ *Med* **b. death**, muerte *f* cerebral; *fig* **b. drain**, fuga *f* de cerebros; *US* **b. trust**, consejeros *mpl* del gobierno; **b. tumour**, tumor *m* cerebral; **b. wave**, idea *f* genial; **electronic b.**, cerebro *m* electrónico. **2** *fam* **brains**, inteligencia *f*; **to have b.**, ser inteligente, tener mucho seso. ■ **b. trust**, asociación *f* de expertos. **3** *Culin* **brains**, sesos *mpl*. **II** *vtr fam* **to b. sb**, romperle la crisma a algn.

brainchild ['breɪntʃaɪld] *n* invento *m*, idea *f* genial, genialidad *f*.

brainless ['breɪnlɪs] *adj* tonto,-a, memo,-a.

brainpower ['breɪnpaʊə'] *n* capacidad *f* intelectual.

brainstorm ['breɪnstɔːm] *n* **1** *(outburst)* arranque *m*. **2** *(brain wave)* genialidad *f*, llvia *f* de ideas.

brainstorming ['breɪnstɔːmɪŋ] *n* brainstorming *m*.

brainwash ['breɪnwɒʃ] *vtr* lavar el cerebro a; **she's been brainwashed**, le han lavado el cerebro.

brainwashing ['breɪnwɒʃɪŋ] *n* lavado *m* de cerebro.

brainy ['breɪnɪ] *adj (brainier, brainiest) fam* listo,-a, inteligente.

braise [breɪz] *vtr Culin (meat)* cocer a fuego lento.

brake¹ [breɪk] **I** *n Aut (also pl)* freno *m*; **to apply/release the brakes**, frenar/soltar el freno. ■ **b. blocks**, pastillas *fpl* del freno; **b. drum**, tambor *m* del freno; **b. fluid**, líquido *m* para frenos; **b. light**, luz *f* de freno; **b. lining**, guarnición *f* del freno; **b. shoe**, zapata *f* del freno. **II** *vi* frenar, echar el freno.

brake² [breɪk] *n Bot (bracken)* helecho *m*; *(thicket)* matorral *m*.

braking ['breɪkɪŋ] *n* frenado *m*. ■ *Aut* **b. distance**, distancia *f* de seguridad.

bramble ['bræmbəl] *n Bot* zarza *f*, zarzamora *f*.

brambling ['bræmblɪŋ] *n Orn* pinzón *m* real.

bran [bræn] *n* salvado *m*, afrecho *m*.

branch [brɑːntʃ] **I** *n* **1** *(of tree, family)* rama *f*; *(of road, railway)* ramal *m*; *(of river)* brazo *m*; *(of science, industry, arts)* rama *f*, ramo *m*. **2** *Com* **b. (office)**, sucursal *f*. **II** *vi* *(road)* bifurcarse. ◆ **branch off** *vi* desviarse; **the road branches off to the left,** la carretera se desvía hacia la izquierda. ◆ **branch out** *vi* diversificarse; **they have branched out into insurance,** han ampliado su campo de acción a los seguros.

brand [brænd] **I** *n* **1** *Com* marca *f*. ■ **b. image,** imagen *m* de marca; **b. name,** marca *f* de fábrica. **2** *(type)* clase *f*; **he has his own b. of humour,** tiene un sentido del humor muy particular. **3** *(on cattle)* hierro *m*. **II** *vtr* **1** *(animal)* marcar con hierro candente; *fig* **to b. sb for life,** dejar marcado a algn para toda la vida. **2** *(label)* tildar; **to b. sb a traitor,** tildar a algn de traidor.

branding-iron ['brændɪŋaɪən] *n* hierro *m* candente *or* de marcar.

brandish ['brændɪʃ] *vtr* **1** *(weapon)* blandir. **2** *fig (threat etc)* esgrimir.

brand-new [brænd'njuː] *adj* flamante, completamente nuevo,-a.

brandy ['brændɪ] *n* coñac *m*, brandy *m*; **cherry b.,** aguardiente *m* de cerezas.

brash [bræʃ] *adj* **1** *(impudent)* descarado,-a, insolente. **2** *(reckless)* temerario,-a. **3** *(loud, showy)* chillón,-ona.

brass [brɑːs] *n* **1** *(metal)* latón *m*; *fig* **to be as bold as b.,** tener mucha cara; *fig* **the top b.,** los peces gordos; *GB fam* **it's not worth a b. farthing,** no vale un real; *fam* **to get down to b. tacks,** ir al grano. ■ **b. rubbing,** calco *m* sacado de una placa de latón. **2** *sl (money)* pasta *f*, guita *f*, *Am* plata *f*. **3** *Mus* instrumentos *mpl* de metal, metal *m*. ■ **b. band,** banda *f*, charanga *f*, fanfarria *f*.

brassiere ['bræzɪəʳ] *n* sostén *m*, sujetador *m*.

brassy ['bræsɪ] *adj (brassier, brassiest)* **1** *(of brass)* de latón. **2** *(harsh)* estridente. **3** *(brazen)* descarado,-a.

brat [bræt] *n fam* mocoso,-a *m,f*.

bravado [brə'vɑːdəʊ] *n (pl bravadoes or bravados)* bravata *f*, baladronada *f*, fanfarronada *f*.

brave [breɪv] **I** *adj* valiente, valeroso,-a; **a b. attempt,** un intento valeroso. **II** *US* **(Indian) b.,** guerrero *m* indio. **III** *vtr* **1** *face (danger)* hacer frente a. **2** *(defy) (death)* desafiar. ◆ **bravely** *adv* valientemente.

bravery ['breɪvərɪ] *n* valentía *f*, valor *m*, arrojo *m*.

bravo [brɑː'vəʊ] *interj* ¡bravo!

brawl [brɔːl] **I** *n* pendencia *f*, reyerta *f*. **II** *vi* pelearse.

brawler ['brɔːləʳ] *n* pendenciero,-a *m,f*, alborotador,-a *m,f*.

brawn [brɔːn] *n* **1** *(strength)* fuerza *f* física. **2** *Culin GB* carne *f* de cerdo adobada.

brawny ['brɔːnɪ] *adj (brawnier, brawniest)* musculoso,-a, fornido,-a.

bray [breɪ] **I** *n (of donkey)* rebuzno *m*. **II** *vi* rebuznar.

brazen ['breɪzən] *adj* **1** *(metal)* de latón. **2** *(shameless)* descarado,-a.

brazier ['breɪzɪəʳ] *n (brass-worker)* brasero *m*.

Brazil [brə'zɪl] *n* (el) Brasil.

brazil [brə'zɪl] *n* **b. nut,** nuez *f* del Brasil.

Brazilian [brə'zɪlɪən] *adj & n* brasileño,-a *(m, f)*, *Am* brasilero,-a *(m, f)*.

breach [briːtʃ] **I** *n* **1** *(in wall)* brecha *f*; *fig* **to step into the b.,** echar una mano (en una situación difícil). **2** *(violation etc)* incumplimiento *m*; **b. of confidence,** abuso *m* de confianza; **b. of contract,** incumplimiento de contrato; **b. of faith,** falta *f* de lealtad; **b. of promise,** incumplimiento de una promesa; **b. of the law,** violación *f* de la ley; **b. of the peace,** alteración *f* del orden público. **3** *(break in relations)* ruptura *f*. **II** *vtr (law, contract)* violar.

bread [bred] *n* **1** pan *m*; **a loaf of b.,** un pan, una barra de pan; **b. and butter,** pan con mantequilla; **piece of b.,** pedazo *m* de pan; **sliced b.,** pan de molde; **slice of b.,** rebanada *f* de pan; **stale b.,** pan duro; **unleavened b.,** pan ácimo; **white b.,** pan blanco *or* candeal; **wholemeal b.,** pan integral; *fig* **our daily b.,** el pan nuestro de cada día; *fig* **to earn one's daily b.,** ganarse el pan de cada día; *fig* **to know which side one's b. is buttered on,** saber dónde aprieta el zapato, saber qué terreno se pisa. ■ *Culin* **b. sauce,** salsa *f* bechamel con pan rallado. **2** *sl (money)* pasta *f*, guita *f*, parné *m*, *Am* plata *f*.

bread-and-butter [bredən'bʌtəʳ] *adj* **1** *(reliable) (player)* seguro,-a. **2** *(expressing gratitude)* **b.-a.-b. letter,** carta *f* de agradecimiento.

breadbasket ['bredbɑːskɪt] *n* cesta *f* del pan.

breadboard ['bredbɔːd] *n* tabla *f* (para cortar el pan).

breadcrumb ['bredkrʌm] *n* **1** miga *f* de pan. **2** **breadcrumbs,** *Culin* pan *m* sing rallado.

breadfruit ['bredfruːt] *n (pl breadfruits or breadfruit) Bot (tree)* árbol *m* del pan; *(fruit)* fruto *m* del árbol del pan.

breadline ['bredlaɪn] *n fam* miseria *f*; **to be on the b.,** vivir en la miseria.

breadth [bredθ] *n* **1** *(width)* anchura *f*, ancho *m*; **it is two metres in b.,** tiene dos metros de ancho. **2** *(extent)* amplitud *f*.

breadwinner ['bredwɪnəʳ] *n* cabeza *mf* de familia, el *or* la que gana el pan.

break [breɪk] **I** *vtr (pt broke; pp broken)* **1** *(gen)* romper; **he broke his glasses,** se le rompieron las gafas; *Med* **to b. a leg,** fracturarse la pierna; *Sport* **to b. a record,** batir un récord; **to b. cover,** salir al descubierto; **to b. even,** no tener ni ganancias ni pérdidas; **to b. open a door,** derribar una puerta; *Av* **to b. the sound barrier,** cruzar la barrera del sonido; *fig* **to b. one's back,** matarse a trabajar; *fig* **to b. sb's heart,** partirle el corazón a algn; *fig* **to b. the ice,** romper el hielo. **2** *(fail to keep)* faltar a; **to b. a contract,** romper un contrato; **to b. a promise,** faltar a una promesa; **to b. one's word,** faltar a su palabra; **to b. the law,** violar la ley. **3** *(destroy)* destrozar; *Fin* arruinar; **to b. a rebellion,** sofocar una rebelión; *Pol* **to b. a strike,** romper una huelga; **to b. sb's health,** quebrantar la salud de algn; **to b. the bank,** hacer saltar la banca. **4** *(interrupt)* interrumpir; **to b. (short) a journey/one's holidays,** cortar *or* interrumpir un viaje/ las vacaciones; **to b. silence,** romper el silencio. **5** *(decipher) (code)* descifrar. **6** *(cushion, soften) (fall, blow)* amortiguar. **7** *(disclose)* desvelar; **she broke the news to him,** le comunicó la noticia. **II** *vi* **1** *(gen)* romperse; *(clouds)* dispersarse; *(waves)* romper; **it fell and broke,** se cayó y se rompió. **2** *(storm)* estallar. **3** *(voice)* cambiar. **4** *(health)* resentirse, quebrantarse. **5** *(day)* rayar, romper; **when day breaks,** al rayar el alba. **6** *(news, story)* propalarse, divulgarse, propagarse. **7** *Rad* separarse. **III** *n* **1** *(split, fracture)* rotura *f*; *(crack)* grieta *f*; *(opening)* abertura *f*; *(in the clouds)* claro *m*. ■ **b. dance,** break *(dance) f*; **b. of day,** amanecer *m*. **2** *(in relationship)* ruptura *f*. **3** *(pause)* pausa *f*, descanso *m*; *(in a journey)* alto *m*; *(at school)* recreo *m*; **to take a b.,** descansar un rato; *(holiday)* tomar unos días libres; **without a b.,** sin parar. **4** *fam (chance)* oportunidad *f*; **a lucky b.,** un golpe de suerte; **give me a b.!,** ¡deja de fastidiarme, quieres! **5** *Elec* corte *m*, interrupción *f*. ◆ **break away** *vi* **1** *(become separate)* desprenderse, separarse **(from,** de). **2** *(escape)* escaparse. ◆ **break down I** *vtr* **1** *(knock down) (door etc)* derribar. **2** *(weaken) (resistence)* minar, acabar con. **3** *Fin (prices)* desglosar. **II** *vi* **1** *Aut* tener una avería; **we broke down on the motorway,** el coche se nos averió en la autopista. **2** *(end) (resistence)* acabar con. **3** *(health)* debilitarse, *(weep)* ponerse a llorar. ◆ **break in I** *vtr* acostumbrar; **to b. in a horse,** domar un caballo; **to b. in a new employee,** iniciar en su trabajo a un empleado nuevo; **to b. in new shoes,** acostumbrarse a unos zapatos nuevos. **II** *vi (burglar)* entrar por la fuerza, allanar. ◆ **break into** *vtr* **1** *(burgle) (house)* entrar por la fuerza en, forzar, allanar; *(safe)* forzar. **2** *(begin)* irrumpir en; **to b. into song,** ponerse a cantar. ◆ **break off I** *vtr* **1** *(detach)* romper, cortar. **2** *fig* romper; **to b. off negotiations,** romper las negociaciones; **to b. off an engagement,** romper un compromiso. **II** *vi* **1** *(become* *detached*) desprenderse. **2** *(talks)* interrumpirse. **3** *(stop)* pararse. ◆ **break out** *vi* **1** *(prisoners)* escaparse. **2** *(war, epidemic, fire)* estallar; *Med* **to b. out in a rash,** salirle a uno una erupción (en la piel). ◆ **break through I** *vtr* **1** *(make one's way through) (crowd)* abrirse camino *or* paso por; *(barricade)* atravesar; *(cordon)* romper. **2** *(sun) (clouds, fog)* atravesar, filtrarse a través de. **II** *vi* abrirse camino *or* paso. ◆ **break up I** *vtr* **1** *(object)* romper; *(earth)* mullir; *(car)* desguazar. **2** *(disperse) (crowd)* disolver. **II** *vi* **1** romperse, hacerse pedazos. **2** disolverse; *(meeting)* levantarse. **3** *(marriage, relationship)* fracasar; *(couple)* separarse. **4** *Educ* terminar; **the schools b. up next week,** las vacaciones empiezan la semana que viene. ◆ **break with** *vtr (past, family)* romper con.

breakable ['breɪkəbəl] **I** *adj* frágil, quebradizo,-a. **II breakables** *npl* objetos *mpl* frágiles.

breakage ['breɪkɪdʒ] *n* **1** *(breaking)* rotura *f.* **2 breakages,** *(broken articles)* objetos *mpl* rotos.

breakaway ['breɪkəweɪ] *adj* disidente; **b. group,** grupo de escisión.

break-dance ['breɪkdɑːns] *vi* bailar el break (dance).

breakdown ['breɪkdaʊn] *n* **1** *Aut* avería *f*; **b. truck,** grúa *f*, camión *m* grúa. **2** *(crisis)* crisis *f*; *Med* **(nervous) b.,** crisis *f* nerviosa. **3** *(in communications)* ruptura *f*; **there was a b. in talks,** hubo una ruptura en las negociaciones. **4** *(analysis)* análisis *m*; *Fin* desglose *m*; **price b.,** desglose de precios.

breaker ['breɪkəʳ] *n* **1** *(large wave)* ola *f* grande. **2** *Tech (crusher)* trituradora *f*. **3** *Elec (switch)* interruptor *m* automático. **4** *Rad sl* radioaficionado,-a *m, f*.

breakfast ['brekfəst] **I** *n* desayuno *m*; **he likes b. in bed,** le gusta desayunar en la cama; **she only has a cup of tea for b.,** sólo desayuna una taza de té; **to have b.,** desayunar. **II** *vi* desayunar.

break-in ['breɪkɪn] *n (burglary)* robo *m* (con allanamiento de morada).

breaking ['breɪkɪŋ] *n* **1** rotura *f*. ■ **b. point,** punto *m* de ruptura; **my patience was at b. point,** no podía más. **2** *Jur* **b. and entering,** allanamiento *m* de morada. **3** *Jur (of law)* violación *f*.

breakneck ['breɪknek] *adj (speed, pace)* de vértigo.

break-out ['breɪkaʊt] *n (from prison)* fuga *f*.

breakthrough ['breɪkθruː] *n (major achievement)* adelanto *m*, avance *m*; **it was an important b. in the treatment of burns,** fue un avance importante en el tratamiento de las quemaduras.

break-up ['breɪkʌp] *n (disintegration)* desintegración *f*; *(of empire)* desmembramiento *m*; *(of marriage, relationship)* fracaso *m*; *(of couple)* separación *f*; *(of talks)* ruptura *f*.

breakwater ['breɪkwɔːtəʳ] *n* rompeolas *m inv*.

bream [briːm] *n inv Zool* brema *f*. ■ **Couch's sea b.,** pagro *m*, pargo *m*; **gilt-head b.,** dorada *f*; **Ray's b.,** japuta *f*, palometa *f*; **red b.,** besugo *m*.

breast [brest] *n* **1** *(chest)* pecho *m*; *(of woman)* pecho *m*, seno *m*; *(of chicken etc)* pechuga *f*; **b. pocket,** bolsillo *m* de pecho; *fig* **to make a clean b. of it,** dar la cara. **2** *(of hill)* repecho *m*.

breastbone ['brestbəʊn] *n Anat* esternón *m*.

breast-fed ['brestfed] **I** *pt & pp see* **breast-feed. II** *adj (baby)* criado,-a con el pecho.

breast-feed ['brestfiːd] *vtr (pt & pp* **breast-fed***) (baby)* dar el pecho a, amamantar a.

breast-feeding ['brestfiːdɪŋ] *n* amamantamiento *m*.

breaststroke ['breststrəʊk] *n Swimming* braza *f*.

breath [breθ] *n* **1** *(gen)* aliento *m*; *(breathing)* respiración *f*; **bad b.,** mal aliento; **in the same b.,** al mismo tiempo; **out of b.,** sin aliento; **take a deep b.,** respire hondo; **to catch one's b.,** recobrar el aliento; **to draw b.,** respirar; **to get one's b. back,** recobrar el aliento *or* la respiración; **under one's b.,** en voz baja; *fig* **to take sb's b. away,**

dejar pasmado a algn; *fig* **to waste one's b.,** gastar saliva en balde. ■ *Aut* **b. test,** prueba *f* del alcohol. **2** *(gust)* soplo *m* (de aire); **to go out for a b. of air,** salir a tomar el aire; *fig* **her presence was like a b. of fresh air,** su presencia fue como una bocanada de aire fresco.

breathalyze ['breθəlaɪz] *vtr* hacer la prueba del alcohol a.

Breathalyzer® ['breθəlaɪzəʳ] *n GB* alcohómetro *m*, alcoholímetro *m*.

breathe [briːð] **I** *vtr (air etc)* respirar; **to b. again, b. a sigh of relief,** dar un suspiro de alivio; **to b. heavily,** resoplar; **to b. one's last,** exhalar el último suspiro; *fig* **don't b. a word of it!,** ¡no digas ni una palabra a nadie!; ¡no digas ni mu! **II** *vi* respirar; **he's still breathing,** vive aún. aún respira; **to b. in,** aspirar; **to b. out,** espirar; *fig* **now we can b. again,** ya podemos estar tranquilos; *fig* **to b. down sb's neck,** atosigar a algn.

breather ['briːðəʳ] *n fam (rest)* (momento *m* de) respiro *m*, descanso *m*; **give me a b.,** déjame respirar un momento; **to take a b.,** tomarse un descanso *or* un respiro.

breathing ['briːðɪŋ] *n* respiración *f*. ■ **b. apparatus,** equipo *m* respiratorio; **b. space,** pausa *f*, respiro *m*.

breathless ['breθlɪs] *adj* sin aliento, jadeante.

breathtaking ['breθteɪkɪŋ] *adj (scenery etc)* impresionante, asombroso,-a.

bred [bred] *pt & pp see* **breed.**

breech [briːtʃ] *n* **1** *(of gun)* recámara *f*. **2** *Med* **b. baby,** niño *m* que nace de nalgas.

breeches ['brɪtʃɪz, 'briːtʃɪz] *npl (gen)* bombachos *mpl*. ■ **knee b., riding b.,** pantalones *mpl* de montar.

breech-loading ['briːtʃləʊdɪŋ] *adj (gun)* de retrocarga.

breed [briːd] **I** *n (of animal)* raza *f*. **2** *fig (class)* clase *f*, género *m*; **a new b. of writers,** una nueva generación de escritores. **II** *vtr (pt & pp* **bred***)* **1** *(animals)* criar. **2** *fig (ideas)* engendrar; *prov* **familiarity breeds contempt,** la confianza hace perder el respeto, donde hay confianza da asco. **III** *vi (animals)* criar.

breeder ['briːdəʳ] *n* **1** *(person)* criador,-a *m, f*. **2** *(animal)* reproductor,-a *m, f*. **3** *Tech* **(fast) b. reactor,** reactor *m* generador.

breeding ['briːdɪŋ] *n* **1** *(of animals)* cría *f*. ■ **b. farm, b. ground,** criadero *m*; *fig (for activity, behaviour)* origen *m*. **2** *(of person)* educación *f*; **(good) b.,** buena crianza *f*; **to lack b.,** carecer de educación.

breeze [briːz] **I** *n* brisa *f*; **sea b.,** brisa marina. ■ *Constr* **b. block,** bloque *m* de cemento. **II** *vi* **to b. in/out,** entrar/ salir despreocupadamente.

breezy ['briːzɪ] *adj (breezier, breeziest)* **1** *(weather)* ventoso,-a. **2** *(person, attitude)* despreocupado,-a.

Bren gun ['brengʌn] *n Mil* fusil *m* ametrallador.

brethren ['breðrɪn] *npl Rel* hermanos *mpl*.

Breton ['bretən] **I** *adj & n* bretón,-ona *(m, f)*. **II** *n (language)* bretón *m*.

breve [briːv] *n Ling Mus* breve *f*.

breviary ['brevjərɪ] *n Rel* breviario *m*.

brevity ['brevɪtɪ] *n* brevedad *f*.

brew [bruː] **I** *vtr* **1** *(beer)* hacer, elaborar. **2** *Culin (hot drink)* preparar. **II** *vi* **1** *fig (crisis etc)* tramar. **II** *vi* **1** *(tea)* reposar; **let the tea b.,** deja reposar el té. **2** *fig* prepararse; **a storm is brewing,** se prepara una tormenta; *fam* **something's brewing,** algo se está cociendo. **III** *n* **1** *(of tea)* infusión *f*; *fam (of beer)* birra *f*. **2** *(magic potion)* brebaje *m*; *(strange mixture)* mezcolanza *f*.

brewer ['bruːəʳ] *n* cervecero,-a *m, f*. ■ **b.'s yeast,** levadura *f* de cerveza.

brewery ['bruərɪ] *n* fábrica *f* de cerveza, cervecería *f*.

brewing ['bruːɪŋ] **I** *adj* cervecero,-a; **the b. industry,** la industria cervecera. **II** *n (of beer)* elaboración *f* de la cerveza.

briar ['braɪəʳ] *n Bot* brezo *m*. ■ **b. pipe,** pipa *f* de brezo.

bribe [braɪb] **I** *vtr* sobornar. **II** *n* soborno *m; to take á b. from sb*, dejarse sobornar por algn.

bribery ['braɪbərɪ] *n (process)* soborno *m.*

bric-a-brac ['brɪkəbræk] *n* baratijas *fpl*, chucherías *fpl.*

brick [brɪk] **I** *n* **1** *Constr* ladrillo *m;* **b. wall,** muro *m* de ladrillo; **solid b.,** ladrillo macizo; *fam* **to come down on sb like a ton of bricks,** echar una bronca de miedo a algn; *GB fam* **to drop a b.,** meter la pata. **2** *GB (child's block)* cubo *m* (de madera). **3** *(of ice, ice cream)* bloque *m.* **4** *fam (reliable person)* persona *f* de confianza. **II** *vtr* **to b. (in, over, up),** tapiar con ladrillos.

brickbat ['brɪkbæt] *n* **1** trozo *m* de ladrillo. **2** *(criticism)* crítica *f.*

bricklayer ['brɪkleɪəʳ] *n* albañil *m.*

brickwork ['brɪkwɜːk] *n* ladrillos *mpl,* enladrillado *m.*

bridal ['braɪdəl] *adj* nupcial. ■ **b. suite,** suite *f* nupcial.

bride [braɪd] *n (on wedding day)* novia *f, (newly-married woman)* recién casada *f;* **the b. and groom,** los novios.

bridegroom ['braɪdgruːm] *n (on wedding day)* novio *m;* *(newly-married man)* recién casado *m.*

bridesmaid ['braɪdzmeɪd] *n* dama *f* de honor.

bridge¹ [brɪdʒ] **I** *n (over river, of violin, for teeth)* puente *m; (of nose)* caballete *m; (of ship)* puente *m* de mando; **suspension b.,** puente colgante. **II** *vtr* **1** *(river)* tender un puente sobre. **2** *(distances etc)* acortar; *(gap)* llenar; *Fin* **bridging loan,** crédito *m* a corto plazo.

bridge² [brɪdʒ] *n Cards* bridge *m.*

bridgehead ['brɪdʒhed] *n Mil* cabeza *f* de puente.

bridle ['braɪdəl] **I** *n* brida *f; (bit)* freno *m;* **b. path,** camino *m* de herradura. **II** *vtr (horse)* embridar, poner la brida a.

brief [briːf] **I** *adj* **1** *(short)* breve; **a b. pause,** una breve pausa; **a b. stay,** una estancia corta. **2** *(concise)* conciso,-a. **II** *n* **1** *(report)* informe *m; (summary)* resumen *m;* **in b.,** en resumen. **2** *Jur* expediente *m.* **3** *Mil* instrucciones *fpl.* **4** *Rel (letter)* breve *m.* **5 briefs,** *(for men)* calzoncillos *mpl,* slip *m sing; (for women)* bragas *fpl.* **III** *vtr* **1** *(inform)* informar. **2** *(instruct)* dar instrucciones a. ◆ **briefly** *adv* brevemente; **as b. as possible,** con la mayor brevedad (posible).

briefcase ['briːfkeɪs] *n* cartera *f,* portafolios *mpl.*

briefing ['briːfɪŋ] *n* **1** *(instructions)* instrucciones *fpl.* **2** *(meeting)* reunión *f* informativa.

briefness ['briːfnɪs] *n* brevedad *f.*

brier ['braɪəʳ] *n see* **briar.**

brig¹ [brɪg] *n Naut* bergantín *m.*

brig² [brɪg] *Mil abbr of* **Brigadier,** General *m* de Brigada, Gral. Brig.

brigade [brɪ'geɪd] *n Mil* brigada *f.*

brigadier [brɪgə'dɪəʳ] *n Mil* general *m* de brigada.

brigand ['brɪgənd] *n* bandido *m,* bandolero *m.*

bright [braɪt] *adj* **1** *(light, sun, eyes)* brillante; *(colour)* vivo,-a; *(day)* claro,-a, despejado,-a. **2** *(cheerful)* alegre, muy animado,-a; **b. and early,** muy temprano; **to look on the b. side,** mirar el lado bueno de las cosas. **3** *(clever)* listo,-a, despierto,-a, espabilado,-a; **a b. idea,** una idea luminosa; *fam* **a b. spark,** un espabilado. **4** *(promising)* prometedor,-a; **a b. future,** un futuro prometedor, un brillante porvenir. ◆ **brightly** *adv* brillantemente; *(cleverly)* inteligentemente.

brighten ['braɪtən] *vi* **1** *(prospects)* mejorarse. **2** *(face, eyes)* iluminarse. ◆ **brighten up I** *vtr* **1** *(make more attractive)* hacer más alegre; **the new carpet brightens up the room,** la alfombra nueva anima mucho la habitación. **2** *(polish metal)* pulir. **II** *vi* **1** *(weather)* aclararse, despejarse. **2** *(person)* animarse.

brightness ['braɪtnɪs] *n* **1** *(light)* luminosidad *f,* intensidad *f; (sun)* resplandor *m; (of day)* claridad *f; (colour)* viveza *f.* **2** *(cleverness)* inteligencia *f.*

brilliance ['brɪljəns] *n* **1** *(light)* brillo *m; (colour)* viveza *f.* **2** *(of person)* brillantez *f.*

brilliant ['brɪljənt] **I** *adj* **1** *(light)* brillante, reluciente. **2** *(person)* brillante, admirable; *(idea)* luminoso,-a, genial; **a b. writer,** un escritor brillante. **3** *fam (very good)* estupendo,-a, fantástico,-a. **II** *n (diamond)* brillante *m.*

brilliantine ['brɪljəntiːn] *n Hairdr* brillantina *f.*

brim [brɪm] **I** *n* **1** *(of cup etc)* borde *m;* **full to the b.,** lleno hasta el borde. **2** *(of hat)* ala *f.* **II** *vi* rebosar **(with,** de); **her eyes brimmed with tears,** las lagrimas cegaban sus ojos; **to be brimming with happiness,** estar rebosante de alegría. ◆ **brim over** rebosar.

brimstone ['brɪmstəʊn] *n Min* azufre *m; lit* **fire and b.,** el infierno.

brine [braɪn] *n* salmuera *f.*

bring [brɪŋ] *vtr (pt & pp* **brought) 1** *(carry sth to sb)* traer; **b. me a cup of coffee,** tráigame un café; **to b. bad luck,** traer mala suerte; **to b. news,** traer noticias. **2** *(take sth or sb with you)* traer; **could you b. that book tomorrow?,** ¿podrías traerme el libro mañana?; **he brought his camera,** se trajo la máquina de hacer fotos; **she brought her boyfriend to the party,** trajo a su novio a la fiesta. ■ **b.-and-buy sale,** venta *f* de artículos de segunda mano or de fabricación casera. **3** *(to take to a different position)* llevar; **Tina brought her hand to her head,** Tina se llevó la mano a la cabeza. **4** *(cause)* llevar, provocar; **he brought it upon himself,** se lo buscó; **the experience brought her to suicide,** aquella experiencia la llevó al suicidio; **the war brought hunger to many homes,** la guerra llevó el hambre a muchos hogares; **what brings you here?,** ¿qué te trae por aquí? **5** *(persuade)* persuadir, convencer; **how did they b. themselves to do it?,** ¿cómo llegaron a hacerlo?; **I can't b. myself to do it,** no puedo resignarme a hacerlo; **she can't b. herself to believe it,** no le cabe en la cabeza. **6** *(lead)* llevar, conducir; **the path brings you to a wood,** el camino lleva a un bosque; **this now brings us to the question of inflation,** esto nos conduce a hablar de la inflación. **7** *Jur* **to b. an action against,** acusar; **to b. a complaint,** hacer una reclamación; **to b. evidence against,** presentar pruebas contra. **8** *(sell for)* vender; **this old car will b. about £50,** este coche viejo se venderá por unas £50. ◆ **bring about** *vtr* causar, provocar, ocasionar; **to b. about a change,** efectuar un cambio. ◆ **bring along** *vtr* traer. ◆ **bring back** *vtr* **1** *(return)* devolver. **2** *(reintroduce)* volver a introducir; **they are trying to b. back the mini-skirt,** quieren poner de moda la minifalda otra vez. **3** *(make one remember)* traerle a la memoria; **it brings back my school days,** me recuerda los días del colegio. ◆ **bring down** *vtr* **1** *(from upstairs)* bajar (algo); **b. down the trunk from the attic,** baja el baúl del desván. **2** *(destroy)* derribar; **to b. down a government/a dictator,** derribar un gobierno/un dictador; *Theat* **to b. the house down,** hacer que el teatro se venga abajo con los aplausos. **3** *(reduce)* rebajar; **to b. down prices,** hacer bajar los precios. ◆ **bring forward** *vtr* **1** *(arrange to happen earlier)* adelantar. **2** *(present)* presentar; **she brought forward some good ideas,** presentó algunas ideas buenas. **3** *Fin (in accounts)* pasar a otra cuenta; **brought forward,** suma y sigue. ◆ **bring in** *vtr* **1** *(yield)* dar; **tourism brings in £7 million a year,** el turismo proporciona £7 millones cada año. **2** *(show in)* hacer entrar. **3** *(introduce a law, custom, etc)* introducir; *(a fashion)* lanzar. **4** *Agr (collect)* recoger. **5** *Jur (verdict)* pronunciar. ◆ **bring off** *vtr* lograr, conseguir. ◆ **bring on** *vtr (cause an illness)* causar, provocar. ◆ **bring out** *vtr* **1** *(publish)* publicar, sacar un libro. **2** *(reveal) (error, colour)* recalcar; **that woman brings out the worst in me,** esa mujer despierta lo peor que hay en mí. **3** *(draw out)* ayudar a algn a tener confianza en sí mismo. ◆ **bring round** *vtr* **1** *(revive)* hacer volver en sí. **2** *(persuade)* convencer, persuadir; **to b. sb round to your point of view,** convencer a algn, poner a algn de tu lado. ◆ **bring to** *vtr* reanimar, hacer volver en sí. ◆ **bring up** *vtr* **1** *(care for, educate)* criar, educar; **he was brought up by his grandmother,** lo crió su abuela. **2** *(raise a subject)* plantear. **3** *(vomit)* devolver.

brink [brɪŋk] *n* (*edge*) borde *m*; *fig* **on the b. of ruin,** al borde de la ruina; **on the b. of tears,** a punto de llorar.

brinkmanship ['brɪŋkmənʃɪp] *n Pol* política *f* de cuerda floja.

briny ['braɪnɪ] *adj* salado,-a.

briquette [brɪ'ket] *n* (*coal, peat*) briqueta *f*.

brisk [brɪsk] *adj* enérgico,-a; (*pace*) rápido,-a; (*trade*) activo,-a; (*weather*) fresco,-a.

briskness ['brɪsknɪs] *n* energía *f*; (*pace*) ligereza *f*; (*trade*) actividad *f*.

bristle ['brɪsəl] **I** *n* (*hair*) cerda *f*. **II** *vi* **1** erizarse, ponerse de punta. **2** (*to show anger*) enfurecer (**at,** -); **she bristled at the suggestion,** mostró su enfado ante tal sugerencia. ◆ **bristle with** *vtr* (*be full of*) estar lleno,-a de, erizar; **bristling with difficulties,** sembrado *or* lleno de dificultades; **the street was bristling with policemen,** la calle estaba llena de policía.

Brit [brɪt] *n* **1** *abbr of* **British. 2** *fam* británico,-a *m,f*.

Britain ['brɪtən] *n* (**Great**) **B.,** Gran Bretaña.

British ['brɪtɪʃ] **I** *adj* británico,-a; **the B. Isles,** las Islas Británicas. **II the B.** *npl* los británicos.

Britisher ['brɪtɪʃəʳ] *n US* británico,-a *m,f*.

Briton ['brɪtən] *n Lit Hist* britano,-a *m,f*, británico,-a *m,f*.

brittle ['brɪtəl] *adj* quebradizo,-a, frágil.

brittleness ['brɪtəlnɪs] *n* fragilidad *f*.

broach [brəʊtʃ] *vtr* **1** (*subject*) abordar, sacar a colación. **2** *arch* (*barrel, bottle*) abrir.

broad [brɔːd] **I** *adj* **1** (*wide*) ancho,-a; (*large*) extenso,-a; **a b. smile,** una sonrisa abierta; *US Sport* **b. jump,** salto *m* de longitud; **she has a b. range of interests,** tiene intereses muy variados; *fig* **it's as b. as it's long,** da lo mismo. **2** (*clear*) obvio,-a; **a b. hint,** una indirecta inconfundible. **3** (*daylight*) pleno,-a. **4** (*not detailed*) general, básico,-a; **a b. outline,** un esquema general; **in the b. sense,** en sentido amplio. **5** (*accent*) marcado,-a, cerrado,-a; **in a b. Italian accent,** en un marcado acento italiano. **II** *n US sl* (*woman*) tía *f*, pájara *f*. ◆ **broadly** *adv* en general, en términos generales; **b. speaking,** hablando en términos generales.

broadcast ['brɔːdkɑːst] *Rad TV* **I** *n* emisión *f*; **live b.,** retransmisión *f* en directo; **repeat b.,** reposición *f*. **II** *vtr* (*pt & pp* **broadcast** *or* **broadcasted**) **1** *Rad TV* emitir, transmitir. **2** (*make widely known*) propagar, difundir.

broadcaster ['brɔːdkɑːstəʳ] *n* locutor,-a *m,f*.

broadcasting ['brɔːdkɑːstɪŋ] *n Rad* radiodifusión *f*; *TV* transmisión *f*. ■ *Rad* **b. station,** emisora *f*.

broaden ['brɔːdən] *vtr* **1** ensanchar. **2** ampliar; **to b. one's horizons,** ampliar horizontes; **travel broadens the mind,** viajar amplia los horizontes.

broad-minded [brɔːd'maɪndɪd] *adj* liberal, tolerante, de miras amplias.

broad-mindedness [brɔːd'maɪndɪdnɪs] *n* tolerancia *f*, amplitud *f* de miras.

broadness ['brɔːdnɪs] *n* anchura *f*.

broadsheet ['brɔːdʃiːt] *n* folleto *m*.

broad-shouldered [brɔːd'ʃəʊldəd] *adj* ancho,-a de espaldas.

broadside ['brɔːdsaɪd] *n* **1** (*side of ship*) costado *m*. **2** (*volley of shots*) andanada *f*; **to fire a b.,** soltar una andanada. **3** (*insults*) andanada *f*, reprensión *f*.

brocade [brəʊ'keɪd] *n Tex* brocado *m*.

broccoli ['brɒkəlɪ] *n Bot* brécol *m*, brócoli *m*.

brochette [brɒ'ʃet] *n Culin* (*skewer*) brocheta *f*, broqueta *f*, pinchito *m*.

brochure ['brəʊʃəʳ, 'brəʊʃjʊəʳ] *n* folleto *m*.

brogue[1] [brəʊg] *n* zapato *m* grueso.

brogue[2] [brəʊg] *n* acento *m* (irlandés) muy marcado.

broil [brɔɪl] *vtr Culin US* asar a la parrilla.

broiler ['brɔɪləʳ] *n Culin* pollo *m*.

broke [brəʊk] **I** *pt see* **break. II** *adj fam* **to be (flat) b.,** estar sin blanca, no tener ni un clavo.

broken ['brəʊkən] **I** *pp see* **break. II** *adj* **1** (*stick, cup, etc*) roto,-a; (*tool, machinery*) estropeado,-a; (*bone*) fracturado,-a; (*promise*) roto,-a; (*sleep*) interrumpido,-a. **2** (*home*) deshecho,-a; (*man, woman*) destrozado,-a; (*language*) chapurreado,-a; (*ground*) accidentado,-a, desnivelado,-a; **to speak b. English,** chapurrear el inglés.

broken-down ['brəʊkəndaʊn] *adj* (*car, engine*) averiado,-a; (*machine*) estropeado,-a.

broken-hearted [brəʊkən'hɑːtɪd] *adj fig* con el corazón destrozado.

broker ['brəʊkəʳ] *n Fin* corredor *m*, agente *mf* de Bolsa, comisionista *mf*. ■ **insurance b.,** agente *mf* de seguros.

brokerage ['brəʊkərɪdʒ] *n Fin* corretaje *m*.

brolly ['brɒlɪ] *n fam* paraguas *m inv*.

bromide ['brəʊmaɪd] *n Chem* bromuro *m*; *fig fml* **please do not come out with those old bromides,** no me vengan con las mismas historias de siempre.

bromine ['brəʊmiːn] *n Chem* bromo *m*.

bronchial ['brɒŋkɪəl] *adj Anat* bronquial; **b. tubes,** bronquios *mpl*.

bronchitic [brɒŋ'kɪtɪk] *adj Med* bronquítico,-a.

bronchitis [brɒŋ'kaɪtɪs] *n Med* bronquitis *f*.

bronze [brɒnz] **I** *n* bronce *m*. ■ **B. Age,** Edad *f* de Bronce. **II** *adj* **1** (*material*) de bronce. **2** (*colour*) bronceado,-a.

bronzed [brɒnzd] *adj* (*suntanned*) bronceado,-a.

brooch [brəʊtʃ] *n* broche *m*, alfiler *m*.

brood [bruːd] **I** *n* (*birds*) cría *f*, nidada *f*; *hum* (*children*) prole *m*. **II** *vi* (*hen*) empollar; *fig* (*ponder*) rumiar; **dark clouds were brooding over the city,** oscuras nubes se cernían sobre la cuidad; *fig* **to b. over a problem,** darle vueltas a un problema.

broody ['bruːdɪ] *adj* **1 b. hen,** gallina *f* clueca; *fam* (*women*) con ganas de tener hijos. **2** (*pensive*) pensativo,-a. **3** (*moody*) melancólico,-a.

brook[1] [brʊk] *n* arroyo *m*.

brook[2] [brʊk] *vtr* (*usu in negative*) soportar, aguantar; **she will b. no interference,** no tolerará ni la más mínima ingerencia.

broom [bruːm] *n* **1** (*sweeping-brush*) escoba *f*; *fig* **a new b.,** una persona con nuevas ideas. **2** *Bot* retama *f*, hiniesta *f*.

broomstick ['bruːmstɪk] *n* palo *m* de escoba.

Bros *Com abbr of* **Brothers,** Hermanos *mpl*, Hnos.

broth [brɒθ] *n Culin* caldo *m*.

brothel ['brɒθəl] *n* burdel *m*.

brother ['brʌðəʳ] *n* **1** hermano *m*; **brothers and sisters,** hermanos; **older b.,** hermano mayor; **younger b.,** hermano menor. **2** (*colleague*) colega *m*, compañero *m*; (*comrade*) camarada *f*. **3** *Rel* hermano *m*.

brotherhood ['brʌðəhʊd] *n* **1** (*condition of brother*) fraternidad *f*, hermandad *f*. **2** (*association*) gremio *m*; *Rel* cofradía *f*, hermandad *f*.

brother-in-law ['brʌðərɪnlɔː] *n* (*pl* **brothers-in-law**) cuñado *m*, hermano *m* político.

brotherly ['brʌðəlɪ] *adj* fraternal, fraterno,-a; **b. love,** amor fraternal.

brought [brɔːt] *pt & pp see* **bring.**

brow [braʊ] *n* **1** (*forehead*) frente *f*. **2** (*eyebrow*) ceja *f*. **3** (*of hill*) cima *f*, cumbre *f*.

browbeat ['braʊbiːt] *vtr* (*pt* **browbeat**; *pp* **browbeaten**) intimidar a algn; **to b. sb into doing sth,** obligar a algn a hacer algo.

brown [braʊn] **I** *adj* **1** marrón, pardo,-a; (*hair, eyes*) castaño,-a. ■ **b. bread,** pan *m* integral; **b. paper,** papel *m* de estraza; **b. sugar,** azúcar *m & f* moreno,-a. **2** (*suntanned*) moreno,-a; **to go b.,** ponerse moreno; **as b.**

as a berry, muy moreno. **II** *n* marrón *m*; *(hair, eyes)* castaño *m*. **III** *vtr* **1** *Culin* dorar. **2** *(tan)* broncear, poner moreno.

browned-off [braʊnd'ɒf] *adj fam* estar hasta las narices *or* hasta la coronilla **(with,** de).

Brownie ['braʊnɪ] *n (in Guide Movement)* niña *f* exploradora.

brownie ['braʊnɪ] *n US Culin* bizcocho *m* de chocolate con nueces.

brownish ['braʊnɪʃ] *adj* pardusco,-a.

brownout ['braʊnaʊt] *n US* apagón *m* parcial.

browse [braʊz] **I** *vi* **1** *(animal) (grass)* pacer; *(leaves)* ramonear. **2** *(person in shop)* mirar; *(through book, magazine)* hojear; **I spend hours browsing in bookshops,** me paso horas en las librerías hojeando libros. **II** *n* ojeada *f*; **to have a b.,** dar un vistazo *or* una ojeada **(in,** a).

bruise [bruːz] **I** *n* morado *m*, contusión *f*, magulladura *f*, cardenal *m*; **I've got a b.,** me ha salido un morado. **II** *vtr (body)* contusionar, magullar; *(fruit)* estropear, machucar; *fig (feelings)* herir; **I feel bruised and upset by his accusation,** me siento herido y afectado por su acusación. **III** *vi (body)* magullarse; *(fruit)* estropearse.

bruiser ['bruːsəʳ] *n fam* matón *m*.

brunch ['brʌntʃ] *n* brunch *m*, combinación *f* de desayuno y almuerzo.

Brunei [bruː'naɪ] *n* Brunei.

brunette [bruː'net] *adj & n (woman)* morena *(f)*.

brunt [brʌnt] *n* lo peor; **to bear** *or* **take the b.,** llevar el peso, aguantar: **we bore the b. of the expense,** llevamos la mayor parte del gasto.

brush¹ [brʌʃ] **I** *n* **1** *(for hair, teeth, clothes)* cepillo *m*; *Art* pincel *m*; *(for house-painting)* brocha *f*. ■ **shaving b.,** brocha *f* de afeitar; **scrubbing b.,** cepillo *m* de fregar. **2** *(act of brushing)* cepillado *m*. **3** *fig* **to have a b. with the law,** tener un roce con la policía. **II** *vtr* **1** cepillar; **to b. one's hair,** peinarse; **to b. one's teeth,** limpiarse los dientes. **2** *(touch lightly)* rozar la pared; **her hair brushed his cheek,** su pelo rozó su mejilla. **III** *vi* rozar al pasar **(against,** -). ◆ **brush aside** *vtr* dejar de lado. ◆ **brush off** *vtr* ignorar. ◆ **brush up** *vtr* mejorar, revisar; **to b. up one's French,** volver a estudiar francés.

brush² [brʌʃ] *n (undergrowth)* broza *f*, maleza *f*.

brush-off ['brʌʃɒf] *n fam* **to give sb the b.-o.,** mandar a algn a paseo.

brushwood ['brʌʃwʊd] *n* maleza *f*.

brusque [bruːsk, brʊsk] *adj (person)* brusco,-a; *(words)* áspero,-a.

brusqueness ['bruːsknɪs, 'brʊsknɪs] *n* brusquedad *f*.

Brussels ['brʌsəlz] *n* Bruselas.

brutal ['bruːtəl] *adj* brutal, cruel; *fig* **the b. truth,** la cruel verdad.

brutality [bruː'tælɪtɪ] *n* brutalidad *f*; *(behaviour)* crueldad *f*.

brute [bruːt] **I** *adj* bruto,-a, brutal; **b. force,** fuerza bruta. **II** *n (animal)* bruto *m*, bestia *mf*; *(person)* bestia *f*; *fam* **a b. of a job,** un trabajo de locos.

brutish ['bruːtɪʃ] *adj* **1** *(savage)* bestial. **2** *(rough)* brutal. **3** *(stupid)* bruto,-a.

BSc [biːes'siː], *US* **BS** [biː'es] *abbr of* **Bachelor of Science,** Licenciado,-a *m, f* en Ciencias.

BST [biːes'tiː] *abbr of* **British Summer Time,** hora *f* británica de verano.

BT [biː'tiː] *abbr of* **British Telecom,** Telecomunicaciones *fpl* británicas.

Bt *abbr of* **Baronet,** baronet *m*.

BTA [biːtiː'eɪ] *abbr of* **British Tourist Authority.**

Bthu, Btu *abbr of* **British Thermal Unit,** unidad *f* calorífica británica, BTU *f*.

bubble ['bʌbəl] **I** *n* burbuja *f*. ■ **b. bath,** espuma *f* de baño; **b. gum,** chicle *m*; **soap b.,** pompa *f* de jabón. **II** *vi* burbujear; *Culin* borbotear; *fig* **to b. over with happiness,** rebosar de alegría.

bubble-and-squeak [bʌbələn'skwiːk] *n GB Culin* guiso *m* de col, patatas y carne.

bubbly ['bʌblɪ] **I** *adj (bubblier, bubbliest)* efervescente, con burbujas; **she has a b. personality,** tiene una personalidad muy vivaz. **II** *n fam* champán *m*, cava *m*.

bubonic [bjuː'bɒnɪk] *adj Med* bubónico,-a. ■ **b. plague,** peste *f* bubónica.

buccaneer [bʌkə'nɪəʳ] *n* bucanero *m*.

Bucharest [bʌkə'rest] *n* Bucarest.

buck¹ [bʌk] **I** *n* **1** *Zool (male species)* macho *m*; *(male deer)* ciervo *m*; *(male goat)* macho *m* cabrío; *fam* **to pass the b. to sb,** echarle el muerto a algn. **2** *Gymn* potro *m*. **3** *(young man)* galán *m*. **II** *vi (horse)* corcovear. **III** *vtr fam (avoid)* esquivar. ◆ **buck up I** *vtr fam* **b. your ideas up, laddie!,** ¡espabílate chico! **II** *vi (cheer up)* animarse.

buck² [bʌk] *n US fam* dólar *m*; **to make a fast** *or* **a quick b.,** hacer dinero rápido.

bucket ['bʌkɪt] **I** *n* cubo *m*; **a b. of water,** un cubo de agua; *fam* **to kick the b.,** estirar la pata, guiñarla; *fam* **it rained buckets,** llovía a cántaros; *fam* **she cried buckets,** lloraba como una Magdalena. ■ *Aut* **b. seat,** asiento *m* envolvente; **b. shop,** agencia *f* de viajes que vende billetes de avión a bajo precio. **II** *vi fam (of rain)* llover a cántaros **(down,** -); **it's been bucketing down all day,** ha llovido a cántaros todo el día.

bucketful ['bʌkɪtfʊl] *n* cubo *m*; **a b. of water,** un cubo lleno de agua.

buckle ['bʌkəl] **I** *n (on belt, shoe)* hebilla *f*. **II** *vtr* abrochar con hebilla. **III** *vi* **1** *(wall, metal)* combarse, torcerse. **2** *(knees)* doblarse. ◆ **buckle down** *vi fam* dedicarse **(to,** a), concentrarse **(to,** en); **to b. down to work,** ponerse a trabajar en serio.

buckshee [bʌk'ʃiː] *fam arch* **I** *adj* gratuito,-a. **II** *adv* gratis.

buckshot ['bʌkʃɒt] *n* perdigón *m*, posta *f*.

buckskin ['bʌkskɪn] *n* ante *m*.

bucktooth ['bʌktuːθ] *n (pl buckteeth* ['bʌktiːθ]) diente *m* saliente.

buckwheat ['bʌkwiːt] *n Bot* alforfón *m*.

bucolic [bjuː'kɒlɪk] *adj* bucólico,-a.

bud [bʌd] **I** *n Bot (shoot)* brote *m*; *(flower)* capullo *m*. **II** *vi Bot* brotar; *fig* florecer.

Budapest [bjuːdə'pest] *n* Budapest.

Buddha ['budə] *n Rel* Buda *m*.

Buddhism ['budɪzəm] *n Rel* budismo *m*.

Buddhist ['budɪst] *adj & n Rel* budista *(mf)*.

budding ['bʌdɪŋ] *adj fam* en ciernes; **a b. gymnast,** una gymnasta que promete.

buddy ['bʌdɪ] *n US fam* compañero *m*, amigote *m*, compinche *m*.

budge [bʌdʒ] *vi* **I** *(move)* moverse; **this screw won't b.,** este tornillo no se mueve. **2** *(yield)* ceder; **she won't b.,** no cederá.

budgerigar ['bʌdʒərɪgɑːʳ] *n Orn* periquito *m*.

budget ['bʌdʒɪt] **I** *n* presupuesto *m*; *Pol* **the B.,** el presupuesto estatal. ■ **b. account,** cuenta *f* presupuestaria. **II** *vi* hacer un presupuesto **(for,** para).

budgetary ['bʌdʒətərɪ] *adj* presupuestario,-a; **b. control,** control presupuestario.

budgie ['bʌdʒɪ] *n fam see* **budgerigar.**

buff¹ [bʌf] **I** *n* **1** *(leather)* piel *f* de búfalo *or* de ante; *fam arch* **in the b.,** en cueros. **2** *(colour)* amarillo *m*, color *m* de ante. **II** *adj* amarillo,-a, de color de ante. **III** *vtr* dar brillo.

buff² [bʌf] *n fam (enthusiast)* aficionado,-a *m, f*, entusiasta *mf*. ■ **film b.,** cinéfilo,-a *m, f*.

buffalo [ˈbʌfələʊ] *n Zool* (*pl* **buffaloes** *or* **buffalo**) búfalo *m.*

buffer[1] [ˈbʌfəʳ] I *n* 1 (*device*) amortiguador *m*; *Rail* tope *m*; *US Aut* parachoques *m inv.* ■ *Pol* **b. state**, estado *m* tapón; **b. zone**, zona *f* intermedia. 2 *Comput* memoria *f* intermedia. 3 *Chem* regulador *m.* II *vtr* (*insulate from shock*) amortiguar.

buffer[2] [ˈbʌfəʳ] *n fam* **old b.**, viejo *m* chocho.

buffet[1] [ˈbʊfeɪ] *n* 1 (*snack bar*) bar *m*; (*at railway station*) cantina *f.* ■ *Rail* **b. car**, coche *m* restaurante. 2 (*self-service meal*) bufet *m* libre. 3 *Furn* (*sideboard*) aparador *m*, cristalera *f.*

buffet[2] [ˈbʌfɪt] I *vtr* (*hit*) golpear; **the ship was buffeted by the waves**, las olas golpeaban el barco. II *n* (*fist*) golpe *m*; (*hand*) puñetazo *m.*

buffoon [bəˈfuːn] *n* bufón *m*, payaso *m.*

buffoonery [bəˈfuːnərɪ] *n* payasada *f*, payasadas *fpl.*

bug [bʌg] I *n* 1 (*insect*) bicho *m*, insecto *m.* 2 *fam* (*microbe*) microbio *m.* ■ **the flu b.**, el virus de la gripe. 3 (*hidden microphone*) micrófono *m* oculto. 4 *fam* (*enthusiasm*) afición *f*; **he's caught the photography b.**, le ha dado por la fotografía. 5 *Comput* error *m.* II *vtr* (*pt & pp* **bugged**) *fam* 1 (*in spying*) **to b. a room**, ocultar micrófonos en una habitación; *Tel* **to b. a telephone**, intervenir *or* pinchar el teléfono. ■ **bugging device**, aparato *m* para realizar escuchas telefónicas. 2 (*annoy*) fastidiar, molestar; **what's bugging her?**, ¿qué mosca la ha picado?, ¿qué le pasa?

bugbear [ˈbʌgbeəʳ] *n* tormento *m*, pesadilla *f.*

bugger [ˈbʌgəʳ] I *n* 1 sodomita *m.* 2 *sl offens* (*person*) cabrón,-ona *m,f*, gilipollas *mf inv*; **you stupid b.!**, ¡qué gilipollas eres!; *hum* **you lucky b.!**, ¡menuda suerte tienes, macho! 3 (*thing*) coñazo *m*; **this computer is a right b. to work with**, trabajar con este ordenador es un verdadero coñazo. II *interj sl offens* ¡joder!; **b. it!**, ¡joder!, ¡mierda! III *vtr sl* sodomizar. ◆ **bugger about** *vulg* I *vi* hacer gilipolladas *or* chorradas, hacer el gilipollas; **stop buggering about and do your work**, deja de hacer chorradas y ponte a trabajar. II *vtr* hacer la puñeta; **they really buggered him about**, se las hicieron pasar canutas. ◆ **bugger off** *vi sl offens* largarse, pirarse; **b. off!**, ¡vete a la mierda! ◆ **bugger up** *vtr sl vulg* joder, jorobar; **the strike really buggered up our holiday**, la huelga nos jodió las vacaciones.

buggery [ˈbʌgərɪ] *n* sodomía *f.*

buggy [ˈbʌgɪ] *n* 1 (*carriage*) calesa *f*, buggy *m.* 2 (*baby's pushchair*) cochecito *m* de niño.

bugle [ˈbjuːgəl] *n Mus* bugle *m.*

bug-ridden [ˈbʌgrɪdən] *adj* lleno,-a de bichos.

build [bɪld] I *vtr* (*pt & pp* **built**) construir; (*nest*) hacer; **English-built**, de fabricación inglesa; **to b. a society**, fundar una sociedad. II *n* (*physique*) tipo *m*, constitución *f*, físico *m.* ◆ **build up** *vtr* 1 (*cover with buildings*) urbanizar. 2 (*accumulate*) (*traffic*) aumentar; **to b. up a collection**, hacer una colección; **to b. up a reputation**, labrarse una buena reputación.

builder [ˈbɪldəʳ] *n* constructor,-a *m*, *f*, (*contractor*) contratista *mf.*

building [ˈbɪldɪŋ] *n* edificio *m*, construcción *f.* ■ **b. site**, solar *m*; (*under construction*) obra *f*; **b. society**, sociedad *f* hipotecaria.

build-up [ˈbɪldʌp] *n* 1 (*accumulation*) aumento *m*; (*gas*) acumulación *f*; *Mil* (*troops*) concentración *f.* 2 (*publicity*) propaganda *f.*

built [bɪlt] *pt & pp see* **build**

built-in [bɪltˈɪn] *adj* 1 *Carp* empotrado,-a; **b.-in cupboard**, armario *m* empotrado. 2 (*incorporated*) incorporado,-a; **this system has b. safeguards**, este sistema lleva medidas de seguridad incorporadas.

built-up [bɪltˈʌp] *adj* urbanizado,-a; **a b.-up area**, una zona urbanizada.

bulb [bʌlb] *n* 1 *Bot* bulbo *m.* 2 *Elec* (*lightbulb*) bombilla *f.*

bulbous [ˈbʌlbəs] *adj* bulboso,-a.

Bulgaria [bʌlˈgeərɪə] *n* Bulgaria.

Bulgarian [bʌlˈgeərɪən] I *adj* búlgaro,-a. II *n* 1 (*person*) búlgaro,-a *m,f.* 2 (*language*) búlgaro *m.*

bulge [bʌldʒ] I *n* 1 protuberancia *f*; (*in pocket*) bulto *m.* 2 (*increase*) aumento *m*; **the population b.**, el rápido aumento de población. II *vi* (*swell*) hincharse; (*be full*) estar repleto,-a; **his pockets were bulging with sweets**, tenía los bolsillos llenos de caramelos.

bulging [ˈbʌldʒɪŋ] *adj* abultado,-a; **b. eyes**, ojos saltones *or* desorbitados.

bulk [bʌlk] I *n* 1 (*mass*) masa *f*, volumen *m*; *Com* (*goods*) **in b.**, a granel, suelto,-a, al por mayor; **to buy in b.**, comprar algo en grandes cantidades *or* al por mayor. 2 (*greater part*) mayor parte *f*, mayoría *f*; **the b. of the people stayed in their seats**, la mayoría de la gente permaneció en sus asientos. II *vi Lit* **to b. large**, parecer grande.

bulk-buying [bʌlkˈbaɪɪŋ] *n Com* compra *f* en grandes cantidades *or* al por mayor.

bulkhead [ˈbʌlkhed] *n Naut* mamparo *m.*

bulkiness [ˈbʌlkɪnɪs] *n* volumen *m*, magnitud *f.*

bulky [ˈbʌlkɪ] *adj* (*bulkier*, *bulkiest*) 1 (*large*) voluminoso,-a, pesado,-a. 2 (*difficult to handle*) de difícil manejo.

bull[1] [bʊl] *n* 1 *Zool* toro *m*; *fig* **to take the b. by the horns**, coger el toro por los cuernos; **like a b. in a china shop**, como una elefante en una cristalería. ■ **b. elephant**, elephante *m* macho. 2 (*speculator*) *Fin* alcista *mf.* 3 *sl* (*rubbish*) tonterías *fpl*; **it's a load of b.**, no son más que tonterías.

bull[2] [bʊl] *n Rel* (*papal announcement*) bula *f.*

bulldog [ˈbʊldɒg] *n Zool* buldog *m.* ■ *Com* **b. clip**, pinza *f* sujetapapeles.

bulldoze [ˈbʊldəʊz] *vtr Const* (*land*) nivelar; (*building*) derribar; *fam* **to b. sb into doing sth**, forzar a algn a hacer algo; **to b. one's way through a crowd**, abrirse paso a codazos entre una muchedumbre.

bulldozer [ˈbʊldəʊzəʳ] *n* bulldozer *m.*

bullet [ˈbʊlɪt] *n* bala *f*; **plastic b.**, bala de plástico. ■ **b. wound**, balazo *m.*

bulletin [ˈbʊlɪtɪn] *n* boletín *m*, comunicado *m.* ■ *Rad TV* **news b.**, (*radio*) boletín *m* de noticias; (*television*) telediario *m.*

bullet-proof [ˈbʊlɪtpruːf] *adj* a prueba de balas; **b.-p. vest**, chaleco *m* antibalas.

bullfight [ˈbʊlfaɪt] *n* corrida *f* de toros.

bullfighter [ˈbʊlfaɪtəʳ] *n* torero,-a *m,f.*

bullfighting [ˈbʊlfaɪtɪŋ] *n* los toros; (*art*) tauromaquia *f*; **he loves b.**, le encantan los toros.

bullfinch [ˈbʊlfɪntʃ] *n Orn* camachuelo *m* común.

bullfrog [ˈbʊlfrɒg] *n Zool* rana *f* toro.

bullion [ˈbʊljən] *n* (*gold*, *silver*) lingote *m.*

bullish [ˈbʊlɪʃ] *adj Fin* (*market*) en alza.

bullock [ˈbʊlək] *n Zool* buey *m.*

bullring [ˈbʊlrɪŋ] *n* plaza *f* de toros.

bull's-eye [ˈbʊlzaɪ] *n* (*of target*) centro *m* del blanco; **to score a b.-e.**, dar en el blanco.

bullshit [ˈbʊlʃɪt] *vulg* I *n* gilipolleces *fpl*, chorradas *fpl*; **that's b.!**, eso son chorradas. II *vi* decir gilipolleces.

bully [ˈbʊlɪ] I *n* matón *m.* II *vtr* (*pt & pp* **bullied**) (*terrorize*) intimidar; (*bulldoze*) tiranizar. III *interj iron* **b. for you!**, ¡bravo!, ¡a mí qué!

bullying [ˈbʊlɪŋ] *n* intimidación *f.*

bully-off [bʊlɪˈɒf] *n Sport* (*hockey*) saque *m.*

bulrush [ˈbʊlrʌʃ] *n Bot* anea *f*, espadaña *f.*

bulwark [ˈbʊlwək] *n* baluarte *m*, bastión *m*; (*small*) luneta *f.*

bum[1] [bʌm] *n fam* (*bottom*) culo *m.*

bum[2] [bʌm] I *n* 1 *US fam* (*tramp*) vagabundo *m.* 2 *fam* (*idler*, *good-for-nothing*) holgazán,-ana *m,f*, vago,-a *m,f.* 3 *fam* (*incompetent*) **he is a b. of a writer**, como escritor es muy malo. II *adj fam* (*poor quality*) malo,-a, de mala calidad; *(useless)* inútil; *(damaged)* dañado,-a, estropeado,-a. **III** *vi (pt & pp bummed) fam* gorrear; **he bummed a pencil off me,** me gorreó un lápiz. ◆ **bum around** *vi fam* vagabundear, vaguear.

bumble ['bʌmbəl] *vi* **1** *(move)* andar a tropezones. **2** *(speak)* murmurar, refunfuñar.

bumblebee ['bʌmbəlbiː] *n Ent* abejorro *m*.

bumbling ['bʌmblɪŋ] *adj* torpe.

bumf [bʌmf] *n fam see* **bumph.**

bump [bʌmp] **I** *n* **1** *(swelling)* chichón *m*; *(lump)* abolladura *f*, bollo *m*; *(on road etc)* bache *m*. **2** *(blow)* choque *m*, golpe *m*. **3** *(jolt)* sacudida *f*. **II** *vtr* golpear; **to b. one's head,** darse un golpe en la cabeza; **to b. one's head against the door,** dar con la cabeza contra la puerta. **III** *vi* chocar, darse un golpe **(into,** contra). ◆ **bump into** *vtr (meet)* tropezar con, encontrarse a; **fancy bumping into you here!,** ¡qué casualidad encontrarte aquí! ◆ **bump off** *vtr sl* liquidar, matar; **she bumped off her husband and ran off with the money,** mató a su marido y escapó con el dinero. ◆ **bump up** *vtr fam* aumentar.

bumper ['bʌmpə'] **I** *adj* abundante; **a b. crop,** una cosecha abundante; **b. edition,** edición *f* especial. **II** *n Aut* parachoques *m inv*.

bumph [bʌmf] *n fam* papeleo *m*.

bumpkin ['bʌmpkɪn] *n* paleto *m*, palurdo *m*.

bumptious ['bʌmpʃəs] *adj* presuntuoso,-a, engreído,-a, creído,-a.

bumpy ['bʌmpɪ] *adj (bumpier, bumpiest) (road)* lleno,-a de baches; *(journey, flight)* muy zarandeado,-a *or* sacudido,-a.

bun [bʌn] *n* **1** *Culin (bread)* panecillo *m*; *(sweet)* bollo *m*; *(small cake)* magdalena *f*; *fig vulg* **she's got a b. in the oven,** esta preñada. **2** *Hairdr* moño *m*.

bunch [bʌntʃ] **I** *n (of herbs, keys)* manojo *m*; *(of flowers)* ramo *m*, ramillete *m*; *(of grapes)* racimo *m*; *(of people)* grupo *m*; *(gang)* pandilla *f*; **the best of a bad b.,** el único del grupo que se salva. **II** *vi* juntarse, agruparse **(together,** -).

bundle ['bʌndəl] **I** *n (of clothes)* bulto *m*, fardo *m*; *(of papers)* fajo *m*; *(of wood)* haz *m*; *fam* **to be a b. of nerves,** ser un manojo de nervios. **II** *vtr* **1** *(make a bundle)* liar, atar; **to b. up clothes,** meter ropa en un hatillo. **2** *(push)* empujar; **the police bundled the thief into the car,** la policía obligó al ladrón a meterse en el coche. ◆ **bundle off** *vi* despachar, mandar; **he was bundled off to stay with friends,** se lo sacaron de encima mandándolo a casa de unos amigos.

bung [bʌŋ] **I** *n* tapón *m*. **II** *vtr* **1** *fam (throw)* largar, arrojar; **b. it over here,** tíramelo. **2** *fam (put)* meter, poner; **b. it here,** ponlo aquí. ◆ **bung up** *vtr fam* atascar.

bungalow ['bʌŋgələʊ] *n* chalet *m*, chalé *m*.

bunged up ['bʌŋdʌp] *adj fam (pipe)* atascado,-a; *(nose)* tapado,-a; *(person)* acatarrado,-a.

bungle ['bʌŋgəl] *vtr* chapucear, chafallar.

bungler ['bʌŋglə'] *n* chapucero,-a *m, f*.

bungling ['bʌŋglɪŋ] **I** *adj* chapucero,-a; *(inaptitude)* torpe. **II** *n* torpeza *f*.

bunion ['bʌnjən] *n* juanete *m*.

bunk¹ [bʌŋk] *n (bed)* litera *f*.

bunk² [bʌŋk] *n sl (nonsense)* tonterías *fpl*.

bunk³ [bʌŋk] *n* **to do a b.,** pirárselas. ◆ **bunk off** *vi sl (run away)* largarse, abrirse, pirarse; *(play truant)* hacer las campanas.

bunker ['bʌŋkə'] *n* **1** *(coal)* carbonera *f*. **2** *Mil* búnker *m*, refugio *m* subterráneo. **3** *Golf* búnker *m*, trampa *f* de arena.

bunkum ['bʌŋkəm] *n US (nonsense)* tonterías *fpl*.

bunny ['bʌnɪ] *n fam (baby talk)* **b. (rabbit),** conejito *m*. ■ **b. girl,** camarera *f* vestida de conejito.

bunting¹ ['bʌntɪŋ] *n (material)* lanilla *f*; *(flags)* banderas *fpl*; *Naut* empavesada *f*.

bunting² ['bʌntɪŋ] *n Orn* escribano *m*. ■ **cirl b.,** escribano *m* soteño; **corn b.,** escribano *m* triguero; **ortolan b.,** escribano *m* hortelano; **reed b.,** escribano *m* palustre; **rock b.,** escribano *m* montesino.

buoy [bɔɪ] **I** *n Naut* boya *f*. **II** *vtr* **1** sostener, mantener a flote **(up,** a). **2** *Naut* señalar con boyas. ◆ **buoy up** *vtr* alentar, animar; **he did his best to b. her up,** hizo todo lo posible para animarla.

buoyancy ['bɔɪənsɪ] *n* **1** *(of object)* flotabilidad *f*. **2** *Fin (of market, prices)* tendencia *f* alcista. **3** *(optimism)* optimismo *m*.

buoyant ['bɔɪənt] *adj* **1** *(object)* flotante, boyante. **2** *Fin (economy)* con tendencia alcista. **3** *(optimistic)* optimista.

burble ['bɜːbəl] *vi* **1** *(stream)* murmurar; *(baby)* hacer gorgoritos, balbucear. **2** *(talk quickly and unclearly)* farfullar, mascullar; **she burbled her thanks and left,** farfulló su agradecimiento y se fue.

burden ['bɜːdən] **I** *n* **1** *(load)* carga *f*; **beast of b.,** bestia *f* de carga; *Jur* **b. of proof,** carga de la prueba. **2** *fig* carga *f*, peso *m*; **to be a b. to sb,** ser una carga para algn. **II** *vtr* cargar **(with,** con).

burdensome ['bɜːdənsəm] *adj fml* oneroso,-a.

bureau ['bjʊərəʊ] *n (pl bureaus or bureaux)* **1** *(desk)* escritorio *m*, mesa *f*. **2** *(office)* agenda *f*, oficina *f*. **3** *US (chest of drawers)* cómoda *f*. **4** *US Pol* departamento *m* del Estado, agencia *f* del gobierno.

bureaucracy [bjʊə'rɒkrəsɪ] *n* burocracia *f*.

bureaucrat ['bjʊərəkræt] *n* burócrata *mf*.

bureaucratic [bjʊərə'krætɪk] *adj* burocrático,-a.

burgeon ['bɜːdʒən] *vi Bot* brotar, retoñar; *fig Lit* crecer, florecer.

burger ['bɜːgə'] *n fam abbr of* **hamburger.**

burglar ['bɜːglə'] *n (of houses and shops)* ladrón,-ona *m, f*. ■ **b. alarm,** alarma *f* antirrobo.

burglarize ['bɜːgləraɪz] *vtr US* robar.

burglar-proof ['bɜːgləpruːf] *adj* a prueba de robo.

burglary ['bɜːglərɪ] *n* robo *m* con allanamiento de morada.

burgle ['bɜːgəl] *vtr* robar una casa *or* un edificio.

burial ['berɪəl] *n* entierro *m*. ■ **b. ground,** cementerio *m*, camposanto *m*.

Burkina-Faso [bɜːkiːnə'fæsəʊ] *n* Burkina Faso.

burlap ['bɜːlæp] *n Tex* arpillera *f*.

burlesque [bɜː'lesk] **I** *adj* burlesco,-a. **II** *n Lit* género *m* burlesco.

burly ['bɜːlɪ] *adj (burlier, burliest)* fornido,-a, fuerte.

Burma ['bɜːmə] *n* Birmania.

Burmese [bɜː'miːz] **I** *adj* birmano,-a. **II** *n (pl Burmese)* **1** *(person)* birmano,-a *m, f*. **2** *(language)* birmano *m*.

burn [bɜːn] **I** *n* quemadura *f*. **II** *vtr (pt & pp burnt or burned)* quemar; **she burnt her hand,** se quemó la mano; **to be burned to death,** morir carbonizado,-a; *fam* **to b. the midnight oil,** quemarse las cejas. **III** *vi* **1** *(fire)* arder; *(building)* arder, quemarse; *Culin* quemarse. **2** *(lamp, light)* estar encendido,-a. **3** *(of sore)* escocer. ◆ **burn down I** *vtr (building)* incendiar. **II** *vi* incendiarse. ◆ **burn out** *vtr* **1** *(of fire)* extinguirse. **2** *(of machines)* desgastarse, dejar de funcionar. **3** *(of people)* quemarse; **you'll b. yourself out if you carry on working so hard,** si trabajas así acabarás quemado. ◆ **burn up I** *vtr* quemar energía. **II** *vi (rocket, etc)* consumirse completamente.

burner ['bɜːnə'] *n* quemador *m*; *fam fig* **to put sth on the back b.,** dejar algo a un lado, aparcar algo. ■ **Bunsen b.,** quemador *m* Bunsen.

burning ['bɜːnɪŋ] **I** *adj* **1** *(on fire)* incendiado,-a; *(hot)* abrasador,-a. **2** *(passionate)* apasionado,-a, ardiente; **b. desire,** deseo ardiente. **3** *(crucial, intense)* vital; **a b. question,** una cuestión candente. **II** *n (combustion)* combustión *f*; **there's a smell of b.,** huele a quemado.

burnt [bɜ:nt] I *pt & pp see* **burn**. II *adj Culin* quemado,- a; **b. almonds**, almendras *fpl* tostadas.

burnt-out [bɜ:nt'aʊt] *adj* **1** *(volcano, etc)* apagado,-a. **2** *fig (worn-out) (person)* quemado,-a; *(passion)* consumido,-a.

burp[bɜ:p] I *n* eructo *m* II *vi* eructar, regoldar. III *vtr* **to b. a baby,** hacer eructar a un bebé.

burr¹ [bɜ:ʳ] *n Bot* erizo *m*.

burr² [bɜ:ʳ] *n* **1** *(humming)* zumbido *m*. **2** *(pronunciation)* pronunciación *f* fuerte de la r; **she speaks with a West-Country b.,** tiene un marcado acento del West Country.

burrow ['bʌrəʊ] I *n* madriguera *f*; *(for rabbits)* conejera *f*. II *vi* **1** hacer una madriguera; *fig* **to b. into an affair,** escudriñar un asunto. **2** *(search)* hurgar; **she burrowed around in the drawer looking for the other glove,** removió todo el cajón buscando el otro guante.

bursar ['bɜ:səʳ] *n Univ* tesorero,-a *m,f.*

bursary ['bɜ:sərɪ] *n* beca *f.*

burst [bɜ:st] I *n* **1** *(explosion)* estallido *m*, explosión *f*; *(of tyre)* reventón *m*. **2** *(sudden outbreak) (activity, speed)* arranque *m*; *(rage)* arrebato *m*; *(applause)* salva *f*; *Mil* **b. of gunfire,** ráfaga *f* de tiros; **b. of laughter,** carcajada *f*. II *vtr (pt & pp burst) (balloon)* reventar; *fig* **the river b. its banks,** el río se salió de madre. III *vi* **1** *(balloon, tyre, boil, pipe)* reventarse; *(shell)* estallar. **2** *(dam)* romperse. **3** *(enter suddenly)* irrumpir (**into,** en). ◆ **burst into** *vi* empezar a; **to b. into tears,** echarse a llorar, deshacerse en lágrimas; **to b. into laughter,** echarse a reír. ◆ **burst open** *vi* abrirse violentamente. ◆ **burst out** *vi* **1** *(shout)* gritar, exclamar. **2** empezar a; **to b. out laughing,** echarse a reír.

bursting ['bɜ:stɪŋ] *adj* estar lleno,-a a reventar; **the bar was b. with people,** había un montón de gente en el bar; *fam* **to be b. to do sth,** reventar por hacer algo, ansiar hacer algo; **I'm b. to tell you,** reviento si no te lo digo.

Burundi [bə'rʊndɪ] *n* Burundi.

Burundian [bə'rʊndɪən] *adj & n* burundés,-esa *(m,f).*

bury ['berɪ] *vtr (pt & pp buried)* **1** *(inter)* enterrar. **2** *(hide)* esconder, ocultar; **to be buried in thought,** estar absorto en pensamientos; **to b. oneself in the country,** refugiarse en el campo.

bus [bʌs] I *n (pl buses, US busses)* autobús *m, Arg* ómnibus *m, Cuba PR* guagua *f, Mex* camión *m*. ■ **b. conductor,** cobrador *m*, revisor *m*; **b. driver,** conductor,-a *m,f*; **b. station,** estación *f* de autobuses; **b. stop,** parada *f* de autobús. II *vtr (pt & pp bused, US bussed)* llevar *or* trasladar en autobús.

bush [bʊʃ] *n* **1** *Bot (shrub)* arbusto *m*, matorral *m*; *fig* **to beat about the b.,** andarse con rodeos, andarse por las ramas. **2** *Austral* **the b.,** el monte. ■ *fam* **b. telegraph,** radio *f* macuto.

bushed [bʊʃt] *adj fam (exhausted)* molido,-a, reventado,-a.

bushel ['bʊʃəl] *n (measure) GB* = 36,35 litros, *US* = 35,23 litros; *fig* **to hide one's light under a b.,** ser muy modesto.

bushman ['bʊʃmən] *n (pl bushmen)* bosquimán *m*.

bushy ['bʊʃɪ] *adj* espeso,-a, tupido,-a; **b. eyebrows,** cejas tupidas.

business ['bɪznɪs] *n* **1** *(commerce)* negocio *m*, negocios *mpl*; **big b.,** los grandes negocios; **b. is good,** los negocios andan bien; **how's b.?,** ¿cómo andan los negocios?; **to be away on b.,** estar de viaje de negocios; **to do b. with sb,** negociar con algn; **to go into b.,** dedicarse a los negocios. ■ **b. deal,** negocio *m*; **b. hours,** horas *fpl* de oficina, horas *fpl* hábiles *or* laborables; **b. relations,** relaciones *fpl* comerciales; **b. trip,** viaje *m* de negocios. **2** *(firm)* negocio *m*, empresa *f*; **family b.,** empresa familiar. **3** *(matter)* asunto *m*, cuestión *f*; **a dreadful b.,** un asunto lamentable; **I mean b.,** estoy hablando en serio; **it's no b. of mine,** no es asunto mío; **the b. of the day,** el orden del día; **to make it one's b. to ...,** encargarse de ...; **to get down to b.,** ir al grano; **to go about one's b.,** ocuparse de sus asuntos; **what a b.!,** ¡qué lío!; *fam* **like nobody's b.,** muy bien; *fam* **mind your own b.,** no te metas donde no te llaman.

businesslike ['bɪznɪslaɪk] *adj (practical)* práctico,-a, eficiente; *(methodical)* metódico,-a; *(serious)* serio,-a.

businessman ['bɪznɪsmən] *n (pl businessmen)* hombre *m* de negocios, empresario *m*.

businesswoman ['bɪznɪswʊmən] *n (pl businesswomen* ['bɪznɪswɪmɪn]*)* mujer *f* de negocios, empresaria *f.*

busk [bʌsk] *vi GB* cantar *or* tocar música en la calle.

busker ['bʌskəʳ] *n fam* músico,-a *m, f* callejero,-a *or* ambulante.

busman ['bʌsmən] *n fam* **b.'s holiday,** día *m* de fiesta en el que uno tiene que hacer el mismo trabajo que de costumbre.

bust¹ [bʌst] *n* **1** *(of woman)* pecho *m*, busto *m*. **2** *Art (sculpture)* busto *m*.

bust² [bʌst] I *vtr* **1** *fam (damage)* estropear; *(break)* destrozar. **2** *sl (person)* trincar; *(place)* hacer una redada; **to b. sb for possession of drugs,** pescar a algn por posesión ilegal de drogas. II *adj* **1** *fam (burst)* reventado,-a; *(damaged)* estropeado,-a; *(broken)* destrozado,-a. **2** *fam (bankrupt)* **to go b.,** quebrar.

bustard ['bʌstəd] *n Orn* **great b.,** avutarda *f*; **little b.,** sisón *m*.

bustle¹ ['bʌsəl] I *n (activity, noise)* bullicio *m*; animación *f*. II *vi* ir y venir (**about,** -).

bustle² ['bʌsəl] *n arch* polisón *m*.

bustling ['bʌslɪŋ] *adj* bullicioso,-a.

bust-up ['bʌstʌp] *n fam* riña *f*, pelea *f*; **to have a b.,** *(fight)* pelearse; *(break a relationship)* romper.

busy ['bɪzɪ] I *adj* **1** *(person)* ocupado,-a, atareado,-a; *(day)* lleno,-a; *(life)* ajetreado,-a; *(street)* concurrido,-a, bullicioso,-a, **to be as b. as a bee,** estar ocupadísimo; **to keep oneself b.,** mantenerse ocupado. **2** *esp US Tel (line)* ocupado,-a; **b. signal,** señal *f* de comunicando. II *vtr (pt & pp busied)* occuparse, dedicarse; **to b. oneself doing sth,** ocuparse en hacer algo.

busybody ['bɪzɪbɒdɪ] *n* entrometido,-a *m,f.*

but [bʌt] I *conj* **1** pero; **b. yet,** pero, a pesar de todo; **poor b. honest,** pobre pero honrado. **2** *(after negative)* sino: **not two b. three,** no dos sino tres; **she's not Spanish b. Portuguese,** no es española sino portuguesa. **3** que; **there's no doubt b. he's guilty,** no hay duda de que es culpable; **we can b. try,** al menos podemos intentarlo. **4 b. for her we would have drowned,** si no hubiera sido por ella, nos habríamos ahogado. II *adv* no más que, sólo, solamente; **had we b. known,** si lo hubiéramos sabido, de haberlo sabido; **he is b. a child,** no es más que un niño. III *prep* salvo, excepto, menos; **everyone b. her,** todos menos ella; **he's anything b. handsome,** es todo menos guapo; **the last b. one,** el penúltimo. IV **buts** *npl* peros *mpl*; **ifs and b.,** pegas *fpl*; **stop all your ifs and b.!,** ¡no pongas más pegas!; **no b.,** no hay peros que valgan.

butane ['bju:teɪn] *n Chem* butano *m*. ■ **b. gas,** gas *m* butano.

butch [bʊtʃ] *adj* **1** *fam offens (woman)* hombruno,-a. **2** *(man) fam* macho.

butcher ['bʊtʃəʳ] I *n* carnicero,-a *m,f*; *fig* carnicero,-a; **b.'s (shop),** carnicería *f*. II *vtr (animals)* matar; *(people)* matar, asesinar.

butcher's ['bʊtʃəz] *n sl* mirada; **let's have a b.,** déjame ver.

butchery ['bʊtʃərɪ] *n* **1** *(work)* carnicería *f*. **2** *(killing)* matanza *f*, carnicería *f.*

butler ['bʌtləʳ] *n* mayordomo *m.*

butt¹ [bʌt] *n* **1** *(end)* extremo *m*; *(of rifle)* culata *f*; *(of cigarette)* colilla *f*. **2** *(target)* blanco *m*; **he was the b. of all the jokes,** era el blanco de todas las bromas. **3** *US sl (bottom)* culo *m.*

butt² [bʌt] I *n (blow with head)* cabezazo *m*. II *vtr* **1** *(strike with head or horns)* topetar. **2** *(shove)* **to b. your way somewhere,** abrirte paso. ◆ **butt in** *vi* entrar en la conversación.

butt³ [bʌt] *n (barrel)* tonel *m.*

butter ['bʌtə'] **I** n mantequilla f; **he always looks as if b. wouldn't melt in his mouth,** siempre se hace la mosquita muerta. ■ **b. dish,** mantequera f. **II** vtr (bread) untar pan con mantequilla; (vegetables) aderezar con mantequilla. ◆ **butter up** vtr dar coba a algn.

buttercup ['bʌtəkʌp] n Bot ranúnculo m, botón m de oro.

butterfingered ['bʌtəfɪŋgəd] adj fam torpe, patoso,-a.

butterfingers ['bʌtəfɪŋgəz] n fam manazas mf inv.

butterfly ['bʌtəflaɪ] n **1** Ent mariposa f; fig **to have butterflies,** tener los nervios de punta, estar muy nervioso. **2** Swimming mariposa f.

buttermilk ['bʌtəmɪlk] n suero m de la leche.

buttock ['bʌtək] n nalga f; **buttocks,** nalgas fpl, trasero m; (of horse) grupa f.

button ['bʌtən] **I** n **1** Sew botón m. **2** (on machine, etc) botón m, pulsador m; **press the b.,** apriete el botón. **3** US (badge) chapa f. **II** vtr **to b. (up),** abrocharse.

buttonhole ['bʌtənhəʊl] **I** n **1** Sew ojal m. **2** (flower) flor f que se lleva en el ojal. **II** vtr fig (detain) enganchar a.

buttress ['bʌtrɪs] **I** n **1** Arch contrafuerte m. ■ **flying b.,** arbotante m. **2** (support) apoyo m, sostén m. **II** vtr Arch apuntalar, reforzar; fig reforzar, apoyar.

butty ['bʌtɪ] n fam (sandwich) bocata f.

buxom ['bʌksəm] adj (woman) (big breasts) pechugona; (robust) macizorra, rolliza.

buy [baɪ] **I** n (purchase) compra f; **a good b.,** una ganga. **II** vtr (pt & pp bought) **1** comprar; **she bought that car from a neighbour,** compró ese coche a un vecino. **2** (bribe) comprar, sobornar. **3** sl (believe) tragar, aceptar, creer; **he won't b. it,** no colará. ◆ **buy off** vtr sobornar, comprar. ◆ **buy out** vtr adquirir la parte de; **he borrowed money to b. out his partner,** pidió dinero para adquirir la parte de negocio de su socio. ◆ **buy up** vtr comprar en grandes cantidades.

buyer ['baɪə'] n comprador,-a m,f; Com **it's a b.'s market,** es un mercado que favorece al comprador. ■ **chief b.,** jefe m de compras.

buzz [bʌz] **I** n **1** (of bee) zumbido m; (of conversation) rumor m, runruneo m. **2** fam (telephone call) telefonazo m; **to give sb a b.,** hacer una llamada a algn. **3** sl **skating gives me a real b.,** esto de patinar me pone a cien. **II** vtr fam (telephone) dar un toque. **III** vi (bee, room, head) zumbar; fam **b. off!,** ¡lárgate!

buzzard ['bʌzəd] n Orn ratonero m común, águila f ratonera; US (vulture) buitre m.

buzzer ['bʌzə'] n zumbador m.

buzzing ['bʌzɪŋ] n zumbido m.

by [baɪ] **I** prep **1** (indicating agent) por; **composed by Bach,** compuesto,-a por Bach; **it was built b. her father,** fue construido por su padre. **2** (via) por; **he left by the back door,** salió por la puerta trasera. **3** (manner) por; **by car,** en coche; **by chance,** por casualidad; **by heart,** de memoria; **by oneself,** solo,-a; **by rail,** en tren; **made by hand,** hecho a mano; **you can obtain a ticket by filling in the compon,** puede conseguir una entrada llenando el cupón. **4** (amount) por; **little by little,** poco a poco; **they are sold by the dozen,** se venden por docenas; **to be paid by the hour,** cobrar por horas. **5** (extent) **by far,** con mucho; **he won by a foot,** ganó por un pie. **6** (beside) al lado de, junto a; **side by side,** juntos, uno al lado del otro; **sit by me,** siéntate a mi lado. **7** (past) **to walk by a building,** pasar por delante de un edificio. **8** (not later than) para; **by now,** ya; **by then,** para entonces; **we have to be there by nine,** tenemos que estar allí para las nueve. **9** (during) de; **by day,** de día; **by night,** de noche. **10** (in an oath) por; **by God!,** ¡por Dios!; **she swears by herbal remedies,** tiene una fe ciega en las hierbas medicinales. **11** Math por; **to multiply six by four,** multiplicar seis por cuatro. **12** (according to) según; **to go by the rules,** actuar según las reglas. **13** (origin) English **by blood,** de sangre inglesa; **he had two children by his first wife,** tuvo dos hijos con su primera esposa. **14** (rate) **bit by bit,** poco a poco; **day by day,** día a día, día tras día. **15** (quoting something) con, por; **what do you mean by that?,** ¿qué quieres decir con eso?; **by 'Lesley' I assumed she meant Lesley Dent,** ∶ ∍ ʋuse que por 'Lesley' quería decir Lesley Dent. **16** (in measurements) por; **the room is twenty metres by ten,** la habitación hace veinte metros por diez. **II** adv (past) **to go by,** pasar; **she just walked by,** pasó de largo. **2 by and by,** con el tiempo.

bye [baɪ] n fam ¡adiós!, ¡hasta luego! **2 by the b.** por cierto, a propósito.

bye-bye ['baɪbaɪ] n fam ¡adiós!, ¡hasta luego!

by-election ['baɪɪlekʃən] n Pol elección f parcial.

bygone [:qxbaɪɡɒn] **I** adj pasado,-a. **II bygones** npl let **b. be b.,** lo pasado pasado está.

by-law ['baɪlɔː] n ley f municipal.

bypass ['baɪpɑːs] **I** n **1** (road) carretera f de circunvalación. **2** Med **b. surgery,** cirugía f de by-pass. **II** vtr evitar; **let's b. Bristol, as we are in a hurry,** como tenemos prisa no entramos en Bristol; **she bypassed the normal procedures by writing directly to the director,** escribió al director desestimando el sistema usual.

by-product ['baɪprɒdʌkt] n Chem Ind derivado m, subproducto m; fig consecuencia f.

byre [baɪə'] n arch establo m para vacas.

by-road ['baɪrəʊd] n carretera f secundaria.

bystander ['baɪstændə'] n espectador,-a m,f, mirón,-a m,f.

byte [baɪt] n Comput byte m, octeto m.

by-way ['baɪweɪ] n carretera f secundaria.

byword ['baɪwɜːd] n **1** (perfect example) sinónimo m; **the film became a b. for modernity,** la película se convirtió en un sinónimo de modernidad. **2** (common saying) decir m.

Byzantine [bɪ'zæntaɪn, baɪ'zæntaɪn] adj & n bizantino,-a (m,f).

C

C, c [siː] n **1** (the letter) C, c f. **2** Mus do m.

C1 abbr of **Celsius,** Celsius, C. **2** abbr of **Centigrade,** centígrado m, C.

c1 abbr of **cent(s),** céntimo(s) m(pl). **2** abbr of **century,** siglo m, s. **3** abbr of **circa** (about, approximately), hacia, h. **4** abbr of **copyright,** propiedad f literaria, copyright m, c.

c/a abbr of **current account,** cuenta f corriente, c/c.

cab [kæb] n US taxi m; **by c.,** en taxi. ■ **c. driver,** taxista mf.

cabaret ['kæbəreɪ] n cabaret m; **is there a c.?,** ¿hay espectáculo?

cabbage ['kæbɪdʒ] n col f, repollo m, berza f; **red c.,** (col f) lombarda f. ■ Ent **c. white,** mariposa f de la col.

cabbie ['kæbɪ] n US fam taxista mf.

cabin ['kæbɪn] n **1** (hut) choza f; **log c.,** cabaña f. **2** Naut camarote m. ■ **c. cruiser,** yate m de motor. **3** (of lorry, plane) cabina f.

cabinet ['kæbɪnɪt] n **1** Furn (gen) armario m; (glass-fronted) vitrina f; **filing c.,** archivador m; **kitchen c.,** armario de cocina. **2** (in government) gabinete m ministerial, consejo m de ministros; **c. meeting,** consejo m de ministros; **shadow c.,** portavoces mpl de la oposición.

cable ['keɪbəl] **I** *n* **1** cable *m*. ■ **c. car,** funicular *m*; **c. TV,** televisión *f* por cable. **2** *(message)* cable *m*, cablegrama *m*. **II** *vtr & vi* cablegrafiar, telegrafiar.

caboodle [kə'buːdəl] *n fam* **the whole c.,** y toda la pesca.

cacao [kə'kɑːəʊ] *n Bot* cacao *m*.

cache [kæʃ] *n* depósito *m* secreto.

cack-handed [kæk'hændɪd] *adj fam* torpe.

cackle ['kækəl] **I** *vi* (hen) cacarear; *(person)* tener la risa tonta. **II** *n (of hen)* cacareo *m*; *(of person)* risa *f* tonta; *fam* **cut the c.,** corta el rollo.

cactus ['kæktəs] *n (pl cactuses or cacti* ['kæktaɪ]*) Bot* cactus *m*.

CAD [kæd] *abbr of* **computer-aided** *or* **-assisted design** *or* **draughting,** diseño *m* con ayuda de ordenador.

cad [kæd] *n GB fam* canalla *m*.

cadaverous [kə'dævərəs] *adj* cadavérico,-a.

caddie ['kædɪ] *n Golf* cadi *m*. ■ **c. car, c. cart,** carrito *m* de golf.

caddy ['kædɪ] *n GB* cajita *f* or lata *f* donde se guarda el té.

cadence ['keɪdəns] *n* cadencia *f*.

cadenza [ke'denzə] *n* cadencia *f*.

cadet [kə'det] *n Mil* cadete *m*. ■ **c. school,** escuela *f* militar.

cadge [kædʒ] *fam* **I** *vtr (cigarettes etc)* gorronear; **to c. a lift from sb,** conseguir que algn te lleve en coche; **to c. money from sb,** darle un sablazo a algn. **II** *vi (gen)* gorronear; *(involving money)* dar un sablazo, sablear.

cadger ['kædʒər] *n GB* gorrón,-ona *m,f*.

cadmium ['kædmɪəm] *n Chem* cadmio *m*.

Caesarean [siː'zeərɪən] *n Med* cesárea *f*; **she had a c.,** le hicieron una cesárea. ■ **C. section,** operación *f* cesárea.

café ['kæfeɪ] *n* cafetería *f*.

cafeteria [kæfɪ'tɪərɪə] *n* cafetería *f*, autoservicio *m*.

caffeine ['kæfiːn] *n* cafeína *f*; **c.-free,** descafeinado,-a.

caftan ['kæftæn] *n see* **kaftan**.

cage [keɪdʒ] **I** *n* **1** *(for bird etc)* jaula *f*. **2** *Min* ascensor *m*. **II** *vtr* enjaular; *fig* **to feel caged in,** sentirse enjaulado,-a, tener claustrofobia.

cagey ['keɪdʒɪ] *adj (cagier, cagiest) fam* reservado,-a, disimulado,-a.

cagoule [kə'guːl] *n (garment)* canguro *m*.

cahoots [kə'huːts] *npl US fam* **to be in c. with sb,** haber confabulado con algn.

cairn [keən] *n* **1** *(monument)* monumento *m* formado de piedras apiladas. **2** *(boundary marker)* hito *m* formado por piedras.

Cairo ['kaɪrəʊ] *n* (el) Cairo.

cajole [kə'dʒəʊl] *vtr* engatusar; **he cajoled me into lending him money,** me engatusó para que le prestara dinero.

cajolery [kə'dʒəʊlərɪ] *n* engatusamiento *m*.

cake [keɪk] **I** *n* **1** *Culin* pastel *m*, tarta *f*, torta *f*; *fam fig* **it's a piece of c.,** está chupado; *fam fig* **to sell like hot cakes,** venderse como rosquillas; *prov* **you can't have your c. and eat it,** tiene que ser una cosa u otra. ■ **birthday c.,** pastel *m* de cumpleaños; **c. shop,** pastelería *f*; **fish c.,** medallón *m* or croqueta *f* de pescado; **fruit c.,** plum cake *m*; **sponge c.,** bizcocho *m*. **2** *(of soap)* pastilla *f*. **II** *vi (mud)* endurecerse; **caked with ...,** cubierto,-a de ... .

CAL [kæl] *abbr of* **computer-aided** *or* **-assisted learning,** instrucción *f* or aprendizaje *m* con ayuda de ordenador.

cal *abbr of* **calorie(s),** caloría(s) *f (pl)*, cal.

calamine ['kæləmaɪn] *n* calamina *f*.

calamitous [kə'læmɪtəs] *adj* calamitoso,-a.

calamity [kə'læmɪtɪ] *n* calamidad *f*.

calcification [kælsɪfɪ'keɪʃən] *n* calcificación *f*.

calcify ['kælsɪfaɪ] **I** *vtr (pt & pp calcified)* calcificar. **II** *vi* calcificarse.

calcium ['kælsɪəm] *n Chem* calcio *m*.

calculate ['kælkjʊleɪt] **I** *vtr* calcular; **it was calculated to upset the plans,** se planeó con la intención de estropear los planes. **II** *vi* contar **(on,** con).

calculated ['kælkjʊleɪtɪd] *adj* deliberado,-a, premeditado,-a.

calculating ['kælkjʊleɪtɪŋ] *adj* **1 c. machine,** calculador *m*, calculadora *f*. **2** *pej (person)* interesado,-a.

calculation [kælkjʊ'leɪʃən] *n* cálculo *m*.

calculator ['kælkjʊleɪtər] *n* calculador *m*, calculadora *f*. ■ **pocket c.,** calculadora *f* de bolsillo.

calculus ['kælkjʊləs] *n* **1** *(pl calculuses) Math* cálculo *m* matemático. **2** *(pl calculi* ['kælkjʊlaɪ]*) Med* cálculo *m*.

caldron ['kɔːldrən] *n see* **cauldron**.

calendar ['kælɪndər] *n* calendario *m*. ■ **c. year,** año *m* civil.

calf[1] [kɑːf] *n (pl calves* [kɑːvz]*) Zool* **1** *(of cattle)* becerro,-a *m, f*, ternero,-a *m, f*; **a cow in c.,** una vaca preñada. **2** *(of other animals)* cría *f*.

calf[2] [kɑːf] *n (pl calves* [kɑːvz]*) Anat* pantorrilla *f*.

calfskin ['kɑːfskɪn] *n* piel *f* de becerro.

caliber ['kælɪbər] *n US see* **calibre**.

calibrate ['kælɪbreɪt] *vtr (gun)* calibrar; *(thermometer)* graduar.

calibre ['kælɪbər] *n* **1** *(of gun)* calibre *m*. **2** *fig (of person)* calibre *m*.

calico ['kælɪkəʊ] *n (pl calicos or calicoes) Tex* calicó *m*.

Californian [kælɪ'fɔːnɪən] *adj & n* californiano,-a *(m,f)*.

calipers ['kælɪpəz] *npl US see* **callipers**.

calisthenics [kælɪs'θenɪks] *n US see* **callisthenics**.

call [kɔːl] **I** *vtr* **1** *(gen)* llamar; **c. me at eight o'clock,** llámame a las ocho; **to c. sb a liar,** llamar a algn embustero; **to c. sb names,** poner verde a algn; **what's he called?,** ¿cómo se llama?; *fam* **let's c. it a day,** vamos a dar esto por terminado, vamos a dejarlo; *fam* **let's c. it £1,** dejémoslo en una libra. **2** *(summon) (meeting etc)* convocar; **to c. sth to mind,** traer algo a la memoria. **3** *Tel* **to c. sb (up),** llamar a algn (por teléfono); **c. 999 in an emergency,** en caso de emergencia llamar al 999. **4** *(expose)* **to c. sb's bluff,** devolver la pelota a algn. **II** *vi* **1** *(gen)* llamar; **to c. out for help,** gritar pidiendo socorro *or* ayuda. **2** *Tel* llamar; **who's calling?,** ¿de parte de quién? **3** *(visit)* pasar; **to c. at sb's (house),** pasar por casa de algn; **to c. for sth/sb,** pasar a recoger algo/a algn; **to c. (in) on sb,** ir a ver a algn. **4** *(trains)* parar, hacer parada; **this train calls at every station,** este tren para en todas las estaciones. **5** *(require)* **to c. for,** *(food)* pedir; *(measures, courage)* exigir; **that wasn't called for,** eso no estaba justificado. **III** *n* **1** *(gen)* llamada *f*, grito *m*; **a c. for help,** un grito de socorro; **give me a c. when dinner is ready,** llámame cuando esté lista la comida. ■ *Rad* **c. sign,** indicativo *m*; *Theat* **curtain c.,** salida *f* (a escena para recibir aplausos). **2** *(of bird)* reclamo *m*. **3** *(short visit)* visita *f*; **to pay** *or* **make a c. on sb,** visitar a *or* ir a ver a algn; *fam* **to pay a c.,** cambiar el agua a las aceitunas. ■ *Naut* **port of c.,** puerto *m* de escala. **4** *Tel* **(phone) c.,** llamada *f* (telefónica *or* por teléfono). ■ **c. box,** cabina *f* telefónica; **trunk c.,** conferencia *f* (interurbana). *Fin (demand)* solicitud *f*; **money payable on c.,** dinero *m* (pagadero) a la vista; *fig* **I have too many calls on my time,** tengo demasiadas obligaciones. **6** *Med* **to be on c.,** estar de guardia. **7** *(need)* motivo *m*; **there's no c. for you to worry,** no hay motivo para que te preocupes. ◆ **call away** *vtr* **to be called away on business,** tener que ausentarse por motivos de trabajo. ◆ **call back I** *vtr* **1** *(phone in reply)* llamar; *(phone again)* llamar otra vez. **2** *Pol* cesar. **II** *vi (phone in reply)* llamar; *(phone again)* llamar otra vez; *(visit again)* volver. ◆ **call in I** *vtr* **1** *(doctor, police)* llamar. **2** *(coins etc)* retirar de circulación; **to c. in a loan,** exigir el pago de un empréstito. **II** *vi* **1** *(visit)* ir a ver, visitar. **2** *Naut* hacer escala (**at,** en). ◆ **call off** *vtr* **1** *(strike etc)* suspender. **2** *(dog)* llamar. ◆ **call on** *vtr* **1** *(visit)* visitar, ir a ver a. **2** *to c.* **on** *or* **upon sb for support,** recurrir *or* acudir a algn en busca de apoyo. ◆ **call out I** *vtr* **1** *(shout)* gritar. **2** *(summon) (troops)* hacer intervenir, sacar a la calle; *(doctor)* hacer venir; *(workers)* llamar a la huelga. **II** *vi* gritar; **to c. out for sth,** pedir algo en voz alta. ◆ **call up** *vtr* **1** *Tel* llamar. **2** *Mil* llamar a filas, reclutar.

callboy ['kɔːlbɔɪ] *n Theat* traspunte *m.*

caller ['kɔːləʳ] *n* **1** *(visitor)* visitante *mf,* visita *f.* **2** *Tel* persona *f* que llama.

calligrapher [kə'lɪgrəfəʳ] *n* calígrafo,-a *m,f.*

calligraphy [kə'lɪgrəfɪ] *n* caligrafía *f.*

calling ['kɔːlɪŋ] *n* vocación *f,* llamada *f.*

callipers ['kælɪpəz] *npl* **1** *Tech* calibrador *m sing.* **2** *Med* aparato *m sing* ortopédico.

callisthenics [kælɪs'θenɪks] *n* gimnasia *f* sueca.

callous ['kæləs] *adj* insensible, duro,-a. ◆ **callously** *adv* con dureza.

callousness ['kæləsnɪs] *n* insensibilidad *f,* dureza *f.*

call-up ['kɔːlʌp] *n Mil* llamamiento *m* a filas, reclutamiento *m.*

callus ['kæləs] *n (pl calluses) Med* callo *m.*

calm [kɑːm] **I** *adj* **1** *(still) (weather)* en calma; *(sea)* en calma, sereno,-a. **2** *(relaxed)* sosegado,-a, tranquilo,-a; **keep c.!,** ¡tranquilo,-a!, ¡calma! **II** *n* **1** *(of weather, sea)* calma *f.* **2** *(tranquility)* serenidad *f,* sosiego *m,* tranquilidad *f.* **III** *vtr* calmar, sosegar, tranquilizar. **IV** *vi* **to c. (down),** calmarse, sosegarse, tranquilizarse. ◆ **calmly** *adv* con calma, tranquilamente.

calmness ['kɑːmnɪs] *n* calma *f,* sosiego *m,* tranquilidad *f.*

Calor Gas® ['kæləgæs] *n* (gas *m*) butano *m.*

calorie *n,* **calory** ['kælərɪ] *n* caloría *f.*

calorific [kælə'rɪfɪk] *adj* calorífico,-a.

calumny ['kæləmnɪ] *n (gen)* calumnia *f; Jur* difamación *f.*

calvary ['kælvərɪ] *n Rel* calvario *f.*

calve [kɑːv] *vi* parir (un becerro).

calves [kɑːvz] *npl* see **calf¹, calf².**

calypso [kə'lɪpsəʊ] *n (pl calypsos) Mus* calipso *m.*

cam [kæm] *n Tech* leva *f.*

camaraderie [kæmə'rɑːdərɪ] *n* compañerismo *m.*

camber ['kæmbəʳ] *n* combadura *f,* convexidad *f.*

Cambodia [kæm'bəʊdɪə] *n* Camboya.

Cambodian [kæm'bəʊdɪən] *adj & n* camboyano,-a *(m,f).*

came [keɪm] *pt see* **come.**

camel ['kæməl] **I** *n* **1** *Zool* camello,-a *m,f.* **2** *(colour)* color *m* leonado. **II** *adj (colour)* leonado,-a.

camelhair ['kæməlheəʳ] *n* pelo *m* de camello.

camellia [kə'miːlɪə] *n Bot* camelia *f.*

cameo ['kæmɪəʊ] *n (pl cameos)* camafeo *m.*

camera ['kæmərə] *n* **1** *Phot* cámara *f or* máquina *f* fotográfica; *Cin TV* cámara *f; Jur* **in c.,** a puerta cerrada.

cameraman ['kæmərəmən] *n (pl cameramen)* cámara *mf.*

Cameroon [kæmə'ruːn] *n* Camerún.

Cameroonian [kæmə'ruːnɪən] *adj & n* camerunés,-esa *(m,f).*

camomile ['kæməmaɪl] *n Bot* camomila *f,* manzanilla *f;* **c. tea,** (infusión *f* de) manzanilla *f.*

camouflage ['kæməflɑːʒ] **I** *n* camuflaje *m.* **II** *vtr* camuflar.

camp¹ [kæmp] **I** *n* campamento *m;* **to break** *or* **strike c.,** levantar el campamento. ■ *Mil* **army c.,** campamento militar; **c. bed,** cama *f* plegable; **c. follower,** vivandero,-a; **c. site,** camping *m,* campamento *m;* **holiday c.,** colonia *f* de verano *or* de vacaciones. **II** *vi* **to c. (out),** acampar; **to go camping,** ir de camping.

camp² [kæmp] *adj fam* **1** *(effeminate)* afeminado,-a; *(affected)* amanerado,-a. **2** *(homosexual)* marica. **3** *(style)* cursi.

campaign [kæm'peɪn] **I** *n* campaña *f;* **election c.,** campaña electoral; **publicity c.,** campaña publicitaria. **II** *vi* **to c. for sb/sth,** hacer una campaña en pro de *or* en favor de algn/de algo.

campaigner [kæm'peɪnəʳ] *n (gen)* defensor,-a *m,f* (**for,** de); *Pol* militante *mf.*

camper ['kæmpəʳ] *n* **1** *(person)* campista *mf.* **2** *US (vehicle)* caravana *f.*

campfire ['kæmpfaɪəʳ] *n* fogata *f.*

camphor ['kæmfəʳ] *n Chem* alcanfor *m.*

camping ['kæmpɪŋ] *n* **c. ground, c. site,** camping *m,* campamento *m.*

campus ['kæmpəs] *n (pl campuses)* campus *m,* ciudad *f* universitaria.

camshaft ['kæmʃɑːft] *n Tech* árbol *m* de levas.

can¹ [kæn] *v aux (pt could)* **1** *(be able to)* poder; **he could have come,** podría haber venido; **I'll phone you as soon as I c.,** te llamaré en cuanto pueda; **she can't do it,** no puede hacerlo. **2** *(know how to)* saber; **I c. drive,** sé conducir; **they couldn't speak French,** no sabían francés. **3** *(be permitted to)* poder; **he cannot** *or* **can't go out tonight,** no le dejan salir esta noche. **4** *(be possible or likely)* poder; **she could have forgotten,** puede (ser) que la haya olvidado; **they can't be very poor,** no deben ser muy pobres; **what c. it be?,** ¿qué será?, ¿qué podrá ser? **5** *(not translated)* **c. I have two coffees, please,** dos cafés, por favor; **you can't be serious!,** ¡no hablarás en serio!

can² [kæn] **I** *n* **1** *(container) (of oil etc)* bidón *m.* ■ *US* **trash c.,** cubo *m* de la basura; **watering c.,** regadera *f.* **2** *US (tin)* lata *f,* bote *m;* **a c. of beer/beans,** una lata de cerveza/judías; *fam fig* **to carry the c.,** pagar el pato. **II** *vtr (pt & pp canned)* **1** *(fish, fruit)* envasar, enlatar. **2** *US fam* desestimar, pasar de; **they canned the whole idea,** decidieron olvidarlo todo.

Canada ['kænədə] *n* Canadá.

Canadian [kə'neɪdɪən] *adj & n* canadiense *(mf).*

canal [kə'næl] *n Anat Geog* canal *m.*

canary [kə'neərɪ] **I** *n Orn* canario *m.* **II** *adj (colour)* **c. yellow,** amarillo vivo.

Canary Islands [kə'neərɪaɪləndz] *npl* (Islas *fpl*) Canarias *fpl.*

cancel ['kænsəl] **I** *vtr (pt & pp cancelled, US canceled)* **1** *(train, contract)* cancelar; *Com* anular. **2** *(revoke) (permission)* retirar; *(decree)* revocar. **3** *(stamp)* matasellar. **II** *vi* **to c. out,** anular, contrarrestar; **they c. each other out,** se anulan mutuamente.

cancellation [kænsɪ'leɪʃən] *n (gen)* cancelación *f; Com* anulación *f.*

cancer ['kænsəʳ] *n* **1** *Med* cáncer *m;* **breast c.,** cáncer de mama; **c. research,** cancerología *f.* **2** *Astrol Astron* **C.,** Cáncer *m; Geog* **tropic of C.,** trópico *m* de Cáncer.

cancerous ['kænsərəs] *adj* canceroso,-a.

candelabra [kændɪ'lɑːbrə] *n* candelabro *m.*

candid ['kændɪd] *adj* franco,-a, sincero,-a; **he's being less than c.,** oculta algo. ■ **c. camera,** cámara *f* indiscreta. ◆ **candidly** *adv* con franqueza.

candidacy ['kændɪdəsɪ] *n* candidatura *f.*

candidate ['kændɪdeɪt, 'kændɪdɪt] *n* **1** *(in election, for job)* candidato,-a *m,f.* **2** *(in examination)* opositor,-a *m,f.*

candidature ['kændɪdətʃəʳ] *n see* **candidacy.**

candied ['kændɪd] *adj Culin* escarchado,-a, confitado,-a.

candle ['kændəl] *n (gen)* vela *f; (in church)* cirio *m;* **to light/blow out a c.,** encender/apagar una vela; *fig* **to burn the c. at both ends,** trabajar a marchas forzadas; *fam* **she can't hold a c. to him,** ella no tiene ni punto de comparación con él. ■ **c. grease,** sebo *m.*

candlelight ['kændəllaɪt] *n* luz *f* de vela; **by c.,** a la luz de las velas.

Candlemas ['kændəlməs] *n Rel* candelaria *f*.

candlestick ['kændəlstɪk] *n (gen)* candelero *m*, palmatoria *f*; *(in church)* cirial *m*.

candlewick ['kændəlwɪk] *n* 1 *Tex* tela *f* afelpada. 2 *(wick)* pábilo *m*, mecha *f*.

candour, *US* **candor** ['kændəʳ] *n* franqueza *f*, sinceridad *f*.

candy ['kændɪ] *n US* caramelo *m*. ■ **c. store,** confitería *f*.

candyfloss ['kændɪflɒs] *n GB (sweet)* algodón *m*.

candy-striped ['kændɪstraɪpt] *adj* de rayas multicolores.

cane [keɪn] **I** *n* 1 *Bot* caña *f*. ■ **c. sugar,** azúcar *m* de caña; **raspberry c.,** frambueso *m*. 2 *Furn* mimbre *m*, junco *m*. ■ **c. chair,** silla *f* de mimbre. 3 *(walking stick)* bastón *m*; *(for punishment)* palmeta *f*. **II** *vtr* castigar con la palmeta.

canine ['keɪnaɪn] *adj* 1 *Zool* canino,-a. 2 *Dent* **c. tooth,** colmillo *m*.

caning ['keɪnɪŋ] *n* castigo *m* con la palmeta.

canister ['kænɪstəʳ] *n* bote *m*.

canker ['kæŋkəʳ] *n Med* chancro *m*; *fig* cáncer *m*.

canned [kænd] *adj* 1 enlatado,-a, envasado,-a; **c. beer,** cerveza enlatada; **c. foods,** conservas *fpl*. 2 *fam pej sl* **music,** música *f* grabada. 3 *sl (drunk)* mamado,-a.

cannery ['kænərɪ] *n* fábrica *f* de conservas.

cannibal ['kænɪbəl] *adj & n* caníbal *(mf)*, antropófago,-a *(m,f)*.

cannibalize ['kænɪbəlaɪz] *vtr (machinery)* desmontar para utilizar de nuevo las piezas.

canning ['kænɪŋ] *n* enlatado *m*. ■ *US* **c. factory,** fábrica *f* de conservas; **c. industry,** industria *f* conservera.

cannon ['kænən] **I** *n (pl cannons or cannon)* 1 *(in aircraft)* cañón *m* antiaéreo. 2 *Hist* cañón *m*; *fig iron* **c. fodder,** carne *f* de cañón. 3 *Bill* carambola *f*. **II** *vi* chocar **(into,** contra).

cannonball ['kænənbɔːl] *n* bala *f* de cañón.

cannot ['kænɒt, kæ'nɒt] *v aux see* **can**[1].

canoe [kə'nuː] *n (gen)* canoa *f*; *Sport* piragua *f*.

canon ['kænən] *n Rel (decree, rule)* canon *m*.

canopy ['kænəpɪ] *n* 1 *(over head)* dosel *m*; *(ceremonial)* palio *m*. 2 *(awning)* toldo *m*. 3 *Av* carlinga *f*.

cant [kænt] *n* 1 *(platitudes)* hipocresías *fpl*. 2 *(jargon)* jerga *f*.

can't [kɑːnt] *v aux see* **can**[1].

Cantab [kæn'tæb] *abbr of* **Cantabrigiensis** (of Cambridge University), de la Universidad de Cambridge.

Cantabrigian [kæntə'brɪdʒɪən] *adj & n* nativo,-a *(m,f)* *or* habitante *(mf)* de Cambridge.

cantankerous [kæn'tæŋkərəs] *adj* intratable, irascible.

canteen [kæn'tiːn] *n* 1 *(restaurant)* cantina *f*. 2 *(set of cutlery)* juego *m* de cubiertos. 3 *(flask)* cantimplora *f*.

canter ['kæntəʳ] *Equit* **I** *n* medio galope *m*. **II** *vi* ir a medio galope.

cantilever ['kæntɪliːvəʳ] *n Archit* voladizo *m*. ■ **c. bridge,** puente *m* con voladizos.

canvas ['kænvəs] *n* 1 *Tex* lona *f*. 2 *(painting)* lienzo *m*. 3 **under c.,** *(in tent)* bajo lona; *Naut* con velamen desplegado.

canvass ['kænvəs] *vi* 1 *Pol* hacer propaganda electoral. 2 *Com* hacer promoción, buscar clientes.

canvasser ['kænvəsəʳ] *n* 1 *Pol* persona *f* que hace propaganda electoral. 2 *Com* promotor,-a *m, f* de un producto.

canyon ['kænjən] *n Geog* cañón *m*; **the Grand C.,** el Gran Cañón.

cap [kæp] **I** *n* 1 *(men's)* gorro *m*; *fig* **c. in hand,** con el sombrero en la mano; *prov* **if the c. fits, wear it,** el que se pica ajos come *or* si te das por aludido,-a peor para ti. 2 *(soldier's)* gorra *f*; *(academic)* birrete *m*; *(nurse's)* cofia *f*;

(cardinal's) capelo *m*. 3 *GB Sport* **to get** *or* **win a c. for England,** ser seleccionado,-a para el equipo de Inglaterra. 4 *(cover) (of pen)* capuchón *m*; *(of bottle)* chapa *f*. 5 *Mech Geog* casquete *m*. 6 *(for toy pistol)* fulminante *m*. 7 *Mat* **(Dutch) c.,** diafragma *m*. **II** *vtr (pt & pp capped)* 1 *(hills etc)* coronar; *(bottle)* poner la chapa a; *fig* **to c. it all,** para colmo; *fam* **to c. sb's joke,** contar un chiste todavía mejor. 2 *GB Sport* seleccionar.

capability [keɪpə'bɪlɪtɪ] *n* habilidad *f*; **it was beyond my capabilities,** estaba fuera de mis posibilidades.

capable ['keɪpəbəl] *adj* 1 *(skilful)* competente, hábil. 2 *(able)* capaz **(of, de).**

capacious [kə'peɪʃəs] *adj* espacioso,-a.

capacitor [kə'pæsɪtəʳ] *n Elec* condensador *m* gerente.

capacity [kə'pæsɪtɪ] *n* 1 *(of container)* capacidad *f*, cabida *f*; *Aut* **engine c.,** cilindrada *f*. 2 *(of bus, theatre)* capacidad *f*; **a seating c. of 300,** capacidad *or* cabida para 300 personas; **there was a c. crowd,** estaba totalmente lleno de gente; **to be filled to c.,** estar al completo 3 *(ability)* capacidad *f* **(for,** de); **at full c.,** a pleno rendimiento. 4 *(position)* puesto *m*; **in her c. as manageress,** en su calidad de gerente.

cape[1] [keɪp] *n (garment)* capa *f*.

cape[2] [keɪp] *n Geog* cabo *m*, promontorio *m*. ■ **C. Horn,** Cabo *m* de Hornos; **C. Town,** Ciudad del Cabo; **C. Verde,** Cabo Verde; **C. Verdean,** caboverdiano,-a *m,f*.

caper[1] ['keɪpəʳ] **I** *n* 1 *(jump)* brinco *m*. 2 *(prank)* travesura *f*. **II** *vi (jump about)* brincar.

caper[2] ['keɪpəʳ] *n* 1 *Culin* alcaparra *f*. 2 *Bot* alcaparro *m*.

capercaillie [kæpə'keɪljɪ] *n Orn* urogallo *m*.

capillary [kə'pɪlərɪ] *adj & n* capilar *(m)*.

capital[1] ['kæpɪtəl] *n* 1 *(town)* capital *f*. 2 *Fin* capital *m*; *fig* **to make c. (out) of sth,** sacar provecho de algo. ■ **c. expenditure,** inversión *f* de capital; *GB* **c. transfer tax,** impuesto *m* sobre sucesiones. 3 *(letter)* mayúscula *f*. **II** *adj* 1 *(city)* capital. 2 *Jur (punishment)* capital. 3 *(very serious)* grave. 4 *(primary)* primordial, prioritario,-a. 5 *(letter)* mayúscula; **c. C,** C mayúscula.

capital[2] ['kæpɪtəl] *n Archit* capitel *m*.

capitalism ['kæpɪtəlɪzəm] *n* capitalismo *m*.

capitalist ['kæpɪtəlɪst] *adj & n* capitalista *(mf)*.

capitalize ['kæpɪtəlaɪz] **I** *vi Fin* capitalizar; *fig* **to c. on sth,** sacar provecho o beneficio de algo. **II** *vtr (letter)* escribir con mayúscula.

capitulate [kə'pɪtjuleɪt] *vi* capitular.

capo ['keɪpəʊ] *n (pl capos) Mus* traste *m*.

capon ['keɪpən] *n* capón *m*.

caprice [kə'priːs] *n* capricho *m*.

capricious [kə'prɪʃəs] *adj* caprichoso,-a.

Capricorn ['kæprɪkɔːn] *n Astrol Astron* Capricornio *m*; *Geog* **tropic of C.,** trópico *m* de Capricornio.

capsicum ['kæpsɪkəm] *n Bot* pimiento *m*.

capsize [kæp'saɪz] **I** *vtr Naut* hacer zozobrar. **II** *vi* zozobrar.

capstan ['kæpstən] *n Naut* cabrestante *m*.

capsule ['kæpsjuːl] *n* cápsula *f*. ■ **space c.,** cápsula *f* espacial.

Capt *Mil Naut abbr of* **Captain,** Capitán *m*, Cap.

captain ['kæptɪn] **I** *n* 1 *Naut Av* capitán *m*. 2 *Sport* capitán,-ana *m,f*. **II** *vtr* capitanear.

captaincy ['kæptɪnsɪ] *n* capitanía *f*.

caption ['kæpʃən] *n* 1 *(under picture)* leyenda *f*. 2 *Cin* subtítulo *m*.

captivate ['kæptɪveɪt] *vtr* cautivar.

captivating ['kæptɪveɪtɪŋ] *adj* encantador,-a, seductor,-a.

captive ['kæptɪv] **I** *n* cautivo,-a *m,f*. **II** *adj* 1 cautivo,-a; **to hold sb c.,** poner *or* mantener a algn en cautiverio. 2 *fig* fascinado,-a; **a c. audience,** un auditorio que escucha sin querer.

captivity [kæp'tɪvɪtɪ] *n* cautiverio *m*.

capture ['kæptʃəʳ] I *vtr* 1 *(fugitive)* capturar, apresar; *Mil (town)* tomar. 2 *Com (market)* acaparar. 3 *fig (mood etc)* captar. II *n* 1 *(seizure) (of fugitive)* captura *f*, apresamiento *m*; *(of town)* toma *f*. 2 *(person)* prisionero,-a *m,f*.

car [kɑːʳ] *n* 1 *Aut* coche *m*, automóvil *m*, *Am* carro *m*; **racing c.**, coche de carreras. ■ **c. ferry**, transbordador *m* para coches; *GB* **c. park**, parking *m*, aparcamiento *m*; **c. wash**, túnel *m* de lavado. 2 *GB Rail* coche *m*, vagón *m*. ■ **dining c.**, coche *m* restaurante; **sleeping c.**, coche *m* cama.

carafe [kə'ræf, kə'rɑːf] *n* garrafa *f*.

caramel ['kærəmel] *n Culin* 1 azúcar *m* quemado; **c. custard**, flan *m*. 2 *(sweet)* caramelo *m*.

carat, *US* **karat** ['kærət] *n* kilate *m*; **24-c. gold**, oro de 24 kilates.

caravan ['kærəvæn] *n* 1 *(vehicle)* remolque *m*, caravana *f*. 2 *(in the desert)* caravana *f*.

caravel ['kærəvel] *n Naut* carabela *f*.

caraway ['kærəweɪ] *n* 1 *Bot* alcaravea *f*. 2 *Culin* **c. seed**, carví *m*.

carbohydrate [kɑː'bəʊ'haɪdreɪt] *n* 1 hidrato *m* de carbono, carbohidrato *m*. 2 **carbohydrates**, *(in diet)* féculas *fpl*.

carbolic [kɑː'bɒlɪk] *adj Chem* **c. acid**, fenol *m*.

carbon ['kɑːbən] *n Chem* carbono *m*. ■ **c. copy**, copia *f* hecha con papel carbón; *fig* copia *f* exacta; **c. dioxide**, bióxido *m* or dióxido *m* de carbono; **c. paper**, papel *m* carbón.

carbonated ['kɑːbəneɪtɪd] *adj (drink)* efervescente.

carbonize ['kɑːbənaɪz] *vtr* carbonizar.

carboy ['kɑːbɔɪ] *n* bombona *f*.

carbuncle ['kɑːbʌŋkəl] *n* 1 *(gem)* granate *m*. 2 *Med* carbunco *m*.

carburettor [kɑːbju'retəʳ], *US* **carburetor** ['kɑːbjureɪtəʳ] *n Aut* carburador *m*.

carcass ['kɑːkəs] *n* 1 res *f* muerta; *(at butcher's)* res *f* abierta en canal. 2 *Archit Naut* armazón *m*. 3 *fam pej* cadáver *m*.

carcinogenic [kɑːsɪnə'dʒenɪk] *adj Med* cancerígeno,-a, carcinógeno,-a.

card¹ [kɑːd] *n* 1 *(gen)* tarjeta *f*; *(piece of cardboard)* cartulina *f*; **birthday/visiting c.**, tarjeta de cumpleaños/ de visita. 2 *(in file)* ficha *f*; *(identity, membership)* carnet *m*; *Ind fig* **to get one's cards**, ser despedido,-a. ■ **c. index**, fichero *m*; *Com* **credit c.**, tarjeta *f* de crédito. 3 *Cards* **game of cards**, partida *f* (de cartas); **pack of cards**, baraja *f*, naipes *mpl*, cartas *fpl*; **(playing) c.**, naipe *m*, carta *f*; *fig* **on the cards**, *US* **in the cards**, previsto; *fig* **to lay one's cards on the table**, poner las cartas boca arriba; *fig* **to play one's cards right**, jugar bien sus cartas. ■ **c. table**, mesa *f* de juego; **c. trick**, truco *m* con las cartas. 4 *fam fig* **he's a real c.**, este tío es la monda.

card² [kɑːd] *vtr (wool)* cardar.

Card *Rel abbr of* **Cardinal**, Cardenal *m*, Card.

cardamom ['kɑːdəməm] *n*, **cardamon** ['kɑːdəmən] *n Bot* cardamono *m*.

cardboard ['kɑːdbɔːd] *n* cartón *m*. ■ **c. box**, caja *f* de cartón; **c. cutout**, recortable *m*.

cardiac ['kɑːdɪæk] *adj* cardíaco,-a; **c. arrest**, paro cardíaco.

cardigan ['kɑːdɪɡən] *n* rebeca *f*, chaqueta *f* de punto.

cardinal ['kɑːdɪnəl] I *n Rel* cardenal *m*. II *adj* cardinal; **c. numbers**, números *mpl* cardinales.

cardiologist [kɑːdɪ'ɒlədʒɪst] *n Med* cardiólogo,-a *m,f*.

cardiology [kɑːdɪ'ɒlədʒɪ] *n Med* cardiología *f*.

cardsharp ['kɑːdʃɑːp] *n*, **cardsharper** ['kɑːdʃɑːpəʳ] *n* fullero,-a *m,f*, tramposo,-a *m,f* (en el juego de cartas).

care [keəʳ] I *vi* 1 *(be concerned)* preocuparse *(about, por)*, importar; **he cares very much about social issues**, le preocupan mucho los asuntos sociales; **I don't c. (at all)**, no me importa (en absoluto); **she only cares about money**, sólo le interesa el dinero; *fam* **for all I c.**, me trae sin cuidado; *fam* **he couldn't c. less**, le importa un bledo. 2 *(like, want)* gustar; **would you c. to go to the theatre tonight?**, ¿te gustaría ir al teatro esta noche? II *n* 1 *(attention, protection)* cuidado *m*, atención *f*; *(on letter)* **'c. of ...'**, 'al cuidado de ...'; **medical c.**, asistencia *f* médica; *Jur* **to take (a child) into c.**, poner (a un niño) bajo la custodia de una institución; **to take c. of**, *(child etc)* cuidar; *(business, matters)* ocuparse de, hacerse cargo de; **under the doctor's c.**, al cuidado del médico; *sl* **I'll take c. of him**, ya me encargaré de él. 2 *(carefulness)* cuidado *m*; *(on parcel)* **'handle with c.'**, 'frágil'; **take c.**, *(be careful)* ten cuidado; *(as farewell)* ¡cuídate!; **take c. not to spill your tea**, ten cuidado de no derramar el té. 3 *(worry)* preocupación *f*; **free of c.**, sin preocupaciones; **he hasn't a c. in the world**, no hay nada que le preocupe. ◆ **care for** *vtr* 1 *(look after)* cuidar; **well cared for**, bien cuidado,-a. 2 *(like, want)* gustar, interesar; **I don't c. much for television**, la televisión no me interesa mucho; **she really cares for him**, él le importa mucho; **would you c. for a coffee?**, ¿te apetece un café?

career [kə'rɪəʳ] I *n (profession)* carrera *f*; **a c. in medicine**, una carrera en medicina. II *vi* correr a toda velocidad.

carefree ['keəfriː] *adj* despreocupado,-a.

careful ['keəfʊl] *adj (painstaking)* cuidadoso,-a; *(cautious)* prudente; **a c. examination of sth**, un examen minucioso de algo; **be c.!**, ¡ojo!, ¡cuidado!; **be c. not to drop it**, procura no dejarlo caer; **c. with one's money**, ahorrador,-a; *pej* tacaño,-a; **to be c.**, tener cuidado; **you can't be too c.**, hay que andar con mucho cuidado. ◆ **carefully** *adv (painstakingly)* cuidadosamente; *(cautiously)* con cuidado, con precaución.

careless ['keəlɪs] *adj* descuidado,-a, despreocupado,-a; *(about clothes, appearance)* desaliñado,-a; *(driving etc)* negligente; **a c. mistake**, un descuido. ◆ **carelessly** *adv* descuidadamente, a la ligera.

carelessness ['keəlɪsnɪs] *n* descuido *m*, despreocupación *f*.

caress [kə'res] I *n* caricia *f*. II *vtr* acariciar.

caretaker ['keəteɪkəʳ] *n (in school, business, premises)* bedel,-a *m, f*; *(in block of flats)* portero,-a *m, f*. ■ **c. government**, gobierno *m* provisional.

careworn ['keəwɔːn] *adj* agobiado,-a (de preocupaciones).

cargo ['kɑːɡəʊ] *n (pl* **cargoes** *or* **cargos)** carga *f*, cargamento *m*. ■ *Naut* **c. boat**, buque *m* de carga, carguero *m*.

Caribbean [kærɪ'bɪən, *US* kə'rɪbɪən] *adj* caribe, caribeño,-a; **the C. (Sea)**, el Mar de las Antillas.

caribou ['kærɪbuː] *n Zool* caribú *m*.

caricature ['kærɪkətjʊəʳ] I *n* caricatura *f*. II *vtr* caricaturizar.

caricaturist ['kærɪkətjʊərɪst] *n* caricaturista *mf*.

caries ['keərɪiːz] *n inv Dent* caries *f*.

caring ['keərɪŋ] *adj* solícito,-a, dedicado,-a.

carmine ['kɑːmaɪn] I *n* carmín *m*. II *adj* carmín, carmíneo,-a.

carnage ['kɑːnɪdʒ] *n fig* carnicería *f*.

carnal ['kɑːnəl] *adj* carnal.

carnation [kɑː'neɪʃən] *n Bot* clavel *m*.

carnival ['kɑːnɪvəl] *n* carnaval *m*.

carnivore ['kɑːnɪvɔːʳ] *n Zool* carnívoro,-a *m,f*.

carnivorous [kɑː'nɪvərəs] *adj Zool* carnívoro,-a.

carol ['kærəl] *n Mus* villancico *m*.

carouse [kə'raʊz] *vi* ir de juerga.

carousel [kærə'sel] *n US* tiovivo *m*.

carp¹ [kɑːp] *n (pl* **carp** *or* **carps)** *(fish)* carpa *f*.

carp² [kɑːp] *vi* refunfuñar, criticar.

Carpathians [kɑː'peɪθɪənz] *npl* (Montes *mpl*) Cárpatos *mpl*.

carpenter ['kɑːpɪntəʳ] n carpintero,-a m,f.

carpentry ['kɑːpɪntrɪ] n carpintería f.

carpet ['kɑːpɪt] I n alfombra f; **fitted c.**, moqueta f; fig **to roll out the red c. for sb**, acoger a algn con la máxima ceremonia; fam **to be on the c.**, tener que aguantar una reprimenda. ■ **c. slippers**, zapatillas fpl. II vtr alfombrar; fig **carpeted with flowers**, cubierto,-a de flores; fam fig **to c. sb**, echar una bronca a algn.

carpetbagger ['kɑːpɪtbæɡəʳ] n US Pol candidato,-a m,f electoral no oriundo,-a (de la zona que pretende representar).

carpeting ['kɑːpɪtɪŋ] n alfombrado m; **wall-to-wall c.**, moqueta f.

carport ['kɑːpɔːt] n cobertizo m para coches.

carriage ['kærɪdʒ] n 1 (horse-drawn) carruaje m; Rail vagón m, coche m; (of gun) cureña f; (of typewriter) carro m. 2 (of goods) porte m, transporte m. ■ **c. forward**, cobro m al destinatario; **c. free**, franco m de porte. 3 (bearing) porte m.

carriageway ['kærɪdʒweɪ] n GB carril m, calzada f; **dual c.**, carretera f de dos carriles en cada sentido.

carrier ['kærɪəʳ] n 1 (company, person) transportista mf; (on bicycle) portaequipajes m inv. ■ Av **aircraft c.**, portaaviones m inv; GB **c. bag**, bolsa f de plástico or de papel; **c. pigeon**, paloma f mensajera. 2 Med portador,-a m,f.

carrion ['kærɪən] n carroña f.

carrot ['kærət] n zanahoria f.

carroty ['kærətɪ] adj fam (hair) rojizo,-a.

carry ['kærɪ] I vtr (pt & pp **carried**) I (gen) llevar; (money, passport, gun) llevar (encima); Com (goods, load) transportar; (electricity) conducir; Archit (load) sostener; **she carries herself very nicely**, tiene buen porte; fig **to c. a joke too far**, llevar una broma demasiado lejos. 2 (have, bear) llevar; (stock) tener; (responsibility, penalty) conllevar, implicar; Press **the newspaper carried the story on the front page**, el periódico publicó la noticia en primera página; fig **that argument doesn't c. any weight**, ese argumento se cae por sí solo. 3 Math (in multiplication etc) llevar. 4 Parl (vote etc) ganar; **the motion was carried**, se aprobó la moción. 5 Med (disease) ser portador,-a de; (in pregnancy) **she's carrying twins**, está embarazada de gemelos. 6 fig (spread) extender; **he carried his style of music to the West**, extendió su estilo musical a Occidente. II vi (sound, voice) oírse, tener alcance. ◆ **carry away** vtr llevarse; **to get carried away**, exaltarse; fam desmadrarse. ◆ **carry forward** vtr Com llevar a la columna or página siguiente; **carried forward**, suma y sigue. ◆ **carry off** vtr (prize) llevarse; fam **to c. it off** (well), salir airoso,-a. ◆ **carry on** I vtr continuar; (conversation) mantener; (business) llevar, dirigir. II vi 1 continuar, seguir adelante; **c. on!**, ¡continúa!; ¡adelante! 2 fam (make a fuss) hacer una escena, exaltarse; **don't c. on about it**, ¡no te enrolles! 3 fam (have liaison) **to c. on with sb**, estar liado,-a con algn. ◆ **carry out** vtr (plan, work) llevar a cabo, realizar; (test) verificar; (threat) cumplir; (repair) hacer. ◆ **carry through** vtr (complete) completar, finalizar.

carryall ['kærɔːl] n US bolsa f de viaje.

carrycot ['kærɪkɒt] n cuna f portátil or plegable.

carry-on ['kærɪ'ɒn] n GB fam follón m, lío m; **what a c.-on!**, ¡menudo lío!

carsick ['kɑːsɪk] adj mareado,-a (en el coche); **he always gets c.**, siempre se marea en coche.

cart [kɑːt] I n (horse-drawn) carro m; (handcart) carretilla f; prov **to put the c. before the horse**, empezar la casa por el tejado. II vtr I carretear, acarrear. 2 fam **to c. about**, llevar; **she spends Saturdays carting the children about**, se pasa los sábados llevando y trayendo a los niños. ◆ **cart off** vtr fam llevarse a la fuerza.

carte blanche [kɑːt'blɑːntʃ] n carta f blanca.

cartel [kɑː'tel] n Ind Fin cártel m.

carthorse ['kɑːthɔːs] n caballo m de tiro.

Carthaginian [kɑːθə'dʒɪnɪən] adj & n cartaginense (mf).

cartilage ['kɑːtɪlɪdʒ] n Anat cartílago m.

cartload ['kɑːtləʊd] n carretada f.

cartographer [kɑː'tɒɡrəfəʳ] n cartógrafo,-a m,f.

cartography [kɑː'tɒɡrəfɪ] n cartografía f.

carton ['kɑːtən] n 1 (of cream, yoghurt) bote m; **a c. of cigarettes**, un cartón de tabaco.

cartoon [kɑː'tuːn] n 1 viñeta f; (strip) tira f cómica, historieta f. 2 Art cartón m. 3 (animated) dibujos mpl animados.

cartoonist [kɑː'tuːnɪst] n caricaturista mf, dibujante mf.

cartridge ['kɑːtrɪdʒ] n 1 Mil cartucho m; **blank c.**, cartucho sin bala or de fogueo. ■ **c. belt**, canana f, cartuchera f. 2 (for pen) recambio m. ■ **c. paper**, papel m guarro. 3 (for camera) cartucho m.

cartwheel ['kɑːtwiːl] n 1 rueda f de carreta. 2 Gymn voltereta f; **to turn cartwheels**, hacer volteretas.

carve [kɑːv] vtr 1 (wood) tallar; (stone, metal) cincelar, esculpir. 2 (meat) trinchar.

carver ['kɑːvəʳ] n 1 Art (of wood) tallista mf; (of stone) escultor,-a m,f. 2 (knife) cuchillo m de trinchar.

cascade [kæs'keɪd] I n cascada f. II vi caer a torrentes.

case¹ [keɪs] n 1 (gen) caso m; **a c. in point**, un buen ejemplo; **in any c.**, en todo or en cualquier caso, de todas formas; **in c. of doubt**, en caso de duda; **just in c.**, por si acaso; **to make out a c. for sth**, exponer los argumentos en favor de algo. 2 Med caso m; **a c. of whooping cough**, un caso de tosferina. ■ **c. history**, historial m clínico. 3 Jur causa f, proceso m; **the c. for the defence/prosecution**, la defensa/acusación. ■ **c. law**, ley f de casos, jurisprudencia f. 4 Ling caso m; **the genitive c.**, el (caso) genitivo. 5 fam (person) caso m; **he's a c.**, es (todo) un caso.

case² [keɪs] I n 1 (suitcase) maleta f; (small) estuche m; (soft) funda f. ■ **cigarette c.**, cigarrera f; Furn **glass c.**, vitrina f; **pillow c.**, funda f (de almohada); **spectacle c.**, funda f de gafas; **watch c.**, estuche m de reloj. 2 (box) caja f; **a c. of wine**, una caja de botellas de vino. 3 Print Typ caja f; **lower c.**, caja baja, minúscula f; **upper c.**, caja alta, mayúscula f. II vtr sl **to c. the joint**, reconocer el terreno.

casement ['keɪsmənt] n ventana f de bisagras.

caseworker ['keɪswɜːkəʳ] n asistente,-a m,f social.

cash [kæʃ] I n dinero m efectivo, metálico m; **hard c.**, metálico; **petty c.**, dinero para gastos menores; **to be short of c.**, tener poco dinero; **to pay at the c. desk**, pagar en (la) caja; **to pay c.**, pagar al contado or en efectivo. ■ **c. desk**, caja f; Fin **c. flow**, movimiento m or flujo m de efectivo; **c. on delivery**, entrega f contra reembolso; **c. register**, caja f registradora. II vtr (cheque) cobrar, hacer efectivo,-a. ◆ **cash in** I vtr fam fig **to c. in on sth**, sacar provecho de algo. II vtr hacer efectivo,-a. ◆ **cash up** vi GB rendir cuentas.

cash-and-carry [kæʃən'kærɪ] adj & adv de venta al por mayor y pago al contado.

cashew ['kæʃuː] n **c. (nut)**, anarcado m.

cashier¹ [kæ'ʃɪəʳ] n cajero,-a m,f.

cashier² [kæ'ʃɪəʳ] vtr Mil dar de baja a.

cashmere ['kæʃmɪəʳ] I n Tex cachemira f. II adj de cachemira.

casino [kə'siːnəʊ] n (pl **casinos**) casino m.

cask [kɑːsk] n tonel m, barril m.

casket ['kɑːskɪt] n 1 (small box) cofre m. 2 (coffin) ataúd m.

Caspian ['kæspɪən] adj **C. Sea**, Mar Caspio.

cassava [kə'sɑːvə] n Bot mandioca f.

casserole ['kæsərəʊl] n 1 (dish) cacerola f. 2 Culin guisado m; **chicken c.**, pollo a la cazuela.

cassette [kæ'set] n casete f. ■ **c. recorder**, casete m.

cassock ['kæsək] n Rel sotana f.

cast [kɑːst] **I** *vtr* (*pt & pp* **cast**) **1** (*throw*) (*net, fishing line*) echar, arrojar; (*shadow, light*) proyectar; (*dice*) tirar; **to c. a glance at sb/sth**, volver la mirada hacia algn/algo; *Naut* **to c. anchor**, echar el ancla; **to c. a spell on sb**, hechizar a algn; *fig* **to c. one's eye over sth**, echar una ojeada a algo. **2** (*of vote*) emitir. **3** (*of snake*) **to c. its skin**, mudar la piel. **4** *fig* (*set, put*) poner; **to c. doubts on sth**, poner algo en duda; **to c. suspicion on sb**, levantar sospechas sobre algn; *fig* **the die is c.**, la suerte está echada. **5** *Tech* (*of metal*) moldear, vaciar. ■ **c. iron**, hierro *m* fundido *or* colado. **6** *Theat* (*play*) hacer el reparto de; **to c. an actor for the part of ...**, asignar a un actor el papel de ... . **II** *n* **1** (*throw*) lanzamiento *m*. **2** *Tech* (*mould*) molde *m*; (*product*) pieza *f*. **3** *Med* (*plaster*) **c.**, escayola *f*; **to have a c. in one's eye**, tener un defecto ocular. **4** *Theat* reparto *m*; **c. list**, reparto *m*, lista *f* de actores. ◆ **cast about for, cast around for** *vi* buscar, andar buscando. ◆ **cast away** *vtr Naut* **to be c. away**, naufragar. ◆ **cast off I** *vtr* (*clothes*) desechar, deshacerse de. **II** *vi* **1** *Knit* cerrar los puntos. **2** *Naut* soltar (las) amarras. ◆ **cast on** *vi Knit* montar los puntos.

castanets [kæstə'nets] *npl* castañuelas *fpl*.

castaway ['kɑːstəweɪ] *n* náufrago,-a *m,f*.

caste [kɑːst] *n* casta *f*.

caster ['kɑːstə'] *n* **1 c. sugar**, azúcar *m* molido muy fino. **2** (*wheel*) ruedecilla *f*.

castigate ['kæstɪɡeɪt] *vtr fml* castigar.

Castile [kæ'stiːl] *n* Castilla.

Castilian [kæ'stɪljən] **I** *adj* castellano,-a. **II** *n* **1** (*person*) castellano,-a *m,f*. **2** (*language*) **C. (Spanish)**, castellano *m*.

casting ['kɑːstɪŋ] *n* **1** *Tech* vaciado *m*. **2** *Theat* reparto *m* de papeles. **3 c. vote**, voto *m* de calidad.

cast-iron ['kɑːstaɪən] *adj* de hierro fundido *or* colado; *fig* irrefutable.

castle ['kɑːsəl] **I** *n* **1** castillo *m*; *fig* **castles in the air**, castillos en el aire. **2** *Chess* torre *f*. **II** *vi Chess* enrocar.

cast-off ['kɑːstɒf] *adj* desechado,-a.

castoffs ['kɑːstɒfs] *npl* ropa *f* sing vieja.

castor[1] ['kɑːstə'] *n Zool* castor *m*. ■ **c. oil**, aceite *m* de ricino.

castor[2] ['kɑːstə'] *n see* **caster**.

castrate [kæ'streɪt] *vtr* castrar.

castration [kæ'streɪʃən] *n* castración *f*.

casual ['kæʒjʊəl] *adj* **1** (*meeting etc*) casual, fortuito,-a. **2** (*worker*) ocasional, temporero,-a. **3** (*clothes, shoes*) (de) sport. **4** (*unimportant*) casual, de paso; **a c. remark**, un comentario sin importancia. **5** (*not serious*) despreocupado,-a, informal; **he has a c. attitude to life**, le trae todo sin cuidado. ◆ **casually** *adv* de paso, sin darle importancia.

casualty ['kæʒjʊəltɪ] *n* **1** *Mil* baja *f*; **casualties**, pérdidas *fpl*. **2** (*injured*) herido,-a *m, f*; *Med* **c. (department)**, departamento *m* de traumatología.

CAT [siːeɪ'tiː] *GB abbr of* **College of Advanced Technology**, ≈ colegio *m* de formación profesional.

cat [kæt] *n Zool* gato,-a *m,f*; **the c. family**, los felinos; *fig* **to be like a c. on a hot tin roof** *or* **on hot bricks**, estar sobre ascuas, estar como un flan; *fig* **to let the c. out of the bag**, descubrir el pastel; *fig* **to play c. and mouse with sb**, jugar con algn al gato y el ratón; *fig* **to put the c. among the pigeons**, meter los perros en danza; *fam* **there isn't room to swing a c.**, no cabe ni un alfiler; *fam fig* **it's raining cats and dogs**, llueve a cántaros. ■ **c. burglar**, ladrón *m* que escala edificios para robar.

cataclysm ['kætəklɪzəm] *n* cataclismo *m*.

catacombs ['kætəkuːmz] *npl* catacumbas *fpl*.

Catalan ['kætələn] **I** *adj* catalán,-ana. **II** *n* **1** (*person*) catalán,-ana *m,f*. **2** (*language*) catalán *m*.

catalogue, *US* **catalog** ['kætəlɒɡ] **I** *n* catálogo *m*. **II** *vtr* catalogar.

Catalonia [kætə'ləʊnɪə] *n* Cataluña.

Catalonian [kætə'ləʊnɪən] *adj* catalán,-ana.

catalyst ['kætəlɪst] *n* catalizador *m*.

catamaran [kætəmə'ræn] *n Naut* catamarán *m*.

catapult ['kætəpʌlt] **I** *n* **1** (*toy*) tiragomas *m inv*, tirador *m*. **2** (*for aircraft*) catapulta *f*. **II** *vtr* (*aircraft*) catapultar. **III** *vi* salir disparado,-a.

cataract ['kætərækt] *n Med* catarata *f*.

catarrh [kə'tɑː'] *n Med* catarro *m*.

catastrophe [kə'tæstrəfɪ] *n* catástrofe *f*.

catastrophic [kætə'strɒfɪk] *adj* catastrófico,-a.

catcall ['kætkɔːl] *n* (*in theatre etc*) silbido *m*, silbo *m*.

catch [kætʃ] **I** *vtr* (*pt & pp* **caught**) **I** (*grasp, take, capture*) coger, alcanzar; (*fish*) pescar; (*mouse etc*) coger, atrapar; (*thief*) coger; **the bullet c. her in the heart**, la bala le alcanzó en el corazón; **to c. fire**, prender fuego, incendiarse, encenderse; **to c. hold of**, agarrar, echar mano a; **to c. one's finger in a door**, pillarse el dedo en una puerta; **to c. sb's eye**, captar la atención de algn; **to c. sight of**, entrever; *fam* **you'll c. it!**, ¡te vas a ganar una bronca! **2** (*surprise*) pillar, sorprender; **to c. sb doing sth**, pillar *or* sorprender a algn haciendo algo; **to get caught in a storm/the traffic**, pillarle a uno una tormenta/el tráfico. **3** (*train, bus*) coger, agarrar, tomar; (*person*) pillar, dar con; **I caught him as he was leaving the office**, lo pillé saliendo de la oficina. **4** (*understand, hear*) entender, oír; **I didn't quite c. that**, no lo he entendido bien. **5** *Med* **to c. a cold**, coger un resfriado; **to c. one's breath**, (*hold*) contener la respiración; (*recover*) recuperar el aliento. **II** *vi* (*sleeve etc*) engancharse (**on**, en); (*fire*) encenderse. **III** *n* **1** (*of ball*) parada *f*; (*of fish*) presa *f*, captura *f*. **2** (*on door*) pestillo *m*. **3** (*drawback*) pega *f*; **c. question**, pega *f*; **c.-22**, círculo *m* vicioso. **4** (*slogan*) **c. phrase**, slogan *m*. **5** (*game*) juego *m* de pelota. ◆ **catch at** *vtr* agarrarse de, asirse a. ◆ **catch on** *vi fam* **1** (*become popular*) ganar popularidad. **2** (*understand*) entender, caer en la cuenta. ◆ **catch out** *vtr fam* **to c. sb out**, pillar a algn cometiendo una falta. ◆ **catch up** *vi* **1** (*reach*) **to c. up (with) sb**, alcanzar a algn. **2** (*make up for lost ground*) (*with news*) ponerse al corriente (**on**, de); **to c. up on sleep**, recuperar el sueño perdido; **to c. up with work**, ponerse al día de trabajo.

catcher ['kætʃə'] *n Sport* receptor,-a *m,f* (de pelota).

catching ['kætʃɪŋ] *adj* **1** (*disease*) contagioso,-a. **2** (*attractive*) atractivo,-a, llamativo,-a.

catchment ['kætʃmənt] *n* captación *f*; **c. area of a hospital/school**, zona *f* de captación de un hospital/una escuela.

catchword ['kætʃwɜːd] *n* slogan *m*, lema *m*, reclamo *m*.

catchy ['kætʃɪ] *adj* (**catchier, catchiest**) *fam* (*tune*) pegadizo,-a.

catechism ['kætɪkɪzəm] *n Rel* catequismo *m*.

categoric(al) [kætɪ'ɡɒrɪk(əl)] *adj* categórico,-a.

categorize ['kætɪɡəraɪz] *vtr* categorizar, clasificar.

category ['kætɪɡərɪ] *n* categoría *f*.

cater ['keɪtə'] *vi* **1** (*at wedding etc*) proveer comida. **2 to c. for**, (*taste, needs*) atender a; **a TV channel that caters for minority groups**, un canal de televisión dirigido a los grupos minoritarios.

caterer ['keɪtərə'] *n* proveedor,-a *m,f*.

catering ['keɪtərɪŋ] *n* (*gen*) abastecimiento *m* (de comidas por encargo); (*on plane*) catering *m*.

caterpillar ['kætəpɪlə'] *n* **1** *Ent* oruga *f*. **2 c. (tractor)**, tractor *m* de oruga.

caterwaul ['kætəwɔːl] *vi* maullar, berrear.

catfish ['kætfɪʃ] *n* (*fish*) barbo *m*.

catgut ['kætɡʌt] *n* **1** *Mus* cuerda *f* de tripa. **2** *Med* catgut *m*.

Cath *abbr of* **Catholic**, católico,-a *m,f*.

catharsis [kə'θɑːsɪs] *n* catarsis *f*.

cathedral [kə'θiːdrəl] *n* catedral *f*; **c. city**, ciudad *f* catedralicia.

Catherine wheel ['kæθrɪnwi:l] *n (firework)* rueda *f*.

catheter ['kæθɪtəʳ] *n Med* catéter *m*.

cathode ['kæθəʊd] *n* cátodo *m*. ■ **c. ray,** rayo *m* catódico; **c.-ray tube,** tubo *m* de rayos catódicos.

Catholic ['kæθəlɪk] *adj & n Rel* católico,-a *(m,f)*.

catholic ['kæθəlɪk] *adj (universal)* católico,-a, liberal; **we have c. tastes,** nos gusta todo.

Catholicism [kə'θɒlɪsɪzəm] *n Rel* catolicismo *m*.

catkin ['kætkɪn] *n Bot* candelilla *f*, amento *m*.

catnap ['kætnæp] *n* siesta *f* corta, cabezadilla *f*.

Catseye® ['kætsaɪ] *n GB* catafaro *m*.

catsuit ['kætsu:t] *n (clothing)* mono *m*.

cattle ['kætəl] *npl* ganado *m* vacuno; *(roadsign)* '**c. crossing'**, 'paso de ganado'. ■ **c. market,** mercado *m* de ganado; **c. shed,** cobertizo *m* para ganado; **c. show,** feria *f* de ganado.

cattle-grid ['kætəlgrɪd] *n* reja *f*, rejilla *f*.

cattleman ['kætəlmən] *n (pl cattlemen)* ganadero *m*.

catty ['kætɪ] *adj (cattier, cattiest) fam (remark)* malintencionado,-a; *(person)* malicioso,-a, criticón,-ona.

catwalk ['kætwɔ:k] *n* pasarela *f*.

Caucasian [kɔ:'keɪzɪən] *adj & n* **1** *(from the Caucasus)* caucasiano,-a *(m,f)*. **2** *(by race)* caucásico,-a *(m,f)*.

Caucasus ['kɔ:kəsəs] *n* Cáucaso *m*.

caucus ['kɔ:kəs] *n (pl caucuses) Pol* comité *m* central, ejecutiva *f*.

caught [kɔ:t] *pt & pp see* **catch.**

cauldron ['kɔ:ldrən] *n* caldero *m*.

cauliflower ['kɒlɪflaʊəʳ] *n* **1** *Bot* coliflor *f*. **2** *Box* **c. ear,** oreja *f* deformada por los golpes.

causality [kɔ:'zælɪtɪ] *n* causalidad *f*.

cause [kɔ:z] I *n* **1** *(origin)* causa *f*; **the causes of poverty,** las causas de la pobreza. **2** *(reason)* motivo *m*, razón *f*; **she has no c. for complaint** *or* **to complain,** no tiene motivos para quejarse; **to have good c. for doing sth,** tener razón en hacer algo, tener motivo para hacer algo. **3** *(purpose)* causa *f*; **for a good c.,** por una buena causa. **4** *Jur* pleito *m*, causa *f*. II *vtr* causar; **to c. damage/anxiety,** causar daño/ansiedad; **to c. sb to do sth,** hacer que algn haga algo; **it caused him to miss the train,** le hizo perder el tren.

causeway ['kɔ:zweɪ] *n* carretera *f* elevada.

caustic ['kɔ:stɪk] *adj* cáustico,-a; *fig* **a c. remark,** un comentario mordaz. ■ **c. soda,** sosa *f* or soda *f* cáustica.

cauterization [kɔ:təraɪ'zeɪʃən] *n Med* cauterización *f*.

cauterize ['kɔ:təraɪz] *vtr Med* cauterizar.

caution ['kɔ:ʃən] I *n* **1** *(care, wariness)* precaución *f*, cautela *f*, prudencia *f*. **2** *(warning)* aviso *m*, advertencia *f*. **3** *GB Jur* represión *f*; **to give sb a c.,** amonestar a algn. II *vtr* advertir, amonestar.

cautionary ['kɔ:ʃənərɪ] *adj* admonitorio,-a; **c. tales,** cuentos morales.

cautious ['kɔ:ʃəs] *adj* cauteloso,-a, cauto,-a, prudente. ◆ **cautiously** *adv* cautelosamente, con precaución *or* prudencia.

cautiousness ['kɔ:ʃəsnɪs] *n* precaución *f*, prudencia *f*, cautela *f*.

cavalcade [kævəl'keɪd] *n (gen)* desfile *m*; *(on horseback)* cabalgata *f*.

cavalier [kævə'lɪəʳ] I *adj (manner)* arrogante. II *n* caballero *m*.

cavalry ['kævəlrɪ] *n Mil* caballería *f*.

cavalryman ['kævəlrɪmən] *n (pl cavalrymen) Mil* soldado *m* de caballería.

cave [keɪv] ■ **c. dweller,** cavernícola *mf*, troglodita *mf*; **c. paintings,** pinturas *fpl* rupestres *or* prehistóricas. ◆ **cave in** *vi (roof etc)* derrumbarse, hundirse.

caveman ['keɪvmæn] *n (pl cavemen* ['keɪvmen]*)* hombre *m* de las cavernas.

cavern ['kævən] *n* caverna *f*.

cavernous ['kævənəs] *adj* cavernoso,-a.

caviar(e) ['kævɪɑ:ʳ] *n* caviar *m*.

cavil ['kævɪl] *vi (pt & pp cavilled, US caviled)* poner reparos *or* pegas **(at, about,** a).

caving ['keɪvɪŋ] *vi* espeleología *f*.

cavity ['kævɪtɪ] *n* **1** *(hole)* cavidad *f*. ■ *Constr* **c. wall,** pared *f* de tabique doble. **2** *Dent* caries *f inv*.

cavort [kə'vɔ:t] *vi* retozar, brincar.

caw [kɔ:] I *n* graznido *m*. II *vi* graznar.

cayenne [keɪ'en] *n Culin* **c. (pepper),** (pimienta *f* de) cayena *f*.

cayman ['keɪmən] *n* **1** *(pl caymans) Zool* caimán *m*. **2 C. Islands,** Islas *fpl* Cayman.

CB [si:'bi:] *Rad abbr* **Citizens' Band,** banda *f* ciudadana, CB.

CBI [si:bi:'aɪ] *GB abbr of* **Confederation of British Industry,** ≈ Confederación *f* Española de Organizaciones Empresariales, **CEOE.**

cc [si:'si:] **1** *Com abbr of* **carbon copy (to),** copia *f* a papel carbón (a). **2** *abbr of* **cubic centimetre(s),** centímetro(s) *m(pl)* cúbico(s), cc.

CD [si:'di:] *abbr of* **compact disc,** disco *m* compacto, compact disc *m*, CD.

Cdr *Mil abbr of* **Commander,** Comandante *m*, Cte.

Cdre *Mil abbr of* **Commodore,** Comodoro *m*.

CE *Rel abbr of* **Church of England,** Iglesia *f* Anglicana.

cease [si:s] I *vtr* suspender, cesar; *Mil* **c. fire,** cesar el fuego. II *vi* cesar; **to c. doing** *or* **to do sth,** dejar de hacer algo.

cease-fire [si:s'faɪəʳ] *n Mil* alto *m* el fuego.

ceaseless ['si:slɪs] *adj* incesante.

cedar ['si:dəʳ] *n Bot* cedro *m*. ■ **Atlas c.,** cedro *m* del atlas; **c. of Lebanon,** cedro *m* del Líbano; **western red c.,** tuya *f* gigante.

cede [si:d] *vtr Jur* ceder.

cedilla [sɪ'dɪlə] *n Ling* cedilla *f*.

ceiling ['si:lɪŋ] *n* **1** techo *m*; *fam fig* **to hit the c.,** ponerse negro,-a. **2** *(limit)* tope *m*, límite *m*. ■ *Com* **c. price,** precio *m* tope.

celebrate ['selɪbreɪt] I *vtr (occasion)* celebrar, conmemorar; *Rel* **to c. Mass,** celebrar la misa. II *vi* divertirse; **let's c.,** vamos a celebrarlo *or* festejarlo.

celebrated ['selɪbreɪtɪd] *adj* famoso,-a, célebre.

celebration [selɪ'breɪʃən] *n* **1** celebración *f*; **in c.,** para celebrar; **this calls for a c.,** esto hay que celebrarlo *or* festejarlo. **2 celebrations,** festividades *fpl*, festejos *mpl*.

celebrity [sɪ'lebrɪtɪ] *n* celebridad *f*, personaje *m* famoso.

celery ['selərɪ] *n* apio *m*.

celestial [sɪ'lestɪəl] *adj* **1** *(heavenly)* celestial. **2** *Astron* celeste; **c. navigation,** navegación *f* astronómica.

celibacy ['selɪbəsɪ] *n* celibato *m*.

celibate ['selɪbɪt] *adj & n* célibe *(mf)*.

cell [sel] *n* **1** *(in prison, monastery)* celda *f*. **2** *(of honeycomb)* celdilla *f*. **3** *Biol Pol* célula *f*. **4** *Elec* pila *f*.

cellar ['selə'] *n* **1** *(basement)* sótano *m*. **2** *(for wine)* bodega *f*.

cellist ['tʃelɪst] *n Mus* violoncelista *mf*.

cello ['tʃeləʊ] *n (pl cellos) Mus* violoncelo *m*.

cellophane ['seləfeɪn] *n* celofán *m*.

cellular ['seljʊlə'] *adj* celular.

celluloid ['seljʊlɔɪd] *n* celuloide *m*.

cellulose ['seljʊləʊs] *n* celulosa *f*.

Celsius ['selsɪəs] *adj* Celsio.

Celt [kelt, selt] *n* celta *mf*.

Celtic ['keltɪk, 'seltɪk] **I** *n (language)* celta *m*. **II** *adj* celta.

cement [sɪ'ment] **I** *n* cemento *m*; **c. mixer,** hormigonera *f*. **II** *vtr Constr (bind)* unir con cemento; *(cover)* revestir de cemento; *fig (friendship)* cimentar.

cemetery ['semɪtrɪ] *n* cementerio *m*.

cenotaph ['senətɑːf] *n* cenotafio *m*.

censer ['sensə'] *n Rel* incensario *m*.

censor ['sensə'] **I** *n* censor,-a *m,f*. **II** *vtr* censurar.

censorship ['sensəʃɪp] *n* censura *f*.

censure ['senʃə'] **I** *n* censura *f*; **vote of c.,** voto de censura. **II** *vtr* censurar.

census ['sensəs] *n (pl censuses)* censo *m*, padrón *m*; **to take a c.,** realizar un censo.

cent [sent] *n* **1** centavo *m*, céntimo *m*. **2 per c.,** por ciento.

centaur ['sentɔː'] *n Myth* centauro *m*.

centenarian [sentɪ'neərɪən] *n* centenario,-a *m,f*.

centenary [sen'tiːnərɪ] *n* centenario *m*.

centennial [sen'tenɪəl] *adj & n* centenario,-a *(m)*.

center ['sentə'] *n & vtr US see* **centre.**

centerfold ['sentəfəʊld] *n US see* **centrefold.**

centigrade ['sentɪgreɪd] *adj* centígrado,-a; **37°C.,** 37 grados centígrados.

centigram(me) ['sentɪgræm] *n* centigramo *m*.

centilitre, *US* **centiliter** ['sentɪliːtə'] *n* centilitro *m*.

centimetre, *US* **centimeter** ['sentɪmiːtə'] *n* centímetro *m*.

centipede ['sentɪpiːd] *n Ent* ciempiés *m inv*.

central ['sentrəl] *adj* central; *Pol* **c. government,** gobierno central; **c. heating,** calefacción central; **the c. character,** el personaje principal. ■ **C. African,** centroafricano,-a *m, f*, **C. African Repubic,** República Centroafricana; **C. America,** Centroamérica; **C. American,** centroamericano,-a *m, f*. ◆ **centrally** *adv* **c. heated,** con calefacción central; **c. situated,** céntrico,-a.

centralize ['sentrəlaɪz] *vtr* centralizar.

centre ['sentə'] **I** *n* **1** *(gen)* centro *m*; **town c.,** centro de la ciudad. ■ *Ftb* **c. forward,** delantero *m* centro; *Ftb* **c. half,** medio *m* centro; *Pol* **c. party,** partido *m* centrista *or* de centro. **2 shopping c.,** centro *m* comercial; **sports c.,** centro *m* deportivo; **arts c.,** centro *m* cultural. **3** *fig* **c. of interest/attention,** centro *m* de interés/de todas las miradas. **II** *vtr (attention etc)* centrar, concentrar **(on, upon,** en, sobre).

centrefold ['sentəfəʊld] *n (of magazine)* página *f* central.

centrepiece ['sentəpiːs] *n* centro *m* de mesa; *fig* atracción *f* principal.

centrifugal [sen'trɪfjʊgəl, 'sentrɪfjuːgəl] *adj* centrífugo,-a.

centripetal [sen'trɪpɪtəl, 'sentrɪpɪːtəl] *adj* centrípeto,-a.

centrist ['sentrɪst] *adj & n Pol* centrista *(mf)*.

centurion [sen'tjʊərɪən] *n Hist* centurión *m*.

century ['sentʃərɪ] *n* **1** siglo *m*; **the nineteenth c.,** el siglo diecinueve. **2** *Cricket (score)* centena *f*.

ceramic [sɪ'ræmɪk] **I** *n* cerámica *f*. **II** *adj* de cerámica; **c. tile,** azulejo *m*, teja *f*.

ceramics [sɪ'ræmɪks] *n sing Art* cerámica *f*.

cereal ['sɪərɪəl] *n* cereal *m*; **breakfast c.,** cereales *mpl* para el desayuno.

cerebral ['serɪbrəl, sɪ'riːbrəl] *adj* **1** *Med* cerebral; **c. palsy,** parálisis cerebral. **2** *(person)* cerebral.

ceremonial [serɪ'məʊnɪəl] **I** *adj* ceremonioso,-a, formal. **II** *n* ceremonial *m*.

ceremonious [serɪ'məʊnɪəs] *adj* ceremonioso,-a.

cert [sɜːt] *n fam* **it's a dead c.,** no puede fallar, no cabe duda.

CertEd [sɜːt'ed] *GB Educ abbr of* **Certificate in Education,** título *m* de profesor.

certain ['sɜːtən] **I** *adj* **1** *(sure)* seguro,-a; **he's c. to win,** no cabe duda que ganará; **I'm c. she didn't pay,** estoy seguro,-a (de) que no ha pagado; **to make c. of sth,** asegurarse de algo. **2** *(moderate)* cierto,-a; **to a c. extent,** hasta cierto punto. **3** *(not known)* cierto,-a; **a c. Miss Ward,** una tal señorita Ward; **for c. reasons,** por razones desconocidas. **4** *(true)* cierto,-a, verdadero,-a. **II** *adv* **for c.,** seguro; **to know for c.,** sé a ciencia cierta, sé con toda seguridad. ◆ **certainly** *adv* naturalmente, desde luego, por supuesto; **c. not,** por supuesto que no, de ninguna manera, ni hablar.

certainty ['sɜːtəntɪ] *n (gen)* certeza *f*; *(assurance)* seguridad *f*.

certifiable ['sɜːtɪfaɪəbəl] *adj* **1** certificable. **2** *Med* demente.

certificate [sə'tɪfɪkɪt] *n* **1** *(gen)* certificado *m*; *Educ* diploma *m*; **birth c.,** partida *f* de nacimiento; **death c.,** certificado *m* de defunción; **medical c.,** certificado médico. **2** *Fin* **savings c.,** bono *m* de ahorro.

certified ['sɜːtɪfaɪd] *adj (gen)* certificado,-a; *(copy)* legalizado,-a.

certify ['sɜːtɪfaɪ] *vtr (pt & pp **certified**)* certificar; **this is to c. that ...,** certifico que ...; **to c. sb (as being) insane,** declarar enfermo,-a mental a algn.

certitude ['sɜːtɪtjuːd] *n* certeza *f*.

cervical ['sɜːvɪkəl, sə'vaɪkəl] *adj* **1** *(neck)* cervical. **2** *(uterus)* del útero; **c. cancer,** cáncer del útero; **c. smear,** frotis cervical.

cervix ['sɜːvɪks] *n (pl **cervixes** or **cervices** [sə'vaɪsɪːz])* *Anat* **1** *(uterus)* cuello *m* del útero. **2** *(neck)* cerviz *f*, cuello *m*.

Cesarian [sɪ'zeərɪən] *n US see* **Caesarean.**

cessation [se'seɪʃən] *n (of hostilities etc)* cese *m*.

cesspit ['sespɪt] *n*, **cesspool** ['sespuːl] *n* pozo *m* negro.

Ceylon [sɪ'lɒn] *n* Ceilán.

Ceylonese [selə'niːz] *adj & n* ceilanés,-esa *(m,f)*.

cf *abbr of* **confer** (compare), compárese, cfr.

CFE [siːef'iː] *GB Educ abbr of* **College of Further Education,** instituto *m* de estudios superiores.

ch *abbr of* **chapter,** capítulo *m*, cap., c.

Chad [tʃæd] *n* Chad.

Chadian ['tʃædɪən] *adj & n* chadiano,-a *(m,f)*.

chafe [tʃeɪf] **I** *vtr* **1** *(make sore)* rozar, excoriar. **2** *(warm up)* calentar. **II** *vi* **1** *(skin)* irritarse. **2** *(person)* irritarse **(at,** a causa de).

chaff¹ [tʃɑːf] *n* barcia *f*, granzas *fpl*; *(fodder)* paja *f*, *fig* **to separate the wheat from the c.,** separar el grano de la paja.

chaff² [tʃɑːf] *vtr* burlarse de.

chaffinch ['tʃæfɪntʃ] *n Orn* pinzón *m* vulgar.

chagrin ['ʃægrɪn] *n* disgusto *m*, desilusión *f*.

chain [tʃeɪn] **I** *n (gen)* cadena *f*, *fig (of events)* serie *f*; **c. of mountains,** cordillera *f*; *Com* **supermarket c.,** cadena de supermercados; *(people)* **to make a c.,** formar una cadena humana; *(in WC)* **to pull the c.,** tirar de la cadena. ■ *US* **c. gang,** cadena *f* de presidiarios; **c. letter,** cadena *f* de cartas; **c. mail,** cota *f* de malla; **c. reaction,** reacción *f* en cadena; **c. saw,** sierra *f* mecánica; *Knit* **c. stitch,** cadeneta *f*. **II** *vtr* **to c. (up),** encadenar.

chain-smoke ['tʃeɪnsməʊk] *vi* fumar un pitillo tras otro.

chair [tʃeə'] **I** *n* **1** *Furn* silla *f*; *(with arms)* sillón *m*, butaca *f*; **high c.,** trono *m*; **please take a c.,** siéntese por favor. ■ *Ski* **c. lift,** telesilla *m*. **2** *(position)* presidencia *f*; *Univ* cátedra *f*; **to address the c.,** dirigirse al presidente; **to be in the c.,** to take the c. (at a meeting),** presidir (una reunión). **II** *vtr (meeting)* presidir.

chairman ['tʃeəmən] *n (pl **chairmen**)* presidente *m*.

chairmanship ['tʃeəmənʃɪp] *n* presidencia *f*.

chairperson ['tʃeəpɜːsən] *n* presidente,-a *m, f*.

chairwoman ['tʃeəwʊmən] n (pl **chairwomen** ['tʃeəwɪmɪn]) presidenta f.

Chaldean [kæl'diːən] adj & n Hist caldeo,-a (m,f).

chalet ['ʃæleɪ] n chalet m, chalé m.

chalice ['tʃælɪs] n cáliz m.

chalk [tʃɔːk] I n Min creta f, roca f caliza; (for writing) tiza f; GB fam **not by a long c.**, ni mucho menos, ni por mucho; fam **they are as different as c. and cheese**, se parecen como un huevo a una manzana. II vtr **to c. (out)**, (area etc) marcar con tiza; (plan) trazar. ◆ **chalk up** vtr fam (victory) apuntarse; **c. it up to me!**, ¡ponlo en mi cuenta!

chalky ['tʃɔːkɪ] adj (**chalkier, chalkiest**) cretáceo,-a, calcáreo,-a.

challenge ['tʃælɪndʒ] I vtr 1 (to game of football etc) retar, desafiar; **to c. sb to do sth**, retar a algn a que haga algo. 2 (person, authority) poner a prueba; (statement) poner en duda. 3 Mil dar el alto or quién vive a. 4 Jur recusar. II n 1 (gen) reto m, desafío m; Sport desafío m; **the job will be a real c. to her**, el trabajo pondrá a prueba sus cualidades; **to take up a c.**, aceptar un reto. 2 Mil quién vive m. 3 Jur recusación f.

challenger ['tʃælɪndʒəʳ] n- desafiador,-a m, f; Sport aspirante mf a un título.

challenging ['tʃælɪndʒɪŋ] adj (idea) provocativo,-a; (task) que presenta un reto or un desafío.

chamber ['tʃeɪmbəʳ] n 1 (hall) cámara f; Parl **Lower/Upper C.**, cámara baja/alta; **C. of Commerce**, Cámara de Comercio. 2 Mus **c. music**, música f de cámara. 3 (of gun) recámara f. 4 GB Jur **chambers**, despacho m sing, gabinete m sing.

chambermaid ['tʃeɪmbəmeɪd] n doncella f, camarera f.

chamberpot ['tʃeɪmbəpɒt] n orinal m.

chameleon [kə'miːlɪən] n Zool camaleón m.

chamois ['ʃæmwɑː] n inv 1 Zool gamuza f. 2 ['ʃæmɪ] **c. (leather)**, gamuza f.

champ¹ [tʃæmp] I vtr (fodder) mascar. II vi fam mordisquear; fig **to c. at the bit**, comerle a uno la impaciencia.

champ² [tʃæmp] n fam campeón,-ona m,f.

champagne [ʃæm'peɪn] n (French) champán m; (from Catalonia) cava m.

champion ['tʃæmpɪən] I n campeón,-ona m, f; **a c. swimmer**, un campeón de natación; **word c.**, campeón mundial; fig **c. of human rights**, defensor,-a de los derechos humanos. II vtr fig (cause) defender.

championship ['tʃæmpɪənʃɪp] n Sport campeonato m.

chance [tʃɑːns] I n 1 (fate, fortune) casualidad f, azar m; **by c.**, por casualidad; **games of c.**, juegos dé azar; **on the c.**, por si acaso; **to take a c.**, arriesgarse, correr un riesgo; **I'm not taking any chances**, no quiero arriesgarme. ■ **c. discovery**, descubrimiento m fortuito; **c. meeting**, encuentro m casual. 2 (likelihood) posibilidad f; **I don't stand a c.**, I've got no c., no tengo ni la más remota posibilidad; **(the) chances are that ...**, lo más posible es que ... . 3 (opportunity) oportunidad f; **to have an eye for the main c.**, cuidar de sus propios intereses; **to miss a c.**, perder una oportunidad. II vi **to c. on or upon**, encontrar por casualidad; **to c. to do sth**, hacer algo por casualidad; **I chanced to look**, miré por casualidad. III vtr arriesgar; fam **let's c. it**, vamos a arriesgarnos.

chancel ['tʃɑːnsəl] n Archit Rel presbiterio m.

chancellor ['tʃɑːnsələʳ] n 1 Pol (head of state, in embassy) canciller m. 2 GB Univ rector,-a m,f. 3 GB **C. of the Exchequer**, ministro,-a m,f de Hacienda.

chancy ['tʃɑːnsɪ] adj (**chancier, chanciest**) fam arriesgado,-a.

chandelier [ʃændɪ'lɪəʳ] n araña f (de luces).

change [tʃeɪndʒ] I vtr cambiar (de); Aut **to c. gear**, cambiar de marcha or de velocidad; **to c. one's mind/the subject**, cambiar de opinión/de tema; **to c. pesetas into**

dollars, cambiar pesetas en dólares; **to c. places with sb**, cambiarse de sitio con algn; Mil **to c. the guard**, cambiar la guardia; **to c. trains**, transbordar, cambiar de tren; **to get changed**, mudarse, cambiarse de ropa; fig **to c. hands**, cambiar de dueño,-a. II vi cambiar, cambiarse; Rail **all c.!**, ¡cambio de tren!; **I think he's changed**, le veo cambiado; **to c. for the better/worse**, mejorar/empeorar; **to c. into**, convertirse or transformarse en. III n 1 cambio m; **c. for the better/worse**, cambio beneficioso/ desventajoso; **c. of address/occupation**, cambio de domicilio/trabajo; **c. of clothes**, muda f de ropa; **for a c.**, para variar; Aut **gear c.**, cambio de velocidades; **to ring the changes**, variar; fig **c. of heart**, cambio de parecer; fig **c. of scene**, cambio de aires; euph **the c. of life**, la menopausia. 2 (money) cambio m; **keep the c.**, quédese con la vuelta; **small c.**, cambio m, suelto m; **to give c. for a pound**, cambiar una libra; fam **you won't get much c. out of him**, no esperes gran cosa de él. ◆ **change down** vi Aut reducir (marcha). ◆ **change over** vi cambiarse; GB Sport cambiar de campo. ◆ **change up** vi Aut cambiar a una velocidad or marcha superior.

changeable ['tʃeɪndʒəbəl] adj (weather) variable; (person) inconstante, voluble.

changeless ['tʃeɪndʒlɪs] adj inmutable.

changeover ['tʃeɪndʒəʊvəʳ] n 1 (gen) conversión f. 2 Mil cambio m, relevo m (de la guardia). 3 Sport (of runner etc) relevo m.

changing ['tʃeɪndʒɪŋ] I n 1 (gen) cambio m. ■ Sport **c. room**, vestuario m. 2 Mil cambio m, relevo m (de la guardia). II adj cambiante.

channel ['tʃænəl] I n 1 Geog canal m; (bed of river) cauce m, lecho m. ■ **the C. Islands**, las Islas Anglonormandas; **the English C.**, el Canal de la Mancha. 2 Admin vía f, conducto m; **c. of communication**, vía de comunicación; **through the official channels**, por los conductos oficiales. 3 TV Rad canal m, cadena f. II vtr (pt & pp **channelled**, US **channeled**) fig (ideas etc) canalizar, encauzar.

chant [tʃɑːnt] I n 1 Rel canto m litúrgico, cántico m. 2 (of demonstrators) slogan m. II vtr & vi 1 Rel cantar (cánticos). 2 (demonstrators) corear, repetir.

chaos ['keɪɒs] n caos m.

chaotic [keɪ'ɒtɪk] adj caótico,-a.

chap¹ [tʃæp] n fam chico m, tío m; **a good c.**, un tío fenomenal or fantástico.

chap² abbr of **chapter**, capítulo m, cap., c.

chapel ['tʃæpəl] n Rel capilla f; **c. of rest**, capilla ardiente.

chaperon(e) ['ʃæpərəʊn] I n carabina f, dama f de compañía. II vtr fam ir de carabina con.

chaplain ['tʃæplɪn] n Rel capellán m.

chapter ['tʃæptəʳ] n 1 capítulo m; fig serie f; **to quote c. and verse**, citar palabra por palabra. 2 Rel cabildo m.

chapterhouse ['tʃæptəhaʊs] n Rel sala f capitular.

char¹ [tʃɑːʳ] I vtr (pt & pp **charred**) chamuscar, carbonizar. II vi chamuscarse, carbonizarse.

char² [tʃɑːʳ] GB fam I n asistenta f, interina f. II vi (pt & pp **charred**) trabajar de asistenta.

character ['kærɪktəʳ] n 1 carácter m; **a person of good c.**, una persona de buena reputación; **to have a lot of c.**, tener mucho carácter or mucha personalidad; **to have a strong c.**, tener un carácter fuerte; fig **to be in/out of c.**, conformar/no conformar al tipo; fam **she's quite a c.**, es todo un carácter. 2 fam (person) tipo m; **a suspicious c.**, un tipo de mucho cuidado. 3 Theat personaje m. 4 (letter) carácter m.

characteristic [kærɪktə'rɪstɪk] I n característica f. II adj característico,-a.

characterization [kærɪktəraɪ'zeɪʃən] n caracterización f.

characterize ['kærɪktəraɪz] vtr caracterizar.

characterless ['kærɪktəlɪs] adj de poco carácter.

charade [ʃə'rɑːd] n 1 GB farsa f. 2 **charades**, (game) charadas fpl.

charcoal ['tʃɑːkəʊl] n Min carbón m vegetal. ■ Art c. **drawing,** carboncillo m, dibujo m al carboncillo; (colour) **c. grey,** gris m marengo or oscuro.

chard [tʃɑːd] n Bot acelga f.

charge [tʃɑːdʒ] I vtr 1 cobrar; Com **c. it to my account,** cárguelo en mi cuenta; **how much do you c.?,** ¿cuánto cobra?; **they c. £10 an hour,** cobran 10 libras la hora. 2 Jur acusar; **to c. sb with a crime,** acusar a algn de un crimen. 3 Mil atacar, cargar contra. 4 Elec (battery) cargar. II vi 1 Elec (battery) cargar. 2 Mil atacar, cargar. 3 **to c. about,** andar a lo loco; **to c. in,** entrar alocadamente. III n 1 (cost) precio m; **bank charges,** comisión f (por servicio bancario); **extra c.,** suplemento m; **free of c.,** gratis, sin gasto alguno; **service c.,** servicio m. ■ **c. account,** cuenta f corriente. 2 (responsibility) cargo m; **to be in c. of,** estar a cargo de; **to take c. of,** hacerse cargo de; **who is in c.?,** ¿quién es el encargado?; fig **a nanny and her c.,** una niñera y el niño a su cargo. 3 Jur cargo m, acusación f; **to bring a c. against sb,** formular una acusación contra algn; **to face a c. of ...,** responder a una acusación de ... . 4 Mil (explosive) carga f explosiva; (by cavalry) carga f. 5 Elec carga f.

chargeable ['tʃɑːdʒəbəl] adj (expenses, debts) **c. to,** a cargo de.

charged [tʃɑːdʒd] adj Elec cargado,-a; fig (issue) emotivo,-a; **emotionally c.,** con una carga afectiva.

chargé d'affaires [ʃɑːʒeɪdæˈfeəʳ] n (pl **chargés d'affaires)** Pol encargado,-a m, f de negocios.

charger ['tʃɑːdʒəʳ] n 1 Elec cargador m. 2 (horse) caballo m de guerra.

chariot ['tʃærɪət] n carro m (de guerra).

charisma [kəˈrɪzmə] n carisma m.

charismatic [kærɪzˈmætɪk] adj carismático,-a.

charitable ['tʃærɪtəbəl] adj 1 (person) caritativo,-a; (attitude) comprensivo,-a. 2 (work, organization) benéfico,-a.

charity ['tʃærɪtɪ] n 1 caridad f; **to do sth out of c.,** hacer algo por caridad; prov **c. begins at home,** la caridad empieza por uno mismo. 2 (organization) institución f benéfica.

charlady ['tʃɑːleɪdɪ] n GB mujer f de la limpieza, asistenta f.

charlatan ['ʃɑːlətən] n (doctor) curandero,-a m, f.

charm [tʃɑːm] I n 1 (quality) encanto m. 2 (spell) hechizo m; **lucky c.,** amuleto m; **to work like a c.,** funcionar a las mil maravillas. ■ **c. bracelet,** pulsera f de dijes. II vtr encantar; fig **she can c. the birds off the trees,** es muy coqueta.

charmer ['tʃɑːməʳ] n 1 fam atractivo,-a m, f, simpático,-a m, f, encantador,-a m, f. 2 (of snakes) encantador,-a m, f.

charming ['tʃɑːmɪŋ] adj encantador,-a.

chart [tʃɑːt] I n 1 Naut carta f de marear; Av carta f de navegación. 2 (giving information) tabla f; (graph) gráfico m. ■ Med **temperature c.,** gráfico m de temperaturas; **weather c.,** mapa m meteorológico or del tiempo. 3 Mus **the charts,** la lista de éxitos, el hit parade. II vtr 1 Av Naut (on map) trazar. 2 (information) poner en un gráfico or una tabla.

charter ['tʃɑːtəʳ] I n 1 (of institution) estatutos mpl; (of company) carta f de privilegios; (of rights) carta f. 2 Av Naut fletamento m; **c. flight,** vuelo m chárter. II vtr (plane, boat) fletar.

chartered accountant [tʃɑːtədəˈkaʊntənt] n GB contable mf diplomado,-a.

charwoman ['tʃɑːwʊmən] n (pl **charwomen** ['tʃɑːwɪmɪn]) GB see **charlady.**

chary ['tʃeərɪ] adj (charier, chariest) fam (wary) cauteloso,-a, cauto,-a; **to be c. of doing sth,** tener cuidado al hacer algo.

chase [tʃeɪs] I vtr perseguir; (hunt) cazar. II vi fam **to c. about** or **around,** correr de un lado para otro. III n persecución f; (hunt) caza f; **to give c. to sb,** dar caza a algn; fig **a wild goose c.,** una empresa descabellada.

chaser ['tʃeɪsəʳ] n 1 fam fig copita f (de licor) que se toma después de cerveza. 2 (that chases) perseguidor,-a m, f.

chasm ['kæzəm] n Geog sima f; fig abismo m.

chassis ['ʃæsɪ] n (pl **chassis** ['ʃæsɪz]) Aut chasis m inv.

chaste [tʃeɪst] adj casto,-a; (style) sobrio,-a.

chasten ['tʃeɪsən] vtr (punish) castigar.

chastise [tʃæsˈtaɪz] vtr castigar.

chastisement ['tʃæstɪzmənt, tʃæsˈtaɪzmənt] n castigo m.

chastity ['tʃæstɪtɪ] n castidad f.

chat [tʃæt] I n charla f; **I'll have a c. with him,** hablaré con él un ratito; GB Rad TV **c. show,** coloquio m, entrevista f. II vi (pt & pp **chatted)** charlar, dar palique; **chatting away,** dando palique. ◆ **chat up** vtr fam (intentar) ligar con algn.

chattels ['tʃætəlz] npl Jur bienes mpl muebles.

chatter ['tʃætəʳ] I vi (person) chacharear, parlotear; (bird) piar, gorjear; (teeth) castañetear; (monkeys) chillar. II n (of person) cháchara f, parloteo m; (of birds) gorjeo m; (of teeth) castañeteo m; (of monkeys) chillidos mpl.

chatterbox ['tʃætəbɒks] n fam parlanchín,-ina m, f.

chatty ['tʃætɪ] adj (chattier, chattiest) parlanchín,-ina, hablador,-a.

chauffeur ['ʃəʊfəʳ, ʃəʊˈfɜːʳ] n chófer m, chofer m.

chauvinism ['ʃəʊvɪnɪzəm] n chovinismo m, chauvinismo m; **male c.,** machismo m.

chauvinist ['ʃəʊvɪnɪst] adj & n chovinista (mf), chauvinista (mf); **male c.,** machista m.

cheap [tʃiːp] I adj barato,-a; (fare) económico,-a; (joke) fácil; fig pej (contemptible) vil, bajo,-a; **to be c.,** ser barato,-a, estar a buen precio; fig **to feel c.,** avergonzarse, sentir vergüenza; fam **c. and nasty,** barato,-a (y malo,-a); fam **dirt c.,** tirado,-a, baratísimo,-a. II n GB fam **on the c.,** en plan barato; **to get sth on the c.,** conseguir algo muy barato. III adv barato. ◆ **cheaply** adv barato, en plan económico or barato.

cheapen ['tʃiːpən] vtr abaratar, rebajar el precio de; fig degradar, rebajar.

cheapness ['tʃiːpnɪs] n baratura f, lo barato.

cheat [tʃiːt] I vtr engañar; **to c. sb out of sth,** estafar algo a algn. II vi 1 (at games) hacer trampa. 2 fam (husband, wife) poner cuernos (on, a). III n (trickster) tramposo,-a m, f, fullero,-a m, f; (involving money) estafador,-a m, f.

cheating ['tʃiːtɪŋ] n (trickery) trampa f, fullería f; (involving money) estafa f, timo m.

check [tʃek] I vtr visar, repasar; (facts, statement) comprobar; (passports, tickets) revisar, controlar; (luggage at Customs) registrar; Aut (tyres, oil) revisar; **to c. sth against a list,** cotejar or comparar algo con una lista. 2 (anger, impulse) contener, refrenar; (growth, progress) retrasar, retardar. 3 (stop, control) detener; **to keep in c.,** (disease, feelings) contener, controlar; (enemy) mantener a raya; **to keep imports in c.,** poner freno a **las importaciones.** 4 Chess dar jaque a. II vi mirar, comprobar; **I have to c. to see if I locked the car,** tengo que comprobar si he cerrado el coche. III n 1 (of documents, goods, people) revisión f; (of results, facts) comprobación f, verificación f; **a c. on all people leaving the country,** una revisión de todas las personas que salgan del país. ■ **c. list,** lista f de cotejo. 2 Chess jaque m. 3 (pattern) cuadro m. 4 US see **cheque.** ◆ **check in** vi (at airport) facturar; (at hotel) registrarse (at, en). ◆ **check off** vtr ir tachando (de una lista); **c. the names off as I read them out,** tacha los nombres a medida que los vaya leyendo. ◆ **check out** vi (of hotel) dejar el hotel, pagar la cuenta y marcharse. II vtr (facts) verificar. ◆ **check up** vi **to c. up on sb,** hacer averiguaciones sobre algn; **to c. up on sth,** averiguar or comprobar algo.

checked [tʃekt] adj a cuadros; **c. material,** tela a cuadros.

checker ['tʃekəʳ] n US (cashier) cajero,-a m, f.

checkerboard ['tʃekəbɔːd] *n US see* **chequerboard**

checkered ['tʃekəd] *adj US see* **chequered.**

checkers ['tʃekəz] *n US (game)* damas *fpl.*

check-in ['tʃekɪn] *n* registro *m;* **c.-in desk,** recepción *f.*

checkmate ['tʃekmeɪt] **I** *n Chess* jaque mate *m.* **II** *vtr Chess* dar mate a; *fig* poner en un callejón sin salida.

checkout ['tʃekaʊt] *n (counter)* caja *f.*

checkpoint ['tʃekpɔɪnt] *n* control *m;* **she passed the c. with no difficulty,** pasó el control sin problemas.

checkup ['tʃekʌp] *n Med* chequeo *m,* examen *m* médico.

cheek [tʃiːk] **I** *n* 1 *Anat* mejilla *f; fig* **c. by jowl,** lado a lado; *fig* **to say sth tongue in c.,** decir algo para burlarse; *fig* **to turn the other c.,** dar la otra mejilla. 2 *fam (nerve)* jeta *f,* cara *f;* **to have the c. of the devil,** tener jeta, ser un caradura; **what (a) c.!,** ¡vaya jeta! **II** *vtr fam* insolentarse con.

cheekbone ['tʃiːkbəʊn] *n* pómulo *m.*

cheeky ['tʃiːkɪ] *adj (cheekier, cheekiest) fam* fresco,-a, insolente, descarado,-a.

cheep [tʃiːp] **I** *n (of bird)* pío *m,* piada *f,* gorjeo *m.* **II** *vi* piar, gorjear.

cheer [tʃɪə] **I** *vi* aplaudir, aclamar. **II** *vtr* 1 *(applaud with shouts)* vitorear, aclamar, ovacionar. 2 *(make hopeful)* animar. **III** *n* viva *m,* vítor *m;* **loud cheers,** una ovación cerrada; **three cheers,** tres hurras; **to the cheers of the crowd,** a los aplausos del público; *fam* **cheers!,** *(thank you)* gracias; *(goodbye)* adiós; *(before drinking)* ¡salud! ◆ **cheer on** *vtr (athlete)* alentar. ◆ **cheer up** *vi* alegrarse, animarse; **c. up!,** ¡ánimo!, ¡alegra esa cara! **II** *vtr* **to c. sb up,** alegrar *or* animar a algn; **your letter cheered me up,** tu carta me dio ánimos.

cheerful ['tʃɪəful] *adj* 1 *(person)* alegre, animado,-a. 2 *(place, colour)* alegre; *(tune, conversation)* animado,-a. 3 *(willing)* contento,-a. ◆ **cheerfully** *adv* alegremente, con buena disposición.

cheerfulness ['tʃɪəfulnɪs] *n* alegría *f.*

cheering ['tʃɪərɪŋ] *n* ovaciones *fpl,* vítores *mpl.*

cheerio [tʃɪərɪ'əʊ] *interj GB fam* ¡adiós!, ¡hasta luego!

cheerleader ['tʃɪəliːdə] *n* persona *f* que inicia los vítores (en un partido).

cheerless ['tʃɪəlɪs] *adj (place)* triste; *(day)* melancólico,-a, triste.

cheery ['tʃɪərɪ] *adj (cheerier, cheeriest)* alegre, optimista. ◆ **cheerily** *adv* de buen humor.

cheese [tʃiːz] *n Culin* queso *m;* **a piece of c.,** un trozo de queso; *fam (for photograph)* **say c.!,** ¡una sonrisa para la prensa! ◼ **cottage c.,** requesón *m.*

cheesecake ['tʃiːzkeɪk] *n Culin* tarta *f* de queso.

cheesecloth ['tʃiːzklɒθ] *n Tex* estopilla *f.*

cheesed off [tʃiːzd'ɒf] *adj GB fam* **to be c. off,** estar harto,-a *or* desencantado,-a.

cheeseparing ['tʃiːzpeərɪŋ] **I** *adj* tacaño,-a. **II** *n* tacañería *f.*

cheetah ['tʃiːtə] *n Zool* guepardo *m.*

chef [ʃef] *n* chef *m.*

chemical ['kemɪkəl] **I** *n* sustancia *f* química, producto *m* químico. **II** *adj* químico,-a.

chemist ['kemɪst] *n* 1 *Chem* químico,-a *m, f.* 2 *GB* **c.'s (shop),** farmacia *f;* **dispensing c.,** farmacéutico,-a *m, f.*

chemistry ['kemɪstrɪ] *n* química *f.*

cheque [tʃek] *n Fin* cheque *m,* talón *m;* **a c. for £50,** un cheque de cincuenta libras; **blank c.,** cheque en blanco; **to pay by c.,** pagar con (un) cheque. ◼ **c. book,** talonario *m* (de cheques); **c. card,** tarjeta *f* de identificación bancaria; **traveller's c.,** cheque de viaje.

chequerboard ['tʃekəbɔːd] *n* tablero *m* de damas.

chequered ['tʃekəd] *adj (cloth)* a cuadros; *fig* **a c. career,** una carrera con altibajos. ◼ *Sport* **c. flag,** bandera *f* a cuadros.

cherish ['tʃerɪʃ] *vtr* 1 *(person)* querer, tenerle mucho cariño a. 2 *fig (hopes etc)* abrigar.

cherry ['tʃerɪ] *n Bot* cereza *f.* ◼ **c. red,** *(colour)* rojo *m* cereza; **c. brandy,** licor *m* de cerezas; **c. tree,** cerezo *m.*

cherub ['tʃerəb] *n (pl* **cherubs** *or* **cherubim** ['tʃerəbɪm]) querubín *m.*

cherubic [tʃe'ruːbɪk] *adj* de querubín, de ángel.

chervil ['tʃɜːvɪl] *n Bot* cerafolio *m.*

chess [tʃes] *n* ajedrez *m;* **game of c.,** partida *f* de ajedrez; **to play c.,** jugar al ajedrez.

chessboard ['tʃesbɔːd] *n* tablero *m* de ajedrez.

chessman ['tʃesmən] *(pl* **chessmen**) pieza *f* de ajedrez.

chesspiece ['tʃespiːs] *n* pieza *f* de ajedrez.

chest [tʃest] *n* 1 *Anat* pecho *m; fig* **to get sth off one's c.,** desahogarse. 2 *(for linen)* arca *f; (for valuables)* cofre *m; (for shipping)* baúl *m,* caja *f;* **tea c.,** cajón *m* de té. ◼ *Furn* **c. of drawers,** cómoda *f.*

chestnut ['tʃesnʌt] *n* 1 *Bot (tree, wood, colour)* castaño *m; (nut)* castaña *f.* ◼ **horse c.,** castaño *m* de las Indias; **Spanish c., sweet c.,** castaño *m.* 2 *(horse)* alazán,-ana *m, f.* 3 *fam (joke)* **an old c.,** un chiste gastado.

chesty ['tʃestɪ] *adj (chestier, chestiest)* 1 bronquítico,-a; **a c. cough,** una tos de pecho. 2 *fam (woman)* pechugona.

chevron ['ʃevrən] *n Mil* galón *m.*

chew [tʃuː] *vtr* masticar, mascar; **to c. the cud,** rumiar; *fam fig* **to c. sth over,** darle vueltas a algo.

chewing gum ['tʃuːɪŋgʌm] *n* chicle *m,* goma *f* de mascar.

chewy ['tʃuːɪ] *adj (chewier, chewiest)* enganchoso,-a, difícil de masticar *or* mascar.

chic [ʃiːk] **I** *adj* elegante. **II** *n* elegancia *f.*

chick [tʃɪk] *n* pollito *m.*

chicken ['tʃɪkɪn] **I** *n* 1 pollo *m; fam* **she's no c.,** tiene sus años; *prov* **don't count your chickens before they hatch** *or* **are hatched,** no hagas como en el cuento de la lechera. ◼ *sl* **c. feed,** una miseria; **c. farming,** avicultura *f; Culin* **c. stock,** caldo *m* de gallina. 2 *sl (coward)* gallina *f.* **II** *adj sl (cowardly)* gallina. **III** *vi fam* **to c. out,** rajarse (por miedo).

chickenpox ['tʃɪkɪnpɒks] *n Med* varicela *f.*

chickpea ['tʃɪkpiː] *n Culin* garbanzo *m.*

chickweed ['tʃɪkwiːd] *n Bot* pamplina *f.*

chicory ['tʃɪkərɪ] *n* achicoria *f.*

chide [tʃaɪd] *vtr (pt* **chided** *or* **chid** [tʃɪd]; *pp* **chided** *or* **chidden** ['tʃɪdən]) regañar, reprender.

chief [tʃiːf] **I** *n (gen)* jefe *m; (of tribe)* cacique *m; Mil* **c. of staff,** jefe *m* del estado mayor; **commander in c.,** comandante *m* en jefe. **II** *adj* principal; **the c. engineer,** el ingeniero principal. ◆ **chiefly** *adv (above all)* sobre todo; *(mainly)* principalmente.

chieftain ['tʃiːftən] *n* cacique *m,* jefe *m.*

chiffchaff ['tʃɪftʃæf] *n Orn* mosquitero *m* común.

chiffon [ʃɪ'fɒn, 'ʃɪfɒn] *n Tex* gasa *f.*

chihuahua [tʃɪ'wɑːwə] *n Zool* chihuahua *m.*

chilblain ['tʃɪlbleɪn] *n Med* sabañón *m.*

child [tʃaɪld] *n (pl* **children**) niño,-a *m, f; (son)* hijo *m; (daughter)* hija *f;* **children's books,** libros *mpl* para niños; **children's stories,** cuentos *mpl* infantiles; *fam* **that's c.'s play,** eso es un juego de niños. ◼ **c. minder,** persona *f* que cuida niños en su propia casa.

childbirth ['tʃaɪldbɜːθ] *n* parto *m,* alumbramiento *m;* **in c.,** de parto.

childhood ['tʃaɪldhʊd] *n* infancia *f,* niñez *f;* **in one's second c.,** en la segunda infancia.

childish ['tʃaɪldɪʃ] *adj* pueril; **don't be c.!,** ¡no seas niño!

childlike ['tʃaɪldlaɪk] *adj* infantil, ingenuo,-a.

children ['tʃɪldrən] *npl see* **child.**

Chile ['tʃɪlɪ] *n* Chile *m.*

Chilean ['tʃɪlɪən] *adj & n* chileno,-a (*m,f*).

chill [tʃɪl] **I** *n* **1** *Med* resfriado *m*; **to catch a c.**, resfriarse, enfriarse, coger frío. **2** *(coldness)* fresco *m*, frío *m*; **there's a c. in the air**, hace fresquito; **to take the c. off sth**, entibiar *or* templar algo; *fig* **to cast a c. over sb**, caer como un jarro de agua fría sobre algn. **II** *adj (wind etc)* frío,-a. **III** *vtr (meat)* refrigerar; *(wine)* enfriar; *fig* **to be chilled to the bone**, estar helado,-a de frío.

chil(l)i ['tʃɪlɪ] *n (pl chil(l)ies) Culin* chile *m*.

chilling ['tʃɪlɪŋ] *adj* glacial; *fig (story, crime)* espeluznante.

chilly ['tʃɪlɪ] *adj (chillier, chilliest)* frío,-a; **to feel c.**, sentir *or* tener frío; *fig* **a c. reception**, una acogida fría.

chime [tʃaɪm] **I** *n* carillón *m*; *(peal)* repique *m* de campanas. **II** *vtr (bells)* tocar; *(clock)* dar; **the bell chimed six**, las campanas tocaron las seis. **III** *vi (bell)* repicar, tañer; *(clock)* sonar. ◆ **chime in** *vi fam* intervenir, intrometerse.

chimney ['tʃɪmnɪ] *n* chimenea *f*; *fam* **he smokes like a c.**, fuma como un carretero. ■ **c. stack**, fuste *m*; **c. sweep**, deshollinador *m*.

chimneypot ['tʃɪmnɪpɒt] *n* cañón *m*.

chimp [tʃɪmp] *n*, **chimpanzee** [tʃɪmpæn'ziː] *n Zool* chimpancé *m*.

chin [tʃɪn] *n* barbilla *f*, mentón *m*; **double c.**, papada *f*; *fam* **keep your c. up**, no te desanimes.

China ['tʃaɪnə] *n* **1** *(People's Republic of)* **C.**, (República *f* Popular de la) China. **2** *Bot* **C. tree**, jabonero *m* de la China.

china ['tʃaɪnə] *n* loza *f*; **bone c.**, porcelana *f*.

Chinese [tʃaɪ'niːz] **I** *adj* chino,-a; **C. lantern**, farolillo *m* de papel. **II** *n* **1** *(person)* chino,-a *m,f*. **2** *(language)* chino *m*.

Chink [tʃɪŋk] *n sl pej* chino,-a *m,f*.

chink¹ [tʃɪŋk] *n (opening)* resquicio *m*; *(crack)* grieta *f*.

chink² [tʃɪŋk] **I** *vtr (glasses, coins)* hacer sonar *or* tintinear. **II** *vi* sonar, tintinear. **III** *n* tintineo *m*.

chintz [tʃɪnts] *n Tex* chintz *m*.

chinwag ['tʃɪnwæg] *n GB fam* charla *f*.

chip [tʃɪp] **I** *n* **1** *(of wood)* astilla *f*; *(of stone)* lasca *f*; *(of china)* pedacito *m*, trocito *m*; *(in cup, dish)* desportilladura *f*; *(in furniture)* astilladura *f*; *fam fig* **a c. off the old block**, de tal palo tal astilla; *fam* **to have a c. on one's shoulder**, estar amargado,-a. **2** *GB Culin* **chips**, patatas *fpl* fritas. ■ *GB fam* **chip shop**, tienda *f* que vende pescado y patatas fritas para llevar. **3** *Tech Comput* **silicon c.**, chip *m*. **4** *(in gambling)* ficha *f*; *fam fig* **when the chips are down**, a la hora de la verdad. **II** *vtr (pt & pp chipped) (wood)* astillar; *(stone)* resquebrajar; *(china, glass)* desportillar, resquebrajar; *(paint)* descascarillar, desconchar. **III** *vi (wood)* astillarse; *(stones)* resquebrajarse; *(china, glass)* desportillarse; *(paint)* descascarillarse, desconcharse. ◆ **chip in** *vi fam* **1** meterse, saltar y decir algo. **2** *(with money)* contribuir, poner algo.

chipboard ['tʃɪpbɔːd] *n Carp* aglomerado *m*, madera *f* aglomerada.

chipmunk ['tʃɪpmʌŋk] *n Zool* ardilla *f* listada.

chiropodist [kɪ'rɒpədɪst] *n* podólogo,-a *m,f*, pedicuro,-a *m,f*, callista *mf*.

chiropody [kɪ'rɒpədɪ] *n Med* pedicura *f*.

chirp [tʃɜːp] **I** *vi (birds)* gorjear; *(insects)* chirriar, cantar. **II** *n (of birds)* gorjeo *m*; *(of insects)* chirrido *m*.

chisel ['tʃɪzəl] **I** *n* cincel *m*. **II** *vtr (pt & pp chiselled, US chiseled)* **1** cincelar. **2** *sl* timar, estafar.

chit¹ [tʃɪt] *n* nota *f*; *(small invoice)* vale *m*.

chit² [tʃɪt] *n pej* mocoso,-a *m,f*.

chitchat ['tʃɪttʃæt] *n fam* palique *m*, habladurías *fpl*.

chivalrous ['ʃɪvəlrəs] *adj* caballeroso,-a.

chivalry ['ʃɪvəlrɪ] *n* **1** *(bravery etc)* caballerosidad *f*. **2** *Hist* caballería *f*.

chives [tʃaɪvz] *npl Bot* cebolleta *f sing*.

chloride ['klɔːraɪd] *n Chem* cloruro *m*.

chlorinate ['klɔːrɪneɪt] *vtr* tratar con cloro.

chlorine ['klɔːriːn] *n* cloro *m*.

chloroform ['klɒrəfɔːm] *n Chem* cloroformo *m*.

chlorophyll, *US* **chlorophyl** ['klɒrəfɪl] *n Biol* clorofila *f*.

choc-ice ['tʃɒkaɪs] *n* helado *m* cubierto de chocolate.

chock [tʃɒk] *n* calzo *m*, cuña *f*.

chock-a-block [tʃɒkə'blɒk] *adj fam*, **chock-full** [tʃɒk'fʊl] *adj fam* hasta los topes, de bote en bote.

chocolate ['tʃɒkəlɪt] **I** *n* **1** chocolate *m*; **bar of c.**, chocolatina *f*, tableta *f* de chocolate; **drinking c.**, chocolate *m* (en taza). **2 chocolates**, bombones *mpl*; **a box of c.**, una caja de bombones. **II** *adj (cake etc)* de chocolate; *(colour)* de color chocolate.

choice [tʃɔɪs] **I** *n* elección *f*, selección *f*; **a big** *or* **wide c.**, un gran surtido; **by c.**, por gusto; **she's my c. for the post**, es la candidata que yo recomiendo para el puesto; **to make a c.**, escoger, elegir. **II** *adj* selecto,-a, de primera calidad.

choir ['kwaɪəʳ] *n Mus* coro *m*, coral *f*.

choirboy ['kwaɪəbɔɪ] *n Mus* niño *m* de coro.

choirmaster ['kwaɪəmɑːstəʳ] *n* **1** *Mus* director *m* de coro. **2** *(in church)* maestro *m* de capilla.

choke [tʃəʊk] **I** *vtr* **1** *(person)* ahogar, asfixiar. **2** *(obstruct)* obstruir, atascar. **II** *vi* ahogarse, asfixiarse; **to c. on food**, atragantarse con la comida. **III** *n Aut* stárter *m*. ◆ **choke back** *vtr (anger, tears)* contener, tragarse.

choker ['tʃəʊkəʳ] *n* gargantilla *f*.

cholera ['kɒlərə] *n Med* cólera *m*.

cholesterol [kə'lestərɒl] *n* colesterol *m*.

choose [tʃuːz] **I** *vtr (pt chose; pp chosen)* **1** *(select)* escoger, elegir; **to c. sb to be** *or* **as a candidate**, designar a algn como candidato,-a; *fig* **the chosen few**, los elegidos. **2** *(decide)* optar por, decidir; **he chose not to do anything**, decidió no hacer nada. **II** *vi* escoger, elegir; **do as you c.**, haz lo que quieras; **there's little to c. between them**, son muy parecidos, tanto monta monta tanto; **there's little** *or* **not much to c. from**, no hay dónde escoger.

choos(e)y ['tʃuːzɪ] *adj (choosier, choosiest) fam* exigente, difícil de complacer.

chop¹ [tʃɒp] **I** *vtr (pt & pp chopped)* **1** *(wood, branch)* cortar; **to c. a branch off a tree**, cortar una rama de un árbol; **to c. a tree down**, talar *or* cortar un árbol; **to c. sth up**, cortar algo en pedazos. **2** *Culin (meat, onions)* cortar a pedacitos. **II** *n* **1** *(blow)* tajo *m*, golpe *m*; *(with axe)* hachazo *m*; *fam* **to get the c.**, ser despedido,-a (del trabajo). **2** *Culin* chuleta *f*; **pork c.**, chuleta de cerdo.

chop² [tʃɒp] *vi (pt & pp chopped)* cambiar bruscamente; **to c. and change**, cambiar *or* estar cambiando como el viento.

chopper ['tʃɒpəʳ] *n* **1** cuchilla *f* de carnicero. **2** *fam* helicóptero *m*.

choppy ['tʃɒpɪ] *adj (choppier, choppiest) (sea)* picado,-a.

chopsticks ['tʃɒpstɪks] *npl* palillos *mpl*.

choral ['kɔːrəl] *adj Mus* coral; **c. society**, orfeón *m*.

chorale [kɒ'rɑːl] *n Mus* coral *m*.

chord¹ [kɔːd] *n* **1** *Math* cuerda *f*. **2** *fig (response)* **it strikes a c.**, (me) suena; *fig* **to touch the right c.**, conmover (a algn). **3** *Anat see* **cord**.

chord² [kɔːd] *n Mus (group of sounds)* acorde *m*.

chore [tʃɔːʳ] *n* quehacer *m*, tarea *f*; **to do the chores**, hacer la limpieza de la casa.

choreographer [kɒrɪ'ɒgrəfəʳ] *n* coreógrafo,-a *m,f*.

choreography [kɒrɪ'ɒgrəfɪ] *n* coreografía *f*.

chorister ['kɒrɪstəʳ] *n* corista *mf*.

chortle ['tʃɔːtəl] **I** *vi* reírse, reír con ganas. **II** *n* risa *f* alegre.

chorus ['kɔːrəs] *n (pl **choruses**) Mus Theat* coro *m; (in a song)* estribillo *m;* in **c.**, a coro; **there was a c. of protest,** todos protestaron a la vez. ■ **c. girl,** corista *f.*

chose [tʃəʊz] *pt see* **choose.**

chosen ['tʃəʊzən] *pp see* **choose.**

chough [tʃʌf] *n Orn* chova *f* piquirroja.

chowder ['tʃaʊdəʳ] *n US Culin* crema *f* de almejas *or* de pescado.

Christ [kraɪst] *n Rel* Cristo *m*, Jesucristo *m.*

christen ['krɪsən] *vtr Rel* bautizar.

christening ['krɪsənɪŋ] *n Rel (sacrament)* bautismo *m; (celebration)* bautizo *m.*

Christian ['krɪstʃən] *Rel* I *adj* cristiano,-a; **c. name,** nombre *m* de pila. II *n* cristiano,-a *m, f.*

Christianity [krɪstɪˈænɪtɪ] *n Rel* cristianismo *m.*

Christmas ['krɪsməs] *n* Navidad *f;* at **C.**, por Navidades; **Father C.,** Papá Noel *m,* Santa Claus *m;* **merry C.,** feliz Navidad. ■ **C. card,** tarjeta *f* de Navidad; **C. carol,** villancico *m;* **C. Day,** día *m* de Navidad; **C. Eve,** Nochebuena *f.*

chrome [krəʊm] *n* cromo *m.*

chromium ['krəʊmɪəm] *n Chem* cromo *m; Tech* **c. plated,** cromado,-a. ■ *Tech* **c. plating,** cromado *m.*

chromosome ['krəʊməsəʊm] *n Biol* cromosoma *m.*

chronic ['krɒnɪk] *adj* 1 crónico,-a; **to suffer from c. ill health,** tener mala salud. 2 *fam* horroroso,-a, fatal.

chronicle ['krɒnɪkəl] I *n* crónica *f.* II *vtr* hacer la crónica de.

chronicler ['krɒnɪkləʳ] *n* cronista *mf.*

chronological [krɒnəˈlɒdʒɪkəl] *adj* cronológico,-a.

chronometer [krəˈnɒmɪtəʳ] *n* cronómetro *m.*

chrysalis ['krɪsəlɪs] *n (pl **chrysalises**) Ent* crisálida *f.*

chrysanthemum [krɪˈsænθəməm] *n Bot* crisantemo *m.*

chub [tʃʌb] *n (fish)* cacho *m.*

chubby ['tʃʌbɪ] *adj (**chubbier, chubbiest**)* llenito,-a, gordinflón,-ona; **c. cheeked,** mofletudo,-a.

chuck [tʃʌk] *vtr fam* tirar; **c. it (in)!,** ¡déjalo!, ¡deja eso!; **to c. one's job in *or* up,** dejar el trabajo; **to c. sb out,** echar a algn; *(from work)* poner a algn de patitas en la calle; **to c. sth away *or* out,** tirar algo.

chuckle ['tʃʌkəl] I *vi* reír en silencio. II *n* sonrisita *f.*

chug [tʃʌg] *vi (pt & pp **chugged**) (engine)* resoplar; *(while moving)* traquetear.

chum [tʃʌm] *n* compinche *mf,* compañero,-a *m, f.*

chummy ['tʃʌmɪ] *adj (**chummier, chummiest**) fam* simpático,-a; **to be c. with sb,** ser amigo,-a de algn; **they're very c.,** son carne y uña.

chump [tʃʌmp] *n* 1 *fam (idiot)* imbécil *m.* 2 *(of meat)* **c. chop,** chuletón *m.* 3 *GB sl (head)* coco *m;* **to be off one's c.,** estar mal de la azotea.

chunk [tʃʌŋk] *n fam* cacho *m,* pedazo *m.*

chunky ['tʃʌŋkɪ] *adj (**chunkier, chunkiest**) (wood)* grueso,-a; *(marmalade)* con pedazos de fruta.

church [tʃɜːtʃ] *n* iglesia *f;* **to go to c.,** ir al oficio *or* a misa; *fig* **to enter the c.,** hacerse cura *or* pastor *or* monja. ■ **c. hall,** sala *f* parroquial; **C. of England,** Iglesia *f* Anglicana.

churchgoer ['tʃɜːtʃgəʊəʳ] *n Rel* practicante *mf.*

churchwarden [tʃɜːtʃˈwɔːdən] *n C of E* capillero *m.*

churchyard ['tʃɜːtʃjɑːd] *n* cementerio *m,* campo *m* santo.

churlish ['tʃɜːlɪʃ] *adj* grosero,-a, maleducado,-a.

churlishness ['tʃɜːlɪʃnɪs] *n* grosería *f,* mala educación *f.*

churn [tʃɜːn] *n* 1 *(for butter)* mantequera *f.* 2 *GB (for milk)* lechera *f.* II *vtr (butter)* hacer; *(cream)* batir. III *vi* revolverse, agitarse. ◆ **churn out** *vtr fam* producir en serie. ◆ **churn up** *vtr* revolver, agitar.

chute [ʃuːt] *n* 1 *(channel)* conducto *m.* 2 *(slide)* tobogán *m.*

chutney ['tʃʌtnɪ] *n Culin* conserva *f* (de frutas) picante.

CIA [siːaɪˈeɪ] *US abbr of* **Central Intelligence Agency,** Agencia *f* Central de Información, CIA *f.*

cicada [sɪˈkɑːdə] *n (pl **cicadas** or **cicadae** [sɪˈkɑːdiː]) Ent* cigarra *f.*

CID [siːaɪˈdiː] *GB abbr of* **Criminal Investigation Department,** ≈ Brigada *f* de Investigación Criminal, BIC.

cider ['saɪdəʳ] *n* sidra *f.*

cig [sɪg] *n (abbr of **cigarette**) fam* pitillo *m.*

cigar [sɪˈgɑːʳ] *n* puro *m,* cigarro *m.*

cigarette [sɪgəˈret] *n* cigarrillo *m;* **a packet/carton of cigarettes,** un paquete/un cartón de tabaco. ■ **c. case,** pitillera *f;* **c. end,** colilla *f;* **c. holder,** boquilla *f;* **c. lighter,** mechero *m,* encendedor *m.*

C-in-C [siːɪnˈsiː] *Mil abbr of* **Commander-in-Chief,** Comandante *m* en jefe.

cinch [sɪntʃ] *n fam* **it's a c.,** está chupado *or* tirado.

cinder ['sɪndəʳ] *n* ceniza *f,* pavesa *f.*

Cinderella [sɪndəˈrelə] *n* Cenicienta *f.*

cine camera ['sɪnɪkæmərə] *n GB* cámara *f* cinematográfica.

cinema ['sɪnɪmə] *n* cine *m.*

cinnamon ['sɪnəmən] *n* canela *f.*

cipher ['saɪfəʳ] *n* 1 *(numeral)* cifra *f; (code)* código *m;* **in c.,** cifrado,-a. 2 *fig (nonentity)* cero *m* a la izquierda, don nadie *m.*

circa ['sɜːkə] *prep* hacia, alrededor de.

circle ['sɜːkəl] I *n* 1 *(shape)* círculo *m; Geom* circunferencia *f; (of people)* corro *m;* **fig to go round in circles,** dar muchas vueltas. 2 *(cycle)* ciclo *m; fig* **to come full c.,** completar un ciclo; *fig* **vicious c.,** círculo *m* vicioso. 3 *(group)* círculo *m;* **a c. of friends,** un círculo de amigos; **in business circles,** en el mundo de los negocios. 4 *Theat* piso *m;* **upper c.,** segundo piso. 5 *US* **traffic c.,** glorieta *f.* II *vtr (in a circle round)* rodear; *(move round)* dar la vuelta a. III *vi* dar vueltas.

circuit ['sɜːkɪt] *n* 1 *(journey round)* recorrido *m;* **to make a c.,** recorrer. 2 *Elec* circuito *m; Sport* **short c.,** cortocircuito *m.* ■ **c. breaker,** cortacircuitos *m inv.* 3 *Sport (events)* liga *f; GB (racing track)* circuito *m.* 4 *Cin Theat* cadena *f.* 5 *GB Jur* distrito *m;* **c. judge,** juez *mf* de distrito.

circuitous [səˈkjuːɪtəs] *adj* indirecto,-a, tortuoso,-a.

circular ['sɜːkjʊləʳ] I *adj* circular; **c. saw,** sierra circular; **c. tour,** circuito *m.* II *n* circular *f.*

circulate ['sɜːkjʊleɪt] I *vtr (news)* hacer circular. II *vi* circular; **circulating library,** biblioteca *f* ambulante.

circulation [sɜːkjʊˈleɪʃən] *n* 1 *(of blood)* circulación *f.* 2 *Press (of newspaper)* tirada *f; (of news)* difusión *f.*

circumcise ['sɜːkəmsaɪz] *vtr Med* circuncidar.

circumcision [sɜːkəmˈsɪʒən] *n Med* circuncisión *f.*

circumference [səˈkʌmfərəns] *n* circunferencia *f.*

circumflex ['sɜːkəmfleks] *n* circumflejo *m.*

circumlocution [sɜːkəmləˈkjuːʃən] *n* circunloquio *m.*

circumnavigate [sɜːkəmˈnævɪgeɪt] *vtr* circunnavegar.

circumscribe ['sɜːkəmskraɪb] *vtr* 1 *(restrict)* restringir, limitar. 2 *Geom* circunscribir.

circumspect ['sɜːkəmspekt] *adj* circunspecto,-a, prudente, cauteloso,-a.

circumstance ['sɜːkəmstəns] *n (gen pl)* circunstancia *f;* **in *or* under no circumstances,** en ningún caso, bajo ningún concepto; **in the circumstances,** dadas las circunstancias; **it depends on your circumstances,** depende de tu situación económica.

circumstantial [sɜːkəmˈstænʃəl] *adj (gen)* circunstancial; *(report)* circunstanciado,-a.

circumvent [sɜːkəmˈvent] *vtr fig (law)* burlar; *(plans)* frustrar.

circus ['sɜːkəs] *n (pl **circuses**)* 1 circo *m.* 2 *GB (part of town)* glorieta *f,* plaza *f* redonda.

cirrhosis [sɪ'rəʊsɪs] *n Med* cirrosis *f*.

cistern ['sɪstən] *n* cisterna *f*.

citadel ['sɪtədəl] *n* ciudadela *f*; *fig* bastión *f*.

citation [saɪ'teɪʃən] *n* **1** *(quotation)* cita *f*. **2** *Mil (award)* mención *f*. **3** *Jur (summons)* citación *f*.

cite [saɪt] *vtr* **1** *(quote)* citar. **2** *Mil* mencionar.

citizen ['sɪtɪzən] *n (native)* ciudadano,-a *m,f*, súbdito,-a *m,f*.

citizenship ['sɪtɪzənʃɪp] *n* ciudadanía *f*.

citric ['sɪtrɪk] *adj* cítrico,-a; **c. acid,** ácido cítrico.

citr(o)us ['sɪtrəs] *adj* cítrico,-a; **c. fruit,** agrios *mpl*, cítricos *mpl*.

city ['sɪtɪ] *n* **1** *(town)* ciudad *f*. ■ **c. centre,** centro *m* de la ciudad; **c. hall,** ayuntamiento *m*. **2** *Fin* **the C.,** el centro financiero de Londres.

civic ['sɪvɪk] *adj* cívico,-a; **c. authorities,** autoridades municipales; *GB* **c. centre,** centro cívico; **c. duties,** obligaciones cívicas.

civics ['sɪvɪks] *npl* educación *f* cívica.

civil ['sɪvəl] *adj* **1** *(non-military etc)* civil. ■ **c. defence,** defensa *f* civil; **c. disobedience,** resistencia *f* pasiva; **c. law,** derecho *m* civil; **c. rights,** derechos *mpl* civiles; *Pol* **c. servant,** funcionario,-a *m,f*; *Pol* **c. service,** administración *f* pública. **2** *(polite)* cortés, educado,-a.

civilian [sɪ'vɪljən] *adj & n* civil *(mf)*.

civility [sɪ'vɪlɪtɪ] *n* cortesía *f*.

civilization [sɪvɪlaɪ'zeɪʃən] *n* civilización *f*.

civilize ['sɪvɪlaɪz] *vtr* civilizar.

cl *abbr of* **centilitre(s),** centilitro(s) *m(pl)*, cl.

clad [klæd] *lit* I *pt & pp see* **clothe.** II *adj* vestido,-a.

claim [kleɪm] I *vtr* **1** *(property, benefits, rights)* reclamar; *Jur (compensation)* exigir. **2** *(assert)* afirmar, alegar, sostener. II *n* **1** *(demand)* reclamación *f*; *Ins* demanda *f* de indemnización, reclamación; *Jur* demanda, reclamación judicial; *Jur* **to lay c. to sth,** reclamar el derecho a algo; **to make a c. for,** reclamar; **to put in a c.,** reclamar una indemnización; **to put in a c. for damages,** demandar por daños. **2** *(right)* derecho *m*; **to have a c. on sth,** tener derecho a algo; *fig* **his only c. to fame is ...,** su único mérito es ... . **3** *(assertion)* pretensión *f*, afirmación *f*; **he made a c. to be a millionaire,** alegó que era millonario. **4** *Min* concesión *f*.

claimant ['kleɪmənt] *n (gen)* reclamante *mf*, pretendiente *mf*; *Jur* demandante *mf*.

clairvoyance [kleə'vɔɪəns] *n* clarividencia *f*.

clairvoyant [kleə'vɔɪənt] *n* clarividente *mf*.

clam [klæm] *n Zool* almeja *f*. ♦ **clam up** *vi (pt & pp clammed)* *fam* callarse.

clamber ['klæmbə'] *vi* trepar *(over,* por).

clammy ['klæmɪ] *adj (clammier, clammiest) (weather)* húmedo,-a, bochornoso,-a; *(hands)* pegajoso,-a.

clamor ['klæmə'] *n US see* **clamour.**

clamorous ['klæmərəs] *adj (demand)* clamoroso,-a; *(crowd)* vociferante.

clamour ['klæmə'] I *n* clamor *m*, griterío *m*. II *vi* clamar, vociferar; **to c. for,** *(things)* pedir a gritos; *(justice)* clamar por.

clamp [klæmp] I *n Carp* tornillo *m* de banco; *Tech* abrazadera *f*; **wheel c.,** cepo *m*. II *vtr* sujetar con abrazaderas. ♦ **clamp down on** *vtr (restrict)* restringir; *(supress)* suprimir.

clampdown ['klæmpdaʊn] *n* restricción *f*.

clan [klæn] *n* clan *m*.

clandestine [klæn'destɪn] *adj* clandestino,-a.

clang [klæŋ] I *vi* sonar. II *vtr* hacer sonar. III *n* sonido *m* metálico.

clanger ['klæŋə'] *n fam* metedura *f* de pata; **to drop a c.,** meter la pata.

clank [klæŋk] I *n* sonido *m* seco y metálico. II *vtr (chains)* hacer sonar. III *vi* sonar.

clannish ['klænɪʃ] *adj* exclusivista.

clansman ['klænzmən] *n (pl* **clansmen***)* miembro *m* de un clan.

clap¹ [klæp] I *vtr (pt & pp* **clapped***)* **1** *(person, performance)* aplaudir; **to c. one's hands,** aplaudir; **to c. sb on the back,** dar a algn una palmada en la espalda. **2** *fam* **to c. eyes on,** ver; **to c. sb in prison,** meter a algn en chirona. II *vi* aplaudir; **to c. to the music,** seguir la música con las palmas. III *n* **1** *(with hands)* palmada *f*; **to give sb a c.,** aplaudir a algn. **2** *(light blow)* palmada *f*, golpecito *m* con la mano. **3** *(noise)* ruido *m* seco; **a c. of thunder,** un trueno.

clap² [klæp] *n sl* gonorrea *f*.

clapped-out [klæpt'aʊt] *adj GB Austral fam* rendido,-a.

clapper ['klæpə'] *n* badajo *m*.

clapping ['klæpɪŋ] *n* aplausos *mpl*.

claptrap ['klæptræp] *n fam* disparates *mpl*.

claret ['klærət] *n* **1** *GB (wine)* clarete *m*. **2** *(colour)* burdeos *m*.

clarification [klærɪfɪ'keɪʃən] *n* aclaración *f*, clarificación *f*.

clarify ['klærɪfaɪ] *vtr (pt & pp* **clarified***)* aclarar, clarificar.

clarinet [klærɪ'net] *n Mus* clarinete *m*.

clarity ['klærɪtɪ] *n* claridad *f*.

clash [klæʃ] I *vi* **1** *(cymbals)* sonar; *(swords)* chocar; *fig* hacer ruido; **to c. with sb,** estar en desacuerdo con algn. **2** *(colours)* desentonar. **3** *(dates)* coincidir. II *n* **1** *(sound)* sonido *m*, ruido *m*; **the c. of cymbals,** el sonido de los platillos; *fig* **a border c.,** un encuentro fronterizo. **2** *(fight)* choque *m*, encuentro *m*; *fig (conflict)* conflicto *m*, desacuerdo *m*; **a c. of interest,** un conflicto de intereses.

clasp [klɑːsp] I *n* **1** *(on belt)* cierre *m*, hebilla *f*; *(on necklace)* broche *m*. **2** *(grasp)* apretón *m*. ■ **c. knife,** navaja *f*. II *vtr (object)* agarrar, asir; **to c. hands,** juntar las manos.

class [klɑːs] I *n* **1** *(kind)* clase *f*, especie *f*, género *m*; *Biol* **a c. of mammal,** una clase de mamífero; *fig* **in a c. of its own,** sin par or igual. **2** *(in society)* clase *f*; **he's working c.,** es de la clase obrera. ■ *Pol* **c. struggle,** lucha *f* de clases; **social c.,** clase *f* social; **middle c.,** clase *f* media, burguesía *f*; **upper c.,** aristocracia *f*. **3** *Educ* clase *f*; *US Educ* **c. of '84,** promoción *f* de 1984; **evening classes,** clases nocturnas; *GB Educ* **first-c. honours degree,** título *m* con sobresaliente; **she's in my c.,** está en or es de mi clase. **4** *(of travel)* clase *f*; *Rail* **first/second c. ticket,** billete *m* de primera/segunda (clase); **tourist c.,** clase *f* turista. II *vtr* clasificar.

class-conscious [klɑːs'kɒnʃəs] *adj* clasista, con conciencia de clase.

classic ['klæsɪk] I *adj* clásico,-a. II *n* **1** *(author)* autor *m* clásico; *(work)* obra *f* clásica. **2 the classics,** *(literature)* las obras clásicas, los clásicos; *(languages)* clásicas *fpl*.

classical ['klæsɪkəl] *adj* clásico,-a.

classification [klæsɪfɪ'keɪʃən] *n* clasificación *f*.

classified ['klæsɪfaɪd] *adj (information)* secreto,-a; *Press* **c. advertisements,** anuncios *mpl* por palabras.

classify ['klæsɪfaɪ] *vtr (pt & pp* **classified***)* clasificar.

classless ['klɑːslɪs] *adj* sin clases.

classmate ['klɑːsmeɪt] *n* compañero,-a *m,f* de clase.

classroom ['klɑːsruːm] *n* aula *f*, clase *f*.

classy ['klɑːsɪ] *adj (classier, classiest) sl* con clase, elegante.

clatter ['klætə'] I *vi (pots etc)* hacer ruido; *(things falling)* hacer estrépito; *(machinery)* traquetear; *(hoofs)* chacolotear. II *n (of pots etc)* ruido *m*; *(of things falling)* estrépito *m*; *(of machinery)* traqueteo *m*; *(of hoofs)* chacoloteo *m*.

clause [klɔːz] *n Ling Jur* cláusula *f*.

claustrophobia [klɔːstrə'fəʊbɪə] *n* claustrofobia *f*.

claustrophobic [klɔːstrə'fəʊbɪk] *adj (person)* que padece claustrofobia; *(situation)* claustrofóbico,-a, que produce claustrofobia.

clavicle ['klævɪkəl] *n Anat* clavícula *f*.

claw [klɔ:] **I** *n* **1** *Zool* (*of bird, lion*) garra *f*; (*of cat*) uña *f*; (*of crab*) pinza *f*. **2 c. hammer,** martillo *m* de orejas. **II** *vtr* agarrar, arañar; (*tear*) desgarrar. ◆ **claw at** *vtr* agarrar, arañar. ◆ **claw back** *vtr* (*money*) lograr recuperar.

clay [kleɪ] *n* arcilla *f*. ■ **c. pigeon,** plato *m*; **c. pigeon shooting,** tiro *m* al plato.

clean [kli:n] **I** *adj* **1** (*not dirty*) limpio,-a. **2** (*unmarked, pure*) correcto,-a, sin defecto; **a c. copy,** una copia en limpio; **they gave him a c. bill of health,** lo declararon en perfecto estado de salud; **to have a c. record,** no tener antecedentes penales; **to have a c. (driving) licence,** no haber cometido infracciones (de tráfico). **3** (*shape*) limpio,-a; **a c. cut,** un corte limpio; **the building has c. lines,** el edificio tiene unas líneas bien definidas. **4** (*not obscene*) decente; **keep it c.!,** ¡nada de groserías! **5** *fig* to **make a c. breast of it,** contarlo todo; **to make a c. sweep of it,** arrasar. **II** *adv* **1** limpiamente; *Sport* **to play c.,** jugar limpio; *fam* **to come c.,** confesarlo todo. **2** *fam* por completo; **it went c. through the middle,** pasó justo por el medio; **they got c. away,** desaparecieron por completo. **III** *vtr* (*room*) limpiar; **to c. one's teeth,** lavarse los dientes. **IV** *n* limpieza *f*; **to give sth a c.,** limpiar algo. ◆ **clean out** *vtr* **1** (*room*) limpiar a fondo. **2** *sl* (*leave broke*) dejar limpio a *or* sin blanca. ◆ **clean up** *vtr & vi* limpiar.

clean-cut ['kli:nkʌt] *adj* **1** (*person*) limpio,-a, pulcro,-a. **2** (*decision*) claro,-a, bien definido,-a.

cleaner ['kli:nə'] *n* (*person*) encargado,-a *m, f* de la limpieza; *fam fig* **to take sb to the c.'s,** dejar limpio,-a *or* sin blanca a algn. ■ **c.'s (shop),** tintorería *f*.

cleaning ['kli:nɪŋ] *n* limpieza *f*. ■ **c. lady,** asistenta *f*, mujer *f* de la limpieza.

cleanliness ['klenlɪnɪs] *n* limpieza *f*.

cleanse [klenz] *vtr* limpiar.

clean-shaven [kli:n'ʃeɪvən] *adj* (*man*) sin barba ni bigote.

cleansing ['klenzɪŋ] *n* limpieza *f*. ■ **c. lotion,** leche *f* limpiadora.

clear [klɪə'] **I** *adj* **1** (*image, handwriting, instruction*) claro,-a; (*road, view, day*) despejado,-a; **c. conscience,** conciencia *f* limpia; *Culin* **c. soup,** consomé *m*. **2** (*obvious, certain*) claro,-a; **have I made myself c.?,** ¿me explico (con claridad)?; **it's c. to me that ...,** me parece evidente que ...; **to make sth c.,** aclarar algo; *fam* **I'm not very c. about it,** no me aclaro. **3** (*complete, definite*) neto,-a, absoluto,-a; **c. majority,** mayoría absoluta; **c. profit,** beneficio *m* neto; **he earns a c. £150 a week,** gana 150 libras semanales limpias; **three c. days,** tres días completos. **4** (*free*) libre; **c. of,** libre de; **when the coast is c.,** cuando el campo esté libre. **II** *adv* **1** claramente; *fig* **loud and c.,** claramente. **2** (*away*) **stand c.!,** ¡apártese!; **to keep** *or* **stay c. of,** evitar, apartarse de. **III** *n* **in the c.,** (*from danger*) fuera de peligro; (*from suspicion*) fuera de toda sospecha. **IV** *vtr* **1** (*snow*) limpiar; (*room*) vaciar; (*pipe*) desatascar; *Com* (*stock, debt*) liquidar; **to c. one's throat,** aclararse la garganta; **to c. the table,** quitar la mesa; **to c. the way,** abrir (el) camino; *fig* **to c. the air,** aclarar las cosas. **2** (*authorize*) autorizar; **c. it with the boss,** pregúntaselo al jefe. **3** (*pass*) pasar por encima de; *Sport* (*hurdle*) salvar, saltar sin tocar; **to c. customs,** pasar por la aduana. **4** *Jur* descargar; **to c. sb of a charge,** exculpar a algn de un delito. **V** *vi* (*weather, sky*) despejarse. ◆ **clear away** *vtr* (*dishes, etc*) quitar. ◆ **clear off I** *vtr* (*debts*) liquidar. **II** *vi fam* largarse; **c. off!,** ¡largo!, ¡fuera (de aquí)! ◆ **clear out I** *vtr* (*room*) limpiar a fondo; (*cupboard*) vaciar; (*old clothes*) tirar. **II** *vi fam* largarse. ◆ **clear up I** *vtr* **1** (*tidy*) recoger; (*arrange*) ordenar, poner en orden. **2** (*mystery*) resolver; (*misunderstanding*) aclarar. **II** *vi* **1** (*tidy up*) recoger. **2** (*weather*) despejarse; (*illness, problem*) desaparecer. ◆

clearly *adv* **1** claramente, con claridad; *fig* **to see c.,** entender bien. **2** (*at start of sentence*) evidentemente.

clearance ['klɪərəns] *n* **1** (*of area*) despeje *m*. ■ *Com* **c. sale,** liquidación *f* (de existencias). **2** (*space*) espacio *m* libre. **3** (*authorization*) autorización *f*.

clear-cut [klɪə'kʌt] *adj* claro,-a, bien definido,-a.

clear-headed [klɪə'hedɪd] *adj* lúcido,-a, perspicaz.

clearing ['klɪərɪŋ] *n* **1** (*in wood*) claro *m*. **2** (*of rubbish*) limpieza *f*; (*of pipe*) desatasco *m*. **3** *Fin* (*of cheque*) compensación *f*.

clearness ['klɪənɪs] *n* claridad *f*.

clear-sighted [klɪə'saɪtɪd] *adj fig* clarividente, perspicaz.

clearway ['klɪəweɪ] *n GB Aut* carretera *f* donde está prohibido parar.

cleavage ['kli:vɪdʒ] *n* **1** *fam* (*in dress*) escote *m*. **2** (*split*) división *f*.

cleave¹ [kli:v] *vtr* (*pt* **cleft, cleaved** *or* **clove;** *pp* **cleft, cleaved** *or* **cloven**) dividir, partir (por la mitad).

cleave² [kli:v] *vi* (*cling*) adherirse (**to, a**).

cleaver ['kli:və'] *n* cuchillo *f* de carnicero.

clef [klef] *n Mus* clave *f*; **bass/treble c.,** clave de fa/de sol.

cleft [kleft] **I** *pt & pp see* **cleave¹.** **II** *n* hendidura *f*, grieta *f*. ■ *Med* **c. palate,** fisura *f* del paladar.

clematis ['klemətɪs] *n Bot* clemátide *f*.

clemency ['klemənsɪ] *n* clemencia *f*; **to appeal for c.,** pedir clemencia.

clementine ['kleməntaɪn] *n* clementina *f*.

clench [klentʃ] *vtr* (*teeth, fist*) apretar; **with clenched fist,** con el puño cerrado.

clergy ['klɜ:dʒɪ] *n Rel* clero *m*.

clergyman ['klɜ:dʒɪmən] *n* (*pl* **clergymen**) *Rel* clérigo *m*.

cleric ['klerɪk] *n Rel* eclesiástico *m*.

clerical ['klerɪkəl] *adj* **1** *Rel* clerical, eclesiástico,-a. ■ **c. collar,** alzacuello *m*. **2** *Admin* de oficina. ■ **c. staff,** oficinistas *mfpl*.

clerk [klɑ:k, *US* klɜ:rk] *n* **1** (*office worker*) oficinista *mf*; *Admin* funcionario,-a *m,f*. ■ **bank c.,** empleado,-a *m,f* de banco; *Jur* **c. of the court,** secretario,-a *m,f* de juzgado; *Constr* **c. of the works,** maestro *m* de obras. **2** *US Com* dependiente,-a *m,f*, vendedor,-a *m,f*.

clever ['klevə'] *adj* **1** (*person*) inteligente, listo,-a, espabilado,-a; **c. at maths,** fuerte en matemáticas; **she's c. with her hands,** tiene mucha destreza manual; **that was/wasn't very c. of you,** lo hiciste muy bien/mal; **to be c. at sth,** tener habilidad *or* aptitud para algo; *fam* **he's too c. by half,** se pasa de listo. ■ *fam* **c. Dick,** sabiondo,-a *m,f*, sabelotodo *mf*. **2** (*argument*) ingenioso,-a, astuto,-a. ◆ **cleverly** *adv* con inteligencia; (*skilfully*) hábilmente.

cleverness ['klevənɪs] *n* **1** (*intelligence*) inteligencia *f*, (*skill*) habilidad *f*. **2** (*of argument*) ingenio *m*.

cliché ['kli:ʃeɪ] *n* cliché *m*, lugar *m* común.

click [klɪk] **I** *n* (*sound*) clic *m*; (*with the tongue*) chasquido *m* **II** *vtr* (*tongue*) chasquear, **to c. one's heels,** taconear **III** *vt* **1** (*realize*) captar; **suddenly I clicked,** de pronto caí en la cuenta **2** *fam* congeniar, **they clicked at once,** enseguida congeniaron.

clicking ['klɪkɪŋ] *n* chasquido *m*

client ['klaɪənt] *n* cliente *mf*

clientele [kli:ɒn'tel] *n* clientela *f*.

cliff [klɪf] *n* acantilado *m*, precipicio *m*.

cliffhanger ['klɪfhæŋə'] *n* momento *m* de suspense

climate ['klaɪmɪt] *n* clima *m*

climatic [klaɪ'mætɪk] *adj* climático,-a

climax ['klaɪmæks] *n* **1** (*peak*) clímax *m*, punto *m* culminante **2** (*sexual*) orgasmo *m*

climb [klaɪm] **I** *vtr* trepar a, subir a; **to c. a ladder,** subir una escalera, **to c. a mountain,** subir una montaña, *Sport* escalar una montaña, **to c. (up) a tree,** trepar a un árbol. **II**

vi subir, trepar, *(plants)* trepar, *Av* subir, *(sun)* ascender, *fig (socially)* ascender, subir **III** *n* subida *f*, ascensión *f* ◆ **climb down** *vi* bajar, *fig* volverse atrás.

climber ['klaɪmə'] *n* **1** *Sport* alpinista *mf* **2** *Bot* enredadera *f* **3** *fig* **social c.**, arribista *mf*

climbing ['klaɪmɪŋ] *n* *Sport* montañismo *m*, alpinismo *m* ■ **c. frame**, barras *fpl*.

clinch [klɪntʃ] **I** *vtr* resolver; **to c. a deal**, cerrar un trato, *fam* **that clinches it!**, ¡ni una palabra más!, ¡se acabó! **II** *n sl* abrazo *m* apasionado

cling [klɪŋ] *vi* *(pt & pp* **clung***)* *(hang on)* agarrarse, *(clothes)* ajustarse, *(smell)* pegarse; **to c. together**, unirse, *fig* **to c. to an opinion**, seguir fiel a una opinión

clinging ['klɪŋɪŋ] *adj* *(child)* enmadrado,-a, *(person)* pegajoso,-a; *(clothing)* ceñido,-a, ajustado,-a

clingy ['klɪŋɪ] *adj (clingier, clingiest) see* **clinging.**

clinic ['klɪnɪk] *n Med* **1** *(in state hospital)* ambulatorio *m*, dispensario *m*. **2** *(specialized)* clínica *f*; **dental c.**, clínica dental.

clinical ['klɪnɪkəl] *adj* **1** *Med* clínico,-a, **c. thermometer**, termómetro *m* clínico **2** *(detached)* imparcial, frío,-a.

clink[1] [klɪŋk] **I** *vt* tintinear. **II** *vtr* **to c. glasses (with sb)**, chocar copas *or* hacer chinchín (con algn) **III** *n (of keys, glasses)* tintineo *m*

clink[2] [klɪŋk] *n sl* chirona *f*, trena *f*.

clinker ['klɪŋkə'] *n* escoria *f* de hulla.

clip[1] [klɪp] **I** *vtr (pt & pp* **clipped***)* **1** *(cut)* cortar; *(sheep's wool)* esquilar; *(ticket)* picar, *fig* **to c. sb's wings**, cortar las alas a algn **2** *fam* dar un cachete a **II** *n* **1** *Cin (of film)* extracto *m*, escenas *fpl*. **2** *(with scissors)* tijeretada *f*. **3** *fam* cachete *m*.

clip[2] [klɪp] **I** *n (for hair)* pasador *m*, clip *m*, *(for paper)* clip *m*, sujetapapeles *m inv*, *(brooch)* alfiler *m* de pecho, clip *m*. **II** *vtr (pt & pp* **clipped***)* sujetar (con un clip)

clip-on ['klɪpɒn] *adj (earrings etc)* de clip

clipped [klɪpt] *adj fig (speech)* entrecortado,-a

clipper ['klɪpə'] *n Naut* clíper *m*.

clippers ['klɪpəz] *npl (for hair)* maquinilla *f* para cortar el pelo, *(for nails)* cortaúñas *m inv*; *(for hedge)* tijeras *fpl* de podar.

clipping ['klɪpɪŋ] *n* recorte *m*

clique [kliːk, klɪk] *n pej* camarilla *f*.

cliqu(e)y ['kliːkɪ] *adj*, **cliquish** ['kliːkɪʃ] *adj pej* exclusivista

clitoris ['klɪtərɪs] *n Anat* clítoris *m*.

cloak [kləʊk] **I** *n (garment)* capa *f*, *fig* pretexto *m*; **under the c. of**, so capa de. **II** *vtr* encubrir; **to c. in secrecy**, rodear de secreto.

cloak-and-dagger [kləʊkən'dægə'] *adj (gen)* clandestino,-a; *(films, books)* de capa y espada, de espías

cloakroom ['kləʊkruːm] *n* guardarropa *m*; *euph (toilets)* servicios *mpl*

clobber[1] ['klɒbə'] *vtr fam* **to c. sb**, dar una paliza a algn

clobber[2] ['klɒbə'] *n GB sl* trastos *mpl*, cachivaches *mpl*

clock [klɒk] **I** *n* reloj *m*, **it's five o'c.**, son las cinco; **to put the c. forward/back**, adelantar/atrasar el reloj, **to work round the c.**, trabajar día y noche. ■ **alarm c.**, despertador *m*; **grandfather c.**, reloj *m* de pie. **II** *vtr (race)* cronometrar. ◆ **clock in, clock on** *vi* fichar, llegar al trabajo ◆ **clock off, clock out** *vi* fichar a la salida. ◆ **clock up** *vtr (mileage)* hacer

clock-watcher ['klɒkwɒtʃə'] *n fam* empleado,-a *m,f* que sólo piensa en salir del trabajo.

clockwise ['klɒkwaɪz] *adj & adv* en el sentido de las agujas del reloj.

clockwork ['klɒkwɜːk] *n* mecanismo *m*, *fig* **to go like c.**, ir sobre ruedas ■ **c. toy**, juguete *m* de cuerda

clod [klɒd] *n* terrón *m*

clodhoppers ['klɒdhɒpəz] *npl fam* zapatones *mpl*.

clog [klɒg] **I** *vtr (pt & pp* **clogged***)* obstruir, *(pipe)* atascar, **to get clogged up**, atascarse. **II** *vi* **to c. (up)**, obstruirse, atascarse **III** *n (footwear)* zueco *m*

cloister ['klɔɪstə'] *n* claustro *m*.

close[1] [kləʊs] **I** *adj* **1** *(in space, time)* cercano,-a; *(print, weave)* compacto,-a; *(encounter)* cara a cara; *(contact)* directo,-a, **c. to**, cerca de, **c. together**, juntos; *fig* **at c. quarters**, de cerca; *fig* **we had a c. shave**, nos libramos por los pelos **2** *(of relationships)* cercano,-a; **c. friends**, amigos íntimos, **c. relative**, pariente cercano, **they're very c.**, están muy unidos *or* muy compenetrados. **3** *(careful)(inspection, examination)* detallado,-a, *(watch)* atento,-a; *(translation)* fiel, exacto,-a; **to pay c. attention**, prestar mucha atención **4** *(resemblance)* muy parecido,-a; *(contest, match, finish)* reñido,-a. **5** *(room, air)* cargado,-a; *(weather)* sofocante, bochornoso,-a. **6** *(secretive)* reservado,-a; **she's very c.**, es muy reservada, **to be c. about sth**, ser reacio a hablar de algo **7** *(mean)* tacaño,-a. **8** *(hunting)* **c. season**, veda *f* **II** *adv* cerca; **they live c. by** *or* **c. at hand**, viven cerca; **to come closer together**, acercarse, **to follow c. behind sb**, seguir a algn de cerca; **to stand c. together**, estar apretados,-as; *fig* **to be c. on forty**, andar rondando los cuarenta. ◆ **closely** *adv* **1** *(tightly, extremely)* estrechamente, muy; **c. connected**, estrechamente relacionado,-a, *(election, match)* **c. contested**, muy reñido,-a; *(people)* **they are c. related**, son parientes próximos; **they c. resemble each other**, se parecen muchísimo. **2** *(attentively)* con atención; **to follow (events) c.**, seguir *or* observar de cerca (los acontecimientos); **to watch/ listen c.**, observar/escuchar atentamente.

close[2] [kləʊz] **I** *vtr* **1** *(shut)* cerrar, *Com* **closing time**, hora *f* del cierre (del comercio); *Aut* 'road closed to traffic', 'carretera cerrada al tráfico'; *Mil* **to c. ranks**, cerrar filas, *fig* **to c. one's eyes to sth**, cerrar los ojos a algo. **2** *(end)* concluir, terminar, cerrar; *(meeting)* levantar; **the closing lines of the play**, el final de la obra. **3** *Fin Com* cerrar; **to c. a deal**, cerrar un trato; **to c. an account**, cerrar *or* liquidar una cuenta. **II** *vi* **1** *(shut)* cerrar, cerrarse. **2** *(end)* concluirse, terminarse. **III** *n* fin *m*, final *m*, conclusión *f*; **to bring to a c.**, concluir, terminar; **to draw to a c.**, tocar a su fin. ◆ **close down I** *vtr (business)* cerrar. **II** *vi (business)* cerrar; *Rad TV (broadcast)* cerrar. ◆ **close in** *vi* **1** *(days)* acortarse; *(night)* caer. **2** **to c. in on sb**, rodear a algn. ◆ **close up I** *vtr (business)* cerrar del todo. **II** *vi* cerrarse; *(wound)* cicatrizar; *Mil (ranks)* apretarse.

closed [kləʊzd] *adj* cerrado,-a; *fig* **a c. book**, un tema que se desconoce. ■ **c. circuit television**, televisión *f* por circuito cerrado; *Ind* **c. shop**, empresa *f* que emplea solamente a miembros de un sindicato.

close-down ['kləʊzdaʊn] *n* cierre *m*.

close-fitting [kləʊs'fɪtɪŋ] *adj (garment)* ajustado,-a, ceñido,-a.

close-knit [kləʊs'nɪt] *adj fig* unido,-a.

closeness ['kləʊsnɪs] *n* **1** *(nearness)* proximidad *f*; *(of connection, relationship)* intimidad *f*; *(of translation)* fidelidad *f*; *(of weather)* falta *f* de aire.

close-set [kləʊs'set] *adj* **c.-s. eyes**, ojos *mpl* muy juntos.

closet ['klɒzɪt] **I** *n US* armario *m*. **II** *vtr fig* **to be closeted with sb**, estar encerrado,-a con algn; **to c. oneself**, recluirse.

close-up ['kləʊsʌp] *n Phot* primer plano *m*; *fig* retrato *m*.

closing ['kləʊzɪŋ] *n* cierre *m*; *Com* **early c. day**, día *m* de cierre temprano. ■ *Fin* **c. price**, precio *m* al cierre; **c. time**, hora *f* de cerrar.

closure ['kləʊʒə'] *n* cierre *m*.

clot [klɒt] **I** *n* **1** *(of blood)* coágulo *m*; *Med* **c. on the brain**, embolia *f* cerebral. **2** *GB fam* tonto,-a *m,f*, bobo,-a *m,f*. **II** *vi (pt & pp* **clotted***)* coagularse, cuajar; *Culin* **clotted cream**, nata *f* cuajada.

cloth [klɒθ] *n (pl cloths* [klɒθs, klɒðz]*) (gen)* tela *f*, paño *m*; *(rag)* trapo *m*; *(tablecloth)* mantel *m*. ■ *Print* **c. binding,** encuadernación *f* en tela.

clothe [kləʊð] *vtr (pt & pp clothed or clad)* vestir **(in, with,** de); *fig* revestir, cubrir **(in, with,** de).

clothes [kləʊðz] *npl* ropa *f sing*, vestidos *mpl*; **in plain c.,** de paisano; **to put on/take off one's c.,** ponerse/quitarse la ropa; **with one's c. on/off,** vestido,-a/desnudo,-a. ■ **c. brush,** cepillo *m* de la ropa; **c. hanger,** percha *f*, colgador *m*; **c. horse,** tendedero *m* plegable; **c. line,** tendedero *m*; **c. peg,** pinza *f*.

clothing ['kləʊðɪŋ] *n* ropa *f*; **article of c.,** prenda *f* de vestir; **the c. industry,** la industria de la confección.

cloud [klaʊd] **I** *n* nube *f*; *fig* **a c. of insects,** una nube de insectos; *fig* **to be under a c.,** estar bajo sospecha; *fam* **to be on c. nine,** estar en el séptimo cielo; *prov* **every c. has a silver lining,** no hay mal que por bien no venga. **II** *vtr* nublar, anublar; **eyes clouded with tears,** ojos nublados *or* empañados de lágrimas; *fig* **to c. the issue,** complicar el asunto. **III** *vi (sky)* **to c. over,** nublarse.

cloudburst ['klaʊdbɜːst] *n Meteor* chaparrón *m*.

cloudiness ['klaʊdɪnɪs] *n* nubosidad *f*.

cloudy ['klaʊdɪ] *adj (cloudier, cloudiest)* **1** *(sky)* nublado,-a. **2** *(liquid)* turbio,-a.

clout [klaʊt] *fam* **I** *n* **1** *(blow)* tortazo *m*. **2** *(influence)* influencia *f*, fuerza *f*. **II** *vtr* dar *or* arrear un tortazo a.

clove¹ [kləʊv] *n Bot Culin (spice)* clavo *m*.

clove² [kləʊv] *n Culin (of garlic)* diente *f*.

clove³ [kləʊv] *pt see* **cleave¹.**

cloven ['kləʊvən] **I** *pp see* **cleave¹.** **II** *adj* **c. hoof,** pezuña *f* hendida.

clover ['kləʊvəʳ] *n Bot* trébol *m*; *fam* **to be in c.,** vivir como un rey.

cloverleaf ['kləʊvəliːf] *n (pl cloverleaves* ['kləʊvəliːvz]*) Bot* hoja *f* de trébol.

clown [klaʊn] **I** *n* payaso *m*. **II** *vi* **to c. (about** *or* **around),** hacer el payaso.

clowning ['klaʊnɪŋ] *n* payasadas *fpl*.

cloy [klɔɪ] *vi* empalagar.

club [klʌb] **I** *n* **1** *(society)* club *m*, círculo *m*; **sports c.,** club deportivo; **youth c.,** club juvenil; *fam* **join the c.!,** ¡ya somos dos! **2** *(heavy stick)* garrote *m*, porra *f*; *Golf* palo *m*. ■ *Med* **c. foot,** pie *m* zopo. **3** *Cards (English pack)* trébol *m*; *(Spanish pack)* bastos *mpl*. **4** *Culin* **c. sandwich,** sandwich *m* doble. **II** *vtr (pt & pp clubbed)* aporrear, dar *or* pegar garrotazos a. **III** *vi* **to c. together,** pagar entre varios.

clubhouse ['klʌbhaʊs] *n Sport* sede *f* de un club.

cluck [klʌk] **I** *n* cloqueo *m*. **II** *vi* cloquear.

clue [kluː] *n (sign)* indicio *m*; *(to mystery)* pista *f*; *(in crossword)* clave *f*, *fam* **I haven't a c.,** no tengo (ni) idea, no tengo la menor idea; *pej* **he hasn't a c.,** es muy despistado, no se entera. ◆ **clue up** *vtr fam* poner al tanto; **to be clued up,** estar al tanto.

clueless ['kluːlɪs] *adj* despistado,-a, que no se entera de nada.

clump [klʌmp] **I** *n* **1** *(of trees)* grupo *m*; *(of plants)* mata *f*, macizo *m*. **2** *(noise)* ruido *m* de pisadas. **II** *vi* andar ruidosamente.

clumsiness ['klʌmsɪnɪs] *n* desmaña *f*, torpeza *f*.

clumsy ['klʌmsɪ] *adj (clumsier, clumsiest)* desmañado,-a, torpe; *(awkward)* tosco,-a, basto,-a.

clung [klʌŋ] *pt & pp see* **cling.**

cluster ['klʌstəʳ] **I** *n (of trees, stars)* grupo *m*; *(of grapes)* racimo *m*; *(of plants)* macizo *m*; *(of flowers)* ramillete *m*. **II** *vi* agruparse **(round,** en torno a).

clutch [klʌtʃ] **I** *vtr (bag)* agarrar; *(child, doll)* estrechar; **to c. at,** echar mano a, tratar de agarrar; *fig* **to c. at straws,** aferrarse a cualquier cosa. **II** *n* **1** *Aut* embrague

m; **to let in/out the c.,** embragar/desembragar. **2** *(hold)* agarrón *m*; *fig* **to fall into sb's clutches,** caer en las garras de algn.

clutter ['klʌtəʳ] **I** *vtr* **to c. (up),** llenar, atestar; **cluttered up with books,** atestado,-a de libros. **II** *n* desorden *m*, revoltijo *m*; **in a c.,** desordenado,-a, revuelto,-a.

cm *abbr of* **centimetre(s),** centímetro(s), cm.

CND [siː'en'diː] *GB abbr of* **Campaign for Nuclear Disarmament,** campaña *f* para el desarme nuclear.

CO [siː'əʊ] *Mil abbr of* **Commanding Officer,** Comandante *m*, Cte.

Co **1** *Com abbr of* **Company,** Compañía *f*, C., Cª, Cía. **2** *abbr of* **County,** condado *m*.

co- [kəʊ] *pref* co-; **coauthor,** coautor,-a *m, f*; **codriver,** copiloto *mf*; **copilot,** copiloto *m*.

c/o [siː'əʊ] *abbr of* **care of,** en casa de, c/d.

coach [kəʊtʃ] **I** *n* **1** *Aut* autocar *m*; *(carriage)* carruaje *m*. ■ **c. tour,** excursión *f* en autocar. **2** *Rail* coche *m*, vagón *m*. **3** *Sport* entrenador,-a *m, f*; *Educ (tutor)* profesor,-a *m, f* particular. **II** *vtr Sport* entrenar; *Educ* clases particulares a, preparar.

coach-builder ['kəʊtʃbɪldəʳ] *n* carrocero,-a *m, f*.

coachwork ['kəʊtʃwɜːk] *n* carrocería *f*.

coagulant [kəʊ'ægjʊlənt] *n Med* coagulante *m*.

coagulate [kəʊ'ægjʊleɪt] **I** *vtr* coagular. **II** *vi* coagularse.

coagulation [kəʊægjʊ'leɪʃən] *n* coagulación *f*.

coal [kəʊl] *n Min* carbón *m*, hulla *f*; *fig* **to carry coals to Newcastle,** llevar leña al monte; *fig* **to haul sb over the coals,** echar un rapapolvo a algn. ■ **c. bunker,** carbonera *f*; **c. gas,** gas *m* de hulla; **c. merchant,** carbonero *m*; **c. mine,** mina *f* de carbón; **c. mining,** explotación *f* hullera; **c. scuttle,** cubo *m* para el carbón; **c. tar,** alquitrán *m* de hulla.

coalesce [kəʊə'les] *vi* fundirse; *(unite)* unirse.

coalfield ['kəʊlfiːld] *n Min* yacimiento *m* de carbón.

coalition [kəʊə'lɪʃən] *n Pol* coalición *f*.

coarse [kɔːs] *adj* **1** *(material)* basto,-a, tosco,-a; *(skin)* áspero,-a; *(salt)* grueso,-a. **2** *(language)* grosero,-a, ordinario,-a.

coarse-grained ['kɔːsɡreɪnd] *adj* de grano grueso.

coarseness ['kɔːsnɪs] *n (gen)* tosquedad *f*; *(of manner)* grosería *f*, ordinariez *f*.

coast [kəʊst] **I** *n* costa *f*, litoral *m*; *fam* **the c. is clear,** no hay moros en la costa. **II** *vi Aut* ir en punto muerto; *(on bicycle)* deslizarse sin pedalear.

coastal ['kəʊstəl] *adj* costero,-a.

coaster ['kəʊstəʳ] *n* **1** *GB Naut* barco *m* de cabotaje. **2** *(mat)* salvamanteles *m inv*.

coastguard ['kəʊstɡɑːd] *n* guardacostas *m inv*.

coastline ['kəʊstlaɪn] *n* litoral *m*, costa *f*.

coat [kəʊt] **I** *n* **1** *(overcoat)* abrigo *m*; *(short)* chaquetón *m*. ■ **c. hanger,** percha *f*. **2** *(of animal)* pelo *m*, pelaje *m*. **3** *(of paint)* mano *f*, capa *f*. **4** *Herald* **c. of arms,** escudo *m* de armas. **II** *vtr (with,* de); *(with liquid)* bañar **(with,** en); *Culin (with egg, flour)* rebozar **(with,** con).

coating ['kəʊtɪŋ] *n* capa *f*, baño *m*.

coax [kəʊks] *vtr* engatusar; **to c. sb into doing sth,** engatusar a algn para que haga algo; **to c. sth out of sb,** sonsacar algo a algn.

coaxing ['kəʊksɪŋ] *n* zalamerías *fpl*, halagos *mpl*.

cob [kɒb] *n* mazorca *f*.

cobalt ['kəʊbɔːlt] *n Chem* cobalto *m*. ■ **c. blue,** azul *m* cobalto.

cobble ['kɒbəl] *n* adoquín *m*.

cobbled ['kɒbəld] *adj* adoquinado,-a.

cobbler ['kɒbləʳ] *n* zapatero *m*.

cobblers ['kɒbləz] *npl GB sl vulg (balls)* huevos *mpl*; **a load of old c.**, *(nonsense)* chorradas *fpl*, gilipolleces *fpl*; *(film etc)* una birria, un asco.

cobra ['kəʊbrə] *n Zool* cobra *f*.

cobweb ['kɒbweb] *n* telaraña *f*.

cocaine [kə'keɪn] *n* cocaína *f*.

cock [kɒk] **I** *n* 1 *Orn* gallo *m*; *(male bird)* macho *m*; **c. sparrow**, gorrión *m* macho; *fig* **c. and bull story**, cuento *m* chino. 2 *(on gun)* percutor *m*, percusor *m*. 3 *sl vulg (penis)* polla *f*. **II** *vtr (gun)* amartillar; *(ears)* erguir; *fam* **to c. a snook at sb**, burlarse de algn. ◆ **cock up** *vtr GB sl* chapucear.

cockade [kɒ'keɪd] *n Mil* escarapela *f*.

cock-a-doodle-doo [kɒkədu:də'du:] *interj* quiquiriquí.

cock-a-hoop [kɒkə'hu:p] *adj fam* contento,-a como unas pascuas.

cock-a-leekie [kɒkə'li:kɪ] *n Scot Culin* sopa *f* de pollo y puerros.

cockatoo [kɒkə'tu:, 'kɒkətu:] *n Orn* cacatúa *f*.

cockcrow ['kɒkkrəʊ] *n* canto *m* del gallo; **at c.**, al amanecer.

cocked [kɒkt] *adj (hat)* de tres picos; *sl* **to knock sb into a c. hat**, dar cien vueltas a algn.

cocker ['kɒkə'] *n Zool* **c. spaniel**, cocker *m*.

cockerel ['kɒkərəl] *n Orn* gallo *m* joven.

cockeyed ['kɒkaɪd] *adj fam (lopsided)* torcido,-a; *(scheme)* disparatado,-a.

cockle ['kɒkəl] *n* berberecho *m*; *fig* **it warmed the cockles of my heart**, me llenó de alegría.

cockney ['kɒknɪ] **I** *adj* del East End londinense. **II** *n* persona *f* del East End londinense.

cockpit ['kɒkpɪt] *n* cabina *f* del piloto, carlinga *f*.

cockroach ['kɒkrəʊtʃ] *n Ent* cucaracha *f*.

cockscomb ['kɒkskəʊm] *n* cresta *f* de gallo.

cocksure [kɒk'ʃʊə'] *adj* presumido,-a, creído,-a.

cocktail ['kɒkteɪl] *n* 1 *Culin* cóctel *m*. ■ **c. lounge**, bar *m*; **c. party**, cóctel *m*, aperitivo *m*; **fruit c.**, macedonia *f* de frutas; **prawn c.**, cóctel *m* de gambas. 2 **Molotov c.**, cóctel *m* Molotov.

cockup ['kɒkʌp] *n GB sl* chapuza *f*, chapucería *f*.

cocky ['kɒkɪ] *adj (cockier, cockiest) fam* creído,-a.

cocoa ['kəʊkəʊ] *n* cacao *m*. ■ **c. butter**, manteca *f* de cacao.

coconut ['kəʊkənʌt] *n* 1 *(fruit)* coco *m*. ■ *Bot* **c. palm**, cocotero *m*. 2 *(fibre)* fibra *f* de coco. ■ **c. matting**, estera *f* de fibra de coco.

cocoon [kə'ku:n] *n Ent* capullo *m*.

COD [si:əʊ'di:] *GB abbr of* **cash on delivery**, *US* **collect (payment) on delivery**, pagar contra reembolso, cóbrese a la entrega, **CAE**.

cod [kɒd] *n (pl cod or cods) (fish)* bacalao *m*. ■ **c. liver oil**, aceite *m* de hígado de bacalao; **salt c.**, bacalao *m* seco.

coddle ['kɒdəl] *vtr* 1 *(child)* mimar. 2 *Culin (eggs)* escaldar.

code [kəʊd] **I** *n* 1 *(gen)* código *m*; **c. of conduct**, ética *f* profesional; *Aut* **highway c.**, código de la circulación. 2 *(symbol)* clave *f*; **Morse c.**, alfabeto *m* Morse; **secret c.**, clave secreta; **to break a c.**, descifrar una clave. 3 *Tel* **c. (number)**, *US* **area c. (number)**, prefijo *m*; **postal c. (number)**, *US* **area c. (number)**, prefijo *m*; **postal c.**, código *m* postal. **II** *vtr (message)* cifrar, poner en clave.

codfish ['kɒdfɪʃ] *n (fish)* bacalao *m*.

codify ['kəʊdɪfaɪ] *vtr (pt & pp codified)* codificar.

codswallop ['kɒdzwɒləp] *n GB sl* chorradas *fpl*, estupideces *fpl*.

co-ed [kəʊ'ed] *fam* **I** *adj* mixto,-a. **II** *n* colegio *m* mixto.

coeducation [kəʊedjʊ'keɪʃən] *n* enseñanza *f* mixta.

coeducational [kəʊedjʊ'keɪʃənəl] *adj* mixto,-a.

coefficient [kəʊɪ'fɪʃənt] *n Math* coeficiente *m*.

coerce [kəʊ'ɜːs] *vtr* coaccionar; **to c. sb into doing sth**, coaccionar a algn a que haga algo.

coercion [kəʊ'ɜːʃən] *n* coacción *f*.

coercive [kəʊ'ɜːsɪv] *adj* coercitivo,-a.

coexist [kəʊɪg'zɪst] *vi* coexistir.

coexistence [kəʊɪg'zɪstəns] *n* coexistencia *f*.

C of E [si:əv'i:] *Rel abbr of* **Church of England**, Iglesia *f* Anglicana.

coffee ['kɒfɪ] *n* café *m*. ■ **black c.**, café *m* solo; **c. bar**, cafetería *f*, snack bar *m*; **c. break**, descanso *m*; **c. cup**, taza *f* para café; **c. grinder**, **c. mill**, molinillo *m* de café; **c. shop**, cafetería *f*, café *m*; **c. table**, mesita *f* de café; **high roast c.**, café *m* torrefacto; **instant c.**, café *m* instantáneo; **white c.**, café *m* con leche.

coffeepot ['kɒfɪpɒt] *n* cafetera *f*.

coffer ['kɒfə'] *n* arca *f*, caja *f* de caudales.

coffin ['kɒfɪn] *n* ataúd *m*.

cog [kɒg] *n Tech* diente *m*; *fig* **to be just a c. in the machine**, no ser más que una pieza del mecanismo.

cogent ['kəʊdʒənt] *adj* lógico,-a, válido,-a.

cognac ['kɒnjæk] *n* coñac *m*.

cogwheel ['kɒgwi:l] *n Tech* rueda *f* dentada.

cohabit [kəʊ'hæbɪt] *vi* cohabitar.

cohabitation [kəʊhæbɪ'teɪʃən] *n* cohabitación *f*.

cohere [kəʊ'hɪə'] *vi* adherirse; *fig* ser coherente, concordar.

coherent [kəʊ'hɪərənt] *adj* coherente, lógico,-a.

cohesion [kəʊ'hi:ʒən] *n* cohesión *f*.

cohesive [kəʊ'hi:sɪv] *adj* adherente, cohesivo,-a.

coil [kɔɪl] **I** *vtr* **to c. (up)**, enrollar. **II** *vi (snake)* enroscarse; **to c. up**, hacerse un ovillo. **III** *n* 1 *(loop)* vuelta *f*; *(of rope)* rollo *m*; *(of hair)* rizo *m*; *(of smoke)* espiral *f*. ■ **c. spring**, muelle *m* en espiral. 2 *Med (contraceptive)* espiral *f*. 3 *Elec* carrete *m*, bobina *f*.

coin [kɔɪn] **I** *n* moneda *f*; **to toss a c.**, echar a cara o cruz. **II** *vtr* 1 *(money)* acuñar. 2 *(invent) (word)* crear; *fig* **to c. a phrase**, por así decirlo or como se suele decir.

coinage ['kɔɪnɪdʒ] *n* moneda *f*, sistema *m* monetario.

coincide [kəʊɪn'saɪd] *vi* coincidir (**with**, con).

coincidence [kəʊ'ɪnsɪdəns] *n* coincidencia *f*.

coincidental [kəʊɪnsɪ'dentəl] *adj* casual. ◆ **coincidentally** *adv* por casualidad or coincidencia, casualmente.

coin-op ['kɔɪnɒp] *n fam* lavandería *f* automática.

coitus ['kɔɪtəs] *n* coito *m*.

Coke® [kəʊk] *n (abbr of Coca-Cola®) fam* coca *f*.

coke¹ [kəʊk] *n (coal)* coque *m*.

coke² [kəʊk] *n (abbr of cocaine) sl* coca *f*.

col 1 *abbr of* **colour**, color *m*. **2** *abbr of* **column**, columna *f*, col.

Col *Mil abbr of* **Colonel**, Coronel *m*, Cnel.

colander ['kʌləndə'] *n* colador *m*.

cold [kəʊld] **I** *adj* 1 *(gen)* frío,-a; **I'm c.**, tengo frío; **it's c.**, *(weather)* hace frío; *(thing)* está frío,-a; **to get c.**, enfriarse; *fig* **as c. as ice**, helado,-a; *fig* **to get or have c. feet (about doing sth)**, entrarle miedo a algn (de hacer algo); *fam fig* **to put into c. storage**, aplazar, dejar en suspenso. ■ **c. cream**, crema *f* hidratante; *Meteor* **c. front**, frente *m* frío; **c. meats**, fiambres *mpl*; **c. storage**, conservación *f* en frío. 2 *fig (unenthusiastic)* indiferente; **it leaves me c.**, me tiene igual. 3 *fig (unemotional, unfriendly)* frío,-a; **in c. blood**, a sangre fría; **to give sb the c. shoulder**, tratar a algn con frialdad. ■ *fig* **c. comfort**, poco consuelo *m*; *Pol* **c. war**, guerra *f* fría. 4 *(unconscious)* inconsciente; **to knock sb out c.**, dejar a algn inconsciente (de un golpe). **II** *n* 1 frío *m*; **to feel the c.**, ser friolero,-a; *fig* **to be left out in the c.**, quedarse al margen. 2 *Med* resfriado *m*; **to catch a c.**, coger un resfriado, resfriarse, acatarrarse; **to have a c.**, estar resfriado,-a or acatarrado,-a. ■ **c. sore**, herpes *m*.

cold-blooded [kəʊld'blʌdɪd] *adj* **1** *(animal)* de sangre fría. **2** *fig (person)* frío,-a, insensible; *(crime)* a sangre fría, premeditado,-a.

cold-hearted [kəʊld'hɑːtɪd] *adj* frío,-a, insensible.

coldness ['kəʊldnɪs] *n* frialdad *f*.

coleslaw ['kəʊlslɔː] *n Culin* ensalada *f* de col.

colic ['kɒlɪc] *n Med* cólico *m*.

colitis [kɒ'laɪtɪs] *n Med* colitis *f*.

collaborate [kə'læbəreɪt] *vi* colaborar (**with**, con).

collaboration [kəlæbə'reɪʃən] *n* colaboración *f*.

collaborator [kə'læbəreɪtəʳ] *n* colaborador,-a *m, f; Pol* colaboracionista *mf*.

collage [kɒ'lɑːʒ] *n Art* collage *m*.

collapse [kə'læps] **I** *vi* **1** *(break down)* derrumbarse; *(cave in)* hundirse, venirse abajo. **2** *fig (currency, prices)* caer en picado. **3** *Med* sufrir un colapso. **4** *(table, tent)* plegarse. **II** *vtr (table)* plegar. **III** *n* **1** *(breaking down)* derrumbamiento *m; (caving in)* hundimiento *m*. **2** *fig (of currency, prices)* caída *f* en picado. **3** *Med* colapso *m*.

collapsible [kə'læpsəbəl] *adj* plegable, desmontable.

collar ['kɒləʳ] **I** *n (of garment)* cuello *m; (for dog)* collar *m*; **detachable c.**, cuello falso; *fig* **blue c. worker**, obrero *m* industrial; *fig* **hot under the c.**, enfadado,-a, indignado,-a. **II** *vtr fam* pescar, agarrar.

collarbone ['kɒləbəʊn] *n Anat* clavícula *f*.

collate [kɒ'leɪt] *vtr* cotejar.

collateral [kɒ'lætərəl] **I** *n Fin* garantía *f* subsidiaria. **II** *adj* colateral.

collation [kɒ'leɪʃən] *n* cotejo *m*.

colleague ['kɒliːg] *n* colega *mf*.

collect [kə'lekt] **I** *vtr* **1** *(gather)* recoger; *fig* **to c. one's thoughts**, poner en orden sus ideas. **2** *(stamps, records)* coleccionar. **3** *Fin (taxes etc)* recaudar. **II** *vi* **1** *(people)* reunirse, congregarse. **2** *(for charity)* hacer una colecta (**for**, para). **III** *adv US Tel* a cobro revertido; **to call c.**, llamar a cobro revertido.

collected [kə'lektɪd] *adj* **1** *(composed)* sosegado,-a, tranquilo,-a. **2** *Lit* **c. works**, obras *fpl* completas.

collection [kə'lekʃən] *n* **1** *(of mail)* recogida *f; (of money)* colecta *f*; **to make** *or* **take up a c.**, hacer *or* efectuar una colecta. **2** *(of stamps)* colección *f*. **3** *(of taxes)* recaudación *f*. **4** *(group) (of people)* grupo *m; (heap)* montón *m*.

collective [kə'lektɪv] **I** *adj (ownership, efforts)* colectivo,-a. ■ *Ind* **c. bargaining**, negociaciones *fpl* colectivas; **c. farm**, (granja *f*) cooperativa *f*. **II** *n (group)* comunidad *f; (business)* cooperativa *f*.

collector [kə'lektəʳ] *n* **1** *(of stamps etc)* coleccionista *mf*. ■ **c.'s item, c.'s piece**, pieza *f* de coleccionista. **2** *Fin* **tax c.**, recaudador,-a *m, f* (de impuestos). **3** *(on bus etc)* **ticket c.**, cobrador,-a *m, f*.

college ['kɒlɪdʒ] *n Educ (school)* colegio *m*, escuela *f; (of university)* colegio mayor; **c. of further education**, escuela de formación profesional; **military c.**, escuela militar; **teachers' training c.**, escuela normal; **technical c.**, escuela de formación profesional.

collide [kə'laɪd] *vi* chocar, colisionar; *fig* estar en conflicto (**with**, con).

collie ['kɒlɪ] *n Zool* perro *m* pastor escocés, collie *m*.

collier ['kɒlɪəʳ] *n GB Min* minero *m*.

colliery ['kɒljərɪ] *n GB Min* mina *f* de carbón.

collision [kə'lɪʒən] *n* choque *m*, colisión *f*.

colloquial [kə'ləʊkwɪəl] *adj* coloquial, familiar.

colloquialism [kə'ləʊkwɪəlɪzəm] *n* expresión *f* coloquial.

collusion [kə'luːʒən] *n* colusión *f*, conspiración *f*; **to act in c. with sb**, conspirar con algn.

collywobbles ['kɒlɪwɒbəlz] *npl sl (upset stomach)* retortijones *mpl; fig* **I've got the c.**, estoy muy nervioso,-a.

Cologne [kə'ləʊn] *n* Colonia.

cologne [kə'ləʊn] *n (agua f de)* colonia *f*.

Colombia [kə'lɒmbɪə] *n* Colombia.

Colombian [kə'lɒmbɪən] *adj & n* colombiano,-a *(m, f)*.

colon[1] ['kəʊlən] *n Typ* dos puntos *mpl*.

colon[2] ['kəʊlən] *n (pl colons or cola* ['kəʊlə]*) Anat* colon *m*.

colonel ['kɜːnəl] *n Mil* coronel *m*.

colonial [kə'ləʊnɪəl] **I** *adj* colonial; **c. rule**, gobierno colonial. **II** *n (person)* colono,-a *m, f*.

colonialism [kə'ləʊnɪəlɪzəm] *n* colonialismo *m*.

colonialist [kə'ləʊnɪəlɪst] *adj & n* colonialista *(mf)*.

colonist ['kɒlənɪst] *n* colonizador,-a *m, f*.

colonization [kɒlənaɪ'zeɪʃən] *n* colonización *f*.

colonize ['kɒlənaɪz] *vtr* colonizar.

colonnade [kɒlə'neɪd] *n Archit* columnata *f*.

colony ['kɒlənɪ] *n* colonia *f*.

color ['kʌləʳ] *n & vtr & vi US see* **colour**.

color-blind ['kʌləblaɪnd] *adj US see* **colour-blind**.

colored ['kʌləd] *adj US see* **coloured**.

colorful ['kʌləfʊl] *adj US see* **colourful**.

coloring ['kʌlərɪŋ] *n US see* **colouring**.

colorless ['kʌləlɪs] *adj US see* **colourless**.

colossal [kə'lɒsəl] *adj* colosal.

colour ['kʌləʳ] **I** *n* **1** *(gen)* color *m*; **in full c.**, a todo color; **to have no c.**, estar pálido,-a; **what c. is it?**, ¿de qué color es?; *fig* **to be/feel off c.**, no encontrarse/sentirse bien; *fig* **to lose c.**, palidecer; *fam* **let's see the c. of your money!**, ¡a ver, saca el dinero! ■ **c. blindness**, daltonismo *m*; **c. film**, película *f* en color; **c. printing**, cromolitografía *f*; **c. scheme**, combinación *f* de colores; **c. television**, televisión *f* en color; *Art* **water c.**, acuarela *f*. **2** *(race)* color *m*. ■ **c. bar**, discriminación *f* racial; **c. problem**, problema *m* del racismo. **3 colours**, *GB Sport* colores *mpl; Mil (flag)* bandera *f* sing, enseña *f* sing; *Mil* **to salute the c.**, saludar la bandera; *fig* **to pass (an examination) with flying c.**, salir airoso,-a *or* victorioso,-a de un examen; *fig* **to show oneself in one's true c.**, mostrarse como uno es de verdad. **II** *vtr* colorear; **to c. sth red**, colorear algo en rojo. **III** *vi* **to c. (up)**, ruborizarse.

colour-blind ['kʌləblaɪnd] *adj* daltónico,-a.

Coloured ['kʌləd] **I** *n* persona *f* de color. **II** *adj* de color.

coloured ['kʌləd] *adj (photograph)* en color; **straw-c.**, de color paja.

colourful ['kʌləfʊl] *adj* **1** *(with colour)* lleno,-a de color, vistoso,-a. **2** *fig (vivid)* vivo,-a, lleno,-a de colorido; *(person)* pintoresco,-a.

colouring ['kʌlərɪŋ] *n (colour)* tinta *m*, colorido *m; (dye)* colorante *m*.

colourless ['kʌləlɪs] *adj* incoloro,-a, sin color; *fig* soso,-a; **a c. life**, una vida gris.

colt [kəʊlt] *n* potro *m*.

column ['kɒləm] *n* columna *f*. ■ *Press* **gossip c.**, ecos *mpl* mundanos; *Anat* **spinal c.**, columna *f* vertebral.

columnist ['kɒləmnɪst] *n Press* columnista *mf*.

coma ['kəʊmə] *n Med* coma *m*; **to go into a c.**, caer en coma.

comatose ['kəʊmətəʊs] *adj* en estado comatoso.

comb [kəʊm] **I** *n* **1** peine *m*. **2** *Orn* cresta *f*. **3** *(honeycomb)* panal *m*. **II** *vtr* **1** peinar; **to c. one's hair**, peinarse. **2** *fig (area etc)* peinar, registrar a fondo.

combat ['kɒmbæt] **I** *n* combate *m*. ■ *Mil* **c. duty**, servicio *m* de frente; **single c.**, duelo *m*. **II** *vtr (enemy, disease)* combatir. **III** *vi* combatir (**against**, contra).

combatant ['kɒmbətənt] *n* combatiente *mf*.

combination [kɒmbɪ'neɪʃən] *n (gen)* combinación *f; (of people)* asociación *f*. ■ **c. lock**, cerradura *f* de combinación.

combine [kəm'baɪn] **I** *vtr* combinar; **to c. business with pleasure**, combinar el trabajo con la diversión. **II** *vi (gen)* combinarse; *(companies)* asociarse; *(people)* unirse; *(workers)* sindicarse. **III** ['kɒmbaɪn] *n* **1** *Com* asociación *f*. **2** *Agr* **c. harvester**, cosechadora *f*.

combined [kəm'baɪnd] *adj* combinado,-a, conjunto,-a; **c. efforts**, esfuerzos combinados; *Mil* **c. operations**, operaciones conjuntas.

combustible [kəm'bʌstəbəl] *adj* combustible.

combustion [kəm'bʌstʃən] *n* combustión *f*. ■ **c. chamber**, cámara *f* de combustión; **c. engine**, motor *m* de combustión.

come [kʌm] *vi (pt came; pp come)* **1** *(gen)* venir; *(arrive)* llegar; **c. and see us soon**, ven a vernos pronto; **c. here**, ven aquí; **c. with me**, ven conmigo; **coming!**, ¡voy!; **he comes every day**, viene cada día; **to c. and go**, ir y venir; **who comes next?**, ¿quién va ahora?; *fig* **in years to c.**, en el futuro; *fig* **to take things as they c.**, tomarse las cosas con calma; *fig* **I could see it coming**, lo veía venir; *fam* **you had it coming to you**, te lo merecías. **2** *(travel)* venir; **she's c. a long way**, viene desde lejos; *fig* ha progresado mucho. **3** *(appear)* venir, aparecer; **it comes in three colours**, viene en tres colores; **that comes on page ten**, eso se encuentra en la página diez; *fig* **that comes easy to me**, eso lo encuentro fácil. **4** *(become)* **to c. apart/undone**, desatarse/soltarse. **5** *(occur, happen)* suceder; **how does the door c. to be open?**, ¿cómo es que la puerta está abierta?; **nothing good will c. of it**, acabará *or* terminará mal; **nothing much came of it**, resultó ser poca cosa; **that's what comes of being too impatient**, es lo que pasa por ser demasiado impaciente; *fam* **how c.?**, ¿cómo es eso? **6** *(become aware of)* llegar a pensar; **I came to believe that ...**, llegué a creer que ...; **now that I c. to think of it**, ahora que lo pienso. **7** *fam* **c. again?**, ¿cómo?; **c. now!**, **don't exaggerate**, ¡anda!, no exageres. **8** *(subjunctive use)* **c. spring**, cuando venga la primavera; *fig* **c. what may**, pase lo que pase. **9** *sl (have orgasm)* correrse. ◆ **come about** *vi* ocurrir, suceder; **how did it c. about that ...?**, ¿cómo ocurrió que ...? ◆ **come across I** *vtr (thing)* encontrar por casualidad; **to c. across sb**, encontrarse con algn por casualidad, tropezar con algn. **II** *vi* **1** cruzar, atravesar. **2** *fig* **to c. across well/badly**, causar buena/mala impresión. ◆ **come after** *vtr & vi* seguir. ◆ **come along** *vi* **1** *(arrive)* venir, llegar; **c. along!**, ¡venga!, ¡date prisa! **2** *(make progress)* ir bien, progresar. ◆ **come at** *vtr (attack)* atacar. ◆ **come away** *vi (leave)* salir; *(part)* separarse, desprenderse (**from**, de); **c. away from there!**, ¡quítate de allí! ◆ **come back** *vi* **1** *(return)* volver; **to c. back to what I was saying**, volviendo a lo que decía. **2** *US (retort)* replicar (**at**, a). ◆ **come before** *vtr* **1** preceder. **2** *Jur (court)* comparecer ante. ◆ **come by** *vtr* adquirir, conseguir. ◆ **come down I** *vi* **1** bajar. **II** *vi (gen)* bajar; *Av* aterrizar; *(rain)* caer; *(prices)* bajar; *(building)* venirse abajo, ser derribado,-a; **it comes down to the ground**, llega hasta el suelo; **to c. down with the flu**, coger la gripe; *fig* **to c. down in the world**, venir a menos; *fig* **to c. down on sb's side**, ponerse de parte de algn. ◆ **come forward** *vi (advance)* avanzar; *(volunteer)* ofrecerse, presentarse. ◆ **come in** *vi* **1** *(enter)* entrar; **c. in!**, ¡pase!, ¡adelante! **2** *(arrive) (train)* llegar; *(tide)* crecer, subir; *Athlet* **to c. in first/second**, llegar el primero/segundo; *fam fig* **where do I c. in?**, y yo ¿qué pinto? **3** *(prove to be)* resultar; **to c. in handy** *or* **useful**, venir bien, ser útil. **4** **to c. in for**, ser objeto de; **to c. in for criticism**, ser blanco de críticas. ◆ **come into** *vtr* **1** *(enter)* entrar en; *Jur* **to c. into force**, entrar en vigor; *fig* **I said the first thing that came into my head**, dije lo primero que me vino a la cabeza; *fig* **to c. into the world**, venir al mundo. **2** *(inherit)* heredar. ◆ **come off I** *vtr (fall from)* caerse de; **to c. off a horse**, caerse de un caballo; *fam* **c. off it!**, ¡venga ya!, ¡no te pases! **II** *vi* **1** *(fall)* caerse; *(stain, lid)* quitarse; *(button)* caerse, despegarse. **2** *fam (take place)* pasar, ocurrir; *(succeed)* tener éxito; **to c. off badly**, salir mal. ◆ **come on** *vi* **1** *(hurry)* darse prisa; **c. on!**, ¡venga!, ¡date prisa! **2** *(make progress)* ir bien, progresar. **3** *(actor)* entrar en escena. **4** *(rain,*

illness) comenzar; **I have a cold coming on**, tengo síntomas de resfriado; **it came on to rain**, se puso a llover. ◆ **come out** *vi* **1** *(gen)* salir (**of**, de), mostrarse; *(sun, book)* salir, aparecer; *(product)* estrenarse; *(facts)* revelarse. **2** *(appear) (on stage)* entrar en escena; *(in society)* presentarse en sociedad. **3** *(be removed) (stain)* quitarse; *(colour)* desteñir. **4** *(declare oneself)* declararse; **to c. out against/in favour of sth**, declararse en contra/a favor de algo; *GB Ind* **to c. out (on strike)**, hacer huelga, declararse en huelga; **to c. out with a remark**, soltar un comentario. **5** *(turn out)* resultar, salir; **the photos didn't c. out very well**, las fotos no han salido muy bien; *Educ* **to c. out on top**, ser el primero (de la clase). **6** *(be covered with)* **to c. out in a rash**, salirle a uno una erupción *or* un sarpullido. ◆ **come over I** *vi* venir, llegar (**from**, de); *fig* **I've c. over to your way of thinking**, me has convencido; *fig* **to c. over well/badly**, causar buena/mala impresión; *fam* **to c. over faint** *or* **funny**, marearse, sentirse indispuesto,-a. **II** *vtr* **1** *(hill etc)* aparecer en lo alto de. **2** *fam (feeling)* pasar; **what's c. over you?**, ¿qué te pasa? ◆ **come round I** *vtr (corner)* dar la vuelta a. **II** *vi* **1** *(visit etc)* venir; *(festival)* volver; **c. round on Monday**, ven a verme el lunes. **2** *(regain consciousness)* volver en sí. **3** *(accept)* **to c. round to sb's way of thinking**, dejarse convencer por algn. ◆ **come through I** *vtr* **1** *(cross)* atravesar, cruzar. **2** *fig (illness)* recuperarse de; *(operation, accident)* sobrevivir, salir con vida de. **II** *vi* **1** *(message)* llegar. **2** *fig (from illness)* recuperarse; *(from operation, accident)* sobrevivir, salir con vida. ◆ **come to I** *vi* **1** *(regain consciousness)* volver en sí. **II** *vtr* **1** **to c. to one's senses**, volver en sí; *fig* recobrar la razón. **2** *(amount to)* costar; **how much does it c. to?**, ¿cuánto es?; **the lunch came to £30**, la comida costó 30 libras en total. **3** *(arrive at, reach)* llegar a; **it came to my notice that ...**, me enteré de que ...; **it comes to the same thing**, viene a ser lo mismo; **the idea came to me that ...**, me vino a la mente que ...; **to c. to an end**, terminar, acabar; **what are things coming to?**, ¿a dónde irá a parar todo esto?; *fig* **if it comes to that**, si hace falta; *fig* **when it comes to religion**, en cuanto a la religión; *fam* **c. to that**, a propósito. ◆ **come under** *vtr* **1** *Jur (person)* estar bajo la jurisdicción de. **2** *(be part of)* estar comprendido,-a en; *fig* **to c. under fire from sb**, ser criticado,-a por algn; *fig* **to c. under sb's influence**, caer bajo la influencia de algn. ◆ **come up I** *vtr* subir. **II** *vi* **1** *(rise)* subir; *(approach)* acercarse (**to**, a); **the water came up to his knees**, el agua le llegaba hasta las rodillas. **2** *(arise) (difficulty, question)* presentarse, surgir; *(number)* salir; **something's c. up**, ha surgido algo; **to c. up with a solution**, encontrar una solución; **to c. up against problems**, encontrarse con problemas. **3** *(rise) (plants)* brotar; *(sun)* salir. **4** **to c. up to**, igualar; **to c. up to sb's expectations**, satisfacer a algn. **5** *Jur* **to c. up before the courts**, *(person)* comparecer ante el tribunal; *(case)* llegar ante el tribunal. **6** *fam (of food)* **three chips, coming up!**, ¡van tres de patatas fritas! ◆ **come upon** *vtr see* **come across**.

comeback ['kʌmbæk] *n fam* **1** *(of person)* reaparición *f*; **to make a c.**, reaparecer. **2** *(answer)* réplica *f*, respuesta *f*.

comedian [kə'miːdɪən] *n* cómico *m*.

comedienne [kəmiːdɪ'en] *n* cómica *f*.

comedown ['kʌmdaʊn] *n fam* desilusión *f*, revés *m*.

comedy ['kɒmɪdɪ] *n* comedia *f*.

comer ['kʌməʳ] *n* asistente *mf*; **first c.**, primero,-a *m,f* (en llegar); **open to all comers**, abierto a todos los que quieran asistir.

comet ['kɒmɪt] *n Astron* cometa *m*.

comeuppance [kʌm'ʌpəns] *n fam* merecido *m*; **to get one's c.**, llevarse su merecido.

comfort ['kʌmfət] **I** *n* **1** *(well-being)* comodidad *f*; **creature comforts**, comodidades *fpl*; **to live in c.**, vivir cómodamente. ■ *US* **c. station**, servicios *mpl*, aseos *mpl*. **2** *(consolation)* consuelo *m*; **to take c. in** *or* **from sth**, consolarse con algo; *fig* **cold c.**, triste consuelo. **II** *vtr* consolar.

comfortable ['kʌmfətəbəl] *adj (chair, clothes, etc)* cómodo,-a; *(atmosphere, temperature)* agradable; *Med (patient)* tranquilo,-a; **he doesn't feel c. with us,** no se encuentra a gusto con nosotros; **it's so c. here,** aquí se está de maravilla; **make yourself c.,** ponte cómodo,-a; *fig* **to win by a c. majority,** ganar por amplia mayoría; *fam* **c. income,** buenos ingresos, ◆ **comfortably** *adv* cómodamente; *fam* **to be c. off,** vivir cómodamente.

comforter ['kʌmfətəʳ] *n* **1** *(person)* consolador,-a *m,f*. **2** *GB (scarf)* bufanda *f.* **3** *(dummy)* chupete *m.* **4** *US* edredón *m.*

comforting ['kʌmfətɪŋ] *adj (gen)* consolador,-a; *(news)* alentador,-a, reconfortante.

comfortless ['kʌmfətlɪs] *adj* incómodo,-a.

comfy ['kʌmfɪ] *adj (comfier, comfiest) fam* cómodo,-a.

comic ['kɒmɪk] **I** *adj* cómico,-a. ■ *Theat* **c. opera,** ópera *f* bufa; **c. strip,** tira *f* cómica, historieta *f.* **II** *n* **1** *(person)* cómico,-a *m,f.* **2** *Press* tebeo *m.*

comical ['kɒmɪkəl] *adj* cómico,-a.

coming ['kʌmɪŋ] **I** *adj (day, year)* próximo,-a; *(generation)* venidero,-a, futuro,-a. **II** *n* venida *f*, llegada *f*; **comings and goings,** idas y venidas; *fig* **c. and going,** ajetreo *m*, vaivén *m.*

comma ['kɒmə] *n Ling* coma *f.* ■ **inverted c.,** comilla *f.*

command [kə'mɑːnd] **I** *vt* **1** *(order)* mandar, ordenar; *Mil* mandar; **to c. sb to do sth,** ordenar a algn que haga algo. **2** *(respect)* imponer, infundir; *(sympathy)* merecer; *(money, resources)* disponer de; **it commanded a high price,** se vendió muy caro; **to c. a view,** tener vista. **II** *vi* mandar. **III** *n* **1** *(order)* orden *f*, *(authority)* mando *m*; **to be at sb's c.,** estar a las órdenes de algn; **to have /take c. of,** tener/tomar el mando de; **under his c.,** a su mando. **2** *(of language)* dominio *m*; **she has many languages at her c.,** domina muchos idiomas. **3** *(disposal)* disposición *f*; **to have a lot of money at one's c.,** disponer de mucho dinero.

commandant ['kɒməndænt] *n Mil* comandante *m.*

commandeer [kɒmən'dɪəʳ] *vt* requisar.

commander [kə'mɑːndəʳ] *n Mil* comandante *m*; *Naut* capitán *m* de fragata. ■ *Mil* **c. in chief,** comandante *m* en jefe.

commanding [kə'mɑːndɪŋ] *adj* dominante. ■ *Mil* **c. officer,** comandante *m.*

commandment [kə'mɑːndmənt] *n* mandamiento *m.*

commando [kə'mɑːndəʊ] *n (pl commandos or commandoes) Mil* comando *m.*

commemorate [kə'meməreɪt] *vt* conmemorar.

commemoration [kəmemə'reɪʃən] *n* conmemoración *f.*

commemorative [kə'memərətɪv] *adj* conmemorativo,-a.

commence [kə'mens] *vt & vi fml* comenzar.

commencement [kə'mensmənt] *n* **1** *fml* comienzo *m.* **2** *US Univ* ceremonia *f* de graduación.

commend [kə'mend] *vt* **1** *(praise)* alabar, elogiar. **2** *(entrust)* encomendar. **3** *(recommend)* recomendar; **it has little to c. it,** poco se puede decir a su favor.

commendable [kə'mendəbəl] *adj* encomiable, recomendable.

commendation [kɒmen'deɪʃən] *n* **1** *(praise)* elogio *m*, encomio *m.* **2** *US (award)* medalla *f.*

commensurate [kə'menʃərɪt] *adj* proporcional, equiparable; **c. to or with,** en proporción con; **salary c. with experience,** salario según experiencia.

comment ['kɒment] **I** *n* comentario *m*, observación *f*; **no c.,** sin comentario; **to cause c.,** dar lugar a comentarios; **to make a c.,** hacer un comentario *or* una observación. **II** *vi* hacer comentarios; **to c. on sth,** comentar algo, hacer comentarios sobre algo.

commentary ['kɒməntərɪ] *n* comentario *m.*

commentate ['kɒmənteɪt] *vi Rad TV* comentar, retransmitir.

commentator ['kɒmənteɪtəʳ] *n Rad TV* comentarista *mf.*

commerce ['kɒmɜːs] *n* comercio *m.*

commercial [kə'mɜːʃəl] **I** *adj* comercial, mercantil. ■ **c. art,** arte *m* publicitario; **c. college,** escuela *f* de estudios administrativos; **c. traveller,** viajante *mf* de comercio. **II** *n TV* spot *m*, anuncio *m* televisivo.

commercialize [kə'mɜːʃəlaɪz] *vt* comercializar.

commie ['kɒmɪ] *adj & n fam pej* rojo,-a *(m,f).*

commiserate [kə'mɪzəreɪt] *vi* compadecerse **(with,** de).

commiseration [kəmɪzə'reɪʃən] *n* conmiseración *f.*

commissar ['kɒmɪsɑːʳ] *n Pol* comisario *m.*

commissariat [kɒmɪ'seərɪət] *n Mil* intendencia *f.*

commission [kə'mɪʃən] **I** *n* **1** *Mil (officer's)* despacho *m* (de oficial); **into/out of c.,** en/fuera de servicio. **2** *(of enquiry)* comisión *f*; *(job)* encargo *m.* **3** *(payment)* comisión *f*; **to sell (goods) on c.,** vender (productos) a comisión. **II** *vt* **1** *Mil* nombrar. **2** *(order)* encargar; **to c. sb to do sth,** encargar a algn que haga algo. **3** *Naut* poner en servicio.

commissionaire [kəmɪʃə'neəʳ] *n GB* portero *m*, conserje *m.*

commissioner [kə'mɪʃənəʳ] *n (official)* comisario *m*; *Jur* **C. for Oaths,** ≈ notario *m*; **c. of police,** comisario *m* jefe de policía.

commit [kə'mɪt] *vt (pt & pp committed)* **1** *(crime)* cometer; **to c. suicide,** suicidarse. **2** *(dedicate, give)* dedicar; **to c. oneself (to do sth),** comprometerse (a hacer algo). **3** *(entrust)* **to c. sth to memory,** aprender algo de memoria; **to c. sth to sb's care,** confiar algo a algn. **4** *Jur* **to c. for trial,** citar ante los tribunales; **to c. to prison,** encarcelar.

commitment [kə'mɪtmənt] *n* compromiso *m*, obligación *f.*

committal [kə'mɪtəl] *n* **1** *(burial)* entierro *m.* **2** *Jur* **c. to prison,** encarcelamiento *m.*

committed [kə'mɪtɪd] *adj* comprometido,-a.

committee [kə'mɪtɪ] *n* comisión *f*, comité *m*; **parliamentary c.,** comisión parlamentaria; **to sit on a c.,** ser miembro de una comisión *or* de un comité.

commode [kə'məʊd] *n Furn (chair)* silla *f* conorinal; *(chest of drawers)* cómoda *f.*

commodious [kə'məʊdɪəs] *adj* espacioso,-a.

commodity [kə'mɒdɪtɪ] *n Com* artículo *m*, producto *m*; **a basic c.,** un artículo de primera necesidad.

commodore ['kɒmədɔːʳ] *n Naut* comodoro *m.*

common ['kɒmən] **I** *adj* **1** *(shared)* común; **to have sth in c. with sb,** tener algo en común con algn; **c. belief,** creencia general; **that's c. knowledge,** eso lo sabe todo el mundo. ■ *Math* **c. denominator,** denominador *m* común; **c. factor,** factor *m* común; *Jur* **c. law,** derecho *m* consuetudinario; **C. Market,** Mercado *m* Común; *GB Educ* **c. room,** sala *f* de profesores *or* de estudiantes. **2** *(ordinary)* corriente, frecuente; **a c. event,** un hecho corriente; **the c. people,** la gente corriente; *fam* **c. or garden,** normal y corriente. ■ *Med* **c. cold,** resfriado *m* común; *Ling* **c. noun,** nombre *m* común. **3** *(vulgar)* ordinario,-a, maleducado,-a. **II** *n (land)* campo *m or* terreno *m* comunal.

commoner ['kɒmənəʳ] *n* plebeyo,-a *m,f.*

commonplace ['kɒmənpleɪs] **I** *adj* ordinario,-a, corriente. **II** *n (remark)* tópico *m*, lugar *m* común.

Commons ['kɒmənz] *npl GB* **the (House of) C.,** (la Cámara de) los Comunes.

Commonwealth ['kɒmənwelθ] *n GB* **the C.,** la Mancomunidad Británica.

commotion [kə'məʊʃən] *n* conmoción *f*, alboroto *m*, confusión *f*; **to cause a c.,** armar un escándalo.

communal ['kɒmjʊnəl] *adj* comunal, comunitario,-a.

commune[1] [kə'mjuːn] *vi (converse)* conversar; *(with nature)* estar en comunión **(with,** con).

commune² ['kɒmjuːn] n comuna f, comunidad f.

communicable [kə'mjuːnɪkəbəl] adj Med transmisible.

communicant [kə'mjuːnɪkənt] n Rel comulgante mf.

communicate [kə'mjuːnɪkeɪt] I vi 1 (people) comunicarse (**with**, con). 2 (rooms) comunicarse; **communicating door**, puerta f que comunica. II vtr comunicar.

communication [kəmjuːnɪ'keɪʃən] n 1 (gen) comunicación f; **radio c.**, comunicación por radio. 2 (message) comunicado m. 3 GB Rail **c. cord**, timbre m de alarma.

communicative [kə'mjuːnɪkətɪv] adj comunicativo,-a.

communion [kə'mjuːnjən] n comunión f; Rel **to take c.**, comulgar.

communiqué [kə'mjuːnɪkeɪ] n comunicado m oficial.

communism ['kɒmjʊnɪzəm] n Pol comunismo m.

communist ['kɒmjʊnɪst] adj & n comunista (mf).

community [kə'mjuːnɪtɪ] n (gen) comunidad f; (people) colectividad f; **the immigrant c.**, la comunidad de inmigrantes; **the local c.**, el vecindario. ▪ **c. centre**, centro m social; **c. singing**, canto m colectivo; **c. spirit**, espíritu m comunitario.

commute [kə'mjuːt] I vi viajar diariamente al lugar de trabajo. II vtr Jur conmutar.

commuter [kə'mjuːtəʳ] n persona f que viaja diariamente al lugar de trabajo.

Comoros ['kɒmərəʊz] n Comoras.

compact¹ [kəm'pækt] I adj (gen) compacto,-a; (style) conciso,-a. ▪ **c. disc**, disco m compacto. II ['kɒmpækt] n (for powder) polvera f.

compact² ['kɒmpækt] n Pol pacto m, convenio m.

companion [kəm'pænjən] n 1 (mate) compañero,-a m, f. ▪ **lady's c.**, señora f de compañía. 2 (handbook) guía f.

companionable [kəm'pænjənəbəl] adj sociable, agradable.

companionship [kəm'pænjənʃɪp] n compañerismo m.

company ['kʌmpənɪ] n 1 (gen) compañía f; **to keep sb c.**, hacer compañía a algn; **she's good c. for me**, me hace mucha compañía; **to part c. with sb**, separarse de algn; **we're expecting c.**, esperamos visita; fig **to get into bad c.**, andar con malas compañías. 2 Com empresa f, compañía f; **Smith & C.**, Smith y Compañía. ▪ **c. car**, coche m de la empresa. 3 Mil Theat compañía f; Naut **ship's c.**, tripulación f.

comparable ['kɒmpərəbəl] adj comparable (**to**, **with**, con).

comparative [kəm'pærətɪv] I adj (gen) comparativo,-a; (relative) relativo,-a; (subject) comparado,-a; **a c. study**, un estudio comparativo; **he's a c. stranger**, es prácticamente un desconocido; Ling **the c. form**, el comparativo. II n Ling comparativo m. ◆ **comparatively** adv relativamente.

compare [kəm'peəʳ] I vtr comparar (**to**, **with**, con); (as) **compared with**, en comparación con; fig **to c. notes**, cambiar impresiones. II vi comparar, compararse; **to c. favourably with sth**, no desmerecer de algo, no perder por comparación con algo. III n **beyond c.**, sin comparación.

comparison [kəm'pærɪsən] n comparación f; **by** or **in c.**, en comparación; **there's no c.**, no se puede comparar, no tiene ni punto de comparación.

compartment [kəm'pɑːtmənt] n 1 (section) compartimiento m; Naut **watertight c.**, compartimiento estanco. 2 Rail departamento m.

compass ['kʌmpəs] n 1 (for finding direction) brújula f. 2 Geom (**pair of**) **compasses**, compás m. 3 fig (range) espectro m, límites mpl.

compassion [kəm'pæʃən] n compasión f.

compassionate [kəm'pæʃənət] adj compasivo,-a. ▪ Mil **c. leave**, permiso m por asuntos personales. ◆ **compassionately** adv con compasión.

compatibility [kəmpætə'bɪlɪtɪ] n compatibilidad f.

compatible [kəm'pætəbəl] adj compatible (**with**, con).

compatriot [kəm'pætrɪət] n compatriota mf.

compel [kəm'pel] vtr (pt & pp **compelled**) 1 (oblige) obligar; **to c. sb to do sth**, obligar a algn a hacer algo; **to be compelled to do sth**, verse obligado,-a a hacer algo. 2 (demand) (respect) imponer; (admiration) despertar.

compelling [kəm'pelɪŋ] adj irresistible; **a c. reason**, una razón apremiante.

compendium [kəm'pendɪəm] n (pl **compendiums** or **compendia** [kəm'pendɪə]) compendio m.

compensate ['kɒmpenseɪt] I vtr compensar; **to c. sb for sth**, indemnizar a algn de algo. II vi compensar; **to c. for sth**, compensar algo.

compensation [kɒmpen'seɪʃən] n (gen) compensación f; (for loss) indemnización f.

compere ['kɒmpeəʳ] GB I n presentador,-a m, f, animador,-a m, f. II vtr presentar.

compete [kəm'piːt] vi competir; **to c. for a prize**, competir por un premio; **to c. with sb**, competir con algn.

competence ['kɒmpɪtəns] n 1 (ability) competencia f, aptitud f. 2 Jur (of court etc) competencia f.

competent ['kɒmpɪtənt] adj 1 (person) competente, apto,-a. 2 Jur competente.

competition [kɒmpɪ'tɪʃən] n 1 (contest) concurso m, competición f. 2 Com competencia f; **fierce c.**, competencia feroz; **in c. with**, en competencia con.

competitive [kəm'petɪtɪv] adj 1 (person) que tiene espíritu competitivo. ▪ **c. examination**, oposición f. 2 Com (price, goods) competitivo,-a.

competitor [kəm'petɪtəʳ] n competidor,-a m, f.

compilation [kɒmpɪ'leɪʃən] n compilación f, recopilación f.

compile [kəm'paɪl] vtr compilar, recopilar.

complacency [kəm'pleɪsənsɪ] n complacencia f.

complacent [kəm'pleɪsənt] adj satisfecho,-a de sí mismo,-a, suficiente; **a c. attitude**, una actitud de complacencia. ◆ **complacently** adv de modo satisfecho.

complain [kəm'pleɪn] vi quejarse (**of**, **about**, de); I **can't** or **mustn't c.**, no me puedo quejar.

complaint [kəm'pleɪnt] n 1 (gen) queja f; Com reclamación f; **reason for c.**, motivo m de queja. 2 Jur demanda f; **to lodge a c.**, presentar or entablar una demanda. 3 Med enfermedad f.

complement ['kɒmplɪmənt] I n 1 Ling Math complemento m. 2 Mil efectivos mpl; Naut dotación f; **a full c.**, la totalidad. II vtr complementar.

complementary [kɒmplɪ'mentərɪ] adj complementario,-a.

complete [kəm'pliːt] I adj 1 (entire) completo,-a; **is the work c. now?**, ¿está terminado ya el trabajo?; **the c. works of Shakespeare**, las obras completas de Shakespeare. 2 (absolute) total; **he's a c. idiot**, es tonto de remate; **she's a c. stranger**, es totalmente desconocida. II vtr completar, rellenar; **to c. a form**, rellenar un formulario. ◆ **completely** adv completamente, por completo.

completion [kəm'pliːʃən] n finalización f, terminación f; **near c.**, casi terminado,-a; **on c.**, en cuanto se termine; Jur **on c. of contract**, cuando se haya firmado el contrato.

complex ['kɒmpleks] I adj complejo,-a. II n 1 (group) complejo m; **industrial c.**, complejo industrial. 2 Psych complejo m; **inferiority c.**, complejo de inferioridad.

complexion [kəm'plekʃən] n tez f, cutis m; fig **that puts a different c. on things**, así la cosa cambia de aspecto.

complexity [kəm'pleksɪtɪ] n complejidad f.

compliance [kəm'plaɪəns] n conformidad f, acuerdo m; **in c. with a request**, en or de conformidad con una solicitud; **in c. with the law**, de acuerdo con la ley.

compliant [kəm'plaɪənt] *adj* sumiso,-a.

complicate ['kɒmplɪkeɪt] *vtr* complicar.

complicated ['kɒmplɪkeɪtɪd] *adj* complicado,-a.

complication [kɒmplɪ'keɪʃən] *n* complicación *f*.

complicity [kəm'plɪsɪtɪ] *n* complicidad *f*.

compliment ['kɒmplɪmənt] **I** *n* **1** *(praise)* cumplido *m*; **to pay sb a c.,** hacerle un cumplido a algn. **2 compliments,** saludos *mpl*; **to send sb one's c.,** dar sus recuerdos *or* saludos a algn; **with my c.,** de mi parte. **II** ['kɒmplɪment] *vtr* felicitar; **to c. sb on sth,** felicitar a algn por algo.

complimentary [kɒmplɪ'mentərɪ] *adj* **1** *(praising)* elogioso,-a. **2** *(free)* gratis; **c. copy (of a book),** ejemplar gratis; **c. ticket,** invitación *f*.

comply [kəm'plaɪ] *vi* (*pt & pp* **complied**) obedecer; **to c. with,** *(order)* cumplir con; *(request)* acceder a.

component [kəm'pəʊnənt] **I** *n* componente *m*. **II** *adj* componente; **c. part,** parte *f*, componente *m*.

compose [kəm'pəʊz] *vtr & vi* **1** *Mus Print* componer; **to be composed of,** componerse de. **2** *(calm)* **to c. oneself,** calmarse, serenarse.

composed [kəm'pəʊzd] *adj* *(calm)* sereno,-a, tranquilo,-a.

composer [kəm'pəʊzəʳ] *n Mus Print* compositor,-a *m,f*.

composite ['kɒmpəzɪt] *adj* compuesto,-a.

composition [kɒmpə'zɪʃən] *n (gen)* composición *f*; *Educ (essay)* redacción *f*.

compositor [kəm'pɒzɪtəʳ] *n Print* cajista *mf*.

compos mentis [kɒmpəs'mentɪs] *adj* **to be c. m.,** estar en su sano juicio.

compost ['kɒmpɒst] *n Agr* abono *m*.

composure [kəm'pəʊʒəʳ] *n* calma *f*, serenidad *f*.

compound¹ ['kɒmpaʊnd] **I** *n Chem Ling* compuesto *m*. **II** [kəm'paʊnd] *vtr (things)* componer, combinar; *(problem)* agravar; **compounded of,** compuesto,-a de. **III** ['kɒmpaʊnd] *adj* compuesto,-a; *Med (fracture)* complicado,-a; *(word)* compuesto,-a. ■ *Fin* **c. interest,** intereses *mpl* compuestos.

compound² ['kɒmpaʊnd] *n (enclosure)* recinto *m*.

comprehend [kɒmprɪ'hend] *vtr* comprender.

comprehensible [kɒmprɪ'hensəbəl] *adj* comprensible.

comprehension [kɒmprɪ'henʃən] *n* comprensión *f*; **that's beyond my c.,** no llego a entenderlo.

comprehensive [kɒmprɪ'hensɪv] **I** *adj* **1** *(broad) (view, knowledge)* amplio,-a; *(study, description)* detallado,-a, global. **2** *Ins* a todo riesgo. **3** *GB Educ* **c. school,** ≈ instituto *m* de segunda enseñanza. **II** *n GB Educ* ≈ instituto *m* de segunda enseñanza.

compress [kəm'pres] **I** *vtr (squeeze)* comprimir; *fig (text)* condensar. **II** ['kɒmpres] *n Med* compresa *f*.

compression [kəm'preʃən] *n* compresión *f*.

compressor [kəm'presəʳ] *n* compresor *m*.

comprise [kəm'praɪz] *vtr (include)* comprender; *(consist of)* constar de.

compromise ['kɒmprəmaɪz] **I** *n* acuerdo *m*, término *m* medio; **the art of c.,** el arte de la negociación; **to reach a c.,** llegar a un acuerdo. **II** *vi* llegar a un acuerdo, transigir. **III** *vtr (person)* comprometer; **to c. oneself,** comprometerse.

compromising ['kɒmprəmaɪzɪŋ] *adj* comprometido,-a.

compulsion [kəm'pʌlʃən] *n* obligación *f*, coacción *f*; **under c.,** bajo coacción.

compulsive [kəm'pʌlsɪv] *adj* compulsivo,-a.

compulsory [kəm'pʌlsərɪ] *adj* obligatorio,-a.

compunction [kəm'pʌŋkʃən] *n* remordimiento *m*; **without c.,** sin escrúpulos.

computation [kɒmpjʊ'teɪʃən] *n* cálculo *m*.

compute [kəm'pjuːt] *vtr & vi* calcular.

computer [kəm'pjuːtəʳ] *n* ordenador *m*, computadora *f*. ■ **c. programmer,** programador,-a *m,f* de ordenadores; **c. science,** informática *f*; **personal c.,** ordenador *m* personal.

computerization [kəmpjuːtəraɪ'zeɪʃən] *n* automatización *f*, informatización *f*.

computerize [kəm'pjuːtəraɪz] *vtr* automatizar, informatizar.

computing [kəm'pjuːtɪŋ] *n* informática *f*.

comrade ['kɒmreɪd] *n* **1** *(companion)* compañero,-a *m,f*. **2** *Pol* camarada *mf*.

comradeship ['kɒmreɪdʃɪp] *n* camaradería *f*.

Con *GB Pol abbr of* **Conservative,** conservador,-a *m,f*.

con¹ [kɒn] *sl* **I** *vtr* (*pt & pp* **conned**) estafar, timar; **I've been conned!,** ¡me han timado! **II** *n* estafa *f*, camelo *m*. ■ **c. man,** estafador *m*; **c. trick,** estafa *f*, camelo *m*.

con² [kɒn] *n fam* contra *m*; **the pros and cons,** los pros y los contras.

concave ['kɒnkeɪv] *adj* cóncavo,-a.

conceal [kən'siːl] *vtr (gen)* ocultar **(from,** de); *(facts)* encubrir; *fig (emotions)* disimular.

concealed [kən'siːld] *adj* oculto,-a; **c. lighting,** luz indirecta.

concealment [kən'siːlmənt] *n* ocultación *f*, encubrimiento *m*; **in c.,** oculto,-a.

concede [kən'siːd] *vtr (gen)* conceder; **to c. defeat,** admitir la derrota, rendirse; **to c. victory,** conceder la victoria.

conceit [kən'siːt] *n* presunción *f*, vanidad *f*.

conceited [kən'siːtɪd] *adj* presuntuoso,-a, engreído,-a, vano,-a.

conceivable [kən'siːvəbəl] *adj* concebible. ◆ **conceivably** *adv* posiblemente; **she may c. have done it,** es posible que lo haya hecho.

conceive [kən'siːv] **I** *vtr* **1** *(child, idea)* concebir. **2** *(understand)* comprender. **II** *vi* **to c. of,** concebir, imaginarse.

concentrate ['kɒnsəntreɪt] **I** *vtr* concentrar. **I** *vi* concentrarse; **to c. on sth,** concentrarse en algo, aplicarse a algo. **III** *n* concentrado *m*.

concentrated ['kɒnsəntreɪtɪd] *adj (gen)* concentrado,-a; *(efforts)* intenso,-a.

concentration [kɒnsən'treɪʃən] *n* concentración *f*. ■ **c. camp,** campo *m* de concentración.

concentric [kən'sentrɪk] *adj* concéntrico,-a.

concept ['kɒnsept] *n* concepto *m*.

conception [kən'sepʃən] *n Med* concepción *f*; *fig (understanding)* concepto *m*, idea *f*.

concern [kən'sɜːn] **I** *vtr* **1** *(affect)* concernir, involucrar, afectar; **as far as I'm concerned,** por lo que a mí se refiere; **it doesn't c. me,** no me afecta; **'to whom it may c.',** 'a quien corresponda'; **where your interests are concerned,** en cuanto a tus intereses. **2** *(worry)* preocupar; **to c. oneself about or with,** preocuparse por, tomarse interés en. **II** *n* **1** *(affair)* interés *m*; **it's no c. of mine,** no es asunto mío; **what c. is it of yours?,** ¿a ti qué te importa? **2** *(worry)* preocupación *f*, inquietud *f*; **there's no cause for c.,** no hay motivo para preocuparse; **to show c.,** mostrar preocupación. **3** *Com (business)* negocio *m*; **a going c.,** un negocio en marcha.

concerned [kən'sɜːnd] *adj* **1** *(affected)* afectado,-a, involucrado,-a; **everybody c.,** los interesados; **the person c.,** la persona a la cual nos referimos. **2** *(worried)* preocupado,-a **(about,** por).

concerning [kən'sɜːnɪŋ] *prep* referente a, con respecto a, en cuanto a.

concert ['kɒnsət, 'kɒnsɜːt] *n* **1** *Mus* concierto *m* ■ **c. hall,** sala *f* de conciertos. **2** *fig* acuerdo *m*; **in c. with,** de acuerdo con.

concerted [kən'sɜːtɪd] *adj* concertado,-a.

concertina [kɒnsə'tiːnə] *n Mus* concertina *f*.

concerto [kən'tʃeətəʊ] *n* (*pl* **concertos** *or* **concerti** [kən'tʃeɑti]) *Mus* concierto *m*.

concession [kən'seʃən] *n* 1 (*gen*) concesión *f*, privilegio *m*; **tax c.**, privilegio fiscal. 2 *Com* reducción *f*.

concessionary [kən'seʃənərɪ] *adj* 1 (*gen*) concesionario,-a. 2 *Com* (*price*) rebajado,-a.

conciliate [kən'sɪlɪeɪt] *vtr* conciliar.

conciliation [kənsɪlɪ'eɪʃən] *n* conciliación *f*.

conciliatory [kən'sɪljətərɪ] *adj* (*gen*) conciliador,-a; (*procedure*) conciliatorio,-a.

concise [kən'saɪs] *adj* conciso,-a. ◆ **concisely** *adv* con concisión.

concision [kən'sɪʒən] *n* concisión *f*, brevedad *f*.

conclave ['kɒnkleɪv] *n RC* cónclave *m*.

conclude [kən'kluːd] I *vtr* (*finish*) concluir, terminar. II *vi* 1 (*finish*) concluir. 2 (*deduce*) concluir, llegar a una conclusión.

concluding [kən'kluːdɪŋ] *adj* final, concluyente.

conclusion [kən'kluːʒən] *n* 1 (*resolution*) conclusión *f*; **a foregone c.**, un final *or* un desenlace anticipado; **to reach a c.**, llegar a una conclusión; *in c.*, en conclusión.

conclusive [kən'kluːsɪv] *adj* concluyente.

concoct [kən'kɒkt] *vtr* (*dish*) confeccionar; *fig* (*lie, plan*) fraguar, urdir; *fig* (*excuse*) inventar.

concoction [kən'kɒkʃən] *n* (*mixture*) mezcolanza *f*, *pej* (*brew*) brebaje *m*.

concord ['kɒŋkɔːd] *n* concordia *f*, armonía *f*.

concordance [kən'kɔːdəns] *n* 1 (*harmony*) concordancia *f*. 2 (*book*) concordancias *fpl*.

concourse ['kɒŋkɔːs] *n* 1 (*of people*) concurrencia *f*, concurso *m*. 2 *Rail* explanada *f*.

concrete ['kɒnkriːt] I *n* hormigón *m*. ■ **c. mixer**, hormigonera *f*; **reinforced c.**, hormigón *m or* cemento *m* armado. II *adj* 1 (*definite*) específico,-a, concreto,-a. 2 (*made of concrete*) de hormigón.

concur [kən'kɜːʳ] *vi* (*pt & pp* **concurred**) 1 (*agree*) **to c. with**, estar de acuerdo con. 2 (*coincide*) coincidir, concurrir.

concurrence [kən'kʌrəns] *n* 1 (*agreement*) acuerdo *m*, conformidad *f*. 2 (*of events etc*) concurrencia *f*, concurso *m*.

concurrent [kən'kʌrənt] *adj* concurrente, simultáneo,-a. ◆ **concurrently** *adv* simultáneamente.

concussion [kən'kʌʃən] *n Med* conmoción *f* cerebral.

condemn [kən'dem] *vtr* (*gen*) condenar; (*house*) declarar en ruina; **the condemned cell**, la celda de los condenados a muerte; **to c. sb to death**, condenar a muerte a algn.

condemnation [kɒndem'neɪʃən] *n* condena *f*.

condensation [kɒnden'seɪʃən] *n* (*gen*) condensación *f*; (*on glass*) vaho *m*.

condense [kən'dens] I *vtr* condensar. II *vi* condensarse.

condensed [kən'denst] *adj* (*gen*) condensado,-a; *fig* (*reduced*) resumido,-a; **c. milk**, leche condensada.

condensor [kən'densəʳ] *n Tech* condensador *m*.

condescend [kɒndɪ'send] *vi* condescender, dignarse; **to c. to sb**, tratar a algn con condescendencia.

condescending [kɒndɪ'sendɪŋ] *adj* condescendiente; **he's very c.**, se da aires de superioridad.

condiment ['kɒndɪmənt] *n* condimento *m*.

condition [kən'dɪʃən] *n* 1 (*state*) condición *f*, estado *m*; **to be in good/bad c.**, estar en buen/mal estado; **to be in no c. to do sth**, no estar en condiciones de hacer algo. 2 (*requirement*) condición *f*; **on c. that ...**, a condición de que ...; **on no c.**, de ningún modo; **on one c.**, con una condición; **to make a c.**, poner una condición. 3 *Med* **heart c.**, enfermedad *f* cardíaca; **to be out of c.**, no estar

en forma. 4 **conditions**, (*circumstances*) circunstancias *fpl*; **under favourable c.**, en condiciones ventajosas. ■ **weather c.**, condiciones *fpl* atmosféricas; **working c.**, condiciones *fpl* de trabajo. II *vtr* condicionar.

conditional [kən'dɪʃənəl] *adj* condicional; *Ling* **c. clause**, oración condicional.

conditioner [kən'dɪʃənəʳ] *n* acondicionador *m*; **hair c.**, (crema *f*) suavizante *m* (para el pelo).

condolences [kən'dəʊlənsɪz] *npl* pésame *m sing*; **please accept my c.**, le acompaño en el sentimiento; **to send one's c.**, dar el pésame.

condom ['kɒndəm] *n* preservativo *m*, condón *m*.

condominium [kɒndə'mɪnɪəm] *n* (*pl* **condominiums**) condominio *m*.

condone [kən'dəʊn] *vtr* consentir, perdonar.

condor ['kɒndɔːʳ] *n Zool* cóndor *m*.

conducive [kən'djuːsɪv] *adj* conducente; **to be c. to sth**, favorecer algo.

conduct ['kɒndʌkt] I *n* (*behaviour*) conducta *f*, comportamiento *m*; (*management*) dirección *f*. II [kən'dʌkt] *vtr* (*lead*) guiar, conducir; (*business*) conducir, dirigir; (*orchestra*) dirigir; **a conducted tour**, una visita acompañada; **to c. oneself**, comportarse, portarse. III *vi Mus* dirigir.

conduction [kən'dʌkʃən] *n Phys* conducción *f*.

conductor [kən'dʌktəʳ] *n* 1 (*on bus*) cobrador *m*. 2 *US Rail* revisor,-a *m, f*. 3 *Mus* director,-a *m, f*. 4 *Phys* conductor *m*.

conductress [kən'dʌktrɪs] *n* (*on bus*) cobradora *f*.

cone [kəʊn] *n* 1 *Geom* cono *m*; **c.-shaped**, en forma de cono. ■ **ice-cream c.**, cucurucho *m*. 2 *Bot* piña *f*.

confab ['kɒnfæb] *n fam* plática *f*, charla *f*.

confectioner [kən'fekʃənəʳ] *n* confitero,-a *m, f*; **c.'s (shop)**, confitería *f*; *US* **confectioners' sugar**, azúcar *m* glas.

confectionery [kən'fekʃənərɪ] *n* dulces *mpl*.

confederacy [kən'fedərəsɪ] *n* confederación *f*.

confederate [kən'fedərɪt] I *adj* confederado,-a. II *n* confederado *m*; *Jur* cómplice *m*. III [kən'fedəreɪt] *vtr* confederar. IV *vi* confederarse.

confederation [kənfedə'reɪʃən] *n* confederación *f*.

confer ['kən'fɜːʳ] I *vtr* (*pt & pp* **conferred**) conferir; **to c. a title on sb**, conferir *or* otorgar un título sobre algn. II *vi* consultar (**about**, sobre).

conference ['kɒnfərəns] *n* conferencia *f*.

confess [kən'fes] I *vi* confesar; *Rel* **to c. (oneself)**, confesarse. II *vtr* confesar, admitir; **to c. to having done sth**, confesar haber hecho algo.

confession [kən'feʃən] *n* confesión *f*; **on his own c.**, según su propia confesión; *Rel* **to go to c.**, confesarse.

confessional [kən'feʃənəl] *n Rel* confesionario *m*.

confessor [kən'fesəʳ] *n Rel* confesor *m*.

confetti [kən'fetɪ] *n* confeti *m*.

confidant [kɒnfɪ'dænt] *n* confidente *m*.

confidante [kɒnfɪ'dænt] *n* confidenta *f*.

confide [kən'faɪd] I *vtr* confiar. II *vi* confiarse; **to c. in sb**, confiar en *or* fiarse de algn.

confidence ['kɒnfɪdəns] *n* 1 (*trust*) confianza *f*; **to have every c. in sb**, tener absoluta confianza en algn; **to take sb into one's c.**, depositar su confianza en algn; *Pol* **vote of c./no c.**, voto *m* de confianza/de censura. ■ *fam* **c. trick**, engaño *m*, camelo *m*. 2 (*self-assurance*) confianza *f*; **self-c.**, confianza *or* seguridad *f* en sí mismo,-a. 3 (*secret*) confidencia *f*; **in c.**, en confianza; **to exchange confidences**, hacerse confidencias.

confident ['kɒnfɪdənt] *adj* seguro,-a; **a c. smile**, una sonrisa confiada; **in a c. tone**, en un tono seguro *or* de seguridad. ◆ **confidently** *adv* con seguridad.

confidential [kɒnfɪ'denʃəl] *adj (secret)* confidencial; *(entrusted)* de confianza. ◆ **confidentially** *adv* confidencialmente, en confianza.

confine [kən'faɪn] *vtr* encerrar; *fig* limitar; **confined space,** espacio *m* reducido; **he's confined to bed,** tiene que guardar cama; *fig* **to c. oneself to sth,** limitarse a algo.

confinement [kən'faɪnmənt] *n* **1** *(prison)* prisión *f*, reclusión *f*; **to be in solitary c.,** estar incomunicado,-a. **2** *Med* parto *m*.

confirm [kən'fɜːm] *vtr (verify, assert)* confirmar; *(ratify)* ratificar.

confirmation [kɒnfə'meɪʃən] *n* confirmación *f*.

confirmed [kən'fɜːmd] *adj* empedernido,-a, inveterado,-a.

confiscate ['kɒnfɪskeɪt] *vtr* confiscar.

confiscation [kɒnfɪs'keɪʃən] *n (gen)* confiscación *f*; *Com* comiso *m*, decomiso *m*.

conflagration [kɒnflə'greɪʃən] *n* conflagración *f*, incendio *m*.

conflict ['kɒnflɪkt] **I** *n* conflicto *m*. **II** [kən'flɪkt] *vi* estar en desacuerdo *or* oposición (**with,** con), chocar (**with,** con).

conflicting [kən'flɪktɪŋ] *adj (reports, evidence)* contradictorio,-a; *(views)* incompatible, contrario,-a.

confluence ['kɒnfluəns] *n* confluencia *f*.

conform [kən'fɔːm] *vi* conformarse; **to c. to** *or* **with,** *(customs)* ajustarse a; *(rules)* someterse a.

conformist [kən'fɔːmɪst] *adj* & *n* conformista *(mf)*.

conformity [kən'fɔːmɪtɪ] *n* conformidad *f*; **in c. with,** conforme a, en conformidad con.

confound [kən'faʊnd] *vtr* **1** *(bewilder)* confundir, desconcertar. **2** [kɒn'faʊnd] *(damn)* **c. it!,** ¡maldito sea!; **you confounded fool!,** ¡imbécil!

confront [kən'frʌnt] *vtr (enemy, problem)* confrontar, hacer frente a, plantar cara a.

confrontation [kɒnfrʌn'teɪʃən] *n* confrontación *f*.

confuse [kən'fjuːz] *vtr (person)* despistar, hacer confuso,-a; *(thing)* confundir (**with,** con); **to get confused,** confundirse, hacerse un lío.

confused [kən'fjuːzd] *adj (person)* confundido,-a, despistado,-a; *(mind, ideas)* confuso,-a.

confusing [kən'fjuːzɪŋ] *adj* confuso,-a.

confusion [kən'fjuːʒən] *n (gen)* confusión *f*, desconcierto *m*; *(of person)* despiste *m*; **to throw into c.,** confundir, desconcertar.

congeal [kən'dʒiːl] **I** *vtr* coagular. **II** *vi* coagularse.

congenial [kən'dʒiːnjəl] *adj (atmosphere etc)* agradable; *(person)* simpático,-a, amable.

congenital [kən'dʒenɪtəl] *adj* congénito,-a.

conger ['kɒŋgəʳ] *n Zool* **c. eel,** congrio *m*.

congested [kən'dʒestɪd] *adj* **1** *(street)* repleto,-a *or* lleno,-a de gente; *(city)* superpoblado,-a. **2** *Med* congestionado,-a.

congestion [kən'dʒestʃən] *n* **1** *(traffic)* retención *f*, aglomeración *f*. **2** *Med* congestión *f*.

conglomeration [kənglɒmə'reɪʃən] *n* conglomeración *f*.

Congo ['kɒŋgəʊ] *n* Congo.

Congolese [kɒŋgə'liːz] *adj* & *n* congoleño,-a *(m,f)*.

congratulate [kən'grætjʊleɪt] *vtr* felicitar, dar la enhorabuena a.

congratulations [kəngrætjʊ'leɪʃənz] *npl* felicitaciones *fpl*, enhorabuena *f sing*; **c.!,** ¡felicidades!; **to offer c.,** dar la enhorabuena.

congratulatory [kən'grætjʊlətərɪ] *adj* de felicitación.

congregate ['kɒŋgrɪgeɪt] *vi* congregarse.

congregation [kɒŋgrɪ'geɪʃən] *n (group)* congregación *f*; *Rel* fieles *mpl*, feligreses *mpl*.

congress ['kɒŋgres] *n* congreso *m*; *US* **C.,** el Congreso.

congressional [kən'greʃənəl] *adj* del congreso.

Congressman ['kɒŋgresmən] *n (pl* **Congressmen)** miembro *m* del Congreso, congresista *m*.

Congresswoman ['kɒŋgreswʊmən] *n (pl* **Congresswomen** ['kɒŋgreswɪmɪn]*)* miembro *f* del Congreso, congresista *f*.

conical ['kɒnɪkəl] *adj* cónico,-a.

conifer ['kɒnɪfəʳ] *n Bot* conífera *f*.

coniferous [kɒ'nɪfərəs] *adj* conífero,-a.

conjectural [kən'dʒektʃərəl] *adj* conjetural.

conjecture [kən'dʒektʃəʳ] **I** *n* conjetura *f*, suposición *f*. **II** *vtr* conjeturar, suponer. **III** *vi* hacer conjeturas.

conjugal ['kɒndʒʊgəl] *adj* conyugal.

conjugate ['kɒndʒʊgeɪt] *vtr* conjugar.

conjugation [kɒndʒʊ'geɪʃən] *n* conjugación *f*.

conjunction [kən'dʒʌŋkʃən] *n* conjunción *f*; *fig* **in c. with,** conjuntamente con.

conjunctivitis [kəndʒʌŋktɪ'vaɪtɪs] *n Med* conjuntivitis *f*.

conjure ['kʌndʒəʳ] **I** *vtr* **to c. (up),** *(magician)* hacer aparecer; *fig (memories etc)* evocar. **II** *vi* hacer juegos de manos; *fig* **a name to c. with,** un nombre todopoderoso.

conjurer ['kʌndʒərəʳ] *n* prestidigitador,-a *m,f*.

conjuring ['kʌndʒərɪŋ] *n* **c. (tricks),** juegos *mpl* de manos.

conjuror ['kʌndʒərəʳ] *n see* **conjurer.**

conk [kɒŋk] *sl* **I** *vtr* pegarle una piña a. **II** *n (nose)* napias *fpl*, narices *fpl*. ◆ **conk out** *vi fam* averiarse.

conker ['kɒŋkəʳ] *n fam* castaña *f* (de las Indias).

connect [kə'nekt] **I** *vtr (join)* juntar, unir; *(wires, cables)* empalmar; *(two cities)* unir, conectar; *fig* **to be connected by marriage,** estar emparentado,-a por matrimonio. **2** *Tech (instal)* instalar; *Elec (to power supply)* enchufar, conectar. **3** *Tel (call)* conectar; *Tel (person)* poner (en comunicación). **4** *fig (associate)* asociar; **are they connected?,** ¿tienen alguna relación entre sí? **II** *vi* unirse; *(rooms)* comunicarse; *(train, flight)* enlazar *or* empalmar (**with,** con).

connected [kə'nektɪd] *adj (gen)* unido,-a, conectado,-a; *(events)* relacionado,-a; *fig* **to be well c.,** *(person)* tener muchos contactos; *fam* tener enchufe.

connection [kə'nekʃən] *n* **1** *(joint)* juntura *f*, unión *f*. **2** *Elec Tech* conexión *f*, empalme *m*. **3** *Tel* instalación *f*, conexión *f*. **4** *Rail* correspondencia *f*. **5** *fig (of ideas)* relación *f*; *(regarding)* **in c. with,** con respecto a. **6** *fig (person)* contacto *m*; *fam* **to have connections,** tener enchufe.

conned [kɒnd] *pt* & *pp see* **con**[1].

connexion [kə'nekʃən] *n see* **connection.**

connivance [kə'naɪvəns] *n* connivencia *f*, complicidad *f*.

connive [kə'naɪv] *vi* conspirar; **to c. at,** hacer la vista gorda con.

connoisseur [kɒnɪ'sɜːʳ] *n* conocedor,-a *m,f*.

connotation [kɒnə'teɪʃən] *n* connotación *f*.

conquer ['kɒŋkəʳ] *vtr (enemy, bad habit)* vencer; *(country)* conquistar.

conquering ['kɒŋkərɪŋ] *adj* victorioso,-a, conquistador,-a.

conqueror ['kɒŋkərəʳ] *n* conquistador *m*, vencedor *m*.

conquest ['kɒŋkwest] *n* conquista *f*.

consanguinity [kɒnsæŋ'gwɪnɪtɪ] *n* consanguinidad *f*.

conscience ['kɒnʃəns] *n* conciencia *f*; **to have a clear** *or* **easy c.,** tener la conciencia limpia; **to have a guilty c.,** sentirse culpable; *fig* **to have sth on one's c.,** llevar *or* tener un peso en la conciencia.

conscience-stricken ['kɒnʃənsstrɪkən] *adj* lleno,-a de remordimientos.

conscientious [kɒnʃɪ'enʃəs] *adj* concienzudo,-a. ■ *Mil* **c. objector,** objetor,-a *m, f* de conciencia. ◆ **conscientiously** *adv* concienzudamente, a conciencia.

conscientiousness [kɒnʃɪ'enʃəsnɪs] *n* escrupulosidad *f*.

conscious ['kɒnʃəs] *adj* **1** *Med* consciente; **to become c.,** volver en sí. **2** *(aware)* consciente; *(choice etc)* deliberadora,-a, intencional.

consciousness ['kɒnʃəsnɪs] *n* **1** *Med* conocimiento *m*; **to lose/regain c.,** perder/recuperar el conocimiento. **2** *(awareness)* consciencia *f*.

conscript ['kɒnskrɪpt] *Mil* **I** *n* recluta *m*. **II** [kən'skrɪpt] *vtr* reclutar.

conscription [kən'skrɪpʃən] *n* servicio *m* militar obligatorio.

consecrate ['kɒnsɪkreɪt] *vtr Rel* consagrar.

consecration [kɒnsɪ'kreɪʃən] *n Rel* consagración *f*.

consecutive [kən'sekjʊtɪv] *adj* consecutivo; **on four c. days,** cuatro días seguidos

consensus [kən'sensəs] *n* consenso *m*; **the c. of opinion,** la opinión general.

consent [kən'sent] **I** *n* consentimiento *m*; **age of c.** edad *f* núbil; **by common c.,** de común acuerdo. **II** *vi* consentir **(to, en); I c.,** lo consiento.

consequence ['kɒnsɪkwəns] *n* consecuencia *f*; **in c.,** por consiguiente; **to take the consequences,** aceptar las consecuencias; *fig* **it's of no c.,** no tiene importancia.

consequent ['kɒnsɪkwənt] *adj* consiguiente; **c. on** *or* **upon,** consecutivo,-a. ◆ **consequently** *adv* por consiguiente, en consecuencia.

consequential [kɒnsɪ'kwenʃəl] *adj* consecuente.

conservation [kɒnsə'veɪʃən] *n* conservación *f*. ■ **c. area,** zona *f* protegida.

conservationist [kɒnsə'veɪʃənɪst] *n* ecologista *mf*.

conservatism [kən'sɜːvətɪzəm] *n Pol* conservadurismo *m*.

conservative [kən'sɜːvətɪv] **I** *adj (estimate etc)* moderado,-a, cauteloso,-a, prudente. **II** *adj* & *n Pol* **C.,** conservador,-a *(m,f)*.

conservatoire [kən'sɜːvətwɑːʳ] *n Mus* conservatorio *m*.

conservatory [kən'sɜːvətrɪ] *n* **1** *(greenhouse)* invernadero *m*. **2** *Mus* conservatorio *m*.

conserve [kən'sɜːv] **I** *vtr* **1** *(guard)* conservar; **to c. one's strength,** reservar las fuerzas, reservarse. **2** *Culin* poner en conserva. **II** ['kɒnsɜːv] *n Culin* conserva *f*.

consider [kən'sɪdəʳ] *vtr* **1** *(ponder on)* considerar; **all things considered,** pensándolo bien; **to c. doing sth,** pensar hacer algo. **2** *(keep in mind)* tener en cuenta. **3** *(regard, judge)* considerar; **he's considered to be an expert,** le tienen por experto; **I c. myself happy,** me considero feliz; *fam* **c. it done!,** ¡dalo por hecho!

considerable [kən'sɪdərəbəl] *adj* considerable. ◆ **considerably** *adv* bastante; **this car is c. cheaper,** este coche es mucho más barato.

considerate [kən'sɪdərɪt] *adj* considerado,-a, atento,-a.

consideration [kənsɪdə'reɪʃən] *n* consideración *f*; **out of c. for,** en consideración a; **the matter is under c.,** se está estudiando *or* examinando el asunto; **without due c.,** sin reflexión

considered [kən'sɪdəd] *adj* considerado,-a; **my c. opinion,** mi opinión después de pensarlo bien.

considering [kən'sɪdərɪŋ] **1** *prep* teniendo en cuenta. **II** *adv fam* **it's not so bad,** no está tan mal, después de todo.

consign [kən'saɪn] *vtr Com (goods)* consignar; *fig* entregar, enviar.

consignment [kən'saɪnmənt] *n Com* envío *m*, remesa *f*. ■ **c. note,** talón *m* de expedición.

consist [kən'sɪst] *vi* consistir; **to c. of,** consistir en, constar de.

consistency [kən'sɪstənsɪ] *n* **1** *(of actions)* consecuencia *f*, lógica *f*. **2** *(of mixture)* consistencia *f*.

consistent [kən'sɪstənt] *adj* consecuente, lógico,-a; **c. with,** consecuente *or* de acuerdo con.

consolation [kɒnsə'leɪʃən] *n* consuelo *m*, consolación *f*. ■ **c. prize,** premio *m* de consolación.

console¹ [kən'səʊl] *vtr* consolar.

console² ['kɒnsəʊl] *n Mus Tech* consola *f*.

consolidate [kən'sɒlɪdeɪt] **I** *vtr* consolidar. **II** *vi* consolidarse.

consolidation [kənsɒlɪ'deɪʃən] *n* consolidación *f*.

consoling [kən'səʊlɪŋ] *adj* consolador,-a, reconfortante.

consommé ['kɒnsɒmeɪ, kən'sɒmeɪ] *n Culin* consomé *m*, caldo *m*.

consonant ['kɒnsənənt] *n Ling* consonante *f*.

consort [kən'sɔːt] **I** *vi* asociarse **(with,** con). **II** ['kɒnsɔːt] *n* consorte *mf*. ■ **prince c.,** príncipe *m* consorte.

consortium [kən'sɔːtɪəm] *n (pl* **consortia** [kən'sɔːtɪə]) consorcio *m*.

conspicuous [kən'spɪkjʊəs] *adj (striking)* llamativo,-a; *(easily seen)* visible; *(colour)* chillón,-ona; *(mistake, difference)* evidente; *(remarkable)* que destaca; **in a c. position,** a la vista de todos; **to make oneself c.,** llamar la atención; *fig* **to be c. by one's absence,** brillar por su ausencia.

conspiracy [kən'spɪrəsɪ] *n* conspiración *f*, conjura *f*.

conspirator [kən'spɪrətəʳ] *n* conspirador,-a *m,f*.

conspiratorial [kənspɪrə'tɔːrɪəl] *adj* conspirador,-a.

conspire [kən'spaɪəʳ] *vi* conspirar **(against,** contra); *fig* **everything conspired against him,** todo se volvió en contra suya.

constable ['kʌnstəbəl] *n* policía *m*, guardia *m*; **chief c.,** jefe *m* de policía.

constabulary [kən'stæbjʊlərɪ] *n GB* comisaría *f*, policía *f*.

constancy ['kɒnstənsɪ] *n* constancia *f*.

constant ['kɒnstənt] **I** *adj (fixed)* constante, estable. **2** *(continuous)* incesante, continuo,-a. **3** *(loyal)* fiel, leal. **II** *n Math Phys* constante *f*.

Constantinople [kɒnstæntɪ'nəʊpəl] *n Hist* Constantinopla.

constellation [kɒnstɪ'leɪʃən] *n Astron* constelación *f*.

consternation [kɒnstə'neɪʃən] *n* consternación *f*; **in c.,** consternado,-a.

constipate ['kɒnstɪpeɪt] *vtr* estreñir; **to be constipated,** sufrir estreñimiento.

constipation [kɒnstɪ'peɪʃən] *n* estreñimiento *m*.

constituency [kən'stɪtjʊənsɪ] *n Pol* circunscripción *f* electoral.

constituent [kən'stɪtjʊənt] **I** *adj (component)* constituyente, constitutivo,-a. **II** *n* **1** *(part)* componente *m*. **2** *Pol* votante *mf*, elector,-a *m,f*.

constitute ['kɒnstɪtjuːt] *vtr* constituir.

constitution [kɒnstɪ'tjuːʃən] *n* constitución *f*.

constitutional [kɒnstɪ'tjuːʃənəl] **I** *adj* constitucional. **II** *n (walk)* paseo *m*. ◆ **constitutionally** *adv* según la constitución.

constrained [kən'streɪnd] *adj* **1** *(obliged)* obligado,-a; **to feel c. to do sth,** sentirse obligado,-a a hacer algo. **2** *(unnatural)* forzado,-a.

constraint [kən'streɪnt] *n* coacción *f*; **to feel** *or* **show c. in sb's presence,** sentirse coartado,-a ante algn.

constrict [kən'strɪkt] *vtr* apretar, oprimir, restringir.

constriction [kən'strɪkʃən] *n* constricción *f*.

construct [kən'strʌkt] *vtr* construir.

construction [kən'strʌkʃən] *n* **1** *(act, building)* construcción *f*; **under c.,** en construcción. **2** *fig (interpretation)* interpretación *f*; **to put a wrong c. on sth,** interpretar mal algo.

constructive [kən'strʌktɪv] *adj* constructivo,-a.

constructor [kən'strʌktəʳ] *n* constructor *m*.

construe [kən'struː] *vtr* interpretar.

consul ['kɒnsəl] *n Pol* cónsul *mf*.

consular ['kɒnsjʊləʳ] *adj Pol* consular.

consulate ['kɒnsjʊlɪt] *n Pol* consulado *m*.

consult [kən'sʌlt] *vtr & vi* consultar (**about,** sobre); **to c. with sb,** consultar con algn.

consultant [kən'sʌltənt] *n* **1** *Med* especialista *mf*. **2** *Com Ind* consultor,-a *m*,*f*, asesor,-a *m*,*f*.

consultation [kɒnsəl'teɪʃən] *n* consulta *f*.

consultative [kən'sʌltətɪv] *adj* consultivo,-a.

consulting [kən'sʌltɪŋ] *adj* **1** *Med* **c. room,** consulta *f*. **2** *Com Ind* asesor,-a; **c. engineer,** ingeniero *m* asesor.

consume [kən'sju:m] *vtr* consumir; **consumed by fire,** consumido,-a *or* devorado,-a por las llamas; *fig* **to be consumed with envy/jealousy,** estar muerto,-a de envidia/de celos.

consumer [kən'sju:mə'] *n* consumidor,-a *m*, *f*. ■ **c. advice,** orientación *f* al consumidor; **c. goods,** bienes *mpl* de consumo.

consuming [kən'sju:mɪŋ] *adj fig* arrollador,-a, devorador,-a.

consummate ['kɒnsəmeɪt] **I** *vtr* consumar. **II** ['kɒnsəmɪt] *adj* consumado,-a, completo,-a.

consummation [kɒnsə'meɪʃən] *n* consumación *f*.

consumption [kən'sʌmpʃən] *n* **1** *(of food, energy)* consumo *m*; **fit for c.,** apto,-a para el consumo. **2** *Med* tisis *f*.

cont. 1 *abbr of* **contents,** contenido *m*. **2** *abbr* of **continued,** sigue.

contact ['kɒntækt] **I** *n* **1** *(gen)* contacto *m*; **to be in c. with,** estar en contacto con; **to make c. with,** *(touch)* tocar; *fig* establecer contacto con, entrar en contacto con. ■ **c. lenses,** lentes *fpl* de contacto, lentillas *fpl*. **2.** *(person)* contacto *m*, relación *f*; **she has a lot of contacts,** tiene muchos contactos. **II** *vtr* ponerse en contacto con, comunicar con.

contagion [kən'teɪdʒən] *n* contagio *m*.

contagious [kən'teɪdʒəs] *adj* contagioso,-a.

contain [kən'teɪn] *vtr* **1** *(hold)* contener. **2** *(restrain)* reprimir; **to c. oneself,** contenerse.

container [kən'teɪnə'] *n* **1** *(box, package)* recipiente *m*, caja *f*; *(wrapping)* envase *m*. **2** *Com* container *m*.

contaminate [kən'tæmɪneɪt] *vtr* contaminar.

contamination [kəntæmɪ'neɪʃən] *n* contaminación *f*.

contd. *abbr of* **continued,** sigue.

contemplate ['kɒntəmpleɪt] *vtr* **1** *(consider)* considerar, pensar en. **2** *(look at)* contemplar.

contemplation [kɒntəm'pleɪʃən] *n* contemplación *f*; **deep in c.,** absorto,-a, ensimismado,-a.

contemplative ['kɒntəmpleɪtɪv, kən'templətɪv] *adj* contemplativo,-a.

contemporaneous [kəntempə'reɪnɪəs] *adj* contemporáneo,-a.

contemporary [kən'temprəri] *adj & n* contemporáneo,-a *(m,f)*.

contempt [kən'tempt] *n* desprecio *m*; **to hold in c.,** despreciar. ■ *Jur* **c. of court,** desacato *m* a los tribunales.

contemptible [kən'temptəbəl] *adj* despreciable.

contemptuous [kən'temptjʊəs] *adj* despectivo,-a, despreciativo,-a.

contend [kən'tend] **I** *vi* contender, competir; **to c. for a prize/a position,** competir por un premio/una posición; *fig* **there are many problems to c. with,** se han planteado muchos problemas. **II** *vtr* sostener, afirmar.

contender [kən'tendə'] *n* contendiente *mf*.

content¹ ['kɒntent] *n* *(of book, pocket)* contenido *m*; **alcohol c.,** grado *m* de alcohol; **some cereals have a high fibre c.,** algunos cereales contienen mucha fibra; **table of contents,** índice *m* de materias.

content² [kən'tent] **I** *adj* contento,-a, satisfecho,-a; **he's quite c. to stay in the background,** se conforma con quedarse en segundo plano. **II** *vtr* contentar; **to c.**

oneself, contentarse (**with,** con). **III** *n* contento *n*; **to one's heart's c.,** hasta quedar satisfecho,-a, todo lo que uno quiera.

contented [kən'tentɪd] *adj* contento,-a, satisfecho,-a; **a c. smile,** una sonrisa de contento *or* de satisfacción.

contention [kən'tenʃən] *n* **1** *(dispute)* controversia *f*; *fig* **bone of c.,** manzana *f* de la discordia. **2** *(point)* punto *m* de vista; **my c. is that ...,** mi opinión es que ... .

contentious [kən'tenʃəs] *adj* contencioso,-a.

contentment [kən'tentmənt] *n* contento *m*.

contest ['kɒntest] **I** *n Sport* competición *f*, prueba *f*; *(of music)* concurso *m*; *fig* **it was a c. of wills,** fue una lucha de poderes. **II** [kən'test] *vtr* **1** *(question, matter)* rebatir, refutar; *(decision, verdict)* impugnar; *fig (will)* disputar. **2** *Pol (seat)* luchar por.

contestant [kən'testənt] *n* concursante *mf*.

context ['kɒntekst] *n* contexto *m*.

continent ['kɒntɪnənt] *n* continente *m*; **(on) the C.,** (en) Europa.

continental [kɒntɪ'nentəl] *adj* **1** *Geol* continental; **c. climate,** clima continental; **c. shelf,** plataforma continental. **2** *GB* **C.,** europeo,-a. ■ **c. breakfast,** desayuno *m* continental; **c. quilt,** edredón *m* de pluma.

contingency [kən'tɪndʒənsɪ] *n* contingencia *f*, eventualidad *f*; **c. plans,** planes *mpl* para casos de emergencia.

contingent [kən'tɪndʒənt] **I** *adj* contingente, fortuito,-a; **c. on** *or* **upon,** dependiente de. **II** *n* **1** *Mil (of troops)* contingente *m*. **2** *(group)* representación *f*.

continual [kən'tɪnjʊəl] *adj* continuo,-a, constante.

continuance [kən'tɪnjʊəns] *n* *(gen)* continuación *f*; *(duration)* duración *f*.

continuation [kəntɪnjʊ'eɪʃən] *n* *(sequel etc)* continuación *f*; *(extension)* prolongación *f*.

continue [kən'tɪnju:] *vtr & vi* continuar, seguir; **please c.,** siga, por favor; **to c. to do sth,** seguir *or* continuar haciendo algo; **'to be continued',** 'continuará'.

continuity [kɒntɪ'nju:ɪtɪ] *n* continuidad *f*. ■ *Cin* **c. girl/man,** secretaria *f* secretario *m* de rodaje.

continuous [kən'tɪnjʊəs] *adj* continuo,-a; *Cin* **c. performance,** sesión continua.

contort [kən'tɔ:t] *vtr (body)* retorcer; *(face)* contraer.

contorted [kən'tɔ:tɪd] *adj* contorsionado,-a, retorcido,-a.

contortion [kən'tɔ:ʃən] *n* contorsión *f*.

contortionist [kən'tɔ:ʃənɪst] *n* contorsionista *mf*.

contour ['kɒntʊə'] *n* contorno *m*. ■ **c. line,** línea *f* de nivel; **c. map,** mapa *m* topográfico.

contraband ['kɒntrəbænd] *n* contrabando *m*.

contraception [kɒntrə'sepʃən] *n* anticoncepción *f*.

contraceptive [kɒntrə'septɪv] **I** *adj* anticonceptivo,-a. **II** *n* anticonceptivo *m*.

contract [kən'trækt] **I** *vi* **1** *Phys* contraerse. **2** *(make agreement)* hacer un contrato; **to c. to do sth,** comprometerse por contrato a hacer algo. **II** *vtr (marriage, illness, debts)* contraer. **III** ['kɒntrækt] *n* contrato *m*; **breach of c.,** incumplimiento *m* de contrato; **to enter into a c.,** hacer un contrato. ■ *Bridge* **c. bridge,** contrato *m*; **marriage c.,** capitulaciones *fpl* matrimoniales. ◆ **contract out** *vi GB* optar por no hacer algo; **to c. out of a pension scheme,** optar por no participar en un sistema de pensión.

contraction [kən'trækʃən] *n Phys* contracción *f*.

contractor [kən'træktə'] *n Constr* contratista *mf*.

contractual [kən'træktjʊəl] *adj* contractual.

contradict [kɒntrə'dɪkt] *vtr* contradecir; *(deny)* desmentir.

contradiction [kɒntrə'dɪkʃən] *n* contradicción *f*; **it's a c. in terms,** no tiene lógica.

contradictory [kɒntrə'dɪktəri] *adj* contradictorio,-a.

contralto [kən'træltəʊ] *n* (*pl* **contraltos** or **contralti** [kən'træltɪ]) *Mus* (*voice*) contralto *m*; (*singer*) contralto *f*.

contraption [kən'træpʃən] *n fam* invento *m*, cacharro *m*.

contrariness [kən'treərɪnɪs] *n* terquedad *f*, obstinación *f*.

contrary ['kɒntrərɪ] **I** *adj* **1** contrario,-a, en contra; **a c. wind**, un viento contrario. **2** [kən'treərɪ] terco,-a, obstinado,-a, que siempre lleva la contraria. **II** *n* contrario *m*; **on the c.**, todo lo contrario, al contrario; **unless I tell you to the c.**, a menos que te diga lo contrario. **III** *adv* contrariamente, en contra de; **c. to common belief**, en contra de lo que se suele creer.

contrast [kən'trɑːst] **I** *vi* contrastar, distinguirse. **II** ['kɒntrɑːst] *n* contraste *m*; **to be in c. to** or **with**, contrastar con.

contrasting [kən'trɑːstɪŋ] *adj* opuesto,-a.

contravene [kɒntrə'viːn] *vtr Jur* contravenir.

contravention [kɒntrə'venʃən] *n Jur* contravención *f*.

contribute [kən'trɪbjuːt] **I** *vtr* (*money*) contribuir; (*one's share*) pagar; (*ideas, information*) aportar. **II** *vi* **1** (*gen*) contribuir; (*in discussion*) participar. **2** *Press* colaborar (**to**, en).

contribution [kɒntrɪ'bjuːʃən] *n* **1** (*of money*) contribución *f*; (*of ideas etc*) aportación *f*. **2** *Press* colaboración *f*.

contributor [kən'trɪbjuːtə'] *n* **1** (*to fund*) contribuyente *mf*. **2** (*to newspaper*) colaborador,-a *m,f*.

contributory [kən'trɪbjuːtərɪ] *adj* contribuyente; **to be a c. cause of sth**, contribuir a algo. ■ *Jur* **c. negligence**, responsabilidad *f* de la víctima; *Ins* **c. pension scheme**, plan *m* privado de jubilación para los trabajadores de una empresa.

contrite [kən'traɪt, 'kɒntraɪt] *adj* contrito,-a.

contrition [kən'trɪʃən] *n Rel* contrición *f*.

contrivance [kən'traɪvəns] *n* **1** (*device*) artefacto *m*, invento *m*. **2** (*plan*) estratagema *f*.

contrive [kən'traɪv] **I** *vtr* inventar, idear. **II** *vi* **to c. to do sth**, buscar la forma de hacer algo.

contrived [kən'traɪvd] *adj* artificial, forzado,-a.

control [kən'trəʊl] **I** *vtr* (*pt & pp* **controlled**) **1** (*gen*) controlar; (*person*) dominar, ejercer control sobre; (*animal*) dominar; (*vehicle*) manejar. **2** (*feelings*) gobernar; **to c. oneself** or **one's temper**, controlarse. **II** *n* **1** (*power*) control *m*, mando *m*, dominio *m*; (*authority*) autoridad *f*; *Sport* dominio *m*; **birth c.**, control de natalidad; **circumstances beyond our c.**, circunstancias fuera de nuestro control; **out of c.**, fuera de control; **parental c.**, autoridad de los padres; **the situation is under c.**, la situación está bajo control; **to be in c.**, estar al mando or a cargo; (*situation*) **to be under c.**, estar bajo control; (*fire, disease etc*) **to bring under c.**, conseguir controlar; **to go out of c.**, descontrolarse; **to keep a dog under c.**, controlar un perro; **to lose c.**, perder el control, perder los estribos; **we brought the fire under c.**, conseguimos controlar el fuego. ■ **c. group**, grupo *m* de control. **2** *Tech* control *m*, mando *m*. ■ **remote c.**, control *m* or mando *m* a distancia. **3** *Aut Av* (*device*) mando *m*; *Rad TV* botón *m* de control; **dual controls**, doble mando *m sing*; **to take over the controls**, *Aut* tomar el volante; *Av* tomar los mandos. ■ **c. panel**, tablero *m* de instrumentos; **c. room**, sala *f* de control; *Av* **c. tower**, torre *f* de control; **volume c.**, botón *m* del volumen.

controller [kən'trəʊlə'] *n* **1** *Admin Fin* interventor,-a *m,f*. **2** *Rad TV* director,-a *m,f* de programación; *Av* **air traffic c.**, controlador,-a *m,f* del tráfico aéreo.

controlling [kən'trəʊlɪŋ] *adj* controlador,-a; *Com* **c. interest**, participación *f* mayoritaria.

controversial [kɒntrə'vɜːʃəl] *adj* controvertido,-a, polémico,-a.

controversy ['kɒntrəvɜːsɪ, kən'trɒvəsɪ] *n* controversia *f*, polémica *f*.

contusion [kən'tjuːʒən] *n Med* contusión *f*.

conundrum [kə'nʌndrəm] *n fml* enigma *m*, problema *m*.

conurbation [kɒnɜː'beɪʃən] *n* conurbación *f*.

convalesce [kɒnvə'les] *vi* convalecer.

convalescence [kɒnvə'lesəns] *n* convalecencia *f*.

convalescent [kɒnvə'lesənt] *adj* convaleciente; **c. home**, clínica *f* de reposo.

convection [kən'vekʃən] *n Phys Meteor* convección *f*.

convector [kən'vektə'] *n* estufa *f* de convección.

convene [kən'viːn] **I** *vtr* (*meeting*) convocar. **II** *vi* reunirse.

convenience [kən'viːnɪəns] *n* (*suitability*) conveniencia *f*, comodidad *f*; **all modern conveniences**, todas las comodidades; **at your c.**, cuando le convenga; **at your earliest c.**, tan pronto como le sea posible; *fig* **to make a c. of sb**, abusar (la amabilidad) de algn. ■ **c. food**, comida *f* precocinada; *GB euph* **public conveniences**, aseos *mpl* públicos.

convenient [kən'viːnɪənt] *adj* (*time, arrangement*) conveniente, oportuno,-a; (*place*) bien situado,-a; **if it is c. for you**, si te conviene, si te viene bien.

convent ['kɒnvənt] *n Rel* convento *m*.

convention [kən'venʃən] *n* **1** (*conference*) convención *f*, congreso *m*. **2** (*custom*) convención *f*. **3** (*treaty*) convención *f*.

conventional [kən'venʃənəl] *adj* convencional, clásico,-a.

converge [kən'vɜːdʒ] *vi* convergir (**on**, en).

convergent [kən'vɜːdʒənt] *adj* convergente.

conversant [kən'vɜːsənt] *adj fml* familiarizado,-a; **to be c. with a subject**, ser versado,-a en una materia; **to become c. with**, familiarizarse con.

conversation [kɒnvə'seɪʃən] *n* conversación *f*, **in c.**, conversando.

conversational [kɒnvə'seɪʃənəl] *adj* coloquial; **c. English**, inglés coloquial; **c. style**, estilo familiar.

conversationalist [kɒnvə'seɪʃənəlɪst] *n* hablador,-a *m, f*; **to be a good c.**, brillar en la conversación.

converse¹ [kən'vɜːs] *vi* conversar, hablar.

converse² ['kɒnvɜːs] **I** *adj* opuesto,-a. **II the c.** *n* lo opuesto. ◆ **conversely** *adv* a la inversa.

conversion [kən'vɜːʃən] *n* **1** *Math Rel* conversión *f* (**to**, a; **into**, en). ■ *Math* **c. table**, tabla *f* de conversión. **2** (*of house etc*) reconstrucción *f*. **3** *Rugby* transformación *f*.

convert [kən'vɜːt] **I** *vtr* **1** (*gen*) convertir. **2** *Rugby* transformar. **II** *vi* convertirse; **a settee that converts into a bed**, un sofá que se convierte en cama. **III** ['kɒnvɜːt] *n Rel* converso,-a *m, f*.

converter [kən'vɜːtə'] *n Tech Elec* convertidor *m*, transformador *m*.

convertible [kən'vɜːtəbəl] **I** *adj* **1** (*gen*) convertible. **2** *Aut* descapotable. **II** *n Aut* descapotable *m*.

convex ['kɒnveks, kɒn'veks] *adj* convexo,-a.

convey [kən'veɪ] *vtr* **1** (*transport, carry*) transportar, llevar. **2** (*communicate*) (*sound*) transmitir; (*idea*) comunicar, expresar. **3** *Jur* preparar escrituras de traspaso.

conveyance [kən'veɪəns] *n* **1** (*carrying*) transporte *m*, transmisión *f*. **2** (*means*) transporte *m*, vehículo *m*.

conveyancing [kən'veɪənsɪŋ] *n Jur* preparación *f* de escrituras de traspaso.

conveyor [kən'veɪə'] *n* (*person*) transportista *mf*. ■ *Tech* **c. belt**, cinta *f* transportadora.

convict [kən'vɪkt] **I** *vtr* declarar culpable (**of**, de), condenar. **II** ['kɒnvɪkt] *n* presidiario,-a *m,f*.

conviction [kən'vɪkʃən] *n* **1** (*belief*) creencia *f*, convicción *f*; **to carry c.**, convencer. **2** *Jur* condena *f*; **he has no previous convictions**, no tiene antecedentes penales.

convince [kən'vɪns] *vtr* convencer; **to c. sb to do sth**, convencer a algn para que haga algo.

convincing [kən'vɪnsɪŋ] *adj* convincente. ◆ **convincingly** *adv* con convicción.

convivial [kən'vɪvɪəl] *adj* (*sociable*) sociable; (*festive*) jovial, festivo,-a.

conviviality [kənvɪvɪ'ælɪtɪ] *n* alegría *f*, jovialidad *f*.

convocation [kɒnvə'keɪʃən] *n* **1** (*gen*) convocatoria *f*. **2** *GB Univ* asamblea *f*.

convoke [kən'vəʊk] *vtr* convocar.

convoluted ['kɒnvəluːtɪd] *adj* **1** (*argument*) complejo,-a. **2** *Bot* (*leaf*) enrollado,-a.

convoy ['kɒnvɔɪ] **I** *n* convoy *m*; **in** or **under c.**, bajo escolta. **II** *vtr* escoltar.

convulse [kən'vʌls] *vtr* convulsionar; **her face was convulsed with pain**, tenía la cara distorsionada por el dolor; *fam* **to be convulsed with laughter**, troncharse de risa.

convulsion [kən'vʌlʃən] *n* convulsión *f*; *fam* **convulsions of laughter**, ataques *mpl* de risa.

convulsive [kən'vʌlsɪv] *adj* convulsivo,-a.

coo [kuː] *vi* (*baby*) gorjear; (*pigeon*) arrullar.

cooing ['kuːɪŋ] *n* (*of baby*) gorjeos *mpl*; (*of pigeon*) arrullo *m*.

cook [kʊk] **I** *vtr* (*chicken, potatoes*) cocinar, guisar; (*food, dinner*) preparar, hacer; **how long do you c. the meat (for)?**, ¿cuánto tiempo pones a cocer la carne?; *fam* **to c. up an excuse**, inventarse una excusa; *sl* **to c. the books**, falsificar las cuentas. **II** *vi* (*person*) cocinar, guisar, cocer; (*food*) cocerse; **c. slowly**, cocer a fuego lento; **I can't c.**, no sé guisar; *fam* **what's cooking?**, ¿cómo está el rancho? **III** *n Culin* cocinero,-a *m*, *f*; **he's a good c.**, guisa bien.

cookbook ['kʊkbʊk] *n US* libro *m* de cocina.

cooker ['kʊkə^r] *n* **1** (*apparatus*) cocina *f*. ■ **gas c.**, cocina *f* de gas. **2** *GB* (*apple*) manzana *f* ácida para cocinar.

cookery ['kʊkərɪ] *n* cocina *f*. ■ **c. book**, libro *m* de cocina.

cookie ['kʊkɪ] *n US* galleta *f*.

cooking ['kʊkɪŋ] **I** *n* cocina *f*; **home c.**, comida casera. **II** *adj* **c. apple**, manzana *f* ácida para cocinar.

cookout ['kʊkaʊt] *n US* barbacoa *f*.

cool [kuːl] **I** *adj* **1** (*gen*) fresco,-a; (*drink*) refrescante; (*weather*) **it's c.**, hace fresquito; **it's getting cooler**, está refrescando, refresca. **2** *fig* (*calm*) tranquilo,-a; (*reserved*) frío,-a; **a c. reception**, una acogida fría; **c. as a cucumber**, fresco,-a como una lechuga; **keep c.!**, ¡tranquilo,-a! **3** *fam* (*cheeky*) fresco,-a, descarado,-a; **a c. £10,000**, la friolera de 10.000 libras; **he's a c. customer**, es un fresco *or* un caradura. **II** *n* **1** (*coolness*) fresco *m*; **the c. of the evening**, el frescor de la tarde. **2** *sl* calma *f*; **to lose** *or* **blow one's c.**, perder la calma. **III** *vtr* (*room, air*) refrescar; (*drink*) enfriar; *fam* **to c. one's heels**, hacer antesala. **IV** *vi* enfriarse; **to c. down**, (*engine, feelings*) enfriarse; (*person*) calmarse. **V** *adv fam* **to play it c.**, hacer como si nada. ◆ **cool off** *vi fig* (*person*) calmarse; (*feelings*) enfriarse. ◆ **coolly** *adv* **1** (*gen*) fríamente. **2** *fam* (*cheekily*) descaradamente.

coolant ['kuːlənt] *n* líquido *m* refrigerante.

cooler ['kuːlə^r] *n* **1** (*box*) nevera *f* portátil. **2** *sl* chirona *f*.

cooling ['kuːlɪŋ] *n Tech* refrigeración *f*, enfriamiento *m*. ■ **c. system**, sistema *m* de refrigeración; *fig* **c.-off period**, período *m* de reflexión.

coolness ['kuːlnɪs] *n* **1** (*of air etc*) frescor *m*. **2** *fig* (*calmness*) calma *f*, frialdad *f*; (*composure*) sangre *f* fría. **3** *fam* frescura *f*.

coop [kuːp] **I** *n* gallinero *m*. **II** *vtr* **to c. (up)**, encerrar.

co-op ['kəʊɒp] *n abbr of* **co-operative**, cooperativa *f*.

co-operate [kəʊ'ɒpəreɪt] *vi* cooperar, colaborar.

co-operation [kəʊɒpə'reɪʃən] *n* cooperación *f*.

co-operative [kəʊ'ɒpərətɪv] **I** *adj* **1** (*helpful*) cooperador,-a. **2** (*society*) cooperativo,-a. ■ **c. farm**, cooperativa *f* agrícola. **II** *n* cooperativa *f*.

co-opt [kəʊ'ɒpt] *vtr fml* nombrar como nuevo miembro.

co-ordinate [kəʊ'ɔːdɪneɪt] **I** *vtr* coordinar. **II** [kəʊ'ɔːdɪnɪt] *n* **1** *Math* coordenada *f*. **2 co-ordinates**, (*clothes*) conjunto *m sing*.

co-ordination [kəʊɔːdɪ'neɪʃən] *n* coordinación *f*.

co-ordinator [kəʊ'ɔːdɪneɪtə^r] *n* coordinador,-a *m*, *f*.

coot [kuːt] *n Orn* focha *f* común.

cop¹ [kɒp] *sl* **I** *n* (*policeman*) poli *m*. **II** *vtr* (*pt & pp copped*) pillar, pescar; **you'll c. it**, te vas a ganar una buena. ◆ **cop out** *vi* rajarse.

cop² [kɒp] *n GB sl* (*value*) **it's not much c.**, no es nada del otro jueves.

cope [kəʊp] *vi* adaptarse, arreglárselas; **she's coping well**, se las arregla *or* apaña bien; **to c. with**, (*person, work*) poder con; (*problem*) hacer frente a.

Copenhagen [kəʊpən'heɪgən] *n* Copenhague.

copier ['kɒpɪə^r] *n* copiadora *f*.

copilot ['kəʊpaɪlət] *n Av* copiloto *m*.

copious ['kəʊpɪəs] *adj* copioso,-a, abundante.

copper¹ ['kɒpə^r] **I** *n* **1** *Min* cobre *m*. **2** *fam* (*money*) perra *f*, pela *f*; **it cost only a few coppers**, me costó cuatro perras. **II** *adj* (*colour*) cobrizo,-a. ■ *Bot* **c. beech**, haya *f* de hoja oscura.

copper² ['kɒpə^r] *n sl* poli *m*; **the coppers**, la pasma.

copperplate ['kɒpəpleɪt] *n* **1** (*plate*) lámina *f* de cobre. **2** (*print*) grabado *m* en cobre. **3 c. (writing)**, letra *f* caligrafiada.

coppice ['kɒpɪs] *n*, **copse** [kɒps] *n* arboleda *f*, bosquecillo *m*.

copulate ['kɒpjʊleɪt] *vi* copular.

copulation [kɒpjʊ'leɪʃən] *n* copulación *f*.

copy ['kɒpɪ] **I** *n* **1** (*reproduction*) copia *f*. ■ **rough c.**, borrador *m*. **2** (*of book, magazine*) ejemplar *m*. **3** *Print* manuscrito *m*. **4** *Press fam* tema *m*, asunto *m*; **it makes good c.**, es un asunto de interés. **II** *vtr* (*pt & pp copied*) (*notes*) copiar; (*imitate*) copiar, imitar; **to c. out a letter**, copiar una carta. **III** *vi* (*gen*) copiar; (*in exam*) copiar.

copybook ['kɒpɪbʊk] *n* cuaderno *m* (de caligrafía); *fam* **to blot one's c.**, manchar su reputación.

copycat ['kɒpɪkæt] *n fam* copión,-ona *m*, *f*.

copyright ['kɒpɪraɪt] *n* derechos *mpl* de autor, propiedad *f* literaria *or* intelectual.

copywriter ['kɒpɪraɪtə^r] *n* redactor,-a *m*, *f* de textos publicitarios.

cor [kɔː^r] *interj GB sl* **c.!**, ¡ostras!, ¡toma!

coral ['kɒrəl] *n* coral *m*. ■ **c. island**, isla *f* coralina; **c. reef**, arrecife *m* de coral; **C. Sea**, Mar *m* del Coral.

cord [kɔːd] *n* **1** (*string, rope*) cuerda *f*; *Elec* cordón *m*. ■ *Anat* **spinal c.**, médula *f* espinal; **umbilical c.**, cordón *m* umbilical; **vocal cords**, cuerdas *fpl* vocales. **2** *Tex* (*corduroy*) pana *f*; (*garment*) **cords**, pantalones *mpl* de pana.

cordial ['kɔːdɪəl] **I** *adj* cordial, afectuoso,-a. **II** *n* (*drink*) licor *m*.

cordon ['kɔːdən] **I** *n* cordón *m*. **II** *vtr* acordonar; **to c. off a street**, acordonar *or* aislar una calle.

corduroy ['kɔːdərɔɪ] *n Tex* pana *f*.

core [kɔː^r] **I** *n* (*of apple, pear*) corazón *m*; *Elec Tech* núcleo *m*; *Pol fig* **hard c.**, los incondicionales; *fig* **to the c.**, hasta la médula. **II** *vtr* (*apple*) quitarle el corazón a.

corer ['kɔːrə^r] *n Culin* deshuesadora *f*.

coriander [kɒrɪ'ændə^r] *n Bot* coriandro *m*, culantro *m*.

cork [kɔːk] **I** *n* **1** (*material*) corcho *m*. ■ *Bot* **c. oak**, alcornoque *m*. **2** (*stopper*) corcho *m*, tapón *m*; **to pull the c. out of a bottle**, descorchar una botella. **II** *vtr* (*bottle*) poner el corcho a, taponar.

corked [kɔːkt] *adj* que sabe a corcho.

corkscrew ['kɔːkskruː] *n* sacacorchos *m inv*.

cormorant ['kɔ:mərənt] *n Orn* cormorán *m* grande.

corn¹ [kɔ:n] *n (grain)* granos *mpl; (seed)* cereal *m; (maize)* maíz *m;* **c. oil,** aceite de maíz; **c. on the cob,** mazorca *f* de maíz.

corn² [kɔ:n] *n Med* callo *m; GB fam* **to tread on sb's corns,** disgustar *or* ofender a algn.

corncob ['kɔ:nkɒb] *n* mazorca *f* de maíz.

corncrake ['kɔ:nkreɪk] *n Orn* guión *m* de codornices.

cornea ['kɔ:nɪə] *n Anat* córnea *f.*

corner ['kɔ:nəʳ] **I** *n* **1** *(of street)* esquina *f; (bend in road)* curva *f,* recodo *m; (of table)* esquina *f,* pico *m;* **(just) round the c.,** a la vuelta de la esquina; **out of the c. of one's eye,** con el rabillo del ojo; *fig* **from all corners of the world,** de todos los rincones del mundo; *fig* **to cut corners,** tomar un atajo. ■ *Ftb* **c. kick,** córner *m;* **c. shop,** tienda *f* pequeña de barrio. **2** *(of room)* rincón *m; fig* **to be in a tight c.,** estar en un aprieto; *fig* **to drive sb into a c.,** arrinconar *or* acorralar a algn. ■ **c. table,** mesa *f* rinconera. **3** *Com* monopolio *m.* **II** *vtr* **1** *(enemy)* arrinconar, acorralar. **2** *Com (market)* acaparar, monopolizar. **III** *vi Aut* tomar una curva.

cornerstone ['kɔ:nəstəʊn] *n* piedra *f* angular; *fig* base *f.*

cornet ['kɔ:nɪt] *n* **1** *Mus* corneta *f.* **2** *GB (for ice cream)* cucurucho *m.*

cornfield ['kɔ:nfi:ld] *n* **1** *GB* trigal *m.* **2** *US* campo *m* de maíz.

cornflakes ['kɔ:nfleɪks] *npl* copos *mpl* de maíz.

cornflour ['kɔ:nflaʊəʳ] *n* harina *f* de maíz, maicena *f.*

cornflower ['kɔ:nflaʊəʳ] *n Bot* aciano *m,* azulina *f.*

cornice ['kɔ:nɪs] *n Archit* cornisa *f.*

Cornish ['kɔ:nɪʃ] *adj* de Cornualles. ■ *Culin* **C. pasty,** empanadilla *f* de carne picada *y* verduras.

cornstarch ['kɔ:nstɑ:tʃ] *n US see* **cornflour.**

Cornwall ['kɔ:nwəl] *n* Cornualles.

corny ['kɔ:nɪ] *adj (cornier, corniest) fam (joke)* gastado,-a, rancio,-a; *(film)* hortera.

corolla [kə'rɒlə] *n Bot* corola *f.*

corollary [kə'rɒlərɪ] *n* corolario *m.*

coronary ['kɒrənərɪ] *Med* **I** *adj* coronario,-a; **c. thrombosis,** trombosis coronaria. **II** *n* trombosis *f* coronaria.

coronation [kɒrə'neɪʃən] *n* coronación *f.*

coroner ['kɒrənəʳ] *n Jur* juez *mf* de instrucción.

Corp 1 *Mil abbr of* **corporal,** cabo *m* **2** *US abbr of* **Corporation,** sociedad *f* anónima, S.A.

corporal¹ ['kɔ:pərəl] *adj* corporal; **c. punishment,** castigo corporal.

corporal² ['kɔ:pərəl] *n Mil* cabo *m.*

corporate ['kɔ:pərɪt] *adj* corporativo,-a; **c. body,** corporación *f;* **c. responsibility/action,** responsabilidad/ acción colectiva.

corporation [kɔ:pə'reɪʃən] *n* **1** *(business)* sociedad *f* anónima. **2** *Admin (of city)* **(municipal) c.,** ayuntamiento *m.*

corps [kɔ:ʳ] *n (pl* **corps** [kɔ:z]) cuerpo *m; Mil* **the medical c.,** el cuerpo médico.

corpse [kɔ:ps] *n* cadáver *m.*

corpulence ['kɔ:pjʊləns] *n* corpulencia *f.*

corpulent ['kɔ:pjʊlənt] *adj* corpulento,-a.

corpuscle ['kɔ:pʌsəl] *n* corpúsculo *m,* glóbulo *m.*

corral [kə'rɑ:l] *n US* corral *m.*

correct [kə'rekt] **I** *vtr* **1** *(mistake)* corregir, rectificar. **2** *(child etc)* reprender. **II** *adj* **1** *(free from error)* correcto,-a, exacto,-a; **you're quite c.,** tienes toda la razón. **2** *(behaviour)* formal.

correction [kə'rekʃən] *n* corrección *f.*

corrective [kə'rektɪv] *adj* correctivo,-a.

correctness [kə'rektnɪs] *n* **1** *(accuracy)* exactitud *f.* **2** *(of behaviour)* formalidad *f.*

correlate ['kɒrəleɪt] **I** *vtr* poner en correlación, correlacionar. **II** *vi* tener *or* guardar correlación **(with,** con).

correlation [kɒrə'leɪʃən] *n* correlación *f.*

correspond [kɒrɪ'spɒnd] *vi* **1** *(one thing with another)* corresponder; **A corresponds with B, A** y B se corresponden; **to c. to,** equivaler a. **2** *(by letter)* escribirse, mantener correspondencia; **they c., se** escriben; **to c. with sb,** mantener correspondencia con algn.

correspondence [kɒrɪ'spɒndəns] *n* **1** *(between two things)* correspondencia *f.* **2** *(letters)* correo *m.* ■ **c. course,** curso *m* por correspondencia.

correspondent [kɒrɪ'spɒndənt] *n Press* corresponsal *mf.* ■ **special c.,** enviado,-a *m, f* especial.

corresponding [kɒrɪ'spɒndɪŋ] *adj (gen)* correspondiente; *(in accordance with)* conforme. ◆ **correspondingly** *adv* igualmente.

corridor ['kɒrɪdɔ:ʳ] *n* pasillo *m,* corredor *m; fig* **the corridors of power,** las altas esferas del poder.

corroborate [kə'rɒbəreɪt] *vtr* corroborar.

corroboration [kərɒbə'reɪʃən] *n* corroboración *f.*

corrode [kə'rəʊd] **I** *vtr* corroer. **II** *vi* corroerse.

corrosion [kə'rəʊʒən] *n* corrosión *f.*

corrosive [kə'rəʊsɪv] **I** *adj* corrosivo,-a. **II** *n* sustancia *f* corrosiva.

corrugate ['kɒrʊgeɪt] *vtr Tech* ondular; **corrugated iron,** hierro ondulado.

corrupt [kə'rʌpt] **I** *adj (person)* corrompido,-a, corrupto,-a; *(actions)* deshonesto,-a; **c. practices,** corrupción *f sing.* **II** *vtr & vi* corromper.

corruption [kə'rʌpʃən] *n,* **corruptness** [kə'rʌptnɪs] *n* corrupción *f.*

corset ['kɔ:sɪt] *n (garment)* faja *f.*

Corsica ['kɔ:sɪkə] *n* Córcega.

Corsican ['kɔ:sɪkən] *adj & n* corso,-a *(m, f).*

cortège [kɔ:'teɪʒ] *n* cortejo *m,* comitiva *f.*

cortisone ['kɔ:tɪzəʊn] *n* cortisona *f.*

Corunna [ke'rʌnə] *n* La Coruña.

cos¹ [kɒs] *n* **c. (lettuce),** lechuga *f* romana.

cos² *Math abbr of* **cosine,** coseno *m,* cos.

cosh [kɒʃ] *GB* **I** *n* porra *f.* **II** *vtr* dar un porrazo a, aporrear.

cosmetic [kɒz'metɪk] **I** *n* producto *m* de belleza, cosmético *m.* **II** *adj* cosmético,-a; **c. surgery,** cirugía plástica.

cosmic ['kɒzmɪk] *adj* cósmico,-a; **c. rays,** rayos cósmicos.

cosmonaut ['kɒzmənɔ:t] *n Astron* cosmonauta *mf.*

cosmopolitan [kɒzmə'pɒlɪtən] *adj* cosmopolita.

cosmos ['kɒzmɒs] *n* cosmos *m.*

cosset ['kɒsɪt] *vtr* mimar.

cost [kɒst] **I** *n (price)* precio *m,* costo *m,* coste *m; (expense)* gasto *m;* **at c. price,** a precio de coste; **c. of living,** coste de vida; **the c. of running a car,** los gastos de mantenimiento de un coche; *Jur* **to pay costs,** pagar las costas; **whatever the c.,** cueste lo que cueste; *fig* **to count the c.,** considerar las desventajas. **II** *vtr & vi (pt & pp cost)* costar, valer; **how much does it c?,** ¿cuánto cuesta?, ¿cuánto vale?; **it c. me £50 to have the car repaired,** me costó 50 libras arreglar el coche; **whatever it costs,** cueste lo que cueste; *fig* **it costs the earth,** cuesta una fortuna *or* un riñón. **III** *vtr (pt & pp costed) Com Ind* calcular el coste de.

co-star ['kəʊstɑ:ʳ] *Cin Theat* **I** *n* coprotagonista *mf.* **II** *vi (pt & pp co-starred)* **to c. with sb,** coprotagonizar con algn.

Costa Rica [kɒstə'ri:kə] *n* Costa Rica.

Costa Rican [kɒstə'ri:kən] *adj & n* costarricense *(mf).*

cost-effective [kɒstɪ'fektɪv] *adj* rentable.

costing ['kɒstɪŋ] *n Com Ind* cálculo *m* de coste.

costliness ['kɒstlɪnɪs] *n (in price)* alto precio *m; (in value)* lujo *m.*

costly ['kɒstlɪ] *adj (costlier, costliest) (dear)* costoso,-a, caro,-a; *(valuable)* costoso,-a.

costume ['kɒstjuːm] *n* traje *m.* ■ **bathing** *or* **swimming c.,** bañador *m;* **c. ball,** baile *m* de disfraces; **c. jewellery,** bisutería *f;* **fancy dress c.,** disfraz *m;* **national c.,** traje *m* típico.

cosy ['kəʊzɪ] *I adj (cosier, cosiest) (room, atmosphere)* acogedor,-a; *(bed)* calentito,-a; **it's c. in here,** aquí se está bien. **II** *n* **tea/egg c.,** cubierta *f* para tetera/huevo pasado por agua.

cot [kɒt] *n* cuna *f.* ■ *Med* **c. death (syndrome),** muerte *f* inexplicable de un bebé en la cuna.

cottage ['kɒtɪdʒ] *n (gen)* casa *f* de campo; *US (for holiday)* chalet *m.* ■ *Culin* **c. cheese,** requesón *m; GB* **c. hospital,** hospital *m* rural; **c. industry,** industria *f* casera; *GB Culin* **c. pie,** pastel *m* de carne picada con puré de patatas.

cotton ['kɒtən] *n* **1** *Bot* algodonero *m; Tex* algodón *m;* **the c. industry,** la industria algodonera. ■ **c. dress,** vestido *m* de algodón; **c. wool,** algodón *m* hidrófilo, guata *f.* **2** *(thread)* hilo *m.* ◆ **cotton on** *vi fam* **to c. on to sth,** caer en la cuenta de algo.

couch [kaʊtʃ] *I n Furn* canapé *m,* sofá *m; (in surgery)* camilla *f.* **II** *vtr* expresar, formular.

couchette [kuː'ʃet] *n Rail* litera *f.*

cough [kɒf] *I vi* toser. **II** *n* tos *f;* **to have a (bad) c.,** tener (mucha) tos. ■ **c. drop,** pastilla *f* para la tos; **c. mixture,** jarabe *m* para la tos. ◆ **cough up** *I vtr* escupir; *fam* **to c. up the money,** soltar la pasta. **II** *vi* escupir; *fam* **c. up!,** ¡suéltalo!

could [kʊd] *v aux* see **can**¹.

council ['kaʊnsəl] *n* **1** *(assembly, body)* consejo *m.* ■ *GB* **c. house,** vivienda *f* de protección oficial; **town** *or* **city c.,** consejo *m* municipal, ayuntamiento *m.* **2** *Rel* concilio *m.*

councillor, *US* **councilor** ['kaʊnsələʳ] *n* concejal *mf.*

counsel ['kaʊnsəl] *I n* **1** *(advice)* consejo *m;* **to take c. with sb,** consultar con algn; *fig* **to keep one's own c.,** guardar silencio. **2** *Jur (barrister)* abogado,-a *m,f;* **c. for the defence,** abogado defensor; **c. for the prosecution,** fiscal *mf.* **II** *vtr* aconsejar.

counselling, *US* **counseling** ['kaʊnsəlɪŋ] *n* orientación *f.*

counsellor, *US* **counselor** ['kaʊnsələʳ] *n* **1** *(adviser)* asesor,-a *m,f.* **2** *US Jur* abogado,-a *m,f.*

count¹ [kaʊnt] *I vtr* **1** *(gen)* contar; **six not counting the dog,** seis sin contar el perro. **2** *fig (consider)* considerar; **to c. one's blessings, to c. oneself lucky,** considerarse afortunado,-a. **II** *vi* contar; *(be valid)* valer; **counting from tomorrow,** a partir de mañana; **he doesn't c.,** él no cuenta *or* no tiene importancia; **that doesn't c.,** eso no vale; **to c. to ten,** contar hasta diez; *fig* **to c. against sb,** perjudicar a algn. **III** *n* **1** *(gen)* cuenta *f; (total)* recuento *m;* **to keep/lose c. of sth,** llevar/perder la cuenta de algo. ■ *Med* **blood c.,** recuento *m* de hemoglobina. **2** *Box* **to be out for the c.,** estar fuera de combate. **3** *Jur* cargo *m,* acusación *f.* ◆ **count in** *vtr fam* incluir, contar con; **c. me in!,** ¡yo me apunto! ◆ **count on, count upon** *vtr* contar con. ◆ **count out** *vtr* **1** *(banknotes)* contar uno por uno. **2** *fam* no contar con; **c. me out!,** ¡no cuentes conmigo!

count² [kaʊnt] *n (nobleman)* conde *m.*

countdown ['kaʊntdaʊn] *n* cuenta *f* atrás.

countenance ['kaʊntɪnəns] *I n* **1** *(face)* semblante *m,* rostro *m.* **2** *(composure)* compostura *f.* **II** *vtr* aprobar, dar aprobación a.

counter¹ ['kaʊntəʳ] *n* **1** *(in shop)* mostrador *m; (in bank)* ventanilla *f;* **to buy a medicine over the c.,** comprar un medicamento sin receta médica; *fig* **under the c.,** clandestinamente. **2** *(in board games)* ficha *f.*

counter² ['kaʊntəʳ] *n* contador *m.*

counter³ ['kaʊntəʳ] *I adv* en contra; **c. to,** en contra de; **to run c. to,** ir en contra de. **II** *vtr (attack)* contestar a; *(blow)* parar; *(tendency)* contrarrestar. **III** *vi* contestar, replicar.

counteract [kaʊntər'ækt] *vtr* contrarrestar.

counterattack ['kaʊntərətæk] **I** *n* contraataque *m.* **II** *vtr & vi* contraatacar.

counterbalance ['kaʊntəbæləns] **I** *n* contrapeso *m.* **II** [kaʊntə'bæləns] *vtr* contrapesar, equilibrar.

counterclockwise [kaʊntə'klɒkwaɪz] *adj & adv US* en sentido contrario a las agujas del reloj.

counterespionage [kaʊntər'espɪənɑːʒ] *n* contraespionaje *m.*

counterfeit ['kaʊntəfɪt] **I** *adj* falsificado,-a; **c. coin,** moneda falsa. **II** *n* falsificación *f.* **III** *vtr* falsificar.

counterfoil ['kaʊntəfɔɪl] *n GB (of cheque)* matriz *f.*

counterintelligence [kaʊntərɪn'telɪdʒəns] *n* contraespionaje *m.*

countermand [kaʊntə'mɑːnd] *vtr (command)* revocar; *Com (order)* anular.

countermeasure ['kaʊntəmeʒəʳ] *n* contramedida *f.*

counteroffensive ['kaʊntərəfensɪv] *n Mil* contraofensiva *f.*

counterpane ['kaʊntəpeɪn] *n* cubrecama *m,* colcha *f.*

counterpart ['kaʊntəpɑːt] *n* homólogo,-a *m,f,* colega *mf.*

counterpoint ['kaʊntəpɔɪnt] *n Mus* contrapunto *m.*

counterproductive [kaʊntəprə'dʌktɪv] *adj* contraproducente.

counter-revolution [kaʊntərevə'luːʃən] *n Pol* contrarrevolución *f.*

counter-revolutionary [kaʊntərevə'luːʃənərɪ] *adj* contrarrevolucionario,-a.

countersign ['kaʊntəsaɪn] *vtr* refrendar.

countess ['kaʊntɪs] *n* condesa *f.*

countless ['kaʊntlɪs] *adj* innumerable, incontable.

country ['kʌntrɪ] *n* **1** *(state, nation)* país *m;* **native c.,** patria *f; Pol* **fig to go to the c.,** celebrar elecciones generales. **2** *(rural area)* campo *m.* ■ **c. and western (music),** música *f* country; **c. dancing,** baile *m* country; **c. seat,** finca *f,* hacienda *f.*

countryfolk ['kʌntrɪfəʊk] *n* gente *f* del campo.

countryman ['kʌntrɪmən] *n (pl countrymen)* **1** *(rural)* hombre *m* del campo. **2** *(compatriot)* compatriota *m.*

countryside ['kʌntrɪsaɪd] *n (area)* campo *m; (scenery)* paisaje *m.*

countrywoman ['kʌntrɪwʊmən] *n (pl countrywomen* ['kʌntrɪwɪmɪn]*)* **1** *(rural)* mujer *f* del campo. **2** *(compatriot)* compatriota *f.*

county ['kaʊntɪ] *n* condado *m.* ■ **c. town,** capital *f* de un condado.

coup [kuː] *n* golpe *m.* ■ *Pol* **c. d'état,** golpe *m* de estado.

coupé ['kuːpeɪ] *n Aut* cupé *m.*

couple ['kʌpəl] *I n* **1** *(people)* pareja *f;* **a married c.,** un matrimonio; **a young c.,** una pareja joven. **2** *(things)* par *m;* **a c.,** un par; *fam* **a c. of times,** un par de veces; *fam* **when he's had a c.,** cuando ha bebido más de la cuenta. **II** *vtr Tech (wagons)* enganchar; *fig* **coupled with,** junto a. **III** *vi (mate)* aparearse.

couplet ['kʌplɪt] *n Lit (verso m)* pareado *m.*

coupling ['kʌplɪŋ] *n Rail* enganche *m.*

coupon ['kuːpɒn] *n* **1** *(gen)* cupón *m.* **2** *GB Ftb* boleto *m.*

courage ['kʌrɪdʒ] *n* coraje *m,* valor *m,* valentía *f;* **he has the c. of his convictions,** tiene el valor de atenerse a sus principios.

courageous [kə'reɪdʒəs] *adj* valeroso,-a, valiente.

courgette [kʊə'ʒet] *n Culin* calabacín *m.*

courier ['kʊərɪəʳ] *n* **1** *(messenger)* mensajero,-a *m,f.* **2** *(guide)* guía *mf* turístico,-a.

course [kɔ:s] **I** n **1** (onward movement) curso m, marcha f; (direction) curso m, dirección f; Naut rumbo m; (of river) curso m; Av trayectoria f; **to be on/off c.,** seguir/perder el rumbo; **to change c.,** cambiar de rumbo or dirección; **to set c.,** poner rumbo. **2** fig curso m, marcha f; (of illness) desarrollo m; **his c. of action was to ...,** su opción fue ...; **in due c.,** a su debido tiempo; **in the c. of construction,** en vías de construcción; **in the c. of our conversation,** mientras hablábamos; **in the c. of time,** en el tiempo; **let things take their c.,** deja que todo siga su curso; **that will happen as a matter of c.,** eso ya vendrá por sí solo; **the c. of events,** el curso de los acontecimientos. **3** (set, series) ciclo m, serie f; (of lectures) ciclo m; **a c. of treatment,** un tratamiento. **4** Educ (year-long) curso m; (short) cursillo m; Univ asignatura f; **refresher c.,** cursillo de reciclaje; **to take a c.,** seguir or hacer un curso. **5** Constr hilada f. **6** Sport (for golf) campo m; (for racing) pista f; (for horse-racing) hipódromo m. **7** Culin plato m; **first c.,** entrada f, primer plato m. **8** of c., claro, naturalmente, por supuesto; **of c. not!,** ¡claro que no! **II** vi (liquid) correr, fluir.

court [kɔ:t] **I** n **1** Jur tribunal m; **high c.,** tribunal supremo; **to settle out of c.,** llegar a un acuerdo sin ir a juicio; **to take sb to c.,** llevar a algn a los tribunales. ■ Mil **c. martial,** consejo m de guerra; GB **c. of inquiry,** comisión f de investigación; **c. of justice,** tribunal m de justicia; **c. order,** orden f judicial. **2** (royal) corte f. ■ **c. shoe,** escarpín m. **3** Sport pista f, cancha f. **II** vtr (woman) festejar a, hacer la corte a; fig **to c. and spark,** pelar la pava; fig **to c. danger,** buscar el peligro; fig **to c. disaster,** exponerse al desastre. **III** vi (couple) llevar or tener relaciones.

courteous ['kɜ:tɪəs] adj cortés, fino,-a, educado,-a. ◆ **courteously** adv cortésmente, con cortesía.

courtesy ['kɜ:tɪsɪ] n **1** (politeness) cortesía f, educación f; **he didn't have the c. to visit her,** no tuvo la atención de visitarla. **2** (favour) permiso m; **by c. of,** con permiso de. **3** Aut **c. light,** luz f interior.

courthouse ['kɔ:thaʊs] n Jur palacio m de justicia.

courtier ['kɔ:tɪər] n cortesano m.

court-martial ['kɔ:tmɑ:ʃəl] vtr (pt & pp **court -martialled,** US **court-martialed**) someter a consejo de guerra.

courtroom ['kɔ:tru:m] n Jur sala f de justicia.

courtship ['kɔ:tʃɪp] n (of people) noviazgo m; (of animals) cortejo m.

courtyard ['kɔ:tjɑ:d] n patio m.

cousin ['kʌzən] n primo,-a m, f; **first c.,** primo,-a hermano,-a.

cove [kəʊv] n Geog cala f, ensenada f.

covenant ['kʌvənənt] **I** n Jur convenio m, pacto m. **II** vi convenir (**with sb,** con algn), comprometerse (**to do sth,** a hacer algo).

Coventry ['kʌvəntrɪ] n fam **to send sb to C.,** hacer el vacío a algn.

cover ['kʌvər] **I** vtr **1** cubrir (**with,** de); (floor, furniture) revestir (**with,** de); (with lid) tapar; (book) forrar. **2** (hide) cubrir, disimular; fig **to c. one's tracks,** no dejar rastro. **3** (protect) abrigar, proteger; **to c. oneself,** protegerse a sí mismo. **4** (financially) cubrir; **£10 should c. it,** con diez libras habrá bastante; **to c. expenses,** cubrir gastos. **5** (distance) recorrer, cubrir; **to c. a great deal of ground,** hacer mucho camino. **6** Ins asegurar, cubrir (**contra** riesgos); **he's covered against fire,** tiene un seguro antiincendios. **7** Journ investigar, hacer un reportaje sobre. **8** (deal with) tratar, abarcar. **9** (include) incluir, comprender; **to c. all eventualities,** tener en cuenta todas las eventualidades. **10** (aim at) apuntar a; **to c. sb with a revolver,** apuntar a algn con una pistola. **11** Sport (player) marcar. **II** vi **to c. for sb,** encubrir a algn. **III** n **1** (gen) cubierta f; (lid) tapa f; (on bed) manta f, colcha f; (of chair, typewriter) funda f. **2** (of book) tapa f, cubierta f; (of magazine) portada f; fig **to read a book from c. to c.,** leer un libro de cabo a rabo. ■ **c. girl,** modelo f de revista. **3** (in restaurant) cubierto m. ■ **c. charge,** precio m del cubierto. **4** (envelope) sobre m; **under separate c.,** por

separado. **5** Ins **full c.,** cobertura f completa. ■ GB **c. note,** seguro m provisional. **6** fig (protection) abrigo m, protección f. ◆ **cover up I** vtr cubrir. **2** fig (crime) encubrir; (truth) disimular. **II** vi **1** (person) abrigarse, taparse. **2** fig **to c. up for sb,** encubrir a algn.

coverage ['kʌvərɪdʒ] n **1** Journ reportaje m (**of,** sobre); **news c.,** reportaje m. **2** Ins cobertura f.

coveralls ['kʌvərɔ:lz] npl US (garment) mono m sing.

covering ['kʌvərɪŋ] **I** n cubierta f, envoltura f. **II** adj (letter) explicatorio,-a.

coverlet ['kʌvəlɪt] n sobrecama m, colcha f.

covert ['kʌvət] adj disimulado,-a, secreto,-a.

cover-up ['kʌvərʌp] n disimulo m, encubrimiento m.

covet ['kʌvɪt] vtr codiciar.

covetous ['kʌvɪtəs] adj codicioso,-a.

cow[1] [kaʊ] n **1** Zool vaca f; (of elephant, seal) hembra f; fam **till the cows come home,** hasta que las ranas echen pelo. ■ **c. shed,** establo m. **2** pej (woman) arpía f, bruja f.

cow[2] [kaʊ] vtr intimidar, acobardar.

coward ['kaʊəd] n cobarde mf.

cowardice ['kaʊədɪs] n cobardía f.

cowardly ['kaʊədlɪ] adj cobarde.

cowboy ['kaʊbɔɪ] n vaquero m.

cower ['kaʊər] vi agacharse; (with fear) encogerse.

cowhide ['kaʊhaɪd] n piel f de vaca, cuero m.

cowl [kaʊl] n **1** (hood) capucha f. **2** (of chimney) sombrerete m.

cowslip ['kaʊslɪp] n Bot primavera f, prímula f.

cox [kɒks] **I** n timonel m. **II** vtr (boat) gobernar. **III** vi servir de timonel.

coy [kɔɪ] adj (shy) tímido,-a; (demure) coquetón,-ona. ◆ **coyly** adv tímidamente.

cozy ['kəʊzɪ] adj US see **cosy.**

CP [si:'pi:] Pol abbr of **Communist Party,** Partido m Comunista, PC.

crab [kræb] n **1** Zool cangrejo m. ■ **fiddler c.,** nécora f; **spider c.,** centolla f. **2** Bot **c. apple,** manzana f silvestre.

crabbed ['kræbɪd] adj **1** (irritable) irritable, tosco,-a. **2** (handwriting) apretado,-a.

crabby ['kræbɪ] adj (**crabbier, crabbiest**) fam **to be c.,** tener mala leche.

crack [kræk] **I** vtr **1** (break) (cup) rajar; Med (bone) fracturar; (nut) cascar; (safe) forzar; (head) golpearse. **2** (whip) hacer restallar. **3** fig (problem) dar con la solución de; (clue) descifrar; (joke) contar, soltar. **II** vi **1** (glass) rajarse, resquebrajarse; (wall) agrietarse. **2** (whip) restallar; (voice) cascarse. **3** fam **to get cracking on or with sth,** ponerse a hacer algo; **get cracking!,** ¡a trabajar!, ¡manos a la obra! **III** n **1** (in cup) raja f; (in ice, wall, ground) grieta f. **2** (of whip) restallido m; (of gun) detonación f; fam fig **he had a fair c. of the whip,** ha tenido su oportunidad. **3** fam (blow) golpetazo m; **a c. on the head,** un tostón en la cabeza. **4** fam (attempt) intento m; **to have a c. at sth,** intentar hacer algo. **5** sl (wisecrack) réplica f aguda. **6** sl (drug) crack m. **7** **the c. of dawn,** el amanecer. **IV** adj sl bestial, de primera; **a c. shot,** un tirador de primera. ◆ **crack down on** vtr castigar. ◆ **crack up I** vi (pathway etc) agrietarse; fam fig (person) desquiciarse, venirse abajo. **II** vtr fam poner por los cielos; **it's not all that it's cracked up to be,** no es tan bueno,-a como se dice.

crackbrained ['krækbreɪnd] adj fam, **cracked** [krækt] adj fam chalado,-a, chiflado,-a.

cracker ['krækər] n **1** (biscuit) galleta f seca. **2** (firework) buscapiés m inv.

crackers ['krækəz] adj fam see **crackbrained.**

crackle ['krækəl] **I** vi crujir, chasquear. **II** n crujido m, chasquido m.

crackling ['kræklɪŋ] *n Culin* chicharrones *mpl*, cortezas *fpl* de cerdo.

crackpot ['krækpɒt] I *n* chiflado,-a *m,f.* II *adj (person)* chiflado,-a; *(idea)* excéntrico,-a, desorbitado,-a.

cradle ['kreɪdəl] I *n (baby's)* cuna *f; Tel* soporte *m; Constr* andamio *m* volante; *fig* **the c. of civilization**, la cuna de la civilización; *fig* **from the c. to the grave**, toda la vida. II *vtr (baby)* acunar (en los brazos).

craft ['krɑːft] *n* **1** *(occupation)* oficio *m; (art)* arte *m; (skill)* destreza *f*, habilidad *f;* **arts and crafts**, artesanía *f.* **2** *(cunning)* astucia *f*, maña *f.* **3** *Naut* embarcación *f.*

craftiness ['krɑːftɪnɪs] *n* astucia *f*, maña *f.*

craftsman ['krɑːftsmən] *n (pl craftsmen)* artesano *m.*

craftsmanship ['krɑːftsmənʃɪp] *n* arte *m*, artificio *m.*

crafty ['krɑːftɪ] *adj (craftier, craftiest)* astuto,-a, taimado,-a. ◆ **craftily** *adv* astutamente, con astucia *or* maña.

crag [kræg] *n* peña *f*, peñasco *m.*

craggy ['krægɪ] *adj (craggier, craggiest)* **1** *(place)* peñascoso,-a, escarpado,-a. **2** *(face)* de facciones marcadas.

crake [kreɪk] *n Orn* polluela *f.*

cram [kræm] **1** *vtr (pt & pp crammed)* **1** *(room etc)* atestar, henchir, atiborrar; **crammed with people**, llenísimo,-a de gente; **to c. oneself with food**, atiborrarse de comida. **2** *Educ fam (subject)* empollar. II *vi Educ fam* empollar.

cram-full [kræm'fʊl] *adj fam* atiborrado,-a, atestado,-a.

cramp¹ [kræmp] *n Med* calambre *m;* **cramps**, *(gen)* retortijones *mpl; (menstrual)* molestias *fpl* menstruales.

cramp² [kræmp] *vtr (restrict)* limitar; *(development)* poner trabas a; **to be cramped for space**, estar abarrotado,-a; *fam fig* **to c. sb's style**, cortar el vuelo a algn.

cramped [kræmpt] *adj* **1** *(place)* atestado,-a, abarrotado,-a. **2** *(writing)* apretado,-a.

cranberry ['krænbərɪ] *n Bot* arándano *m.*

crane [kreɪn] I *n* **1** *Zool* grulla *f* común. **2** *(device)* grúa *f.* **3** *Ent* **c. fly**, típula *f.* II *vtr* estirar; **to c. one's neck (to see sth)**, estirar el cuello (para ver algo).

cranium ['kreɪnɪəm] *n (pl craniums or crania* ['kreɪnɪə]*) Anat* cráneo *m.*

crank [kræŋk] I *n* **1** *Tech* cigüeñal *m.* **2** *Tech (starting handle)* manivela *f.* **3** *fam (eccentric)* maniático,-a *m,f*, pájaro *m* raro. II *vtr* **to c. (up)**, *(engine)* arrancar con la manivela.

crankshaft ['kræŋkʃɑːft] *n Tech* árbol *m* del cigüeñal.

cranky ['kræŋkɪ] *adj (crankier, crankiest) fam* excéntrico,-a, chiflado,-a.

cranny ['krænɪ] *n* grieta *f*, *fig* **in every nook and c.**, en todos los rincones.

crap [kræp] *n fam* mierda *f.*

crash [kræʃ] I *vtr* **1** **to c. one's car**, tener un accidente con el coche. **2** *fam* colarse; **she crashed the party**, se coló en la fiesta. II *vi* **1** *(car, plane)* estrellarse; *(collide)* chocar; **to c. into**, estrellarse contra, chocar con *or* contra. **2** *Com* quebrar, hundirse. **3** *sl* **to c. (out)**, quedarse roque. III *n* **1** *(noise)* estrépito *m;* **c.!**, ¡patapún! **2** *(collision)* choque *m*, colisión *f;* **car/plane c.**, accidente *m* de coche/avión. ■ **c. barrier**, barrera *f; fig* **c. course**, curso *m* intensivo; *fig* **c. diet**, régimen *m* riguroso; **c. helmet**, casco *m* protector. **3** *Com* quiebra *f.*

crashing ['kræʃɪŋ] *adj fam* enorme; **c. bore**, pelma *mf*, pelmazo *mf.*

crash-land [kræʃ'lænd] *vi Av* hacer un aterrizaje forzoso.

crass [kræs] *adj (person)* grosero,-a; *(ignorance)* indisculpable, garrafal.

crate [kreɪt] I *n* caja *f*, cajón *m* (para embalaje). II *vtr* embalar.

crater ['kreɪtə'] *n Geol* cráter *m.*

cravat [krə'væt] *n* pañuelo *m* (de hombre).

crave [kreɪv] *vi* ansiar; **to c. for sth**, ansiar algo; *(in pregnancy)* antojar algo.

craving ['kreɪvɪŋ] *n (gen)* ansia *f; (in pregnancy)* antojo *m.*

crawfish ['krɔːfɪʃ] *n (fish)* langosta *f.*

crawl [krɔːl] I *vi (baby)* gatear; *(insect)* arrastrarse; *(vehicle)* avanzar lentamente; *fig* **to be crawling with vermin**, estar plagado,-a de bichos; *fig* **to c. to sb**, arrastrarse a los pies de algn, lamer a algn; *fam fig* **it makes my flesh c.**, me pone los pelos de punta. II *n* **1** *Aut* velocidad *f* lenta; **to go at a c.**, ir *or* avanzar lentamente. **2** *Swimming* crol *m;* **to do the c.**, nadar crol.

crawler ['krɔːlə'] *n sl* cobista *mf*, adulador,-a *m,f.*

crayfish ['kreɪfɪʃ] *n Zool* cangrejo *m* de río.

crayon ['kreɪɒn] I *n* pastel *m*, lápiz *m* pastel. ■ *Art* **c. drawing**, dibujo *m* al pastel. II *vtr* dibujar al pastel.

craze [kreɪz] *n* manía *f*, moda *f;* **it's the latest c.**, es la última moda, es lo que se lleva.

crazed [kreɪzd] *adj* loco,-a *(with*, de*)*; **half c.**, medio loco,-a.

craziness ['kreɪzɪnɪs] *n fam* locura *f.*

crazy ['kreɪzɪ] *adj (crazier, craziest) fam* loco,-a, chalado,-a; **like c.**, como un,-a loco,-a; **to drive sb c.**, volver loco a algn. ■ *GB sl* **c. paving**, pavimento *m* en mosaico. ◆ **crazily** *adv* locamente.

creak [kriːk] I *vi (floor, stairs)* crujir, hacer un crujido; *(hinge)* chirriar. II *n (of floorboards, new boots)* crujido *m; (of hinge)* chirrido *m.*

creaky ['kriːkɪ] *adj (creakier, creakiest) (floor)* que cruje; *(hinge)* chirriante.

cream [kriːm] I *n* **1** *(of milk)* nata *f;* **c. coloured**, color crema; **c. of chicken soup**, crema *f* de pollo; **whipped c.**, nata montada; *fig* **the c.**, la flor y nata. ■ **c. cheese**, queso *m* cremoso; **double c.**, nata *f* para montar. **2** *(cosmetic)* crema *f;* **face/hand c.**, crema para el cutis/las manos. II *vtr* **1** *(milk)* desnatar. **2** *Culin* batir; **c. the butter and sugar**, batir la mantequilla con el azúcar. ◆ **creamed potatoes**, puré *m* de patatas. ◆ **cream off** *vtr fig* seleccionar.

creamery ['kriːmərɪ] *n* lechería *f*, mantequería *f.*

creamy ['kriːmɪ] *adj (creamier, creamiest)* cremoso,-a.

crease [kriːs] I *n* **1** *(wrinkle)* arruga *f; (fold)* pliegue *m; (on trousers)* raya *f.* II *vtr (clothes)* arrugar; *(with iron)* hacer la raya. III *vi* arrugarse.

create [kriː'eɪt] I *vtr* **1** *(gen)* crear; *(sensation)* producir; *(difficulties)* crear; **to c. a diversion**, distraer la atención. **2** *(appoint)* nombrar. II *vi GB sl* armar un jaleo.

creation [kriː'eɪʃən] *n* creación *f.*

creative [kriː'eɪtɪv] *adj* **1** *(person)* creativo,-a. **2** *(work)* original.

creativity [kriːeɪ'tɪvɪtɪ] *n* creatividad *f.*

creator [kriː'eɪtə'] *n* creador,-a *m,f.*

creature ['kriːtʃə'] *n* I *(animal)* criatura *f.* **2** *(human being)* ser *m;* **c. of habit**, esclavo,-a *m, f* de los hábitos. ■ **c. comforts**, comodidades *fpl:*

crèche [kreɪʃ, kreʃ] *n* guardería *f.*

credence ['kriːdəns] *n* crédito *m;* **to give c. to**, dar crédito a.

credentials [krɪ'denʃəlz] *npl* credenciales *fpl.*

credibility [kredɪ'bɪlɪtɪ] *n* credibilidad *f.* ■ **c. gap**, falta *f* de credibilidad.

credible ['kredɪbəl] *adj* creíble.

credit ['kredɪt] I *n* **1** *Com* crédito *m; (in accountancy)* haber *m;* **c. and debit**, debe y haber; **on c.**, a crédito. ■ **c. card**, tarjeta *f* de crédito; **c. sales**, ventas *fpl* a crédito; **c. squeeze**, restricciones *fpl* al crédito. **2** *(acknowledgement)* reconocimiento *m;* **to give c. to sb for sth**, reconocer algo a algn; *fig* **c. where c. is due**, reconocimiento al mérito. **3** *(benefit)* honor *m;* **it does you c.**, puedes estar orgulloso,-a; **to be a c. to**, hacer honor a. **4** *C in TV* **credits,** ficha *f sing* técnica. **5** *US Univ* punto *m*, crédito *m*. **II** *vtr* **1** *Com (sum to sb's account)* abonar, acreditar. **2** *(believe)* creer; **you wouldn't c. it!,** ¡no te lo creerías! **3** *fig* atribuir; **he was credited with the invention of the new machine,** se le atribuyó el invento de la nueva máquina; **to c. sb with common sense,** creer que algn tiene sentido común.

creditable ['krɛdɪtəbəl] *adj* loable, digno,-a de crédito.

creditor ['krɛdɪtəʳ] *n Com* acreedor,-a *m,f*.

credulity [krɪ'dju:lɪtɪ] *n* credulidad *f*.

credulous ['krɛdjʊləs] *adj* crédulo,-a.

creed [kri:d] *n* credo *m*.

creek [kri:k] *n* **1** *GB* cala *f*. **2** *US Austral* riachuelo *m*; *sl* **to be up the c.,** estar jodido,-a.

creel [kri:l] *n* nasa *f*.

creep [kri:p] **I** *vi (pt & pp* **crept)** *(insect)* arrastrarse, trepar; *(cat)* deslizarse (sigilosamente); *(plant)* trepar; *Med* **creeping paralysis,** parálisis *f* progresiva; **to c. in /out of a house,** entrar/salir sigilosamente de una casa; **to c. up on sb,** sorprender a algn; *fig* **it made my flesh c.,** me dio escalofríos; *fig* **middle age is creeping up on me,** me estoy haciendo mayor. **II** *n fam* **1** *(person)* pelotillero *mf*, pelota *mf*. **2 to give sb the creeps,** hacerle poner la carne de gallina a algn, dar asco a algn.

creeper ['kri:pəʳ] *n Bot* trepadora *f*.

creepy ['kri:pɪ] *adj (creepier, creepiest) fam* horripilante, espeluznante.

creepy-crawly ['kri:pɪ'krɔ:lɪ] *n GB fam* bicho *m*.

cremate [krɪ'meɪt] *vtr* incinerar.

cremation [krɪ'meɪʃən] *n* incineración *f*.

crematorium [kremə'tɔ:rɪəm] *n (pl* **crematoriums** *or* **crematoria** [kremə'tɔ:rɪə])** *(horno m)* crematorio *m*.

creole ['kri:əʊl] **I** *adj* criollo,-a. **II** *n* **1** *(person)* criollo,-a *m,f*. **2** *(language)* criollo *m*.

creosote ['krɪəsəʊt] *n Chem* creosota *f*.

crepe [kreɪp] *n* **1** *Tex* crepé *m*, crespón *m*. **2 c. paper,** papel *m* crespón.

crept [krept] *pt & pp see* **creep.**

crescendo [krɪ'ʃendəʊ] *n Mus* crescendo *m*.

crescent ['krɛsənt] **I** *n (shape)* medialuna *f*; *GB (street)* calle *f* en medialuna. **II** *adj* creciente; **c. moon,** luna creciente.

cress [kres] *n Bot* berro *m*.

crest [krest] *n* **1** *(of cock, wave)* cresta *f*; *(on helmet)* penacho *m*, cimera *f*; *(of hill)* cima *f*. **2** *Herald* blasón *m*.

crested ['krestɪd] *adj* crestado,-a.

crestfallen ['krestfɔ:lən] *adj* abatido,-a, desanimado,-a.

Cretan ['kri:tən] *adj* cretense.

Crete [kri:t] *n* Creta.

cretin ['kretɪn] *n* cretino,-a *m,f*.

cretinous ['kretɪnəs] *adj* cretino,-a.

crevasse [krɪ'væs] *n* grieta *f*, fisura *f*.

crevice ['krevɪs] *n* grieta *f*, raja *f*, hendedura *f*.

crew¹ [kru:] **I** *n Av Naut* tripulación *f*; *(team)* equipo *m*; *fam* banda *f*; *Cin* **camera c.,** equipo *m* de filmación; *Hairdr* **c. cut,** corte *m* al rape; **c.-neck sweater,** jersey *m* con cuello redondo; **ground c.,** personal *m* de tierra. **III** *vi* tripular.

crew² [kru:] *pt see* **crow².**

crib [krɪb] *n* **1** *(manger)* pesebre *m*; *(for baby)* cuna *f*. **2** *fam (plagiarism)* hurto *m*, plagio *m*. **II** *vtr (pt & pp* **cribbed)** *fam* **1** *(steal)* hurtar. **2** *(copy)* copiar, plagiar.

crick [krɪk] *n fam (in the neck)* tortícolis *f*.

cricket¹ ['krɪkɪt] *n Ent* grillo *m*.

cricket² ['krɪkɪt] *n Sport* cricket *m*; *fam* **that's not c.,** eso no se hace. ■ **c. ball,** pelota *f* de cricket; **c. bat,** paleta *f* de cricket.

cricketer ['krɪkɪtəʳ] *n Sport* jugador,-a *m,f* de cricket.

crikey ['kraɪkɪ] *interj sl* ¡mecachis!, ¡ostras!

crime [kraɪm] *n Jur* delito *m*; **to prevent c.,** prevenir la criminalidad. ■ **c. fiction,** novelas *fpl* policíacas.

criminal ['krɪmɪnəl] *adj & n* criminal *(mf)*; **C. Investigation Department,** ≈ Brigada *f* de Investigación Criminal; **c. law,** derecho *m* penal; **c. offender,** infractor,-a *m,f*; **c. record,** antecedentes *mpl* penales.

criminology [krɪmɪ'nɒlədʒɪ] *n* criminología *f*.

crimp [krɪmp] *vtr (hair)* rizar (con tenacillas).

crimson ['krɪmzən] *adj & n* carmesí *(m)*.

cringe [krɪndʒ] *vi* abatirse, encogerse; **to c. before sb,** rebajarse ante algn.

cringing ['krɪndʒɪŋ] *adj (behaviour)* servil; *(gesture)* de servilismo.

crinkle ['krɪŋkəl] **I** *vtr (gen)* fruncir, arrugar; *(paper)* hacer pliegues en. **II** *vi* arrugarse, plegarse.

crinkly ['krɪŋklɪ] *adj (crinklier, crinkliest)* fruncido,-a, arrugado,-a; *(paper)* con pliegues.

cripple ['krɪpəl] **I** *n* lisiado,-a *m,f*, mutilado,-a *m,f*. **II** *vtr* mutilar, dejar cojo,-a; *fig* paralizar.

crippled ['krɪpəld] *adj* tullido,-a, lisiado,-a.

crisis ['kraɪsɪs] *n (pl* **crises** ['kraɪsi:z]) crisis *f inv*.

crisp [krɪsp] **I** *adj (toast, biscuit, snow)* crujiente; *(lettuce)* fresco,-a, tierno,-a; *(banknote)* nuevo,-a; *(air, weather)* frío,-a y seco,-a; *fig (style)* directo,-a, resuelto,-a. **II** *n GB Culin (potato)* **c.,** patata *f* frita (de churrería); **burnt to a c.,** achicharrado,-a. ◆ **crisply** *adv* decididamente.

crispbread ['krɪspbred] *n Culin* biscote® *m*.

crispy ['krɪspɪ] *adj (crispier, crispiest) (crisp)* crujiente.

crisscross ['krɪskrɒs] **I** *vi* entrecruzarse. **II** *vtr* entrecruzar. **III** *n* líneas *fpl* entrecruzadas.

criterion [kraɪ'tɪərɪən] *n (pl* **criterions** *or* **criteria** [kraɪ'tɪərɪə]) criterio *m*.

critic ['krɪtɪk] *n* **1** *Art Theat* crítico,-a *m,f*. **2** *(of person)* criticón,-ona *m,f*.

critical ['krɪtɪkəl] *adj* **1** *(judging, analytical)* crítico,-a; **a c. remark,** un comentario de crítica; **to be c. of sb,** criticar a algn. **2** *(crucial)* crítico,-a, crucial, decisivo,-a. ◆ **critically** *adv* críticamente; **c. ill,** gravemente enfermo,-a.

criticism ['krɪtɪsɪzəm] *n* crítica *f*; **he doesn't like c.,** no le gusta que le critiquen; **literary c.,** crítica literaria.

criticize ['krɪtɪsaɪz] *vtr* criticar.

critique [krɪ'ti:k] *n Lit Philos* crítica *f*.

croak [krəʊk] **I** *n* **1** *(of frog)* canto *m*; *(of raven)* graznido *m*. **2** *(of person)* voz *f* ronca. **II** *vi* **1** *(frog)* croar; *(raven)* graznar. **2** *(person)* hablar con voz ronca. **3** *sl (die)* estirar la pata.

crochet ['krəʊʃeɪ] *Knit* **I** *vtr* hacer a ganchillo. **II** *vi* hacer ganchillo. **III** *n* ganchillo *m*. ■ **c. hook,** aguja *f* de ganchillo.

crock¹ [krɒk] *n (pot)* cántaro *m*.

crock² [krɒk] *n GB sl (old person)* carca *mf*, carroza *mf*; *(car)* trasto *m*, cacharro *m*.

crockery ['krɒkərɪ] *n* loza *f*.

crocodile ['krɒkədaɪl] *n* **1** *Zool* cocodrilo *m*; *fig* **c. tears,** lágrimas *fpl* de cocodrilo. **2** *GB fam (line)* fila *f* (de niños) de dos en dos.

crocus ['krəʊkəs] *n Bot* azafrán *m*.

crone [krəʊn] *n* vieja *f*, bruja *f*.

crony ['krəʊnɪ] *n* amiguete *m*, compinche *mf*.

crook [krʊk] **I** *n* **1** gancho *m*; *(of shepherd)* cayado *m*. **2** *fam* caco *m*, delincuente *mf*. **II** *vtr (arm)* doblar.

crooked ['krʊkɪd] *adj* **1** *(stick, bridge)* torcido,-a; *(path)* tortuoso,-a. **2** *fam (dishonest)* deshonesto,-a.

croon [kru:n] *vtr & vi* canturrear.

crooner ['kru:nəʳ] *n* cantante *m* de música ligera.

crop [krɒp] **I** n **1** cultivo m; (harvest) cosecha f; (of hair) mata f. **2** (of bird) buche m. **3** (whip) fusta f. **II** vtr (pt & pp cropped) (hair) rapar, cortar al rape; (grass) pacer. ◆ **crop up** vi fam surgir, presentarse.

croquet ['krəʊkeɪ] n Sport croquet n.

cross [krɒs] **I** n **1** cruz f; fig cruz f, calvario m. ■ **Red C.,** Cruz f Roja. **2** (breeds, animals) cruce m. **3** Sew sesgo m; **cut on the c.,** cortado,-a al sesgo. **4** Math **c. section,** sección f transversal. **II** vtr **1** (street) cruzar, atravesar; (legs) cruzar; (cheque) cruzar; **it crossed my mind that ...,** se me ocurrió que ...; fam **to keep one's fingers crossed,** tocar madera. ■ Tel **crossed line,** mala comunicación f. **2** Rel santiguar(se); **to c. oneself,** hacer la señal de la cruz; fam **c. my heart!,** ¡te lo juro! **3** (thwart) contrariar. **III** vi (gen) cruzar; (roads) cruzarse; **to c. from Dover to Calais,** hacer la travesía de Dover a calais; **to c. into another country,** pasar la frontera a otro país; **to c. over,** atravesar, cruzar, pasar. **IV** adj **1** transversal; fig **they are at c. purposes,** hay un malentendido entre ellos. **2** (angry) de mal humor, enfadado,-a; **to get c. with sb,** enfadarse con algn. ◆ **cross off, cross out** vtr tachar, rayar. ◆ **crossly** adv de mal humor.

crossbar ['krɒsbɑːʳ] n travesaño m.

crossbill ['krɒsbɪl] n Orn piquituerto m (común).

crossbow ['krɒsbəʊ] n ballesta f.

crossbred ['krɒsbred] **I** pt & pp see **crossbreed. II** adj híbrido,-a.

crossbreed ['krɒsbriːd] **I** n mestizo m. **II** vtr (pt & pp crossbred) cruzar.

crosscheck ['krɒstʃek] **I** vtr comprobar por otro sistema. **II** n comprobación f adicional.

cross-country ['krɒskʌntrɪ] **I** adj **1** campo través. **2** Sport de cros. ■ Sport **c.-c. race,** cros m. **III** [krɒs'kʌntrɪ] adv campo través.

cross-examination [krɒsɪgzæmɪ'neɪʃən] n Jur interrogatorio m.

cross-examine [krɒsɪg'zæmɪn] vtr Jur (witness) interrogar.

cross-eyed ['krɒsaɪd] adj bizco,-a.

crossfire ['krɒsfaɪəʳ] n Mil fuego m cruzado.

crossing ['krɒsɪŋ] n cruce m. ■ **pedestrian c.,** paso m de peatones; **sea c.,** travesía f.

cross-legged [krɒs'legɪd] adj con las piernas cruzadas.

cross-reference [krɒs'refərəns] n remisión f.

crossroads ['krɒsrəʊdz] n encrucijada f.

crosswind ['krɒswɪnd] n viento m lateral.

crosswise ['krɒswaɪz] adv transversal, de través.

crossword ['krɒswɜːd] n **c. (puzzzle),** crucigrama m.

crotch [krɒtʃ] n (of body, garment) entrepierna f.

crotchet ['krɒtʃɪt] n Mus negra f.

crotchety ['krɒtʃɪtɪ] adj fam cascarrabias inv, gruñón,-ona.

crouch [kraʊtʃ] vi **to c. (down),** agacharse.

croup [kruːp] n Med crup m.

croupier ['kruːpɪə] n (in casino) crupié mf, crupier mf.

crow[1] [krəʊ] n Orn cuervo m; fig **as the c. flies,** en línea recta; US fig **to eat c.,** humillarse. ■ **carrion c.,** corneja f negra; **c.'s-feet,** patas fpl de gallo; Naut **c.'s-nest,** vigía f.

crow[2] [krəʊ] **I** vi (pt crowed or crew; pp crowed) **1** (cock) cantar; (person) **to c. over sth,** jactarse de algo. **2** (baby) balbucir. **II** n (cry of bird) canto m.

crowbar ['krəʊbɑːʳ] n palanca f.

crowd [kraʊd] **I** n **1** multitud f, muchedumbre f, gentío m; **the c.,** el populacho; **to push through the c.,** abrirse paso por entre la muchedumbre; fig **to follow the c.,** seguir a la mayoría; fam **he's a real c. puller,** atrae a las masas. ■ Cin **c. secne,** escena f de masas. **2** fam (gang) pandilla f. **II** vtr (streets, area) llenar, atestar. **III** vi apiñarse, aglomerarse; **to c. in/out,** entrar/salir en tropel; **to c. round sb,** apiñarse alrededor de algn.

crowded ['kraʊdɪd] adj atestado,-a, lleno,-a; **the animals were c. together,** los animales estaban todos apiñados.

crown [kraʊn] **I** n **1** (headdress) corona f; (garland) guirnalda f; **the c. jewels,** las joyas de la corona. ■ GB Jur **c. court,** tribunal m superior; **C. Prince,** príncipe m heredero. **2** Anat coronilla f; (of hat, tree) copa f; Dent corona f. **II** vtr **1** (king, queen) coronar; **crowned heads,** testas coronadas. **2** Dent poner una corona a. **3** fam **to c. sb,** dar un golpe en la cabeza a algn; fam fig **to c. it all,** y para colmo, y para más inri.

crowning ['kraʊnɪŋ] **I** adj supremo,-a, **II** n coronación f.

crucial ['kruːʃəl] adj crucial, decisivo,-a, crítico,-a.

crucible ['kruːsɪbəl] n crisol m.

crucifix ['kruːsɪfɪks] n crucifijo m.

crucifixion [kruːsɪ'fɪkʃən] n crucifixión f.

crucify ['kruːsɪfaɪ] vtr (pt & pp crucified) crucificar.

crude [kruːd] adj **1** (manners, style) tosco,-a, grosero,-a. **2** (unrefined) (oil) crudo,-a; (tool) primitivo,-a. ◆ **crudely** adv con crudeza, con tosquedad.

crudeness ['kruːdnɪs] n, **crudity** ['kruːdɪtɪ] n crudeza f, tosquedad f.

cruel [kruːəl] adj cruel (to, con). ◆ **cruelly** adv cruelmente, con crueldad.

cruelty ['kruːəltɪ] n crueldad f (to, hacia).

cruet ['kruːɪt] n Culin **c. set,** vinagreras fpl.

cruise [kruːz] **I** vi **1** Naut hacer un crucero. **2** Aut viajar or circular a velocidad constante; Av Naut viajar a velocidad de crucero. **3** fam ir de ligue. **II** n **1** Naut crucero m. **2** Mil **c. missile,** misil m teledirigido.

cruiser ['kruːzəʳ] n Naut (barco m) crucero m.

cruising ['kruːzɪŋ] adj **c. speed,** Aut velocidad f constante; Av velocidad de crucero.

crumb [krʌm] n miga f, migaja f; fig **a c. of comfort,** una pizca de consuelo.

crumble ['krʌmbəl] **I** vtr (bread) desmigar, desmenuzar. **II** vi (wall, building) desmoronarse; (empire) derrumbarse; fig (hopes) desvanecerse.

crumbly ['krʌmblɪ] adj (crumblier, crumbliest) (bread, cake) que se desmigaja.

crummy ['krʌmɪ] adj (crummier, crummiest) fam chungo,-a.

crumpet ['krʌmpɪt] n GB Culin clase f de crepe grueso que se puede tostar.

crumple ['krʌmpəl] **I** vtr (paper) estrujar; (clothes) arrugar. **II** vi (material) arrugarse, estrujarse.

crunch [krʌntʃ] **I** vtr (food) ronchar, mascar; (with feet, tyres) hacer crujir. **II** vi ronchar, crujir. **III** n (of snow, gravel) crujido m; fam **when it comes to the c.,** a la hora de la verdad.

crunchy ['krʌntʃɪ] adj (crunchier, crunchiest) crujiente, que cruje.

crusade [kruː'seɪd] **I** n cruzada f. **II** vi **to c. for/against,** hacer una cruzada or campaña a favor/en contra de.

crusader [kruː'seɪdəʳ] n Hist cruzado m; (champion) campeón,-ona m,f.

crush [krʌʃ] **I** vtr **1** (mash, squash) aplastar; (wrinkle) arrugar; (grind) moler; (squeeze) exprimir; fig **to c. people into a train,** apiñar gente en un tren. **2** fig (defeat utterly) aplastar. **II** vi (clothes) arrugarse, ajarse; fig **to c. into a car,** apretujarse en un coche. **III** n **1** (of people) gentío m, aglomeración f. **2** Culin jugo m; **orange c.,** naranjada f. **3** fam enamoramiento m; **to have a c. on sb,** estar loco,-a perdido,-a por algn.

crushing ['krʌʃɪŋ] adj fig (defeat, reply) aplastante.

crust [krʌst] n **1** (of bread) corteza f, cuscurro m; (of pastry) pasta f. **2** Geol (of earth) corteza f.

crustacean [krʌ'steɪʃən] adj & n Zool crustáceo,-a (m).

crusty ['krʌstɪ] adj (**crustier, crustiest**) **1** (bread) crujiente. **2** fig (person) brusco,-a, áspero,-a, irritable.

crutch [krʌtʃ] n **1** Med muleta f; fig apoyo m. **2** GB see **crotch**.

crux [krʌks] n (pl **cruxes** or **cruces** ['kru:si:z]) quid m, meollo m; **the c. of the matter**, el quid de la cuestión.

cry [kraɪ] **I** vi (pt & pp **cried**) **1** gritar; **to c. for help**, pedir socorro a voces. **2** (weep) llorar; **to c. over sth**, lamentarse por algo; **to c. with joy**, llorar de alegría; fig **to c. for the moon**, pedir peras al olmo; prov **don't c. over spilt milk**, a lo hecho, pecho. **II** vtr **1** gritar; **'it's true!' he cried**, '¡es cierto!' gritó; fig **to c. wolf**, dar una falsa alarma. **2** fig **to c. one's eyes out**, llorar a lágrima viva. **III** n **1** grito m; **to give a c.**, gritar; fig **it's a far c. from ...**, tiene poco que ver con ... . **2** (weep) llanto m; **to have a good c.**, desahogarse llorando. ◆ **cry down** vtr despreciar, desacreditar. ◆ **cry off** vi fam volverse atrás, rajarse. ◆ **cry out** vi gritar; **to c. out against**, clamar contra; **to c. out for sth**, pedir algo a gritos.

crybaby ['kraɪbeɪbɪ] n niño,-a m,f llorón,-ona.

crying ['kraɪɪŋ] **I** n **1** (shouts) gritos mpl. **2** (weeping) llanto m. **II** adj **1** (child) que llora. **2** fig (need) urgente, apremiante; (injustice) que clama al cielo; **it's a c. shame**, es una vergüenza.

crypt [krɪpt] n Rel cripta f.

cryptic ['krɪptɪk] adj enigmático,-a.

crystal ['krɪstəl] n **1** cristal m; **a c. vase**, un florero de cristal. ■ **c. ball**, bola f de cristal; **c. gazing**, predicciones fpl que se hacen mirando una bola de cristal.

crystal-clear [krɪstəl'klɪə'] adj claro,-a como el agua.

crystalline ['krɪstəlaɪn] adj cristalino,-a.

crystallize ['krɪstəlaɪz] **I** vtr cristalizar; **crystallized fruits**, frutas fpl confitadas. **II** vi cristalizarse.

ct 1 abbr of **carat**, quilate m, quil. **2** abbr of **cent**, céntimo m, centavo m.

cu abbr of **cubic**, cúbico,-a.

cub [kʌb] n **1** (animal) cachorro m. **2** (junior scout) niño m explorador.

Cuba ['kju:bə] n Cuba.

Cuban ['kju:bən] adj & n cubano,-a (m,f).

cubbyhole ['kʌbɪhəʊl] n chiribitil m.

cube [kju:b] **I** n **1** (shape) cubo m; (of sugar) terrón m; Culin **stock c.**, pastilla f de caldo. **2** Math cubo m. ■ **c. root**, raíz f cúbica. **II** vtr **1** Math elevar al cubo. **2** Culin cortar en dados.

cubic ['kju:bɪk] adj cúbico,-a; **c. centimetre**, centímetro cúbico.

cubicle ['kju:bɪkəl] n (gen) cubículo m; (at swimming pool) caseta f.

cubism ['kju:bɪzəm] n Art cubismo m.

cuckoo ['kuku:] n Orn cuco m común; (call) cucú m. ■ **c. clock**, reloj m de cuco. **II** adj fam lelo,-a, majareta.

cucumber ['kju:kʌmbə'] n Culin pepino m.

cud [kʌd] n **to chew the c.**, rumiar.

cuddle ['kʌdəl] **I** vtr abrazar, acariciar; (baby) acunar (en los brazos). **II** vi abrazarse; **to c. up to sb**, acurrucarse contra algn. **III** n abrazo m afectuoso or amoroso.

cuddly ['kʌdlɪ] adj (**cuddlier, cuddliest**) (child) mimoso,-a; **c. toy**, muñeco m de peluche.

cudgel ['kʌdʒəl] n porra f; fig **to take up the cudgels for sb**, salir en defensa de algn.

cue¹ [kju:] n Theat pie m; fig **to take one's c. from sb**, seguir la corriente a algn. ◆ **cue in** vtr indicar a, hacer una señal a.

cue² [kju:] n Bill taco m. ■ **c. ball**, bola f blanca or con que se juega.

cuff¹ [kʌf] n (of sleeve) puño m; US (of trousers) dobladillo m; fig **to do sth off the c.**, improvisar.

cuff² [kʌf] **I** vtr abofetear. **II** n bofetada f.

cufflinks ['kʌflɪŋks] npl (for shirt) gemelos mpl.

cul-de-sac ['kʌldəsæk] n (pl **cul-de-sacs**) calle f sin salida.

culinary ['kʌlɪnərɪ] adj culinario,-a.

cull [kʌl] **I** vtr **1** (choose) escoger. **2** (take out) (animals) eliminar. **II** n (of animals) eliminación f.

culminate ['kʌlmɪneɪt] vi culminar; **to c. in**, terminar en.

culmination [kʌlmɪ'neɪʃən] n culminación f, punto m culminante, apogeo m.

culottes [kju:'lɒts] npl (garment) falda-pantalón f sing.

culpability [kʌlpə'bɪlɪtɪ] n culpabilidad f.

culpable ['kʌlpəbəl] adj culpable.

culprit ['kʌlprɪt] n Jur culpable mf.

cult [kʌlt] n culto m. ■ **c. figure**, ídolo m.

cultivate ['kʌltɪveɪt] vtr cultivar.

cultivated ['kʌltɪveɪtɪd] adj **1** (person) culto,-a. **2** (grown, tended) cultivado,-a.

cultivation [kʌltɪ'veɪʃən] n cultivo m (de la tierra).

cultivator ['kʌltɪveɪtə'] n **1** (person) cultivador,-a m,f. **2** Tech cultivador m.

cultural ['kʌltʃərəl] adj cultural.

culture ['kʌltʃə'] n **1** cultura f; **ancient c.**, cultura de la antigüedad. **2** Biol cultivo m.

cultured ['kʌltʃəd] adj see **cultivated**.

cumbersome ['kʌmbəsəm] adj (awkward) incómodo,-a; (bulky) voluminoso,-a.

cum(m)in ['kʌmɪn] n Bot comino m.

cumulative ['kju:mjʊlətɪv] adj acumulativo,-a.

cunning ['kʌnɪŋ] **I** adj astuto,-a, mañoso,-a. **II** n astucia f, maña f. ◆ **cunningly** adv con astucia or maña.

cunt [kʌnt] n offens coño m.

cup [kʌp] **I** n **1** taza f; **a c. of tea**, un té; fam **it's not everyone's c. of tea**, no es lo que les gusta a todos. **2** Sport copa f. ■ **C. Final**, final f de copa; **c. tie**, partido m de copa. **II** vtr (pt & pp **cupped**) (hands) ahuecar (**round**, alrededor de).

cupboard ['kʌbəd] n Furn (for clothes, books) armario m; (on wall) alacena f; (for crockery) aparador m.

cupful ['kʌpfʊl] n taza f (llena).

Cupid ['kju:pɪd] n Cupido m.

cupidity [kju:'pɪdɪtɪ] n codicia f.

cupola ['kju:pələ] n Archit cúpula f.

cuppa ['kʌpə] n GB fam **a c.**, un té.

cur [kɜ:'] n **1** (dog) perro m de mala raza. **2** (person) canalla m.

curable ['kjʊərəbəl] adj curable.

curate ['kjʊərɪt] n C of E cura m coadjutor.

curative ['kjʊərətɪv] adj & n curativo,-a (m).

curator [kjʊə'reɪtə'] n (of museum) conservador,-a m,f, director,-a m,f.

curb [kɜ:b] **I** n **1** (for horse) barbada f; fig **to put a c. on**, poner freno a. **2** (kerb) bordillo m (de la acera). **II** vtr (horse) refrenar; fig (public spending) contener; fig (emotions) controlar.

curd [kɜ:d] n Culin cuajada f; **lemon c.**, crema f de limón.

curdle ['kɜ:dəl] **I** vtr (milk) cuajar. **II** vi (milk) cuajarse; (sauce) cortarse; fig **his blood curdled**, se le heló la sangre en las venas.

cure [kjʊə'] **I** vtr **1** (illness) curar; (habit) quitar. **2** (fish) curar; (hide) curtir. **II** n (remedy) cura f, remedio m; (recovery) curación f, cura f.

cure-all ['kjʊərɔ:l] n panacea f.

curettage [kjʊərɪ'tɑ:ʒ] n Med raspado m.

curfew ['kɜ:fju:] n toque m de queda.

curiosity [kjʊərɪ'ɒsɪtɪ] n curiosidad f.

curious ['kjʊərɪəs] *adj* **1** *(inquisitive)* curioso,-a. **2** *(odd)* extraño,-a, singular; *(object)* curioso,-a, interesante; **the c. thing is that ...**, lo curioso es que ... . ◆ **curiously** *adv* curiosamente; **c. enough**, aunque parezca mentira.

curl [kɜːl] **I** *vtr (hair)* rizar; *(lip)* fruncir. **II** *vi (hair)* rizarse; *(smoke)* formar una espiral; *(dry leaves)* enrollarse; *(wave)* encresparse. **III** *n (of hair)* rizo *m*; *(of smoke)* espiral *f*, voluta *f*; **soft c.**, bucle *m*; **with a c. of the lips**, con una mueca. ◆ **curl up** *vi* enroscarse, acurrucarse; *fam* **to c. up with a good book**, echarse acurrucado,-a leyendo un libro interesante.

curlew ['kɜːljuː] *n Orn* zarapito *m* real. ■ **stone c.**, alcaraván *m*.

curling ['kɜːlɪŋ] **I** *n Sport* curling *m*. **II** *adj Hairdr* **c. tongs**, tenacillas *fpl* de rizar el pelo.

curly ['kɜːlɪ] *adj (curlier, curliest) (hair)* rizado,-a.

currant ['kʌrənt] *n* **1** *Culin (dried grape)* pasa *f* (de Corinto); **c. bun**, bollo *m* con pasas. **2** *(fruit, on bush)* grosella *f*; **c. bush**, grosellero *m*.

currency ['kʌrənsɪ] *n* **1** moneda *f*; **foreign c.**, divisa *f*, moneda extranjera; **hard c.**, divisa fuerte. **2** *(acceptance)* aceptación *f*; *(idea etc)* **to gain c.**, ganar fuerza, irse extendiendo.

current ['kʌrənt] **I** *adj* **1** *(opinions, beliefs, tendency)* general; *(word, phrase)* actual; *(year, month)* en curso. ■ **c. affairs**, actualidad *f sing* (política); *Fin* **c. assets**, activo *m sing* disponible. **2** *Fin (bank account)* corriente. **3** *Press (latest)* **the c. issue** *or* **number**, el último número. **II** *n* **1** *(of gas, air, water)* corriente *f*; *Elec* **alternating/direct c.**, corriente alterna/continua. **2** *(trend)* corriente *f*. ◆ **currently** *adv* actualmente, en la actualidad.

curriculum [kə'rɪkjʊləm] *n (pl curriculums or curricula* [kə'rɪkjʊlə]) *Educ* plan *m* de estudios. ■ **c. vitae**, currículum *m* (vitae).

curry¹ ['kʌrɪ] **I** *n Culin* curry *m*; **chicken c.**, pollo *m* al curry. **II** *vtr (pt & pp curried)* preparar *or* guisar al curry.

curry² ['kʌrɪ] *vtr (pt & pp curried)* **to c. favour with sb**, congraciarse *or* insinuarse con algn.

currycomb ['kʌrɪkəʊm] *n* almohaza *f*.

curse [kɜːs] **I** *n* maldición *f*; *(oath)* palabrota *f*; *fig* azote *m*, plaga *f*; *fam (woman)* **to have the c.**, tener la regla. **II** *vtr* maldecir; *fig (illness)* **to be cursed with**, sufrir de. **III** *vi* blasfemar, maldecir; **to c. at sb**, maldecir a algn.

cursed [kɜːst] *adj* maldito,-a.

cursory ['kɜːsərɪ] *adj (glance, reading)* rápido,-a, superficial. ◆ **cursorily** *adv* precipitadamente, superficialmente.

curt [kɜːt] *adj* brusco,-a, seco,-a.

curtail [kɜː'teɪl] *vtr (expenses)* reducir; *(text)* acortar, abreviar.

curtain ['kɜːtən] **I** *n* cortina *f*; *Theat* telón *m*; *fig (of smoke, fog)* velo *m*; **to draw the curtains**, correr las cortinas; **to drop/raise the c.**, bajar/alzar el telón; *Pol fig* **the Iron C.**, el telón de acero; *fam* **take care or it'll be curtains for us**, ten cuidado o será nuestra perdición. ■ *Theat* **c. call**, llamada *f* a escena; **c. ring**, anillo *m* (de cortina); **c. rod**, varilla *f* de la cortina. **II** *vtr* poner cortinas a; **to c. off (an area)**, esconder *or* dividir (una zona) con una cortina.

curts(e)y ['kɜːtsɪ] **I** *n* reverencia *f*. **II** *vi (pt & pp curtseyed or curtsied)* hacer una reverencia (**to**, a).

curvaceous [kɜː'veɪʃəs] *adj fam (woman)* cachas *inv*.

curvature ['kɜːvətʃəʳ] *n* curvatura *f*; *Med (of the spine)* encorvamiento *m*.

curve [kɜːv] **I** *n (in road etc)* curva *f*; *(of woman)* redondez *f*; *Aut* **to take a c.**, doblar una curva. **II** *vtr* encorvar. **III** *vi (road, river)* torcer, describir una curva.

curved [kɜːvd] *adj* curvo,-a, encorvado,-a.

cushion ['kʊʃən] **I** *n* cojín *m*; *(large)* almohadón *m*; *(of billiard table)* banda *f*. ■ *Tech* **air c.**, colchón *m* de aire; **c. cover**, funda *f* de almohadón *or* de cojín. **II** *vtr* **1** poner cojines a; **cushioned seat**, asiento *m* con almohadilla. **2** *fig (person)* proteger; *(blow)* suavizar; *(defeat, setback)* mitigar.

cushy ['kʊʃɪ] *adj (cushier, cushiest) fam (job, life)* fácil, cómodo,-a; **a c. number**, un chollo.

cussedness ['kʌsɪdnɪs] *n fam* terquedad *f*; **out of sheer c.**, por narices.

custard ['kʌstəd] *n* **1** *Culin* natillas *fpl*. ■ **c. powder**, polvos *mpl* para natillas. **2** *(fruit)* **c. apple**, chirimoya *f*.

custodian [kʌs'təʊdɪən] *n (of public building)* conserje *mf*, guarda *mf*.

custody ['kʌstədɪ] *n* custodia *f*; *Jur* **in c.**, bajo custodia; **to take into c.**, detener.

custom ['kʌstəm] *n* **1** *(habit, tradition)* costumbre *f*, hábito *m*. **2** *Com (patronage)* clientela *f*; **to lose c.**, perder clientes *or* clientela; **to withdraw one's c. from a shop**, dejar de ser cliente de una tienda.

customary ['kʌstəmərɪ] *adj* acostumbrado,-a, habitual.

custom-built [kʌstəm'bɪlt] *adj* hecho,-a por encargo.

customer ['kʌstəməʳ] *n* cliente *mf*; *fam* **an odd c.**, un tipo raro.

customize ['kʌstəmaɪz] *vtr* personalizar, hacer por encargo.

custom-made [kʌstəm'meɪd] *adj (suit etc)* hecho,-a a la medida.

customs ['kʌstəmz] *n sing or pl* aduana *f*; **to go through c.**, pasar la aduana. ■ **c. duty**, derechos *mpl* de aduana; **c. officer**, agente *mf* de aduana; **c. post**, puesto *m* aduanero.

cut [kʌt] **I** *vtr (pt & pp cut)* **1** cortar; *(stone)* tallar; *(film)* hacer cortes en; *(record)* grabar; **he's cutting a tooth**, está saliendo un diente; *Aut* **to c. a corner**, tomar una curva muy cerrada; **to c. one's finger**, cortarse el dedo; **to c. one's hair**, cortarse el pelo (uno mismo); **to c. one's way through the jungle**, abrirse paso por la selva; **to c. short a visit**, acortar una visita; **to have one's hair c.**, hacerse cortar el pelo; *fig* **that cuts no ice**, no convence; *fig* **to c. a long story short**, en resumidas cuentas; *fig* **to c. corners**, recortar presupuestos; *fig* **to c. it fine**, llegar *or* contar con el tiempo justo; *fig* **to c. sb to the quick**, herir a algn en lo más vivo. **2** *(reduce)* reducir, rebajar; **to c. one's losses**, cortar por lo sano. **3** *(divide up)* dividir, partir; **to c. a cake into four**, dividir un pastel en cuatro (partes). **4** *(cards)* cortar. **5** *fig* **to c. sb dead**, negarse a saludar a algn. **II** *n* **1** *Elec Med* corte *m*; *(in skin)* cortadura *f*; *(wound)* herida *f*; *(with knife)* cuchillada *f*; *fig* **a short c.**, un atajo; *fig* **the c. and thrust of politics**, la esgrima política. **2** *(part cut off)* parte *f*, *(of meat)* clase *f* de carne; *fam* **to get one's c.**, recibir su parte; *fam* **a c. of the profits**, una parte de los beneficios. ■ *Culin* **cold cuts**, fiambres *mpl*. **3** *(reduction)* reducción *f*; *Press (deletion)* corte *m*. **4** *(of clothes, hair)* corte *m*. **5** *(insult)* desaire *m*, corte *m*. **6** *Cin* corte *m*. **7** *fig* **to be above sb**, estar por encima de algn. **III** *adj* cortado,-a; *(price)* reducido,-a; **well c.** *(clothes)* de buen corte; *fig* **c. and dried**, convenido,-a de antemano. ■ **c. glass**, cristal *m* tallado. **IV** *vi* **1** cortar; **this cuts easily**, tela que se corta fácilmente; *fig* **that cuts both ways**, es un arma de dos filos; *fam fig* **to c. loose**, romper con todo. **2** *Cin* **c.!**, ¡corten!; **to c. to the next scene**, pasar a la siguiente escena. **3** **to c. across the fields**, coger un atajo campo través. ◆ **cut back** *vt (tree)* talar; *(plant)* podar; *(expenses)* reducir; *(production)* disminuir. ◆ **cut down** *vtr (tree)* talar, cortar; *(spending)* **to c. down on**, reducir; **to c. down on smoking**, fumar menos. ◆ **cut in** *vi (in conversation)* interrumpir; *(driver)* adelantar bruscamente. ◆ **cut off** *vtr (water supply etc)* cortar; *(place)* aislar; *(leg)* amputar; *(hair)* excluir; *Tel* **I've been c. off**, me han cortado (la comunicación); *fig* **to c. sb off without a penny**, desheredar a algn; *fig* **to feel c. off**, sentirse aislado,-a. ◆ **cut out** *vtr* **1** *(from newspaper)* recortar; *Sew (dress)* cortar; *(person)* **to be c. out for sth**, estar hecho,-a para algo; *fam* **he's got his work c. out,** tiene cantidad de trabajo. **2** *(exclude, delete)* suprimir; **to c. out alcohol,** dejar el alcohol; *fam* **c. that out!,** ¡basta ya! **II** *vi (engine)* calarse, pararse. ◆ **cut up I** *vtr* cortar en pedazos, partir; *Culin* cortar a pedacitos; *fam* **he's very c. up about it,** está profundamente afectado por ello. **II** *vi* **to c. up rough,** enfadarse, ponerse agresivo,-a.

cutaneous [kjuːˈteɪnɪəs] *adj* cutáneo,-a.

cutback [ˈkʌtbæk] *n* reducción *f* **(in,** de).

cute [kjuːt] *adj* mono,-a, lindo,-a; *US fam* listillo,-a.

cuticle [ˈkjuːtɪkəl] *n* cutícula *f.* ■ **c. remover,** crema *f* o líquido *m* para quitar la cutícula.

cutlery [ˈkʌtlərɪ] *n* cubiertos *mpl,* cubertería *f sing.*

cutlet [ˈkʌtlɪt] *n Culin* chuleta *f.*

cut-price [kʌtˈpraɪs] *adj (article)* a precio rebajado; *(shop)* de rebajas.

cutter [ˈkʌtəʳ] *n* **1** *(person)* cortador,-a *m, f; (of gems)* lapidario,-a *m, f; (of stone)* cantero *m.* **2** *Naut* cúter *m,* patrullero *m.*

cutthroat [ˈkʌtθrəʊt] **I** *n* asesino,-a *m, f,* matón *m.* **II** *adj (cruel)* cruel; *(fierce)* feroz.

cutting [ˈkʌtɪŋ] **I** *n (from newspaper)* recorte *m; Bot* esqueje *m; Tex* retal *m; Rail* tajo *m.* ■ *Cin* **c. room,** sala *f* de montaje. **II** *adj (edge)* cortante; *fig (wind)* penetrante; *fig (remark)* mordaz.

cuttlefish [ˈkʌtəlfɪʃ] *n Zool* jibia *f,* sepia *f.*

CV, cv [siːˈviː] *abbr of* **curriculum vitae,** currículum *m* (vitae).

cwt. *abbr of* **hundredweight,** quintal *m.*

cyanide [ˈsaɪənaɪd] *n Chem* cianuro *m.*

cyclamen [ˈsɪkləmən] *n Bot* ciclamen *m.*

cycle [ˈsaɪkəl] **I** *n* **1** *(of events)* ciclo *m.* **2** *(bicycle)* bicicleta *f; (motorcycle)* moto *f.* ■ **c. track,** pista *f* para bicicletas; **c. racing track,** velódromo *m.* **II** *vi* ir en bicicleta.

cyclic(al) [ˈsaɪklɪk(əl), ˈsɪklɪk(əl)] *adj* cíclico,-a.

cycling [ˈsaɪklɪŋ] *n* ciclismo *m.*

cyclist [ˈsaɪklɪst] *n* ciclista *mf.*

cyclone [ˈsaɪkləʊn] *n Meteor* ciclón *m.*

cygnet [ˈsɪgnɪt] *n Orn* pollo *m* de cisne.

cylinder [ˈsɪlɪndəʳ] *n* **1** *Geom Tech* cilindro *m.* **2** *(for gas)* bombona *f;* **oxygen c.,** balón *m* de oxígeno.

cylindrical [sɪˈlɪndrɪkəl] *adj* cilíndrico,-a.

cymbal [ˈsɪmbəl] *n Mus* címbalo *m,* platillo *m.*

cynic [ˈsɪnɪk] *n* cínico,-a *m, f.*

cynical [ˈsɪnɪkəl] *adj* cínico,-a.

cynicism [ˈsɪnɪsɪzəm] *n* cinismo *m.*

cypress [ˈsaɪprəs] *n Bot* ciprés *m.* ■ **Italian c.,** ciprés *m;* **swamp c.,** ciprés de los pantanos.

Cypriot [ˈsɪprɪət] *adj & n* chipriota *(mf).*

Cyprus [ˈsaɪprəs] *n* Chipre.

cyst [sɪst] *n Med* quiste *m.*

cystitis [sɪˈstaɪtɪs] *n Med* cistitis *f.*

czar [zɑːʳ] *n* zar *m.*

Czech [tʃek] **I** *adj* checo,-a. **II** *n* **1** *(person)* checo,-a *m, f.* **2** *(language)* checo *m.*

Czechoslovak [tʃekəʊˈsləʊvæk] *adj & n* checoslovaco,-a *(m, f).*

Czechoslovakia [tʃekəʊsləʊˈvækɪə] *n* Checoslovaquia.

Czechoslovakian [tʃekəʊsləʊˈvækɪən] *adj & n see* **Czechoslovak**

D

D, d [diː] *n (the letter)* D, d *f.*

D [diː] *n Mus* re *m.*

'd = would; had; **he'd seen,** había visto; **I'd have gone,** habría ido.

D.A. [diːˈeɪ] *US Jur abbr of* **District Attorney,** fiscal *mf.*

dab¹ [dæb] **I** *n* **1** *(small quantity)* toque *m.* **2** *GB fam* **dabs,** *(fingerprints)* huellas *fpl* digitales. **II** *vtr (pt & pp dabbed)* **1** *(apply)* aplicar. **2** *(touch lightly)* tocar ligeramente; *(split liquid)* frotar.

dab² [dæb] *n (fish)* ≈ acedia *f.*

dab³ [dæb] *n GB fam* **to be a d. hand,** ser un manitas.

dabble [ˈdæbəl] **I** *vi* interesarse superficialmente, tener afición; **to d. in politics,** meterse en política. **II** *vtr (in water)* chapotear.

dabbler [ˈdæblə] *n pej* pseudoaficionado,-a *m, f,* amateur *mf; (in politics)* politiquero,-a *m, f.*

dachshund [ˈdækshʊnd] *n* perro *m* salchicha.

dad [dæd] *n fam,* **daddy** [ˈdædɪ] *n fam* papá *m,* papi *m.*

daddy-longlegs [dædɪˈlɒŋlegz] *n inv Ent GB fam* típula *f.*

daffodil [ˈdæfədɪl] *n Bot* narciso *m.*

daft [dɑːft] *adj GB fam (person)* chalado,-a, majareta; *(action, idea)* tonto,-a; **to be d. about sb/sth,** estar loco,-a por algn/algo.

dagger [ˈdægəʳ] *n* puñal *m,* daga *f; fig* **to be at daggers drawn** con algn, estar a matar (con algn); *fig* **to look daggers at sb,** fulminar a algn con la mirada.

dago [ˈdeɪgəʊ] *n (pl dagos or dagoes) sl offens* persona *f* de raza latina.

dahlia [ˈdeɪljə] *n Bot* dalia *f.*

daily [ˈdeɪlɪ] **I** *adj* diario,-a, cotidiano,-a; **our d. bread,** el pan nuestro de cada día. **II** *adv* diariamente, a diario; **three times d.,** tres veces al día. **III** *n* **1** *(newspaper)* diario *m.* **2** *GB fam (cleaning lady)* asistenta *f.*

dainty [ˈdeɪntɪ] **I** *adj (daintier, daintiest)* **1** *(lace, china, flower)* delicado,-a, fino,-a. **2** *(child)* precioso,-a; *(figure, manners)* exquisito,-a. **II** **dainties** *npl (sweets)* golosinas *fpl.*

dairy [ˈdeərɪ] *n (on farm)* vaquería *f; (shop)* lechería *f;* **d. farming,** industria *f* lechera. **d. produce,** productos *mpl* lácteos.

dais [ˈdeɪɪs] *n (in hall etc)* tarima *f; (in official ceremony)* estrado *m.*

daisy [ˈdeɪzɪ] *n Bot* margarita *f; fam hum* **to be pushing up the daisies,** estar criando malvas. ■ **d. chain,** collar *m* de margaritas.

daisywheel [ˈdeɪzɪwiːl] *n (typewriter, printer)* margarita *f.*

dale [deɪl] *n lit* valle *m,* hondonada *f.*

dally [ˈdælɪ] *vi (pt & pp dallied) (be slow)* tardar **(over,** en); *(waste time)* perder el tiempo; **don't d. about,** no te entretengas. ◆ **dally with** *vtr (idea, thought)* acariciar; *dated (person)* flirtear con, coquetear con.

Dalmatian [dælˈmeɪʃən] *n Zool* perro *m* dálmata, dálmata *m.*

dam¹ [dæm] **I** *n (barrier)* dique *m; (lake)* embalse *m,* presa *f.* **II** *vtr (pt & pp dammed) (water)* embalsar, represar, estancar; **to d. (up) a river,** construir una presa sobre un río. ◆ **dam up** *vtr fig (emotion)* contener, reprimir.

dam² [dæm] *n Zool (of lamb etc)* madre *f.*

damage ['dæmɪdʒ] **I** *n* **l** *(gen)* daño *m*; *(to health, reputation)* perjuicio *m*; *(to relationship)* deterioro *m*; *esp GB fam* **what's the d.?**, la dolorosa, por favor. **2** *Jur* **damages**, daños *mpl* y perjuicios *mpl*. **II** *vtr (harm)* dañar, hacer daño a; *(spoil)* estropear; *(undermine)* perjudicar, causar deterioro en.

damaging ['dæmɪdʒɪŋ] *adj* perjudicial.

damask ['dæməsk] *n Tex* damasco *m*.

dame [deɪm] *n* **I** *US fam* mujer *f*, tía *f*. **2** *(title)* dama *f*. **3** *Theat (in pantomime)* vieja *f*.

damn [dæm] **I** *vtr (gen)* condenar; *fam* (**I'm**) **damned if I know**, (no tengo) ni idea. **II** *interj fam* **d.** (**it**)!, ¡maldito,-a sea!; **well, I'm** *or* **I'll be damned!**, ¡vaya por Dios!; ¡mecachis! **III** *n fam* **I don't give a d.**, me importa un rábano *or* un bledo. **IV** *adj fam* maldito,-a, condenado,-a; **it's a d. nuisance!**, ¡vaya lata! **V** *adv fam* muy, sumainente; **I was d. lucky**, tuve muchísima suerte; **you know d. well what I mean**, sabes de sobra lo que quiero decir.

damnation [dæm'neɪʃən] **I** *n Rel* condenación *f*. **II** *interj see* ¡maldito,-a sea!

damned [dæmd] **I** *adj see* **damn IV**. **II** *adv see* **damn V**. **III the d.** *npl Rel* los condenados.

damnedest ['dæmdɪst] *n fam* **to do one's d. to ...**, hacer todo lo posible para ... .

damning ['dæmɪŋ] *adj* **1** *(proof, evidence)* indiscutible, irrefutable. **2** *(remark, criticism)* mordaz.

damp [dæmp] **I** *adj (gen)* húmedo,-a; *(wet)* mojado,-a. **II** *n* humedad *f*. **III** *vtr* **1** *(for ironing)* humedecer. **2 to d.** (**down**), *(fire)* sofocar; *fig (violence)* reducir, frenar; *(enthusiasm)* desalentar.

dampcourse ['dæmpkɔːs] *n Constr* aislante *m* hidrófugo.

dampen ['dæmpən] *vtr* humedecer; *fig* **reducir**, frenar.

damper ['dæmpə'] *n* **1** *(in chimney)* regulador *m* de tiro. **2** *Mus* sordina *f*. **3** *fam fig (restraint)* freno *m*; *fig* **to put a d. on sth**, poner freno a algo.

damsel ['dæmzəl] *n lit* doncella *f*; **d. in distress**, chica *f* en apuros.

damson ['dæmzən] *n Bot (fruit)* ciruela *f* damascena; *(tree)* ciruelo *m* damasceno.

dance [dɑːns] **I** *n (gen)* baile *m*; *(classical, tribal)* danza *f*; *(formal)* baile *m* de etiqueta; *GB fam fig* **to lead sb a** (**merry**) **d.**, traer a algn al retortero. ▪ **d. band**, orquesta *f* de baile; **d. floor**, pista *f* de baile; **d. hall**, salón *m* de baile. **II** *vi* **1** *(gen)* bailar; **to d. about**, dar saltos, brincar. **2** *(leaves, waves)* danzar, agitarse, moverse. **III** *vtr (gen)* bailar; *GB fig* **to d. attendance on sb**, desvivirse por complacer a algn.

dancer ['dɑːnsə'] *n (by profession)* bailarín,-ina *m, f*; *(of flamenco)* bailador,-a *m, f*; *(person dancing)* bailador,-a *m, f*.

dancing ['dɑːnsɪŋ] *adj* de baile; *fig (eyes)* que baila. ▪ **d. girl**, corista *f*.

dandelion ['dændɪlaɪən] *n Bot* diente *m* de león.

dandruff ['dændrəf] *n* caspa *f*.

dandy ['dændɪ] **I** *n pej* dandy *m*, petimetre *m*. **II** *adj US fam* estupendo,-a; **fine and d.**, perfecto, de perlas.

Dane [deɪn] *n* danés,-esa *m, f*.

danger ['deɪndʒə'] *n* **I** *(risk)* riesgo *m*; **there was a** *or* **some d. of war**, amenazaba la posibilidad de una guerra. **2** *(peril)* peligro *m*; **'d.', 'peligro'**; **out of d.**, fuera de peligro; *Med* **to be on the d. list**, estar en estado crítico, estar grave. ▪ **d. money**, prima *f* de peligrosidad.

dangerous ['deɪndʒərəs] *adj (gen)* peligroso,-a; *(risky)* arriesgado,-a; *(harmful)* nocivo,-a; *(illness)* grave. ◆ **dangerously** *adv (gen)* peligrosamente.

dangle ['dæŋgəl] **I** *vi (hang)* colgar, pender; *(swing)* balancearse; *fam* **to keep sb dangling**, tener a algn pendiente. **II** *vtr (arms, legs)* colgar; *(bait)* dejar

colgado,-a; *(swing)* balancear en el *aire*; *fig* **bonuses were dangled before the workers**, se intentaba persuadir a los trabajadores ofreciéndoles primas.

Danish ['deɪnɪʃ] **I** *adj* danés,-esa. ▪ *Culin* **D. pastry**, brioche *m* danés. **II** *n* **1** *pl* **the D.**, los daneses. **2** *(language)* danés *m*.

dank [dæŋk] *adj* húmedo,-a y malsano,-a.

dapper ['dæpə'] *adj* pulcro,-a, aseado,-a.

dappled ['dæpəld] *adj (shade)* moteado,-a; *(horse)* rodado,-a.

dapple-grey [dæpəl'greɪ] *adj & n (horse)* tordo,-a *(m, f)*.

dare [deə'] **I** *vi* atreverse, osar; **don't you d.** (**to**) **tell him!**, ¡no se te ocurra decírselo!; **he d. not** *or* **he doesn't d. be late**, no se atreve a llegar tarde; **how d. you!**, ¿cómo te atreves?, ¡qué cara tienes!; *esp GB* **I d. say**, quizás, posiblemente; *iron* ya (lo creo). **II** *vtr (challenge)* desafiar; **hit me —I d. you!**, ¡pégame! —¡a que no te atreves! **III** *n* desafío *m*, reto *m*; **I did it as a d.**, me lo tomé como un desafío.

daredevil ['deədevəl] *adj & n* atrevido,-a *(m, f)*, temerario,-a *(m, f)*.

daring ['deərɪŋ] **I** *adj* **1** *(bold)* audaz, osado,-a, atrevido,-a. **2** *(unconventional)* original; *(shocking)* atrevido,-a. **II** *n* atrevimiento *m*, osadía *f*.

dark [dɑːk] **I** *adj* **1** *(unlit)* oscuro,-a; **it gets d. by five**, a las cinco y es de noche. **2** *(colour)* oscuro,-a; *(hair, complexion)* moreno,-a; *(eyes)* negro,-a; *(glasses)* oscuro,-a. **3** *fig (gloomy)* triste; *(future)* negro,-a, tenebroso,-a; *(forebodings)* sombrío,-a. ▪ **D. Ages**, la Edad de las tinieblas. **4** *fig (secret)* secreto,-a, misterioso,-a, oscuro,-a; *fig* **to be a d. horse**, ser una incógnita. **5** *fig (sinister)* siniestro,-a, tenebroso,-a. **II** *n* **1** *(darkness)* oscuridad *f*, tinieblas *fpl*; **before/after d.**, antes/después del anochecer. **2** *fig* **to be in the d.** (**about sth**), estar a oscuras *or* estar en tinieblas (sobre algo), no saber nada (sobre algo); **to keep sb in the d.** (**about sth**), no dar a conocer (algo) a algn.

darken ['dɑːkən] **I** *vtr (sky)* oscurecer; *(room, colour)* hacer más oscuro,-a; *fig* **don't you darken my door again!**, ¡no vuelvas nunca a pisar (el umbral de) mi casa! **II** *vi (gen)* oscurecerse, ponerse más oscuro,-a; *(sky)* nublarse; *fig (face, eyes)* ensombrecerse.

darkish ['dɑːkɪʃ] *adj (colour)* tirando a *or* bastante oscuro,-a; *(complexion, hair)* tirando a *or* bastante moreno,-a.

darkness ['dɑːknɪs] *n* oscuridad *f*, tinieblas *fpl*; **in d.**, a oscuras.

darkroom ['dɑːkruːm] *n Phot* cuarto *m* oscuro, cámara *f* oscura.

darky *n*, **darkie** ['dɑːkɪ] *n offens* negrito,-a *m, f*.

darling ['dɑːlɪŋ] **I** *n* querido,-a *m, f*, cariño *m*, amor *m*; *fig* **she's the d. of the press**, es la favorita de los periodistas; *fam* **be a d. and get me a drink**, sé bueno,-a y tráeme algo para beber. **II** *adj* **1** *(loved)* querido,-a. **2** *fam (charming)* encantador,-a, precioso,-a; **what a d. little baby!**, ¡qué monada de criatura!

darn¹ [dɑːn] **I** *vtr (sock etc)* zurcir. **II** *n (in sock etc)* zurcido *m*.

darn² [dɑːn] **I** *vtr fam euph see* **damn I**. **II** *adj fam euph see* **damn IV**. **III** *interj fam euph see* **damn II**.

darning ['dɑːnɪŋ] *n* **1** *(act)* zurcidura *f*. ▪ **d. needle**, aguja *f* de zurcir. **2** *(before)* cosas *fpl* por zurcir; *(after)* cosas *fpl* zurcidas.

dart [dɑːt] **I** *n* **1** *(missile)* dardo *m*, rehilete *m*. **2** *(sudden rush)* movimiento *m* rápido; **to make a d. for sth**, lanzarse *or* precipitarse hacia algo. **3** *(in sewing)* pinza *f*. **4 darts**, *sing (game)* dardos *mpl*. **II** *vi (rush suddenly)* lanzarse, precipitarse; *(run about)* corretear; *(fly about)* revolotear; **to d. in/out**, entrar/salir corriendo. **II** *vtr (look, glance)* echar un vistazo.

dartboard ['dɑːtbɔːd] *n* blanco *m* de tiro.

dash¹ [dæʃ] **I** n **1** (rush) carrera f; fam **to make a d. for it,** echarse a correr. **2** esp US (race) sprint m, esprint m. **3** (small amount) poco m, poquito m; (of salt, spice) pizca f; (of liquid) chorrillo m, chorrito m, gota f; fig nota f, toque m. **4** Typ raya f; (hyphen) guión m; (in Morse) raya f. **5** (vitality) brío m, dinamismo m; (style) elegancia f; fig **to cut a d.,** causar sensación. **II** vtr **1** (throw) lanzar, arrojar; **to d. sth to the ground,** tirar algo al suelo. **2** (smash) estrellar, romper; **to d. sth to pieces,** hacer algo añicos; fig **to dash sb's hopes,** desvanecer las esperanzas de algn. **III** vi **1** (rush) correr; **to d. around** or **about,** correr de un lado a otro; **to d. away** or **out,** salir corriendo or disparado,-a; fam **I must d.!,** ¡me voy pitando! **2** (waves etc) **to d. against/over,** estrellarse or romper contra/ sobre. ◆ **dash off I** vtr (letter, note) escribir a la carrera. **II** vi salir corriendo o disparado,-a.

dash² [dæʃ] interj GB fam ¡mecachis!

dashboard ['dæʃbɔːd] n Aut salpicadero m.

dashing ['dæʃɪŋ] adj (appearance) garboso,-a, gallardo,-a; (performance) dinámico,-a, lleno,-a de brío.

data ['deɪtə, 'dɑːtə] npl datos mpl, información f. ■ Comput **d. bank** or **base,** banco m de datos; **d. capture,** recolección f de datos; Comput **d. processing** (act) proceso m de datos; (science) informática f.

date¹ [deɪt] **I** n **1** fecha f; **at a later d.,** más tarde; **out of d.,** (ideas) desusado,-a, pasado,-a de moda; (expression) desusado,-a; (invalid) caducado,-a, vencido,-a; **to d.,** hasta la fecha; **what's the d. today?,** ¿a qué fecha estamos hoy?; fig **to be up to d.** (on sth), estar al tanto or estar al corriente (de algo). ■ **closing d.,** fecha f tope or límite; **d. of birth,** fecha f de nacimiento; **d. stamp,** sello m de fecha; (on foods) **sell-by d.,** fecha f de caducidad. **2** (social event) compromiso m; fam (with girl, boy) cita f. ■ **blind d.,** cita f a ciegas. **2** US fam (person dated) ligue m; **who's your d.?,** ¿con quién sales?, ¿con quién tienes cita? **II** vtr **1** (ruins etc) datar. **2** (person) demostrar la edad de, hacer parecer mayor. **3** US fam (girlfriend, boyfriend) salir con; (for fun) ligarse a. **III** vi (ideas) quedar anticuado,-a, pasar de moda; (expression) caer en desuso. **IV** vtr **to d.** (back or from), remontar a, datar de.

date² [deɪt] n (fruit) dátil m. ■ **d. palm,** datilera f, palmera f datilera.

dated ['deɪtɪd] adj (ideas) anticuado,-a; (fashion) pasado,-a de moda; (expression) desusado,-a.

dative ['deɪtɪv] n Ling dativo m; **d. case,** caso m dativo.

daub [dɔːb] **I** vtr (with mud, paint, ink) embadurnar (**with,** con, de); (with oil, grease) untar (**with,** con). **II** vi fam (paint badly) pintorrear, pintarrajear.

daughter ['dɔːtə'] n hija f; **baby d.,** nena f, hijita f; **only d.,** hija f única; fig **she was a true d. of her times,** era hija de su tiempo. ■ Biol **d. cell,** célula f hija.

daughter-in-law ['dɔːtərɪnlɔː] n (pl **daughters-in-law**) nuera f, hija f política.

daunt [dɔːnt] vtr intimidar, desanimar, desalentar.

daunting ['dɔːntɪŋ] adj desalentador,-a, que inspira miedo.

dauntless ['dɔːntlɪs] adj esp lit intrépido,-a, impávido,-a.

dawdle ['dɔːdəl] vi fam (walking) andar despacio; (waste time) perder el tiempo, entretenerse.

dawn [dɔːn] **I** n **1** alba f, amanecer m, aurora f; **at (the) break of d.,** al rayar el alba; fig **to work from d. till dusk,** trabajar de sol a sol. ■ **d. chorus,** canto m de los pájaros al amanecer. **2** fig (birth) amanecer m, albores mpl (**of,** de). **II** vi **1** (day) amanecer. **2** fig (age, hope) comenzar, nacer. **3** fig (truth) **to d.** (**on** or **upon**), comprender poco a poco; **suddenly it dawned on him that ...,** de repente se dio cuenta or cayó en la cuenta de que ... .

day [deɪ] n **1** (24 hours) día m; **any d. now,** cualquier día de éstos, de un día a otro; **d. after d., d. in, d. out,** día tras día; **d. by d.,** diariamente, día a día; **every d.,** todos los días, a diario; **every other d.,** cada dos días, un día sí y otro no; **from one d. to the next,** de un día para otro; **from this d. onward(s),** de hoy en adelante; **good d.!,** ¡buenos días!; **in a few days' time,** dentro de unos días; **once a d.,** una vez al día; **one (fine) d., some d., one of these days,** un día de éstos; **(on) the next** or **following d.,** el or al día siguiente; **the d. after tomorrow,** pasado mañana; **the d. before yesterday,** anteayer; **the d. that ...,** el día en que ...; **the other d.,** el otro día; **this very d.,** hoy mismo; **two years ago to the d.,** hoy hace dos años; fig **to live from d. to d.,** vivir al día; fig **to win the d.,** llevarse la palma; fam **from d. one,** desde el primer momento; fam **he's forty if he's a d.,** tendrá los cuarenta años cumplidos; fam **that'll be the d.!,** ¡cuándo las ranas críen pelos será!; fam **to call it a d.,** (finish) dar por acabado un trabajo; (give up) darse por vencido,-a; fam **today was one of those days,** hoy todo ha salido mal; fam **to make sb's d.,** poner contento,-a a algn. ■ **Christmas D.,** día m de Navidad; GB (on train, bus, etc) **d. return** (ticket), billete m de ida y vuelta para el mismo día; **d. trip,** excursión f de un día. **2** (period of daylight) día m; **a winter's d.,** un día de invierno; **by d.,** de día; **d. and night,** continuamente, de día y de noche; **we had a d. in the country,** fuimos un día de campo; **what an awful d.!,** ¡qué día más malo! ■ GB **d. care,** servicio m de guardería (infantil); **d. nursery,** guardería f (infantil); Ind (time, staff) **d. shift,** turno m de día. **3** (period of work) jornada f; **an eight-hour d.,** una jornada de ocho horas; **paid by the d.,** pagado,-a a jornal; esp US **to work days,** trabajar de día; fig **it's all in a d.'s work,** son gajes del oficio. ■ **d. off,** día m de fiesta. **4** (era) época f; **in (the) olden days,** antaño; **in those days,** en aquellos tiempos; **the best poet of his d.,** el mejor poeta de su tiempo; **the good old days,** los buenos tiempos de antaño; **these days, in this d. and age,** hoy (en) día; fig **he's had his d. as an athlete,** ya no sirve para ser atleta; fig **it's still early days,** aún es temprano.

dayboy ['deɪbɔɪ] n esp GB Educ externo m.

daybreak ['deɪbreɪk] n amanecer m, alba f; **at d.,** al amanecer, al alba.

daydream ['deɪdriːm] **I** n (reverie) ensueño m; (vain, hope) fantasía f, ilusión f. **II** vi (have reverie) soñar despierto,-a; (hope vainly) hacerse ilusiones.

daygirl ['deɪgɜːl] n GB Educ externa f.

daylight ['deɪlaɪt] n **1** (sunlight) luz f del día; **in broad d.,** en pleno día; **in** or **by d.,** de día; **it's still d.,** aún es de día; fig **to (begin to) see d.,** (empezar a) ver las cosas claras; esp GB fam fig **it's d. robbery!,** ¡es un robo or una estafa! **2** fam **to beat/knock the (living) daylights out of sb,** darle/ pegarle a algn una paliza tremenda; **to scare the (living) daylights out of sb,** pegarle a algn un susto de muerte.

daytime ['deɪtaɪm] n día m; **in the d.,** de día.

day-to-day ['deɪtədeɪ] adj cotidiano,-a, diario,-a.

daze [deɪz] **I** n aturdimiento m; **in a d.,** aturdido,-a, atontado,-a. **II** vtr aturdir, atontar.

dazed [deɪzd] adj aturdido,-a, atontado,-a.

dazzle ['dæzəl] **I** n (momentary blindness) deslumbramiento m; (brightness) resplandor m. **II** vtr deslumbrar.

dB Tech abbr of **decibel(s),** decibel(es), decibelio(s) m(pl), dB.

D-day ['diːdeɪ] n día m D.

deacon ['diːkən] n diácono m.

deaconess ['diːkənıs] n diaconisa f.

deactivate [diːˈæktɪveɪt] vtr desactivar.

dead [ded] **I** adj **1** (gen) muerto,-a; (matter) inerte; **d. woman,** muerta f; **he was shot d.,** le mataron de un tiro or a tiros; **to be d.,** estar muerto,-a; **to drop (down) d.,** caer muerto,-a; fig **to be d. to the world,** (asleep) estar dormido,-a con un tronco; (unconscious) estar sin sentido; fam **drop d.!,** ¡vete al cuerno!; fam **I wouldn't be seen d. in that hat!,** no me pondría ese sombrero por nada del mundo; fam **to be d. and buried, to be d. as a doornail,** estar muerto,-a y bien muerto,-a; fam fig **I'm absolutely d.!,** ¡estoy muerto,-a!, ¡estoy agotado,-a!; fam *fig* **over my d. body!,** ¡moriré antes!; *fam fig* **to be d. from the neck up,** estar más torpe que un arado. ■ **d. body,** cadáver *m*; *fam fig* **d. duck,** fracaso *m* total; **d. man,** muerto *m*; **d. march,** marcha *f* fúnebre; **d. weight,** peso *m* muerto; **the D. Sea,** el Mar Muerto. 2 *(match)* calado,-a; *(machine)* averiado,-a; *(telephone)* cortado,-a. 3 *(out of use) (language)* muerto,-a; *(custom)* desusado,-a; *(topic, issue)* agotado,-a. 4 *(numb)* entumecido,-a; *(limb, foot, etc)* adormecido,-a; **my leg's gone d.,** se me ha dormido la pierna. 5 *(total) (silence, secrecy)* total, completo,-a, absoluto,-a; **to come to a d. stop,** pararse en seco. ■ **d. end,** callejón *m* sin salida; *fig* **d.-end job,** trabajo *m* sin porvenir; *Sport* **d. heat,** empate *m*, final *m* reñido; *fam* **d. loss,** nulidad *f*, inútil *m*, birria *f*. II *adv* 1 *(totally)* completamente, absolutamente, totalmente; *fam* **d. drunk,** borracho,-a perdido,-a; *fam* **easy,** sumamente fácil; *Aut* **'d. slow',** 'al paso'; *fam* **to be d. (set) against sth,** oponerse totalmente a algo; *fam* **to be set on sth/ on doing sth,** empeñarse en algo/en hacer algo; *fam* **you're d. right,** tienes toda la razón. 2 *(exactly)* justo; **d. in the centre,** justo *or* precisamente en medio; **d. on time,** a la hora en punto. 3 *(suddenly)* abruptamente; **to stop d.,** pararse en seco. 4 *(very)* muy; *fam* **d. beat, d. tired,** muerto,-a, rendido,-a; *fam* **it's d. easy!,** ¡está chupado,-a! III *n* 1 **the d.,** *pl* los muertos. 2 *(depths)* **at d. of night,** a altas horas de la noche; **in the d. of winter,** en pleno invierno.

deadbeat ['dedbi:t] I *n US fam (drop-out)* pasota *mf*. II *adj fam (tired)* reventado,-a, hecho,-a polvo.

deaden ['dedən] *vtr (impact, noise)* amortiguar; *fig (pain, feeling)* calmar, aliviar.

deadline ['dedlaɪn] *n (date)* fecha *f* tope; *(time)* hora *f* tope; **to meet a d.,** acabar *or* entregar un trabajo dentro del plazo; **to work to deadlines,** respetar plazos.

deadlock ['dedlɒk] *n* punto *m* muerto, callejón *m* sin salida; **the talks reached d.,** las discusiones llegaron a un punto muerto.

deadly ['dedlɪ] I *adj (deadlier, deadliest)* 1 *(gen)* mortal; *(weapon, gas)* mortífero,-a; *(aim)* certero,-a; *Rel* **the seven d. sins,** los siete pecados capitales. 2 *(absolute)* completo,-a, total; **d. silence,** silencio de muerte. 3 *fam (very dull)* aburridísimo,-a. II *adv (extremely)* terriblemente, sumamente; **d. boring,** aburridísimo,-a.

deadpan ['dedpæn] *fam* I *adj* 1 *(face)* sin expresión, inexpresivo,-a. 2 *(humour, grin)* socarrón,-ona, guasón,-ona. II *adv* 1 *(look)* sin expresión. 2 *(act)* de una manera socarrona.

deadwood ['dedwʊd] *n fig* persona *f or* cosa *f* inútil; **to prune out the d.,** *(in organization)* echar al personal que ya no sirve; *(in text)* quitar el material que sobra.

deaf [def] I *adj* sordo,-a; **to be d. in one ear,** estar sordo,-a de un oído; **to go d.,** quedarse sordo,-a; *fig* **to turn a d. ear,** hacerse el sordo; *fam* **to be stone d., be as d. as a (door)post,** estar más sordo,-a que una tapia. ■ **d. mute,** sordomudo,-a *m,f*. II **the d.** *npl* los sordos; **the d. and dumb,** los sordomudos.

deaf-aid ['defeɪd] *n GB* audífono *m*.

deaf-and-dumb [defən'dʌm] *adj* sordomudo,-a.

deafen ['defən] *vtr* ensordecer.

deafening ['defənɪŋ] *adj* ensordecedor,-a.

deafness ['defnɪs] *n* sordera *f*.

deal¹ [di:l] *n* madera *f* de abeto *or* de pino.

deal² [di:l] I *n* 1 *Com Pol* trato *m*, pacto *m*; **a new d. for nurses,** un programa de reformas para enfermeras; **business d.,** negocio *m*, transacción *f*; **fair** *or* **square d.,** trato *m* justo; **the's on/off,** vale/no vale el trato; **to do** *or* **make a d. with sb,** *(transaction)* hacer *or* cerrar un trato con algn; *(agreement)* pactar algo con algn, llegar a un acuerdo con algn; *iron* **big d.!,** ¡vaya cosa!; *fam* **it's a d.!,** ¡trato hecho!, ¡de acuerdo!; *fam fig* **he got a rough** *or* **raw d. from life,** la vida le trató mal. 2 *(amount)* cantidad *f*; **a good** *or* **great d. (of sth),** una gran parte *o* cantidad (de algo); **a good d. slower,** mucho más despacio; **it means a**

good d. to me, me importa mucho, significa mucho para mí; *fig* **to make a great d. of sb,** tratar a algn con mucha atención. 3 *Cards* reparto *m*; **it's your d.,** te toca a ti repartir. II *vtr (pt & pp dealt)* 1 *Cards* repartir **(to,** a), dar **(to,** a). 2 *(give)* dar; **to d. sb a blow,** asestarle un golpe a algn; *fig* **the article dealt a blow for freedom,** el artículo ganó la batalla de la libertad. III *vi Cards* repartir, dar. ◆ **deal in** *vtr (goods)* comerciar en, tratar en; *(illegal drugs)* traficar en *or* con. ◆ **deal out** *vtr Cards* repartir, dar; *fig* repartir. ◆ **deal with** *vtr* 1 *(firm, person)* tratar con. 2 *(subject, problem)* abordar, ocuparse de, encargarse de; *Com (order)* despachar; **it's not to be dealt with lightly,** no se debe tomar a la ligera. 3 *(subject, theme)* tratar de.

dealer ['di:lər] *n* 1 *Com (in goods)* comerciante *mf*, negociante *mf*; *(in illegal drugs)* traficante *mf*. 2 *Cards* repartidor,-a *m,f*.

dealings ['di:lɪŋz] *npl* 1 *(relations)* trato *m sing*, relaciones *fpl* personales; **to have d. with sb,** tener trato con algn. 2 *Com (transactions)* negocios *mpl*, transacciones *fpl*.

dealt [delt] *pt & pp see* deal².

dean [di:n] *n* 1 *Rel* deán *m*. 2 *Univ* decano *m*.

dear [dɪər] I *adj* 1 *(loved)* querido,-a; **a d. friend,** un amigo *or* una amiga entrañable; **my dearest wife,** mi queridísima mujer; **to hold sth/sb d.,** apreciar mucho algo/a algn, tener cariño a algo/algn. 2 *(in letter)* Querido,-a; *fam* **D. Andrew,** Querido Andrew; *fml* **D. Madam,** Estimada señora; *fml* **D. Sir(s),** Muy señor(es) mío(s). 3 *(precious)* **it is very d. to me,** le tengo un gran cariño. 4 *GB (expensive)* caro,-a; *(price)* elevado,-a. II *adv (buy, sell)* caro; *fig* **it cost me d.,** me costó caro. III *n* querido,-a *m,f*, cariño *m*, cielo *m*, chato,-a *m,f*; *GB* **be a d. and hold this,** sé bueno,-a y aguántame esto; **my d.,** mi vida, mi amor; **she's a d.,** es un amor *or* un cielo *or* un encanto; **(you) poor d.!,** ¡pobrecito,-a! ■ *fam (woman)* **old d.,** viejecita *f*. IV *interj* **oh d.!, d. me!,** *(surprise)* ¡vaya por Dios!, ¡caramba!; *(disappointment)* ¡qué pena!, ¡qué lástima! ◆ **dearly** *adv* mucho, muchísimo; **he loved her d.,** la tenía gran cariño; **I'd d. love to know,** me encantaría saberlo; *fig* **he paid d. for his mistake,** su error le costó caro.

dearie *n*, **deary** ['dɪərɪ] *n GB fam* querido,-a *m,f*, chato,-a *m,f*.

dearth [dɜːθ] *n fml* escasez *f*, falta *f*, carencia *f*.

death [deθ] *n* 1 *(gen)* muerte *f*; *fml* fallecimiento *m*, defunción *f*; **to bleed to d.,** morir desangrado,-a; **to die a natural/violent d.,** morir de muerte natural/violenta; **to fight to the d.,** luchar hasta la muerte; **to put sb to death,** matar *or* dar muerte a algn; **to sentence** *or* **condemn sb to death,** condenar a algn a muerte; *fig* **he works his employees to d.,** hace trabajar muy duro a sus trabajadores; *fig* **that subject's been done to d.,** es un tema muy trillado; *fig* **to be at d.'s door,** estar a las puertas de la muerte; *fam* **he drank himself to d.,** drink was the d. of him, le mató la bebida; *fam* **to be bored to d.,** aburrirse como una ostra; *fam* **to catch one's d. (of cold),** pelarse de frío; *fam* **to be scared** *or* **frightened to d.,** estar muerto,-a de miedo; *fam* **to worry oneself to d.,** estar muy preocupado,-a; *fam fig* **to be sick to d. of sb/ sth,** estar hasta la coronilla de algo/algn; *fam fig* **to look like d. warmed up,** parecer un muerto viviente *or* un cadaver; *fam fig* **you'll be the d. of me!,** ¡me vas a matar! ■ **d. cell,** celda *f* de los condenados a muerte; *Jur* **d. certificate,** certificado *m* de defunción; *fig* **d. knell,** golpe *m* de gracia; **d. mask,** mascarilla *f*; *Jur* **d. penalty, d. sentence,** pena *f* de muerte; **d. rate,** índice *m* de mortalidad; **d. rattle,** estertor *m* de la muerte; **d. squad,** brigada *f* de muerte; **d. throes,** agonía *f*; *fig* **the firm was in its d. throes,** la empresa estaba a punto de irse a pique; **d. toll,** mortandad *f*, número *m* de muertos *or* de víctimas; *Psych* **d. wish,** ganas *fpl* de morir. 2 *fig (end)* fin *m*.

deathbed ['deθbed] *n* lecho *m* de muerte; **to be on one's d.,** estar en el lecho de muerte.

deathblow ['deθbləʊ] n golpe m mortal.

deathly ['deθlɪ] adj *(deathlier, deathliest) (silence)* sepulcral; *(pallor)* cadavérico,-a, de muerte; **d. pale,** pálido,-a como un muerto.

deathtrap ['deθtræp] n fam *(place)* lugar m peligroso.

deathwatch ['deθwɒtʃ] n velatorio m. ■ *Ent* **d. beetle,** escarabajo m del reloj de la muerte.

deb [deb] n fam abbr of **debutante**

debacle [deɪ'bɑːkəl] n debacle f, desastre m, catástrofe f.

debar [dɪ'bɑːʳ] vtr *(pt & pp debarred) fml* excluir, prohibir, privar.

debase [dɪ'beɪs] vtr 1 *(coinage)* alterar. 2 fig desvalorizar, envilecer, degradar; *(meaning, word)* quitar el sentido de; **to d. oneself,** rebajarse o humillarse.

debasement [dɪ'beɪsmənt] n desvalorización f.

debate [dɪ'beɪt] I n *(gen)* debate m; **a heated d.,** una discusión acalorada; **it's a matter for d., the matter is open to d.,** se podría discutir la cuestión. II vtr 1 *(discuss)* debatir, discutir. 2 *(wonder about)* considerar, dar vueltas a; **to d. (with oneself) whether ...,** preguntarse si .... III vi discutir; **to d. on or about sth,** discutir sobre algo.

debat(e)able [dɪ'beɪtəbəl] adj discutible.

debater [dɪ'beɪtəʳ] n participante mf en un debate.

debating [dɪ'beɪtɪŋ] n debate m, discusión f. ■ **d. society,** grupo m de discusión, tertulia f.

debauch [dɪ'bɔːtʃ] vtr fml corromper, pervertir, seducir.

debauched [dɪ'bɔːtʃt] adj *(person)* libertino,-a, inmoral; *(life, behaviour)* vicioso,-a, licencioso,-a.

debauchery [dɪ'bɔːtʃərɪ] n libertinaje m, corrupción f.

debilitate [dɪ'bɪlɪteɪt] vtr *(weaken)* debilitar; *(exhaust)* agotar.

debilitating [dɪ'bɪlɪteɪtɪŋ] adj *(gen)* debilitante; *(heat, climate)* agotador,-a.

debility [dɪ'bɪlɪtɪ] n decaimiento m, abatimiento m.

debit ['debɪt] I n *Fin* débito m. ■ **d. balance,** saldo m negativo. II vtr *(account, person)* cargar en cuenta; **to d. £20 against Mr Jones, d. Mr Jones with £20,** cargar la suma de veinte libras en la cuenta del Sr. Jones.

debonair [debə'neəʳ] adj *(cheerful)* alegre, despreocupado,-a; *(elegant)* garboso,-a, elegante; *(polite)* cortés; *(pleasant)* afable.

debrief [diː'briːf] vtr interrogar, pedir un informe de.

debriefing [diː'briːfɪŋ] n informe m.

debris ['debriː, 'deɪbriː] n sing *(of building)* escombros mpl; *(of vehicle)* restos mpl.

debt [det] n deuda f; **to be deeply in d.,** cargado,-a de deudas; **to get into d., to run up debts,** contraer deudas; **to pay (off) one's debts,** saldar las deudas; fig **to be in sb's d.,** estar en deuda con algn. ■ **national d.,** deuda f pública.

debtor ['detəʳ] n deudor,-a m, f.

debug [diː'bʌg] vtr *(pt & pp debugged)* 1 *Comput (program)* eliminar fallos de. 2 *(telephone, room)* quitar micrófonos ocultos de.

debunk [diː'bʌŋk] vtr fam *(idea, belief)* desacreditar, desprestigiar; *(institution)* desmitificar; *(expose)* desenmascarar.

debut ['debjuː, 'deɪbjuː] n debut m; **to make one's d.,** debutar, estrenarse.

debutante ['debjutɑːnt] n debutante f.

Dec abbr of **December,** diciembre m, dic.

decade [de'keɪd, 'dekeɪd] n decenio m, década f.

decadence ['dekədəns] n decadencia f.

decadent ['dekədənt] adj decadente.

decaffeinated [diː'kæfɪneɪtɪd] adj descafeinado,-a.

decalitre, US **decaliter** ['dekəliːtəʳ] n decalitro m.

decametre, US **decameter** ['dekəmiːtəʳ] n decámetro m.

decamp [dɪ'kæmp] vi fam *(go away)* largarse, pirárselas.

decant [dɪ'kænt] vtr decantar.

decanter [dɪ'kæntəʳ] n jarra f, jarro m.

decapitate [dɪ'kæpɪteɪt] vtr decapitar.

decapitation [dɪkæpɪ'teɪʃən] n decapitación f.

decathlon [dɪ'kæθlɒn] n *Sport* decatlón m.

decay [dɪ'keɪ] I n *(of food, body)* descomposición f, putrefacción f; *(of teeth)* caries f inv; *(of buildings)* ruina f, deterioro m, desmoronamiento m; fig decadencia f, corrupción f; fig **to fall into d.,** entrar en decadencia. II vi *(gen)* descomponerse, pudrirse; *(teeth)* cariarse, picarse; *(buildings)* deteriorarse, desmoronarse; fig corromperse, estar en decadencia. III vtr *(teeth)* cariar.

decease [dɪ'siːs] n fml fallecimiento m, defunción f.

deceased [dɪ'siːst] fml I adj difunto,-a, fallecido,-a. II n **the d.,** sing el difunto, la difunta, el fallecido, la fallecida; pl los difuntos, los fallecidos, las difuntas, los fallecidos.

deceit [dɪ'siːt] n 1 *(dishonesty)* falta f de honradez, falsedad f. 2 *(trick)* engaño m, mentira f.

deceitful [dɪ'siːtfʊl] adj *(person)* falso,-a, embustero,-a, mentiroso,-a; *(words)* falso,-a, mentiroso,-a; *(behaviour)* falso,-a, engañoso,-a.

deceitfulness [dɪ'siːtfʊlnɪs] n falsedad f.

deceive [dɪ'siːv] vtr *(mislead)* engañar; *(lie to)* mentir; **to d. oneself,** engañarse; **to d. sb into doing sth,** engañar a algn para que haga algo.

decelerate [diː'seləreɪt] vi reducir la velocidad, desacelerar.

December [dɪ'sembəʳ] n diciembre m; *see also* **May.**

decency ['diːsənsɪ] n 1 *(seemliness)* decencia f, decoro m; *(modesty)* pudor m; *(morality)* moralidad f; **to have a or some sense of d.,** tener sentido del decoro. 2 *(politeness)* educación f, cortesía f; **he did have the d. to apologize,** tuvo suficiente educación como para disculparse; **to do sth out of common d.,** hacer algo por cumplir.

decent ['diːsənt] adj 1 *(dress, behaviour)* decente; *(person)* honrado,-a, bueno,-a, decente; **to do the d. thing,** hacer lo correcto; fam *(dressed)* **are you d. yet?,** ¿estás presentable ya? 2 *(meal, wage)* adecuado,-a, decente; *(price)* razonable. 3 fam *(kind)* simpático,-a, bueno,-a; **it's very d. of you to help,** es muy amable de tu parte ayudar. ◆ **decently** adv 1 *(honourably)* decentemente, honradamente. 2 *(adequately)* adecuadamente. 3 fam *(kindly)* con amabilidad.

decentralization [diːsentrəlaɪ'zeɪʃən] n descentralización f.

decentralize [diː'sentrəlaɪz] I vtr descentralizar; **to become decentralized,** descentralizarse. II vi descentralizarse.

deception [dɪ'sepʃən] n *(act, trick)* engaño m; *(lie)* mentira f.

deceptive [dɪ'septɪv] adj engañoso,-a, falso,-a. ◆ **deceptively** adv **it looks d. simple,** parece engañosamente sencillo,-a.

decibel ['desɪbel] n *Tech* decibel m, decibelio m.

decide [dɪ'saɪd] I vtr 1 *(gen)* decidir; **I can't d. which one to choose,** no sé cuál escoger; **that was what decided me,** *(determined)* fue eso lo que me hizo tomar la decisión; *(convinced)* fue eso lo que me convenció; **to d. to do sth,** decidir o determinar hacer algo. 2 *(matter, question)* resolver, determinar; **that move decided the outcome,** esa jugada determinó el resultado. II vi *(reach decision)* decidirse, tomar una decisión; **it's for you to d.,** tú eres quien decide; **to d. against sth,** decidirse en contra de algo; **to d. in favour of sth,** optar por algo. ◆ **decide on** vtr *(choose)* optar por.

decided [dɪ'saɪdɪd] adj 1 *(noticeable)* marcado,-a, claro,-a. 2 *(resolute)* decidido,-a, resuelto,-a; *(views)* categórico,-a. ◆ **decidedly** adv fml 1 *(clearly)* indudablemente, sin duda; **he's d. better,** se encuentra francamente mejor. 2 *(resolutely)* decididamente, con resolución.

deciding [dɪ'saɪdɪŋ] adj decisivo,-a.

deciduous [dɪˈsɪdjʊːəs] *adj Bot* de hoja caduca.

decilitre, *US* **deciliter** [ˈdesɪliːtəʳ] *n* decilitro *m*.

decimal [ˈdesɪməl] I *adj* decimal; **to six d. places**, hasta la sexta cifra. ■ **d. point**, coma *f* (de fracción decimal). II *n* decimal *m*.

decimalize [ˈdesɪməlaɪz] *vtr GB* convertir al sistema decimal.

decimalization [desɪməlaɪˈzeɪʃən] *n GB* conversión *f* al sistema decimal.

decimate [ˈdesɪmeɪt] *vtr* diezmar.

decimation [desɪˈmeɪʃən] *n* reducción *f* catastrófica.

decimetre, *US* **decimeter** [ˈdesɪmiːtəʳ] *n* decímetro *m*.

decipher [dɪˈsaɪfəʳ] *vtr* descifrar.

decision [dɪˈsɪʒən] *n* 1 *(conclusion)* decisión *f*; *Jur* fallo *m*; **to come to** or **reach a d.**, llegar a una decisión; **to take** or **make a d.**, tomar una decisión. 2 *(resolution)* resolución *f*, determinación *f*.

decisive [dɪˈsaɪsɪv] *adj* 1 *(resolute)* decidido,-a, resuelto,-a, firme. 2 *(conclusive)* decisivo,-a.

decisiveness [dɪˈsaɪsɪvnɪs] *n* resolución *f*, firmeza *f*, determinación *f*.

deck [dek] I *n* 1 *(of ship)* cubierta *f*; **below decks**, en la bodega; **on/below d.**, en/bajo cubierta. ■ **d. chair**, tumbona *f*. 2 *(of bus, coach)* piso *m*; **top d.**, piso de arriba. 3 *esp US* *(of cards)* baraja *f*. 4 *(of record player)* plato *m*, platina *f*. ■ **cassette d.**, platina *f*. II *vtr* **to d. out**, adornar, decorar; **she decked herself (out) in all her finery**, se puso de punta en blanco.

declaim [dɪˈkleɪm] *vtr & vi fml* declamar.

declamatory [dɪˈklæmətərɪ] *adj fml* declamatorio,-a.

declaration [dekləˈreɪʃən] *n* declaración *f*.

declare [dɪˈkleəʳ] I *vtr (gen)* declarar; *(winner, innocence)* proclamar; *(war)* declarar; *(decision)* manifestar; *(in customs)* **have you anything to d.?**, ¿tiene vd. algo que declarar? II *vi* 1 I **(do) d.!**, ¡vaya por Dios!, ¡no me digas! 2 pronunciarse; **to d. against/for**, pronunciarse en contra de/a favor de.

declared [dɪˈkleəd] *adj (opponent, supporter)* declarado,-a, reconocido,-a; *(intention)* manifiesto,-a.

declassify [diːˈklæsɪfaɪ] *vtr (pt & pp declassified)* *(information etc)* levantar el secreto oficial de.

declension [dɪˈklenʃən] *n Ling* declinación *f*.

decline [dɪˈklaɪn] I *n* 1 *(decrease)* disminución *f*; *(amount)* baja *f*; **to be on the d.**, *(gen)* ir disminuyendo, ser menos frecuente; *(traditions etc)* ir perdiéndose; *(prestige etc)* ir a menos. 2 *(deterioration)* deterioro *m*, decadencia *f*; *(of health)* empeoramiento *m*; *(empire etc)* ocaso *m*; **to go** or **fall into d.**, empezar a decaer. II *vi* 1 *(decrease)* disminuir; *(strength etc)* declinar; *(amount)* bajar; *(business)* ir de baja. 2 *(deteriorate)* deteriorarse; *(health)* empeorarse. 3 *(refuse)* negarse. 4 *Ling* declinarse. III *vtr* 1 *(refuse)* rehusar, rechazar; *(offer, invitation)* declinar. 2 *Ling* declinar.

declining [dɪˈklaɪnɪŋ] *adj (decreasing)* disminuyendo; *(deteriorating)* deteriorando.

declutch [dɪˈklʌtʃ] *vi Aut* desembragar.

decode [diːˈkəʊd] *vtr* descifrar.

decolonize [diːˈkɒlənaɪz] *vtr* descolonizar.

decompose [diːkəmˈpəʊz] I *vtr* 1 *(rot)* descomponer, pudrir. 2 *Chem (separate)* descomponer. II *vi* 1 *(rot)* descomponerse, pudrirse. 2 *Chem (separate)* descomponerse.

decomposition [diːkɒmpəˈzɪʃən] *n* descomposición *f*, putrefacción *f*.

decompression [diːkəmˈpreʃən] *n* descompresión *f*. ■ **d. chamber**, cámara *f* de descompresión; **d. sickness**, aeroembolismo *m*.

decongestant [diːkənˈdʒestənt] *adj & n* descongestionante *(m)*.

decontaminate [diːkənˈtæmɪneɪt] *vtr* descontaminar.

decontamination [diːkəntæmɪˈneɪʃən] *n* descontaminación *f*.

décor [ˈdeɪkɔːʳ] *n*, **decor** [ˈdekɔːʳ] *n* decoración *f*; *Theat* decorado *m*.

decorate [ˈdekəreɪt] I *vtr* 1 *(adorn)* decorar, adornar **(with**, con). 2 *(paint)* pintar; *(wallpaper)* empapelar. 3 *(honour)* condecorar. II *vi (paint)* pintar; *(wallpaper)* empapelar.

decorating [ˈdekəreɪtɪŋ] *n* decoración *f*; *(painting)* pintura *f*; *(wallpapering)* empapelamiento *m*.

decoration [dekəˈreɪʃən] *n* 1 *(decor)* decoración *f*. ■ **Christmas decorations**, adornos *mpl* navideños. 2 *(medal)* condecoración *f*.

decorative [ˈdekərətɪv] *adj* decorativo,-a, ornamental.

decorator [ˈdekəreɪtəʳ] *n* 1 decorador,-a *m*, *f*; *(painter)* pintor,-a *m*, *f*; *(paperhanger)* empapelador,-a *m*, *f*. 2 *(designer)* interiorista *mf*.

decorous [ˈdekərəs] *adj fml* decoroso,-a, correcto,-a.

decorum [dɪˈkɔːrəm] *n* decoro *m*.

decoy [ˈdiːkɔɪ] I *n* 1 *(bird)* cimbel *m*; *(artificial bird)* señuelo *m*. 2 *fig* señuelo *m*. II *vtr (person, ship, etc)* atraer con señuelo **(into**, a).

decrease [ˈdiːkriːs] I *n (strength)* disminución *f*, decrecimiento *m*; *(price, temperature)* baja *f*; *Fin* merma *f*; *(weight, speed, size)* reducción *f*; **to be on the d.**, ir disminuyendo. II [dɪˈkriːs] *vi (gen)* disminuir; *(strength, intensity)* menguar; *(price, temperature)* bajar; *Knit* menguar, perder valor; *(weight, speed, size)* reducir; *Knit* menguar. III *vtr (gen)* disminuir, reducir; *(price, temperatures)* bajar; *Knit* menguar.

decreasing [dɪˈkriːsɪŋ] *adj* decreciente.

decree [dɪˈkriː] I *n* 1 *Pol Rel* decreto *m*; **to issue a d.**, promulgar un decreto. 2 *esp US Jur* sentencia *f*. ■ **d. absolute**, sentencia *f* definitiva de divorcio; **d. nisi**, sentencia *f* provisional de divorcio. II *vtr Pol Rel* decretar, pronunciar.

decrepit [dɪˈkrepɪt] *adj* decrépito,-a.

decry [dɪˈkraɪ] *vtr fml* censurar, criticar.

dedicate [ˈdedɪkeɪt] *vtr (gen)* consagrar, dedicar; **to d. oneself/one's life to science**, dedicarse/dedicar su vida a la ciencia.

dedicated [ˈdedɪkeɪtɪd] *adj* ardiente, convencido,-a; **d. to**, entregado,-a a.

dedication [dedɪˈkeɪʃən] *n* 1 *(act)* consagración *f*, dedicación *f*. 2 *(commitment)* entrega *f*, compromiso *m*. 3 *(in book, on music)* dedicatoria *f*.

deduce [dɪˈdjuːs] *vtr fml* deducir, inferir, concluir **(from**, de).

deduct [dɪˈdʌkt] *vtr* restar, descontar, deducir **(from**, de).

deductible [dɪˈdʌktəbəl] *adj* deducible **(from**, de).

deduction [dɪˈdʌkʃən] *n* 1 *(conclusion)* conclusión *f*, deducción *f*; *(reasoning)* deducción *f*. 2 *(subtraction)* deducción *f*, descuento *m*.

deductive [dɪˈdʌktɪv] *adj* deductivo,-a.

deed [diːd] *n* 1 *lit (act)* acto *m*; *(feat)* hazaña *f*, proeza *f*; *fam* **to do one's good d. for the day**, hacer su buena obra diaria. 2 *Jur* escritura *f*; *esp GB* **to do sth by d. poll**, hacer algo por escritura legal. ■ **d. box**, caja *f* de caudales, caja *f* fuerte; **title deeds**, título *m sing* de propiedad.

deejay [ˈdiːdʒeɪ] *n fam* pinchadiscos *mf inv*, discjockey *mf*.

deem [diːm] *vtr fml* considerar, juzgar.

deep [diːp] I *adj* 1 *(well, river, etc)* profundo,-a, hondo,-a; *(wrinkle, gash)* profundo,-a; *(breath)* hondo,-a; **it's ten metres d.**, tiene diez metros de profundidad; *fam fig* **to be thrown in at the d. end**, hacer algo por primera vez; *fam fig* **to go off the d. end**, salirse de casillas, perder los estribos 2 *(shelf etc)* de fondo, *(hem, border)* ancho,-a 3 *(sound, voice)* grave, bajo,-a, *(disgrace, shame)* grande, *(silence, mystery)* profundo,-a, completo,-a, *(interest)* vivo,-a, *(mourning)* riguroso,-a, *(sigh)* hondo,-a 4 *(colour)* oscuro,-a **5** *(serious)* grave, serio,-a, *fam* pseudofilosófico,-a **II** *adv* **1** *(down)* profundamente, **to dig d.,** cavar hondo, **he thrust his hand d. into his pocket,** metió la mano hasta el fondo del bolsillo, **to sleep d.,** dormir profundamente, *fig* **d. down (inside me), I knew he was right,** en *or* para mis adentros, sabía que tenía razón, *fig* **to be d. in thought,** estar absorto,-a, estar ensimismado,-a **2** *(back)* lejos, **d. in the woods,** en lo más profundo del bosque, **to look d. into sb's eyes,** penetrar a algn con la mirada, *fig* **nine d.,** de nueve en fondo **III** *n lit* **the d.,** el piélago ◆ **deeply** *vtr* **1** *(gen)* profundamente, *(breathe)* hondo, **to be d. in debt,** estar cargado,-a de deudas **2** *(very)* muy, profundamente, sumamente, **I was d. hurt,** me hirió *or* me tocó en lo vivo

deepen ['diːpən] **I** *vtr* *(well etc)* profundizar, ahondar, *fig (knowledge etc)* aumentar, *(colour, emotion)* intensificar, *(sound, voice)* hacer más grave **II** *vi* *(river etc)* hacerse más hondo *or* profundo, *fig (knowledge etc)* aumentarse, *(colour, emotion)* intensificarse, *(sound, voice)* hacerse más grave

deep-freeze [diːp'friːz] **I** *n* congelador *m* **II** *vtr* *(pt deep-froze* [diːp'frəʊz]*, pp deep-frozen* [diːp'frəʊzən]*) (food)* congelar

deep-fry [diːp'fraɪ] *vtr (pt & pp deep-fried)* freír en mucho aceite

deep-rooted [diːp'ruːtɪd] *adj fig* profundo,-a, arraigado,-a

deep-sea ['diːpsiː] *adj (fishing)* de altura *f*, *(fish)* de aguas profundas, de alta mar

deep-seated [diːp'siːtɪd] *adj fig* profundo,-a, arraigado,-a

deep-set [diːp'set] *adj (eyes)* hundido,-a

deer [dɪər] *n inv Zool* ciervo *m*, venado *m* ■ **red d.,** ciervo *m* común

deface [dɪ'feɪs] *vtr (break)* mutilar, *(mark)* desfigurar con garabatos, *(tear)* desgarrar

de facto [deɪ'fæktəʊ] *adj & adv fml* de hecho

defamation [defə'meɪʃən] *n fml* difamación *f*

defamatory [dɪ'fæmətərɪ] *adj fml* difamatorio,-a

defame [dɪ'feɪm] *vtr fml* difamar

default [dɪ'fɔːlt] **I** *vi* **1** *(not act)* faltar a sus compromisos, incumplir un acuerdo *or* una promesa **2** *(not appear) Sport* no comparecer por incomparecencia, *Jur* estar en rebeldía **3** *(not pay)* suspender pagos **II** *n* **1** *(failure to act)* omisión *f*, negligencia *f* **2** *(failure to pay)* incumplimiento *m* de pago **3** *(failure to appear) Jur* rebeldía *f*, *fml* ausencia *f*, **in d. of,** a falta de, en ausencia de, *Sport* **to win by d.,** ganar por incomparecencia del adversario

defaulter [dɪ'fɔːltər] *n (on loan, rent)* moroso,-a *mf*, *Jur Mil* rebelde *mf*

defeat [dɪ'fiːt] **I** *vtr* **1** *(gen)* derrotar, vencer, *(motion, bill)* rechazar **2** *fig* frustrar, **to d. an outrage,** hacer fracasar un atentado **II** *n* **1** *(of army, team)* derrota *f*, *(of motion)* rechazo *m* **2** *fig* fracaso *m*

defeatism [dɪ'fiːtɪzəm] *n* derrotismo *m*

defeatist [dɪ'fiːtɪst] *adj & n* derrotista *(mf)*

defecate ['defɪkeɪt] *vi fml* defecar

defecation [defɪ'keɪʃən] *n fml* defecación *f*

defect ['diːfekt] **I** *n (gen)* defecto *m*, *(flaw)* desperfecto *m* **II** [dɪ'fekt] *vi* desertar **(from,** de)*, (from country)* huir

defection [dɪ'fekʃən] *n (from or to party)* deserción *f*, defección *f*, *(from or to country)* huida *f*, fuga *f*

defective [dɪ'fektɪv] *adj* **1** *(faulty)* defectuoso,-a, *(flawed)* con desperfectos, *(lacking)* incompleto,-a, deficiente **2** *Ling* defectivo,-a

defector [dɪ'fektər] *n Pol* tránsfuga *mf*, trásfuga *mf*

defence [dɪ'fens] *n* **1** *(gen)* defensa *f*, *(of rights, wildlife)* protección *f*, **d. against air attack,** protección *f* antiaérea, **to act in self-d.,** actuar en defensa propia, **the Ministry of D.,** el Ministerio de Defensa, **to come to sb's d.,** salir en defensa de algn ■ *Physiol & Psych* **d. mechanism,** mecanismo *m* de defensa, **d. spending,** gastos *mpl*

militares **2** *usu sing Jur* defensa *f*, **counsel for the d.,** abogado,-a *m, f* defensor,-a **3** *Sport* GB [dɪ'fens], *US* ['diːfens] **the d.,** la defensa

defenceless [dɪ'fenslɪs] *adj* indefenso,-a

defend [dɪ'fend] *vtr* **1** *(gen)* defender **(from,** de, **against,** contra)*, (rights, wildlife)* proteger **(from,** de, **against,** contra)*,* **to d. oneself,** defenderse **2** *Jur (accused, case)* defender **3** *(claim, action, decision)* defender, vindicar, justificar

defendant [dɪ'fendənt] *n Jur* demandado,-a *m, f,* acusado,-a *m, f*

defender [dɪ'fendə] *n (gen)* defensor,-a *m, f, Sport* defensa *mf*

defending [dɪ'fendɪŋ] *adj* **1** *Sport* defensor,-a, **d. champion,** campeón,-ona *m, f* titular **2** *Jur* **d. counsel,** abogado,-a *m, f* defensor,-a

defense [dɪ'fens, 'diːfens] *n US see* **defence.**

defenseless [dɪ'fenslɪs] *adj US see* **defenceless.**

defensible [dɪ'fensəbəl] *adj* defendible, justificable

defensive [dɪ'fensɪv] *adj* defensivo,-a, **to be on the d.,** estar a la defensiva

defer¹ [dɪ'fɜː] *vtr (pt & pp deferred)* aplazar, retrasar

defer² [dɪ'fɜː] *vt (pt & pp deferred)* **to d. to sth/sb,** deferir a algo/a algn

deference ['defərəns] *n fml* deferencia *f*, respeto *m*, consideración *f*, **out of** *or* **in d. to sth/sb,** por respeto *or* por deferencia a algo/a algn

deferential [defə'renʃəl] *adj fml* deferente, respetuoso,-a

deferment [dɪ'fɜːmənt] *n*, **deferral** [dɪ'fɜːrəl] *n fml* aplazamiento *m*

defiance [dɪ'faɪəns] *n* **1** *(challenge)* desafío *m*, **in d. of,** a despecho de **2** *(resistence)* resistencia *f*, oposición *f*

defiant [dɪ'faɪənt] *adj (challenging)* de desafío, provocador,-a, *(bold)* insolente

deficiency [dɪ'fɪʃənsɪ] *n* **1** *(lack)* deficiencia *f*, falta *f*, carencia *f*. **2** *(shortcoming)* defecto *m*

deficient [dɪ'fɪʃənt] *adj* deficiente, **to be d. in sth,** carecer de algo, estar falto,-a de algo

deficit ['defɪsɪt] *n Com Fin* déficit *m*

defile¹ [dɪ'faɪl] *vtr fml* **1** *(water)* contaminar, *(mind)* corromper, *(honour)* manchar; *(memory)* profanar, *(woman)* deshonrar **2** *(desecrate)* profanar

defile² [dɪ'faɪl, 'diːfaɪl] *n* desfiladero *m*

definable [dɪ'faɪnəbəl] *adj* definible

define [dɪ'faɪn] *vtr* **1** *(explain)* definir, explicar, *(functions, duties, powers)* delimitar. **2** *(show clearly)* definir, perfilar

definite ['defɪnɪt] *adj* **1** *(clear)* claro,-a, preciso,-a, categórico,-a; *(improvement, progress)* notable. **2** *(date, place)* determinado,-a, fijo,-a; **is it d.?,** ¿es seguro?; **it's quite d. that ...,** no hay *or* no cabe ninguna duda que ... . **3** *Ling* **d. article,** artículo *m* determinado. ◆ **definitely I** *adv (without doubt)* sin duda, seguramente; **he was d. drunk,** no cabe duda que estaba borracho; **I'm d. going,** yo voy, seguro. **II** *interj* ¡desde luego!, ¡claro que sí!, ¡por supuesto!

definition [defɪ'nɪʃən] *n* **1** *(explanation)* definición *f*; **by d.,** por definición. **2** *(clarity)* nitidez *f*.

definitive [dɪ'fɪnɪtɪv] *adj* definitivo,-a.

deflate [dɪ'fleɪt] **I** *vtr* **1** *(tyre, balloon)* desinflar, deshinchar. **2** *fig* rebajar; *fig* **to d. sb,** hacer bajar los humos a algn; *fig* **to feel deflated,** sentirse desilusionado,-a. **3** *Econ* reducir la inflación. **II** *vi* **1** *(tyre, balloon)* desinflarse, deshincharse. **2** *Econ* sufrir la deflación.

deflation [dɪ'fleɪʃən] *n* **1** *Econ* deflación *f*. **2** *fig (disappointment)* decepción *f*, desilusión *f*.

deflationary [dɪ'fleɪʃənərɪ] *adj Econ* deflacionista, deflacionario,-a.

deflect [dɪ'flekt] **I** *vtr (gen)* desviar; *fig (attention)* desviar, distraer. **II** *vi (gen)* desviarse.

deflection [dɪ'flekʃən] *n* desviación *f*.

deflower [diː'flaʊəʳ] *vtr lit (of virginity)* desflorar, desvirgar.

defoliant [diː'fəʊlɪənt] *n Tech* defoliante *m*.

defoliate [diː'fəʊlɪeɪt] *vtr* defoliar, deshojar.

deforestation [diːfɒrɪs'teɪʃən] *n* deforestación *f*.

deform [dɪ'fɔːm] *vtr* deformar, desfigurar.

deformation [diːfɔː'meɪʃən] *n* deformación *f*.

deformed [dɪ'fɔːmd] *adj* deforme.

deformity [dɪ'fɔːmɪtɪ] *n* deformidad *f*.

defraud [dɪ'frɔːd] *vtr* estafar.

defrost [diː'frɒst] **I** *vtr* **1** *(freezer, food)* descongelar. **2** *US (windscreen)* desempañar, **II** *vi* descongelarse.

deft [deft] *adj (skilful)* hábil, diestro,-a; *(adroit)* experto,-a.

defunct [dɪ'fʌŋkt] *adj (person)* difunto,-a; *(thing)* en desuso.

defuse [diː'fjuːz] *vtr (bomb)* desactivar; *fig* **to d. a situation,** reducir la tensión de una situación.

defy [dɪ'faɪ] *vtr (pt & pp defied)* **1** *(person)* desafiar; *(law, order)* desobedecer, contravenir. **2** *(challenge)* retar, desafiar; *fig* **it defies reason,** se escapa a la razón.

degeneracy [dɪ'dʒenərəsɪ] *n* degeneración *f*, decadencia *f*.

degenerate [dɪ'dʒenəreɪt] **I** *vi* degenerar **(into,** en). **II** [dɪ'dʒenərɪt] *adj & n* degenerado,-a *(m,f)*.

degeneration [dɪdʒenə'reɪʃən] *n* degeneración *f*.

degenerative [dɪ'dʒenərətɪv] *adj* degenerativo,-a.

degrade [dɪ'greɪd] *vtr* degradar, envilecer; **to d. oneself by doing sth,** rebajarse a hacer algo.

degrading [dɪ'greɪdɪŋ] *adj* degradante.

degree [dɪ'griː] *n* **1** *(unit of measurement)* grado *m*. **2** *(amount, extent)* grado *m*, cantidad *f*; **a certain d. of skill,** una cierta habilidad; **it involves a high d. of risk,** es sumamente arriesgado,-a; **to some d.,** hasta cierto punto. **3** *(stage)* punto *m*, etapa *m*; **first-d. burns,** quemaduras *fpl* de primer grado; **to do sth by degrees,** hacer algo poco a poco o paso a paso. **4** *(qualification)* título *m*; **first d.,** licenciatura *f*; **higher d.,** *(of Master)* licenciatura *f* superior; *(of doctor)* doctorado *m*; **honorary d.,** doctorado *m* 'honoris causa'; **to have/take a d. in science,** ser licenciado,-a/licenciarse en ciencias.

dehydrate [diːhaɪ'dreɪt] *vtr* deshidratar.

dehydrated [diːhaɪ'dreɪtɪd] *adj (person)* deshidratado,-a; *(milk)* en polvo; *(vegetables)* seco,-a.

dehydration [diːhaɪ'dreɪʃən] *n* deshidratación *f*.

de-ice [diː'aɪs] *vtr* quitar el hielo a, deshelar.

de-icer [diː'aɪsəʳ] *n (device)* dispositivo *m* anticongelante; *(chemical)* anticongelante *m*.

deify ['deɪɪfaɪ] *vtr (pt & pp deified)* deificar.

deign [deɪn] *vi* dignarse.

deity ['deɪɪtɪ] *n* deidad *f*.

dejected [dɪ'dʒektɪd] *adj* desalentado,-a, desanimado,-a, abatido,-a. ♦ **dejectedly** *adv* con desánimo.

dejection [dɪ'dʒekʃən] *n* desaliento *m*, desánimo *m*, abatimiento *m*.

dekko ['dekəʊ] *n GB fam* ojeada *f*; **let's have a d. at the menu,** echemos un vistazo al menú.

delay [dɪ'leɪ] **I** *vtr* **1** *(make late) (flight, train)* retrasar; *(person)* entretener; *(fuse, bomb, camera shutter)* **delayed action,** acción *f* retardada. **2** *(defer)* aplazar; *(payment)* demorar, aplazar, diferir. **II** *vi (be late)* tardar; **don't d.!,** ¡no te entretengas!; **to d. in doing sth,** demorarse en hacer algo. **III** *n (gen)* retraso *m*, demora *f*; *(to traffic)* atasco *m*, embotellamiento *m*; **trains are subject to d.,** es posible que los trenes lleguen con retraso.

delaying [dɪ'leɪɪŋ] *adj* dilatorio,-a, prorrogativo,-a.

delectable [dɪ'lektəbəl] *adj lit* delicioso,-a.

delegate ['delɪgɪt] **I** *n* delegado,-a *m,f*. ■ **conference d.,** congresista *mf*. **II** ['delɪgeɪt] *vtr* **1** *(command, responsibility)* delegar **(to,** en). **2** *(to representative)* delegar; **to d. sb to do sth,** encargar a algn que haga algo. **III** *vi* delegar responsabilidad.

delegation [delɪ'geɪʃən] *n* delegación *f*.

delete [dɪ'liːt] *vtr (cross out)* tachar **(from,** de); *(remove)* suprimir **(from,** de).

deletion [dɪ'liːʃən] *n (crossing out)* tachadura *f*; *(removal)* supresión *f*.

deleterious [delɪ'tɪərɪəs] *adj fml* nocivo,-a.

deliberate [dɪ'lɪbərɪt] **I** *adj* **1** *(intentional)* deliberado,-a, intencionado,-a; *(studied)* premeditado,-a; **was it d.?,** ¿fue a propósito? **2** *(careful)* prudente; *(unhurried)* pausado,-a, lento,-a. **II** [dɪ'lɪbəreɪt] *vtr (consider)* deliberar, considerar, examinar. **III** *vi (consider)* deliberar, reflexionar **(on, about,** sobre). ♦ **deliberately** *adv* **1** *(intentionally)* a propósito, adrede. **2** *(carefully)* prudentemente; *(unhurriedly)* pausadamente; **to speak d.,** ser pausado,-a en el hablar.

deliberation [dɪlɪbə'reɪʃən] *n* **1** *esp pl (consideration)* deliberación *f*, consideración *f*; **our deliberations produced little result,** nuestras discusiones tuvieron poco resultado. **2** *(care)* cuidado *m*; *(unhurriedness)* pausa *f*, lentitud *f*.

delicacy ['delɪkəsɪ] *n* **1** *(exquisiteness)* delicadeza *f*. **2** *(fragility) (of glass etc)* fragilidad *f*; *fig (of health)* debilidad *f*. **3** *(sensitivity)* lo delicado. **4** *(tact)* delicadeza *f*, consideración *f*, atención *f*, gentileza *f*. **5** *(food)* manjar *m* (exquisito *or* delicioso).

delicate ['delɪkɪt] *adj* **1** *(exquisite) (gen)* delicado,-a; *(embroidery, handiwork)* fino,-a; *(touch)* ligero,-a. **2** *(fragile) (china etc)* frágil,-a; *fig (health)* delicado,-a. **3** *(sensitive) (question, matter)* delicado,-a; *(instrument)* sensible; *(sense of smell or taste)* fino,-a. **4** *(subtle) (colour)* suave; *(flavour)* delicado,-a, fino,-a; *(perfume)* delicado,-a. ♦ **delicately** *adv* **1** *(exquisitely)* delicadamente, con finura. **2** *(tactfully)* con delicadeza *or* consideración. **3** *(precisely)* con sensibilidad.

delicious [dɪ'lɪʃəs] *adj (food)* delicioso,-a; *(taste, smell)* exquisito,-a; *fig (feeling)* agradable; **it's d.!,** ¡está buenísimo,-a *or* riquísimo,-a!

delight [dɪ'laɪt] **I** *n* **1** *(great pleasure)* gusto *m*, placer *m*, alegría *f*; **to take a d. in sth,** encantarle algo. **2** *(source of pleasure)* encanto *m*, delicia *f*; **that player's a d. to watch,** da gusto ver ese jugador. **II** *vtr* encantar, dar gusto, deleitar. **III** *vi* **to d. in doing sth,** encantar hacer algo, deleitarse en *or* con hacer algo.

delighted [dɪ'laɪtɪd] *adj (gen)* encantado,-a, contentísimo,-a; *(smile, shout)* de alegría; **d. to meet you,** encantado,-a (de conocerle), mucho gusto (de conocerle); **I am d. with** *or* **by the result,** el resultado me pone muy contento,-a; **I'm d. to see you,** me alegro mucho de verte.

delightful [dɪ'laɪtfʊl] *adj (house, person, film)* encantador,-a; *(view, person)* muy agradable; *(meal, weather, conversation)* delicioso,-a; **how d.!,** ¡qué delicia! ♦ **delightfully** *adv* de una manera encantadora, deliciosamente.

delineate [dɪ'lɪnɪeɪt] *vtr fml (outline)* delinear, esbozar, perfilar; *fig (describe) (plan, argument)* perfilar, describir *or* explicar con todo detalle.

delinquency [dɪ'lɪŋkwənsɪ] *n* delincuencia *f*. ■ **juvenile d.,** delincuencia *f* juvenil.

delinquent [dɪ'lɪŋkwənt] *adj & n* delincuente *(mf)*.

delirious [dɪ'lɪrɪəs] *adj* **1** *Med* delirante; **to be d.,** delirar, tener delirios, desvariar. **2** *fig (audience)* muy entusiasmado,-a *or* emocionado,-a; **to be d. with joy,** estar loco,-a de alegría.

delirium [dɪ'lɪrɪəm] *n (pl deliriums or deliria* [dɪ'lɪrɪə]*) Med & fig* delirio *m*, desvarío *m*.

deliver [dɪ'lɪvəʳ] *vtr* **1** *(take, mail)* *(goods)* repartir, entregar **(to**, a); *(message)* dar **(to**, a); *(order)* despachar **(to**, a); *(order)* **to d. the goods**, cumplir con la obligación. **2** *(give)* *(kick, push, blow)* dar; *Sport* *(shot, fast ball)* lanzar; *(speech, sermon, verdict)* pronunciar; *(lecture)* dar. **3** *Med* *(baby)* asistir al parto; *fml* **she was delivered of a son**, dio a luz un niño; **the baby was delivered safely**, el niño nació sano. **4** *fml* *(rescue)* liberar, rescatar **(from**, de). **5** *(fulfill)* cumplir.

deliverance [dɪ'lɪvərəns] *n fml* liberación *f*, rescate *m*.

delivery [dɪ'lɪvərɪ] *n* **1** *(of goods)* reparto *m*, entrega *f*; *(of mail)* reparto *m*; **cash on d.**, entrega *f* contra reembolso; **special d.**, correo *m* urgente; **to take d. of an order**, recibir un pedido. ∎ **d. boy**, recadero *m*, chico *m* de los recados; **d. man**, repartidor *m*; **d. note**, albaran *m* de entrega; **d. service**, servicio *m* a domicilio; *GB* **d. van**, furgoneta *f* de reparto. **2** *(of speech etc)* declamacion *f*, pronunciación *f*, modo *m* de hablar. **3** *(of baby)* parto *m*, alumbramiento *m*. ∎ **d. room**, sala *f* de partos.

dell [del] *n Lit* valle *m* pequeño.

delphinium [del'fɪnɪəm] *n Bot* espuela *f* de caballero.

delta ['deltə] *n* **1** *(Greek letter)* delta *f*. **2** *Geog* delta *m*; **the Nile d.**, el delta del Nilo.

delude [dɪ'luːd] *vtr* engañar; **don't d. yourself**, no te hagas ilusiones, no te dejes engañar; **to d. sb into doing sth**, engañar a algn para que haga algo.

deluge ['deljuːdʒ] I *n* *(flood)* inundación *f*; *(rain)* diluvio *m*; *fig* *(of questions, complaints)* avalancha *f*, alud *m*. II *vtr* *(flood)* inundar; *fig* inundar **(with**, de), abrumar **(with**, con); **I was deluged with enquiries**, me llovieron las preguntas.

delusion [dɪ'luːʒən] *n* **1** *(state, act)* engaño *m*. **2** *(false belief)* ilusión *f* (falsa); **delusions of grandeur**, delirios *mpl* de grandeza; **he was under the d. that ...**, pensaba equivocadamente que ...; *Psych* **to suffer from delusions**, tener alucinaciones.

delusive [dɪ'luːsɪv] *adj* **1** *(misleading)* engañoso,-a. **2** *(illusory)* ilusorio,-a.

de luxe [də'lʌks, də'lʊks] *adj* de lujo *inv*.

delve [delv] *vi* **1** *(search)* *(bag, pocket)* hurgar **(into**, en). **2** *(gen)* investigar; *(subject)* profundizar, ahondar **(into**, en); *(past, private affairs)* escarbar **(into**, en).

demagogue, *US* **demagog** ['deməgɒg] *n Pol pej* demagogo,-a *m*,*f*.

demand [dɪ'mɑːnd] I *n* **1** *(request)* *(gen)* solicitud *f*; *(for pay rise, rights, etc)* reclamación *f*; *(need)* necesidad *f*; **by popular d.**, a petición del público; **final d.**, ultimo aviso *m*; **on d.**, a petición. **2** *(claim)* exigencia *f*; **the work makes great demands on me**, me absorbe totalmente el trabajo; **to be in d.**, ser solicitado,-a; **to make demands on sb**, pedir mucho de algn. **3** *Econ* demanda *f*; **there's a big d. for this product**, este producto tiene mucha demanda. II *vtr* **1** *(request firmly)* *(gen)* exigir; *(pay rise, rights)* reclamar; **to d. that ...**, insistir en que ... . **2** *(need)* exigir, requerir.

demanding [dɪ'mɑːndɪŋ] *adj* **1** *(hard to please)* exigente. **2** *(wearing)* agotador,-a.

demarcation [diːmɑː'keɪʃən] *n* demarcación *f*. ∎ *Ind* **d. dispute**, conflicto *m* (laboral) de competencias; **d. line**, línea *f* de demarcación.

demean [dɪ'miːn] *vtr fml* **to d. oneself**, rebajarse; **I won't d. myself by accepting**, no me voy a humillar por aceptar.

demeaning [dɪ'miːnɪŋ] *adj fml* humillante, vergonzoso,-a.

demeanour, *US* **demeanor** [dɪ'miːnəʳ] *n fml* **1** *(behaviour)* comportamiento *m*, conducta *f*. **2** *(bearing)* porte *m*.

demented [dɪ'mentɪd] *adj Med* demente, trastornado,-a; *fam* loco,-a.

dementia [dɪ'menʃɪə] *n Med* demencia *f*. ∎ **senile d.**, demencia *f* senil.

demerara [demə'reərə] *n* **d. (sugar)**, azúcar *m* & *f* moreno,-a.

demerit [diː'merɪt] *n fml* demérito *m*, defecto *m*; **the merits and demerits of the system**, las ventajas y desventajas del sistema.

demi- ['demɪ] *pref* medio-, semi-; *Myth* **d.-god**, semidiós *m*.

demise [dɪ'maɪz] *n fml* *(death)* fallecimiento *m*, defunción *f*; *(of institution)* desaparición *f*, *fig* *(of ambition etc)* fracaso *m*.

demist [diː'mɪst] *vtr Aut* desempañar.

demo ['deməʊ] *n* *(pl demos)* *fam* manifestación *f*.

demob [diː'mɒb] *vtr* *(pt & pp demobbed)* *Mil fam abbr of* **demobilize**, desmovilizar.

demobilize [diː'məʊbɪlaɪz] *vtr* desmovilizar.

democracy [dɪ'mɒkrəsɪ] *n* democracia *f*.

democrat ['deməkræt] *n* demócrata *mf*; *Pol* **Christian D.**, democratacristiano,-a *m*,*f*; **Social D.**, socialdemócrata *mf*.

democratic [demə'krætɪk] *adj* democrático,-a; *US Pol* **D. party**, partido *m* demócrata. ◆ **democratically** *adv* democráticamente, con democracia.

demography [dɪ'mɒgrəfɪ] *n* demografía *f*.

demolish [dɪ'mɒlɪʃ] *vtr* *(building etc)* derribar, echar abajo, demoler; *fig* *(theory, proposal)* echar por tierra, destruir.

demolition [demə'lɪʃən] *n* demolición *f*, derribo *m*. ∎ **d. squad**, equipo *m* de demolición.

demon ['diːmən] *n* **1** *(devil, bad child)* demonio *m*, diablo *m*. **2** *fam* *(energetic person)* fiera *f*; *(skilful person)* hacha *m*.

demoniac [dɪ'məʊnɪæk] *adj*, **demoniacal** [diːmə'naɪəkəl] *adj* *(person)* endemoniado,-a, demoniaco,-a; *(laughter, urge)* demoniaco,-a, diabólico,-a.

demonstrable [dɪ'mɒnstrəbəl] *adj* demostrable. ◆ **demonstrably** *adv* claramente.

demonstrate ['demənstreɪt] I *vtr* **1** *(gen)* demostrar, probar; **to d. one's affection**, dar prueba de su cariño. **2** *(explain)* *(procedure, system)* demostrar, explicar; **he demonstrates microwave ovens**, enseña cómo funcionan los hornos microondas. II *vi* *Pol* manifestarse, hacer una manifestación.

demonstration [demən'streɪʃən] *n* **1** *(proof)* demostración *f*, prueba *f*. **2** *(explanation)* demostración *f*, explicación *f*. **3** *Pol* *(march)* manifestación *f*; **to hold** *or* **stage a d.**, manifestarse, hacer una manifestación.

demonstrative [dɪ'mɒnstrətɪv] I *adj* franco,-a, expansivo,-a, que muestra sus sentimientos. II *n Ling* demostrativo *m*. ∎ **d. pronoun**, pronombre *m* demostrativo.

demonstrator ['demənstreɪtəʳ] *n* **1** *Pol* manifestante *mf*. **2** *Com* persona *f* que hace demostraciones.

demoralize [dɪ'mɒrəlaɪz] *vtr* desmoralizar; **to be** *or* **become demoralized**, desmoralizarse.

demoralizing [dɪ'mɒrəlaɪzɪŋ] *adj* desmoralizador,-a, desmoralizante.

demote [dɪ'məʊt] *vtr* rebajar de graduación *or* de categoría; *Mil* degradar.

demotion [dɪ'məʊʃən] *n* reducción *f* de categoría; *Mil* degradación *f*.

demur [dɪ'mɜːʳ] *fml* I *vi* *(pt & pp demurred)* *(object)* oponerse, objetar; *(be reluctant)* vacilar **(at**, ante); **I demurred at paying the bill**, puse reparos a pagar la cuenta. II *n* *without d.*, sin reparo(s) *m(pl)*.

demure [dɪ'mjʊəʳ] *adj* **1** *(reserved)* *(person)* recatado,-a; *(behaviour)* tímido,-a, discreto,-a. **2** *(affected, coy)* remilgado,-a. ◆ **demurely** *adv* **1** con recato, discretamente. **2** con remilgos.

demystify [diː'mɪstɪfaɪ] *vtr* *(pt & pp demystified)* desembrollar, aclarar.

den [den] *n* **1** *(of lions, wolves, etc)* guarida *f*; *fig* **d. of vice** *or* **iniquity**, antro *m* de perdición. **2** *fam* *(study)* estudio *m*.

denial [dɪ'naɪəl] *n* **1** (*repudiation*) (*of charge*) mentís *m inv*, desmentido *m*; **he issued a firm d. of the report,** desmintió rotundamente el informe. **2** (*refusal*) (*of rights*) denegación *f*; (*of request*) negativa *f*, rechazo *m*. **3** (*rejection*) (*of doctrine, principles*) negación *f*.

denier ['denɪə'] *n Tex* denier *m*.

denigrate ['denɪgreɪt] *vtr fml* denigrar.

denim ['denɪm] *n Tex* **1** dril *m*; **d. skirt,** falda *f* tejana. **2** **denims,** tejanos *mpl*, pantalón *m sing* vaquero, vaqueros *mpl*; **a pair of blue d.,** unos tejanos *or* vaqueros azules.

denizen ['denɪzən] *n lit* habitante *mf*.

Denmark ['denmɑːk] *n* Dinamarca.

denomination [dɪnɒmɪ'neɪʃən] *n* **1** *Rel* confesión *f*, secta *f*. **2** *Fin* (*of coins*) valor *m*.

denominational [dɪnɒmɪ'neɪʃənəl] *adj Rel* confesional.

denominator [dɪ'nɒmɪneɪtə'] *n Math* denominador *m*. ◼ **common d.,** común denominador *m*.

denote [dɪ'nəʊt] *vtr* **1** (*show*) (*illness, satisfaction*) indicar, denotar; (*position, exit, weight*) marcar. **2** (*mean*) significar.

denouement [deɪ'nuːmɒn] *n* desenlace *m*.

denounce [dɪ'naʊns] *vtr* censurar, denunciar; **she denounced him as a fraud,** le acusó de ser un impostor.

dense [dens] *adj* **1** (*jungle etc*) denso,-a, cerrado,-a; (*crowd*) numeroso,-a. **2** (*thick*) (*fog etc*) espeso,-a. **3** *fam* (*stupid*) torpe, estúpido,-a. ◆ **densely** *adv* densamente.

density ['densɪtɪ] *n* densidad *f*; **the d. of the fog,** lo espeso de la niebla.

dent [dent] **I** *n* (*in metal*) abolladura *f*; (*in cushion, pillow*) hueco *m*; *fig* **the trip made a d. in her savings,** el viaje mermó sus ahorros. **II** *vtr* (*car*) abollar; (*cushion*) hacer un hueco en; *fig* **to d. sb's confidence,** hacer que algn pierda la confianza.

dental ['dentəl] *adj* dental; **d. floss,** hilo *m* dental; **d. hygienist,** ayudante *mf or* asistente *mf* de dentista. ◼ **d. surgeon,** odontólogo,-a *m, f*; **d. surgery,** (*place*) consultorio *m* odontológico, clínica *f* dental; (*treatment*) cirugía *f* dental.

dentist ['dentɪst] *n* dentista *mf*.

dentistry ['dentɪstrɪ] *n* odontología *f*.

denture ['dentʃə'] *n usu pl* dentadura *f* postiza.

denude [dɪ'njuːd] *vtr* despojar (**of,** de); **hillsides denuded of soil,** laderas erosionadas.

denunciation [dɪnʌnsɪ'eɪʃən] *n* denuncia *f*, condena *f*, censura *f*.

deny [dɪ'naɪ] *vtr* (*pt & pp* **denied**) **1** (*repudiate*) negar; (*rumour, report*) desmentir; (*charge*) rechazar; **he denied knowing her** *or* **that he knew her,** afirmó que no la conocía; **there's no denying that ...,** no se puede negar que .... **2** (*refuse*) negar, privar; **he denies her nothing,** le consiente todo; **I was denied access,** no me permitieron entrar; **to d. sb his** *or* **her rights,** privar a algn de sus derechos. **3** *arch* (*disown*) (*person*) desconocer, negar a; (*faith*) rechazar.

deodorant [diː'əʊdərənt] *n* desodorante *m*.

deodorize [diː'əʊdəraɪz] *vtr* desodorizar.

dep *abbr of* **departure, departs, departing** *or* **departed,** salida *f*, sale, saliendo *or* salió.

depart [dɪ'pɑːt] *vi* (*leave*) marcharse, irse (**from,** de); *fig* (*deviate*) (*from subject*) desviarse (**from,** de); (*from routine*) salirse (**from,** de).

departed [dɪ'pɑːtɪd] *euph* **I** *adj* difunto,-a. **II the d.,** *n sing or pl* el difunto, la difunta, los difuntos, las difuntas.

department [dɪ'pɑːtmənt] *n* **1** (*division*) (*in office, bank, etc*) sección *f*, servicio *m*; (*in hospital*) departamento *m*; (*in shop*) sección *f*, departamento *m*; (*in university etc*) departamento *m*, facultad *f*; (*in government*) ministerio *m*, departamento *m*. ◼ *Com* **accounts/sales d.,** (sección *f* de) contabilidad *f*/ventas *fpl*; **d. store,** grandes almacenes *mpl*. **2** *fam* (*responsibility*) campo *m*, esfera *f*; **pets aren't my d.,** no me toca a mí cuidar los animales domésticos.

departmental [diːpɑːt'mentəl] *adj* departamental.

departure [dɪ'pɑːtʃə'] *n* **1** (*leaving*) márcha *f*, partida *f*. ◼ (*at airport, station*) **d. board,** tablón *m* de salidas; *Av* **d. lounge,** sala *f* de embarque; **d. times,** horas *fpl* de salida. **2** *fig* (*from routine*) salida *f* (**from,** de); (*from previous policy*) reorientación *f*.

depend [dɪ'pend] *vi* **1** (*rely*) fiarse (**on, upon,** de); **a friend you can d. on,** un amigo *or* una amiga de confianza; **he'll forget, (you can) d. on it!,** ¡se olvidará, puedes estar seguro,-a! **2** *impers* (*be determined by*) depender (**on, upon,** de); **it depends on the weather,** según el tiempo que haga; **that** *or* **it all depends,** según, eso depende.

dependable [dɪ'pendəbəl] *adj* (*person*) responsable, fiable, digno,-a de confianza; (*income*) seguro,-a; (*car, machine*) fiable.

dependant, *US* **dependent** [dɪ'pendənt] *n* dependiente *mf*.

dependence [dɪ'pendəns] *n* **1** (*need*) dependencia *f*. **2** (*trust*) confianza *f*.

dependency [dɪ'pendənsɪ] *n Pol* dependencia *f*.

dependent [dɪ'pendənt] **I** *adj* **1** (*reliant*) dependiente; *Pol* **d. territories,** territorios *mpl* anexos; **to be d. on sth,** depender de algo. **2** *Ling* subordinado,-a. ◼ **d. clause,** oración *f* subordinada. **II** *n US see* **dependant.**

depict [dɪ'pɪkt] *vtr Art* representar, pintar, retratar; *fig* describir, retratar.

depilatory [dɪ'pɪlətərɪ] *n* depilatorio *m*. ◼ **d. cream,** crema *f* depilatoria.

deplete [dɪ'pliːt] *vtr fml* reducir.

depletion [dɪ'pliːʃən] *n fml* reducción *f*.

deplorable [dɪ'plɔːrəbəl] *adj* lamentable, deplorable.

deplore [dɪ'plɔː'] *vtr* lamentar, deplorar.

deploy [dɪ'plɔɪ] *vtr Mil* (*troops, ships etc*) desplegar; *fig* (*staff, resources*) utilizar.

depopulate [diː'pɒpjʊleɪt] *vtr* despoblar.

deport [dɪ'pɔːt] *vtr* expulsar, deportar (**from,** de; **to,** a).

deportation [diːpɔː'teɪʃən] *n* expulsión *f*, deportación *f*. ◼ **d. order,** orden *f* de expulsión.

deportment [dɪ'pɔːtmənt] *n fml* porte *m*.

depose [dɪ'pəʊz] **I** *vtr* (*leader, president*) deponer, destituir; (*king*) destronar. **II** *vi Jur* declarar, prestar declaración, deponer.

deposit [dɪ'pɒzɪt] **I** *n* **1** (*gen*) sedimento *m*; *Min* yacimiento *m*; (*wine*) poso *m*, heces *mpl*, *Chem* precipitado *m*. **2** (*in bank etc*) depósito *m*. ◼ **d. account,** cuenta *f* de ahorros. **3** *Com* (*on purchase*) señal *f*; (*on rented car, property*) depósito *m*; (*on house purchase*) entrada *f*; **to put a d. on sth,** dejar una señal para algo. **II** *vtr* **1** (*leave*) depositar. **2** (*put down*) depositar, poner, colocar; **the taxi deposited me at the door,** el taxi me dejó en la puerta. **3** (*store*) (*valuables etc*) depositar; (*luggage*) dejar en consigna. **4** (*pay*) (*into account*) ingresar; (*towards sth*) pagar un depósito de.

deposition [depə'zɪʃən] *n* **1** (*of leader, president*) deposición *f*, destitución *f*; (*king*) destronamiento *m*. **2** *Jur* (*of witness*) declaración *f*.

depositor [dɪ'pɒzɪtə'] *n* depositante *mf*.

depot ['depəʊ] *n* **1** *gen* almacén *m*; *Mil* depósito *m*; (*bus garage*) cochera *f* (de autobuses); (*rail siding*) depósito *m* de locomotoras. **2** *US* (*bus station*) estación *f* de autobuses; (*railway station*) estación *f* de ferrocarriles.

deprave [dɪ'preɪv] *vtr* depravar.

depraved [dɪ'preɪvd] *adj* (*person*) depravado,-a.

depravity [dɪ'prævɪtɪ] *n* depravación *f*.

deprecate ['deprɪkeɪt] *vtr fml* desaprobar, censurar.

deprecatory ['deprɪkətərɪ] *adj* desaprobatorio,-a.

depreciate [dɪ'priːʃɪeɪt] *vi* depreciarse.

depreciation [dɪpriːʃɪ'eɪʃən] *n* depreciación *f*, desvalorización *f*.

depress [dɪ'pres] *vtr* 1 *(discourage)* deprimir, desanimar, desalentar. 2 *Econ (reduce) (profits)* reducir; *(trade)* dificultar; *(prices, wages)* disminuir, hacer bajar. 3 *fml (press down) (switch, lever, etc)* apretar; *(clutch, piano pedal)* pisar.

depressed [dɪ'prest] *adj* 1 *(person)* deprimido,-a, desanimado,-a, desalentado,-a; **to get d.,** desanimarse. 2 *Econ (area) (market)* or *(stockmarket)* paralizado,-a, en crisis. 3 *(surface)* hundido,-a, deprimido,-a.

depressing [dɪ'presɪŋ] *adj* deprimente; **I find it d.,** me deprime.

depression [dɪ'preʃən] *n* 1 *(low spirits)* depresión *f*. 2 *Econ* crisis *f inv* económica. 3 *(hollow)* depresión *f*. 4 *Meteor* depresión *f*.

depressive [dɪ'presɪv] *adj* depresivo,-a.

deprivation [deprɪ'veɪʃən] *n (hardship)* privación *f*; *(loss)* perdida *f*.

deprive [dɪ'praɪv] *vtr (gen)* privar **(of,** de); *(of office)* destituir **(of,** de).

deprived [dɪ'praɪvd] *adj* pobre, necesitado,-a.

Dept *abbr of* **Department,** departamento *m*, dpt, dpto; *(in store)* sección *f*.

depth [depθ] *n* 1 *(of pond, hole)* profundidad *f*; *(of cupboard, shelf)* fondo *m*; *(of hem, border)* ancho *m*; **to be** or **get out of one's d.,** *(in water)* perder pie; *fig (in conversation etc)* meterse en camisa de once varas. ■ *Mil* **d. charge,** carga *f* de profundidad. 2 *fig (of emotion, colour, gaze)* intensidad *f*; *(of shame, anxiety, silence, mystery)* profundidad *f*; *(of thought)* complejidad *f*; **in the depths of the forest,** en el corazón del bosque; **in the depths of night,** a altas horas de la noche; **in the depths of winter,** en pleno invierno; **to be in the depths of despair,** estar completamente desesperado,-a; **to study sth in d.,** estudiar algo a fondo.

deputation [depjʊ'teɪʃən] *n inv* delegación *f*.

depute [dɪ'pjuːt] *vtr fml (reponsibility, power)* delegar **(to,** en); *(person)* diputar.

deputy ['depjʊtɪ] *n* 1 *(substitute)* suplente *mf*, sustituto,-a *m*, *f*. ■ **d. chairman,** vicepresidente *m*; **d. director,** director,-a *m*, *f* adjunto,-a; *Educ* **d. head,** subdirector,-a *m*, *f*. 2 *Pol (representative)* diputado,-a *m*, *f*.

derail [dɪ'reɪl] *vtr* hacer descarrilar.

deranged [dɪ'reɪndʒd] *adj* trastornado,-a, loco,-a.

derby ['dɑːbɪ] *n* 1 *Sport* prueba *f*; **donkey d.,** carrera *f* de burros; *GB* **the D.,** carrera *f* (anual) clásica de caballos. 2 ['dɜːrbɪ] *US* sombrero *m* hongo, bombín *m*.

derelict ['derɪlɪkt] *adj* abandonado,-a, en ruinas.

dereliction [derɪ'lɪkʃən] *n (ruin)* abandono *m*; *fml* **d. of duty,** incumplimiento *m* del deber.

deride [dɪ'raɪd] *vtr* ridiculizar, burlarse, mofarse.

derision [dɪ'rɪʒən] *n* mofa *f*, burla *f*; **his views met with d.,** se mofaron de sus opiniones; **laugh of d.,** risa *f* burlona.

derisive [dɪ'raɪsɪv] *adj* burlón,-ona, irónico,-a.

derisory [dɪ'raɪsərɪ] *adj* irrisorio,-a, ridículo,-a.

derivation [derɪ'veɪʃən] *n* derivación *f*.

derivative [de'rɪvətɪv] **I** *adj (art, writing)* sin originalidad, poco original. **II** *n (of word, substance)* derivado *m*.

derive [dɪ'raɪv] *fml* **I** *vtr* sacar; **I d. comfort from my family,** la familia es un consuelo para mí. **II** *vi (word)* derivarse **(from,** de); *(skill)* provenir **(from, de).**

dermatitis [dɜːmə'taɪtɪs] *n Med* dermatitis *f*.

dermatology [dɜːmə'tɒlədʒɪ] *n Med* dermatología *f*.

derogatory [dɪ'rɒgətərɪ] *adj (remark, article)* despectivo,-a; *(meaning)* peyorativo,-a.

derrick ['derɪk] *n* 1 *Naut (crane)* grúa *f*. 2 *Petrol* torre *f* de perforación.

DES [diːiː'es] *GB abbr of* **Department of Education and Science,** ≈ Ministerio *m* de Educación y Ciencia, MEC *m*.

descant ['deskænt] *n Mus* contrapunto *m*.

descend [dɪ'send] **I** *vi* 1 *(come or go down) (gen)* bajar, descender; *fig* **night descended,** se hizo de noche. 2 **to d. on,** *(invade) (enemy)* caer sobre, atacar; *(area)* invadir; *fig* **they descended on us at lunchtime,** se dejaron caer por casa a la hora del almuerzo. 3 *(lower yourself) (gossip, rudeness)* rebajarse **(to,** a); **to d. to telling lies,** recurrir a mentiras. 4 *(be related to)* descender. **II** *vtr (stairs)* bajar.

descendant [dɪ'sendənt] *n* descendiente *mf*.

descent [dɪ'sent] *n* 1 *(way down)* descenso *m*, bajada *f*. 2 *(degeneration)* caída *f*; **d. into poverty,** caída en la miseria. 3 *(slope)* declive *m*, pendiente *f*. 4 *(ancestry)* ascendencia *f*, familia *f*; **she is of Russian d.,** es de ascendencia rusa. 5 *(attack)* incursión *f*.

describe [dɪ'skraɪb] *vtr* 1 describir; **d. him to me,** cuéntame cómo es; **I wouldn't d. her as an expert,** no la calificaría de experta. 2 *Tech (arc, circle)* trazar.

description [dɪ'skrɪpʃən] *n* 1 *(portrayal, account)* descripción *f*; **it was painful beyond d.,** el dolor era indescriptible; **to beggar** or **defy d.,** superar la descripción. 2 *(type)* clase *f*; **fish of all descriptions,** peces de toda clase; **transport of some d.,** algún medio de transporte.

descriptive [dɪ'skrɪptɪv] *adj* descriptivo,-a.

desecrate ['desɪkreɪt] *vtr* profanar.

desecration [desɪ'kreɪʃən] *n* profanación *f*.

desegregate [diː'segrɪgeɪt] *vtr* suprimir la segregación racial.

desert[1] ['dezət] *n* desierto *m*; **the Sahara D.,** el desierto del Sáhara. ■ **d. island,** isla *f* desierta.

desert[2] [dɪ'zɜːt] **I** *vtr (place, family)* abandonar; *(political party, attributes)* desertar; *fam* **you've deserted us!,** ¡nos has abandonado! **II** *vi Mil* desertar **(from,** de).

deserter [dɪ'zɜːtə*ʳ*] *n Mil* desertor,-a *m*, *f*.

desertion [dɪ'zɜːʃən] *n (gen)* abandono *m*; *Pol* defección *f*; *Mil* deserción *f*; *Jur* **divorce on the grounds of d.,** divorcio *m* por abandono del domicilio conyugal.

deserts [dɪ'zɜːts] *npl* merecido *m*; **to get one's just d.,** llevarse su merecido.

deserve [dɪ'zɜːv] *vtr (rest, punishment)* merecer; *(prize, praise)* ser digno,-a de; **she got what she deserved,** se llevó su merecido.

deservedly [dɪ'zɜːvɪdlɪ] *adv* con (toda) razón.

deserving [dɪ'zɜːvɪŋ] *adj (person)* de valía, que vale; *(action, cause)* meritorio,-a; *fml* **to be d. of praise/blame,** ser digno,-a de elogio/censura.

desiccated ['desɪkeɪtɪd] *adj fml (gen)* desecado,-a; *(skin)* deshidratado,-a. ■ *Culin* **d. coconut,** coco *m* rallado.

design [dɪ'zaɪn] **I** *n* 1 *Art* diseño *m*, dibujo *m*; **fashion d.,** creación *f* or diseño *m* de modas. 2 *(preliminary plan) (of building, vehicle)* plano *m*; *(of dress etc)* patrón *m*; *(of painting, sculpture)* boceto *m*; *(of course, test, computer program)* modelo *m*. 3 *(general arrangement, form)* diseño *m*; *(of room, city centre)* disposición *f*; **the d. of the car was wrong,** el coche estaba mal concebido; **the overall d.,** el concepto or la idea general. 4 *(decoration, pattern)* dibujo *m*, diseño *m*, motivo *m* ornamental or decorativo. 5 *fig (scheme)* plan *m*, intención *f*, proyecto *m*; **was it by accident or by d.?,** ¿ocurrió por casualidad o bien a propósito?; *fam* **to have designs on sth/sb,** tener puestas las miras en algo/en algn. **II** *vtr* 1 *(draw, create) (gen)* diseñar; *(fashions)* crear. 2 *(intend, plan)* concebir; **the oven is designed to switch itself off,** el horno está programado para autodesconectarse. **III** *vi Art* diseñar.

designate ['dezɪgneɪt] **I** *vtr* 1 *(appoint)* designar, nombrar. 2 *fml (mark, show) (boundary)* señalar, indicar. **II** ['dezɪgnɪt] *adj* designado,-a, nombrado,-a.

designation [dezɪg'neɪʃən] *n fml* 1 *(appointment)* nombramiento *m*; **his d. as minister,** su designación como ministro. 2 *(title)* denominación *f*.

designer [dɪ'zaɪnəʳ] n Art diseñador,-a m, f. ■ **d. jeans/ shoes,** pantalones mpl/zapatos mpl de marca; Tex **dress** or **fashion d.,** diseñador,-a m, f de modas, modisto,-a m, f; Cin Theat **set d.,** escenógrafo,-a m, f.

designing [dɪ'zaɪnɪŋ] adj pej intrigante.

desirable [dɪ'zaɪərəbəl] adj 1 (attractive) (asset, position, offer) atractivo,-a; (residence) de alto standing; (woman) deseable, seductora. 2 (advisable) conveniente, prudente; **it is d. that safety helmets should be worn,** es aconsejable llevar casco de seguridad; **make what changes you think are d.,** haga los cambios que le parezcan oportunos.

desire [dɪ'zaɪəʳ] I n 1 (longing) deseo m, anhelo m, ansia f; (sexual longing) deseo m, instinto m sexual. 2 (wish) deseo m; **I haven't the slightest d. to go,** no me apetece nada ir. II vtr 1 (long for) desear, anhelar, ansiar; (person) desear. 2 (wish for) desear; iron **it leaves much** or **a lot** or **a great deal to be desired,** deja mucho que desear.

desirous [dɪ'zaɪərəs] adj fml deseoso,-a.

desist [dɪ'zɪst] vi fml desistir (**from,** de); **to d. from smoking,** abstenerse de fumar.

desk [desk] n (in school) pupitre m; (in office etc) escritorio m. ■ **cash d.,** caja f; US (in hotel) **d. clerk,** recepcionista mf; **d. job, d. work,** trabajo m de oficina; **information d.,** (oficina f de) información f; **news d.,** redacción f; **reception d.,** recepción f.

desolate ['desəlɪt] I adj 1 (uninhabited) deshabitado,-a, desierto,-a, desocupado,-a, despoblado,-a, solitario,-a; (barren) yermo,-a, desolado,-a. 2 (person) (forlon) desconsolado,-a, afligido,-a; (friendless) solitario,-a. II ['desəleɪt] vtr lit desolar.

desolation [desə'leɪʃən] n 1 (of place) desolación f; (by destruction) asolamiento m. 2 (of person) desconsuelo m, aflicción f; **to feel a sense of d.,** sentirse abandonado,-a.

despair [dɪ'speəʳ] I n desesperación f; **to drive sb to d.,** desesperar a algn; fig **he's the d. of his parents,** es una cruz para sus padres. II vi desesperar(se), perder la esperanza (**of,** de); **don't d.!,** ¡no te desanimes!, ¡ánimo!

despairing [dɪ'speərɪŋ] adj de desesperación, desperado,-a. ◆ **despairingly** adv con desesperación.

despatch [dɪ'spætʃ] n & vtr see **dispatch.**

desperate ['despərɪt] adj 1 (reckless) desesperado,-a; (sight, struggle) encarnizado,-a; **to do something d.,** cometer un acto de desesperación; **to get d.,** estar a punto de desesperarse. 2 (critical, extreme) (situation) desesperado,-a, grave; (need) urgente, apremiante; (conditions) malísimo,-a; **to be d. for sth/to do sth,** necesitar algo/hacer algo con gran urgencia. ◆ **desperately** adv (recklessly) desesperadamente; (struggle) encarnizadamente; (ill) gravemente, de gravedad; (in love) locamente; (difficult, serious) sumamente; **he was d. in need of sleep,** le hacía muchísima falta dormir.

desperation [despə'reɪʃən] n desesperación f; **in d.,** a la desesperada; **the children drove her to d.,** los niños la volvían loca.

despicable [dɪ'spɪkəbəl] adj (person, act) despreciable, vil; (behaviour) indigno,-a. ◆ **despicably** adv de una manera despreciable or vil.

despise [dɪ'spaɪz] vtr despreciar, menospreciar.

despite [dɪ'spaɪt] prep fml a pesar de.

despondent [dɪ'spɒndənt] adj abatido,-a, desanimado,-a, desalentado,-a. ◆ **despondently** adv con desánimo, sin entusiasmo.

despot ['despɒt] n déspota mf.

despotism ['despətɪzəm] n despotismo m.

dessert [dɪ'zɜːt] n Culin postre m. ■ **d. wine,** vino m dulce.

dessertspoon [dɪ'zɜːtspuːn] n 1 cuchara f de postre. 2 **d.(ful),** (measure) cucharada f de postre.

destination [destɪ'neɪʃən] n destino m.

destined ['destɪnd] adj 1 (meant, fated) destinado,-a; **he was d. to be king,** estaba llamado a ser rey; **she was d. to meet him,** el destino quiso que lo conociera; **the attempt was d. to fail,** el atentado estaba condenado al fracaso. 2 (bound) con destino (**for,** a).

destiny ['destɪnɪ] n destino m, sino m.

destitute ['destɪtjuːt] adj indigente; **to be d.,** estar en la miseria.

destitution [destɪ'tjuːʃən] n indigencia f; **in d.,** en la miseria.

destroy [dɪ'strɔɪ] vtr 1 (building, letter, area) destruir; (vehicle, old furniture) destrozar; (plans, hopes, chances) destruir, destrozar; (health, career, reputation) destruir, arruinar. 2 euph (kill) (sick or unwanted animal) matar, abatir; (insects, pests, vermin) aniquilar.

destroyer [dɪ'strɔɪəʳ] n Naut destructor m.

destruction [dɪ'strʌkʃən] n (gen) destrucción f, ruina f; **the d. caused by floods,** los destrozos or daños causados por las inundaciones.

destructive [dɪ'strʌktɪv] adj (gale, fire, etc) destructor,-a; (power, tendency) destructivo,-a; (child) destrozón,-ona; (criticism) destructivo,-a, perjudicial.

destructiveness [dɪ'strʌktɪvnɪs] n (of gale etc) poder m destructor, destructividad f; (of criticism) poder m destructivo.

desultory ['desəltərɪ] adj fml 1 (fitful, unplanned) (attempts) irregular; **he worked in a d. way,** trabajaba sin orden ni concierto. 2 (random) (remark, conversation) inconexo,-a, vago,-a. ◆ **desultorily** adv (randomly) vagamente.

detach [dɪ'tætʃ] vtr (remove) separar, quitar (**from,** de); Mil destacar (**from,** de); **she detached herself from the group,** se apartó del grupo.

detachable [dɪ'tætʃəbəl] adj (gen) separable (**from,** de); (collar) postizo,-a.

detached [dɪ'tætʃt] adj 1 (separated) separado,-a, suelto,-a. ■ **d. house,** casa f independiente; Med **d. retina,** retina f desprendida. 2 (impartial) objetivo,-a, desinteresado,-a, imparcial; (unemotional) indiferente.

detachment [dɪ'tætʃmənt] n 1 (impartiality) objetividad f, imparcialidad f; (aloofness) desapego m; **an air of d.,** un aire de indiferencia. 2 Mil destacamento m.

detail ['diːteɪl] I n 1 (item, particulars) detalle m, pormenor m; **attention to d.,** preocupación f por los detalles; **to have an eye for d.,** fijarse en los detalles; **without going into detail(s), we won the match,** sin entrar en detalles or pormenores, ganamos el partido. 2 **details,** (information) información f sing; **please send full d. of your activities,** rogamos envíe información completa sobre sus actividades. 3 Mil destacamento m. II vtr 1 (list) detallar, enumerar. 2 Mil (appoint) destacar; **to d. sb for sth/to do sth,** destacar a algn para algo/para hacer algo.

detailed ['diːteɪld] adj (description) detallado,-a, minucioso,-a, pormenorizado,-a.

detain [dɪ'teɪn] vtr 1 Jur (hold) detener. 2 (delay) retener; **I won't d. you any longer,** no le entretengo más.

detainee [diːteɪ'niː] n Jur detenido,-a m, f; Pol preso,-a m, f.

detect [dɪ'tekt] vtr 1 (error, movement) advertir, detectar; (sarcasm, difference) notar; (smell, sound) percibir. 2 (discover) (substance, fraud) descubrir; (enemy ship) detectar; (position) localizar.

detectable [dɪ'tektəbəl] adj (difference, flaw) detectable; **a barely d. scent of roses,** un perfume de rosas que apenas se percibía.

detection [dɪ'tekʃən] n 1 (noticing) (of error, substance) descubrimiento m; (of smell, sound) percepción f; **to escape d.,** pasar inadvertido,-a. 2 (discovery) (of criminal) descubrimiento m; (of enemy ship) detección f; **police d. work,** averiguaciones fpl or investigaciones fpl policiales.

detective [dɪ'tektɪv] *n* detective *mf*. ■ **d. story**, novela *f* policíaca; **d. work**, investigaciones *fpl*.

detector [dɪ'tektəʳ] *n* aparato *m* detector. ■ **metal d.**, detector *m* de metales.

detention [dɪ'tenʃən] *n* (*of suspect etc*) detención *f*, arresto *m*; *Educ* **to give/get d.**, castigar/quedar castigado,-a. ■ *Jur* **d. centre**, centro *m* de internamiento.

deter [dɪ'tɜːr] *vtr* (*pt & pp* **deterred**) (*dissuade*) disuadir (**from**, de); (*stop*) impedir, hacer desistir (**from**, de); **he was not deterred**, no se desanimaba.

detergent [dɪ'tɜːdʒənt] *n* detergente *m*.

deteriorate [dɪ'tɪərɪəreɪt] *vi* (*gen*) deteriorar, empeorar; (*substance, friendship*) deteriorarse.

deterioration [dɪtɪərɪə'reɪʃən] *n* (*gen*) empeoramiento *m*; (*of substance, friendship*) deterioro *m*.

determination [dɪtɜːmɪ'neɪʃən] *n* **1** (*resolution*) resolución *f*, decisión *f*, determinación *f*; **with an air of d.**, con un aire decidido. **2** (*settling*) determinación *f*.

determine [dɪ'tɜːmɪn] *vtr* **1** (*find out*) (*cause, meaning*) determinar, averiguar; (*position, speed*) determinar, calcular. **2** (*settle*) (*date, price*) fijar, determinar, (*limit, boundary*) determinar, definir. **3** (*influence*) (*reaction, expenditure*) determinar, condicionar. **4** *fml* (*decide*) determinar, decidir, resolver.

determined [dɪ'tɜːmɪnd] *adj* (*person*) decidido,-a, resuelto,-a; (*attempt, effort*) enérgico,-a, persistente.

deterrent [dɪ'terənt] **I** *adj* disuasivo,-a, disuasorio,-a. **II** *n* fuerza *f* de disuasión, fuerza *f* disuasoria *or* disuasiva; **to act as a d.**, disuadir, servir como fuerza disuasoria. ■ *Mil* **nuclear d.**, arma *f* nuclear disuasoria.

detest [dɪ'test] *vtr* detestar, odiar, aborrecer.

detestable [dɪ'testəbəl] *adj* detestable, odioso,-a.

detestation [di:tes'teɪʃən] *n* odio *m*, aborrecimiento *m*.

dethrone [dɪ'θrəʊn] *vtr* destronar.

detonate ['detəneɪt] **I** *vtr* hacer detonar, hacer estallar, hacer explotar. **II** *vi* detonar, estallar, explotar.

detonation [detə'neɪʃən] *n* detonación *f*, explosión *f*.

detonator ['detəneɪtəʳ] *n* detonador *m*.

detour ['di:tʊəʳ] *n* desvío *m*; **to make a d.**, dar un rodeo.

detract [dɪ'trækt] *vi* quitar mérito (**from**, a).

detractor [dɪ'træktəʳ] *n* detractor,-a *m,f*.

detriment ['detrɪmənt] *n* *fml* detrimento *m* (**to**, de), perjuicio *m* (**to**, de).

detrimental [detrɪ'mentəl] *adj fml* (*gen*) perjudicial (**to**, para); (*noxious*) nocivo,-a (**to**, para).

detritus [dɪ'traɪtəs] *n Geol & fig* detrito *m*, detritus *m inv*.

deuce [dju:s] *n Ten* cuarenta iguales *mpl*.

devaluation [di:vælju:'eɪʃən] *n* devaluación *f*, desvalorización *f*.

devalue [di:'vælju:] *vtr* devaluar, desvalorizar.

devastate ['devəsteɪt] *vtr* **1** (*city, area*) devastar, asolar, destruir. **2** *fig* (*person*) anonadar, apabullar; **he was devastated by the news**, se quedó *or* se sintió anonado por la noticia.

devastating ['devəsteɪtɪŋ] *adj* **1** (*storm, fire*) devastador,-a, asolador,-a; (*wind, flood*) arrollador,-a. **2** *fig* (*argument*) apabullante, abrumador,-a; (*charm, beauty*) fatal; *fam* **you look d.!**, ¡estás guapísimo,-a!, ¡estás irresistible! ◆ **devastatingly** *adv* (*witty, simple*) extraordinariamente.

devastation [devə'steɪʃən] *n* devastación *f*, asolación *f*, asolamiento *m*.

develop [dɪ'veləp] **I** *vtr* **1** (*cultivate*) (*gen*) desarrollar; (*trade, arts*) fomentar; (*skill, system*) perfeccionar. **2** (*start*) (*roots*) echar; (*plan, programme*) elaborar, formar; (*illness*) contraer, coger; **he soon developed spots**, pronto le empezaron a salir granos. **3** *fml* (*acquire*) (*talent, interest*) mostrar; (*habit*) contraer, adquirir; (*tendency*) revelar, manifestar; (*accent*) contraer; **to d. a**

taste/hatred for sth, cogerle gusto/odio a algo. **4** (*exploit*) (*natural resources*) aprovechar, explotar; (*region*) desarrollar, explotar; *Constr* (*site, area*) urbanizar; **the area will be developed soon**, próximamente se urbanizará esta zona. **5** *Phot* revelar. **II** *vi* **1** (*grow*) (*body, muscles, industry*) desarrollarse; (*system*) perfeccionarse; (*feeling, interest*) aumentar, crecer; (*plot, theme*) elaborarse; **it developed from friendship into love**, se transformó de amistad en amor. **2** *fml* (*appear*) aparecer; (*situation*) producirse.

developer [dɪ'veləpəʳ] *n* **1** *Phot* revelador *m*. **2** *Constr* (**property**) **d.**, inmobiliaria *f*, empresa *f* constructora.

development [dɪ'veləpmənt] *n* **1** (*growth*) desarrollo *m*; (*of trade, arts*) fomento *m*; (*of skill, system*) perfección *f*; (*of plot, theme, plan*) elaboración *f*, (*of character, writer*) formación *f*; **at the peak** *or* **height of d.**, en pleno desarrollo. **2** (*advance*) avance *m*; **the latest developments in science**, los últimos descubrimientos de la ciencia. **3** (*change*) cambio *m*; (*in situation, policy, attitude*) dirección *f*, rumbo *m*; **let's await developments**, esperemos a ver lo que pasa; **there are no new developments**, no hay ninguna novedad. **4** (*exploitation*) explotación *f*, aprovechamiento *m*. **5** *Constr* urbanización *f*. ■ *GB* **d. area**, zona *f* de reindustrialización; **housing d.**, conjunto *m* residencial.

developmental [dɪveləp'mentəl] *adj* de desarrollo.

deviance ['di:vɪəns] *n* desviación *f*.

deviant ['di:vɪənt] **I** *adj* (*behaviour, action*) anormal, irregular; (*sexuality*) pervertido,-a. **II** *n* pervertido,-a *m,f*.

deviate ['di:vɪeɪt] *vi* desviarse (**from**, de).

deviation [di:vɪ'eɪʃən] *n* (*from norm, route*) desviación *f* (**from**, de); (*from truth*) alejamiento *m*; **sexual d.**, perversión *f* sexual.

device [dɪ'vaɪs] *n* **1** (*object*) (*gen*) aparato *m*; (*mechanism*) mecanismo *m*. ■ **electronic d.**, dispositivo *m* electrónico; **explosive d.**, artefacto *m* explosivo; **orthopaedic d.**, aparato *m* ortopédico. **2** (*trick, scheme*) ardid *m*, estratagema *f*, plan *m*; **to leave sb to his own devices**, dejar que algn se las apañe solo.

devil ['devəl] *n* **1** (*evil spirit*) diablo *m*, demonio *m*; **d.'s advocate**, abogado,-a *m,f* del diablo; **the D.**, el Diablo, el Demonio; *fig* **between the d. and the deep blue sea**, entre la espada y la pared; *fam* **d.'s (the (very) d. to fix**, es dificilísimo de arreglar; *fam* **talk** *or* **speak of the d.!**, ¡hablando del rey de Roma!; *fam* **to have the luck of the d.**, desafiar a la suerte y tener éxito; *fam* **to run/work like the d.**, correr/trabajar como un loco,-a; *fam* **where the d. did you put it?**, ¿dónde demonios lo pusiste?; *prov* **better the d. you know**, más vale malo conocido. **2** *fam* **go on, be a d.!**, ¡anda!, ¡atrévete!; (*child*) **little d.**, diablillo *m*; **poor d.**, (*unlucky person*) pobre *mf*, pobre diablo *m*; (*wretched person*) desgraciado,-a *m, f*; **you lucky d.!**, ¡vaya suerte que tienes! **3** *fam* **he had a** *or* **the d. of a job selling his car**, sudó tinta para vender su coche; **it's a d. of a problem**, menudo problemón.

devilish ['devəlɪʃ] *adj* **1** (*wicked*) malvado,-a, diabólico,-a. **2** (*difficult*) diabólico,-a. ◆ **devilishly** *adv fam* muy, sumamente; **we were d. lucky**, tuvimos una gran suerte.

devilry ['devəlrɪ] *n* diablura *f*; **to be full of d.**, ser de la piel del diablo.

devious ['di:vɪəs] *adj* **1** (*winding*) (*path etc*) tortuoso,-a. **2** *esp pej* (*not straight forward*) (*person*) tortuoso,-a, taimado,-a, falso,-a; (*mind*) tortuoso,-a; (*process, argument*) intrincado,-a, enrevesado,-a; **by d. means**, (*complicated*) por medios complicados; (*underhand*) por medios poco limpios; **she's very d.**, disimula *or* finge a la perfección.

deviousness ['di:vɪəsnɪs] *n* (*of person*) tortuosidad *f*, falsedad *f*; (*of argument*) intrincamiento *m*.

devise [dɪ'vaɪs] *vtr* idear, concebir, inventar.

devoid [dɪ'vɔɪd] *adj* desprovisto,-a (**of**, de); **d. of interest**, falto,-a de interés.

devolution [diːvəˈluːʃən] *n Pol* transmisión *f* de poderes; **the nationalists want d.,** los nacionalistas quieren la autonomía.

devolve [dɪˈvɒlv] **I** *vtr Pol* delegar; *(autonomy)* descentralizar; **to d. government on** *or* **to the regions,** dar autonomía a las regiones. **II** *vi (duty, task)* **to d. on sth/ sb,** recaer sobre algo/algn, corresponder a algo/algn.

devote [dɪˈvəʊt] *vtr* dedicar; **she devoted her life to helping the poor,** consagró su vida a la ayuda de los pobres.

devoted [dɪˈvəʊtɪd] *adj* fiel, leal (**to,** a); **he's d. to sport,** tiene gran afición al deporte; **to be d. to sb,** tenerle mucho cariño a algn.

devotee [devəˈtiː] *n* **1** *(of religion)* devoto,-a *m, f.* **2** *(of theatre, sport)* aficionado,-a *m, f; Pol* partidario,-a *m, f.*

devotion [dɪˈvəʊʃən] *n* **1** *(to friend, master)* lealtad *f,* fidelidad *f; (to family, wife)* cariño *m,* afecto *m,* amor *m; (to research, cause)* dedicación *f,* entrega *f;* **d. to duty,** cumplimiento *m* fiel de su deber. **2** *Rel* devoción *f,* fervor *m;* **devotions,** oraciones *fpl;* **he was at his devotions,** rezaba.

devour [dɪˈvaʊəʳ] *vtr (meal)* devorar, zampar; *(prey, book)* devorar; *fig* **I was devoured by jealousy,** me devoraban *or* me consumían los celos.

devout [dɪˈvaʊt] *adj Rel* devoto,-a; *(prayer, hope)* sincero,-a. ◆ **devoutly** *adv* con devoción.

dew [djuː] *n* rocío *m.*

dewy [ˈdjuːɪ] *adj (dewier, dewiest)* rociado,-a, cubierto,-a de rocío.

dewy-eyed [djuːrˈaɪd] *adj fig (innocent)* inocente, ingenuo,-a; *(loving)* romántico,-a, sentimental.

dexterity [dekˈsterɪtɪ] *n (of hands, fingers)* destreza *f,* habilidad *f; (of movement)* agilidad *f.*

dext(e)rous [ˈdekstrəs] *adj (skilful)* diestro,-a, hábil; *(agile)* ágil.

DHSS [diːeɪtʃesˈes] *abbr of* **Department of Health and Social Services,** Departamento *m* de Sanidad y Servicios Sociales.

diabetes [daɪəˈbiːtiːz, daɪəˈbiːtɪs] *n Med* diabetes *f.*

diabetic [daɪəˈbetɪk] *Med* **1** *adj (person)* diabético,-a; *(diet, treatment)* para diabéticos. **II** *n* diabético,-a *m, f.*

diabolical [daɪəˈbɒlɪkəl] *adj* **1** *(evil)* diabólico,-a. **2** *fam (difficult)* diabólico,-a; *(unbearable) (noise, delay, weather)* insoportable, espantoso,-a.

diagnose [ˈdaɪəgnəʊz] *vtr Med (condition)* diagnosticar; *fig (fault)* descubrir; **his illness was diagnosed as hepatitis,** le diagnosticaron una hepatitis.

diagnosis [daɪəgˈnəʊsɪs] *n (pl* **diagnoses** [daɪəgˈnəʊsiːz]*) Med* diagnóstico *m;* **to make** *or* **give a d.,** hacer un diagnóstico.

diagnostic [daɪəgˈnɒstɪk] *adj Med* diagnóstico,-a.

diagonal [daɪˈægənəl] *adj & n* diagonal *(f).* ◆ **diagonally** *adv (cut)* en diagonal; *(go across)* diagonalmente.

diagram [ˈdaɪəgræm] *n (gen)* diagrama *m; (of process, system)* esquema *m; (of workings)* gráfico *m,* plano *m.*

dial [ˈdaɪəl, daɪl] **I** *n (of clock, barometer)* esfera *f; (of radio, time-switch)* dial *m,* cuadrante *m; (of telephone)* disco *m,* dial *m; (of machine)* botón *m* selector. **II** *vi & vtr (pt & pp* **dialled,** *US* **dialed)** *Tel* marcar; *(operator)* llamar; **to d. a wrong number,** equivocarse de número. ■ **dialling code,** prefijo *m;* **dialling tone,** señal *f* de marcar.

dialect [ˈdaɪəlekt] *n Ling* dialecto *m.*

dialectic(s) [daɪəˈlektɪk(s)] *n* dialéctica *f.*

dialogue, *US* **dialog** [ˈdaɪəlɒg] *n* diálogo *m.*

dialysis [daɪˈælɪsɪs] *n Med* diálisis *f.*

diameter [daɪˈæmɪtəʳ] *n* diámetro *m*

diametrically [daɪəˈmetrɪkəlɪ] *adv* diametralmente.

diamond [ˈdaɪəmənd] *n* **1** diamante *m,* brillante *m; fig* **rough d.,** diamante *m* (en) bruto. ■ **d. jubilee,** sexagésimo aniversario *m;* **d. wedding,** bodas *fpl* de diamante. **2** *(shape)* rombo *m.* **3** *Cards* diamante *m.*

diaper [ˈdaɪəpəʳ] *n US* pañal *m.*

diaphragm [ˈdaɪəfræm] *n Med Anat* diafragma *m.*

diarrhoea, *US* **diarrhea** [daɪəˈrɪə] *n* diarrea *f.*

diary [ˈdaɪərɪ] *n* **1** *(of thoughts, events)* diario *m;* **to keep a d.,** llevar un diario. **2** *GB (for appointments)* agenda *f.* ■ **desk d.,** agenda *f* de sobremesa.

dice [daɪs] **I** *npl* dados *mpl;* **to play d.,** jugar a los dados. **II** *vtr Culin* cortar en cuadritos; *fig* **to d. with death,** jugar con la muerte.

dicey [ˈdaɪsɪ] *adj (dicier, diciest) fam (risky)* arriesgado,-a; *(dangerous)* peligroso,-a; *(uncertain)* dudoso,-a.

dichotomy [daɪˈkɒtəmɪ] *n fml* dicotomía *f.*

dicta [ˈdɪktə] *npl see* **dictum.**

dictate [dɪkˈteɪt] **I** *vtr* **1** *(letter)* dictar. **2** *(order)* dar. **II** *vi (order about)* dar órdenes; **I won't be dictated to!,** ¡a mí no me manda nadie! **III** [ˈdɪkteɪt] *n (order)* mandato *m,* orden *f; fig* **the dictates of conscience,** los dictados de la conciencia.

dictation [dɪkˈteɪʃən] *n* **1** *(of letter, passage)* dictado *m;* **to take d.,** escribir al dictado. **2** *(by authority)* mandato *m.*

dictator [dɪkˈteɪtəʳ] *n* dictador,-a *m, f.*

dictatorial [dɪktəˈtɔːrɪəl] *adj* dictatorial.

dictatorship [dɪkˈteɪtəʃɪp] *n* dictadura *f.*

diction [ˈdɪkʃən] *n* dicción *f.*

dictionary [ˈdɪkʃənərɪ] *n* diccionario *m.* ■ **French d.,** diccionario *m* de francés.

dictum [ˈdɪktəm] *n (pl* **dictums** *or* **dicta) 1** *(formal statement)* afirmación *f,* declaración *f; Jur* dictamen *m.* **2** *(saying)* dicho *m.*

did [dɪd] *pt see* **do.**

diddle [ˈdɪdəl] *vtr fam* estafar, timar; **to d. sb out of sth,** sacar algo a algn con maña.

die¹ [daɪ] *vi (pt & pp* **died) 1** *(person, animal, plant)* morir, morirse; **to be dying,** estar agonizando,-a; *fam fig* **I nearly died!, I could have died!,** *(of laughter)* ¡me moría *or* me mondaba de risa!; *(of shock, shame)* ¡me moría!; *fam fig* **to be dying for sth/to do sth,** morirse por algo/de ganas de hacer algo. **2** *fig (light, flame)* extinguirse, agonizar; *(day, wave)* morir; *(feeling)* morir, desaparecer; *(smile)* desaparecer; *fig (habit, custom)* **to d. hard,** tardar en desaparecer. **3** *(machine, engine)* calarse, pararse; *(battery)* agotarse; *Tel* **the phone** *or* **the line died,** la línea se cortó. ◆ **die away** *vi (sound)* desvanecerse. ◆ **die back** *vi (plant)* morir hasta las raíces. ◆ **die down** *vi (fire)* extinguirse, apagarse; *(wind, storm)* amainar; *(noise, excitement)* disminuir. ◆ **die off** *vi (members of group, family relations)* morir uno por uno. ◆ **die out** *vi (tribe, species)* extinguirse, perderse.

die² [daɪ] *n* **1** *(pl* **dies)** *(for coins)* cuño *m,* troquel *m; fig* **the d. is cast,** la suerte está echada. **2** *(pl* **dice)** *arch* dado *m.*

die-hard [ˈdaɪhɑːd] *n* reaccionario,-a *m, f,* intransigente *mf.*

diesel [ˈdiːzəl] *n* **1** *(oil, fuel)* gasoil *m,* gasóleo *m.* ■ **d. engine,** motor *m* diesel. **2** *fam (vehicle)* vehículo *m* diesel.

diet [ˈdaɪət] **I** *n* **1** *(normal food)* alimentación *f,* dieta *f.* **2** *(selected food)* régimen *m; Med* dieta *f;* **to be** *or* **go on a d.,** estar a régimen. **II** *vi* estar a régimen *or* a dieta.

dietary [ˈdaɪətərɪ] *adj* alimenticio,-a, dietético,-a; *(products)* de régimen; *Med* de dieta.

dietician [daɪˈtɪʃən] *n Med* especialista *mf* en dietética.

differ [ˈdɪfəʳ] *vi* **1** *(be unlike)* ser distinto,-a, diferir. **2** *(disagree)* discrepar; **to agree to d.,** quedarse cada uno con la suya; *fml* **I beg to d.,** permítame decir que no estoy de acuerdo.

difference ['dɪfərəns] *n* 1 *(dissimilarity)* diferencia *f*; **a job with a d.,** un trabajo fuera de lo normal; **it makes no d. (to me),** (me) da lo mismo, (me) da igual; **what d. does it make?,** ¿qué más da? 2 *(disagreement)* desacuerdo *m*; **to settle one's differences,** llegar a un acuerdo.

different ['dɪfərənt] *adj* 1 *(unlike)* diferente, distinto,-a; **that's quite a d. matter,** ésa es otra cuestión, eso es harina de otro costal; **you look d.,** pareces otro,-a. 2 *(several)* distinto,-a; **I spoke to d. people,** hablé con varias personas. ◆ **differently** *adv* de otra manera.

differential [dɪfə'renʃəl] *n Econ Mat* diferencial *f*; *GB* **pay differentials,** diferencia *f sing* salarial. ■ *Aut* **d. (gear),** diferencial *f*.

differentiate [dɪfə'renʃɪeɪt] I *vtr* distinguir, diferenciar **(from,** de). II *vi* distinguir **(between,** entre).

difficult ['dɪfɪkəlt] *adj (gen)* difícil; **I find it d. to believe (that ...),** me cuesta creer (que ...); **to make life d. for sb,** hacerle la vida imposible a algn.

difficulty ['dɪfɪkəltɪ] *n (trouble)* dificultad *f*; *(problem)* problema *m*; **to be in difficulties,** estar en un apuro *or* un aprieto; **to get into difficulties,** meterse en un lío; **to make difficulties,** crear problemas, poner pegas; **with d.,** difícilmente, a duras penas; **without d.,** fácilmente, sin problema *or* problemas.

diffidence ['dɪfɪdəns] *n* timidez *f*, falta *f* de confianza en uno,-a mismo,-a.

diffident ['dɪfɪdənt] *adj* tímido,-a.

diffuse [dɪ'fjuːs] I *adj* 1 *(light)* difuso, -a; *fig (feeling)* vago,-a. 2 *pej (style, writer)* prolijo,-a. II [dɪ'fjuːz] *vtr (light, perfume)* difundir; *(heat)* desprender; *fig (knowledge)* difundir, extender. III [dɪ'fjuːz] *vi* difundirse.

diffusion [dɪ'fjuːʒən] *n* difusión *f*.

dig [dɪg] I *n* 1 *(poke)* codazo *m*. 2 *fam (gibe)* pulla *f*, *(hint)* indirecta *f*. 3 *Archeol* excavación *f*. 3 **digs,** *GB (lodgings)* alojamiento *m sing*; *(room)* habitación *f sing* alquilada. II *vtr (pt & pp* **dug)** 1 *(earth, well)* cavar; *(tunnel, trench)* excavar; *(hole)* hacer; *(potatoes etc)* sacar; *fig* **to d. one's own grave,** cavar la (propia) tumba. 2 *(thrust)* clavar, hincar; **I dug my feet into the sand,** hundí los pies en la arena; *fig* **to d. sb in the ribs,** darle un codazo a algn; *fam fig* **to d. one's heels in,** mantenerse en sus trece. 3 *fam (enjoy)* molar, gustar; *(understand)* ligar, comprender. III *vi (person)* cavar, excavar; *(animal)* escarbar; *Archeol Tech* excavar. ◆ **dig in** I *vtr* 1 *(compost etc)* enterrar. 2 *Mil* **to d. oneself in,** atrincherarse; *fam fig* **we're well dug into our new home,** estamos bien instalados en nuestra casa nueva. II *vi* 1 *Mil* atrincherarse. 2 *GB fam (start eating)* empezar a comer; *(serve oneself)* servirse; **d. in!,** ¡al ataque!, ¡a comer! ◆ **dig out** *vtr (trapped person)* sacar, desenterrar; *fig (old suit etc)* sacar, desenterrar; *fig (information)* encontrar, descubrir. ◆ **dig up** *vtr (weeds)* arrancar; *(buried object)* desenterrar; *(lawn)* roturar; *(pavement, road)* levantar; *fig (scandal, facts)* sacar a relucir.

digest ['daɪdʒest] I *n (summary)* resumen *m*. II [dɪ'dʒest] *vtr (food)* digerir; *fig (facts, novel)* digerir, asimilar.

digestible [dɪ'dʒestəbəl] *adj* digerible, digestible.

digestion [dɪ'dʒestʃən] *n* digestión *f*.

digestive [dɪ'dʒestɪv] *adj* digestivo,-a. ■ *GB* **d. biscuit,** galleta *f* integral; **d. system,** aparato *m* digestivo.

digger ['dɪgər] *n (machine)* excavadora *f*, *(person)* excavador,-a *m,f*.

digit ['dɪdʒɪt] *n* 1 *Math* dígito *m*. 2 *fml Anat (finger, toe)* dedo *m*; *(thumb)* pulgar *m*.

digital ['dɪdʒɪtəl] *adj Math & Anat* digital.

dignified ['dɪgnɪfaɪd] *adj (manner)* solemne, serio,-a; *(appearance)* majestuoso,-a, señorial.

dignify ['dɪgnɪfaɪ] *vtr (pt & pp* **dignified)** dignificar.

dignitary ['dɪgnɪtərɪ] *n fml* dignatario *m*.

dignity ['dɪgnɪtɪ] *n* dignidad *f*; **to stand on one's d.,** hacerse respetar.

digress [daɪ'gres] *vi fml* apartarse **(from,** de), desviarse **(from,** de).

digression [daɪ'greʃən] *n fml* digresión *f*.

dike [daɪk] *n US see* **dyke.**

dilapidated [dɪ'læpɪdeɪtɪd] *adj (gen)* en mal estado, muy estropeado,-a; *(ruined)* derruido,-a; *(falling apart)* desvencijado,-a.

dilapidation [dɪlæpɪ'deɪʃən] *n (gen)* mal estado *m*; *(ruin)* estado *m* ruinoso.

dilate [daɪ'leɪt] I *vi* dilatarse. II *vtr* dilatar.

dilatory ['dɪlətərɪ] *adj fml* lento,-a, tardo,-a; **to be d. in** *or* **about doing sth,** tardar en hacer algo.

dilemma [dɪ'lemə, daɪ'lemə] *n* dilema *m*; *fig* **to be on the horns of a d.,** estar entre la espada y la pared.

dilettante [dɪlɪ'tɑːntɪ] *n (pl* **dilettantes** *or* **dilettanti** [dɪlɪ'tɑːntiː]*)* diletante *mf*.

diligence ['dɪlɪdʒəns] *n* diligencia *f*.

diligent ['dɪlɪdʒənt] *adj (worker, student)* diligente, aplicado,-a, concienzudo,-a; *(inquiries, search)* minucioso,-a, esmerado,-a.

dill [dɪl] *n Bot* eneldo *m*.

dilute [daɪ'luːt] I *vtr* diluir; *(wine, milk)* aguar; *fig (effect, influence)* atenuar, suavizar. II *vi* diluirse. III *adj (solution)* diluido,-a.

dilution [daɪ'luːʃən] *n (of liquid)* dilución *f*, *fig (of effect)* atenuación *f*.

dim [dɪm] I *adj (***dimmer, dimmest)** 1 *(light)* difuso,-a, débil, tenue; *(room, street)* oscuro,-a; *(outline)* borroso,-a; *(eyesight)* defectuoso,-a; *fig (memory)* vago,-a, lejano,-a; *fig (prospects, future)* sombrío,-a; **his eyes are growing d.,** le falla la vista; *fam* **to take a d. view of sth,** ver algo con malos ojos. 2 *fam (stupid)* torpe, tonto,-a. II *vtr (pt & pp* **dimmed)** *(light)* bajar; *(sight, eyes)* nublar, empañar; *fig (memory)* borrar, difuminar; *fig (joy, hope)* apagar. III *vi (light)* bajarse; *(daylight)* oscurecerse; *(sight, eyes)* nublarse, empañarse; *fig (memory)* borrarse, difuminarse; *fig (joy)* apagarse. ◆ **dimly** *adv* vagamente, de una manera confusa.

dime [daɪm] *n US* moneda *f* de diez centavos; *fam fig* **they're a d. a dozen,** los hay a porrillo. ■ **d. store,** tienda *f* de baratijas.

dimension [daɪ'menʃən] *n* dimensión *f*.

dimensional [daɪ'menʃənəl] *adj* dimensional.

diminish [dɪ'mɪnɪʃ] I *vtr* 1 *(size, number)* disminuir, reducir. ■ *Jur* **diminished responsibility,** responsabilidad *f* disminuida. 2 *(person, importance)* rebajar, menospreciar. II *vi (size, number)* disminuir, reducirse.

diminution [dɪmɪ'njuːʃən] *n fml* disminución *f*, reducción *f*.

diminutive [dɪ'mɪnjʊtɪv] I *adj fml* diminuto,-a. II *n Ling* diminutivo *m*.

dimmer ['dɪmər] *n Elec* **d. (switch),** regulador *m* de voltaje.

dimness ['dɪmnɪs] *n* 1 *(of light)* palidez *f*; *(of room)* oscuridad *f*, *fig (of memory)* imprecisión *f*. 2 *(of shape)* lo borroso; *(of eyesight)* debilidad *f*. 3 *fam (of person)* torpeza *f*.

dimple ['dɪmpəl] *n* hoyuelo *m*.

dimwit ['dɪmwɪt] *n fam* tonto,-a *m, f*, mentecato,-a *m, f*, imbécil *mf*.

din [dɪn] I *n (of crowd)* alboroto *m*; *(of machinery)* ruido *m* ensordecedor. II *vi (pt & pp* **dinned)** *fam* **to d. sth into sb,** meterle algo en la cabeza a algn.

dine [daɪn] *vi fml* cenar; **to d. on** *or* **off caviar,** cenar caviar; **to d. out,** cenar fuera, salir a cenar; **to wine and d. sb,** invitar a algn a comer *or* a cenar.

diner ['daɪnər] *n* 1 *(person)* comensal *mf*. 2 *US (restaurant)* restaurante *m* barato.

ding-dong ['dɪŋdɒŋ] I *n* **1** *(sound)* din dan *m*, din don *m*. **2** *fam (quarrel)* riña *f*; *(fight)* pelea *f*. **II** *adj fam (argument, contest)* reñido,-a, disputado,-a.

dinghy ['dɪŋɪ] *n Naut* bote *m*. ■ **(rubber) d.,** bote *m* neumático; **(sailing) d.,** bote *m* con vela.

dingy ['dɪndʒɪ] *adj* **(dingier, dingiest) 1** *(street, house)* oscuro,-a, sórdido,-a. **2** *(dirty)* sucio,-a. **3** *(colour)* desteñido,-a, descolorido,-a.

diningcar ['daɪnɪŋkɑːʳ] *n Rail* vagón *m* restaurante.

diningroom ['daɪnɪŋruːm] *n* comedor *m*.

dinner ['dɪnəʳ] *n (at midday)* comida *f*; *(in evening)* cena *f*; *fml* **to attend a d.,** asistir a una cena. ■ **d. jacket,** smoking *m*; **d. service,** vajilla *f*; **d. table,** mesa *f* de comedor.

dinosaur ['daɪnəsɔːʳ] *n* dinosaurio *m*.

dint [dɪnt] *n* **by d. of,** a fuerza de.

diocese ['daɪəsɪs] *n Rel* diócesis *f inv*.

dioxide [daɪˈɒksaɪd] *n Chem* bióxido *m*, dióxido *m*.

dip [dɪp] I *n* **1** *fam (quick bathe)* chapuzón *m*. **2** *(drop) (of road, land)* pendiente *f*, declive *m*; *(in ground)* depresión *f*; *(of price, temperature)* caída *f*. **3** *(for sheep)* baño *m* desinfectante. **4** *Culin (sauce)* salsa *f*. **II** *vtr (pt & pp dipped)* **1** *(put into liquid)* bañar; *(pen)* mojar; *(spoon, hand)* meter. **2** *(disinfect) (sheep)* bañar en desinfectante. **3** *GB Aut* **to d. one's lights,** poner luces de cruce. **III** *vi (drop) (road, land)* bajar; *Av* bajar en picado; *(prices, temperature)* bajar; **the sun dipped below the horizon,** el sol desapareció bajo el horizonte. ◆ **dip into** *vtr* **1** *(savings, capital)* echar mano de. **2** *(book, magazine)* hojear.

DipEd [dɪp'ed] *GB abbr of* **Diploma in Education,** título *m* de profesor,-a.

diphtheria [dɪpˈθɪərɪə] *n Med* difteria *f*.

diphthong ['dɪfθɒŋ] *n Ling* diptongo *m*.

diploma [dɪˈpləʊmə] *n* diploma *m*.

diplomacy [dɪˈpləʊməsɪ] *n Pol & fig* diplomacia *f*; *(tact)* tacto *m*, discreción *f*.

diplomat ['dɪpləmæt] *n Pol & fig* diplomático,-a *m*, *f*.

diplomatic [dɪpləˈmætɪk] *adj Pol & fig* diplomático,-a. ■ *GB* **d. bag,** valija *f* diplomática; **d. corps,** cuerpo *m* diplomático.

dipper ['dɪpəʳ] *n* **1** *(for sherry etc)* venencia *f*; *(for soup etc)* cazo *m*, cacillo *m*. **2** *Orn* mirlo *m* acuático.

dipsomania [dɪpsəʊˈmeɪnɪə] *n Med* dipsomanía *f*.

dipsomaniac [dɪpsəʊˈmeɪnɪæk] *n Med* dipsómano,-a *m*, *f*, dipsomaníaco,-a *m*, *f*.

dipstick ['dɪpstɪk] *n Aut* indicador *m* de nivel del aceite.

Dir *abbr of* **Director,** Director,-a *m*, *f*, Dir.

dire [daɪəʳ] *adj* **1** *(urgent)* extremo,-a, urgente. **2** *(serious)* fatal, grave; **to be in d. straits,** estar en una situación desesperada. **3** *(terrible)* espantoso,-a, terrible.

direct [dɪˈrekt, 'daɪrekt] **I** *adj* **1** *(route, flight, link)* directo,-a. **2** *(result, action)* directo,-a, inmediato,-a; **to be a d. descendent of sb,** ser descendiente por línea directa de algn. ■ *Elec* **d. current,** corriente *f* continua; *Ling* **d. speech,** estilo *m* directo. **3** *(person, manner)* franco,-a, sincero,-a. **4** *(exact)* exacto,-a; **the d. opposite (of sth),** todo *or* exactamente lo contrario (de algo); *fig* **to make** *or* **score a d. hit,** dar en el blanco. **II** *adv (go, write)* directamente; *(broadcast)* en directo. **III** *vtr* **1** *(send)* dirigir; **can you d. me to a bank?,** ¿me puede indicar dónde hay un banco? **2** *(control)* dirigir. **3** *fml (order)* mandar, ordenar.

direction [dɪˈrekʃən, daɪˈrekʃən] *n* **1** *(way)* dirección *f*; **in every d., in all directions,** en todas direcciones; **sense of d.,** sentido *m* de la orientación; *fig* **a step in the right d.,** un paso hacia adelante. **2** *(control)* dirección *f*; **under the d. of,** bajo la dirección de. **3 directions,** *(to place)* señas *fpl*; **d. for use,** instrucciones *fpl* de uso, modo *m* de empleo.

directional [dɪˈrekʃənəl, daɪˈrekʃənəl] *adj Tech* direccional.

directive [dɪˈrektɪv, daɪˈrektɪv] *n fml* directiva *f*, directriz *f*.

directly [dɪˈrektlɪ, daɪˈrektlɪ] **I** *adv* **1** *(above, opposite, etc)* exactamente, justo. **2** *(speak)* sinceramente, directamente. **4** *(come)* en seguida, dentro de poco. **II** *conj fam* en cuanto, tan pronto como.

directness [dɪˈrektnɪs, daɪˈreknɪs] *n* franqueza *f*, sinceridad *f*.

director [dɪˈrektər, daɪˈrektəʳ] *n* **1** *(of operation, company)* director,-a *m*, *f*; **board of directors,** consejo *m* de administración, (junta *f*) directiva *f*. ■ **managing d.,** director,-a *m*, *f*, gerente *mf*. **2** *(of film, programme)* director,-a *m*, *f*. ■ *GB Jur* **D. of Public Prosecutions,** Fiscal *mf* General del Estado.

directorate [dɪˈrektərɪt, daɪˈrektərɪt] *n* consejo *m* de administración, (junta *f*) directiva *f*.

directorship [dɪˈrektəʃɪp, daɪˈrektəʃɪp] *n* cargo *m* de director.

directory [dɪˈrektərɪ, daɪˈrektərɪ] *n Tel* guía *f* telefónica. ■ *Tel* **d. enquiries,** (servicio *m* de) información *f*; **(street) d.,** callejero *m*.

dirge [dɜːdʒ] *n* canto *m* fúnebre.

dirt [dɜːt] *n* **1** *(dirtiness)* suciedad *f*; *(filth, grime)* mugre *f*; *(grease)* porquería *f*; *(mud)* barro *m*; *fam fig* **to treat sb like d.,** tratar a algn como a una zapatilla. **2** *(earth)* tierra *f*. ■ **d. road,** pista *f* de tierra; *Sport* **d. track,** pista *f* de ceniza. **3** *fam (obscenity)* porquerías *fpl*; *(scandal)* chisme *m*.

dirt-cheap [dɜːtˈtʃiːp] *adv & adj fam* tirado,-a.

dirtiness ['dɜːtɪnɪs] *n* suciedad *f*.

dirty ['dɜːtɪ] **I** *adj* **(dirtier, dirtiest) 1** *(not clean)* sucio,-a; *(muddy)* embarrado,-a; **a d. mark,** una mancha; **to get d.,** ensuciarse. **2** *(dishonest)* sucio,-a, deshonesto,-a; *(dealer)* sin escrúpulos; *(player, fighter)* sucio,-a, tramposo,-a; *fam* **to do the d. on sb,** hacer a algn una mala jugada. **3** *fam (night, weather)* borrascoso,-a, de perros; *(thief)* vil, despreciable; **to give sb a d. look,** fulminar a algn con la mirada. **4** *(story, joke)* verde; *(mind, sense of humour)* pervertido,-a. ■ **d. word,** palabrota *f*; *(insult)* insulto *m*; **d. old man,** viejo *m* verde; *fam* **d. weekend,** aventura *f* de fin de semana. **III** *vtr (pt & pp dirtied)* ensuciar. **IV** *adv GB fam* **1** *(play, fight)* sucio. **2** *(intensifier)* muy; **a d. great hole,** un agujero enorme.

dis- [dɪs] *pref* des-; **disconnected,** desconectado,-a; **disgrace,** desgracia *f*.

disability [dɪsəˈbɪlɪtɪ] *n* **1** *(handicap)* desventaja *f*, hándicap *m*. **2** *(state)* incapacidad *f* (física *or* mental), invalidez *f*. ■ **d. allowance, d. pension,** pensión *f* por invalidez.

disable [dɪsˈeɪbəl] *vtr* **1** *(physically)* dejar imposibilitado,-a; *(mentally)* dejar incapacitado,-a. **2** *(ship, gun)* inutilizar.

disabled [dɪsˈeɪbəld] **I** *adj* minusválido,-a. **II the d.** *npl* los minusválidos.

disabuse [dɪsəˈbjuːz] *vtr fml* desengañar.

disadvantage [dɪsədˈvɑːntɪdʒ] *n* desventaja *f*; *(obstacle)* inconveniente *m*; **to be at a d.,** estar en inferioridad de condiciones.

disadvantaged [dɪsədˈvɑːntɪdʒd] *adj* desheredado,-a, discriminado,-a.

disadvantageous [dɪsædvɑːnˈteɪdʒəs] *adj* desfavorable.

disaffectal [dɪsəˈfektɪd] *adj* desafecto,-a.

disaffection [dɪsəˈfekʃən] *n* desafección *f*.

disagree [dɪsəˈɡriː] *vi* **1** *(differ)* no estar de acuerdo (**with,** con); **to d. on** *or* **over** *or* **about sth,** reñir por algo. **2** *(not match)* discrepar (**with,** de, con), no corresponder (**with,** a). **3** *(upset) (climate)* no convenir (**with,** a); *(food)* sentar mal (**with,** -).

disagreable [dɪsəˈɡriəbəl] *adj* desagradable.

disagreement [dɪsə'griːmənt] *n* **1** *(difference)*, desacuerdo *m*; *(argument)* riña *f*. altercado *m*. **2** *(non-correspondence)* discrepancia *f*, disconformidad *f*.

disallow [dɪsə'laʊ] *vtr fml (goal)* anular; *(objection)* rechazar.

disappear [dɪsə'pɪəʳ] *vi* desaparecer; *fam (person)* esfumarse; **to d. from view,** perderse de vista.

disappearance [dɪsə'pɪərəns] *n* desaparición *f*.

disappoint [dɪsə'pɔɪnt] *vtr (person)* decepcionar, defraudar, desilusionar; *(hope, ambition)* frustrar.

disappointed [dɪsə'pɔɪntɪd] *adj (person)* decepcionado,-a, desilusionado,-a; *(hope, ambition)* frustrado,-a; **to be d. in sth,** sufrir *or* llevarse un desengaño con algo.

disappointing [dɪsə'pɔɪntɪŋ] *adj* decepcionante.

disappointment [dɪsə'pɔɪntmənt] *n* decepción *f*, desilusión *f*.

disapproval [dɪsə'pruːvəl] *n* desaprobación *f*.

disapprove [dɪsə'pruːv] *vi* desaprobar.

disapproving [dɪsə'pruːvɪŋ] *adj* de desaprobación.

disarm [dɪs'ɑːm] **I** *vtr* desarmar. **II** *vi (country)* desarmarse.

disarmament [dɪs'ɑːməmənt] *n* desarme *m*.

disarming [dɪs'ɑːmɪŋ] *adj fig* que desarma.

disarray [dɪsə'reɪ] *n fml* **in d.,** *(room, papers)* en desorden; *(hair)* desarreglado,-a, desaliñado,-a; *(thoughts)* confuso,-a.

disaster [dɪ'zɑːstəʳ] *n* desastre *f*, catástrofe *f*.

disastrous [dɪ'zɑːstrəs] *adj* desastroso,-a, catastrófico,-a.

disavow [dɪsə'vaʊ] *vtr fml* negar, rechazar.

disband [dɪs'bænd] **I** *vtr (group)* disolver, deshacer; *(army)* licenciar. **II** *vi (group)* disolverse, deshacerse; *(army)* licenciarse.

disbelief [dɪsbɪ'liːf] *n* incredulidad *f*.

disbelieve [dɪsbɪ'liːv] *vtr fml* no creer, dudar.

disburse [dɪs'bɜːs] *vtr fml* desembolsar.

disbursement [dɪs'bɜːsmənt] *n* desembolso *m*.

disc [dɪsk] *n* disco *m*; *Comput* disquete. ■ *Mus* **d. jockey,** disc-jockey *mf*, pinchadiscos *mf inv*.

discard [dɪs'kɑːd] *vtr (old things)* desechar, deshacerse de; *(idea, plan)* descartar, desechar, rechazar; *(playing card)* descartarse de.

discern [dɪ'sɜːn] *vtr fml (shape)* percibir, distinguir; *(merit, difference)* distinguir, discernir; *(truth)* darse cuenta de.

discernible [dɪ'sɜːnəbəl] *adj (shape)* visible; *(merit)* perceptible.

discerning [dɪ'sɜːnɪŋ] *adj (person)* perspicaz; *(taste)* refinado,-a.

discernment [dɪ'sɜːnmənt] *n (perception)* discernimiento *m*, perspicacia *f*; *(judgement)* buen criterio *m*.

discharge [dɪs'tʃɑːdʒ] *fml* **I** *vtr* **1** *(release)* verter; *(electric current, cargo)* descargar; *(smoke, pus)* echar, emitir; **factories d. waste into the sea,** las fábricas vierten los residuos en el mar. **2** *(allow to go) (prisoner)* liberar, soltar; *(patient)* dar de alta; *(soldier etc)* licenciar; *(injured soldier etc)* dar de baja; *(dismiss)* despedir. **3** *(pay)* saldar. **4** *(fulfil)* cumplir. **II** *vi* **1** *(release) (sewer, pipe)* verter, desembocar; *(chimney)* emitir; *(wound)* supurar. **III** ['dɪstʃɑːdʒ] *n* **1** *(of electric current, load)* descarga *f*; *(of smoke)* emisión *f*; *(of gases)* escape *m*; *(of waste)* vertido *m*; *(of wound)* supuración *f*. **2** *(of prisoner)* liberación *f*, puesta *f* en libertad; *(of patient)* alta *f*; *(of soldier etc)* licencia *f* (absoluta); *(of dismissal)* despido *m*. **3** *(of debt)* descargo *m*, pago *m*. **4** *(of duty)* cumplimiento *m*; **in the d. of her duties,** en el ejercicio de sus funciones.

disciple [dɪ'saɪpəl] *n* discípulo,-a *m,f*.

disciplinary ['dɪsɪplɪnərɪ] *adj* disciplinario,-a.

discipline [dɪsɪplɪn] **I** *n* **1** *(training, behaviour)* disciplina *f*; **self-d.,** autodisciplina *f*. **2** *(punishment)* castigo *m*. **3** *fml (subject)* disciplina *f*. **II** *vtr* **1** *(punish) (child)* castigar; *(worker)* sancionar; *(official)* expedientar. **2** *(train)* disciplinar.

disclaim [dɪs'kleɪm] *vtr fml (knowledge, responsibility)* negar tener; *(credit)* renunciar a, rechazar.

disclaimer [dɪs'kleɪməʳ] *n fml (in contract etc)* (nota *f* de) rectificación *f*; *(denial)* renuncia *f*.

disclose [dɪs'kləʊz] *vtr* **1** *(reveal)* revelar, dar a conocer. **2** *(show)* mostrar, dejar ver.

disclosure [dɪs'kləʊʒəʳ] *n (revelation)* revelación *f*.

disco ['dɪskəʊ] *n (pl* discos*) (abbr of* discotheque*) fam* disco *f*, discoteca *f*.

discoloration [dɪskʌlə'reɪʃən] *n* descoloramiento *m*.

discolour, US **discolor** [dɪs'kʌləʳ] **I** *vtr* descolorar. **II** *vi* descolorarse.

discomfiture [dɪs'kʌmfɪtʃəʳ] *n fml* desconcierto *m*.

discomfort [dɪs'kʌmfət] *n* **1** *(lack of comfort)* incomodidad *f*. **2** *(pain)* malestar *m*, molestia *f*. **3** *(unease)* inquietud *f*, preocupación *f*.

disconcert [dɪskən'sɜːt] *vtr* desconcertar, perturbar.

disconcerting [dɪskən'sɜːtɪŋ] *adj* desconcertante.

disconnect [dɪskə'nekt] *vtr (gen)* desconectar **(from,** de); *(gas or electricity supply)* cortar.

disconnected [dɪskə'nektɪd] *adj (speech)* deshilvanado,-a; *(thoughts)* inconexo,-a.

disconsolate [dɪs'kɒnsəlɪt] *adj (gen)* desconsolado,-a; *(look)* abatido,-a.

discontent [dɪskən'tent] *n* descontento *m*, disgusto *m*.

discontented [dɪskən'tentɪd] *adj* descontento,-a, disgustado,-a.

discontentment [dɪskən'tentmənt] *n see* **discontent.**

discontinue [dɪskən'tɪnjuː] *vtr fml (gen)* abandonar; *(work)* interrumpir, suspender; *Com* **discontinued line,** restos *mpl* de serie.

discontinuity [dɪskɒntɪ'njuːɪtɪ] *n* discontinuidad *f*; *fml* interrupción *f*.

discontinuous [dɪskən'tɪnjʊəs] *adj* discontinuo,-a, interrumpido,-a.

discord ['dɪskɔːd] *n* **1** *fml* discordia *f*, disensión *f*. **2** *Mus* disonancia *f*.

discordant [dɪs'kɔːdənt] *adj* **1** *(views)* discordante; *(personalities)* discorde. **2** *Mus* discordante.

discotheque ['dɪskətek] *n* discoteca *f*.

discount ['dɪskaʊnt] **I** *n* descuento *m*; **a ten percent d., a d. of ten percent,** un descuento de diez por ciento. **II** [dɪs'kaʊnt] *vtr* **1** *(price)* hacer descuento de, rebajar. **2** *(view, suggestion, possibility)* descartar.

discourage [dɪs'kʌrɪdʒ] *vtr* **1** *(dishearten)* desanimar, desalentar. **2** *(deter) (investment)* no fomentar; *(advances)* rechazar, resistirse a; *(bad habit)* hacer desistir de.

discouragement [dɪs'kʌrɪdʒmənt] *n* **1** *(depression)* desánimo *m*, desaliento *m*. **2** *(dissuasion)* desaprobación *f*. **3** *(obstacle)* obstáculo *m*.

discouraging [dɪs'kʌrɪdʒɪŋ] *adj* desalentador,-a, desmoralizador,-a.

discourse ['dɪskɔːs, dɪs'kɔːs] *fml* **I** *n (spoken)* discurso *m*, plática *f*; *(written)* discurso *m*, tratado *m*. **II** [dɪs'kɔːs] *vtr* disertar **(on,** sobre), conversar **(on,** sobre).

discourteous [dɪs'kɜːtɪəs] *adj fml* maleducado,-a, descortés,-esa.

discourtesy [dɪs'kɜːtɪsɪ] *n fml* descortesía *f*, falta *f* de educación.

discover [dɪ'skʌvəʳ] *vtr (gen)* descubrir; *(missing person, object)* encontrar, hallar; *(mistake, loss)* darse cuenta de; *(secret reason)* aprender, enterarse de.

discovery [dɪ'skʌvərɪ] *n* descubrimiento *m*.

discredit [dɪs'kredɪt] **I** *n* descrédito *m*. **II** *vtr (person, régime)* desacreditar, desprestigiar; *(idea, theory)* poner en duda.

discreditable [dɪs'kredɪtəbəl] *adj* indigno,-a, vergonzoso,-a.

discreet [dɪ'skriːt] *adj (gen)* discreto,-a; *(distance, silence)* prudente; *(hat, house)* modesto,-a.

discrepancy [dɪ'skrepənsɪ] *n (stories, facts)* discrepancia *f* (**between**, entre); *(figures)* diferencia *f* (**between**, entre).

discrete [dɪs'kriːt] *adj fml* discreto,-a.

discretion [dɪ'skreʃən] *n (gen)* discreción *f*; *(prudence)* prudencia *f*; **at the d. of ...**, a juicio de ...; **use your own d.**, haz lo que te parezca (bien).

discretionary [dɪ'skreʃənərɪ] *adj fml* discrecional.

discriminate [dɪ'skrɪmɪneɪt] **I** *vtr* distinguir (**from**, de). **II** *vi* discriminar (**between**, entre); **to d. against sth/sb**, discriminar algo/a algn; **to d. in favour of sth/sb**, dar un trato preferencial a algo/a algn.

discriminating [dɪ'skrɪmɪneɪtɪŋ] *adj (person)* entendido,-a, exigente; *(taste)* refinado,-a, fino,-a.

discrimination [dɪskrɪmɪ'neɪʃən] *n* **1** *(bias)* discriminación *f*. **2** *(distinction)* diferenciación *f*, distinción *f*. **3** *(taste)* juicio *m*, buen gusto *m*, discernimiento *m*.

discriminatory [dɪ'skrɪmɪnətərɪ] *adj* discriminatorio,-a.

discursive [dɪ'skɜːsɪv] *adj* divagador,-a.

discus ['dɪskəs] *n (pl discuses or disci* ['dɪskaɪ]*) Sport* disco *m*.

discuss [dɪ'skʌs] *vtr* **1** *(talk about)* discutir; *(in writing)* tratar de; **to d. sth in detail**, examinar algo a fondo. **2** *(debate)* discutir.

discussion [dɪ'skʌʃən] *n* discusión *f*.

disdain [dɪs'deɪn] *fml* **I** *n* desdén *m*, desprecio *m*. **II** *vtr* desdeñar, despreciar; **he disdained to notice me**, no se dignó a hacerme caso.

disdainful [dɪs'deɪnful] *adj fml* desdeñoso,-a, despectivo,-a.

disease [dɪ'ziːz] *n* enfermedad *f*; *fig* mal *m*, enfermedad *f*.

diseased [dɪ'ziːzd] *adj* enfermo,-a.

disembark [dɪsɪm'bɑːk] *vtr & vi* desembarcar (**from**, de).

disembarkation [dɪsɪmbɑː'keɪʃən] *n (of people)* desembarco *m*; *(of goods)* desembarque *m*.

disembodied [dɪsɪm'bɒdɪd] *adj* incorpóreo,-a.

disembowel [dɪsɪm'bauəl] *vtr (pt & pp disembowelled, US disemboweled)* desentrañar, destripar.

disenchanted [dɪsɪn'tʃɑːntɪd] *adj* desencantado,-a, desilusionado,-a.

disenchantment [dɪsɪn'tʃɑːntmənt] *n* desencanto *m*, desilusión *f*.

disengage [dɪsɪn'geɪdʒ] **I** *vtr* **1** *(free)* desprender, soltar. **2** *(clutch, gears)* desembragar. **II** *vi (troops)* retirar (**from**, de).

disentangle [dɪsɪn'tæŋgəl] *vtr* desenmarañar, desenredar.

disfavour, *US* **disfavor** [dɪs'feɪvə^r] *n fml* desaprobación *f*; **to fall into d.**, caer en desgracia.

disfigure [dɪs'fɪgə^r] *vtr* desfigurar.

disfigurement [dɪs'fɪgəmənt] *n* desfiguración *f*.

disgorge [dɪs'gɔːdʒ] *vtr (liquid, waste)* verter; *(smoke, fumes)* emitir.

disgrace [dɪs'greɪs] **I** *n* **1** *(loss of favour)* desgracia *f*; **to be in d.**, *(official etc)* estar desacreditado,-a; *(child)* estar castigado,-a; **to fall into d.**, caer en desgracia. **2** *(shame)* vergüenza *f*, escándalo *m*. **II** *vtr (family, name)* deshonrar, desacreditar.

disgraceful [dɪs'greɪsful] *adj* vergonzoso,-a; **it's d!**, ¡es una vergüenza!, ¡es un escándalo!

disgruntled [dɪs'grʌntəld] *adj (person, expression) (sulky)* contrariado,-a, disgustado,-a; *(bad-tempered)* malhumorado,-a.

disguise [dɪs'gaɪz] **I** *n* disfraz *m*; **in d.**, disfrazado,-a; *fig* **it's a blessing in d.**, no hay mal que por bien no venga. **II** *vtr* **1** *(person)* disfrazar (**as**, de); *(voice, handwriting)* cambiar. **2** *(feelings, views)* disfrazar, disimular, esconder; **there's no disguising the fact that ...**, no se puede ocultar que ... .

disgust [dɪs'gʌst] **I** *n* **1** *(loathing)* repugnancia *f*, asco *m*; **to fill sb with d.**, repugnar a *or* dar asco a algn. **2** *(strong disapproval)* indignación *f*. **II** *vtr* **1** *(revolt)* repugnar, dar asco a. **2** *(disapprove)* indignar, disgustar; **I'm disgusted with** *or* **at your rudeness**, tu falta de educación me indigna.

disgusting [dɪs'gʌstɪŋ] *adj* **1** *(loathsome) (sight, habit)* asqueroso,-a, repugnante; *(smell)* nauseabundo,-a; *(behaviour, state of affairs)* desagradable, intolerable, reprobable. **2** *fam (weather)* asqueroso,-a, horrible.

dish [dɪʃ] *n* **1** *(for serving)* fuente *f*; *(course)* plato *m*; **to wash** *or* **do the dishes**, fregar los platos. **2** *fam (attractive man, woman)* bombón *m*. ◆ **dish out** *vtr fam (food)* servir; *(books, passes, advice)* repartir; **to d. it out (to sb)**, *(punish)* castigar (a algn); *(criticize)* criticar (a algn). ◆ **dish up** *vtr (meal)* servir.

dishcloth ['dɪʃklɒθ] *n* trapo *m* de fregar.

dishearten [dɪs'hɑːtən] *vtr* desanimar, descorazonar, desalentar.

disheartening [dɪs'hɑːtənɪŋ] *adj* desalentador,-a.

dishevelled, *US* **disheveled** [dɪ'ʃevəld] *adj (hair)* despeinado,-a, *(appearance, clothes)* desaliñado,-a, desarreglado,-a.

dishonest [dɪs'ɒnɪst] *adj (person, behaviour)* poco honrado,-a, deshonesto,-a; *(means)* fraudulento,-a.

dishonesty [dɪs'ɒnɪstɪ] *n (of person, behaviour)* falta *f* de honradez; *(of means)* fraude *m*.

dishonour, *US* **dishonor** [dɪs'ɒnə^r] **I** *n fml* deshonra *f*. **II** *vtr* **1** *(family, name)* deshonrar. **2** *(cheque)* rechazar, negarse a pagar.

dishonourable, *US* **dishonorable** [dɪs'ɒnərəbəl] *adj* deshonroso,-a.

dishtowel ['dɪʃtauəl] *n US* trapo *m* de cocina.

dishwasher ['dɪʃwɒʃə^r] *n (machine)* lavaplatos *m inv*, lavavajillas *m inv*; *(person)* lavaplatos *mf inv*.

dishy ['dɪʃɪ] *adj (dishier, dishiest) GB fam* guapo,-a; **he's really d.**, está buenísimo, está como un tren.

disillusion [dɪsɪ'luːʒən] **I** *n* desilusión *f*. **II** *vtr* desilusionar.

disillusionment [dɪsɪ'luːʒənmənt] *n* desilusión *f*.

disincentive [dɪsɪn'sentɪv] *n* freno *m*.

disinclination [dɪsɪnklɪ'neɪʃən] *n* aversión *f*.

disinfect [dɪsɪn'fekt] *vtr* desinfectar.

disinfectant [dɪsɪn'fektənt] *n* desinfectante *m*.

disingenuous [dɪsɪn'dʒenjʊəs] *adj* falso,-a, poco sincero,-a.

disinherit [dɪsɪn'herɪt] *vtr* desheredar.

disintegrate [dɪs'ɪntɪgreɪt] *vi* desintegrarse.

disintegration [dɪsɪntɪ'greɪʃən] *n* desintegración *f*.

disinter [dɪsɪn'tɜː^r] *vtr fml* desenterrar.

disinterested [dɪs'ɪntrɪstɪd] *adj* desinteresado,-a, imparcial, objetivo,-a.

disjointed [dɪs'dʒɔɪntɪd] *adj* inconexo,-a, sin relación.

disk [dɪsk] *n US* disco *m*; *Comput* disquete *m*. ■ **d. drive**, disquetera *f*.

diskette [dɪs'ket] *n Comput* disquete *m*.

dislike [dɪs'laɪk] **I** *n* antipatía *f*, aversión *f* (**for, of, a**, hacia). **II** *vtr* tener antipatía *or* aversión a *or* hacia; **I d. her intensely**, me cae muy mal *or* gorda.

dislocate ['dɪsləkeɪt] *vtr* **1** *(joint)* dislocar; **he dislocated his hip**, se dislocó *or* se desencajó la cadera. **2** *fig (routine, plan)* trastornar, desarreglar.

dislocation [dɪslə'keɪʃən] *n* dislocación *f*.

dislodge [dɪs'lɒdʒ] *vtr* desalojar, sacar.

disloyal [dɪs'lɔɪəl] *adj* desleal.

disloyalty [dɪs'lɔɪəltɪ] *n* deslealtad *f*.

dismal ['dɪzməl] *adj* **1** *(gloomy) (prospect)* sombrío,-a; *(place, weather)* deprimente; *(person)* triste. **2** *(hopeless)* lamentable.

dismantle [dɪs'mæntəl] **I** *vtr (tent, clock)* desarmar, desmontar; *fig (company, system)* desmantelar. **II** *vi (tent, clock)* desarmarse, desmontarse.

dismay [dɪs'meɪ] **I** *n* consternación *f*. **II** *vtr (concern)* consternar; *(discourage)* desanimar, desalentar.

dismember [dɪs'membər] *vtr* desmembrar.

dismiss [dɪs'mɪs] *vtr* **1** *(put aside) (idea etc)* descartar; *(thought)* alejar; *(subject)* despachar. **2** *fml (sack) (employee)* despedir; *(official)* destituir. **3** *(send away) (gen)* dar permiso para retirarse; *(butler etc)* despedir; *(troops)* hacer romper filas; **the teacher dismissed the class**, el profesor dio por terminada la clase. **4** *(reject)* rechazar; *Jur* desestimar; *Jur (case, charge)* sobreseer.

dismissal [dɪs'mɪsəl] *n* **1** *(of idea, suggestion)* descarte *m*, abandono *m*. **2** *(of employee)* despido *m*; *(of official)* destitución *f*. **3** *(of claim)* rechazo *m*; *Jur* desestimación *f*.

dismissive [dɪs'mɪsɪv] *adj* despectivo,-a.

dismount [dɪs'maʊnt] *vi fml* desmontarse, apearse **(from,** de).

disobedience [dɪsə'biːdɪəns] *n* desobediencia *f*.

disobedient [dɪsə'biːdɪənt] *adj* desobediente.

disobey [dɪsə'beɪ] *vtr & vi (person)* desobedecer; *(law, rules)* contravenir, violar.

disobliging [dɪsə'blaɪdʒɪŋ] *adj fml (unhelpful)* poco complaciente; *(unpleasant)* desagradable.

disorder [dɪs'ɔːdər] *n* **1** *(untidiness)* desorden *m*. **2** *(riot)* disturbio *m*, desórdenes *mpl*. **3** *(ailment) (of stomach etc)* indisposición *f*; *(of mind)* trastorno *m* (nervioso); *(of speech)* defecto *m*.

disordered [dɪs'ɔːdəd] *adj* **1** *(untidy)* desordenado,-a, desarreglado,-a. **2** *(malfunctioning) (stomach)* indispuesto,-a; *(mind)* enfermo,-a, trastornado,-a.

disorderly [dɪs'ɔːdəlɪ] *adj* **1** *(untidy)* desordenado,-a, desarreglado,-a. **2** *(unruly)* desordenado,-a; *(meeting)* alborotado,-a; *(conduct)* escandaloso,-a. ■ *Jur* **d. house**, casa *f* de lenocinio.

disorganized [dɪs'ɔːgənaɪzd] *adj (person)* desorganizado,-a; *(schedule, system)* desorganizado,-a, caótico,-a.

disorient [dɪs'ɔːrɪent] *vtr*, **disorientate** [dɪs'ɔːrɪenteɪt] *vtr* desorientar.

disown [dɪs'əʊn] *vtr* desconocer.

disparage [dɪ'spærɪdʒ] *vtr* menospreciar, despreciar.

disparaging [dɪ'spærɪdʒɪŋ] *adj* despectivo,-a.

disparate ['dɪspərɪt] *adj fml* dispar, diferente.

disparity [dɪ'spærɪtɪ] *n fml* disparidad *f*.

dispassionate [dɪs'pæʃənɪt] *adj* desapasionado,-a.

dispatch [dɪ'spætʃ] **I** *n* **1** *(message)* mensaje *m*; *(official message)* despacho *m*; *(journalist's report)* noticia *m*, reportaje *m*; *(military message)* parte *m*. ■ *Admin* **d. box**, cartera *f*; **d. case**, portafolios *m inv*; **d. rider**, mensajero *m*. **2** *(sending) (of mail, parcel)* envío *m*; *(of goods)* consignación *f*; *(of courier, message)* despacho *m*, envío *m*. **3** *fml (speed)* prontitud *f*; **to act with d.**, obrar con diligencia. **II** *vtr* **1** *(send) (mail, parcel)* expedir, remitir, enviar; *(goods)* expedir, consignar; *(courier, message)* despachar, enviar. **2** *fam (finish quickly) (food)* zampar; *(job, business)* despachar. **3** *euph (kill)* despachar, matar.

dispel [dɪ'spel] *vtr (pt & pp dispelled)* disipar.

dispensable [dɪ'spensəbəl] *adj* innecesario,-a, superfluo,-a.

dispensary [dɪ'spensərɪ] *n* dispensario *m*.

dispensation [dɪspen'seɪʃən] *n* **1** *fml (handing out)* administración *f*. **2** *(exemption)* exención *f*; *Rel* dispensa *f*.

dispense [dɪ'spens] *vtr* **1** *(supplies, funds)* repartir, distribuir; *fig (justice)* administrar; *fig (favours)* conceder. **2** *Pharm* preparar y despachar. ◆ **dispense with** *vi* **1** *(do without)* prescindir de, pasar sin. **2** *(make unnecessary)* eliminar la necesidad de.

dispenser [dɪ'spensər] *n* máquina *f* expendedora. ■ **cash d.**, cajero *m* automático; **soap d.**, dosificador *m* de jabón.

dispensing chemist [dɪspensɪŋ'kemɪst] *n GB* farmacéutico,-a *m*,*f*.

dispersal [dɪ'spɜːsəl] *n* dispersión *f*.

disperse [dɪ'spɜːs] **I** *vtr* dispersar. **II** *vi* dispersarse; *(fog)* disiparse.

dispirited [dɪ'spɪrɪtɪd] *adj* abatido,-a, desanimado,-a, desalentado,-a.

displace [dɪs'pleɪs] *vtr* **1** *(gen)* desplazar; *(bone)* dislocar. ■ **displaced person**, refugiado,-a *m*, *f*. **2** *(supplant)* sustituir, reemplazar; *(official)* destituir.

displacement [dɪs'pleɪsmənt] *n* **1** *(removal)* desplazamiento *m*. **2** *(supplanting)* sustitución *f*, reemplazo *m*. **3** *Tech* desplazamiento *m*.

display [dɪ'spleɪ] **I** *n* **1** *(of paintings, goods)* exposición *f*; *Comput* visualización *f*; *(of feelings, skills)* demostración *f*; *(of strength, force)* despliegue *m*, exhibición *f*. ■ *Comput* **d. terminal**, terminal *f* de ordenador; **d. window**, escaparate *m*; *Mil* **military d.**, desfile *m* or despliegue *m* militar. **II** *vtr* **1** *(gen)* mostrar; *(china, medals)* exhibir; *(goods)* exponer; *(advert)* colocar; *Comput* visualizar. **2** *fig fml (feelings)* demostrar, manifestar; *(skill, courage)* mostrar.

displease [dɪs'pliːz] *vtr fml* disgustar, desagradar, contrariar; *(offend)* ofender.

displeasure [dɪs'pleʒər] *n fml* disgusto *m*, desagrado *m*; **to voice one's d.**, expresar la desaprobación.

disport [dɪ'spɔːt] *vtr fml* **to d. oneself**, entretenerse.

disposable [dɪ'spəʊzəbəl] *adj* **1** *(throwaway)* desechable, de usar y tirar. **2** *(available)* disponible.

disposal [dɪ'spəʊzəl] *n* **1** *(removal)* eliminación *f*. ■ **bomb d.**, desactivación *f* de artefactos explosivos; **waste d.**, recogida *f* de basuras; **waste d. unit**, trituradora *f* de basura. **2** *(availability)* disponibilidad *f*; **at my d.**, a mi disposición. **3** *fml (arrangement)* disposición *f*. **4** *(sale)* venta *f*; *(of property)* traspaso *m*.

dispose [dɪ'spəʊz] **I** *vi* **to d. of,** *(remove)* eliminar; *(rubbish)* tirar; *(unwanted object)* deshacerse de; *(argument)* echar por tierra; *(problem, matter)* resolver; *(sell)* vender; *(property)* traspasar; *(free time)* emplear; *euph (kill)* liquidar, despachar. **II** *vtr fml (arrange)* disponer.

disposed [dɪ'spəʊzd] *adj (inclined)* dispuesto,-a.

disposition [dɪspə'zɪʃən] *n* **1** *(temperament)* carácter *m*, genio *m*, naturaleza *f*. **2** *(readiness)* predisposición *f*. **3** *fml (arrangement)* disposición *f*.

dispossess [dɪspə'zes] *fml* **I** **the dispossessed** *npl* los desposeídos. **II** *vtr* desposeer **(of,** de).

disproportion [dɪsprə'pɔːʃən] *n* desproporción *f*.

disproportionate [dɪsprə'pɔːʃənɪt] *adj* desproporcionado,-a **(to,** a).

disprove [dɪs'pruːv] *vtr* refutar.

dispute ['dɪspjuːt] **I** *n* **1** *(disagreement)* discusión *f*, controversia *f*; **beyond** *or* **without d.**, indiscutiblemente. **2** *(quarrel)* disputa *f*. ■ **industrial d.**, conflicto *m* laboral. **II** [dɪ'spjuːt] *vtr* **1** *(claim, right)* refutar. **2** *(territory)* disputar. **3** *(matter, question)* discutir; **a hotly disputed affair**, un asunto muy controvertido. **III** *vi* discutir **(about, over,** de, sobre).

disqualification [dɪskwɒlɪfɪ'keɪʃən] *n* descalificación *f*.

disqualify [dɪs'kwɒlɪfaɪ] *vtr (pt & pp disqualified)* **1** *Sport* descalificar. **2** *(make ineligible)* incapacitar.

disquiet [dɪs'kwaɪət] *n* preocupación *f*, inquietud *f*.

disquieting [dɪsˈkwaɪətɪŋ] *adj* preocupante, inquietante.

disquisition [dɪskwɪˈzɪʃən] *n fml* disquisición *f*, razonamiento *m*.

disregard [dɪsrɪˈgɑːd] **I** *n (lack of concern)* indiferencia *f*; *(for risk, safety)* despreocupación *f*. **II** *vtr* descuidar; *(ignore)* ignorar.

disrepair [dɪsrɪˈpeəʳ] *n* mal estado *m*; **in (a state of) d.,** en mal estado; *(building)* que amenaza ruina; *(road)* carretera *f* muy bacheada; **to fall into d.,** deteriorarse.

disreputable [dɪsˈrepjʊtəbəl] *adj (person, area)* de mala fama; *(behaviour)* vergonzoso,-a, lamentable; *(clothes)* asqueroso,-a.

disrepute [dɪsrɪˈpjuːt] *n* mala fama *f*, oprobio *m*.

disrespect [dɪsrɪˈspekt] *n* falta *f* de respeto.

disrespectful [dɪsrɪˈspektfʊl] *adj* irrespetuoso,-a.

disrobe [dɪsˈrəʊb] *vi fml* desvestirse, desnudarse.

disrupt [dɪsˈrʌpt] *vtr (meeting, traffic)* interrumpir; *(order)* trastornar; *(schedule etc)* desbaratar.

disruption [dɪsˈrʌpʃən] *n (of meeting, traffic)* interrupción *f*; *(of order)* trastorno *m*; *(of schedule etc)* desbaratamiento *m*.

disruptive [dɪsˈrʌptɪv] *adj (behaviour, influence)* perjudicial, nocivo,-a; *(person)* que trastorna *or* desorganiza todo.

dissatisfaction [dɪssætɪsˈfækʃən] *n* descontento *m*, insatisfacción *f*.

dissatisfied [dɪsˈsætɪsfaɪd] *adj* descontento,-a, insatisfecho,-a.

dissect [dɪˈsekt, daɪˈsekt] *vtr* disecar.

dissemble [dɪˈsembəl] *vi fml* disimular.

disseminate [dɪˈsemɪneɪt] *vtr fml* diseminar, difundir, propagar.

dissemination [dɪsemɪˈneɪʃən] *n fml* diseminación *f*, difusión *f*, propagación *f*.

dissension [dɪˈsenʃən] *n* disensión *f*, discordia *f*.

dissent [dɪˈsent] **I** *n* disenso *m*, disentimiento *m*. **II** *vi* disentir **(from,** de).

dissenter [dɪˈsentəʳ] *n Rel* disidente *mf*.

dissertation [dɪsəˈteɪʃən] *n (gen)* disertación *f*; *(for master's degree)* tesina *f* **(on,** sobre).

disservice [dɪsˈsɜːvɪs] *n* perjuicio *m*; **to do sth/sb a d.,** perjudicar algo/a algn.

dissident [ˈdɪsɪdənt] *adj & n Pol* disidente *(mf)*.

dissimilar [dɪˈsɪmɪləʳ] *adj* distinto,-a, diferente.

dissimilarity [dɪsɪmɪˈlærɪtɪ] *n* desemejanza *f*, diferencia *f*.

dissimulation [dɪsɪmjʊˈleɪʃən] *n fml* disimulo *m*, disimulación *f*.

dissipate [ˈdɪsɪpeɪt] **I** *vtr* **1** *(clear)* disipar; *(crowd)* dispersar; *fig (doubt, fear)* disipar, desvanecer. **2** *(waste)* derrochar. **II** *vi (fog, cloud)* disiparse; *(crowd)* dispersarse; *fig (doubt, fear)* disiparse, desvanecerse.

dissipated [ˈdɪsɪpeɪtɪd] *adj* disoluto,-a.

dissipation [dɪsɪˈpeɪʃən] *n* **1** *(clearing)* disipación *f*. **2** *(waste)* derroche *m*. **3** *(debauchery)* disolución *f*, libertinaje *m*.

dissociate [dɪˈsəʊʃɪeɪt] *vtr* separar.

dissolute [ˈdɪsəluːt] *adj* disoluto,-a.

dissolution [dɪsəˈluːʃən] *n* disolución *f*; *(of agreement)* rescisión *f*.

dissolve [dɪˈzɒlv] **I** *vtr* disolver. **II** *vi* **1** *(disintegrate)* disolverse; *fig* **to d. in** *or* **into tears/laughter,** deshacerse en lágrimas/en risa. **2** *(disappear)* desvanecerse, esfumarse.

dissuade [dɪˈsweɪd] *vtr* disuadir **(from,** de).

distance [ˈdɪstəns] **I** *n* **1** *(gen)* distancia *f*; **at a (good) d.,** (bastante) lejos; **in the d.,** a lo lejos, en la lejanía; *fam* **it's no d. to the beach,** la playa está a la vuelta de la esquina *or* está a dos pasos; *fam (in race, competition)* **to go/stay**
the d., acabar/completar la prueba. **2** *fig (coldness)* distancia *f*; **to keep sb at a d.,** tratar a algn con frialdad. **II** *vtr* distanciarse, alejarse.

distant [ˈdɪstənt] *adj* **1** *(place)* distante, lejano,-a, remoto,-a, apartado,-a; *(time)* lejano,-a; *(look)* distraído,-a; *(cousin etc)* lejano,-a. **2** *fig (aloof)* distante, frío,-a. ◆
distantly *adv (see, hear)* a lo lejos, de lejos; *(smile)* con frialdad; *(absent-mindedly)* distraídamente.

distaste [dɪsˈteɪst] *n* aversión *f*.

distasteful [dɪsˈteɪstfʊl] *adj (joke)* de mal gusto; *(idea)* desagradable.

distemper¹ [dɪsˈtempəʳ] *n Art* temple *m*.

distemper² [dɪsˈtempəʳ] *n Vet* moquillo *m*.

distend [dɪˈstend] *fml* **I** *vtr* dilatar. **II** *vi* dilatarse.

distil, *US* **distill** [dɪsˈtɪl] *vtr (pt & pp **distilled**)* destilar.

distillation [dɪstɪˈleɪʃən] *n* destilación *f*.

distiller [dɪˈstɪləʳ] *n* destilador,-a *m*,*f*.

distillery [dɪˈstɪlərɪ] *n* destilería *f*.

distinct [dɪˈstɪŋkt] *adj* **1** *(different)* diferente, distinto,-a; **as d. from,** a diferencia de. **2** *(smell, likeness, change)* marcado,-a; *(idea, sign, intention)* claro,-a, evidente; *(tendency)* bien determinado,-a.

distinction [dɪˈstɪŋkʃən] *n* **1** *(difference)* diferencia *f*. **2** *(excellence)* distinción *f*; **a man of d.,** un,-a experto,-a notable *or* distinguido,-a; *iron* **I had the d. of coming last,** tuvo el gran honor de llegar el último. **3** *Educ* sobresaliente *m*; **he got two distinctions,** sacó dos sobresalientes.

distinctive [dɪˈstɪŋktɪv] *adj* distintivo,-a.

distinguish [dɪˈstɪŋgwɪʃ] **I** *vtr* **1** *(differentiate)* distinguir **(from,** de). **2** *(see, hear, taste)* notar, percibir. **3** *(bring honour to)* distinguirse, descollar, destacar. **II** *vi (differentiate)* distinguirse.

distinguishable [dɪˈstɪŋgwɪʃəbəl] *adj* distinguible.

distinguished [dɪˈstɪŋgwɪʃt] *adj (appearance)* distinguido,-a; *(career, position)* distinguido,-a, eminente.

distinguishing [dɪˈstɪŋgwɪʃɪŋ] *adj* distintivo,-a, característico,-a.

distort [dɪˈstɔːt] *vtr* **1** *(misrepresent)* deformar, desfigurar; *(words)* distorsionar. **2** *(contort)* distorsionar; *(shape, object)* deformar.

distortion [dɪˈstɔːʃən] *n* **1** *(of case, motive, truth)* deformación *f*, distorsión *f*. **2** *(of sound, image)* distorsión *f*; *(of shape)* deformación *f*; *(of features)* alteración *f*.

distract [dɪˈstrækt] *vtr (person)* distraer; *(attention)* distraer, desviar, apartar.

distracted [dɪˈstræktɪd] *adj* distraído,-a.

distracting [dɪˈstræktɪŋ] *adj* **1** *(amusing)* que distrae, ameno,-a. **2** *(annoying)* molesto,-a.

distraction [dɪˈstrækʃən] *n* **1** *(interruption)* interrupción *f*, distracción *f*. **2** *(amusement)* distracción *f*, entretenimiento *m*, diversión *f*. **3** *(confusion)* confusión *f*; **to drive sb to d.,** sacar a algn de quicio; **to love sb to d.,** ester loco,-a por algn.

distraught [dɪˈstrɔːt] *adj (anguished)* afligido,-a; *(upset)* turbado,-a; *(crazed)* trastornado,-a, enloquecido,-a.

distress [dɪˈstres] **I** *n* **1** *(mental)* aflicción *f*, angustia *f*; *(physical)* dolor *m*; *(exhaustion)* agotamiento *m*. **2** *(poverty)* miseria *f*; **in economic d.,** en un apuro económico. **3** *(danger)* peligro *m*. ■ **d. call, d. signal,** señal *f* de socorro. **II** *vtr (upset)* dar pena a.

distressing [dɪˈstresɪŋ] *adj* penoso,-a.

distribute [dɪˈstrɪbjuːt] *vtr* distribuir, repartir.

distribution [dɪstrɪˈbjuːʃən] *n* distribución *f*.

distributor [dɪˈstrɪbjutəʳ] *n* **1** *Com* distribuidor,-a *m*,*f*. **2** *Aut* delco *m*.

district ['dɪstrɪkt] *n (of country)* región *f; (of town, city)* barrio *m*, distrito *m*. ▪ *US Jur* **d. attorney,** fiscal *m (de un distrito judicial);* **d. council,** municipio *m;* **d. nurse,** practicante *mf;* **federal d.,** distrito *m* federal; **postal d.,** distrito *m* postal.

distrust [dɪs'trʌst] **I** *n* desconfianza *f,* recelo *m.* **II** *vtr* desconfiar, recelar.

distrustful [dɪs'trʌstful] *adj* desconfiado,-a, receloso,-a.

disturb [dɪ'stɜːb] *vtr* **1** *(inconvenience)* molestar, estorbar; **'do not d.',** 'se ruega no molestar'. **2** *(silence)* romper; *(sleep)* interrumpir; *Jur* **to d. the peace,** alterar el orden público. **3** *(worry)* perturbar, inquietar, preocupar. **4** *(disarrange) (papers)* desordenar; *(lake, grass)* agitar, mover.

disturbance [dɪ'stɜːbəns] *n* **1** *(worry)* preocupación *f,* inquietud *f; (nuisance)* molestia *f.* **2** *(of routine)* alteración *f; (of plans)* desarreglo *m.* **3** *(commotion)* disturbio *m,* alboroto *m.*

disturbed [dɪ'stɜːbd] *adj* desequilibrado,-a, inestable.

disturbing [dɪ'stɜːbɪŋ] *adj* inquietante.

disunity [dɪs'juːnɪtɪ] *n* desunión *f.*

disuse [dɪs'juːs] *n* desuso *m.*

disused [dɪs'juːzd] *adj* abandonado,-a.

ditch [dɪtʃ] **I** *n (gen)* zanja *f; (at roadside)* cuneta *f; (for irrigation)* acequia *f; (round earthworks)* foso *m;* **to make a last-d. attempt to do sth,** hacer un último esfuerzo para conseguir algo. **II** *vtr fam (plane)* hacer un amerizaje forzoso; *(plan, friend)* abandonar; *(relationship, lover)* deshacerse de.

dither ['dɪðəʳ] *fam GB* **I** *n* confusión *f.* **II** *vi* vacilar, titubear; **stop dithering about!,** ¡decídete ya de una vez!

ditto ['dɪtəʊ] **I** *n (pl dittos) (in list)* ídem *m.* **II** *adv fam* lo mismo, ídem; **I love chocolate —d.,** me encanta el chocolate -a mí también.

ditty ['dɪtɪ] *n* cantinela *f.*

diurnal [daɪ'ɜːnəl] *adj* diurno,-a.

divan [dɪ'væn] *n Furn* diván *m.* ▪ **d. (bed),** cama *f* turca.

dive [daɪv] **I** *n* **1** *(into water)* zambullida *f; (of diver)* buceo *m; (of submarine, whale)* inmersión *f; (of plane)* picado *m; (of bird)* descenso *m; Sport* salto *m.* **2** *fam (bar etc)* antro *m.* **II** *vi (US pt also dove)* **1** *(to plunge)* zambullirse, tirarse; *(plane)* bajar en picado; *Sport* saltar; *fig* **he dived into the discussion,** se metió de lleno en la discusión. **2** *(diver)* bucear; *(submarine, whale)* sumergirse. **3** *(person, animal)* meterse rápidamente, precipitarse hacia; **he dived for the phone,** se precipitó hacia el teléfono; *fig* **she dived into her pocket,** se metió la mano rápidamente en el bolsillo. ◆ **dive in** *vi fam (eat)* **d. in!,** ¡a comer!, ¡al ataque!

diver ['daɪvəʳ] *n* **1** *(person)* buceador,-a *m, f; (professional)* buzo *m; Sport* saltador,-a *m, f.* **2** *Orn* colimbo *m.* ▪ **black-throated d.,** colimbo *m* ártico; **great northern d.,** colimbo *m* grande; **red-throated d.,** colimbo *m* chico.

diverge [daɪ'vɜːdʒ] *vi* divergir; *(roads etc)* bifurcarse.

divergence [daɪ'vɜːdʒəns] *n* divergencia *f.*

divergent [daɪ'vɜːdʒənt] *adj* divergente.

diverse [daɪ'vɜːs] *adj* **1** *(varied)* diverso,-a, variado,-a. **2** *(different)* distinto,-a, diferente.

diversify [daɪ'vɜːsɪfaɪ] **I** *vtr (pt & pp diversified)* diversificar. **II** *vi* diversificarse.

diversion [daɪ'vɜːʃən] *n* **1** *(distraction)* distracción *f.* **2** *GB (detour)* desvío *m.*

diversity [daɪ'vɜːsɪtɪ] *n* diversidad *f,* variedad *f.*

divert [daɪ'vɜːt] *vtr* desviar.

divest [daɪ'vest] *vtr* **to d. sb of sth,** quitar algo a algn, desvestir a algn de algo; *fig* despojar a algn de algo.

divide [dɪ'vaɪd] **I** *vtr* **1** *(separate)* dividir, separar; *(classify)* dividir, clasificar, agrupar; **to d. sth in two** *or* **in half,** partir algo por la mitad. **2** *(share)* dividir, repartir. **3** *Math* dividir; **d. 40 by 8,** cuarenta dividido entre *or* por

ocho. **II** *vi* **1** *(separate) (road, stream)* dividirse, bifurcarse. **2** *fig (disagree)* dividirse, enfrentarse; *prov* **d. and rule,** divide y vencerás. **3** *GB Parl* votar. **III** *n* **1** *fml (split)* división *f,* diferencia *f.* **2** *US Geog* línea *f* divisoria de las aguas.

dividend ['dɪvɪdend] *n Com* dividendo *m; fig* beneficio *m,* provecho *m.*

dividers [dɪ'vaɪdəz] *npl* compás *m sing* de puntas.

divination [dɪvɪ'neɪʃən] *n* adivinación *f,* futurología *f.*

divine [dɪ'vaɪn] *adj (gen)* divino,-a; *fam fig (dress, house)* divino,-a, precioso,-a.

diving board ['daɪvɪŋbɔːd] *n* trampolín *m.*

divinity [dɪ'vɪnɪtɪ] *n* **1** *(subject)* teología *f.* **2** *(quality, personage)* divinidad *f.*

divisible [dɪ'vɪzəbəl] *adj* divisible.

division [dɪ'vɪʒən] *n* **1** *(separation)* división *f,* separación *f; (classification)* clasificación *f.* **2** *(sharing)* división *f,* reparto *m.* ▪ **d. of labour,** división *f or* distribución *f* del trabajo. **3** *(of organization)* sección *f; Mil* división *f.* **4** *Math* división *f.* **5** *GB Parl* votación *f* (secreta). **6** *Ftb* división *f.*

divisional [dɪ'vɪʒənəl] *adj (gen)* divisional; *Mil* de división.

divisive [dɪ'vaɪsɪv] *adj* divisivo,-a.

divorce [dɪ'vɔːs] **I** *n* divorcio *m; fig* divorcio *m;* **to get a d.,** obtener el divorcio; **to start d. proceedings,** iniciar los trámites de divorcio. **II** *vtr* divorciar; *fig* divorciar, separar; **she divorced him,** se divorció de él. **III** *vi* divorciarse.

divorcé [dɪ'vɔːseɪ] *n,* **divorcée** [dɪvɔː'siː] *n* divorciado,-a *m, f.*

divulge [daɪ'vʌldʒ] *vtr fml* divulgar, revelar.

dizziness ['dɪzɪnɪs] *n (sickness)* mareo *m; (giddiness)* vértigo *m.*

dizzy ['dɪzɪ] *adj (dizzier, dizziest)* **1** *(person) (unwell, giddy)* mareado,-a. **2** *(height, pace)* vertiginoso,-a.

DIY [diːaɪ'waɪ] *GB abbr of* **do-it-yourself,** bricolaje *m.*

DJ *fam* **1** *GB abbr of* **dinner jacket,** smoking *m.* **2** *abbr of* **disc jockey,** pinchadiscos *m inv,* disc-jockey *mf.*

Djibouti [dʒɪ'buːtɪ] *n* Djibouti, Yibuti.

DLitt [diː'lɪt] *abbr of* **Doctor of Letters,** Doctor,-a *m, f* en Letras.

DNA [diːen'eɪ] *Chem abbr of* **deoxyribonucleic acid,** ácido *m* desoxirribonucleico, ADN *m.*

do [duː, *unstressed* du, də] **I** *v aux (3rd person sing pres does; pt did; pp done)* **1** *(in negatives and questions) (not traslated in Span)* **do you drive?,** ¿tienes carnet de conducir?; **don't you want to come?,** ¿no quieres venir?; **he does not** *or* **doesn't smoke,** no fuma. **2** *(emphatic) (not translated in Span)* **do come with us!,** ¡ánimo, vente con nosotros!; **I do like your bag,** me encanta tu bolso. **3** *(substituting main verb) (in sentence) (not translated in Span)* **I don't believe him —neither do I,** no le creo —yo tampoco; **I'll go if you do,** si vas tú, voy yo; **I think it's dear, but he doesn't,** a mí me parece caro pero a él no; **who went? —I did,** ¿quién asistió? —yo. **4** *(in question tags)* **he refused, didn't he?,** dijo que no, ¿verdad?; **I don't like it, do you?,** a mí no me gusta, ¿y a ti? **II** *vtr* **1** *(gen)* hacer; *(task)* realizar, llevar a cabo; *(puzzle)* solucionar; *(duty)* cumplir con; **are you doing anything?,** ¿estás ocupado,-a?; **he did nothing but laugh,** no hizo más que reír; **that dress doesn't do much for you,** ese vestido no te favorece; **to do business with sb,** hacer negocios con algn; **to do one's best** *or* **all one can,** hacer todo lo posible; **to do sth again,** volver a hacer algo; **to do sth for sb,** hacer algo por algn; **to do the cooking/cleaning,** cocinar/limpiar; **we must do something about it,** tenemos que ocuparnos de ello; **what can I do about it?,** ¿qué quieres que haga?; **what can I do for you?,** ¿en qué puedo servirle?; **what do you do (for a living)?,** ¿a qué te dedicas?, ¿en qué trabajas?;

what's to be done?, ¿qué se puede hacer?; *fam* **he's done it!,** ¡lo ha conseguido!; *fam* **you've done it now!,** ¡buena la has hecho!; *fam* **well done!,** ¡enhorabuena!, ¡muy bien!; *prov* **what's done is done,** a lo hecho, pecho. **2** *(produce, make, offer) (film)* hacer; *(meat, food)* producir; **do you do sportswear?,** ¿aquí venden *or* tienen ropa de deporte? **3** *(study)* estudiar. **4** *(suffice)* bastar; **ten will do us,** con diez tenemos suficiente *or* bastante. **5** *(tour, visit)* recorrer, visitar, ver. **6** *Aut (speed)* ir a; *(distance)* recorrer; **we were doing eighty,** íbamos a ochenta. **7** *GB fam (injure)* **I'll do you if you don't shut up!,** ¡como no te calles te voy a dar! **8** *GB fam* **I've been done!,** ¡me han timado! **III** *vi* **1** *(act, perform, function)* hacer, actuar; **do as I tell you,** haz lo que te digo; **you did right,** hiciste bien. **2** *(proceed)* **he did badly in the exams,** los exámenes le fueron mal; **how are you doing?,** ¿qué tal?, ¿cómo te van las cosas?; **how do you do?,** *(greeting)* ¿cómo está usted?; *(answer)* mucho gusto, encantado,-a (de conocerle); **to do well,** *(person)* tener éxito, salir adelante; *(business)* ir bien. **3** *(suffice)* bastar; **will five pounds do?,** ¿tendrás suficiente *or* bastante con cinco libras?; *fam* **that will do!,** ¡basta ya!, ¡ya está bien! **4** *(be suitable)* servir; **this cushion will do for** *or* as a pillow, este cojín servirá de almohada; **this won't do,** esto no puede ser. **IV** *n* *(pl dos or do's* [du:z]*) fam* **1** *GB (party)* fiesta *f*, guateque *m*; *(gathering)* celebración *f*; *(event)* ceremonia *f*. **2** **do's and don'ts,** reglas *fpl* de conducta. ◆ **do away with** *vtr* **1** *(abolish)* abolir, suprimir; *(discard)* deshacerse de. **2** *(kill)* asesinar. ◆ **do down** *vtr fam* **1** *(humiliate)* hacer quedar mal, rebajar. **2** *(cheat)* estafar, timar. ◆ **do for** *fam* **I** *vtr (destroy, ruin)* arruinar, destrozar; *fig* **I'm done for if I don't finish this,** estoy perdido,-a si no acabo esto. **II** *vi* llevar la casa a; **Amanda has been doing for them since their mother died,** Amanda lleva la casa desde que murió su madre. ◆ **do in** *vtr sl* **1** *(kill)* matar, cargarse. **2** *(exhaust)* agotar; **I'm done in,** estoy hecho,-a polvo. ◆ **do out** *vtr fam* **1** *GB (clean)* limpiar a fondo; *(decorate)* decorar. **2 to do sb out of sth,** quitarle algo a algn por engaño. ◆ **do over** *vtr fam* **1** *US (repeat)* repetir, volver a hacer, hacer de nuevo. **2** *(redecorate)* decorar. **3** *GB (thrash)* dar una paliza a. ◆ **do up** *vtr* **1** *(wrap)* envolver. **2** *(fasten) (belt etc)* abrochar; *(laces)* atar. **3** *(dress up)* arreglar; **she was really done up,** se había puesto guapísima. **4** *fam (redecorate)* renovar, decorar. ◆ **do with** *vtr* **1** *(need)* **I could do with a rest,** un descanso me vendría muy bien *or* no me vendría nada mal. **2** *(concern)* **to have** *or* **be to do with,** tener que ver con, tratarse de. ◆ **do without** *vtr* pasar sin, prescindir de; **I can't do without your help,** no puedo pasar sin tu ayuda.

doc [dɒk] *n (abbr of doctor) fam* doctor *m*.

docile ['dəʊsaɪl] *adj (person)* dócil, sumiso,-a; *(animal)* manso,-a.

dock¹ [dɒk] **I** *n Naut (gen)* muelle *m*; *(for cargo)* dársena *f*; **to work on** *or* **at the docks,** trabajar en el puerto. ■ **dry d.,** dique *m* seco. **II** *vtr* **1** *(ship)* atracar **(at,** en). **2** *(spacecraft)* acoplar. **III** *vi* **1** *(ship)* atracar. **2** *(spacecraft)* acoplarse.

dock² [dɒk] *n (tail)* cola *f*, rabo *m*. **II** *vtr* **1** *(tail)* descolar, cortar la cola a. **2** *(reduce)* deducir, descontar.

dock³ [dɒk] *n Jur* the *d.,* el banquillo (de los acusados).

docker ['dɒkə'] *n* estibador *m*.

docket ['dɒkɪt] *GB* **I** *n (label)* rótulo *m*, etiqueta *f*. ■ **customs d.,** recibo *m* de aduanas. **II** *vtr* rotular.

dockland ['dɒklænd] *n* zona *f* del puerto.

dockyard ['dɒkjɑːd] *n* astillero *m*.

doctor ['dɒktə'] **I** *n* **1** *Med* médico,-a *m,f*, doctor,-a *m,f*; **D. Jane Wells,** la doctora Jane Wells. ■ **family d.,** médico,-a *m,f* de cabecera. **2** *Univ* doctor,-a *m,f*; **D. of Law,** doctor en derecho. **II** *vtr* **1** *pej (tamper with) (figures, bill)* falsificar; *(text)* arreglar, amañar; *(food, drink)* adulterar. **2** *GB (castrate)* castrar, esterilizar.

doctoral ['dɒktərəl] *adj* doctoral.

doctorate ['dɒktərɪt] *n Educ* doctorado *m*.

doctrinal [dɒk'traɪnəl] *adj* doctrinal.

doctrine ['dɒktrɪn] *n* doctrina *f*.

document ['dɒkjʊmənt] **I** *n (gen)* documento *m*. ■ **legal d.,** escritura *f* (pública); **travel documents,** documentación *f* para viajar. **II** *vtr* documentar.

documentary [dɒkjʊ'mentərɪ] *adj & n* documental *(m)*.

documentation [dɒkjʊmen'teɪʃən] *n* documentación *f*.

dodder ['dɒdə'] *vi fam (of old person)* andar con paso inseguro.

doddle ['dɒdəl] *n GB fam* pan *m* comido; **it's a d.!,** ¡está chupado!

dodge [dɒdʒ] **I** *vtr* **1** *(avoid) (blow etc)* esquivar; *(pursuer)* despistar, dar esquinazo a; *(queue etc)* evitar; *fig* evitar, esquivar, soslayar. **2** *fam (evade) (tax)* evadir; *(class, meeting)* fumarse; *(punishment, commitment)* librarse *or* zafarse de. **II** *vi (move aside)* echarse a un lado. **III** *n* **1** *(movement)* regate *m*, evasión *f*. **2** *fam (trick)* truco *m*, astucia *f*; **to be up to all the dodges,** sabérselas todas. ■ **tax d.,** elusión *f* fiscal *or* de impuestos.

Dodgem® ['dɒdʒəm] *n fam* **d. (car),** auto *m* de choque.

dodgy ['dɒdʒɪ] *adj (dodgier, dodgiest) GB fam* **1** *(risky)* arriesgado,-a; *(tricky)* difícil, problemático,-a. **2** *(person)* poco honesto,-a, que no es de fiar.

dodo ['dəʊdəʊ] *n (pl dodos or dodoes) Orn* dodo *m*; *fam fig* **as dead as a d.,** muerto y bien muerto.

doe [dəʊ] *n inv (of deer)* gama *f*; *(of rabbit)* coneja *f*; *(of hare)* liebre *f*.

DOE [di:əʊ'i:] *GB abbr of Department of the Environment,* Departamento *m* del Medio Ambiente.

doer ['du:ə'] *n fam* persona *f* dinámica.

does [dʌz] *3rd person sing pres see do.*

doesn't ['dʌzənt] = **does not**

dog [dɒg] **I** *n* **1** *Zool* perro,-a *m, f*; **to d.-paddle,** nadar como los perros; *fig* **d. eat d.,** competencia *f* despiadada; *fig* **not to have a d.'s chance,** no tener ni la más remota posibilidad; *GB fam* **to be dressed (up) like a d.'s dinner,** estar hecho,-a un cromo; *US fam* **to put on the d.,** darse pisto; *fam fig* **a d.'s life,** una vida de perros; *prov* **every d. has his day,** a cada cerdo le llega su San Martín; *prov* **let sleeping dogs lie,** las cosas como están; *prov* **you can't teach an old d. new tricks,** loro viejo no aprende a hablar. ■ **d. collar,** *(of dog)* collar *m* de perro; *Rel fam* alzacuello *m*; **d. show,** exhibición *f* canina; **guard d.,** perro *m* guardián; **pedigree d.,** perro *m* de raza. **2** *(male canine)* macho *m*; *(fox)* zorro *m*; *(wolf)* lobo *m*. **3** *GB Sport fam* **the dogs,** carreras *fpl* de galgos; *fig* **to go to the dogs,** arruinarse. **4** *fam (fellow)* **dirty d.,** canalla *m*, sinvergüenza *m*; **lucky d.,** tío *m* con suerte. **5** *US fam (disappointment)* desastre *m*, fracaso *m*. **II** *vtr (pt & pp dogged) (pursue)* seguir de cerca, acosar; **to d. sb's footsteps,** seguir los pasos de algn; *fig* **dogged by bad luck,** perseguido,-a por la mala suerte.

dogcart ['dɒgkɑːt] *n* coche *m* de un solo caballo.

dog-eared ['dɒgɪəd] *adj (newspaper, book)* con los bordes de la páginas doblados; *(shabby)* sobado,-a.

dogfight ['dɒgfaɪt] *n* **1** *Av* combate *m* aéreo. **2** *(between dogs)* pelea *f* entre perros; *fig* altercado *m*.

dogfish ['dɒgfɪʃ] *n inv cazón m*, perro *m* marino.

dogged ['dɒgɪd] *adj (refusal)* obstinado,-a; *(determination)* tenaz, persistente.

doggerel ['dɒgərəl] *n sing Lit* aleluyas *fpl*.

doggie ['dɒgɪ] *n see* **doggy.**

doggo ['dɒgəʊ] *adv GB fam* **to lie d.,** permanecer escondido,-a.

doggone ['dɒgɒn] *adj US fam euph see* **damned.**

doggy ['dɒgɪ] **I** *n (child's talk)* perrito,-a *m, f*. ■ **d. bag,** bolsa *f* para el perro. **II** *adj (fond of dogs)* aficionado,-a a los perros.

doghouse ['dɒghaʊs] *n US fam* perrera *f*; *fig* **to be in the d.,** tener la negra.

dogma ['dɒgmə] n (pl **dogmas** or **dogmata** ['dɒgmətə]) Rel Pol dogma m.

dogmatic [dɒg'mætɪk] adj dogmático,-a.

do-gooder [duːˈgʊdər] n fam persona f bien intencionada.

dogsbody ['dɒgzbɒdɪ] n GB fam (drudge) burro m de carga.

dog-tired ['dɒgtaɪəd] adj fam rendido,-a, hecho,-a polvo.

doh [dəʊ] n Mus do m.

doily ['dɔɪlɪ] n (of paper) tapete m decorativo (de papel).

doing ['duːɪŋ] n 1 (action) obra f; **it was none of my d.,** yo no tuve nada que ver; fig **it took some d.,** costó trabajo hacerlo. **2 doings,** (activities) actividades fpl.

do-it-yourself [duːɪtjəˈself] n bricolaje m. ■ **do-it-y. shop,** tienda f de bricolaje.

doldrums ['dɒldrəmz] npl fam fig **to be in the d.,** (person) estar deprimido,-a or abatido,-a; (business, trade) estar estancado,-a.

dole [dəʊl] I n GB fam **the d.,** el paro; **to be** or **go on the d.,** estar en el paro. ■ fig **d. queue,** los parados, II vtr **to d. (out),** repartir.

doleful ['dəʊlfʊl] adj triste, afligido,-a.

doll [dɒl] I n 1 (toy) muñeca f. 2 US sl (girl) muñeca f. II vtr sl (girl etc) **to d. oneself up,** ponerse guapa, arreglarse.

dollar ['dɒlər] n dólar m. ■ **d. bill,** billete m de un dólar.

dollop ['dɒləp] n fam cucharada f; (of ice cream) porción f.

dolly ['dɒlɪ] n 1 (child's talk) muñeca f. 2 GB sl **d. (bird),** muñeca f.

Dolomites ['dɒləmaɪts] npl the **D.,** las Dolomitas.

dolphin ['dɒlfɪn] n Zool delfín m.

dolt [dəʊlt] n idiota mf, tonto,-a m,f, mentecato,-a m,f.

domain [dəˈmeɪn] n 1 (sphere) campo m, esfera f; **that's not my d.,** no es de mi competencia. 2 (territory) dominio m.

dome [dəʊm] n Archit (roof) cúpula f; (ceiling) bóveda f; fam fig (head) coronilla f.

domestic [dəˈmestɪk] I adj 1 (appliance, pet) doméstico,-a; **d. bliss,** felicidad conyugal; **d. troubles,** problemas familiares. ■ Educ **d. science,** economía f doméstica. 2 (home-loving) hogareño,-a, casero,-a. 3 (national) (flight, news) nacional; (trade, policy) interior. II n **d. (help),** servicio m doméstico.

domesticate [dəˈmestɪkeɪt] vtr 1 (animal) domesticar; (plant) aclimatar. 2 (make home-loving) volver hogareño,-a or casero,-a.

domesticity [dəʊmeˈstɪsɪtɪ] n vida f casera.

domicile ['dɒmɪsaɪl] n Jur domicilio m.

dominance ['dɒmɪnəns] n dominio m, control m.

dominant ['dɒmɪnənt] adj dominante.

dominate ['dɒmɪneɪt] vtr & vi dominar.

domineering [dɒmɪˈnɪərɪŋ] adj pej dominante, autoritario,-a; (woman) marimandona.

Dominica [dəˈmɪnɪkə] n Dominica.

Dominican [dəˈmɪnɪkən] adj & n 1 (of Dominica) dominicano,-a (m, f). ■ **D. Republic,** República f Dominicana. 2 Rel dominicano,-a (m,f).

dominion [dəˈmɪnjən] n dominio m.

domino ['dɒmɪnəʊ] n (pl **dominoes**) (piece) ficha f de dominó; (game) **dominoes,** dominó m sing.

don[1] [dɒn] vtr (pt & pp **donned**) fml ponerse.

don[2] [dɒn] n GB Univ catedrático,-a m,f.

donate [dəʊˈneɪt] vtr (money) hacer un donativo de; (books, clothes) donar; (property) hacer donación de.

donation [dəʊˈneɪʃən] n 1 (gift) donativo m. 2 (act) donación f.

done [dʌn] I pp see **do.** II adj 1 (finished) terminado,-a, acabado,-a, completado,-a; **I'm** or **I've d. with the matter,** no quiero tener más que ver con el asunto; **it's over and d. with,** se acabó; fam **d.!,** ¡trato hecho! 2 fam (tired) rendido,-a, agotado,-a. 3 (cooked) (meat) hecho,-a; (vegetables) cocido,-a; **d. to a turn,** en su punto. 4 GB (acceptable) **it's not d. to ...,** es de mal gusto ...; **it's the d. thing,** es de rigor, es lo que se hace.

donkey ['dɒŋkɪ] n (animal, person) burro,-a m,f; fam **I haven't seen you for d.'s years,** hace siglos que no te veo. ■ GB fig **d. jacket,** chaqueta f gruesa de obrero.

donor ['dəʊnər] n donante m.

don't [dəʊnt] ≈ **do not.**

donut ['dəʊnʌt] n US see **doughnut.**

doodle ['duːdəl] fam I vi (write) garabatear (distraídamente); (draw) hacer dibujos. II n (writing) garabato m; (drawing) dibujo m.

doom [duːm] I n (fate) destino m (funesto); (ruin) perdición f; (death) muerte f. II vtr usu pass (destine) destinar; (condemn) condenar; **doomed to failure,** condenado,-a al fracaso.

doomsday ['duːmzdeɪ] n Rel día m del juicio final; fam fig **till D.,** para siempre.

door [dɔːr] n 1 (entrance) puerta f; **front/back d.,** puerta principal/trasera; **to answer the d.,** ir a abrir la puerta; **to be at the d.,** estar en la puerta; **to be on the d.,** hacer de portero; **to knock at the d.,** llamar a la puerta; **to see sb to the d.,** acompañar a algn hasta la puerta or la salida; **to slam the d.,** dar un portazo; fig **behind closed doors,** a puerta cerrada; fig **to get in by the back d.,** colarse por la puerta falsa; fig **to lay sth at sb's d.,** echar la culpa de algo a algn; fig **to show sb the d.,** echar a algn (a la calle); fig **to shut** or **slam the d. in sb's face,** darle a algn con la puerta en las narices. ■ **d. handle,** manilla f (de la puerta); **d. knocker,** picaporte m; **revolving d.,** puerta f giratoria; **sliding d.,** puerta f corredera. 2 (house, building) casa f, puerta f; **next d. (to),** (en) la casa de al lado (de); **two doors up/down (the street),** en la segunda casa calle arriba/abajo.

doorbell ['dɔːbel] n timbre m (de la puerta).

doorknob ['dɔːnɒb] n pomo m (de la puerta).

doorman ['dɔːmən] n (pl **doormen**) portero m.

doormat ['dɔːmæt] n felpudo m, esterilla f; fam fig (person) trapo m.

doornail ['dɔːneɪl] n fam **as dead as a d.,** muerto,-a y bien muerto,-a.

doorstep ['dɔːstep] n peldaño m; fig **on one's d.,** al lado de casa.

doorstop ['dɔːstɒp] n (to prevent over-opening) tope m (de puerta); (to prop open) cuña f (de puerta).

door-to-door [dɔːtəˈdɔːr] adj a domicilio.

doorway ['dɔːweɪ] n portal m, entrada f; **he stood in the d.,** se quedó en la puerta.

dope [dəʊp] I n 1 sl (illegal drug) chocolate m; **to take** or **be on d.,** drogarse. ■ **d. addict,** drogadicto,-a m,f. 2 fam (person) imbécil mf, pelmazo mf. 3 fam (news) información f confidencial, soplo m. II vtr (food, drink) adulterar con drogas; Sport (athlete, horse) drogar, dopar.

dop(e)y ['dəʊpɪ] adj (dopier, dopiest) fam 1 (sleepy) medio dormido,-a; (fuddled) atontado,-a. 2 sl (silly) torpe, tonto,-a.

Dordogne [dɔːˈdɒn] n Dordoña.

dorm [dɔːm] n fam abbr of **dormitory.**

dormant ['dɔːmənt] adj (gen) inactivo,-a; fig (rivalry) latente; fig **the idea lay d. in her mind,** le bullía la idea en la cabeza.

dormer ['dɔːmər] n **d. (window),** buhardilla f.

dormitory ['dɔːmɪtərɪ] n 1 (in school, hostel) dormitorio m. ■ GB **d. suburb** or **town,** ciudad f dormitorio. 2 US (in university) residencia f, colegio m mayor.

dorsal ['dɔːsəl] adj Anat dorsal.

dosage ['dəʊsɪdʒ] n fml (amount) dosis f inv; (on medicine bottle) posología f.

dose [dəʊs] I n dosis f inv; fig **a nasty d. of flu**, un ataque fuerte de gripe, II vtr (patient) medicar; **he's always dosing himself (up) with pills**, siempre se está automedicando con pastillas.

doss [dɒs] vi GB sl dormir, clapar; **I'll just d. (down) on the sofa**, me echaré a dormir or me acostaré en el sofá.

dosser ['dɒsəʳ] n GB sl vago,-a m,f, gandul,-a m,f.

dosshouse ['dɒshaʊs] n GB sl pensión f barata or de mala muerte.

dossier ['dɒsɪeɪ] n expediente m, dossier m; **to keep a d. on sth/sb**, abrir un expediente sobre algo/a algn.

dot [dɒt] I n punto m; **at two on the d.**, **on the d. of two**, a las dos en punto; fam **the year d.**, el año de la pera. II vtr (pt & pp **dotted**) 1 (letter) poner el punto a; fam **to d. one's i's and cross one's t's**, poner los puntos sobre las íes. 2 (scatter) esparcir, desparramar; **fields dotted with daisies**, campos salpicados de margaritas.

dotage ['dəʊtɪdʒ] n chochez f; **to be in one's d.**, estar chocho,-a.

dote [dəʊt] vi chochear.

double ['dʌbəl] I adj (gen) doble; Tel **d. six five nine**, sesenta y seis cincuenta y nueve; **he's d. my age**, me dobla la edad; **it's d. the price**, cuesta dos veces más; **to reach d. figures**, ascender a una cantidad de dos cifras; **written with a d. 't'**, escrito,-a con dos tes; GB fam **it's d. Dutch to me**, me suena a chino; fam **to do a d. take**, reaccionar tarde. ■ **d. agent**, agente mf doble; Mus **d. bass**, contrabajo m; **d. bed**, cama f de matrimonio; Cin Theat **d. bill**, programa m doble; **d. check**, segundo repaso m, segunda verificación f or revisión f; **d. chin**, papada f; GB **d. cream**, nata f para montar; **d. glazing**, ventana f doble; **d. standard**, doble moral m; **d. talk**, palabras fpl ambiguas; **d. time**, (pay) paga f doble; (time) horas fpl extra. II adv doble; **sheets folded by d.**, sábanas dobladas por la mitad; **to be bent d.**, estar encorvado,-a. III n 1 (lookalike) imagen f viva, vivo retrato m; Cin Theat (substitute) doble m. 2 (amount) doble m; **to earn d.**, ganar el doble, ganar dos veces más; fam **at** or **on the d.**, enseguida, corriendo. 3 Ten **doubles**, partido n sing de dobles; **men's/ladies' d.**, partido de dobles masculino/femenino. IV vtr 1 (gen) doblar, duplicar; fig (efforts) redoblar. 2 (bend, fold) doblar; **she doubled (back or over) the sheet**, dobló la sábana para hacer reborde. V vi 1 (increase) doblarse, duplicarse. 2 (serve) **to d. as sth/sb**, hacer las veces de algo/de algn. 3 (turn sharply) girar bruscamente. ◆ **double back** vi **to d. back on one's tracks**, volver sobre sus pasos. ◆ **double up I** vtr (bend) doblar; **to be doubled up with** or **in pain**, retorcerse de dolor. II vi 1 (bend) doblarse; **to d. up with laughter**, mondarse or partirse de risa. 2 (share room) compartir la habitación (with, con).

double-barrelled, US **double-barreled** ['dʌbəlbærəld] adj 1 (gun) de dos cañones. 2 GB (surname) compuesto,-a.

double-breasted ['dʌbəlbrestɪd] adj (garment) cruzado,-a.

double-check [dʌbəl'tʃek] vtr & vi repasar or verificar or revisar dos veces.

double-cross [dʌbəl'krɒs] fam I vtr engañar, traicionar. II n engaño m, traición f.

double-dealing [dʌbəl'diːlɪŋ] n fig duplicidad f, doblez f.

double-decker [dʌbəl'dekəʳ] n 1 GB **d.-d. (bus)**, autobús m de dos pisos. 2 US fam **d.-d. (sandwich)**, sandwich m doble.

double-edged [dʌbəl'edʒd] adj de doble filo.

double-jointed [dʌbəl'dʒɔɪntɪd] adj con articulaciones dobles.

double-park [dʌbəl'pɑːk] vtr & vi Aut aparcar en doble fila.

doubt [daʊt] I n (gen) duda f; (uncertainty) incertidumbre f; **beyond (all reasonable) d.**, sin duda alguna, fuera de (toda) duda; **if** or **when in d.**, en caso de duda; **no d.**, sin duda, seguramente; **there's no d. about it**, no cabe la menor duda; **there's some d. whether he'll go**, no se sabe si irá; **to be in d. about sth**, dudar algo; **to be in d., be open to d.**, (fact, integrity) ser dudoso,-a; (outcome) ser incierto,-a; **to cast d. on sth**, poner algo en duda or en tela de juicio. II vtr 1 (distrust) dudar de, desconfiar de. 2 (not be sure of) dudar; **I d. if** or **whether he'll come**, dudo que or no creo que venga; **I very much d. it**, lo dudo mucho.

doubter ['daʊtəʳ] n Pol Rel escéptico,-a m,f.

doubtful ['daʊtful] adj 1 (uncertain) (future) dudoso,-a incierto,-a; (look, feeling) dubitativo,-a, de duda; **I'm a bit d. about it**, no me convence del todo; **it's d. whether ...**, no se sabe seguro si ... . 2 (questionable) dudoso,-a, sospechoso,-a.

doubtless ['daʊtlɪs] I adv sin duda, seguramente. II adj indudable.

douche [duːʃ] n Med (process) irrigación f; (instrument) irrigador m.

dough [dəʊ] n 1 Culin (for bread) masa f; (for pastries) pasta f. 2 sl (money) pasta f.

doughnut ['dəʊnʌt] n rosquilla f, dónut® m. ■ **jam/cream d.**, rosquilla f rellena de mermelada/nata.

dour [dʊəʳ] adj hosco,-a.

Douro ['dʊərəʊ] n the D., el Duero.

douse [daʊs] vtr 1 (soak) mojar. 2 (extinguish) apagar.

dove¹ [dʌv] n paloma f. ■ **collared d.**, tórtola f turca; **stock d.**, paloma f zurita; **turtle d.**, tórtola f común.

dove² [dəʊv] pt US see **dive**.

dovetail ['dʌvteɪl] I n Tech **d. (joint)**, cola f de milano. II vtr fig (plans) sincronizar.

dowager ['daʊədʒəʳ] n 1 (widower) viuda f (de un noble); **d. countess**, condesa f viuda. 2 fam vieja dama f.

dowdy ['daʊdɪ] adj (dowdier, dowdiest) sin gracia, poco elegante or atractivo,-a.

dowel ['daʊəl] n Carp clavija f.

down¹ [daʊn] I prep 1 (to or at a lower level) (hacia) abajo; **d. the hill/river**, cuesta/río abajo; **he ran a finger d. the list**, recorrió la lista con el dedo; **to go d. the road**, bajar la calle. 2 (along) por; **cut it d. the middle**, córtalo por la mitad. II adv 1 (to lower level) (hacia) abajo; (to floor) al suelo; (to ground) a tierra; **to drink sth d.**, beberse hasta la última gota de algo; **to fall d.**, caerse; **to go d.**, (price, person) bajar; (sun) ponerse; fig **to come d. in the world**, venir a menos. 2 (at lower level) abajo; **d. here/there**, aquí/allí abajo; **face d.**, boca abajo; **he's just d. from Scotland**, acaba de llegar de Escocia; fig **he can't keep food d.**, no retiene la comida; fig **to be d. with a cold**, estar resfriado,-a; fam fig **to feel d.**, estar deprimido,-a. ■ fam fig **d. under**, Australia f, Nueva Zelanda f. 3 (of smaller size, volume) **I'm d. to my last stamp**, no me queda más que un solo sello; **sales are d. by five percent**, las ventas han bajado un cinco por ciento; **the tyres are d.**, los neumáticos están desinflados; **to put prices d.**, reducir los precios; fig **I'm one pound d.**, me falta una libra. 4 (in writing) **I'm d. for the French course**, me he matriculado para el cursillo de francés; **to take** or **write sth d.**, apuntar algo; **to be d. in writing**, estar puesto,-a por escrito. 5 (in succession) **d. through the ages**, a través de los siglos; **from 1800 d. to the present day**, desde 1800 hasta el día de hoy. 6 (as payment) **to pay ten pounds d.**, pagar diez libras al contado como paga y señal. III adj 1 (train) que va hacia las afueras; (escalator, draught) de bajada. 2 (payment) al contado; (on property) de entrada. IV vtr 1 (knock over) derribar; (defeat) derrotar. 2 fam (drink) tomarse de un trago; (food) zamparse. V n 1 (misfortune) desgracia f; **ups and downs**, altibajos mpl, vicisitudes fpl. 2 fam (dislike) **to have a d. on sb**, guardarle rencor a algn, tenerle manía a algn. VI interj **d.!**, (to dog) ¡quieto!; **d. with taxes!**, ¡abajo los impuestos!

down² [daʊn] *n* **1** *(on bird)* plumón *m*. **2** *(on cheek, peach)* pelusa *f*, pelusilla *f*; *(on body)* vello *m*.

down-and-out ['daʊnənaʊt] **I** *adj* en las últimas. **II** *n (pl* **down-and-outs)** vagabundo,-a *m, f*.

downbeat ['daʊnbiːt] *adj fam (gloomy)* triste, deprimido,-a.

downcast ['daʊnkɑːst] *adj* abatido,-a, desalentado,-a; **with d. eyes,** con los ojos bajos.

downer ['daʊnəʳ] *n sl (drug)* calmante *m*, sedante *m*; *fig* **to be on a d.,** estar depre.

downfall ['daʊnfɔːl] *n (of régime)* caída *f*; *(of person)* perdición *f*, ruina *f*.

downgrade ['daʊngreɪd] *vtr* degradar.

downhearted [daʊn'hɑːtɪd] *adj* desalentado,-a, descorazonado,-a.

downhill [daʊn'hɪl] **I** *adj (road etc)* en pendiente; *(skiing)* de descenso; *fam* **after his first exam, the rest were all d.,** después del primer examen, los demás le fueron sobre ruedas. **II** *adv (slide)* cuesta abajo; **to go d.,** *(gen)* ir cuesta abajo; *fig (person, health)* desmejorar; *fig (standards)* perderse.

down-market [daʊn'mɑːkɪt] *adj Com* barato,-a, de baja calidad.

downpour ['daʊnpɔːʳ] *n* chaparrón *m*, aguacero *m*.

downright ['daʊnraɪt] *fam* **I** *adj (blunt)* tajante; *(categorical)* categórico,-a; **a d. fool,** un tonto de remate; **it's a d. lie,** es una mentira y gorda. **II** *adv (totally)* completamente.

downstairs [daʊn'steəz] **I** *adv* abajo; *(to ground floor)* a la planta baja; **to go d.,** bajar la escalera. **II** *adj (rooms) (on ground floor)* de la planta baja.

downstream [daʊn'striːm] *adv* río abajo.

down-to-earth [daʊntʊ'ɜːθ] *adj* práctico,-a, realista.

downtown [daʊn'taʊn] *US* **I** *adv* al *or* en el centro (de la ciudad). **II** *adj* céntrico,-a; **d. New York,** el centro de Nueva York.

downtrodden ['daʊntrɒdən] *adj* oprimido,-a, pisoteado,-a.

downturn ['daʊntɜːn] *n* baja *f*, reducción *f*.

downward ['daʊnwəd] *adj (slope)* descendente; *(look)* hacia abajo; *Fin (tendency)* a la baja.

downward(s) ['daʊnwəd(z)] *adv (gen)* hacia abajo; **face d.,** boca abajo.

dowry ['daʊərɪ] *n* dote *f*.

dowse [daʊs] *vtr see* **douse.**

doyl(e)y ['dɔɪlɪ] *n see* **doily.**

doz *abbr of* **dozen,** docena *f*, doc.

doze [daʊz] **I** *vi* dormitar, echar una cabezada. **II** *n* cabezada *f*; **to have a d.,** echar una cabezada. ◆ **doze off** *vi* quedarse dormido,-a, dormirse.

dozen ['dʌzən] *n* docena *f*; **half a d./a d. eggs,** media docena/una docena de huevos; **twenty pence a d.,** veinte peniques la docena; *fam* **dozens of,** *(times)* miles de, cantidad de; *(things, people)* un montón de.

DPh, DPhil *abbr of* **Doctor of Philosophy,** Doctor,-a *m, f* en Filosofía.

DPP [diːpiː'piː] *GB Jur abbr of* **Director of Public Prosecutions,** Director,-a *m, f* del Ministerio Público *or* Fiscal.

Dr *Med Univ abbr of* **Doctor,** Doctor,-a *m, f*, Dr., Dra.

drab [dræb] *adj (drabber, drabbest)* **1** *(ugly)* feo,-a; *(dreary)* monótono,-a, gris. **2** *(colour)* pardo,-a.

drachma ['drækmə] *n (pl* **drachmas** *or* **drachmae** ['drækmiː]) *(coin)* dracma *f*.

Draconian [drə'kəʊnɪən] *adj pej* draconiano,-a.

draft [drɑːft] **I** *n* **1** *(of letter, speech)* borrador *m*; *(of plot)* esbozo *m*, bosquejo *m*. **2** *(bill of exchange)* letra *f* de cambio, giro *m*. **3** *US* servicio *m* militar obligatorio. ■ **d.**

dodger, prófugo *m*. **4** *US see* **draught. II** *vtr* **1** *(letter)* hacer un borrador de; *(novel)* esbozar, bosquejar. **2** *US Mil* reclutar.

draftsman ['drɑːftsmən] *n (pl* **draftsmen)** *US see* **draughtsman.**

draftsmanship ['drɑːftsmənʃɪp] *n US see* **draughtsmanship.**

drafty ['drɑːftɪ] *adj (draftier, draftiest) US see* **draughty.**

drag [dræg] **I** *vtr (pt & pp* **dragged) 1** *(pull)* arrastrar; **to d. sb out of bed,** sacar a algn de la cama; *fig* **to d. one's feet** *or* **heels (over sth),** dar largas a (algo); *fig* **we couldn't d. ourselves away from the scene,** nos fue imposible marcharnos del lugar. **2** *(trawl)* dragar, rastrear. **II** *vi* **1** *(trail, be pulled)* arrastrarse. **2** *(go slowly) (person)* rezagarse, quedarse atrás; *(film, time)* hacerse largo,-a. **III** *n* **1** *Tech (force)* resistencia *f* (aerodinámica); *fig (hindrance)* estorbo *m*; **to be a d. on progress,** poner trabas al progreso. **2** *fam (nuisance)* lata *f*; **the party was a d.,** la fiesta fue un rollo. **3** *fam (on cigarette etc)* calada *f*, chupada *f*. **4** *sl (man)* **to be in d.,** ir vestido de mujer. ■ **d. artist,** travesti *mf*, travestí *mf*. **5** *US sl (street)* calle *f*. ◆ **drag off,** **drag away** *vtr* llevar *or* llevarse arrastrando. ◆ **drag down** *vtr (depress)* deprimir, hundir. ◆ **drag in** *vtr (subject)* arrastrar por los cabellos; **don't d. me into it,** a mí no me metas. ◆ **drag on** *vi (war, strike)* prolongarse, hacerse in terminable. ◆ **drag out** *vtr (speech, meeting)* alargar, prolongar. ◆ **drag up** *vtr fam* **1** *(revive)* sacar a relucir. **2** *GB (child)* criar a la buena de Dios.

dragon ['drægən] *n Myth* dragón *m*; *fam fig (woman)* bruja *f*.

dragonfly ['drægənflaɪ] *n* libélula *f*.

dragoon [drə'guːn] **I** *n Mil* dragón *m*. **II** *vtr* **to d. sb into doing sth,** obligar a algn a hacer algo.

drain [dreɪn] **I** *n* **1** *(pipe) (for* water) desagüe *m*, desaguadero *m*; *(for sewage)* alcantarilla *f*; **the drains,** el alcantarillado. **2** *(grating)* alcantarilla *f*, sumidero *m*; *fam fig* **to go down the d.,** *(money)* esfumarse; *(work)* echarse a perder; *(business)* fracasar. **3** *fig (on energy)* pérdida *f*, disminución *f* **(on,** de); **the boys are a d. on her strength,** los niños le dejan agotada. **II** *vtr* **1** *(dry out) (marsh etc)* avenar; *(reservoir, region)* desecar, desaguar. **2 to d. (off),** *(glasses etc)* escurrir; *(person)* drenar. **3** *(empty) (radiator)* vaciar; *(glass)* apurar; *fig (wound, capital, etc)* agotar. **III** *vi* **1** *(crockery etc)* escurrirse; **the colour drained from her cheeks,** quedó pálida. **2 to d. (away),** *(liquid)* irse; *fig (run out)* agotarse; *fig (disappear)* desaparecer.

drainage ['dreɪnɪdʒ] *n (of marsh etc)* avenamiento *m*; *(of reservoir, region)* desagüe *m*, desecación *f*; *(of town etc)* alcantarillado *m*; *(of building)* desagüe *m*.

drainpipe ['dreɪnpaɪp] *n* tubo *m* de desagüe.

drake [dreɪk] *n Orn* pato *m* (macho).

dram [dræm] *n fam* trago *m* (de whisky).

drama ['drɑːmə] *n* **1** *(play)* obra *f* de teatro, drama *m*; *fig* drama; *fig* **human d.,** drama humano. **2** *Lit (subject)* teatro *m*.

dramatic [drə'mætɪk] *adj* **1** *(change, reduction)* impresionante, notable; *(moment)* emocionante; *(entrance)* teatral, afectado,-a. **2** *Theat* dramático,-a, teatral.

dramatics [drə'mætɪks] *n (acting)* teatro *m*; *esp pej* afectación *f*.

dramatist ['dræmətɪst] *n* dramaturgo,-a *m, f*.

dramatization [dræmətaɪ'zeɪʃən] *n* adaptación *f* teatral, dramatización *f*.

dramatize ['dræmətaɪz] **I** *vtr* **1** *(adapt)* hacer una adaptación teatral de. **2** *pej (exaggerate)* dramatizar. **II** *vi pej* dramatizar, exagerar.

drank [dræŋk] *pt see* **drink.**

drape [dreɪp] **I** *vtr* **1** *(cloth)* drapear; **chairs draped with** *or* **in sheets,** sillas cubiertas con sábanas. **2** *(part of body)* dejar colgado,-a. **II** *n* **1** *(of fabric)* caída *f*. **2** *US* cortina *f*.

draper ['dreɪpəʳ] *n GB* pañero,-a *m, f*; **d.'s (shop),** pañería *f*.

drapery ['dreɪpərɪ] *n* **1** *(fabric)* tela *f*; *(hanging)* colgadura *f*. **2** *GB (goods)* pañería *f*. **3** *esp pl US* cortina *f*.

drastic ['dræstɪk] *adj* **1** *(severe)* drástico,-a, severo,-a. **2** *(important)* radical, importante.

draught [drɑːft] **I** *n* **1** *(of cold air)* corriente *f* (deaire); **to make a d.,** hacer aire. **2** *(of liquid)* trago *m*. **3 d. (beer),** cerveza *f* de barril; **on d.,** a presión. **4** *GB (in game)* dama *f*, pieza *f*; **draughts,** *(game)* damas *fpl*. **5** *Naut* calado *m*. **II** *adj* **1** *(animal)* de tiro. **2** *(beer)* de barril, a presión.

draughtboard ['drɑːftbɔːd] *n GB* tablero *m* de damas, damero *m*.

draughtsman ['drɑːftsmən] *n (pl **draughtsmen**)* delineante *mf*.

draughtsmanship ['drɑːftsmənʃɪp] *n (drawing)* dibujo *m* lineal; *(skill)* ejecución *f* gráfica.

draughty ['drɑːftɪ] *adj (**draughtier, draughtiest**)* lleno,-a de corrientes de aire.

draw [drɔː] **I** *vtr (pt **drew**; pp **drawn**)* **1** *(sketch) (picture)* dibujar; *(line, circle)* trazar; *(map)* hacer. **2** *(pull) (cart)* tirar de; *(train, carriage)* arrastrar; *(curtains) (open)* descorrer; *(close)* correr; *(blinds)* bajar; **he drew his hand over his eyes,** se pasó la mano por los ojos; *fig* **I was drawn into the discussion,** me envolvieron en la discusión. **3** *(take out) (remove, withdraw)* sacar, extraer; *(salary, wage)* cobrar; *Fin (cheque)* librar, extender; **to d. blood,** hacer sangrar. **4** *(attract) (crowd)* atraer; *(response)* provocar; *(attention)* llamar. **5** *(derive)* atraer; *fig (strength)* sacar. **6** *Sport (equalize)* empatar. **7** *(take in) (breath)* aspirar, respirar; *fig* **to have no time to d. breath,** estar ocupadísimo,-a. **8** *(choose)* escoger; **to d. lots,** echar a suertes; *fam fig* **to d. a blank,** seguir sin saber algo. **9** *(formulate) (comparison)* hacer; *(conclusion)* sacar. **II** *vi* **1** *(sketch)* dibujar. **2** *(move)* moverse, desplazarse; **the train drew into/out of the station,** el tren entró en/salió de la estación; **to d. apart (from),** separarse (de); *fig* echarse atrás (de); **to d. to an end,** acabarse; **to d. towards** *or* **near,** acercarse (a). **3** *(equalize)* empatar; **they drew two all,** empataron a dos. **4** *(produce draught) (chimney)* tirar. **III** *n* **1** *(raffle)* sorteo *m*; **the luck of the d.,** toca a quien toca. **2** *(score)* empate *m*. **3** *fig (attraction)* atracción *f*. ◆ **draw in** *vi (days)* acortarse, hacerse más corto,-a. ◆ **draw on** *vtr* **1** *(exploit) (savings)* utilizar, recurrir a; *(experience)* aprovecharse de. **2** *(suck)* chupar. ◆ **draw out** *vtr* **1** *(make long)* alargar. **2** *(encourage to speak)* hacer hablar, desatar la lengua. **3** *(withdraw)* sacar. ◆ **draw up** *vtr* **1** *(contract)* preparar, hacer; *(plan)* esbozar. **2** *(straighten up)* enderezarse.

drawback ['drɔːbæk] *n* desventaja *f*, inconveniente *m*.

drawbridge ['drɔːbrɪdʒ] *n* puente *m* levadizo.

drawer ['drɔːəʳ] *n* cajón *m*; **chest of drawers,** cómoda *f*.

drawers [drɔːz] *npl arch (for men)* calzoncillos *mpl*; *(for women)* bragas *fpl*.

drawing ['drɔːɪŋ] *n (picture, skill)* dibujo *m*; **rough d.,** esbozo *m*; *fam fig* **to go back to the d. board,** volver a empezar, empezar de nuevo. ■ **d. board,** tablero *m* de dibujo; **charcoal d.,** dibujo al carbón; *GB* **d. pin,** chincheta *f*; *fml* **d. room,** sala *f* de estar, salón *m*.

drawl [drɔːl] **I** *vtr & vi* hablar arrastrando las palabras. **II** *n* voz *f* cansina; *US* **a Southern d.,** un acento sureño.

drawn [drɔːn] **I** *pp see* **draw. II** *adj (tired)* cansado,-a, ojeroso,-a; *(worried)* preocupado,-a.

drawstring ['drɔːstrɪŋ] *n* cordón *m*. ■ **d. waist,** cintura *f* (de pantalón etc) que se cierra con cordón.

dread [dred] **I** *vtr* temer, tener pavor a. **II** *n* temor *m*, pavor *m*.

dreadful ['dredfʊl] *adj* **1** *(shocking)* espantoso,-a, terrible, atroz. **2** *fam (awful)* fatal, malísimo,-a; **how d.!,** ¡qué horror! ◆ **dreadfully** *adv fam (horribly)* terriblemente; *(very)* muy, sumamente; **it was d. hot,** hacía un calor espantoso.

dream [driːm] **I** *n* **1** *(while asleep)* sueño *m*; *fig (hope)* sueño *m* (dorado), deseo *m*, ilusión *f*; **bad d.,** pesadilla *f*; **to have a d. about sth/sb,** soñar con algo/algn; *fig* **a d. come true,** un sueño hecho realidad; *fig* **she was happy beyond her wildest dreams,** era más feliz de lo que jamás había soñado. **2** *(while awake)* ensueño *m*; **to go round in a d.,** tener la cabeza en las nubes. ■ **d. world,** mundo *m* de en sueño. **3** *fam (marvel)* encanto *m*, maravilla *f*; **things turned out like a d.,** todo salió a las mil maravillas. **II** *vtr (pt & pp **dreamed** or **dreamt**)* soñar, imaginar. **III** *vi* soñar *(of, about, con)*; *fam* **I wouldn't d. of it!,** ¡ni pensarlo! ◆ **dream up** *vtr fam pej (excuse)* inventarse; *(plan)* idear.

dreamer ['driːməʳ] *n* soñador,-a *m, f*, visionario,-a *m, f*.

dreamlike ['driːmlaɪk] *adj (state)* de ensueño.

dreamt [dremt] *pt & pp see* **dream.**

dreamy ['driːmɪ] *adj (**dreamier, dreamiest**)* **1** *(absentminded)* distraído,-a. **2** *(dreamlike) (state)* de ensueño; *(vision)* nebuloso,-a. **3** *fam (wonderful)* maravilloso,-a, encantador,-a.

dreary ['drɪərɪ] *adj (**drearier, dreariest**)* **1** *(gloomy)* melancólico,-a, triste, deprimente. **2** *fam (boring)* aburrido,-a, pesado,-a.

dredge [dredʒ] *vtr & vi* dragar, rastrear. ◆ **dredge up** *vtr* **1** *(body)* sacar del agua. **2** *fam fig* sacar a relucir.

dredger ['dredʒəʳ] *n Naut* draga *f*.

dregs [dregz] *npl (of tea etc)* heces *fpl*, sedimento *m sing*, poso *m sing*; *fig* **the d. of society,** la hez de la sociedad.

drench [drentʃ] *vtr (person, clothes)* empapar, mojar; **to be drenched to the skin,** estar calado,-a hasta los huesos.

Dresden ['drezdən] *n* Dresde.

dress [dres] **I** *n* **1** *(frock)* vestido *m*. ■ **wedding d.,** traje *m* de novia. **2** *(clothing)* ropa *f*, vestimenta *f*. ■ *Theat* **d. circle,** piso *m* principal; *Theat* **d. rehearsal,** ensayo *m* general; **d. shirt,** camisa *f* de etiqueta; **evening d.,** *(men)* traje *m* de etiqueta; *(women)* traje *m* de noche; **fancy d.,** disfraz *m*. **II** *vtr* **1** *(person)* vestir; **he was dressed in a grey suit,** llevaba (puesto) un traje gris; **to be dressed in green/silk,** ir (vestido,-a) de verde/seda. **2** *Culin (salad)* aliñar; *(poultry, crab)* aderezar. **3** *Med (wound)* vendar. **4** *(shop window)* arreglar, decorar. **III** *vi* vestirse. ◆ **dress down I** *vtr (rebuke)* echar una bronca a; *(scold)* regañar. **II** *vi GB* vestirse de una manera informal. ◆ **dress up I** *vi (child)* disfrazarse (**as,** de); *(partygoer)* ponerse *or* ir de tiros largos, ponerse guapo,-a; *fam* **to be dressed up to the nines,** ir de punta en blanco. **II** *vtr fig (truth)* disfrazar, hacer más aceptable.

dresser ['dresəʳ] *n* **1** *GB (in kitchen)* aparador *m*. **2** *US (in bedroom)* tocador *m*. **3** *Theat* ayudante *mf* de camerino. **4** *fam* **a smart/shabby d.,** uno *or* una que viste bien/mal.

dressing ['dresɪŋ] *n* **1** *Med (bandage)* vendaje *m*. **2** *Culin* **(salad) d.,** aliño *m*. **3** *(clothing)* **d. gown,** bata *f*; **d. room,** *Theat* camarino *m*; *Sport* vestuario *m*; **d. table,** tocador *m*.

dressing-down [dresɪŋ'daʊn] *n* **to give sb. a d.-d.,** echarle una bronca *or* un rapapolvo a algn.

dressmaker ['dresmeɪkəʳ] *n* modista *mf*.

dressmaking ['dresmeɪkɪŋ] *n* costura *f*.

dressy ['dresɪ] *adj (**dressier, dressiest**)* **1** *(elegant)* elegante, vistoso,-a. **2** *pej (person)* emperifollado,-a.

drew [druː] *pt see* **draw.**

dribble ['drɪbəl] **I** *vi* **1** *(baby)* babear. **2** *(liquid)* gotear; *fig* **the pupils dribbled into class,** los alumnos fueron entrando en la clase en pequeños grupos. **II** *vtr* **1** *(saliva etc)* dejar caer; **the baby dribbled milk down its chin,** al niño le caía la leche por la barbilla. **2** *Sport (ball)* driblar. **III** *n (saliva)* saliva *f*, baba *f*; *(of water, blood)* gotas *fpl*, hilo *m*.

dribs and drabs [drɪbzən'dræbz] *npl fam* **in d. a. d.,** poquito a poco, en pequeñas cantidades.

dried [draɪd] *adj (fruit)* seco,-a; *(milk)* en polvo.

drier ['draɪəʳ] *n see* **dryer.**

drift [drɪft] I *vi* 1 *(boat)* dejarse llevar por la corriente; **the yacht drifted out to sea,** el yate iba a la deriva hacia alta mar. 2 *fig (government)* ir a la deriva; *(person)* ir *or* vivir sin rumbo, vagar; **the conversation began to d.,** la conversación empezó a apartarse del tema; **the pupils drifted away,** los alumnos se marcharon poco a poco. 3 *(snow etc)* amontonarse. II *vtr* amontonar. III *n* 1 *(flow)* flujo *m,* dirección *f; fig (of people)* desplazamiento *m; (of events)* tendencia *f,* movimiento *m.* 2 *(of snow)* ventisquero *m; (of sand, cloud)* montón *m.* 3 *fig (meaning)* significado *m,* idea *f.*

drifter ['drɪftə'] *n* 1 *fam fig* persona *f* sin ocupación fija. 2 *Naut* trainera *f.*

driftwood ['drɪftwʊd] *n* madera *f* flotante.

drill[1] [drɪl] I *n* 1 *(handtool)* taladro *m;* *Min (machine)* barreno *m,* barrena *f.* ■ **dentist's d.,** fresa *f;* **pneumatic d.,** taladradora *f.* 2 *esp Mil* instrucción *f.* ■ **fire d.,** procedimiento *m* en caso de incendio; **safety d.,** instrucciones *fpl* de seguridad. II *vtr* 1 *(wood etc)* taladrar; *(hole)* agujerear. 2 *(train) (soldier)* instruir; **to d. pupils in pronunciation,** hacer ejercicios de pronunciación con los alumnos; *fig* **to d. sth into sb,** hacer que algn entienda algo a fuerza de repetición. III *vi* 1 *(by hand)* taladrar; *(for oil, coal)* perforar, sondar. 2 *Mil* entrenarse.

drill[2] [drɪl] *n Tex* dril *m.*

drily ['draɪlɪ] *adv see* **dryly.**

drink [drɪŋk] I *vtr (pt* **drank;** *pp* **drunk)** 1 *(gen)* beber; *fig* **he drank himself into a stupor,** bebió hasta perder el conocimiento; *fam* **to d. sb under the table,** aguantar más bebiendo que otro. 2 *fig* **to d. (in),** *(scene)* apreciar; *(success)* saborear. II *vi* beber; **to have sth to d.,** tomarse algo; **to d. to sth/sb,** brindar por algo/algn; *fam fig* **to d. like a fish,** beber como un cosaco. III *n* 1 *(gen)* bebida *f; (alcoholic)* copa *f;* **I gave the dog a d.,** di de beber al perro; **let's have a d.!,** ¡vamos a tomar una copita!; **to take to d.,** darse a la bebida. ■ **soft d.,** refresco *m.* 2 *fam* **the d.,** el *or* la mar.

drinkable ['drɪŋkəbəl] *adj (water)* potable; *(wine, beer)* agradable al paladar.

drinker [drɪŋkə'] *n* bebedor,-a *m, f;* **hard** *or* **heavy d.,** bebedor,-a empedernido,-a.

drinking ['drɪŋkɪŋ] *n* 1 *(drunkenness)* bebida *f.* 2 **d. water,** agua *f* potable; **d. fountain,** fuente *f* de agua potable.

drip [drɪp] I *n* 1 *(gen)* goteo *m.* 2 *Med* gota a gota *m inv.* 3 *fam (person)* necio,-a *m, f.* II *vi (pt & pp* **dripped)** gotear; **he was dripping with sweat,** el sudor le caía a gotas. III *vtr* dejar caer gota a gota.

drip-dry ['drɪpdraɪ] *adj* que no necesita planchado.

dripping ['drɪpɪŋ] I *n Culin* pringue *m & f,* grasa *f* de carne asada. II *adv* **d. wet,** chorreando; **I'm d.!,** ¡estoy calado,-a hasta los huesos!

drive [draɪv] I *vtr (pt* **drove;** *pp* **driven)** 1 *(operate) (vehicle)* conducir, *Am* manejar; *(person)* llevar *or* traer (en coche); **I'll d. you home,** te llevaré a casa; **to d. a bus,** ser conductor de autobús. 2 *(power)* hacer funcionar, poner en movimiento; **driven by nuclear power,** impulsado,-a por energía nuclear. 3 *(propel) (cattle etc)* arrear; *(enemy)* acosar; *(ball)* mandar; **inflation drives prices up,** la inflación hace subir los precios; **rain drove us back,** la lluvia nos hizo volver atrás. 4 *(strike in) (stake)* hincar; *(rail)* clavar; *fig* **the accident drove it home to me that ...,** el accidente me hizo comprender que ... . 5 *(compel)* forzar, obligar; **he drives himself too hard,** trabaja demasiado; **to d. sb mad,** volver loco,-a a algn; **to d. sb to crime/despair,** llevar a algn al crimen/a la desesperación. 6 **to d. (off),** repeler, rechazar. II *vi Aut* conducir, *Am* manejar; **can you d.?,** ¿sabes conducir?; **we drove home,** fuimos a casa en coche. III *n* 1 *(trip)* paseo *m* en coche; **to go for a d.,** dar una vuelta en coche; **it's an hour's d. (away),** es una hora en coche. 2 *(private road)* calle *f; (to house)* camino *m* de entrada. 3 *(transmission)* transmisión *f;* *Aut* tracción *f;* *Aut* **left-hand d.,**

conducción *f* por la izquierda. ■ **d. shaft,** eje *m* de transmisión. 4 *Golf* golpe *m* inicial; *Ten* golpe *m* fuerte. 5 *(campaign)* campaña *f.* ■ *Com* **sales d.,** promoción *f.* 6 *(need)* necesidad *f, (energy)* energía *f,* vigor *m,* fuerza *f,* dinamismo *m.* ■ **sex d.,** instinto *m* sexual. ◆ **drive at** *vtr fig* insinuar; **what are you driving at?,** ¿qué insinúas?, ¿qué quieres decir?

drive-in ['draɪvɪn] *n US* 1 *(cinema)* autocine *m.* 2 **d.-in bank,** autobanco *m.*

driven ['drɪvən] *pp see* **drive.**

driver [draɪvə'] *n (of car, bus)* conductor,-a *m, f; (of taxi)* taxista *mf; (of train)* maquinista *mf; (of lorry)* camionero,-a *m, f; (of racing car)* piloto *mf,* corredor,-a *m, f;* *US* **d.'s license,** carnet *m or* permiso *m* de conducir.

driveway ['draɪvweɪ] *n (to house)* camino *m* de entrada.

driving ['draɪvɪŋ] *adj* 1 *Aut* **d. licence,** carnet *m or* permiso *m* de conducir; **d. school,** autoescuela *f;* **d. test,** examen *m* de conducir. 2 *(rain, wind)* que azota. 3 *fig (force)* motriz; *(personality)* dinámico,-a.

drizzle ['drɪzəl] I *n* llovizna *f.* II *vi* lloviznar.

droll [drəʊl] *adj* 1 *(amusing)* gracioso,-a, cómico,-a. 2 *(odd)* curioso,-a, extraño,-a.

dromedary ['drɒmədərɪ] *n Zool* dromedario *m.*

drone[1] [drəʊn] *n Ent* zángano *m.*

drone[2] [drəʊn] I *vi (plane, bee)* zumbar; *fig* **to d. on,** hablar monótonamente. II *n (noise) (of bee, engine)* zumbido *m; (of traffic)* ruido *m* sordo, runruneo *m.*

droop [dru:p] *vi (flower)* marchitarse; *(shoulders)* encorvarse; *(eyelids)* caerse; *(head)* inclinarse; *fig* **her spirits drooped,** se desanimó.

droopy ['dru:pɪ] *adj (droopier, droopiest)* caído,-a.

drop [drɒp] I *n* 1 *(liquid)* gota *f; fig* **a d. in the ocean,** una gota de agua en el mar; *fam fig* **to have had a d. too much,** haber bebido más de la cuenta. ■ **eye drops,** colirio *m sing.* 2 *(sweet)* pastilla *f.* 3 *(descent)* desnivel *m.* 4 *(fall)* caída *f; (in price)* bajada *f; (in sales)* disminución *f; (in temperature)* descenso *m; fig* **at the d. of a hat,** sin más ni más. 5 *US fam* lugar *m* de reparto *or* de recogida. 6 *(airdrop)* lanzamiento *m.* II *vtr (pt & pp* **dropped)** 1 *(let fall)* dejar caer; *(let go of)* soltar; *(lower)* bajar; *(launch)* lanzar; *(reduce)* disminuir; **don't d. it!,** ¡que no se te caiga!; **to d. a hint,** soltar una indirecta; *GB fam fig* **to d. a brick** *or* **a clanger,** hacer una plancha, meter la pata. 2 *fam (leave)* dejar; **I'll d. you (off) here,** te dejo aquí. 3 *(abandon) (subject, charge)* dejar, abandonar; *(idea, plan)* abandonar, renunciar a; *fam (boyfriend etc)* plantar, dejar plantado,-a; *fam (friend)* dejar de ver; **let's d. the subject,** cambiemos de tema; **the matter was dropped,** ahí quedó el asunto; *fam* **d. it!,** ¡basta ya!, ¡ya está bien! 4 *(omit) (spoken syllable, word)* no pronunciar, comerse; *(written syllable, word)* omitir; *Sport* **he was dropped from the team,** le echaron del equipo; *Ling* **the article is dropped,** no se usa el artículo. 5 *Mus* perder. 6 *Knit* soltar. III *vi* 1 *(fall) (object)* caerse; *(person)* dejarse caer; *(voice, price, temperature)* bajar; *(wind)* amainar; *(speed)* disminuir; **to d. dead,** caerse muerto,-a; **to d. to one's knees,** arrodillarse; *fam* **d. dead!,** ¡vete a la porra!; *fam* **I'm fit to d.!,** ¡estoy hecho,-a polvo! 2 *(descend)* bajar, descender. ◆ **drop away** *vi (interest)* disminuir. ◆ **drop by, drop in, drop round** *fam* I *vi (visit)* dejarse caer, pasar (at, por). II *vtr (deliver)* dejar en casa de (algn). ◆ **drop off** *vi* 1 *fam (fall asleep)* quedarse dormido,-a, echar una cabezada. 2 *see* **drop away.** ◆ **drop out** *vi (leave) (school, college)* dejar los estudios; *(society)* marginarse; *(match, competition)* retirarse; **he dropped out of the class,** dejó el curso sin acabar. ◆ **drop round** *vi & vtr see* **drop by.**

droplet ['drɒplɪt] *n* gotita *f.*

dropout ['drɒpaʊt] *n fam pej (from school)* estudiante *mf* que no termina el curso; *(from society)* marginado,-a *m, f.*

dropper ['drɒpə'] *n Med* cuentagotas *m inv.*

droppings ['drɒpɪŋz] *npl* excrementos *mpl,* cagadas *fpl.*

dropsy ['drɒpsɪ] *n Med* hidropesía *f.*

drought [draʊt] n sequía f.

drove [drəʊv] I pt see **drive**. II (of cattle) manada f; fig (of people) multitud f; fig **in droves**, en manada.

drown [draʊn] I vtr **1** (gen) ahogar; fig **to d. one's sorrows**, ahogar las penas. **2** (place) inundar, anegar. **3** pej (food) ahogar; **a salad drowned in or with oil**, una ensalada que nadaba en aceite. **4** (sound) ahogar; **we were drowned out by the music**, no nos podíamos oír por culpa de la música. II vi (person, animal) ahogarse; **he (was) drowned**, murió ahogado.

drowse [draʊz] vi **to d. off**, adormilarse.

drowsiness ['draʊzɪnɪs] n somnolencia f.

drowsy ['draʊzɪ] adj (**drowsier, drowsiest**) **1** (person, yawn) soñoliento,-a; **to feel d.**, tener ganas de dormir. **2** (murmur, scene) soporífero,-a.

drudge [drʌdʒ] n pej (housewife) esclavo f de la casa; (employee) esclavo,-a m,f del trabajo.

drudgery ['drʌdʒərɪ] n trabajo m duro y pesado.

drug [drʌg] I n **1** (medicine) medicamento m, medicina f. **2** (narcotic) droga f, estupefaciente m, narcótico m; **to be on or take drugs**, drogarse. ■ **d. addict**, drogadicto,-a m, f; **d. addiction**, drogadicción f; **d. pusher**, traficante mf de drogas; **d. squad**, brigada f de estupefacientes. II vtr (pt & pp **drugged**) (person, animal) drogar; (food, drink) echar una droga en, adulterar con drogas.

druggist ['drʌgɪst] n US farmacéutico,-a m,f.

drugstore ['drʌgstɔːʳ] n US establecimiento m donde se compran medicamentos, periódicos, etc.

drum [drʌm] I n **1** (instrument) tambor m; **to play the drums**, tocar la batería. ■ Mil **d. major**, tambor m mayor; US **d. majorette**, majorette f. **2** (container) bidón m. **3** Tech tambor m. II vi (pt & pp **drummed**) fig (rain, fingers, hooves) tabalear. III vtr fig **1** (tap) tamborilear, tabalear. **2** fig **to d. sth into sb**, meterle algo en la cabeza de algn a fuerza de repetirlo. ◆ **drum up** vtr fam (votes) solicitar; (business) fomentar, atraer; (support) buscar.

drumbeat ['drʌmbiːt] n Mus toque m del tambor.

drummer ['drʌməʳ] n Mus (in band) tambor mf; (in pop group) batería mf.

drumstick ['drʌmstɪk] n **1** Mus baqueta f, palillo m (de tambor). **2** Culin muslo m (de ave).

drunk [drʌŋk] **1** pp see **drink** II adj **1** borracho,-a; fig borracho,-a, ebrio,-a; Jur **to be d. and disorderly**, comportarse escandalosamente estando borracho,-a; **to get d.**, emborracharse; fam **to be dead or blind d.**, estar como una cuba, estar trompa; fig **d. with happiness**, embriagado,-a de alegría. III n borracho,-a m,f.

drunkard ['drʌŋkəd] n borracho,-a m,f.

dry [draɪ] I adj (**drier, driest** or **dryer, dryest**) **1** (gen) seco,-a; **it was a d. day**, hacía un tiempo seco. **2** (wine etc) seco,-a. **3** (wry) agudo,-a. **4** fam (thirsty) sediento,-a. II vtr (pt & pp **dried**) secar. III vi **to d. (off)**, secar, secarse. ◆ **dryly** adv (coldly) secamente; (humorously) con humor, con guasa.

dry-clean [draɪ'kliːn] vtr limpiar or lavar en seco.

dryer ['draɪəʳ] n secadora f.

DSc [diːes'siː] abbr of **Doctor of Science**, Doctor,-a m,f en Ciencias, Dr. en Cien.

DT [diː'tiː] abbr of **delirium tremens** (trembling delirium), delírium m tremens, DT.

DTI [diːtiːaɪ] GB abbr of **Department of Trade and Industry**.

dub[1] [dʌb] vtr (pt & pp **dubbed**) (subtitle) doblar (**into**, a).

dub[2] [dʌb] vtr (pt & pp **dubbed**) **1** (give nickname) apodar. **2** (knight) armar.

dubbing ['dʌbɪŋ] n Cin doblaje m.

dubious ['djuːbɪəs] adj **1** (doubtful) (morals, activities) dudoso,-a, sospechoso,-a; (compliment) ambiguo,-a, equívoco,-a. **2** (doubting) dudoso,-a, indeciso,-a; **to be d. about sth**, tener dudas sobre algo.

Dublin ['dʌblɪn] n Dublín.

Dubliner ['dʌblɪnəʳ] adj & n dublinés,-esa (m,f).

ducal ['djuːkəl] adj ducal.

duchess ['dʌtʃɪs] n duquesa f.

duchy ['dʌtʃɪ] n ducado m.

duck[1] [dʌk] n Orn pato,-a m,f; Culin pato m; fig **to play ducks and drakes**, hacer saltar piedras planas sobre el agua; fam fig **criticism was like water off a d.'s back to him**, las críticas le eran indiferentes; fam fig **like a d. to water**, como el pez en el agua. ■ Orn **mandarin d.**, pato m mandarín; fig **sitting d.**, víctima f propiciatoria.

duck[2] [dʌk] I vtr **1** (bow down) (head) agachar. **2** (submerge) zambullir. **3** (evade) esquivar; fig eludir. II vi **1** (bow down) agacharse; **he ducked behind the door**, se escondió detrás de la puerta. **2** (go under water) zambullirse. **3** (evade blow) esquivar. **4** fam **to d. (out)**, rajarse.

duckling ['dʌklɪŋ] n Orn Culin patito m.

duct [dʌkt] n (for fuel etc) conducto m; Anat canal m, conducto m.

dud [dʌd] fam I adj **1** (tool, machine) (useless) inútil, que no sirve; (defective) defectuoso,-a, estropeado,-a. **2** (banknote) falso,-a; (cheque) sin fondos. II n (useless thing) trasto m inútil, engañifa f; (person) desastre m; **this tape's a d.**, esta cinta no sirve.

dude [djuːd] n US fam **1** (city-dweller) ciudadano m. ■ **d. ranch**, rancho m or hacienda f para turistas. **2** (type) tío,-a m,f.

dudgeon ['dʌdʒən] n fml **in high d.**, muy enojado,-a.

due [djuː] I adj **1** (expected) esperado,-a; **I'm due for a rise**, me toca una subida de sueldo; **the train is d. (to arrive) at ten**, el tren debe llegar a las diez; **when's the baby d.?**, ¿para cuándo esperas tener el niño? **2** fml (proper) debido,-a; **after d. consideration**, con las debidas consideraciones; **in d. course**, a su debido tiempo. **3** (owing) pagadero,-a; **how much are you d. or is d. to you?**, ¿cuánto te deben?; (payment) **to become d.**, vencer. ■ **d. date**, vencimiento m, plazo m. **4** to be d. to, deberse a, ser causado,-a por. II adv (north etc) derecho hacia. III n **1** to give sb his or her d.**, dar a algn su merecido, ser justo,-a con algn. **2 dues**, (fee) cuota f sing.

duel ['djuːəl] I n duelo m. II vi (pt & pp **duelld**, US **dueled**) batirse en duelo (**with**, con).

duet [djuː'et] n Mus dúo m, duelo m; **to play/sing a d.**, tocar/cantar a dúo.

duff [dʌf] adj GB sl (defective) defectuoso,-a, estropeado,-a; (useless) inútil, que no sirve. ◆ **duff up** vtr GB sl (beat up) dar una paliza a.

duffel ['dʌfəl] n **d. bag**, petate m; **d. coat**, trenca f.

duffer ['dʌfəʳ] n fam (hopeless person) zoquete m; **he's a d. at Latin**, es un desastre para el latín.

dug [dʌg] pt & pp see **dig**.

dugout ['dʌgaʊt] n **1** (canoe) piragua f. **2** Mil (shelter) refugio m subterráneo.

duke [djuːk] n duque m.

dukedom ['djuːkdəm] n ducado m.

dull [dʌl] I adj **1** (uninteresting) (job) monótono,-a, pesado,-a; (person, life, film) pesado,-a, aburrido,-a, soso,-a; (place) aburrido,-a, sin interés. **2** (not bright) (light, colour) apagado,-a; (weather, day) gris, triste; (sky) cubierto,-a. **3** (muffled) sordo,-a, amortiguado,-a; fig (ache, pain) sordo,-a. **4** fig (slow-witted) torpe, lerdo,-a. II vtr **1** (deaden) (pain) aliviar; (sound) amortiguar. **2** fig (faculty) embotar.

duly ['djuːlɪ] adv fml **1** (properly) debidamente; **I d. paid my share**, pagué mi parte como era debido. **2** (as expected) como era de esperar; (in due course) a su debido tiempo.

dumb [dʌm] I adj **1** Med (unspeaking) mudo,-a; **deaf and d.**, sordomudo,-a; fig **to be struck d. (with surprise)**, quedarse de una pieza. ■ (lift) **d. waiter**, montaplatos m *inv.* **2** *fam (stupid)* tonto,-a, estúpido,-a; **to act d.,** hacerse el tonto. ■ *pej* **d. blonde,** rubia *f* sosa. **II the d.** *npl* los mudos. ◆ **dumbly** *adv* sin decir nada.

dumbbell ['dʌmbel] *n* **1** *Sport* pesa *f*. **2** *US fam* tonto,-a *m,f*, imbécil *mf*.

dumbfounded [dʌm'faʊndɪd] *adj*, **dumbstruck** ['dʌmstrʌk] *adj* pasmado,-a.

dummy ['dʌmɪ] *n* **1** *(sham)* substituto *m*, imitación *f*. ■ **d. run,** ensayo *m*, prueba *f*. **2** *(model) (in shop window)* maniquí *m*; *(of ventriloquist)* muñeco *m*. **3** *GB (comforter)* chupete *m*. **4** *Cards* **d. (hand),** mano *f* muerta. **5** *fam (fool)* tonto,-a *m,f*.

dump [dʌmp] **I** *n* **1** *(tip) (for refuse)* vertedero *m*, basurero *m*; *(for old cars)* cementerio *m* (de coches). **2** *fam pej (place)* lugar *m* de mala muerte; *(town)* poblacho *m*; *(dwelling)* tugurio *m*. **3** *Mil (store)* depósito *m*. **II** *vtr* **1** *(unload) (rubbish)* verter; *(truck contents)* descargar. ■ **d. truck,** volquete *m*. **2** *(leave)* dejar, abandonar, tirar; *fam (boyfriend etc)* plantar; *fam (passenger)* dejar; *Com (goods)* inundar el mercado con. **3** *Comput (transfer)* copiar de memoria interna, vaciar de memoria.

dumper-truck ['dʌmpətrʌk] *n* volquete *m*.

dumping ['dʌmpɪŋ] *n* vertido *m*. ■ *(tip)* **d. ground,** vertedero *m*, basurero *m*.

dumpling ['dʌmplɪŋ] *n Culin (in stew)* bola *f* de masa hervida; *(as dessert)* (tipo *m* de) budín *m* relleno.

dumps [dʌmps] *npl fam* **to be (down) in the d.,** estar pocho,-a *or* deprimido,-a.

dumpy ['dʌmpɪ] *adj (dumpier, dumpiest) fam* rechoncho,-a, regordete.

dunce [dʌns] *n fam* tonto,-a *m,f*.

dune [djuːn] *n (sand)* **d.,** duna *f*.

dung [dʌŋ] *n (of horse, cow)* excrementos *mpl*; *(as manure)* estiércol *m*.

dungarees [dʌŋgə'riːz] *npl (overalls)* mono *m sing*; *(fashion garment, playsuit)* peto *m sing*.

dungeon ['dʌndʒən] *n* calabozo *m*, mazmorra *f*.

dunk [dʌŋk] *vtr fam (bread, biscuit)* mojar.

dunlin ['dʌnlɪn] *n Orn* correlimos *m inv* común.

dunnock ['dʌnək] *n Orn* acentor *m* común.

duo ['djuːəʊ] *n (pl duos) Mus* dúo *m*, duet *m*; *fam* pareja *f*.

duodenal [djuːə'diːnəl] *adj Anat* duodenal.

dupe [djuːp] **I** *vtr* engañar, timar, **to d. sb into doing sth,** embaucar a algn para que haga algo. **II** *n* ingenuo,-a *m,f*, simple *mf*.

duplex ['djuːpleks] *n US (house)* casa *f* adosada. ■ *US* **d. apartment,** dúplex *m inv*.

duplicate ['djuːplɪkeɪt] **I** *vtr* **1** *(copy) (document, key)* sacar copia(s) de, duplicar; *(film, tape)* reproducir. **2** *(repeat) (work)* repetir; *(reproduce)* reproducir. **II** ['djuːplɪkɪt] *n (copy)* copia *f*, duplicado *m*; **in d.,** por duplicado.

duplicator ['djuːplɪkeɪtər] *n* multicopista *m*.

duplication [djuːplɪ'keɪʃən] *n* repetición *f*.

duplicity [djuː'plɪsɪtɪ] *n fml* doblez *f*, falsedad *f*, duplicidad *f*.

durability [djʊərə'bɪlɪtɪ] *n* durabilidad *f*.

durable ['djʊərəbəl] *adj* duradero,-a.

duration [djʊ'reɪʃən] *n fml* duración *f*.

duress [djʊ'res] *n fml* coacción *f*.

during ['djʊərɪŋ] *prep* durante; **I work d. the day,** trabajo de día.

dusk [dʌsk] *n fml* crepúsculo *m*; **at d.,** al anochecer.

dust [dʌst] **I** *n (gen)* polvo *m*; *fig* **to allow the d. to settle,** esperar que se calme la borrasca; *fam* **to bite the d.,** *(person)* morder el polvo; *(plan)* irse a pique. ■ **coal d.,** polvo *m* de carbón; *Geog* **d. bowl,** región *f* de sequía, zona *f* semi-árida; **d. cloud,** polvareda *f*; *(of book)* **d. cover, d.**

jacket, sobrecubierta *f*. **II** *vtr* **1** *(room, furniture)* quitar el polvo a; **to d. oneself off** *or* **down,** sacudirse el polvo. **2** *(cake, plant)* espolvorear.

dustbin ['dʌstbɪn] *n GB* cubo *m* de la basura.

dustcart ['dʌstkɑːt] *n GB* camión *m* de la basura.

duster ['dʌstər] *n (for housework)* trapo *m or* paño *m* (para quitar el polvo); *(for blackboard)* borrador *m*. ■ **feather d.,** plumero *m*.

dustman ['dʌstmən] *n (pl dustmen) GB* basurero *m*.

dustpan ['dʌstpæn] *n* recogedor *m*.

dust-up ['dʌstʌp] *n GB fam (fight)* pelea *f*, riña *f*; *(argument)* discusión *f*, altercado *m*.

dusty ['dʌstɪ] *adj (dustier, dustiest)* **1** *(track)* polvoriento,-a; *(room)* lleno,-a de polvo; *(clothes etc)* cubierto,-a de polvo; *fig* **d. answer,** evasiva *f*. **2** *(colour)* ceniciento,-a.

Dutch [dʌtʃ] **I** *adj* holandés,-esa. ■ *fig* **D. cap,** diafragma *m*; *Culin* **D. cheese,** queso *m* de bola; *fam* **D. courage,** valor *m* que da la bebida. **II** *n* **1** *pl* **the D.,** los holandeses. **2** *(language)* holandés *m*. **III** *adv fig* **to go D. (with sb),** pagar cada uno lo suyo, pagar a escote.

Dutchman ['dʌtʃmən] *n (pl Dutchmen)* holandés *m*; *fam* **if that car starts, I'm a D.,** que me maten si ese coche arranca.

Dutchwoman ['dʌtʃwʊmən] *n (pl Dutchwomen* ['dʌtʃwɪmɪn]*)* holandesa *f*.

dutiable ['djuːtɪəbəl] *adj (goods)* sujeto,-a a derechos de aduanas.

duty ['djuːtɪ] *n* **1** *(obligation)* deber *m*, obligación *f*; **he went out of a sense of d.,** asistió para cumplir *or* por cumplido; **to do one's d.,** cumplir con su deber. **2** *(task)* función *f*, cometido *m*; **to make it one's d. to ...,** encargarse de ...; **to take up one's duties,** entrar en funciones. **3** *(availability)* **to be on d.,** *(gen)* estar de servicio; *Admin* estar de turno; *Med Mil* estar de guardia; **to do night d.,** tener el turno de noche. **4** *(tax)* impuesto *m*. ■ **customs d.,** derechos *mpl* de aduana, aranceles *mpl*; **stamp d.,** póliza *f*.

duty-bound ['djuːtɪbaʊnd] *adj* moralmente obligado,-a.

duty-free ['djuːtɪfriː] **I** *adj (shop, goods)* libre de impuestos. **II** *adv* sin pagar impuestos. **III** *n* duty-free *m*.

duvet ['duːveɪ] *n* edredón *m*. ■ **d. cover,** funda *f* (de edredón).

DV [diː'viː] *abbr of* *Deo volente* (God willing), Dios mediante, D.m.

dwarf [dwɔːf] **I** *n (pl dwarfs or dwarves* [dwɔːvz]*)* **1** *(person)* enano,-a *m,f*. **2** *Bot* **d. geranium,** geranio *m* enano. **II** *vtr* achicar, hacer parecer pequeño,-a.

dwell [dwel] *vi (pt & pp dwelled or dwelt) fml* morar, vivir. ◆ **dwell on, dwell upon** *vtr* hablar extensamente de; **let's not d. on it,** olvidémoslo, cambiemos de tema.

dweller ['dwelər] *n* habitante *mf*. ■ **cave d.,** cavernícola *mf*.

dwelling ['dwelɪŋ] *n fml & hum* morada *f*, vivienda *f*.

dwelt [dwelt] *pt & pp see* **dwell.**

dwindle ['dwɪndəl] *vi* menguar, disminuir; **to d. away to nothing,** quedar reducido,-a a nada.

dwindling [dwɪndlɪŋ] *adj (interest, number)* cada vez más reducido,-a; *(capital)* en disminución *f*.

dye [daɪ] **1** *n (substance)* tinte *m*, colorante *m*. **II** *vtr (pres p dyeing; pt & pp dyed) (gen)* teñir; **to d. one's hair black,** teñirse el pelo de negro.

dyed-in-the-wool [daɪdɪnðə'wʊl] *adj pej* acérrimo,-a, inflexible, intransigente.

dying ['daɪɪŋ] **I** *adj (person)* moribundo,-a *m,f*, agonizante *mf*; *fig (custom)* en vías de desaparición; **to my d. day,** hasta que me muera. **II the d.** *npl* los moribundos, los agonizantes.

dyke [daɪk] *n* **1** *(bank)* dique *m*, barrera *m*; *(causeway)* terraplén *m*. **2** *sl offens (lesbian)* tortillera *f*.

dynamic [daɪˈnæmɪk] I *adj Phys & fig* dinámico,-a; *(person)* dinámico,-a, emprendedor,-a. II *n Tech* dinámica *f*.

dynamics [daɪˈnæmɪks] *n Phys* dinámica *f*.

dynamism [ˈdaɪnəmɪzəm] *n fig* dinamismo *m*, energía *f*.

dynamite [ˈdaɪnəmaɪt] I *n* dinamita *f*; *fam fig (star, news)* sensación *f*; **his ideas are political d.,** sus ideas son políticamente explosivas. II *vtr (building)* dinamitar, volar con dinamita.

dynamo [ˈdaɪnəməʊ] *n (pl dynamos) Elec & fig* dínamo *m*, dinamo *m*.

dynasty [ˈdɪnəstɪ] *n* dinastía *f*.

dysentery [ˈdɪsəntrɪ] *n Med* disentería *f*.

dyslexia [dɪsˈleksɪə] *n Med* dislexia *f*.

dystrophy [ˈdɪstrəfɪ] *n Med* distrofia *f*; **muscular d.,** distrofia muscular.

E

E, e [iː] *n* **1** *(the letter)* E, e *f*. **2** *Mus* mi *m*. ■ **E flat,** mi *m* bemol.

E *abbr of* **East,** Este, E.

each [iːtʃ] I *adj* cada; **e. and every one (of us),** todos y cada uno de nosotros; **e. day/month,** todos los días/ meses; **e. person,** cada cual; **e. time I see him,** cada vez que lo veo. II *pron* **1** cada uno,-a; **e. to his own,** cada uno a lo suyo; **two pounds e.,** dos libras cada uno; **we bought one e.,** nos compramos uno cada uno. **2** *(mutual)* **e. other,** a cada uno, el uno al otro; **they hate e. other,** se odian; **we write to e. other,** nos escribimos.

eager [ˈiːgəʳ] *adj* **1** *(anxious)* impaciente, ansioso; **e. to begin,** impaciente por empezar. **2** *(desirous)* deseoso,-a; **e. to please,** deseoso de quedar bien; **to be e. for success,** codiciar el éxito. **3** *(keen)* apremiante; **he gave me an e. look,** me dirigió una mirada apremiante. ■ *fam* **e. beaver,** trabajador,-a *m*,*f* incansable. ◆ **eagerly** *adv* **1** *(anxiously)* con impaciencia. **2** *(keenly)* con afán *or* ilusión.

eagerness [ˈiːgənɪs] *n* **1** *(anxiety)* impaciencia *f*. **2** *(enthusiasm)* afán *m*, ilusión *f*.

eagle [ˈiːgəl] *n Zool* águila *f*.

eagle-eyed [iːgəlˈaɪd] *adj* que tiene vista de lince.

eaglet [ˈiːglɪt] *n Zool* aguilucho *m*.

ear [ɪəʳ] *n* **1** *Anat* oreja *f*; *(sense of hearing)* oído *m*; *Mus* **to have a good e.,** tener buen oído; **to play sth by e.,** tocar algo de oído; *fig* **in one e. and out the other,** por un oído entra y por otro sale; *fig* **to be all ears,** ser todo oídos; *fig* **to keep one's e. to the ground,** estar al corriente; *fam* **up to one's ears,** hasta aquí; *fam* **I'm up to my ears in work,** estoy agobiado de trabajo. ■ *Med* **e., nose, and throat specialist,** otorrinolaringólogo,-a *m*, *f*. **2** *Bot (of corn)* espiga *f*; **e. of wheat/barley,** espiga de trigo/cebada.

earache [ˈɪəreɪk] *n* dolor *m* de oídos; *fam* **to give sb e.,** dar dolor de cabeza a algn.

eardrum [ˈɪədrʌm] *n Anat* tímpano *m*.

earful [ˈɪəfʊl] *n fam* **to give sb an e.,** decirle a algn cuatro verdades.

earl [ɜːl] *n* conde *m*.

earldom [ˈɜːldəm] *n* condado *m*.

earlobe [ˈɪələʊb] *n Anat* lóbulo *m*.

early [ˈɜːlɪ] *(earlier, earliest)* I *adj* **1** *(before the usual time)* temprano,-a, prematuro,-a; **due to his e. arrival,** debido a que llegó antes de lo previsto; **e. death,** muerte prematura; **to book e.,** reservar con tiempo; **to have an e. night,** acostarse pronto; **you're e.!,** ¡qué pronto has venido! ■ **e. bird** *or* **riser,** madrugador,-a *m*,*f*. **2** *(at first stage, period)* **at an e. age,** siendo joven; **e. Gothic,** Gótico primitivo; **e. on,** al principio; **e. strawberries,** fresas tempranas; **e. train,** tren que sale temprano; **e. work,** obra de juventud; **in her e. forties,** a los cuarenta y pocos; **it's still e. days,** aún es pronto; *prov* **the e. bird catches the worm,** a quien madruga Dios le ayuda. ■ **e. man,** el hombre primitivo; **e. warning system,** sistema *m* de alerta roja. **3** *(in the near future)* **an e. reply,** una respuesta pronta; **at the earliest,** cuanto antes; **at the earliest opportunity,** lo antes posible; **could I have an earlier date?,** ¿no podría ser antes? II *adv* **1** *(before the expected time)* temprano, pronto; **earlier on,** antes; **five minutes e.,** con cinco minutos de adelanto; **to leave e.,** irse pronto. **2** *(near the beginning)* **as e. as 1914,** ya en 1914; **as e. as possible,** tan pronto como sea posible; **e. on in the book,** al comienzo del libro; **in e. July,** a principios de julio.

earmark [ˈɪəmɑːk] *vtr* destinar, reservar (**for,** para, a).

earn [ɜːn] *vtr* **1** *(money)* ganar; **money well earned,** dinero bien merecido; **to e. one's living,** ganarse la vida. **2** *(obtain, get as deserved)* ganarse; **it earned him the respect of ...,** le valió el respeto de ...; **to e. a place at university,** conseguir una plaza en la universidad. **3** *Fin* **to e. interest,** cobrar interés *or* intereses.

earnest [ˈɜːnɪst] I *adj* serio,-a, formal. II **n in e.,** de veras, en serio; **he said it in e.,** lo dijo en serio. ◆ **earnestly** *adv* **1** *(sincerely)* seriamente. **2** *(zealously)* con gran interés.

earnestness [ˈɜːnɪstnɪs] *n* seriedad *f*; **in all e.,** muy seriamente.

earnings [ˈɜːnɪŋz] *npl* ingresos *mpl*.

earpiece [ˈɪəpiːs] *n* auricular *m*.

earplug [ˈɪəplʌg] *n* tapón *m* (para los oídos).

earring [ˈɪərɪŋ] *n* pendiente *m*.

earshot [ˈɪəʃɒt] *n* **out of e.,** fuera del alcance del oído; **within e.,** al alcance del oído.

earth [ɜːθ] I *n* **1** *(gen)* tierra *f*; *fig* **he promised the e.,** prometió el oro y el moro; *fig* **it costs the e.,** cuesta un ojo de la cara; *fig* **to go down to e.,** tocar de pies en el suelo; tener los pies en el suelo; *fig* **to be the salt of the e.,** ser de fiar; *fig* **to come down to e.,** despertarse; *fam* **where/why one e ...?,** ¿de dónde/porqué demonios ...? **2** *(of fox, badger)* madriguera *f*; **to run to e.,** acorralar. **3** *Elec* toma *f* de tierra. II *vtr (electricity)* conectar a tierra.

earthen [ˈɜːðən] *adj* **1** *(gen)* de tierra. **2** *(of clay)* de arcilla, de barro.

earthenware [ˈɜːðənweəʳ] I *n* loza *f*. II *adj* de barro.

earthly [ˈɜːθlɪ] *adj (worldly)* material, terrenal; *fam* **it's no e. use,** no sirve absolutamente para nada; *fam* **we don't have an e. (chance),** no tenemos la más mínima posibilidad.

earthquake [ˈɜːθkweɪk] *n* terremoto *m*.

earthshattering [ˈɜːθʃætərɪŋ] *adj* trascendental; **e. news,** noticia bomba.

earthworm [ˈɜːθwɜːm] *n Zool* lombriz *f*.

earthy [ˈɜːθɪ] *adj (earthier, earthiest)* **1** *(of colour, taste)* terroso,-a. **2** *(bawdy)* tosco,-a, grosero,-a.

earwig [ˈɪəwɪg] *n Ent* tijereta *f*.

ease [iːz] I *n* **1** *(freedom from discomfort)* calma *f*, tranquilidad *f*; *Mil* posición *f* de descanso; **at e.,** relajado,-a; **to set sb's mind at e.,** tranquilizar a algn; **to**

take one's e., ponerse cómodo. **2** *(lack of difficulty)* facilidad *f;* **with e.,** con facilidad. **3** *(affluence)* comodidad *f;* **a life of e.,** una vida cómoda *or* fácil. **4** *(lack of restraint)* **e. of manner,** naturalidad *f,* desenvoltura *f,* espontaneidad *f.* **II** *vtr* **1** *(pain)* aliviar. **2** *(move gently)* deslizar, correr. ◆ **ease off, ease up** *vi* **1** *(decrease)* ceder, disminuir. **2** *(slow down)* ir más despacio.

easel ['iːzəl] *n* caballete *m.*

easiness ['iːzɪnɪs] *n* **1** *(simplicity)* facilidad *f.* **2** *(of manner etc)* naturalidad *f.*

east [iːst] **I** *n* este *m.* ■ **the Far E.,** el Lejano Oriente; **the Middle E.,** el Oriente Medio. **II** *adj* este, del este, oriental; **E. Germany,** Alemania Oriental. **III** *adv* en dirección este, al *or* hacia el este; **heading e.,** rumbo al este; **to face** *or* **look e.,** estar orientado al este.

eastbound ['iːstbaʊnd] *adj* con rumbo al este, dirección este.

Easter ['iːstə] *n* Semana *f* Santa, Pascua *f.* ■ **E. egg,** huevo *m* de Pascua; **E. Sunday,** Domingo *m* de Pascua *or* de Resurrección.

easterly ['iːstəlɪ] *adj* **1** *(from the east)* del este; **e. wind,** viento del este. **2** *(to the east)* hacia al este; **in an e. direction,** en dirección este.

eastern ['iːstən] *adj* oriental, del este; *Pol* **E. Bloc countries,** los países del Este.

eastward ['iːstwəd] *adj & adv* hacia el este.

eastwards ['iːstwədz] *adv* hacia el este.

easy ['iːzɪ] *(easier, easiest)* **I** *adj* **1** *(simple)* fácil sencillo,-a; **e. to please,** poco exigente; *fam* **it's as e. as pie,** es pan comido, está chupado. ■ *Com* **e. payments, e. terms,** facilidades *fpl* de pago. **2** *(unworried, comfortable)* cómodo,-a, tranquilo,-a; **at an e. pace,** con calma, tranquilamente; **e. life,** vida tranquila *or* cómoda; **in e. stages,** poco a poco, de forma escalonada; **to have an e. mind,** estar tranquilo; *fig* **to be on e. street,** no tener problemas económicos; *fam* **to be e.,** dar igual, ser indiferente; *fam* **I'm e.!,** me da lo mismo. ■ **e. chair,** butacón *m.* **4** *(colour)* agradable; **e. on the eyes,** agradable a la vista. **II** *adv* **go e. on the cakes/wine,** deja algún pastel/algo de vino; **go e. with that knife,** ten cuidado con ese cuchillo; **it's easier said than done,** es más fácil decirlo que hacerlo; *fam* **to take things e.,** tomarse la vida con calma; *fam* **take it e.!,** ¡tranquilo! ◆ **easily** *adv* **1** fácilmente. **2** *(beyond question)* **e. the best,** con mucho el mejor.

easy-going [iːzɪ'gəʊɪŋ] *adj* **1** *(calm)* tranquilo,-a. **2** *(lax)* despreocupado,-a; *(undemanding)* poco exigente.

eat [iːt] *(pt ate* [et, eɪt], *pp eaten)* *vtr (gen)* comer; **to e. one's breakfast,** desayunar; *fig* **he had them eating out of his hand,** comían en la palma de su mano; *fig* **to e. one's heart out,** consumirse de pena; *fig* **to e. one's words,** tragarse lo dicho; *fam* **what's eating you?,** ¿qué mosca te ha picado?; *fam* **to e. like a horse,** comer como una vaca. ◆ **eat away** *vtr (gen)* desgastar; *(metal)* corroer. ◆ **eat into** *vtr* **1** *(wood)* roer. **2** *fig (savings)* consumir. ◆ **eat out** *vi* comer fuera. ◆ **eat up** *vtr* **1** *(meal)* terminar. **2** *fig (petrol)* consumir; *(miles)* tragar; *(money)* llevarse, tragar.

eatable ['iːtəbəl] *adj* comible, comestible.

eaten ['iːtən] *pp see* **eat.**

eater ['iːtə'] *n (fam)* **to be a big e.,** ser de buen comer, ser comilón,-ona; **to be a slow e.,** ser lento,-a comiendo.

eau de Cologne [əʊdəkə'ləʊn] *n* colonia *f,* agua *f* de colonia.

eaves [iːvz] *npl* alero *m sing.*

eavesdrop ['iːvzdrɒp] *vi (pt & pp eavesdropped)* escuchar disimuladamente.

eavesdropper ['iːvzdrɒpə'] *n* curioso,-a *m,f.*

ebb [eb] **I** *n* reflujo *m;* **e. and flow,** flujo y reflujo; *fig* **to be at a low e.,** estar decaído. **II** *vi* **1** *(tide)* bajar; **to e. and flow,** subir y bajar. **2** *fig* **to e. away,** decaer, disminuir.

ebony ['ebənɪ] **I** *n Bot* ébano *m.* **II** *adj* de ébano.

ebullience [ɪ'bʌljəns] *n* exaltación *f,* entusiamo *m.*

ebullient [ɪ'bʌljənt] *adj* exaltado,-a, entusiasta.

eccentric [ɪk'sentrɪk] **I** *adj* **1** *(person)* excéntrico,-a, estrafalario,-a, extravagante. **2** *Math (circle)* excéntrico. **II** *n (person)* excéntrico,-a *m,f,* persona *f* extravagante.

eccentricity [eksen'trɪsɪtɪ] *n* excentricidad *f,* extravagancia *f.*

ecclesiastic [ɪkliːzɪ'æstɪk] **I** *adj* eclesiástico,-a. **II** *n* eclesiástico *m,* clérigo *m,* sacerdote *m.*

ecclesiastical [ɪkliːzɪ'æstɪkəl] *adj* eclesiástico,-a.

echelon ['eʃəlɒn] *n (status)* nivel *m,* escalafón *m; Mil* **in e.,** en escalafón.

echo ['ekəʊ] **I** *n (pl echoes)* eco *m.* ■ **e. chamber,** cámara *f* acústica; **e. sounder,** sonda *f* acústica. **II** *vtr (repeat)* repetir; **to e. sb's words,** repetir las palabras de algn; **to e. sb's opinions,** hacerse eco de las opiniones de algn. **III** *vi* resonar, hacer eco.

éclair [eɪ'kleə, ɪ'kleə] *n Culin (cake)* palo *m* de nata, pastel *m* petisú; **chocolate e.,** bombón *m* de chocolate y caramelo.

eclectic [ɪ'klektɪk] *adj* ecléctico,-a.

eclecticism [ɪ'klektɪsɪzəm] *n* eclecticismo *m.*

eclipse [ɪ'klɪps] **I** *n* eclipse *m.* **II** *vtr* eclipsar.

ecological [iːkə'lɒdʒɪkəl] *adj* ecológico,-a. ◆ **ecologically** *adv* ecológicamente.

ecologist [ɪ'kɒlədʒɪst] *n* ecólogo,-a *m,f,* ecologista *mf.*

ecology [ɪ'kɒlədʒɪ] *n* ecología *f.*

economic [iːkə'nɒmɪk] *adj (gen)* económico,-a; *(profitable)* rentable.

economical [iːkə'nɒmɪkəl] *adj (gen)* económico,-a; *(cheap)* barato,-a; **to be e. with sth,** economizar en algo. ◆ **economically** *adv* económicamente.

economics [iːkə'nɒmɪks] *n sing* **1** *(science)* economía *f; Educ* (ciencias *fpl*) económicas *fpl.* **2** *(financial aspect)* aspecto *m* económico.

economist [ɪ'kɒnəmɪst] *n* economista *mf.*

economize [ɪ'kɒnəmaɪz] *vi* economizar, ahorrar.

economy [ɪ'kɒnəmɪ] *n* **1** *(science)* economía *f; Pol* **the e.,** la economía, el sistema económico. ■ **black e.,** economía *f* sumergida. **2** *(saving)* economía *f.* *Av* **e. class,** (clase *f*) turista *f;* **I always fly e. class,** siempre viajo en clase turista; *Com* **e. sized,** de tamaño familiar; **that's a false e.,** esto no es un ahorro.

ecosystem [iːkəsɪstəm] *n* ecosistema *m.*

ecstasy ['ekstəsɪ] *n* éxtasis *m;* **to go into ecstasies over,** extasiarse ante.

ecstatic [ek'stætɪk] *adj* extático,-a.

Ecuador ['ekwədɔː'] *n* Ecuador *m.*

ecumenical [iːkju'menɪkəl] *adj* ecuménico,-a.

eczema ['eksɪmə] *n Med* eczema *mf.*

ed. [ed] **1** *abbr of* **edition,** edición *f,* ed. **2** *abbr of* **editor,** editor,-a *m,f.* **3** *abbr of* **edited,** editado,-a.

eddy ['edɪ] **I** *n* remolino *m.* **II** *vi (pt & pp eddied)* formar remolinos, arremolinarse.

Eden ['iːdən] *n* Edén *m.*

edge [edʒ] **I** *n* borde *m; (of knife)* filo *m; (of coin)* canto *m; (end)* extremidad *f; (of water)* orilla *f;* **a knife with a blunt e.,** un cuchillo con el canto desafilado; **he lives on the e. of town,** vive en las afueras de la ciudad; **to have the e. on** *or* **over sb,** llevar ventaja a algn; **to take the e. off one's appetite,** quitar el hambre; *fig* **to be on e.,** tener los nervios de punta; *fig* **to set sb's teeth on e.,** crispar los nervios a algn; *sl* **to live on the e.,** vivir peligrosamente. **II** *vtr Sew* ribetear; **to e. with lace,** poner un borde de encaje. **III** *vi* **to e. closer,** acercarse lentamente; **to e. forward,** avanzar poco a poco; *fig (prices)* **to e. up** subir gradualmente. ◆ **edge out** *vtr (displace)* eliminar, apartar; **to e. sb out,** empujar a algn, poner la zancadilla a algn.

edgeways ['edʒweɪz] adv de lado; fig **I couldn't get a word in e.,** no pude meter baza.

edging ['edʒɪŋ] n borde m; Sew ribete m.

edgy ['edʒɪ] adj (edgier, edgiest) nervioso,-a.

edible ['edɪbəl] adj comestible.

edict ['iːdɪkt] Hist n edicto m; Jur decreto m.

edification [edɪfɪ'keɪʃən] n edificación f.

edifice ['edɪfɪs] n gran edificio m; fig **the whole c. of his argument fell down,** su argumento se vino abajo.

edify ['edɪfaɪ] vtr (pt & pp **edified**) edificar.

edifying ['edɪfaɪŋ] adj edificante.

Edinburgh ['edɪnbrə] n Edimburgo.

edit ['edɪt] vtr **1** (prepare for printing) preparar para la imprenta. **2** (rewrite) corregir; **to e. sth out,** suprimir algo. **3** Press dirigir la redacción de, ser redactor,-a de. **4** Cin Rad TV montar; (cut) cortar, reducir.

edition [ɪ'dɪʃən] n edición f; **first e.,** primera edición.

editor ['edɪtəʳ] n **1** (of book) editor,-a m,f, autor,-a m,f de la edición. **2** Press redactor,-a m,f; **e. in chief,** redactor,-a jefe; (newspaper) director,-a m,f. **3** Cin TV montador,-a m,f.

editorial [edɪ'tɔːrɪəl] **I** adj editorial; **e. staff,** redacción f. **II** n editorial m.

educate ['edjʊkeɪt] vtr educar; **he was educated in Italy,** se formó en Italia; **she was educated at Oxford University,** estudió en la universidad de Oxford.

educated ['edjʊkeɪtɪd] adj culto,-a, cultivado,-a; **e. speech,** lenguaje m culto.

education [edjʊ'keɪʃən] n **1** (teaching, schooling) enseñanza f; **she received a good e.,** recibió una buena preparación. ■ **adult e.,** enseñanza f para adultos; **further e.,** enseñanza f superior; **primary/secondary e.,** enseñanza f primaria/secundaria; **Ministry of E.,** Ministerio m de Educación. **2** (training) formación f. **3** (studies) estudios mpl. **4** (culture) cultura f.

educational [edjʊ'keɪʃənəl] adj educativo,-a, educacional; ■ **e. film,** película educativa; **e. publisher,** editor,-a de libros de texto. ■ **e. reform,** reforma f educativa.

education(al)ist [edjʊ'keɪʃən(əl)ɪst] n pedagogo,-a m,f, educador,-a m,f.

educator ['edjʊkeɪtəʳ] n educador,-a m,f, pedagogo,-a m,f.

Edwardian [ed'wɔːdɪən] adj eduardiano,-a.

eel [iːl] n Zool anguila f.

eerie ['ɪərɪ] adj (eerier, eeriest) siniestro,-a, escalofriante.

efface [ɪ'feɪs] vtr borrar.

effect [ɪ'fekt] **I** n **1** (gen) efecto m; **in e.,** efectivamente; **to come into e.,** entrar en vigor; **to have an e. on,** afectar a; **to have the desired e.,** producir el efecto esperado; **to no e.,** sin resultado alguno; **to take e.,** (drug) surtir efecto; (law) entrar en vigor; **words to that e.,** algo por el estilo. **2** (impression) impresión f, efecto m; fig **for e.,** para impresionar. **3** effects, efectos mpl. ■ **personal e.,** enseres mpl personales; **side e.,** efectos mpl secundarios; **sound e.,** efectos mpl sonoros; **special e.,** efectos mpl especiales. **II** vtr (produce) efectuar; (cause) provocar.

effective [ɪ'fektɪv] adj **1** (successful) eficaz; **to be e.,** ser eficaz. **2** (active, real) efectivo,-a; **e. power,** poder efectivo. **3** (impressive) impresionante. **4** (striking) llamativo,-a. ◆ **effectively** adv **1** (successfully) eficazmente. **2** (in fact) en efecto, de hecho.

effectuate [ɪ'fektjʊeɪt] vt efectuar, realizar, llevar a cabo.

effeminacy [ɪ'femɪnəsɪ] n afeminación f, afeminamiento m.

effeminate [ɪ'femɪnɪt] adj afeminado,-a.

effervesce [efə'ves] vi Chem **1** entrar en efervescencia. **2** ser efervescente.

effervescence [efə'vesəns] n efervescencia f.

effervescent [efə'vesənt] adj efervescente.

effete [ɪ'fiːt] adj débil, cansado,-a, agotado,-a.

efficacious [efɪ'keɪʃəs] adj eficaz.

efficacy ['efɪkəsɪ] n eficacia f.

efficiency [ɪ'fɪʃənsɪ] n **1** (of person) eficacia f, eficiencia f, competencia f. **2** (of machine) rendimiento m.

efficient [ɪ'fɪʃənt] adj **1** (person) eficaz, eficiente, competente. **2** (system, method) eficaz, eficiente. **3** (machine) de buen rendimiento.

effigy ['efɪdʒɪ] n efigie f.

effluent ['efluənt] n aguas fpl residuales, vertidos mpl, residuos mpl.

effort ['efət] n **1** (gen) esfuerzo m; **to make an e.,** hacer un esfuerzo, esforzarse. **2** (attempt) tentativa f, intento m, conato m; **it was a good e.,** fue un buen intento.

effortless ['efətlɪs] adj fácil, sin esfuerzo. ◆ **effortlessly** adv fácilmente, sin esfuerzo.

effrontery [ɪ'frʌntərɪ] n descaro m, desfachatez f, desvergüenza f.

effusion [ɪ'fjuːʒən] n efusión f.

effusive [ɪ'fjuːsɪv] adj efusivo,-a. ◆ **effusively** adv efusivamente.

eg [iːdʒiː] abbr of **exempli gratia** (for example), por ejemplo, p. ej.

egalitarian [ɪgælɪ'teərɪən] adj igualitario,-a.

egalitarianism [ɪgælɪ'teərɪənɪzəm] n igualitarismo m.

egg [eg] **I** n huevo m; fig **to be a bad e.,** ser una mala persona; fam **to have e. on one's face,** quedar en ridículo; fam fig **to put all one's eggs in one basket,** jugárselo todo a una carta. ■ Culin **boiled e.,** huevo m pasado por agua; **e. cup,** huevera f; **e. custard,** natillas fpl; **e. timer,** reloj m de arena; **e. white,** clara f de huevo; **e. yolk,** yema f de huevo; **fried e.,** huevo m frito; fig **nest e.,** ahorrillos mpl; **poached e.,** huevo m escalfado; **scrambled eggs,** huevos mpl revueltos. **II** vtr **to e. sb on (to do sth),** empujar or animar a algn (a hacer algo).

egghead ['eghed] n pej intelectual mf.

eggnog [eg'nɒg] n Culin ponche m de huevo.

eggplant ['egplɑːnt] n Bot berenjena f.

egg-shaped ['egʃeɪpt] adj ovoide.

eggshell ['egʃel] n cáscara f de huevo; (paint) **e. finish,** acabado m mate.

egg-whisk ['egwɪsk] n Culin batidor m.

ego ['iːgəʊ, 'egəʊ] n **1** Psychol ego m. ■ **alter e.,** alter ego m; fam **e. trip,** autobombo m. **2** fam amor m propio; **to boost sb's e.,** levantar la moral a algn; **to deflate sb's e.,** bajar los humos a algn; **to have a big e.,** tener mucho ego.

egocentric(al) [iːgəʊ'sentrɪk(əl)] adj egocéntrico,-a.

egoism ['iːgəʊɪzəm] n egoísmo m.

egoist ['iːgəʊɪst] n egoísta mf.

egotism ['iːgəʊtɪzəm] n egotismo m.

egotist ['iːgəʊtɪst] n egotista mf.

egotistic(al) [iːgəʊ'tɪstɪk(əl)] adj egotista.

Egypt ['iːdʒɪpt] n Egipto.

Egyptian ['iːdʒɪpʃən] adj & n egipcio,-a (m,f).

eiderdown ['aɪdədaʊn] n edredón m.

eight [eɪt] **I** adj ocho inv. **II** n ocho m inv; fam **to have one over the e.,** llevar una copa de más; see also **seven.**

eighteen [er'tiːn] **I** adj dieciocho inv. **II** n dieciocho m inv; see also **seven.**

eighteenth [er'tiːnθ] **I** adj decimoctavo,-a. **II** n **1** (in series) decimoctavo,-a m,f. **2** (fraction) decimoctavo m, decimoctava parte f; see also **seventh.**

eighth [eɪtθ] **I** adj octavo,-a. **II** n **1** (in series) octavo,-a m, f. **2** (fraction) octavo m, octava parte f; see also **seventh.**

eightieth ['eɪtɪɪθ] **I** adj octogésimo,-a. **II** n **1** (in series) octogésimo,-a m,f. **2** (fraction) octogavo m, octogésima parte f; see also **seventh**.

eighty ['eɪtɪ] **I** adj ochenta inv. **II** n ochenta m inv; see also **seven**.

Eire ['eərə] n Eire.

either ['aɪðər, 'iːðər] **I** pron **1** (affirmative) cualquiera; **e. of them will do**, cualquiera de los dos sirve; **e. of us**, cualquiera de nosotros dos. **2** (negative) ninguno, ninguna, ni el uno ni el otro, ni la una ni la otra; **I don't want e. of them**, no quiero ninguno de los dos. **II** adj (both) cada, los dos, las dos; **on e. side**, en ambos lados, a cada lado; **in e. case**, en cualquier de los dos casos. **III** conj o; **e. ... or ...,** o ... o ...; **e. Friday or Saturday**, o (bien) el viernes o el sábado; **you e. like it or you don't**, o te gusta o no te gusta. **IV** adv (after negative) tampoco; **I don't want to do it e.**, yo tampoco quiero hacerlo, yo no quiero hacerlo tampoco.

ejaculate [ɪ'dʒækjuleɪt] vi **1** Physiol eyacular. **2** (exclaim) exclamar.

ejaculation [ɪdʒækjuˈleɪʃən] n **1** Physiol eyaculación f. **2** (exclamation) exclamación f.

eject [ɪ'dʒekt] **I** vtr expulsar, echar. **II** vi Av eyectar, eyectarse.

ejection [ɪ'dʒekʃən] n **1** expulsión f. **2** Av eyección f.

ejector [ɪ'dʒektər] n Av **e. seat**, asiento m eyectable.

eke [iːk] vtr **to e. out a living**, ganarse la vida a duras penas.

elaborate [ɪ'læbəreɪt] **I** vtr **1** (devise) elaborar, desarrollar; **to e. a plan**, elaborar un proyecto. **2** (explain) explicar detalladamente. **II** vi explicarse; **to e. on sth**, explicar algo con más detalles; **he refused to e.**, se negó a dar más detalles. **III** [ɪ'læbərɪt] adj **1** (complicated) complicado,-a. **2** (detailed) detallado,-a; (of style, work of art) trabajado,-a, esmerada,-a. ♦ **elaborately** adv **1** (complicated) de modo complicado. **2** (in detail) detalladamente. **3** (carefully) cuidadosamente.

elaboration [ɪlæbə'reɪʃən] n elaboración f.

élan [eɪ'lɑːn, eɪ'læn] n brío m, vivacidad f, impetuosidad f.

elapse [ɪ'læps] vi transcurrir, pasar.

elastic [ɪ'læstɪk] **I** adj elástico,-a; fig flexible. ■ **e. band**, goma f elástica. **II** n elástico m.

elasticity [ɪlæ'stɪsɪtɪ] n elasticidad f; fig flexibilidad f.

Elastoplast® [ɪ'lɑːstəplɑːst] n tirita® f.

elated [ɪ'leɪtɪd] adj eufórico,-a, satisfecho,-a, muy contento,-a.

elation [ɪ'leɪʃən] n júbilo m, regocijo m, euforia f.

elbow ['elbəʊ] **I** n **1** Anat codo m; fig **e. grease**, sudor m; fig **e. room**, espacio m, sitio m. **2** (bend) recodo m. **II** vtr **to e. one's way through**, abrirse paso a codazos; **to e. sb**, dar un codazo a algn; fig **to e. sb out**, empujar or echar a algn.

elder¹ ['eldər] **I** adj mayor; **e. statesman** viejo estadista; **my e. brother**, mi hermano mayor. **II** n (respected person) mayor m; **the village elders**, los ancianos del pueblo; **you must respect your elders**, hay que respetar a tus mayores.

elder² ['eldər] n Bot saúco m.

elderberry ['eldəberɪ] n Bot baya f del saúco.

elderly ['eldəlɪ] adj anciano,-a; **the e.**, los ancianos.

eldest ['eldɪst] **I** adj mayor; **their e. sister**, su hermana mayor. **II** n el or la mayor; **my e. has gone to work in London**, mi hijo o hija mayor (se) ha ido a trabajar a Londres.

elect [ɪ'lekt] **I** vtr **1** Pol elegir. **2** (choose) decidir; **he elected not to go on holiday**, decidió no ir de vacaciones. **II** adj electo,-a; **the president e.**, el presidente electo. **III** **the e.** npl los elegidos.

election [ɪ'lekʃən] n elección f; **to hold an e.**, convocar elecciones. ■ **general e.**, elecciones fpl generales. **II** adj electoral. ■ **e. campaign**, campaña f electoral.

electioneering [ɪlekʃəˈnɪərɪŋ] **1** adj electoralista. **II** n electoralismo m.

elector [ɪ'lektər] n elector,-a m,f.

electoral [ɪ'lektərəl] adj electoral. ■ **e. roll, e. register**, censo m electoral.

electorate [ɪ'lektərɪt] n electorado m.

Electra [ɪ'lektrə] n Electra f; Psych **E. complex**, complejo m de Electra.

electric [ɪ'lektrɪk] adj **1** eléctrico,-a. ■ **e. blanket**, manta f eléctrica; **e. chair**, silla f eléctrica; **e. motor**, electromotor m; **e. shock**, electrochock m, electrochoque m; **to get an e. shock**, recibir una descarga eléctrica; **e. storm**, tormenta f eléctrica. **2** fig electrizante; **the atmosphere was e.**, había electricidad en el ambiente.

electrical [ɪ'lektrɪkəl] adj eléctrico,-a. ■ **e. engineer**, ingeniero,-a m, f electrotécnico,-a; **e. engineering**, ingeniería f eléctrica, electrotecnia f. ♦ **electrically** adv por electricidad; **e. operated** or **powered**, electroaccionado,-a.

electrician [ɪlek'trɪʃən] n electricista mf.

electricity [ɪlek'trɪsɪtɪ] n electricidad f. ■ **e. supply**, suministro m eléctrico.

electrics [ɪ'lektrɪks] npl (house) instalación f sing eléctrica; (equipment, apparatus) sistema m sing eléctrico.

electrification [ɪlektrɪfɪ'keɪʃən] n electrificación f.

electrify [ɪ'lektrɪfaɪ] vtr (pt & pp **electrified**) **1** (provide supply) electrificar; **they are going to e. the railway network**, van a electrificar la red ferroviaria. **2** fig (excite) electrizar.

electrifying [ɪ'lektrɪfaɪɪŋ] adj fig electrizante.

electrocardiogram [ɪlektrəʊ'kɑːdɪəʊgræm] n Med electrocardiograma m.

electrocardiograph [ɪlektrəʊ'kɑːdɪəgrɑːf] n electrocardiógrafo m.

electrocute [ɪ'lektrəkjuːt] vtr electrocutar; **she was electrocuted**, se electrocutó.

electrode [ɪ'lektrəʊd] n electrodo m.

electroencephalogram [ɪlektrəʊen'sefələgræm] n Med electroencefalograma m.

electroencephalograph [ɪlektrəʊen'sefələgrɑːf] n Med electroencefalógrafo m.

electrolysis [ɪlek'trɒlɪsɪs] n electrólisis f.

electrolyte [ɪ'lektrəʊlaɪt] n electrólito m.

electrolyze [ɪ'lektrəʊlaɪz] vtr electrolizar.

electromagnet [ɪlektrəʊ'mægnɪt] n electroimán m.

electromagnetic [ɪlektrəʊmæg'netɪk] adj electromagnético,-a. ■ **e. field**, campo m electromagnético.

electron [ɪ'lektrɒn] n electrón m. ■ **e. microscope**, microscopio m electrónico.

electronic [ɪlek'trɒnɪk] adj electrónico,-a.

electronics [ɪlek'trɒnɪks] n **1** (science) electrónica f. **2** (of machine) componentes mpl electrónicos.

elegance ['elɪgəns] n elegancia f.

elegant ['elɪgənt] adj elegante. ♦ **elegantly** adv con elegancia.

elegy ['elɪdʒɪ] n Lit elegía f.

element ['elɪmənt] n **1** (gen) elemento m; **an e. of surprise**, un elemento de sorpresa; **the human e.**, el factor humano. **2** (part of a whole) parte f, componente m; **an e. of truth**, una parte de verdad; **the reactionary elements of the party**, la fracción reaccionaria del partido. **3** (electrical) resistencia f. **4** Chem elemento m. **5** Meteor **the elements**, los elementos, las fuerzas de la naturaleza; fig **to brave the e.**, hacer frente a los elementos; fam fig **to be in one's element**, estar en su elemento.

elemental [elɪ'mənt əl] adj elemental, básico,-a.

elementary [elɪ'mentərɪ] adj **1** (basic) elemental, fundamental; **e. arithmetic**, matemáticas elementales. ■ Educ **e. school**, escuela f primaria. **2** (not developed) rudimentario,-a. **3** (easy) fácil.

elephant ['elɪfənt] *n Zool* elefante *m*; **cow e.**, elefanta *f*; *fig* **white e.**, cosa *f* inútil; *fam* **to have a memory like an e.**, tener una memoria de elefante.

elephantiasis [elɪfən'taɪəsɪs] *n Med* elefantiasis *f*.

elephantine [eh'fæntaɪn] *adj* **1** *(huge)* mastodóntico,-a, descomunal. **2** *(clumsy)* torpe, patoso,-a.

elevate ['elɪveɪt] *vtr* **1** *(mind, tone of conversation)* elevar. **2** *(in rank)* ascender, promover.

elevated ['elɪveɪtɪd] *adj* elevado,-a.

elevation [elɪ'veɪʃən] *n* **1** elevación *f*. **2** *(in rank)* ascenso *m*. **3** *Archit* alzado *m*. **4** *Rel* **the E.**, la Ascensión. **5** *Geog (hill)* elevación *f*; *(above sea level)* altitud *f*.

elevator ['elɪveɪtəʳ] *n* **1** *US* ascensor *m*. ■ **goods e.**, montacargas *m inv*. **2** *Av* timón *m* de profundidad.

eleven [ɪ'levən] **I** *adj* once *inv*. **II** *n* once *m inv*; *Sport* equipo *m*, once *m*; *see also* **seven.**

eleven-plus [ɪ'levənplʌs] *n Educ* examen *m* de ingreso a un **grammar school.**

elevenses [ɪ'levənzɪz] *npl fam* bocadillo *m* de las once.

eleventh [ɪ'levənθ] **I** *adj* undécimo,-a, onceavo,-a; *fig* **at the e. hour**, en el último momento. **II** *n* **1** *(in series)* undécimo,-a *m,f*. **2** *(fraction)* undécima parte *f*; *see also* **seventh.**

elf [elf] *n (pl elves* [elvz]*)* elfo *m*.

elfish ['elfɪʃ] *adj* travieso,-a, malicioso,-a.

elicit [ɪ'lɪsɪt] *vtr* provocar, obtener.

elide [ɪ'laɪd] *vtr Ling* elidir.

eligibility [elɪdʒə'bɪlɪtɪ] *n* elegibilidad *f*, idoneidad *f*.

eligible ['elɪdʒəbl] *adj (fulfilling requirements)* idóneo,-a, apto,-a; **an e. young man**, un buen partido; **he isn't e. to vote**, no tiene derecho al voto; **you are e. for a grant**, tienes derecho a una beca, cumples los requisitos para obtener una beca.

eliminate [ɪ'lɪmɪneɪt] *vtr* eliminar.

elimination [ɪlɪmɪ'neɪʃən] *n* eliminación *f*.

eliminatory [ɪ'lɪmɪnətərɪ] *adj* eliminatorio,-a; *Sport* **e. round**, eliminatoria *f*.

elision [ɪ'lɪʒən] *n Ling Lit* elisión *f*.

élite [ɪ'liːt] *n* elite *f*.

élitism [ɪ'liːtɪzəm] *n* elitismo *m*.

élitist [ɪ'liːtɪst] *adj* elitista.

elixir [ɪ'lɪksəʳ] *n* elixir *m*.

Elizabethan [ɪlɪzə'biːθən] *adj & n* isabelino,-a *(m,f)*.

elk [elk] *n Zool* alce *m*.

ellipsis [ɪ'lɪpsɪs] *n (pl ellipses* [ɪ'lɪpsiːz]*)* *Ling Lit* elipsis *f*.

elm [elm] *n Bot* olmo *m*. ■ **Dutch e. disease**, grafiosis *f*, enfermedad *f* holandesa del olmo.

elocution [elə'kjuːʃən] *n* elocución *f*.

elongate [iː'lɒŋgeɪt] *vtr* alargar, extender.

elope [ɪ'ləʊp] *vi* fugarse para casarse.

elopement [ɪ'ləʊpmənt] *n* fuga *f* para casarse.

eloquence ['eləkwəns] *n* elocuencia *f*.

eloquent ['eləkwənt] *adj* elocuente.

else [els] *adv* **1** más, otro,-a; **anyone e.**, alguien más; **anything e.?**, ¿algo más?; **everything e.**, todo lo demás; **no-one e.**, nadie más; **someone e.**, otro,-a; **something e.**, otra cosa, algo más; **somewhere e.**, en otra parte; **what e.?**, ¿qué más?; **where e.?**, ¿en qué otro sitio? **2** *fam (otherwise)* **or e.**, si no; **do as I tell you or e.**, haz lo que te digo, si no (ya verás).

elsewhere [els'weəʳ] *adv* en otro sitio, en otra parte.

elucidate [ɪ'luːsɪdeɪt] *vtr* aclarar, dilucidar, poner en claro.

elucidation [ɪluːsɪ'deɪʃən] *n* aclaración *f*, dilucidación *f*.

elude [ɪ'luːd] *vtr* **1** *(escape)* eludir, escapar; **his name eludes me**, no consigo acordarme de su nombre. **2** *(avoid)* esquivar.

elusive [ɪ'luːsɪv] *adj* **1** *(difficult to find)* esquivo,-a, escurridizo,-a. **2** *(evasive)* evasivo,-a.

elver ['elvəʳ] *n Zool* angula *f*.

emaciated [ɪ'meɪsɪeɪtɪd] *adj (body)* enflaquecido,-a; *(of face)* demacrado,-a; **to become e.**, *(go thin)* enflaquecer; *(waste away)* demacrarse.

emaciation [ɪmeɪsɪ'eɪʃən] *n (of body)* enflaquecimiento *m*; *(of face)* demacración *f*.

emanate ['eməneɪt] *vi* emanar **(from**, de), provenir **(from**, de).

emancipate [ɪ'mænsɪpeɪt] *vtr* emancipar.

emancipation [ɪmænsɪ'peɪʃən] *n* emancipación *f*.

emasculate [ɪ'mæskjʊleɪt] *vtr* **1** *(debilitate, weaken)* debilitar. **2** *Med (castrate)* emacular, castrar.

emasculation [ɪmæskjʊ'leɪʃən] *n* emasculación *f*, castración *f*.

embalm [ɪm'bɑːm] *vtr* embalsamar.

embalmer [ɪm'bɑːməʳ] *n* embalsamador,-a *m,f*.

embankment [ɪm'bæŋkmənt] *n* **1** *(de tierra)* terraplén *m*. **2** *(river)* dique *m*.

embargo [em'bɑːgəʊ] **I** *n (pl embargoes)* prohibición *f*, embargo *m*; **to put an e. on sth**, prohibir algo. **II** *vtr (pt & pp embargoed)* **1** *(forbid)* prohibir. **2** *(seize)* embargar.

embark [em'bɑːk] **I** *vtr (merchandize)* embarcar. **II** *vi (boat, ship)* embarcar, embarcarse; *fig* **to e. upon**, emprender.

embarkation [embɑː'keɪʃən] *n* embarque *m*.

embarrass [ɪm'bærəs] *vtr* avergonzar, azorar.

embarrassed [ɪm'bærəst] *adj* avergonzado,-a.

embarrassing [ɪm'bærəsɪŋ] *adj* embarazoso,-a, violento,-a; **it's an e. situation**, es una situación violenta.

embarrassment [ɪm'bærəsmənt] *n* vergüenza *f*; **to be an e. to sb**, hacer pasar vergüenza a algn.

embassy ['embəsɪ] *n* embajada *f*.

embed [ɪm'bed] *vtr (pt & pp embedded)* **1** *(jewels etc)* incrustar. **2** *fig* fijar, grabar; **it's embedded in my memory**, lo tengo grabado en la mente.

embellish [ɪm'belɪʃ] *vtr (decorate)* adornar, embellecer; *fig (story, facts)* adornar.

embellishment [ɪm'belɪʃmənt] *n* adorno *m*.

ember ['embəʳ] *n* brasa *f*, ascua *f*, rescoldo *m*.

embezzle [ɪm'bezəl] *vtr* desfalcar, malversar.

embezzlement [ɪm'bezəlmənt] *n* desfalco *m*, malversación *f*.

embezzler [ɪm'bezələʳ] *n* desfalcador,-a *m, f*, malversador,-a *m,f*.

embitter [ɪm'bɪtəʳ] *vtr* amargar.

embittered [ɪm'bɪtəd] *adj* amargado,-a, resentido,-a.

emblem ['embləm] *n* emblema *m*.

embodiment [ɪm'bɒdɪmənt] *n* encarnación *f*, personificación *f*.

embody [ɪm'bɒdɪ] *vtr (pt & pp embodied)* **1** *(include)* incorporar, abarcar. **2** *(personify)* encarnar, personificar.

embolism ['embəlɪzəm] *n Med* embolia *f*.

emboss [ɪm'bɒs] *vtr (gen)* grabar en relieve; *(leather, metal)* repujar.

embossed [ɪm'bɒst] *adj (gen)* en relieve; *(leather, metal)* repujado,-a; **e. letterhead**, membrete *m* en relieve.

embrace [ɪm'breɪs] **I** *vtr* **1** *(gen)* abrazar. **2** *(occasion)* aprovechar. **3** *(accept)* aceptar, adoptar. **4** *(cover, include)* abarcar. **II** *vi* abrazarse; **they embraced**, se abrazaron. **III** *n* abrazo *m*.

embroider [ɪm'brɔɪdəʳ] *vtr* **1** *Sew* bordar. **2** *fig (story, truth)* adornar, embellecer.

embroidery [ɪm'brɔɪdərɪ] *n* **1** *Sew* bordado *m*. **2** *fig* adorno *m*.

embroil [ɪm'brɔɪl] *vtr* enredar, liar; **to become embroiled in sth,** enredarse en algo, liarse en algo.

embryo ['embrɪəʊ] *n* embrión *m*.

embryonic [embrɪ'ɒnɪk] *adj fig* embrionario,-a.

emend [ɪ'mend] *vtr* corregir, enmendar.

emendation [i:men'deɪʃən] *n* corrección *f*, enmienda *f*.

emerald ['emərəld] **I** *n* (*stone*) esmeralda *f*; (*colour*) esmeralda *m*. **II** *adj* (color) esmeralda; **the E. Isle,** Irlanda.

emerge [ɪ'mɜːdʒ] *vi* (*gen*) salir; (*problem*) surgir; **it emerged that ...,** resultó que ... .

emergence [ɪ'mɜːdʒəns] *n* aparición *f*, surgimiento *m*.

emergency [ɪ'mɜːdʒənsɪ] *n* **1** (*gen*) emergencia *f*; **in an e.,** en caso de emergencia. ■ **e. exit,** salida *f* de emergencia; *Av* **e. landing,** aterrizaje *m* forzoso; **e. measures,** medidas *fpl* de urgencia; *Aut* **e. stop,** frenazo *m* en seco; *Pol* **state of e.,** estado *m* de excepción. **2** *Med* urgencia *f*, caso *m* de urgencia.

emergent [ɪ'mɜːdʒənt] *adj* emergente. ■ **e. nation,** país *m* en vías de desarrollo.

emeritus [ɪ'merɪtəs] *adj* emérito,-a.

emery ['emərɪ] *n* esmeril *m*. ■ **e. board,** lima *f* de uñas.

emetic [ɪ'metɪk] **I** *adj* emético,-a, vomitivo,-a. **II** *n* emético *m*, vomitivo *m*.

emigrant ['emɪgrənt] *n* emigrante *mf*.

emigrate ['emɪgreɪt] *vi* emigrar.

emigration [emɪ'greɪʃən] *n* emigración *f*.

émigré ['emɪgreɪ] *n* emigrado,-a *m,f*.

eminence ['emɪnəns] *n* eminencia *f*; *Rel* **Your/His E.,** Su Eminencia; *fig* **grey e.,** eminencia gris.

eminent ['emɪnənt] *adj* (*distinguished*) eminente; (*outstanding*) destacado,-a.

emirate ['emɪrɪt] *n* emirato *m*.

emissary ['emɪsərɪ] *n* emisario,-a *m,f*.

emission [ɪ'mɪʃən] *n* emisión *f*.

emit [ɪ'mɪt] *vtr (pt & pp emitted)* (*signals*) emitir; (*smells*) despedir; (*sound*) producir.

emolument [ɪ'mɒljʊmənt] *n* (*gen pl*) emolumentos *mpl*, honorarios *mpl*.

emotion [ɪ'məʊʃən] *n* emoción *f*.

emotional [ɪ'məʊʃənəl] *adj* **1** (*concerning the emotions*) emocional, sensible. **2** (*moving*) emotivo,-a, conmovedor,-a.

emotionalism [ɪ'məʊʃənəlɪzəm] *n* emotividad *f*, sentimentalismo *m*, sensiblería *f*.

emotive [ɪ'məʊtɪv] *adj* emotivo,-a.

empathy ['empəθɪ] *n* empatía *f*.

emperor ['empərəʳ] *n* emperador *m*.

emphasis ['emfəsɪs] *n (pl emphases* ['emfəsi:z]*)* énfasis *m*; **in this school the e. is on languages,** en este colegio ponemos especial énfasis en los idiomas; **to put** *or* **place e. on sth,** hacer hincapié en algo, subrayar algo, poner algo de relieve.

emphasize ['emfəsaɪz] *vtr (give importance to)* subrayar, hacer hincapié en; (*specify*) poner de relieve; (*insist*) insistir; (*highlight*) hacer resaltar; **I must e. that ...,** debo insistir que ...; **the dress emphasizes her figure,** el vestido realza su figura.

emphatic [em'fætɪk] *adj* (*forceful*) enfático,-a, enérgico,-a; (*convinced*) categórico,-a; **e. denial,** negación rotunda; **he was most e.,** fue muy categórico. ◆ **emphatically** *adv* enfáticamente, enérgicamente, categóricamente.

empire ['empaɪəʳ] *n* imperio *m*; **the British/Roman E.,** el Imperio Británico/Romano.

empirical [em'pɪrɪkəl] *adj* empírico,-a.

empiricism [em'pɪrɪsɪzəm] *n* empirismo *m*.

emplacement [em'pleɪsmənt] *n* emplazamiento *m*.

employ [ɪm'plɔɪ] **I** *vtr* **1** (*worker*) emplear, contratar. **2** (*make use of*) emplear, usar. **3** (*time*) ocupar. **II** *n* empleo *m*; **to be in the e. of sb,** ser empleado de algn.

employee [em'plɔɪi:, emplɔɪ'i:] *n* empleado,-a *m,f*.

employer [ɪm'plɔɪəʳ] *n* empresario,-a *m,f*, patrón,-ona *m,f*.

employment [ɪm'plɔɪmənt] *n* empleo *m*, trabajo *m*. ■ **e. agency,** agencia *f* de colocaciones; **e. exchange,** bolsa *f* de trabajo; **full e.,** pleno empleo *m*.

emporium [em'pɔːrɪəm] *n* (*pl* **emporia** [em'pɔːrɪə]) emporio *m*, almacén *m*.

empower [ɪm'paʊəʳ] *vtr* autorizar, habilitar.

empress ['emprɪs] *n* emperatriz *f*.

emptiness ['emptɪnɪs] *n* vacío *m*.

empty ['emptɪ] **I** *adj* (*emptier, emptiest*) vacío,-a; **an e. house,** una casa deshabitada; **an e. look,** una mirada vacía; **to do sth on an e. stomach,** hacer algo en ayunas *or* con el estómago vacío. ■ **e. promises,** promesas *fpl* vanas. **II** *vtr* vaciar. **III** *vi* **1** (*gen*) vaciarse. **2** (*of river*) desembocar (*into*, en). **IV empties** *npl* envases *mpl*, cascos *mpl*.

empty-handed [emptɪ'hændɪd] *adj* con las manos vacías.

empty-headed [emptɪ'hedɪd] *adj* **1** (*dim-witted*) tonto,-a, cabeza hueca *or* de chorlito. **2** (*frivolous*) frívolo,-a.

emu ['iːmjuː] *n Orn* emú *m*.

emulate ['emjʊleɪt] *vtr* emular.

emulation [emjʊ'leɪʃən] *n* emulación *f*.

emulsification [ɪmʌlsɪfɪ'keɪʃən] *n* emulsificación *f*.

emulsify [ɪ'mʌlsɪfaɪ] *vtr (pt & pp emulsified)* emulsionar.

emulsion [ɪ'mʌlʃən] *n* emulsión *f*. ■ **e. paint,** pintura *f* mate.

enable [ɪn'eɪbəl] *vtr* permitir.

enact [ɪn'ækt] *vtr* (*play*) representar; (*law, scene*) promulgar.

enamel [ɪ'næməl] **I** *n* esmalte *m*. **II** *vtr* (*pt & pp* **enamelled,** US **enameled**) esmaltar.

enamoured, US **enamored** [ɪ'næməd] *adj* enamorado,-a; **to be e. of** *or* **by sth,** encantarle algo a algn.

encamp [ɪn'kæmp] *vt* acampar.

encampment [ɪn'kæmpmənt] *n Mil* campamento *m*.

encapsulate [ɪn'kæpsjʊleɪt] *vtr* encapsular, encerrar.

encase [ɪn'keɪs] *vtr* encajonar, encerrar; **to be encased in,** estar revestido de.

encephalitis [ensefə'laɪtɪs] *n Med* encefalitis *f*.

enchant [ɪn'tʃɑːnt] *vtr* (*gen*) encantar, cautivar; (*cast spell on*) hechizar.

enchanter [ɪn'tʃɑːntəʳ] *n* hechicero *m*.

enchanting [ɪn'tʃɑːntɪŋ] *adj* encantador,-a.

enchantment [ɪn'tʃɑːntmənt] *n* encanto *m*, hechizo *m*.

enchantress [ɪn'tʃɑːntrɪs] *n* hechicera *f*.

encircle [ɪn'sɜːkəl] *vtr* rodear, cercar.

enclave ['enkleɪv] *n* enclave *m*.

enclose [ɪn'kləʊz] *vtr* **1** (*surround*) rodear, cercar. **2** (*fenced in*) encerrar; *Rel* **an enclosed order,** una orden de clausura. **3** (*in an envelope*) adjuntar; **enclosed herewith,** adjunto *or* a la presente; **please find enclosed,** le enviamos adjunto *or* anexo; **the enclosed document,** el documento adjunto.

enclosure [ɪn'kləʊʒəʳ] *n* **1** (*act*) cercamiento *m*, encierro *m*. **2** (*fenced area*) cercado *m*. **3** (*in an envelope*) documento *m* adjunto, anexo *m*. **4** (*stadium*) general *f*. **5** (*racecourse*) recinto *m*.

encompass [ɪn'kʌmpəs] *vtr* abarcar.

encore ['ɒŋkɔː] **I** *interj* ¡otra!, ¡bis! **II** *n* repetición *f*, bis *m*; **to give an e.,** repetir, bisar.

encounter [ɪn'kaʊntəʳ] **I** *n* (*fight, meeting*) encuentro *m*. **II** *vtr* (*meet*) encontrar, encontrarse con; (*problems*) tropezar con.

encourage [ɪn'kʌrɪdʒ] *vtr* **1** (*urge*) animar. **2** (*help to develop*) fomentar, favorecer.

encouragement [ɪnˈkʌrɪdʒmənt] *n* estímulo *m*, aliento *m*.

encouraging [ɪnˈkʌrɪdʒɪŋ] *adj (smile)* alentador,-a; *(news)* prometedor,-a, halagüeño,-a.

encroach [ɪnˈkrəʊtʃ] *vtr* **to e. on,** *(territory)* invadir; *(rights)* usurpar, abusar; *(time, freedom)* quitar.

encroachment [ɪnˈkrəʊtʃmənt] *n* invasión *f*, usurpación *f*.

encrusted [ɪnˈkrʌstɪd] *adj* incrustado,-a (**with,** de).

encumber [ɪnˈkʌmbəʳ] *vtr (impede)* estorbar; *(debts)* gravar.

encumbrance [ɪnˈkʌmbrəns] *n* estorbo *m*; *Fin Jur* gravamen *m*.

encyclical [ɪnˈsɪklɪkəl] *n Rel* encíclica *f*.

encyclop(a)edia [ensaɪkləʊˈpiːdɪə] *n* enciclopedia *f*.

encyclop(a)edic [ensaɪkləʊˈpiːdɪk] *adj* enciclopédico,-a.

end [end] **I** *n* **1** *(of stick)* punta *f*; *(street)* final *m*; *(table)* extremo *m*; *fig* **to jump in at the deep e.,** meterse de cabeza; *fig* **to make ends meet,** llegar a final de mes; *fig* **to make one's hair stand on e.,** ponersele el pelo en punta; *fam* **to get the wrong e. of the stick,** tomar el rábano de las hojas. **2** *(conclusion)* fin *m*, final *m*; **in the e.,** al final; **for hours/weeks on e.,** hora/semana tras hora/semana; **no e. of problems,** un sinfín de problemas, cantidad de problemas; **there's no e. to it,** esto no se acaba nunca; **that's the e.!,** ¡es el colmo!; **to bring an e. to sth,** poner fin a algo, acabar con algo; **to draw to an e.,** acabarse; **to put an e. to,** acabar con; *fig* **the e. of the line** *or* **road,** el acabóse; *fig* **to the bitter e.,** hasta el último suspiro. **3** *(aim)* objetivo *m*, fin *m*; **to achieve one's e.,** alcanzar su objetivo; **to no e.,** en vano; **the e. justifies the means,** el fin justifica los medios. ■ **e. product,** producto *m* final; **loose ends,** cabos *mpl* sueltos. **4** *(remnants)* resto *m*, cabo *m*; **cigarette e.,** colilla *f*. **II** *vtr* acabar, terminar, concluir; *fam* **to e. it all,** suicidarse. **III** *vi* acabarse, terminarse; **at what time does the film e.?,** ¿a qué hora (se) termina la película? ◆ **end up** *vi* terminar, acabar; **he'll e. up with no money,** acabará sin dinero; **it ended up in the dustbin,** fue a parar en el cubo de la basura; **to e. up doing sth,** terminar por hacer algo.

endanger [ɪnˈdeɪndʒəʳ] *vtr* poner en peligro.

endangered [ɪnˈdeɪndʒəd] *adj Zool* en peligro; **e. species,** especie *f* en peligro de extinción).

endearing [ɪnˈdɪərɪŋ] *adj* simpático,-a, atractivo,-a.

endearment [ɪnˈdɪəmənt] *n* palabra *f* or frase *f* cariñosa.

endeavour, *US* **endeavor** [ɪnˈdevəʳ] **I** *n* esfuerzo *m*, empeño *m*. **II** *vtr* intentar, procurar; **to e. to do sth,** procurar hacer algo.

endemic [enˈdemɪk] *adj* endémico,-a.

ending [ˈendɪŋ] *n* final *m*.

endive [ˈendaɪv] *n Bot* **1** endibia *f*. **2** *US* escarola *f*.

endless [ˈendlɪs] *adj (wait etc)* interminable, eterno,-a, sin fin; *(resources)* inagotable.

endocrine [ˈendəʊkrɪn] *adj* endocrino,-a. ■ **e. gland,** glándula *f* endocrina.

endocrinologist [endəʊkrɪˈnɒlədʒɪst] *n* endocrinólogo,-a *m*, *f*.

endocrinology [endəʊkrɪˈnɒlədʒɪ] *n* endocrinología *f*.

endorse [ɪnˈdɔːs] *vtr* **I** *Fin* endosar. **2** *(approve)* aprobar; *(support)* apoyar.

endorsement [ɪnˈdɔːsmənt] *n* **1** *Fin* endoso *m*. **2** *Aut* nota *f* de sanción. **3** *(approval)* aprobación *f*; *(support)* respaldo *m*, apoyo *m*.

endow [ɪnˈdaʊ] *vtr* dotar; **to be endowed with,** estar dotado,-a de.

endowment [ɪnˈdaʊmənt] *n* *(donation)* donación *f*. ■ *Ins* **e. policy,** póliza *f* diferida.

endpaper [ˈendpeɪpəʳ] *n Print* guarda *f*.

endurance [ɪnˈdjʊərəns] *n* resistencia *f*. ■ **e. test,** prueba *f* de resistencia.

endure [ɪnˈdjʊəʳ] **I** *vtr (bear)* aguantar, soportar. **II** *vi (last)* durar, perdurar.

enduring [ɪnˈdjʊərɪŋ] *adj* duradero,-a.

enema [ˈenɪmə] *n Med* enema *m*.

enemy [ˈenəmɪ] *adj & n* enemigo,-a *(m, f)*; **to make enemies,** hacerse enemigos. ■ *Mil* **e. forces,** fuerzas *fpl* enemigas.

energetic [enəˈdʒetɪk] *adj* enérgico,-a. ◆ **energetically** *adv* enérgicamente.

energy [ˈenədʒɪ] *n* energía *f*; **to save e.,** ahorrar energía. ■ **e. crisis,** crisis *f* energética.

enervate [ˈenəveɪt] *vtr* enervar, debilitar.

enervating [ˈenəveɪtɪŋ] *adj* enervador,-a, enervante.

enfold [ɪnˈfəʊld] *vtr* envolver.

enforce [ɪnˈfɔːs] *vtr (law)* hacer cumplir; *(compel)* imponer; *(argument)* reforzar, enfatizar.

enforcement [ɪnˈfɔːsmənt] *n* aplicación *f*.

enfranchise [ɪnˈfræntʃaɪz] *vtr Pol* conceder el derecho de votar; *(slave)* liberar.

engage [ɪnˈgeɪdʒ] *vtr* **1** *(hire)* contratar. **2** *(attention)* atraer, llamar. **3** *(conversation)* entablar. **4** *Tech* engranar; *Aut* **to e. the clutch,** embragar.

engaged [ɪnˈgeɪdʒd] *adj* **1** *(to be married)* prometido,-a; **to get e.,** prometerse. **2** *(busy)* ocupado,-a; *Tel* **it's e.,** está comunicando.

engagement [ɪnˈgeɪdʒmənt] *n* **1** *(to be married)* petición *f* de mano; *(period)* noviazgo *m*. ■ **e. ring,** anillo *m* de compromiso. **2** *(business appointment)* cita *f*; **prior e.,** cita *f* previa. **3** *Mil* combate *m*.

engaging [ɪnˈgeɪdʒɪŋ] *adj* simpático,-a, atractivo,-a, agradable.

engender [ɪnˈdʒendəʳ] *vtr* engendrar.

engine [ˈendʒɪn] *n* **1** *(combustion)* motor *m*. ■ **e. room,** sala *f* de máquinas; **steam e.,** máquina *f* de vapor. **2** *Rail* locomotora *f*. ■ **e. driver,** maquinista *mf*; **fire e.,** coche *m* de bomberos.

engineer [endʒɪˈnɪəʳ] **I** *n* **1** ingeniero,-a *m*, *f*. ■ **civil e.,** ingeniero *m* de caminos; **chemical e.,** ingeniero *m* químico. **2** *US Rail* maquinista *mf*. **II** *vtr fig (contrive)* maquinar, tramar.

engineering [endʒɪˈnɪərɪŋ] *n* ingeniería *f*. ■ **electrical e.,** electrotecnia *f*; **civil e.,** ingeniería *f* civil.

England [ˈɪŋglənd] *n* Inglaterra *f*.

English [ˈɪŋglɪʃ] **I** *adj* inglés,-esa. **II** *n* **1** *(language)* inglés *m*. **2** *pl* **the E.,** los ingleses.

Englishman [ˈɪŋglɪʃmən] *n (pl Englishmen)* inglés *m*.

English-speaking [ˈɪŋglɪʃspiːkɪŋ] *adj* de habla inglesa.

Englishwoman [ˈɪŋglɪʃwʊmən] *n (pl Englishwomen* [ˈɪŋglɪʃwɪmɪn]*)* inglesa *f*.

engorged [ɪnˈgɔːdʒd] *adj Med* congestionado,-a.

engrave [ɪnˈgreɪv] *vtr* grabar.

engraver [ɪnˈgreɪvəʳ] *n* grabador,-a *m*, *f*.

engraving [ɪnˈgreɪvɪŋ] *n* **1** *(art)* grabación *f*. **2** *(picture, plate)* grabado *m*.

engrossed [ɪnˈgrəʊst] *adj* absorto,-a (**in,** en).

engrossing [ɪnˈgrəʊsɪŋ] *adj* fascinante, apasionante.

engulf [ɪnˈgʌlf] *vtr* tragarse, sumergir, hundir.

engulfed [ɪnˈgʌlft] *adj* hundido,-a (**in,** en).

enhance [ɪnˈhɑːns] *vtr (beauty)* realzar; *(power)* aumentar; *(chances)* mejorar.

enigma [ɪˈnɪgmə] *n* enigma *m*.

enigmatic [ɪnɪgˈmætɪk] *adj* enigmático,-a.

enjoy [ɪnˈdʒɔɪ] **I** *vtr* **1** *(take pleasure)* disfrutar de; **did you e. the film?,** ¿te gustó la película?; **to e. oneself,** pasarlo bien, divertirse. **2** *(benefit from)* gozar de; **to e. good health,** gozar de buena salud. **II** *vi US* **e.!,** ¡qué lo pases bien!

enjoyable [ɪn'dʒɔɪəbəl] *adj* agradable, divertido,-a.

enjoyment [ɪn'dʒɔɪmənt] *n* placer *m*, gusto *m*; **to spoil sb's e.,** quitarle el gusto a algn.

enlarge [ɪn'lɑːdʒ] I *vtr* extender, ampliar; *Phot* ampliar. II *vi* ampliarse; **to e. upon a subject,** extenderse sobre un tema.

enlargement [ɪn'lɑːdʒmənt] *n Phot* ampliación *f*.

enlarger [ɪn'lɑːdʒə^r] *n Phot* ampliadora *f*.

enlighten [ɪn'laɪtən] *vtr* iluminar; **to e. sb on sth,** aclararle algo a algn.

enlightened [ɪn'laɪtənd] *adj* 1 *(leaned)* culto,-a; *(informed)* bien informado,-a. 2 *Hist* ilustrado,-a; **e. despotism,** despotismo ilustrado.

enlightenment [ɪn'laɪtənmənt] *n* aclaración *f*; **the Age of E.,** el Siglo de las Luces.

enlist [ɪn'lɪst] I *vtr Mil* reclutar; **to e. sb's help,** conseguir ayuda de algn. II *vi Mil* alistarse.

enlisted [ɪn'lɪstɪd] *adj* alistado,-a: *US* **e. man,** soldado raso, soldado de tropa.

enliven [ɪn'laɪvən] *vtr* animar, avivar.

en masse [ɒn'mæs] *adv* en masa.

enmesh [ɪn'meʃ] *vtr* enredar.

enmity ['enmɪtɪ] *n* enemistad *f*, hostilidad *f*.

enormity [ɪ'nɔːmɪtɪ] *n* 1 *(hugeness)* enormidad *f*, inmensidad *f*. 2 *(atrocity)* atrocidad *f*, monstruosidad *f*.

enormous [ɪ'nɔːməs] *adj* enorme, inmenso,-a, descomunal. ◆ **enormously** *adv* enormemente; **I enjoyed myself e.,** lo pasé genial.

enough [ɪ'nʌf] I *adj* bastante, suficiente; **e. books,** bastantes libros; **e. money,** bastante dinero; **have we got e. petrol?,** ¿tenemos suficiente gasolina? II *adv* bastante; **fair e.,** de acuerdo; **large e.,** bastante grande; **oddly** *or* **curiously e. ...,** lo curioso es que ...; **sure e.,** en efecto, sin duda alguna. III *n* lo bastante, lo suficiente; **e. to live on,** lo suficiente para vivir; **it isn't e.,** no basta; **more than e.,** más que suficiente; *fam* **e. is e.,** ya está, ¡basta!; *fam* **I've had e.!,** estoy harto!

en passant [ɒnpæ'sɒn] *adv* de paso.

enquire [ɪn'kwaɪə^r] *vi (information)* preguntar; *Jur* **to e. into a case,** investigar un caso.

enquiry [ɪn'kwaɪərɪ] *n* 1 *(question)* pregunta *f*; **enquiries,** información *f*; **to make an e.,** preguntar. 2 *(investigation)* investigación *f*; **they conducted an e. into the affair,** investigaron el asunto.

enrage [ɪn'reɪdʒ] *vtr* enfurecer.

enrich [ɪn'rɪtʃ] *vtr* enriquecer; **enriched with vitamin C,** enriquecido con vitamina C.

enrol, *US* **enroll** [ɪn'rəʊl] *(pt & pp* **enrolled)** I *vtr* matricular. II *vi* matricularse, inscribirse, apuntarse.

enrolment, *US* **enrollment** [ɪn'rəʊlmənt] *n* matrícula *f*.

en route [ɒn'ruːt] *adv* en *or* por el camino; **en r. to Soria,** camino de Soria.

ensemble [ɒn'sɒmbəl] *n Mus* conjunto *m*.

enshrine [ɪn'ʃraɪn] *vtr fig* conservar religiosamente.

ensign ['ensaɪn] *n* bandera *f*, pabellón *m*.

enslave [ɪn'sleɪv] *vtr* esclavizar.

enslavement [ɪn'sleɪvmənt] *n* esclavitud *f*.

ensue [ɪn'sjuː] *vi* 1 *(follow)* seguir. 2 *(result)* resultar **(from,** de).

ensuing [ɪn'sjuːɪŋ] *adj* consiguiente, subsiguiente.

ensure [ɪn'ʃʊə^r] *vtr* asegurar.

entail [ɪn'teɪl] *vtr* 1 *(give rise to)* ocasionar, acarrear. 2 *(involve)* suponer, implicar. 3 *Jur* vincular.

entangle [ɪn'tæŋgəl] *vtr (general)* enredar; **he became entangled in the net,** se enredó en la red; *fig* **to get entangled in sth,** enredarse en algo; *fig* **they became entangled in political affairs,** se vieron involucrados en asuntos políticos.

entanglement [ɪn'tæŋgəlmənt] *n* enredo *m*; *fig* complicación *f*.

enter ['entə^r] I *vtr* 1 *(go into)* entrar en; *fig (join)* ingresar en, hacerse socio de. 2 *(write down)* apuntar, anotar, dar entrada a. 3 *(register)* inscribir; **to e. a car for a race,** inscribir un coche en una carrera; **to e. one's name for a course,** matricularse en un curso. 4 *Comput* dar entrada a. II *vi* entrar; **to e. for a race,** tomar parte en *or* participar en una carrera. ◆ **enter into** *vtr* 1 *(agreement)* concertar, firmar; *(negotiations)* iniciar **(with,** con); *(bargain)* cerrar. 2 *(relations)* establecer **(with,** con); *(marriage)* contraer **(with,** con). 3 *(conversation)* entablar **(with,** con).

enterprise ['entəpraɪz] *n* empresa *f*; **a dangerous e.,** una empresa peligrosa; **a man of e.,** un hombre de empresa. ■ **free e.,** libre empresa *f*; **private e.,** iniciativa *f* privada; *(as a whole)* el sector privado; *(capitalism)* capitalismo *m*; **public e.,** el sector público.

enterprising ['entəpraɪzɪŋ] *adj* emprendedor,-a.

entertain [entə'teɪn] I *vtr* I *(amuse)* divertir. 2 *(consider)* considerar; **to e. an idea,** abrigar una idea; **to e. a proposal,** estudiar una propuesta; **to e. the hope that ...,** abrigar la esperanza que .... II *vi* tener invitados; **they e. a lot,** invitan con mucha frecuencia.

entertainer [entə'teɪnə^r] *n* 1 *(gen)* animador,-a *m*, *f*. 2 *Theat* artista *mf*.

entertaining [entə'teɪnɪŋ] I *adj* divertido,-a, entretenido,-a. II *n* **the secretary has to do a lot of e.,** la secretaria tiene que hacer muchas relaciones públicas.

entertainment [entə'teɪnmənt] *n* 1 *(gen)* diversión *f*, entretenimiento *m*. ■ **e. allowance,** gastos *mpl* de representación. 2 *Theat* espectáculo *m*.

enthral, *US* **enthrall** [ɪn'θrɔːl] *vtr (pt & pp* **enthralled)** cautivar.

enthralling [ɪn'θrɔːlɪŋ] *adj* cautivador,-a, fascinante.

enthrone [ɪn'θrəʊn] *vtr* entronizar.

enthronement [ɪn'θrəʊnmənt] *n* entronización *f*.

enthuse [ɪn'θjuːz] I *vi* entusiasmarse **(over,** por). II *vtr* estimular, animar.

enthusiasm [ɪn'θjuːzɪæzəm] *n* entusiasmo *m*.

enthusiast [ɪn'θjuːzɪæst] *n* entusiasta *mf*, apasionado,-a *m*, *f*; **she's a real opera e.,** es una entusiasta de la ópera.

enthusiastic [ɪnθjuːzɪ'æstɪk] *adj* 1 *(person)* entusiasta; **to be e. about sth,** entusiasmarse por algo. 2 *(praise)* entusiástico,-a, caluroso,-a; **an e. welcome,** un recibimiento caluroso. ◆ **enthusiastically** *adv* con entusiasmo, entusiasmado,-a.

entice [ɪn'taɪs] *vtr* seducir, atraer.

enticing [ɪn'taɪsɪŋ] *adj* atractivo,-a, tentador,-a.

entire [ɪn'taɪə^r] *adj* entero,-a, todo,-a; **it wasn't an e. success,** no fue un éxito absoluto; **the e. community,** la comunidad entera; **the e. population,** toda la población. ◆ **entirely** *adv* 1 *(completely)* enteramente, totalmente, I **e. agree,** estoy totalmente de acuerdo. 2 *(solely)* únicamente, exclusivamente; **the group was made up e. of Germans,** el grupo estaba formado exclusivamente de alemanes

entirety [ɪn'taɪərɪtɪ] *n* totalidad *f*, **in its e.,** en su totalidad

entitle [ɪn'taɪtəl] *vtr* 1 *(allow)* dar derecho a, **it will e. you to travel free,** le dará derecho a viajar gratis; **to be entitled to,** tener derecho a 2 *(book etc)* titular, **the film was entitled ...,** la película se titulaba

entitlement [ɪn'taɪtəlmənt] *n* derecho *m*

entity ['entɪtɪ] *n* entidad *f*

entomologist [entə'mɒlədʒɪst] *n* entomólogo,-a *m*,*f*

entomology [entə'mɒlədʒɪ] *n* entomología *f*

entourage [ɒntʊ'rɑːʒ] *n* séquito *m*

entrails ['entreɪlz] *npl Anat* tripas *fpl*, *fig* entrañas *fpl*

entrance[1] ['entrəns] *n* 1 *(act of entering)* entrada *f*, *Theat* entrada *f* en escena, aparición *f*; **to make one's e.,** entrar en escena ■ **e. fee,** *(museum etc)* entrada *f*, *(organization)* cuota *f*, inscripción *f* 2 *(door)* entrada *f*, puerta *f* ■ **e. hall,**

vestíbulo *m*, **main e.**, puerta *f* principal. **3** *(admission)* admisión *f*, ingreso *m* ■ **e. examination,** examen *m* de ingreso

entrance² [ɪnˈtrɑːns] *vtr* arrebatar, extasiar, encantar

entranced [ɪnˈtrɑːnst] *adj (delighted)* encantado,-a, *(ecstatic)* extasiado,-a

entrancing [ɪnˈtrɑːnsɪŋ] *adj* fascinante, encantador,-a

entrant [ˈentrənt] *n (competition)* participante *mf*, *(applicant)* aspirante *mf*

entreat [ɪnˈtriːt] *vtr fml* suplicar, rogar, **I entreated them not to do it,** les rogué que no lo hicieran

entreaty [ɪnˈtriːtɪ] *n* súplica *f*, ruego *m*

entrée [ˈɒntreɪ] *n Culin* **1** entremés *m*, entrada *f* **2** *US* plato *m* fuerte

entrench [ɪnˈtrentʃ] *vtr fig* reafirmar, consolidar.

entrenched [ɪnˈtrentʃt] *adj* firmemente enraizado,-a

entrepreneur [ɒntrəprəˈnɜːᵣ] *n* **1** *(business person)* empresario,-a *m,f* **2** *(middle person)* intermediario,-a *m,f*

entrepreneurial [ɒntrəprəˈnɜːrɪəl] *adj* empresarial

entrust [ɪnˈtrʌst] *vtr* encargar **(with,** de)**, to e. sth to sb,** dejar algo al cuidado de algn

entry [ˈentrɪ] *n* **1** *(entrance)* entrada *f* ■ *Jur* **forcible e.,** allanamiento *m* de morada, *Aut* **no e.,** dirección *f* prohibida **2** *(in dictionary)* entrada *f*, artículo *m* **3** *(competition)* participante ■ **e. fee,** *(museum etc)* entrada *f*, *(organization)* cuota *f*, inscripción *f*

entwine [ɪnˈtwaɪn] **I** *vtr* entrelazar **II** *vi* **to become entwined,** entrelazarse, enredarse

enumerate [ɪˈnjuːməreɪt] *vtr* enumerar

enumeration [ɪnjuːməˈreɪʃən] *n* enumeración *f*

enunciate [ɪˈnʌnsɪeɪt] *vtr Ling* pronunciar, articular

envelop [ɪnˈveləp] *vtr* envolver

envelope [ˈenvələʊp] *n* **1** *(letters)* sobre *m*; *(cover)* funda *f*, **airmail e.,** sobre de avión **2** *Av* envoltura *f*

enviable [ˈenvɪəbəl] *adj* envidiable

envious [ˈenvɪəs] *adj* envidioso,-a, **to feel e.,** tener envidia. ◆ **enviously** *adv* con envidia, envidiosamente

environment [ɪnˈvaɪərənmənt] *n Ecol* medio ambiente *m*; *(surroundings)* ambiente *m*, *fig* contexto *m*

environmental [ɪnvaɪərənˈmentəl] *adj Ecol* del medio ambiente, ambiental, *fig* contextual, **e. pollution,** contaminación *f* del medio ambiente

environs [ɪnˈvaɪrənz] *npl* alrededores *mpl*

envisage [ɪnˈvɪzɪdʒ] *vtr* **1** *(imagine)* imaginarse **2** *(foresee)* prever; **I don't e. going before Christmas,** no pienso ir antes de Navidad

envision [ɪnˈvɪʒən] *vtr* imaginar

envoy [ˈenvɔɪ] *n* enviado,-a *m, f*, **special e.,** enviado especial

envy [ˈenvɪ] **I** *n* envidia *f*, **to be green with e.,** estar corroído por la envidia, **to be the envy of,** ser la envidia de **II** *vtr* envidiar, tener envidia de.

enzyme [ˈenzaɪm] *n Biol* enzima *m*

epaulet(te) [ˈepəlet] *n Mil* charretera *f*, hombrera *f*

ephemeral [ɪˈfemərəl] *adj* efímero,-a.

epic [ˈepɪk] **I** *n* epopeya *f* **II** *adj* épico,-a, **it reached e. proportions,** alcanzó dimensiones colosales.

epicentre, *US* **epicenter** [ˈepɪsentəᵣ] *n* epicentro *m*

epicure [ˈepɪkjʊəᵣ] *n fml* gastrónomo,-a *m,f*

epicurean [epɪkjʊˈriːən] *adj & n fml* epicúreo,-a *(m,f)*

epidemic [epɪˈdemɪk] **I** *n Med* epidemia *f*, *fig (wave)* ola *f* **II** *adj* epidémico,-a

epidermis [epɪˈdɜːmɪs] *n* epidermis *f*

epiglottis [epɪˈglɒtɪs] *n Anat* epiglotis *f*.

epigram [ˈepɪɡræm] *n Lit* epigrama *m*.

epilepsy [ˈepɪlepsɪ] *n Med* epilepsia *f*.

epileptic [epɪˈleptɪk] *adj & n Med* epiléptico,-a *(m,f)*.

epilogue, *US* **epilog** [ˈepɪlɒɡ] *n* epílogo *m*.

Epiphany [ɪˈpɪfənɪ] *n Rel* Epifanía *f*, Día *m* de Reyes

episcopal [ɪˈpɪskəpəl] *adj* episcopal

episcopalian [ɪpɪskəˈpeɪlɪən] *adj & n* episcopaliano,-a *(m,f)*

episode [ˈepɪsəʊd] *n* episodio *m*, *TV* capítulo *m*

episodic [epɪˈsɒdɪk] *adj* episódico,-a

epistle [ɪˈpɪsəl] *n* epístola *f*; *Rel* **the E. to the Ephesians,** la Epístola a los Efesios

epitaph [ˈepɪtɑːf] *n* epitafio *m*

epithet [ˈepɪθet] *n Ling* epíteto *m*

epitome [ɪˈpɪtəmɪ] *n fml* personificación *f*, **she was the e. of generosity,** era la personificación de la generosidad

epitomize [ɪˈpɪtəmaɪz] *vtr fml* personificar, ejemplificar.

epoch [ˈiːpɒk] *n* época *f*

epoch-making [ˈiːpɒkmeɪkɪŋ] *adj* histórico,-a

equable [ˈekwəbəl] *adj* **1** *(person)* ecuánime **2** *(climate)* uniforme, regular

equal [ˈiːkwəl] **I** *adj* igual, **of e. value,** de igual valor, **other things being e.,** si todo sigue igual, **she doesn't feel e. to going to the party,** no se siente con fuerzas para ir a la fiesta; **to be e. to the occasion,** estar a la altura de las circunstancias, **with e. indifference,** con la misma indiferencia ■ **e. distance,** equidistancia *f*, **e. opportunities employer,** empresa *f* que contrata sin ningún tipo de discriminación; **e. pay,** igualdad *f* de salarios; **e. rights,** igualdad *f* de derechos. **II** *n* igual *mf*; **to treat sb as an e.,** tratar a algn de igual a igual. **III** *vtr (pt & pp* **equalled,** *US* **equaled)** **1** *Math* ser igual a, equivaler; **three and two equals five,** tres más dos son cinco. ■ **equals sign,** signo *m* igual. **2** *(match)* igualar; **very few people can e. him at diplomacy,** muy pocos le igualan en la diplomacia. ◆ **equally** *adv* igualmente; **e. pretty,** igual de bonito; **to share sth e.,** dividir algo en partes iguales.

equality [iːˈkwɒlɪtɪ] *n* igualdad *f*.

equalize [ˈiːkwəlaɪz] **I** *vi Ftb* igualar, empatar. **II** *vtr* igualar.

equalizer [ˈiːkwəlaɪzəᵣ] *n Ftb* gol *m* del empate, igualada *f*.

equanimity [ekwəˈnɪmɪtɪ] *n* ecuanimidad *f*.

equate [ɪˈkweɪt] *vtr* equiparar, comparar **(to,** a, con).

equation [ɪˈkweɪʒən, ɪˈkweɪʃən] *n Math* ecuación *f*; **simple e.,** ecuación de primer grado.

equator [ɪˈkweɪtəᵣ] *n Geog* ecuador *m*.

equatorial [ekwəˈtɔːrɪəl] *adj* ecuatorial.

equerry [ˈekwərɪ] *n* caballerizo *m* de la casa real.

equestrian [ɪˈkwestrɪən] **I** *adj* ecuestre. **II** *n (man)* jinete *m*; *(woman)* amazona *f*.

equidistant [iːkwɪˈdɪstənt] *adj* equidistante.

equilateral [iːkwɪˈlætərəl] *adj* equilátero,-a. ■ **e. triangle,** triángulo *m* equilátero.

equilibrium [iːkwɪˈlɪbrɪəm] *n* equilibrio *m*.

equine [ˈekwaɪn] *adj* equino,-a.

equinox [ˈiːkwɪnɒks] *n Astron* equinoccio *m*. ■ **autumnal e.,** equinoccio *m* de otoño; **vernal e.,** equinoccio *m* de primavera.

equip [ɪˈkwɪp] *vtr (pt & pp* **equipped)** *(supply)* equipar **(with,** con); *(person)* proveer **(with,** de).

equipment [ɪˈkwɪpmənt] *n (materials)* equipo *m*; *(act of equipping)* aprovisionamiento *m*, equipamiento *m*. ■ **office e.,** material *m* de oficina.

equipped [ɪˈkwɪpt] *adj (machine)* estar dotado,-a de; *(person)* estar provisto,-a de; **he was ill e. to deal with them,** no estaba preparado para enfrentarse con ellos.

equitable [ˈekwɪtəbəl] *adj* equitativo,-a.

equities [ˈekwɪtɪz] *npl Fin* acciones *fpl* ordinarias.

equity ['ekwɪtɪ] *n* **1** *(general)* equidad *f*. **2** *GB* E., Sindicato *m* de actores.

equivalence [ɪ'kwɪvələns] *n* equivalencia *f*.

equivalent [ɪ'kwɪvələnt] **I** *adj* equivalente; **to be e. to,** equivaler a, ser equivalente a. **II** *n* equivalencia *f*.

equivocal [ɪ'kwɪvəkəl] *adj* equívoco,-a.

era ['ɪərə] *n* era *f*.

eradicate [ɪ'rædɪkeɪt] *vtr (eliminate)* erradicar; *(take out)* extirpar; *(uproot)* desarraigar.

eradication [ɪrædɪ'kaɪʃən] *n* extirpación *f*, destrucción *f*, aniquilación *f*.

erase [ɪ'reɪz] *vtr* borrar.

eraser [ɪ'reɪzəʳ] *n* goma *f* de borrar.

erasure [ɪ'reɪʒə] *n fml* borradura *f*.

erect [ɪ'rekt] **I** *adj* **1** *(upright)* erguido,-a, derecho,-a; **to hold one's head e.,** levantar la cabeza. **2** *(penis)* erecto,-a. **II** *vtr (monument)* levantar, erigir.

erection [ɪ'rekʃən] *n* **1** *(building)* construcción *f*. **2** *(penis)* erección *f*.

ergonomics [ɜːgəʊ'nɒmɪks] *n* ergonomía *f*.

ermine ['ɜːmɪn] *n* armiño *m*.

erode [ɪ'rəʊd] *vtr* **1** *Geol (rock, soil)* erosionar. **2** *(metal)* corroer, desgastar; *fig (power, confidence)* perder.

erogenous [ɪ'rɒdʒɪnəs] *adj* erógeno,-a. ■ **e. zones,** zonas *fpl* erógenas.

erosion [ɪ'rəʊʒən] *n* **1** *Geol* erosión *f*. **2** *(metal)* corrosión *f*, desgaste *m*; *fig* desgaste *f*.

erotic [ɪ'rɒtɪk] *adj* erótico,-a.

eroticism [ɪ'rɒtɪsɪzəm] *n* erotismo *m*.

err [ɜːʳ] *vi* errar; **to e. on the side of ...,** pecar por exceso de ... .

errand ['erənd] *n* recado *m*; **to run an e.,** hacer un recado. ■ **e. boy,** recadero *m*.

errata [ɪ'rɑːtə] *npl Typ* **e** *f sing* de erratas; *see* **erratum.**

erratic [ɪ'rætɪk] **I** *adj* **1** *(performance, behaviour)* irregular; *(weather)* muy variable. **2** *(person)* caprichoso,-a. **II** *n Geol* errático *m*. ◆ **erratically** *adv* de manera irregular.

erratum [ɪ'rɑːtəm] *n (pl* **errata)** *Typ* errata *f*.

erroneous [ɪ'rəʊnɪəs] *adj* erróneo,-a, equivocado,-a.

error ['erəʳ] *n* error *m*, equivocación *f*; **he saw the e. of his ways,** reconoció sus errores; **in e.,** por error; **typing e.,** falta de mecanografía.

error-free ['erəfriː] *adj* sin error.

Erse [ɜːs] *n* gaélico *m* irlandés.

erstwhile ['ɜːstwaɪl] **I** *adj* antiguo,-a. **II** *adv arch* antiguamente.

eruct [ɪ'rʌt] *vi* eructar.

erudite ['erʊdaɪt] *adj* & *n* erudito,-a *(m,f)*.

erudition [erʊ'dɪʃən] *n* erudición *f*.

erupt [ɪ'rʌpt] *vi* **1** *(volcano)* entrar en erupción; *(sudden movement)* irrumpir; *(violence)* estallar; **to e. in anger,** montar en cólera. **2** *Med (rash)* brotar; *(tooth)* salir.

eruption [ɪ'rʌpʃən] *n* **1** *(volcano)* erupción *f*; *(violence)* estallido *m*, explosión *f*. **2** *Med* erupción *f*.

escalate ['eskəleɪt] **I** *vtr* **1** *(war)* agravar, intensificar. **2** *(prices)* aumentar. **II** *vi* **1** *(war)* agravarse, intensificarse. **2** *(prices)* aumentarse. **3** *(change)* convertirse (**into,** en).

escalation [eskə'leɪʃən] *n* **1** *(of war)* agravación *f*, intensificación *f*, escalada *f*. **2** *(of prices)* subida *f*, aumento *m*.

escalator ['eskəleɪtəʳ] *n* escalera *f* mecánica.

escalope ['eskəlɒp] *n Culin* escalopa *f*, escalope *m*.

escapade ['eskəpeɪd] *n* aventura *f*.

escape [ɪs'keɪp] **I** *n* **1** *(flight)* huída *f*, fuga *f*; **to make one's e.,** escaparse; *fam* **to have a narrow e.,** salvarse por los pelos. ■ *Jur* **e. clause,** cláusula *f* de excepción; *Av Naut* **e.**

hatch, escotilla *f* de salvamento; **e. route,** vía *f* de escape; **fire e.,** escalera *f* de incendios. **2** *(gas)* fuga *f*, escape *m*. ■ **e. valve,** válvula *f* de escape. **II** *vi* **1** escaparse, huir. **2** *(gas)* escapar. **III** *vtr* **1** *(avoid)* evitar, huir de; **he narrowly escaped being hit,** se libró del golpe por poco; **to e. punishment,** librarse del castigo. **2** *fig (elude)* escaparse; **her name escapes me,** ahora mismo no recuerdo su nombre; **it escaped my notice,** me pasó desapercibido; **nothing escapes him,** no se le escapa nada.

escapee [ɪskeɪ'piː] *n* fugitivo,-a *m,f*.

escapism [ɪ'skeɪpɪzəm] *n* evasión *f*; **this novel is pure e.,** esta novela es pura evasión.

escapist [ɪ'skeɪpɪst] **I** *adj* de evasión, evasionista. **II** *n* soñador,-a *m,f*, escapista *mf*.

escarpment [ɪ'skɑːpmənt] *n (fortress)* escarpa *f*; *(slope)* escarpadura *f*, escarpa *f*.

eschew [ɪs'tʃuː] *vtr* evitar, abstenerse.

escort [ɪ'eskɔːt] **I** *n* **1** *(companion)* acompañante *mf*. **2** *(military, police)* escolta *f*; **under police e.,** escoltado,-a por la policía. **II** [ɪs'kɔːt] *vtr* **1** *(accompany)* acompañar; **to e. sb home,** acompañar a algn a casa. **2** *(protect)* escoltar.

Eskimo ['eskɪməʊ] *adj* & *n (pl* **Eskimos** *or* **Eskimo)** esquimal *(mf)*.

esophagus [iː'sɒfəgəs] *n (pl* **esophagi** [iː'sɒfədʒaɪ]*) US Anat* esófago *m*.

esoteric [esəʊ'terɪk] *adj* esotérico,-a.

ESP [iːes'piː] **1** *abbr of* **extrasensory perception,** percepción *f* extrasensorial. **2** *abbr of* **English for Specific Purposes,** *(cursos mpl* de) inglés *m* especializado.

espadrille [espə'drɪl] *n* alpargata *f*.

espagnolette [espænjə'let] *n* falleba *f*.

especial [ɪ'speʃəl] *adj* especial, particular; **of e. importance,** de especial importancia. ◆ **especially** *adv* especialmente, sobre todo.

esperantist [espə'ræntɪst] *n* esperantista *mf*.

Esperanto [espə'ræntəʊ] *n* esperanto *m*.

espionage ['espɪɒnɑːʒ] *n* espionaje *m*.

esplanade [esplə'neɪd] *n* paseo *m* marítimo.

espouse [ɪ'spaʊz] *vtr fml* **1** *(cause)* abrazar, adoptar. **2** *(marry)* casarse con.

espresso [e'spresəʊ] *n* café *m*. ■ **e. coffee,** café *m* exprés.

esprit de corps [espriːdə'kɔːʳ] *n* espíritu *m* de camadería, fraternidad *f*.

esquire [ɪ'skwaɪəʳ] *n GB* señor *m*; **Timothy Whiteman E.,** Sr. Don Timothy Whiteman.

essay ['eseɪ] **I** *n* **1** *Educ* redacción *f*, composición *f*. **2** *Lit* ensayo *m*. **3** *(attempt)* intento *m*. **II** [e'seɪ] *vtr* **1** *(test)* probar. **2** *(attempt)* intentar.

essayist ['eseɪɪst] *n Lit* ensayista *mf*.

essence ['esəns] *n* **1** *(fundamental)* esencia *f*; **in e.,** esencialmente; **of the e.,** lo esencial, lo imprescindible; **speed is of the e.,** la rapidez es esencial; **the e. of the matter,** el quid de la cuestión. **2** *(perfume)* esencia *f*, perfume *m*.

essential [ɪ'senʃəl] **I** *adj* esencial, fundamental, imprescindible. **II** *n* **1** *(fundamental)* elemento *m* esencial. **2** *(vital)* necesidad *f* básica. **3 essentials,** substancia *f sing*. ◆ **essentially** *adv* esencialmente, fundamentalmente.

EST [iːes'tiː] *US abbr of* **Eastern Standard Time,** hora *f* del meridiano 75 al oeste de Greenwich.

establish [ɪ'stæblɪʃ] *vtr* **1** *(found)* establecer, fundar, crear; *(business)* montar; *(habit)* consolidar; *(theory)* sentar; **to e. a precedent,** sentar un precedente; **to e. oneself,** establecerse; **to e. one's rights,** hacer constar sus derechos. **2** *Jur* **to e. a fact/sb's innocence,** probar un hecho/la inocencia de algn; **to e. the truth,** demostrar la verdad.

established [ɪ'stæblɪʃt] *adj (person)* establecido,-a; *(habit)* arraigado,-a, consolidado,-a; *(fact)* conocido,-a. ■ **e. church,** iglesia *f* oficial del Estado.

establishment [ɪ'stæblɪʃmənt] *n* **1** *(creation)* establecimiento *m*. **2** *Com* negocio *m*, establecimiento *m*. **3** *Pol* the E., el sistema.

estate [ɪ'steɪt] *n* **1** *(land)* finca *f*. ■ *GB* **e. agent,** *(person)* agente *mf* inmobiliario,-a; *(office)* agencia *f* inmobiliaria; *Aut GB* **e. car,** coche *m* modelo familiar. **2** zona *f* urbanizada. ■ **council e.,** viviendas *fpl* de protección oficial; **housing e.,** urbanización *f*; **industrial e.,** polígono *m* industrial; **trading e.,** zona *f* comercial. **3** *(property)* propiedad *f*, bienes *mpl*. **4** *(inheritance)* herencia *f*.

esteem [ɪ'stiːm] **I** *n* aprecio *m*, respeto *m*; **to hold sb in great e.,** apreciar mucho a algn. **II** *vtr* **1** *(person)* apreciar a. **2** *(regard)* considerar.

esteemed [ɪ'stiːmd] *adj* apreciado,-a, estimado,-a.

esthetic [es'θetɪk] *adj US* estético,-a.

esthetics [es'θetɪks] *n US* estética *f*.

estimate ['estɪmɪt] **I** *n (calculation)* cálculo *m*; **rough e.,** cálculo aproximado; *(likely cost of work)* presupuesto *m*. **II** ['estɪmeɪt] *vtr* calcular; *fig* pensar, creer.

estimation [estɪ'meɪʃən] *n* **1** *(opinion)* juicio *m*, opinión *f*; **in my e.,** a mi juicio. **2** *(esteem)* estima *f*.

estrange [ɪ'streɪndʒ] *vtr* alejar; **to become estranged,** alejarse **(from,** de).

estrangement [ɪ'streɪndʒmənt] *n fml* alejamiento *m*; **the e. from his wife,** el alejamiento de su mujer.

estrogen ['iːstrədʒən] *n US Biol* estrógeno *m*.

estuary ['estjʊərɪ] *n Geog* estuario *m*.

ETA [iːtiː'eɪ] *abbr of* **estimated time of arrival,** hora *f* prevista de llegada.

etch [etʃ] *vtr Art* grabar al agua fuerte.

etching ['etʃɪŋ] *n Art* aguafuerte *m*.

eternal [ɪ'tɜːnəl] *adj* eterno,-a, incesante. ■ **e. triangle,** triángulo *m* amoroso. ◆ **eternally** *adv* eternamente, siempre.

eternity [ɪ'tɜːnɪtɪ] *n* eternidad *f*.

ethane ['iːθeɪn, 'eθeɪn] *n Chem* etano *m*.

ethanol ['eθənɒl, 'iːθənɒl] *n Chem* etanol *m*.

ether ['iːθəʳ] *n Chem* éter *m*.

ethereal [ɪ'θɪərɪəl] *adj* etéreo,-a.

ethic ['eθɪk] *n* ética *f*.

ethical ['eθɪkəl] *adj* ético,-a. ◆ **ethically** *adv* éticamente.

ethics ['eθɪks] *n* ética *f*, moralidad *f*; **medical e.,** ética profesional médica.

Ethiopia [iːθɪ'əʊpɪə] *n* Etiopía.

Ethiopian [iːθɪ'əʊpɪən] *adj & n* etíope *(mf)*.

ethnic ['eθnɪk] *adj* étnico,-a; **e. minority,** minoría *f* étnica.

ethnographer [eθ'nɒgəfəʳ] *n* etnógrafo,-a *m,f*.

ethnography [eθ'nɒgrəfɪ] *n* etnografía *f*.

ethnologist [eθ'nɒlədʒɪst] *n* etnólogo,-a *m,f*.

ethnology [eθ'nɒlədʒɪ] *n* etnología *f*.

ethos ['iːθɒs] *n* carácter *m* distintivo.

ethyl ['iːθaɪl, 'eθɪl] *n Chem* etilo *m*. ■ **e. alcohol,** alcohol *m* etílico.

ethylene ['eθɪliːn] *n Chem* etileno *m*.

etiquette ['etɪket] *n* protocolo *m*, etiqueta *f*, buenos modales *mpl*; **professional e.,** ética *f* profesional.

etymological [etɪmə'lɒdʒɪkəl] *adj* etimológico,-a.

etymologist [etɪ'mɒlədʒɪst] *n* etimólogo,-a *m,f*.

etymology [etɪ'mɒlədʒɪ] *n* etimología *f*.

eucalyptus [juːkə'lɪptəs] *n Bot* eucalipto *m*.

Eucharist ['juːkərɪst] *n Rel* Eucaristía *f*.

eulogize ['juːlədʒaɪz] *vtr* elogiar.

eulogy ['juːlədʒɪ] *n* elogio *m*.

eunuch ['juːnək] *n* eunuco *m*.

euphemism ['juːfɪmɪzəm] *n* eufemismo *m*.

euphemistic [juːfɪ'mɪstɪk] *adj* eufemístico,-a.

euphonic [juː'fɒnɪk] *adj* eufónico,-a.

euphony ['juːfənɪ] *n* eufonía *f*.

euphoria [juː'fɔːrɪə] *n* euforia *f*.

euphoric [juː'fɒrɪk] *adj* eufórico,-a.

Eurasian [jʊə'reɪʒən] *adj & n* euroasiático,-a *(m,f)*.

eureka [jʊ'riːkə] *interj* ¡eureka!

eurhythmics [juː'rɪðmɪks] *n US* gimnasia *f* rítmica.

Eurocheque ['jʊərəʊtʃek] *n* eurocheque *m*. ■ **E. card,** tarjeta *f* de eurocheque.

eurocommunism [jʊərəʊ'kɒmjʊnɪzəm] *n Pol* eurocomunismo *m*.

Eurocrat ['jʊərəkræt] *n* eurócrata *mf*.

Eurocurrency ['jʊərəʊkʌrənsɪ] *n Fin* eurodivisa *f*.

eurodollar ['jʊərəʊdɒləʳ] *n Fin* eurodólar *m*.

euro-MP ['jʊərəʊempiː] *n Pol* eurodiputado,-a *m,f*.

Europe ['jʊərəp] *n* Europa.

European [jʊərə'pɪən] *adj & n* europeo,-a *(m, f)*. ■ **E. Economic Community,** Comunidad *f* Económica Europea.

Eustachian tube [juːsteɪʃən'tjuːb] *n Anat* trompa *f* de Eustaquio.

euthanasia [juːθə'neɪzɪə] *n* eutanasia *f*.

evacuate [ɪ'vækjʊeɪt] *vtr* evacuar, desalojar.

evacuation [ɪvækjʊ'eɪʃən] *n* evacuación *f*, desalojamiento *m*.

evacuee [ɪvækjʊ'iː] *n* evacuado,-a *m,f*.

evade [ɪ'veɪd] *vtr* evadir, evitar; **to e. the issue,** eludir la cuestión.

evaluate [ɪ'væljʊeɪt] *vtr* **1** *(calculate)* evaluar, calcular; **to e. damages,** juzgar la cuantía de los daños. **2** *Math* hallar el valor numérico de.

evaluation [ɪvælju'eɪʃən] *n* evaluación *f*.

evanescent [evə'nesənt] *adj* evanescente.

evangelical [iːvæn'dʒelɪkəl] *adj Rel* evangélico,-a.

evangelism [ɪ'vændʒɪlɪzəm] *n Rel* **1** evangelio *m*. **2** evangelismo *m*.

evangelist [ɪ'vændʒɪlɪst] *n Rel* evangelista *mf*; **Saint John the E.,** San Juan Evangelista.

evangelize [ɪ'vændʒɪlaɪz] *vtr* evangelizar.

evaporate [ɪ'væpəreɪt] **I** *vtr* evaporar. ■ **evaporated milk,** leche *f* evaporada. **II** *vi* evaporarse; *fig* desvanecerse.

evaporation [ɪvæpə'reɪʃən] *n* evaporación *f*.

evasion [ɪ'veɪʒən] *n* **1** *(gen)* evasión *f*. ■ **e. of duty,** incumplimiento *m* del deber; **tax e.,** evasión *f* fiscal *or* capital. **2** *(evasive answer)* evasiva *f*.

evasive [ɪ'veɪsɪv] *adj* evasivo,-a.

eve [iːv] *n* víspera *f*; **on the e. of,** en vísperas de.

even ['iːvən] **I** *adj* **1** *(smooth)* liso,-a; *(level)* llano,-a. **2** *(regular)* regular, uniforme; **e. temper,** carácter apacible; **to keep an e. pace,** mantener un ritmo constante. **3** *(equally balanced)* igual, igualado,-a; *(Sport)* **to be e.,** estar igualado,-a empatar; *Fin* **to break e.,** cubrir gastos; **to get e. with sb,** desquitarse con algn; **to stand an e. chance,** tener tantas posibilidades de éxito como de fracaso. **4** *(number)* par; **odd or e.,** par o impar. **5** *(at the same level)* a nivel. **6** *(quantity)* exacto,-a, redondo,-a. **II** *adv* **1** incluso, hasta, aun; **e. now,** incluso ahora; **e. so,** aun así; **e. the children knew,** hasta los niños lo sabían; **e. when it rains,** incluso cuando llueve. **2** *(negative)* ni siquiera; **she can't e. write her name,** ni siquiera sabe escribir su nombre; **without e. speaking,** sin hablar siquiera. **3** *(before comparative)* aun, todavía; **that**

would be e. **worse**, eso sería aun peor. **4 e. as**, en el mismo momento en que, mientras; **e. as he wrote the letter**, mientras escribía la carta; **e. if**, incluso si; **e. though**, aunque, aun cuando. **III** *vtr* nivelar, igualar; *fig* **to e. a score with sb**, desquitarse con algn. ◆ **evenly** *adv* **1** *(uniformly)* de modo uniforme. **2** *(fairly)* equitativamente, igualmente. **3** *(tone of voice)* en el mismo tono.

even-handed [iːvən'hændɪd] *adj* imparcial.

evening ['iːvnɪŋ] *n* **1** *(early)* tarde *f*; *(late)* noche *f*; **in the e.**, por la tarde; **tomorrow e.**, mañana por la tarde; **yesterday e.**, ayer por la tarde. ■ *Educ* **e. class**, clase *f* nocturna; **e. dress**, *(man)* traje *m* de etiqueta; *(woman)* traje *m* de noche; **e. paper**, periódico *m* de la tarde; *Cin Theat* **e. perfomance**, función *f* de noche; *Rel* **e. service**, misa *f* vespertina. **2** *(greeting)* **good e.!**, *(early)* ¡buenas tardes!; *(late)* ¡buenas noches!

evenness ['iːvənnɪs] *n* **1** *(equal)* uniformidad *f*. **2** *(fairness)* ecuanimidad *f*.

evensong ['iːvənsɒŋ] *n Rel* vísperas *fpl*.

event [ɪ'vent] *n* **1** *(happening)* suceso *m*, acontecimiento *m*; **in the normal course of events**, si todo sigue su curso normal; **it was quite an e.**, fue todo un acontecimiento; **programme of events**, programa *m* de actos. **2** *(case)* caso *m*; **at all events**, en todo caso; **in the e. of fire**, en caso de incendio; **in the e. of his refusing**, en (el) caso de que no acepte. **3** *Sport* prueba *f*. ■ **track events**, atletismo *m* en pista.

eventful [ɪ'ventfʊl] *adj* lleno,-a de acontecimientos, agitado,-a; **an e. day**, *(busy)* un día agitado; *(memorable)* un día memorable.

eventual [ɪ'ventʃʊəl] *adj* **1** *(ultimate)* final; *(resulting)* consiguiente; *(possible)* posible. ◆ **eventually** *adv* finalmente, con el tiempo; **we e. managed to find a telephone box**, finalmente encontramos una cabina telefónica.

eventuality [ventʃʊ'ælɪtɪ] *n* eventualidad *f*; **to prepare for all eventualities**, prepararse para cualquier eventualidad.

ever ['evəʳ] *adv* **1** *(never)* nunca, jamás; **nothing e. happens**, nunca pasa nada; **stronger than e.**, más fuerte que nunca. **2** *(interrogative) (sometimes)* alguna vez; **have you e. been there?**, ¿has estado allí alguna vez?; *fam* **did you e.?**, ¡habrase visto! **3** *(always)* siempre; **for e.**, para siempre; **for e. and e.**, para siempre jamás; **Scotland for e.!**, ¡viva Escocia! **4** *(emphasis)* **how e. did you manage it?**, ¿cómo diablos lo conseguiste?; **what e. shall we do now?**, ¿qué demonios hacemos ahora?; **why e. not?**, ¿por qué no?; *fam* **e. so, e. such**, muy; **e. so difficult**, terriblemente difícil; **e. so little**, muy poco; **thank you e. so much**, muchísimas gracias.

evergreen ['evəgriːn] *Bot* **I** *adj* de hoja perenne. **II** *n* árbol *m* or planta *f* de hoja perenne. ■ **e. oak**, encina *f*.

everlasting [evə'lɑːstɪŋ] *adj* eterno,-a, perpetuo,-a.

evermore [evə'mɔːʳ] *adv* eternamente; **for e.**, para siempre.

every ['evrɪ] *adj* **1** *(each)* cada; **e. now and then**, de vez en cuando; **e. other day**, cada dos días. **2** *(all)* todos,-as; **e. citizen**, todo ciudadano, todos los ciudadanos; **e. day**, todos los días; **e. Saturday**, todos los sábados. **3** *(intensive)* **I have e. confidence in her**, tengo plena confianza en ella; **you had e. right to be angry**, tenías todo el derecho a estar enfadado.

everybody ['evrɪbɒdɪ] *pron* todo el mundo, todos,-as.

everyday ['evrɪdeɪ] *adj* diario,-a, de todos los días; corriente; **an e. occurrence**, un suceso cotidiano; **it's an e. event**, es un suceso ordinario. ■ **e. clothes**, ropa *f* de todos los días.

everyone ['evrɪwʌn] *pron* todo el mundo, todos,-as.

everything ['evrɪθɪŋ] *pron* todo; **e. needs washing**, hace falta lavarlo todo; **he eats e.**, come de todo; **she means e. to me**, ella lo es todo para mí.

everywhere ['evrɪweəʳ] *adv* en todas partes, por todas partes.

evict [ɪ'vikt] *vtr* desahuciar.

eviction [ɪ'vɪkʃən] *n* desahucio *m*.

evidence ['evɪdəns] **I** *n* **1** *(proof)* evidencia *f*; **there is no e. against her**, no hay ninguna prueba en contra suya. **2** *Jur* testimonio *m*, declaración *f*; **to call sb in e.**, llamar a algn como testigo; **to give e.**, prestar declaración, declarar como testigo; **to turn King's** or **Queen's e.**, *US* **to turn state's e.**, delatar a un cómplice. **3** *(sign)* indicio *m*, señal *f*; **in e.**, visible; **to be in e.**, estar a la vista, hacerse notar. **II** *vtr* **1** *(prove)* demostrar, probar. **2** *Jur (witness)* declarar; *(to give proof)* justificar.

evident ['evɪdənt] *adj* evidente, patente, manifiesto,-a. ◆ **evidently** *adv* evidentemente, al parecer.

evil ['iːvəl] **I** *adj* **1** *(wicked)* malo,-a, malvado,-a. **2** *(harmful)* malo,-a, nocivo,-a. **3** *(unfortunate)* aciago,-a, de mal agüero. **4** *(nasty)* geniudo,-a; **he's got an e. temper**, tiene muy mal genio. **II** *n* mal *m*; **to speak e. of sb**, hablar mal de algn.

evil-doer ['iːvəldʊəʳ] *n* persona *f* malvada.

evil-minded [iːvəl'maɪndɪd] *adj* malvado,-a, malpensado,-a.

evocation [evə'keɪʃən] *n* evocación *f*.

evocative [ɪ'vɒkətɪv] *adj* evocador,-a.

evoke [ɪ'vəʊk] *vtr* evocar, provocar.

evolution [iːvə'luːʃən] *n* **1** evolución *f*; **the Darwinian theory of e.**, la teoría de la evolución de Darwin. **2** *Biol* desarrollo *m*.

evolutionary [iːvə'luːʃənərɪ] *adj* evolutivo,-a.

evolve [ɪ'vɒlv] **I** *vi* *(species)* evolucionar; *(ideas)* desarrollarse. **II** *vtr* **1** *(gen)* desarrollar. **2** *(gas, heat)* desprender.

evolvement [ɪ'vɒlvmənt] *n (of ideas, plans)* desarrollo *m*; *(of gas, heat)* desprendimiento *m*.

ewe [juː] *n Zool* oveja *f*.

ex[1] [eks] *prep* **1 e. dividend**, sin dividendo, sin cupón. **2 e. factory**, franco fábrica.

ex[2] [eks] *n* **her e.**, su ex marido; **his e.**, su ex mujer.

ex- [eks] *pref* ex, antiguo,-a; **ex-minister**, ex ministro *m*.

exacerbate [ɪg'zæsəbeɪt] *vtr* exacerbar, agravar.

exact [ɪg'zækt] **I** *adj (accurate, precise)* exacto,-a; *(of description, definition)* preciso,-a; **an e. mind**, una mente clara or precisa; **this e. spot**, ese mismo lugar. **II** *vtr* exigir. ◆ **exactly** *adv* exactamente; precisamente; **e.!**, ¡exacto!

exacting [ɪg'zæktɪŋ] *adj* exigente.

exactitude [ɪg'zæktɪtjuːd] *n* exactitud *f*.

exactness [ɪg'zæktnəs] *n* exactitud *f*.

exaggerate [ɪg'zædʒəreɪt] *vi & vtr* exagerar.

exaggerated [ɪg'zædʒəreɪtɪd] *adj* exagerado,-a.

exaggeration [ɪgzædʒə'reɪʃən] *n* exageración *f*.

exalt [ɪg'zɔːlt] *vtr fml* exaltar.

exaltation [egzɔːl'teɪʃən] *n fml* exaltación *f*.

exam [ɪg'zæm] *n Educ fam* examen *m*.

examination [ɪgzæmɪ'neɪʃən] *n* **1** *Educ* examen *m*; **to sit an e.**, hacer un examen; **to take an e.**, examinarse. ■ **entrance e.**, examen *m* de ingreso. **2** *Med* reconocimiento *m*. **3** *Jur* interrogatorio *m*.

examine [ɪg'zæmɪn] *vtr* **1** *(education)* examinar; *(customs)* registrar. **2** *Med* hacer un reconocimiento médico. **3** *Jur (witness)* interrogar.

examinee [ɪgzæmɪ'niː] *n* examinado,-a *m,f*.

examiner [ɪg'zæmɪnəʳ] *n* examinador,-a *m,f*.

example [ɪg'zɑːmpəl] *n (gen)* ejemplo *m*; *(specimen)* ejemplar *m*; **for e.**, por ejemplo; **to make an e. of sb**, dar un castigo ejemplar a algn; **to set an e.**, dar ejemplo.

exasperate [ɪɡ'zɑːspəreɪt] *vtr* exasperar.

exasperated [ɪɡ'zɑːspəreɪtɪd] *adj* exasperado,-a.

exasperation [ɪɡzɑːspə'reɪʃən] *n* exasperación *f*.

excavate ['ekskəveɪt] *vtr* excavar.

excavation [ekskə'veɪʃən] *n* excavación *f*.

excavator ['ekskəveɪtəʳ] *n* **1** (*machine*) excavadora *f*. **2** (*person*) excavador,-a *m*,*f*.

exceed [ek'siːd] *vtr* exceder, sobrepasar; **to e. one's income,** gastar más de lo que uno gana. ■ **exceedingly** *adv* extremadamente, sumamente; **e. pleased,** contentísimo,-a.

excel [ɪk'sel] (*pt & pp* **excelled**) **I** *vi* sobresalir. **II** *vtr* superar; **to e. oneself,** superarse.

excellence ['eksələns] *n* excelencia *f*.

excellency ['eksələnsɪ] *n* excelencia *f*; **His E.,** Su Excelencia.

excellent ['eksələnt] *adj* excelente, sobresaliente.

excelsior [ɪk'selsɪɔːʳ] *n US* virutas *fpl*.

except [ɪk'sept] **I** *prep* excepto, salvo, con la excepción de; **e. for the little ones,** excepto los pequeños; **e. that ...,** sólo que ..., salvo que ... . **II** *vtr* excluir; **present company excepted,** exceptuando a los aquí presentes.

exception [ɪk'sepʃən] *n* **1** (*gen*) excepción *f*; **the e. proves the rule,** la excepción confirma la regla; **to make an e. of,** hacer una excepción de, exceptuar; **with the e. of,** a excepción de; **without e.,** sin excepción. **2** (*objection*) objeción *f*; **to take e. to sth,** ofenderse por algo.

exceptionable [ɪk'sepʃənəbəl] *adj* censurable.

exceptional [ɪk'sepʃənəl] *adj* excepcional, extraordinario,-a.

excerpt [ek'sɜːpt] *n* extracto *m*.

excess [ɪk'ses] **I** *n* exceso *m*; **in e.,** en exceso; **in e. of,** superior a; **to eat to e.,** comer con exceso. **II** *adj* ['ekses] excedente. ■ *Av* **e. baggage,** exceso *m* de equipaje; *Econ* **e. demand,** exceso *m* de demanda; *Rail* **e. fare,** suplemento *m*; **e. postage,** franqueo *m* excesivo; **e. profits tax,** impuestos *mpl* sobre beneficios excesivos; *Econ* **e. supply,** exceso *m* de oferta.

excessive [ɪk'sesɪv] *adj* excesivo,-a. ◆ **excessively** *adv* excesivamente, en exceso.

exchange [ɪks'tʃeɪndʒ] **I** *n* **1** (*gen*) cambio *m*, intercambio *m*; **e. of ideas,** intercambio de ideas; **in e. for,** a cambio de. **2** *Fin* cambio *m*. ■ **bill of e.,** letra *f* de cambio; **foreign e.,** divisas *fpl*; **E. control,** control *m* de divisas; **rate of e.,** tipo *m* de cambio. **3** *Hist* lonja *f*. ■ **corn e.,** lonja *f* de granos; *GB* **labour e.,** oficina *f* de desempleo, bolsa *f* de trabajo; *Fin* **Stock E.,** Bolsa *f*. **4** *Tel* (**telephone**) **e.,** central *f* telefónica. **II** *vtr* **1** (*gen*) cambiar; **to e. blows,** golpearse; **to e. greetings,** saludarse; **to e. words,** cruzar unas palabras. **2** (*prisoners*) canjear.

exchangeable [ɪks'tʃeɪndʒəbəl] *adj* cambiable, canjeable.

exchequer [ɪks'tʃekəʳ] *n GB* **1 the E.,** Hacienda *f*. ■ **Chancellor of the E.,** Ministro *m* de Hacienda. **2** tesoro *m* público.

ex gratia [eks'greɪʃə] *adj fml* (*payment*) pago *m* discrecional.

excise[1] ['eksaɪz] *n* impuesto *m* sobre el consumo. ■ **E. duty,** derechos *mpl* de aduana; *GB* **the Commissioners of Customs and E.,** ≈ Oficina *f* de Control de Derechos de Aduana y de Importación; **E. officer,** agente *mf* de aduana.

excise[2] [ɪk'saɪz] *vtr* extirpar.

excision [ɪk'sɪʒən] *n Med* extirpación *f*, excisión *f*.

excitable [ɪk'saɪtəbəl] *adj* (*temperamental*) excitable; (*nervous*) nervioso,-a.

excite [ɪk'saɪt] *vtr* **1** (*stimulate*) excitar; **to get excited,** ponerse nervioso,-a. **2** (*move*) emocionar. **3** (*enthuse*) entusiasmar; **don't get too excited about it,** no te hagas

demasiadas ilusiones; **to get excited,** entusiasmarse. **4** (*arouse*) provocar, levantar, despertar; **his speech excited suspicion,** su discurso provocó sospechas.

excitement [ɪk'saɪtmənt] *n* **1** (*stimulation*) excitación *f*. **2** (*emotion*) emoción *f*. **3** (*commotion*) agitación *f*, revuelo *m*; **to cause great e.,** causar sensación; **what's all the e. about?,** ¿a qué se debe tanto alboroto?

exciting [ɪk'saɪtɪŋ] *adj* apasionante, emocionante; **how e.!,** ¡qué ilusión!

exclaim [ɪk'skleɪm] **1** *vi* exclamar. **II** *vtr* gritar.

exclamation [eksklə'meɪʃən] *n* exclamación *f*. ■ **e. mark,** *US* **e. point,** signo *m* de admiración.

exclamatory [ɪk'sklæmətərɪ] *adj* exclamatorio,-a.

exclude [ɪk'skluːd] *vtr* **1** (*to leave out*) excluir. **2** (*club*) no admitir.

excluding [ɪk'sluːdɪŋ] *prep* excepto, con exclusión de.

exclusion [ɪk'sluːʒən] *n* exclusión *f*; **to the e. of,** con exclusión de.

exclusive [ɪk'sluːsɪv] **I** *adj* **1** (*sole*) exclusivo,-a. ■ **e. interview,** entrevista *f* en exclusiva; **e. rights,** derechos *mpl* exclusivos. **2** (*select*) selecto,-a; (*club*) cerrado,-a. **II** *n Press* exclusiva *f*. **III** *adv* **e. of,** excluyendo, sin tener en cuenta. ◆ **exclusively** *adv* exclusivamente.

excommunicate [ekskə'mjuːnɪkeɪt] *vtr Rel* excomulgar.

excommunication [ekskəmjuːnɪ'keɪʃən] *n* excomunión *f*.

excrement ['ekskrɪmənt] *n* excremento *m*.

excrescence [ɪk'skresəns] *n* excrecencia *f*.

excreta [ɪk'skriːtəl] *npl* excrementos *mpl*.

excrete [ɪk'skriːt] *vtr* excretar.

excretion [ɪk'skriːʃən] *n* excreción *f*.

excruciating [ɪk'skruːʃieɪtɪŋ] *adj* insoportable. ◆ **excruciatingly** *adv* atrozmente, horriblemente; **it's e. funny,** es para morirse de risa.

excursion [ɪk'skɜːʃən] *n* excursión *f*. ■ **e. ticket,** billete *m* reducido.

excursionist [ɪk'skɜːʃənɪst] *n* excursionista *mf*.

excusable [ɪk'skjuːzəbəl] *adj* perdonable, disculpable.

excuse [ɪk'skjuːz] **I** *vtr* **1** (*forgive*) perdonar, disculpar; **e. me!,** ¡oiga, por favor!, con permiso; **e. my saying so,** perdone mi atrevimiento; **may I be excused for a moment?,** ¿puedo salir un momento? **2** (*exempt*) dispensar, eximir; *Mil* rebajar; **he was excused kitchen duty,** lo rebajaron del servicio de cocina. **3** (*justify*) justificar; **that does not e. your behaviour,** eso no justifica su comportamiento. **II** [ɪk'skjuːs] *n* excusa *f*; **to make an e.,** dar excusas.

ex-directory [eksdɪ'rektərɪ] *adj Tel* que no se encuentra en la guía telefónica; **the Minister's number is ex-d.,** el número de teléfono del Ministro no figura en el listín.

execrable ['eksɪkrəbəl] *adj fml* (*abysmal*) execrable; (*awful*) abominablee.

execute ['eksɪkjuːt] *vtr* **1** (*carry out*) ejecutar; (*order*) cumplir; (*task*) realizar, llevar a cabo. **2** *Jur* cumplir; **to e. a will,** cumplir un testamento. **3** (*put to death*) ejecutar. **4** *Mus* interpretar.

execution [eksɪ'kjuːʃən] *n* **1** (*carrying out*) ejecución *f*; (*of order*) cumplimiento *m*; (*of task*) realización *f*. **2** *Jur* cumplimiento *m*. **3** (*putting to death*) ejecución *f*. **4** *Mus* interpretación *f*.

executioner [eksɪ'kjuːʃənəʳ] *n* verdugo *m*.

executive [ɪɡ'zekjʊtɪv] **I** *adj* ejecutivo,-a. ■ **E. Board,** consejo *m* de dirección; *US* **E. officer,** segundo comandante *m*; **e. power,** poder *m* ejecutivo. **II** *n* ejecutivo,-a *m*,*f*.

executor [ɪɡ'zekjʊtəʳ] *n Jur* albacea *m*.

executrix [ɪɡ'zekjʊtrɪks] *n Jur* albacea *f*.

exemplary [ɪɡ'zemplərɪ] *adj* ejemplar; **an e. pupil,** un alumno ejemplar.

exemplify [ɪg'zemplɪfaɪ] *vtr (pt & pp exemplified)* ejemplificar, servir de ejemplo para.

exempt [ɪg'zempt] **I** *vtr* eximir, dispensar **(from,** de); **he was exempted from national service,** le eximieron del servicio militar. **II** *adj* exento,-a, libre; **e. from tax,** libre de impuesto; **e. from taxation,** exento,-a de impuestos.

exemption [ɪg'zempʃən] *n* exención *f* **(from,** de).

exercise ['eksəsaɪz] **I** *n* ejercicio *m*; **to take e.,** hacer ejercicio, hacer deporte. ■ *Educ* **e. book,** cuaderno *m*. **II** *vtr* **1** *(influence, rights, duties)* ejercer; **to e. care,** tener cuidado, proceder con cuidado. **2** *(dog)* sacar de paseo. **3** *(mind)* inquietar; **this matter has much exercised the minds of scientists,** este asunto ha inquietado mucho a los científicos. **III** *vi* hacer ejercicio, entrenarse.

exert [ɪg'zɜːt] *vtr (influence)* ejercer; **to e. oneself,** esforzarse.

exertion [ɪg'zɜːʃən] *n* esfuerzo *m*, esfuerzo excesivo.

exhale [eks'heɪl] *vtr (breathe)* exhalar; *(smell)* despedir.

exhaust [ɪg'zɔːst] **I** *vtr* **1** *(tire)* agotar; **to e. oneself,** agotarse. **2** *(use up)* agotar; **we have exhausted all the possibilities,** hemos agotado todas las posibilidades. **3** *(empty)* vaciar. **II** *n (gases)* gases *mpl* de combustión; *(pipe)* escape *m*. ■ *Aut* **e. pipe,** tubo *m* de escape; **e. valve,** válvula *f* de escape.

exhausted [ɪg'zɔːstɪd] *adj* agotado,-a.

exhausting [ɪg'zɔːstɪŋ] *adj* agotador,-a.

exhaustion [ɪg'zɔːstʃən] *n* agotamiento *m*.

exhaustive [ɪg'zɔːstɪv] *adj* exhaustivo,-a, completo,-a; **an e. inquiry,** una investigación minuciosa.

exhibit [ɪg'zɪbɪt] **I** *n* **1** *Art* objeto *m* expuesto. **2** *Jur* prueba *f* instrumental. **II** *vtr* **1** *Art* exponer. **2** *(manifest)* mostrar, presentar.

exhibition [eksɪ'bɪʃən] *n* **1** *(display)* muestra *f*, demostración *f*; **to make on e. of oneself,** hacer el ridículo. **2** *Art* exposición *f*; **to be an e.,** estar actualmente expuesto,-a. **3** *Com (trade fair)* feria *f*.

exhibitionism [eksɪ'bɪʃənɪzəm] *n* exhibicionismo *m*.

exhibitionist [eksɪ'bɪʃənɪst] *adj & n* exhibicionista *(mf)*.

exhibitor [ɪg'zɪbɪtə'] *n* expositor,-a *m,f*.

exhilarate [ɪg'zɪləreɪt] *vtr* alegrar, levantar el ánimo, animar.

exhilarated [ɪg'zɪləreɪtɪd] *adj* muy animado,-a.

exhilarating [ɪg'zɪləreɪtɪŋ] *adj* estimulante.

exhilaration [ɪgzɪlə'reɪʃən] *n* regocijo *m*, alegría *f*.

exhort [ɪg'zɔːt] *vtr* exhortar.

exhumation [ekshjuː'meɪʃən] *n* exhumación *f*.

exhume [eks'hjuːm] *vtr* exhumar, desenterrar.

exigency ['eksɪdʒənsɪ, ɪg'zɪdʒənsɪ] *n (need)* exigencia *f*; *(emergency)* caso *m* de emergencia.

exigent ['eksɪdʒənt] *adj (demanding)* exigente; *(urgent)* urgente.

exiguous [ɪg'zɪgjʊəs] *adj* exiguo,-a.

exile ['eksaɪl] **I** *n* **1** *(banishment)* exilio *m*, destierro *m*. **2** *(person)* exiliado,-a *m, f*. ■ **tax e.,** exiliado,-a voluntario,-a para evitar los impuestos. **II** *vtr* exiliar, desterrar.

exist [ɪg'zɪst] *vi* **1** *(gen)* existir. **2** *(stay alive)* subsistir; **to e. on bread,** subsistir a base de pan.

existence [ɪg'zɪstəns] *n* existencia *f*; **to be in e.,** existir; **to come into e.,** nacer.

existential [egzɪ'stenʃəl] *adj Philos* existencial.

existentialism [egzɪ'stenʃəlɪzəm] *n Philos* existencialismo *m*.

existentialist [egzɪ'stenʃəlɪst] *adj & n Philos* existencialista *(mf)*.

existing [eg'zɪstɪŋ] *adj* existente, actual; **in the e. circumstances,** en las circunstancias actuales.

exit ['eksɪt] **I** *n* **1** *(gen)* salida *f*. ■ **emergency e.,** salida *f* de emergencia; **e. visa,** visado *m* de salida; **fire e.,** salida *f* de emergencia. **2** *Theat* salida *f*, mutis *m*; **to make one's e.,** salir. **II** *vi Theat* salir (de escena), hacer mutis; **e. Macbeth,** sale Macbeth.

ex officio [eksə'fɪʃɪəʊ] *adj & adv* ex-oficio.

exodus ['eksədəs] *n* éxodo *m*; *fam* **there was a general e.,** se fueron todos.

exogamy [ek'sɒgəmɪ] *n* exogamia *f*.

exonerate [ɪg'zɒnəreɪt] *vtr fml* exonerar, dispensar **(from,** de).

exoneration [ɪgzɒnə'reɪʃən] *n fml* exoneración *f*, dispensa *f*.

exorbitant [ɪg'zɔːbɪtənt] *adj* exorbitante, desorbitado,-a, excesivo,-a.

exorcise ['eksɔːsaɪz] *vtr (demon)* exorcizar; *fig (memory)* borrar de la memoria.

exorcism ['eksɔːsɪsəm] *n* exorcismo *m*.

exorcist ['eksɔːsɪst] *n* exorcista *mf*.

exotic [ɪg'zɒtɪk] *adj* exótico,-a.

expand [ɪk'spænd] **I** *vtr* **1** *(enlarge)* ampliar; **he expanded his business,** amplió su negocio. **2** *(gas, metal)* dilatar. **II** *vi* **1** *(grow)* ampliarse, crecer. **2** *(metal)* dilatarse. **3** *(become more friendly)* abrirse. ◆ **expand on** *vtr* ampliar; **could you e. on your theory a little?,** ¿podría ampliar un poco su teoría?

expanding [ɪk'spændɪŋ] *adj* en expansión.

expanse [ɪk'spæns] *n* extensión *f*.

expansion [ɪk'spænʃən] *n* **1** *(size)* ampliación *f*, expansión *f*. **2** *(gas, metal)* dilatación *f*. **3** *(trade)* desarrollo *m*.

expansionism [ɪk'spænʃənɪzəm] *n* expansionismo *m*.

expansive [ɪk'spænsɪv] *adj* expansivo,-a, comunicativo,-a.

expatriate [eks'pætrɪt] **I** *adj & n* expatriado,-a *(m,f)*. **II** [eks'pætrɪeɪt] *vtr* expatriar, desterrar.

expatriation [ekspætrɪ'eɪʃən] *n* expatriación *f*.

expect [ɪk'spekt] **I** *vtr* **1** *(anticipate)* esperar; **I expected as much,** ya me lo esperaba; **I fully expected to see them,** estaba seguro de verlos; **I half-expected that to happen,** suponía que iba a ocurrir; **I knew what to e.,** sabía a qué atenerme. **2** *(demand)* esperar, contar con; **I e. you to be punctual,** cuento con que seas puntual; **I wouldn't have expected such behaviour from her,** no esperaba tal comportamiento por su parte. **3** *(suppose)* suponer, imaginar; **I e. she's in the office,** me imagino que estará en la oficina; **I e. so,** supongo que sí. **II** *vi fam* **to be expecting,** estar embarazada.

expectancy [ɪk'spektənsɪ] *n* expectación *f*. ■ **life e.,** esperanza *f* de vida.

expectant [ɪk'spektənt] *adj* ilusionado,-a. ■ **e. mother,** mujer *f* embarazada.

expectation [ekspek'teɪʃən] *n* esperanza *f*; **beyond e.,** por encima de lo esperado; **contrary to e., against e.,** contrariamente a lo que se esperaba; **in e. of,** con la esperanza de; **not to come up to sb's expectations, to fall short of sb's expectations,** no alcanzar las expectativas de algn.

expectorant [ɪk'spektərənt] *n* expectorante *m*.

expectorate [ɪk'spektəreɪt] *vtr* expectorar, escupir.

expediency [ɪk'spiːdɪənsɪ] *n* conveniencia *f*, oportunidad *f*.

expedient [ɪk'spiːdɪənt] **I** *adj* conveniente, oportuno,-a. **II** *n* expediente *m*, recurso *m*.

expedite ['ekspɪdaɪt] *vtr* **1** *(speed up)* acelerar. **2** *(business)* despachar.

expedition [ekspɪ'dɪʃən] *n* expedición *f*. ■ **rescue e.,** expedición *f* de salvamento.

expeditionary [ekspɪ'dɪʃənərɪ] *adj* expedicionario,-a. ■ **e. force,** cuerpo *m* expedicionario.

expeditious [ekspɪ'dɪʃəs] *adj* expeditivo,-a.

expel [ɪk'spel] *vtr* (*pt & pp* **expelled**) expulsar.

expend [ɪk'spend] *vtr* gastar, emplear.

expendable [ɪk'spendəbəl] *adj* prescindible.

expenditure [ɪk'spendɪtʃəʳ] *n* gasto *m*, desembolso *m*.

expense [ɪk'spens] *n* gasto *m*; **all expenses paid,** con todos los gastos pagados; **at great e.,** pagándolo caro; **he went on the trip at his own e.,** pagó el viaje de su propio bolsillo; **to go to a lot of e.,** gastar mucho dinero; **to spare no e.,** no escatimar gastos; *fig* **at my e.,** a costa mía; *fig* **at the e. of,** a expensas de, a costa de. ■ *Com* **e. account,** cuenta *f* de gastos de representación.

expensive [ɪk'spensɪv] *adj* caro,-a, costoso,-a; *fig* **it was an e. mistake,** el error costó muy caro.

experience [ɪk'spɪərɪəns] **I** *n* experiencia *f*; **an unforgettable e.,** una experiencia inolvidable; **he has a lot of e. as a doctor,** es un médico con mucha experiencia. **II** *vtr* (*sensation, situation*) experimentar; (*difficulty*) padecer, tener; (*loss*) sufrir.

experienced [ɪk'spɪərɪənst] *adj* experimentado,-a, con experiencia (**at, in,** en); **you've got to be very e.,** se necesita mucha experiencia.

experiment [ɪk'sperɪmənt] **I** *n* experimento *m*; **as an e.,** como experimento. **II** *vi* experimentar, hacer experimentos (**on, with,** con).

experimental [ɪksperɪ'mentəl] *adj* experimental.

expert ['ekspɜːt] **I** *adj* experto,-a; **e. opinion,** opinión de un experto. **II** *n* experto,-a *m, f*, especialista *mf*; **to be an e. on the subject,** ser experto,-a en la materia. ■ *Comput* **e. system,** sistema *m* experto. ◆ **expertly** *adv* expertamente.

expertise [ekspɜː'tiːz] *n* pericia *f*, habilidad *f*, competencia *f*.

expiate ['ekspɪeɪt] *vtr fml* expiar.

expiation [ekspɪ'eɪʃən] *n fml* expiación *f*.

expire [ɪk'spaɪəʳ] *vi* **1** *euph* (*die*) expirar; (*come to an end*) terminar. **2** *Com Ins* vencer; (*of ticket*) caducar. **3** (*breathe out*) espirar.

expiry [ɪk'spaɪərɪ] *n* expiración *f*, terminación *f*; (*bill of exchange*) vencimiento *m*. ■ **e. date,** fecha *f* de caducidad.

explain [ɪk'spleɪn] **I** *vtr* (*gen*) explicar; (*clarify*) aclarar; **that explains it,** así se explica; **to e. oneself,** explicarse, justificarse. **II** *vi* explicarse. ◆ **explain away** *vtr* dar razones por, justificar; **he found it difficult to e. away the high number of accidents,** le fue difícil justificar el gran número de accidentes.

explanation [eksplə'neɪʃən] *n* (*gen*) explicación *f*; (*clarification*) aclaración *f*.

explanatory [ɪk'splænətərɪ] *adj* explicativo,-a, aclaratorio,-a.

expletive [ɪk'spliːtɪv] *n fml* taco *m*, palabrota *f*.

explicable [ɪk'splɪkəbəl] *adj* explicable.

explicit [ɪk'splɪsɪt] *adj* explícito,-a. ◆ **explicitly** *adv* explícitamente.

explode [ɪk'spləʊd] **I** *vtr* **1** (*bomb*) hacer explotar; (*mine*) hacer volar. **2** *fig* (*theory*) refutar; (*rumour*) desmentir. **II** *vi* **1** (*bomb*) estallar, explotar; *fig* **to e. with** *or* **in anger,** montar en cólera; *fig* **to e. with** *or* **into laughter,** estallar de risa.

exploit ['eksplɔɪt] **I** *n* proeza *f*, hazaña *f*. **II** [ek'splɔɪt] *vtr* explotar, aprovecharse de.

exploitation [eksplɔɪ'teɪʃən] *n* explotación *f*.

exploration [eksplə'reɪʃən] *n* exploración *f*.

exploratory [ek'splɒrətərɪ] *adj* exploratorio,-a.

explore [ɪk'splɔːʳ] *vtr* explorar.

explorer [ɪk'splɔːrəʳ] *n* explorador,-a *m, f*.

explosion [ɪk'spləʊʒən] *n* explosión *f*; **e. of anger,** ataque *m* de rabia *or* genio. ■ **population e.,** explosión *f* demográfica.

explosive [ɪk'spləʊsɪv] **I** *adj* explosivo,-a; *fig* **he's got an e. temper,** se enfurece por cualquier cosa. ■ **e. issue,** asunto *m* delicado. **II** *n* explosivo *m*.

exponent [ɪk'spəʊnənt] *n* **1** (*gen*) exponente *m*; (*supporter*) defensor,-a *m, f*; (*expert*) experto,-a *m, f*; **he is the leading e. of the theory,** es el principal defensor de la teoría. **2** (*performer*) intérprete *mf*. **3** *Math* exponente *m*.

export [ɪk'spɔːt] **I** *vtr* exportar. **II** ['ekspɔːt] *n* **1** *Com* (*trade*) exportación *f*. ■ **e. duty,** aranceles *mpl* de exportación; **e. licence,** licencia *f* de exportación; **e. subsidy,** ayudas *fpl* a la exportación. **2** *Com* (*commodity*) artículo *m* de exportación.

exportation [ekspɔː'teɪʃən] *n* exportación *f*.

exporter [eks'pɔːtəʳ] *n* exportador,-a *m, f*.

exporting [eks'pɔːtɪŋ] *adj* exportador,-a.

expose [ɪk'spəʊz] *vtr* **1** (*uncover*) exponer; (*secret*) revelar; (*plot*) descubrir; **to e. oneself,** exhibirse desnudo; (*habitually*) practicar el exhibicionismo; **to e. oneself to danger,** exponerse al peligro. **2** *Phot* exponer.

exposé [eks'pəʊzeɪ] *n* revelación *f*, desenmascaramiento *m*.

exposed [ɪk'spəʊzd] *adj* (*shown*) expuesto,-a. **2** (*house, place*) desabrigado,-a, al descubierto.

exposition [ekspə'zɪʃən] *n* **1** (*exhibition*) exposición *f*. **2** (*account*) explicación *f*.

expostulate [ɪk'spɒstjʊleɪt] *vi fml* protestar, discutir, reconvenir.

exposure [ɪk'spəʊʒəʳ] *n* **1** (*light, cold, heat*) exposición *f*; **to die of e.,** morir de frío. **2** *Phot* fotografía *f*. ■ **e. meter,** fotómetro *m*; **e. time,** tiempo *m* de exposición. **3** (*reveal*) revelación *f*; (*criminal*) descubrimiento *m*; **fear of e.,** temor *m* al escándalo. ■ **indecent e.,** exhibicionismo *m*. **4** (*house*) situación *f*, orientación *f*.

expound [ɪk'spaʊnd] *vtr* exponer.

express [ɪk'spres] **I** *adj* **1** (*explicit*) expreso,-a, claro,-a; **for the e. purpose of ...,** con el propósito expreso de ... . **2** *GB* (*letter, parcel*) urgente; **send it by e. delivery,** envíalo por correo urgente. ■ *Rail* **e. train,** expreso *m*. **II** *n Rail* expreso *m*. **III** *vtr* **1** (*opinion*) expresar; (*speak, write thoughts*) expresarse. **2** (*fruit juice*) exprimir. **IV** *adv* urgente; **send it e.,** mándalo urgente. ◆ **expressly** *adv fml* expresamente.

expression [ɪk'spreʃən] *n* expresión *f*; *Math* señal *f*.

expressive [ɪk'spresɪv] *adj* expresivo,-a.

expropriate [eks'prəʊprɪeɪt] *vtr* expropiar.

expropriation [eksprəʊprɪ'eɪʃən] *n* expropiación *f*.

expulsion [ɪk'spʌlʃən] *n* expulsión *n f*.

expurgate ['ekspɜːgeɪt] *vtr* expurgar.

expurgation [ekspɜː'geɪʃən] *n* expurgación *f*.

exquisite [ɪk'skwɪzɪt] *adj* exquisito,-a, perfecto,-a. ◆ **exquisitely** *adv* exquisitamente.

ex-serviceman [eks'sɜːvɪsmən] *n* (*pl* **ex-servicemen**) *Mil* ex combatiente *m*.

extant [ek'stænt] *adj* existente.

extempore [ɪk'stempərɪ] **I** *adj fml* improvisado,-a. **II** *adv* de improviso, improvisadamente.

extemporize [ɪk'stempəraɪz] *vtr & vi fml* improvisar.

extend [ɪk'stend] **I** *vtr* **1** (*space*) (*enlarge*) ampliar; (*lengthen*) alargar; (*increase*) augmentar; **she wants to e. her country house,** quiere ampliar su casa de campo; *fig* **the prohibition was extended to cover cigarettes,** extendieron la prohibición a los cigarrillos. **2** (*give, offer*) rendir, dar; **he extended the letter to the manager,** hizo entrega de la carta al director; **to e. an invitation to sb,** invitar a algn; **to e. a welcome to sb,** recibir a algn. **3** (*time*) (*prolong*) prolongar, alargar; **I asked them to e. my travel insurance,** solicité que prorrogaran el seguro de viaje; **regular maintenance extends a car's life,** el mantenimiento regular alarga la vida de un coche; **to e. a stay,** prolongar una estancia. **II** *vi* **1** (*stretch*) extenderse;

his lands extended as far as the great desert, sus tierras se extendían hasta el gran desierto. **2** *(last)* extenderse, prolongarse, durar, alargarse; **the winter extended well into March,** el invierno se alargó hasta bien entrado marzo.

extension [ɪk'stenʃən] *n* **1** *(gen)* extensión *f*, prolongación *f*; *(of time)* prórroga *f*. **2** *Tel* extensión; **e. 33 please,** con la extensión 33 por favor. **3** *Constr* anexo *m*.

extensive [ɪk'stensɪv] *adj (length, quality)* extenso,-a; *(space)* amplio,-a. ◆ **extensively** *adv* **1** *(widely)* extensamente. **2** *(frequently)* frecuentemente, con frecuencia.

extent [ɪk'stent] *n* **1** *(area)* extensión *f*. **2** *(degree)* punto *m*; **to a certain e.,** hasta cierto punto; **to a large e.,** en gran parte; **to a lesser e.,** en menor grado; **to such an e.,** hasta tal punto. **3** *(limit)* límite *m*; **I've reached the e. of my patience,** he llegado al límite de mi paciencia.

extenuating [ɪk'stenjʊeɪtɪŋ] *adj Jur* atenuante. ■ **e. circumstances,** circunstancias *fpl* atenuantes.

exterior [ɪk'stɪərɪəʳ] **I** *adj* exterior, externo,-a. **II** *n* exterior *m*.

exterminate [ɪk'stɜ:mɪneɪt] *vtr* exterminar.

extermination [ɪkstɜ:mɪ'neɪʃən] *n* exterminación *f*, exterminio *m*.

exterminator [ɪk'stɜ:mɪneɪtəʳ] *n* exterminador,-a *m,f*.

external [ek'stɜ:nəl] *adj* **1** *(gen)* externo,-a, exterior; *Med* **for e. use only,** sólo para uso externo. ■ *Pol* **e. affairs,** asuntos *mpl* exteriores. **2** *Univ* por libre.

extinct [ɪk'stɪŋkt] *adj* **1** *(species)* extinguido,-a; **to become e.,** extinguirse. **2** *(volcano)* extinguido,-a, apagado,-a.

extinction [ɪk'stɪŋkʃən] *n* extinción *f*.

extinguish [ɪk'stɪŋgwɪʃ] *vtr* extinguir, apagar.

extinguisher [ɪk'stɪŋgwɪʃəʳ] *n* extintor *m*.

extirpate ['ekstəpeɪt] *vtr* extirpar.

extol, *US* **extoll** [ɪk'stəʊl] *vtr (pt & pp extolled)* ensalzar, alabar.

extort [ɪk'stɔ:t] *vtr (promise, confession)* arrancar; *(money)* sacar.

extortion [ɪk'stɔ:ʃən] *n (of money)* extorsión *f*.

extortionate [ɪk'stɔ:ʃənɪt] *adj* exorbitante, desorbitado,-a.

extra ['ekstrə] **I** *adj* extra, más; *(spare)* de sobra; **e. charge,** suplemento *m*; **I've got two e. tickets,** me sobran dos entradas; **the wine is e.,** el vino se cobra aparte, el vino no está incluido. **II** *adv* extra; **e. fine,** finísimo, extra fino; **e. strong,** fortísimo, extra fuerte. **III** *n* **1** *(additional charge)* suplemento *m*. **2** *Cin* extra *mf*. **3** *(newspaper)* edición *f* especial.

extract ['ekstrækt] **I** *n* **1** extracto *m*; **meat e.,** extracto de carne. **2** *(book)* extracto *m*, trozo *m*. **II** [ɪk'strækt] *vtr (tooth, information)* extraer, sacar; *(confession)* arrancar.

extraction [ɪk'strækʃən] *n* **1** extracción *f*. **2** *(descent)* origen *m*; **to be of Spanish e.,** ser de origen español.

extractor [ɪk'stræktəʳ] *n* extractor *m*. ■ **e. fan,** extractor *m* de humos.

extracurricular [ekstrəkə'rɪkjʊləʳ] *adj Educ* extraescolar, fuera del programa de estudios.

extradite ['ekstrədaɪt] *vtr* extraditar, extradir.

extradition [ekstr'dɪʃən] *n* extradición *f*.

extramarital [ekstrə'mærɪtəl] *adj* fuera del matrimonio, extramatrimonial.

extramural [ekstrə'mjʊərəl] *adj Univ* **e. course,** curso *m* para estudiantes libres.

extraneous [ɪk'streɪnɪəs] *adj fml* ajeno,-a, extraño,-a.

extraordinary [ɪk'strɔ:dənərɪ] *adj* **1** *(special, additional)* extraordinario,-a, fuera de lo común. **2** *(strange)* raro,-a; **what an e. thing!,** ¡qué cosa más rara! ◆ **extraordinarily** *adv* extraordinariamente.

extrapolate [ɪk'stræpəleɪt] *vtr* **1** *Math* extrapolar. **2** *(guess)* extrapolar.

extrapolation [ɪkstræpə'leɪʃən] *n* extrapolación *f*.

extravagance [ɪk'strævɪgəns] *n (spending)* derroche *m*, despilfarro *m*; *(behaviour)* extravagancia *f*, exageración *f*.

extravagant [ɪk'strævɪgənt] *adj (wasteful)* derrochador,-a, despilfarrador,-a; *(excessive)* exagerado,-a; *(luxurious)* lujoso,-a, suntuoso,-a.

extravaganza [ɪkstrævə'gænzə] *n Theat* farsa *f*, fantasía *f*.

extreme [ɪk'stri:m] **I** *adj* extremo,-a; **an e. case,** un caso excepcional; **to hold e. views,** tener opiniones muy radicales. ■ *Rel* **E. Unction,** Extremaunción *f*. **II** *n* extremo *m*; **in the e.,** en sumo grado, en extremo; **to go from one e. to the other,** pasar de un extremo a otro; **to go to extremes,** llegar a extremos. ◆ **extremely** *adv* extremadamente, sumamente; **e. annoyed/pleased,** enfadadísimo,-a/contentísimo,-a; **I'm e. sorry,** lo siento de veras.

extremism [ɪk'stri:mɪzəm] *n* extremismo *m*.

extremist [ɪk'stri:mɪst] *n* extremista *mf*.

extremity [ɪk'stremɪtɪ] *n* **1** *(extreme)* extremidad *f*, extremo *m*. **2** **extremities,** *(hands, feet)* extremidades *fpl*.

extricate ['ekstrɪkeɪt] *vtr* librar, sacar; **to e. oneself,** lograr salir (**from,** de).

extrovert [ekstrəvɜ:t] *adj & n* extrovertido,-a *(m,f)*.

extrude [ɪk'stru:d] **I** *vi (squeeze)* inquibir; *(force out)* hacer salir. **II** *vtr Tech* expulsar.

exuberance [ɪg'zju:bərəns] *n (effusiveness)* exuberancia *f*; *(vitality)* euforia *f*.

exuberant [ɪg'zju:bərənt] *adj (excessive)* exuberante; *(energetic)* eufórico,-a.

exude [ɪg'zju:d] *vtr & vi (sweat, sap)* exudar, rezumar; *fig* rebosar.

exult [ɪg'zʌlt] *vi* regocijarse.

exultant [ɪg'zʌltənt] *adj* jubiloso,-a, regocijado,-a, triunfante.

exultation [ɪgzʌl'teɪʃən] *n* exultación *f*, júbilo *m*.

eye [aɪ] **I** *n* **1** *Anat* ojo *m*; *fig* **anyone with half an e. can see she's wrong,** cualquiera con dos dedos de frente puede ver que está equivocada; *fig* **as far as the e. can see,** hasta donde alcanza la vista; *fig* **before** *or* **under my very eyes,** delante de mis propios ojos; *fig* **I couldn't believe my eyes,** no podía creerlo; *fig* **in the eyes of,** según; *fig* **in the eyes of the Law this is illegal,** según la Ley esto es ilegal; *fig* **in the mind's e.,** en la imaginación; *fig* **in the twinkling of an e.,** en un abrir y cerrar de ojos; *fig* **my e. fell upon ...,** me di cuenta de ...; *fig* **not to take one's eyes off sb/sth,** no quitar la vista de encima a algn/algo; *fig* **to be very much in the public e.,** aparecer mucho en público; *fig* **to catch sb's e.,** llamar la atención a algn; *fig* **to do sth with one's eyes open,** hacer algo sabiendo lo que le espera a uno; *fig* **to have an e. for,** tener buen ojo para; *fig* **to have eyes in the back of one's head,** saber *or* darse cuenta de todo; *fig* **to make eyes at sb,** dirigir miraditas a algn; *fig* **to my e.,** en mi opinión; *fig* **to only have eyes for ...,** sólo tener ojos para ...; *fig* **to open sb's eyes,** abrirle los ojos a algn; *fig* **to shut one's eyes to sth,** hacer la vista gorda a algo; *fig* **to see e. to e. with sb,** estar de acuerdo con algn; *fig* **to turn a blind e.,** hacer la vista gorda **(to,** a); *fig* **with an e. to,** con el propósito de, con miras a; *fig* **with the naked e.,** a simple vista; *fam* **to keep an e. on sb/sth,** vigilar a algn/algo; *fam* **to keep an e. out for sb/sth,** tener un ojo pendiente de algn/algo; *fam* **to keep one's eyes peeled** *or* **skinned,** estar ojo alerta; *fam fig* **I'm up to my eyes in work,** estoy hasta aquí de trabajo; *prov* **an e. for an e. (a tooth for a tooth),** ojo por ojo (diente por diente). ■ **black e.,** ojo *m* a la funerala; **glass e.,** ojo *m* de cristal; **private e.,** detective *mf* privado,-a. **2** *(of needle, potato, hurricane)* ojo *m*. **II** *vtr* mirar, observar; **to e. sb up and down,** mirar a algn de arriba abajo.

eyeball ['aɪbɔːl] *n Anat* globo *m* ocular.

eyebrow ['aɪbraʊ] *n Anat* ceja *f*.

eyecatching ['aɪkætʃɪŋ] *adj* llamativo,-a.

eyeful ['aɪfʊl] *n fam* **to get an e.,** echar un vistazo.

eyeglass ['aɪglɑːs] *n* monóculo *m*.

eyelash ['aɪlæʃ] *n Anat* pestaña *f*.

eyelet ['aɪlɪt] *n* ojete *m*.

eyelid ['aɪlɪd] *n Anat* párpado *m*.

eyeliner ['aɪlaɪnə] *n* lápiz *m* de ojos.

eye-opener ['aɪəʊpənə^r] *n* revelación *f*, gran sorpresa *f*.

eyepatch ['aɪpætʃ] *n* parche *m*.

eyepiece ['aɪpiːs] *n* ocular *m*.

eyeshade ['aɪʃeɪd] *n* visera *f*.

eyeshadow ['aɪʃædəʊ] *n* sombra *f* de ojos.

eyesight ['aɪsaɪt] *n* vista *f*; **my e. is failing,** me está fallando la vista.

eyesore ['aɪsɔː^r] *n* monstruosidad *f*; **to be an e.,** ofender a la vista.

eyestrain ['aɪstreɪn] *n* vista *f* cansada; **to suffer from e.,** tener la vista cansada.

eyetooth ['aɪtuːθ] *n (pl eyeteeth* ['aɪtiːθ]*) Anat* colmillo *m*; *fam* **I would give my eyeteeth to ...,** daría un ojo de la cara por ... .

eyewash ['aɪwɒʃ] *n Med* colirio *m*; *fam* **it's all e.,** eso son disparates.

eyewitness ['aɪwɪtnɪs] *n* testigo *mf* ocular.

eyrie ['ɪərɪ, 'aɪərɪ] *n* aguilera *f*.

F

F, f [ef] *n* **1** *(the letter)* F, f *f*. **2** *Mus* fa *m*.

F [ef] *abbr of* **Fahrenheit,** Fahrenheit, F.

f [ef] *Ling abbr of* **feminine,** femenino, f.

FA [ef'eɪ] **1** *GB Sport abbr of* **Football Association,** Federación *f* de fútbol. **2** *vulg offens abbr of* **fuck all,** *(virtually nothing)* una mierda; *(absolutely nothing)* ni una mierda.

fab [fæb] *adj (abbr of fabulous)* guai, chachi.

fable ['feɪbəl] *n* fábula *f*; **Aesop's fables,** fábulas de Esopo.

fabled ['feɪbəld] *adj* **1** fabulado,-a; **ghosts are f. to appear at midnight,** cuenta la leyenda que los fantasmas aparecen a media noche. **2** ficticio,-a.

fabric ['fæbrɪk] *n* **1** *Tex* tela *f*, tejido *m*. **2** *Constr* fábrica *f*, estructura *f*; *fig* **the f. of society,** la estructura de la sociedad.

fabricate ['fæbrɪkeɪt] *vtr* **1** *(build, invent)* fabricar; *(story, lie)* inventar. **2** *(forge)* falsificar.

fabrication [fæbrɪ'keɪʃən] *n fig* invención *f*; **it is pure f.,** es pura invención *or* ficción.

fabulous ['fæbjʊləs] *adj* fabuloso,-a.

façade, facade [fə'sɑːd, fæ'sɑːd] *n Archit* fachada *f*; *fig* **it's all a f.,** es pura fachada.

face [feɪs] **I** *n* **1** *Anat* cara *f*, rostro *m*; **a serious f.,** una cara seria; **a smiling f.,** un semblante risueño; **f. to f.,** cara a cara; **he never forgets a f.,** es muy buen fisonomista; **I told him to his f.,** se lo dije en la cara; **she laughed in my f.,** se me rió en la cara; **she slammed the door in my f.,** me dió con la puerta en las narices; **shut your f.!,** ¡cierra el pico!; **to look sb in the f.,** mirarle a algn a la cara; *fig* **to fall flat on one's f.,** caerse de bruces; *fig* **to show one's f.,** asomar la cara. ■ **f. cloth,** paño *m*; **f. cream,** crema *f* de belleza; **f. pack,** mascarilla *f* facial. **2** *(expression)* cara *f*, expresión *f*; **to pull a long f.,** poner una cara larga; **to keep a straight f.,** mantenerse serio,-a; **to pull faces,** hacer muecas. **3** *(surface)* superficie *f*; *(card, coin)* cara *f*; *(dial)* cuadrante *m*; *(watch)* esfera *f*; *(cliff)* cara *f*; *(world)* faz *f*, superficie *f*; *(cards)* **f. down,** boca abajo; **f. up,** boca arriba; *(fig)* **in the f. of danger,** ante el peligro. ■ **coal f.,** frente *m* de carbón; **f. value,** valor *m* nominal; **f. worker,** minero *m* del frente. **4** *(appearance)* aspecto *m*; **on the f. of it,** a primera vista; **to lose f.,** desprestigiarse; **to save f.,** salvar las apariencias; **to take sth at f. value,** entender algo sólo en su sentido literal. **II** *vtr* **1** *(building etc) (look onto)* dar a, mirar hacia; *(be opposite)* estar enfrente de. **2** *(confront)* encontrarse delante de; **the country is facing a crisis,** el país se halla frente a una crisis; **the problem facing us,** el problema que se nos plantea; **we are faced with the prospect of ...,** nos encontramos ante la perspectiva de ... . **3** *(meet resolutely)* hacer frente a; **he won't f. the facts,** no quiere enfrentarse con la realidad; **let's f. it,** hay que reconocerlo; **to f. up to,** hacer cara a, enfrentarse con, afrontar; **to f. the consequences,** afrontar las consecuencias; *fam* **to f. the music,** dar la cara. **4** *(tolerate)* soportar, aguantar; **I can't f. another meat pie,** no puedo con otra empanada. **5** *Constr (wall)* revestir **(with,** de). **6** *Sew* forrar **(with,** de). **III** *vi* **f. this way,** vuélvase de este lado; **to f. on to,** dar a; **to f. towards,** mirar hacia.

face-ache ['feɪseɪk] **1** *n (pain)* neuralgia *f*. **2** *sl (ugly person)* feto *m*.

faceless ['feɪslɪs] *adj* sin cara, anónimo,-a.

facelift ['feɪslɪft] *n* **1** *Med* lifting *m*. **2** *fig (building)* renovación *f*, modernización *f*.

face-saving ['feɪsseɪvɪŋ] *adj* **f.-s. exercise,** maniobra *f* para salvar las apariencias.

facet ['fæsɪt] *n* faceta *f*, aspecto *m*.

facetious [fə'siːʃəs] *adj* bromista, chistoso,-a, gracioso,-a.

facial ['feɪʃəl] **I** *adj* facial. **II** *n* tratamiento *m* facial.

facile ['fæsaɪl] *adj (easy)* fácil; *(simplistic)* superficial.

facilitate [fə'sɪlɪteɪt] *vtr* facilitar

facility [fə'sɪlɪtɪ] *n* **1** *(ease)* facilidad *f* **2** **facilities,** *(means)* facilidades *fpl* ■ **credit f.,** facilidades *fpl* de crédito **3** **facilities,** *(rooms, equipment)* instalaciones *fpl* ■ **cooking f.,** derecho *m* a cocina, **sports f.,** instalaciones *fpl* deportivas

facing [feɪsɪŋ] **I** *n* **1** *Constr* revestimiento *m* **2** *Sew* guarnición *f* **3** **facings,** vueltas *fpl* **II** *adj* de enfrente, **f. page,** página *f* opuesta

facsimile [fæk'sɪmɪlɪ] **I** *n* **1** *(exact copy)* facsímil *m*, facsímile *m* **2** *(message)* facsímil *m*, telefax *m*, fax *m* **3** *(machine)* facsímil *m*, fax *m* **II** *vtr* mandar *or* enviar por fax

fact [fækt] *n* **1** *(event, happening)* hecho *m*, **a story based on f.,** una historia basada en un hecho real, **as a matter of f.,** de hecho, **facts and figures,** datos *mpl* y cifras *fpl*, **hard facts,** hechos *mpl* innegables; **the f. that he confessed,** el hecho de que confesara, **to stick to facts,** atenerse a los hechos **2** *(reality)* realidad *f*, **f. and fiction,** lo real y lo ficticio, **in f., in point of f.,** en realidad, **it is a f. of life that ...,** es un hecho ineludible que ..., **the f. is that ...,** el hecho es que ..., **the f. remains that ...,** sigue siendo un hecho que ..., *euph* **the facts of life,** el misterio de la vida, **we know for a f. that ...,** sabemos a ciencia cierta que

fact-finding ['fæktfaɪndɪŋ] *adj* investigador,-a, **a f.-f. mission,** una misión investigadora

faction[1] ['fækʃən] *n (group)* facción *f*

faction[2] ['fækʃən] *n Lit fam* historia *f* novelada, reportaje *m* novelado

factitive ['fæktɪtɪv] *adj Ling* factitivo,-a

factor ['fæktəʳ] *n* 1 *(element)* factor *m* 2 *Math* factor *m*, **highest common f.**, máximo *m* común divisor

factory ['fæktərɪ] *n* fábrica *f* ■ **f. worker**, obrero,-a *m*,*f*, operario,-a *m*, **f.** de fábrica

factorize ['fæktəraɪz] *vtr Math* dividir en factores

factotum [fæk'təʊtəm] *n* factótum *m*

factual ['fæktʃʊəl] *adj* factual, objetivo,-a, **a f. analysis**, un análisis de los hechos, **a f. error**, un error de hecho

faculty ['fækəltɪ] *n* 1 *(power)* facultad *f*, **he has all his faculties**, tiene todas sus facultades 2 *Univ* facultad *f* 3 *US Univ* profesorado *m*, cuerpo *m* docente

fad [fæd] *n fam* 1 *(fashion, craze)* moda *f* pasajera 2 *(whim)* capricho *m*, *(mania)* manía *f*

faddy ['fædɪ] *adj (faddier, faddiest)* fam caprichoso,-a

fade [feɪd] I *vtr (colours, material)* descolorar, destñir II *vt* 1 *(colour, material)* descolorarse, desteñirse 2 *(flower)* marchitarse 3 *(light)* apagarse ◆ **fade away** *vt* desvanecerse, **all hope has faded away**, todas las esperanzas se desvanecieron ◆ **fade in** *vtr*, **fade out** *vtr Cin TV* fundir

faded ['feɪdɪd] *adj* 1 *(colour, material)* descolorido,-a, desteñido,-a 2 *(flower)* marchito,-a

fade-in ['feɪdɪn] *n*, **fade-out** ['feɪdaʊt] *n Cin TV* fundido *m*

fag [fæg] *n sl* 1 *(nuisance)* pesadez *f*, lata *f*, **what a f.!**, ¡qué latazo! 2 *fam (cigarette)* pitillo *m* 3 *US sl (homosexual)* marica *m* 4 *GB Sch sl* fámulo *m*

fag-end ['fægend] *n fam* colilla *f*

fagged [fægd] *adj sl* rendido,-a, molido,-a

faggot ['fægət] *n* 1 *(wood)* haz *m* de leña 2 *Culin* albondiguilla *f* 3 *US sl offens* marica *m*

Fahrenheit ['færənhaɪt] *n* Fahrenheit *m*, **ten degrees F.**, diez grados Fahrenheit

fail [feɪl] I *n* 1 *Educ* suspenso *m* 2 *(definitely)* **without f.**, sin falta II *vtr* 1 *(let down)* fallar, **his memory failed him**, le falló la memoria, **words f. me**, no encuentro palabras 2 *Educ (exam)* suspender, **she failed biology**, la suspendieron en biología III *vt* 1 *(show, film)* fracasar, fallar, *(brakes, lights)* fallar, *(crops)* perderse, **the attempt failed**, el intento fracasó 2 *Com (business)* quebrar, **it can't f.**, no puede fallar, **if all else fails**, si te falla todo 3 *Educ* suspender, ser suspendido,-a 4 *(to be unable)* no lograr, **he failed to score**, no logró marcar, **I f. to see why**, no veo por qué 5 *(forget, neglect)* dejar de, **don't f. to come**, no deje de venir, **she never fails to attend**, nunca falta 6 *(health)* deteriorarse, **her sight is failing**, le falla la vista, **his heart failed**, le falló el corazón

failed [feɪld] *adj* fracasado,-a, **a f. actress**, una actriz fracasada

failing ['feɪlɪŋ] I *n* 1 *(shortcoming)* defecto *m* 2 *(weakness)* debilidad *f*, flaqueza *f* II *prep* a falta de

fail-safe ['feɪlseɪf] *adj* **f.-s. device**, dispositivo *m* de seguridad

failure ['feɪljə] *n* 1 fracaso *m*, malogro *m*, **the meal was a complete f.**, la comida fue un fracaso total 2 *Com* quiebra *f* 3 *Educ* suspenso *m* 4 *(person)* fracasado,-a *m*,*f*, **he was a f. as a writer**, como escritor fue un fracaso 5 *Tech (breakdown)* fallo *m*, avería *f* ■ **brake f.**, fallo *m* de los frenos, **power f.**, apagón *m*, *Med* **heart f.**, paro *m* cardíaco 6 *(inability, neglect)* **her f. to answer the question**, el hecho de que no contestara a la pregunta, **f. to attend will be punished**, se castigará la falta de asistencia, **f. to observe the rules**, incumplimiento *m* de las reglas

fain [feɪn] *adv poet* de buena gana, **I would f. have stayed at home**, me habría quedado en casa tranquilamente

faint [feɪnt] I *adj* 1 *(sound, voice)* débil, tenue, *(colour)* pálido,-a, *(outline)* borroso,-a, *(idea, recollection)* vago,-a, **a f. resemblance**, un ligero parecido, **f. hope**, pocas esperanzas, **I haven't the faintest idea**, no tengo la más

mínima idea 2 *Med (giddy)* mareado,-a, **to feel f.**, sentirse mareado,-a II *Med* desmayo *m* III *vt Med* desmayarse ◆ **faintly** *adv (with little strength)* débilmente, *(unclear)* vagamente

faint-hearted [feɪnt'hɑːtɪd] *adj* pusilánime, temeroso,-a

faintness ['feɪntnɪs] *n* 1 debilidad *f*, falta *f* de claridad 2 *Med* desmayo *m*, desfallecimiento *m*

fair¹ [feəʳ] I *adj* 1 *(impartial)* imparcial, *(just)* justo,-a, equitativo,-a, **I have had my f. share of problems**, yo ya tenido bastantes problemas, **I paid my f. share**, pagué mi parte, **it's not f.**, no hay derecho, **to give sb a f. hearing**, escuchar imparcialmente a algn, **to give sb a f. warning**, avisar debidamente a algn *fam* **f. do's**, seamos justos *fam* **f. enough!**, ¡vale! ■ **f. play**, juego *m* limpio 2 *(hair, skin)* rubio,-a, *(complexion)* blanco,-a 3 *Meteor* bueno,-a, bonancible, *fig* **a f. weather friend**, un amigo de circunstancias 4 *Lit (beautiful)* bello,-a, hermoso,-a, **the f. sex**, el bello sexo 5 *(quite good)* **a f. number**, un buen número, **he has a f. chance**, tiene bastantes probabilidades, *fam* **f. to middling**, mediano, regular 6 **f. copy**, versión *f* definitiva II *adv* **it hit me f. and square on the chin**, me dio en pleno mentón, **they beat us f. and square**, nos ganaron merecidamente, **to play f.**, jugar limpio. ◆ **fairly** *adv* 1 *(justly)* justamente, con equidad 2 *(moderately)* bastante, **f. rich**, bastante rico,-a 3 *fam (really, utterly)* **it's f. tipping it down**, ciertamente llueve mucho.

fair² [feəʳ] *n* feria *f*. ■ **trade f.**, feria *f* de muestras.

fairground ['feəgraʊnd] *n* real *m* de la feria.

fair-haired [feə'heəd] *adj* rubio,-a.

fairness ['feənɪs] *n* 1 *(justice)* justicia *f*, equidad *f*; **in all f.**, para ser justo,-a. 2 *(hair)* color *m* rubio; *(complexion)* blancura *f*, palidez *f*.

fair-sized [feə'saɪzd] *adj* bastante grande.

fair-skinned [feə'skɪnd] *adj* de piel blanca *or* pálida.

fairway ['feəweɪ] *n Golf* calle *f*.

fairy ['feərɪ] *n* 1 hada *f*. ■ **f. godmother**, hada *f* madrina; **f. tale**, cuento *m* de hadas; **f. tale ending**, desenlace *m* feliz. 2 *sl offens* marica *m*.

fairyland ['feərɪlænd] *n fig* lugar *m* de ensueño.

fairy-lights ['feərɪlaɪts] *npl* bombillas *fpl* de colorines.

fait accompli [feɪtə'kɒmpliː] *n (pl* **faits accomplis** [feɪtsə'kɒmpliː]) *fml* hecho *m* consumado.

faith [feɪθ] *n* 1 *Rel* fe *f*; **the Catholic f.**, la fe católica. 2 *(trust)* fe *f*, confianza *f*; **in good/bad f.**, de buena/mala fe; **to break f. with sb**, ser desleal a algn; **to have f. in sb**, tener fe *or* confiar en algn.

faithful ['feɪθfʊl] I *adj* 1 *(loyal)* fiel, leal *(to*, a, con). 2 *(accurate)* fiel, exacto. II **the f.** *npl Rel* los fieles. ◆ **faithfully** *adv* 1 *(loyally)* fielmente, lealmente. 2 *(accurately)* fielmente. 3 *(in letter)* **yours f.**, le saluda atentamente.

faithfulness ['feɪθfʊlnɪs] *n* 1 *(loyalty)* fidelidad *f*, lealtad *f* *(to*, a). 2 *(accuracy)* fidelidad *f*, exactitud *f*.

faith-healer ['feɪθhiːlə] *n* curandero,-a *m*,*f* por fe.

faith-healing ['feɪθhiːlɪŋ] *n* curación *f* por fe.

fake [feɪk] I *adj* falso,-a, falsificado,-a. II *n* 1 *(object)* falsificación *f*, copia *f*. 2 *(person)* impostor,-a *m*, *f*, farsante *mf*, tramposo,-a *m*,*f*. III *vtr* 1 *(forge)* falsificar. 2 *(feign)* fingir, simular. IV *vi (pretend)* fingir, simular.

falcon ['fɔːlkən] *n Orn* halcón *m*.

Falklands ['fɔːkləndz] *npl* **the F.**, las (Islas) Malvinas.

fall [fɔːl] I *n* 1 caída *f*. ■ *US fam* **f. guy**, cabeza *f* de turco. 2 *Pol (of government, politician, empire)* caída *f* 3 *(of rock)* desprendimiento *m*; **f. of snow**, nevada *f*. 4 *(decrease)* baja *f*, disminución *f*; **an unexpected f. in prices**, un inesperado descenso de los precios. 5 *US* otoño *m*; **in the f.**, en otoño. 6 *(usu pl)* cascada *f*; **Niagara Falls**, las cataratas del Niágara. II *vi (pt fell; pp fallen)* 1 caer, caerse; **she fell off her bicycle**, se cayó de la bicicleta; **the stress falls on the first syllable**, el acento cae en la primera sílaba; **they f. into two categories,** se dividen en dos categorías; *fig* **Christmas Day falls on a Sunday,** el día de Navidad cae en domingo; *fig* **night was falling,** anochecía; *fig* **to f. from grace,** caer en desgracia; *fig* **to f. into line,** aceptar las reglas; *fig* **to f. into sb's hands,** caer en manos de algn; *fig* **to f. prey to,** ser víctima de; *fig* **to f. short,** no alcanzar (**of,** -). **2** *(in battle)* caer. **3** *(temperature, prices)* bajar. **4** *(become)* **to f. asleep,** dormirse; **to f. ill,** caer enfermo,-a; **to f. in love,** enamorarse; **to f. to pieces,** hacerse pedazos. ◆ **fall about** *vi* troncharse *or* mondarse *or* partirse de risa. ◆ **fall away** *vi* desaparecer. ◆ **fall back** *vi* *Mil* retirarse. ◆ **fall back on** *vtr* *(resort to)* echar mano a, recurrir a. ◆ **fall behind** *vi* *(in race)* quedarse atrás; **to f. behind with one's work,** retrasarse en el trabajo. ◆ **fall down** *vi* **1** *(picture etc)* caerse. **2** *(building)* derrumbarse, hundirse. **3** *(argument)* fallar. ◆ **fall for** *vtr* **1** *(fall in love with)* enamorarse de, prendarse de. **2** *(to be tricked by)* dejarse engañar por; *fam* **she fell for it,** picó, se lo tragó. ◆ **fall in** *vi* **1** *(roof)* desplomarse, caerse. **2** *Mil* formar filas, ponerse en fila. ◆ **fall off** *vi* **1** *(drop off)* caer; **her ring fell off,** se le cayó el anillo. **2** *(part)* desprenderse. **3** *(diminish)* bajar, disminuir, decaer; **sales have fallen off,** las ventas han bajado. ◆ **fall out** *vi* **1** *(hair)* caerse. **2** *Mil* romper filas. **3** *(quarrel)* pelearse, reñirse (**with,** con). ◆ **fall over** *vi* **1** caer, caerse. **2** *fig* **to f. over oneself to do sth,** volcarse en algo. ◆ **fall through** *vi* *(plan)* fracasar.

fallacious [fə'leɪʃəs] *adj fml* falso,-a, erróneo,-a.

fallacy ['fæləsɪ] *n* falacia *f*.

fallen ['fɔːlən] **I** *pp see* **fall. II** *adj* **1** caído,-a. **2** *(dishonoured)* perdido,-a, deshonrado,-a. **III the f.** *npl Mil* los caídos.

fallible ['fælɪbəl] *adj* falible.

fallibility [fælɪ'bɪlɪtɪ] *n* falibilidad *f*.

Fallopian [fə'ləupɪən] *adj Anat* **F. tube,** trompa *f* de Falopio.

fall-out ['fɔːlaut] *n* **(radioactive) f.,** lluvia *f* radioactiva. ■ **f. shelter,** refugio *m* antiatómico.

fallow ['fæləu] **1** *adj Agr* en barbecho; **to lie f.,** estar en barbecho. **2** *Zool* **f. deer,** gamo *m*.

false [fɔːls] *adj* falso,-a; **f. statement,** declaración *f* falsa; *Mus* **f. note,** nota falsa; **f. step,** paso *m* en falso; **under f. pretences,** por fraude. ■ *Sport* **f. start,** salida *f* nula; **f. teeth,** dentadura *f* postiza; **f. alarm,** falsa alarma *f*; **f. bottom,** doble fondo *m*. ◆ **falsely** *adv* falsamente.

falsehood ['fɔːlshud] *n* *(lies)* falsedad *f*, mentira *f*.

falseness ['fɔːlsnɪs] *n* *(fake)* falsedad *f*.

falsetto [fɔːl'setəu] *n* *(pl falsettos)* *Mus* falsete *m*. ■ **a f. voice,** una voz de falsete.

falsies ['fɔːlsɪz] *npl fam (breasts)* postizos *mpl*, rellenos *mpl*.

falsification [fɔːlsɪfɪ'keɪʃən] *n* falsificación *f*.

falsify ['fɔːlsɪfaɪ] *vt* *(pt & pp falsified)* *(records, accounts)* falsificar; *(misrepresent)* *(story, issue)* falsear.

falter ['fɔːltə'] *vi* *(hesitate)* titubear, vacilar; *(voice)* fallar.

faltering ['fɔːltərɪŋ] *adj* titubeante, vacilante; **with f. voice,** con voz temblorosa.

fame [feɪm] *n* fama *f*

famed [feɪmd] *adj* famoso,-a, célebre (**for,** por).

familiar [fə'mɪlɪə'] *adj* **1** *(common, usual)* familiar, conocido,-a; **his face is f.,** su cara me suena; **it's the old f. story,** es la misma historia de siempre. **2** *(aware, knowledgeable)* al corriente; **to make oneself f. with sth,** familiarizarse con algo; **I'm f. with the details,** estoy al corriente de los detalles. **3** *(intimacy)* **to be on f. terms with sb,** tener confianza con algn; **to get too f. with sb,** tomarse demasiadas libertades con algn.

familiarity [fəmɪlɪ'ærɪtɪ] *n* **1** *(awareness, knowledge)* familiaridad *f* (**with,** con), conocimiento *m* (**with,** de). **2** *(intimacy)* familiaridad *f*, confianza *f*; *prov* **f. breeds contempt,** el que no te conozca que te compre.

familiarize [fə'mɪljəraɪz] *vtr* **I** *(become acquainted)* familiarizarse (**with,** con). **2** *(divulge)* popularizar; **the press have familiarized the word 'yuppie',** la prensa ha popularizado la palabra 'yuppie'.

family ['fæmɪlɪ] *n* familia *f*; **she is one of the f.,** es como de la familia; *fam* **it runs in the f.,** viene de familia; *fam* **to be in the f. way,** estar en estado. ■ **f. allowance,** subsidio *m* familiar; **f. doctor,** médico *m* de cabecera; **f. life,** vida *f* familiar; **f. man,** hombre *m* hogareño; *US* **f. name,** apellido *m*; **f. planning,** planificación *f* familiar; **f. ties,** lazos *mpl* familiares; **f. tree,** árbol *m* genealógico.

famine ['fæmɪn] *n* hambre *f*, escasez *f* de alimentos.

famished ['fæmɪʃt] *adj fam* muerto,-a de hambre.

famous ['feɪməs] *adj* célebre, famoso,-a (**for,** por). ◆ **famously** *adv fam* estupendamente; **they get on f.,** se llevan estupendamente bien.

fan [fæn] **I** *n* **1** abanico *m*; *Elec* ventilador *m*. ■ *Aut* **f. belt,** correa *f* del ventilador; **f. heater,** estufa *f* de aire. **2** *(person)* aficionado,-a *m*,*f*; *(of pop star, entertainer, etc)* admirador,-a *m*,*f*; **a cinema f.,** un aficionado al cine. ■ **f. club,** club *m* de admiradores; **f. mail,** cartas *fpl* de los admiradores; **football f.,** hincha *mf*. **II** *vtr* **1** abanicar; **to f. oneself,** abanicarse. **2** *(fire)* avivar. **3** *fig (passions)* atizar, avivar. ◆ **fan out** *vi (troops)* desplegarse en abanico.

fanlight ['fænlaɪt] *n Arch* claraboya *f*.

fanatic [fə'nætɪk] *adj & n* fanático,-a *(m, f)*.

fanatical [fə'nætɪkəl] *adj* fanático,-a.

fanaticism [fə'nætɪsɪzəm] *n* fanatismo *m*.

fancier ['fænsɪə'] *n* aficionado-a *m*, *f*; **pigeon f.,** colombófilo,-a *m*,*f*.

fanciful ['fænsɪful] *adj* **1** *(person)* caprichoso,-a, poco realista. **2** *(idea)* fantástico,-a.

fancy ['fænsɪ] **I** *adj (fancier, fanciest)* de fantasía; *pej* **a f. car,** un coche muy pero. ■ **f. dress,** disfraz *m*; **in f. dress,** disfrazado,-a; **f. dress ball,** baile *m* de disfraces; **f. cakes,** pasteles *mpl* finos; **f. goods,** artículos *mpl* de fantasía; **f. prices,** precios *mpl* exorbitantes. **II** *n* **1** *(imagination)* fantasía *f*, imaginación *f*; **flights of f.,** ilusiones *fpl*; *fam* **it tickled my f.,** me cayó en gracia. **2** *(whim)* capricho *m*, antojo *m*; **to take a f. to sb,** cogerle cariño a algn; **to take a f. to sth,** encapricharse con algo; **what takes your f.?,** ¿qué se le antoja? ◆ **f. man** amigo *m*, amante *m*; **f. woman,** amiga *f*, amante *f*. **III** *vtr (pt & pp fancied)* **1** *(imagine)* imaginar, figurarse; *fam* **(just) f. that!,** ¡fíjate!; *fam* **f. Liverpool losing!,** parece mentira que baya perdido el Liverpool; *fam* **f. seeing you here!,** ¡qué casualidad verte por aquí! **2** *(like, want)* apetecer; **do you f. a drink?,** ¿te apetece una copa?; **take whatever you f.,** coja lo que quiera; *fam* **I f. her,** esta chica me gusta. **4** *(think highly of)* **I don't f. her chances,** no creo que tenga muchas posibilidades. **IV** *vr fam* **to f. oneself,** ser creído,-a *or* presumido,-a; **he fancies himself as a singer,** se las da de cantante.

fancy-free [fænsɪ'friː] *adj* sin compromiso; *fam* **footloose and f.-f.,** soltero,-a *m*,*f* y sin compromiso.

fanfare ['fænfeə'] *n Mus* fanfarria *f*, toque *m* de trompetas.

fang [fæŋ] *n Zool* colmillo *m*.

fanny ['fænɪ] *n* **1** *GB vulg* coño *m*. **2** *US sl* pompis *m*, culo *m*.

fantasize ['fæntəsaɪz] *vi* fantasear.

fantasy ['fæntəsɪ] *n* fantasía *f*.

fantastic [fæn'tæstɪk] *adj* fantástico,-a, fabuloso,-a.

far [fɑː'] *(farther or further, farthest or furthest)* **I** *adj* **1** *(distant)* lejano,-a; *fig* **it's a f. cry from student life,** dista mucho de la vida estudiantil. ■ **the F. East,** el Lejano Oriente. **2** *(more remote)* **at the f. side,** en el lado opuesto; **at the f. end,** en el otro extremo. **3** *Pol (extreme)* extrema; **the f. left,** la extrema izquierda. **II** *adv* **1** *(distant)* lejos; **as f. as the eye can see,** hasta donde alcanza la vista; **f. and wide,** por todas partes; **f. off,** a lo lejos; **farther back/forward,** más atrás/adelante; **farther north/south,** más al norte/sur; **how f. is it?,** ¿a qué distancia está?; **how f. is**

it to Cardiff?, ¿cuánto hay de aquí a Cardiff?; **how much farther is it?**, ¿cuánto camino nos queda?; **not f. from here**, no muy lejos de aquí; **very f.**, lejísimos; *fig* **as f. as I can**, en lo que puedo; **as f. as I'm concerned**, por lo que a mí respecta *or* me toca; **as f. as I know**, que yo sepa; **as f. as possible**, en lo posible; *fig* **f. from complaining, he seemed pleased**, lejos de quejarse, parecía contento; *fig* **he went so f. as to swear**, llegó a jurar; *fig* **how f. can we believe him?**, ¿hasta qué punto podemos creerle?; *fig* **I'm f. from satisfied**, no estoy satisfecho,-a ni mucho menos; *fig* **in so f. as ...**, en la medida en que ...; *fig* **ten pounds won't go f.**, diez libras no alcanzarán para mucho; *fam* **she will go f.**, llegará lejos; *fam* **to be f. away**, estar en las nubes; *fam* **to go too f.**, pasarse de la raya, propasarse. **2** *(in time)* **as f. back as I can remember**, hasta donde alcanza mi memoria; **as f. back as the fifties**, ya en los años cincuenta; **f. into the night**, hasta muy entrada la noche; **so f.**, hasta ahora, hasta aquí; **so f. so good**, por ahora bien; **so f. this year**, en lo que va de año. **3** *(much)* mucho; **by f.**, con mucho; **by f. the best**, con mucho el mejor; **f. beyond**, mucho más allá; **f. cleverer**, mucho más listo,-a; **f. too much**, demasiado; **you're not f. wrong**, casi aciertas; *fam* **f. gone**, borracho,-a.

faraway ['fɑːrəweɪ] *adj* lejano,-a, remoto,-a; **a f. look**, una mirada distraída.

farce [fɑːs] *n Theat* farsa *f*; *fig* farsa *f*; **what a f.!**, ¡menudo cuento!

farcical ['fɑːsɪkəl] *adj* absurdo,-a, ridículo,-a.

fare [feə^r] **I** *n* **1** *(ticket price)* tarifa *f*, precio *m* del billete *or* del viaje; *(for boat)* pasaje *m*; **fares please!**, ¡billetes por favor!; **half f.**, medio billete. **2** *(passenger)* viajero,-a *m,f*, pasajero-a *m,f*. **3** *(food)* comida *f*. ■ **bill of f.**, lista *f* de platos, menú *m*. **II** *(progress)* *vi* irle a algn; **how did you f.?**, ¿qué tal te fue?

farewell [feə'wel] **I** *interj arch* ¡adiós! **II** *n* despedida *f*; **to bid sb f.**, despedirse de algn. ■ **f. dinner**, cena *f* de despedida; **f. speech**, discurso *m* de despedida.

far-fetched [fɑː'fetʃt] *adj* rebuscado,-a, inverosímil.

far-flung [fɑː'flʌŋ] *adj* **1** *(distant)* lejano,-a. **2** *(widespread)* vasto,-a.

farm [fɑːm] **I** *n* granja *f*, *Am* hacienda *f*. ■ **f. labourer**, peón *m*, labriego,-a *m,f*; **f. produce**, productos *mpl* agrícolas; **fish f.**, criadero *m*, piscifactoría *f*. **II** *vtr* cultivar, labrar. **III** *vi* cultivar la tierra. ◆ **farm out** *vtr* encargar fuera.

farmer ['fɑːmə^r] *n* agricultor,-a *m,f*, granjero,-a *m,f*, *Am* hacendado,-a *m,f*.

farmhand ['fɑːmhænd] *n* peón *m*, labriego,-a *m,f*.

farmhouse ['fɑːmhaʊs] *n* granja *f*, casa *f* de labranza, *Am* hacienda *f*

farming ['fɑːmɪŋ] **I** *n* **1** *(agriculture)* agricultura *f*. **2** *(the land)* cultivo *m*, labranza *f*. **II** *adj* agrícola.

farmyard ['fɑːmjɑːd] *n* corral *m*.

far-off [fɑː'rɒf] *adj* lejano,-a, remoto,-a.

far-reaching [fɑː'riːtʃɪŋ] *adj* de gran alcance.

farrier ['færɪə^r] *n* herrero *m*.

far-sighted [fɑː'saɪtɪd] *adj* **1** *(person)* con visión de futuro, calculador,-a. **2** *(plan)* planeado,-a, con miras al futuro.

far-sightedness [fɑː'saɪtɪdnɪs] *n* visión *f* de futuro, perspicacia *f*.

fart [fɑːt] *vulg* **I** *n* pedo *m*. **II** *vi* echarse *or* tirarse un pedo.

farther ['fɑːðə^r] *adj & adv comp see* **far**.

farthest ['fɑːðɪst] *adj & adv superl see* **far**.

farthing ['fɑːðɪŋ] *n Hist* cuarto *m* de penique; *fam* **it isn't worth a brass f.**, no vale un real.

fascinate ['fæsɪneɪt] *vtr* fascinar.

fascinating ['fæsɪneɪtɪŋ] *adj* fascinador,-a, fascinante.

fascination [fæsɪ'neɪʃən] *n* fascinación *f*.

fascism ['fæʃɪzəm] *n Pol* fascismo *m*.

fascist ['fæʃɪst] *adj & n Pol* fascista *(mf)*.

fashion ['fæʃən] **I** *n* **1** *(manner)* manera *f*, modo *m*; **in her own f.**, a su manera; *(somehow)* **after a f.**, más o menos; *(in the manner of)* **after the f. of Dickens**, imitando a Dickens. **2** *(latest style)* moda *f*; **it's all the f.**, está muy de moda; **this year waistcoats are the f.**, este año se llevan mucho los chalecos; **to be a slave to f.**, ser un esclavo de la moda; **to be in f.**, estar de moda; **to be out of f.**, no estar de moda; **to come into f.**, ponerse de moda; **to go out of f.**, pasar de moda. ■ **f. designer**, diseñador,-a *m,f* de modas; **f. magazine**, revista *f* de modas; **f. parade**, desfile *m* de modelos. **II** *vtr (metal)* labrar; *(clay)* formar.

fashionable ['fæʃənəbəl] *adj* **1** de moda; **to be f.**, estar de moda. **2** *(area, hotel, resort)* elegante, de buen tono.

fast[1] [fɑːst] **I** *adj* **1** *(quick)* rápido,-a, veloz; **the f. train**, el tren rápido; *Aut* **the f. lane**, el carril de alta velocidad; *fig* **to live in the f. lane**, vivir deprisa; **at a f. and furious pace**, a una velocidad vertiginosa; *fam* **to be a f. worker**, ser un ligón; *fam* **to pull a f. one on sb**, jugarle una mala pasada a algn. ■ **f. woman**, (mujer *f*) ligera *f* de cascos. **2** *(tight, inflexible)* firme; seguro,-a; **hard and f. rules**, reglas estrictas. **3** *(colour)* sólido,-a. **4** *(clock)* adelantado,-a. **II** *adv* **1** rápidamente, deprisa; **how f.?**, ¿a qué velocidad? **to drive f.**, correr; *fam* **not so f.!**, ¡un momento! **2** *(securely)* firmemente; **f. asleep**, profundamente dormido,-a; **stuck f.**, bien pegado,-a; *fig (with determination)* **to stand f.**, mantenerse firme.

fast[2] [fɑːst] **I** *n* ayuno *m*. **II** *vi* ayunar.

fasten ['fɑːsən] **I** *vtr* **1** *(attach)* sujetar; *(fix)* fijar; **to f. one's eyes on**, fijar los ojos en. **2** *(do up, secure)* *(belt)* abrochar; *(bag, suitcase)* asegurar; *(shoe laces)* atar; *(window)* echar el pestillo; *(papers)* **to f. (together)**, sujetar. **II** *vi (door)* cerrarse; *(dress)* abrocharse; *fig* **to f. on to**, apropiarse de.

fastener ['fɑːsənə^r] *n* **1** *(window)* cierre *m*. **2** *(necklace, dress)* cierre *m*, broche *m*. ■ **zip f.**, cremallera *f*.

fastidious [fæ'stɪdɪəs] *adj* quisquilloso,-a, melindroso,-a.

fastidiousness [fæs'tɪdɪəsnɪs] *n* mellindres *mpl*, remilgos *mpl*.

fat [fæt] **I** *adj (fatter, fattest)* **1** gordo,-a; **to get f.**, engordar. **2** *(thick)* grueso,-a. **3** *(meat)* que tiene mucha grasa. **4** *fig (profit)* hermoso,-a, jugoso,-a; *fam fig* **that was a f. lot of good!**, ¡pues sí que ha valido de mucho!; **that was a f. lot of help!**, ¡valiente ayuda! **II** *n* grasa *f*, *fam* **the f.'s in the fire**, se va a armar la de Dios; *fig* **to live off the f. of the land**, vivir a cuerpo de rey. ■ **cooking f.**, manteca *f* de cerdo; *US sl* **f. cat**, pez *m* gordo.

fatty ['fætɪ] **I** *adj* **1** *(food)* graso,-a. **2** *Anat (tissue)* adiposo,-a. **II** *n fam (person)* gordinflón,-ona *m,f*.

fatal ['feɪtəl] *adj* **1** *(accident, illness, blow)* mortal. **2** *(ill-fated)* fatal, funesto,-a. **3** *(fateful)* fatídico,-a. ◆ **fatally** *adv* mortalmente; **f. wounded**, mortalmente herido.

fatalist ['feɪtəlɪst] *n* fatalista *mf*.

fatalistic [feɪtə'lɪstɪk] *adj* fatalista.

fatality [fə'tælɪtɪ] *n* víctima *f* mortal; **there were no fatalities**, no hubo muertos.

fate [feɪt] *n* **1** *(destiny)* destino *m*, suerte *f*; **his f. is decided**, su suerte está decidida; **let us see what f. has in store**, veamos lo que nos depara la suerte; **to meet one's f.**, encontrarse uno con su destino; **to tempt f.**, tentar a la suerte. **2** *Myth* **the Fates**, las Parcas.

fated ['feɪtɪd] *adj* **1** condenado,-a. **2** *(cursed)* maldito,-a.

fat-free ['fætfriː] *adj* **a f.-f. diet**, un régimen sin grasas.

fateful ['feɪtfʊl] *adj* fatídico,-a, aciago,-a; **on this f. day in 1936**, este día aciago en 1936.

father ['fɑːðə^r] **I** *n* **1** padre *m*; **my f. and mother**, mis padres; **to be a f. to sb**, ser un padre para algn; *prov* **like f. like son**, de tal palo, tal astilla. ■ **F. Christmas**, Papá *m* Noel. **2** *Rel* padre *m*; **F. McSweeney**, el padre McSweeney; **Our F.**, Padre Nuestro; **the Holy F.**, el Santo Padre. **II** *vtr* engendrar.

fatherhood ['fɑːðəhʊd] *n* paternidad *f*.

father-in-law ['fɑːðərinlɔː] *n* (*pl* **fathers-in-law**) suegro *m*.

fatherland ['fɑːðəlænd] *n* patria *f*.

fatherly ['fɑːðəli] *adj* paternal.

fathom ['fæðəm] **I** *n Naut* (*measure*) braza *f*. **II** *vtr* comprender, penetrar en. ◆ **fathom out** *vtr* averiguar, comprobar; **I can't f. it out,** no me lo explico; **to f. out a mystery,** desentrañar un misterio.

fatigue [fə'tiːg] **I** *n* 1 (*tiredness*) fatiga *f*, cansancio *m*. ■ *Tech* **metal f.,** fatiga *f* del metal. 2 *Mil* faena *f*. ■ **f. dress,** traje *m* de faena. **II** *vtr* fatigar, cansar a.

fatso ['fætsəʊ] *n* (*pl* **fatsos** or **fatsoes**) *fam offens* gordo,-a *m,f*.

fatted ['fætɪd] *adj fig* cebado,-a; **to kill the f. calf,** echar la casa por la ventana.

fatten ['fætən] *vtr* (*animal*) cebar; (*person*) engordar.

fattening ['fætənɪŋ] *adj* que hace engordar; **milk is f.,** la leche engorda.

fatuous ['fætjʊəs] *adj* fatuo,-a, necio,-a.

faucet ['fɔːsɪt] *n US* grifo *m*.

fault [fɔːlt] **I** *n* 1 (*defect*) defecto *m*; **generous to a f.,** generoso,-a en exceso; **he has many faults,** tiene muchos defectos. 2 (*in merchandise*) defecto *m*, desperfecto *m*; **to find f. with,** poner reparos a; **to pick f. with sb,** criticar a algn. 3 (*culpability*) culpa *f*; **it's their f.,** es culpa suya; **to be at f.,** tener la culpa; **whose f. is it?,** ¿quién tiene la culpa? 4 (*mistake*) error *m*, falta *f*. 5 *Geol* falla *f*. 6 *Tennis* falta *f*. **II** *vtr* criticar; **her attitude cannot be faulted,** su conducta es intachable.

fault-finding ['fɔːltfaɪndɪŋ] *adj* criticón,-ona.

faultless ['fɔːltlɪs] *adj* intachable, impecable, perfecto,-a. ◆ **faultlessly** *adv* perfectamente.

faulty ['fɔːlti] *adj* defectuoso,-a

fauna ['fɔːnə] *n* (*pl* **faunas** or **faunae** ['fɔːniː]) *Zool* fauna *f*

faux pas [fəʊ'pɑː] *n inv fml* (*mistake*) paso *m* en falso; (*blunder*) metedura *f* de pata

favour, *US* **favor** ['feɪvəʳ] **I** *n* 1 (*approval*) favor *m*, **to be in f. of doing sth,** estar a favor de hacer algo, **to be in f. with sb,** gozar del favor de algn; **to fall out of f. with sb,** perder el favor de algn, to vote in f. of sth, votar a favor de algo 2 (*service*) favor *m*; **to ask sb a f.,** pedirle un favor a algn; *fam* **do me a f.!,** ¡venga ya!; **do me a f. and shut up,** hazme el favor de callarte 3 (*advantage*) favor, **an error in my f.,** un error a mi favor; **1-0 in our f.,** 1-0 a favor nuestro **II** *vtr* 1 (*bias*) favorecer a algn, *prov* **fortune favours the brave,** la fortuna sonríe a los audaces. 2 (*approve*) estar a favor de

favourable, *US* **favorable** ['feɪvərəbəl] *adj* favorable, propicio,-a ◆ **favourably,** *US* **favorably** *adv* favorablemente, **f. disposed towards sb,** bien dispuesto hacia algn

favoured, *US* **favored** ['feɪvəd] *adj* 1 favorecido,-a; **the f. few,** la minoría selecta 2 (*endowed*) dotado,-a (**with,** de)

favourite, *US* **favorite** ['feɪvərɪt] **1** *adj* favorito,-a, preferido,-a, predilecto,-a. **II** *n Sport* favorito,-a *m,f*

favouritism, *US* **favoritism** ['feɪvərɪtɪzəm] *n* favoritismo *m*

fawn¹ [fɔːn] **I** *adj* (de) color café claro **II** *n* 1 *Zool* cervato *m* 2 color *m* café claro.

fawn² [fɔːn] *vi* 1 (*dog*) hacer fiestas (**on,** a) 2 (*person*) adular (**on,** a), lisonjear (**on,** a)

fawning ['fɔːnɪŋ] *adj* adulador,-a, lisonjero,-a, servil

fax [fæks] **I** *n* 1 (*message*) facsímil *m*, telefax *m*, fax *m* 2 (*machine*) facsímil *m*, fax *m* **II** *vtr* mandar *or* enviar por fax

FC [ef'siː] *GB Sport abbr of* **Football Club,** Club *m* de Fútbol, CF.

fealty ['fiːəltɪ] *n* fidelidad *f*; **to swear f.,** jurar fidelidad.

fear [fɪəʳ] **I** *n* miedo *m*, temor *m*, **for f. of losing,** por temor a perder; **have no f.!,** ¡no temas!; **1 ran for f. that it might rain,** corrí por miedo de que lloviera, **there's no f. of that happening,** no hay peligro de que ocurra eso; **to go in f. of one's life,** temer por su vida, *fam* **no f.!,** ¡ni pensarlo! *fam fig* **to put the f. of God into sb,** darle un susto mortal a algn **II** *vtr* temer, tener miedo, **he's to be feared,** es de temer, **1 f. it's too late,** me temo que ya es tarde; **to f. the worst,** temer lo peor **III** *vi* temer (**for,** por)

fearful ['fɪəfʊl] *adj* 1 (*person*) temeroso,-a 2 (*frightening*) horrible, espantoso,-a

fearless ['fɪəlɪs] *adj* intrépido,-a, impávido,-a. ◆ **fearlessly** *adv* con intrepidez

fearlessness ['fɪəlɪsnɪs] *n* intrepidez *f*, impavidez *f*

fearsome ['fɪəsəm] *adj* terrible, espantoso,-a

feasible ['fiːzəbəl] *adj* 1 (*practicable*) factible; (*possible*) viable 2 (*plausible*) verosímil

feasibility [fiːzə'bɪlɪtɪ] *n* viabilidad *f* ■ **f. study,** estudio *m* de viabilidad

feast [fiːst] **I** *n* 1 banquete *m*, festín *m*, *fam* comilona *f*, guateque *m* 2 *Rel* **f. day,** día *m* de fiesta ■ **movable f.,** fiesta *f* movible **II** *vtr* festejar, *fig* **to f. one's eyes on sth,** regalarse la vista con algo **III** *vi* banquetear, *fig* **to f. on sth,** regalarse con algo.

feat [fiːt] *n* proeza *f*, hazaña *f*, **f. of endurance,** prueba *f* de resistencia

feather ['feðə] **I** *n* pluma *f*, *fig* **that's a f. in his cap,** es un triunfo para él; *fig* **they're birds of a f.,** son de la misma calaña, *fam* **you could have knocked me down with a f.,** me quedé patidifuso,-a; *prov* **birds of a f. flock together,** Dios los cría y ellos se juntan ■ **f. bed,** colchón *m* de plumas; **f. duster,** plumero *m* **II** *vtr fam* **to f. one's nest,** hacer su agosto.

feather-brained ['feðəbreɪnd] *adj* despistado,-a, insensato,-a.

featherweight ['feðəweɪt] *n Box* peso *m* pluma

feature ['fiːtʃəʳ] **I** *n* 1 (*face*) rasgo *m*, facción *f*, **he has typically Basque features,** sus facciones son típicamente vascas 2 (*characteristic*) rasgo *m*, característica *f* 3 *Cin* **f. film,** largometraje *m*. 4 *Press* crónica *f* especial ■ **f. writer,** cronista *mf* **II** *vtr* 1 (*give prominence to*) poner de relieve. 2 *Cin* tener como protagonista, **the film features Cantinflas,** es una película de Cantinflas **III** *vi* 1 (*appear*) constar, figurar, **his name features in the list,** su nombre figura en la lista 2 (*in film*) figurar.

featureless ['fiːtʃəlɪs] *adj* monótono,-a

Feb [feb] *abbr of* **February,** febrero *m*, feb

February ['febrʊərɪ] *n* febrero *m*, **in F.,** en febrero; *see also* **May.**

feckless ['feklɪs] *adj* débil, incapaz.

Fed [fed] *n US sl* agente *mf* de FBI.

fed [fed] **I** *pt & pp see* **feed. II f. up** *adj fam* harto,-a (**with,** de)

federal ['fedərəl] *adj* federal

federation [fedə'reɪʃən] *n* federación *f*.

fee [fiː] *n* (*lawyer, doctor*) honorarios *mpl*, **what are your fees?,** ¿cuánto cobra por visita? ■ **entrance f.,** entrada *f*, **membership f.,** cuota *f* de socio; **retaining f.,** anticipo *m*; *Ftb* **transfer f.,** prima *f* de traslado, *Univ* **tuition fees,** derechos *mpl* de matrícula.

feeble ['fiːbəl] *adj* (*person*) débil; (*excuse, argument*) de poco peso, (*voice, light*) ténue, débil

feeble-minded [fiːbəl'maɪndɪd] *adj* imbécil, mentecato,-a

feebleness ['fiːbəlnɪs] *n* debilidad *f*

feed [fiːd] **I** *vtr* (*pt & pp* **fed**) 1 (*give food to*) dar de comer a, alimentar, *fig* (*fire, passions*) alimentar, cebar, **to f. a baby,** (*breast-feed*) amamantar a un bebé, (*with bottle*) dar el biberón a un bebé 2 *Comput Elec* alimentar, suministrar **3** *(insert)* introducir, **to f. a parking meter,** meter monedas en un parquímetro, **to f. data into a computer,** introducir datos en un ordenador **II** *vi* comer **(on, -),** alimentarse **(on, -);** *(cows, sheep)* pacer **III** *n* **1** *(food, meal)* comida *f; fam* comilona *f.* ■ *Agr* **cattle f.,** pienso *m* **2** *Tech* alimentación *f.* ■ **f. pipe,** tubo *m* de alimentación ◆ **feed up** *vtr (animal)* cebar, *(make fat)* engordar

feedback ['fiːdbæk] *n* **1** *Comput Elec* realimentación *f* **2** *fig* reacción *f,* impresion *f*

feeder ['fiːdə'] *n Tech* alimentador *m*

feeding ['fiːdɪŋ] *n* alimentación *f* ■ **f. bottle,** biberón *m*

feel [fiːl] **I** *vi (pt & pp felt)* **1** *(emotion, sensation)* sentir, experimentar, **f. free to return,** vuelva cuando quiera, **how does it f. to be rich?,** ¿qué se siente al ser rico,-a?, **how do you f.?,** ¿qué tal te encuentras?, **I f. bad about it,** me da pena, **I f. like a new man,** me siento como nuevo, **I f.** (sorry) **for him,** le compadezco; **I'm not feeling myself,** no me encuentro del todo bien; **they felt the wind on their faces,** sentían el viento en sus caras, **to f. happy,** sentirse feliz, **to f. cold/sleepy,** tener frío/sueño, *fam* **to f. up to sth,** sentirse con ánimos *or* con fuerzas para hacer algo **2** *(seem)* parecer, **it felt good to do nothing,** daba gusto no hacer nada, **your hand feels cold,** tienes la mano fría, **it feels like leather,** parece piel **it feels like rain,** parece que va a llover, **it feels like summer,** parece verano **3** *(perceive, sense)* sentir **he feels uncomfortable,** se siente incómodo, **the atmosphere felt tense,** el ambiente era tenso **4** *(opinion)* opinar, pensar, **how do you f. about this?,** ¿qué opinas de esto?, **I f. sure that ...,** estoy seguro,-a de que ..., **they f. strongly about apartheid,** tienen opiniones muy concretas sobre el apartheid **5** *(fancy)* apetecer **I f. like an ice cream,** me apetece un helado, **to f. like doing sth,** tener ganas de hacer algo. **II** *vtr* **1** *(touch)* tocar, palpar, **f. my hand,** toca mi mano, **to f. one's way,** andar a tientas, *fig* tantear el terreno **2** *(believe, sense)* sentir, tener la impresion, **she felt a failure,** se siente hundida, **we f. it is our duty,** creemos que es nuestro deber **3** *(notice)* notar, apreciar, **we won't f. the effects of this until next year,** no notaremos los efectos hasta el año que viene. **III** *n* **1** *(touch, sensation)* tacto *m,* **I recognize it by the f.,** lo reconozco al tacto, *fig* **to get the f. for sth,** acostumbrarse a algo, cogerle el truco a algo **2** *(atmosphere)* ambiente *m,* **this place has a certain f. about it,** este lugar tiene una atmósfera especial ◆ **feel for** *vtr* **1** *(search for)* buscar, **he felt around in the dark for the light switch,** buscó el interruptor de la luz a tientas en la oscuridad, **she felt for her keys in her bag,** buscó sus llaves en la bolsa **2** *(have sympathy for)* sentirlo mucho, **I f. for you,** lo siento mucho por ti

feeler ['fiːlə'] *n Ent* antena *f fig* **to put one's feelers out,** tantear el terreno

feeling ['fiːlɪŋ] **I** *n* **1** *(emotion)* sentimiento *m,* emoción *f,* **a f. of guilt,** sentimiento de culpabilidad, **ill f.,** resentimiento *m,* rencor *m* **2** *(concern, compassion)* compasión *f,* ternura *f,* **to have no f.,** ser duro,-a *or* insensible **3** *(impression)* impresión *f,* **I had the f. that ...,** tuve la impresión de que ... . **4** *(consciousness, sensitivity)* sensibilidad *f,* **artistic f.,** sensibilidad artística **he has a f. for music,** tiene sensibilidad para la música, **he has no f. in his fingers,** no tiene sensibilidad en los dedos, **the pianist played with a lot of f.,** el pianist tocó con mucho sentimiento **5** *(opinion)* sentir *m,* opinión *f,* **the general f. is that ...,** la opinión general es que ..., **to express one's feelings,** expresar sus opiniones **6 feelings,** sentimientos *mpl fig* **f. ran high,** la gente estaba exaltada, *fam* **no hard f.,** no nos guardemos rencor **7 feelings,** *(thoughts)* sentimientos *mpl* pensamientos *mpl,* **to have mixed f.,** tener sentimientos enfrentados **to hide one's f,** ocultar sus sentimientos **II** *adj* sensible, compasivo,-a, **a f. person,** una persona compasiva

fee-paying ['fiːpeɪɪŋ] *adj (school)* de pago

feet [fiːt] *npl see* **foot.**

feign [feɪn] *vtr* fingir, aparentar, **to f. illness,** fingirse enfermo,-a

feint [feɪnt] *Sport* **1** *n* finta *f* **II** *vi* fintar

feline ['fiːlaɪn] *Zool adj & n* felino,-a *(m,f)*

fell[1] [fel] *pt see* **fall.**

fell[2] [fel] *adj (fierce)* feroz, **at one f. swoop,** de un solo golpe

fell[3] [fel] *n GB Geog (hill)* monte *m, (moor)* páramo *m*

fell[4] [fel] *vtr (cut down) (trees)* talar, *fig (enemy)* matar, derribar

fell[5] [fel] *n (animal)* piel *f*

felling ['felɪŋ] *n* tala *f*

fellow ['feləʊ] *n* **1** *(companion)* compañero,-a *m, f,* camarada *mf,* **come in, my dear f.!,** ¡adelante, hombre!, *fig* **to be hail f. well met with sb,** tratar a la gente con falsa simpatía ■ **f. citizen,** conciudadano,-a *m, f,* **f. countryman, f. countrywoman,** compatriota *mf,* **f. men,** prójimos *mpl,* **f. passenger/student/worker,** compañero,-a *m, f,* de viaje/estudios trabajo **2** *fam (chap, guy)* tipo *m,* tío *m,* **a strange f.,** un tío raro, **poor f.!,** ¡pobrecito! **3** *(of society)* socio,-a *m, f* **4** *Univ* miembro *mf* del claustro de profesores

fellowship ['feləʊʃɪp] *n* **1** *(comradeship)* compañerismo *m* camaradería *f* **2** *(organization)* asociación *f,* sociedad *f* **3** *Univ (scholarship)* beca *f*

felon ['felən] *n Jur* criminal *mf*

felony ['felənɪ] *n* crimen *m,* delito *m* mayor

felt[1] [felt] *pt & pp see* **feel.**

felt[2] [felt] *n Tex* fieltro *m,* **f. hat,** sombrero *m* de fieltro

felt-tip(ped) ['felttɪp(t)] *adj* **f.-t. pen,** rotulador *m*

fem *Ling abbr of* **feminine,** femenino, f

female ['fiːmeɪl] **I** *adj* **1** *Zool* hembra, **a f. giraffe,** una jirafa hembra, **a f. hedgehog,** un erizo hembra **2** *femenino,-a de mujer,* **the f. sex,** el sexo femenino **a f. voice,** una voz de mujer **II** *n* **1** *Zool* hembra *f* **2** *(woman)* mujer *f, (girl)* chica *f* ■ **f. suffrage,** sufragio *m* femenino

feminine ['femɪnɪn] **I** *adj* femenino,-a **II** *n Ling* femenino *m*

femininity [femɪ'nɪnɪtɪ] *n* feminidad *f*

feminism ['femɪnɪzəm] *n* feminismo *m*

feminist ['femɪnɪst] *adj & n* feminista *(mf)*

femur ['fiːmə'] *n (pl* **femurs** *or* **femora** ['femərə]*) Anat* fémur *m*

fen [fen] *n Geog* pantano *m*

fence [fens] **I** *n* **1** cerca *f,* valla *f, Equit* valla *f, fig* **to sit on the f.,** ver los toros desde la barrera **2** *sl* perista *mf* **II** *vi Sport* practicar la esgrima. ◆ **fence in** *vtr* meter en un cercado ◆ **fence off** *vtr* separar mediante cercas

fencer ['fensə'] *n* jugador,-a *m, f* de esgrima

fencing ['fensɪŋ] *n* **1** *(surround)* cercado *m,* vallado *m* **2** *(material)* material *m* para cercas **3** *Sport* esgrima *f* ■ **f. foil,** florete *m*

fend [fend] *vi* **to f. for oneself,** valerse por sí mismo. ◆ **fend off** *vtr (blow)* parar, desviar, *(question)* esquivar, *(attack)* rechazar

fender ['fendə'] *n* **I** *(fireplace)* pantalla *f* **2** *US Aut* parachoques *m inv* **3** *Naut* defensa *f*

fennel ['fenəl] *n Bot* hinojo *m*

ferment ['fɜːment] **I** *n* fermento *m fig* **in a state of f.,** agitado,-a. **II** ['fɜːment] *vtr & vi* fermentar

fermentation [fɜːmen'teɪʃən] *n* fermentación *f*

fern [fɜːn] *n Bot* helecho *m*

ferocious [fə'rəʊʃəs] *adj* feroz

ferocity [fə'rɒsɪtɪ] *n* ferocidad *f*

ferret ['ferɪt] **I** *n Zool* hurón *m.* **II** *vt fam* huronear, husmear. ◆ **ferret out** *vtr fam* conseguir, descubrir

ferrous ['ferəs] *adj* de hierro, ferroso,-a, **f. metals,** metales ferrosos

ferry ['ferɪ] **I** n **1** (small) barca f de pasaje. **2** (large, for cars) transbordador m, ferry m. **II** vtr transportar

ferryman ['ferɪmən] n (pl **ferrymen**) barquero m

fertile ['fɜːtaɪl] adj fértil, fecundo,-a; fig fértil, fecundo,-a; **a f. imagination**, una imaginación fecunda.

fertility [fə'tɪlɪtɪ] n (of soil) fertilidad f, fecundidad f; (of living thing) fertilidad. ■ **f. drug**, medicamento m contra la esterilidad.

fertilization [fɜːtɪlaɪ'zeɪʃən] n **1** (soil) fertilización f. **2** Biol fecundación f.

fertilize ['fɜːtɪlaɪz] vtr **1** (soil) fertilizar, abonar. **2** (egg) fecundar.

fertilizer ['fɜːtɪlaɪzə'] n Agr abono m, fertilizante m.

fervent ['fɜːvənt] adj ferviente, fervoroso,-a.

fervid ['fɜːvɪd] adj exaltado,-a, apasionado,-a.

fervour, US **fervor** ['fɜːvə'] n fervor m.

fester ['festə'] vi Med supurar, enconarse.

festival ['festɪvəl] n (event) festival m; (celebration) fiesta f. ■ **film f.**, festival m de cine; Rel **harvest f.**, fiesta f (de acción de gracias) de la cosecha.

festive ['festɪv] adj festivo,-a; **the f. season**, las fiestas de Navidad.

festivity [fes'tɪvɪtɪ] n **1** ficesta f. **2 the festivities**, las fiestas, los festejos.

festoon [fe'stuːn] **I** n guirnalda f, festón m. **II** vtr adornar.

fetal ['fiːtəl] adj US see **foetal**.

fetch [fetʃ] **I** vtr **1** (go and get) buscar, ir a buscar, ir por. **2** (bring) traer; **why did you f. me?**, ¿para qué me has hecho venir?; (to dog) **f.!**, ¡busca!; **to f. and carry for sb**, ser el machaca de algn. **3** (sell for) alcanzar; **how much did it f.?**, ¿por cuánto se vendió?

fetching ['fetʃɪŋ] adj atractivo,-a.

fete [feɪt] **I** n fiesta f. **II** vtr festejar.

fetid ['fetɪd, 'fiːtɪd] adj fétido,-a, hediondo,-a.

fetish ['fetɪʃ, 'fiːtɪʃ] n fetiche m; fig veneración f, culto m.

fetishism ['fetɪʃɪzəm, 'fiːtɪʃɪzəm] n fetichismo m.

fetishist ['fetɪʃɪst, 'fiːtɪʃɪst] n fetichista mf.

fetlock ['fetlɒk] n Zool espolón m.

fetter ['fetə'] **I** n (usu pl) grillos mpl, cadenas fpl; **to be in fetters**, estar encadenado,-a. **II** vtr encadenar.

fettle ['fetəl] n fam condición f, forma f; **in fine f.**, (health) en plena forma; (spirit) de buen humor.

fetus ['fiːtəs] n US see **foetus**.

feud [fjuːd] **I** n enemistad f duradera; **family f.**, disensión f familiar. **II** vi disentir, pelear.

feudal ['fjuːdəl] adj feudal.

feudalism ['fjuːdəlɪzəm] n feudalismo m.

fever ['fiːvə'] n Med fiebre f; fig fiebre; **to have a f.**, tener fiebre; **gambling f.**, la fiebre del juego.

feverish ['fiːvərɪʃ] adj Med febril, calenturiento,-a; fig febril; **to be f.**, tener fiebre; **f. excitement**, emoción febril.

feverishness ['fiːvərɪʃnɪs] n estado m febril.

few [fjuː] **I** adj **1** (small number) **for the past f. years**, durante estos últimos años; **in the next f. days**, dentro de unos días. **2** (not many) pocos,-as; **he has f. friends**, tiene pocos amigos; **he is one of the f. people who know**, es uno de los pocos que saben. **3** (some) algunos,-as, unos,-as cuantos,-as; **a f. books**, unos or algunos libros; **she has fewer books than I thought**, tiene menos libros de lo que pensaba; **quite a f.**, un buen número. **4** (rare) muy pocos,-as; **f. and far between**, escaso,-a, raro,-a. **5 as f. as**, solamente. **II** pron **1** (not many) pocos,-as; **f. finish**, son raros los que terminan; **few of them**, pocos de entre ellos; **there are too f.**, no hay suficientes; **there are precious f. of them left**, quedan muy pocos; **the fewer the better**, cuantos menos mejor. **2** (some) **a f.**, algunos,-as, unos,-as cuantos,-as; **a f. of them**, algunos de ellos; **I've**

only **a f. left**, sólo me quedan unos cuantos; **the chosen f.**, los seleccionados, la crema; **there were no fewer than ten**, había no menos de diez; **who has the fewest?**, ¿quién tiene menos?; fam **to have a f. too many**, haber bebido unas copas de más.

fiancé [fɪ'ænseɪ] n novio m, prometido m.

fiancée [fɪ'ænseɪ] n novia f, prometida f.

fiasco [fɪ'æskəʊ] n (pl **fiascos**) fiasco m, fracaso m.

fib [fɪb] fam **I** n bola f, trola f. **II** vi (pt & pp **fibbed**) contar bolas, decir trolas.

fibber ['fɪbə'] n fam mentiroso,-a m,f, trolero,-a m,f.

fibre, US **fiber** ['faɪbə'] n fibra f. ■ **man-made f.**, fibra f artificial; fig **moral f.**, nervio m, carácter m.

fibreglass, US **fiberglass** ['faɪbəglɑːs] n fibra f de vidrio.

fibrositis [faɪbrə'saɪtɪs] n Med fibromatosis f.

fibrous ['faɪbrəs] adj fibroso,-a.

fickle ['fɪkəl] adj inconstante, voluble.

fickleness ['fɪkəlnɪs] n inconstancia f, volubilidad f.

fiction ['fɪkʃən] n **1** Lit novela f, narrativa f; **works of f.**, novelas fpl. **2** (invention) ficción f.

fictional ['fɪkʃənəl] adj **1** Lit novelesco,-a. **2** (imaginative) ficticio,-a.

fictitious [fɪk'tɪʃəs] adj ficticio,-a, fingido,-a.

fiddle ['fɪdəl] fam **I** n **1** violín m; fig **to play** or **be second f.**, ser de segunda categoría; prov **as fit as a f.**, más sano,-a que una manzana, fuerte como un roble. **2** (shady deal) estafa f, trampa f; **he's on the f.**, está haciendo trampas. ■ **tax f.**, evasión f fiscal. **II** vtr **1** estafar. **2** (accounts) falsificar. **III** vi tocar el violín. ◆ **fiddle about, fiddle around** vi **1** perder tiempo. **2** juguetear (**with**, con).

fiddler ['fɪdlə'] n fam **1** violinista mf. **2** tramposo,-a m,f, (money) chanchullero,-a m,f.

fiddly ['fɪdlɪ] adj fam delicado,-a, poco manejable.

fidelity [fɪ'delətɪ] n fidelidad f. ■ **high f.**, alta fidelidad f.

fidget ['fɪdʒɪt] **I** vi moverse, no poder estarse quieto,-a; **stop fidgeting!**, ¡estáte quieto! **II** vtr jugar (**with**, con). **III** n argadillo,-a m,f.

fidgety ['fɪdʒɪtɪ] adj inquieto,-a.

field [fiːld] **I** n **1** (meadow) campo m, prado m. **2** Mil campo m; **in the f.**, en campaña; fig **to have a f. day**, disfrutar de lo lindo. ■ **f. day**, día m de maniobras; **f. glasses**, gemelos mpl (de campaña); **f. marshal**, mariscal m de campo; **f. of battle**, campo m de batalla. **3** Sport campo m; **to take the f.**, salir al campo. ■ **playing f.**, campo m de deportes. **4** Geol Min yacimiento m, yacimientos mpl. ■ **oil f.**, yacimiento m petrolífero. **5** Elec Phys campo m. ■ Opt **f. of vision**, campo m visual. **6** (subject, area) campo m, terreno m; **it's outside my f.**, no es de mi competencia; **the f. of medicine**, el campo de la medicina; **what's your f.?**, ¿cuál es su especialidad? ■ **f. trip**, viaje m de estudios; **f. work**, trabajo m de campo. **II** vtr Sport **1** (ball) parar y devolver. **2** (present) presentar; **to f. a strong team**, presentar un equipo fuerte. **III** vi Sport **1** parar y devolver la pelota. **2** jugar en campo.

fielder ['fiːldə'] n Sport jugador,-a m,f, que no batea, fildeador,-a m,f.

fieldfare ['fiːldfeə'] n Orn zorzal m real.

fieldmouse ['fiːldmaʊs] n (pl **fieldmice** ['fiːldmaɪs]) Zool ratón m del campo.

fiend [fiːnd] n **1** (devil) demonio m, diablo m. **2** fam (fanatic) fanático,-a m,f; **she's a fresh air f.**, es una fanática del aire fresco.

fiendish ['fiːndɪʃ] adj fam (cruel) diabólico,-a, malvado,-a, fig (difficult) enrevesado,-a.

fierce [fɪəs] adj **1** (of animal, look) feroz. **2** (of argument) acalorado,-a. **3** (of heat, competition) intenso,-a, fuerte. **4** (of wind) fuerte, violento,-a.

fierceness ['fɪəsnɪs] n **1** (animal, look) ferocidad f. **2** (heat, competition) intensidad f. **3** (wind) fuerza f.

fiery ['faɪərɪ] *adj (temper)* fogoso,-a; *(speech)* acalorado,-a; *(colour)* encendido,-a.

fife [faɪf] *n Mus* pífano *m*.

fifteen [fɪf'tiːn] **I** *adj* quince *inv*; **f. books,** quince libros; **she is f.,** tiene quince años. **II** *n* 1 quince *m inv*. 2 Rugby equipo *m*; *see also* **seven.**

fifteenth [fɪf'tiːnθ] **I** *adj* decimoquinto,-a; **the f. of August,** el quince de agosto. **II** *n* 1 *(in series)* decimoquinto,-a *m*,*f*. 2 *(fraction)* quinzavo *m*; *see also* **seventh.**

fifth [fɪfθ] **I** *adj* quinto,-a; *pol* **f. column,** quinta columna; **the f. of May,** el cinco de mayo. **II** *n* 1 *(in series)* quintó,-a *m*,*f*. 2 *(fraction)* quinto *m*; *see also* **seventh.**

fifth-former ['fɪfθfɔːməʳ] *n GB Sch* alumno,-a *m*, *f* del quinto curso.

fiftieth ['fɪftɪɪθ] **I** *adj* quincuagésimo,-a *m*, *f*. **II** *n* 1 *(in series)* quincuagésimo,-a *m*, *f*. **II** *n* 1 *(fraction)* cincuentavo *m*; *see also* **seventh.**

fifty ['fɪftɪ] **I** *adj* cincuenta *inv*; **the Fifties,** los años cincuenta; **she's in her fifties,** tiene unos cincuenta años; *fam* **a f.-f. chance,** una probabilidad del cincuenta por ciento; *fam* **to go f.-f.,** ir a medias. **II** *n* cincuenta *m inv*; *see also* **seventy** *and* **seven.**

fig¹ [fɪg] *n Bot* 1 *(fruit)* higo *m*; *fam* **I don't give** *or* **care a f.,** me importa un pimiento *or* comino. 2 *(tree)* higuera *f*.

fig² [fɪg] *abbr of* **figure,** figura *f*, fig.

fight [faɪt] **I** *vtr (pt & pp fought)* 1 *(physical violence)* pelear(se) (**with,** con), luchar (**with,** con); *Box* pelear (**against,** contra); *Taur* lidiar; *fig (corruption, decision)* combatir, luchar (**against,** contra); **to f. one's way through (the crowds),** luchar por abrirse camino (entre la multitud); *fig* **to f. a losing battle,** luchar por una causa perdida. 2 *Mil (battle)* librar; *(war)* hacer. 3 *(contest)* recurrir contra, presentar un recurso contra; **to f. a case,** defenderse contra un cargo *or* un pleito. **II** *vi* 1 pelear(se), luchar; *Box* pelear, combatir. 2 *(quarrel)* pelearse, reñir; **to f. over sth,** disputarse la posesión de algo. 3 *fig (struggle)* luchar (**for/against,** por/contra); **to f. on,** seguir luchando; **to f. for one's life,** luchar por la vida; **to f. shy of,** evitar. **III** *n* 1 *(physical violence)* pelea *f*, lucha *f*; *Box* combate *m*; **a f. to the death,** una lucha a muerte; **to pick a f. with sb,** meterse con algn; **to start a f.,** armar una pelea. 2 *(quarrel)* pelea *f*, riña *f*. 3 *fig (struggle)* lucha *f*; **the f. against poverty,** la lucha contra la pobreza. 4 *(spirit)* combatividad *f*; **there's no f. left in him,** no le queda ánimo para luchar. ◆ **fight back I** *vtr (tears)* contener. **II** *vi* 1 *(recover a position)* resistir. 2 *(in argument)* defenderse. ◆ **fight off** *vtr* 1 *(attack)* rechazar. 2 *fig (illness)* cortar. ◆ **fight out** *vtr* discutir; **a meeting with management to f. out the overtime issue,** una reunión con la dirección para llegar a una decisión sobre las horas extras.

fighter ['faɪtəʳ] *n* 1 *(person)* combatiente *mf*. *Box* púgil *m*. 2 *fig* luchador,-a *m*, *f*. ■ *Av* **f. (plane),** (avión *m* de) caza *m*; **f. bomber,** cazabombardero *m*; **f. pilot,** piloto *m* de caza.

fighting ['faɪtɪŋ] **I** *adj* **he's got a f. chance,** tiene verdaderas posibilidades; **to be f. fit,** estar en plena forma. **II** *n* lucha *f*, pelea *f*.

fig-leaf ['fɪgliːf] *n (pl fig-leaves* ['fɪgliːvz]*)* hoja *f* de parra.

figment ['fɪgmənt] *n* **it's a f. of your imagination,** es un producto de tu imaginación.

figurative ['fɪgərətɪv] *adj* figurado,-a. ◆ **figuratively** *adv* **f. speaking,** en sentido figurado.

figure ['fɪgəʳ, *US* 'fɪgjəʳ] **I** *n* 1 *(form, outline)* forma *f*, silueta *f*; **a human f.,** una figura humana. ■ **f. skating,** patinaje *m* artístico. 2 *(body shape)* figura *f*; **a fine f. of a man,** un hombre bien plantado; **she has a good f.,** tiene buen tipo; **to keep a good f.,** guardar la línea. 3 *(bearing)* **to cut a fine f.,** tener buena presencia. 4 *(character)* figura *f*, personaje *m*; **she was a key f. in the negotiations,** fue una figura clave en las negociaciones. 5 *(statue)* figura *f*. 6 *(in book)* grabado *m*, dibujo *m*. 7 *Ling* **f. of speech,** figura *f* retórica. 8 *Geom* figura *f*. 9 *Math* cifra *f*, guarismo *m*; **in round figures,** en números redondos; **he's good at figures,** se le dan bien los números; *fam* **to put a f. to sth,** ponerle precio a algo. ■ *TV* **viewing figures,** cifras *fpl* de los telespectadores. **II** *vtr US fam* imaginarse, suponer; **I f. it's time to go,** me imagino que ya es hora dé marchar. **III** *vi* 1 *(appear)* figurar, constar; **his name figures on the list,** su nombre figura en la lista. 2 *US fam (make sense)* **that figures,** eso tiene sentido. ◆ **figure on** *vtr US* esperar, contar con. ◆ **figure out** *vtr fam (person)* comprender; *(problem)* resolver; **I can't f. it out,** no me lo explico.

figurehead ['fɪgəhed] *n Naut* mascarón *m* de proa; *fig* figura *f* decorativa.

Fiji ['fiːdʒiː, fiːˈdʒiː] *n* Fiji.

Fijian [fiːˈdʒiːən] *n* fijiano,-a *m*, *f*.

filament ['fɪləmənt] *n Elec* filamento *m*.

filch [fɪltʃ] *n Elec* filamento *m*.

file [faɪl] **I** *n* 1 *(tool)* lima *f*. 2 *(folder)* carpeta *f*. 3 *(archive)* archivo *m*, expediente *m*; **to be on f.,** estar archivado,-a. ■ **card-index f.,** fichero *m*; **police f.,** archivos *mpl* policiales. 4 *Comput* archivo *m*. 5 *(line)* fila *m*; **in single f.,** en fila india. **II** *vtr* 1 *(smooth)* limar; **to f. one's nails,** limarse las uñas. 2 *(put away)* archivar; *(in card-index)* fichar. 3 *Jur* presentar; **to f. a petition for divorce,** entablar demanda de divorcio. **III** *vi Mil* **to f. past,** desfilar.

filet ['fɪlɪt] *n US see* **fillet.**

filibuster ['fɪlɪbʌstəʳ] **I** *n US Pol* filibustero,-a m, *f*, obstruccionista *mf*. **II** *vi* practicar el filibusterismo. **III** *vtr (law, project)* obstruir.

filibustering ['fɪlɪbʌstərɪŋ] *n US Pol* filibusterismo *m*, obstruccionismo *m*.

filigree ['fɪlɪgriː] *n* filigrana *f*.

filing ['faɪlɪŋ] *n* 1 clasificación *f*. ■ **f. cabinet,** archivador *m*, clasificador *m*; *(for cards)* fichero *m*; **f. clerk,** archivero,-a *m*, *f*. 2 **filings,** limaduras *fpl*.

Filipino [fɪlɪ'piːnəu] *n* filipino,-a *m*, *f*.

fill [fɪl] **I** *vtr* 1 *(space)* llenar (**with,** de); **to f. a glass,** llenar un vaso; **to f. a gap,** llenar un vacío. 2 *(time)* llenar, ocupar. 3 *(post, requirements)* cubrir. 4 *(to load)* cargar. 5 *Culin* rellenar. 6 *Dent* empastar. **II** *vi* llenarse (**with,** de); **his eyes filled with tears,** sus ojos se llenaron de lágrimas. **III** *n lit* saciedad *f*; **to eat one's f.,** comer hasta hartarse; *fam* **I've had my f. of him,** estoy harto,-a de él. ◆ **fill in I** *vtr* 1 *(space, hole)* rellenar; **to f. in a form,** rellenar un formulario. 2 *(inform) fam* poner al corriente (**on,** de); **could you f. me in on the affair?,** ¿me podrías poner al corriente del asunto? 3 *(time)* pasar; **how shall we f. in the afternoon?,** ¿cómo vamos a pasar la tarde? **II** *vi* sustituir; **to f. in for sb,** sustituir a algn. ◆ **fill out I** *vtr US (form)* llenar. **II** *vi fam* engordar. ◆ **fill up I** *vtr* 1 llenar hasta arriba; *Aut fam* **f. her up!,** ¡llénelo! 2 *(application form)* llenar. **II** *vi* llenarse; **the room filled up quickly,** la sala se llenó rápidamente; *Aut* **to f. up with petrol,** llenar el depósito de gasolina.

filler ['fɪləʳ] *n (for cracks)* masilla *f*; *(increase size)* relleno *m*.

fillet ['fɪlɪt] *n Culin* filete *m*; **f. of sole,** filete de lenguado; **f. steak,** filete *m*. **II** *vtr* cortar en filetes.

filling ['fɪlɪŋ] **I** *adj* que llena mucho; **rice is very f.,** el arroz llena mucho. **II** *n* 1 *(stuffing)* relleno *m*; *Culin* **cake with lemon f.,** pastel *m* relleno de limón. ■ *GB Aut* **f. station,** gasolinera *f*. 2 *Dent* empaste *m*.

fillip ['fɪlɪp] *n fam* estímulo *m*.

filly ['fɪlɪ] *n Zool* potra *f*.

film [fɪlm] **I** *n* 1 *Cin* película *f*, filme(e) *m*; **on f.,** filmado,-a, en película. ■ **f. industry,** industria *f* cinematográfica; **f. star,** estrella *f* de cine; **f. studio,** estudio *m* de cine; **silent f.,** película *f* muda. 2 *(of dust, oil)* capa *f*. 3 *Phot* película *f*. ■ **colour f.,** película *f* en color. **II** *vtr Cin* filmar. **III** *vi Cin* rodar. ◆ **film over** *vtr* nublarse.

film-strip ['fɪlmstrɪp] n cortometraje m.

filter ['fɪltər] I n 1 filtro m. ■ Phot colour f., filtro m de color; Aut oil f., filtro m de aceite. 2 Aut (traffic light) flecha f. ■ f. lane, carril m de acceso. II vtr filtrar; the sun filtered through the curtains, el sol se filtraba entre las cortinas. III vi Aut to f. to the left/right, girar a la izquierda/derecha. ◆ filter through vi fig filtrar (to, a); the news filtered through, se filtraron las noticias.

filter-tip ['fɪltətɪp] n 1 (of cigarette) boquilla f, filtro m. 2 (cigarette) cigarrillo m con filtro.

filth [fɪlθ] n 1 (dirt) porquería f, suciedad f. 2 fig (language, thoughts) porquerías fpl, marranadas fpl. 3 sl bofia f, pasma f, maderos mpl.

filthy ['fɪlθɪ] adj (filthier, filthiest) 1 (dirty) puerco,-a, asqueroso,-a, sucio,-a. 2 (obscene) obsceno,-a, grosero,-a; a f. mind, una mente sucia.

fin [fɪn] n Zool Av aleta f.

final ['faɪnəl] I adj 1 (last) último,-a, final; f. call, último aviso; Sport the f. score, el resultado final; (payment) f. demand, último aviso m de pago. 2 (definitive) definitivo,-a; and that's f., y no hay más que hablar. II n 1 Sport final f. ■ cup f., final f de la copa. 2 Univ finals, exámenes mpl finales or de fin de curso. ◆ finally adv 1 (lastly) por último, finalmente. 2 (at last) por fin. 3 (definitively) definitivamente.

finale [fɪ'nɑːlɪ] n Mus final m; fig grand f., apoteosis f.

finalist ['faɪnəlɪst] n finalista mf.

finalize ['faɪnəlaɪz] vtr (plans, arrangements) ultimar; (date) fijar.

finance ['faɪnæns, fɪ'næns] I n 1 finanzas fpl. ■ f. company, sociedad f financiera; high f., altas finanzas fpl; Minister of F., ministro,-a m,f de Economía; public f., hacienda f pública. 2 finances, fondos mpl. II vtr financiar.

financial [faɪ'nænʃəl, fɪ'nænʃəl] adj financiero,-a. ■ f. affairs, asuntos mpl financieros; f. crisis, crisis f económica; f. reform, reforma f fiscal; f. success, éxito m financiero; f. year, año m económico.

financier [faɪ'nænsɪə', fɪ'nænsɪə'] n financiero,-a m,f.

financing ['faɪnænsɪŋ, fɪ'nænsɪŋ] n financiación f.

finch [fɪntʃ] n Orn pinzón m.

find [faɪnd] I vtr (pt & pp found) 1 (locate) encontrar; I couldn't f. him, no pude localizarlo; they were nowhere to be found, no los encontramos en ningún sitio. 2 (think) encontrar; I f. her very nice, la encuentro muy simpática; we f. the car a bit small, el coche nos resulta un poco pequeño. 3 (end up) venir a parar; this found its way into my bag, esto vino a parar a mi bolso; we found ourselves without a car, nos encontramos sin coche. 4 (discover) descubrir; it has been found that ..., se ha comprobado que ...; you'll f. that I'm right, ya verás cómo llevo razón. 5 Jur declarar; to f. sb guilty/not guilty, declarar culpable/inocente a algn. 6 (obtain, manage) encontrar, conseguir; he found his way in, logró introducirse; he's been working there for one week and hasn't found his feet yet, lleva una semana trabajando allí y todavía no se ha situado; I can't f. the courage to tell him, no tengo valor para decírselo; I found him a job, le encontré un trabajo; I found it impossible to get away, me resultó imposible irme; to f. one's tongue, soltarse a hablar; to f. one's way, encontrar el camino. 7 arch thirty pounds, all found, treinta libras, todo incluido. II n hallazgo m. ◆ find out I vtr 1 (enquire) averiguar; f. out his address, averigüe or entérese de su dirección; I phoned to f. out the dates, llamé para preguntar las fechas. 2 (discover) descubrir; I found out that he had lied, descubrí que había mentido; to f. sb out, descubrirle el juego a algn. II vi 1 (enquire) averiguar; to f. out about sth, informarse sobre algo. 2 (discover) enterarse; when I found out ..., cuando lo supe ...

findings ['faɪndɪŋz] npl conclusiones fpl, resultados mpl.

fine [faɪn] I n multa f. II vtr multar; he was fined ten pounds, le pusieron una multa de diez libras. III adj 1 (delicate etc) fino,-a. 2 (subtle) sutil; a f. distinction, una diferencia sutil; he's got it down to a f. art, lo hace a la perfección; not to put too f. a point on it, hablando sin rodeos. 3 (excellent) excelente; a f. effort, un gran esfuerzo; a f. pianist, un excelente pianista; a f. piece of work, un trabajo excelente; f. clothes, ropa elegante. 4 (weather) bueno; it was f., hacía buen tiempo. 5 the f. arts, las bellas artes. 6 (all right) bien; I'm f., estoy bien; that's f. by me, me parece muy bien. 7 iron a f. mess, menudo lío; you're a f. friend, ¡vaya amigo estás hecho!; you're a f. one!, ¡estás tú bueno!; you're a f. one to talk!, ¡mira quién habla! IV adv 1 fam muy bien; it suits me f., me viene muy bien; the patient's doing f., el enfermo va muy bien; fig to cut it f., ser muy justo de tiempo, llegar con el tiempo justo. V interj ¡vale! ◆ finely adv 1 (small pieces) finamente; f. chopped, picado fino. 2 Tech Aut (delicately) f. tuned, a punto. 3 (elegantly) f. dressed, vestido,-a con elegancia.

finery ['faɪnərɪ] n galas fpl; in all her f., vestida con sus mejores galas.

finesse [fɪ'nes] n 1 (delicacy) finura f, delicadeza f. 2 (cunning) astucia f; (tact) sutileza f.

finger ['fɪŋɡər] I n Anat dedo m (de la mano); fam he didn't lift a f. to help, no movió ni un dedo para ayudar; fam I didn't lay a f. on her, no la toqué en absoluto; GB fam pull your f. out!, ¡muévete!; fam to have a f. in every pie, estar metido,-a en todo; fam to keep one's fingers crossed, esperar que todo salga bien; fam to put two fingers up, hacer un corte de mangas; fam you've put your f. on it, has dado en el clavo. ■ f. bowl, lavadedos m inv; index f., dedo m índice; little f., dedo m meñique; middle f., dedo m corazón. II vtr tocar; pej manosear.

fingernail ['fɪŋɡəneɪl] n uña f.

fingerprint ['fɪŋɡəprɪnt] I n huella f digital or dactilar. II vtr tomar las huellas digitales.

fingertip ['fɪŋɡətɪp] n punta f or yema f del dedo; fig to have sth at one's fingertips, saberse algo al dedillo.

finicky ['fɪnɪkɪ] adj 1 (person) quisquilloso,-a, melindroso,-a. 2 (job) delicado,-a.

finish ['fɪnɪʃ] I n 1 (end) fin m, conclusión f; (of race) llegada f; a close f., un final muy reñido; a fight to the f., una lucha hasta el final; to be in at the f., estar presente en el final. 2 (surface) acabado m. ■ matt/glossy f., acabado m mate/brillo. II vtr 1 (complete) acabar, terminar. 2 (use up, eat up) acabar, agotar; f. (up) your potatoes, cómete las patatas. 3 fam (exhaust) agotar. III vi acabar, terminar; she finished by saying ..., terminó diciendo ...; she has finished with her boyfriend, ha roto con el novio; to f. doing sth, terminar de hacer algo; Sport to f. second, llegar el segundo. ◆ finish off I vtr 1 (complete) terminar completamente. 2 (use up) acabar, terminar; let's f. off the wine, acabemos el vino. 3 (kill) fam rematar, despachar. II vi acabar. ◆ finish up I vtr acabar, agotar. II vi ir a parar; she finished up in jail, fue a parar a la cárcel.

finished ['fɪnɪʃt] adj 1 (product) acabado,-a; hand f., acabado a mano. 2 fam (exhausted) agotado,-a, rendido,-a. 3 fam (burnt-out) quemado,-a; he's f. as a footballer, como futbolista está acabado.

finishing ['fɪnɪʃɪŋ] adj to put the f. touch(es) to sth, darle los últimos toques a algo. ■ Sport f. line or post, (línea f de) meta f; f. school, escuela f privada de modales para señoritas.

finite ['faɪnaɪt] adj finito,-a. ■ Ling f. verb, verbo m conjugable.

Finland ['fɪnlənd] n Finlandia.

Finn [fɪn] n finlandés,-esa m,f.

Finnish ['fɪnɪʃ] I adj finlandés,-esa. II n (language) finlandés m.

fiord [fjɔːd, 'fiːɔːd] n Geog fiordo m.

fir [fɜː] n Bot abeto m. ■ Douglas f., abeto m de Douglas; silver f., abeto m (blanco).

fire ['faɪəʳ] **I** n 1 fuego m; **to light a f.**, encender un fuego; **to sit by the f.**, sentarse al calor de la lumbre. 2 (accident etc) incendio m, fuego m; **f.!**, ¡fuego!; **to be on f.**, estar ardiendo o en llamas; **to catch f.**, incendiarse; **to set f. to sth**, prenderle fuego a algo, incendiar algo; fig **to get on like a house on f.**, hacer muy buenas migas; fig **to play with f.**, jugar con fuego. ▪ **f. alarm**, alarma f de incendios; **f. brigade**, (cuerpo m de) bomberos mpl; **f. door**, puerta f cortafuegos; **f. drill**, ensayo m para caso de incendio; **f. engine**, coche m de bomberos; **f. escape**, escalera f de incendios; **f. exit**, salida f de emergencia; **f. extinguisher**, extintor m; **f. fighting**, extinción f de incendios; **f. fighting equipment**, equipo m contra incendios; **f. insurance**, seguro m contra incendios; **f. raiser**, incendiario,-a m,f; **f. station**, parque m de bomberos. 3 (heater) estufa f. ▪ **electric/gas f.**, estufa f eléctrica/de gas. 4 Mil fuego m; **heavy f.**, fuego nutrido; Mil **to come under f.**, estar bajo el fuego; fig ser el blanco de las críticas; **to open f.**, abrir fuego. **II** vtr 1 (discharge) (arm) disparar (**at**, a); (rocket) lanzar; fig **to f. questions at sb**, bombardear a algn a preguntas. 2 fam (dismiss) despedir; **she was fired after they caught her stealing**, le despidieron después de encontrarla robando. 3 (pottery) cocer. **III** vi 1 (shoot) disparar, hacer fuego (**at**, sobre); **f.!**, ¡fuego! 2 Aut encenderse. 3 fig **f. away!**, ¡adelante!

firearm ['faɪərɑːm] n arma f de fuego.

firebrand ['faɪəbrænd] n 1 tea f. 2 (person) revoltoso,-a m,f.

firebreak ['faɪəbreɪk] n cortafuego m.

firecracker ['faɪəkrækəʳ] n petardo m.

firecrest ['faɪəkrest] n Orn reyezuelo m listado.

fire-fighter ['faɪəfaɪtəʳ] n US bombero m.

fireguard ['faɪəgɑːd] n pantalla f (de chimenea).

firelighter ['faɪəlaɪtəʳ] n (to start a fire) astilla f para encender el fuego; (firebrand) tea f.

fireman ['faɪəmən] n (pl firemen) bombero m.

fireplace ['faɪəpleɪs] n (whole structure) chimenea f; (hearth) hogar m.

fireproof ['faɪəpruːf] adj incombustible.

fireside ['faɪəsaɪd] n hogar m; **by the f.**, al calor de la lumbre. ▪ **f. chair**, sillón m; **f. chat**, tertulia f.

firewood ['faɪəwʊd] n leña f.

fireworks ['faɪəwɜːks] npl fuegos mpl artificiales; fig **there will be f.**, se va a armar la gorda.

firing ['faɪərɪŋ] n Mil tiroteo m. ▪ **f. line**, línea f de fuego; **f. squad**, pelotón m de fusilamiento.

firm [fɜːm] **I** adj 1 firme, sólido,-a; **f. decision**, firme decisión f; **f. foundation**, base f sólida; **f. offer**, oferta f en firme; **to stand f.**, mantenerse firme. 2 (strict) **to be f. with sb**, tratar a algn con firmeza; **to rule with a f. hand**, gobernar con mano dura. **II** n Com empresa f, firma f. ◆ **firmly** adv firmemente.

firmness ['fɜːmnɪs] n firmeza f.

first [fɜːst] **I** adj primero,-a; (before masculine singular noun) primer; **at f. sight**, a primera vista; **Charles the F.**, Carlos Primero; **for the f. time**, por primera vez; **f. thing in the morning**, a primera hora de la mañana; **in the f. place**, en primer lugar. ▪ Univ **f. degree**, licenciatura f; **f. edition**, primera edición f; **f. floor**, primer piso m, US planta f baja; Aut **f. gear**, primera f (marcha); **f. name**, nombre m de pila; Theat **f. night**, noche f de estreno; Jur **f. offender**, delincuente mf sin antecedentes penales. **II** adv (before anything else) primero; **finish your work f.**, primero acaba el trabajo; **f. and foremost**, ante todo; **f. of all**, en primer lugar; **f. things f.**, primero es lo primero; **her career comes f.**, para ella su carrera es lo primero; **I'd die f.!**, ¡antes morir!; Sport **to come f.**, llegar el primero o la primera; (in exam) sacar la mejor nota; **when I f. saw her**, cuando la vi por primera vez. **III** n 1 **the f.**, el primero, la primera; **to be the f. to do sth**, ser el primero o la primera en hacer algo; **the f. of April**, el uno o el primero de abril; fam **f. come, f. served**, los primeros primero. ▪ Med **f. aid**, primeros

auxilios mpl; **f. aid box**, botiquín m. 2 (at the beginning) **at f.**, al principio; **from the (very) f.**, desde el principio. 3 Aut primera f (marcha); **in f.**, en primera. 4 Univ **to get a f.**, sacar un sobresaliente. ◆ **firstly** adv primero, en primer lugar.

first-born ['fɜːstbɔːn] n primogénito,-a m, f.

first-class ['fɜːstklɑːs] **I** adj de primera clase; **f.-c. hotel**, hotel de primera categoría; **f.-c. sportsman**, deportista fuera de serie; **f.-c. ticket**, billete de primera clase. **II first class** [fɜːst'klɑːs] adv Rail en primera; **to travel f. c.**, viajar en primera.

first-former ['fɜːstfɔːməʳ] n GB Sch alumno,-a del primer curso.

first-hand ['fɜːsthænd] adv & adj de primera mano; **f.-h. information**, información f de primera mano.

first-rate ['fɜːstreɪt] adj excelente, de primera.

fiscal ['fɪskəl] adj fiscal.

fish [fɪʃ] **I** n (pl fish or fishes) 1 Zool pez m; fig **he's a queer f.**, es un tipo raro; fig **like a f. out of water**, como pez fuera del agua; fam **to drink like a f.**, beber como una esponja. ▪ **f. hook**, anzuelo m; **f. shop**, pescadería f; US Canada **f. stick**, palito m de pescado; **f. tank**, pecera f. 2 Culin pescado m; **f. and chips**, pescado frito con patatas fritas. **II** vi pescar; **to f. for trout**, pescar truchas; fig **to f. in one's pocket for sth**, buscar algo en el bolsillo; fig **to f. a sock out of the drawer**, sacar un calcetín del cajón; fig **to f. for compliments**, buscar los elogios.

fishbone ['fɪʃbəʊn] n espina f, raspa f.

fishcake ['fɪʃkeɪk] n Culin medallón m de pescado y patata.

fisherman ['fɪʃəmən] n (pl fishermen) pescador m.

fishery ['fɪʃərɪ] n pesquería f, pesquera f.

fishfinger [fɪʃ'fɪŋgəʳ] n Culin palito m de pescado.

fishing ['fɪʃɪŋ] n pesca f; **to go f.**, ir de pesca. ▪ **deep-sea f.**, pesca f de altura; **f. net**, red f de pesca; **f. rod**, caña f de pescar; **f. tackle**, aparejo m de pescar.

fish-knife ['fɪʃnaɪf] n (pl fish-knives ['fɪʃnaɪvz]) cuchillo m de pescado.

fishmonger ['fɪʃmʌŋgəʳ] n GB pescadero,-a m, f; **fishmonger's (shop)**, pescadería f.

fishnet ['fɪʃnet] n malla f. ▪ **f. tighs**, leotardo m de malla gruesa.

fishwife ['fɪʃwaɪf] n (pl fishwives ['fɪʃwaɪvz]) fig pej verdulera f.

fishy ['fɪʃɪ] adj (fishier, fishiest) de pescado; **f. smell**, olor a pescado; fam fig **there's something f. going on**, aquí hay gato encerrado.

fission ['fɪʃən] n Phys fisión f.

fissure ['fɪʃəʳ] n 1 grieta f. 2 Anat fisura f.

fist [fɪst] n puño m; **to shake one's f. at sb**, amenazar a algn con el puño.

fistful ['fɪstful] n puñado m.

fit¹ [fɪt] **I** vtr (pt & pp fitted) 1 (correct size) ir bien a; **that suit doesn't f.**, ese traje no te entalla; **to f. like a glove**, (clothes) entallar muy bien; (others) ir muy bien. 2 Sew probar; **he is being fitted for a jacket**, le están probando una chaqueta. 3 (slot) encajar, poner; **this key doesn't f. the lock**, esta llave no es de esta cerradura. 4 (put, install) poner, colocar; **a car fitted with a radio**, un coche provisto de radio; **to have a shelf fitted**, hacer colocar un estante. 5 fig (correspond) encajar con, estar de acuerdo con; **she doesn't f. the description**, no responde a la descripción. 6 (suitable) encajar; fml **to f. sb for sth**, capacitar a algn para algo. **II** vi 1 (right size) caber; **all my belongings f. into the room**, todas mis pertenencias caben en la habitación; **the door doesn't f. properly**, la puerta no ajusta bien; **these trousers f. well**, estos pantalones se ponen muy bien. 2 (correspond) cuadrar; **the facts don't f.**, los hechos no cuadran; fig **his lace didn't f.**, no encajó. **III** adj 1 (suitable) apto,-a, adecuado,-a (**for**, para); **a feast f. for a king**, un banquete digno de un rey; **are you f. to drive?**, ¿estás en condiciones de conducir?; **is he a f. person for the job?**,

¿es la persona adecuada para el puesto?; **she's not f. to teach,** no vale para la enseñanza; **that's all he's f. for,** no sirve para nada más; **to see** *or* **think f. to do sth,** juzgar oportuno hacer algo. 2 *(healthy)* en forma, en plena forma; **to get/keep fit,** ponerse/mantenerse en forma; *prov* **f. as a fiddle,** más sano,-a que una manzana, fuerte como un roble. 3 *fam (ready)* a punto de; **he was f. to start laughing,** estaba con la risa a punto de explotar. **IV** *n* 1 ajuste *m*; *Sew* corte *m*; **to be a good f.,** encajar bien; **the jacket is a good f.,** la americana te viene bien. ◆ **fit in I** *vi* 1 *(match)* adaptarse; **he didn't f. in with his colleagues,** no encajó con sus compañeros de trabajo. 2 *(tally)* cuadrar **(with,** con)**; her story didn't f. in with the rest,** su historia no cuadraba con las otras; **it's all fitting into place,** ahora empiezo a entenderlo. **II** *vtr (find time for)* encontrar un hueco para; **the director tried to f. me in on Monday,** el director intentó encontrar un hueco para verme el lunes; **we couldn't f. it all in,** no tuvimos tiempo para todo. ◆ **fit out** *vtr* equipar; **they fitted him out for the expedition,** le equiparon para la expedición; **they fitted out the office,** amueblaron el despacho.

fit² [fɪt] *n* 1 *Med* ataque *m*, acceso *m*; **a f. of coughing,** un acceso de tos; **epileptic f.,** ataque epiléptico; *fam* **he'll have a f.,** le va a dar un ataque. 2 *fig* ataque *m*, arrebato *m*; **f. of anger,** arranque *m* de cólera; **f. of enthusiasm,** arrebato *m* de entusiasmo; **f. of jealously,** ataque *or* arrebato *m* de celos; *fig* **by fits and starts,** a trompicones; **to go into fits of laughter,** troncharse de risa.

fitful ['fɪtful] *adj* irregular, discontinuo,-a. ◆ **fitfully** *adv* a rachas.

fitness ['fɪtnɪs] *n* 1 *(aptitude)* aptitud *f*, capacidad *f*. 2 *(health)* (buen) estado *m* físico. ■ *Sport* **f. test,** examen *m* de forma física.

fitted ['fɪtɪd] *adj* empotrado,-a. ■ **f. carpet,** moqueta *f*; **f. cupboard,** armario *m* empotrado.

fitter ['fɪtə'] *n* ajustador,-a *m*, *f*.

fitting ['fɪtɪŋ] **I** *adj (appropiate)* apropiado,-a, oportuno,-a; **it was f. that he,** era justo que ganara. **II** *n* 1 *(dress)* prueba *f*. ■ **f. room,** probador *m*. 2 *(usu pl)* accesorio *m*; **light fittings,** apliques *mpl* eléctricos; **bathroom fittings,** sanitarios *mpl*.

five [faɪv] **I** *adj* cinco *inv*; **f. cups,** cinco tazas; **f. hundred,** quinientos,-as; **f. thousand men,** cinco mil hombres; **f.-day week,** semana *f* laboral de cinco días. **II** *n* cinco *m inv*; *see also* **seven.**

fiver ['faɪvə'] *n fam* billete *m* de cinco libras *or* dólares.

five-star ['faɪvstɑː'] *adj* de cinco estrellas; **f.-s. hotel,** hotel *m* de cinco estrellas.

five-year ['faɪvjɪə'] *adj* que dura cinco años; **f.-y. plan,** plan *m* quinquenal.

fix [fɪks] **I** *n* 1 *fam (difficulty)* aprieto *m*, apuro *m*; **to be in a f.,** estar en un apuro. 2 *(drugs) sl* dosis *f*. **II** *vtr* 1 *(fasten)* fijar, asegurar; *fig* fijar (**on,** en); **she fixed her eyes on me,** clavó sus ojos en mí; *fig* **they fixed the blame on me,** me echaron la culpa. 2 *(establish) (date, price)* fijar; *(limit)* señalar; **let's f. a price,** fijemos un precio. 3 *(arrange)* arreglar; **he'll f. it with the boss,** se las arreglará con el jefe; *fam* **how are you fixed for money?,** ¿qué tal andas de dinero?; **there's nothing fixed yet,** no hay nada decidido todavía. 4 *Sport (dishonestly)* amañar; **the game was fixed for them to win,** les arreglaron el partido para que ganasen. 5 *(repair)* arreglar, componer. 6 *US (food, drink)* preparar. 7 *Phot* fijar. 8 *(tidy)* arreglar; **she fixed her hair,** se arregló el pelo. ◆ **fix up** *vtr (arrange)* arreglar; **it's all fixed up,** ya está todo arreglado; **to f. sb up with sth,** proveer a algn de algo.

fixation [fɪk'seɪʃən] *n* idea *f* fija, obsesión *f*; **to have a f. about sth.,** estar obsesionado,-a por algo.

fixed [fɪkst] *adj* 1 fijo,-a; **of no f. abode,** sin domicilio fijo. 2 *fam* amañado,-a. ■ **f. match,** un partido arreglado.

fixer ['fɪksə'] *n Phot* fijador *m*.

fixture ['fɪkstʃə'] *n* 1 *Sport* encuentro *m*. 2 **fixtures,** *(in building)* accesorios *mpl*.

fizz [fɪz] **I** *n* burbujeo *m*. **II** *vi* burbujear.

fizziness ['fɪzɪnɪs] *n* efervescencia *f*.

fizzle ['fɪzəl] *vi (hiss)* chisporrotear. ◆ **fizzle out** *vi* quedar en nada; **their interest in the matter fizzled out within a week,** su interés en el tema se desvaneció en una semana.

fizzy ['fɪzɪ] *adj (fizzier, fizziest) (water)* gaseoso,-a, con gas; *(wine)* espumoso,-a.

fjord [fjɔːd, 'fiːɔːd] *n Geog* fiordo *m*.

flab [flæb] *n fam* michelines *mpl*.

flabbergasted ['flæbəgɑːstɪd] *adj* pasmado,-a; **I was f.,** quedé pasmado,-a.

flabby ['flæbɪ] *adj (flabbier, flabbiest)* fofo,-a.

flaccid ['flæsɪd] *adj* flácido,-a.

flag [flæg] **I** *n* 1 bandera *f*; *Naut* pabellón *m*; *fig* **to show the f.,** hacer acto de presencia; **to keep the f. flying,** ser patriótico,-a, representar a alguien a su propio país. 2 *(for charity)* banderita *f*. ■ **f. day,** día *m* de la banderita. **II** *vtr (pt & pp flagged) (mark)* señalar; *fig* **to f. down a car,** hacer señales a un coche para que pare. **III** *vi (interest)* decaer; *(conversation)* languidecer; **after working on the same material his attention began to f.,** después de trabajar el mismo material su atención empezó a decaer.

flagellate ['flædʒəleɪt] *vtr fml* flagelar.

flagon ['flægən] *n (jug)* jarro *m*; *(bottle)* botella *f* grande.

flagpole ['flægpəʊl] *n* asta *f* de bandera.

flagrant ['fleɪɡrənt] *adj* flagrante.

flagship ['flægʃɪp] *n Naut* buque insignia *m*.

flagstone ['flægstəʊn] *n* losa *f*.

flair [fleə'] *n* instinto *m*, facilidad *f*, talento *m*, don *m*; **he has a f. for languages,** tiene un don especial para los idiomas.

flak [flæk] *n* 1 *Mil* fuego *m* antiáreo. 2 *fam* críticas *fpl* negativas; **the decision came in for a lot of f.,** la decisión fue duramente criticada.

flake [fleɪk] **I** *n (of snow)* copo *m*; *(of skin, soap)* escama *f*; *(of paint)* desconchón *m*. **II** *vi (skin)* descamarse; *(paint)* desconcharse. ◆ **flake out** *vi fam* caer rendido,-a; **I ran 5 miles and then flaked out,** corrí 5 millas y después no me tenía en pie.

flaky ['fleɪkɪ] *adj (flakier, flakiest)* que se desconcha. ■ *Culin* **f. pastry,** hojaldre *m*.

flamboyant [flæm'bɔɪənt] *adj* llamativo,-a, extravagante.

flame [fleɪm] *n* llama *f*; **to go up in flames,** incendiarse; **to burst into flames,** estallar en llamas; *fam* **an old f.,** un antiguo amor.

flameproof ['fleɪmpruːf] *adj* ininflamable, ignífugo,-a.

flaming ['fleɪmɪŋ] *adj* 1 llameante. 2 *fam* condenado,-a, maldito,-a; **where's the f. key?,** ¿dónde está la maldita llave?

flamingo [flə'mɪŋgəʊ] *n (pl flamingos or flamingoes) Orn* flamenco *m*.

flammable ['flæməbəl] *adj* inflamable.

flan [flæn] *n Culin* tarta *f* rellena; **fruit f.,** tarta de fruta.

Flanders ['flɑːndəz] *n* Flandes.

flange [flændʒ] *n* pestaña *f*, reborde *m*.

flank [flæŋk] **I** *n* 1 *(of animal)* ijada *f*, ijar *m*. 2 *Mil* flanco *m*. **II** *vtr* flanquear, bordear; **the road was flanked with** *or* **by trees,** la carretera estaba bordeada de árboles.

flannel ['flænəl] *n* 1 *Tex* franela *f*. ■ **f. trousers,** pantalón *m* de franela. 2 *GB (face cloth)* toallita *f*.

flap [flæp] **I** *vtr (pt & pp flapped) (wings, arms)* batir. **II** *vi* 1 *(wings)* aletear; *(flag)* ondear. 2 *fam* inquietarse. **III** *n* 1 *(of envelope, book, pocket)* solapa *f*; *(of tent)* faldón *m*. ■ **cat f.,** gatera *f*. 2 *(of wing)* alerón *m*. 3 *fam* pánico *m*; **to get into a f.,** ponerse nervioso,-a.

flapjack ['flæpdʒæk] *n Culin* 1 *GB (biscuit)* galleta *f*. 2 *US (pancake)* hojuela *f*, tortita *f*.

flare [fleə^r] **I** *n* 1 (*flame*) llamarada *f*. 2 *Mil Naut* bengala *f*, cohete *m* de señales. **II** *vi* 1 (*fire*) llamear. 2 *fig* (*person*) encolerizarse. 3 (*trouble*) estallar.

flared [fleəd] *adj* acampanado,-a; **f. trousers,** pantalones *mpl* acampanados.

flash [flæʃ] **I** *n* 1 (*of light*) destello *m*; **f. of lightning,** relámpago *m*; *fig* **quick as a f.,** como un relámpago; *fig* **in a f.,** en un decir Jesús. ■ **f. flood,** inundación *f* repentina. 2 (*burst*) ráfaga *f*; **a f. in the pan,** un triunfo or éxito fugaz; *fig* **f. of inspiration,** momento *m* de inspiración. 3 *Rad TV* (**news**) **f.,** flash *m*, noticia *f* de última hora. 4 *Phot* flash *m*. **II** *adj sl* chulo,-a, guay. **III** *vtr* 1 (*shine torch, light*) dirigir; (*shine*) brillar. 2 *Rad TV* transmitir. 3 (*show quickly*) **he flashed his card,** enseñó rápidamente su carnet. **IV** *vi* 1 (*sudden light*) destellar; (*shine*) brillar. 2 (*move quickly*) mover muy rapidamente; **a car flashed past,** un coche pasó como un rayo; *fig* **it flashed across** or **through** or **into my mind that ...,** se me ocurrió de repente que ... .

flashback ['flæʃbæk] *n Cin Lit* escena *f* retrospectiva.

flashcube ['flæʃkjuːb] *n Phot* cubo *m* flash.

flasher ['flæʃə^r] *n sl* exhibicionista *m*.

flashing ['flæʃɪŋ] *adj* (*light*) intermitente.

flashlight ['flæʃlaɪt] *n* 1 *US* (*torch*) linterna *f*. 2 *GB Phot* flash *m*.

flashy ['flæʃɪ] *adj* (*flashier, flashiest*) *fam* chillón,-a, ostentoso,-a.

flask [flɑːsk, flæsk] *n* 1 frasco *m*; *Chem* matraz *m*. 2 (**thermos**) **f.,** termo *m*.

flat [flæt] **I** *adj* (*flatter, flattest*) 1 (*surface*) llano,-a, plano,-a; **to lay sth f.,** tender algo; **to lie f.,** tenderse. ■ **f. feet,** pies *mpl* planos. 2 (*beer*) sin gas. 3 *Aut* (*battery*) descargado,-a; (*tyre*) desinflado,-a. 4 (*rate*) fijo,-a. ■ **f. rate,** precio *m* fijo. 5 (*categorical*) rotundo,-a; **a f. refusal,** una negativa rotunda. 6 (*dull*) monótono,-a, soso,-a; **a f. party,** una fiesta sosa. 7 *Mus* bemol; **B. f.,** si *m* bemol. **II** *adv* 1 **to fall f. on one's face,** caerse de bruces. 2 (*exactly*) **in ten seconds f.,** en diez segundos justos. 3 *fam* **to be f. broke,** estar sin blanca; *fam* **to go f. out,** ir a todo gas. **III** *n* 1 superficie *f* plana. 2 (*apartment*) piso *m*; **block of flats,** bloque *m* de pisos. 3 *US Aut* pinchazo *m*. 4 *Geog* **mud flats,** marismas *fpl*. ◆ **flatly** *adv* categóricamente, rotundamente.

flat-chested [flæt'tʃestɪd] *adj* de poco pecho, liso,-a.

flat-footed [flæt'futɪd] *adj* **to be f.-f.,** tener los pies planos.

flatlet ['flætlɪt] *n GB* piso *m* pequeño, apartamento *m*.

flatmate ['flætmeɪt] *n GB* compañero,-a *m, f* de piso.

flatness ['flætnəs] *n* 1 (*of surface*) lo llano. 2 (*dullness*) monotonía *f*, sosería *f*.

flatten ['flætən] *vtr* 1 (*make level*) allanar, aplanar. 2 (*crush*) aplastar.

flatter ['flætə^r] *vtr* 1 adular, halagar; **I am flattered to be invited,** me siento halagado,-a por su invitación. 2 (*clothes, portrait*) favorecer; **that hairstyle flatters her,** ese peinado le favorece mucho. 3 **to f. oneself,** hacerse ilusiones; **don't f. yourself,** no te hagas ilusiones.

flatterer ['flætərə^r] *n* adulador,-a *m, f*.

flattering ['flætərɪŋ] *adj* 1 (*words*) halagüeño,-a, lisonjero,-a. 2 (*dress, portrait*) favorecedor,-a, que favorece.

flattery ['flætərɪ] *n* adulación *f*, halago *m*.

flatulence ['flætjuləns] *n* flatulencia *f*.

flaunt [flɔːnt] *vtr* ostentar, hacer alarde de; **to f. oneself,** pavonearse.

flautist ['flɔːtɪst] *n* flautista *mf*.

flavour, *US* **flavor** ['fleɪvə^r] **I** *n* 1 sabor *m*; *fig* (*feel*) atmósfera *f*; **there's a strange f. about this place,** hay una estraña atmósfera en este lugar. **II** *vtr Culin* sazonar (**with,** con), condimentar (**with,** con).

flavoured, *US* **flavored** ['fleɪvəd] *adj* con sabor a; **strawberry f. ice cream,** helado *m* con sabor a fresa.

flavouring, *US* **flavoring** ['fleɪvərɪŋ] *n Culin* condimento *m*, aderezo *m*; **artificial f.,** aroma *m* artificial.

flaw [flɔː] *n* (*failing*) defecto *m*; (*fault*) desperfecto *m*.

flawless ['flɔːlɪs] *adj* (*immaculate*) sin defecto, sin tacha, perfecto,-a.

flax [flæks] *n Bot* lino *m*.

flaxen ['flæksən] *adj* (*hair*) (de color) rubio pajizo.

flay [fleɪ] *vtr* 1 (*flog*) desollar; (*animal*) despellejar. 2 *fig* (*argument*) criticar; **to f. sb alive,** desollar a algn vivo,-a.

flea [fliː] *n Ent* pulga *f*. ■ **f. market,** rastro *m*, mercado *m* de trastos viejos; *GB fam pej* **f. pit,** cine *m* or teatro *m* de mala muerte.

fleabag ['fliːbæg] *n* 1 *GB fam pej* cochino,-a *m, f*. 2 *US* hotelucho *m*.

fleabite ['fliːbaɪt] *n* picadura *f* de pulga.

flea-bitten ['fliːbɪtən] *adj* sucio,-a, desaharrapado,-a.

fleck [flek] *n* (*speck*) mota *f*, punto *m*.

flecked [flekt] *adj* (*speckled*) moteado,-a; (*spattered*) salpicado,-a (**with,** de).

fled [fled] *pt & pp see* **flee.**

fledg(e)ling ['fledʒlɪŋ] **I** *n Orn* volantón *m*, volandero *m*. **II** *adj fig* novato,-a.

flee [fliː] **I** *vtr* (*pt & pp* **fled**) huir; **to f. the country,** huir del país. **II** *vi* huir (**from,** de); **city dwellers f. to the coast in the summer,** los habitantes de la ciudad huyen hacia la costa en verano.

fleece [fliːs] **I** *n* 1 (*sheep's coat*) lana *f*. 2 (*sheared*) vellón *m*; *Myth* **the Golden F.,** el Vellocino de Oro. **II** *vtr fam* (*cheat*) desollar, desplumar.

fleecy ['fliːsɪ] *adj* (*fleecier, fleeciest*) 1 (*woollen*) lanoso,-a. 2 (*soft, fluffy*) suave; **f. clouds,** nubes *fpl* aborregadas.

fleet[1] [fliːt] *n Naut* flota *f*. ■ **fishing f.,** flota *f* pesquera; (*of cars*) escuadra *f*; *GB* **F. Air Arm,** Armada *f* Aérea de la Flota.

fleet[2] [fliːt] *adj poet* rápido,-a, veloz; **f. of foot,** de pies ligeros.

fleeting ['fliːtɪŋ] *adj* (*brief, passing*) fugaz, efímero,-a. ◆ **fleetingly** *adv* fugazmente.

Flemish ['flemɪʃ] **I** *adj* flamenco,-a. **II** *n* (*language*) flamenco *m*.

flesh [fleʃ] *n* 1 carne *f*; *fig* **I saw David Bowie in the f.,** ví a David Bowie en persona; *fig* (*kin*) **she's your own f. and blood,** es de tu propia sangre; *fig* **the pleasures of the f.,** los placeres de la carne; *fig* **to be of f. and blood,** ser de carne y hueso; *fig* (*fill out*) **to put f. on sth,** dar forma a algo. ■ **f. wound,** le rida *f* superficial. 2 (*of fruit*) carne *f*, pulpa *f*.

flesh-coloured ['fleʃkʌləd] *adj* de color carne.

fleshy ['fleʃɪ] *adj* (*fleshier, fleshiest*) carnoso,-a.

flew [fluː] *pt see* **fly.**

flex [fleks] **I** *n GB Elec* cable *m*. **II** *vtr* (*body, knees*) doblar; (*muscles*) flexionar.

flexible ['fleksɪbəl] *adj* flexible.

flexibility [fleksɪ'bɪlɪtɪ] *n* flexibilidad *f*.

flexitime ['fleksɪtaɪm] *n* horario *m* flexible.

flick[1] [flɪk] **I** *n* 1 (*jerk*) movimiento *m* rápido or brusco; (*finger*) capirotazo *m*; **with the flick of a wrist,** con un movimiento rápido de la muñeca; **with a f. of the tail,** de un coletazo; **at the f. of a switch,** solo con apretar un botón. 2 *sl* **the flicks,** (*cinema*) el cine. **II** *vtr* 1 (*button, switch*) darle al interruptor. 2 (*whip*) chasquear. 3 (*finger*) dar un capirotazo; **to f. sth at sb,** tirarle algo a algn con un capirotazo. ◆ **flick off** *vtr* (*brush*) sacudirse de encima; (*ash*) tirar; (*light*) apagar. ◆ **flick on** *vtr* (*light*) encender. ◆ **flick through** *vi* (*book etc*) hojear.

flicker ['flɪkə^r] **I** *n* 1 (*gen*) parpadeo *m*; (*light*) titileo *m*. 2 *fig* (*trace*) indicio *m*, rastro *m*; **a f. of hope,** una pizca de esperanza; **not a f. of interest,** ni un ápice de interés. **II** *vi* (*eyes*) parpadear; (*flame*) vacilar, titular.

flick-knife ['flɪknaɪf] *n (pl flick-knives* ['flɪknaɪvz]*)* navaja *f* automática.

flier ['flaɪə^r] *n Av* aviador,-a *m,f.* ■ *fig* **high f.,** ambicioso,- a *m,f.*

flight [flaɪt] *n* **1** vuelo *m;* **how long is the f.?,** ¿cuánto dura el vuelo?; **is there a f. to Malaga?,** ¿hay algún vuelo a Málaga?; *fig* **f. of fancy,** vuelo *m* de la imaginación. ■ **charter f.,** vuelo *m* chárter; **f. path,** trayectoria *f* de vuelo; **f. recorder,** registrador *m* de vuelo. **2** *(of ball)* trayectoria *f.* **3** *(flock of birds)* bandada *f.* **4** *(running away)* huida *f,* fuga *f; (fleeing)* **to take f.,** darse a la fuga. **5** *(of stairs)* tramo *m;* **the office is three flights up,** el despacho está tres pisos más arriba.

flight-deck ['flaɪtdek] *n Av* **1** *(carrier)* cubierta *f* de vuelo. **2** *(cockpit)* cabina *f* del piloto.

flightiness ['flaɪtɪnɪs] *n* ligereza *f.*

flightless ['flaɪtlɪs] *adj Zool* **f. bird,** ave *f* no voladora.

flighty ['flaɪtɪ] *adj (flightier, flightiest)* casquivano,-a.

flimsy ['flɪmzɪ] I *adj (flimsier, flimsiest)* **1** *(cloth)* ligero,-a; *(paper)* fino,-a. **2** *(structure)* poco sólido,-a. **3** *(excuse)* flojo,-a, malo,-a. II *n* papel *m* cebolla.

flimsiness ['flɪmzɪnɪs] *n* **1** *(thinness)* ligereza *f,* finura *f.* **2** *(brittleness)* fragilidad *f.*

flinch [flɪntʃ] *vi* **1** *(wince)* estremecerse, conmover; **without flinching,** sin pestañear. **2** *(shun)* esquivar, evitar; **to f. from sth,** retroceder ante algo.

fling [flɪŋ] I *vtr (pt & pp flung) (hurl, toss)* arrojar, tirar; **he flung his hat onto the table,** lanzó su sombrero sobre la mesa; **she flung herself into his arms,** se dejó caer en sus brazos; **to f. a door open,** abrir una puerta de golpe; **to f. oneself at sb,** arrojarse sobre algn; **to f. sb out,** echar a algn a patadas; *fig* **she flung insults at him,** le lanzó una sarta de insultos; *fig* **to f. oneself into sth,** entregarse a algo. II *n* **1** *(throw)* lanzamiento *m.* **2** *fam (good time)* juerga *f;* **to have one last f.,** correrse la última juerga. **3** *fam (affair)* lío *m;* **to have a f.,** echar una cana al aire. ◆ **fling off** *vtr (clothes)* quitarse rápidamente. ◆ **fling on** *vtr (clothes)* ponerse rápidamente. ◆ **fling out** *vtr* tirar; **we flung out all the old furniture,** tiramos todos los muebles viejos.

flint [flɪnt] *n* **1** *(stone)* pedernal *m,* sílex *m.* **2** *(in cigarette lighter)* piedra *f* de mechero.

flintlock ['flɪntlɒk] *n (gun)* escopeta *f* or fusil *m* de chispa.

flip [flɪp] I *(flick)* capirotazo *m,* capirote *m,* papirotazo *m.* ■ **f. side,** *(of record)* cara *f* B. II *interj GB fam* ¡ostras! III *vtr (pt & pp flipped)* **1** *(toss)* tirar or echar (al aire); **to f. a coin,** echar a cara o cruz. **2** *(flick) (button, switch)* darle al interruptor. IV *vi fam (freak)* perder los estribos.

flip-flop ['flɪpflɒp] *n* **1** *Comput* báscula *f* biestable, flip-flop *m.* **2** *(footwear)* chancleta *f.*

flippancy ['flɪpənsɪ] *n (frivolity)* livianidad *f,* ligereza *f,* falta *f* de seriedad.

flippant ['flɪpənt] *adj (frivolous)* liviano,-a, ligero,-a, poco serio,-a.

flipper ['flɪpə^r] *n* aleta *f.*

flirt [flɜːt] I *n* coqueto,-a *m,f,* ligón,-a *m,f.* II *vi* flirtear, coquetear; *fig* **to f. with an idea,** acariciar una idea; **to f. with death,** jugar con la muerte.

flirtation [flɜː'teɪʃən] *n* flirteo *m,* coqueteo *m,* ligue *m.*

flirtatious [flɜː'teɪʃəs] *adj* coqueto,-a.

flit [flɪt] I *n fam* escapada *f;* **to do a moonlight f.,** irse a la chita callando. II *vi (pt & pp flitted) (buzz, whizz)* revolotear; **to f. in and out,** ir y venir sin hacer ruido.

float [fləʊt] I *n* **1** *Fishing* corcho *m,* flotador *m.* **2** *(Swimming)* flotador *m.* **3** *(money)* cambio *m.* **4** *(in procession)* carroza *f.* ■ **milk f.,** furgoneta *f* de repartir la leche. II *vtr* **1** poner a flote. **2** *Fin (shares)* emitir; *(currency, business)* hacer flotar. III *vi (on float)* flotar; **to f. to the surface,** salir a la superficie; *(glide)* **she floated into the room,** entró en la habitación elegantemente. ◆ **float around** *vi (rumour)* circular.

floating ['fləʊtɪŋ] *adj* flotante; *(population)* flotante; *Pol (voter)* indeciso,-a. ■ *Tech* **f. axle,** eje *m* flotante; *Fin* **f. currency,** moneda *f* flotante.

flock [flɒk] I *n* **1** *Zool* rebaño *m; Orn* bandada *f.* **2** *Rel (congregation)* grey *f.* **3** *(crowd)* multitud *f,* tropel *m.* **4** *Tex* borra *f.* II *vi* acudir en masa; **to f. together,** congregarse, reunirse; *fig* **they flocked to the exhibition,** acudieron en masa *or* tropel a la exposición.

floe [fləʊ] *n* témpano *m* (de hielo).

flog [flɒg] *vtr (pt & pp flogged)* **1** azotar; *fam fig (idea)* **flogged to death,** pasado,-a de moda, demasiado usado,-a; *fam fig* **to f. a dead horse,** querer hacer lo imposible; *fam fig* **to f. oneself to death,** matarse trabajando. **2** *sl (sell)* vender.

flogging ['flɒgɪŋ] *n* azotaina *f,* paliza *f.*

flood [flʌd] I *n* inundación *f; (of river)* riada *f; fig (of people)* torrente *m,* riada *f,* tropel *m; (of light)* torrente *m,* chorro *m.* II *vtr* inundar; **to be flooded,** inundarse; *fig* inundar; *Com* **to f. the market with products,** inundar el mercado de productos. III *vi (river)* desbordarse; *(of to)* **f. in,** entrar a raudales; **letters came flooding in,** hubo una avalancha de cartas.

floodgate ['flʌdgeɪt] *n* compuerta *f.*

flooding ['flʌdɪŋ] *n* inundaciones *fpl.*

floodlight ['flʌdlaɪt] *n Elec* foco *m.*

floodlit ['flʌdlɪt] *adj* iluminado,-a con focos.

floor [flɔː^r] I *n* **1** *(of room)* suelo *m,* piso *m;* **to take the f.,** salir a bailar. ■ **dance f.,** pista *f* de baile; **f. polish,** cera *f* (de suelos). **2** *Geog (of ocean, forest, etc)* fondo *m.* **3** *(storey)* piso *m.* ■ **first f.,** *GB* primer piso *m. US* planta *f* baja. **f. show,** espectáculo *m* de cabaret; **ground f.,** planta *f* baja. **4** *Parl* hemiciclo *m.* II *vtr (knock down)* derribar; *fig* dejar perplejo,-a.

floorboard ['flɔːbɔːd] *n* tabla *f* (del suelo).

floorcloth ['flɔːklɒθ] *n* bayeta *f.*

flop [flɒp] I *n fam* fracaso *m.* II *vi (pt & pp flopped)* **1** abalanzarse, arrojarse; **to f. down on the bed,** tumbarse en la cama. **2** *fam* fracasar.

floppy ['flɒpɪ] *adj (floppier, floppiest)* blando,-a; flojo,-a. ■ *Comput* **f. disc,** disco *m* flexible, disquete *m.*

flora ['flɔːrə] *n Bot* flora *f.*

floral ['flɔːrəl] *adj* floral.

Florence ['flɒrəns] *n* Florencia.

florentine ['flɒrəntaɪn] *adj & n* florentino,-a *(m,f).*

florid ['flɒrɪd] *adj fml* **1** *(style etc)* florido,-a, recargado,-a. **2** *(complexion)* rojizo,-a.

florist ['flɒrɪst] *n* florista *mf;* **f.'s,** floristería *f.*

flotation [fləʊ'teɪʃən] *n (buoyancy)* flotabilidad *f.*

flotilla [flə'tɪlə] *n Naut* flotilla *f.*

flotsam ['flɒtsəm] *n Naut* **f. and jetsam,** desechos *mpl* arrojados al mar; *fig* gente *f sing* sin oficio ni beneficio.

flounce¹ [flaʊns] I *n* gesto *m* exagerado *or* de enfado. II *vi* moverse desahogadamente; **to f. in/out,** entrar/salir airadamente.

flounce² [flaʊns] *n Sew* volante *m.*

flounder¹ ['flaʊndə^r] *n (fish)* platija *f.*

flounder² ['flaʊndə^r] *vi* **1** *(struggle)* forcejear; *fig* enredarse. **2** *(dither)* no saber que decir *or* hacer; *fig* vacilar.

flour ['flaʊə^r] *n* harina *f.* ■ **f. mill,** molino *m* de harina.

flourish ['flʌrɪʃ] I *n* **1** *(gesture)* ademán *m,* gesto *m;* **he entered the room with a f.,** entró en la habitación haciendo un gesto teatral. **2** *(of sword)* floreo *m; (under signature)* rúbrica *f; (in writing)* plumada *f.* **3** *Mus (on guitar)* floreo *m; (fanfare)* toque *m* de trompeta. **4** *(speech, singing)* floritura *f.* II *vtr* **1** *(brandish, wave)* agitar, ondear. **2** *Mus* florear. **3** *(speech, writings)* adornar. III *vi* **1** *(thrive, bloom)* prosperar, florecer. **2** *(plant)* crecer, medrar.

flourishing ['flʌrɪʃɪŋ] *adj* floreciente, próspero,-a.

flout [flaʊt] *vtr Jur* desacatar.

flow [fləʊ] **I** *n* **1** flujo *m*; *(of river)* corriente *f*; *(of tide)* flujo *m*; **he interrupted me when I was in full f.,** me interrumpió en pleno discurso. **2** *(of traffic)* circulación *f*. **3** *Fin (of capital)* movimiento *m*. **4** *(of people, goods)* afluencia *f*; **to go along with the f.,** seguir la corriente. **II** *vi* **1** *(blood, river, etc)* fluir, manar; **the Douro flows into the Atlantic,** el Duero desemboca en el Atlántico. **2** *(sea)* subir. **3** *(traffic)* circular. **4** *fig (ideas, information, people)* correr. ■ **f. chart,** diagrama *m* de flujo; *Comput* organigrama *m*.

flower ['flaʊəʳ] **I** *n* **1** *Bot* flor *f*; **in f.,** en flor; **bunch of flowers,** ramo *m* de flores. ■ **f. bed,** arriate *m*, parterre *m*; **f. show,** exposición *f* de flores. **2** *fig* flor *f*; **in the f. of youth,** en la flor de la juventud. **II** *vi (blossom, bloom)* florecer.

flowered ['flaʊəd] *adj (patterned)* floreado,-a.

flowering ['flaʊərɪŋ] **I** *adj* **f. plant,** planta *f* florida. **II** *n fig (blossoming)* floración *f*, florecimiento *m*.

flowerpot ['flaʊəpɒt] *n* maceta *f*, tiesto *m*.

flowery ['flaʊrɪ] *adj (pattern)* de flores; *fig (elaborate style)* florido,-a; **a f. apron,** un delantal de flores.

flowing ['fləʊɪŋ] *adj (water)* que fluye; *(hair)* suelto,-a; *(dress)* de mucho vuelo; *(style)* fluido,-a, suelto,-a; *(shape, movement)* natural.

flown [fləʊn] *pp see* **fly.**

flu [fluː] *n (abbr of influenza)* gripe *f*.

fluctuate ['flʌktjʊeɪt] *vi* fluctuar.

fluctuating ['flʌktjʊeɪtɪŋ] *adj* fluctuante.

fluctuation [flʌktjʊ'eɪʃən] *n* fluctuación *f*, variación *f*.

flue [fluː] *n Archit* conducto *m* de humos; *(chimney)* cañón *m*; *(stove)* orificios *mpl* de ventilación.

fluency ['fluːənsɪ] *n* fluidez *f*; **f. in Russian,** dominio *m* del ruso.

fluent ['fluːənt] *adj* **1** *(articulate, eloquent)* fluido,-a, elocuente. **2** *(languages)* **he speaks f. German,** habla el alemán con soltura.

fluff [flʌf] **I** *n (down, material)* pelusa *f*. **II** *vtr fam* hacer algo mal, hacer algo a destiempo; *Theat (bungle)* equivocar; **to f. one's lines,** equivocarse en su papel. ◆ **fluff up, fluff out** *vtr (cushion)* sacudir; *(hair, feathers)* encrespar, erizar, ensortijar; **the cock fluffed up his feathers,** el gallo se encrespó.

fluffy ['flʌfɪ] *adj (fluffier, fluffiest) (pillow)* mullido,-a; *(toy)* de peluche; *(cake)* esponjoso,-a.

fluid ['fluːɪd] **I** *adj* **1** *(movement, shape)* natural, con soltura. **2** *(flexible, variable)* flexible; *(politics etc)* incierto,-a. **II** *n* fluido *m*, líquido *m*. ■ **f. mechanics,** mecánica *f* de fluidos; **f. ounce,** onza *f* líquida.

fluidity [fluː'ɪdɪtɪ] *n* fluidez *f*; *(movement, shape)* soltura *f*.

fluke [fluːk] *n fam* chiripa *f*, churra *f*; **by a f.,** por *or* de chiripa.

fluk(e)y ['fluːkɪ] *adj (flukier, flukiest) fam (lucky)* **a f. goal,** un gol de churro *or* por churra.

flummox ['flʌməks] *vtr fam* desconcertar, despistar; **his question left me flummoxed,** su pregunta me dejó parado,-a.

flung [flʌŋ] *pt & pp see* **fling.**

flunk [flʌŋk] *vtr & vi esp US Canada NZ fam* catear, suspender; **I've flunked history,** me han suspendido en historia. ◆ **flunk out** *vi fam* suspender; **if you don't study you're gonna f. out,** si no empollas vas a catear.

flunk(e)y ['flʌŋkɪ] *n* **1** *fam* mayordomo *m*, lacayo *m*. **2** *pej (sycophant)* lameculos *mf inv*, pelota *mf*.

fluorescence [flʊə'resəns] *n* fluorescencia *f*.

fluorescent [flʊə'resənt] *adj (glowing)* fluorescente. ■ **f. lighting,** alumbrado *m* fluorescente.

fluoride ['flʊəraɪd] *n Chem* fluoruro *m*.

flurry ['flʌrɪ] *n* **1** *(wind)* ráfaga *f*; *(whirl)* **f. of snow,** nevato *m*. **2** *fig (bustle, excitement)* agitación *f*; **a f. of terrorism,** una oleada de terrorismo.

flush [flʌʃ] **I** *adj* **1** *(level)* nivelado,-a; **f. with,** a ras de. **2** *fam (replete)* desahogado,-a; **to be f.,** andar bien de dinero. **II** *n* **1** *(blush)* rubor *m*; *Med* **hot flushes,** sofocos *mpl*; **f. of anger,** acceso *m* de cólera; **in the first f. of victory,** en la euforia inicial de la victoria. **2** *Cards (poker)* color *m*. ■ **Royal f.,** escalera *f* real. **III** *vtr* **1** *(clean)* limpiar con agua; **to f. the lavatory,** tirar la cadena (del wáter); **to f. sth down the lavatory,** tirar algo al wáter. **2** *Hunt Mil (enemy, prey)* hacer salir; **the police flushed out the kidnappers,** la policía hizo salir a los secuestradores. **IV** *vi* **1** **the loo won't f.,** la cisterna del wáter no funciona. **2** *(blush)* ruborizarse; **to f. with anger,** ponerse rojo,-a de ira.

flushed [flʌʃt] *adj (cheeks)* rojo,-a, encendido,-a; *fig* **f. with success,** emocionado,-a ante el éxito.

fluster ['flʌstəʳ] *vtr (bother)* molestar, marear; **to get flustered,** ponerse nervioso,-a.

flute [fluːt] *n Mus* flauta *f*.

fluted ['fluːtɪd] *adj Archit* acanalado,-a.

flutist ['fluːtɪs] *n US* flautista *mf*.

flutter ['flʌtəʳ] **I** *vi* **1** *(leaves, birds)* revolotear; *fig (flit)* **she fluttered about the room,** revoloteaba por la habitación. **2** *(flag)* ondear. **II** *vtr* **to f. one's eyelashes,** parpadear. **III** *n (flap)* agitación *f*; **to be in a f.,** estar nervioso,-a. **2** *fam (gambling)* apuesta *f* pequeña.

fluvial ['fluːvɪəl] *adj* fluvial.

flux [flʌks] *n (flow)* flujo *m*; *(instability)* inestabilidad *f*; *fig* **to be in a state of f.,** estar cambiando constantemente.

fly[1] [flaɪ] **I** *vtr (pt flew; pp flown)* **1** *Av* pilotar. **2** *Av (merchandize, troops)* transportar. **3** *(travel)* sobrevolar; **to f. the Atlantic,** sobrevolar el Atlántico. **4** *(hoist)* izar. **5** *(kite)* hacer volar. **II** *vi* **1** *(bird, plane)* volar; *fig* **the bird has flown,** el pájaro voló. **2** *(go by plane)* ir en avión. **3** *(flag)* estar izado,-a. **4** *(sparks)* saltar; **the door flew open,** la puerta se abrió de golpe. **5** atacar, insultar; **to f. into a rage,** montar en cólera; **to let f. at sb,** asestarle un golpe a algn, empezar a insultar a algn; *fam fig* **to f. off the handle,** salirse de sus casillas. **6** *(rush)* irse volando; **I must f.,** me voy volando; **the train flew past,** el tren pasó volando. **7** *(fall)* caerse; *fam* **to go flying,** caerse; **he slipped and went flying,** resbaló y se cayó; *fam* **to send sb flying,** mandar a algn por los aires. **III** *n* **1** *(also f. sheet) (paper)* hoja *f* suelta; *(of tent)* doble techo *m*. **2** flies, bragueta *f sing*.

fly[2] [flaɪ] *n* **1** *Ent* mosca *f*; *fig* **she wouldn't hurt a f.,** es incapaz de matar una mosca; *fam fig* **there are no flies on him,** no se chupa el dedo; *fam fig* **they're dropping like flies,** caen como moscas. ■ **f. spray,** spray *m* matamoscas, matamoscas *m inv*. **2** *Fishing (bait)* mosca *f*.

fly[3] [flaɪ] *adj GB fam* avispado,-a, astuto,-a.

flyby ['flaɪbaɪ] *n (pl flybys) US Av* desfile *m* aéreo.

fly-by-night ['flaɪbaɪnaɪt] *adj fam* de poca confianza, pesetero,-a.

flycatcher ['flaɪkætʃəʳ] *n Orn* papamoscas *m inv*. ■ **pied f.,** papamoscas *m inv* cerrojillo; **spotted f.,** papamoscas *m inv* gris.

flyer ['flaɪəʳ] *n see* **flier.**

fly-fishing ['flaɪfɪʃɪŋ] *n Fishing* pesca *f* con moscas *or* al lanzado.

flying ['flaɪɪŋ] **I** *adj (soaring)* volante; *(rapid)* rápido,-a; *Sport* **a f. start,** una salida lanzada; **a f. visit,** una visita relámpago; *fig* **to come out of an affair with f. colours,** salir airoso,-a de un asunto; *fig* **to get off to a f. start,** empezar con buen pie. ■ *Archit* **f. buttress,** arbotante *m*; *Austral* **f. doctor,** médico *m* que viaja en avión para visitar a sus pacientes; **f. fish,** pez *m* volador; **f. picket,** piquete *m* (informativo); **f. saucer,** platillo *m* volante; **f. squad,** patrulla *f* volante. **II** *n* **1** *(action)* vuelo *m*. **2**

(aviation) aviación *f*; **fear of f.,** miedo *m* a volar. ■ **f. school,** escuela *f* de aviación; **f. hours,** horas *fpl* de vuelo.

flyleaf ['flaɪliːf] *n (pl flyleaves* ['flaɪliːvz]*) (of book)* guarda *f*.

flyover ['flaɪəʊvəʳ] *n* paso *m* elevado.

flypaper ['flaɪpeɪpəʳ] *n* tira *f* de papel matamoscas, matamoscas *m inv*.

flypast ['flaɪpɑːst] *n GB Av* desfile *m* aéreo.

flyweight ['flaɪweɪt] *n Box* peso *m* mosca.

foal [fəʊl] *Zool* I *n* potro,-a *m,f*; *(mare)* **in f.,** preñada. II *vi (mare)* parir.

foam [fəʊm] I *n (froth)* espuma *f*. ■ **f. bath,** espuma *f* de baño; **f. rubber,** (goma) espuma *f*; **shaving f.,** espuma *f* de afeitar. II *vi (bubble)* hacer espuma; *(froth)* **to f. at the mouth,** echar espumarajos; *fig* echar espumarajos de cólera.

foamy ['fəʊmɪ] *adj (foamier, foamiest)* espumoso,-a.

fob [fɒb] I *n (chain)* cadenilla *f* de reloj. II *vtr (pt & pp fobbed) fam* engañar; **to f. sb off with excuses,** darle largas a algn. ◆ **fob off** *vtr fam* colocar (**on,** a); *(unload on)* **he fobbed off his old radio on a stranger,** le colocó su radio vieja a un desconocido.

focal ['fəʊkəl] *adj* focal. ■ *Opt* **f. point,** foco *m*; *fig* punto *m* de referencia.

focus ['fəʊkəs] I *vtr (pt & pp focused or focussed)* centrarse (**on,** en), fijarse (**on,** en); **all eyes focused on him,** todas las miradas recayeron sobre él. II *vi* enfocar; **to f. on sth,** *Phot* enfocar algo; *fig* centrarse en algo. III *n* 1 *(pl focuses or focusses or foci* ['fəʊsaɪ]*) Phys Opt* foco *m*; **to be in f./out of f.,** estar enfocado,-a/desenfocado,-a. 2 *fig* foco *m*, centro *m*; **to be the f. of attention,** ser el centro de la atención.

focus(s)ing ['fəʊkəsɪŋ] *n* enfoque *m*.

fodder ['fɒdəʳ] *n* forraje *m*, pienso *m*. ■ *fig iron* **cannon f.,** carne *f* de cañón.

foe [fəʊ] *n fml* enemigo,-a *m,f*.

foetal ['fiːtəl] *adj* fetal; **f. position,** posición *f* fetal.

foetus ['fiːtəs] *n Biol* feto *m*.

fog [fɒg] I *n* niebla *f*, bruma *f*, neblina *f*. II *vtr (pt & pp fogged) (glass)* empañar; *fig* **to f. the issue,** complicar el asunto. ◆ **fog up** *vi* empañarse.

fogbound ['fɒgbaʊnd] *adj* inmovilizado,-a *or* paralizado,-a por la niebla.

fogey ['fəʊgɪ] *n (pl fogeys) fam* carca *mf*, persona *f* chapada a la antigua; **old f.,** cascarrabias *mf inv*.

foggy ['fɒgɪ] *adj (foggier, foggiest)* nubloso,-a, brumoso,-a; **a f. day,** un día de niebla; **it is f.,** hay niebla; *fam* **I haven't the foggiest (idea),** no tengo la más mínima idea.

foghorn ['fɒghɔːn] *n Naut* sirena *f* (de niebla).

foglamp ['fɒglæmp] *n, US* **foglight** ['fɒglaɪt] *n Aut* faro *m* antiniebla.

foible ['fɔɪbəl] *n (peculiarity)* extravagancia *f*; *(fad)* manía *f*; *(weakness)* punto *m* flaco, debilidad *f*.

foil [fɔɪl] I *n* 1 *Metal* hoja *f* de metal. ■ **aluminium f.,** papel *m* de aluminio; *fam* papel *m* de plata. 2 *Fenc* florete *m*. 3 *contraste m*; **to act as a f. to,** hacer resaltar, realzar. II *vtr (plot)* frustrar.

foist [fɔɪst] *vtr fam* coaccionar; **to f. sth on sb,** colocarle algo a algn; **to f. oneself on sb,** pegarse a algn.

fold [fəʊld] I *n* 1 *(for sheep)* redil *m*, aprisco *m*. 2 *(crease)* pliegue *m*. II *vtr* plegar, doblar; **to f. up a chair,** plegar una silla; **to f. one's arms,** cruzar los brazos. III *vi* **to f. (up),** *(chair etc)* plegarse, doblarse; *Com* quebrar.

folder ['fəʊldəʳ] *n* carpeta *f*.

folding ['fəʊldɪŋ] *adj* plegable. ■ **f. ladder,** escalera *f* de tijera; **f. table,** mesa *f* plegable.

foliage ['fəʊlɪɪdʒ] *n Bot* follaje *m*.

folio ['fəʊlɪəʊ] *n* 1 *(sheet)* folio *m*. 2 *(volume)* libro *m* en folio.

folk [fəʊk] I *npl* 1 *(people)* gente *f*; **old f.,** la gente mayor. 2 *fam* **folks,** *(friends)* amigos *mpl*; **hello f.!,** ¿qué tal chicos? 3 *fam* **folks,** *(family)* padres *mpl*; **one's f.,** la familia. II *adj* popular; **f. customs,** costumbres populares; **f. music,** música folk; **f. singer,** cantante de música folk; **f. song,** canción tradicional, canción folk.

folklore ['fəʊklɔː] *n* folklore *m*.

follow ['fɒləʊ] I *vtr (gen)* seguir; *(pursue)* perseguir; *(film, events)* seguir; *(advice, example, orders, etc)* seguir; *(understand)* comprender; *(way of life)* llevar; *(hobby, faith)* seguir; *(profession)* ejercer; **do yon f. the rock scene?,** ¿te interesa el rock?; *Ftb* **he follows Hull City,** es un seguidor del Hull City; **I don't f. (you),** no (te) entiendo; **she is being followed,** la están siguiendo; **they f. a life of total abstinence,** llevan una vida de abstinencia total; *fam* **f. your nose,** sigue todo recto. II *vi* 1 *(come after, ensue)* seguir; **as follows,** a saber; **to f. close behind,** seguir muy cerca; **and to f., a delicious paella,** y a continuación, una deliciosa paella. 2 *(result)* resultar; **it follows that ...,** resulta que ..., se sigue que ...; **that doesn't f.,** eso no es lógico. 3 *(understand)* entender, comprender, seguir; **do you f.?,** ¿entiendes?, ¿me sigues? ◆ **follow about, follow around** *vtr* seguir por todas partes. ◆ **follow on** *vi* 1 venir detrás. 2 *(result)* ser la consecuencia lógica (**from,** de). ◆ **follow out** *vtr (plan)* ejecutar. ◆ **follow through, follow up** *vtr (idea)* llevar a cabo; *(clue)* investigar.

follower ['fɒləʊəʳ] *n* seguidor,-a *m,f*, partidario,-a *m,f*.

following ['fɒləʊɪŋ] I *adj* siguiente; **listen to the f.,** escuche lo siguiente; **the f. day,** al día siguiente. II *n* seguidores *mpl*, partidarios *mpl*, admiradores *mpl*; **he has a large f.,** tiene muchos admiradores.

follow-my-leader [fɒləʊmaɪˈliːdəʳ] *n* juego *m* de seguir al rey.

follow-up ['fɒləʊʌp] *n* continuación *f*.

folly ['fɒlɪ] *n* locura *f*, desatino *m*.

foment [fəˈment] *vtr* instigar.

fond [fɒnd] *adj* 1 *(loving)* cariñoso,-a, tierno,-a. 2 *(partial to)* aficionado,-a; **to be f. of sb,** tenerle mucho cariño a algn; **she is f. of music,** tiene afición a la música; **to be f. of doing sth,** ser aficionado,-a a hacer algo. 3 *(hope)* fervoroso,-a. ◆ **fondly** *adv (naïvely)* ingenuamente; **I f. believed that we could win,** creí ingenuamente que podíamos ganar.

fondness ['fɒndnɪs] *n* 1 *(love)* cariño *m* (**for,** a). 2 *(liking)* afición *f* (**for,** a).

fondle ['fɒndəl] *vtr* acariciar.

fondue ['fɒndjuː] *n Culin* fondue *f*.

font [fɒnt] *n Rel* pila *f*.

food [fuːd] *n* comida *f*, alimento *m*; **f. and drink,** comida y bebida *f*; **I like Greek f.,** me gusta la comida griega; **I'm off my f.,** he perdido el apetito; *fig* **to give sb f. for thought,** darle a algn en qué pensar. ■ *Ecol* **f. chain,** cadena *f* trófica *or* alimentaria; **f. department,** sección *f* de alimentación; **f. poisoning,** intoxicación *f* alimenticia; **f. supplies,** víveres *mpl*.

foodstuffs ['fuːdstʌfs] *npl* alimentos *mpl*, productos *mpl* alimenticios.

fool [fuːl] I *n* 1 tonto,-a *m,f*, imbécil *mf*; **don't be a f.,** no seas tonto,-a; **to feel a f.,** sentirse ridículo,-a; **to make a f. of sb,** poner a algn en ridículo; **to play the f.,** hacer el tonto. ■ **f.'s errand,** trabajo *m* inútil; **f.'s paradise,** mundo *m* irreal *or* de ensueño. 2 *Culin* ≈ mousse *f* de fruta. 3 *(jester)* bufón,-ona *m,f*. II *US adj* tonto,-a; **what a f. thing to say,** ¡vaya estupidez decir aquello! III *vtr (deceive)* engañar. IV *vi* 1 *(joke)* bromear. 2 *(mess around)* **to f. about** *or* **around,** hacer el tonto.

foolhardy ['fuːlhɑːdɪ] *adj (foolhardier, foolhardiest)* temerario,-a; *(person)* intrépido,-a.

foolish ['fuːlɪʃ] *adj (silly)* tonto,-a; *(unwise)* estúpido,-a; **that would be f.,** eso sería imprudente; **to do sth f.,** hacer una tontería; **to look f.,** parecer ridículo,-a.

foolishness ['fuːlɪʃnɪs] *n* estupidez *f.*

foolproof ['fuːlpruːf] *adj (plan, method, device)* infalible; **a f. machine,** una máquina fácil de usar y segura.

foolscap ['fuːlskæp] *n Print* pliego *m*, folio *m.*

foot [fʊt] **I** *n (pl feet* [fiːt]) **1** *Anat* pie *m; Zool* pata *f;* **to be on one's feet,** estar de pie; *(after illness)* levantarse; **to go on f.,** ir a pie *o* andando; **to leap to one's feet,** levantarse de un salto; **to set f. in,** entrar; **wipe your feet,** límpiate los pies; *fig* **he didn't put a f. wrong,** no se equivocó; *fig* **to drag one's feet,** hacerse el remolón *or* el roncero; *fig* **to fall on one's feet,** tener buena suerte; *fig* **to find one's feet,** acostumbrarse, situarse; *fig* **to have one's feet on the ground,** ser realista; *fig* **to put one's best f. forward,** esmerarse; *fig* **to stand on one's own two feet,** valerse por si mismo, ser independiente; *fam fig* **to get off on the wrong f.,** empezar con mal pie; *fam fig* **to have** *or* **get cold feet,** tener miedo; *fam fig* **to put one's f. down,** *(control)* imponerse; *(car)* pisar a fondo; *fam fig* **to put one's f. in it,** meter la pata; *fam fig* **to put one's feet up,** descansar. ■ **f. soldier,** soldado *m* de infantería. **2** *(of stairs, hill)* pie *m;* **at the f. of the page,** a pie de página; **at the f. of the bed,** a los pies de la cama. **3** *(of shoe, stocking)* pie *m.* **4** *Mus* pie *m.* **5** *(in poetry)* pie *m.* **II** *vtr* **1** to **f. it,** ir a pie. **2** *(pay)* pagar; **to f. the bill,** pagar la cuenta.

footage ['fʊtɪdʒ] *n Cin* metraje *m.*

foot-and-mouth disease [fʊtən'maʊθdɪziːz] *n* fiebre *f* aftosa.

football ['fʊtbɔːl] *n* **1** *(soccer)* fútbol *m.* ■ **bar f.,** futbolín *m;* **f. ground,** campo *m* de fútbol; **f. match,** partido *m* de fútbol; **f. pools,** quinielas *fpl.* **2** *(ball)* balón *m.*

footballer ['fʊtbɔːləʳ] *n* futbolista *mf.*

footbridge ['fʊtbrɪdʒ] *n* puente *m* para peatones.

foothills ['fʊthɪlz] *npl Geog* estribaciones *fpl.*

foothold ['fʊthəʊld] *n* hueco *m* para apoyar el pie; *fig* **to gain a f.,** afianzarse en una posición.

footing ['fʊtɪŋ] *n* **1** *(balance)* equilibrio *m;* **to lose one's f.,** perder el equilibrio. **2** *fig* base *f*, nivel *m;* **on a friendly f.,** en plan amistoso; **on an equal f.,** en igualdad.

footlights ['fʊtlaɪts] *npl Theat* candilejas *fpl.*

footling ['fʊtlɪŋ] *adj arch* fútil, trivial.

footman ['fʊtmən] *n (pl footmen)* lacayo *m.*

footnote ['fʊtnəʊt] *n* nota *f* a pie de página.

footpath ['fʊtpɑːθ] *n (track)* sendero *m*, camino *m.*

footprint ['fʊtprɪnt] *n* huella *f*, pisada *f.*

footrest ['fʊtrest] *n (on motorbike)* reposapiés *m inv.*

footsore ['fʊtsɔːʳ] *adj* con los pies doloridos.

footstep ['fʊtstep] *n* paso *m*, pisada *f; fig* **to follow in sb's footsteps,** seguir los pasos de algn, imitar a algn.

footwear ['fʊtweəʳ] *n* calzado *m.*

footwork ['fʊtwɜːk] *n Sport* juego *m* de pies.

fop [fɒp] *n arch* lechuguino *m.*

foppish ['fɒpɪʃ] *adj arch* afeminado,-a.

for [fɔːʳ] **I** *prep* **1** *(intended)* para; **curtains f. the bedroom,** cortinas para el dormitorio; **f. sale,** en venta; **it's not f. eating,** no es para comer; **it's time f. bed,** es hora de acostarse. **2** *(representing)* por; **a cheque f. ten pounds,** un cheque *(por valor)* de diez libras; **'fag' is slang f. cigarette,** en argot cigarillo es pitillo; **J f. John,** J de Juan; **the MP f. Oxford,** el diputado por Oxford; **what's the Spanish f. 'rivet'?,** ¿cómo se dice 'rivet' en español? **3** *(purpose)* para; **it's good f. the digestion,** es bueno para la digestión; **this knob is f. the volume,** este botón es el del volumen; **to study f. an exam,** estudiar para un examen; **what's this f.?,** ¿para qué sirve esto? **4** *(because of)* por; **but f. that,** a no ser por eso; **famous f. its cuisine,** famoso,-a por su cocina; **I couldn't hear f. the noise,** no pude oír nada por el ruido; **if it weren't f.**

him, si no fuera por él; **to jump f. joy,** saltar de alegría. **5** *(on behalf of)* por; **I can do it f. myself,** puedo hacerlo yo solo; **I speak f. everybody,** hablo por todos; **open the door f. me,** ábreme la puerta; **the campaign f. peace,** la campaña por la paz; **to die f. one's country,** morir por la patria; **will you do it f. me?,** ¿lo harás por mí? **6** *(during)* por, durante; **I hadn't seen him f. two years,** hacía dos años que no le veía; **I lent it to her f. a year,** se lo presté por un año; **I shall stay f. two weeks,** me quedaré dos semanas; **I was ill f. a month,** estuve enfermo,-a durante un mes; **I've been here f. three months,** hace tres meses que estoy aquí; **she has been studying f. a year,** lleva un año estudiando. **7** *(distance)* por; **I walked f. ten kilometres,** caminé diez kilómetros. **8** *(at a point in time)* para; **can you do it f. tomorrow?,** ¿puedes hacerlo para mañana?; **f. my birthday,** para mi cumpleaños; **f. the first/last time,** por primera/última vez; **we have a meeting arranged f. next Thursday,** hemos convenido un mítin para el jueves que viene. **9** *(destination)* para; **he left f. France,** partió para Francia; **the train f. London,** el tren para *or* de Londres. **10** *(amount of money)* por; **I got the car f. five hundred pounds,** conseguí el coche por quinientas libras; **the painting went f. six million,** la pintura se vendió por seis millones. **11** *(in favour of)* en favor de; **are yon in f. or against?,** ¿estás a favor o en contra?; **I'm all f. telling the truth,** soy partidario,-a de decir la verdad, **to vote f. sb** *or* **sth,** votar por algn *or* algo, **we argued f. a stop to the violence,** insistimos en la necesidad de acabar con la violencia; **who's f. a drink?,** ¿quién quiere una copa? **12** *(to obtain)* para, **f. further details apply to ...,** para mayor información diríjanse a ..., **to run f. the bus,** correr para coger el autobús, **to send sb f. water,** mandar a algn a por agua **13** *(with respect to, concerning)* en cuanto a, **are you all right f. money?,** ¿qué tal andas de dinero?, **as f. him,** en cuanto a él; **f. all I care,** por mí; **f. all I know,** que yo sepa, **f. all the good it has done us,** teniendo en cuenta de lo poco que nos ha servido, **f. one thing,** para empezar. **14** *(despite)* a pesar de, **f. all his faults,** con *or* a pesar de todos sus defectos, **f. all that,** aún así, con todo y eso, **he's tall f. his age,** está muy alto para su edad **15** *(instead of)* por, **can you go f. me?,** puede ir por mí? **16** *(towards)* hacia, por, **affection f. sb,** cariño hacia algn; **his love f. you,** su amor por ti, **respect f. sb,** respeto para algn **17** *(as regards)* **to leave sb f. dead,** dar a algn por muerto,-a, **what do you use f. fuel?,** ¿qué utilizan como combustible? **18** *(in exchange)* por, **f. every success there are two failures,** por cada éxito hay dos fracasos, **to exchange one thing f. another,** cambiar una cosa por otra, **to buy/sell sth f. five pounds,** comprar/vender algo por cinco libras **19** *(+ object + infin)* **there's no reason f. us to quarrel,** no hay motivo para que riñamos, **he signalled f. the car to stop,** hizo señas al coche para que parara, **it's time f. you to go,** es hora de que os marchéis, **it's best f. you to leave,** más vale que te vayas, **it would be a pity f. you to resign,** sería una lástima que dimitieras; **it's easy f. him to say that,** le es fácil decir eso **20** *(exclamation)* **oh f. a drink!,** ¡ojalá tuviera una copa!, **that's politicians f. you!,** ¡mira cómo son los políticos!, *fam* **you'll be f. it!,** ¡te la vas a cargar! **II** *conj (since, as)* ya que, puesto que

forage ['fɒrɪdʒ] **I** *n Agr* forraje *m.* **II** *vi* hurgar, fisgar, **to f. about in a drawer,** hurgar en un cajón

foray ['fɒreɪ] *n* **1** *(raid)* correría *f*, incursión *f;* *(plundering)* saqueo *m* **2** *(excursion)* ecursión *f.*

forbade [fɔː'beɪd] *pt see* **forbid.**

forbear [fɔː'beəʳ] *vtr (pt forbore, pp forborne)* abstenerse (**from,** de)

forbearance [fɔː'beərəns] *n* paciencia *f*, comprensión *f*

forbid [fə'bɪd] *vtr (pt forbade; pp forbidden* [fə'bɪdən]) prohibir, *Rel* **forbidden fruit,** fruta *f* prohibida, **smoking is forbidden,** está prohibido fumar, **to f. sb to do sth,** prohibirle a algn hacer algo

forbidding [fə'bɪdɪŋ] *adj* **1** *(stern)* severo,-a, *(bleak)* inhóspito,-a **2** *(task)* difícil, peligroso,-a

forbore [fɔː'bɔːʳ] *pt,* **forborne** [fɔː'bɔːn] *pp see* **forbear.**

force [fɔːs] **I** *n* **1** fuerza *f*, **by f. of habit**, por la fuerza de la costumbre, **the f. of the earthquake**, la fuerza del terramoto, **the forces of nature**, las fuerza de la naturaleza **2** *(strength)* fuerza *f*, **brute f.**, fuerza bruta, **to join forces**, unirse **3** *(violence)* **by f.**, a *or* por la fuerza, **by sheer f.**, a viva fuerza **4** *Mil* cuerpo *m* ■ **the (armed) forces**, las fuerzas armadas; **the police f.**, la policía, *Ind* **labour f.**, mano *f* de obra, **to turn up in f.**, llegar en gran número **5** *(law etc)* **to come into f.**, entrar en vigor **II** *vtr* **1** *(oblige, coerce)* forzar, obligar, **I was forced to do it**, me obligaron a hacerlo, **to f. sb to do sth**, forzar a algn a hacer algo, **to f. sth on sb**, obligar a algn a aceptar algo **2** *(break open, prise)* forzar ◆ **force back** *vtr* **1** *(enemy)* hacer retroceder **2** *(tears, emotions)* contener ◆ **force down** *vtr* **1** *(plane)* obligar a aterrizar **2** *(food)* tragar a duras penas.

forced [fɔːst] *adj* **1** *(labour, march)* forzado,-a. ■ *Av* **f. landing**, aterrizaje *m* forzoso **2** *(smile, laugh)* forzado,-a

force-feed [ˈfɔːsfiːd] *vtr (pt & pp* **force-fed** [ˈfɔːsfed]*)* alimentar a la fuerza

forceful [ˈfɔːsful] *adj* **1** *(person, manner)* enérgico,-a, contundente **2** *(argument)* convincente

forcible [ˈfɔːsəbəl] *adj Jur* **f. entry**, allanamiento *m* de morada ◆ **forcibly** *adv* a *or* por la fuerza.

forceps [ˈfɔːseps] *npl Med* fórceps *m sing*; *Dent* gatillo *m sing*

ford [fɔːd] *Geog* **I** *n* vado *m* **II** *vtr* vadear.

fore¹ [fɔːʳ] **I** *adj Naut* delantero,-a; **f. and aft**, de popa a proa **II** *n* parte *f* delantera; *fig* **to come to the f.**, empezar a destacar

fore² [fɔːʳ] *interj Golf* ¡atención!

forearm [ˈfɔːrɑːm] *n Anat* antebrazo *m*

forebear [ˈfɔːbeəʳ] *n (usu pl)* antepasado *m*

foreboding [fɔːˈbəʊdɪŋ] *n* presentimiento *m*

forecast [ˈfɔːkɑːst] **I** *n* previsión *f*; pronóstico *m*. ■ **weather f.**, parte *m* meteorológico. **II** *vtr (pt & pp* **forecast** *or* **forecasted***)* pronosticar.

forecourt [ˈfɔːkɔːt] *n (of garage)* área *f* de servicio.

forefathers [ˈfɔːfɑːðəz] *npl* antepasados *mpl*

forefront [ˈfɔːfrʌnt] *n* vanguardia *f*; **to be in the f.**, estar a la vanguardia

forego [fɔːˈgəʊ] *vtr fml (pt* **forewent**; *pp* **foregone***)* sacrificar; **she forewent her holiday to be with her family**, no se marchó de vacaciones para estar con su familia

foregoing [fɔːˈgəʊwɪŋ] *adj* precedente, *(aforementioned)* susodicho,-a.

foregone [ˈfɔːgɒn] **I** *pp of* **forego**. **II** *adj* **a f. conclusion**, un resultado inevitable

foreground [ˈfɔːgraʊnd] *n* primer plano *m*.

forehead [fɒrɪd, ˈfɔːhed] *n Anat* frente *f*

foreign [ˈfɒrɪn] *adj* **1** *(from abroad)* extranjero,-a; **f. language**, lengua extranjera, **f. travel**, viajes al *or* en el extranjero ■ **the F. Legion**, la Legión Extranjera; *Fin* **f. exchange**, divisas *fpl*. **2** *(trade, policy)* exterior, **the F. Office**, el Ministerio de Asuntos Exteriores. **3** *(strange, extraneous)* ajeno,-a; *Med* **f. body**, cuerpo extraño.

foreigner [ˈfɒrɪnəʳ] *n* extranjero,-a *m,f*

foreman [ˈfɔːmən] *n (pl* **foremen***)* **1** *Ind* capataz *m*. **2** *Jur* presidente *m* del jurado

foremost [ˈfɔːməʊst] *adj* primero,-a, principal, **first and f.**, ante todo

forename [ˈfɔːneɪm] *n* nombre *m* de pila

forensic [fəˈrensɪk] *adj* forense; **f. medicine**, medicina *f* forense

forerunner [ˈfɔːrʌnəʳ] *n* precursor,-a *m,f*

foresaw [fɔːˈsɔː] *pt see* **foresee**.

foresee [fɔːˈsiː] *vtr (pt* **foresaw***, pp* **foreseen***)* prever.

foreseeable [fɔːˈsiːəbəl] *adj* previsible, **in the f. future**, en un futuro próximo, **for the f. future**, por mucho tiempo

foreseen [fɔːˈsiːn] *pp see* **foresee**.

foreshadow [fɔːˈʃædəʊ] *vtr* presagiar, anunciar

foresight [ˈfɔːsaɪt] *n* previsión *f*, **lack of f.**, imprevisión *f*, **to have f.**, ser previsor,-a

foreskin [ˈfɔːskɪn] *n Anat* prepucio *m*

forest [ˈfɒrɪst] *n (large)* selva *f*; *(small)* bosque *m*. ■ **f. fire**, incendio *m* forestal.

forestall [fɔːˈstɔːl] *vtr (plan)* anticiparse; *(danger)* prevenir.

forester [ˈfɒrɪstəʳ] *n* guardabosques *m inv*.

forestry [ˈfɒrɪstrɪ] *n* silvicultura *f*, selvicultura *f*.

foretaste [ˈfɔːteɪst] *n* anticipo *m*, anticipación *f* **(of**, de).

foretell [fɔːˈtel] *vtr (pt & pp* **foretold***)* presagiar, pronosticar.

forethought [ˈfɔːθɔːt] *n* previsión *f*; *Jur* premeditación *f*.

foretold [fɔːˈtəʊld] *pt & pp see* **foretell**.

forever [fəˈrevəʳ] *adv* **1** *(eternally)* siempre. **2** *(for good)* para siempre. **3** *fam (ages)* siglos *mpl*, mucho tiempo; **I've been reading this book f.**, llevo siglos leyendo este libro. **4** *(constantly)* siempre; **they're f. digging up the roads**, no paran de hacer obras. **5** *(long live)* ¡viva!; **Liverpool f.!**, ¡viva el Liverpool!

forewarn [fɔːˈwɔːn] *vtr* prevenir; *prov* **forewarned is forearmed**, hombre prevenido vale por dos.

forewent [fɔːˈwent] *pt see* **forego**

forewoman [ˈfɔːwʊmən] *n (pl* **forewomen** [ˈfɔːwɪmɪn]*)* **1** *Ind* encargada *f*. **2** *Jur* presidenta *f* del jurado.

foreword [ˈfɔːwɜːd] *n lit* prefacio *m*, prólogo *m*.

forfeit [ˈfɔːfɪt] **I** *adj* perdido,-a. **II** *n (penalty)* pena *f*, multa *f (in games)* prenda *f*; **to pay a f.**, pagar prenda. **III** *vtr* perder; *(declare)* comisar; **he was forced to f. all his property**, tuvo que renunciar a todas sus propiedades.

forfeiture [ˈfɔːfeɪtʃəʳ] *n* pérdida *f*.

forgave [fəˈgeɪv] *pt see* **forgive**.

forge [fɔːdʒ] **I** *n* **1** *(fire)* fragua *f*. **2** *(blacksmith's)* herrería *f*. **II** *vtr* **1** *(counterfeit)* falsificar. **2** forjar; fig **to f. a friendship/an alliance**, forjar una amistad/una alianza, **III** *vi* **to f. ahead**, hacer grandes progresos.

forger [ˈfɔːdʒəʳ] *n* falsificador,-a *m,f*.

forgery [ˈfɔːdʒərɪ] *n* falsificación *f*.

forget [fəˈget] **I** *vtr (pt* **forgot***; pp* **forgotten***)*, olvidar, olvidarse de; **and don't you f. it!**, ¡no lo olvides!; **f. it!**, ¡déjalo!; **I forgot that ...**, olvidé que ..., se me olvidó que ...; **I forgot to close the window**, se me olvidó cerrar la ventana; **I shall never f. you**, nunca me olvidaré de ti; **I've forgotten my key**, he olvidado la llave; **never to be forgotten**, inolvidable; **not forgetting ...**, sin olvidar ...; **to f. how to do sth**, olvidar cómo se hace algo; **to f. oneself**, perder los estribos, no poderse contener. **II** *vi* olvidar; **I f.**, no me acuerdo; **it's hard to f.**, es difícil olvidarlo.

forgetful [fəˈgetful] *adj* olvidadizo,-a, despistado,-a.

forgetfulness [fəˈgetfulnɪs] *n* falta *f* de memoria; *(overlook)* despiste *m*.

forget-me-not [fəˈgetmɪnɒt] *n Bot* nomeolvides *f inv*.

forgivable [fəˈgɪvəbəl] *adj* perdonable.

forgive [fəˈgɪv] *vtr (pt* **forgave***; pp* **forgiven** [fəˈgɪvən]*)* *(pardon)* perdonar, excusar; **f. my brother's impoliteness**, disculpe la mala educación de mi hermano; **to f. sb sth**, perdonarle algo a algn.

forgiveness [fəˈgɪvnɪs] *n* **1** *(pardon)* perdón *m*. **2** *(mercy)* clemencia *f*.

forgiving [fəˈgɪvɪŋ] *adj* **1** *(easy-going)* dispuesto,-a a perdonar. **2** *(merciful)* clemente.

forgo [fɔːˈgəʊ] *vtr (pt* **forwent***; pp* **forgone** [fɔːˈgɒn]*) see* **forego**.

forgot [fəˈgɒt] *pt*, **forgotten** [fəˈgɒtən] *pp see* **forget**.

fork [fɔːk] **I** n 1 *Agr* horca f, horquilla f. 2 (*cutlery*) tenedor m. 3 *Cycl* horquilla f. 4 (*in road*) bifurcación f. 5 *Mus* **tuning f.**, diapasón m. **II** vi (*of roads*) bifurcarse. ◆ **fork out** vtr *fam* (*money*) aflojar, soltar.

forked [fɔːkt] *adj* bifurcado,-a. ■ *Meteor* **f. lightning**, relámpago m en zigzag.

fork-lift truck [fɔːklɪf'trʌk] n carretilla f elevadora de horquilla.

forlorn [fə'lɔːn] *adj* 1 (*forsaken*) abandonado,-a. 2 (*desolate, wretched*) triste, melancólico,-a. 3 (*without hope*) desesperado,-a.

form [fɔːm] **I** n 1 (*type*) clase f, tipo m. 2 (*shape*) forma f; **in book f.**, en forma de libro; **in the f. of a cross**, en forma de cruz; **what f. does the disease take?**, ¿cómo se manifiesta la enfermedad? 3 (*formality*) formas fpl; **for f.'s sake**, para guardar las formas; **it's bad f.**, es de mala educación. 4 (*document*) formulario m; **application f.**, formulario m de solicitud. 5 (*condition*) forma f; **to be on f. /on top f./off f.**, estar en forma/en plena forma/en baja forma; (*mood*) **to be in good f.**, estar de buen humor; **true to f.**, como es de esperar. 6 *Educ* clase f; **the first/second f.**, el primer/segundo grado. 7 (*bench*) banco m. 8 (*style*) forma f; **sculpture is an ancient art f.**, la escultura es una forma de arte muy antigua. 9 *Ling* forma f. **II** vtr formar; **to f. a ring**, formar un corro; **to f. a government**, formar un gobierno; **to f. an impression**, formarse una impresión; **to f. part of sth**, formar parte de algo. **III** vi formarse; **a crowd formed outside the town hall**, se juntó una multitud frente al ayuntamiento.

formal [ˈfɔːməl] *adj* 1 (*public, official*) formal, oficial; **a f. application**, una solicitud en forma; **f. education**, educación convencional. 2 (*conventional*) (*party, dress*) de etiqueta; (*visit*) de cumplido. 3 (*ordered*) formal, ordenador,-a. 4 (*person, language*) formalista, ceremonioso,-a. ◆ **formally** *adv* formalmente, oficialmente; **f. dressed**, vestido,-a de etiqueta.

formality [fɔː'mælɪtɪ] n *Admin* formalidad f; **it's just a f.**, son sólo formalidades.

format [ˈfɔːmæt] **I** n formato m. **II** vtr (*pt & pp* **formatted**) *Comput* formatear.

formation [fɔː'meɪʃən] n (*arrangement*) formación f; (*development*) formación f; (*establishment*) creación f. ■ *Av* **f. flying**, vuelo m en formación; *Mil* **in battle f.**, en formación de combate.

formative [ˈfɔːmətɪv] *adj* formativo,-a; **f. years**, años mpl de formación.

former [ˈfɔːmə] *adj* 1 (*time*) anterior; **f. glories**, glorias pasadas. 2 (*former time*) antiguo,-a; (*person*) ex; **the f. champion**, el excampeón; **the hotel was a f. convent**, el hotel era un antiguo convento. 3 (*first*) aquél, aquélla, primero,-a; **Peter and Lisa came, the f. wearing a hat**, vinieron Peter y Lisa, aquél llevaba sombrero. ◆ **formerly** *adv* antiguamente.

Formica® [fɔː'maɪkə] n formica® f.

formidable [ˈfɔːmɪdəbəl] *adj* (*prodigious*) formidable; (*daunting, intimidating*) terrible.

formula [ˈfɔːmjʊlə] n (*pl* **formulae** [ˈfɔːmjʊliː] *or* **formulas**) fórmula f.

formulate [ˈfɔːmjʊleɪt] vtr formular.

fornicate [ˈfɔːnɪkeɪt] vtr *fml* fornicar.

forsake [fə'seɪk] vtr (*pt* **forsook** [fɔː'sʊk]; *pp* **forsaken** [fɔː'seɪkən]) *Lit* 1 (*abandon, desert*) abandonar. 2 (*give up*) renunciar a.

fort [fɔːt] n *Mil* fortaleza f, fuerte m; *fam fig* **to hold the f.**, quedarse vigilando.

forte [ˈfɔːteɪ] **I** n (*strong point*) fuerte m; **music is not my f.**, la música no es mi fuerte. **II** *adv Mus* forte.

forth [fɔːθ] *adv fml* **and so f.**, y así sucesivamente; **to go back and f.**, ir de acá para allá; (*onwards*) **from that day f.**, desde aquel día en adelante; *fnl* **to set f.**, ponerse en camino.

forthcoming [fɔːθ'kʌmɪŋ] *adj* 1 (*event*) próximo,-a, de próxima aparición. 2 (*available*) **no money was f.**, no hubo oferta de dinero. 3 (*communicative*) communicativo,-a; **he wasn't very f.**, estaba poco dispuesto a hablar.

forthright [ˈfɔːθraɪt] *adj* (*blunt, frank*) franco,-a; (*direct*) directo,-a.

fortieth [ˈfɔːtɪəθ] **I** *adj* cuadragésimo,-a. **II** n 1 (*in series*) cuadragésimo,-a m, f. 2 (*fraction*) cuarentavo m; *see also* **seventh**.

fortification [fɔːtɪfɪ'keɪʃən] n *Mil* fortificación f.

fortify [ˈfɔːtɪfaɪ] vtr (*pt & pp* **fortified**) *Mil* fortificar; *fig* fortalecer; **fortified wine**, vino m licoroso.

fortitude [ˈfɔːtɪtjuːd] n fortaleza f, fuerza f.

fortnight [ˈfɔːtnaɪt] n *GB* quince días mpl, quincena f; **a f.'s holiday**, dos semanas de vacaciones.

fortnightly [ˈfɔːtnaɪtlɪ] *GB* **I** *adj* quincenal. **II** *adv* cada quince días.

fortress [ˈfɔːtrɪs] n fortaleza f, fuerte m; (*city*) plaza f fuerte.

fortuitous [fɔː'tjuːɪtəs] *adj fml* (*accidental*) accidental, casual; (*lucky*) fortuito,-a.

fortunate [ˈfɔːtʃənɪt] *adj* afortunado,-a; **she was f.**, tuvo suerte; **it was f. that he came**, fue una suerte que viniera; **how f.!**, ¡qué suerte! ◆ **fortunately** *adv* afortunadamente, por suerte *or* fortuna.

fortune [ˈfɔːtʃən] n 1 (*luck*) suerte f; **he had the good f. to escape**, tuvo la suerte de escapar. 2 (*fate*) fortuna f; **the wheel of f.**, la rueda de la fortuna; **to tell sb's f.**, decir *or* echar la buenaventura a algn; *fml* **f. smiled on them**, la suerte les sonrió. ■ *US* **f. cookie**, galleta f de la buenaventura. 3 (*money*) fortuna f; **to make one's f.**, hacer (una) fortuna; *fam* **it cost a f.**, costó un dineral; *fam* **to be worth a f.**, valer una fortuna.

fortune-teller [ˈfɔːtʃəntelə] n echador,-a m, f de la buenaventura, adivino,-a m, f.

forty [ˈfɔːtɪ] **I** *adj* cuarenta inv; *fam* **to have f. winks**, echar una siestecita. **II** n cuarenta m inv; *see also* **seventy** and **seven**.

forum [ˈfɔːrəm] n (*pl* **forums** *or* **fora** [ˈfɔːrə]) foro m.

forward [ˈfɔːwəd] **I** *adv* 1 (*also* **forwards**) (*direction and movement*) hacia adelante; **leaning f.**, inclinado,-a hacia delante; **to go f.**, ir hacia adelante; **to step f.**, dar un paso adelante. 2 *fig* **carried f.**, suma y sigue; **to come f. (with help)**, ofrecerse (para ayudar). 3 (*time*) **from this day f.**, de ahora *or* de aquí en adelante; **to bring sth f.**, adelantar algo; **to look f. to sth**, esperar algo con ilusión; **to put the clock f.**, adelantar el reloj. 4 *Naut* hacia la proa. **II** *adj* 1 (*movement*) hacia adelante; **a f. movemeat**, un movimiento hacia adelante; (*position*) delantero,-a, frontal; **the f. section**, la sección delantera. ■ *Admin Com* **f. planning**, planificación f a largo plazo. 2 (*person*) fresco,-a, descarado,-a. **III** n *Sport* delantero,-a m, f. **IV** vtr 1 (*send on*) remitir; **please f.**, remítase al destinatario. 2 *fml* (*send goods*) expedir, enviar; **the goods will be forwarded on receipt of payment**, se enviarán las mercancías contra recibo del pago. 3 *fml* (*further*) adelantar, fomentar; **he tried to f. his career by ...**, intentó promocionarse hacienda ... .

forward-looking [ˈfɔːwədlʊkɪŋ] *adj* previsor,-a.

forwent [fɔː'went] *pt see* **forego**.

fossil [ˈfɒsəl] n fósil m. ■ **f. fuel**, combustible m fósil.

fossilized [ˈfɒsɪlaɪzd] *adj* fosilizado,-a.

foster [ˈfɒstə] **I** vtr 1 (*child*) criar. 2 *fml* (*cherish*) (*hopes, ideas*) abrigar; (*promote*) (*relations, business*) fomentar. **II** *adj* adoptivo,-a. ■ **f. child**, hijo,-a m, f adoptivo,-a; **f. father**, padre m adoptivo; **f. mother**, madre f adoptiva; **f. parents**, padres mpl adoptivos.

fought [fɔːt] *pt & pp see* **fight**.

foul [faʊl] **I** *adj* 1 (*smell*) fétido,-a; (*taste*) asqueroso,-a. 2 *lit* (*deed*) vil, atroz; **f. temper** *or* **weather**, humor m *or* tiempo *m* de perros. **3** (*language*) grosero,-a, obsceno,-a. **4** (*illegal*) **by fair means or f.,** por las buenas o por las malas, por fas o por nefas; **to fall f. of the law,** tener líos con la policía. ■ *Sport* **f. play,** juego *m* sucio; *Jur* **f. play is suspected,** se sospecha que se haya cometido un acto criminal. **II** *n Sport* falta *f*. **III** *vtr* **1** (*dirty*) ensuciar; (*air*) contaminar. **2** (*block a device*) atascar; (*get entangled with a net*) enredarse. **3** *Sport* cometer una falta. ◆ **foul up** *vtr fam* estropear, fastidiar; **he fouled up the whole plan,** echó por tierra todo el plan.

foul-mouthed [faʊl'maʊðd] *adj* malhablado,-a.

foul-smelling [faʊl'smelɪŋ] *adj* hediondo,-a.

found[1] [faʊnd] *pt & pp see* **find.**

found[2] [faʊnd] *vtr* **1** (*establish*) fundar. **2** (*base*) fundar, fundamentar (on, en); **founded on fact,** basado,-a en hechos.

found[3] [faʊnd] *vtr Tech* fundir.

foundation [faʊn'deɪʃən] *n* **1** (*establishment*) fundación *f*. ■ **f. stone,** primera piedra *f*. **2** (*basis*) fundamento *m*, base *f*; **without f.,** sin fundamento. ■ **f. course,** curso *m* común. **3** (*cosmetic*) **f. (cream),** maquillaje *m* de fondo. **4** *Constr* **foundations,** cimientos *mpl*; **to lay the foundations,** poner los cimientos.

founder[1] [faʊndə^r] *n* fundador,-a *m,f*.

founder[2] [faʊndə^r] *vi* **1** *fml* (*sink*) hundirse, irse a pique. **2** *fig* (*plan, hopes*) fracasar, malograrse; **the project foundered because of a lack of finance,** el proyecto se malogró por falta de financiación.

foundling [faʊndlɪŋ] *n lit* expósito,-a *m,f*.

foundry [faʊndrɪ] *n Ind* fundición *f*.

fount[1] [faʊnt] *n Print* fuente *f*.

fount[2] [faʊnt] *n Lit fig* fuente *f*; **it was the f. of all knowledge,** era la fuente de todos los conocimientos.

fountain [faʊntɪn] *n* (*structure*) fuente *f*; (*jet*) surtidor *m*; **drinking f.,** fuente de agua potable. ■ **f. pen,** pluma *f* estilográfica.

four [fɔː^r] **I** *adj* cuatro *inv*; **to the f. corners of the earth,** de una punta a otra del mundo. **II** *n* cuatro *m inv*; **on all fours,** a gatas; *see also* **seven.**

four-door [fɔːdɔː^r] *adj Aut* de cuatro puertas.

foureyes [fɔːraɪz] *n sl pej* cuatrojos *mf inv*.

four-letter [fɔːletə^r] *adj* **f. word,** palabrota *f*, taco *m*.

four-poster [fɔː'pəʊstə^r] *n* **f.-p. (bed),** cama *f* con colgadura.

foursome [fɔːsəm] *n* grupo *m* de cuatro personas.

fourteen [fɔː'tiːn] **I** *adj* catorce *inv*. **II** *n* catorce *m inv*; *see also* **seven.**

fourteenth [fɔː'tiːnθ] **I** *adj* decimocuarto,-a; **the f. century,** el siglo catorce. **II** *n* **1** (*in series*) decimocuarto,-a *m,f*. **2** (*fraction*) catorceavo *m*; *see also* **seventh.**

fourth [fɔːθ] **I** *adj* cuarto,-a; **the f. of June,** el cuatro de junio. **II** *n* **1** (*in series*) cuarto,-a *m,f*. **2** (*fraction*) cuarto *m*. **3** *Aut* cuarta velocidad; *see also* **seventh.**

fourth-former [fɔːθfɔːmə^r] *n GB Sch* alumno,-a *m,f* del cuarto curso.

fowl [faʊl] *n aves fpl* de corral.

fox [fɒks] **I** *n* **1** *Zool* zorro,-a *m,f*; **f. hunt,** caza *f* de zorros. **2** *fig pej* zorro *m*. **II** *vtr* **1** (*perplex*) dejar perplejo,-a, desorientar. **2** (*deceive*) engañar.

foxglove [fɒksglʌv] *n Bot* digital *f*, dedalera *f*.

foxhound [fɒkshaʊnd] *n Zool* perro *m* raposero.

foxtrot [fɒkstrɒt] *n Mus* fox-trot *m*.

foxy [fɒksɪ] *adj* (*foxier, foxiest*) *fam* astuto,-a, zorro,-a.

foyer [fɔɪer, 'fɔɪe] *n Cin Theat* vestíbulo *m*; *US* (*house*) vestíbulo *m*.

Fr 1 *Rel abbr of* **Father,** Padre *m*, P., Pe. **2** *abbr of* **French,** francés,-esa, fr.

fracas [fræka:] *n* gresca *f*, reyerta *f*.

fraction [frækʃən] *n Math* fracción *f*, quebrado *m*; **a f. of a second,** una fracción de segundo; **a f. smaller,** un poquitín más pequeño.

fractional [frækʃənəl] *adj* fraccional; *fig* ínfimo,-a. ◆ **fractionally** *adv* ligeramente.

fracture [fræktʃə^r] *Med Tech* **I** *n* fractura *f*. **II** *vtr* fracturar; **to f. a leg,** fracturarse una pierna. **III** *vi* fracturarse.

fragile [frædʒaɪl] *adj* **1** frágil; **this glass is f.,** esta copa es frágil. **2** *fig* (*health*) frágil, delicado,-a; **the morning after the party he felt f.,** al día siguiente de la fiesta se encontraba mal.

fragility [frædʒɪlɪtɪ] *n* fragilidad *f*.

fragment [frægmənt] **I** *n* fragmento *m*. **II** *vi* [fræg'ment] fragmentarse.

fragmentary [frægməntərɪ] *adj* fragmentario,-a.

fragrance [freɪgrəns] *n* fragancia *f*, aroma *m*, perfume *m*.

fragrant [freɪgrənt] *adj* fragante, aromatico,-a.

frail [freɪl] *adj* frágil, delicado,-a.

frailty [freɪltɪ] *n* fragilidad *f*, delicadeza *f*; **human frailties,** las flaquezas humanas.

frame [freɪm] **I** *n* **1** (*window, door, picture*) marco *m*; (*building, machine*) armazón *f*; (*bed*) armadura *f*; (*bicycle*) cuadro *m*; (*spectacles*) montura *f*; *fig* **f. of mind,** estado *m* de ánimo. **2** (*human, animal*) cuerpo *m*. **3** *Cin TV* fotograma *m*. **4** (*snooker*) jugada *f*, set *m*. **II** *vtr* **1** (*picture*) enmarcar; *fig* **a doorway framed by roses,** una puerta encuadrada por rosas. **2** (*formulate a question*) formular; (*a plan*) elaborar. **3** *fam* (*innocent person*) incriminar.

framework [freɪmwɜːk] *n* (*structure*) armazón *f*; *fig* estructura *f*; **within the f. of ...,** dentro del marco de ... .

franc [fræŋk] *n Fin* franco *m*.

France [frɑːns] *n* Francia *f*.

franchise [fræntʃaɪz] *n* **1** *Pol* derecho *m* al voto. **2** *Com* concesión *f*, franquicia *f*.

Frank [fræŋk] *n Hist* franco,-a *m,f*.

frank [fræŋk] **I** *adj* franco,-a, sincero,-a. **II** *vtr* (*mail*) franquear. ◆ **frankly** *adv* francamente.

Frankfurt [fræŋkfɜːt] *n* Francfort.

franking [fræŋkɪŋ] *n* franqueo *m*. ■ **f. machine,** máquina *f* franqueadora.

frankness [fræŋknɪs] *n* franqueza *f*.

frantic [fræntɪk] *adj* (*anxious*) desesperado,-a; (*hectic*) frenético,-a; **to be f. with worry,** estar preocupadísimo,-a. ◆ **frantically** *adv* desesperadamente; **shouting f.,** gritando como un loco *or* un poseso.

fraternal [frə'tɜːnəl] *adj* fraterno,-a, fraternal.

fraternity [frə'tɜːnɪtɪ] *n* **1** (*brotherliness*) fraternidad *f*. **2** (*society*) asociación *f*; *Rel* hermandad *f*, cofradía *f*; *US Univ* club *m* de estudiantes.

fraternize [frætənaɪz] *vi* fraternizar (with, con).

fratricide [frætrɪsaɪd, 'freɪtrɪsaɪd] *n fml Jur* (*action*) fratricidio *m*; (*person*) fratricida *mf*.

fraud [frɔːd] *n* **1** (*act*) fraude *m*, engaño *m*. **2** *Jur* fraude *m*. **3** (*person*) impostor,-a *m,f*.

fraudulent [frɔːdjʊlənt] *adj* fraudulento,-a.

fraught [frɔːt] *adj* **1** (*full*) lleno,-a (with, de), cargado,-a (with, de); **f. with difficulties,** cargado,-a de dificultades. **2** (*tense*) nervioso,-a.

fray[1] [freɪ] *vi* **1** (*cloth*) deshilacharse. **2** (*temper*) crisparse; **his temper frequently frayed,** se irritaba a menudo.

fray[2] [freɪ] *n* combate *m*; *fig* **to enter the f.,** salir a la palestra.

frayed [freɪd] *adj* (*cloth*) deshilachado,-a; (*temper*) crispado,-a; **to have f. nerves,** tener los nervios crispados.

frazzle ['fræzəl] *n fam* **to be worn to a f.,** estar hecho,-a polvo; **burnt to a f.,** carbonizado,-a, quemado,-a; **she was burnt to a f. in the midday sun,** se achicharró bajo el sol del mediodía.

freak [fri:k] **I** *n* **1** *(monster)* monstruo *m*; **a f. of nature,** un accidente de la naturaleza. **2** *sl (eccentric)* estrafalario,-a *m,f*. **3** *sl (fan)* fanático,-a *m,f*; **she's a jazz f.,** es una fanática del jazz. **II** *adj* **1** *(unexpected)* inesperado,-a, imprevisto,-a; **f. result,** resultado inesperado. **2** *(unusual)* insólito,-a, extraño,-a; **f. storm,** tormenta insólita. ◆ **freak out** *vi sl* fliparse, alucinarse.

freakish ['fri:kɪʃ] *adj* **1** *(unexpected)* inesperado,-a, imprevisto,-a. **2** *(unusual)* insólito,-a, extraño,-a. **3** *(abnormal)* anormal, monstruoso,-a. **4** *(eccentric)* estrafalario,-a, excéntrico,-a.

freckle ['frekəl] *n* peca *f*.

freckled ['frekəld] *adj* pecoso,-a, lleno,-a de pecas.

freckly ['freklɪ] *adj* pecoso,-a, lleno,-a de pecas.

free [fri:] **I** *adj* **1** libre; **as f. as a bird,** libre como un pájaro; **feel f.!,** ¡con toda confianza!; **of his own f. will,** por voluntad propia; **to be f. to do sth,** ser libre de hacer algo; **to give sb a f. hand,** darle carta blanca a algn; **to set sb f.,** poner en libertad a algn, liberar a algn; **to work f.,** soltarse. ■ **f. access,** entrada *f* libre; **f. fall,** caída *f* libre; *Ftb* **f. kick,** golpe *m* franco, saque *m* de falta; **f. love,** amor *m* libre; **f. speech,** libertad *f* de expresión; **f. will,** libre albedrío *m*; **f. translation,** traducción *f* libre; **the f. world,** el mundo libre. **2** *Com* **f. trade,** libre cambio *m*; **f. port,** puerto *m* franco. **3** *(not occupied)* libre; **when will you be f.?,** ¿cuándo estará libre?; **is that seat f.?,** ¿está libre ese asiento? **4** *(gratis)* **f. time,** tiempo *m* libre. **4** *(gratis)* **f. (of charge),** gratuito,-a, gratis; **admission f.,** entrada *f* gratuita *or* libre; **f. gift,** obsequio *m*; **f. sample,** muestra *f* gratuita; **f. gift,** obsequio *m*; **f. pass,** pase *m*. **5** *(exempt)* libre **(from,** de); **trouble f.,** sin problemas. **6** *(generous)* generoso,-a; **she's too f. with her money,** es una manirrota. **7** *(relaxed)* desenvuelto,-a; **f. and easy,** despreocupado,-a. **II** *adv* **1** *(gratis)* gratis, gratuitamente; **to travel f.,** viajar gratis *or* de balde; *fam* **for f.,** gratis. **2** *(loose)* suelto,-a; **the dogs run f. in the garden,** los perros andan sueltos *or* libres en el jardín. **III** *vtr* **1** *(liberate)* poner en libertad; *(release)* liberar. **2** *(let loose, work loose)* soltar. **3** *(untie)* soltar, desatar. **4** *(exempt)* eximir **(from,** de). ◆ **freely** *adv* **1** *(without limitation)* libremente; **to come and go f.,** ir y venir con toda libertad. **2** *(openly)* abiertamente, francamente. **3** *(without payment)* gratis, gratuitamente; **you can travel f.,** puedes viajar gratis.

freedom ['fri:dəm] *n* **1** *(liberty)* libertad *f*; **f. of choice,** libertad de elección; **f. of the press,** libertad de prensa; **to have complete f. to do sth,** tener plena libertad para hacer algo; **f. of the city,** ciudadanía *f* de honor. ■ **f. fighter,** luchador,-a *m,f* por la libertad. **2** *(exemption)* exención *f*.

free-for-all ['fri:fərɔ:l] *n* pelea *f*, riña *f*.

freehand ['fri:hænd] *adv* a mano alzada; **to draw f.,** dibujar a mano alzada.

freehold ['fri:həʊld] *Jur* **I** *n* derecho *m* de dominio absoluto. **II** *adj* en propiedad absoluta.

freelance ['fri:lɑ:ns] **I** *adj* independiente. **II** *n* persona *f* que trabaja por cuenta propia. **III** *vi* trabajar por su cuenta.

freeloader ['fri:ləʊdəʳ] *n fam* gorrón,-a *m,f*.

freemason ['fri:meɪsən] *n* francmasón,-ona *m,f*, masón,-ona *m,f*.

freemasonry ['fri:meɪsənrɪ] *n* francmasonería *f*, masonería *f*.

free-range ['fri:reɪndʒ] *adj GB* de granja; **f.-r. eggs,** huevos *mpl* de granja.

freestanding [fri:'stændɪŋ] *adj* independiente.

free-style ['fri:staɪl] *n Swimming* estilo *m* libre; **the hundred metres f.-s.,** los cien metros libres.

freethinker [fri:'θɪŋkəʳ] *n* librepensador,-a *m,f*.

freeway ['fri:weɪ] *n US* autopista *f*.

freewheel [fri:'wi:l] *vi* **1** *Cycl* andar a rueda libre. **2** *Aut* ir en punto muerto.

freeze [fri:z] **I** *vtr* *(pt froze; pp frozen)* **1** *(liquid, food)* congelar. **2** *Econ (money)* congelar. **3** *Cin TV (image)* congelar. **II** *n Meteor* helada *f*. ■ *Econ* **price f.,** congelación *f* de precios. **III** *vi* **1** *(liquid)* helarse; *(food)* congelarse; **I'm freezing,** estoy helado,-a; **to f. to death,** morirse de frío. **2** *fig (stand still)* quedarse inmóvil; *(from shock)* quedarse paralizado,-a ◆ **freeze over, freeze up** helarse.

freeze-dried ['fri:zdraɪd] *adj* liofilizado,-a; **f.-d. coffee,** café liofilizado.

freeze-dry ['fri:zdraɪ] *vtr* *(pt & pp freeze-dried)* liofilizar.

freezer ['fri:zəʳ] *n* congelador *m*.

freezing ['fri:zɪŋ] **I** *adj* **1** *Meteor* glacial; **f. fog,** niebla *f* glacial; *fam* **it's f. cold,** hace un frío que pela. **2** *Phys* **f. point,** punto *m* de congelación; **above/below f. point,** sobre/bajo cero. **II** *n* *(of food, prices)* congelación *f*.

freight [freɪt] *n* **1** *(transport)* transporte *m*. ■ air/sea f., transporte *m* aéreo/marítimo de mercancías. **2** *(goods)* flete *m*, carga *f*. ■ *US.* **f. car,** wagon *m* de mercancías; **f. train,** tren *m* de mercancías; **f. plane,** avión *m* de carga. **3** *(price)* flete *m*.

freighter ['freɪtəʳ] *n Av Naut* buque *m or* avión *m* de carga, carguero *m*.

French [frentʃ] **I** *adj* francés,-esa; **to take F. leave,** despedirse a la francesa. ■ **F. bean,** judía *f* verde; **F. dressing,** vinagreta *f*; *US* **F. fries,** patatas *fpl* fritas; **F. Horn,** trompa *f* de pistones; **F. kiss,** beso *m* de película; *sl* **F. letter,** condón *m*; **F. window,** puerta *f* vidriera. **II** *n* **1** *(language)* francés *m*; **F. teacher,** profesor,-a *m, f* de francés. **2** *pl* **the F.,** los franceses.

French-Canadian [frentʃkə'neɪdɪən] **I** *adj* franco canadiense. **II** **F. C.** *n* francocanadiense *mf*.

Frenchman ['frentʃmən] *n (pl Frenchmen)* francés *m*.

French-speaking ['frentʃspi:kɪŋ] *adj* de habla francesa, francófono,-a.

Frenchwoman ['frentʃwʊmən] *n (pl Frenchwomen* ['frentʃwɪmɪn]*)* francesa *f*.

frenetic [frɪ'netɪk] *adj* frenético,-a.

frenzied ['frenzid] *adj* **1** *(wild)* frenético,-a. **2** *(mad)* enloquecido,-a.

frenzy ['frenzi] *n* frenesí *m*; **to be in a f.,** estar frenético,-a.

frequency ['fri:kwənsɪ] *n* **1** *(rate)* frecuencia *f*. **2** *Rad* frecuencia *f*; **high/low f.,** alta/baja frecuencia.

frequent ['fri:kwənt] **I** *adj* frecuente, habitual. **II** [frɪ'kwent] *vtr (visit)* frecuentar. ◆ **frequently** *adv* frecuentemente, con frecuencia, a menudo.

fresco ['freskəʊ] *n (pl frescoes) Art* fresco *m*.

fresh [freʃ] **I** *adj* **1** *(new)* nuevo,-a; **f. clues,** nuevos indicios; **open a f. packet,** abre otro paquete; **to make a f. start,** volver a empezar. **2** *(recent)* fresco,-a; **have you got any f. news?,** ¿traes noticias frescas? **3** *(air)* puro,-a; **in the f. air,** al aire libre. **4** *(not salt)* dulce; **f. water,** agua *f* dulce. **5** *(not tired)* fresco,-a; **as f. as a daisy,** tan fresco,-a como una rosa. **6** *(not frozen, untreated)* natural, fresco,-a; **f. egg,** huevos frescos; **f. bread,** pan del día. **7** *(complexion)* sano,-a. **8** *fam (cheeky)* fresco,-a, carota; **don't get f. with me!,** ¡basta de familiaridades! **II** *adv* recién; **f. from university,** recién salido,-a de la universidad, ◆ **freshly** *adv* recién, recientemente; **f. made sandwiches,** bocadillos recién preparados.

freshen ['freʃən] *vi (wind)* refrescar. ◆ **freshen up** *vi* lavarse y arreglarse, asearse.

fresher ['freʃəʳ] *n,* **freshman** ['freʃmən] *n (pl freshmen) n Univ* estudiante *mf* de primer año, novato,-a *m,f*.

freshness ['freʃnɪs] *n* **1** *(brightness)* frescura *f*. **2** *(newness)* novedad *f*.

freshwater ['freʃwɔ:təʳ] *adj* de agua dulce.

fret¹ [fret] *vi (pt & pp **fretted**) (worry)* preocuparse (**about**, por).

fret² [fret] *n Mus (guitar)* traste *m*.

fretful ['fretful] *adj* **1** *(worried)* preocupado,-a. **2** *(complaining)* quejumbroso,-a. **3** *(tearful)* lloroso,-a.

fretsaw ['fretsɔː] *n* segueta *f*, sierra *f* de calar.

fretwork ['fretwɜːk] *n* calado *m*.

Freudian ['frɔɪdɪən] *adj* freudiano,-a; **F. slip**, lapsus *m* freudiano.

FRG [efɑːˈdʒiː] *abbr of* **Federal Republic of Germany**, República *f* Federal de Alemania, RFA *f*.

Fri *abbr of* **Friday,** viernes *m*, viern.

friar ['fraɪəʳ] *n Rel* fraile *m*.

fricative ['frɪkətɪv] *Ling* **I** *adj* fricativo,-a. **II** *n* fricativa *f*.

friction ['frɪkʃən] *n (resistance, conflict)* fricción *f*; *(chafing)* roce *m*.

Friday ['fraɪdɪ] *n* viernes *m*; **on F.**, el viernes; **on Fridays**, los viernes; **Good F.,** Viernes Santo; *see also* **Saturday.**

fridge [frɪdʒ] *n (abbr of refrigerator) fam* nevera *f*, frigorífico *m*.

fried [fraɪd] *adj* frito,-a; **f. egg**, huevo frito.

friend [frend] *n* amigo,-a *m,f*, compañero,-a *m,f*, amistad *f*; **a family f.**, un amigo de la familia; **a f. in need is a f. indeed,** en la necesidad se conoce a los amigos; **a f. of mine,** un,-a amigo,-a mío,-a; **a school f.**, un,-a compañero,-a de clase; **he has lots of friends,** tiene muchos amigos *or* muchas amistades; **she's friends with John,** es amiga de John; **to have friends in high places,** tener enchufes; **to make friends with sb,** trabar amistad con algn; *(after a quarrel)* **to make friends again,** hacer las paces; **we're just good friends,** sólo somos amigos.

friendliness ['frendlɪnɪs] *n* amabilidad *f*, simpatía *f*.

friendly ['frendlɪ] *adj (friendlier, friendliest)* **1** *(person)* simpático,-a, amable; **she's very f.**, es muy simpático; **they became f.**, se hicieron amigos; **to be on f. terms with sb,** estar en buenos términos con algn. **2** *(atmosphere)* acogedor,-a. **3** de amigo; **f. advice,** consejo *m* de amigo; **f. nation,** nación *f* amiga. **4** *GB Sport* **f. match,** partido *m* amistoso.

friendship ['frendʃɪp] *n* amistad *f*, relación *f*.

Friesian ['friːʒən] *adj & n* frisón,-ona *(m,f)*.

frieze [friːz] *n Art* friso *m*.

frigate ['frɪgɪt] *n Naut* fragata *f*.

frigging ['frɪgɪŋ] *adj vulg* jodido,-a, puto,-a.

fright [fraɪt] *n* **1** *(fear)* miedo *m*; **to take f.,** asustarse. **2** *(shock)* susto *m*; **to get a f.,** pegarse un susto; **to give sb a f.**, darle un susto a algn; **the f. of one's life,** un susto de muerte. **3** *fam (person)* adefesio *m*; **she looks a f.,** está hecha un adefesio.

frighten ['fraɪtən] *vtr* asustar, espantar; **to f. the life/wits out of sb,** dar un susto de muerte a algn. ◆ **frighten away, frighten off** *vtr* espantar, ahuyentar.

frightened ['fraɪtənd] *adj* asustado,-a; **easily f.**, asustadizo,-a; **f. to death,** muerto,-a de miedo; **to be f. of sb,** tenerle miedo a algn; **to be f. to do sth,** tener miedo de hacer algo.

frightening ['fraɪtənɪŋ] *adj* espantoso,-a.

frightful ['fraɪtful] *adj* espantoso,-a, horroroso,-a; **I'm in a f. hurry,** tengo una prisa tremenda. ◆ **frightfully** *adv* tremendamente, terriblemente; **I'm f. sorry,** lo siento muchísimo.

frigid ['frɪdʒɪd] *adj* **1** *Med* frígido,-a. **2** *(climate)* glacial, muy frío,-a; *fig (manner, atmosphere)* glacial.

frigidity [frɪˈdʒɪtɪ] *n Med* frigidez *f*.

frill [frɪl] *n* **1** *(dress)* volante *m*. **2** *fig* **frills**, *(decorations)* adornos *mpl*; *(extras)* pretensiones *fpl*; **with no f.,** sencillo,-a, sin adornos; **with all the f.**, con toda la pompa.

frilly ['frɪlɪ] *adj (dress etc)* con volantes.

fringe [frɪndʒ] **I** *n* **1** *Hairdr* flequillo *m*. **2** *Tex* fleco *m*. **3** *(edge)* borde *m*; *(of city)* periferia *f*; *fig* **on the f. of society,** al margen de la sociedad; **the lunatic f.,** los elementos fanáticos. ■ **f. group,** grupo *m* marginal; **f. theatre,** teatro *m* experimental; **f. benefits,** extras *mpl*. **II** *vtr* **1** *Sew* poner un fleco. **2** *fig (border)* bordear; **a lake fringed by trees,** un lago rodeado de árboles.

Frisbee® ['frɪzbɪ] *n* frisbee® *m*.

Frisian ['frɪʒən] *adj & n* frisón,-ona *(m,f)*.

frisk [frɪsk] **I** *vtr (search)* registrar, cachear. **II** *vi (frolic)* retozar, juguetear, corretear.

frisky ['frɪskɪ] *adj (friskier, friskiest)* **1** *(children, animals)* retozón,-a, juguetón,-a. **2** *(adult)* vivo,-a, vital.

fritter ['frɪtəʳ] *n Culin* buñuelo *m*; **apple f.**, buñuelo *m* de manzana. ◆ **fritter away** *vtr* malgastar.

frivolity [frɪˈvɒlɪtɪ] *n* frivolidad *f*.

frivolous ['frɪvələs] *adj (flippant)* frívolo,-a; *(useless)* sin importancia.

frizz [frɪz] **I** *n* pelo *m* crespo *or* rizado. **II** *vtr* rizarse.

frizzy ['frɪzɪ] *adj (frizzier, frizziest)* crespo,-a, muy rizado,-a.

frock [frɒk] *n* vestido *m*. ■ **f. coat,** levita *f*.

Frog [frɒg] *n sl pey* gabacho,-a *m,f*, franchute,-a *m,f*.

frog [frɒg] *n Zool* rana *f*; **frogs' legs,** ancas *fpl* de rana; *fig* **to have a f. in one's throat,** tener carraspera.

frogman ['frɒgmən] *n (pl **frogmen**)* hombre *m* rana.

frogmarch ['frɒgmɑːtʃ] *vtr* llevar a algn a la fuerza sujetándole los brazos; llevar a algn en volandas.

frogspawn ['frɒgspɔːn] *n* huevos *mpl* de rana.

frolic ['frɒlɪk] *vi* retozar, juguetear.

from [frɒm, *unstressed* frəm] *prep* **1** *(time)* desde, a partir de; **f. her childhood onwards,** desde la infancia; **f. now on,** a partir de ahora; **f. one o'clock to two o'clock,** desde la una hasta las dos; **f. that time onwards,** desde entonces, desde aquel momento; **f. time to time,** de vez en cuando. **2** *(price, number)* desde, de; **dresses f. five pounds,** vestidos *mpl* desde cinco libras; **choose a number f. one to ten,** elige un número del uno a diez. **3** *(source, origin)* de; **a letter f. her father,** una carta de su padre; **f. a woman's point of view,** desde el punto de vista de una mujer; **English into Spanish,** del inglés al español; **f. far and wide,** desde los lugares más remotos; **f. head to foot,** de los pies a la cabeza; **he's f. Malaga,** es de Málaga; **I heard it f. Daniel,** me lo dijo Daniel; **she jumped (down) f. the wall,** saltó del muro; **the train f. Bilbao,** el tren procedente de Bilbao; **things went f. bad to worse,** las cosas fueron de mal en peor; **tell her f. me that ...,** dile de mi parte que ...; **to go f. door to door,** ir de puerta en puerta. **4** *(distance)* de; **the town is four miles f. the coast,** el pueblo está a cuatro millas de la costa. **5** *(out of)* de; **bread is made f. flour,** el pan se hace con harina; **he recited the poem f. memory,** recitó el poema de memoria. **6** *(remove, subtract)* a; **he took the book f. the child,** le quitó el libro al niño; *Math* **take three f. five,** restar tres a cinco. **7** *(according to)* según, por; **f. what the author said,** según lo que dijo el autor; **speaking f. my own experience,** hablando por experiencia propia. **8** *(position)* desde, de; **f. here,** desde aquí; **f. the top of the mountain,** desde la cima de la montaña. **9** *(distinguish)* entre; **can you tell margarine f. butter?,** ¿puedes distinguir entre la margarina y la mantequilla?

frond [frɒnd] *n* fronda *f*.

front [frʌnt] **I** *n* **1** *(general)* parte *f* delantera; **from the f.,** por delante, de frente; **in f. of,** delante de; **in f.,** delante; *fam* **up f.,** con antelación; *fam* **we want the money up f.,** primero, queremos ver el dinero. **2** *(of building)* fachada *f*. **3** *Mil Pol* frente *m*; **he was sent to the f.,** lo mandaron al frente; **popular f.,** frente *m* popular. **4** *Meteor* frente *m*; **cold f.,** frente *m* frío. **5** *(seaside)* paseo *m* marítimo. **6** *(activity)* asunto *m*; **has she made any progress on the work f.?,** ¿ha progresado en el trabajo? **7** *fig (cover)* she put on a brave f., hizo de tripas corazón; they **used him as a f.** for smuggling **heroin,** lo utilizaban como una tapadera para pasar heroína. II *adj* delantero,-a, de delante. ▪ *Parl* f. **bench,** primera fila de escaños donde se sientan los ministros del Gobierno o de la Oposición; *Parl* f. **bencher,** ministro,-a *m, f* (del Gobierno o de la Oposición) que se sienta en la primera fila de escaños; f. **door,** puerta *f* principal *or* de entrada; f. **room,** salón *m*; *Aut* f. **seat,** asiento *m* de delante *or* delantero. III *vi* to f. **on(to),** dar a; **the house fronts onto the river,** la casa da al río.

frontage ['frʌntɪdʒ] *n* fachada *f*.

frontal ['frʌntəl] *adj* frontal; f. **attack,** ataque *m* frontal.

frontier ['frʌntɪər] I *n* frontera *f*; *fig* the **frontiers of scientific knowledge,** las fronteras de la ciencia. II *adj* fronterizo,-a; f. **post,** puesto *m* fronterizo.

frontispiece ['frʌntɪspiːs] *n* frontispicio *m*.

front-page ['frʌntpeɪdʒ] *adj* de primera página; **f.-p. news,** noticias *fpl* de primera plana.

frost [frɒst] I *n* 1 (*covering*) escarcha *f*. 2 (*freezing*) helada *f*. II *vi* 1 helarse. 2 *US Culin* recubrir con azúcar glas. ◆ **frost over** *vi* escarchar, helar.

frostbite ['frɒstbaɪt] *n Med* congelación *f*.

frostbitten ['frɒstbɪtən] *adj Med* congelado,-a; **her fingers were f.,** tenía los dedos congelados.

frosted ['frɒstɪd] *adj* 1 (*glass*) esmerilado,-a. 2 *US Culin* recubierto,-a de azúcar glas.

frostiness ['frɒstɪnɪs] *n fig* frialdad *f*.

frosty ['frɒstɪ] *adj* (*frostier, frostiest*) 1 (*weather*) de helada; **a f. night,** una noche de helada. 2 *fig* glacial; **a f. reception,** una acogida glacial.

froth [frɒθ] I *n* 1 (*gen*) espuma *f*. 2 (*from mouth*) espumarajos *mpl*. II *vi* espumar; **to f. at the mouth,** echar espumarajos por la boca.

frothy ['frɒθɪ] *adj* (*frothier, frothiest*) espumoso,-a, con mucha espuma.

frown [fraʊn] I *vi* fruncir el ceño; **he frowned as he read the latest news,** frunció el ceño al leer las últimas noticias. II *n* ceño *m*. ◆ **frown upon** *vtr* desaprobar; **his behaviour was frowned upon,** desaprobaron su comportamiento.

froze [frəʊz] *pt see* **freeze.**

frozen ['frəʊzən] I *pp see* **freeze.** II *adj* 1 (*liquid, lake*) helado,-a; *fam* **I'm f. stiff,** estoy helado,-a; *fam* **my feet are f.,** tengo los pies helados. 2 (*food*) congelado,-a; f. **peas,** guisantes *mpl* congelados.

FRS [efɑːr'es] *GB abbr of* **Fellow of the Royal Society,** Socio *m* de la Real Sociedad.

frugal ['fruːgəl] *adj* frugal; **she lived a f. life,** llevaba una vida austera; **we sat down to a f. supper,** tuvimos una cena frugal.

frugality [fruː'gælɪtɪ] *n* frugalidad *f*.

fruit [fruːt] I *n* 1 *Bot* fruto *m*; **to bear f.,** dar fruto; f. **tree,** árbol *m* frutal. 2 (*for eating*) fruta *f*; **there's f. for dessert,** de postre tenemos fruta. ▪ f. **bowl,** frutero *m*; f. **cake,** pastel *m* con fruto seco; f. **dish,** frutero *m*; f. **machine,** máquina *f* tragaperras; f. **salad,** macedonia *f* de frutas. 3 **fruits,** (*rewards*) frutos *mpl*; **to reap the f.** of such hard **work,** cosechar los frutos de tan duro trabajo. II *vtr* dar fruto.

fruitful ['fruːtful] *adj* fructífero,-a; *fig* provechoso,-a.

fruition [fruː'ɪʃən] *n fml* fruición *f*; **to come to f.,** realizarse.

fruitless ['fruːtlɪs] *adj* infructuoso,-a, inútil, vano,-a; **a f. task,** un trabajo infructuoso.

fruity ['fruːtɪ] *adj* (*fruitier, fruitiest*) 1 (*taste*) con sabor a fruta. 2 *fam* (*voice*) pastoso,-a. 3 *fam* (*joke*) picante, verde.

frump [frʌmp] *n fam* (*woman*) adefesio *m*.

frumpish ['frʌmpɪʃ] *adj* 1 (*old-fashioned*) anticuado,-a, pasado,-a de moda. 2 (*ideas*) chapado,-a a la antigua.

frustate [frʌ'streɪt] *vtr* frustrar; **the bad weather frustrated our plans,** el mal tiempo frustró nuestros planes.

frustrated [frʌ'streɪtɪd] *adj* frustrado,-a; **he felt f.,** se sentía frustrado.

frustration [frʌ'streɪʃən] *n* frustración *f*.

fry[1] [fraɪ] I *vtr* (*pt & pp* **fried**) freír. II *vi* freírse; *fig* asarse; *fig* **you'll f. in this sun without suncream,** te achicharrarás bajo este sol sin crema bronceadora.

fry[2] [fraɪ] *npl* (*fish*) alevines *mpl*; (*children*) gente *f* menuda; **small f.,** gente *f* de poca monta.

frying pan ['fraɪɪŋpæn] *n*, *US* **fry-pan** ['fraɪpæn] *n* sartén *f*; **to jump out of the frying p. into the fire,** salir de Guatemala y entrar en Guatepeor.

fry-up ['fraɪʌp] *n GB fam* fritada *f*, fritanga *f*.

ft 1 *abbr of* **foot,** pie *m*. 2 *abbr of* **feet,** pies *mpl*.

fuchsia ['fjuːʃə] *n Bot* fucsia *f*.

fuck [fʌk] *vulg* I *vtr & vi* joder, follar; f. **(it)!,** ¡joder!; f. **you!,** ¡que te jodas! II *n* **I don't give a f.,** me importa un carajo *or* una mierda; f. **all, sweet F.A.,** ni hostias. ◆ **fuck off** *vi* largarse, pirarse, abrirse; f. **off!,** ¡vete a la mierda! ◆ **fuck up** *vtr* joder, jorobar; **the poor bloke's really fucked up,** está muy jodido el pobre tío.

fucker ['fʌkər] *n US vulg* cabrón *m*.

fucking ['fʌkɪŋ] *vulg* I *adj* f. **idiot!,** ¡gilipollas!; **where are my f. keys?,** ¿dónde coño están las llaves? II *adv* (*intensifier*) **a f. good film,** una película de puta madre.

fuddy-duddy ['fʌdɪdʌdɪ] *n* persona *f* chapada a la antigua.

fudge [fʌdʒ] I *n Culin* dulce *m* hecho con azúcar, leche y mantequilla. II *vtr* 1 (*fiddle*) amañar. 2 (*dodge*) eludir; **to f. the issue,** eludir el problema.

fuel ['fjuːəl] I *n* 1 combustible *m*; (*for engines*) carburante *m*; *fig* **to add f. to the fire,** echar leña al fuego. ▪ f. **tank,** depósito *m* de combustible. II *vtr* (*pt & pp* **fuelled,** *US* **fueled**) 1 (*plane*) abastecer de combustible; (*car*) echar gasolina; *fig* (*ambition*) estimular; *fig* (*difficult situation*) empeorar. III *vi* repostar.

fug ['fʌg] *n GB fam* aire *m* viciado.

fugitive ['fjuːdʒɪtɪv] I *n fml* fugitivo,-a *m, f*, prófugo,-a *m, f*. II *adj* (*fleeing*) fugitivo,-a; *fig* (*transient*) fugaz, efímero,-a, pasajero,-a.

fugue [fjuːg] *n Mus* fuga *f*.

fulcrum ['fʌlkrəm] *n* (*pl* **fulcrums** *or* **fulcra** ['fʌlkrə]) *Tech* fulcro *m*, punto *m* de apoyo.

fulfil, *US* **fulfill** [fʊl'fɪl] *vtr* (*pt & pp* **fulfilled**) 1 (*carry out*) (*task, ambition*) realizar; (*promise*) cumplir; (*role, function*) desempeñar. 2 (*satisfy requirements, wishes*) satisfacer.

fulfilment, *US* **fulfillment** [fʊl'fɪlmənt] *n* 1 (*of ambition*) realización *f*; **a sense of f.,** un sentimiento de realización. 2 (*of duty, promise*) cumplimiento *m*.

full [fʊl] I *adj* 1 (*filled*) lleno,-a; **don't talk with your mouth f.,** no hables con la boca llena; f. **of,** lleno,-a de; f. **of beans,** rebosante de salud *or* de alegría; f. **of gratitude,** muy agradecido,-a; f. **to the brim,** lleno,-a hasta los topes; **I'm f. (up),** no puedo más; **the bottle is f.,** la botella está llena; **to be f. of oneself,** ser un,-a engreído,-a; **to lead a very f. life,** llevar una vida muy ajetreada. 2 (*complete, entire*) completo,-a; **at f. speed,** a toda velocidad; f. **particulars,** todos los detalles; f. **report,** informe completo; f. **text,** texto íntegro; **in f. uniform,** de uniforme completo; **the hotel is f.,** el hotel está completo; **to come f. circle,** volver al punto de partida; *fam* f. **blast,** a todo gas; *fam* **in f. swing,** en pleno auge. ▪ f. **board,** pensión *f* completa; f. **employment,** pleno empleo *m*; *Theat* f. **house,** agotadas las localidades; f. **moon,** luna *f* llena; f. **stop,** punto *m*, punto *m* y seguido *or* aparte. 3 (*parts of body*) (*face*) lleno,-a; (*figure*) relleno,-a. 4 (*clothes*) (*loose-fitting*) ancho,-a; (*too big*) flojo,-a; f. **skirt,** falda *f* con vuelo; f. **sleeve,** manga *f* ancha. II *n* **in f.,** en su totalidad; **name in f.,** nombre y apellidos completos; **the bill must be paid in f.,** hay que pagar la factura en su totalidad; **to enjoy life to the f.,** disfrutar al máximo de la vida. **III** *adv* **f. well,** perfectamente, muy bien. ◆ **fully** *adv* completamente, enteramente; **I f. agree with you,** estoy completamente de acuerdo contigo.

fullback ['fʊlbæk] *n Sport* defensa *m* central; *(rugby)* zaguero *m*.

full-blown [fʊl'bləʊn] *adj* autentico,-a.

full-bodied [fʊl'bɒdɪd] *adj (wine)* con cuerpo.

full-grown [fʊl'grəʊn] *adj* **1** *(tree)* crecido,-a. **2** *(person, animal)* adulto,-a.

full-length ['fʊleŋθ] *adj* **1** *(film)* de largo metraje. ■ **f.-l. feature film,** largometraje *m*. **2** *(mirror, portrait)* de cuerpo entero; *(skirt)* largo,-a.

fullness ['fʊlnɪs] *n* **1** *(abundance)* plenitud *f*, abundancia *f*; *Lit & fam* **in the f. of time,** con el tiempo. **2** *(of skirt)* amplitud *f*.

full-page [fʊl'peɪdʒ] *adj* de una página; **f.-p. advertisement,** un anuncio que ocupa una página entera.

full-scale ['fʊlskeɪl] *adj* **1** *(model etc)* de tamaño natural. **2** *(thorough)* completo,-a, total; **f.-s. search,** registro *m* a fondo, búsqueda *f* minuciosa; **f.-s. war,** guerra *f* generalizada *or* total.

full-time ['fʊltaɪm] **I** *adj* de jornada completa; **looking after two children is a f.-t. job,** cuidar a dos niños requiere una dedicación total. **II f. t.** *adv* **to work f. t.,** hacer una jornada completa.

fully fledged ['fʊlfledʒd] *adj* hecho,-a y derecho,-a.

fully-grown [fʊlɪ'grəʊn] *adj see* **full-grown.**

fulmar ['fʊlmə^r] *n Orn* fulmar *m*.

fulsome ['fʊlsəm] *adj fml* excesivo,-a, exagerado,-a.

fumble ['fʌmbəl] *vi* hurgar; **to f. for sth,** buscar algo a tientas; **to f. with sth,** manejar algo con torpeza.

fume [fjuːm] **I** *n (usu pl)* humo *m*, vapores *mpl*. **II** *vi* echar humo; *fig* **she was fuming (with rage),** estaba que se subía por las paredes.

fumigate ['fjuːmɪgeɪt] *vtr* fumigar.

fumigation [fjuːmɪ'geɪʃən] *n* fumigación *f*.

fun [fʌn] **I** *n* **1** *(amusement)* diversión *f*; **figure of f.,** hazmerreír *m*; **have f.!,** ¡que lo pases muy bien!; **in** *or* **for f.,** en broma; **to have f.,** divertirse, pasarlo bien; **to make f. of** *or* **to poke f. at sb,** reírse de algn; *fam* **to have f. and games,** pasárselo en grande. **2** *(amusing)* gracia *f*; **I can't see the f. in it,** no le veo la gracia. **II** *adj* divertido,-a; **he's great f.,** es muy divertido; *US fam* **f. clothes,** ropa graciosa; *US fam* **to have a f. time,** pasarlo bomba.

function ['fʌŋkʃən] **I** *n* **1** *(purpose)* función *f*; **to fulfil a f.,** desempeñar una función; **in my f. as treasurer,** en mi calidad de tesorero,-a. **2** *(working)* funcionamiento *m*. **3** *(ceremony)* acto *m*, ceremonia *f*; *(party)* recepción *f*. **4** *Comput Math* función *f*. **II** *vi* funcionar.

functional ['fʌŋkʃənəl] *adj* funcional, práctico,-a; **f. clothes,** ropa práctica.

functionary ['fʌŋkʃənəri] *n* funcionario,-a *m,f*.

fund [fʌnd] **I** *n* **1** *Com* fondo *m*; **school building f.,** fondo para la construcción del colegio. ■ **International Monetary F.,** Fondo Monetario Internacional. **2** *fig (source)* fuente *f*; **f. of wisdom,** fuente *f* de sabiduría. **3** **funds,** fondos *mpl*; *(securities)* fondos *mpl* públicos. **III** *vtr (finance)* patrocinar.

fundamental [fʌndə'mentəl] **I** *adj (central, basic)* fundamental, básico,-a; *(elementary)* elemental. **II** **fundamentals** *npl* los fundamentos; **they need to know the f. before setting sail,** es necesario conocer las cuatro reglas básicas antes de lanzarse a la mar.

fundamentalism [fʌndə'mentəlɪzəm] *n Rel* fundamentalismo *m*.

funeral ['fjuːnərəl] *n* entierro *m*, funerales *mpl*; **to attend sb's f.,** asistir a los funerales de algn; *fam fig* **that's her f.,** allá ella *or* con su pan se lo coma. ■ **f. march,** marcha *f*

fúnebre; *US* **f. parlor,** funeraria *f*; **f. procession,** cortejo *m* fúnebre; **f. service,** misa *f* de cuerpo presente; **state f.,** exequias *fpl* nacionales.

funereal [fjuː'nɪərɪəl] *adj* fúnebre.

funfair ['fʌnfeə^r] *n GB* feria *f*, parque *m* de atracciones.

fungous ['fʌŋɡəs] *adj* fungoso,-a.

fungus ['fʌŋɡəs] *n (pl* **funguses** *or* **fungus** *or* **fungi** ['fʌŋɡiː or 'fʌŋɡaɪ]) **1** *Bot* hongo *m*. **2** *Med* fungo *m*.

funicular [fjuː'nɪkjʊlə^r] *adj & n* funicular *(m)*

funky ['fʌŋki] *adj (funkier, funkiest) Mus* vibrante.

funnel ['fʌnəl] **I** *n* **1** *(for liquids)* embudo *m*. **2** *Naut* chimenea *f*. **II** *vtr* **1** verter por un embudo. **2** *fig (channel funds, energy)* encauzar.

funny ['fʌni] *adj (funnier, funniest)* **1** *(peculiar, strange)* raro,-a, extraño,-a; **he's a f. character,** es un tipo raro; **that's f., I can't remember,** ¡qué raro! no lo recuerdo; **the f. thing about it is that ...,** lo curioso del caso es que ...; **the heat made her feel f.,** el calor le hizo sentirse mal. **2** *(amusing)* divertido,-a, gracioso,-a; **I found it very f.,** me hizo mucha gracia; **are you trying to be f.?,** ¿me estás tomando el pelo?; **don't get f. with me!,** ¡no te hagas el gracioso conmigo! ■ **f. bone,** hueso *m* de la alegría. **3** *(malfunction) fam* estropeado,-a; **the radio's gone f.,** la radio se ha estropeado. **4** *fam (ill)* enfermo,-a, mal; **I feel a bit f.,** me encuentro un poco mal. **5** *fam (dishonest)* dudoso,-a; **f. business,** negocios *mpl* sucios; **I don't want any f. business round here,** no quiero lios por aquí. ◆ **funnily** *adv fam* de forma estraña; **f. enough,** aunque parezca extraño.

fur [fɜː^r] **I** *n* **1** *(of living animal)* pelo *m*, pelaje *m*. **2** *(of dead animal)* piel *f*. **3** *(in kettle)* sarro *m*; *(on tongue)* sarro *m*, saburra *f*. **II** *adj* de piel, de pieles; **f. coat,** abrigo *m* de pieles. **III** *vi (pt & pp* **furred)** calcificarse; **an iron furs (up) if you don't clean it regularly,** una plancha se calcifica si no la limpias a menudo.

furious ['fjʊərɪəs] *adj* **1** *(angry)* furioso,-a; **to be f. with sb,** estar muy enfadado,-a con algn. **2** *(vigorous)* violento,-a, furioso,-a; **she was in a f. mood,** estaba de un humor de perros.

furlong ['fɜːlɒŋ] *n (measurement)* ≈ 201 metros.

furnace ['fɜːnɪs] *n* horno *m*; **blast f.,** alto horno.

furnish ['fɜːnɪʃ] *vtr* **1** *(house)* amueblar **(with,** con); **furnished bedsitter,** estudio amueblado. **2** *fml (supply) (food)* suministrar, proveer; *(details)* facilitar, proporcionar.

furnishings ['fɜːnɪʃɪŋz] *npl* **1** muebles *mpl*, mobiliario *m*. **2** *(fittings)* accesorios *mpl*.

furniture ['fɜːnɪtʃə^r] *n* muebles *mpl*, mobiliario *m*; **a piece of f.,** un mueble. ■ **f. polish,** cera *f* para muebles; **f. shop,** tienda *f* de muebles; **f. remover,** agente *m* de mudanzas; **f. van,** camión *m* de mudanzas.

furore [fjʊ'rɔːri] *US* **furor** ['fjʊərɔː^r] *n* ola *f* de protestas *or* de entusiasmo.

furrier ['fʌrɪə^r] *n* peletero,-a *m,f*.

furrow ['fʌrəʊ] **I** *n* **1** *Agr* surco *m*. **2** *(on forehead)* arruga *f*. **II** *vtr* **1** *Agr* surcar. **2** *(forehead)* arrugar.

furry ['fɜːri] *adj (furrier, furriest)* **1** *(hairy)* peludo,-a. **2** *(tongue, kettle)* sarroso,-a.

further ['fɜːðə^r] **I** *adj see also* **far. 1** *(new)* nuevo,-a; **until f. notice,** hasta nuevo aviso; **until f. orders,** hasta nueva orden. **2** *(additional)* otro,-a, adicional; **f. detail,** más detalles; **we have no f. use for it,** ya no nos sirve. **3** *(later)* posterior, ulterior. ■ **f. education,** estudios *mpl* superiores. **II** *adv* **1** *(more)* más; **f. back,** más allá; **f. along,** más adelante; **she heard nothing f.,** no volvió a saber nada más; **to go f. into sth,** estudiar algo más a fondo; **nothing was f. from my thoughts,** nada estaba más lejos de mi pensamiento. **2** *fml Com* con referencia, referente; **f. to your letter of the 9th,** con referencia a su carta del 9 del corriente. **3** *fml (besides)* además; **I disagree with the new company policy, and f., it does not cover any of the points discussed initially,** no estoy de acuerdo con la nueva política de la empresa y además no incluye ninguno de los puntos acordados inicialmente. **III** *vtr (peace, development)* fomentar, promover.

furthermore ['fɜːðəmɔːʳ] *adv fml* además.

furthermost ['fɜːðəməʊst] *adj Lit* más lejano,-a.

furthest ['fɜːðɪst] *adj see* **far**, más, más lejano,-a.

furtive ['fɜːtɪv] *adj* furtivo,-a.

fury ['fjʊərɪ] *n* **1** *(rage)* furia *f*, furor *m*. **2** *(energy)* furor *m*; **to work like f.**, trabajar como un loco. **3** *Myth* **the Furies**, las Furias.

furze [fɜːz] *n Bot* aulaga *f*.

fuse [fjuːz] **I** *n* **1** *Elec* fusible *m*, plomo *m*; **f. box**, caja *f* de fusibles. **2** *(of bomb) (lead)* mecha *f*; *(detonator)* espoleta *f*; **to light the f.**, encender la mecha. **II** *vi* **1** *Elec* fundirse; **the lights fused**, se fundieron los plomos. **2** *fig (merge)* fusionarse; **the two organizations fused after the talks**, las dos organizaciones se fusionaron después de las negociaciones. **3** *(melt)* fundirse. **III** *vtr* **1** *Elec* fundir los plomos; **if you're not careful you'll f. the lights**, si no vas con cuidado fundirás los plomos. **2** *fig (merge)* fusionarse. **3** *(melt)* fundir.

fuselage ['fjuːzɪlɑːʒ] *n Av* fuselaje *m*.

fusilier [fjuːzɪ'lɪəʳ] *n Mil* fusilero *m*.

fusillade [fjuːzɪ'leɪd] *n* tiroteo *m*; *fig (questions, criticisms)* lluvia *f*.

fusion ['fjuːʒən] *n* fusión *f*.

fuss [fʌs] **I** *n* **1** *(commotion)* jaleo *m*, alboroto *m*; **what's all the f. about?**, ¿por qué tanto jaleo?; **to kick up a f.**, armar un escándalo; *fig* **a lot of f. about nothing**, mucho ruido y

pocas nueces. **2** *(complaints)* quejas *fpl*; **stop making a f.**, deja ya de quejarte; **there's no need to make such a f.**, no es para tanto. **3** *(attention)* atenciones *fpl*; **to make a f.**, mimar; **he always makes a real f. of Maggie**, se deshace por Maggie. **II** *vi* preocuparse **(about**, por). ◆ **fuss over** *vtr* mimar excesivamente, preocuparse excesivamente por.

fusspot ['fʌspɒt] *n fam* quisquilloso,-a *m,f*, tiquismiquis *mf*.

fussy ['fʌsɪ] *adj* **(fussier, fussiest)** *(nitpicking)* quisquilloso,-a; *(thorough)* exigente.

fusty ['fʌstɪ] *adj* **(fustier, fustiest)** **1** *(old-fashioned)* chapado,-a a la antigua. **2** *(musty)* mohoso,-a.

futile ['fjuːtaɪl] *adj* inútil, vano,-a.

futility [fjuː'tɪlɪtɪ] *n* inutilidad *f*.

future ['fjuːtʃəʳ] **I** *n* **1** futuro *m*, porvenir *m*; **in the f.**, en el futuro, en lo sucesivo; **in the near f.**, en un futuro próximo; **in the not too distant f.**, en un futuro no muy lejano; **that job has no f.**, ese trabajo no tiene porvenir; **we'll be more careful in f.**, de aquí en adelante tendremos más cuidado. **2** *Ling* futuro *m*. **3** *Fin* **futures**, futuros *mpl*. **II** *adj* futuro,-a; **her f. husband**, su futuro marido.

futuristic [fjuːtʃə'rɪstɪk] *adj* futurista.

fuzz[1] [fʌz] *n (hair)* vello *m*. **II** *vtr* rizar.

fuzz[2] [fʌz] *n sl (police)* **the f**, la bofia.

fuzzy ['fʌzɪ] *adj* **(fuzzier, fuzziest)** **1** *fam (hair)* muy rizado,-a. **2** *(blurred)* borroso,-a; **the photo was f.**, la foto era borrosa.

fwd *abbr of* **forward(s)**, adelante.

G

G, g [dʒiː] *n* **1** *(the letter)* G, g *f*. **2 G**, *Mus* sol *m*; **G major**, sol *m* mayor.

g [dʒiː] *abbr of* **gram(s), gramme(s)**, gramo(s) *m(pl)*, g.

gab [gæb] *fam* **I** *vtr (pt & pp gabbed)* charlar. **II** *n* palique *m*; **to have the gift of the g.**, tener un pico de oro.

gabardine ['gæbədiːn, gæbə'diːn] *n* gabardina *f*, impermeable *m*.

gabble ['gæbəl] **I** *n* chapurreo *m*, farfulla *f*. **II** *vi* chapurrear, hablar atropelladamente, farfullar.

gaberdine ['gæbədiːn] *n see* **gabardine.**

gable ['geɪbəl] *n Archit* aguilón *m*, gablete *m*; **g. end**, hastial *m*.

Gabon [gə'bɒn] *n* Gabón.

Gabonese [gæbə'niːz] *adj & n* gabonés,-esa *(m,f)*.

gad [gæd] *vi (pt & pp gadded)* **to g. about**, callejear.

gadabout ['gædəbaʊt] *n fam* callejero,-a *m,f*, azotacalles *mf inv*, juerguista *mf*.

gadfly ['gædflaɪ] *n Ent* tábano *m*.

gadget ['gædʒɪt] *n* artilugio *m*, aparato *m*, dispositivo *m*; *fam* chisme *m*.

gadgetry ['gædʒɪtrɪ] *n* artilugios *mpl*; *fam* chismes *mpl*.

gadwall ['gædwɔːl] *n Orn* ánade *m* friso.

Gaelic ['geɪlɪk] **I** *adj* gaélico,-a. **II** *n (language)* gaélico *m*.

gaff[1] [gæf] *n Fishing* garfio *m*.

gaff[2] [gæf] *n fam* disparate *m*; **to blow the g.**, descubrir el pastel.

gaffe [gæf] *n* metedura *f* de pata, plancha *f*, planchazo *m*, patinazo *m*; **to make a g.**, meter la pata, patinar.

gaffer ['gæfəʳ] *n GB fam* **1** *(boss)* jefe *m*. **2** *(man)* tío *m*.

gag [gæg] **I** *n* **1** *(for the mouth)* mordaza *f*. **2** *fam Theat* morcilla *f*; *(joke)* gag *m*, chiste *m*. **II** *vtr (pt & pp gagged)*

amordazar; **they tied him up and gagged him**, le ataron y le amordazaron. **III** *vi* tener náuseas.

gaga ['gɑːgɑː] *adj fam* chocho,-a.

gage [geɪdʒ] *n & vtr US see* **gauge.**

gaggle ['gægəl] *n* manada *f*; **g. of geese**, manada de ocas; *fig* **a g. of journalists**, una horda de periodistas.

gaiety ['geɪətɪ] *n* alegría *f*, regocijo *m*, animación *f*.

gaily ['geɪlɪ] *adv* alegremente; **g. coloured**, de colores vivos *or* alegres.

gain [geɪn] **I** *n* **1** *(profit)* ganancia *f*, beneficio *m*; **they hoped to make a financial g. from the company**, esperaban obtener beneficios de la compañía. **2** *(increase)* aumento *m*; **weight g.**, aumento de peso. **II** *vtr* **1** *(obtain)* ganar; **what did he g. from such hard work?**, ¿qué consiguió con tanto esfuerzo?; *fig* **to g. ground**, ganar terreno. **2** *(increase)* incrementar, aumentar; **to g. speed**, ganar velocidad, acelerar; **to g. weight**, aumentar de peso. **III** *vi (clock)* adelantar.

gainful ['geɪnfʊl] *adj fam* beneficioso,-a, lucrativo,-a. ◆ **gainfully** *adv* **to be g. employed**, tener un trabajo remunerado.

gainsay [geɪn'seɪ] *vtr (pt & pp gainsaid)* *fml (gen negative)* negar; **there's no gainsaying they were right**, no se puede negar que tenían razón *or* estaban en lo cierto.

gait [geɪt] *n* porte *m*, manera *f* de andar, andares *mpl*.

gaiter ['geɪtəʳ] *n (gen pl)* polaina *f*.

gal[1] [gæl] *n fam* chavala *f*, chica *f*, muchacha *f*, tía *f*.

gal[2] [gæl] *(pl gal or gals) abbr of* **gallon**, galón *m*.

gala ['gɑːlə, 'geɪlə] *n* gala *f*, fiesta *f*; *Sport* **swimming g.**, festival *m* de natación.

galactic [gə'læktɪk] *adj* galáctico,-a.

Galapagos [gəˈlæpəgəs] *n* **the G. Islands,** las Islas Galápagos.

galaxy [ˈgæləksɪ] *n Astron* galaxia *f*.

gale [geɪl] *n* vendaval *m*, viento *m* fuerte; *fig* **gales of laughter,** carcajadas *fpl*.

Galician [gəˈlɪʃɪən, gəˈlɪʃən] **I** *adj* gallego,-a. **II** *n* **1** *(person)* gallego,-a *m,f*. **2** *(language)* gallego *m*.

gall¹ [gɔːl] **I** *n fam* descaro *m*, caradura *f*. **II** *vtr* molestar, irritar.

gall² [gæl] *abbr of* **gallon,** *see* **gal²**

gallant [ˈgælənt] *adj* **1** *(brave)* valiente. **2** *(also* [gəˈlænt]*) (chivalrous)* galante.

gallantry [ˈgæləntrɪ] *n* **1** *(bravery)* valentía *f*, gallardía *f*, valor *m*. **2** *(politeness)* galantería *f*.

galleon [ˈgælɪən] *n Naut* galeón *m*.

gallery [ˈgælərɪ] *n* **1** *(gen)* galería *f*; **art g.,** galería de arte. **2** *Theat* gallinero *m*; **to play to the g.,** actuar para la galería. **3** *Parl (court)* tribuna *f*. **4** *(mine)* galería *f*.

galley [ˈgælɪ] *n* **1** *Naut (ship)* galera *f*; **g. slave,** galeote *m*. **2** *Naut (kitchen)* cocina *f*. **3** *Print* **g. (proof),** galerada *f*.

Gallic [ˈgælɪk] *adj fml (French)* francés,-esa; *(of Gaul)* gálico,-a.

Gallicism [ˈgælɪsɪzəm] *n Ling* galicismo *m*.

galling [ˈgɔːlɪŋ] *adj* irritante.

gallivant [ˈgælɪvænt] *vi fam* callejear.

gallon [ˈgælən] *n* galón *m* (≈ 4,55 litros; *US* 3,79 litros).

gallop [ˈgæləp] **I** *n* galope *m*; **at a g.,** al galope; **at full g.,** a galope tendido. **II** *vi* galopar, ir al galope; **to g. away,** alejarse al galope.

galloping [ˈgæləpɪŋ] *adj* galopante. ▪ *Med* **g. consumption,** tisis *f* galopante.

gallows [ˈgæləʊz] *npl* horca *f sing*, patíbulo *m sing*, cadalso *m sing*.

gallstone [ˈgɔːlstəʊn] *n Med* cálculo *m* biliar.

Gallup poll [ˈgæləppəʊl] *n* encuesta *f*, sondeo *m*.

galore [gəˈlɔːʳ] *adv fam* en cantidad, en abundancia; **money g.,** dinero en abundancia; **whisky g.,** whisky a granel.

galosh [gəˈlɒʃ] *n* chanclo *m*.

galumph [ˈgəˈlʌmf] *vi fam* corretear; **to g. about,** dar saltos de alegría.

galvanize [ˈgælvənaɪz] *vtr (metal)* galvanizar; *fig* **to g. sb into action,** galvanizar a algn.

galvanization [gælvənaɪˈzeɪʃən] *n* galvanización *f*.

galvanized [ˈgælvənaɪzd] *adj* galvanizado,-a.

Gambia [ˈgæmbɪə] *n* Gambia.

Gambian [ˈgæmbɪən] *adj & n* gambiano,-a *(m,f)*.

gambit [ˈgæmbɪt] *n* **1** *Chess* gambito *m*. **2** *fig (move)* táctica *f*, maniobra *f*, estratagema *f*.

gamble [ˈgæmbəl] **I** *n* **1** *(risk)* riesgo *m*; *(risky undertaking)* empresa *f* arriesgada; **they took a real g. when they decided to employ him,** arriesgaron mucho cuando decidieron contratarlo. **2** *(bet, wager)* jugada *f*, apuesta *f*. **II** *vi* **1** *(bet)* jugar; **to g. away a fortune,** perder una fortuna en el juego. **2** *(take a risk)* arriesgarse; **they gambled on the assumption that nobody would come,** tomaron el riesgo de pensar que nadie vendría.

gambler [ˈgæmbləʳ] *n* jugador,-a *m,f*.

gambling [ˈgæmblɪŋ] *n* juego *m*. ▪ **g. house,** casa *f* de juego.

gambol [ˈgæmbəl] *vi (pt & pp* **gambolled,** *US* **gamboled)** saltar, brincar.

game [geɪm] **I** *n* **1** *(gen)* juego *m*; **g. of chance,** juego de azar; *fig* **the g. is up,** se acabó; *fig* **to give the g. away,** enseñar las cartas; *fig* **to play the g.,** jugar limpio; *fig* **two can play at that g.,** donde las dan las toman; *fig* **what's his g.?,** ¿qué pretende? **2** *(match etc)* partido *m*; *(bridge)* partida *f*; **to be off one's g.,** no estar en forma. **3 games,**

Sport juegos *mpl*; *GB Sch* educación *f* física; **Olympic G.,** Juegos Olímpicos, Olimpiadas *fpl*. **4** *(hunting)* caza *f*; *fig* presa *f*; **big g.,** caza mayor; **g. bag,** morral *m*; **g. reserve,** coto *m* de caza; *fig* **he was easy g.,** fue una presa fácil; *fig* **to play silly games,** hacer el tonto. **II** *adj (ready)* listo,-a; **g. for,** listo,-a para, preparado,-a para; **g. for anything,** listo,-a para todo. ◆ **gamely** *adv* resueltamente.

gamekeeper [ˈgeɪmkiːpəʳ] *n* guardabosque *mf*.

gamma [ˈgæmə] *n* gamma *f*. ▪ *Biol* **g. globulin,** gammaglobulina *f*; *Phys* **g. rays,** rayos *mpl* gamma.

gammon [ˈgæmən] *n GB* jamón *m* ahumado *or* curado.

gammy [ˈgæmɪ] *adj (gammier, gammiest) GB fam* lisiado,-a, tullido,-a; **g. leg,** pierna *f* coja.

gamut [ˈgæmət] *n* gama *f*, serie *f*; **to run the g. of ...,** experimentar todas las posibilidades de ... .

gander [ˈgændəʳ] *n Orn* ganso *m*.

gang [gæŋ] *n (of criminals)* banda *f*; *(of youths)* pandilla *f*; *(of workers)* cuadrilla *f*, brigada *f*, equipo *m*; *fam (of friends)* grupo *m*, pandilla *f*, cuadrilla *f*. ◆ **gang up** *vi fam* unirse **(on,** contra), confabularse **(on,** contra).

ganger [ˈgæŋəʳ] *n GB fam* capataz *m*.

Ganges [ˈgændʒiːz] *n* **the G.,** el Ganges.

gangland [ˈgæŋlænd] *n fam* hampa *f*, submundo *m*, bajos fondos *mpl*.

gangling [ˈgæŋglɪŋ] *adj fam* larguirucho,-a.

ganglion [ˈgæŋglɪən] *n Med* ganglio *m*.

gangplank [ˈgæŋplæŋk] *n Naut* plancha *f*.

gangrene [ˈgæŋgriːn] *n Med* gangrena *f*.

gangrenous [ˈgæŋgrɪnəs] *adj* gangrenoso,-a; **to go g.,** gangrenarse.

gangster [ˈgæŋstəʳ] *n* gángster *m*.

gangway [ˈgæŋweɪ] *n Naut Theat* pasarela *f*, pasillo *m*; **g.!,** ¡abran paso!

gannet [ˈgænɪt] *n Orn* alcatraz *m*; *fig* comilón *m*.

gantry [ˈgæntrɪ] *n* **1** *Tech* puente *m* transversal. ▪ **g. crane,** grúa *f* de pórtico. **2** *Astronaut* torre *f* de lanzamiento. **3** *(for barrel)* caballete *m*.

gaol [dʒeɪl] *n & vtr GB see* **jail.**

gap [gæp] *n* **1** *(hole)* abertura *f*, hueco *m*; *(crack)* brecha *f*; *(space)* espacio *m*; *(blank space)* blanco *m*; *(in traffic)* claro *m*; **to bridge** *or* **fill a g.,** rellenar un hueco. **2** *Geol* desfiladero *m*. **3** *(in time)* intervalo *m*; *(emptiness)* vacío *m*. **4** *(gulf)* diferencia *f*; **age g.,** diferencia de edades; *Econ* **trade g.,** déficit *m* comercial. **5** *(deficiency)* laguna *f*; **there were gaps in his knowledge of English,** su inglés presentaba ciertas lagunas.

gape [geɪp] *vi (person)* quedarse boquiabierto,-a, mirar boquiabierto,-a; *(thing)* abrir, quedar abierto,-a.

gaping [ˈgeɪpɪŋ] *adj* profundo,-a; **a g. wound,** una herida tremenda *or* profunda.

garage [ˈgærɑːʒ, ˈgærɪdʒ] *n* **1** garaje *m*. ▪ **g. sale,** venta *f* de trastos viejos. **2** *(for repairs)* taller *m* mecánico. **3** *(filling station)* gasolinera *f*, estación *f* de servicio.

garb [gɑːb] *n fml* atuendo *m*, atavío *m*.

garbage [ˈgɑːbɪdʒ] *n* **1** *US* basura *f*. ▪ **g. can,** cubo *m* de la basura; **g. truck,** camión *m* de la basura. **2** *fig* tonterías *fpl*, majaderías *fpl*.

garbled [ˈgɑːbəld] *adj* embrollado,-a; **g. account,** relato confuso; **she left a g. message,** dejó un recado incomprensible.

garden [ˈgɑːdən] **I** *n* jardín *m*. ▪ **g. centre,** centro *m* de jardinería, vivero *m*, plantel *m*; **G. of Eden,** Edén *m*; **g. party,** recepción *f* al aire libre; **vegetable g.,** huerto *m*. **II** *vi (usually continuous)* cuidar el jardín; **John's gardening,** John está trabajando en el jardín.

gardener [ˈgɑːdənəʳ] *n* jardinero,-a *m,f*.

gardening [ˈgɑːdənɪŋ] *n* jardinería *f*; **his mother does the g.,** su madre es la que cuida el jardín.

gardenia [gɑːˈdiːnɪə] *n Bot* gardenia *f*.

garfish ['gɑːfɪʃ] *n (fish)* aguja *f*.

gargle ['gɑːgəl] **I** *n* **1** *(act)* gárgaras *fpl*. **2** *(liquid)* gargarismo *m*. **II** *vi* hacer gárgaras, gargarizar.

gargoyle ['gɑːgɔɪl] *n Archit* gárgola *f*.

garish ['geərɪʃ] *adj (colour)* chillón,-ona, llamativo,-a; *(light)* cegador,-a, deslumbrante.

garland ['gɑːlənd] **I** *n* guirnalda *f*. **II** *vtr* adornar con guirnaldas.

garlic ['gɑːlɪk] *n Culin Hortic* ajo *m*; **a clove of g.,** un diente de ajo; **prawns in g.,** gambas *fpl* al ajillo.

garment ['gɑːmənt] *n* prenda *f*.

garnet ['gɑːnɪt] *n Min* granate *m*.

garnish ['gɑːnɪʃ] *Culin* **I** *n* guarnición *f*. **II** *vtr* guarnecer.

Garonne [gæ'rɒn] *n* Garona.

garret ['gærɪt] *n* buhardilla *f*, ático *m*.

garrison ['gærɪsən] *Mil* **I** *n* guarnición *f*; **g. town,** ciudad *f* de guarnición. **II** *vtr* guarnecer; **to g. a town,** guarnecer una ciudad; **to g. troops in a town,** acuartelar tropas en una ciudad.

garrotte [gə'rɒt] **I** *n* garrote *m*. **II** *vtr* dar garrote a, ejecutar con garrote.

garrulous ['gærʊləs] *adj* gárrulo,-a, locuaz, parlanchín,-ina.

garter ['gɑːtər] *n* **1** liga *f*. ■ **g. belt,** liguero *m*. **2 the Order of the G.,** la Orden de la Jarretera.

gas [gæs] **I** *n (pl* **gases** *or* **gasses) 1** *(substance)* gas *m*. ■ **Calor g.,** gas *m* butano; **g. chamber,** cámara *f* de gas; **g. cooker,** cocina *f* de gas; **g. fire,** estufa *f* de gas; **g. mask,** careta *f* antigás; **g. meter,** contador *m* del gas; **g. ring,** hornillo *m* de gas; **natural g.,** gas *m* natural; **tear g.,** gas *m* lacrimógeno. **2** *Dent Med* anestesia *f*; **I had g.,** me anestesiaron. ■ **laughing g.,** gas *m* hilarante. **3** *US* gasolina *f*; **g. station,** gasolinera *f*; *fam* **step on the g.!,** ¡pisa a fondo!; *sl* **g. guzzler,** coche *m* que tiene un alto consumo de gasolina, coche que chupa mucha gasolina. **4** *fam* **it was a real g.,** lo pasamos bomba. **II** *vtr (pt & pp* **gassed)** *(asphyxiate)* asfixiar con gas. **III** *vi fam (talk)* charlotear, darle a la sinhueso.

gasbag ['gæsbæg] *n fam offens* cotorra *f*.

gaseous ['gæsɪəs, 'gæʃɪəs] *adj* gaseoso,-a.

gash [gæʃ] **I** *n* herida *f* profunda. **II** *vtr* hacer un corte en; **he gashed his forehead,** se hizo una herida en la frente.

gasket ['gæskɪt] *n Tech* junta *f*; *fam* **to blow a g.,** salirse de sus casillas.

gasoline ['gæsəliːn] *n US* gasolina *f*.

gasometer [gæs'ɒmɪtər] *n* gasómetro *m*.

gasp [gɑːsp] **I** *n* **1** *(cry)* grito *m*. **2** *(breath)* boqueada *f*; *fig* **to be at one's last g.,** estar en las últimas. **II** *vi* **1** *(in surprise)* quedar boquiabierto,-a. **2** *(breathe)* jadear; **to g. for air,** hacer esfuerzos para respirar.

gassy ['gæsɪ] *adj (gassier, gassiest)* gaseoso,-a.

gastric ['gæstrɪk] *adj* gástrico,-a; *Med* **g. flu,** fiebre *f* gástrica; **g. juice,** jugo *m* gástrico; **g. ulcer,** úlcera *f* gástrica.

gastritis [gæs'traɪtɪs] *n Med* gastritis *f*.

gastro-enteritis [gæstrəʊentə'raɪtɪs] *n Med* gastroenteritis *f*.

gastronome ['gæstrənəʊm] *n* gastrónomo,-a *m,f*.

gastronomic [gæstrə'nɒmɪk] *adj* gastronómico,-a.

gastronomy [gæs'trɒnəmɪ] *n* gastronomía *f*.

gasworks ['gæswɜːks] *n* fábrica *f* de gas.

gate [geɪt] *n* **1** *(door)* puerta *f*, verja *f*; **garden g.,** puerta de jardín. **2** *(at airport)* puerta *f*. **3** *(at football ground etc)* entrada *f*; **g. (money),** taquilla *f*, recaudación *f*. **4** *Sport (attendance)* entrada *f*.

gateau ['gætəʊ] *n (pl* **gateaux** ['gætəʊz]*) Culin* pastel *m* con nata.

gatecrash ['geɪtkræʃ] *vtr & vi fam* colarse, entrar de gorra.

gatecrasher ['geɪtkræʃər] *n fam* persona *f* que se cuela.

gatepost ['geɪtpəʊst] *n* poste *m*; *fam fig* **between you, me and the g.,** entre nosotros.

gateway ['geɪtweɪ] *n* entrada *f*, puerta *f*; *fig* camino *m*, pasaporte *m*; *fig* **the g. to success,** el camino *or* pasaporte hacía el éxito.

gather ['gæðə] **I** *vtr* **1** *(collect)* juntar; *(pick)* coger; *(pick up)* recoger. **2** *(bring together)* reunir, juntar. **3** *(harvest)* cosechar. **4** *(gain)* ganar, cobrar; **to g. speed,** ir ganando velocidad; **to g. strength,** cobrar fuerzas. **5** *(understand)* suponer deducir; **I g. that ...,** tengo entendido que ... . **6** *Sew* fruncir. **II** *vi* **1** *(come together)* reunirse, juntarse. **2** *(form)* formarse; **a crowd gathered,** se formó una muchedumbre; **a storm is gathering,** amenaza tormenta. ♦ **gather round** *vi* acercarse, agruparse. ♦ **gather up** *vtr* recoger.

gathering ['gæðərɪŋ] **I** *adj* creciente; **g. darkness,** oscuridad *f* creciente; **g. gloom,** tristeza *f* creciente. **II** *n* reunión *f*; **a family g.,** una reunión familiar.

gauche [gəʊʃ] *adj* **1** *(clumsy)* torpe, desmañado,-a. **2** *(tactless)* sin tacto, torpe.

gaucheness ['gəʊʃnɪs] *n* **1** *(clumsiness)* torpeza *f*. **2** *(tactlessness)* falta *f* de tacto, falta *f* de delicadeza.

gaudy ['gɔːdɪ] *adj (gaudier, gaudiest)* chillón,-ona, llamativo,-a. ♦ **gaudily** *adv* llamativamente; **g. dressed,** vestido,-a de forma llamativa.

gauge [geɪdʒ] **I** *n* **1** *(measure)* medida *f* estándar; *(of gun, wire)* calibre *m*. **2** *Rail* ancho *m* de vía; **narrow g.,** de vía estrecha. **3** *(calibrator)* indicador *m*, calibre *m*, calibrador *m*; **oil g.,** indicador *m* del nivel de aceite; **tyre g.,** manómetro *m* para neumáticos. **4** *fig (indication)* indicación *f*, muestra *f*. **II** *vtr* **1** *(measure)* medir, calibrar. **2** *fig (judge)* calcular, determinar, juzgar.

Gaul [gɔːl] *n Hist* **1** *(country)* Galia. **2** *(inhabitant)* galo,-a *m,f*.

gaunt [gɔːnt] *adj* **1** *(lean)* demacrado,-a. **2** *(desolate)* lúgubre.

gauntlet ['gɔːntlɪt] *n Hist* guantelete *m*; *(glove)* guante *m*; *fig* **to run the g. of ...,** estar sometido,-a a ...; *fig* **to take up the g.,** recoger el guante; *fig* **to throw down the g.,** arrojar el guante.

gauze [gɔːz] *n* gasa *f*.

gave [geɪv] *pt see* **give**.

gavel ['gævəl] *n* martillo *m*.

gawk [gɔːk] *vi fam* papar moscas, mirar a las musarañas; **to g. at,** mirar con cara de tonto,-a.

gawky ['gɔːkɪ] *adj (gawkier, gawkiest)* desgarbado,-a.

gay [geɪ] **I** *adj* **1** *(homosexual)* gay, homosexual; *(woman)* lesbiana; **the G. Liberation Movement,** el Movimiento Gay. **2** *(happy)* alegre; **g. bachelor,** soltero *m* libre y sin compromiso. **II** *n (man)* gay *m*, homosexual *m*; *(woman)* lesbiana *f*.

gaze [geɪz] **I** *n* mirada *f* fija. **II** *vi* mirar fijamente.

gazebo [gə'ziːbəʊ] *n (pl* **gazebos** *or* **gazeboes)** belvedere *m*.

gazelle [gə'zel] *n (pl* **gazelles** *or* **gazelle)** *Zool* gacela *f*.

gazette [gə'zet] *n* gaceta *f*; *US* periódico *m*.

gazump [gə'zʌmp] *vi GB fam* romper un compromiso de venta para vender a un precio más alto.

GB [dʒiː'biː] *abbr of* **Great Britain,** Gran Bretaña.

GCE [dʒiːsiː'iː] *abbr of* **General Certificate of Education (A-Level),** ≈ Curso *m* de Orientación Universitaria, COU *m*.

GCSE [dʒiːsiːes'iː] *abbr of* **General Certificate of Secondary Education,** ≈ Bachillerato *m* Unificado Polivalente, BUP *m*.

Gdns *abbr of* **Gardens,** ≈ calle *f sing*, c/.

GDP [dʒiːdiː'piː] *Econ abbr of* **gross domestic product,** producto *m* interior bruto, PIB *m*.

GDR [dʒiːdiːɑː] *abbr of* **German Democratic Republic,** República Democrática Alemana *or* de Alemania, RDA.

gear [gɪə^r] **I** *n* **1** *(equipment)* equipo *m*. ■ **camping g.**, equipo *m* de acampada; **fishing g.**, aparejo *m* de pesca; *Av* **landing g.**, tren *m* de aterrizaje. **2** *fam (belongings)* efectos *mpl* personales. **3** *fam (clothing)* ropa *f*; **punk g.**, ropa punk. **4** *Tech* engranaje *m*. **5** *Aut* velocidad *f*, marcha *f*; **out of g.**, en punto muerto; **to change g.**, cambiar de velocidad. ■ **first g.**, primera *f* (velocidad *f*); **g. lever**, palanca *f* de cambio. **II** *vtr* ajustar, adaptar; **a policy geared to the needs of the people**, una política adaptada a las necesidades del pueblo.

gearbox ['gɪəbɒks] *n Aut* caja *f* de cambios.

gearstick, ['gɪəstɪk], *US* **gearshift** ['gɪəʃɪft] *n Aut* palanca *f* de cambio.

gee [dʒiː] *interj* **1** *US fam* ¡caramba!, ¡ostras! **2** *(to horse)* **g. up!**, ¡arre!

gee-gee ['dʒiːdʒiː] *n fam* caballito *m*.

geese [giːs] *npl see* **goose**.

geezer ['giːzə^r] *n fam* tío *m*; **an old g.**, un viejo.

gel [dʒel] **I** *n* **1** *Chem* gel *m*. **2** *Hairdr* gomina *f*, fijador *m*. **II** *vi (pt & pp gelled)* **1** *Chem* gelificarse. **2** *fig (ideas etc)* cuajar. **III** *vtr Hairdr* engominar; **to g. one's hair**, engominarse el pelo.

gelatin ['dʒelətɪn] *n*, **gelatine** ['dʒelətiːn] *n* gelatina *f*.

gelatinous [dʒɪ'lætɪnəs] *adj* gelatinoso,-a.

geld [geld] *vtr* capar, castrar.

gelding ['geldɪŋ] *n* caballo *m* castrado.

gelignite ['dʒelɪgnaɪt] *n* gelignita *f*, gelinita *f*.

gem [dʒem] *n* **1** *(jewel)* piedra *f* preciosa, gema *f*. **2** *fig (person)* joya *f*, alhaja *f*.

Gemini ['dʒeminaɪ] *n Astrol Astron* Géminis *m sing*.

gen¹ [dʒen] *n fam* información *f*, datos *mpl*; **to get the g. on sth**, informarse sobre algo.

gen² [dʒen] *Mil abbr of* **General**, General *m*, Gral., Genl.

gender ['dʒendə] *n Ling* género *m*.

gene [dʒiːn] *n Biol* gene *m*, gen *m*.

genealogical [dʒiːnɪə'lɒdʒɪkəl] *adj* genealógico,-a.

genealogist [dʒiːnɪ'ælədʒɪst] *n* genealogista *mf*.

genealogy [dʒiːnɪ'ælədʒɪ] *n* genealogía *f*.

general ['dʒenərəl] **I** *adj* general; **a g. idea**, una idea general; **as a g. rule**, por regla general; **a word in g. use**, una palabra de uso corriente; **g. knowledge**, conocimientos generales; **g. store**, tienda de comestibles; **in g.**, en general, generalmente; **in the g. interest**, en beneficio de todos, para el bien de todos; **the g. public**, el público. ■ *Pol* **G. Assembly**, Asamblea *f* General; *Med* **g. practice**, medicina *f* general; *Med* **g. practitioner (GP)**, médico *m* de cabecera. **II** *n Mil* general *m*. ◆ **generally** *adv* generalmente, por lo general, en general; **g. speaking**, hablando en términos generales.

generality [dʒenə'rælɪtɪ] *n* generalidad *f*.

generalization [dʒenərəlaɪ'zerʃən] *n* generalización *f*.

generalize ['dʒenərəlaɪz] *vtr & vi* generalizar.

general-purpose ['dʒenərəl'pɜːpəs] *adj* de uso general.

generate ['dʒenəreɪt] *vtr* **1** *Elec* generar. **2** *fig (produce)* generar, engendrar, producir.

generating ['dʒenəreɪtɪŋ] *adj* generador,-a; **g. station**, central generadora.

generation [dʒenə'reɪʃən] *n* generación *f*; **from g. to g.**, de generación en generación; **the younger g.**, los jóvenes, la juventud, la nueva generación. ■ **g. gap**, abismo *m* or conflicto *m* or diferencia *f* generacional.

generator ['dʒenəreɪtə^r] *n Elec* generador *m*.

generic [dʒɪ'nerɪk] *adj* genérico,-a.

generosity [dʒenə'rɒsɪtɪ] *n* generosidad *f*.

generous ['dʒenərəs] *adj (lavish)* generoso,-a; *(plentiful)* copioso,-a; **a g. helping**, una buena ración. ◆ **generously** *adv* generosamente.

Genesis ['dʒenɪsɪs] *n Rel* Génesis *m*.

genesis ['dʒenɪsɪs] *n (pl geneses* ['dʒenɪsiːz]*)* génesis *f*, origen *m*.

genetic [dʒɪ'netɪk] *adj* genético,-a.

geneticist [dʒɪ'netɪsɪst] *n* genetista *mf*.

genetics [dʒɪ'netɪks] *n* genética *f*.

Geneva [dʒɪ'niːvə] *n* Ginebra.

Genevan [dʒɪ'niːvən] *adj & n* ginebrino,-a *(m,f)*.

genial ['dʒiːnɪəl, 'dʒiːnjəl] *adj* cordial, amable, simpático,-a.

geniality [dʒiːnɪ'ælɪtɪ] *n* cordialidad *f*, amabilidad *f*, simpatía *f*.

genie ['dʒiːnɪ] *n* duende *m*, genio *m*.

genital ['dʒenɪtəl] *adj* genital.

genitals ['dʒenɪtəlz] *npl* órganos *mpl* genitales.

genitive ['dʒenɪtɪv] *adj & n Ling* genitivo *(m)*.

genius ['dʒiːnjəs, 'dʒiːnɪəs] *n (pl geniuses)* **1** *(person)* genio *m*; **a work of g.**, una obra genial; **to be a g.**, ser un genio. **2** *(gift)* don *m*; **to have a g. for business**, tener un don especial para los negocios.

Genoa ['dʒenəʊə] *n* Génova.

genocide ['dʒenəʊsaɪd] *n* genocidio *m*.

Genoese [dʒenəʊ'iːz] *adj & n*, **Genovese** [dʒenə'viːz] *adj & n* genovés,-esa *(m,f)*.

genre ['ʒɑːnrə] *n Art Lit* género *m*; **dramatic g.**, género dramático.

gent [dʒent] *n (abbr of gentleman) fam* señor *m*, caballero *m*; *Com* **gents' footwear**, calzado *m* para caballero; **the gents**, los servicios (de caballeros); **where's the gents?**, ¿dónde están los servicios (de caballeros)?

genteel [dʒen'tiːl] *adj (refined)* fino,-a, distinguido,-a; *pej* afectado,-a, cursi.

Gentile ['dʒentaɪl] **I** *adj (not Jew)* no judío,-a; *(Christian)* cristiano,-a; *(pagan)* pagano,-a, gentil. **II** *n (not Jewish)* no judío,-a *m, f*; *(Christian)* cristiano,-a *m, f*; *(pagan)* pagano,-a *m, f*, gentil *mf*.

gentle ['dʒentəl] *adj* **1** *(person)* dulce, tierno,-a; *(breeze)* suave; *(movement)* suave, palisado,-a. **2** *(noble)* noble; **of g. birth**, de buena cuna. ◆ **gently** *(movement)* con cuidado.

gentleness ['dʒentəlnɪs] *n (mildness)* ternura *f*; *(kindness)* amabilidad *f*.

gentleman [dʒentəlmən] *n (pl gentlemen)* caballero *m*; **g.'s agreement**, acuerdo *m* entre caballeros; **he's a real g.**, es todo un caballero; **ladies and gentlemen!**, ¡señoras y señores!

gentry ['dʒentrɪ] *n* pequeña nobleza *f*, alta burguesía *f*.

genuflect ['dʒenju:flekt] *vi Rel* hacer una genuflexión.

genuflection *n*, **genuflexion** [dʒenju:'flekʃən] *n* genuflexión *f*.

genuine ['dʒenjuɪn] *adj* **1** *(authentic, true)* auténtico,-a, genuino,-a, verdadero,-a; **the painting was discovered to be g.**, el cuadro resultó ser un original. **2** *(sincere)* sincero,-a; **his feelings for her were g.**, sus sentimientos hacía ella eran sinceros; **they were g. people**, era buena gente. ◆ **genuinely** *adv* auténticamente, realmente, sinceramente; **they were g. surprised**, estaban realmente sorprendidos.

genus ['dʒiːnəs] *n (pl genuses or genera* ['dʒenərə]*) Biol* género *m*.

geocentric [dʒiːəʊ'sentrɪk] *adj* geocéntrico,-a.

geodesic [dʒiːəʊ'diːzɪk] *adj Geom* geodésico,-a.

geographer [dʒɪ'ɒgrəfə^r] *n* geógrafo,-a *m, f*.

geographic(al) [dʒɪə'græfɪk(əl)] *adj* geográfico,-a.

geography [dʒɪ'ɒgrəfɪ, 'dʒɒgrəfɪ] *n* geografía *f*.

geologic(al) [dʒɪə'lɒdʒɪk(əl)] *adj* geológico,-a.

geologist [dʒɪ'ɒlədʒɪst] *n* geólogo,-a *m, f*.

geology [dʒɪ'ɒlədʒɪ] *n* geología *f*.

geomagnetic [dʒiːəʊmæg'netɪk] *adj* geomagnético,-a.
geometric(al) [dʒɪə'metrɪk(əl)] *adj* geométrico,-a.
geometrician [dʒɪɒmɪ'trɪʃən] *n* geómetra *mf*.
geometry [dʒɪ'ɒmɪtrɪ] *n* geometría *f*.
geomorphic [dʒiːəʊ'mɔːfɪk] *adj Geol* geomórfico,-a.
geophysical [dʒiːəʊ'fɪzɪkəl] *adj* geofísico,-a.
geophysics [dʒiːəʊ'fɪzɪks] *n* geofísica *f*.
geopolitical [dʒiːəʊpə'lɪtɪkəl] *adj* geopolítico,-a.
geopolitics [dʒiːəʊ'pɒlɪtɪks] *n* geopolítica *f*.
Georgia ['dʒɔːdʒə] *n* Georgia.
Georgian ['dʒɔːdʒən] *adj & n* georgiano,-a (*m,f*).
georgic ['dʒɔːdʒɪk] *n Lit* geórgica *f*.
geranium [dʒɪ'reɪnɪəm] *n Bot* geranio *m*.
gerbil ['dʒɜːbɪl] *n Zool* gerbo *m*, jerbo *m*.
geriatric [dʒerɪ'ætrɪk] *adj Med* geriátrico,-a.
geriatrician [dʒerɪə'trɪʃən] *n Med* geriatra *mf*.
geriatrics [dʒerɪ'ætrɪks] *n Med* geriatría *f*.
germ [dʒɜːm] *n* **1** *Biol* germen *m*; *fig* germen *m*, principio *m*; **wheat g.,** germen del trigo. **2** *Med* microbio *m*. ■ **g. warfare,** guerra *f* bacteriológica.
German ['dʒɜːmən] **I** *adj* **1** (*from Germany*) alemán,-ana; germano,-a. **2** *Med* **G. measles,** rubeola *f*. **II** *n* **1** (*from Germany*) alemán,-ana *m, f*, germano,-a *m, f*; (*East*) germanooriental *mf*; (*West*) germanooccidental *mf*. **2** (*language*) alemán *m*.
Germanic [dʒɜː'mænɪk] *adj* germánico,-a, germano,-a.
Germany ['dʒɜːmənɪ] *n* Alemania; **East G.,** Alemania Oriental, Alemania del Este; **West G.,** Alemania Occidental.
germ-free ['dʒɜːmfriː] *adj* esterilizado,-a.
germicidal [dʒɜːmɪ'saɪdəl] *adj* germicida.
germicide ['dʒɜːmɪsaɪd] *n* germicida *m*.
germinate ['dʒɜːmɪneɪt] *vi* germinar.
germination [dʒɜːmɪ'neɪʃən] *n* germinación *f*.
gerontocracy [dʒerɒn'tɒkrəsɪ] *n Pol* gerontocracia *f*.
gerontologist [dʒerɒn'tɒlədʒɪst] *n Med* gerontólogo,-a *m,f*.
gerontology [dʒerɒn'tɒlədʒɪ] *n Med* gerontología *f*.
gerund ['dʒerənd] *n Ling* gerundio *m*.
gestate ['dʒesteɪt] *vi* gestar.
gestation [dʒe'steɪʃən] *n* gestación *f*.
gestatorial [dʒestə'tɔːrɪəl] *adj* **g. chair,** silla *f* gestatoria.
gesticulate [dʒe'stɪkjuleɪt] *vi* gesticular.
gesticulation [dʒestɪkjʊ'leɪʃən] *n* gesticulación *f*.
gesture ['dʒestʃəʳ] **I** *n* gesto *m*, ademán *m*; *fig* gesto *m*, detalle *m*; **as a g. of friendship,** en señal de amistad; **it's an empty g.,** es pura formalidad. **II** *vi* gesticular, hacer gestos.
get [get] **I** *vtr* (*pt & pp* **got,** *pp US also* **gotten**) **1** (*obtain, acquire*) obtener, conseguir; **he got the best marks in the class,** obtuvo las mejores notas de la clase; **I got it for nothing,** me lo dieron gratis; **she got a first in her degree,** sacó una matrícula en la carrera; **she got a job at the school,** obtuvo un trabajo en el colegio; **to g. a bank loan,** obtener un crédito; **to g. a divorce,** obtener el divorcio; **to g. one's own way,** salirse con la suya. **2** (*earn*) ganar; **he gets paid on Fridays,** cobra los viernes. **3** (*fetch*) traer; **g. my coat,** tráigame el abrigo; **g. the police!,** ¡llama a la policía! **4** (*receive*) recibir; **he got a prize for the best picture,** recibió un premio por el mejor cuadro; **she got chocolates for Christmas,** le regalaron bombones por Navidad; *fam* **he got the sack,** le despidieron; *fam* **she got five years for armed robbery,** le echaron cinco años por robo a mano armada. **5** (*catch*) coger. **6** *Tel* **can you g. me New York?,** ¿me puede poner con Nueva York?; **g. me Mr Brown,** póngame con el Sr. Brown. **7** (*prepare*) preparar; **can I g. you a drink?,** ¿quiere beber algo?, ¿le pongo algo para beber?; **to g.**

lunch, preparar la comida. **8** (*ask*) pedir; **g. him to call me,** dile que me llame. **9** (*make do sth*) conseguir; **I can't g. the radio to work,** no consigo arreglar la radio; **they got him to return the money,** le convencieron para que devolviese el dinero; **to g. sb to agree to sth,** conseguir que algn acepte algo. **10** (*have sth done*) **he must g. his hair cut,** tiene que cortarse el pelo; **they got the house painted,** hicieron pintar la casa. **11** (*wound*) dar, alcanzar; **they got him in the chest,** le dieron en el pecho. **12 have got, have got to,** *see* **have. 13** *fam* (*understand*) entender, ligar; **I don't g. it,** no lo entiendo; **do you g. the joke?,** ¿entiendes la broma? **14** *fam* (*record*) **did you g. that?,** ¿lo ha apuntado? **II** *vi* **1** (*become*) ponerse; **to g. angry,** ponerse furioso,-a, enfadarse; **to g. dark,** anochecer; **to g. dressed,** vestirse; **to g. drunk,** emborracharse; **to g. late,** hacerse tarde; **to g. married,** casarse; **to g. used to doing sth,** acostumbrarse a hacer algo; **to g. wet,** mojarse. **2** (*go*) ir; **can you g. there by train?,** ¿se puede ir en tren?; *fig* **we are not getting anywhere,** así no vamos a ninguna parte; *fam* **where has he got to?,** ¿dónde se ha metido? **3** (*arrive*) llegar; **she'll g. here at three,** llegará a las tres. **4** (*come to*) **to g. to,** llegar a; **to g. to know sb,** llegar a conocer a algn; **we got to like him in the end,** llegamos a quererle al final; **when I got to know ...,** al enterarme ... . ◆ **get about** *vi* **1** (*person*) desplazarse. **2** (*news etc*) difundirse. ◆ **get across** *vtr* **1** (*cross*) (*street*) cruzar; (*bridge*) atravesar. **2** (*idea etc*) hacer comprender. ◆ **get ahead** *vi* adelantar, progresar. ◆ **get along** *vi* (*leave*) marcharse; **I'll have to be getting along,** tengo que marcharme. **2** (*manage*) arreglárselas; **to g. along without sb,** pasarse sin algo; *fam* **g. along with you!,** ¡déjate de memeces! ◆ **get around** *vi* **1** (*person*) desplazarse; (*travel*) viajar. **2** (*news*) difundirse. ◆ **get around to I** *vi* tener tiempo para; **I never got around to doing it,** al final no lo hice. **II** *vtr* (*problem*) evitar. ◆ **get at** *vtr* **1** (*reach*) alcanzar; **I can't g. at it,** no lo alcanzo, no llego a cogerlo. **2** (*ascertain*) descubrir; **they want to g. at the truth,** quieren descubrir la verdad. **3** (*insinuate*) insinuar; **what are you getting at?,** ¿qué estás insinuando?, ¿a dónde quieres llegar? **4** (*criticize*) (*tease*) meterse con; **she's always getting at me,** siempre me está pinchando. ◆ **get away** *vi* escaparse; *fam* **to g. away from it all,** alejarse del mundanal ruido. ◆ **get away with** *vi* salir impune; **she got away with stealing the money,** salió impune del robo. ◆ **get back I** *vi* **1** (*return*) regresar, volver; **they got b. at nine,** regresaron a las nueve. **2** (*move backwards*) **g. back!,** ¡atrás! **II** *vtr* (*recover money, strength, etc*) recuperar; *fam* **to g. one's own back on sb,** vengarse de algn. ◆ **get behind** *vi* atrasarse. ◆ **get by** *vi* **1** (*manage*) arreglárselas; **she can g. by in French,** sabe defenderse en francés. **2** (*pass*) pasar; **let me g. by,** déjame pasar. ◆ **get down I** *vtr* (*depress*) deprimir; **don't let it g. you down,** no te desanimes. **II** *vi* (*descend*) bajar; **g. down off the table!,** ¡bájate de la mesa!; **to g. down on one's knees,** arrodillarse. ◆ **get down to** *vi* ponerse a; **to g. down to work,** ponerse a trabajar; **to g. down to the facts,** ir al grano. ◆ **get in** *vi* **1** (*arrive*) llegar; **when the train gets in,** cuando llegue el tren. **2** *Pol* ser elegido,-a; **the labour party got in at the last elections,** el partido laborista ganó las últimas elecciones. **II** *vtr* **1** (*buy*) comprar; **to g. in a supply of sth,** hacer provisión de algo. **2** (*collect*) recoger, recolectar; **they wanted to g. the harvest in,** querían recoger la cosecha; *fam* **he couldn't g. a word in edgeways,** no pudo meter baza. ◆ **get into** *vtr* **1** *Pol* salir electo,-a *or* elegido,-a; **to g. into parliament,** ser elegido,-a diputado,-a. **2** *fig* adquirir; **to g. into bad habits,** adquirir malas costumbres; **to g. into trouble,** meterse en un lío; *fam* **what's got into him?,** ¿qué mosca le ha picado? ◆ **get off I** *vtr* **1** (*bus, train, etc*) bajarse de. **2** (*remove*) quitarse; **he couldn't g. the paint off his trousers,** no podía quitar la pintura de los pantalones; *fig* **to g. sth off one's hands,** quitarse algo de encima. **II** *vi* **1** bajarse; **he got off the table,** se bajó de la mesa; *fam* **to tell sb where to g. off,** mandar a algn a hacer puñetas; *fam* **g. off!,** ¡fuera! **2** (*depart*) salir; **I must be getting off now,** tengo que irme.

3 *(begin)* empezar; **to g. off to a good start,** empezar bien *or* con buen pie; *fig* **I couldn't g. off to sleep,** no pude conciliar el sueño. **4** *(escape)* escaparse; **to g. off lightly,** salir bien librado,-a. ◆ **get off with** *vtr* ligar; **Richard got off with Anne on Saturday night,** Richard ligó con Anne el sábado por la noche. ◆ **get on I** *vtr (board)* subir a, subirse a. **II** *vi* **1** *(board)* subirse. **2** *(make progress)* hacer progresos; *(succeed)* tener éxito; **how are you getting on?,** ¿qué tal estás?, ¿cómo te van las cosas? **3** *(have good relationship)* llevarse bien; **to g. on well with sb,** llevarse bien con algn; **we g. on well together,** nos entendemos muy bien. **4** *(continue)* seguir; **to g. on with one's work,** seguir trabajando. **5** *(time)* **it's getting on for eleven,** son casi las once; **she's getting on in years,** está envejeciendo; **time's getting on,** se está haciendo tarde. ◆ **get on to** *vtr* **1** *(find a person)* localizar; *(find out)* descubrir; **you should g. on to her straight away,** deberías localizarla enseguida, deberías ponerte en contacto con ella enseguida. **2** *(continue)* pasar a; **let's now g. on to the question of pay,** ahora tratemos la cuestión de dinero. ◆ **get out I** *vtr (object)* sacar; *(nail)* arrancar; *(stain)* quitar. **II** *vi* **1** *(room, building, etc)* salir (**of,** de); *(train)* bajar, bajarse (**of,** de). **2** *(escape)* escaparse (**of,** de); **to g. out of an obligation,** librarse de un compromiso. **3** *(stop)* dejar; **to g. out of the habit of doing sth,** perder la costumbre de hacer algo. **4** *(news etc)* difundirse; *(secret)* hacerse público. ◆ **get over** *vtr* **1** *(recover from) (illness)* recuperarse; *(loss)* sobreponerse; **I can't g. over him,** no le puedo olvidar; **you'll g. over it,** con el tiempo se le pasará. **2** *(overcome) (obstacle)* salvar; *(difficulty)* vencer. **3** *(convey)* hacer comprender, comunicar. ◆ **get over with** *vtr* acabar; **to g. sth over with,** acabar con algo. ◆ **get round** *vtr* **1** *(problem)* salvar; *(difficulty)* vencer. **2** *(rule, law)* soslayar, evitar. **3** *(news)* difundirse; **if news gets round about this, we'll suffer,** si se difunden noticias sobre esto, tendremos problemas. **4** *(win over)* persuadir, convencer; **she knows how to g. round him,** sabe cómo, llevarlo. ◆ **get round to** *vi* llegar a hacer algo; **if I g. round to it,** si tengo tiempo. **get through I** *vi* **1** *(message, news)* llegar. **2** *Educ* aprobar; *Sport* **to g. through to the final,** llegar a la final. **3** *Tel* **to g. through to sb,** conseguir comunicar con algn. **4** *(law)* aprobar; **if this law gets through ...,** si aprueban esta ley ... . **II** *vtr* **1** *(finish)* acabar, terminar; **to g. through a lot of work,** trabajar mucho. **2** *(consume)* consumir; **he got through fifty pounds in two days,** se gastó cincuenta libras en dos días; **we got through a bottle of milk,** nos bebimos una botella entera de leche. **3** *Educ (pass)* aprobar; **to g. through an exam,** aprobar un examen. **4** *(make understand)* hacer entender *or* comprender; **I can't g. it through to her that ...,** no consigo hacerle comprender que ... . ◆ **get together I** *vi* *(people)* juntarse, reunirse. **II** *vtr* **1** *(people)* juntar, reunir; **he got them all together before making the announcement,** reunió a todos antes de anunciarlo. **2** *(assemble)* montar; **they got the whole machine together,** consiguieron montar la máquina. **3** *(money)* recoger; **they managed to g. enough money together to go on holiday,** reunieron suficiente dinero para irse de vacaciones. ◆ **get up I** *vi (rise)* levantarse; **to g. up out of bed,** levantarse de la cama. **II** *vtr* **1** *(wake up)* despertar; **get me up at six,** despiértame a las seis. **2** *(disguise)* **to g. oneself up as ...,** disfrazarse de ..., vestirse de ...; **he was got up as a clown,** iba disfrazado de payaso. **3** *(organize)* montar, organizar. ◆ **get up to** *vi* hacer; **to g. up to mischief,** hacer de las suyas; **what are they getting up to?,** ¿qué estarán haciendo?

get-at-able [get'ætəbəl] *adj fam* accesible.

getaway ['getəweɪ] *n* fuga *f*; **to make one's g.,** fugarse. ■ **g. car,** coche *m* utilizado en una fuga.

get-together ['getəgeðə'] *n (meeting)* reunión *f*; *(party)* fiesta *f*.

get-up ['getʌp] *n fam* atuendo *m*, atavío *m*; *(disguise)* disfraz *m*.

get-well card [get'welkɑːd] *n* tarjeta *f* con la inscripción 'qué te mejores'.

geyser ['giːzə, *US* 'gaɪzəʳ] *n* **1** *Geog* géiser *m*. **2** *(water heater)* calentador *m* de agua.

Ghana ['gɑːnə] *n* Ghana.

Ghanian ['gɑːnɪən] *adj & n*, **Ghanaian** [gɑː'neɪən] *adj & n* ghanés,-esa *(m,f)*.

ghastly ['gɑːstlɪ] *adj (ghastlier, ghastliest)* horrible, horroroso,-a, espantoso,-a, atroz.

Ghent [gent] *n* Gante.

gherkin ['gɜːkɪn] *n* pepinillo *m*.

ghetto ['getəʊ] *n (pl ghettos or ghettoes)* ghetto *m*, gueto *m*.

ghost [gəʊst] **I** *n* **1** fantasma *m*; *fig* **not the g. of a chance,** ni la más remota posibilidad; *fam* **to give up the g.,** entregar el alma. ■ **g. story,** cuento *m* de fantasmas; **g. town,** pueblo *m* abandonado *or* fantasma. **2** *Rel* **the Holy G.,** el Espíritu Santo. **II** *vtr Lit* hacer de negro; **to g. a book for sb,** escribir un libro para otro.

ghostly ['gəʊstlɪ] *adj* fantasmal, espectral.

ghost-write ['gəʊstraɪt] *vtr Lit* escribir para otro, hacer de negro.

ghost-writer ['gəʊstraɪtə'] *n Lit* negro,-a *m,f*.

ghoul [guːl] *n* **1** *(evil spirit)* espíritu *m* maligno. **2** *(person)* persona *f* de gustos macabros.

ghoulish ['guːlɪʃ] *adj* macabro,-a.

GHQ [dʒiːeɪtʃ'kjuː] *abbr of* **General Headquarters,** Cuartel *m* General.

giant ['dʒaɪənt] **I** *n* gigante *m*. **II** *adj* gigante, gigantesco,-a.

Gib [dʒɪb] *n fam (abbr of Gibraltar)* Gibraltar.

gibberish ['dʒɪbərɪʃ] *n* galimatías *m inv*.

gibbet ['dʒɪbɪt] *n* horca *f*.

gibbon ['gɪbən] *n Zool* gibón *m*.

gibe [dʒaɪb] **I** *n* mofa *f*, comentario *m* sarcástico, sarcasmo *m*. **II** *vi* mofarse (**at,** de), burlarse (**at,** de).

giblets ['dʒɪblɪts] *npl* menudillos *mpl*.

Gibraltar [dʒɪ'brɔːltə'] *n* Gibraltar; **the Rock of G.,** el Peñón de Gibraltar; **the Straits of G.,** el Estrecho de Gibraltar.

Gibraltarian [dʒɪbrɔːl'teərɪən] *adj & n* gibraltareño,-a *(m,f)*.

giddiness ['gɪdɪnɪs] *n* mareo *m*, vértigo *m*.

giddy ['gɪdɪ] *adj (giddier, giddiest)* mareado,-a; **it makes me g.,** me da vértigo; **to feel g.,** sentirse mareado,-a.

gift [gɪft] *n* **1** *(present)* regalo *m*; *Com* obsequio *m*. **2** *(give-away)* ganga *f*; **g. shop,** tienda *f* de artículos de regalo; **g. token,** vale *m*; **that car was a g. at that price,** ese coche te ha salido que ni regalado; *fam fig* **he thinks he's God's g.,** se cree el Rey del Mambo; *prov* **never look a g. horse in the mouth,** a caballo regalado no le mires el diente. **3** *(talent)* don *m*; **to have a g. for music,** estar muy dotado,-a para la música; *fam* **to have the g. of the gab,** tener un pico de oro.

gifted ['gɪftɪd] *adj* dotado,-a.

gift-wrapped ['gɪftræpt] *adj* envuelto,-a para regalo.

gig [gɪg] *n sl Mus* actuación *f*.

gigantic [dʒaɪ'gæntɪk] *adj* gigantesco,-a, descomunal.

giggle ['gɪgəl] **I** *n* **1** *(chuckle)* risita *f*, risa *f* tonta; **I got the giggles,** me dio la risa. **2** *(lark)* broma *f*, diversión *f*; **the film's a right g.,** la película es divertida; **we all dressed up like clowns for a g.,** nos disfrazamos de payaso para reír un rato. **II** *vi* reírse tontamente.

gigolo ['dʒɪgələʊ] *n (pl gigolos)* gigolo *m*.

gild [gɪld] *vtr (pt & pp gilded or gilt)* dorar; *fig* **to g. the lily,** *(gen)* sobrecargar; *(decoration)* poner demasiadas florituras a.

gill¹ [dʒɪl] *n (measurement)* medida *f* de líquidos (≈ 0,142 litro).

gill² [gɪl] *n (of fish)* branquia *f*, agalla *f*; *fam* **to look pale** *o* **green about the gills**, tener mala cara.

gilt [gɪlt] **I** *adj* dorado,-a. **II** *n (colour)* dorado *m*.

gilt-edged ['gɪltedʒd] *adj Fin* **g.-e. securities**, valores *mpl* de máxima garantía.

gimlet ['gɪmlɪt] *n Tech* barrena *f* de cola, broca *f*.

gimmick ['gɪmɪk] *n (action)* truco *m*; *(device)* reclamo *m*; **advertising g.**, reclamo *m* publicitario.

gimmicky ['gɪmɪkɪ] *adj* con truco, superficial.

gin [dʒɪn] *n* ginebra *f*; **g. and tonic**, gin tonic *m*.

ginger ['dʒɪndʒə*ʳ*] **I** *n* **1** *Bot* jengibre *m*; **g. ale**, ginger ale *m*. **2** *Pol* **g. group**, grupo *m* de presión. **II** *adj* **1** de jengibre. **2** *(hair)* pelirrojo,-a.

gingerbread ['dʒɪndʒəbred] *n* pan *m* *o* galleta *f* de jengibre.

gingerly ['dʒɪndʒəlɪ] *adv* cautelosamente.

gingernut ['dʒɪndʒənʌt] *n* galleta *f* de jengibre.

gingersnap ['dʒɪndʒəsnæp] *n US* galleta *f* de jengibre.

gingham ['gɪŋəm] *n Tex* guinga *f*, guingán *m*.

gingivitis [dʒɪndʒɪ'vaɪtɪs] *n Med* gingivitis *f*.

gipsy ['dʒɪpsɪ] *adj & n* gitano,-a *(m,f)*.

giraffe [dʒɪ'rɑːf] *n Zool* jirafa *f*.

gird [gɜːd] *vtr (pt & pp* **girded** *or* **girt)** **1** *(fasten)* ceñir. **2** *(for fight etc)* prepararse; *fig* **to g. up one's loins**, prepararse para la lucha. **3** *(encircle)* rodear.

girder ['gɜːdə*ʳ*] *n Constr* viga *f*.

girdle ['gɜːdəl] **I** *n* **1** *(clothes)* faja *f*. **2** *Anat* **pelvic g.**, pelvis *f*. **II** *vtr Lit* rodear.

girl [gɜːl] *n* **1** *(gen)* chica *f*, muchacha *f*, joven *f*; *(child)* niña *f*; **g. Friday**, chica *f* para todo; **g. guide**, *US* **g. scout**, exploradora *f*. **2** *(daughter)* hija *f*. **3** *(pupil)* alumna *f*; **old girls' reunion**, reunión *f* de las antiguas alumnas. **4** *(sweetheart)* novia *f*.

girlfriend ['gɜːlfrend] *n* **1** *(fiancée)* novia *f*. **2** *(companion)* amiga *f*, compañera *f*.

girlhood ['gɜːlhʊd] *n (childhood)* niñez *f*; *(youth)* juventud *f*.

girlie ['gɜːlɪ] *adj fam* **g. magazines**, revistas *fpl* de destape.

girlish ['gɜːlɪʃ] *adj* **1** *(of girl)* de niña. **2** *(effeminate)* afeminado,-a.

giro ['dʒaɪrəʊ] *n GB* giro *m* (postal). ■ **g. account**, cuenta *f* de giros postales; **g. (cheque)**, cheque *m* de giros postales.

girt [gɜːt] *pt & pp* see **gird**.

gist [dʒɪst] *n* esencia *f*, lo esencial; **did you get the g. of what he was saying?**, ¿cogiste la idea de lo que decía?; **the g. of the matter**, el quid de la cuestión.

give [gɪv] **I** *n (elasticity)* elasticidad *f*. **II** *vtr (pt* **gave***; pp* **given)** **1** *(gen)* dar; **to g. a cry**, lanzar un grito; **to g. a sigh**, dar un suspiro; **to g. a start**, asustarse, pegar un salto; **to g. sth a shake**, sacudir algo. **2** *(deliver, pass on)* entregar; *Tel* **could you please g. me Anne Smith**, póngame con Anne Smith, por favor; **g. him our love**, dale un abrazo de nuestra parte; **to g. sb a message**, dar un recado a algn; **to g. sb a present**, regalar algo a algn; **to g. sth to sb**, dar algo a algn. **3** *(provide)* dar, suministrar; **to g. sb sth to eat**, dar de comer a algn; **to g. sb one's support**, apoyar a algn; *fig* **to g. one's word**, dar su palabra. **4** *(pay)* pagar, dar; **how much did he g. for it?**, ¿cuánto pagó por ello?; *fig* **I'd g. anything to go**, daría cualquier cosa por poder ir. **5** *(perform etc)* *(concert etc)* dar; *(speech)* pronunciar; **g. us a song!**, ¡cántanos algo! **6** *(dedicate)* dedicar, consagrar; **to g. same thought to a matter**, reflexionar sobre un asunto. **7** *(grant)* otorgar; **to g. sb one's attention**, prestar atención a algn. **8** *(cause)* ocasionar, causar; **to g. sb to understand that ...**, dar a entender a algn que ... . **9** *(yield)* ceder; *fam* **I'll g. you that**, te doy la razón. **10 to g. way**, *Aut* ceder el paso; *fig* ceder, conceder; *(ground)* hundirse; *(ladder)* romperse; *(legs)* doblarse; **'g. way',**

'ceda el paso'. **11** *(expressions)* *fam* **don't g. me that!**, ¡no me vengas con esas!; *fam* **g. roe English cooking every time**, para mí no hay nada como la cocina inglesa; *fam* **I'll g. you (what for)!**, ¡te vas a enterar! **III** *vi* **1** *(concede)* conceder; **to g. and take**, hacer concesiones mutuas; **to g. as good as one gets**, devolver golpe por golpe. **2** *(yield)* ceder; *(cloth, elastic)* dar de sí. ◆ **give away** *vtr* **1** *(gen)* distribuir, repartir; *(present)* regalar; *(prize)* entregar; *fam fig* **to g. the bride away**, llevar a la novia al altar. **2** *(disclose, divulge)* revelar, descubrir; **to g. the game away**, descubrir el pastel. **3** *(betray)* traicionar, denunciar; **his smile gave him away**, su sonrisa le traicionó. ◆ **give back** *vtr (return)* devolver. ◆ **give in** *vi* **1** *(admit defeat)* darse por vencido,-a; *(surrender)* rendirse; **I g. in!**, ¡me rindo! **2** *(yield)* ceder; **to g. in to**, ceder ante. **II** *vtr (hand in)* entregar. ◆ **give off** *vtr (smell, heat, etc)* despedir, emitir. ◆ **give onto** *vi* dar a; **her apartment gives onto a rubbish tip**, su piso da a un vertedero de basuras. ◆ **give out I** *vtr* **1** *(distribute)* distribuir, repartir. **2** *(announce)* anunciar. **II** *vi (supplies)* agotarse; *(break down)* sufrir una avería; *fam fig* **my patience is giving out**, se me está acabando la paciencia. ◆ **give over** *vtr (hand over)* entregar; *(devote)* dedicar; **land given over to agriculture**, terreno dedicado a la agricultura; *fam* **g. over!**, ¡basta ya! ◆ **give up I** *vtr* **1** *(renounce)* dejar; *(idea)* abandonar, renunciar a; **to g. up smoking**, dejar de fumar. **2** *(betray)* traicionar; **my friends would never g. me up**, mis amigos nunca me traicionarían. **3** *(abandon)* dar; **the victims were given up for dead**, se dieron las víctimas por muertos. **II** *vi* **1** *(admit defeat)* darse por vencido,-a, rendirse; *(life)* dar; **don't g. up**, no te desanimes; **I g. up!**, ¡me rindo! **many young men gave up their lives for their country**, muchos jóvenes dieron su vida por el país. **2** *(hand over)* entregar; **to g. oneself up to the police**, entregarse a la policía. ◆ **give up on** *vtr* desistir; **he gave up on the idea of becoming a successful writer**, abandonó la idea de ser un escritor famoso. ◆ **give up to** *vtr* dedicarse enteramente; **she gave her whole life up to helping the needy**, entregó su vida a ayudar a los necesitados.

giveaway ['gɪvəweɪ] *n* **1** *(disclosure)* revelación *f* involuntaria; *fam* **it's a dead g.**, salta a la vista. **2** *(gift)* regalo *m*; **g. price**, precio *m* de saldo; **when I bought that I got a chocolate as a g.**, cuando compré esto me dieron una chocolatina de regalo.

given ['gɪvn] **I** *pp* see **give**. **II** *adj* **1** *(particular, fixed)* dado,-a; **at a g. time**, en un momento determinado; **g. name**, nombre *m* de pila. **2** *(inclined, prone)* **g. to**, dado,-a a, propenso,-a a. **III** *conj* **1** *(considering)* dado,-a; **g. his resources, he's done pretty well**, teniendo en cuenta sus medios lo ha hecho bastante bien. **2** *(if)* si; **g. the chance, he could do just as well as the others**, si tuviera la oportunidad, lo podría hacer tan bien como los otros.

gizmo ['gɪzməʊ] *n fam* chisme *m*.

gizzard ['gɪzəd] *n (of bird)* molleja *f*.

Gk *abbr of* **Greek**, griego,-a *m*,*f*.

glacé ['glæseɪ] *adj Culin* escarchado,-a; **g. cherry**, cereza *f* confitada.

glacial ['gleɪsɪəl] *adj* **1** *Geol* glaciar; **g. deposits**, depósitos *mpl* glaciares. **2** *(icy)* glacial; *fig (cold)* glacial; **g. wind**, viento *m* glacial; *fig* **g. look**, mirada *f* glacial.

glacier ['glæsɪə*ʳ*] *n Geol* glaciar *m*.

glad [glæd] *adj* **(gladder, gladdest)** *(delighted)* contento,-a; *(happy)* alegre; **he'll be only too g. to help you**, tendrá mucho gusto en ayudarle; **I'm g. you came**, me alegro de que hayas venido; **to be g.**, alegrarse. ■ **g. rags**, ropa *f* de fiesta. ◆ **gladly** *adv* con mucho gusto.

gladden ['glædən] *vtr* alegrar.

glade [gleɪd] *n (clearing)* claro *m*; **a g. in the forest**, un claro en el bosque.

gladiator ['glædɪeɪtə*ʳ*] *n Hist* gladiador *m*.

gladness ['glædnɪs]*(delight)* satisfacción *f; (happiness)* alegría *f.*

gladiolus [glædɪ'əʊləs] *n (pl **gladioli** [glædɪ'əʊlaɪ]) Bot* gladiolo *m.*

glamor ['glæməʳ] *n US see* **glamour.**

glamorize ['glæməraɪz] *vtr* embellecer, hacer más atractivo,-a; **films can sometimes g. war,** en algunas ocasiones, el cine puede hacer que la guerra resulte atractiva.

glamorous ['glæmərəs] *adj* 1 *(attractive, stunning)* atractivo,-a, encantador,-a; **his wife looked very g. in her silk dress,** su esposa estaba muy llamativa con el vestido de seda. 2 *(fashionable)* prestigioso,-a; **the group played many g. venues,** el grupo actuó en muchos locales prestigiosos.

glamour ['glæməʳ] *n* 1 *(attraction)* atractivo *m; (charm)* encanto *m;* **a g. girl,** una belleza. 2 *(beauty)* belleza *f* sofisticada.

glance [glɑːns] *I n* mirada *f*, vistazo *m*, ojeada *f;* **at a g.,** de un vistazo; **at first g.,** a primera vista. **II** *vi* 1 *(look)* echar una mirada *or* un vistazo *or* una ojeada **(at,** a); **to g. sideways,** mirar de reojo. 2 *(newspaper etc)* **to g. through,** ojear. ◆ **glance off** *vtr (ball etc)* rebotar de.

glancing ['glɑːnsɪn] *adj (blow)* oblicuo,-a.

gland [glænd] *n Anat* glándula *f.*

glandular [glændjʊləʳ] *adj* glandular. ■ *Med* **g. fever,** mononucleosis *f* infecciosa.

glare [gleəʳ] *I n* 1 *(light)* luz *f* deslumbrante; *Aut (dazzle)* deslumbramiento *m.* 2 *(look)* mirada *f* feroz. **II** *vi* 1 *(dazzle)* deslumbrar. 2. *(look)* lanzar una mirada furiosa, mirar airadamente **(at,** a).

glaring ['gleərɪn] *adj* 1 *(light)* deslumbrante; *(colour)* chillón,-ona. 2 *(obvious)* evidente; **a g. mistake,** un error que salta a la vista.

glass [glɑːs] *n (pl **glasses**)* 1 *(material)* vidrio *m;* **pane of g.,** cristal *m; prov* **people who live in g. houses shouldn't throw stones,** el que esté libre de pecado que tire la pimera piedra. ■ **cut g.,** cristal *m* tallado; **g. bead,** abalorio *m;* **g. case,** campana *f* de cristal; **g. door,** puerta *f* de cristal; **g. eye,** ojo *m* de cristal; **g. fibre,** fibra *f* de vidrio; **g. industry,** industria *f* del vidrio; **stained g.,** vidrio *m* de color. 2 *(drinking vessel)* vaso *m;* **a g. of water,** un vaso de agua; **wine g.,** copa *f*(para vino). 3 *arch* **looking g.,** espejo *m.* 4 *(barometer)* barómetro *m.* 5 **glasses,** gafas *fpl*, lentes *mpl;* **to wear g.,** llevar gafas. ■ **field g.,** gemelos *mpl.*

glass-blower ['glɑːsbləʊəʳ] *n* soplador,-a *m, f* de vidrio.

glass-blowing ['glɑːsbləʊɪn] *n* soplado *m* de vidrio.

glasshouse ['glɑːshaʊs] *n* 1 *Hort* invernadero *m.* 2 *sl Mil* prisión *f* militar.

glassware ['glɑːsweəʳ] *n* cristalería *f.*

glassy ['glɑːsɪ] *adj (glassier, glassiest)* 1 *(like glass)* vítreo,-a; *(water)* cristalino,-a. 2 *fig (eyes)* vidrioso,-a.

glaucoma [glɔː'kəʊmə] *n Med* glaucoma *m.*

glaze [gleɪz] *I (varnish)* barniz *m; (for pottery)* vidriado *m.* **II** *vtr* 1 *(windows)* poner cristales. 2 *(varnish)* barnizar; *(ceramics)* vidriar. 3 *Culin* glasear.

glazed [gleɪzd] *adj (eyes)* de mirada ausente.

glazier ['gleɪzɪəʳ] *n* vidriero,-a *m, f.*

glazing ['gleɪzɪn] *n* cristales *mpl;* **double g.,** doble cristal *m.*

gleam [gliːm] *I n* 1 destello *m.* 2 *fig (glimmer)* rayo *m;* **a g. of hope,** un rayo de esperanza. **II** *vi* brillar, relucir.

gleaming ['gliːmɪn] *adj* brillante, reluciente.

glean [gliːn] *vtr* 1 *Agr* espigar. 2 *fig (cull)* recoger, cosechar; **we gleaned very little information from the lecture,** pudimos extraer muy poca información de la conferencia.

glee [gliː] *n* 1 *(delight)* alegría *f*, júbilo *m*, regocijo *m.* 2 *Mus* **g. club,** coral *f.*

gleeful ['gliːfʊl] *adj* alegre, jubiloso,-a. ◆ **gleefully** *adv* con alegría, con júbilo.

glen [glen] *n Scot Ir Geog* cañada *f.*

glib [glɪb] *adj (glibber, glibbest) pej (person)* de mucha labia.

glide [glaɪd] *vi* 1 *(slip, slide)* deslizarse. 2 *Av* planear.

glider ['glaɪdəʳ] *n Av* planeador *m.*

gliding ['glaɪdɪn] *n Av* planeo *m; Sport* vuelo *m* sin motor.

glimmer ['glɪməʳ] *I n* 1 *(light)* luz *f* tenue. 2*(reflection)* reflejo *m.* 3 *fig (trace)* resquicio *m*, indicio *m;* **g. of hope,** resquicio de esperanza. **II** *vi* 1 *(shine)* brillar tenuemente. 2 *(water)* espejear, relucir.

glimpse [glɪmps] *I n* vislumbre *f*, visión *f* momentánea; **to catch a g. of,** vislumbrar. **II** *vtr (catch sight of)* vislumbrar, entrever; *(perceive)* darse cuenta, comprender; **he glimpsed a difficult week ahead,** vio que le esperaba una semana muy difícil.

glint [glɪnt] *I n (twinkle)* destello *m*, centelleo *m;* **he had a g. in his eye,** le brillaban los ojos. **II** *vi (glisten)* destellar, centellear.

glisten ['glɪsən] *vi* relucir, brillar.

glitter ['glɪtəʳ] *I n* brillo *m.* **II** *vi* relucir, brillar; *prov* **all that glitters is not gold,** no es oro todo lo que reluce.

glittering ['glɪtərɪn] *adj* reluciente, brillante, resplandeciente.

gloat [gləʊt] *vi* jactarse; *(news)* saborear; **to g. over another's misfortune,** recrearse con la desgracia de otro.

global ['gləʊbəl] *adj* 1 *(of the world)* mundial. 2 *(overall)* global; **g. view,** vista *f* global, vista *f* de conjunto.

globe [gləʊb] *n* 1 globo *m*, esfera *f; Elec* **g. lampshade,** globo *m.* 2 *(earth)* globo *m* terrestre; *(model)* globo *m* (terráquio).

globe-trotter ['gləʊbtrɒtəʳ] *n* trotamundos *mf inv.*

globular ['glɒbjʊləʳ] *adj* globular.

globule ['glɒbjuːl] *n (droplet)* glóbulo *m.*

gloom [gluːm] *n* 1 *(obscurity)* penumbra *f.* 2 *(melancholy)* melancolía *f*, tristeza *f.* 3 *(pessimism)* desolación *f*, pesimísmo *m.*

gloomy ['gluːmɪ] *adj (gloomier, gloomiest)* 1 *(dark)* oscuro,-a, tenebroso,-a; *(weather)* gris. 2 *(dismal)* deprimente. 3 *(dispondent)* pesimista, desalentador,-a; *(sad)* melancólico,-a, triste; **the future looks g.,** el futuro pinta negro; **to feel g.,** verlo todo negro.

glorified ['glɔːrɪfaɪd] *adj pej* pretencioso,-a; **the castle was just a g. old house,** resultó ser una casa con pretensiones de castillo.

glorify ['glɔːrɪfaɪ] *vtr (pt & pp **glorified**) (God)* glorificar; *(extol)* alabar.

glorious ['glɔːrɪəs] *adj (momentous)* glorioso,-a; *(splendid)* magnífico,-a, espléndido,-a; **the weather is g. at the moment,** hace un tiempo espléndido.

glory ['glɔːrɪ] *I n (gen)* gloria *f; fig (splendour)* esplendor *m; fig (triumph)* triunfo *m;* **to be in one's g.,** estar en la gloria; **to live on past glories,** vivir de glorias pasadas. **II** *vi (pt & pp **gloried**)* **to g. in sth,** jactarse de algo.

gloss [glɒs] *I n* 1 *(explanation)* glosa *f.* 2 *(sheen)* brillo *m; fig (polish)* lustre *m.* ■ **g. (paint),** pintura *f* brillante *or* esmalte. **II** *vi* glosar. ◆ **gloss over** *vtr fig* encubrir.

glossary ['glɒsərɪ] *n* glosario *m.*

glossy ['glɒsɪ] *adj (glossier, glossiest)* lustroso,-a, brillante. ■ *Press* **g. magazine,** revista *f* de lujo.

glottis ['glɒtɪs] *n Anat* glotis *f.*

glove [glʌv] *n* guante *m; fig* **to fit like a g.,** sentar como un guante. ■ *Aut* **g. compartment,** guantera *f;* **g. puppet,** polichinela *f*, pulchinela *f.*

glow [gləʊ] *I n* 1 *(of jewel)* brillo *m; (of fire, metal)* incandescencia *f; (of sun)* arrebol *m; (heat)* calor *m; (light)* luz *f.* 2 *(in cheeks)* rubor *m.* 3 *fig (thrill)* bienestar *m*, satisfacción *f.* **II** *vi* 1 *(jewel, sun)* brillar; *(fire)* arder; *(metal)* estar al rojo vivo. 2 *fig* rebosar de; **to g. with health,** rebosar de salud.

glower ['glaʊə'] *vi* poner cara de enfadado,-a, fruncir el ceño.

glowing ['gləʊɪŋ] *adj* **1** *(fire, metal)* incandescente; *(metal)* al rojo vivo; *(fire, colour)* vivo,-a; *(light)* brillante. **2** *(cheeks)* encendido,-a. **3** *(report)* entusiasta; *(style)* cálido,-a.

glowworm ['gləʊwɜːm] *n Zool* luciérnaga *f*, gusano *m* de luz.

glucose ['gluːkəʊz] *n Chem* glucosa *f*.

glue [gluː] **I** *n* pegamento *m*, cola *f*; *(drug)* **to sniff g.,** inhalar cola. **II** *vtr* pegar **(to,** a); **to g. sth together,** pegar algo; *fam fig* **his eyes were glued to the screen,** tenía los ojos pegados a la pantalla.

glue-sniffing ['gluːsnɪfɪŋ] *n* inhalación *f* de cola.

glum [glʌm] *adj* **(glummer, glummest)** triste, abatido,-a; desanimado,-a; **don't look so g.,** no estés tan serio,-a. ◆ **glumly** *adv* con desánimo.

glut [glʌt] **I** *n* superabundancia *f*, exceso *m*. **II** *vtr (pt & pp* **glutted)** **1** *(swamp)* saturar. **2** *(overeat)* hartarse, saciar; **the market is glutted with bifi equipment,** el mercado está invadido de equipos de alta fidelidad.

glutinous ['gluːtɪnəs] *adj* pegajoso,-a, glutinoso,-a.

glutton ['glʌtən] *n* glotón,-ona *m, f*; *fam fig* **he's a g. for punishment, he studies ten hours a day,** es un masoquista, estudia diez horas cada día; *fam fig* **to be a g. for work,** ser un trabajador incansable.

gluttonous ['glʌtənəs] *adj* glotón,-ona, goloso,-a.

gluttony ['glʌtənɪ] *n* glotonería *f*, gula *f*.

glycerine, *US* **glycerin** ['glɪsərɪn] *n* glicerina *f*.

gm *abbr of* **gram,** gramo *m*, gr.

GMT [dʒiːemˈtiː] *abbr of* **Greenwich Mean Time,** Hora *f* media de Greenwich, GMT.

gnarled [nɑːld] *adj* nudoso,-a.

gnash [næʃ] *vtr* chirriar, rechinar; **to g. one's teeth,** hacer rechinar los dientes.

gnat [næt] *n Ent* mosquito *m*.

gnaw [nɔː] *vtr & vi (chew)* roer; *fig (nag)* corroer; **he had a great sense of sadness gnawing away inside,** una terrible sensación de tristeza le corroía por dentro.

gnawing ['nɔːɪŋ] *adj (hunger, anxiety)* constante; *(pain)* insistente.

GNP [dʒiːenˈpiː] *Econ abbr of* **gross national product,** producto *m* nacional bruto, PNB *m*.

gnome [nəʊm] *n* gnomo *m*.

go [gəʊ] **I** *vi (3rd person sing pres* **goes**; *pt* **went**; *pp* **gone) 1** *(gen)* ir; **to come and go,** ir y venir; **to go by car/by train/on foot,** ir en coche/en tren/a pie; **to go for a walk,** (ir a) dar un paseo; **to g. on a journey,** ir de viaje; **to go shopping,** ir de compras; **to go to Scotland,** ir a Escocia; **to go to the cinema,** ir al cine; **you go first,** vete tú primero; *fig* **to go too far,** ir demasiado lejos, pasarse (de la raya); *fig* **I wouldn't go so far as to say that,** yo no diría tanto. **2** *(depart)* irse, marcharse; *(train, bus)* salir; **let's go!,** ¡vámonos!; **we must be going,** tenemos que irnos; *Sport* **ready, steady, go!,** ¡preparados, listos, ya! **3** *(disappear)* desaparecer; **her voice has gone,** se ha quedado afónica; **my umbrella has gone,** he desaparecido mi paraguas; **these flowers will have to go,** habrá que tirar estas flores. **4** *(function)* funcionar, marchar; *(car)* marchar; **it goes at 50 miles an hour,** alcanza 50 millas por hora; **to make an engine go,** hacer funcionar un motor; *fig* **to get things going,** poner las cosas en marcha; *fig* **to keep going,** mantenerse a flote. **5** *(sell)* venderse; **going, going, gone!,** ¡a la una, a las dos, a las tres!; **it went for £10,** se vendió por 10 libras; **shoes going cheap,** zapatos a precios de rebaja. **6** *(become)* quedarse, volverse; **to go blind,** quedarse ciego,-a; **to go mad,** volverse loco,-a; **to go red,** ruborizarse. **7** *(progress)* ir, marchar, andar; **everything went well,** todo salió bien; **how did the meeting go?,** ¿qué tal la reunión?; **how's it going?,** ¿cómo va todo?, qué tal te van

las cosas?; **I hope it goes well for you,** que te vaya bien; **the way things are going,** tal como van las cosas. **8** *(future)* **to be going to,** *(in the future)* ir a; *(on the point of)* estar a punto de; **she's just going to leave,** va a salir; **we were just going to do it now,** estábamos a punto de hacerlo. **9** *(fit)* caber; **it won't go into the box,** no cabe en la caja; **three into two won't go,** dos dividido entre tres no cabe. **10** *(be kept)* guardarse; **where do the cups go?,** ¿dónde se guardan las tazas? **11** *(be available)* quedar; **I'll take whatever's going,** me conformo con lo que hay; **is there any tea going?** ¿queda algo de té?; **there are few jobs going,** hay poco trabajo. **12** *(be acceptable)* valer; **anything goes,** todo vale, todo está permitido; **that goes without saying,** eso es evidente. **13** *(break)* romperse; *(yield)* ceder; *(blow)* fundirse; **the fuses went,** se fundieron los plomos; **to go at the seams,** descoserse. **14** *(make) (noise, gesture)* hacer; **go like this with your hands,** haz así con las manos; **how does that song go?,** ¿cómo hace aquella canción?; **it went bang,** hizo pum. **15** *(time)* pasar; **it's just gone seven,** acaban de dar las siete; **there are only two weeks to go,** sólo (nos) quedan dos semanas; **time goes (by) so quickly,** el tiempo pasa volando; *fam* **she's six months gone,** está embarazada de seis meses. **16** *(be won)* ganar; **the prize went to Paul,** el premio fue a parar a Paul. **17** *(be inherited)* pasar **(to,** a); **the house went to her daughter,** la casa pasó a su hija. **18** *(say)* decir; **and I went ...,** y yo dije ...; **as the saying goes,** según el dicho; **there he goes again,** otra vez con la misma canción. **19** *(release)* soltar; **to let sth go,** soltar algo; *fam fig* **to let oneself go,** *(lose inhibitions)* dejarse llevar; *(neglect appearance)* descuidarse. **20** *(have a turn)* tocar; **it's my turn to go,** ahora me toca a mí. **II** *vtr* **1** *(travel, cover)* hacer, recorrer; **they went six miles,** hicieron seis millas. **2** **to go it alone,** apañárselas solo; **to go one better than sb,** superar a algn. **III** *n* **1** *(energy)* energía *f*, dinamismo *m*; **he's always on the go,** no para nunca; **it's all go!,** ¡no hay quien pare!; **she's got lots of go,** tiene mucha marcha. **2** *(try)* intento *m*; **to have a go at sth,** probar suerte con algo. **3** *(turn)* turno *m*; **it's your go,** te toca a ti. **4** *(success)* **to make a go of sth,** tener éxito en algo; **no go,** nada que hacer. **5** *(fashion)* moda *f*; **it's all the go,** está muy de moda. **6** *(start)* principio *m*; **I knew from the word go,** lo sabía desde el principio. **7** *(criticism)* crítica *f*; **to have a go at sb,** criticar a algn. ◆ **go about I** *vtr* **1** *(task)* emprender; **how do you go about it?,** ¿cómo hay que hacerlo? **2** *(regular activity)* continuar; **to go about one's business,** ocuparse de sus asuntos. **II** *vi* **1** *(circulate)* circular; *(rumour)* correr; *(illness)* haber, correr. **2** *Naut* virar. ◆ **go after** *vtr (pursue)* perseguir, andar tras. ◆ **go against** *vi (oppose)* ir en contra de; *(verdict)* ser desfavorable a. ◆ **go ahead I** *vi* **1** *(proceed)* proceder; **go ahead!,** ¡adelante!; **to go ahead with a scheme,** llevar un proyecto adelante. **2** *(precede)* preceder; **we'll go on ahead,** iremos delante. ◆ **go along** *vtr* **1** *(street etc)* pasar por. **2** *(progress)* progresar; **things are going along fine,** las cosas van muy bien; *fam* **I made it up as I went along,** lo iba pensando a medida que lo hacía. ◆ **go along with** *vi* **1** *(agree)* estar de acuerdo con. **2** *(accompany)* acompañar. ◆ **go around** *vi* **1** *(rumour)* correr; *(illness)* haber, correr. **2** *(suffice)* llegar, haber; **there's enough to go around,** hay para todos. **3** *(associate oneself)* salir, acompañar; **I don't like the people they go around with,** no me gusta la gente cón la que salen. **4** *(habit)* estar continuamente; **she was always going around talking about people behind their backs,** siempre estaba criticando a la gente a sus espaldas. ◆ **go at** *vi fig (attack)* atacar; **he went at the wine,** se abalanzó sobre el vino. ◆ **go away** *vi* marcharse. ◆ **go back** *vi* **1** *(return)* volver, regresar. **2** *fig (date from)* datar de; **the church goes back to the Middle Ages,** la iglesia data de la Edad Medieval. ◆ **go back on** *vi (break)* no cumplir; **to go back on one's word,** faltar a su palabra. ◆ **go back to** *vi (resume)* volver a. ◆ **go before** *vi* **1** *(precede)* preceder. **2** *(in court) (person, matter)* presentarse. ◆ **go by** *vi (elapse)* pasar; **as time goes by,** con el tiempo; **in days gone by,** en otros tiempos. ◆ **go down** *vi* **1** *(gen)* ir; *(descend)* bajar;

(sun) ponerse; *(ship)* hundirse; **to go down on all fours,** gatear. **2** *(tyre)* desincharse. **3** *(diminish)* disminuir; *(temperature)* bajar; **to go down in value,** perder su valor. **4** *(be received)* ser acogido,-a; **to go down well,** ser bien acogido,-a. **5** *GB Univ* dejar la universidad. ♦ **go down as** *vi (record, remember)* considerar; **this moment will go down as an important one in this country's history,** este momento pasará a la historia. ♦ **go down with** *vi (contract)* pillar, coger; **to go down with flu,** coger una gripe. ♦ **go for** *vtr* **1** *(attack)* lanzarse sobre, atacar; *fam fig* **go for it!,** ¡a por ello! **2** *(fetch)* ir por, ir a buscar. **3** *fam (favour, like)* gustar; **I don't go much for that,** eso no me dice gran cosa. **4** *fam* valer para; **that goes for me too,** esto también va por mí. ♦ **go in** *vi (enter)* entrar; *(sun)* esconderse. ♦ **go in for** *vtr (exam)* presentarse a; *(pastime, hobby)* dedicarse a; *fam* **we don't go in for that sort of thing,** esas cosas no nos van. ♦ **go into** *vtr* **1** *(enter)* entrar en; **to go into fits of laughter,** troncharse de risa; **to go into journalism,** dedicarse al periodismo. **2** *(study)* examinar; *(matter)* investigar. **3** *(energy, money)* invertir; **a lot of money went into the project,** se invirtió mucho dinero en el proyecto. **4** *(crash)* chocar; **my car went into yours,** choqué contra tu coche. ♦ **go off I** *vi* **1** *(leave)* irse, marcharse; *Theat* hacer mutis; **she went off to post a letter,** salió a echar una carta. **2** *(bomb)* explotar; *(gun)* dispararse; *(alarm)* sonar. **3** *(food)* estropearse, pasarse; *(milk)* cortarse. **4** *(event)* salir; **it went off very well,** salió muy bien; **it went off without a hitch,** transcurrió sin problemas. **5** *fam (go to sleep)* dormirse. **II** *vtr fam* **to go off sth,** perder el gusto o el interés por algo; **I've gone off him,** ya no me gusta. ♦ **go off with** *vi fam (elope)* escaparse con un,-a amante. ♦ **go on I** *vi* **1** *(continue)* seguir, continuar; **after University she went on to work in the media,** después de la universidad pasó a trabajar en los medios de comunicación; *fam* **to go on talking,** seguir hablando; *fam* **to go on and on about sth,** machacar un tema; *(complain)* quejarse constantemente de algo; *fam* **don't go on!,** ¡no insistas!; *fam* **she's always going on about it,** siempre está con la misma canción; *fam* **to go on at sb,** dar el tostón a algn. **2** *(happen, take place)* pasar, ocurrir; **what's going on?,** ¿qué pasa? **3** *(time)* transcurrir, pasar; **as time goes on I get more impatient,** a medida que pasa el tiempo me voy impacientando más. **4** *(light etc)* encenderse; **the heating goes on automatically at eight o'clock,** la calefacción se enciende automáticamente a las ocho. **5** *(age)* estar a punto de cumplir; **he's sixteen going on seventeen,** estar a punto de cumplir los diecisiete. **6** *(for the purpose of)* bastar; **this is enough to be going on with,** de momento esto va bien así. **7** *fam* **go on!,** *(incredulity)* ¡no me digas!, ¡vaya!; *(persuasion)* ¡venga!, ¡adelante! ♦ **go out** *vi* **1** *(leave)* salir; **she doesn't go out much,** apenas sale; **to go out for a meal,** comer o cenar fuera; **to go out on strike,** declararse en huelga. **2** *(boy and girl)* salir juntos. **3** *(fire, light)* apagarse. **4** *(tide)* bajar. **5** *(información)* propagarse; *TV Rad* transmitir, retransmitir; **the film goes out on Friday on BBC 1,** la película se emite el viernes por el canal 1 de la BBC. **6 to go (all) out,** *(set out)* ir a por todas; **they went all out to win,** hicieron todo lo posible para ganar. **7** *Sport (cup-tie)* perder la eliminatoria. ♦ **go over** *vtr* **1** *(approach)* acercarse a; **they came over to help us,** se acercaron para ayudarnos. **2** *(revise)* repasar. ♦ **go over to** *vi* **1** *(desert)* traicionar; **to go over to the enemy,** pasarse al enemigo. **2** *(switch to)* cambiar a, pasar a; **in the seventies we went over to the decimal system,** en los años setenta pasamos a usar el sistema decimal. ♦ **go round** *vi* **1** *(revolve)* girar, dar vueltas. **2 to go round to sb's house,** pasar por casa de algn. ♦ **go through I** *vi* **1** *(endure)* resistir, sufrir; **after their divorce they went through a lot,** lo pasaron muy mal después del divorcio. **2** *(bill, law)* ser aprobado,-a; *(deal)* ser concluido,-a, ser llevado,-a a cabo. **II** *vtr* **1** *(examine)* examinar; *(search)* registrar; **to go through sb's pockets,** registrar los bolsillos a algn. **2** *(rehearse)* ensayar. **3** *(spend)* gastar; **he went through five hundred pounds on his holidays,** se gastó 500 libras en sus vacaciones. **4** *(list, plan, story, etc)* explicar. **5** *Sport (cup-*

tie) pasar la eliminatoria. ♦ **go through with** *vi* llevar algo a cabo; **I don't think I can go through with this marriage,** no creo que pueda llevar bien esto de la boda. ♦ **go towards** *vi* contribuir a; **this money will go towards the down payment for the house,** este dinero se reserva para el pago de la casa. ♦ **go under** *vi* **1** *(ship)* hundirse. **2** *(business)* fracasar. ♦ **go up** *vi* **1** *(price, temperature, stairs)* subir. **2** *Univ* ingresar en la universidad. **3** *(approach)* acercarse; **to go up to sb,** acercarse a algn. **4** *(go)* ir; **they always go up the pub before Sunday lunch,** siempre se acercan al pub los domingos a mediodía. **5** *(in a lift etc)* subir. **6** *(explode)* explotar; **the oil refinery could go up any minute,** la refinería puede explotar en cualquier momento; **to go up in flames,** quemarse. **7** *Theat (curtain)* levantar; **the curtain goes up at seven thirty,** se levanta el telón a las siete y media. **8** *Sport (be promoted)* subir, promocionarse; **United went up with City,** el United se promocionó junto al City. ♦ **go with** *vi* **1** *(accompany)* ir con; **the car goes with the job,** el coche va con el puesto. **2** *(colours)* hacer juego con, armonizar con. **3** *fam (sexually)* ir con, dormir con. ♦ **go without** *vtr* **1** pasarse sin, prescindir de; **I couldn't go a day without seeing her,** no podía pasar un día sin verla; **if there's no bread we'll have to go without,** tendremos que prescindir del pan si no lo hay. **2** *fam* **that goes without saying,** eso es evidente.

goad [gəʊd] *vtr* aguijonear; **to g. sb into doing sth,** acosar a algn para que haga algo. ♦ **goad on** *vtr (spur on)* incitar.

go-ahead ['gəʊəhed] *fam* **I** *n* luz *f* verde; **to give sb the go-a.,** dar luz verde a algn. **II** *adj (enterprising)* dinámico,-a, emprendedor,-a.

goal [gəʊl] *n* **1** *Sport* gol *m*; **to score a g.,** marcar un gol. ■ *Ftb* **g. area,** área *f* de meta; **g. kick,** saque *m* de puerta; **g. line,** línea *f* meta; **(g.) post,** poste *m*; **g. posts,** portería *f*; **g. scorer,** goleador,-a *m, f*, **leading g. scorer,** pichichi *m*. **2** *(aim, objective)* meta *f*, objetivo *m*, fin *m*.

goalie ['gəʊlɪ] *n Sport fam* portero,-a *m, f*, guardameta *mf*, meta *mf*, cancerbero *m*.

goalkeeper ['gəʊliːpəʳ] *n Sport* portero,-a *m, f*, guardameta *mf*.

goat [gəʊt] *n Zool (female)* cabra *f*; **he-g.,** macho *m* cabrío; **old g.,** viejo,-a *m, f* pesado,-a; *fam* **it gets my g.,** me pone negro,-a, me saca de quicio; *fam* **to act** o **play the g.,** hacer el indio, hacer el ganso.

goatee [gəʊ'tiː] *n* perilla *f*.

goatherd ['gəʊthɜːd] *n* cabrero,-a *m, f*.

goatskin ['gəʊtskɪn] *n* piel *f* de cabra.

gob¹ [gɒb] *n GB sl* boca *f*; **shut your g.!,** ¡cierra el pico!, ¡cállate la boca!

gob² [gɒb] *GB sl* **I** *n* lapo *f*, sipiajo *m*. **II** *vi* escupir.

gobble¹ ['gɒbəl] *vtr (food)* engullir.

gobble² ['gɒbəl] *vi (turkey)* gluglutear.

gobbledegook *n*, **gobbledygook** ['gɒbəldɪguːk] *n fam* parrafada *f*; **the minister just gave us a mouthful of g.,** el ministro sólo soltó una parrafada incomprensible.

go-between ['gəʊbɪtwiːn] *n* **1** *(mediator)* intermediario,-a *m, f*, mediator,-a *m, f*. **2** *Lit (between lovers)* alcahueta *f*.

goblet ['gɒblɪt] *n* copa *f*.

goblin ['gɒblɪn] *n* duende *m*.

gobstopper ['gɒbstɒpəʳ] *n GB* caramelo *m* grande y redondo.

goby ['gəʊbɪ] *n (fish)* chanquete *m*.

go-cart ['gəʊkɑːt] *n* **1** *(toy)* coche *m* de juguete. **2** *(handcart)* carretilla *f* de mano.

god [gɒd] *n* **1** dios *m*; **for G.'s sake!,** ¡por Dios!; **G.,** Dios; **(my) G.!,** ¡Dios mío!; **G. forbid,** ¡no lo permita Dios!; **G. only knows,** sabe Dios; **G. willing,** si Dios quiere. **2** *Theat fam* **the gods,** el gallinero.

godchild ['gɒdtʃaɪld] *n (pl godchildren* ['gɒdtʃɪldrən]*)* ahijado,-a *m, f*.

goddaughter ['gɒddɔːtə'] *n* ahijada *f*.

goddess ['gɒdɪs] *n* diosa *f*.

godfather ['gɒdfɑːðə'] *n* padrino *m*.

God-fearing ['gɒdfɪərɪŋ] *adj* timorato,-a, que teme a Dios.

godforsaken ['gɒdfəseɪkən] *adj (person)* dejado,-a de la mano de Dios; *(place)* poco interesante, remoto,-a.

godless ['gɒdlɪs] *adj* 1 *(wicked)* descreído,-a. 2 *(atheist)* ateo,-a.

godmother ['gɒdmʌðə'] *n* madrina *f*.

godparents ['gɒdpeərənts] *npl* padrinos *mpl*.

godsend ['gɒdsend] *n* regalo *m* inesperado; **those twelve pounds were a g.**, los doce libras me vinieron como llovidas del cielo.

godson ['gɒdsʌn] *n* ahijado *m*.

godwit ['gɒdwɪt] *n Orn* aguja *f*.

go-getter ['gəʊgetə'] *n fam* ambicioso,-a *m,f*.

goggle ['gɒgəl] I *vi* salirse los ojos de órbita; **to g. at sth**, mirar algo con ojos desorbitados; *TV fam* **the g. box**, la caja tonta.

goggles ['gɒgəlz] *npl* gafas *fpl* protectoras; **don't forget your g. if you go swimming**, si vas a la piscina, no te olvides las gafas.

going ['gəʊɪŋ] I *adj* 1 *(price)* actual, corriente; **the g. rate**, el precio medio. 2 *(business)* **a g. concern**, un negocio que marcha bien. 3 **to get** *or* **be g.**, marcharse; **we must be g.**, tenemos que irnos. 4 **to keep g.**, resistir, aguantar. II *n* 1 *(departure)* ida *f*, salida *f*. 2 *(pace)* paso *m*, ritmo *m*; **that was good g.!**, ¡qué rápido!; *fam* **when the g. gets tough the tough get g.**, cuando las cosas se ponen difíciles la reacción del valiente es hacerles frente. 3 *(condition of terrain)* estado *m* del camino; *fig* **the g. was rough**, encontraron muchos obstáculos; *fig* **to get out while the g. is good**, dejar de hacer algo antes que sea demasiado tarde.

going-over [gəʊɪŋ'əʊvə'] *n fam* 1 *(check)* inspección *f*. 2 *(beating)* paliza *f*; **to give sb a g.-o.**, darle una paliza a algn.

goings-on [gəʊɪŋz'ɒn] *npl fam* actividades *fpl*, tejemanejes *mpl*.

goitre, *US* **goiter** ['gɔɪtə'] *n Med* bocio *m*.

go-kart ['gəʊkɑːt] *n Sport* kart *m*.

gold [gəʊld] I *n (metal)* oro *m*; *(colour)* dorado *m*; **the g. rush**, la fiebre del oro; *fig* **to have a heart of g.**, tener un corazón de oro. ■ **g. digger**, buscador,-a *m, f* de oro; **g. dust**, oro *m* en polvo; **g. leaf**, pan *m* de oro; **g. medal**, medalla *f* de oro; **g. mine**, mina *f* de oro; **g. plate**, vajilla *f* de oro; **g. reserves**, reservas *fpl* de oro; *(colour)* oro, dorado,-a. II *adj* de oro; *(colour)* oro, dorado,-a.

goldcrest ['gəʊldkrest] *n Orn* reyezuelo *m* sencillo.

golden ['gəʊldən] *adj* de oro; *(colour)* dorado,-a; *fig* **a g. opportunity**, una excelente oportunidad. ■ *Myth* **G. Age**, Edad *f* de Oro; *Span* Siglo *m* de Oro; *Orn* **g. eagle**, águila *f* real; *fig* **g. handshake**, indemnización *f* de despido; **g. wedding**, bodas *fpl* de oro; *Myth* **the G. Fleece**, el Vellocino de oro.

goldfinch ['gəʊldfɪntʃ] *n Orn* jilguero *m*.

goldfish ['gəʊldfɪʃ] *n (pl goldfish or goldfishes)* pez *m* de colores. ■ **g. bowl**, pecera *f*.

gold-plated ['gəʊld'pleɪtɪd] *adj* dorado,-a, chapado,-a en oro.

goldsmith ['gəʊldsmɪθ] *n* orfebre *m*.

golf [gɒlf] *n Sport* golf *m*; **to play g.**, jugar al golf. ■ **g. ball**, pelota *f* de golf; **g. club**, *(stick)* palo *m* de golf; *(place)* club *m* de golf; **g. course**, campo *m* de golf.

golfer ['gɒlfə'] *n Sport* golfista *mf*, jugador,-a *m,f* de golf.

golfing ['gɒlfɪŋ] I *adj* de golf; **g. holiday**, vacaciones para jugar al golf. II *n* jugar al golf; **their husbands go g. every weekend**, sus maridos van a jugar al golf cada fin de semana.

golly ['gɒlɪ] *interj* ¡vaya!; *fam* **by g.**, sea como sea; **by g. I'm going to have a good time**, sea como sea me lo voy a pasar bien.

gondola ['gɒndələ] *n* góndola *f*.

gondolier [gɒndə'lɪə'] *n* gondolero *m*.

gone [gɒn] I *pp see* **go**. II *adj* desaparecido,-a; **g. are the days when you can walk the streets at night safely**, quedan lejos los tiempos en los que se podía caminar por las calles de noche con seguridad. III *prep* **it'll be g. six by the time he gets here**, serán las seis pasadas cuando llegue.

goner ['gɒnə'] *n fam* enfermo *m* terminal.

gong [gɒŋ] *n* gong *m*, batintín *m*.

gonorrhoea, *US* **gonorrhea** [gɒnə'rɪə] *n Med* gonorrea *f*.

goo [guː] *n fam* 1 *(gunge)* sustancia *f* pegajosa. 2 *fig (sentimentality)* sentimentalismo *m*.

good [gʊd] I *adj (better, best)* 1 *(of positive or pleasing qualities) (before noun)* buen,-a; *(after noun)* bueno,-a; *(land)* bueno,-a, rico,-a, fértil; **a g. book**, un buen libro; **g. afternoon**, **g. evening**, buenas tardes; **g. morning**, buenos días; **g. night**, buenas noches; **it looks g.**, tiene buen aspecto *or* buena pinta; **it's too g. to be true**, es demasiado bueno para ser cierto; **it was g. to get your letter**, me hizo mucha ilusión recibir tu carta; **that's a g. one!**, ¡qué chiste más bueno!; **this cake is very g.**, este pastel está riquísimo; **to be as g. as new**, estar como nuevo,-a; **to feel g.**, sentirse bien; **to have a g. time**, pasarlo bien; **to smell g.**, oler bien; **with all g. wishes**, con mis *or* nuestros mejores deseos. ■ *Rel* **G. Friday**, Viernes *m* Santo. 2 *(person) (kind)* amable; *(generous)* generoso,-a; **it's very g. of you**, es muy amable de tu parte; **to be g. to sb**, ser amable con algn; **would you be g. enough to open the window?**, ¿sería tan amable de abrir la ventana? 3 *(beneficial)* bueno,-a; *(healthy)* sano,-a; **to drink more than is g. for one**, beber más de la cuenta; **yoghurt is g. for you**, el yogur es muy sano. 4 *(well-behaved)* bueno,-a; *(morally correct)* correcto,-a, responsable; **be g.!**, ¡pórtate bien!; **you can trust her, she's a g. woman**, puedes confiar en ella, es una buena mujer; *fam* **fig her son was as g. as gold**, su hijo se portó como un ángel. 5 *(skilled)* bueno,-a, hábil; **he's g. at languages**, tiene facilidad para las idiomas; **she's g. with her hands**, es muy hábil con las manos; **they're g. with children**, tienen don para los niños. 6 *(attractive)* bueno,-a, bonito,-a; **g. handwriting**, buena letra; **he's earning g. money**, gana un buen sueldo; **red looks g. on you**, el rojo te favorece mucho; **she has a very g. figure**, tiene un tipo estupendo. ■ **g. looks**, atractivo *m sing*, belleza *f sing*. 7 *(valid)* válido,-a; **it's as g. as an offer**, equivale a una oferta; **it's as g. a way as any**, es una manera como otra cualquiera; **she's as g. as you**, ella vale tanto como tú. 8 *(at least)* como mínimo, por lo menos; **a g. 50 kilometres**, unos 50 kilómetros por lo menos. 9 *(considerable)* bueno,-a; *(sufficient)* bastante; **a g. amount of food**, bastante comida; **a g. many people**, bastante gente; **to give sb a g. telling off**, echar una bronca a algn; **to give sth a g. clean**, limpiar algo a fondo; **we waited a g. while**, esperamos un buen rato. 10 *(just, fair)* **to give as g. as one gets**, devolver golpe por golpe; **to make g.**, *(injustice)* reparar; *(loss)* compensar; *(one's word)* cumplir; *(succeed in life)* triunfar. 11 *(reliable)* de confianza, bueno,-a; **a g. butcher's**, una carnicería de confianza. 12 *(satisfying)* bueno,-a; **a g. rest**, un buen descanso. 13 *(propitious)* bueno,-a, propicio,-a; **a g. time to go on holiday**, un buen momento para ir de vacaciones. 14 *(honourable)* bueno,-a; **she comes from a g. family**, es de buena familia. 15 *(suitable)* bueno,-a; **a g. pair of gloves and a g. coat**, unos buenos guantes y un buen abrigo. 16 *(character)* bueno,-a, agradable; **he's in a g. mood**, está de buen humor. II *n* 1 *(gen)* bien *m*; **g. and evil**, el bien y el mal; **he's up to no g.**, está tramando algo malo; **to come to no g.**, acabar mal; **to do g.**, hacer el bien. 2 *(people)* the **g.**, los buenos *mpl*; **he's no g. as a doctor**, no es buen médico. 3 *(advantage)* bien *m*, provecho *m*; **for the common g.**, en bien de todos; **for**

your own g., para tu propio bien; **if it's any g.**, si te sirve de algo; **it's no g. waiting**, no sirve de nada esperar; **it will do you g.**, te hará bien; **what's the g. of that?**, ¿de qué sirve eso?; *fam* **to be on to a g. thing**, tenerlo bien montado. **4** *Jur* **goods**, *(possessions)* bienes *mpl.* ◼ **consumer g.**, bienes *mpl* de consumo; **g. and chattels**, muebles y enseres *mpl*, efectos *mpl* personales. **5** *Com* **goods**, artículos *mpl*, géneros *mpl*, mercancías *fpl*; **knitted g.**, género *m* de punto; artículos; *fam* **to deliver the g.**, cumplir su palabra. ◼ **g. train**, tren *m* de mercancías. **III** *adv (forever)* **she's gone for g.**, se ha ido para siempre. **IV** *interj* **g.!**, ¡bravo!, ¡muy bien!

goodbye ['gʊdbaɪ] **I** *interj* ¡adiós! **II** *n* adiós *m*, despedida *f*; **to say g. to sb**, despedirse de algn.

good-for-nothing ['gʊdfənʌθɪŋ] *adj & n* inútil *(mf)*.

good-hearted [gʊd'hɑːtɪd] *adj* de buen corazón, bueno,-a.

good-humoured [gʊd'hjuːməd] *adj* de buen humor.

good-looking [gʊd'lʊkɪŋ] *adj* guapo,-a; **he's very g.-l.**, es muy guapo.

good-natured [gʊd'neɪtʃəd] *adj* amable, bondadoso,-a.

goodness ['gʊdnɪs] *n* **1** *(of heart)* bondad *f*; **my g.!**, ¡Dios mío!, ¡madre mía!; **thank g.!**, ¡gracias a Dios!; **for g. sake!**, ¡por Dios!; **I wish to g. you'd shut up!**, ¡ojalá te callaras! **2** *(quality)* calidad *f*

good-tempered [gʊd'tempəd] *adj* de buen carácter; *(pleasant)* apacible.

goodwill [gʊd'wɪl] *n* **1** buena voluntad *f*. **2** *Com (reputation)* buen nombre *m*.

goody ['gʊdɪ] **I** *n fam* **1** *Cin* el bueno; **the goodies and the baddies**, los buenos y los malos. **2** *Culin* dulce *m*, golosina *f*. **II** *interj (baby-talk)* **g.!**, ¡qué bien!

goody-goody [gʊdɪgʊdɪ] *adj & n fam (pl goody-goodies)* mosquita *f* muerta, santurrón,-ona *(m,f)*.

gooey ['guːɪ] *adj (gooier, gooiest) fam* **1** *(sticky)* pegajoso,-a. **2** *fig (slushy)* sentimental, sentimentaloide.

goof [guːf] *US fam* **I** *n (person)* bobo,-a *m, f*; *(thing)* metadura *f* de pata. **II** *vi (blunder)* meter la pata. ◆ **goof off** *vi (skive)* perder el tiempo.

goofy ['guːfɪ] *adj (goofier, goofiest) fam* **1** *(of teeth)* dentudo,-a; **to have g. teeth**, tener dientes de conejo. **2** *US (crazy)* alocado,-a, estúpido,-a.

goosander [guːˈsændəʳ] *n Orn* serreta *f* grande.

goon [guːn] *n fam* **1** *GB (clown)* tonto,-a, imbécil. **2** *US (thug)* sicario *m*.

goose [guːs] *n (pl geese* [giːs]) **1** *Orn* ganso *m*, oca *f*; *fig* **the golden g.**, la gallina de los huevos de oro; *fam fig* **to cook sb's g.**, hacerle la pascua a algn. ◼ **barnacle g.**, barnacla *f* cariblanca; **Canada g.**, barnacla *f* canadiense; **greylag g.**, ánsar *m* común. **2** *fam (silly person)* tonto,-a *m,f*, bobo,-a *m,f*.

gooseberry [gʊzbərɪ, 'guːsbərɪ] *n Bot* uva *f* espina, grosella *f* espinosa; *fam* **to play g.**, hacer de carabina. ◼ **g. bush**, grosellero *m* espinoso.

gooseflesh ['guːsfleʃ] *n*, **goosepimples** ['guːspɪmpəlz] *npl* carne *f* de gallina; **the cold air raised g. on her arms**, con el aire frío se le puso la carne de gallina.

goose-step ['guːsstep] *Mil* **I** *n* paso *m* de la oca. **II** *vi* ir a paso de la oca.

Gordian ['gɔːdɪən] *adj fml* **G. knot**, nudo *m* gordiano, problema *m* grave.

gore¹ [gɔːʳ] *n* sangre *f* derramada.

gore² [gɔːʳ] *vtr Taur* cornear, dar cornadas a.

gorge [gɔːdʒ] **I** *n Geog* desfiladero *m*, garganta *f*. **II** *vtr & vi (food)* **to g. (oneself)**, atiborrarse **(on**, de), hartarse **(on**, de).

gorgeous ['gɔːdʒəs] *adj (fantastic)* magnífico,-a, estupendo,-a; *(marvellous)* espléndido,-a; *(person)* atractivo,-a, guapo,-a.

gorilla [gəˈrɪlə] *n Zool* gorila *m*.

gormless ['gɔːmlɪs] *adj GB fam* memo,-a, tonto,-a.

gorse [gɔːs] *n Bot* tojo *m*, aulaga *f*.

gory ['gɔːrɪ] *adj (gorier, goriest)* sangriento,-a; **a g. horror film**, una película sangrienta *or* de vísceras; **I'd rather you spared me the g. details**, puedes ahorrarte los detalles escabrosos.

gosh [gɒʃ] *interj fam* ¡cielos!, ¡caray!

goshawk ['gɒshɔːk] *n Orn* azor *m*.

gosling ['gɒzlɪŋ] *n* ansarón *m*.

go-slow [gəʊˈsləʊ] *n* huelga *f* de celo.

gospel ['gɒspəl] *n Rel* **the G.**, el Evangelio; **the G. according to Saint Mark**, el Evangelio según San Marcos; *fam* **it's the g. truth**, es la pura verdad.

gossamer ['gɒsəməʳ] *n* **1** *(cobweb)* telaraña *f*. **2** *Tex* gasa *f*.

gossip ['gɒsɪp] **I** *n* **1** *(rumour)* cotilleo *m*, chismorreo *m*, comadreo *m*. ◼ *Press* **g. column**, ecos *mpl* de sociedad. **2** *(person)* chismoso,-a *m, f*, cotilla *mf*. **II** *vi (natter)* cotillear, chismorrear, contar chismes.

gossipy ['gɒsɪpɪ] *adj fam (style)* familiar; *(person)* chismoso,-a.

got [gɒt] *pt & pp see* **get**.

Goth [gɒθ] *n Hist* godo,-a *m,f*.

Gothic ['gɒθɪk] *adj* **1** *(race)* godo,-a. **2** *Art* gótico,-a.

gotten ['gɒtən] *US pp see* **get**.

gouache [guˈɑːʃ] *n Art* aguada *f*, pintura *f* a la aguada.

gouge [gaʊdʒ] **I** *n Carp* gubia *f*. **II** *vi Carp* **to g. out**, escoplear con gubia; *fig* **to g. out sb's eyes**, arrancarle los ojos a algn.

gourd [gʊəd] *n* calabaza *f*.

gourmand ['gʊəmənd] *n* goloso,-a *m,f*, glotón,-ona *m,f*.

gourmet ['gʊəmeɪ] *n* gourmet *mf*, gastrónomo,-a *m,f*.

gout [gaʊt] *n Med* gota *f*.

Gov 1 *abbr of* **Governor**, Gobernador,-a *m,f*, Gobr. **2** *abbr of* **Government**, Gobierno *m*, Gob, Gobno.

govern ['gʌvən] *vtr* **1** *(gen)* gobernar. **2** *(determine)* dictar, guiar.

governess ['gʌvənɪs] *n* institutriz *f*.

governing ['gʌvənɪŋ] *adj* gobernante, gobernador,-a; **g. body**, consejo *m* de administración.

government ['gʌvənmənt] *n* **I** *n* gobierno *m*; **local g.**, gobierno municipal. **II** *adj* del gobierno, del Estado, gubernamental.

governmental [gʌvən'mentəl] *adj* gubernamental.

governor ['gʌvənəʳ] *n* **1** *(ruler)* gobernador,-a *m,f*. **2** *(of prison)* director,-a *m,f*. **3** *(of school)* administrador,-a *m,f*. **4** *fam* jefe *m*.

Govt *abbr of* **Government**, Gobierno *m*, Gob, Gobno.

gown [gaʊn] *n* **1** *(dress)* vestido *m* largo; **dressing g.**, bata *f*. **2** *Jur Univ (robe)* toga *f*.

GP [dʒiːˈpiː] *Med abbr of* **general practioner**, médico,-a *m,f* de cabecera.

GPO [dʒiːpiːˈəʊ] *GB abbr of* **General Post Office**, Oficina *f* Central de Correos.

grab [græb] **I** *n* agarrón *m*; **to make a g. for sth**, intentar agarrar algo; *fam* **to be up for grabs**, estar libre, estar disponible. **II** *vtr (pt & pp grabbed)* **1** *(gen)* agarrar, coger; **to g. hold of sb**, agarrarse a algn; *fam* **the police grabbed him**, le pilló la policía. **2** *fig* pillar; **I think I'll g. a few hours sleep before I go out**, creo que antes de salir me echaré una siesta. **3** *fig (interest)* hacer ilusion; **how does that g. you?**, ¿qué te parece?; **the idea of going to Egypt really grabbed him**, la idea de ir a Egipto le estusiasmaba.

grace [greɪs] **I** *n* **1** *(favour)* gracia *f*; **by the g. of God**, por la gracia de Dios; **in a state of g.**, en estado de gracia; *fig* **to fall from g.**, caer en desgracia. **2** *(prayer)* bendición *f* de la mesa; **to say g.**, bendecir la mesa. **3** *(courtesy)* cortesía *f*, delicadeza *f*; **he had the g. to apologize**, tuvo la cortesía de pedir perdón; **it's her saving g.,** es lo que la salva; **to do sth with good g.,** hacer algo de buena gana. **4** *(delay, reprieve)* plazo *m*, demora *f*; **five days' g.,** un plazo de cinco días. **5** *(refinement, elegance)* gracia *f*, elegancia *f*; *(tact)* tacto *m*. **6** *(in title)* **Your G.,** *(gen)* (Su) Excelencia; *(bishop)* (Su) Ilustrísima. **7 graces,** *(manners)* buenos modales *mpl*. **II** *vtr* **1** *(adorn)* adornar. **2** *(honour)* honrar.

graceful ['greisful] *adj (beautiful)* lleno,-a de gracia, elegante; *(movement)* garboso,-a. ◆ **gracefully** *adv* **1** *(beautifully)* con gracia, con elegancia. **2** *(accept, decline)* con cortesía.

gracefulness ['greisfulnis] *n* gracia *f*.

gracious ['greiʃəs] *adj* **1** *(elegant)* elegante; **g. living,** vida *f* elegante *or* de lujo. **2** *(courteous)* cortés, educado,-a. **3** *(kind)* amable. **II** *interj* **good g. (me)!, goodness g.!,** ¡santo cielo! ◆ **graciously** *adv* **1** *(elegantly)* elegantemente. **2** *(kindly)* amablemente.

graciousness ['greiʃəsnis] *n* **1** *(elegance)* elegancia *f*. **2** *(affability)* amabilidad *f*.

gradation [grə'deiʃən] *n* gradación *f*.

grade [greid] **I** *n* **1** *(degree, quality)* grado *m*; *(rank)* categoría *f*; *Mil* rango *m*. **2** *Educ (mark)* nota *f*; **to get good grades,** sacar buenas notas. **3** *US Educ (class, form)* clase *f*; *US* **g. school,** escuela primaria. **4** *(level)* nivel *m*; **to make the g.,** llegar al nivel deseado, tener éxito, triunfar. **5** *US (slope)* pendiente *f*. **6** *US Rail* **g. crossing,** paso *m* a nivel. **II** *vtr (classify)* clasificar.

gradient ['greidiənt] *n (graph)* declive *m*; *(hill)* cuesta *f*, pendiente *f*; **a g. of one in five,** una pendiente de veinte por ciento.

gradual ['grædjuəl] *adj* gradual, progresivo,-a. ◆ **gradually** *adv* poco a poco, progresivamente.

graduate ['grædjuit] **I** *n Educ* titulado,-a *m*, *f*; *(with diploma)* diplomado,-a *m*, *f*; *Univ* graduado,-a *m*, *f*, licenciado,-a *m*, *f*. ■ *US* **g. school,** escuela *f* para graduados. **II** *vi* ['grædjueit] **1** *Educ* sacarse el título; *(with a diploma)* diplomarse (**in,** en); *Univ* licenciarse, graduarse (**in,** en). **2** *(progress)* pasar a; **start with a small one and then g. to a bigger one,** empezar con uno pequeño *y* después pasar a uno mayor.

graduation [grædju'eiʃən] *n (gen)* graduación *f*; *Univ* **g. ceremony,** ceremonia *f* de entrega de los títulos.

graffiti [græ'fi:ti:] *npl* grafiti *mpl*.

graft [grɑ:ft] **I** *n* **1** *Agr Med* injerto *m*. ■ **skin g.,** injerto *m* de piel. **2** *fam (work)* trabajo *m*; **it was hard g.,** trabajamos duro. **3** *US (bribery)* soborno *m*. **II** *vtr Agr Med* injertar (**on to,** en). **III** *vi fam* trabajar duro.

Grail [greil] *n Lit* grial *m*; **the Holy G.,** el Santo Grial.

grain [grein] *n* **1** *(cereals)* cereales *mpl*. **2** *(seed, particle)* grano *m*; *fig* **there's not a g. of truth in it,** no tiene ni pizca de verdad. **3** *(in wood)* fibra *f*; *(in stone)* veta *f*; *(in leather)* flor *f*; *fig* **to go against the g.,** *(gen)* ir a contrapelo; *fig* ir en contra de la naturaleza de algn.

gram [græm] *n* gramo *m*.

grammar ['græmər] *n* gramática *f*; **English g.,** la gramática inglesa. ■ **g. (book),** libro *m* de gramática; **g. school,** instituto *m* de segunda enseñanza.

grammarian [grə'meəriən] *n* gramático,-a *m*, *f*.

grammatical [grə'mætikəl] *adj* gramatical, gramático,-a. ◆ **grammatically** *adv* gramaticalmente.

gramme [græm] *n* gramo *m*.

gramophone ['græməfəun] *n* gramófono *m*, gramola *f*.

granary ['grænəri] *n Agr* granero *m*.

grand [grænd] **I** *adj* **1** *(gen)* grande; *(before sing noun)* gran; **g. ideas,** grandes ideas. ■ **G. Canary,** Gran Canaria *f*; *Jur* **g. jury,** gran jurado *m*; **g. piano,** piano *m* de cola; *Aut* **G. Prix,** Gran Premio *m*. **2** *(splendid)* grandioso,-a, magnífico,-a; *(impressive)* impresionante. **3** *(complete)* global. ■ **g. total,** total *m*. **4** *fam (wonderful)* estupendo,-a, fenomenal; **that would be g.!,** ¡eso sería

estupendo!; **to have a g. time,** pasarlo en grande. **II** *n* **1** *(piano)* piano *m* de cola. **2** *sl* mil libras *fpl*, *US* mil dólares *mpl*.

grandchild ['græntʃaild] *n* *(pl* **grandchildren** ['græntʃildrən]*)* nieto,-a *m*, *f*.

granddad ['grændæd] *n fam* abuelito *m*.

granddaughter ['grændɔ:tər] *n* nieta *f*.

grandeur ['grændʒər] *n* grandeza *f*, grandiosidad *f*.

grandfather ['grænfɑ:ðər] *n* abuelo *m*. ■ **g. clock,** reloj *m* de caja.

grandiose ['grændiəus] *adj* grandioso,-a, imponente.

grandma ['grænmɑ:] *n fam* abuelita *f*.

grandmaster ['grændmɑ:stər] *n Chess* gran maestro *m*.

grandmother ['grænmʌðər] *n* abuela *f*.

grandpa ['grænpɑ:] *n fam* abuelito *m*.

grandparents ['grænpeərənts] *npl* abuelos *mpl*.

grandson ['grænsʌn] *n* nieto *m*.

grandstand ['grændstænd] *n Sport* tribuna *f*.

grange [greindʒ] *n* finca *f*, cortijo *m*.

granite ['grænit] *n Min* granito *m*.

granite-like ['grænitlaik] *adj Min* granítico,-a.

granny ['græni] *n fam* abuelita *f*.

grant [grɑ:nt] **I** *vtr* **1** *(allow) (interview etc)* conceder. **2** *(concede, bestow)* conceder, otorgar. **3** *(admit)* admitir, reconocer; **I g. that you were right,** reconozco que tenías razón; **to take sb for granted,** no apreciar a algn en lo que vale; **to take sth for granted,** dar algo por sentado. **II** *n Educ* beca *f*; *(subsidy)* subvención *f*.

granular ['grænjulər] *adj* granular.

granulate ['grænjuleit] **I** *vtr Chem* granular. **II** *vi* granularse.

granulated ['grænjuleitid] *adj* granulado,-a. ■ **g. sugar,** azúcar *m* granulado.

granulation [grænju'leiʃən] *n* granulación *f*.

granule ['grænju:l] *n* gránulo *m*.

grape [greip] *n Bot* uva *f*; **a bunch of grapes,** un racimo de uvas; *fam* **sour grapes!,** ¡te aguantas! ■ **g. harvest,** vendimia *f*; **g. juice,** zumo *m* de uva, mosto *m*.

grapefruit ['greipfru:t] *n* *(pl* **grapefruit** *or* **grapefruits***)* pomelo *m*.

grapevine ['greipvain] *n Bot* vid *f*; *(against wall)* parra *f*; *fam* **I heard it on** *or* **through the g.,** me enteré por ahí.

graph [grɑ:f, græf] *n* gráfica *f*. ■ **g. paper,** papel *m* cuadriculado.

graphic ['græfik] *adj* gráfico,-a. ■ **g. arts,** artes *fpl* gráficas; **g. designer,** grafista *mf*.

graphics ['græfiks] *n* **1** *(study)* grafismo *m*. **2** *pl Comput* gráficas *fpl*.

graphite ['græfait] *n Min* grafito *m*.

graphologist [græ'fɒlədʒist] *n* grafólogo,-a *m*, *f*.

graphology [græ'fɒlədʒi] *n* grafología *f*.

grapple ['græpəl] **I** *vi (struggle)* luchar cuerpo a cuerpo (**with,** con); *fig* **to g. with a problem,** intentar resolver un problema. **II** *n (hook)* garfio *m*.

grasp [grɑ:sp] **I** *vtr* **1** *(seize)* agarrar, asir. **2** *(understand)* comprender, captar. **II** *n* **1** *(grip)* asimiento *m*; *(clasp)* apretón *m*; **to have a strong g.,** agarrar muy fuerte; **to lose one's g.,** soltarse. **2** *(understanding)* comprensión *f*, alcance *m*; **it's beyond my g.,** está fuera de mi alcance; **to have a good g. of sth,** comprender algo bien, dominar algo; **within sb's g.,** al alcance de algn.

grasping [grɑ:spɪŋ] *adj* ávaro,-a, codicioso,-a.

grass [grɑ:s] **I** *n* **1** *(plant)* hierba *f*, yerba *f*; *(lawn)* césped *m*; *(pasture)* pasto *m*; **'keep off the g.',** 'prohibido pisar el césped'; *fig* **he doesn't let the g. grow under his feet,** no pierde el tiempo. ■ **Ten g. court,** pista *f* de hierba; *Sport* **g. hockey,** hockey *m* sobre hierba; *Pol* **g. roots,**

base *f* (popular); *Zool* **g. snake,** culebra *f*; **g. widow,** mujer *f* cuyo marido está ausente; **g. widower,** hombre *m* cuya mujer está ausente; *(for the summer)* Rodríguez *m*. **2** *sl (drug)* hierba *f*, maría *f*. **II** *vi GB sl* soplar, chivarse **(on,** a). ◆ **grass over** *vi* cubrirse de hierba *or* yerba.

grasshopper ['grɑːshɒpəʳ] *n* saltamontes *m inv*.

grassland ['grɑːslænd] *n* prado *m*, pasto *m*.

grass-roots ['grɑːsruːts] *adj* Pol de base; **at g.-r. level,** a nivel popular; **g.-r. militant,** militante *mf* de base.

grassy ['grɑːsɪ] *adj (grassier, grassiest)* cubierto,-a de hierba.

grate¹ [greɪt] **I** *vtr* **1** *Culin* rallar. **2** *(teeth etc)* hacer rechinar. **II** *vi* chirriar; *(teeth)* rechinar; *fig* **to g. on one's nerves,** crisparle a uno los nervios.

grate² [greɪt] *n* **1** *(in fireplace etc)* rejilla *f*. **2** *(fireplace)* chimenea *f*. **3** *Constr* rejilla *f*, reja *f*.

grateful ['greɪtful] *adj (person)* agradecido,-a; *(letter etc)* de agradecimiento; **I am very g. to you,** te lo agradezco mucho, te estoy muy agradecido,-a; **to be g. for,** agradecer; **with g. thanks,** con agradecimiento. ◆ **gratefully** *adv* con agradecimiento.

grater ['greɪtəʳ] *n Culin* rallador *m*.

gratification [grætɪfɪ'keɪʃən] *n* **1** *(pleasure)* placer *m*, satisfacción *f*. **2** *fig (reward)* recompensa *f*, gratificación *f*.

gratify ['grætɪfaɪ] *vtr (pt & pp gratified)* **1** *(please)* complacer, gratificar. **2** *(yield to)* sucumbir a.

gratifying ['grætɪfaɪɪŋ] *adj* grato,-a, gratificante.

gratin ['grætɪn] *n Culin* gratén *m*; **au g.,** al gratén.

grating¹ ['greɪtɪŋ] *n* rejilla *f*, reja *f*.

grating² ['greɪtɪŋ] *adj (noise)* chirriante, rechinante; *(voice)* chillón,-ona; *(tone)* áspero,-a.

gratis ['greɪtɪs, 'grætɪs] *adv* gratis.

gratitude ['grætɪtjuːd] *n* agradecimiento *m*, gratitud *f*.

gratuitous [grə'tjuːɪtəs] *adj* gratuito,-a. ◆ **gratuitously** *adv* gratuitamente.

gratuitousness [grə'tjuːɪtəsnɪs] *n* gratuidad *f*.

gratuity [grə'tjuːɪtɪ] *n (reward)* gratificación *f*; *(tip)* propina *f*.

grave¹ [greɪv] *n (tomb)* sepultura *f*, sepulcro *m*, tumba *f*; *fig* **to make sb turn over in his** *or* **her grave,** hacer que algn se retuerza en su tumba; *fam* **to have one foot in the g.,** tener un pie en la tumba, estar en las últimas.

grave² [greɪv] *adj* **1** *(serious)* *(look etc)* serio,-a; *(situation)* grave. **2** [grɑːv] *Ling* grave; **g. accent,** acento grave. ◆ **gravely** *adv* gravemente.

gravedigger ['greɪvdɪgəʳ] *n* sepulturero *m*, enterrador *m*.

gravel ['grævəl] *n* grava *f*, gravilla *f*, guijo *m*; **g. path,** camino *m* de grava.

gravestone ['greɪvstəun] *n* lápida *f* sepulcral *or* mortuoria.

graveyard ['greɪvjɑːd] *n* cementerio *m*.

gravitate ['grævɪteɪt] *vi* **1** *Phys* gravitar. **2** *fig (be drawn)* sentirse atraído,-a **(towards,** por).

gravitation [grævɪ'teɪʃən] *n Phys* gravitación *f*.

gravity ['grævɪtɪ] *n* **1** *Phys* gravedad *f*; **the law of g.,** la ley de la gravedad. ■ **centre of g.,** centro *m* de gravedad; **specific g.,** peso *m* específico. **2** *(of situation)* gravedad *f*.

gravy ['greɪvɪ] *n Culin* salsa *f*, jugo *m* (de la carne). ■ **g. boat,** salsera *f*; *sl* **g. train,** chollo *m*.

gray [greɪ] *adj & n US see* **grey.**

grayling ['greɪlɪŋ] *n Orn* tímalo *m*.

graze¹ [greɪz] *vi* pacer, pastar.

graze² [greɪz] **I** *vtr* rasguñar, rozar, arañar. **II** *n* rasguño *m*, roce *m*, arañazo *m*.

grazing ['greɪzɪŋ] *n* (tierra *f* de) pasto *m*.

grease [griːs, griːz] **I** *n* grasa *f*. ■ **g. gun,** pistola *f* engrasadora, engrasador *m*. **II** *vtr Tech* engrasar, untar; *sl* **to g. sb's palm,** untar a algn.

greasepaint ['griːspeɪnt] *n Theat* maquillaje *m*.

greaseproof ['griːspruːf] *adj* impermeable a la grasa; **g. paper,** papel *m* graso.

greasy ['griːsɪ, 'griːzɪ] *adj (greasier, greasiest)* **1** *(oily)* grasiento,-a; *(hair, food)* graso,-a. ■ *sl* **g. spoon,** restaurante *m* de mala muerte. **2** *(slippery)* resbaladizo,-a. **3** *fam (ingratiating)* cobista, pelota.

great [greɪt] **I** *adj* **1** *(big, large)* grande; *(before sing noun)* gran; *(pain, heat)* fuerte, intenso,-a; *(determination)* fuerte; **a g. many,** muchos,-as; **a g. number of,** un gran número de. ■ **G. Britain,** Gran Bretaña; *Zool* **G. Dane,** gran danés *m*. **2** *(important)* grande, importante; **a g. writer,** un gran escritor; **the G. War,** la Gran Guerra, la Primera Guerra Mundial. **3** *fam (excellent)* estupendo,-a, magnífico,-a; **g.!,** ¡estupendo!; **he's g. at tennis,** juega al tenis de maravilla; **she's a g. one for museums,** le encantan los museos; **there was a g. big crash,** se oyó un ruido de narices; **to have a g. time,** pasarlo en grande. **II** *n (person)* grande *m*. **III** *adv fam* muy bien, estupendamente; **she's doing just g.,** le va todo muy bien. ◆ **greatly** *adv* muy, mucho; **it is g. improved,** ha mejorado mucho; **you are g. mistaken,** estás muy equivocado,-a.

great-aunt [greɪt'ɑːnt] *n* tía *f* abuela.

greatcoat ['greɪtkəut] *n* abrigo *m*, gabán *m*.

great-grandchild [greɪt'græntʃaɪld] *n (pl great-grandchildren* [greɪt'græntʃɪldrən]*)* bisnieto,-a *m*, *f*, biznieto,-a *m*, *f*.

great-granddaughter [greɪt'grændɔːtəʳ] *n* bisnieta *f*, biznieta *f*.

great-grandfather [greɪt'grænfɑːðəʳ] *n* bisabuelo *m*.

great-grandmother [greɪt'grænmʌðəʳ] *n* bisabuela *f*.

great-grandson [greɪt'grænsʌn] *n* bisnieto *m*, biznieto *m*.

great-great-grandfather [greɪtgreɪt'grænfɑːðəʳ] *n* tatarabuelo *m*.

great-great-grandmother [greɪtgreɪt'grænmʌðəʳ] *n* tatarabuela *f*.

greatness ['greɪtnɪs] *n (importance)* grandeza *f*; *(size)* magnitud *f*.

great-uncle [greɪt'ʌŋkəl] *n* tío *m* abuelo.

grebe [griːb] *n Orn* somormujo *m*. ■ **great creasted g.,** somormujo *m* lavanco; **little g.,** zampullín *m* chico *or* común; **red-necked g.,** somormujo *m* cuellirrojo.

Greece [griːs] *n* Grecia.

greed [griːd] *n,* **greediness** ['griːdɪnɪs] *n* **1** *(for food)* gula *f*, glotonería *f*. **2** *(for money)* codicia *f*, avaricia *f*.

greedy ['griːdɪ] *adj (greedier, greediest)* **1** *(for food)* glotón,-ona, goloso,-a. **2** *(for money)* codicioso,-a, ávido,-a **(for,** de).

Greek [griːk] **I** *adj* griego,-a. **II** *n* **1** *(person)* griego,-a *m*, *f*; **the G.,** los griegos. **2** *(language)* griego *m*; **ancient/ modern G.,** griego clásico/moderno; *fam* **it's (all) G. to me,** me suena a chino.

green [griːn] *n* **1** *(colour)* verde *m*. **2** *(stretch of grass)* césped *m*; *Golf* campo *m*, green *m*. ■ **village g.,** terreno comunal, plaza *f* (del pueblo). **3** **greens,** *(vegetables)* verdura *f sing*, verduras *fpl*. **II** *adj* **1** *(colour)* verde; *fig* **to give a project the g. light,** dar luz verde a un proyecto; *fig* **to have g. fingers,** *US* **have a g. thumb,** tener buena mano para las plantas. ■ **g. bean,** judía *f* verde; **g. belt,** zona *f* verde; *Ins* **g. card,** carta *f* verde; **g. pepper,** pimiento *m* verde; **g. salad,** ensalada *f* verde. **2** *(unripe)* verde; *(uncured)* sin curar. **3** *(pale)* pálido,-a, lívido,-a; **to go** *or* **turn g.,** ponerse pálido,-a. **4** *(jealous)* envidioso,-a; **she was g. with envy,** se la comía la envidia. **5** *(inexperienced)* verde, novato,-a; *(gullible)* crédulo,-a, ingenuo,-a. **6** *Pol (ecologist)* verde; **G. party,** Partido *m* Verde, Partido *m* Ecologista.

greenback ['griːnbæk] *n US sl (any bill)* papiro *m*; *(green bill)* verde *m*, lechuga *f*.

greenery ['griːnərɪ] n verde m, follaje m.

green-eyed ['griːnaɪd] adj fig envidioso,-a, celoso,-a.

greenfinch ['griːnfɪntʃ] n Orn verderón m común.

greenfly ['griːnflaɪ] n pulgón m.

greengage ['griːngeɪdʒ] n Bot ciruela f claudia.

greengrocer ['griːngrəʊsər] n GB verdulero,-a m, f, frutero,-a m, f; **g.'s (shop)**, verdulería f, frutería f.

greenhorn ['griːnhɔːn] n novato,-a m, f.

greenhouse ['griːnhaʊs] n invernadero m. ■ Meteor **g. effect**, efecto m invernadero.

greenish ['griːnɪʃ] adj verdoso,-a.

Greenland ['griːnlənd] n Groenlandia. ■ **G. Sea**, Mar m de Groenlandia.

Greenlander ['griːnləndər] n groenlandés,-esa m, f.

Greenlandic [griːn'lændɪk] adj groenlandés,-esa.

greenness ['griːnnɪs] n verdor m.

greenroom ['griːnruːm] n Theat camerino m.

Greenwich ['grɪnɪdʒ, 'grenɪtʃ] n **G. (Mean) Time (GMT)**, la hora media de Greenwich.

greet [griːt] vtr 1 (wave at) saludar. 2 (receive) recibir; (welcome) dar la bienvenida a.

greeting ['griːtɪŋ] n 1 (gen) saludo m; **greetings on your birthday!**, ¡felicidades en el día de tu cumpleaños!; **greetings to all!**, ¡saludos a todos!, ¡recuerdos a todos! ■ **greetings card**, tarjeta f de felicitación. 2 (reception) recibimiento m; (welcome) bienvenida f.

gregarious [grɪ'geərɪəs] adj gregario,-a, sociable.

Gregorian [grɪ'gɔːrɪən] adj gregoriano,-a. ■ Mus **G. chant**, canto m gregoriano.

gremlin ['gremlɪn] n duende m.

Grenada [gre'neɪdə] n Granada.

grenade [grɪ'neɪd] n Mil granada f. ■ **hand g.**, granada f de mano.

Grenadian [gre'neɪdɪən] adj & n granadino,-a (m, f).

grenadier [grenə'dɪər] n Mil granadero m.

grenadine¹ [grenə'diːn] n Tex granadina f.

grenadine² ['grenədiːn] n (syrup) granadina f.

grew [gruː] pt see **grow**.

grey [greɪ] I adj 1 (colour) gris; (hair) cano,-a; (sky) nublado,-a; **to go g.**, (sky) nublarse; (hair) encanecer, volverse cano. ■ **g. matter**, materia f gris. 2 (gloomy) gris, triste. II n 1 (colour) gris m. 2 (horse) caballo m tordo.

grey-haired ['greɪheəd] adj de pelo cano, canoso,-a.

greyhound ['greɪhaʊnd] n Zool galgo m.

greyish ['greɪʃ] adj (gen) grisáceo,-a; (hair) entrecano,-a.

grid [grɪd] n 1 (on map etc) cuadrícula f. 2 Tech (of electricity, water, etc) red f nacional de suministro. 3 see **gridiron**.

griddle ['grɪdəl] n Culin plancha f.

gridiron ['grɪdaɪən] n 1 Culin parrilla f. 2 US Ftb campo m de fútbol.

grief [griːf] n dolor m, pena f; fam **to come to g.**, (car, driver) sufrir un accidente; (plans) irse al traste; fam **good g.!**, ¡Dios mío!

grief-stricken ['griːfstrɪkən] adj desconsolado,-a.

grievance ['griːvəns] n 1 (wrong) motivo m de queja, agravio m. 2 (resentment) queja f; **to air one's grievances**, desahogarse.

grieve [griːv] I vtr apenar, dar pena; **it grieves me to hear it**, me da pena saberlo. II vi apenarse, afligirse; **to g. for sb**, llorar la muerte de algn; **to g. over sth**, lamentar algo.

grievous ['griːvəs] adj (loss) cruel, penoso,-a; (injury etc) fuerte, doloroso,-a; (offence) grave. ■ Jur **g. bodily harm**, lesiones fpl corporales graves (de pronóstico reservado).

griffin ['grɪfɪn] n Myth grifo m.

grill [grɪl] I vtr 1 Culin asar a la parrilla; **grilled steak**, bistec m a la parrilla. 2 fam (interrogate) interrogar duramente. II n 1 (gridiron) parrilla f; (over cooker) parrilla f, grill m. 2 Culin (dish) parrillada f, asado m a la parrilla; **mixed g.**, parrillada f de carne.

grill(e) [grɪl] n (grating) reja f, verja f, enrejado m; (latticework) rejilla f. ■ Aut **radiator g.**, calandra f.

grillroom ['grɪlruːm] n (restaurant) asador m.

grim [grɪm] adj (grimmer, grimmest) 1 (sinister) macabro,-a; (landscape) lúgubre; (smile, laughter) sardónico,-a. 2 (manner) severo,-a; (expression) ceñudo,-a. 3 (resolute) inflexible, inexorable; **he held on like g. death**, se agarró como si su vida dependiera de ello; **with g. determination**, con una voluntad de hierro. 4 fam (unpleasant) desagradable; **g. reality**, la dura realidad; **to feel g.**, encontrarse fatal. ◆ **grimly** adv 1 (derisively) sardónicamente. 2 (resolutely) inexorablemente.

grimace [grɪ'meɪs, US 'grɪməs] I n mueca f. II vi hacer una mueca.

grime [graɪm] n mugre f, suciedad f.

grimy ['graɪmɪ] adj (grimier, grimiest) mugriento,-a, sucio,-a.

grin [grɪn] I vi (pt & pp grinned) sonreír abiertamente; fam **to g. and bear it**, poner al mal tiempo buena cara II n sonrisa f abierta, (ironic) sonrisa f burlona

grind [graɪnd] I vtr (pt & pp ground) (mill) moler, (crush) triturar, (sharpen) afilar, **to g. one's teeth**, hacer rechinar los dientes; fig **to have an axe to g.**, tener intereses personales II vi 1 rechinar; fig **to g. to a halt**, (vehicle) pararse ruidosamente, (production etc) pararse poco a poco. 2 fam (swot) empollar, machacar III n 1 fam (routine) trabajo m pesado; **the daily g.**, la rutina cotidiana, **what a g.!**, ¡qué rollo!, ¡qué lata! 2 US sl (swot) empollón,-ona m, f ◆ **grind down** vtr fig (oppress) oprimir, **to g. down the opposition**, acabar con la oposición ◆ **grind out** vtr 1 (words) decir gruñendo 2 (tune) machacar

grinder ['graɪndər] n (for coffee, pepper) molinillo m; (crusher) trituradora f.

grinding ['graɪndɪŋ] n rechinamiento m

grindstone ['graɪndstəʊn] n muela f; fig **to keep one's nose to the g.**, trabajar sin levantar cabeza

gringo ['grɪŋgəʊ] n (pl gringos) pej gringo,-a m, f

grip [grɪp] I n 1 (hold) asimiento m, (handshake) apretón m, (of tyre) adherencia f, **to have a firm g. on sth**, agarrar bien algo 2 fig (control) dominio m, control m, **get a g. on yourself!**, ¡tranquilízate!; **to come** or **get to grips with a problem**, superar un problema; **to lose one's g.**, perder el control 2 (handle) asidero m, (of weapon) empuñadura f 3 (travel bag) bolsa f de viaje, maletín m 4 (hairgrip) pasador m, horquilla f. II vtr (pt & pp gripped) 1 (gen) agarrar, asir, (weapon) empuñar, (hand) apretar 2 fig (film, story) captar la atención de; **to be gripped by fear**, ser presa del miedo III vi (tyres) adherirse a la carretera

gripe [graɪp] I vi fam (complain) quejarse, refunfuñar II n 1 Med (pain) retortijón m, cólico m ■ GB **g. water**, calmante m para el cólico infantil 2 fam (complaint) queja f

gripping ['grɪpɪŋ] adj (film, story) apasionante.

grisly ['grɪzlɪ] adj (grislier, grisliest) espeluznante, horripilante

grist [grɪst] n grano m, fam **it's all g. to the mill**, todo ayuda

gristle ['grɪsəl] n cartílago m, ternilla f.

gristly ['grɪsəlɪ] adj (gristlier, gristliest) cartilaginoso,-a, ternilloso,-a

grit [grɪt] I n 1 (sand) arena f, (gravel) grava f 2 (sandstone) arenisca f, asperón m 3 fam (courage) valor m; **she's got g.**, tiene agallas II vtr (pt & pp gritted) 1 (cover with grit) cubrir de arena or grava 2 fig hacer rechinar, **to g. one's teeth**, apretar los dientes

grits [grɪts] *npl US Culin* (**hominy**) **g.,** maíz *m sing* molido

gritty ['grɪtɪ] *adj* (**grittier, grittiest**) **1** (*courageous*) valiente, duro,-a **2** (*sandy*) arenoso,-a, (*gravelly*) cubierto,-a de grava.

grizzle ['grɪzəl] *vi GB fam* **1** (*whine*) lloriquear **2** (*complain*) refunfuñar

grizzled ['grɪzəld] *adj* gris, entrecano,-a, canoso,-a

grizzly ['grɪzlɪ] *adj* (**grizzlier, grizzliest**) gris, pardo,-a ■ *Zool* **g. bear,** oso *m* pardo

groan [grəʊn] **I** *n* **1** (*of pain*) gemido *m*, (*tree etc*) crujido *m* **2** *fam* (*of disapproval*) gruñido *m* **II** *vi* **1** (*in pain*) gemir; (*plank, table*) crujir **2** *fam* (complain) quejarse (**about,** de), gruñir

grocer ['grəʊsəʳ] *n* tendero,-a *m*, *f*, **g.'s** (**shop**), tienda *f* de ultramarinos, colmado *m*

groceries ['grəʊsərɪz] *npl* comestibles *mpl*

grocery ['grəʊsərɪ] *n* (*shop*) tienda *f* de ultramarinos, colmado *m* ■ *US* **g. store,** supermercado *m*

grog [grɒg] *n* grog *m*, ponche *m*

groggy ['grɒgɪ] *adj* (**groggier, groggiest**) *fam* **1** *Box* grogui, *fig* (*unsteady*) grogui, atontado,-a; (*reeling*) tambaleante **2** (*weak*) débil

groin [grɔɪn] *n* **1** *Anat* ingle *f* **2** *US see* **groyne.**

groom [gru:m] **I** *n* **1** (*for horses*) mozo *m* de cuadra **2** (*bridegroom*) novio *m* **II** *vtr* (*horse*) almohazar; (*clothes, appearance*) cuidar; **well groomed,** bien arreglado,-a, *fig* **to g. sb for a post,** preparar a algn para un puesto

groove [gru:v] *n* (*furrow etc*) ranura *f*, (*of record*) surco *m*

groovy ['gru:vɪ] *adj* (**groovier, grooviest**) *sl dated* chupi, chuli

grope [grəʊp] *vi* **1** (*search about*) andar a tientas, **to g. for sth,** buscar algo a tientas **2** *sl* (*fondle*) meter mano, sobar

gross [grəʊs] **I** *adj* **1** (*coarse*) basto,-a, grosero,-a; (*joke*) verde. **2** (*fat*) muy gordo,-a, obeso,-a **3** (*flagrant*) (*injustice*) flagrante, (*ignorance*) craso,-a. **4** *Com Econ* (*profit, weight, income*) bruto,-a. ■ **g. national product,** producto *m* nacional bruto. **II** *n* **1** (*pl* **gross**) (*unit*) gruesa *f*, doce docenas *fpl*, *Com* **by the g.,** (al) por mayor, en grueso **2** (*pl* **grosses**) totalidad *f* **III** *vtr* (*gain*) recaudar (en bruto), **he grosses £20,000 a year,** tiene unos ingresos brutos de 20 mil libras al año ◆ **gross out** *vtr US sl* revolver el estómago ◆ **grossly** *adv* enormemente, **g. exaggerated,** muy exagerado, **g. unfair,** totalmente injusto

grotesque [grəʊ'tesk] *adj* grotesco,-a

grotto ['grɒtəʊ] *n* (*pl* **grottos** *or* **grottoes**) gruta *f*

grotty ['grɒtɪ] *adj* (**grottier, grottiest**) *GB sl* sucio,-a, asqueroso,-a, de mala muerte, **to feel g.,** encontrarse fatal

grouch [graʊtʃ] **I** *vi fam* refunfuñar, quejarse **II** *n* (*person*) gruñón,-ona *m*, *f*, cascarrabias *mf*

grouchy ['graʊtʃɪ] *adj* (**grouchier, grouchiest**) refunfuñón,-ona, quejica

ground¹ [graʊnd] **I** *n* **1** (*surface*) suelo *m*, tierra *f*; **at g. level,** al nivel del suelo; **stony g.,** suelo pedregoso, **to fall to the g.,** caer al suelo; **to get off the g.,** (*plane*) despegar, *fig* (*scheme*) realizarse; **to sit on the g.,** sentarse en el suelo, **to touch g.,** tocar fondo, *fig* **above g.,** vivo,-a, *fig* **to go to g.,** esconderse; *GB fam* **it suits me down to the g.,** me viene de perlas ■ *Av* **g. control,** control *m* de tierra; **g. floor,** planta *f* baja, *Av* **g. staff,** personal *m* de tierra; **g. swell,** mar *m* de fondo, *fig* marejada *f* **2** (*terrain*) terreno *m*; **to gain/lose g.,** ganar/perder terreno; *fig* **to break new** *or* **fresh g.,** abrir nuevos horizontes, *fig* **to hold** *or* **stand one's g.,** mantenerse firme. ■ **breeding g.,** semillero *m*, *fig* **football g.,** campo *m* de fútbol, estadio *m* **3** *US Elec* tierra *f*, toma *f* de tierra. **4 grounds,** (*gardens*) jardines *mpl*, parque *m sing* **5 grounds,** (*reason*) motivo *m sing*, razón *f sing*, **g. for divorce,** motivo de divorcio, **on health g.,** por motivos de salud **6 grounds,** (*sediment*) poso *m sing*, sedimento *m sing* **II** *vtr* **1** *Av* obligar a quedarse en tierra,

Naut varar **2** *US Elec* conectar con tierra **3** (*teach*) enseñar los conocimientos básicos, **to be well grounded in,** ser muy entendido,-a en

ground² [graʊnd] **I** *pt & pp see* **grind. II** *adj* (*coffee*) molido,-a. *US* (*meat*) picado,-a

groundhog ['graʊndhɒg] *n Zool* marmota *f*. ■ *US* **G. Day,** día *m* dos de febrero.

grounding ['graʊndɪŋ] *n* base *f*, conocimiento *m*; **to have a good g. in,** tener buenos conocimientos de.

groundless ['graʊndlɪs] *adj* sin fundamento, infundado,-a.

groundnut ['graʊndnʌt] *n GB* cacahuete *m*.

groundsheet ['graʊndʃi:t] *n* tela *f* impermeable.

groundsman ['graʊndzmən] *n* (*pl* **groundsmen**) *Sport* encargado *m* de campo.

groundwork ['graʊndwɜ:k] *n* trabajo *m* preparatorio *or* preliminar.

group [gru:p] **I** *n* (*gen*) grupo *m*, conjunto *m*. ■ *Med* **blood g.,** grupo *m* sanguíneo; *Med* **g. practice,** gabinete *m* médico; *Psychol* **g. therapy,** psicoterapia *f* de grupo; *Pol* **pressure g.,** grupo *m* de presión. **II** *vtr* agrupar, juntar (**into,** en). **III** *vi* **to g. (together),** agruparse, juntarse.

grouper ['gru:pəʳ] *n* (*fish*) mero *m*.

groupie ['gru:pɪ] *n sl* fan *mf* que intenta ligar con los miembros de un grupo de rock.

grouse¹ [graʊs] *n* (*pl* **grouse** *or* **grouses**) *Orn* urogallo *m*. ■ **red g.,** lagópodo *m* escocés.

grouse² [graʊs] *fam* **I** *vi* quejarse (**about,** de). **II** *n* queja *f*, motivo *m* de queja.

grout [graʊt] *n Constr* lechada *f*.

grove [grəʊv] *n* arboleda *f*, bosquecillo *m*; **orange g.,** naranjal *m*.

grovel ['grɒvəl] *vi* (*pt & pp* **grovelled**) (*humble*) humillarse, rebajarse (**to,** ante); (*crawl*) arrastrarse (**to,** ante).

grovelling, *US* **groveling** ['grɒvəlɪŋ] *adj* servil, rastrero,-a.

grow [grəʊ] **I** *vtr* (*pt* **grew**; *pp* **grown**) (*cultivate*) cultivar; **to g. a beard,** dejarse (crecer) la barba. **II** *vi* **1** (*gen*) crecer; (*increase*) aumentar. **2** (*become*) hacerse, volverse; **to g. accustomed to,** acostumbrarse a; **to g. dark,** oscurecer; **to g. into a woman,** hacerse mujer; **to g. old,** envejecer. ◆ **grow on** *vtr* llegar a gustar. ◆ **grow out of** *vtr* **1** (*become too big for*) **he's grown out of his shirt,** se le ha quedado pequeña la camisa. **2** *fig* (*phase etc*) superar. ◆ **grow up** *vi* (*become adult*) crecer, hacerse mayor; **they grew up together,** se criaron juntos; *fam* **g. up!,** ¡no seas tan infantil!

grower ['grəʊəʳ] *n* cultivador,-a *m*, *f*.

growing ['grəʊɪŋ] *adj* (*child*) que crece; (*problem etc*) creciente; **he's a g. boy,** el niño crece cada día más. ■ **g. paints,** *Med* dolores *mpl* producidos por el crecimiento; *fig* problemas *mpl* iniciales.

growl [graʊl] **I** *vi* **1** (*dog*) gruñir. **2** (*person*) refunfuñar. **II** *vtr* decir refunfuñando. **III** *n* gruñido *m*.

growling ['graʊlɪŋ] *n* gruñidos *mpl*.

grown [grəʊn] **I** *pp see* **grow. II** *adj* crecido,-a, adulto,-a.

grown-up ['grəʊnʌp] *adj & n* adulto,-a (*m*, *f*); **the grown-ups,** los mayores.

growth [grəʊθ] *n* **1** (*gen*) crecimiento *m*; (*increase*) aumento *m*; (*development*) desarrollo *m*; **economic g.,** desarrollo económico; **three days' g. of beard,** barba *f* de tres días. **2** *Med* bulto *m*, tumor *m*.

groyne [grɔɪn] *n* espigón *m*.

grub [grʌb] **I** *vi* (*pt & pp* **grubbed**) **to g. about** *or* **around,** hurgar, rebuscar (**in,** entre). **II** *n* **1** (*larva*) larva *f*, gusano *m*. **2** *sl* (*food*) manduca *f*, papeo *m*; **g.'s up!,** ¡a comer! **3** *fam* (*drudge*) chupatintas *mf inv*.

grubbiness ['grʌbɪnɪs] *n* suciedad *f*.

grubby ['grʌbɪ] *adj* (**grubbier, grubbiest**) sucio,-a, mugriento,-a.

grudge [grʌdʒ] **I** *n* rencor *m*, resentimiento *m*; **to bear sb a g.**, guardar rencor a algn. **II** *vtr* **1** *(give unwillingly)* dar a regañadientes. **2** *(envy)* envidiar; **he grudges me my success**, me envidia el éxito.

grudgingly ['grʌdʒɪŋlɪ] *adv* a regañadientes, de mala gana.

gruel ['gruːəl] *n Culin* gachas *fpl*.

gruelling, *US* **grueling** ['gruːəlɪŋ] *adj* agotador,-a, duro,-a, penoso,-a.

gruesome ['gruːsəm] *adj* espantoso,-a, horrible, horripilante.

gruff [grʌf] *adj (manner)* brusco,-a; *(voice)* áspero,-a. ◆ **gruffly** *adv* en un tono brusco.

gruffness ['grʌfnɪs] *n* brusquedad *f*, aspereza *f*.

grumble ['grʌmbəl] **I** *vi* quejarse (**about,** de), refunfuñar. **II** *n* queja *f*; **to have a g. about sth**, quejarse de algo.

grumbler ['grʌmblə'] *n* refunfuñón,-ona *m*, *f*, quejica *mf*, gruñón,-ona *m*, *f*.

grumbling ['grʌmblɪŋ] **I** *adj* gruñón,-ona, refunfuñón,-ona; *fam* **g. appendix**, apendicitis *f* crónica. **II** *n* quejas *fpl*.

grumpy ['grʌmpɪ] *adj (grumpier, grumpiest)* gruñón,-ona, malhumorado,-a. ◆ **grumpily** *adv* con mal humor, de mala gana.

grunt [grʌnt] **I** *vi* gruñir. **II** *vtr* decir gruñendo, **III** *n* gruñido *m*.

gryphon ['grɪfɪn] *n see* **griffin**.

Guadaloupe [gwɑːdə'luːp] *n* Guadalupe.

Guam [gwɑːm] *n* Guam.

guarantee [gærən'tiː] **I** *n (gen)* garantía *f*, *(certificate)* certificado *m* de garantía; *Com* **a six-month g.**, una garantía de seis meses; **there's no g. that they will come**, no hay ninguna garantía de que vengan; **under g.**, bajo garantía. **II** *vtr (gen)* garantizar; *(assure)* asegurar; *(take responsibility for)* responder de; **I can't g. it**, no te lo puedo asegurar; **it is guaranteed for five years**, está garantizado por cinco años.

guarantor [gærən'tɔː'] *n* garante *mf*.

guard [gɑːd] **I** *vtr* **1** *(protect)* defender, proteger; *(keep watch over)* vigilar; **a closely guarded secret**, un secreto bien guardado. **2** *(control)* guardar. **II** *vi* protegerse (**against,** de, contra); **g. against doing that**, guárdate de hacer eso. **III** *n* **1** *(act)* guardia *f*; **to be on g.**, estar de guardia; **to be on one's g.**, estar en guardia; **to catch sb off bis g.**, coger desprevenido a algn; **to put sb on his g.**, poner en guardia a algn. **2** *Mil (sentry)* guardia *mf*; *(body of sentries)* guardia *f*; **g. of honour**, guardia de honor; **the changing of the g.**, el relevo de la guardia; **the Guards**, la guardia; **to mount** *or* **stand g.**, montar la guardia. ■ **g. dog**, perro *m* guardián. **3** *GB Rail* jefe *m* de tren. ■ **g.'s van**, furgón *m* de cola. **4** *(on machine)* seguro *m*, dispositivo *m* de seguridad. ■ **fire g.**, pantalla *f*.

guarded ['gɑːdɪd] *adj* cauteloso,-a, precavido,-a. ◆ **guardedly** *adv* cautelosamente, con cautela.

guardhouse ['gɑːdhaʊs] *n Mil* **1** *(headquarters)* cuerpo *m* de guardia. **2** *(prison)* prisión *f* militar.

guardian ['gɑːdɪən] *n* **1** *(defender)* guardián,-ana. *m*, *f*. ■ **g. angel**, ángel *m* de la guarda. **2** *Jur (of minor)* tutor,-a *m*, *f*.

guardrail ['gɑːdreɪl] *n* barandilla *f*.

guardsman ['gɑːdzmən] *n (pl guardsmen) Mil* guardia *m*.

Guatemala [gwɑːtə'mɑːlə] *n* Guatemala.

Guatemalan [gwɑːtə'mɑːlən] *adj & n* guatemalteco,-a *(m, f)*.

guava ['gwɑːvə] *n Bot* guayaba *f*. ■ **g. tree**, guayabo *m*.

gudgeon[1] ['gʌdʒən] *n (fish)* gobio *m*.

gudgeon[2] ['gʌdʒən] *n Tech (of axle)* gorrón *m*.

Guernsey ['gɜːnzɪ] *n* Guernesey.

guer(r)illa [gə'rɪlə] *n* guerrillero,-a *m*, *f*. ■ **g. warfare**, guerra *f* de guerrillas.

guess [ges] **I** *vtr & vi* **1** *(gen)* adivinar; **g. what happened today!**, ¡adivina lo que ha pasado hoy!; **I guessed as much**, me lo imaginaba; **to g. right/wrong**, acertar/no acertar; **to keep sb guessing**, mantener a algn en la incertidumbre. **2** *US fam* creer, pensar, suponer; **I g. so**, supongo que sí. **II** *n (gen)* conjetura *f*, suposición *f*; *(estimate)* cálculo *m*, suposición *f*; **at a rough g.**, a ojo de buen cubero; **have a g.!**, ¡a ver si aciertas!; **it's anyone's g.**, no se sabe; **to have** *or* **make a g.**, intentar adivinar.

gues(s)timate ['gestɪmɪt] *n fam* cálculo *m* aproximado.

guesswork ['gesw3ːk] *n* conjetura *f*; **it's all g.**, es pura conjetura.

guest [gest] *n (at home)* invitado,-a *m*, *f*; *(in hotel)* cliente,-a *m*, *f*, huésped,-a *m*, *f*; **g. of honour**, invitado,-a de honor; *fam* **be my g.!**, ¡estás en tu casa! ■ **g. artist**, artista *mf* invitado,-a; **g. room**, cuarto *m* de los invitados.

guesthouse ['gesthaʊs] *n* casa *f* de huéspedes.

guffaw [gʌ'fɔː] **I** *n* carcajada *f*. **II** *vi* reírse a carcajadas.

Guiana [gaɪ'ænə] *n* Guayana. ■ **French G.**, Guayana Francesa.

Guianian [gaɪ'ænən] *adj & n*, **Guianese** [gaɪə'niːz] *adj & n* guayanés,-esa *(m, f)*.

guidance ['gaɪdəns] *n* orientación *f*, consejos *mpl*; **for your g.**, a título de información; *Educ* **vocational g.**, orientación profesional.

guide [gaɪd] **I** *vtr* guiar, orientar, dirigir; **to be guided by**, dejarse guiar por. **II** *n* **1** *(person)* guía *mf*. ■ *GB* **girl g.**, exploradora *f*; **g. dog**, perro *m* lazarillo. **2** *(guidebook)* guía *f*. **3** *(example)* ejemplo *m*; **it's a rough g.**, es una aproximación; **reason is my g.**, me dejo guiar por la razón.

guidebook ['gaɪdbʊk] *n* guía *f*.

guided ['gaɪdɪd] *adj* dirigido,-a; **g. tour**, visita con guía. ■ *Mil* **g. missile**, misil *m* teledirigido.

guideline ['gaɪdlaɪn] *n* directiva *f*, directriz *f*, pauta *f*; **to serve as a g.**, servir de gobierno *or* de directriz.

guiding ['gaɪdɪŋ] *adj* que sirve de guía; *(principle)* directivo,-a; *fig* **g. light**, **g. star**, lumbrera *f*.

guild [gɪld] *n* gremio *m*.

guile [gaɪl] *n (cleverness)* sagacidad *f*; *(cunning)* astucia *f*.

guileless ['gaɪllɪs] *adj* inocente. ingenuo,-a.

guillemot ['gɪlɪmɒt] *n Orn* arao *m* común.

guillotine ['gɪlətiːn] **I** *n* guillotina *f*. **II** *vtr* guillotinar.

guilt [gɪlt] *n* **1** *(gen)* culpa *f*; **g. feelings**, sentimiento de culpabilidad. **2** *Jur* culpabilidad *f*.

guilty ['gɪltɪ] *adj (guiltier, guiltiest)* culpable (**of,** de); **to feel g.**, sentirse culpable; **to have a g. conscience**, remorderle a uno la conciencia; *Jur* **to plead g./not g.**, declararse culpable/inocente.

Guinea ['gɪnɪ] *n* Guinea; *fig* **to act as a g. pig**, servir de conejillo de Indias. ■ **Equatorial G.**, Guinea Ecuatorial; **g. fowl**, gallina *f* de Guinea; *Zool* **g pig**, conejillo *m* de Indias, cobaya *m*; cobayo *m*.

guinea ['gɪnɪ] *n (coin)* guinea *f* (= 21 chelines).

Guinea-Bissau [gɪnɪbɪ'saʊ] *n* Guinea Bissau.

Guinean ['gɪnɪən] *adj & n* guineano,-a *(m, f)*.

guipure [gɪ'pjʊə'] *n Tex* guipur *m*.

guise [gaɪz] *n* apariencia *f*; **under the g. of**, so pretexto de.

guitar [gɪ'tɑː'] *n Mus* guitarra *f*.

guitarist [gɪ'tɑːrɪst] *n Mus* guitarrista *mf*, guitarra *mf*.

gulf [gʌlf] *n* **1** *Geog* golfo *m*. ■ **G. of Bothnia**, Golfo *m* de Botnia; **G. of Guinea**, Golfo *m* de Guinea; **G. of Lions**, Golfo *m* de León; **G. of Mexico**, Golfo *m* de Méjico; **G. Stream**, corriente *f* del Golfo de Méjico; **Persian G.**, golfo *m* Pérsico. **2** *fig* abismo *m*.

gull [gʌl] *n Orn* gaviota *f*. ■ **black-headed g.**, gaviota *f* reidora; **common g.**, gaviota *f* cana; **herring g.**, gaviota *f* argéntea; **little g.**, gaviota *f* enana.

gull(e)y ['gʌlɪ] *n (pl gulleys or gullies)* barranco *m*, hondonada *f*.

gullibility [gʌlə'bɪlɪtɪ] *n* credulidad *f*, tragaderas *fpl*.

gullible ['gʌləbəl] *adj* crédulo,-a.

gulp [gʌlp] I *n* trago *m*; **in one g.,** de un trago. II *vtr* tragar; **to g. back tears,** tragarse las lágrimas; **to g. sth down,** *(drink)* tomarse algo de un trago; *(food)* engullir algo. III *vi* **1** *(swallow air)* tragar aire. **2** *fig (with year)* tragar saliva.

gum¹ [gʌm] I *n* **1** *(natural substance)* goma *f*, chicle *m*. ■ **chewing g.,** chicle *m*, goma *f* de mascar; **g. arabic,** goma *f* arábiga. **2** *(glue)* goma *f*, pegamento *m*. **3** *Bot (gumtree)* gomero *m*. ■ **sweet g.,** ocozol *m*, liquidámbar *m* americano. II *vtr (pt & pp gummed)* pegar con goma. ◆ **gum up** *vtr fam* estropear.

gum² [gʌm] *n Anat* encía *f*.

gumboil ['gʌmbɔɪl] *n Med* flemón *m*.

gumboots ['gʌmbuːts] *npl* botas *fpl* de agua.

gummed [gʌmd] *adj* engomado,-a, gomoso,-a.

gummy ['gʌmɪ] *adj (gummier, gummiest)* **1** *(sticky)* pegajoso,-a. **2** *(gummed)* engomado,-a, gomoso,-a.

gumption ['gʌmpʃən] *n GB fam* caletre *m*, mollera *f*, cacumen *m*.

gumtree ['gʌmtriː] *n Bot* gomero *m*; *fam* **to be up a g.,** estar en un aprieto.

gun [gʌn] I *n (gen)* arma *f* de fuego; *(handgun)* pistola *f*, revólver *m*; *(rifle)* fusil *m*, rifle *m*, escopeta *f*; *(cannon)* cañón *m*; **he was carrying a g.,** iba armado; *fam* **the big guns,** los peces gordos; *fam* **to jump the g.,** adelantarse; *fam* **to stick to one's guns,** mantenerse en sus trece; *sl* **to go great guns,** ir a toda pastilla. ■ **g. carriage,** cureña *f*; **g. dog,** perro *m* de caza; **g. licence,** licencia *f* de armas; **machine g.,** ametralladora *f*; **spray g.,** pistola *f*, pulverizador *m*; **sub-machine-g.,** metralleta *f*. II *vtr (pt & pp gunned) Aut (engine)* hacer zumbar. ◆ **gun down** *vtr* matar a tiros. ◆ **gun for** *vtr (hunt down)* ir a la caza de.

gunboat ['gʌnbəʊt] *n Naut* cañonero *m*, (lancha *f*) cañonera *f*. ■ *fig* **g. diplomacy,** diplomacia *f* de cañón.

gunfire ['gʌnfaɪəʳ] *n (gen)* fuego *m*, tiros *mpl*; *(shellfire)* cañoneo *m*; *(shooting)* tiroteo *m*.

gunman ['gʌnmən] *n (pl gunmen)* pistolero *m*, gángster *m*.

gunner ['gʌnəʳ] *n Mil* artillero *m*.

gunnery ['gʌnərɪ] *n Mil* artillería *f*.

gunpoint ['gʌnpɔɪnt] *n* **at g.,** a punta de pistola.

gunpowder ['gʌnpaʊdəʳ] *n* pólvora *f*.

gunrunner ['gʌnrʌnəʳ] *n* traficante *mf* de armas.

gunrunning ['gʌnrʌnɪŋ] *n* tráfico *m* de armas.

gunshot ['gʌnʃɒt] *n* disparo *m*, tiro *m*. ■ **g. wounds,** heridas *fpl* de bala.

gunsmith ['gʌnsmɪθ] *n* armero *m*.

gunwale ['gʌnəl] *n Naut* regala *f*, borda *f*.

gurnard ['gɜːnəd] *n (pl gurnard or gurnards) (fish)* red *g.,* arete *m*, cuco *m*, rubio *m*.

gurgle ['gɜːgəl] I *vi (baby)* gorjear; *(liquid, gas)* gorgotear; *(stream)* murmurar. II *n (of baby)* gorjeo *m*; *(of liquid, gas)* gorgoteo *m*. gluglú *m*; *(of stream)* murmullo *m*.

guru ['guruː, 'guːruː] *n* gurú *m*.

gush [gʌʃ] I *vi* **1** brotar *or* salir a borbotones, borbotear. **2** *fig* **to g. over sb,** enjabonar a algn. II *n* **1** *(of water etc)* chorro *m*; *(of words)* torrente *m*. **2** *fig* efusión *f*, sentimentalismo *m*.

gushing ['gʌʃɪŋ] *adj* **1** *(liquid, gas)* que brota, que sale a chorros. **2** *fig (person)* efusivo,-a.

gusset ['gʌsɪt] *n Sew* escudete *m*.

gust [gʌst] *n (of wind)* ráfaga *f*, racha *f*; *(of rain)* chaparrón *m*.

gusto ['gʌstəʊ] *n* entusiasmo *m*, placer *m*; **to eat with g.,** comer con ganas.

gusty ['gʌstɪ] *adj (gustier, gustiest) (wind)* racheado,-a.

gut [gʌt] I *n* **1** *Anat (intestine)* intestino *m*, tripa *f*. **2** *(catgut)* cuerda *f* de tripa. **3** guts, *(entrails)* entrañas *fpl*, tripas *fpl*. **4** guts, *sl* agallas *fpl*; **to have g.,** tener agallas; *fam* **she hates his g.,** no lo puede ni ver; *fam* **to sweat *or* work one's g. out,** dejarse la piel en algo, trabajar como un negro. II *vtr (pt & pp gutted)* **1** *(fish etc)* destripar, limpiar. **2** *(destroy)* destruir por dentro; **fire gutted the building,** el fuego destruyó el interior del edificio. III *adj fam* visceral; **g. reaction,** reacción visceral.

gutsy ['gʌtsɪ] *adj (gutsier, gutsiest) sl (courageous)* con agallas; *(determined)* lanzado,-a.

gutta-percha [gʌtə'pɜːtʃə] *n* gutapercha *f*.

gutter ['gʌtəʳ] I *n (in street)* arroyo *m*, cuneta *f*; *(on roof)* canal *m*, canalón *m*; *fig* **the g.,** los barrios bajos; *fig* **to rise from the g.,** salir del arroyo *or* de la nada. ■ *Press fig* **g. press,** prensa *f* amarilla. II *vi (candle)* derretirse.

guttural ['gʌtərəl] *adj* gutural.

guy¹ [gaɪ] *n fam* tipo *m*, tio *m*; **he's a great g.,** es un chico estupendo. ■ *fam* **g. fawkes,** *fig* tío *m* duro, matón *m*; **wise g.,** sabihondo *m*. sabelotodo *m inv*.

guy² [gaɪ] *n (rope)* viento *m*, cuerda *f*.

Guyana [gaɪ'ænə] *n* Guyana.

Guyanan [gaɪ'ænən] *adj & n*, **Guyanese** [gaɪə'niːz] *adj & n* guyanés,-esa *(m, f)* guayanés,-esa.

guzzle ['gʌzəl] *vtr & vi fam (food etc)* engullirse, zamparse, tragarse; *(car)* tragar mucho.

guzzler ['gʌzləʳ] *n fam (person)* tragón,-ona *m, f*; comilón,-ona *m, f*, glotón,-ona *m, f*; *(car)* que traga mucho.

gym [dʒɪm] *fam* I *(gymnasium)* gimnasio *m*. **2** *(gymnastics)* gimnasia *f*. ■ **g. shoes,** zapatillas *fpl* de deporte.

gymkhana [dʒɪm'kɑːnə] *n Equit* gymkhana *f*.

gymnasium [dʒɪm'neɪzɪəm] *n (pl gymnasiums or gymnasia* [dʒɪm'neɪzɪə]*)* gimnasio *m*.

gymnast ['dʒɪmnæst] *n* gimnasta *mf*.

gymnastic [dʒɪm'næstɪk] *adj* gimnástico,-a.

gymnastics [dʒɪm'næstɪks] *n* gimnasia *f*.

gynaecological, *US* **gynecological** [gaɪnɪkə'lɒdʒɪkəl] *adj Med* ginecológico,-a.

gynaecologist, *US* **gynecologist** [gaɪnɪ'kɒlədʒɪst] *n Med* ginecólogo,-a *m, f*.

gynaecology, *US* **gynecology** [gaɪnɪ'kɒlədʒɪ] *n Med* ginecología *f*.

gyp [dʒɪp] *sl* I *vtr (pt & pp gypped)* engatusar. II *n* robo *m*, timo *m*.

gypsum ['dʒɪpsəm] *n* yeso *m*.

gypsy ['dʒɪpsɪ] *adj & n* gitano,-a *(m, f)*.

gyrate [dʒaɪ'reɪt] *vi* girar, dar vueltas.

gyration [dʒaɪ'reɪʃən] *n* giro *m*, vuelta *f*.

gyratory ['dʒaɪrətərɪ] *adj* giratorio,-a.

gyrocompass ['dʒaɪrəʊkʌmpəs] *n* girocompás *m*.

gyroscope ['dʒaɪrəskəʊp] *n* giroscopio *m*, giróscopo *m*.

gyroscopic [dʒaɪrə'skɒpɪk] *adj* giroscópico,-a.

gyrostat ['dʒaɪrəʊstæt] *n see* **gyroscope.**

H

H, h [eɪtʃ] *n (the letter)* H, h *f*.

H *abbr of* **hydrogen**, hidrógeno *m*, H.

ha *abbr of* **hectare**, hectárea *f*, ha.

haberdasher ['hæbədæʃəʳ] *n* **1** *GB (shopkeeper)* mercero,-a *m*,*f*; *(shop)* **h.'s,** mercería *f*. **2** *US (shop)* tienda *f* de ropa para caballeros.

haberdashery [hæbə'dæʃərɪ] *n* **1** *GB* artículos *mpl* de mercería. **2** *US* ropa *f* masculina.

habit ['hæbɪt] *n* **1** *(custom)* hábito *m*, costumbre *f*; **bad h.,** vicio *m*; **out of h.,** por costumbre; **to be in the h. of,** tener la costumbre de; **to get into the h. of,** coger la costumbre de, acostumbrarse a; **to get out of the h. of,** perder la costumbre de; **to kick the h.,** dejar un vicio; **to make a h. of sth,** hacer de algo una costumbre. **2** *(garment) Rel* hábito *m*.

habitable ['hæbɪtəbəl] *adj* habitable.

habitat ['hæbɪtæt] *n* hábitat *m*.

habitation [hæbɪ'teɪʃən] *n fml* habitación *f*; **unfit for human h.,** inhabitable.

habit-forming ['hæbɪtfɔːmɪŋ] *adj* que crea hábito *or* dependencia.

habitual [hə'bɪtjʊəl] *adj (customary)* habitual, acostumbrado,-a; *(of drinker, smoker, liar)* inveterado,-a, empedernido,-a. ◆ **habitually** *adv* por costumbre, habitualmente.

habituate [hə'bɪtjʊeɪt] *vtr fml* habituarse (**a,** to), acostumbrarse (**a,** to).

habitué [hə'bɪtjʊeɪ] *n fml* parroquiano,-a *m*,*f* habitual.

hack¹ [hæk] **I** *n (cut)* corte *m*, tajo *m*; *(with an axe)* hachazo *m*; *(notch)* mella *f*; *(kick)* patada *f*, puntapié *m*. **II** *vtr (with knife, axe)* cortar, rajar; *(notch)* mellar; *(kick)* dar un puntapié a. ◆ **hack about** *vtr (text, article)* cortar, mutilar. ◆ **hack through** *vtr (work)* hacer una chapuza.

hack² [hæk] **I** *n* **1** *(hired horse)* caballo *m* de alquiler; *(worn-out horse)* rocín *m*, jamelgo *m*. **2** *fam (writer)* escritorzuelo,-a *m*, *f*, *(journalist)* gacetillero,-a *m*, *f*, periodista *mf* de poca categoría. **II** *adj fam (work)* mecánico,-a, rutinario,-a. **III** *vi fam* montar a caballo.

hacking¹ ['hækɪŋ] *adj (cough)* seco,-a, áspero,-a.

hacking² ['hækɪŋ] *adj* de montar. ■ **h. jacket,** chaqueta *f* de montar.

hackles ['hæklz] *npl Zool (of bird)* collar *m*, plumas *fpl* del cuello; *(of mammal)* pelo *m* del cuello; *fig* **to put sb's h. up,** poner negro a algn.

hackneyed ['hæknɪd] *adj* gastado,-a, trillado,-a.

hacksaw ['hæksɔ:] *n* sierra *f* para metales.

had [hæd] *pt & pp see* **have**.

haddock ['hædək] *n (pl* **haddocks** *or* **haddock***) (fish)* abadejo *m*.

haemoglobin [hi:məʊ'gləʊbɪn] *n Med* hemoglobina *f*.

haemophilia [hi:məʊ'fɪlɪə] *n Med* hemofilia *f*.

haemophiliac [hi:məʊ'fɪlɪæk] *adj & n Med* hemofílico,-a *(m,f)*.

haemorrhage ['hemərɪdʒ] *n Med* hemorragia *f*.

haemorrhoids ['hemərɔɪdz] *npl Med* hemorroides *fpl*.

haft [hɑ:ft] *n (of knife)* mango *m*; *(of sword)* puño *m*, empuñadura *f*.

hag [hæg] *n pej* bruja *f*, arpía *f*.

haggard ['hægəd] *adj* ojeroso,-a.

haggis ['hægɪs] *n Scot Culin* guiso hecho con las asaduras del cordero.

haggish ['hægɪʃ] *adj* de bruja.

haggle ['hægəl] *vi* regatear; **to h. over** *or* **about the price of sth,** regatear el precio de algo.

haggling ['hæglɪŋ] *n* regateo *m*.

hagiography [hægɪ'ɒgrəfɪ] *n* hagiografía *f*.

Hague [heɪg] *n* **The H.,** La Haya.

hah [hɑ:] *interj*, **ha ha** [hɑ:'hɑ:] *interj* ¡ja ja!

hail¹ [heɪl] **I** *n Meteor (ice)* granizo *m*; *(storm)* granizada *f*; *fig* **a h. of bullets/insults,** una lluvia de balas/insultos. **II** *vi* granizar.

hail² [heɪl] **I** *n (greeting)* saludo *m*. ■ *Rel* **H. Mary, avemaria** *f*. **II** *vtr* **1** *arch (call)* llamar. **2** *(taxi)* llamar. **3** *(acclaim)* aclamar, proclamar. **III** *vi* **1** *Meteor* granizar. **2** *(originate)* ser nativo,-a **(from,** de), ser **(from,** de).

hailstone ['heɪlstəʊn] *n* granizo *m*.

hailstorm ['heɪlstɔːm] *n* granizada *f*.

hair [heəʳ] *n (strand)* pelo *m*, cabello *m*; *(mass)* pelo *m*, cabellos *npl*, cabellera *f*; *(on arm, leg)* vello *m*; **to have long h.,** tener melena *or* el pelo largo; **to have one's h. cut,** cortarse el pelo; *fig* **to let one's h. down,** desmadrarse; *fig* **to make sb's h. stand on end,** poner los pelos de punta a algn; *fig* **to split hairs,** hilar muy delgado; *fig* **to tear one's h. out,** estar desesperado,-a; *fam* **keep your h. on!,** ¡tranquilo!, ¡no es para tanto!; *fam fig* **it gets in my h.,** lo odio. ■ **h's breadth,** anchura *f* de un pelo; **h. lacquer,** laca *f*; **h. slide,** pasador *m*.

hairband ['heəbænd] *n* cinta *f* (para el pelo).

hairbrush ['heəbrʌʃ] *n* cepillo *m* (para el pelo).

haircut ['heəkʌt] *n* corte *m* de pelo; **to have a h.,** cortarse el pelo.

hairdo ['heədu:] *n fam* peinado *m*.

hairdresser ['heədresəʳ] *n* peluquero,-a *m*,*f*; **h.'s (shop),** peluquería *f*.

hairdressing ['heədresɪŋ] *n (profession)* peluquería *f*.

hairdryer *n*, **hairdrier** ['heədraɪəʳ] *n* secador *m* (de pelo).

hair-grip ['heəgrɪp] *n* horquilla *f*, pasador *m*.

hairless ['heəlɪs] *adj* sin pelo, calvo,-a.

hairline ['heəlaɪn] **I** *adj* muy fino,-a; **a h. crack,** una raja pequeña. **II** *n* nacimiento *m* del pelo; **receding h.,** entradas *fpl*.

hairnet ['heənet] *n* redecilla *f*.

hairpiece ['heəpi:s] *n* postizo *m*, peluquín *m*.

hairpin ['heəpɪn] *n* horquilla *f*. ■ *Aut* **h. bend,** curva *f* muy cerrada.

hair-raising ['heəreɪsɪŋ] *adj* espeluznante, que pone los pelos de punta.

hair-remover ['heərɪmu:vəʳ] *n* depilatorio *m*.

hair-splitting ['heəsplɪtɪŋ] *pej* **I** *adj* sutil. **II** *n* sutilezas *fpl*.

hairspray ['heəspreɪ] *n* laca *f* (para el pelo).

hairstyle ['heəstaɪl] *n* peinado *m*, corte *m* de pelo.

hairy ['heərɪ] *adj (***hairier, hairiest***)* **1** *(with hair)* peludo,-a. **2** *fig (frightening)* enervante, espantoso,-a.

Haiti ['heɪtɪ, hɑ:'i:tɪ] *n* Haití.

Haitian ['heɪʃən, hɑ:'i:ʃən] **1** *adj* haitiano,-a. **II** *n* **1** *(person)* haitiano,-a *m*,*f*. **2** *(language)* haitiano *m*.

hake [heɪk] *n (pl* **hakes** *or* **hake***) (fish)* merluza *f*; *(young)* pescadilla *f*.

halcyon ['hælsɪən] *adj fml* **h. days,** los brillantes y tranquilos días de la juventud.

hale [heɪl] *adj Lit* sano,-a; **h. and hearty,** fuerte y sano.

half [hɑːf] **I** *n* (*pl* **halves**) (*section*) media parte *f*, mitad *f*; *Sport* (*period*) parte *f*, mitad *f*, tiempo *m*; (*position*) medio *m*; **he's four and a h.,** tiene cuatro años y medio; **to cut/rip/break in h.,** cortar/rasgar/romper por la mitad; *fig* **my better** *or* **other h.,** mi media naranja; *fam* **to go halves with sb,** ir a medias con algn; *fam fig* **I've a problem and a h.,** ¡vaya problema que tengo! ■ *Sport* **first/second h.,** primer/segundo tiempo *m*, primera/segunda parte *f* or mitad *f*; *Ftb* **centre h.,** (defensa *m*) central *m*. **II** *adj* medió,-a; **h. a dozen/an hour,** media docena/hora; **he is h. German,** es medio alemán. ■ **h. board,** media pensión *f*; **h. fare,** media tarifa *f*, medio billete *m*; **h. measures,** medias tintas *fpl*; **h. term,** medio trimestre *m*; **h. year,** semestre *m*, medio año *m*. **III** *adv* medio, a medias; **h. asleep,** medio dormido,-a; **h. and h.,** mitad y mitad; *fam* **I was h. expecting you not to come,** casi creía que no ibas a venir; *fam* **would you like a beer? —not h.!,** ¿quieres una cerveza? —¡hombre, claro!; *fam iron* **he's too clever by h.,** es un poco desmasiado listillo, ¿sabes?

half-baked [hɑːfˈbeɪkt] *adj* **1** *Culin* medio cocido,-a. **2** *fig* (*of idea, plan*) mal concebido,-a, poco serio,-a.

half-breed [ˈhɑːfbriːd] *adj & n* mestizo,-a (*m*,*f*).

half-brother [ˈhɑːfbrʌðəʳ] *n* hermanastro *m*.

half-caste [ˈhɑːfkɑːst] *adj & n* mestizo,-a (*m*,*f*).

half-closed [hɑːfkləʊzd] *adj* entreabierto,-a.

half-cock [hɑːfˈkɒk] *n* (*of gun*) **at h.-c.,** con el seguro echado.

half-day [hɑːfˈdeɪ] *n* media jornada *f*.

half-empty [hɑːfˈemptɪ] *adj* medio vacío,-a.

half-hearted [hɑːfˈhɑːtɪd] *adj* poco entusiasta. ◆ **half-heartedly** *adv* sin entusiasmo, sin ganas.

half-hour [hɑːfˈaʊəʳ] *n* media hora *f*. ◆ **half-hourly** *adv* cada media hora.

half-life [ˈhɑːflaɪf] *n Chem* media vida *f*.

half-mast [hɑːfˈmɑːst] *n* **at h.,** a media asta.

half-note [ˈhɑːfnəʊt] *n US Mus* blanca *f*.

halfpenny [ˈhɑːfpenɪ] *n* (*pl* **halfpennies** *or* **halfpence** [ˈhɑːpens]) medio penique *m*.

half-price [hɑːfˈpraɪs] *adv* a mitad de precio.

half-sister [ˈhɑːfsɪstəʳ] *n* hermanastra *f*.

half-time [hɑːfˈtaɪm] *n Sport* descanso *m*.

half-tone [ˈhɑːftəʊn] *n* **1** *Print* medio tono *m*, media tinta *f*. **2** *Mus* semitono *m*.

half-way [ˈhɑːfweɪ] **1** *adj* medio,-a, intermedio,-a; **the h.-w. point,** el punto intermedio. **II** *halfway* [hɑːfˈweɪ] *adv* a medio camino, a mitad de camino; *fig* **to meet sb h.,** llegar a un arreglo con algn.

half-wit [ˈhɑːfwɪt] *n* tonto,-a *m*,*f*, imbécil *mf*.

half-yearly [ˈhɑːfjɪəlɪ] *adj* semestral.

halibut [ˈhælɪbət] *n* (*pl* **halibuts** *or* **halibut**) (*fish*) mero *m*.

hall [hɔːl] *n* **1** (*lobby*) entrada *f*, vestíbulo *m*. ■ **h. stand,** percha *f*. **2** (*building*) sala *f*. ■ *Univ* **h. of residence,** colegio *m* mayor, residencia *f* universitaria; **town** *or* **city h.,** ayuntamiento *m*. **3** (*estate*) mansión *f*, casa *f* de campo señorial.

hallmark [ˈhɔːlmɑːk] *n* **1** (*on gold, silver*) contraste *m*. **2** *fig* sello *m*.

hallo [həˈləʊ] *interj* ¡hola!

hallowed [ˈhæləʊd] *adj* (*holy*) santo,-a, santificado,-a, bendito,-a; *fig* reverenciado,-a; **h. be Thy name,** santificado sea Tu nombre.

Hallowe(')en [hæləʊˈiːn] *n* víspera *f* de Todos los Santos.

hallucinate [həˈluːsɪˈneɪt] *vi* alucinar.

hallucination [həluːsɪˈneɪʃən] *n* alucinación *f*.

hallucinatory [həˈluːsɪnɒtrɪ] *adj* alucinante.

hallucinogenic [həluːsɪnəʊˈdʒenɪk] *adj* alucinógeno,-a.

hallway [ˈhɔːlweɪ] *n* vestíbulo *m*.

halo [ˈheɪləʊ] *n* (*pl* **haloes** *or* **halos**) **1** *Astron* halo *m*. **2** *Rel* aureola *f*.

halt [hɔːlt] **I** *n* (*stop*) alto *m*, parada *f*; **to call a h. to sth,** atajar algo, acabar con algo; **to come to a h.,** (*stop*) pararse; (*interrupt*) interrumpirse. **II** *vtr* parar, detener. **III** *vi* pararse, detenerse. **IV** *interj* ¡alto!

halter [ˈhɔːltəʳ] *n Equit* ronzal *m*, cabestro *m*.

halterneck [ˈhɔːltənek] *adj* vestido *m* escotado por detrás.

halting [ˈhɔːltɪŋ] *adj* (*speech*) vacilante; (*steps*) titubeante.

halve [hɑːv] *vtr* **1** (*cut in half*) partir por la mitad; (*reduce by half*) reducir a la mitad. **2** (*share*) compartir. **3** *Golf* empatar.

halves [hɑːvz] *pl see* **half.**

ham¹ [hæm] *n Culin* jamón *m*. ■ **boiled h.,** jamón *m* cocido *or* en dulce *or* de York; **Parma** *or* **cured h.,** jamón *m* serrano.

ham² [hæm] **I** *n* **1** *Rad* radioaficionado,-a *m*,*f*. **2** *Theat* (*actor*) comicastro,-a *m*, *f*, histrión *m*; (*acting*) histrionismo *m*. **II** *vi* (*pt & pp* **hammed**) *Theat* **to h. (it) up,** sobreactuar.

Hamburg [ˈhæmbɜːg] *n* Hamburgo.

hamburger [ˈhæmbɜːgəʳ] *n Culin* hamburguesa *f*.

ham-fisted [hæmˈfɪstɪd] *adj* torpe; **he's very h.-f,** es un manazas.

hamlet [ˈhæmlɪt] *n* aldea *f*, pueblecito *m*.

hammer [ˈhæməʳ] **I** *n* **1** (*tool*) martillo *m*; *Pol* **the h. and sickle,** la hoz y el martillo; *fig* **to come under the h.,** salir a subasta; *fig* **to fight h. and tongs,** luchar a brazo partido. **2** *Mus* (*of piano*) macillo *m*. **3** (*gun*) percursor *m*. **4** *Sport* lanzamiento *m* de martillo. **II** *vtr* **1** (*gen*) martillar, martillear; (*nail*) clavar; *fig* **to h. home,** insistir sobre *or* en; *fig* **to h. sth into sb,** meterle algo en la cabeza a algn. **2** *fam* (*defeat*) dar una paliza a. **3** (*slate*) machacar; (*criticize*) criticar. **III** *vi* (*gen*) martillar, martillear, dar golpes; **to h. at the door,** golpear la puerta; *fig* **it's been hammering it down,** no ha parado de llover. ◆ **hammer away** *vi* trabajar constantemente. ◆ **hammer out** *vtr* (*agreement*) lograr, alcanzar; **to h. it out,** llegar a un acuerdo.

hammerhead [ˈhæməhed] *n* (*fish*) pez *m* martillo.

hammering [ˈhæmərɪŋ] *n* **1** (*knocking*) martilleo *m*. **2** *fam* paliza *f*; **to give sb a h.,** darle una paliza a algn; **to take a h.,** recibir una paliza.

hammock [ˈhæmək] *n* hamaca *f*; *Naut* coy *m*.

hamper¹ [ˈhæmpəʳ] *n* cesta *f*. ■ **Christmas h.,** cesta *f* de Navidad.

hamper² [ˈhæmpəʳ] *vtr* estorbar, obstaculizar, impedir, dificultar.

hamster [ˈhæmstəʳ] *n Zool* hámster *m*.

hamstring [ˈhæmstrɪŋ] **I** *n Anat* tendón *m* de la corva. **II** *vtr* (*pt & pp* **hamstrung** [ˈhæmstrʌŋ]) limitar, perjudicar.

hand [hænd] **I** *n* **1** mano *f*; **by h.,** a mano; (*close*) **at h.,** a mano, muy cerca; **hands off!,** ¡manos fuera!; **hands up!,** ¡manos arriba!; **on the one/other h.,** por una/otra parte; **to walk h. in h.,** andar cogidos *or* ir de la mano; *fig* **a free h.,** carta *f* blanca; *fig* **to get out of h.,** descontrolarse; *fig* **the job in h.,** lo que nos ocupa; *fig* **to ask for sb's h.,** pedir la mano de algn; *fig* **to be on h.,** estar a mano; *fig* **to bite the h. that feeds you,** cria cuervos y te sacarán los ojos; *fig* **to change hands,** cambiar de manos; *fig* **to do sth out of h.,** hacer algo sin pensarlo; *fig* **to have the upper h.,** llevar ventaja; *fig* **to have a h. in,** intervenir en; *fig* **to have sth to h.,** tener algo a la mano; *fig* **to have time in h.,** sobrarle a uno tiempo; *fig* **to keep one's h. in,** no perder la práctica; *fig* **to know sth like the back of one's h.,** conocer algo como la palma de mano; *fig* **to live from h. to mouth,** vivir al día; *fig* **to play (right) into sb's hands,** ponerse a merced de algn; *fig* **to take sb in h.,** ocuparse de algn; *fig* **to turn one's h. to,** meterse en, dedicarse a; *fig* **to wash one's hands,** lavarse las manos; *fig* **to wait h. and foot on sb,** ser el esclavo de algn; *fig* **to work h. in glove,** colaborar; *fam fig* **to do sth with one's hands tied behind one's back,** hacer algo con las manos cerados; *fam fig* **to have one's hands full,** tener mucho que hacer; *fam fig* **to give** *or* **lend sb a h.,** echarle una mano a algn. ■ **h. grenade,** granada *f* de mano. **2** *(worker)* trabajador,-a *m, f; Naut* tripulante *m;* **all hands on deck!,** ¡toda la tripulación a cubierta! ■ *Agr* **farm h.,** peón *m.* **3** *(of clock etc)* manecilla *f,* aguja *f.* **4** *(applause)* aplauso *m;* **to give sb a big h.,** dedicar a algn una gran ovación. **5** *Cards* mano *f,* partida *f. fig* **to force sb's h.,** forzar la mano a algn; *fig* **to show one's h.,** poner las cartas sobre la mesa. **6** *(handwriting)* letra *f;* **to write by h.,** escribir a mano. **II** *vtr (give)* dar, entregar; *fam fig* **I have to h. it to you,** tengo que reconocerlo. ◆ **hand around** *vtr* repartir, ofrecer, pasar. ◆ **hand back** *vtr* devolver. ◆ **hand down** *vtr* dejar en herencia. ◆ **hand in** *vtr (homework, document)* entregar; *(resignation, notice)* presentar, notificar. ◆ **hand on** *vtr (give)* pasar; *(inherit)* heredar. ◆ **hand out** *vtr* repartir, distribuir. ◆ **hand over** *vtr* entregar. ◆ **hand round** *vtr* repartir.

handbag ['hændbæg] *n* bolso *m.*

handball ['hændbɔːl] *n Sport* balonmano *m.*

handbook ['hændbʊk] *n* manual *m,* guía *f.*

handbrake ['hændbreɪk] *n Aut* freno *m* de mano.

handclap ['hændklæp] *n* aplauso *m.*

handcuff ['hændkʌf] **I** *vtr* esposar. **II handcuffs** *npl* esposas *fpl.*

handful ['hændfʊl] *n* puñado *m.*

handgun ['hændgʌn] *n* pistola *f.*

handicap ['hændɪkæp] *n* **I** *n* **1** *(physical, mental)* menusvalía *f,* disminución *f,* deficiencia *f.* **2** *(Sport)* handicap *m,* desventaja *f.* **II** *vtr (pt & pp **handicapped)* impedir, obstaculizar, handicapar.

handicapped ['hændɪkæpt] **I** *adj* **1** *Med (physically)* minusválido,-a; *(mentally)* retrasado,-a. **2** *Sport* en desventaja. **3** *fig* desfavorecido,-a. **II the h.** *npl* los minusválidos.

handicraft ['hændɪkræft] *n (art)* artesanía *f; (articles)* (objetos *mpl* de) artesanía, artesanado *m.*

handiwork ['hændɪwɜːk] *n (work)* trabajo *m,* obra *f; (craft)* artesanía *f.*

handkerchief ['hæŋkətʃiːf] *n* pañuelo *m.*

handle ['hændəl] **I** *n (of knife)* mango *m; (of cup, bag)* asa *f; (of door, stick)* pomo *m; (of lever)* palanca *f; (of drawer)* tirador *m; fam fig* **to fly off the h.,** salirse de sus casillas. **II** *vtr* **1** *(gen)* manejar, manipular; *(on parcel)* **'h. with care', 'frágil'.** **2** *(situation, subject)* manejar; *(problem, responsibility)* encargarse de; *(people)* tratar; *fam (put up with)* soportar, aguantar. **III** *vi* manejarse; *(car)* comportarse.

handlebar ['hændəlbɑːʳ] *n Cycl* manillar *m.*

handler ['hændləʳ] *n* cuidador,-a *m, f.* ■ **baggage h.,** mozo *m* de equipajes; **dog h.,** cuidador,-a *m, f* de perros.

handmade ['hændmeɪd] *adj* hecho,-a a mano.

handmaiden ['hændmeɪdən] *n* **1** *arch* criada *f.* **2** *fig* algo *m* de segunda.

hand-me-down ['hændmɪdaʊn] *n fam* prenda *f* de segunda mano *or* usada.

hand-out ['hændaʊt] *n* **1** *(leaflet)* folleto *m; Pol* octavilla *f; Press* nota *f or* comunicado *m* de prensa. **2** *(charity)* limosna *f,* caridad *f.*

hand-picked [hænd'pɪkt] *adj* cuidadosamente escogido,-a.

handrail ['hændreɪl] *n* pasamano *m,* barandilla *f.*

handshake ['hændʃeɪk] *n* apretón *m* de manos.

handsome ['hænsəm] *adj* **1** *(of person)* guapo,-a; *(beautiful)* bonito,-a, bello,-a; *(elegant)* elegante. **2** *(substantial)* considerable. ◆ **handsomely** *adv* **1** *(elegantly)* elegantemente, con elegancia. **2** *(substantially)* substancialmente.

handspring ['hændsprɪŋ] *n Gymn* paloma *f.*

handstand ['hændstænd] *n Gymn* pino *m,* vertical *m.*

hand-to-hand ['hændtəhænd] *adj* **h.-to-h. combat,** combate cuerpo a cuerpo.

handwriting ['hændraɪtɪŋ] *n* letra *f.*

handwritten ['hændrɪtən] *adj* escrito,-a a mano.

handy ['hændɪ] *adj (handier, handiest)* **1** *(useful)* útil, práctico,-a; *(nearby)* a mano, cercano,-a; *fam* **to come in h.,** ser útil, venir bien; **to keep h.,** tener a mano. **2** *(dextrous)* hábil.

hang [hæŋ] **I** *vtr (pt & pp hung)* **1** *(gen)* colgar. **2** *(wallpaper)* pegar; *(room)* empapelar, decorar. **3** *(head)* bajar, inclinar. **4** *(pt & pp hanged)* ahorcar. **II** *vi* **1** colgar *(from,* de), pender *(from,* with); *(in air)* flotar; *(material, clothing)* colgar; *fig* **to h. in the air,** flotar en el aire; **the problem was left hanging in the air,** el problema quedó sin solución; *US fam* **h. loose!,** ¡tranqui, tranqui!; *fam fig* **we've got this exam hanging over us,** tenemos pendiente este examen. **2** *(of criminal)* ser ahorcado,-a; **to h. oneself,** ahorcarse, **III** *n* **1** *(of material, clothing)* caída *f.* **2** *fam (trick)* truquillo *m;* **to get the h. of sth,** cogerle el truquillo a algo. ◆ **hang about, hang round** *vi fam* **1** perder el tiempo. **2** *fam (wait)* esperar; **h. about!,** ¡espera! ◆ **hang around** *vi fam* **1** esperar; *fam fig* **he doesn't h. around,** es muy rápido. **2** *fam* frecuentar, andar por. ◆ **hang back** *vi* **1** *(place, race, etc)* quedarse atrás. **2** *fig* vacilar. ◆ **hang down** *vi (of hair)* caer, colgar. ◆ **hang on** *vi* **1** agarrarse; *fig* **we hung on his every word,** estábamos pendientes de cada una de sus palabras. **2** *(wait)* esperar; **h. on!,** ¡espérate!; *US fam* **h. on in there!,** ¡aguanta tío! ◆ **hang onto** *vi* agarrar; *fig* **h. onto it,** guárdalo. ◆ **hang out I** *vtr (washing etc)* colgar, tender. **II** *vi sl (frequent)* frecuentar; **where do they h. out?,** ¿qué lugares frecuentan?; *US fam* **to let it all h. out,** desmadrarse. ◆ **hang together** *vi* **1** *(friends)* mantenerse unidos. **2** *(ideas, argument)* ser coherente. ◆ **hang up** *vtr (coat, picture, telephone)* colgar; *fig* **to h. up one's boots,** colgar las botas.

hangar ['hæŋəʳ] *n Av* hangar *m.*

hanger ['hæŋəʳ] *n* percha *f.*

hanger-on [hæŋər'ɒn] *n (pl hangers-on) fam* lapa *f,* parásito,-a *m, f.*

hang-glider ['hæŋglaɪdəʳ] *n* ala *f* delta.

hang-gliding ['hæŋglaɪdɪŋ] *n* vuelo *m* libre.

hanging ['hæŋɪŋ] **I** *adj* colgante. ■ **h. bridge,** puente *m* colgante. **II** *n* **1** *(execution)* ejecución *f* en la horca. **2** **(wall) h.,** colgadura *f.*

hangman ['hæŋmən] *n (pl hangmen)* verdugo *m.*

hangnail ['hæŋneɪl] *n* padrastro *m,* pellejo *m.*

hang-out ['hæŋaʊt] *n sl (bar etc)* local *m; (pad)* guarida *f.*

hangover ['hæŋəʊvəʳ] *n* **1** *(remnant)* resto *m,* vestigio *m.* **2** *(after drinking)* resaca *f.*

hang-up ['hæŋʌp] *n (pl hang-ups) fam (worries)* preocupación *f,* inhibición *f; (complex)* complejo *m.*

hanker ['hæŋkəʳ] *vi* desear; **to h. after** *or* **for sth,** anhelar *or* ansiar algo.

hankering ['hæŋkərɪŋ] *n* deseo *m,* anhelo *m,* ansia *f.*

hankie *n,* **hanky** ['hæŋkɪ] *n fam* pañuelo *m.*

hanky-panky [hæŋkɪ'pæŋkɪ] *n fam (mal)* rollo *m.*

haphazard [hæp'hæzəd] *adj* caótico,-a, desordenado,-a. ◆ **haphazardly** *adv* sin orden ni concierto.

hapless ['hæplɪs] *adj fml* desdichado,-a, infortunado,-a.

happen ['hæpən] *vi (occur)* suceder, ocurrir, pasar, producirse; **as it happens,** lo que pasa es que; **if you h. to see my friend,** si por casualidad vez a mi amigo; **I h. to know that it is true,** me consta que es verdad.

happening ['hæpənɪŋ] *n* acontecimiento *m*.

happiness ['hæpɪnɪs] *n* felicidad *f*.

happy ['hæpɪ] *adj (happier, happiest) (cheerful)* feliz, contento,-a, alegre; *(fortunate)* afortunado,-a; **h. birthday!**, ¡feliz cumpleaños!; **we're not h. with the decision**, no nos convence la decisión. ■ **h. ending**, desenlace *m* feliz; **h. medium**, término *m* medio. ◆ **happily** *adv (with pleasure)* felizmente, con alegría; *(fortunately)* afortunadamente.

happy-go-lucky [hæpɪgəʊ'lʌkɪ] *adj* despreocupado,-a; **a h.-go-l. fellow**, un viva la virgen.

hara-kiri [hærə'kɪrɪ] *n* harakiri *m*.

harangue [hə'ræŋ] **I** *vtr* arengar. **II** *n* arenga *f*.

harass ['hærəs] *vtr* acosar, atormentar.

harassment ['hærəsmənt, hə'ræsmənt] *n* hostigamiento *m*, acoso *m*.

harbinger ['hɑːbɪndʒəʳ] **I** *n (person)* precursor,-a *m, f*; *(thing)* presagio *m*. **II** *vtr* anunciar, presagiar.

harbour, *US* **harbor** ['hɑːbəʳ] **I** *n* puerto *m*. **II** *vtr* **I** *(criminal)* encubrir. **2** *(doubts, suspicions)* abrigar; **to h. a grudge,** guardar rencor.

hard [hɑːd] **I** *adj* **I** *(not soft)* duro,-a, firme; *(solid)* sólido,-a; *fam fig* **as h. as nails,** más duro que una piedra; *fam fig* **he's a h. nut,** es un hueso duro de roer. ■ *Ten* **h. court,** pista *f* (de tenis) dura; **h. shoulder,** arcén *m*. **2** *(difficult)* difícil, duro,-a; **h. of hearing,** duro,-a de oído; *fig* **we'll be h. pushed** *or* **pressed** *or* **put to finish today,** difícilmente acabaremos hoy; *fam fig* **to be h. up,** estar sin blanca; *fam fig* **to have a h. time,** pasarlo mal. **3** *(harsh, severe)* duro,-a. severo,-a; *(strict)* estricto,-a, rígido,-a; **a h. winter,** un invierno riguroso; *Pol* **to take a h. line,** tomar medidas severas; *fig* **h. and fast,** *(information)* fidedigno,-a; *(rule)* fijo,-a; *fig* **to be h. hit,** resultar gravemente afectado,-a; *fig* **to be h. on sb,** ser severo,-a con algn; *fam fig* **to drive a h. bargain,** ser muy duro,-a negociando. ■ **h. drugs,** droga *f* dura; **h. labour,** trabajos *mpl* forzados; *Pol* **h. left,** extrema izquierda *f*; **h. porn,** pornografía *f* dura; *Pol* **h. right,** extrema derecha *f*; *Com* **h. sell,** promoción *f* de venta agresiva. **4** *(inveterate, incorrigible)* incorregible; **a h. drinker,** un bebedor inveterado; **a h. worker,** un trabajador concienzudo. **5** *(unfortunate)* malo,-a; **h. luck!,** ¡mala suerte! ■ **h. evidence,** pruebas *fpl* definitivas. ■ *Com* **h. cash,** dinero *m* en metálico; *Pol* **h. core,** núcleo *m*; *Com* **h. currency,** divisa *f* fuerte. **II** *adv* **I** *(forcibly)* fuerte. **2** *(with application)* mucho, fijamente, concienzudamente; *fig* **to be h. on sb's heels,** pisar los talones a algn. **3** *(with pain)* con dolor, duramente; **he took it very h.,** fue un golpe muy duro para él; **to be h. done by** ser tratado,-a injustamente.

hardback ['hɑːdbæk] *n Print* edición *f* en tela *or* de tapas duras.

hard-bitten ['hɑːdbɪtən] *adj* tenaz, duro,-a.

hardboard ['hɑːdbɔːd] *n* chapa *f* de madera, contrachapado *m*.

hard-boiled ['hɑːdbɔɪld] *adj* **I** *(of egg)* duro,-a. **2** *fig (of person)* duro,-a, insensible.

hard-core ['hɑːdkɔːʳ] *adj* irreductible, incondicional; **h.-c. supporter,** partidario-a *m, f* acérrimo,-a.

harden ['hɑːdən] **I** *vtr* endurecer; *fig* **to h. sb's heart,** insensibilizar el corazón de algn. **II** *vi* endurecerse.

hardened ['hɑːdənd] *adj* endurecido,-a; *(criminal)* habitual.

hard-headed [hɑːd'hedɪd] *adj* realista, poco sentimental.

hard-hearted [hɑːd'hɑːtɪd] *adj* cruel, insensible.

hardliner [hɑːd'laɪnəʳ] *n Pol* duro,-a *m, f*, partidario,-a *m, f* de la línea dura.

hardly ['hɑːdlɪ] *adv* apenas, casi; **h. anyone/ever,** casi nadie/nunca; **h.!**, ¡qué va!; **he had h. begun when ....,** apenas había comenzado cuando ...; **I can h. believe it,** apenas lo puedo creer.

hardness ['hɑːdnɪs] *n* **I** *(gen)* dureza *f*. **2** *(difficulty)* dificultad *f*. **3** *(insensitivity)* insensibilidad *f*.

hard-nosed [hɑːd'nəʊʃd] *adj fam* realista, poco sentimental.

hard-pressed [hɑːd'prest] *adj* en aprietos.

hardship ['hɑːdʃɪp] *n* privación *f*, apuro *m*.

hardware ['hɑːdweəʳ] *n* **I** *(goods)* ferretería *f*. ■ **h. shop,** ferretería *f*. **2** *Mil* armamento *m*. **3** *Comput* hardware *m*.

hardwearing ['hɑːdweərɪŋ] *adj* duradero,-a, resistente.

hardworking ['hɑːdwɜːkɪŋ] *adj* trabajador,-a.

hardy ['hɑːdɪ] *adj (hardier, hardiest) (of person)* robusto,-a, fuerte; *(of plant)* resistente.

hare [heəʳ] **I** *n (pl hares or hare) Zool* liebre *f*; *fam* **mad as a March h.,** loco,-a como una cabra. **II** *vi* correr muy de prisa; **to h. off** *or* **away,** huir a toda velocidad.

harebrained ['heəbreɪnd] *adj* estúpido,-a, absurdo,-a.

harelip ['heəlɪp] *n Med* labio *m* leporino.

harem [hɑː'riːm] *n* harén *m*.

haricot ['hærɪkəʊ] *n Culin* **h. (bean),** alubia *f*.

hark [hɑːk] *vi arch* escuchar. ◆ **hark back** *vi* recordar.

harlequin ['hɑːlɪkwɪn] *n* arlequín *m*.

harlot ['hɑːlət] *n lit* ramera *f*.

harm [hɑːm] **I** *n* daño *m*, perjuicio *m*; **there's no h. in it,** no hay de malo en ello; **to be out of h's way,** estar a salvo; **you will come to no h.,** no te pasará nada; *fam* **no h. done,** tranquilo, no pasa nada. **II** *vtr* dañar, hace daño a, perjudicar.

harmful ['hɑːmfʌl] *adj* nocivo,-a **(to,** para), perjudicial **(to,** para).

harmless ['hɑːmlɪs] *adj* inocuo,-a, inofensivo,-a.

harmonic [hɑː'mɒnɪk] **I** *adj* armónico,-a. **II** *n* armónico *m*.

harmonica [hɑː'mɒnɪkæ] *n* armónica *f*.

harmonious [hɑː'məʊnɪəs] *adj* armonioso,-a.

harmonize ['hɑːmənaɪz] *vtr & vi* armonizar.

harmony ['hɑːmənɪ] *n* armonía *f*.

harness ['hɑːnɪs] **I** *n (for horse)* guarniciones *fpl*, arreos *mpl*; *fig* **to die in h.,** morir con las botas puestas; *fig* **to work in h.,** colaborar. **II** *vtr* **I** *(horse)* enjaezar, poner los arreos a. **2** *fig (resources, energy, etc)* aprovechar.

harp [hɑːp] *n Mus* arpa *f*. ◆ **harp on** *vi fam* hablar sin parar.

harpist ['hɑːpɪst] *n Mus* arpista *mf*.

harpoon [hɑː'puːn] **I** *n* arpón *m*. **II** *vtr* arponear.

harpsichord ['hɑːpsɪkɔːd] *n Mus* clavicordio *m*.

harpy ['hɑːpɪ] *n lit* arpía *f*.

harrier¹ ['hærɪəʳ] *n* **I** *(hound)* perro *m* de caza. **2** *Sport* corredor,-a *m, f* de cros.

harrier² ['hærɪəʳ] *n Orn* aguilucho *m*.

harrow ['hærəʊ] *n Agr* grada *f*.

harrowing ['hærəʊɪŋ] *adj* angustioso,-a; *(experience)* terrible.

harry ['hærɪ] *vtr (pt & pp harried)* acosar.

harsh [hɑːʃ] *adj (gen)* severo,-a, duro,-a; *(of voice)* áspero,-a; *(of sound)* discordante. ◆ **harshly** *(gen)* severamente, duramente; *(sound)* con discordancia.

harshness ['hɑːʃnɪs] *n (gen)* severidad *f*, dureza *f*; *(hardness, roughness)* aspereza *f*; *(discordancy)* discordancia *f*.

hart [hɑːt] *n Zool* ciervo *m*.

harvest ['hɑːvɪst] **I** *n (gen)* cosecha *f*, siega *f*; *(of grapes)* vendimia *f*; *fig* cosecha *f*. **II** *vtr* cosechar, recoger.

harvester ['hɑːvɪstəʳ] *n* **I** *(person)* segador,-a *m, f*. **2** *(machine)* segadora *f*, cosechadora *f*.

has [hæs] *3rd person sing pres see* **have.**

has-been ['hæzbiːn] *n fam* vieja gloria *f*.

hash¹ [hæʃ] *n* **I** *Culin* sofrito *m* de carne; *fam fig* **to make a h. of sth,** estropear algo.

hash² [hæʃ] *n sl* hachís *m*.

hashish ['hæʃiːʃ] *n* hachís *m*.

hasp [hɑːsp] *n* (*of lock*) cierre *m*; (*of door*) pestillo *m*; (*of window*) falleba *f*.

hassle ['hæsəl] *fam* **I** *n* **1** (*nuisance*) rollo *m*, molestia *f*. **2** (*problem*) problema *m*, lío *m*. **3** (*wrangle*) bronca *f*, discusión *f*. **II** *vtr* molestar, fastidiar; **don't h. me,** déjame en paz.

hassock ['hæsək] *n Rel* cojín *m*.

haste [heɪst] *n fml* prisa *f*, precipitación *f*; **to make h.,** darse prisa; *prov* **more h. less speed,** vístete despacio que tengo prisa.

hasten ['heɪsən] **I** *vtr fml* apresurar, acelerar el paso de. **II** *vi* darse prisa, apresurarse.

hastiness ['heɪstɪnɪs] *n* prisa *f*, precipitación *f*.

hasty ['heɪstɪ] *adj* (*hastier, hastiest*) **1** (*hurried*) apresurado,-a, rápido,-a. **2** (*rash*) precipitado,-a, ligero,-a. ◆ **hastily** *adv* **1** (*quickly*) de prisa. **2** (*rashly*) sin reflexionar, a la ligera, precipitadamente.

hat [hæt] *n* sombrero *m*; *fig* **I'll eat my h. if ...,** que me ahorquen si ...; *fig* **I take my h. off to him,** lo admiro; **to keep sth under one's h.,** guardar un secreto; *fam fig* **that story is old h.,** esa historia es muy vieja; *fam fig* **to talk through one's h.,** decir tonterías.

hatband ['hætbænd] *n* cinta *f* de sombrero.

hatbox ['hætbɒks] *n* sombrerera *f*.

hatch¹ [hætʃ] *n* escotilla *f*; *fam* **down the h.!,** ¡salud! ■ **serving h.,** ventanilla *f*.

hatch² [hætʃ] **I** *vtr* **1** (*of eggs, chicks*) empollar, incubar. **2** *fig* (*scheme, plan*) tramar, idear. **II** *n* (*of chickens*) pollada *f*. ◆ **hatch out** *vi* salirse del huevo, romper el cascarón.

hatchback ['hætʃbæk] *n Aut* coche *m* con portón trasero.

hatchery ['hætʃərɪ] *n* criadero *m*.

hatchet ['hætʃɪt] *n* hacha *f*; *fig* **to bury the h.,** enterrar el hache de guerra, hacer las paces. ■ **h. man,** matón *m*.

hate [heɪt] **I** *n* odio *m*; *fig* **pet h.,** bestia *f* negra. **II** *vtr* **1** (*detest*) odiar, aborrecer, no soportar. **2** (*regret*) lamentar; **I h. to say this but ...,** lamento decirte esto pero ... .

hateful ['heɪtfʌl] *adj* odioso,-a.

hatpin ['hætpɪn] *n* alfiler *m* de sombrero.

hatred ['heɪtrɪd] *n* odio *m*.

hatstand ['hætstænd] *n* percha *f* (para sombreros).

haughtiness ['hɔːtɪnɪs] *n* altanería *f*, arrogancia *f*, altivez *f*.

haughty ['hɔːtɪ] *adj* (*haughtier, haughtiest*) altanero,-a, arrogante, engreído,-a.

haul [hɔːl] **I** *n* **1** (*pull*) tirón *m*, estirón *m*. **2** (*journey*) trayecto *m*. **3** *Fishing* redada *f*. **4** (*loot*) botín *m*. **II** *vtr* **1** (*gen*) tirar; (*drag*) arrastrar; *Naut* halar; (*car*) remolcar. **2** (*transport*) acarrear. ◆ **haul up** *vtr fam* (*to court*) llevar.

haulage ['hɔːlɪdʒ] *n* transporte *m*, acarreo *m*.

haulier ['hɔːljəʳ] *n* transportista *mf*.

haunch [hɔːntʃ] *n* **1** *Anat* cadera *f*; **to sit on one's haunches,** ponerse en cuclillas. **2** *Culin* pernil *m*.

haunt [hɔːnt] **I** *n* lugar *m* predilecto; (*of criminals, animals*) guarida *f*. **II** *vtr* **1** (*of ghost*) aparecer en. **2** *fig* perseguir, atormentar. **3** (*frequent*) frecuentar.

haunted ['hɔːntɪd] *adj* encantado,-a, embrujado,-a.

haunting ['hɔːntɪŋ] *adj* obsesionante.

Havana [hə'vænə] *n* La Habana. ■ **H. cigar,** habano *m*.

have [hæv] *vtr* (*3rd person sing pres has*) (*pt & pp had*) **1** (*possess*) tener; **h. you got a car?,** *US* **do you h. a car?,** ¿tienes coche?; **if you like it h. it,** si te gusta, quédate con él; **we h. jobs at the same school,** trabajamos a la misma escuela; **you h. a way with children,** tienes mucha mano con los niños; *fig* **to put** *or* **give all one has into sth,** hacer todo lo que uno pueda. **2** (*get, experience, suffer*) pasar,

tener; **to h. a fright** *or* **a shock,** asustarse; **to h. a holiday,** tomarse unas vacaciones; *fam fig* **I've had it,** (*be in trouble*) me lo voy a cargar; (*be tired etc*) estoy hecho polvo; *fam fig* **I've had it with smoking,** voy a dejar de fumar porque ya estoy harto; *fam fig* **the radio's had it,** la radio ya no va. **3** (*partake of*) (*drink*) tomar; **to h. a cigarette,** fumarse un cigarrillo; **to h. breakfast/lunch/ tea/dinner,** desayunar/comer/merendar/cenar. **4** (*engage in*) **to h. a bath/shower/shave,** bañarse/ducharse/ afeitarse; **to h. a game of football,** jugar un partido de fútbol; **to h. a nap,** echar la siesta; *GB vulg* **to h. it off** *or* **away,** echar un polvo. **5** (*obligation*) tener que, deber; **to h. to,** tener que, deber; **we h. to speak in French,** debemos hablar francés. **6** (*make happen*) hacer que; **I'll h. someone come round,** haré que venga alguien; **they had me washing up,** tuve que lavar los platos. **7** (*receive*) (*people, mail*) tener, recibir; **to h. people round,** invitar a gente; **you h. my permission,** tienes mi permiso. **8** (*borrow*) pedir prestado; (*use*) utilzar, emplear; **can I h. your pen a moment?,** ¿me dejas tu bolígrafo un momento? **9** (*party, meeting*) hacer, celebrar; **they had an exhibition last year,** montaron una exposición el año pasado. **10** (*give birth*) dar luz a; **to h. a baby,** tener un niño. **11** (*allow, tolerate*) permitir; **we won't h. it,** no lo consentiremos. **12** (*hold*) tener; **he had his head in his hands,** tenía la cabeza entre las manos; *fig* **to h. sth against sb,** tener algo en contra de algn. **13** (*according to*) según; **legend has it that ...,** según la leyenda ... . **14** *fam* (*cheat, deceive*) engañar; **I've been had!,** ¡me han timado! **15** (*preference*) más vale que; **you'd better stay,** más vale que te quedes; *fig* **to h. done with sth,** acabar con algo. **II** *v aux* **1** (*compound*) haber; **I had been waiting for half an hour,** hacía media hora que esperaba, llevaba media hora esperando; **he hasn't eaten yet,** no ha comido aún; **she had broken the window,** había roto el cristal; **we h. lived here for ten years,** hace diez años que vivimos aquí; (*emphatic*) **you h. forgotten your gloves—so I h.!,** te has olvidado los guantes —¡ay, sí!, es verdad; **you haven't swept the floor —I h.!,** no has barrido el suelo —¡sí que lo he barrido! **2** (*have + just*) acabar de; **she's just arrived,** acaba de llegar; **we'd just gone out,** acabábamos de salir. ◆ **have in** *vtr* **1** (*invite*) invitar, recibir; (*call*) llamar. **2** *fam* (*hold against*) guardar rencor; **to h. it in for sb,** tenerla tomada con algn. ◆ **have on** *vtr* **1** (*wear*) llevar puesto,-a, vestir; **to h. nothing on,** estar desnudo,-a. **2** (*plan to do*) tener planeado,-a, tener que hacer; **I h. nothing on,** estoy libre. **3** *fam* (*fool*) engañar; **to h. sb on,** tomarle el pelo a algn. ◆ **have out** *vtr* **1** (*extract*) sacar; **to h. one's appendix out,** operarse de apendicitis. **2** *fam* (*clear up*) arreglar; **to h. it out with sb,** ajustar cuentas con algn. ◆ **have over** *vtr* **1** (*invite*) recibir, invitar. **2** *fam* (*finish*) acabar con; **to h. it over and done with,** acabar con toda la historia. ◆ **have up** *vtr Jur* **to h. sb up for sth,** llevar a algn ante los tribunales por algo, procesar a algn por algo.

haven ['heɪvən] *n* **1** *Naut* puerto *m*. **2** *fig* refugio *m*, asilo *m*; **a h. of peace,** un remanso de paz.

have-nots ['hævnɒts] *npl* desposeídos *mpl*, pobres *mpl*.

haversack ['hævəsæk] *n* mochila *f*.

havoc ['hævək] *n* estragos *mpl*; **to play h. with,** hacer estragos en.

haw [hɔː] *n Bot* baya *f* del espino.

Hawaii [hə'waɪɪ] *n* Hawai.

Hawaiian [hə'waɪən] *adj & n* hawaiano,-a (*m,f*).

hawfinch ['hɔːfɪntʃ] *n Orn* picogordo *m*.

hawk¹ [hɔːk] *n Orn Pol* halcón *m*; *fig* **to have eyes like a h.,** tener ojo de lince.

hawk² [hɔːk] *vtr* **1** (*in the street*) vender en la calle; (*door-to-door*) vender de puerta en puerta. **2** (*gossip, news*) divulgar, pregonar.

hawker ['hɔːkəʳ] *n* vendedor,-a *m*, *f* ambulante.

hawser ['hɔːzəʳ] *n Naut* guindaleza *f*.

hawthorn ['hɔːθɔːn] *n Bot* majuelo *m*, espino *m* albar.

hay [heɪ] *n Bot* heno *m*; **to make h.,** secar la paja; *fam* **to hit the h.,** irse al catre; *prov* **make h. while the sun shines,** la ocasión la pintan calva. ■ *Med* **b. fever,** fiebre *f* del heno.

hayfork ['heɪfɔːk] *n Agr* bieldo *m*.

haymaker ['heɪmeɪkə'] *n* segador,-a *m*,*f*.

haymaking ['heɪmeɪkɪŋ] *n Agr* siega *f* del heno.

haystack ['heɪstæk] *n* almiar *m*; *fig* **to look for a needle in a h.,** buscar una aguja en un pajar.

Haytian ['heɪʃən, haɪ'iːʃən] *adj & n see* **Haitian.**

haywire ['heɪwaɪə'] *adj fam* en desorden, confuso,-a; **to go h.,** *(machine etc)* estropearse; *(person)* volverse loco,-a.

hazard ['hæzəd] **I** *n* **1** *(risk)* peligro *m*, riesgo *m*. **2** *Golf* obstáculo *m*. **II** *vtr fml* arriesgar, poner en peligro; **to h. a guess,** intentar adivinar.

hazardous ['hæzədəs] *adj* arriesgado,-a, peligroso,-a.

haze [heɪz] *n* **1** *(mist)* neblina *f*. **2** *fig (blur)* confusión *f*.

hazel ['heɪzəl] **I** *n Bot (tree)* avellano *m*. **II** *adj (de color)* avellana.

hazelnut ['heɪzəlnʌt] *n Bot* avellana *f*.

hazy ['heɪzɪ] *adj (hazier, haziest)* nebuloso,-a; *fig* vago,-a.
♦ **hazily** *adv* vagamente, con poca claridad.

H-bomb ['eɪtʃbɒm] *n Mil* bomba *f* H.

HE [eɪtʃ'iː] *abbr of* **His** *or* **Her Excellency,** Su Excellencia *mf*, S.E.

he [hiː] **I** *pers pron* él; **he did it,** ha sido él; **he who,** el que. **II** *adj* macho; **he-goat,** macho cabrío.

head [hed] **I** *n* **1** *Anat* cabeza *f*; *(mind)* mente *f*; **from h. to toe,** de pies a cabeza; **she got** *or* **took it into her h. to ...,** se le ocurrió la idea de ...; *fig* **off the top of one's h.,** así de entrada; *fig* **on your own h. be it,** allá te las compongas; *fig* **three pounds a** *or* **per h.,** tres libras por cabeza; *fig* **to be h. over heels in love,** estar locamente enamorado,-a; *fig* **to do sth standing on one's h.,** hacer algo con los ojos cerrados; *fig* **to go over sb's h.,** pasar por encima de algn; *fig* **to keep one's h.,** mantener la calma; *fig* **to keep one's h. above water,** mantenerse a flote; *fig* **to lose one's h.,** perder la cabeza; *fam* **champagne goes to my h.,** el champán se me sube a la cabeza; *fam* **he couldn't get it into his thick h.,** no le entraba en la cabezota; *fam* **success went to his h.,** se le subió el éxito a cabeza; *fam* **to be off one's h.,** estar chiflado,-a; *fam fig* **this philosophy stuff is over my h.,** de todo este rollo de la filosofía no entiendo nada; *fam fig* **to bite sb's h. off,** echar una bronca a algn; *fam fig* **to cry one's h. off,** llorar a moco tendido; *fam fig* **to get one's h. around sth,** alcanzar a comprender algo; **to laugh one's h. off,** reírse a mandíbula batiente; *prov* **two heads are better than one,** cuatro ojos ven más que dos. ■ **crowned h.,** testa *f* coronada; **h. start,** ventaja *f*. **2** *(end, top, etc) (of table)* cabecera *f*; *(of nail, pin, etc)* cabeza *f*; *(of beer)* espuma *f*; *(of arrow)* puma *f*; *(of cabbage)* cogollo *m*; *(of page)* principio *m*; *(of tape recorder)* cabezal *m*; *(of spot, boil)* punta *f*; *(of water, steam)* presión *f*; *fig* **to come to a h.,** llegar a un momento decisivo. **3** *(chief, boss)* cabeza *m*; *(of school, company, etc)* director,-a *m*, *f*; *(of family)* cabeza *f*. ■ *Sch* **h. teacher,** director,-a *m*,*f*. **4** *(cattle)* res *f*. **5** *(of coin)* cara *f*; **heads or tails,** cara o cruz; *fam fig* **I can't make h. or tail of it,** no entiendo ni jota. **6** *Geog (headland)* cabo *m*, punta *f*. **7** *Press* título *m*, titular *m*. **II** *adj* principal. ■ **h. office,** oficina *f* central. **III** *vtr* **1** *(list, company, procession, etc)* encabezar. **2** *Ftb* rematar de cabeza. **3** *(title)* titular. **IV** *vi* dirigirse, ir. ♦ **head for** *vtr* dirigirse hacia; *fig* **they're heading for big trouble,** van a tener muchos problemas. ♦ **head off I** *vi* marcharse, irse. **II** *vtr (divert)* desviar, interceptar; *(avert)* evitar.

headache ['hedeɪk] *n* dolor *m* de cabeza; *fig* quebradero *m* de cabeza.

headband ['hedbænd] *n* cinta *f* (para la cabeza).

headboard ['hedbɔːd] *n* cabecera *f*.

headdress ['heddres] *n* tocado *m*.

header ['hedə'] *n Ftb* cabezazo *m*.

head-first [hed'fɜːst] *adv* de cabeza.

head-hunter ['hedhʌntə'] *n* cazador,-a *m* de cabezas; *fam fig* cazatalentos *mf inv*.

heading ['hedɪŋ] *n (of chapter)* título *m*; *(of letter)* membrete *m*.

headlamp ['hedlæmp] *n Aut* faro *m*.

headland ['hedlənd] *n Geog* punta *f*, cabo *m*.

headlight ['hedlaɪt] *n Aut* faro *m*.

headline ['hedlaɪn] **I** *n* titular *m*; **to hit the headlines,** ser noticia de primera plana. **II** *vtr* poner en los titulares.

headlong ['hedlɒŋ] *adj & adv* de cabeza; **to rush h. into sth,** lanzarse a hacer algo sin pensar.

headmaster [hed'mɑːstə'] *n Sch* director *m*.

headmistress [hed'mɪstrɪs] *n Sch* directora *f*.

head-on ['hedɒn] **I** *adj* frontal; **a h.-on collision,** un choque frontal. **II** [hed'ɒn] *adv* de frente.

headphones ['hedfəʊnz] *npl* auriculares *mpl*, cascos *mpl*.

headquarters ['hedkwɔːtəz] *npl* **1** oficina *f* central, sede *f*. **2** *Mil* cuartel *m* general.

headrest ['hedrest] *n* cabecero *m*, cabezal *m*.

headroom ['hedruːm] *n* altura *f* libre.

headscarf ['hedskɑːf] *n (pl headscarves* ['hedskɑːvz]*)* pañuelo *m*.

headset ['hedset] *n* auriculares *mpl*.

headship ['hedʃɪp] *n Educ* dirección *f*.

headstand ['hedstænd] *n* posición *f* de la cabeza.

headstone ['hedstəʊn] *n* **1** *(gravestone)* lápida *f* mortuoria. **2** *Arch (keystone)* piedra *f* angular.

headstrong ['hedstrɒŋ] *adj* testarudo,-a, cabezota.

headway ['hedweɪ] *n* progreso *m*; **to make h.,** avanzar, progresar.

headwind ['hedwɪnd] *n* viento *m* de proa.

headword ['hedwɜːd] *n* entrada *f*, lema *m*.

heady ['hedɪ] *adj (headier, headiest)* embriagador,-a; **a h. drink,** una bebida fuerte.

heal [hiːl] **I** *vi (of wound)* cicatrizar; **to h. up,** curarse. **II** *vtr (illness)* curar.

healer ['hiːlə'] *n* curador,-a *m*,*f*.

health [helθ] *n* salud *f*; *fig* prosperidad *f*; **to drink (to) sb's h.,** beber a la salud de algn; **to be in good/bad h.,** estar bien/mal de salud; **your good h.!,** ¡salud! ■ **h. centre,** centro *m* médico; **h. farm,** centro *m* para curas de adelgazamiento; **h. foods,** alimentos *mpl* naturales; **h. food shop,** tienda *f* de alimentos naturales; **h. officer,** inspector,-a *m*, *f* de Sanidad; **h. service,** Dirección *f* General de Sanidad; **h. visitor,** enfermero,-a *m*,*f* visitante.

healthful ['helθfʊl] *adj esp US* saludable, sano,-a.

healthy ['helθɪ] *adj (healthier, healthiest) (in good health)* sano,-a; *(good for health)* saludable; *(thriving)* próspero,-a; *(attitude etc)* sensato,-a; *fig* **to have a h. outlook on sth,** tener ideas sanas sobre algo.

heap [hiːp] **I** *n* montón *m*; *fig* **to be at the bottom of the h.,** ser el último mono; *fam* **heaps of,** montones de, cantidad de; *fam* **I've got heaps to do,** tengo muchos cosas que hacer. **II** *vtr* amontonar; *fig (presents, praises)* colmar; *Culin* **a heaped spoonful,** una cucharada colmada.

hear [hɪə'] *vtr (pt & pp heard* [hɜːd]*)* **1** oír; **do you h. (me)?,** ¿me oyes?; **h. h.!,** ¡muy bien!; **to have heard of sb,** haber oído hablar de algn; *fig* **I can't h. myself think,** me van a estallar los oídos; *hum* **have you heard the one about the Englishman who ...?,** ¿conoces el chiste del inglés que ...? **2** *(listen to)* escuchar; **did you h. the ten o'clock news?,** ¿escuchaste las noticias de las diez? **3** *(refuse)* negarse a; **I won't h. of it!,** ¡ni hablar! **4** *(find out)* enterarse; **I've heard he's ill,** me han dicho que está enfermo; **to h. from sb,** tener noticias de algn. **5** *Jur (case)* ver; *(evidence)* oír. ♦ **hear out** *vtr* escuchar hasta el final.

hearer [ˈhɪərər] n oyente mf.

hearing [ˈhɪərɪŋ] n 1 (sense) oído m; **hard of h.**, duro,-a de oído, sordo,-a; **within h. (distance)**, al alcance del oído. ■ **h. aid**, audífono m. 2 Jur audiencia f; fig **to give sb a fair h.**, escuchar a algn, dejar hablar a algn.

hearsay [ˈhɪəseɪ] n rumores mpl.

hearse [hɜːs] n coche m or carroza f fúnebre.

heart [hɑːt] n 1 Anat corazón m; **to have h. trouble**, padecer del corazón. ■ **h. attack**, infarto m de miocardio or de corazón; Med **h. transplant**, trasplante m de corazón. 2 (centre of feelings) corazón m; **a broken h.**, un corazón destrozado or roto; **a change of h.**, un cambio de opinión; **at h.**, en el fondo; **have a h.!**, ¡ten piedad!; **to pour out your h.**, abrir el corazón; **to take sth to h.**, tomarse algo a pecho; **to wear your h. on your sleeve**, llevar el corazón en la mano. 3 (courage and determination) valor m, corazón m; **he had his h. in his mouth**, tenía el alma en un hilo; **her h. sank**, se le cayó el alma a los pies; **his h. wasn't in it**, no ponía interés en ello; **to lose h.**, desanimarse. 4 (character and attitudes) corazón m; **he's a man after my own h.**, es un hombre de los que me gustan; **she's got her h. in the right place**, es buena persona; **to have a good or kind h.**, tener buen corazón. 5 (core, centre) meollo m; (of lettuce) cogollo m; **in the h. of winter**, en pleno invierno; **to get to the h.**, profundizar (of, en). 6 Cards corazón m; **the ace of hearts**, el as de corazones.

heartbeat [ˈhɑːtbiːt] n latido m del corazón.

heart-breaking [ˈhɑːtbreɪkɪŋ] adj que parte el corazón, desgarrador,-a.

heart-broken [ˈhɑːtbrəʊkən] adj hundido,-a; **he's h.-b.**, tiene el corazón destrozado.

heartburn [ˈhɑːtbɜːn] n ardor m de estómago, acedía f.

hearten [ˈhɑːtən] vtr animar.

heartening [ˈhɑːtənɪŋ] adj alentador,-a.

heartfelt [ˈhɑːtfelt] adj sincero,-a; **my h. thanks**, mi sincero agradecimiento.

hearth [hɑːθ] n 1 (of fireplace) chimenea f, hogar m. 2 fml (home) hogar m. ■ **h.-rug**, alfombrilla f que se coloca delante de la chimenea.

heartless [ˈhɑːtlɪs] adj cruel, insensible. ◆ **heartlessly** adv sin corazón, cruelmente.

heart-rending [ˈhɑːtrendɪŋ] adj conmovedor,-a, desgarrador,-a.

heartstrings [ˈhɑːtstrɪŋz] npl corazón m sing; **it tugs at your h.**, llega hasta lo más hondo, toca la fibra sensible.

heartthrob [ˈhɑːtθrɒb] n ídolo m.

heart-to-heart [hɑːttəˈhɑːt] n conversación f íntima y franca.

hearty [ˈhɑːtɪ] adj (heartier, heartiest) (person) francote; (meal) abundante; (welcome) cordial; **to have a h. appetite**, ser de buen comer. ◆ **heartily** adv 1 (enthusiastically) **to welcome h.**, recibir cordialmente; **to laugh h.**, reírse de buena gana. 2 (thoroughly) completamente; fam **I'm h. sick of it**, estoy hasta la coronilla de ello.

heat [hiːt] I n 1 (warmth) calor m; (heating) calefacción f. ■ Med **h. rash**, sarpullido m. 2 Sport eliminatoria f, serie f; **dead h.**, empate m. 3 Zool celo m; **on or in h.**, en celo. II vtr calentar. III vi calentarse. ◆ **heat up** vi 1 (warm up) calentarse. 2 (increase action and excitement) acalorarse; **the atmosphere in the square started to h. up as the demonstrators came closer**, el ambiente de la plaza comenzó a hacerse más tenso a medida que se acercaban los manifestantes.

heated [ˈhiːtɪd] adj 1 (of room) con calefacción. 2 fig (of argument) acalorado,-a; **to become or get h. about sth**, acalorarse por algo.

heater [ˈhiːtər] n calentador m; **gas/water h.**, calentador de gas/agua.

heath [hiːθ] n Bot 1 (land) brezal m. 2 (plant) brezo m.

heathen [ˈhiːðən] adj & n arch pagano,-a (m, f).

heather [ˈheðər] n Bot brezo m.

heating [ˈhiːtɪŋ] n calefacción f. ■ **central h.**, calefacción f central.

heatwave [ˈhiːtweɪv] n ola f de calor.

heave [hiːv] I n (pull) tirón m; (push) empujón m. II vtr 1 (lift) levantar; (haul) tirar; (push) empujar. 2 (throw) lanzar, arrojar; fig **to h. a sigh of relief**, dar un suspiro de alivio. III vi 1 (rise and fall) (gen) subir y bajar; (chest) jadear; **her shoulders heaved with emotion**, sus hombros se movían por la emoción. 2 (retch) tener náuscas. 3 Naut (pt & pp hove) cabecear. ◆ **heave to** vi (pt & pp hove to) Naut ponerse al pairo.

heaven [ˈhevən] I n 1 cielo m; **thank h.!**, ¡gracias a Dios!; **to be in seventh h.**, estar en el séptimo cielo; fam **for heaven's sake!**, ¡por Dios!, fam **h. knows**, ¡no tengo ni idea!; fam **h. knows I've worked hard enough!**, ¡hambre, he trabajado bastante!; fam **to stink to high h.**, heder or oler a perro muerto. 2 fam gloria f, paraíso m; **that hotel is h. on earth**, ese hotel es el paraíso en la tierra. 3 **heavens**, cielo m sing; **the h. opened**, empezó a llover a cántaros. II interj **heavens!**, ¡cielos!; **good heavens!**, ¡por Dios!

heavenly [ˈhevənlɪ] adj celestial; fig divino,-a. ■ Astron **h. body**, cuerpo m celeste.

heaven-sent [hevənˈsent] adj de lo más oportuno,-a, llovido,-a del cielo; **the opportunity is h.-s.**, es la ocasión perfecta.

heavenward(s) [ˈhevənwəd(z)] adv hacia el cielo.

heaviness [ˈhevɪnɪs] n (quality) pesadez f; (weight) peso m.

heavy [ˈhevɪ] I adj (heavier, heaviest) (weight) pesado,-a; (of rain, meal) fuerte, pesado,-a; (of traffic) denso,-a; (of atmosphere) cargado,-a; (of loss, expense) grande; **a h. fine**, una multa grande; **h. going**, duro,-a; **is it h.?**, ¿pesa mucho?; **she is a h. sleeper**, tiene el sueño muy profundo; **to be a h. drinker/smoker**, beber/fumar mucho; **to have a h. heart**, tener el corazón oprimido. ■ **h. industry**, industria f pesada; Mus **h. metal**, rock m duro or heavy. II n sl gorila m. ◆ **heavily** adv pesadamente; **he was fined h.**, le pusieron una multa muy fuerte; **it rained/snowed h.**, llovió/nevó mucho; **the country relied h. on its tourist trade**, el país dependía principalmente de la industria turística; **to sleep h.**, dormir profundamente.

heavy-duty [hevɪˈdjuːtɪ] adj (of clothes, footwear) de faena, resistente; (of machinery) sólido,-a, para grandes cargas.

heavy-handed [hevɪˈhændɪd] adj (clumsy) torpe; (severe) autoritario,-a.

heavyweight [ˈhevɪweɪt] n Box peso m pesado.

Hebrew [ˈhiːbruː] I adj hebreo,-a m, f. II n 1 (person) hebreo,-a. 2 (language) hebreo m.

Hebrides [ˈhebrɪdiːz] npl **the H.**, las (Islas) Hébridas.

heck [hek] interj fam ¡jolín!; fam **a h. of a noise**, un ruido de mil demonios; fam **what the h.!**, ¿qué diablos importa?

heckle [ˈhekəl] vtr Pol Theat interrumpir or provocar.

heckler [ˈheklər] n Pol Theat altercador,-a m, f, follonero,-a m, f.

heckling [ˈheklɪŋ] n Pol Theat altercado m, gresca f.

hectare [ˈhektɑːr] n hectárea f.

hectic [ˈhektɪk] adj agitado,-a; **a h. day**, un día ajetreado.

hectogram [ˈhektəʊgræm] n hectogramo m.

hector [ˈhektər] vtr intimidar, tiranizar.

hectoring [ˈhektərɪŋ] adj tiránico,-a.

hedge [hedʒ] I n seto m vivo; fig barrera f; fig **a h. against inflation**, una barrera contra la inflación. II vtr cercar o separar con un seto; fig **to h. one's bets**, cubrirse. III vi 1 contestar con evasivas. 2 **to be hedged in or around with**, estar rodeado,-a de.

hedgehog [ˈhedʒhɒg] n Zool erizo m.

hedgerow [ˈhedʒrəʊ] n seto m vivo.

heed [hi:d] *fml* **I** *vtr* prestar atención a, hacer caso de. **II** *n* atención *m*; **to pay h. to, take h. of**, hacer caso de.

heedless ['hi:dlɪs] *adj* desatento,-a, despreocupado,-a.
♦ **heedlessly** *adv* despreocupadamente, a la ligera.

hee-haw ['hi:'hɔ:] *n* rebuzno *m*.

heel[1] [hi:l] **I** *n* **1** *Anat* talón *m*; *(of sock, stocking)* talón *m*; *(of shoe)* tacón *m*; *(of palm of hand)* pulpejo *m*; *fig* **to bring sb to h.**, meter a algn en cintura; *fig* **to dig one's heels in**, negarse a cambiar; *fig* **down at h.**, desharrapado,-a; *fig* **head over heels in love**, locamente enamorado,-a; *fig* **to take to one's heels**, darse a la fuga; *fig* **to be on sb's heels**, pisarle los talones a algn; *fam* **to cool** *or* **kick one's heels**, esperar impacientemente. ■ **high heels**, zapatos *mpl* de tacón alto. **2** *sl* sinvergüenza *mf*. **II** *vtr* poner tacón a.

heel[2] [hi:l] *vi Naut* escorar. ♦ **heel over** *vi* ladearse.

heeled [hi:ld] *adj* de tacón; *fam fig* **well-h.**, adinerado,-a.

hefty ['heftɪ] *adj* (**heftier, heftiest**) **1** *(big and powerful)* *(of person)* robusto,-a, fornido,-a; *(of package)* pesado,-a; **a h. punch**, un puñetazo fuerte. **2** *(large amount)* grande; **a h. sum of money**, una fuerte suma.

heifer ['hefə[r]] *n* novilla *f*, vaquilla *f*.

height [haɪt] *n* **1** *(gen)* altura *f*; **to be afraid of heights**, tener vértigo; **to gain/lose h.**, subir/bajar. **2** *(of person)* estatura *f*; **what h. are you?**, ¿cuánto mides? **3** *fig (most intense or successful part)* **it's the h. of fashion**, es la última moda; **the h. of ignorance**, el colmo de la ignorancia. **4** *Geog* cumbre *f*. *Lit* **'Wuthering Heights'**, 'Cumbres Borrascosas'.

heighten ['haɪtən] *vtr (intensify)* realzar; *(increase)* aumentar.

heinous ['heɪnəs] *adj fml* atroz.

heir [eə[r]] *n* heredero *m*; **to be h. to**, ser heredero de. ■ *Jur* **h. apparent**, heredero *m* forzoso; **h. presumptive**, presunto heredero *m*.

heiress ['eərɪs] *n* heredera *f*.

heirloom ['eəlu:m] *n* reliquia *f or* joya *f* de familia.

held [held] *pt* & *pp see* **hold**.

helicopter ['helɪkɒptə[r]] *n* helicóptero *m*.

heliport ['helɪpɔ:t] *n* helipuerto *m*.

helium ['hi:lɪəm] *n Chem* helio *m*.

hell [hel] *n* **1** *(gen)* infierno *m*; **come h. or high water**, pase lo que pase; *fig* **to go h. for leather**, ir como si se le llevara el diablo; *fam* **like h.!**, ¡ni hablar!; *fam* **she gave him h.**, se las hizo pasar canutas; *fam* **there'll be h. to pay**, habrá problemas; *fam* **to play h. with**, estropear; *fam* **what the h. are you doing?**, ¿qué diablos estás haciendo?; *offens* **go** *or* **get to h.!**, ¡vete a hacer puñetas! **2** *fam* **a h. of a**, mucho,-a; **a h. of a noise**, un ruido excesivo; **a h. of a party**, una fiesta estupenda; **one h. of a guy**, un tío genial; **she's had a h. of a day**, ha tenido un día fatal; **they paid a h. of a lot**, pagaron muchísimo dinero; **we had a h. of a time**, *(good time)* lo pasamos bomba; *(bad time)* las pasamos negras.

hell-bent [hel'bent] *adj* empeñado,-a; **he's h.-b. on destruction**, está empeñado en destruirse *or* destruirlo.

hellish ['helɪʃ] *adj fam* infernal. ♦ **hellishly** *adv fam* muy; **a h. difficult job**, una faena muy difícil.

hello [hə'ləʊ, 'heləʊ] *interj* **1** ¡hola! **2** *Tel (answering)* ¡diga!; *(calling)* ¡oiga! **3** *(showing surprise)* ¡vaya!; **hello!, what's this?**, ¡vaya!, ¿qué pasa?

helm [helm] *n Naut* timón *m*; **to be at the h.**, llevar el timón.

helmsman ['helmzmən] *n (pl* **helmsmen**) timonel *m*.

helmet ['helmɪt] *n* casco *m*. ■ **crash h.**, casco *m* protector.

help [help] **I** *n* **1** *(gen)* ayuda *f*; **h.!**, ¡socorro!; **there's no h. for it**, no tenemos más remedio; **to ask for h.**, pedir socorro *or* ayuda. **2** *(daily)* **h.**, asistenta *f*. **II** *vtr* **1** *(gen)* ayudar; **can you h. me?**, ¿me quieres ayudar?; *(in shop etc)* **may I h. you?**, ¿qué desea?; **your advice didn't h. at all**, tus consejos no sirvieron de nada. **2** *(alleviate)* aliviar;

this new medicine will h. your cold, este nuevo medicamente te aliviará el resfriado. **3** *(serve)* **h. yourself!**, ¡sírvete!; **to h. oneself to more food**, servirse más comida; *fam* **he helped himself to my purse**, me birló el monedero. **4** *(assist)* ayudar; **can I h. you up with that case?**, ¿puedo echar una mano para subir esa maleta?; **he helped her into her coat**, la ayudó a ponerse el abrigo. **5** *(avoid)* evitar; **I can't h. it**, no lo puedo remediar; **I couldn't h. laughing**, no pude por menos que reír; **it can't be helped**, no lo podemos evitar. ♦ **help out** *vtr* ayudar; **to h. sb out**, echar una mano a algn.

helper ['helpə[r]] *n* ayudante,-a *m,f*, auxiliar *mf*.

helpful ['helpful] *adj (of person)* amable; *(of thing)* útil, práctico,-a. ♦ **helpfully** *adv* amablemente.

helping ['helpɪŋ] **I** *n* porción *f*, ración *f*; **who wants a second h.?**, ¿quién quiere repetir? **II** *adj* **to give sb a h. hand**, echarle una mano a algn.

helpless ['helplɪs] *adj (defenceless)* desamparado,-a; *(powerless)* incapaz, impotente; **a h. child**, un niño indefenso. ♦ **helplessly** *adv* inútilmente, en vano.

helplessness ['helplɪsnɪs] *n (without defense)* desamparo *m*; *(without power)* impotencia *f*.

Helsinki [hel'sɪŋkɪ] *n* Helsinki.

helter-skelter [heltə'skeltə[r]] **I** *n* tobogán *m*. **II** *adj* atropellado,-a. **III** *adv* atropelladamente, deprisa y corriendo.

hem [hem] **I** *n Sew* dobladillo *m*. **II** *vtr (pt & pp* **hemmed**) *Sew* hacer un dobladillo. ♦ **hem in** *vtr* cercar o rodear.

he-man ['hi:mæn] *n (pl* **he-men** ['hi:men]) machote *m*.

hemisphere ['hemɪsfɪə[r]] *n* hemisferio *m*; **northern/ southern h.**, hemisferio norte/sur.

hemispherical [hemɪs'ferɪkəl] *adj* hemisférico,-a.

hemline ['hemlaɪn] *n* bajo *m*; **hemlines are lower this year**, los vestidos se llevan más largos este año.

hemlock ['hemlɒk] *n Bot* **1** *(plant)* cicuta *f*. **2** *(tree)* tsuga *f*. ■ **eastern h.**, tsuga *f* del Canadá; **western h.**, tsuga *f* heterófila.

hemoglobin [hi:məʊ'gləʊbɪn] *n US Med see* **haemoglobin**.

hemophilia [hi:məʊ'fɪlɪə] *n US Med see* **haemophilia**.

hemophiliac [hi:məʊ'fɪlɪæk] *adj & n US Med see* **haemophiliac**.

hemorrhage ['hemərɪdʒ] *n US Med see* **haemorrhage**.

hemorrhoids ['hemərɔɪdz] *npl US Med see* **haemorrhoids**.

hemp [hemp] *n* **1** *Bot* cáñamo *m*. **2** *(drug)* hachís *m*, marihuana *f*.

hemstitch ['hemstɪtʃ] **I** *n Sew* vainica *f*. **II** *vtr Sew* hacer una vainica.

hen [hen] *n Zool* gallina *f*. ■ *fam* **h. party**, reunión *f* de mujeres.

hence [hens] *adv fml* **1** *(from now)* de aquí a; **six months h.**, de aquí a seis meses. **2** *(consequently)* por lo tanto, de ahí *or* aquí que; **he is upset, h. his long face**, está disgustado, de ahí que tenga cara larga.

henceforth [hens'fɔ:θ] *adv fml* de ahora en adelante.

henchman ['hentʃmən] *n (pl* **henchmen**) *pej* secuaz *m*.

henhouse ['henhaʊs] *n* gallinero *m*.

henna ['henə] *n Bot* alheña *f*.

henpecked ['henpekt] *adj fam* **a h. husband**, un calzonazos.

hepatic [hɪ'pætɪk] *adj Med* hepático,-a.

hepatitis [hepə'taɪtɪs] *n Med* hepatitis *f*.

heptagon ['heptəgən] *n* heptágono *m*.

heptagonal [hep'tægənəl] *adj* heptagonal.

her [hɜ:[r], *unstressed* hə] **I** *poss adj (one thing)* su; *(more than one)* sus; *(to distinguish)* de ella; **are they h. books or his?**, ¿los libros son de ella o de él?; **h. car**, su coche; **h.**

children, sus hijos; **she has cut h. finger,** se ha cortado el dedo. **II** *object pron* **1** *(direct object)* la; **I saw h. recently,** la vi hace poco; **they can't help h.,** no la pueden ayudar. **2** *(indirect object)* le; *(with other third person pronouns)* se; **he gave h. money,** le dio dinero; **they handed it to h.,** se lo entregaron. **3** *(after prep)* ella; **for h.,** para ella; **with h.,** con ella. **4** *(as subject) fam* ella; **look, it's h.!,** ¡mira, es ella!

herald ['herəld] **I** *n* heraldo *m; fig* precursor *m.* **II** *vtr* anunciar.

heraldic [he'rældɪk] *adj* heráldico,-a.

heraldry ['herəldrɪ] *n* heráldica *f.*

herb [hɜːb] *n Bot Culin* hierba *f.* ■ **h. tea,** infusión *f* de hierbas.

herbaceous [hɜː'beɪʃəs] *adj* herbáceo,-a; **h. border,** arriate *m* de plantas.

herbal ['hɜːbəl] *adj* herbario,-a; **h. remedies,** curas *fpl* de hierbas.

herbalist ['hɜːbəlɪst] *n* herbolario,-a *m,f.*

herbicide ['hɜːbɪsaɪd] *n* herbicida *m.*

herbivore ['hɜːbɪvɔː] *n Zool* herbívoro,-a *m,f.*

herbivorous [hɜː'bɪvərəs] *adj Zool* herbívoro,-a.

herd [hɜːd] **I** *n (of cattle)* manada *f; (of goats)* rebaño *m; (of pigs)* piara *f; fig (large group)* manada *f,* multitud *f; fig* **to go with the h.,** ir con las masas. ■ **h. instinct,** instinto *m* gregario. **II** *vtr (collect)* juntar en manada; *(drive forward)* guiar *or* conducir en manada. **III** *vi (of animals)* reunirse rebaño *or* manada; *(of people)* apiñarse; **the tourists were herded into the coach,** los turistas se apiñaron en el autobús.

herdsman ['hɜːdzmən] *n (pl herdsmen) (of cattle)* vaquero *m; (of sheep)* pastor *m.*

here [hɪə] **I** *adv* aquí; **come h.,** ven aquí; **h.!,** ¡presente!; **h. and there,** aquí y allá; **h. goes!,** ¡vamos a ver!; **h. he comes,** ya viene; **here's to success!,** ¡brindemos por el éxito!; **h. you are!,** ¡toma!, ¡ten!; **that's neither h. nor there,** eso no tiene nada que ver. **II** *interj* ¡oye!, ¡oiga!; **look h., you can't do that!,** ¡oiga, qué no se permite hacer eso! **III** *n* the **h. and now,** el presente, el aquí y ahora.

hereafter [hɪər'ɑːftə] *fml* **I** *adv* de ahora en adelante. **II** the **h.** n la otra vida, el más allá.

hereby [hɪə'baɪ] *adv fml* por la presente; **I h. declare that ...,** afirmo por la presente que ... .

hereditary [hɪ'redɪtərɪ] *adj* hereditario,-a.

heredity [hɪ'redɪtɪ] *n* herencia *f.*

herein [hɪər'ɪn] *adv fml (inside)* aquí dentro; *(in document)* aquí mencionado,-a.

heresy ['herəsɪ] *n* herejía *f.*

heretic ['herətɪk] *n* hereje *mf.*

heretical [hɪ'retɪkəl] *adj* herético,-a.

herewith [hɪə'wɪð] *adv fml* adjunto,-a; **the letter enclosed h.,** la carta adjunta.

heritage ['herɪtɪdʒ] *n* patrimonio *m; Jur* herencia *f.*

hermaphrodite [hɜː'mæfrədaɪt] *adj & n* hermafrodita *(mf).*

hermetic [hɜː'metɪk] *adj* hermético,-a. ◆ **hermetically** *adv* herméticamente; **h. sealed,** con cierre hermético.

hermit ['hɜːmɪt] *n* ermitaño,-a *m,f,* eremita *m.* ■ **hermit crab,** ermitaño *m,* paguro *m.*

hermitage ['hɜːmɪtɪdʒ] *n* ermita *f.*

hernia ['hɜːnɪə] *n Med* hernia *f.*

hero ['hɪərəʊ] *n (pl heroes)* héroe *m; (in novel)* personaje *m* principal, protagonista *m.* ■ **h. worship,** idolatría *f.*

heroic [hɪ'rəʊɪk] **I** *adj* heroico,-a. **II heroics** *npl* grandilocuencia *f.* ◆ **heroically** *adv* heroicamente.

heroin ['herəʊɪn] *n* heroína *f.* ■ **h. addict,** heroinómano,-a *m,f.*

heroine ['herəʊɪn] *n* heroína *f; (in novel)* personaje *m* principal, protagonista *f.*

heroism ['herəʊɪzəm] *n* heroísmo *m.*

heron ['herən] *n Orn* garza *f,* garza *f* real. ■ **night h.,** martinete *m;* **purple h.,** garza *f* imperial.

herpes ['hɜːpiːz] *n Med* herpes *m.*

herring ['herɪŋ] *n (pl herring or herrings) Zool* arenque *m; fig* **a red h.,** una divagación, una pista falsa.

herringbone ['herɪŋbəʊn] *n* espiga *f.* ■ **h. tweed,** cheviot *m* de espiga.

hers [hɜːz] *poss pron* **1** *(attribute) (one thing)* suyo,-a; *(more than one)* suyos,-as; *(to distinguish)* de ella; **a friend of h.,** un amigo suyo; **the book is h.,** el libro es suyo *or* de ella; **they are h.** son h., son de ella, no de él. **2** *(noun reference) (one thing)* el suyo, la suya; *(more than one)* los suyos, las suyas; **of all the houses h. is the nicest,** de todas las casas la suya es la más bonita.

herself [hɜː'self] *pers pron* **1** *(reflexive)* se; **she dressed h.,** se vistió; **she wasn't h.,** no se encontraba bien. **2** *(alone)* ella misma; **she did it (by) h.,** lo hizo ella misma *or* por sí sola; **she was by h.,** estaba sola. **3** *(emphatic)* ella misma; **she told me so h.,** eso dijo ella.

hertz [hɜːts] *n Phys* hertz *m,* hercio *m.*

hesitant ['hezɪtənt] *adj* vacilante, indeciso,-a; **h. steps,** pasos *mpl* titubeantes. ◆ **hesitantly** *adv* indecisamente.

hesitate ['hezɪteɪt] *vi* vacilar; **don't h. to call/ask,** llámame/pídemele con toda confianza;, **without hesitating,** sin vacilar.

hesitation [hezɪ'teɪʃən] *n* vacilación *f,* indecisión *f;* **without h.,** sin vacilar.

hessian ['hesɪən] *n* arpillera *f.*

heterogeneous [hetərəʊ'dʒiːnɪəs] *adj* heterogéneo,-a.

heterosexual [hetərəʊ'seksjʊəl] *adj & n* heterosexual *(mf).*

het up [het'ʌp] *adj fam* nervioso,-a; **to get h. up about sth,** ponerse nervioso,-a por algo.

heuristic [hjʊə'rɪstɪk] *adj* heurístico,-a.

hew [hjuː] *vtr (pt hewed; pp hewed or hewn* [hjuːn]) tallar.

hexagon ['heksəgən] *n* hexágono *m.*

hexagonal [hek'sægənəl] *adj* hexagonal.

hey [heɪ] *interj* ¡oye!, ¡oiga!

heyday ['heɪdeɪ] *n* auge *m,* apogeo *m;* **in his h.,** en sus mejores años.

HF [eɪt'ef] *Rad abbr of* **high frequency,** alta frecuencia *f,* AF *f.*

HGV [eɪtdʒiː'viː] *GB Aut abbr of* **heavy goods vehicle,** vehículo *m* de carga pesada.

HH *abbr of* **His** *or* **Her Highness,** Su Alteza, SA.

hi [haɪ] *interj fam* ¡hola!

hiatus [haɪ'eɪtəs] *n (pl hiatuses or hiatus)* **1** *Ling* hiato *m.* **2** *fml* laguna *f,* pausa *f.*

hibernate ['haɪbəneɪt] *vi* hibernar.

hibernation [haɪbə'neɪʃən] *n* hibernación *f.*

hibiscus [haɪ'bɪskəs] *n Bot* hibisco *m.*

hiccough ['hɪkʌp] *n & vi see* **hiccup.**

hiccup ['hɪkʌp] **I** *n* **1** hipo *m;* **to have hiccups,** tener hipo. **2** *fam (minor problem)* pega *f,* fallo *m.* **II** *vi (pt & pp hiccuped, hiccupped)* tener hipo, hipar.

hick [hɪk] *adj & n US fam* cateto,-a *(m, f),* paleto,-a *(m, f).*

hide¹ [haɪd] **I** *vtr (pt hid* [hɪd]; *pp hidden* ['hɪdən]) *(conceal)* esconder; *(obscure)* ocultar; **she hid her feelings,** ocultó sus sentimientos; **to h. the truth from sb,** ocultar la verdad a algn. **II** *vi* esconderse, ocultarse. **III** *n* puesto *m.*

hide² [haɪd] *n (animal skin)* piel *f, fam (of person)* pellejo *m; fig* **I haven't seen h. nor hair of him,** no le he visto el pelo últimamente; *fig* **to have a h. like an elephant,** ser totalmente insensible.

hide-and-seek [haɪdən'siːk] *n* escondite *m;* **to play h.-a.-s.,** jugar al escondite.

hidebound ['haɪdbaʊnd] *adj* chapado,-a a la antigua.

hideous ['hɪdɪəs] *adj* **1** *(horrific)* horroroso,-a; **a h. crime**, un crimen atroz. **2** *(extremely ugly)* espantoso,-a. repelente. ◆ **hideously** *adv* horrorosamente.

hide-out ['haɪdaʊt] *n* escondrijo *m*, escondite *m*.

hiding[1] ['haɪdɪŋ] *n* huida *f*; **to go into h.**, esconderse.

hiding[2] ['haɪdɪŋ] *n fam* paliza *f*; **to give sb a good h.**, darle una buena paliza a algn.

hierarchic(al) [haɪə'rɑːkɪk(əl)] *adj* jerárquico,-a.

hierarchy ['haɪərɑːkɪ] *n* jerarquía *f*.

hieroglyphics [haɪərə'glɪfɪks] *npl* jeroglíficos *mpl*.

hi-fi ['haɪfaɪ] *n* hifi *m*. ■ **hi-fi equipment**, equipo *m* de alta fidelidad.

higgledy-piggledy [hɪgəldɪ'pɪgəldɪ] **I** *adj* desordenado,-a, hecho,-a un lío. **II** *adv* a la buena de Dios.

high [haɪ] **I** *adj* **1** *(tall)* alto,-a; **h. building**, edificio alto; **h. ceiling**, techo alto; **how h. is that wall?**, ¿qué altura tiene esa pared?; **it's three feet h.**, tiene tres pies de alto; *fig* **to leave sb h. and dry**, dejar plantado,-a a algn; *fig* **to search h. and low for sth**, buscar algo por todas partes. ■ **h. chair**, silla *f* alta para niños; *Swimming* **h. diving**, salto *m* de palanca; *Athlet* **h. jump**, salto *m* de altura; *fam fig* **she's in for the h. jump**, se la va a cargar. **2** *(elevated, intense)* alto,-a, elevado,-a; *Med* **h. blood pressure**, presión *or* tensión alta; **h. prices**, precios elevados; *fam* **to be in h. spirits**, estar alegre *or* de buen humor. **3** *(great, important)* alto,-a, importante; **a h. position in life**, un alto standing; **h. wind**, viento *m* fuerte; **to have a h. opinion of sb**, hablar muy bien de algn; **to have friends in h. places**, estar bien relacionado,-a. ■ **H. Commissioner**, Alto Comisario *m*; **H. Court**, Tribunal *m* Supremo; **h. fidelity**, alta fidelidad *f*; **h. priest**, sumo sacerdote *m*; **h. road**, carretera *f* principal; *Educ* **h. school**, instituto *m* de enseñanza media; **h. tea**, meriendacena *f*; **the H. Street**, la Calle Mayor. **4** *Mus (of note)* alto,-a. **5** *(excellent)* bueno,-a; **a h. standard**, un nivel alto; **h. principles**, buenos principios; *fam* **the h. life**, la buena vida; *fam* **to have a h. old time of it**, pasarlo en grande. **6** *(of food)* pasado,-a; *(of game)* manido,-a. **7** *sl (drugged)* olocado,-a, flipado,-a. **II** *adv* alto; **feelings ran h.**, los ánimos estaban exaltados; **to bet** *or* **stake h.**, apostar fuerte; **to fly h.**, volar a gran altura. **III** *n* **1** *(high point)* récord *m*, punto *m* máximo; **to reach an all-time h.**, batir el récord; *fam* **to be on a h.**, estar a las mil maravillas. **2** *US Meteor* temperatura *f* alta.

highball ['haɪbɔːl] *n US* whisky *m or* bourbon *m* con sifón y hielo.

highbrow ['haɪbraʊ] *adj & n* intelectual *(mf)*.

high-class ['haɪklɑːs] *adj* de alta categoría.

higher ['haɪəʳ] *adj* superior. ■ **h. education**, enseñanza *f* superior.

highfalutin(g) [haɪfə'luːtɪŋ] *adj fam* pomposo,-a, presumido,-a, presuntuoso,-a.

high-flier *n*, **high-flyer** [haɪ'flaɪəʳ] *n fig* persona *f* ambiciosa.

high-flying ['haɪflaɪɪŋ] *adj fig* ambicioso,-a.

high-frecuency [haɪ'friːkwənsɪ] *adj Rad* de alta frecuencia.

high-handed [haɪ'hændɪd] *adj* autoritario,-a, despótico,-a.

high-heeled ['haɪhiːld] *adj* de tacón alto.

highland ['haɪlənd] **I** *adj* montañoso,-a. ■ **h. cattle**, ganado *m* vacuno de las montañas. **II highlands** *npl Geog* tierras *npl* altas.

highlander ['haɪləndəʳ] *n* montañés,-esa *m,f*.

highlight ['haɪlaɪt] **I** *n* **1** *Art* toque *m* de luz. **2** *Hairdr* reflejo *m*. **3** *(the most interesting)* atracción *f* principal. **II** *vtr* **1** hacer resaltar, destacar; **the talk highlighted the problem**, el discurso puso de relieve el problema. **2** *(a text)* marcar un texto con un rotulador fosforescente.

highly ['haɪlɪ] *adv* **1** *(very)* muy, sumamente; **h. pleased**, muy contento,-a; *Culin* **h. seasoned**, muy picante. **2** *(favourably)* muy bien; **to speak h. of sb**, hablar muy bien de algn.

highly-strung [haɪlɪ'strʌŋ] *adj* muy nervioso,-a, hipertenso,-a.

high-minded [haɪ'maɪndɪd] *adj* noble, magnánimo,-a; *pej* altivo,-a.

Highness ['haɪnɪs] *n* alteza *mf*; **Your H.**, Su Alteza.

high-pitched ['haɪpɪtʃt] *adj* estridente, agudo,-a.

high-powered ['haɪpaʊəd] *adj (of engine)* de gran potencia; *(of person)* dinámico,-a.

high-ranking ['haɪræŋkɪŋ] *adj* superior, de alta categoría; **h. official**, alto funcionario.

high-rise ['haɪraɪz] *adj* **h.-r. building**, rascacielos *m inv*.

high-speed ['haɪspiːd] *adj & adv* rápido,-a, de gran velocidad; *Phot* **h. lens**, objetivo ultrarrápido; *Rail* **h. train**, supertrén *m*.

high-spirited ['haɪspɪrɪtɪd] *adj (of person)* muy animado,-a; *(of horse)* fogoso,-a.

highway ['haɪweɪ] *n US* carretera *f*, autopista *f*. ■ *GB* **H. Code**, código *m* de la circulación.

highwayman ['haɪweɪmən] *n* (*pl* **highwaymen**) salteador *m* de caminos, bandido *m*.

hijack ['haɪdʒæk] **I** *vtr* secuestrar. **II** *n* secuestro *m*.

hijacker ['haɪdʒækəʳ] *n* secuestrador,-a *m, f; (of planes)* pirata *mf* del aire.

hijacking ['haɪdʒækɪŋ] *n* secuestro *m*.

hike [haɪk] **I** *n* **1** *(walk)* excursión *f*; **to go for** *or* **on a h.**, hacer una excursión a pie. **2** *US* aumento *m* de precio. **II** *vi* ir de excursión, hacer una excursión.

hiker ['haɪkəʳ] *n* excursionista *mf*.

hiking ['haɪkɪŋ] *n* **to go h.**, hacer una excursión.

hilarious [hɪ'leərɪəs] *adj* graciosísimo,-a, hilarante, para morirse de risa. ◆ **hilariously** *adv* hilarantemente; **h. funny**, graciosísimo,-a.

hilarity [hɪ'lærɪtɪ] *n* hilaridad *f*.

hill [hɪl] *n* **1** colina *f*, cerro *m*; *fam* **as old as the hills**, más viejo que Matusalén. **2** *(slope)* cuesta *f*.

hillbilly ['hɪlbɪlɪ] *n US pej* paleto,-a *m,f*.

hillock ['hɪlək] *n (small hill)* collado *m*, colina *f* pequeña; *(mound)* montículo *m*.

hillside ['hɪlsaɪd] *n* ladera *f*.

hilltop ['hɪltɒp] *n* cima *f* de una colina.

hilly ['hɪlɪ] *adj (hillier, hilliest)* accidentado,-a.

hilt [hɪlt] *n* puño *m*, empuñadura *f*; *fam* **I'll support you up to the h.**, daré mi apoyo total; *fam* **mortgaged up to the h.**, hipotecado al máximo.

him [hɪm] *object pron* **1** *(direct object)* lo, le; **hit h.!**, ¡pégale!; **she loves h.**, lo quiere. **2** *(indirect object)* le; *(with other third person pronouns)* se; **give h. the money**, dale el dinero; **give it to h.**, dáselo; **I gave h. my book**, le di mi libro. **3** *(after prep)* él; **he had no money on h.**, no llevaba dinero encima; **he took his luggage with h.**, se llevó el equipaje; **it's not like h. to say that**, no es muy propio de él decir eso. **4** *(as subject) fam* él; **it's h.**, es él.

Himalayas [hɪmə'leɪəz, hɪ'mɑːljəz] *npl* **the H.**, el Himalaya *sing*.

himself [hɪm'self] *pers pron* **1** *(reflexive)* se; **he hurt h.**, se hizo daño; **he's not h. today**, hoy no se encuentra bien. **2** *(unaided, alone)* solo, por sí mismo; **he lives by h.**, vive solo. **3** *(emphatic)* él mismo; **he said so h.**, eso dijo él.

hind[1] [haɪnd] *adj* trasero,-a; **h. legs**, patas traseras; *fam* **to talk the h. legs off a donkey**, hablar por los codos.

hind[2] [haɪnd] *n Zool* cierva *f*.

hinder ['hɪndəʳ] *vtr* dificultar, entorpecer, estorbar; **h. sb from doing sth.**, impedir a algn hacer algo; **noise hinders my concentration**, el ruido me impide concentrarme; **the rain hindered our journey**, la lluvia dificultó nuestro viaje.

hindquarters ['haɪndkwɔːtəz] *npl* cuartos *mpl* traseros.

hindrance ['hɪndrəns] *n* obstáculo *m*, estorbo *m*.

hindsight ['haɪndsaɪt] *n* retrospectiva *f*.

Hindu [hɪn'du:, 'hɪndu:] *adj* & *n* hindú (*mf*).

Hinduism ['hɪnduːɪzəm] *n* hinduismo *m*.

hinge [hɪndʒ] **I** *n* **1** bisagra *f*, gozne *m*; fig eje *m*. **2** *Philat* fijasellos *m inv*. **II** *vtr* engoznar. ◆ **hinge on** *vtr* depender; **everything hinged on his reaction**, todo dependía de su reacción.

hinged ['hɪndʒd] *adj* de bisagra.

hint [hɪnt] **I** *n* **1** (*indirect suggestion*) indirecta *f*; **to drop a h.**, lanzar *or* tirar una indirecta; **to take the h.**, darse por aludido. **2** (*clue*) pista *f*; **give us a h.**, danos una pista. **3** (*sign, trace*) pizca *f*; Culin **a h. of garlic**, una pizca de ajo; **there wasn't the slightest h. of cold**, no hacía ni pizca de frío. **4** (*advice*) sugerencia *f*, consejo *m*; **hints for travellers**, consejos para el viajero. **II** *vi* **1** (*suggest indirectly*) lanzar *or* soltar indirectas. **2** (*imply*) insinuar algo; **he hinted at a possible change in policy**, aludió a un posible cambio de política; **what was she hinting at?**, ¿qué estaba insinuando?

hinterland ['hɪntəlænd] *n Geog* interior *m*.

hip¹ [hɪp] *n Anat* cadera *f*. ■ **h. bath**, baño *m* de asiento; **h. flask**, petaca *f*.

hip² [hɪp] *n Bot* escaramujo *m*.

hip³ [hɪp] *adj sl* en la onda, marchoso,-a.

hip⁴ [hɪp] *interj* **h., h., hooray!**, ¡hurra!, ¡viva!

hipbone ['hɪpbəʊn] *n Anat* hueso *m* de la cadera.

hippie ['hɪpɪ] *adj* & *n fam* hippy (*mf*).

hippo ['hɪpəʊ] *n fam* hipopótamo *m*.

hippopotamus [hɪpə'pɒtəməs] *n* (*pl* **hippopotamus** *or* **hippopotami** [hɪpə'pɒtəmaɪ]) *Zool* hipopótamo *m*.

hippy ['hɪpɪ] *adj* & *n fam see* **hippie**.

hire ['haɪəʳ] **I** *n* alquiler *m*; **bicycles for h.**, se alquilan bicicletas; **taxi for h.**, taxi *m* libre. ■ **car h.**, alquiler *m* de coches; **h. purchase**, compra *f* a plazos; **we bought it on h. purchase**, lo compramos a plazos. **II** *vtr* **1** (*rent*) alquilar; **we hired skates**, alquilamos patines. **2** (*employ*) contratar; **they hired her for the job**, la contrataron para el puesto. ◆ **hire out** *vtr* (*car, tools, etc*) aquilar; (*people*) contratar.

hired ['haɪəd] *adj* alquilado,-a, de alquiler; *Jur* **h. assassin**, asesino a sueldo.

hireling ['haɪəlɪŋ] *n pej* mercenario,-a *m,f*.

hirsute ['hɜːsjuːt] *adj fml* hirsuto,-a.

his [hɪz] **I** *poss adj* (*one thing*) su; (*more than one*) sus; (*to distinguish*) de él; **h. book**, su libro; **h. house**, su casa; **h. friends**, sus amigos; **he washed h. face**, se lavó la cara; **he broke h. leg**, se rompió la pierna; **is it h. dog or hers?**, ¿el perro es de él o de ella? **II** *poss pron* **1** (*attribute*) (*one thing*) suyo,-a; (*more than one*) suyos,-as; (*to distinguish*) de él; **is the umbrella h. or hers?**, ¿el paraguas es de él o de ella?; **the cigarettes are h.**, el tabaco es suyo. **2** (*noun reference*) (*one thing*) el suyo, la suya; (*more than one*) los suyos, las suyas; **my car is blue and h. is red**, mi coche es azul y el suyo es rojo.

Hispanic [hɪ'spænɪk] **I** *adj* hispánico,-a. **II** *n US* hispano,-a *m,f*, latino,-a *m,f*.

Hispaniola [hɪspæn'jəʊlə] *n* la Española.

Hispanicist [hɪs'pænɪsɪst] *n* hispanista *mf*.

hiss [hɪs] **I** *n* (*gen*) siseo *m*; (*of steam*) silbido *m*; *Theat* silbido *m*. **II** *vtr* sisear, silbar; *Theat* **the actors were booed and hissed**, silbaron y abuchearon a los actores.

hissing ['hɪsɪŋ] *n* (*gen*) siseo *m*; (*of steam*) silbido *m*; **a h. noise**, un pitido.

histamine ['hɪstəmiːn] *n Biol* histamina *f*.

histology [hɪ'stɒlədʒɪ] *n Med* histología *f*.

historian [hɪ'stɔːrɪən] *n* historiador,-a *m,f*.

historic [hɪ'stɒrɪk] *adj* histórico,-a; **a(n) h. day**, un día memorable.

historical [hɪ'stɒrɪkəl] *adj* histórico,-a. ■ **h. novel**, novela *f* histórica. ◆ **historically** *adv* históricamente.

history ['hɪstərɪ] *n* historia *f*; **to go down in h.**, pasar a la historia; *Med* **to have a h. of ...**, haber tenido *or* sufrido ... . ■ **H. of Art**, Historia *f* del Arte.

hit [hɪt] **I** *n* **1** (*blow*) golpe *m*. **2** (*shot*) tiro *m*; *Mil* impacto *m*; **direct h.**, impacto directo. ■ **h. list**, lista *f* negra; *fam* **h. man**, asesino *m* sueldo. **3** (*success*) éxito *m*, acierto *m*; **he made a h. with them**, les cayó muy simpático; **smash h.**, exitazo *m*, éxito rotundo. ■ **h. musical**, comedia *f* musical con éxito; **h. parade**, hit-parade *m*, lista *f* de éxitos; **h. record**, disco *m* con éxito. **4** *fig* (*damaging remark*) pulla *f*. **II** *vtr* (*pt* & *pp* **hit**) **1** (*strike*) golpear, pegar; **he h. me**, me pegó; **he was h. in the leg**, le dieron en la pierna; **she h. the dog with the stick**, le pegó un bastonazo al perro; **the car h. the kerb**, el coche chocó contra el bordillo; **to h. sth back**, devolver; *fig* **it suddenly h. me**, de repente me di cuenta; *fig* **to h. the nail on the head**, dar en clavo; *fam fig* **it hits you in the eye**, salta a la vista; *fam fig* **to h. below the belt**, dar un golpe bajo; *fam fig* **to h. it off with sb**, caer bien a algn; *fam fig* **to h. the bottle**, darse a la bebida; *fam fig* **to h. the roof**, poner el grito en el cielo; *fam* **to h. the hay**, irse al catre. **2** (*affect badly*) afectar; **the company was h. by high inflation**, la empresa sufrió a causa de la alta inflación. **3** (*reach*) alcanzar; **to h. the headlines**, ser noticia; *fam* **to h. the road**, irse, ponerse en camino; *fam* **we h. bad weather**, nos tocó mal tiempo. ◆ **hit back** *vi* **1** (*strike in return*) devolver los golpes. **2** (*reply to criticism*) vengarse. ◆ **hit on, hit upon** *vtr* dar con; **they h. on an interesting solution**, dieron con una solución interesante; **we h. on the idea of ...**, se nos ocurrió la idea de ... . ◆ **hit out** *vi* **1** (*try to hit*) atacar; **to h. out at sb**, atacar a algn. **2** (*attack verbally*) atacar.

hit-and-miss [hɪtən'mɪs] *adj* al azar, casual.

hit-and-run [hɪtən'rʌn] *adj Aut* que se da a la fuga; **h.-a.-r. driver**, conductor que atropella a algn y no para.

hitch [hɪtʃ] **I** *n* obstáculo *m*, dificultad *f*; **a technical h.**, un incidente técnico; **without a h.**, sin problema alguno. **II** *vtr* **1** (*fasten*) atar; **they hitched on another wagon**, añadieron otro vagón. **2** *fam* (*hitchhike*) hacer autostop *or* dedo; **they hitched a lift into town**, llegaron a dedo a la ciudad. ◆ **hitch up** *vtr* remangar; **to h. up one's trousers**, arremangarse los pantalones.

hitched ['hɪtʃt] *adj fam* **to get h.**, casarse.

hitch-hike ['hɪtʃhaɪk] *vi* hacer autostop *or* dedo.

hitch-hiker ['hɪtʃhaɪkəʳ] *n* autostopista *mf*.

hither ['hɪðəʳ] *adv arch* acá; **h. and thither**, acá y acullá.

hitherto [hɪðə'tuː] *adv fml* hasta ahora, hasta la fecha.

hit-or-miss [hɪtɔː'mɪs] *adj* al azar, casual.

Hittite ['hɪtaɪt] **I** *adj* & *n* hitita (*mf*). **II** *n Ling* hitita *m*.

HIV [eɪtʃaɪ'viː] *Med abbr of* **human immunodeficiency virus**, virus *m* de inmunodeficiencia humano; **to be diagnosed H. positive/negative**, dar seropositivo,-a seronegativo,-a en la prueba del SIDA.

hive [haɪv] *n* colmena *f*; *fig* lugar *m* muy activo. ◆ **hive off** *vtr* separar; **to h. sth off from sth else**, separar una cosa de otra.

hives [haɪvz] *npl Med* urticaria *f*.

HM *abbr of* **His** *or* **Her Majesty**, Su Majestad *mf*, SM.

HMI [eɪtʃem'aɪ] *GB Educ abbr of* **His/Her Majesty's Inspector (of schools)**, Inspector,-a *m, f* oficial de escuelas y colegios.

HMS [eɪtʃem'es] *GB Naut abbr of* (*on warships*) **His/Her Majesty's Ship**, Barco *m* de Su Majestad.

HNC [eɪtʃen'siː] *GB Educ abbr of* **Higher National Certificate**, certificado *m* de formación profesional.

HND [eɪtʃen'diː] *GB Educ abbr of* **Higher National Diploma**, diploma *m* de formación profesional.

hoard [hɔːd] **I** *n* (*provisions*) reservas *fpl*; (*money, jewels etc*) tesoro *m*; *fam* **a h. of things**, un montón de cosas. **II** *vtr* (*objects*) acumular, amontonar; (*money*) atesorar.

hoarder ['hɔːdəʳ] *n* acumulador,-a *m,f*.

hoarding ['hɔːdɪŋ] n 1 (billboard) valla f publicitaria. 2 Constr (temporary fence) valla f.

hoarfrost ['hɔːfrɒst] n escarcha f.

hoarse [hɔːs] adj ronco,-a; **to be h.**, tener la voz ronca. ◆ **hoarsely** adv roncamente.

hoarseness ['hɔːsnɪs] n ronquera f.

hoary ['hɔːrɪ] adj (hoarier, hoariest) 1 Lit (of hair) cano,-a, canoso,-a. 2 (very old) viejo,-a; **a h. old joke**, un chiste muy pasado.

hoax [həʊks] I n (joke) broma f pesada; (trick) engaño m; **to play a h. on sb**, gastarle una broma a algn. II vtr gastar una broma a, engañar.

hob [hɒb] n 1 (of cooker) encimera f. 2 (by fireplace) repisa f.

hobble ['hɒbəl] I (walk with difficulty) vi andar con dificultad, cojear. II (fetter) (animal) manear.

hobby¹ ['hɒbɪ] n hobby m, pasatie npo m favorito; **his h. is carpentry**, dedica su tiempo libre a la carpintería.

hobby² ['hɒbɪ] n Orn alcotán m.

hobbyhorse ['hɒbɪhɔːs] n 1 (toy) caballito m de juguete. 2 fig (fixed idea) caballo m de batalla, tema m preferido; **he's on his h. again**, ya sacó el tema de siempre.

hobgoblin [hɒb'gɒblɪn] n duende m.

hobnailed ['hɒbneɪld] adj claveteado,-a, con clavos; **h. boots**, botas de clavos.

hobnob ['hɒbnɒb] vi fam codearse; **to h. with the rich**, codearse con los ricos.

hobo ['həʊbəʊ] n US (pl hobos or hoboes) vagabundo,-a m,f.

hock¹ [hɒk] n Anat Zool jarrete m.

hock² [hɒk] n vino m del Rin.

hock³ [hɒk] US fam I vtr empeñar. II n in h., empeñado,-a.

hockey ['hɒkɪ] n Sport hockey m. ■ **field h.**, hockey m sobre hierba.

hocus-pocus [həʊkəs'pəʊkəs] n trampa f.

hod [hɒd] n capacho m de albañil. ■ **h. carrier**, peón m de albañil.

hoe [həʊ] I n azada f, azadón m. II vtr azadonar.

hog [hɒg] n 1 (castrated male pig) cerdo m, puerco m, marrano m, Am chancho m; fam **to go the whole h.**, liarse la manta a la cabeza. 2 fam pej (undesirable person) indeseable mf. II vtr (pt & pp hogged) fam acaparar; **to h. the limelight**, monopolizar la atención.

Hogmanay [hɒgmə'neɪ] n Scot Nochevieja f.

hogwash ['hɒgwɒʃ] n inv fam tonterías fpl, disparates mpl.

hoi polloi [hɔɪpə'lɔɪ] n inv pej **the h. p.**, la gentuza, el populacho.

hoist [hɔɪst] I n 1 (crane) grúa f. 2 (lift) montacargas m inv. II vtr levantar, subir; **to h. the flag**, izar la bandera.

hoity-toity [hɔɪtɪ'tɔɪtɪ] adj fam pej presumido,-a.

hold [həʊld] I vtr (pt & pp held) 1 (keep in hand) aguantar, tener (en la mano), asir, sostener; (grip) agarrar; (support) (weight etc) soportar, aguantar; (opinion) sostener; **h. my books**, aguántame los libros; **to h. sb**, abrazar a algn; **to h. sb's hand**, cogerle la mano a algn; Aut **to h. the road**, agarrarse a la carretera; fig **she can h. her own in French**, se defiende en francés; fig **to h. one's head high**, mantener la cabeza alta. 2 (contain) dar cabida a; **the chapel holds a hundred people**, caben cien personas en la capilla; **the jug holds a litre**, la jarra tiene capacidad para un litro; fig **to h. water**, resultar cierto o válido; fig **who knows what the future holds**, quién sabe lo que nos espera en el futuro. 3 (have) (meeting etc) celebrar; (conversation) mantener; **the concert was held in the school**, el concierto se celebró en el colegio. 4 (reserve) guardar, reservar; **they will h. our tickets until this afternoon**, nos guardarán las entradas hasta esta tarde. 5 (occupy) ocupar; **to h. office**, ocupar un puesto or un

cargo. 6 (consider) considerar; **I h. you responsible**, te considero responsable. 7 (restrain) retener; **he was held for two hours at the police station**, estuvo detenido durante dos horas en la comisaría; **to h. one's breath**, contener la respiración; **to h. one's tongue**, callarse; **to h. sb hostage**, retener a algn como rehén; fig **there was no holding her**, no había manera de disuadirle; **it was it!**, ¡espera! 8 Tel **to h. the line**, mantenerse al habla, no colgar. II vi 1 (of rope etc) aguantar, resistir. 2 fig (of offer, promise) ser válido,-a, valer; **the rules h. (good) for everyone**, las reglas valen para todos. III n 1 (grip) asimiento m; **to catch or get h. of**, coger, agarrar; fig **to get h. of**, encontrar, localizar; **can you get h. of a newspaper?**, ¿puedes conseguir un periódico?; **where can I get h. of you?**, ¿dónde te puedo localizar? 2 (control) control m; **to have a firm h. on spending**, controlar rigurosamente los gastos; **to have a h. over sb**, influir mucho en algn, tener control sobre algn. 3 Wrest llave f. 4 Naut bodega f. ◆ **hold back I** vtr 1 (restrain) (crowd) contener; (feelings) reprimir; (truth) ocultar; (suspect) retener. 2 (store) guardar. II vi 1 (hesitate) vacilar, no atreverse. 2 (abstain) abstenerse. ◆ **hold down** vtr 1 (control) dominar. 2 fam (job) desempeñar; **she couldn't h. down a job**, perdía todos los empleos. ◆ **hold forth** vi hablar detenidamente (on, sobre). ◆ **hold off I** vtr (keep apart) mantener a distancia. II vi (refrain) refrenarse, retenerse; **he held off from buying new shares**, aplazó or postergó la compra de nuevas acciones; **I hope the rain holds off**, espero que no llueva. ◆ **hold on** vi 1 (keep a firm grasp) agarrarse bien; **h. on tight!**, ¡agárrate fuerte! 2 (wait) esperar; Tel **h. on!**, ¡no cuelgue! ◆ **hold out I** vtr (hand etc) ofrecer, tender. II vi 1 (last) (of things) durar; (of person) resistir; **will supplies h. out?**, ¿nos llegarán or alcanzarán las provisiones? 2 **to h. out for**, insistir en; **they held out for more pay**, persistieron en su demanda de aumento de sueldo. ◆ **hold over** vtr (meeting etc) aplazar. ◆ **hold up** vtr 1 (attack and rob) (train) asaltar; (bank etc) atracar. 2 (delay) retrasar; **we were held up for half an hour**, sufrimos media hora de retraso. 3 (raise) levantar; **h. your hand up**, levanta la mano. 4 (support) (weight) sostener, sujetar. ◆ **hold with** vtr estar de acuerdo con; **I don't h. with such ideas**, no comulgo con esas ideas.

holdall ['həʊldɔːl] n GB bolsa f de viaje.

holdback ['həʊldbæk] n fig inconveniente m.

holder ['həʊldə] n 1 (handle) asidero m. 2 (receptacle) receptáculo m, recipiente m. ■ **cigarette h.**, boquilla f. 3 (owner) poseedor,-a m, f; (bearer) portador,-a m, f; (of passport) titular mf. ■ Sport **record h.**, plusmarquista mf, recordman mf.

holding ['həʊldɪŋ] I n 1 (property) propiedad f; (land) terreno m, propiedad f. 2 Fin valor m en cartera. ■ **h. company**, holding m. II adj de control.

hold-up ['həʊldʌp] n 1 (robbery) atraco m. 2 (delay) retraso m; (in traffic) atasco m.

hole [həʊl] I n 1 (small) agujero m; (large) hoyo m; (in the road) bache m; sl **to be in a h.**, estar en un apuro. 2 Golf hoyo m. ■ **h. in one**, hoyo m en uno. 3 sl (of place) antro m. II vi Golf meter la pelota en el hoyo. ◆ **hole up** vi (animal) hibernar; fig esconderse.

holiday ['hɒlɪdeɪ] n 1 (one day) día m de fiesta, día m festivo; **Monday is a h.**, el lunes es fiesta. ■ **h. atmosphere**, ambiente m festivo. 2 GB (several days) vacaciones fpl; **paid holidays**, vacaciones pagadas; **to be/go on h.**, estar/ir de vacaciones; **to take a h.**, coger unas vacaciones; **we usually spend our summer holidays in France**, solemos veranear en Francia. ■ **h. pay**, paga f extra (de vacaciones); **h. resort**, lugar m turístico. II vi GB (gen) pasar las vacaciones; (in summer) veranear.

holiday-maker ['hɒlɪdeɪmeɪkə] n GB (gen) turista mf; (in summer) veraneante mf.

holier-than-thou ['həʊlɪəðən'ðaʊ] adj gazmoño,-a.

holiness ['həʊlɪnɪs] n Rel santidad f; **His H. Pope John Paul II**, Su Santidad el Papa Juan Pablo II.

holistic [həʊ'lɪstɪk] *adj* holístico,-a; **h. medicine**, medicina holística.

Holland ['hɒlənd] *n* Holanda.

hollandaise [hɒlən'deɪz] *adj* Culin **h. sauce**, salsa *f* holandesa.

hollow ['hɒləʊ] I *adj* 1 *(sound, object)* hueco,-a. 2 *(cheeks, eyes)* hundido,-a. 3 *fig (insincere)* falso,-a; *(empty)* vacío,-a; **a h. laugh**, una risa falsa; **h. promises**, promesas vacías. II *n (gen)* hueco *m*; *Geog* hondonada *f*. III *vtr* **to h. (out)**, vaciar, hacer un hueco en.

holly ['hɒlɪ] *n Bot* acebo *m*.

hollyhock ['hɒlɪhɒk] *n Bot* malvarrosa *f*.

holocaust ['hɒləkɔːst] *n* holocausto *m*; **nuclear h.**, holocausto nuclear.

holograph ['hɒləɡrɑːf] *n* hológrafo *m*, ológrafo *m*.

holster ['həʊlstəʳ] *n* pistolera *f*.

holy ['həʊlɪ] *adj Rel* 1 *(sacred)* sagrado,-a, santo,-a. ■ **H. Communion**, Sagrada Comunión *f*; **H. Ghost**, Espíritu *m* Santo; **H. Land**, Tierra *f* Santa; **h. orders**, órdenes *fpl* sagradas; **H. See**, Santa Sede *f*; **H. Week**, Semana *f* Santa. 2 *(blessed) (of bread, water)* bendito,-a.

homage ['hɒmɪdʒ] *n* homenaje *m*; **to pay** or **do h.** to sb, rendir homenaje a algn.

home [həʊm] I *n* 1 *(house)* casa *f*, hogar *m*; *fml* domicilio *m*; **at h.**, en casa; *fig* a gusto; **h. sweet h.**, hogar dulce hogar; *fig* **a h. from h.**, un segundo hogar; *fig* **make yourself at h.!**, ¡estás en tu casa!; *fig* **to feel at h.**, estar a gusto. 2 *(institution)* asilo *m*. ■ **nursing h.**, clínica *f*; **old people's h.**, asilo *m* or residencia *f* de ancianos. 3 *(country etc)* tierra *f*, patria *f*; **he is far from h.**, está lejos de su tierra. 4 *Zool* hábitat *m*. 5 *Sport* casa *f*; **to play at h.**, jugar en casa. ■ *US Baseb* **h. base**, **h. plate**, base *f* del bateador; **h. run**, carrera *f* completa. II *adj* 1 *(domestic)* casero,-a, del hogar; **h. cooking**, cocina casera; **h. comforts**, comodidades del hogar. ■ *GB* **h. help**, asistenta *f*; **h. life**, vida *f* de familia. 2 *Pol* interior, del interior; **h. affairs**, asuntos interiores. ■ *GB* **H. Office**, Ministerio *m* del Interior; **h. rule**, autonomía *f*; *GB* **H. Secretary**, Ministro,-a *m*, *f* del Interior. 3 *(native)* natal; **h. town**, pueblo natal, patria chica. 4 *Sport* de or en casa; **h. game**, partido en casa; **h. team**, equipo de casa. III *adv* en casa, a casa, de casa; **to be (at) h.**, estar en casa; **to go h.**, irse or volver a casa; **to leave h.**, irse de casa; *fig* **to bring sth h. to sb**, hacer comprender algo a algn; *fam* **it's nothing to write h. about**, no es nada del otro jueves.

homecoming ['həʊmkʌmɪŋ] *n* regreso *m* a casa.

home-grown ['həʊmɡrəʊn] *adj (produced in the region)* del país; *(in one's garden)* de cosecha propia, casero,-a.

homeland ['həʊmlænd] *n (gen)* patria *f*; *(birthplace)* tierra *f* natal.

homeless ['həʊmlɪs] I *adj* sin techo. II **the h.** *npl* los sin techo.

home-loving ['həʊmlʌvɪŋ] *adj* casero,-a, hogareño,-a.

homely ['həʊmlɪ] *adj (homelier, homeliest)* 1 *GB (warm, domesticated) (of person)* casero,-a; *(of atmosphere)* familiar. 2 *US (unattractive)* sin atractivo, feo,-a.

home-made ['həʊmmeɪd] *adj* hecho,-a en casa, de fabricación casera.

homeopath ['həʊmɪəpæθ] *n US Med see* **homoeopath**.

homeopathy [həʊmɪ'ɒpəθɪ] *n US Med see* **homoeopathy**.

homesick ['həʊmsɪk] *adj* nostálgico,-a; **to be h.**, tener morriña; **to be h. for one's family**, echar en falta a la familia.

homesickness ['həʊmsɪknɪs] *n* nostalgia *f*, morriña *f*.

homestead ['həʊmsted] *n* granja *f*, *Am* estancia *f*, *Am* hacienda *f*.

homeward(s) ['həʊmwəd(z)] *adv* hacia casa.

homework ['həʊmwɜːk] *n* deberes *mpl*; **to do one's h.**, hacer los deberes; **what do we have for h.?**, ¿qué tenemos de deberes?

homicidal [hɒmɪ'saɪdəl] *adj* homicida.

homicide ['hɒmɪsaɪd] *n* I *(crime)* homicidio *m*. 2 *(criminal)* homicida *mf*.

homily ['hɒmɪlɪ] *n* homilía *f*.

homing ['həʊmɪŋ] *adj* 1 *Mil* buscador,-a; **h. device**, cabeza *f* buscadora. 2 *Zool* **h. pigeon**, paloma *f* mensajera.

homoeopath ['həʊmɪəpæθ] *n Med* homeópata *mf*.

homoeopathy [həʊmɪ'ɒpəθɪ] *n Med* homeopatía *f*.

homogeneous [hɒmə'dʒiːnɪəs] *adj* homogéneo,-a.

homogenization [hɒmɒdʒɪnaɪ'zeɪʃən] *n* homogeneización *f*.

homogenize [hɒ'mɒdʒɪnaɪz] *vtr* homogeneizar; **homogenized milk**, leche homogeneizada.

homogenous [hə'mɒdʒɪnəs] *adj see* **homogeneous**.

homologate [hɒ'mɒləɡeɪt] *vtr* homologar.

homological [həʊmə'lɒdʒɪkəl] *adj*, **homologous** [həʊ'mɒləɡəs] *adj* homólogo,-a.

homology [həʊ'mɒlədʒɪ] *n* homología *f*.

homonym ['hɒmənɪm] *n* homónimo *m*.

homophone ['hɒməfəʊn] *n* homófono *m*.

homosexual [həʊməʊ'seksjʊəl] *adj & n* homosexual *(mf)*.

homosexuality [həʊməʊseksjʊ'ælɪtɪ] *n* homosexualidad *f*.

Hon 1 *abbr of* **Honorary**, *(member)* honorario,-a; *(Secretary, Treasurer)* no remunerado,-a. 2 *abbr of* **Honourable**, ilustre señor,-a.

Honduran [hɒn'djʊərən] *adj & n* hondureño,-a *(m, f)*.

Honduras [hɒn'djʊərəs] *n* Honduras.

hone [həʊn] I *n* piedra *n* de afilar. II *vtr* afilar.

honest ['ɒnɪst] I *adj* 1 *(trustworthy)* honrado,-a, recto,-a; **an h. face**, una cara abierta; *fam* **to do an h. day's work**, hacer una buena jornada. 2 *(sincere)* sincero,-a, franco,-a; **give me your h. opinion**, dime sinceramente lo que opinas; **the h. truth**, la pura verdad; **to be h., I don't know what to say**, sinceramente, no sé qué decir. 3 *(fair)* justo,-a, decente. II *adv fam* **h. (to God)!**, ¡te lo prometo! ◆ **honestly** *adv (fairly etc)* honradamente; *(question)* ¿de verdad?; *(exclamation)* ¡hay que ver!; *fig* de verdad, a decir verdad; **h., it doesn't matter**, de verdad or créeme, no tiene importancia; **h., it's the truth**, es la verdad, te lo juro.

honesty ['ɒnɪstɪ] *n* honradez *f*, rectitud *f*.

honey ['hʌnɪ] *n* 1 *(substance)* miel *f*. 2 *US fam (endearment)* cariño *m*.

honeycomb ['hʌnɪkəʊm] *n* panal *m*.

honeyed ['hʌnɪd] *adj* meloso,-a, dulzón,-a; **h. words**, palabras melosas or dulces.

honeymoon ['hʌnɪmuːn] I *n* luna *f* de miel, viaje *m* de novios. II *vi* pasar la luna de miel, hacer el viaje de novios.

honeymooner ['hʌnɪmuːnəʳ] *n* recién casado,-a *m*, *f*.

honeysuckle ['hʌnɪsʌkəl] *n Bot* madreselva *f*.

honied ['hʌnɪd] *adj see* **honeyed**.

honk [hɒŋk] I *n* 1 *(of goose)* graznido *m*. 2 *(of car horn)* bocinazo *m*. II *vi* 1 *(goose)* graznar. 2 *Aut* tocar la bocina. III *vtr (car horn)* tocar.

honky ['hɒŋkɪ] *n US sl pej* blanco,-a *m*, *f*.

honor ['ɒnəʳ] *n & vtr US see* **honour**.

honorable ['ɒnərəbəl] *adj US see* **honourable**.

honorarium [ɒnə'reərɪəm] *n (pl* **honorariums** or **honoraria** [ɒnə'reərɪə]*)* honorarios *mpl*.

honorary ['ɒnərərɪ] *adj (of member)* honorario,-a; *(of duties)* honorífico,-a; *Univ* **to receive an h. degree**, ser nombrado,-a doctor,-a honoris causa.

honour ['ɒnəʳ] I *n* 1 *(virtue)* honor *m*, honra *f*; **in h. of**, en honor de; **to defend one's h.**, defender su honra; **to do h. to**, *(pay homage to)* rendir honores a; *(be a credit to)* honrar; **to do to honours,** hacer los honores; **to have the h. of doing sth,** tener el honor de hacer algo. **2** (*title*) **Her H., His H., Your H.,** Su Señoría *f.* **3** *Mil* **honours,** honores *mpl.* **4 Honours degree,** licenciatura *f* superior. **II** *vtr* **1** (*respect*) honrar. **2** (*fulfil obligation*) cumplir; *Fin* **to h. a cheque,** aceptar y pagar un talón bancario; **to h. one's word,** cumplir con su palabra.

honourable ['ɒnərəbəl] *adj* **1** (*of person*) honrado,-a; *Parl* **the h. gentleman,** el ilustre diputado. **2** (*of actions*) honorífico,-a, honroso,-a; **h. mention,** mención honorífica.

Hons [ɒnz] *GB Educ abbr of* **Honours,** Licenciado *m* Superior.

hooch [huːtʃ] *n sl see* **hootch.**

hood¹ [hʊd] *n* **1** (*of garment*) capucha *f*; **Little Red Riding H.,** Caperucita *f* Roja. **2** (*of car, pram*) capota *f.* **3** (*of falcon*) capirote *m,* capillo *m.* **4** *US Aut* (*bonnet*) capó *m.*

hood² [hʊd] *n esp US sl abbr of* **hoodlum.**

hooded ['hʊdɪd] *adj* (*of person, garment*) con capucha; **a h. bank robber,** un atracador encapuchado. **2** (*of falcon*) encapirotado,-a.

hoodlum ['huːdləm] *n US* matón *m.*

hoodwink ['hʊdwɪŋk] *vtr* engañar; **I've been hoodwinked,** me han tomado el pelo.

hoof [huːf] *n* (*pl* **hoofs** *or* **hooves** [huːvz]) (*of horse*) casco *m*; (*of cow, sheep*) pezuña *f.* **II** *vtr sl* **to h. it,** ir a pata, ir con el coche de San Fernando.

hoofed [huːft] *adj* ungulado,-a.

hoofer ['huːfər] *n US sl* bailarín,-ina *m,f* de claqué.

hoo-ha ['huːhaː] *n fam* follón *m*; **there was a great h.-ha,** se armó un follón enorme.

hook [hʊk] **I** *n* **1** (*gen*) gancho *m*; *Knit* **crochet h.,** ganchillo *m*; *Sew* **hooks and eyes,** corchetes *mpl*; *Tel* **to take the phone off the h.,** descolgar el teléfono; *fig* **by h. or (by) crook,** por las buenas o por las malas; *sl* **off the h.,** limpio,-a; *sl* **on the h.,** (*waiting*) a la espera; (*in trouble*) en la mierda. **2** *Fishing* anzuelo *m.* **3** *Box* gancho *m.* **II** *vtr* **1** (*fasten*) enganchar; **her skirt got hooked on a nail,** se le enganchó la falda en un clavo. **2** (*of bull etc*) clavar. **3** *Fishing* pescar, coger. **4** *Box* pegar haciendo un gancho. **5** *sl* (*steal*) birlar, mangar. ◆ **hook up** *vtr & vi Rad TV Comput* conectar (**with,** con).

hooka(h) ['hʊkə] *n* narguile *m.*

hooked [hʊkt] *adj* **1** (*hook-shaped*) ganchudo,-a; (*nose*) aquilino,-a. **2** *sl* (*attracted*) prendado,-a, encariñado,-a; (*addicted*) enganchado,-a (**on,** a); **to get h.,** engancharse; **he's h. on heroin,** está enganchado al caballo.

hooker ['hʊkər] *n* **1** *Rugby* talonador,-a *m,f.* **2** *US sl* puta *f.*

hook(e)y ['hʊkɪ] *n US Canada NZ fam* **to play h.,** hacer campana.

hook-up ['hʊkʌp] *n* **1** *Comput* conexión *f.* **2** *Rad TV* emisión *f* transmitida a varios lugares.

hooligan ['huːlɪgən] *n sl* gamberro,-a *m, f,* delincuente *mf.*

hooliganism ['huːlɪgənɪzəm] *n sl* gamberrismo *m,* delincuencia *f.*

hoop [huːp] *n* (*gen*) aro *m*; (*of barrel*) fleje *m*; (*of wheel*) llanta *f, fig* **to put sb through the hoops,** hacérselo pasar mal a algn.

hoopoe ['huːpuː] *n Orn* abubilla *f.*

hoorah [huːˈraː] *interj,* **hooray** [huːˈreɪ] *interj* ¡hurra!

hoot [huːt] **I** *n* **1** (*of owl, train, wind*) ululato *m*; *fam* **hoots of laughter,** carcajadas *fpl,* risotadas *fpl; fam* **I don't care a h.,** me importa un pepino. **2** (*of car horn*) bocinazo *m.* **3** *fam* cosa *f or* persona *f* divertida; *fam* **it was a h.,** fue divertidísimo. **II** *vi* **1** (*of owl*) ulular. **2** (*of car*) dar un bocinazo, tocar la bocina; (*of train*) silbar; (*of siren*) pitar.

hootch [huːtʃ] *n sl* aguardiente *m.*

hooter ['huːtər] *n* **1** *esp GB* (*of car*) bocina *f*; (*siren*) sirena *f.* **2** *GB sl* (*nose*) narizota *f.*

Hoover® ['huːvər] *GB* **I** *n* aspiradora *f.* **II** *vtr* **to h.,** pasar la aspiradora a.

hop¹ [hɒp] **I** *vi* (*pt & pp* **hopped**) saltar, dar saltitos; **to h. on the leg,** andar a la pata coja; *fam* **h. in!,** (*into car*) ¡sube!; *fam* **to h. on the bus/train,** subirse al autobús/ tren. **II** *vtr* **1** *US fam* (*train etc*) coger. **2** *GB* **sl h. it!,** ¡lárgate!, ¡esfúmate! **3** *Av* cruzar. **III** *n* **1** (*small jump*) brinco *m,* saltito *m*; **in one h.,** de un salto; *fam* **to be on the h.,** estar muy atareado,-a; *GB fam* **to catch sb on the h.,** coger desprevenido,-a a algn. **2** *fam* (*dance*) baile *m,* bailongo *m.* **3** *Av fam* vuelo *m* corto.

hop² [hɒp] *n Bot* lúpulo *m.*

hope [həʊp] **I** *n* (*gen*) esperanza *f*; (*false*) ilusión *f*; **don't build up your hopes,** no te hagas ilusiones; **to have high hopes,** tener grandes esperanzas; **to have little h. of doing sth,** tener pocas posibilidades de hacer algo; *fam* **not a h.!, some h.!,** ¡ni hablar!, ¡qué va! ■ *US* **h. chest,** ajuar *m.* **II** *vtr & vi* esperar; **I h. not,** espero que no; **I h. so,** espero que sí; **I h. to have an answer tomorrow,** espero tener una respuesta para mañana; **I'm hoping for a letter,** espero carta; **we h. you're well,** esperamos que estés bien.

hopeful ['həʊpfʊl] **I** *adj* (*confident*) optimista; (*promising*) esperanzador,-a, prometedor,-a; **she's h. that ...,** tiene esperanzas de que ... . **II** *n* persona *f* que promete; **young h.,** joven *mf* promesa. ◆ **hopefully** *adv* **1** (*confidently*) con esperanza, con optimismo. **2** *fam* (*it is hoped*) esperamos, se espera; **h., the weather will be fine,** se espera que haga buen tiempo.

hopeless ['həʊplɪs] *adj* desesperado,-a; **a h. case,** un caso perdido; **it's h.,** es imposible; *fam* **to be h. at sports,** ser negado,-a para los deportes. ◆ **hopelessly** *adv* sin esperanza, desesperadamente; **h. in love,** locamente enamorado,-a; **h. lost,** completamente perdido,-a.

hopper ['hɒpər] *n* (*funnel*) tolva *f.*

hop-picker ['hɒppɪkər] *n* recogedor,-a *m,f* de lúpulo.

hop-picking ['hɒppɪkɪŋ] *n* cosecha *f* del lúpulo.

hopping ['hɒpɪŋ] **I** *n* saltos *mpl,* brincos *mpl.* **II** *adj fam* **h. mad,** rabioso,-a; **she's h. mad,** está que trina, está que bota.

hopscotch ['hɒpskɒtʃ] *n* infernáculo *m.*

horde [hɔːd] *n* **1** (*crowd*) multitud *f.* **2** (*nomadic group*) horda *f.*

horizon [həˈraɪzən] *n* horizonte *m.*

horizontal [hɒrɪˈzɒntəl] *adj* horizontal. ◆ **horizontally** *adv* horizontalmente.

hormonal [hɔːˈməʊnəl] *adj* hormonal.

hormone ['hɔːməʊn] *n Biol* hormona *f,* hormón *m.*

horn [hɔːn] *n* **1** *Zool* cuerno *m,* asta *f*; (*of snail*) tentáculo *m; fig* **to take the bull by the horns,** agarrar *or* coger el toro por los cuernos. **2** *Mus* (*gen*) instrumento *m* de viento; (*primitive*) cuerno *m*; *fam* trompeta *f; fig* **on the horns of a dilemma,** entre la espada y la pared; *US fig* **to blow one's own h.,** vanagloriarse. ■ **French h.,** trompa *f*; **hunting h.,** cuerno *m* de caza. **3** (*of gramophone*) pabellón *m,* bocina *f.* **4** *Aut* bocina *f*; **to honk** *or* **sound the h.,** dar un bocinazo. **5** *GB sl vulg* erección *f.*

hornbeam ['hɔːnbiːm] *n Bot* carpe *m.*

horned [hɔːnd] *adj* (*of cattle etc*) con cuernos.

hornet ['hɔːnɪt] *n Ent* avispón *m*; *fig* **to stir up a h.'s nest,** meterse en un avispero.

hornpipe ['hɔːnpaɪp] *n* **1** *Mus* (*instrument*) chirimía *f.* **2** *GB* (*dance*) baile *m* folklórico marinero.

horn-rimmed ['hɔːnrɪmd] *adj* (*spectacles*) con montura de concha.

horny ['hɔːnɪ] *adj* (**hornier, horniest**) **1** (*of hands*) calloso,-a. **2** *sl* (*sexually aroused*) caliente, cachondo,-a.

horology [hɒˈrɒlədʒɪ] *n* relojería *f.*

horoscope ['hɒrəskəʊp] *n* horóscopo *m.*

horrendous [hɒˈrendəs] *adj* horrendo,-a, horroroso,-a.

horrible ['hɒrəbəl] *adj* horrible, horroroso,-a; **the weather was h.,** hizo un tiempo horroroso; *fam* **what a h. man!,** ¡qué hombre más antipático! ◆ **horribly** *adv* horriblemente; **it was h. hot,** hacía un calor insoportable.

horrid ['hɒrɪd] *adj* (*horrible*) horrible, horroroso,-a; (*unkind*) antipático,-a.

horrific [hə'rɪfɪk] *adj* horrendo,-a.

horrify ['hɒrɪfaɪ] *vtr* (*pt & pp* **horrified**) espantar, horrorizar; **she was horrified at the thought,** se horrorizaba sólo de pensarlo.

horror ['hɒrəʳ] *n* horror *m*, terror *m*; **it fills me with h.,** me llena de temor; **to have a h. of sth,** tener horror a algo; *fam* **a little h.,** un diablillo. ■ **h. film,** película *f* de miedo *or* de terror.

horrors ['hɒrəz] *interj* ¡qué horror!

horror-stricken ['hɒrəstrɪkən] *adj*, **horrorstruck** ['hɒrəstrʌk] *adj* horrorizado,-a;

hors d'oeuvre [ɔː'dɜːvr] *n* (*pl* **hors d'oeuvre** *or* **hors d'oeuvres**) *Culin* entremés *m*.

horse [hɔːs] **I** *n* **1** *Zool* caballo *m*; *fig* **hold your horses!,** ¡echa el freno!, ¡alto ahí! *fig* **to beat** *or* **flog a dead h.,** machacar en hierro frío; *fig* **to get sth straight from the h.'s mouth,** saber algo de buena tinta; *fam fig* **to get on one's high h.,** darse ínfulas. ■ **h. doctor,** veterinario *m*; *Zool* **h. family,** grupo *m* *or* familia *f* de los ecuestres; **h. race,** carrera *f* de caballos; *fig* **h. sense,** sentido *m* común. **2** *Gymn* potro *m*. **3** *Tech* caballete *m*. **4** *Bot* **h. chestnut,** (*tree*) castaño *m* de Indias; (*fruit*) castaña *f* de Indias. **5** *sl* (*heroin*) caballo *m*. **II** *vi fam* **to h. around** *or* **about,** hacer el indio.

horseback ['hɔːsbæk] *n* **on h.,** a caballo. ■ *US Canada* **h. riding,** equitación *f*.

horsebox ['hɔːsbɒks] *n GB* furgón *m* para caballos.

horseflesh ['hɔːsfleʃ] *n* carne *f* de caballo.

horsefly ['hɔːsflaɪ] *n Ent* tábano *m*.

horsehair ['hɔːsheəʳ] *n* crin *m* (de caballo). ■ **h. mattress,** colchón *m* de crin (de caballo).

horseman ['hɔːsmən] *n* (*pl* **horsemen**) jinete *m*, caballista *m*; (*professional*) yoquey *m*.

horsemanship ['hɔːsmənʃɪp] *n* equitación *f*.

horseplay ['hɔːspleɪ] *n* payasadas *fpl*; **to indulge in h.,** hacer el payaso.

horsepower ['hɔːspaʊəʳ] *n Aut* caballo *m* (de vapor).

horseradish ['hɔːsrædɪʃ] *n Bot* rábano *m* rusticano.

horseshoe ['hɔːsʃuː] *n* herradura *f*.

horsewoman ['hɔːswʊmən] *n* (*pl* **horsewomen** ['hɔːswɪmɪn]) amazona *f*, caballista *f*.

hors(e)y ['hɔːsɪ] *adj* (*horsier, horsiest*) **1** (*horse-like*) caballuno,-a; **h. features,** rasgos caballunos. **2** (*interested in horses*) aficionado,-a a los caballos.

horticultural [hɔːtɪ'kʌltʃərəl] *adj* hortícola, hortelano,-a.

horticulture ['hɔːtɪkʌltʃəʳ] *n* horticultura *f*.

hose¹ [həʊz] **I** *n* (*pipe*) manguera *f*. **II** *vtr* **to h.** (**down**), (*with water*) regar con una manguera; (*wash*) lavar con una manguera.

hose² [həʊz] *n* (*pl* **hose** *or* **hosen** ['həʊzən]) (*socks*) calcetines *mpl*; (*stockings*) medias *fpl*.

hosiery ['həʊzɪərɪ] *n Com* medias *fpl* y calcetines *mpl*.

hospice ['hɒspɪs] *n* residencia *f* geriátrica *or* de ancianos.

hospitable ['hɒspɪtəbəl, hɒ'spɪtəbəl] *adj* hospitalario,-a; **h. atmosphere,** ambiente *m* acogedor. ◆ **hospitably** *adv* con hospitalidad.

hospital ['hɒspɪtəl] *n* hospital *m*.

hospitality [hɒspɪ'tælɪtɪ] *n* hospitalidad *f*.

hospitalize ['hɒspɪtəlaɪz] *vtr* hospitalizar.

Host [həʊst] *n Rel* hostia *f*.

host¹ [həʊst] **I** *n* **1** (*at home*) anfitrión *m*. **2** *Theat TV* presentador *m*. **3** *Biot Zool* huésped *m*. **II** *vtr Theat TV* (*show*) presentar.

host² [həʊst] *n* (*large number*) montón *m*; **a h. of things,** la tira de cosas.

hostage ['hɒstɪdʒ] *n* rehén *m*; **to hold sb h.,** tener a algn como rehén.

hostel ['hɒstəl] *n* hostal *m*, residencia *f*. ■ **youth h.,** albergue *m* para la juventud.

hostess ['həʊstɪs] *n* **1** (*at home etc*) anfitriona *f*. **2** (*in club*) camarera *f*. **3** *Theat TV* presentadora *f*. **4** *Av* (*air*) **h.,** azafata *f*.

hostile ['hɒstaɪl] *adj* hostil, enemigo,-a; **to be h. to change,** ser hostil a los cambios.

hostility [hɒ'stɪlɪtɪ] *n* hostilidad *f*; *Mil* **hostilities have now ceased,** han cesado las hostilidades.

hot [hɒt] *adj* (*hotter, hottest*) **1** (*gen*) caliente; **h. water,** agua caliente; *fig* **to blow h. and cold,** cambiar continuamente de actitud. ■ *Tel fig* **h. line,** teléfono *m* rojo; *US Aut sl* **h. rod,** bólido *m*; (*nightclub*) **h. spot,** club *m* nocturno. **2** *Meteor* caluroso,-a; **it's very h.,** hace mucho calor; **to feel h.,** tener calor. ■ *fig* **h. air,** palabrería *f*. **3** *Culin* (*not cold*) caliente; **h. meals,** comidas calientes. ■ **h. dog,** perrito *m* caliente. **4** *Culin* (*spicy*) caliente; **h. sauce,** salsa picante; **not a very h. chicken curry,** un pollo al curry no muy picante. **5** (*temper*) fuerte; (*anger*) rabioso,-a, colérico,-a; *fam* **to get h. under the collar,** ponerse nervioso,-a. **6** *fam* (*fresh*) de última hora; **h. news,** noticia *f* de última hora. **7** *fam* (*good*) bueno,-a, enterado,-a; **ask Frank, he's h. on that subject,** pregúntaselo a Frank, sabe bastante de eso; **it's not so h.,** no mata; **she's h. stuff,** está buena, está como un tren. **8** (*popular*) popular; **a very h. play,** una obra muy taquillera. **9** (*dangerous*) peligroso,-a; *fig* **to get oneself into h. water,** meterse en un lío; *fig* **to make things h. for sb,** hacerle la vida difícil a algn. ◆ *fam* **h. potato,** asunto *m* delicado; *fam* **h. seat,** primera fila *f*; *fam* **h. spot,** punto *m* caliente. ◆ **hot up** *vi fam* sucederse rápidamente; **things are hotting up,** la cosa se está poniendo al rojo vivo.

hotbed ['hɒtbed] *n fig* hervidero *m*.

hot-blooded ['hɒtblʌdɪd] *adj* de sangre caliente; *fig* **to be h.-b.,** tener la sangre caliente.

hotch-potch ['hɒtpɒtʃ] *n fam* mezcolanza *f*, batiburrillo *m*.

hotel [həʊ'tel] *n* hotel *m*.

hotelier [həʊ'teljeʳ] *n*, **hotel-keeper** [həʊ'telkiːpəʳ] *n* hotelero,-a *m,f*.

hotfoot ['hɒtfʊt] *adv* a toda prisa.

hothead ['hɒthed] *n fam* cabeza *mf* loca.

hot-headed [hɒt'hedɪd] *adj* impetuoso,-a, impulsivo,-a.

hothouse ['hɒthaʊs] *n Hortic* invernadero *m*.

hotplate ['hɒtpleɪt] *n* (*cooker*) placa *f* de cocina; (*to keep food warm*) calientaplatos *m inv*.

hotpot ['hɒtpɒt] *n GB Culin* estofado *m*.

hotshot ['hɒtʃɒt] *n US sl* as *m*, hacha *m*.

hot-tempered [hɒt'tempəd] *adj* de genio vivo.

hot-water ['hɒtwɔːtəʳ] *adj* de agua caliente. ■ **h.-w. bottle,** bolsa *f* de agua caliente.

hound [haʊnd] *n Zool* perro *m* de caza. **II** *vtr* acosar, perseguir; **he was hounded by the press,** fue acosado por la prensa.

hour ['aʊəʳ] *n* hora *f*; **a quarter of an h.,** un cuarto de hora; **every h.,** cada hora; **half an h.,** media hora; **on the h.,** a la hora en punto; **60 miles an h.,** 60 millas por hora; **the clock struck the h.,** el reloj dio la hora; **to be paid by the h.,** cobrar por horas; **what are the visiting hours?,** ¿cuáles son las horas de visita?; *fig* **his h. had come,** había llegado su hora; *fig* **the small hours,** la madrugada; *fig* **to take hours to do sth,** tardar horas en hacer algo; *fig* **until all hours (of the night),** hasta la madrugada. ■ **h. hand,** manecilla *f*; **lunch h.,** hora *f* de comer; **rush h.,** hora *f* punta.

hourly ['aʊəlɪ] **I** *adj* cada hora; **an h. train service,** un tren cada hora. **II** *adv* por horas; **to be paid h.,** cobrar por horas.

house [haʊs] **I** *n* **1** *(gen)* casa *f*; *fml* domicilio *m*; **at my h.**, en mi casa; **doll's h.**, casa de muñecas; **to move h.**, mudarse de casa, trasladarse; *fig* **on the h.**, cortesía de la casa; *fig* **to keep open h.**, ser muy hospitalario,-a; *fam* **to get on with sb like a h. on fire**, llevarse de maravilla con algn. ■ *GB* **h. agent**, agente *m* inmobiliario; *Jur* **h. arrest**, arresto *m* domiciliario; **h. guest**, invitado,-a *m*, *f* de la casa; *Med* **h. physician**, interno,-a *m*, *f*; **h. plant**, planta *f* de interior; *Med* **h. surgeon**, cirujano *m* interno. **2** *Pol* cámara *f*. ■ **H. of Commons**, Cámara *f* de los Comunes; **H. of Lords**, Cámara *f* de los Lores; *US* **H. of Representatives**, Cámara *f* de Representantes; **Houses of Parliament**, Parlamento *m*. **3** *(company)* empresa *f*. ■ **publishing h.**, editorial *f*. **4** *Theat* Sala *f*; *fig* **to bring the h. down**, ser un exitazo. ■ **first h.**, primera sesión *f*; **full h.**, lleno *m*; **'h. full'**, 'agotadas las localidades'. **II** [haʊz] *vtr (gen)* alojar; *(give housing to)* proveer de vivienda; *(store)* guardar; *(fit)* dar cabida a.

houseboat ['haʊsbəʊt] *n* casa *f* flotante.

housebreaker ['haʊsbreɪkə'] *n* ladrón,-ona *m*, *f*.

housebreaking ['haʊsbreɪkɪŋ] *n* *Jur* allanamiento *m* de morada.

housecoat ['haʊskəʊt] *n* bata *f*.

houseful ['haʊsfʊl] *n* **we have a h. of guests**, tenemos la casa llena de invitados.

household ['haʊshəʊld] *n* casa *f*, hogar *m*; *fig* **to become a h. name**, ser archiconocido,-a *or* popular. ■ **h. expenses**, gastos *mpl* de la casa; **h. products**, productos *mpl* domésticos.

householder ['haʊshəʊldə'] *n* dueño,-a *m*, *f* de la casa.

househusband ['haʊshʌzbənd] *n* *fam* hombre *m* que hace de ama de casa.

housekeeper ['haʊski:pə'] *n* ama *f* de llaves.

housekeeping ['haʊski:pɪŋ] *n* administración *f* de la casa. ■ **h. money**, dinero *m* para los gastos de casa.

housemaid ['haʊsmeɪd] *n* criada *f*. ■ *Med* **h.'s knee**, hidrartrosis *f*.

houseman ['haʊsmən] *n* *(pl* **housemen***)* *Med* interno *m*.

housemaster ['haʊsmɑ:stə'] *n* *Educ* tutor *m*.

housemistress ['haʊsmɪstrɪs] *n* *Educ* tutora *f*.

houseroom ['haʊsru:m] *n* sitio *m* en casa; **I wouldn't give it h.**, no lo tendría ni en casa.

house-to-house [haʊstə'haʊs] *adj* de casa en casa; **h.-to-h. salesman**, vendedor a domicilio.

house-train ['haʊstreɪn] *vtr (pet)* educar.

house-warming ['haʊswɔ:mɪŋ] *n* **h.-w. (party)**, fiesta *f* que se da al estrenar casa.

housewife ['haʊswaɪf] *n* ama *f* de casa.

housework ['haʊswɜ:k] *n* trabajo *m* doméstico, quehaceres *mpl* domésticos.

housing ['haʊzɪŋ] *n* vivienda *f*. ■ **h. estate**, urbanización *f*; *Pol* **Ministry of H.**, Ministerio *m* de la Vivienda.

hove [həʊv] *pt* & *pp see* **heave**.

hovel ['hʌvəl, 'hɒvəl] *n* casucha *f*, tugurio *m*, chabola *f*.

hover ['hɒvə'] *vi* **1** *(bird)* cernerse; *(aircraft)* permanecer inmóvil (en el aire); **the eagle hovered over its prey**, el águila se cernía sobre su presa. **2** *(person)* cernerse; **to h. between one thing and another**, vacilar entre una cosa y otra.

hovercraft ['hɒvəkrɑ:ft] *n* *Naut* hovercraft *m*.

how [haʊ] *adv* **1** *(direct question)* ¿cómo?; **h. are you?**, ¿cómo estás?; **h. did it happen?**, ¿cómo ocurrió?; **h. do you do**, mucho gusto; *fam* **and h.!**, ¡y tanto!; *fam* **h. come?**, ¿por qué?; *fam* **h.'s that for an answer?**, ¿qué te parece? **2** *(indirect question)* cómo; **I don't know h. to tell you**, no sé cómo decírtelo. **3** *(very)* qué; *fam* ¡qué divertido!; **h. long the film was!**, ¡qué larga que fue la película! **4** *(suggestion)* **h. about ...?**, ¿y si ...?; **h. about a stroll?**, ¿qué te parece un paseo?; **h. about going out to lunch?**, ¿y si saliésemos a comer? **5** *(quantity)* cuánto; **h.**

old is she?, ¿cuántos años tiene?, ¿qué edad tiene?; **h. tall are you?**, ¿cuánto mides de altura? **6** *(quantity)* **h. many?**, ¿cuántos,-as?; **h. much?**, ¿cuánto,-a?; **I don't know h. many people there were**, no sé cuánta gente había.

howdy ['haʊdɪ] *interj US fam* ¡qué hay?, ¿qué tal?, ¡hola!

however [haʊ'evə'] *adv* **1** *(nevertheless)* no obstante, sin embargo; **h., he was right**, sin embargo, tenía razón. **2** *(with adjective)* por; **h. difficult it may be**, por difícil que sea; **h. much**, por más que, por mucho que (+ *subj*); **h. much you insist ...**, por más que insistas ... . **3** *(how)* ¿cómo?; **h. did you manage to do it?**, ¿cómo diablos conseguiste hacerlo?

howl [haʊl] **I** *n* **1** *(cry)* aullido *m*. **2** *sl (funny thing, person)* **to be a h.**, ser la monda. **II** *vi* aullar; *fam* **to h. with laughter**, reír a carcajadas. ◆ **howl down** *vtr* abuchear.

howler ['haʊlə'] *n* *fam* despiste *m*; **to make a h.**, cometer una falta garrafal.

howling ['haʊlɪŋ] *n* *(of dogs, wolves)* aullido *m*; *(of wind)* rumor *m*.

HP, hp [eɪt∫'pi:] **I** *GB abbr of* **hire purchase**, compra *f* a plazos. **2** *abbr of* **horsepower**, **caballos** *mpl* de vapor, cv *mpl*.

HQ [eɪt∫'kju:] *Mil abbr of* **headquarters**, cuartel *m* general; *fig* centro *m* de operaciones.

hr *(pl* **hrs***)* *abbr of* **hour**, hora *f*, h.

HRH [eɪt∫ɑ:r'eɪt∫] *abbr of* **His/Her Royal Highness**, Su Alteza *mf* Real, **S.A.R.**

hub [hʌb] *n* **1** *Aut* cubo *m*. **2** *fig* eje *m*, centro *m*.

hubbub ['hʌbʌb] *n* alboroto *m*, jaleo *m*.

hubby ['hʌbɪ] *n* *fam* marido *m*.

hubcap ['hʌbkæp] *n* *Aut* tapacubos *m inv*.

huckleberry ['hʌkəlberɪ] *n* *Bot* arándano *m*.

huddle ['hʌdəl] **I** *n* grupo *m*; **a h. of people**, un grupo cerrado de gente; *fam* **to go into a h. about sth**, conferenciar en secreto sobre algo. **II** *vi* **to h. (up** *or* **together)**, acurrucarse.

Hudson Bay [hʌdsən'beɪ] *n* Bahía *f* de Hudson.

hue[hju:] *n (colour)* tinte *m*; *(shade)* matiz *m*; *fig* color *m*.

hue[2] [hju:] *n* **h. and cry**, fuerte protesta *f*.

huff [hʌf] **I** *n* enfado *m*; **to be in a h.**, estar de mala uva. **II** *vi* **to h. (and puff)**, resoplar.

huffy ['hʌfɪ] *adj (huffier, huffiest)* enojadizo,-a, malhumorado,-a.

hug [hʌg] **I** *vtr (pt* & *pp* **hugged***)* **1** abrazar, dar un abrazo a; *fig* **to h. oneself**, sentirse satisfecho,-a de sí mismo,-a. **2** *fig (coast, kerb)* pegarse a. **II** *n* abrazo *m*.

huge [hju:dʒ] *adj* enorme; **a h. building**, un edificio inmenso; **a h. success**, un exitazo. ◆ **hugely** *adv* enormemente.

huh [hʌ] *interj (showing surprise)* ¡vaya!, ¡caramba!; *(inquiry)* ¿eh?, ¿qué?

hulk [hʌlk] *n* **1** *Naut* casco *m*. **2** *(thing, person)* armatoste *m*.

hulking ['hʌlkɪŋ] *adj* grueso,-a, pesado,-a.

hull [hʌl] **I** *n* **1** *Naut* casco *m*. **2** *Bot (shell)* cáscara *f*; *(pod)* vaina *f*. **II** *vtr (fruit, peas)* desvainar.

hullaballoo [hʌləbə'lu:] *n* *fam* follón *m*, escándalo *m*, jaleo *m*.

hullo ['hʌ'ləʊ] *inter GB* ¡hola!; *Tel (when answering)* ¿diga?, ¿dígame?; *(when phoning)* ¡oiga!, ¡óigame!

hum [hʌm] **I** *vtr (pt* & *pp* **hummed***)* *(tune)* tararear. **II** *vi* **1** *(of bees, engine)* zumbar; *(sing)* tararear; *fig* **to h. and haw**, vacilar al hablar. **2** *sl (smell)* apestar. **III** *n (of bees)* zumbido *m*.

human ['hju:mən] *adj* humano,-a; **h. race**, raza *f* humana. ■ **h. being**, ser *m* humano. **II** *n* ser *m* humano. ◆ **humanly** *adv* humanamente; **to do everything h. possible**, hacer todo lo posible.

humane [hju:'meɪn] *adj* humano,-a; **toward a more h. society,** hacia una sociedad más humana. ■ *Univ* **h. studies,** humanidades *fpl.* ◆ **humanely** *adv* con humanidad, de una forma humana.

humanism ['hju:mənɪzəm] *n* humanismo *m*.

humanist ['hju:mənɪst] *adj & n* humanista *(mf)*.

humanitarian [hju:mænɪ'teərɪən] **1** *adj* humanitario,-a, filantrópico,-a. **II** *n* filántropo,-a *m,f*.

humanity [hju:'mænɪtɪ] *n* **1** *(mankind)* género *m* humano, raza *f* humana. **2** *(virtue)* humanidad *f.* **3** *Univ* **the humanities,** las humanidades.

humanoid ['hju:mənɔɪd] *n* humanoide *mf*.

humble ['hʌmbəl] **I** *adj* humilde; **in my h. opinion,** en mi modesta opinión; *fig* **to eat h. pie,** reconocer su error. **II** *vi* humillar. ◆ **humbly** *adv* humildemente.

humbleness ['hʌmbəlnɪs] *n* humildad *f*.

humbug ['hʌmbʌg] *n* **1** *fam (trick)* burla *f*, camelo *m*; **it's all h.,** son tonterías. **2** *(trickster)* embaucador,-a *m, f*, camelista *mf*, farsante *mf.* **3** *GB* **(mint) h.,** caramelo *m* de menta.

humdrum ['hʌmdrʌm] *adj* monótono,-a, aburrido,-a.

humerus ['hju:mərəs] *n (pl* **humeri** ['hju:mərai]*) Anat* húmero *m*.

humid ['hju:mɪd] *adj* húmedo,-a.

humidifier [hju:'mɪdɪfaɪə'] *n* humidificador *m*.

humidity [hju:'mɪdɪtɪ] *n* humedad *f*.

humiliate [hju:'mɪlɪeɪt] *vtr* humillar.

humiliation [hju:mɪlɪ'eɪʃən] *n* humillación *f*.

humility [hju:'mɪlɪtɪ] *n see* **humbleness**.

hummingbird ['hʌmɪŋbɜ:d] *n Orn* colibrí *m*.

humorist ['hju:mərɪst] *n* humorista *mf*.

humor ['hju:mə'] *n US see* **humour**.

humorous ['hju:mərəs] *adj (of writer)* humorístico,-a; *(of person, story)* gracioso,-a, divertido,-a.

humour ['hju:mə'] **I** *n* **1** humor *m*; **to see the h. in sth,** vere la gracia a algo. ■ **sense of h.,** sentido *m* del humor. **2** *(mood)* humor *m*; **ill/good h.,** mal/buen humor; **out of h.,** de mal humor; **to be in good/bad h.,** estar de buen/mal humor. **II** *vtr* seguir el humor a.

hump [hʌmp] **I** *n* **1** *(on back)* joroba *f*; *GB fam* **to have the h.,** estar deprimido,-a or chafado,-a. **2** *(small hill)* montículo *m.* **II** *vtr GB sl* cargar (a la espalda); **to h. coal,** cargar carbón.

humpback ['hʌmpbæk] *n* jorobado,-a *m,f.* ■ *GB Constr* **h. bridge,** puente *m* peraltado.

humus ['hju:məs] *n Agr* mantillo *m*, humus *m*.

Hun [hʌn] *n Hist* huno,-a *m,f*.

hunch [hʌntʃ] **I** *n fam* presentimiento *m*; **to act on one's hunches,** actuar por intuición; **to have a h.,** tener una corazonada. **II** *vtr* **to h. one's back,** encorvarse.

hunchback ['hʌntʃbæk] *n (person)* jorobado,-a *m,f*.

hundred ['hʌndrəd] **I** *n (pl* **hundred** or **hundreds)** cien *m*, ciento *m*; *(rough number)* centenar *m*; **a h. and twenty-five books,** ciento veinticinco libros; **by the hundreds,** a centenares; **five h.,** quinientos; **hundreds of soldiers,** centenares de soldados; **hundreds of trees,** cientos de árboles; **she lived in the sixteen hundreds,** vivió en el siglo dieciséis; **to live to be a h.,** llegar a los cien años. **II** *adj (inv)*; **a h. people,** cien personas; **a h. per cent,** cien por cien; **two h. chairs,** doscientas sillas; *fig* **to agree one h. per cent with sb,** estar totalmente de acuerdo con algn.

hundredth ['hʌndrədθ] **I** *adj* centésimo,-a; **for the h. time,** por centésima vez. **II** *n* centésimo *m*, centésima parte *f*.

hundredweight ['hʌndrədweɪt] *n (pl* **hundredweight** or **hundredweights)** ciento doce libras *fpl (≈ quindal m)*

hung [hʌŋ] **I** *pt & pp see* **hang**. **II** *adj* **1 h. jury,** jurado *m* cuyos miembros no se ponen de acuerdo. **2** *fam* **h. over,** con resaca; **he's still h. over from yesterday,** aún tiene

resaca de lo de ayer. **3** *fam* **h. up,** acomplejado,-a; *sl* **h. up on sb/sth,** obsesionado,-a con algn/algo. **4** *sl (man)* **well h.,** bien dotado.

Hungarian [hʌŋ'geərɪən] *adj & n* húngaro,-a *(m, f)*.

Hungary ['hʌŋgərɪ] *n* Hungría.

hunger ['hʌŋgə'] **I** *n* hambre *f.* ■ **h. strike,** huelga *f* de hambre. **II** *vi fig* tener bambre, estar hambriento,-a **(for,** de); ansiar **(for** *or* **after,** -).

hungry ['hʌŋgrɪ] *adj (***hungrier, hungriest)** hambriento,-a; **to be h.,** tener hambre; **to go h.,** pasar hambre; **to make h.,** dar hambre a, abrir el apetito a.

hunk [hʌŋk] *n* **1** *(large piece)* trozo *m* grueso, buen pedazo *m*; **a h. of bread,** un buen pedazo de pan. **2** *sl* **a h. (of a man),** un machote.

hunt [hʌnt] **I** *vtr* cazar. **II** *vi* **1** *(for game)* cazar. **2** *(search)* buscar; **to h. for sth/sb,** buscar algo/a algn; *fam* **we hunted high and low for it,** lo buscamos por todas partes. **III** *n* **1** *(gen)* caza *f; (expedition)* partida *f* de caza. **2** *(search)* búsqueda *f*; **they're on the h. for the killer,** van en busca del asesino. ◆ **hunt down** *vtr* perseguir, ir a la caza de. ◆ **hunt out, hunt up** *vtr (look for)* buscar; *(find)* encontrar.

hunter ['hʌntə'] *n* **1** *(person)* cazador,-a *m,f*; *fig* **bargain h.,** persona *f* que busca gangas en las rebajas; *fig* **fortune h.,** *(gen)* aventurero *m*; *(through marriage)* cazadotes *m inv*. **2** *Zool (horse)* caballo *m* de caza.

hunting ['hʌntɪŋ] *n (gen)* caza *f; (expedition)* cacería *f; fig* **a happy h. ground for stamp collectors,** un buen mercado para los coleccionistas de sellos. ■ **fox h.,** caza *f* del zorro; **h. ground,** terreno *m* or coto *m* de caza; **h. knife,** navaja *f* de monte.

huntsman ['hʌntsmən] *n (pl* **huntsmen)** cazador *m*.

hurdle ['hɜ:dəl] **I** *n* **1** *Athlet* valla *f*; **the 100 metres hurdles,** los 100 metros obstáculos. **2** *fig* obstáculo *m*. **II** *vtr Athlet (barrier etc)* saltar.

hurdler ['hɜ:dlə'] *n Athlet* corredor,-a *m,f* de obstáculos.

hurdling ['hɜ:dlɪŋ] *n Athlet* carrera *f* de obstáculos.

hurdy-gurdy ['hɜ:dɪgɜ:dɪ] *n Mus* organillo *m*.

hurl [hɜ:l] *vtr (object)* arrojar, lanzar; **to h. oneself,** tirarse **(from,** de); *fig* **to h. abuse at sb,** soltar una retahíla de insultos a algn, decir de todo a algn.

hurling ['hɜ:lɪŋ] *n Sport* juego *m* irlandés parecido al hockey y al lacrosse.

hurly-burly ['hɜ:lɪbɜ:lɪ] *n fam* alboroto *m*.

hurrah [hʊ'rɑ:] *interj* **hurray** [hʊ'reɪ] *interj* ¡hurra!, ¡olé!; **h. for John!,** ¡viva John!

hurricane ['hʌrɪkən, 'hʌrɪkeɪn] *n* huracán *m*. ■ **h. lamp,** farol *m*.

hurried [hʌrɪd] *adj* apresurado,-a, hecho,-a de prisa; **a h. letter,** una carta escrita deprisa; **a h. visit,** una visita apresurada. ◆ **hurriedly** *adv* deprisa, apresuradamente.

hurry ['hʌrɪ] **I** *vi (pt & pp* **hurried)** darse prisa, apresurarse; **he hurried through his work,** trabajó a toda prisa; **h. (up)!,** ¡date prisa! **II** *vtr* meter prisa; **don't h. us,** no nos metas prisa; **he was hurried (off) to hospital,** le llevaron urgentemente al hospital; **to h. a meal,** comer deprisa. **II** *n* prisa *f*; **are you in a h. for it?,** ¿le corre prisa?; **there's no h. for it,** no corre prisa; **to be in a h.,** tener prisa; **to do sth in a h.,** hacer algo de prisa; **to leave in a h.,** salir corriendo; **what's your h.?,** ¿tanta prisa tienes?; *fig* **I won't do it again in a h.,** la próxima vez me lo pensaré dos veces.

hurt [hɜ:t] **I** *vtr (pp & pt* **hurt)** **1** *(physically)* hacer daño a; *(wound)* herir; **she has h. her foot,** se ha hecho daño en el pie; **to h. oneself,** hacerse daño, lastimarse. **2** *(mentally)* herir, ofender; **her words h. me,** sus palabras me hirieron; **to h. sb's feelings,** ofender a algn. **II** *vi* **1** *(physically)* doler; **my arm hurts,** me duele el brazo; **where does it h. most?,** ¿dónde le duele más? **2** *(mentally)* escocer, doler; **the truth always hurts,** la verdad siempre duele. **3** *fam* venir or ir mal; **it doesn't h.**

to go out once in a while, no viene mal salir de vez en cuando; **it wouldn't h. for you to help,** no iría mal que echaras una mano. **III** *n* **1** *(physical)* herida *f.* **2** *(mental)* daño *m,* mal *m.* **IV** *adj* **1** *(physically)* herido,-a. **2** *(mentally)* dolido,-a; **a h. look,** una mirada dolida.

hurtful ['hɜːtfʊl] *adj* doloroso,-a, hiriente; **a h. remark,** una observación hiriente.

hurtle ['hɜːtəl] **I** *vi* lanzarse, precipitarse; **to h. down,** precipitarse *or* caer violentamente. **II** *vtr* lanzar.

husband ['hʌzbənd] *n* marido *m,* esposo *m.*

husbandry ['hʌzbəndrɪ] *n* agricultura *f.*

hush [hʌʃ] **I** *vtr* callar, silenciar; **to h. sth up,** echar tierra a un asunto. **II** *n* silencio *m.* ■ *sl* **h. money,** soborno *m,* cohecho *m.* **III** *interj* ¡silencio!, ¡chito!

hush-hush [hʌʃ'hʌʃ] *adj fam* confidencial, secreto,-a.

husk [hʌsk] **I** *n (of nuts, cereals)* cáscara *f; (of peas, beans)* vaina *f.* **II** *vtr* pelar.

huskiness ['hʌskɪnɪs] *n* ronquera *f.*

husky¹ ['hʌskɪ] *adj (huskier, huskiest)* ronco,-a; **a h. voice,** una voz profunda.

husky² ['hʌskɪ] *n Zool* perro *m* esquimal.

hussar [hʊ'zɑː] *n Mil* húsar *m.*

hussy ['hʌzɪ, 'hʌsɪ] *n fam (woman)* iresca *f.*

hustings ['hʌstɪŋz] *npl Pol* **1** *(platform)* tribuna *f sing* electoral. **2** *(election)* elecciones *fpl;* **at the h.,** durante la campaña electoral.

hustle ['hʌsəl] **I** *vtr* **1** *(jostle)* empujar, dar empujones. **2** *fam* apurar, apremiar. **3** *sl* apañarse, hacerse con. **II** *n* apaño *m,* bullicio *m;* **h. and bustle,** ajetreo *m.*

hustler ['hʌslə'] *n* **1** *(swindler)* estafador,-a *m,f,* timador,-a *m,f.* **2** *US sl (female prostitute)* puta *f.*

hut [hʌt] *n (gen)* cabaña *f; (garden shed)* cobertizo *m; Mil* barraca *f.*

hutch [hʌtʃ] *n* **1** *(cage)* jaula *f.* ■ **rabbit h.,** conejera *f.* **2** *fam pej* ratonera *f.*

hyacinth ['haɪəsɪnθ] *n Bot* jacinto *m.*

hybrid ['haɪbrɪd] *adj & n* híbrido,-a *(m, f).*

hydrangea [haɪ'dreɪndʒə] *n Bot* hortensia *f.*

hydrant ['haɪdrənt] *n* boca *f* de riego. ■ **fire h.,** boca *f* de incendio.

hydraulic [haɪ'drɒlɪk] *adj* hidráulico,-a; **h. power,** fuerza hidráulica. ■ **h. brake,** freno *m* hidráulico; **h. suspension** suspensión *f* hidráulica.

hydraulics [haɪ'drɒlɪks] *n* hidráulica *f.*

hydric ['haɪdrɪk] *adj* hídrico,-a.

hydro¹ ['haɪdrəʊ] *n (pl hydros) GB (spa)* balneario *m,* estación *f* termal.

hydro² ['haɪdrəʊ] *adj abbr of* **hydroelectric.**

hydrocarbon [haɪdrəʊ'kɑːbən] *n Chem* hidrocarburo *m.*

hydrochloric [haɪdrəʊ'klɒrɪk] *adj Chem* clorhídrico,-a. ■ **h. acid,** ácido *m* clorhídrico.

hydroelectric [haɪdrəʊɪ'lektrɪk] *adj* hidroeléctrico,-a. ■ **h. power station,** central *f* hidroeléctrica.

hydroelectricity [haɪdrəʊɪlek'trɪsɪtɪ] *n* hidroelectricidad *f.*

hydrofoil ['haɪdrəfɔɪl] *n* hidroala *f.*

hydrogen ['haɪdrɪdʒən] *n Chem* hidrógeno *m.* ■ **h. bomb,** bomba *f* de hidrógeno; **h. chloride,** ácido *m* clorhídrico; **h. peroxide,** agua *f* oxigenada.

hydrographer [haɪ'drɒgrəfə'] *n* hidrógrafo,-a *m,f.*

hydrography [haɪ'drɒgrəfɪ] *n* hidrografía *f.*

hydrolysis [haɪ'drɒlɪsɪs] *n Chem* hidrólisis *f.*

hydrophobia [haɪdrə'fəʊbɪə] *n Med* hidrofobia *f.*

hydroplane ['haɪdrəʊpleɪn] *n Av* hidroavión *m,* hidroplano *m.*

hydroponics [haɪdrəʊ'pɒnɪks] *n* hidroponía *f.*

hydrotherapy [haɪdrəʊ'θerəpɪ] *n Med* hidroterapia *f.*

hyena [haɪ'iːnə] *n Zool* hiena *f.* ■ **laughing h.,** hiena *f* manchada.

hygiene ['haɪdʒiːn] *n* higiene *f.*

hygienic [haɪ'dʒiːnɪk] *adj* higiénico,-a.

hygrometer [haɪ'grɒmɪtə'] *n* higrómetro *m.*

hymen ['haɪmen] *n Anat* himen *m.*

hymn [hɪm] *n* himno *m.* ■ **h. book,** cantoral *m.*

hymnal ['hɪmnəl] *n* cantoral *m.*

hype¹ [haɪp] *sl* **I** *vi* **to h. (up),** *(shoot up)* chutarse; *(get high)* colocarse. **II** *vtr* estimular, excitar; *fig* **hyped up,** excitado,-a.

hype² [haɪp] *n sl* campaña *f* publicitaria, movida *f.*

hyper- ['haɪpə'] *pref* hiper-; **hyperactive,** hiperactivo,-a.

hyperbola [haɪ'pɜːbələ] *n (pl hyperbolas or hyperbole* [haɪ'pɜːbəliː]*)* hipérbola *f.*

hyperbole [haɪ'pɜːbəlɪ] *n* hipérbole *f.*

hypercritical [haɪpə'krɪtɪkəl] *adj* hipercrítico,-a.

hypermarket ['haɪpəmɑːkɪt] *n GB* hipermercado *m.*

hypersensitive [haɪpə'sensɪtɪv] *adj* hipersensible.

hypertension [haɪpə'tenʃən] *n Med* hipertensión *f.*

hyphen ['haɪfən] *n* guión *m.*

hyphenate ['haɪfəneɪt] *vtr (gen)* escribir con guión; *(write together)* unir con guión; *(separate)* separar con guión.

hypnosis [hɪp'nəʊsɪs] *n (pl hypnoses* [hɪp'nəʊsiːz]*) Med* hipnosis *f.*

hypnotic [hɪp'nɒtɪk] *adj* hipnótico,-a.

hypnotism ['hɪpnətɪzəm] *n* hipnotismo *m.*

hypnotist ['hɪpnətɪst] *n* hipnotizador,-a *m,f.*

hypnotize ['hɪpnətaɪz] *vtr* hipnotizar.

hypo ['haɪpəʊ] *n Phot* fijador *m.*

hypo- ['haɪpəʊ] *pref* hipo-.

hypoallergenic [haɪpəʊælɜː'dʒenɪk] *adj (cosmetics etc)* hipoalérgico,-a.

hypochondria [haɪpə'kɒndrɪə] *n* hipocondría *f.*

hypochondriac [haɪpə'kɒndrɪæk] *adj & n* hipocondríaco,-a *(m, f).*

hypocrisy [hɪ'pɒkrəsɪ] *n* hipocresía *f.*

hypocrite ['hɪpəkrɪt] *n* hipócrita *mf.*

hypocritical [hɪpə'krɪtɪkəl] *adj* hipócrita.

hypodermic [haɪpə'dɜːmɪk] *adj Med* hipodérmico,-a; **h. needle/syringe,** aguja/jennga hipodérmica.

hypotension [haɪpəʊ'tenʃən] *n Med* hipotensión *f.*

hypotenuse [haɪ'pɒtɪnjuːz] *n Geom* hipotenusa *f.*

hypothermia [haɪpəʊ'θɜːmɪə] *n Med* hipotermia *f.*

hypothesis [haɪ'pɒθɪsɪs] *n (pl hypotheses* [haɪ'pɒθɪsiːz]*)* hipótesis *f.*

hypothetic(al) [haɪpə'θetɪk(əl)] *adj* hipotético,-a

hysterectomy [hɪstə'rektəmɪ] *n Med* histerectomía *f.*

hysteria [hɪ'stɪərɪə] *n Psych* histeria *f.*

hysterical [hɪ'sterɪkəl] *adj* histérico,-a, **h. laughter,** risa convulsiva. ◆ **hysterically** *adv* histéricamente

hysterics [hɪ'sterɪks] *n or npl* **1** *(attack)* ataque *m* de histeria. **2** *fam (of laughter)* ataque *m* de risa; **to have h.,** mondarse de risa.

HZ *abbr of* **hertz,** hercio(s) *m(pl),* Hz.

I

I, i [aɪ] n (the letter) I, i f

I [aɪ] pers pron yo, **I know her,** la conozco; **I know him but you don't,** yo lo conozco pero tú no

IATA [aɪ'ɑːtə] abbr of **International Air Transport Association,** Asociación f del Transporte Aéreo Internacional, IATA f.

IBA [aɪbiː'eɪ] GB abbr of **Independent Broadcasting Authority,** compañía f independiente de radiodifusión.

Iberia [aɪ'bɪərɪə] n Iberia.

Iberian [aɪ'bɪərɪən] **I** adj ibérico,-a. **II** n Hist (person) ibero,-a m, f.

ICBM [aɪsiːbiː'em] Mil abbr of **intercontinental ballistic missile,** proyectil m balístico intercontinental, PBI m.

ice [aɪs] **I** n (frozen water) hielo m, (ice cream) helado m; **a lemon ice,** un helado de limón; fig **my feet are like i.,** tengo los pies helados, fig **to break the i.,** romper el hielo; fig **to cut tittle** or **no i. with sb,** dejar frío,-a a algn, fig **to put** or **keep sth on i.,** (project) postergar algo, (suggestion, idea) tener algo de reserva; fig **to skate on thin i.,** pisar un terreno resbaladizo. ■ **black i.,** hielo m invisible; **i. axe,** pico m or piqueta f (de alpinista), **i. cream,** helado m; **i.-cream parlour,** heladería f, **i. cube,** cubito m de hielo; **i. floe,** témpano m, **i. hockey,** hockey m sobre hielo; **i. lolly,** polo m; **i. pack,** bolsa f de hielo; **i. rink,** pista f de patinaje; **i. show,** espectáculo m sobre hielo, **i. skate,** patín m de cuchilla. **II** vtr **1** (drink) poner hielo en. **2** (cake etc) alcorzar, glasear ◆ **ice over, ice up** vi (pond etc) helarse, (windscreen, plane wings) cubrirse de hielo

iceberg ['aɪsbɜːg] n iceberg m, témpano m

icebound ['aɪsbaʊnd] adj (harbour, road) obstruido,-a or bloqueado,-a por el hielo, (ship) atrapado,-a por el hielo

icebox ['aɪsbɒks] n **1** (compartment of fridge) congelador m. **2** US (fridge) nevera f, frigorífico m

icebreaker ['aɪsbreɪkə'] n Naut rompehielos m inv.

icecap ['aɪskæp] n casquete m glaciar

ice-cold ['aɪskəʊld] adj helado,-a

iced [aɪst] adj **1** (drink) con hielo **2** (cake etc) glaseado,-a

Iceland ['aɪslənd] n Islandia

Icelander ['aɪsləndə'] n islandés,-esa m, f

Icelandic [aɪs'lændɪk] **I** adj islandés,-esa. **II** n (language) islandés m

ice-skate ['aɪsskeɪt] vi patinar sobre hielo

ice-skater ['aɪsskeɪtə'] n patinador,-a m, f sobre hielo.

ice-skating ['aɪsskeɪtɪŋ] n patinaje m sobre hielo.

icicle ['aɪsɪkəl] n carámbano m

icing ['aɪsɪŋ] n Culin alcorza f, azúcar m glas, fig **the i. on the cake,** remate m, guinda f. ■ **i. sugar,** azúcar m glas or lustre

icon ['aɪkɒn] n icono m.

iconoclast [aɪ'kɒnəklæst] n iconoclasta mf

iconoclastic [aɪkɒnə'klæstɪk] adj iconoclasta

icy ['aɪsɪ] adj (icier, iciest) **1** (road etc) helado,-a, cubierto,-a de hielo. **2** fig (hands, feet) helado,-a; (wrind, smile) glacial.

ID [aɪ'diː] US abbr of **identification, identity,** identificación f, identidad f; **ID card,** documento m nacional de identidad, DNI m.

I'd [aɪd] = **I would, I had.**

idea [aɪ'dɪə] n **1** (thought) idea f; (opinion) idea f, opinión f, (concept) concepto m; **I haven't the faintest** or **foggiest i.,** no tengo ni la menor or la más mínima idea; **I've got an i.,** tengo una idea, se me ocurre una idea, **the (very) i. of it!,** ¡vaya or qué ocurrencia!, **to put ideas into sb's head,** meter ideas en la cabeza a algn, **vague i.,** ligera idea, **what gave you that i.?,** ¿cómo se te ocurrió pensar eso? **2** (aim) idea f, intención f, **the i. is to save money,** la idea es ahorrar dinero; fam **that's the i.!,** ¡eso es! ¡así se hace!, fam **what's the big i.?,** ¿a qué viene eso? **3** (impression) impresión f, idea f, **some i. (of) what it's about,** una idea aproximada de lo que se trata, **to have an i. that ...,** tener la impresión (de) que

ideal [aɪ'dɪəl] **I** adj ideal **II** n **1** (example) ideal m (of, de). **2** (principle) ideal m, principio m. ◆ **ideally** adv **1** (perfectly) idealmente, perfectamente, **they're i. suited (to each other),** forman una pareja perfecta, están hechos el uno para el otro. **2** (in the best conditions) en el mejor de los casos, de ser posible, si es posible; **i., we should start now,** lo ideal sería que empezáramos ahora.

idealism [aɪ'dɪəlɪzəm] n idealismo m

idealist [aɪ'dɪəlɪst] n idealista mf

idealistic [aɪdɪə'lɪstɪk] adj idealista

idealize [aɪ'dɪəlaɪz] vtr idealizar

identical [aɪ'dentɪkəl] adj idéntico,-a

identification [aɪdentɪfɪ'keɪʃən] n **1** (gen) identificación f. ■ GB **i. parade,** rueda f de identificación or reconocimiento. **2** (papers etc) documentación f

identify [aɪ'dentɪfaɪ] **I** vtr (pt & pp identified) **1** (suspect, body) identificar; **he was identified with the Labour Party,** se le relacionaba con el partido laborista. **2** (cause, source) descubrir, averiguar. **II** vi (hero, cause) identificarse (**with,** con).

identikit® [aɪ'dentɪkɪt] n **1. picture,** retrato m robot.

identity [aɪ'dentɪtɪ] n identidad f. ■ **i. card,** carné m de identidad; **proof of i.,** prueba f de identidad.

ideological [aɪdɪə'lɒdʒɪkəl] adj ideológico,-a.

ideology [aɪdɪ'ɒlədʒɪ] n ideología f.

idiocy ['ɪdɪəsɪ] n idiotez f.

idiom ['ɪdɪəm] n **1** (expression) modismo m, locución f, frase f hecha. **2** fig (style) lenguaje m, estilo m.

idiomatic [ɪdɪə'mætɪk] adj idiomático,-a; **i. expression,** modismo m, locución f, frase f hecha.

idiosyncrasy [ɪdɪəʊ'sɪŋkrəsɪ] n idiosincrasia f.

idiosyncratic [ɪdɪəsɪŋ'krætɪk] adj idiosincrásico,-a.

idiot ['ɪdɪət] n **1** (stupid person) idiota mf, tonto,-a m, f, imbécil mf. **2** Med pej (imbecile) idiota mf, subnormal mf.

idiotic [ɪdɪ'ɒtɪk] adj (person, behaviour) idiota, imbécil, tonto,-a; (joke, plan) estúpido,-a.

idle ['aɪdəl] **I** adj **1** (lazy) perezoso,-a, holgazán,-ana, vago,-a; fam **he's bone i.,** no da golpe. **2** (at leisure) ocioso,-a; **i. moment,** momento m libre; **I went out of i. curiosity,** fui por pura curiosidad. **3** (not working) (person) desempleado,-a, sin trabajo; (machinery) parado,-a; (capital) improductivo,-a. **4** (gossip, talk) frívolo,-a; (threat, hope) vano,-a; (fear, suspicion) infundado,-a. **II** vi (engine) funcionar en vacío. ◆ **idle away** vtr (time) desperdiciar.

idleness ['aɪdəlnɪs] n **1** (laziness) pereza f, holgazanería f, vagancia f. **2** (leisure) ociosidad f. **3** (unemployment) desempleo m, paro m; (stoppage) paro m. **4** (groundlessness) falta f de base; (of gossip etc) frivolidad f; (of threat etc) futilidad f.

idol [aɪdəl] n ídolo m.

idolatry [aɪ'dɒlətrɪ] n idolatría f.

idolize ['aɪdəlaɪz] vtr idolatrar.

idyll ['ɪdɪl] *n* idilio *m*.

idyllic [ɪ'dɪlɪk] *adj* idílico,-a.

ie *abbr of* **id est** (that is to say), esto es, a saber, i.e.

if [ɪf] **I** *conj* **1** *(supposing)* si; **as if**, como si; **as if by magic**, como por ensalmo; **it's not as if I'm rich**, no soy rico, ni mucho menos; **if at all**, si acaso; **if ever**, raras veces, por no decir nunca; **if I were rich**, si fuera rico,-a; **if necessary**, (en) caso de que sea necesario; **if not**, sino; **if so**, si es así, de ser así; **if I were you**, yo en tu lugar, yo que tú; **I would appreciate it if you could come**, te agradecería que vinieras; **she's tall if anything**, es más bien alta. **2** *(whenever)* si, cuandoquiera que; **if you need help, ask**, siempre que necesites ayuda, pídela. **3** *(although)* aunque, si bien; **the film's good, if a bit long**, la película es buena aunque un poco larga. **4** *(whether)* si; **I don't know if I can go**, no sé si puedo ir. **5** *(in exclamations)* **if only I'd known!**, ¡si lo hubiera sabido!, ¡de haberlo sabido!; **if only she were here!**, ¡ojalá estuviera aquí!; **well, if it isn't David!**, ¡pero si es David! **II** *n* **ifs and buts**, pegas *fpl*; **it's a big if**, es muy dudoso.

iffy ['ɪfɪ] *adj fam* dudoso,-a.

igloo ['ɪgluː] *n* (*pl igloos*) iglú *m*.

ignite [ɪg'naɪt] **I** *vtr* encender, prender fuego a. **II** *vi* encenderse, prender.

ignition [ɪg'nɪʃən] *n* ignición *f*; *Aut* encendido *m*, arranque *m*. **■ i. key**, llave *f* de contacto.

ignoble [ɪg'nəʊbəl] *adj* innoble, vil, infame.

ignominious [ɪgnə'mɪnɪəs] *adj* ignominioso,-a, vergonzoso,-a.

ignominy ['ɪgnəmɪnɪ] *n fml* ignominia *f*, oprobio *m*.

ignoramus [ɪgnə'reɪməs] *n* ignorante *mf*.

ignorance ['ɪgnərəns] *n* ignorancia *f*; **to be in i. of sth**, ignorar *or* desconocer *or* no saber algo; **to keep sb in i. of sth**, ocultarle algo a algn, tener a algn en la ignorancia (de algo).

ignorant ['ɪgnərənt] *adj* ignorante (**of**, de); **to be i. of the facts**, ignorar *or* desconocer los hechos.

ignore [ɪg'nɔː'] *vtr* *(warning, remark)* no hacer caso de, hacer caso omiso de; *(behaviour, fact)* pasar por alto; *(letter, message)* dejar sin contestar; **whenever we met, he ignored me**, siempre que nos encontrábamos, solía hacer como si no me viera.

iguana [ɪ'gwɑːnə] *n Zool* iguana *f*.

ilk [ɪlk] *n* **of that i.**, de esa clase *or* índole.

ill [ɪl] **I** *adj* **1** *(sick)* enfermo,-a; **to fall** *or* **be taken i.**, caer *or* ponerse enfermo,-a; **to feel i.**, encontrarse *or* sentirse mal; **to look i.**, hacer mala cara, tener mal aspecto. **2** *(bad)* malo,-a; **i. feeling**, resentimiento; **i. will**, mala voluntad; **I bear you no i. will**, no le guardo ningún rencor; **to suffer from i. health**, estar mal de salud, ser enfermizo,-a; *prov* **it's an i. wind (that blows nobody any good)**, no hay mal que por bien no venga. **II** *n* *(evil)* mal *m*; *(misfortune)* desgracia *f*. **III** *adv* difícilmente; **I can i. afford it**, a duras penas puedo permitírmelo; **to be i. received**, ser mal recibido,-a.

I'll [aɪl] ≈ **I shall**; **I will**.

ill-advised [ɪləd'vaɪzd] *adj (person)* mal aconsejado,-a, imprudente; *(act, remark)* desatinado,-a, poco acertado,-a; **you'd be i.-a. to go**, harías mal en ir.

ill-bred [ɪl'bred] *adj* maleducado,-a, malcriado,-a.

ill-considered [ɪlkən'sɪdəd] *adj* poco pensado,-a, imprudente.

ill-disposed [ɪldɪ'spəʊzd] *adj* mal *or* poco dispuesto,-a; **to be i.-d. towards sb**, tenerla tomada con algn.

illegal [ɪ'liːgəl] *adj* ilegal.

illegality [ɪlɪ'gælɪtɪ] *n* ilegalidad *f*.

illegible [ɪ'ledʒɪbəl] *adj* ilegible.

illegitimacy [ɪlɪ'dʒɪtɪməsɪ] *n* ilegitimidad *f*.

illegitimate [ɪlɪ'dʒɪtɪmɪt] *adj* ilegítimo,-a.

ill-equipped [ɪlɪ'kwɪpt] *adj* mal equipado,-a; *fig* mal preparado,-a.

ill-fated [ɪl'feɪtɪd] *adj* fatal, desdichado,-a, desafortunado,-a.

ill-founded [ɪl'faʊndɪd] *adj (fear, suspicion)* infundado,-a; *(hope, ambition)* vano,-a.

ill-gotten [ɪl'gɒtən] *adj fml* **i.-g. gains**, bienes *mpl* mal adquiridos.

illicit [ɪ'lɪsɪt] *adj* ilícito,-a.

illiteracy [ɪ'lɪtərəsɪ] *n* analfabetismo *m*.

illiterate [ɪ'lɪtərɪt] **I** *adj* **1**(*person*) *(unlettered)* analfabeto,-a; *fam (uneducate)* ignorante, inculto,-a. **2** *(style)* *(poor)* inculto,-a, pobre. **II** *n* *(unlettered person)* analfabeto,-a *m*, *f*.

illness ['ɪlnɪs] *n* enfermedad *f*.

illogical [ɪ'lɒdʒɪkəl] *adj* ilógico,-a.

ill-suited [ɪl'suːtɪd] *adj* que no congenian.

ill-timed [ɪl'taɪmd] *adj* inoportuno,-a.

ill-treat [ɪl'triːt] *vtr* maltratar.

ill-treatment [ɪl'triːtmənt] *n* malos tratos *mpl*, maltrato *m*.

illuminate [ɪ'luːmɪneɪt] *vtr* **1** *(light up)* iluminar, alumbrar. **2** *fig (clarify)* aclarar. **3** *(manuscript)* iluminar.

illuminating [ɪ'luːmɪneɪtɪŋ] *adj (experience, book)* instructivo,-a; *(remark)* revelador,-a.

illumination [ɪluːmɪ'neɪʃən] *n* **1** *(lighting up)* iluminación *f*, alumbrado *m*. **2** *fig (clarification)* aclaración *f*. **3** *GB* **illuminations**, *(coloured lights)* iluminación *f sing*. **4** *(of manuscript)* iluminación *f*.

illusion [ɪ'luːʒən] *n* ilusión *f*; **to be under the i. that ...**, estar equivocado,-a *or* engañarse pensando que ... .

illusive [ɪ'luːsɪv] *adj*, **illusory** [ɪ'luːsərɪ] *adj* ilusorio,-a.

illustrate ['ɪləstreɪt] *vtr (gen)* ilustrar; *fig (point, theory)* aclarar.

illustration [ɪlə'streɪʃən] *(gen)* ilustración *f*; *fig (clarification)* aclaración *f*; *(example)* ejemplo *m*.

illustrative ['ɪləstrətɪv] *adj (gen)* ilustrativo,-a, ilustrador,-a; *fig (example)* aclaratorio,-a.

illustrator ['ɪləstreɪtə'] *n* ilustrador,-a *m*, *f*.

illustrious [ɪ'lʌstrɪəs] *adj* ilustre.

ILO [aɪel'əʊ] *abbr of* **International Labour Organization**, Organización *f* Internacional del Trabajo, OIT *f*.

I'm [aɪm] = **I am**.

image ['ɪmɪdʒ] *n* **1** *(gen)* imagen *f*; *fam* **he's the living** *or* **spitting i. of his father**, es el vivo retrato de su padre. **2** *(reputation)* imagen *f*, fama *f*, reputación *f*.

imagery ['ɪmɪdʒərɪ] *n Lit* imágenes *fpl*.

imaginable [ɪ'mædʒɪnəbəl] *adj* imaginable, concebible.

imaginary [ɪ'mædʒɪnərɪ] *adj* imaginario,-a.

imagination [ɪmædʒɪ'neɪʃən] *n (gen)* imaginación *f*; *(inventiveness)* inventiva *f*; **don't let your i. run away with you**, no te dejes llevar por la imaginación; **it's a figment of your i.**, son imaginaciones tuyas.

imaginative [ɪ'mædʒɪnətɪv] *adj (person)* imaginativo,-a, de gran inventiva; *(writing, decor)* lleno,-a de imaginación *or* fantasía.

imagine [ɪ'mædʒɪn] *vtr* **1** *(visualize)* imaginar; **I can't i. what it is**, no tengo ni idea de lo que es. **2** *(think)* suponer, figurarse, imaginarse; **just i.!**, ¡imagínate!, ¡fíjate!

imbalance [ɪm'bæləns] *n* falta *f* de equilibrio, desequilibrio *m*.

imbecile ['ɪmbɪsiːl] *n* imbécil *mf*.

imbibe [ɪm'baɪb] *vtr* **1** *fml (alcohol etc)* beber. **2** *fig (ideas, knowledge)* asimilar, empaparse de, absorber.

imbue [ɪm'bjuː] *vtr fml* **to i. sb with sth**, imbuir a algn de algo; **imbued with hope**, lleno,-a de esperanza.

IMF [aɪem'ef] *Econ abbr of* **International Monetary Fund**, Fondo *m* Monetario Internacional, FMI *m*.

imitate ['ɪmɪteɪt] *vtr (gen)* imitar, copiar; *pej* parodiar, remedar.

imitation [ɪmɪ'teɪʃən] **I** *n (gen)* imitación *f*, copia *f*; *pej* parodia *f*, remedo *m*; *Com* **'beware of imitations'**, 'desconfíe de las imitaciones'. **II** *adj* de imitación.

imitative ['ɪmɪtətɪv] *adj* imitativo,-a.

imitator ['ɪmɪteɪtəʳ] *n* imitador,-a *m,f*.

immaculate [ɪ'mækjʊlɪt] *adj (clean)* inmaculado,-a; *(tidy)* perfectamente ordenado,-a; *(clothes, appearance)* impecable; *(work)* perfecto,-a; *Rel* the **1. Conception,** la Inmaculada Concepción, la Purísima.

immaterial [ɪmə'tɪərɪəl] *adj* irrelevante; **it's i. to me whether ...,** me trae sin cuidado *or* me es indiferente si ...; **my views are i.,** lo que opino yo no tiene nada que ver *or* no viene al caso.

immature [ɪmə'tjʊəʳ] *adj* inmaduro,-a.

immaturity [ɪmə'tjʊərɪtɪ] *n* inmadurez *f*, falta *f* de madurez.

immeasurable [ɪ'meʒərəbəl] *adj* inconmensurable, incalculable.

immediacy [ɪ'miːdɪəsɪ] *n* **1** *(urgency)* urgencia *f*, carácter *m* urgente. **2** *(closeness)* inmediación *f*, proximidad *f*.

immediate [ɪ'miːdɪət] *adj* **1** *(instant)* inmediato,-a; *(urgent)* urgente; **i. need,** primera necesidad; **to have i. rapport (with sb),** simpatizar en seguida (con algn); **to take i. action,** actuar inmediatamente. **2** *(close)* (area, family) cercano,-a, próximo,-a; *(danger)* inminente; **the i. vicinity,** las inmediaciones. **3** *(direct)* (cause) primero,-a, principal; *(heir)* en línea directa. ◆ **immediately I** *adv* **1** *(at once)* inmediatamente, de inmediato, en seguida, en el acto; **i. after arriving,** inmediatamente después de llegar; **I i. left,** acto seguido, me marché. **2** *(directly)* directamente; **i. in front of/behind,** directamente delante/detrás. **II** *conj* en cuanto, tan pronto como; **i. I sat down, the waiter came,** en cuanto me senté vino el camarero.

immemorial [ɪmɪ'mɔːrɪəl] *adj* inmemorial.

immense [ɪ'mens] *adj* inmenso,-a, enorme. ◆ **immensely** *adv (rich, gifted)* enormemente; *(interesting, difficult)* sumamente; **to enjoy oneself i.,** disfrutar muchísimo, pasarlo en grande.

immensity [ɪ'mensɪtɪ] *n* inmensidad *f*.

immerse [ɪ'mɜːs] *vtr* sumergir, hundir (**in,** en); *fig* **to be immersed in one's work,** estar absorto,-a en el trabajo.

immersion [ɪ'mɜːʃən] *n (in water etc)* inmersión *f*, sumersión *f*; *fig (in work etc)* absorción *f*, enfrascamiento *m*. ■ **i. course,** cursillo *m* intensivo; *GB* **i. heater,** calentador *m* de inmersión.

immigrant ['ɪmɪgrənt] *adj & n* inmigrante *(mf)*.

immigration [ɪmɪ'greɪʃən] *n* inmigración *f*.

imminence ['ɪmɪnəns] *n fml* inminencia *f*.

imminent ['ɪmɪnənt] *adj* inminente.

immobile [ɪ'məʊbaɪl] *adj* inmóvil, sin movimiento.

immobility [ɪməʊ'bɪlɪtɪ] *n* inmovilidad *f*.

immobilize [ɪ'məʊbɪlaɪz] *vtr* inmovilizar; *fig* **he was immobilized by lack of funds,** su proyecto estaba paralizado por falta de fondos.

immoderate [ɪ'mɒdərɪt] *adj fml (views, conduct)* desmedido,-a; *(desire, appetite)* descomunal, desaforado,-a; *(demands)* excesivo,-a.

immodest [ɪ'mɒdɪst] *adj* **1** *(indecent)* indecente; *(act)* desvergonzado,-a, descarado,-a, impúdico,-a. **2** *(presumptuous)* presumido,-a, creído,-a, engreído,-a.

immodesty [ɪ'mɒdɪstɪ] *n* **1** *(indecency)* indecencia *f*, falta *f* de pudor; *(of act)* descaro *m*. **2** *(presumption)* presunción *f*, engreimiento *m*.

immoral [ɪ'mɒrəl] *adj* inmoral; **i. earnings,** ganancias *fpl* ilícitas.

immorality [ɪmə'rælɪtɪ] *n* inmoralidad *f*.

immortal [ɪ'mɔːtəl] *adj (soul, god)* inmortal; *(fame, memory)* imperecedero,-a. perdurable.

immortality [ɪmɔː'tælɪtɪ] *n* inmortalidad *f*.

immortalize [ɪ'mɔːtəlaɪz] *vtr* inmortalizar.

immovable [ɪ'muːvəbəl] *adj* **1** *(fixed)* inamovible; *(feast)* fijo,-a. **2** *fig (person)* inconmovible, inflexible; *(impassive)* impasible, inmutable.

immune [ɪ'mjuːn] *adj (gen)* inmune; *(exempt)* exento,-a; **to be i. from attack,** no correr riesgo de set atacado,-a.

immunity [ɪ'mjuːnɪtɪ] *n (gen)* inmunidad *f*; *(exemption)* exención *f*. ■ **diplomatic i.,** inmunidad *f* diplomática.

immunization [ɪmjʊnəˈɪzeɪʃən] *n Med* inmunización *f*.

immunize ['ɪmjʊnaɪz] *vtr Med* inmunizar (**against,** contra).

immutable [ɪ'mjuːtəbəl] *adj fml* inmutable, inalterable.

imp [ɪmp] *n (small devil)* diablillo *m*, duendecillo *m*; *fig (mischievous child)* diablillo *m*, pillo,-a *m,f*.

impact ['ɪmpækt] *n (gen)* impacto *m*; *(crash)* choque *m*; *(influence)* efecto *m*; **on i.,** al chocar; *fig* **the poem had** *or* **made a great i. on me,** el poema me produjo un gran impacto, el poema me impresionó mucho.

impacted [ɪm'æktɪd] *adj (tooth)* impactado,-a.

impair [ɪm'peəʳ] *vtr (health, efforts)* perjudicar, debilitar; *(sight etc)* dañar; *(quality)* alterar; *(efficiency)* disminuir.

impale [ɪm'peɪl] *vtr (with sword etc)* atravesar.

impart [ɪm'pɑːt] *vtr fml (news, information)* comunicar, hacer saber; *(skill, knowledge)* impartir, transmitir; *(flavour)* desprender.

impartial [ɪm'pɑːʃəl] *adj* imparcial.

impartiality [ɪmpɑːʃɪ'ælɪtɪ] *n* imparcialidad *f*.

impassable [ɪm'pɑːsəbəl] *adj (road, ground)* intransitable, impracticable; *(barrier)* infranqueable.

impasse [æm'pɑːs] *n* impasse *m*, punto *m* muerto.

impassioned [ɪm'pæʃənd] *adj (gen)* apasionado,-a, exaltado,-a; *(debate)* acalorado,-a.

impassive [ɪm'pæsɪv] *adj (expressionless)* impasible, impávido,-a, imperturbable; *(indifferent)* indiferente.

impatience [ɪm'peɪʃəns] *n* impaciencia *f*.

impatient [ɪm'peɪʃənt] *adj (intolerant)* impaciente; *(fretful)* irritable, nervioso,-a; *(eager)* impaciente, ansioso,-a; **to get i. with sb,** perder la paciencia con algn.

impeach [ɪm'piːtʃ] *vtr* **1** *Jur (denounce)* acusar, denunciar; *(try)* procesar. **2** *(question)* poner en tela de juicio.

impeachment [ɪm'piːtʃmənt] *n Jur* denuncia *f*, acusación *f*; *(trial)* proceso *m*.

impeccable [ɪm'pekəbəl] *adj* impecable.

impecunious [ɪmpɪ'kjuːnɪəs] *adj* falto,-a de dinero, necesitado,-a.

impede [ɪm'piːd] *vtr (prevent)* impedir; *(hinder)* estorbar, dificultar; *(obstruct)* poner obstáculos *or* trabas a.

impediment [ɪm'pedɪmənt] *n (gen)* impedimento *m*; *(obstacle)* estorbo *m*, obstáculo *m*; **speech i.,** defecto *m* del habla.

impel [ɪm'pel] *vtr (pt & pp impelled) (compel)* obligar (**to,** a); *(urge)* incitar (**to,** a).

impending [ɪm'pendɪŋ] *adj fml* inminente.

impenetrable [ɪm'penɪtrəbəl] *adj (gen)* impenetrable; *fig (mystery, thoughts)* insondable; *(character, smile)* inescrutable.

imperative [ɪm'perətɪv] **I** *adj* **1** *fml (gen)* imperativo,-a; *(tone, voice)* imperioso,-a. **2** *(urgent)* urgente, apremiante. **3** *(authoritative)* perentorio,-a, autoritario,-a. **4** *Ling* imperativo,-a. **II** *n Ling* imperativo *m*.

imperceptible [ɪmpə'septəbəl] *adj (gen)* imperceptible; *(difference, change)* insensible.

imperfect [ɪm'pɜːfɪkt] **I** *adj* **1** *(gen)* imperfecto,-a; *(goods, sight)* defectuoso,-a. **2** *Ling* imperfecto,-a. **II** *n Ling* imperfecto *m*.

imperfection [ˌɪmpəˈfekʃən] n imperfección f, defecto m.

imperial [ɪmˈpɪərɪəl] adj 1 (power etc) imperial. 2 (weight, measure) **i. gallon,** galón m británico or inglés (= 4,543 litres).

imperialism [ɪmˈpɪərɪəlɪzəm] n imperialismo m.

imperialist [ɪmˈpɪərɪəlɪst] adj & n imperialista (mf).

imperil [ɪmˈperɪl] vtr (pt & pp **imperilled,** US **imperiled**) fml poner en peligro, arriesgar.

imperious [ɪmˈpɪərɪəs] adj imperioso,-a, autoritario,-a.

imperishable [ɪmˈperɪʃəbəl] adj imperecedero,-a.

impermeable [ɪmˈpɜːmɪəbəl] adj impermeable.

impersonal [ɪmˈpɜːsənəl] adj impersonal.

impersonate [ɪmˈpɜːsəneɪt] vtr (gen) hacerse pasar por; (famous people) imitar.

impersonation [ɪmpɜːsəˈneɪʃən] n imitación f.

impersonator [ɪmˈpɜːsəneɪtəʳ] n imitador,-a m,f.

impertinence [ɪmˈpɜːtɪnəns] n impertinencia f, descaro m.

impertinent [ɪmˈpɜːtɪnənt] adj impertinente, descarado,-a.

imperturbable [ɪmpəˈtɜːbəbəl] adj imperturbable.

impervious [ɪmˈpɜːvɪəs] adj 1 (rock etc) impermeable. 2 fig (person) insensible (**to,** a); **to be i. to reason,** no atender a razones.

impetuosity [ɪmpetjʊˈɒsɪtɪ] n impetuosidad f.

impetuous [ɪmˈpetjʊəs] adj impetuoso,-a, impulsivo,-a, irreflexivo,-a.

impetus [ˈɪmpɪtəs] n ímpetu m; fig impulso m.

impinge [ɪmˈpɪndʒ] vi fml afectar (**on,** a), repercutir (**on,** en), hacerse sentir (**on,** en).

impish [ˈɪmpɪʃ] adj travieso,-a, pícaro,-a.

implacable [ɪmˈplækəbəl] adj implacable.

implant [ɪmˈplɑːnt] I vtr 1 Med (tissue, hormone) implantar, injertar. 2 fig (principles, ideas) inculcar. II [ɪmˈplɑːnt] n Med implantación f, injerto m.

implausible [ɪmˈplɔːzəbəl] adj inverosímil, poco probable.

implement [ˈɪmplɪmənt] I n (tool) herramienta f; (instrument) instrumento m. ■ **farm implements,** aperos mpl de labranza. II [ˈɪmplɪment] vtr (decision, plan) llevar a cabo, realizar, poner en práctica; (promise) cumplir; (law, policy) aplicar.

implicate [ˈɪmplɪkeɪt] vtr implicar (**in,** en), comprometer (**in,** en).

implication [ɪmplɪˈkeɪʃən] n (gen) implicación f; (consequence) consecuencia f.

implicit [ɪmˈplɪsɪt] adj 1 (implied) implícito,-a, tácito,-a. 2 (belief, trust) absoluto,-a; (faith, obedience) incondicional, ciego,-a.

implied [ɪmˈplaɪd] adj implícito,-a, tácito,-a.

implore [ɪmˈplɔːʳ] vtr implorar, suplicar.

imploring [ɪmˈplɔːrɪŋ] adj suplicante, de súplica. ◆ **imploringly** adv (look) de modo suplicante; (beg) en tono suplicante.

imply [ɪmˈplaɪ] vtr (pt & pp **implied**) 1 (involve) implicar, presuponer, suponer. 2 (hint) insinuar, dar a entender; (mean) significar, querer decir.

impolite [ɪmpəˈlaɪt] adj maleducado,-a, descortés.

impoliteness [ɪmpəˈlaɪtnəs] n mala educación f, falta f de educación, descortesía f.

imponderable [ɪmˈpɒndərəbəl] I adj imponderable. II **imponderables** npl imponderables mpl.

import [ˈɪmpɔːt] I n 1 Com (gen pl) (commodity) artículo m importado, importación f; (act) importación f. ■ **i. duty,** derechos mpl de importación. 2 fml (meaning) sentido m, significado m. 3 fml (importance) importancia f. II [ˈɪmpɔːt] vtr Com importar.

importance [ɪmˈpɔːtəns] n (gen) importancia f; (standing) envergadura f; **a matter of the utmost i.,** un asunto de suma importancia; **he's full of his own i.,** se

cree muy importante, es muy engreído; **of little i.,** de poca monta or importancia; **to attach great i. to sth,** dar or otorgar mucha importancia a algo.

important [ɪmˈpɔːtənt] adj (gen) importante; (influential) de envergadura; **it's not i.,** no importa, no tiene importancia. ◆ **importantly** adv 1 (speak, say) **rather an i.,** es pedir demasiado; **would it be an i. if ...?,** ¿le molestaría si ...? dándose aires. 2 **it's hard work and more i., badly-paid,** el trabajo es difícil y, lo que es más, rinde poco.

importer [ɪmˈpɔːtəʳ] n Com importador,-a m,f.

importunate [ɪmˈpɔːtjunɪt] adj fml importuno,-a, molesto,-a.

importune [ɪmˈpɔːtjuːn] vtr importunar, molestar.

impose [ɪmˈpəʊz] I vtr (force upon) imponer (**on, upon,** a). II vi (take advantage of) **to i. on** or **upon,** abusar de, aprovecharse de.

imposing [ɪmˈpəʊzɪŋ] adj imponente, impresionante.

imposition [ɪmpəˈzɪʃən] n 1 (of tax, fine, beliefs) imposición f. 2 (unfair demand) imposición f, abuso m; **it's rather an i.,** es pedir demasiado; **would it be an i. if ...?,** ¿le molestaría si ...?

impossibility [ɪmpɒsəˈbɪlɪtɪ] n imposibilidad f.

impossible [ɪmˈpɒsəbəl] I adj (gen) imposible; (person) insoportable, inaguantable; **it's not i. that ...,** existe la posibilidad de que ...; **to make life i. for sb,** hacerle la vida imposible a algn. II **the i.** n lo imposible; **to ask** or **to do the i.,** pedir or hacer lo imposible. ◆ **impossibly** adv (gen) de manera insoportable; **i. difficult,** de una dificultad insuperable; **the train was i. late,** el tren llevaba un retraso increíble; **to behave i.,** comportarse de una manera insoportable.

impostor, US **imposter** [ɪmˈpɒstəʳ] n impostor,-a m,f.

impotent [ˈɪmpətənt] adj impotente.

impound [ɪmˈpaʊnd] vtr Jur confiscar, incautarse, embargar.

impoverished [ɪmˈpɒvərɪʃt] adj (person, country) empobrecido,-a, necesitado,-a; (soil, resources) agotado,-a.

impracticable [ɪmˈpræktɪkəbəl] adj no factible, irrealizable, impracticable.

impractical [ɪmˈpræktɪkəl] adj (person) poco or nada práctico,-a; (project, solution, etc) poco viable or factible.

imprecise [ɪmprɪˈsaɪs] adj impreciso,-a.

imprecision [ɪmprɪˈsɪʒən] n imprecisión f, falta f de precisión.

impregnable [ɪmˈpregnəbəl] adj (fortress) inexpugnable; fig (position) inexpugnable, invulnerable.

impregnate [ˈɪmpregneɪt] vtr 1 (soak) impregnar (**with,** de), empapar (**with,** de). 2 fml (fertilize) fecundar.

impresario [ɪmprəˈsɑːrɪəʊ] n (pl **impresarios**) empresario,-a m,f.

impress [ɪmˈpres] vtr 1 (make an impression on) impresionar; **I was not impressed with the film,** la película me dejó frío,-a; **to i. sb favourably/unfavourably,** hacerle or causarle a algn buena/buena/mala impresión. 2 (mark) imprimir, marcar (**into, on,** en); (pattern) estampar (**into, on,** en); fig **her advice remained impressed on my mind,** sus consejos quedaron grabados en mi memoria; fig **to i. sth on sb,** convencer a algn de la importancia de algo.

impression [ɪmˈpreʃən] n 1 (gen) impresión f; **good/bad i.,** buena/mala impresión; **to be under** or **have the i. that ...,** tener la impresión de que ...; **what's your i. of her?,** ¿qué te parece ella?; **to give the i. of ...,** dar la impresión de ... . 2 (imprint) impresión f, marca f, señal f; (in snow etc) huella f; (in wax, plaster) hueco m. 3 (imitation) imitación f; **to do impressions,** hacer imitaciones. 5 Print (printing) impresión f; (number of copies) edición f, tirada f.

impressionable [ɪmˈpreʃənəbəl] adj impresionable.

Impressionism [ɪmˈpreʃənɪzəm] n Art impresionismo m.

impressionist [ɪmˈpreʃənɪst] *adj & n Art* impresionista *(mf)*.

impressionistic [ɪmpreʃənˈɪstɪk] *adj Art* impresionista.

impressive [ɪmˈpresɪv] *adj* impresionante.

imprint I [ɪmˈprɪnt] *vtr (mark)* dejar huella, marcar **(on, in,** en); *(stamp)* imprimir, estampar **(on, in,** en); *fig* **his words were imprinted on my mind,** sus palabras quedaron grabadas en mi memoria. **II** [ˈɪmprɪnt] *n* **1** *(mark)* marca *f*, *(left by foot etc)* huella *f*; *(stamp)* marca *f*, sello *m*. **2** *(publisher's name)* pie *m* de imprenta.

imprison [ɪmˈprɪzən] *vtr* encarcelar, meter en la cárcel.

imprisonment [ɪmˈprɪzənmənt] *n* encarcelamiento *m*. ■ **life i.,** cadena *f* perpetua.

improbability [ɪmprɒbəˈbɪlɪtɪ] *n (of event)* improbabilidad *f*; *(of story, explanation)* inverosimilitud *f*.

improbable [ɪmˈprɒbəbəl] *adj (event)* improbable; *(story, explanation)* inverosímil.

impromptu [ɪmˈprɒmptjuː] **I** *adj (speech, party)* improvisado,-a; *(visit, trip)* imprevisto,-a. **II** *adv (spontaneously)* improvisadamente, sin preparación; *(unexpectedly)* de improviso, de repente.

improper [ɪmˈprɒpəʳ] *adj* **1** *(gen)* impropio,-a; *(conditions, method)* inadecuado,-a. **2** *(indecent)* indecente, indecoroso,-a; *(behaviour, suggestion)* deshonesto,-a. **3** *(wrong)* *(use, diagnosis)* incorrecto,-a. ◆ **improperly** *adv* **1** *(dress, behave)* impropiamente. **2** *(speak)* mal; *(behave)* con indecencia, deshonestamente. **3** *(use, diagnose)* incorrectamente.

impropriety [ɪmprəˈpraɪɪtɪ] *n fml* impropiedad *f*, falta *f* de decoro.

improve [ɪmˈpruːv] **I** *vtr* **1** *(make better)* mejorar; *(looks, appearance)* favorecer, caer bien; *(beauty)* realzar; *(skill, knowledge)* perfeccionar; *(property)* hacer mejoras en; *(mind)* cultivar. **2** *(increase)* aumentar; **to i. one's chances,** tener más probabilidades or posibilidades. **II** *vi* **1** *(become better)* mejorar, mejorarse; *(skill, knowledge)* perfeccionarse; **to i. with keeping,** mejorar con el tiempo. **2** *(increase)* aumentar, subir. ◆ **improve on** *vtr (gen)* superar, sobrepasar; *(offer, bid)* sobrepujar; **can you i. on my suggestion?,** ¿se le ocurre algo mejor?

improvement [ɪmˈpruːvmənt] *n* **1** *(making better)* mejora *f*, mejoramiento *m*; *(in aim, skill)* perfeccionamiento *m*; **home improvements,** reformas *fpl* domésticas; **my new car is an i. on my old one,** mi coche nuevo es mejor que el que tenía antes; **there's room for i.,** deja algo que desear; **to show (signs of) i.,** hacer progresos, ir mejorando. **2** *(increase)* aumento *m*.

improvident [ɪmˈprɒvɪdənt] *adj fml* **1** *(wasteful)* derrochador,-a, despilfarrador,-a, pródigo,-a. **2** *(lacking foresight)* imprevisor,-a.

improvisation [ɪmprəvaɪˈzeɪʃən] *n* improvisación *f*.

improvise [ˈɪmprəvaɪz] *vtr & vi* improvisar.

imprudent [ɪmˈpruːdənt] *adj* imprudente.

impudence [ˈɪmpjʊdəns] *n* insolencia *f*, frescura *f*, descaro *m*.

impudent [ˈɪmpjʊdənt] *adj* insolente, fresco,-a, descarado,-a.

impugn [ɪmˈpjuːn] *vtr fml* impugnar.

impulse [ˈɪmpʌls] *n (gen)* impulso *m*; *fig* impulso *m*, estímulo *m*; **to act on (an) i.,** dejarse llevar por un impulso; **to give in** or **to yield to an i.,** obedecer or ceder a un impulso. ■ *Com* **i. buy,** compra *f* por impulso.

impulsive [ɪmˈpʌlsɪv] *adj* impulsivo,-a, irreflexivo,-a.

impunity [ɪmˈpjuːnɪtɪ] *n* impunidad *f*; **to break the law with i.,** romper or quebrantar la ley impunemente or con impunidad.

impure [ɪmˈpjʊəʳ] *adj* **1** *(acts)* impuro,-a; *(thoughts, motives)* impúdico,-a, deshonesto,-a. **2** *(air, water, etc)* contaminado; *(milk, oil, etc)* adulterado,-a.

impurity [ɪmˈpjʊərɪtɪ] *n* **1** *(of act)* deshonestidad *f*, falta *f* de pudor. **2** *(gen pl)* *(in air, substance)* impureza *f*.

impute [ɪmˈpjuːt] *vtr. fml* **to i. sth to sth/sb,** *(crime, blame)* imputar or achacar algo a algo/algn; *(false motives)* atribuir algo a algo/algn.

in¹ (*pl* **in** or **ins**) *abbr of* **inch(es),** pulgada(s) *f(pl)*.

in² [ɪn] **I** *prep* **1** *(place)* en; *(within)* dentro de; **a pain in one's back,** un dolor de espalda; **in bed,** en la cama; **in England,** en Inglaterra; **in prison,** en la cárcel; **in the distance,** a lo lejos; **in the wardrobe,** en el armario; **the light in the kitchen,** la luz de la cocina. **2** *(motion)* en; **I threw it in the fire,** lo eché al fuego; **put it in your bag,** métolo en tu bolso; **she arrived in Paris,** llegó a París; **he fell in the river,** se cayó al río. **3** *(time)* *(during)* en, durante; **I haven't seen her in years,** hace años que no la veo; **in May,** en mayo; **in my youth,** en mi juventud; **in 1945** en 1945; **in spring,** en primavera; **in the daytime,** durante el día; **in the morning,** por la mañana; **at ten in the morning,** a las diez de la mañana; **in the sixties,** en los sesenta. **4** *(time)* *(within)* dentro de; **I arrived in time,** llegué a tiempo; **phone me in ten minutes,** llámame dentro de diez minutos. **5** *(time)* *(after)* al cabo de; **in a while he returned,** volvió al cabo de un rato; **you'll learn in time,** con el tiempo aprenderás. **6** *(manner)* en; **in all honesty,** con toda franqueza; **in alphabetical order,** en orden alfabético; **in a loud voice,** en voz alta; **in cash,** en efectivo, en metálico; **in fashion,** de moda; **in French,** en francés; **in an odd way,** de una manera rara; **in this way,** de este modo; **in rows,** en filas; **in writing,** por escrito; **packed in sixes,** envasado en cajas de seis; **they arrived in (their) thousands,** llegaron a millares; **write in pencil,** escribe con lápiz. **7** *(wearing)* en; **dressed in blue,** vestido,-a de azul; **in jeans,** en tejanos or vaqueros; **in uniform,** de uniforme; **the man in a tie,** el señor de la corbata; **you look good in black,** el negro te sienta bien. **8** *(weather)* a, en; **in darkness,** en la oscuridad; **in daylight,** a la luz del día; **in the rain,** bajo la lluvia; **in the shade,** a la sombra; **in the sun,** al sol; **in this heat,** con este calor. **9** *(state, condition)* en; **blind in the right eye,** ciego,-a del ojo derecho; **carved in wood,** tallado,-a en madera; **he's in his sixties,** anda por los sesenta; **in a good/bad mood,** de buen/mal humor; **in bloom** or **flower,** en flor; **in danger,** en peligro; **in love,** enamorado,-a; **in good/bad condition,** en buenas/malas condiciones; **in public/private,** en público/privado; **in silence,** en silencio; **to live in poverty,** vivir en la miseria. **10** *(ratio, measurement, numbers)* de; **cut in half,** cortado,-a por la mitad; **in threes,** de tres en tres; **one in six,** uno de cada seis; **ten pence in the pound,** diez peniques por libra; **two metres in length width/depth/height,** dos metros de largo/ancho/profundo/alto; **we were ten in number,** éramos diez. **11** *(profession)* en; **to be in insurance,** trabajar en seguros; **to be in medicine,** dedicarse a la medicina; **to be in the army,** ser militar. **12** *(person)* en; **he has it in him to win,** es capaz de ganar; **you have a good friend in me,** en mí tienes un buen amigo. **13** *(after superlative)* de; **the smallest car in the world,** el coche más pequeño del mundo. **14** *(before present participle)* al; **in so doing,** con ello, gracias a ello; **in spending so much,** al gastar tanto. **15** *(phrases)* **in all,** en total; **in itself/himself/herself,** en sí; **in that ...,** dado que ..., ya que .... **II** *adv* **all in,** *(price etc)* todo incluido; **in here/there,** aquí/allí dentro; **let's go in,** vamos adentro; **on the way in,** al entrar; **to be in,** *(at home)* estar (en casa); *(at work)* estar; *(train, plane, etc)* haber llegado; *(tide)* estar alta; *Sport (ball)* estar en juego; *(harvest)* estar recogido,-a; *Pol (in power)* estar en el poder; *fam (in fashion)* estar de moda; **aplications must be in by the 3rd,** el plazo para presentar las solicitudes finaliza el día 3; **my luck is in,** estoy de suerte; **to go in and out,** entrar y salir; **to invite sb in,** invitar a algn a entrar; *fam* **to be all in,** estar agotado,-a or rendido,-a; *fam* **to be** or **get in on sth,** estar al tanto de or enterado,-a de algo; *fam* **to be** or **keep (well) in with sb,** tener (mucha) confianza con algn; *fam* **to have it in for sb,** tenerla tomada con algn; *fam* **we're in for a storm,** vamos a tener tormenta; *fam* **you're**

in for a surprise, te espera una sorpresa; *fam* **you're in for it!,** ¡la que te espera! **III** *adj fam* **1** *(fashionable) (place)* de moda; *(clothes, jewellery)* del último grito; **the in crowd to be with,** la gente in *or* de moda con la que hay que codearse. **2** *(private)* particular; **an in joke,** una broma privada. **IV** *n fam* **ins and outs,** detalles *mpl*, complicaciones *fpl*; **without going into all the ins and outs of the matter ...,** sin entrar en los pormenores del caso ... .

inability [ɪnəˈbɪlɪtɪ] *n* incapacidad *f*.

inaccessibility [ɪnæksesəˈbɪlɪtɪ] *n* inaccesibilidad *f*.

inaccessible [ɪnækˈsesəbəl] *adj* inaccesible.

inaccuracy [ɪnˈækjʊrəsɪ] *n (gen)* inexactitud *f*; *(gen pl)* error *m*, incorrección *f*.

inaccurate [ɪnˈækjʊrɪt] *adj (gen)* inexacto,-a; *(statement)* erróneo,-a; *(figures, total)* incorrecto,-a.

inaction [ɪnˈækʃən] *n* inacción *f*.

inactive [ɪnˈæktɪv] *adj* inactivo,-a.

inactivity [ɪnækˈtɪvɪtɪ] *n* inactividad *f*.

inadequacy [ɪnˈædɪkwəsɪ] *n* **1** *(lack)* insuficiencia *f*. **2** *(inability)* incompetencia *f*, incapacidad *f*. **3** *(defect)* defecto *m*, imperfección *f*.

inadequate [ɪnˈædɪkwɪt] *adj* **1** *(lacking)* insuficiente. **2** *(not capable)* incapaz, incompetente; *(unsuitable)* inadecuado,-a; **socially i.,** inadaptado,-a. **3** *(defective)* defectuoso,-a, imperfecto,-a.

inadmissible [ɪnədˈmɪsəbəl] *adj* inadmisible, intolerable; *Jur (evidence etc)* improcedente.

inadvertent [ɪnədˈvɜːtənt] *adj* involuntario,-a. ◆ **inadvertently** *adv* involuntariamente, sin querer.

inadvisable [ɪnədˈvaɪzəbəl] *adj* imprudente, inconveniente, poco aconsejable.

inalienable [ɪnˈeɪljənəbəl] *adj fml (right)* inalienable.

inane [ɪˈneɪn] *adj (comment etc)* necio,-a, fatuo,-a; *(question, conversation)* tonto,-a, estúpido,-a.

inanimate [ɪnˈænɪmɪt] *adj* inanimado,-a.

inanity [ɪˈnænɪtɪ] *n (of comment etc)* necedad *f*, fatuidad *f*; *(of question, conversation)* tontería,*f*, estupidez *f*.

inapplicable [ɪnəˈplɪkəbəl] *adj* inaplicable **(to,** a); **delete where i.,** táchese lo que no proceda.

inappropriate [ɪnəˈprəʊprɪɪt] *adj (time, remark)* inoportuno,-a, inconveniente; *(clothes, behaviour)* no *or* poco apropiado,-a, impropio,-a; **it would be i. for you to attend,** no estaría bien que vd. asistiera.

inapt [ɪnˈæpt] *adj fml* inadecuado,-a, impropio,-a.

inarticulate [ɪnɑːˈtɪkjʊlɪt] *adj (cry, sound)* inarticulado,-a; *(words)* mal pronunciado,-a; **he was i. with rage,** se puso tan furioso que apenas podía hablar.

inasmuch as [ɪnəzˈmʌtʃəz] *conj fml* **1** *(since, because)* puesto que, visto que, ya que. **2** *(in so far as)* en la medida en que, en tanto que.

inattention [ɪnəˈtenʃən] *n* inatención *f*, desatención *f*, falta *f* de atención.

inattentive [ɪnəˈtentɪv] *adj* desatento,-a, poco atento,-a, distraído,-a.

inaudible [ɪnˈɔːdəbəl] *adj* inaudible, imperceptible.

inaugural [ɪnˈɔːgjʊrəl] *adj* inaugural, de apertura, de inauguración.

inaugurate [ɪnˈɔːgjʊreɪt] *vtr* **1** *(event, scheme)* inaugurar. **2** *(president etc)* investir; **he was inaugurated president,** fue investido como presidente.

inauguration [ɪnɔːgjʊˈreɪʃən] *n* **1** *(of event, scheme)* inauguración *f*. **2** *(of president etc)* toma *f* de posesión, investidura *f*.

inauspicious [ɪnɔːˈspɪʃəs] *adj fml (start, moment)* poco propicio,-a, -a; *(circumstances)* desfavorable, adverso,-a.

inborn [ˈɪnbɔːn] *adj* innato,-a.

inbred [ˈɪnbred] *adj* **1** *(quality)* innato,-a. **2** *(family)* endogámico,-a, nacido,-a de padres consanguíneos.

Inc, inc *US Com abbr of* **Incorporated,** ≈ sociedad *f* anónima, S.A.

Inca [ˈɪŋkə] **I** *adj* inca, incaico,-a, incásico,-a. **II** *n* inca *mf*.

incalculable [ɪnˈkælkjʊləbəl] *adj (loss, assets)* incalculable; *(mood)* imprevisible.

incandescent [ɪnkænˈdesənt] *adj* incandescente.

incantation [ɪnkænˈteɪʃən] *n* conjuro *m*.

incapable [ɪnˈkeɪpəbəl] *adj* **1** *(unable)* incapaz **(of,** de). **2** *(incompetent)* incompetente.

incapacitate [ɪnkəˈpæsɪteɪt] *vtr fml* incapacitar **(for,** para).

incapacity [ɪnkəˈpæsɪtɪ] *n* incapacidad *f*.

incarcerate [ɪnˈkɑːsəreɪt] *vtr fml* encarcelar.

incarceration [ɪnkɑːsəˈreɪʃən] *n fml* encarcelamiento *m*, encarcelación *f*.

incarnate [ɪnˈkɑːneɪt] *adj* encarnado,-a; **beauty i.,** la belleza personificada; **the devil i.,** el mismísimo diablo.

incarnation [ɪnkɑːˈneɪʃən] *n* encarnación *f*.

incendiary [ɪnˈsendɪərɪ] **I** *adj* incendiario,-a. **II** *n* **1** *(bomb)* bomba *f* incendiaria, **2** *(person)* incendiario,-a *m*,*f*, pirómano,-a *m*,*f*.

incense¹ [ˈɪnsens] *n* incienso *m*.

incense² [ɪnˈsens] *vtr* enfurecer, poner furioso,-a, sacar de quicio.

incentive [ɪnˈsentɪv] *n* **1** *(stimulus)* incentivo *m*, estímulo *m*, aliciente *m*; **to give sb an i.,** incentivar a algn. **2** *(payment)* incentivo *m*, plus *m or* prima *f* de rendimiento.

inception [ɪnˈsepʃən] *n fml* comienzo *m*, principio *m*.

incessant [ɪnˈsesənt] *adj (rain, noise)* incesante, ininterrumpido,-a; *(complaints, demands)* constante, continuo,-a. ◆ **incessantly** *adv* sin cesar *or* parar.

incest [ˈɪnsest] *n* incesto *m*.

incestuous [ɪnˈsestjʊəs] *adj* incestuoso,-a; *fig (profession, group)* endogámico,-a, cerrado,-a.

inch [ɪntʃ] *n* pulgada *f* (= 2,54 cm); *fig* **he's every i. a hero,** es todo un héroe; *fig* **I know every i. of the city,** conozco todos los rincones de la ciudad; *fig* **i. by i.,** poco a poco; *fig* **she wouldn't budge** *or* **give an i.,** no quería ceder ni un ápice; *fig* **the car missed me by inches,** por poco me atropelló el coche; *prov* **give him an i. and he'll take a mile** *or* **a yard,** le das la mano y te coge *or* se toma el pie. ◆ **inch along,** inch forward *vtr & vi* avanzar poco a poco. ◆ **inch through** *vtr & vi* pasar poco a poco.

incidence [ˈɪnsɪdəns] *n* frecuencia *f*, extensión *f*.

incident [ˈɪnsɪdənt] *n* incidente *m*, incidencia *f*; **the visit passed (off) without i.,** la visita se desarrolló sin incidentes.

incidental [ɪnsɪˈdentəl] **I** *adj (accessory)* incidental, accesorio,-a, secundario,-a; *(risk, danger)* inherente **(to,** a), propio,-a **(to,** de); **i. music,** música *f* de fondo. **II** **incidentals** *npl (gastos mpl)* imprevistos *mpl* ◆ **incidentally** *adv* a propósito, dicho sea de paso, por cierto.

incinerate [ɪnˈsɪnəreɪt] *vtr* incinerar, quemar.

incineration [ɪnsɪnəˈreɪʃən] *n* incineración *f*, quema *f*.

incinerator [ɪnˈsɪnəreɪtəʳ] *n* incinerador *m*.

incipient [ɪnˈsɪpɪənt] *adj fml* incipiente.

incision [ɪnˈsɪʒən] *n Med* incisión *f*.

incisive [ɪnˈsaɪsɪv] *adj (comment)* incisivo,-a, mordaz, agudo,-a; *(reply)* tajante; *(mind)* penetrante.

incisor [ɪnˈsaɪzəʳ] *n* diente *m* incisivo, incisivo *m*.

incite [ɪnˈsaɪt] *vtr (violence)* incitar, provocar, instigar **(to,** a); *(crowd)* incitar, provocar **(to,** a); **to i. sb to do sth,** incitar a algn a hacer algo.

incitement [ɪnˈsaɪtmənt] *n* incitación *f*, provocación *f*, instigación *f*.

incivility [ɪnsɪˈvɪlɪtɪ] *n fml* descortesía *f*, falta *f* de cortesía.

inclement [ɪnˈklemənt] *adj fml (weather)* inclemente.

inclination [ɪnklɪ'neɪʃən] *n* **1** *(tendency)* inclinación *f*, tendencia *f* (**to**, a); **he shows no i. to leave**, no da señales de querer marcharse; **my i. is to stay**, yo prefiero quedarme. **2** *(slope)* inclinación *f*, pendiente *f*. **3** *(bow)* inclinación *f*.

incline [ɪn'klaɪn] **I** *vtr* **1** *(tend)* tender a, tener tendencia a, inclinarse por; **if you feel so inclined**, si quieres; **it is romantic but I'm that way inclined**, es romántico pero es que yo soy así; **she's inclined to be mean**, tiene tendencia a la tacañería. **2** *(head)* inclinar, bajar; *(body)* inclinar. **II** *vi (slope)* inclinarse, estar inclinado,-a. **III** [ɪn'klaɪn, 'ɪnklaɪn] *n (slope)* pendiente *f*, inclinación *f*; **steep i.**, cuesta *f* empinada.

include [ɪn'kluːd] *vtr (gen)* incluir (**in**, en); *(in range, series, price)* comprender (**in**, en); *(in list, cast, etc)* figurar (**in**, en); **the team includes two women**, el equipo incluye dos mujeres; **he lost everything, his wallet included**, perdió todo incluso su cartera.

including [ɪn'kluːdɪŋ] *prep* incluso, inclusive; **I stayed up to and i. Friday**, me quedé hasta el viernes inclusive; **there are five desserts, i. ice cream**, hay cinco postres, incluido helado; **we have six children i. the baby**, tenemos seis hijos contando el bebé.

inclusion [ɪn'kluːʒən] *n* inclusión *f*.

inclusive [ɪn'kluːsɪv] *adj* inclusivo,-a; **all-i. price**, precio *m* (con) todo incluido; **pages six to ten i.**, de la página seis a la diez, ambas inclusive; **the rent is i. of bills**, el alquiler incluye el importe de las facturas.

incognito [ɪnkɒg'niːtəʊ] **I** *n* incógnito,-a *m*, *f*. **II** *adv (travel etc)* de incógnito.

incoherence [ɪnkəʊ'hɪərəns] *n* incoherencia *f*; *(of speech)* ininteligibilidad *f*.

incoherent [ɪnkəʊ'hɪərənt] *adj* **1** *(unconnected)* incoherente, inconexo,-a, deshilvanado,-a. **2** *(unintelligible)* incoherente, ininteligible.

income ['ɪnkʌm] *n (gen)* ingresos *mpl*; *(from investment)* réditos *mpl*; **earned i.**, ingresos profesionales *or* salariales; **I live on a monthly i. of £800**, vivo de un sueldo de ochocientas libras mensuales; **to live within one's i.**, vivir de acuerdo con lo que se gana; **unearned** *or* **private i.**, rentas *fpl* particulares. ■ **i. tax**, impuesto *m* sobre la renta; **i. tax return**, declaración *f* de impuestos.

incoming ['ɪnkʌmɪŋ] *adj (flight, train)* de llegada; *(passenger)* que llega; *(president, government)* nuevo,-a; recién elegido,-a; *(tide)* ascendente; *(mail, message, call)* recibido,-a.

incommunicado [ɪnkəmjuːnɪ'kɑːdəʊ] *adj* incomunicado,-a.

incomparable [ɪn'kɒmpərəbəl] *adj* incomparable, inigualable, sin par. ◆ **incomparably** *adv* sin comparación; **i. better than ...**, muchísimo mejor que ... .

incompatibility [ɪnkəmpætə'bɪlɪti] *n* incompatibilidad *f*; **divorce on grounds of i.**, divorcio *m* por incompatibilidad de caracteres.

incompatible [ɪnkəm'pætəbəl] *adj* incompatible (**with**, con).

incompetence [ɪn'kɒmpɪtəns] *n* incompetencia *f*, incapacidad *f*, ineptitud *f*.

incompetent [ɪn'kɒmpɪtənt] *adj* incompetente, incapaz, inepto,-a.

incomplete [ɪnkəm'pliːt] *adj (series, account)* incompleto,-a; *(task)* inacabado,-a, sin terminar.

incomprehensible [ɪnkɒmprɪ'hensəbəl] *adj* incomprensible.

incomprehension [ɪnkɒmprɪ'henʃən] *n* incomprensión *f*.

inconceivable [ɪnkən'siːvəbəl] *adj* inconcebible.

inconclusive [ɪnkən'kluːsɪv] *adj (debate, vote, meeting)* no decisivo,-a; *(reasoning)* poco convincente; *(proof)* no concluyente.

incongruity [ɪnkɒŋ'gruːɪti] *n* incongruencia *f*.

incongruous [ɪn'kɒŋgruəs] *adj* incongruente, incongruo,-a, fuera de lugar.

inconsequential [ɪnkɒnsɪ'kwənʃəl] *adj* de poca importancia, sin trascendencia.

inconsiderable [ɪnkən'sɪdərəbəl] *adj* insignificante.

inconsiderate [ɪnkən'sɪdərɪt] *adj* desconsiderado,-a, inconsiderado,-a, desatento,-a; **how i. of you!**, ¡qué falta de consideración por tu parte!

inconsistency [ɪnkən'sɪstənsi] *n (gen)* inconsecuencia *f*, inconsistencia *f*, falta *f* de lógica; *(contradiction)* contradicción *f*.

inconsistent [ɪnkən'sɪstənt] *adj (gen)* inconsecuente, inconsistente; *(contradictory)* contradictorio,-a, ilógico,-a; **your evidence is i. with the facts**, su testimonio no concuerda con los hechos.

inconsolable [ɪnkən'səʊəbəl] *adj* inconsolable, desconsolado,-a.

inconspicuous [ɪnkən'spɪkjʊəs] *adj (not noticeable)* que pasa desapercibido,-a *or* inadvertido,-a; *(discrete)* discreto,-a; **to make oneself i.**, pasar desapercibido, no llamar la atención.

incontinence [ɪn'kɒntɪnəns] *n Med* incontinencia *f*.

incontinent [ɪn'kɒntɪnənt] *adj Med* incontinente.

incontrovertible [ɪnkɒntrə'vɜːtəbəl] *adj fml* incontrovertible.

inconvenience [ɪnkən'viːnɪəns] **I** *n (gen)* inconveniente *f*; *(annoyance)* molestia *f*, incomodidad *f*; *(difficulty)* dificultad *f*; **to put sb to i.**, molestar *or* incomodar a algn; **to go to great i.**, sufrir muchos inconvenientes. **II** *vtr (annoy)* molestar, causar molestia a; *(cause difficulty)* incomodar.

inconvenient [ɪnkən'viːnɪənt] *adj (gen)* molesto,-a; *(place)* mal situado,-a; *(time)* inoportuno,-a, mal escogido,-a; *(arrangement, design)* poco práctico,-a.

incorporate [ɪn'kɔːpəreɪt] *vtr (integrate)* incorporar (**in**, **into**, a); *(include)* incluir (**in**, **into**, en); *(contain)* contener; **a lawyer was incorporated into the team**, se incorporó un abogado al equipo.

incorporated [ɪn'kɔːpəreɪtɪd] *adj US Com* **i. company**, sociedad *f* anónima.

incorrect [ɪnkə'rekt] *adj* **1** *(answer)* incorrecto,-a, equivocado,-a; *(view)* erróneo,-a; **you're i. in thinking that ...**, te equivocas al pensar que ... . **2** *(behaviour)* incorrecto,-a; *(dress)* impropio,-a, inadecuado,-a.

incorrigible [ɪn'kɒrɪdʒəbəl] *adj* incorregible.

increase ['ɪnkriːs] **I** *n (gen)* aumento *m*; *(in number, birthrate)* incremento *in*; *(in price, temperature)* subida *f*, alza *f*; **to be on the i.**, estar en aumento *or* en alza. **II** [ɪn'kriːs] *vtr (gen)* aumentar; *(price, temperature)* subir; **to i. one's efforts**, redoblar sus esfuerzos; **to i. one's speed**, acelerar el paso. **III** *vi (gen)* aumentar; *(temperature)* subir; **to i. in price**, subir *or* aumentar de precio; **to i. in weight/size**, aumentar en peso/tamaño.

increasing [ɪn'kriːsɪŋ] *adj* creciente. ◆ **increasingly** *adv* cada vez más.

incredible [ɪn'kredəbəl] *adj* increíble; **it's i. that ...**, parece mentira que ... .

incredulity [ɪnkrɪ'djuːlɪti] *n* incredulidad *f*.

incredulous [ɪn'kredjʊləs] *adj* incrédulo,-a; **i. smile**, sonrisa *f* de incredulidad.

increment ['ɪnkrɪmənt] *n* aumento *m*, incremento *m*. ■ **unearned i.**, plusvalía *f*.

incriminate [ɪn'krɪmɪneɪt] *vtr* incriminar, inculpar.

incriminating [ɪn'krɪmɪneɪtɪŋ] *adj* incriminatorio,-a, incriminador,-a.

incubate ['ɪnkjʊbeɪt] *vtr & vi (egg)* incubar, empollar; *(virus)* incubar.

incubation [ɪnkjʊ'beɪʃən] *n* incubación *f*.

incubator ['ɪnkjʊbeɪtəʳ] *n* incubadora *f*.

inculcate ['ɪnkʌlkeɪt] *vtr fml* inculcar (**in,** en).

incumbent [ɪn'kʌmbənt] **I** *n (gen)* titular *mf*. **II** *adj fml* **to be i. on sb to do sth,** incumbir *or* corresponder a algn hacer algo.

incur [ɪn'kɜːʳ] *vtr (pt & pp incurred) (blame, displeasure)* incurrir en; *(risk)* correr; *(debt, expenses)* contraer; *(loss)* sufrir.

incurable [ɪn'kjʊərəbəl] *adj (disease)* incurable; *fig (loss)* irremediable; *(optimist)* incorregible.

incursion [ɪn'kɜːʃən] *n* incursión *f*.

Ind *GB Pol abbr of* **Independent,** independiente *(mf).*

indebted [ɪn'detɪd] *adj (gen)* endeudado,-a; *fig (grateful)* agradecido,-a; *fig* **I am i. to you for your help,** le agradezco su ayuda; *fig* **to be i. to sb,** estar en deuda con algn.

indebtedness [ɪn'detɪdnɪs] *n (gen)* deuda *f*; *fig* agradecimiento *m*.

indecency [ɪn'diːsənsɪ] *n* indecencia *f*, obscenidad *f*.

indecent [ɪn'diːsənt] *adj* indecente, indecoroso,-a. ▪ *Jur* **i. assault,** atentado *m* contra el pudor; *Jur* **i. exposure,** exhibicionismo *m*.

indecipherable [ɪndɪ'saɪfərəbəl] *adj fml* indescifrable.

indecision [ɪndɪ'sɪʒən] *n* indecisión *f*, irresolución *f*.

indecisive [ɪndɪ'saɪsɪv] *adj* **1** *(person, manner)* indeciso,-a, irresoluto,-a. **2** *(evidence, victory)* poco concluyente, no decisivo,-a.

indeed [ɪn'diːd] *adv* **1** *fml (in fact)* efectivamente, en efecto, realmente, en realidad; **I was i. late but ...,** de acuerdo que llegué tarde pero ... . **2** *(intensifying use)* realmente; **I'm very sorry i.,** lo siento de veras *or* de verdad; **it's very hard i.,** es sumamente *or* verdaderamente difícil; **look at my new car! —car i.!, it's a banger!,** mira mi coche nuevo — ¿coche dices?, ¡pues sí es una cafetera!; **thank you very much i.,** muchísimas gracias; **that is i. a problem,** eso sí (que) es un problema; **you'll come then? —i. I won't!,** ¿entonces, vendrás? —¡ni hablar!, ¡claro que no!

indefatigable [ɪndɪ'fætɪgəbəl] *adj fml* incansable, infatigable.

indefensible [ɪndɪ'fensəbəl] *adj* **1** *(place)* indefenso,-a, indefendible, indefensible, indefensable. **2** *fig (view)* insostenible; *(behaviour)* injustificable, inexcusable.

indefinable [ɪndɪ'faɪnəbəl] *adj* indefinible.

indefinite [ɪn'defɪnɪt] *adj* **1** *(vague)* indefinido,-a, vago,-a, impreciso,-a. **2** *(indeterminate)* indefinido,-a, indeterminado,-a; **i. strike,** huelga indefinida. **3** *Ling* indefinido,-a, indeterminado,-a.

indelible [ɪn'deləbəl] *adj* indeleble, imborrable.

indelicate [ɪn'delɪkɪt] *adj* **1** *(indecent)* indelicado,-a, poco delicado,-a. **2** *(tactless)* indiscreto,-a.

indemnify [ɪn'demnɪfaɪ] *vtr (pt & pp indemnified)* indemnizar (**for,** de, por).

indemnity [ɪn'demnɪtɪ] *n* **1** *(insurance)* indemnidad *f*. **2** *(compensation)* indemnización *f*, reparación *f*, compensación *f*.

indent [ɪn'dent] **I** *vtr Typ* sangrar. **II** *vi GB Com* **to i. for sth,** hacer un pedido de algo.

indentation [ɪnden'teɪʃən] *n* **1** *Typ* sangría *f*. **2** *(of edge)* muesca *f*; *(of coastline)* quebradura *f*; *(of surface)* depresión *f*, hundimiento *m*, abolladura *f*.

indented [ɪn'dentɪd] *adj* **1** *Typ* sangrado,-a. **2** *(coastline)* quebrado,-a; *(surface)* abollado,-a.

independence [ɪndɪ'pendəns] *n* independencia *f*. ▪ *US* **I. Day,** día *m* de la Independencia *(4 July).*

independent [ɪndɪ'pendənt] *adj* independiente; *GB* **i. school,** colegio *m* no subvencionado por el estado; **to become i.,** independizarse; **to have i. means,** vivir de renta.

in-depth ['ɪndepθ] *adj* minucioso,-a, exhaustivo,-a.

indescribable [ɪndɪ'skraɪbəbəl] *adj (gen)* indescriptible; *(spectacle, grandeur)* inenarrable; *(emotion)* indecible.

indestructible [ɪndɪ'strʌktəbəl] *adj* indestructible.

indeterminable [ɪndɪ'tɜːmɪnəbəl] *adj* indeterminable.

indeterminate [ɪndɪ'tɜːmɪnɪt] *adj* indeterminado,-a.

index ['ɪndeks] **I** *n (pl indexes or indices)* **1** *(in book etc)* índice *m*; *(in library)* índice *m*, catálogo *m*. ▪ **card i.,** fichero *m*; **i. card,** ficha *f*. **2** *Math* índice *m*, exponente *m*; *Econ* índice *m*; **cost-of-living i.,** índice del coste de la vida. **3** *(forefinger)* **i. finger,** dedo *m* índice. **II** *vtr (book etc)* poner un índice a; *(collection)* catalogar, clasificar.

index-linked ['ɪndekslɪŋkt] *adj* sujeto,-a al aumento del coste de la vida.

India ['ɪndɪə] *n* (la) India.

Indian ['ɪndɪən] **I** *adj (of America)* indio,-a, amerindio,-a; *(of India)* indio,-a, hindú. ▪ **I. elephant,** elefante *m* asiático; **I. ink,** tinta *f* china; **I. Ocean,** Océano *m* Índico; **I. Summer,** veranillo *m* de San Martín. **II** *n (person) (of America)* indio,-a *m, f*, amerindio,-a *m, f*; *(of India)* indio,-a *m, f*, hindú *mf*. ▪ **Red I.,** piel roja *mf*; **West I.,** antillano,-a *m, f*.

indicate ['ɪndɪkeɪt] **I** *vtr* indicar. **II** *vi Aut* poner el intermitente; **to i. left/right,** indicar a la izquierda/derecha.

indication [ɪndɪ'keɪʃən] *n* indicio *m*, señal *f*; **there's every i. that** *or* **all the indications are that he'll win,** todo hace suponer que ganará; **this gives some i. of his strength,** esto da una idea de su fuerza.

indicative [ɪn'dɪkətɪv] **I** *adj* indicativo,-a. **II** *n Ling* indicativo *m*.

indicator ['ɪndɪkeɪtəʳ] *n (gen)* indicador *m*; *Aut* intermitente *m*.

indices ['ɪndɪsiːz] *npl see* **index.**

indict [ɪn'daɪt] *vtr Jur* acusar (**for,** de), procesar (**for,** por).

indictable [ɪn'daɪtəbəl] *adj Jur* encausable, procesable.

indictment [ɪn'daɪtmənt] *n Jur* acusación *f*, procesamiento *m*; **to bring an i. against sb,** procesar a algn; *fig* **a damning i. of his books,** una crítica feroz de sus libros.

indifference [ɪn'dɪfərəns] *n* indiferencia *f*.

indifferent [ɪn'dɪfərənt] *adj* **1** *(uninterested)* indiferente; **it's quite i. to me,** me trae sin cuidado. **2** *(mediocre)* pobre, regular.

indigenous [ɪn'dɪdʒɪnəs] *adj fml* indígena, nativo,-a.

indigestible [ɪndɪ'dʒestəbəl] *adj* indigesto,-a; *fig* **this book is very i.,** este libro es muy indigesto.

indigestion [ɪndɪ'dʒestʃən] *n* indigestión *f*, empacho *m*; **milk gives me i.,** la leche no me indigesta, la leche me sienta mal; **to suffer from i.,** tener una indigestión *or* un empacho; **you'll get i.!,** ¡te vas a indigestar!

indignant [ɪn'dɪgnənt] *adj (person)* indignado,-a; *(look, tone)* de indignación; **to get i. about sth,** indignarse por algo.

indignation [ɪndɪg'neɪʃən] *n* indignación *f*.

indignity [ɪn'dɪgnɪtɪ] *n* indignidad *f*.

indigo ['ɪndɪgəʊ] **I** *n (pl indigos or indigoes)* añil *m*. **II** *adj* (de color) añil.

indirect [ɪndɪ'rekt, ɪndaɪ'rekt] *adj* indirecto,-a. ▪ *Ling* **i. speech,** estilo *m* indirecto; **i. taxation,** impuestos *mpl* indirectos.

indiscreet [ɪndɪ'skriːt] *adj* indiscreto,-a, poco discreto,-a, imprudente.

indiscretion [ɪndɪ'skreʃən] *n* indiscreción *f*, imprudencia *f*.

indiscriminate [ɪndɪ'skrɪmɪnɪt] *adj (punishment, shooting)* indiscriminado,-a; *(praise, reading)* sin criterio, sin discernimiento.

indispensable [ɪndɪ'spensəbəl] *adj* indispensable, imprescindible.

indisposed [ɪndɪ'spəʊzd] *adj fml* **1** *(ill)* indispuesto,-a. **2** *(disinclined)* poco dispuesto,-a; **i. to help,** con pocas ganas de ayudar.

indisposition [ɪndɪspə'zɪʃən] *n fml* indisposición *f*.

indisputable [ɪndɪ'spjuːtəbəl] *adj* indiscutible, incontestable, irrefutable.

indissoluble [ɪndɪ'sɒljʊbəl] *adj fml* indisoluble.

indistinct [ɪndɪ'stɪŋkt] *adj (gen)* indistinto,-a; *(memory)* confuso,-a; vago,-a; *(shape etc)* borroso,-a.

indistinguishable [ɪndɪ'stɪŋgwɪʃəbəl] *adj* indistinguible.

individual [ɪndɪ'vɪdjʊəl] **I** *adj* **1** *(separate)* individual; *(for one)* particular, propio,-a; *(personal)* personal; **each i. note,** cada una de las notas, cada nota por separado. **2** *(characteristic)* personal, particular; *(original)* original; **she has a highly i. style of dressing,** es muy original en el vestir. **II** *n fam (person)* individuo *m*, tipo *m*, tío,-a *m*, *f*; **private i.,** particular *m*.

individualist [ɪndɪ'vɪdjʊəlɪst] *n* individualista *mf*.

indivisible [ɪndɪ'vɪzəbəl] *adj Math* indivisible.

Indo- ['ɪndəʊ] *pref* indo-.

indoctrinate [ɪn'dɒktrɪneɪt] *vtr* adoctrinar.

indoctrination [ɪndɒktrɪ'neɪʃən] *n* adoctrinamiento *m*.

indolent ['ɪndələnt] *adj fml* indolente, perezoso,-a.

indomitable [ɪn'dɒmɪtəbəl] *adj fml* indomable, indómito,-a.

Indonesia [ɪndəʊ'niːzɪə] *n* Indonesia.

Indonesian [ɪndəʊ'niːzɪən] **I** *adj* indonesio,-a. **II** *n* **1** *(person)* indonesio,-a *m*, *f*. **2** *(language)* indonesio *m*.

indoor ['ɪndɔː'] *adj (aerial, plant)* interior; *(clothes, shoes)* de andar por casa, casero,-a; *(hobby)* casero,-a. **■ i. football,** fútbol *m* sala; **i. games,** juegos *mpl* de salón; **i. pool,** piscina *f* cubierta.

indoors [ɪn'dɔːz] *adv (inside)* dentro (de casa); *(at home)* en casa; **i. the house had been painted,** el interior de la casa había sido pintado; **let's go i.,** vamos adentro; **to stay i.,** quedarse en casa.

induce [ɪn'djuːs] *vtr* **1** *(persuade)* inducir, persuadir. **2** *(cause)* producir, causar; *Med (labour)* provocar.

inducement [ɪn'djuːsmənt] *n* incentivo *m*, estímulo *m*, aliciente *m*; **as an added i.,** para mayor estímulo; **material inducements,** incentivo *m sing* económico.

induction [ɪn'dʌkʃən] *n* **1** *Med (of labour)* provocación *f*. **2** *Elec* inducción *f*. **3** *(reasoning)* inducción *f*. **4** *Educ* introducción *f*.

inductive [ɪn'dʌktɪv] *adj* inductivo,-a.

indulge [ɪn'dʌldʒ] **I** *vtr* **1** *(child etc)* mimar, consentir; *(person)* complacer; **to i. oneself,** darse gusto. **2** *(whim)* ceder a, consentir, satisfacer; *(passion)* dar rienda suelta a. **II** *vi* **1** *fam (drink)* beber (demasiado). **2** *(luxuries)* darse el gusto **(in,** de), complacerse **(in,** en); *(vices)* entregarse **(in,** a), abandonarse a **(in,** a); **to i. in a nap,** permitirse el lujo de una siesta.

indulgence [ɪn'dʌldʒəns] *n* **1** *(of child etc)* mimo *m*, consentimiento *m*; *(of attitude)* indulgencia *f*, tolerancia *f*. **2** *(of whim)* satisfacción *f*, gratificación *f*; **to allow or permit oneself small indulgences,** permitirse pequeños lujos; *fam* **it's sheer self-i.!,** ¡es puro vicio!

indulgent [ɪn'dʌldʒənt] *adj* indulgente.

industrial [ɪn'dʌstrɪəl] *adj (gen)* industrial; *(accident)* de trabajo, laboral; *(disease)* profesional; *GB* **to take i. action,** declararse en huelga. **■** *GB* **i. dispute,** conflicto *m* laboral; **i. estate,** polígono *m* or zona *f* industrial; **i. relations,** relaciones *fpl* laborales; **i. unrest,** conflictividad *f* laboral; **i. waste,** residuos *mpl* industriales.

industrialist [ɪn'dʌstrɪəlɪst] *n* industrial *mf*, empresario,-a *m*, *f*.

industrialize [ɪn'dʌstrɪəlaɪz] **I** *vtr (country, area)* industrializar; **to become industrialized,** industrializarse. **II** *vi* industrializarse.

industrious [ɪn'dʌstrɪəs] *adj* trabajador,-a.

industry ['ɪndəstrɪ] *n* **1** *(business)* industria *f*. **■** **heavy i.,** industria *f* pesada; **light i.,** industria *f* ligera; **steel i.,** industria *f* siderúrgica. **2** *(diligence)* diligencia *f*, aplicación *f*.

inebriated [ɪn'iːbrɪeɪtɪd] *adj* ebrio,-a, embriagado,-a.

inedible [ɪn'edəbəl] *adj* incomible, incomestible.

ineffable [ɪn'efəbəl] *adj fml* inefable.

ineffective [ɪnɪ'fektɪv] *adj (cure, method)* ineficaz, inútil; *(person)* incapaz, incompetente; **the strike was i.,** la huelga no surtió efecto.

ineffectiveness [ɪnɪ'fektɪvnɪs] *n (of cure, method)* ineficacia *f*; *(of person)* incapacidad *f*, incompetencia *f*.

ineffectual [ɪnɪ'fektʃʊəl] *adj (aim, protest)* ineficaz, inútil; *(person)* incapaz, incompetente.

inefficiency [ɪnɪ'fɪʃənsɪ] *n (gen)* ineficacia *f*; *(of person)* ineptitud *f*, incompetencia *f*.

inefficient [ɪnɪ'fɪʃənt] *adj (gen)* ineficaz, ineficiente; *(person)* inepto,-a, poco eficiente.

inelegant [ɪn'elɪgənt] *adj* poco elegante.

ineligible [ɪn'elɪdʒəbəl] *adj* inelegible **(for,** para); **to be i. to vote,** no tener el derecho al voto.

inept [ɪn'ept] *adj* **1** *(person)* inepto,-a; *(treatment, attempt)* inepto,-a, inapropiado,-a. **2** *(absurd) (remark, behaviour)* estúpido,-a.

ineptitude [ɪn'eptɪtjuːd] *n* ineptitud *f*, incapacidad *f*.

inequality [ɪnɪ'kwɒlɪtɪ] *n* desigualdad *f*.

inequitable [ɪn'ekwɪtəbəl] *adj fml* injusto,-a.

inert [ɪn'ɜːt] *adj* **1** *Chem (gas etc)* inerte. **2** *(position)* inerte, inmóvil.

inertia [ɪn'ɜːʃə] *n* inercia *f*.

inescapable [ɪnɪ'skeɪpəbəl] *adj* ineludible, inevitable.

inessential [ɪnɪ'senʃəl] **I** *adj* no esencial, innecesario,-a. **II** **inessentials** *npl* detalles *mpl* or cosas *fpl* sin importancia.

inestimable [ɪn'estɪməbəl] *adj (gen)* inestimable; *(value, cost)* incalculable.

inevitability [ɪnevɪtə'bɪlɪtɪ] *n* inevitabilidad *f*.

inevitable [ɪn'evɪtəbəl] *adj* inevitable; *fam* **his i. jokes,** sus chistes de siempre.

inexact [ɪnɪg'zækt] *adj* inexacto,-a.

inexcusable [ɪnɪk'skjuːzəbəl] *adj* inexcusable, imperdonable, injustificable.

inexhaustible [ɪnɪg'zɔːstəbəl] *adj* inagotable.

inexorable [ɪn'eksərəbəl] *adj fml* inexorable.

inexpensive [ɪnɪk'spensɪv] *adj* económico,-a, barato,-a.

inexperience [ɪnɪk'spɪərɪəns] *n* inexperiencia *f*, falta *f* de experiencia.

inexperienced [ɪnɪk'spɪərɪənst] *adj* inexperto,-a.

inexpert [ɪn'ekspɜːt] *adj* inexperto,-a, inhábil, torpe.

inexplicable [ɪnɪk'splɪkəbəl] *adj* inexplicable.

inexpressible [ɪnɪk'spresəbəl] *adj fml* inexpresable, indecible, inefable.

inexpressive [ɪnɪk'spresɪv] *adj* inexpresivo,-a.

infallibility [ɪnfælə'bɪlɪtɪ] *n* infalibilidad *f*.

infallible [ɪn'fæləbəl] *adj* infalible.

infamous ['ɪnfəməs] *adj* infame, ruin.

infamy ['ɪnfəmɪ] *n* infamia *f*.

infancy ['ɪnfənsɪ] *n (childhood)* infancia *f*, niñez *f*; *fig (first stage)* infancia *f*; **a nation in its i.,** una nación joven.

infant ['ɪnfənt] *n* niño,-a *m*, *f*, criatura *f*. **■** *GB* **i. school,** parvulario *m*.

infanticide [ɪn'fæntɪsaɪd] *n (murder)* infanticidio *m*; *(murderer)* infanticida *mf*.

infantile ['ɪnfəntaɪl] *adj* infantil.

infantry ['ɪnfəntrɪ] *n Mil* infantería *f*.

infantryman ['ɪnfəntrɪmən] *n (pl infantrymen)* *Mil* soldado *m* de infantería.

infatuated [ɪn'fætjʊeɪtɪd] *adj* encaprichado,-a.

infatuation [ɪnfætjʊ'eɪʃən] *n* encaprichamiento *m*.

infect [ɪnˈfekt] *vtr (cut, spot)* infectar; *(food, water)* contaminar; *(person)* contagiar; *fig* **she infected us with her optimism,** nos contagió su optimismo.

infection [ɪnˈfekʃən] *n (of cut etc)* infección *f*; *(of air, food)* contaminación *f*; *(with illness)* infección *f*, contagio *m*; **source of i.,** foco *m* infeccioso *or* de infección.

infectious [ɪnˈfekʃəs] *adj (disease)* infeccioso,-a, contagioso,-a; *fig* contagioso,-a.

infer [ɪnˈfɜːʳ] *vtr (pt & pp* **inferred)** inferir **(from,** de), deducir **(from,** de).

inference [ˈɪnfərəns] *n* inferencia *f*; **to draw inferences from sth,** sacar conclusiones de algo.

inferior [ɪnˈfɪərɪəʳ] **I** *adj* inferior **(to,** a). **II** *n pej* inferior *mf*.

inferiority [ɪnfɪərɪˈɒrɪtɪ] *n* inferioridad *f*.

infernal [ɪnˈfɜːnəl] *adj* infernal.

inferno [ɪnˈfɜːnəʊ] *n (pl* **infernos)** *lit* infierno *m*; *fig* **the house was a raging i.,** la casa ardía en llamas.

infertile [ɪnˈfɜːtaɪl] *adj* estéril.

infertility [ɪnfəˈtɪlɪtɪ] *n* esterilidad *f*.

infest [ɪnˈfest] *vtr* infestar, plagar **(with,** de); **shark-infested seas,** mares *mpl* infestados de tiburones.

infestation [ɪnfesˈteɪʃən] *n* infestación *f*, plaga *f*.

infidelity [ɪnfɪˈdelɪtɪ] *n* infidelidad *f*.

infighting [ˈɪnfaɪtɪŋ] *n fig* luchas *fpl* internas.

infiltrate [ˈɪnfɪltreɪt] *vtr* infiltrarse **(into,** en).

infiltration [ɪnfɪlˈtreɪʃən] *n* infiltración *f*.

infiltrator [ˈɪnfɪltreɪtəʳ] *n* infiltrado,-a *m,f*, espía *mf*.

infinite [ˈɪnfɪnɪt] *adj (gen)* infinito,-a; *(love, patience, etc)* sin límites; **an i. variety of jobs,** un sinfín de empleos. ◆ **infinitely** *adv* infinitamente; **i. better,** muchísimo mejor; **i. tiny,** pequeñísimo,-a.

infinitesimal [ɪnfɪnɪˈtesɪməl] *adj* infinitesimal, infinitéstmo,-a.

infinitive [ɪnˈfɪnɪtɪv] *n Ling* infinitivo *m*.

infinity [ɪnˈfɪnɪtɪ] *n (gen)* infinidad *f*; *Math* infinito *m*.

infirm [ɪnˈfɜːm] **I** *adj (ailing)* enfermizo,-a; *(weak)* débil, endeble. **II the i.** *npl* los inválidos.

infirmary [ɪnˈfɜːmərɪ] *n (hospital)* hospital *m*, clínica *f*; *(in monastery etc)* enfermería *f*.

infirmity [ɪnˈfɜːmɪtɪ] *n fml (ailment)* enfermedad *f*; *(weakness)* debilidad *f*; **the infirmities of old age,** los achaques de la vejez.

inflame [ɪnˈfleɪm] *vtr (anger passion)* encender, inflamar; *(curiosity)* avivar; *(crowd)* excitar; **to be inflamed with rage,** rabiar.

inflamed [ɪnˈfleɪmd] *adj Med* inflamado,-a; **to become i.,** inflamarse.

inflammable [ɪnˈflæməbəl] *adj (material, fuel)* inflamable; *fig (situation)* explosivo,-a.

inflammation [ɪnfləˈmeɪʃən] *n Med* inflamación *f*.

inflammatory [ɪnˈflæmətərɪ] *adj* incendiario,-a.

inflatable [ɪnˈfleɪtəbəl] *adj* inflable.

inflate [ɪnˈfleɪt] **I** *vtr (tyre etc)* hinchar, inflar; *fig (prices)* inflar. **II** *vi* hincharse, inflarse.

inflated [ɪnˈfleɪtɪd] *adj* **1** *(tyre etc)* hinchado,-a, inflado,-a; *fig (prices)* inflacionista, inflacionario,-a. **2** *pej (view, idea)* exagerado,-a; **to have an i. opinion of oneself,** ser muy engreído,-a.

inflation [ɪnˈfleɪʃən] *n Econ* inflación *f*.

inflationary [ɪnˈfleɪʃənərɪ] *adj Econ* inflacionista, inflacionario,-a.

inflect [ɪnˈflekt] **I** *vtr* **1** *(voice)* modular. **2** *Ling (noun)* declinar; *(verb)* conjugar. **II** *vi* **1** *(voice)* modularse. **2** *Ling (noun)* declinarse; *(verb)* conjugarse.

inflected [ɪnˈflektɪd] *adj Ling* flexional.

inflection [ɪnˈflekʃən] *n Ling* inflexión *f*, flexión *f*.

inflexibility [ɪnfleksəˈbɪlɪtɪ] *n* inflexibilidad *f*.

inflexible [ɪnˈfleksəbəl] *adj* inflexible.

inflexion [ɪnˈflekʃən] *n see* inflection.

inflict [ɪnˈflɪkt] *vtr (blow)* dar, asestar **(on,** a); *(damage, wound, suffering)* causar **(on,** a); *(punishment, defeat)* infligir, imponer **(on,** a); *(view, opinion)* imponer **(on,** a); **to i. oneself** *or* **one's company on sb,** imponer su presencia a algn.

in-flight [ˈɪnflaɪt] *adj Av (meal, entertainment)* durante el vuelo.

influence [ˈɪnfluəns] **I** *n* influencia *f*; **to have** *or* **be a strong i. on sb,** tener mucha influencia sobre algn; **under the i. of drink/drugs,** bajo la influencia del alcohol/de las drogas; *fam* **to be under the i.,** llevar una copa de más. **II** *vtr* influir en *or* con; **to be easily influenced,** ser influenciable.

influential [ɪnfluˈenʃəl] *adj* influyente, acreditado,-a.

influenza [ɪnfluˈenzə] *n Med* gripe *f*.

influx [ˈɪnflʌks] *n* afluencia *f*, oleada *f*.

info [ˈɪnfəʊ] *n (abbr of* **information)** *fam* información *f*.

inform [ɪnˈfɔːm] **I** *vtr (gen)* informar, notificar **(of, about,** de, sobre); *(police)* avisar **(of, about,** de); **keep me informed,** téngame al corriente. **II** *vi* **to i. against** *or* **on,** denunciar, delatar.

informal [ɪnˈfɔːməl] *adj* **1** *(occasion, behaviour)* sin ceremonia, sin etiqueta, informal; *(discussion)* entre amigos, de confianza; *(language, treatment)* familiar. **2** *(unofficial)* extraoficial, no oficial.

informality [ɪnfɔːˈmælɪtɪ] *n* **1** *(of occasion, behaviour)* sencillez *f*; *(of treatment)* familiaridad *f*. **2** *(of announcement)* carácter *m* no oficial.

informant [ɪnˈfɔːmənt] *n fml* informante *mf*.

information [ɪnfəˈmeɪʃən] *n (gen)* información *f*; *(details)* detalles *mpl*; *(facts, computer data)* datos *mpl*; *(knowledge)* conocimientos *mpl*; *(news)* noticias *fpl*; **a piece of i.,** una información, un dato. ■ **classified i.,** información *f* secreta *or* reservada; **i. bureau,** centro *m* de información; **i. desk,** información *f*; *Comput* **i. technology,** informática *f*.

informative [ɪnˈfɔːmətɪv] *adj* informativo,-a.

informed [ɪnˈfɔːmd] *adj (gen)* informado,-a, enterado,-a; *(up-to-date)* al corriente, al tanto; **i. guess,** suposición *f* bien fundada.

informer [ɪnˈfɔːməʳ] *n (gen)* delator,-a *m,f*, *(to the police)* informador,-a *m,f*, soplón,-ona *m,f*, chivato,-a *m,f*.

infra dig [ɪnfrəˈdɪg] *adj phr (behaviour, situation)* indigno,-a; *(clothes)* impropio,-a.

infrared [ɪnfrəˈred] *adj* infrarrojo,-a.

infrastructure [ˈɪnfrəstrʌktʃəʳ] *n* infraestructura *f*.

infrequent [ɪnˈfriːkwənt] *adj fml* poco frecuente, raro,-a.

infringe [ɪnˈfrɪndʒ] **I** *vtr fml (law, rule)* infringir, transgredir, violar; *(copyright)* no respetar. **II** *vi* **to i. on** *or* **upon,** *(rights)* violar, usurpar; *(privacy)* invadir, estorbar.

infringement [ɪnˈfrɪndʒmənt] *n fml (of law, rule)* infracción *f*, transgresión *f*, violación *f*; *(of rights)* violación *f*, usurpación *f*.

infuriate [ɪnˈfjʊərɪeɪt] *vtr* poner furioso,-a, enfurecer; **you i. me!,** ¡me pones negro,-a!, ¡me sacas de quicio!

infuriating [ɪnˈfjʊərɪeɪtɪŋ] *adj* exasperante.

infuse [ɪnˈfjuːz] *vtr* **1** *(herbs, tea)* hacer una infusión de. **2** *fig (courage etc)* infundir.

infusion [ɪnˈfjuːʒən] *n (drink)* infusión *f*, tisana *f*.

ingenious [ɪnˈdʒiːnɪəs] *adj (skilful)* ingenioso,-a; *(inspired)* genial.

ingenuity [ɪndʒɪˈnjuːɪtɪ] *n* ingenio *m*, ingeniosidad *f*, inventiva *f*; **to test one's i.,** aguzar el ingenio.

ingenuous [ɪnˈdʒenjuəs] *adj* ingenuo,-a.

ingot [ˈɪŋgət] *n* lingote *m*.

ingrained [ɪnˈgreɪnd] *adj (dirt)* incrustado,-a; *fig (habit, belief)* arraigado,-a.

ingratiate [ɪnˈgreɪʃɪeɪt] *vtr pej* **to i. oneself with sb,** darle coba a algn.

ingratiating [ɪnˈgreɪʃɪeɪtɪŋ] *adj* zalamero,-a obsequioso,-a.

ingratitude [ɪnˈgrætɪtjuːd] *n* ingratitud *f.*

ingredient [ɪnˈgriːdɪənt] *n Culin* ingrediente *m; fig* componente *m,* elemento *m.*

ingrowing [ˈɪngrəʊɪŋ] *adj* **i. nail.,** uñero *m,* uña *f* encarnada.

inhabit [ɪnˈhæbɪt] *vtr fml* vivir en, habitar, ocupar, poblar.

inhabitant [ɪnˈhæbɪtənt] *n* habitante *mf.*

inhalant [ɪnˈheɪlənt] *n* inhalación *f,* medicamento *m* para inhalar.

inhale [ɪnˈheɪl] **I** *vtr (gas, vapour)* inhalar; *(air)* aspirar, respirar; *(cigarette smoke)* tragar. **II** *vi (smoker)* tragar el humo; *(patient)* aspirar, respirar.

inhaler [ɪnˈheɪləʳ] *n* inhalador *m.*

inherent [ɪnˈhɪərənt] *adj* inherente, intrínseco,-a; **the risks i. in climbing,** los riesgos propios del montañismo.

inherit [ɪnˈherɪt] *vtr* heredar **(from,** de).

inheritance [ɪnˈherɪtəns] *n (wealth, title)* herencia *f; (act)* sucesión *f;* **to come into an i.,** heredar.

inhibit [ɪnˈhɪbɪt] *vtr (freedom, activity)* limitar, restringir; *(feeling, reaction)* reprimir, inhibir; *(person)* cohibir; *(sales, growth)* limitar; **to i. sb from doing sth,** impedir a algn de hacer algo.

inhibited [ɪnˈhɪbɪtɪd] *adj* cohibido,-a.

inhibition [ɪnhɪˈbɪʃən] *n* cohibición *f,* inhibición *f.*

inhospitable [ɪnhɒˈspɪtəbəl] *adj (gen)* inhospitalario,-a; *(climate, place)* inhóspito,-a.

inhuman [ɪnˈhjuːmən] *adj,* **inhumane** [ɪnhjuːˈmeɪn] *adj* inhumano,-a.

inhumanity [ɪnhjuːˈmænɪtɪ] *n* falta *f* de humanidad, inhumanidad *f.*

inimical [ɪˈnɪmɪkəl] *adj fml (person)* hostil; *(conditions, methods)* desfavorable; *(interest)* perjudicial.

inimitable [ɪˈnɪmɪtəbəl] *adj* inimitable.

iniquitous [ɪˈnɪkwɪtəs] *adj fml* inicuo,-a, injusto,-a.

iniquity [ɪˈnɪkwɪtɪ] *n fml* iniquidad *f,* injusticia *f.*

initial [ɪˈnɪʃəl] **I** *adj* inicial, primero,-a; **in the i. stages,** al principio. **II** *n* 1 inicial *f,* letra *f* inicial. 2 initials, *(of name)* iniciales *fpl; (of abbreviation etc)* siglas *fpl.* **III** *vtr (pt & pp* **initialled,** *US* **initialed)** firmar con las iniciales. ◆ **initially** *adv* al principio, en primer lugar.

initiate [ɪˈnɪʃɪeɪt] *vtr* 1 *(gen)* iniciar; *(struggle, talks)* iniciar, entablar; *(plan, reform)* promover; *(lawsuit)* entablar. 2 *(admit) (into society)* admitir **(into,** en); *(into knowledge)* iniciar **(into,** en).

initiation [ɪnɪʃɪˈeɪʃən] *n* 1 *(start)* iniciación *f,* principio *m.* 2 *(admission)* admisión *f,* iniciación *f.*

initiative [ɪˈnɪʃətɪv] *n* iniciativa *f;* **on one's own i.,** por iniciativa propia.

inject [ɪnˈdʒekt] *vtr* 1 *(drug etc)* inyectar; *(person)* poner una inyección a; **to i. sb with a vaccine,** vacunar a algn. 2 *fig (capital)* invertir; *(life, hope)* infundir.

injection [ɪnˈdʒekʃən] *n* 1 *Med* inyección *f;* **to give sb an i.,** poner una inyección a algn. 2 *fig (of capital)* inversión *f; (of life, hope)* inyección *f.*

injudicious [ɪndʒʊˈdɪʃəs] *adj fml* poco discreto,-a, imprudente.

injunction [ɪnˈdʒʌŋkʃən] *n Jur* interdicto *m,* entredicho *m;* **to issue/take out an i.,** dar/obtener una orden *or un* mandato.

injure [ˈɪndʒəʳ] *vtr* 1 *(gen)* herir, lesionar, lastimar; **to i. oneself,** hacerse daño. 2 *fig (feelings)* herir; *(health, economy, reputation)* perjudicar.

injured [ˈɪndʒəd] **I** *adj* 1 *(gen)* lesionado,-a, lastimado,-a, herido,-a. 2 *fig (feelings)* herido,-a; *(look, tone)* ofendido,-a. **II the i.** *npl* los heridos.

injurious [ɪnˈdʒʊərɪəs] *adj fml* perjudicial.

injury [ˈɪndʒərɪ] *n* 1 *(hunt)* herida *f,* lesión *f;* **to do oneself an i.,** hacerse daño, lastimarse. ■ *Sport* **i. time,** (tiempo *m* de) descuento *m.* 2 *fig (harm)* daño *m,* perjuicio *m.*

injustice [ɪnˈdʒʌstɪs] *n* injusticia *f;* **to do sb an i.,** ser injusto,-a con algn.

ink [ɪŋk] *n* tinta *f.* ■ **invisible i.,** tinta *f* simpática. ◆ **ink in** *vtr* repasar con tinta.

inkling [ˈɪŋklɪŋ] *n (idea)* idea *f,* noción *f,* impresión *f; (suspicion)* sospecha *f; (sign)* señal *m,* indicio *m;* **I hadn't an i. that he was married,** no tenía la menor idea de que estaba casado.

inkpad [ˈɪŋkpæd] *n* almohadilla *f.*

inkwell [ˈɪŋkwel] *n* tintero *m.*

inky [ˈɪŋkɪ] *adj (inkier, inkiest)* 1 *(fingers etc)* manchado,-a de tinta. 2 *fig (night etc)* negro,-a.

inlaid [ɪnˈleɪd] **I** *-pt & pp see* **inlay. II** *adj (wood)* taraceado,-a; *(iron, gold)* damasquinado,-a; *(marquetry)* adornado,-a con marquetería; *(ivory, gems)* incrustado,-a.

inland [ˈɪnlənd] **I** *adj* (del) interior. ■ *GB* **I. Revenue.,** Hacienda *f.* **II** [ɪnˈlænd] *adv* 1 *(live)* en el interior. 2 *(travel)* tierra adentro, hacia el interior.

in-laws [ˈɪnlɔːz] *npl fam* familia *f sing* política.

inlay [ˈɪnleɪ] **I** *n* 1 *(in wood)* taracea *f; (in metal)* damasquinado *m; (of marquetry)* marquetería *f.* 2 *(in tooth)* empaste *m.* **II** [ɪnˈleɪ] *vtr (pt & pp* **inlaid)** *(wood)* taracear; *(iron, gold)* damasquinar; *(ivory, gem)* incrustar.

inlet [ˈɪnlet] *n* 1 *(in coastline)* ensenada *f,* cala *f; (between islands)* brazo *m* de mar. 2 *(in pipe, machine)* entrada *f,* admisión *f.*

inmate [ˈɪnmeɪt] *n (gen)* residente *mf,* habitante *mf; (of prison)* preso,-a *m, f,* interno,-a *m, f; (of hospital)* enfermo,-a *m, f,* hospitalizado,-a *m, f; (of asylum, camp)* internado,-a *m, f.*

inmost [ˈɪnməʊst] *adj see* **innermost.**

inn [ɪn] *n (with lodging)* posada *f,* mesón *m,* fonda *f; (in country)* venta *f; (pub)* taberna *f.*

innards [ˈɪnədz] *npl* entrañas *fpl,* tripas *fpl.*

innate [ɪˈneɪt] *adj* innato,-a.

inner [ˈɪnəʳ] *adj* 1 *(room, region)* interior; *(structure, organization)* interno,-a. ■ **i. city,** centro *m* de una ciudad; **i. ear,** oído *m* interno; **i. tube,** cámara *f* de aire. 2 *fig (thoughts, feelings)* interior, íntimo,-a; *(peace etc)* profundo,-a.

innermost [ˈɪnəməʊst] *adj* 1 *(room, recess)* más interior. 2 *fig (thoughts, feelings)* más íntimo,-a, más secreto,-a.

innings [ˈɪnɪŋz] *n Crick* entrada *f,* turno *m; GB fam fig* **to have had a good i.,** haber disfrutado de una vida larga y feliz.

innkeeper [ˈɪnkiːpəʳ] *n arch (of lodging house)* posadero,-a *m, f* mesonero, *m, f; (of pub)* tabernero,-a *m, f.*

innocence [ˈɪnəsəns] *n* inocencia *f.*

innocent [ˈɪnəsənt] *adj & n* inocente *(mf).*

innocuous [ɪˈnɒkjʊəs] *adj* inocuo,-a, inofensivo,-a.

innovate [ˈɪnəveɪt] *vi* innovar.

innovation [ɪnəˈveɪʃən] *n* innovación *f,* novedad *f.*

innovative [ˈɪnəvətɪv] *adj,* **innovatory** [ɪnəˈveɪtərɪ] *adj* innovador,-a.

innovator [ˈɪnəveɪtəʳ] *n* innovador,-a *m, f.*

innuendo [ɪnjuˈendəʊ] *n (pl* **innuendoes** *or* **innuendos)** indirecta *f,* insinuación *f.*

innumerable [ɪˈnjuːmərəbəl] *adj* innumerable.

inoculate [ɪˈnɒkjʊleɪt] *vtr* inocular, vacunar.

inoculation [ɪnɒkjʊˈleɪʃən] *n* inoculación *f,* vacuna *f.*

inoffensive [ɪnəˈfensɪv] *adj* inofensivo,-a.

inoperable [ɪnˈɒpərəbəl] *adj Med* inoperable.

inoperative [ɪnˈɒpərətɪv] *adj* inoperante.

inopportune [ɪn'ɒpətjuːn, ɪnɒpə'tjuːn] *adj* inoportuno,-a.

inordinate [ɪ'nɔːdɪnɪt] *adj fml* **1** *(uncontrolled)* desmesurado,-a, desmedido,-a. **2** *(excessive)* excesivo,-a.

inorganic [ɪnɔː'gænɪk] *adj* inorgánico,-a.

inpatient ['ɪnpeɪʃənt] *n* interno,-a *m,f*, internado,-a *m,f*.

input ['ɪnput] **I** *n 1 (of capital, resources)* inversión *f*; *(of power)* entrada *f*; *Comput (of data)* input *m*. **II** *(pt & pp* **input)** *vtr Comput* entrar, introducir.

inquest ['ɪnkwest] *n* encuesta *f* judicial; *fam fig* investigación *f*.

inquire [ɪn'kwaɪəʳ] **I** *vtr (ask)* preguntar; *(find out)* averiguar, informarse de; *fml* se lo **i.**, preguntar algo a algn. **II** *vi (ask)* preguntar **(about,** por); *(find out)* informarse **(about,** de), pedir informes **(about,** sobre); **'i. within'**, 'razón aquí'. ◆ **inquire after** *vtr (person, person's heath)* preguntar por. ◆ **inquire into** *vtr (case, matter)* investigar, indagar.

inquiring [ɪn'kwaɪərɪŋ] *adj (look etc)* de interrogación; *(mind)* curioso,-a, inquisidor,-a.

inquiry [ɪn'kwaɪərɪ] *n* **1** *(question)* pregunta *f*; **'all inquiries to ...'**, 'dirigirse a ...'; **'inquiries'**, 'información'; **to make inquiries (about sth)**, pedir informes (sobre algo). ■ **i. desk**, información *f*. **2** *(investigation)* investigación *f*, encuesta *f*; **to set up** *or* **open an i.**, abrir una investigación; **we are making inquiries**, estamos investigando.

inquisition [ɪnkwɪ'zɪʃən] *n* investigación *f*, inquisición *f*; *Hist* **the (Spanish) I.**, la Inquisición.

inquisitive [ɪn'kwɪzɪtɪv] *adj (curious)* curioso,-a, inquisidor,-a; *(questioning)* preguntón,-ona. ◆ **inquisitively** *adv* con curiosidad.

inroads ['ɪnrəʊdz] *npl* **the firm is making i. into the market**, la empresa está ganando terreno *or* se está abriendo camino en el mercado; **to make i. on one's free time**, quitarle a uno sus horas libres; **to make i. into one's capital**, reducir *or* mermar su capital.

insane [ɪn'seɪn] **I** *adj (person)* loco,-a, demente; *(act)* insensato,-a; **to go i.**, enloquecer, volverse loco,-a; *fig* **to drive sb i.**, volver loco,-a a algn; *fam* **what an i. idea!**, ¡vaya locura! **II the i.** *npl* los enfermos mentales. ◆ **insanely** *adv fig* **i. jealous**, loco,-a de celos.

insanitary [ɪn'sænɪtərɪ] *adj* insalubre, antihigiénico,-a.

insanity [ɪn'sænɪtɪ] *n* **1** *Med (madness)* demencia *f*, locura *f*. **2** *fig (stupidity)* locura *f*, insensatez *f*.

insatiable [ɪn'seɪʃəbəl] *adj* insaciable.

inscribe [ɪn'skraɪb] *vtr fml (tombstone)* inscribir, grabar; *(book, photo)* dedicar; *(name, initials)* inscribir.

inscription [ɪn'skrɪpʃən] *n (on stone, coin)* inscripción *f*; *(in book, on photo)* dedicatoria *f*.

inscrutable [ɪn'skruːtəbəl] *adj* inescrutable, insondable, impenetrable.

insect ['ɪnsekt] *n* insecto *m*. ■ **i. bite**, picadura *f*.

insecticide [ɪn'sektɪsaɪd] *n* insecticida *m*.

insecure [ɪnsɪ'kjʊəʳ] *adj* inseguro,-a.

insecurity [ɪnsɪ'kjʊərɪtɪ] *n* inseguridad *f*.

inseminate [ɪn'semɪneɪt] *vtr* inseminar.

insensible [ɪn'sensəbəl] *adj fml* **1** *(unconscious)* inconsciente, sin conocimiento. **2** *(unaware)* inconsciente. **3** *(unfeeling)* insensible.

insensitive [ɪn'sensɪtɪv] *adj* insensible.

insensitivity [ɪnsensɪ'tɪvɪtɪ] *n* insensibilidad *f*.

inseparable [ɪn'sepərəbəl] *adj* inseparable.

insert ['ɪnsɜːt] **I** *n (in journal etc)* encarte *m*. **II** [ɪn'sɜːt] *vtr (gen)* introducir, meter **(in, into,** en); *(clause, text)* incluir, insertar **(in, into,** en); *(advertisement)* poner **(in, into,** en).

insertion [ɪn'sɜːʃən] *n (gen)* introducción *f*; *(of clause, text)* inclusión *f*, inserción *f*; *(in newspaper)* anuncio *m*.

inset ['ɪnset] *n (in map, picture)* recuadro *m*.

inshore ['ɪnʃɔːʳ] **I** *adj (fishing, navigation)* costero,-a; *(wind)* de mar. **II** [ɪn'ʃɔːʳ] *adv (fish, sail)* cerca de la costa; *(blow)* hacia la costa.

inside [ɪn'saɪd] **I** *n* **1** interior *m*, parte *f* interior; **gloves with fur on the i.**, guantes *mpl* forrados de piel; **on/from the i.**, por/de dentro; **to know sb i. out**, conocer muy bien a algn; **to know sth i. out**, conocer algo al dedillo; *Aut* **to overtake on the i.**, *(in Britain)* adelantar por la izquierda; *(in the US, Europe, etc)* adelantar por la derecha; **to turn sth i. out**, volver algo al revés; *fam* **someone on the i. told me**, me lo dijo alguien de dentro. **2** *fam* **insides**, tripas *fpl*. **II** ['ɪnsaɪd] *adj* interior; *Sport* **i. forward**, interior *mf*; *Aut* **i. lane**, carril *m* interior; *Sport* **i. left/right**, interior *mf* izquierda/derecha; *fam* **i. information**, información *f* confidencial *or* privilegiada; *fam* **i. story**, *(of scandal)* revelaciones *fpl* íntimas; *(of event)* relato *m* de uno de los protagonistas; *fam* **the robbery was an i. job**, el robo fue organizado por alguien de dentro. **III** [ɪn'saɪd] *adv (be, stay)* dentro, adentro; *(run etc)* hacia *or* para adentro; **please come** *or* **step i.**, pase, por favor; **to come** *or* **go i.**, entrar; **we looked i. and outside**, miramos por dentro y por fuera; *fig* **to feel funny i.**, tener una sensación rara en el estómago; *GB fam* **he spent a year i.**, pasó un año en chirona. **IV** *prep* **1** *(place)* dentro de; *Aut* **to be travelling i.**, **the speed limit**, circular dentro del límite de velocidad. **2** *fam* **i. (of)**, *(time)* en menos de, dentro de.

insider [ɪn'saɪdəʳ] *n* persona *f* enterada. ■ *Jur Fin* **i. dealing** *or* **trading**, uso *m* indebido de información privilegiada y confidencial para operaciones comerciales.

insidious [ɪn'sɪdɪəs] *adj* insidioso,-a.

insight ['ɪnsaɪt] *n* **1** *(perception)* penetración *f*, perspicacia *f*. **2** *(understanding)* idea *f*; **to get an i. into sth**, hacerse una idea de algo.

insignia [ɪn'sɪgnɪə] *n inv* insignia *f*.

insignificance [ɪnsɪg'nɪfɪkəns] *n* insignificancia *f*.

insignificant [ɪnsɪg'nɪfɪkənt] *adj* insignificante.

insincere [ɪnsɪn'sɪəʳ] *adj* poco sincero,-a, insincero,-a, falso,-a.

insincerity [ɪnsɪn'serɪtɪ] *n* falta *f* de sinceridad, insinceridad *f*, falsedad *f*.

insinuate [ɪn'sɪnjʊeɪt] *vtr* **1** *(hint)* insinuar, dar a entender. **2** *(ingratiate)* insinuarse.

insinuation [ɪnsɪnjʊ'eɪʃən] *n* insinuación *f*, indirecta *f*.

insipid [ɪn'sɪpɪd] *adj* insípido,-a, soso,-a, insulso,-a.

insist [ɪn'sɪst] **1** *vi (gen)* insistir **(on, upon,** en); *(argue)* obstinarse **(on, upon,** en); **I i. on coming**, insisto en ir. **II** *vtr* insistir; **to i. that ...**, insistir en que ... .

insistence [ɪn'sɪstəns] *n* insistencia *f*, empeño *m*; **at my i.**, ante mi insistencia.

insistent [ɪn'sɪstənt] *adj* **1** *(person)* insistente, obstinado,-a; **I was most i. about it**, insistí mucho en ello. **2** *(demand, noise)* persistente.

in so far as [ɪnsəʊ'fɑːrəz] *adv* en la medida en que, en tanto que.

insole ['ɪnsəʊl] *n (of shoe)* plantilla *f*.

insolence ['ɪnsələns] *n* insolencia *f*, descaro *m*, frescura *f*.

insolent ['ɪnsələnt] *adj* insolente, descarado,-a, fresco,-a.

insoluble [ɪn'sɒljʊbəl] *adj* insoluble, indisoluble.

insolvency [ɪn'sɒlvənsɪ] *n* insolvencia *f*.

insolvent [ɪn'sɒlvənt] *adj* insolvente.

insomnia [ɪn'sɒmnɪə] *n* insomnio *m*.

insomniac [ɪn'sɒmnɪæk] *n* insomne *mf*.

insomuch as [ɪnsəʊ'mʌtʃəz] *adv phr* **1** *(inasmuch as)* puesto que, visto que, ya que. **2** *(to such extent)* hasta tal punto que.

insouciance [ɪn'suːsɪəns] *n fml* despreocupación *f*, indiferencia *f*.

Insp *abbr of* **Inspector,** Inspector,-a *m,f,* Inspec.

inspect [ɪn'spekt] *vtr* **1** *(gen)* inspeccionar, examinar, revisar; *(luggage etc)* registrar. **2** *(troops)* pasar revista a; *(school)* inspeccionar.

inspection [ɪn'spekʃən] *n* **1** *(gen)* inspección *f,* examen *m,* revisión *f; (of luggage etc)* registro *m;* **to make a detailed i. of sth,** examinar algo minuciosamente. **2** *(of troops)* revista *f; (of school)* (visita *f* de) inspección *f.*

inspector [ɪn'spektəʳ] *n (gen)* inspector,-a *m,f; (on bus, train)* revisor,-a *m, f.* ■ **police i.,** inspector,-a *m, f* de policía; **tax i.,** inspector,-a *m, f* de hacienda.

inspectorate [ɪn'spektərɪt] *n* cuerpo *m* de inspectores.

inspiration [ɪnspɪ'reɪʃən] *n* inspiración *f;* **to get** *or* **draw i. from sb/sth,** inspirarse en algn/algo.

inspire [ɪn'spaɪəʳ] *vtr* **1** *(feeling, novel)* inspirar; **to i. respect in sb, to i. sb with respect,** infundir respeto a algn. **2** *(effort)* estimular, animar; **it inspired me to try harder,** me animó a esforzarme más.

inspired [ɪn'spaɪəd] *adj* inspirado,-a.

inspiring [ɪn'spaɪərɪŋ] *adj* inspirador,-a.

Inst *abbr of* **Institute,** Instituto *m,* Inst.

instability [ɪnstə'bɪlɪtɪ] *n* inestabilidad *f.*

install, *US* **instal** [ɪn'stɔːl] *vtr (pp & pp installed)* **1** *(fit)* instalar; *fml* **to i. oneself in an armchair,** instalarse en un sillón. **2** *(appoint)* nombrar.

installation [ɪnstə'leɪʃən] *n* **1** *(of equipment)* instalación *f.* **2** *(appointment)* nombramiento *m.*

instalment *US* **installment** [ɪn'stɔːlmənt] *n* **1** *(of payment)* plazo *m;* **to pay by** *or* **in instalments,** pagar a plazos. ■ **annual i.,** anualidad *f; US* **i. plan,** venta *f or* compra *f* a plazos; **monthly i.,** mensualidad *f.* **2** *(of novel, programme)* entrega *f; (of journal)* fascículo *m.*

instance ['ɪnstəns] *n* ejemplo *m;* caso *m;* **for i.,** por ejemplo; **in the first i.,** en primer lugar; **in this i.,** en este caso.

instant ['ɪnstənt] **I** *n (moment)* instante *m,* momento *m;* **do it this i.!,** ¡hazlo ahora mismo!; **in an i.,** *(soon)* de un momento a otro; *(quickly)* en un instante; **not an i. too soon,** justo a tiempo; **the i. I saw you,** en cuanto te vi. **II** *adj (gen)* inmediato,-a; *(coffee, meal)* instantáneo,-a. ◆ **took an i. liking to him,** me cayó bien enseguida. ◆ **instantly** *adv* inmediatamente, al instante; **he died i.,** su muerte fue instantánea.

instantaneous [ɪnstən'teɪnɪəs] *adj* instantáneo,-a.

instead [ɪn'sted] **I** *adv* en lugar de eso, en cambio. **II** *prep* **i. of,** en vez de, en lugar de; **I went i. of her,** fui yo en su lugar.

instep ['ɪnstep] *n* empeine *m.*

instigate ['ɪnstɪgeɪt] *vtr* instigar.

instigation [ɪnstɪ'geɪʃən] *n* instigación *f.*

instigator ['ɪnstɪgeɪtəʳ] *n* instigador,-a *m,f.*

instil, *US* **instill** [ɪn'stɪl] *vtr (pt & pp instilled) (idea, habit)* inculcar **(in,** a, en); *(courage, respect)* infundir **(in,** a).

instinct ['ɪnstɪŋkt] *n* instinto *m;* **to have an i. for sth/for doing sth,** tener un don para algo/para hacer algo.

instinctive [ɪn'stɪŋktɪv] *adj* instintivo,-a, intuitivo,-a.

institute ['ɪnstɪtjuːt] **I** *n (gen)* instituto *m; (centre)* centro *m; (professional body)* asociación *f,* colegio *m.* **II** *vtr fml* **1** *(system, rules)* establezer; *(society)* fundar, empezar. **2** *(start)* iniciar, empezar; *(proceedings)* entablar.

institution [ɪnstɪ'tjuːʃən] *n* **1** *(act)* institución *f,* creación *f.* **2** *(organization)* institución *f;* organismo *m.* **3** *(home)* asilo *m; (asylum)* manicomio *m.* **4** *(habit, custom)* institución *f;* tradición *f.*

institutional [ɪnstɪ'tjuːʃənəl] *adj* institucional.

institutionalize [ɪnstɪ'tjuːʃənəlaɪz] *vtr* **1** *(practice)* institucionalizar. **2** *(person)* meter en un asilo *or* manicomio.

instruct [ɪn'strʌkt] *vtr* **1** *(teach)* instruir, enseñar. **2** *(order)* mandar; **I am instructed to say that ...,** me han encargado decir que ... .

instruction [ɪn'strʌkʃən] *n* **1** *(teaching)* instrucción *f,* enseñanza *f;* **driving i.,** clases *fpl* de conducir. **2 instructions,** instrucciones *fpl;* **'instructions for use',** 'modo de empleo'; **on the instructions of the boss,** por orden del jefe.

instructive [ɪn'strʌktɪv] *adj* instructivo,-a, formativo,-a.

instructor [ɪn'strʌktəʳ] *n (gen)* instructor,-a *m, f; (of driving)* profesor,-a *m,f; (of sport)* monitor,-a *m,f.*

instructress [ɪn'strʌktrɪs] *n (gen)* instructora *f; (of driving)* profesora *f; (of sport)* monitora *f.*

instrument ['ɪnstrəmənt] *n* instrumento *m.* ■ *Aut Av Naut* **i. panel,** tablero *m* de mandos.

instrumental [ɪnstrə'mentəl] *adj* **1** *Mus* instrumental. **2** *fml* **to be i. in sth/in doing sth,** contribuir decisivamente a algo/a hacer algo.

instrumentalist [ɪnstrə'mentəlɪst] *n Mus* instrumentista *mf.*

instrumentation [ɪnstrəmen'teɪʃən] *n* **1** *Aut Av Naut* instrumentos *mpl.* **2** *Mus* instrumentación *f.*

insubordinate [ɪnsə'bɔːdɪnɪt] *adj* insubordinado,-a, indisciplinado,-a.

insubordination [ɪnsəbɔːdɪ'neɪʃən] *n* insubordinación *f,* indisciplina *f.*

insubstancial [ɪnsəb'stænʃəl] *adj (gen)* insubstancial; *(meal)* poco nutritivo,-a; *(structure)* poco sólido,-a, poco seguro,-a; *(evidence)* flojo,-a.

insufferable [ɪn'sʌfərəbəl] *adj* insoportable, inaguantable, insufrible. ◆ **insufferably** *adv* **i. rude,** extremadamente grosero,-a.

insufficient [ɪnsə'fɪʃənt] *adj* insuficiente.

insular ['ɪnsjʊləʳ] *adj* **1** *Geog* insular. **2** *fig pej* estrecho,-a de miras.

insularity [ɪnsjʊ'lærɪtɪ] *n* **1** *Geog* insularidad *f.* **2** *fig pej* estrechez *f* de miras.

insulate ['ɪnsjʊleɪt] *vtr* aislar **(against, from,** de).

insulating tape ['ɪnsjʊleɪtɪŋteɪp] *n Elec* cinta *f* aislante.

insulation [ɪnsjʊ'leɪʃən] *n* aislamiento *m.*

insulin ['ɪnsjʊlɪn] *n* insulina *f.*

insult ['ɪnsʌlt] **I** *n (words)* insulto *m; (action)* afrenta *f,* ofensa *f,* ultraje *m; fig* **to add i. to injury,** para colmo. **II** [ɪn'sʌlt] *n vtr* insultar, ofender.

insulting [ɪn'sʌltɪŋ] *adj* insultante, ofensivo,-a.

insuperable [ɪn'suːpərəbəl] *adj* insuperable.

insurance [ɪn'ʃʊərəns] *n* seguro *m;* **to take out i.,** hacerse *or* contratar un seguro. ■ **fire i.,** seguro *m* contra incendios; **fully comprehensive i.,** seguro *m* a todo riesgo; **i. broker,** agente *mf* de seguros; **i. company,** compañía *f* de seguros; **i. cover,** cobertura *f* del seguro; **i. policy,** póliza *f* (de seguro); **i. premium,** prima *f* (de seguro); **i. value,** valor *m* asegurado; **life i.,** seguro *m* de vida; **private health i.,** seguro *m* médico privado; **third party i.,** seguro *m* a terceros.

insure [ɪn'ʃʊəʳ] *vtr* asegurar **(against,** contra); **to i. oneself** *or* **one's life,** hacerse un seguro de vida.

insured [ɪn'ʃʊəd] *adj & n* asegurado,-a *m, f).*

insurer [ɪn'ʃʊərəʳ] *n* asegurador,-a *m,f.*

insurgent [ɪn'sɜːdʒənt] *adj & n* insurgente *(mf),* insurrecto,-a *m, f).*

insurmountable [ɪnsə'maʊtəbəl] *adj (problem etc)* insuperable; *(barrier)* infranqueable.

insurrection [ɪnsə'rekʃən] *n* insurreción *f.*

intact [ɪn'tækt] *adj* intacto,-a.

intake ['ɪnteɪk] *n* **1** *Tech (of air, water)* entrada *f; (of electricity, water, gas)* toma *f.* **2** *(of food, calories)* consumo *m.* **3** *(of students, recruits)* número *m* de admitidos *or* inscritos.

intangible [ɪn'tændʒɪbəl] *adj* intangible.

integer ['ɪntɪdʒəʳ] *n Math* (número *m*) entero *m*.

integral ['ɪntɪɡrəl] **I** *adj* **1** *(intrinsic)* integrante. **2** *(whole)* íntegro,-a. **3** *Math* integral. **II** *n Math* integral *f*.

integrate ['ɪntɪɡreɪt] **I** *vtr* integrar (**into, with,** en), incorporar (**into, with,** a). **II** *vi* integrarse (**into, with,** en), incorporarse (**into, with,** a).

integrated ['ɪntɪɡreɪtɪd] *adj* integrado,-a.

integration [ɪntɪ'ɡreɪʃən] *n* integración *f*.

integrity [ɪn'teɡrɪtɪ] *n* integridad *f*, honradez *f*.

intellect ['ɪntɪlekt] *n* inteligencia *f*, intelecto *m*.

intellectual [ɪntɪ'lektʃʊəl] *adj & n* intelectual *(mf)*.

intelligence [ɪn'telɪdʒəns] *n* **1** *(gen)* inteligencia *f*. ■ *Comput* **artificial i.,** inteligencia *f* artificial; **i. quotient,** cociente *m* intelectual. **2** *(information)* espionaje *m*, información *f*. ■ **i. officer,** oficial *m* del servicio de información.

intelligent [ɪn'telɪdʒənt] *adj* inteligente.

intelligentsia [ɪntelɪ'dʒentsɪə] *n* intelectualidad *f*.

intelligible [ɪn'telɪdʒəbəl] *adj* inteligible,comprensible.

intemperate [ɪn'tempərɪt] *adj fml (behaviour; habits)* inmoderado,-a; *(drunkard)* dado,-a a la bebida; *(climate)* riguroso, -a.

intend [ɪn'tend] *vtr* **1** *(mean)* tener la intención de, proponerse, querer; **I i. you to be happy,** quiero que seas feliz; **I intended no harm,** no lo hice con mala intención; **it was intended as a joke,** era sólo una broma; **to i. to do sth, i doing sth,** tener el propósito de hacer algo; **was that intended?,** ¿fue intencionado? **2** *(destine for)* **to i. sth for sb,** destinar algo a algn; **that place was intended for me,** ese sitio estaba reservado para mí; **the film is intended for children,** la película es para niños.

intended [ɪn'tendɪd] **I** *adj* **1** *(deliberate)* intencionado,-a, deliberado,-a. **2** *(planned)* previsto,-a, proyectado,-a; **it had the i. effect,** consiguió el efecto deseado. **II** *n arch* prometido,-a *m,f*.

intense [ɪn'tens] *adj (gen)* intenso,-a, fuerte; *(look)* penetrante; *(person)* muy serio,-a; *(difficulty)* enorme, sumo,-a. ◆ **intensely** *adv (extremely)* enormemente, sumamente; **to dislike sb i.,** tener una fuerte aversión a algn.

intensify [ɪn'tensɪfaɪ] **I** *vtr (pt & pp intensified) (search)* intensificar; *(effort)* redoblar; *(production, pollution)* aumentar. **II** *vi* intensificarse, aumentar.

intensity [ɪn'tensɪtɪ] *n* intensidad *f*.

intensive [ɪn'tensɪv] *adj (course, farming)* intensivo,-a; *(activity, study)* profundo,-a. ■ *Med* **i. care unit,** unidad *f* de vigilancia intensiva.

intent [ɪn'tent] **I** *adj* **1** *(absorbed)* absorto,-a; *(gaze etc)* atento,-a. **2** *(resolved)* decidido,-a; **to be i. on doing sth,** estar resuelto,-a *or* decidido,-a a hacer algo. **II** *n fml* intención *f*, propósito *m*; **to all intents and purposes,** a todos los efectos.

intention [ɪn'tenʃən] *n* intención *f*, propósito *m*.

intentional [ɪn'tenʃənəl] *adj* deliberado,-a, intencional; **it wasn't i.,** fue sin querer. ◆ **intentionally** *adv* a propósito, adrede.

inter [ɪn'tɜːʳ] *vtr (pt & pp interred) fml* enterrar.

inter- ['ɪntəʳ] *pref* inter-, entre-.

interact [ɪntər'ækt] *vi* actuar recíprocamente, interactuar.

interaction [ɪntər'ækʃən] *n* interacción *f*.

interactive [ɪntər'æktɪv] *adj* interactivo,-a.

intercede [ɪntə'siːd] *vi* interceder (**with,** con).

intercept [ɪntə'sept] *vtr* interceptar.

interception [ɪntə'sepʃən] *n* interceptación *f*.

interceptor [ɪntə'septəʳ] *n Av* avión *m* interceptor.

intercession [ɪntə'seʃən] *n* intercesión *f*, mediación *f*.

interchange ['ɪntətʃeɪndʒ] **I** *n* **1** *(exchange)* intercambio *m*. **2** *(on motorway)* cruce *m*. **II** [ɪntə'tʃeɪndʒ] *vtr* intercambiar (**with,** con).

interchangeable [ɪntə'tʃeɪndʒəbəl] *adj* intercambiable.

intercity [ɪntə'sɪtɪ] *adj Rail* interurbano,-a, de largo recorrido.

intercom ['ɪntəkɒm] *n* interfono *m*.

interconnect [ɪntəkə'nekt] *vtr* interconectar.

intercontinental [ɪntəkɒntɪ'nentəl] *adj* intercontinental. ■ **i. ballistic missile,** misil *m* balístico intercontinental.

intercourse ['ɪntəkɔːs] *n* **1** *(dealings)* trato *m*. **2** *(sexual)* relaciones *fpl* sexuales, coito *m*.

interdependent [ɪntədɪ'pendənt] *adj* interdependiente.

interest ['ɪntrɪst] **I** *n* **1** *(curiosity)* interés *m*; **is this of i. to you?,** ¿te interesa esto?; **my main i. is travel,** viajar es lo que más me interesa; **to have** *or* **take an i. in sb/sth,** interesarse por algn/algo; **to lose i. in sth/in doing sth,** perder el interés por algo/en hacer algo. **2** *(advantage)* provecho *m*, beneficio *m*; **in the i. of peace,** en pro de la paz; **it's not in my (best) i.,** yo no salgo ganando; **to act in one's own i.,** obrar en beneficio propio; **to have a vested i. in sth,** tener interés personal en algo. **3** *Com (share)* participación *f*, interés *m*; **he has a controlling i. in the firm,** tiene la mayor parte de las acciones de la empresa. **4** *Fin* interés *m*, rédito *m*; **a loan at six per cent i.,** un préstamo a un interés del seis por ciento; **i.-free loan,** préstamo sin intereses. ■ **i. rate,** tipo *m* de interés; **simple/compound i.,** interés *m* simple/compuesto. **II** *vtr* interesar; **to be interested in sth/sb,** interesarse en *or* por algn/algo; *fml* **can I i. you in a drink?,** ¿le gustaría tomar algo?

interested ['ɪntrɪstɪd] *adj* interesado,-a.

interesting ['ɪntrɪstɪŋ] *adj* interesante. ◆ **interestingly** *adv* **i. enough ...,** lo curioso (del caso) es que ... .

interface ['ɪntəfeɪs] *n* interface *f*, *fig* terreno *m* común.

interfere [ɪntə'fɪəʳ] *vi* **1** *(meddle)* entrometerse, meterse (in, en; **between,** entre); **to i. with,** *(hinder)* dificultar; *(spoil)* estropear; *(prevent)* impedir; **don't i. with my papers,** no toques mis papeles. **2** *Rad TV* interferir (**with,** con). **3** *euph (person)* abusar (**with,** de).

interference [ɪntə'fɪərəns] *n* **1** *(meddling)* intromisión *f*, entrometimiento *m*, injerencia *f*. **2** *(hindrance)* dificultad *f*, estorbo *m*. **3** *Rad TV* interferencia *f*.

interfering [ɪntə'fɪərɪŋ] *adj* entrometido,-a.

interim ['ɪntərɪm] **I** *n fml* **in the i.,** en el ínterin, mientras tanto. **II** *adj* interino,-a, provisional.

interior [ɪn'tɪərɪəʳ] **I** *adj (gen)* interior. **II** *n* interior *m*, parte *f* interior. ■ **i. design,** interiorismo *m*; **i. designer,** interiorista *mf*.

interject [ɪntə'dʒekt] *vtr* interponer.

interjection [ɪntə'dʒekʃən] *n* **1** *(act, remark)* interposición *f*. **2** *Ling* interjección *f*.

interlink [ɪntə'lɪŋk] *vtr* entrelazar.

interlock [ɪntə'lɒk] **1** *vtr (fingers)* entrelazar; *(cogs)* engranar; *(units, parts)* enganchar. **II** *vi (fingers)* entrelazarse; *(cogs)* engranarse; *(units)* engancharse.

interlocutor [ɪntə'lɒkjʊtəʳ] *n fml* interlocutor,-a *m,f*.

interloper ['ɪntələupəʳ] *n* intruso,-a *m,f*.

interlude ['ɪntəluːd] *n* **1** *(break)* intervalo *m*, pausa *f*. **2** *Cin Theat* descanso *m*, intermedio *m*; *Mus* interludio *m*.

intermarriage [ɪntə'mærɪdʒ] *n* *(within family)* matrimonio *m* entre parientes; *(between races, tribes, etc)* matrimonio *m* mixto.

intermediary [ɪntə'miːdɪərɪ] *n* intermediario,-a *m,f*.

intermediate [ɪntə'miːdɪət] *adj* intermedio,-a.

interment [ɪn'tɜːmənt] *n fml* entierro *m*.

interminable [ɪn'tɜːmɪnəbəl] *adj* inacabable, interminable, sin fin.

intermingle [ɪntəˈmɪŋɡəl] *vi* entremezclarse.

intermisson [ɪntəˈmɪʃən] *n US Cin Mus Theat* descanso *m*, intermedio *m*.

intermittent [ɪntəˈmɪtənt] *adj* intermitente.

intern [ɪnˈtɜːn] I *vtr* internar, recluir. II [ˈɪntɜːn] *n US Med interno*,-a *m*,*f*.

internal [ɪnˈtɜːnəl] *adj* 1 (gen), interior; *(dispute,injury)* interno,-a. 2 *pol (domestic)* interior; *US* I. **Revenue**, ≈ Hacienda *f*. ◆ **internally** *adv* interiormente; *Med* 'not to be taken i.', 'euso externo'.

international [ɪntəˈnæʃənəl] I *adj* internacional; **the i. date line**, la línea de cambio de fecha. II *n Sport (player)* internacional *mf*; *(match)* partido *m* internacional.

internee [ɪntɜːˈniː] *n* preso,-a, *m*,*f*, interno,-a *m*,*f*.

internment [ɪnˈtɜːnmənt] *n* internamiento *m*.

interpersonal [ɪntəˈpɜːsənəl] *adj* interpersonal.

interplay [ˈɪntəpleɪ] *n* interacción *f*.

interpolate [ɪnˈtɜːpəleɪt] *vtr fml* interpolar, intercalar.

interpose [ɪntəˈpəʊz] *vtr fml* interponer.

interpret [ɪnˈtɜːprɪt] I *vtr (gen)* interpretar; *(understand)* interpretar, entender. II *vi* actuar or hacer de intérprete.

interpretation [ɪntɜːprɪˈteɪʃən] *n* interpretación *f*.

interpreter [ɪnˈtɜːprɪtər] *n* intérprete *mf*.

interrelated [ɪntərɪˈleɪtɪd] *adj* estrechamente relacionado,-a.

interrogate [ɪnˈtərəɡeɪt] *vtr* interrogar.

interrogation [ɪntərəˈɡeɪʃən] *n* errogatorio *m*.

interrogative [ɪntəˈrɒɡətɪv] *Ling* I *adj* interrogativo,-a. II *n (word)* palabra *f* interrogativa; *(phrase)* oración *f* interrogativa.

interrogator [ɪnˈterəɡeɪtər] *n* interrogador,-a *m*,*f*.

interrupt [ɪntəˈrʌpt] *vtr & vi* interrumpir.

interruption [ɪntəˈrʌpʃən] *n* interrupción *f*.

intersect [ɪntəˈsekt] I *vtr* 1 *(road etc)* cortar, cruzar. 2 *Geom* intersecar. II *vi* I*(road etc)* cruzarse. 2 *Geom* intersecarse.

intersection [ɪntəˈsekʃən] *n* I *(crossroads)* cruce *m*; *(junction)* bocacalle *f*. 2 *(act)* intersección *f*.

intersperse [ɪntəˈspɜːs] *vtr* esparcir, entremezclar; **sunny intervals interspersed with showers**, claros con intervalos de lluvia.

interstate [ˈɪntəsteɪt] *adj esp US* interestatal, entre estados.

intertwine [ɪntəˈtwaɪn] I *vtr* entrelazar (**with**, con). II *vi* entrelazarse (**with**, con).

interval [ˈɪntəvəl] *n* 1 *(of time, space)* intervalo *m* (**between**, entre); **at intervals**, *(time, space)* a intervalos; *(time)* de vez en cuando. 2 *GB Cin Mus Theat* descanso *m*, intermedio *m*. 3 *Mus* intervalo *m*.

intervene [ɪntəˈviːn] *vi* 1 *(person)* intervenir (**in**, en). 2 *(event)* sobrevenir, ocurrir. 3 *(time)* transcurrir, mediar.

intervention [ɪntəˈvenʃən] *n* intervención *f*.

interview [ˈɪntəvjuː] I *n (gen)* entrevista *f*; *(by media)* interviú *f*; **to give an i.**, conceder una entrevista. II *vtr* entrevistar.

interviewee [ɪntəvjuːˈiː] *n* entrevistado,-a *m*,*f*.

interviewer [ˈɪntəvjuːər] *n* entrevistador,-a *m*,*f*.

interweave [ɪntəˈwiːv] *vtr (pt interwove* [ɪntəˈwəʊv]*; pp interwoven* [ɪntəˈwəʊvən]*)* entretejer.

intestate [ɪnˈtesteɪt] *adj* intestado,-a.

intestinal [ɪnˈtestɪnəl] *adj* intestinal.

intestine [ɪnˈtestɪn] *n (gen pl)* intestino *m*. ■ **large/small i.**, intestino *m* grueso/delgado.

intimacy [ˈɪntɪməsɪ] *n (closeness)* intimidad *f*, familiaridad *f*; *euph (sex)* relación *f* íntima; *(act, remark)* intimacies, intimidades *fpl*.

intimate¹ [ˈɪntɪmɪt] I *adj (gen)* íntimo,-a; *(knowledge)* profundo,-a; **to be i. with sb**, *(friendly)* intimar con algn; *euph (having sex)* tener relaciones (íntimas) con algn. II *n (person)* a migo,-a *m*,*f* íntimo,-a.

intimate² [ˈɪntɪmeɪt] *vtr fml* insinuar, dar a entender.

intimation [ɪntɪˈmeɪʃən] *n fml (sign)* indicio *m*; *(hint)* sugerencia *f*, indircta *f*; **to have an i. of sth**, presentir algo.

intimidate [ɪnˈtɪmɪdeɪt] *vtr* intimidar; **to i. sb into doing sth**, convencer a algn con amenazas de que haga algo.

intimidating [ɪnˈtɪmɪdeɪtɪŋ] *adj* atemorizante, amenazador,-a.

intimidation [ɪntɪmɪˈdeɪʃən] *n* intimidación *f*.

into [ˈɪntuː, *unstressed* ˈɪntə] *prep* 1 *(motion)* en, dentro de, a, contra, con; **he fell i. the water**, se cayó al agua; *(met by chance)* **I bumped i. a friend**, me topé con un amigo; **it crashed i. a tree**, chocó contra un árbol; **to get i. a car/train**, subir a un coche/tren; **to get i. a house**, entrar en una casa; **to go i. town**, ir al centro. 2 *(state, condition)* en, a; **buds develop i. flowers**, los capullos se convierten en flores; **he grew i. a man**, se hizo un hombre; **to burst i. tears**, deshacerse en lágrimas; **to change pounds i. pesetas**, cambiar libras en *or* por pesetas; **to translate sth i. French**, traducir algo al francés. 3 *(time, age)* **she's well i. her fifties**, tiene los cincuenta bien cumplidos; **to work i. the night**, trabajar hasta muy avanzada la noche. 4 *Math* **to divide sth i. three**, dividir algo en *or* entre tres; **two i. ten goes five**, diez entre dos caben a *or* son cinco. 5 *fam* **to be i. sth**, ser aficionado,-a de algo; **I'm i. cycling**, me chifla *or* me encanta el ciclismo.

intolerable [ɪnˈtɒlərəbəl] *adj* intolerable, inaceptable, inadmisible, inaguantable.

intolerance [ɪnˈtɒlərəns] *n* intolerancia *f*, intransigencia *f*.

intolerant [ɪnˈtɒlərənt] *adj* intolerante, intransigente.

intonation [ɪntəʊˈneɪʃən] *n* entonación *f*.

intoxicated [ɪnˈtɒksɪkeɪtɪd] *adj (drunk)* borracho,-a, ebrio,-a.

intoxicating [ɪnˈtɒksɪkeɪtɪŋ] *adj (inebriating)* embriagador,-a. ■ **i. liquor**, bebida *f* alcohólica.

intoxication [ɪntɒksɪˈkeɪʃən] *n (drunkenness)* embriaguez *f*, borrachera *f*.

intractable [ɪnˈtræktəbəl] *adj fml (person)* intratable; *(problem)* insoluble.

intransigence [ɪnˈtrænsɪdʒəns] *n fml* intransigencia *f*, intolerancia *f*.

intransigent [ɪnˈtrænsɪdʒənt] *adj fml* intransigente, intolerante.

intransitive [ɪnˈtrænsɪtɪv] *adj* Ling intransitivo,-a.

intrauterine [ɪntrəˈjuːtəraɪn] *adj Med* intrauterino,-a. ■ **i. device**, dispositivo *m* intrauterino.

intravenous [ɪntrəˈviːnəs] *adj Med* intravenoso,-a.

in-tray [ˈɪntreɪ] *n* bandeja *f* de asuntos pendientes.

intrepid [ɪnˈtrepɪd] *adj* intrépido,-a, audaz.

intricacy [ˈɪntrɪkəsɪ] *n (gen pl)* complejidad *f*.

intricate [ˈɪntrɪkɪt] *adj* intrincado,-a, complejo,-a, complicado,-a.

intrigue [ɪnˈtriːɡ, ˈɪntriːɡ] I *n* intriga *f*; *hum* **amorous intrigues**, amoríos *mpl*, aventuras *fpl*. II [ɪnˈtriːɡ] *vtr* intrigar, fascinar. III *vi* intrigar, conspirar, tramar, maquinar (**against**, contra).

intriguing [ɪnˈtriːɡɪŋ] *adj* intrigante, fascinante, curioso,-a.

intrinsic [ɪnˈtrɪnsɪk] *adj fml* intrínseco,-a.

intro [ˈɪntrəʊ] *n (abbr of* **introduction**) *fam* presentación *f*.

introduce [ɪntrəˈdjuːs] *vtr* 1 *(person, programme)* presentar (**to**, a); **let me i. my son**, permítame presentar a mi hijo, le presento a mi hijo. 2 *(bring in)* introducir (**into**, **to**, en); *Com (range, producir)* lanzar (**into**, **to**, a); *Pol (act, law)* presentar; *(topic, question)* proponer, sugerir, plantear.

introduction [ɪntrə'dʌkʃən] n 1 *(of person, programme)* presentación f; *(in book, speech)* introducción f; **letter of i.,** carta f de recomendación; **my i. to art,** mi iniciación f en el arte; *fam* **to make** or **do the intro-ductions,** hacer las presentaciones. **2** *(bringing in)* introducción f; *Com (of product)* lanzamiento m; *Pol (of act)* presentation f; *(of topic)* planteamiento m.

introductory [ɪntrə'dʌktərɪ] adj *(gen)* introductorio,-a; *(remarks)* preliminar; *Com (price, offer)* de lanzamiento.

introspection [ɪntrə'spekʃən] n introspección f.

introspective [ɪntrə'spektɪv] adj introspectivo,-a.

introvert ['ɪntrəvɜːt] n introvertido,-a m,f.

introverted ['ɪntrəvɜːtɪd] adj introvertido,-a.

intrude [ɪn'truːd] vi *(interfere)* entrometerse, inmiscuirse **(into, on,** en); *(disturb)* estorbar; **I don't wish to i. (on you),** no quiero molestar(te).

intruder [ɪn'truːdə^r] n intruso,-a m,f.

intrusion [ɪn'truːʒən] n *(into place)* intrusion f; *(on privacy, mood)* invasión f.

intrusive [ɪn'truːsɪv] adj *(neighbour etc)* entrometido,-a; *(presence, noise)* que molesta or estorba.

intuition [ɪntjʊ'ɪʃən] n intuición f.

intuitive [ɪn'tjuːɪtɪv] adj intuitivo,-a.

inundate ['ɪnʌndeɪt] vtr inundar **(with,** de); *fig* **we were inundated with complaints,** recibimos un montón de quejas.

inure [ɪ'njʊə^r] vtr fml acostumbrar **(to,** a), habituar **(to,** a).

invade [ɪn'veɪd] vtr invadir.

invader [ɪn'veɪdə^r] n invasor,-a m,f.

invalid¹ ['ɪnvəlɪd] n *(disabled person)* inválido,-a m, f, minusválido,-a m,f; *(sick person)* enfermo,-a m,f. ■ **i. chair,** silla f de ruedas.

invalid² [ɪn'vælɪd] adj inválido,-a, no válido,-a, nulo,-a.

invalidate [ɪn'vælɪdeɪt] vtr *(result, agreement)* invalidar, anular; *(argument)* refutar, demostrar el error de.

invaluable [ɪn'væljʊəbəl] adj inestimable, inapreciable.

invariable [ɪn'veərɪəbəl] adj invariable, constante.

invasion [ɪn'veɪʒən] n invasión f.

invective [ɪn'vektɪv] n fml invectiva f, improperio m.

inveigh [ɪn'veɪ] vi fml **to i. against sb/sth,** censurar or condenar algn/algo.

inveigle [ɪn'viːgəl, ɪn'veɪgəl] vtr fml **to i. sb into sth/into doing sth,** embaucar or persuadir a algn para que haga algo.

invent [ɪn'vent] vtr inventar.

invention [ɪn'venʃən] n 1 *(machine etc)* invento m, invención f. **2** *(creativity)* invención f, fantasía f; *(lie)* mentira f.

inventive [ɪn'ventɪv] adj inventivo,-a.

inventiveness [ɪn'ventɪvnɪs] n inventiva f.

inventor [ɪn'ventə^r] n inventor,-a m,f.

inventory ['ɪnvəntərɪ] n inventario m; **to draw up an i. of sth,** inventariar algo.

inverse [ɪn'vɜːs] fml I adj inverso,-a. II **the i.** n lo inverso, lo contrario.

inversion [ɪn'vɜːʃən] n inversión f.

invert [ɪn'vɜːt] vtr invertir, volver del revés.

invertebrate [ɪn'vɜːtɪbrɪt] Zool I adj invertebrado,-a. II n invertebrado m.

inverted [ɪn'vɜːtɪd] adj **i. commas,** comillas fpl; **in i. commas,** entre comillas.

invest [ɪn'vest] I vtr 1 *(money)* invertir **(in,** en); *fig (time, energy)* emplear, invertir **(in,** en). **2** fml *(right, power, etc)* investir; **to i. sb with sth,** conferir algo a algn. II vi hacer una inversión, invertir dinero **(in,** en); *fam* **I must i. in a new watch,** me tengo que comprar un reloj nuevo.

investigate [ɪn'vestɪgeɪt] vtr *(crime, subject)* investigar; *(cause, possibility)* examinar, estudiar.

investigation [ɪnvestɪ'geɪʃən] n *(of crime, subject)* investigación f; *(of cause, possibility)* examinen m, estudio m.

investigative [ɪn'vestgətɪv] adj investigador,-a. ■ *Press* **i. journalism,** periodismo m de investigación.

investigator [ɪn'vestɪgeɪtə^r] n investigador,-a m, f. ■ **private i.,** detective m privado.

investiture [ɪn'vestɪtʃə^r] n investidura f.

investment [ɪn'vestmənt] n inversión f.

investor [ɪn'vestə^r] n inversor,-a m,f, inversionista mf.

inveterate [ɪn'vetərɪt] adj empedernido,-a.

invidious [ɪn'vɪdɪəs] adj *(gen)* odioso,-a; *(task, role)* ingrato,-a, desagradable; *(comparison, choice)* injusto,-a.

invigilate [ɪn'vɪdʒɪleɪt] vtr & vi GB *(exam)* vigilar.

invigilator [ɪn'vɪdʒɪleɪtə^r] n GB *(in exam)* vigilante mf.

invigorated [ɪn'vɪgəreɪtɪd] adj tonificado,-a, vigorizado,-a.

invigorating [ɪn'vɪgəreɪtɪŋ] adj tónico,-a, vigorizante, estimulante.

invincible [ɪn'vɪnsəbəl] adj invencible.

inviolable [ɪn'vaɪələbəl] adj fml inviolable.

inviolate [ɪn'vaɪəlɪt] adj fml inviolado,-a; **to remain i.,** permanecer intacto,-a.

invisible [ɪn'vɪzəbəl] adj invisible.

invitation [ɪnvɪ'teɪʃən] n invitación f.

invite [ɪn'vaɪt] I vtr 1 *(guest)* invitar, convidar **(to,** a); *(candidate, participant)* pedir, invitar; **to i. sb over** or **round for supper,** invitar a algn a casa a cenar; **I was invited for interview,** me pidieron que fuera a entrevistarme con ellos. **2** *(comments, questions, offers)* solicitar; *(criticism, disaster)* provocar; **to i. trouble,** buscarse problemas. II [ɪn'vaɪt] n fam invitación f.

inviting [ɪn'vaɪtɪŋ] adj *(attractive)* atractivo,-a, tentador,-a, atrayente; *(food)* apetitoso,-a.

invoice ['ɪnvɔɪs] *Com* I n factura f; **to draw up** or **make out an i.,** extender una factura. II vtr facturar.

invoke [ɪn'vəʊk] vtr fml invocar.

involuntary [ɪn'vɒləntərɪ] adj involuntario,-a, sin querer.

involve [ɪn'vɒlv] vtr 1 *(concern)* implicar, comprometer, involucrar **(in,** en); **I don't want to get involved in your problems,** no quiero mezclarme en tus líos; **is there money involved?,** ¿hay dinero de por medio?; **the changes don't i. me,** los cambios no me afectan; **the issues involved,** las cuestiones en juego; **the people involved,** los interesados; **to be involved in an accident,** sufrir un accidente; **to be deeply involved in sth,** estar muy metido,-a en algo. **2** *(email)* suponer, implicar **(in,** en); *(trouble, risk)* acarrear; **the post involves travel,** el puesto exige viajar; **what's involved?,** ¿de qué se trata?

involved [ɪn'vɒlvd] adj 1 *(complicated)* complicado,-a, complejo,-a, enrevesado,-a. **2** fam *(romantically attached)* enredado,-a.

involvement [ɪn'vɒlvmənt] n 1 *(participation)* participación f; *(in crime)* implicación f, complicidad f; *(in scandal)* compromiso m; **American i. in Nicaragua,** intervención f americana en Nicaragua. **2** fam *(romance)* enredo m.

invulnerable [ɪn'vʌlnərəbəl] adj invulnerable.

inward ['ɪnwəd] I adj interior. II adv see **inwards.** ◆ **inwardly** adv interiormente, por dentro; **to laugh i.,** reír para sus adentros.

inwards ['ɪnwədz] adv hacia dentro.

iodine ['aɪədiːn] n yodo m.

ion ['aɪən] n ion m.

ionian [aɪ'əʊnɪən] adj I. **Sea,** Mar Jónico.

iota [ai'əʊtə] *n* pizca *f*, ápice *m*.

IOU [aiəʊ'juː] *abbr of* **I owe you,** pagaré *m*.

IPA [aipi:'ei] *abbr of* **International Phonetic Alphabet,** Alfabeto *m* Fonético Internacional, AFI *m*.

IQ [ai'kjuː] *abbr of* **intelligence quotient,** coeficiente *m* de inteligencia, CI *m*.

IRA [aiɑ:'rei] *abbr of* **Irish Republican Army,** Ejército *m* Republicano irlandés, IRA *m*.

Iran [i'rɑːn] *n* Irán.

Iranian [i'reiniən] **I** *adj* iraní *mf*. **II** *n* 1 *(person)* iraní *mf*. 2 *(language)* iraní *m*.

Iraq [i'rɑːk] *n* Irak.

Iraqi [i'rɑːki] *adj & n* iraquí *(mf)*.

irascible [i'ræsibəl] *adj fml* irascible, colérico,-a.

irate [ai'reit] *adj* airado,-a, furioso,-a.

IRBM [aiɑ:bi:'em] *Mil abbr of* **intermediate-range ballistic missile,** proyectil *m* balístico de alcance intermedio, PBAI *m*.

ire ['aiər] *n lit* ira *f*, cólera *f*.

Ireland ['aiələnd] *n* Irlanda. ■ **Northern I,** Irlanda del Norte; **Republic of I.,** República de Irlanda.

iridescent [iri'desənt] *adj fml* iridiscente, irisado,-a.

iris ['aiəris] *n* 1 *Anat* iris *m inv*. 2 *Bot* lirio *m*.

Irish ['aiəriʃ] **I** *adj* irlandés,-esa. ■ **I. coffee,** café *m* irlandés; **I. Sea,** Mar *m* de Irlanda; **I. setter,** setter *m* irlandés. **II** *n* 1 *(language)* irlandés *m*. 2 *pl* the **I.,** los irlandeses.

Irishman ['aiəriʃmən] *n (pl Irishmen)* irlandés *m*.

Irishwoman ['aiəriʃwʊmən] *n (pl Irishwomen* ['aiəriʃwimin] *)* irlandesa *f*.

irk [ɜːk] *vtr* fastidiar, molestar.

irksome ['ɜːksəm] *adj* fastidioso,-a, molesto,-a; **how i.!,** ¡qué lata!

iron ['aiən] **I** *n* 1 *Min* hierro *m*; **the i. and steel industry,** la industria siderúrgica; *fig* **a will of i., an i. will,** una voluntad de hierro; *fig* **to have an i. constitution,** ser de hierro; *fig* **to have several/too many irons in the fire,** traer varias/ demasiadas cosas entre manos; *prov* **strike while the i. is hot,** a hierro candente batir de repente. ■ **cast i.,** hierro *m* colado; *Pol* **I. Curtain,** Telón *m* de Acero; **i. foundry,** fundición *f* (de hierro); **fire i. lung,** pulmón *m* de acero; **i. ore,** mineral *m* de hierro; **scrap i.,** chatarra *f*; **wrought i.,** hierro *m* forjado. 2 *(for clothes)* plancha *f*. ■ **steam i.,** plancha *f* de vapor. 3 *(for golf)* hierro *m*. 4 **irons,** *(fetters)* grillos *mpl*, grilletes *mpl*; **to clap sb in i.,** encadenar a algn. **II** *vtr (clothes)* planchar. ◆ **iron out** *vtr* 1 *(crease)* planchar. 2 *fam fig (problem)* resolver; *(objection)* quitar.

ironic(al) [ai'rɒnik(ə)l] *adj* irónico,-a.

ironing ['aiəniŋ] *n* 1 *(act)* **to do the i.,** planchar, ■ **i. board,** tabla *f* de planchar. 2 *(clothes to be ironed)* ropa *f* por planchar; *(clothes ironed)* ropa *f* planchada.

ironmonger ['aiənmʌŋgər] *n GB* ferretero,-a *m,f*. ■ **i.'s (shop),** ferretería *f*.

irony ['aiərəni] *n* ironía *f*; **the i. (of it) is that ...,** lo más curioso *or* gracioso es que ... .

irradiate [i'reidieit] *vtr Med* irradiar.

irrational [i'ræʃənəl] *adj* irracional.

irreconcilable [irekən'sailəbəl] irreconciliable, inconciliable.

irredeemable [iri'diːməbəl] *adj fml (gen)* irredimible, irremediable; *(fault)* irreparable, incorregible.

irrefutable [iri'fjuːtəbəl] *adj fml* irrefutable.

irregular [i'regjʊlər] *adj* 1 *(gen)* irregular; *(abnormal)* anormal. 2 *(uneven)* desigual.

irregularity [iregjʊ'læriti] *n* 1 *(abnormality)* irregularidad *f*. 2 *(unevenness)* desigualdad *f*.

irrelevance [i'reləvəns] *n*, **irrelevancy** [i'reləvənsi] *n* 1 *(state)* falta *f* de pertinencia. 2 *(remark)* observación *f* fuera de lugar *or* que no viene al caso.

irrelevant [i'reləvənt] *adj* no pertinente, ajeno,-a; **i. remark,** comentario *m* fuera de lugar; **that's i.,** eso no viene al caso *or* no tiene nada que ver.

irreligious [iri'lidʒəs] *adj fml* irreligioso,-a.

irreparable [i'repərəbəl] *adj* irreparable.

irreplaceable [iri'pleisəbəl] *adj* irremplazable, insustituible.

irrepressible [iri'presəbəl] *adj* incontenible, incontrolable.

irreproachable [iri'prəʊtʃəbəl] *adj fml* irreprochable, intachable.

irresistible [iri'zistəbəl] *adj* irresistible.

irresolute [i'rezəluːt] *adj fml* indeciso,-a, vacilante, irresoluto,-a.

irrespective [iri'spektiv] *adj* **i. of,** sin tomar en consideración, sin tener en cuenta.

irresponsible [iri'spɒnsəbəl] *adj* irresponsable.

irretrievable [iri'triːvəbəl] *adj (object)* irrecuperable; *(mistake, harm)* irreparable; *(loss, situation)* irremediable.

irreverence [i'revərəns] *n* irreverencia *f*, falta *f* de respeto.

irreverent [i'revərənt] *adj* irreverente, irrespetuoso,-a.

irreversible [iri'vɜːsəbəl] *adj (process)* irreversible; *(judgement, decision)* irrevocable.

irrevocable [i'revəkəbəl] *adj* irrevocable, inalterable.

irrigate ['irigeit] *vtr Agr* regar, irrigar.

irrigation [iri'geiʃən] *n Agr* riego *m*, irrigación *f*. ■ **i. channel,** acequia *f*, canal *m* de riego; **i. system,** sistema *m* de regadío.

irritable ['iritəbəl] *adj* irritable, de mal humor.

irritant ['iritənt] *n* 1 *Med* agente *m* irritante. 2 *fig fml* motivo *m* de irritación, molestia *f*.

irritate ['iriteit] *vtr* 1 *(annoy)* irritar, fastidiar, molestar. 2 *Med* irritar, inflamar.

irritating ['iriteitiŋ] *adj* 1 *(habit, delay)* irritante, fastidioso,-a, molesto,-a. 2 *Med* irritante.

irritation [iri'teiʃən] *n* 1 *(annoyance)* fastidio *m*, molestia *f*; *(ill humour)* mal humor *m*. 2 *Med* irritación *f*.

is [iz] *3rd person sing pres see* **be.**

Islam ['izlɑːm] *n* Islam *m*.

Islamic [iz'læmik] *adj* islámico,-a.

island ['ailənd] *n* isla *f*; *Aut* **(traffic) i,** isla *f*, refugio *m*.

islander ['ailəndər] *n* isleño,-a *m,f*.

isle [ail] *n lit* isla *f*; **the British Isles,** las Islas Británicas.

isn't ['izənt] = **is not.**

isolate ['aisəleit] *vtr* aislar **(from,** de).

isolated ['aisəleitid] *adj* aislado,-a.

isolation [aisə'leiʃən] *n* aislamiento *m*; **to deal with sth in i.,** tratar algo por separado; **to live in i.,** vivir aislado,-a. ■ *Med* **i. ward,** pabellón *m* *or* sala *f* de aislamiento *or* de enfermedades contagiosas.

isolationism [aisə'leiʃənizəm] *n Pol* aislacionismo *m*.

isotope ['aisətəʊp] *n* isótopo *m*.

Israel ['izreiəl] *n* Israel.

Israeli [iz'reili] **I** *adj* israelí. **II** *n (pl Israelis)* israelí *mf*.

Israelite ['izriəlait] *adj & n Hist* israelita *(mf)*.

issue ['iʃjuː] **I** *n* 1 *(matter)* cuestión *f*, asunto *m*, tema *m*, **let's not make an i. of it,** no riñamos por esto; **side i.,** cuestión secundaria; **the point at i.,** el tema en discusión; **to avoid** *or* **evade the i.,** andar con rodeos; **to cloud** *or* **confuse the i.,** complicar la cosa; **to face the i.,** hacer frente al problema; **to force the i.,** forzar una decisión; **to raise an i.,** plantear un tema; **to take i. with sb (over sth),** manifestar su desacuerdo con algn (en algo). 2 *(of book)* tirada *f*; *(of banknotes, stamps)* emisión *f*; *(of passport)* expedición *f*. 3 *(copy) (of journal etc)* ejemplar *m*; **back i.,** número *m* atrasado. 4 *(of equipment, supplies)* distribución *f*, reparto *m*. 5 *fml (outcome)* resultado *m*, consecuencia *f*. 6 *Jur (off-spring)* prole *f*, descendencia *f*; **to die without i.,** morir sin descendencia **II** *vtr* **1** *(book)* publicar; *(banknotes, stamps)* emitir; *(passport)* expedir. **2** *(equipment, supplies)* distribuir, repartir; **to i. sb with sth** *or* **sth to sb,** suministrar algo a algn. **3** *(order, instructions)* dar; *Jur (warrant)* dictar. **III** *vi fml (blood)* brotar **(from,** de); *(smoke)* salir **(from,** de).

Istanbul [ɪstæn'buːl] *n* Estambul.

isthmus ['ɪsməs] *n* istmo *m*.

IT [aɪ'tiː] *Comput abbr of* **information technology,** informática *f*.

it [ɪt] *pers pron* **1** *(subject)* él, ella, ello *(often omitted)*; **it's here,** está aquí. **2** *(direct object)* lo, la; **I don't believe it,** no me lo creo; **I liked the house and bought it,** me gustó la casa y la compré. **3** *(indirect object)* le; **give it a kick,** dale una patada. **4** *(after prep)* él, ella, ello; **are you afraid of it?,** ¿te da miedo?; **I saw the beach and ran towards it,** vi la playa y fui corriendo hacia ella; **we'll talk about it later,** ya hablaremos de ello. **5** *(abstract)* ello; **let's get down to it!,** ¡vamos a ello! **6** *(impersonal)* **he had a bad time of it,** lo pasó mal; **it's late,** es tarde; **it's me,** soy yo; **it's raining,** llueve, está lloviendo; **it's said that ...,** se dice que ...; **it's two miles to town,** son dos millas de aquí al pueblo; **how's it going?,** ¿qué tal?; **that's it!,** *(agreeing)* ¡eso mismo!, ¡precisamente!; *(finishing)* ¡se acabó!; *(disapproving)* ¡basta ya!; **the worst of it is that ...,** lo peor del caso es que ..., **this is it!,** ¡ha llegado la hora *or* el momento!; **who is it?,** ¿quién es?; *fam* **she thinks she's it,** se da mucho tono.

Italian [ɪ'tæljən] **I** *adj* italiano,-a. **II** *n* **1** *(person)* italiano,-a *m*,*f*. **2** *(language)* italiano *m*.

italic [ɪ'tælɪk] *n Typ* cursiva *f*; **i. script,** letra *f* cursiva.

Italy ['ɪtəlɪ] *n* Italia.

itch [ɪtʃ] **I** *n* picor *m*, picazón *f*; *fig* **an i. to travel,** unas ganas locas de viajar. **II** *vi* **1** *(skin)* picar; **my hand itches,** me pica la mano. **2** *fig* anhelar; *fam* **to be itching for sth/ to do sth,** estar impaciente por *or* tener muchas ganas de algo/hacer algo.

itchy ['ɪtʃɪ] *adj (itchier, itchiest) (scalp, material)* que pica; **I've got an i. nose,** me pica la nariz; *fam fig* **to have i. feet,** *(travel)* tener muchas ganas de viajar; *(move off or away)* tener muchas ganas de largarse.

item ['aɪtəm] *n* **1** *(object) (in list)* artículo *m*; *(in collection)* pieza *f*; **i. of clothing,** prenda *f* de vestir. **2** *(subject) (on agenda)* punto *m*, asunto *m*; *(on bill)* partida *f*, asiento *m*, *(in show)* número *m*; **news i.,** noticia *f*.

itemize ['aɪtəmaɪz] *vtr (contents)* hacer una lista de; *(bill)* detallar.

itinerant [ɪ'tɪnərənt] *adj fml* itinerante, ambulante.

itinerary [aɪ'tɪnərərɪ] *n* itinerario *m*, ruta *f*.

it'll ['ɪtəl] = **it will.**

its [ɪts] *poss adj (one thing)* su; *(more than one)* sus; **the bear hurt i. paw,** el oso se lastimó la pata; **the club and i. members,** el club y sus socios.

itself [ɪt'self] *pers pron* **1** *(reflexive)* se; **the cat scratched i.,** el gato se arañó. **2** *(emphatic)* él *or* ella *or* ello mismo,-a; *(after prep)* sí (mismo,-a); **in i.,** en sí, de por sí; **it works by i.,** funciona solo,-a; **she's kindness i.,** es la bondad misma.

ITV [aɪtiː'viː] *GB abbr of* **Independent Television,** television *f* independiente, ITV *f*.

IUD [aɪjuː'diː] **IUCD** [aɪjuːsiː'diː] *Med abbrs of* **Intrauterine (contraceptive) device,** dispositivo *m* intrauterino, DIU *m*.

ivory ['aɪvərɪ] *n (substance)* marfil *m*; *(colour)* color *m* marfil. ■ **I. Costa,** Costa *f* de Marfil.

ivy ['aɪvɪ] *n* **1** *Bot* hiedra *f*, yedra *f*. **2** *US* **I. League,** grupo *m* de ocho universidades privadas y de categoría del Nordeste.

J

J, j [dʒeɪ] *n (the letter)* J, j *f*.

jab [dʒæb] **I** *n* **1** *(stab)* pinchazo *m*; *(poke)* golpe *m* seco; *(with elbow)* codazo *m*. **2** *fam (injection)* pinchazo *m*. **II** *vtr (pt & pp jabbed) (with sharp object)* pinchar; *(with fist)* dar un puñetazo a; *(with elbow)* dar un codazo a.

jabber ['dʒæbə'] *fam* **I** *vtr* decir atropelladamente, farfullar. **II** *vi (chatter)* charlotear, charlar; *(speak quickly)* farfullar, chapurrear, hablar atropelladamente.

jacaranda [dʒækə'rændə] *n Bot* jacarandá *m*.

Jack [dʒæk] *n (dimin of John)* Juanito *m*; **every man J.,** todo quisque; *fam* **I'm all right, J.,** ande yo caliente y ríase la gente.

jack [dʒæk] *n* **1** *Aut* gato *m*; *Tech* cric *m*. **2** *Cards* sota *f*; *(Spanish pack)* sota *f*. **3** *(bowls)* boliche *m*. **4** *Naut* bandera *f* de proa, pabellón *m*. ◆ **Jack in** *vtr GB fam* dejar. ◆ **jack up** *vtr Aut* levantar (con el gato); *fig (prices)* aumentar.

jackal ['dʒækɔːl] *n Zool* chacal *m*.

jackass ['dʒækæs] *n fam* burro,-a *m*,*f*, imbécil *mf*.

jackboot ['dʒækbuːt] *n* **1** *Mil* bota *f* militar. **2** *fam fig* represión *f*, tiranía *f*.

jackdaw ['dʒækdɔː] *n Orn* grajilla *f*.

jacket ['dʒækɪt] *n* **1** *(clothing)* chaqueta *f*; *(of suit)* americana *f*; *(bomber jacket)* cazadora *f*; **bed j.,** mañanita *f*; **dinner j.,** esmoquin **m**, smoking *m*. **2** *(of book)* sobrecubierta *f*. **3** *US (record)* funda *f*. **4** *Culin* **j. potatoes** patatas *fpl* al horno.

jackhammer ['dʒækhæmə'] *n* martillo *m* perforador.

jack-in-the-box ['dʒækɪndʒəbɒks] *n (pl jack-in-the-boxes)* caja *f* sorpresa.

jack-knife ['dʒæknaɪf] **I** *n (pl jack-knives* ['dʒæknaɪvz]*)* navaja *f*. **II** *vi (of lorry)* colear.

jack-of-all-trades [dʒækəv'ɔːltreɪdz] *n (pl jacks-of-all-trades)* persona *f* mañosa *or* de muchos oficios; **j.-of-a.-t., master of none,** hombre de muchos oficios, maestro de ninguno.

jackpot ['dʒækpɒt] *n (premio m)* gordo *m*; *fam* **I hit the j.,** me tocó el premio gordo.

Jacobean [dʒækə'bɪən] *adj* jacobita.

Jacobin ['dʒækəbɪn] *adj & n* jacobino,-a *(m, f)*.

Jacuzzi® [dʒə'kuːzɪ] *n (pl Jacuzzis)* jacuzzi® *m*, baño *m* de burbujas.

jade [dʒeɪd] *n Min* jade *m*.

jaded ['dʒeɪdɪd] *adj* **1** *(tired)* agotado,-a, molido,-a. **2** *(of palate)* hastiado,-a, saciado,-a, harto,-a.

jagged ['dʒægɪd] *adj* dentado,-a, mellado,-a.

jaguar ['dʒægjʊə'] *n Zool* jaguar *m*.

jail [dʒeɪl] **I** *n* cárcel *f*, prisión *f*; **to be in j.,** estar en la cárcel, estar encarcelado,-a; **to go to j.,** ir a la cárcel. **II** *vtr* encarcelar, meter en la cárcel.

jailbird ['dʒeɪlbɜːd] *n fam (preso,-a m, f)* reincidente *mf*.

jailbreak ['dʒeɪlbreɪk] *n* fuga *f*, evasión *f*.

jailer ['dʒeɪlə'] *n* carcelero,-a *m*,*f*.

jailhouse ['dʒeɪlhaʊs] *n US* cárcel *f*.

jailor ['dʒeɪlə'] *n see* **jailer**

Jakarta [dʒə'kɑːtə] *n* Yakarta.

jalop (p)y [dʒə'lɒpɪ] *n fam Aut* cacharro *m*.

jam¹ [dʒæm] *n Culin* mermelada *f*; *fam* **that's money for j.,** ¡qué chollo! ■ **j. roll,** rollo *m* de bizcocho con mermelada.

jam² [dʒæm] **I** *n* **1** *(blockage)* atasco *m*; **traffic j.,** embotellamiento *m*, atasco *m*. **2** *fam (fix)* apuro *m*; **in a j.,** en un apuro. **3** *Mus* **j. session,** sesión *f* de jazz improvisado. **II** *vtr (pt & pp jammed)* **1** *(cram)* meter a la fuerza, embutir. **2** *(block)* atascar, obstruir; *Rad (transmission)* interferir. **III** *vi* **1** *(of door)* atrancarse; *(of brakes)* agarrotarse. **2** *Mus* tocar en una sesión de jazz improvisado. ◆ **jam on** *vtr Aut* **to j. on the brakes,** frenar en seco.

Jamaica [dʒə'meɪkə] *n* Jamaica.

Jamaican [dʒə'meɪkən] *adj & n* jamaicano,-a *(m, f),* jamaiquino,-a *(m, f).*

jamb [dʒæm] *n* jamba *f.*

jamboree [dʒæmbə'riː] *n* **1** *(scout meeting)* congreso *m* internacional de exploradores. **2** *fam (party)* juerga *f.*

jammed [dʒæmd] *adj* atestado,-a, relleno,-a; **j. with people,** atestado,-a de gente; **j. with things,** atiborrado,-a de cosas.

jamming [ˈdʒæmɪŋ] *n Rad* interferencia *f*

jammy [ˈdʒæmɪ] *adj (jammier, jammiest)* **1** *GB fam (lucky)* **what a j. shot!,** ¡vaya churra!; **you j. bugger!,** ¡qué suerte tienes tío! **2** *fam* pegajoso,-a, pringoso,-a.

jam-packed [dʒæmˈpækt] *adj fam (people)* atestado,-a; *(things)* atiborrado,-a.

Jan [dʒæn] *abbr of* **January,** enero *m*, ene, eno.

jangle [ˈdʒæŋɡəl] **I** *vtr (keys etc)* hacer sonar. **II** *vi* tintinear.

janitor [ˈdʒænɪtəʳ] *n US Scot* portero *m*, conserje *m*.

January [ˈdʒænjʊərɪ] *n* enero *m*; *see also* **May.**

Japanese [dʒæpəˈniːz] **I** *adj* japonés,-esa, nipón,-ona; **the J.,** los japoneses. **II** *n (person)* japonés,- esa *m, f,* nipón,-ona *m, f; (language)* japonés *m.*

Japan [dʒəˈpæn] *n* (el) Japón; **the Sea of J.,** el Mar del Japón.

jape [dʒeɪp] **I** *n* broma *f.* **II** *vi* bromear.

jar¹ [dʒɑːʳ] *n* **1** *(glass)* tarro *m*, pote *m; (earthenware)* tinaja *f; (jug)* jarra *f.* **2** *GB fam* **to have a j.,** tomar una caña *or* copa.

jar² [dʒɑːʳ] *vi (pt & pp jarred)* **1** *(sounds)* chirriar; *fig* **to j. on one's nerves,** ponerle a uno los nervios de punta, crispar los nervios a uno. **2** *(of colours, appearance)* chocar, desentonar.

jarring [ˈdʒɑːrɪŋ] *adj* **1** *(of sounds)* discordante, disonante. **2** *(of colours)* que chocan *or* desentonan. **3** *(of opinion)* discorde, discordante.

jargon [ˈdʒɑːɡən] *n* jerga *f*, argot *m*, jerigonza *f*; **political j.,** jerga política.

jasmin(e) [ˈdʒæzmɪn] *n Bot* jazmín *m.*

jasper [ˈdʒæspəʳ] *n Min* jaspe *m.*

jaundice [ˈdʒɔːndɪs] *n Med* ictericia *f.*

jaundiced [ˈdʒɔːndɪst] *adj* **1** *Med* ictérico,-a. **2** *fig (bitter)* amargado,-a, resentido,-a; **to take a j. view of things,** ver las cosas por el lado malo.

jaunt [dʒɔːnt] **I** *n* **1** *(walk)* paseo *m.* **2** *(trip)* excursión *f,* viaje *m* corto. **II** *vi (walk)* pasear; *(go on a trip)* viajar.

jauntiness [ˈdʒɔːntɪnɪs] *n* **1** *(sprightliness)* garbo *m.* **2** *(liveliness)* viveza *f.* **3** *(ease)* desenvoltura *f.*

jaunty [ˈdʒɔːntɪ] *adj (jauntier, jauntiest)* **1** *(sprightly)* garboso,-a; **j. gait,** paso airoso. **2** *(lively)* vivaz. **3** *(easy-going)* desenvuelto,-a; **a j. manner,** un aire desenvuelto.

Java [ˈdʒɑːvə] *n* Java.

Javanese [dʒɑːvəˈniːz] *adj & n* javanés,-esa *(m, f);* **the j.,** los javaneses.

javelin [ˈdʒævəlɪn] *n Sport* jabalina *f;* **j. throwing,** lanzamiento *m* de jabalina.

jaw [dʒɔː] **I** *n* **1** *Anat* mandíbula *f, Zool* mandíbula *f,* quijada *f; fig* **the jaws of death,** las garras de la muerte. **2** *Tech* **jaws,** mordaza *f sing.* **II** *vi fam* charlar, estar de palique, darle a la sinhueso.

jawbone [ˈdʒɔːbəʊn] *n Anat* maxilar *m*, mandíbula *f.*

jay [dʒeɪ] *n Orn* arrendajo *m* (común).

jaywalker [ˈdʒeɪwɔːkəʳ] *n* peatón *m* imprudente.

jazz [dʒæz] **I** *n Mus* jazz *m*; **modern j.,** jazz moderno; *fam* **and all that j.,** y otras hierbas, etcétera, etcétera, y demás. ■ **j. band,** conjunto *m* de jazz. **II** *adj* de jazz, jazzístico,-a. ◆ **jazz up** *vtr* alegrar; *(premises)* arreglar, modernizar; **she turned up all jazzed up,** se presentó vestida de forma muy llamativa.

jazzman [ˈdʒæzmæn] *n (pl jazzmen* [ˈdʒæzmæn]*)* músico *m* de jazz.

jazzy [ˈdʒæzɪ] *adj (jazzier, jazziest) fam* **1** *(showy)* llamativo,-a. **2** *(brightly coloured)* de colores chillones. **3** *Mus* del estilo de jazz, jazzístico,-a.

jealous [ˈdʒeləs] *adj* **1** *(gen)* celoso,-a; **to be j. of ...,** tener celos de .... **2** *(envious)* envidioso,-a. ◆ **jealously** *adv* **1** *(gen)* celosamente. **2** *(enviously)* con envidia.

jealousy [ˈdʒeləsɪ] *n* **1** *(resentment)* celos *mpl.* **2** *(envy)* envidia *f,* celos *mpl.*

jeans [dʒiːnz] *npl* vaqueros *mpl,* tejanos *mpl.*

jeep [dʒiːp] *n Aut* jeep *m,* todo terreno *m inv.*

jeer [dʒɪəʳ] **I** *n* **1** *(boo)* abucheo *m; (mocking)* mofa *f,* burla *f.* **2 jeers,** *(insults)* insultos *mpl.* **II** *vi (boo)* abuchear; *(mock)* burlarse.

jeering [ˈdʒɪərɪŋ] **I** *adj* burlón,-ona, sarcástico,-a. **II** *n (booing)* abucheo *m; (mocking)* mofa *f,* burla *f.*

jeeze [dʒiːz] *interj US sl* ¡jolín!, ¡caray!

Jehovah [dʒɪˈhəʊvə] *n Rel* Jehová *m.* ■ **J.'s Witness,** testigo *mf* de Jehová.

jejunum [dʒɪˈdʒuːnəm] *n Anat* yeyuno *m.*

jell [dʒel] *n see* **gel.**

jellied [ˈdʒelɪd] *adj Culin* en gelatina.

Jello® *n* [ˈdʒeləʊ] *(pl Jellos) US* jalea *f.*

jelly [ˈdʒelɪ] *n* **1** *(gelatine)* gelatina *f.* **2** *(of meat)* gelatina *f* de carne; *(sweet dessert)* jalea *f.* ■ **j. bean,** *US* pastilla *f* de goma. **3** *fig* tembleque *m;* **when he saw her, his legs turned to j.,** cuando la vió, las piernas empezaron a temblarle.

jellyfish [ˈdʒelɪfɪʃ] *n (pl jellyfish or jellyfishes) Zool* medusa *f.*

jemmy [ˈdʒemɪ] *n* palanqueta *f.*

jeopardize [ˈdʒepədaɪz] *vtr* poner en peligro, arriesgar; *(agreement etc)* comprometer.

jeopardy [ˈdʒepədɪ] *n* riesgo *m*, peligro *m*.

Jericho [ˈdʒerɪkəʊ] *n* Jericó.

jerk¹ [dʒɜːk] **I** *n* **1** *(jolt)* sacudida *f.* **2** *(pull)* tirón *m.* **3** *pej (idiot)* majadero,-a *m,f,* imbécil *mf; (nuisance)* pelmazo,-a *m, f.* **II** *vtr* **1** *(shake)* sacudir. **2** *(pull)* tirar; **to j. oneself free,** soltarse de un tirón. **III** *vi (move suddenly)* dar una sacudida; **the car jerked forward,** el coche avanzaba a tirones. ◆ **jerk off** *vi vulg* hacerse una paja.

jerk² [dʒɜːk] *n Culin* cecina *f.*

jerky¹ [ˈdʒɜːkɪ] *adj (jerkier, jerkiest) (movement)* espasmódico,-a nervioso,-a.

jerky² [ˈdʒɜːkɪ] *n Culin see* **jerk².**

jerkin [ˈdʒɜːkɪn] *n* **1** *Hist* jubón *m.* **2** *(sleeveless)* chaleco *m.*

Jerry [ˈdʒerɪ] *n fam* alemán *m; (soldier)* soldado *m* alemán.

jerry-builder [ˈdʒerɪbɪldəʳ] *n Constr* chapucero,-a *m,f.*

jerry-built [ˈdʒerɪbɪlt] *adj* chapucero,-a, construido,-a de cualquier manera.

Jersey [ˈdʒɜːzɪ] *n* **1** *(island)* Jersey. **2** *Zool* vaca *f.*

jersey [ˈdʒɜːzɪ] *n* **1** *(sweater)* jersey *m,* suéter *m.* **2** *Tex* tejido *m* de punto.

Jerusalem [dʒəˈruːsələm] *n* **1** *(city)* Jerusalén. **2** *Hortic* **J. artichoke,** aguaturma *f,* pataca *f.*

jest [dʒest] **I** *n* **1** *(fun, joking)* burla *f,* broma *f;* **spoken in j.,** dicho,-a en broma. **2** *(joke)* chiste *m.* **II** *vi* bromear.

jester [ˈdʒestəʳ] *n* bromista *mf; Hist* bufón *m.*

Jesuit ['dʒezjʊɪt] *adj* & *n Rel* jesuita *(m)*; **J. school,** colegio *m* de jesuitas.

Jesus ['dʒiːzəs] *n* Jesús *m*; **J. Christ,** Jesucristo *m*; offens **J. Christ!,** ¡joder!

jet¹ [dʒet] **I** *n* **1** *(stream of water)* chorro *m*. **2** *(water spout)* surtidor *m*; **gas j.,** mechero *m* de gas. ■ *Meteor* **j. stream,** corriente *f* a chorro. **3** *Av* reactor *m*; **j. propelled,** de propulsión a reacción *or* chorro. ■ **j. engine,** reactor *m*; **j. lag,** desfase *m* horario. **II** *vi (pt & pp jetted) fam* viajar, volar.

jet² [dʒet] *n Min* azabache *m*; **j. black,** negro,-a como el azabache.

jetsam ['dʒetsəm] *n Naut* echazón *m*, carga *f* arrojada al mar; *fig* desechos *mpl*.

jet-set ['dʒetset] *n* **the j.-s.,** la alta sociedad, la jetset.

jetsom ['dʒetsəm] *n see* **jetsam.**

jettison ['dʒetɪsən] *vtr Naut* echar al mar; *fig* deshacerse de, tirar; *(project etc)* abandonar.

jetty ['dʒetɪ] *n Naut* muelle *m*, malecón *m*.

Jew [dʒuː] *n* judío,-a *m,f*.

jewel ['dʒuːəl] *n* **1** *(ornament)* joya *f*, alhaja *f*; *(stone)* piedra *f* preciosa; *(in watch)* rubí *m*. **2** *fig (person)* joya *f*, perla *f*.

jeweller, *US* **jeweler** ['dʒuːələʳ] *n* joyero,-a m, *f*, **j.'s (shop),** joyería *f*.

jewellery, *US* **jewelry** ['dʒuːəlrɪ] *n* joyas *fpl*, alhajas *fpl*; **costume j.,** bisutería *f*.

Jewess ['dʒuːɪs] *n* judía *f*.

Jewish ['dʒuːɪʃ] *adj* judío,-a.

Jewry ['dʒʊərɪ] *n fml (people)* los Judíos, el Pueblo Judio; *(religion)* judaísmo *m*.

jew's-harp [dʒuːz'hɑːp] *n Mus* birimbao *m*.

jib¹ [dʒɪp] *vi (pt & pp jibbed)* **1** *(of horse)* plantarse. **2** *GB (of person)* resistirse, oponerse.

jib² [dʒɪp] *n* **1** *Tech (of crane)* aguijón *m*. **2** *Naut* foque *m*. ■ **j. boom,** botalón *m*.

jibe [dʒaɪb] *n* & *vi see* **gibe.**

jiffy ['dʒɪfɪ] *n fam* momento *m*, instante *m*; **in a j.,** en un santiamén; **just a j.!,** ¡un momento! ■ **j. bag®,** sobre *m* acolchado.

jig [dʒɪg] **I** *n* **1** *Mus* giga *f*. **2** *Tech* calibre *m*, gálibo *m*. **II** *vi (pt & pp jigged)* bailar.

jiggery-pokery [dʒɪgərɪ'pəʊkərɪ] *n GB fam* tejemaneje *m*, trampas *fpl*.

jiggle ['dʒɪgəl] **I** *vtr* sacudir, dar meneos a, menear. **II** *vi* to **j. about,** menearse.

jigsaw ['dʒɪgsɔː] *n* **1** *(puzzle)* rompecabezas *m inv*. **2** *Tech* sierra *f* de vaivén.

jilt [dʒɪlt] *vtr fam* dejar plantado,-a, dar calabazas a.

jimjams ['dʒɪmdʒæmz] *npl fam* nervios *mpl*, mieditis *f sing*.

jimmy ['dʒɪmɪ] *n US see* **jemmy.**

jingle ['dʒɪŋgəl] **I** *n* **1** *(sound)* tintineo *m*. **2** *Rad TV* canción *f* que acompaña un anuncio. **II** *vtr* hacer sonar. **III** *vi* tintinear.

jingling ['dʒɪŋglɪŋ] *n* tintineo *m*.

jingo ['dʒɪŋgəʊ] *n* patriotero,-a *m,f*, jingoísta *mf*; **by j.!,** ¡pardiez!, ¡caray!

jingoism ['dʒɪŋgəʊɪzəm] *n* patriotería *f*, jingoísmo *m*.

jingoistic [dʒɪŋgəʊ'ɪstɪk] *adj* patriotero-a, jingoísta.

jink [dʒɪŋk] *vi fam* zigzaguear.

jinks [dʒɪŋks] *npl* juerga *f sing*; **high j.,** jolgorio *m sing*; **to get up to high j.,** ponerse en plan de juerga.

jinx [dʒɪŋks] **I** *n fam (person)* gafe *mf*, cenizo *m*; **to be a j.,** *(person)* ser un gafe; *(bad luck)* ser mala suerte; **to put a j. on,** traer mala suerte a, echar el gafe a. **II** *vtr* gafar.

jinxed [dʒɪŋkst] *adj fam* gafado,-a.

jitters ['dʒɪtəz] *npl* **the j.,** nervios *mpl*; **to get/have the j.,** ponerse nervioso,-a/estar nervioso,-a, tener miedo *or* canguelo.

jittery ['dʒɪtərɪ] *adj* nervioso,-a, **to be j.,** tener miedo *or* canguelo.

jive [dʒaɪv] *Mus* **I** *n* swing *m*. **II** *vi* bailar el swing.

Jnr *US abbr of* **Junior,** hijo, el más joven.

job [dʒɒb] *n* **1** *(piece of work)* trabajo *m*; *(task)* tarea *f*; **to do a j.,** hacer un trabajo; **to do a good j.,** hacer un buen trabajo; **to do odd jobs,** hacer trabajillos; **to give sth *or* sb up as a bad j.,** darse por vencido,-a; **to make a good/bad j. of sth,** hacer algo bien/mal; **to make the best of a bad j.,** poner a mal tiempo buena cara; **you should be on the j.,** deberías estar trabajando en este momento; *fam* **just the j.!,** ¡perfecto! ¡justo lo que nos hacía falta! ■ **odd j. man,** hombre *m* que hace de todo. **2** *(occupation, post)* (puesto *m* de) trabajo *m*, empleo *m*; *(trade)* oficio *m*; **he's got a j. as a waiter,** trabaja de camarero; **to have a good j.,** tener un buen puesto; **to have j. satisfaction,** sentirse realizado,-a en su trabajo; **to look for a j.,** buscar empleo; **to lose one's j.,** perder el empleo; **she knows her j.,** conoce (bien) su oficio; *GB fam* **jobs for the boys,** enchufismo *m*. ■ **j. centre,** oficina *f* de empleo; **j. hunting,** búsqueda *f* de empleo; **j. sharing,** trabajo *m* compartido a tiempo partido. **3** *fam (difficult task)* esfuerzo *m*, trabajo *m*; **we had a j. to ...,** nos costó (trabajo) ... . **4** *fam (robbery)* golpe *m*, robo *m*. **5** *(duty)* deber *m*; **it's his j. to ...,** él está encargado de ... . **6** *fam (state of affairs)* suerte *f*; **it's a good j.!,** ¡menos mal!; **it's a good j. that ...,** menos mal que ... . **7** *fam (specimen)* modelo *m*; **that motorbike's a lovely j.,** esa moto es una máquina finísima. **8** *fam (finished piece of work)* trabajo *m*, obra *f*; **he did a good paint j. on the house,** hizo un buen trabajo pintando la casa.

jobber ['dʒɒbəʳ] *n* **1** *(middleman)* intermediario,-a *m,f*. **2** *(Stock Exchange)* corredor,-a m, *f* de Bolsa.

jobbing ['dʒɒbɪŋ] *adj* temporal. ■ *Print* **j. printer,** impresor *m* que se dedica al mundo comercial.

jobless ['dʒɒblɪs] *adj* sin trabajo, desocupado,-a, parado,-a.

job lot [dʒɒb'lɒt] *n* lote *m* mixto vendido a bajo precio.

jockey ['dʒɒkɪ] **I** *n* jinete *m*, jockey *m*. **II** *vi* luchar para conseguir una posición aventajada; *(in hierarchy)* ascender, escalar; **to j. for position,** escalar puestos.

jockstrap ['dʒɒkstræp] *n* suspensorio *m*.

jocose [dʒə'kəʊs] *adj* jocoso,-a, gracioso,-a, divertido,-a.

jocular ['dʒɒkjʊləʳ] *adj* jocoso,-a, gracioso,-a.

jodhpurs ['dʒɒdpəz] *npl Equit* pantalón *m sing* de montar.

jog [dʒɒg] **I** *n* **1** trote *m*; **slow j.,** trote corto; *Sport* **to go for a j.,** hacer footing. **II** *vtr (pt & pp jugged)* empujar; *fig (memory)* refrescar; **to j. sb's elbow,** dar un golpe en el codo a algn. **III** *vi* **1** *Sport* hacer footing; **to j. along *or* on,** andar a trote corto. **2** *fig (progress slowly)* avanzar poco a poco; *fig (manage)* ir tirando.

jogger ['dʒɒgəʳ] *n Sport* persona *f* que practica el footing.

jogging ['dʒɒgɪŋ] *n Sport* footing *m*; **to go j.,** hacer footing.

Johannesburg [dʒəʊ'hænɪsbɜːg] *n* Johannesburgo.

John [dʒɒn] *n* **1** Juan *m*; **J. Bull,** personificación *f* de Inglaterra; **J. the Baptist,** San Juan Bautista. **2** *(fish)* **J. Dory,** pez *m* de San Pedro.

john [dʒɒn] *n US fam* wáter *m*, retrete *m*, servicio *m*.

join [dʒɔɪn] **I** *vtr* **1** *(gen)* juntar; **they joined the tables,** juntaron las mesas; **to j. forces with sb,** unir fuerzas con algn. **2** *(of road)* empalmar con; *(of river)* desembocar en; **the road joins the motorway here,** la carretera empalma con la autopista aquí. **3** *(meet, accompany)* reunirse con; **will you j. us for a drink?,** ¿quiere tomar una copa con nonostro? **4** *(take one's place in) (team, group)* unirse; *(institution)* entrar; *(army)* alistarse; **Mr Serrano joined the company last month,** Sr. Serrano entró en la compañía el mes pasado. **5** *(become a member of) (party)* afiliarse a; *(club)* hacerse socio,-a de. **II** *vi* **1** *(gen)* unirse. **2** *(of roads)* empalmar; *(of rivers)* confluir; **the Wharfe and the Ouse j. near Cawood,** el Wharfe y el Ouse confluyen cerca de Cawood. **3** *(become a member) (party)* afiliarse;

(club) hacerse socio,-a. **III** *n* 1 *(gen)* juntura *f*. 2 *Sew* costura *f*. ◆ **join in** *vtr & vi (game etc)* participar, tomar parte; *(debate, discussion)* intervenir; **they all joined in the singing,** todos se pusieron a cantar. ◆ **join up I** *vtr (of two things)* juntar. **II** *vi* 1 *(of roads)* unirse. 2 *Mil* alistarse.

joiner ['dʒɔɪnəʳ] *n GB* carpintero,-a *m,f*.

joinery ['dʒɔɪnərɪ] *n* carpintería *f*.

joint [dʒɔɪnt] **I** *n* 1 *(gen)* juntura *f*, unión *f*; *Tech* articulación *f*; *(woodwork, pipes)* ensambladura *f*; *Anat* articulación *f*; **out of j.,** dislocado,-a; **to put sb's nose out of j.,** partirle las narices a algn. 2 *Culin (piece of meat)* corte *m* de carne para asar; *(once roasted)* asado *m*. 3 *sl (nightclub etc)* garito *m*, antro *m*. 4 *sl (drug)* porro *m*. **II** *vtr Culin (chicken etc)* descuartizar. **III** *adj* colectivo,-a. ■ **j. (bank) account,** cuenta *f* (bancaria) conjunta; **j. agreement,** acuerdo *m* mutuo; **j. author,** coautor,-a *m, f*; **j. effort,** esfuerzo *m* colectivo; **j. ownership,** copropiedad *f*; **j. statement,** declaración *f* conjunta; **j. venture,** empresa *f* común. ◆ **jointly** *adv* conjuntamente, en común.

jointed ['dʒɔɪntɪd] *adj* articulado,-a.

joist ['dʒɔɪst] *n Archit* vigueta *f*.

joke [dʒəʊk] **I** *n* 1 *(funny story)* chiste *m*; *(prank)* broma *f*; **he can't take a j.,** no sabe aguantar una broma; **it's getting beyond a j.,** está pasando de castaño a oscuro, ya no tiene gracia; **she did it for a j.,** lo hizo en broma; **to make a j. of everything,** reírse de todo; **to play a practical j. on sb,** gastarle una broma pesada a algn; **to tell a j.,** contar un chiste; *fam* **it's no j.,** no tiene gracia. 2 *fam (person, thing)* hazmerreír *m*, payaso,-a *m, f*; *fam* **the j. is on you,** tú pagarás el pato. **II** *vi* estar de broma; **I'm not joking,** lo digo en serio; **joking apart,** bromas aparte; **to j. about sth,** reírse de algo; **you must be joking!,** ¡no hablarás en serio!

joker ['dʒəʊkəʳ] *n* **I** *(clown)* bromista *mf*, guasón,-a *m,f*. 2 *Cards* comodín *m*.

jokingly ['dʒəʊkɪŋlɪ] *adv* en broma.

jolly ['dʒɒlɪ] **I** *adj (jollier, jolliest)* 1 *(happy)* jovial, alegre. 2 *(tipsy)* piripi, achispado,-a. **II** *adv fam* 1 *(very)* **it was j. cold,** hacía mucho frío; **j. good!,** ¡muy bien!; **j. useful,** de lo más práctico; **she played j. well,** jugó muy bien. 2 **j. well,** *(really)* decididamente; **I'm j. well not going,** desde luego, yo no voy. **III** *vtr* animar; **to j. sb along,** animar a algn.

jolt [dʒəʊlt] **I** *n* 1 *(jerk)* sacudida *f*; *(pull)* tirón *m*. 2 *fig (fright)* susto *m*; **it gave me a j.,** me pegó un susto. **II** *vi* moverse a sacudidas; **the car jolted along,** el coche iba dando botes. **III** *vtr (usually passive)* sacudir; **she was jolted out of her daydreaming by a sudden scream,** un grito repentino la hizo volver a la realidad.

Jordan ['dʒɔːdən] *n* 1 *(river)* Jordán *m*. 2 *(country)* Jordania.

Jordanian [dʒɔː'deɪnɪən] *adj & n* jordano,-a *(m, f)*.

joss-stick ['dʒɒstɪk] *n* varita *f* de incienso, pebete *m*.

jostle ['dʒɒsəl] *vtr & vi* 1 *(bump)* empujar, dar empujones; **he jostled his way through the crowd,** se abrió paso a empujones entre la multitud. 2 *(compete)* competir; **they jostled for the prize,** compitieron para el premio.

jot [dʒɒt] **I** *n* jota *f*, pizca *f*; **I don't care a j.,** me importa en bledo; **not a j.,** ni jota. **II** *vtr (pt & pp jotted)* apuntar, anotar. ◆ **jot down** *vtr* apuntar, anotar.

jotter ['dʒɒtəʳ] *n GB* bloc *m*.

jottings ['dʒɒtɪŋz] *npl* notas *fpl*, apuntes *mpl*.

joule [dʒuːl] *n Elec Phys* julio *m*.

journal ['dʒɜːnəl] *n* 1 *(periodical)* boletín *m*, revista *f*. 2 *(diary)* diario *m*. 3 *(newspaper)* periódico *m*.

journalese [dʒɜːnə'liːz] *n* jerga *f* periodística, lenguaje *m* periodístico.

journalism ['dʒɜːnəlɪzəm] *n* periodismo *m*.

journalist ['dʒɜːnəlɪst] *n* periodista *mf*.

journalistic [dʒɜːnə'lɪstɪk] *adj* periodístico,-a.

journey ['dʒɜːnɪ] **I** *n* 1 *(trip)* viaje *m*; **to go on a j.,** salir de viaje. 2 *(distance)* trayecto *m*; **a 20 mile j.,** un trayecto de 20 millas; **it's a two day j. from here,** son dos días de viaje desde aquí. **II** *vi fml* viajar.

joust [dʒaʊst] *vi Hist* justar, justear.

jovial ['dʒəʊvɪəl] *adj* jovial.

jowl [dʒaʊl] *n (of animal)* quijada *f*; *fig* **cheek by j.,** muy unidos,-as.

joy [dʒɔɪ] *n* 1 *(happiness)* alegría *f*. 2 *(pleasure)* placer *m*; **it's a j. to see him,** da gusto verle. 3 *fam (luck, use)* suerte *f*; **you won't get any j. out of it, it doesn't work,** no conseguirás nada, no funciona.

joyful ['dʒɔɪfʊl] *adj* alegre, contento,-a.

joyless ['dʒɔɪlɪs] *adj* triste.

joyous ['dʒɔɪəs] *adj lit* alegre, apenado,-a.

joyride ['dʒɔɪraɪd] *n fam* paseo *m* en un coche robado.

joystick ['dʒɔɪstɪk] *n* 1 *Av* palanca *f* de mando. 2 *(of video game)* joystick *m*.

JP [dʒeɪ'piː] *Jur abbr of* **Justice of the Peace,** juez *m* de paz.

Jr *abbr see* **Jnr.**

jubilant ['dʒuːbɪlənt] *adj* jubiloso,-a, alborozado,-a.

jubilation [dʒuːbɪ'leɪʃən] *n* júbilo *m*, regocijo *m*, alborozo *m*.

jubilee ['dʒuːbɪliː] *n* festejos *mpl*; **golden j.,** *(general sense)* quincuagésimo aniversario *m*; *(wedding anniversary)* bodas *fpl* de oro.

Judaic(al) [dʒuː'deɪɪk(əl)] *adj* judaico,-a.

Judaism ['dʒuːdeɪɪzəm] *n* judaísmo *m*.

Judas ['dʒuːdəs] *n* **J. tree,** árbol *m* del amor *or* de Judas, ciclamor *m*.

judder ['dʒʌdəʳ] *vi* dar sacudidas, dar botes, vibrar.

judge [dʒʌdʒ] **I** *n Jur* juez *mf*, jueza *f*; *(competition)* jurado *m*; **to be a good j.,** saber juzgar; **to be a good j. of character,** saber juzgar a las personas. **II** *vtr* 1 *Jur (case)* juzgar; *(accused)* declarar. 2 *(estimate, consider)* calcular, considerar; **he judged the distance badly,** calculó mal la distancia; **I j. him the best,** le considero el mejor; **I j. him to be about 45,** le calculo unos 45 años. 3 *(competition)* adjudicar, decidir; **she judged the poetry competition,** fue miembro del jurado en el concurso de poesía. 4 *(assess)* juzgar; **never j. a person just by their appearance,** no juzgues nunca a una persona sólo por su aspecto. **III** *vi* juzgar, formarse una opinión sobre; **judging from what you say,** a juzgar por lo que dices.

judg(e)ment ['dʒʌdʒmənt] *n* 1 *Jur (sentence)* sentencia *f*, fallo *m*; **to pass j.,** pronunciar sentencia; **to sit in j. on a case,** deliberar en un juicio. 2 *(opinion)* juicio *m*, opinión *f*; **to do sth against one's better j.,** hacer algo sin estar completamente convencido; **to pass j.,** comentar, opinar **(on,** sobre); **to reserve j.,** no opinar **(on,** sobre), reservarse la opinión; **to the best of my j.,** por lo que puedo juzgar, a mi entender. 3 *(ability)* discernimiento *m*, buen juicio *m*; **a person of sound j.,** una persona con capacidad de juicio. 4 *Jur (trial)* juicio *m*; **the Last J.,** el Juicio Final.

judicial [dʒuː'dɪʃəl] *adj* judicial; **j. inquiry,** investigación *f* judicial.

judiciary [dʒuː'dɪʃɪərɪ] *n* magistratura *f*, judicatura *f*.

judicious [dʒuː'dɪʃəs] *adj fml* juicioso,-a, sensato,-a.

judiciousness [dʒuː'dɪʃəsnɪs] *n fml* juicio *m*, sensatez *f*, sentido *m* común.

judo ['dʒuːdəʊ] *n* judo *m*.

judoka ['dʒuːdəʊkæ] *n* judoka *mf*.

jug [dʒʌg] *n* 1 *GB (container)* jarra *f*; **milk j.,** jarra de leche. 2 *sl (prison)* chirona *f*, talego *m*; **in j.,** en chirona. **II** *vtr Culin* estofar; **jugged hare,** estofado *m* de liebre.

juggernaut ['dʒʌgənɔːt] *n GB Aut* camión *m* pesado.

juggle ['dʒʌgəl] *vi* 1 *(perform)* hacer juegos malabares **(with,** con). 2 *fig (organize)* reorganizar; **to j. (with) figures,** jugar con las cifras.

juggler ['dʒʌɡlə'] *n* malabarista *mf*.

jugular ['dʒʌɡjulə'] *adj* Anat yugular *f*.

juice [dʒu:s] *n* **1** (*gen*) jugo *m*; (*of citrus fruits*) zumo *m*; **tomato j.**, jugo de tomate; **gastric j.**, jugo gastrico. **2** *fam sl (petrol)* gasolina *f*. **3** Anat **juices**, jugos *mpl*; **digestive j.**, jugos digestivos.

juiciness ['dʒu:sɪnɪs] *n* jugosidad *f*.

juicy ['dʒu:sɪ] *adj* (*juicier, juiciest*) **I** (*succulent*) jugoso,-a; **j. orange**, naranja jugosa. **2** *fam fig* verde, picante; **a j. story**, una historia picante.

jukebox ['dʒu:kbɒks] *n* máquina *f* de discos.

Jul *abbr of* **July**, julio *m*, jul.

July [dʒu:'laɪ, dʒə'laɪ, dʒu'laɪ] *n* julio *m*; **in J.**, en julio; *see also* **May**.

jumble ['dʒʌmbəl] **I** *n* revoltijo *m*, revoltillo *m*, mezcolanza *f*. ■ **j. sale**, bazar *m* or mercadillo *m* de caridad. **II** *vtr* mezclar, hacer un revoltillo.

jumbo ['dʒʌmbəʊ] **I** *adj* enorme, gigante. **II** *n* **1** *Av* **j. (jet)**, jumbo *m*. **2** *Zool fam* elefante *m*.

jump [dʒʌmp] **I** *n* **1** (*leap*) salto *m*; *Sport* **the horse cleared the third j.**, el caballo pasó el tercer obstáculo. ■ **high j.**, salto *m* de altura; **j. leads**, cables *mpl* de emergencia; **j. suit**, mono *m*; **long j.**, salto *m* de longitud; *US* **j. rope**, comba *f*. **2** (*sudden increase*) salto *m*, subida *f* repentina; **there was a sudden j. in prices in December**, hubo una subida repentina de los precios en diciembre. **3** (*step*) paso *m*; **they made a huge j. forward in the plans for the pedestrian precinct**, dieron un paso gigante para adelantar el proyecto de la zona peatonal. **II** *vi* **1** (*leap*) saltar, dar un salto; *Aut* **j. in!**, ¡sube!; **he jumped into the taxi**, subió de un salto al taxi; **Ingrid jumped off the wall**, Ingrid saltó del muro; **to j. down from a wall**, bajarse de un muro; **to j. into the water**, tirarse al agua; **to j. out of the window**, tirarse por la ventana; **to j. up and down**, dar brincos; *fig* **to j. for joy**, saltar de alegría; *fig* **to j. from one subject to another**, saltar de un tema a otro; *fig* **to j. to conclusions**, sacar conclusiones precipitadas; *fam* **j. to it!**, ¡hazlo ya!; *fam fig* **to j. down sb's throat**, echarle una bronca *or* un rapapolvo a algn. **2** *fig* (*start*) sobresaltarse; **he jumped out of his skin when he heard the noise**, se pegó un susto de muerte cuando oyó el ruido; **her heart jumped when she saw the telegram**, el corazón le dio un vuelco cuando vio el telegrama; **to make sb j.**, darle un susto a algn, asustar a algn. **3** (*increase*) dar un salto, aumentar de golpe; **the price of petrol jumped sharply last month**, el precio de gasolina aumentó bruscamente el mes pasado. **III** *vtr* **1** (*leap*) saltar; **the horse jumped the fence**, el caballo saltó la valla; **to j. the gun**, *Sport* tomar la salida en falso; *fam fig* precipitarse; *GB* **to j. the queue**, colarse. **2** *Equit* hacer saltar; **to j. a horse over a fence**, hacer saltar una valla a un caballo. **3** (*miss out*) saltarse; **he jumped the question**, se saltó la pregunta. **4** (*of train*) *fam* **to j. a train**, coger un tren sin pagar. **5** *Aut fam* saltarse; **to j. the lights**, saltarse el semáforo. ◆ **jump at** *vtr* aceptar sin pensarlo; **she jumped at the offer**, aceptó la oferta sin pensarlo. ◆ **jump on** *vtr* criticar, reñir; **she jumped on me for telling Sylvia**, me riñó por habérselo contado a Sylvia.

jumped-up ['dʒʌmptʌp] *adj* GB arribista, advenedizo,-a.

jumper ['dʒʌmpə'] *n* **1** GB (*sweater*) jersey *m*. **2** *US* (*dress*) pichi *m*, falda *f* con peto.

jumpiness ['dʒʌmpɪnɪs] *n fam* nerviosismo *m*.

jump-jet ['dʒʌmpdʒet] *n Av* avión *m* or reactor *m* de despegue vertical.

jumpy ['dʒʌmpɪ] *adj* (*jumpier, jumpiest*) *fam* nervioso,-a.

Jun 1 *abbr of* **June**, junio *m*, jun. **2** *abbr see* **Jnr**.

junction ['dʒʌŋkʃən] *n* **1** (*of roads*) cruce *m*. **2** Rail Elec empalme *m*. ■ **j. box**, caja *f* de empalme.

juncture ['dʒʌŋktʃə'] *n fml* coyuntura *f*; **at this j.**, en esta coyuntura.

June [dʒu:n] *n* junio *m*; **(on) 5th J.**, el cinco de junio; *see also* **May**.

jungle ['dʒʌŋɡəl] *n* jungla *f*, selva *f*; *fig* laberinto *m*; **the concrete j.**, la jungla de asfalto.

junior ['dʒu:nɪə'] **I** *adj* **1** (*son of*) hijo; **David Hughes j.**, David Hughes hijo. **2** (*young*) *Educ* **j. school**, escuela de EGB (=Enseñanza General Básica); *Sport* **j. team**, equipo juvenil. **3** (*lower in rank*) subalterno,-a; **j. officer**, oficial subalterno; **j. members**, miembros *mpl* de menor antigüedad *or* más recientes. **II** *n* **1** (*person of lower rank*) subalterno,-a *m, f*. **2** (*younger person*) menor *mf*; **she's my j. by five years**, tiene cinco años menos que yo, le llevo cinco años. **3** *GB Educ* alumno,-a *m, f* de EGB; *US* estudiante *mf* de penúltimo año.

juniper ['dʒu:nɪpə'] *n Bot* enebro *m*, junípero *m*. ■ **Chinese golden j.**, enebro *m* de la China.

junk [dʒʌŋk] *n* **1** *fam* (*old furniture etc*) trastos *mpl*. ■ *fam* **j. food**, comida *f* de plástico; **j. heap**, vertedero *m*; **j. mail**, propaganda *f* (por correo); **j. shop**, baratillo *m*, tienda *f* de artículos usados. **2** (*boat*) junco *m*. **3** (*drug*) *sl* heroína *f*.

junkie ['dʒʌŋkɪ] *n sl* yonqui *mf*.

junket ['dʒʌŋkɪt] *n* **1** *Culin* requesón *m*, cuajada *f*. **2** *US Canada* (*visit*) visita *f* oficial.

junketing ['dʒʌŋkɪtɪŋ] *n fam* fiesta *f*; **to go j.**, irse de fiesta.

junky ['dʒʌŋkɪ] *n see* **junkie**.

junta ['dʒʌntə, 'dʒʊntə, *US* 'hʊntə] *n Mil Pol* junta *f*, junta *f* militar.

Jupiter ['dʒu:pɪtə'] *n Astron Myth* Júpiter *m*.

jurisdiction [dʒʊərɪs'dɪkʃən] *n fml* jurisdicción *f*; **it doesn't come within our j.**, no es de nuestra competencia.

jurisprudence [dʒʊərɪs'pru:dəns] *n fml* jurisprudencia *f*.

jurist ['dʒʊərɪst] *n fml* jurista *mf*.

juror ['dʒʊərə'] *n* jurado,-a *m, f*, miembro *m* de un jurado.

jury ['dʒʊərɪ] *n* jurado *m*, tribunal *m*; **to serve on a j.**, ser miembro de un jurado. ■ **j. box**, tribuna *f* del jurado, banco *m* del jurado.

just [dʒʌst] **I** *adj* (*fair*) justo,-a; (*deserved*) merecido,-a; *fml* (*well-founded*) justificado,-a; **a j. sentence**, una sentencia justa; **a j. war**, una guerra justificada; **it is only j. that ...**, es justo que ...; **it was a j. reward for all his hard work**, fue un justo premio a todos sus esfuerzos. **II** *adv* **1** (*recently*) **to have j.**, acabar de; **he had j. arrived**, acababa de llegar; **the film has j. started**, la película acaba de empezar. **2** (*at this very moment*) ahora mismo, en este momento; **a plane is j. taking off**, un avión está despegando en este mismo momento; **he was j. leaving when Rosa arrived**, estaba a punto de salir cuando llegó Rosa; **I'm j. coming!**, ¡ya voy!; **I'm j. leaving**, me marcho ahora mismo; **j. as ...**, cuando ..., justo al ...; **j. as I shut the door I realized I had left my keys inside**, justo al cerrar la puerta me di cuenta de que había dejado las llaves en el interior; **j. as I thought**, me lo figuraba; **j. as I was leaving**, en el momento en que me marchaba. **3** (*only*) solamente, nada más, sólo; **he is j. a boy**, no es más que un niño; **j. in case**, por si acaso; **j. those with tickets**, únicamente los que llevan billetes; **these are j. a few examples of his work**, estas son sólo algunas muestras de su trabajo; **they are j. good friends**, sólo son buenos amigos; **j. a minute** *or* **a moment** *or* **a second!**, ¡un momento! **4** (*barely, very nearly*) por poco; **I j. managed it**, por poco no lo consigo; **I only j. caught the bus**, cogí el autobús por los pelos; **j. about**, casi; **j. enough**, justo lo suficiente; **we'll j. make it**, llegaremos justo a tiempo. **5** (*emphatic*) **he's so good-looking —isn't he j.!**, ¡es tan guapo! —¡ya lo creo!; **it's j. fantastic!**, ¡es sencillamente fantástico!; **she's j. marvellous**, es un encanto de mujer; **you'll j. have to wait**, tendrás que esperar. **6** (*exactly*) exactamente, justamente, justo; **it's j. what I wanted**, es exactamente lo que quería; **she likes everything j. so**, le gusta tenerlo todo perfecto; **that's j. it!**, ¡precisamente!; *fam* **it's j. my luck**, vaya mala suerte tengo. **7** (*equally*) tan, igual de; **my car's j. as fast as yours**, mi coche es tan rápido como el tuyo. **III** **the j.** *npl* los, justos. ◆ **justly** *adv* justamente, con justicia; **she was j. famous**, alcanzó merecida fama.

justice ['dʒʌstɪs] n 1 (fairness) justicia f; **he was brought to j.**, lo llevaron ante los tribunales; **let j. be done**, que se haga justicia; **the portrait doesn't do her j.**, el retrato no le hace justicia; **we did j. to the fantastic lunch**, correspondimos lo mejor que pudimos a tan fantástica comida; **you didn't do yourself j. in the interview**, no diste lo mejor de ti en la entrevista. 3 US (judge, magistrate) juez mf; GB **J. of the Peace**, juez de paz; GB **Mr J. Burke**, el juez Burke.

justifiable ['dʒʌstɪfaɪəbəl] adj justificable.

justification [dʒʌstɪfɪ'keɪʃən] n 1 (defence) justificación f, razón f; **in j. of**, en defensa de. 2 Print justificación f.

justified ['dʒʌstɪfaɪd] adj 1(right) justificado,-a; **to be j. in doing sth**, tener razón en hacer algo. 2 Print justificado,-a.

justify ['dʒʌstɪfaɪ] vtr (pt & pp **justified**) 1 (explain) justificar; **he justified what he had done**, justificó lo que había hecho. 2 Print justificar.

justness ['dʒʌstnɪs] n (fairness) justicia f.

jut [dʒʌt] vi (pt & pp **jutted**) sobresalir; **to j. out from**, sobresalir de; **to j. out over**, proyectarse sobre.

Jute [dʒuːt] n Hist yuto,-a m,f.

jute [dʒuːt] n Bot yute m.

juvenile ['dʒuːvənaɪl] I adj 1 (young) juvenil; Jur **j. court**, tribunal de menores; **j. delinquent**, delincuente juvenil. 2 (immature) infantil; **don't be so j.!**, ¡no seas tan infantil! II n menor mf, joven mf, adolescente mf.

juxtapose [dʒʌkstə'pəʊz] vtr yuxtaponer.

juxtaposition [dʒʌkstəpə'zɪʃən] n yuxtaposición f.

K

K, k [keɪ] n (the letter) K, k f.

k [keɪ] abbr of **kilo**, kilo m, kilogramo m, kg.

Kabul [kə'bʊl, 'kɑ:bəl] n Kabul.

kaftan ['kæftæn] n caftán m.

Kaiser ['kaɪzə'] n káiser m.

kale [keɪl] n col f rizada.

kaleidoscope [kə'laɪdəskəʊp] n caleidoscopio m.

kamikaze [kæmɪ'kɑːzɪ] adj & n kamikaze (mf).

Kampuchea [kæmpʊ'tʃɪə] n Kampuchea.

kangaroo ['kæŋgə'ruː] n Zool canguro m. ■ **k. court**, tribunal m desautorizado.

kaolin ['keɪəlɪn] n Min caolín m.

kapok ['keɪpɒk] n kapok m.

kaput [kə'pʊt] adj fam estropeado,-a; (plan) fastidiado,-a; **my car's k.**, tengo el coche estropeado.

karat ['kærət] n US quilate m.

karate [kə'rɑːtɪ] n Sport kárate m.

Kashmir [kæʃ'mɪə'] n Cachemira.

Kat(h)mandu [kætmæn'duː] n Katmandú.

kayak ['kaɪæk] n kayac m.

KC [keɪ'siː] GB Jur abbr of **King's Counsel**, abogado,-a m,f del Estado.

kebab [kə'bæb] n Culin pincho m moruno, brocheta f.

keel [kiːl] n Naut quilla f; fig **to be on an even k.**, estar en equilibrio. ◆ **keel over** vi (boat) zozobrar; fam (person) desmayarse.

keen¹ [kiːn] adj 1 (eager) entusiasta; **he's a k. golfer, he's k. on golf**, es muy aficionado al golf; fam **he's k. on your sister**, le gusta tu hermana. 2 (intense) profundo,-a; **she took a k. interest in international affairs**, tomó un gran interés por los asuntos internacionales. 3 (sharp, acute) (mind, senses) agudo,-a; (look) penetrante; (wind) cortante; (blade) afilado,-a; (competition) fuerte. 4 (price) competitivo,-a. ◆ **keenly** adv (intensely) profundamente; (eagerly) con entusiasmo.

keen² [kiːn] vi arch lamentar.

keenness ['kiːnnɪs] n 1 (enthusiasm) entusiasmo m, afición f. 2 (intensity) intensidad f, fuerza f. 3 (sharpness) agudeza f, penetración f.

keep [kiːp] I n 1 (maintenance) manutención f; **to earn one's k.**, ganarse el cocido or el pan. 2 (tower) torreón m. 3 fam **for keeps**, para siempre. II vtr (pt & pp **kept**) 1 (cause to remain) tener, mantener; (letters, memories, silence) guardar; **to k. one's looks**, conservarse bien; **to k. sb awake**, mantener despierto a algn; **to k. sb informed**, tener a algn al corriente; **to k. sb in the dark about sth**, ocultarle algo a algn; **to k. sth in mind**, tener a algo en cuenta or en mente. 2 (retain possession of) quedarse; **he can't k. a job for more than six months**, es incapaz de conservar un trabajo más de seis meses; **k. it, it's for you**, quédatelo, es tuyo; **k. the change**, qué dese con el cambio. 3 (detain) detener, retener; **the rain kept them at home**, la lluvia les retuvo en casa; **to k. sb waiting**, hacer esperar a algn. 4 (maintain, support) mantener; (animals) criar; **badly kept road**, carretera en mal estado. 5 (observe, fulfil) (the law) observar; (a promise) cumplir; (holidays) guardar. 6 (conceal, reserve) (secret, place) guardar; **k. this to yourself**, no se lo digas a nadie. 7 (write) (diary, accounts) llevar; Educ **to k. the register**, pasar lista. 8 (prevent, delay) impedir; **I don't know what kept me from slapping him**, no sé qué me impidió darle una bofetada; **the noise keeps me from sleeping**, el ruido me impide dormir. 9 (own, manage) tener; (shop, hotel) llevar; **to k. house**, llevar la casa. 10 (stock) tener, vender; **we don't k. cigars**, no vendemos puros. III vi 1 (remain) seguir; **k. calm!**, ¡tranquilo,-a!; **k. quiet!**, ¡cállate!; **k. still!**, ¡estáte quieto,-a!; **to k. fit**, mantenerse en forma; **to k. going**, seguir adelante; fig ir tirando; **to k. in touch**, no perder el contacto; **to k. smiling**, seguir sonriendo. 2 (do frequently) no dejar de; **he keeps phoning me**, no deja de llamarme; **she keeps forgetting her keys**, siempre se olvida las llaves. 3 (food) conservarse. ◆ **keep at** vi (persevere) perseverar; (force) insistir en; **k. at it!**, ¡no te desanimes!; **the boss kept us at it all day**, el jefe nos hizo trabajar en ello todo el día. ◆ **keep away** I vtr mantener a distancia. II vi mantenerse a distancia; **to k. away from drink**, abstenerse de beber. ◆ **keep back** vtr 1 (hold back) (enemy) contener; **his ill-health kept him back at school**, su mala salud le impidió progresar en el colegio. 2 (withhold) (truth, information) ocultar, callar; (money, food, etc) retener. ◆ **keep down** vtr 1 (limit) limitar; **to k. expenses down**, limitar los gastos; **to k. prices down**, mantener los precios bajos. 2 (oppress) contener. 3 (prevent vomiting) **I can't even k. water down**, vomito hasta el agua que bebo. ◆ **keep in** vtr (detain) no dejar salir, impedir salir a; **he was kept in after school**, le dejaron castigado. ◆ **keep in with** vi cultivar la amistad de. ◆ **keep off** vtr & vi (bar from) prohibir; (prevent from touch or reference) no tocar; (avoid consuming) no comer, no beber; **k. off the grass**, prohibido pisar la hierba; **please k. off that subject**, le ruego que no toque ese tema; **the rain kept off**, no llegó a llover. ◆ **keep on** I vtr 1 (clothes etc) no quitarse; **to k. an eye on sth/sb**, vigilar algo/a algn; fam **k. your shirt on!**, ¡no pierdas la calma! 2 (continue to employ) no despedir a. II vi (continue to do) seguir; **she kept on walking**, siguió andando. ◆ **keep on about** vtr fam pej no parar; **he keeps on about money,** no para de hablar del dinero. ◆ **keep on at** *vtr fam* no dejar tranquilo. ◆ **keep out I** *vtr* no dejar pasar. **II** *vi* no entrar; **k. out!,** ¡prohibida la entrada! ◆ **keep out of** *vtr* evitar; **I kept out of trouble,** evité líos; **k. out of this!,** ¡no te metas en esto! ◆ **keep to** *vtr & vi* **1** *(observe) (law, promise)* cumplir; **to k. sb to his promise,** obligar a algn a cumplir lo prometido; **to k. to a resolution,** mantenerse firme en un propósito. **2** *(restrict)* limitarse a; **k. to the point!,** ¡ciñete a la cuestión! **3** *(remain, stay)* quedarse; **he kept to his room all day,** se quedó en su cuarto todo el día; **to k. oneself to oneself,** no relacionarse con la gente; **to k. to the left,** circular por la izquierda. ◆ **keep up I** *vtr* **1** mantener; **to k. up appearances,** guardar las apariencias; **to k. up the pace,** mantener el ritmo. **2** *(continue)* seguir; *fam* **k. it up!,** ¡sigue así! **3** *(prevent from sleeping)* mantener despierto,-a; **I mustn't k. you up,** ya debe ser tarde para ti. ◆ **keep up with** *vtr* mantenerse; **to k. up with the times,** estar al día; *fig* **to k. up with the Joneses,** no ser menos que el vecino.

keeper ['kiːpə'] *n* guarda *mf*, vigilante *m*; *(in library, record office)* archivero,-a *m*, *f*; *(in museum)* conservador,-a *m, f*.

keeping ['kiːpɪŋ] *n* **1** *(care)* cargo *m*, cuidado *m*; **in sb's k.,** al cuidado de algn; **to be in safe k.,** estar en buenas manos. **2** *(appropriate)* **in k. with,** en armonía con; **out of k. with,** en desacuerdo con.

keepsake ['kiːpseɪk] *n* recuerdo *m*.

keg [keg] *n* barril *m*.

kennel ['kenəl] *n* **1** *(hut)* caseta *f* para perros. **2 kennels,** *(for breeding)* granja *f sing* de perros; *(for boarding)* hotel *m sing* de perros.

Kenya ['kenjə, 'kiːnjə] *n* Kenia.

Kenyan ['kenjən, 'kiːnjən] *adj & n* keniata *(mf)*, keniano,-a *(m, f)*.

kept [kept] *pt & pp see* **keep.**

kerb [kɜːb] *n* bordillo *m*; *Aut* **to hit the k.,** chocar contra el bordillo.

kerchief ['kɜːtʃɪf] *n arch* pañuelo *m*.

kerfuffle [kə'fʌfəl] *n fam* jaleo *m*.

kernel ['kɜːnəl] *n (of fruit, nut)* pepita *f*; *(of wheat)* grano *m*; *fig* **the k. of the matter,** el meollo de la cuestión.

kerosene *n*, **kerosine** ['kerəsiːn] *n US* queroseno *m*. ■ **k. lamp,** lámpara *f* de petróleo.

kestrel ['kestrəl] *n Orn* cernícalo *m* vulgar.

ketch [ketʃ] *n Naut* queche *m*.

ketchup ['ketʃəp] *n* ketchup *m*, salsa *f* de tomate.

kettle ['ketəl] *n* tetera *f*; *fig* **a fine k. of fish!,** ¡menudo lío!; *fam* **that's a different k. of fish,** eso es harina de otro costal. ■ **electric k.,** tetera *f* eléctrica.

kettle-drum ['ketəldrʌm] *n Mus* timbal *m*.

key [kiː] **I** *n* **1** *(for lock)* llave *f*. ■ **k. money,** depósito *m*; **k. ring,** llavero *m*. **2** *(to code, mystery)* clave *f*. **3** *(of piano, typewriter, computer)* tecla *f*. **4** *Mus* tono *m*; **minor k.,** tono *m* menor; **to play off k.,** desafinar. **5** *Geog* cayo *m*. **II** *adj* clave; **k. industry,** industria clave. ◆ **key in** *vtr Comput* introducir.

keyboard ['kiːbɔːd] *n* teclado *m*.

keyed up [kiːd'ʌp] *adj* nervioso,-a, excitado,-a.

keyhole ['kiːhəul] *n* ojo *m* de la cerradura.

keynote ['kiːnəut] *n Mus* tónica *f*; *fig* nota *f* dominante.

keypunch ['kiːpʌntʃ] *n US Comput* perforadora *f*.

keystone ['kiːstəun] *n Archit* piedra *f* clave; *fig* piedra *f* angular.

kg *abbr of* **kilogram(s),** kilogramo(s) *m(pl)*, kg.

khaki ['kæːkɪ] *adj & n* caqui *(m)*.

Khart(o)um [kɑː'tuːm] *n* Jartum.

kHz *Rad abbr of* **kilohertz,** kilohercio(s) *m(pl)*, kHz.

kibbutz [kɪbʊts] *n (pl kibbutzim* [kɪbʊ'tsiːm]) kibutz *m*.

kick [kɪk] **I** *n* **1** *(a blow) (from animal)* coz *f*; *(from person)* patada *f*, puntapié *m*; *(from gun)* culatazo *m*; *fig* **to get a k. in the teeth,** darse con un canto en las narices; *fam* **a drink with a k. in it,** una bebida explosiva. ■ *Aut* **k. starter,** arranque *m*, pedal *m* de arranque. **2** *fam (pleasure, thrill)* **I get a k. out of it,** disfruto con ello; **to do sth for kicks,** hacer algo por el simple placer de hacerlo. **II** *vi (animal)* cocear; *(person)* dar patadas; *(gun)* dar un culatazo; *fam* **alive and kicking,** vivito y coleando. **III** *vtr* dar un puntapié a; **to k. the ball,** chutar (el balón); *fig* **to k. sb when they are down,** dar la puntilla *or* rematar a algn; *fig* **to k. up a fuss** *or* **a row,** armar un escándalo; **that I could k. myself,** ¡qué imbécil soy!; *fam* **to k. a habit,** dejar un vicio; *fam* **to k. the bucket,** estirar la pata. ◆ **kick about** *vi fam (lie unnoticed, unused)* andar por ahí. ◆ **kick against** *vtr (react)* saltar, reaccionar. ◆ **kick around** *fam* **I** *vi (lie unnoticed, unused)* andar por ahí. **II** *vtr (consider) (ideas, suggestions)* dar vueltas a. ◆ **kick off** *vi fam* empezar; *Ftb* sacar. ◆ **kick out** *vtr* echar a patadas, expulsar. ◆ **kick up** *vtr fam (fuss, row)* armar.

kickback ['kɪkbæk] *n* **1** *(of gun)* culatazo *m*. **2** *fam* soborno *m*.

kick-off ['kɪkɒf] *n Ftb* saque *m* inicial.

kid¹ [kɪd] *n* **1** *Zool* cabrito *m*; **k. gloves,** guantes de cabritilla; *fig* **to handle sb with k. gloves,** tratar a algn con guante blanco. **2** *fam* niño,-a *m, f*, chiquillo,-a *m, f*; **my k. brother,** mi hermano pequeño; **that's k.'s stuff,** eso está chupado, es cosa de niños. **3** *fam* **the kids,** los críos, los chiquillos.

kid² ['kɪd] *vtr & vi (pt & pp* **kidded)** *fam* **1** *(joke)* estar de broma, tomar el pelo; **no kidding!,** va en serio, no es broma; **you're kidding!,** ¡no me digas! **2** *(fool)* **to k. oneself,** hacerse ilusiones.

kidnap ['kɪdnæp] *vtr (pt & pp* **kidnapped)** secuestrar, raptar.

kidnapper ['kɪdnæpə'] *n* secuestrador,-a *m, f*, raptor,-a *m, f*.

kidnapping ['kɪdnæpɪŋ] *n* secuestro *m*, rapto *m*.

kidney ['kɪdnɪ] *n Anat Culin* riñón *m*. ■ *Med* **k. machine,** riñón *m* artificial; *Med* **k. stone,** cálculo *m* renal.

kill [kɪl] **I** *n (act)* matanza *f*; *(animal)* pieza *f*; *fig* **to be in at the k.,** ser testigo. **II** *vtr* **1** *(gen)* matar; **to k. oneself,** suicidarse, matarse; *fig* **to k. time,** pasar el rato, matar el tiempo; *fig* **to k. two birds with one stone,** matar dos pájaros de un tiro; *fig* **to k. with kindness,** proteger excesivamente; *fam* **to k. oneself laughing,** morirse de risa. **2** *fam (hurt)* doler mucho; **my feet are killing me,** ¡ay, cómo me duelen los pies! **3** *fam (stop)* acabar; **that mistake has killed his chances,** ese error ha acabado con sus posibilidades. ◆ **kill off** *vtr* exterminar, liquidar.

killer ['kɪlə'] *n* asesino,-a *m, f*. ■ **k. whale,** orca *f*.

killing ['kɪlɪŋ] **I** *n* matanza *f*, asesinato *m*; *fig* **to make a k.,** forrarse de dinero. **II** *adj fam* **1** *(tiring)* agotador,-a. **2** *(funny)* para morirse, divertidísimo,-a.

killjoy ['kɪldʒɔɪ] *n* aguafiestas *mf inv*.

kiln [kɪln] *n* horno *m*.

kilo ['kiːləu] *n* kilo *m*.

kilogram(me) ['kɪləugræm] *n* kilogramo *m*.

kilohertz ['kɪləuhɜːts] *n* kilohercio *m*.

kilometre, *US* **kilometer** [kɪ'lɒmɪtə'] *n* kilómetro *m*.

kilowatt ['kɪləuwɒt] *n* kilovatio *m*.

kilt [kɪlt] *n* falda *f* escocesa, kilt *m*.

kimono [kɪ'məunəu] *n* quimono *m*, kimono *m*.

kin [kɪn] *n* familiares *mpl*, parientes *mpl*; **next of k.,** parientes *m(pl)* más cercanos.

kind¹ [kaɪnd] **I** *n* **1** *(gen)* tipo *m*, clase *f*; **all kinds of,** toda clase de; **chicha is a k. of beer,** la chicha es una especie de cerveza; **nothing of the k.,** nada por el estilo; **they are the k. you can eat,** son de los que se puede comer; **they are two of a k.,** son tal para cual; **what k. of car?,** ¿qué tipo de coche? **2 in k.,** *(payment)* en especie; *(similar treatment)* con la misma moneda. **II** *adv fam* **k. of,** en cierta manera; **I feel k. of sorry for him,** en cierta manera le compadezco; **I k. of expected it,** me lo temía; **she's k. of tired,** está algo cansada.

kind² [kaɪnd] *adj* amable, simpático,-a; **it's very k. of you,** es usted muy amable; **fml would you be so k. as to ...?,** ¿me haría usted el favor de ...? ◆ **kindly** *adv* amablemente.

kindergarten ['kɪndəgɑːtən] *n* parvulario *m,* jardín *m* de infancia.

kind-hearted [kaɪnd'hɑːtɪd] *adj* bondadoso,-a, de buen corazón.

kindle ['kɪndəl] *vtr (fire)* encender; *fig (emotion, interest, etc)* encender, despertar.

kindling ['kɪndlɪŋ] *n* leña *f.*

kindliness ['kaɪndlɪnɪs] *n* bondad *f,* amabilidad *f.*

kindly ['kaɪndlɪ] **I** *adj (kindlier, kindliest)* amable, bondadoso,-a. **II** *adv fml (please)* por favor; **k. remit a cheque,** sírvase enviar cheque; **to look k. on,** aprobar.

kindness ['kaɪndnɪs] *n* bondad *f,* amabilidad *f;* **to do sb a k.,** hacerle un favor a algn.

kindred ['kɪndrɪd] **I** *adj* **1** *(related)* emparentado,-a; **k. languages,** idiomas emparentados. **2** *(similar)* semejante, afín; **k. spirits,** almas *fpl* gemelas. **II** *n arch* familiares *mpl.*

kinetic [kɪ'netɪk] *adj* cinéticoa,-a.

king [kɪŋ] *n (gen)* rey *m; (draughts)* dama *f;* **K. John,** el rey Juan; **the three kings,** los Reyes Magos.

kingdom ['kɪŋdəm] *n* reino *m;* **the animal k.,** el reino animal.

kingfisher ['kɪŋfɪʃəʳ] *n Orn* martín *m* pescador.

kingpin ['kɪŋpɪn] *n Tech* clavija *f* maestra; *fig* persona *f* clave.

king-size ['kɪŋsaɪz] *adj* extralargo,-a.

kink [kɪŋk] *n (in rope, thread)* coca *f,* retorcimiento *m; (in hair)* rizo *m; (peculiarity)* manía *f.*

kinky ['kɪŋkɪ] *adj (kinkier, kinkiest) fam (strange)* raro,-a; *(sexually)* pervertido,-a.

kinship ['kɪnʃɪp] *n* parentesco *m.*

kiosk ['kiːɒsk] *n* quiosco *m.*

kip [kɪp] **I** *n fam* **to have a k.,** echar una cabezada. **II** *vi fam* **to k. (down),** dormir.

kiss [kɪs] **I** *n* beso *m;* **the k. of life,** el boca a boca. **II** *vtr* besar; **he kissed the child good night,** besó al niño al darle las buenas noches; *fam* **to k. sth goodbye,** dar un beso de despedida a algo. **III** *vi* besarse.

kit [kɪt] *n* **1** *(equipment, gear)* equipo *m; Mil* avíos *mpl,* pertrechos *mpl.* ■ **first-aid k.,** botiquín *m;* **tool k.,** caja *f* de herramientas. **2** *(clothing)* ropa *f.* ■ **riding k.,** traje *m* de montar. **3** *(toy model)* maqueta *f,* kit *m.* ◆ **kit out** *vtr* equipar.

kitbag ['kɪtbæg] *n Mil Naut* mochila *f.*

kitchen ['kɪtʃɪn] *n* cocina *f.* ■ **k. sink,** fregadero *m; fig* **they took everything but the k. sink,** sólo les faltó llevarse las paredes; **k. unit,** módulo *m* de cocina.

kitchenware ['kɪtʃɪnweəʳ] *n* batería *f* de cocina.

kite [kaɪt] *n* **1** *Orn* milano *m.* ■ **red k.,** milano *m* real. **2** *(toy)* cometa *f; fig* **to fly a k.,** sondear la opinión.

kith [kɪθ] *n* **k. and kin,** *arch* parientes *mpl* y amigos *mpl.*

kitten ['kɪtən] *n* gatito,-a *m, f; fam* **I nearly had kittens,** casi me muero del susto.

kittiwake ['kɪtɪweɪk] *n Orn* gaviota *f* tridáctila.

kitty¹ ['kɪtɪ] *n fam* minino,-a *m,f.*

kitty² ['kɪtɪ] *n (moneybox)* hucha *f; Cards* bote *m.*

kiwi ['kiːwiː] **I** *n* **1** *Orn* kiwi *m.* **2** *(fruit)* kiwi *m.* **3** *(person) fam* neozelandés,-esa *m, f.* **II** *adj fam* neozelandés,-esa.

kleptomania [kleptəʊ'meɪnɪə] *n* cleptomanía *f.*

kleptomaniac [kleptəʊ'meɪnɪæk] *n* cleptómano,-a *m, f.*

km *(pl km or kms) abbr of* **kilometre(s),** kilómetro(s) *m (pl),* km.

knack [næk] *n* maña *f,* truco *m;* **to get the k. of doing sth,** cogerle el tranquillo *or* el truquillo a algo.

knacker ['nækəʳ] *n* matarife *m.*

knackered ['nækəd] *adj fam* **to be k.,** estar reventado,-a.

knapsack ['næpsæk] *n arch* mochila *f.*

knave [neɪv] *n Cards (English pack)* jota *f; (Spanish pack)* sota *f.*

knead [niːd] *vtr* dar masaje; *(bread etc)* amasar.

knee [niː] **I** *n* **1** *Anat* rodilla *f;* **on one's knees,** de rodillas; *fig* **to bring sb to their knees,** humillar a algn. **2** *(of trousers)* rodillera *f.* **II** *vtr* dar un rodillazo a.

kneecap ['niːkæp] **I** *n Anat* rótula *f.* **II** *vtr* romper la rótula.

knee-deep ['niːdiːp] *adj* que llega hasta las rodillas; **he was k. in water,** estaba metido en el agua hasta las rodillas.

kneel [niːl] *vi (pt & pp* **knelt) to k. (down),** arrodillarse.

knee-length ['niːleŋθ] *adj* largo,-a hasta las rodillas; **a k.-l. skirt,** una falda hasta la rodilla.

knees-up ['niːsʌp] *n inv fam* fiesta *f,* juerga *f.*

knell [nel] *n lit* toque *m* de difuntos.

knelt [nelt] *pt & pp see* **kneel.**

knew [njuː] *pt see* **know.**

knickerbockers ['nɪkəbɒkəz] *npl* bombachos *mpl.*

knickers ['nɪkəz] *npl* **1** *(for women)* bragas *fpl; fam* **to get your k. in a twist,** ponerse negro,-a. **2** *US* bombachos *mpl.*

knick-knack ['nɪknæk] *n* chuchería *f.*

knife [naɪf] **I** *n (pl* **knives** [naɪvz]) cuchillo *m; fig* **on a k. edge,** pendiendo de un hilo; *fam* **to get one's k. into sb,** tenérsela jurada a algn. **II** *vtr* apuñalar, dar una puñalada a.

knight [naɪt] **I** *n Hist* caballero *m; Chess* caballo *m.* **II** *vtr* armar caballero.

knighthood ['naɪthʊd] *n* **1** *(rank)* título *m* de caballero. **2** *(body of knights)* caballería *f.*

knit [nɪt] **I** *vtr (pt & pp* **knitted** *or* **knit) 1** *(with wool etc)* tejer. **2** *(join)* juntar **(together,** -); *fig* **to k. one's brow,** fruncir el entrecejo *or* el ceño. **II** *vi* **1** hacer punto, hacer calceta, tejer, tricotar. **2** *Med (bone)* soldarse.

knitting ['nɪtɪŋ] *n* punto *m,* calceta *f.* ■ **k. machine,** máquina *f* de tejer, tricotosa *f;* **k. needle,** aguja *f* de tejer.

knit-wear ['nɪtweəʳ] *n* géneros *mpl* de punto.

knob [nɒb] *n* **1** *(of stick)* puño *m,* pomo *m; (of drawer)* tirador *m; (control button)* botón *m.* **2** *(small portion)* trozo *m,* porción *f.*

knobbly [nɒblɪ] *adj (knobblier, knobbliest)* nudoso,-a; **k. knees,** rodillas huesudas.

knock [nɒk] **I** *n* **1** *(sound, blow)* golpe *m;* **k., k., k.!,** ¡toc, toc, toc!; **there was a k. at the door,** llamaron a la puerta; **to get a nasty k.,** darse un buen golpe. **2** *fig* revés *m.* **II** *vtr* **1** *(strike)* golpear; **to k. a hole in sth,** abrir un agujero en algo; *fig* **to k. one's head against a brick wall,** darse de cabeza contra la pared; *fig* **to k. sb for six,** dejar pasmado,- a a algn. **2** *fam (criticize)* criticar. **III** *vi* **1** chocar **(against, into,** contra); *(at door)* llamar **(at,** a); *fam* **she's knocking on 70,** tiene casi 70 años. **2** *Aut (make a noise)* golpetear. ◆ **knock about, knock around I** *vtr* **1** pegar, maltratar. **2** *(discuss) (ideas etc)* discutir. **II** *vi fam* **to be present)** andar por ahí; **she has knocked about a bit,** ha vivido mucho. ◆ **knock back** *vtr fam* **1** *(drink)* beber de un trago. **2** *(cost)* costar. ◆ **knock down** *vtr* **1** *(demolish)* derribar. **2** *Aut (hit)* atropellar; **he was knocked down by a car,** le atropelló un coche. **3** *(reduce price)* rebajar. ◆ **knock off I** *vtr* **1** tirar; **she knocked the vase off the table,** tiró el florero de la mesa. **2** *(reduce)* hacer una rebaja, rebajar; **he knocked five pounds off it,** lo rebajó en cinco libras. **3** *fam (steal)* mangar, birlar. **4** *sl (kill)* **to k. sb off,** liquidar a algn. **5** *fam exclam* **k. it off!,** ¡basta ya! **II** *vi fam* largarse; **they k. off at five,** se piran a las cinco. ◆ **knock out** *vtr* **1** *(make unconscious)* dejar sin conocimiento; *Box* poner fuera de combate, derrotar por K.O., noquear. **2** *(surprise)* dejar pasmado,-a; **she was knocked out by the**

news, se quedó de una pieza al oírlo. ◆ **knock over** *vtr* volcar; *Aut* atropellar. ◆ **knock up** I *vtr* **1** *fam (wake)* despertar. **2** *(make)* hacer deprisa. **3** *US fam offens (make pregnant)* dejar preñada. II *vi Ten* pelotear.

knocker ['nɒkə^r] *n* aldaba *f*.

knock-kneed [nɒk'ni:d] *adj* patizambo,-a.

knockout ['nɒkaʊt] I *n* **1** *Box* K.O. *m*, fuera de combate *m*, knock-out *m*. **2** *fam* maravilla *f*; **she's a k.,** es guapísima. II *adj* **1** *Box* **k. blow,** golpe *m* que pone fuera de combate. **2** *Sport* **k. competition,** competición *f* de pruebas eliminatorias.

knoll [nəʊl] *n lit* loma *f*, montículo *m*.

knot [nɒt] I *n* **1** *(gen)* nudo *m*; *(in ribbon)* lazo *m*; *(group)* grupo *m*; *fig* **to tie oneself up in knots,** hacerse un lío. **2** *Naut (sea mile)* nudo *m*. II *vtr* anudar; **the rope must be knotted,** hay que anudar la cuerda, hay que hacer un nudo a la cuerda.

knotty ['nɒtɪ] *adj (knottier, knottiest)* nudoso,-a; *fig* **a k. problem,** un problema espinoso.

know [nəʊ] I *vtr & vi (pt knew; pp known)* **1** *(have knowledge or information of)* saber; **as far as I k.,** que yo sepa; **how should I k.!,** ¡yo qué sé!; **I don't k. about that,** eso no te lo puedo decir; **if only I'd known,** de haberlo sabido antes; **not that I k. of,** que yo sepa no; **not to k. the first thing about sth,** no saber ni jota de algo; **she knows how to ski,** sabe esquiar; **sth worth knowing,** algo que merece la pena saber; **to get to k. sth,** enterarse de algo; **to k. better than to do sth,** guardarse bien de hacer algo; **to k. one's own mind,** saber lo que se quiere; **to k. sth by heart,** saber algo de memoria; **to k. too much,** saber más de la cuenta; **to let sb k.,** avisar al algn; *fam* **Heaven knows!,** ¡sabe Dios! **2** *(be acquainted with)* conocer; **he has known better days,** ha conocido tiempos mejores; **to k. sb by sight,** conocer a algn de vista; *fam* **I don't k. him from Adam,** no tengo ni idea de quién es; **we got to k. each other at the party,** nos conocimos én la fiesta. **3** *(understand)* entender; **I don't k. a thing about cars,** no entiendo nada de coches; **she was a very clever person, yon k.,** era muy inteligente, ¿entiendes? II *n fam* **to be in the k.,** estar en el ajo.

knowable ['nəʊəbəl] *adj* conocible.

know-all ['nəʊɔːl] *n fam* sabelotodo *mf*, sabihondo,-a *m,f*.

know-how ['nəʊhaʊw] *n fam* conocimiento *m* práctico.

knowing ['nəʊɪŋ] *adj (shrewd)* astuto,-a; *(deliberate)* deliberado,-a; **a k. smile,** una sonrisa de complicidad. ◆ **knowingly** *adv (shrewd)* a sabiendas; *(deliberately)* deliberadamente.

know-it-all ['nəʊɪtɔːl] *n US fam* sabelotodo *mf*.

knowledge ['nɒlɪdʒ] *n* **1** *(understanding)* conocimiento *m*; **he has no k. of good and evil,** no tiene conocimiento del bien o del mal; **it's a matter of common k.,** es de sobra sabido; **lack of k.,** falta *f* de conocimiento; **not to my k.,** que yo sepa no; **without my k.,** sin saberlo yo. **2** *(learning)* conocimientos *mpl*; **my k. of German is poor,** mis conocimientos del alemán son escasos; **scientific k.,** conocimientos científicos; **to have a thorough k. of a subject,** conocer un tema a fondo; **to improve one's k.,** aumentar los conocimientos.

knowledgeable ['nɒlɪdʒəbəl] *adj* erudito,-a; **to be k. about a subject,** ser muy entendido,-a en un tema. ◆ **knowledgeably** *adv* eruditamente.

known [nəʊn] I *pp* of **know.** II *adj* conocido,-a.

knuckle ['nʌkəl] *n Anat* nudillo *m*; *Culin* hueso *m*; *fam* **near the k.,** rayando la indecencia. ◆ **knuckle down** *vi fam* ponerse a trabajar o estudiar en serio. ◆ **knuckle under** *vi fam* pasar por el aro.

knuckleduster ['nʌkəldʌstə^r] *n* puño *m* americano.

KO [keɪ'əʊ] *Box fam abbr of* **knockout,** fuera de combate *m*, K.O. *m*.

koala [kəʊ'ɑːlə] *n Zool* koala *m*.

kookie *adj*, **kooky** ['kʊkɪ] *adj (kookier, kookiest) US fam* chalado,-a, chiflado,-a.

Koran [kɔː'rɑːn] *n Rel* Corán *m*.

Korea [kə'rɪːə] *n* Corea.

Korean [kə'rɪːən] *adj & n* coreano,-a *(m, f)*.

kosher ['kəʊʃə^r] *adj* conforme a la ley judaica; *fam* correcto,-a.

kph [keɪpiː'eɪtʃ] *abbr of* **kilometres per hour,** kilómetros *mpl* por hora, Km/h, km/h.

Kraut [kraʊt] *n sl offens* boche *mf*.

krypton ['krɪptɒn] *n Chem* kriptón *m*.

kudos ['kjuːdɒs] *n* prestigio *m*.

Kurd [kɜːd] *n* curdo,-a *m,f*.

Kurdish ['kɜːdɪʃ] I *adj* curdo,-a. II *n (language)* curdo *m*.

Kurdistan [kɜːdɪ'stɑːn] *n* Kurdistán.

Kuwait [kʊ'weɪt] *n* Kuwait.

Kuwaiti [kʊ'weɪtɪ] *adj & n* kuwaití *(mf)*.

kW *abbr of* **kilowatt(s),** kilovatio(s) *m(pl)*, Kw, kw.

kWh *abbr of* **kilowat(s)-hour,** kilovatios-hora *m (pl)*, Kw/h, kw/h.

L

L, l [el] *n (the letter)* L, l *f*.

L *Aut abbr of* **Learner driver,** ≈ conductor *m* en prácticas.

Lab *abbr of* **Labour,** laborista.

lab [læb] *n fam abbr of* **laboratory,** laboratorio *m*.

label ['leɪbəl] I *n* **1** *(tag)* etiqueta *f*. ■ *Mus* **record l.,** — casa *f* discográfica. **2** *fig* etiqueta *f*, calificación *f*, clasificación *f*. II *vtr (pt & pp labelled, US labeled)* **1** *(parcel)* poner etiqueta a, etiquetar. **2** *fig* calificar, clasificar.

labial ['leɪbɪəl] *adj Ling* labial.

labor ['leɪbə^r] *n & vi US Austral see* **labour.**

laboratory [lə'bɒrətərɪ, *US* 'læbrətɔːrɪ] *n* laboratorio *m*. ■ **l. assistant,** ayudante *m,f* de laboratorio.

labored ['leɪbəd] *adj US Austral see* **laboured.**

laborer ['leɪbərə^r] *n US Austral see* **labourer.**

labor-intensive [leɪbərɪn'tensɪv] *adj US Austral see* **labour-intensive.**

laborious [lə'bɔːrɪəs] *adj* laborioso,-a, penoso,-a, difícil.

labor-saving ['leɪbərseɪvɪŋ] *adj US Austral see* **labour-saving.**

labour ['leɪbə^r] I *n* **1** *(work)* trabajo *m*; *(task, job)* labor *f*, tarea *f*, faena *f*; **l. of love,** trabajo *m* placentero o agradable. ■ *Jur* **hard l.,** trabajos *mpl* forzados or forzosos; **l. camp,** campo *m* de trabajos. forzados or forzosos. **2** *Ind (workforce)* mano *f* de obra. ■ **l. costs,** coste *m* de la mano de obra; **skilled l.,** mano *f* de obra especializada. **3 labours,** *(efforts)* esfuerzos *mpl*. **4** *Pol* **L. (Party),** el Partido Laborista, los laboristas. **5** *Med (childbirth)* parto *m*; **to be in l.,** estar de parto. ■ **l. pains,** dolores *mpl* or contracciones *fpl* del parto. II *adj Ind* laboral; **l. relations/ disputes,** relaciones/conflictos laborales. ■ *US* **L. Day,** Día *m* del Trabajador; *GB* **L. Exchange,** Bolsa *f* de Trabajo; **l. force,** mano *f* de obra; *US* **l. laws,** legislación *f* laboral; **l. market,** mercado *m* laboral; *US* **l. union,** sindicato *m*. III *vi* **1** *(work)* trabajar (duro); *fig* **to l. under a delusion,** hacerse ilusiones, estar equivocado,-a. **2**

(move etc) (person) avanzar penosamente; *(engine)* funcionar con dificultad. **IV** *vtr (stress, linger on)* machacar; *(a point)* insistir en.

laboured ['leɪbəd] *adj* **1** *(breathing)* fatigoso,-a. **2** *(style)* trabajoso,-a, forzado,-a.

labourer ['leɪbərəʳ] *n (on roads etc)* peón *m.* ■ **farm l.**, peón *m* agrícola, jornalero,-a *m,f*, bracero,-a *m,f*.

labour-intensive [leɪbərɪn'tensɪv] *adj* con mucha mano de obra.

labour-saving [leɪbəseɪvɪŋ] *adj* que ahorra trabajo; *(in kitchen)* **l.-s. devices**, electrodomésticos *mpl*.

laburnum [lə'bɜːnəm] *n Bot* laburno *m*, codeso *m*.

labyrinth ['læbərɪnθ] *n* laberinto *m*.

lace [leɪs] **I** *n* **1** *(fabric)* encaje *m*. **2 laces**, cordones *mpl*. **II** *vtr* **1** *(tie)* atar; *(shoes)* atarse los cordones. **2** *(add spirits to)* echar licor *(with, a)*. ◆ **lace up** *vtr* atar con cordones.

lacerate ['læsəreɪt] *vtr Med* lacerar.

laceration [læsə'reɪʃən] *n* laceración *f*.

lace-up ['leɪsʌp] **I** *adj (shoes etc)* con cordones. **II lace-ups** *npl* zapatos *mpl* de cordones.

lachrymose ['lækrɪməʊs, 'lækrɪməʊz] *adi* llorón,-ona.

lack [læk] **I** *n* falta *f*, carencia *f*, escasez *f*; **for l. of**, por falta de, a falta de; **there is no l. of enthusiasm**, entusiasmo no falta. **II** *vtr* faltarle a uno, carecer de, no tener. **III** *vi* faltar, carecer; **she lacked for nothing**, no le hacía falta nada.

lackadaisical [lækə'deɪzɪkəl] *adj (lazy)* perezoso,-a, vago,-a; *(distracted)* distraído,-a, despistado,-a; *(indifferent)* indiferente, apático,-a.

lackey ['lækɪ] *n pej* lacayo *n*.

lacklustre, US **lackluster** ['læklʌstəʳ] *adj (eyes)* apagado,-a, sin brillo; *(performance)* inexpresivo,-a, sin brillo.

laconic [lə'kɒnɪk] *adj* lacónico,-a.

lacquer ['lækəʳ] **I** *n Constr* laca *f*; *(hair)* laca *f* para el pelo. **II** *vtr (furniture)* pintar con laca; *(hair)* poner laca.

lacrosse [lə'krɒs] *n Sport* lacrosse *f*.

lactation [læk'teɪʃən] *n* lactancia *f*.

lactic ['læktɪk] *adj* láctico,-a. ■ **l. acid** ácido *m* láctico.

lactose ['læktəʊs, 'læktəʊz] *n Chem* lactosa *f*.

lacuna [lə'kjuːnə] *n (pl lacunae* [lə'kjuːniː] *or lacunas)* laguna *f*.

lacy ['leɪsɪ] *adj (lacier, laciest) (real)* de encaje; *(artificial)* parecido,-a al encaje.

lad [læd] *n fam* chaval *m*, muchacho *m*, chico *m*, joven *m*; **come on, lads!**, ¡vamos, muchachos!; *fam* **the lads**, los amigotes, la pandilla. ■ **(stable) l.**, mozo *m* de cuadra.

ladder ['lædəʳ] **I** *n* **1** escalera *f* (de mano); *fig* escala *f*, jerarquía *f*; *fig* **the evolutionary/social l.**, la escala evolutiva/social. ■ **rope l.**, escalera *f* de cuerda. **2** *(in stocking)* carrera *f*. **II** *vtr (stocking)* hacer una carrera. **III** *vi (stocking)* hacerse una carrera.

laddie ['lædɪ] *n esp Scot fam* chaval *m*, muchacho *m*, chico *m*, joven *m*.

laden ['leɪdən] *adj* cargado,-a *(with*, de).

lading ['leɪdɪŋ] *n Com* flete *m*, mercancías *fpl*; **bill of l.**, conocimiento *m* de embarque.

ladle ['leɪdəl] **I** *n Culin* cucharón *n*. **II** *vtr Culin* servir con cucharón; *fig (advice, duties)* repartir. ◆ **ladle out** *vtr* repartir.

lady ['leɪdɪ] *n* señora *f*, dama *f*; *Pol* **First L.**, primera dama; *(WC)* **'Ladies'**, 'Señoras', 'Damas'; **ladies and gentlemen!**, ¡señoras y señores!; *(title)* **L. Brown**, Lady Brown; **l. doctor**, médica, doctora; *Theat* **leading l.**, primera actriz; *Rel* **Our L.**, Nuestra Señora; *fam* **l. friend**, amiguita; *fam* **ladies' man**, hombre mujeriego; *fam pej* **who does she think she is, L. Muck?**, no sé quién se cree que es.

ladybird ['leɪdɪbɜːd] *n*, US Canada **ladybug** ['leɪdɪbʌg] *n Ent* mariquita *f*, vaca *f* de San Antón.

lady-in-waiting [leɪdɪɪn'weɪtɪŋ] *n (pl ladies-in-waiting)* dama *f* de honor.

lady-killer ['leɪdɪkɪləʳ] *n* ladrón *n* de corazones, tenorio *m*, donjuán *m*.

ladylike ['leɪdɪlaɪk] *adj* elegante, fino,-a, distinguido,-a.

ladyship ['leɪdɪʃɪp] *n* señoría *f*; **Her L., Your L.**, su señoría.

lag [læg] **I** *n* **1** *(delay)* retraso *m*; **time l.**, retraso *m*, demora *f*. **2** *sl (convict)* presidiario *m*; **old l.**, reincidente *m*. **II** *vi (pt & pp lagged)* rezagarse; **to l. (behind)**, quedarse atrás, retrasarse, rezagarse. **III** *vtr Tech* revestir.

lager ['lɑːgəʳ] *n* cerveza *f* rubia.

lagging ['lægɪŋ] *n Tech* revestimiento *m* (calorífugo).

lagoon [lə'guːn] *n* laguna *f*.

laid [leɪd] *pt & pp* **lay**.

laid-back [leɪd'bæk] *adj fam* tranquilo,-a, suave.

lain [leɪn] *pp* of **lie**.

lair [leəʳ] *n* guarida *f*.

laird [leəd] *n Scot (landowner)* terrateniente *m*.

laissez-faire [leɪseɪ'feəʳ] *n Pol* política *f* de no injerencia *or* no intervención.

laity ['leɪɪtɪ] *n Rel* **the l.**, los seglares, los laicos, los legos.

lake [leɪk] *n* lago *m*.

lama ['lɑːmə] *n Rel* lama *m*.

lamb [læm] **I** *n (animal)* cordero *m*; *(meat)* carne *f* de cordero; *fam* **poor l.!**, ¡pobrecito! ■ **l. chop**, chuleta *f* de cordero; **l.'s wool**, lana *f* de cordero. **II** *vi (sheep)* parir.

lambskin ['læmskɪn] *n* piel *f* de cordero.

lamb's-wool ['læmswʊl] *adj* de lana de cordero, de lambswool.

lame [leɪm] *adj* **1** *(person, animal)* cojo,-a; **to be l.**, *(temporarily)* estar cojo,-a; *(permanently)* ser cojo,-a; **l. in one leg**, cojo,-a de una pierna. ■ *(person)* **l. duck**, incapaz *mf*. **2** *fig (excuse)* poco convincente, débil; *(argument)* flojo,-a; *(business)* fallido,-a. ◆ **lamely** *adv fig* sin convicción.

lameness ['leɪmnɪs] *n* cojera *f*, *fig* falta *f* de convicción, debilidad *f*.

lament [lə'ment] **I** *n (grief)* lamento *n*; *Mus* endecha *f*. **II** *vtr (death)* llorar, lamentar. **III** *vi* llorar **(for**, a), lamentarse **(over**, de).

lamentable ['læməntəbəl] *adj* lamentable, deplorable.

lamentation [læmən'teɪʃən] *n* lamentación *f*, lamento *m*.

lamented [lə'mentɪd] *adj* llorado,-a.

laminate ['læmɪneɪt] **I** *vtr* laminar. **II** *n* laminado *m*.

laminated ['læmɪneɪtɪd] *adj (metal)* laminado,-a; *(glass)* inastillable; *(paper)* plastificado,-a.

lamp [læmp] *n (gen)* lámpara *f*; *Aut Rail* faro *m*. ■ **street l.**, farol *m*, farola *f*; **sun l.**, lámpara *f* UVA *or* de rayos ultravioletas; **table l.**, lámpara *f* de mesa.

lamplight ['læmplaɪt] *n* luz *f* de lámpara.

lamplit ['læmplɪt] *n* illuminado,-a con luz de lámpara.

lampoon [læm'puːn] *n* pasquín *m*, sátira *f*. **II** *vtr* satirizar.

lamp-post ['læmppəʊst] *n* (poste *m* de) farol *m*, farola *f*.

lamprey ['læmprɪ] *n (fish)* lamprea *f*.

lampshade ['læmpʃeɪd] *n* pantalla *f*.

lance [lɑːns] **I** *n* **1** *(weapon)* lanza *f*. ■ *GB Mil* **l. corporal**, cabo *n* interino. **2** *Med* lanceta *f*. **II** *vtr Med* abrir con lanceta.

lancet ['lɑːnsɪt] *n Med* lanceta *f*.

land [lænd] **I** *n* **1** *(gen)* tierra *f*; *(soil)* suelo *m*, tierra *f*; **by l.**, por tierra; *Naut* **l. ahoy!**, ¡tierra a la vista!; **on dry l.**, en tierra firme; *fig* **to see how the l. lies**, tantear el terreno. ■ **farm l.**, tierras *fpl* de cultivo; *Mil* **l. forces**, ejército *m* de tierra; **l. mass**, gran extensión *f* de tierra; **l. reform**, reforma *f* agraria; **waste l.**, tierra *f* baldía. **2** *(country)* país *m*, tierra *f*; *fig (world)* mundo *m*; **foreign lands,** tierras extranjeras; *fig* **the l. of milk and honey,** (la tierra de) Jauja; *fam fig* **to be in the l. of the living,** seguir entre los vivos. ■ **native l.,** tierra *f* natal, patria *f*. **3** *(property)* tierras *fpl*; *(estate)* finca *f*, estancia *f*, hacienda *f*. ■ **l. register,** registro *m* de la propiedad; **piece of l.,** terreno *m*; **plot of l.,** parcela *f*. II *vtr* **1** *(touch down)* hacer aterrizar. **2** *(disembark)* desembarcar; *(unload)* descargar. **3** *Fishing (catch)* sacar peces del agua, pescar. **4** *fam (succeed in obtaining)* conseguir; *(prize, contract, etc)* ganar, conseguir, obtener. **5** *fam (put in jail)* llevar; **she got landed with the job,** tuvo que cargar con el paquete; **to l. sb in trouble,** causarle problemas a algn. **6** *fam (hit)* arrear; *(blow)* asestar. III *vi* **1** *(plane)* aterrizar; *(bird)* posarse; *Av* **to l. on the moon,** alunizar. **2** *(disembark)* desembarcar. **3** *(after jumping, falling)* caer **(in,** sobre); *fig* salir adelante; *fig* **to l. on one's feet,** caer de pies. ◆ **land up** *vi fam* ir a parar.

landed ['lændɪd] *adj* hacendado,-a. ■ **l. gentry,** los terratenientes; **l. property,** bienes *mpl* raíces.

landing ['lændɪŋ] *n* **1** *(of staircase)* descansillo *m*, rellano *m*. **2** *(of plane)* aterrizaje *m*. ■ **crash l.,** aterrizaje *m* de emergencia; **forced l.,** aterrizaje forzoso; **l. gear,** tren *m* de aterrizaje; **l. strip,** pista *f* de aterrizaje. **3** *(of passengers, troops)* desembarco *m*. ■ **l. card,** tarjeta *f* de inmigración, *Mil* **l. craft,** lancha *f* or barcaza *f* de desembarco; **l. net,** salabre *m*; **l. stage,** desembarcadero *m*. **4** *Naut* embarcadero *m*.

landlady ['lændleɪdɪ] *n (of flat, land)* dueña *f*, propietaria *f*; *(of boarding house)* patrona *f*; *(of pub)* dueña *f*.

landlocked ['lændlɒkt] *adj (lack)* rodeado,-a de tierra; *(country)* sin salida al mar, interior.

landlord ['lændlɔːd] *n (of flat, land)* dueño *m*, propietario *m*; *(of pub)* patrón *m*, dueño *m*.

landmark ['lændmɑːk] *n* **1** *Geog Naut* señal *f*, marca *f*; *(well-known place)* lugar *m* muy conocido *or* famoso. **2** *fig* hito *m*.

landmine ['lændmaɪn] *n Mil* mina *f* (de tierra).

landowner ['lændəʊnə'] *n* terrateniente *mf*, propietario,-a *m*,*f*, hacendado,-a *m*,*f*.

landscape ['lændskeɪp] I *n* paisaje *m*. ■ **l. gardener,** jardinero,-a *m*, *f* paisajista; **l. gardening,** jardinería *f* paisajista; *Art* **l. painter,** paisajista *mf*; **l. painting,** paisaje *m*. II *vtr* ajardinar.

landslide ['lændslaɪd] *n Geol* desprendimiento *m or* corrimiento *m* de tierras. ◆ *Pol* **l. victory,** triunfo *m* arrollador, victoria *f* arrolladora.

landward ['lændwəd] *adj* hacia la tierra.

lane [leɪn] *n* **1** *(in country)* camino *m*, sendero *m*, vereda *f*; *(in town)* callejuela *f*, callejón *m*. **2** *(of motorway)* carril *m*, vía *f*. ■ **bus l.,** carril-bus *m*. **3** *Sport* calle *f*. **4** *Naut* ruta *f*. ■ **shipping l.,** ruta *f* marítima.

language ['læŋgwɪdʒ] *n* **1** *(faculty, style, terminology)* lenguaje *m*; **bad l.,** palabrotas *fpl*; **scientific l.,** lenguaje científico; **to use bad l.,** ser mal hablado,-a; **watch your l.!,** ¡cuida tu lenguaje!; *fig* **we speak the same l.,** hablamos el mismo idioma. **2** *(of a country)* idioma *m*, lengua *f*; **dead l.,** lengua muerta; **the English l.,** el (idioma) inglés; **we study l. and literature,** estudiamos lengua y literatura. ■ **language l.,** laboratorio *m* de idiomas; **l. school,** escuela *f* or academia *f* de idiomas.

languid ['læŋgwɪd] *adj* lánguido,-a.

languish ['læŋgwɪʃ] *vi (for love)* languidecer; *(project, plan, etc)* quedar abandonado,-a, consumirse; *(in prison)* pudrirse.

languishing ['læŋgwɪʃɪŋ] *adj* lánguido,-a; *(attitude)* relajado,-a.

languor ['læŋgə'] *n* languidez *f*.

languorous ['læŋgərəs] *adj* lánguido,-a.

lank [læŋk] *adj (hair)* lacio,-a.

lanky ['læŋkɪ] *adj (lankier, lankiest)* larguirucho,-a.

lanolin(e) ['lænəlɪn] *n* lanolina *f*.

lantern ['læntən] *n* farol *m*, linterna *f*.

lantern-jawed ['læntəndʒɔːd] *adj fam* chupado,-a de cara.

Laos [laʊz, laʊs] *n* Laos.

Laotian ['laʊʃɪən] I *adj* laosiano,-a. II *n (person)* laosiano,-a *m*, *f*; *(language)* laosiano *m*.

lap¹ [læp] *n Anat* regazo *m*; *(knees)* rodillas *fpl*; *(skirt)* falda *f*; *fig* **it's in the l. of the gods,** está en manos de los dioses; *fig* **to live in the l. of luxury,** vivir rodeado,-a de lujo or como un pachá.

lap² [læp] I *n Sport (circuit)* vuelta *f*; *(of journey)* etapa *f*, escala *f*; *fig* trecho *m*, etapa. ■ **l. of honour,** vuelta *f* de honor. II *vtr* & *vi (pt* & *pp* **lapped)** *Sport (overtake)* doblar; *(go round)* girar, dar la vuelta.

lap³ [læp] I *vtr (pt* & *pp* **lapped)** *(cat)* beber a lengüetadas. II *vi (waves)* lamer, besar. ◆ **lap up** *vtr* **1** *(cat)* beber a lengüetadas. **2** *fig (wallow in)* disfrutar con; *(flattery)* recibir con estusiasmo. **3** *fig (belive)* tragar.

lapdog ['læpdɒg] *n* perrito *m* faldero.

lapping ['læpɪŋ] *n (of cat)* lamedura *f*, lametón *m*, lametazo *m*; *(of waves)* chapoteo *m*,

lapel [lə'pel] *n (of jacket, coat)* solapa *f*.

Lapland ['læplænd] *n* Laponia.

Laplander ['læplændə'] *n* lapón,-ona *m*,*f*.

Lapp [læp] I *adj* lapón,-ona. II *n (language)* lapón *m*.

lapse [læps] I *n* **1** *(of time)* lapso *m*, intervalo *m*. **2** *(error)* error *m*, desliz *m*; *(when speaking)* lapso *m*, lapsus *m*; *(of memory)* fallo *m*. II *vi* **1** *(time) (pass)* pasar, transcurrir. **2** *(contract, subcription) (expire)* caducar. **3** *(person) (err)* cometer un error, equivocarse; *(fall back)* caer **(into,** en); **to l. into silence,** quedarse callado,-a. **4** *Rel* perder la fe.

lapsed [læpst] *adj* **1** *(contract etc)* caducado,-a. **2** *(Catholic)* no practicante.

lapwing ['læpwɪŋ] *n Orn* avefría *f*.

larceny ['lɑːsənɪ] *n GB Jur* latrocinio *m*; *US* robo *m*, hurto *m*; **grand l.,** robo importante; **petty l.,** robo de menor cuantía.

larch [lɑːtʃ] *n Bot* alerce *m*.

lard [lɑːd] I *n Culin* manteca *f* de cerdo. II *vtr* **1** *Culin* poner manteca. **2** *fig pej (speech, style)* cargar, recargar.

larder ['lɑːdə'] *n* despensa *f*; *fam* **to raid the l.,** saquear la dispensa.

large [lɑːdʒ] I *adj* **1** *(gen)* grande; *(amount, sum)* importante, considerable; *(meal, harvest)* abundante; *(family)* numeroso,-a; *Com* **the l. size,** la talla grande; *fig* **as l. as life,** en persona; *fig* **to be larger than life,** ser exagerado,-a. **2** *(extensive)* amplio,-a, extenso,-a; **by and l.,** por lo general. II *n (prisoner etc)* **to be at l.,** estar libre *or* en libertad, andar suelto,-a; **the public at l.,** el público en general. ◆ **largely** *adv (mainly)* en gran parte; *(chiefly)* principalmente.

largeness ['lɑːdʒnɪs] *n* **1** *(size)* gran tamaño *m*, magnitud *f*, amplitud *f*. **2** *(importance)* importancia *f*.

large-scale ['lɑːdʒskeɪl] *adj (project, problem, etc)* de gran escala; *(map)* a gran escala.

largesse [lɑː'dʒes] *n fml (generosity)* generosidad *f*.

lark¹ [lɑːk] *n Orn* alondra *f*; *fig* **to rise** *or* **be up with the l.,** madrugar. ■ **calandra l.,** calandria *f* (común); **sky l.,** alondra *f* común; **wood l.,** totovía *f*.

lark² [lɑːk] *n fam* **1** *(joke)* broma *f*; **what a l.!,** ¡qué divertido!, ¡qué risa! **2** *(stupid thing)* tontería *f*. ◆ **lark about, lark around** *vi fam* hacer el tonto.

larkspur ['lɑːkspɜː'] *n Bot* espuela *f* de caballero.

larva ['lɑːvə] *n (pl larvae* ['lɑːviː]) larva *f*.

laryngitis [lærɪn'dʒaɪtɪs] *n Med* laringitis *f*.

larynx ['lærɪŋks] *n Anat* laringe *f*.

lascivious [lə'sɪvɪəs] *adj* lascivo,-a, lujurioso,-a

lasciviousness [lə'sɪviːəsnɪs] *n* lascivia *f*, lujuria *f*.

laser ['leɪzə'] *n* láser *m*.

lash [læʃ] **I** *n* **1** *(eyelash)* pestaña *f*. **2** *(whip)* látigo *m*; *(thong)* tralla *f*. **3** *(blow with whip)* latigazo *m*, azote *m*. **4** *(tail)* coletazo *m*. **II** *vt* **1** *(beat)* azotar. **2** *(rain, hail)* caer con fuerza; *(sea)* azotar. **3** *(lay into)* criticar. **4** *(tail)* dar coletazos. **5** *(tie, bound)* atar. ◆ **lash down** *vtr (fasten)* atar, sujetar; *Naut* amarrar. ◆ **lash out** *vi* **1** *(with fists)* repartir golpes a diestro y siniestro; *(verbally)* criticar (**at**, a). **2** *fam (spending spree)* tirar la casa por la ventana; **to l. out on sth**, permitirse el lujo de comprar algo.

lashing ['læʃɪŋ] *n* **1** *(beating)* azotes *mpl*; *(whipping)* flagelación *f*. **2** *(rope)* cuerda *f*, maroma *f*. **3** **lashings of**, *fam* montones de, la tira de.

lass [læs] *n fam* chavala *f*, muchacha *f*, chica *f*, joven *f*.

lassitude ['læsɪtjuːd] *n* lasitud *f*.

lasso [læ'suː] **I** *n (pl lassos or lassoes)* lazo *m*. **II** *vtr* coger con el lazo, lazar.

last[1] [lɑːst] **I** *adj* **1** *(final)* último,-a, final; **she would be the l. person to do sth like that,** eso me lo esperaría de cualquiera menos a ella; *Rel* **the L. Judgement,** el Juicio Final; *Rel* **the l. rites,** extremaunción *f*; *fam* **if it's the l. thing I do,** aunque sea lo último que haga; *fam* **the l. straw,** el colmo. **2** *(most recent)* último,-a; **the l. time,** la última vez. **3** *(past)* pasado,-a; *(previous)* anterior; **l. but one,** penúltimo,-a; **l. month/Sunday,** el mes/domingo pasado; **l. night,** anoche, ayer por la noche; **l. week,** la semana pasada; **the night before l.,** anteanoche; **the year before l.,** hace dos años. **II** *adv* **1** *(last occasion)* por última vez; **the last I heard ...,** lo último que sé ...; **when I l. saw her,** la última vez que la vi. **2** *(at the end)* en último lugar; *(in race etc)* último; **at (long) l.,** por fin, finalmente; **last but not least,** el último en orden pero no en importancia; **to come l.,** llegar el último. **3** *(until the end)* **to the last,** hasta el final. **III** *n* **1** *(in queue)* el último, la última; **the l. of the wine/cheese,** (todo) lo que queda del vino/queso; **to have seen the l. of sb,** haber visto a algn por última vez; **we'll never hear the l. of it,** esto no nos lo dejarán olvidar nunca; *fig* **to breathe one's l.,** dar el último suspiro. **IV** *vi* **1** *(time)* durar; *(suffer, hold out)* aguantar, resistir. **2** *(money, food) (be enough for)* llegar, alcanzar. **V** *vtr (time)* durar. ◆ **last out** *vi* **1** *(continue)* durar; *(hold out)* aguantar, resistir. **2** *(be enough for)* llegar, alcanzar. ◆ **lastly** *adv* por último, finalmente.

last[2] [lɑːst] *n (shoemaker's)* horma *f*.

last-ditch ['lɑːstdɪtʃ] *adj (effort, attempt)* último,-a; *(desperate)* desesperado,-a.

lasting ['lɑːstɪŋ] *adj* duradero,-a, perdurable.

last-minute ['lɑːstmɪnɪt] *adj* de última hora.

latch [lætʃ] *n* picaporte *m*, pestillo *m*. ◆ **latch onto** *vi (cling)* pegarse; **to l. onto sb,** pegarse a algn; **to l. onto an idea,** agarrarse *or* aferrarse a una idea.

latchkey ['lætʃkiː] *n fam* llavín *m*. ■ **l. child,** niño *m* cuyos padres trabajan.

late [leɪt] **I** *adj* **1** *(not on time)* tardío,-a; *(hour)* avanzado,-a; *(arrival)* tardío,-a; **to be five minutes l.,** llegar con cinco minutos de retraso; **to be l.,** *(not arrive on time)* llegar tarde; *(be detained)* retrasarse; **to be l. in doing sth,** tardar en hacer algo. **2** *(far on in time)* tarde; **in l. autumn,** a finales del otoño; **in the l. afternoon,** a última hora de la tarde; **in the l. nineteenth century,** a finales del siglo diecinueve; **it's getting l.,** se hace tarde; **she's in her l. twenties,** tiene casi treinta años, ronda los treinta; **to keep l. hours,** acostarse tarde. **3** *(dead)* difunto,-a, fallecido,-a, finado,-a. **II** *adv* **1** *(not on time)* tarde; **to arrive l.,** llegar tarde; *prov* **better l. than never,** más vale tarde que nunca. **2** *(far on in time)* tarde; **l. at night,** a altas horas de la noche; **l. into the night,** hasta muy entrada la noche; **l. in life,** a una edad avanzada; **to stay up l.,** acostarse muy tarde; *fam fig* **it's a bit l. in the day,** ya es tarde. **3** *(recently)* recién; **as l. as 1950,** todavía en 1950; **as l. as yesterday,** ayer mismo; **of l.,** últimamente, reciente-

mente. ◆ **lately** *adv* últimamente, recientemente; **until l.,** hasta hace poco.

latecomer ['leɪtkʌmə'] *n* tardón,-ona *m,f*.

lateness ['leɪtnɪs] *n* **1** *(of person, train)* retraso *m*; *(of delivery)* atraso *m*. **2** *(of hour)* avanzado.

late-night ['leɪtnaɪt] *adj* de noche, de madrugada; **the l.-n. film,** la película de media noche *or* de madrugada, la sesión golfa.

latent ['leɪtənt] *adj* **1** *(heat, infection)* latente. **2** *(desire etc)* oculto,-a.

later ['leɪtə'] **I** *adj (comp of late)* **1** *(subsequent)* más tarde; **at a l. stage,** más adelante; **in her l. novels,** en sus novelas posteriores. **2** *(more recent)* más reciente. **II** *adv (comp of late)* más tarde, después; **five years l.,** cinco años después; **I'll do it l.,** lo haré luego; **l. on,** más adelante, más tarde, después; **no l. than Monday,** el lunes a más tardar; **see you l.!,** ¡hasta luego!; **sooner or l.,** tarde o temprano.

lateral ['lætərəl] *adj* lateral.

latest ['leɪtɪst] **I** *adj (superl of late) (most recent)* último,-a, más reciente. **II** *n* **1** lo último; **have you heard the l.?,** ¿te enteraste de lo último?; **it's the l. in kitchen furniture,** es el último grito en muebles de cocina. **2** *(final date)* **Friday at the l.,** el viernes a más tardar.

latex ['leɪteks] *n (pl latexes or latices* ['lætɪsiːz]*) Bot* látex *m*.

lath [lɑːθ] *n* listón *m*.

lathe [leɪð] *n Tech* torno *m*. ■ **l. operator,** tornero,-a *m,f*.

lather ['lɑːðə'] **I** *n* **1** *(of soap)* espuma *f*. **2** *(horse's sweat)* sudor *m*; *fam* **to work oneself into a l.,** ponerse histérico,-a. **II** *vtr (with soap)* enjabonar. **III** *vi* enjabonarse, sacar espuma.

Latin ['lætɪn] **I** *adj & n* latino,-a *(m, f)*; **the L. Quarter,** el barrio latino; **L. America,** América *f* Latina, Latinoamérica *f*; **L. American,** latinoamericano,-a *(m, f)*. **II** *n (language)* latín *m*.

latitude ['lætɪtjuːd] *n* latitud *f*.

latrine [lə'triːn] *n* letrina *f*, retrete *n*.

latter ['lætə'] **I** *adj* **1** *(last)* último,-a. **2** *(second of two)* segundo,-a; **the l. half of the week,** la segunda mitad de la semana. **II** *pron* éste,-a; **the former ... the l. ...,** aquél *or* aquélla ... éste *or* ésta ... .

latter-day ['lætədeɪ] *adj* moderno,-a, actual, de hoy.

lattice ['lætɪs] *n* enrejado *m*, rejilla *f*, celosía *f*. ■ **l. window,** ventana *f* de celosía.

latticework ['lætɪswɜːk] *n* enrejado *m*.

laud [lɔːd] *vtr arch* alabar, elogiar.

laudable ['lɔːdəbəl] *adj* loable.

laudanum ['lɔːdənəm] *n* láudano *m*.

laugh [lɑːf] **I** *n (gen)* risa *f*; *(guffaw)* carcajada *f*; **to do sth for a l.** *or* **for laughs,** hacer algo en broma *or* para divertirse; **to have a good l.,** reírse mucho; *fig* **to have the last l.,** ser el último en reír; *fam* **what a l.!,** ¡qué risa!; *fam fig* **he's a good l.,** es muy divertido. **II** *vi* reír, reírse; **it makes me l.,** me da risa; **to burst out laughing,** echarse a reír; *fam* **to l. all the way to bank,** regocijarse de un éxito económico; *fam* **you've got to l., haven't you?,** es mejor tomárselo a risa; *fam fig* **to l. on the other side of one's face,** arrepentirse; *fam fig* **to l. one's head off,** partirse de risa; *prov* **he who laughs last laughs longest,** quien ríe el último ríe mejor. ◆ **laugh at** *vi* **to l. at sb/sth,** reírse de algn/algo. ◆ **laugh about** *vi* **to l. about sb/sth,** reírse de algn/algo. ◆ **laugh off** *vtr* tomar a risa.

laughable ['lɑːfəbəl] *adj (situation, suggestion)* ridículo,-a, absurdo,-a; *(amount, offer)* irrisorio,-a.

laughing ['lɑːfɪŋ] **I** *adj* risueño,-a; **it's no l. matter,** no es para tomárselo a risa. ■ **l. gas,** gas *m* hilarante. **II** *n (gen)* risas *fpl*; *(loud)* carjadas *fpl*. ◆ **laughingly** *adv* **1** *(cheerfully)* con risas. **2** *(absurdly)* absurdamente, risiblemente.

laughing-stock ['lɑːfɪŋstɒk] *n* hazmerreír *m inv*.

laughter [ˈlɑːftəʳ] n risa f.

launch [lɔːntʃ] I n 1 (vessel) lancha f. 2 see **launching**. II vtr 1 (rocket, new product) lanzar. 2 (ship, bat) botar; (lifeboat) echar al mar. 3 (film, play) estrenar. 4 (company) crear, fundar. 5 Mil desatar, iniciar; fig (scheme) iniciar; (attack) iniciar (**against**, contra). ◆ **launch into** vtr (speech etc) lanzarse a, enfrascarse en. ◆ **launch out into** or **on** vtr emprender, lanzarse a.

launcher [ˈlɔːntʃəʳ] n Mil lanzador m. ■ **grenade l.**, lanzagranadas m inv; **rocket l.**, lanzacohetes m inv.

launching [ˈlɔːntʃɪŋ] n 1 (of rocket, new product) lanzamiento m; fig (trigger, catalyst) trampolín m. ■ **l. pad**, plataforma f de lanzamiento. 2 (of ship) botadura f. ■ **l. ramp**, rampa f de lanzamiento. 3 (of film, play) estreno m. 4 (of new company) creación f, fundación f.

launchpad [ˈlɔːntʃpæd] n plataforma f de lanzamiento.

launder [ˈlɔːndəʳ] vtr 1 (wash and iron) lavar y planchar. 2 fig (money) blanquear.

Launderette® [lɔːndəˈret] n, US **Laundromat**® [lɔːndrəmæt] n lavandería f automática.

laundry [ˈlɔːndrɪ] n 1 (place) lavandería f. 2 (dirty clothes or linen) ropa f sucia, colada f; (clean clothes) ropa f lavada; **to do the l.**, lavar la ropa. ■ **l. basket**, cesto m de la ropa sucia.

laurel [ˈlɒrəl] n Bot laurel m. ■ **l. wreath**, corona f de laureles; fam fig **to rest on one's laurels**, dormirse en los laureles.

lava [ˈlɑːvə] n lava f.

lavatory [ˈlævətərɪ] n 1 (toilet) excusado m, water m. ■ **l. paper**, papel m higiénico. 2 (room) baño m, lavabo m, **pubic l.**, servicios mpl, aseos mpl.

lavender [ˈlævəndəʳ] I n Bot espliego m, lavanda f. ■ **l. water**, agua f de lavanda. II adj (colour) de color lavanda.

lavish [ˈlævɪʃ] I adj 1 (generous) pródigo,-a, generoso,-a. 2 (abundant) abundante. 3 (luxurious, extravagant) lujoso,-a, espléndido,-a. II vtr (praise) colmar (**on**, de); (care, attention) prodigar (**on**, a).

law [lɔː] n 1 (governing customs, actions) ley f; **by** or **in l.**, según la ley; **l. and order**, el orden público; **to be above the l.**, estar por encima de la ley; **to go to l.**, recurrir a la justicia; **to keep within the l.**, obrar según la ley; **to lay down the l.**, dictar la ley; fig **to be a l. unto oneself**, dictar sus propias leyes; fig **to take the l. into one's own hands**, tomarse la justicia por su mano. 2 (as subject) derecho m; civil/criminal, derecho civil/penal. ■ **l. court**, tribunal m de justicia; US **l. school**, facultad f de derecho. 3 Philos Phys ley f. 4 fam **the l.**, la poli, la bofia, la pasma.

law-abiding [ˈlɔːəbaɪdɪŋ] adj observante or respetuoso,-a de la ley.

law-breaker [ˈlɔːbreɪkəʳ] n infractor,-a, m,f or violador,-a m,f de la ley.

law-breaking [ˈlɔːbreɪkɪŋ] n infracción f or violación f de la ley.

lawful [ˈlɔːfʊl] adj (gen) legal; (permitted by law) lícito,-a; (legitimate) legítimo,-a.

lawless [ˈlɔːlɪs] adj (without law) ilegal; (law-breaking) anárquico,-a; (ungovernable) ingobernable.

lawlessness [ˈlɔːlɪsnɪs] n anarquía f, desorden m.

lawmaker [ˈlɔːmeɪkəʳ] n legislador,-a m,f.

lawn [lɔːn] n 1 (grass) césped m. ■ Sport **l. tennis**, tenis m sobre hierba. 2 Tex linón m.

lawnmower [ˈlɔːnməʊəʳ] n cortacéspedes m inv.

lawsuit [ˈlɔːsjuːt] n pleito m, juicio m, proceso m.

lawyer [ˈlɔːjəʳ] n abogado,-a m,f; Ind **labour l.**, abogado,-a m,f laboralista; **l.'s office**, bufete m de abogados; **l.'s fees**, honorarios mpl de abogado,-a.

lax [læks] adj 1 (not strict) laxo,-a, relajado,-a; (not demanding) poco exigente. 2 (careless) descuidado,-a; (negligent) negligente. 3 (loose, not taut) suelto,-a, flojo,-a.

laxative [ˈlæksətɪv] adj & n laxante (m).

laxity [ˈlæksɪtɪ] n 1 (lacking stricture) laxitud f, relajación f, relajamiento m; (undemanding) falta f de exigencia. 2 (carelessness) descuido m; (negligence) negligencia f.

lay¹ [leɪ] adj 1 Rel seglar, laico,-a. ■ **l. preacher**, predicador,-a m, f seglar. 2 (non-specialist) lego,-a, profano,-a.

lay² [leɪ] I vtr (pt & pp **laid**) 1 (place, put) poner, colocar; (bricks, carpet) poner; (cable, trap) tender; (basis, foundations) echar; (bomb) colocar; (child) acostar; fam **don't l. a finger on it!**, ¡no lo toques!; fam fig **I've never laid eyes on him before**, es la primera vez que lo veo; fam fig **just wait until I lay my hands on him!**, espera a que lo pille or atrape. 2 (prepare) preparar; (fire) hacer; (table) poner; (curse) lanzar. 3 (leave) dejar; (trail) dejar; **to l. oneself open to criticism**, exponerse a las críticas. 4 (eggs) poner. 5 vulg follar. 6 (set down) asentar; (bet) hacer; (charge) acusar; (blame) echar; (emphasis) hacer; **to l. claim to sth**, hacer valer su derecho a algo. II vi (hen) poner huevos. III n vulg la persona con la cual uno se acuesta. ◆ **lay aside** vtr (gen) dejar a un lado; (principles) dejar de lado; fig (emotions, feelings) olvidar. ◆ **lay before** vtr (plan, accusation, etc) presentar. ◆ **lay by** vtr (save) guardar; (money) ahorrar. ◆ **lay down** vtr 1 (put down) posar, dejar a un lado; (let go) dejar, soltar. 2 (title etc) renunciar. 3 (surrender) deponer; **to l. down one's arms**, rendir or deponer las armas; lit **to l. down one's life for sb**, dar la vida por algn. 4 (plan) formular. 5 (establish, dictate) fijar, imponer; (principles, guidelines) sentar. ◆ **lay in** vtr (store up) proveerse de, abastecerse de. ◆ **lay into** vtr fam (attack) (physically) dar una paliza a; (verbally) arremeter contra. ◆ **lay off** I vtr 1 (dismiss, make redundant) despedir. 2 fam (cease) dejar de. II vtr & vi fam dejar en paz; **l. off!**, ¡deja de fastidiarme!, ¡ya está bien!, ya vale, ¿no? ◆ **lay on** vtr 1 (provide) proveer de; (coach) entregar; (food) preparar. 2 (spread) poner, aplicar; fam fig (flatter) hacer la pelota, adular; fam (exaggerate) **to l. it on (thick)**, cargar las tintas, exagerar; fam **to l. one on sb**, pegar a algn. 3 fam GB (trick) engañar, timar; **to l. one on sb**, hacer una jugarreta a algn. ◆ **lay out** vtr 1 (open out) extender, tender, desplegar. 2 (arrange) disponer, distribuir, colocar; (body) amortajar. 3 (ideas, information) presentar, exponer. 4 (plan) (road) trazar; (garden) diseñar. 5 fam (spend money) gastar; desembolsar. 6 fam (knock out) derribar, turbar. ◆ **lay over** vi US hacer noche. ◆ **lay up** vtr 1 (store) guardar, almacenar. 2 (accumulate) acumular, amasar; **to l. up trouble for oneself**, crearse problemas. 3 fam hacer, guardar cama; **to be laid up**, tener que guardar cama, estar enfermo,-a.

lay³ [leɪ] pt of **lie²**.

lay⁴ [leɪ] n Lit arch (ballad) romance m.

layabout [ˈleɪəbaʊt] n fam holgazán,-ana m,f, gandul,-a m,f, vago,-a m,f.

lay-by [ˈleɪbaɪ] n Aut área f de descanso.

layer [ˈleɪəʳ] I n 1 (of paint etc) capa f, (of rock) estrato m. 2 (hen) gallina f ponedora. II vtr Hairdr hacer un corte escalonado a.

layman [ˈleɪmən] n (pl **laymen**) 1 Rel seglar m, laico,-a m, f. 2 (non-specialist) lego,-a m,f, profano,-a m,f.

lay-off [ˈleɪɒf] n despido m.

layout [ˈleɪaʊt] n 1 (arrangement) disposición f, distribución f; (presentation) presentación f; Typ composición f, formato m. 2 (plan) diseño m, trazado m.

laywoman [ˈleɪwʊmən] n (pl **laywomen** [ˈleɪwɪmɪn]) 1 Rel seglar f, laica f. 2 (non-specialist) lega f, profana f.

laze [leɪz] vi holgazanear, gandulear. ◆ **laze about**, **laze around** vi no hacer nada.

laziness [ˈleɪzɪnɪs] n pereza f, holgazanería f, gandulería f.

lazy [ˈleɪzɪ] adj (lazier, laziest) perezoso,-a, holgazán,-ana, vago,-a; **at a l. pace**, a paso lento.

lazybones [ˈleɪzɪbaʊnz] n inv fam perezoso,-a m, f, gandul,-a m,f, vago,-a m,f.

lb *abbr of* **pound,** libra *f*.

Ld *abbr of* **Lord,** Lord *m*.

lead¹ [led] *n* **1** *(metal)* plomo *m*; *fam* **to swing the l.,** gandulear. ■ *Med* **l. poisoning,** saturnismo *m*; **white l.,** albayalde *m*, plomo *m* blanco. **2** *sl (bullets)* plomo *m*. **3** *(in pencil)* mina *f*.

lead² [li:d] **I** *n* **1** *(front position)* delantera *f*; *(advantage)* ventaja *f*; **to be in the l.,** ir en cabeza; **to take the l.,** *(race)* ponerse a la cabeza, tomar la delantera; *(score)* adelantarse. **2** *(clue)* pista *f*. **3** *Theat (principal role)* primer papel *m*. ■ **l. singer,** cantante *mf* principal. **4** *Cards* mano *f*: **it's your l.,** es tu turno; *fig* **to follow sb's l.,** seguirle el ejemplo de algn. **5** *(leash)* correa *f*. **6** *Elec* cable *m*. **II** *vtr (pt & pp* **led)** **1** *(conduct)* llevar, conducir, dirigir; **to l. the way,** enseñar el camino. **2** *(be the leader of)* dirigir, encabezar, liderar; *GB Mus (orchestra)* ser el primer violín de; *US* dirigir; *fig* **to l. the field,** ir en cabeza. **3** *(influence)* llevar a, inducir a; **she is easily led,** se deja llevar fácilmente; **this leads me to believe that,** esto me lleva a creer que. **4** *(life)* llevar; **to l. a dog's life,** llevar una vida de perros. **5** *Cards* salir con. **III** *vi* **1** *(road)* llevar, conducir, ir **(to,** a); *(door)* dar **(to,** a). **2** *(go first)* ir delante; *(in procession)* ir a la cabeza; *(in race)* llevar la delantera. **3** *Cards* salir. **4** *(result in)* resultar en; **to l. to,** resultar en, llevar a; **it led to nothing,** no llevó a nada. ◆ **lead away** *vtr* llevar. ◆ **lead off** *vi* **1** *(road, corridor, etc)* llevar a, conducir a; *(room, door)* dar a; *(street)* desembocar en. **2** *(conversation, performance, etc)* empezar. ◆ **lead on I** *vi (go ahead)* ir adelante; **l. on!,** ¡adelante! **II** *vtr (deceive)* engañar, timar. ◆ **lead up to** *vtr* llevar a, conducir a.

leaded ['ledɪd] *adj (window)* emplomado,-a.

leaden ['ledən] *adj Lit (of lead)* de plomo; *(sky)* plomizo,-a; *(food)* pesado,-a.

leader ['li:dər] *n* **1** *(of party etc)* jefe,-a *m*, *f*, líder *mf*, dirigente *mf*; *(race)* líder; **she was a born l.,** nació para mandar. **2** *Mus (of orchestra) GB* primer violín *m*; *US* director,-a *m*, *f*. **3** *Press* editorial *m*, artículo *m* de fondo.

leadership ['li:dəʃɪp] *n* **1** *(command)* dirección *f*, mando *m*; *Pol* liderato *m*, liderazgo *m*; *fig* dotes *mpl* de mando. **2** *(leaders)* dirigentes *mpl*, dirección *f*.

lead-free ['ledfri:] *adj (petrol, paint)* sin plomo.

lead-in ['li:dɪn] *n TV Rad* introducción *f*, presentación *f*.

leading ['li:dɪŋ] *adj* **1** *(most important)* principal, primero,-a. ■ *Press* **l. article,** artículo *m* de fondo, editorial *m*. **2** *(outstanding)* destacado,-a, notable; *fam* **the l. light,** el cerebro gris. **3 l. question,** pregunta *f* tendenciosa.

leaf [li:f] *n (pl* **leaves** [li:vz])* **1** *(of plant)* hoja *f*; **gold l.,** pan *m* de oro; **to be in/come into l.,** tener/echar hojas. **2** *(of book)* hoja *f*, página *f*; *fig* **to take a l. out of sb's book,** tomar el ejemplo de algn; **to turn over a new l.,** hacer borrón y cuenta nueva, volver la página. **3** *(of table)* hoja *f* abatible. ◆ **leaf through** *vtr* hojear.

leaflet ['li:flɪt] **I** *n (single sheet)* octavilla *f*, panfleto *m*; *(brochure)* folleto *m*. **II** *vtr* distribuir octavillas *or* folletos.

leafy ['li:fɪ] *adj (leafier, leafiest)* frondoso,-a.

league [li:g] *n* **1** *(alliance)* liga *f*, alianza *f*; *(association)* sociedad *f*; **L. of Nations,** Sociedad de las Naciones; *fam* **to be in l. with sb,** estar conchabado,-a con algn. **2** *Sport* liga *f*; *fam* **they are in a completely different l.,** no hay comparación entre los dos. ■ **l. championship,** campeonato *m* de liga. **3** *(measure)* legua *f*.

leak [li:k] **I** *n* **1** *(hole)* agujero *m*; *(in roof)* gotera *f*; *(in boat)* vía *f* de agua. **2** *(escape) (of gas, liquid)* fuga *f*, escape *m*; *(of information)* filtración *f*. **3** *fam* meada *f*. **II** *vi* **1** *(container)* tener un agujero; *(pipe)* tener un escape; *(roof)* gotear; *(boat)* hacer agua; *(shoes)* dejar entrar el agua. **2** *(gas, liquid)* salirse, fugarse, escaparse; *(information)* filtrarse; *(news)* trascender. **III** *vtr* **1** *(pipe etc)* dejar salir, dejar escapar. **2** *(information, secret, etc)* filtrarse, pasar información **(to,** a).

leakage ['li:kɪdʒ] *n (loss)* pérdida *f*.

leaky ['li:kɪ] *adj (leakier, leakiest) (container)* agujereado,-a; *(roof)* que tiene goteras; *(ship)* que hace agua; *(shoes)* que dejan entrar el agua.

lean¹ [li:n] *adj (meat)* magro,-a, sin grasa; *(person)* flaco,-a, delgado,-a; *(harvest)* malo,-a, escaso,-a; *fig* **the l. years,** los años de escasez, las vacas flacas.

lean² [li:n] **I** *vi (pt & pp* **leaned** *or* **leant) 1** *(building, tree)* inclinarse, ladearse. **2** *(for support)* apoyarse; **to l. on/ against,** apoyarse en/contra; *fig* **to l. on** *or* **upon sb,** *(pressurize)* presionar a algn; *(depend)* depender de algn. **II** *vtr (ladder, bicycle, etc)* apoyar, recostar **(on,** en). ◆ **lean back** *vi* reclinarse, recostarse. ◆ **lean forward** *vi* inclinarse hacia delante. ◆ **lean out** *vi* asomarse. ◆ **lean over** *vi* inclinarse.

leaning ['li:nɪŋ] **I** *adj* inclinado,-a. **II** *n fig (tendency)* inclinación *f*, tendencia *f*, propensión *f*.

leant [lent] *pt & pp see* **lean.**

lean-to ['li:ntu:] *n (hut)* cobertizo *m*.

leap [li:p] **I** *n (jump)* salto *m*, brinco *m*; *fig* salto *m*, paso *m*; **a l. forward** *or* **ahead,** un paso hacia adelante, un avance; *fig* **a l. in the dark,** un salto en el vacío. ■ **l. year,** año *m* bisiesto. **II** *vi (pt & pp* **leaped** *or* **leapt)** *(jump)* saltar, brincar; **to l. for joy,** dar saltos de alegría; **to l. over a fence,** saltarse una valla; **to l. to one's feet,** levantarse de un salto; *fig* **her heart leapt,** su corazón dio un vuelco; *fig* **Jones leapt from tenth to fourth;** Jones dio un salto de la décima a la cuarta posición; *fig* **the words leapt off the page at me,** las palabras saltaba a la vista. ◆ **leap at** *vi fig (gen)* aprovechar; *(chance)* no dejar escapar. ◆ **leap up** *vi* **1** *(person) (off ground)* saltar; *(to one's feet)* levantarse de un salto. **2** *(flame)* brotar, saltar.

leapfrog ['li:pfrɒg] **I** *n* pídola *f*. **II** *vi (pt & pp* **leap-frogged)** jugar a la pídola.

leapt [lept] *pt & pp see* **leap.**

learn [lɜːn] *vtr (pt & pp* **learned** *or* **learnt) 1** *(in school etc)* aprender; **to l. (how) to ski,** aprender a esquiar; **to l. sth by heart,** aprenderse algo de memoria. **2** *(find out about)* enterarse de, saber. **II** *vi* **1** *(in school etc)* estudiar, aprender; **to l. from experience,** aprender por experiencia; **to l. by** *o* **from one's mistakes, to l. the hard way,** aprender de sus errores. **2** *(find out)* enterarse; **to l. about** *o* **of,** enterarse de, saber.

learned ['lɜːnɪd] *adj (person)* culto,-a, erudito,-a, leído,-a; *(journal etc)* erudito,-a.

learner ['lɜːnər] *n (beginner)* principiante *mf*; *(student)* estudiante *mf*; *Aut* **l. driver,** aprendiz,-a *m*, *f* de conductor; **to be a slow l.,** tener dificultades para aprender.

learning ['lɜːnɪŋ] *n (knowledge)* conocimientos *mpl*; *(erudition)* saber *m*.

learnt [lɜːnt] *pt & pp see* **learn.**

lease [li:s] **I** *n* contrato *m* de arrendamiento; *fig* **to give sb a new l. on life,** dar nueva vida a algn. **II** *vtr* arrendar; *(rent)* alquilar.

leasehold ['li:shəʊld] **I** *n* derechos *mpl* de arrendamiento. **II** *adj (property)* arrendado,-a.

leasing ['li:sɪŋ] *n* **1** *(gen)* arrendamiento *m*, arriendo *m*; *(renting)* alquiler *m*. **2** *Fin* leasing *m*.

leash [li:ʃ] *n* correa *f*.

least [li:st] *(superl of* **little) I** *adj* menor, mínimo,-a; **he has the l. time,** él es quien menos tiempo tiene. **II** *adv* menos; **it's the l. known of his novels,** es su novela menos conocida; **l. of all him,** él menos que nadie; **they are the ones who go l.,** son ellos quienes van menos. **III** *n* lo menos; **at l.,** por lo menos; *(in number)* al menos; **it's the l. we can do,** es lo menos que podemos hacer; **not in the l.!,** ¡en absoluto!, ¡no faltaba más!, ¡cómo no!; **not in the l.,** en lo más mínimo; **that's the l. of my worries,** eso es lo de menos; **to say the l.,** por no decir más.

leather ['leðər] **I** *n* piel *f* cuero *m*. ■ **patent l.,** charol *m*. **II** *adj* de piel, de cuero.

leathery ['leðərɪ] *adj (skin)* curtido,-a; *(meat)* correoso,-a.

leave¹ [li:v] **I** *vtr (pt & pp left)* **1** *(go away from)* dejar, abandonar; *(go out of)* salir de; **he left his wife to live with his mistress,** abandonó a su mujer para ir a vivir con su amante; **he left school at 16,** dejó de estudiar a los 16 años; **I usually l. home at 8,** normalmente salgo de casa a las ocho; **she left home after a family row,** se marchó de casa después de una discusión familiar; **the car left the road,** el coche se salió de la carretera; **they left him to his fate,** lo abandonaron a su suerte; **to l. the table,** levantarse de la mesa. **2** *(allow to remain)* dejar; **it leaves much to be desired,** deja mucho que desear; **l. her to herself,** déjala que lo haga a su manera; **l. him alone!,** *fam* **l. him be!,** ¡déjale en paz!; **she leaves the cleaning to me,** a mí me deja encargarme de la limpieza; **to l. a tip/ a message,** dejar una propina/un recado; **to l. the door open,** dejar la puerta abierta; *fam* **l. it to me,** yo me encargo; *fam* **let's l. it at that!,** ¡dejémoslo así! **3** *(bequeath)* dejar, legar. **4** *(be survived by)* dejar; **he leaves a wife and three children,** deja una viuda y tres hijos. **5** *(forget)* dejarse, olvidarse; **he left his umbrella on the bus,** se dejó el paraguas en el autobús. **6** *Math* dar; **3 from 9 leaves 6,** 9 menos 3 son 6, de 3 a 9 van 6. **7 to be left,** quedar; **I have two biscuits left,** me quedan dos galletas; **it's all the money we have left,** es todo el dinero que nos queda; **there's nobody/nothing left,** no queda nadie/nada. **8 to be left over,** sobrar; **there are three serviettes left over,** sobran tres servilletas. **II** *vi (go away)* irse, marcharse; *(go out)* salir; **he left without saying goodbye,** se fue sin despedirse; **the train is leaving in five minutes,** el tren sale dentro de cinco minutos. ◆ **leave about** *vtr* dejar tirado,-a; **he always leaves his clothes about,** siempre deja la ropa tirada por ahí. ◆ **leave behind** *vtr* **1** *(gen)* dejar atrás. **2** *(forget)* dejarse, olvidarse. ◆ **leave off** *vtr* **1** *(stop)* dejar de; **to l. off smoking,** dejar de fumar. **2** *(clothes)* dejar de llevar. **II** *vi (finish)* acabar; **where did we l. off?,** ¿dónde acabamos? ◆ **leave on** *vtr* **1** *(clothes)* dejar puesto,-a. **2** *(lights, radio)* dejar encendido,-a. ◆ **leave out** *vtr* **1** *(keep in the open)* dejar fuera; *(put out) (books, clothes, etc)* dejar a mano; *(food, meal, etc)* dejar preparado,-a; **you shouldn't l. the car out in the rain,** no deberías dejar el coche a la intemperie cuando llueve. **2** *(omit)* omitir, saltarse; *fig* **to feel left out,** sentirse excluido,-a.

leave² [li:v] *n* **1** *(permission)* permiso *m*; **by or with your l.,** con su permiso; **without so much as a by your l.,** sin pedir permiso a nadie. **2** *(time off)* vacaciones *fpl*; *Mil* permiso *m*; **annual l.,** vacaciones anuales; *Mil* **to be on l.,** estar de permiso; **to go on sick l.,** darse de baja por enfermedad. ■ **l. of absence,** excedencia *f*; **maternity l.,** baja *f* por maternidad; **sick l.,** baja *f* por enfermedad. **3** *(farewell)* despedida *f*; **to take one's l. of sb,** despedirse de algn; *fig* **to take French l.,** despedirse a la francesa; *fig* **to take l. of one's senses,** perder la razón *or* la cabeza.

leaven ['levən] **n, leavening** ['levənɪŋ] *n* levadura *f*.

leaves [li:vz] *npl see* **leaf**.

leave-taking ['li:vteɪkɪŋ] *n* despedida *f*.

Lebanese [lebə'ni:z] *adj & n* libanés,-esa, *(m,f)*.

Lebanon ['lebənən] *n* (the) L., (el) Líbano.

lecherous ['letʃərəs] *adj* lascivo,-a, lujurioso,-a.

lechery ['letʃərɪ] *n* lascivia *f*, lujuria *f*.

lectern ['lektən] *n (gen)* atril *m*; *(in church)* facistol *m*.

lecture ['lektʃəʳ] **I** *n* **1** *(by visiting speaker)* conferencia *f*, charla *f*; *Univ* clase *f*; **to give a l.,** dar una conferencia (**on,** sobre). ■ **l. hall, l. room, l. theatre,** *(gen)* sala *f* de conferencias; *Univ* aula *f*; **l. notes,** apuntes *mpl*. **2** *(reproof)* sermón *m*, reprimenda *f*. **II** *vi (visiting speaker)* dar una conferencia *or* conferencias; *Univ* dar clases; **he lectured on animal life,** dio una conferencia sobre la vida animal; **she lectures to advanced students,** da clases a los alumnos más avanzados. **III** *vtr (reproach)* sermonear;

echar una reprimenda; **they were lectured for being late,** les echaron una reprimenda por haber llegado tarde.

lecturer ['lektʃərəʳ] *n (visiting speaker)* conferenciante *mf*; *Univ* profesor,-a *m,f*.

lectureship ['lektʃəʃɪp] *n Univ* cargo *m* de profesor.

led [led] *pt & pp see* **lead²**.

ledge [ledʒ] *n* **1** *(shelf)* repisa *f*; *(of window)* antepecho *m*, alféizar *m*. **2** *(on mountain)* saliente *m*.

ledger ['ledʒəʳ] *n Com* libro *m* mayor.

lee [li:] **I** *n* **1** *Naut* sotavento *m*, socaire *m*. **2** *fig* abrigo *m*; **in the l. of,** al abrigo de. **II** *adj Naut* de sotavento.

leech [li:tʃ] *n* **1** *Zool* sanguijuela *f*. **2** *fig (person)* sanguijuela *f*, parásito,-a *m,f*; **to cling like a l.,** pegarse como una lapa.

leek [li:k] *n Bot* puerro *m*.

leer [lɪəʳ] **I** *vi* mirar con lascivia, echar una mirada lasciva. **II** *n* mirada *f* lasciva.

leery ['lɪərɪ] *adj (leerier, leeriest)* *sl* **1** *(suspicious)* receloso,-a. **2** *(wary)* cauteloso,-a; **to be l. of,** tener cuidado con.

lees [li:z] *npl* heces *fpl*, poso *m*.

leeward ['li:wəd] *Naut* **I** *adj* de sotavento; **L. Islands,** Islas de Sotavento. **II** *n* sotavento *m*. **III** *adv* a sotavento.

leeway ['li:weɪ] *n* **1** *(freedom)* libertad *f*; **this gives me a certain amount of l.,** esto me da cierto margen de libertad. **2** *Naut Av* deriva *f*. **3** *fig (backlog)* tiempo *m* perdido, atraso *m*; **to make up l.,** recuperar el tiempo perdido.

left¹ [left] **I** *adj* **1** *(gen)* izquierdo,-a. **2** *Pol* de izquierdas. ■ **L. wing,** izquierda *f*. **II** *adv* a la izquierda, hacia la izquierda; **turn l. at the lights,** gira a la izquierda después del semáforo. **III** *n* **1** *(gen)* izquierda *f*; **on the l.,** a mano izquierda. **2** *Pol* izquierda *f*; **the far L.,** la extrema izquierda; **to be on the L.,** ser de izquierdas.

left² [left] *pt & pp see* **leave¹**.

left-hand ['lefthænd] *adj* izquierdo,-a; *Aut* **l.-h. drive,** con el volante a la izquierda; **on the l.-h. side,** a mano izquierda.

left-handed [left'hændɪd] *adj* **1** *(person)* zurdo,-a; *(object)* para zurdos; **l.-h. scissors,** tijeras para zurdos. **2** *(ambiguous)* de doble filo, ambiguo,-a.

left-hander [left'hændəʳ] *n* **1** *(blow)* golpe *m* con la izquierda. **2** *(person)* zurdo,-a *m,f*.

leftist ['leftɪst] *adj & n* izquierdista *(mf)*.

left-luggage [left'lʌgɪdʒ] *n GB* **l.-l. office,** consigna *f*.

leftover ['leftəʊvəʳ] *n* sobrante, restante, de sobras. **II** **leftovers** *npl* sobras *fpl*, restos *mpl*.

left-wing ['leftwɪŋ] *adj* de izquierdas, izquierdista.

lefty ['leftɪ] *n fam Pol* izquierdista *mf*, izquierdoso,-a *m,f*.

leg [leg] *n* **1** *(of person)* pierna *f*; *(of animal)* pata *f*, *Culin (of lamb)* pierna *f*; *(of chicken)* muslo *m*; *(of table, chair)* pata *f*, pie *m*; *(of trousers)* pernera *f*; **to give sb a l. up,** ayudar a algn a subir; **to stretch one's legs,** estirar las piernas; *fig* **he hasn't got a l. to stand on,** no tiene en qué basarse; *fig* **to be on one's last legs,** estar en las últimas; *fam* **to shake a l.,** *(hurry)* espabilarse; *(dance)* bailotear; *fam* **to show a l.,** levantarse por la mañana; *fam fig* **to pull sb's l.,** tomar el pelo a algn. **2** *(stage)* etapa *f*. **II** *vtr (pt & pp legged) fam* **to l. it,** *(walk)* ir a pata; *(rush)* ir volando.

legacy ['legəsɪ] *n* herencia *f*, legado *m*; *fig* herencia *f*, patrimonio *m*.

legal ['li:gəl] *adj* **1** *(gen)* legal; *(legitimate)* legítimo,-a; *(permitted by law)* lícito,-a. ■ **l. tender,** moneda *f* de curso legal. **2** *(relating to the law)* jurídico,-a, legal; **the l. profession,** la abogacía; **to take l. action against sb,** entablar un pleito contra algn. ■ **l. adviser,** asesor *m* jurídico, asesoría *f* jurídica; **l. aid,** asesoramiento *m* jurídico para los pobres; **l. costs,** costas *fpl*, *US* **l. holiday,** fiesta *f* nacional. ◆ **legally** *adv* legalmente; **l. responsible,** responsable ante la ley.

legalistic [li:gə'lɪstɪk] *adj* legalista.

legality [lɪ'gælɪtɪ] *n* legalidad *f*.

legalize ['li:gəlaɪz] *vtr* legalizar.

legate ['legɪt] *n Rel* legado *m*.

legend ['ledʒənd] *n* leyenda *f*, *fig* **to become a l. in one's own time**, ser una leyenda viva.

legendary ['ledʒəndərɪ] *adj* legendario,-a.

leggings ['legɪŋz] *npl* polainas *fpl*.

leggy ['legɪ] *adj* (**leggier, leggiest**) **1** (*long-legged*) zanquilargo,-a. patilargo,-a; (*with shapely legs*) con bonitas piernas. **2** (*plant*) muy crecido,-a.

legibility [ledʒə'bɪlɪtɪ] *n* legibilidad *f*.

legible ['ledʒəbəl] *adj* legible.

legion ['li:dʒən] *n* legión *f*; **the Foreign L.,** la Legión Extranjera.

legionnaire [li:ʒə'neəʳ] *legionario m*. ■ *Med* **l.'s disease,** enfermedad *f* del legionario.

legislate ['ledʒɪsleɪt] *vi* legislar.

legislation [ledʒɪs'leɪʃən] *n* legislación *f*.

legislative ['ledʒɪslətɪv] *adj* legislativo,-a.

legislator ['ledʒɪsleɪtəʳ] *n* legislador,-a *m,f*.

legislature ['ledʒɪsleɪtʃəʳ] *n* asamblea *f* legislativa, legislatura *f*.

legitimacy [lɪ'dʒɪtɪməsɪ] *n* legitimidad *f*.

legitimate [lɪ'dʒɪtɪmɪt] *adj* legítimo,-a; (*valid*) válido,-a.

legitimize [lɪ'dʒɪtɪmaɪz] *vtr* legitimar.

legless ['legləs] *adj fam* (*drunk*) trompa, ciego,-a.

leg-pull ['legpʌl] *n GB fam* broma *f*, tomadura *f* de pelo.

legroom ['legruːm] *n* espacio *m* para las piernas.

legume ['legjuːm, lɪ'gjuːm] *n Bot* legumbre *f*.

leg-warmers ['legwɔːməz] *npl* calientapiernas *fpl*.

leisure ['leʒəʳ, *US* 'liːʒəʳ] *n* ocio *m*, tiempo *m* libre; **at l.,** (*with free time*) con tiempo libre; (*calmly*) con calma; **do it at your l.,** hazlo cuando tengas tiempo; **to live a life of l.,** vivir como un rey. ■ **l. activities,** pasatiempos *mpl*; **l. centre,** centro *m* de deportes *or* de actividades culturales.

leisurely ['leʒəlɪ, *US* 'liːʒəlɪ] *adj* (*unhurried*) con calma, sin prisa; (*slow*) lento,-a.

leitmotif *n* **leitmotiv** ['laɪtməʊtiːf] *n* leitmotiv *m*, tema *m* central.

lemming ['lemɪŋ] *n Zool* lemming *m*.

lemon ['lemən] **I** *n* **1** (*fruit*) limón *m*. ■ **l. cheese, l. curd,** crema *f* de limón; **l. ice,** granizado *m* de limón; **l. juice,** zumo *m* de limón; *GB* **l. squash,** limonada *f*; **l. squeezer,** exprimidor *m*, exprimelimones *m inv*; **l. tea,** té *m* con limón; **l. tree,** limonero *m*. **2** *sl* (*halfwit*) primo,-a *m,f*. **3** *sl* (*old car*) cacharro *m*. **II** *adj* (*colour*) de color limón.

lemonade [lemə'neɪd] *n* limonada *f*.

lend [lend] *vtr* (*pt & pp* **lent**) (*money etc*) prestar, dejar; *fig* (*impart, contribute*) dar, prestar, dotar de; **can you l. me your pen?,** ¿me dejas tu bolígrafo?; **her ideas lent intelligence to the meeting,** sus ideas dotaron de inteligencia a la reunión; **to l. oneself** *or* **itself to sth,** prestarse a *or* para algo; *fam* **can you l. me a hand?,** ¿me echas una mano?; *fam fig* **to l. an ear to sb,** escuchar a algn.

lending ['lendɪŋ] *n* **l. library,** biblioteca *f* pública.

length [leŋkθ, leŋθ] *n* **1** (*dimension*) longitud *f*, largo *m*; **it is five metres in l.** tiene *or* mide cinco metros de largo; **what l. is it?,** ¿cuánto tiene *or* mide de largo?; *fig* **throughout the l. and breadth of the country,** a lo largo y ancho del país. **2** (*duration*) duración *f*; **for what l. of time?,** ¿por cuánto tiempo?; **the l. of a visit,** la duración de una visita. **3** (*piece*) (*of string, tubing*) trozo *m*; (*of cloth*) largo *m*. **4** (*distance*) largo *m*, distancia *f*; (*of swimming pool*) largo *m*; (*stretch of road*) tramo *m*; **she walked the l. of the river,** anduvo a lo largo del río; *Sport* **to win by a l.,** ganar por un largo; *fig* **to go to any lengths to achieve sth,** hacer lo que sea para conseguir algo; *fig* **to go to**

great lengths, tomarse mucha molestia; *fig* **to keep sb at arm's l.,** mantener las distancias con algn. **5 at l.,** (*finally*) finalmente, a la larga; (*in depth*) a fondo, con detalle; **to explain sth at l.,** explicar algo con todo detalle; **to talk at l.,** hablar largo y tendido.

lengthen ['leŋkθən, 'leŋθən] **I** *vtr* **1** (*skirt etc*) alargar. **2** (*lifetime*) prolongar, extender. **II** *vi* **1** (*skirt etc*) alargarse. **2** (*lifetime*) prolongarse; (*days*) crecer.

lengthways ['leŋθweɪz] *adv*, **lengthwise** ['leŋθwaɪz] *adv* a lo largo, longitudinalmente.

lengthy ['leŋkθɪ, 'leŋθɪ] *adj* (**lengthier, lengthiest**) (*gen*) largo,-a; (*film, illness*) de larga duración; (*meeting, discussion*) prolongado,-a.

lenience ['liːnɪəns] *n*, **leniency** ['liːnɪənsɪ] *n* lenidad *f*, clemencia *f*, indulgencia *f*.

lenient ['liːnɪənt] *adj* indulgente.

Leningrad ['lenɪngræd] *n* Leningrado.

lens [lenz] *n* **1** (*of eye*) cristalino *m*. **2** (*of spectacles*) lente *m or f*. ■ **contact lenses,** lentes *mpl* de contacto, lentillas *fpl*. **2** *Phot* objetivo *m*.

Lent [lent] *n Rel* Cuaresma *f*.

lent [lent] *pt & pp see* **lend.**

lentil ['lentɪl] *n Bot* lenteja *f*; **l. soup,** sopa de lentejas.

Leo ['liːəʊ] *n Astrol Astron* Leo *m*, León *m*.

leopard ['lepəd] *n Zool* leopardo *m*.

leotard ['liːətɑːd] *n* (*for dance, gym*) leotardo *m*, malla *f*, maillot *m*; (*as underwear*) leotardo *m*.

leper ['lepəʳ] *n Med* leproso,-a *m,f*.

leprechaun ['leprəkɔːn] *n Ir* duende *m*.

leprosy ['leprəsɪ] *n Med* lepra *f*.

leprous ['leprəs] *adj Med* leproso,-a.

lesbian ['lezbɪən] *adj & n* lesbiana (*f*).

lesion ['liːʒən] *n Med* lesión *f*.

Lesotho [lɪ'suːtʊ, lə'səʊtəʊ] *n* Lesotho.

less [les] **I** *adj* (*comp of* **little**) menos; **he is earning l. money than last year,** gana menos dinero que el año pasado. **II** *pron* menos; **at a price of l. than ten pence,** a un precio inferior a diez peniques; **in l. than an hour,** en menos de una hora; **nothing l. than,** nada menos que; **the l. said about it, the better,** cuanto menos se diga mejor; **they see l. of each other these days,** se ven menos estos días; *fam* **it was signed by the President, no l.,** lo firmó el mismísimo presidente. **III** *adv* menos; **l. and l.,** cada vez menos; **she's l. intelligent than her brother,** es menos inteligente que su hermano; **still l.,** menos aún; *fig* **to think l. of,** tener en menos consideración. **IV** *prep* menos; **a year l. two days,** un año menos dos días; **she earns a hundred pounds, l. tax,** gana cien libras, sin descontar los impuestos.

lessee [le'siː] *n* arrendatario,-a *m,f*.

lessen ['lesən] **I** *vtr* disminuir, reducir. **II** *vi* disminuir, reducirse.

lessening ['lesənɪŋ] *n* disminución *f*, reducción *f*.

lesser ['lesəʳ] *adj* menor; **to a l. extent,** en menor grado; **to choose the l. of two evils,** escoger el mal menor.

lesson ['lesən] *n* **1** clase *f*, lección *f*; **Spanish lessons,** clases de español; *fig* **let that be a l. to you,** que eso te sirva de lección. **2** *Rel* lectura *f*.

lessor ['lesɔːʳ, le'sɔːʳ] *n* arrendador,-a *m,f*.

lest [lest] *conj fml* **1** (*in order not to*) para (que) no; **l. we forget,** para que no lo olvidemos. **2** (*for fear that*) por miedo a que; **he kept quiet l. he should be discovered,** no hizo ruido por miedo a que le descubrieran.

let¹ [let] **I** *vtr* (*pt & pp* **let**) **1** (*allow*) dejar, permitir; **he l. me borrow his car,** me dejó el coche; **l. me know if you want one,** avísame si quieres uno; **to l. go of sth,** soltar algo; **to l. loose,** soltar, dejar suelto,-a; **to l. sb by,** dejar pasar a algn; **to l. sb know,** avisar a algn; *fig* **to l., oneself go,** dejarse ir. **2** (*rent out*) alquilar; **'to l.',** 'se alquila'. **3** *Med* (*blood*) sangrar. **4 l. alone,** ni mucho menos; **he can't walk, l. alone run,** no puede andar, ni mucho menos correr. **II** *v aux* **l. him wait,** que espere; **l. me alone!, l. me be!,** ¡déjame en paz!; **I. me go!,** ¡suéltame!; **l. me tell you sth,** déjame decirte una cosa; **l. us pray,** oremos; **l.'s go!,** ¡vamos!, ¡vámonos!; **l.'s see,** a ver; **l. X equal Y,** pongamos que X es igual a Y. **III** *n GB (renting of house etc)* alquiler *m;* **short l.,** alquiler de corto plazo. ◆ **let down** *vtr* **1** *(lower)* bajar; *(lengthen)* alargar; *fam fig* **to l. one's hair down,** desmelenarse, echar una cana al aire. **2** *(deflate)* desinflar, deshinchar. **3** *(fail)* fallar, defraudar, decepcionar; **the car l. us down,** nos falló el coche; **to be l. down,** llevarse un chasco *or* un disgusto; **to feel l. down,** sentirse defraudado,-a. ◆ **let in** *vtr* **1** *(admit)* dejar entrar, hacer pasar; **her mother l. me in,** me abrió su madre; **these shoes l. the water in,** estos zapatos dejan entrar el agua; **to l. oneself in,** abrir la puerta uno,-a mismo,-a. **2 to l. oneself in for,** meterse en; **to l. oneself in for trouble,** meterse en un lío. **3 to l. in on,** revelar; **to l. sb in on a secret,** revelar un secreto a algn. ◆ **let off** *vtr* **1** *(leave off)* dejar; **could you l. me off at the station?,** ¿puedes dejarme en la estación? **2** *(bomb)* hacer explotar; *(fireworks)* hacer estallar. **3** *(liquid, air)* soltar, emitir; *fam fig* **to l. off steam,** desfogarse, desahogarse. **4** *fam* **to l. sb off** *(pardon)* perdonar; *(free)* dejar en libertad; **he was l. off with a warning,** le dejaron marcharse tras una amonestación. ◆ **let on** *vi fam (pretend)* hacer ver; *(reveal)* contar, revelar; **don't l. on, will you?,** no digas nada, por favor; **he l. on that he knew nothing,** hizo ver que no sabía nada. ◆ **let out** *vtr* **1** *(release)* *(prisoner)* soltar, poner en libertad; *(news)* divulgar; *(secret)* revelar; *fam* **that lets me out,** eso me deja limpio. **2** *(air, water)* dejar salir; **to l. air out of a tyre,** desinflar un neumático. **3** *(sound, cry)* soltar. **4** *Sew (widen)* ensanchar. **5** *(rent out)* alquilar. ◆ **let through** *vtr* dejar pasar. ◆ **let up** *vi* cesar, parar; **when will this rain l. up?,** ¿cuándo dejará de llover?; *fam* **l. up on me, will you?,** déjame en paz, ¿quieres?

let² [let] *n Ten* let *m.*

letdown ['letdaʊn] *n* decepción *f,* chasco *m;* **what a l.!,** ¡qué desilusión!

lethal ['li:θəl] *adj* mortal, letal.

lethargic [lɪ'θɑ:dʒɪk] *adj* letárgico,-a, aletargado,-a.

lethargy ['leθədʒɪ] *n* letargo *m,*

letter ['letə'] *n* **1** *(of alphabet)* letra *f;* **the l. 'S',** la letra 'S'; *fig* **to the l.,** al pie de la letra. ■ **capital l.,** mayúscula *f;* **small l.,** minúscula *f.* **2** *(written message)* carta *f;* **covering l.,** carta adjunta; **registered l., carta certificada.** ■ *GB* **l. box,** buzón *m; GB.* **l. card,** carta-tarjeta *f;* **l. of attorney,** poderes *mpl; Com* **l. of credit,** carta *f* de crédito; **l. of introduction,** carta *f* de presentación *or* de recomendación. **3 letters,** *(learning)* letras *fpl;* **man of l.,** hombre *m* de letras.

letter-carrier ['letəkæriə'] *n US* cartero,-a *m,f.*

letterhead ['letəhed] *n* membrete *m.*

lettering ['letərɪŋ] *n* inscripción *f,* rótulo *m.*

letter-opener ['letərəʊpenə'] *n* abrecartas *m inv.*

letterpress ['letəpres] *n* **1** *(method)* impresión *f* tipográfica. **2** *(text)* texto *m* impreso.

letter-writer ['letəraɪtə'] *n* escritor,-a *m, f* de cartas; **he isn't much of a l.-w.,** no es muy amigo de escribir cartas.

lettuce ['letɪs] *n Bot* lechuga *f.*

let-up ['letʌp] *n fam* descanso *m,* tregua *f,* respiro *m.*

leukaemia, *US* **leukemia** [lu:'ki:mɪə] *n Mea* leucemia *f.*

levee ['levɪ] *n US* dique *m.*

level ['levəl] **I** *adj* **1** *(flat)* *(surface, ground)* llano,-a, plano,-a; *(even)* uniforme; *Math* nivelado,-a; *(equal)* igual, parejo,-a, igualado,-a; *Culin* **a l. spoonful of,** una cucharada rasa de; **to be l. with,** estar a la altura de; **to draw l.,** igualar (with, a); *fig* **to do one's l. best,** hacer todo lo posible. ■ *GB Rail* **l. crossing,** paso *m* a nivel. **2** *(steady)* *(temperature)* estable; *(tone)* uniforme; *fig* **to keep a l. head,** no perder la cabeza. **II** *vtr (pt & pp* **levelled,** *US* **leveled) 1** *(make level)* nivelar, allanar. **2** *(raze)* rasar, igualar, arrasar. **3** *(aim)* dirigir; **to l.**

a blow at sb, asestar un golpe a algn; **to l. a weapon at sb,** apuntar un arma a algn; *fig* **to l. an accusation against sb,** dirigir una acusación a algn. **4** *(survey)* nivelar. **III** *n* **1** *(horizontal plane)* nivel *m;* **at sea l.,** a nivel del mar; **to be on a l. with,** estar al mismo nivel que; *fig* **to find one's (own) l.,** estar con los suyos; *fam* **to be on the l.,** *(be honest)* ser de fiar; *(be truthful)* decir la verdad, hablar en serio. **2** *(instrument)* nivel *m.* ■ *Constr* **spirit l.,** nivel *m* (de burbuja de aire). ◆ **level off, level out** *vi* **1** *(ground)* nivelarse. **2** *(prices)* estabilizarse. **3** *(aircraft)* enderezarse, recuperar la estabilidad. ◆ **level with** *vtr fam* ser franco,-a con.

level-headed [levəl'hedɪd] *adj* sensato,-a, equilibrado,-a.

lever ['li:və'] **I** *n* palanca *f.* **II** *vtr* apalancar; **to l. sth out,** alzar algo con palanca.

leverage ['li:vərɪdʒ] *n* apalancamiento *m; fig (influence)* influencia *f.*

leveret ['levərɪt] *n Zool* lebrato *m.*

levitate ['levɪteɪt] **I** *vtr* hacer levitar. **II** *vi* levitar.

levitation [levɪ'teɪʃən] *n* levitación *f.*

levity ['levɪtɪ] *n* ligereza *f,* frivolidad *f.*

levy ['levɪ] **1** *vtr (pt & pp* **levied)** *(impose, collect)* *(tax)* recaudar; *(fine)* imponer. **II** *n (of tax)* recaudación *f; (of fine)* imposición *f.*

lewd [lu:d] *adj (person)* lascivo,-a lujurioso,-a; *(story, song)* obsceno,-a; *(joke)* verde.

lewdness ['lu:dnɪʃ] *n (of person)* lascivia *f; (of song etc)* obscenidad *f.*

lexical ['leksɪkəl] *adj* léxico,-a.

lexicographer [leksɪ'kɒgrəfə'] *n* lexicógrafo,-a *m,f.*

lexicography [leksɪ'kɒgrəfɪ] *n* lexicografía *f.*

lexicology [leksɪ'kɒlədʒɪ] *n* lexicología *f.*

LF [el'ef] *Rad abbr of* **low frequency,** frecuencia *f* baja, FB *f.*

lh *abbr of* **left hand,** (mano *f*) izquierda *f.*

liability [laɪə'bɪlɪtɪ] *n* **1** *Jur (responsibility)* responsabilidad *f.* **2** *(handicap)* estorbo *m,* carga *f; fam* **he's a real l.,** es un cero a la izquierda. **3 liabilities,** *Fin (debts)* deudas *fpl,* pasivo *m sing;* **assets and l.,** activo *m sing* y pasivo *m sing.*

liable ['laɪəbəl] *adj* **1** *Jur (responsible)* responsable; *(susceptible)* sujeto,-a, obligado,-a; **he is l. for military service,** está obligado a hacer el servicio militar; **l. to a fine,** expuesto,-a a una multa; **l. to duties,** sujeto a impuestos; **to be l. for,** ser responsable de, responder de. **2** *(likely)* propenso,-a; **to be l. to do sth,** tener tendencia a hacer algo, ser propenso,-a a hacer algo; **he's l. to change his mind,** puede que cambie de idea; **it's l. to happen,** es muy probable que así suceda.

liaise [lɪ'eɪz] *vi* comunicarse (**with,** con), establecer contacto (**with,** con).

liaison [lɪ'eɪzɒn] *n* **1** *(coordination)* enlace *m,* coordinación *f.* ■ **l. committee,** comité *m* de enlace; **l. officer,** oficial *mf* de enlace. **2** *(love affair)* aventura *f,* amorío *m.*

liar ['laɪə'] *n* mentiroso,-a *m,f,* embustero,-a *m,f.*

lib [lɪb] *n fam abbr of* **liberation.**

libel ['laɪbəl] *Jur* **I** *n (defamation)* difamación *f,* calumnia *f; (written)* libelo *m.* ■ **l. suit,** pleito *m* por difamación. **II** *vtr (pt & pp* **libelled,** *US* **libeled)** difamar, calumniar.

libellous, *US* **libelous** ['laɪbələs] *adj* difamatorio,-a, calumnioso,-a.

liberal ['lɪbərəl] **I** *adj* **1** *(gen)* liberal. ■ *GB* **l. arts,** letras *fpl; Pol* **L. Party,** Partido *m* Liberal. **2** *(abundant)* abundante. **II** *n Pol* **L.,** liberal *mf.*

liberalism ['lɪbərəlɪzəm] *n* liberalismo *m.*

liberalize ['lɪbərəlaɪz] *vtr* liberalizar.

liberal-minded ['lɪbərəlmaɪndɪd] *adj* liberal, tolerante, de amplias miras.

liberate ['lɪbəreɪt] *vtr (gen)* liberar; *(prisoner etc)* poner en libertad, libertar; **liberated woman,** mujer liberada.

liberation [lɪbə'reɪʃən] n liberación f. ■ Rel **l. theology**, teología f de la liberación; **women's l.**, liberación f de la mujer.

liberator ['lɪbəreɪtəʳ] n liberador,-a m,f, libertador,-a m,f.

Liberia [laɪ'bɪərɪə] n Liberia.

Liberian [laɪ'bɪərɪən] adj & n liberiano,-a (m,f).

libertine ['lɪbəti:n] adj & n libertino,-a (m,f).

libertinism ['lɪbəti:nɪzəm] n libertinaje m.

liberty ['lɪbətɪ] n libertad f; **at l.**, libre, en libertad; **to be at l. to say sth**, ser libre de decir algo, tener derecho a decir algo; **to take liberties with sb**, tomarse libertades con algn; **to take the l. of doing sth**, tomarse la libertad de hacer algo; fam **what a l.!**, ¡qué cara!

libido [lɪ'bi:dəʊ] n (pl libidos) libido f.

Libra ['li:brə] n Astrol Astron Libra f.

librarian [laɪ'breərɪən] n bibliotecario,-a m,f.

library ['laɪbrərɪ] n biblioteca f. ■ **l. book**, libro m de biblioteca; **l. ticket**, carnet m de biblioteca; **mobile l.**, biblioteca f móvil, bibliobús m; **newspaper l.**, hemeroteca f; **public l.**, biblioteca f pública; **reference l.**, biblioteca f de consulta.

libretto [lɪ'bretəʊ] n (pl librettos or libretti [lɪ'breti:]) Mus libreto m.

Libya ['lɪbɪə] n Libia.

Libyan ['lɪbɪən] adj & n libio,-a (m,f).

lice [laɪs] npl see **louse**.

licence ['laɪsəns] n 1 (permit) licencia f, permiso m. ■ **driving l.**, carnet m de conducir; **gun l.**, licencia f de armas; Aut **l. number**, matrícula f; US Aut **l. plate**, (placa f de) matrícula f. 2 (freedom) libertad f; (excessive freedom) licencia f. ■ **poetic l.**, licencia f poética.

license ['laɪsəns] I vtr licenciar, dar licencia autorizar. II n US see **licence**.

licensed ['laɪsənst] adj autorizado,-a; **l. premises**, local m autorizado para la venta de bebidas alcohólicas.

licensee [laɪsən'si:] n (gen) concesionario,-a m, f; (of pub) dueño,-a m,f.

licentious [laɪ'senʃəs] adj licencioso,-a, disoluto,-a.

lichen ['laɪkən, 'lɪtʃən] n Bot liquen m.

lick [lɪk] I vtr 1 lamer; to **l. one's lips**, relamerse; fam **to l. sth into shape**, poner algo a punto; fam fig **to l. sb's boots**, hacer la pelota a algn. 2 fam (beat) dar una paliza a. II n lamedura f, lengüetada f; fam **a l. of paint**, una mano de pintura; fam **at full l.**, a todo gas; fam **to give oneself a l. and a promise**, lavarse rápidamente.

licking ['lɪkɪŋ] n paliza f.

licorice ['lɪkərɪs, 'lɪkərɪʃ] n US see **liquorice**.

lid [lɪd] n 1 (cover) tapa f, tapadera f; GB fam **that puts the (tin) l. on it!**, ¡eso ya es el colmo!; fam fig **to take the l. off a scandal**, destapar un escándalo; sl **to flip one's l.**, volverse majara. 2 (of eye) párpado m.

lie¹ [laɪ] I vi (pt & pp lied) mentir; fam **to l. one's head off**, mentir como un bellaco. II n mentira f; **it's a pack of lies**, es pura mentira; **to give the l. to**, desmentir; **to tell lies**, mentir. ■ **l. detector**, detector m de mentiras; fig **white l.**, mentira f piadosa.

lie² [laɪ] I vi (pt lay; pp lain) 1 (act) echarse, acostarse, tumbarse, tenderse; (state) estar echado,-a, estar acostado,-a, estar tumbado,-a, estar tendido,-a; (be buried) yacer. 2 (be situated) estar, encontrarse, hallarse, situarse; **the city lies to the north**, la ciudad está al norte; **the fault lies with him**, la culpa es suya; **the problem lies in her intransigence**, el problema está en or radica en su intransigencia; **the valley lay before us**, el valle se extendía ante nosotros. 3 (remain) quedarse; **to l. still**, quedarse inmóvil; fig **to l. low**, permanecer escondido. II n (position) posición f, situación f; (direction) dirección f, orientación f; **the l. of the land**, la topografía del terreno; fig el estado de las cosas. ◆ **lie about, lie around** vi (person) estar tumbado,-a; (things) estar tirado,-a. ◆ **lie**

back vi (in an armchair) recostarse. ◆ **lie down** vi acostarse, echarse, tumbarse, tenderse; fig **to take sth lying down**, aceptar algo sin chistar. ◆ **lie in** vi fam (stay in bed) levantarse tarde.

Liechtenstein ['lɪktənstaɪn] n Liechtenstein.

lie-down ['laɪdaʊn] n descanso m, siesta f.

lie-in ['laɪɪn] n fam **to have a l.-in**, levantarse tarde.

lieu [lju:, lu:] n lugar m; **in l. of**, en lugar de.

Lieut, Lt Mil abbr of **Lieutenant**, Teniente m, Tenᵗᵉ., Tte.

lieutenant [lef'tenənt, US lu:'tenənt] n 1 Mil teniente m. ■ **l. colonel**, teniente m coronel; **l. general**, teniente m general. 2 (non-military) lugarteniente m.

life [laɪf] n (pl lives [laɪvz]) 1 (gen) vida f; **human l.**, la vida humana; **it's a matter of l. and death**, es cuestión de vida o muerte; **to bring sb back to l.**, resucitar a algn; **to come to l.**, cobrar vida; fig **for dear l.**, con toda la fuerza, a más no poder; fam **as large as l.**, de carne y hueso. ■ **l. belt**, cinturón m salvavidas; **l. cycle**, ciclo m vital; **l. force**, fuerza f vital; **l. imprisonment**, cadena f perpetua; **l. insurance**, seguro m de vida; **l. jacket**, chaleco m salvavidas; **l. style**, estilo m de vida. 2 (individual) vida f; **at my time of l.**, a mi edad; **his early l.**, su juventud; **run for your l.!**, ¡sálvese quien pueda!; **to take one's own l.**, suicidarse; **to take sb's l.**, matar a algn; fig **he had the time of his l.**, se lo pasó como nunca; fam **he can't play the piano to save his l.**, es un negado para el piano; fam **never in my l. have I seen such a thing**, en mi vida he visto tal cosa; fam **not on your l.!**, ¡ni hablar! ■ **l. story**, biografía f. 3 (way of life) vida f; **urban l.**, la vida urbana; fig **to see l.**, ver mundo; fam **how's l.?**, ¿qué tal (la vida)?; fam **this is the l.!**, ¡esto sí que es vivir!; fam **to lead the l. of Riley**, pegarse la gran vida. 4 (of machine, battery) vida f, duración f. 5 (liveliness) vida f, vitalidad f, vivacidad f; fam fig **to be the l. (and soul) of the party**, ser el alma de la fiesta. 5 Art **still l.**, bodegón m, naturaleza f muerta.

life-and-death ['laɪfəndeθ] adj a vida o muerte; **l.-and-d. struggle**, lucha a vida o muerte.

lifeblood ['laɪfblʌd] n sangre f vital; fig alma f, nervio m.

lifeboat ['laɪfbəʊt] n (on ship) bote m salvavidas; (on shore) lancha f de socorro.

lifeguard ['laɪfgɑ:d] n socorrista mf.

lifeless ['laɪflɪs] adj sin vida, exánime, inánime.

lifelike ['laɪflaɪk] adj (gen) natural; (portrait) fiel.

lifeline ['laɪflaɪn] n (rope) cuerda f de salvamento; fig cordón m umbilical.

lifelong ['laɪflɒŋ] adj de toda la vida, de siempre.

life-saving ['laɪfseɪvɪŋ] I n socorrismo m, salvamento m. II adj de salvamento.

life-size(d) ['laɪfsaɪz(d)] adj (de) tamaño natural.

lifetime ['laɪftaɪm] n vida f; **in his l.**, durante su vida; **it's the chance of a l.**, es una ocasión única; fam **never in a l.!**, ¡nunca en la vida!; fam **we had to wait a l.**, tuvimos que esperar una eternidad.

lift [lɪft] vtr 1 (raise) (weight) levantar; (head etc) levantar, alzar; (baby) levantar en brazos; (take up) subir; (pick up) coger; fam **he never lifts a finger in the house**, no mueve ni un dedo para ayudar en casa. 2 Av Mil (troops) transportar. 3 (ban, restriction) levantar. 4 fam (steal) birlar; (plagiarize) copiar, plagiar. II vi (disappear) disiparse. III n 1 (act) levantamiento m. 2 GB (elevator) ascensor m. ■ **goods l.**, montacargas m inv; **l. attendant**, ascensorista mf; **l. shaft**, hueco m del ascensor; **ski l.**, telesquí m. 3 (free ride) **to give sb a l.**, llevar a algn en coche; **to hitch a l.**, hacer autostop. 4 fig (boost) estímulo m; **the news gave her a l.**, la noticia le subió la moral. ◆ **lift down** vtr bajar. ◆ **lift off** I vtr levantar, quitar. II vi Astronaut despegar. ◆ **lift out** vtr sacar. ◆ **lift up** vtr levantar, alzar; fig (spirits) exaltar, elevar.

lift-off ['lɪftɒf] n Astronaut despegue m.

ligament ['lɪgəmənt] n Anat ligamento m.

light

limb

light¹ [laɪt] **I** *n* **1** (*gen*) luz *f*; **against the l.**, a trasluz; **by the l. of the moon**, a la luz de la luna; **electric l.**, luz eléctrica; **to stand in sb's l.**, quitarle la luz a algn; *fig* **in the l. of**, en vista de; *fig* **to bring sth to l.**, sacar algo a luz; *fig* **to come to l.**, salir a luz; *fig* **to see things in a new l.**, ver las cosas bajo otro aspecto. ■ **l. bulb**, bombilla *f*; *Phot* **l. meter**, fotómetro *m*; *Comput* **l. pen**, lápiz *m* óptico; **l. year**, año *m* luz. **2** (*lamp*) luz *f*, lámpara *f*; (*traffic light*) semáforo *m*; *Aut* (*headlight*) faro *m*; **the lights were (at) green**, el semáforo estaba en verde; **to turn on the l.**, encender la luz; *fam fig* **to go out like a l.**, quedarse roque. ◆ *Aut* **parking lights**, luces *fpl* de estacionamiento; *Aut* **tail lights**, pilotos *mpl*; **traffic lights**, semáforo *m sing*. **4** (*flame*) fuego *m*, lumbre *f*; **to set l. to sth**, prender fuego a algo; **to strike a l.**, encender una cerilla; *fam* **have you got a l.?**, ¿tiene fuego? **II** *vtr* (*pt & pp* **lighted** *or* **lit**) **1** (*illuminate*) iluminar, alumbrar. **2** (*ignite*) encender. **III** *vi* (*fire*) encenderse, prenderse. **IV** *adj* **1** (*bright*) claro,-a; **it's growing l.**, se hace de día. **2** (*not dark*) (*colour, eyes*) claro,-a, pálido,-a; (*hair*) rubio,-a; (*complexion*) blanco,-a; **l. green**, verde claro. ◆ **light up l.** *vtr* iluminar, alumbrar. **II** *vi* **1** iluminarse. **2** *fam* encender un cigarrillo.

light² [laɪt] **I** *adj* (*not heavy*) ligero,-a; (*rain*) fino,-a; (*breeze*) suave; *fig* (*wound, sentence, etc*) leve; **l. ale**, cerveza clara; *fig* **to be a l. sleeper**, tener el sueño ligero; *fig* **to be l. on one's feet**, ser ligero,-a de pies; *fig* **to make l. of sth**, dar poca importancia a algo; *fig* **with a l. heart**, con el corazón alegre; *fam* **to be l. on sth**, andar mal de algo. ■ *fig* **l. fingers**, uñas *fpl* largas; *Mil* **l. horse**, caballería *f* ligera; **l. opera**, opereta *f*; **l. reading**, lectura *f* fácil. **II** *adv* **to travel l.**, ir ligero,-a de equipaje, viajar con poco equipaje. ◆ **lightly** *adv* **1** (*not heavily*) ligeramente; **l. clad**, ligero,-a de ropa. **2** (*not seriously*) a la ligera; **to get off l.**, salir casi indemne; **to take sth l.**, tomar algo de ligera.

lighten¹ [ˈlaɪtən] **I** *vtr* **1** (*colour*) aclarar. **2** (*iluminate*) iluminar. **II** *vi* (*colour*) aclararse.

lighten² [ˈlaɪtən] *vtr* **1** (*weight*) aligerar. **2** *fig* (*mitigate*) aliviar, mitigar; (*heart*) alegrar.

lighter¹ [ˈlaɪtə] *n* (*cigarette*) l., encendedor *m*, mechero *m*.

lighter² [ˈlaɪtə] *n Naut* (*barge*) barcaza *f*, gabarra *f*.

light-fingered [ˈlaɪtˈfɪŋgəd] *adj* de uñas largas.

light-footed [ˈlaɪtfʊtɪd] *adj* ligero,-a de pies.

light-haired [ˈlaɪtheəd] *adj* rubio,-a, de pelo claro.

light-headed [laɪtˈhedɪd] *adj* **1** (*dizzy*) mareado,-a. **2** (*frivolous*) frívolo,-a.

light-hearted [ˈlaɪthɑːtɪd] *adj* alegre, despreocupado,-a.

lighthouse [ˈlaɪthaʊs] *n* faro *m*. ■ **l. keeper**, farero,-a *m,f*.

lighting [ˈlaɪtɪŋ] *n* **1** (*act*) iluminación *f*. **2** (*system*) alumbrado *m*.

lightness¹ [ˈlaɪtnɪs] *n* (*brightness*) (*of room*) luminosidad *f*, claridad *f*; (*of colour*) claridad *f*.

lightness² [ˈlaɪtnɪs] *n* (*of weight*) ligereza *f*.

lightning [ˈlaɪtnɪŋ] *n* (*flash*) relámpago *m*; (*stroke*) rayo *m*; *fig* **as quick as l.**, **like l.**, como un rayo. ■ **l. conductor**, **l. rod**, pararrayos *m inv*; **l. strike**, huelga *f* relámpago; **l. visit**, visita *f* relámpago.

lightweight [ˈlaɪtweɪt] **I** *adj* **1** (*suit etc*) ligero,-a. **2** *Box* de peso ligero. **II** *n Box* peso *m* ligero.

Ligurian [lɪˈgjʊərɪən] *adj* L. Sea, Mar Ligur.

like¹ [laɪk] *adj* **1** (*similar*) parecido,-a, semejante, similar; **umbrellas, walking-sticks and l. objects**, paraguas, bastones y otros objetos parecidos; *fig* **they are as l. as two peas (in a pod)**, son como dos gotas de agua. **2** (*equal*) igual, equivalente; *Elec* **l. poles**, polos iguales. **II** *adv* **1** (*likely*) probable; (**as**) **l. as not**, a lo mejor, probablemente. **2** *fam* (*as it were*) como; **because he's an orphan l.**, porque es huérfano, ¿sabes?; **he looked scared, l.**, parecía como asustado. **III** *prep* **1** (*similar to*) como, parecido,-a a; (*the same as*) igual que; **he thinks l. us**, piensa como nosotros; **it costs something l. £50**, cuesta alrededor de las 50 libras; **it looks l. a bullet wound**, parece un balazo; **it looks l. rain**, parece que va a

llover; **it's not l. her to do that**, no es propio de ella hacer eso; **it's nothing l. Rioja wine**, no se parece en nada al vino de Rioja; **I've never seen anything l. it**, nunca he visto cosa igual; **l. that**, así; **people l. that**, ese tipo de gente; **she's l. her mother**, se parece a su madre; **something l. that**, algo por el estilo; **that's just l. a man!**, ¡eso es muy típico de los hombres!; **the actual profit is more l. forty per cent**, el beneficio real es más bien del cuarenta por ciento; **what's he l.?**, ¿cómo es?, ¿qué tal es?; **what's the weather l.?**, ¿qué tiempo hace?; *fam* **that's more l. it!**, ¡así es!, ¡así se hace!; *prov* **l. father l. son**, de tal palo tal astilla. **2** **to feel l.**, tener ganas de; **he doesn't feel l. dancing**, no tiene ganas de bailar; **I feel l. a change**, me apetece un cambio. **IV** *n* cosa *f* parecida; **brushes, combs and the l.**, cepillos, peines y cosas por el estilo; **it's too good for the likes of him**, es demasiado bueno para personas como él; **I've never seen the l. of it**, nunca he visto cosa igual.

like² [laɪk] **I** *vtr* **1** (*take pleasure in*) (*person, thing*) gustar; (*friend*) tener cariño a; **do you l. chocolate?**, ¿te gusta el chocolate?; **he likes dancing**, le gusta bailar; **how do you l. London?**, ¿qué (tal) te parece Londres?; **I don't l. him at all**, ése no me gusta nada, ése me cae muy mal; **she likes children**, le gustan los niños; **they l. each other**, se caen bien; **to l. sth better**, preferir; *fam iron* **well, I l. that!**, ¡qué cara! **2** (*want, wish*) querer, gustar; (*prefer*) preferir; **how do you l. your coffee?**, ¿cómo quiere el café?; **I didn't l. to disturb them**, no quería molestarles; **I should l. a chat with your father**, me gustaría hablar con tu padre; **whether you l. it or not**, quieras o no (quieras), te guste o no te guste; **would you l. a drink?**, ¿quieres tomar algo?, ¿te apetece tomar algo?; **would you l. him to wait?**, ¿quiere que espere? **II** *vi* querer, gustar; **as you l.**, como quieras; **if you l.**, si quieres; **whenever you l.**, cuando quieras. **III** *n* gusto *m*; **likes and dislikes**, gustos, preferencias.

likeable [ˈlaɪkəbəl] *adj* simpático,-a, agradable.

likelihood [ˈlaɪklɪhʊd] *n*, **likeliness** [ˈlaɪklɪnɪs] *n* probabilidad *f*; **in all l.**, con toda probabilidad; **there's little l. of finding it**, es poco probable que lo encontremos.

likely [ˈlaɪklɪ] **I** *adj* (*likelier, likeliest*) probable; **a l. outcome**, un resultado probable; **he's l. to cause trouble**, es probable que cause problemas; **he's the man most l. to succeed in the job**, es el hombre más indicado para el trabajo; *fam iron* **that's a l. story!**, ¡esto es puro cuento!; **where are you l. to be this afternoon?**, ¿dónde piensas estar esta tarde? **II** *adv* probablemente; **as l. as not**, a lo mejor; **not l.!**, ¡ni hablar!

like-minded [laɪkˈmaɪndɪd] *adj* de la misma opinión.

liken [ˈlaɪkən] *vtr* comparar (**to**, con).

likeness [ˈlaɪknɪs] *n* **1** (*similarity*) semejanza *f*, parecido *m*; **in his l.**, a su semejanza. ■ **family l.**, aire *m* de familia. **2** (*portrait*) retrato *m*.

likewise [ˈlaɪkwaɪz] *adv* **1** (*also*) también, asimismo. **2** (*the same*) lo mismo, igualmente; **to do l.**, hacer lo mismo.

liking [ˈlaɪkɪŋ] *n* (*for thing*) gusto *m*, afición *f*; (*for person*) simpatía *f*; (*for friend*) cariño *m*; **is it to your l.?**, ¿te gusta?; **to take a l. to sth**, tomar gusto a algo; **to take a l. to sb**, tomar *or* coger cariño a algn; **to have a l. for sth**, ser aficionado,-a a algo.

lilac [ˈlaɪlək] *n* **1** *Bot* lila *f*. **2** (*colour*) lila *m*. **II** *adj* lila, de color lila.

Lilo® [ˈlaɪləʊ] *n* (*pl Lilos*) colchón *m* inflable *or* de aire.

lilt [lɪlt] *n* (*in voice*) melodía *f*; (*in song*) ritmo *m* alegre.

lilting [ˈlɪltɪŋ] *adj* (*voice*) melodioso,-a, cantarín,-ina; (*song*) rítmico,-a.

lily [ˈlɪlɪ] *n Bot* lirio *m*, azucena *f*. ■ **l. of the valley**, lirio de los valles, muguete *m*; **water l.**, nenúfar *m*.

lily-livered [ˈlɪlɪlɪvəd] *adj* cobarde, miedoso,-a.

limb [lɪm] *n* **1** *Anat* miembro *m*. **2** (*of tree*) rama *f*; *fig* **to be out on a l.**, (*in danger*) estar en peligro; *GB* (*isolated*) estar aislado,-a.

244

limber ['lɪmbəʳ] *adj* (*person*) ágil; (*thing*) flexible. ◆ **limber up** I *vi* 1 *Sport* entrar en calor. 2 *fig* prepararse, entrenarse (**for**, para). II *vtr* calentar.

limbo ['lɪmbəʊ] *n* (*pl* **limbos**) 1 *Rel* limbo *m*. 2 *fig* olvido *m*; **to be** *or* **remain in l.**, caer en el olvido.

lime¹ [laɪm] *n Chem* cal *f*.

lime² [laɪm] *n Bot* (*citrus fruit*) lima *f*; (*citrus tree*) limero *m*. ■ **l. juice**, lima *f*.

lime³ [laɪm] *n Bot* (*linden*) tilo *m*. ■ **broad-leaved l.**, tilo *m* de hoja grande; **European l.**, tilo *m* común; **silver l.**, tilo *m* plateado; **weeping silver l.**, tilo *m* péndulo.

lime-green ['laɪmgri:n] *adj* de color verde lima.

limekiln ['laɪmkɪln] *n* calera *f*, horno *m* de cal.

limelight ['laɪmlaɪt] *n* luz *f* de calcio; *fig* **to be in the l.**, estar en el candelero, ser el centro de la atención pública.

limerick ['lɪmərɪk] *n* quintilla *f* humorística.

limestone ['laɪmstəʊn] *n* piedra *f* caliza.

limey ['laɪmɪ] *n US Canada fam* inglés,-esa *m*, *f*.

limit ['lɪmɪt] I *n* 1 (*boundary*) límite *m*, frontera *f*; **to be off limits**, estar en zona prohibida. 2 (*restriction*) límite *m*; (*maximum*) máximo *m*; (*minimum*) mínimo *m*; *Aut* **speed l.**, límite *m* de velocidad; *Aut* **'speed limit 40'**, 'velocidad máxima 40'; **within limits**, dentro de ciertos límites; *fam* **that's the l.!**, ¡eso es el colmo!; *fam* **you really are the l.!**, ¡eres imposible! II *vtr* (*restrict*) limitar, restringir; **she has limited herself to two slices of bread a day**, ya no se permite más de dos rebanadas de pan al día.

limitation [lɪmɪ'teɪʃən] *n* limitación *f*, restricción *f*.

limited ['lɪmɪtɪd] *adj* limitado,-a, restringido,-a. ■ **l. edition**, edición *f* limitada; *GB Com* **l. (liability) company**, sociedad *f* limitada, sociedad *f* anónima.

limiting ['lɪmɪtɪŋ] *adj* restrictivo,-a.

limitless ['lɪmɪtlɪs] *adj* ilimitado,-a, sin límites.

limousine ['lɪməzi:n, lɪmə'zi:n] *n Aut* limousine *f*, limusina *f*.

limp¹ [lɪmp] I *vi* cojear. II *n* cojera *f*; **to walk with a l.**, cojear.

limp² [lɪmp] *adj* 1 (*floppy*) flojo,-a, fláccido,-a, fofo,-a; (*relaxed*) relajado,-a; **let your body go l.**, relaja el cuerpo. 2 (*weak*) débil. ◆ **limply** *adv* (*weakly*) lánguidamente.

limpet ['lɪmpɪt] *n* 1 *Zool* lapa *f*. 2 *Mil* **l. mine**, mina *f* magnética.

limpid ['lɪmpɪd] *adj* límpido,-a, claro,-a.

linchpin ['lɪntʃpɪn] *n* 1 *Tech* pezonera *f*. 2 *fig* eje *m*, pieza *f* clave.

linctus ['lɪŋktəs] *n* (*pl* **linctuses**) jarabe *m* para la tos.

linden ['lɪndən] *n Bot* tilo *m*.

line¹ [laɪn] *n* 1 (*gen*) línea *f*; (*made with pen etc*) raya *f*; **to draw a l. under sth**, subrayar algo; *fig* **to draw the l. at sth**, decir basta a algo; *fig* **to know where to draw the l.**, saber cuándo hay que parar. ■ **l. drawing**, dibujo *m* lineal. 2 (*of writing*) línea *f*, renglón *m*; (*of poetry*) verso *m*; **new l.**, punto y aparte; *Theat* **to learn one's lines**, aprenderse el papel; *fig* **to read between the lines**, leer entre líneas; *fam* **to give sb four lines**, mándame cuatro líneas. *Typ* **l. spacer**, interlineador *m*. 3 (*of descent*) línea *f*, linaje *m*. 4 (*row*) fila *f*, línea *f*; (*of trees*) hilera *f*; *US* (*queue*) cola *f*; *US* **to stand in l.**, hacer cola; *fig* **he's in l. for presidency**, está bien situado en la carrera por la presidencia; *fig* **to be in l.**, corresponder, coincidir (**with**, con); *fig* **to be out of l.**, no corresponder, no coincidir (**with**, con); *fam* **to step out of l.**, salirse de las reglas. ■ *Ind* **assembly l.**, línea *f* de montaje. 4 (*rope*) cuerda *f*; (*wire*) cable *m*. ■ **fishing l.**, sedal *m*, hilo *m*; **washing l.**, cuerda *f* para tender la ropa. 5 *Tel* (*line*) línea *f*; **hold the l.!**, ¡no cuelgue!, ¡no se retire! ■ *fig* **hot l.**, teléfono *m* rojo. 6 (*route*) vía *f*; *GB Rail* (*track*) vía *f*, línea *f*; **lines of communication**, vías de comunicación; *fig* **to reach** *or* **come to the end of the l.**, llegar al final. ■ *GB Rail*

branch l., ramal *m*. 7 (*boundary*) límite *m*; *Sport* (*on court, field*) línea *f*. ■ *US* **State l.**, límite *m* de un Estado. 8 *Mil* línea *f*; **l. of fire**, línea de fuego; **to be in the front l.**, estar en primera línea. 9 (*company*) empresa *f*, compañía *f*; **bus l.**, línea *f* de autobuses; **shipping l.**, compañía naviera. 10 *fig* (*course, direction*) línea *f*; **l. of argument**, argumento *m*; **l. of vision**, campo *m* visual; **sth along these lines**, algo por el estilo; **to be in l. with**, ser conforme a; **to be on the right lines**, ir por buen camino; **to take a strong l. on sth**, tener una actitud firme sobre algo; **to toe the (party) l.**, seguir la línea (del partido); *fig* **all along the l.**, (*at every stage*) desde el principio; (*in detail*) con todo detalle. 11 *fam* (*speciality*) especialidad *f*, rama *f*; **it's not my l.**, no es lo mío; **what's his l.?**, ¿qué hace? 12 (*range of goods*) surtido *m*; *Com* **it is a new l.**, es una línea nueva. 13 *fam* (*story*) rollo *m*, cuento *m*; **don't give me that l.**, no me vengas otra vez con ese rollo. 14 *sl* (*of cocaine etc*) línea *f*.

line² [laɪn] I *vtr* 1 *Tech* (*pipe etc*) revestir; *Sew* forrar; (*walls*) llenar; *fam* **to l. one's pockets**, forrarse. 2 (*border*) bordear (**with**, con). ◆ **line up** I *vtr* 1 (*arrange in rows*) poner en fila. 2 (*organize*) organizar; **he has something lined up for this evening**, tiene algo organizado para esta noche. II *vi* (*people*) ponerse en fila; (*troops*) formar; (*in queue*) hacer cola.

lineage ['lɪnɪɪdʒ] *n* linaje *m*.

linear ['lɪnɪəʳ] *adj* (*gen*) lineal; (*of length*) de longitud; **l. perspective**, perspectiva lineal.

lined [laɪnd] I *pt* & *pp* see **line²**. II *adj* 1 (*paper*) rayado,-a; (*face*) arrugado,-a. 2 (*garment*) forrado,-a, con forro.

linen ['lɪnɪn] *n* lino *m*.

liner¹ ['laɪnəʳ] *n Naut* transatlántico *m*.

liner² ['laɪnəʳ] *n* (*lining*) forro *m*, revestimiento *m*. ■ **dustbin l.**, bolsa *f* de la basura; **nappy l.**, metedor *m*.

linesman ['laɪnzmən] *n* (*pl* **linesmen**) *Sport* juez *m* de línea.

line-up ['laɪnʌp] *n Sport* formación *f*, alineación *f*. ■ *Theat* **star l.-up**, reparto *m* estelar.

linen ['lɪnɪn] *n* 1 (*cloth*) lino *m*, lino *m*. 2 ropa *f*; (*sheets, tablecloths, etc*) ropa blanca, lencería *f*; *fig* **don't wash your dirty l. in public**, los trapos sucios se lavan en casa. ■ **bed l.**, ropa *f* de cama; **dirty l.**, ropa *f* sucia; **l. basket**, cesto *m* de la ropa sucia; **l. room**, lencería *f*; **table l.**, mantelería *f*.

linger ['lɪŋgəʳ] *vi* (*gen*) tardar; (*dawdle*) rezagarse; (*smell, doubt*) persistir, tardar en desaparecer; *fig* (*memory*) perdurar; **to l. over doing sth**, tardar en hacer algo.

lingerie ['lænʒəri:] *n fml* ropa *f* íntima, ropa *f* interior (de mujer).

lingering ['lɪŋgərɪŋ] *adj* (*death*) lento,-a; (*doubt*) persistente; (*look*) fijo,-a.

lingo ['lɪŋgəʊ] *n* (*pl* **lingoes**) *fam* 1 (*language*) lengua *f*, idioma *m*. 2 (*jargon*) jerga *f*.

lingua ['lɪŋgwə] *n* (*pl* **linguas** *or* **linguae** ['lɪŋgwi:]) *Ling* **l. franca**, lingua *f* franca.

linguist ['lɪŋgwɪst] *n* 1 (*specialist in linguistics*) lingüista *mf*. 2 *fam* (*speaker of various languages*) políglota *mf*.

linguistic [lɪŋ'gwɪstɪk] *adj* lingüístico,-a.

linguistics [lɪŋ'gwɪstɪks] *n* lingüística *f*.

liniment ['lɪnɪmənt] *n* linimento *m*.

lining ['laɪnɪŋ] *n Tech* (*of pipes etc*) revestimiento *m* interior; (*of garment*) forro *m*.

link [lɪŋk] I *n* 1 (*of chain*) eslabón *m*; *fig* **missing l.**, eslabón perdido; *fig* **weak l.**, punto *m* débil. 2 (*connection*) conexión *f*, enlace *m*; *fig* (*tie*) lazo *m*, vínculo *m*; **air/rail l.**, enlace aéreo/ferroviario; **cultural/economic links**, lazos culturales/económicos. 3 **links**, campo *m sing* de golf. II *vtr* (*join*) unir, enlazar, conectar; *fig* unir, vincular, relacionar; **to l. arms**, tomarse del brazo. ◆ **link up** *vi* (*gen*) unirse, conectarse; (*meet*) encontrarse, reunirse; (*spaceships*) acoplarse.

linkage ['lɪŋkɪdʒ] *n* (*act*) conexión *f*, concatenación *f*.

linkman ['lɪŋkmən] n (pl **linkmen**) TV Radio presentador m.

link-up ['lɪŋkʌp] n Tel TV enlace m, conexión f; (meeting) encuentro m, reunión f; (of spaceships) acoplamiento m.

linnet ['lɪnɪt] n Orn pardillo m.

lino ['laɪnəʊ] n fam linóleo m, linóleum m.

linoleum [lɪ'nəʊlɪəm] n linóleo m, linóleum m.

linseed ['lɪnsiːd] n linaza f.

lint [lɪnt] n Med hilas fpl.

lintel ['lɪntəl] n Archit dintel m.

lion ['laɪən] n Zool león m; fig the l.'s share, la parte del león.

lioness ['laɪənɪs] n Zool leona f.

lion-hearted [laɪən'hɑːtɪd] adj valiente.

lip [lɪp] n 1 Anat labio m; to lick one's lips, relamerse los labios; fig his name is on everybody's lips, todos hablan de él; fig my lips are sealed, soy una tumba; fig to bite one's l., disimular, morderse la lengua; fig to keep a stiff upper l., no inmutarse, poner al mal tiempo buen cara. 2 fam (cheek) impertinencia f; less of your l.!, ¡basta de impertinencias! 3 (of jug) pico m.

lip-read ['lɪpriːd] vtr & vi (pt & pp **lip-read** ['lɪpred]) leer en los labios.

lip-reading ['lɪpriːdɪŋ] n lectura f en los labios.

lip-service ['lɪpsɜːvɪs] n jarabé m de pico, palabrería f.

lipstick ['lɪpstɪk] n barra f de labios, lápiz m de labios.

liquefy ['lɪkwɪfaɪ] 1 vtr (pt & pp **liquefied**) licuar. II vi licuarse.

liqueur [lɪ'kjʊəʳ] n licor m.

liquid ['lɪkwɪd] I adj líquido,-a; fig (eyes) claro,-a. ■ Fin l. assets, activo m líquido. II n líquido m.

liquidate ['lɪkwɪdeɪt] vtr Fin liquidar; euph (murder) liquidar.

liquidation [lɪkwɪ'deɪʃən] n Fin liquidación f; to go into l., entrar en liquidación.

liquidator ['lɪkwɪdeɪtəʳ] n Fin liquidador,-a m,f.

liquidity [lɪ'kwɪdɪtɪ] n Fin liquidez f.

liquidize ['lɪkwɪdaɪz] vtr Culin licuar.

liquidizer ['lɪkwɪdaɪzəʳ] n Culin licuadora f.

liquor ['lɪkəʳ] n US alcohol m, bebidas fpl alcohólicas; hard l., bebida fpl de alta graduación alcohólica. ■ l. store, bodega f, tienda f de bebidas alcohólicas.

liquorice ['lɪkərɪs, 'lɪkərɪʃ] n regaliz m.

Lisbon ['lɪzbən] n Lisboa.

lisp [lɪsp] I n ceceo m. II vi cecear.

lissom(e) ['lɪsəm] adj lit esbelto,-a, elegante.

list¹ [lɪst] I n (gen) lista f; (catalogue) catálogo m; Med to be on the danger l., estar grave; fig to enter the lists, entrar en acción. ■ Com l. price, precio m de catálogo; price/waiting l., lista f de precios/espera; wine l., carta f de vinos. II vtr (make a list of) hacer una lista de; (put on a list) poner en una lista; it is not listed, no figura en la lista; Archit listed building, edificio de interés histórico.

list² [lɪst] Naut I n escora f. II vi escorar.

listen ['lɪsən] vi (gen) escuchar, oír; (pay attention) prestar atención, hacer caso; fig l., ¡escucha!, ¡oye!; to l. to reason, atender a razones. ◆ **listen in** vi (telephone etc) escuchar, espiar. ◆ **listen out (for)** vi estar atento,-a a.

listener ['lɪsənəʳ] n oyente mf; (to the radio) radioyente mf, radioescucha mf.

listing ['lɪstɪŋ] n listado m.

listless ['lɪstlɪs] adj decaído,-a, apático,-a.

listlessness ['lɪstlɪsnɪs] n apatía f, desgana f.

lit [lɪt] pt & pp see **light¹**.

Lit. [lɪt] fam abbr of **Literature**, literatura f.

litany ['lɪtənɪ] n letanía f.

liter ['liːtəʳ] n US see **litre**.

literacy ['lɪtərəsɪ] n alfabetización f.

literal ['lɪtərəl] adj literal. ◆ **literally** adv literalmente; (really) verdaderamente, auténticamente.

literary ['lɪtərərɪ] adj literario,-a.

literate ['lɪtərɪt] adj alfabetizado,-a.

literature ['lɪtərɪtʃəʳ] n 1 (writings) literatura f. 2 (secondary) bibliografía f. 3 fam (bumph etc) folleto m informativo.

lithe [laɪð] adj fml ágil.

lithograph ['lɪθəgrɑːf] n litografía f.

lithographer [lɪ'θɒgrəfəʳ] n litógrafo,-a m,f.

lithography [lɪ'θɒgrəfɪ] n litografía f.

Lithuania [lɪθjʊ'eɪnɪə] n Lituania.

Lithuanian [lɪθjʊ'eɪnɪən] I adj lituano,-a. II n (person) lituano,-a m,f, (language) lituano m.

litigant ['lɪtɪgənt] n litigante mf.

litigate ['lɪtɪgeɪt] I vi Jur litigar. II vtr Jur pleitear.

litigation [lɪtɪ'geɪʃən] n Jur litigio m, pleito m.

litmus ['lɪtməs] n Chem l. paper, papel m de tornasol; fig l. test, prueba f contundente.

litre ['liːtəʳ] n litro m.

litter ['lɪtəʳ] I n 1 (rubbish) basura f; (papers) papeles mpl. ■ l. basket, l. bin, papelera f. 2 Zool (off-spring) camada f. 3 (stretcher) camilla f. 4 (for animals) (to sleep) cesto m (para dormir); (to defecate) pajaza f. II vtr ensuciar; books and magazines littered the floor, el suelo estaba lleno de libros y revistas.

litterbug ['lɪtəbʌg] n US Canada see **litterlout**.

littered ['lɪtəd] adj cubierto,-a (with, de), lleno,-a (with, de).

litterlout ['lɪtəlaʊt] n persona f que tira papeles en la vía pública.

little ['lɪtəl] I adj 1 (small) pequeño,-a; a l. dog, un perrito; a l. house, una casita; do you fancy a l. drink?, ¿quieres un trago de algo?; fam poor l. thing!, ¡pobrecillo! ■ l. finger, dedo m meñique. 2 (not much) poco,-a; a l. cheese, un poco de queso; he has l. money, tiene poco dinero. 3 (young) pequeño,-a; I have three l. girls, tengo tres niñas pequeñas. II pron poco m; l. by l., poco a poco; l. or nothing, casi nada; save me a l., guárdame un poco; stay a l. (bit) longer, quédate un ratito más. III adv poco; as l. as possible, lo menos posible; I see her very l., la veo muy poco; l. did she know that ..., no tenía la menor idea de que ...; they were a l. surprised, se quedaron algo sorprendidos.

littoral ['lɪtərəl] adj Geog litoral.

liturgical [lɪ'tɜːdʒɪkəl] adj litúrgico,-a.

liturgy ['lɪtədʒɪ] n liturgia f.

livable ['lɪvəbəl] adj (house) habitante; (life) llevadero,-a.

live¹ [lɪv] I vi vivir; as long as I l., mientras yo viva; long l. the King!, ¡viva el Rey!; to l. and learn, vivir para ver; to l. and let l., vivir y dejar vivir. II vtr vivir; to l. an interesting life, llevar o tener una vida interesante; to l. a lie, vivir en la mentira; to l. a part, identificarse con un personaje. ◆ **live by** vi adherirse a, seguir los dictados de. ◆ **live down** vtr conseguir que se olvide. ◆ **live for** vi vivir para. ◆ **live in** vi (student) ser interno,-a; (maid) vivir con la familia; he has a l.-in girlfriend, vive con su novia. ◆ **live off** vi vivir de, alimentarse de; to l. off the land, vivir de la tierra; to l. off the state, vivir del cuento. ◆ **live on** I vtr (food, money, etc) vivir de. II vi 1 (memory) persistir. 2 (survive) sobrevivivir. ◆ **live out I** vtr (finish) acabar; to l. out one's days, acabarse le uno sus días. 2 (student) ser externo,-a; (maid) no vivir con la familia. 3 fam to l. out of a suitcase, ir de hotel en hotel; fam to l. out of cans, vivir (a base) de latas. ◆ **live through** vi vivir (durante). ◆ **live together** vi fam vivir juntos. ◆ **live up** vtr fam pasarlo bien; to l. it up, pegarse la gran vida. ◆ **live up to** vtr (promises) cumplir con; (principles) vivir de acuerdo con; (expectations) no ser lo que se esperaba. ◆ **live with** vi I vivir con. 2 fig (accept) aceptar.

live² [laɪv] **I** *adj* **1** *(living)* vivo,-a; **a real l. prince,** un príncipe de verdad; *fig* **a l. issue,** un tema de actualidad *or* candente. **2** *TV Rad* en directo, en vivo. **3** *Mil (ammunition)* real; *(bomb)* sin explotar; *Elec (wire)* con corriente; *fam* **he's a real l. wire!,** ¡éste no para nunca! **II** *adv (broadcast, perform)* en directo, en vivo.

livelihood ['laɪvlɪhʊd] *n* sustento *m*; **to carn one's l.,** ganarse la vida.

liveliness ['laɪvlɪnɪs] *n (person)* viveza *f*, vivacidad *f*; *(event)* animación *f*.

lively ['laɪvlɪ] *adj (livelier, liveliest) (person)* vivo,-a, enérgico,-a; *(place)* animado,-a; *fig (interest)* estusiasmado,-a; *fam* **look l.!,** ¡date prisa!; *fam* **things are getting l.,** las cosa se están poniendo interesantes.

liven ['laɪvən] **I** *vtr* **to l. (up),** animar. **II** *vi* animarse.

liver ['lɪvəʳ] *n Anat Culin* hígado *m*.

liverish ['lɪvərɪʃ] *adj fam* enfermo,-a.

livery ['lɪvərɪ] *n* librea *f*.

livestock ['laɪvstɒk] *n (cattle)* ganado *m*; **l. farming,** ganadería *f*.

livid ['lɪvɪd] *adj* **1** *(palid)* lívido,-a; *(lead-coloured)* plomizo,-a. **2** *fam (angry)* furioso,-a.

living ['lɪvɪŋ] **I** *adj* vivo,-a; *lit* **l. death,** enterrado,-a, en vida; **not a l. soul,** ni un alma; **the greatest l. poet, el mejor poeta** contemporáneo. **II** *n* **1** vida *f*; **clean l.,** vida respetable; **l. conditions,** condiciones de vida; **l. expenses,** dietas; **l. space,** espacio vital; **to earn** *or* **make one's l.,** ganarse la vida; **what does she do for a l.?,** ¿cómo se gana la vida? ■ **l. room,** sala *f* de estar, living *m*; **l. standards,** nivel *m* de vida; **l. wage,** sueldo *m* mínimo. **2** *(alive)* vivo *m*; **the l.,** los vivos; *fam fig* **she's still in the land of the l.,** sigue viva. **3** *Rel* beneficio *m*.

lizard ['lɪzəd] *n Zool (large)* lagarto *m*; *(small)* lagartija *f*.

llama ['lɑːmə] *n Zool* llama *f*.

loach [ləʊtʃ] *n (fish)* lobo *m*. ■ **spined l.,** lobo *m* de río; **stone l.,** lobo *m* franco.

load [ləʊd] **I** *n (cargo etc)* carga *f*; *(weight)* peso *m*; *Elec Tech* carga *f*; **to lighten the l.,** aligerar la carga; *fig* **you have taken a l. off my mind,** me has quitado un peso de encima; *fam* **get a l. of this!,** ¡fíjate en esto!; *fam* **loads (of),** montones de, un montón de; **I've got loads to tell you,** tengo un montón de cosas que contarte; *fam* **that's a l. of rubbish!,** ¡no son más que tonterías! **II** *vtr* cargar. **III** *vi* cargar. ◆ **load down** *vtr* cargar; *fig (work, worries)* estar agobiado,-a de. ◆ **load up** *vi & vtr* cargar.

loaded ['ləʊdɪd] *adj* **1** cargado,-a (**with,** de); **we were l. down with presents,** íbamos cargados de regalos; *fig* **a l. question,** una pregunta tendenciosa. **2** *fam* rico,-a; **to be l.,** estar forrado,-a. **3** *(dice)* trucado,-a; *fig* **the dice are l. against me,** tengo pocas posibilidades.

loading ['ləʊdɪŋ] *n (gen)* carga *f*; **l. bay,** cargadero *m*.

loaf¹ [ləʊf] *(pl loaves)* **1** pan *m*; *(unsliced)* barra *f* de pan; *(sliced)* pan *m* de molde. **2** *fam* mollera *f*; **use your l.!,** ¿para qué tienes la cabeza?

loaf² [ləʊf] *vi* **to l. (about** *or* **around),** holgazanear, gandulear.

loafer ['ləʊfəʳ] *n fam* **1** *(person)* holgazán,-ana *m, f,* gandul,-a *m, f,* vago,-a *m, f.* **2** *US* **loafers,** *(shoes)* mocasines *mpl.*

loan [ləʊn] **I** *n (gen)* préstamo *m*; *Fin* empréstito *m*; **on l.,** prestado,-a; *(footballer)* cedido,-a; *Fin* **to raise a l.,** hacer un empréstito. ■ **l. shark,** prestamista *mf*; **l. word,** préstamo *m* (lingüístico). **II** *vtr* prestar.

loath [ləʊθ] *adj* reacio,-a; **to be l. to do sth,** estar poco dispuesto,-a a hacer algo.

loathe [ləʊð] *vtr* aborrecer, odiar.

loathing ['ləʊðɪŋ] *n* aborrecimiento *m*, odio *m*.

loathsome ['ləʊðsəm] *adj* odioso,-a, repugnante, asqueroso,-a.

loaves [ləʊvz] *npl see* **loaf.**

lob [lɒb] **I** *n Ten* lob *m*. **II** *vtr* **1** *(pt & pp lobbed)* *Ten* hacer un lob. **2** *fam (throw)* lanzar, tirar.

lobby ['lɒbɪ] **I** *n* **1** *(entrance hall)* vestíbulo *m*. **2** *(pressure group)* grupo *m* de presión, lobby *m*; *(campaign)* campaña *f*. **II** *vtr (pt & pp lobbied)* presionar; **to l. an MP,** ejercer presiones sobre un diputado. **III** *vi* ejercer presiones, cabildear.

lobbyist ['lɒbɪɪst] *n Pol* activista *mf* de un grupo de presión.

lobe [ləʊb] *n Anat* lóbulo *m*.

lobotomy [ləʊ'bɒtəmɪ] *n Med* lobotomía *f*.

lobster ['lɒbstəʳ] *n (pl lobster or lobsters) Zool* bogavante *m*. ■ **Norway l.,** cigala *f*; **l. pot,** nasa *f*, langostera *f*; **spiny l.,** langosta *f*.

local ['ləʊkəl] **I** *adj (gen)* local; *(person)* del pueblo, del barrio; *(wine)* de la región, del país. ■ *Med* **l. anaesthetic,** anestésico *m* local; *Tel* **l. call,** llamada *f* urbana; **l. colour,** ambientación *f*; **l. government,** gobierno *m* municipal; **l. time,** hora *f* local. **II** *n fam* **1** *(person)* vecino,-a *m, f*; **the locals,** los vecinos, la gente *sing* del barrio. **2** *GB (pub)* bar *m del* barrio. ◆ **locally** *adv* en *or* de la localidad, en el *or* del lugar.

locale [ləʊ'kɑːl] *n fml (place)* lugar *m*; *(scene)* escenario *m*.

locality [ləʊ'kælɪtɪ] *n* localidad *f*.

localize ['ləʊkəlaɪz] *vtr fml* localizar.

locate [ləʊ'keɪt] *vtr fml* **1** *(situate)* situar, ubicar. **2** *(find)* localizar, encontrar.

location [ləʊ'keɪʃən] *n* **1** *(place)* lugar *m*, situación *f*. **2** *(placing)* ubicación *f*. **3** *(pinpointing)* localizar con exactitud, indicar con precisión. **4** *Cin* **l. shots,** exteriores *mpl*; **they're on l. in Australia,** están rodando en Australia.

loc. cit. [lɒk'sɪt] *abbr of* **loco citato** (in the place cited), en el lugar citado, loc. cit., l. c.

loch [lɒx, lɒk] *n Scot Geog* lago *m*.

loci ['ləʊsaɪ] *npl of* **locus.**

lock¹ [lɒk] **I** *n* **1** *(on door, drawer, etc)* cerradura *f*; *(bolt)* cerrojo *m*; *(padlock)* candado *m*; *Aut (on steering wheel)* retén *m*; **to force the l.,** forzar la cerradura; **under l. and key,** bajo llave, bajo siete llaves; *fam* **l. stock, and barrel,** completamente. **2** *(on canal)* esclusa *f*. **3** *Wrest* llave *f.* **4** *Aut (steering)* ángulo *m* de giro. **II** *vtr* cerrar con llave *or* cerrojo *or* candado; *fig* **they were locked in each other's arms,** quedaron fuertemente abrazados. **III** *vi (door etc)* cerrarse; *(wheels)* trabarse. ◆ **lock away** *vtr* guardar bajo llave. ◆ **lock in** *vtr (prisoners etc)* encerrar. ◆ **lock out** *vtr* **1** *(gen)* cerrar la puerta a, dejar fuera a; **I've locked myself out,** he olvidado la llave dentro. **2** *Ind* declarar el cierre patronal, declarar el lockout. ◆ **lock up** *vtr (house)* cerrar; *(valuables)* dejar bajo llave; *(jail)* meter en la cárcel.

lock² [lɒk] *n lit (of hair)* mecha *f*, mechón *m*.

locker ['lɒkəʳ] *n* **1** *(cupboard)* armario *m* ropero, taquilla *f*. ■ **l. room,** vestuario *m* con armarios roperos. **2** *(chest)* cajón *m*.

locket ['lɒkɪt] *n (with picture)* medallón *m*; *(with hair)* guardapelo *m*.

lockout ['lɒkaʊt] *n Ind* cierre *m* patronal, lockout *m*.

locksmith ['lɒksmɪθ] *n* cerrajero *m*.

lockup ['lɒkʌp] *n US (prison)* cárcel *f*; *(garage)* garaje *m* alejado de la casa; *(shop)* tienda *f* pequeña.

locomotion [ləʊkə'məʊʃən] *n* locomoción *f*.

locomotive [ləʊkə'məʊtɪv] *n Rail* locomotora *f*.

locum ['ləʊkəm] *n* suplente *mf*.

locus ['ləʊkəs] *n (pl loci)* lugar *m*.

locust ['ləʊkəst] *n Ent* langosta *f*.

locution [ləʊ'kjuːʃən] *n Ling* locución *f*.

lodge [lɒdʒ] **I** *n* **1** *(gamekeeper's)* casa *f* del guarda; *(porter's)* portería *f*; *(hunter's)* refugio *m*. **2** *(masonic)* logia *f*. **3** *(beaver's den)* madriguera *f*. **II** *vtr* **1** *(accommodate)* alojar, hospedar. **2** *(complaint)* presentar. **III** *vi* **1** *(live)* alojarse, hospedarse. **2** *(jam, become fixed)* posarse, meterse (**in**, en); *fig* **he had strange thoughts lodged in his mind**, tenía algunas estrañas ideas metidas en la cabeza.

lodger ['lɒdʒəʳ] *n* huésped,-a *m,f*.

lodging ['lɒdʒɪŋ] *n* alojamiento *m*, hospedaje *m*. ■ **l. house**, casa *f* de huéspedes.

loft [lɒft] **1** *n (attic)* desván *m*, buhardilla *f*. ■ *Agr* **hay l.**, pajar *m*. **II** *vi Sport (ball)* lanzar al aire.

lofty ['lɒftɪ] *adj (loftier, loftiest) lit* **1** *(high)* alto,-a; *fig (sentiments etc)* altivo,-a. **2** *pej (haughty)* arrogante, altivo,-a.

log [lɒg] **I** *n* **1** tronco *m*, troza *f*; *(for fuel)* leño *m*; *fig* **to sleep like a l.**, dormir como un tronco. ■ **l. cabin**, cabaña *f* de troncos. **2** *(book) Naut* diario *m* de a bordo; *Admin* diario *m* de vuelo. **3** *Math fam* logaritmo *m*. **II** *vtr (pt & pp logged) (record)* registrar, apuntar. ◆ **log in, log on** *vi Comput* entrar (en sistema). ◆ **log out, log off** *vi Comput* salir (del sistema), abandonar el sistema.

loganberry ['ləʊgənbərɪ] *n Bot (fruit)* zarza *f* frambuesa *or* de Logan.

logarithm ['lɒgərɪðəm] *n Math* logaritmo *m*.

log-book ['lɒgbʊk] *n Naut* diario *m* de a bordo; *Av* diario *m* de vuelo; *Aut* documentación *f* (del coche).

loggerheads ['lɒgəhedz] *npl* **to be at l. with sb**, estar a mal con algn.

logic ['lɒdʒɪk] *n* lógica *f*.

logical ['lɒdʒɪkəl] *adj* lógico,-a.

logician [lɒ'dʒɪʃən] *n* lógico,-a *m,f*.

logistic(al) [lə'dʒɪstɪk(əl)] *adj* logístico,-a.

logistics [lə'dʒɪstɪks] *npl* logística *f*.

logo ['ləʊgəʊ] *n*, **logotype** ['ləʊgəʊtaɪp] *n* logotipo *m*.

loin [lɔɪn] *n* **1** *(of animal)* ijada *f*, ijar *m*; *fig* **to gird up one's loins**, prepararse para la lucha. **2** *Culin (of pork)* lomo *m*; *(of beef)* solomillo *m*.

loincloth ['lɔɪnklɒθ] *n* taparrabos *m inv*.

Loire [lwɑː'] *n* Loira.

loiter ['lɔɪtəʳ] *vi (hang about)* holgazanear; *(lag behind)* rezagarse; retrasarse; *(prowl)* merodear.

loiterer ['lɔɪtərəʳ] *n* gandul *mf*, holgazán,-ana *m, f*; *(suspicious person)* merodeador,-a *m, f*.

loll [lɒl] *vi (tongue, head)* colgar. ◆ **loll about, loll around** *vi (sit lazily)* repantigarse; *(laze about)* holgazanear, hacer el vago, no dar golpe.

lollipop ['lɒlɪpɒp] *n* pirulí *m*, chupachup® *m*; **ice(d) l.**, polo *m*. ■ *GB fam* **l. lady** *or* **man**, guardia *mf* (que para el tráfico para que puedan cruzar los colegiales).

lollop ['lɒləp] *vi fam* moverse torpe y lentamente.

lolly ['lɒlɪ] *n fam* **1** *(sweet)* pirulí *m*. chupachup® *m*; **ice(d) l.**, polo *m*. **2** *fam (money)* pasta *f*.

London ['lʌndən] **I** *n* Londres. **II** *adj* londinense, de Londres.

Londoner ['lʌndənəʳ] *n* londinense *mf*.

lone [ləʊn] *adj (solitary)* solitario,-a; *(single)* solo,-a, único,-a.

loneliness ['ləʊnlɪnɪs] *n* soledad *f*.

lonely ['ləʊnlɪ] *adj (lonelier, loneliest)* **1** *(person)* solo,-a, solitario,-a. ■ **l. hearts club**, agencia *f* matrimonial. **2** *(place)* solitario,-a, aislado,-a.

loner ['ləʊnəʳ] *n* solitario,-a *m,f*.

lonesome ['ləʊnsəm] *adj US see* **lonely**.

long¹ [lɒŋ] **I** *adj* **1** *(size, distance)* largo,-a; **how l. is the table?**, ¿cuánto tiene de largo la mesa?; **it's three metres l.**, tiene tres metros de largo; *Sport* **l. jump**, salto de longitud; **the l. way round**, el camino más largo; *fig* **to pull a l. face**, poner cara larga. **2** *(time)* mucho,-a; **a l.**

time, mucho tiempo; **at l. last**, por fin; **how l. is the film?**, ¿cuánto tiempo dura la película?; **we were a l. time in getting here**, tardamos mucho en llegar. ■ **l. life milk**, leche *f* de larga conservación. **II** *adv* mucho, mucho tiempo; **all day l.**, todo el día; **as l. as the exhibition lasts**, mientras dure la exposición; **as l.** *or* **so l. as you don't mind**, con tal que no te importe; **before l.**, dentro de poco; **(for) how much longer is he going to stay?**, ¿cuánto tiempo más va a quedarse?; **how l. have you been here?**, ¿cuánto tiempo llevas aquí?; **how l. did you live in Spain?**, ¿durante cuánto tiempo viviste en España?; **I can't wait any longer**, no puedo esperar más; **keep it as l. as you like**, quédatelo el tiempo que quieras; *fam* **so l.!**, ¡hasta luego! **III** *n* **the l. and the short of the matter**, los pormenores del asunto.

long² [lɒŋ] *vi* **to l. for,** *(yearn)* desear con ansia, anhelar; *(nostalgically)* añorar con ansia; **to l. to do sth**, tener muchas ganas de hacer algo.

long³ [lɒŋ] *Geog abbr of* **longitude**, longitud *f*, long.

longboat ['lɒŋbəʊt] *n Naut* chalupa *f*, lancha *f*.

longbow ['lɒŋbəʊ] *n Mil* arco *m*.

long-distance ['lɒŋdɪstəns] *adj* de larga distancia. ■ *Tel* **l.-d. call**, conferencia *f* interurbana; *Sport* **l.-d. runner**, corredor,-a *m, f* de fondo.

long-drawn-out [lɒŋdrɔːn'aʊt] *adj* interminable.

longevity [lɒn'dʒevɪtɪ] *n* longevidad *f*.

longhand ['lɒŋhænd] *n* escritura *f* a mano.

longing ['lɒŋɪŋ] *n (desire)* deseo *m*, ansia *f*, anhelo *m*; *(nostalgia)* nostalgia *f*, añoranza *f*. ◆ **longingly** *adv (with desire)* ansiosamente; *(nostalgically)* con nostalgia.

longish ['lɒŋɪʃ] *adj fam* bastante largo,-a, más bien largo,-a.

longitude ['lɒndʒɪtjuːd] *n* longitud *f*.

longitudinal [lɒndʒɪ'tjuːdɪnəl] *adj* longitudinal.

long johns ['lɒŋdʒɒnz] *npl* calzones *mpl* largos.

long-playing ['lɒŋpleɪɪŋ] *adj* de larga duración; **l.-p. record**, elepé *m*.

long-range ['lɒŋreɪndʒ] *adj* **1** *(missile etc)* de largo alcance. **2** *(weather forecast)* de largo plazo; *fam (plans etc)* para las próximas semanas, para los meses que vienen.

longshoreman ['lɒŋʃɔːmən] *n (pl* **longshoremen)** estibador *m*, descargador *m* de muelle.

long-sighted [lɒŋ'saɪtɪd] *adj* **1** *Med* présbita. **2** *fig* previsor,-a, perspicaz.

long-standing ['lɒŋstændɪŋ] *adj* viejo,-a, antiguo,-a, de hace mucho tiempo.

long-suffering ['lɒŋsʌfrɪŋ] *adj* sufrido,-a.

long-term ['lɒŋtɜːm] *adj* a largo plazo.

longtime ['lɒŋtaɪm] *adj* viejo,-a antiguo,-a, de hace mucho tiempo.

long-winded [lɒŋ'wɪndɪd] *adj (person)* prolijo,-a, pedante; *(story)* interminable.

loo [luː] *n fam* excusado *m*, wáter *n*, baño *m*, servicios *mpl*.

loofah ['luːfə] *n* esponja *f* de lufa.

look [lʊk] **I** *n* **1** *(glance)* mirada *f*; **have** *or* **take a l. in the cupboard**, mira en el armario; **he had a strange l. in his eye**, tenía una mirada extraña; **let me have** *or* **take a l.**, déjeme ver; **to have a l. around a place**, visitar un lugar; **to have a l. for sth**, buscar algo; **to have** *or* **take a l. at**, *(peep)* echar una mirada *or* vistazo a; *(examine)* examinar. **2** *(appearance)* aspecto *m*, apariencia *f*; **by the l. of him**, a juzgar por su aspecto; **by the l. of things**, según parece; **I don't like the l. of it**, me da mala espina. **3** *(fashion)* moda *f*, estilo *m*. **4** *(good)* **looks**, belleza *f*; **he had it all: looks, money, and prospects**, lo tenía todo; era guapo, tenía dinero y buen futuro; **she has her mother's looks**, es tan guapa como su madre. **II** *vi* **1** *(glance etc)* mirar; *fam* **l. here!**, ¡oye!; *prov* **l. before you leap**, antes de que te cases mira lo que haces. **2** *(seem)* parecer; **he looks well,** tiene buena cara; **it looks delicious,** tiene un aspecto buenísimo; **how does the hat l.?,** ¿qué te parece el sombrero?; **it looks good on you,** te va muy bien; **she looks tired,** parece cansada; *fam* **l. lively!,** ¡espabílate! 3 *(be similar)* parecer; **it looks like rain,** parece que va a llover; **she looks like her father,** se parece a su padre. III *vtr* 1 *(gen)* mirar; **to l. sb in the face,** mirar a algn a la cara; **to l. sb up and down,** mirar a algn de arriba abajo. 2 *(seem)* parecer; **she doesn't l. herself today,** tiene mala cara hoy. ◆ **look after** *vtr (pay attention)* cuidar a, cuidar de, ocuparse de; *(supervise)* vigilar; **l. after yourself!,** ¡cuídate!; *fam iron* **he can l. after himself,** sabe arreglárselas. ◆ **look ahead** *vi* mirar hacia adelante; *fig* mirar al futuro. ◆ **look at** *vtr* mirar; *fig* **it depends on how you l. at it,** depende de como se enfoca la cuestión; *fig* **to l. at him, you wouldn't think he was rich,** no tiene aspecto de persona rica; *fig* **whichever way you l. at it,** desde cualquier punto de vista. ◆ **look away** *vi* apartar la mirada. ◆ **look back** *vi* 1 mirar hacia atrás; *fig* **since then he has never looked back,** desde entonces le ha ido prosperando. 2 *(remember)* recordar. ◆ **look down** *vi* bajar la mirada; *fig* **to l. down on sth/sb,** despreciar algo/a algn. ◆ **look for** *vtr* 1 *(search)* buscar. 2 *(expect)* esperar; **we're looking for two points,** esperamos ganar los dos puntos. ◆ **look forward to** *vtr* esperar con ansia; *(in letter)* **I l. forward to hearing from you,** espero noticias suyas. ◆ **look in** *vi (visit)* hacer una visita rápida; **to l. in on sb,** pasar por casa de algn. ◆ **look into** *vtr* examinar, estudiar, investigar. ◆ **look on I** *vtr (consider)* considerar. **II** *vi (not participate etc)* mirar, hacer de espectador,-a. ◆ **look onto** *vi* dar a. ◆ **look out I** *vi* 1 *(window etc)* mirar por; **the bedroom looks out onto the garden,** el dormitorio da al jardín. 2 *(take care)* **l. out!,** ¡cuidado!, ¡ojo! ◆ **look out for** *vi* 1 *(await)* esperar, estar alerta; **l. out for that film,** estate al tanto de cuando hacen esta película. 2 *fam* **to l. out for oneself,** velar por los intereses propios. ◆ **look over** *vtr (examine)* revisar, examinar; *(place)* inspeccionar, registrar. ◆ **look round I** *vi (gen)* mirar alrededor; *(turn head)* volver la cabeza; **don't l. round!,** ¡no mires atrás!; **to l. round for sb,** buscar a algn. **II** *vtr (visit) (city etc)* visitar, recorrer. ◆ **look through I** *vtr (window etc)* mirar por; *fam fig* **he just looked through me,** me pasó de largo. 2 *(leaf through)* hojear; *(examine)* examinar, revisar; *(check)* registrar. ◆ **look to** *vi* 1 *(take care of)* cuidar de, velar por, ocuparse de. 2 *(turn to)* recurrir a, contar con; **they always looked to their father for advice,** siempre buscaban los consejos de su padre. 3 *(make sure)* asegurar; **l. to it that you get here on time,** asegúrate de que llegues a tiempo. 4 *(foresee)* contemplar; **certain ecologists l. to the future with great pessimism,** ciertos ecologistas tienen una visión muy pesimista del futuro. ◆ **look up I** *vi* 1 *(glance upwards)* alzar la vista. 2 *fam (improve)* mejorar; **things are looking up,** se nota una mejora en las cosas. II *vtr* 1 *(look for)* buscar; **he looked the word up (in a dictionary),** buscó la palabra en un diccionario. 2 *(visit)* ver, ir a visitar; **when I go to Madrid I'll l. him up,** cuando vaya a Madrid iré a verle. ◆ **look upon** *vi (consider)* considerar. ◆ **look up to** *vi (person)* respetar.

lookalike ['lʊkəlaɪk] *n* sosia *m.*

looker ['lʊkə^r] *n* 1 **l. (on),** espectador,-a *m,f.* 2 *(woman)* belleza *f.*

look-in ['lʊkɪn] *n fam* ocasión *f,* oportunidad *f;* **he won't get a l.-in,** no le harán ni caso.

lookout ['lʊkaʊt] *n* 1 *(person)* centinela *mf,* guardia *mf.* 2 *(place)* mirador *m,* atalaya *f.* 3 *(watch)* **to be on the l. for,** estar al acecho de; **to keep a l.,** estar ojo avizor. 4 *fam* problema *m;* **that's his l.!,** ¡eso es asunto suyo!, ¡allá él!

loom¹ [luːm] *n* telar *m.*

loom² [luːm] *vi (stand tall)* surgir, aparecer; *fig (threaten)* amenazar; **to l. large,** cobrar mucha importancia. ◆ **loom up** *vi (problems, buildings, etc)* surgir.

loony ['luːnɪ] *adj (loonier, looniest) fam* loco,-a, chiflado,-a. ■ **l. bin,** manicomio *m.*

loop [luːp] **I** *n* 1 *(in rope)* lazo *m,* lazada *f.* 2 *(contraceptive)* esterilete *m.* 3 *Comput* bucle *m.* **II** *vtr* 1 encordar; **to l. a rope around sth,** pasar una cuerda alrededor de algo. 2 *Av* hacer una vuelta de campana. **III** *vi (road etc)* serpentear.

loophole ['luːphəʊl] *n* 1 *(in wall)* aspillera *f.* 2 *fig (in law etc)* escapatoria *f;* **tax l.,** laguna *f* impositiva.

loopy ['luːpɪ] *adj (loopier, loopiest) fam* loco,-a, chiflado,-a.

loose [luːs] **I** *adj* 1 *(not secure) (knot, rope, screw)* flojo,-a, holgado,-a; *(tooth)* que se mueve; *(bowels)* suelto,-a; *(papers, hair)* suelto,-a; *(tongue)* suelto,-a, desatado,-a; *(clothes)* suelto,-a; *(baggy)* holgado,-a; **l. skin,** carnes *fpl* fofas; **to break l.,** escaparse; **to come l.,** *(shoelace etc)* desatarse; *(part)* desprenderse; **to cut** *or* **let l.,** soltar, dejar; **to set sb l.,** soltar a algn, poner en libertad a algn; *US fam* **to stay** *or* **hang l.,** relajarse; *fig* **to tie up l. ends,** no dejar cabo suelto; *fam* **to be at a l. end,** no saber qué hacer para distraerse. ■ **l. cover,** funda *f;* **l. end,** cabo *m* suelto. 2 *(not packaged) (goods)* suelto,-a, a granel; **l. tobacco,** tabaco *m* en hebras; **l. change,** suelto *m,* dinero *m* suelto. 3 *(not connected) Elec* desconectado,-a; *fig (ideas)* inconexo,-a. 4 *(not exact)* inexacto,-a, vago,a; *(translation)* libre. 5 *(lax)* relajado,-a; **a l. woman,** una mujer fácil; **l. living,** vida *f* alegre. **II** *n fam (prisoner etc)* **to be on the l.,** andar suelto,-a. **III** *vtr lit* 1 *(animal, person)* dejar en libertad, soltar. 2 *(bring about)* provocar. ◆ **loosely** *adv* 1 *(approximately)* aproximadamente. 2 *(vaguely)* vagamente.

loose-fitting [luːs'fɪtɪŋ] *adj (gen)* suelto,-a; *(clothes)* holgado,-a, amplio,-a.

loose-leaf [luːs'liːf] *adj (album, folder)* de hojas sueltas.

loosen ['luːsən] *vtr* 1 *(slacken)* aflojar, soltar; *(belt)* desabrochar; *fig (restrictions)* flexibilizar 2 *(untie)* desatar; *fig* **the wine loosened his tongue,** el vino te hizo hablar más de la cuenta. **II** *vi* 1 *(slacken)* aflojarse, soltarse. 2 *(become untied)* desatarse. ◆ **loosen up** *vi* 1 *Sport* desentumecerse. 2 *fam (relax)* relajarse.

looseness ['luːsnɪs] *n* 1 *(of knot, rope)* aflojamiento *m,* soltura *f.* 2 *(of clothes)* holgura *f.* 3 *(of morals, discipline)* relajamiento *m.* 4 *(vagueness)* vaguedad *f,* falta *f* de precisión.

loot [luːt] **I** *n* 1 *(booty)* botín *m.* 2 *arch fam (money)* pasta *f.* **II** *vtr* saquear.

looter ['luːtə^r] *n* saqueador,-a *m,f.*

looting ['luːtɪŋ] *n* saqueo *m.*

lop [lɒp] *vtr (pt & pp lopped)* podar; **to l. branches off a tree,** podar un árbol. ◆ **lop off** *vtr* cortar.

lope [ləʊp] **I** *vi* andar a zancador *or* con paso largo. **II** *n* zancada *f,* paso *m* largo.

lop-eared ['lɒpɪəd] *adj* de orejas gachas.

lopsided [lɒp'saɪdɪd] *adj (gen)* ladeado,-a, torcido,-a; *(table)* cojo,-a; *(view)* descentrado,-a.

loquacious [lɒ'kweɪʃəs] *adj fml* locuaz.

loquacity [lɒ'kwæsɪtɪ] *n fml* locuacidad *f.*

lord [lɔːd] **I** *n* 1 *(ruler)* señor *m; (British peer)* lord *m; Parl* **the House of Lords,** la Cámara de los Lores; **the L. Mayor,** el señor alcalde; *fig* **to live like a l.,** vivir a cuerpo de rey *or* como un pachá. 2 *Rel* **the L.,** El Señor; **good L.!,** ¡Dios mío!; **the L.'s Prayer,** el Padrenuestro. 3 *Jur (judge)* señoría *mf;* **yes, my l.,** sí, señoría. **II** *vtr* **to l. it over sb,** tratar despóticamente a algn.

lordship ['lɔːdʃɪp] *n GB* señoría *f,* señorío *m;* **His L., Your L.,** su señoría.

lore [lɔː^r] *n* saber *m* popular, tradición *f.*

lorry ['lɒrɪ] *n GB* camión *m; fam fig* **to fall off the back of a l.,** ser robado,-a. ■ **l. driver,** camionero,-a *m,f;* **l. load,** carga *f.*

lose [luːz] **I** *vtr (pt & pp lost)* 1 *(gen)* perder; **to l. one's way,** perderse; *fig* **to l. face,** perder prestigio *or* carisma; *fig* **to l. one's voice,** quedarse afónico; *fam fig* **we're**

losing sight of the problem, nos estamos desviando del problema; *fam fig* **you've got nothing to l.,** no tienes nada que perder. **2** *(wipe out)* destrozar; **to be lost at sea,** perecer en el mar. **3** *(shed)* perder; **she's lost 6 kilos,** ha adelgazado 6 kilos; **to l. weight,** perder peso, adelgazar; **the patient has lost a lot of blood,** el paciente ha perdido mucha sangre. **4** *(be dismissed)* costar, hacer perder; **his attitude lost him the job,** su actitud le costó el puesto de trabajo. **5** *(make a loss)* perder. **6** *(through death)* perder; **to l. a child,** perder a un hijo; **to l. one's life,** perder la vida, perecer. **6** *(time)* perder; *(clock, watch)* atrasar; **his alarm clock loses 3 minutes a day,** su despertador se atrasa 3 minutos por día. **II** *vi* **1** *(gen)* perder; **to l. to sb,** perder contra algn; **to l. out,** salir perdiendo; **United lost 6-0,** el United perdió 6-0. **2** *(clock, watch)* atrasarse. ◆ **lose out (to)** *vi* sufrir a costa de.

loser ['luːzə^r] *n* perdedor,-a *m, f;* **to be a good/bad l.,** saber/no saber perder; *fam* **she's a born l.,** tiene mala suerte; *fam* **to be on a l.,** tener todas las de perder.

losing ['luːzɪŋ] *adj (team etc)* vencido,-a, derrotado,-a; **to be on the l. side,** ser entre los perdedores; *fig* **to fight a l. battle,** luchar por una causa perdida.

loss [lɒs] *n (gen)* pérdida *f;* **heat/weight l.,** pérdida de calor/peso; **l. of memory/vision,** pérdida de memoria/vista; **there was a great l. of life,** hubo muchas víctimas; *Com* **to make a l.,** perder; *Com* **to sell sth at a l.,** vender algo con pérdida; *fig* **to be at a l.,** estar perdido,-a *or* desorientado,-a; *fig* **to be at a l. for words,** quedarse de una pieza; **to be at a l. what to do,** no saber qué hacer; *fig* **to cut one's losses,** reducir pérdidas; *fam* **it's your l.,** sales perdiendo tú; *fam* **she's a dead l.,** es un desastre *or* una calamidad.

lost [lɒst] **I** *pt & pp see* **lose. II** *adj* **1** *(gen)* perdido,-a; **to get l.,** perderse; **to mak up for l. time,** recuperar el tiempo perdido; *fam* **get l.!,** ¡vete a la porra! ◼ **l. cause,** causa *f* perdida; **l. property,** objetos *mpl* perdidos; **l. property office,** *US* **l. and found department,** oficina *f* de objetos perdidos. **2** *(disoriented)* desorientado,-a; *(distracted)* distraído,-a, despistado,-a; **to be l. for words,** quedarse de una pieza; **to be l. in thought,** estar ensimismado,-a. **3** *(wasted)* inútil.

lot [lɒt] *n* **1** *(fortune, fate)* suerte *f,* destino *m; fig* **the common l.,** la suerte común; *fig* **to throw in one's l. with sb,** unirse a la suerte de algn. **2** *(for choosing)* sorteo *m;* **to draw** *or* **cast lots for sth,** sortear algo, echar algo a suertes. **3** *US (plot of land)* parcela *f,* terreno *m.* ◼ *US* **parking l.,** aparcamiento *m.* **4** *(in an auction)* lote *m.* **5** *fam (group of people)* grupo *m* de gente; **are you l. coming tonight?,** ¿vosotros venís esta tarde?; **the whole l. of you,** todos vosotros; **they never speak to us l.,** nunca hablan connosotros; **they're a nice l.,** es gente maja. **6** *(everything)* todo *m;* **he ate the l.,** se lo comió todo; **that's the l.,** eso es todo. **7** *(large amount, number)* **a l. of,** *(much)* mucho,-a; *(many)* muchos,-as; **a l. of people,** mucha gente, muchas personas; **he feels a l. better,** se encuentra mucho mejor; **she reads a l.,** lee mucho; **such a l. of,** tanto,-a, tantos,-as; **thanks a l.!,** ¡muchísimas gracias!; *iron* ¡y gracias!; **what a l. of children!,** ¡cuántos niños! **8** *fam* **lots of,** un montón de, montones de, cantidad de, la mar de; **lots of concentration,** mucha concentración.

loth [ləʊθ] *adj see* **loath.**

lotion ['ləʊʃən] *n* loción *f.*

lottery ['lɒtərɪ] *n* lotería *f.* ◼ **l. ticket,** billete *m.*

lotto ['lɒtəʊ] *n (boardgame)* lotería *f.*

lotus ['ləʊtəs] *n Bot* loto *m.* ◼ **l. position,** postura *f* del loto.

lotus-eater ['ləʊtəsiːtə^r] *n* vividor,-a *m.f.*

loud [laʊd] **I** *adj* **1** *(voice)* alto,-a, fuerte; *(noise)* fuerte; *(laugh)* estrepitoso,-a; *(applause)* clamoroso,-a; *(protests, party)* ruidoso,-a; *fig* **I can hear you l. and clear,** te oigo perfectamente. **2** *(flashy) (colour)* chillón,-ona, llamativo,-a. **3** *(vulgar) (behaviour etc)* de mal gusto, cursi, hortera. **II** *adv* alto, fuerte; **to say/read/think out l.,** decir/leer/pensar en voz alta.

loud-hailer [laʊd'heɪlə^r] *n* megáfono *m.*

loudmouth ['laʊdmaʊθ] *n pej* gritón,-ona *m, f; (mujer)* verdulera *f.*

loud-mouthed ['laʊdmaʊθt] *adj* gritón,-ona.

loudness ['laʊdnɪs] *n (of noise)* fuerza *f,* intensidad *f.*

loudspeaker [laʊd'spiːkə^r] *n* altavoz *m.*

lounge [laʊndʒ] **I** *n GB (sitting-room)* salón *m,* sala *f* de estar; *(in pub)* salón *m.* ◼ **departure l.,** sala *f* de espera. **II** *vi* holgazanear, gandulear; **to l. on the sofa,** repantigarse en el sofá. ◆ **lounge about** *vi* holgazanear, gandulear.

lounger ['laʊndʒə^r] *n* tumbona *f.*

louse [laʊs] *n* **1** *(pl* **lice** [laɪs]) *(insect)* piojo *m.* **2** *(pl* **louses)** *fam (person)* canalla *mf,* sinvergüenza *mf.* ◆ **louse up** *vtr fam, (spoil)* echar a perder, estropear.

Lousiana [luːɪzɪ'ænə] *n* Luisiana *f.*

lousy ['laʊzɪ] *adj (lousier, lousiest) fam (dreadful)* pésimo,-a, malísimo,-a, fatal; **a l. day,** un día de perros; **a l. trick,** una cochinada; **I feel l.,** me encuentro fatal.

lout [laʊt] *n* bruto *m,* patán *m.*

loutish ['laʊtɪʃ] *adj* bruto,-a.

louvre, *US* **louver** ['luːvə^r] *n* persiana *f.*

lovable ['lʌvəbəl] *adj* adorable, encantador,-a.

love [lʌv] **I** *n* **1** amor *m,* cariño *m* (for, por), *(passion)* pasión *f* (for, por), afición *f* (for, a); **for the l. of it,** por amor al arte; **give my l. to David,** dale un abrazo de mi parte a David; **it was l. at first sight,** fue un flechazo; **not for l. or money,** por nada del mundo; **to be in l. with sb,** estar enamorado,-a de algn; **to fall in l.,** enamorarse; **to make l.,** hacer el amor; *dated* **to make l. to sb,** hacer la corte a algn; *(in letter)* **(with) l. (from) Mary,** un abrazo afectuoso, Mary; *fig* **there's no l. lost between them,** no se pueden *ver.* ◼ **l. affair,** amorío *m; euph* **l. child,** hijo,-a *m, f* natural; **l. letter/story,** carta *f*/historia *f* de amor; **l. life,** vida *f* sentimental; *(sexual)* vida *f* sexual. **2** *(person)* amor *m* cariño *m; fam* chato,-a *m.f;* **my l.,** mi amor, amor mío; *fam* **thanks, l.,** gracias, chato,-a. **3** *Ten (nil)* **forty l.,** cuarenta a cero. **II** *vtr* querer a, amar a. **II** *vtr* querer a, amar a; *(sport etc)* ser muy aficionado,-a a; **he loves cooking,** le encanta cocinar; **we'd l. to go with you,** nos gustaría mucho acompañaros.

lovebirds ['lʌvbɜːdz] *npl iron* enamorados *mpl,* tortolitos *mpl.*

loveless ['lʌvlɪs] *adj* sin amor.

loveliness ['lʌvlɪnɪs] *n* encanto *m,* belleza *f.*

lovely ['lʌvlɪ] *adj (lovelier, loveliest) (pleasing, charming)* encantador,-a; *(beautiful)* hermoso,-a, precioso,-a; *(delicious)* delicioso,-a, riquísimo,-a; **we had a l. time,** lo pasamos en grande.

love-making ['lʌvmeɪkɪŋ] *n* **1** *(courtship)* galanteo *m.* **2** *(sexual intercourse)* relaciones *fpl* sexuales.

lover ['lʌvə^r] *n* **1** *(sexual partner)* amante *mf.* **2** *(enthusiast)* amante *mf,* aficionado,-a *m,f,* amigo,-a *m,f;* **he's a l. of fine food,** es un amante de la buena comida.

lovesick ['lʌvsɪk] *adj* enfermo,-a de amor.

lovey-dovey [lʌvɪ'dʌvɪ] *adj iron* zalamero,-a, empalagoso,-a

loving ['lʌvɪŋ] *adj (affectionate)* cariñoso,-a, afectuoso,a; *(in letter)* **your l. daughter, Emma,** un abrazo afectuoso de tu hija Emma.

low[1] ['ləʊ] **I** *adj* **1** *(not high)* bajo,-a; *(bridge, voice, sun)* bajo,-a; *(neckline)* escotado,-a; *(tide, level)* bajo,-a; *Culin* **cook on a l. light** *or* **gas,** cocinar a fuego lento; *fig* **to keep a l. profile,** ser discreto,-a. ◼ *Geog* **the L. Countries,** los Países Bajos. **2** *(in number or quantity)* bajo,-a, poco,-a; **l. prices,** precios bajos; **l. tar cigarettes,** cigarrillos bajos en nicotina; **l. temperatures,** temperaturas bajas; **we're l. on supplies,** no tenemos muchos provisiones. **3** *(poor)* pobre, bajo,-a; **a l. standard of living,** un bajo nivel de vida. **4** *(battery)* gastado,-a. ◼ **l. frequency,** baja frecuencia *f*. **5** *(depressed)* deprimido,-a; **morale among the soldiers was l.**, había muy poco entusiasmo entre los soldados; **to feel l.**, sentirse deprimido,-a. **6** *(reprehensible)* malo,-a; **a l. trick**, una mala jugada. **II** *adv* bajo; **our supplies are running l.**, se nos están acabando las provisiones; **to aim l.**, apuntar bajo; **to fly l.**, volar bajo; *fig* **to be laid l. with flu**, tener que guardar cama a causa de la gripe; *fig* **to lie l.**, permanecer escondido,-a. **III** *n* **1** *Meteor* depresión *f*, área *f* de baja presión. **2** *(low point)* punto *m* más bajo; **to reach an all-time l.**, tocar fondo.

low² [ləʊ] *vi (cow)* mugir.

lowbrow ['ləʊbraʊ] **I** *adj* poco culto,-a. **II** *n* persona *f* de poca cultura.

low-down ['ləʊdaʊn] *adj* bajo,-a, vil.

lowdown ['ləʊdaʊn] *n fam* pormenores *mpl*; **to give sb the l. on sth**, dar informes confidenciales a algn sobre algo.

lower ['ləʊə'] **I** *adj (comp of low)* inferior; **the l. law**, la mandíbula inferior. ▪ *Typ* **l. case**, caja *f* baja, minúscula *f*; **l. class**, clase *f* baja. **II** *adv comp see* **low**. **III** *vtr* **1** *(voice, radio)* bajar; *(lifeboat)* lanzar; *(flag)* arriar. **2** *(reduce)* reducir, bajar, disminuir; *(price)* rebajar, bajar; *fig* **to l. oneself**, rebajarse. **3** *(weaken)* debilitar.

lower-class ['ləʊəklɑːs] *adj* de clase baja.

lowest ['ləʊɪst] **I** *adj (superl of low)* más bajo,-a; *(price, speed)* mínimo,-a. ▪ *Math* **l. common denominator**, mínimo común denominador *m*. **II** *n* mínimo *m*; **at the l.**, como mínimo; *fig* **the l. of the low**, lo peor que hay.

low-key [ləʊ'kiː] *adj (calm)* de baja intensidad; *(informal)* sin ceremonia.

lowlands ['ləʊləndz] *npl* tierras *fpl* bajas; *Geog* **the L.**, las Tierras Bajas de Escocia.

low-level ['ləʊlevəl] *adj* de bajo nivel.

lowly ['ləʊlɪ] *adj (lowlier, lowliest)* humilde, modesto,-a.

low-necked ['ləʊnekt] *adj (dress)* escotado,-a, con escote.

low-pitched ['ləʊpɪtʃt] *adj* grave.

low-spirited [ləʊ'spɪrɪtɪd] *adj* desanimado,-a.

loyal ['lɔɪəl] *adj* leal, fiel.

loyalist ['lɔɪəlɪst] *n* leal *mf*; *Hist* legitimista *mf*.

loyalty ['lɔɪəltɪ] *n* lealtad *f*, fidelidad *f*.

lozenge ['lɒzɪndʒ] *n* **1** *Med* pastilla *f*. **2** *Geom* rombo *m*.

LP [el'piː] *abbr of* **long-playing record**, disco *m* de larga duración, LP *m*.

L-plate ['elpleɪt] *n GB Aut* (placa *f* de) la ele.

LSD [eles'diː] *abbr of* **lysergic acid diethylamide**, dietilamida *f* del ácido lisérgico, LSD *m*.

Lt *abbr see* **Lieut**.

Ltd *GB Com abbr of* **Limited (Liability)**, (responsabilidad *f*) Limitada, Ltda.

lubricant ['luːbrɪkənt] *n* lubricante *m*, lubrificante *m*.

lubricate ['luːbrɪkeɪt] *vtr (gen)* lubricar; *(engine)* engrasar.

lubrication [luːbrɪ'keɪʃən] *n* engrase *m*.

lubricious [luː'brɪʃəs] *adj lit* lascivo,-a, lujurioso,-a.

lucerne [luː'sɜːn] *n Bot* alfalfa *f* brasileña.

lucid ['luːsɪd] *adj* lúcido,-a, claro,-a.

lucidity [luː'sɪdɪtɪ] *n* lucidez *f*, claridad *f*.

luck [lʌk] *n* suerte *f*; **bad** *or* **hard** *or* **tough l.!**, mala suerte!; **good l.!**, ¡(buena) suerte!; **no such l.!**, ¡ojalá!; **this pen brings me good l.**, este bolígrafo me da buena suerte; **to be in l.**, estar de suerte, estar con suerte; **to be down on one's l.**, tener muy mala suerte; **to be out of l.**, estar de malas; *fig* **as I. would have it ...**, la suerte quiso que ...; *fig* **to have l. on one's side**, tener la suerte de su parte; *fig* **to push one's l.**, tentar la suerte; *fig* **to try one's l.**, probar fortuna; *fam* **any l.?**, ¿qué?, ¿cómo te ha ido?; *fam* **I've got to do the dishes, worse l.**, ¡vaya suerte que

tengo! me toca hacer los platos; *fam* **with any** *or* **a bit of l., he'll phone this evening,** con un poco de suerte llamará esta tarde.

luckless ['lʌklɪs] *adj fml* infortunado,-a, desgraciado,-a, desafortunado,-a.

lucky ['lʌkɪ] *adj (luckier, luckiest) (person)* afortunado,-a, que tiene suerte; *(day)* favorable, de buen agüero; *(move)* oportuno,-a; *(charm)* que trae suerte; **a l. break**, una oportunidad; **how l.!**, ¡qué suerte!; **I'm wearing my l. shirt**, visto mi camisa de la suerte; **it's your l. day !**, hoy estás de suerte; **to be born l.**, haber nacido,-a con buena estrella; **to have a l. escape**, escaparse por los pelos; **you'll be l. to get the job**, no veo muy claro que consigas el trabajo; *fig* **third time l.**, a la tercera va la vencida; *fam* **l. you!, l. devil!**, ¡que suerte tienes!; *fam* **l. you phoned when you did**, menos mal que llamaste; *fam fig* **to thank one's l. stars**, dar gracias a Dios; *fam iron* **you'll be l.!, you should be so l.!**, ¡ya veremos! ▪ *GB* **l. dip**, caja *f* de las sorpresas. ◆ **luckily** *adv* por suerte afortunadamente.

lucrative ['luːkrətɪv] *adj* lucrativo,-a.

ludicrous ['luːdɪkrəs] *adj* absurdo,-a, ridículo,-a.

ludo ['luːdəʊ] *n (game)* parchís *m*.

lug [lʌg] *vtr (pt & pp lugged) fam (heave)* arrastrar, transportar con dificultad.

luggage ['lʌgɪdʒ] *n* equipaje *m*. ▪ **l. rack,** *Aut* baca *f*, portaequipajes *m inv*; *Rail* red *f* redecilla *f*; *Rail* **l. van,** furgón *m* de equipaje.

lughole ['lʌghəʊl] *n usu pl GB fam* oreja *f*.

lugubrious [lʊ'guːbrɪəs] *adj lit* lúgubre.

lukewarm ['luːkwɔːm] *adj (water etc)* tibio,-a; *fig (reception etc)* poco entusiasta.

lull [lʌl] **I** *n (in storm, wind)* calma *f*, recalmón *m*; *(in activity, fighting)* respiro *m*, tregua *f*; *fig* **the l. before the storm**, una tensa calma que anuncia la tempestad. **II** *vtr (cause to sleep, relax, etc)* adormecer; *(deceive)* **to l. sb into a false sense of security**, infundir una falsa seguridad a algn.

lullaby ['lʌləbaɪ] *n* canción *f* de cuna, nana *f*, arrullo *m*.

lumbago [lʌm'beɪgəʊ] *n Med* lumbago *m*.

lumbar ['lʌmbə'] *adj Anat* lumbar.

lumber ['lʌmbə'] **I** *n* **1** *GB (junk)* trastos *mpl* viejos. ▪ **l. room**, trastero *m*. **2** *US (timber)* maderos *mpl*, madera *f*. **II** *vtr* **1** *(encumber)* abarrotar, atestar **(with,** de). **2** *fam* cargar **(with,** de); **he lumbered me with his little brother**, tuve que cargar con el hermano pequeño. **2** *US (fell) (trees)* talar. **III** *vi* **to l.** *(about or along)*, *(move clumsily)* moverse pesadamente.

lumberjack ['lʌmbədʒæk] *n* leñador *m*.

lumberyard ['lʌmbəjɑːd] *n* almacén *m* de madera.

luminary ['luːmɪnərɪ] *n lit* luminario,-a *m,f*.

luminosity [luːmɪ'nɒsɪtɪ] *n lit* luminosidad *f*.

luminous ['luːmɪnəs] *adj* luminoso,-a.

lump [lʌmp] **I** *n* **1** *(of coal etc)* trozo *m*, pedazo *m*; *(of sugar, earth)* terrón *m*; *(in sauce)* grumo *m*; *Med (swelling)* bulto *m*, protuberancia *f*; *fam fig (in throat)* nudo *m*. ▪ **l. sum**, cantidad *f* global, suma *f* global. **2** *fam (person)* bobo,-a *m,f*. **II** *vtr fam (endure)* aguantar; **he'll just have to l. it**, que se aguante. ◆ **lump together** *vtr* juntar, agrupar, amontonar.

lumpy ['lʌmpɪ] *adj (lumpier, lumpiest) (bed)* lleno,-a de bultos; *(sauce)* grumoso,-a lleno,-a de grumos; *Culin* **to go l.**, hacerse grumos.

lunacy ['luːnəsɪ] *n* locura *f*; *fam* **it's sheer l.!**, ¡es una locura!

lunar ['luːnə'] *adj* lunar. ▪ **l. eclipse**, eclipse *m* lunar; *Astronaut* **l. landing**, alunizaje *m*; **l. month**, mes *m* lunar.

lunatic ['luːnətɪk] *adj & n* loco,-a *(m, f)*. ▪ **l. asylum**, manicomio *m*; *pej* **the l. fringe**, el sector más radical *y* fanático.

lunch [lʌnʃ] **I** n comida f, almuerzo m; **to have l.,** comer, almorzar. ■ **l. hour,** hora f de comer; GB **pub l.,** comida f servida en pub. **II** vi comer, almorzar.

luncheon ['lʌntʃən] n arch fml comida f, almuerzo m. ■ **l. voucher,** vale m de comida; **(pork) l. meat,** carne f de cerdo troceada, chopped m.

lunchtime ['lʌntʃtaɪm] n hora f de comer or del almuerzo.

lung [lʌŋ] n pulmón m. ■ Med **iron l.,** pulmón m de acero; **l. cancer,** cáncer m del pulmón.

lunge [lʌndʒ] **I** n **1** arremetida f, embestida f. **2** Fenc estocada f. **II** vi **1** (also **l. forward**) arremeter, lanzarse; **to l. (out) at sb,** arremeter contra algn, abalanzarse sobre algn. **2** Fenc atacar.

lupin, US **lupine** ['luːpɪn] n Bot altramuz m, lupino m.

lurch [lɜːtʃ] **I** n **1** (of vehicle) sacudida f, bandazo m; (person) tambaleo m. **2** fam **to leave sb in the l.,** dejar plantado,-a a algn. **II** vi (vehicle) dar sacudidas, dar bandazos; (person) tambalearse; **to l. along,** (vehicle) ir dando sacudidas or bandazos; (person) ir tambaleándose.

lure [luəʳ] **I** n **1** (decoy) señuelo m; (bait) cebo m. **2** fig (charm) aliciente m, atractivo m. **II** vtr atraer or convencer con engaños; **nothing could l. him away from the game,** era imposible distraerlo del partido.

lurid ['luərɪd] adj **1** (gruesome) espeluznante, horripilante. **2** (sensational) sensacionalista. **3** (gaudy) chillón,-ona.

lurk [lɜːk] vi **1** (lie in wait) estar al acecho. **2** (hidden) esconderse, estar escondido,-a; fig **a doubt still lurked in his mind,** aún le atormentaba una duda.

luscious ['lʌʃəs] adj (food) delicioso,-a, exquisito,-a; (person) encantador,-a.

lush [lʌʃ] adj (vegetation) exuberante; (places, life, etc) lujoso,-a.

lust [lʌst] **I** n **1** (sexual desire) lujuria f. **2** (craving) ansia f; (greed) codicia f. **II** vi **to l. after sth/sb,** codiciar algo/ desear a algn.

luster ['lʌstəʳ] n US see **lustre**.

lustful ['lʌstful] adj lujurioso,-a, lascivo,-a; (look) lleno,-a de deseo.

lustre ['lʌstəʳ] n lustre m, brillo m.

lustrous ['lʌstrəs] adj lustroso,-a, brillante.

lusty ['lʌstɪ] adj (lustier, lustiest) (person) fuerte, robusto,-a; (cry) fuerte.

lute [luːt] n Mus laúd m.

lutist ['luːtɪst] n tañedor,-a m, f de laúd.

Lutheranism ['luːθərənɪzəm] n Hist luteranismo m.

Luxembourg ['lʌksəmbɜːg] n Luxemburgo.

Luxembourger ['lʌksəmbɜːgəʳ] n luxemburgués,-esa m, f.

luxuriance [lʌg'zjuərɪəns] n (plants) exuberancia f; (hair etc) abundancia f.

luxuriant [lʌg'zjuərɪənt] adj (plants) exuberante; (hair etc) abundante.

luxuriate [lʌg'zjuərɪeɪt] vi disfrutar; **to l. in,** deleitarse con.

luxurious [lʌg'zjuərɪəs] adj lujoso,-a, de lujo.

luxury ['lʌkʃərɪ] n **1** (gen) lujo m; **l. flat,** piso m de lujo. ■ **l. goods,** artículos mpl de lujo. **2** (article) artículo m de lujo.

LW Rad abbr of **long wave,** onda f larga. OL f.

lychee ['laɪtʃiː] n lichi m.

lying ['laɪɪŋ] **I** adj mentiroso,-a, falso,-a. **II** n mentira f, mentiras fpl.

lymph [lɪmf] n Anat linfa f. ■ **l. gland,** glándula f linfática.

lymphatic [lɪm'fætɪk] adj linfático,-a.

lynch [lɪntʃ] vtr linchar.

lynching ['lɪntʃɪŋ] n linchamiento m.

lynx [lɪŋks] n Zool lince m.

lynx-eyed ['lɪŋksaɪd] adj con ojos de lince.

lyre [laɪəʳ] n Mus lira f.

lyric ['lɪrɪk] **I** adj lírico,-a. **II** n **1** (poem) poema m lírico. **2** **lyrics,** (words of song) letra f sing.

lyrical ['lɪrɪkəl] adj lírico,-a; fam **to wax l. about sth,** entusiasmarse por algo.

lyricism ['lɪrɪsɪzəm] n lirismo m.

lyricist ['lɪrɪsɪst] n letrista mf.

M

M, m [em] n (the letter) M, m f.

M 1 (on clothes etc) abbr of **medium (size)**, (talla f) mediana. **2** [em] GB abbr of **motorway,** autopista f, A f.

m 1 (on forms etc) abbr of **male,** varón m, v. **2** (on forms etc) abbr of **married,** casado,-a, c. **3** (also masc) Ling abbr of **masculine,** masculino m, m. **4** (distance, radio) abbr of **metre(s),** metro(s) m(pl), m. **5** abbr of **million(s),** millón m, millones mpl, m.

MA [em'eɪ] abbr of **Master of Arts.**

ma [mɑː] n fam (mother) mamá f.

ma'am [mæm, mɑːm] n fml señora f.

macabre [mə'kɑːbrə] adj macabro,-a.

macaroon [mækə'ruːn] n Culin mostachón m.

macaw [mə'kɔː] n Orn guacamayo m, ara m.

mac(c)aroni [mækə'rəʊnɪ] n Culin macarrones mpl. ■ **m. cheese,** macarrones mpl al gratén.

mace¹ [meɪs] n (club, ceremonial staff) maza f. ■ **m. bearer,** macero m.

mace² [meɪs] n (spice) macis f inv.

macerate ['mæsəreɪt] **I** vtr macerar. **II** vi macerarse.

maceration [mæsə'reɪʃən] n maceración f.

Mach [mæk, mɑːk] n Av **M. (number),** (número m de) Mach m.

machete [mə'tʃeɪtɪ] n machete m.

Machiavellian [mækɪə'velɪən] adj maquiavélico,-a.

machinations [mækɪ'neɪʃənz] npl intrigas fpl, maquinaciones fpl.

machine [mə'ʃiːn] **I** n (gen) máquina f, aparato m; (machinery) maquinaria f; fig **they treat you like machines,** te tratan como si fueras una máquina. ■ **drinks m.,** distribuidor m automático de bebidas; **fruit m.,** máquina f tragaperras; **m. gun,** ametralladora f; Comput **m. language,** lenguaje m máquina **m. shop,** taller m de máquinas; **m. tool,** máquina f herramienta; **sewing m.,** máquina f de coser; **washing m.,** lavadora f. **II** vtr Tech trabajar a máquina; Sew coser a máquina.

machine-gun [mə'ʃiːngʌn] vtr (pt & pp **machine-gunned**) ametrallar.

machine-readable [məʃiːn'riːdəbəl] adj Comput (text, data) para ser leído,-a en máquina.

machinery [mə'ʃiːnərɪ] n (machines) maquinaria f; (workings of machine) mecanismo m; fig **the bureaucratic m.,** la maquinaria burocrática.

machinist [mə'ʃiːnɪst] *n Tech* operario,-a *m, f*, mecánico,-a *m,f.*

macho ['mætʃəʊ] **I** *adj (virile etc)* viril, macho; *(male chauvinist)* machista. **II** *n (pl machos)* macho *m*; *pej* machista *m.*

mac(k) [mæk] *n GB fam abbr of* **mackintosh**

mackerel ['mækrəl] *n (pl mackerel or mackerels) (fish)* caballa *f.*

mac(k)intosh ['mækɪntɒʃ] *n* impermeable *m.*

macramé [mə'krɑːmɪ] *n* macramé *m.*

macrobiotic [mækrəʊbaɪ'ɒtɪk] *adj* macrobiótico,-a.

macrocosm ['mækrəkɒzəm] *n* macrocosmo *m.*

macroeconomics [mækrəʊiːkə'nɒmɪks] *n* macroeconomía *f.*

mad [mæd] *adj (madder, maddest)* **1** *(insane)* loco,-a, demente; *fig* loco,-a; *(animal)* furioso,-a *(dog)* rabioso,-a; **to be m.**, estar loco,-a; **to drive sb m.,** volver loco,-a a algn; **to go m.,** volverse loco,-a, enloquecer; **you must be m.!,** ¿estás loco?; **as m. as a hatter** *or* **as a March hare,** más loco que una cabra. **2** *(foolish)* loco,-a; *(idea, plan)* disparatado,-a, insensato,-a. **3** *fam (enthusiastic)* chiflado,-a; **to be m. about** *or* **on sth/sb,** estar loco,-a por algo/algn, chiflarse por algo/algn. **4** *fam (angry)* enfadado,-a; **hopping m.,** furioso,-a; **to be m. with** *or* **at sb,** estar enfadado,-a con algn. **5** *(wild, uncontrolled) (gallop, race, etc)* desenfrenado,-a, frenético,-a; **to be in a m. rush,** ir como un loco, ir a toda prisa. ◆ **madly** *adv* **1** *(gen)* como un loco, locamente. **2** *(hurriedly)* apresuradamente, precipitadamente; *(frantically)* desesperadamente. **3** *fam (intensely, extremely)* terriblemente; **it's m. expensive,** es carísimo; **to be m. in love with sb,** estar locamente *or* perdidamente enamorado,-a de algn.

madam ['mædəm] *n* **1** señora *f*; *(in letter)* **Dear M.,** Muy señora mía, Estimada señora. **2** *(brothel-keeper)* patrona *f*, ama *f.* **3** *fam (girl)* **a little m.,** una niña precoz; *pej* una niña sabihonda.

madcap ['mædkæp] *adj (idea, plan, etc)* disparatado,-a, descabellado-a.

madden ['mædən] *vtr (infuriate)* volver loco,-a, enfurecer.

maddening ['mædənɪŋ] *adv (infuriating)* exasperante, enloquecedor; **it's m.,** es para volverse loco,-a.

made [meɪd] *pt & pp see* **make.**

Madeira [mə'dɪərə] *n* **1** *(island)* Madeira. **2** *(wine)* madeira *m*, madera *m.* ■ *Culin* **M. cake,** bizcocho *m.*

made-to-measure [meɪdtə'meʒəʳ] *adj (suit, curtains, etc)* hecho,-a a (la) medida.

made-up ['meɪdʌp] *adj* **1** *(face, person)* maquillado,-a; *(eyes, lips)* pintado,-a. **2** *(story, excuse)* inventado,-a.

madhouse ['mædhaʊs] *n fam (mental hospital)* manicomio *m*; *fig* casa *f* de locos.

madman ['mædmən] *n (pl madmen)* loco *m.*

madness ['mædnɪs] *n (insanity)* locura *f*, demencia *f*; *fig* locura *f*; **it's sheer m.,** es una locura *or* un desvarío.

Madonna [mə'dɒnə] *n* Virgen *f.*

madrigal ['mædrɪgəl] *n Mus* madrigal *m.*

madwoman ['mædwʊmən] *n (pl madwomen* ['mædwɪmɪn]*)* loca *f.*

maelstrom ['meɪlstrəʊm] *n* remolino *m*, torbellino *m.*

maestro ['maɪstrəʊ] *n (pl maestros)* maestro *m.*

Mafia ['mæfɪə] *n* mafia *f.*

mag [mæg] *n (abbr of magazine) fam* revista *f.*

magazine [mægə'ziːn] *n* **1** *(periodical)* revista *f.* **2** *(in rifle)* recámara *f.* **3** *Mil (storehouse)* almacén *m*; *(for explosives)* polvorín *m*; *Naut* santabárbara *f*, pañol *m* de municiones.

magenta [mə'dʒentə] **I** *n* magenta *f.* **II** *adj (de color)* magenta *inv.*

maggot ['mægət] *n Zool* larva *f*, cresa *f*, gusano *m.*

maggoty ['mægətɪ] *adj* agusanado,-a, gusaniento,-a.

Magi ['meɪdʒaɪ] *npl Rel* **the M.,** los Reyes Magos.

magic ['mædʒɪk] **I** *n* magia *f*; **as if by m.,** como por arte de magia. ■ **black m.,** magia *f* negra. **II** *adj* **1** mágico,-a; **m. spell,** hechizo *m*, encanto *m*. ■ **m. wand,** varita *f* mágica. **2** *fam (wonderful)* estupendo,-a, fantástico,-a.

magical ['mædʒɪkəl] *adj* mágico,-a.

magician [mə'dʒɪʃən] *n* **1** *(wizard)* mago,-a *m, f.* **2** *(conjuror)* prestigiditador,-a *m, f*, ilusionista *mf.*

magisterial [mædʒɪ'stɪərɪəl] *adj* magistral.

magistrate ['mædʒɪstreɪt] *n Jur* magistrado,-a *m, f*, juez *mf.* ■ **magistrates' court,** juzgado *m* de primera instancia.

magnanimity [mægnə'nɪmɪtɪ] *n* magnanimidad *f.*

magnanimous [mæg'nænɪməs] *adj* magnánimo,-a.

magnate ['mægneɪt] *n* magnate *m.*

magnesia [mæg'niːʒə] *n Chem* magnesia *f.*

magnesium [mæg'niːzɪəm] *n Chem* magnesio *m.*

magnet ['mægnɪt] *n* imán *m.*

magnetic [mæg'netɪk] *adj (force, field, etc)* magnético,-a; *fig (personality)* carismático,-a, magnético,-a. ■ **m. compass,** brújula *f*; **m. field,** campo *m* magnético; **m. north,** norte *m* magnético; **m. tape,** cinta *f* magnetofónica.

magnetism ['mægnɪtɪzəm] *n (force)* magnetismo *m*; *fig (of personality)* magnetismo *m*, carisma *m.*

magnetize ['mægnɪtaɪz] *vtr (object)* magnetizar, imanar, imantar; *fig (person)* magnetizar.

magnification [mægnɪfɪ'keɪʃən] *n* aumento m, ampliación *f.*

magnificence [mæg'nɪfɪsəns] *n* magnificencia *f*, esplendor *m.*

magnificent [mæg'nɪfɪsənt] *adj* magníco,-a, espléndido,-a; *(sumptuous)* suntuoso,-a.

magnify ['mægnɪfaɪ] *vtr (pt & pp magnified)* **1** *(enlarge)* aumentar, ampliar. **2** *fig (exaggerate)* exagerar.

magnifying glass ['mægnɪfaɪɪŋglɑːs] *n* lupa *f.*

magnitude ['mægnɪtjuːd] *n (gen)* magnitud *f*; *fig (importance)* magnitud *f*, envergadura *f*; **a problem of the first m.,** un problema de mucha envergadura.

magnolia [mæg'nəʊlɪə] *n Bot* **1** *(tree)* magnolio *m.* **2** *(flower)* magnolia *f.*

magpie ['mægpaɪ] *n Orn* urraca *f.*

mahogany [mə'hɒgənɪ] **I** *n* caoba *f.* **II** *adj* de caoba.

maid [meɪd] *n* **1** *(servant)* criada *f*, sirvienta *f*, *Am* mucama *f*; *(in hotel)* camarera *f.* ■ **m. of honour,** dama *f* de honor. **2** *lit (young girl)* doncella *f*; *pej* **old m.,** solterona *f.*

maiden ['meɪdən] **I** *n lit (young girl)* doncella *f.* **II** *adj* **1** *(unmarried)* soltera; **m. aunt,** tía soltera. ■ **m. name,** apellido *m* de soltera. **2** *(voyage, flight)* inaugural. ■ *Parl* **m. speech,** primer discurso *m* (de un parlamentario en el Parlamento).

mail¹ [meɪl] **I** *n* correo *m*; **by m.,** por correo. ■ **air m.,** correo *m* aéreo; *Com* **m. order,** venta *f* por correo; **m. train,** tren *m* correo. **II** *vtr (post)* echar al buzón; *(send)* enviar *or* mandar por correo.

mail² [meɪl] *n* malla *f.* ■ **coat of m.,** cota *f* de malla.

mailbag ['meɪlbæg] *n* valija *f*, saca *f* de correo.

mailbox ['meɪlbɒks] *n US* buzón *m.*

mailing list ['meɪlɪŋlɪst] *n Com* lista *f* de direcciones.

mailmen ['meɪlmæn] *n (pl mailmen* ['meɪlmen]*) US* cartero *m.*

maim [meɪm] *vtr* mutilar, lisiar.

main [meɪn] **I** *adj (problem, idea, floor, door, etc)* principal; *(square, mast, sail)* mayor; *(office)* central; **the m. body of the army,** el grueso del ejército; **the m. thing**

is to keep calm, lo esencial *or* lo más importante es mantener la calma. ■ *Archit* **m. beam,** viga *f* maestra; *Culin* **m. course,** plato *m* principal; *Aut* **m. road,** carretera *f* principal; **m. street,** calle *f* mayor. II **n** 1 *(pipe, wire)* conducto *m* principal; *(sewer)* colector *m;* **the mains,** *(water or gas system)* cañería *f* principal *or* maestra; *Elec* la red eléctrica; **a radio that works on battery or mains,** una radio que funciona con pilas o con corriente; **to turn off the water at the mains,** cerrar la llave principal del agua. 2 **in the m.,** *(on the whole)* en general, por regla general; *(for the most part)* en su mayoría. ◆ **mainly** *adv (chiefly)* principalmente, sobre todo; *(for the most part)* en su mayoría.

mainframe ['meɪnfreɪm] *n Comput* **m. computer,** unidad *f* central, torre *f.*

mainland ['meɪnlənd] *n* continente *m;* **m. Europe,** la Europa continental; **to reach the m.,** llegar a tierra firme.

main-line ['meɪnlaɪn] *adj Rail (train, station)* interurbano,-a.

mainsail ['meɪnseɪl] *n Naut* vela *f* mayor.

mainspring ['meɪnsprɪŋ] *n (of clock)* muelle *m* real; *fig* motivo *m or* razón *f* principal.

mainstay ['meɪnsteɪ] *n Naut* estay *m* mayor; *fig* sustento *m,* sostén *m.*

mainstream ['meɪnstriːm] *n* corriente *f* principal; **m. ideology,** la manera de pensar convencional, la ideología dominante.

maintain [meɪn'teɪn] *vtr* 1 *(preserve) (order, balance)* mantener; *(living standard, conversation)* sostener; *(silence, appearances)* guardar; *(custom)* conservar; *(road, building, car, machine)* conservar en buen estado. 2 *(support one's family etc)* mantener, sustentar. 3 *(claim, assert)* mantener, sostener; **she maintains that it is untrue,** sostiene que no es verdad.

maintenance ['meɪntənəns] *n* 1 *(gen)* mantenimiento *m.* ■ **m. costs,** gastos *mpl* de mantenimiento; **m. man,** encargado *m* de mantenimiento. 2 *Jur (divorce allowance)* pensión *f.*

maisonette [meɪzə'net] *n* dúplex *m.*

maize [meɪz] *n* maíz *m.*

majestic [mə'dʒestɪk] *adj* majestuoso,-a.

majesty ['mædʒɪstɪ] *n* majestad *f;* **Her M. the Queen,** Su Graciosa Majestad.

major ['meɪdʒəʳ] **I** *adj* 1 *(gen)* principal, mayor; *(contribution, operation)* importante, considerable; *(issue)* de mucha envergadura; *(illness)* grave. 2 *Mus (scale etc)* mayor; **in C m.,** en do mayor. II **n** 1 *Mil* comandante *m.* ■ **m. general,** general *m* de división. 2 *US Univ* especialidad *f.* III *vi US Univ* **to m. in,** especializarse en; **he wants to m. in medieval literature,** quiere especializarse en literatura medieval.

Majorca [mə'dʒɔːkə] *n* Mallorca.

Majorcan [mə'dʒɔːkən] *adj & n* mallorquín,-ina *(m,f).*

majority [mə'dʒɒrɪtɪ] *n* 1 mayoría *f;* **he won by a m. vote,** ganó por mayoría; **in the m. of cases,** en la mayoría de los casos. ■ *Pol* **m. rule,** gobierno *m* mayoritario. 2 *Jur* **age of m.,** mayoría *f* de edad.

make [meɪk] *(pt & pp* **made) I** *vtr* 1 *(gen)* hacer; *(build)* construir; *(manufacture)* fabricar, elaborar; *(create)* crear; *(clothes, curtains)* confeccionar; *(meal)* preparar; *(plans, journey, statement)* hacer; *(payment)* efectuar; *(speech)* pronunciar; *(decision)* tomar; *(mistake)* cometer; **'made in Ireland',** 'fabricado en Irlanda'; **made of gold,** de oro; **to be made of,** estar hecho,-a *or* compuesto,-a de, ser de; **to m. a noise,** hacer ruido; **to m. love,** hacer el amor **(to,** con); *fig* **to m. a clean breast of sth,** confesar algo. 2 *(render)* hacer, poner, volver; *(convert)* convertir, transformar **(into,** en); *(appoint)* hacer, nombrar; **he made it clear that ...,** dejó claro que ...; **it makes me sad,** me pone triste; **it makes you look taller,** te hace (parecer) más alto; **m. yourself at home,** estás en tu casa; **to m. a fool of sb,** dejar *or* poner en

ridículo a algn; **to m. sb happy,** hacer feliz a algn. 3 *(force, compel)* hacer, obligar; *(cause)* hacer, causar; **to m. do with sth,** arreglárselas con algo; **to m. sb do sth,** obligar a algn a hacer algo; **what makes you say that?,** ¿por qué dices eso? 4 *(earn)* ganar; *(profits)* sacar; **he makes £200 a week,** gana 200 libras a la semana; **to m. a living,** ganarse la vida; **to m. a name for oneself,** hacerse famoso,-a; *fig* **to m. the best of sth,** sacar partido de algo. 5 *(have qualities of)* ser, servir de; **it makes interesting reading,** es interesante de leer; **she'll m. a good teacher,** será una buena profesora. 6 *(amount to)* ser, hacer, equivaler a; **5 and 5 m. 10,** 5 y 5 son 10. 7 *(calculate, reckon)* calcular; **I m. it £20 in all,** calculo que son 20 libras en total; **what time do you m. it?,** ¿qué hora tienes? 8 *(think)* pensar, opinar; **what do you m. of his behaviour?,** ¿qué te parece su conducta? 9 **I don't know what to m. of it,** no lo acabo de entender; **it doesn't m. sense,** no tiene sentido. 9 *(reach)* alcanzar, llegar a; *(achieve)* alcanzar, conseguir; **she's made it!,** ¡lo ha conseguido!; **we just made it to the airport,** llegamos al aeropuerto con el tiempo justo; *sl* **to m. it with sb,** conseguir acostarse con algn. 10 *(assure future or success of)* **it will m. or break her,** será su consagración o su ruina; **that novel made him,** esa novela lo consagró; **you've got it made!,** ¡tienes el éxito asegurado! 11 **to m. an early start,** empezar temprano; **to m. a fresh start,** volver a empezar. II *vi* 1 *(gen)* hacer; **to m. certain** *or* **sure of sth,** asegurarse de algo; **to m. good,** triunfar; **to m. merry,** divertirse. 2 *(move)* dirigirse; **to m. after sb,** perseguir a algn; **to m. at sb,** abalanzarse sobre algn; **to m. towards a place,** dirigirse hacia un lugar. 3 *(appear to)* hacer como, simular; **she made as if to leave,** hizo como si quisiera marcharse. III *n* 1 *(brand)* marca *f;* **of German m.,** de fabricación alemana. 2 *fam* **to be on the m.,** *(seeking profit)* andar tras el dinero; *(seeking success)* ir a por todas; *(full of self-interest)* barrer para adentro; *(in search of sex)* andar buscando aventuras. ◆ **make for** *vtr* 1 *(move towards)* dirigirse hacia; *(attack)* atacar a, abalanzarse sobre. 2 *(result in)* crear; *(contribute to)* contribuir a; **this makes for less work,** esto genera menos trabajo. ◆ **make out I** *vtr* 1 *(write out) (list, receipt)* hacer; *(report)* redactar; *(cheque)* extender. 2 *(see, perceive)* distinguir, divisar; *(writing)* descifrar. 3 *(understand)* comprender, entender. 4 *(claim)* pretender; **she made out that she was a nurse,** se hizo pasar por enfermera. 5 *(present)* presentar; **to m. out a case for doing sth,** presentar sus argumentos para hacer algo. II *vi (manage)* arreglárselas, apañárselas; *(get on)* **how did you m. out?,** ¿qué tal te fue? ◆ **make up I** *vtr* 1 *(put together) (parcel, list)* hacer; *(prescription, bed)* preparar; *(dress, curtains)* confeccionar, hacer; *Typ (page)* componer; *(assemble)* montar; **to m. sth up into a parcel,** empaquetar algo. 2 *(invent)* inventar; **the whole thing is made up!,** ¡es puro cuento! 3 *(apply cosmetics to)* maquillar; *(one's face)* maquillarse, pintarse; **to m. oneself up,** maquillarse, pintarse. 4 *(complete quantity, sum)* completar. 5 *(compensate for) (loss)* compensar; *(deficit)* cubrir; *(lack)* suplir; *(lost time, ground)* recuperar. 6 *(constitute)* componer, integrar, formar; *(represent)* representar; **the committee is made up of six teachers,** el comité está compuesto de seis profesores; **they m. up 10 per cent of the population,** representan un 10 por ciento de la población. 7 **to m. up a quarrel, m. it up (with sb),** hacer las paces (con algn), reconciliarse (con algn). 8 **to m. up one's mind,** decidirse. II *vi* 1 *(friends)* hacer las paces, reconciliarse. 2 *(apply cosmetics)* maquillarse, pintarse. ◆ **make up for** *vtr (loss, damage)* compensar; *(lost time)* recuperar; *(lack)* suplir. ◆ **make up to** *vtr* 1 **to m. up to sb,** *(try to gain favour with)* congraciarse con algn; *(flatter)* halagar a algn. 2 **to m. it up to sb for sth,** compensar *or* indemnizar a algn por algo.

make-believe ['meɪkbɪliːv] **I** *n (fantasy)* fantasía *f,* invención *f; (pretence)* simulación *f,* fingimiento *m;* **that story is just m.-b.,** esa historia es pura fantasía; **to live in**

a world of m.-b., vivir en un mundo de ensueño. **II** adj (world) imaginario,-a, falso,-a; (game, toy) de mentirijillas.

maker ['meɪkə'] n 1 (manufacturer) fabricante mf; (builder) constructor,-a m,f, **the makers,** los fabricantes, la fábrica. **2 the M.,** el Creador; euph **to meet one's M.,** morirse.

makeshift ['meɪkʃɪft] adj (improvised) improvisado,-a; (temporary) provisional, temporal.

make-up ['meɪkʌp] n 1 (cosmetics) maquillaje m. ■ **m.-up bag,** neceser m; **m.-up remover,** desmaquillador m. **2** (composition) (of team etc) composición f; (structure) estructura f; (character) carácter m, temperamento m. **3** Print (of page, book) compaginación f. **4** Sew confección f.

making ['meɪkɪŋ] n 1 (manufacture) fabricación f; (of clothes) confección f; (of bridge, machinery, etc) construcción f; (of post) creación f; (preparation) preparación f, elaboración f; **it is history in the m.,** eso pasará a la historia; **the film was three years in the m.,** se tardó tres años en hacer la película; **the novel was the m. of her,** la novela marcó el inicio de su éxito. **2 to have the makings of ...,** tener las características para llegar a ser ...; **he has the makings of a politician,** tiene madera de político.

malachite ['mæləkaɪt] n Min malaquita f.

maladjusted [mælə'dʒʌstɪd] adj Psych inadaptado,-a.

maladjustment [mælə'dʒʌstmənt] n Psych inadaptación f.

malady ['mælədɪ] n mal m, enfermedad f.

malaise [mæ'leɪz] n Med & fig malestar m.

malapropism ['mæləprɒpɪzəm] n equivocación f de palabras; (on purpose) equívoco m.

malaria [mə'leərɪə] n Med paludismo m, malaria f.

Malay [mə'leɪ] **I** adj malayo,-a. **II** n 1 (person) malayo,-a m,f. **2** (language) malayo m.

Malaysia [mə'leɪzɪə] n Malasia.

Malaysian [mə'leɪzɪən] adj & n malasio,-a (m,f).

male [meɪl] **I** adj (animal, plant) macho; (person, child) varón; (sex) masculino; Tech (screw, plug) macho; (ward, attire) de hombres; (manly) varonil, viril. ■ pej **m. chauvinism,** machismo m; **m. nurse,** enfermero m. **II** n (person) varón m; (animal, plant) macho m.

malevolence [mə'levələns] n malevolencia f.

malevolent [mə'levələnt] adj malévolo,-a.

malformation [mælfɔː'meɪʃən] n malformación f, deformidad f.

malformed [mæl'fɔːmd] adj malformado,-a, deforme.

malfunction [mæl'fʌŋkʃən] **I** n mal funcionamiento m, funcionamiento m defectuoso. **II** vi funcionar mal or defectuosamente.

malice ['mælɪs] n (wickedness) malicia f; (evil intent) maldad f; (bitterness) rencor m; **to bear sb m.,** guardar rencor a algn; Jur **with m. aforethought,** con premeditación.

malicious [mə'lɪʃəs] adj (wicked) malévolo,-a; (bitter) rencoroso,-a.

malign [mə'laɪn] **I** adj maligno,-a, malévolo,-a; (influence) perjudicial. **II** vtr (slander) calumniar, difamar, hablar mal de.

malignant [mə'lɪgnənt] adj 1 (person) malvado,-a, malo,-a; (influence) maligno,-a; (action) perjudicial. **2** Med (tumour, disease) maligno,-a.

malinger [mə'lɪŋgə'] vi fingirse enfermo,-a.

malingerer [mə'lɪŋgərə'] n enfermo,-a. m, f fingido,-a, calandria mf.

mall [mɔːl, mæl] n US (shopping centre) centro m comercial (peatonal).

mallard ['mælɑːd] n (pl mallard or mallards) Orn ánade m real.

malleable ['mælɪəbəl] adj (metal) maleable; fig (person) dócil.

mallet ['mælɪt] n mazo m.

mallow ['mæləʊ] n Bot malva f.

malnourished [mæl'nʌrɪʃt] adj desnutrido,-a.

malnutrition [mælnjuː'trɪʃən] n desnutrición f.

malpractice [mæl'præktɪs] n Jur procedimiento m ilegal; Med negligencia f.

malt [mɔːlt] **I** n (grain) malta f. ■ **m. whisky,** whisky m de malta. **II** vtr (grain) hacer germinar.

Malta ['mɔːltə] n Malta.

malted ['mɔːltɪd] adj malteado,-a.

Maltese [mɔːl'tiːz] adj & n maltés,-esa (m,f).

mammal ['mæməl] n Zool mamífero m.

mammary ['mæmərɪ] adj Anat mamario,-a. ■ **m. gland,** mama f.

mammography [mæ'mɒgrəfɪ] n mamografía f.

mammoth ['mæməθ] **I** n Zool mamut m. **II** adj (huge) descomunal, gigantesco,-a; Com **'m. reductions',** 'super rebajas'.

mammy ['mæmɪ] n esp Ir & US fam mamá f.

Man [mæn] n **the Isle of M.,** la Isla de Man.

man [mæn] **I** n (pl men) **1** (adult male person) hombre m; **old m.,** viejo m; US **the men's room,** el servicio de caballeros; **the navy will make a m. of him,** la marina le hará un hombre; **young m.,** joven m; fig **a m. about town,** un gran vividor; fig **a m. of the world,** un hombre de mundo; fig **the m. in the street,** el hombre de la calle; fig **to be a family m.,** (with children etc) ser padre de familia; (home-loving) ser muy casero; fig **to be m. enough for ...,** ser lo suficientemente hombre como para ... . ■ **best m.,** padrino m de boda; **m. Friday,** factótum m; fam **dirty old m.,** viejo m verde. **2** (humanity) **M.,** el Hombre; (person) hombre m; (human being) ser m humano; **all men are equal,** todos los hombres son iguales. ■ **Stone Age m.,** el hombre de la Edad de Piedra. **3** (person, type) hombre m, persona f; **he's a Bristol m.,** es de Bristol; **he's the best m. for the job,** es el más indicado para el puesto; fig **as one m.,** todos a la vez; fig **he's a m. of his word,** es hombre de palabra; fig **they are patriots to a m.,** todos sin excepción son patriotas; fig **to be one's own m.,** ser dueño de sí mismo. **4** (husband) hombre m, marido m; (boyfriend) compañero m; (partner) pareja f; **to live together as m. and wife,** vivir como marido y mujer. **5** (male worker) hombre m, empleado m; (in factory) obrero m; (servant) criado m; (butler) mayordomo m; (soldier) soldado m; **our m. in Madrid,** nuestro representante en Madrid; fig **right-hand m.,** brazo m derecho. **6** Chess pieza f; Draughts ficha f. **II** vtr (pt & pp manned) (boat, plane) tripular; (post) servir; (gun) manejar; **m. the lifeboats!,** ¡todos a los botes!; **manned flight,** vuelo m tripulado; **the telephone is manned 24 hours a day,** el teléfono está en servicio las 24 horas del día. **III** interj fam ¡hombre!, ¡tío!, ¡macho!

manacles ['mænəkəlz] npl esposas fpl, grillos mpl.

manage ['mænɪdʒ] **I** vtr **1** (company) dirigir, llevar, administrar; (property) administrar; (household) llevar; (money, affairs) manejar; (child, person) llevar, manejar; (animal) domar. **2** (succeed) conseguir; **to m. to do sth,** lograr hacer algo; **to m. to get sth,** conseguir algo; **can you m. to do it?,** ¿lo puedes hacer? **II** vi **1** (cope physically) poder; **can you m.?,** ¿puedes con eso?; **could you m. another piece of cake?,** ¿te apetece otro trozo de pastel?; **I can m., thanks,** ya puedo, gracias. **2** (cope esp financially) arreglárselas, apañárselas; **to m. on very little money,** arreglárselas or apañarse con muy poco dinero; **to m. without sth,** prescindir de algo; **we're managing,** vamos tirando.

manageable ['mænɪdʒəbəl] adj manejable.

management ['mænɪdʒmənt] n 1 (of company, project, etc) dirección f, administración f, gestión f. ■ **m. studies,**

administración *f* de empresas. **2** *(people in charge)* dirección *f*, gerencia *f*; *(board of directors)* junta *f* directiva, consejo *m* de administración; **the M. and the workers,** la patronal y los trabajadores; **under new m.,** bajo nueva dirección.

manager ['mænɪdʒə'] *n* **1** *(of company, bank)* director,-a *m,f*, gerente *mf*; *(of estate)* administrador,-a *m,f*; *(head of department)* jefe,-a *m, f*. **2** *(of actor, pop group, etc)* manager *m*. **3** *Sport (of football team)* director *m* técnico, manager *m*; *(trainer)* entrenador *m*.

manageress [mænɪdʒə'res] *n (of shop, restaurant)* encargada *f*, jefa *f*; *(head of department)* jefa *f*; *(of company)* directora *f*, gerente *f*.

managerial [mænɪ'dʒɪərɪəl] *adj* directivo,-a, administrador,-a; **m. staff,** personal directivo *or* gerente.

managing ['mænɪdʒɪŋ] *adj* directivo,-a. ■ **m. director,** director,-a *m, f* gerente; **m. editor,** jefe,-a *m, f* de redacción, redactor,-a *m,f* jefe.

Mancunian [mæn'kju:nɪən] **I** *adj* de Manchester. **II** *n* habitante *mf* de Manchester.

mandarin ['mændərɪn] *n* **I** *Bot* **m. (orange),** mandarina *f*. **2** *(Chinese language)* M., mandarín *m*. **3** *pej (official)* mandarín *m*.

mandate ['mændeɪt] *n* mandato *m*.

mandatory ['mændətərɪ] *adj fml (compulsory)* obligatorio,-a.

mandible ['mændɪbəl] *n Anat* mandíbula *f*.

mandolin(e) ['mændəlɪn] *n Mus* mandolina *f*.

mandrake ['mændreɪk] *n Bot* mandrágora *f*.

mane [meɪn] *n (of horse)* crin *f*; *(of lion)* melena *f*.

maneuver [mə'nu:və'] *n & vt US see* **manoeuvre.**

maneuverable [mə'nu:vərəbəl] *adj US see* **manoeuvrable.**

manfully ['mænfʊlɪ] *adv* valientemente.

manganese [mæŋgə'ni:z] *n Chem* manganeso *m*.

mange [meɪndʒ] *n Med* sarna *f*.

manger ['meɪndʒə'] *n (trough)* pesebre *m*; *fig* **to be a dog in the m.,** ser el perro del hortelano.

mangetout [mɒnʒ'tu:] *n Bot* **m. (pea),** guisante *m* mollar.

mangle¹ ['mæŋgəl] *n (for wringing)* escurridor *m*, rodillo *m*.

mangle² ['mæŋgəl] *vtr (crush)* aplastar; *(destroy by cutting)* destrozar, despedazar; *fig* **a mangled version of events,** una versión mutilada de los hechos.

mango ['mæŋgəʊ] *n (pl mongoes or mangos) Bot (tree, fruit)* mango *m*.

mangy ['meɪndʒɪ] *adj (mangier, mangiest) (animal)* sarnoso,-a; *fam (carpet)* raído,-a.

manhandle ['mænhændəl] *vtr* **1** *(person)* maltratar. **2** *(large obect)* manipular.

manhole ['mænhəʊl] *n* boca *f* de acceso. ■ **m. cover,** *(in roof, boiler room)* tapa *f* de registro; *(in street)* recubrimiento *m*; *(of sewer)* tapa *f* de alcantarilla.

manhood ['mænhʊd] *n* **1** *(state)* madurez *f*; *(age of majority)* mayoría *f* de edad; **to reach m.,** llegar a la edad viril. **2** *(manly qualities)* virilidad *f*, hombría *f*. **3** *(men collectively)* hombres *mpl*.

manhunt ['mænhʌnt] *n* persecución *f*.

mania ['meɪnɪə] *n Psych & fig* manía *f*.

maniac ['meɪnɪæk] *n* **1** *Psych* maníaco,-a *m,f*; *fam* loco,-a *m,f*. ■ **sex m.,** obseso *m* sexual. **2** *fam (enthusiast, fan)* fanático,-a *m,f*.

maniacal [mə'naɪəkəl] *adj Psych* maníaco,-a; *fig* loco,-a.

manic ['mænɪk] *adj* maníaco,-a; **m. depression,** depresión maníaca.

manic-depressive [mænɪkdɪ'presɪv] *n Psych* **I** *adj (illness)* maníaco,-a depresivo,-a. **II** *n* maníaco,-a *m, f* depresivo,-a.

manicure ['mænɪkjʊə'] **I** *n* manicura *f*; **to give sb a m.,** hacer la manicura a algn. **II** *vtr* **to m. one's nails,** arreglarse las uñas.

manicurist ['mænɪkjʊərɪst] *n* manicuro,-a *m,f*.

manifest ['mænɪfest] *fml* **I** *adj (obvious)* manifiesto,-a, evidente. **II** *vtr (show)* manifestar.

manifestation [mænɪfe'steɪʃən] *n fml* manifestación *f*.

manifesto [mænɪ'festəʊ] *n (pl manifestos or manifestoes) Pol* manifiesto *m*.

manifold ['mænɪfəʊld] **I** *adj fml (many)* múltiples; *(varied)* diversos,-as, variados,-as. **II** *n Aut* colector *m* de escape.

manipulate [mə'nɪpjʊleɪt] *vtr* **1** *(machine, vehicle, etc)* manipular, manejar; *(knob, lever)* accionar; *Med (bones)* dar masajes a. **2** *fig* manipular; *(accounts etc)* falsificar.

manipulation [mənɪpjʊ'leɪʃən] *n* **1** *(of machine, vehicle, etc)* manipulación *f*, manejo *m*; *(of knob, lever)* accionamiento *m*; *Med (of bones)* masaje *m*. **2** *fig* manipulación *f*; *(of accounts etc)* manipulación *f*, falseamiento *m*.

mankind [mæn'kaɪnd] *n* la humanidad, el género humano, los hombres.

manliness ['mænlɪnɪs] *n* virilidad *f*, hombría *f*.

manly ['mænlɪ] *adj (manlier, manliest)* varonil, viril, macho.

man-made ['mænmeɪd] *adj (disaster)* provocado,-a por el hombre; *(lake)* artificial; *(fibres, fabric)* sintético,-a.

manned [mænd] *adj (ship, aircraft, etc)* tripulado,-a.

mannequin ['mænɪkɪn] *n* **1** *(dummy)* maniquí *m*. **2** *(fashion model)* modelo *f*.

manner ['mænə'] *n* **1** *(way, method)* manera *f*, modo *m*; **in this m.,** de esta manera, así; **in a m. of speaking,** por así decirlo, hasta cierto punto. **2** *(way of behaving)* forma *f* de ser, comportamiento *m*; **to have an easy m.,** tener un aire desenvuelto; *(of doctor)* bedside m., trato *m*. **3** *fml (type, class)* clase *f*, suerte *f*, índole *f*; **all m. of gifts,** toda clase de regalos. **4** *(social behaviour)* **manners,** modales *mpl*, educación *f sing*; **(good) m.,** buenos modales *mpl*. **bad m.,** falta *f sing* de educación. **5 manners,** *(of society)* costumbres *fpl*.

mannered ['mænəd] *adj fml (affected)* amanerado,-a, afectado-a.

mannerism ['mænərɪzəm] *n (gesture)* gesto *m*; *(affectation)* amaneramiento *m*.

mannerly ['mænəlɪ] *adj* cortés, (bien) educado,-a, formal.

mannish ['mænɪʃ] *adj (appearance, behaviour, etc)* hombruno,-a.

manoeuvrable [mə'nu:vərəbəl] *adj* manejable.

manoeuvre [mə'nu:və'] **I** *n* **1** *(gen)* maniobra *f*. **2** *fig (scheme)* maniobra *f*, estratagema *f*. **II** *vtr (gen)* maniobrar; *(person)* manejar, manipular; **to m. sth into position,** poner algo en posición. **III** *vi* maniobrar; *fig* **we need room to m.,** necesitamos un amplio margen de actuación.

manometer [mə'nɒmɪtə'] *n* manómetro *m*.

manor ['mænə'] *n (estate)* señorío *m*. ■ **m. house,** casa *f* solariega.

manpower ['mænpaʊə'] *n Ind* mano *f* de obra; *Mil* soldados *mpl*.

manservant ['mænsɜ:vənt] *n (pl menservants* ['mensɜ:vənts]*)* criado *m*, sirviente *m*.

mansion ['mænʃən] *n* casa *f* grande; *(in country)* casa *f* solariega.

manslaughter ['mænslɔ:tə'] *n Jur* homicidio *m* involuntario.

mantelpiece ['mæntəlpi:s] *n (shelf)* repisa *f* de chimenea; *(fireplace)* chimenea *f*.

mantle ['mæntəl] *n* **1** *(cloak)* capa *f*. **2** *fig* manto *m*; *(layer)* capa *f*; **beneath a m. of snow,** bajo una capa de nieve.

man-to-man [mæntə'mæn] *adj* de hombre a hombre.

manual ['mænjʊəl] **I** *adj (work etc)* manual. **II** *n (handbook)* manual *m*. ◆ **manually** *adv* a mano, manualmente.

manufacture [mænjuˈfæktʃəʳ] **I** *vtr (gen)* fabricar; *(clothing)* confeccionar; *(foodstuffs)* elaborar; *fig (excuse)* inventar. **II** *n (gen)* fabricación *f*; *(of clothing)* confección *f*; *(of foodstuffs)* elaboración *f*.

manufacturer [mænjuˈfæktʃərəʳ] *n (maker)* fabricante *mf*.

manure [məˈnjʊəʳ] **I** *n* abono *m*, estiércol *m*; **m. heap,** estercolero *m*. **II** *vtr* abonar, estercolar.

manuscript ['mænjʊskrɪpt] *n* manuscrito *m*; *(original text)* texto *m* original.

many ['menɪ] **I** *adj (more, most)* mucho,-a, muchos,-as; **a good** *or* **great m. citizens,** muchísimos,-as ciudadanos, un gran número de ciudadanos; **as m. ... as ...,** tantos,-as ... como ...; **as m. books as records,** tantos libros como discos; **how m. days?,** ¿cuántos días?; **m. people,** muchas personas, mucha gente muchos; **m. things,** muchas cosas; **m. times, m. a time,** muchas veces; **not m. books,** pocos *or* no muchos libros; **one too m.,** uno de más, uno de sobra; **so m. flowers!,** ¡cuántas flores!; **too m.,** demasiados,-as; *fam* **he has had one too m.,** ha tomado una copa de más. **II** *pron* muchos,-as; **m. came,** vinieron muchos. **III** *n* muchos,-as *mpl, fpl*; **the m.,** la mayoría.

many-sided ['menɪsaɪdɪd] *adj* **1** *(figure)* multilateral, de muchos lados. **2** *fig (personality, talent)* polifacético,-a; *(question)* complejo,-a.

map [mæp] **I** *n (of country, region)* mapa *m*; *(of town, bus, tube)* plano *m*; **m. of the world,** mapamundi *m*; *fig* **this will put our village on the m.,** esto dará a conocer nuestro pueblo; *fam* **his house is right off the m.,** su casa está en el quinto pino. ■ **weather m.,** carta *f* meteorológica. **II** *vtr (pt & pp mapped) (area)* trazar un mapa de. ◆ **map out** *vtr (route)* trazar en un mapa; *fig (future etc)* proyectar, planear, organizar.

mapmaker ['mæpmeɪkəʳ] *n* cartógrafo,-a *m, f*.

mapmaking ['mæpmeɪkɪŋ] *n* cartografía *f*.

maple ['meɪpəl] *n (tree, wood)* arce *m*. ■ **m. syrup,** jarabe *m* de arce.

mar [mɑːʳ] *vtr (pt & pp marred) (spoil)* estropear, echar a perder; **to m. sb's enjoyment,** aguarle la fiesta a algn.

marathon ['mærəθən] **I** *n* maratón *m*. **II** *adj fig (speech etc)* maratoniano,-a, larguísimo,-a.

marauder [məˈrɔːdəʳ] *n* merodeador,-a *m, f*.

marauding [məˈrɔːdɪŋ] *adj* merodeador,-a.

marble ['mɑːbəl] **I** *n* **1** *(stone, statue)* mármol *m*. **2** *(glass ball)* canica *f*; **to play marbles,** jugar a canicas; *fig* **fam to have lost one's marbles,** estar chiflado,-a. **II** *adj (floor, statue, etc)* de mármol; *(industry)* del mármol. ■ **m. cutter,** marmolista *mf*; **m. quarry,** cantera *f* de mármol.

March [mɑːtʃ] *n* marzo *m*; *see also* **May.**

march [mɑːtʃ] **I** *n* **1** *Mil* marcha *f*; *(walk)* caminata *f*; **it's three days' m. from here,** está a tres días de marcha; **to be on the m.,** estar en marcha; *fig* **to steal a m. on sb,** tomar la delantera a algn. **2** *(demonstration)* manifestación *f*; **a peace m.,** una manifestación a favor de la paz. **3** *(of time, events)* marcha *f*, paso *m*. **4** *Mus* marcha *f*. ■ **wedding m.,** marcha *f* nupcial. **II** *vi* **1** *Mil* marchar, hacer una marcha; *(walk)* marchar, caminar; **forward** *or* **quick m.!,** ¡frente!, ¡ar!; **to m. in,** entrar decidido,-a; **to m. out,** salir enfadado,-a; **to m. straight up to sb,** abordar a algn; *Mil* **to m. past,** desfilar. **2** *(demonstrate)* manifestarse, hacer una manifestación. **III** *vtr Mil* hacer marchar; **they marched him off to prison,** se lo llevaron a la cárcel; **to m. sb off,** llevarse a algn.

marcher ['mɑːtʃəʳ] *n (in demonstration)* manifestante *mf*.

marching orders ['mɑːtʃɪŋɔːdəz] *npl fam* **to give sb his** *or* **her m. o.,** despedir a algn.

march past ['mɑːtʃpɑːst] *n Mil* desfile *m*.

mare [meəʳ] *n Zool* yegua *f*.

margarine [mɑːdʒəˈriːn] *n*, **marge** [mɑːdʒ] *n fam* margarina *f*.

margin ['mɑːdʒɪn] *n* **1** *(on page)* margen *m*; **in the m.,** al margen. **2** *fig* margen *m*, límite *m*; **to win by a narrow m.,** ganar por poco. ■ **m. of error,** margen *m* de error; *Com* **profit m.,** margen *m* de beneficio.

marginal ['mɑːdzɪnəl] *adj (gen)* marginal; *(improvement)* escaso,-a, pequeño,-a; **m. note,** nota *f* al margen. ■ *Pol* **m. seat,** escaño *m* pendiente (para decidir la mayoría absoluta). ◆ **marginally** *adv* ligeramente.

marigold ['mærɪɡəʊld] *n Bot* maravilla *f*, caléndula *f*.

marijuana *n*, **marihuana** [mærɪˈhwɑːnə] *n* marihuana *f*, marijuana *f*.

marina [məˈriːnə] *n* puerto *m* deportivo.

marinade [mærɪˈneɪd] *Culin* **I** *n* adobo *m*. **II** *vtr* ['mærɪneɪd] *see* **marinate.**

marinate ['mærɪneɪt] *vtr Culin* adobar.

marine [məˈriːn] **I** *adj (life, flora, etc)* marino,-a, marítimo,-a. ■ **m. engineer,** ingeniero,-a *m, f* naval; **m. insurance,** seguro *m* marítimo, **II** *n (person)* soldado *m* de infantería de marina; *GB* **the Marines,** *US* **the M. Corps,** la infantería de marina.

mariner ['mærɪnəʳ] *n* marinero *m*.

marionette [mærɪəˈnet] *n* marioneta *f*. títere *m*.

marital ['mærɪtəl] *adj (relations, problems)* matrimonial, marital; *(bliss)* conyugal. ■ **m. status,** estado *m* civil.

maritime ['mærɪtaɪm] *adj* marítimo,-a.

marjoram ['mɑːdʒərəm] *n Bot* mejorana *f*.

mark [mɑːk] **I** *n* **1** *(trace)* huella *f*; *(left by blow etc)* señal *f*; *(stain)* mancha *f*; *(distinguishing marks,* señas *fpl* de identidad; *fig* **to leave one's m.,** dejar su impronta; *fig* **to make one's m.,** distinguirse. **2** *(symbol)* signo *m*, señal *f*; *(instead of signature)* cruz *f*. ■ **punctuation m.,** signo *m* de puntuación. **3** *(sign, token)* señal *f*, marca *f*; *(indication)* indicio *m*; *(proof)* prueba *f*; **as a m. of respect,** en señal de respeto. **4** *Sch (in exam etc)* nota *f*, calificación *f*; *Sport (of score)* tanto *m*; **to get high marks in English,** sacar una buena nota en inglés. **5** *(target)* blanco *m*; *(aim)* objetivo *m*; **to hit the m.,** dar en el blanco; *fig* dar en el clavo, acertar; *fig* **to be up to the m.,** estar a la altura (de las circunstancias); *fig* **to be wide of the m.,** estar lejos de la verdad. **6** *Sport* línea *f* de salida; **on your marks!, get set!, go!,** ¡preparados!, ¡listos!, ¡ya! **7** *Com (brand, trade name)* marca *f*; *(label)* etiqueta *f*. **8** *Tech (model)* serie *f*; **a M. 3 engine,** un motor de tercera serie. **II** *vtr* **1** *(make mark on)* marcar; *(stain)* manchar. **2** *(indicate)* señalar, indicar; *(show)* mostrar, revelar; **it marks a change of direction,** indica un cambio de dirección. **3** *(exam, exercise) (correct)* corregir; *(give mark to)* puntuar, calificar; *(student)* dar notas a. **4** *Com (add price)* indicar el precio de, poner precio a; *(label)* poner etiqueta a; **'10% off marked price',** 'descuento del 10% sobre el precio indicado'. **5** *(pay attention to)* fijarse en, prestar atención a; **m. my words,** fíjate en lo que te digo. **6** *Sport (opponent)* marcar. **7** *Mil* **to m. time,** marcar el paso; *fig (kill time)* hacer tiempo; *(await one's chance)* esperar el momento oportuno. ◆ **mark down** *vtr 1 (note down)* apuntar. **2** *Com (price)* rebajar; *(goods)* rebajar el precio de. ◆ **mark off** *vtr* **1** *(separate)* separar, dividir, distinguir; *(area)* delimitar. **2** *(tick off)* poner una señal a; *(cross out)* tachar. ◆ **mark out** *vtr* **1** *(area)* delimitar; *(boundary)* trazar; *(field)* jalonar. **2** *(single out)* distinguir; **to m. sb out for,** destinar a algn a. ◆ **mark up** *vtr (price)* aumentar.

mark² [mɑːk] *n (unit of currency)* marco *m*.

markdown ['mɑːkdaʊn] *n (of price)* rebaja *f*.

marked [mɑːkt] *adj* **1** *(noticeable)* marcado,-a, acusado,-a; *(improvement, increase)* sensible, apreciable. **2** **he is a m. man,** lo tienen fichado. ◆ **markedly** ['mɑːkɪdlɪ] *adv (different)* marcadamente, acusadamente; *(better)* sensiblemente.

marker ['mɑːkəʳ] n 1 *(stake, pole)* jalón m. 2 *(bookmark)* registro m. 3 *Sport (person)* marcador,-a m, f. 4 *Educ (person)* examinador,-a m, f. 5 *(pen)* marcador m, rotulador m.

market ['mɑːkɪt] I n 1 *(place)* mercado m; **Monday is m. day,** el lunes hay mercado; **to go to m.,** ir al mercado *or fam* a la plaza. ■ **flea m.,** rastrillo m; mercadillo m; **m. garden,** *(small)* huerto m; *(large)* huerta f; **m. town,** población f con mercado. 2 *(trade)* mercado m; *(demand)* salida f, mercado m, demanda f; **to be on the m.,** estar a la *or* en venta; *(product)* **to come on to the m.,** salir al mercado, ponerse en venta. ■ **black m.,** mercado m negro; **domestic m., home m.,** mercado m interior *or* nacional; **m. forces,** tendencias fpl del mercado; **m. price,** precio m de mercado; **m. research,** estudio m de mercado; **open m.,** mercado m libre; **overseas m.,** mercado m exterior; **the Common M.,** el Mercado Común. 3 *Fin* **stock m.,** bolsa f *or* mercado m (de valores); **to play the stock m.,** jugar a la bolsa. II vtr *(sell)* poner en venta, vender; *(launch)* lanzar al mercado; *(find outlet for)* dar salida a; *(promote)* promocionar.

marketable ['mɑːkɪtəbəl] adj vendible, comerciable.

marketing ['mɑːkɪtɪŋ] n marketing m, mercadotecnia f. ■ **m. director,** director,-a m, f de marketing; **m. strategy,** estrategia f comercial.

marketplace ['mɑːkɪtpleɪs] n *(gen)* mercado m; *(square)* plaza f.

marksman ['mɑːksmən] n *(pl* **marksmen***)* tirador m.

marksmanship ['mɑːksmənʃɪp] n puntería f.

mark-up ['mɑːkʌp] n *Com (increase)* subida f, aumento m; *(profit margin)* margen m de beneficio *or* comercial.

marmalade ['mɑːməleɪd] n mermelada f (de cítricos).

maroon [mə'ruːn] I n *(color)* granate m. II adj *(de color)* granate.

marooned [mə'ruːnd] adj abandonado,-a, bloqueado,-a; **m. by the snow,** bloqueado,-a por la nieve.

marquee [mɑː'kiː] n *(awning)* carpa f, entoldado m, toldo m.

marquetry ['mɑːkɪtrɪ] n marquetería f, taracea f.

marquess n, **marquis** ['mɑːkwɪs] n marqués m.

marriage ['mærɪdʒ] n *(state, institution)* matrimonio m; *(wedding)* boda f, casamiento m, enlace m matrimonial; **an uncle by m.,** un tío político. ■ **m. bureau,** agencia f matrimonial; **m. certificate,** certificado m de matrimonio; **m. of convenience,** matrimonio m de conveniencia.

marriageable ['mærɪdʒəbəl] adj casadero,-a, en edad de casarse.

married ['mærɪd] adj *(person, status)* casado,-a; **to be m.,** estar casado,-a **(to,** con); **to get m.,** casarse **(to,** con). ■ **m. life,** vida f matrimonial *or* conyugal; *(of woman)* **m. name,** apellido m de casada.

marrow ['mærəʊ] n 1 *Anat* **(bone) m.,** médula f, tuétano m; *fig* meollo m; *fig* **to be frozen to the m.,** estar helado,-a hasta los tuétanos. 2 *Bot* **(vegetable) m.,** calabacín m.

marrowbone ['mærəʊbəʊn] n *Culin* caña f de vaca.

marry ['mærɪ] vtr *(pt & pp* **married***) (take in marriage)* casarse con; *(give in marriage)* casar **(to,** con); *(unite in marriage)* casar; *fig* **to m. (up),** unir. ◆ **marry into** vi emparentarse vía matrimonio; **to m. into a wealthy family,** emparentarse con una familia adinerada. ◆ **marry off** vtr casar a; **to m. off one's daughters,** casar a sus hijas.

Mars [mɑːz] n *Astrol Astron Myth* Marte m.

marsh [mɑːʃ] n *(bog)* pantano m. ■ **salt m.,** marisma f.

marshal ['mɑːʃəl] I n 1 *Mil* mariscal m. 2 *GB (sports event, demonstration)* oficial mf. 3 *US (sheriff)* sherif m, alguacil m. 4 *US (of police department)* jefe m de policía; *(of fire department)* jefe m de bomberos. II vtr *(pt & pp* **marshalled,** *US* **marshaled)** 1 *Mil* formar. 2 *(facts, arguments, etc)* ordenar, poner en orden.

marshland ['mɑːʃlənd] n tierra f pantanosa, pantanal m.

marshmallow [mɑːʃ'mæləʊ] n 1 *Bot* malvavisco m. 2 *(sweet)* esponja f, bombón m de merengue blando.

marshy ['mɑːʃɪ] adj **(marshier, marshiest)** pantanoso,-a.

marsupial [mɑː'suːpɪəl] adj & n *Zool* marsupial *(m).*

martial ['mɑːʃəl] adj marcial. ■ **m. arts,** artes fpl marciales; **m. law,** ley f marcial.

Martian ['mɑːʃən] adj & n marciano,-a *(m, f).*

martin ['mɑːtɪn] n *Orn* avión m.

Martini® [mɑː'tiːnɪ] n vermut m, Martíni® m.

Martinique [mɑːtɪ'niːk] n La Martinica.

martyr ['mɑːtəʳ] I n mártir mf; *fig* **to make a m. of oneself,** dárselas de mártir. II vtr martirizar.

martyrdom ['mɑːtədəm] n martirio m.

marvel ['mɑːvəl] I n maravilla f; *fig* **it's a m. he survived,** es un milagro que sobreviviera. II vi **to m. at,** maravillarse, asombrarse. III vtr *(pt & pp* **marvelled,** *US* **marveled)** **to m. that ...,** maravillarse que ... + *subj*; **I m. at the fact that he can work so much,** me sorprende *or* maravilla que pueda trabajar tanto.

marvellous, *US* **marvelous** ['mɑːvələs] adj maravilloso,-a, estupendo,-a; **how m.!,** ¡qué bien!, ¡fantástico!

Marxism ['mɑːksɪzəm] n *Pol* marxismo m.

Marxist ['mɑːksɪst] adj & n *Pol* marxista *(mf).*

marzipan ['mɑːzɪpæn] n *Culin* mazapán m, pasta f de almendras.

mascara [mæ'skɑːrə] n rímel m.

mascot ['mæskət] n mascota f.

masculine ['mæskjulɪn] I adj masculino,-a; *(woman)* hombruna. II n *Ling* masculino m.

masculinity [mæskjʊ'lɪnɪtɪ] n masculinidad f.

mash [mæʃ] I n 1 *fam Culin* puré m de patatas. 2 *(for poultry, cattle, etc)* afrecho n II vtr **to m. (up),** *(crush)* triturar, machacar; *Culin* hacer un puré de; **mashed potatoes,** puré m de patatas.

mask [mɑːsk] I n *(gen)* máscara f; *(disguise)* disfraz m; *Med* mascarilla f; *(face pack)* mascarilla f. ■ **gas m.,** máscara antigás; **oxygen m.,** máscara f de oxígeno. II vtr enmascarar; *fig (conceal)* encubrir, ocultar **(from,** de).

masked [mɑːskt] adj enmascarado,-a. ■ **m. bail,** baile m de disfraces *or* de máscaras.

masking tape ['mɑːskɪŋteɪp] n cinta f adhesiva.

masochism ['mæsəkɪzəm] n masoquismo m.

masochist ['mæsəkɪst] adj & n masoquista *(mf).*

masochistic [mæsə'kɪstɪk] adj masoquista.

mason ['meɪsən] n 1 *(builder)* albañil m. 2 *(freemason)* masón m, francmasón m.

masonic [mə'sɒnɪk] adj masónico,-a.

masonry ['meɪsənrɪ] n *(stonework)* albañilería f, construcción f.

masquerade [mæskə'reɪd] I n *(pretence)* farsa f, mascarada f, falacia f. II vi disfrazarse; **to m. as a policeman,** disfrazarse de *or* hacerse pasar por policía.

mass¹ [mæs] n *Rel* misa f; **to hear m.** oír misa; **to say m.,** decir misa. ■ **Low M.,** misa f rezada; **Midnight M.,** misa f del gallo; **Requiem M.,** misa f de réquiem *or* difuntos.

mass² [mæs] I n 1 *(gen)* masa f; **atomic m.,** masa atómica. 2 *(large quantity)* montón m; *(of people)* multitud f; **masses of clothes,** montones de ropa; **the m. of people,** la mayoría de gente. 3 **the masses,** la masa, la gente en general. II adj masivo,-a, multitudinario,-a; **a m. protest,** una protesta multitudinaria. ■ **m. grave,** fosa f común; **m. hysteria,** histeria f colectiva; **m. media,** medios mpl de comunicación (de masas); **m. production,** fabricación f en serie. III vi *(crowd)* congregarse, reunirse en gran número; *Mil (troops)* concentrarse; *(clouds)* amontonarse.

massacre ['mæsəkə^r] **I** *n* masacre *f*, **matanza** *f*, carnicería *f*. **II** *vtr* asesinar en masa, **masacrar.**

massage ['mæsɑːʒ, mæ'sɑːdʒ] **I** *n* masaje *m*. **II** *vtr* **1** dar masajes a. **2** *fig (figures, fact)* manipular, falsificar.

masseur [mæ'sɜː^r] *n* masajista *m*.

masseuse [mæ'sɜːz] *n* masajista *f*.

massive ['mæsɪv] *adj* **1** *(solid, weighty)* macizo,-a, sólido,-a. **2** *(huge)* enorme, descomunal; **a m. majority,** una mayoría aplastante. **3** *(imposing)* imponente.

mass-produce ['mæsprə'djuːs] *vtr* fabricar en serie.

mast [mɑːst] *n* **1** *Naut* mástil *m*, palo *m*. **2** *Rad TV* torre *f*, poste *m*.

mastectomy [mæ'stektəmɪ] *n Med* mastectomía *f*.

master ['mɑːstə^r] **I** *n* **1** *(of dog, servant)* amo *m*; *(of household)* señor *m*; *(owner)* dueño *m*; **the m. of the house,** el señor de la casa; *fig* **to be m. of the situation,** dominar la situación; *fig* **to be one's own m.,** ser dueño de sí mismo. ◼ **m. of ceremonies,** maestro *m* de ceremonias. **2** *Naut (of ship)* capitán *m*; *(of fishing boat)* patrón *m*. **3** *GB (teacher)* maestro *m*, profesor *m*; **music m.,** profesor de música. **4** *Univ* **m.'s degree,** licenciatura *f* con tesina. **5** *(expert)* maestro *m*. **6** *arch (boy)* **the young m.,** el señorito; *(as title)* **M. James Brown,** el señor James Brown. **II** *adj* **1** *(original)* original. ◼ **m. copy,** original *m*; **m. key,** llave *f* maestra; **m. switch,** interruptor *m* central. **2** *(expert)* experto,-a, maestro,-a. ◼ **m. baker,** maestro *m* panadero; **m. builder,** maestro *m* de obras, contratista *mf*. **III** *vtr* **1** *(control) (person, situation, etc)* dominar; *(overcome)* superar, vencer. **2** *(learn) (subject, skill)* llegar a dominar; *(craft)* llegar a ser experto en; **she will never m. the cello,** no llegará nunca a dominar el violoncelo.

masterful ['mɑːstəful] *adj* **1** autoritario,-a; *(imperious)* imperioso,-a; *(personality)* dominante. **2** *(showing great skill)* magistral.

masterly ['mɑːstəlɪ] *adj* magistral, genial; **in a m. way,** con gran maestría, magistralmente.

mastermind ['mɑːstəmaɪnd] **I** *n (person)* cerebro *m*, genio *m*. **II** *vtr (crime, operation)* dirigir, ser el cerebro de.

masterpiece ['mɑːstəpiːs] *n* obra *f* maestra.

masterstroke ['mɑːstəstrəʊk] *n* golpe *m* maestro.

mastery ['mɑːstərɪ] *n* **1** *(control)* dominio *m* (**of,** de); *(supremacy)* supremacía *f*, superioridad *f*; **to gain the m. of** *or* **over,** llegar a dominar. **2** *(skill, expertise)* maestría *f*.

masticate ['mæstɪkeɪt] *vtr & vi* masticar.

mastiff ['mæstɪf] *n (dog)* mastín *m*.

mastitis [mæ'staɪtɪs] *n Med* mastitis *f inv*.

masturbate ['mæstəbeɪt] **I** *vtr* masturbar. **II** *vi* masturbarse.

masturbation [mæstə'beɪʃən] *n* masturbación *f*.

mat¹ [mæt] *n* **1** *(rug)* alfombrilla *f*; *(doormat)* felpudo *m*; *(rush mat)* estera *f*; *(table mat)* salvamanteles *m inv*; *(drink mat)* posavasos *m inv*; *(under vase etc)* tapete *m*; *Sport* colchoneta *f*. **2 a m. of hair,** una mata de pelos.

mat² [mæt] *adj* mate.

match¹ [mætʃ] *n* cerilla *f*, fósforo *m*; **box of matches,** caja *f* de cerillas; **to strike a m.,** encender una cerilla.

match² [mætʃ] **I** *n* **1** *Sport* partido *m*, encuentro *m*; *Box* combate *m*; *Ten* match *m*. **2** *(equal)* igual *mf*; **he's no m. for his brother,** no puede competir con su hermano; **she's more than a m. for you,** te da cien vueltas; *fig* **to meet one's m.,** encontrar uno la horma de su zapato. **3** *(colours, clothes, etc)* **to be a good m.,** hacer juego, armonizar; **the gloves are a good m. for the hat,** los guantes hacen juego con el sombrero. **4** *(marriage)* matrimonio *m*, casamiento *m*; **they are a good m.,** hacen buena pareja. **II** *vtr* **1** *(equal, be the equal of)* igualar; **there is nobody to m. him,** no tiene par. **2** *(be in harmony with) (gen)* armonizar; **they are well matched,** *(teams)* van iguales *or* igualados; *(couple)* hacen buena pareja. **3** *(colours, clothes, etc)* hacer juego con, combinar con,

casar con; *(pair of socks, gloves)* emparejar con, casar con; **the blouse does not m. the skirt,** la blusa y la falda no hacen juego. **4** *(compare)* equiparar; **to m. X with Y,** equiparar X con Y. **5** *(confront)* enfrentar; **to m. one team against another,** enfrentar un equipo contra otro. **III** *vi* **1** *(harmonize)* hacer juego, estar a tono; **with handbag to m.,** con (un) bolso a juego. **2 to m. up to,** *(equal)* corresponder a; *(live up to)* estar a la altura de.

matchbox ['mætʃbɒks] *n* caja *f* de cerillas.

matching ['mætʃɪŋ] *adj (jacket etc)* que hace juego.

matchless ['mætʃlɪs] *adj* sin par, sin igual.

matchmaker ['mætʃmeɪkə^r] *n* casamentero,-a *m,f*.

mate¹ [meɪt] **I** *n* **1** *(school companion, fellow worker)* companero,-a *m,f*, camarada *mf*, colega *mf*; *fam (friend)* amigo,-a *m,f*, compinche *mf*; *fam* **many thanks, m.!,** ¡muchas gracias, macho! **2** *Zool (male)* macho *m*; *(female)* hembra *f*. **3** *(assistant)* ayudante *mf*; aprendiz,-a *m,f*; **plumber's m.,** ayudante *or* aprendiz de fontanero. **4** *Naut* piloto *m*; **first/second m.,** primer/segundo oficial *m*. **II** *vtr Zool* acoplar, aparear. **III** *vi Zool* acoplarse, aparearse.

mate² [meɪt] *C u ss* **I** *n* mate *m*. **II** *vtr* dar jaque mate a.

material [mə't ɔrɪəl] **I** *n* **1** *(substance)* materia *f*; *fig* **he's artist m.,** tiene madera de artista. **2** *(cloth)* tejido *m*, tela *f*. **3** *(ideas, information)* material *m*, datos *mpl*, documentación *f*; **teaching m.,** material (para usar en clase). **4 materials,** *(ingredients, equipment)* material *msing*, materiales *mpl*; **building m.,** materiales para la construcción. **II** *adj* **1** importante, substancial; *Jur* **m. evidence,** prueba substancial *or* pertinente. **2** *(not spiritual)* material; **m. world,** mundo material. ◆ **materially** *adv* **1** *(physically)* materialmente. **2** *(essentially)* esencialmente, en esencia. **3** *(noticeably)* sensiblemente; *(significantly)* considerablemente.

materialism [mə'tɪərɪəlɪzəm] *n* materialismo *m*.

materialist [mə'tɪərɪəlɪst] *adj & n* materialista (*mf*).

materialistic [mətɪərɪə'lɪstɪk] *adj* materialista.

materialize [mə'tɪərɪəlaɪz] *vi* **1** *(hopes)* realizarse, hacerse realidad; *(plan, idea)* concretarse, tomar forma. **2** *(appear, show up)* aparecer, presentarse.

maternal [mə'tɜːnəl] *adj (motherly)* maternal; *(uncle etc)* materno,-a.

maternity [mə'tɜːnɪtɪ] *n* maternidad *f*. ◼ **m. benefit,** subsidio *m* por maternidad; **m. dress,** vestido *m* premamá; **m. hospital,** maternidad *f*; **m. leave,** baja *f* por maternidad.

mat(e)y ['meɪtɪ] *adj (matier, matiest) fam (person)* simpático,-a, bonachón,-ona.

math [mæθ] *n US see* **maths.**

mathematical [mæθə'mætɪkəl] *adj* matemático,-a; **to have a m. brain,** estar dotado,-a para las matemáticas.

mathematician [mæθəmə'tɪʃən] *n* matemático,-a *m,f*.

mathematics [mæθə'mætɪks] *n* matemáticas *fpl*.

maths [mæθs] *n fam* mates *fpl*, matemáticas *fpl*.

matinée ['mætɪneɪ] *n Cin* sesión *f* de tarde; *Theat* función *f* de tarde.

mating ['meɪtɪŋ] *n Zool* acoplamiento *m*, apareamiento *m*. ◼ **m. call,** reclamo *m*; **m. season,** época *f* de celo.

matins ['mætɪnz] *npl Rel* maitines *mpl*.

matriarch ['meɪtrɪɑːk] *n* matriarca *f*.

matriarchal ['meɪtrɪɑːkəl] *adj* matriarcal.

matriarchy ['meɪtrɪɑːkɪ] *n* matriarcado *m*.

matricide ['mætrɪsaɪd] *n (act)* matricidio *m*.

matriculate [mə'trɪkjuleɪt] *Univ* **I** *vtr* matricular. **II** *vi* matricularse.

matriculation [mətrɪkjuˈleɪʃən] *n Univ* matrícula *f*, matriculación *f*; *(entrance exam)* examen *m* de selectividad.

matrimonial [mætrɪ'məunɪəl] *adj* matrimonial.

matrimony ['mætrɪmənɪ] n matrimonio m; (married life) vida f conyugal.

matrix ['meɪtrɪks] n (pl **matrixes** or **matrices** ['meɪtrɪsiːz]) matriz f.

matron ['meɪtrən] n 1 (in hospital) enfermera f jefe or jefa. 2 (in school) ama f de llaves. 3 (older married woman) matrona f.

matronly ['meɪtrənlɪ] adj madura y recia.

matt [mæt] adj (colour, surface) mate.

matted ['mætɪd] adj enmarañado,-a.

matter ['mætər] n 1 (substance) materia f, sustancia f. ■ **grey m.**, materia f gris; **printed m.**, impresos mpl; **reading m.**, lecturas fpl, material m de lectura. 2 Med (pus) pus m. 3 (content) contenido m; **subject m.**, tema m. 4 (affair, question) asunto m, cuestión f; **as a m. of course**, por rutina; **as a m. of fact**, en realidad; **as matters stand**, tal y como están las cosas; **business matters**, negocios mpl; **it's a m. of five minutes**, es cuestión or cosa de cinco minutos; **it's no laughing m.**, no es cosa de risa; **that's another m.**, eso es otra cosa; **to make matters worse**, para colmo de desgracias. 5 (problem, difficulty) problema m; **there's something the m.**, pasa algo; **there's something the m. with my foot**, me pasa algo en el pie; **there's nothing the m. with him**, no le pasa nada; **what's the m.?**, ¿qué pasa?, ¿qué ocurre?; **what's the m. with her?**, ¿qué le pasa? 6 (importance) **no m.!**, ¡no importa!; **no m. what he does**, haga lo que haga; **no m. when**, no importa cuando; **no m. where you go**, dondequiera que vayas; **no m. how clever he is**, por muy inteligente que sea; **no m. how much you work**, por mucho que trabajes; **no m. how**, como sea. II vi (be important) importar; **it doesn't m.**, no importa, da igual; **what does it m.?**, ¿y qué?

matter-of-fact ['mætərəvfækt] adj (person) práctico,-a, realista; (account) realista; (style) prosaico,-a; (voice) impersonal.

matting ['mætɪŋ] n estera f.

mattress ['mætrɪs] n colchón f.

mature [mə'tʃʊər] I adj maduro,-a; Fin vencido,-a. II vi madurar; Fin vencer. III vtr madurar.

maturity [mə'tʃʊərɪtɪ] n madurez f.

maudlin ['mɔːdlɪn] adj (sentimental) sensiblero,-a; (tearful) llorón,-ona.

maul [mɔːl] vtr 1 (wound) herir, agredir; **he was mauled by a lion**, fue agredido por un león. 2 (handle roughly) maltratar. 3 fig (criticize) vapulear.

maundy ['mɔːndɪ] n Rel lavatorio m. ■ **M. Thursday**, Jueves m Santo.

Mauritius [mə'rɪʃəs] n Mauricio.

mausoleum [mɔːsə'lɪəm] n mausoleo m.

mauve [məʊv] adj & n (colour) malva (m).

maverick ['mævərɪk] adj & n inconformista (mf); Pol disidente (mf).

mavis ['meɪvɪs] n Orn zorzal m charlo.

mawkish ['mɔːkɪʃ] adj sensiblero,-a, empalagoso,-a.

max [mæks] abbr of **maximum**, máximo m, max.

maxim ['mæksɪm] n máxima f.

maximize ['mæksɪmaɪz] vtr llevar al máximo, maximizar.

maximum ['mæksɪməm] I n (pl **maximums** or **maxima** ['mæksɪmə]) máximo m, máximum m; **as a m.**, como máximo; **to the m.**, al máximo. II adj máximo,-a; **m. speed**, velocidad f máxima.

May [meɪ] n mayo m; **at the beginning/end of M.**, a principios/finales de mayo; **during M.**, durante el mes de mayo; **each** or **every M.**, todos los años en mayo; **in M.**, en mayo; **in the middle of M.**, a mediados de mayo; **last/next M.**, en mayo del año pasado/del año que viene; **(on) the first/sixteenth of M.**, el primero/dieciséis de mayo; **she was born on 16th M. 1964**, nació el 16 de mayo de 1964. ■ **M. Day**, el Primero or el Uno de Mayo.

may¹ [meɪ] v aux (pt **might**) 1 (possibility, probability) poder, ser posible; **be that as it m.**, sea como sea; **come what m.**, pase lo que pase; **he m.** or **might come**, puede que venga, es posible que venga, a lo mejor viene; **he m.** or **might have forgotten**, puede que se haya olvidado; **I m.** or **might be wrong**, quizás esté equivocado,-a; **I'm afraid you m.** or **might be late**, me temo que llegarás tarde; **you m.** or **might as well stay**, más vale que te quedes; **you might have said something (to me)!**, ¡habérmelo dicho (antes)!; **work as she might**, por mucho que trabajara. 2 (permission) poder; **if I m.**, si me lo permite; **m. I?**, ¿me permite?; **m. I come in?**, ¿se puede (entrar or pasar)?; **m. we go now?**, ¿podemos irnos ya?; **you m. smoke**, pueden fumar. 3 (wish) ojalá (+ subj); **m. you always be happy!**, ¡ojalá seas siempre feliz!, ¡que siempre seas feliz!; **we hoped it might last**, esperábamos que durase.

may² [meɪ] n Bot 1 (blossom) flor f de espino. 2 (tree) espino m.

maybe ['meɪbiː] adv quizá, quizás, tal vez; **m. she'll phone today**, quizá or quizás or tal vez llame hoy, a lo mejor llama hoy.

Mayday ['meɪdeɪ] n Av Naut señal f de socorro, SOS m.

mayfly ['meɪflaɪ] n Ent cachipolla f, efímera f.

mayhem ['meɪhem] n (disturbance) alboroto m, bullicio m; (havoc) estragos mpl.

mayonnaise [meɪə'neɪz] n Culin mayonesa f, mahonesa f.

mayor [meər] n (man) alcalde m; (woman) alcaldesa f.

mayoress ['meərɪs] n alcaldesa f.

maypole ['meɪpəʊl] n mayo m.

maze [meɪz] n laberinto m.

MB [em'biː] abbr of **Bachelor of Medicine**, licenciado,-a m, f en Medicina, Lic. en Med.

MC [em'siː] abbr of **Master of Ceremonies**, maestro m de ceremonias.

MCC [emsiː'siː] GB Sport abbr of **Marylebone Cricket Club**, consejo m de administración del cricket en Inglaterra.

MD [em'diː] 1 abbr of **Doctor of Medicine**, doctor,-a m, f en Medicina, Dr. en Medicina. 2 fam abbr of **Managing Director**, director,-a m, f gerente.

me¹ [miː] pron 1 (as object) me; **he gave it to me, he gave me it**, me lo dio; **listen to me**, escúchame; **she knows me**, me conoce. 2 (after prep) mí; **it's for me**, es para mí; **with me**, conmigo. 3 (emphatic) yo; **it's me**, soy yo; **it's me, Alyson**, soy Alyson; **what about me?**, ¿y yo, qué?

me² [miː] n Mus mi m.

meadow ['medəʊ] n prado m, pradera f.

meagre, US **meager** ['miːgər] adj escaso,-a, exiguo,-a.

meal¹ [miːl] n (flour) harina f.

meal² [miːl] n (food) comida f; **to have a m.**, comer; fam fig **to make a m. of sth**, recrearse en algo. ■ US **m. ticket**, vale m or cupón m de comida.

mealtime [miːltaɪm] n hora f de comer.

mealy ['miːlɪ] adj (mealier, mealiest) (floury) harinoso,-a.

mealy-mouthed [miːlɪ'maʊðd] adj pej evasivo,-a, embustero,-a; **stop being m-m. about it!**, ¡déjate ya de rodeos!

mean¹ [miːn] vtr (pt & pp **meant**) 1 (signify) significar, querer decir; **'casa' means 'house'**, 'casa' significa 'house'; **that name means nothing to me**, ese nombre no me suena; **this clock means a lot to me**, este reloj significa mucho para mí; **what does 'gullible' m.?**, ¿qué quiere decir 'gullible'?; **what do you m. by that?**, ¿qué quieres decir con eso? 2 (intend) pensar, tener la intención de; (wish) querer; **he meant to do it tomorrow**, tenía pensado hacerlo mañana; **I m. it**, (te) lo digo en serio; **she didn't m. to do it**, lo hizo sin querer; **she was meant to arrive on the 7th**, tenía que or debía llegar el día 7; **they m. well**, tienen buenas intenciones;

to m. business, hablar *or* actuar en serio. **3** *(involve, entail)* suponer, implicar; **it means an outlay of £500,** supone una inversión de 500 libras. **4** *(refer to)* referirse a; **do you m. me?,** ¿te refieres a mí? **5** *(destine)* destinar **(for,** a, para); **his remarks were meant for your mother,** sus observaciones iban dirigidas a tu madre; **they are meant for each other,** están hechos el uno para el otro.

mean² [mi:n] *adj (meaner, meanest)* **1** *(miserly)* tacaño,-a, agarrado,-a; **to be m. with one's money,** mirar mucho por su dinero. **2** *(unkind)* malo,-a; *(petty)* mezquino,-a; *US (bad-tempered)* malhumorado,-a; **a m. trick,** una mala pasada *or* jugada; **don't be so m.!,** ¡no seas tan malo!; **to be m. to sb,** tratar mal a algn. **3** *(inferior)* pobre, mediocre; *(origins)* humilde, pobre. **4 no m.,** *(difficult achievements)* difícil, hazañoso,-a; *(excellent)* de primera; **it was no m. feat,** fue toda una hazaña; **she's no m. photographer,** es una excelente fotógrafa, es una fotógrafa de primera.

mean³ [mi:n] **I** *adj (average)* medio,-a; **m. temperature,** temperatura *f* media. **II** *n* **1** *(average)* promedio *m; Math* media *f.* **2** *(middle term)* término medio.

meander [mɪ'ændə'] **I** *vi (river)* serpentear; *(person)* vagar, andar sin rumbo fijo; *fig (digress)* divagar. **II** meandro *m.*

meanderings [mɪ'ændərɪŋz] *npl fig (digressions)* divagaciones *fpl.*

meaning ['mi:nɪŋ] *n* **1** *(sense of word etc)* sentido *m,* significado *m; (in dictionary)* acepción *f;* **double m.,** doble sentido; **what is the m. of 'gazump'?,** ¿qué significa 'gazump'?, ¿qué quiere decir 'gazump'?; **what's the m. of this?,** y esto, ¿qué quiere decir?; *fam* **do you get my m.?,** ¿entiendes lo que te quiero decir? **2** *fig* sentido *m;* **a world without m.,** un mundo sin sentido.

meaningful ['mi:nɪŋfʊl] *adj* significativo,-a.

meaningless ['mi:nɪŋlɪs] *adj* sin sentido, que carece de sentido; *(absurd)* absurdo,-a.

meanness ['mi:nnɪs] *n* **1** *(miserliness)* tacañería *f,* mezquindad *f.* **2** *(nastiness)* mezquindad *f,* maldad *f.*

means [mi:nz] *n* **1** *sing or pl (method)* medio *m,* manera *f;* **a m. of transport,** un medio de transporte; **by fair m. or foul,** por las buenas o por las malas; **by m. of,** por medio de, mediante; **the end does not justify m.,** el fin no justifica los medios. **2** *pl (resources, wealth)* medios *mpl* (de vida), recursos *mpl* (económicos); **a woman of m.,** una mujer acaudalada; **to live beyond one's m.,** vivir por encima de sus posibilidades. ■ **m. test,** comprobación *f* de medios de vida. **3 by all m.!,** ¡por supuesto!, ¡naturalmente!; **by all m. telephone him,** no dejes de llamarle; **by no m.,** de ningún modo, de ninguna manera; **by any m.,** de cualquier modo.

meant [ment] *pt & pp see* **mean¹.**

meantime ['mi:ntaɪm] **I** *adv* mientras tanto, entretanto. **II** *n* **in the m.,** mientras tanto.

meanwhile ['mi:nwaɪl] *adv* mientras tanto, entretanto.

measles ['mi:zəlz] *n Med* sarampión *m.* ■ **German m.,** rubeola *f.*

measly ['mi:zlɪ] *adj (measlier, measliest) fam* miserable, mezquino,-a.

measurable ['meʒərəbəl] *adj* mensurable, medible.

measure ['meʒə'] **I** *n* **1** *(system)* medida *f;* **liquid m.,** medida para líquidos; **square/cubic m.,** medida de superficie/de volumen. **2** *(ruler)* regla *f;* metro *m.* ■ **tape m.,** cinta *f* métrica, metro *m.* **3** *(measured amount)* medida *f;* **to give full m.,** dar la medida exacta; *fig* **for good m.,** para estar seguro,-a. **4** *(degree, extent)* **in some m.,** hasta cierto punto; **she had a m. of success,** tuvo cierto éxito. **5** *Mus* compás *m,* ritmo *m.* **6** *(step, remedy)* medida *f;* **safety measures,** medidas de seguridad. **II** *vtr (object, area)* medir; *(person)* tomar las medidas de. ◆ **measure off** *vtr (area)* medir. ◆ **measure up** *vi* to **m. (up) (to sth),** estar a la altura (de algo); **he didn't m. up,** no estuvo a la altura de las circunstancias.

measured ['meʒəd] *adj (step)* estudiado,-a; *(tone)* mesurado,-a; *(statement)* prudente, circunspecto,-a; *(language)* moderado,-a, comedido,-a.

measurement ['meʒəmənt] *n* **1** *(act of measuring)* medición *f.* **2** *(length etc)* medida *f;* **to take sb's measurements,** tomarle las medidas a algn.

measuring ['meʒərɪŋ] *n* medición *f.* ■ **m. tape,** cinta *f* métrica, metro *m.*

meat [mi:t] *n* **1** carne *f;* **cold m.,** fiambre *m; fig* **it is m. and drink to them,** es lo que más les gusta. ■ *Culin* **m. pie,** empanada *f* de carne. **2** *fig* esencia *f,* jugo *m.*

meatball ['mi:tbɔ:l] *n Culin* albóndiga *f.*

meaty ['mi:tɪ] *adj (meatier, meatiest)* **1** carnoso,-a; **m. smell,** olor *m* a carne. **2** *fig (story)* jugoso,-a, sustancioso,-a.

Mecca ['mekə] *n* la Meca.

mechanic [mɪ'kænɪk] *n (person)* mecánico,-a *m,f.*

mechanical [mɪ'kænɪkəl] *adj* mecánico,-a; *fig (behaviour)* mecánico,-a, maquinal. ■ **m. engineer,** ingeniero,-a *m,f* mecánico,-a *or* industrial.

mechanics [mɪ'kænɪks] *n* **1** *sing (science)* mecánica *f.* **2** *pl (technical aspects)* mecanismo *m sing; fig* **the m. of politics,** los mecanismos de la política.

mechanism ['mekənɪzəm] *n* mecanismo *m.*

mechanization [mekənaɪ'zeɪʃən] *n* mecanización *f.*

mechanize ['mekənaɪz] *vtr* mecanizar.

MEd [em'ed] *abbr of* **Master of Education.**

medal ['medəl] *n* medalla *f;* **gold/silver/bronze m.,** medalla de oro/plata/bronce.

medallion [mɪ'dæljən] *n* medallón *m.*

medallist, *US* **medalist** ['medəlɪst] *n Sport* medalla *f,* campeón *m;* **he was the 1988 Olympic gold m.,** fue medalla de oro en los juegos olímpicos de 1988.

meddle ['medəl] *vi* entrometerse **(in,** en); **to m.with sth,** manosear algo.

meddler ['medlə'] *n* entrometido,-a *m,f.*

meddlesome ['medəlsəm] *adj,* **meddling** ['medəlɪŋ] *adj* entrometido,-a.

media ['mi:dɪə] *npl* medios *mpl* de comunicación. ■ **m. coverage,** cobertura *f* periodística; **m. man,** periodista *m; Univ* **m. studies,** ciencias *fpl* de la información, periodismo *m.*

median ['mi:dɪən] **I** *adj* mediano,-a. **II** *n Geom (line)* mediana *f; (quantity)* valor *m* mediano.

mediate ['mi:dɪeɪt] *vi* mediar **(between,** entre; **in,** en).

mediation [mi:dɪ'eɪʃən] *n* mediación *f.*

mediator ['mi:dɪeɪtə'] *n* mediador,-a *m,f.*

medic ['medɪk] *n fam (doctor)* médico,-a *m, f; Univ* estudiante *mf* de medicina.

medical ['medɪkəl] **I** *adj (treatment, profession)* médico,-a; *(book, student)* de medicina. ■ **m. examination,** reconocimiento *m* médico; *US* **m. examiner,** médico,-a *m, f* forense; **m. practitioner,** médico,-a *m, f; Univ* **m. school,** Facultad *f* de Medicina. **II** *n* reconocimiento *m* médico.

medicated ['medɪkeɪtɪd] *adj (shampoo etc)* medicinal.

medication [medɪ'keɪʃən] *n* medicación *f.*

medicinal [me'dɪsɪnəl] *adj* medicinal.

medicine ['medsɪn, 'medɪsɪn] *n* **1** *(science)* medicina *f.* **2** *(drugs etc)* medicina *f,* medicamento *m; fig* **to give sb a taste of his own m.,** pagar a algn con la misma moneda. ■ **m. chest,** botiquín *m.*

medieval [medɪ'i:vəl] *adj* medieval.

mediocre [mi:dɪ'əʊkə'] *adj* mediocre.

mediocrity [mi:dɪ'ɒkrɪtɪ] *n* mediocridad *f.*

meditate ['medɪteɪt] **I** *vi* meditar, reflexionar **(on,** sobre), **II** *vtr* meditar.

meditation [medɪ'teɪʃən] *n* meditación *f.*

meditative ['medɪtətɪv] *adj* meditabundo,-a, meditativo,-a.

Mediterranean [medɪtə'reɪnɪən] I *adj* mediterráneo,-a. II the M. *n* el Mediterráneo.

medium ['mi:dɪəm] I *adj* (*average*) mediano,-a, regular; **of m. height,** de estatura mediana. ■ *Rad* **m. wave,** onda *f* media. II *n* (*pl* **media**) 1 (*means*) medio *m*; (*to express ideas etc*) medio de expresión; **the media,** los medios de comunicación; **through the m. of,** por medio de. 2 (*environment*) medio *m* ambiente. 3 **to strike a happy m,,** hallar el punto justo. 4 (*pl* **mediums**) (*spiritualist*) médium *mf*.

medium-dry [mi:dɪəm'draɪ] *adj* (*wines*) semiseco,-a.

medium-sized [mi:dɪəm'saɪzd] *adj* de tamaño mediano.

medlar ['medlə'] *n Bot* níspero *m*.

medley ['medlɪ] *n* 1 (*miscellany*) miscelánea *f*; (*mixture*) mezcla *f*; (*of articles*) surtido *m*. 2 *Mus* popurrí *m*.

meek [mi:k] *adj* manso,-a, sumiso,-a, dócil; (*humble*) humilde; **to be m. and mild,** ser un corderito.

meekness ['mi:knɪs] *n* mansedumbre *f*, docilidad *f*; (*humility*) humildad *f*.

meet [mi:t] I *vtr* (*pt & pp* **met**) 1 (*person*) (*by chance*) encontrar, encontrarse con; (*by arrangement*) reunirse con, citarse; (*in formal meeting*) entrevistarse con; (*see*) ver; (*pass in street etc*) cruzar *or* topar con; *fig* **to m. sb halfway,** llegar a un acuerdo con algn. 2 (*get to know*) conocer; **I'd like you to m. my mother,** quiero presentarte a mi madre; **pleased to m. you!,** ¡encantado,- a de conocerle!, ¡mucho gusto! 3 (*await arrival of*) esperar; (*collect*) ir *or* venir a buscar; (*receive*) recibir, ir a recibir; **she'll m. us at the airport,** irá a buscarnos al aeropuerto. 4 (*bus, train, etc*) tener conexión con, empalmar. 5 (*danger, difficulty*) encontrar; (*opponent*) enfrentarse con; **to m. one's death,** encontrar la muerte, morir. 6 (*satisfy*) satisfacer; (*obligations*) cumplir con; (*expenses*) costear, hacer frente a, correr con; (*bill, debt*) pagar; (*deficit*) cubrir. 7 **to m. sb's eye,** cruzarse las miradas; *fig* **there's more to this than meets the eye,** es más difícil de lo que parece. II *vi* 1 (*people*) (*by chance*) encontrarse; (*by arrangement*) verse, reunirse; (*formal meeting*) entrevistarse; **we've arranged to m. tomorrow,** hemos quedado en vernos mañana; **until we m. again!,** ¡hasta la vista!, ¡hasta luego! 2 (*get to know each other*) conocerse; **they met at school,** se conocieron en la escuela. 3 *Sport* enfrentarse. 4 (*join*) unirse; (*rivers*) confluir; (*roads, railway lines*) empalmar; **our eyes met,** nuestras miradas se cruzaron; *fam* **to make ends m.,** llegar a fin de mes. III *n* 1 *Sport* reunión *f*. 2 (*hunting*) partida *f* de caza. ◆ **meet up** *vi fam* (*by chance*) encontrar, encontrarse (**with,** con); (*by arrangement*) reunirse (**with,** con). ◆ **meet with** *vtr* 1 (*difficulty, problem*) encontrar, tropezar con; (*loss, accident*) sufrir; (*success*) tener; **she met with a warm welcome,** fue acogida calurosamente. 2 *esp US* (*person*) reunirse con.

meeting ['mi:tɪŋ] *n* 1 (*chance encounter*) encuentro *m*; (*prearranged*) cita *f*; (*formal*) entrevista *f*. 2 (*of club, committee, etc*) reunión *f*; (*of assembly*) sesión *f*; (*of shareholders, creditors*) junta *f*, *Pol* (*rally*) mitin *m*; **to hold a m.,** celebrar una reunión *or* una sesión; **to open/ close a m.,** abrir/levantar la sesión. ■ **annual general m.,** junta *f* general anual; **business m.,** reunión *f* de negocios; *Educ* **staff m.,** claustro *m*. 3 *Sport* encuentro *m*. 4 (*of two rivers*) confluencia *f*.

meeting place ['mi:tɪŋpleɪs] *n* lugar *m* de encuentro *or* de reunión.

megabyte ['megəbaɪt] *n Comput* megabyte *m*, megaocteto *m*.

megahertz ['megəhɜːts] *n* megahercio *m*.

megalith ['megəlɪθ] *n* megalito *m*.

megalomania [megələʊ'meɪnɪə] *adj & n* megalómano,-a (*m,f*).

megaphone ['megəfəʊn] *n* megáfono *m*, altavoz *m*.

megawatt ['megəwɒt] *n* megavatio *m*.

megrim ['mi:grɪm] *n* (*fish*) gallo *m*.

melamine ['meləmi:n] *n* melamina *f*.

melancholic [melən'kɒlɪk] *adj* melancólico,-a.

melancholy ['melənkəlɪ] I *n* melancolía *f*. II *adj* melancólico,-a.

melanin ['melənɪn] *n* melanina *f*.

mêlée ['meleɪ] *n* (*of people*) tumulto *m*, gentío *m*; (*fight*) pelea *f* confusa.

mellifluous [me'lɪfluəs] *adj* melifluo,-a.

mellow ['meləʊ] I *adj* maduro,-a; (*wines*) añejo,-a; (*colour, voice*) suave; (*person*) apacible, tierno-a. II *vi* (*fruit*) madurar; (*colour, voice*) suavizarse; (*person*) enternecerse, ablandarse; **he has mellowed with age,** ha madurado con los años.

melodic [mɪ'lɒdɪk] *adj* melódico,-a.

melodious [mɪ'ləʊdɪəs] *adj* melodioso,-a.

melodrama ['melədrɑːmə] *n* melodrama *m*.

melodramatic [melədrə'mætɪk] *adj* melodramático,-a.

melody ['melədɪ] *n* melodía *f*.

melon ['melən] *n* (*honeydew etc*) melón *m*; (*watermelon*) sandía *f*.

melt [melt] I *vtr* (*snow*) derretir; (*metal*) fundir; *fig* (*sb's heart*) ablandar. II *vi* (*snow*) derretirse; (*metal*) fundirse; *fig* ablandarse; **it melts in one's mouth,** se derrite en la boca; **to m. into tears,** deshacerse en lágrimas. ◆ **melt away** *vi* (*snow*) derretirse; *fig* (*money*) desaparecer; *fig* (*confidence*) desvanecerse, esfumarse. ◆ **melt down** *vtr* (*metal*) fundir.

melting ['meltɪŋ] *n* 1 (*of snow*) derretimiento *m*; (*of metal*) fundición *f*; **m. point,** punto *m* de fusión. 2 **m. pot,** crisol *m*; *fig* **it's in the m. pot,** está por decidir.

member ['membə'] *n* 1 (*person*) miembro *mf*; (*of society*) miembro *mf*, socio,-a *m, f*; (*of party, union*) miembro *mf*, afiliado,-a *m, f*; **'members only',** 'sólo para socios'. ■ *Pol* **active m.,** militante *mf*; **M. of Parliament (MP),** diputado,-a *m, f*; **m. of staff,** empleado,-a *m, f*; (*teacher*) profesor,-a *m, f*. 2 *Anat* miembro *m*. ■ **made m.,** miembro *m* viril.

membership ['membəʃɪp] *n* 1 (*state*) calidad *f* de socio *or* miembro; (*entry*) ingreso *m*; *Pol* afiliación *f*. ■ **m. card,** carnet *m* de socio; **m. (fee),** cuota *f* de socio. 2 (*members*) socios *mpl*, miembros *mpl*; (*number of members*) número *m* de socios *or* miembros; *Pol* **the active m.,** la militancia, **what is the m.?,** ¿cuántos socios hay?

membrane ['membreɪn] *n* membrana *f*; **mucus m.,** membrana mucosa.

memento [mə'mentəʊ] *n* (*pl* **mementos** *or* **mementoes**) recuerdo *m*, recordatorio *m*.

memo ['meməʊ] *n* (*pl* **memos**) (*abbr of* **memorandum**) 1 (*official note*) memorándum *m*. 2 (*personal note*) nota *f*, apunte *m*. ■ **m. pad,** bloc *m* de notas.

memoir ['memwɑː'] *n* (*essay*) memoria *f*; (*biography*) **memoirs,** memorias *fpl*, autobiografía *f*.

memorabilia [memərə'bɪlɪə] *npl* (*things*) recuerdos *mpl*.

memorable ['memərəbəl] *adj* memorable.

memorandum [memə'rændəm] *n* (*pl* **memorandums** *or* **memoranda**) 1 *Pol Com* memorándum *m*. 2 (*personal note*) nota *f*, apunte *m*.

memorial [mɪ'mɔːrɪəl] I *adj* (*plaque etc*) conmemorativo,-a. II *n* monumento *m* conmemorativo; **war m.,** monumento a los Caídos. ■ *US* **M. Day,** Día *m* de Conmemoración a los Caidos.

memorize ['meməraɪz] *vtr* memorizar, aprender de memoria.

memory ['memərɪ] *n* 1 (*faculty, computers*) memoria *f*; *Med* **loss of m.,** amnesia *f*; **to have a good/bad m.,** tener buena/ mala memoria; **to play sth from m.,** tocar algo de memoria. 2 (*recollection*) recuerdo *m*; **childhood memories,** recuerdos de la infancia; **in m. of,** en memoria de.

men [men] *npl see* **man.**

menace ['menɪs] **I** *n* **1** *(threat)* an enaza *f; (danger)* peligro *m*. **2** *fam (nuisance) (thing)* lata *f; (person)* pesado,-a *m, f*. **II** *vtr* amenazar.

menacing ['menɪsɪŋ] *adj* amenazador,-a.

menagerie [mɪ'nædʒərɪ] *n* casa *f* de fieras; *(zoo)* zoo *m*.

mend [mend] **I** *vtr* **1** *(repair)* reparar, arreglar; *(clothes)* remendar; *(socks etc)* zurcir. **2** *(reform)* **to m. one's ways,** enmendarse, reformarse. **II** *vi (recover)* mejorarse, reponerse. **II** *n (patch)* remiendo *m; (darn)* zurcido *m; fig* **to be on the m.,** estar *or* ir mejorando.

mendacious [men'deɪʃəs] *adj fml* mendaz, mentiroso,-a.

mending ['mendɪŋ] *n* **1** *(repair)* reparación *f*, arreglo *m; (darning)* zurcido *m*. **2** *(clothes for mending)* ropa *f* por remendar *or* zurcir.

menfolk ['menfəʊk] *npl fam* **the m.,** los hombres.

menial ['mi:nɪəl] **I** *adj (task)* servil, bajo,-a. **II** *n (servant)* criado,-a *m, f*.

meningitis [menɪn'dʒaɪtɪs] *n Med* meningitis *f*.

menopausal [menə'pɔ:zəl] *adj* menopáusico,-a.

menopause ['menəpɔ:z] *n* menopausia *f*.

menstrual ['menstrʊəl] *adj* menstrual. ■ **m. cycle,** ciclo *m* menstrual.

menstruate ['menstrʊeɪt] *vi* menstruar.

menstruation [menstrʊ'eɪʃən] *n* menstruación *f*, regla *f*.

menswear ['menzweəʳ] *n Com* ropa *f* de caballero.

mental ['mentəl] *adj* **1** *(of the mind)* mental. ■ **m. age,** edad *f* mental; **m. arithmetic,** cálculo *m* mental; **m. home, m. hospital,** hospital *m* psiquiátrico; **m. illness,** enfermedad *f* mental; **m. patient,** enfermo,-a *m, f* mental; **m. strain,** tensión *f* nerviosa. **2** *fam (crazy)* chalado,-a, tocado,-a. ◆ **mentally** *adv* mentalmente; **to be m. handicapped,** ser un,-a disminuido,-a psíquico,-a; **to be m. ill,** padecer una enfermedad mental.

mentality [men'tælɪtɪ] *n* mentalidad *f*.

menthol ['menθɒl] *n* mentol *m*. **II** *adj (sweet)* de menta; *(cigarette)* mentolado,-a.

mention ['menʃən] **I** *n* mención *f*. **II** *vtr* mencionar, hacer mención de, aludir a; *Jur (in will)* mencionar; **don't m. it!,** ¡de nada!, ¡no hay de qué!, ¡no faltaba más!; **I need hardly m. that ...,** huelga decir que ... .

mentor ['mentɔ:ʳ] *n* mentor *m*.

menu ['menju:] *n* **1** *(card)* carta *f; (fixed meal)* menú *m;* **today's m.,** menú del día. **2** *Comput* menú *m*.

meow [mɪ'aʊ] **I** *n* maullido *m*, miau *m*. **II** *vi* maullar.

MEP [emi:'pi:] *abbr* of **Member of the European Parliament,** miembro *mf* del Parlamento Europeo.

mercantile ['mɜ:kəntaɪl] *adj* mercantil, comercial.

mercenary ['mɜ:sɪnərɪ] *adj & n* mercenario,-a *(m, f)*.

merchandise ['mɜ:tʃəndaɪz] *n* mercancías *fpl*, géneros *mpl*.

merchant ['mɜ:tʃənt] *n Com Fin (trades)* comerciante *mf*, negociante *mf; (retailer)* detallista *mf*, minorista *mf; (shopkeeper)* tendero,-a *m, f; arch* mercader *m*. ■ **m. bank,** banco *m* comercial; **m. navy,** marina *f* mercante.

merciful ['mɜ:sɪfʊl] *adj* misericordioso,-a, demente, compasivo,-a **(towards,** con). ◆ **mercifully** *adv* con compasión; *(fortunately)* afortunadamente.

merciless ['mɜ:sɪlɪs] *adj* despiadado,-a, sin piedad.

mercurial [mɜ:'kjʊərɪəl] *adj (person, temperament)* voluble, volátil.

Mercury ['mɜ:kjʊrɪ] *n Myth Astron* Mercurio *m*.

mercury ['mɜ:kjʊrɪ] *n* mercurio *m*, azogue *m*.

mercy ['mɜ:sɪ] *n* **1** *(compassion)* misericordia *f*, clemencia *f*, compasión *f;* **to be at the m. of sth/sb,** estar a la merced de algn/algn; **to beg for m.,** pedir clemencia; **to have m. on sb,** tener compasión de algn. **2** *fam (good fortune)* suerte *f;* **it's a m. that more people weren't**

injured, es una suerte que no hubiera más heridos. ■ **m. killing,** eutanasia *f*.

mere [mɪəʳ] *adj* mero,-a, simple, puro,-a. ◆ **merely** *adv* simplemente, solamente.

meretricious [merɪ'trɪʃəs] *adj fml (flashy)* de oropel, de relumbrón; *(deceptive)* engañoso,-a.

merganser [mɜ:'gænsəʳ] *n Orn* serreta *f* mediana.

merge [mɜ:dʒ] **I** *vtr (blend)* unir, combinar **(with,** con); *Com (firms)* fusionar; *(roads)* empalmar; **to m. into the background,** perderse de vista. **II** *vi* unirse, combinarse; *Com (firms)* fusionarse.

merger ['mɜ:dʒəʳ] *n Com* fusión *f*.

meridian [mə'rɪdɪən] *n Astron Geog* meridiano *m*.

meringue [mə'ræŋ] *n Culin* merengue *m*.

merit ['merɪt] **I** *n* **1** *(worth)* mérito *m*. **2** *(advantage)* ventaja *f*, mérito *m;* **to look into the merits of sth,** examinar los pros y los contras de algo. **II** *vtr (deserve)* merecer; **the plan merits consideration,** el plan es digno de consideración.

meritocracy [merɪ'tɒkrəsɪ] *n* meritocracia *f*.

merlin ['mɜ:lɪn] *n Orn* esmerejón.

mermaid ['mɜ:meɪd] *n* sirena *f*.

merman ['mɜ:mæn] *n (pl mermen* ['mɜ:men]*)* tritón *m*.

merriment ['merɪmənt] *n* alegría *f*, regocijo *m*.

merry ['merɪ] *adj (merrier, merriest)* alegre; *(amusing)* divertido,-a, gracioso,-a; *fam (tipsy)* alegre, achispado,-a; **m. Christmas!,** ¡felices Navidades!; **the more the merrier,** cuantos,-as más mejor. ◆ **merrily** *adv* alegremente.

merry-go-round ['merɪgəʊraʊnd] *n* tiovivo *m*, caballitos *mpl*.

merry-making ['merɪmeɪkɪŋ] *n (fun)* juerga *f; (party)* fiesta *f*.

mesh [meʃ] **I** *n* **1** *Tex* malla *f; fig* red *f*. ■ **wire m.,** tela *f* metálica. **2** *Tech* engranaje *m*. **II** *vtr Tech* engranar; *(fit)* encajar.

mesmerize ['mezməraɪz] *vtr* hipnotizar.

mess [mes] **I** *n* **1** *(confusion)* confusión *f; (disorder)* desorden *m;* **the house is a m.,** la casa está patas arriba; *fig* **he's a complete m.,** es un desastre. **2** *(difficult situation, mix-up)* lío *m*, follón *m;* **to get into a m.,** meterse en un lío *or* un aprieto; **to make a m. of one's life,** fracasar en la vida; **what a m.!,** ¡vaya lío!, ¡vaya follón! **3** *(dirt)* suciedad *f; euph (faeces)* porquería *f;* **to make a m. of one's clothes,** ensuciarse la ropa. **4** *Mil (food)* rancho *m*, comida *f*. **5** *Mil (room)* comedor *m*. **II** *vtr* **to m. one's pants,** cagarse encima. ◆ **mess about, mess around** *fam* **I** *vtr* fastidiar. **II** *vi* **1** *(act the fool)* hacer el primo. **2** *(idle)* gandulear; *(kill time)* matar el rato; *(potter about)* entretenerse. ◆ **mess about with** *vtr (fiddle with)* tocar, manosear; **to m. about with sb,** *(have affair with)* tener un lío *or* estar liado,-a con algn. ◆ **mess up** *vtr fam (untidy)* desordenar, dejar en desorden; *(dirty)* ensuciar; *fam (spoil)* estropear, echar a perder.

message ['mesɪdʒ] *n* **1** *(communication)* recado *m;* **to leave a m.,** dejar un recado. **2** *(of story, film, etc)* mensaje *m; fam* **to get the m.,** comprender.

messenger ['mesɪndʒəʳ] *n* mensajero,-a *m, f*. ■ **m. boy,** chico *m* de los recados.

Messiah [mɪ'saɪə] *n* Mesías *m*.

messianic [mesɪ'ænɪk] *adj* mesiánico,-a.

Messrs ['mesəz] *Com abbr of pl of* **Mr,** Señores *mpl*, Sres.

mess-up ['mesʌp] *n fam* lío *m*, follón *m*.

messy ['mesɪ] *adj (messier, messiest)* **1** *(untidy)* desordenado,-a, en desorden. **2** *(confused)* confuso,-a; *(involved)* lioso,-a, enredado,-a. **3** *(dirty)* sucio,-a.

met [met] *pt & pp see* **meet.**

metabolic [metə'bɒlɪk] *adj* metabólico,-a.

metabolism [me'tæbəlɪzəm] *n* metabolismo *m*.

metabolize [me'tæbəlaɪz] *vtr* metabolizar.

metal ['met əl] **I** n **1** metal m. ■ **m. detector,** detector m de metales; **m. polish,** limpiametales m inv. **2** (on road) grava f; **sheet m.,** lámina f de metal. **II** adj metálico,-a, de metal.

metallic [mɪ'tælɪk] adj metálico,-a. ■ **m. blue,** (colour) azul m metalizado.

metallurgist [me'tælədʒɪst] n metalúrgico,-a m,f.

metallurgy [me'tælədʒɪ] n metalurgia f.

metalwork ['metəlwɜːk] n **1** (craft) metalistería f. **2** (objects) objetos mpl de metal.

metamorphosis [metə'mɔːfəsɪs] n (pl **metamorphoses** [metə'mɔːfəsiːz]) metamorfosis f.

metaphor ['metəfəʳ, 'metəfɔːʳ] n metáfora f.

metaphoric(al) [metə'fɒrɪk(əl)] adj metafórico,-a.

metaphysical [metə'fɪzɪkəl] adj metafísico,-a.

metaphysics [metə'fɪzɪks] n metafísica f.

mete [miːt] vtr **to m. out,** (justice, rewards) repartir; (punishment) imponer.

meteor ['miːtɪəʳ] n bólido m.

meteoric [miːtɪ'ɒrɪk] adj meteórico,-a; fig **his m. rise to fame,** su meteórico ascenso a la fama.

meteorite ['miːtɪəraɪt] n meteorito m, aerolito m.

meteorological [miːtɪərə'lɒdʒɪkəl] adj meteorológico,-a.

meteorologist [miːtɪə'rɒlədʒɪst] n meteorólogo,-a m,f.

meteorology [miːtɪə'rɒlədʒɪ] n meteorología f.

meter¹ ['miːtəʳ] n contador m. ■ **gas/electricity m.,** contador m de gas/electricidad; **parking m.,** parquímetro m.

meter² ['miːtəʳ] n US see **metre.**

methane ['miːθeɪn] n Chem metano m.

method ['meθəd] n (manner, way) método m; (technique) técnica f; fam **there's m. in her madness,** es menos loca de lo que parece.

methodical [mɪ'θɒdɪkəl] adj metódico,-a, ordenado,-a.

Methodism ['meθədɪzəm] n Rel metodismo m.

Methodist ['meθədɪst] adj & n Rel metodista (mf).

methodology [meθə'dɒlədʒɪ] n metodología f.

meths [meθs] n fam abbr of **methylated spirits.**

Methuselah [mə'θjuːzələ] n Matusalén m; hum **as old as M.,** más viejo,-a que Matusalén.

methylated spirits [meθɪleɪtɪd'spɪrɪts] n alcohol m metilado or desnaturalizado.

meticulous [mə'tɪkjuləs] adj meticuloso,-a, minucioso,-a.

metre ['miːtəʳ] n metro m; **cubic/square m.,** metro cúbico/cuadrado.

metric ['metrɪk] adj métrico,-a. ■ **m. ton,** tonelada f métrica.

metrication [metrɪ'keɪʃən] n adopción f del sistema métrico.

metronome ['metrənəʊm] n metrónomo m.

metropolis [mɪ'trɒpəlɪs] n metrópoli f.

metropolitan [metrə'pɒlɪtən] adj metropolitano,-a.

mettle ['metəl] n ánimo m, valor m.

mew [mjuː] vi (cat) maullar, miar.

mewing ['mjuːɪŋ] n maullido m.

mews [mjuːz] n (street, yard) calleluela f. ■ **m. flat/house,** apartamento m/casa f de lujo en unas caballerizas reconvertidas.

Mexican ['meksɪkən] adj & n mejicano,-a (m, f), mexicano,-a (m,f).

Mexico ['meksɪkəʊ] n Méjico, México.

mezzanine ['mezəniːn] n **m. (floor),** entresuelo m.

MF abbr of **medium frequency,** frecuencia f modulada, FM f.

mg abbr of **milligram(s), milligramme(s),** miligramo(s) m(pl).

Mgr Rel abbr of **Monsignor,** Monseñor m, Mons.

MHz abbr of **megahertz,** megahercio(s) m(pl), MHz.

mi [miː] n Mus mi m.

miaow [miː'aʊ] **I** vi (cat) maullar, miar. **II** interj ¡miau! **III** n maullido m, miau m.

mice [maɪs] npl see **mouse.**

mickey ['mɪkɪ] n fam **to take the m.** (out of sb), tomar el pelo (a algn).

microbe ['maɪkrəʊb] n microbio m.

microbiologist [maɪkrəʊbaɪ'ɒlədʒɪst] n microbiólogo,-a m,f.

microbiology [maɪkrəʊbaɪ'ɒlədʒɪ] n microbiología f.

microchip ['maɪkrəʊtʃɪp] n Comput microchip m, microplaqueta f.

microcomputer [maɪkrəʊkəm'pjuːtəʳ] n microordenador m, microcomputador m.

microcosm ['maɪkrəʊkɒzəm] n microcosmo m.

microdot ['maɪkrəʊdɒt] n micropunto m.

microelectronics [maɪkrəʊɪlek'trɒnɪks] n microelectrónica f.

microfiche ['maɪkrəʊfiːʃ] n microficha f.

microfilm ['maɪkrəʊfɪlm] n microfilm m. ■ **m. reader,** lector m óptico.

microphone ['maɪkrəfəʊn] n micrófono m.

microprocessor [maɪkrəʊ'prəʊsesəʳ] n microprocesador m.

microscope ['maɪkrəskəʊp] n microscopio m.

microscopic [maɪkrə'skɒpɪk] adj microscópico,-a.

microsurgery [maɪkrəʊ'sɜːdʒərɪ] n microcirugía f.

microwave ['maɪkrəʊweɪv] n microonda f. ■ **m. oven,** (horno m de) microondas m inv.

mid [mɪd] adj medio,-a; **(in) m. afternoon,** a media tarde; **(in) m. April,** a mediados de abril; **in the m. ninteen-sixties,** a mediados de los sesenta; **to be in one's m. thirties,** tener unos treinta y cinco años.

midair [mɪd'eəʳ] adj (collision, explosion) en el aire; fig **to leave sth in m.,** dejar algo sin resolver.

midday [mɪd'deɪ] **I** n mediodía m; **at m.,** a mediodía. **II** adj de mediodía.

middle ['mɪdəl] **I** adj (central) de en medio; (medium) mediano,-a; **m. age,** mediana edad f; **the M. Ages,** la Edad Media; **the m. class,** la clase media. **II** n **1** (centre) centro m, medio m; (half-way point) mitad f; **in the m. of,** en medio de, en el centro de; **in the m. of August,** a mediados de agosto; **in the m. of winter,** en pleno invierno; **to be in the m. of doing sth,** estar metido en faena; fam **in the m. of nowhere,** en el quinto pino. **2** fam (waist) cintura f.

middle-aged [mɪdəl'eɪdʒd] adj de mediana edad.

middle-class [mɪdəl'klɑːs] adj de la clase media; (bourgeois) burgués,-esa.

middleman ['mɪdəlmæn] n (pl **middlemen** ['mɪdəlmen]) Com intermediario m.

middle-of-the-road [mɪdələvðə'rəʊd] adj (politics, views) moderado,-a.

middle-size(d) ['mɪdəlsaɪz(d)] adj de tamaño mediano.

middleweight ['mɪdəlweɪt] n Box peso m medio.

middling ['mɪdlɪŋ] adj mediano,-a, regular.

midfield [mɪd'fiːld] n Sport centrocampo m. ■ **m. player,** centrocampista mf.

midfielder [mɪd'fiːldəʳ] n Sport centrocampista mf.

midge [mɪdʒ] n mosca f enana.

midget ['mɪdʒɪt] **I** n enano,-a m, f. **II** adj (very small) diminuto,-a, pequeñísimo,-a; (miniature) en miniatura.

Midlands ['mɪdləndz] npl the M., la región central de Inglaterra.

midnight ['mɪdnaɪt] *n* medianoche *f; fam fig* **to burn the m. oil,** quemarse las pestañas.

midriff ['mɪdrɪf] *n Anat* diafragma *m*.

midshipman ['mɪdʃɪpmən] *n (pl midshipmen) Naut* guardia *m* marina.

midst [mɪdst] *prep* en medio de; **in our/their m.,** entre nosotros/ellos; **in the m. of,** en medio de.

midstream [mɪd'striːm] *n* **in m.,** *(river)* en medio de la corriente; *(way)* a mitad de camino.

midsummer [mɪd'sʌmə^r] *n* pleno verano *m*. ■ **M.'s Day,** Día *m* de San Juan (24 de junio).

midway ['mɪdweɪ] **I** *adv* a medio camino, a mitad del camino. **II** *adj (point etc)* intermedio,-a.

midweek ['mɪdwiːk] **I** *adv* entre semana. **II** *adj (match, flight, etc)* de entre semana.

midwife ['mɪdwaɪf] *n (pl midwives ['mɪdwaɪvz])* comadrona *f*; partera *f*.

midwifery ['mɪdwɪfərɪ] *n Med* obstetricia *f*.

midwinter [mɪd'wɪntə^r] **I** *n* pleno invierno *m*. **II** *adj* de pleno invierno.

miff [mɪf] *vtr fam* ofender, disgustar; **she was quite miffed about it,** le sentó bastante mal.

might¹ [maɪt] *v aux see* **may.**

might² [maɪt] *n fml* fuerza *f*, poder *m*; **with m. and main,** a más no poder.

mighty ['maɪtɪ] **I** *adj (mightier, mightiest)* **1** *(strong)* fuerte; *(powerful)* poderoso,-a. **2** *(great)* enorme. **II** *adv US fam (very)* muy; **a m. long journey,** un viaje muy largo *or* larguísimo.

migraine ['miːɡreɪn, 'maɪɡreɪn] *n* jaqueca *f*.

migrant ['maɪɡrənt] **I** *adj* migratorio,-a, emigrante. **II** *n* **1** *n (person)* emigrante *mf; (bird)* ave *f* migratoria. **2** *Austral* inmigrante *mf*.

migrate [maɪ'ɡreɪt] *vi* emigrar.

migration [maɪ'ɡreɪʃən] *n* migración *f*.

migratory ['maɪɡrətərɪ] *adj* migratoria,-a.

mike [maɪk] *n fam (abbr of microphone)* micro *m*.

mil 1 *(pl ml) abbr of* **mile,** milla *f*. **2** *abbr of* **millilitre(s),** mililitro(s) *m(pl)*, ml.

mild [maɪld] **I** *adj (person, character)* apacible, dulce; *(climate, weather)* templado,-a; *(punishment)* leve; *(beer)* ligero,-a; *(tobacco, taste)* suave. **II** *n fam* cerveza *f* ligera. ◆ **mildly** *adv (softly, gently)* suavemente; *(slightly)* ligeramente; **and that's putting it m.,** y esto es decir poco.

mildew ['mɪldjuː] *n* moho *m; (on plants)* añublo *m; (on vine)* mildiu *m*.

mildness ['maɪldnɪs] *n (of person, character)* apacibilidad *f*, suavidad *f*, dulzura *f; (of climate, weather, taste)* suavidad *f; (of punishment)* levedad *f*.

mile [maɪl] *n* milla *f; Aut* **miles to the gallon,** millas por galón; *fig* **it stands out a m.,** se ve a la legua; *fam* **it's miles away,** está lejísimos; *fam* **this is miles better,** este es muchísimo mejor. ■ **nautical m.,** milla marina.

mileage ['maɪlɪdʒ] *n* distancia *f* en millas; *Aut* kilometraje *m*; **a car with a low m.,** un coche con pocos kilometros; *fig* **to get a lot of m. out of sth,** sacarle mucho partido a algo.

mil(e)ometer [maɪ'lɒmɪtə^r] *n Aut* cuentakilómetros *m inv*.

milestone ['maɪlstəʊn] *n* hito *m*, mojón *m; fig* hito *m*.

milieu [miː'ljɜː] *n (pl milieux or milieus)* medio *m* ambiente *m*, entorno *m*.

militant ['mɪlɪtənt] *adj & n Pol* militante *(mf)*.

militarism ['mɪlɪtərɪzəm] *n* militarismo *m*.

militarist ['mɪlɪtərɪst] *n* militarista *mf*.

militaristic [mɪlɪtə'rɪstɪk] *adj* militarista.

military ['mɪlɪtərɪ] **I** *adj* militar; **to do one's m. service,** hacer el servicio militar. **II the m.** *npl* los militares, las fuerzas armadas.

militate ['mɪlɪteɪt] *vi fig* **to m. against/in favour of,** militar en contra/a favor de.

militia [mɪ'lɪʃə] *n* milicia *f*.

militiaman [mɪ'lɪʃəmən] *n (pl militiamen)* miliciano *m*.

milk [mɪlk] **I** *n* leche *f; fig* **it's no use crying over split m.,** a lo hecho, pecho. ■ **condensed m.,** leche *f* condensada; **m. chocolate,** chocolate *m* con leche; **m. churn,** lechera *f*; **m. products,** productos *mpl* lácteos; **m. shake,** batido *m* (de leche); **m. tooth,** diente *m* de leche; **powdered m.,** leche *f* en polvo; **skimmed m.,** leche *f* descremada *or* desnatada. **II** *vtr* **1** ordeñar. **2** *fam* chupar; **they milked him of all his money,** le chuparon hasta el último céntimo.

milking ['mɪlkɪŋ] *n* ordeño *m*. ■ **m. machine,** ordeñadora *f* mecánica.

milkman ['mɪlkmən] *n (pl milkmen)* lechero *m*, repartidor *m* de la leche.

milky ['mɪlkɪ] *adj (milkier, milkiest)* lechoso,-a, lácteo; *(colour)* pálido,-a; **a m. coffee,** un café con mucha leche. ■ *Astron* **M. Way,** Vía *f* Láctea.

mill [mɪl] **I** *n* **1** *(grinder)* molino *m; (for coffee, pepper)* molinillo *m; Tech (for metals)* fresadora *f; fig* **they put me through the m.,** me hicieron pasarlas moradas. **2** *(factory)* fábrica *f*; **cotton m.,** hilandería *f*; **paper/steel m.,** fábrica de papel/acero. **II** *vtr (grind)* moler; *Tech (metals)* fresar. ◆ **mill about, mill around** *vi (crowd)* arremolinarse, apiñarse.

millennium [mɪ'lenɪəm] *n (pl milleniums or milenia [mɪ'lenɪə])* milenio *m*, milenario *m*.

miller ['mɪlə^r] *n* **1** molinero,-a *m*,*f*. **2** *(fish)* **m.'s thumb,** cabezudo *m*.

millet ['mɪlɪt] *n Bot* mijo *m*.

millibar ['mɪlɪbɑː^r] *n* milibar *m*.

milligram(me) ['mɪlɪɡræm] *n* miligramo *m*.

millilitre, *US* **milliliter** ['mɪlɪliːtə^r] *n* mililitro *m*.

millimetre, *US* **millimeter** ['mɪlɪmɪ^r] *n* milímetro *m*.

milliner ['mɪlɪnə^r] *n* sombrerero,-a *m*, *f*; **m.'s (shop),** sombrerería *f*, tienda *f* de sombreros.

millinery ['mɪlɪnərɪ] *n (hats)* sombreros *mpl* de señora.

million ['mɪljən] *n* millón *m; fig* **one m. pounds,** un millón de libras; **two m. women,** dos millones de mujeres; *fam* **millions of,** millones de.

millionaire [mɪljə'neə^r] *n* millonario,-a *m*,*f*.

millionth ['mɪljənθ] *adj & n* millonésimo,-a *(m, f); fam* **for the m. time,** por enésima vez.

millipede ['mɪlɪpiːd] *n Ent* milpiés *m inv*.

millstone ['mɪlstəʊn] *n* muela *f*, rueda *f* de molino; *fig* **it's a m. round his neck,** es su cruz.

mime [maɪm] **I** *n (art)* mímica *f; (play, performance)* pantomima *f*. **II** *vtr* imitar, remedar.

mimic ['mɪmɪk] **I** *n (imitator)* mímico,-a *m*,*f*, remedador,-a *m*,*f*. **II** *adj* mímico,-a; **m. art,** mímica *f*. **III** *vtr (pt & pp mimicked)* imitar, remedar.

mimicry ['mɪmɪkrɪ] *n (art)* mímica *f; (imitation)* imitación *f*, remedo *m*.

mimosa [mɪ'məʊzə] *n Bot* mimosa *f*.

minaret ['mɪnəret] *n* alminar *m*, minarete *m*.

mince [mɪns] **I** *n (meat)* carne *f* picada. ■ *Culin* **m. pie,** pastel *m* de picadillo de fruta. **II** *vtr (meat etc)* picar; *fig* **he doesn't m. his words,** no tiene pelos en la lengua. **III** *vi (walk)* **to m. (along),** andar con pasos menuditos.

mincemeat ['mɪnsmiːt] *n (dried fruit)* conserva *f* de picadillo de fruta; *US (meat)* carne *f* picada.

mincer ['mɪnsə^r] *n (machine)* máquina *f* de picar carne, picadora *f* de carne.

mincing ['mɪnsɪŋ] *adj (step)* menudito,-a.

mind [maɪnd] **I** *n* **1** *(intellect)* mente *f; (intelligence)* inteligencia *f*; **peace of m.,** tranquilidad *f* de espíritu; **state of m.,** estado *m* de ánimo. **2** *(mentality)* mentalidad *f*; **open m.,** mentalidad abierta. **3** *(brain)* cabeza *f*, cerebro *m*; **I can't get it out of my m.,** no me lo puedo quitar de la cabeza; **to speak one's m.,** hablar sin rodeos; **what kind of car do you have in m.?,** ¿en qué clase de coche estás pensando? 4 *(sanity)* juicio *m*; **to lose one's m.,** perder el juicio. 4 *(opinion)* opinión *f*, parecer *m*; **to be in two minds about sth,** estar indeciso,-a; **to chance one's m.,** cambiar de opinión *or* parecer; **to make up one's m.,** decidirse; **to my m.,** a mi parecer. 6 *(intention)* intención *f*, propósito *m*; **to have a m. to do sth,** tener intención de hacer algo. 7 *(memory)* recuerdo *m*, memoria *f*; **it slipped my m.,** lo olvidé por completo; **to bear sth in m.,** tener algo en cuenta; **to bring/call sth to m.,** recordar algo, traer algo a la memoria. **II** *vtr* **1** *(look after)* *(child)* cuidar; *(house)* vigilar. **2** *(heed)* hacer caso de; *(be careful of)* tener cuidado con; **m. the step!,** ¡ojo con el peldaño!; **m. your own business!,** ¡no te metas donde no te llaman! **3** *(object to)* tener inconveniente en; **I don't m. going,** no tengo inconveniente en ir; **I wouldn't m. a cup of coffee,** me vendría bien un café; **never m.,** no importa. **III** *vi* **1** *(be careful)* tener cuidado; **m. (out)!,** ¡cuidado!, ¡ojo!; **m. you ...,** la verdad es que ...; **m. you, he is fifty,** ten en cuente que tiene cincuenta años; *fam* **never you m.!,** ¿a ti qué te importa? **2** *(object, express reluctance)* importar; **do you m. if I open the window?,** ¿le molesta *or* importa que abre la ventana?; **never m.,** *(don't worry)* no te preocupes; *(it doesn't matter)* no importa. ◆ **mind out** *vi* tener cuidado; **m. out!,** ¡cuidado!, ¡ojo!

mind-boggling ['maɪndbɒgəlɪŋ] *adj fam* alucinante, acojonante.

-minded ['maɪndɪd] *adj suff* **fair-m.,** imparcial; **single-m.,** resuelto,-a.

minder ['maɪndər] *n* **1** *fam (bodyguard)* guardaespaldas *m inv*, gorila *m*. **2** *(for child)* niñera *f*; *(babysitter)* canguro *mf*.

mindful ['maɪndful] *adj* consciente.

mindless ['maɪndlɪs] *adj* estúpido,-a, absurdo,-a; **to be m. of danger,** ser inconsciente del peligro.

mind-reader ['maɪndriːdər] *n* adivinador,-a *m*, *f* de pensamientos.

mind-reading ['maɪndriːdɪŋ] *n* adivinación *f* de pensamientos.

mine[1] [maɪn] *poss pron* (el) mío,-a, (la) mía, (los) míos, (las) mías, lo mío; **a friend of m.,** un amigo mío; **these gloves are m.,** estos guantes son míos; **which is m.?,** ¿cuál es el mío?

mine[2] [maɪn] *I n* **1** mina *f*. ■ **coal/gold m.,** mina *f* de carbón/de oro; **m. shaft,** pozo *m* de extracción. **2** *Mil Naut* mina *f*; *fig* **he's a m. of information,** es un pozo *or* una mina de información. **II** *vtr* **1** *(coal etc)* extraer. **2** *Mil Naut (road, waterway)* sembrar minas en; *(ship) (blow up)* volar con minas.

minefield ['maɪnfiːld] *n* campo *m* de minas.

minelayer ['maɪnleɪər] *n Naut (ship)* minador *m*.

miner ['maɪnər] *n* minero,-a *m*,*f*.

mineral ['mɪnərəl] *I adj* mineral. ■ **m. water,** agua *f* mineral. **II** *n* mineral *m*.

mineralogy [mɪnə'rælədʒɪ] *n* mineralogía *f*.

minesweeper ['maɪnswiːpər] *n Naut* dragaminas *m inv*.

mingle ['mɪŋgəl] *I vtr* mezclar. **II** *vi* mezclarse; *(sounds etc)* confundirse.

mini ['mɪnɪ] *n (skirt)* minifalda *f*.

miniature ['mɪnɪtʃər] *I n* miniatura *f*; **in m.,** en miniatura. **II** *adj* (en) miniatura; *(very small)* diminuto,-a. ■ **m. golf,** minigolf *m*, golf *m* miniatura.

minibus ['mɪnɪbʌs] *n* microbús *m*.

minicab ['mɪnɪkæb] *n* microtaxi *m*.

minim ['mɪnɪm] *n Mus* mínima *f*, blanca *f*.

minimal ['mɪnɪməl] *adj* mínimo,-a.

minimize ['mɪnɪmaɪz] *vtr (problems, dangers)* minimizar, reducir al mínimo.

minimum ['mɪnɪməm] *I adj* mínimo,-a; *Econ* **m. wage,** salario *m* mínimo. **II** *n (pl minima)* mínimo *m*, mínimum *m*; **with a m. of effort,** con el mínimo esfuerzo.

mining ['maɪnɪŋ] *I n* **1** minería *f*, explotación *f* de minas. **2** *Mil Naut* minado *m*. **II** *adj (industry, town)* minero,-a. ■ **m. engineer,** ingeniero,-a *m*,*f* de minas.

minion ['mɪnjən] *n* servidor *m*; *(favourite)* paniguado *m*.

miniskirt ['mɪnɪskɜːt] *n* minifalda *f*.

minister ['mɪnɪstər] *I n Pol* ministro,-a *m*,*f*; **the M. for Health,** el ministro de Sanidad. ■ **Prime M.,** primer,-a ministro,-a *m*,*f*. **2** *Rel* pastor,-a *m*,*f*. **II** *vi* **to m. to sb,** atender *or* cuidar a algn.

ministerial [mɪnɪ'stɪərɪəl] *adj Pol* ministerial; **m. office,** cargo *m* de ministro.

ministry ['mɪnɪstrɪ] *n* **1** *Pol* ministerio *m*; **M. of Transport,** Ministerio de Transportes (Públicos). **2** *Rel* sacerdocio *m*; **to enter the m.,** *(Catholics)* hacerse sacerdote; *(Protestants)* hacerse pastor.

mink [mɪŋk] *n (animal, fur)* visón *m*. ■ **m. coat,** abrigo *m* de visón.

minnow ['mɪnəʊ] *n (fish)* piscardo *m*.

minor ['maɪnər] *I adj* **1** *(smaller, lesser)* menor, más pequeño,-a. **2** *(unimportant)* sin importancia, insignificante; *(defect)* pequeño,-a; *(role, interest)* secundario,-a; *(party)* minoritario,-a; **m. expenses,** gastos *mpl* menudos. **3** *Mus* menor; **G m.,** Sol *m* menor; **m. key,** tono *m* menor. **II** *n* **1** *Jur* menor *mf* de edad. **2** *Mus* tono *m* menor. **3** *US Univ* asignatura *f* secundaria.

Minorca [mɪ'nɔːkə] *n* Menorca.

Minorcan [mɪ'nɔːkən] *adj* & *n* menorquín,-ina *(m*,*f)*.

minority [maɪ'nɒrɪtɪ] *n* **1** *(smaller part, small group)* minoría *f*. **2** *Jur* minoría *f* de edad. **II** *adj (government, interest, etc)* minoritario,-a.

minstrel ['mɪnstrəl] *n* juglar *m*, trovador *m*.

mint[1] [mɪnt] *I n* **1** *Fin* **the M.,** la Casa de la Moneda; **in m. condition,** en perfecto estado; *fam* **to be worth a m.,** valer un dineral. **II** *vtr (coin, words)* acuñar.

mint[2] [mɪnt] *n* **1** *Bot* menta *f*. **2** *(sweet)* pastilla *f* de menta.

minuet [mɪnjʊ'et] *n Mus* minué *m*.

minus ['maɪnəs] *I prep Math* menor; **5 m. 3,** 5 menos 3; **m. 10 degrees,** 10 grados bajo cero. **2** *fam (without)* sin; **he came back m. his wife,** volvió sin su mujer. **II** *adj (quanity, number)* negativo,-a. **III** *n (quanity)* cantidad *f* negativa; **m. (sign),** signo *m* de menos.

minuscule ['mɪnəskjuːl] *adj* minúsculo,-a.

minute[1] ['mɪnɪt] *n* **1** *(of time)* minuto *m*; **at the last m.,** a última hora; **(10 minutes) past 3,** las 3 y 10 (minutos); **just a m.,** *(espera)* un momento; **she could arrive any m. now,** llegará de un momento a otro; **this very m.,** ahora mismo. ■ *(on clock)* **m. hand,** minutero *m*. **2** *(note)* nota *f*, minuta *f*; **the minutes of the meeting,** el acta de reunión.

minute[2] [maɪ'njuːt] *adj (tiny)* diminuto,-a, minúsculo-a; *(careful, exact)* minucioso,-a, detallado,-a.

minutiae [mɪ'njuːʃiː] *npl* pequeños detalles *mpl*.

miracle ['mɪrəkəl] *n* milagro *m*; **by a m.,** de *or* por milagro; **it's a m. that she survived,** es un milagro que haya sobrevivido; **to work miracles,** hacer milagros.

miraculous [mɪ'rækjʊləs] *adj* milagroso,-a; **to have a m. escape,** salvarse de milagro. ◆ **miraculously** *adv* milagrosamente, por milagro.

mirage [mɪ'rɑːʒ] *n* espejismo *m*.

mire [maɪər] *n (mud)* fango *m*, lodo *m*; *(muddy place)* lodazal *m*.

mirror ['mɪrər] *I n* espejo *m*; *fig* espejo *m*, reflejo *m*; **to look at oneself in the m.,** mirarse en el espejo. ■ **driving m., rear-view m.,** retrovisor *m*; **m. image,** réplica *f*. **II** *vtr* reflejar.

mirth [mɜːθ] *n (jollity)* alegría *f*; *(laughter)* risas *fpl*.

misadventure [mɪsəd'ventʃəʳ] *n* desgracia *f*; *Jur* **death by m.,** muerte *f* accidental.

misanthrope ['mɪzənθrəʊp] *n*, **misanthropist** [mɪ'zænθrəpɪst] *n* misántropo,-a *m,f*.

misapprehend ['mɪsæprɪ'hend] *vtr* comprender *or* entender mal.

misapprehension [mɪsæprɪ'henʃən] *n* malentendido *m*, equivocación *f*.

misappropriate [mɪsə'prəʊprɪeɪt] *vtr (funds)* malversar.

misappropriation ['mɪsəprəʊprɪ'eɪʃən] *n (of funds)* malversación *f*.

misbehave [mɪsbɪ'heɪv] *vi* portarse *or* comportarse mal.

misbehaviour, *US* **misbehavior** [mɪsbɪ'heɪvjəʳ] *n* mala conducta *f*, mal comportamiento *m*.

miscalculate [mɪs'kælkjʊleɪt] *vtr & vi* calcular mal.

miscalculation [mɪskælkjʊ'leɪʃən] *n* cálculo *m* erróneo, error *m* de cálculo; *fig* error *m*, desacierto *m*, equivocación *f*.

miscarriage [mɪs'kærɪdʒ] *n* **1** *Med* aborto *m* (espontáneo). **2 m. of justice,** error *m* judicial.

miscarry [mɪs'kærɪ] *vi (pt & pp **miscarried**)* **1** *Med* abortar (espontáneamente). **2** *fig (plan)* fracasar.

miscast [mɪs'kɑːst] *vtr (pt & pp **miscast**) (actor)* dar un papel poco apropiado a.

miscellaneous [mɪsɪ'leɪnɪəs] *adj* misceláneo,-a, variado,-a; **m. expenses,** gastos *mpl* diversos.

miscellany [mɪ'selənɪ] *n* miscelánea *f*; *(of poems etc)* antología *f*.

mischance [mɪs'tʃɑːns] *n* mala suerte *f*, desgracia *f*.

mischief ['mɪstʃɪf] *n* **1** *(naughtiness)* travesura *f*, diablura *f*; **she's full of m.,** es muy traviesa; **to get into** *or* **up to m.,** hacer diabluras *or* travesuras. **2** *(evil)* malicia *f*, maldad *f*. **3** *fam (harm)* daño *m*, mal *m*; **to do oneself a m.,** hacerse daño.

mischievous ['mɪstʃɪvəs] *adj* **1** *(naughty)* travieso,-a; *(playful)* juguetón,-ona. **2** *(wicked)* malicioso,-a.

misconception [mɪskən'sepʃən] *n* concepto *m* erróneo *or* falso.

misconduct [mɪs'kɒndʌkt] *n (misbehaviour)* mala conducta *f*; *Com* mala administración *f*; *(adultery)* adulterio *m*; **professional m.,** error *m* profesional.

misconstruction [mɪskən'strʌkʃən] *n* mala interpretación *f*.

misconstrue [mɪskən'struː] *vtr* interpretar mal.

miscount [mɪs'kaʊnt] *vtr (votes etc)* contar mal.

misdeed [mɪs'diːd] *n* delito *m*, fechoría *f*.

misdemeanour, *US* **misdemeanor** [mɪsdɪ'miːnəʳ] *n (misdeed)* fechoría *f*; *Jur* delito *m* menor.

misdirect [mɪsdɪ'rekt] *vtr (letter)* poner mal las señas en; *(operation)* dirigir mal; *(person)* orientar *or* informar mal; *(energies, efforts)* encaminar *or* encauzar mal.

miser ['maɪzəʳ] *n* avaro,-a *m,f*.

miserable ['mɪzərəbəl] *adj* **1** *(sad)* triste, deprimido,-a; *(unfortunate)* desgraciado,-a; **it makes me m.,** me deprime muchísimo. **2** *(unpleasant)* desagradable; *(weather)* malo,-a; *(wretched, pathetic)* miserable, lamentable. **3** *(paltry)* despreciable, miserable. ◆ **miserably** *adv* **1** *(sadly)* tristemente; *(unfortunately)* desgraciadamente. **2** *(pathetically)* miserablemente, lamentablemente.

miserly ['maɪzəlɪ] *adj* avaro,-a, tacaño,-a.

misery ['mɪzərɪ] *n* **1** *(sadness)* tristeza *f*, *(wretchedness)* desgracia *f*, desdicha *f*; **to make sb's life a m.,** amargarle la vida a algn. **2** *(suffering)* sufrimiento *m*, dolor *m*; **to put an animal out of its m.,** acortarle la agonía a un animal; *fig hum* **go on, tell me, put me out of my m.,** anda, dímelo, no me hagas esperar más. **3** *(poverty)* pobreza *f*, miseria *f*. **4** *fam (person)* aguafiestas *mf*; **what a m. you are!,** ¡qué pesado eres!

misfire [mɪs'faɪəʳ] *vi (gun, car, plan)* fallar.

misfit ['mɪsfɪt] *n (person)* inadaptado,-a *m, f*; *(outcast)* marginado,-a *m, f*.

misfortune [mɪs'fɔːtʃən] *n* desgracia *f*, infortunio *m*; *(bad luck)* mala suerte *f*.

misgiving [mɪs'gɪvɪŋ] *n (doubt)* duda *f*, recelo *m*; *(fear)* temor *m*.

misguided [mɪs'gaɪdɪd] *adj* equivocado,-a, desacertado,-a.

mishandle [mɪs'hændəl] *vtr* llevar *or* manejar mal.

mishap ['mɪshæp] *n* desgracia *f*, contratiempo *m*, accidente *m*; **without m.,** sin novedad.

mishear [mɪs'hɪəʳ] *vtr & vi (pt & pp **misheard** [mɪs'hɜːd])* oír mal.

mishmash ['mɪʃmæʃ] *n fam* batiburrillo *m*, mezcolanza *f*.

misinform [mɪsɪn'fɔːm] *vtr* informar mal.

misinformation [mɪsɪnfə'meɪʃən] *n* falsa información *f*.

misinterpret [mɪsɪn'tɜːprɪt] *vtr* interpretar mal.

misinterpretation [mɪsɪntɜːprɪ'teɪʃən] *n* mala interpretación *f*.

misjudge [mɪs'dʒʌdʒ] *vtr (person, situation)* juzgar mal; *(distance etc)* calcular mal.

mislay [mɪs'leɪ] *vtr (pt & pp **mislaid** [mɪs'leɪd])* extraviar, perder.

mislead [mɪs'liːd] *vtr (pt & pp **misled**)* despistar, desorientar; *(deliberately)* engañar.

misleading [mɪs'liːdɪŋ] *adj (erroneous)* erróneo,-a; *(deliberately)* engañoso,-a.

misled [mɪs'led] *pt & pp see* **mislead**.

mismanage [mɪs'mænɪdʒ] *vtr* manejar mal, administrar mal.

mismanagement [mɪs'mænɪdʒmənt] *n* mal manejo *m*, mala administración *f*.

misnomer [mɪs'nəʊməʳ] *n* nombre *m* equivocado *or* inapropiado.

misogynist [mɪs'ɒdʒɪnɪst] *n* misógino,-a *m, f*.

misplace [mɪs'pleɪs] *vtr* **1** *(trust, affection)* encauzar mal. **2** *(lose)* extraviar, perder.

misplaced [mɪ'spleɪst] *adj* **1** *(trust, affection)* inapropiado,-a, equivocado,-a; *(remark)* fuera de lugar. **2** *(lost)* extraviado,-a, perdido,-a.

misprint ['mɪsprɪnt] *n* errata *f*, error *m* de imprenta.

mispronounce [mɪsprə'naʊns] *vtr* pronunciar mal.

mispronounciation [mɪsprənʌnsɪ'eɪʃən] *n* mala pronunciación *f*.

misquotation [mɪskwəʊ'teɪʃən] *n* cita *f* incorrecta *or* equivocada.

misread [mɪs'riːd] *vtr (pt & pp **misread** [mɪs'red])* leer mal; *(misinterpret)* interpretar mal.

misrepresent [mɪsreprɪ'zent] *vtr (facts)* falsificar, desvirtuar; *(words)* tergiversar, desvirtuar.

misrepresentation [mɪsreprɪzen'teɪʃən] *n* falsificación *f*, tergiversación *f*.

miss¹ [mɪs] *n* señorita *f*; **M. Fitzpatrick,** la señorita Fitzpatrick; **M. World,** Miss *f* Mundo; **thank you, m.,** gracias, señorita.

miss² [mɪs] **I** *n* **l** *(throw etc)* fallo *m*; *(shot)* tiro *m* errado; *(failure)* fracaso *m*; *fig* desacierto *m*. **2** *fam* **to give sth a m.,** no asistir; **I'll give the party a m.,** paso de ir a la fiesta. **II** *vtr* **1** *(throw etc)* fallar; *(shot)* errar. **2** *(fail to catch) (train etc)* perder; *(fail to see, hear, understand) (joke)* no entender; *(opportunity)* perder, dejar pasar; **I missed what you said,** no oí lo que dijiste; **you didn't m. much!,** ¡no te perdiste gran cosa!; **you have missed the point,** no has captado la idea; *fig* **to m. the boat,** perder el tren *or* la ocasión. **3** *(avoid)* evitar; **that car just missed me,** por poco me atropella ese coche. **4** *(not attend)* no asistir a; **to m. class,** faltar a clase. **5** *(omit,* *skip)* saltarse; *(disregard)* pasar por alto; **you missed a page,** te saltaste una página. **6** *(sth just lost)* echar en falta; *(person)* echar de menos; *(homeland)* añorar. **III** *vi* **1** *(throw etc)* fallar; *(shot)* errar. **2** *(fail to attend)* faltar. **3** *Aut (engine)* fallar. **4** *(be lacking)* faltar; **is anything missing?,** ¿falta algo? ◆ **miss out I** *vtr (omit)* saltarse; *(disregard)* pasar por alto. **II** *vi (opportunity etc)* **to m. out on,** perderse, dejar pasar.

missal ['mɪsəl] *n Rel* misal *m.*

misshapen [mɪs'ʃeɪpən] *adj (badly formed)* deforme; *(out of shape)* deformado,-a.

missile ['mɪsaɪl], *US* ['mɪsəl] *n Mil* misil *m; (object thrown)* proyectil *m.*■ **m. launcher,** lanzamisiles *m inv.*

missing ['mɪsɪŋ] *adj (lost)* perdido,-a, extraviado,-a; *(disappeared)* desaparecido,-a; *(absent)* ausente; **m. link,** eslabón *m* perdido; **m. person,** desaparecido,-a *m,f;* **three cups are m.,** faltan tres tazas.

mission ['mɪʃən] *n* misión *f; Astronaut* **m. control,** centro *m* de control.

missionary ['mɪʃənərɪ] **I** *adj* misional. **II** *n Rel* misionero,-a *m,f.*

missis ['mɪsɪs] *n fam (wife)* **the m.,** la parienta.

missive ['mɪsɪv] *n* misiva *f.*

misspell [mɪs'spel] *vtr (pt & pp misspelled or misspelt* [mɪs'spelt]*) (write)* escribir mal; *(say)* deletrear mal.

misspent [mɪsspent] *adj (youth)* malgastado,-a.

mist [mɪst] **I** *n (fog)* niebla *f; (thin)* neblina *f,* calina *f; (at sea)* bruma *f; (on window etc)* vaho *m; fig (of tears etc)* velo *m.* **II** *vi* **to m. over** *or* **up,** *(countryside)* cubrirse de neblina; *(window etc)* empañarse; *fig (eyes)* llenarse de lágrimas.

mistake [mɪ'steɪk] **I** *n* equivocación *f,* error *m; (oversight)* descuido *m; (in test etc)* falta *f;* **by m.,** por equivocación *or* descuido; *(unintentionally)* sin querer; **make no m. about it!,** ¡que quede bien claro!; **to make a m.,** equivocarse, cometer un error. ■ **spelling m.,** falta *f* de ortografía. **II** *vtr (pt mistook; pp mistaken)* **1** *(meaning, intention)* entender *or* interpretar mal. **2** *(confuse)* confundir; **to m. Jack for Bill,** confundir a Jack con Bill.

mistaken [mɪ'steɪkən] **I** *pp see* **mistake. II** *adj* equivocado,-a, erróneo,-a; **you are m.,** estás equivocado,-a.

mister ['mɪstər] *n* **1** señor *m.* **2** *fam* señor *m,* caballero *m.*

mistime [mɪs'taɪm] *vtr* **to m. sth,** hacer algo a deshora *or* a destiempo.

mistletoe ['mɪsltəʊ] *n Bot* muérdago *m.*

mistook [mɪ'stʊk] *pt see* **mistake.**

mistreat [mɪs'triːt] *vtr* maltratar, tratar mal.

mistress ['mɪstrɪs] *n* **1** *(of house, servant)* señora *f,* ama *f; (of dog)* dueña *f.* **2** *(lover)* amante *f,* querida *f.* **3** *(teacher) (primary school)* maestra *f; (secondary school)* profesora *f.*

mistrust [mɪs'trʌst] **I** *n* desconfianza *f,* recelo *m.* **II** *vtr* desconfiar de, dudar de.

mistrustful [mɪs'trʌstfʊl] *adj* desconfiado,-a, receloso,-a; **to be m. of sth/sb,** desconfiar de algo/algn.

misty ['mɪstɪ] *adj (mistier, mistiest) (weather)* nublado,-a, de niebla; *(window etc)* empañado,-a.

misunderstand [mɪsʌndə'stænd] *vtr & vi (pt & pp misundertood)* entender *or* comprender mal.

misunderstanding [mɪsʌndə'stændɪŋ] *n* malentendido *m; (mistake)* equivocacion *f; (disagreement)* desacuerdo *m,* desavenencia *f.*

misunderstood [mɪsʌndə'stʊd] *pt & pp see* **misunderstand. II** *adj (thing)* mal entendido,-a; *(person)* incomprendido,-a.

misuse [mɪs'juːs] **I** *n (of tool, resources, word)* mal uso *m,* mal empleo *m; (of funds)* malversación *f; (of authority, power)* abuso *m.* **II** [mɪs'juːz] *vtr (tool, resources, word)* utilizar *or* emplear mal; *(funds)* malversar; *(authority, power)* abusar de.

mite [maɪt] *n* **1** *(insect)* ácaro *m,* acárido *m.* **2** *(small child)* chiquillo,-a *m,f,* criatura *f.* **3** *(small amount)* pizca *f, fam* **he's a m. tired,** está cansadito.

miter ['maɪtər] *n US see* **mitre.**

mitigate ['mɪtɪgeɪt] *vtr* mitigar, aliviar; *Jur* **mitigating circumstances,** circunstancias *fpl* atenuantes.

mitigation [mɪtɪ'geɪʃən] *n* mitigación *f,* alivio *m; Jur* **to plead sth in m.,** alegar algo como atenuante.

mitre ['maɪtər] *n* **1** *Rel* mitra *f.* **2** *Carp* **m. (joint),** inglete *m.*

mitt [mɪt] *n* manopla *f;* **baseball m.,** guante *m* de béisbol; **oven m.,** manopla de cocina.

mitten ['mɪtən] *n* manopla *f; (fingerless glove)* mitón *m.*

mix [mɪks] **I** *n* mezcla *f; Culin* **cake m.,** preparado *m* para hacer un pastel. **II** *vtr* mezclar, combinar; *(paste, concrete)* amasar, mezclar; *Culin (ingredients)* mezclar; *(eggs)* batir; *(cocktail)* preparar; **to m. business with pleasure,** compaginar los negocios con la diversión. **III** *vi (blend)* mezclarse **(with,** con); *(go well together)* ir bien juntos; *(socially, people)* llevarse *or* entenderse bien; *fig* **oil and water don't m.,** el queso y el chocolate no se comen juntos. ◆ **mix in** *vtr* incorporar, añadir. ◆ **mix up** *vtr* **1** *(mix well) (ingredients)* mezclar bien. **2** *(confuse, muddle up) (person)* confundir **(with,** con); *(papers)* revolver; **to get all mixed up,** hacerse un lío. **3** *(involve)* implicar; **to be mixed up in sth,** estar metido,-a *or* enredado,-a en algo; **to get mixed up with sb,** liarse con algn.

mixed [mɪkst] *adj (assorted)* surtido,-a; *(varied)* variado,-a; *(education, school)* mixto,-a; *(feelings)* contradictorio,-a; *(salad)* mixto,-a; *(weather)* variable; *Sport* **m. doubles,** dobles *mpl* mixtos; *Culin* **m. grill,** parrillada *f.*

mixed-up [mɪkst'ʌp] *adj (objects, papers, etc)* revuelto,-a; *(person)* confuso,-a, desorientado,-a.

mixer ['mɪksər] *n* **1** *Culin* mezcladora *f,* batidora *f.* **2** *Constr* **concrete m.,** hormigonera *f.* **3** *Cin TV* mezclador,-a *m,f.* **4** *(person)* **to be a good m.,** tener don de gentes.

mixture ['mɪkstʃər] *n* mezcla *f.* ■ *Med* **cough m.,** jarabe *m* para la tos.

mix-up ['mɪksʌp] *n fam (confusion)* confusión *f,* lío *m,* enredo *m.*

mizzle ['mɪzəl] **I** *n* llovizna *f.* **II** *vi* lloviznar.

MLitt [em'lɪt] *Educ abbr of* **Master of Letters.**

mm *abbr of* **millimetre(s),** milímetro(s), *m(pl),* mm.

mnemonic [nɪ'mɒnɪk] **I** *adj* mnemotécnico,-a. **II** *n* mnemotécnica *f,* nemotécnica *f.*

MO [em'əʊ] *abbr of* **Medical Officer,** médico,-a *m, f* militar.

moan [məʊn] **I** *n* **1** *(groan)* gemido *m,* quejido *m.* **2** *(complaint)* queja *f.* **II** *vi* **1** *(groan)* gemir. **2** *(complain)* quejarse **(about,** de).

moaning ['məʊnɪŋ] *n* **1** *(groaning)* gemidos *mpl; (of wind in trees)* susurro *m.* **2** *(complaining)* quejas *fpl.*

moat [məʊt] *n* foso *m.*

mob [mɒb] **I** *n (crowds)* multitud *f,* muchedumbre *f,* gentío *m; (gang)* pandilla *f; (riff-raff)* gentuza *f,* chusma *f; US sl (Mafia)* **the M.,** la mafia; **m. rule,** ley *f* de la calle; **the m.,** el populacho. **II** *vtr (pt & pp mobbed) (crowd around)* acosar, rodear; *(attack)* asaltar, atropellar.

mobile ['məʊbaɪl, *US* 'məʊbəl] **I** *adj* móvil, movible; **are you m.?** ¿tienes coche?; **m. home,** caravana *f,* remolque *m.* **II** *n (hanging ornament)* móvil *m.*

mobility [məʊ'bɪlɪtɪ] *n* movilidad *f.*

mobilization [məʊbɪlaɪ'zeɪʃən] *n* movilización *f.*

mobilize ['məʊbɪlaɪz] *vtr (troops, support)* movilizar.

mobster ['mɒbstər] *n US fam* gángster *m.*

moccasin ['mɒkəsɪn] *n (shoe)* mocasín *m.*

mocha ['mɒkə] *n* moca *m.*

mock [mɒk] **I** adj **1** (feelings) fingido,-a simulado,-a; (modesty) falso,-a. **2** (objects) de imitación. **3** (events) de prueba; **m. battle,** simulacro m de batalla. **II** vtr (make fun of) burlarse or mofarse de; (mimic) imitar. **III** vi burlarse, mofarse (**at,** de).

mockery ['mɒkəri] n **1** (ridicule, derision) burla f, mofa f. **2** (travesty) parodia f; (farce) farsa f; **it makes a m. of the whole system,** esto pone el sistema en ridículo.

mocking ['mɒkɪŋ] adj burlón,-ona.

mockingbird ['mɒkɪŋbɜːd] n Orn sinsonte m.

mock-up ['mɒkʌp] (model) maqueta f, modelo m a escala.

MOD [eməʊ'diː] GB abbr of **Ministry of Defence,** Ministerio m de Defensa.

mode [məʊd] n **1** (manner, way) modo m, estilo m. **2** (fashion) moda f.

model ['mɒdəl] **I** n **1** (solid representation) modelo m; (scale) **m.,** maqueta f. **2** (design) figurín m; (pattern) patrón m, modelo m. **3** (fashion model) modelo mf, maniquí mf. **4** (of car, machine, etc) modelo m. **5** fig (perfect example) modelo m; **to act as a m. for,** servir de pauta a. **II** adj **1** (railway, car) en miniatura, de juguete; **m. aeroplane,** aeromodelo m. **2** (teacher, friend) ejemplar. **3** (factory, school) modelo; **m. home,** casa f piloto. **III** vtr (pt & pp **modelled,** US **modeled**) **1** (clay etc) modelar. **2** (clothes) presentar. **3** fig imitar, copiar; **A is modelled on B,** A se ha inspirado en B; **to m. oneself on sb,** seguir el ejemplo de algn. **IV** vi **1** (make clay models etc) modelar. **2** (work as fashion model) trabajar de modelo; (pose for artist) posar.

modelling, US **modeling** ['mɒdəlɪŋ] n **1** (of clay etc) modelado m. **2** (profession) profesión f de modelo.

modem ['məʊdem] n Comput modem m.

moderate¹ ['mɒdərɪt] **I** adj (gen) moderado,-a; (reasonable) razonable; (price) módico,-a; (average) regular, mediano,-a; (talent, ability) mediocre; (climate) templado,-a; **to be a m. drinker,** beber con moderación. **II** n Pol moderado,-a m, f, centrista mf. ◆ **moderately** adv (expensive, good) medianamente; (eat, drink) con moderación.

moderate² ['mɒdəreɪt] **I** vtr (demands, speed, etc) moderar. **II** vi **1** (diminish) moderarse; (wind, storm) calmarse, amainar. **2** (act as moderator) arbitrar, servir de moderador.

moderation [mɒdə'reɪʃən] n moderación f; **in m.,** con moderación.

moderator ['mɒdəreɪtə'] n (mediator) moderador,-a m, f, árbitro m.

modern ['mɒdən] adj moderno,-a; (history, literature) contemporáneo,-a; **m. languages,** lenguas fpl modernas.

modernism ['mɒdənɪzəm] n modernismo m.

modernist ['mɒdənɪst] adj & n modernista (mf).

modernity [mɒ'dɜːnɪti] n modernidad f.

modernización [mɒdənaɪˈzeɪʃən] n modernización f.

modernize ['mɒdənaɪz] **I** vtr modernizar. **II** vi modernizarse.

modest ['mɒdɪst] adj **1** modesto,-a, humilde. **2** (chaste) púdico,-a, recatado,-a. **3** (small) (sum of money, house, etc) modesto,-a, pequeño,-a; (price) módico,-a; (success) discreto,-a.

modesty ['mɒdɪsti] n **1** (humility) modestia f, humildad f. **2** (chastity) pudor m, recato m.

modicum ['mɒdɪkəm] n a **m. of,** una pizca de, un mínimo de; **it requires a m. of know-how,** requiere un mínimo de conocimientos.

modification [mɒdɪfɪ'keɪʃən] n modificación f.

modify ['mɒdɪfaɪ] vtr (pt & pp **modified**) modificar.

modulate ['mɒdjuleɪt] vtr modular.

modulation [mɒdjʊ'leɪʃən] n modulación f. ■ Rad **frequency m.,** frecuencia f modulada.

module ['mɒdjuːl] n módulo m.

mogul ['məʊgʌl] n magnate m.

mohair ['məʊheə'] n mohair m.

Mohammedan [məʊ'hæmɪdən] adj & n musulmán,-ana (m, f).

moist [mɔɪst] adj húmedo,-a; (wet) ligeramente mojado,-a.

moisten ['mɔɪsən] vtr humedecer; (wet) mojar ligeramente.

moisture ['mɔɪstʃə'] n (dampness) humedad f; (on glass) vaho m.

moisturize ['mɔɪstʃəraɪz] vtr (air) humedecer; (skin) hidratar; **moisturizing cream,** crema f hidratante.

moisturizer ['mɔɪstʃəraɪzə'] n crema f or leche f hidratante.

molar ['məʊlə'] n muela f.

molasses [mə'læsɪz] n melaza f.

mold [məʊld] n US see **mould.**

molder ['məʊldə'] vi US see **moulder.**

molding ['məʊldɪŋ] n US see **moulding.**

moldy ['məʊldɪ] adj US see **mouldy.**

mole¹ [məʊl] n (beauty spot) lunar m.

mole² [məʊl] n **1** (animal) topo m. **2** (spy) agente mf clandestino,-a, infiltrado,-a m, f.

molecular [məʊ'lekjʊlə'] adj molecular.

molecule ['mɒlɪkjuːl] n molécula f.

molehill ['məʊlhɪl] n topera f; fig **to make a mountain out of a m.,** hacer una montaña de un grano de arena.

molest [mə'lest] vtr (annoy) importunar, acosar, vejar; Jur (sexually assault) acosar (sexualmente).

mollify ['mɒlɪfaɪ] vtr (pt & pp **mollified**) aplacar, calmar, apaciguar.

mollusc, US **mollusk** ['mɒləsk] n Zool molusco m.

mollycoddle ['mɒlɪkɒdəl] vtr fam mimar, consentir.

Molotov cocktail [mɒlətɒf'kɒkteɪl] n cóctel m Molotov.

molt [məʊlt] vi US see **moult.**

molten ['məʊltən] adj fundido,-a, derretido,-a; **m. lava,** lava líquida.

mom [mɒm] n US fam mamá f.

moment ['məʊmənt] n **1** (instant) momento m, instante m; **a m. ago,** hace un momento; **at the m.,** en este momento; **at the last m.,** a última hora; **for the m.,** de momento; **I've just this m. seen them,** acabo de verles ahora mismo; **in a m.,** dentro de un momento; **to expect sb at any m.,** esperar a algn de un momento a otro. **2** (significance) importancia f, trascendencia f; **of great m.,** de gran importancia.

momentary ['məʊməntərɪ] adj momentáneo,-a. ◆ **momentarily** adv **1** (for a short time) momentáneamente. **2** (soon) de un momento a otro. **3** US (very soon) dentro de poco.

momentous [məʊ'mentəs] adj trascendental.

momentum [məʊ'mentəm] n (pl **momentums** or **momento** [məʊ'məntə]) Phys momento m; (speed) ímpetu m, velocidad f; fig ímpetu m, impulso m; **to gather m.,** cobrar velocidad.

mommy ['mɒmɪ] n US fam mamá f.

Mon abbr of **Monday,** lunes m, lun.

Monaco ['mɒnəkəʊ] n Mónaco.

monarch ['mɒnək] n monarca m.

monarchical [mə'nɑːkɪkəl] n monárquico,-a.

monarchist ['mɒnəkɪst] adj & n monárquico,-a (m, f).

monarchy ['mɒnəkɪ] n monarquía f.

monastery ['mɒnəstərɪ] n monasterio m.

monastic [mə'næstɪk] adj monástico,-a.

Monday ['mʌndɪ] n lunes m; see also **Saturday.**

Monegasque [mɒnə'gæsk] adj & n monegasco,-a (m, f).

monetarism ['mʌnɪtərɪzəm] n monetarismo m.

monetarist ['mʌnɪtərɪst] *adj & n* monetarista *(mf)*.

monetary ['mʌnɪtərɪ] *adj* monetario,-a.

money ['mʌnɪ] *n* dinero *m*; *(coin, currency)* moneda *f*; **pubic moneys** *or* **monies**, fondos *mpl* públicos; **to be worth a lot of m.**, *(person)* ser rico,-a, tener mucho dinero; *(thing)* valer mucho dinero; **to get one's m.'s worth**, sacar partido del dinero; **to make m.**, *(person)* ganar *or* hacer dinero; *(business etc)* rendir bien; **to put m. on**, apostar por; *fig* **I'd put my m. on her**, yo apostaría por ella; *fam* **it's m. for old rope**, es dinero regalado; *fam* **to be in the m.**, estar bien de dinero; *fam* **to be made of m., to be rolling in m.**, estar forrado,-a (de dinero). ■ **paper m.**, papel *m* moneda; **m. market**, mercado *m* de valores; **m. order**, giro *m* postal; **ready m.**, dinero *m* contante; **spending m.**, dinero *m* para gastos personales.

moneybags ['mʌnɪbægz] *n fam* ricachón,-ona *m,f*.

moneybox ['mʌnɪbɒks] *n* hucha *f*.

moneyed ['mʌnɪd] *adj* adinerado,-a, rico,-a.

moneylender ['mʌnɪlendə'] *n* prestamista *mf*.

moneylending ['mʌnɪlendɪŋ] *n* préstamo *m*.

moneymaker ['mʌnɪmeɪkə'] *n* **1** *(product, business)* negocio *m* rentable. **2** *fam pey (person)* pesetero,-a *m,f*.

moneymaking ['mʌnɪmeɪkɪŋ] **I** *adj (business)* rentable, lucrativo,-a. **II** *n* ganancia *f*.

money-spinner ['mʌnɪspɪnə'] *n fam see* **money-maker 1**.

Mongol ['mɒŋgɒl] **I** *adj* mongol,-a. **II** *n* **1** *(person)* mongol,-a *m,f*, mogol,-a *m,f*. **2** *(language)* mongol *m*, mogol *m*.

Mongolia [mɒŋ'gəʊlɪə] *n* Mongolia.

Mongolian [mɒŋ'gəʊlɪən] *adj & n* mongol,-a *(m,f)*.

mongolism ['mɒŋgəlɪzəm] *n* mongolismo *m*.

mongoose ['mɒŋguːs] *n (pl mongooses)* *Zool* mangosta *f*.

mongrel ['mʌŋgrəl] *n (dog)* perro *m* mestizo; *pey* perro *m* callejero.

monied ['mʌnɪd] *adj see* **moneyed**.

monitor ['mɒnɪtə'] **I** *n* **1** *Rad (person)* escucha *mf*. **2** *TV Tech Med (screen)* monitor *m*. **3** *Sch (prefect)* delegado,-a *m,f*, responsable *mf*. **II** *vtr* **1** *(radio broadcast)* escuchar. **2** *(check)* controlar; *(progress, events)* seguir de cerca.

monitoring ['mɒnɪtərɪŋ] *n* **1** *(of radio broadcast)* escucha *f*; **m. station**, estación *f* de escucha. **2** *(checking)* control *m*.

monk [mʌŋk] *n* monje *m*.

monkey ['mʌŋkɪ] *n* mono *m*, mico *m*; **female m.**, mona *f*, mica *f*; *fam (child)* **little m.**, diablillo *m*. ■ *fam* **m. business**, *(mischief)* travesuras *fpl*; *(swindle)* trampas *fpl*; **m. nut**, cacahuete *m*; *fam (mischief)* **m. tricks**, diabluras *fpl*, travesuras *fpl*; **m. wrench**, llave *f* inglesa. ◆ **monkey about monkey around** *vi fam* hacer tonterías, hacer el tonto; **to m. about** *or* **around with sth**, juguetear con algo.

monochrome ['mɒnəkrəʊm] **I** *adj* monocromo,-a; *(television, photo)* en blanco y negro. **II** *n* monocromía *f*.

monocle ['mɒnəkəl] *n* monóculo *m*.

monogamous [mɒ'nɒgəməs] *adj* monógamo,-a.

monogamy [mɒ'nɒgəmɪ] *n* monogamía *f*.

monogram ['mɒnəgræm] *n* monograma *m*.

monolith ['mɒnəlɪθ] *n* monolito *m*.

monologue, *US* **monolog** ['mɒnəlɒg] *n* monólogo *m*.

monoplane ['mɒnəʊpleɪn] *n* monoplano *m*.

monopolize [mə'nɒpəlaɪz] *vtr* **1** *Fin* monopolizar. **2** *(attention etc)* acaparar.

monopoly [mə'nɒpəlɪ] *n* monopolio *m*.

monorail ['mɒnəʊreɪl] *n (train, system)* monorriel *m*, monocarril *m*.

monosyllabic [mɒnəsɪ'læbɪk] *adj (word)* monosílabo,-a; *(language, remark)* monosilábico,-a.

monosyllable ['mɒnə'sɪləbəl] *n* monosílabo *m*.

monotone ['mɒnətəʊn] *n* **in a m.**, con una voz monótona.

monotonous [mə'nɒtənəs] *adj* monótono,-a.

monotony [mə'nɒtənɪ] *n* monotonía *f*.

monoxide [mɒ'nɒksaɪd] *n Chem* monóxido *m*. ■ **carbon m.**, monóxido *m* de carbono.

monsoon [mɒn'suːn] *n Meteor* monzón *m*; **m. rains**, lluvias *fpl* monzónicas.

monster ['mɒnstə'] **I** *n* monstruo *m*. **II** *adj fam (huge)* enorme, gigantesco,-a.

monstrosity [mɒn'strɒsɪtɪ] *n* monstruosidad *f*.

monstrous ['mɒnstrəs] *adj* **1** *(huge)* enorme, gigantesco,-a; *(hideous)* monstruoso,-a. **2** *(outrageous)* escandaloso,-a, monstruoso,-a; *(unfair)* injusto,-a; **it's m. that ...**, es una vergüenza que ... .

montage ['mɒntɑːʒ] *n Cin Phot* montaje *m*.

Monte Carlo [mɒntɪ'kɑːləʊ] *n* Montecarlo.

month [mʌnθ] *n* mes *m*; **a m. today**, de aquí a un mes; **calendar m.**, mes civil; **every m.**, cada mes, todos los meses; **in the m. of June**, en el mes de junio; **last/next m.**, el mes pasado/que viene; **m.'s pay**, sueldo *m* mensual, mensualidad *f*; **once a m.**, una vez al mes; **the l0th of this m.**, el 10 del corriente; *fam* **never in a m. of Sundays**, nunca jamás.

monthly ['mʌnθlɪ] **I** *adj* mensual; **m. instalment** *or* **payment**, mensualidad *f*; *Rail etc* **m. ticket**, abono *m* mensual. **II** *n (periodical)* revista *f* mensual. **III** *adv (every month)* mensualmente, cada mes; *(pay)* al mes.

monument ['mɒnjʊmənt] *n* monumento *m*.

monumental [mɒnʊ'məntəl] *adj* **1** monumental; **m. mason**, marmolista *mf*. **2** *fam (huge)* enorme, monumental; **a m. blunder**, una metedura de pata garrafal.

moo [muː] **I** *n (of cow)* mugido *m*. **II** *vi* mugir.

mooch [muːtʃ] **I** *vi fam* **to m. about** *or* **around**, vagar, divagar. **II** *vtr US sl* **to m. sth off sb**, *(cadge)* gorrear algo a algn; *(steal)* birlar algo a algn.

mood[1] [muːd] *n Ling* modo *m*.

mood[2] [muːd] *n* humor *m*; **he's in one of his moods**, está de malas; **to be in a good/bad m.**, estar de buen/mal humor; **to be in the m. for (doing) sth**, tener ganas de *or* estar de humor para (hacer) algo; **I'm not in the m. for jokes**, no estoy para bromas.

moodiness ['muːdɪnɪs] *n (changeable moods)* cambios *mpl* de humor; *(bad mood)* mal humor *m*; *(sadness)* melancolía *f*.

moody ['muːdɪ] *adj (moodier, moodiest) (changeable)* de humor cambiadizo, lunático,-a; *(badtempered)* malhumorado,-a; *(sad)* melancólico,-a; **she's very m.**, siempre está con caras largas.

moon [muːn] **I** *n* luna *f*; *fig* **once in a blue m.**, de higos a brevas; **to be over the m.**, estar en el séptimo cielo. ■ **full/new m.**, luna llena/nueva. **II** *adj* lunar. ■ **m. buggy**, vehículo *m* lunar; **m. landing**, alunizaje *m*. **III** *vi* **to m. about** *or* **around**, perder el tiempo, mirar a las musarañas.

moonbeam ['muːnbiːm] *n* rayo *m* de luna.

moonlight ['muːnlaɪt] **I** *n* claro *m* de luna, luz *f* de la luna; **by m., in the m.**, a la luz de la luna; **it was m.**, había luna; *fam* **to do a m. flit**, largarse a la chita callando. **II** *vi fam* estar pluriempleado,-a.

moonlighter ['muːnlaɪtə'] *n fam* pluriempleado,-a *m,f*.

moonlighting ['muːnlaɪtɪŋ] *n fam* pluriempleo *m*.

moonlit ['muːnlɪt] *adj (landscape etc)* iluminado,-a por la luna; *(night)* de luna.

moonshine ['muːnʃaɪn] *n* **1** *(nonsense)* bobadas *fpl*, pamplinas *fpl*. **2** *US (alcohol)* licor *m* destilado ilegalmente.

moonstone ['muːnstəʊn] *n Min* piedra *f* de la luna, adularia *f*.

moonstruck ['muːnstrʌk] *adj fam (crazy)* chiflado,-a, tocado,-a.

Moor [mʊəʳ] *n* moro,-a *m, f*.

moor¹ [mʊəʳ] *n (heath)* brezal *m*, páramo *m*.

moor² [mʊəʳ, mɔːʳ] *vtr Naut (with ropes)* amarrar; *(with anchor)* anclar.

moorhen ['mʊəhen] *n Orn* polla *f* de agua.

mooring ['mʊərɪŋ] *n* **1** *(place)* amarradero *m*. **2 moorings,** *(ropes etc)* amarras *fpl*.

Moorish ['mʊərɪʃ] *adj* moro,-a.

moorland ['mʊələnd] *n* brezal *m*, páramo *m*.

moose ['muːs] *n inv Zool* alce *m*.

moot ['muːt] **I** *adj* **it's a m. point,** es discutible (**whether,** si). **II** *vtr (suggest)* plantear, proponer, sugerir; **it has been mooted that ...,** se ha sugerido que ... .

mop [mɒp] **I** *n (for floor)* fregona *f*, fregasuelos *m inv*; *fam* **m. of hair,** melena *f*, mata *f* de pelo. **II** *vtr (pt & pp mopped) (floor)* fregar, limpiar; **to m. one's brow,** enjugarse la frente. ◆ **mop up** *vtr* **1** *(spilt liquids)* limpiar, enjugar; *(dry up)* secar; *fig (profits, funds)* llevarse. **2** *Mil (enemy forces)* acabar con, rematar.

mope [məʊp] *vi* estar deprimido,-a *or* abatido,-a. ◆ **mope about, mope around** *vi* andar abatido,-a.

moped ['məʊped] *n* ciclomotor *m*, vespa *f*.

mopping-up [mɒpɪŋ'ʌp] *n Mil* **m.-up operation,** operación *f* de limpieza.

moral ['mɒrəl] **I** *adj* moral; **m. victory,** victoria moral. **II** *n* **1** *(of story)* moraleja *f*. **2 morals,** *(standards)* moral *f sing*, moralidad *f sing*. ◆ **morally** *adv* moralmente; **m. right/wrong,** moral/inmoral.

morale [mə'rɑːl] *n* moral *f*, estado *m* de ánimo; **her m. was very low,** estaba muy baja de moral; **to raise sb's m.,** subirle la moral a algn.

moralistic [mɒrə'lɪstɪk] *adj* moralizador,-a.

morality [mə'rælɪtɪ] *n* moralidad *f*.

moralize ['mɒrəlaɪz] *vi* moralizar.

morass [mə'ræs] *n (marsh)* cenagal *m*, pantano *m*; *fig (mess)* lío *m*, embrollo *m*; **a m. of details,** un laberinto *o* un mar de detalles.

moratorium [mɒrə'tɔːrɪəm] *n (pl moratoriums or moratoria* [mɒrə'tɔːrɪə]*)* moratoria *f*.

morbid ['mɔːbid] *adj Med* mórbido,-a; *(mind)* morboso,-a, enfermizo,-a; *(curiosity)* malsano,-a; *(depressed)* pesimista.

morbidness ['mɔːbɪdnɪs] *n (medical, of mind)* morbosidad *f*; *(depression)* pesimismo *m*.

mordant ['mɔːdənt] *adj (criticism etc)* mordaz.

more [mɔːʳ] **I** *adj* más; **and what is m.,** y además, y lo que es más; **is there any m. tea?,** ¿queda más té?; **I've no m. money,** no me queda más dinero; **m. people,** más gente; **no m. crying!,** ¡deja ya de llorar! **II** *pron* más; **how many m.?,** ¿cuántos más?; **I need some m.,** necesito más; **it's m. than enough,** basta y sobra; **many/much m.,** muchos,-as/mucho más; **m. than a hundred,** más de cien; **the m. he has, the m. he wants,** cuanto más tiene más quiere; **to see m. of sb,** ver a algn más a menudo. **III** *adv* más; **I won't do it any m.,** no lo volveré a hacer; **it's m. than a little suprising,** es bastante sorprendente; **m. and m. difficult,** cada vez más difícil; **m. or less the same,** más o menos igual; **once m.,** una vez más; **she doesn't live here any m.,** ya no vive aquí; **still m.,** todavía más.

moreover [mɔː'rəʊvəʳ] *adv* además, por otra parte.

mores ['mɔːreɪz] *npl fml* costumbres *fpl*, tradiciones *fpl*.

morgue [mɔːg] *n* depósito *m* de cadáveres.

moribund ['mɒrɪbʌnd] *adj* moribundo,-a.

morning ['mɔːnɪŋ] **I** *n* mañana *f*; *(before dawn)* madrugada *f*; **early in the m.,** muy de mañana; **in the m.,** por la mañana; **in the early hours of the m.,** de madrugada; **on Monday mornings,** los lunes por la mañana; **tomorrow m.,** mañana por la mañana; *(greeting)* **good m.!,** ¡buenos días!; *fam* **to have the m.-after feeling,** tener resaca. **II** *adj (walk, breeze)* matutino,-a, de la mañana. ■ **m.-after pill,** *(contraceptive)* píldora *f* abortiva; **m. dress,** chaqué *m*; **m. paper,** diario *m* de la mañana; **m. sickness,** náuseas *fpl* del embarazo; **m. star,** lucero *m* del alba, estrella *f* matutina.

mornings ['mɔːnɪŋs] *adv* por la mañana.

Moroccan [mə'rɒkən] *adj & n* marroquí *(mf)*.

Morocco [mə'rɒkəʊ] *n* Marruecos.

moron ['mɔːrɒn] *n* **1** *Med* retrasado,-a *m, f* mental. **2** *fam* imbécil *mf*, idiota *mf*.

morose [mə'rəʊs] *adj* malhumorado,-a, hosco,-a.

morpheme ['mɔːfiːm] *n Ling* morfema *m*.

morphia ['mɔːfɪə] *n*, **morphine** ['mɔːfiːn] *n* morfina *f*.

morphology [mɔː'fɒlədʒɪ] *n Biol Ling* morfología *f*.

Morse [mɔːs] *n* **M. (code),** (alfabeto *m*) Morse *m*.

morsel ['mɔːsəl] *n (of food)* bocado *m*; *fig* trozo *m*, fragmento *m*.

mortal ['mɔːtəl] **I** *adj* mortal; *(human)* humanó,-a; **m. remains,** restos *mpl* mortales; *Rel* **m. sin,** pecado *m* mortal. **II** *n* mortal *mf*. ◆ **mortally** *adv (offended etc)* mortalmente; **m. wounded,** herido,-a de muerte.

mortality [mɔː'tælɪtɪ] *n* **1** *(condition)* mortalidad *f*. **2** *(number of deaths)* mortalidad *f*; **infant m.,** la mortalidad infantil; **m. (rate),** índice *m* or tasa *f* de mortalidad. **3** *(number of victims)* mortandad *f*.

mortar ['mɔːtəʳ] **I** *n* **1** *Constr (cement)* mortero *m*, argamasa *f*; *fig* **to put one's money in bricks and m.,** invertir dinero en asuntos inmobiliarios. **2** *Mil (gun)* mortero *m*. **3** *(bowl)* mortero *m*, almirez *m*; **pestle and m.,** maja *f* y mortero. **II** *vtr Mil* bombardear con morteros.

mortarboard ['mɔːtəbɔːd] *n Univ (cap)* birrete *m*.

mortgage ['mɔːgɪdʒ] **I** *n* hipoteca *f*; **m. repayment,** pago *m* hipotecario; **to pay off a m.,** levantar *or* redimir una hipoteca. **II** *vtr (property, one's future)* hipotecar.

mortice ['mɔːtɪs] *n see* **mortise.**

mortician [mɔː'tɪʃən] *n US* empresario,-a *m, f* de pompas fúnebres.

mortification [mɔːtɪfɪ'keɪʃən] *n* mortificación *f*.

mortify ['mɔːtɪfaɪ] *vtr (pt & pp mortified) fam* mortificar; *fam* **I was mortified,** me sentí avergonzado,-a.

mortise ['mɔːtɪs] *n Carp* muesca *f*, mortaja *f*; **m. lock,** cerradura *f* embutida.

mortuary ['mɔːtʃʊərɪ] *n* depósito *m* de cadáveres.

mosaic [mə'zeɪɪk] *n* mosaico *m*; **m. floor,** suelo *m* de mosaico.

Moscow ['mɒskəʊ, *US* 'mɒskaʊ] *n* Moscú.

Moses ['məʊzɪz] *n* Moisés *m*. ■ **M. basket,** moisés *m*.

Moslem ['mɒzləm] *adj & n* musulmán,-ana *(m, f)*.

mosque [mɒsk] *n* mezquita *f*.

mosquito [mɒs'kiːtəʊ] *n (pl mosquitoes or mosquitos) Ent* mosquito *m*; **m. bite,** picadura *f* de mosquito. ■ **m. net,** mosquitero *m*, mosquitera *f*.

moss [mɒs] *n Bot* musgo *m*. ■ *Knit* **m. stitch,** punto *m* de arroz.

mossy ['mɒsɪ] *adj (mossier, mossiest)* musgoso,-a, cubierto,-a de musgo.

most [məʊst] **I** *adj (superl of much, many)* **1** *(greatest in quantity etc)* más; **this house suffered (the) m. damage,** esta casa fue la más afectada; **who made (the) m. mistakes?,** quién cometió más errores? **2** *(the majority of)* la mayoría de, la mayor parte de; **for the m. part,** por lo general; **m. of the time,** la mayor parte del tiempo; **m. people,** la mayoría de la gente. **II** *pron* **1** *(greatest part)* la mayor parte; **m. of it is finished,** la mayor parte está terminada. **2** *(greatest number or* *amount)* lo máximo, lo más; **there were 50 at the (very) m.,** había 50 como máximo; **to make the m. of sth,** aprovechar algo al máximo. **3** *(the majority of people)* la mayoría; **m. voted in favour,** la mayoría votó a favor. **III** *adv* (*superl of much*) **1** *(to form superl)* más; **the m. intelligent student in the class,** el estudiante más inteligente de la clase. **2** *(to the greatest degree)* más; **what I like m.,** lo que más me gusta. **3** *(very)* muy, de lo más; **a m. amusing speech,** un discurso de lo más divertido; **m. likely,** muy probablemente; *(especially)* **m. of all,** sobre todo; **she'll m. likely come,** es muy probable que venga; **you have been m. kind,** usted ha sido muy amable. **4** *US fam* casi; **m. everyone,** casi todos. ◆ **mostly** *adv* **1** *(chiefly)* principalmente, en su mayor parte. **2** *(generally)* generalmente; *(usually)* normalmente.

MOT [eməʊ'tiː] *GB abbr of* **Ministry of Transport,** Ministerio *m* de Trasporte; **MOT test,** inspección *f* técnica de vehículos, ITV.

motel [mə'tel] *n* motel *m*.

moth [mɒθ] *n* mariposa *f* nocturna. ▪ **clothes m.,** polilla *f*.

mothball ['mɒθbɔːl] *n* bola *f* de naftalina.

motheaten ['mɒθiːtən] *adj* apolillado,-a.

mother ['mʌðəʳ] **I** *n* **1** madre *f*; **m. love,** amor *m* materno *or* maternal; **unmarried m.,** madre soltera. ▪ **m. country,** patria *f*, madre patria *f*; **M. Nature,** Madre *f* Naturaleza; **M.'s Day,** Día *m* de la Madre; **m.'s help,** niñera *f*; **m. tongue,** lengua *f* materna. **2** *Rel* madre *f*; **M. Superior,** madre superior; **M. Teresa,** la Madre Teresa. **II** *vtr (care for)* cuidar como una madre; *pej (spoil)* mimar.

motherhood ['mʌðəhʊd] *n* maternidad *f*.

mother-in-law ['mʌðərɪnlɔː] *n* (*pl* **mothers-in-law**) suegra *f*.

mothering ['mʌðərɪŋ] *n* cuidados *mpl* maternales. ▪ **M. Sunday,** Día *m* de la Madre.

motherland ['mʌðəlænd] *n* patria *f*, madre patria *f*.

motherless ['mʌðəlɪs] *adj* huérfano,-a de madre.

motherly ['mʌðəlɪ] *adj* maternal.

mother-of-pearl [mʌðərəv'pɜːl] *n* madreperla *f*, nácar *m*.

mother-to-be [mʌðətə'biː] *n* (*pl* **mothers-to-be**) futura madre *f*.

mothproof ['mɒθpruːf] *adj* a prueba de polillas.

motif [məʊ'tiːf] *n Art Mus* motivo *m*; *(embroidered etc)* adorno *m*; *fig (main subject)* tema *m*.

motion ['məʊʃən] **I** *n* **1** *(movement)* movimiento *m*; *Cin* **in slow m.,** a cámara lenta; **to be in m.,** estar en marcha; *fig* **to go through the motions,** hacer algo como es debido pero sin convicción. ▪ *Cin* **m. pictures,** el cine; **m. sickness,** mareo *m*. **2** *(gesture)* ademán *m*, señal *f*. **3** *Pol etc (proposal)* moción *f*; **to carry a m.,** aprobar una moción; **to second a m.,** apoyar una moción. **2** *(bowel movement)* evacuación *f* del vientre. **II** *vtr & vi* hacer señas; **to m. (to) sb to do sth,** hacer señas a algn para que haga algo.

motionless ['məʊʃənlɪs] *adj* inmóvil.

motivate ['məʊtɪveɪt] *vtr* motivar.

motivation [məʊtɪ'veɪʃən] *n* motivación *f*.

motive ['məʊtɪv] **I** *adj* motor, motora *or* motriz. ▪ **m. power,** fuerza *f* motriz. **II** *n (reason)* motivo *m*; *Jur* móvil *m*; **with the best of motives,** con la mejor intención.

motiveless ['məʊtɪvlɪs] *adj* sin motivo.

motley ['mɒtlɪ] *adj* (*motlier, motliest*) **1** *(multicoloured)* abigarrado,-a, variopinto,-a. **2** *(varied)* diverso,-a, variado,-a, heterogéneo,-a.

motocross ['məʊtəkrɒs] *n Sport* motocross *m*, motocrós *m*.

motor ['məʊtəʳ] *n (engine)* motor *m*; *fam (car)* coche *m*, automóvil *m*; **the m. trade,** la industria del automóvil. ▪ **m. oil,** aceite *m* para motores; **m. racing,** carreras *fpl* de coches; **m. show,** salón *m* del automóvil.

motorbike ['məʊtəbaɪk] *n fam* motocicleta *f*, moto *f*.

motorboat ['məʊtəbəʊt] *n* (lancha) motora *f*.

motorcade ['məʊtəkeɪd] *n* desfile *m* de coches *or* vehículos.

motorcar ['məʊtəkɑːʳ] *n* coche *m*, automóvil *m*.

motorcoach ['məʊtəkəʊtʃ] *n* autocar *m*.

motorcycle ['məʊtəsaɪkəl] *n* motocicleta *f*.

motorcyclist ['məʊtəsaɪklɪst] *n* motociclista *mf*.

motoring ['məʊtərɪŋ] **I** *adj* automovilístico,-a, del automóvil; **m. accident,** accidente *m* automovilístico; **m. holiday,** vacaciones *fpl* en coche. **II** *n* automovilismo *m*.

motorist ['məʊtərɪst] *n* automovilista *mf*, conductor,-a *m*, *f* (de coche).

motorize ['məʊtəraɪz] *vtr* motorizar.

motorized ['məʊtəraɪzd] *adj* motorizado,-a.

motorman ['məʊtəmən] *n* (*pl* **motormen**) *(train driver)* maquinista *m*, conductor *m*.

motorway ['məʊtəweɪ] *n GB* autopista *f*.

mottled ['mɒtəld] *adj (skin, animal)* con manchas; *(surface)* moteado,-a, jaspeado,-a.

motto ['mɒtəʊ] *n* (*pl* **mottoes** *or* **mottos**) lema *m*.

mould¹, *US* **mold** [məʊld] *n (fungus)* moho *m*.

mould², *US* **mold** [məʊld] **I** *n Art Culin Tech* molde *m*; *fig* carácter *m*, temple *m*; **cast in the same m.,** cortado,-a con el mismo patrón. **II** *vtr (figure)* moldear; *(clay)* modelar; *fig* **to m. oneself on sb,** tomar a algn como modelo.

moulder, *US* **molder** ['məʊldəʳ] *vi* **to m. (away),** desmoronarse.

moulding, *US* **molding** ['məʊldɪŋ] *n Archit* moldura *f*.

mouldy, *US* **moldy** ['məʊldɪ] *adj* (*mouldier, mouldiest*) **1** mohoso,-a, enmohecido,-a; **to go m.,** enmohecerse; **to smell m.,** oler a moho *or* humedad. **2** *GB sl* cochino,-a, miserable.

moult [məʊlt] *vi (feathers, skin)* mudar.

mound [maʊnd] *n* **1** *(of earth)* montón *m*; *(small hill)* montículo *m*. **2** *fig (pile)* montón *m*.

mount¹ [maʊnt] *n (mountain)* monte *m*; **M. Everest** (Monte) Everest *m*.

mount² [maʊnt] **I** *n* **1** *(horse)* montura *f*. **2** *(base, support)* soporte *m*, base *f*; *(for photograph)* marco *m*; *(for jewel)* engaste *m*, montura *f*. **II** *vtr* **1** *(horse)* subirse *or* montar a; *(bicycle)* subir a, montar en; **the car mounted the pavement,** el coche se subió a la acera. **2** *(exhibition)* montar; *(campaign)* organizar, lanzar. **3** *(photograph)* enmarcar; *(jewel)* engastar, montar. **4** *Mil* **to m. guard,** montar la guardia. **III** *vi* **1** *(go up)* subir; *(get on horse, bike)* montar. **2** *(increase)* subir, aumentar. ◆ **mount up** *vi (increase)* subir, aumentar; *(accumulate)* amontonarse, acumularse.

mountain ['maʊntɪn] **I** *n* montaña *f*; *fig (pile)* montaña *f*, montón *m*. **II** *adj* de montaña, montañés,-esa; *(country)* montañoso,-a. ▪ *Bot* **m. ash,** serbal *m*; **m. bike,** bicicleta *f* de montaña; *Zool* **m. lion,** puma *m*; **m. range,** sierra *f*, cordillera *f*; **m. sickness,** mal *m* de montaña.

mountaineer [maʊntɪ'nɪəʳ] *n* alpinista *mf*, *Am* andinista *mf*.

mountaineering [maʊntɪ'nɪərɪŋ] *n* alpinismo *m*, *Am* andinismo *m*.

mountainous ['maʊntɪnəs] *adj (region)* montañoso,-a; *fig* enorme.

mounted ['maʊntɪd] *adj* montado,-a; **the m. police,** la policía montada.

mourn [mɔːn] *vtr & vi* **to m. (for) sb,** llorar la muerte de algn.

mourner ['mɔːnəʳ] *n* doliente *mf*.

mournful ['mɔːnfʊl] *adj (person)* triste, afligido,-a; *(voice, tone)* triste, lúgubre.

mourning ['mɔːnɪŋ] *n* luto *m*, duelo *m*; **to be dressed in m.,** ir vestido,-a de luto; **to be in m.** for sb, estar de luto por algn; **to go into m.,** ponerse de luto.

mouse [maʊs] n (pl **mice**) **1** Zool ratón m. **2** Comput ratón m.

mousetrap ['maʊstræp] n ratonera f.

mousse [muːs] n **1** Culin mousse f. **2** Hairdr **(styling) m.,** espuma f (moldeadora).

moustache [mə'staːʃ] n bigote(s) m(pl).

mousy ['maʊsɪ] adj (**mousier, mousiest**) **1** (colour) pardusco,-a; (hair) castaño claro. **2** (shy) tímido,-a.

mouth [maʊθ] **I** n (pl **mouths** [maʊðz]) **1** Anat boca f; fig **I got it straight from the horse's m.,** lo sé de buena tinta; fig **it made my m. water,** se me hizo la boca agua; fig **she has five mouths to feed,** tiene cinco bocas que alimentar; fig **to keep one's m. shut,** no decir esta boca es mía; fam **shut your m.!,** ¡cállate la boca!; ¡cierra el pico!; fam **to be down in the m.,** estar deprimido,-a; fam **to have a big m.,** ser un bocazas; fam **to shoot one's m. off,** hablar más de la cuenta. **2** (of bottle) boca f; (of tube) abertura f; (of cave, tunnel, etc) boca f, entrada f; (of river) desembocadura f. **II** vtr [maʊð] (words) pronunciar, articular; (in affected manner) pronunciar con afectación; (insults) proferir. **III** vi mover los labios. ◆ **mouth off** vi fam **to m. off about sth,** echar un discurso sobre algo, hacerse el enterado en algo.

mouthful ['maʊθfʊl] n (of food) bocado m; (of drink) sorbo m; (of air) bocanada f; (name etc) **to be a bit of a m.,** ser largo o difícil de pronunciar; fam **to give sb a m.,** poner verde a algn.

mouth organ ['maʊθɔːgən] n Mus armónica f.

mouthpiece ['maʊθpiːs] n **1** Mus boquilla f. **2** (of telephone) micrófono m. **3** fig (spokesman) portavoz m.

mouth-to-mouth [maʊθtə'maʊθ] adj **m.-to-m. resuscitation,** boca a boca m.

mouthwash ['maʊθwɒʃ] n enjuage m bucal.

mouthwatering ['maʊθwɔːtərɪŋ] adj muy apetitoso,-a, que se le hace a uno la boca agua.

movable ['muːvəbəl] adj movible, móvil.

move [muːv] **I** n **1** (movement) movimiento m; **to be on the m.,** (to travel) viajar, desplazarse; fig (army, country) estar en marcha; fig (to be busy) estar muy ocupado,-a, no parar; **we must make a m.,** debemos irnos ya; fam **get a m. on!,** ¡date prisa! **2** (games) jugada f; (turn) turno m; **whose m. is it?,** ¿a quién le toca jugar? **3** (step) paso m; (course of action) medida f; **to make the first m.,** dar el primer paso; **what is the next m.?,** ¿qué hay que hacer ahora? **4** (transfer to new home) mudanza f, traslado m; (to new job) traslado m. **II** vtr **1** (gen) mover; (furniture etc) cambiar de sitio; (steering wheel) girar; (transfer) trasladar; **m. that motorbike off the lawn!,** ¡quita esa moto del césped!; **to m. house,** mudarse (de casa), trasladarse; **to m. job,** cambiar de trabajo; **to m. sth closer,** acercar algo. **2** (in games) mover, jugar. **3** (incite, motivate) inducir, mover; (persuade) persuadir; **I won't be moved,** no me harán cambiar de parecer; **to m. sb to tears,** hacer llorar a algn. **4** (affect emotionally) conmover; **she is easily moved,** es muy sensible. **5** (resolution etc) proponer; **I m. that the meeting be closed,** propongo que se cierre la reunión. **III** vi **1** (change position) moverse, trasladarse, desplazarse; (change house) mudarse (de casa); (change post, department, etc) trasladarse; **don't m.!,** ¡no te muevas!; **m. out of the way!,** ¡quítate de en medio!; **to m. to another seat/job,** cambiar de asiento/trabajo; **keep moving!,** ¡circulen! **2** (be moving) estar en marcha o en movimiento; **to start moving,** ponerse en marcha. **3** (travel, go) ir; **it moves at high speed,** va a gran velocidad. **4** (leave) irse, marcharse; **it's time we were moving,** es hora de irnos. **5** (games) jugar, hacer una jugada; (game piece) moverse. **6** (take action) tomar medidas. **7** (progress) hacer progresos, adelantar. ◆ **move about, move around I** vtr (object) cambiar de sitio o lugar; (employee) trasladar. **II** vi (be restless) moverse mucho; (walk o fro etc) ir y venir, ir de acá para allá; (travel) viajar de un lugar a otro; **to m. about freely,** circular libremente. ◆ **move along I** vtr (move forward) hacer avanzar, adelantar; (keep moving) hacer circular. **II** vi (move

forward) avanzar, adelantarse; (keep moving) circular; **m. along!,** (to crowd) ¡circulen!; (to person on bench) ¡córrete!, ¡haz sitio! ◆ **move away I** vtr (object, person) alejar, apartar **(from,** de). **II** vi **1** (move aside etc) alejarse, apartarse. **2** (leave) irse, marcharse. **3** (change house) mudarse (de casa). ◆ **move back I** vtr **1** (object) mover hacia atrás; (crowd etc) hacer retroceder. **2** (to original place) volver. **II** vi **1** (withdraw, retreat) retroceder, retirarse. **2** (to original place) volver. ◆ **move down I** vtr (person, object) bajar. **II** vi bajar. ◆ **move forward I** vtr **1** (person, vehicle, etc) avanzar, adelantar. **2** (clock) adelantar. **II** vi avanzar, adelantarse. ◆ **move in I** vtr (object) (furniture into new home etc) instalar. **II** vi **1** (into new home) instalarse. **2** (police etc) (approach) acercarse; **to m. in on,** acercarse a, avanzar hacia. ◆ **move off I** vtr (remove from) sacar o quitar de. **II** vi **1** (go away) irse, marcharse; (train) salir. **2** (set off) ponerse en camino; (car, train) arrancar. ◆ **move on I** vtr **1** (keep moving) (people, cars, etc) circular. **2** (hands of clock) adelantar. **II** vi **1** (keep moving) (people, cars) circular; **m. on, please!,** ¡circulen! **2** (go forward) avanzar; (time) pasar, transcurrir. ◆ **move out I** vtr (object) sacar; (troops) retirar. **II** vi **1** (leave) irse, marcharse; (troops) retirarse. **2** (leave house) mudarse. **3** Aut **to m. out in order to overtake,** salirse para adelantar. ◆ **move over I** vtr correr. **II** vi correrse; **m. over!,** ¡córrete! ◆ **move up I** vtr **1** (object, person) subir; (bring closer) acercar. **2** fig (promote) ascender; (pupil) **to be moved up,** pasar a la clase superior. **II** vi **1** (go up) subir. **2** fig (be promoted) ser ascendido,-a, ascender. **3** (move along) correrse.

moveable ['muːvəbəl] adj see **movable.**

movement ['muːvmənt] n **1** (act, motion) movimiento m; (gesture with hand etc) gesto m, ademán m; **back and forth m.,** vaivén m; **to watch sb's movements,** vigilar los movimientos or las actividades de algn. **2** (transport) transporte m; (of goods, employees) traslado m; (of troops) desplazamiento m. **3** Pol Lit movimiento m; (trend) tendencia f, corriente f; **the feminist m.,** el movimiento feminista. **4** Com (of stock market) actividad f; (of prices) su riación f. **5** Tech (workings) (of clock, machine) mecanismo m. **6** Mus (of symphony etc) movimiento m, tempo m, tiempo m. **7** Med (of bowels) evacuación f.

mover ['muːvə'] n **1** fam **she's a lovely m.,** tiene mucho garbo. **2** (in meeting etc) proponedor,-a. **3** US mozo m de mudanzas.

movie ['muːvɪ] n US película f; **to go to the movies,** ir al cine. ◆ **m. star,** estrella f de cine.

moviegoer ['muːvɪɡəʊə'] n US aficionado,-a m, f al cine.

moving ['muːvɪŋ] adj **1** (that moves) móvil; (in motion) en movimiento; (car etc) en marcha. ◆ **m. staircase,** escalera f mecánica. **2** (causing motion) motor,-a, motriz; fig (motivating) instigador,-a, promotor. **3** fig (touching) conmovedor,-a.

mow [məʊ] vtr (pt **mowed;** pp **mown** or **mowed**) (lawn) cortar, segar; (corn, wheat) segar; fig (kill etc) **to m. down,** matar, segar.

mower ['məʊə'] n (for lawn) segadora f, cortacésped m & f; Agr segadora f.

mown [məʊn] pp see **mow.**

Mozambique [məʊzəm'biːk] n Mozambique.

Mozarab [məʊ'zærəb] n mozárabe mf.

MP [em'piː] **1** abbr of **Member of Parliament,** miembro mf de la Cámara de los Comunes. **2** fam abbr of **Military Police,** policía f militar.

mpg [empiː'dʒiː] abbr of **miles per gallon,** ≈ litros de gasolina a los cien kilómetros.

mph [empiː'eɪtʃ] abbr of **miles per hour,** millas fpl por hora.

MPhil [em'fɪl] abbr of **Master of Philosophy.**

Mr ['mɪstə'] abbr of **mister,** señor m, Sr.

MRBM [eməːbiːˈem] *Mil abbr of* **medium-range balistic missile,** proyectil *m* balístico de alcance intermedio, PBAI.

Mrs [ˈmɪsɪs] *abbr* señora *f*, Sra.

MS, ms [emˈes] *abbr of* **manuscript,** manuscrito *m*, ms.

Ms [məz] *abbr* señora *f*, Sra, señorita *f*, Srta.

MSc [emesˈsiː] *abbr of* **Master of Science.**

Mt *abbr of* **Mount, Mountain,** monte *m*, montaña *f*.

mth *abbr of* **month,** mes *m*, m/.

much [mʌtʃ] (*more, most*) **I** *adj* mucho,-a; **add twice as m. flour,** añade el doble de harina; **as . ... m as,** tanto,-a ... como; **as m. wine as you like,** tanto vino como quieras; **how m. chocolate?,** ¿cuánto chocolate?; **m. admiration,** mucha admiración; **so m.,** tanto,-a; **so m. suffering,** tanto sufrimiento; **too m.,** demasiado,-a; *(at end of letter)* **m. love,** un fuerte abrazo. **II** *adv* mucho; **as m. as,** tanto como; **as m. as you like,** todo lo que quieras; **as m. as possible,** todo lo posible; **how m.?,** ¿cuánto?; **how m. is it?,** ¿cuánto es?, ¿cuánto vale?; **m. better/worse,** mucho mejor/peor; **m. as I hate him,** por mucho que le odie; **m. more,** mucho más; **m. to my surprise,** para gran sorpresa mía; **so m. the better,** ¡tanto mejor!; **thank you very m.,** muchísimas gracias; **they are m. the same,** son más o menos iguales; **too m.,** demasiado; **10 kilos too m.,** 10 kilos de más; **very m.,** muchísimo; **without so m. as,** sin siquiera; *fam* **that's a bit m.!,** ¡eso ya es el colmo! **III** *pron* mucho; **I'll say this m. for her,** tiene eso en su favor; **I thought as m.,** lo suponía; **it's not up to m.,** no vale gran cosa; **m. of the town was destroyed,** gran parte de la ciudad quedó destrozada; **m. remains to be done,** queda mucho por hacer; **they don't see m. of each other,** se ven muy poco; **there isn't that m. of it,** no hay tanto; **to be not m. of sth,** *(no good)* no ser muy bueno,-a en algo; *(no kind)* no ser muy aficionado,-a a algo; **to make m. of sth,** dar mucha importancia a algo.

muchness [mʌtʃnɪs] *n fam* **it's much of a m.,** viene a ser lo mismo.

muck [mʌk] *n* **1** *(dirt)* suciedad *f*; *(mud)* lodo *m*; *(manure)* estiércol *m*; *fam* caca *f*. **2** *fig* porquería *f*; **to make a m. of sth,** echar algo a perder. ◆ **muck about, muck around** *fam* **I** *vi (idle)* gandulear, perder el tiempo; *(play the fool)* hacer el tonto; *(fiddle with)* **to m. about with sth,** manosear algo, juguetear con algo. **II** *vtr* **to m. sb about,** fastidiar a algn. ◆ **muck in** *vi fam (help)* echar una mano. ◆ **muck out** *vtr (stable)* limpiar. ◆ **muck up** *vtr* **1** *(dirty)* ensuciar. **2** *fig (spoil)* echar a perder; *(fail to achieve)* no conseguir, fracasar.

muckraking [ˈmʌkreɪkɪŋ] *n fam* cotilleo *m*.

muck-up [ˈmʌkʌp] *n fam (bungle)* chapuza; *(mess)* follón *m*, lío *m*.

mucky [ˈmʌki] *adj* (*muckier, muckiest*) *(dirty)* sucio,-a; *(muddy)* lodoso,-a.

mucous [ˈmjuːkəs] *adj* mucoso,-a. ■ **m. membrane,** membrana *f* mucosa.

mucus [ˈmjuːkəs] *n* moco *m*, mocosidad *f*.

mud [mʌd] *n* lodo *m*, barro *m*; *(thick)* fango *m*; *fig hum* **it's as clear as m.,** no queda nada claro; *fam* **her name is m.,** tiene muy mala fama; **to throw** *or* **sling m. at sb,** poner a algn por los suelos. ■ **m. bath,** baño *m* de lodo; **m. flat,** marisma *f*.

mudbank [ˈmʌdbæŋk] *n* banco *m* de arena.

muddle [ˈmʌdəl] **I** *n (mess)* desorden *m*; *fig (mix-up)* confusión *f*, embrollo *m*, lío *m*; **to be in a m.,** *(things)* estar en desorden; *(person)* estar hecho un lío; **to get into a m.,** *(things)* quedar en desorden; *(person)* hacerse un lío; **there was a m. over the dates,** hubo un lío con las fechas. **II** *vtr* **to m. (up),** *(person, facts)* confundir; **to get muddled up,** liarse, hacerse un lío. ◆ **muddle along** *vi* actuar a la buena de Dios *or* al tuntún. ◆ **muddle through** *vi* arreglárselas, ingeniárselas.

muddle-headed [ˈmʌdəlhedɪd] *adj (person)* despistado,-a; *(plan, ideas)* confuso,-a.

muddy [ˈmʌdɪ] *adj* (*muddier, muddiest*) *(path etc)* lodoso,-a fangoso,-a; *(hands, shoes, etc)* lleno,-a *or* cubierto,-a de barro *or* de lodo; *(river)* cenagoso,-a; *(liquid)* turbio,-a; *(complexion, colour)* terroso,-a.

mudguard [ˈmʌdgɑːd] *n (on car, bicycle, etc)* guardabarros *m inv*.

muff¹ [mʌf] *n (for hands)* manguito *m*; **ear muffs,** orejeras *fpl*.

muff² [mʌf] *vtr fam* pifiar; **to m. it (up),** estropearlo, echarlo a perder.

muffin [ˈmʌfɪn] *n Culin* panecillo *m*.

muffle [ˈmʌfəl] *vtr* **1** *(sound)* an ortiguar, ensordecer. **2** *(person)* **to m. (up),** abrigar; *(with scarf, hat)* embozar.

muffled [ˈmʌfəld] *adj (sound)* sordo,-a.

muffler [ˈmʌflər] *n* **1** *(scarf)* bufanda *f*. **2** *US Aut* silenciador *m*.

mufti [ˈmʌftɪ] *n Mil etc* **in m.,** vestido,-a de paisano.

mug¹ [mʌg] *n (large cup)* taza *f* alta, tazón *m*; *(beer tankard)* jarra *f*.

mug² [mʌg] **I** *n fam* **1** *(fool)* tonto,-a *m,f*; **it's a m.'s game,** es cosa de tontos. **2** *(face)* jeta *f*, hocico *m*. **II** *vtr (pt & pp mugged)* *(attack)* atracar, asaltar. ◆ **mug up** *vi fam* empollar; **to m. up (on) a subject,** empollar una asignatura.

mugger [ˈmʌgər] *n (attacker)* asaltante *mf*.

mugging [ˈmʌgɪŋ] *n (attack)* asalto *m*.

muggy [ˈmʌgɪ] *adj* (*muggier, muggiest*) *(weather)* bochornoso,-a.

mugshot [ˈmʌgʃɒt] *n fam (esp taken by police)* foto *f* de la cara.

mulatto [mjuːˈlætəʊ] *n (pl mulattos or mulattoes)* mulato,-a *m,f*.

mulberry [ˈmʌlbərɪ] *n* **1** *(fruit)* mora *f*. **2** *(tree)* morera *f*, moral *m*. **3** *(colour)* morado *m*.

mulch [mʌltʃ] *n Agr* abono *m*, pajote *m*.

mule¹ [mjuːl] *n (animal)* mulo,-a *m, f*; *fig (person)* **as stubborn as a m.,** más terco,-a que una mula.

mule² [mjuːl] *n (slipper)* chinela *f*.

mulish [mjuːlɪʃ] *adj* terco,-a, testarudo,-a.

mull [mʌl] *vtr (wine)* calentar con especias; **mulled wine,** vino *m* caliente con especias. ◆ **mull over** *vi* **to m. over a matter,** reflexionar sobre *or* reconsiderar un asunto.

mullet [ˈmʌlɪt] *n (pt mullet or mullets)* *(fish)* **grey m.,** mújol *m*; **red m.,** salmonete *m*.

multiaccess [mʌltɪˈækses] *n Comput* acceso *m* múltiple; **m. system,** sistema *m* multiacceso *or* de acceso múltiple.

multicoloured, *US* **multicolored** [ˈmʌltɪkʌləd] *adj* multicolor.

multifarious [mʌltɪˈfeərɪəs] *adj* múltiple, vario,-a, diverso,-a.

multilingual [mʌltɪˈlɪŋgwəl] *adj* plurilingüe.

multimillionaire [mʌltɪmɪljəˈneər] *n* multimillonario,-a *m,f*.

multinational [mʌltɪˈnæʃənəl] **I** *adj* multinacional.**II** *n* multinacional *f*.

multiple [ˈmʌltɪpəl] **I** *adj* múltiple; *Aut* **m. pile-up,** colisión *f* múltiple. ■ *Med* **m. sclerosis,** esclerosis *f* en placas *or* múltiple. **II** *n Math* múltiplo *m*.

multiplication [mʌltɪplɪˈkeɪʃən] *n* multiplicación *f*. ■ **m. sign,** signo *m* de multiplicar; **m. table,** tabla *f* de multiplicar.

multiplicity [mʌltɪˈplɪsɪtɪ] *n* multiplicidad *f*.

multiply [ˈmʌltɪplaɪ] **I** *vtr (pt & pp multiplied) Math* multiplicar (**by,** por). **II** *vi (reproduce)* multiplicarse.

multipurpose [mʌltɪˈpɜːpəs] *adj* multiuso *inv*.

multiracial [mʌltɪˈreɪʃəl] *adj* multirracial.

multistorey [mʌltɪˈstɔːrɪ] *adj (building)* de varios pisos; **m. car park,** parking *m* de varias plantas.

multitude ['mʌltɪtjuːd] *n (crowd)* multitud *f*, muchedumbre *f*.

mum¹ [mʌm] *n fam* mamá *f*.

mum² [mʌm] *adj* **to keep m.,** no decir ni pío, guardar silencio.

mumble ['mʌmbəl] *vtr & vi* musitar, hablar entre dientes.

mumbo jumbo [mʌmbəʊ'dʒʌmbəʊ] *n (pl mumbo jumbos) (gibberish)* galimatías *f inv.*

mummify ['mʌmɪfaɪ] *vtr (pt & pp mummified)* momificar.

mummy¹ ['mʌmɪ] *n (body)* momia *f.*

mummy² ['mʌmɪ] *n fam (mother)* mamá *f*, mamy *f.*

mumps [mʌmps] *n Med* paperas *fpl.*

munch [mʌntʃ] *vtr & vi* mascar, masticar.

mundane [mʌn'deɪn] *adj* **1** *(worldly)* mundano,-a. **2** *pej (ordinary)* vulgar, banal; *(job, life)* rutinario,-a.

municipal [mjuː'nɪsɪpəl] *adj* municipal.

municipality [mjuːnɪsɪ'pælɪtɪ] *n* municipio *m.*

munitions [mjuː'nɪʃənz] *npl* municiones *fpl.*

mural ['mjʊərəl] **I** *adj* mural. **II** *n* pintura *f* mural, mural *m.*

murder ['mɜːdəʳ] **I** *n* **1** asesinato *m*, homicidio *m*; **m. case,** caso *m* de homicidio; **the m. weapon,** el arma homicida. **2** *fam* **it was m.!,** ¡vaya pesadilla!; **she cried blue m.,** gritó como si la estuvieran matando; **they get away with m.,** hacen lo que les da la gana. **II** *vtr* **1** *(kill)* asesinar, matar. **2** *fam fig (song etc)* destrozar, estropear.

murderer ['mɜːdərəʳ] *n* asesino *m*, homicida *m.*

murderess ['mɜːdərɪs] *n* asesina *f*, homicida *f.*

murderous ['mɜːdərəs] *adj (look, thoughts)* asesino,-a, homicida.

murky ['mɜːkɪ] *adj (murkier, murkiest)* **1** *(gen)* oscura,-a, tenebroso,-a; *(water)* turbio,-a; *(weather)* nublado,-a; *(night)* de niebla. **2** *fig (business)* turbio,-a; *(past)* tenebroso,-a.

murmur ['mɜːməʳ] **I** *n* **1** *(of voice, stream)* murmullo *m*, susurro *m*; *(of traffic)* rumor *m*. ■ *Med* **heart m.,** soplo *m* cardíaco. **2** *(complaint)* queja *f*; **he did it without a m.,** lo hizo sin rechistar. **II** *vtr & vi* murmurar.

muscle ['mʌsəl] **I** *n* músculo *m*; **m. power,** fuerza *f*; **he didn't move a m.,** ni se inmutó. **II** *vi fam* **to m. in on sth,** entrometerse en asuntos ajenos.

Muscovite ['mʌskəvaɪt] *adj & n* moscovita *(mf).*

muscular ['mʌskjʊləʳ] *adj (pain, tissue)* muscular; *(person)* musculoso,-a.

Muse [mjuːz] *n Myth* musa *f.*

muse [mjuːz] *vi* **to m. on** *or* **about sth,** meditar algo, reflexionar sobre algo.

museum [mjuː'zɪəm] *n* museo *m.*

mush [mʌʃ] *n (soft)* papilla *f*; *(porridge)* gachas *fpl*; *fam (food overcooked)* mazacote *m.*

mushroom ['mʌʃruːm] **I** *n Bot* seta *f*, hongo *m*; *Culin* champiñón *m*. **II** *vi fig (grow quickly)* crecer de la noche a la mañana; *(spread)* multiplicarse.

mushy ['mʌʃɪ] *adj (mushier, mushiest)* **1** *(food)* blando,-a, en papilla; **m. peas,** puré *m* de guisantes. **2** *fam (sentimental)* sentimentaloide.

music ['mjuːzɪk] *n* música *f*; **to set a work to m.,** poner música a una obra; *fig* **to face the m.,** dar la cara. ■ **chamber m.,** música de cámara; **m. box,** caja *f* de música; **m. hall,** teatro *m* de variedades; **m. lover,** melómano,-a *m,f*; **m. score,** partitura *f*; **m. stand,** atril *m*; **piped m.,** música *f* ambiental.

musical ['mjuːzɪkəl] **I** *adj* musical, de música; **to be m.,** *(gifted)* estar dotado,-a para la música; *(fond of music)* ser aficionado,-a a la música; **to have a m. ear,** tener buen oído para la música. ■ **m. instrument,** instrumento *m* musical. **II** *n* comedia *f* musical.

musician [mjuː'zɪʃən] *n* músico,-a *m,f.*

musicologist [mjuːzɪ'kɒlədʒɪst] *n* musicólogo,-a *m,f*, musicógrafo,-a *m,f.*

musings ['mjuːzɪŋz] *npl* meditaciones *fpl*, reflexiones *fpl.*

musk [mʌsk] *n (substance)* almizcle *m.*

musket ['mʌskɪt] *n* mosquete *m.*

musketeer [mʌskɪ'tɪəʳ] *n* mosquetero *m.*

Muslim ['muzlɪm] *adj & n* musulmán,-ana *(m,f).*

muslin ['mʌzlɪn] *n* muselina *f.*

musquash ['mʌskwɒʃ] *n Zool* ratón *m* amizclero, desmán *m.*

mussel ['mʌsəl] *n Zool* mejillón *m*. ■ **m. bed,** criadero *m* de mejillones.

must¹ [mʌst] *n (of grapes)* mosto *m.*

must² [mʌst] *n (mould)* moho *m*; *(smell)* olor *m* a humedad.

must³ [mʌst] **I** *v aux* **1** *(necessity, obligation)* deber, tener que; **if I m.,** si no hay más remedio; **one m. eat to live,** hay que comer para vivir; **you m. arrive on time,** tienes que *or* debes llegar a la hora; **you m. not do that again,** no lo vuelvas a hacer. **2** *(probability)* deber de; **he m. be ill,** debe de estar enfermo; **it m. be four o'clock,** serán las cuatro. **II** *n fam* necesidad *f*; **this gadget is an absolute m. for do-it-yourself fanatics,** es un aparato imprescindible para los aficionados al bricolage.

mustache [mə'stɑːʃ] *n US see* **moustache.**

mustard ['mʌstəd] *n Bot Culin* mostaza *f*. ■ **m. pot,** mostacera *f.*

muster ['mʌstəʳ] **I** *n Mil etc (gathering)* asamblea *f*; *(inspection)* revista *f*, *fig* **to pass m.,** ser aceptable. **II** *vtr (supporters)* reunir; *(troops)* formar; *fig* **to m. (up) courage** *or* **strength,** cobrar fuerzas. **III** *vi (supporters)* reunirse, juntarse; *(troops)* formar.

mustiness ['mʌstɪnɪs] *n* olor *m* a humedad.

mustn't ['mʌsənt] = **must not.**

musty ['mʌstɪ] *adj (mustier, mustiest)* que huele a cerrado *or* a humedad.

mutate [mjuː'teɪt] **I** *vtr* mudar, transformar. **II** *vi* sufrir mutación, transformarse.

mutation [mjuː'teɪʃən] *n* mutación *f.*

mute ['mjuːt] **I** *adj (person, letter, etc)* mudo,-a. **II** *n* **1** *(person)* mudo,-a *m,f*. ■ **deaf m.,** sordomudo,-a *m,f*. **2** *Mus* sordina *f.*

muted ['mjuːtɪd] *adj (sound)* sordo,-a, apagado,-a; *(colour)* suave, apagado,-a.

mutilate ['mjuːtɪleɪt] *vtr* mutilar.

mutilation [mjuːtɪ'leɪʃən] *n* mutilación *f.*

mutineer [mjuːtɪ'nɪəʳ] *n* amotinado,-a *m,f.*

mutinous ['mjuːtɪnəs] *adj* amotinado,-a; *fig* rebelde.

mutiny ['mjuːtɪnɪ] **I** *n* motín *m*, rebelión *f*. **II** *vi* amotinarse, rebelarse.

mutt [mʌt] *n fam* **1** *(dog)* perro *m* callejero. **2** *(person)* estúpido,-a *m,f.*

mutter ['mʌtəʳ] **I** *n (mumble)* murmullo *m*. **II** *vtr* murmurar, decir entre dientes. **III** *vi (angrily)* refunfuñar.

muttering ['mʌtərɪŋ] *n* rezongo *m*, refunfuño *m.*

mutton ['mʌtən] *n Culin* cordero *m*; **shoulder of m.,** paletilla *f* de cordero.

mutual ['mjuːtʃʊəl] *adj (help, love, etc)* mutuo,-a, recíproco,-a; *(common, shared)* común; **by m. consent,** de común acuerdo; **our m. friend George,** nuestro (común) amigo George; **the feeling is m.,** lo mismo digo yo. ■ *US* **m. fund,** fondo *m* común de inversión; **m. insurance,** seguro *m* mutuo; **m. benefit society,** mutualidad *f*, mutua *f*. ■ **mutually** *adv* mutuamente; **at a m. agreed time,** a una hora convenida entre los dos.

Muzak® ['mjuːzæk] *n* hilo *m* musical®.

muzzle ['mʌzəl] **I** *n* **1** *(snout)* hocico *m*. **2** *(device)* bozal *m*; *(of gun)* boca *f*. **II** *vtr (dog)* abozalar, poner un bozal a; *fig (person, press, etc)* amordazar.

muzzy ['mʌzɪ] *adj (muzzier, muzziest)* **1** *(dizzy)* mareado,-a; *(groggy)* atontado,-a; *(tipsy)* achispado,-a. **2** *(blurred)* borroso,-a.

MW *abbr of* **medium wave,** onda *f* media, OM *f*.

my [maɪ] **I** *poss adj* mi; **I washed my hair,** me lavé el pelo; **my cousins,** mis primos; **my father,** mi padre; **my own car,** mi propio coche; **one of my friends,** un amigo mío; **she twisted my arm,** me torció el brazo. **II** *interj* ¡caramba!, ¡caray!

myopia [maɪˈəʊpɪə] *n* miopía *f*.

myopic [maɪˈɒpɪk] *adj* miope.

myriad [ˈmɪrɪəd] *n lit* miríada *f*.

myrrh [mɜːʳ] *n* mirra *f*.

myrtle [ˈmɜːtəl] *n Bot* arrayán *m*, mirto *m*.

myself [maɪˈself] *pers pron* **1** *(emphatic)* yo mismo,-a; **I did it all by m.,** lo hice yo solo; **I saw it (for) m.,** yo mismo lo vi; **my husband and m.,** mi marido y yo. **2** *(reflexive)* me; **I hurt m.,** me hice daño. **3** *(after prep)* mí (mismo,-a); **I kept it for m.,** lo guardé para mí; **I said to m.,** me dije para mí.

mysterious [mɪˈstɪərɪəs] *adj* misterioso,-a. ◆ **mysteriously** *adv* misteriosamente.

mystery [ˈmɪstərɪ] *n* misterio *m*; **it's a m. to me how he managed to do it,** no entiendo cómo consiguió hacerlo. ■ *Rel* **m. play,** auto *m* sacramental, misterio *m*.

mystic [ˈmɪstɪk] *adj & n* místico,-a *(m,f)*.

mystical [ˈmɪstɪkəl] *adj* místico,-a.

mysticism [ˈmɪstɪsɪzəm] *n* misticismo *m*; *Lit* mística *f*.

mystify [ˈmɪstɪfaɪ] *vtr (pt & pp mystified)* dejar perplejo,-a, desconcertar; **I was completely mystified,** me quedé pasmado,-a.

mystique [mɪˈstiːk] *n* mística *f*; **there's no m. about it,** no tiene secretos.

myth [mɪθ] *n* mito *m*; *(illusion)* **it's a complete m.,** es pura fantasía.

mythical [ˈmɪθɪkəl] *adj* mítico,-a; *(imagined)* imaginario,-a, fantástico,-a.

mythological [mɪθəˈlɒdʒɪkəl] *adj* mitológico,-a.

mythology [mɪˈθɒlədʒɪ] *n* mitología *f*.

myxomatosis [mɪksəməˈtəʊsɪs] *n* mixomatosis *f*.

N

N, n [en] *n (the letter)* N, n *f*.

N *abbr of* **North,** Norte, N.

n 1 *abbr of* **name,** nombre *m*, n. **2** *Ling abbr of* **neuter,** neutro *m*, n.

NAAFI [ˈnæfɪ] *GB Mil abbr of* **Navy, Army and Air Force Institutes,** servicio *m* de tiendas y cantinas para las fuerzas armadas.

nab [næb] *vtr (pt & pp nabbed) fam* pescar, pillar.

nacre [ˈneɪkəʳ] *n* nácar *m*, madreperla *f*.

nadir [ˈnædɪəʳ] *n* **1** *Astron* nadir *m*. **2** *fig* punto *m* más bajo.

naff [næf] *adj GB sl* chungo,-a; **a n. film,** un bodrio de película.

nag¹ [næg] *n (horse)* rocín *m*.

nag² [næg] **I** *n (person)* gruñón,-ona *m,f*, regañón,-ona *m,f*. **II** *vtr (pt & pp nagged) (annoy)* fastidiar, molestar; *(constantly complain)* dar la tabarra. **III** *vi* quejarse.

nagger [ˈnægəʳ] *n* regañón,-ona *m,f*.

nagging [ˈnægɪŋ] **I** *adj* **1** *(complaining)* gruñón,-ona, regañón,-ona. **2** *(persistent)* continuo,-a; **a n. pain,** un dolor continuo. **II** *n* quejas *fpl*.

nail [neɪl] **I** *n* **1** *(of finger, toe)* uña *f*; **to bite/clip/trim one's nails,** comerse/cortarse/arreglarse las uñas; *fig* **to be as hard as nails,** *(tough)* ser muy fuerte *or* resistente; *(unsympathetic)* tener el corazón de piedra. ■ **n. clippers,** cortaúñas *m inv*; **n. polish, n. varnish,** esmalte *m or* laca *f* de uñas. **2** *(metal)* clavo *m*; *fig* **to hit the n. on the head,** dar en el clavo. **II** *vtr* **1** clavar, sujetar con clavos; **they nailed the picture to the wall,** clavaron el cuadro en la pared. **2** *fam (catch, trap)* pillar, coger.

nailbrush [ˈneɪlbrʌʃ] *n* cepillo *m* de uñas.

nailfile [ˈneɪlfaɪl] *n* lima *f* de uñas.

nail-scissors [ˈneɪlsɪzəz] *npl* tijeras *fpl* de uñas.

naïve [naɪˈiːv] *adj* ingenuo,-a.

naivety [naɪˈiːvtɪ] *n* ingenuidad *f*.

naked [ˈneɪkɪd] *adj (body)* desnudo,-a; *(light)* sin pantalla; *(flame)* sin protección; **n. from the waist up/down,** desnudo de cintura para arriba/abajo; **barely visible to the n. eye,** apenas visible a simple vista; *fig* **the n. truth,** la pura verdad.

nakedness [ˈneɪkɪdnɪs] *n* desnudez *f*.

namby-pamby [næmbɪˈpæmbɪ] *adj & n* ñoño,-a *(m,f)*.

name [neɪm] **I** *n* **1** nombre *m*; *(surname)* apellido *m*; **what's your n.?,** ¿cómo te llamas?; **the house is in my father's n.,** la casa está a nombre de mi padre; **this is a democracy in n. only,** esto de democracia tiene solamente el nombre; **to call sb names,** poner verde a algn; **to put one's n. down,** apuntarse. ■ **n. day,** santo *m*; **proper n.,** nombre *m* propio; **stage n.,** nombre *m* artístico. **2** *(reputation)* fama *f*, reputación *f*; **she's a big n. in the fashion world,** es una de las grandes figuras de la moda; **to have a bad/good n.,** tener mala/buena reputación; **to make a n. for oneself,** hacerse famoso,-a. **II** *vtr* **1** llamar, bautizar; **they named the ship 'Coronia',** bautizaron el buque con el nombre de 'Coronia'. **2** *(appoint)* nombrar; **he was named Chief of Police,** lo nombraron Jefe de Policía. **3** *(mention)* mencionar; **to be named in a list,** figurar en una lista.

name-dropping [ˈneɪmdrɒpɪŋ] *n fam* **to go in for n.-d.,** dárselas de conocer a gente importante.

nameless [ˈneɪmlɪs] *adj* anónimo,-a; **to remain n.,** permanecer en el anonimato.

namely [ˈneɪmlɪ] *adv* a saber.

nameplate [ˈneɪmpleɪt] *n* placa *f* con el nombre.

namesake [ˈneɪmseɪk] *n* tocayo,-a *m,f*.

Namibia [nəˈmɪbɪə] *n* Namibia.

Namibian [nəˈmɪbɪən] *adj & n* namibia,-a *(m,f)*.

naming [ˈneɪmɪŋ] *n* **1** elección *f* de un nombre. **2** *(appointment)* nombramiento *m*.

nan [næn] *n (baby talk)* yaya *f*.

nancy [ˈnænsɪ] *n fam* afeminado *m*. ■ **n. boy,** mariquita *m*.

nanna [ˈnænə] *n see* **nan.**

nanny [ˈnænɪ] *n* niñera *f*.

nanny goat [ˈnænɪgəʊt] *n Zool fam* cabra *f*.

nap¹ [næp] **I** *n (sleep)* siesta *f*; **to take** *or* **have a n.,** echar la *or* una siesta. **II** *vi (pt & pp napped)* dormir la siesta; *fig* **to catch sb napping,** coger a algn desprevenido.

nap² [næp] *n Tex* lanilla *f*, pelusa *f*.

napalm [ˈneɪpɑːm] *n* napalm *m*.

nape [neɪp] *n Anat* nuca *f*, cogote *m*.

naphtha [ˈnæfθə] *n Chem* nafta *f*.

naphthalene ['næfθəli:n] *n Chem* naftalina *f*.

napkin ['næpkɪn] *n* (**table**) **n.**, servilleta *f*. ■ **n. ring**, servilletero *m*.

Naples ['neɪpəlz] *n* Nápoles.

Napoleonic [nəpəʊlɪ'ɒnɪk] *adj* napoleónico,-a.

napper ['næpə'] *n GB fam* coco *m*.

nappy ['næpɪ] *n* pañal *m*.

narcissism ['nɑ:sɪsɪzəm] *n* narcisismo *m*.

narcissist ['nɑ:sɪsɪst] *n* narcisista *mf*.

narcissistic [nɑ:sɪ'sɪstɪk] *adj* narcisista.

narcissus [nɑ:'sɪsəs] *n* (*pl* **narcissi** [nɑ:'sɪsaɪ] *or* **narcissuses** [nɑ:'sɪsəsɪz]) *Bot* narciso *m*.

narcotic [nɑ:'kɒtɪk] **I** *adj* narcótico,-a. **II** *n* (*usu pl*) narcótico *m*, estupefaciente *m*.

nark [nɑ:k] *sl* **I** *n* soplón,-ona *m*, *f*, chivato,-a *m*, *f*. **II** *vtr* (*annoy*) fastidiar. **III** *vi* (*inform the police*) dar el chivatazo.

narrate [nə'reɪt] *vtr* narrar, relatar.

narration [nə'reɪʃən] *n* narración *f*, relato *m*.

narrative ['nærətɪv] **I** *n Lit* narrativa *f*; (*story*) narración *f*. **II** *adj* narrativo,-a.

narrator [nə'reɪtə'] *n* narrador,-a *m*, *f*.

narrow ['nærəʊ] **I** *adj* **1** (*passage, road, etc*) estrecho,-a, angosto,-a. **2** (*restricted*) reducido,-a, restringido,-a, limitado,-a; **a n. circle of friends**, un círculo reducido de amigos; **in the narrowest sense of the word**, en el sentido más estricto de la palabra; **a n. majority**, una mayoría escasa; **to have a n. escape**, escaparse *or* librarse por los pelos. **3** (*person*) de miras estrechas, cerrado,-a. **II narrows** *npl* (*in river*) estrecho *m sing*. **III** *vi* **1** estrecharse, hacerse más estrecho. **2 to n. down to**, reducirse a. **IV** *vtr* estrechar, hacer más estrecho. ◆ **narrowly** *adv* **1** (*closely*) de cerca, minuciosamente. **2** (*by a small margin*) por poco; **he n. avoided bitting the tree**, faltó muy poco para que chocase contra el árbol. ◆ **narrow down** *vtr* reducir, limitar; **our choice was narrowed down to four applicants**, tuvimos que escoger entre los cuatro candidatos que quedaban.

narrow-gauge ['nærəʊgeɪdʒ] *adj* (*railway*) de vía estrecha.

narrow-minded [nærəʊ'maɪndɪd] *adj* de miras estrechas.

narrow-mindedness [nærəʊ'maɪndɪdnɪs] *n* estrechez *f* de miras.

narrowness ['nærəʊnɪs] *n* estrechez *f*.

narwhal ['nɑ:wəl] *n Zool* narval *m*.

NASA ['næsə] *US abbr of* **National Aeronautics and Space Administration**, Administración *f* Nacional de Aeronáutica y del Espacio, NASA *f*.

nasal ['neɪzəl] *adj* nasal; **a n. voice**, una voz gangosa.

nastiness ['nɑ:stɪnɪs] *n* **1** (*unpleasantness*) carácter *m* desagradable. **2** (*maliciousness*) mala intención *f*.

nasturtium [nə'stɜ:ʃəm] *n Bot* capuchina *f*.

nasty ['nɑ:stɪ] *adj* (**nastier, nastiest**) **1** (*unpleasant*) desagradable; **a n. business**, un asunto feo; **a n. habit**, una mala costumbre; **a n. remark**, una observación desagradable; **a n. smell**, un olor desagradable; **a n. trick**, una mala jugada *or* pasada; **cheap and n.**, hortera; **to smell n.**, oler mal; **to taste n.**, tener mal sabor; (*weather, situation*) **to turn n.**, ponerse feo; **to have a n. mind**, ser un mal pensado *or* una mal pensada. **2** (*dirty*) sucio,-a, asqueroso,-a. **3** (*indecent*) obsceno,-a. **4** (*unfriendly*) antipático,-a; (*malicious*) mal intencionado,-a, malévolo,-a; *fam* **he's a n. piece of work**, es un asco de tío. **5** (*dangerous*) peligroso,-a; (*illness, accident*) grave; **a n. bend**, una curva peligrosa; **a n. wound**, una herida fea.

nation ['neɪʃən] *n* nación *f*.

national ['næʃnəl] **I** *adj* nacional. ■ **n. anthem**, himno *m* nacional; **n. debt**, deuda *f* pública; **n. grid**, red *f* nacional de electricidad; **n. insurance**, seguridad *f* social; **n. park**, parque *m* nacional; *GB Mil* **n. service**, servicio *m* militar. **II** *n* súbdito,-a *m*, *f*.

nationalism ['næʃnəlɪzəm] *n* nacionalismo *m*.

nationalist ['næʃnəlɪst] *adj & n* nacionalista (*mf*).

nationality [næʃə'nælɪtɪ] *n* nacionalidad *f*.

nationalization [næʃnəlaɪ'zeɪʃən] *n* nacionalización *f*.

nationalize ['næʃnəlaɪz] *vtr* nacionalizar.

nationwide ['neɪʃənwaɪd] *adj* de ámbito nacional; **n. appeal**, llamamiento a toda la nación; **n. tour**, viaje por todo el país; **n. scandal**, escándalo nacional.

native ['neɪtɪv] **I** *adj* **1** (*place*) natal; **n. city**, ciudad natal; **n. land**, patria *f*; **n. language**, lengua materna. **2** (*innate*) innato,-a. **3** (*plant, animal*) originario,-a (**to**, de). **II** *n* nativo,-a *m*, *f*, natural *mf*; **she's a n. of Edinburgh**, es natural de Edimburgo; (*original inhabitant*) indígena *mf*.

Nativity [nə'tɪvɪtɪ] *n Rel* Natividad *f*; (*Christmas*) Navidad *f*.

NATO, Nato ['neɪtəʊ] *abbr of* **North Atlantic Treaty Organization**, Organización *f* del Tratado del Atlántico Norte, OTAN *f*.

natter ['nætə'] *fam* **I** *vi* charlar. **II** *n* charla *f*; **to have a n.**, charlar, pegar la hebra.

natty ['nætɪ] *adj* (**nattier, nattiest**) *fam* **1** (*clothes*) elegante; **to be a n. dresser**, vestir bien. **2** (*gadget etc*) ingenioso,-a. ◆ **nattily** *adv* (*smartly*) elegantemente; **n. dressed**, bien vestido.

natural ['nætʃərəl] **I** *adj* **1** natural. ■ **n. gas**, gas *m* natural; **n. language**, lenguaje *m* natural; **n. resources**, recursos *mpl* naturales. **2** (*normal*) normal; **it's only n. that ...**, es lógico que ... . ■ **n. childbirth**, parto *m* natural; **n. death**, muerte *f* natural. **3** (*born*) nato,-a; **a n. actor**, un actor nato. **4** (*unaffected*) sencillo,-a, natural. **II** *n* **1** (*person*) she's a n. for the job, es la persona ideal para el trabajo. **2** *Mus* becuadro *m*. ◆ **naturally** *adv* **1** (*of course*) naturalmente, por supuesto, desde luego. **2** (*by nature*) por naturaleza. **3** (*in a relaxed manner*) con naturalidad.

naturalism ['nætʃərəlɪzəm] *n* naturalismo *m*.

naturalist ['nætʃərəlɪst] *adj & n* naturalista (*mf*).

naturalization [nætʃərəlaɪ'zeɪʃən] *n* (*of person*) naturalización *f*. ■ **n. papers**, carta *f* sing de ciudadanía.

nature ['neɪtʃə'] *n* **1** naturaleza *f*. ■ **Mother N.**, la Madre Naturaleza; **n. lover**, amante *mf* de la naturaleza; **n. reserve**, reserva *f* natural; **n. study**, historia *f* natural. **2** (*character*) naturaleza *f* carácter *m*; **by n.**, por naturaleza; **it is in his n. to be kind**, es bondadoso por naturaleza; ■ **human n.**, la naturaleza humana. **3** (*sort, kind*) índole *f*, género *m*, clase *f*; **things of this n.**, cosas de esta índole.

naturism ['neɪtʃərɪzəm] *n* naturismo *m*.

naturist ['neɪtʃərɪst] *n* naturista *mf*.

naught [nɔ:t] *n* nada *f*; **to bring to n.**, frustrar; **to come to n.**, fracasar.

naughtiness ['nɔ:tɪnɪs] *n* **1** (*behaviour*) mala conducta *f*, desobediencia *f*. **2** (*of story*) picardía *f*.

naughty ['nɔ:tɪ] *adj* (**naughtier, naughtiest**) **1** (*child*) travieso,-a. **2** (*risqué*) atrevido,-a, picante. ◆ **naughtily** *adv* **to behave n.**, portarse mal.

Nauru [nɑ:'u:ru:] *n* Nauru.

Nauruan [nɑ:'u:ru:ən] *adj & n* nauruano,-a (*m*, *f*).

nausea ['nɔ:zɪə] *n* **1** *Med* (*sickness*) náusea *f*. **2** *fig* (*disgust*) asco *m*.

nauseate ['nɔ:zɪeɪt] *vtr* **1** *Med* (*sickness*) dar náuseas. **2** (*disgust*) dar asco a.

nauseating ['nɔ:zɪeɪtɪŋ] *adj* nauseabundo,-a, repugnante.

nautical ['nɔ:tɪkəl] *adj* náutico,-a; **n. mile**, milla marítima.

naval ['neɪvəl] *adj* naval. ■ **n. attaché**, agregado *m* naval; **n. base**, base *f* naval; **n. officer**, oficial *mf* de marina; **n. power**, potencia *f* marítima *or* naval.

Navarre [nəˈvɑːʳ] n Navarra.

Navarrese [nævəˈriːz] adj & n navarro,-a (m,f).

nave [neɪv] n Arch nave f.

navel [ˈneɪvəl] n Anat ombligo m. ■ **n. orange,** naranja f navel.

navigable [ˈnævɪgəbəl] adj (river) navegable.

navigate [ˈnævɪgeɪt] I vtr 1 Naut (river) navegar por. 2 Naut (ship) gobernar; Av (aircraft) pilotar. II vi 1 Naut navegar. 2 Aut (rally driving) hacer de copiloto.

navigation [nævɪˈgeɪʃən] n Naut navegación f. ■ **n. laws,** código m marítimo.

navigator [ˈnævɪgeɪtəʳ] n 1 Naut navegante mf, oficial mf de derrota. 2 Aut Av copiloto mf.

navvy [ˈnævɪ] n peón m.

navy [ˈneɪvɪ] n 1 marina f. ■ **merchant n.,** marina f mercante; **N. Department,** Ministerio m de la Marina; **n. blue,** azul m marino; **a n. blue skirt,** una falda azul marino. 2 (fleet) flota f, armada f.

Nazi [ˈnɑːtsɪ] adj & n nazi (mf).

Nazism [ˈnɑːtsɪzəm] nazismo m.

NB, nb [enˈbiː] abbr of **nota bene** (note well), observa bien, N.B.

NBC [enbiːˈsiː] US abbr of **National Broadcasting Company,** sociedad f nacional de radiodifusión, NBC f.

NCO [ensiːˈəʊ] GB Mil abbr of **non-commissioned officer,** suboficial mf.

NE abbr of **North-East,** nordeste, NE.

neap [niːp] n **n. (tide),** marea f muerta.

Neapolitan [nɪəˈpɒlɪtən] adj & n napolitano,-a (m,f).

near [nɪəʳ] I adj 1 (space) cercano,-a; **the nearest stop,** la parada más cercana; **the nearest way,** el camino más corto. ■ Aut **the n. side,** el lado del pasajero. 2 (time) próximo,-a; **in the n. future,** en un futuro próximo. 3 fig cercano,-a; **a n. relation,** un pariente cercano; **it was a n. thing,** poco faltó; **one's nearest and dearest,** los más íntimos. II adv (space) cerca; **do you live n.?,** ¿vives cerca?; **far and n.,** por todas partes; **n. at hand,** a un paso, a mano; (degree) **the hotel is nowhere n. as good as it appears in the brochure,** el hotel está muy lejos de ser tan bueno como parece en el folleto; (close) **that's n. enough,** (ya) vale, está bien, III prep cerca de; **n. death,** cerca de la muerte; **n. here,** cerca de aquí, aquí cerca; **the end of the film,** hacia el final de la película. IV vtr acercarse a; **she's nearing retirement,** está a punto de jubilarse; **the ship is nearing port,** el barco se está acercando al puerto. ◆ **nearly** adv casi; **I n. died,** por poco me mucrio; **it's n. seven,** son casi las siete; **very n.,** casi, casi; **we haven't n. enough to buy her a present,** no alcanza ni con mucho para comprarle un regalo.

near-sighted [nɪəˈsaɪtɪd] adj miope, corto,-a de vista.

near-sightedness [nɪəˈsaɪtɪdnɪs] n miopía f.

neat [niːt] adj 1 (room etc) ordenado,-a, limpio,-a; (handwriting) claro,-a; (person) (appearance) pulcro,-a; (habits) ordenado,-a; **n. and tidy,** bienordenado,-a. 2 (clever) hábil, ingenioso,-a; **a n. trick,** un truco ingenioso. 3 (whisky etc) solo,-a. 4 US fam (fine) chulo,-a, guapo,-a. ◆ **neatly** adv 1 (carefully) cuidadosamente, con esmero. 2 (cleverly) hábilmente.

nearby [nɪəˈbaɪ] I adj cereano,-a II adv cerca.

nearness [ˈnɪənɪs] n proximidad f.

neatness [ˈniːtnɪs] n esmero m, pulcritud f.

nebula [ˈnebjʊlə] n (pl **nebulae** [ˈnebjʊliː]) Astron nebulosa f.

nebulous [ˈnebjʊləs] adj Astron nebuloso,-a; fig vago,-a, impreciso,-a.

necessary [ˈnesɪsərɪ] I adj 1 (essential) necesario,-a, esencial; **absolutely n.,** imprescindible; **is it n. that we all go?** or **is it n. for all of us to go?,** ¿es necesario que vayamos todos?; **to do what is n.,** hacer todo lo necesario or lo que haga falta; **to do no more than is n.,** no hacer

más que lo (mínimo) indispensable; **if n.,** si es preciso. 2 (unavoidable) inevitable; **the n. consequence,** la consecuencia inevitable. II n lo necesario, lo esencial; **to do the n.,** hacer lo necesario. ◆ **necessarily** [nesɪˈserəlɪ] adv necesariamente, por fuerza.

necessitate [nɪˈsesɪteɪt] vtr necesitar, exigir, requerir.

necessitous [nɪˈsesɪtəs] adj necesitado,-a, indigente.

necessity [nɪˈsesɪtɪ] n 1 necesidad f; **in case of n.,** en caso de necesidad or urgencia; **out of n.,** por necesidad; **to make a virtue of n.,** hacer de la necesidad una virtud; prov **n. is the mother of invention,** la necesidad aviva el ingenio. 2 (article) requisito m indispensable; **a phone is a n. these days,** hoy en día el teléfono es indispensable. 3 **necessities,** artículos mpl de primera necesidad.

neck [nek] I n 1 Anat cuello m; (of animal) pescuezo m; **to be n. and n.,** ir parejos; **to be up to one's n. in debt,** estar hasta el cuello de deudas; **to break one's n. working,** matarse trabajando; **to crane one's n.,** estirar el cuello; **to risk one's n.,** jugarse el tipo or el cuello; **to stick one's n. out,** arriesgarse; (in horse racing) **to win/lose by a n.,** ganar/perder por una cabeza; **to wring sb's n.,** retorcerle el pescuezo a algn. ■ **stiff n.,** tortícolis f. 2 (of garment) cuello m. ■ **low n.,** escote m; **roll n.,** cuello m vuelto or de cisne; **V n.,** cuello m de pico. 3 (of bottle) cuello m. 4 (of guitar) mástil m. 5 Geog istmo m. II vi fam (kiss) besuquearse, morrearse; (caress, hug) magrearse.

necking [ˈnekɪŋ] n fam (kissing) besuqueo m, morreo m; (caressing, hugging) magreo m.

necklace [ˈneklɪs] n collar m.

neckline [ˈneklaɪn] n (of dress) escote m.

necktie [ˈnektaɪ] n corbata f.

nectar [ˈnektəʳ] n néctar m.

nectarine [ˈnektəriːn] n nectarina f.

née [neɪ] adj de soltera; **Mrs Williams, n. Brown,** Sra. Williams, de soltera Brown.

need [niːd] I n 1 necesidad f; **basic needs,** necesidades elementales; **if n. be,** si fuera necesario; **there's no n. for you to do that,** no hace falta que hagas eso; **the urgent n. for ...,** la acuciante necesidad de ...; **to be in n. of,** necesitar. 2 (poverty) indigencia f, necesidad f; **to be in n.,** estar necesitado; **to help a friend in n.,** sacar a un amigo de un apuro. II vtr 1 necesitar; **I didn't n. to pay, it was free,** no tuve que pagar, era gratis; **I n. a break,** necesito un descanso; **I n. to see him,** tengo que verle; **they n. to be told everything,** hay que decirles or explicárselo todo; fam **that's all I n.,** sólo me faltaba eso; fam **what she needs is a good ticking off,** lo que le hace falta es una buena bronca. 2 (require) requerir, exigir; **it's a job that needs patience,** es un trabajo que requiere paciencia. III aux v tener que, deber; **n. he go?,** ¿tiene que ir?; **n. you shout so much?,** ¿tienes que gritar tanto?; **yon needn't have bothered to come, you could have phoned,** no tenías que haberte molestado en venir, podrías haber llamado; **you needn't wait,** no hace falta que esperes.

needful [ˈniːdfʊl] adj necesario,-a; **to do what is n.,** hacer lo necesario.

needle [ˈniːdəl] I n 1 (gen) aguja f; **to look for a n. in a haystack,** buscar una aguja en un pajar; **to thread a n.,** enhebrar una aguja. 2 Bot hoja f; **the ground was covered with pine needles,** la tierra estaba cubierta de pinaza. 3 fam (friction) pique m; GB **to get the n.,** picarse. II vtr fam pinchar; **he's always needling me,** nunca me deja en paz.

needless [ˈniːdlɪs] adj innecesario,-a, inútil; **n. violence,** violencia gratuita; **n. to say,** ni que decir tiene que, huelga decir. ◆ **needlessly** adv innecesariamente, iuútilmente.

needlework [ˈniːdlwɜːk] n (sewiig) costura f, (embroidery) bordado m.

needs [niːdz] adv necesariamente, forzosamente; **if n. must,** si hace falta.

needy [ˈniːdɪ] I adj (needier, neediest) necesitado,-a. II **the n.** npl los necesitados.

ne'er-do-well [ˈneəduːwel] n vago,-a m,f.

nefarious [nɪˈfeərɪəs] *adj* infame.

neg *abbr of* **negative**, negativo,-a, negat.

negate [nɪˈgeɪt] *vtr* **I** *(deny)* negar. **2** *(nullify)* anular, invalidar.

negation [nɪˈgeɪʃən] *n* negación *f*.

negative [ˈnegətɪv] **I** *adj* negativo,-a. ■ **n. result**, resultado *m* negativo; **n. criticism**, crítica *f* negativa. **II** *n* **1** *Ling* negación *f*; **to reply in the n.**, contestar con una negativa. **2** *Phot* negativo *m*. **3** *Math* término *m* negativo. ◆ **negatively** *adv* negativamente.

neglect [nɪˈglekt] **I** *vtr* **1** *(not look after)* descuidar, desatender; **to n. one's health/house**, descuidar la salud/la casa; **to n. one's appearance**, no arreglarse, dejarse ir; **to n. one's friends**, olvidarse de los amigos. **2** *(omit to do)* no cumplir con, faltar a; **to n. one's duty/obligations**, no cumplir con su deber/sus obligaciones. **II** *n* negligencia *f*, descuido *m*, dejadez *f*; **in a state of n.**, abandonado,-a, descuidado,-a; **n. of duty**, incumplimiento de su deber; **through n.**, por negligencia.

neglectful [nɪˈglektfʊl] *adj* descuidado,-a, negligente.

negligée [ˈneglɪʒeɪ] *n* salto *m* de cama, negligé *m*.

negligence [ˈneglɪdʒəns] *n* negligencia *f*, descuido *m*.

negligent [ˈneglɪdʒənt] *adj* descuidado,-a, negligente.

negligible [ˈneglɪdʒɪbəl] *adj* insignificante.

negotiable [nɪˈgəʊʃəbəl] *adj* **1** negociable. **2** *fig (obstacle)* superable.

negotiate [nɪˈgəʊʃɪeɪt] **I** *vtr* **1** *(treaty, contract)* negociar. **2** *Fin (sale, han)* gestionar; *(bill of exchange)* negociar. **3** *fig (obstacle)* salvar, franquear; **to n. a bend**, tomar una curva. **II** *vi* negociar; **he refused to n. with the terrorists**, se negó a negociar con los terroristas.

negotiation [nɪgəʊʃɪˈeɪʃən] *n* negociación *f*; **to open negotiations**, entablar negociaciones; **under n.**, en negociación.

negotiator [nɪˈgəʊʃɪeɪtə*r*] *n* negociador,-a *m,f*.

negro [ˈniːgrəʊ] **I** *adj* negro,-a. **II** *n (pl* **negroes)** negro,-a *m,f*.

negroid [ˈniːgrɔɪd] *adj* negroide.

neigh [neɪ] **I** *n* relincho *m*. **II** *vi* relinchar.

neighbour, *US* **neighbor** [ˈneɪbə*r*] *n* vecino,-a *m, f*; *Rel* prójimo *m*; **Britain's neighbours**, los países vecinos a Gran Bretaña.

neighbourhood, *US* **neighborhood** [ˈneɪbəhʊd] *n* **1** *(district)* vecindad *f*, barrio *m*; *(people)* vecindario *m*. **2** *(of amotunt)* **in the n. of**, alrededor de, aproximadamente.

neighbouring, *US* **neighboring** [ˈneɪbərɪŋ] *adj* vecino,-a; **n. country**, país vecino.

neighbourly, *US* **neighborly** [ˈneɪbəlɪ] *adj* amable, de buen vecino.

neither [ˈnaɪðə*r*, ˈniːðə*r*] **I** *adj & pron* ninguno de los dos, ninguna de las dos; **n. candidate is good enongh**, ninguno de los candidatos es suficientemente bueno; **n. (of them) has come**, ninguno de los dos ha venido. **II** *adv & conj* **1** ni; **n. ... nor**, ni ... ni; **n. young nor old**, ni joven ni viejo; **n. you nor I**, ni tú ni yo; **fig it's n. here nor there**, no viene al caso. **2** tampoco; **she was not there and n. was her sister**, ella no estaba, ni su hermana tampoco.

neoclassical [niːəʊˈklæsɪkəl] *adj* neoclásico,-a.

neoclassicism [niːəʊˈklæsɪsɪzəm] *n* neoclasicismo *m*.

neolithic [niːəʊˈlɪθɪk] *adj* neolítico,-a.

neologism [niːˈɒlədʒɪzəm] *n* neologismo *m*.

neon [ˈniːɒn] *n* neón *m*. ■ **n. sign**, letrero *m* de neón.

Nepal [nɪˈpɔːl] *n* Nepal.

Nepalese [nepəˈliːz] *adj & n* nepalés,-esa *(m,f)*; **the N.**, los nepaleses.

nephew [ˈnevjuː, ˈnefjuː] *n* sobrino *m*.

nephritis [nɪˈfraɪtɪs] *n* nefritis *f*.

nepotism [ˈnepətɪzəm] *n* nepotismo *m*.

nerve [nɜːv] *n* **1** *Anat* nervio *m*; **to be a bundle of nerves**, estar hecho un manojo de nervios; **to get on sb's nerves**, poner los nervios de punta a algn, poner nervioso a algn; **to have nerves of steel**, tener nervios de acero. ■ **n. cell**, neurona *f*; **n. centre**, *Anat* centro *m* nervioso; *fig* punto *m* neurálgico; **n. gas**, gas *m* nervioso. **2** *(courage)* valor *m*; **to lose one's n.**, rajarse. **3** *fam (cheek)* cara *f*, descaro *m*, caradura *f*; **he had the n. to phone me**, tuvo el des caro de llamarme por teléfono; **what a n.!**, ¡qué cara!

nerve-racking [ˈnɜːvrækɪŋ] *adj* crispante, exasperante.

nervous [ˈnɜːvəs] *adj* **1** *Anat* nervioso,-a. ■ **n. breakdown**, depresión *f* nerviosa; **n. system**, sistema *m* nervioso. **2** *(on edge)* nervioso,-a. **3** *(afraid)* miedoso,-a; **to be n.**, tener miedo. **4** *(timid)* tímido,-a. ◆ **nervously** *adv* nerviosamente, con miedo.

nervousness [ˈnɜːvəsnɪs] *n* *(edginess)* nerviosismo *m*, nerviosidad *f*; *(fear)* miedo *m*.

nervy [ˈnɜːvɪ] *adj (nervier, nerviest) fam* nervioso,-a.

nest [nest] **I** *n* **1** *Orn* nido *m*; *(hen's)* nidal, *m*; *(wasps')* avispero *m*; *(animal's)* madriguera *f*, *fig* punto *m* de **n.**, hacer su agosto. ■ **n. egg**, ahorros *mpl*, ahorrillos *mpl*. **2** *fig (shelter)* nido *m*, refugio *m*. ■ **machine-gun n.**, nido *m* de ametralladoras. **3** *Furn* **n. of tables**, mesas *fpl* de nido. **II** *vi* **1** *(birds)* anidar. **2** *(egg collector)* ir a buscar nidos.

nestle [ˈnesəl] **I** *vtr* recostar; **to n. one's head against sb's shoulder**, recostar la cabeza contra el hombro de algn. **II** *vi* **I** *(settle comfortably)* acomodarse, arrellanarse; **to n. up to sb**, apretarse contra algn. **2** *(lie sheltered)* esconderse, ocultarse.

net¹ [net] *n* **1** red *f*; *Sport* red, malla *f*. ■ **fishing n.**, red *f* de pescar; **hair n.**, redecilla *f*; **landing n.**, manga *m*; **mosquito n.**, mosquitero *m*; **n. curtains**, visillos *mpl*. **2** *(trap)* red *f*, trampa *f*. **II** *vtr (pt & pp* **netted)** coger con red; **Fish** pescar con red.

net² [net] **I** *adj* neto,-a; **n. price/profit/weight**, precio/beneficio/peso neto. **II** *vtr (pt & pp* **netted)** *(earn)* ganar neto; **he netted 100,000 dollars**, ganó cien mil dólares netos.

netball [ˈnetbɔːl] *n* *Sport* baloncesto *m* femenino.

Netherlands [ˈneðələndz] *npl* **the N.**, Holanda, los Países Bajos.

netting [ˈnetɪŋ] *n* redes *fpl*, malla *f*. ■ **wire n.**, alambrera *f*.

nettle [ˈnetəl] **I** *n* *Bot* ortiga *f*. ■ **n. rash**, urticaria *f*. **II** *vtr fam* irritar, fastidiar, molestar.

network [ˈnetwɜːk] *n* red *f*; **road/rail n.**, red de carreteras/ferrocarriles.

neuralgia [njʊəˈrældʒə] *n Med* neuralgia *f*.

neuritis [njʊəˈraɪtɪs] *n Med* neuritis *f*.

neurological [njʊərəˈlɒdʒɪkəl] *adj Med* neurológico,-a.

neurologist [njʊəˈrɒlədʒɪst] *n Med* neurólogo,-a *m,f*.

neurology [njʊəˈrɒlədʒɪ] *n Med* neurología *f*.

neurosis [njʊəˈrəʊsɪs] *n (pl* **neuroses** [njʊəˈrəʊsiːz]*) Med* neurosis *f*.

neurotic [njʊˈrɒtɪk] *adj & n Med* neurótico,-a *(m, f)*.

neuter [ˈnjuːtə*r*] **I** *adj* neutro,-a. **II** *n Ling* neutro *m*. **III** *vtr (geld)* castrar.

neutral [ˈnjuːtrəl] **I** *adj* neutro,-a; *Pol* **to remain n.**, permanecer neutral. **II** *n Aut* punto *m* muerto.

neutrality [njuːˈtrælətɪ] *n* neutralidad *f*.

neutralize [ˈnjuːtrəlaɪz] *vtr* neutralizar.

neutron [ˈnjuːtrɒn] *n Phys* neutrón *m*. ■ **n. bomb**, bomba *f* de neutrones.

never [ˈnevə*r*] *adv* nunca, jamás; **he n. complains**, nunca se queja; **n. again**, nunca más, nunca jamás; **n. in all my life have I seen anything like it**, jamás en la vida he visto nada parecido; *fam* **n. mind**, da igual, no importa; *fam* **that will n. do!**, ¡eso es inaceptable!; *fam* **you n. forgot your keys!**, ¡no me digas que te olvidaste tas llaves!; *fam* **well, I n. (did)!**, ¡no me digas!

never-ending [nevər'endıŋ] *adj* sin fin, interminable.

never-never [nevə'nevə'] *n fam* **to buy sth on the n.-n.**, comprar algo a plazos. ■ **n.-n. land**, tierra *f* de Jauja.

nevermore [nevə'mɔːᶜ] *adj* nunca más.

nevertheless [nevəðə'les] *adv* sin embargo, no obstante.

new [njuː] *adj* nuevo,-a; **a n. car/dress/suit**, un coche/ vestido/traje nuevo; **as good as n.**, como nuevo; **I'm n. to this job**, soy nuevo en este trabajo. ■ **n. baby**, recién nacido *m*; **N. Delhi**, Nueva Delhi; **N. England**, Nueva Inglaterra; **N. Englander**, nativo,-a *m,f or* habitante *mf* de Nueva Inglaterra; **N. Guinea**, Nueva Guinea; **N. Hampshire**, Nueva Hampshire; **N. Jersey**, Nueva Jersey; **n. moon**, luna *f* nueva; **N. Orleans**, Nueva Orleáns; **n. potatoes**, patatas *fpl* nuevas; **N. South Wales**, Nueva Gales del Sur; **N. Year**, Año *m* nuevo; **N. Year's Day**, día *m* del Año nuevo; **N. Year's Eve**, Noche *f* vieja, Nochevieja *f*; **N. York**, Nueva York; **N. Yorker**, neoyorquino,-a *m, f*; **N. Zealand**, Nueva Zelanda; **N. Zealander**, neocelandés,-esa *m, f*. ◆ **newly** *adv* recién, recientemente; **a n. painted house**, una casa recién pintada.

newborn ['njuːbɔːn] *adj* recién nacido,-a.

newcomer ['njuːkʌmə'] *n* recién llegado,-a *m,f*.

newfangled ['njuːfæŋɡəld] *adj* novedoso,-a; **n.-f. ideas**, ideas novedosas.

Newfoundland ['njuːfəndlənd] *n* Terranova.

newish ['njuːıʃ] *adj fam* casi nuevo,-a.

newlywed ['njuːlıwed] *n* recién casado,-a *m,f*.

news [njuːz] *n* noticias *fpl*; **a piece of n.**, una noticia; **it's in the n.**, es noticia; **the n.**, *TV* el telediario; *Rad* el diario hablado; **to break the n. to sb**, dar una (mala) noticia a algn; *fam* **it's n. to me**, ahora me entero; *prov* **no n. is good n.**, sin noticias, buenas noticias. ■ **n. agency**, agencia *f* de prensa *or* de información; **n. bulletin**, noticiario *m*, boletín *m* informativo; **n. conference**, rueda *f* de prensa; **n. correspondent**, corresponsal *mf* de prensa; **n. clipping**, recorte *m* de periódico; **n. item**, noticia *f*.

newsagent ['njuːzeıdʒənt] *n* vendedor,-a *m, f* de periódicos.

newscaster ['njuːzkɑːstə'] *n* *TV* locutor,-a *m, f* del telediario; *Rad* locutor,-a *m, f* del diario hablado.

newsflash ['njuːzflæʃ] *n* noticia *f* de última hora.

newsletter ['njuːzletə'] *n* boletín *m* informativo.

newspaper ['njuːzpeıpə'] *n* periódico *m*, diario *m*.

newsprint ['njuːzprınt] *n* papel *m* de periódico.

newsreader ['njuːzriːdə'] *TV Rad* presentador,-a *m, f* de los informativos.

newsreel ['njuːzriːl] *n* noticiario *m*.

newsroom ['njuːzrʊm] *n* sala *f* de redacción.

news-stand ['njuːzstænd] *n* quiosco *m*, puesto *m* de periódicos.

newsworthy ['njuːzwɜːðı] *adj* de interés periodístico.

newsy ['njuːzı] *adj* *(newsier, newsiest)* *fam* **a n. letter**, una carta llena de noticias.

newt [njuːt] *n Zool* tritón *m*.

next [nekst] **I** *adj* **1** *(place)* vecino,-a, de al lado; **the n. room**, la habitación de al lado. **2** *(time)* próximo,-a; **the n. time**, la próxima vez; **the n. day**, el día siguiente; **n. day**, al día siguiente; **n. Friday**, el viernes que viene; **n. week**, la semana que viene; **the week after n.**, dentro de dos semanas. **3** *(order)* siguiente, próximo,-a; **the n. page**, la página siguiente; **the n. stop**, la próxima parada; **n. of kin**, pariente *m* más cercano; **who's n.?**, ¿quién es el siguiente? **II** *adv* **1** después, luego; **what did you do n.?**, ¿que hiciste luego?; **what shall we do n.?**, ¿qué hacemos ahora? **2** *(next time)* la próxima vez; **when n. we meet**, la próxima vez que nos veamos. **III** *prep* **n. to**, al lado de, junto a; **n. to nothing**, casi nada.

next door [neks'dɔːᶜ] *adj & adv* de al lado; **our n.-d. neighbour**, el vecino *or* la vecina de al lado; **the house n. d.**, la casa de al lado; **they live n. d.**, viven en la casa de al lado.

NHS [eneıtʃ'es] *GB abbr of* **National Health Service**, ≈ Seguridad *f* Social, SS *f*.

niacin ['naıəsın] *n* niacina *f*.

nib [nıb] *n* plumilla *f*.

nibble ['nıbəl] **I** *vtr & vi* mordisquear; *(of fish)* picar; **to n. at sth**, mordisquear algo. **II** *n* **1** *(bite)* mordisco *m*. **2** *(small piece)* pedacito *m*; **a n. of cheese**, un trocito de queso.

nibs [nıbz] *n fam iron* **his n.**, su señoría.

Nicaragua [nıkə'ræɡjʊə, nıkə'rɑːɡwə] *n* Nicaragua.

Nicaraguan [nıkə'ræɡjʊən, nıkə'rɑːɡwən] *adj & n* nicaragüense *(mf)*.

Nice [niːs] *n* Niza.

nice [naıs] *adj* **1** *(pleasant) (person)* simpático,-a, amable, majo,-a; *(thing)* agradable, bueno,-a; **a n. meal**, una buena comida; **a n. day**, un día agradable; **how n. of you!**, ¡qué amable eres!; **n. weather**, buen tiempo; **n. and cool/ warm**, fresquito,-a/calentito,-a; **to smell/taste n.**, oler/ saber bien. **2** *(pretty)* bonito,-a, mono,-a, *SA m* lindo,-a; **a n. house**, una casa bonita. **3** *iron* menudo,-a; **a n. mess you've made!**, ¡menudo lío has hecho!, ¡buena la has hecho! **3** *(subtle)* sutil; **a n. distinction**, una distinción sutil. **4** *(exact)* **these shoes are a n. fit**, estos zapatos me sientan muy bien. ◆ **nicely** *adv* muy bien; **that will do n.**, así está muy bien; **she's doing n.**, va bien.

nice-looking [naıs'lʊkıŋ] *adj* guapo,-a, mono,-a.

nicety ['naısıtı] *n* **1** *(subtlety)* sutileza *f*, detalle *m*. **2** **niceties**, *(refinements)* lujos *mpl*, detalles *mpl*.

niche [niːtʃ] *n* **1** hornacina *f*, nicho *m*. **2** *fig* hueco *m*; **to carve out a n. for oneself**, hacerse un hueco.

Nick [nık] *n dimin of* **Nicholas**; **Old N.**, el diablo.

nick¹ [nık] **I** *n* **1** *(notch)* muesca *f*, corte *m*; *(cut)* corte *m*, rasguño *m*; *fam* **in the n. of time**, en el momento preciso. **2** *GB sl (prison)* **the n.**, chirona *f*, talego *m*. **II** *vtr sl (steal)* mangar, birlar, afanar. **2** *(arrest)* pillar, pescar.

nick² [nık] *n sl* **in good/poor n.**, en buenas/malas condiciones.

nickel ['nıkəl] *n* **1** níquel *m*. ■ **n. silver**, metal *m* blanco. **2** *US* moneda *f* de cinco centavos.

nicker ['nıkə'] *n inv GB sl* libra *f* esterlina.

nickname ['nıkneım] **1** *n* *(derisory)* apodo *m*, mote *m*; *(affectionate)* diminutivo *m*. **II** *vtr* apodar, poner de apodo; **he was nicknamed 'Fatty'** le apodaron 'el Gordo'.

nicotine ['nıkətiːn] *n* nicotina *f*.

niece [niːs] *n* sobrina *f*.

niff [nıf] *GB fam* **I** *n* tufo *m*. **II** *vtr* tufar.

niffy ['nıfı] *adj GB fam* maloliente.

nifty ['nıftı] *adj (niftier, niftiest)* **1** *(smart)* elegante, chulo,-a. **2** *(quick)* rápido,-a; *(agile)* ágil. **3** *(ingenious)* ingenioso,-a.

Niger ['naıdʒə'] *n* Níger.

Nigeria [naı'dʒıərıə] *n* Nigeria.

Nigerian [naı'dʒıərıən] *adj & n* nigeriano,-a *(m,f)*.

Nigerien [niː'ʒeərıən] *adj & n* nigeriano,-a *(m,f)*.

niggardly ['nıɡədlı] *adj (miserly)* tacaño,-a, avaro,-a; *(meagre)* exiguo,-a.

nigger ['nıɡə'] *n offens* negro,-a *m,f*.

niggle ['nıɡəl] *vi* reparar en nimiedades *or* pequeñeces.

niggling ['nıɡəlıŋ] *adj (trifling)* insignificante, de poca monta; *(irritating)* molesto,-a.

night [naıt] *n* noche *f*; **all n.**, toda la noche; **at n.**, de noche; **last n.**, anoche; **last at n.**, avanzada *or* bien entrada la noche; **the n. before last**, anteanoche, antes de anoche;

tomorrow n., mañana por la noche; **to have a n. out,** salir por la noche. ■ **first n.,** estreno *m*; **n. court,** juzgado *m* de guardia; **n. life,** vida *f* nocturna; **n. owl,** trasnochador,-a *m*, *f*; **n. school,** escuela *f* nocturna; **n. shift,** turno *m* de noche.

nightcap ['naɪtkæp] *n* bebida *f* antes de acostarse.

nightclub ['naɪtklʌb] *n* club *m* nocturno, sala *f* de fiestas.

nightdress ['naɪtdres] *n* camisón *m*.

nightfall ['naɪtfɔːl] *n* anochecer *m*; **at n.,** al anochecer, al caer la noche.

nightgown ['naɪtgaʊn] *n*, **nightie** ['naɪtɪ] *n fam* camisón *m*.

nightingale ['naɪtɪŋgeɪl] *n Orn* ruiseñor *m*.

nightjar ['naɪtdʒɑː'] *n Orn* chotacabras *m inv*.

nightlife ['naɪtlaɪf] *n* ambiente *m* nocturno; **there's not much n. here,** no hay mucha marcha (nocturna) aquí.

nightlight ['naɪtlaɪt] *n* lamparilla *f*.

nightly ['naɪtlɪ] **I** *adj* **1** *(at night)* nocturno,-a, de noche. **2** *(every night)* de cada noche. **II** *adv* cada noche, todas las noches.

nightmare ['naɪtmeə'] *n* pesadilla *f*.

nights [naɪts] *adv fam* de noche, por la noche; **to work n.,** trabajar de noche.

nightshade ['naɪtʃeɪd] *n Bot* hierba *f* mora. ■ **deadly n.,** belladona *f*.

nightspot ['naɪtspɒt] *n* club *m* nocturno, sala *f* de fiestas.

night-time ['naɪttaɪm] *n* noche *f*; **at n.,** por la noche.

nihilism ['naɪɪlɪzəm] *n* nihilismo *m*.

nihilistic [naɪɪ'lɪstɪk] *adj* nihilista.

nil [nɪl] *n* nada *f*; *Sport* cero *m*; **we won two n.,** ganamos dos a cero.

Nile [naɪl] *n* the N., el Nilo.

nimble ['nɪmbəl] *adj* ágil, rápido,-a; **n. feet,** pies ágiles.

nincornpoop ['nɪŋkəmpuːp] *n fam* memo,-a *m*, *f*, tonto,-a *m*, *f*.

nine [naɪn] **I** *adj* nueve *inv*; **n. hundred,** novecientos,-as; **n. thousand pounds,** nueve mil libras; **n. times,** nueve veces; **n. times out of ten,** en el noventa por ciento de los casos. **II** *n* nueve *m inv*; *fam* **dressed up to the nines,** de punta en blanco; *see also* **seven.**

ninepins ['naɪnpɪnz] *npl* bolos *mpl*, juego *m* de bolos; **they went down like n.,** cayeron como moscas.

nineteen [naɪn'tiːn] *adj & n* diecinueve *(m) inv*; **to talk n. to the dozen,** hablar por los codos; *see also* **seven.**

nineteenth [naɪn'tiːnθ] *adj* decimonoveno,-a. ■ *Golf sl* **the n. hole,** el bar; *see also* **seventh.**

ninety ['naɪntɪ] *adj & n* noventa *(m) inv*; **n.-nine times out of a hundred,** casi siempre; **the nineties,** los (años) noventa; *see also* **seventy.**

ninth [naɪnθ] **I** *adj* noveno,-a. **II** *n* **1** *(in series)* noveno,-a *m*, *f*. **2** *(fraction)* noveno *m*; *see also* **seventh.**

Nip [nɪp] *n sl offens* japonés,-esa *m*, *f*, nipón,-ona *m*, *f*.

nip[1] [nɪp] **I** *vtr (pt & pp nipped)* **1** *(pinch)* pellizcar. **2** *(bite)* morder; **to n. sth in the bud,** cortar algo de raíz. **II** *vi fam* **to n. in/out/up,** entrar/salir/subir un momento; **n. across to the shop,** ve un momento a la tienda. **III** *n* **1** *(pinch)* pellizco *m*. **2** *(bite)* mordisco *m*, mordedura *f*; *fig* **there's a n. in the air,** hace frío.

nip[2] [nɪp] *n (of drink)* trago *m*; **a n. of brandy,** un trago de coñac.

nipper ['nɪpə'] *n fam* chaval,-a *m*, *f*, chiquillo,-a *m*, *f*.

nipple ['nɪpəl] *n* **1** *Anat (female)* pezón *m*; *(male)* tetilla *f*. **2** *(teat)* tetina *f*, boquilla *f*. **3** *Tech* **(greasing) n.,** pezón *m* de engrase.

nippy ['nɪpɪ] *adj (nippier, nippiest) fam* **1** *(quick)* rápido,-a; **look n.!,** ¡date prisa! **2** *(cold)* fresquito,-a; **it's a bit n. today,** hoy hace fresquito.

nirvana [nɪə'vɑːnə] *n Rel* nirvana *f*.

nit[1] [nɪt] *n Zool* liendre *f*.

nit[2] [nɪt] *n fam* imbécil *mf*.

nit-picking ['nɪtpɪkɪŋ] *adj fam* quisquill oso,-a; **n. details,** nimiedades *fpl*.

nitrate ['naɪtreɪt] *n Chem* nitrato *m*.

nitric ['naɪtrɪk] *adj Chem* nítrico,-a. ■ **n. acid,** ácido *m* nítrico.

nitride ['naɪtraɪd] *n Chem* nituro *m*.

nitrite ['naɪtraɪt] *n Chem* nitrito *m*.

nitrogen ['naɪtrədʒən] *n Chem* nitrógeno *m*.

nitroglycerin(e) [naɪtrəʊ'glɪsəriːn] *n Chem* nitro-glicerina *f*.

nitrous ['naɪtrəs] *adj* nitroso,-a.

nitty-gritty [nɪtɪ'grɪtɪ] *n fam* **to get down to the n.-g.,** ir al grano.

nitwit ['nɪtwɪt] *n fam* imbécil *mf*.

no [nəʊ] **I** *adj* ninguno,-a; **I have no idea,** no tengo (ni) idea; **it's no good** *or* **use,** no vale la pena; **make no mistake about it,** no lo dudes; *Aut* **'no parking',** 'prohibido aparcar'; **no sensible person,** ninguna persona razonable; **no two are the same,** no hay dos (que sean) iguales; **she has no children,** no tiene hijos; **she's no genius,** no es ningún genio; **there is no such thing as ...,** no existe ...; **there's no changing your mind now,** ya no puedes cambiar de idea; *fam* **n. end of ...,** un mogollón *or* montón de ...; *fam* **no way!,** ¡ni hablar! **II** *n* no *m*; **ayes and noes,** votos a favor y votos en contra; **she won't take no for an answer,** no se dará por vencida, no aceptará un no por respuesta. **III** *adv* no; **come here! —no!,** ¡ven aquí! —¡no!; **it's no better than before,** no esté mejor que antes; **no longer,** ya no; **no less than,** no menos de; **to say no,** decir que no.

no. *(pl nos.) abbr* of **number,** número *m*, n.°, núm.

Noah ['nəʊə] *n Rel* Noé *m*. ■ **N.'s ark,** el arca *f* de Noé.

nob [nɒb] *n fam* pez *m* gordo.

nobble ['nɒbəl] *vtr sl* **1** *(drug)* drogar. **2** *(bribe)* sobornar. **3** *(steal)* mangar, birlar. **4** *(catch)* pillar, pescar.

nobility [nəʊ'bɪlɪtɪ] *n* nobleza *f*.

noble ['nəʊbəl] **I** *adj* **1** *(aristocratic)* noble; **of n. birth,** de noble cuna; **of n. descent,** de noble alcurnia. **2** *(sentiment)* noble; *(gesture)* magnánimo,-a. **3** *(impressive)* magnífico,-a, grandioso,-a. **II** *n (in feudal system)* noble *m*.

nobleman ['nəʊbəlmən] *n (pl noblemen)* noble *m*.

noblewoman ['nəʊbəlwʊmən] *n (pl noblewomen* ['nəʊbəlwɪmɪn]) noble *f*.

nobody ['nəʊbədɪ] **I** *pron* nadie; **I told n.,** no se lo dije a nadie; **n. came,** no vino nadie; **n. else,** nadie más; **n. knows the answer,** no conoce la respuesta nadie. **II** *n* nadie *m*; **he's a n.,** es un don nadie.

no-claims ['nəʊkleɪmz] *adj Ins* **no-c. bonus,** prima de no siniestrabilidad.

nocturnal [nɒk'tɜːnəl] *adj* nocturno,-a.

nod [nɒd] **I** *n* **1** *(in greeting)* saludo *m* con la cabeza. **2** *(in agreement)* señal *f* de asentimiento; *GB fam* **a n.'s as good as a wink,** a buen entendedor pocas palabras bastan. **3 the land of N.,** el mundo de los sueños. **II** *vi (pt & pp nodded)* **1** *(in greeting)* saludar con la cabeza. **2** *(in agreement)* asentir con la cabeza. **III** *vtr* **to n. one's head,** inclinar la cabeza; *(in agreement)* asentir con la cabeza. ◆ **nod off** *vi* quedarse dormido-a, dormirse.

nodding ['nɒdɪŋ] *adj* **to have a n. acquaintance with sb,** conocer a algn de vista.

node [nəʊd] *n* **1** *Bot* nudo *m*. **2** *Anat Med* nodo *m*.

nodule ['nɒdjuːl] *n* nódulo *m*.

no-go [nəʊ'gəʊ] *adj* **no-go area,** zona *f* prohibida.

no-hoper [nəʊ'həʊpə'] *n fam* inútil *mf*.

nohow ['nəʊhaʊ] *adv* de ninguna manera.

noise [nɔɪz] *n* **1** ruido *m*; **to make a n.,** hacer ruido. ■ **background n.,** ruido *m* de fondo. **2** *fam* **a big n.,** un pez gordo.

noiseless ['nɔɪzlɪs] *adj* silencioso,-a, sin ruido. ◆ **noiselessly** *adv* silenciosamente.

noiseproof ['nɔɪzpruːf] *adj* insonorizado,-a.

noisy ['nɔɪzɪ] *adj (noisier, noisiest)* ruidoso,-a; **n. machine/street,** máquina/calle ruidosa; **a n. crowd,** una muchedumbre bulliciosa.

nomad ['nəʊmæd] *n* nómada *mf*.

nomadic [nəʊ'mædɪk] *adj* nómada.

no-man's-land ['nəʊmænzlænd] *n* tierra *f* de nadie.

nomenclature ['nəʊ'menklətʃəʳ] *n* nomenclatura *f*.

nominal ['nɒmɪnəl] *adj* 1 nominal. 2 *(payment, rent)* simbólico,-a. ◆ **nominally** *adv* nominalmente, de nombre solamente.

nominate ['nɒmɪneɪt] *vtr* 1 *(propose)* designar, proponer. 2 *(appoint)* nombrar.

nomination [nɒmɪ'neɪʃən] *n* 1 *(proposal)* propuesta *f*; **to accept/support a n.,** aceptar/apoyar una candidatura. 2 *(appointment)* nombramiento *m*.

nominative ['nɒmɪnətɪv] *n Ling* nominativo *m*.

nominee [nɒmɪ'niː] *n* nominado,-a, *m*, *f*, persona *f* propuesta.

non- [nɒn] *pref* no; **n.-Catholic,** no católico,-a.

non-aggression [nɒnə'greʃən] *n Pol* no agresión *f*. ■ **n.-a. pact,** pacto *m* de no agresión.

non-alcoholic [nɒnælkə'hɒlɪk] *adj* no alcohólico,-a, sin alcohol.

non-aligned [nɒnə'laɪnd] *adj Pol* no alineado,-a. ■ **n.-a. countries,** países *mpl* no alineados.

nonagon ['nɒnəgɒn] *n Geom* eneágono *m*.

nonchalance ['nɒnʃələns] *n (indifference)* indiferencia *f*; *(calmness)* imperturbabilidad *f*.

nonchalant ['nɒnʃələnt] *adj (indifferent)* indiferente; *(calm)* imperturbable, impasible.

noncombatant [nɒn'kɒmbətənt] *adj & n* no combatiente *(mf)*.

noncommissioned ['nɒnkəmɪʃənd] *adj Mil* **n. officer,** suboficial *m*.

noncommittal ['nɒnkəmɪtəl] *adj* evasivo,-a, que no compromete a nada; **a n. reply,** una respuesta poco comprometedora.

nonconductor [nɒnkən'dʌktəʳ] *n Elec Phys* aislante *m*.

nonconformist [nɒnkən'fɔːmɪst] *n* inconformista *mf*.

noncontributory [nɒnkən'trɪbjʊtərɪ] *adj* **a n. pension scheme,** un plan de jubilación pagado por la empresa.

nondescript ['nɒndɪskrɪpt] *adj* indescriptible, inclasificable; *(uninteresting)* soso,-a, anodino,-a; **n. music,** una música cualquiera.

none [nʌn] **I** *pron* ninguno,-a; **I know n. of them,** no conozco a ninguno de ellos; **it is n. of her business,** no tiene nada que ver con ella, no es asunto suyo; **n. at all,** nada en absoluto; **n. of that in here!,** ¡nada de esto aquí dentro!; **n. of the records is his,** ninguno de los discos es suyo; **n. other than ...,** nada menos que ... . **II** *adv* de ningún modo, de ninguna manera; **she's n. the worse for it,** no se ha visto afectada *or* perjudicada por ello; **n. too soon,** a buena hora.

nonentity [nɒ'nentɪtɪ] *n (person)* nulidad *f*, cero *m* a la izquierda.

nonetheless [nʌnðə'les] *adv* no obstante, sin embargo.

nonevent [nɒnɪ'vent] *n* fracaso *m*; **the concert turned out to be a n.,** aquello ni fue concierto ni fue nada.

nonexistent [nɒnɪg'zɪstənt] *adj* inexistente.

nonfattening [nɒn'fætənɪŋ] *adj* que no engorda.

nonfiction [nɒn'fɪkʃən] *n* literatura *f* no novelesca.

nonmember [nɒn'membəʳ] *n* no socio,-a *m*,*f*.

no-nonsense [nəʊ'nɒnsens] *adj (person)* recto,-a, serio,-a.

nonpayment [nɒn'peɪmənt] *n* falta *f* de pago.

nonplussed [nɒn'plʌst] *adj* perplejo,-a, anonadado,-a.

non-profit-making [nɒn'prɒfɪtmeɪkɪŋ] *adj (organization)* sin fin lucrativo.

nonresident [nɒn'rezɪdənt] *n* no residente *mf*.

nonreturnable [nɒnrɪ'tɜːnəbəl] *adj* no retornable.

nonsense ['nɒnsəns] *n* tonterías *fpl*, disparates *mpl*; **to talk n.,** decir tonterías; **that's n.,** eso es absurdo.

nonsensical [nɒn'sensɪkəl] *adj* absurdo,-a.

nonsmoker [nɒn'sməʊkəʳ] *n* no fumador,-a *m*,*f*, persona *f* que no fuma.

nonstarter [nɒn'stɑːtəʳ] *n* **to be a n.,** *Sport (competitor)* quedar descalificado,-a; *fig (person)* ser imposible.

nonstick [nɒn'stɪk] *adj (pan etc)* antiadherente.

nonstop [nɒn'stɒp] **I** *adj (train)* directo,-a; *(flight)* sin escalas. **II** *adv* sin parar; **to talk n.,** hablar sin parar, no parar de hablar; **to fly n.,** volar sin hacer escalas.

nontaxable [nɒn'tæksəbəl] *adj* exento,-a de impuestos, no imponible.

nontoxic [nɒn'tɒksɪk] *adj* no tóxico,-a.

noodles ['nuːdəlz] *npl Culin* fideos *mpl*.

nook [nʊk] *n* rincón *m*, recoveco *m*.

noon [nuːn] *n* mediodía *m*; **at n.,** a mediodía.

noonday ['nuːndeɪ] *n* **the n. sun,** el sol de mediodía.

no-one ['nəʊwʌn] *pron* nadie; **n. came,** no vino nadie.

noose [nuːs] *n* lazo *m*; *(hangman's)* soga *f*; *fig* **to have one's head in the n.,** estar con la soga al cuello.

nor [nɔːʳ] *conj* ni, ni tampoco; **neither ... n.,** ni ... ni; **neither you n. I,** ni tú ni yo; **he neither drinks n. smokes,** ni fuma ni bebe; **n. do I,** (ni) yo tampoco.

Nordic ['nɔːdɪk] *adj* nórdico,-a.

norm [nɔːm] *n* norma *f*; **to deviate from the n.,** salirse de lo normal *or* de la norma.

normal ['nɔːməl] **I** *adj* normal; **a n. person,** una persona normal. **II** *n* lo normal; **below n.,** por debajo de lo normal.

normality [nɔː'mælɪtɪ] *n* normalidad *f*.

normalization [nɔːməlaɪ'zeɪʃən] *n* normalización *f*.

normally ['nɔːməlɪ] *adv* normalmente.

Norman ['nɔːmən] *adj & n* normando,-a *(m,f)*.

Normandy ['nɔːməndɪ] *n* Normandía.

Norse [nɔːs] *Hist* **I** *adj* nórdico,-a. **II** *n (language)* nórdico *m*.

Norseman ['nɔːsmən] *n (pl Norsemen) Hist* vikingo *m*.

north [nɔːθ] **I** *n* norte *m*; **the N.,** el norte. ■ **N. America,** América del Norte, Norteamérica; **N. Pole,** Polo *m* Norte; **N. Sea,** Mar *m* del Norte. **II** *adj* hacia el norte, al norte; **to face n.,** dar al norte. **III** *adj* del norte; **the n. coast,** la costa del norte; **n. wind,** viento del norte.

northbound ['nɔːθbaʊnd] *adj* con dirección norte; **a n. train,** un tren que viaja hacia el norte.

northeast [nɔːθ'iːst] *n* nordeste *m*, noreste *m*.

northeasterly [nɔːθ'iːstəlɪ] *adj*, **northeastern** [nɔːθ'iːstən] *adj* del nordeste.

northerly ['nɔːðəlɪ] *adj* norte, del norte; **n. wind,** viento del norte; **in a n. direction,** en dirección norte; **the most n. point,** el punto más septentrional.

northern ['nɔːðən] *adj* del norte, septentrional. ■ **n. hemisphere,** hemisferio *m* norte; **N. Ireland,** Irlanda del Norte; **N. Irishman,** norirlandés *m*; **N. Irshwoman,** norirladesa *f*; **n. lights,** aurora *f sing* boreal.

northerner ['nɔːðənəʳ] *n* norteño,-a, *mf*.

northward ['nɔːθwəd] *adj & adv* hacia el norte.

northwest [nɔːθ'west] *n* noroeste *m*.

northwesterly [nɔːθ'westəlɪ] *adj*, **northwestern** [nɔːθ'westən] *adj* del noroeste.

Norway ['nɔːweɪ] *n* Noruega.

Northwegian [nɔː'wiːdʒən] I *adj* noruego,-a. ■ **N. Sea,** Mar *m* de Noruega. II *n* 1 *(person)* noruego,-a *m*, *f*. 2 *(language)* noruego *m*.

nose [nəʊz] I *n* 1 *Anat* nariz *f*; **my n. is bleeding,** me sangra la nariz; **to blow one's n.,** sonarse; *fig (right)* **under sb's n.,** delante de las propias narices de algn; *fig* **to be as plain as the n. on one's face,** estar tan claro como el agua; *fig* **to lead sb by the n.,** manejar a algn a su antojo; *GB fam* **to get up sb's n.,** fastidiar *or* jorobar a algn; *fam* **to keep one's n. clean,** no meterse en líos; *fam* **to pay through the n.,** pagar un dineral; *fam* **to poke** *or* **stick one's n. into sth,** meter la nariz *or* las narices en algo; *fam* **to turn one's n. up at sth,** despreciar algo. 2 *(sense of smell)* olfato *m*. 3 *(of car, plane)* morro *m*; **the cars stood n. to tail,** los coches estaban parados en una caravana. II *vi* avanzar poco a poco; **the car nosed (out) into the street,** el coche asomó el morro para salir a la calle. ◆ **nose out** *vtr (animal)* olfatear; *fig (secret)* averiguar. ◆ **nose about, nose around** *vi* curiosear.

nosebag ['nəʊzbæg] *n* morral *m*.

nosebleed ['nəʊzbliːd] *n* hemorragia *f* nasal.

nosedive ['nəʊzdaɪv] *Av* I *n* picado *m*. II *vi* descender en picado.

nosegay ['nəʊzgeɪ] *n* ramillete *m* de flores.

nosey-parker ['nəʊzɪ'pɑːkəʳ] *n fam* entrometido,-a *m*, *f*, metomentodo *mf*.

nosh [nɒʃ] *n sl* papeo *m*, manducatoria *f*.

nostalgia [nɒ'stældʒə] *n* nostalgia *f*.

nostalgic [nɒ'stældʒɪk] *adj* nostálgico,-a.

nostril ['nɒstrɪl] *n Anat* orificio *m* nasal.

nosy ['nəʊzɪ] *adj (nosier, nosiest) fam* entrometido,-a.

not [nɒt] *adv* no; **certainly n.,** de ninguna manera; **he's n. in today,** hoy no está; **I'm n. sorry to leave,** no siento nada irme; **n. at all,** en absoluto; **thank you — n. at all,** gracias —no hay de qué, de nada; **n. one, but many,** no uno sino muchos; **n. one (of them) said thank you,** nadie me dio las gracias; **n. that I don't want to come,** no es que no quiera ir; **n. too well,** bastante mal; **n. without reason,** no sin razón; *fam* **n. likely!,** ¡ni hablar!

notable ['nəʊtəbəl] *adj* notable; **a n. success,** un éxito notable. ◆ **notably** *adv* notablemente; **n. well done,** admirablemente bien hecho; **she was n. absent,** brilló por su ausencia.

notary ['nəʊtərɪ] *n* notario *m*.

notation [nəʊ'teɪʃən] *n Mus* notación *f*.

notch [nɒtʃ] I *n* muesca *f*, corte *m*. II *vtr* hacer una muesca, marcar con muescas. ◆ **notch up** *vtr fig* **to n. up a victory,** apuntarse una victoria *or* un tanto.

note [nəʊt] I *n* 1 *Mus* nota *f*; *(hint)* tono *m*, nota *f*; **a n. of bitterness,** un tono de amargura. 2 *Mus (key)* tecla *f*; **the black/white notes,** las teclas negras/blancas; *fig* **to strike the right n.,** acertar, hacer *or* decir lo apropiado. 3 *(on paper)* nota *f*; **I sent her a n.,** le envié una nota; **there's a n. in the margin,** hay una nota en el margen. 4 *(notice)* **to take n. of,** prestar atención a; **worthy of n.,** digno de mención. 5 *Fin* billete *m* de banco; **a ten pound n.,** un billete de diez libras. 6 **notes,** apuntes *mpl*; **I'll have to look it up in my n.,** tendré que mirarlo en mis apuntes; **to take n.,** tomar apuntes. II *vtr* 1 *(write down)* apuntar, anotar; **she noted the details in her diary,** apuntó los detalles en su agenda. 2 *(see, notice)* notar, advertir, fijarse; **his reaction was noted by everyone,** todos advirtieron su reacción.

notebook ['nəʊtbʊk] *n* cuaderno *m*, libreta *f*.

noted ['nəʊtɪd] *adj* notable, célebre; **she was n. for her strength,** era famosa por su fuerza.

notepad ['nəʊtpæd] *n* bloc *m* de notas.

notepaper ['nəʊtpeɪpəʳ] *n* papel *m* de cartas *or* de escribir.

noteworthy ['nəʊtwɜːðɪ] *adj* digno,-a de mención.

nothing ['nʌθɪŋ] I *n* nada; no ... nada; **for n.,** gratis; **it's n.,** no es nada; **it's n. to be proud of,** no es como para estar orgulloso; **it's n. to do with you,** no tiene nada que ver contigo; **n. else,** nada más; **n. happened today,** hoy no pasó nada; **n. more,** nada más; **sweet nothings,** ternezas *fpl*; **there's n. in it,** no es cierto; *fam* **n. much,** poca cosa; *fam* **there's n. to it,** es facilísimo; *sl* **n. doing,** ni hablar. II *adv* de ninguna manera, de ningún modo; **it's n. like as good as ...,** no tiene ni (punto de) comparación con ...; **she looks n. like her sister,** no se parece en nada a su hermana.

nothingness ['nʌθɪŋnɪs] *n* nada *f*.

notice ['nəʊtɪs] I *n* 1 *(warning)* aviso *m*; **a month's n.,** un mes de plazo; **he gave a month's n.,** presentó la dimisión con un mes de antelación; **at a moment's n.,** sin antelación; **at short n.,** con poca antelación; **until further n.,** hasta nuevo aviso; **without n.,** sin previo aviso. ■ **n. to quit,** notificación *f* para desocupar una vivienda *or* un local. 2 *(attention)* atención *f*; **it escaped my n.,** se me escapó; **to come to one's n.,** llegar al conocimiento de uno; **to take no n. of sth,** no hacer caso de algo; **to take n. of sth,** prestar atención a algo. 3 *(announcement)* anuncio *m*; **she put a n. in the shop window,** puso un anuncio en el escaparate de la tienda. 4 *(sign)* letrero *m*, aviso *m*; **the n. says 'keep off the grass',** el letrero dice 'prohibido pisar el césped'. 5 *(review)* reseña *f*. II *vtr* darse cuenta de, fijarse en, notar; **he didn't n.,** no se dio cuenta; **I didn't n. the new curtains,** no me fijé en las cortinas nuevas; **she noticed nothing strange,** no notó nada extraño.

noticeable ['nəʊtɪsəbəl] *adj* que se nota, evidente; **the stain isn't very n.,** la mancha no se nota mucho; **it's hardly n.,** casi no se nota; **a n. change,** un cambio evidente.

noticeboard ['nəʊtɪsbɔːd] *n* tablón *m* de anuncios.

notifiable [nəʊtɪ'faɪəbəl] *adj Med (disease)* de declaración médica obligatoria.

notification [nəʊtɪfɪ'keɪʃən] *n* aviso *m*, notificación *f*.

notify ['nəʊtɪfaɪ] *vtr (pt & pp notified)* avisar, notificar; **she was notified that her car had been found,** le notificaron que el coche había aparecido; **to n. the police of a burglary,** denunciar un robo a la policía.

notion ['nəʊʃən] *n* 1 idea *f*, concepto *m*, noción *f*; **he had little n. of what was being said,** tenía muy poca idea de lo que se estaba diciendo; **her n. of friendship is different from mine,** su concepto de la amistad es diferente del mío. 2 *(whim)* capricho *m*. 3 *US Sew* **notions,** artículos *mpl* de mercería.

notional ['nəʊʃənəl] *adj* 1 *(vague)* teórico,-a. 2 *(imaginary)* imaginario,-a.

notoriety [nəʊtə'raɪətɪ] *n* mala fama *f*, mala reputación *f*.

notorious [nəʊ'tɔːrɪəs] *adj* célebre, muy conocido,-a; **a n. criminal,** un criminal célebre. ◆ **notoriously** *adv* notoriamente; **they were n. ill-equipped,** era de todos sabido que iban mal equipados.

notwithstanding [nɒtwɪθ'stændɪŋ] I *prep* a pesar de. II *adv* sin embargo, no obstante.

nougat ['nuːgɑː] *n* turrón *m* blando.

nought [nɔːt] *n* cero *m*; **n. point five,** cero coma cinco. ■ **noughts and crosses,** tres en raya *m*.

noun [naʊn] *n Ling* nombre *m*, sustantivo *m*. ■ **proper n.,** nombre *m* propio.

nourish ['nʌrɪʃ] *vtr* 1 alimentar, nutrir. 2 *fig (hopes)* abrigar.

nourishing ['nʌrɪʃɪŋ] *adj* nutritivo,-a, alimenticio,-a.

nourishment ['nʌrɪʃmənt] *n* alimentación *f*, nutrición *f*.

nous [naʊs] *n GB fam* cacumen *m*.

Nov *abbr of* **November,** noviembre *m*, nov, novbre.

Nova Scotia [nəʊvə'skəʊʃə] *n* Nueva Escocia.

novel¹ ['nɒvəl] *n* novela *f*.

novel² ['nɒvəl] *adj* original, novedoso,-a.

novelist ['nɒvəlɪst] *n* novelista *mf*.

novelty ['nɒvəltɪ] *n* **1** *(thing, idea)* novedad *f*; **the n. of the situation,** la novedad de la situación; **the n. will soon wear off,** pronto dejará de ser una novedad. **2** *(trinket)* novedad *f*, fantasía *f*.

November [nəʊ'vembəʳ] *n* noviembre *m*; **(on) the fifth of N.,** el cinco de noviembre; *see also* **May.**

novice ['nɒvɪs] *n* **1** *(beginner)* novato,-a *m,f*, principiante *mf*. **2** *Rel* novicio,-a *m,f*.

now [naʊ] *adv* **1** *(at this moment)* ahora; **from n. on,** de ahora en adelante; **it's my turn n.,** ahora me toca a mí; **just n., right n.,** ahora mismo; **n. and then, n. and again,** de vez en cuando. **2** *(for events in past)* ya, entonces; **everything was n. ready,** ya estaba todo a punto. **3** *(at present, these days)* actualmente, hoy (en) día. **4** *(not related to time)* **n. (then),** ahora bien; **n. then, what's the problem?,** ¿veamos, cuál es el problema?'; **n., n.!,** ¡vamos!, ¡ya está bien! **II** *conj* **n. (that),** ahora que, ya que; **n. that she is going to school,** ahora que va al colegio; **n. that you mention it,** ya que lo mencionas. **3** *n* **until n.,** hasta ahora; **he'll be home by n.,** ya habrá llegado a casa; **goodbye for n.,** ¡hasta pronto!; **four days from n.,** dentro de cuatro días.

nowadays ['naʊədeɪz] *adv* hoy, hoy (en) día, actualmente.

nowhere ['nəʊweəʳ] *adv* en ningún lugar, en ningún sitio, en ninguna parte; **it's n. to be seen,** no está en ninguna parte; **he's n. near the end,** le falta mucho para terminar; **that will get you n.,** eso no te servirá de nada; *fam* **she lives in the middle of n.,** vive en el quinto pino; **n. else,** en ninguna otra parte; **to come out of n.,** salir de la nada.

noxious ['nɒkʃəs] *adj* nocivo,-a, perjudicial.

nozzle ['nɒzəl] *n* boca *f*, boquilla *f*.

nr *abbr of* **near,** cerca de.

NSPCC [enespi:si:'si:] *GB abbr of* **National Society for the Prevention of Cruelty to Children,** sociedad *f* nacional para la protección de los niños.

NT *GB abbr of* **National Trust,** organización que vela por el patrimonio nacional.

nth [enθ] *adj* **for the n. time,** por enésima vez.

Nth *abbr of* **North,** norte, N.

nuance [nju:'ɑ:ns] *n* matiz *m*.

nub [nʌb] *n* nudo *m*, meollo *m*; **the n. of the matter,** el quid de la cuestión.

nubile ['nju:baɪl] *adj f* núbil, casadera.

nuclear ['nju:klɪəʳ] *adj* nuclear. ■ **n. arms,** armas *fpl* nucleares; **n. disarmament,** desarme *m* nuclear; **n. fission,** fisión *f* nuclear; **n. power,** energía *f* nuclear; **n. power station,** central *f* nuclear; **n. winter,** invierno *m* nuclear.

nucleic [nju:'kli:ɪk] *adj Biol Chem* nucleico,-a; **n. acid,** ácido *m* nucleico.

nucleus ['nju:klɪəs] *n (pl nuclei* ['nju:klɪaɪ]*)* núcleo *m*.

nude [nju:d] **I** *adj* desnudo,-a. **II** *n Art Phot* desnudo *m*; **in the n.,** desnudo,-a.

nudge [nʌdʒ] **I** *vtr* dar un codazo a. **II** *n* codazo *m*.

nudism ['nju:dɪzəm] *n* nudismo *m*.

nudist ['nju:dɪst] *adj & n* nudista *(mf)*. ■ **n. colony,** colonia *f* nudista.

nudity ['nju:dɪtɪ] *n* desnudez *f*.

nugget ['nʌgɪt] *n Min* pepita *f*; **gold n.,** pepita de oro.

nuisance ['nju:səns] *n* **1** molestia *f*, fastidio *m*, pesadez *f*; **this weather is a n.,** este tiempo es una pesadez; **what a n.!,** ¡qué lata! **2** *(person)* pesado,-a *m, f*; **make a n. of oneself,** dar la lata, ponerse pesado.

nuke [nju:k] *sl* **I** *n* **1** *(bomb)* bomba *f* nuclear *or* atómica. **2** *(power station)* central *f* nuclear. **II** *vtr* atacar con armas nucleares.

null [nʌl] *adj* nulo,-a; **n. and void,** nulo y sin valor.

nullify ['nʌlɪfaɪ] *vtr (pt & pp **nullified**)* anular.

numb [nʌm] **I** *adj* **1** *(without feeling)* entumecido,-a; **my leg has gone n.,** se me ha dormido la pierna; **n. with cold,** entumecido de frío. **2** *fig (unable to move)* paralizado,-a, petrificado,-a; **n. with fear,** paralizado de miedo. **II** *vtr* **1** *(with cold)* entumecer (de frío); *(with anaesthetic)* adormecer. **2** *fig (paralyse)* paralizar, dejar helado.

number ['nʌmbəʳ] **I** *n* **1** *Math* número *m*; **odd/even n.,** número impar/par; **in round numbers,** en números redondos. **2** *(quantity)* **a n. of people,** varias personas; **a large n. of,** un gran número de. **3** *(of page, house, etc)* número *m*; **she lives at n. four,** vive en el (número) cuatro; *Tel* **have you got my n.?,** ¿tienes mi (número de) teléfono?; *Tel* **you've got the wrong n.,** se ha equivocado de número. **4 to be n. one,** ser el primero *or* el mejor *or* el número uno; **to look after n. one,** barrer para adentro. **5** *Press (issue)* número *m*; **the June n.,** el número de junio; **back n.,** número atrasado. **6** *fam (clothing)* modelo *m*; **Kathy was wearing a black lace n.,** Kathy llevaba un modelo de encaje negro. **7** *fam (job etc)* **a cushy n.,** un chollo. **8** *Mus Theat* número *m*. **II** *vtr* **1** *(put a number on)* numerar, poner número a; **the seats are numbered,** los asientos llevan número. **2** *(count)* contar; **his days are numbered,** tiene los días contados; **I n. you among my friends,** te cuento entre mis amigos.

numberplate ['nʌmbəpleɪt] *n GB Aut* placa *f* de la matrícula.

numbness ['nʌmnɪs] *n* **1** *(loss of feeling)* entumecimiento *m*. **2** *fig* parálisis *f*.

numbskull ['nʌmskʌl] *n* tonto,-a *m,f*, imbécil *mf*.

numeracy ['nju:mərəsɪ] *n* conocimiento *m* básico de las matemáticas.

numeral ['nju:mərəl] *n* número *m*, cifra *f*; **Roman numerals,** números romanos.

numerate ['nju:mərət] *adj* **to be n.,** tener un conocimiento básico de matemáticas.

numerical [nju:'merɪkəl] *adj* numérico,-a; **in n. order,** por orden numérico. ◆ **numerically** *adv* numéricamente; **the enemy was n. superior,** el enemigo era numéricamente superior.

numerous ['nju:mərəs] *adj* numeroso,-a; **n. friends,** numerosos *or* muchos amigos; **on n. occasions,** en innumerables ocasiones.

numismatic [nju:mɪz'mætɪk] *adj* numismático,-a.

numismatics [nju:mɪz'mætɪks] *n* numismática *f*.

numismatist [nju:'mɪzmətɪst] *n* numismático,-a *m,f*.

nun [nʌn] *n* monja *f*.

nuncio ['nʌnsɪəʊ] *n Rel* nuncio *m*.

nunlike ['nʌnlaɪk] *adj* monjil.

nunnery ['nʌnərɪ] *n* convento *m*.

nuptial ['nʌpʃəl] **I** *adj* nupcial; **n. mass,** misa *f* nupcial. **II** **nuptials** *npl hum* casamiento *m*, boda *f*.

nurse [nɜ:s] **I** *n* enfermera *f*; **children's n.,** niñera *f*, **male n.,** enfermero *m*. **II** *vtr* **1** *(look after)* cuidar, atender; **to n. sb back to health,** cuidar a algn durante una enfermedad; **to n. a cold,** curarse un resfriado. **2** *(baby)* acunar, mecer en los brazos; **he nursed his swollen ankle,** cuidó de su tobillo hinchado. **3** *(suckle)* amamantar, criar. **4** *fig (harbour)* guardar; **to n. a grievance,** guardar rencor.

nursemaid ['nɜ:smeɪd] *n* niñera *f*.

nursery ['nɜ:sərɪ] *n* **1** *(in house)* cuarto *m* de los niños. ■ **n. rhyme,** poema *m* infantil. **2** *(institution)* guardería *f*. ■ **day n.,** guardería *f*; **n. school,** parvulario *m*, jardín *m* de infancia. **3** *fig* semillero *m*, vivero *m*. **4** *Sport* **n. slopes,** pistas *fpl* para principiantes. **5** *Hortic* vivero *m*.

nurseryman ['nɜ:sərɪmən] *n (pl nurserymen)* encargado *m* de un vivero, arbolista *m*.

nursing ['nɜ:sɪŋ] **I** *adj* **1** *(mother)* que amamanta. **2** *Med* **n. home,** clínica *f*; **n. staff,** enfermeros *mpl* y enfermeras *fpl*, personal *m* sanitario. **II** *n* profesión *f* de enfermero,-a.

nurture ['nɜːtʃəʳ] *vtr* nutrir, alimentar.

nut [nʌt] *n* 1 (*fruit*) fruto *m* seco; *fig* **a tough n. to crack,** un hueso duro de roer. 2 *sl (head)* coco *m*, chola *f*, melón *m*; **he's off his n.,** está chalado. 3 *sl (mad person)* loco,-a *m*, *f*, chalado,-a *m*, *f*. 4 *Tech* tuerca *f*; **nuts and bolts,** tuercas y pernios.

nut-brown ['nʌtbraʊn] *adj* castaño,-a, (de) color avellana.

nutcase ['nʌtkeɪs] *n sl* loco,-a *m*, *f*, chalado,-a *m*, *f*.

nutcracker ['nʌtkrækəʳ] *n* cascanueces *m inv*.

nuthatch ['nʌthætʃ] *n Orn* trepador *m* azul.

nutmeg ['nʌtmeg] *n* nuez *f* moscada.

nutrient ['njuːtrɪənt] I *adj* nutritivo,-a. II *n* alimento *m* nutritivo, sustancia *f* nutritiva.

nutrition [njuːˈtrɪʃən] *n* nutrición *f*, alimentación *f*.

nutritious [njuːˈtrɪʃəs] *adj* nutritivo,-a, alimenticio,-a.

nuts [nʌts] *adj* chalado,-a; **to go n.,** volverse loco; **he's n. about motorbikes,** las motos le chiflan.

nutshell ['nʌtʃel] *n* cáscara *f*; *fig* **in a n.,** en pocas palabras.

nutter ['nʌtəʳ] *n sl* loco,-a *m*, *f*, chalado,-a *m*, *f*.

nutty ['nʌtɪ] *adj (nuttier, nuttiest)* 1 *Culin* que sabe a nuez. 2 *sl (crazy)* loco,-a, chalado,-a.

nuzzle ['nʌzəl] *vi* **to n. up to,** arrimarse a.

NW *abbr of* **North-West,** noroeste, NO.

NY *abbr of* **New York,** Nueva York.

nylon ['naɪlɒn] I *n* 1 (*material*) nilón *m*, nailon *m*. 2 **nylons,** medias *fpl* de nilón. II *adj* de nilón.

nymph [nɪmf] *n Myth* ninfa *f*.

nymphomania [nɪmfəˈmeɪnɪə] *n* ninfomanía *f*.

nymphomaniac [nɪmfəˈmeɪnɪæk] *n* ninfómana *f*.

NZ *abbr of* **New Zealand,** Nueva Zelanda.

O

O, o [əʊ] *n* 1 (*the letter*) O, o *f*. 2 *Math Tel* cero *m*; **3.01 (three point nought one),** 3,01 (tres coma cero uno).

oaf [əʊf] *n* patán *m*, palurdo,-a *m*, *f*, zoquete *m*, *f*.

oak [əʊk] *n Bot* roble *m*. ■ **common o.,** carballo *m*, carvallo *m*; **cork o.,** alcornoque *m*; **evergreen** *or* **holm o.,** encina *f*; **o. apple,** agalla *f*; **red o.,** roble *m* americano; **sessile o.,** roble *m* albar.

oaken ['əʊkən] *adj* de roble.

OAP [əʊeɪˈpiː] *GB fam abbr of* **old-age pensioner,** pensionista *mf*.

oar [ɔːʳ] *n* 1 (*pole*) remo *m*; *fig* **to put** *or* **stick one's o. in,** entrometerse; *fig* **to rest on one's oars,** dormirse en los laureles. 2 (*person*) remero,-a *m*, *f*.

oarsman ['ɔːzmən] *n* (*pl oarsmen*) remero *m*.

oasis [əʊˈeɪsɪs] *n* (*pl oases* [əʊˈeɪsiːz]) oasis *m inv*.

oat [əʊt] *n Bot* 1 avena *f*. 2 **oats,** avena *f sing*; *fig* **to sow one's wild o.,** correrla; *US fam* **to feel one's o.,** (*feel exuberant*) sentirse en la gloria. ■ **rolled o.,** copos *mpl* de avena.

oatcake ['əʊtkeɪk] *n* torta *f* de avena.

oath [əʊθ] *n* (*pl oaths* [əʊðz]) 1 *Jur* juramento *m*; **o. of allegiance,** juramento de fidelidad; **to swear** *or* **take an o.,** prestar juramento; *fam* **on my o.,** palabra de honor. 2 (*blasphemy*) blasfemia *f*; (*swearword*) palabrota *f*.

oatmeal ['əʊtmiːl] *n* 1 (*meal*) harina *f* de avena. 2 *US* (*porridge*) copos *mpl* de avena.

obdurate ['ɒbdjʊrɪt] *adj* (*obstinate*) obstinado,-a, terco,-a; (*unyielding*) inflexible, duro,-a.

obedience [əˈbiːdɪəns] *n* obediencia *f*.

obedient [əˈbiːdɪənt] *adj* obediente.

obelisk ['ɒbɪlɪsk] *n* obelisco *m*.

obese [əʊˈbiːs] *adj* obeso,-a.

obesity [əʊˈbiːsɪtɪ] *n* obesidad *f*.

obey [əˈbeɪ] *vtr* (*gen*) obedecer; (*law*) cumplir; (*need*) responder a.

obfuscate ['ɒbfʌskeɪt] *vtr* ofuscar, oscurecer.

obituary [əˈbɪtjʊərɪ] *n* necrología *f*, nota *f* necrológica. ■ **o. column,** sección *f* necrológica.

object¹ ['ɒbdʒɪkt] *n* 1 (*thing*) objeto *m*, cosa *f*. ■ *Opt* **o. glass,** objetivo *m*. 2 (*aim, purpose*) fin *m*, objeto *m*, objetivo *m*; **with this o.,** con este fin. ■ **o. lesson,** ejemplo *m* práctico. 3 *fam* (*focus of feelings etc*) objeto *m*; **he's an o. of pity,** da lástima, es un triste espectáculo; **she's an o. of affection,** inspira afecto. 4 (*obstacle*) inconveniente *m*;

money is no o., el dinero no es inconveniente. 5 *Ling* complemento *m*, objeto *m*; **direct o.,** complemento directo.

object² [əbˈdʒekt] I *vtr* objetar. II *vi* oponerse, poner reparos (**to,** a); **everyone objected to the decision,** todos se opusieron a la decisión; *fig* **do you o. to my smoking?,** ¿le molesta que fume?

objection [əbˈdʒekʃən] *n* 1 (*argument against*) objeción *f*, reparo *m*; **she raised no objections,** no puso reparo alguno; **to take o.,** molestarse (**to,** por). 2 (*drawback*) inconveniente *m*, obstáculo *m*; **provided there's no o.,** si no hay inconveniente.

objectionable [əbˈdʒekʃənəbəl] *adj* (*unacceptable*) inaceptable; (*unpleasant*) ofensivo,-a, desagradable; **o. remarks,** observaciones inadmisibles.

objective [əbˈdʒektɪv] I *adj* objetivo,-a. II *n* 1 (*aim*) fin *m*, objetivo *m*. 2 *Opt Phot* objetivo *m*.

objector [əbˈdʒektəʳ] *n* objetante *mf*, objetor,-a *m*, *f*. ■ **conscientious o.,** objetor,-a *m*, *f* de conciencia.

obligation [ɒblɪˈgeɪʃən] *n* obligación *f*; **to be under an o. to sb,** estarle muy agradecido,-a a algn; **to meet one's obligations,** cumplir las obligaciones. ■ *Rel* **day of o.,** fiesta *f* de guardar.

obligatory [ɒˈblɪgətərɪ] *adj* obligatorio,-a.

oblige [əˈblaɪdʒ] *vtr* 1 (*compel*) obligar; **I'm obliged to do it,** me veo obligado,-a a hacerlo. 2 (*do a favour for*) ayudar a, hacer un favor a; **can you o. me with a pound?,** ¿podrías prestarme una libra? 3 (*be grateful*) **to be obliged,** estar agradecido,-a; **I'm much obliged to you,** le estoy muy agradecido.

obliging [əˈblaɪdʒɪŋ] *adj* complaciente, amable.

oblique [əˈbliːk] *adj* oblicuo,-a, inclinado,-a; *fig* **an o. reference,** una alusión indirecta.

obliterate [əˈblɪtəreɪt] *vtr* 1 (*efface*) borrar, obliterar. 2 (*eliminate*) eliminar; (*destroy*) destruir, arrasar.

obliteration [əblɪtəˈreɪʃən] *n* 1 (*effacing*) borradura *f*. 2 (*elimination*) eliminación *f*; (*destruction*) destrucción *f*.

oblivion [əˈblɪvɪən] *n* 1 olvido *m*; **to sink into o.,** caer en el olvido. 2 *Jur* amnistía *f*.

oblivious [əˈblɪvɪəs] *adj* inconsciente.

oblong ['ɒblɒŋ] 1 *adj* oblongo,-a, rectangular. II *n* rectángulo *m*.

obnoxious [əbˈnɒkʃəs] *adj* (*of person*) repugnante, odioso,-a; (*of smell*) nocivo,-a, repugnante.

oboe ['əʊbəʊ] *n Mus* oboe *m*.

oboist ['əʊbəʊɪst] *n* oboe *m*, oboísta *mf*.

obscene [əb'si:n] *adj* obsceno,-a, indecente, escabroso,-a.

obscenity [əb'senɪtɪ] *n* obscenidad *f*, indecencia *f*.

obscure [əb'skjʊəʳ] **I** *adj* **1** *(unclear)* oscuro,-a, obscuro,-a; *(vague)* confuso,-a, vago,-a; *(hidden)* recóndito,-a. **2** *(unimportant) (writer etc)* desconocido,-a. **3** *(dark)* oscuro,-a, obscuro,-a. **II** *vtr* **1** *(make unclear)* ofuscar, obscurecer. **2** *(cover)* oscurecer, obscurecer.

obscurity [əb'skjʊərɪtɪ] *n* oscuridad *f*, obscuridad *f*.

obsequious [əb'si:kwɪəs] *adj* servil.

observable [əb'zɜ:vəbəl] *adj* visible, observable, apreciable.

observance [əb'zɜ:vəns] *n* **1** observancia *f*. **2** *Rel* **observances**, prácticas *fpl* religiosas.

observant [əb'zɜ:vənt] *adj* observador,-a, atento,-a.

observation [ɒbzə'veɪʃən] *n* *(watching)* observación *f*; *(surveillance)* vigilancia *f*; **to escape o.**, pasar inadvertido,-a. ■ *Mil* **o. post**, puesto *m* de observación. **2** *(remark)* observación *f*, comentario *m*; **to make an o.**, hacer un comen ario.

observatory [əb'zɜ:vətɒrɪ] *n* **1** *Astron* observatorio *m*. **2** *(lookout)* mirador *m*.

observe [əb'zɜ:v] *vtr* **1** *(watch)* observar; *(in surveillance)* vigilar; **she observes things keenly**, se fija mucho en las cosas. **2** *(remark)* observar, señalar; **as Mr Brown has observed**, como ha señalado el Sr. Brown. **3** *(notice)* notar, observar. **4** *(keep)* guardar, respetar.

observer [əb'zɜ:vəʳ] *n* observador,-a *m*, *f*.

obsess [əb'ses] *vtr* obsesionar; **to be obsessed**, estar obsesionado,-a, obsesionarse **(with, by,** con).

obsession [əb'seʃən] *n* obsesión *f*, idea *f* fija.

obsessive [əb'sesɪv] *adj* obsesivo,-a.

obsolescent [ɒbsə'lesənt] *adj* obsolescente.

obsolete ['ɒbsəli:t, ɒbsə'li:t] *adj* obsoleto,-a, caído,-a en desuso.

obstacle ['ɒbstəkəl] *n* obstáculo *m*; *fig* obstáculo *m*, impedimento *m*, inconveniente *m*. ■ *Sport* **o. race**, carrera *f* de obstáculos.

obstetric(al) [ɒb'stetrɪk(əl)] *adj* obstétrico,-a.

obstetrician [ɒbste'trɪʃən] *n* tocólogo,-a *m*, *f*, obstetra *mf*.

obstetrics [ɒb'stetrɪks] *n* *Med* obstetricia *f*, tocología *f*.

obstinacy ['ɒbstɪnəsɪ] *n* obstinación *f*, terquedad *f*, tenacidad *f*.

obstinate ['ɒbstɪnɪt] *adj* **1** *(of person)* obstinado, a, tenaz, terco,-a. **2** *Med (of pain)* persistente; *(of illness)* rebelde.

obstruct [əb'strʌkt] *vtr* **1** *(block) (passage)* obstruir, estorbar; *(pipe etc)* atascar, obstruir; *(view)* tapar; *Med* obstruir. **2** *(hinder)* estorbar; *(progress)* dificultar; *Parl* **to o. a bill**, obstaculizar la aprobación de un proyecto de ley; *Sport* **to o. a player**, bloquear a un jugador.

obstruction [əb'strʌkʃən] *n* **1** *(gen)* obstrucción *f*. **2** *(hindrance)* estorbo *m*, obstáculo *m*.

obstructive [əb'strʌktɪv] *adj* obstructor,-a; **o. tactics**, tácticas de obstrucción.

obtain [əb'teɪn] **I** *vtr (acquire)* obtener, conseguir. **II** *vi (be valid)* prevalecer, regir.

obtainable [əb'teɪnəbəl] *adj* obtenible; **only o. at chemists**, de venta exclusiva en farmacias.

obtrude [əb'tru:d] **I** *vi (interfere)* entrometerse, imponerse. **II** *vtr* **1** *(impose)* imponer. **2** *(push out)* extender.

obtrusive [əb'tru:sɪv] *adj* **1** *(interfering)* entrometido,-a. **2** *(noticeable)* llamativo,-a; *(smell)* penetrante.

obtuse [əb'tju:s] *adj* **I** *(slow)* obtuso,-a, lento,-a, torpe. **2** *Geom* obtuso,-a; **o. triangle**, triángulo obtusángulo.

obverse ['ɒbvɜ:s] **I** *adj* del anverso. **II** *n* anverso *m*.

obviate ['ɒbvɪeɪt] *vtr (counter) (difficulty etc)* obviar; *(danger)* evitar.

obvious ['ɒbvɪəs] *adj* obvio,-a, evidente, manifiesto,-a; **an o. fact**, un hecho patente; **it's the o. thing to do**, es lo más indicado. ◆ **obviously** *adv* evidentemente, claramente; **o.!**, ¡claro!, ¡por supuesto!; **she is o. not telling the truth**, es evidente que no está diciendo la verdad.

occasion [ə'keɪʒən] **I** *n* **1** *(gen)* ocasión *f*; **on o.**, en ocasiones, de vez en cuando; **on the o. of**, con motivo de; **to rise to the o.**, ponerse a la altura de las circmstancias. **2** *(opportunity)* ocasión *f*, oportunidad *f*; **to take o. to do sth**, aprovechar la oportunidad para hacer algo. **3** *(event)* acontecimiento *m*; **let's make it an o.!**, ¡vamos a celebrarlo! **4** *(cause)* motivo *m*; **I have no o. for complaint**, no tengo motivo de queja. **II** *vtr* ocasionar, causar.

occasional [ə'keɪʒənəl] *adj* **1** *(not frequent)* esporádico,-a, eventual; *Meteor* **o. showers in Galicia**, chubascos aislados en Galicia. **2** *(on special occasions)* en *o* para ocasiones especiales. ◆ **occasionally** *adv* de vez en cuando, en ocasiones.

occlusion [ə'klu:ʒən] *n* oclusión *f*.

occult [ɒ'kʌlt, 'ɒkʌlt] **I** *adj* oculto,-a. **II the o.** *n* las ciencias ocultas, lo oculto.

occupant ['ɒkjʊpənt] *n* ocupante *mf*; *(tenant)* inquilino,-a *m*, *f*.

occupation [ɒkjʊ'peɪʃən] *n* **1** *(job, profession)* profesión *f*, ocupación *f*. **2** *(task)* trabajo *m*. **3** *(of building, house, country)* ocupación *f*; **army of o.**, ejército de ocupación.

occupational [ɒkjʊ'peɪʃənəl] *adj* profesional, laboral, de oficio; **o. hazards**, gajes del oficio.

occupied ['ɒkjʊpaɪd] *adj* ocupado,-a; **to keep one's mind o. doing sth**, distraerse haciendo algo.

occupier ['ɒkjʊpaɪəʳ] *n* *GB* ocupante *mf*; *(tenant)* inquilino,-a *m*, *f*.

occupy ['ɒkjʊpaɪ] *vtr (pt & pp occupied)* **1** *(live in)* ocupar, habitar, vivir en. **2** *(fill)* emplear, ocupar; **to o. one's time in doing sth**, dedicar su tiempo a hacer algo. **3** *(take possession of)* ocupar, tomar posesión de.

occur [ə'kɜ:ʳ] *vi (pt & pp occurred)* **1** *(happen) (of event)* ocurrir, suceder, acaecer; *(of change)* producirse; **if another opportunity occurs**, si se presenta otra ocasión. **2** *(be found)* encontrarse, existir. **3** *(come to mind)* ocurrir, ocurrirse, ofrecerse; **it occurred to me that ...**, se me ocurrió que ... .

occurence [ə'kʌrəns] *n* **1** *(event)* acontecimiento *m*, suceso *m*; **an everyday o.**, un hecho cotidiano; **it's a common o.**, ocurre con frecuencia. **2** *(occurring)* reincidencia *f*; **that's a habit of frequent o.**, es un hábito que se muestra con frecuencia.

ocean ['əʊʃən] *n* **1** océano *m*. ■ **o. currents**, corrientes *fpl* oceánicas. **2** *fig (wave)* ola *f*, oleada *f*; **an o. of protests**, una oleada de protestas; *fam* **oceans of**, la mar de, montones de.

ocean-going ['əʊʃəngəʊɪŋ] *adj* de alta mar.

Oceania [əʊʃɪ'ɑ:nɪə] *n* Oceanía.

Oceanian [əʊʃɪ'ɑ:nɪən] **I** *adj* de Oceanía. **II** *n* persona *f* de Oceanía.

oceanic [əʊʃɪ'ænɪk] *adj* oceánico,-a; **o. ridge**, cresta oceánica.

oceanography [əʊʃə'nɒgrəfɪ] *n* oceanografía *f*.

ocelot ['ɒsɪlɒt, 'əʊsɪlɒt] *n* *Zool* ocelote *m*.

ochre, *US* **ocher** ['əʊkəʳ] **I** *n* ocre *m*, sil *m*. ■ **red o.**, almagre *m*; **yellow o.**, ocre *m* amarillo. **II** *adj* (de color) ocre.

o'clock [ə'klɒk] *adv* (it's) **one o'c.**, (es) la una; (it's) **two o'c.**, (son) las dos; **the train leaves at six o'c.**, el tren sale a las seis.

Oct *abbr of* **October**, octubre *m*, oct.

octagon ['ɒktəgən] *n Geom* octágono *m*, octógono *m*.

octagonal [ɒk'tægənəl] *adj* octagonal, octogonal.

octane ['ɒkteɪn] *n* octano *m*. ■ **high-o. petrol**, supercarburante *m*; **o. number**, octanaje *m*.

octave ['ɒktɪv] *n* octava *f*.

octet [ɒk'tet] *n Mus* octeto *m*.

October [ɒk'təʊbəʳ] *n* octubre *m*; **in O**, en octubre; **(on) the sixth of O.**, el seis de octubre; *see also* **May.**

octogenarian [ɒktəʊdʒɪ'neərɪən] *adj & n* octogenario,-a (*m,f*), ochentón,-ona (*m,f*).

octopus ['ɒktəpəs] *n Zool* pulpo *m*.

octosyllable ['ɒktə'sɪləbəl] *n* octosílabo *m*.

odd [ɒd] **I** *adj* **1** (*strange*) raro,-a, extraño,-a; **the o. thing is that ...**, lo raro es que ... . **2** (*occasional*) esporádico,-a, eventual; **at o. times**, de vez en cuando; **he writes the o. letter to me**, me escribe de vez en cuando; **the o. customer**, algún que otro cliente; **o. job**, trabajillo *m*. **3** (*extra*) adicional, de más; **a few o. coins**, algunas monedas sueltas; *fig* **to be the o. man out**, estar de más. **4** *Math* (*not even*) impar; **1 and 3 are o. numbers**, el 1 y el 3 son números impares. **5** (*unpaired*) desparejado,-a, suelto,-a; **an o. sock**, un calcetín suelto. **II** *adv* y pico; **there were twenty o. students there**, había unos veinte y tantos alumnos. **III** *n* (*number*) non *m*, impar *m*; **odds and evens**, pares y nones. ◆ **oddly** *adv* de manera extraña, extrañamente; **o. enough**, por extraño que parezca.

oddball ['ɒdbɔ:l] *fam* **I** *n* pájaro *m* raro, estrafalario,-a *m,f*. **II** *adj* estrafalario,-a.

oddity ['ɒdɪtɪ] *n* **1** (*thing*) cosa *f* rara, curiosidad *f*; (*person*) estrafalario,-a *m*, *f*. **2** (*quality*) rareza *f*, peculiaridad *f*.

odd-jobman ['ɒdʒɒbmən] *n* chapucero *m*, chapuzas *m inv*.

oddness ['ɒdnɪs] *n* (*strangeness*) rareza *f*, peculiaridad *f*; (*eccentricity*) extravagancia *f*.

odds [ɒdz] *npl* **1** (*chances*) probabilidades *fpl*, posibilidades *fpl*; **he's fighting against the o.**, lleva las de perder, está luchando contra fuerzas mayores; **the o. are in her favour**, ella lleva ventaja; **the o. are that ...**, lo más probable es que (+ *subj*). **2** (*in betting*) puntos *mpl* de ventaja; **the o. are five to one**, las apuestas están cinco a uno; **to give** *or* **lay o.**, ofrecer puntos de ventaja. **3** *GB* (*difference*) diferencia *f*; **it makes no o.**, da lo mismo; *fig* **to be at o. with sb**, estar peleado,-a *or* reñido,-a con algn; *fam* **what's the o.?**, ¿qué más da? **4 o. and ends**, (*small things*) cositas *fpl*, cosillas *fpl*; (*trinkets*) cachivaches *mpl*, chucherías *fpl*.

odds-on ['ɒdzɒn] *adj* seguro,-a; **o.-on favourite**, (*horse*) caballo favorito; (*person*) favorito,-a *m,f*; **o.-on victory**, victoria segura.

ode [əʊd] *n* oda *f*.

odious ['əʊdɪəs] *adj* odioso,-a, repugnante.

odium ['əʊdɪəm] *n* **1** (*dislike, disapproval*) reprobación *f*, rechazo *m*. **2** (*hatred*) odio *m*.

odometer [ɒ'dɒmɪtəʳ, əʊ'dɒmɪtəʳ] *n Aut* ≈ cuentakilómetros *m inv*.

odontologist [ɒdɒn'tɒlədʒɪst] *n* odontólogo,-a *m,f*.

odontology [ɒdɒn'tɒlədʒɪ] *n* odontología *f*.

odour, *US* **odor** ['əʊdəʳ] *n* **1** (*smell*) olor *m*; (*fragance*) perfume *m*, fragancia *f*. **2** *fig* consideración *f*; **to be in good/bad o. with sb**, estar bien/mal visto,-a por algn.

odourless, *US* **odorless** ['əʊdəlɪs] *adj* inodoro,-a.

odyssey ['ɒdɪsɪ] *n* odisea *f*.

OECD [əʊi:si:'di:] *abbr of* **Organization for Economic Co-operation and Development**, ≈ Organización *f* para la Cooperación y el Desarrollo Económico, OCDE *f*.

Oedipus ['i:dɪpəs] *n* Edipo *m*. ■ **O. complex**, complejo *m* de Edipo.

oenology [i:'nɒlədʒɪ] *n* enología *f*.

oesophagus [i:'sɒfəgəs] *n* (*pl* **oesophagi** [i:'sɒfəgaɪ]) *Anat* esófago *m*.

of [ɒv, *unstressed* əv] *prep* **I** (*belonging to, part of*) de; **a friend of mine**, un amigo mío; **a friend of my mother's**, un amigo de mi madre; **it's no business of yours**, no es asunto tuyo; **the end of the novel**, el final de la novela; **the Queen of England**, la reina de Inglaterra. **2** (*containing*) de; **a bottle of wine**, una botella de vino. **3** (*origin*) de; **of good family**, de buena familia. **4** (*by*) de, por; **beloved of all**, amado,-a por todos; **the works of Shakespeare**, las obras de Shakespeare. **5** (*quantity*) de; **there are four of us**, somos cuatro; **there were twenty of them**, fueron veinte; **two of them**, dos de ellos. **6** (*from*) de; *US* **a quarter of seven**, las siete menos cuarto; **free of**, libre de; **south of**, al sur de; **within a year of his death**, al año de su muerte. **7** (*material*) de; **a dress (made) of silk**, un vestido de seda. **8** (*apposition*) de; **the city of Lisbon**, la ciudad de Lisboa; **the topic of pollution**, el asunto de la contaminación. **9** (*characteristic*) de; **a man of no importance**, un hombre de poca monta; **it's wrong of him not to come**, hace mal en no venir; **that fool of a sergeant**, el imbécil del sargento; **that's typical of her**, es muy propio de ella; **that's very cruel of him**, es muy cruel por su parte; **that's very kind of you**, es usted muy amable. **10** (*with adj*) de; **hard of hearing**, duro,-a de oído; **tired/guilty of sth**, cansado,-a/culpable de algo. **11** (*after superlative*) de; **king of kings**, rey de reyes; **the bravest of them**, el más valiente (de todos ellos); **the thing she wanted most of all**, lo que más quería; **you, of all people**, precisamente tú. **12** (*cause*) por, de; **because of**, a causa de; **of necessity**, por necesidad; **to die of hunger**, morir de hambre. **13** (*concerning, about*) de, sobre; **to dream of sth/sb**, soñar con algo/algn; **to think of sb**, pensar en algn; **what do you think of her?**, ¿qué opinas de ella?; **what of it?**, ¿y qué? **14** (*with dates*) de; **the seventh of July**, el siete de julio.

off [ɒf] **I** *prep* **1** (*movement*) de; **she fell o. her horse**, se cayó del caballo; **take it o. the table**, quítalo de la mesa; **there's a button o. my jacket**, le falta un botón a mi chaqueta. **2** (*removal*) de; **I'll take sth o. the price for you**, se lo rebajaré un poco. **3** (*distance, situation*) de; **a few kilometres o. the coast**, a unos kilómetros de la costa; **a house o. the road**, una casa apartada de la carretera; *Naut* **o. Calais**, a la altura de Calais. **4** (*away from*) fuera de; **the ship went o. course**, el barco se desvió; *Sport* **to be o. form**, no estar en forma. **5** (*not inclined towards*) **I'm o. wine**, he perdido el gusto al vino. **6** (*free from*) libre de; **he took two days o. work**, se tomó dos días libres; **I'm o. duty today**, libro hoy; *fig* **o. the record**, extraoficialmente. **II** *adv* **1** (*disengaged*) **he turned o. the radio**, apagó la radio. **2** (*absent*) fuera; **I can't take time o.**, no puedo faltar al trabajo; **I have a day o.**, tengo un día libre; **she's o. on Mondays**, los lunes no viene *or* no trabaja; **to be o. sick**, estar de baja por enfermedad. **3** (*completely*) del todo, completamente; **this will kill o. any extra germs**, esto rematará cualquier germen restante. **4** (*away*) (*distance*) **his arrival is three days o.**, faltan tres días para su llegada; **six miles o.**, a seis millas; *Theat* **voice o.**, voz en off. **5** (*departure*) **I'm o. to London**, me voy a Londres; **o. we go**, vámonos; **she ran o.**, se fue corriendo; *Sport* **they're o.!**, ¡ya han salido! **6** (*removal*) **ten per cent o.**, un descuento del diez por ciento; **to take one's shoes o.**, quitarse los zapatos. **7** (*not fresh*) (*food*) pasado,-a, malo,-a. **8 hands o.!**, ¡fuera las manos! **9 right o.**, acto seguido. **III** *adj* **1** (*disconnected*) (*of gas etc*) apagado,-a; (*of water*) cortado,-a. **2** (*cancelled*) cancelado,-a, suspendido,-a; **their engagement is o.**, han roto el compromiso. **3** (*low*) bajo,-a; (*unsatisfactory*) malo,-a; **on the o. chance**, por si acaso; **the o. season**, la temporada baja. ■ **o. chance**, posibilidad *f*. **4** (*equipped, situated*) parado,-a, situado,-a; **how are you o. for money?**, ¿cómo andas de dinero?; **to be badly o.**, andar mal de dinero; **you're better/worse**

o. like that, así estas mejor/peor. **5** *(gone bad) (of meat, fish)* malo,-a, pasado,-a; *(of milk)* agrio,-a, cortado,-a.

offal ['ɒf əl] *n (of chicken etc)* menudillos *mpl; (of cattle, pigs)* asaduras *fpl,* menudos *mpl.*

offbeat ['ɒfbi:t] *adj* excéntrico,-a, poco convencional.

off-centre, *US* **off-center** ['ɒfsentə'] *adj* descentrado,-a.

off-colour, *US* **off-color** ['ɒfkʌlə'] *adj* **1** *GB (ill)* indispuesto,-a, malo,-a. **2** *(risqué)* indecente, verde.

offence [ə'fens] *n* **1** *Jur* delito *m.* ■ **minor o.,** infracción *f;* **second o.,** reincidencia *f.* **2** *(insult)* ofensa *f;* **no o. meant,** sin intención de ofenderle; **to give o.,** ofender; **to take o. at sth,** sentirse ofendido,-a por algo, ofenderse por algo. **3** *Mil (attack)* ofensiva *f,* ataque *m.*

offend [ə'fend] *vtr* **1** *(hurt)* ofender; **to be easily offended,** ser muy susceptible. **2** *(disgust)* disgustar, repeler.

offender [ə'fendə'] *n* **1** *Jur (criminal)* delincuente *mf,* infractor,-a *m,f.* **2** *(insulter)* ofensor,-a *m,f.*

offense [ə'fens] *n US see* **offence.**

offensive [ə'fensɪv] **I** *adj* **1** *(insulting)* ofensivo,-a, insultante. **2** *(repulsive)* repugnante. **3** *Mil* ofensivo,-a. **II** *n Mil* ofensiva *f.*

offer ['ɒfə'] **I** *vtr* **1** *(gen)* ofrecer; **to o. to do a job,** ofrecerse para hacer un trabajo. **2** *(propose)* proponer. **3** *(provide)* proporcionar. **4** *(bid)* ofrecer. **5** *Rel* ofrecer, ofrendar. **II** *vi* **1** *(arise)* presentarse. **2** *(propose marriage)* proponer el matrimonio. **III** *n* **1** *(gen)* oferta *f,* ofrecimiento *m; (proposal)* propuesta *f;* **o. of marriage,** proposición *f* de matrimonio. **2** *(bid)* oferta *f;* **any offers?,** ¿hay alguna oferta?, ¿le(s) interesa?; *Com* **on o.,** de oferta.

offering ['ɒfərɪŋ] *n* **1** *(gen)* ofrecimiento *m; (gift)* regalo *m;* **a peace o.,** una prenda de paz. **2** *Rel* ofrenda *f;* **burnt o.,** holocausto *m.*

offertory ['ɒfətərɪ] *n Rel* **1** ofertorio *m.* **2** *(collection)* colecta *f.*

offhand [ɒfhænd] **I** *adj* **1** *(abrupt)* brusco,-a; *(inconsiderate)* descortés, desatento,-a, desconsiderado,-a; **in an o. way,** sin ceremonias. **2** *(impromptu)* improvisado,-a. **II** *adv* de improviso; **I don't know o.,** así sin pensarlo, no lo sé.

office ['ɒfɪs] *n* **1** *(room)* despacho *m,* oficina *f; (building)* oficina *f.* ■ **box o.,** taquilla *f;* **head o.,** sede *f* central; **lawyer's o.,** bufete *m;* **o. boy,** recadero *m;* **o. hours,** horas *fpl* de oficina; **o. work,** trabajo *m* de oficina; **o. worker,** oficinista *mf.* **2** *GB Pol* ministerio *m.* ■ **Foreign O.,** Ministerio *m* de Asuntos Exteriores. **3** *US (federal agency)* agencia *f* gubernamental. **4** *(position)* cargo *m;* **to hold o.,** ocupar un cargo; **to leave o.,** dimitir; **to seek o.,** pretender *or* aspirar a un cargo. **5** *Pol (portfolio)* cartera *f* de ministro; **to be in o.,** estar en el poder.

officer ['ɒfɪsə'] *n* **1** *Mil* oficial *mf.* ■ **customs o.,** aduanero,-a *m,f.* **2** **(police) o.,** policía *mf,* agente *mf* de policía. **3** *Admin* oficial *mf,* funcionario,-a *m,f;* **Medical O. of Health,** jefe,-a *m,f* de Sanidad. **4** *(of company, society)* director,-a *m,f.*

official [ə'fɪʃəl] **I** *adj* oficial. **II** *n* oficial *mf,* funcionario,-a *m,f.*

officialese [əfɪʃə'li:z] *n* jerga *f* burocrática.

officiate [ə'fɪʃɪeɪt] *vi* **1** *(gen)* ejercer; **to o. as,** ejercer de. **2** *Rel* oficiar.

officious [ə'fɪʃəs] *adj (ready)* oficioso,-a; *(obtrusive)* entrometido,-a.

offish ['ɒfɪʃ] *adj fam* altivo,-a, distante.

off-key ['ɒfki:] *adj Mus (out of tune)* desafinado,-a. **2** *fig (discordant)* desentonado,-a, discordante.

off-licence ['ɒflaɪsəns] *n GB* establecimiento *m* de venta de bebidas alcohólicas.

off-peak ['ɒfpi:k] *adj Elec Tel* reducido,-a; **o.-p. charge,** tarifa reducida; *(transport)* **the o.-p. hours,** las horas de menos tránsito.

offprint ['ɒfprɪnt] *n Print* separata *f.*

off-putting ['ɒfpʊtɪŋ] *adj GB fam* desconcertante, chocante.

offset ['ɒfset] **I** *n* **1** *(counterbalance)* compensación *f.* **2** *Print* offset *m.* **II** [ɒf'set] *vtr (pt & pp* offset) **1** *(balance out)* compensar. **2** *Print* imprimir en offset.

offshoot ['ɒfʃu:t] *n* **1** *Bot* renuevo *m,* vástago *m.* **2** *fig (of organization)* ramificación *f; (of discussion)* consecuencia *f,* resultado *m.*

offshore [ɒf'ʃɔ:'] **I** *adj* **1** *(from the coast) (breeze etc)* terral, que sopla de tierra. **2** *(off the coast)* offshore, costa afuera. ■ *Petrol* **o. drilling,** perforación *f* costa afuera. **3** *(overseas)* en el extranjero; **o. investment,** inversión en el extranjero. **II** *adv* mar adentro.

offside [ɒf'saɪd] **I** *adj & adv Ftb* fuera de juego, offside, orsay. **II** *n Aut (with left-hand drive)* lado *m* derecho; *(with right-hand drive)* lado *m* izquierdo.

offspring ['ɒfsprɪŋ] *n inv* **1** *(child)* vástago *m,* descendiente *mf; (children)* progenitura *f,* descendencia *f.* **2** *fig* consecuencia *f,* resultado *m.*

offstage [ɒf'steɪdʒ] *adj & adv* entre bastidores.

off-the-record [ɒfθə'rekəd] *adj* extraoficial, oficioso,-a.

off-white ['ɒfwaɪt] *adj* blancuzco,-a, blanquecino,-a.

oft [ɒft] *adv lit abbr of* **often.**

often ['ɒfən, 'ɒftən] *adv* a menudo, con frecuencia; **as o. as not,** con bastante regularidad; **every so o.,** de vez en cuando, regularmente; **more o. than not,** la mayoría de las veces.

ogle ['əʊgəl] *vtr & vi* **to o. (at) sb,** comerse a algn con los ojos.

ogre ['əʊgə'] *n* ogro *m.*

oh [əʊ] *interj* ¡oh!, ¡ay!; **oh, my God!,** ¡Dios mío!; **oh, really?,** ¿de veras?

OHMS [əʊeɪtʃem'es] *GB abbr of* **On His/Her Majesty's Service,** en el servicio de su majestad.

oil [ɔɪl] **I** *n* **1** *(gen)* aceite *m; fig* **to pour o. on troubled waters,** templar los ánimos. ■ **cooking o.,** aceite *m* comestible *or* para cocinar; **lubricating o.,** aceite *m* lubricante; **o. drum,** bidón *m; Aut* **o. gauge,** indicador *m* (del nivel) del aceite; *Aut* **o. gun,** bomba *f* de engrase; **o. lamp,** lámpara *f* de aceite, quinqué *m;* **o. slick,** mancha *f* de aceite, marea *f* negra; **olive o.,** aceite *m* de oliva. **2** *Petrol* petróleo *m;* **crude o.,** crudo *m;* **the o. industry,** la industria petrolera; **to strike o.,** encontrar petróleo. ■ **o. rig,** plataforma *f* petrolera; **o. tanker,** petrolero *m.* **3** *Art (painting)* óleo *m,* pintura *f* al óleo; *fam fig* **she's no o. painting,** no es exactamente una belleza. ■ **o. colour, o. paint,** óleo *m; (picture)* **o. painting,** cuadro *m* al óleo, óleo *m.* **II** *vtr* engrasar, lubricar, lubrificar; *fig* **to o. the wheels,** preparar el terreno; *fam* **to o. sb's palm,** untar la mano a algn.

oil-bearing ['ɔɪlbeərɪŋ] *adj Petrol* petrolífero,-a.

oilcan ['ɔɪlkæn] *n Aut* aceitera *f.*

oilcloth ['ɔɪlklɒθ] *n* hule *m.*

oilfield ['ɔɪlfi:ld] *n Petrol* yacimiento *m* petrolífero.

oilfired ['ɔɪlfaɪəd] *adj* de fuel-oil.

oilskin ['ɔɪlskɪn] *n* **1** hule *m.* **2 oilskins,** chubasquero *m sing,* traje *m sing* de hule.

oily ['ɔɪlɪ] *adj (oilier, oiliest) (gen)* aceitoso,-a, grasiento,-a; *(hair, skin)* graso,-a.

ointment ['ɔɪntmənt] *n* ungüento *m,* pomada *f.*

O.K., okay [əʊ'keɪ] *fam* **I** *interj* ¡vale!, ¡de acuerdo! **II** *adj* correcto,-a, bien; **is it O.K. if ...?,** ¿está bien si ...? **III** *n* visto *m* bueno, aprobación *f;* **to give the O.K.,** dar el visto bueno. **IV** *vtr (pt & pp O.K.ed or okayed)* dar el visto bueno a.

old [əʊld] **I** *adj* **1** *(gen)* viejo,-a; *(worn)* viejo,-a, usado,-a; *(of wine)* añejo,-a; *(stale) (of bread)* duro,-a; *(of food)* pasado,-a, malo,-a; **an o. man,** un hombre mayor, un anciano; **to grow o.,** envejecer; *fam* **my o. man,** *(father)* mi viejo; *(husband)* mi media naranja. ■ **o. age**, vejez *f*; **o.-age pensioner**, pensionista *mf*; **o. maid**, soltera *f*, *fam pej* solterona *f*; **o. wives' tale**, cuento m de viejas. **2** *(age)* edad *f*, años *mpl*; **how o. are you?**, ¿cuántos años tienes?, ¿qué edad tienes?; **she's five years o.**, tiene cinco años; **she's o. enough to do it**, ya tiene edad para hacerlo. **3** *GB (former)* **o. boy**, antiguo alumno, exalumno. **4** *(earlier)* antiguo,-a. ■ **o. country**, madre patria *f*; *Rel* **O. Testament**, Antiguo Testamento *m*. **5** *(long-established, experienced)* viejo,-a; **an o. dodge**, un viejo truco; **an o. friend**, un viejo amigo. ■ **o. hand, o. stager**, veterano,-a *m,f*. **6** *(cherished)* **good o. John!**, ¡el bueno de John! **7** *fam (intensifying)* **any o. how**, de cualquier manera; **any o. thing**, cualquier cosa. **II** *n* pasado *m*; **of o.**, de antaño. **2 the o.**, los viejos, los áncianos.

olden ['əʊldən] *adj lit* antiguo,-a; **in o. times**, en tiempos antiguos, antaño.

older ['əʊldəʳ] *I adj comp of* **old II** *adj (elder)* mayor.

old-established [əʊldɪ'stæblɪʃt] *adj* antiguo,-a.

old-fashioned [əʊld'fæʃənd] *adj (outdated)* chapado,-a a la antigua, anticuado,-a; *(unfashionable)* anticuado,-a, pasado,-a de moda.

old-time ['əʊldtaɪm] *adj* antiguo,-a.

old-timer [əʊld'taɪməʳ] *n* **1** *(old hand)* veterano,-a *m,f*. **2** *US fam (old man)* viejo *m*.

old-world ['əʊldwɜːld] *adj* tradicional, de los tiempos antiguos.

oleander [əʊlɪ'ændəʳ] *n Bot* adelfa *f*.

olfactory [ɒl'fæktərɪ, ɒl'fæktrɪ] **I** *adj* olfativo,-a, olfatorio,-a. **II** *n (nerve)* nervio m olfativo.

oligarchy ['ɒlɪgɑːkɪ] *n* oligarquía *f*.

olive ['ɒlɪv] **I** *n* **1** *(tree)* olivo *m*; *fig* **to hold out the o. branch**, proponer una reconciliación. ■ **o. grove**, olivar *m*. **2** *(fruit)* aceituna *f*, oliva *f*; **stuffed olives**, aceitunas rellenas. **3** *(wood)* olivo *m*. **4** *(colour)* **o. (green)**, verde *m* oliva. **II** *adj (olive-growing)* olivarero,-a.

olive-growing ['ɒlɪvgrəʊɪŋ] *adj* olivarero,-a.

Olympiad [ə'lɪmpɪæd] *n* Olimpíada *f*, Olimpiada *f*.

Olympic [ə'lɪmpɪk] **I** *adj* olímpico,-a. ■ **O. Games**, Juegos *mpl* Olímpicos. **II the Olympics** *pl* los Juegos Olímpicos, la Olimpíada.

Oman [əʊ'mɑːn] *n* Omán.

Omani [əʊ'mɑːnɪ] *adj & n* omaní *(mf)*.

omelette, *US* **omelet** ['ɒmlɪt] *n Culin* tortilla *f*; **Spanish o.**, tortilla española *or* de patatas.

omen ['əʊmen] *n* presagio *m*, agüero *m*, augurio *m*; **it's a good o.**, es un buen presagio; *fig* **bird of ill o.**, pájaro agorero *or* de mal agüero.

ominous ['ɒmɪnəs] *adj (foreboding evil)* de mal agüero, siniestro,-a; *(prophetic)* agorero,-a, inquietante. ◆ **ominously** *adv* de modo amenazante.

omission [əʊ'mɪʃən] *n* omisión *f*, *fig* olvido *m*, descuido *m*.

omit [əʊ'mɪt] *vtr (pt & pp omitted) (gen)* omitir; *(overlook)* pasar por alto, dejarse; *(forget)* olvidarse.

omnibus ['ɒmnɪbʌs, 'ɒmnɪbəs] *n (vehicle)* ómnibus *m*, autobús *m*. ■ *Print* **o. volume**, antología *f*.

omnipotence [ɒm'nɪpətəns] *n* omnipotencia *f*.

omnipotent [ɒm'nɪpətənt] **I** *adj* omnipotente. **II the O.** *n* el Todopoderoso.

omniscient [ɒm'nɪsɪənt] *adj* omnisciente.

omnivorus [ɒm'nɪvərəs] *adj* omnívoro,-a.

on [ɒn] **I** *prep* **1** *(position) (on top of)* sobre, encima de, en; **I hit him on the head**, le di un golpe en la cabeza; **it's on the table**, está encima de *or* sobre *or* en la mesa; **on page four**, en la página cuatro; *fig* **to swear on the Bible**, jurar por la Biblia; *fam* **have you got any money on you?**, ¿llevas dinero? **2** *(alongside)* en; **a town on the coast**, un pueblo en la costa; **on shore**, en tierra. **3** *(attached to)* **a puppet on a string**, un títere colgado de

un hilo; **hanging on a nail/the wall**, colgado de un clavo/la pared. **4** *(direction)* en, a; **on the right**, a la derecha; **on the way**, en el camino; **on this side of the road**, de este lado de la carretera. **5** *(time)* **on April 3rd, on 3rd of April**, el tres de abril; **on a sunny day**, un día de sol; **on Monday**, el lunes; **on that occasion**, en aquella ocasión; **on the following day**, al día siguiente; **on the morning of the crime**, la mañana del crimen; **on time**, a tiempo. **6** *(relayed through)* en; **I heard it on the radio**, lo oí en la radio; **to play sth on the piano**, tocar algo al piano; **what's on TV?**, ¿qué ponen en la tele?; *fam* **she's on the phone**, está al teléfono. **7** *(at the time of)* a; **on his arrival**, al llegar él; **on leaving the office**, al salir de la oficina; **on second thoughts**, pensándolo bien. **8** *(support, subsistence)* **she lives on bread**, vive de pan; **to be on a diet**, estar a régimen; **to be on drugs**, drogarse; **to be on the pill**, tomar la píldora; **to depend on**, depender de. **9** *(transport)* en, a; **on foot**, a pie; **on horseback**, a caballo; **on the train/plane**, en el tren/ avión; **on wheels**, sobre ruedas. **10** *(state, process)* en, de; **on hoilday**, de vacaciones; **on purpose**, adrede, a propósito; **on sale**, en venta; **on strike**, en huelga; **she is here on business**, está aquí por negocios; **to be on duty**, estar de guardia; **to be on fire**, arder, estar en llamas; **to go out on an errand**, salir a hacer un recado. **11** *(regarding)* sobre; **a lecture on numismatics**, una conferencia sobre la numismática; **the new tax on tobacco**, el nuevo impuesto sobre el tabaco; **they congratulated him on his success**, le felicitaron por su éxito. **12** *(under)* bajo; **on condition that ...**, a condición de que ... *(+ subj)*; *Jur* **on a charge of**, acusado,-a de; **on no account**, bajo ningún concepto, de ninguna manera; **on pain of death**, so pena de muerte. **13** *(against)* contra; **an attack on the government**, un ataque contra el Gobierno; **they marched on Washington**, hicieron una marcha sobre Washington; *fam* **the police have nothing on him**, la policía no tiene ningún cargo contra él. **14** *fam (manner)* **on the cheap**, en plan barato; **on the sly**, a escondidas, a hurtadillas. **15** *fam (in detriment to)* **he told on me**, se chivó; **the car conked out on him**, el coche se le escoñó. **16** *(working for)* **he's on the Daily Telegraph**, trabaja para el Daily Telegraph; **to be on the staff**, estar en plantilla. **II** *adv* **1** *(functioning)* **to be on**, *(of TV, radio, light)* estar encendido,-a; *(of engine)* estar en marcha; **to put the brake on**, echar el freno. **2** *(covering)* encima, puesto; **she had a coat on**, llevaba un abrigo puesto; **on with your boots!**, ¡ponte las botas! **3** **to have nothing on**, estar *or* ir desnudo,-a. **3** *Cin TV Theat* en cartelera; **that film was on last week**, pusieron esa película la semana pasada; **what's on at the theatre?**, ¿qué dan en el teatro?; *fam* **have you anything on tonight?**, ¿tienes algún plan para esta noche? **4** *(continued activity)* **and so on**, y así sucesivamente; **go on!**, ¡sigue!; **he talks on and on**, habla sin parar; **she's always going on about her boss**, se pasa el día hablando de su jefe; **to work on**, seguir trabajando. **5** *(time)* **from that day on**, a partir de aquel día; **later on**, más tarde; **he's getting on**, se está haciendo viejo; **it's getting on for ten**, son casi las diez; **well on in April**, muy entrado el mes de abril; **well on in years**, entrado en años. **6** *fig* **to get on to sb**, ponerse en contacto con algn; **to have sb on**, tomarle el pelo a algn. **III** *adj fam* **1** *(of actor)* **to be on**, salir a escena. **2** *(definitely planned)* previsto,-a; **the party's on for Friday**, la fiesta se hará el viernes; **you're on!**, ¡trato hecho! **3** *(charged to)* **the drinks are on me**, invito yo; **the drinks are on the house**, invita la casa. **4** *(tolerable, practicable)* **that attitude isn't on**, esa actitud no vale. **5** *fam* **to be on at**, dar la lata a; **she's always on at me**, no para de pincharme, me tiene manía. **6** **on to**, enterado,-a de; **the police are on to him**, la policía le tiene fichado.

onanism ['əʊnənɪzəm] *n* onanismo *m*.

once [wʌns] **I** *adv* **1** *(one time)* una vez; **not o.**, ni una sola vez; **o. a week**, una vez por semana; **o. in a while**, de vez en cuando; **o. more**, una vez más; **o. or twice**, un par de veces, una o dos veces; *fig* **o. and for all**, de una vez por todas; *fig* **o. in a blue moon,** de Pascuas a Ramos; *prov* **o. a ... always a ...,** genio y figura hasta la sepultura. **2** *(formerly)* antes, en otro tiempo; **o. (upon a time) there was,** érase una vez; **the o. famous actress,** la antes famosa actriz. **3** *at* **o.,** en seguida, inmediatamente; **all at o.,** de repente; **don't speak all at o.,** no habléis todos a la vez. **II** *conj* una vez que, en cuanto; **o. you've seen it,** una vez que lo hayas visto.

once-over ['wʌnsəʊvə^r] *n fam* vistazo *m*.

oncology [ɒŋ'kɒlədʒɪ] *n Med* oncología *f*.

oncoming ['ɒnkʌmɪŋ] *adj (of event)* venidero,-a, futuro,-a; *(of car, traffic)* que viene en dirección contraria.

one [wʌn] **I** *adj* **1** *(a single)* un, una; **for o. thing,** primero; **o. book,** un libro. **2** *(only)* único,-a; **the o. and only,** el único, la única; **the o. way of doing it,** la única manera de hacerlo; *fig* **neither o. thing nor the other,** ni una cosa ni otra. **3** *(same)* mismo,-a; **all in o.,** en una (sola) pieza; **it's all o.,** es lo mismo; **o. and the same,** el mismo, la misma; *fig* **it's all o. to me,** me da igual; *fig* **to be made o.,** unirse en matrimonio. **4** *(indefinite)* un, una; **he'll come back o. day,** un día volverá, volverá algún día; **o. stormy night,** una noche de tormenta. **II** *dem pron* **any o.,** cualquiera; **that o.,** ése, ésa; *(distant)* aquél, aquélla; **the blue ones,** los azules, las azules; **the little ones,** los pequeños, las pequeñas; **the o. on the table,** el *or* la que está encima de la mesa; **the ones that, the ones which,** los *or* las que; **the ones you want,** los *or* las que quieras; **the red o.,** el rojo, la roja; **this o.,** éste, ésta; **which o.?,** ¿cuál?; **which ones?,** ¿cuáles?; *fam* **he's a sharp o.,** no se le escapa ni una; *fam* **that's a good o.!,** ¡ésa sí que es buena!; *fam* **you're a o.!,** ¡eres un caso! **III** *indef pron* **1** uno,-a *m*, *f*; **he's o. of the family,** es de la familia; **I, for o., am against it,** yo, por lo menos, estoy en contra; **I'm not o. to complain,** no soy de los que se quejan; **o. at a time,** de uno en uno; **o. by o.,** uno por uno, uno tras otro; *fig* **many a o.,** mucha gente; *fig* **o. and all,** todo el mundo; *fam* **I landed him o.,** le pegué un tortazo *or* una; *fam* **to have o. for the road,** echar la espuela *or* el último trago. **2** *(indefinite person)* uno,-a *m*, *f*; **o. has to fight,** uno tiene que luchar, hay que luchar; **o. never knows,** nunca se sabe; **to cut o's finger,** cortarse el dedo; **to give o.'s opinion,** dar su opinión; *fig* **it's enough to kill o.,** es como para morirse. **3** *o.* **another,** el uno al otro; **they help o. another,** se ayudan mutuamente; **they love o. another,** se quieren. **IV** *n (digit)* uno *m*; **a hundred and o.,** ciento uno; **at o. o'clock,** a la una; **there's only o. left,** sólo queda uno; **o. of two things,** una de dos.

one-act ['wʌnækt] *adj (of play)* de un (solo) acto.

one-armed ['wʌnɑːmd] *adj* manco,-a; *fig* **o.-a. bandit,** máquina *f* tragaperras.

one-eyed ['wʌnaɪd] *adj* tuerto,-a.

one-handed ['wʌnhændɪd] **I** *adj (one-armed)* manco,-a. **2** *(solitary)* solitario,-a. **II** *adv* con una mano.

one-horse ['wʌnhɔːs] *adj pej* de poca monta; **o.-h. town,** pueblucho *m*.

one-legged ['wʌnlegɪd] *adj* cojo,-a, con una sola pierna.

one-man ['wʌnmæn] *adj* individual, de un solo hombre; **a o.-m. show,** un espectáculo con un solo artista; *fig* **to be a o.-m. show,** llevarse la palma.

oneness ['wʌnɪs] *n* unidad *f*.

one-night ['wʌnaɪt] *adj* **o.-n. stand,** *Theat* representación *f* única; *(encounter)* ligue *m* de una sola noche.

one-off ['wʌnɒf] *adj GB fam* único,-a, fuera de serie, irrepetible.

one-parent ['wʌnpeərənt] *adj* **o.-p. family,** familia en que sólo hay padre o madre.

one-piece ['wʌnpiːs] *adj* de una sola pieza.

onerous ['ɒnərəs, 'əʊnərəs] *adj* oneroso,-a; **an o. duty,** una carga pesada.

oneself [wʌn'self] *pron (pl oneselves* [wʌn'selvz]) **1** *(reflexive)* uno,-a mismo,-a *m*, *f*, sí mismo,-a *m*, *f*; **to speak of o.,** hablar de sí mismo,-a; **to talk to o.,** hablar para sí,

hablar a solas; **to wash o.,** lavarse. **2** *(alone)* uno,-a mismo,-a *m*, *f*; **by o.,** solo,-a; **one must do it o.,** hay que hacérselo uno mismo. **3** *(one's usual self)* el *or* la de siempre; **one isn't o. after such a shock,** un golpe así trastorna a uno.

one-sided ['wʌnsaɪdɪd] *adj (bargain)* desigual; *(judgement)* parcial; *(decision)* unilateral.

one-storey(ed) ['wʌnstɔːrɪ(d)] *adj* de una planta; **o.-s. house,** casa de planta baja.

one-time ['wʌntaɪm] *adj* antiguo,-a, ex-; **o. mayor of,** exalcalde de.

one-to-one ['wʌntəwʌn] *adj* de uno a uno; **on a o.-to-o. basis,** con una correspondencia mutua.

one-track ['wʌntræk] *adj fam* **to have a o.-t. mind,** ser monomaníaco,-a, no pensar más que en una cosa.

one-way ['wʌnweɪ] *adj* **1** *(of ticket)* de ida. **2** *(of street)* de dirección única; *fig (agreement etc)* sin compromiso.

ongoing ['ɒngəʊɪŋ] *adj* **1** *(in progress)* en curso, actual. **2** *(developing)* en desarrollo.

onion ['ʌnjən] *n* cebolla *f*; *GB sl* **to know one's onions,** saber lo que se trae entre manos. ■ **o. soup,** sopa *f* de cebolla; **spring o.,** cebollino *m*, cebolleta *f*.

onionskin ['ʌnjənskɪn] *n* papel *m* cebolla.

onlooker ['ɒnlʊkə^r] *n* espectador,-a *m*, *f*, mirón,-ona *m*, *f*; **there was a group of onlookers,** hubo un grupo de gente que miraba.

only ['əʊnlɪ] **I** *adj* único,-a; **his one o. hope,** su única esperanza; **I'm the o. one to receive a prize,** soy el único que recibo un premio; **o. son,** hijo único. **II** *adv* **1** solamente, sólo; **I o. touched it,** no hice más que tocarlo; **I've o. got three,** sólo tengo tres; **'staff o.',** "reservado al personal"; **you've o. to ask for it,** no tienes más que pedirlo. **2** *(not earlier than)* apenas; **he has o. just left,** acaba de marcharse hace un momento; **o. yesterday,** ayer mismo. **3** **if o., I knew!,** ¡ojalá lo supiera! **4** *(as intensifier)* **o. too glad!,** ¡con mucho gusto!; **o. too pleased to,** encantado,-a de. **III** *conj* pero; **I would do it, o. I can't,** lo haría, pero no puedo.

ono [əʊen'əʊ] *GB abbr of* **or nearest offer,** u oferta aproximada.

onomatopoeia [ɒnəmætə'piːə] *n* onomatopeya *f*.

onrush ['ɒnrʌʃ] *n (of people)* riada *f*, oleada *f*; *(of water)* riada *f*.

onset ['ɒnset] *n* **1** *(attack)* asalto *m*, arremetida *f*. **2** *(start)* comienzo *m*, principio *m*.

onslaught ['ɒnslɔːt] *n* ataque *m* violento, embestida *f*.

onto ['ɒntʊ, *unstressed* 'ɒntə] *prep see* **on.**

onus ['əʊnəs] *n (pl onuses)* responsabilidad *f*; **the o. is upon you to find a solution,** a ti te incumbe encontrar una solución.

onward ['ɒnwəd] *adj* progresivo,-a, hacia adelante.

onward(s) ['ɒnwəd(z)] *adv* a partir de, en adelante; **from this time on,** de ahora en adelante.

onyx ['ɒnɪks] *n Min* ónice *m*.

oodles ['uːdəlz] *npl fam* montones *mpl*; **o. of money,** un montón de dinero.

oomph [ʊmf] *n fam (enthusiasm)* nervio *m*, vigor *m*; *(sex appeal)* atractivo *m* sexual, sex-appeal *m*.

ooze[1] [uːz] **I** *vi* rezumar; **blood was oozing from the wound,** brotaba sangre de la herida. **II** *vtr* rebosar; **she oozes confidence,** rebosa confianza.

ooze[2] [uːz] *n (mud)* cieno *m*.

op [ɒp] *n* **1** *Med abbr of* **operation.** **2** *Mil (abbr of operation)* **ops,** maniobras *fpl*.

opal ['əʊpəl] *n Min* ópalo *m*.

opalescent ['əʊpə'lesənt] *adj* opalescente.

opaque [əʊ'peɪk] *adj* opaco,-a.

op cit [ɒp'sɪt] *abbr of* **opere citato** (in the work cited), en la obra citada, ob. cit., op. cit.

OPEC ['əʊpek] *abbr of* **Organization of Petroleum Exporting Countries,** Organización *f* de los Países Exportadores de Petróleo, OPEP *f*.

open ['əʊpən] **I** *adj* **1** *(not closed)* *(gen)* abierto,-a; *(of wound)* abierto,-a, sin cicatrizar; **half o.,** entreabierto; **wide o.,** abierto de par en par. **2** *(not enclosed)* abierto,-a; **in the o. air,** al aire libre, al descubierto; **o. field,** descampado *m*; **o. view,** vista despejada. ◼ **o. prison,** prisión *f* de régimen abierto. **3** *(extended)* abierto,-a, extendido,-a; *fig* **with o. arms,** con los brazos abiertos. **4** *(not covered)* *(of car etc)* descubierto,-a; *(of pan)* destapado,-a. **5** *(admitting customers, visitors)* abierto,-a; **o. to the public,** abierto al público; *fig* **to keep o. house,** tener las puertas abiertas a todo el mundo. ◼ *US* **o. house,** fiesta *f* de inauguración de residencia; *Jur* **o. court,** juicio *m* a puerta abierta. **6** *(not restricted)* abierto,-a, libre; **o. competition,** concurso libre; **o. letter,** carta abierta. ◼ *(hunting)* **o. season,** temporada *f* de caza; **o. shop,** empresa *f* de sindicación libre; **O. University,** Universidad *f* a Distancia. **7** *(unengaged)* libre. **8** *(not hidden)* abierto,-a, franco,-a; **o. admiration,** franca admiración; **o. secret,** secreto a voces; **to be o. with sb,** ser sincero,-a con algn. **9** *(available)* *(of post, job)* vacante. **10** *(undecided)* sin decidir; **an o. question,** una cuestión sin resolver; **let's leave it o.,** dejémoslo sin concretar; *Av Rail* **o. ticket,** billete abierto. ◼ *Jur* **o. verdict,** veredicto *m* inconcluso. **11** *(blatant)* manifiesto,-a, patente. **12** *(not biased)* sin prejuicios; **to keep an o. mind,** no tener prejuicios. **13** *(liable, susceptible)* abierto,-a; **I am o. to suggestions,** acepto cualquier sugerencia; *Sport* **o. goal,** gol cantado; **o. to attack,** expuesto,-a a los ataques; **o. to criticism,** que da lugar a críticas. **14** *Fin (cheque, account)* abierto,-a. **II** *vtr* **1** *(gen)* abrir; *(unfold)* desplegar; *Mil* **to o. fire,** abrir fuego; *Mil* **to o. ranks,** romper filas; *fig* **to o. one's heart to sb,** sincerarse con algn. **2** *(inaugurate, initiate)* *(shop)* abrir; *(exhibition etc)* inaugurar; *(negotiations)* iniciar; *(conversation)* entablar; *Fin (account)* abrir. **III** *vi* **1** *(gen)* abrir, abrirse; **the bank opens at ten,** el banco abre a las diez. **2** *(render accessible)* dar a; **is there an exit opening on the street?,** ¿hay una salida a la calle? **3** *(appear in view)* abrirse. **4** *(start)* empezar, comenzar; *Theat Cin* estrenarse; **the story opens with a murder,** la historia comienza con un asesinato. **5** *Cards* abrir **(with,** de)**. IV** *n* **1** *(open air)* campo *m*, aire *m* libre; **in the o.,** al aire libre, al raso; *fig* **to bring into the o.,** hacer público; *fig* **to come into the o.,** declarar abiertamente. **2** *Sport* open *m*. ◆ **open out I** *vtr* abrir, desplegar, desdoblar. **II** *vi (of flowers)* abrirse; *(of view)* extenderse. ◆ **open up I** *vtr* **1** *(market etc)* abrir; *(possibilities)* crear. **2** *Aut fam* dar gas, acelerar. **II** *vi* **1** *(gen)* abrirse; **open u. up!,** ¡ábreme!; ¡abre la puerta! **2** *(start)* empezar, comenzar, miciarse. **3** *(talk freely)* hablar con franqueza. **4** *(become more lively)* animarse. ◆ **openly** *adv (gen)* abiertamente; *(publicly)* públicamente, en público.

open-air ['əʊpəneə'] *adj* al aire libre.

open-and-shut [əʊpən'ænd'ʃʌt] *adj* claro,-a, evidente; **o.-a.-s. case,** un caso evidente.

opencast ['əʊpənkɑːst] *adj GB Min* a cielo abierto.

open-door ['əʊpəndɔːr'] *adj Ind* no proteccionista.

open-ended [əʊpən'endɪd] *adj (gen)* sin límites; *(contract)* ilimitado,-a.

opener ['əʊpənə'] *n* abridor *m*; **bottle o.,** abrebotellas *m inv*; **tin o.,** *US* **can o.,** abrelatas *m inv*.

open-heart ['əʊpənhɑːt] *adj Med* de corazón abierto.

open-hearted [əʊpən'hɑːtɪd] *adj* abierto,-a, sincero,-a.

opening ['əʊpənɪŋ] *n* **1** *(act)* apertura *f*; *Cin Theat* estreno *m*; **formal o.,** inauguración *f*. ◼ *Theat* **o. night,** noche *f* de estreno; *Fin* **o. price,** cotización *f* inicial; **o. speech,** discurso *m* inaugural; *GB (in pub)* **o. time,** hora *f* en que abren los bares. **2** *(beginning)* comienzo *m*. **3** *(aperture)* abertura *f*; *(gap)* brecha *f*; *US (in forest)* claro *m*. **4** *Com (chance)* salida *f*, oportunidad *f*. **5** *(vacancy)* puesto *m* vacante, vacante *f*.

open-minded [əʊpən'maɪndɪd] *adj* de mente abierta, sin prejuicios.

open-mindedness [əʊpən'maɪndɪdnɪs] *n* falta *f* de prejuicios.

open-mouthed [əʊpən'maʊθt] *adj* boquiabierto,-a.

openness ['əʊpənnɪs] *n* franqueza *f*.

open-plan ['əʊpənplæn] *adj Archit (office etc)* abierto,-a.

opera¹ ['ɒpərə] *n Mus* ópera *f*. ◼ **o. glasses,** prismáticos *mpl*, gemelos *mpl*; **o. house,** ópera *f*, teatro *m* de la ópera; **o. singer,** cantante *mf* de ópera.

opera² ['ɒpərə] *npl see* **opus.**

operand ['ɒpərænd] *n Comput* operando *m*.

operate ['ɒpəreɪt] **I** *vi* **1** *(function)* funcionar. **2** *(act)* obrar, actuar. **3** *Med* operar, hacer una intervención quirúrgica, intervenir; **to o. on sb for appendicitis,** operar a algn de apendicitis. **II** *vtr* **1** *(switch on)* accionar; *(control)* hacer funcionar, manejar. **2** *(manage)* *(business)* dirigir; *(mine)* explotar.

operatic [ɒpə'rætɪk] *adj* de ópera, operístico,-a.

operating ['ɒpəreɪtɪŋ] *n* **1** *Com Ind* operación *f*, funcionamiento *m*. ◼ **o. costs,** gastos *mpl* de funcionamiento. **2** *Med* operación *f*. ◼ **o. table,** mesa *f* de operaciones; **o. theatre,** *US* **o. theater,** quirófano *m*.

operation [ɒpə'reɪʃən] *n* **1** *(of machine)* funcionamiento *m*; *(by person)* manejo *m*; **to be in o.,** *(of machine)* estar funcionando *or* en funcionamiento; *(of law)* estar vigente *or* en vigor. **2** *Math* operación *f*. **3** *Mil* operación *f*, maniobra *f*. **4** *Med* operación *f*, intervención *f* quirúrgica; **to undergo an o. for,** ser operado,-a de.

operational [ɒpə'reɪʃənəl] *adj* **1** *(of operations)* de operaciones. **2** *(ready for use)* operativo,-a, listo,-a para usar; *(in use)* en funcionamiento; **to be o.,** estar en funcionamiento. **3** *Mil* operacional, de servicio.

operative ['ɒpərətɪv] **I** *adj* **1** *Jur (in force)* vigente; **to become o.,** entrar en vigor. **2** *(significant)* clave, significativo,-a; **the o. word,** la palabra clave. **3** *Med* operatorio,-a. **II** *n* operario,-a *m,f*.

operator ['ɒpəreɪtə'] *n* **1** *Ind* operario,-a *m, f*. **2** *Tel* operador,-a *m, f*, telefonista *mf*; *Av Mil* **radio o.,** radiotelegrafista *mf*. **3** *(dealer)* negociante *mf*, agente *m*; **tour o.,** agente de viajes; *fam* **a slick o.,** un tipo aprovechado. **4** *Math* operador *m*.

operetta [ɒpə'retə] *n Mus* opereta *f*.

ophthalmology [ɒfθæl'mɒlədʒɪ] *n Med* oftalmología *f*.

opinion [ə'pɪnjən] *n* **1** *(belief)* opinión *f*; **in my o.,** a mi parecer, en mi opinión, a mi juicio; **it's a matter of o.,** es cuestión de opiniones; **to be of the o. that ...,** opinar qué ...; **to give one's o.,** dar su opinión. **2** *(evaluation, estimation)* opinión *f*, concepto *m*; **to have a high/low o. of sb,** tener buen/mal concepto de algn; **public o.,** la opinión pública; **what's your o. of him?,** ¿qué piensas de él? ◼ **o. poll,** encuesta *f*, sondeo *m*.

opinionated [ə'pɪnjəneɪtɪd] *adj (obstinate)* terco,-a, testarudo,-a; *(dogmatic)* dogmático,-a.

opium ['əʊpɪəm] *n* opio *m*. ◼ **o. addict,** opiómano,-a *m,f*, adicto,-a *m, f* al opio; **o. den,** fumadero *m* de opio.

opossum [ə'pɒsəm] *n Zool* zarigüeya *f*.

opp *abbr of* **opposite,** enfrente.

opponent [ə'pəʊnənt] *n* adversario,-a *m,f*, contrincante *mf*.

opportune ['ɒpətjuːn] *adj* oportuno,-a, propicio,-a; **an o. moment,** un momento oportuno.

opportunist [ɒpə'tjuːnɪst] *adj & n* oportunista *(mf)*.

opportunity [ɒpə'tjuːnɪtɪ] *n* **1** *(gen)* oportunidad *f*, ocasión *f*; **if I get an o.,** si se me presenta la ocasión; **to miss an o.,** perder una oportunidad. ◼ **equal o.,** igualdad *f* de oportunidades. **2** *(prospect)* perspectiva *f*; *(advert)* 'excellent opportunities for promotion', 'excelentes perspectivas de promoción'.

oppose [ə'pəʊz] *vtr* oponerse a, ser contrario,-a a; *Pol* **to o. the motion,** oponerse a la moción.

opposed [ə'pəuzd] *adj* **1** opuesto,-a, contrario,-a; **to be o. to** sth, estar en contra de algo, oponerse a algo. **2** **as o. to**, comparado,-a con, en comparación con.

opposing [ə'pəuzɪŋ] *adj* contrario,-a, adversario,-a; *Mil* **the o. forces**, las fuerzas enemigas; *Sport* **the o. team**, el equipo adversario.

opposite ['ɒpəzɪt, 'ɒpəsɪt] **I** *adj* **1** *(facing)* de enfrente; *(page)* contiguo,-a; **the house o.**, la casa de enfrente. **2** *(contrary)* opuesto,-a, contrario,-a, contrapuesto,-a; **at the o. end**, en el extremo opuesto; **in the o. direction**, en dirección contraria; **o. poles**, polos opuestos; **to take the o. view**, tomar la actitud contraria. ■ **o. number**, colega *mf*, homólogo,-a *m,f*; **o. sex**, sexo *m* opuesto. **II** *n* antítesis *f*, contraposición *f*; **quite the o.!**, ¡al contrario!; **she's the o. of her brother**, es la antítesis de su hermano. **III** *prep* enfrente de, frente a; **o. (to) the butcher's**, frente a la carnicería. **IV** *adv* enfrente, the church is o., la iglesia está enfrente.

opposition [ɒpə'zɪʃən] *n* **1** *(resistance)* oposición *f*, resistencia *f*; **they met with no o.**, no encontraron resistencia. **2** *(contrast)* contradicción *f*, contraposición *f*; **in o. to**, en contra de, contrario a. **3** *Pol* **the o.,** la oposición; **the o. party**, el partido de la oposición; **to be in o.**, ser de la oposición.

oppress [ə'pres] *vtr* **1** oprimir. **2** *fig (of anxiety etc)* agobiar, oprimir.

oppression [ə'preʃən] *n* **1** opresión *f*. **2** *fig (of anxiety etc)* agobio *m*.

oppressive [ə'presɪv] *adj* **1** *(gen)* opresivo,-a. **2** *(of atmosphere)* agobiante; *(of heat)* sofocante.

opt [ɒpt] *vi* optar; **to o. for**, optar por; **we opted to decline the invitation**, optamos por no ir. ◆ **opt out** *vi* desentenderse (**of,** de).

optative ['ɒptətɪv] **I** *adj* optativo,-a. **II** *n Ling* modo *m* optativo.

optic ['ɒptɪk] *adj* óptico,-a; *Anat* **o. nerve**, nervio óptico.

optical ['ɒptɪkəl] *adj* óptico,-a; **o. fibre**, fibra óptica; **o. illusion**, ilusión óptica.

optician [ɒp'tɪʃən] *n* óptico,-a *m,f*.

optics ['ɒptɪks] *n* óptica *f*.

optimism ['ɒptɪmɪzəm] *n* optimismo *m*.

optimist ['ɒptɪmɪst] *n* optimista *mf*.

optimistic(al) [ɒptɪ'mɪstɪk(əl)] *adj* optimista. ◆ **optimistically** *adv* con optimismo.

optimize ['ɒptɪmaɪz] *vtr* aprovechar al máximo, optimizar.

optimum ['ɒptɪməm] **I** *n (pl* **optimums** *or* **optima** ['ɒptɪmə])* grado *m* óptimo. **II** *adj* óptimo,-a; **o. conditions**, condiciones óptimas.

option ['ɒpʃən] *n* opción *f*; **I have no o.**, no tengo más remedio; **to keep** *or* **leave one's options open**, no comprometerse; **with the o. on**, con opción a.

optional ['ɒpʃənəl] *adj* optativo,-a, facultativo,-a. ■ *Com* **o. extras**, extras *mpl* opcionales; *Educ* **o. subject**, (asignatura *f*) optativa *f*.

opulence ['ɒpjʊləns] *n* opulencia *f*.

or [ɔːˈ, *unstressed* ə] *conj* **1** o; *(before a word beginning o or* ho) u; **keep still or I'll shoot**, no se mueva o disparo; **or else**, si no, o bien; **tell me whether you like it or not**, dime si te gusta o no; **ten kilometres or so**, unos diez kilómetros; **you may have either a bun or a piece of cake**, puedes tomarte (o) una madalena o un trozo de pastel. **2** *(with negative)* ni; **he can't read or write**, no sabe leer ni escribir; **without money or lunggage**, sin dinero ni equipaje; *see also* **nor**.

oracle ['ɒrəkəl] *n* oráculo *m*.

oral ['ɔːrəl, 'ɒrəl] **I** *adj* oral; **o. contraceptive**, anticonceptivo oral; **o. hygiene**, higiene bucal; *Med* **o. vaccine**, vacuna por vía oral. **II** *n* examen *m* oral. ◆ **orally** *adv* oralmente; *Pharm* **to be taken o.**, por vía oral.

orange ['ɒrɪndʒ] **I** *n* **1** *(fruit)* naranja *f*. ■ *Bot* **o. blossom**, azahar *m*; *Bot* **o. grove**, naranjal *m*; **o. juice**, zumo *m* de naranja; **o. tree**, naranjo *m*. **2** *(colour)* naranja *m*. **II** *adj* naranja *inv*, de color naranja.

orangeade [ɒrɪndʒ'eɪd] *n* naranjada *f*.

orang-outang [ɔːˈræŋuːˈtæŋ] *n Zool* orangután *m*.

oration [ɔː'reɪʃən] *n* oración *f*, discurso *m*.

orator ['ɒrətəˈ] *n* orador,-a *m,f*.

oratorical [ɒrə'tɒrɪkəl] *adj* oratorio,-a.

oratory¹ ['ɒrətərɪ] *n (art of speaking)* oratoria *f*.

oratory² ['ɒrətərɪ] *n Rel (chapel)* oratorio *m*, capilla *f*.

orbit ['ɔːbɪt] **I** *n* **1** *Astron* órbita *f*; **to go into o.**, entrar en órbita; **to put a satellite into o.**, poner un satélite en órbita. **2** *fig* ámbito *m*, esfera *f*, órbita *f*; **the Russian o.,** la esfera de influencia soviética. **II** *vtr* girar alrededor de. **III** *vi* orbitar, girar.

orbital ['ɔːbɪtəl] *adj* orbital, orbitario,-a.

orchard ['ɔːtʃəd] *n* huerto *m*. ■ **apple o.**, manzanal *m*.

orchestra ['ɔːkɪstrə] *n Mus* orquesta *f*. ■ **chamber o.**, orquesta *f* de cámara; **o. pit**, orquesta *f*, foso *m*.

orchestral [ɔː'kestrəl] *adj* orquestal.

orchestration [ɔːkɪ'streɪʃən] *n* orquestación *f*.

orchid ['ɔːkɪd] *n Bot* orquídea *f*.

ordain [ɔː'deɪn] *vtr* **1** *Rel* ordenar; **to be ordained**, ordenarse. **2** *(decree)* decretar, ordenar; **it was ordained by fate**, el destino quiso que fuera así.

ordeal [ɔː'diːl] *n* mala experiencia *f*, sufrimiento *m*.

order ['ɔːdəˈ] **I** *n* **1** *(sequence)* orden *m*, serie *f*; **in alphabetical o.**, por orden alfabético; **in o. of importance**, por orden de importancia; **in the wrong o., out of o.**, sin orden; **to put in** *or* **into o.**, poner en orden, ordenar. **2** *(condition)* estado *m*, condiciones *fpl*; **in good o.**, en buen estado, en condiciones; **is your passport in o.?**, ¿tienes el pasaporte en regla?; **'out of o.'**, 'no funciona'. **3** *(peace)* orden *m*; **law and o.**, orden público; **to call to o.**, llamar al orden. **4** *(class etc)* clase *f*; **the lower orders**, las clases bajas, el proletariado. **5** *Biol* orden *m*. **6** *(command)* orden *f*; **to give orders**, dar órdenes; **until further orders**, hasta nueva orden; **we received an o. to withdraw**, recibimos órdenes de retirarnos; *fig* **to be the o. of the day**, estar a la orden del día. ■ *Jur* **court o.**, orden *f* judicial; **extradition o.**, orden *f* de extradición. **7** *(commission, instruction)* pedido *m*, encargo *m*; **to be on o.**, estar pedido *or* encargado; **to place an o. with sb**, hacer un pedido a algn; **to o.**, a (la) medida; *fam* **that's a tall o.**, eso es mucho pedir. ■ **o. form**, hoja *f* de pedido; **postal o.**, giro *m* postal. **8** *Rel* orden *f*; **to take (holy) orders**, ordenarse (sacerdote). **9** *Hist (medal)* condecoración *f*; *(title)* orden *f*. **10** *Archit* orden *m*. **11** *(quality)* calidad *f*, categoría *f*; **of the highest o.**, de primer orden, de primera calidad. **12** *(kind)* índole *f*, tipo *m*. **13** **in the o. of**, del orden de, alrededor de, aproximadamente. **14** **in o. that**, para que, a fin de que; **in o. that she should arrive on time**, para que llegara a tiempo; **in o. to** *(+ infin)*, para, a fin de *(+ infin)*. **II** *vtr* **1** *(command)* ordenar, mandar; **she ordered me into the car**, me ordenó que entrara en el coche; *Sport* **to o. a player off**, expulsar a un jugador; **to o. sb about** *or* **around**, mangonear a algn, gobernar a algn; **to o. sb to do sth**, mandar *or* ordenar a algn hacer algo. **2** *(request)* pedir; *Com* pedir, encargar; **to o. a dish**, pedir un plato. **3** *(organize)* ordenar, poner en orden. **III** *interj* ¡orden!; **o. in the court!**, ¡orden en la sala!

orderliness ['ɔːdəlɪnɪs] *n* orden *m*, disciplina *f*.

orderly ['ɔːdəlɪ] **I** *adj* **1** *(tidy etc)* ordenado,-a; **he's very o.**, es muy metódico. **2** *(obeying)* disciplinado,-a. **II** *n* **1** *Med* enfermero *m*. **2** *Mil* ordenanza *m*. ■ **o. room**, oficina *f*.

ordinal ['ɔːdɪnəl] *adj & n* ordinal *(m)*.

ordinance ['ɔːdɪnəns] *n fml* ordenanza *f*, decreto *m*.

ordinary ['ɔːdənrɪ] **I** *adj (usual, normal)* usual, normal; *(average)* corriente, común; **an o. guy,** un tipo corriente; **in the o. way,** en la forma habitual, de la manera usual; **the o. citizen,** el ciudadano de a pie, el hombre de la calle; **the o. Spaniard,** el español medio. ■ *Naut* **o. seaman,** marinero *m*; *GB* **o. shares,** acciones *fpl* ordinarias. **II the o.,** *n* lo corriente, lo normal; **above the o.,** sobresaliente; **out of the o.,** fuera de lo común, excepcional, extraordinario,-a.

ordinate ['ɔːdɪnɪt] *n Math* ordenada *f*.

ordination [ɔːdɪ'neɪʃən] *n* ordenación *f*.

ordnance ['ɔːdnəns] *n GB* **O. Survey,** servicio *m* oficial de topografía y cartografía.

ore [ɔːr] *n Min* mineral *m*, mena *f*. ■ **iron o.,** mineral *m* de hierro.

oregano [ɒrɪ'gɑːnəʊ] *n Bot* orégano *m*.

organ ['ɔːgən] *n* **1** *Mus* órgano *m*. ■ **barrel o.,** organillo *m*. **2** *Anat* órgano *m*. **3** *(agency)* órgano *m*; *(periodical)* órgano *m*, boletín *m*; **the party o.,** el órgano del partido.

organ-grinder ['ɔːgəngraɪndər] *n* organillero,-a *m,f*.

organic [ɔː'gænɪk] *adj* orgánico,-a; **o. chemistry,** química orgánica.

organism ['ɔːgənɪʒəm] *n* organismo *m*.

organist ['ɔːgənɪst] *n Mus* organista *mf*.

organization [ɔːgənaɪ'zeɪʃən] *n* organización *f*.

organize ['ɔːgənaɪz] *vtr* organizar; **to get organized,** organizarse.

organizer ['ɔːgənaɪzər] *n* organizador,-a *m,f*.

orgasm ['ɔːgæzəm] *n* orgasmo *m*.

orgy ['ɔːdʒɪ] *n* orgía *f*; *fig* **an o. of colour,** una explosión de colores.

orient ['ɔːrɪənt] *n* **the O.,** el Oriente.

Oriental [ɔːrɪ'entəl] *adj & n* oriental *(mf)*.

orientate ['ɔːrɪenteɪt] *vtr* orientar.

orientation [ɔːrɪen'teɪʃən] *n* orientación *f*.

orifice ['ɒrɪfɪs] *n* orificio *m*.

origin ['ɒrɪdʒɪn] *n* origen *m*; **country of o.,** país natal *or* de origen.

original [ə'rɪdʒɪnəl] **I** *adj* **1** *(first)* primero,-a, original; **the o. inhabitants,** los primeros habitantes. ■ *Rel* **o. sin,** pecado *m* original. **2** *(novel)* original, genuino,-a. **II** *n* original *m*; **the o. is in the Prado,** el original está en el Prado; **to read Cervantes in the o.,** leer a Cervantes en versión original. ◆ **originally** *adv* **1** *(at first)* en un principio, originariamente. **2** *(with originality)* con originalidad.

originality [ərɪdʒɪ'nælɪtɪ] *n* originalidad *f*.

originate [ə'rɪdʒɪneɪt] **I** *vtr* originar, crear, dar lugar a. **II** *vi* **to o. from** *or* **in,** tener su origen en, provenir de.

oriole ['ɔːrɪəʊl] *n Orn* **(golden) o.,** oropéndola *f*.

Orkneys ['ɔːknɪz] *npl* (Islas) Orcadas.

ornament ['ɔːnəmənt] **I** *n* ornamento *m*, adorno *m*. **II** *vtr* adornar, engalanar.

ornamental [ɔːnə'mentəl] *adj* ornamental, decorativo,-a.

ornate [ɔː'neɪt] *adj* *(gen)* vistoso,-a; *(style)* sobre-cargado,-a.

ornithology [ɔːnɪ'θɒlədʒɪ] *n* ornitología *f*.

orphan ['ɔːfən] **I** *n* huérfano,-a *m,f*. **II** *vtr* dejar huérfano,-a; **she was orphaned,** quedó huérfana.

orphanage ['ɔːfənɪdʒ] *n* orfanato *m*.

orthodontics [ɔːθəʊ'dɒntɪks] *n* ortodoncia *f*.

orthodox ['ɔːθədɒks] *adj* ortodoxo,-a.

orthodoxy ['ɔːθədɒksɪ] *n* ortodoxia *f*.

orthography [ɔː'θɒgrəfɪ] *n* ortografía *f*.

orthopaedics, *US* **orthopedics** [ɔːθəʊ'piːdɪks] *n* ortopedia *f*.

orthopaedist, *US* **orthopedist** [ɔːθəʊ'piːdɪst] *n* ortopedista *mf*.

OS [əʊ'es] **1** *Naut abbr of* **ordinary seaman,** marinero *m*. **2** *GB Geol abbr of* **Ordnance Survey,** servicio *m* oficial de topografía y cartografía. **3** *abbr of* **outsize,** (talla *f*) extra grande *f*.

oscillate ['ɒsɪleɪt] *vi* oscilar; *fig* oscilar, variar.

osier ['əʊʒɪər] *n* mimbre *m*. ■ **o. bed,** mimbrera *f*.

Oslo ['ɒzləʊ] *n* Oslo.

osmosis [ɒz'məʊsɪs] *n* ósmosis *f*, osmosis *f*.

osprey ['ɒsprɪ, 'ɒspreɪ] *n Orn* águila *f* pescadora.

ossification [ɒsɪfɪ'keɪʃən] *n* osificación *f*.

ossify ['ɒsɪfaɪ] *vi (pt & pp ossified)* osificarse.

ostensible [ɒ'stensɪbəl] *adj* **1** *(apparent)* ostensible. **2** *(pretended)* aparentado,-a, fingido,-a.

ostentation [ɒsten'teɪʃən] *n* ostentación *f*.

ostentatious [ɒsten'teɪʃəs] *adj* ostentoso,-a.

ostracism ['ɒstrəsɪzəm] *n* ostracismo *m*.

ostracize ['ɒstrəsaɪz] *vtr (from society)* condenar al ostracismo; *(from group)* aislar, excluir.

ostrich ['ɒstrɪtʃ] *n Orn* avestruz *m*.

other ['ʌðər] **I** *adj* **1** *(gen)* otro,-a; **any o. member,** cualquier otro miembro; **every o. day,** cada dos días; **on the o. hand,** por otra parte, por otro lado; **o. people have seen it,** otros lo han visto; **o. people's property,** los bienes ajenos; **the o. four,** los otros cuatro; **the o. one,** el otro, la otra; **the o. thing,** lo otro. **2 or o.,** u otro,-a; **he must be somewhere or o.,** debe de estar en alguna parte; **one or o. of us,** alguno de nosotros. **II** *pron* otro,-a *m,f*; **many others,** otros muchos; **one after the o.,** uno tras otro; **the others,** los otros, los demás; **we see each o. quite often,** nos vemos con bastante frecuencia. **III** *adv* distinto,-a, diferente; **she can't be o. than what she is,** ella no puede ser de otra manera.

otherwise ['ʌðəwaɪz] **I** *adv* **1** *(if not)* si no, de no ser así; **o. you'll have to do it on your own,** si no, tendrás que hacerlo solo. **2** *(differently)* de otra manera; **except where o. stated,** excepto cuando se indique lo contrario; **he couldn't do o.,** no podía obrar de otra manera; **if she's not o. engaged,** si no tiene otro compromiso. **3** *(in other respects)* por lo demás; **he's o. quite sane,** aparte de eso está en su sano juicio. **II** *adj* distinto,-a; **the truth is o.,** la verdad es bastante distina.

otherworldly [ʌðə'wɜːldlɪ] *adj* alejado,-a de este mundo, espiritual.

otter ['ɒtər] *n (pl otters or otter) Zool* nutria *f*.

Ottoman ['ɒtəmən] *adj & n* otomán,-ana *(m,f)*, otomano,-a *(m,f)*.

ottoman ['ɒtəmən] *n Furn* otomana *f*.

OU [əʊ'juː] *GB abbr of* **Open University,** Universidad *f* Nacional de Educación a Distancia, UNED *f*.

ouch [aʊtʃ] *interj* ¡ay!

ought [ɔːt] *v aux* **1** *(obligation)* deber; **I thought I o. to tell you,** creí que debía decírtelo; **she o. to do it,** debería hacerlo; **to behave as one o.,** comportarse como es debido; **you oughtn't to eat so many cakes,** no deberías comer tantos pasteles. **2** *(vague desirability)* tener que, deber; **you o. to see the exhibition,** deberías ver la exposición; **you o. to have seen it!,** ¡si lo hubieras visto! **3** *(expectation)* **he o. to pass the exam,** seguramente aprobará el examen; **that o. to do,** con eso bastará.

ounce [aʊns] *n* onza *f*; *fig* **he hasn't an o. of courage,** no tiene ni pizca de valentía.

our [aʊər] *poss adj* nuestro,-a; **o. daughter,** nuestra hija; **o. friends,** nuestros amigos; **it's one of o. books,** es un libro nuestro. ■ *Rel* **O. Father,** Padre nuestro *m*; *Rel* **O. Lady,** Nuestra Señora *f*.

ours [aʊəz] *poss pron* **1** (el) nuestro, (la) nuestra; **have you seen o.?,** ¿has visto el nuestro?; **this table is o.,** esta mesa es nuestra. **2 of o.,** nuestro,-a; **a friend of o.,** un amigo nuestro.

ourselves [aʊə'selvz] *pers pron pl* **1** *(reflexive)* nos; **we can serve o.**, nos podemos servir. **2** *(emphatic)* nosotros mismos, nosotras mismas; **we did it o.**, lo hicimos nosotros mismos; **we o. are to blame**, la culpa es nuestra. **3 by o.**, a solas; **all by o.**, completamente solos.

oust [aʊst] *vtr* **1** *(from a post)* desbancar. **2** *(from property etc)* expulsar, desalojar.

out [aʊt] **I** *adv* **1** *(outside, away)* fuera; **o. you go!**, ¡vete!; **he's o. and about again**, ya está bien otra vez; **a long way o.** *(of town)*, muy lejos (de la ciudad); **o. at sea**, en alta mar; **o. there**, ahí fuera; *Naut* **the voyage o.**, la ida; **to go o.**, salir; **to throw sth o.**, tirar algo (a la basura); **'way o.'**, 'salida'. **2** *(clearly)* claramente; **I told him straight o.**, se lo dije muy claramente; **o. loud**, en voz alta. **3** *(to the end)* hasta el final; **hear me o.**, escúchame hasta el final. **4 o. of**, *(place)* fuera de; **get o. of here!**, ¡sal de aquí!; **move o. of the way!**, ¡quítate de en medio!; **o. of danger**, fuera de peligro; **she's o. of town**, está fuera de la ciudad; **to get money o. of sb**, sacarle dinero a algn; **to go o. of the room**, salir de la habitación; *fig* **to feel o. of it**, sentirse aislado; *fam* **you must be o. of your mind**, estás mal de la cabeza, estás loco; *sl* **to be o. of it**, no estar al tanto, no enterarse; *prov* **o. of sight, o. of mind**, ojos que no ven, corazón que no siente. **5 o. of**, *fig* fuera de; **o. of control**, fuera de control, descontrolado,-a; **o. of date**, *(expired)* caducado,-a; *(old-fashioned)* pasado,-a de moda; **o. of focus**, desenfocado,-a; *Pol* **o. of office**, fuera del poder; **'o. of order'**, 'no funciona'; **o. of print**, agotado,-a. **6 o. of**, *(cause, motive)* por; **he did it o. of spite**, lo hizo por despecho; **o. of respect**, por respeto. **7 o. of**, *(made from)* de; **made o. of wood**, hecho,-a de madera. **8 o. of**, *(short of, without)* sin; **I'm o. of money**, se me ha acabado el dinero, estoy sin dinero; **o. of breath**, sin aliento; **to be o. of practice**, faltarle práctica a algn; **to be o. of work**, estar parado,-a *or* sin empleo; **we're o. of milk**, nos hemos quedado sin leche, se nos ha acabado la leche. **9 o. of**, *(among)* entre; **forty o. of fifty**, cuarenta de cada cincuenta; **one o. of many**, uno entre otros muchos. **II** *adj* **1** *(in view)* **the sun is o.**, ha salido el sol. **2** *(unfashionable)* pasado,-a de moda; **hats are o. this year**, los sombreros no se llevan este año. **3** *(not lit)* apagado,-a; **the fire is o.**, se ha apagado el fuego. **4** *(not working)* estropeado,-a; **the TV's o.**, la tele no va. **5** *(unconscious)* inconsciente; **to be o. cold**, haber perdido completamente el conocimiento. **6** *(not in)* **she's o.**, ha salido, no está. **7** *(intent)* **to be o. for** *or* **to**, buscar; **he's o. for your blood**, va a por ti; **I'm not o. to do that**, no es ése mi propósito. **8** *(on strike)* en huelga. **9** *(published)* publicado,-a; *(made public)* público,-a; **the book is just o.**, el libro acaba de salir; **the secret is o.**, el secreto ha salido a luz. **10** *Sport (ball)* fuera de juego; *(player)* eliminado,-a; *Box* fuera de combate. **11** *(used up)* agotado,-a, terminado,-a; **the paper is o.**, se ha terminado el papel. **12** *(inaccurate)* equivocado,-a; **I wasn't far o.**, no andaba muy equivocado; **to be o. in one's calculations**, equivocarse en los cálculos. **13** *(not in office)* fuera del poder. **14** *(completed)* acabado,-a, terminado,-a; **before the week is o.**, antes de acabar la semana. **15** *(in flower)* en flor. **III** *prep* **1** *(out of)* por; **he jumped o. the window**, saltó por la ventana; **she ran o. the door**, salió corriendo por la puerta. **IV** *n fig* **the ins and outs of the matter**, los pormenores del asunto. **V** *interj* ¡fuera!; *fam* **o. with it!**, ¡suéltalo ya!

outage ['aʊtɪdʒ] *n Elec* **power o.**, corte *m or* interrupción *f* del servicio eléctrico.

out-and-out ['aʊtənaʊt] *adj* empedernido,-a, redomado,-a; **he's an o.-a.-o. liar**, es un mentiroso empedernido.

outbid [aʊt'bɪd] *vtr (pt* **outbid**; *pp* **outbid** *or* **outbidden** [aʊt'bɪdən]) *(at auction)* pujar más alto que, ofrecer más que.

outboard ['aʊtbɔːd] *adj Naut* **o. motor**, motor *m* fueraborda, fuera borda *m*.

outbreak ['aʊtbreɪk] *n (of war)* comienzo *m*; *(of spots)* erupción *f*; *(of disease)* brote *m*, epidemia *f*; *(of violence)* ola *f*; *(of anger)* arrebato *m*; **at the o. of war**, cuando estalló la guerra.

outbuilding ['aʊtbɪldɪŋ] *n (gen)* dependencia *f*; *(shed)* cobertizo *m*.

outburst ['aʊtbɜːst] *n (of anger)* explosión *f*, arrebato *m*; *(of generosity)* arranque *m*; **there was an o. of applause**, irrumpieron en aplausos.

outcast ['aʊtkɑːst] *n* marginado,-a *m,f*, proscrito,-a *m,f*.

outcome ['aʊtkʌm] *n* resultado *m*.

outcrop ['aʊtkrɒp] *n Geol* afloramiento *m*.

outcry ['aʊtkraɪ] *n* protesta *f*; **there was an o.**, hubo fuertes protestas.

outdated [aʊt'deɪtɪd] *adj* anticuado,-a, obsoleto,-a.

outdid [aʊt'dɪd] *pl see* **outdo**.

outdistance [aʊt'dɪstəns] *vtr* dejar atrás.

outdo [aʊt'duː] *vtr (pt* **outdid** [aʊt'dɪd]; *pp* **outdone** [aʊt'dʌn]) exceder; *fig* ganar; **not to be outdone**, para no ser menos; **to o. sb**, poderle a algn.

outdoor ['aʊtdɔː'] *adj* **1** *(gen)* exterior, al aire libre; **o. swimming pool**, piscina descubierta; **the o. life**, la vida al aire libre. ■ *Phot* **o. shot**, exterior *m*. **2** *(of clothes)* de calle.

outdoors [aʊt'dɔːz] **I** *adv* fuera; **to eat o.**, comer al aire libre. **II the (great) o.** *n* el aire libre, la naturaleza.

outer ['aʊtə'] *adj* exterior, externo,-a; **o. garments**, ropa exterior; **the o. suburbs**, las afueras. ■ **o. space**, espacio *m* sideral.

outfit ['aʊtfɪt] *n* **1** *(kit, equipment)* equipo *m*; **tool o.**, juego *m* de herramientas. **2** *(set of clothes)* conjunto *m*; *(uniform)* uniforme *m*. **3** *fam (group)* grupo *m*, equipo *m*.

outfox [aʊt'fɒks] *vtr* ser más listo,-a que.

outgoing ['aʊtgəʊɪŋ] **I** *adj* **1** *(departing)* saliente. **2** *(sociable)* sociable, extrovertido,-a. **II outgoings** *npl* gastos *mpl*.

outgrow [aʊt'grəʊ] *vtr (pt* **outgrew** [aʊt'gruː]; *pp* **outgrown** [aʊt'grəʊn]) quedársele pequeño,-a; *(of habit)* superar; **he's outgrowing all his clothes**, toda la ropa se le está quedando pequeña; **she'll o. it**, se le pasará con la edad.

outhouse ['aʊthaʊs] *n see* **outbuilding**.

outing ['aʊtɪŋ] *n* excursión *f*.

outlandish [aʊt'lændɪʃ] *adj* extravagante, estrafalario,-a.

outlast [aʊt'lɑːst] *vtr (gen)* durar más que; *(outlive)* sobrevivir a.

outlaw ['aʊtlɔː] **I** *n* proscrito,-a *m,f*. **II** *vtr (ban)* prohibir.

outlet ['aʊtlet, 'aʊtlɪt] *n* **1** *(opening)* salida *f*. **2** *(for emotions)* válvula *f* de escape. **3** *Com* mercado *m*, salida *f*. **4** *(for water)* desagüe *m*.

outline ['aʊtlaɪn] **I** *n* **1** *(draft)* bosquejo *m*. **2** *(résumé)* resumen *m*. **3** *(outer line)* contorno *m*; *(silhouette)* perfil *m*. **4** *Art (sketch)* boceto *m*, esbozo *m*; *(of map)* trazado *m*. **II** *vtr* **1** *(draw lines of)* perfilar; **to be outlined against the sky**, perfilarse en el cielo. **2** *(summarize)* hacer un resumen de, resumir. **3** *(describe roughly)* trazar las líneas generales de.

outlive [aʊt'lɪv] *vtr (person, experience)* sobrevivir a.

outlook ['aʊtlʊk] *n* **1** *(point of view)* punto *m* de vista; *(attitude)* enfoque *m*. **2** *(prospect)* perspectiva *f*, panorama *m*; *Meteor* previsión *f*; **the o. is not very promising**, no es un panorama muy esperanzador.

outlying ['aʊtlaɪɪŋ] *adj (remote)* alejado,-a, aislado,-a; *(suburban)* periférico,-a; **o. districts**, barrios periféricos.

outmanoeuvre, *US* **outmaneuver** [aʊtmə'nuːvə'] *vtr* superar estratégicamente.

outmoded [aʊt'məʊdɪd] *adj* anticuado,-a, pasado,-a de moda.

outnumber [aʊt'nʌmbə'] *vtr* exceder en número; **we were outnumbered by them**, eran más que nosotros.

out-of-doors [aʊtəv'dɔːz] *adv see* **outdoors I**.

out-of-the-way [aʊtəvðə'weɪ] *adj* **1** *(distant)* apartado,-a, aislado,-a. **2** *(uncommon)* poco corriente, insólito,-a.

outpatient ['aʊtpeɪʃənt] *n Med* paciente *mf* externo,-a; **outpatients' department,** departamento de consulta externa.

outpost ['aʊtpəʊst] *n Mil* avanzada *f*; *(at frontier)* puesto *m* fronterizo.

output ['aʊtpʊt] *n* **1** *(gen)* producción *f*; *(of machine)* rendimiento *m*. **2** *Elec* potencia *f*. **3** *Comput* salida *f*.

outrage ['aʊtreɪdʒ] **I** *n* ultraje *m*, agravio *m*; **an o. against humanity,** un atentado contra la humanidad; **it's an o.!,** ¡es un escándalo! **II** *vtr* ultrajar, agraviar; **to be outraged by sth,** indignarse por algo.

outrageous [aʊt'reɪdʒəs] *adj (gen)* indignante; *(crime)* atroz; *(behaviour)* escandaloso,-a; *(clothes)* extravagante; *(price)* exorbitante. ◆ **outrageously** *adv* de manera indignante; **o. expensive,** terriblemente caro.

outright ['aʊtraɪt] **I** *adj* **I** *(absolute)* absoluto,-a, total; **the o. winner,** el ganador indiscutible. **2** *(straightforward)* directo,-a. **II** [aʊt'raɪt] *adv* **1** *(completely)* por completo; **to buy sth o.,** comprar algo en su totalidad. **2** *(directly)* directamente, sin reserva. **3** *(immediately)* en el acto.

outset ['aʊtset] *n* comienzo *m*, principio *m*; **from the o.,** de entrada, desde el principio.

outside [aʊt'saɪd] **I** *prep* **1** *(gen)* fuera de; **o. the house,** fuera de la casa. **2** *(beyond)* más allá de, fuera de; **o. office hours,** fuera de las horas de trabajo. **3** *(other than)* aparte de. **II** ['aʊtsaɪd] *adj* **1** *(exterior)* exterior, externo,-a; **the o. world,** el mundo exterior; *fig* **an o. opinion,** una opinión ajena. ■ *Rad TV* **o. broadcast,** emisión *f* desde fuera de los estudios. **2** *(remote)* remoto,-a. **III** [aʊt'saɪd] *adv* fuera, afuera; **she's o.,** está fuera. **IV** *n* exterior *m*, parte *f* exterior; **from the o.,** desde fuera; **on the o.,** por fuera; *fam* **at the o.,** como mucho, como máximo.

outsider [aʊt'saɪdər] *n* **1** *(stranger)* extraño,-a *m, f*, forastero-a *m, f*; *(intruder)* intruso,-a *m, f*. **2** *(unlikely winner) (horse)* caballo *m* que no es el favorito; *Pol (person)* candidato,-a *m, f* con pocas posibilidades de ganar.

outsize(d) ['aʊtsaɪz(d)] *adj (vegetables etc)* de gran tamaño; *(clothes)* de talla muy grande.

outskirts ['aʊtskɜːts] *npl (of town)* afueras *fpl*.

outsmart [aʊt'smɑːt] *vtr fam* burlar, engañar.

outspoken [aʊt'spəʊkən] *adj* directo,-a, abierto,-a; **to be very o.,** no tener pelos en la lengua.

outstanding [aʊt'stændɪŋ] *adj (exceptional)* destacado,-a, notable, sobresaliente; **an o. success,** un éxito rotundo. **2** *(unpaid)* sin pagar, pendiente; *(unresolved)* pendiente, por hacer.

outstretched [aʊt'stretʃt] *adj* extendido,-a.

outvote [aʊt'vəʊt] *vtr (person)* derrotar; *(proposal etc)* vencer; **to be outvoted,** perder la votación.

outward ['aʊtwəd] *adj* **1** *(external)* exterior, externo,-a. **2** *(of ship, voyage)* de ida; **the o. journey,** el viaje de ida. ◆ **outwardly** *adv* **1** *(apparently)* aparentemente; **o. calm,** tranquilo en apariencia. **2** *(externally)* por fuera.

outward(s) ['aʊtwəd(z)] *adv* hacia fuera, hacia afuera.

outweigh [aʊt'weɪ] *vtr* **1** *(prevail over)* prevalecer sobre, ser de más peso que. **2** *(weigh more than)* pesar más que.

ouzel ['uːzəl] *n Orn* **water o.,** mirlo *m* acuático.

ova ['əʊvə] *npl see* **ovum.**

oval ['əʊvəl] **I** *adj* oval, ovalado,-a. **II** *n* óvalo *m*.

ovary ['əʊvərɪ] *n Anat* ovario *m*.

ovation [əʊ'veɪʃən] *n* ovación *f*; **to give sb a standing o.,** tributar una ovación a algn, ovacionar a algn (puestos de pie).

oven ['ʌvən] *n* horno *m*; *Cook* **bake in a slow o.,** cocer a baja temperatura.

ovenproof ['ʌvənpruːf] *adj (dish etc)* refractario,-a.

over ['əʊvər] **I** *prep* **1** *(above)* encima de; **her name is o. the door,** su nombre está escrito encima de la puerta; **the plane flew o. the afflicted area,** el avión voló por encima de la zona afectada; *fig* **what came o. you?,** ¿qué te pasó?, ¿por qué reaccionaste así? **2** *(on top of)* sobre, encima de; **he put on a sweater o. his shirt,** se puso un jersey encima de la camisa. **3** *(across)* al otro lado de; **o. the border,** al otro lado de la frontera; **the bridge o. the river,** el puente que cruza el río; **the house o. the road,** la casa de enfrente. **4** *(during)* durante; **o. the last fifty years,** en los últimos cincuenta años; **o. the weekend,** durante el fin de semana; **she told me o. dinner,** me lo dijo durante la cena. **5** *(throughout)* por; **to travel o. France,** viajar por Francia. **6 all o.,** por todo,-a; **all o. the house,** por toda la casa; **famous all o. the world,** famoso en el mundo entero; *fig* **to be all o. sb,** deshacerse en atenciones con algn. **7** *(by the agency of)* por; **o. the phone,** por teléfono; **o. the radio,** por la radio. **8** *(more than)* más de; **men o. twenty-five,** hombres mayores de veinticinco años; **o. a century ago,** hace más de un siglo; **o. and above,** además de; **o. sixty pounds,** más de sesenta libras. **9** *(about)* por; **to fight o. sth,** pelearse por algo. **10** *(recovered from)* recuperado,-a de; **he isn't o. the flu yet,** aún no se ha repuesto de la gripe. **II** *adv* **1** *(above, across)* **to flow o.,** rebosar; **to cross o.,** cruzar (la calle). **2** *(downwards)* **to fall o.,** caerse; **to lean o.,** inclinarse. **3** *(somewhere else)* **o. there,** allá; *Rad* **o. to you,** corto; **why don't you come o. tomorrow?,** ¿por qué no vienes a casa mañana? **4** *(throughout)* por; **all o.,** en *or* por todas partes; **all the world o.,** en el mundo entero; **I ache all o.,** me duele todo. **5** *(more)* más; **children of ten and o.,** niños mayores de diez años; **there are about two hundred people or o.,** hay unas doscientas personas o más. **6** *(again)* otra vez; **o. and o. (again),** repetidas veces, una y otra vez; **to do sth o. (again),** volver a hacer algo; **to start all o. again,** volver a empezar; **twice o.,** dos veces seguidas. **7** *(in excess)* de más; **it's two ounces o.,** pesa dos onzas de más, sobran dos onzas. **III** *adj* **1** *(finished)* acabado,-a, terminado,-a; **it's (all) o.,** se acabó; **the danger is o.,** ha pasado el peligro; **the performance is o.,** la función ha terminado; **to get sth o. with,** acabar con algo de una vez. **2** *(remaining)* sobrante; **keep what is left o.,** quédate con lo que sobra. **IV** *n Cricket* serie *f* de seis saques.

over- ['əʊvə'] *pref* sobre-, super-.

overact [əʊvər'ækt] *vtr & vi Theat* exagerar.

overall ['əʊvərɔːl] **I** *adj* total, global; **the o. price,** el precio global. **II** [əʊvər'ɔːl] *adv (on the whole)* por lo general, en conjunto. **III** ['əʊvərɔːl] *n* **1** *GB* guardapolvo *m*, bata *f*. **2 overalls,** mono *m sing*.

overambitious [əʊvəræm'bɪʃəs] *adj* demasiado ambicioso,-a.

overanxious [əʊvər'æŋkʃəs] *adj (too eager)* demasiado *or* excesivamente ansioso,-a; **don't get too o. about buying the house,** no le des tantas vueltas a eso de comprar la casa.

overate [əʊvər'eɪt] *pt see* **overeat.**

overawe [əʊvər'ɔː] *vtr* intimidar; **to be overawed,** sobrecogerse.

overbearing [əʊvə'beərɪŋ] *adj (domineering)* dominante, autoritario,-a; *(important)* significativo,-a.

overblown [əʊvə'bləʊn] *adj* pomposo,-a, exagerado,-a.

overboard ['əʊvəbɔːd] *adv* por la borda; **man o.!,** ¡hombre al agua!; **to fall o.,** caer al agua; *fam* **to go o.,** pasarse; *fam* **to go o. for sth,** chiflarse por algo.

overburden [əʊvə'bɜːdən] *vtr* sobrecargar, agobiar **(with,** de).

overcame [əʊvə'keɪm] *pt see* **overcome.**

overcast ['əʊvəkɑːst] *adj Meteor* nuboso,-a, nublado,-a, cubierto,-a.

overcharge [əʊvə'tʃɑːdʒ] *vtr* **I** *(charge too much)* cobrar demasiado. **2** *(overload)* sobrecargar.

overcoat ['əʊvəkəʊt] *n* abrigo *m*.

overcome [əʊvə'kʌm] *vtr (pt overcame; pp overcome)* **1** *(conquer)* vencer; **we shall o.,** venceremos. **2** *(overwhelm)* agobiar, abrumar; **he was o. by grief,** estaba deshecho por el dolor; **the fireman was o. by smoke,** el bombero perdió el conocimiento a causa del humo. **3** *(surmount)* salvar, superar.

overconfident [əʊvə'kɒnfɪdənt] *adj* presumido,-a, creído,-a.

overcrowded [əʊvə'kraudɪd] *adj (of room)* abarrotado,-a, atestado,-a (de gente); *(of country)* superpoblado,-a.

overcrowding [əʊvə'kraudɪŋ] *n (of prisons etc)* hacinamiento *m*; *(of country)* superpoblación *f*.

overdeveloped [əʊvədɪ'veləpt] *adj* **1** superdesarrollado,-a. **2** *Phot* sobreprocesado,-a.

overdevelopment [əʊvədɪ'veləpmənt] *n* desarrollo *m* excesivo.

overdo [əʊvə'duː] *vtr (pt overdid* [əʊvə'dɪd]*; pp overdone)* **1** *(carry too far)* exagerar; *jam don't o. it,* no te pases. **2** *Cook* cocer *or* asar demasiado.

overdone [əʊvə'dʌn] **I** *pp see* **overdo. II** *adj (of meat)* muy hecho,-a.

overdose ['əʊvədəʊs] *n* sobredosis *f*.

overdraft ['əʊvədrɑːft] *n Fin (draft)* giro *m* en descubierto, sobregiro *m*; *(amount)* saldo *m* deudor.

overdraw [əʊvə'drɔː] *vtr (pt overdrew* [əʊvə'druː]*; pp overdrawn* [əʊvə'drɔːn]*) Fin* girar en descubierto; **to be overdrawn,** tener la cuenta en descubierto.

overdue [əʊvə'djuː] *adj (of rent, train, etc)* atrasado,-a; *(of reform)* largamente esperado,-a; *Com* vencido y sin pagar.

overeat [əʊvər'iːt] *vi (pt overate; pp overeaten* [əʊvər'iːtən]*)* comer en exceso.

overestimate [əʊvər'estɪmeɪt] **I** *vtr* sobreestimar. **II** [əʊvər'estɪmɪt] *n* sobreestimación *f*.

overexertion [əʊvərɪg'zɜːʃən] *n* esfuerzo *m* excesivo.

overexposure [əʊvərɪks'pəʊʒər] *n Phot* sobreexposición *f*.

overfeed [əʊvə'fiːd] *vtr (pt & pp overfed* [əʊvə'fed]*)* sobrealimentar.

overflew [əʊvə'fluː] *pt see* **overfly.**

overflow [əʊvə'fləʊ] **I** *vi (river)* desbordarse; *(cup etc)* derramarse; *fig* **to o. with joy,** rebosar de alegría. **II** ['əʊvəfləʊ] *n* **1** *(of river etc)* desbordamiento *m*; *(smaller)* derrame *m*. ■ **o. pipe,** cañería *f* de desagüe. **2** *fig* exceso *m*. ■ **o. meeting,** reunión *f* suplementaria; **population o.,** exceso *m* de población. **3** *Comput* sobrecarga *f*.

overfly [əʊvə'flaɪ] *vtr (pt overflew; pp overflown* [əʊvə'fləʊn]*)* sobrevolar.

overgrown ['əʊvəgrəʊn] *adj* **1** *(with grass etc)* cubierto,-a (de hierba). **2** *(in size)* demasiado grande.

overhang [əʊvə'hæŋ] **I** *vtr (pt & pp overhung) (project over)* sobresalir por encima de; *(hang over)* colgar por encima de. **II** *n* proyección *f*.

overhaul [əʊvə'hɔːl] **I** *vtr Mech* revisar. **II** ['əʊvəhɔːl] *n (gen)* revisión *f* y reparación *f*.

overhead ['əʊvəhed] **I** *adj* (por) encima de la cabeza; **o. cable,** cable aéreo. **II** [əʊvə'hed] *adv* arriba, por encima de la cabeza.

overheads ['əʊvəhedz] *npl Com* gastos *mpl* generales *or* indirectos.

overhear [əʊvə'hɪər] *vtr (pt & pp overheard* [əʊvə'hɜːd]*)* oír por casualidad *or* sin querer.

overheat [əʊvə'hiːt] *vi* recalentarse, calentarse demasiado.

overhung [əʊvə'hʌŋ] *pt & pp see* **overhang.**

overjoyed [əʊvə'dʒɔɪd] *adj* rebosante de alegría; **he was o.,** no cabía en sí de contento.

overland ['əʊvəlænd] *adj & adv* por tierra.

overlap [əʊvə'læp] **I** *vi (pt & pp overlapped)* superponerse; *fig* **our plans o.,** nuestros planes coinciden parcialmente. **II** *n* superposición *f*; *fig* coincidencia *f*.

overleaf [əʊvə'liːf] *adv* al dorso; **see o.,** véase al dorso.

overload [əʊvə'ləʊd] **I** *vtr* sobrecargar. **II** *n* sobrecarga *f*.

overlook [əʊvə'lʊk] *vtr* **1** *(fail to notice)* pasar por alto, dejar pasar; **to o. an error,** dejar pasar un error. **2** *(ignore)* no hacer caso de; **we'll o. it this time,** esta vez haremos la vista gorda. **3** *(have a view of)* dar a, tener vista a; **the house overlooks the park,** la casa da al parque. **4** *(supervise) (job)* supervisar; *(person)* vigilar.

overly ['əʊvəlɪ] *adv* demasiado; **I'm not o. impressed,** no estoy del todo convencido.

overnight [əʊvə'naɪt] **I** *adv* **1** *(during the night)* por la noche; **we stayed there o.,** pasamos la noche allí; **will this meat keep o.?,** ¿se conservará esta carne hasta mañana? **2** *(suddenly)* de la noche a la mañana. **II** ['əʊvənaɪt] *adj* **1** *(of one night)* de (una) noche; **o. bag,** bolsa de viaje; **o. journey,** viaje de noche; **o. stay,** estancia de una (sola) noche. **2** *(sudden)* repentino,-a; **to be an o. success,** saltar a la fama de la noche a la mañana.

overpaid [əʊvə'peɪd] *pt & pp see* **overpay.**

overpass ['əʊvəpæs] *n Aut* paso *m* elevado.

overpay [əʊvə'peɪ] *vtr (pt & pp overpaid)* pagar demasiado.

overpower [əʊvə'paʊər] *vtr* **1** *(subdue)* vencer, dominar. **2** *(affect strongly)* sofocar, abrumar, agobiar.

overproduce [əʊvəprə'djuːs] *vtr* producir en exceso.

overproduction [əʊvəprə'dʌkʃən] *n* superproducción *f*.

overran [əʊvə'ræn] *pt see* **overrun.**

overrate [əʊvə'reɪt] *vtr* sobreestimar, supervalorar; **an overrated restaurant,** un restaurante que no merece la buena fama que tiene.

overreach [əʊvə'riːtʃ] *vtr* **to o. oneself,** extralimitarse.

override [əʊvə'raɪd] *vtr (pt overrode; pp overridden* [əʊvə'rɪdən]*)* **1** *(disregard)* hacer caso omiso de, no tener en cuenta. **2** *(annul)* invalidar, anular. **3** *(be more important than)* contar más que.

overriding [əʊvə'raɪdɪŋ] *adj* principal, decisivo,-a; *(importance)* primordial; *(need)* imperioso,-a.

overrode [əʊvə'rəʊd] *pt see* **override.**

overrule [əʊvə'ruːl] *vtr* invalidar, descalificar; *Jur* denegar.

overrun [əʊvə'rʌn] **I** *vtr (pt overran; pp overrun)* **1** *(invade)* invadir; **a garden o. with weeds,** un jardín invadido por la mala hierba. **2** *(extend beyond)* exceder, rebasar. **II** *vi* rebasar el tiempo previsto.

oversaw [əʊvə'sɔː] *pt see* **oversee.**

overseas [əʊvə'siːz] **I** *adv* en ultramar; **to go o.,** ir al extranjero; **to live o.,** vivir en el extranjero. **II** ['əʊvəsiːz] *adj* de ultramar; *(of person)* extranjero,-a; *(of trade)* exterior; **our o. office,** nuestra sucursal en el extranjero.

oversee [əʊvə'siː] *vtr (pt oversaw; pp overseen* [əʊvə'siːn]*)* supervisar.

overseer [əʊvə'siːər] *n (gen)* supervisor,-a *m,f*; *(foreman)* capataz *m*.

overshadow [əʊvə'ʃædəʊ] *vtr fig* hacer sombra a, eclipsar.

overshoot [əʊvə'ʃuːt] *vtr (pt & pp overshot* [əʊvə'ʃɒt]*) Aut* **to o. a turning,** pasarse un cruce; *Av* **to o. the runway,** *(in the air)* aterrizar más allá de la pista; *(on land)* quedarse demasiado tiempo en la pista; *fig* **to o. the mark,** pasarse de la raya.

oversight ['əʊvəsaɪt] *n* descuido *m*; **through o.,** por descuido.

oversimplify [əʊvə'sɪmplɪfaɪ] *vtr (pt & pp oversimplified)* simplificar demasiado.

oversize(d) [əʊvə'saɪz(d)] *adj* demasiado grande.

oversleep [əʊvə'sliːp] *vi (pt & pp overslept* [əʊvə'slept]*)* dormirse, no despertar a tiempo.

overspend [əʊvə'spend] *vi (pt & pp overspent* [əʊvə'slept]*)* gastar demasiado *or* más de la cuenta.

overspill ['əʊvəspɪl] *n (population)* exceso *m* de población.

overstate [əʊvə'steɪt] *vtr* exagerar.

overstep [əʊvə'step] *vtr (pt & pp overstepped)* pasar de; *fig* **to o. the mark,** pasarse de la raya.

overt ['əʊvɜːt, əʊ'vɜːt] *adj* **1** *(observable)* manifiesto,-a, patente. **2** *Jur (deliberate)* abierto,-a. ◆ **overtly** *adv* abiertamente.

overtake [əʊvə'teɪk] *vtr (pt overtook; pp overtaken)* **1** *GB Aut* adelantar, *SAm* rebasar. **2** *(pass)* adelantarse a; *(surpass)* superar a. **3** *(catch unawares)* sorprender. **4** *(catch up with)* alcanzar.

overtax [əʊvə'tæks] *vtr* **1** *Fin* gravar en exceso. **2** *fig* exigir demasiado a.

over-the-counter [əʊvəðə'kaʊntər] *adj Pharm* **o.-t.-c. drugs,** medicamentos que se pueden adquirir sin receta médica.

overthrow [əʊvə'θrəʊ] *vtr (pt overthrew* [əʊvə'θruː]*; pp overthrown* [əʊvə'θrəʊn]*) (government etc)* derribar, derrocar; *(project)* enervar, destruir.

overtime ['əʊvətaɪm] **I** *n* **1** horas *fpl* extras. **2** *US Sport* prórroga *f*. **II** *adv* **to work o.,** hacer horas extras.

overtone ['əʊvətəʊn] *n* insinuación *f*, alusión *f*.

overtook [əʊvə'tʊk] *pt see* **overtake.**

overture ['əʊvətjʊə'] *n* **1** *Mus* obertura *f*. **2** *(proposal)* propuesta *f*; **peace overtures,** propuestas de paz. **3** *(introduction)* introducción *f*.

overturn [əʊvə'tɜːn] **I** *vtr (car etc)* volcar; *(boat)* hacer zozobrar. **II** *vi (of car etc)* volcar; *(of boat)* zozobrar.

overweight [əʊvə'weɪt] *adj* demasiado pesado,-a; **he's five pounds o.,** pesa cinco libras de más; **to be o.,** *(gen)* pesar demasiado; *(person)* estar gordo,-a.

overwhelm [əʊvə'welm] *vtr* **1** *(overcome)* aplastar, arrollar; *(overpower)* abrumar; **to be overwhelmed with joy,** rebosar de alegría; **we were overwhelmed by the news,** nos quedamos de piedra al saber la noticia. **2** *(cover over)* inundar, sumergir.

overwhelming [əʊvə'welmɪŋ] *adj (defeat)* aplastante, arrollador,-a; *(desire etc)* irresistible; **o. majority,** mayoría aplastante.

overwork [əʊvə'wɜːk] **I** *vi* trabajar demasiado. **II** *vtr (person)* forzar, hacer trabajar demasiado; *(excuse etc)* abusar de.

overworked [əʊvə'wɜːkt] *adj* forzado,-a; **an o. expression,** una expresión muy gastada.

overwrought [əʊvə'rɔːt] *adj* **1** *(tense)* muy nervioso,-a, con los nervios crispados. **2** *(too elaborate)* forzado,-a.

ovulate ['ɒvjʊleɪt] *vi* ovular.

ovulation [ɒvjʊ'leɪʃən] *n* ovulación *f*.

ovum ['əʊvəm] *n (pl ova) Biol* óvulo *m*.

owe [əʊ] *vtr* deber; **I o. my life to you,** te debo la vida; **I still o. you for the petrol,** aún te debo lo de la gasolina; **she owes her fortune to hard work,** se ha hecho rica a base de trabajar duro.

owing ['əʊɪŋ] *adj* **1** *(due)* **the money o. to me,** el dinero que se me debe. **2 o. to,** debido a, a causa de; **o. to the rain,** a causa de la lluvia.

owl [aʊl] *n* **1** *Orn* lechuza *f*, búho *m*. ■ **barn o.,** lechuza *f* común; **eagle o.,** búho *m* real; **little o.,** mochuelo *m* común. **2** *fig* **night o.,** ave *f* nocturna.

owlet ['aʊlɪt] *n Orn* mochuelo *m*.

own [əʊn] **I** *adj* propio,-a; **his o. money,** su propio dinero; **in my o. time,** en mi tiempo libre; **it's his o. fault,** es culpa suya; **she makes all her o. clothes,** se hace toda la ropa ella misma. **II** *pron* **1** **my o., your o., his o., etc,** lo mío, lo tuyo, lo suyo, etc; **for reasons of her o.,** por razones personales; **he has a copy of his o.,** tiene su propio ejemplar; **the house is my o.,** la casa es mía; **this fruit has a flavour all its o.,** esta fruta tiene un sabor inconfundible; *fig* **he can hold his o.,** se defiende, sabe, defenderse; *fig* **to come into one's o.,** *(fulfil oneself)* realizarse; *(receive recognition)* ser reconocido,-a; *fam* **to get one's o. back,** vengarse, tomarse la revancha. **2 on one's o.,** *(without help)* uno,-a mismo,-a; *(alone)* solo,-a; **he did it on his o.,** lo hizo él mismo; **I was left on my o.,** me dejaron solo. **III** *vtr* poseer, ser dueño,-a de; **he owns three newspapers,** es propietario de tres periódicos; **who owns this plot of land?,** ¿a quién pertenece esta parcela? ◆ **own up** *vtr* **to o. up (to),** confesar, admitir; **to o. up to a mistake,** reconocer un error.

owner ['əʊnər] *n* propietario,-a *m*, *f*, dueño,-a *m*, *f*, poseedor,-a *m*, *f*; **'cars parked here at owners' risk',** 'la empresa no se hace responsable de los vehículos aparcados aquí'. ■ **joint o.,** copropietario,-a *m*, *f*.

ownership ['əʊnəʃɪp] *n* propiedad *f*, posesión *f*; **under new o.,** bajo nueva dirección.

ox [ɒks] *n (pl oxen)* buey *m*.

oxcart ['ɒkskɑːt] *n* carro *m* de bueyes.

oxen ['ɒksən] *npl see* **ox.**

Oxfam ['ɒksfæm] *abbr* **Oxford Committee for Famine Relief.**

oxide ['ɒksaɪd] *n Chem* óxido *m*.

oxidize ['ɒksɪdaɪz] **1** *vtr* oxidar. **II** *vi* oxidarse.

Oxon ['ɒksən] *abbr of* **Oxoniensis** *(of Oxford University),* de (la Universidad de) Oxford.

oxtail ['ɒksteɪl] *n* rabo *m* de buey.

oxyacetylene [ɒksɪə'setɪliːn] *n Chem* oxiacetileno *m*. ■ **o. torch,** soplete *m* oxiacetilénico; **o. welding,** soldadura *f* oxiacetilénica.

oxygen ['ɒksɪdʒən] *n Chem* oxígeno *m*. ■ **o. mask,** máscara *f* de oxígeno.

oyster ['ɔɪstər] *n (fish)* ostra *f*; **the o. industry,** la industria ostrícola. ■ **o. bed o. farm,** criadero *m* de ostras; *(colour)* **o. pink,** rosa *m* salmón.

oystercatcher ['ɔɪstəkætʃər] *n Orn* ostrero *m*.

oz *(pl oz or ozs) abbr of* **ounce(s),** onza(s) *f(pl)*, oz *f*.

ozone ['əʊzəʊn] *n Chem* ozono *m*. ■ **o. layer,** capa *f* del ozono.

P

P, p [piː] *n (the letter)* P, p *f*; *fam* **to mind one's p's and q's,** andar con cuidado.

P *Aut abbr of* **Parking,** aparcamiento *m*, P.

P 1 *(pl pp) abbr of* **page,** página *f*, pág.. p. **2** [piː] *GB fam abbr of* **penny, pence,** penique(s) *m(pl)*.

PA [piːˈeɪ] **1** *fam abbr of* **personal assistant,** ayudante *mf* personal. **2** *abbr of* **Press Association,** asociación *f* nacional de prensa. **3** *abbr of* **public-address (system),** megafonía *f*, sistema *m* de altavoces.

pa *abbr of* **per annum** (per year), al año.

pace [peɪs] **I** *n (step)* paso *m*; *(speed)* marcha *f*, velocidad *f*, ritmo *m*; **at a brisk p.,** a buen paso; **20 paces away,** a 20 pasos; **to keep p. with,** seguir a; *fig* avanzar al mismo ritmo que; **to quicken one's p.,** acelerar el paso; **to set the p.,** marcar el paso a; *fig* marcar la pauta. **II** *vtr* **1** *(room, floor)* ir de un lado a otro de. **2** *(runner)* marcar el paso a. **III** *vi* **to p. up and down,** ir de un lado a otro.

pacemaker [ˈpeɪsmeɪkə^r] *n* **1** *Sport* liebre *f*. **2** *Med* marcapasos *m inv*.

Pacific [pəˈsɪfɪk] *adj* **the P. (Ocean),** el (océano) Pacífico.

pacifier [ˈpæsɪfaɪə^r] *n US* chupete *m*.

pacifism [ˈpæsɪfɪzəm] *n* pacifismo *m*.

pacifist [ˈpæsɪfɪst] *adj & n* pacifista *(mf)*.

pacify [ˈpæsɪfaɪ] *vtr (pt & pp pacified) (person)* calmar, tranquilizar; *(country)* pacificar.

pack¹ [pæk] **I** *n* **1** *(parcel)* paquete *m*; *(bundle)* bulto *m*; *(rucksack)* mochila *f*; *(on animal)* albarda *f*, *fam* **to tell a p. of lies,** contar una sarta de mentiras. ■ **p. ice,** banco *m* de hielo. **2** *US (of cigarettes)* paquete *m*, cajetilla *f*. **3** *GB (of cards)* baraja *f*. **4** *(of thieves)* banda *f*; *(of wolves, dogs)* manada *f*; *(of hounds)* jauría *f*. **5** *Med* emplasto *m*, compresa *f*; **face (or mud) p.,** mascarilla *f* (de lodo). **II** *vtr* **1** *(goods)* embalar, envasar, empaquetar; **packed lunch,** comida *f* fría para llevar. **2** *(things in suitcase)* poner; **to p. one's bags,** hacer las maletas; *fig* marcharse. **3** *(fill)* atestar, llenar; *(people)* meter; **the room was packed,** la sala estaba abarrotada; *fig* **to be packed in like sardines,** estar apretados como sardinas. **4** *(press down) (snow, soil)* apretar. **5** *fam Box* **to p. a hard punch,** pegar duro; *fig* jugar fuerte. **III** *vi* **1** *(prepare baggage)* hacer las maletas *or* el equipaje; *fam* **to send sb packing,** mandar a paseo a algn. **2** *(people)* apiñarse, apretarse **(into,** en). ♦ **pack in** *vtr fam* **1** *(give up)* dejar; **p. it in!,** ¡déjalo ya! **2** *(pull in)* atraer; **the show is really packing them in,** este espectáculo atrae a muchísimas personas. ♦ **pack off** *vtr fam* enviar, mandar; **to p. a child off to bed,** mandar a un niño a la cama. ♦ **pack up I** *vtr* **1** *(belongings)* meter en la maleta. **2** *(give up)* dejar; **she packed up smoking,** ha dejado de fumar, ya no fuma. **II** *vi fam* **1** *(stop working)* terminar. **2** *(machine etc)* estropearse, pararse.

pack² [pæk] *vtr (meeting, jury)* amañar, llenar de partidarios.

package [ˈpækɪdʒ] **I** *n* **1** *(parcel)* paquete *m*; *(bundle)* bulto *m*. ■ *fig* **p. holiday, p. tour,** viaje *m* organizado todo incluido. **2** *(of proposals etc)* paquete *m*; *(agreement)* acuerdo *m*, convenio *m*. ■ **p. deal,** convenio *m* general. **II** *vtr (goods)* envasar, embalar.

packaging [ˈpækɪdʒɪŋ] *n* envase *m*, embalaje *m*.

packer [ˈpækə^r] *n* empaquetador,-a *m,f*, embalador,-a *m,f*.

packet [ˈpækɪt] *n* **1** *(box)* cajita *f*, paquete *m*; *(of cigarettes)* cajetilla *f*; *(bag)* bolsa *f*; *(envelope)* sobre *m*. **2** *fam (fortune)* dineral *m*; **to cost a p.,** costar un riñón *or* un ojo de la cara; **to make a p.,** ganar una fortuna.

packhorse [ˈpækhɔːs] *n* caballo *m* de carga.

packing [ˈpækɪŋ] *n* envase *m*, embalaje *m*; **p. case,** caja *f* de embalar; **to do one's p.,** hacer las maletas.

pact [pækt] *n* pacto *m*; **to make a p. with sb,** pactar con algn.

pad¹ [pæd] **I** *n* **1** *(gen)* almohadilla *f*, cojinete *m*; *(of brake)* zapata *f*; *(filling)* relleno *m*. ■ **knee p.,** rodillera *f*; **sanitary p.,** compresa *f*; **shin p.,** espinillera *f*; **shoulder p.,** hombrera *f*. **2** *(of paper)* bloc *m*, taco *m*. ■ **blotting p.,** papel *m* secante; **writing p.,** bloc *m* de cartas. **3** *(platform)* plataforma *f*. ■ **launch p.,** plataforma *f* de lanzamiento. **4** *Zool Anat* almohadilla *f*. **5** *Bot (large leaf)* hoja *f* grande. **6** *fam* casa *f*, piso *m*; **bachelor p.,** piso de soltero. **II** *vtr (pt & pp padded) (chair, wall)* rellenar, acolchar; *(shoulders of garment)* poner hombreras a. ♦ **pad out** *vtr fig (speech etc)* meter paja en.

pad² [pæd] *vi (pt & pp padded)* **to p. about** *or* **around,** andar sin hacer ruido.

padded [ˈpædɪd] *adj (shoulders of garment)* con hombreras; *(cell)* acolchado,-a.

padding [ˈpædɪŋ] *n* **1** *(material)* relleno *m*, acolchado *m*. **2** *fig (in speech etc)* paja *f*.

paddle¹ [ˈpædəl] **I** *n (oar)* pala *f*, remo *m*, canalete *m*; *Tech (blade on wheel)* alabe *m*, paleta *f*; *(flat tool)* pala *f*. ■ **p. boat** *or* **steamer,** vapor *m* de ruedas. **II** *vtr (boat, canoe)* remar con pala *or* canalete en; *fig* **to p. one's own canoe,** arreglárselas solo,-a. **III** *vi (in boat)* remar con pala *or* canalete.

paddle² [ˈpædəl] **I** *vi* chapotear, mojarse los pies. **II** *n* chapoteo *m*; **to go for** *or* **have a p.,** chapotear, mojarse los pies.

paddling pool [ˈpædəlɪŋpuːl] *n* piscina *f* para niños.

paddock [ˈpædək] *n (field)* potrero *m*; *(in race course)* paddock *m*.

paddy [ˈpædɪ] *n* arrozal *m*.

padlock [ˈpædlɒk] **I** *n* candado *m*. **II** *vtr* cerrar con candado.

padre [ˈpɑːdrɪ] *n Mil Naut fam* capellán *m*.

paediatric [piːdɪˈætrɪk] *adj* pediátrico,-a.

paediatrician [piːdɪəˈtrɪʃən] *n* pediatra *mf*.

paediatrics [piːdɪˈætrɪks] *n* pediatría *f*.

pagan [ˈpeɪɡən] *adj & n* pagano,-a *(m,f)*.

page¹ [peɪdʒ] **I** *n* **1** *(servant, at wedding)* paje *m*; *(of knight)* escudero *m*. **2** *(at club)* botones *m inv*. **II** *vtr (call)* llamar por altavoz.

page² [peɪdʒ] *n (of book)* página *f*; *(of newspaper)* plana *f*; **front p. news,** noticias *fpl* de primera plana; **on p. six,** en la página seis.

pageant [ˈpædʒənt] *n (show)* espectáculo *m*; *(procession)* desfile *m*; *(on horses)* cabalgata *f*.

pageantry [ˈpædʒəntrɪ] *n* pompa *f*, boato *m*.

pageboy [ˈpeɪdʒbɔɪ] *n* **I** *(servant, at wedding)* paje *m*; *Hairdr* **p. hairstyle,** peinado *m* estilo paje. **2** *(in hotel)* botones *m inv*.

pagoda [pəˈɡəʊdə] *n* pagoda *f*.

paid [peɪd] **I** *pt & pp see* **pay. II** *adj* pagado,-a; *fig* **to put p. to sth,** acabar con algo.

paid-up [peɪdˈʌp] *adj*, *US* **paid-in** [peɪdˈɪn] *adj (member)* que ha pagado las cuotas.

pail [peɪl] *n (gen)* cubo *m*; *(child's)* cubito *m*.

pain [peɪn] *n* **1** *(gen) (grief)* sufrimiento *m*; **a severe p.,** un dolor agudo; **aches and pains,** achaques *mpl*; **I have a p. in my chest,** me duele el pecho; **to be in great p.,** sufrir mucho; **where is the p.?,** ¿dónde te duele?; *fam* **he's a p. (in the neck),** es un pesado *or* un pelmazo. **2** *(punishment)* pena *f*; **on p. of death,** so pena de muerte. **3** pains, esfuerzos *mpl*, esmero *m sing*; **to take p. over sth,** esforzarse *or* esmerarse en algo. **II** *vtr (gen)* doler; *(grieve)* dar pena a, apenar; **it pains me to see her like this,** me da pena verla así.

pained [peɪnd] *adj* afligido,-a, disgustado,-a ofendido,-a

painful ['peɪnfʊl] *adj* **1** *(physically)* doloroso,-a dolorido,-a; *(mentally)* angustioso,-a; **it's my p. duty to tell you,** es mi doloroso deber decírselo; **it's p. to watch them,** da pena verles. **2** *fam (very bad)* malísimo,-a, pésimo,-a. ◆ **painfully** *adv* **1** *(with pain)* dolorosamente, con dolor; **p. shy,** lastimosamente tímido,-a. **2** *fam* lamentablemente, terriblemente.

painkiller ['peɪnkɪlə'] *n* analgésico *m*, calmante *m*.

painless ['peɪnlɪs] *adj (childbirth)* indoloro,-a, sin dolor; *fig* sin esfuerzos *or* dificultades. ◆ **painlessly** *adv* sin causar dolor; *fig* sin hacer esfuerzos.

painstaking ['peɪnzteɪkɪŋ] *adj (person)* cuidadoso,-a, concienzudo,-a; *(care, research)* esmerado,-a.

paint [peɪnt] **I** *n* pintura *f*; **coat of p.,** capa *f* de pintura; **'wet paint',** 'recién pintado'. ■ **p. remover,** quitapinturas *m inv*; **p. spray,** pistola *f* (de pintar). **II** *vtr* pintar; **to p. one's face,** pintarse la cara; **to p. sth white,** pintar algo de blanco; *fig* **he isn't as black as he is painted,** no es tan fiero el león como lo pintan; *fig* **to p. the town red,** irse de juerga. **III** *vi* pintar, ser pintor,-a.

paintbox ['peɪntbɒks] *n* caja *f* de pinturas.

paintbrush ['peɪntbrʌʃ] *n Art* pincel *m*; *(for walls)* brocha *f*.

painter¹ ['peɪntə'] *n Art* pintor,-a *m,f*; *(decorator)* pintor,-a *m,f* (de brocha gorda).

painter² ['peɪntə'] *n Naut* amarra *f*.

painting ['peɪntɪŋ] *n Art (picture)* pintura *f*, cuadro *m*; *(activity)* pintura *f*; **oil p.,** pintura al óleo; **p. and decorating,** (pintura y) decoración *f* del hogar; **she likes p.,** le gusta pintar.

paint stripper ['peɪntstrɪpə'] *n* quitapinturas *f inv*

paintwork ['peɪntwɜːk] *n* pintura *f*.

pair [peə'] **I** *n (of gloves, socks, shoes)* par *m*; *(of people, cards)* pareja *f*; **a p. of scissors,** unas tijeras; **a p. of pyjamas,** un pijama; **a p. of trousers,** un pantalón, unos pantalones; **to make a p.,** hacer juego *or* pareja. **II** *vtr (animals)* aparear; *(people)* emparejar. **III** *vi (animals)* aparearse; *(people)* emparejarse, formar pareja. ◆ **pair off I** *vtr* emparejar. **II** *vi* emparejarse, formar pareja (**with,** con).

pajamas [pə'dʒæməz] *npl US see* **pyjamas.**

Pakistan [paːkɪ'staːn] *n* Paquistán, Pakistán.

Pakistani [paːkɪ'staːnɪ] *adj & n* paquistaní *(mf)*, pakistaní *(mf)*.

pal [pæl] *n fam* amigo,-a *m,f*, colega *mf*.

palace ['pælɪs] *n* palacio *m*.

palatable ['pælətəbəl] *adj (tasty)* sabroso,-a; *fig (acceptable)* aceptable.

palatal ['pælətəl] *adj & n* palatal *(f)*.

palate ['pælɪt] *n* paladar *m*.

palatial [pə'leɪʃəl] *adj* magnífico,-a, suntuoso,-a.

palaver [pə'laːvə'] *n fam* lío *m*, follón *m*; **what a p.!,** ¡qué follón!

pale¹ [peɪl] **I** *adj (complexion, skin)* pálido,-a; *(colour)* claro,-a; *(light)* débil, tenue; **to go** *or* **turn p.,** ponerse pálido,-a, palidecer. ■ **p. ale,** cerveza *f* rubia. **IV** *vi* palidecer.

pale² [peɪl] *n* estaca *f*; *fig* **to be beyond the p.,** ser inaceptable.

paleness ['peɪlnɪs] *n* palidez *f*.

Palestine ['pælɪstaɪn] *n* Palestina.

Palestinian [pælɪ'stɪnɪən] *adj & n* palestino,-a *(m,f)*.

palette ['pælɪt] *n* paleta *f*. ■ **p. knife,** espátula *f*.

paling ['peɪlɪŋ] *n* estacada *f*, valla *f*.

palisade [pælɪ'seɪd] *n* **1** *(fence)* palizada *f*, estacada *f*. **2** *US* **palisades,** *(cliffs)* acantilado *m sing*.

pall¹ [pɔːl] *n (on coffin)* paño *m* mortuorio; *fig (covering)* manto *m*; *(of smoke)* cortina *f*.

pall² [pɔːl] *vi* dejar de gustar, cansar, aburrir; **it never palls,** nunca cansa.

pallbearer ['pɔːlbeərə'] *n* portador,-a *m,f* del féretro.

pallet ['pælɪt] *n* **1** *Tech* plataforma *f* de carga. **2** *(bed)* jergón *m*.

palliative ['pælɪətɪv] *n* paliativo *m*.

pallid ['pælɪd] *adj* pálido,-a.

pallor ['pælə'] *n* palidez *f*.

pally ['pælɪ] *adj (pallier, palliest)* amigo,-a; **to be p. with sb,** ser amigo,-a de algn; **we're very p.,** somos muy amigos.

palm¹ [paːm] *n Bot (tree)* palmera *f*; *(leaf, branch)* palma *f*. ■ **coconut p.,** cocotero *m*; **date p.,** palma *f* datilera; **P. Sunday,** domingo *m* de Ramos.

palm² [paːm] *n Anat* palma *f*; **to read sb's p.,** leer la mano a algn; *fig* **to have sb in the p. of one's hand,** tener a algn en la palma de la mano; *fam* **to grease sb's p.,** untar la mano a algn. ◆ **palm off** *vtr* **to p. sth off onto sb,** colocar *or* endosar algo a algn.

palmist ['paːmɪst] *n* quiromántico,-a *m,f*.

palmistry ['paːmɪstrɪ] *n* quiromancia *f*.

palpable ['pælpəbəl] *adj* palpable.

palpate ['pælpeɪt] *vtr Med* palpar.

palpitate ['pælpɪteɪt] *vi* palpitar.

palpitation [pælpɪ'teɪʃən] *n* palpitación *f*.

paltry ['pɔːltrɪ] *adj (paltrier, paltriest)* insignificante.

pampas ['pæmpəz] *npl Geog* pampa *f sing*.

pamper ['pæmpə'] *vtr* mimar, consentir.

pamphlet ['pæmflɪt] *n* folleto *m*.

pan¹ [pæn] **I** *n* **1** *(saucepan)* cazuela *f*, cacerola *f*; *fam* **pots and pans,** batería *f sing* (de cocina). ■ **frying p.,** sartén *f*. **2** *(of scales)* platillo *m*. **3** *(of lavatory)* taza *f*. **II** *vtr (pt & pp panned)* **1** *(gold)* lavar con batea. **2** *fam (critize)* dejar por los suelos. **III** *vi* extraer oro. ◆ **pan out** *vi (turn out)* salir; *(be successful)* salir bien.

pan² [pæn] *vtr & vi (pt & pp panned) Cin* tomar vistas panorámicas.

pan- [pæn] *pref* pan; **pan-American,** panamericano,-a.

panacea [pænə'sɪə] *n* panacea *f*.

panache [pə'næʃ] *n* garbo *m*, salero *m*.

Panama ['pænəmaː] *n* Panamá; **P. Canal,** Canal *m* de Panamá.

panama ['pænəmaː] *n* **p. (hat),** panamá *m*.

Panamanian [pænə'meɪnɪən] *adj & n* panameño,-a *(m,f)*.

pancake ['pænkeɪk] *n Culin* crepe *f*. ■ **P. Day,** martes *m* de carnaval; *Av* **p. landing,** aterrizaje *m* de emergencia.

panchromatic [pænkrəʊ'mætɪk] *adj* pancromático,-a.

pancreas ['pæŋkrɪəs] *n Anat* páncreas *m*.

panda ['pændə] *n Zool* panda *m*. ■ *GB* **p. car,** coche *m* patrulla.

pandemonium [pændɪ'məʊnɪəm] *n* jaleo *m*, desmadre *m*; **there was p.,** había mucho jaleo.

pander ['pændə'] *vi (person)* consentir (**to,** a), complacer (**to,** a); *(wishes)* acceder (**to,** a).

pandora [pæn'dɔːrə] *n (fish)* pagel *m*.

p and p, p & p [piːən'piː] *GB Com abbr* **of (cost of) postage and packing,** gastos *mpl* de embalaje y envío.

pane [peɪn] *n* cristal *m*, vidrio *m*.

panel ['pænəl] *n* **1** *(of wall, door)* panel *m*; *(flat surface)* tablero *m*, tabla *f*; *(of control, instruments)* tablero *m*; *(of ceiling)* artesón *m*. ■ *Aut* **p. beater,** planchista *mf*; **p. pin,**

clavo *m or* alfiler *m* de espiga. **2** *(team)* equipo *m*; *(jury)* jurado *m*; *Rad TV(contestants)* concursantes *mpl*; **p. game,** concurso *m* por equipos.

panelled, *US* **paneled** ['pænəld] *adj (door, wall)* con paneles; *(ceiling)* artesonado,-a.

panelling, *US* **paneling** ['pænəlɪŋ] *n (of door, wall)* paneles *mpl*; *(of ceiling)* artesonado *m*.

panellist, *US* **panelist** ['pænəlɪst] *n (judge)* miembro *mf* del jurado; *Rad TV (contestant)* concursante *mf*.

pang [pæŋ] *n (of pain, hunger)* punzada *f*; *(of childbirth)* dolores *mpl*; *fig (of conscience)* remordimiento *m*.

panic ['pænɪk] **I** *n* pánico *m*, miedo *m*; **the crowd was thrown into a p.,** el pánico cundió entre la gente; **to get into a p.,** dejarse llevar por el pánico *or* el miedo; *fig* **to push the p. button,** dejarse llevar por el pánico; **it was p. stations,** cundió el pánico. **II** *vi (pt & pp panicked)* aterrarse, entrar el pánico; **I panicked,** me entró el pánico. **III** *vtr* aterrar, infundir pánico a.

panicky ['pænɪkɪ] *adj* asustadizo,-a; **to get p.,** dejarse llevar por el pánico *or* el miedo.

panic-stricken ['pænɪkstrɪkən] *adj* preso,-a de pánico, aterrado,-a.

pannier ['pænɪəʳ] *n (for animal)* alforja *f*; *(for bicycle)* bolsa *f*.

panorama [pænə'rɑːmə] *n (view)* panorama *m*; *Cin Phot* panorámica *f*.

panoramic [pænə'ræmɪk] *adj* panorámico,-a.

panpipes ['pænpaɪps] *npl Mus* siringa *f sing*.

pansy ['pænzɪ] *n* **1** Bot pensamiento *m*. **2** *fam (effeminate man)* mariquita *m*.

pant [pænt] **I** *n* jadeo *m*, resoplido *m*. **II** *vi* jadear, resoplar; **to p.** for breath, intentar recobrar el aliento.

pantechnicon [pæn'teknɪkən] *n* camión *m* de mudanzas.

pantheon ['pænθɪɒn] *n Archit* panteón *m*.

panther ['pænθəʳ] *n Zool* pantera *f*.

panties ['pæntɪz] *npl* bragas *fpl*, braguitas *fpl*; **a pair of p.,** unas braguitas.

pantomime ['pæntəmaɪm] *n Theat (play)* función *f* musical navideña; *(mime)* pantomima *f*.

pantry ['pæntrɪ] *n* despensa *f*.

pants [pænts] *npl (underpants) (ladies')* bragas *fpl*; *(men's)* calzoncillos *mpl*; *US (trousers)* pantalones *mpl*, pantalón *m sing*; **a pair of p.,** *(men's)* unos calzoncillos; *US* unos pantalones; *(ladies')* unas bragas.

pantyhose ['pæntɪhəʊz] *npl (tights)* medias *fpl* panties; *(woollen)* leotardos *mpl*.

papa [pə'pɑː] *n* papá *m*.

papacy ['peɪpəsɪ] *n* papado *m*, pontificado *m*.

papal ['peɪpəl] *adj* papal ponificio,-a.

papaya [pə'paɪə] *n (tree)* papayo *m*; *(fruit)* papaya *f*.

paper ['peɪpəʳ] **I** *n* **I** *(material)* papel *m*; **a piece/sheet of p.,** un trozo/una hoja de papel; **to put sth down on p.,** poner algo por escrito; *fig* **it isn't worth the p. it's written on,** es papel mojado; *fig* **on p.,** en teoría, sobre el papel. ■ **brown p.,** papel *m* de estraza; **cigarette p.,** papel *m* de fumar; **p. mill,** fábrica *f* de papel; **p. money,** papel *m* moneda; **toilet p.,** papel *m* higiénico; **wrapping p.,** papel *m* de envolver; **writing p.,** papel *m* de escribir. **2** *Educ Univ (examination)* examen *m*; *(test)* prueba *f*; *(essay)* trabajo *m* (escrito); **to write a p. on a subject,** hacer un trabajo sobre un tema. ■ **question p.,** cuestionario *m*; **written p.,** examen *m* escrito. **3** *Pol* libro *m*; **white p.,** libro blanco. **4** *(newspaper)* periódico *m*, diario *m*; **to write for a p.,** hacer de *or* ser periodista; **the papers,** los periódicos, la prensa. ■ **p. round,** reparto *m* de periódicos; **p. shop,** tienda *f* de periódicos; **weekly p.,** semanario *m*. **5 papers,** *(documents)* papeles *mpl*, documentos *mpl*. ■ *Mil* **call-up p.,** llamamiento *m sing* a filas; **identity p.,** documentación *f sing*. **II** *vtr (wall, room)* empapelar.

paperback ['peɪpəbæk] *n* libro *m* en rústica.

paperboy ['peɪpəbɔɪ] *n* repartidor *m* de periódicos.

paperclip ['peɪpəklɪp] *n* clip *m*, sujetapapeles *m inv*.

papergirl ['peɪpəgɜːl] *n* repartidora *f* de periódicos.

paperknife ['peɪpənaɪf] *n* cortapapeles *m inv*.

paperweight ['peɪpəweɪt] *n* pisapapeles *m inv*.

paperwork ['peɪpəwɜːk] *n* papeleo *m*.

papery ['peɪpərɪ] *adj* parecido,-a al papel.

papier-mâché [pæpjeɪ'mæʃeɪ] *n* cartón *m* piedra.

papist ['peɪpɪst] *adj & n* papista *(mf)*.

paprika ['pæprɪkə] *n* pimentón *m* molido, paprika *f*.

Papua ['pæpjʊə] *n* Papúa. ■ **P. New Guinea,** Papúa Nueva Guinea.

Papuan ['pæpjʊən] *adj & n* papú,-a *(m,f)*.

par [pɑːʳ] *n (parity)* igualdad *f*; *Fin* par *f*; *Golf* par *m*; *Golf* **three under p.,** tres bajo par; *fig* **it's p. for the course,** es lo normal en estos casos; *fig* **to be on a p. with sb,** estar en igualdad de condiciones con algn; *fig* **to feel under** *or* **below p.,** sentirse mal, estar en baja forma.

para ['pærə] *abbr of* **paragraph,** párrafo *m*, párr.

parable ['pærəbəl] *n* parábola *f*.

parabolic [pærə'bɒlɪk] *adj* parabólico,-a.

parachute ['pærəʃuːt] **I** *n* paracaídas *m inv*. ■ **p. jump,** salto *m* en paracaídas. **II** *vtr (person, provisions, etc)* lanzar en paracaídas. **III** *vi* **to p. (down),** saltar *or* lanzarse en paracaídas.

parachutist ['pærəʃuːtɪst] *n* paracaidista *mf*.

parade [pə'reɪd] **I** *n* **1** *(procession)* desfile *m*; **carnival/ fashion p.,** desfile de carrozas/de modelos; *Mil* **to be on p.,** pasar revista. ■ **shopping p.,** área *f* comercial; **p. ground,** plaza *f* de armas. **2** *fig (display)* alarde *m*; **to make a p. of sth,** hacer alarde de algo. **II** *vtr* **I** *Mil* hacer desfilar. **2** *fig (flaunt) (knowledge, wealth)* alardear de, hacer alarde de. **III** *vi (troops)* pasar revista; *(demonstrators, procession)* desfilar. ◆ **parade about, parade around** *vi (show off)* pavonearse.

paradigm ['pærədaɪm] *n* paradigma *m*.

paradigmatic [pærədɪg'mætɪk] *adj* paradigmático,-a.

paradise ['pærədaɪs] *n* paraíso *m*; *fig* **it's sheer p.,** es un paraíso terrenal.

paradox ['pærədɒks] *n* paradoja *f*.

paradoxical [pærə'dɒksɪkəl] *adj* paradójico,-a.

paraffin ['pærəfɪn] *n* parafina *f*. ■ **liquid p.,** aceite *m* de parafina; **p. heater,** estufa *f* de parafina; **p. lamp,** lámpara *f* de petróleo, quinqué *m*; **p. wax,** parafina *f*.

paragon ['pærəgən] *n* modelo *m*, dechado *m*.

paragraph ['pærəgrɑːf] *n* párrafo *m*; **new p.,** punto y aparte.

Paraguay ['pærəgwaɪ] *n* Paraguay.

Paraguayan [pærə'gwaɪən] *adj & n* paraguayo,-a *(m,f)*.

parakeet ['pærəkiːt] *n Orn* periquito *m*, perico *m*.

parallel ['pærəlel] **I** *adj* paralelo,-a **(to, with,** con); *fig* comparable, análogo,-a **(to, with,** a); **to be/ run p. with sth,** ser/correr paralelo,-a a algo. ■ *Sport* **p. bars,** (barras *fpl*) paralelas *fpl*. **II** *n Geog* paralelo *m*; *Geom* paralela *f*; *fig* paralelo *m*; *fig* **to draw a p. between two things,** establecer un paralelo entre dos cosas; **without p.,** sin comparación. **III** *vtr fig* ser paralelo,-a a, correr paralelo,-a a.

parallelogram [pærə'leləgræm] *n Geom* paralelogramo *m*.

paralysis [pə'rælɪsɪs] *n (pl paralyses* [pə'rælɪsiːz]*) Med* parálisis *f*; *fig* paralización *f*.

paralytic [pærə'lɪtɪk] **I** *adj Med* paralítico,-a; *fam* **to be p.,** estar como una cuba. **II** *n* paralítico,-a *m,f*.

paralyse, *US* **paralyze** ['pærəlaɪz] *vtr* paralizar; **the strike paralysed the railway system,** la huelga paralizó la red ferroviaria; **to be paralysed in both legs,** estar paralizado,-a de ambas piernas; *fig* **to be paralysed with fear,** quedarse paralizado de miedo.

parameter [pə'ræmɪtəʳ] *n* parámetro *m*.
paramilitary [pærə'mɪlɪtərɪ] *adj* paramilitar.
paramount ['pærəmaunt] *adj* supremo,-a; **of p. importance,** de suma importancia.
paranoia [pærə'nɔɪə] *n Med* paranoia *f*.
paranoiac [pærə'nɔɪɪk] *adj & n*, **paranoid** ['pærənɔɪd] *adj & n* paranoico,-a (*m*,*f*).
paranormal [pærə'nɔːməl] *adj* paranormal.
parapet ['pærəpɪt] *n* parapeto *m*.
paraphernalia [pærəfə'neɪlɪə] *n* parafernalia *f*.
paraphrase ['pærəfreɪz] **I** *n* paráfrasis *f inv*. **II** *vtr* parafrasear.
paraplegia [pærə'pliːdʒə] *n Med* paraplejía *f*.
paraplegic [pærə'pliːdʒɪk] *adj & n Med* parapléjico,-a (*m*,*f*).
parasite ['pærəsaɪt] *n* parásito,-a *m*,*f*.
parasitic(al) [pærə'sɪtɪk(əl)] *adj* parásito,-a, parasitario,-a.
parasol ['pærəsɒl] *n* sombrilla *f*.
paratrooper ['pærətruːpəʳ] *n Mil* paracaidista *mf*.
paratroops ['pærətruːps] *npl Mil* paracaidistas *mpl*.
parboil ['pɑːbɔɪl] *vtr* cocer a medias, sancochar.
parcel ['pɑːsəl] **I** *n* **1** (*package*) paquete *m*. ■ **p. bomb,** paquete *m* bomba; **p. post,** servicio *m* de paquetes postales. **2** (*piece of land*) parcela *f*, *fig* **to be part and p. of sth,** formar parte esencial de algo. **II** *vtr* **to p. up,** envolver, empaquetar, embalar. ◆ **parcel out** *vtr* repartir, distribuir.
parched [pɑːtʃt] *adj* (*land*) abrasado,-a, reseco,-a; (*lips, mouth*) seco,-a; *fig* **to be p.,** estar muerto,-a de sed.
parchment ['pɑːtʃmənt] *n* pergamino *m*. ■ **p. paper,** papel *m* pergamino.
pardon ['pɑːdən] **I** *n* (*forgiveness*) perdón *m*; *Jur* indulto *m*; **I beg your p.,** (Vd.) perdone; **(I beg your) p.?,** ¿cómo (dice)?; **to ask for p.,** pedir perdón. **II** *vtr* (*forgive*) perdonar, disculpar; **p. me!,** ¡Vd. perdone!; **p. me interrupting but ...,** perdone que le interrumpa pero ...; **to p. sb sth,** perdonar algo a algn.
pardonable ['pɑːdənəbəl] *adj* perdonable, disculpable.
pare [peəʳ] *vtr* (*fruit*) pelar, mondar; (*nails*) cortar. ◆ **pare down** *vtr* (*reduce*) reducir.
parent ['peərənt] *n* (*father*) padre *m*; (*mother*) madre *f*; **parents,** padres *mpl*; **the p. company,** la casa *f* madre.
parentage ['peərəntɪdʒ] *n* familia *f*, origen *m*; **of humble p.,** de padres humildes.
parental [pə'rentəl] *adj* (*paternal*) paterno,-a; (*maternal*) materno,-a; **p. guidance,** consejos *mpl* paternales.
parenthesis [pə'renθɪsɪs] *n* (*pl* **parentheses** [pə'renθɪsiːz]) paréntesis *m inv*; **in p.,** entre paréntesis.
parenthetical [pærən'θetɪkəl] *adj* entre paréntesis.
parenthood ['peərənthʊd] *n* paternidad *f*, maternidad *f*; **planned p.,** planificación *f* familiar; **the joys of p.,** la alegría de tener hijos.
par excellence [pɑːr'eksələns] *adv* por excelencia.
pariah [pə'raɪə] *n* paria *m*.
parings ['peərɪŋz] *npl* mondaduras *fpl*.
Paris ['pærɪs] *n* París.
parish ['pærɪʃ] *n Rel* parroquia *f*; (*civil*) municipio *m*. ■ **p. council,** consejo *m* parroquial *or* municipal; **p. priest,** párroco *m*.
parishioner [pə'rɪʃənəʳ] *n* feligrés,-esa *m*,*f*.
Parisian [pə'rɪzɪən] *adj & n* parisino,-a (*m*,*f*), parisiense (*mf*).
parity ['pærɪtɪ] *n* (*equality*) igualdad *f*; *Fin* (*of shares*) paridad *f*.
park [pɑːk] **I** *n* parque *m*, jardín *m* (público). ■ **amusement p.,** parque *m* de atracciones; **car p.,** aparcamiento *m*, parking *m*; **national p.,** parque *m* nacional; **p. bench,**

banco *m* del parque. **II** *vtr* (*car*) aparcar; *fam* **p. yourself down here,** siéntate aquí.
parka ['pɑːkə] *n* anorak *m*.
parking ['pɑːkɪŋ] *n* aparcamiento *m*, estacionamiento *m*; **'no p.',** 'prohibido aparcar'. ■ **p. attendant,** guardacoches *mf inv*; **p. lights,** luces *fpl* de estacionamiento; *US* **p. lot,** aparcamiento *m*, parking *m*; **p. meter,** parquímetro *m*; **p. offence,** multa *f* por estacionamiento incorrecto; **p. space,** aparcamiento *m*.
parkland ['pɑːklænd] *n* prado *m*.
parkway ['pɑːkweɪ] *n US* alameda *f*, paseo *m*, avenida *f*.
parky ['pɑːkɪ] *adj* (**parkier, parkiest**) *GB fam* fresco,-a; **it's a bit p.,** hace fresquito.
parlance ['pɑːləns] *n* lenguaje *m*.
parley ['pɑːlɪ] **I** *n* parlamento *m*. **II** *vi* parlamentar.
parliament ['pɑːləmənt] *n* parlamento *m*; **to get into p.,** ser elegido,-a diputado,-a. ■ **Houses of P.,** parlamento *m*; **Member of P.,** diputado,-a *m*,*f*.
parliamentarian [pɑːləmən'teərɪən] *n* parlamentario,-a *m*,*f*.
parliamentary [pɑːlə'mentərɪ] *adj* parlamentario,-a.
parlour, *US* **parlor** ['pɑːləʳ] *n* (*in house*) salón *m*, salita *f*; (*shop*) salón tienda *f*. ■ **funeral p.,** funeraria *f*.
parochial [pə'rəʊkɪəl] *adj* **1** (*of parish*) parroquial. **2** *pej* (*narrow-minded*) de miras estrechas, pueblerino,-a.
parody ['pærədɪ] **I** *n* parodia *f*. **II** *vtr* (*pt & pp* **parodied**) parodiar.
parole [pə'rəʊl] **I** *n Jur* libertad *f* condicional *or* bajo palabra; **to be on p.,** estar libre bajo palabra. **II** *vtr* (*prisoner*) poner en libertad condicional *or* bajo palabra.
paroxysm ['pærəksɪzəm] *n* paroxismo *m*.
parquet ['pɑːkeɪ] *n* parqué *m*. ■ **p. floor,** suelo *m* de parqué.
parrot ['pærət] *n* loro *m*, papagayo *m*; *fig* **to repeat sth p. fashion,** repetir algo como un loro.
parry ['pærɪ] *vtr* (*pt & pp* **parried**) (*blow*) parar, desviar; *fig* (*question etc*) esquivar, eludir.
parse [pɑːz] *vtr* (*sentence*) analizar gramaticalmente.
parsimonious [pɑːsɪ'məʊnɪəs] *adj* tacaño,-a, parco,-a.
parsley ['pɑːslɪ] *n Bot* perejil *m*.
parsnip ['pɑːsnɪp] *n Bot* chirivía *f*.
parson ['pɑːsən] *n* (*vicar*) cura *m*, párroco *m*. ■ *Culin* **p.'s nose,** rabadilla *f* (de pollo).
parsonage ['pɑːsənɪdʒ] *n* casa *f* parroquial, parroquia *f*.
part [pɑːt] **I** *n* **1** (*portion, proportion, section*) parte *f*; (*piece*) parte, trozo *m*; *Rad TV* (*episode*) capítulo *m*; *Tech* pieza *f*; **a tenth p.,** una décima parte; **for the most p.,** en la mayor parte; *Cin Lit* **in p. two,** en la segunda parte; *Ling* **parts of speech,** partes de la oración; *Anat euph* **private parts,** partes pudendas; **she was away for the best p. of a week,** estaba fuera durante la mayor parte de la semana; **spare parts,** piezas de recambio; **the funniest/saddest p. of it is that ...,** lo más gracioso/triste del caso es que ...; *Culin* **two parts water to one p. wine,** dos partes de agua y una de vino. ■ **p. owner,** copropietario,-a *m*, *f*. **2** (*role, participation*) papel *m*, parte *f*; *Cin Theat* (*play*): **bit p.,** papel secundario; **to look the p.,** encajar bien en el papel; **to play a p. in a film/play,** hacer un papel en una película/una obra de teatro; **to play a p. in sth,** tener algo que ver con algo; **to take p. in sth,** participar en algo; *fig* **a man of many parts,** un hombre de mucho talento; *fig* **I want no p. in it,** no quiero saber nada de ello. **3** (*area, place*) parte *f*, lugar *m*; **in foreign parts,** en el extranjero; **in these parts,** por estos lugares. **4** (*side*) parte *f*; **for my p.,** en cuanto a mí, por mi parte; **it was an oversight on the p. of my wife,** fue un descuido por parte de mi mujer; **to take sb's p.,** tomar partido por algn, apoyar a algn; **to take sth in good p.,** tomarse bien algo. **II** *adj* (*partial*) parcial; **the pullover is p. wool,** el

jersey tiene una parte de lana; **to take sth in p. exchange,** aceptar algo como parte de un pago. III *adv (partly)* en parte; **he's p. Scottish, p. Spanish,** es mitad escocés, mitad español. IV *vtr (separate)* separar; **they were parted during the war,** la guerra los separó; **to p. company with sb,** *(leave)* despedirse de algn; *(quarrel)* reñir con algn; **to p. one's hair,** hacerse la raya (en el pelo). V *vi (separate)* separarse; *(say good bye)* despedirse; **to p. (as) friends,** se separaron amistosamente. ◆ **part with** *vi* separarse de; **I'm sorry to have to p. with it,** siento perderlo *or* perderla. ◆ **partly** *adv (in part)* en parte, parcialmente; *(in a sense)* en cierto sentido; **p. cooked,** cocido,-a a medias; **we are p. to blame,** somos culpables en parte.

partake [pɑːˈteɪk] *vi (pt* **partook;** *pp* **partaken** [pɑːˈteɪkən]) *fml* **to p. of,** *(food)* comer; *(drink)* beber.

partial [ˈpɑːʃəl] *adj* parcial; **to be p. to sth,** ser aficionado,-a a algo. ◆ **partially** *adv (partly)* parcialmente; *(with bias)* con parcialidad.

partiality [pɑːʃɪˈælɪtɪ] *n (bias)* parcialidad *f*; *(liking)* afición *f*, gusto *m*.

participant [pɑːˈtɪsɪpənt] *n (gen)* participante *mf*; *(in competition)* concursante *mf*.

participate [pɑːˈtɪsɪpeɪt] *vi* participar **(in,** en).

participation [pɑːtɪsɪˈpeɪʃən] *n* participación *f*.

participle [ˈpɑːtɪsɪpəl] *n* participio *m*. ■ **past p.,** participio *m* pasado; **present p.,** participio *m* presente.

particle [ˈpɑːtɪkəl] *n* partícula *f*.

particular [pəˈtɪkjʊləʳ] I *adj* 1 *(special)* particular, especial; **for no p. reason,** sin ninguna razón especial; **in this p. case,** en este caso concreto; **it's of p. interest,** es de especial interés; **nothing in p.,** nada de especial; **that p. person,** esa persona en particular. 2 *(fussy)* exigente; **I'm not p.,** me da igual; **she's very p. about her food,** es muy especial para la comida. II **particulars** *npl (details)* detalles *mpl*, pormenores *mpl*; **to receive full p. about sth,** recibir información detallada sobre algo; **to take down sb's p.,** tomar nota de los datos personales de algn. ◆ **particularly** *adv (especially)* particularmente, especialmente; **I'm p. fond of peaches,** me encantan los melocotones.

particularize [pəˈtɪkjʊləraɪz] I *vtr* particularizar, especificar. II *vi* entrar en detalles.

parting [ˈpɑːtɪŋ] I *n* 1 *(separation)* separación *f*, despedida *f*; *fig* **the p. of the ways,** el momento de la separación *or* la despedida. 2 *(in hair)* raya *f*. II *adj* de despedida; **a p. kiss,** un beso de despedida; **his p. words were ...,** sus palabras al despedirse fueron ...; *fig* **p. shot,** último comentario *m*, golpe *m* de gracia.

partisan [pɑːtɪˈzæn, ˈpɑːtɪzæn] I *n Mil* guerrillero,-a *m*, *f*; *(supporter)* partidario,-a *m*, *f*. II *adj Mil* guerrillero,-a; *(supporter)* partidario,-a; *(of party)* partidista.

partition [pɑːˈtɪʃən] I *n* 1 *(wall)* tabique *m*; **glass p.,** tabique de cristal. 2 *(of country)* partición *f*, división *f*. II *vtr (country)* partir, dividir. ◆ **partition off** *vtr (room)* dividir *or* separar con tabiques.

partner [ˈpɑːtnəʳ] I *n* 1 *(gen)* compañero,-a *m*, *f*; *(dancing, in tennis)* pareja *f*; *(husband)* marido *m*; *(wife)* mujer *f*. 2 *Com* socio,-a *m*, *f*, asociado,-a *m*, *f*. II *vtr* acompañar, ser pareja de.

partnership [ˈpɑːtnəʃɪp] *n* 1 *(marriage, relationship)* vida *f* en común. 2 *Com* sociedad *f*, asociación *f*; *Com* **to go into p. with sb,** asociarse con algn.

partook [pɑːˈtʊk] *pt see* **partake.**

partridge [ˈpɑːtrɪdʒ] *n Orn* perdiz *f* pardilla. ■ **rough-legged p.,** perdiz *f* común.

part-time [pɑːtˈtaɪm] I *adj (work etc)* de media jornada. II *adv* media jornada, a tiempo parcial.

party [ˈpɑːtɪ] I *n* 1 *(celebration)* fiesta *f*; **to give** *or* **have** *or* **throw a p.,** organizar una fiesta; **to give a dinner p.,** invitar a gente a cenar. ■ **birthday p.,** fiesta *f* de cumpleaños; **tea p.,** merienda *f*. 2 *(group)* grupo *m*. ■

rescue p., equipo *m* de rescate. 3 *Pol* partido *m*. ■ **Conservative/Labour P.,** partido *m* Conservador/Socialista; **p. leader,** secretario,-a *m*, *f* general del partido; **p. political broadcast,** emisión *f* de propaganda política. 4 *Jur* parte *f*; interesado,-a *m*, *f*; **guilty/innocent p.,** el *or* la culpable/inocente; **to be a p. to a crime,** ser cómplice *mf* en un delito. II *adj (clothes, atmosphere)* de fiesta, de gala; *Tel* **p. line,** línea *f* compartida; **p. wall,** pared *f* medianera.

pass [pɑːs] I *n* 1 *Geog (mountain)* puerto *m*, desfiladero *m*. 2 *(official permit)* permiso *m*, pase *m*; **rail/bus p.,** abono *m or* pase *m* de tren/autobús. 3 *(in exam)* aprobado *m*; **to get a p. in French,** sacar un aprobado en francés. 4 *Sport* pase *m*; *Ftb* **to make a p. with the ball,** hacer un pase con *or* pasar la pelota. 5 *fam* **to make a p. at sb,** intentar ligar con algn. II *vtr* 1 *(go past)* pasar; *(border)* cruzar, atravesar; *Aut (overtake)* adelantar; **to p. the police station,** pasar por delante de la comisaría; **we passed him in the street,** nos cruzamos con él por la calle. 2 *(go, move)* pasar; *Sport (ball)* pasar; **to p. sb a chair, p. a chair to sb,** pasar una silla a algn; **p. the salt, please,** ¿me puedes pasar la sal, por favor? 3 *(exam)* aprobar; *(motion, plan, law)* aprobar; **to p. sb as fit for work,** dar a algn de alta; *Jur* **to p. sentence,** fallar, dictar sentencia; **to p. the censors,** pasar la censura. 4 *(time)* pasar; **it helps to p. the time,** ayuda a pasar el rato; **to p. the time of day with sb,** pasar el rato con algn. 5 *(express)* expresar; **to p. an opinion,** dar una opinión; **to p. a remark,** hacer una observación *or* un comentario. 6 *(expel)* **to p. water,** orinar; **to p. wind,** tener gases. III *vi* 1 *(move past)* pasar; *(procession)* desfilar; *Aut (car)* adelantar; *(people)* cruzarse; *Sport* hacer un pase; **we passed on the stairs,** nos cruzamos en la escalera. 2 *(go, move)* pasar; *(pain)* remitir; *(anger, storm)* pasar, desaparecer; *(opportunity)* perderse; *(memory)* olvidarse; *(time)* pasar; **time passes quickly,** el tiempo pasa rápido; **to p. into oblivion,** caer en el olvido; **to p. out of sight,** perderse a la vista. 3 *(happen)* pasar, ocurrir; **all that has passed,** todo lo que ha pasado *or* ocurrido; **it came to p. that ...,** resultó que ... 4 *(be accepted)* pasar por; **let it p.,** déjalo pasar; **what passes for good manners,** lo que se considera buena educación. 5 *(in exam)* aprobar, ser aprobado,-a. ◆ **pass away** *vi euph* pasar a mejor vida. ◆ **pass by** I *vtr* pasar de largo; **life has passed him by,** ha disfrutado poco de la vida. II *vi* pasar cerca (de). ◆ **pass down** *vtr (hand down)* pasar, transmitir. ◆ **pass for** *vtr* **she could p. for our sister,** podría pasar por nuestra hermana. ◆ **pass off** I *vtr* hacer pasar; **to p. oneself off as sth,** hacerse pasar por algo; **to p. sth/sb off as sth,** hacer pasar a algn/algo por algo. II *vi (happen)* pasar, transcurrir. ◆ **pass on** I *vtr (hand on)* pasar, transmitir. II *vi* 1 *euph (die)* pasar a mejor vida. 2 *(proceed)* pasar a. ◆ **pass out** *vi* 1 *(faint)* desmayarse, perder el conocimiento. 2 *Mil* graduarse. ◆ **pass over** *vtr* 1 *(bridge, land, etc)* atravesar, cruzar; *(aircraft)* volar por. 2 *(disregard)* pasar por alto, hacer caso omiso de; **she was passed over in favour of her sister,** eligieron a su hermana en vez de a ella. ◆ **pass through** I *vtr (place)* pasar por, atravesar; *(barrier, border)* cruzar. II *vi* estar de paso; **I'm just passing through,** sólo estoy de paso. ◆ **pass up** *vtr (opportunity)* renunciar; *(offer)* rechazar.

passable [ˈpɑːsəbəl] *adj* 1 *(road, bridge)* transitable. 2 *(acceptable)* pasable, aceptable. ◆ **passably** *adv* aceptablemente; **p. good,** bastante bueno,-a.

passage [ˈpæsɪdʒ] *n* 1 *(in street)* pasaje *m*; *(alleyway)* callejón *m*; *(hallway)* pasillo *m*. 2 *(travelling)* paso *m*, tránsito *m*; *Naut* travesía *f*; **to grant sb a safe p.,** darle a algn un salvoconducto; *fig* **the p. of time,** el paso del tiempo. 3 *Mus Lit (piece)* pasaje *m*, trozo *m*.

passageway [ˈpæsɪdʒweɪ] *n (interior)* pasillo *m*; *(exterior)* pasaje *m*.

passbook [ˈpɑːsbʊk] *n* libreta *f* de banco.

passé [ˈpæseɪ] *adj* pasado,-a de moda.

passenger [ˈpæsɪndʒəʳ] *n* pasajero,-a *m*, *f*, viajero,-a *m*, *f*.

passer-by [pɑːsə'baɪ] n (pl **passers-by**) transeúnte mf.

passing ['pɑːsɪŋ] I n 1 (of car, train) paso m; (of time) transcurso m; paso m; Aut (overtaking) adelantamiento m; **to mention sth in p.**, mencionar algo de pasada. **2** (of law) aprobación f. II adj (car etc) que pasa; (glance) rápido,-a; (thought) pasajero,-a; **a p. remark,** una observación hecha de pasada.

passion ['pæʃ ən] n (gen) pasión f; (vehemence) ardor m, vehemencia f; crimen of p., crimen m pasional; **he has a p. for opera,** le apasiona la ópera; Rel **the P.,** la Pasión. ■ **p. fruit,** granadilla f.

passionate ['pæʃ ənɪt] adj (gen) apasionado,-a; (vehement) ardiente, vehemente.

passionflower ['pæʃ ənflaʊə'] n Bot pasionaria f.

passive ['pæsɪv] I adj pasivo,-a. II n Ling (voz f) pasiva f. ◆ **passively** adv (gen) pasivamente; Ling en voz pasiva.

passkey ['pɑːskiː] n llave f maestra.

passover ['pɑːsəʊvə'] n Rel Pascua f de los judíos.

passport ['pɑːspɔːt] n pasaporte m.

password ['pɑːswɜːd] n contraseña f.

past [pɑːst] I n pasado m; **in the p.,** en el pasado, antes; **it's a thing of the p.,** pertenece al pasado; **the p.,** (time) el pasado; (events) (tense) el pretérito, el pasado; **to have a p.,** tener antecedentes. II adj (gen) pasado,-a; (former) anterior; **in p. years,** en años anteriores; **in the p. weeks,** en las últimas semanas; **to be a p. master at sth,** ser experto,-a en algo. ■ Ling **p. participle,** participio m pasado; **p. tense,** pretérito m, pasado m. III adv por delante; **to drive p.,** pasar en coche; **to run/walk p.,** pasar corriendo/andando. IV prep (beyond) más allá de; (more than) más de; **he's p. forty,** pasa de los cuarenta (años); **it's five p. ten,** son las diez y cinco; **it's just p. the postbox,** está un poco más allá del buzón; **quarter/half p. two,** las dos y cuarto/media; fam **I'm p. caring,** me trae sin cuidado; fam **I wouldn't put it p. him,** soy capaz de cualquier cosa, no me extraña viniendo de él; fam **she's p. going to discotheques,** ya no tiene edad para ir de discotecas; fam **to be p. it,** estar muy carroza.

pasta ['pæstə] n pasta f, pastas fpl.

paste [peɪst] I n 1 (gen) pasta f; (glue) engrudo m; Culin pasta f; **anchovy p.,** pasta de anchoas; **tomato p.,** tomate m concentrado. **2** (jewellery) bisutería f. II vtr (stick) pegar; (put paste on) engomar, encolar; **to p. sth onto a wall,** pegar algo a una pared.

pasteboard ['peɪstbɔːd] n cartón m.

pastel ['pæst əl] I n (chalk) pastel m; (drawing) pintura f al pastel; (colour) color m pastel. II adj (drawing) al pastel; (colour) pastel.

pasteurization [pæstʃəraɪ'zeɪʃən] n pasteurización f.

pasteurized ['pæstʃəraɪzd] adj pasteurizado,-a.

pastiche [pæ'stiːʃ] n pastiche m.

pastille ['pæstɪl] n pastilla f.

pastime ['pɑːstaɪm] n pasatiempo m.

pasting ['peɪstɪŋ] n fam paliza f; **to give sb a p.,** dar una paliza a algn.

pastor ['pɑːstə'] n Rel pastor m.

pastoral ['pɑːstərəl] adj pastoril, pastoral.

pastry ['peɪstrɪ] n (dough) pasta f; (cake) pastel m; **pastries,** pasteles, pastas.

pasture ['pɑːstʃə'] I n pasto m; **to put cattle out to p.,** pastorear or apacentar el ganado; fig **to put sth out to p.,** tirar algo, deshacerse de algo; fig **to move on to pastures new,** buscar nuevos terrenos. ■ **p. land,** pradera f. II vtr apacentar. III vi pacer.

pasty[1] ['pæstɪ] n Culin empanada f, pastel m de carne.

pasty[2] ['peɪstɪ] adj (pastier, pastiest) pálido,-a, blancuzco,-a.

Pat abbr of **patent** (number), patente f, Pat.

pat[1] [pæt] I n 1 (touch) toque m; (caress) caricia f; (tap) golpecito m, palmadita f; **to give a dog a p.,** acariciar a un perro; **to give sb a p. on the back,** dar a algn una palmadita en la espalda; fig (congratulate) felicitar a algn. **2** (of butter) porción f. II vtr (pt & pp patted) (touch) tocar; (caress) acariciar; (tap) dar una palmadita en; **to p. sb on the back,** dar a algn palmaditas en la espalda; fig felicitar a algn.

pat[2] [pæt] I adv de memoria; **to learn sth off p.,** aprender algo de memoria; **to know sth off p.,** saber algo al dedillo. II adj (answer) (glib) fácil; (appropriate) apropiado,-a; **to give a p. answer,** dar una respuesta fácil.

patch [pætʃ] n 1 (piece of material) parche m; (of land) terreno m; (of colour) mancha f; (of sky) trozo m; (of road) trecho m; fig **to go through/to hit a bad p.,** pasar por/tener una mala racha; fam **the film isn't a p. on the book,** no se puede comparar la película con el libro. **2** (hole, garment) poner un parche en. ◆ **patch up** vtr 1 (garment) poner un parche en; fig **a patched-up job,** una chapuza. **2** (marriage, quarrel) reconciliarse.

patchwork ['pætʃwɜːk] I n labor f de retales. II adj (quilt etc) hecho,-a con retales distintos.

patchy ['pætʃɪ] adj (patchier, patchiest) 1 (colour, performance) desigual. **2** (knowledge) incompleto,-a, parcial.

pâté ['pæteɪ] n paté m, foie gras m.

patent ['peɪt ənt] I n Com patente f; **to take out a p. on sth,** sacar una patente de algo. II adj 1 (obvious) patente, evidente. **2** Com (patented) patentado,-a. ■ **p. medicine,** específico m. III vtr Com patentar. ◆ **patently** adv (obviously) evidentemente; **it is p. obvious,** está clarísimo.

patent[2] ['peɪt ənt] n charol m. ■ **p. leather,** charol m; **p. leather shoes,** zapatos de charol.

paternal [pə'tɜːnəl] adj (fatherly) paternal; (through father's line) paterno,-a; **p. grandmother,** abuela f paterna.

paternalism [pə'tɜːnəlɪzəm] adj paternalista.

paternalistic [pətɜːnə'lɪstɪk] adj paternalista.

paternity [pə'tɜːnɪtɪ] n paternidad f. ■ Jur **p. suit,** demanda f de paternidad.

path [pɑːθ] n (pl **paths** [pɑːðz]) camino m, sendero m; (route) rumbo m, ruta f; (of bullet, missile) trayectoria f; **to clear a p. through the forest,** abrir camino por el bosque; fig **to be on the right p.,** ir bien encaminado,-a; fig **to lead sb up the garden p.,** llevar a algn al huerto.

pathetic [pə'θetɪk] adj (rousing pity) patético,-a; fam (hopeless) malísimo,-a, pésimo,-a; **she was a p. sight,** daba lástima or pena verla así; **the music was p.,** la música era malísima. ◆ **pathetically** adv patéticamente; fam que da lástima or pena; **p. thin,** tan flaco,-a que da lástima.

pathological [pæθə'lɒdʒɪkəl] adj patológico,-a.

pathologist [pə'θɒlədʒɪst] n patólogo,-a m,f.

pathology [pə'θɒlədʒɪ] n patología f.

pathos ['peɪθɒs] n patetismo m.

pathway ['pɑːθweɪ] n camino m, sendero m.

patience ['peɪʃəns] n 1 (quality) paciencia f; **to lose one's p. with sb,** perder la paciencia con algn; **to try sb's p.,** poner a la prueba la paciencia a algn; **you need p. for that,** para eso hace falta tener paciencia. **2** Cards solitario m; **to play p.,** hacer solitarios.

patient ['peɪʃənt] I adj paciente, sufrido,-a; **to be p. with sb** tener paciencia con algn. II n paciente mf, enfermo,-a m,f. ◆ **patiently** adv pacientemente, con paciencia.

patina ['pætɪnə] n pátina f.

patio ['pætɪəʊ] n patio m.

patriarch ['peɪtrɪɑːk] n patriarca m.

patriarchal [peɪtrɪ'ɑːkəl] adj patriarcal.

patrimony ['pætrɪmənɪ] *n* patrimonio *m*.

patriot ['peɪtrɪət] *n* patriota *mf*.

patriotic [pætrɪ'ɒtɪk] *adj (person)* patriota; *(speech, act)* patriótico,-a.

patriotism ['pætrɪətɪzəm] *n* patriotismo *m*.

patrol [pə'trəʊl] **I** *n* patrulla *f*; **to be on p.,** estar de patrulla. ■ **p. car,** coche *m* patrulla; **p. leader,** jefe,-a *m,f* de patrulla. **II** *vtr (pt & pp patrolled) (area)* estar de patrulla en, patrullar por. **III** *vi* patrullar; *fig* **to p. up and down,** pasearse de un lado a otro.

patrolman [pə'trəʊlmən] *n (pl patrolmen) Anat* patrullero *m*; *US (policeman)* guardia *m*, policía *m*.

patron ['peɪtrən] *n* **1** *(benefactor)* patrón,-ona *m, f*; *(of charity, cause)* patrocinador,-a *m, f*; *(of arts)* mecenas *m inv*. ■ **p. saint,** (santo,-a *m, f)* patrón,-ona *m, f*. **2** *Com (customer)* cliente,-a *m, f* habitual.

patronage ['pætrənɪdʒ] *n* **1** *(of charity, cause)* patrocinio *m*; *(of arts etc)* mecenazgo *m*; *pej (in politics, business)* enchufe *m*; **under the p. of,** patrocinado,-a por. **2** *Com (customers)* clientela *f* habitual.

patronize ['pætrənaɪz] *vtr* **1** *(arts etc)* fomentar, proteger. **2** *Com (shop)* ser cliente,-a *m, f* habitual de; *(club etc)* frecuentar. **3** *pej (treat condescendingly)* tratar con condescendencia.

patronizing ['pætrənaɪzɪŋ] *adj pej* condescendiente.

patter[1] ['pætə`] **I** *n (noise) (of rain)* repiqueteo *m*, tamborileo *m*; *(of feet)* pasito *m*. **II** *vi (rain)* repiquetear, tamborilear; *(feet, person)* trotar, corretear.

patter[2] ['pætə`] *n fam* parloteo *m*, labia *f*.

pattern ['pætən] *n (model)* modelo *m*, patrón *m*; *Sew* patrón; *(design)* diseño *m*, dibujo *m*; *(on material)* estampado *m*; *(sample)* muestra *f*; *fig (of behaviour)* modelo *m*; *fig* **the p. of events,** el curso de los acontecimientos. ■ **p. book,** libro *m* de muestras, muestrario *m*; *Sew* catálogo *m* de modas.

patterned ['pætənd] *adj (gen)* decorado,-a con dibujos; *(material)* estampado,-a.

paunch [pɔːntʃ] *n* barriga *f*, panza *f*; **to have a p.,** tener barriga *or* panza.

pauper ['pɔːpə`] *n* pobre *mf*. ■ **p.'s grave,** fosa *f* común.

pause [pɔːz] **I** *n (gen)* pausa *f*; *(silence)* silencio *m*; *(rest)* descanso *m*; **there was a p. in the conversation,** la conversación se interrumpió por un instante. **II** *vi (gen)* hacer una pausa; *(be silent)* callarse; *(rest)* descansar; **she paused for breath,** se paró para recobrar el aliento.

pave [peɪv] *vtr (road)* pavimentar; *(courtyard, floor)* embaldosar, enlosar; *(with stones)* empedrar, adoquinar; *fig* **to p. the way for sb/sth,** preparar el terreno para algn/algo.

pavement ['peɪvmənt] *n (along street)* acera *f*; *US (road surface)* calzada *f*, pavimento *m*.

pavilion [pə'vɪljən] *n* **1** *(at exhibition)* pabellón *m*. **2** *GB Sport (changing rooms)* vestuarios *mpl*.

paving ['peɪvɪŋ] *n (on road)* pavimento *m*; *(on courtyard, floor)* embaldosado *m*, enlosado *m*; *(with stones)* empedrado *m*, adoquinado *m*. ■ **p. stone,** baldosa *f*, losa *f*.

paw [pɔː] **I** *n Zool (foot)* pata *f*; *(claw) (of cat)* garra *f*; *(of lion)* zarpa *f*; *fam (hand)* manaza *f*. **II** *vtr* **1** *(animal)* tocar con la pata; *(lion)* dar zarpazos; *(horse)* **to p. the ground,** piafar. **2** *pej (person)* manosear, sobar.

pawn[1] [pɔːn] *n Chess* peón *m*; *fig* **to be sb's p.,** ser el juguete de algn.

pawn[2] [pɔːn] **I** *n* prenda *f*; **to put sth in p.,** dejar *or* entregar algo en prenda, empeñar algo. **II** *vtr* empeñar.

pawnbroker ['pɔːnbrəʊkə`] *n* prestamista *mf*; **p.'s (shop),** monte *m* de piedad, casa *f* de empeños.

pawnshop ['pɔːnʃɒp] *n* monte *m* de piedad, casa *f* de empeños.

pay [peɪ] **I** *n (wages)* paga *f*, sueldo *m*, salario *m*; **equal p.,** igualdad *f* de salarios; **holidays with p.,** vacaciones *fpl* pagadas; **to be in sb's p.,** ser empleado,-a de algn. ■ **overtime p.,** paga *f* extraordinaria; **p. packet,** sobre *m* de la paga; **p. rise,** aumento *m* del sueldo; **p. slip,** hoja *f* de salario. **II** *vtr (pt & pp paid)* **1** *(gen)* pagar; **how much did you p. for this?,** ¿cuánto pagaste por esto?; **to be** *or* **get paid,** cobrar; **to be well/badly paid,** estar bien/mal pagado,-a; **to p. interest/dividends,** dar interés/beneficios; **to p. money into an account,** ingresar dinero en una cuenta; **to p. one's way,** pagar su parte; **to p. sb money,** pagar dinero a algn; **to p. sb to do sth,** pagar a algn para que haga algo; **when will you be paid?,** ¿cuándo cobrarás *or* te pagarán? **2** *(give, make) (attention)* prestar; *(homage)* rendir; *(visit)* hacer; **to p. one's respects to sb,** saludar a algn; **to p. sb a compliment,** halagar a algn. **3** *(be profitable)* compensar; **it paid him to do it,** le compensó hacerlo; *fig* **it pays you to be honest,** te compensa *or* vale la pena ser honrado,-a. **III** *vi* **1** *(gen)* pagar; **to p. by cash/cheque,** pagar al contado *or* en efectivo/con talón; **to p. for sth,** pagar (por) algo; **to p. for sb to do sth** *or* **for sth to be done,** pagar para que algn haga algo; **they paid for us to attend,** nos pagaron para que asistiéramos; **to p. in advance/instalments,** pagar por adelantado/a plazos; *fam* **to p. through the nose for sth,** pagar un dineral por algo. **2** *fig (suffer)* pagar; **you'll p. for this!,** ¡me las pagarás! **3** *(be profitable)* ser factible *or* rentable; **the business doesn't p.,** el negocio no es rentable; *fig* **crime doesn't p.,** el crimen no compensa. ◆ **pay back** *vtr (money)* devolver, reembolsar; *fig* **to p. sb back,** vengarse de algn, pagar a algn con la misma moneda. ◆ **pay in** *vtr (money, cheque)* ingresar. ◆ **pay off I** *vtr (debt)* liquidar, saldar; *(loan)* pagar; *(mortgage)* cancelar; **to p. sth off in instalments,** pagar algo a plazos; *Ind* **to p. off an employee,** despedir a un empleado con una indemnización. **II** *vi (be successful)* dar resultado; **the plan paid off,** el proyecto dio buen resultado. ◆ **pay out** *vtr* **1** *(spend) (money)* desembolsar, gastar (**on,** en); **to p. out money to sb,** pagar dinero a algn. **2** *Naut (rope)* soltar. ◆ **pay up I** *vtr (bill, debt)* liquidar, saldar. **II** *vi* pagar.

payable ['peɪəbəl] *adj* pagadero,-a; **to make a cheque p. to sb,** extender un talón a favor de algn.

paybed ['peɪbed] *n (in hospital)* cama *f* de pago.

paycheque ['peɪtʃek] *n* sueldo *m*.

payday ['peɪdeɪ] *n* día *m* de pago.

PAYE [piːeɪwɑːiː] *GB abbr of* **pay as you earn,** retención *f* fiscal sobre el sueldo.

payee [peɪ'iː] *n* portador,-a *m, f*, beneficiario,-a *m, f*.

paying ['peɪɪŋ] *adj* de pago; **p. guest,** huésped,-a *m, f* de pago.

paymaster ['peɪmɑːstə`] *n* oficial *m* pagador.

payment ['peɪmənt] *n (paying)* pago *m*; *(amount paid)* pago *m*, remuneración *f*; *(expense)* desembolso *m*; *(of cheque)* cobro *m*; **on p. of £10,** mediante pago de *or* pagando 10 libras; **to do sth without p.,** hacer algo gratis *or* sin cobrar. ■ **advance p.,** anticipo *m*; **cash p.,** pago *m* al contado *or* en efectivo; **deferred p., p. by instalments,** pago *m* a plazos; **down p.,** entrada *f*; **monthly p.,** mensualidad *f*, pago *m* mensual; **yearly p.,** anualidad *f*, pago *m* anual.

payoff ['peɪɒf] *n* **1** *(of debt)* liquidación *f*; *(reward)* recompensa *f*. **2** *fam (bribe)* soborno *m*. **3** *fam (outcome)* desenlace *m*.

payroll ['peɪrəʊl] *n* nómina *f*; **to be on a firm's p.,** estar en la nómina de una empresa.

PC [piː'siː] *(pl PCs) GB abbr of* **Police Constable,** (agente *mf* de) policía *mf*.

pc 1 *abbr of* **per cent,** por ciento, p.c. **2** [piː'siː] *fam abbr of* **postcard,** (tarjeta *f)* postal *f*. **3** *Comput abbr of* **personal computer,** ordenador *m* personal, PC.

pct *US abbr of* **per cent,** por ciento, p.c.

pd *abbr of* **paid,** pagado,-a.

PE [piːˈiː] *abbr of* **physical education,** educación *f* física.

pea [piː] *n Bot* guisante *m*; *fig* **to be as like as two peas in a pod,** ser *or* parecerse como dos gotas de agua. ■ **sweet p.,** guisante *m* de olor.

peace [piːs] *n (gen)* paz *f*; *(calm)* tranquilidad *f*; **at** *or* **in p.,** en paz; **leave us in p.,** déjanos en paz; **p. of mind,** tranquilidad de espíritu; **p. and quiet,** tranquilidad, sosiego *m*; **to keep the p.,** mantener la paz; *Jur* mantener el orden; **to make p.,** *(people)* hacer las paces; *(countries)* firmar la paz. ■ **p. conference,** conferencia *f* de paz; **p. march,** marcha *f* por la paz *or* pacifista; *fig* **p. offering,** prenda *f* de paz; **p. talks,** conversaciones *fpl* por la paz; **p. treaty,** tratado *m* de paz.

peaceable [ˈpiːsəbəl] *adj* pacífico,-a.

peaceful [ˈpiːsfʊl] *adj (non-violent)* pacífico,-a; *(calm)* tranquilo,-a, sosegado,-a.

peace-keeping [ˈpiːskiːpɪŋ] *adj* pacificador,-a. ■ **p.-k. forces,** fuerzas *fpl* de pacificación.

peace-loving [ˈpiːslʌvɪŋ] *adj* amante de la paz, pacífico,-a.

peacemaker [ˈpiːsmeɪkəʳ] *n* pacificador,-a *m*,*f*.

peacetime [ˈpiːstaɪm] *n* tiempos *mpl* de paz.

peach [piːtʃ] **I** *n* **1** *Bot (fruit)* melocotón *m*; *fam* **she's a p.,** es una monada. ■ **p. tree,** melocotonero *m*. **2** *(colour)* color *m* de melocotón. **II** *adj* de color melocotón.

peacock [ˈpiːkɒk] *n* pavo *m* real.

peahen [ˈpiːhen] *n* pava *f* real.

peak [piːk] *n* **1** *(of cap)* visera *f*. **2** *(of mountain)* pico *m*; *(summit)* cima *f*, cumbre *f*. **3** *fig (highest point)* cumbre *f*, cúspide *f*; *(climax)* apogeo *m*; **she was at the p. of her career,** estaba en pleno apogeo de su carrera. ■ **p. hours,** horas *fpl* punta; *Elec* **p. period,** horas *fpl* de mayor consumo; *Ind* **p. output,** máxima producción *f*, máximo rendimiento *m*; **p. season,** temporada *f* alta.

peaked [piːkt] *adj (cap)* con visera.

peaky [ˈpiːki] *adj (peakier, peakiest)* *fam* pálido,-a, paliducho,-a; **to look p.,** estar paliducho,-a, tener la cara pálida.

peal [piːl] **I** *n (of bells)* repique *m*; **p. of thunder,** trueno *m*; **peals of laughter,** carcajadas *fpl*. **II** *vtr (also* **p. out)** *(bells)* repicar, tocar a vuelo. **III** *vi (bells)* repicar, tocar a vuelo; *(thunder)* retumbar; *(organ)* sonar.

peanut [ˈpiːnʌt] *n* cacahuete *m*; *fam* **it's peanuts,** son migajas. ■ **p. butter,** mantequilla *f or* manteca *f* de cacahuete; **p. oil,** aceite *m* de cacahuete.

pear [peəʳ] *n (tree)* peral *m*; *(fruit)* pera *f*.

pearl [pɜːl] **I** *n* perla *f*; **real/cultured pearls,** perlas finas/ cultivadas; **mother of p.,** nácar *m*, madreperla *f*; **string of pearls, p. necklace,** collar *m* de perlas; *fig* **pearls of wisdom,** joyas *fpl* de sabiduría; **to cast pearls before swine,** echar margaritas a los cerdos. **II** *adj (necklace etc)* de perlas; *(button)* de nácar *or* madreperla; **p. barley,** cebada *f* perlada; **p. diver,** pescador,-a *m*,*f* de perlas; **p. oyster,** ostra *f* perlífera.

pearly [ˈpɜːli] *adj (pearlier, pearliest) (colour)* nacarado,-a; *hum* **the P. Gates,** las puertas del paraíso.

pear-shaped [ˈpɜːʃeɪpt] *adj* en forma de pera.

peasant [ˈpezənt] *adj & n* campesino,-a *(m,f)*.

peat [piːt] *n* turba *f*. ■ **p. bog,** turbera *f*.

peaty [ˈpiːti] *adj (peatier, peatiest)* turboso,-a.

pebble [ˈpebəl] *n* guijarro *m*, china *f*; *fam* **you're not the only one on the beach,** no eres el único que cuenta.

pebbledash [ˈpebəldæʃ] *n* empedrado *m*.

pebbly [ˈpebli] *adj (pebblier, pebbliest) (stony)* pedregoso,-a; *(beach)* guijarroso,-a.

pecan [prˈkæn] *n (tree)* pacanero *m*; *(nut)* pacana *f*.

peccadillo [pekəˈdɪləʊ] *n (pl* **peccadilloes** *or* **peccadillos)** pecadillo *m*, vicio *m* pequeño.

peccary [ˈpekəri] *n Zool* pecarí *m*.

peck [pek] **I** *n (of bird)* picotazo *m*; *fam (little kiss)* besito *m*. **II** *vtr (bird)* picotear; *fam (kiss)* dar un besito a. **III** *vi (bird)* picotear; **to p. at sth,** picotear algo; **to p. at one's food,** picar la comida.

pecker [ˈpekəʳ] *n sl* **keep your p. up!,** ¡ánimo!, ¡no te desanimes!

pecking order [ˈpekɪŋɔːdəʳ] *n fig* jerarquía *f*.

peckish [ˈpekɪʃ] *adj fam* algo hambriento,-a; **to feel p.,** empezar a tener hambre.

pectin [ˈpektɪn] *n* pectina *f*.

peculiar [prˈkjuːlɪəʳ] *adj* **1** *(strange)* extraño,-a, raro,-a; *(unwell)* indispuesto,-a; **to feel p.,** sentirse mal; **what a p. taste!,** ¡qué sabor más raro! **2** *(particular)* característico,-a, peculiar, propio,-a; **customs p. to this region,** costumbres propias de esta región. ◆ **peculiarly** *adv (strangely)* de una forma extraña *or* rara; *(especially)* particularmente.

peculiarity [pɪkjuːlɪˈærɪti] *n* **1** *(oddity)* rareza *f*, cosa *f* extraña. **2** *(characteristic)* característica *f*, peculiaridad *f*, particularidad *f*.

pecuniary [prˈkjuːnɪəri] *adj* pecuniario,-a; **p. problems,** problemas de dinero.

pedagogical [pedəˈɡɒdʒɪkəl] *adj* pedagógico,-a.

pedagogy [ˈpedəɡɒdʒi] *n* pedagogía *f*.

pedal [ˈpedəl] **I** *n* pedal *m*. ■ *Aut* **clutch p.,** pedal *m* del embrague; **loud p.,** pedal *m* fuerte; *Mus* **soft p.,** sordina *f*; **p. bin,** cubo *m* de la basura con pedal; **p. boat,** hidropedal *m*; **p. car,** cochecito *m* con pedales. **II** *vtr (pt & pp* **pedalled)** *(bicycle, boat, etc)* impulsar pedaleando. **III** *vi* pedalear.

pedant [ˈpedənt] *n* pedante *mf*.

pedantic [prˈdæntɪk] *adj* pedante.

pedantry [ˈpedəntri] *n* pedantería *f*.

peddle [ˈpedəl] *vtr & vi Com* vender de puerta en puerta; **to p. drugs,** traficar con drogas.

peddler [ˈpedləʳ] *n* **1** *(pusher)* traficante *mf* de drogas. **2** *US see* **pedlar.**

pederast [ˈpedəræst] *n* pederasta *m*.

pedestal [ˈpedɪstəl] *n* pedestal *m*, basa *f*; *fig* **to put sb on a p.,** poner a algn sobre un pedestal. ■ **p. lamp,** lámpara *f* de pie.

pedestrian [prˈdestrɪən] **1** *n* peatón,-ona *m*, *f*. ■ **p. crossing,** paso *m* de peatones; **p. precinct,** zona *f* peatonal. **II** *adj (dull)* pedestre, prosaico,-a.

pediatric [piːdiˈætrɪk] *adj US see* **paediatric.**

pediatrician [piːdiəˈtrɪʃən] *n US see* **paediatrician.**

pediatrics [piːdiˈætrɪks] *n US see* **paediatrics.**

pedicure [ˈpedɪkjʊəʳ] *n* pedicura *f*, quiropedia *f*.

pedigree [ˈpedɪɡriː] **I** *n (ancestry)* linaje *m*; *(family tree)* árbol *m* genealógico; *(of animal)* pedigrí *m*. **II** *adj (animal)* de raza, de casta.

pedlar [ˈpedləʳ] *n Com* vendedor,-a *m*, *f* ambulante.

pee [piː] *fam* **I** *n* pis *m*; **to have a p.,** hacer pis. **II** *vi* hacer pis.

peek [piːk] **I** *n* mirada *f* rápida, ojeada *f*; **to have** *or* **take a p. at sth,** echar una ojeada a algo, mirar algo a hurtadillas. **II** *vi* **to p. at sth,** echar una ojeada a algo, mirar algo a hurtadillas.

peel [piːl] **I** *n (skin)* piel *f*, mondadura *f*; *(of orange, lemon)* corteza *f*; **candied p.,** piel confitada. **II** *vtr (fruit etc)* pelar, quitar la piel *or* la corteza de; *fam* **to keep one's eyes peeled,** estar ojo avizor. **III** *vi (paint)* desconcharse; *(wallpaper)* despegarse; *(skin, person)* pelarse; **her back was peeling,** se le pelaba la espalda. ◆ **peel back** *vtr (layers etc)* quitar, despegar. ◆ **peel off** **I** *vtr (skin of fruit)* pelar, quitar la piel *or* corteza de; *fam (clothes)* quitarse. **II** *vi (paint)* desconcharse; *(wallpaper)* despegarse; *(clothes)* desnudarse.

peeler [ˈpiːləʳ] *n (tool)* mondador *m*; *(machine)* máquina *f* de pelar. ■ **p. peeler,** pelapatatas *m inv*.

peelings ['pi:lɪŋz] *npl* peladuras *fpl*, mondaduras *fpl*.

peep¹ [pi:p] **I** *n (sound)* pío *m*; *fig* **there hasn't been a p. out of them all day,** no han dicho ni pío en todo el día.

peep² [pi:p] **I** *n (glance)* ojeada *f*, vistazo *m*; *(furtive look)* mirada *f* furtiva; **to have** *or* **take a p. at sth,** echar una ojeada *or* un vistazo a algo. **II** *vi* **to p. at sth,** echar una ojeada *or* un vistazo a algo; **to p. through the keyhole,** mirar *or* espiar por el ojo de la cerradura; **to p. out from behind sth,** dejarse ver detrás de algo.

peephole ['pi:phəʊl] *n* mirilla *f*.

peeping Tom [pi:pɪŋ'tɒm] *n pej* mirón *m*.

peepshow ['pi:pʃəʊ] *n* mundonuevo *m*.

peer¹ [pɪəʳ] *n* **1** *(noble)* par *m*; **to be made a p.,** adquirir un título de nobleza. **2** *(contemporary)* par *mf*, igual *mf*. ■ **p. group,** grupo *m* parejo.

peer² [pɪəʳ] *vi (look closely)* mirar detenidamente; *(shortsightedly)* mirar con ojos de miope; **to p. over a wall,** echar un vistazo por un muro.

peerage ['pɪərɪdʒ] *n* título *m* de nobleza; **to give sb a p.,** otorgar a algn un título de nobleza.

peeress ['pɪərɪs] *n* paresa *f*.

peerless ['pɪəlɪs] *adj* sin par, sin igual, incomparable.

peeved [pi:vd] *adj fam* fastidiado,-a, de mal humor; **to be p. about sth,** estar fastidiado,-a *or* de malhumor por algo.

peevish ['pi:vɪʃ] *adj* malhumorado,-a. ◆ **peevishly** *adv* con mal humor, malhumoradamente.

peewit ['pi:wɪt] *n Orn* avefría *f*.

peg [peg] **I** *n Tech* clavija *f*; *(for coat, hat)* percha *f*, gancho *m*, colgador *m*; **to buy clothes off the p.,** comprar la ropa hecha; *fam fig* **to take sb down a p. or two,** bajar los humos a algn. ■ **clothes p.,** pinza *f*; **tent p.,** estaca *f*; *Mus* **tuning p.,** clavija *f*. **II** *vtr (pt & pp pegged) (clothes)* tender; *(tent)* fijar con estacas; *Fin (prices)* fijar, estabilizar. ◆ **peg away at** *vtr fam* machacar. ◆ **peg down** *vtr (tent)* sujetar con estacas. ◆ **peg out I** *vtr (clothes)* tender; *(boundary)* marcar con estacas. **II** *vi fam (die)* estirar la pata.

pegging ['pegɪŋ] *n Sport* **to be level p.,** estar igualados,-as.

pejorative [pɪ'dʒɒrətɪv] *adj* peyorativo,-a, despectivo,-a.

Pekinese [pi:kə'ni:z] *adj & n* pequinés,-esa *(m,f)*.

Peking [pi:'kɪŋ] *n* Pekín.

pelican ['pelɪkən] *n Orn* pelícano *m*. ■ *GB* **p. crossing,** paso *m* de peatones.

pellet ['pelɪt] *n (small ball)* bolita *f*; *(for gun)* perdigón *m*; *Med* píldora *f*.

pell-mell [pel'mel] *adv* en confusión, en tropel.

pelmet ['pelmɪt] *n* galería *f* de cortina.

pelt¹ [pelt] *n (skin)* piel *f*, pellejo *m*.

pelt² [pelt] **I** *vtr* arrojar, tirar; **to p. sb with sth,** tirar algo a algn; **he was pelted with stones,** lo apedrearon; **he was pelted with abuse,** le cubrieron de insultos. **II** *vi fam* **1** *(rain)* **it's pelting (down),** llueve a cántaros. **2** *(rush)* **to p. along,** ir disparado,-a *or* como una flecha.

pelvic ['pelvɪk] *adj* pélvico,-a.

pelvis ['pelvɪs] *n* pelvis *f*.

pen¹ [pen] **I** *n (gen)* pluma *f*; *(ballpoint pen)* bolígrafo *m*; *(biro®)* bic® *m*; **to put p. to paper,** tomar la pluma, escribir. ■ **felt-tip p.,** rotulador *m*; **fountain p.,** estilográfica *f*; **p. name,** seudónimo *m*. **II** *vtr (pt & pp penned) (letter)* escribir; *(article)* redactar.

pen² [pen] **I** *n (for animals)* corral *m*; *(for sheep)* aprisco *m*, redil *m*; *(for bulls)* toril *m*; *(for children)* parque *m* de niños. **II** *vtr* **to p. in,** encerrar, acorralar.

pen³ [pen] *n (abbr of penitentiary) US fam (prison)* chirona *f*.

penal ['pi:nəl] *adj* penal. ■ **p. code,** código *m* penal; **p. offence,** infracción *f* penal; **p. servitude,** trabajos *mpl* forzados.

penalize ['pi:nəlaɪz] *vtr (punish)* castigar; *Sport* penalizar; *(handicap)* perjudicar; **the policy penalizes the poor,** la política perjudica a los pobres.

penalty ['penəltɪ] *n (punishment)* pena *f*, castigo *m*; *Sport* castigo *m*; *Ftb* penalti *m*; *fig (handicap)* desventaja *f*; **on p. of death,** so pena de muerte; **to pay the p. for sth,** cargar con *or* pagar las consecuencias de algo. ■ **death p.,** pena *m* de muerte; *Ftb* **p. area,** área *f* de castigo; *Jur* **p. clause,** cláusula *f* de penalización; *Ftb* **p. goal,** gol *m* de penalti; *Ftb* **p. kick,** penalti *m*.

penance ['penəns] *n* penitencia *f*; **to do p. for sth,** hacer penitencia por algo.

pence [pens] *npl see* **penny.**

penchant ['pɒnʃɒn] *n* inclinación *f*, predilección *f*; **to have a p. for sth,** tener una predilección por algo.

pencil ['pensəl] **I** *n* lápiz *m*; **to write in p.,** escribir a lápiz. ■ **p. case,** estuche *m* de lápices, plumero *m*; **p. drawing,** dibujo *m* a lápiz; **p. sharpener,** sacapuntas *m inv*. **II** *vtr* **to p. in,** *(write)* escribir con lápiz; *(draw)* dibujar (con lápiz).

pendant ['pendənt] *n* colgante *m*, medallón *m*.

pending ['pendɪŋ] **I** *adj* pendiente; **to be p.,** estar pendiente, estar en trámites. **II** *prep (while)* mientras; *(until)* hasta; **p. a decision,** hasta que se tome una decisión; **p. their arrival,** hasta que lleguen.

pendulum ['pendjʊləm] *n* péndulo *m*.

penetrate ['penɪtreɪt] **I** *vtr (go through)* penetrar por; *(infiltrate)* infiltrar; *fig (reach)* llegar hasta. **II** *vi (go through)* atravesar; *(get inside)* penetrar; *(permeate)* trascender; *fig (be understood)* entrar, penetrar.

penetrating ['penɪtreɪtɪŋ] *adj (look, thought)* penetrante; *(smell)* trascendente; *(mind)* perspicaz; *(sound)* agudo,-a.

penetration [penɪ'treɪʃən] *n (gen)* penetración *f*; *(permeation)* trascendencia *f*; *fig (entry)* entrada *f*.

penfriend ['penfrend] *n* amigo,-a *m,f* por carta.

penguin ['peŋgwɪn] *n Orn* pingüino *m*.

penicillin [penɪ'sɪlɪn] *n Med* penicilina *f*.

peninsula [pɪ'nɪnsjʊlə] *n* península *f*; **the Iberian P.,** la Península Ibérica.

peninsular [pɪ'nɪnsjʊləʳ] *adj* peninsular; *Hist* **the P. War,** la guerra de la Independencia de España.

penis ['pi:nɪs] *n Anat* pene *m*.

penitence ['penɪtəns] *n Rel* penitencia *f*; *(repentance)* arrepentimiento *m*.

penitent ['penɪtənt] **I** *adj Rel* penitente; *(repentant)* arrepentido,-a. **II** *n Rel* penitente *mf*.

penitentiary [penɪ'tenʃərɪ] *n US* penitenciaría *f*, cárcel *f*, penal *m*.

penknife ['pennaɪf] *n (pl penknives* ['pennaɪvz]*)* navaja *f*, cortaplumas *m inv*.

penniless ['penɪlɪs] *adj* sin dinero, arruinado,-a; **to be p.,** estar sin un duro.

Pennines ['penaɪnz] *n* **the P.,** los (montes) Peninos.

penny ['penɪ] *n (pl pennies, pence* [pens]*)* penique *m*; **a ten/twenty pence piece,** una moneda de diez/veinte peniques; **he dropped three pennies,** dejó caer tres peniques; **in for a p., in for a pound,** preso por mil, preso por mil quinientos; **they haven't got a p. to their name,** están sin un duro; **to cost a pretty p.,** costar un dineral; *fig* **the p. dropped,** cayó en la cuenta; *fig* **he turns up like a bad p.,** mala hierba nunca muere; *euph* **to spend a p.,** ir a los servicios; *fam* **they are two a p.,** están muy vistos,-as.

penny-pinching ['penɪpɪntʃɪŋ] *adj* tacaño,-a.

penpal ['penpæl] *n US see* **penfriend.**

pension ['penʃən] *n* pensión *f*; **to draw one's p.,** cobrar la pensión. ■ **old age p.,** pensión *f* de vejez; **retirement p.,** jubilación *f*, pensión *f*; **p. fund,** caja *f* de pensiones; **p. scheme,** plan *m* de jubilación. ◆ **pension off** *vtr* jubilar.

pensioner ['penʃənəʳ] *n* pensionista *mf*, jubilado,-a *m,f*.

pensive ['pensɪv] adj (deep in thought) pensativo,-a; (melancholy) melancólico,-a. ◆ **pensively** adv con aire pensativo or melancólico.

pentagon ['pentəgɒn] n pentágono m; US Pol **the P.,** el Pentágono.

pentathlon [pen'tæθlən] n pentatlón m.

Pentecost ['pentɪkɒst] n Rel Pentecostés m.

penthouse ['penthaʊs] n ático m, sobreático m.

pent-up ['pentʌp] adj (confined) encerrado,-a; (repressed) reprimido,-a.

penultimate [pɪ'nʌltɪmɪt] adj & n penúltimo,-a (m, f).

penury ['penjʊrɪ] n miseria f, pobreza f; **to live in p.,** vivir en la miseria.

peony ['piːənɪ] n Bot peonía f.

people ['piːpəl] I npl 1 (gen) gente f sing; (individuals) personas fpl; **many p.,** mucha gente, muchas personas; **Mary of all p.!,** María, ¿quién lo diría?; **old p.,** los viejos or ancianos, la gente vieja; **old p.'s home,** asilo m de ancianos; **other p.,** los demás, otras personas; **p. say that ...,** se dice que ...; **some p.,** algunas personas; **some p. have all the luck!,** ¡algunos nacen de pie!; **there were 500 p.,** había 500 personas; **what a lot of p.!,** ¡cuánta gente!; **young p.,** los jóvenes, la juventud la gente joven. **2** (citizens) ciudadanos mpl; (inhabitants) habitantes mpl; **city/country p.,** la gente de la ciudad/del campo; **government by the p.,** el gobierno del pueblo; **the p.,** el pueblo; **the p. of Scotland,** los habitantes de Escocia, los escoceses. ■ **p.'s tribunal,** tribunal m popular or del pueblo. **3** (family) familia f, gente f; **his p.,** los suyos. **4** (nation) pueblo m, nación f; **the Mexican p.,** el pueblo mejicano. II vtr poblar.

pep [pep] n fam ánimo m, energía f. ■ **p. pill,** estimulante m; **p. talk,** discurso m enardecedor. ◆ **pep up** vtr fam (pt & pp **pepped**) (gen) animar; (person) dar ánimos a.

pepper ['pepə'] I n (spice) pimienta f; (fruit) pimiento m. ■ **black/white p.,** pimienta f negra/blanca; **p. pot,** pimentero m; **red/green p.,** pimiento m rojo/verde; **sweet p.,** pimiento m morrón; **p. mill,** molinillo m de pimienta. II vtr Culin echar pimienta a; fig **peppered with,** salpicado,-a de; **peppered with bullets,** acribillado,-a a balazos.

peppercorn ['pepəkɔːn] n grano m de pimienta.

peppermint ['pepəmɪnt] n Bot hierbabuena f, menta f; (sweet) caramelo m or pastilla f de menta. ■ **p. tea,** infusión f de menta.

peppery ['pepərɪ] adj (food) con mucha pimienta; (spicy) picante; fig (person) colérico,-a, enojadizo,-a.

peptic ['peptɪk] n Med péptico,-a. ■ **p. ulcer,** úlcera f estomacal.

per [pɜː'] prep por; **as p. usual,** como de costumbre; **as p. your advice,** según tus consejos; **5 times p. week,** 5 veces a la semana; **p. cent,** por ciento; **100 p. cent,** cien por cien; **p. day/annum,** al or por día/año; **p. head** or **cápita** or **person,** por cabeza, cada uno.

perceive [pə'siːv] vtr (see) percibir, ver; (realize) darse cuenta de; (notice) notar.

percentage [pə'sentɪdʒ] n porcentaje m; **to get a p. on the sales,** recibir un tanto por ciento de las ventas.

perceptible [pə'septəbəl] adj (visible) perceptible, visible; (audible) audible; (noticeable) sensible. ◆ **perceptibly** adv (visibly) visiblemente; (audibly) audiblemente; (noticeably) sensiblemente.

perception [pə'sepʃən] n percepción f.

perceptive [pə'septɪv] adj perspicaz.

perch¹ [pɜːtʃ] n (fish) perca f.

perch² [pɜːtʃ] I n (for bird) percha f, fig (pedestal) posición f elevada, pedestal m. II vtr poner or colocar arriba; **perched on a rock,** encaramado,-a en una roca. III vi (bird) posarse (**on,** en); (person) colocarse en una posición elevada.

percolate ['pɜːkəleɪt] I vtr filtrar. ■ **percolated coffee,** café m filtro. II vi (gen) filtrarse.

percolator ['pɜːkəleɪtə'] n cafetera f de filtro.

percussion [pə'kʌʃən] n percusión f; **p. instrument,** instrumento m de percusión.

percussionist [pə'kʌʃənɪst] n percusionista mf.

peregrine falcon [perɪgrɪn'fɔːlkən] n Orn halcón m peregrino.

peremptory [pə'remptərɪ] adj perentorio,-a.

perennial [pə'renɪəl] I n Bot planta f perenne. II adj (plant) perenne; (youthfulness) eterno,-a.

perfect ['pɜːfɪkt] I adj 1 (gen) perfecto,-a; (behaviour reputation) intachable. ■ Mus **p. pitch,** tono m perfecto. 2 (ideal) idóneo,-a. 3 (absolute, utter) (fool) perdido,-a; (gentleman) consumado,-a; (waste of time) auténtico,-a; **he's a p. stranger to us,** nos es totalmente desconocido. 4 Ling **p. tense,** tiempo m perfecto. II n Ling perfecto m. III ['pɜːfekt] vtr perfeccionar. ◆ **perfectly** adv (faultlessly) perfectamente; (absolutely) completamente; **p. obvious,** clarísimo; **you're p. right,** tienes toda la razón.

perfection [pə'fekʃən] n perfección f; **done to p.,** hecho,-a a la perfección.

perfectionist [pə'fekʃənɪst] n perfeccionista mf.

perfidious [pə'fɪdɪəs] adj pérfido,-a.

perforate ['pɜːfəreɪt] vtr perforar. ■ **perforated line,** línea f perforada; Med **perforated ulcer,** úlcera f perforada.

perforation [pɜːfə'reɪʃən] n Med perforación f; (on stamps etc) perforado m.

perform [pə'fɔːm] I vtr 1 (task, work) ejecutar, cumplir, realizar. 2 Mus (piece of music) tocar, interpretar; (song) cantar; Theat (play) representar, dar. II vi 1 (machine) funcionar, marchar; (car etc) andar, ir; (person) trabajar. 2 Mus tocar, interpretar; Theat (actor) actuar; (company) dar una representación; (in circus, show) hacer un número.

performance [pə'fɔːməns] n 1 (of task etc) ejecución f, cumplimiento m, realización f. 2 Mus interpretación f; Theat representación f; (in circus, show) número m; Sport (team etc) actuación f; **a great p. by Arsenal,** una magnífica actuación del Arsenal; fam **what a p.!,** ¡vaya lío! 3 (of machine etc) funcionamiento m, rendimiento m.

performer [pə'fɔːmə'] n Mus intérprete mf, Theat artista mf, actor m, actriz f.

perfume ['pɜːfjuːm] I n perfume m. II vtr [pə'fjuːm] perfumar, echar perfume a.

perfumery [pə'fjuːmərɪ] n perfumería f.

perfunctory [pə'fʌŋktərɪ] adj (action) superficial; (person) negligente.

perhaps [pə'hæps, præps] adv tal vez, quizá, quizás; **p./p. not,** puede que sí/no; **p. she'll come,** quizás vendrá, puede que venga.

peril ['perɪl] n (risk) riesgo m; (danger) peligro m; **at your own p.,** por su cuenta y riesgo.

perilous ['perɪləs] adj (risky) arriesgado,-a; (dangerous) peligroso,-a. ◆ **perilously** adv peligrosamente; **we came p. close to falling,** por poco nos caemos.

perimeter [pə'rɪmɪtə'] n perímetro m.

period ['pɪərɪəd] I n 1 (length of time) período m, época f; (stage) etapa f; **for a p. of three years,** durante (un período de) tres años; Meteor **sunny periods,** claros mpl; **the holiday p.,** el período or la temporada de vacaciones; **the post-war p.,** la posguerra; **the Romantic p.,** la época romántica. 2 Educ (class) clase f; **free p.,** hora f libre. 3 Ling (full stop) punto m. 4 (menstruation) (menstrual) **p.,** regla f, período m; **to have one's p.,** tener el período. ■ **p. pains,** dismenorrea f sing. II adj (dress) de época; (furniture) de época, clásico,-a.

periodic [pɪərɪ'ɒdɪk] adj periódico,-a. ■ Chem **p. table,** cuadro m de elementos. ◆ **periodically** adv de vez en cuando.

periodical [pɪərɪˈɒdɪkəl] **I** *adj* periódico,-a. **II** *n* revista *f*.

peripatetic [perɪpəˈtetɪk] *adj* peripatético,-a.

peripheral [pəˈrɪfərəl] *adj* periférico,-a.

periphery [pəˈrɪfərɪ] *n* periferia *f*.

periscope [ˈperɪskəʊp] *n* periscopio *m*.

perish [ˈperɪʃ] *vi* 1 (*person*) fallecer, perecer. 2 (*material*) echarse a perder, estropearse.

perishable [ˈperɪʃəbəl] **I** *adj* perecedero,-a. **II perishables** *npl* productos *mpl* perecederos.

perishing [ˈperɪʃɪŋ] *adj fam* **it's p.**, hace un frío que pela.

peritonitis [perɪtəˈnaɪtɪs] *n Med* peritonitis *f inv*.

periwinkle [ˈperɪwɪŋkəl] *n Bot* vincapervinca *f*; *Zool* caracol *m* de mar, bígaro *m*.

perjure [ˈpɜːdʒəʳ] *vtr* **to p. oneself**, jurar en falso, perjurar.

perjury [ˈpɜːdʒərɪ] *n* perjurio *m*; **to commit p.**, cometer perjurio.

perk [pɜːk] *n fam* beneficio *m*, gaje *m*. ◆ **perk up I** *vtr* (*liven up*) animar, levantar el ánimo; **to p. one-self up**, animarse. **II** *vi* (*person*) animarse; (*after illness*) reponerse.

perky [ˈpɜːkɪ] *adj* (*perkier, perkiest*) animado,-a, alegre.

perm [pɜːm] **I** *n* (*abbr of permanent wave*) permanente *f*; **to have a p.**, hacerse la permanente. **II** *vtr* **to p. sb's hair**, hacer la permanente a algn; **to have one's hair permed**, hacerse la permanente.

permanence [ˈpɜːmənəns] *n*, **permanency** [ˈpɜːmənənsɪ] *n* permanencia *f*.

permanent [ˈpɜːmənənt] *adj* (*lasting*) permanente, duradero,-a; (*address, job*) fijo,-a. ■ **p. wave**, permanente *f*. ◆ **permanently** *adv* (*forever*) permanentemente; (*always*) siempre.

permanganate [pəˈmæŋgənɪt] *n* permanganato *m*.

permeate [ˈpɜːmɪeɪt] *vtr & vi* penetrar, trascender (**through**, por); *fig* extenderse por.

permissible [pəˈmɪsəbəl] *adj* admisible, lícito,-a; **it's not p.**, no se permite.

permission [pəˈmɪʃən] *n* (*gen*) permiso *m*; (*authorization*) autorización *f*; **to ask for p. to do sth**, pedir permiso para hacer algo; **to give sb p. to do sth**, autorizar a algn para que haga algo; **with your p.**, con su permiso.

permissive [pəˈmɪsɪv] *adj* permisivo,-a.

permit [ˈpɜːmɪt] **I** *n* (*gen*) permiso *m*; *Com* permiso, licencia *f*; (*pass*) pase *m*. ■ **import/export p.**, licencia *f* de importación/exportación; **residence p.**, permiso *m* de residencia. **II** [pəˈmɪt] *vtr* (*pt & pp permitted*) (*gen*) permitir; (*authorize*) autorizar; **to p. sb to do sth**, permitir *or* autorizar a algn hacer algo. **III** [pəˈmɪt] *vi* permitir; **weather permitting**, si el tiempo lo permite.

permutation [pɜːmjuˈteɪʃən] *n* permutación *f*.

pernicious [pəˈnɪʃəs] *adj* nocivo,-a, perjudicial; *Med* pernicioso,-a.

pernickety [pəˈnɪkətɪ] *adj fam* (*person*) quisquilloso,-a; (*job*) delicado,-a.

peroxide [pəˈrɒksaɪd] *n* peróxido *m*. ■ **hydrogen p.**, agua *f* oxigenada.

perpendicular [pɜːpənˈdɪkjʊləʳ] **I** *adj* (*gen*) perpendicular; (*cliff*) vertical. **II** *n* perpendicular *f*.

perpetrate [ˈpɜːpɪtreɪt] *vtr* (*crime*) perpetrar, cometer.

perpetrator [ˈpɜːpɪtreɪtəʳ] *n* (*of crime*) autor,-a *m,f*.

perpetual [pəˈpetʃʊəl] *adj* (*constant*) continuo,-a; (*endless*) interminable; (*eternal*) perpetuo,-a; eterno,-a. ◆ **perpetually** *adv* (*constantly*) continuamente; (*eternally*) perpetuamente, eternamente.

perpetuate [pəˈpetʃʊeɪt] *vtr* perˢeᵃr.

perpetuity [pɜːpɪˈtjuːɪtɪ] *n* perpetuidad *f*; **in p.**, a perpetuidad.

perplex [pəˈpleks] *vtr* dejar perplejo,-a *or* confuso,-a.

perplexed [pəˈplekst] *adj* perplejo,-a, confuso,-a; **we were p. by her refusal**, su negativa nos dejó perplejos.

perplexing [pəˈpleksɪŋ] *adj* que deja perplejo,-a *or* confuso,-a.

perplexity [pəˈpleksɪtɪ] *n* perplejidad *f*, confusión *f*.

pers 1 *abbr of* **person**, persona *f*. 2 *abbr of* **personal**, personal *m*.

persecute [ˈpɜːsɪkjuːt] *vtr* (*for political, religious reasons*) perseguir; (*harass*) atormentar, acosar.

persecution [pɜːsɪˈkjuːʃən] *n* persecución *f*. ■ *Psych* **p. complex**, complejo *m* persecutorio.

persecutor [ˈpɜːsɪkjuːtəʳ] *n* perseguidor,-a *m,f*.

perseverance [pɜːsɪˈvɪərəns] *n* perseverancia *f*, persistencia *f*.

persevere [pɜːsɪˈvɪəʳ] *vi* perseverar, persistir; **to p. with sth/at doing sth**, perseverar en algo/en hacer algo.

persevering [pɜːsɪˈvɪərɪŋ] *adj* perseverante.

Persian [ˈpɜːʃən] *adj* persa. ■ **P. Gulf**, golfo *m* Pérsico.

persist [pəˈsɪst] *vi* (*insist*) empeñarse (**in**, en); (*endure*) persistir; (*rain*) continuar; **to p. in doing sth**, empeñarse en hacer algo.

persistence [pəˈsɪstəns] *n* (*insistence*) empeño *m*; (*durability*) persistencia *f*.

persistent [pəˈsɪstənt] *adj* (*person*) perseverante; (*cough, smell, etc*) persistente; (*attempts, warnings, etc*) (*continuous*) continuo,-a; (*continual*) constante. ■ **p. offender**, reincidente *mf*. ◆ **persistently** *adv* (*determinedly*) con empeño; (*continually*) continuamente, constantemente.

person [ˈpɜːsən] *n* (*pl* **people** [ˈpiːpəl]) persona *f*; (*individual*) individuo *m*, tipo *m*, *Tel* **a p. to p. call**, una llamada persona a persona; *Ling* **first p. singular/plural**, primera persona del singular/plural; **in p.**, en persona.

personable [ˈpɜːsənəbəl] *adj* (*handsome*) bien parecido,-a; (*pleasant*) amable.

personage [ˈpɜːsənɪdʒ] *n* personaje *m*.

personal [ˈpɜːsənəl] *adj* 1 (*private*) personal, particular; (*friend, life, hygiene*) íntimo,-a. ■ *Tel* **p. call**, llamada *f* particular; **p. column**, anuncios *mpl* personales; **p. effects**, efectos *mpl* personales; *Ling* **p. pronoun**, pronombre *m* personal. 2 (*in person*) en persona; **to give sth one's p. attention**, encargarse personalmente de algo, atender algo personalmente; **to make a p. appearance**, hacer acto de presencia. 3 *pej* (*indiscreet*) indiscreto,-a; **to get p. about sth**, hacer alusiones personales acerca de algo; **to make p. remarks**, ser indiscreto,-a. ◆ **personally** *adv* (*for my part*) personalmente; (*in person*) en persona; **don't take it p.**, no lo tomes como algo personal; **p., I think ...**, en cuanto a mí, pienso que ... .

personality [pɜːsəˈnælɪtɪ] *n* 1 (*nature*) personalidad *f*. 2 (*famous person*) personaje *m*.

personification [pɜːsɒnɪfɪˈkeɪʃən] *n* personificación *f*; **she's the p. of patience**, es la paciencia personificada.

personify [pɜːˈsɒnɪfaɪ] *vtr* personificar, encarnar.

personnel [pɜːsəˈnel] *n* personal *m*. ■ **p. department**, departamento *m* de personal; **p. manager, p. officer**, jefe,-a *m,f* de personal.

perspective [pəˈspektɪv] *n* perspectiva *f*; **to get** *or* **keep sth in p.**, ver algo en perspectiva *or* objetivamente.

Perspex® [ˈpɜːspeks] *n* plexiglás® *m*.

perspicacious [pɜːspɪˈkeɪʃəs] *adj* perspicaz.

perspicacity [pɜːspɪˈkæsɪtɪ] *n* perspicacia *f*.

perspiration [pɜːspəˈreɪʃən] *n* transpiración *f*, sudor *m*; **to be bathed in p.**, estar bañado,-a en sudor.

perspire [pəˈspaɪəʳ] *vi* transpirar, sudar.

persuade [pəˈsweɪd] *vtr* persuadir, convencer; **he isn't easily persuaded**, no se deja convencer fácilmente; **to p. sb not to do sth**, disuadir a algn de hacer algo; **to p. sb to do sth**, persuadir *or* convencer a algn para que haga algo.

persuasion [pə'sweɪʒən] *n* **1** *(act)* persuasión *f.* **2** *(persuasiveness)* persuasiva*f*; **to use p. on sb,** persuadir a algn. ■ **powers of p.,** poder *m sing* de persuasión. **3** *Pol Rel (opinion, belief)* credo *m*; *Art (movement)* tendencia*f.*

persuasive [pə'sweɪsəv] *adj* persuasivo,-a, convincente.
 ◆ **persuasively** *adv* de mo lo persuasivo *or* convincente.

pert [pɜːt] *adj (girl etc)* pizpireta, coqueto,-a.

pertain [pə'teɪn] *vi* estar relacionado,-a (**to**, con).

pertinence ['pɜːtɪnəns] *n* pertinencia*f.*

pertinent ['pɜːtɪnənt] *adj (relevant)* pertinente; **p. to,** relacionado,-a con, a propósito de.

perturb [pə'tɜːb] *vtr* inquietar, perturbar.

perturbing [pə'tɜːbɪŋ] *adj* inquietante, perturbador,-a.

Peru [pə'ruː] *n* Perú.

perusal [pə'ruːzəl] *n (reading with care)* lectura*f* detenida; *(browsing leisurely)* lectura*f* rápida *or* por encima.

peruse [pə'ruːz] *vtr (read with care)* leer detenidamente; *(browse through)* leer rápidamente *or* por encima.

Peruvian [pə'ruːvɪən] *adj* & *n* peruano,-a *(m,f).*

pervade [pɜː'veɪd] *vtr (smell)* penetrar, extenderse por; *(light)* difundirse por; *fig (influence)* extenderse por.

pervasive [pɜː'veɪsɪv] *adj (smell)* penetrante; *(influence)* extendido,-a.

perverse [pə'vɜːs] *adj (wicked)* perverso,-a; *(stubborn)* terco,-a; *(contrary)* puñetero,-a. ◆ **perversely** *adv (wickedly)* por perversidad; *(stubbornly)* tercamente; *(contrarily)* por llevar la contraria.

perversion [pə'vɜːʃən] *n Med Psych* perversión *f*; *(of justice, truth)* tergiversación *f.*

perversity [pə'vɜːsɪtɪ] *n (wickedness)* perversidad *f*; *(stubbornness)* terquedad *f.*

pervert ['pɜːvɜːt] **I** *n Med Psych* pervertido,-a *m, f (sexual).* **II** [pə'vɜːt] *vtr (gen)* pervertir; *(justice, truth)* tergiversar, desvirtuar.

pessary ['pesərɪ] *n* pesario *m.*

pessimism ['pesɪmɪzəm] *n* pesimismo *m.*

pessimist ['pesɪmɪst] *n* pesimista *mf.*

pessimistic [pesɪ'mɪstɪk] *adj* pesimista; **to be p. about sth,** ser pesimista en cuanto a algo. ◆ **pessimistically** *adv* con pesimismo.

pest [pest] *n* **1** *Zool* insecto *m or* animal *m* nocivo, bicho *m*; *Bot* planta*f* nociva. ■ **p. control,** control *m* de plagas. **2** *fam (person)* pelma *mf*; *(thing)* lata *f.*

pester ['pestər] *vtr* molestar, fastidiar.

pesticide ['pestɪsaɪd] *n* pesticida *f.*

pestilence ['pestɪləns] *n* pestilencia*f*, plaga*f.*

pestilent ['pestɪlənt] *adj* latoso,-a.

pestle ['pesəl] *n* maja *f*, mano *f* (de mortero *or* almirez).

pet [pet] **I** *n (animal)* **1** animal *m or* pájaro *m* doméstico. ■ **p. shop,** tienda *f* de animales. **2** *(favourite)* preferido,-a *m, f.* ■ **teacher's p.,** alumno,-a *m, f* preferido,-a *or* enchufado,-a del maestro *or* de la maestra. **3** *fam (dear)* cariño *m*, chato,-a *m,f*; **he's a p.,** es un cielo. **II** *adj* **1** *(tame)* domesticado,-a. **2** *(favourite)* preferido,-a, favorito,-a. ■ **p. hate,** bestia *f* negra; **p. name,** rombre *m* cariñoso; **p. subject,** tema *m* preferido, manía *f.* **III** *vtr (spoil) (child)* mimar, consentir; *(caress)* acariciar. **IV** *vi (sexually)* besuquearse.

petal ['petəl] *n* pétalo *m.*

peter ['piːtər] *vi* **to p. out,** *(gen)* acabarse, agotarse; *(supplies)* irse agotando; *(plans)* quedar en agua de borrajas; *(engine)* pararse.

petite [pə'tiːt] *adj (woman)* menuda, chiquita.

petitior [pɪ'tɪʃən] **I** *n* petición *f*, solicitud *f*, demanda *f.* ■ **divorce p.,** demanda *f* de divorcio. **II** *vtr* presentar una solicitud a. **III** *vi* **to p. for sth,** solicitar algo; **to p. for divorce,** pedir el divorcio.

petrel ['petrəl] *n Orn* paíño *m.*

petrify ['petrɪfaɪ] *vtr (pt* & *pp* **petrified)** *lit* petrificar; *fig* horrorizar, paralizar; *fig* **they were petrified,** se quedaron de piedra.

petrochemical [petrəʊ'kemɪkəl] **I** *adj* petroquímico,-a. **II** *n* producto *m* petroquímico.

petrodollar ['petrəʊdɒlər] *n* petrodólar *m.*

petrol ['petrəl] *n* gasolina *f*; *Aut* **to be heavy on p.,** gastar mucha gasolina; *Aut* **to run out of p.,** quedarse sin gasolina. ■ **high-octane p.,** supercarburante *m*, gasolina *f* súper; **p. bomb,** bomba *f* de petróleo; **p. can,** bidón *m* de gasolina; **p. pump,** surtidor *m* de gasolina; **p. station,** gasolinera *f*; **p. tank,** depósito *m* de gasolina.

petroleum [pə'trəʊlɪəm] *n* petróleo *m.* ■ **p. jelly,** vaselina *f*; **p. products,** productos *mpl* petrolíferos.

petticoat ['petɪkəʊt] *n (waist slip)* enaguas *fpl*; *(full length slip)* combinación *f.*

pettiness ['petɪnɪs] *n* mezquindad *f.*

petty ['petɪ] *adj (pettier, pettiest) (trivial)* insignificante, sin importancia; *(small-minded)* mezquino,-a. ■ **p. cash,** dinero *m* para gastos pequeños; **p. officer,** sargento *m* de marina.

petulance ['petjʊləns] *n* mal humor *m.*

petulant ['petjʊlənt] *adj* malhumorado,-a. ◆ **petulantly** *adv* de mal humor.

petunia [pɪ'tjuːnɪə] *n Bot* petunia *f.*

pew [pjuː] *n* banco *m* de iglesia; *fam* **take a p.!,** ¡siéntate!

pewter ['pjuːtər] *n* peltre *m.*

phalarope ['fælərəʊp] *n Orn* falaropo *m.*

phallic ['fælɪk] *adj* fálico,-a.

phallus ['fæləs] *n* falo *m.*

phantom ['fæntəm] *adj* & *n* fantasma *(m).*

Pharaoh ['feərəʊ] *n* faraón *m.*

pharmaceutical [fɑːmə'sjuːtɪkəl] *adj* farmacéutico,-a.

pharmacist ['fɑːməsɪst] *n* farmacéutico,-a *m,f.*

pharmacology [fɑːmə'kɒlədʒɪ] *n* farmacología *f.*

pharmacy ['fɑːməsɪ] *n* farmacia *f.*

pharyngitis [færɪn'dʒaɪtɪs] *n* faringitis *f.*

pharynx ['færɪŋks] *n* faringe *f.*

phase [feɪz] **I** *n (gen)* fase *f*; *fig (stage)* etapa *f*; **to be out of p.,** estar fuera de fase, estar desfasado,-a. **II** *vtr* **to p. sth in/out,** introducir/retirar algo progresivamente.

PhD [piːeɪtʃ'diː] *abbr* of **Doctor of Philosophy,** Doctor,-a *m, f* en Filosofía.

pheasant ['fezənt] *n Orn* faisán *m* (vulgar).

phenix ['fiːnɪks] *n US see* **phoenix.**

phenobarbitone [fiːnəʊ'bɑːbɪtəʊn] *n* fenobarbitona *f.*

phenomenal [fɪ'nɒmɪnəl] *adj* fenomenal.

phenomenon [fɪ'nɒmɪnən] *n (pl* **phenomenons** *or* **phenomena** [fɪ'nɒmɪnə]) fenómeno *m.*

phew [fjuː] *interj* ¡uf!

phial ['faɪəl] *n* frasco *m.*

philanderer [fɪ'lændərər] *n fml* tenorio *m.*

philanthropic [fɪlən'θrɒpɪk] *adj* filantrópico,-a.

philanthropist [fɪ'lænθrəpɪst] *n* filántropo,-a *m,f.*

philanthropy [fɪ'lænθrəpɪ] *n* filantropía *f.*

philately [fɪ'lætəlɪ] *n* filatelia *f.*

philharmonic [fɪlhɑː'mɒnɪk] *adj* filarmónico,-a.

Philippine ['fɪlɪpiːn] *adj* & *n* filipino,-a *(m,f).*

Philippines ['fɪlɪpiːnz] *n* **the P.,** las (Islas) Filipinas.

Philistine ['fɪlɪstaɪn] *n* filisteo,-a *m,f.*

philology [fɪ'lɒlədʒɪ] *n* filología *f.*

philologist [fɪ'lɒlədʒɪst] *n* filólogo,-a *m,f.*

philosopher [fɪ'lɒsəfər] *n* filósofo,-a *m,f.*

philosophical [fɪlə'sɒfɪkəl] *adj (argument)* filosófico,-a; *(person)* filósofo,-a; **to have a p. attitude towards sth,** tener una actitud resignada frente a algo.

philolosophize [fɪ'lɒsəfaɪz] *vi* filosofar.

philosophy [fɪ'lɒsəfɪ] *n* filosofía *f*.

phlegm [flem] *n* flema *f*.

phlegmatic [fleg'mætɪk] *adj* flemático,-a. ◆ **phlegmatically** *adv* con mucha flema, tranquilamente.

phobia ['fəʊbɪə] *n* fobia *f*.

Phoenicia [fə'niːʃɪə] *n* Fenicia.

Phoenician [fə'niːʃən] *adj & n* fenicio,-a *(m,f)*.

phoenix ['fiːnɪks] *n Myth* fénix *m*.

phone [fəʊn] *n see* **telephone.**

phone-in ['fəʊnɪn] *n fam* programa *m* de radio *or* televisión con línea telefónica abierta.

phoneme ['fəʊniːm] *n* fonema *m*.

phonetic [fə'netɪk] **I** *adj* fonético,-a. **II phonetics** *n* fonética *f sing*.

phoney ['fəʊnɪ] **I** *adj (phonier, phoniest) (thing)* falso,-a; *(person)* farsante. **II** *n (thing)* camelo *m*; *(person)* farsante *mf*.

phonograph ['fəʊnəɡrɑːf] *n US* tocadiscos *m inv*.

phonology [fə'nɒlədʒɪ] *n* fonología *f*.

phosphate ['fɒsfeɪt] *n* fosfato *m*.

phosphorescent [fɒsfə'resənt] *adj* fosforescente.

phosphorus ['fɒsfərəs] *n* fósforo *m*.

photo ['fəʊtəʊ] *n (abbr of* **photograph)** foto *f*.

photocopier ['fəʊtəʊkɒpɪəʳ] *n* fotocopiadora *f*.

photocopy ['fəʊtəʊkɒpɪ] **I** *n* fotocopia *f*. **II** *vtr (pt & pp photocopied)* fotocopiar.

photoelectric [fəʊtəʊɪ'lektrɪk] *adj* fotoeléctrico,-a. ■ **p. cell,** célula *f* fotoeléctrica, fotocélula *f*.

photogenic [fəʊtəʊ'dʒenɪk] *adj* fotogénico,-a.

photograph ['fəʊtəɡræf, 'fəʊtəɡrɑːf] **I** *n* fotografía *f*; *fam* foto *f*; **black and white/colour p.,** fotografía en blanco y negro/en color; **to take a p. of sb/sth,** hacer *or* sacar una fotografía de algn/algo; **to have one's p. taken,** sacarse una fotografía. ■ **p. album,** álbum *m* de fotos. **II** *vtr* fotografiar, hacer *or* sacar fotografías *or* fotos de.

photographer [fə'tɒɡrəfəʳ] *n* fotógrafo,-a *m,f*.

photographic [fəʊtə'ɡræfɪk] *adj* fotográfico,-a.

photography [fə'tɒɡrəfɪ] *n* fotografía *f*.

photosensitive [fəʊtəʊ'sensɪtɪv] *adj* fotosensible.

photostat ['fəʊtəʊstæt] *n* fotostato *m*.

photosynthesis [fəʊtəʊ'sɪnθɪsɪs] *n* fotosíntesis *f inv*.

phrasal verb [freɪzəl'vɜːb] *n* verbo *m* preposicional *or* adverbial.

phrase [freɪz] **I** *n (thing, saying)* frase *f*, locución *f*; *Mus* frase. ■ **p. book,** libro *m* de frases *or* expresiones; **stock p.,** frase *f* hecha. **II** *vtr (express)* expresar; *Mus* frasear.

phraseology [freɪzɪ'ɒlədʒɪ] *n* fraseología *f*.

phrasing ['freɪzɪŋ] *n Mus* fraseo *m*.

phrenology [frɪ'nɒlədʒɪ] *n* frenología *f*.

Phrygian ['frɪdʒɪən] *adj & n* frigio,-a *(m,f)*.

physical ['fɪzɪkəl] **I** *adj (of the body)* físico,-a; *(of the world)* material; *(of physics)* físico,-a. ■ **p. education,** educación *f* física; **p. examination,** reconocimiento *m* físico; **p. exercises** *or* **jerks,** ejercicios *mpl* físicos. **II** *n fam* reconocimiento *m* físico. ◆ **physically** *adv* físicamente; **it's p. impossible,** es materialmente imposible; **p. handicapped,** minusválido,-a; **the p. handicapped,** los minusválidos; **to be p. fit,** estar en forma.

physician [fɪ'zɪʃən] *n* médico,-a *m,f*.

physicist ['fɪzɪsɪst] *n* físico,-a *m,f*.

physics ['fɪzɪks] *n* física *f*.

physiological [fɪzɪə'lɒdʒɪkəl] *adj* fisiológico,-a.

physiology [fɪzɪ'ɒlədʒɪ] *n* fisiología *f*.

physiotherapist [fɪzɪəʊ'θerəpɪst] *n* fisioterapeuta *mf*.

physiotherapy [fɪzɪəʊ'θerəpɪ] *n* fisioterapia *f*.

physique [fɪ'ziːk] *n* físico *m*.

pianist ['pɪənɪst] *n* pianista *mf*.

piano [pɪ'ænəʊ] *n* piano *m*; **to play the p.,** tocar al piano. ■ **baby grand p.,** piano *m* de media cola; **grand p.,** piano *m* de cola; **p. accordion,** acordeón/piano *m*; **p. stool,** taburete *m* de piano; **p. tuner,** afinador,-a *m,f* de pianos; **upright p.,** piano *m* vertical.

piccolo ['pɪkələʊ] *n Mus* flautín *m*.

pick [pɪk] **I** *n* **1** *(tool)* pico *m*, piqueta *f*. **2** *(choice)* elección *f*; **the p. of the bunch,** lo mejor; **take your p.,** elige *or* escoge el que quieras. **II** *vtr* **1** *(choose)* elegir, escoger; *(team)* seleccionar; *fig* **to p. a winner,** elegir *or* escoger bien. **2** *(flowers, fruit)* coger, recoger. **3** *(scratch)* escarbar, hurgar; *(pimple etc)* rasgarse; **to p. one's nose,** hurgarse la nariz; **to p. one's teeth,** mondarse *or* escarbarse los dientes (con un palillo); **to p. the bones of a chicken,** chupar los huesos de un pollo; *fig* **to p. holes in sth,** encontrar defectos en algo; *fig* **to p. sb's brains,** explotar los conocimientos de algn. **4** *(steal)* robar; **to p. sb's pocket,** robar algo del bolsillo dc algn. **5** *(lock)* forzar. **6** *US (pluck)* desplumar. **7** *Mus (guitar, violin)* puntear. **8 to p. a fight** *or* **quarrel with sb,** buscar camorra con algn. **III** *vi* **to p. at one's food,** comer sin ganas, picar la comida; **to p. and choose,** ser muy exigente. ◆ **pick off** *vtr* **1** *(remove)* quitar. **2** *(shoot)* matar uno a uno. ◆ **pick on** *vtr (persecute)* meterse con; **they always p. on her,** siempre se meten con ella. ◆ **pick out** *vtr* **1** *(choose)* elegir, escoger. **2** *(distinguish, see) (identify)* identificar; *(recognize)* reconocer. **3** *Mus (tune)* buscar, tocar de oído. ◆ **pick up I** *vtr* **1** *(object on floor etc)* recoger, levantar; *(child)* coger; *(telephone)* descolgar; *Knit (stitches)* coger; **this tonic will p. you up,** este tónico te fortalecerá; **to p. oneself up,** levantarse, ponerse de pie; *fig* reponerse; *fig* **to p. up the bill,** quedarse con *or* pagar la cuenta; *fig* **to p. up the pieces,** volver a empezar después de un fracaso. **2** *(collect) (apples, toys, etc)* recoger; *(shopping, person)* buscar, recoger; **to p. up a hitchhiker,** coger a un autostopista; *fam* **to p. up a boy on the beach,** ligar con un chico en la playa. **3** *(increase)* aumentar; *(points)* ganar; **to p. up speed,** acelerar la marcha. **4** *(acquire)* conseguir, encontrar; *(learn)* aprender. **5** *Rad TV (station)* captar. **II** *vi* **1** *(improve) (health, situation)* mejorarse, ir mejorando; *(prices)* subir. **2** *(continue)* seguir; **we picked up where he had left off,** seguimos donde él lo había dejado.

pickaxe, *US* **pickax** ['pɪkæks] *n* piqueta *f*, piocha *f*, zapapico *m*.

picket ['pɪkɪt] **I** *n* **1** *(stick)* estaca *f*. **2** *Ind (strikers)* piquete *m*; *Mil (sentry)* piquete; **to be on p. duty,** estar de guardia. ■ **p. fence,** vallado *m*; **p. line,** piquete *m*. **II** *vtr* piquetear. **III** *vi* hacer piquete.

pickings ['pɪkɪŋz] *npl (leftovers)* restos *mpl*, sobras *fpl*; *(profits)* ganancias *fpl*.

pickle ['pɪkəl] **I** *n* **1** *Culin* adobo *m*, escabeche *m*. **2** *fam (mess)* lío *m*, apuro *m*; **to be in a p.,** estar en un apuro. **II** *vtr Culin* conservar en adobo *or* escabeche. ■ **pickled onions,** cebollas *fpl* en vinagre.

picklock ['pɪklɒk] *n* ganzúa *f*.

pick-me-up ['pɪkmiːʌp] *n Med* tónico *m*, reconstituyente *m*.

pickpocket ['pɪkpɒkɪt] *n* carterista *mf*, ratero,-a *m,f*.

pick-up ['pɪkʌp] *n* **1** *(on record player)* **p.-up (arm),** brazo *m* (del tocadiscos). **2 p.-up (truck),** furgoneta *f*. **3** *US (acceleration)* aceleración *f*. **4** *fam* ligue *m*.

picnic ['pɪknɪk] *n* comida *f* campestre *or* de campo, picnic *m*; **to go on a p.,** hacer comida de campo, ir a comer al campo; *fam* **fig it was no p.,** no fue nada fácil. ■ **p. basket,** cesta *f* para picnic. **II** *vi (pt & pp* **picnicked)** hacer una comida campestre *or* de campo.

picnicker ['pɪknɪkə^r] *n* excursionista *mf*.

Pict [pɪkt] *n Hist* picto,-a *m,f*.

pictorial [pɪk'tɔːrɪəl] *adj (magazine)* ilustrado,-a.

picture ['pɪktʃə^r] **I** *n* **1** *(painting)* cuadro *m; (drawing)* dibujo *m; (portrait)* retrato *m; (photo)* foto *f; (illustration)* ilustración *f*, lámina *f*; **to draw a p.**, hacer un dibujo; **to paint a p.**, pintar un cuadro; **to take a p. of sb**, sacar una foto a algn; *fig* **pretty as a p.**, monísimo,-a; *fig* **she's the p. of health**, rebosa de salud. ■ **p. book**, libro *m* ilustrado; **p. frame**, marco *m*; **p. gallery**, galería *f* de arte; **p. postcard**, tarjeta *f* postal; **p. window**, ventanal *m*. **2** *TV* imagen *m; Cin* película *f*; **to go to the pictures**, ir al cine. **3** *(mental image)* imagen *f*; *fig* **the other side of the p.**, la otra cara de la moneda; *fig* **to paint a black p. of sth**, pintar algo muy negro; *fig* **to put sb in the p.**, poner a algn al corriente; *fam fig* **do you get the p.?**, ¿entiendes? **II** *vtr (imagine)* imaginarse, figurarse; **I can p. it as if it were yesterday**, lo recuerdo como si fuera ayer.

picturesque [pɪktʃə'resk] *adj* pintoresco,-a.

pidgin ['pɪdʒɪn] *adj* macarrónico,-a. ■ **p. English**, inglés *m* macarrónico.

pie [paɪ] *n (of fruit)* tarta *f*, pastel *m; (of meat etc)* pastel, empanada *f; (pasty)* empanadilla *f*; *fig* **it's p. in the sky**, es pura fantasía.

piece [piːs] *n* **1** *(of food) (large)* pedazo *m*; trozo *m; (small)* cacho *m; (of paper, wood)* trozo *m; (of grass)* fragmento *m; (of one's work)* muestra *f; (part)* pieza *f*; **a 56 p. dinner service**, una vajilla de 56 piezas; **a 500 p. jigsaw**, un rompecabezas de 500 piezas; **a p. of advice**, un consejo; **a p. of carelessness**, un descuido; **a p. of furniture**, un mueble; **a p. of land**, *(for building)* una parcela; *(for farming)* un terreno; **a p. of luck**, un golpe de suerte; **a p. of luggage**, un bulto; **a p. of news**, una noticia; **a p. of work**, un trabajo; **in one p.**, en un solo trozo; *fig* sano,-a y salvo,-a; **she arrived in one p.**, llegó sana y salva; **to be in pieces**, *(broken)* estar hecho,-a pedazos; *(dismantled)* estar desmontado,-a; **to break sth into pieces**, hacer algo pedazos; **to pull** *or* **tear sth to pieces**, hacer algo trizas; **to take sth to pieces**, desmontar algo; *fig (criticize)* dejar algo por los suelos; *fig* **to give sb a p. of one's mind**, decir cuatro verdades a algn; *fig* **to go to pieces**, *(business etc)* venirse abajo; *(person)* perder el control (de sí mismo); *fig* **to say one's p.**, decir su parte; *fam* **it's a p. of cake**, es pan comido. **2** *Lit Mus* obra *f*, pieza *f*; **a p. of music/poetry**, una obra musical/un poema; **a 20 p. orchestra**, una orquesta de 20 músicos. **3** *(coin)* moneda *f*; **a 10 pence p.**, una moneda de 10 peniques. **4** *(in chess)* pieza *f*; *(in draughts)* ficha *f*. ◆ **piece together** *vtr (facts)* reconstruir; *(evidence)* atar cabos; *(jigsaw)* hacer.

piecemeal ['piːsmiːl] *adv (by degrees)* poco a poco, a etapas; *(unsystematically)* desordenadamente.

piecework ['piːswɜːk] *n* trabajo *m* a destajo; **to be on p.**, trabajar a destajo.

pieceworker ['piːswɜːkə^r] *n* trabajador,-a *m,f* a destajo.

pied [paɪd] *adj* de varios colores.

pier [pɪə^r] *n* **1** *(jetty)* embarcadero *m*, muelle *m; (promenade)* paseo *m*, rompeolas, *m inv*. **2** *Archit (of bridge)* pila *f*, estribo *m*.

pierce [pɪəs] *vtr (with sharp instrument)* perforar, agujerear; *(with drill)* taladrar; *(penetrate)* penetrar en; *fig* trascender; **to have one's ears pierced**, hacerse los agujeros en las orejas.

piercing ['pɪəsɪŋ] *adj (sound etc)* penetrante, agudo,-a.

piety ['paɪɪtɪ] *n* piedad *f*.

pig [pɪg] *n* **I** *Zool* cerdo *m*, marrano *m; fam (person)* puerco *m*, cochino *m; (glutton)* glotón,-ona *m,f*, tragón,-ona *m,f*; *fig* **he bought a p. in a poke**, le dieron gato por liebre; *fam* **to make a p. of oneself**, ponerse las botas. ■ **p. farm**, granja *f* porcina; **sucking p.**, lechón *m*, cochinillo *m*. **2** *(ingot)* lingote *m*. ■ **p. iron**, hierro *m* en lingotes. **3** *sl offens (policeman)* madero *m*; **the pigs**, la bofia, la pasma. ◆ **pig out** *vi US fam* ponerse las botas.

pigeon ['pɪdʒɪn] *n (gen)* paloma *f*; *Culin Sport* pichón *m; fam* **that's your p.**, eso es asunto tuyo. ■ **clay p. shooting**, tiro *m*, al pichón; **homing p.**, paloma *f* mensajera; **p. breeding**, colombofilia *f*; **p. fancier**, colombófilo,-a *m,f*.

pigeonhole ['pɪdʒɪnhəʊl] **I** *n* casilla *f*. **II** *vtr* encasillar, clasificar.

pigeon-toed [pɪdʒɪn'təʊd] *adj* patituerto,-a.

piggery ['pɪgərɪ] *n (farm)* granja *f* porcina; *(sty)* pocilga *f*.

piggy ['pɪgɪ] *n* cerdito *m*. ■ **p. bank**, hucha *f* en forma de cerdito.

piggyback ['pɪgɪbæk] *n & adv* **to give sb a p.** *or* **carry sb p.**, llevar a algn a cuestas.

pigheaded [pɪg'hedɪd] *adj* terco,-a, cabezota.

piglet ['pɪglɪt] *n* cerdito *m*, lechón *m*, cochinillo *m*.

pigment ['pɪgmənt] *n* pigmento *m*.

pigmentation [pɪgmən'teɪʃən] *n* pigmentación *f*.

pigmy ['pɪgmɪ] *n see* **pygmy**.

pigskin ['pɪgskɪn] *n* piel *f* de cerdo.

pigsty ['pɪgstaɪ] *n* pocilga *f*.

pigtail ['pɪgteɪl] *n* trenza *f*; *(Chinese, bullfighter's)* coleta *f*.

pike [paɪk] *n (fish)* lucio *m*.

pilchard ['pɪltʃəd] *n* sardina *f*.

pile[1] [paɪl] **I** *n* **1** *(of books, things)* montón *m*; **to put things into a p.**, amontonar cosas; *fig* **to make one's p.**, hacer fortuna, forrarse; *fam* **piles of work**, montones de trabajo. **2** *fam (building)* caserón *m*. **II** *vtr* amontonar; **a plate piled with food**, un plato colmado de comida. **III** *vi* **to p. into**, amontonarse *or* meterse en; **to p. on/off a bus**, subir a/bajar de un autobús en tropel. ◆ **pile on** *vtr fam* **to p. it on**, *(exaggerate)* exagerar, recargar las tintas. ◆ **pile up** **I** *vtr (books, clothes)* amontonar; *(riches, debts)* acumular. **II** *vi* amontonarse, acumularse.

pile[2] [paɪl] *n (on carpet)* pelo *m*; **thick p.**, pelo largo.

pile[3] [paɪl] *n Archit* pilar *m*, pilote *m*.

pile-driver ['paɪldraɪvə^r] *n* martinete *m*.

piles [paɪlz] *npl Med* almorranas *fpl*, hemorroides *fpl*.

pile-up ['paɪlʌp] *n Aut* choque *m* en cadena.

pilfer ['pɪlfə^r] *vtr & vi* hurtar.

pilgrim ['pɪlgrɪm] *n* peregrino,-a *m,f*.

pilgrimage ['pɪlgrɪmɪdʒ] *n* peregrinación *f*, romería *f*; **to go on** *or* **make a p.**, ir en peregrinación *or* en romería.

pill [pɪl] *n* píldora *f*, pastilla *f*; **to be on** *or* **take the p.**, tomar la píldora (anticonceptiva).

pillage ['pɪlɪdʒ] **I** *n* pillaje *m*, saqueo *m*. **II** *vtr & vi* pillar, saquear.

pillar ['pɪlə^r] *n Archit* pilar *m*, columna *f; (of smoke etc)* columna; **to go from p. to post**, ir de Herodes a Pilatos. ■ **p. box**, buzón *m*.

pillion ['pɪljən] *n* asiento *m* trasero (de una moto); **to ride p.**, ir sentado,-a detrás.

pillory ['pɪlərɪ] **I** *n* picota *f*. **II** *vtr (pt & pp pilloried)* poner en la picota; *fig* dejar en ridículo.

pillow ['pɪləʊ] *n* almohada *f*.

pillowcase ['pɪləʊkeɪs] *n*, **pillowslip** ['pɪləʊslɪp] *n* funda *f* de almohada.

pilot ['paɪlət] **I** *n* piloto *m*. **II** *adj (trial)* piloto *inv*, experimental. ■ **p. light**, piloto *m*; **p. scheme**, proyecto *m* piloto. **III** *vtr (aircraft, boat)* pilotar; *fig* **to p. sth through**, llevar algo a buen término.

pimonto [pɪ'mentəʊ] *n Culin* pimiento *m* morrón.

pimp [pɪmp] *n* chulo *m*.

pimple ['pɪmpəl] *n (gen)* grano *m; (blackhead)* espinilla *f*.

pimply ['pɪmplɪ] *adj (pimplier, pimpliest)* cubierto,-a de granos.

pin [pɪn] **I** *n (gen)* alfiler *m; Med* clavo *m; Tech* clavija *f; (wooden peg)* espiga *f*, *(bolt)* perno *m; Elec (in plug)* polo *m*; *(in grenade)* percutor *m*; *Bowling* bolo *m*; *US (brooch)* broche *m*; *fig* **as neat as a new p.,** limpio,-a como un espejo; *fig* **you could have heard a p. drop,** se podía oír el vuelo de una mosca; *fam* **for two pins I'd have walked out!,** ¡por poco me marcho! ■ **drawing p.,** chincheta *f*; **hair p.,** horquilla *f*; **p. money,** alfileres *mpl*; **pins and needles,** hormigueo *m*; **rolling p.,** rodillo *m*; **safety p.,** imperdible *m*; *Elec* **three p. plug,** clavija *f* de tres patillas. **II** *vtr (pt & pp pinned) (notice on board etc)* clavar con chinchetas; *(garment etc)* sujetar con alfileres; **to p. a hem,** prender un dobladillo con alfileres; **to p. sb against a wall,** tener a algn contra una pared; *fig* **to p. one's hopes on sth,** poner sus esperanzas en algo; *fam* **to p. a crime on sb,** endosar un delito a algn. ◆ **pin down** *vtr* sujetar; *fig* **to p. sb down,** hacer que algn se comprometa. ◆ **pin up** *vtr (notice etc)* clavar con chinchetas; *(hem etc)* prender con alfileres; *(hair)* recoger.

pinafore ['pɪnəfɔːʳ] *n (apron)* delantal *m*. ■ **p. dress,** pichi *m*.

pinball ['pɪnbɔːl] *n* flipper *m*, millón *m*.

pincers ['pɪnsəz] *npl (on crab, lobster, etc)* pinzas *fpl*; *(tool)* tenazas *fpl*.

pinch [pɪntʃ] **I** *n* **1** *(nip)* pellizco *m*; **to give sb a p.,** pellizcar a algn. **2** *fig (hardship)* apuro *m*; **at a p.,** en caso de apuro; **to feel the p.,** pasar apuros or estrecheces. **3** *(small amount)* pizca *f*; **p. of salt,** pizca de sal; *fig* **to take sth with a p. of salt,** admitir algo con reservas. **II** *vtr* **1** *(nip)* pellizcar; **these shoes p. my feet,** no me zapatos me aprietan (los pies). **2** *fam (steal)* birlar, robar. **3** *fam (arrest)* pescar. **III** *vi (shoes)* apretar; **to p. and scrape,** escatimar gastos.

pinched [pɪntʃt] *adj* **1** *(face)* cansado,-a; **p. with cold,** muerto,-a de frío; **to look p.,** tener mala cara. **2** *(short)* **p. for time/money,** escaso,-a de tiempo/dinero.

pincushion ['pɪnkuʃən] *n* acerico *m*.

pine¹ [paɪn] *n* pino *m*. ■ **p. cone,** piña *f*; **p. forest,** pinar *m*; **p. needle,** aguja *f* de pino; **p. tree,** pino *m*; *Scots* **p.,** pino *m* albar; **stone p.,** pino *m* manso or piñonero.

pine² [paɪn] *vi* **to p.** (away), consumirse, morirse de pena; **to p. for sth/sb,** añorar algo/a algn.

pineapple ['paɪnæpəl] *n* piña *f*.

ping [pɪŋ] *n (sound)* sonido *m* metálico; *(of bullet)* silbido *m*. **II** *vi (gen)* hacer un sonido metálico; *(bullet)* silbar.

ping-pong ['pɪŋpɒŋ] *n* ping-pong *m*, tenis *m* de mesa.

pinion ['pɪnjən] *n Tech* piñón *m*.

pink¹ [pɪŋk] **I** *n* **1** *(colour)* rosa *m*; **to be in the p. (of health),** rebosar de salud. **2** *Bot* clavel *m*. **II** *adj (colour)* rosa *inv*; *Pol fam* rojillo,-a; **to go** or **turn p.,** ponerse colorado,-a.

pink² [pɪŋk] **I** *vtr Sew* cortar con tijeras dentadas. **II** *vi Aut* picar.

pinkie ['pɪŋkɪ] *n Scot US fam* dedo *m* meñique.

pinking shears ['pɪŋkɪŋʃiːəz] *npl* tijeras *fpl* dentadas.

pinkish ['pɪŋkɪʃ] *adj* rosáceo,-a.

pinnacle ['pɪnəkəl] *n (of building)* pináculo *m*; *(of mountain)* cima *f*, pico *m*; *fig (of success)* cumbre *f*.

pinny ['pɪnɪ] *n fam (abbr of pinafore)* delantal *m*.

pinpoint ['pɪnpɔɪnt] *vtr* señalar.

pinprick ['pɪnprɪk] *n* pinchazo *m*.

pinstripe ['pɪnstraɪp] *adj* a rayas.

pint [paɪnt] *n (measure)* pinta *f*; *fam* **a p. (of beer),** una cerveza; **to go for a p.,** salir a tomar una copa.

pinta ['paɪntə] *n fam* pinta *f* de leche.

pintail ['pɪnteɪl] *n Orn* ánade *m* rabudo.

pint-sized ['paɪntsaɪzd] *adj* muy pequeño,-a, minúsculo,-a.

pioneer [paɪə'nɪəʳ] **I** *n (settler)* pionero,-a *m*, *f*; *(forerunner)* precursor,-a *m*,*f*. **II** *vtr* promover, iniciar.

pioneering [paɪə'nɪərɪŋ] *adj* pionero,-a.

pious ['paɪəs] *adj* piadoso,-a, devoto,-a; *pej* beato,-a; **a p. hope,** un deseo bienintencionado. ◆ **piously** *adv* piadosamente, con piedad.

pip¹ [pɪp] *n (seed)* pepita *f*; *(of sunflower)* pipa *f*.

pip² [pɪp] **1** *(sound)* señal *f* (corta). **2** *fam (on dice, dominoes)* punto *m*; *(on uniform)* estrella *f*. **3** *fam* **to give sb the p.,** sacar a algn de quicio.

pip³ [pɪp] *vtr (pt & pp pipped)* **to p. sb at the post,** ganar a algn en el último momento; **to be pipped at the post,** perder por un pelo.

pipe [paɪp] **I** *n* **1** *(for water, gas, etc)* conducto *m*, tubería *f*. **2** *Mus (flute)* flauta *f*; *(of organ)* caramillo *m*; *Scot fam* **the pipes,** la gaita. **3** *(for smoking)* pipa *f*; **to smoke a p.,** fumar en pipa; *fam* **put that in your p. and smoke it!,** ¡chúpate ésa! **■ p. cleaner,** limpiapipas *m inv*; *fig* **p. dream,** sueño *m* imposible. **II** *vtr* **1** *(water)* llevar or transportar por tubería; *(oil)* transportar por oleoducto; *Culin (cream etc)* poner con manga; **piped music,** hilo *m* musical. **2** *Mus* tocar la flauta; *(with bagpipes)* tocar en gaita. ◆ **pipe down** *vi fam* callarse. ◆ **pipe up** *vi fam* hacerse oír.

pipeline ['paɪplaɪn] *n (for water)* tubería *f*, cañería *f*; *(for gas)* gasoducto *m*; *(for oil)* oleoducto *m*; *fig* **it's in the p.,** está en trámites.

piper ['paɪpəʳ] *n* gaitero,-a *m*,*f*.

piping ['paɪpɪŋ] **I** *n* **1** *(for water, gas, etc)* tubería *f*, cañería *f*. **2** *Sew* ribete *m*. **3** *Culin (on cake)* adorno *m*. **4** *Mus* música *f* de gaita. **II** *adj* **p. hot,** bien caliente.

pipit ['pɪpɪt] *n Orn* bisbita *m*. **■ meadow/tawny/tree p.,** bisbita *m* común/campestre/arbóreo.

piquancy ['piːkənsɪ] *n* gusto *m* picante.

piquant ['piːkənt] *adj (taste)* picante; *(fig)* intrigante, estimulante.

pique [piːk] **I** *n* resentimiento *m*, despecho *m*; **to do sth in a fit of p.,** hacer algo por resentimiento. **II** *vtr* picar, herir.

piracy ['paɪərəsɪ] *n* piratería *f*.

piranha [pɪ'rɑːnjə] *n (fish)* piraña *f*.

pirate ['paɪrɪt] **I** *n* pirata *m*. **■ p. edition,** edición *f* pirata; **p. radio,** emisora *f* pirata; **p. ship,** barco *m* pirata.

pirouette [pɪrʊ'et] **I** *n* pirueta *f*. **II** *vi* piruetear, hacer piruetas.

Pisces ['paɪsiːz] *n Astrol Astron* Piscis *m*.

piss [pɪs] *sl* **I** *vi* mear. **II** *n* meada *f*; *fig* **to take the p. out of sb,** cachondearse de algn.

pissed [pɪst] *adj sl (drunk)* borracho,-a; **p. off with sth,** hasta las narices de algo.

pistachio [pɪs'tɑːʃɪəʊ] *n (pt pistachios) (nut)* pistacho *m*. **■ p. tree,** pistachero *m*.

pistol ['pɪstəl] *n* pistola *f*; **at p. point,** a punta de pistola. **■ p. shot,** tiro *m* de pistola, pistoletazo *m*; *Sport* **starting p.,** pistola *f* (para dar la señal de salida).

piston ['pɪstən] *n* pistón *m*, émbolo *m*. **■ p. ring,** aro *m* de pistón; **p. rod,** biela *f*.

pit¹ [pɪt] **I** *n* **1** *(hole)* hoyo *m*, foso *m*; *(large)* hoya *f*; *(of stomach)* boca *f*. **■ orchestra p.,** foso *m* de la orquesta. **2** *(coal mine)* mina *f* de carbón; **to work down the p.,** trabajar en las minas. **3** *Theat* patio *m* de butacas, platea *f*. **4** *(mark on surface)* hoyo *m*, picadura *f*. **5** *Aut (in garage)* foso *m* de inspección; *(in motor racing)* box *m*, box *m*. **6** *(hell)* **the p.,** el infierno. **7** *fam (bed)* catre *m*. **II** *vtr (pt & pp pitted)* **1** *(mark)* llenar de hoyos, picar; **pitted with,** picado,-a de. **2** *(oppose, challenge)* **to p. one's strength** or **wits against sth,** medirse con algn.

pit² [pɪt] *US* **I** *n (seed)* pepita *f*; *(stone)* hueso *m*. **II** *vtr (pt & pp pitted)* quitar las pepitas a, deshuesar.

pitapat ['pɪtəpæt] *adv* **to go p.,** *(rain)* repiquetear; *(feet, heart)* golpetear.

pitch¹ [pɪtʃ] **I** *vtr* **1** *Mus (sound)* entonar; *(instrument)* afinar; *fig* **the speech was pitched at a simple level,** el discurso tuvo un tono asequible. **2** *(throw)* lanzar, arrojar. **3** *(tent)* armar. **II** *vi* **1** *(aircraft, ship)* **to p. and**

toss, cabecear. **2** *(fall)* **to p. forward,** caerse hacia adelante. **III** *n* **1** *Mus (of sound)* tono *m*; *(of instrument)* diapasón *m*; **to have perfect p.,** tener el oído perfecto. **2** *(degree)* grado *m*; *(level)* nivel *m*; **it reached such a p. that ...,** llegó a tal punto *or* tal extremo que ... . **3** *(of aircraft, ship)* cabeceo *m*. **4** *Sport (field)* campo *m*, terreno *m*. **5** *(stall) (in market etc)* puesto *m*; *fig (reserved place)* terreno *m*; **to queer sb's p.,** estropear los planes a algn. **6** *(slope of roof)* pendiente *f*. **7** *(throw)* lanzamiento *m*. ◆ **pitch in** *vi fam* echar una mano. ◆ **pitch into** *vtr (attack) (physically)* atacar; *(verbally)* criticar.

pitch² [pɪtʃ] *n (tar)* brea *f*, pez *f*.

pitch-black [pɪtʃ'blæk] *adj*, **pitch-dark** [pɪtʃ'dɑːk] *adj* negro,-a como la boca de lobo.

pitched [pɪtʃt] *adj* **1** *(roof)* pendiente. **2 p. battle,** batalla *f*.

pitcher¹ ['pɪtʃə'] *n (container)* cántaro *m*, jarro *m*.

pitcher² ['pɪtʃə'] *n Baseb* pítcher *m*.

pitchfork ['pɪtʃfɔːk] **I** *n* horca *f*. **II** *vtr fig* **to p. sb into doing sth,** forzar a algn a hacer algo sin ser preparado.

piteous ['pɪtɪəs] *adj* lastimoso,-a.

pitfall ['pɪtfɔːl] *n (difficulty)* dificultad *f*; *(obstacle)* obstáculo *m*; *(danger)* peligro *m*.

pith [pɪθ] *n (of bone, plant)* médula *f*; *(of orange)* piel *f* blanca; *fig (essence)* meollo *m*. ■ **p. helmet,** salacot *m*.

pithead ['pɪthed] *n Min* bocamina *f*.

pithy ['pɪθɪ] *adj* **(pithier, pithiest)** *(bone, plant)* meduloso,-a; *fig (advice, argument)* contundente.

pitiful ['pɪtɪful] *adj (producing pity)* lastimoso,-a, que da lástima; *(terrible)* lamentable, pésimo,-a. ◆ **pitifully** *adv* que da pena; **she's p. thin,** está tan delgada que da pena verla.

pitiless ['pɪtɪlɪs] *adj* despiadado,-a, implacable.

pittance ['pɪtəns] *n* miseria *f*.

pitter-patter [pɪtə'pætə'] *n* repiqueteo *m*; **to go p.-p.,** repiquetear.

pituitary [pɪ'tjuːɪtərɪ] *adj* **p. gland,** glándula *f* pituitaria.

pity ['pɪtɪ] **I** *n* **1** *(compassion, sorrow)* compasión *f*, piedad *f*; **for p.'s sake!,** ¡por amor de Dios!; **to have** *or* **take p. on sb,** compadecerse de algn. **2** *(regret)* lástima *f*, pena *f*; **it's a p. he didn't pass,** es una pena que no aprobó; **more's the p.,** tanto peor; **what's a p.!,** ¡qué pena!, ¡qué lástima! **II** *vtr (pt & pp pitied)* compadecerse de, sentir pena por; **I p. them,** me dan pena.

pitying ['pɪtɪɪŋ] *adj* compasivo,-a.

pivot ['pɪvət] **I** *n* pivote *m*. **II** *vi* girar sobre su eje; *fig* **to p. on sth,** depender de algo, girar sobre algo.

pixie ['pɪksɪ] *n* duendecillo *m*.

pizza ['piːtsə] *n* pizza *f*. ■ **p. parlour,** pizzería *f*.

Pk *abbr of* **Park,** parque *m*.

pkt *abbr of* **packet,** paquete *m*.

placard ['plækɑːd] *n* pancarta *f*.

placate [plə'keɪt] *vtr* aplacar, apaciguar, calmar.

place [pleɪs] **I** *n* **1** *(position)* sitio *m*, lugar *m*; *(area)* área *f*; *(in book)* página *f*; *(in queue)* turno *m*; **in p. of Mary, in Mary's p.,** en el lugar de María; **in your p. I'd have gone,** yo en tu lugar habría ido; **there's no p. for that here,** eso está de más aquí; **there's no p. like home,** como tu casa no hay dos; **to be in/out of p.,** estar en/fuera de su sitio; **to go from p. to p.,** ir *or* andar de un lugar a otro; **to hold sth in p.,** sujetar algo; **to put sth back in its p.,** devolver algo a su sitio; **to take p.,** tener lugar; *fig* **to put sb in his p.,** poner a algn en su lugar; **you'll go places,** irás lejos; *fam* **all over the p.,** por todas partes; *fam* **here's the p.,** aquí estamos. **2** *(seat)* sitio *m*, plaza *f*; *(space)* espacio *m*; *Theat* localidad *f*; *(on bus)* asiento *m*; *(at university, on course)* plaza; *(at table)* plaza *f*; *(place setting)* cubierto *m*; **to change places with sb,** intercambiar sitios con algn; **to feel out of p.,** encontrarse fuera de lugar; **to lay a p. at table for sb,** poner un cubierto para algn; **to get a p. at university,** ser

aceptado,-a para ingresar en la universidad; **to take sb's p.,** sustituir a algn. ■ **p. mat,** individual *m*. **3** *fig (suitable occasion)* sitio *m*, lugar *m*; **this isn't the p. to discuss religion,** este no es el lugar más indicado para hablar de religión. **4** *(position on scale)* posición *f*, lugar *m*; *(social position)* lugar, rango *m*; *(in argument)* lugar; **in the first/second p.,** en el primer/segundo lugar; **people in high places,** gente *f* influyente; **to finish in last p.,** llegar el último; **to take first/second p.,** ganar el primer/segundo lugar; *fig* **it isn't your p. to give advice,** no te incumbe a ti dar consejos; *fig* **to have friends in high places,** tener enchufes; *fig* **to know one's p.,** conocer su lugar. ■ *Math* **decimal p.,** punto *m* decimal. **5** *(house)* casa *f*; *(building)* lugar *m*, sitio *m*; **come round to our p. for coffee,** pasa por casa a tomar café; **we're going to his p.,** vamos a su casa. ■ **p. of residence,** domicilio *m*; **p. of work,** lugar *m* de trabajo; **p. of worship,** *(church)* iglesia *f*; *(temple)* templo *m*. **6** *(square, street)* plaza *f*. **II** *vtr* **1** *(put)* poner, colocar; **p. the books on the shelves,** coloca los libros en la estantería; **she placed a vase on the table,** puso un florero en la mesa; **to be well/better placed to do sth,** estar en buena/mejor situación para hacer algo; **to p. in order of preference,** poner en orden de preferencia; *fig* **it places me in an awkward position,** me pone en una situación difícil o delicada. **2** *Com* **to p. a bet,** hacer una apuesta, apostar; **to p. an order with sb,** hacer un pedido a algn. **3** *(face, person)* recordar; **I know the face but I can't p. him,** reconozco la cara pero no sé de qué. **4** *(in job)* colocar en un empleo.

placebo [plə'siːbəʊ] *n (pl placebos or placeboes) Med* placebo *m*.

placement ['pleɪsmənt] *n* colocación *f*.

placenta [plə'sentə] *n (pl placentas or placentae* [plə'sentiː]*)* placenta *f*.

placid ['plæsɪd] *adj* apacible, tranquilo,-a.

plagiarism ['pleɪdʒərɪzəm] *n* plagio *m*.

plagiarize ['pleɪdʒəraɪz] *vtr* plagiar.

plague [pleɪg] **I** *n (of insects etc)* plaga *f*; *Med* peste *f*; *fig* **to avoid sth like the p.,** evitar algo por todos los medios. **II** *vtr* **to p. sb with requests,** acosar a algn a peticiones.

plaice [pleɪs] *n inv (fish)* platija *f*.

plaid [plæd, pleɪd] **I** *n (cloth)* tejido *m* escocés. **II** *adj (shawl)* de cuadros. ■ **p. skirt,** falda *f* escocesa.

plain [pleɪn] **I** *adj* **1** *(clear)* claro,-a, evidente; obvio,-a; **her attitude made it p. that she wasn't interested,** su actitud puso de manifiesto que no estaba interesada; **it was p. that he was mistaken,** quedó claro que estaba equivocado; *fig* **he likes p. speaking,** le gusta hablar con franqueza; *fam* **as p. as the nose on your face,** más claro no puede ser. ■ **p. language,** palabras *fpl* claras. **2** *(simple)* sencillo,-a; *(chocolate)* amargo,-a; *(flour)* sin levadura; *(material)* de un solo color; *(paper)* liso,-a; *(person)* llano,-a; *(stitch)* a la derecha; **in p. clothes,** vestido,-a de paisano; **the p. truth,** la verdad lisa y llana. **3** *(unattractive)* sin atractivo *or* encanto. **4** *(complete)* total; **it's p. foolishness,** es una auténtica locura. **II** *n* **1** *(in knitting)* punto *m* a la derecha. **2** *Geog* llanura *f*, llano *m*. ◆ **plainly** *adv (clearly)* claramente; *(simply)* sencillamente; **to speak p.,** hablar con franqueza.

plainness ['pleɪnnɪs] *n (clearness)* claridad *f*; *(simplicity)* sencillez *f*; *(unattractiveness)* falta *f* de atractivo *or* encanto.

plain-spoken [pleɪn'spəʊkən] *adj* franco,-a.

plaintiff ['pleɪntɪf] *n* demandante *mf*, querellante *mf*.

plaintive ['pleɪntɪv] *adj* lastimero,-a, triste.

plait [plæt] **I** *n* trenza *f*. **II** *vtr* trenzar.

plan [plæn] **I** *n* **1** *(scheme)* plan *m*, proyecto *m*; **everything went according to p.,** todo salió como estaba previsto; **to draw up a p.,** elaborar *or* hacer un proyecto; **to have a change of p.,** cambiar de planes; **to make plans,** hacer proyectos; *fam* **the best p. would be to attend,** lo mejor sería asistir. ■ **development p.,** plan *m* de desarrollo;

five-year p., plan *m* quinquenal. **2** *(drawing, diagram)* plano *m*. **II** *vtr (pt & pp **planned**) (make plans for) (future etc)* planear, proyectar; *(design, draw up plans for) (economy)* planificar; *(house etc)* hacer los planos de; *(intend)* pensar, tener la intención de; **it wasn't planned,** no estaba previsto; **to p. one's family,** planificarse la familia; **we p. to go out,** pensamos salir. **III** *vi* hacer planes; **she hadn't planned for so many guests,** no había previsto tantos invitados; **to p. for the future,** hacer planes *or* proyectos para el futuro; **to p. on doing sth,** contar con hacer algo.

plane¹ [pleɪn] **I** *n* **1** *Art Math* plano *m*; *fig* nivel *m*. **2** *fam* avión *m*. **II** *adj Geom* plano,-a. **III** *vi (glide)* planear.

plane² [pleɪn] **I** *n (tool)* cepillo *m*. **II** *vtr* cepillar.

plane³ [pleɪn] *n Bot* **p. (tree),** plátano *m*. ■ **London p.,** plátano *a* comun; **Oriental p.,** plátano *m* oriental.

planet ['plænɪt] *n* planeta *m*.

planetarium [plænɪ'teərɪəm] *n (pl **planetariums** or **planetaria** [plænɪ'teərɪə])* planetario *m*.

planetary ['plænɪt ərɪ] *adj* planetario,-a.

plank [plæŋk] *n (piece of wood)* tabla *f*, tablón *m*; *fig (principle)* punto *m*.

plankton ['plæŋktən] *n* plankton *m*.

planner ['plænə'] *n* planificador,-a *m, f*. ■ **town p.,** urbanista *mf*.

planning ['plænɪŋ] *n* planificación *f*. ■ **family p.,** planificación *f* familiar; **p. committee,** servicio *m* de planning; **p. permission,** permiso *m* de construcción *or* de obras; **town p.,** urbanismo *m*.

plant¹ [plɑːnt] **I** *n Bot* planta *f*. ■ **p. life,** flora *f*; **p. pot,** maceta *f*, tiesto *m*. **II** *vtr (flowers etc)* plantar; *(seeds, vegetables)* sembrar; *(bomb)* poner, colocar; *fig* **to p. an idea in sb's mind,** introducir una idea en la mente de algn; **to p. sth on sb,** endosarle algo a algn.

plant² [plɑːnt] *n Ind (factory)* planta *f*, fábrica *f*; *(machinery)* equipo *m*, maquinaria *f*.

plantain ['plæntɪn] *n Bot* llantén *m*.

plantation [plæn'teɪʃən] *n* plantación *f*; *Am* hacienda *f*.

planter ['plɑːntə'] *n (person)* plantador,-a *m, f*; *(machine)* plantadora *f*.

plaque [plæk] *n* placa *f*.

plasma ['plæzmə] *n* plasma *m*.

plaster ['plɑːstə'] **I** *n Constr* yeso *m*, argamasa *f*; *Med* escayola *f*; *GB* **sticking p.,** esparadrapo *m*, tirita *f*; **to have one's leg in p.,** tener la pierna escayolada. ■ **p. cast,** *Art* vaciado *m* de yeso; *Med* enyesado *m*; **p. of Paris,** yeso *m* mate. **II** *vtr* **1** *Constr* enyesar, enlucir. **2** *fig (cover)* cubrir; **the wall was plastered with slogans,** la pared estaba cubierta de pintadas.

plasterboard ['plɑːstəbɔːd] *n* cartón *m* yeso.

plastered ['plɑːstəd] *adj sl* borracho,-a, trompa.

plasterer ['plɑːstərə'] *n* yesero,-a *m, f*.

plastic ['plæstɪk, 'plɑːstɪk] **I** *n* plástico *m*, materia *f* plástica; **plastics,** materiales *mpl* plásticos; **the plastics industry,** la industria del plástico. **II** *(cup, bag, etc)* de plástico; **it's p.,** es de plástico; **the p. arts,** las artes plásticas. ■ **p. bomb, p. explosive,** plástico *m*; **p. surgery,** cirugía *f* plástica; **p. surgeon,** especialista *mf* en cirugía plástica.

Plasticine® ['plæstɪsiːn] *n* arcilla *f* de moldear, plastilina *f*.

plate [pleɪt] **I** *n* **1** *(dish)* plato *m*; *(plateful)* plato lleno **(of,** de); *(for church offering)* platillo *m*, bandeja *f*; *fam fig* **it was handed to him on a p.,** se lo dieron en bandeja de plata; *fig* **to have a lot on one's p.,** tener mucha faena. ■ **p. rack,** escurreplatos *m inv*. **2** *(sheet)* placa *f*. ■ *Elec* **hot p.,** placa *f* eléctrica; **gold/silver p.,** chapa *f* de oro/de plata; *(tableware)* vajilla *f* de oro/de plata; *Aut* **number p.,** matrícula *f*, placa *f*; **p. glass,** vidrio *m or* cristal *m* cilindrado. **3** *Print (illustration)* grabado *m*, lámina *f*. **4** **dental p.,** dentadura *f* postiza. **II** *vtr* chapar; *(with gold)*

dorar; *(with silver)* platear; **gold/silver/chromium plated,** chapado,-a en oro/en plata/de cromo.

plateau ['plætəʊ] *n (pl **plateaus** or **plateaux** ['plætəʊz])* meseta *f*.

platform ['plætfɔːm] *n* **1** *(gen)* plataforma *f*; *(stage)* estrado *m*; *(at meeting)* tribuna *f*; *Rail* andén *m*, vía *f*. ■ **p. ticket,** billete *m* de andén. **2** *Pol (programme)* programa *m*.

platinum ['plætɪnəm] *n* platino *m*. ■ **p.-blond hair,** pelo *m* rubio platino.

platitude ['plætɪtjuːd] *n* lugar *m* común, tópico *m*.

Platonic [plə'tɒnɪk] *adj* platónico,-a.

platoon [plə'tuːn] *n Mil* pelotón *m*.

platter ['plætə'] *n (dish)* fuente *f*.

plausible ['plɔːzəbəl] *adj (excuse, argument)* admisible, plausible.

play [pleɪ] **I** *vtr* **1** *(game, sport)* jugar a; **to p. a game of cards,** echar una partida de cartas; **to p. ball,** jugar a la pelota; *fig* cooperar; **to p. cards,** jugar a las cartas *or* a los naipes; **to p. hide-and-seek/chess/football,** jugar al escondite/al ajedrez/al fútbol; **to p. games,** jugar; *Fin* **to p. the Stock Exchange,** jugar a la Bolsa; *fig* **stop playing games!,** ¡basta de tomar el pelo!; *fig* **if you p. your cards right,** si te espabilas; *fam* **to p. a trick on sb,** gastar una broma a algn; *fam* **to p. a dirty trick on sb,** jugar una mala pasada a algn; *fam* **to p. it cool,** tomárselo con calma. **2** *Sport (position)* jugar de; *(team)* jugar contra; **Spain played Scotland,** España jugó contra Escocia; **they played her in the team,** la seleccionaron para el equipo; **to p. a shot,** *(football)* tirar; *(golf, tennis)* golpear. **3** *Mus (instrument, tune)* tocar; **to p. a record/tape,** poner un disco/cassette; **to p. sth by ear,** tocar algo de oído; **to p. the piano/guitar,** tocar el piano/la guitarra; *fig* **you'll have to p. it by ear,** tendrás que improvisar. **4** *Theat (part)* hacer (el papel) de; *(play)* representar; **to p. Ophelia,** hacer de Ofelia; *fig* **to p. a part in sth,** intervenir *or* participar en algo; *fig* **to p. the fool,** hacer el indio *or* el tonto. **5** *(aim)* dirigir. **II** *vi* **1** *(of children)* jugar (**with,** con); *(of animals)* juguetear; **to go out to p.,** salir a jugar; **to p. at doctors and nurses,** jugar a médicos y enfermeras; *fig* **to p. with an idea,** dar vueltas a una idea; *fig* **to p. with fire,** jugar con fuego; *fam* **what is she playing at?,** ¿qué pretende? **2** *Sport (at game, gamble)* jugar; **he plays centre-forward,** juega de centro delantero; **to p. against sb,** jugar contra algn; **to p. at cards,** jugar a las cartas *or* a los naipes; **to p. fair,** jugar limpio; **to p. for money,** jugar por dinero; *fig* **to p. for time,** tratar de ganar tiempo; *fig* **to p. into sb's hands,** hacerle el juego a algn. **3** *(joke)* bromear; **he's just playing,** lo hace en broma. **4** *Mus (person)* tocar; *(instrument)* sonar. **5** *Theat (act)* actuar; **to p. in a film,** trabajar en una película; *fig* **to p. to the gallery,** actuar para la galería. **III** *n* **1** *(game, activity)* juego *m*; **a p. on words,** un juego de palabras; **to be at p.,** estar jugando; *fig* **it's child's p.,** es coser y cantar. **2** *Sport* juego *m*; *(match)* partido *m*; **fair/foul p.,** juego limpio/sucio; **p. begins at 3 o'clock,** el partido empieza a las 3; *(ball)* **to be in/out of p.,** estar dentro/fuera de juego. **3** *Theat* obra *f* de teatro; **films and plays,** cine *m sing* y teatro *m sing*. ■ **radio/television p.,** obra *f* para radio/televisión. **4** *Tech & fig (movement)* juego *m*; **there's a lot of p. in the steering wheel,** el volante tiene mucho juego; *fig* **to bring sth into p.,** poner algo en juego; *fig* **to give full p. to one's emotions,** dar rienda suelta a las emociones; *fig* **to make a p. for sth/sb,** intentar conseguir algo/conquistar a algn.
◆ **play about** *vi* juguetear; **to p. about with sth,** juguetear con algo. ◆ **play around** *vi (waste time)* gandulear; *(be unfaithful)* tener líos. ◆ **play along** *vi* **to p. along with sb,** seguirle la corriente *or* la pista a algn. ◆ **play back** *vtr* (volver a) poner. ◆ **play down** *vtr* minimizar, quitar importancia a. ◆ **play off I** *vtr* oponer; **to p. off one thing against another,** oponer una cosa a otra. **II** *vi Sport* jugar un partido de desempate. ◆ **play on I** *vtr* **1** *(take advantage of)* aprovecharse de; *(exploit)* explotar. **2** *(irritate) (nerves etc)* atacar, exacerbar. ◆

play out vtr (game etc) llevar a su fin; fam **to be played out,** estar agotado,-a or rendido,-a. ◆ **play up I** vtr (annoy) dar la lata, fastidiar. **II** vi (child etc) dar guerra; (machine) no funcionar bien.

playbill ['pleɪbɪl] n cartel m.

playboy ['pleɪbɔɪ] n playboy m.

player ['pleɪəʳ] n Sport jugador,-a m,f; Mus músico,-a m,f; Theat (man) actor m; (woman) actriz f. ■ **football p.,** futbolista mf; **guitar p.,** guitarrista mf; **tennis p.,** tenista mf.

playful ['pleɪful] adj (person, animal) juguetón,-ona, travieso,-a; (mood) juguetón,-ona.

playground ['pleɪgraʊnd] n patio m de recreo.

playgroup ['pleɪgru:p] n jardín m de niños or de infancia, guardería f.

playhouse ['pleɪhaʊs] n **1** (theatre) teatro m. **2** (for children) casita f.

playing ['pleɪɪŋ] n juego m, el jugar. ■ **p. card,** carta f, naipe m; **p. field,** campo m de deportes.

playmate ['pleɪmeɪt] n compañero,-a m,f de juego.

play-off ['pleɪɒf] n Sport partido m de desempate.

playpen ['pleɪpen] n corral m or parque m (de niños).

playroom ['pleɪru:m] n cuarto m de juego.

playschool ['pleɪsku:l] n jardín m de infancia, guardería f.

plaything ['pleɪθɪŋ] n juguete m.

playtime ['pleɪtaɪm] n recreo m.

playwright ['pleɪraɪt] n dramaturgo,-a m,f.

PLC, plc [pi:el'si:] GB Com abbr of **Public Limited Company,** Sociedad f Anónima, S.A.

plea [pli:] n (request) petición f, súplica f; (excuse) pretexto m, disculpa f; Jur alegato m; **to enter a p. of not guilty,** declararse inocente. ■ **p. bargaining,** negociación f colectiva.

plead [pli:d] **I** vtr (pt & pp **pleaded** or **plead** [pled]) **1** Jur defender; fig abogar por; **to p. sb's case,** defender en juicio a algn; fig **to p. sb's cause,** defender la causa de algn, hablar por algn. **2** (give excuse) pretender; **to p. ignorance/poverty,** alegar ignorancia/pobreza. **II** vi **1** (beg) rogar, implorar, suplicar; **to p. for mercy,** pedir clemencia. **2** Jur declararse; **to p. for sb,** intervenir a favor de algn; **to p. guilty/not guilty,** declararse culpable/ inocente; **to p. with sb for sth,** rogar a algn que conceda algo; **to p. with sb to do sth,** suplicar a algn que haga algo.

pleading ['pli:dɪŋ] **I** n súplicas fpl (for, a favor de); Jur defensa f, alegato m. **II** adj (voice, look) suplicante.

pleasant ['plezənt] adj (gen) agradable; (person) simpático,-a, amable; (surprise) grato,-a; **it's very p. here,** aquí se está muy bien; **to have a p. time,** pasar un buen rato.

pleasantry ['plezəntrɪ] n cumplido m; **to exchange pleasantries,** intercambiar cumplidos.

please [pli:z] **I** vtr (give pleasure to) gustar, agradar, complacer; (satisfy) satisfacer; **he did it to p. us,** lo hizo para complacernos; **there's no pleasing her,** no hay forma de contentarla; **this will p. you,** esto te gustará; **to p. oneself,** hacer lo que le da la gana; fml **p. God he will come,** si Dios quiere vendrá; fam **p. yourself,** como quieras. **II** vi (give pleasure) complacer; (give satisfaction) satisfacer; **easy/hard to p.,** poco/muy exigente; **to be eager to p.,** estar deseoso,-a de complacer. **III** adv por favor; **come in, p.,** pase, por favor; **may I? —p. do,** ¿me permite? —desde luego; **'p. do not smoke',** 'se ruega no fumar'; **p. don't go,** no te vayas, te lo ruego; **yes, p.,** sí, por favor.

pleased [pli:zd] adj (happy) contento,-a; (satisfied) satisfecho,-a; **I'm p. for you,** me alegro por ti; **I'm p. to see it,** me alegra verlo; **p. to meet you!,** ¡encantado,-a!, ¡mucho gusto!; **to be p. about sth,** alegrarse de algo; **to be p. with oneself,** estar satisfecho,-a de sí mismo,-a; **to be p. with sb/sth,** estar contento,-a con algn/algo; **we are**

p. to inform you that ..., tenemos el gusto de comunicarle que ... .

pleasing ['pli:zɪŋ] adj (pleasant) agradable, grato,-a; (satisfactory) satisfactorio,-a.

pleasurable ['pleʒərəbəl] adj agradable, divertido,-a.

pleasure ['pleʒəʳ] n **1** (feeling of enjoyment) gusto m, placer m; (source of enjoyment) placer; **it gives me great p. to welcome you,** me complace mucho darle la bienvenida; **it's a p. to talk to him,** da gusto hablar con él; **'Mr and Mrs Smith request the p. of your company',** 'los Sres. Smith tienen el gusto de solicitar la compañía de usted'; **the pleasures of the flesh,** los placeres de la carne; **to take great p. in doing sth,** disfrutar mucho haciendo algo; **with p.,** con mucho gusto. ■ **p. boat,** barco m de recreo; **p. cruise,** crucero m; **p. ground,** parque m de atracciones; **p. trip,** excursión f. **2** (will) voluntad f; **at sb's p.,** según la voluntad de algn; GB **to be detained at** or **during her Majesty's P.,** quedar detenido,-a a disposición del Estado.

pleasure-loving ['pleʒəlʌvɪŋ] adj, **pleasure-seeking** ['pleʒəsi:kɪŋ] adj hedonista.

pleat [pli:t] **I** n pliegue m. **II** vtr plisar, hacer pliegues en.

plebeian [plɪ'bi:ən] adj plebeyo,-a; fig ordinario,-a.

plectrum ['plektrəm] n (pl **plectrums** or **plectra** ['plektrə]) púa f, plectro m.

pledge [pledʒ] **I** n (promise) promesa f; (token of love etc) señal f; (security, guarantee) garantía f, prenda f; **as a p. of our friendship,** en señal de nuestra amistad; fig **to take the p.,** hacer la promesa de no beber alcohol. **II** vtr **1** (promise) prometer; **he pledged his support,** prometió su apoyo; **she pledged never to return,** juró no regresar nunca; **to p. sb to secrecy,** hacer jurar a algn guardar el secreto. **2** (pawn) empeñar, dar en prenda.

plenary ['pli:nərɪ, 'plenərɪ] adj plenario,-a; **p. power,** poder absoluto; **p. session,** sesión plenaria.

plenipotentiary [plenɪpə'tenʃərɪ] adj & n plenipotenciario,-a m,f.

plentiful ['plentɪful] adj abundante.

plenty ['plentɪ] **I** n abundancia f; **p. of potatoes,** patatas fpl en abundancia, muchas patatas; **p. of time/money,** tiempo m/dinero m de sobra; **that's p.,** es más que suficiente; **we've got p.,** tenemos de sobra; **years of p.,** años mpl de abundancia. **II** adv US fam **it's p. big enough,** es bastante grande.

pleurisy ['plʊərɪsɪ] n Med pleuresía f.

pliable ['plaɪəbəl] adj flexible.

pliant ['plaɪənt] adj dócil.

pliers ['plaɪəz] npl **(pair of) p.,** alicates mpl, tenazas fpl.

plight [plaɪt] n situación f grave.

plimsolls ['plɪmsəlz] npl GB playeras fpl, zapatos mpl de lona or de tenis.

plinth [plɪnθ] n plinto m.

plod [plɒd] vi (pt & pp **plodded**) andar con paso lento or pesado; **to p. along,** ir andando con paso lento; fig **to p. on,** perseverar; fig **to p. through a report,** estudiar laboriosamente un informe.

plodder ['plɒdəʳ] n trabajador,-a m, f or estudiante mf tenaz.

plodding ['plɒdɪŋ] adj tenaz, laborioso,-a.

plonk¹ [plɒŋk] **I** vtr fam dejar caer; **p. yourself down,** siéntate; **to p. books down on the table,** dejar caer los libros sobre la mesa. **II** n (sound) golpe m seco, ruido m sordo.

plonk² [plɒŋk] n GB fam (cheap wine) vino m, vinaza f.

plop [plɒp] **I** n plaf m; **to go p.,** hacer plaf. **II** vi (pt & pp **plopped**) hacer plaf.

plot¹ [plɒt] **I** n (conspiracy) complot m; Theat Lit (story) argumento m, trama f; fig **the p. thickens,** se complica la trama. **II** vtr (course, position) trazar; (scheme) fraguar. **III** vi conspirar, maquinar, tramar; **to p. to kill sb,** conspirar para matar a algn.

plot² [plɒt] **I** *n Agr* parcela *f*, terreno *m*; **a p. of land,** un terreno, una parcela; *(for building)* un solar. ■ **vegetable p.,** campo *m* de hortalizas.

plough [plaʊ] **I** *n Agr* arado *m*; *Astron* **the P.,** el Carro, la Osa Mayor. **II** *vtr Agr* arar, labrar. **III** *vi* **1** *Agr (till)* arar, labrar. **2** *fig (run)* **the car ploughed through the fencing,** el coche a ravesó la valla; **to p. into sth,** chocar *or* dar fuerte contra algo; *fig* **to p. through a book,** leer un libro con dificultad. ◆ **plough back** *vtr (money, profits)* reinvertir. ◆ **plough up** *vtr (field)* arar, surcar.

ploughman ['plaʊmən] *n (pl* **ploughmen)** arador *m*, labrador *m*. ■ *Culin* **p.'s lunch.** pan *m* y ensalada *f* con queso.

plover ['plʌvəʳ] *n Orn* **common p.,** avefría *f*; **golden p.,** chorlito *m* dorado común; **Kentish p.,** chorlitejo *m* patingro; **little ringed p.,** chorlitejo *m* chico; **ringed p.,** chorlitejo *m* grande.

plow [plaʊ] *n US see* **plough.**

plowman ['plaʊmən] *n (pl* **plowmen)** *US see* **ploughman.**

ploy [plɔɪ] *n* truco *m*, estratagema *f*.

pluck [plʌk] **I** *vtr (gen)* arrancar **(out of, from,** de); *(flowers)* coger; *(chicken etc)* desplumar; *Mus (guitar etc)* puntear; **to p. one's eyebrows,** depilarse las cejas. **II** *n (courage)* valor *m*, ánimo *m*, arrojo *m*. ◆ **pluck up** *vtr* **to p. up courage,** armarse de valor, cobrar ánimos.

plucky ['plʌkɪ] *adj (***pluckier, pluckiest)** valiente.

plug [plʌg] **I** *n* **1** *(in bath, sink, etc)* tapón *m*; *(of cotton wool)* tampón *m*. **2** *Elec* enchufe *m*, clavija *f*; *(socket)* toma *f* de corriente. ■ *Aut* **spark p.,** bujía *f*; **2/3 pin p.,** clavija *f* de dos/tres patillas, clavija *f* bipolar/tripolar. **3** *fam (publicity)* publicidad *f*; **to give sth a p.,** promocionar algo. **II** *vtr (pt & pp* **plugged)** **1** *(hole etc)* tapar; *(tooth)* empastar; *fig* cerrar. **2** *(insert)* introducir; *(plug)* enchufar. **3** *fam (publicize)* dar publicidad a, promocionar; *(push) (idea etc)* hacer hincapié en. ◆ **plug away** *vi* **to p. away at sth,** perseverar en algo. ◆ **plug in** *vtr & vi Elec* enchufar. ◆ **plug up** *vtr (hole etc)* tapar.

plughole ['plʌghəʊl] *n* desagüe *m*, desaguadero *m*.

plum [plʌm] *n (fruit)* ciruela *f*; *(colour)* color *m* ciruela; *fig* **a p. job,** un chollo. ■ *Culin* **p. pudding,** budín *m* de pasas; **p. tree,** ciruelo *m*.

plumage ['pluːmɪdʒ] *n Orn* plumaje *m*.

plumb [plʌm] **I** *n* plomo *m*, plomada *f*. ■ **p. line,** *(in building)* plomada *f*; *(in sea)* sonda *f*. **II** *adj* a plomo, vertical; **out of p.,** torcido,-a, desnivelado,-a. **III** *adv US fam* **it's p. crazy,** es una locura; **p. in the middle,** justo en medio *or* en el centro. **IV** *vtr (depths) (of sea)* sondar; *fig (of mind, soul, etc)* sondear, penetrar; *fig* **to p. the depths of despair,** estar completamente desesperado,-a.

plumber ['plʌməʳ] *n* fontanero,-a *m,f*.

plumbing ['plʌmɪŋ] *n (occupation)* fontanería *f*; *(system)* tubería *f*, cañería *f*.

plume [pluːm] *n* penacho *m*.

plummet ['plʌmɪt] *vi (bird, plane)* caer en picado; *fig (prices)* bajar vertiginosamente; *(morale)* caer a plomo.

plump¹ [plʌmp] *adj (person)* relleno,-a; *(baby)* rechoncho,-a; *(animal)* gordo,-a.

plump² [plʌmp] *vi* **to p. for sth,** optar *or* decidirse por algo. ◆ **plump down** **I** *vtr* dejar caer. **II** *vi* desplomarse. ◆ **plump up** *vtr (cushions)* ahuecar, agitar.

plunder ['plʌndəʳ] **I** *vtr* saquear, pillar. **II** *n (action)* saqueo *m*, pillaje *m*; *(loot)* botín *m*.

plunge [plʌndʒ] **I** *vtr (immerse)* sumergir; *(thrust)* arrojar; **to p. a knife into sth,** clavar *or* hundir un cuchillo en algo; *fig* **to be plunged into despair,** estar hundido,-a en la desesperación. **II** *vi* **1** *(dive) (into water)* lanzarse, tirarse de cabeza, zambullirse; *(ship)* cabecear; *fig (fall)* caer, hundirse; **to p. to one's death,** tener una caída mortal. **2** *Fin (shares, prices)* desplomarse. **III** *n (dive)*

chapuzón *m*, zambullida *f*; *fig (fall)* caída *f*, desplome *m*; **to take the p.,** dar el paso decisivo. ◆ **plunge into** *vtr* sumirse en, lanzarse a.

plunger ['plʌndʒəʳ] *n Tech* émbolo *m*; *(for blocked pipes)* desatascador *m*.

plunging ['plʌndʒɪŋ] *adj (neckline)* escotado,-a.

pluperfect [pluː'pɜːfɪkt] *n Ling* pluscuamperfecto *m*.

plural ['plʊərəl] **I** *adj* plural. **II** *n* plural *m*; **in the p.,** en el plural.

pluralism ['plʊərəlɪzəm] *n* pluralismo *m*.

plurality [plʊə'rælɪtɪ] *n* pluralidad *f*.

plus [plʌs] **I** *prep* más; **there are four of them, p. the children,** son cuatro, más los niños; **three p. four makes seven,** tres más cuatro hacen siete. **II** *adj Math Elec* positivo,-a; **a p. factor,** un factor positivo, *fam* **she's forty p.,** ha pasado de las cuarenta. ■ **p. sign,** signo *m* más. **III** *n Math* signo *m* más; *fig (advantage)* ventaja *f*, factor *m* positivo; *fam* plus *m*.

plush [plʌʃ] **I** *n* felpa *f*, peluche *m*. **II** *adj fam (luxurious)* lujoso,-a.

Pluto ['pluːtəʊ] *n Astron Myth* Plutón *m*.

plutonium [pluː'təʊnɪəm] *n* plutonio *m*.

ply¹ [plaɪ] **I** *vtr (pt & pp* **plied)** **1** *(use) (tool)* manejar, utilizar; *(sea route)* navegar por; **to p. one's trade,** ejercer su oficio *or* profesión. **2** *(overwhelm)* abrumar, acosar; **to p. sb with drinks,** no parar de ofrecer copas a algn; **to p. sb with questions,** acosar a algn con preguntas. **II** *vi (ship)* navegar; **to p. between Majorca and Barcelona,** cubrir la línea *or* ir y venir de Mallorca a Barcelona; **to p. for hire,** ir en busca de clientes.

ply² [plaɪ] *n (of wood)* capa *f*; *(of wool)* cabo *m*. ■ **three-p. wool,** lana *f* de tres cabos.

plywood ['plaɪwʊd] *n* madera *f* contrachapada, contrachapado *m*.

PM [piː'em] *GB fam abbr of* **Prime Minister,** Primer,-a Ministro,-a *m,f*.

p.m. [piː'em] *abbr of* **post meridiem** (after noon), después del mediodía; **at 2 p.m.,** a las dos de la tarde.

PMT [piːem'tiː] *Med fam abbr of* **premenstrual tension,** tensión *f* premenstrual.

pneumatic [njuː'mætɪk] *adj* neumático,-a.

pneumonia [njuː'məʊnɪə] *n Med* pulmonía *f*.

PO [piː'əʊ] **1** *Naut abbr of* **Petty Officer,** contramaestre *m*. **2** *abbr of* **postal order,** giro *m* postal, g.p. **3** *abbr of* **Post Office,** correos *mpl*.

poach¹ [pəʊtʃ] **I** *vtr* **to p. fish/game,** pescar/cazar en vedado; *fig fam (steal)* birlar, quitar. **II** *vi (for fish)* pescar en vedado; *(for game)* cazar en vedado; *fig* **to p. on sb's territory,** pisar los papeles a algn.

poach² [pəʊtʃ] *vtr Culin (egg)* escalfar; *(fish)* hervir; **poached egg,** huevo *m* escalfado.

poacher¹ ['pəʊtʃəʳ] *n (of fish)* pescador *m* furtivo; *(of game)* cazador *m* furtivo.

poacher² ['pəʊtʃəʳ] *n (for eggs)* escalfador *m*.

pochard ['pəʊtʃəd] *n Orn* porrón *m* común.

pocket ['pɒkɪt] *n* **1** *(gen)* bolsillo *m*; **he came in with his hands in his pockets,** entró con las manos metidas en los bolsillos; **to dip into one's p., put one's hand in one's p.,** poner las manos en el bolsillo; **to go through sb's pockets,** vaciar los bolsillos a algn; **to pay for sth out of one's own p.,** pagar algo con su propio dinero; **to turn out one's pockets,** vaciar los bolsillos; *fig* **to be £10 in/ out of p.,** salir ganando/perdiendo 10 libras; *fig* **to have sth/sb in one's p.,** tener algo/a algn en el bolsillo; *fig* **to line one's pockets,** forrarse. ■ **p. dictionary,** diccionario *m* de bolsillo; **p. handkerchief,** pañuelo *m*; **p. money,** dinero *m* de bolsillo. **2** *(area) (of air)* bolsa *f*; *(of resistence)* foco *m*, rincón *m*. **II** *vtr (money)* embolsar, meter en el bolsillo; **to p. the change,** quedarse con el cambio; *fig* **to p. one's pride,** tragarse el orgullo.

pocketbook ['pɒkɪtbʊk] *n US* bolso *m*.

pocketknife ['pɒkɪtnaɪf] *n (pl pocketknives* ['pɒkɪt naɪvz]*)* navaja *f*.

pocket-sized ['pɒkɪtsaɪzd] *adj* (tamaño *m*) de bolsillo.

pockmarked ['pɒkmɑːkt] *adj (face)* picado,-a de viruelas; *(surface)* acribillado,-a de agujeros.

pod [pɒd] *n Bot* vaina *f*.

podgy ['pɒdʒɪ] *adj (podgier, podgiest)* gordinflón,-ona, regordete.

podium ['pəʊdɪəm] *n (pl podiums or podia* ['pəʊdɪə]*)* podio *m*.

poem ['pəʊɪm] *n* poema *m*, poesía *f*.

poet ['pəʊɪt] *n* poeta *mf*.

poetic [pəʊ'etɪk] *adj* poético,-a. ■ **p. justice**, justicia *f* divina; **p. licence**, licencia *f* poética.

poetry ['pəʊɪtrɪ] *n* poesía *f*. ■ **p. reading**, lectura *f* o recital *m* de poesías.

pogrom ['pɒgrəm] *n* pogrom *m*.

poignancy ['pɔɪnjənsɪ] *n* patetismo *m*.

poignant ['pɔɪnjənt] *adj* patético,-a, conmovedor,-a.

point [pɔɪnt] **I** *n* **1** *(sharp end)* punta *f*; **at the p. of a gun**, a mano armada; *(ballet)* **to dance on points**, bailar de puntas; **with a sharp p.**, puntiagudo,-a; *fig* **not to put too fine a p. on it**, hablando sin rodeos *or* con franqueza. **2** *(place)* punto *m*, lugar *m*; **he's outspoken to the p. of being rude**, es franco para no decir grosero; **p. of arrival/departure**, punto de llegada/salida *or* partida; *fig* **p. of contact**, punto de contacto; *fig* **p. of no return**, punto de no volver atrás. **3** *(quality)* cualidad *f*, punto *m*; **good/bad p.**, cualidad buena/mala; **weak/strong p.**, punto débil/fuerte. **4** *(moment)* punto *m*; **at that p.**, entonces, en aquel momento; **at the p. of death**, al borde de la muerte; **from that p. onwards**, desde entonces; **to be on the p. of doing sth**, estar a punto de hacer algo. ■ **boiling/freezing/melting p.**, punto *m* de ebullición/ congelación/fusión. **5** *(score) (in test, sport)* punto *m*, tanto *m*; **to score points**, ganar *or* marcar puntos; *Box* **to win on points**, ganar por puntos. ■ *Ten* **match/set p.**, pelota *f* de match/partido; **penalty p.**, punto *m* de penalti. **6** *(in argument)* punto *m*; **the main p.**, lo esencial, el meollo; **to make one's p.**, insistir en el argumento; **I see** *or* **take your p.**, entiendo lo que quieres decir; **p. taken!**, ¡ya, ya!; **it's a case in p.**, es un ejemplo de esto; **in p. of fact**, de hecho, en realidad; **to stretch a p.**, hacer una excepción. **7** *(purpose)* fin *m*, propósito *m*; **I don't see the p.**, no veo el sentido; **it's to the p.**, viene al caso; **that isn't the p.**, **it's beside the p.**, eso no viene al caso; **there's no p. in going**, no merece la pena ir; **to come** *or* **get to the p.**, llegar al meollo de la cuestión; **to make a p. of doing sth**, poner empeño en hacer algo; **to miss the p. of sth**, no seguir la corriente de algo; **what's the p.?**, ¿para qué?; **what's the p. of it?**, ¿qué sentido tiene? ■ **moot p.**, punto *m* discutible. **8** *(on scale)* punto *m*; *(on compass)* grado *m*, cuarta *f*; *(on thermometer)* punto *m*; *Fin (of shares etc)* entero *m*; *Math* **decimal p.**, punto decimal; **six p. three**, seis coma tres; *Fin* **the index is up 3 points**, el índice ha subido de 3 puntos; *fig* **up to a p.**, hasta cierto punto. **9** *(full stop)* punto *m*. **10** *Geog* punta *f*, cabo *m*. **11** *Elec* **power p.**, toma *f* de corriente. **12** *(police)* **to be on p. duty**, dirigir la circulación. **13 points**, *Aut* platinos *mpl*; *Rail* agujas *fpl*. **II** *vt* **1** *(aim) (gun etc)* apuntar; *(indicate) (way etc)* señalar, indicar; **to p. a gun at sb**, apuntar a algn con una pistola; **to p. one's finger**, señalar con el dedo; **to p. one's toes**, hacer puntas; *fig* **to p. the finger at sb**, acusar a algn; *Lit & fig* **to p. the way**, señalar el camino. **2** *Constr (wall, house)* rejuntar. **III** *vi* señalar, indicar; **the hands of the clock p. to ten o'clock**, las manecillas del reloj marcan las diez; **to p. at sth/sb**, señalar algo/a algn con el dedo; **to p. to** *or* **towards somewhere**, indicar el camino hacia un lugar; *fig* **everything points to her guilt**, todo indica que ella es la culpable. ◆ **point out** *vtr (show)* indicar, señalar; *(mistake)* señalar, hacer notar; *(mention)* hacer notar;

(warn) advertir; **they pointed out that it could be difficult**, advirtieron que podría ser difícil. ◆ **point up** *vtr* destacar, subrayar.

point-blank [pɔɪnt'blæŋk] **I** *adj (shot)* a boca de jarro, a quemarropa; *(question)* hecho,-a de golpe y porrazo; *(refusal)* categórico,-a, rotundo,-a; **to shoot at p.-b. range**, tirar a boca de jarro *or* a quemarropa. **II** *adv (shoot)* a boca de jarro, a quemarropa; *(fire question)* de golpe y porrazo; *(refuse)* categóricamente, rotundamente.

pointed ['pɔɪntɪd] *adj (sharp)* puntiagudo,-a; *fig (comment)* intencionado,-a, significativo,-a; *(cutting)* mordaz. ◆ **pointedly** *adv fig (significantly)* con intención, de un modo significativo; *(cuttingly)* con mordacidad.

pointer ['pɔɪntə'] *n* **1** *(indicator)* indicador *m*, aguja *f*; *(for blackboard, map)* puntero *m*. **2** *Zool (dog)* perro *m* de muestra. **3** *(clue)* indicación *f*; *(piece of advice)* consejo *m*.

pointless ['pɔɪntlɪs] *adj* sin sentido; **it's p.**, carece de sentido; **it would be p. to accept**, no serviría de nada aceptar.

point-to-point [pɔɪnttə'pɔɪnt] *n GB Sport* **p.-to-p. race**, carrera *f*.

poise [pɔɪz] **I** *n (balance)* equilibrio *m*; *(bearing)* porte *m*; *(self-assured)* aplomo *m*. **II** *vtr (hold in balance)* equilibrar, balancear; **to be poised**, estar equilibrado,-a, cernerse; *fig* **to be poised for action**, estar listo,-a para la acción.

poised [pɔɪzd] *adj* sereno,-a.

poison ['pɔɪzən] **I** *n* veneno *m*; **to take p.**, envenenarse; *fam* **what's your p.?**, ¿qué quieres tomar? ■ **p. gas**, gas *m* tóxico; *Bot* **p. ivy**, hiedra *f* venenosa; **p.-pen letter**, anónimo *m* amenazador *or* insultante. **II** *vtr* envenenar, intoxicar; **to p. oneself**, envenenarse; **to p. one's system**, intoxicarse; *fig* **to p. sb's mind**, envenenar la mente de algn.

poisoning ['pɔɪzənɪŋ] *n* envenenamiento *m*, intoxicación *f*; **to die of p.**, morir envenenado,-a *or* intoxicado,-a. ■ **blood p.**, envenenamiento *m* de la sangre; **food p.**, intoxicación *f* por alimentos.

poisonous ['pɔɪzənəs] *adj (plant, snake)* venenoso,-a; *(drugs, gas)* tóxico,-a; *fig (rumour)* pernicioso,-a.

poke [pəʊk] **I** *vtr (with finger or stick)* dar con la punta del dedo *or* del bastón a; **to p. one's head out of the window**, asomar la cabeza por la ventana; **to p. sb in the eye with one's finger**, poner el dedo en el ojo de algn; **to p. sb with one's elbow**, dar un codazo a algn; **to p. the fire**, atizar el fuego; *fig* **to p. fun at sb**, burlarse de algn; *fig* **to p. one's nose into sb else's business**, meterse en asuntos ajenos. **II** *n (jab) (with finger)* empujón *m*, golpe *m*; *(nudge)* codazo *m*; **to give sb a p. in the ribs**, dar a algn un codazo en las costillas; **to give the fire a p.**, atizar el fuego. ◆ **poke about**, **poke around** *vi* **to p. about** *or* **around in sb's handbag**, fisgonear *or* hurgar en el bolso de algn. ◆ **poke out** *vtr (eye)* sacar; **you nearly poked my eye out!**, ¡casi me sacaste el ojo!

poker¹ ['pəʊkə'] *n (for fire)* atizador *m*; *fig* **as stiff as a p.**, más tieso,-a que un palo.

poker² ['pəʊkə'] *n Cards* póquer *m*.

poker-faced ['pəʊkəfeɪst] *adj fam* de rostro impasible.

poky ['pəʊkɪ] *adj (pokier, pokiest) US fam pej* minúsculo,-a; **a p. littte house/room**, una casucha/un cuartucho.

Poland ['pəʊlənd] *n* Polonia.

polar ['pəʊlə'] *adj* polar. ■ **p. bear**, oso *m* polar.

polarity [pəʊ'lærɪtɪ] *n* polaridad *f*.

polarization [pəʊləraɪ'zeɪʃən] *n* polarización *f*.

polarize ['pəʊləraɪz] **I** *vtr* polarizar. **II** *vi* polarizarse.

Polaroid ['pəʊlərɔɪd] *adj* polaroid.

Pole [pəʊl] *n* polaco,-a *m,f*.

pole¹ [pəʊl] *n* palo *m*, estaca *f*; *(for curtain)* bara *f*. ■ *Athlet* **p. vault**, salto *m* de pértiga; **telegraph p.**, poste *m* telegráfico; **tent p.**, palo *m* de tienda; *Athlet* **vaulting p.**, pértiga *f*.

pole² [pəʊl] *n Elec Geog* polo *m*; *fig* **to be poles apart**, ser polos opuestos. ■ **North/South P.**, Polo *m* Norte/Sur; **P. Star**, estrella *f* polar.

poleaxe, *US* **poleax** ['pəʊlæks] *vtr* apalear.

polecat ['pəʊlkæt] *n inv Zool* turón *m*.

polemic [pə'lemɪk] *n* **1** polémica *f*. **2** **polemics**, *(art)* polémica *f sing*.

police [pə'liːs] *n npl* policía *f sing*; **to call the p.**, llamar a la policía; **to join the p.**, meterse de policía. ■ **p. car**, coche *m* patrulla; **p. constable**, guardia *m*, policía *m*; **p. escort**, escolta *f* de policía; **p. force**, cuerpo *m* de policía; **p. headquarters**, jefatura *f* de policía; **p. officer**, guardia *m*, policía *m*; **p. record**, antecedentes *mpl* penales; **p. state**, estado *m* policíaco; **p. station**, comisaría *f*. II *vtr* vigilar, mantener el orden en.

policeman [pə'liːsmən] *n (pl policemen)* guardia *m*, policía *m*.

policewoman [pə'liːswʊmən] *n (pl policewomen* [pə'liːswɪmɪn]*) (mujer f)* policía *f*.

policy ['pɒlɪsɪ] *n* **1** *(course of action)* norma *f*, táctica *f*; *Pol* política *f*; **foreign p.**, política exterior; **it's a good/bad p.**, es buena/mala táctica; **it's a matter of p.**, es cuestión de política; **our p. is to do this**, tenemos por norma hacer esto. **2** *Ins (insurance)* **p.**, póliza *f* (de seguros); **to take out an insurance p.**, hacerse un seguro, sacar una póliza. ■ **p. holder**, asegurado,-a *m*,*f*.

polio ['pəʊlɪəʊ] *n (abbr of poliomyelitis) Med* poliomielitis *f*, polio *f*.

Polish ['pəʊlɪʃ] I *adj* polaco,-a. II *n* **1** *pl* **the P.**, los polacos. **2** *(language)* polaco *m*.

polish ['pɒlɪʃ] I *vtr (metal, stone)* pulir; *(furniture, floors)* encerar; *(nails)* pintar con esmalte; *(shoes)* limpiar; *(silver)* sacar brillo a. II *n* **1** *(cream etc) (for furniture, floors)* cera *f*; *(for shoes)* betún *m*; *(for nails)* esmalte *m*. **2** *(action)* pulimento *m*; **to give one's shoes a p.**, limpiar los zapatos; **to give sth a p.**, dar brillo a algo. **3** *(shine)* brillo *m*, lustre *m*; *fig (refinement)* refinamiento *m*, brillo *m*. ◆ **polish off** *vtr fam (work)* despachar, terminar con; *(food)* tragarse, zamparse. ◆ **polish up** *vtr fig* perfeccionar.

polished ['pɒlɪʃt] *adj (metal, stone, silver)* pulido,-a, lustroso,-a; *(furniture, floors)* encerado,-a; *(nails)* pintado,-a; *(shoes)* limpio,-a; *fig (manners)* refinado,-a; *(style)* pulido,-a; *(performance)* impecable.

polite [pə'laɪt] *adj* cortés, educado,-a; **in p. society**, entre gente educada; **to be p. to sb**, tratar a algn con cortesía *or* educación. ◆ **politely** *adv* cortésmente, educadamente, con cortesía *or* educación.

politeness [pə'laɪtnɪs] *n* cortesía *f*, educación *f*.

politic ['pɒlɪtɪk] *adj* prudente.

political [pə'lɪtɪkəl] *adj* político,-a. ■ **p. asylum**, asilo *m* político; **p. science**, ciencias *fpl* políticas.

politician [pɒlɪ'tɪʃən] *n* político,-a *m*,*f*.

politics ['pɒlɪtɪks] I *n sing (subject)* política *f*; **to go into p.**, dedicarse a la política; **to talk p.**, hablar de política. II *npl (views)* posición *f sing or* postura *f sing* política; **what are his p.?**, ¿cuál es su postura política?

polka ['pɒlkə] *n (pl polkas)* **1** *(dance)* polca *f*. **2** **p. dot**, dibujo *m* de puntos.

poll [pəʊl] I *n* **1** *(voting)* votación *f*; **a defeat at the polls**, una derrota electoral; **a heavy p.**, una votación masiva; **the polls**, las elecciones; **to go to the polls**, acudir a las urnas; **to take a p. on sth**, someter algo a votación. **2** *(survey)* encuesta *f*; *(register)* registro *m*. ■ **opinion p.**, sondeo *m* de opinión; **p. tax**, contribución *f* urbana. II *vtr (votes)* obtener; *(opinion)* sondear.

pollen ['pɒlən] *n* polen *m*. ■ **p. count**, índice *m* de polen en el aire.

pollinate ['pɒlɪneɪt] *vtr* polinizar.

polling ['pəʊlɪŋ] *n* votación *f*. ■ **p. booth**, cabina *f* electoral; **p. station**, centro *m* electoral.

pollute [pə'luːt] *vtr* contaminar, polucionar.

pollution [pə'luːʃən] *n* contaminación *f*, polución *f*; **environmental p.**, contaminación del medio ambiente.

polo ['pəʊləʊ] *n* **1** *Sport* polo *m*. ■ **water p.**, waterpolo *m*, poto *m* acuático. **2** **p. neck sweater**, jersey *m* con cuello vuelto *or* cuello cisne.

poltergeist ['pɒltəgaɪst] *n* duende *m*.

poly ['pɒlɪ] *n GB fam abbr of* **polytechnic**.

poly- ['pɒlɪ] *pref* poli-, multi-.

polyester [pɒlɪ'estə^r] *n* poliéster *m*.

polygamy [pə'lɪgəmɪ] *n* poligamia *f*.

polygamous [pə'lɪgəməs] *adj* polígamo,-a.

polyglot ['pɒlɪglɒt] *adj & n* políglota,-a *(m*,*f)*.

polygon ['pɒlɪgɒn] *n Geom* polígono *m*.

polymer ['pɒlɪmə^r] *n Chem* polímero *m*.

Polynesia [pɒlɪ'niːʒɪə] *n* Polinesia.

polyp ['pɒlɪp] *n Med* pólipo *m*.

polyphonic [pɒlɪ'fɒnɪk] *adj Mus* polifónico,-a.

polystyrene [pɒlɪ'staɪriːn] *n* poliestireno *m*.

polytechnic [pɒlɪ'teknɪk] *n Educ* escuela *f* politécnica, politécnico *m*.

polythene ['pɒlɪθiːn] *n* polietileno *m*. ■ **p. bag**, bolsa *f* de plástico.

polyurethane [pɒlɪ'jʊərəθeɪn] *n* poliuretano *m*.

pomegranate ['pɒmɪgrænɪt] *n Bot (fruit)* granada *f*. ■ **p. tree**, granado *m*.

pommy ['pɒmɪ] *n Austral sl pej* inglés,-esa *m*,*f*.

pomp [pɒmp] *n* pompa *f*.

pompom ['pɒmpɒm] *n*, **pompon** ['pɒmpɒn] *n* borla *f*, pompón *m*.

pomposity [pɒm'pɒsɪtɪ] *n* pomposidad *f*.

pompous ['pɒmpəs] *adj (person)* presumido,-a; *(speech)* rimbombante; *(occasion)* pomposo,-a.

ponce [pɒns] *n GB sl pej* chulo *m*.

poncho ['pɒntʃəʊ] *n (pl ponchos)* poncho *m*.

pond [pɒnd] *n* estanque *m*.

ponder ['pɒndə^r] I *vtr* considerar, sopesar. II *vi* **to p. over sth**, meditar *or* reflexionar sobre algo.

ponderous ['pɒndərəs] *adj* pesado,-a.

pong ['pɒŋ] *GB fam* I *n* hedor *m*, olor *m* a peste. II *vi* heder, oler a peste, apestar.

pontiff ['pɒntɪf] *n* pontífice *m*.

pontificate [pɒn'tɪfɪkeɪt] *vi* pontificar.

pontoon¹ [pɒn'tuːn] *n Constr* pontón *m*. ■ **p. bridge**, puente *m* de pontones.

pontoon² [pɒn'tuːn] *n Cards* veintiuna *f*, siete y medio *m*.

pony ['pəʊnɪ] *n* poney *m*. ■ **p. trekking**, excursión *f* en poney.

ponytail ['pəʊnɪteɪl] *n* cola *f* de caballo.

poodle ['puːdəl] *n Zool* caniche *m*.

poof [pʊf] *n GB sl offens* marica *m*.

pooh [puː] *interj* ¡bah!

pooh-pooh [puː'puː] *vtr* despreciar, descartar.

pool¹ [puːl] *n (of water, oil, etc)* charco *m*; *(pond)* estanque *m*; *(in river)* pozo *m*. ■ **swimming p.**, piscina *f*.

pool² [puːl] I *n* **1** *Com (common fund)* fondo *m* común; *(services)* servicios *mpl* comunes. ■ **car p.**, reserva *f* de coches; **typing p.**, servicio *m* de mecanografía. **2** *US (snooker)* billar *m* americano. **3** **football pools**, quinielas *fpl*; **to do the football p.**, hacer una quiniela. II *vtr (funds)* reunir, juntar; *(ideas, resources)* poner en común.

poor [pʊəʳ, pɔːʳ] **I** *adj (person)* pobre; *(quality)* malo,-a, inferior; *(attempt)* poco satisfactorio,-a; **he was knocked down by a car, p. thing,** le atropelló un coche, el pobre; **p. people,** gente pobre; **to be a p. traveller,** soportar mal los viajes; **to be p. at French,** estar flojo,-a en francés; **to be in p. health,** estar mal de salud; **to have a p. memory,** tener poca memoria; **to have a p. opinion of sth,** tener una opinión poco favorable de algo; *fam* **you p. thing!,** ¡pobrecito! **II the poor** *npl* los pobres.

poorly ['pʊəlɪ, 'pɔːlɪ] **I** *adv (gen)* pobremente; *(badly)* mal; **p. dressed/attended,** mal vestido,-a/asistido,-a. **II** *adj (poorlier, poorliest) (ill)* mal, malo,-a; **to be p.,** estar *or* sentirse mal *or* malo,-a.

pop [pɒp] **I** *vtr (pt & pp popped)* **1** *(burst)* hacer reventar; *(cork)* hacer saltar. **2** *fam* **p. your coat on,** ponte el abrigo; **she popped a chocolate into her mouth,** se metió un bombón en la boca; **to p. one's head out of the window,** asomar la cabeza por la ventana; *fam* **to p. the question,** declararse. **II** *vi* **1** *(burst)* reventar; *(cork)* saltar; **her eyes nearly popped out of her head,** le saltaron los ojos de sorpresa. **2** *fam (go quickly)* **I'm just popping over to Ian's,** voy un momento a casa de Ian. **III** *n* **1** *(noise)* pequeña explosión *f*; **to go p.,** *(burst)* reventar; *(bang)* hacer pum. **2** *fam (drink)* gaseosa *f*. **3** *fam (father)* papá *m*. **4** *Mus fam* música *f* pop. ■ **p. festival,** festival *m* de música pop; **p. singer,** cantante *mf* pop. ◆ **pop in** *vi fam* ir un momento a, pasar por; **p. in and see us,** pásate a hacernos una visita. ◆ **pop off** *vi fam* **1** *(leave)* irse, marcharse. **2** *(die)* palmar.

pop *abbr of* **population,** población *f*.

popcorn ['pɒpkɔːn] *n* palomitas *fpl* de maíz.

pope [pəʊp] *n* papa *m*.

popeyed ['pɒpaɪd] *adj* de ojos saltones.

popgun ['pɒpɡʌn] *n* pistola *f* de juguete (de aire comprimido).

poplar ['pɒpləʳ] *n Bot* álamo *m*. ■ **black p.,** chopo *m* negro; **grey p.,** álamo *m* cano; **Italian black p.,** chopo *m* negro italiano; **Lombardy p.,** chopo *m* lombardo, álamo *m* de Italia.

poplin ['pɒplɪn] *n Tex* popelina *f*.

popper ['pɒpəʳ] *n GB Sew* fam corchete *m*.

poppet ['pɒpɪt] *n fam* cielo *m*, encanto *m*; **she's a p.,** es un cielo; **yes, my p.,** sí, mi vida.

poppy ['pɒpɪ] *n Bot* amapola *f*. ■ **p. seed,** semilla *f* de amapola.

poppycock ['pɒpɪkɒk] *n fam* tonterías *fpl*; **don't talk p.!,** ¡no digas tonterías!

populace ['pɒpjʊləs] *n (people)* pueblo *m*; *(masses)* populacho *m*.

popular ['pɒpjʊləʳ] *adj* **1** *(well-liked)* popular; *(person)* estimado,-a; *(fashionable)* de moda; *(common)* corriente, común; **a p. colour,** un color muy visto; **he's p. with his colleagues,** sus colegas le estiman mucho; **you won't be p. with the neighbours if you do it,** no ganarás la simpatía de los vecinos si lo haces. **2** *(of or for the people)* popular; **by p. request,** a petición del público. ■ **p. opinion,** opinión *f* general; **p. prices,** precios *mpl* populares. ◆ **popularly** *adv* popularmente, generalmente; **it's p. believed that ...,** la mayoría de la gente cree que ... .

popularity [pɒpjʊ'lærɪtɪ] *n* popularidad *f*.

popularize ['pɒpjʊləraɪz] *vtr (music, fashion, etc)* popularizar; *(idea etc) (make understandable)* vulgarizar.

populate ['pɒpjʊleɪt] *vtr* poblar; **thinly populated,** muy poco poblado,-a.

population [pɒpjʊ'leɪʃən] *n* población *f*; **the p. explosion,** la explosión demográfica.

populous ['pɒpjʊləs] *adj* populoso,-a, poblado,-a.

porcelain ['pɔːslɪn] *n* porcelana *f*; **made of p.,** de porcelana. ■ **p. cup,** taza *f* de porcelana.

porch [pɔːtʃ] *n* **1** *(of church)* pórtico *m*; *(of house)* porche *m*, entrada *f*. **2** *US (veranda)* terraza *f*.

porcupine ['pɔːkjʊpaɪn] *n Zool* puerco *m* espín.

pore[1] [pɔːʳ] *vi* **to p. over sth,** engolfarse en algo.

pore[2] [pɔːʳ] *n Anat* poro *m*.

pork [pɔːk] *n* carne *f* de cerdo. ■ **p. butcher,** charcutero,-a *m,f*; **p. chop,** chuleta *f* de cerdo; **p. pie,** empanada *f* de carne de cerdo; **p. sausage,** salchicha *f*.

porn [pɔːn] *n fam (abbr of pornography)* porno *m*; **hard/soft p.,** pornografía *f* dura/blanda.

pornographic [pɔːnə'ɡræfɪk] *adj* pornográfico,-a.

pornography [pɔː'nɒɡrəfɪ] *n* pornografía *f*.

porous ['pɔːrəs] *adj* poroso,-a.

porpoise ['pɔːpəs] *n Zool* marsopa *f*.

porridge ['pɒrɪdʒ] *n Culin* gachas *fpl* de avena. ■ **p. oats,** copos *mpl* de avena (para hacer gachas).

port[1] [pɔːt] *n (town, harbour)* puerto *m*; **to come** *or* **put into p.,** tomar puerto; *fig* **any p. in a storm,** la necesidad carece de ley. ■ **fishing/sea p.,** puerto *m* pesquero/marítimo; **free p.,** puerto *m* franco; **home p.,** puerto *m* de matrícula; **p. of call,** puerto *m* de escala; **P. of Spain,** Puerto España.

port[2] [pɔːt] *n Naut Av (larboard)* babor *m*.

port[3] [pɔːt] *n (wine)* vino *m* de Oporto, oporto *m*.

portable ['pɔːtəbəl] *adj* portátil.

Port-au-Prince [pɔːtəʊ'prɪns] *n* Puerto Príncipe.

portend [pɔː'tend] *vtr fml* augurar, presagiar.

portent ['pɔːtent] *n fml* augurio *m*, presagio *m*.

porter ['pɔːtəʳ] *n* **1** *(in hotel, building, market)* portero,-a *m,f*; *Rail* mozo *m* de estación. **2** *US* mozo *m* de los coches-cama.

portfolio [pɔːt'fəʊlɪəʊ] *n (pl portfolios) (file)* carpeta *f*; *(of artist, politician)* cartera *f*; **minister without p.,** ministro,-a *m,f* sin cartera.

porthole ['pɔːthəʊl] *n Naut* portilla *f*.

portion ['pɔːʃən] *n (part, piece)* parte *f*, porción *f*; *(of food)* ración *f*. ◆ **portion out** *vtr* repartir, distribuir.

portly ['pɔːtlɪ] *adj (portlier, portliest)* corpulento,-a, gordo,-a.

portrait ['pɔːtrɪt, 'pɔːtreɪt] *n* retrato *m*; **to have one's p. painted,** hacerse *(hacer)* un retrato; **to paint sb's p.,** retratar a algn. ■ **p. painter,** retratista *mf*.

portray [pɔː'treɪ] *vtr (paint portrait of)* retratar; *(describe)* pintar, describir; *Theat (character)* representar.

Portugal ['pɔːtjʊɡəl] *n* Portugal.

Portuguese [pɔːtjʊ'ɡiːz] *adj* portugués,-esa, luso,-a. ■ **P. man-of-war,** medusa *f*. **II** *n* **1** *(person)* portugués,-esa *m,f*. **2** *(language)* portugués *m*.

pos *abbr of* **positive,** positivo,-a.

pose [pəʊz] **I** *vtr (problem, question)* plantear; *(threat)* representar. **II** *vi* **1** *(for painting, photograph)* posar. **2** *pej (behave affectedly)* presumir, hacer pose. **3 to p. as,** hacerse pasar por; **he posed as a doctor,** se hizo pasar por médico. **III** *n* **1** *(position, stance)* postura *f*, actitud *f*. **2** *pej (affectation)* pose *f*.

poser[1] ['pəʊzəʳ] *n fam pej (person)* presumido,-a *m,f*.

poser[2] ['pəʊzəʳ] *n (problem)* problema *m*; *(difficult question)* pregunta *f* difícil.

posh [pɒʃ] *GB fam* **I** *adj (hotel, restaurant etc)* elegante, de lujo; *(person)* presumido,-a; *(accent)* afectado,-a. **II** *adv* **to talk p.,** hablar con acento afectado.

position [pə'zɪʃən] **I** *n* **1** *(place)* posición *f*; *(location)* situación *f*; *Sport* posición; **from this/that p.,** desde aquí/allí; *Sport* **what p. does she play?** ¿de qué juega? **2** *(right place)* sitio *m*, lugar *m*; **to be in/out of p.,** estar en su sitio/fuera de lugar; **to hold sth in p.,** sujetar algo; **to put sth into p.,** colocar algo. **3** *(posture, stance)* posición *f*, postura *f*; **in a comfortable p.,** en una postura cómoda; **in a horizontal/vertical p.,** en posición horizontal/vertical. **4** *(on scale, in competition)* posición *f*, lugar *m*; *(rank)* rango m; **a woman of her p.,** una mujer de su categoría social; **in first/last p.,** en primer/último lugar. **5** *(situation)* lugar m, situación f; **put yourself in my p.,** ponte en mi lugar; **the economic/political p.,** la situación económica/política; **to be in an awkward p.,** encontrarse en una situación delicada; **to be in a p. to do sth,** estar en condiciones de hacer algo. **6** *(opinion)* postura f; **you know my p. on this matter,** ya sabes lo que opino sobre este tema. **7** *(job)* puesto m, empleo m; **a p. of responsibility,** un puesto de responsabilidad; **to apply for the p. of cook,** solicitar el puesto de cocinero. **II** *vtr* *(put in place)* colocar; *(troops)* situar; **to p. oneself,** ponerse en posición.

positive ['pɒzɪtɪv] *adj* **1** *(affirmative)* positivo,-a; *(criticism)* constructivo,-a; *Math Ling Elec* positivo,-a; *(person)* dinámico,-a; *(sign)* favorable; *(proof)* incontrovertible; *(refusal)* categórico,-a; *Med* **the tests were p.,** las pruebas resultaron positivas. **2** *(sure, certain)* seguro,-a; **to be p. about sth,** estar seguro,-a de algo. **3** *fam (absolute)* auténtico,-a, verdadero,-a; **it was a p. disaster,** fue un auténtico desastre. ◆ **positively** *adv* **1** *(answer)* en forma positiva; *(think)* positivamente; *(talk)* con convicción. **2** *fam (absolutely)* realmente, verdaderamente; **the food was p. revolting,** la comida daba auténtico asco.

possess [pə'zes] *vtr* **1** *(own)* poseer; **everything she possessed,** todo cuanto tenía. **2** *(take over)* apoderarse de; **what possessed him to buy it?,** ¿cómo se le ocurrió comprarlo?

possessed [pə'zest] *adj* poseído,-a, endemoniado,-a.

possession [pə'zeʃən] *n* **1** *(ownership)* posesión f; *Sport* **to have p. of the ball,** tener el balón *or (in football)* la pelota; **to have sth in one's p.,** tener algo (en su poder); *Jur* **to take p. of sth,** tomar posesión de algo. **2** *(personal property)* posesión f; **her prized p.,** su posesión más estimada; **it was his only p.,** era lo único que tenía, **3 possessions,** bienes *mpl*. **4** *(by evil spirit)* posesión f.

possessive [pə'zesɪv] **I** *adj* posesivo,-a; **to be p. about sth/with sb,** ser posesivo,-a con algo/algn. **II** *n* *Ling* posesivo m.

possessor [pə'zesə^r] *n* poseedor,-a m,f.

possibility [pɒsɪ'bɪlɪtɪ] *n* **1** *(likelihood)* posibilidad f; **it's a p.,** es posible; **it's within the realms of p.,** queda dentro de lo posible; **there's a p. that they'll accept,** existe posibilidad *or* es posible que acepten. **2 possibilities,** *(potential)* potencial m *sing*; **to have p.,** ser prometedor,-a.

possible ['pɒsɪbəl] **I** *adj* posible; **as much as p.,** todo lo posible; **as often as p.,** cuanto más mejor; **as soon as p.,** cuanto antes; **if at all p.,** a ser posible; **it's p. that they'll come,** es posible que vengan; **it's p. to go there,** es posible *or* se puede ir allí; **to make sth p.,** posibilitar algo. **II** *n* **he's a p. for the job,** es un candidato para el puesto. ◆ **possibly** *adv* **1** posiblemente; **as well as I p. can,** lo mejor que pueda; **I can't p. come,** no puedo venir de ninguna manera. **2** *(perhaps)* tal vez, quizás, puede que sí; **will you go? —p.,** ¿irás? — puede que sí.

post¹ [pəʊst] **I** *n* *(of wood)* estaca f, poste m; *Ftb (goalpost)* poste; *fig* **to go from pillar to p.,** ir de la Ceca a la Meca; *GB sl* **to be pipped at the p.,** perder por un pelo. ■ **starting/finishing p.,** línea f de salida/llegada. **II** *vtr* *(fix)* fijar; *(notice)* **'post no bills',** 'prohibido fijar carteles'.

post² [pəʊst] **I** *n* **1** *(position, job)* puesto m, cargo m; **to take up one's p.,** ocupar el puesto. **2** *Mil* puesto m. ■ **frontier p.,** puesto m fronterizo; **last p.,** toque m de retreta. **3** *US trading p.,** factoría f. **II** *vtr* **1** *Mil* enviar, destinar. **2** *(send)* enviar, destinar.

post³ [pəʊst] *GB* **I** *n* *(mail)* correo m; **by p.,** por correo; **by return p.,** a vuelta de correo; **by separate p.,** por correo aparte; **is there any p.?,** ¿hay cartas?; **to catch/miss the p.,** alcanzar/no alcanzar el correo; **to come first/last p.,** venir con el primer/último reparto. ■ **p. office,** oficina f de correos; **P. Office Box,** apartado m de correos; **P. Office Savings Bank,** Caja f Postal de Ahorros; **p. office**

worker, empleado,-a m,f de correos. **II** *vtr* *(letter)* echar al correo; **to p. sth to sb,** mandar algo por correo a algn; *fig* **to keep sb posted about sth,** tener a algn al tanto de algo.

post- [pəʊst] *pref* post-, pos-.

postage ['pəʊstɪdʒ] *n* franqueo m, porte m; **p. paid,** franco de porte. ■ **p. and packing,** gastos *mpl* de envío; **p. stamp,** sello m.

postal ['pəʊstəl] *adj* postal, de correos. ■ **p. district,** distrito m postal; **p. order,** giro m postal; **p. vote,** voto m por correo.

postbag ['pəʊstbæg] *n* *GB (mail)* cartas *fpl*, correspondencia f.

postbox ['pəʊstbɒks] *n* *GB* buzón m.

postcard ['pəʊstkɑːd] *n* tarjeta f postal.

postcode ['pəʊstkəʊd] *n* *GB* código m postal.

postdate [pəʊst'deɪt] *vtr* poner fecha adelantada a.

poster ['pəʊstə^r] *n* cartel m, póster m.

poste restante [pəʊstrɪ'stænt] *n* lista f de correos.

posterior [pɒ'stɪərɪə^r] **I** *n* *hum* trasero m, pompis m. **II** *adj* posterior.

posterity [pɒ'sterɪtɪ] *n* posteridad f.

post-free [pəʊst'friː] *GB* **I** *adj* porte pagado. **II** *adv* a porte pagado.

postgraduate [pəʊst'grædjʊɪt] **I** *n* postgraduado,-a m,f, posgraduado,-a m, f. **II** *adj* de postgraduado *or* posgraduado.

posthaste [pəʊst'heɪst] *adv* a toda prisa.

posthumous ['pɒstjʊməs] *adj* póstumo,-a. ◆ **posthumously** *adv* póstumamente, después de la muerte.

postman ['pəʊstmən] *n* *(pl postmen)* cartero m.

postmark ['pəʊstmɑːk] **I** *n* matasellos m *inv*. **II** *vtr* timbrar, matasellar.

postmaster ['pəʊstmɑːstə^r] *n* administrador m de correos. ■ **p. general,** director m general de correos.

postmistress ['pəʊstmɪstrɪs] *n* administradora f de correos.

postmortem [pəʊst'mɔːtəm] *n* autopsia f.

postnatal [pəʊst'neɪtəl] *adj* postnatal, (de) postparto.

postpone [pəʊst'pəʊn, pə'spəʊn] *vtr* aplazar, posponer.

postponement [pəʊst'pəʊnmənt] *n* aplazamiento m.

postscript ['pəʊsskrɪpt] *n* postdata f, posdata f.

postulate ['pɒstjʊleɪt] *vtr* postular.

posture ['pɒstʃə^r] **I** *n* postura f; *(affected)* pose f. **II** *vi* adoptar una postura; *(affected)* adoptar una pose.

postwar ['pəʊstwɔː^r] *adj* de la postguerra *or* posguerra; **the p. period,** la postguerra, la posguerra.

posy ['pəʊzɪ] *n* ramillete m.

pot [pɒt] **I** *n* *(container)* tarro m, pote m; *(for cooking)* olla f, puchero m; *(for tea)* tetera f; *(for coffee)* cafetera f; *(for flowers)* maceta f, tiesto m; *(ornament)* cacharro m; **pots and pans,** batería f (de cocina); **to take a p. shot at sb,** tirar *or* disparar al azar contra algn; *fam* **to go to p.,** irse al traste; *fam* **to have pots of money,** estar forrado,-a. ■ *Culin* **p. roast,** carne f asada en la olla; **p. shot,** tiro m al azar. **II** *vtr* *(pt &. pp potted)* **1** *(meat etc)* conservar en tarro; *(plant)* meter en maceta *or* tiesto. **2** *(ball)* *(in billiards)* meter en la tronera; *(in golf)* meter en el hoyo.

potable ['pəʊtəbəl] *adj* potable.

potash ['pɒtæʃ] *n* *Chem* potasa f.

potassium [pə'tæsɪəm] *n* *Chem* potasio m.

potato [pə'teɪtəʊ] *n* *(pl potatoes)* patata f; *sl* **hot p.,** patata caliente. ■ **jacket p.,** patata f cocida *or* asada con piel; **mashed p.,** puré m de patatas; **p. crisp,** *US* **p. chip,** patata f frita (de bolsa); **sweet p.,** boniato m.

potbellied ['pɒtbelɪd] *adj* *(fat)* barrigón,-ona; *(malnourished)* de vientre hinchado.

potency ['pəutənsı] *n* potencia *f*, fuerza *f*.

potent ['pəutənt] *adj* potente, fuerte.

potentate ['pəutənteit] *n* potentado *m*.

potential [pə'tenʃəl] **I** *adj* potencial, posible. **II** *n* 1 *(promise)* potencial *m*; **to have p.**, ser prometedor,-a; **to realize one's full p.**, realizarse plenamente. **2** *Elec Math* potencial *m*. ◆ **potentially** *adv* en potencia.

pothole ['pɒthəul] *n Geol* cueva *f*, *(in road)* bache *m*.

potholer ['pɒthəulər] *n GB Sport* espeleólogo,-a *m*, *f*.

potholing ['pɒthəulıŋ] *n GB Sport* espeleología *f*.

potion ['pəuʃən] *n* poción *f*, pócima *f*.

potluck [pɒt'lʌk] *n fam* **to take p.**, conformarse con lo que haya.

potpourri [pəu'puərı] *n* (*pl* *potpourris*) 1 *(of flowers)* pebete *m*; *(of music, poems, etc)* popurrí *m*. 2 *Culin* olla *f* podrida.

potted ['pɒtıd] **I** *pt* & *pp* see **pot**. **II** *adj* *(food)* en conserva; *(plant)* en maceta *or* tiesto; *fam fig* **a p. version**, una versión resumida.

potter¹ ['pɒtər] *n* alfarero,-a *m*, *f*. ■ **p.'s wheel**, torno *m* de alfarero.

potter² ['pɒtər] *vi GB* **to p. about** *or* **around**, entretenerse.

pottery ['pɒtərı] *n* *(craft, place)* alfarería *f*; *(objects)* cerámica *f*, loza *f*. ■ **p. mug**, tazón *m* de barro.

potty¹ ['pɒtı] *adj* (*pottier, pottiest*) *GB fam* chiflado,-a; **to drive sb p.**, volverle loco,-a a algn.

potty² ['pɒtı] *n fam* orinal *m*.

potty-trained ['pɒtıtreind] *adj* *(child)* que ya no necesita llevar pañales.

pouch [pautʃ] *n* 1 *(gen)* bolsa *f* pequeña; *(for ammunition)* morral *m*; *(for tobacco)* petaca *f*. 2 *Zool* bolsa *f* abdominal.

pouf(fe) [puːf] *n* puf *m*.

poulterer ['pəultərər] *n GB* pollero,-a *m*, *f*.

poultice ['pəultıs] *n Med* cataplasma *f*, emplasto *m*.

poultry ['pəultrı] *n* *(live)* aves *fpl* de corral; *(food)* pollos *mpl*, volatería *f*. ■ **p. farm**, granja *f* avícola; **p. farmer**, avicultor,-a *m*, *f*; **p. farming**, avicultura *f*.

pounce [pauns] **I** *vi* **to p. on sb/sth**, echarse encima de algn/algo. **II** *n* salto *m*.

pound¹ [paund] **I** *vtr* *(strike)* aporrear, machacar; **to p. at** *or* **on the door**, golpear la puerta. **II** *vi* 1 *(beat)* resonar; *(heart)* palpitar; *(waves)* romper. 2 *(walk heavily)* andar con paso pesado.

pound² [paund] *n* 1 *(money)* libra *f* (esterlina). ■ **p. note**, billete *m* de una libra. 2 *(weight)* libra *f*; **half a p.**, media libra; **to sell sth by the p.**, vender algo por libras.

pound³ [paund] *n* *(enclosure)* *(for dogs)* perrera *f*; *(for cars)* depósito *m* de coches.

pounding ['paundıŋ] *n* *(of heart)* palpitación *f*; *(of waves)* embate *m*; *fam* **to give sb a p.**, darle una paliza a algn.

pour [pɔːr] **I** *vtr* 1 *(liquid)* echar, verter; *(spill)* derramar; **to p. money into a venture**, invertir mucho dinero en un negocio; **to p. sb a drink**, servirle una copa a algn; *fig* **to p. cold water on a scheme**, poner pegas a un proyecto; *fig* **to p. scorn on sth**, despreciar algo. **II** *vi* *(liquid)* correr, fluir; *(spill)* derramarse; *(of teapot)* echar; **it's pouring with rain**, está lloviendo a cántaros; *fam* **the sweat was pouring off him**, sudaba la gota gorda. ◆ **pour out** *vtr* *(liquid)* echar, verter; *(spill)* derramar; **to p. sb out a drink, p. out a drink for sb**, servirle una copa a algn; *fig* **to p. one's heart out to sb**, desahogarse con algn.

pouring ['pɔːrıŋ] *adj* *(rain)* torrencial; *(custard etc)* para echar; **p. consistency**, consistencia *f* líquida.

pout¹ [paut] **I** *vi* hacer pucheros, poner mala cara. **II** *n* puchero *m*, mala cara *f*.

pout² [paut] *n* *(fish)* faneca *f*.

poverty ['pɒvətı] *n* pobreza *f*; *fig* *(of ideas)* falta *f*, carencia *f*; **extreme p.**, miseria *f*; **to live in p.**, vivir en la miseria.

poverty-stricken ['pɒvətıstrıkən] *adj* necesitado,-a; **to be p.-s.**, vivir en la miseria.

POW [piːəu'dʌbəljuː] *abbr of* **prisoner of war**, prisionero,-a *m*, *f* de guerra.

powder ['paudər] **I** *n* polvo *m*; **to reduce sth to p.**, pulverizar algo, reducir algo a polvo. ■ **p. compact**, polvera *f*; **p. keg**, polvorín *m*; **p. puff**, borla *f*; **p. room**, servicios *mpl* de señora, tocador *m*; **talcum p.**, polvos *mpl* de talco. **II** *vtr* 1 *(reduce to powder)* pulverizar, reducir a polvo. 2 *(put powder on)* **to p. one's nose**, poner polvos en la cara; *euph* ir a los servicios de señora *or* al tocador.

powdered ['paudəd] *adj* *(milk)* en polvo.

powdery ['paudərı] *adj* *(like powder)* polvoriento,-a; *(powdered)* en polvo.

power ['pauər] **I** *n* 1 *(force, strength)* fuerza *f*; *(energy)* energía *f*; **electric/nuclear p.**, energía eléctrica/nuclear; *Elec* **to cut off the p.**, cortar la corriente. ■ **p. point**, enchufe *m*, toma *f* (de corriente); **p. station**, central *f* eléctrica; *Aut* **p. steering**, dirección *f* asistida. 2 *(ability)* poder *m*, capacidad *f*; *(faculty)* facultad *f*; *fig* *(impact)* poder; **to do everything in one's p. to achive sth**, hacer todo lo posible por conseguir algo; **powers of persuasion**, poder de persuasión; **powers of resistance**, poder *or* capacidad de resistencia; **the p. of speech**, la facultad del habla; *fig* **el poder del habla**; *fam* **it did him a p. of good**, le hizo mucho bien. 3 *(authority)* poder *m*, autoridad *f*; *(nation)* potencia *f*; *Jur Pol* poder; *(influence)* influencia *f*; *(right)* derecho *m*; **powers of darkness**, las fuerzas del mal; **the great powers**, las grandes potencias; **the p. of veto**, el derecho de veto; *Pol* **to be in p.**, estar en *or* tener el poder; *Pol* **to come into p.**, subir al poder; **to have p. over sb**, tener influencia sobre algn; **to have sb in one's p.**, tener a algn en su poder; *fig* **the powers that be**, las autoridades. ■ *Jur* **p. of attorney**, poder *m*, procuración *f*. 4 *Tech* potencia *f*, fuerza *f*; *(performance, output)* rendimiento *m*. ■ **p. drill**, taladradora *f* mecánica; **p. saw**, sierra *f* mecánica. 5 *Math* potencia *f*; **two to the p. of four**, dos elevado a la cuarta potencia. **II** *vtr* *(aircraft)* propulsar, impulsar; **powered by jet**, impulsado,-a por motor a reacción; **to be powered by electricity**, funcionar con electricidad.

powerboat ['pauəbəut] *n Naut* motoroa *f*, lancha *f* a motor.

power-driven ['pauədrıvən] *adj Tech* mecánico,-a; *Elec* eléctrico,-a.

powerful ['pauəful] *adj* *(strong)* *(person)* fuerte, fornido,-a; *(influential)* *(person, country)* poderoso,-a; *(remedy)* eficaz; *(engine, machine)* potente; *(emotion)* fuerte; *(speech)* conmovedor,-a, emocionante.

powerhouse ['pauəhaus] *n Elec* central *f* eléctrica; *fig* *(person)* persona *f* dinámica; *fig* *(thing)* fuerza *f* motriz.

powerless ['pauəlıs] *adj* impotente, ineficaz; **I was p. to help**, no pude hacer nada para ayudar.

powwow ['pauwau] *n fam* plática *f*, conferencia *f*.

pox [pɒks] *n Med* viruela *f*; *fam* **the p.**, la sífilis.

poxy ['pɒksı] *adj* (*poxier, poxiest*) *sl* pésimo,-a, malísimo,-a.

pp *abbr of* **pages**, páginas *fpl*, págs., pp.

PR [piː'ɑːr] *abbr of* **public relations**, relaciones *fpl* públicas.

pr 1 *abbr of* **pair**, par *m*. 2 *abbr of* **price**, precio *m*.

practicability [præktıkə'bılıtı] *n* factibilidad *f*.

practicable ['præktıkəbəl] *adj* factible, practicable.

practical ['præktıkəl] **I** *adj* *(gen)* práctico,-a; *(useful)* útil; *(sensible)* sensato,-a, adecuado,-a; *(person)* práctico,-a, realista; **for all p. purposes**, en la práctica. **II** *n* *(lesson)* clase *f* práctica. ◆ **practically** *adv* 1 *(in practice)* en la práctica; **p. speaking**, hablando de la práctica. 2 *(almost)* casi; **I p. did it**, por poco lo hago; **it's p. impossible**, es casi imposible.

practicality [præktɪˈkælɪtɪ] *n (of suggestion, plan)* factibilidad *f*; **practicalities,** detalles *mpl* prácticos.

practice [ˈpræktɪs] I *n* 1 *(custom, habit)* costumbre *f*; **it's their p. to ask for references,** acostumbran a *or* suelen pedir informes; **it's the usual p.,** es la costumbre; **sharp p.,** trampas *fpl*; **to make a p. of doing sth,** tener la costumbre de hacer algo. 2 *(exercise)* práctica *f*, ejercicios *mpl*; *Sport* entrenamiento *m*; *Mus* ensayo *m*, práctica *f*; **it takes years of p.,** requiere años de práctica *or* de entrenamiento; **to be out of p.,** no estar en forma; **to keep in p.,** mantenerse en forma; *prov* **p. makes perfect,** se aprende a base de práctica. ■ **choir p.,** ensayo *m* coral; **piano p.,** *(scales)* ejercicios *mpl* en el piano; *(studies)* estudios *mpl* del piano; *Sport* **p. match,** partido *m* de entrenamiento. 3 *(way of doing sth)* práctica *f*; *Ind (technique)* técnica *f*, métodos *mpl*; **in p.,** en la práctica; **to put sth into p.,** poner algo en práctica. 4 *(exercise of profession)* ejercicio *m*; *(place) (of doctors)* consultorio *m*, consulta *f*, *(of lawyers)* bufete *m*, gabinete *m*; *(clients) (of doctors)* pacientes *mpl*; *(of lawyers)* clientela *f*; *Med* **private p.,** consulta privada; **she's no longer in p.,** ya no practica *or* ejerce; **to be in p.,** *(doctor)* ejercer la medicina; *(lawyer)* ejercer la abogacía; **to set up in p. as a doctor,** establecerse como médico. II *vtr & vi US see* **practise.**

practise [ˈpræktɪs] I *vtr* 1 *(gen)* practicar; *(language, virtue)* practicar; *(method)* seguir; *(principle)* poner en práctica; *Mus Theat* ensayar; *(piano)* estudiar; **to p. one's Spanish on sb,** practicar el español con algn; *fig* **to p. what one preaches,** predicar con el ejemplo. 2 *(profession)* ejercer; **to p. medicine/law,** ejercer la medicina/la abogacía. II *vi* 1 *(gen)* practicar; *Sport* entrenar; *Mus Theat* ensayar. 2 *(doctor)* practicar; *(lawyer)* ejercer.

practised, *US* **practiced** [ˈpræktɪst] *adj (skilled)* experto,-a.

practising, *US* **practicing** [ˈpræktɪsɪŋ] *adj (of doctor etc)* que ejerce; *(Christian etc)* practicante.

practitioner [prækˈtɪʃənəʳ] *n GB Med* **general p.,** médico,-a *m*, *f* de cabecera; **medical p.,** médico,-a *m*, *f*.

pragmatic [prægˈmætɪk] *adj* pragmático,-a.

pragmatics [prægˈmætɪks] *n* pragmática *f*.

pragmatism [ˈprægmətɪzəm] *n* pragmatismo *m*.

pragmatist [ˈprægmətɪst] *n* pragmatista *mf*.

Prague [prɑːg] *n* Praga *f*.

prairie [ˈprɛərɪ] *n (gen)* pradera *f*, *US* llanura *f*, pampa *f*. ■ *Zool* **p. dog,** perro *m* de las praderas.

praise [preɪz] I *n* alabanza *f*, elogio *m*, loa *f*; **I have nothing but p. for what she has done,** sólo tengo elogios para lo que ha hecho; **in p. of sth/sb,** en alabanza de algo/ algn; **p. be to God!,** ¡alabado sea Dios!; *fig* **to sing the praises of sth/sb,** alabar *or* elogiar algo/a algn. II *vtr* alabar, elogiar; **to p. God,** alabar a Dios; *fig* **to p. sb to the skies,** poner a algn por las nubes.

praiseworthy [ˈpreɪzwɜːðɪ] *adj* loable, digno,-a de elogio.

praline [ˈprɑːliːn] *n US Culin* praliné *m*.

pram [præm] *n GB* cochecito *m* de niño.

prance [prɑːns] *vi (horse)* hacer cabriolas, encabritarse; *(person)* **to p. about,** ir pegando brincos; **to p. in/out,** entrar/salir dando brincos.

prang [præŋ] *GB sl* I *n (bombing)* bombardeo *m*; *(accident)* accidente *m*. II *vtr (bomb)* bombardear; *(crash)* estrellar.

prank [præŋk] *n (piece of mischief)* travesura *f*; *(joke)* broma *f*; **to play a p. on sb,** gastar una broma a algn.

prat [præt] *n sl* imbécil *mf*.

prate [preɪt] *vi* decir tonterías.

prattle [ˈprætəl] I *vi* charlar, parlotear. II *n* charla *f*, parloteo *m*.

prawn [prɔːn] *n Zool* gamba *f*.

pray [preɪ] *vi Rel* rezar, orar; **to p. to God that sth might happen,** rogar a Dios para que pase algo; *fam* **he's past praying for,** es un caso perdido; *fam* **we're praying for good weather,** deseamos que haga buen tiempo.

prayer [prɛəʳ] I *n Rel* rezo *m*, oración *f*; *(entreaty)* súplica *f*, ruego *m*; *(in church)* **morning prayers,** maitines *mpl*; **the Lord's P.,** el Padrenuestro; **to say one's prayers,** rezar, orar; *fig* **his prayers were answered,** sus oraciones fueron escuchadas. ■ **evening prayers,** vísperas *fpl*; **p. book,** devocionario *m*, misal *m*; **p. meeting,** reunión *f* para orar juntos.

pre- [priː] *pref* pre-, ante-; **pre-1960,** antes de 1960.

preach [priːtʃ] I *vtr Rel (gospel)* predicar; *(sermon)* dar, hacer. II *vi Rel* predicar; *fig* **to p. to sb,** sermonear a algn.

preacher [ˈpriːtʃəʳ] *n Rel* predicador,-a *m*, *f*; *US (minister)* pastor *m*.

preamble [priːˈæmbəl] *n* preámbulo *m*.

prearrange [priːəˈreɪndʒ] *vtr* arreglar de antemano.

precarious [prɪˈkɛərɪəs] *adj (unstable)* precario,-a; *(dangerous)* peligroso,-a.

precaution [prɪˈkɔːʃən] *n* precaución *f*; **as a p. against illness,** por precaución contra la enfermedad; **to take precautions,** *(gen)* tomar precauciones; *(in sex)* usar contraceptivo; **to take the p. of doing sth,** tomar la precaución de hacer algo.

precautionary [prɪˈkɔːʃənərɪ] *adj* preventivo,-a *(against,* contra).

precede [prɪˈsiːd] *vtr* preceder; **the speech was preceded by an introduction,** el discurso estuvo precedido por una introducción.

precedence [ˈpresɪdəns] *n* preferencia *f*, prioridad *f*; **in order of p.,** por orden de preferencia; **to take p. over sth/ sb,** tener prioridad sobre algo/algn.

precedent [ˈpresɪdənt] *n* precedente *m*; **to create** *or* **set a p.,** sentar un precedente; **without p.,** sin precedente.

preceding [prɪˈsiːdɪŋ] *adj* precedente, anterior; **the week p. the accident,** la semana anterior al accidente.

precept [ˈpriːsept] *n* precepto *m*.

precinct [ˈpriːsɪŋkt] *n (enclosure)* recinto *m*; *US (district)* distrito *m*. ■ **pedestrian/shopping p.,** zona *f* peatonal/ comercial.

precious [ˈpreʃəs] I *adj (valuable)* precioso,-a; *(treasured)* precioso,-a, querido,-a; *iron* maldito,-a; **p. memories,** gratos recuerdos *mpl*; **p. stones,** piedras *fpl* preciosas; *fam* **you and your p. car!,** ¡tú y tu tan querido coche! II *n (term of endearment)* precioso,-a *m*, *f*, cariño *m*; **yes, my p.,** sí, mi vida. III *adv fam* **p. little/few,** muy poco/pocos.

precipice [ˈpresɪpɪs] *n* precipicio *m*; *fig* **to be living on the edge of a p.,** vivir al borde del precipicio.

precipitate [prɪˈsɪpɪteɪt] I *vtr (hasten)* precipitar, provocar; *Chem* precipitar; *fig* arrojar. II *adj* precipitado,-a. III [prɪˈsɪpɪtɪt] *n Chem* precipitado *m*.

precipitation [prɪsɪpɪˈteɪʃən] *n* precipitación *f*.

precipitous [prɪˈsɪpɪtəs] *adj* 1 *(steep)* escarpado,-a. 2 *(hasty)* precipitado,-a.

précis [ˈpreɪsiː] I *n (pl précis* [ˈpreɪsiːz]*)* resumen *m*. II *vtr* resumir, sintetizar.

precise [prɪˈsaɪs] *adj* 1 *(exact)* preciso,-a, exacto,-a; **an hour, 55 minutes to be p.,** una hora, 55 minutos para ser precisos; **at that p. moment,** en aquel preciso *or* mismo momento; **be p.!,** ¡sé preciso,-a!, ¡concreta! 2 *(meticulous)* meticuloso,-a; *pej* quisquilloso,-a. ◆

precisely *adv (exactly)* precisamente, exactamente; *(with precision)* con precisión; **it's p. six o'clock,** son las seis en punto; **p.!,** ¡eso es!, ¡exacto!

precision [prɪˈsɪʒən] *n (exactness)* precisión *f*, exactitud *f*; **lack of p.,** imprecisión *f*. ■ **p. instrument,** instrumento *m* de precisión.

preclude [prɪ'kluːd] *vtr (exclude)* excluir; *(avoid)* evitar; *(prevent)* impedir; **it precludes us from going,** nos impide que vayamos; **to p. any misunderstanding,** para evitar todo malentendido.

precocious [prɪ'kəʊʃəs] *adj* precoz.

precociousness [prɪ'kəʊʃəsnɪs] *n*, **precocity** [prɪ'kɒsɪtɪ] *n* precocidad *f*.

preconceived [priːkən'siːvd] *adj* preconcebido,-a.

preconception [priːkən'sepʃən] *n (idea)* idea *f* preconcebida; *(prejudice)* prejuicio *m*.

precondition [priːkən'dɪʃən] *n* condición *f* previa.

precook [priː'kʊk] *vtr* precocinar.

precursor [prɪ'kɜːsə'] *n* precursor,-a *m,f*.

predate [priː'deɪt] *vtr* **1** *(precede)* preceder, ser anterior a. **2** *(put earlier date on)* poner fecha anterior a, antedatar.

predator ['predətə'] *n* Zool depredador *m*, animal *m* de rapiña.

predatory ['predətərɪ] *adj* Zool predador,-a, de rapiña; *fig (person)* depredador,-a.

predecease [priːdɪ'siːs] *vtr* morir antes que.

predecessor ['priːdɪsesə'] *n (gen)* predecesor,-a *m, f*, antecesor,-a *m,f*; *(ancestor)* antepasado,-a *m,f*.

predestination [priːdestɪ'neɪʃən] *n* predestinación *f*.

predestine [priː'destɪn] *vtr* predestinar.

predetermination [priːdɪtɜːmɪ'neɪʃən] *n* predeterminación *f*.

predetermine [priːdɪ'tɜːmɪn] *vtr* predeterminar.

predicament [prɪ'dɪkəmənt] *n* apuro *m*, aprieto *m*; **to be in a p.,** *(difficult situation)* estar en un apuro; *(dilemma)* estar en un dilema.

predicate ['predɪkeɪt] **I** *vtr* **1** *(state)* afirmar. **2** *(base)* basar; **to be predicated upon sth,** basarse en algo. **II** ['predɪkɪt] *n* Ling predicado *m*.

predict [prɪ'dɪkt] *vtr* predecir, pronosticar.

predictable [prɪ'dɪktəbəl] *adj* previsible; **she's very p.,** actúa siempre de forma previsible. ◆ **predictably** *adv* como era de esperar.

prediction [prɪ'dɪkʃən] *n* predicción *f*, pronóstico *m*.

predispose [priːdɪ'spəʊz] *vtr* predisponer; **to be predisposed to doing sth,** *(conditioned)* estar predispuesto,-a a hacer algo; *(prone)* ser propenso,-a a hacer algo.

predisposition [priːdɪspə'zɪʃən] *n* predisposición *f*, propensión *f* **(to, towards**, a).

predominance [prɪ'dɒmɪnəns] *n* predominio *m*.

predominant [prɪ'dɒmɪnənt] *adj* predominante, prevalente. ◆ **predominantly** *adv (mostly)* en su mayoría.

predominate [prɪ'dɒmɪneɪt] *vi* predominar.

pre-eminence [prɪ'emɪnəns] *n* preeminencia *f*.

pre-eminent [prɪ'emɪnənt] *adj* preeminente.

pre-empt [prɪ'empt] *vtr* adelantarse a.

preen [priːn] *vtr (feathers)* arreglar con el pico; **to p. oneself,** *(bird)* arreglarse las plumas; *fig (person)* pavonearse.

pre-establish [priːɪ'stæblɪʃ] *vtr* establecer de antemano.

pre-established [priːɪ'stæblɪʃt] *adj* preestablecido,-a.

prefab ['priːfæb] *n fam (house)* casa *f* prefabricada.

prefabricated [priː'fæbrɪkeɪtɪd] *adj* prefabricado,-a.

preface ['prefɪs] **I** *n* prólogo *m*, prefacio *m*. **II** *vtr* prologar.

prefect ['priːfekt] *n* **1** GB Educ monitor,-a *m,f*. **2** Admin prefecto *m*.

prefer [prɪ'fɜː'] *vtr* **1** *(pt & pp preferred)* preferir; **he prefers swimming to playing tennis,** prefiere nadar a jugar al tenis; **I p. milk to tea,** prefiero la leche al té, me gusta más la leche que el té; **she would p. us to come**

tomorrow, preferiría que viniéramos mañana; **we p. to stay at home,** preferimos quedarnos en casa. **2** *Jur* presentar; **to p. charges against sb,** acusar a algn.

preferable ['prefərəbəl] *adj* preferible **(to**, a). ◆ **preferably** *adv* preferentemente, de preferencia.

preference ['prefərəns] *n (preferred choice)* preferencia *f*; *(priority)* prioridad *f*; **in order of p.,** en orden de preferencia; **to give p. to sth,** dar prioridad a algo; **to have a p. for sth,** preferir algo; **what's your p.?,** ¿cuál prefieres?

preferential [prefə'renʃəl] *adj* preferente.

prefix ['priːfɪks] *n* Ling prefijo *m*.

pregnancy ['pregnənsɪ] *n* embarazo *m*. ■ **p. test,** prueba *f* del embarazo.

pregnant ['pregnənt] *adj (human)* embarazado,-a; *(animal)* preñado,-a; **to be three months p.,** estar embarazada de tres meses; *fig* **a p. pause,** una pausa significativa.

prehistoric(al) [priːhɪ'stɒrɪk(əl)] *adj* prehistórico,-a.

prehistory [priː'hɪstərɪ] *n* prehistoria *f*.

prejudge [priː'dʒʌdʒ] *vtr (situation)* prejuzgar; *(person)* juzgar de antemano.

prejudice ['predʒʊdɪs] **I** *n* **1** *(bias)* prejuicio *m*; **to have a p. against sth,** estar predispuesto,-a contra algo. **2** *(harm)* perjuicio *m*; *Jur* **without p.,** sin detrimento de sus propios intereses. **II** *vtr* **1** *(bias)* predisponer. **2** *(harm)* perjudicar.

prejudiced ['predʒʊdɪst] *adj* parcial; **to be p. against/in favour of sb/sth,** estar predispuesto,-a contra/a favor de algn/algo.

prejudicial [predʒʊ'dɪʃəl] *adj* perjudicial.

prelate ['prelɪt] *n* Rel prelado *m*.

preliminary [prɪ'lɪmɪnərɪ] **I** *adj (exam, remark)* preliminar; *Sport (round)* eliminatorio,-a. **II** *n* preliminar *m*; **preliminaries,** preliminares *mpl*.

prelude ['preljuːd] *n* preludio *m*; **a p. to sth,** un preludio de algo.

premarital [priː'mærɪtəl] *adj* prematrimonial.

premature [premə'tjʊə', 'premətjʊə'] *adj* prematuro,-a; **you're being a bit p.,** te adelantas un poco. ◆ **prematurely** *adv* antes de tiempo.

premeditate [prɪ'medɪteɪt] *vtr (crime)* premeditar; *(action)* calcular.

premenstrual [priː'menstruəl] *adj* Med **p. tension,** tensión *f* premenstrual.

premier ['premjə'] **I** *n* Pol primer,-a ministro,-a *m,f*. **II** *adj* primer, primero,-a.

premiere ['premɪeə'] *n* Cin estreno *m*.

premise ['premɪs] *n* premisa *f*.

premises ['premɪsɪz] *npl* local *m sing*; **business p.,** local comercial; **licensed p.,** local autorizado para la venta de bebidas alcohólicas; **on/off the p.,** en el/fuera del local.

premium ['priːmɪəm] *n Com Fin Ind* prima *f*; **to be at a p.,** estar sobre la par; *fig* estar muy solicitado,-a *or* cotizado,-a; **to put a p. on sth,** dar un gran valor a algo. ■ **p. bonds,** bonos *mpl* cotizados sobre la par.

premonition [premə'nɪʃən] *n* presentimiento *m*, premonición *f*.

prenatal [priː'neɪtəl] *adj* prenatal.

preoccupation [priːɒkjʊ'peɪʃən] *n* preocupación *f*.

preoccupied [priː'ɒkjʊpaɪd] *adj* preocupado,-a; **to be p. with sth,** preocuparse por algo.

preoccupy [priː'ɒkjʊpaɪ] *vtr (pt & pp preoccupied)* preocupar.

prep [prep] *fam* **1** *abbr of* **preparation,** deberes *mpl*. **2** *abbr of* **preparatory school,** escuela *f* primaria privada (hasta los 13 años).

prepaid [priː'peɪd] **I** *pt & pp see* **prepay. II** *adj* porte pagado.

preparation [prepə'reɪʃən] *n* **1** *(action)* preparación *f*; **in p. for sth,** en preparación para algo. **2** *(plan)* preparativo *m*. **3** *Chem* preparado *m*. **4** *fam Educ* deberes *mpl*.

preparatory [prɪ'pærətərɪ] *adj* preparatorio,-a, preliminar; **p. to doing sth,** como preparativo para hacer algo. ▪ *Educ* **p. school,** escuela *f* primaria privada (hasta los 13 años).

prepare [prɪ'peəʳ] **I** *vtr* *(gen)* preparar; *(document)* redactar; *(attack)* montar; **to p. sb for sth,** preparar a algn para algo; **to p. the way for talks,** preparar el terreno para conversaciones; **to p. to do sth,** prepararse para hacer algo. **II** *vi* prepararse (**for,** para).

prepared [prɪ'peəd] *adj* **1** *(ready)* listo,-a, preparado,-a; **we're all p.,** estamos todos listos. **2** *(willing)* dispuesto,-a; **to be p. to do sth,** estar dispuesto,-a a hacer algo.

prepay [priː'peɪ] *vtr* *(pt & pp prepaid)* pagar por adelantado; **to send sth carriage prepaid,** mandar algo a porte pagado.

prepayment [priː'peɪmənt] *n* pago *m* por adelantado.

preponderance [prɪ'pɒndərəns] *n* preponderancia *f*.

preponderant [prɪ'pɒndərənt] *adj* preponderante.

preposition [prepə'zɪʃən] *n Ling* preposición *f*.

prepossessing [priːpə'zesɪŋ] *adj* agradable, atractivo,-a.

preposterous [prɪ'pɒstərəs] *adj* absurdo,-a, ridículo,-a.

prerecord [priːrɪ'kɔːd] *vtr* pregrabar, grabar de antemano.

prerequisite [priː'rekwɪzɪt] *n* condición *f* previa, requisito *m*.

prerogative [prɪ'rɒgətɪv] *n* prerrogativa *f*, privilegio *m*.

Pres *abbr of* **President,** Presidente *m*, Pres.

Presbyterian [prezbɪ'tɪərɪən] *adj & n Rel* presbíteriano,-a *(m,f)*.

preschool [priː'skuːl] *adj* preescolar.

prescribe [prɪ'skraɪb] *vtr* **1** *(set down)* prescribir, ordenar; **in the prescribed way,** de la forma prescrita. **2** *Med* recetar; *fig (recommend)* recomendar.

prescription [prɪ'skrɪpʃən] *n Med* receta *f* (médica); **it's available only on p.,** se vende sólo con receta médica; **to make up a p.,** preparar una receta.

prescriptive [prɪ'skrɪptɪv] *adj* legal.

presence ['prezəns] *n* *(gen)* presencia *f*; *(attendance)* asistencia *f*; **don't mention it in her p.,** no hables de ello delante de ella; **in the p. of,** en presencia de; **to make one's p. felt,** destacar, hacerse sentir; *fig* **p. of mind,** presencia *f* de ánimo, aplomo *m*, sangre *f* fría.

present[1] ['prezənt] **I** *adj* **1** *(in attendance)* presente; *Ling* **p. tense,** (tiempo *m*) presente *m*; **those p.,** los presentes; **to be p. at,** estar presente en, asistir a. **2** *(current)* actual; **at the p. time,** actualmente; **her p. address,** su domicilio actual. **II** *n* *(time)* presente *m*, actualidad *f*; **at p.,** actualmente; **for the p.,** de momento, por ahora; **up to the p.,** hasta ahora. ◆ **presently** *adv* **1** *(soon)* dentro de poco. **2** *US (now)* ahora.

present[2] [prɪ'zent] **I** *vtr* **1** *(give)* *(as gift)* regalar; *(formally)* obsequiar; *(make presentation)* entregar, hacer la presentación de; **to p. sb with sth,** regalar algo a algn, obsequiar a algn con algo. **2** *(offer)* *(cheque, report, etc)* presentar; *(provide)* *(opportunity)* ofrecer; *(problems etc)* plantear. **3** *(introduce)* *(person)* presentar; **may I p. my brother,** le presento a mi hermano; **to p. oneself,** presentarse. **4** *Rad TV (programme)* presentar. **II** [prezənt] *n (gift)* regalo *m*; *(formal)* obsequio *m*; **to give sb a p.,** hacer un regalo a algn; **to make sb a p. of sth,** regalar algo a algn.

presentable [prɪ'zentəbəl] *adj* presentable, arreglado,-a; **to make oneself p.,** arreglarse.

presentation [prezən'teɪʃən] *n* **1** *(act of giving)* presentación *f*; **on p. of the ticket,** al presentar *or* entregar la entrada; **to make the p.,** hacer la presentación. ▪ **p. ceremony,** ceremonia *f* de entrega. **2** *Rad TV Theat* representación *f*.

present-day ['prezəntdeɪ] *adj* actual, de hoy en día; **p.-d. Britain,** la Gran Bretaña de hoy en día.

presenter [prɪ'zentəʳ] *n Rad* locutor,-a *m*, *f*; *TV* presentador,-a *m*,*f*.

presentiment [prɪ'zentmənt] *n* presentimiento *m*.

preservation [prezə'veɪʃən] *n* **1** *(protection)* conservación *f*, preservación *f*. ▪ **p. order,** orden *f* de preservación. **2** *Culin* conservación *f*.

preservative [prɪ'zɜːvətɪv] *n Culin* conservante *m*.

preserve [prɪ'zɜːv] *vtr* **1** *(keep)* mantener, conservar; **to p. one's dignity/sense of humour,** mantener la dignidad/el sentido del humor. **2** *Culin* conservar, guardar *or* poner en conserva. **II** *n* **1** *(hunting)* coto *m*, vedado *m*; *fig* **to trespass on sb's p.,** meterse en terreno ajeno. **2** *Culin* conserva *f*.

preshrunk [priː'ʃrʌŋk] *adj* ya lavado,-a.

preside [prɪ'zaɪd] *vi* presidir; **to p. at** *or* **over a meeting,** presidir una reunión.

presidency ['prezɪdənsɪ] *n Pol* presidencia *f*; *US Com* dirección *f*.

president ['prezɪdənt] *n Pol* presidente,-a *m*,*f*; *US Com* director,-a *m*,*f*, gerente *mf*.

presidential [prezɪ'denʃəl] *adj Pol* presidencial.

press [pres] **I** *vtr* **1** *(push down)* *(button)* apretar, presionar, pulsar; *(trigger)* presionar; *(keys on typewriter)* pulsar; *(squeeze)* apretar; *(fruit)* exprimir, estrujar; *(grapes)* pisar; *(flowers)* prensar; **he pressed his lips to hers,** la besó en la boca. **2** *(iron)* planchar (a vapor). **3** *(urge)* presionar, instar; *(insist on)* insistir en; **to p. a point,** recalcar un punto; **to p. home an advantage,** aprovecharse de una ventaja; **to p. sb to do sth,** acosar a alga para que haga algo. **4** *Jur* **to p. charges against sb,** demandar a algn. **II** *vi* **1** *(push)* apretar; **p. hard,** aprieta fuerte; **to p. against sb/sth,** apretarse contra algn/algo; **to p. (down) on sth,** hacer presión sobre algo. **2** *(crowd)* apiñarse; *(hurry)* apresurarse; **the crowd pressed towards the stage,** el público se apresuró hacia el escenario. **3** *(urge)* apremiar, insistir en; **time presses,** el tiempo apremia; **to p. for an answer,** exigir una respuesta. **III** *n* **1** *(pressure)* presión *f*; **to give sth a p.,** presionar *or* apretar algo; *(trousers etc)* planchar algo. ▪ **p. stud,** botón *m* de presión. **2** *(machine)* prensa *f*; *Tech* **hydraulic p.,** prensa hidráulica. ▪ **oil/grape p.,** prensa *f* de uvas/aceite; **trouser p.,** prensa *f* para pantalones. **3** *Print* imprenta *f*; **ready for p.,** listo,-a para la impresión; **to go to p.,** entrar en prensa. ▪ **rotary/offset p.,** rotativa *f*/offset *f*. **4** *Press* prensa *f*; **freedom of the p.,** libertad *f* de (la) prensa; **the p.,** la prensa, los periódicos; **to get a good/bad p.,** tener buena/mala prensa. ▪ **p. agency,** oficina *f* de prensa; **p. conference,** conferencia *f* or rueda *f* de (la) prensa; **p. cutting,** recorte *m* de prensa; **p. gallery,** tribuna *f* de prensa. ◆ **press ahead** *vi* **to p. ahead with sth,** seguir adelante con algo. ◆ **press on** *vi* seguir adelante; **p. on!,** ¡adelante!

pressed [prest] *adj* **1** *Culin* embutido,-a; **p. chicken,** embutido *m* de pollo. **2** **to be (hard) p. for,** andar escaso,-a de; **I'd be hard p. to do it,** me costaría mucho hacerlo.

press-gang ['presgæŋ] *vtr fam* **to p.-g. sb into doing sth,** obligar a algn a hacer algo.

pressing ['presɪŋ] *adj* apremiante, urgente.

pressman ['presmən] *n (pl pressmen)* periodista *m*.

pressure ['preʃəʳ] *n* **1** *Phys Tech Elec* presión *f*; *(weight)* peso *m*; *Med Meteor* **high/low p.,** altas/bajas presiones *fpl*; *Med* **to have high/low blood p.,** tener la tensión alta/baja; **to put p. on sth,** hacer presión sobre algo. ▪ **blood p.,** tensión *f* arterial; *Tech* **p. chamber,** cámara *f* de presión; *Culin* **p. cooker,** olla *f* a presión; *Tech* **p. gauge,** manómetro *m*; **p. suit,** traje *m* espacial. **2** *fig* presión *f*; **the pressures of work,** las exigencias del trabajo; **to bring p. (to bear) on sb,** ejercer presión sobre algn; **to work under p.,** trabajar bajo presión.

pressure-cook ['preʃəkʊk] *vtr Culin* cocer en la olla a presión.

pressurize ['preʃəraɪz] *vtr* presurizar; *fig* apremiar, presionar; *Av* **pressurized cabin,** cabina *f* presurizada; *fig* **to p. sb into doing sth,** ejercer presión sobre algn para que haga algo.

prestige [pre'stiːʒ] *n* prestigio *m*.

prestigious [pre'stɪdʒəs] *adj* prestigioso,-a.

presumably [prɪ'zjuːməblɪ] *adv* es presumible *or* de suponer que, se supone que; **p. he's innocent,** se supone que es inocente; **p. they'll come,** se espera que vengan.

presume [prɪ'zjuːm] I *vtr (suppose)* suponer, imaginarse, presumir; **I p. that they will phone,** supongo *or* me imagino que llamarán; **missing, presumed dead,** desaparecido,-a, probablemente muerto,-a; **we p. so/not,** suponemos que sí/no. II *vi* 1 *(suppose)* suponer. 2 *(rely)* **to p. on sb's generosity,** abusar de la generosidad de algn.

presumption [prɪ'zʌmpʃən] *n* 1 *(supposition)* suposición *f*, presunción *f*. 2 *(conceit, boldness)* osadía *f*, presunción *f*.

presumptuous [prɪ'zʌmptjʊəs] *adj* presuntuoso,-a.

presuppose [priːsə'pəʊz] *vtr* presuponer.

presupposition [priːsʌpə'zɪʃən] *n* presuposición *f*.

pretence, *US* **pretense** [prɪ'tens] *n* 1 *(deception)* fingimiento *m*, simulacro *m*; **it's all a p.,** es todo fingido; **to make a p. of doing sth,** fingir hacer algo. 2 *(pretext)* pretexto *m*; *Jur* **false pretences,** estafa *f sing*, fraude *m sing*; **to obtain sth by false pretences,** conseguir algo mediante estafa; **under the p. of friendship,** so pretexto de amistad. 3 *(claim)* pretensión *f*.

pretend [prɪ'tend] I *vtr* 1 *(feign)* fingir, simular, aparentar; **he pretended he couldn't understand us,** fingía no entendernos; **she's pretending to be asleep,** finge estar dormida. 2 *(claim)* pretender; **I don't p. to be an authority on the subject,** no pretendo ser experto en el tema. II *vi (feign)* fingir; **stop pretending!,** ¡déjate de mentiras! III *adj fam* fingido,-a, de mentirijillas.

pretense [prɪ'tens] *n US see* **pretence**.

pretension [prɪ'tenʃən] *n* 1 *(claim)* pretensión *f*. 2 *(showiness)* pretensiones *fpl*, presunción *f*.

pretentious [prɪ'tenʃəs] *adj (showy)* presumido,-a, ostentoso,-a, presuntuoso,-a.

preterite, *US* **preterit** ['pretərɪt] *n Ling* pretérito *m*.

pretext ['priːtekst] *n* pretexto *m*; **on** *or* **under the p. of doing sth,** so pretexto de hacer algo.

pretty ['prɪtɪ] I *adj (prettier, prettiest) (person)* bonito,-a, guapo,-a; *(thing)* bonito,-a, mono,-a; **it isn't a p. sight,** no es nada bonito; *fam* **it cost a p. penny,** costó un dineral. II *adv fam* bastante; **p. easy,** bastante fácil; **p. much the same,** más o menos lo mismo; **p. well finished,** casi terminado,-a.

pretzel ['pretsəl] *n Culin* galleta *f* salada.

prevail [prɪ'veɪl] *vi* 1 *(continue to exist)* predominar, regir; **the customs which prevailed,** las costumbres que regían. 2 *(win through)* prevalecer. 3 *(persuade)* persuadir; **to p. upon** *or* **on sb to do sth,** persuadir *or* convencer a algn para que haga algo.

prevailing [prɪ'veɪlɪŋ] *adj (wind)* predominante; *(opinion)* general, común, predominante; *(condition, fashion)* actual.

prevalent ['prevələnt] *adj (gen)* predominante, general; *(illness)* extendido,-a.

prevaricate [prɪ'værɪkeɪt] *vi* andar con rodeos.

prevarication [prɪværɪ'keɪʃən] *n (gen)* evasivas *fpl*; *Jur* prevaricación *f*.

prevent [prɪ'vent] *vtr (gen)* impedir; *(accident)* evitar; *(illness)* prevenir; **to p. sb from doing sth,** impedir a algn hacer algo; **to p. sth from happening,** evitar que pase algo.

preventable [prɪ'ventəbəl] *adj* evitable.

prevention [prɪ'venʃən] *n* prevención *f*; **p. of accidents,** precauciones *fpl* *or* medidas *fpl* preventivas contra los accidentes; **Society for the P. of Cruelty to Animals/ Children,** Sociedad *f* Protectora de Animales/de Niños; *prov* **p. is better than cure,** más vale prevenir que curar.

preventive [prɪ'ventɪv] *adj* preventivo,-a; **p. medicine,** medicina *f* preventiva.

preview ['priːvjuː] I *n (of film, exhibition, etc)* preestreno *m*; *fig* **to give sb a p. of sth,** permitir a algn ver algo de antemano. II *vtr (of film, exhibition, etc)* ver en preestreno; *fig* ver de antemano.

previous ['priːvɪəs] I *adj* anterior, previo,-a, **a p. engagement,** un compromiso anterior, **on a p. occasion,** en otra ocasión, **the p. afternoon,** la tarde anterior. ◆ *Jur* **p. conviction,** antecedente *m* penal, **p. experience,** conocimientos *mpl* previos II *adv* **p. to going,** antes de ir ◆ **previously** *adv* anteriormente, previamente

prevue ['priːvjuː] *n & vtr US see* **preview**.

prewar ['priːwɔːr] *adj* de antes de la guerra, **the p. period,** la preguerra

prey [preɪ] I *n* presa *f*, *fig* presa, víctima *f*; **bird of p.,** ave *f* de rapiña, *fig* **to fall p. to temptation,** caer en la tentación II *vi* cazar, alimentarse, **to p. on animals,** alimentarse de animales, *fig* **it's been preying on my mind,** me ha estado dando vueltas por la cabeza

price [praɪs] I *n (value)* precio *m*, valor *m*, *(valuation)* valor, **fixed/cash p.,** precio fijo/al contado, **high/low prices,** precios *mpl* altos/bajos, **not at any p.,** por nada del mundo, **peace at any p.,** la paz a cualquier precio, **to go up/down in p.,** subir/bajar de precio, **to pay a high p. for sth,** pagar algo muy caro, **what p. is that coat?,** ¿cuanto cuesta el abrigo?; *fig* **the p. of fame/success,** el precio de la fama/del éxito ▪ **p. control,** control *m* de precios, **p. freeze,** congelación *f* de precios, **p. index,** índice *m* de precios, **p. limit,** tope *m*, precio *m* tope, **p. list,** lista *f* de precios, **p. reduction,** descuento *m*, rebaja *f*, **p. tag,** etiqueta *f* II *vtr (put price on)* poner un precio a; *(value)* poner un precio a, valorar, tasar; *(ask price of)* preguntar el precio de, **it is priced at £10,** vale 10 libras, **to be priced too high/low,** tener una valoración demasiado alta/baja, *Com* **to p. oneself out of the market,** perder clientela por poner precios muy altos

priceless ['praɪslɪs] *adj (invaluable)* que no tiene precio, inestimable, *fam (very funny)* graciosísimo,-a, divertidísimo,-a

pric(e)y ['praɪsɪ] *adj (pricier, priciest) fam* caro,-a

prick [prɪk] I *vtr* 1 *(with pin etc)* picar, **to p. one's finger on sth,** pincharse el dedo con algo, *fig* **her conscience is pricking her,** le remuerde la conciencia 2 *(to p. (up),* levantar, *fig* **to p. up one's ears,** aguzar el oído II *n* 1 *(with pin etc)* pinchazo *m*, *fig* **pricks of conscience,** remordimientos *mpl* 2 *sl (penis)* polla *f*, picha *f*, *sl offens (obnoxious person)* gilipollas *mf inv*

prickle ['prɪkəl] I *n (on plant, animal)* espina *f*, *(spike)* pincho *m*, *(sensation)* picor *m*, comezón *m* II *vtr & vt* pinchar, picar

prickly ['prɪklɪ] *adj (pricklier, prickliest)* espinoso,-a, lleno,-a de pinchos, *(sensation)* de picor, de hormigueo, *fig (touchy)* enojadizo,-a ▪ *Med* **p. heat,** sarpullido *m* por causa del calor, *Bot* **p. pear,** higo *m* chumbo

pride [praɪd] I *n (gen)* orgullo *m*, *(self-respect)* amor *m* propio, *(arrogance)* soberbia *f*, orgullo *m*, **false p.,** vanidad *f*, **he has no p.,** no tiene amor propio, **to take a p. in sth,** enorgullecerse de algo, *fig* **he's the family's p. and joy,** es el orgullo de la familia, *fig* **to take p. of place,** tener el lugar de honor ▪ *Orn* **p. of India,** jabonero *m* de la India II *vtr* **to p. oneself on** *or* **upon doing sth,** enorgullecerse *or* estar orgulloso,-a de hacer algo

priest [priːst] *n* sacerdote *m*, cura *m*

priestess ['priːstɪs] *n* sacerdotisa *f*

priesthood ['priːsthʊd] *n (clergy)* clero *m, (body of priests)* sacerdocio *m*; **to enter the p.,** hacerse *or* ordenarse sacerdote.

priestly ['priːstlɪ] *adj (priestlier, priestliest)* sacerdotal

prig [prɪg] *n* gazmoño,-a *m,f,* mojigato,-a *m,f*

priggish ['prɪgɪʃ] *adj* gazmoño,-a, mojigato,-a

prim [prɪm] *adj (primmer, primmest)* **p. (and proper),** remilgado,-a ◆ **primly** *adv* con remilgo

prima donna [priːmə'dɒnə] *n (pl prima donnas)* diva *f*

prim(a)eval [praɪ'miːvəl] *adj* primitivo,-a, **p. forest,** selva *f* vírgen

prima facie [praɪmə'feɪʃɪ] **I** *adj Jur* **to have a p. f. case,** tener razón a primera vista **II** *adv* a primera vista

primary ['praɪmərɪ] **I** *adj* **1** *(main, chief)* fundamental, principal, **of p. importance,** primordial, de suma importancia **2** *(basic)* primario,-a, **p. colour,** color *m* primario, **p. education/school,** enseñanza *f*/escuela *f* primaria, **p. school teacher,** maestro,-a *m,f* (de escuela) **II** *n Pol* elección *f* primaria ◼ **primarily** *adv* en primer lugar, ante todo, principalmente

primate¹ ['praɪmeɪt] *n Rel* primado *m*

primate² ['praɪmeɪt] *n Zool* primate *m*

prime [praɪm] **I** *adj* **1** *(main, chief)* principal, primer, primero,-a, *(major)* primordial, **of p. importance,** de suma importancia ◼ **P. Minister,** primer,-a ministro,-a *m,f* **2** *(first-rate)* de primera, **in p. condition,** en perfecto estado, **p. meat,** carne *f* de primera (calidad) **3** *Com* **p. cost,** coste *m* de producción **4** *Math* primo,-a, **p. number,** número *m* primo **II** *n* **p. (of life),** flor *f* de la vida; **he has passed his p.,** ya no está en sus mejores años, **to be in the p. of life** *or* **in one's p.,** estar en la flor de la vida **III** *vtr (pump, engine)* cebar, *(surface)* imprimar, preparar; *fig (prepare)* enseñar, preparar, *fig* **they were primed about how to answer,** les enseñaron cómo tenían que contestar, *fam (drunk)* **he was well primed,** estaba medio borracho

primer¹ ['praɪmə'] *n (textbook)* libro *m or* texto *m* elemental ◼ **history p.,** texto *m* de introducción a la historia

primer² ['praɪmə'] *n (paint)* imprimación *f*

primitive ['prɪmɪtɪv] **I** *adj (language, culture)* primitivo,-a, *(method, tool)* rudimentario,-a, básico,-a **II** *n Art (artist)* primitivista *mf; (work)* obra *f* primitivista

primrose ['prɪmrəʊz] **I** *n Bot* primavera *f* **II** *adj* **p. (yellow),** (de color) amarillo claro

primula ['prɪmjʊlə] *n Bot* prímula *f*

Primus® ['praɪməs] *n* hornillo *m* de camping

prince [prɪns] *n* príncipe *m,* **P. Charming,** Príncipe Azul, **p. consort/regent,** príncipe consorte/regente, *fig* **P. of Darkness,** Satanás *m*

princess [prɪn'ses] *n* princesa *f*

principal ['prɪnsɪpəl] **I** *adj* principal **II** *n* **1** *Educ* director,-a *m,f, Theat (in play)* protagonista *mf* principal ◼ *Theat* **p. boy,** primera figura *f* **2** *Fin* capital *m,* principal *m*

principality [prɪnsɪ'pælɪtɪ] *n* principado *m.*

principle ['prɪnsɪpəl] *n (gen)* principio *m, (law)* ley *f,* **a man of principles,** un hombre de principios, **in p.,** en principio, **it's against my principles to do that,** va en contra de mis principios hacer eso; **on p.,** por principio, **to have high principles,** tener principios

print [prɪnt] **I** *vtr* **1** *Print (book etc)* imprimir, *(publish)* publicar; *fig* grabar, **printed matter,** impresos *mpl* **2** *(write)* escribir con letra de imprenta **3** *Tex (fabric)* estampar **4** *Phot* **to p. a negative,** sacar copias de un negativo. **II** *n* **1** *(mark) (of finger, foot)* huella *f; (of type)* impresión *f,* marca *f;* **thumb p.,** huella del pulgar. **2** *Print* letra *f;* **in small/large p.,** con letra pequeña/grande; **to be in/out of p.,** estar en venta/agotado,-a. ◼ **p. run,** tirada *f.* **3** *Tex* estampado *m.* ◼ **p. dress/skirt,** vestido *m* estampado/falda *f* estampada. **4** *Art* grabado *m.* **5** *Phot*

prueba *f,* copia *f;* **to make prints from a negative,** hacer copias de un negativo. ◆ **print out** *vtr Comput* imprimir.

printed ['prɪntɪd] *adj* impreso,-a.

printer ['prɪntə'] *n (person)* impresor,-a *m, f; (machine)* máquina *f* impresora; **p.'s error,** error *m* de imprenta.

printing ['prɪntɪŋ] *n* **1** *Print (industry)* imprenta *f; (process)* impresión *f; (print run)* tirada *f.* ◼ **p. press,** prensa *f;* **p. works,** imprenta *f sing.* **2** *(writing)* letras *fpl* de imprenta.

print-out ['prɪntaʊt] *n Comput* impresión *f.*

prior¹ ['praɪə'] *adj* previo,-a, anterior; **p. to leaving,** antes de salir; **to have a p. claim,** tener prioridad (**to,** sobre); **without p. warning,** sin previo aviso.

prior² ['praɪə'] *n Rel* prior *m.*

priority [praɪ'ɒrɪtɪ] *n* prioridad *f;* **to have** *or* **take p. over sth,** tener prioridad sobre algo; *fam* **to get one's priorities right,** saber lo que más le importa a uno en la vida.

priory ['praɪərɪ] *n Rel* priorato *m.*

prise [praɪz] *vtr* **to p. sth open/off,** abrir/levantar algo con palanca.

prism ['prɪzəm] *n Geom Tech* prisma *f.* ◼ **p. binoculars,** prismáticos *mpl.*

prison ['prɪzən] *n* cárcel *f,* prisión *f;* **to be in p.,** estar en la cárcel; **to be sent to p. for 10 years,** ser condenado,-a a 10 años de cárcel; **to put sb in p. for 5 years,** condenar a algn a 5 años de cárcel. ◼ **p. camp,** campamento *m* para prisioneros; **p. officer,** carcelero,-a *m, f.*

prisoner ['prɪzənə'] *n* preso,-a *m, f; Mil* prisionero,-a *m, f;* **to take/hold sb p.,** tomar preso/detener a algn. ◼ **p. of war,** prisionero,-a *m, f* de guerra.

pristine ['prɪstaɪn, 'prɪstiːn] *adj* prístino,-a.

privacy ['praɪvəsɪ, 'prɪvəsɪ] *n* intimidad *f,* vida *f* privada, privacidad *f;* **in the p. of one's own home,** en la intimidad del hogar; **one's right to p.,** su derecho a la intimidad.

private ['praɪvɪt] **I** *adj (not public)* privado,-a; *(individual)* particular; *(personal)* personal; *(classes)* particular; *(school)* de pago; *(clinic, property)* privado,-a; *(letter, conversation)* confidencial; *(bank account)* personal; **in p.,** en privado; **it's my p. opinion that ...,** por mi parte pienso que ...; **it will be a p. celebration,** se celebrará en la intimidad; **one's p. life,** la vida privada de uno; *(notice)* **'P.',** *(on road)* 'carretera privada'; *(on gate)* 'propiedad privada'; *(on envelope)* 'confidencial'; **to keep sth p.,** no divulgar algo. ◼ **p. citizen,** particular *mf;* **p. detective** *or* **investigator,** *fam* **p. eye,** detective *mf* privado,-a; **p. income,** fortuna *f* personal; *Pol* **p. member's bill,** proyecto *m* de ley propuesto por un diputado independiente; **p. school,** escuela *f* privada; **p. secretary,** secretario,-a *m, f* particular. **II** *n Mil* soldado *m* raso. ◆ **privately** *adv (not publicly)* en privado; *(personally)* personalmente; *(in secret)* en secreto; *(discreetly)* en la intimidad.

privation [praɪ'veɪʃən] *n (hardship)* privación *f; (poverty)* estrechez *f,* privaciones *fpl;* **to suffer p.,** pasar apuros.

privet ['prɪvɪt] *n Bot* alheña *f.*

privilege ['prɪvɪlɪdʒ] *n* privilegio *m; Pol* **parliamentary p.,** inmunidad *f* parlamentaria; **to have the p. of doing sth,** tener el honor *or* el privilegio de hacer algo. **II** *vtr* **to be privileged to do sth,** gozar del honor *or* del privilegio de hacer algo.

privileged ['prɪvɪlɪdʒd] *adj* privilegiado,-a; **the p. few,** unos cuantos privilegiados, la élite.

privy ['prɪvɪ] **I** *adj (privier, priviest)* **1** *(private)* privado,-a; **P. Council/Councillor,** Consejo *m*/Consejero *m* Privado. **2** **to be p. to sth,** estar enterado,-a de algo. **II** *n fam (toilet)* retrete *m.*

prize¹ [praɪz] **I** *n* premio *m;* **to win first p.,** ganar el primer premio; *(in lottery)* **he's won first p.,** le ha tocado el gordo. **II** *adj (first-class)* de primera (categoría *or* clase), selecto,-a; *fam* **a p. idiot,** un tonto de remate. ■ **p. draw,** sorteo *m* con premio; *Box* **p. fight,** combate *m* (de boxeo) profesional. **III** *vtr (value)* apreciar, valorar.

prize² [praiz] *vtr see* **prise.**

prize-giving ['praizgiviŋ] *n* distribución *f* de premios.

prizewinner ['praizwinə'] *n* premiado,-a *m, f, fml* galardonado,-a *m,f.*

pro¹ [prəu] *n* pro *m*; **the pros and cons of an issue,** los pros y los contras de una cuestión.

pro² [prəu] *n (abbr of professional) fam* profesional *mf.*

pro- [prəu] *pref* a favor de, pro-; **they're pro-Common Market,** están a favor del Mercado Común.

probability [probə'biliti] *n* probabilidad *f*; **in all p. they will write,** lo más probable es que escriban.

probable ['probəbəl] *adj* probable. ◆ **probably** *adv* probablemente; **he'll p. phone,** es probable que llame.

probate ['prəubit, 'prəubeit] *n Jur* legalización *f* de un testamento.

probation [prə'beiʃən] *n (in employment)* período *m* de prueba; *Jur* libertad *f* condicional; *Jur* **to be on p.,** estar en libertad condicional; *(at work)* **to be on two months' p.,** trabajar dos meses de prueba. ■ **p. officer,** encargado,-a *m, f* oficial de vigilar a los que están en libertad condicional.

probationary [prə'beiʃənəri] *adj* de prueba; **p. period,** *(in employment)* período *m* de prueba; *Jur* período *m* de libertad condicional.

probationer [prə'beiʃənə'] *n (in employment)* empleado,-a *m, f* a prueba; *Jur* persona *f* en libertad condicional.

probe [prəub] **I** *n* **1** *Med* sonda *f*. **2** *(investigation)* investigación *f*, sondeo *m*. **3** *Astronaut* sonda *f*. ■ **space p.,** sonda *f* espacial. **II** *vtr* **1** *Med* sondar. **2** *(investigate)* investigar, sondear. **3** *Astronaut* sondar, explorar. ◆ **probe into** *vtr* investigar.

probity ['prəubiti] *n* probidad *f.*

problem ['probləm] *n* problema *m*; **it poses many problems for us,** nos crea muchos problemas; **she has a drink p.,** tiene tendencia al alcoholismo; **the unemployment p.,** el problema del desempleo; **we had no p. getting there,** llegamos sin problemas; *fam* **no p.!,** ¡desde luego! ■ **p. child,** niño,-a *m, f* difícil; **p. family,** familia *f* inadaptada; *Press* **p. page,** consultorio *m* sentimental.

problematic(al) [problə'mætik(əl)] *adj* problemático,-a; **it's p.,** hay problemas, tiene sus problemas.

procedure [prə'siːdʒə'] *n (way of acting)* procedimiento *m*; *(legal, business)* gestión *f*, trámite *m*; **the normal p. is as follows,** se suele proceder de la siguiente manera; **what's the p.?,** ¿cómo se suele proceder?

proceed [prə'siːd] *vi* **1** *(go on)* seguir, avanzar, proceder; **to p. to do sth,** empezar a *or* ponerse a hacer algo; **to p. to the next matter,** pasar a la siguiente cuestión; **to p. with caution,** avanzar con cuidado; **to p. with sth,** seguir con algo; **we're not sure how to p.,** no sabemos cómo proceder. **2** *Jur* **to p. against sb,** proceder contra algn.

proceeding [prə'siːdiŋ] *n* **1** *(way of acting)* proceder *m*. **2 proceedings,** *(of meeting)* actas *fpl*; *(measures)* medidas *fpl*; *Jur* proceso *m sing*; **to take legal p. against sb,** proceder contra algn.

proceeds ['prəusiːdz] *npl* beneficios *mpl*, ganancias *fpl.*

process¹ ['prəuses] **I** *n* **1** *(working out)* proceso *m*; *(method)* método *m*, sistema *m*; **chemical/natural p.,** proceso químico/natural; *Metal* **the Bessemer p.,** el proceso de Bessemer; **they were in the p. of moving,** estaban en vías de mudarse. **2** *Jur* proceso *m*. **II** *vtr (information)* tramitar; *(food)* tratar; *Phot (negative)* revelar; *Comput* procesar; **processed cheese,** queso *m* tratado.

process² [prə'ses] *vi (in procession)* desfilar.

processing ['prəusesiŋ] *n (of information)* trámites *mpl*; *(of food)* tratamiento *m*; *Phot (of negative)* revelado *m*; *Comput* tratamiento *m.*

procession [prə'seʃən] *n (of people, floats)* desfile *m*; *Rel* procesión *f.*

proclaim [prə'kleim] *vtr (announce)* proclamar, declarar; **to p. sb king/queen,** proclamar rey/reina a algn; **to p. war/peace,** declarar la guerra/paz.

proclamation [proklə'meiʃən] *n* proclamación *f.*

proclivity [prə'kliviti] *n* inclinación *f*, propensión *f* **(for,** para).

procrastinate [prəu'kræstineit] *vi* aplazar una decisión.

procrastination [prəukræsti'neiʃən] *n* dilación *f.*

procreate ['prəukrieit] *vtr & vi* procrear.

procreation [prəukri'eiʃən] *n* procreación *f.*

procure [prə'kjuə'] **I** *vtr* **1** *(obtain)* conseguir, procurar, lograr; **to p. sth for sb,** conseguir algo para algn. **2** *(for prostitution)* llevar a la prostitución. **II** *vi (for prostitution)* alcahuetear.

prod [prod] **I** *vtr (pt & pp prodded) (with finger, stick, etc)* golpear, pinchar; *(push)* empujar; *fig* empujar; **to p. sb in the ribs,** darle a algn en las costillas; *fig* **she needs prodding,** necesita un estímulo; *fig* **to p. sb into doing sth,** estimular a algn para que haga algo. **II** *n (with finger, stick)* golpecito *m*, pinchazo *m*; *(push)* empuje *m*; **to give sb a p.,** empujar a algn; *fig* **he needs a p.,** le hace falta un empujón.

prodigal ['prodigəl] *adj* pródigo,-a.

prodigious [prə'didʒəs] *adj (wonderful)* prodigioso,-a; *(huge)* enorme.

prodigy ['prodidʒi] *n* prodigio *m*. ■ **child p.,** niño,-a *m,f* prodigio.

produce [prə'djuːs] **I** *vtr (gen)* producir; *Ind* fabricar; *Press* editar; *Theat* dirigir; *Rad TV* realizar; *Cin* producir; *(give birth to)* dar a luz a, **oil producing country,** país *m* productor de petróleo. **2** *(show)* enseñar, presentar; *(bring out)* sacar; **she produced a sweet from her pocket,** se sacó un caramelo del bolsillo. **3** *(cause)* causar, ocasionar. **II** ['prodjuːs] *n Agr* productos *mpl*; **foreign p.,** productos del extranjero; **p. of Spain,** producto *m* de España.

producer [prə'djuːsə'] *n (gen)* productor,-a *m, f*; *Ind* fabricante *mf*; *Theat* director,-a *m, f* de escena; *Rad TV* realizador,-a *m, f*; *Cin* productor,-a *m.f.*

product ['prodʌkt] *n (gen)* producto *m*; *fig* producto *m*, fruto *m*, resultado *m*; **oil products,** productos derivados del petróleo.

production [prə'dʌkʃən] *n* **1** *(gen)* producción *f*; *Ind* fabricación *f*; *Theat* representación *f*; *Rad TV* realización *f*; *Cin* producción *f*; **to put sth into p.,** lanzar algo a la producción; **to take sth out of p.,** retirar algo de la producción. ■ **mass p.,** fabricación *f* en serie; **p. line,** cadena *f* de montaje. **2** *(showing)* presentación *f*; **on p. of one's passport,** al enseñar el pasaporte.

productive [prə'dʌktiv] *adj Agr* productivo,-a, fértil; *fig* **a p. meeting,** una reunión positiva *or* productiva.

productivity [prodʌk'tiviti] *n* productividad *f*; **p. agreement,** acuerdo *m* de productividad; **p. bonus,** bono *m* de productividad.

Prof *abbr of* **Professor,** catedrático,-a *m, f.*

profane [prə'fein] **I** *adj (secular)* profano,-a; *(irreverent)* sacrílego,-a; *(language)* blasfemo,-a. **II** *vtr* profanar.

profanity [prə'fæniti] *n* blasfemia *f.*

profess [prə'fes] *vtr (faith)* profesar; *(opinion)* proclamar, declarar; *(claim)* pretender; **I don't p. to be an authority on the matter,** no pretendo ser experto en el tema.

professed [prə'fest] *adj (Christian etc)* profeso,-a; *(acknowledged)* declarado,-a; *(supposed)* pretendido,-a; supuesto,-a.

profession [prə'feʃən] *n* **1** *(occupation)* profesión *f*; **by p.**, de profesión; **the medical/teaching p.**, los médicos/el profesorado; **the professions**, las profesiones. **2** *(declaration)* declaración *f*, afirmación *f*; **p. of faith**, profesión *f* de fe.

professional [prə'feʃənəl] **I** *adj* **1** *(gen)* profesional; *(soldier)* de profesión; **p. footballer/singer**, futbolista/cantante profesional; **to seek p. advice**, buscar un consejo profesional. **2** *(polished)* *(work)* de gran calidad; *(person)* perito,-a; **her work is very p.**, su trabajo es de una gran calidad. **II** *n* profesional *mf*. ◆ **professionally** *adv* profesionalmente; **he's p. qualified**, tiene un título profesional.

professionalism [prə'feʃənəlɪzəm] *n* profesionalismo *m*.

professor [prə'fesər] *n Univ* catedrático,-a *m*,*f*.

proffer ['prɒfər] *vtr fml (gift etc)* ofrecer; *(thanks)* dar.

proficiency [prə'fɪʃənsɪ] *n (in language)* capacidad *f*; *(in skill)* habilidad *f*, pericia *f*.

proficient [prə'fɪʃənt] *adj (in language)* experto,-a; *(in skill)* hábil, perito,-a.

profile ['prəʊfaɪl] *n* **1** *(of face)* perfil *m*; **in p.**, de perfil; *fig* **to keep a low p.**, procurar pasar desapercibido,-a. **2** *Press* reseña *f* biográfica.

profit ['prɒfɪt] **I** *n* **1** *Com* beneficio *m*, ganancia *f*; **gross/net p.**, beneficio bruto/neto; **to make a p. on sth**, sacar beneficios de algo; **to sell sth at a p.**, vender algo con un margen de ganancias. ■ **p. and loss account**, cuenta *f* de ganancias y pérdidas; **p. margin**, margen *m* de beneficio. **2** *fml (benefit)* provecho *m*; **to turn sth to p.**, sacar provecho de algo. **II** *vi Com* ganar; *fig* sacar provecho; **to p. from sth**, aprovecharse de algo.

profitability [prɒfɪtə'bɪlɪtɪ] *n* rentabilidad *f*.

profitable ['prɒfɪtəbəl] *adj* **1** *Com* rentable. **2** *fig (worthwhile)* provechoso,-a, positivo,-a. ◆ **profitably** *adv* **1** *Com* con rentabilidad. **2** *(worthwhile)* con provecho.

profiteer [prɒfɪ'tɪər] **I** *n* especulador,-a *m*,*f*. **II** *vi* obtener beneficios excesivos.

profit-making ['prɒfɪtmeɪkɪŋ] *adj (business)* rentable; *(charity)* con fines lucrativos; **non-p.-m.**, of sin fines lucrativos.

profit-sharing ['prɒfɪtʃɛərɪŋ] *n (by company)* reparto *m* de los beneficios.

profligate ['prɒflɪgɪt] *adj fml (immoral)* disoluto,-a, libertino,-a; *(wasteful)* despilfarrador,-a.

profound [prə'faʊnd] *adj* profundo,-a, grave, serio,-a.

profundity [prə'fʌndɪtɪ] *n* profundidad *f*.

profuse [prə'fjuːs] *adj* profuso,-a, abundante. ◆ **profusely** *adv* con profusión, abundantemente; **to apologize p.**, disculparse efusivamente; **to sweat p.**, sudar mucho.

profusion [prə'fjuːʒən] *n* profusión *f*, abundancia *f*.

progenitor [prəʊ'dʒenɪtər] *n fml (ancestor)* antepasado,-a *m*,*f*, progenitor,-a, *m*,*f*; *(forerunner)* precursor,-a *m*,*f*.

progeny ['prɒdʒɪnɪ] *n fml* progenie *f*, prole *f*, descendencia *f*.

prognosis [prɒg'nəʊsɪs] *n (pl prognoses) Med* pronóstico *m*; *fig (prediction)* augurio *m*.

prognosticate [prɒg'nɒstɪkeɪt] *vtr fml* pronosticar.

program ['prəʊgræm] *Comput* **I** *n* programa *m*. **II** *vi & vtr (pp & pt programmed)* programar.

programme, *US* **program** ['prəʊgræm] **I** *n (gen)* programa *m*; *(plan)* plan *m*; **p. of activities**, programa de actividades; **what's the p. for today?**, ¿qué plan tenemos para hoy? **II** *vtr (plan)* planear, planificar; **to p. central heating**, regular la calefacción central.

programmer, *US* **programer** ['prəʊgræmər] *n* programador,-a *m*,*f*.

progress ['prəʊgres] **1** *n (advance)* progreso *m*, avance *m*; *(development)* desarrollo *m*; *Med* mejora *f*; **the p. of**

events, el curso de los acontecimientos; **to make good p.**, hacer muchos progresos, avanzar; *Med* mejorar; **work in p.**, trabajo *m* en curso. ■ **p. report**, informe *m* sobre la marcha (del trabajo *or* de los estudios). **II** [prəʊ'gres] *vi (advance)* avanzar; *(develop)* desarrollar; *(improve)* mejorar, hacer progresos, progresar; *Med* mejorar; **as the meeting progressed**, a medida que avanzaba la reunión.

progression [prə'greʃən] *n (advance, development)* progresión *f*, avance *m*; *(series)* serie *f*.

progressive [prə'gresɪv] **I** *adj* **1** *(increasing)* progresivo,-a. **2** *Pol* progresista. **II** *n Pol* progresista *mf*. ◆ **progressively** *adv* progresivamente, poco a poco, de forma progresiva.

prohibit [prə'hɪbɪt] *vtr* prohibir; **'Smoking Prohibited'**, 'Prohibido Fumar'; **to p. sb from doing sth**, prohibir a algn hacer algo; **we were prohibited from entering**, se nos prohibió entrar.

prohibition [prəʊɪ'bɪʃən] *n* prohibición *f*; *US Hist* **the P.**, la Prohibición.

prohibitive [prə'hɪbɪtɪv] *adj* prohibitivo,-a.

project ['prɒdʒekt] **I** *n (gen)* proyecto *m*; *(plan)* plan *m*; *Educ (study)* trabajo *m*, estudio *m*. **II** [prə'dʒekt] *vtr* proyectar, planear. **III** *vi (stick out)* resaltar, sobresalir.

projectile [prə'dʒektaɪl] *n fml* proyectil *m*.

projection [prə'dʒekʃən] *n* **1** *fml (overhang etc)* resalto *m*, saliente *m*. **2** *Cin* proyección *f*. **3** *(forecast)* proyección *f*.

projectionist [prə'dʒekʃənɪst] *n Cin* operador,-a *m*,*f* de cine.

projector [prə'dʒektər] *n Cin* proyector *m*.

prolapse ['prəʊlæps, prəʊ'læps] *n Med* prolapso *m*.

proletarian [prəʊlɪ'tɛərɪən] *adj* proletario,-a.

proletariat [prəʊlɪ'tɜːrɪət] *n* proletariado *m*.

proliferate [prə'lɪfəreɪt] *vi* proliferar.

proliferation [prəlɪfə'reɪʃən] *n* proliferación *f*.

prolific [prə'lɪfɪk] *adj* prolífico,-a.

prolix ['prəʊlɪks, prəʊ'lɪks] *adj fml* prolijo,-a.

prologue, *US* **prolog** ['prəʊlɒg] *n* prólogo *m*.

prolong [prə'lɒŋ] *vtr* alargar, extender, prolongar.

prolongation [prəʊlɒŋ'geɪʃən] *n* extensión *f*, alargamiento *m*, prolongación *f*.

prom [prɒm] *n (abbr of promenade) fam* **1** *(seafront)* paseo *m* marítimo. **2** *(concert)* concierto *m* sinfónico en que parte del público está de pie.

promenade [prɒmə'nɑːd] **I** *n (at seaside)* paseo *m* marítimo. ■ *Naut* **p. deck**, cubierta *f* de paseo. **II** *vi* pasearse.

prominence ['prɒmɪnəns] *n (noticeable)* prominencia *f*; *fig (importance)* importancia *f*.

prominent ['prɒmɪnənt] *adj (standing out)* saliente, prominente; *fig (important)* importante, destacado,-a; *(famous)* famoso,-a, eminente; **to play a p. part in sth**, tener *or* desempeñar un papel importante en algo. ◆ **prominently** *adv (standing out)* muy a la vista; **to figure p. in sth**, destacar en algo.

promiscuity [prɒmɪ'skjuːɪtɪ] *n* promiscuidad *f*.

promiscuous [prə'mɪskjʊəs] *adj* promiscuo,-a.

promise ['prɒmɪs] **I** *n* **1** *(pledge)* promesa *f*; **to break/keep a p.**, faltar a/cumplir una promesa; **to make sb a p.**, prometer algo a algn. **2** *(expectation)* esperanza *f*; **there's p. of an agreement**, hay esperanzas de que se llegará a un acuerdo; **to show p.**, ser prometedor,-a. **II** *vtr (pledge)* prometer; **he promises to come** *or* **that he will come**, promete que vendrá; **I'll do it, I p. you**, lo haré, te lo prometo; **to p. sth to sb**, prometer (dar) algo a algn; *fig* **to p. sb the earth**, prometer la luna a algn. **III** *vi* **1** *(pledge)* prometer; **I p.**, te lo prometo. **2** *(augur)* prometer, augurar; **it promises to be interesting**, promete ser interesante.

promising ['prɒmɪsɪŋ] *adj* prometedor,-a.

promontory ['prɒməntərɪ] *n* promontorio *m*.

promote [prə'məʊt] *vtr* **1** *(in rank)* promover, ascender; *(in league)* hacer subir; **our team has been promoted to the first division,** nuestro equipo ha subido a primera división. **2** *Com (product)* lanzar, promocionar. **3** *(ideas etc)* fomentar.

promoter [prə'məʊtəʳ] *n (gen)* promotor,-a *m, f*; *Com* patrocinador,-a *m, f*.

promotion [prə'məʊʃən] *n* **1** *(in rank)* promoción *f*, ascenso *m*; **to get p.,** of ser ascendido,-a. **2** *Com (of product)* promoción *f*. **3** *(of arts, ideas, etc)* fomento *m*.

prompt [prɒmpt] **I** *adj (quick)* rápido,-a; *(punctual)* puntual; **to be p.,** ser puntual. **II** *adv* en punto; **at 2 o'clock p.,** a las 2 en punto. **III** *vtr* **1** *(motivate)* instar, incitar; **to p. sb to do sth,** instar a algn a hacer algo. **2** *(actor)* apuntar; *(speaker)* alentar. ◆ **promptly** *adv (quickly)* rápidamente; *(punctually)* puntualmente, en punto.

prompter ['prɒmptəʳ] *n Theat* apuntador,-a *m, f*.

prone [prəʊn] *adj* **1** *(inclined)* propenso,-a; **to be p. to sth/to do sth,** ser propenso,-a a algo/a hacer algo. **2** *fml (face down)* boca abajo.

prong [prɒŋ] *n* punta *f*, diente *m*.

pronoun ['prəʊnaʊn] *n Ling* pronombre *m*.

pronounce [prə'naʊns] *vtr* **1** *Ling* pronunciar. **2** *fml (declare)* declarar; **he was pronounced fit for work,** le declararon hábil para trabajar; *Jur* **to p. sentence,** dictar sentencia, pronunciar un fallo. **II** *vi fml* **to p. on sth,** opinar sobre algo.

pronounced [prə'naʊnst] *adj* marcado,-a.

pronouncement [prə'naʊnsmənt] *n fml* declaración *f*.

pronunciation [prənʌnsɪ'eɪʃən] *n* pronunciación *f*.

proof [pruːf] *n* **1** *(evidence)* prueba *f*; *Math* comprobación *f*; *(test)* prueba *f*; **as p. of,** como prueba de; **give me p.,** dame pruebas; **p. of identity,** documentos *mpl* de identidad; *fig* **the p. of the pudding is in the eating,** el movimiento se demuestra andando. **3** *Phot Typ* prueba *f*. **II** *adj* **1** *(secure)* resistente a, a prueba de; **p. against water,** impermeable. **2** *(of alcohol)* graduación *f*; **this rum is 70° p.,** este ron tiene 70 grados. **III** *vtr* impermeabilizar.

proofread ['pruːfriːd] *vtr & vi (pt & pp proofread* ['pruːfred]*)* corregir pruebas de imprenta.

proofreader ['pruːfriːdəʳ] *n* corrector,-a *m, f* de pruebas (de imprenta).

prop[1] [prɒp] **I** *n (support)* puntal *m*; *fig* apoyo *m*, sostén *m*. **II** *vtr (pt & pp propped) (support)* apoyar; *fig* apoyar, sostener; **to p. a bicycle/ladder against a wall,** apoyar una bicicleta/escalera contra la pared. ◆ **prop up** *vtr* apuntalar, apoyar; *fig* fortalecer; **to p. up a wall,** apuntalar una pared; *Fin* **to p. up the pound,** reforzar la libra; *fig* **to p. up a business,** poner un negocio a flote.

prop[2] [prɒp] *n Theat (abbr of property) fam* accesorio *m*.

propaganda [prɒpə'gændə] *n pej* propaganda *f*.

propagate ['prɒpəgeɪt] *fml* **I** *vtr* propagar. **II** *vi* propagarse.

propagation [prɒpə'geɪʃən] *n fml* propagación *f*.

propane ['prəʊpeɪn] *n Chem* propano *m*.

propel [prə'pel] *vtr (pt & pp propelled)* propulsar, impulsar; **to p. sb along,** impulsar a algn; **propelled by electricity,** propulsado,-a por electricidad.

propeller [prə'peləʳ] *n* hélice *f*.

propelling pencil [prəpelɪŋ'pensəl] *n* portaminas *m inv*.

propensity [prə'pensɪtɪ] *n fml* propensión *f*.

proper ['prɒpəʳ] **I** *adj* **1** adecuado,-a, correcto,-a; **p. clothing,** ropa adecuada; **prim and p.,** remilgado,-a; **the p. answer,** la respuesta correcta; **the p. way to do sth,** la manera correcta de proceder; **the p. time,** el momento oportuno. **2** *(real)* real, auténtico,-a; *(actual, exact)* propiamente dicho,-a; **he isn't a p. doctor,** no es médico de verdad; **he's a p. gentleman,** es un caballero de pies a cabeza; **in the p. sense of the word,** en el sentido estricto de la palabra; **outside the city,** fuera de la ciudad propiamente dicha. **3** *(characteristic)* propio,-a; **customs p. to the region,** costumbres propias a la región. **4** *Ling* propio,-a. ■ **p. name, p. noun,** nombre *m* propio. **II** *adv fam* realmente, de verdad; **p. poorly,** malito,-a de verdad. ◆ **properly** *adv* **1** *(appropriately, suitably, correctly)* bien, correctamente; **it wasn't p. closed,** no estaba bien cerrado,-a; **she refused, quite p.,** se negó, y con razón; **to speak p.,** hablar correctamente. **2** *(decently)* correctamente; **he wasn't p. dressed,** no iba correctamente vestido.

property ['prɒpətɪ] *n* **1** *(quality)* propiedad *f*; **medicinal properties,** propiedades medicinales. **2** *(possession)* propiedad *f*, posesión *f*; **it's our p.,** es de nuestra propiedad, nos pertenece; **lost p.,** objetos *mpl* perdidos *or* extraviados; **personal p.,** bienes *mpl*; **public p.,** dominio *m* público. **3** *(land, building)* propiedad *f*; *(estate)* finca *f*; **p. developer,** promotor,-a *m, f* de construcciones; **p. manager,** accesorista *mf*.

prophecy ['prɒfɪsɪ] *n* profecía *f*.

prophesy ['prɒfɪsaɪ] *vtr (pt & pp prophesied) (predict)* predecir; *Rel* profetizar.

prophet ['prɒfɪt] *n* profeta *mf*.

prophetic [prə'fetɪk] *adj* profético,-a.

prophylactic [prɒfɪ'læktɪk] *adj & n* profiláctico,-a *(m)*.

propitiate [prə'pɪʃɪeɪt] *vtr fml* propiciar.

propitious [prə'pɪʃəs] *adj fml* propicio,-a, favorable.

proportion [prə'pɔːʃən] **I** *n* **1** *(ratio)* proporción *f*; *(part, quantity)* parte *f*; **in equal proportions,** en partes iguales; **in p. to or with,** en proporción a; **the p. of men to women,** la proporción entre hombres y mujeres; **to be out of (all) p.,** ser desproporcionado,-a; **to keep a sense of p.,** guardar el sentido de la justa medida. **2** *(dimensions)* **proportions,** dimensiones *fpl*. **II** *vtr* proporcionar.

proportional [prə'pɔːʃənəl] *adj* proporcional **(to,** a), en proporción **(to,** con). ■ *Pol* **p. representation,** representación *f* proporcional.

proportionate [prə'pɔːʃənɪt] *adj* proporcionado,-a, proporcional.

proposal [prə'pəʊzəl] *n (offer)* propuesta *f*, oferta *f*; *(suggestion)* sugerencia *f*; **p. of marriage,** propuesta de matrimonio.

propose [prə'pəʊz] **I** *vtr* **1** *(offer)* proponer; *(suggest)* sugerir; **to p. a toast to sb,** proponer un brindis por algn; **to p. marriage to sb,** hacer una propuesta de matrimonio a algn. **2** *fml (plan, intend)* pretender, pensar; **what do you p. to do?,** ¿qué piensas hacer? **II** *vi* declararse; **to p. to sb,** pedir la mano a algn, declararse a algn.

proposer [prə'pəʊzəʳ] *n* proponente *mf*, autor,-a *m, f* de la proposición.

proposition [prɒpə'zɪʃən] **I** *n* **1** *(offer)* proposición *f*, propuesta *f*; **to make sb a p.,** hacer una propuesta a algn. **2** *Math* proposición *f*. **3** *(business)* trato *m*, negocio *m*; **a paying p.,** un negocio rentable. **II** *vtr* hacer proposiciones (deshonestas) a.

propound [prə'paʊnd] *vtr fml* exponer, plantear.

proprietary [prə'praɪɪtərɪ] *adj fml* patentado,-a.

proprietor [prə'praɪətəʳ] *n* propietario,-a *m, f*, dueño,-a *m, f*.

propriety [prə'praɪətɪ] *n* **1** *(decency)* decoro *m*, decencia *f*; *(suitability)* conveniencia *f*. **2 proprieties,** cánones *mpl* sociales, conveniencias *fpl*.

propulsion [prə'pʌlʃən] *n* propulsión *f*. ■ **jet p.,** propulsión *f* a chorro *or* por reacción.

prosaic [prəʊ'zeɪɪk] *adj* prosaico,-a.

proscribe [prəʊ'skraɪb] *vtr fml* proscribir.

prose [prəʊz] *n* **1** *Lit* prosa *f*. ■ **p. writer,** prosista *mf*. **2** *Educ (translation)* texto *m* para traducir.

prosecute ['prɒsɪkjuːt] vtr Jur procesar, entablar una acción judicial contra.

prosecution [prɒsɪ'kjuːʃən] n 1 Jur (action) proceso m, juicio m; (person) **the p.**, la parte acusadora. ■ **counsel for the p.**, fiscal mf; **witness for the p.**, testigo mf de cargo. 2 (carrying out) realización f.

prosecutor ['prɒsɪkjuːtəʳ] n Jur acusador,-a m,f.

prospect ['prɒspekt] I n (outlook) perspectiva f; (chance, hope) esperanza f, probabilidad f; **future prospects**, perspectivas para el futuro; **there's little p. of that happening**, hay pocas probabilidades de que eso ocurra; **the job has prospects**, es un trabajo con porvenir. II [prə'spekt] vtr explorar. III vi **to p. for gold/oil**, buscar oro/petróleo.

prospective [prə'spektɪv] adj (future) futuro,-a; (possible) eventual, probable.

prospector [prə'spektəʳ] n explorador,-a m, f, prospector,-a m,f. ■ **gold p.**, buscador,-a m,f del oro.

prospectus [prə'spektəs] n prospecto m.

prosper ['prɒspəʳ] vi prosperar.

prosperity [prɒ'sperɪtɪ] n prosperidad f.

prosperous ['prɒspərəs] adj próspero,-a.

prostate ['prɒsteɪt] n próstata f.

prostitute ['prɒstɪtjuːt] I n prostituta f, puta f. ■ **male p.**, puto m. II vtr **to p. oneself**, prostituirse.

prostitution [prɒstɪ'tjuːʃən] n prostitución f.

prostrate ['prɒstreɪt] I adj (face down) boca abajo, postrado,-a; fig (powerless, exhausted) abatido,-a, postrado,-a; **p. with grief**, desconsolado,-a. II [prɒ'streɪt] vtr **to p. oneself**, postrarse.

prostration [prɒs'treɪʃən] n postración f.

protagonist [prəʊ'tægənɪst] n protagonista mf.

protect [prə'tekt] vtr (gen) proteger; (interests etc) salvaguardar; **to p. sb from/against sth**, proteger a algn de/contra algo.

protection [prə'tekʃən] n protección f, amparo m; **to be under sb's p.**, estar protegido,-a or amparado,-a por algn. ■ **p. racket**, chantaje m.

protectionism [prə'tekʃənɪzəm] n proteccionismo m.

protective [prə'tektɪv] adj protector,-a; **p.clothing**, ropa f de protección.

protector [prə'tektəʳ] n (person) protector,-a m,f; (thing) protector m.

protégé(e) ['prəʊteʒeɪ] n protegido,-a m,f.

protein ['prəʊtiːn] n proteína f.

protest ['prəʊtest] I n (gen) protesta f; (complaint) queja f; **to make a p. about sth**, protestar por algo; **under p.**, bajo protesta. ■ **p. march**, manifestación f, marcha f de protesta. II [prə'test] vtr protestar de; **to p. one's innocence**, protestar de su inocencia; US **to p. sth**, protestar por algo. III vi GB protestar; **to p. that ...**, protestar manifestando or diciendo que ...; **to p. about sth**, protestar por algo.

Protestant ['prɒtɪstənt] adj & n Rel protestante (mf).

Protestantism ['prɒtɪstəntɪzəm] n Rel protestantismo m.

protestation [prɒtes'teɪʃən] n fml 1 (protest) protesta f. 2 (declaration) declaración f.

protester [prə'testəʳ] n manifestante mf.

protocol ['prəʊtəkɒl] n protocolo m.

proton ['prəʊtɒn] n Phys protón m.

prototype ['prəʊtətaɪp] n prototipo m.

protracted [prə'træktɪd] adj prolongado,-a, largo,-a.

protractor [prə'træktəʳ] n Geom transportador m.

protrude [prə'truːd] vi fml salir, sobresalir.

protruding [prə'truːdɪŋ] adj saliente, sobresaliente, prominente; **p. eyes**, ojos saltones; **p. teeth**, dientes prominentes.

protuberance [prə'tjuːbərəns] n fml protuberancia f, saliente m.

proud [praʊd] adj 1 (gen) orgulloso,-a; (arrogant) soberbio,-a; **a p. moment**, un momento glorioso; **I'm p. to introduce ...**, tengo el honor de presentar a ...; **to be p. of sth**, estar orgulloso,-a de algo, enorgullecerse or ufanarse de algo; fam **to do sb p.**, tratar a algn a cuerpo de rey. 2 lit (sticking out) saliente, sobresaliente. ◆ **proudly** adv (gen) orgullosamente, con orgullo; (arrogantly) soberbiamente, con soberbia.

prove [pruːv] vtr (pt **proved**; pp **proved** or **proven**) 1 (give evidence of) probar, demostrar; Math comprobar; **history proved him right**, la historia le dio la razón; **the exception proves the rule**, la excepción confirma la regla; **to p. oneself**, dar pruebas de valor; **to p. sb's innocence**, demostrar la inocencia de algn. 2 (turn out) resultar; **it proved to be disastrous**, resultó ser desastroso,-a.

proven ['pruːvən] I pp see **prove**. II adj probado,-a, demostrado,-a; **this is not p.**, esto está por comprobar.

proverb ['prɒvɜːb] n refrán m, proverbio m.

proverbial [prə'vɜːbɪəl] adj proverbial.

provide [prə'vaɪd] I vtr (gen) proporcionar, facilitar; (supplies) suministrar, proveer; **provided with**, provisto,-a de; **the firm will p. you with a car**, la empresa te facilitará or dará un coche; **to p. oneself with sth**, proveerse de algo; **to p. sb with food/water**, suministrar comida/agua a algn. II vi 1 proveer; **God will p.**, Dios proveerá; **to p. against misfortune**, tomar medidas contra cualquier desgracia; **to p. for sb**, mantener a algn; **to p. for the future**, ahorrar para el futuro. 2 Jur estipular; **the law provides that ...**, la ley estipula que ... .

provided [prə'vaɪdɪd] conj **p. (that)**, con tal de que, a condición de que, siempre que.

providence ['prɒvɪdəns] n providencia f.

provindential [prɒvɪ'denʃəl] adj providencial.

providing [prə'vaɪdɪŋ] conj see **provided**.

province ['prɒvɪns] n 1 (region) provincia f; **to live in the provinces**, vivir en provincias. 2 fig (field of knowledge etc) campo m, competencia f; **that's not my p.**, no es de mi competencia.

provincial [prə'vɪnʃəl] I adj provincial; pej provinciano,-a, pueblerino,-a. II n pej (person) provinciano, m,f.

provision [prə'vɪʒən] n 1 (supplying) provisión f; **to. make p. for sb**, atender las necesidades de algn; **to make p. for the future**, ahorrar para el futuro. 2 (supply) suministro m; (food) **provisions**, provisiones fpl víveres mpl. 3 (condition) disposición f; **there is no p. for this in the agreement**, esto no está previsto en el acuerdo; **with the p. that they sell it**, con tal de que lo vendan.

provisional [prə'vɪʒənəl] adj provisional, provisorio,-a.

proviso [prə'vaɪzəʊ] n (pl **provisos** or **provisoes**) **with the p. that**, con tal de que, a condición de que, siempre que.

provocation [prɒvə'keɪʃən] n provocación f; **at the slightest p.**, a la más mínima provocación; **to act under p.**, reaccionar ante una provocación.

provocative [prə'vɒkətɪv] adj provocador,-a, provocativo,-a. ◆ **provocatively** adv de una forma provocadora or provocativa.

provoke [prə'vəʊk] vtr provocar; **he gets angry when provoked**, se enfada cuando lo provocan; **to p. sb to do sth**, provocar a algn a que haga algo.

provoking [prə'vəʊkɪŋ] adj provocador,-a, que provoca.

provost ['prɒvəst] n 1 Scot alcalde m. 2 Univ rector m.

prow [praʊ] n proa f.

prowess ['praʊɪs] n fml habilidad f, capacidad f.

prowl [praʊl] I n merodeo m; **to be on the p.**, merodear, rondar. II vi merodear; fam **to p. about** or **around**, rondar.

prowler ['praʊləʳ] *n fam* merodeador *m*.

proximity [prɒk'sɪmɪtɪ] *n fml* proximidad *f*; **in p. to, in the p. of,** cerca de.

proxy ['prɒksɪ] *n Jur (power)* poderes *mpl*; *(person)* apoderado,-a *m*,*f*, mandatario,-a *m*,*f*; **by p.,** por poderes.

prs *abbr of* **pairs,** pares *mpl*.

prude [pruːd] *n* gazmoño,-a *m*,*f*, mojigato,-a *m*,*f*.

prudence ['pruːdəns] *n fml* prudencia *f*.

prudent ['pruːdənt] *adj fml* prudente.

prudish ['pruːdɪʃ] *adj* remilgado,-a.

prune¹ [pruːn] *n* ciruela *f* pasa.

prune² [pruːn] *vtr Hortic* podar; *fig (text etc)* acortar, expurgar. ■ **pruning knife,** podera *f*.

prurient ['prʊərɪənt] *adj fml* lascivo,-a.

Prussia ['prʌʃə] *n* Prusia.

Prussian ['prʌʃən] *adj & n* prusiano,-a *(m,f)*.

pry [praɪ] *vi (pt & pp pried)* curiosear, husmear; **to p. into sb's affairs,** meterse en asuntos ajenos.

prying ['praɪɪŋ] *adj* entrometido,-a, husmeador,-a.

PS, ps [piːˈes] *abbr of* **post scriptum** (postscript), posdata *f*, P.S., P.D.

psalm [sɑːm] *n Rel* salmo *m*.

pseud [sjuːd] *n fam* farsante *mf*.

pseudo- ['sjuːdəʊ] *pref* pseudo-, seudo-.

pseudonym ['sjuːdənɪm] *n* pseudónimo *m*, seudónimo *m*.

psyche ['saɪkɪ] *n* psique *f*, psiquis *f*.

psychedelic [saɪkɪ'delɪk] *adj* psicodélico,-a; sicodelico,-a.

psychiatric [saɪkɪ'ætrɪk] *adj* psiquiátrico,-a, siquiátrico,-a.

psychiatrist [saɪ'kaɪətrɪst] *n* psiquiatra *mf*, siquiatra *mf*.

psychiatry [saɪ'kaɪətrɪ] *n* psiquiatría *f*, siquiatría *f*.

psychic ['saɪkɪk] **I** *adj* psíquico,-a, síquico,-a; *fam* **you must be p.!,** ¡cómo lo adivinaste! **II** *n (medium)* médium *mf*.

psycho ['saɪkəʊ] *n fam* psicópata *mf*, sicópata *mf*.

psychoanalyse, *US* **psychoanalyze** [saɪkəʊ'ænəlaɪz] *vtr* psicoanalizar, sicoanalizar.

psychoanalysis [saɪkəʊə'nælɪsɪs] *n* psicoanálisis *f*, sicoanálisis *f*.

psychoanalyst [saɪkəʊ'ænəlɪst] *n* psicoanalista *mf*, sicoanalista *mf*.

psychological [saɪkə'lɒdʒɪkəl] *adj* psicológico,-a, sicológico,-a.

psychologist [saɪ'kɒlədʒɪst] *n* psicólogo,-a *m*, *f*, sicologo,-a *m*,*f*.

psychology [saɪ'kɒlədʒɪ] *n* psicología *f*, sicología *f*.

psychopath ['saɪkəʊpæθ] *n* psicópata *mf*, sicópata *mf*.

psychosis [saɪ'kəʊsɪs] *n (pl psychoses* [saɪ'kəʊsiːz]*)* psicosis *f inv*, sicosis *f inv*.

psychosomatic [saɪkəʊsə'mætɪk] *adj* psicosomático,-a, sicosomático,-a.

psychotherapy [saɪkəʊ'θerəpɪ] *n* psicoterapia *f*, sicoterapia *f*.

psychotic [saɪ'kɒtɪk] *adj & n* psicótico,-a *(m, f)*, sicótico,-a *(m,f)*.

PT [piːˈtiː] *abbr of* **physical training,** educación *f* física.

pt *abbr of* **1** *(also Pt)* **part,** parte *f*. **2** *(pl pts)* **pint,** pinta *f*. **3** *(pl pts)* **point,** punto *m*.

PTA [piːtiːˈeɪ] *Educ abbr of* **Parent-Teacher Association,** Asociación *f* de Padres de Familia y Profesores.

Pte *Mil abbr of* **Private,** soldado *m* raso.

PTO, pto [piːtiːˈəʊ] *abbr of* **please turn over,** sigue.

ptarmigan ['tɑːmɪgən] *n Orn* perdiz *f* nival.

pub *n GB fam* bar *m*, pub *m*, taberna *f*.

pub-crawl ['pʌbkrɔːl] *n fam* **to go on a p.-c.,** ir de tascas.

puberty ['pjuːbətɪ] *n* pubertad *f*.

pubescent [pjuːˈbesənt] *adj & n* pubescente *(mf)*.

pubic ['pjuːbɪk] *adj* púbico,-a. ■ **p. hair,** vello *m* púbico.

pubis ['pjuːbɪs] *n Anat* pubis *m*.

public ['pʌblɪk] **I** *adj* público,-a; **in the p. interest,** en interés del estado; **it's p. knowledge,** es del dominio público; **to be in the p. eye,** ser objeto del interés público; *Com* **to go p.,** constituirse en sociedad anónima; **to make sth p.,** hacer público algo. ■ **p. company,** empresa *f* pública; **p. convenience,** servicios *mpl*, aseos *mpl*; **p. holiday,** fiesta *f* nacional; **p. house,** pub *m*, taberna *f*; **p. opinion,** opinión *f* pública; **p. ownership,** titularidad *f* estatal; **p. relations,** relaciones *fpl* públicas; *GB* **p. school,** colegio *m* privado; **p. sector,** sector *m* estatal *or* público; **p. speaking,** declamación *f*; **p. spirit,** civismo *m*; **p. transport,** transporte *m* público. **II the p.** *n* el público; **in p.,** en público; **the British p.,** los británicos.

public-address system [pʌblɪkə'dressɪstəm] *n* megafonía *f*, sistema *m* de altavoces.

publican ['pʌblɪkən] *n* patrón,-ona *m*, *f* de un pub, tabernero,-a *m*,*f*.

publication [pʌblɪ'keɪʃən] *n* publicación *f*. ■ **p. date,** fecha *f* de publicación.

publicity [pʌ'blɪsɪtɪ] *n* publicidad *f*.

publicize ['pʌblɪsaɪz] *vtr (make public)* divulgar, hacer público,-a, dar a conocer; *(advertise)* promocionar, hacer publicidad para.

public-spirited [pʌblɪk'spɪrɪtɪd] *adj* de espíritu cívico.

publish ['pʌblɪʃ] *vtr* publicar, editar; **published weekly,** semanal; **just published,** última novedad, de reciente publicación.

publisher ['pʌblɪʃəʳ] *n (person)* editor,-a *m*,*f*; *(firm)* (casa *f*) editorial *f*.

publishing ['pʌblɪʃɪŋ] *n (business)* industria *f* editorial; **she works in p.,** trabaja en una editorial. ■ **p. company** *or* **house,** casa *f* editorial.

puce [pjuːs] *adj* de color pardo rojizo.

pucker ['pʌkəʳ] **I** *vtr (lips, brow)* fruncir, arrugar. **II** *vi (lips, brow)* fruncirse, arrugarse; *Sew* fruncir.

pudding ['pʊdɪŋ] *n Culin* pudín *m*; *fam (desert)* postre *m*; **what's for p.?,** ¿qué hay de postre? ■ **black p.,** morcilla *f*; **Christmas p.,** pudín *m* a base de frutos secos típico de Navidad; **p. basin,** cuenco *m*; **rice p.,** arroz *m* con leche; **steamed p.,** budín *m*.

puddle ['pʌdəl] *n* charco *m*.

puerile ['pjʊəraɪl] *adj* pueril.

Puerto Rico [pwɜːtəʊ'riːkəʊ] *n* Puerto Rico.

Puerto Rican [pwɜːtəʊ'riːkən] *adj & n* portorriqueño,-a *(m,f)*, portorriqueño,-a *(m,f)*.

puff [pʌf] **I** *n* **1** *(of wind)* soplo *m*, racha *f*; *(of smoke)* bocanada *f*; **to take a p. of a cigarette,** dar una calada a un cigarrillo; *fam* **to be out of p.,** quedarse *or* estar sin aliento. **2 powder p.,** borla *f*. **3** *Culin* **cream p.,** petisú *m*; **p. pastry,** pasta *f* de hojaldre. **II** *vi (person)* jadear, resoplar; *(train)* echar humo *or* vapor; **to p. on one's pipe,** chupar la pipa. **III** *vtr* dar una calada a. ◆ **puff up** *vi* hincharse; *fig* **to be puffed up with pride,** hincharse de orgullo.

puffin ['pʌfɪn] *n Orn* frailecillo *m* (común).

puffy ['pʌfɪ] *adj (puffier, puffiest)* hinchado,-a, inflado,-a.

pug [pʌg] *n Zool* doguillo *m*.

pugnacious [pʌg'neɪʃəs] *adj* pugnaz, agresivo,-a.

pug-nosed ['pʌgnəʊzd] *adj* de nariz chata.

puke [pjuːk] *vi fam* devolver, vomitar.

pull [pʊl] **I** *n* **1** *(tug)* tirón *m*; **to give sth a p.,** dar un tirón a algo. **2** *Tech (of engine)* tracción *f*. **3** *fig (attraction)* atracción *f*; *(influence)* enchufe *m*, influencia *f*; **the p. of the big city,** la atracción de la gran ciudad; **to have p. with sb,** tener influencia sobre algn. **4** *(journey)* trecho *m*; **a long p.,** una tirada; **it was a long p. to the top,** nos costó llegar a la cumbre. **5** *(of bell)* cuerda *f*. **6** *Print* galerada *f*, primera prueba *f*. **II** *vtr* **1** *(tug)* oar un tirón a; *Med* **to p. a muscle,** sufrir un tirón en un músculo; **to p. the trigger of a gun,** apretar el gatillo de una pistola; **to p. sth to pieces,** hacer algo pedazos; *fig* poner algo por los suelos; *fig* **to p. a face,** hacer una mueca; *fig* **to p. strings,** tocar teclas; *fig* **to p. sb's leg,** tomar el pelo a algn; *fam* **p. the other one,** que lo cuentes a tu primo; *fam* **to p. a fast one on sb,** hacer una jugada a algn. **2** *(draw)* tirar, arrastrar; **to p. sth open/ shut,** abrir/cerrar algo de un tirón; **p. your chair up to the fire,** acércate la silla al fuego; **to p. a heavy object,** arrastrar un objeto pesado; *fig* **to p. one's weight,** hacer su parte del trabajo; **to p. the wool over sb's eyes,** engañar a algn. **3** *(draw out)* sacar; **to p. a gun on sb,** amenazar a algn con pistola. **4** *Culin* **to p. a chicken,** desplumar un pollo. **5** *fam (people)* atraer; **the new exhibition pulled in the punters,** la nueva exposición atrajo mucha gente. **III** *vi* **1** *(drag)* tirar; **the car pulls to the right,** el coche tira hacia la derecha; **to p. on one's pipe,** dar chupadas a la pipa. **2** *(move)* **to p. in/out,** entrar en/salir de; **to p. alongside sb,** acercarse a algn. ◆ **pull apart** *vtr (gen)* desmontar; *(separate)* separar; *(break)* hacer pedazos; *fig (critize)* hacer pedazos. ◆ **pull away** *vtr* apartar, separar. **II** *vi (car)* arrancar; *(train)* salir de la estación; *(ship)* desatracar. ◆ **pull back I** *vtr* tirar hacia atrás. **II** *vi* contenerse; *Mil* retirarse. ◆ **pull down** *vtr (building)* derribar; *fig (depress)* deprimir, abatir. ◆ **pull in I** *vtr* **1** *(crowds)* atraer; *fam (money)* aportar. **2** *fam (arrest)* detener. **II** *vi* entrar; *(train)* entrar en la estación; *(stop)* parar. ◆ **pull off I** *vtr fam (carry out)* llevar a cabo; **to p. sth off,** llevar algo a cabo. **II** *vi (vehicle)* salir, arrancar. ◆ **pull out I** *vtr (withdraw)* retirarse. **II** *vi Aut* **to p. out to overtake,** salir para adelantar. ◆ **pull over** *vi* hacerse a un lado. ◆ **pull through** *vi* reponerse, restablecerse. ◆ **pull together I** *vtr* **to p. oneself together,** calmarse, serenarse, tranquilizarse. **II** *vi (cooperate)* tirar en conjunto. ◆ **pull up I** *vtr* **1** *(lift up)* levantar, subir; *(uproot)* desarraigar, sacar; **to p. up one's socks,** subirse los calcetines; *fig* espabilarse; *fig* **to p. up one's roots,** desarraigarse. **2** *(draw close)* acercar. **3** *(scold)* regañar. **II** *vi (stop)* pararse, detenerse.

pullet ['pʊlɪt] *n* pollo *m*.

pulley ['pʊlɪ] *n* polea *f*.

Pullman® ['pʊlmən] *n* coche-cama *m*.

pull-out ['pʊlaʊt] **I** *n Press (supplement)* suplemento *m*. **II** *adj (magazine)* separable; *(leaf of table etc)* extensible.

pullover ['pʊləʊvə'] *n* jersey *m*, pullover *m*.

pulp [pʌlp] **I** *n (of paper, wood)* pasta *f*, pulpa *f*; *(of fruit)* pulpa *f*, *fam fig (book etc)* basura *f*; **to crush sth to a p.,** hacer algo papilla. **II** *vtr* reducir a pulpa.

pulpit ['pʊlpɪt] *n* púlpito *m*.

pulsate [pʌl'seɪt] *vi* vibrar, palpitar.

pulse[1] [pʌls] *n* **1** *Anat* pulso *m*; *(of radio)* pulsación *f*; *fig (rhythm)* compás *m*; **to take sb's p.,** tomar el pulso a algn. **2** pulso *m*.

pulse[2] [pʌls] *n Bot Culin* legumbre *f*.

pulverize ['pʌlvəraɪz] *vtr* pulverizar.

puma ['pjuːmə] *n* puma *m*.

pumice (stone) ['pʌmɪs (stəʊn)] *n* piedra *f* pómez.

pummel ['pʌmǝl] *vtr* *(pt & pp* **pummelled,** *US* **pummeled)** aporrear.

pump[1] [pʌmp] **I** *n* bomba *f*. ■ **petrol p.,** bomba *f* (de gasolina); **stomach p.,** bomba *f* estomacal. **II** *vtr* bombear; **the heart pumps blood,** el corazón bombea la sangre; **to p. air into a tyre,** inflar un neumático con una bomba; **to p. sth in in/out,** meter/sacar algo con una bomba; *fam fig* **to p. money into a venture,** invertir dinero en una empresa; *fam fig* **to p. sb for information,** sonsacar información a algn. ◆ **pump out** *vtr (churn out)* producir; *(empty)* vaciar. ◆ **pump up** *vtr (tyre)* inflar.

pump[2] [pʌmp] *n (for ballet)* zapatilla *f* de ballet; *(for tennis)* zapatilla *f* de tenis; *(for beach)* playera *f*.

pumpkin ['pʌmpkɪn] *n* calabaza *f*.

pun [pʌn] *n* juego *m* de palabras, retruécano *m*.

Punch [pʌntʃ] *n* **P. and Judy show,** teatro *m* de títeres.

punch[1] [pʌntʃ] **I** *n (for making holes)* perforadora *f*, taladro *m*; *(for tickets)* máquina *f* de picar billetes; *(in leather etc)* punzón *m*. **II** *vtr (make hole)* perforar; *(in ticket)* picar; *(in leather)* punzar.

punch[2] [pʌntʃ] **I** *n* **1** *(blow)* puñetazo *m*; *(in boxing)* pegada *f*; *fig* he **doesn't pull any punches,** no tiene pelos en la lengua. **2** *fig (force)* fuerza *f*, empuje *m*; **it lacks p.,** le falta fuerza. ■ **p. line,** remate *m* (de un chiste). **II** *vtr (with fist)* dar un puñetazo a.

punch[3] [pʌntʃ] *n (drink)* ponche *m*.

punchball ['pʌntʃbɔːl] *n Box* saco *m* de arena.

punchbowl ['pʌntʃbəʊl] *n* ponchera *f*.

punch-drunk [pʌntʃ'drʌŋk] *adj* aturdido,-a, grogui.

punching bag ['pʌntʃɪŋbæg] *n US Box* saco *m* de arena.

punch-up ['pʌntʃʌp] *n fam* riña *f*, pelea *f*.

punctilious [pʌŋk'tɪlɪəs] *adj fml* puntilloso,-a, quisquilloso,-a.

punctual ['pʌŋktjʊəl] *adj* puntual; **the train was p.,** el tren llegó a la hora. ◆ **punctually** *adv* puntualmente, en punto.

punctuality [pʌŋktjʊ'ælɪtɪ] *n* puntualidad *f*.

punctuate ['pʌŋktjʊeɪt] *vtr Ling* puntuar; *fig* **to p. a speech with anecdotes,** salpicar un discurso con anécdotas.

punctuation [pʌŋktjʊ'eɪʃən] *n Ling* puntuación *f*. ■ **p. mark,** signo *m* de puntuación.

puncture ['pʌŋktʃə'] **I** *n (in tyre etc)* pinchazo *m*; *Aut* **I've got a p.,** se me ha pinchado una rueda. **II** *vtr (tyre)* pinchar; **to p. the skin,** hacer una punción en la piel. **III** *vi* pincharse.

pundit ['pʌndɪt] *n fam* experto,-a *m,f*.

pungency ['pʌndʒənsɪ] *n (of smell)* acritud *f*; *(of taste)* sabor *m* fuerte *or* picante; *fig (of remark)* mordacidad *f*.

pungent ['pʌndʒənt] *adj (smell)* acre; *(taste)* fuerte, picante; *fig (remark)* mordaz.

punish ['pʌnɪʃ] *vtr* castigar; **to p. sb for doing sth,** castigar a algn por haber hecho algo.

punishable ['pʌnɪʃəbəl] *adj* castigable, punible; *Jur* delictivo,-a.

punishment ['pʌnɪʃmənt] *n* castigo *m*; **to make the p. fit the crime,** adecuar el castigo al crimen; *fig* **the team took a lot of p.,** el equipo sufrió una paliza. ■ **capital p.,** pena *f* de muerte; **corporal p.,** castigo *m* físico.

punk [pʌŋk] *n fam* **1** punk *mf*. ■ **p. music,** música *f* punk. **2** *US* mamón *m*.

punnet ['pʌnɪt] *n* cestita *f*.

punt[1] [pʌnt] **I** *n (boat)* batea *f*. **II** *vtr* dirigir con percha. **III** *vi* ir en batea.

punt[2] [pʌnt] *vi GB (bet)* apostar.

punter ['pʌntə'] *n GB* **1** *(gambler)* jugador,-a *m, f*, apostante *mf*. **2** *(customer)* cliente,-a *m,f*.

puny ['pjuːnɪ] *adj (punier, puniest)* enclenque, endeble.

pup [pʌp] *n* cachorro,-a *m,f*.

pupil[1] ['pjuːpəl] *n Educ* alumno,-a *m,f*.

pupil[2] ['pjuːpəl] *n Anat* pupila *f*.

puppet ['pʌpɪt] *n* títere *m*, marioneta *f*; *fig* títere. ■ *fig* **p. government,** gobierno *m* títere; **p. show,** teatro *m* de títeres *or* de marionetas.

puppy ['pʌpɪ] *n (young dog)* cachorro,-a *m,f*, perrito *m*. ■ *fam* **p. fat,** gordura *f* infantil; *fam* **p. love,** amor *m* adolescente.

purchase ['pɜːtʃɪs] **I** *n* **1** *Com* compra *f*, adquisición *f*. ■ **p. price,** precio *m* de compra; **p. tax,** impuesto *m* sobre la venta. **2** *(hold)* agarre *m*, asidero *m*; **to get a p. on sth,** agarrar algo bien. **II** *vtr Com fml* comprar, adquirir; **purchasing power,** poder *m* adquisitivo.

purchaser ['pɜːtʃɪsə^r] n comprador,-a m,f.

pure [pjʊə^r] adj puro,-a; **it was p. chance,** fue pura casualidad; **p. and simple,** puro,-a y simple. ■ **p. new wool,** pura lana f virgen; **p. science,** ciencia f pura. ◆ **purely** adv simplemente, sencillamente; **p. and simply,** pura y simplemente; **p. for economic reasons,** por motivos económicos nada más.

purebred [pjʊə'bred] I adj de pura sangre, de raza. II ['pjʊəbred] n animal m (de) pura sangre or de raza.

purée ['pjʊəreɪ] I n Culin puré m; **apple p.,** puré de manzana; **tomato p.,** tomate m concentrado. II vtr pasar por el pasapurés, machacar.

purgative ['pɜːgətɪv] adj & n Med purgante (m).

purgatory ['pɜːgətərɪ] n Rel & fig purgatorio m.

purge [pɜːdʒ] I n Med Pol purga f. II vtr Med purgar; Pol purgar, depurar; fig (of thoughts etc) librar (**of, de**).

purify ['pjʊərɪfaɪ] vtr (pt & pp **purified**) purificar.

purl [pɜːl] Knit I n punto m del revés. II vtr hacer punto del revés.

purple ['pɜːpəl] I n (colour) color m morado, púrpura f. II adj morado,-a, purpúreo,-a; **to go** or **turn p. (in the face),** ponerse morado,-a.

purport ['pɜːpɔːt] I n fml sentido m, significado m. II [pɜː'pɔːt] vi fml pretender; **to p. to be sth,** pretender ser algo.

purpose ['pɜːpəs] n 1 (aim, intention) propósito m, intención f; **on p.,** a propósito; **to have a p. in life,** tener una meta or un objetivo en la vida; **to have a sense of p.,** ser firme en tus propósitos; **what's the p. of your visit?,** ¿con qué fin vienes a vernos? 2 (use) uso m, utilidad f; **for all practical purposes, to all intents and purposes,** en la práctica; **for general purposes,** para todos los usos; **it serves no useful p.,** no sirve para nada; **to turn sth to good p.,** aprovechar algo. ◆ **purposely** adv a propósito, adrede.

purpose-built [pɜːpəs'bɪlt] adj construido,-a or hecho,-a a la medida.

purposeful ['pɜːpəsfʊl] adj (resolute) decidido,-a, resoluto,-a; (intentional) intencionado,-a.

purr [pɜː^r] I n (of cat) ronroneo m; (of engine) zumbido m. II vi (cat) ronronear; (engine) zumbar.

purse [pɜːs] I n 1 GB monedero m, portamonedas m inv; fig **to hold the p. strings,** administrar el dinero; prov **you can't make a silk p. out of a sow's ear,** no se puede pedir peras al olmo. 2 US (bag) bolso m, cartera f. 3 (prize money) premio m en metálico f. II vtr **to p. one's lips,** apretarse los labios.

purser ['pɜːsə^r] n Naut contador,-a m,f.

pursue [pə'sjuː] vtr fml 1 (criminal etc) perseguir; (person, animal) seguir; (pleasure, happiness) buscar. 2 (carry out) llevar a cabo; (studies) dedicarse a, seguir; (profession, career) ejercer.

pursuer [pə'sjuːə^r] n fml perseguidor,-a m,f.

pursuit [pə'sjuːt] n 1 (of criminal) persecución f; (of animal) caza f; (of pleasure, happiness) busca f, búsqueda f; **in hot p. (of sb),** pisando los talones a algn; **in p. of fame,** en busca de la fama. 2 (occupation) ocupación f, trabajo m; **leisure p.,** pasatiempo m.

purveyor [pə'veɪə^r] n Com fml proveedor,-a m,f.

pus [pʌs] n pus m.

push [pʊʃ] I n 1 (shove) empujón m, empuje m; **to give sth/sb a p.,** empujar algo/a algn, dar un empujón a algo/algn; fam **at a p.,** caso de necesidad; fam **to give sb the p.,** echar a algn. 2 fig (drive) empuje m, dinamismo m. II vtr 1 (shove) empujar; (bell, button, etc) pulsar, apretar; **to p. one's finger into a hole,** meter el dedo en un agujero; **to p. one's way through the crowd,** abrirse camino a empujones entre la multitud; **to p. the door open/shut,** abrir/cerrar la puerta empujándola; fam **she's pushing forty,** ronda los cuarenta. 3 fig (pressurize) instar, presionar; (harass) apremiar; **don't p. me too far!,** ¡no te pases conmigo!; **to p. oneself too far,** exigirse

demasiado; **to p. sb for payment,** apremiar a algn a hacer algo; **to p. sb into doing sth,** instar or obligar a algn a hacer algo; fam **to be (hard) pushed for time/money,** andar justo,-a de tiempo/dinero. 4 Com fam (product) promover, promocionar; (trade) fomentar; **to p. drugs,** pasar or vender droga; **to p. sales,** hacer una campaña de venta. III vi (shove) empujar; **'Push',** (on door) 'Empujar'; (on bell, button, etc) 'Pulse'; **to p. through the crowd,** abrirse paso or camino entre la multitud. ◆ **push about, push around** vtr fam (bully) intimidar. ◆ **push ahead** vi progresar, avanzar; **to p. ahead with sth,** progresar con algo. ◆ **push aside** vtr (object) apartar; fig (person) hacer caso omiso de. ◆ **push in** I vtr empujar. II vi (interrupt) entrometerse, colarse. ◆ **push off** vi (in boat) desatracar; fam (leave) marcharse; **p. off!,** ¡lárgate! ◆ **push on** vi (continue) seguir adelante. ◆ **push over** vtr (knock over) volcar. ◆ **push through** vtr abrirse paso or camino por or entre.

push-bike ['pʊʃbaɪk] n bicicleta f.

push-button ['pʊʃbʌtən] adj con botón de mando.

pushchair ['pʊʃtʃeə^r] n GB sillita f (de ruedas).

pusher ['pʊʃə^r] n fam (of drugs) camello m.

pushover ['pʊʃəʊvə^r] n fam **it's a p.,** está chupado; **she's a p.,** es un ligue fácil.

push-up ['pʊʃʌp] n US Gymn flexión f de brazos.

pushy ['pʊʃɪ] adj (**pushier, pushiest**) fam agresivo,-a, insistente.

puss [pʊs] n fam, **pussy** ['pʊsɪ] n fam minino m; **p., p.!,** ¡miz, miz!

put [pʊt] vtr (pt & pp **put**) 1 (gen) poner; (place) colocar, fijar; (add) echar, añadir; (insert) meter, introducir; (when packing) coger; **have you p. in any ties?,** ¿has cogido corbatas?; **not to know where to p. oneself,** no saber dónde ponerse or esconderse; **to p. a ball into the net,** meter la pelota en la red; **to p. a bone out of joint,** dislocarse un hueso; **to p. a child to bed,** acostar a un niño; **to p. a coin into a slot,** meter una moneda en una ranura; **to p. a picture up on the wall,** colgar or fijar un cuadro en la pared; **to p. a stop to sth,** prohibir algo, poner término a algo; **to p. an animal out of its misery,** rematar un animal; **to p. money on a horse,** jugarse dinero en un caballo; **to p. one's arms around sb,** abrazar a algn; **to p. one's energy into sth,** concentrarse en (hacer) algo; **to p. one's head on sb's shoulder,** recostar or apoyar la cabeza en el hombro de algn; **to p. one's head round the door,** asomarse por detrás de la puerta; **to p. one's pen through sth,** tachar algo; **to p. one thing before another,** anteponer una cosa a otra; **to p. salt in food,** echar or añadir sal a la comida; **to p. sb on the train/plane,** dejar a algn en el tren/el avión, acompañar a algn al tren/al avión; **to p. sb's mind at ease,** tranquilizar a algn; **to p. sb/sth to the test,** poner a algn/algo a la prueba; **to p. sb to a lot of trouble,** ocasionar a algn muchas molestias; **to p. sth in the dustbin,** echar or tirar algo a la basura; **to p. sth on the table,** poner algo en la mesa; **to p. sth to good use,** hacer buen uso de algo; **to p. the blame on sb,** echar la culpa a algn; **to p. the finishing touches to sth,** dar los últimos toques a algo; fig **to p. one's foot in it,** meter la pata. 2 (ask, present) presentar, exponer; **to p. a proposal to a committee,** someter una propuesta a una comisión; **to p. a question to sb,** hacer una pregunta a algn; Jur **to p. one's case before the jury,** exponer su caso al jurado. 3 (express) expresar, decir; **as you p. it,** como tú lo dices; **to p. it bluntly,** hablando sin rodeos; **to p. it mildly,** por decirlo de alguna manera; **to p. sth into Spanish,** traducir algo al castellano; **to p. sth into words,** expresar algo en palabras; **to p. sth simply,** explicar algo de manera sencilla. 4 (estimate) calcular; **I'd p. his age at thirty,** yo le echaría unos treinta años; **they p. the price at £50,** calcularon que costaría unas 50 libras. 5 Com **to p. a product on the market,** lanzar un producto al mercado. 6 Fin (money) ingresar, poner; (invest) invertir; **to p. money into a bank account,** ingresar dinero en una cuenta. **7** *Sport* **to p. the shot,** lanzar el peso. **III** *vi Naut* **to p. into port,** hacer escala en un puerto; **to p. to sea,** zarpar. **IV** *adv* **to be hard p. to do sth,** costarle mucho hacer algo; **to stay p.,** quedarse quieto,-a. ◆ **put about** *vtr (rumour etc)* hacer correr; **she p. it about that ...,** hizo correr la voz de que ... . ◆ **put across** *vtr* **1** *(idea etc)* comunicar. **2** *fam* **to p. one across on sb,** engañar a algn. ◆ **put aside** *vtr* **1** *(save) (money)* ahorrar; *(time)* reservar; *(food)* guardar, poner a un lado. **2** *fig (forget)* dejar de lado. ◆ **put away** *vtr* **1** *(tidy away)* guardar en su sitio, recoger. **2** *fam (lock up)* encerrar; *(in prison)* meter en la cárcel. **3** *fam (eat)* zamparse. **4** *(save money)* ahorrar. ◆ **put back** *vtr* **1** *(postpone)* aplazar. **2 to p. the clock back,** retrasar la hora; *fig* volver atrás. **3** *fam (drink)* beberse. ◆ **put by** *vtr (save) (money)* ahorrar. ◆ **put down I** *vtr (set down)* dejar; **I couldn't p. the book down,** leí el libro de un tirón. **2** *(suppress)* sofocar; *(humiliate)* humillar; *(criticize)* criticar. **3** *(animal)* rematar. **4** *(write down)* apuntar; **p. it down in writing,** ponlo por escrito; **to p. one's name down on a list,** apuntarse en una lista. **II** *vi (plane)* aterrizar. ◆ **put down for** *vtr (donation)* anotar, apuntar; *(register)* inscribir; **p. us down for £10,** apúntanos por 10 libras; **to p. one's name down for a course,** inscribirse en un curso; **to p. a child down for a school,** matricular a un niño en un colegio. ◆ **put down to** *vtr (attribute)* achacar, atribuir; **to p. sth down to inexperience,** atribuir algo a la falta de experiencia. ◆ **put forward** *vtr (theory)* exponer; *(proposal, suggestion)* hacer; **to p. one's name forward for sth,** presentarse *or* ofrecerse como candidato,-a para algo. ◆ **put in** *vtr* **1** *(install)* instalar. **2** *Agr (seeds)* sembrar. **3** *(complaint, request)* hacer, presentar; *Jur (petition)* presentar; *fig* **to p. in a good word for sb,** hablar a favor de algn. **4** *Pol (candidate)* elegir. **5** *(spend time)* pasar; **to p. in one's time reading,** pasar el tiempo leyendo; **to p. in overtime,** trabajar unas horas extraordinarias. **II** *vi* **1** *Naut* hacer escala **(at,** en). **2** *(apply)* solicitar; **to p. in for a post,** solicitar un puesto; ◆ **put off** *vtr* **1** *(postpone)* aplazar; *fig* **he kept putting off a decision,** no logró decidirse. **2** *(dissuade)* disuadir; **don't be p. off,** no te desanimes; **the smell puts me off eating,** el olor me quita las ganas de comer; **to p. sb off (doing) sth,** disuadir a algn de (hacer) algo; **to p. sb off with an excuse,** quitarse a algn de encima con una excusa. ◆ **put on** *vtr* **1** *(clothes)* poner, ponerse; **to p. clothes on sb,** ponerle ropa a algn; **to p. on one's clothes,** vestirse. **2** *Theat (show)* montar; *(concert)* presentar. **3** *(increase)* aumentar; *(add to)* añadir; **to p. on weight,** aumentar de peso, engordar. **4** *(provide)* poner; **to p. on an extra bus/ train service,** poner un servicio suplementario de autobuses/de trenes. **5** *(switch on) (radio, central heating)* poner; *(light)* encender; *(water, gas)* abrir; **to p. the kettle on,** poner el agua a calentar; *Aut* **to p. on the brakes/handbrake,** frenar/poner el freno de mano. **6** *(pretend)* fingir; **to p. on a straight face,** poner cara de serio,-a; **he's just putting it on,** está disimulando. **7** *(inform)* informar; **to p. sb on to sth,** informar a algn sobre algo. ◆ **put out I** *vtr* **1** *(switch off)* apagar. **2** *(place outside)* sacar; **to p. the cat out,** sacar el gato; **to p. clothes** *or* **washing out to dry,** tender la ropa a secar. **3** *(extend) (arm)* extender; *(tongue)* sacar; *(hand)* tender; **to p. one's head out of a window,** asomarse por una ventana. **4** *Med* dislocar. **5** *(publish) (periodical)* publicar, editar; *(spread) (rumour)* hacer correr, hacer circular. **6** *(extinguish)* apagar. **7** *(annoy)* molestar; *(inconvenience)* incordiar; **I hope I'm not putting you out,** espero que no te moleste. **8** *(anger)* enfadar, enojar; **to be p. out by sb/sth,** enfadarse *or* enojarse con algn por algo. **II** *vi Naut* **to p. out to sea,** hacerse a la mar. ◆ **put over** *vtr fam* comunicar. ◆ **put through** *vtr* **1** *(push*

through) hacer aceptar, forzar; *(law)* hacer aprobar. **2** *Tel (connect)* poner; **p. me through to Pat, please,** póngame con Pat, por favor. **3** *(unpleasant experience)* hacer pasar por. ◆ **put together** *vtr* **1** *(join)* unir, reunir, juntar; **all of them p. together,** todos,-as juntos,-as; *fig* **to p. two and two together,** atar cabos. **2** *(assemble)* armar, montar. ◆ **put up I** *vtr* **1** *(raise)* levantar, subir; *(flag)* izar; *(shelves, picture)* colocar; *(curtains)* colgar; *(building)* construir; *(umbrella)* abrir; *(tent)* armar; **to p. one's hair up,** recogerse el pelo; **p. your hands up!,** ¡manos arriba! **2** *(prices)* subir, aumentar. **3** *(offer)* ofrecer; **to p. sth up for sale,** poner algo a la venta; *Pol* **to p. sb up as a candidate,** presentar a algn como candidato,-a; **to p. up a reward for sth,** ofrecer una recompensa por algo. **4** *(accommodate)* alojar, hospedar. **5** *(resistance)* luchar; **to p. up a fight,** resistirse, ofrecer resistencia. **II** *vi (stay)* alojarse, hospedarse. ◆ **put upon** *vtr (exploit)* explotar; **to p. upon sb,** explotar a algn; **to be p. upon,** dejarse pisotear. ◆ **put up to** *vtr* **to p. sb up to sth,** incitar a algn a hacer algo. ◆ **put up with** *vtr (tolerate)* aguantar, soportar; **to p. up with sth/sb,** aguantar algo/a algn.

putrefy [ˈpjuːtrɪfaɪ] *vi (pp & pt putrefied) fml* podrir, pudrir.

putrid [ˈpjuːtrɪd] *adj fml* podrido,-a.

putsch [pʊtʃ] *n* golpe *m* de estado.

putt [pʌt] *Golf* **I** *n* tiro *m* al hoyo. **II** *vtr & vi* tirar al hoyo.

putter [ˈpʌtəʳ] *n Golf* putter *m*.

putting [ˈpʌtɪŋ] *n Golf* minigolf *m*. ■ **p. green,** minigolf *m*; *(part of golf course)* zona *f* que rodea al hoyo.

putty [ˈpʌtɪ] *n* masilla *f*; *fig* **to be p. in sb's hands,** ser como barro en las manos de algn.

put-up [ˈpʊtʌp] *adj fam* **a p.-up job,** una estafa, un montaje.

puzzle [ˈpʌzəl] **I** *n (game)* puzzle *m*; *(crossword)* crucigrama *m*; *(jigsaw)* rompecabezas *m inv*; *fig (mystery)* misterio *m*, enigma *m*; *(riddle)* acertijo *m*; **it's a p. to me how/why ...,** no entiendo cómo/por qué ... . **II** *vtr* dejar perplejo,-a; **her letter puzzled us,** su carta nos dejó perplejos; **to be puzzled about sth,** no entender algo; **to p. sth out,** lograr entender algo. **III** *vi* **to p. about sth,** dar vueltas a algo (en la cabeza). ◆ **puzzle out** *vtr* resolver; **to p. out a problem,** resolver un problema. ◆ **puzzle over** *vtr* **to p. over sth,** dar vueltas a algo (en la cabeza).

puzzled [ˈpʌzəld] *adj* perplejo,-a; **a p. expression,** una cara de perplejidad.

puzzlement [ˈpʌzəlmənt] *n* perplejidad *f*.

puzzling [ˈpʌzəlɪŋ] *adj* extraño,-a, curioso,-a.

PVC [piːviːˈsiː] *abbr of* **polyvinyl chloride,** cloruro *m* de polivinilo, PVC *m*.

Pvt *US Mil abbr of* **Private,** soldado *m* raso.

PW [piːˈdʌbəljuː] *GB abbr of* **Policewoman,** mujer *f* policía.

pygmy [ˈpɪgmɪ] *n* pigmeo,-a *m,f*; *fig* enano,-a *m,f*.

pyjamas [pəˈdʒɑːməz] *npl* pijama *m sing*.

pylon [ˈpaɪlən] *n* **1** *Elec* poste *m*, torre *f* (de conducción eléctrica). **2** *Archit* pilón *m*, pilar *m*.

pyramid [ˈpɪrəmɪd] *n* pirámide *f*.

pyre [paɪəʳ] *n* hoguera *f*, pira *f*.

Pyrenees [pɪrəˈniːz] *npl* **the P.,** los Pirineos.

Pyrex® [ˈpaɪreks] *n* pírex® *m*.

pyromaniac [paɪərəʊˈmeɪnɪæk] *n* pirómano,-a *m,f*.

pyrotechnics [paɪərəʊˈtekniks] *n* **1** *(gen)* pirotecnia *f*. **2** *pl (fireworks)* fuegos *mpl* artificiales.

python [ˈpaɪθən] *n* pitón *m*.

Q

Q, q [kju:] *n (the letter)* Q, q *f*.

Qatar [kæ'tɑːᵗ] *n* Qatar, Katar.

QC [kjuː'siː] *Brit Jur abbr of* **Queen's Counsel**, abogado,-a *m*, *f* del Estado.

QED [kjuːiː'diː] *Math abbr of* **quod erat demonstrandum** (which was to be proved), lo que había que demostrar.

qt *abbr of* **quart(s)**, cuarto(s) *m(pl)* de galón.

quack [kwæk] **I** *n* **1** *(of duck)* graznido *m*. **2** *fam (doctor)* curandero,-a *m*, *f*. **II** *vi* graznar.

quad [kwɒd] *n fam* **1** *GB (of school, University)* patio *m* interior. **2** *(quadruplet)* cuatrillizo,-a *m*, *f*.

quadrangle ['kwɒdræŋɡəl] *n* **1** *Geom* cuadrángulo *m*. **2** *(courtyard)* patio *m* interior.

quadrant ['kwɒdrənt] *n* cuadrante *m*.

quadraphonic [kwɒdrə'fɒnɪk] *adj* cuadrafónico,-a.

quadratic [kwɒ'drætɪk] *adj Math* cuadrático,-a; **q. equation**, ecuación *f* de segundo grado.

quadrilateral [kwɒdrɪ'lætərəl] *adj & n* cuadrilátero *(m)*.

quadruped ['kwɒdrʊped] *n fml* cuadrúpedo *m*.

quadruple ['kwɒdrʊpəl, kwɒ'druːpəl] **I** *n* cuádruplo *m*. **II** *adj* cuádruple. **III** *vtr* cuadruplicar. **IV** *vi* cuadruplicarse.

quadruplet ['kwɒdrʊplɪt, kwɒ'druːplɪt] *n* cuatrillizo,-a *m*, *f*.

quadruplicate [kwɒ'druːplɪkɪt, kwɒ'druːplɪkeɪt] **I** *adj* cuadruplicado,-a. **II** *n* cuadruplicado *m*; **in q.**, por cuadruplicado. **III** *vtr* [kwɒ'druːplɪkeɪt] cuadruplicar.

quaff [kwɒf, kwɑːf] *vtr* beber a grandes tragos.

quagmire ['kwæɡmaɪəᵗ, 'kwɒɡmaɪəᵗ] *n* **1** *(land)* cenagal *m*. **2** *fig (embarrassing situation)* atolladero *m*.

quail¹ [kweɪl] *n Orn* codorniz *f*.

quail² [kweɪl] *vi fig* encogerse, empequeñecerse; **he quailed at the sight of the sword**, al ver la espada se encogió.

quaint [kweɪnt] *adj (picturesque)* pintoresco,-a; *(original)* singular; *(odd)* extraño,-a, raro,-a; **q. idea**, idea singular; **q. style**, estilo original.

quake [kweɪk] **I** *vi (with fear)* temblar; **to q. at the knees**, temblarle a uno las piernas. **II** *n fam* temblor *m* de tierra.

Quaker ['kweɪkəᵗ] *n Rel* cuáquero,-a *m*, *f*

Quakerism ['kweɪkərɪzəm] *n Rel* cuaquerismo *m*

qualification [kwɒlɪfɪ'keɪʃən] *n* **1** *(ability)* aptitud *f*, **to have/not to have the qualifications to ...**, estar/no estar capacitado,-a para —. **2** *(requirement)* requisito *m*, **she has the right qualifications for the job**, es la persona idónea para el puesto. **3** *(diploma etc)* título *m*. **4** *(reservation)* reserva *f*, **to accept without q.**, aceptar sin reserva. **5** *(restriction)* limitación *f*. **6** *(act of qualifying)* **even after q.** Bill found it difficult to get a job, a Bill le costó encontrar trabajo incluso después de haberse graduado

qualified ['kwɒlɪfaɪd] *adj* **1** capacitado,-a, **to be q. to do sth**, estar capacitado,-a para hacer algo, **q. teacher**, profesor titulado. **2** *(modified)* restringido,-a, limitado,-a, **q. approval**, aprobación condicional.

qualify ['kwɒlɪfaɪ] **I** *vtr (pt & pp qualified)* **1** *(make eligible, entitle)* capacitar, habilitar, **the letter qualified him for membership**, la carta le dio derecho a hacerse socio. **2** *(modify) (report)* modificar, *(declaration)* matizar, *Ling* calificar, **the adjective qualifies the noun**, el adjetivo califica al sustantivo, **would you like to q. what you've just said?**, ¿le importaría puntualizar lo que acaba de decir? **II** *vi* **1** *(obtain diplomas etc)* **to q. as**, sacar

el título de; **she qualified as a doctor**, obtuvo el título de médico, **when did you q.?**, ¿cuándo terminaste la carrera? **2** *(in competition)* quedar clasificado,-a

qualifying ['kwɒlɪfaɪɪŋ] *adj (of round, exam)* eliminatorio,-a

qualitative ['kwɒlɪtətɪv, 'kwɒlɪteɪtɪv] *adj* cualitativo,-a

quality ['kwɒlɪtɪ] *n* **1** *(degree of excellence)* calidad *f*, **of good q.**, de buena calidad, **of poor q.**, de poca calidad, *Com* **q. goods**, géneros *mpl* de calidad ■ **q. control**, control *m* de calidad, **q. newspapers**, prensa *f* no sensacionalista. **2** *(attribute)* cualidad *f*, **he has many good qualities**, tiene muchas cualidades buenas

qualm [kwɑːm] *n* **1** *(scruple)* escrúpulo *m*, **to have no qualms about doing sth**, no tener escrúpulos en hacer algo. **2** *(doubt)* duda *f*, *(worry)* inquietud *f*, ansia *f*; **he has qualms about whether he's doing his work properly**, está intranquilo porque no sabe si da la talla con su trabajo

quandary ['kwɒndərɪ, 'kwɒndrɪ] *n (dilemma)* dilema *m*, *(difficulty)* apuro *m*, **to be in a q.**, estar en un dilema

quango ['kwæŋɡəʊ] *n Pol* organización *f* semi-autónoma paralela

quantify ['kwɒntɪfaɪ] *vtr* cuantificar

quantitative ['kwɒntɪtətɪv, 'kwɒntɪteɪtɪv] *adj* cuantitativo,-a.

quantity ['kwɒntɪtɪ] *n* **1** *(amount)* cantidad *f*; **a small/large q. of ...**, una pequeña/gran cantidad de ..., **in great quantities**, en grandes cantidades, en abundancia, **unknown q.**, incógnita *f*. **2** *Math* cantidad *f*

quantum ['kwɒntəm] *n (pl guanta* ['kwɒntə]*)* **1** *Phys* quantum *m*, **q. theory**, teoría *f* de los quanta. **2** *(amount) fml* cantidad *f*

quarantine ['kwɒrəntiːn] **I** *n* cuarentena *f*, **to be in q.**, estar en cuarentena. **II** *vtr* poner en cuarentena

quarrel ['kwɒrəl] **I** *n* **1** *(argument)* riña *f*, pelea *f*, **to have a big q.**, pelearse, **to pick a q.**, meterse con algn, buscar camorra (con algn). **2** *(disagreement)* desacuerdo *m*, **I have no q. with her**, no tengo queja de ella, no tengo nada contra ella. **II** *vi* **1** *(argue)* pelearse, reñir. **2** **to q. with sth**, discutir algo, poner algo en duda, **she quarrelled with their decision**, les discutió su decisión

quarrelsome ['kwɒrəlsəm] *adj* camorrista, pendenciero,-a

quarry¹ ['kwɒrɪ] *Min* **I** *n* cantera *f*. **II** *vtr (pt & pp quarried)* extraer, sacar

quarry² ['kwɒrɪ] *n* presa *f*, *fig* persona *f* acorralada, **the hunter's dog looked for the q.**, el perro del cazador buscaba la presa

quart [kwɔːt] *n (measurement)* cuarto *m* de galón *(GB =* 1,13 litros, *US =* 0,94 litros*)*.

quarter ['kwɔːtəᵗ] *n* **1** *(fraction)* cuarto *m*, cuarta parte *f*, **a q. of a century**, un cuarto de siglo, **a q. of an hour**, un cuarto de hora, **a q. of a cake**, la cuarta parte de un pastel, **what's a q. of sixteen?**, ¿cuál es la cuarta parte de dieciséis? ■ *US Canada Mus* **q. note**, negra *f*. **2** *(telling the time)* **it's a q.**, *US* **it's a q. of three**, son las tres menos cuarto. **3** *(three months)* trimestre *m*, **he pays the gas bill every q.**, paga la cuenta del gas por trimestres. **4** *GB (weight)* cuarto *m* de libra, **a q. of tea**, un cuarto de libra de té. **5** *US Canada (coin)* cuarto *m* (de dólar), veinticinco centavos *mpl*. **6** *(district)* barrio *m*, **the Latin Q.**, el barrio latino, **the old q.**, el casco antiguo. **7** *(area, people)* **there was criticism from all quarters**, todos lo criticaron. **8** *(of moon)* cuarto *m*, **the first q.**, cuarto creciente, **the last q.**, cuarto menguante. **9** *fig (mercy)* **they gave no q. to the enemy**, no dieron cuartel al enemigo. **10 quarters**, *(lodgings)* alojamiento *m sing*,

Mil **officers' q.**, residencia *f sing* de oficiales, **married q.**, viviendas *fpl* del ejército, **at close q.**, muy cerca II *vtr* **1** *(cut into quarters)* dividir en cuartos; *(reduce)* reducir a la cuarta parte **2** *(accommodate)* alojar **3** *Hist (body)* descuartizar

quarterdeck ['kwɔːtədek] *n Naut* alcázar *m*

quarterfinal ['kwɔːtəfaɪnəl] *n Sport* cuarto *m* de final

quarterfinalist ['kwɔːtefaɪnəlɪst] *n Sport* participante *mf* en el cuarto de final

quarterlight ['kwɔːtəlaɪt] *n GB Aut* ventanilla *f* trasera

quarterly ['kwɔːtəlɪ] I *adj* trimestral. II *n* publicación *f* trimestral. III *adv* trimestralmente, cada tres meses

quartermaster ['kwɔːtəmɑːstəʳ] *n* **1** *Mil* oficial *m* de intendencia. **2** *Naut* cabo *m* de la Marina

quartet(te) [kwɔː'tet] *n Mus* cuarteto *m*

quarto ['kwɔːtəʊ] I *adj (paper size)* en cuarto. II *n (book)* libro *m* en cuarto

quartz [kwɔːts] *n Min* cuarzo *m*; **q. watch**, reloj de cuarzo

quash [kwɒʃ] *vtr* **1** *Jur (sentence)* anular, invalidar. **2** *(uprising)* aplastar, sofocar.

quasi ['kwɑːzɪ, 'kweɪzaɪ, 'kweɪsaɪ] *adv* casi, *Jur* **q. contract**, cuasicontrato *m*

quatrain ['kwɒtreɪn] *n Lit* cuarteto *m*

quaver ['kweɪvəʳ] I *n* **1** *Mus (note)* corchea *f*; *(sound)* trémolo *m*. **2** *(trembling)* temblor *m*. II *n (sound)* temblar, **his voice quavered**, su voz temblaba

quavering ['kweɪvərɪŋ] *adj* tembloroso,-a, trémulo,-a, **q. voice**, voz temblorosa *or* trémula

quay [kiː] *n Naut* muelle *m*

quayside ['kiːsaɪd] *n Naut* muelle *m*.

queasy ['kwiːzɪ] *adj (queasier, queasiest)* mareado,-a; **to feel q.**, *(ill)* sentirse mal, tener náuseas; *(worried)* estar preocupado,-a.

queasiness ['kwiːzɪnɪs] *n* náuseas *fpl*.

Quechua ['ketʃwə] *n (person)* quechua *mf*; *(language)* quechua *m*.

queen [kwiːn] *n* **1** reina *f*; **the Q. Mother**, la reina madre. **2** *Cards Chess* reina *f*. **3** *Ent* reina *f*. **4** *offens* loca *f*, marica *m*.

queenly ['kwiːnlɪ] *adj (queenlier, queenliest)* regio,-a, de reina.

queer [kwɪəʳ] I *adj* **1** *(strange)* extraño,-a, raro,-a; **a q. looking lad**, un chico de aspecto raro. **2** *fam (mad)* loco,-a. **3** *fam (unwell)* mareado,-a; **to feel q.**, no encontrarse bien. **4** *offens* marica, maricón. **5** *GB fam* **in q. street**, en deuda, endeudado,-a. II *n sl pej* marica *m*, maricón *m*. III *vtr fam* **to q. sb's pitch**, fastidiar los planes de algn.

quell [kwel] *vtr* reprimir, sofocar, frenar; **to q. a rebellion**, reprimir *or* sofocar una rebelión.

quench [kwentʃ] *vtr* **1** *(thirst)* saciar. **2** *(fire)* apagar.

querulous ['kwerʊləs, 'kwerjʊləs] *adj fml* quejumbroso,-a; **a q. old lady**, una vieja quejumbrosa.

query ['kwɪərɪ] I *n* **1** *(question)* pregunta *f*. **2** *Ling* signo *m* de interrogación. II *vtr (pt & pp queried) (ask)* preguntar; *(have doubts about)* poner en duda.

quest [kwest] I *n lit* búsqueda *f*, busca *f*; **to go in q. of sth**, ir en busca de algo. II *vi* buscar.

question ['kwestʃən] I *n* **1** *(interrogative)* pregunta *f*; **questions and answers**, preguntas y respuestas; **to ask sb a q.**, hacer una pregunta a algn; **without q.**, sin rechistar; **he did it without q.**, lo hizo sin rechistar; *hum* **to pop the q.**, declararse. ■ **q. mark**, *Ling* signo *m* de interrogación; *fig* interrogante *m*; *Ling* **q. tag**, coletilla *f*. **2** *(problem, issue, matter)* asunto *m*, cuestión *f*, problema *m*; **it's a q. of**, se trata de; **it's a q. of two hours**, es cuestión de dos horas; **it's all a q. of time**, con el tiempo se arreglará; **that's the q.**, he aquí el problema; **the Northern Ireland q.**, el problema de Irlanda del Norte; **the q. of overtime**, el asunto de las horas extras. **3** *(criticism, doubt)* en duda; **beyond q.**, fuera de duda; **in**

q., en duda; **open to q.**, dudoso,-a; **to bring sth into q.**, hacer reflexionar sobre; **to call sth into q.**, poner algo en duda. **4** *(suggestion, possibility)* posibilidad *f*; **out of the q.**, imposible, impensable; **that's out of the q.**, ¡ni hablar¡; **there is no q. of recovering the money now**, ya no hay posibilidad alguna de recuperar el dinero. **5** *Sch (exam)* pregunta *f*, problema *m*. II *vtr* **1** *(ask questions)* hacer preguntas; *(interrogate)* interrogar; **he questioned the boy**, le hizo preguntas al niño; **they are being questioned about the theft**, están interrogándoles sobre el robo. **2** *(query)* poner en duda, dudar de.

questionable ['kwestʃənəbəl] *adj (doubtful)* dudoso,-a; *(debatable)* discutible; **of q. taste**, de gusto dudoso; **it's q. whether he's right**, eso de que tenga razón es discutible

questioner ['kwestʃənəʳ] *n* interrogador,-a *m,f*.

questioning ['kwestʃənɪŋ] *adj* inquisitivo,-a; **a q. look**, una mirada inquisitiva.

questionnaire ['kwestʃə'neəʳ] *n* cuestionario *m*.

queue [kjuː] *GB* I *n* cola *f*; **to jump the q.**, colarse. II *vi* **to q. (up)**, hacer cola; **they queued up for the bus**, hicieron cola para el autobús.

queue-jumper ['kjuːdʒʌmpəʳ] *n fam* persona *f* que se cuela.

quibble ['kwɪbəl] I *n* pega *f*, objeción *f*. II *vi* poner pegas **(with**, a); *fam* buscarle tres pies al gato.

quibbler ['kwɪbələʳ] *n* polemista *mf*, porfiador,-a *m,f*.

quick [kwɪk] I *adj* **1** *(fast)* rápido,-a; **a q. reply**, una respuesta pronta; **a q. sale**, una venta inmediata; **a q. snack**, un tentempié, un bocado; **as q. as lightning** *or* **a flash**, como un rayo *or* una bala *or* una centella; **be q.!**, ¡rápido!, ¡date prisa!; **it's quicker by plane**, se llega antes en avión; *Mil* **q. match!**, ¡de frente!; **the quickest way**, el camino más corto; **to have a q. lunch**, tomar un bocado a la hora de comer; *fam* **to have a q. one**, tomar una copita. **2** *(clever)* espabilado,-a, listo,-a; *(of wit)* agudo,-a; **a q. child**, un niño espabilado *or* despierto. **3** *(hasty)* apresurado,-a, irritable; **he's q. to take offence**, se enfada por nada; **she has a q. temper**, tiene un genio vivo; **to be q. to anger**, tener mal genio. II *n* carne *f* viva; *fig* **to cut sb to the q.**, herir a algn en lo vivo. ◆

quickly *adv* rápido, rápidamente, de prisa.

quick-acting ['kwɪkæktɪŋ] *adj* de acción rápida.

quick-change ['kwɪktʃeɪndʒ] *adj Theat* **q.-c. artist**, transformista *mf*.

quicken ['kwɪkən] I *vtr* **1** *(speed up)* acelerar; **to q. one's pace**, acelerar el paso. **2** *(stimulate)* estimular. II *vi* **1** *(speed up)* acelerarse. **2** *(become stronger)* acrecentarse, aumentarse.

quickening ['kwɪkənɪŋ] *n Med* movimientos *mpl* del feto.

quickie ['kwɪkɪ] *n fam* uno,-a rápido,-a.

quicklime ['kwɪklaɪm] *n* cal *f* viva.

quickness ['kwɪknɪs] *n* **1** *(speed)* rapidez *f*, velocidad *f*. **2** *(of wit)* agudeza *f*, viveza *f*.

quicksand ['kwɪksænd] *n* arenas *fpl* movedizas.

quicksilver ['kwɪksɪlvəʳ] *n* mercurio *m*.

quick-tempered [kwɪk'tempəd] *adj* irascible, de genio vivo.

quick-witted [kwɪk'wɪtɪd] *adj* agudo,-a, listo,-a.

quid[1] [kwɪd] *n GB sl* libra *f* (esterlina); **five q.**, cinco libras.

quid[2] *n* mascada *f* de tabaco.

quiet ['kwaɪət] I *n* **1** *(silence)* silencio *m*. **2** *(calm)* tranquilidad *f*, sosiego *m*. **3** *(secretly)* fam **to do sth on the q.**, hacer algo sin que nadie se entere. II *adj* **1** *(silent)* silencioso,-a; *(of town, street)* tranquilo,-a; **a q. engine**, un motor silencioso; **a q. voice**, una voz suave; **keep q.**; ¡silencio!; **q. footsteps**, pasos silenciosos. **2** *(peaceful, calm)* tranquilo,-a; **she leads a very q. life**, lleva una vida muy tranquila. **3** *Com Fin* apagado,-a; **business is q. today**, hoy hay poco negocio; **the market was q.**, el mercado estaba apagado. **4** *(unobtrusive)* callado,-a; **a q. man,** un hombre reservado; **of a q. disposition,** de carácter reservado. **5** *(secret)* confidencial; **I'd like a q. word with him,** quiero hablarle en privado; **keep (it) q.;** ¡no se lo digas a nadie! **6** *(without fuss, tranquil)* tranquilo,-a; **a q. supper,** una cena sencilla; **it was a q. wedding,** la boda se celebró en la intimidad. **7** *(not showy) (of clothes)* sobrio,-a, poco llamativo,-a; *(of colours)* suave, apagado,-a. **II** *vtr US* silenciar, calmar; **I quieted the children (down),** calmé a los niños. **III** *vi US* calmarse. ◆ **quietly** *adv* **1** *(silently; not noisily)* silenciosamente; *(not loudly)* bajo; **he spoke q.,** habló en voz baja. **2** *(calmly)* tranquilamente. **3** *(discreetly)* discretamente, con discreción. **4** *(simply)* sencillamente.

quieten ['kwaɪətən] **I** *vtr* *(silence)* callar; *(calm)* tranquilizar, calmar. **II** *vi* *(silence)* callarse; *(calm)* calmarse, tranquilizarse. ◆ **quieten down** *GB* **I** *vtr* calmar. **II** *vi* calmarse.

quietism ['kwaɪətɪzəm] *n Rel* quietismo *m*.

quietist ['kwaɪətɪst] *n Rel* quietista *mf*.

quietness ['kwaɪətnɪs] *n* **1** *(silence)* silencio *m*. **2** *(calm)* tranquilidad *f*, sosiego *m*.

quiff [kwɪf] *n GB (of hair)* copete *m*.

quill [kwɪl] *n* **1** *(feather, pen)* pluma *f*. **2** *(of porcupine)* púa *f*.

quilt [kwɪlt] **I** *n* edredón *m*. **II** *vtr* acolchar; **quilted jacket,** chaqueta *f* acolchada.

quin [kwɪn] *n* quintillizo,-a *m*, *f*.

quince [kwɪns] *n Bot Culin* membrillo *m*; **q. jelly,** carne *f* de membrillo.

quinine ['kwɪniːn, *US* 'kwaɪnaɪn] *n* quinina *f*.

quinsy ['kwɪnzɪ] *n Med* anginas *fpl*.

quintessence [kwɪn'tesəns] *n fml* quintaesencia *f*.

quintessential [kwɪntɪ'senʃəl] *adj* fundamental.

quintet(te) [kwɪn'tet] *n Mus* quinteto *m*.

quintuple ['kwɪntjupəl, kwɪn'tjuːpəl] **I** *adj* quíntuplo,-a. **II** *n* quíntuplo *m*. **III** *vtr* quintuplicar.

quintuplet ['kwɪntjuplɪt, kwɪn'tjuːplɪt] *n* quintillizo,-a *m*, *f*.

quip [kwɪp] **I** *n (remark)* salida *f*, ocurrencia *f*; *(joke)* chiste *m*. **II** *vi* bromear.

quire [kwaɪər] *n* mano *f* de papel.

quirk [kwɜːk] *n* **1** *(peculiarity)* manía *f*, rareza *f*. **2** *(of fate)* vicisitud *f*, avatar *m*.

quirky ['kwɜːkɪ] *adj (quirkier, quirkiest)* raro,-a.

quisling ['kwɪzlɪŋ] *n* colaboracionista *mf*, traidor,-a *m*, *f*.

quit [kwɪt] **I** *vtr (pt & pp quitted or esp US quit)* **1** *(leave)* dejar, abandonar; **to q. one's job,** dejar el trabajo; *US* **he's**

q. school, ha dejado los estudios. **2** *(stop)* **q. making that noise!,** ¡deja de hacer ese ruido! **II** *vi* **1** *(go)* irse, marcharse; *(give up)* dimitir. **2** *(cease)* dejar de hacer algo. **III** *adj* **quits** iguales; **let's call it q.,** dejémoslo estar, estar en paces; **to be q.,** estar en paces.

quite [kwaɪt] *adv* **1** *(entirely)* del todo, totalmente; **I q. agree,** estoy totalmente de acuerdo; **I q. understand,** te entiendo perfectamente; **she hasn't q. recovered,** no se ha recuperado del todo; **she's q. right,** tiene toda la razón. **2** *(fairly, rather)* bastante; **it's q. warm,** hace bastante calor; **q. a few,** bastantes; **q. a while,** un buen rato; **q. often,** con bastante frecuencia; **she's q. a good artist,** es bastante buena como artista; **that's q. enough!,** ¡ya basta!, ¡ya está bien! **3** *(exceptional)* excepcional; **he's q. a gentleman,** está hecho un señor; **she's q. a character,** es un tipo original; **to be q. sth.,** es increíble; **you've got q. a voice,** tienes una voz excepcional. **4** *(exactly)* exactamente; **I'm not q. sure,** no estoy exactamente seguro; **it isn't q. what I wanted,** no es exactamente lo que quería; **q. (so)!,** ¡en efecto!, ¡exacto!

quiver¹ ['kwɪvər] **I** *n (trembling) (of lips, voice)* temblor *m*; *(of eyelids)* parpadeo *m*; *(shiver)* estremecimiento *m*. **II** *vi* temblar, estremecerse.

quiver² ['kwɪvər] *n* aljaba *f*, carcaj *m*.

quivering ['kwɪvərɪŋ] *adj* tembloroso,-a.

quixottic [kwɪk'sɒtɪk] *adj* quijotesco,-a.

quiz [kwɪz] **I** *n (pl quizzes)* *Rad TV* concurso *m*. **II** *vtr* hacer preguntas.

quizmaster ['kwɪzmɑːstər] *n* moderador *m*.

quizzical ['kwɪzɪkəl] *adj* **1** *(bemused)* burlón,-ona; **a q. smile,** una sonrisa burlona. **2** *(enquiring)* curioso,-a; **a q. glance,** una mirada llena de curiosidad.

quoin [kɔɪn] *n Archit* piedra *f* angular.

quoit [kɔɪt] *n* **1** *(game)* tejo *m*. **2 quoits,** tejo *m*.

quorum ['kwɔːrəm] *n* quórum *m*.

quota ['kwəʊtə] *n* **1** *(proportional share)* cuota *f*, parte *f*. **2** *(prescribed amount, number)* cupo *m*.

quotation [kwəʊ'teɪʃən] *n* **1** *Lit* cita *f*; **q. marks,** comillas *fpl*. **2** *(Stock Exchange)* cotización *f*.

quote [kwəʊt] **I** *vtr* **1** *(cite)* citar; **can I q. you?,** ¿puedo repetir tus mismas palabras? **2** *Com* **to q. a price,** dar un presupuesto. **3** *(Stock Exchange)* cotizar. **II** *n* **1** *Lit* cita *f*. **2** *Com* presupuesto *m*.

quotidian [kwəʊ'tɪdɪən] *adj fml* cotidiano,-a.

quotient ['kwəʊʃənt] *n* **1** *Math* cociente *m*. **2** *(degree)* grado *m*, coeficiente *m*; **intelligence q.,** coeficiente *m* intelectual.

qv [kjuː'viː] *fml abbr* of **quod vide** (which see), véase, v.

R

R, r [ɑːr] *n (the letter)* R, r *f*, *fam fig* **the three Rs,** lectura, escritura y aritmética.

R 1 *abbr of* **1 Rex** (King), rey *m*. **2** *abbr of* **Regina** (Queen), reina *f*. **3** *Com abbr of* **registered (trademark),** (marca *f*) registrada. **4** *abbr of* **River,** río *m*.

r *abbr of* **right,** derecho,-a, dcho,-a.

RA [ɑːr'eɪ] *GB* **1** *abbr of* **Royal Academy (of Arts),** Real Academia *f* (de las Artes). **2** *abbr of* **Royal Academician,** miembro *mf* de la Real Academia.

rabbi ['ræbaɪ] *n Rel* rabí *m*, rabino *m*.

rabbit ['ræbɪt] **I** *n Zool* conejo,-a *m*, *f*. ▪ **r. hole,** madriguera *f*; **r. hutch,** conejera *f*. **II** *vi fam* enrollarse.

rabble ['ræbəl] *n* multitud *m*, muchedumbre *f*; *pej* **the r.,** la chusma, el populacho.

rabble-rouser ['ræbəlraʊzər] *n pej* demagogo,-a *m*, *f*, agitador,-a *m*, *f*.

rabble-rousing ['ræbəlraʊzɪŋ] *pej* **I** *adj (speech etc)* demagógico,-a. **II** *n (incitement)* demagogia *f*, agitación *f*.

rabid ['ræbɪd, 'reɪbɪd] *adj* **1** *Med* rabioso,-a. **2** *fig (person)* furioso,-a; *(supporter)* fanático,-a.

rabies ['reɪbiːz] *n Med* rabia *f*.

RAC [ɑːreɪ'siː] *GB abbr of* **Royal Automobile Club,** ≈ Real Automóvil Club *m* de España, RACE.

rac(c)oon [rə'kuːn] *n Zool* mapache *m*.

race¹ [reɪs] **I** *n* **1** *Sport* carrera *f*; **long-distance r.,** carrera de larga distancia; **to run a r.,** participar en una carrera; *fig* **r. against time,** carrera contra reloj. ▪ *fig* **arms r.,** carrera *f* de armamentos; **r. meeting,** carreras *fpl* caballos). **2** *(in sea, river)* corriente *f* fuerte. **3** *GB* **the races**, las carreras (de caballos). **II** *vtr* **1** *(compete with)* competir con; **I'll r. you!**, ¡te echo una carrera! **2** *(car, horse)* hacer correr. **3** *(engine)* acelerar. **III** *vi (go quickly)* correr; *(pulse)* acelerarse.

race² [reɪs] *n (people)* raza *f*; **the human r.**, la raza humana. ■ **r. relations**, relaciones *fpl* raciales; **r. riots**, disturbios *mpl* raciales.

racecourse ['reɪskɔːs] *n GB Sport* hipódromo *m*.

racehorse ['reɪshɔːs] *n Sport* caballo *m* de carreras.

racer ['reɪsə'] *n Sport* **1** *(person)* corredor,-a *m*, *f*. **2** *(bicycle)* bicicleta *f* de carreras; *(car)* coche *m* de carreras.

racetrack ['reɪstræk] *n Sport* **1** *(for cars, people, bikes)* pista *f*. **2** *US (for horses)* hipódromo *m*.

racial ['reɪʃəl] *adj* racial; **r. prejudice**, prejuicio *m* racial.

racialism ['reɪʃəlɪzəm] *n arch* racismo *m*.

racialist ['reɪʃəlɪst] *adj & n arch* racista *(mf)*.

racing ['reɪsɪŋ] **I** *n Sport* carreras *fpl*. ■ **horse r.**, carreras *fpl* de caballos. **II** *adj* de carreras; **r. car/bike**, coche *m*/moto *f* de carreras.

racism ['reɪsɪzəm] *n* racismo *m*.

racist ['reɪsɪst] *adj & n* racista *(mf)*.

rack [ræk] *n* **1** *(shelf)* estante *m*; *(for clothes)* percha *f*, perchero *m*. ■ **luggage r.**, portaequipajes *m inv*; **plate r.**, escurreplatos *m inv*; *Aut* **roof r.**, baca *f*. **2** *Hist (for torture)* potro *m*; *fig* **on the r.**, angustiado,-a; *fam* **to go to r. and ruin**, venirse abajo. **3** *Tech* **r. and pinion**, engranaje *m* de cremallera y piñón. ■ *Rail* **r. railway**, (ferrocarril *m* de) cremallera *f*. **II** *vtr lit (torment)* atormentar; *fam fig* **to r. one's brains**, devanarse los sesos.

racket¹ ['rækɪt] *n* **1** *(din)* ruido *m*, alboroto *m*, jaleo *m*; **to kick up a r.**, armar jaleo. **2** *(swindle)* timo *m*, estafa *f*; *(shady business)* chanchullo *m*.

racket² ['rækɪt] *n sport* raqueta *f*.

racketeer [rækə'tɪə'] *n* estafador,-a *m*,*f*, timador,-a *m*,*f*.

racketeering [rækə'tɪərɪŋ] *n* crimen *m* organizado.

raconteur [rækɒn'tɜː'] *n* anecdotista *mf*.

racquet ['rækɪt] *n see* **racket.**

racquetball ['rækɪtbɔːl] *n US Sport* juego *m* parecido al frontón.

racy ['reɪsɪ] *adj (racier, raciest) (lively)* vivo,-a; *(risqué)* atrevido,-a.

RADA ['rɑːdə] *GB abbr of* **Royal Academy of Dramatic Art**, Real Academia *f* de las Artes Dramáticas.

radar ['reɪdɑː'] *n radar m*. ■ **r. operator**, operador,-a *m*,*f* de radar; **r. screen**, pantalla *f* de radar.

radial ['reɪdɪəl] **I** *adj* radial. **II** *n Aut* neumático *m* radial.

radiance ['reɪdɪəns] *n* resplandor *m*.

radiant ['reɪdɪənt] *adj (gen)* radiante, resplandeciente.

radiate ['reɪdɪeɪt] **I** *vtr (gen)* irradiar; *fig* **she radiated happiness**, rebosaba de alegría. **II** *vi Phys* irradiar, emitir radiaciones.

radiation [reɪdɪ'eɪʃən] *n* radiación *f*.

radiator ['reɪdɪeɪtə'] *n* radiador *m*.

radical ['rædɪkəl] **I** *adj* radical. **II** *n* **1** *(person)* radical *mf*. **2** *Chem Math* radical *m*.

radio ['reɪdɪəʊ] **I** *n* radio *f*; **on the r.**, en *or* por la radio. ■ **r. ham**, radioaficionado,-a *m*, *f*; **r. station**, emisora *f* (de radio). **II** *vtr* **to r. sb**, enviar un mensaje a algn por radio.

radioactive [reɪdɪəʊ'æktɪv] *adj* radiactivo,-a, radioactivo,-a.

radioactivity [reɪdɪəʊæk'tɪvɪtɪ] *n* radiactividad *f*, radioactividad *f*.

radiocarbon [reɪdɪəʊ'kɑːbən] *n Chem* radiocarbón *m*.

radio-controlled [reɪdɪəʊkən'trəʊld] *adj* teledirigido,-a.

radiograph ['reɪdɪəʊgrɑːf] *n* radiografía *f*.

radiographer [reɪdɪ'ɒgrəfə'] *n* radiógrafo,-a *m*,*f*.

radiography [reɪdɪ'ɒgrəfɪ] *n* radiografía *f*.

radiologist [reɪdɪ'ɒlədʒɪst] *n* radiólogo,-a *m*,*f*.

radiology [reɪdɪ'ɒlədʒɪ] *n* radiología *f*.

radiotherapist [reɪdɪəʊ'θerəpɪst] *n* radioterapeuta *mf*.

radiotherapy [reɪdɪəʊ'θerəpɪ] *n* radioterapia *f*.

radish ['rædɪʃ] *n Bot* rábano *m*.

radium ['reɪdɪəm] *n Chem* radio *m*. ■ **r. therapy**, radioterapia *f*.

radius ['reɪdɪəs] *n (pl radii* ['reɪdɪaɪ] *or radiuses) Anat Geom* radio *m*; **within a r. of**, en un radio de.

RAF [ɑːreɪ'ef, *fam* ræf] *GB abbr of* **Royal Air Force**, fuerzas *fpl* aéreas británicas.

raffia ['ræfɪə] *n Bot* rafia *f*.

raffle ['ræfəl] **I** *n* sorteo *m*, rifa *f*. **II** *vtr* sortear, rifar.

raft¹ [rɑːft] *n* balsa *f*.

raft² [rɑːft] *n US Canada fam* montón *m*, cantidad *f*; **a r. of things**, cantidad de cosas.

rafter ['rɑːftə'] *n Archit* viga *f*, par *m*.

rag¹ [ræg] **I** *n* **1** *(torn piece)* harapo *m*, andrajo *m*; **in rags**, harapiento,-a; *fig* **from rags to riches**, de la pobreza a la riqueza. ■ **r. doll**, muñeca *f* de trapo. **2** *(for cleaning)* trapo *m*; *GB fam fig* **it was like a red r. to a bull**, era una provocación descarada. **3** *fam* **rags**, *(clothes)* trapos *mpl*; *euph* **the rag trade**, (el ramo de) la confección. **4** *Press* periodicucho *m*.

rag² [ræg] **I** *n (prank)* broma *f* pesada; *GB Univ* función *f* benéfica. **II** *vtr (pt & pp ragged)* gastar bromas a.

ragamuffin ['rægəmʌfɪn] *n* golfillo,-a *m*,*f*, pilluelo,-a *m*,*f*.

rag-and-bone [rægən'bəʊn] *adj GB* **r.-a.-b. man**, trapero *m*.

ragbag ['rægbæg] *n fam* mezcla *f*, barullo *m*.

rage [reɪdʒ] **I** *n (fury)* rabia *f*, cólera *f*; *fam fig (craze)* moda; **it's all the r.**, hace furor. **II** *vi* **1** *(person)* rabiar, estar furioso,-a. **2** *fig (storm, sea)* rugir; *(wind)* bramar.

ragged ['rægɪd] *adj* **1** *(clothes)* hecho,-a jirones. **2** *(person)* harapiento,-a, andrajoso,-a; *fam fig* **to run sb r.**, dejar hecho,-a polvo a algn. **3** *(edge)* dentado,-a, mellado,-a. **4** *fig (uneven)* desigual.

raging ['reɪdʒɪŋ] *adj* **1** *(angry)* furioso,-a. **2** *fig (sea)* embravecido,-a. **3** *(storm)* violento,-a; *(intense)* feroz, tremendo,-a.

raglan ['ræglən] *n* abrigo *m* raglán. ■ **r. sleeve**, manga *f* raglán.

ragtime ['rægtaɪm] *n Mus* ragtime *m*.

ragwort ['rægwɜːt] *n Bot* azuzón *m*, hierba *f* de Santiago.

raid [reɪd] **I** *n* **1** *Mil* incursión *f*, raid *m*. ■ **air r.**, ataque *m* aéreo. **2** *(police)* redada *f*. **3** *(robbery etc)* atraco *m*. **II** *vtr* **1** *Mil (place)* asaltar, hacer una incursión en. **2** *(police)* hacer una redada en. **3** *(rob)* asaltar, atracar; *fam* **to r. the larder**, vaciar la despensa.

raider ['reɪdə'] *n* **1** *(invader)* invasor,-a *m*, *f*. **2** *(thief)* ladrón,-a *m*,*f*.

rail¹ [reɪl] *n* **1** barra *f*. ■ **curtain r.**, barra *f* de cortina; **towel r.**, toallero *m*. **2** *(railing)* baranda *f*, barandilla *f*. **3** *Rail* riel *m*, carril *f*; **by r.**, *(mail)* por ferrocarril; *(travel)* en tren; *fam fig* **to go off the rails**, irse por el mal camino. ■ **r. strike**, huelga *f* de ferroviarios. ◆ **rail in** *vtr (animals, people)* encercar, cercar. ◆ **rail off** *vtr (land)* encercar, cercar.

rail² [reɪl] *vi arch* despotricar **(against**, contra).

rail³ [reɪl] *n Orn* **water r.**, rascón *m*.

railcard ['reɪlkɑːd] *n GB Rail* abono *m*.

railing ['reɪlɪŋ] *n (usu pl)* verja *f*.

railroad ['reɪlrəʊd] *n US* ferrocarril *m*. ■ **r. track**, vía *f* férrea. **II** *vtr fam* **to r. sb into sth**, presionar a algn para que haga algo.

railway ['reɪlweɪ] *n GB* ferrocarril *m*. ■ **r. carriage**, vagón *m*; **r. line**, **r. track**, vía *f* férrea; **r. station**, estación *f* de ferrocarril.

railwayman ['reɪlweɪmən] *n (pl **railwaymen**) GB* ferroviario *m*.

rain [reɪn] **I** *n* **1** lluvia *f*; *fig (of bullets, insults)* lluvia *f*; **in the r.**, bajo la lluvia; *fam* **come r. or shine**, pase lo que pase; *fam* **jas as right as r.**, fresco,-a como una rosa, sano,-a como una manzana. **2 the rains**, *(season)* las lluvias, estación *f* lluviosa. **II** *vtr & vi* llover; **it's raining**, llueve; *fam* **it's raining cats and dogs**, llueve a cántaros; *prov* **it never rains but it pours**, las desgracias nunca vienen solas. ◆ **rain down** *vi fig (criticism etc)* caer encima, llover. ◆ **rain off** *vtr Sport* interrumpir *or* cancelar por la lluvia.

rainbow ['reɪnbəʊ] *n* arco *m* iris.

raincoat ['reɪnkəʊt] *n* impermeable *m*.

raindrop ['reɪndrɒp] *n* gota *f* de lluvia.

rainfall ['reɪnfɔːl] *n (falling of rain)* precipitación *f*; *(amount)* pluviosidad *f*.

rainforest ['reɪnfɒrɪst] *n* selva *f* tropical.

rainproof ['reɪnpruːf] *adj* impermeable.

rainwater ['reɪnwɔːtəʳ] *n* agua *f* de lluvia.

rainy ['reɪnɪ] *adj (rainier, rainiest)* lluvioso,-a; **a r. day**, un día de lluvia; *fig* **to save *or* keep sth for a r. day**, guardar algo para los tiempos difíciles.

raise [reɪz] **I** *n US* aumento *m* (de sueldo). **II** *vtr* **1** *(gen)* levantar; *(glass)* brindar; *(voice)* levantar, subir; *(building, statue)* erigir; *fig (embargo, restriction, etc)* levantar; *fig* **to r. an eyebrow**, hacer un gesto de desaprobación; *fam* **to r. the roof**, armar un follón. **2** *(increase)* aumentar; *Cards* subir; **I'll r. you ten**, igualo y subo diez. **3** *(money, help)* reunir. **4** *(problem, subject)* plantear. **5** *(crops, animals, children)* criar. **6** *Rad* comunicar con. **7** *(smile, laugh)* provocar. **8** *(standards)* mejorar.

raisin ['reɪzən] *n* pasa *f*.

raison d'être [reɪzɒn'detrə] *n fml* razón *f* de ser.

rake¹ [reɪk] **I** *n* **1** *(garden tool)* rastrillo *m*. **2** *(for fire)* hurgón *m*. **II** *vtr* **1** *(leaves)* rastrillar. **2** *(fire)* hurgar. **3** *(with machine gun)* barrer. **4** *(search for)* escudriñar, registrar, hurgar. ◆ **rake in** *vtr fam* forrarse; **he's raking it in**, se está forrando. ◆ **rake over** *vtr (topic, question)* insistir en. ◆ **rake up** *vtr* **1** *(people)* reunir. **2** *(bring up)* sacar a luz; **to r. up the past**, desenterrar el pasado.

rake² [reɪk] *n (dissolute man)* calavera *m*, libertino *m*.

rake³ [reɪk] *n Theat (stage)* inclinación *f*.

raked [reɪkt] *adj Theat (stage)* inclinado,-a.

rake-off ['reɪkɒf] *n sl* tajada *f*, comisión *f*.

rakish¹ ['reɪkɪʃ] *adj (dissolute)* libertino,-a.

rakish² ['reɪkɪʃ] *adj (jaunty)* desenvuelto,-a.

rally ['rælɪ] **I** *n* **1** *(gathering)* reunión *f*; *Pol* mitin *m*; **peace r.**, manifestación *f* pacifista. **2** *Aut* rallye *m*. **3** *Ten* pelota *f*, jugada *f*. **II** *vtr (pt & pp **rallied**) (support, troops)* reunir. **III** *vi (after setback)* reponerse, recuperarse. ◆ **rally round** *vi* unirse, formar una piña.

RAM [ræm] *Comput abbr of* **random access memory**, memoria *f* de acceso aleatorio, RAM.

ram [ræm] **I** *n* **1** *Zool* carnero *m*. ■ *Mil* **battering r.**, ariete *m*. **2** *Tech* maza *f*. **II** *vtr (pt & pp **rammed**)* **1** *(drive into place)* hincar, clavar; *(cram)* embutir; *fam* **to r. sth down sb's throat**, machacar algo a algn; *fam* **to r. sth home**, demostrar algo, hacer algo patente. **2** *(crash into)* chocar con, darse contra.

ramble ['ræmbəl] **I** *n (walk)* paseo *m*, caminata *f*. **II** *vi* **1** *(walk)* pasear, hacer una excursión a pie. **2** *fig (digress)* divagar. **3** *(plant)* trepar.

rambler ['ræmbləʳ] *n* **1** *(person)* excursionista *mf*. **2** *Bot* rosal *m* trepador.

rambling ['ræmblɪŋ] **I** *adj* **1** *(speech, writing)* confuso,-a, enmarañado,-a; *(incoherent)* incoherente. **2** *(house)* laberíntico,-a, lleno,-a de recovecos. **3** *Bot* trepador,-a. **II** **ramblings** *npl (walking)* paseos *mpl*, excursiones *fpl*, caminatas *fpl*; *fig (digressions)* divagaciones *fpl*.

ramification [ræmɪfɪ'keɪʃən] *n* ramificación *f*.

ramp [ræmp] *n* **1** *(sloping surface)* rampa *f*. **2** *Av (movable stairway)* escalerilla *f*; *Aut* **hydraulic r.**, elevador *m* hidráulico.

rampage [ræm'peɪdʒ] **I** *n* destrozos *mpl*; **to be *or* go on the r.**, comportarse violentamente, provocar destrozos. **II** *vi* **to r. about**, comportarse como un loco.

rampant ['ræmpənt] *adj* desenfrenado,-a, incontrolado,-a; **corruption is r.**, la corrupción está muy extendida.

rampart ['ræmpɑːt] *n Archit* muralla *f*.

ramrod ['ræmrɒd] **I** *n Tech* baqueta *f*. **II** *adj* tieso,-a, derecho,-a.

ramshackle ['ræmʃækəl] *adj* destartalado,-a.

ran [ræn] *pt see* **run**.

ranch [rɑːntʃ] *n US* rancho *m*, hacienda *f*.

rancher ['rɑːntʃəʳ] *n US* ranchero,-a *m*, *f*, haciendado,-a *m*, *f*.

rancid ['rænsɪd] *adj* rancio,-a.

rancorous ['ræŋkərəs] *adj fml* rencoroso,-a.

rancour, *US* **rancor** ['ræŋkəʳ] *n fml* rencor *m*.

random ['rændəm] **I** *n* **at r.**, al azar. **II** *adj* fortuito,-a, arbitrario,-a; **r. selection**, selección *f* hecha al azar; **r. shot**, bala *f* perdida.

randy ['rændɪ] *adj (randier, randiest) GB fam* caliente, cachondo,-a.

rang [ræŋ] *pt see* **ring**.

range [reɪndʒ] **I** *n* **1** *(of mountains)* cordillera *f*, sierra *f*. **2** *US (open land)* pradera *f*, dehesa *f*. **3** *(choice, diversity)* gama *f*, surtido *m*, variedad *f*; *(of products)* gama *f*. ■ **price r.**, escala *f* de precios. **4** *Mus* registro *m*. **5** *Mil* **firing r.**, campo *m* de tiro. **6** *(of bullet, gun)* alcance *m*, distancia *f* máxima; **at close r.**, de cerca; **long-/short-r. nuclear missiles**, mísiles *mpl* nucleares de largo/corto alcance. **7** *(capacity, extent)* campo *m*; **r. of vision**, campo de visión. **8** *(vehicles)* autonomía *f*. **9** *Culin* cocina *f* de carbón. **II** *vi* **1** *(extend)* extenderse (**to**, hasta). **2** *(vary)* variar, oscilar; **prices r. from five to twenty pounds**, los precios oscilan entre cinco y veinte libras. **III** *vtr* **1** *(encompass)* abarcar, comprender; *(join together)* reunir, unir. **2** *lit (animals, people)* vagar por, recorrer.

rangefinder ['reɪndʒfaɪndəʳ] *n Mil Phot* telémetro *m*.

ranger ['reɪndʒəʳ] *n* **1** **(forest) r.**, guardabosques *mf inv*. **2** *US (mounted policeman)* policía *m* montado.

Rangoon [ræŋ'guːn] *n* Rangún.

rangy ['reɪndʒɪ] *adj (rangier, rangiest)* **1** *(long-legged)* larguirucho,-a. **2** *(spacious)* amplio,-a.

rank¹ [ræŋk] **I** *n* **1** *Mil (row)* fila *f*; **the ranks**, los soldados rasos; **to break ranks**, romper filas; **to rise from the ranks**, ser ascendido,-a a oficial. ■ *Pol* **the r. and file**, las bases (del partido). **2** *(position in army)* graduación *f*; *dated (in society)* rango *m*, categoría *f*; **to pull r.**, abusar de su autoridad; **what r. is he?**, ¿qué graduación tiene? **3 (taxi) r.**, parada *f* de taxis. **II** *vtr (classify)* clasificar, catalogar. **III** *vi (figure)* estar, figurar; **to r. above/below sb**, ser superior/inferior a algn; **to r. with**, estar al mismo nivel que.

rank² [ræŋk] *adj fml* **1** *(vegetation)* exuberante. **2** *(foul-smelling)* fétido,-a. **3** *(thorough)* total, absoluto,-a, completo,-a; *(injustice)* flagrante.

ranking ['ræŋkɪŋ] *n (position)* clasificación *f*, ranking *m*; **the world r.**, el ranking mundial.

ransack ['rænsæk] *vtr* **1** *(plunder)* saquear. **2** *(rummage)* registrar.

ransom ['rænsəm] **I** *n* rescate *m*; **to hold sb to r.**, pedir rescate por algn; *fig* poner a algn entre la espada y la pared. **II** *vtr (free)* rescatar.

rant [rænt] *vi (shout)* vociferar; *fam* **to r. and rave**, pegar gritos.

rap [ræp] **I** *n* **1** *(sharp blow)* golpe *m* seco; *(on door)* golpecito *m*. **2** *(reprimand)* amonestación *f*, reprimenda *f*; *fam* **to take the r.**, pagar el pato. **3** *Mus* rap *m*. **II** *vtr & vi* *(pt & pp* **rapped)** **1** *(knock)* golpear; **to r. at the door,** llamar a la puerta; *fig* **to r. sb over the knuckles,** regañar a algn. **2** *US fam* charlar. ◆ **rap out** *vtr (order, question, etc)* gritar.

rapacious [rə'peɪʃəs] *adj fml (greedy)* rapaz; *(voracious)* voraz.

rape¹ [reɪp] *Jur* **I** *n* violación *f.* **II** *vtr* violar.

rape² [reɪp] *n Bot* colza *f.*

rape³ [reɪp] *n (skins and stalks of grapes)* orujo *m.*

rapeseed ['reɪpsiːd] *n Bot* semilla *f* de colza. ■ **r. oil,** aceite *m* de colza.

rapid ['ræpɪd] **I** *adj* rápido,-a. **II rapids** *npl (in river)* rápidos *mpl.*

rapidity [rə'pɪdɪtɪ] *n* rapidez *f.*

rapier ['reɪpɪə'] *n Fenc* estoque *m.*

rapist ['reɪpɪst] *n* violador,-a *m,f.*

rapport [ræ'pɔː'] *n* compenetración *f,* entendimiento *m;* **to have a good r.,** compenetrarse bien.

rapt [ræpt] *adj (distracted)* absorto,-a; *(daydreaming)* ensimismado,-a; *(attention)* profundo,-a.

rapture ['ræptʃə'] *n* éxtasis *m,* arrobamiento *m;* **to go into raptures over sth,** extasiarse ante algo.

rapturous ['ræptʃərəs] *adj lit (with ecstasy)* extático,-a, arrobado,-a, *(with enthusiasm)* muy entusiasta; *(welcome)* caluroso,-a.

rare¹ [reə'] *adj* **1** *(uncommon)* raro,-a, poco común; *(exceptional)* excepcional. **2** *(atmosphere)* enrarecido,-a. **3** *fam* estupendo,-a. ◆ **rarely** *adv* raramente, raras veces.

rare² [reə'] *adj Culin (steak)* poco hecho,-a.

rarefied ['reərɪfaɪd] *adj* enrarecido,-a.

rarebit ['reəbɪt] *n Culin* tostada *f* de queso.

raring ['reərɪŋ] *adj fam* ansioso,-a, con ganas; *fam* **to be r. to do sth,** morirse de ganas de hacer algo.

rarity ['reərɪtɪ] *n* rareza *f.*

rascal ['rɑːskəl] *n* **1** *(naughty child)* pillo,-a *m,f,* granuja *mf.* **2** *dated (scoundrel)* sinvergüenza *mf.*

rash¹ [ræʃ] *n* **1** *Med* erupción *f* cutánea, sarpullido *m.* **2** *(spate)* racha *f.*

rash² [ræʃ] *adj (reckless)* impetuoso,-a; *(of words, actions)* precipitado,-a, imprudente. ◆ **rashly** *adv* sin reflexionar, a la ligera.

rashness ['ræʃnɪs] *n (recklessness)* impetuosidad *f;* *(of words, actions)* precipitación *f,* imprudencia *f.*

rasher ['ræʃə'] *n Culin* loncha *f.*

rasp [rɑːsp] **I** *n* **1** *Tech* escofina *f.* **2** *(grating noise)* chirrido *m.* **II** *vtr Tech* raspar, escofinar; *fig* **to r. out,** decir con voz áspera.

rasping ['rɑːspɪŋ] *adj (sound)* chirriante; *(voice)* áspero,-a.

raspberry ['rɑːzbərɪ] *n Bot* **1** *(fruit)* frambuesa *f.* **2** *(plant)* frambueso *m.* **3** *fam* pedorreta *f; (jeer)* **to blow a r. at sb,** hacer pedorretas a algn.

rat [ræt] **I** *n* **1** *Zool* rata *f; fig* **to smell a r.,** olerse algo raro; *fam fig* **to look like a drowned r.,** estar hecho,-a una sopa. ■ **r. poison,** raticida *m.* **2** *fam (scoundrel)* canalla *m.* **II** *vi (pt & pp* **ratted) 1** *(hunt rats)* cazar ratas. **2** *fam (inform)* **to r. on sb,** chivarse de algn, denunciar a algn. **3** *fam (break promise)* romper.

ratchet ['rætʃɪt] *n Tech* trinquete *m.* ■ **r. wheel,** rueda *f* de trinquete.

rate [reɪt] **I** *n* **1** *(ratio)* índice *m,* tasa *f; fam fig* **at any r.,** *(at least)* al menos, por lo menos; *(anyway)* en todo caso; *fam fig* **at this r.,** si las cosas siguen así. **■ birth r.,** tasa *f* de natalidad; **growth r.,** índice *m* de crecimiento. **2** *(cost)* precio *m,* tarifa *f;* **hourly r.,** precio por hora. ■ **postal r.,** tarifa *f* postal; *Fin* **r. of exchange/interest,** tipo *m* de cambio/interés. **3 at the r. of,** *(speed)* a la velocidad *f* de; *(quantity)* a razón de. ■ *Med* **pulse r.,** frecuencia *f* del pulso. **4** *(quality)* categoría *f,* cualidad *f;* **first/second r.,** de primera/segunda categoría. **5** *GB*

rates, impuestos *mpl* municipales. **II** *vtr* **1** *(estimate)* estimar. **2** *(evaluate)* tasar. **3** *(consider)* considerar; **how did you r. the film?,** ¿qué te pareció la película?

rateable ['reɪtəbəl] *adj GB* **r. value,** valor *m* catastral.

ratepayer ['reɪtpeɪə'] *n GB* contribuyente *mf.*

rather ['rɑːðə'] **I** *adv* **1** *(quite)* más bien, bastante; *(very much so)* muy; **he's r. good-looking,** es muy guapo; **it's r. cold,** hace bastante frío; **we r. fancy going,** nos apetece ir. **2** *(more accurately)* mejor dicho; **r. than,** *(instead of)* en vez de; *(more than)* más que; **r. them than me!,** ¡ellos, no yo! **3** *(preference)* **she would r. stay here,** prefiere quedarse aquí. **II** [rɑː'ðɜː'] *interj dated fam* ¡por supuesto!, ¡cómo no!; **do you like it? —r.!,** ¿te gusta? — ¡ya lo creo! *or* ¡por supuesto!

ratification [rætɪfɪ'keɪʃən] *n fml* ratificación *f*

ratify ['rætɪfaɪ] *vtr (pt & pp* **ratified)** *fml* ratificar

rating ['reɪtɪŋ] **1** *(valuation)* tasación *f, (score)* valoración *f.* **2** *TV (programme)* **ratings,** índice *m sing* de audiencia. **3** *Naut* marinero *m* sin graduación

ratio ['reɪʃɪəʊ] *n (pl* **ratios)** razón *f,* proporción *f,* relación *f,* **in direct r. to,** en razón directa con, **in the r. of,** a razón de

ration ['ræʃən] **I** *n* **1** *(allowance)* ración *f,* porción *f,* **to be on rations,** sufrir racionamiento. ■ **r. book,** cartilla *f* de racionamiento. **2 rations,** víveres *mpl.* **II** *vtr* racionar

rational ['ræʃənəl] *adj* racional, lógico,-a.

rationale [ræʃə'nɑːl] *n* base *f,* razón *f* fundamental

rationalize ['ræʃənəlaɪz] *vtr* racionalizar

rationing ['ræʃənɪŋ] *n* racionamiento *m*

ratted ['rætɪd] *adj fam (drunk)* ciego,-a

rattle ['rætəl] **I** *n* **1** *(noise of train, cart)* traqueteo *m; (of metal)* repiqueteo *m, (of glass)* tintineo *m.* **2** *(toy)* sonajero *m, (instrument)* matraca *f.* **3** *(of death)* estertor *m.* **II** *vtr* **1** *(keys, chains)* agitar, hacer sonar. **2** *fam (unsettle)* crispar, poner nervioso,-a, **to get sb rattled,** poner nervioso,-a a algn. **III** *vi (gen)* sonar, *(metal)* repiquetear, *(glass)* tintinear. ◆ **rattle off** *vtr (person)* recitar *or* decir a toda prisa. ◆ **rattle on, rattle away** *vi* parlotear, hablar sin parar. ◆ **rattle through** *vtr (work etc)* terminar rápidamente

rattler ['rætlə'] *n US fam* serpiente *f* de cascabel

rattlesnake ['rætəlsneɪk] *n Zool* serpiente *f* de cascabel

ratty ['rætɪ] *adj (rattier, rattiest) fam* malhumorado,-a

raucous ['rɔːkəs] *adj (hoarse)* ronco,-a, *(shrill)* estridente, chillón,-ona.

raunchy ['rɔːntʃɪ] *adj (raunchier, raunchiest) fam* lascivo,-a

ravage ['rævɪdʒ] *fml* **I** *n (usu pl)* estragos *mpl.* **II** *vtr* asolar, devastar, destrozar.

rave [reɪv] *vi* **1** *(be delirious)* delirar. **2** *(be angry)* enfurecerse **(at,** con). **3** *(speak enthusiastically)* entusiasmarse **(about,** por), **to r. about sth,** poner algo por las nubes. **II** *n* **1** *Mus Theat* **r. review,** crítica *f* muy favorable. **2** *fam (trend)* moda *f.* **III** *adj fam (fashionable)* de moda, enrollado,-a

raven ['reɪvən] *n Orn* cuervo *m,* **r.-haired,** de pelo negro como el azabache

ravenous ['rævənəs] *adj* voraz, **I'm r.,** tengo un hambre que no veo

raver ['reɪvə'] *n GB fam* juerguista *mf*

rave-up ['reɪvʌp] *n fam* juerga *f*

ravine [rə'viːn] *n Geog* barranco *m*

raving ['reɪvɪŋ] **I** *n* **1** *(delirium)* delirio *m, fam* **r. mad,** loco,-a de atar. **2** *(rambling talk)* divagaciones *fpl*

ravish ['rævɪʃ] *vtr* **1** *dated (rape)* violar. **2** *(plunder)* saquear. **3** *fig* encantar, cautivar

ravishing ['rævɪʃɪŋ] *adj (person)* encantador,-a, cautivador,-a

raw [rɔː] **I** *adj* **1** *(uncooked)* crudo,-a. **2** *(not processed)* bruto,-a, *(pure)* puro,-a. ■ **r. material,** materia *f* prima. **3** *(emotions)* instintivo,-a, primario,-a. **4** *(weather)* crudo,-a frío,-a. **5** (*unfair*) injusto,-a; **r. deal**, trato *m* injusto. **6** (*wound*) abierto,-a, **r. flesh**, carne viva. **7** *US* (*inexperienced*) novato,-a, inexperto,-a, bisoño,-a, *Mil* **r. recruits**, novatos *mpl*. **8** (*frank*) franco,-a. **9** (*uncivilized*) tosco,-a. **II** *n* **1** (*tender spot*) carne *f* viva; **to touch sb on the r.**, herir a algn en lo vivo. **2 in the r.**, *fam* (*naked*) en cueros, en pelotas

rawness ['rɔːnɪs] *n* **1** (*of food, weather*) crudeza *f*. **2** *US* (*lack of experience*) falta *f* de experiencia

ray[1] [reɪ] *n* (*light etc*) rayo *m, fig* **r. of hope**, resquicio *m* de esperanza

ray[2] [reɪ] *n* (*fish*) raya *f*

ray[3] [reɪ] *n Mus* (*note*) re *m*

rayon ['reɪɒn] *n Tex* rayón *m*

raze [reɪz] *vtr* arrasar, **to r. a building to the ground**, arrasar un edificio

razor ['reɪzə'] *n* (*wet*) navaja *f* de afeitar; (*electric*) máquinilla *f* de afeitar. ■ **r. blade**, hoja *f* de afeitar

razorbill ['reɪzəbɪl] *n Orn* alca *f* común

razor-sharp [reɪzə'ʃɑːp] *adj* (*knife etc*) muy afilado,-a; *fig* (*mind*) perspicaz

razor-shell ['reɪzəʃel] *n* (*fish*) navaja *f*

razzle ['ræzəl] *n fam* juerga *f*, **to go out on the r.**, ir de marcha, irse de juerga

razzmatazz [ræzmə'tæz] *n fam* jaleo *m*

RC [ɑː'siː] *abbr of* **Roman Catholic**, católico,-a (*m,f*)

Rd *abbr of* **Road**, calle *f*, c/

RE [ɑː'riː] *Sen abbr of* **religious education**, educación *f* religiosa

re [riː] *prep Com* respecto a, con referencia a

reach [riːtʃ] **I** *vtr* **1** (*arrive at*) llegar a, alcanzar; (*grab*) alcanzar, (*agreement*) llegar a, *Dep* **to r. the finals**, llegar a la final. **2** (*contact*) comunicarse, localizar; **where can I r. you?**, ¿dónde te puedo localizar? **II** *vi* (*arrive at*) llegar, alcanzar; (*grab*) alcanzar, **he can't r.**, no llega, **to r. for sth**, intentar coger algo, **to r. out**, extender la mano. **III** *n* **1** (*range*) alcance *m*, out of r., fuera del alcance; **within easy r.**, muy cerca, **within r.**, al alcance. **2** *Box* (*extension*) extensión *f* del brazo. **3 reaches**, (*on a river*) recta *f sing*

react [rɪ'ækt] *vi* reaccionar

reaction [rɪ'ækʃən] *n* reacción *f*.

reactionary [rɪ'ækʃənərɪ] *adj & n* reaccionario,-a (*m,f*)

reactivate [rɪ'æktɪveɪt] *vtr* reactivar

reactive [rɪ'æktɪv] *adj Chem* reactivo,-a.

reactor [rɪ'æktə'] *n Phys* reactor *m*

read [riːd] **I** *n fam* lectura *f*, **to have a quiet r.**, pasar un rato tranquilo leyendo. **II** *vtr* (*pt & pp* **read** [red]) **1** (*book, newspaper, etc*) leer, (*poem*) recitar. **2** (*decipher*) descifrar. **3** (*understand*) entender, (*interpret*) interpretar, **it can be r. both ways**, se puede interpretar de las dos maneras, **to r. sb's lips**, leer los labios de algn, *fig* **to r. between the lines**, leer entre líneas, *fig* **to r. sb's mind**, adivinarle el pensamiento a algn, *fam* **do you r. me?**, ¿me entiendes?, *Rad* ¿me recibe? **4** *Impr* (*proofs*) corregir. **5** *Univ* (*subject*) estudiar. **III** *vi* **1** (*dial*) marcar. **2** (*signpost, text*) decir, poner, **the sign r. 'No Parking'**, el letrero decía 'Prohibido Aparcar' ◆ **read into** (*interpret*) interpretar erróneamente, **don't r. too much into this book**, no busques mensaje en este libro porque no lo hay. ◆ **read out** *vtr* leer en voz alta. ◆ **read up** *vtr* (*subject*) investigar (**on**, -), buscar datos (**on**, sobre).

readable ['riːdəbəl] *adj* **1** (*interesting*) interesante, que vale la pena leerse. **2** (*legible*) legible

reader ['riːdə'] *n* **1** (*of books, newspapers, etc*) lector,-a *m, f*; **she's a keen r.**, lee mucho. **2** (*book*) libro *m* de lectura, **a Russian r.**, un libro de lectura en ruso. **3** *GB Univ* (*man*) profesor *m* adjunto; (*woman*) profesora *f* adjunta. **4** (*microfilm*) lector *m*.

readership ['riːdəʃɪp] *n* **1** *Press* lectores *mpl*. **2** *GB Univ* puesto *m* de profesor,-a adjunto-a.

readiness ['redɪnɪs] *n* **1** (*preparedness*) preparación *f*. **2** (*availability*) disponibilidad *f*. **3** (*swiftness*) rapidez *f*. **4** (*willingness*) buena disposición *f*.

reading ['riːdɪŋ] **I** *n* **1** (*gen*) lectura *f*; **poetry r.**, recital *m* de poesía; **the novel makes excellent r.**, es un libro excelente. **2** (*of gas meter etc*) lectura *f*. **3** *fig* interpretación *f*; **my r. of the situation is that ...**, según yo veo la situación ... . **4** (*laws, bills*) presentación *f*. **II** *adj* de lectura. ■ **r. glasses**, gafas *fpl* de lectura; **r. lamp**., lámpara *f* de leer; **r. matter**, material *m* escrito, bibliografía *f*; **r. room**, sala *f* de lectura.

readjust [riːə'dʒʌst] *vtr* (*gen*) reajustar; (*adapt oneself*) readaptarse.

readjustment [riːə'dʒʌstmənt] *n* (*gen*) reajuste *m*; (*adopting*) readaptación *f*.

ready ['redɪ] **I** *adj* **1** (*prepared*) listo,-a, preparado,-a; **lunch is r.!**, ¡a comer!; *Av* **r. for take-off**, preparado,-a para el despegue; *Sport* **r., steady, go!**, ¡preparados, listos, ya!; **r. when you are!**, ¡cuando quieras!; **we're r. for bed**, nos vamos a la cama. **2** (*about to*) a punto; **r. to**, a punto de. **3** (*quick, convenient*) a mano, (*smile*) fácil; **to be r. with advice**, tener siempre un consejo a punto. ■ **r. cash**, dinero *m* en efectivo. **4** (*willing*) dispuesto,-a. **II readies** *npl fam* (*cash*) pasta *f sing*. **III** *vtr* (*pt & pp* **readied**) **1** (*make ready*) preparar; **the consignment will be readied**, el envío estará listo. **2** *fml* (*person*) prepararse. ◆ **readily** *adv* **1** (*easily*) fácilmente, libremente; **r. available**, disponible en el acto. **2** (*willingly*) de buena gana.

ready-cooked [redɪ'kʊkt] *adj* precocinado,-a; **r.-c. chickens**, pollos *mpl* asados para llevar.

ready-made [redɪ'meɪd] *adj* confeccionado,-a; hecho,-a; **r.-m. clothes**, ropa hecha.

real [rɪəl] **I** *adj* **1** (*not imaginary*) real, verdadero,-a; **in r. life**, en la vida real; *fam* **for r.**, de veras; **this time it's for r.**, esta vez va de veras; **is this bloke for r.?**, ¿pero este tío de qué va? **2** (*genuine*) auténtico,-a, legítimo,-a; **he's a r. friend**, es un auténtico amigo; **r. leather**, piel legítima; *fam* **it's the r. McCoy, it's the r. thing**, es el auténtico *or* la auténtica. **3** *US Com* **r. estate**, bienes *mpl* inmuebles; **r. estate agent**, agente *m* inmobiliario. **II** *adv US fam* (*very*) **r. pleased**, verdaderamente, contento,-a. ◆ **really** *adv* **1** (*truly*) verdaderamente, realmente; **it's r. sad**, es verdaderamente triste; **you r. shouldn't have done it**, no deberías haberlo hecho, de verdad. **2** (*sure*) de verdad; **r.?**, ¿de veras?; **r.!**, ¡no me digas!

realign [riːə'laɪn] *vtr* reordenar, restructurar.

realignment [riːə'laɪnmənt] *n* restructuración *f*.

realism ['rɪəlɪzəm] *n* realismo *m*.

realist ['rɪəlɪst] *n* realista *mf*.

realistic ['rɪəlɪstɪk] *adj* realista.

reality [rɪ'ælɪtɪ] *n* realidad *f*; **in r.**, en realidad.

realizable [rɪə'laɪzəbəl] *adj* realizable.

realize ['rɪəlaɪz] *vtr* **1** (*become aware of*) darse cuenta de; **I didn't r. that ...**, no me di cuenta de que ... . **2** *fml* (*fulfil*) realizarse, hacerse realidad; **to r. one's full potential**, realizarse. **3** *Com* (*assets*) realizar, vender, convertir en efectivo. **4** *Art Lit* realizar.

realization [rɪəlaɪ'zeɪʃən] *n* **1** (*understanding*) comprensión *f*. **2** (*fulfilment*) realización *f*. **3** *Com* realización *f*, venta *f*.

realm [relm] *n fml* **1** (*kingdom*) reino *m*. **2** *fig* (*field*) terreno *m*, esfera *f*, mundo *m*.

ream [riːm] *n* **1** (*of paper*) resma *f*. **2** *fig* **reams**, (*writings*) montones *mpl*, gran cantidad *f sing*.

reanimate [riː'ænɪmeɪt] *vtr* reanimar, resucitar, dar nueva vida a.

reap [riːp] *vtr Agr* cosechar, recoger; *fig* **to r. the benefits**, llevarse los beneficios.

reaper ['riːpə'] *n* **1** (*person*) segador,-a *m, f*. **2** (*machine*) segadora *f*. ■ **r. and binder**, segadora *f* agavilladora.

reappear [riːə'pɪə'] *vi* reaparecer.

reappearance [riːəˈpɪərəns] *n* reaparición *f*.

reappraisal [riːəˈpreɪzəl] *n fml* revaluación *f*.

reappraise [riːəˈpreɪz] *vtr fml* revaluar.

rear¹ [rɪəʳ] **I** *n* 1 *(back part)* parte *f* de atrás, parte *f* posterior; **in the r.,** *Mil* en la retaguardia; **to bring up the r.,** cerrar la marcha. 2 *Aut* parte *f* de atrás. 3 *fam (buttocks)* trasero *m*. **II** *adj* posterior, trasero,-a. ■ **r. entrance,** puerta *f* de atrás; *Naut* **r. admiral,** contralmirante *m*; *Aut* **r. wheel,** rueda *f* trasera.

rear² [rɪəʳ] **I** *vtr* 1 *(breed, raise)* criar. 2 *(build)* erigir; *(lift up)* levantar, alzar; *(head)* levantar; *fig* **corruption reared its ugly head,** la corrupción hizo acto de presencia. **II** *vi (horse)* **to r. up,** encabritarse.

rearguard [ˈrɪəgɑːd] *n Mil* retaguardia *f*; *fig* **r. action,** última tentativa *f*.

rearm [riːˈɑːm] *Mil* **I** *vtr* rearmar. **II** *vi* rearmarse.

rearmament [riːˈɑːməmənt] *n* rearme *m*.

rearmost [ˈrɪəməʊst] *adj (nearest to the back)* último,-a.

rearrange [riːəˈreɪndʒ] *vtr* 1 *(furniture)* colocar de otra manera. 2 *(fix new date)* fijar otra fecha.

rearrangement [riːəˈreɪndʒmənt] *n* reorganización *f*, ajuste *m*.

rear-view [ˈrɪəvjuː] *adj* **r.-v. mirror,** (espejo *m*) retrovisor *m*.

reason [ˈriːzən] **I** *n* 1 *(cause)* motivo *m*, razón *f*; **all the more r. why,** razón de más; **for no r.,** sin razón; **for reasons best known to him,** por razones sólo conocidas por él; **for some r.,** por algún motivo; **for this r.,** por esta razón; **he has r. to think that ...,** tiene motivos para pensar que ...; *fml* **by r. of,** en virtud de. 2 *(good sense)* sentido *m* común, razón *f*; **it stands to r.,** es lógico; **to listen to r.,** atender a razones; **to lose one's r.,** perder la razón; **to see r.,** ver la razón; **within r.,** dentro de lo razonable. **II** *vi* 1 *(be reasonable)* razonar; **to r. with sb,** convencer a algn. 2 *(argue, work out)* razonar, llegar a la conclusión. ◆ **reason out** *vtr* solucionar con lógica.

reasonable [ˈriːzənəbəl] *adj* 1 *(fair)* razonable, moderado,-a. 2 *(sensible)* razonable, sensato,-a. 3 *(average)* regular, pasable. ◆ **reasonably** *adv* 1 *(fairly)* bastante; **it was r. cheap,** era bastante barato,-a. 2 *(sensibly)* sensatamente.

reasoning [ˈriːzənɪŋ] *n* razonamiento *m*; **by your r.,** según tus cálculos.

reassemble [riːəˈsembəl] **I** *vtr (machine etc)* volver a montar. **II** *vi (people, group)* reunirse, volverse a juntar.

reassure [riːəˈʃʊəʳ] *vtr* 1 *(comfort)* tranquilizar. 2 *(restore confidence)* dar confianza a.

reassurance [riːəˈʃʊərəns] *n (comfort)* consuelo *m*; *(words of comfort)* palabras *fpl* tranquilizadoras.

reassuring [riːəˈʃʊərɪŋ] *adj* consolador,-a, tranquilizador,-a; **it's r. (to me) to know that ...,** me tranquiliza saber que ... .

reawaken [riːəˈweɪkən] **I** *vtr (feelings etc)* volver a despertar. **II** *vi (from sleep)* despertar de nuevo.

rebate [ˈriːbeɪt] *n Fin* 1 *(repayment)* devolución *f*, reembolso *m*. ■ **tax r.,** devolución *f* fiscal. 2 *(discount)* descuento *m*, rebaja *f*.

rebel [ˈrebəl] **I** *adj & n* rebelde *(mf)*. **II** [rɪˈbel] *vi* rebelarse, sublevarse **(against,** contra).

rebellion [rɪˈbeljən] *n* rebelión *f*, sublevación *f*.

rebellious [rɪˈbeljəs] *adj* rebelde.

rebirth [riːˈbɜːθ] *n* renacimiento *m*.

reborn [riːˈbɔːn] *adj* **te be r.,** volver a nacer.

rebound [ˈriːbaʊnd] **I** *n (of ball)* rebote *m*; *fig* **to do sth on the r.,** hacer algo de rebote; *fig* **to marry on the r.,** of casarse por despecho. **II** [rɪˈbaʊnd] *vi (ball)* rebotar; *fig (action)* repercutir.

rebuff [rɪˈbʌf] **I** *n* rechazo *m*, desaire *m*; **to suffer a r.,** verse rechazado,-a. **II** *vtr* rechazar, desairar.

rebuild [riːˈbɪld] *vtr (pt & pp rebuilt)* reconstruir.

rebuke [rɪˈbjuːk] **I** *n* reproche *m*, reprensión *f*. **II** *vtr* reprochar, reprender.

rebut [rɪˈbʌt] *vtr (pt & pp rebutted)* refutar.

rebuttal [rɪˈbʌtəl] *n fml* refutación *f*.

recalcitrant [rɪˈkælsɪtrənt] *adj fml* recalcitrante, obstinado,-a.

recall [rɪˈkɔːl] **I** *n* 1 *(soldiers)* llamada *f*. 2 *(revocation)* revocación *f*, anulación *f*. 3 *(memory)* memoria *f*; **beyond or past r.,** sepultado,-a para siempre; **total r.,** gran capacidad de memoria. **II** *vtr* 1 *(soldiers, products, etc)* hacer volver. 2 *(withdraw)* retirar. 3 *(remember)* acordarse, recordar; **as I r.,** tal como yo lo recuerdo.

recant [rɪˈkænt] *vi fml* retractarse.

recap [riːˈkæp] *fam* **I** *vtr & vi (pt & pp recapped)* recapitular, resumir; **to r., en resumen. II** [ˈriːkæp] *n* recapitulación *f*, resumen *m*.

recapitulate [riːkəˈpɪtjʊleɪt] *vtr & vi fml* recapitular, resumir.

recapitulation [riːkəpɪtjʊˈleɪʃən] *n fml* recapitulación *f*, resumen *m*.

recapture [riːˈkæptʃəʳ] **I** *n (of person)* nueva detención *f*; *(of place)* reconquista *f*. **II** *vtr* 1 *(person)* volver a capturar; *(place)* reconquistar. 2 *fig (memory, feeling)* hacer revivir, recuperar.

recast [riːˈkɑːst] *vtr (pt & pp recast)* 1 *(redo)* rehacer. 2 *(metal)* refundir. 3 *Theat (play)* cambiar el reparto; *(actor, actress)* dar otro papel a; **they r. the part of Grimbling,** dieron el papel de Grimbling a otro actor.

recd *Com Fin abbr of* **received,** recibido,-a.

recede [rɪˈsiːd] *vi (withdraw)* retroceder, retirarse; *(fade)* desvanecerse.

receipt [rɪˈsiːt] **I** *n* 1 *(act)* recepción *f*, recibo *m*; **to acknowledge r. of sth,** acusar recibo de algo. 2 *Com (paper)* recibo *m*; **to ask for a r.,** pedir un recibo. 3 **receipts,** *(talkings)* recuadación *f sing*. **II** *vtr Com* dar un recibo por.

receive [rɪˈsiːv] *vtr* 1 *(gen)* recibir. 2 *Jur (stolen goods)* ocultar. 3 *(ceremony)* acoger, recibir; **well/badly received,** bien/mal acogido,-a; *Rel* **to r. sb into the Church,** recibir a algn en el seno de la Iglesia. 4 *TV Rad (transmission)* captar, recibir. 5 *(in club)* aceptar.

receiver [rɪˈsiːvəʳ] *n* 1 *(person)* receptor,-a *m, f*, recibidor,-a *m, f*; *(of letter)* destinario,-a *m, f*. 2 *Jur (of stolen goods)* perista *mf*. 3 *GB Jur* **official r.,** síndico *m*. 4 *Tel* auricular *m*; **to lift/put down the r.,** descolgar/colgar el teléfono. 5 *Rad* receptor *m*.

receiving [rɪˈsiːvɪŋ] *n Jur (stolen goods)* encubrimiento *m*; *fig* **to be on the r. end,** ser la víctima *or* el blanco.

recent [ˈriːsənt] *adj* reciente; **in r. years,** en los últimos años. ◆ **recently** *adv* hace poco, recientemente.

receptacle [rɪˈseptəkəl] *n* receptáculo *m*, recipiente *m*.

reception [rɪˈsepʃən] *n* 1 *(welcome)* recibimiento *m*, acogida *f*. ■ **r. centre,** hogar *m* de beneficencia; **r. room** sala *f* de recepción. 2 *(party)* recepción *f*. ■ **wedding r.,** banquete *m* de bodas. 3 *(in hotel)* **r. (desk),** recepción *f*. 4 *Rad TV* recepción *f*.

receptionist [rɪˈsepʃənɪst] *n* recepcionista *mf*.

receptive [rɪˈseptɪv] *adj* receptivo,-a.

receptor [rɪˈseptəʳ] *n* receptor *m*.

recess [rɪˈses, ˈriːses] *n* 1 *(in a wall)* hueco *m*. 2 *(remote place)* lugar *m* apartado. 3 *(secret place)* escondrijo *m*, recoveco *m*; *fig* **the recesses of the mind,** los recovecos de la mente. 4 *(rest period)* descanso *m*; *US Educ* recreo *m*; *Parl* período *m* de vacaciones. **II** [rɪˈses] *vi Parl* suspender la sesión.

recession [rɪˈseʃən] *n Econ* recesión *f*.

recharge [riːˈtʃɑːdʒ] *vtr Aut (battery)* recargar; *fig* **to r. one's batteries,** recargar las baterías *or* pilas.

rechargeable [riːˈtʃɑːdʒəbəl] *adj* recargable.

recherché [rəˈʃeəʃeɪ] *adj* rebuscado,-a.

recidivism [rɪ'sɪdɪvɪzəm] *n* reincidencia *f*.

recidivist [rɪ'sɪdɪvɪst] *adj & n* reincidente *(mf)*.

recipe ['resɪpɪ] *n* 1 *Culin* receta *f*. 2 *fig (formula)* fórmula *f*; *(secret)* secreto *m*.

recipient [rɪ'sɪpɪənt] *n* 1 *(person)* receptor,-a *m*, *f*. 2 *(of letter)* destinatario,-a *m*, *f*.

reciprocate [rɪ'sɪprəkeɪt] *vtr & vi (gen)* corresponder; *(favour etc)* devolver.

reciprocal [rɪ'sɪprəkəl] *adj* recíproco,-a, mutuo,-a.

recital [rɪ'saɪtəl] *n* recital *m*.

recitation [resɪ'teɪʃən] *n* recitación *f*.

recite [rɪ'saɪt] *vtr & vi* recitar.

reckless ['reklɪs] *adj (unwise)* imprudente; *(fearless)* temerario,-a.

recklessness ['reklɪsnɪs] *n (unwise)* imprudencia *f*; *(fearless)* temeridad *f*.

reckon ['rekən] *vtr & vi* 1 *(calculate)* calcular; *(count)* contar. 2 *fam (think)* creer; *(consider)* considerar; **he reckons he's an expert on the subject,** se considera un experto en el tema. ◆ **reckon in** *vtr* tomar en cuenta, incluir. ◆ **reckon on** *vi* contar con. ◆ **reckon up** *vtr dated* calcular, sumar. ◆ **reckon with** *vtr* tener en cuenta; *fig* **he's a man to be reckoned with,** es un hombre muy poderoso. ◆ **reckon without** *vi* no contar con.

reckoner ['rekənər] *n* **ready r.,** tabla *f* de cálculo.

reckoning ['rekənɪŋ] *n* cálculo *m*, cuenta *f*; **by my r. ...,** según mis cálculos ...; **to be out in one's r.,** equivocarse en las cuentas; *fig* **day of r.,** día *m* del juicio final.

reclaim [rɪ'kleɪm] *vtr* 1 *(recover)* recuperar; *(demand back)* reclamar. 2 *(waste products)* recidir, tratar. 3 *(marshland, desert, etc)* convertir.

reclamation [reklə'meɪʃən] *n* 1 *(act of reclaiming)* reclamación *f*. 2 *(waste products)* reciclaje *m*. 3 *(marshland, desert, etc)* conversión *f* en tierra cultivable.

recline [rɪ'klaɪn] *vi* recostarse, reclinarse.

reclining [rɪ'klaɪnɪŋ] *adj* recostado,-a, reclinado,-a; **r. seat,** asiento *m* con respaldo reclinable.

recluse [rɪ'kluːs] *n* recluso,-a *m*, *f*.

reclusive [re'kluːsɪv] *adj fml* recluso,-a.

recognition [rekəg'nɪʃən] *n (gen)* reconocimiento *m*; *(appreciation)* apreciación *f*; *(acceptance)* acceptación *f*; **in r. of,** en reconocimiento de; **the town has changed beyond all r.,** el puel lo ha cambiado tanto que ahora es irreconocible.

recognizable [rekəg'naɪzəbəl] *adj* reconocible.

recognize ['rekəgnaɪz] *vtr* reconocer.

recognized ['rekəgnaɪzd] *adj (approved)* aprobado,-a.

recoil ['riːkɔɪl] **I** *n (of gun)* culatazo *m*; *(of cannon)* retroceso *m*; *(of spring)* aflojamiento *m*. **II** [rɪ'kɔɪl] *vi* 1 *(gun)* dar un culatazo; *(cannon)* retroceder; *(spring)* aflojarse. 2 *fig (in fear)* asustarse; *(with disgust)* disgustarse, sentir repugnancia por. 3 *fig (rebound)* repercutir.

recollect [rekə'lekt] *vtr fml* acordarse de, recordar.

recollection [rekə'lekʃən] *n* recuerdo *m*; **to the best of my r.,** que yo recuerde.

recommence [riːkə'mens] *vtr & vi* recomenzar, empezar de nuevo.

recommend [rekə'mend] *vtr* recomendar; **he has little to r. him,** poca cosa tiene a su favor; **not to be recommended,** poco aconsejable *or* recomendable.

recommendation [rekəmen'deɪʃən] *n* recomendación *f*.

recompense ['rekəmpens] **I** *n* recompensa *f*; *Jur (for damage)* indemnización *f*. **II** *vtr* recompensar (**for,** por); *Jur* indemnizar.

reconcile ['rekənsaɪl] *vtr* 1 *(two people)* reconciliar; *(two ideas)* conciliar; **to become reconciled,** reconciliarse; **to r. oneself to,** resignarse a, conformarse con.

reconciliation [rekənsɪlɪ'eɪʃən] *n (of two people)* reconciliación *f*; *(of two ideas)* conciliación *f*.

recondite [rɪ'kɒndaɪt, 'rekəndaɪt] *adj fml* recóndito,-a.

recondition [riːkən'dɪʃən] *vtr (engine)* revisar, reparar.

reconnaissance [rɪ'kɒnɪsəns] *n Mil* reconocimiento *m*, exploración *f*.

reconnoitre, US reconnoiter [rekə'nɔɪtər] *vtr Mil* reconocer, explorar.

reconquer [riː'kɒŋkər] *vtr* reconquistar.

reconquest [riː'kɒŋkwest] *n* reconquista *f*.

reconsider [riːkən'sɪdər] *vtr* reconsiderar, considerar de nuevo.

reconsideration [riːkənsɪdə'reɪʃən] *n* reconsideración *f*, revisión *f*.

reconstitute [riː'kɒnstɪtjuːt] *vtr (group, movement, etc)* reconstituir, reorganizar.

reconstruct [riːkən'strʌkt] *vtr* reconstruir.

reconstruction [riːkən'strʌkʃən] *n* reconstrucción *f*.

record ['rekɔːd] **I** *n* 1 *(account)* relación *f*; *(meeting)* actas *fpl*; **for the r.,** para que quede constancia; **off the r.,** confidencialmente; **to go on r.,** declarar públicamente; **to keep a r. of sth,** anotar algo; **to put** *or* **set the r. straight,** dejar las cosas claras. 2 *(document)* documento *m*; **offcial r.,** boletín *m* oficial; **r. of attendance,** registro *m* de asistencia; **public records,** archivos *mpl*. 3 *(case history) Univ* expediente *m* académico; *Med* historial *m* médico; **police r.,** antecedentes *mpl* penales; *(criminal)* **to have a r.,** tener antecedentes. 4 *Mus* disco *m*; **to cut/ make a r.,** grabar un disco. ◆ **r. library,** discoteca *f*; **r. player,** tocadiscos *m inv*. 5 *Sport* récord *m*; **to break a r.,** batir un récord; **to hold the r.,** tener el récord. **II** [rɪ'kɔːd] *vtr* 1 *(relate)* hacer constar; *(note down)* apuntar, anotar. 2 *(record, voice)* grabar. 3 *(thermometer etc)* marcar, registrar.

record-breaking ['rekɔːdbreɪkɪŋ] *adj* que bate todos los récords.

recorded [re'kɔːdɪd] *adj* **r. delivery,** correo *m* certificado; **r. message,** mensaje *m* grabado.

recorder [re'kɔːdər] **1** *(person)* registrador,-a *m*, *f*, archivero,-a *m*, *f*; *Jur* magistrado,-a *m*, *f* municipal. 2 *Mus* flauta *f*. 3 **tape r.,** magnetofón *m*.

recording [re'kɔːdɪŋ] *n* 1 *(writing down)* consignación *f*. 2 *(registering)* registro *m*. ■ **tape r.,** grabación *f*.

recount [rɪ'kaunt] *vtr* 1 *(tell)* contar, relatar. 2 *(count again)* volver a contar.

re-count [riː'kaunt] **I** *vi Pol* hacer un recuento. **II** ['riːkaunt] *n Pol* recuento *m*.

recoup [rɪ'kuːp] *vtr (recover)* recuperar; *(losses)* resarcirse de, recuperar.

recourse [rɪ'kɔːs] *n* recurso *m*; **to have r. to,** recurrir,-a.

recover [rɪ'kʌvər] **I** *vtr (items, time)* recuperar; *(consciousness, composure)* recobrar. **II** *vi (from illness, setback, etc)* reponerse, recuperarse, restablecerse.

re-cover [riː'kʌvər] *vtr (book)* forrar de nuevo; *(furniture)* tapizar de nuevo.

recoverable [rɪ'kʌrəbəl] *adj* recuperable.

recovery [rɪ'kʌvərɪ] *n* 1 *(retrieval)* recuperación *f*. 2 *(improvement)* restablecimiento *m*, recuperación *f*.

re-create [riːkrɪ'eɪt] *vtr* recrear.

recreation [rekrɪ'eɪʃən] *n* 1 diversión *f*, entretenimiento *m*. 2 *Educ (playtime)* recreo *m*. ■ **r. ground,** terreno *m* de juegos.

re-creation [riːkrɪ'eɪʃən] *n* recreación *f*.

recreational [rekrɪ'eɪʃənəl] *adj* recreativo,-a.

recriminate [rɪ'krɪmɪneɪt] *vtr* recriminar, reprochar.

recrimination [rɪkrɪmɪ'neɪʃən] *n* recriminación *f*, reproche *m*.

recriminatory [rɪ'krɪmɪnətərɪ] *adj* recriminatorio,-a.

recruit [rɪ'kruːt] **I** n **1** Mil recluta m. **2** (new member) miembro mf or socio,-a m,f nuevo,-a. **II** vtr (soldiers) reclutar, alistar; (members) admitir; (workers) contratar.

recruitment [rɪ'kruːtmənt] n (soldiers) reclutamiento m; (employees) contratación f.

rectangle ['rektæŋgəl] n Geom rectángulo m.

rectangular [rekt'æŋgjʊləʳ] adj Geom rectangular.

rectify ['rektɪfaɪ] vtr (pt & pp rectified) rectificar, corregir.

rectifiable [rektɪ'faɪəbəl] adj rectificable.

rectitude ['rektɪtjuːd] n fml rectitud f.

rector ['rektəʳ] n **1** Rel párroco m. **2** Scot Educ director,-a m,f.

rectory ['rektərɪ] n rectoría f.

rectum ['rektəm] n (pl rectums or recta ['rektə]) Anat recto m.

recumbent [rɪ'kʌmbənt] adj lit recostado,-a; **r. statue,** estatua f yacente.

recuperate [rɪ'kuːpəreɪt] vi fml reponerse, restablecerse, recuperarse.

recuperation [rɪkuːpə'reɪʃən] n restablecimiento m, recuperación f.

recur [rɪ'kɜːʳ] vi (pt & pp recurred) reproducirse, repetirse.

recurrence [rɪ'kʌrəns] n repetición f, reaparición f.

recurrent [rɪ'kʌrənt] adj **1** periódico,-a. **2** Med recurrente.

recurring [rɪ'kɜːrɪŋ] adj periódico,-a; **two point six r.,** dos coma seis periódico.

recycle [riː'saɪkəl] vtr reciclar.

recycling [riː'saɪklɪŋ] n reciclaje m.

red [red] **I** adj (redder, reddest) (colour) rojo,-a; (person) **as r. as a beetroot,** más rojo,-a que un tomate; **r. alert,** alerta roja; **r. flag,** bandera roja; Traffic **r. light,** semáforo en rojo; **r. wine,** vino tinto; **to go r.,** ponerse colorado,-a; **to have r. hair,** ser pelirrojo,-a; fig **r. herring,** truco m para despistar; fam **to roll out the r. carpet for sb,** recibir a algn con todos los honores. ■ **R. Cross,** Cruz f Roja; **R. Indian,** piel roja mf, **R. Riding Hood,** Caperucita f Roja; **R. Sea,** Mar m Rojo; **r. tape,** papeleo m, trámites mpl. **II** n **1** (colour) rojo m; Fin **to be in the r.,** estar en descubierto or en números rojos; **to make sb see r.,** poner negro,-a a algn. **2** Pol rojo,-a m,f.

redbreast ['redbrest] n Orn petirrojo m.

redbrick ['redbrɪk] adj provincial. ■ **r. university,** universidad f de provincias construida a finales del siglo diecinueve.

redcurrant [red'kʌrənt] n Bot grosella f roja.

redden ['redən] **I** vi (person) enrojecerse, ponerse colorado,-a. **II** vtr (make red) teñir de rojo.

reddish ['redɪʃ] adj rojizo,-a.

redecorate [riː'dekəreɪt] vtr repintar, renovar la decoración.

redeem [rɪ'diːm] vtr **1** (regain) recobrar, rescatar, recuperar; (from pawn) desempeñar; (voucher etc) canjear. **2** (pay off debt) amortizar, cancelar. **3** (fulfil an obligation) cumplir. **4** (compensate) compensar, salvar. **5** Rel redimir.

redeemable [rɪ'diːməbəl] adj **1** (exchanged) canjeable; (from pawn) redimible. **2** (debt) amortizable.

redeemer [rɪ'diːməʳ] n (saviour) redentor,-a m,f; Rel **the R.,** el Redentor.

redeeming [rɪ'diːmɪŋ] adj compensatorio,-a; **his only r. feature,** lo único que le salva.

redemption [rɪ'dempʃən] n fml **1** (of debt) reembolso m, amortización f. **2** Rel redención f, salvación f; **beyond r.,** irredimible.

redeploy [riːdɪ'plɔɪ] vtr Mil transferir.

red-handed [red'hændɪd] adj flagrante; **to catch sb r.-h.,** coger a algn en flagrante delito or con las manos en la masa.

redhead ['redhed] n pelirrojo,-a m,f.

red-hot [red'hɒt] adj **1** (turned red) al rojo vivo, candente; **r.-h. news,** noticia(s) f(pl) de última hora. **2** fam (passionate) fervoroso,-a, ardiente.

redirect [riːdɪ'rekt] vtr **1** (alter) redistribuir; **the government will r. funds to pension schemes,** el gobierno destinará nuevos fondos a los planes de jubilación. **2** (forward) remitir a la nueva dirección.

red-letter [red'letəʳ] adj **r.-l. day,** día m memorable.

red-light [red'laɪt] adj fam **r.-l. district,** barrio m chino, barrios mpl bajos.

redouble [riː'dʌbəl] vtr redoblar, incrementar; **to r. one's efforts,** redoblar los esfuerzos.

redoubt [rɪ'daʊt] n fml **1** (haven) refugio m, amparo m. **2** (stronghold) reducto m, fortaleza f.

redpoll ['redpɒl] n Orn pardillo m sizerín.

redress [rɪ'dres] fml **I** n reparación f, fig desagravio m; **to seek r.,** exigir reparación. **II** vtr (grievance, wrong) reparar; fig **to r. the balance,** equilibrar la balanza.

redshank ['redʃæŋk] n Orn archibebe m común.

redskin ['redskɪn] n piel roja mf.

redstart ['redstɑːt] n Orn colirrojo m real. ■ **black r.,** colirrojo m tizón.

redwing ['redwɪŋ] n Orn zorzal m alirrojo.

reduce [rɪ'djuːs] vtr **1** (make less) reducir; **to r. output,** disminuir la producción. **2** Mil (demote) degradar; **to r. an officer to the ranks,** degradar a un oficial. **3** Culin espesar, trabar; **to r. a sauce,** trabar una salsa. **4** Med recomponer; **to r. a fracture,** recomponer una fractura. **5** (force) forzar; **to r. sb to tears,** hacer llorar a algn; **he was reduced to borrowing money,** se vio en la necesidad de pedir dinero prestado.

reduced [rɪ'djuːst] adj reducido,-a.

reduction [rɪ'dʌkʃən] n (made smaller) reducción f, Com (cut) descuento m, rebaja f; (simplification) simplificación f.

redundancy [rɪ'dʌndənsɪ] n Ind despido m; **r. pay,** indemnización f por despido.

redundant [rɪ'dʌndənt] adj **1** (superfluous) redundante, superfluo,-a. **2** Ind **to be made r.,** perder el empleo; **to make sb r.,** despedir a algn.

reduplicate [rɪ'djuːplɪkeɪt] vtr reduplicar.

reduplication [rɪdjuːplɪ'keɪʃən] n reduplicación f.

redwood ['redwʊd] n Bot secuoya f.

reed [riːd] n **1** Bot caña f. **2** Mus caramillo m; **r. instruments,** instrumentos mpl de lengüeta.

reedy ['riːdɪ] adj (reedier, reediest) **1** (place) lleno,-a de cañas. **2** (sound) aflautado,-a, agudo,-a.

reeducate [riː'edjʊkeɪt] vtr reeducar.

reef [riːf] n **1** Mar arrecife m; **coral r.,** arrecife de coral. **2** Naut (of sail) rizo m; **r. knot,** nudo m de rizo.

reefer ['riːfəʳ] n **1** **r. jacket,** chaquetón m cruzado de lana. **2** sl (drugs) porro m.

reek [riːk] **I** n tufo m, mal olor m. **II** vi apestar; **he reeks of garlic,** huele a ajo que apesta.

reel [riːl] **I** n **1** (spool) bobina f, carrete m; **cotton r.,** carrete de hilo; Cin **to change reels,** cambiar de bobina. **2** Scot Mus danza f tradicional. **II** vi (stagger) tambalearse; **my head was reeling,** la cabeza me daba vueltas. ◆ **reel off** vtr soltar, recitar; **to r. off a list of insults,** soltar una retahíla de insultos; **to r. off a poem,** recitar un poema de un tirón.

re-elect [riːɪ'lekt] vtr reelegir.

re-election [riːɪ'lekʃən] n reelección f.

re-enter [riː'entəʳ] **I** vtr **1** (enter again) volver a entrar. **2** (write again) volver a apuntar. **II** vi (exam) **to r. for an exam,** presentarse a un examen por segunda vez.

re-entry [ri:'entri] *n* vuelta *f*, reingreso *m*.

re-examine [ri:ig'zæmin] *vtr* examinar de nuevo.

ref [ref] *n* 1 *Sport fam abbr of* **referee**, árbitro,-a *m,f.* 2 *Com abbr of* **reference**, referencia *f*, ref.

refectory [ri'fektəri] *n* refectorio *m*, cantina *f*.

refer [ri'fɜ:'] I *vtr (pt & pp referred)* mandar, enviar; **I was referred to a specialist,** me enviaron a un especialista; **they referred me to the manager,** me mandaron hablar con el gerente; **to r. a matter to a tribunal,** remitir un asunto a un tribunal. II *vi* 1 *(allude)* referirse, aludir; **are you referring to me?,** ¿te refieres a mí?; **the article refers to ...,** el artículo hace referencia a ... . 2 *(consult)* consultar; **to r. to one's notes,** consultar los apuntes.

referee [rəfə'ri:] I *n* 1 *Sport* árbitro,-a *m,f.* 2 *(for job application)* garante *mf*. II *vtr Sport* arbitrar.

reference ['refərəns] I *n* 1 *(mention)* referencia *f*, mención *f*; **there's no r. to it,** no se hace mención de ello; **they want to keep it for future r.,** quieren guardarlo para futuras referencias; **with r. to,** referente a, con referencia a. 2 *(in a book)* referencia *f*, nota *f*; **r. mark,** llamada *f.* 3 *(information)* de consulta. ■ **r. book,** libro *m* de consulta; **r. library,** blioteca *f* de consulta. 4 *(character report)* informe *m*, referencia *f*.

referendum [refə'rendəm] *n (pl referendums or referenda* [refə'rendə]) *Pol* referéndum *m*; **to have a r. on a matter,** convocar un referéndum sobre un asunto.

refill ['ri:fil] I *n* 1 *(replacement)* recambio *m*; carga *f.* 2 *fam* otra copa *f*. II [ri:'fil] *vtr (bottle)* rellenar; *(pen, lighter)* recargar.

refillable [ri:'filəbəl] *adj* recargable.

refine [ri'fain] *vtr* refinar.

refined [ri'faind] *adj* 1 *(purified, developed)* refinado,-a. 2 *(genteel)* fino,-a, delicado,-a.

refinement [ri'fainmənt] *n* refinamiento *m*.

refiner [ri'fainə'] *n* refinador,-a *m,f*.

refinery [ri'fainəri] *n* refinería *f*.

refining [ri'fainiŋ] *n* refinado *m*, refinación *f*.

refit ['ri:fit] I *n* reacondicionamiento *m*. II [ri:'fit] *vtr (pt & pp refitted)* reacondicionar.

reflation [ri:'fleiʃən] *n Econ* reflación *f*.

reflect [ri'flekt] I *vtr (light, sound, attitude)* reflejar; **does it r. your opinion?,** ¿refleja tu opinión?; **her face was reflected in the mirror,** su cara se reflejó en el espejo. II *vi* 1 *(think)* reflexionar; **to r. upon sth,** reflexionar *or* meditar sobre algo. 2 *(discredit)* perjudicar, decir mal de.

reflected [ri'flektid] *adj* reflejado,-a.

reflection [ri'flekʃən] *n* 1 *(indication, mirror image)* reflejo *m*. 2 *(thought)* reflexión *f*; **on r.,** pensándolo bien. 3 *(criticism)* crítica *f*; **the fact that you're unemployed is no r. on you,** el que no tengas trabajo no dice nada en contra tuya.

reflector [ri'flektə'] *n* 1 *Astron* reflector *m*. 2 *(vehicle)* catafaro *m*.

reflex ['ri:fleks] *n* reflejo *m*. ■ **r. action,** acto *m* reflejo; *Phot* **r. camera,** cámara *f* réflex.

reflexive [ri'fleksiv] *adj Ling* reflexivo,-a; **r. verb,** verbo *m* reflexivo.

reform [ri'fɔ:m] I *n* reforma *f*. II *vtr* reformar; **he is a reformed character,** se ha reformado.

reformation [refə'meiʃən] *n* reforma *f*.

reformatory [ri'fɔ:mətəri] *n* reformatorio *m*.

reformer [ri'fɔ:mə'] *n* reformador,-a *m,f*.

reformist [ri'fɔ:mist] *adj & n* reformista *(mf)*.

refractory [ri'fræktəri] *adj (person)* refractario,-a.

refrain [ri'frein] I *n Mus* estribillo *m*; *fig* lema *m*. II *vi* abstenerse **(from,** de); **please r. from smoking,** se ruega no fumar.

refresh [ri'freʃ] *vtr* refrescar; **to r. one's memory,** refrescar la memoria; **to r. oneself,** refrescarse.

refresher [ri'freʃə'] *n* **r. course,** cursillo *m* de reciclaje.

refreshing [ri'freʃiŋ] *adj* refrescante; **a r. change,** un cambio muy agradable.

refreshment [ri'freʃmənt] *n* refresco *m*.

refrigerated [ri'fridʒəreitid] *adj* refrigerado,-a.

refrigeration [rifridʒə'reiʃən] *n* refrigeración *f*.

refrigerator [ri'fridʒəreitə'] *n* nevera *f*, frigorífico *m*, refrigerador *m*.

refuel [ri:'fju:əl] *vtr & vi (pt & pp refuelled, US refueled)* repostar combustible; *fig* renovar **to r. emotions,** reavivar emociones; **to stop to r.,** hacer escala para repostar.

refuge ['refju:dʒ] *n (shelter)* refugio *m*, cobijo *m*; **to seek r.,** buscar refugio; **to take r.,** refugiarse.

refugee [refju'dʒi:] *n Pol* refugiado,-a *m,f*.

refund ['ri:fʌnd] I *n* reembolso *m*, devolución *f*; **to demand a r.,** exigir un reembolso. II [ri:'fʌnd] *vtr* reembolsar, devolver.

refurbish [ri:'fɜ:biʃ] *vtr fml (building)* redecorar.

refusal [ri'fju:zəl] *n* negativa *f*; **to have first r. on sth,** tener la primera opción en algo; **to meet with r.,** ser rechazado,-a.

refuse¹ [ri'fju:z] *vtr* 1 *(reject an offer)* rechazar; **he refused my offer of a lift,** no aceptó mi ofrecimiento de que le llevara en coche. 2 *(deny)* negar; **to r. sb sth,** negar algo a algn; **to r. permission,** negar el permiso. II *vi* negarse; **we refused to do it,** nos negamos a hacerlo; **they asked me but I refused,** me lo pidieron pero dije que no.

refuse² ['refju:s] *n* basura *f*; **r. bin,** cubo *m* de la basura; **r. collector,** basurero *m*; **r. dump,** vertedero *m* de basuras.

refutation [refju'teiʃən] *n* refutación *f*, rebatimiento *m*.

refute [ri'fju:t] *vtr* refutar, rebatir.

regain [ri'gein] *vtr* 1 *(recover)* recuperar recobrar; **to r. consciousness,** volver en sí; **to r. possession of,** recuperar la propiedad de; **to r. one's composure,** serenarse. 2 *(reach again)* llegar de nuevo.

regal ['ri:gəl] *adj* regio,-a.

regale [ri'geil] *vtr* agasajar; **they regaled us with presents,** nos agasajaron con regalos.

regalia [ri'geiliə] *npl* galas *fpl*, adornos *mpl*; **in full r.,** luciendo todas sus galas.

regard [ri'gɑ:d] I *n* 1 *(concern)* consideración *f*, respeto *m*; **to have r. for sb's feelings,** respetar los sentimientos de algn; **with** *or* **in r. to,** respecto a; **without r. to,** indiferente a. 2 *(esteem)* estima *f*, respeto *m*; **to hold sb in high r.,** tener a algn en gran estima. 3 **regards,** *(good wishes)* recuerdos *mpl*; **give him my r.,** dale recuerdos de mi parte; *(regarding)* **as r.,** respecto a. II *vtr (consider)* considerar, juzgar; **I r. it as my duty,** lo considero mi deber.

regarding [ri'gɑ:diŋ] *prep* respecto **a; r. our future ...,** respecto a nuestro futuro ... .

regardless [ri'gɑ:dlis] I *prep* a pesar de, sin tener en cuenta; **r. of the expense,** queste lo que cueste; **r. of the outcome,** pase lo que pase. II *adv* a todo coste; **to carry on r.,** seguir a todo coste.

regatta [ri'gætə] *n Naut* regata *f*.

regd *Com abbr of* **registered (trademark),** registrado,-a; *(letter)* certificado,-a.

regency ['ri:dʒənsi] *n* regencia *f*.

regenerate [ri'dʒenəreit] I *vtr* regenerar, reproducir. II *vi* regenerarse.

regeneration [ridʒenə'reiʃən] *n* regeneración *f*.

regent ['ri:dʒənt] *n* regente *mf*.

regime [rei'ʒi:m] *n Pol* régimen *m*; **the present r.,** el régimen actual.

regiment ['redʒimənt] I *n Mil* regimiento *m*; *fig* **a r. of people,** una multitud. II *vtr Mil* regimentar.

regimental [redʒi'mentəl] *adj Mil* del regimiento.

regimentals [redʒɪ'mentəlz] *npl Mil* uniforme *m sing* militar.

regimentation [redʒɪmen'teɪʃən] *n* reglamentación *f.*

region ['riːdʒən] *n* **1** región *f*, territorio *m.* **2 in the r. of,** aproximadamente.

regional ['riːdʒənəl] *adj* regional.

regionalism ['riːdʒənəlɪzəm] *n* regionalismo *m.*

register ['redʒɪstə'] I *n* **1** *(list)* registro *m*, lista *f*; **r. of births, marriage and deaths,** registro civil; **r. of voters,** censo *m* electoral; **to call the r.,** pasar lista. **2** *US Com* contador *m*; **cash r.,** caja *f* registradora. **3** *Mus* registro *m.* **4** *Ling* registro *m.* II *vtr* **1** *(record)* registrar; **to r. the birth of a child,** inscribir el na cimiento de un niño. **2** *(letter, parcel)* certificar; *(baúl)* facturar. **3** *(show)* marcar; **his face registered fear,** en su rostro se reflejaba el miedo; **the thermometer registered forty degrees centigrade,** el ter mómetro marcaba los cuarenta grados. III *vi* **1** *(enter one's name)* inscribirse, registrarse; *Univ* matricularse. **2** *fam* fijarse, sonarse; **his name didn't r. with me,** su nombre no me sonaba.

registered ['redʒɪstəd] *adj* certificado,-a. ■ **r. letter,** carta *f* certificada; **r. nurse,** enfermera *f* titulada; **r. trademark,** marca *f* registrada.

registrar [redʒɪ'strɑːʳ, 'redʒɪstrɑːʳ] *n* **1** *(record keeper)* registrador,-a *m, f.* **2** *(hospital doctor)* interno,-a *m, f.* **3** *Univ* secretario,-a *m, f* general.

registration [redʒɪ'streɪʃən] *n* **1** *(enrolment)* inscripción *f*; *Univ* matrícula *f.* **2** *(of trademark)* registro *m.* **3** *Aut* registro *m.* ■ *GB* **r. number,** matrícula *f.*

registry ['redʒɪstrɪ] *n* registro *m*; **to get married in a r. office,** casarse por lo civil. ■ **r. office,** registro *m* civil.

regress [rɪ'gres] *vi fml* retroceder.

regression [rɪ'greʃən] *n fml* retroceso *m*, regresión *f.*

regressive [rɪ'gresɪv] *adj fml* regresivo,-a.

regret [rɪ'gret] I *n* **1** *(remorse)* remordimiento *m*; *(sadness)* pesar *m.* **2 regrets,** *(excuses)* excusas *fpl*; **to send one's r.,** excusarse; *(remorse)* **to have no r.,** no arrepentirse de nada. II *vtr* *(pt & pp* **regretted)** arrepentirse de, lamentar; **she regrets having gone,** se arrepiente de haberse ido; *(in letter)* **I r. to tell you that ...,** lamento decirle que ... .

regretful [rɪ'gretful] *adj* arrepentido,-a; **to be r. about sth,** arrepentirse de algo.

regrettable [rɪ'gretəbəl] *adj* lamentable. ◆ **regrettably** *adv* lamentablemente; **r. we were late,** desgraciadamente llegamos tarde.

regroup [riː'gruːp] I *vtr* reagrupar. II *vi* reagruparse.

regular ['regjulə'] I *adj* **1** regular; **as r. as clockwork,** con una regularidad cronométrica; **at r. intervals,** a intervalos regulares; **r. pulse,** pulso regular. **2** *(usual)* usual, normal; **do you want it in the large or r. size?,** lo quiere tamaño familiar o tamaño normal?; **r. customer,** *(in shop)* cliente *mf* habitual; *(of bar)* asiduo,-a *m, f.* **3** *(permanent)* permanente; **a r. job,** un trabajo permanente. **4** *(frequent)* frecuente; **the IRA carried out r. bombings,** el IRA llevó a cabo frecuentes atentados con bombas. **5** *(even)* regular; **r. features,** facciones *fpl* regulares. **6** *Ling* regular; **r. verb,** verbo *m* regular. **7** *Mil* **r. army,** tropas *fpl* regulares. **8** *US fam* **a r. guy,** un tío simpático. II *n* **1** *(customer)* cliente *mf* habitual, asiduo,-a *m, f.* **2** *Mil* militar *m* de carrera. ◆ **regularly** *adv* regularmente, con regularidad.

regularity [regjʊ'lærɪtɪ] *n* regularidad *f.*

regularize ['regjʊləraɪz] *vtr* regularizar, normalizar.

regulate ['regjʊleɪt] *vtr* **1** *(control)* regular. **2** *(make rules)* reglamentar.

regulation [regjʊ'leɪʃən] I *n* **1** *(control)* regulación *f*, reglamentación *f.* **2** *(rule)* regla *f.* II *adj* reglamentario,-a.

regulator ['regjʊleɪtə'] *n* regulador,-a *m, f.*

regurgitate [rɪ'gɜːdʒɪteɪt] *vtr* regurgitar, devolver; *fig* repetir maquinalmente.

rehabilitate [riːə'bɪlɪteɪt] *vtr* **1** *(readapt)* rehabilitar, reeducar. **2** *(building etc)* rehabilitar, renovar.

rehabilitation [riːəbɪlɪ'teɪʃən] *n* **1** *(restore)* rehabilitación *f.* **2** *(reeducation)* rehabilitación *f*, reeducación *f.* ■ **r. centre,** centro *m* de reeducación.

rehash ['riːhæʃ] I *n* refrito *m*, refundición *f.* II [riː'hæʃ] *vtr* refundir.

rehearsal [rɪ'hɜːsəl] *n* ensayo *m.* ■ **dress r.,** ensayo general.

rehearse [rɪ'hɜːs] *vtr & vi Theat* ensayar.

reheat [riː'hiːt] *vtr* recalentar.

rehouse [riː'haʊz] *vtr* dar una nueva vivienda a.

reign [reɪn] I *n* reinado *m.* II *vi* reinar; *fig* **chaos reigned,** reinaba el caos.

reigning ['reɪnɪŋ] *adj* actual; **r. champion,** campeón *m* actual.

reimburse [riːɪm'bɜːs] *vtr fml* reembolsar.

reimbursement [riːɪm'bɜːsmənt] *n fml* reembolso *m*, pago *m.*

rein [reɪn] I *n* **1** *(for horse)* rienda *f*; *fig* **he gave free r. to his emotions,** dio rienda suelta a sus emociones; *fig* **to keep sb on a tight r.,** atar corto a algn. **2 reins,** *(for child)* andadores *mpl.*

reincarnation [riːɪnkɑː'neɪʃən] *n* reencarnación *f.*

reindeer ['reɪndɪə'] *n Zool* (*pl* **reindeer** *or* **reindeers**) reno *m.*

reinforce [riːɪn'fɔːs] *vtr* *(strengthen)* reforzar; *(support)* apoyar; *Constr* **reinforced concrete,** hormigón *m* armado.

reinforcement [riːɪn'fɔːsmənt] *n* **1** refuerzo *m*; *Constr* armazón *m.* **2** *Mil* **reinforcements,** refuerzos *mpl.*

reinstate [riːɪn'steɪt] *vtr fml* *(to job)* reincorporar; *(restore)* restaurar.

reinstatement [riːɪn'steɪtmənt] *n fml* *(to job)* reincorporación *f*, reintegración *f*; *(restoration)* restauración *f.*

reissue [riː'ɪʃuː] I *vtr* *(book, record)* reeditar; *(stamp)* volver a emitir. II *n* *(book, record)* nueva edición *f*; *(stamp)* nueva emisión *f.*

reiterate [riː'ɪtəreɪt] *vtr & vi fml* reiterar.

reiteration [riːɪtə'reɪʃən] *n fml* reiteración *f.*

reject ['riːdʒekt] I *n* **1** desecho *m.* **2** *Com* **rejects,** artículos *mpl* defectuosos. II [rɪ'dʒekt] *vtr* *(offer, proposal)* rechazar.

rejection [rɪ'dʒekʃən] *n* rechazo *m*; **to meet with r.,** ser rechazado,-a.

rejoice [rɪ'dʒɔɪs] *vi* alegrarse, regocijarse (**at, over,** de).

rejoicing [rɪ'dʒɔɪsɪŋ] *n* alegría *f*, regocijo *m*; **the r. lasted a week,** las fiestas duraron una semana.

rejoin¹ [rɪ'dʒɔɪn] *vtr* **1** *(join again)* volver a juntar. **2** *(meet again)* reencontrar.

rejoin² [rɪ'dʒɔɪn] *vtr fml* replicar.

rejoinder [rɪ'dʒɔɪndə'] *n fml* réplica *f.*

rejuvenate [rɪ'dʒuːvɪneɪt] *vtr* **1** *(regenerate)* rejuvenecer. **2** *(revitalize)* revitalizar.

rejuvenation [rɪdʒuːvɪ'neɪʃən] *n* **1** *(regeneration)* rejuvenecimiento *m.* **2** *(revitalization)* revitalización *f.*

rekindle [riː'kɪndəl] *vtr fml* volver a encender; *fig* reanimar, reavivar.

relapse [rɪ'læps] I *n* **1** *Med* recaída *f*; **to have a r.,** sufrir una recaída. **2** *fml* reincidencia *f.* II *vi* **1** *Med* recaer. **2** *fml* reincidir, recaer; **to r. into crime,** reincidir en el delito.

relate [rɪ'leɪt] I *vtr* **1** *(connect)* relacionar; **to r. two ideas,** relacionar dos ideas. **2** *(tell)* contar, relatar. II *vi* relacionarse; **I can't r. to him,** no estamos en la misma onda; **to r. to sb,** llevarse bien con algn.

related [rɪ'leɪtɪd] *adj* **1** *(linked)* relacionado,-a (**to,** con); **it is thought that this illness is r. to excess exposure to the sun,** se cree que esta enfermedad guarda, relación con la excesiva exposición al sol. **2** *(of the same family)* **to be r. to sb,** ser pariente de algn. **3** *(of same origen)* de la misma familia; **these languages are r.,** estas lenguas son de la misma familia.

relation [rɪ'leɪʃən] *n* **1** *(link)* relación *f*; **business relations,** relaciones *fpl* comerciales; **in** *or* **with r. to,** con relación a, respecto a; **it bears no r. to what we said,** no tiene nada que ver con to que dijimos. ■ **public relations,** relaciones *fpl* públicas. **2** *(family)* pariente,-a *m,f*; **she's a r. of mine,** es parienta mía.

relationship [rɪ'leɪʃənʃɪp] *n* **1** *(link)* relación *f*; **what is the r. between reading and writing?,** ¿qué relación hay entre la lectura y la ecritura? **2** *(between people)* relaciones *fpl*; **to have a good/bad r. with sb,** llevarse bien/mal con algn.

relative ['relətɪv] **I** *n* pariente,-a *m, f*; **a distant r.,** un pariente lejano. **II** *adj* **1** *(not absolute)* relativo,-a; **everything is r.,** todo es relativo. **2** *Ling* **r. pronoun,** pronombre *m* relativo; **r. clause,** oración *f* de relativo. ◆ **relatively** *adv* relativamente, bastante; **they're r. poor,** son bastante pobres.

relativity [relə'tɪvɪtɪ] *n* relatividad *f*; *Phys* **the theory of r.,** la teoría de la relatividad.

relax [rɪ'læks] **I** *vtr* **1** *(calm)* relajar. **2** *(loosen)* aflojar. **3** *(rules)* suavizar. **II** *vi* relajarse; **r.!,** ¡tranquilízate!

relaxation [ri:læk'seɪʃən] *n* **1** *(rest)* descanso *m*, relajación *f*; **methods of r.,** métodos *mpl* de relajación; **r. period,** período *m* de descanso. **2** *(of rules etc)* relajación *f*, aflojamiento *m*. **3** *(pastime)* distracción *f*; **it's my favourite r.,** es mi distracción predilecta.

relaxed [rɪ'lækst] *adj* *(calm)* relajado,-a; *(peaceful)* tranquilo,-a; **a r. atmosphere,** un ambiente desenfadado.

relaxing [rɪ'læksɪŋ] *adj* relajante; **a r. holiday,** unas vacaciones relajantes.

relay ['ri:leɪ] **I** *m* **1** relevo *m*; *Sport* **r. (race),** carrera *f* de relevos; **100 metres r.,** los 100 metros relevos; **to work in relays,** trabajar por relevos. **2** *Elec* relé *m*, repetidor *m*. **3** *Rad TV (broadcast)* retransmisión *f*. ■ **r. station,** estación *f* repetidora. **II** [rɪ'leɪ] *vtr* **1** *(pass on)* difundir, divulgar. **2** *Rad TV* retransmitir.

release [rɪ'li:s] **I** *n* **1** *(setting free)* liberación *f*, puesta *f* en libertad; *(gas)* escape *m*. **2** *Com* puesta *f* en venta. **3** *Cin* estreno *m*; **on general r.,** en todos los cines. **4** *Mus (record)* emisión *f*. **5** *Press* comunicado *m*. ■ **press r.,** comunicado *m* de prensa. **II** *vtr* **1** *(set free)* liberar, poner en libertad; *(gas)* despedir; *(feelings)* desahogar, descargar; **to r. sb from an obligation,** librar a algn de una obligación. **2** *Com* poner en venta. **3** *Cin* estrenar. **4** *Mus (record)* sacar. **5** *(let go)* soltar; **to r. the handbrake,** soltar el freno de mano; *Phot* **to r. the shutter,** disparar. **6** *(publish)* publicar.

relegate ['relɪgeɪt] *vtr* **1** relegar. **2** *Ftb* **to be relegated,** descender *or* bajar a una división inferior.

relegation [relɪ'geɪʃən] *n* **1** relegación *f*. **2** *Ftb* descenso *m*.

relent [rɪ'lent] *vi fml* ceder, aplacarse.

relentless [rɪ'lentlɪs] *adj* implacable, despiadado,-a, cruel. ◆ **relentlessly** *adv* implacablemente; **it rained r.,** llovió sin cesar.

relevance ['reləvəns] *n* relación *f*, pertinencia *f*.

relevant ['reləvənt] *adj* pertinente (**to,** a); **it is not r.,** no viene al caso; **the r. details,** los detalles pertinentes.

reliable [rɪ'laɪəbəl] *adj* **1** *(person)* de fiar, serio,-a; **he's a r. worker,** es un trabajador muy serio; **she's very r.,** es muy de fiar. **2** *(thing)* de fiar; **a r. car,** un coche seguro; **a r. source,** una fuente fidedigna. ◆ **reliably** *adv* de buena fuente; **to be r. informed that,** saber de buena fuente que.

reliability [rɪlaɪə'bɪlɪtɪ] *n* **1** *(of person)* formalidad *f*, seriedad *f*. **2** *(of thing)* seguridad *f*.

reliance [rɪ'laɪəns] *n* dependencia *f*.

reliant [rɪ'laɪənt] *adj* **to be r. on,** depender de.

relic ['relɪk] *n* **1** *Rel* reliquia *f*. **2** *(reminder of past)* vestigio *m*; recuerdo *m*. **3** **relics,** *(human remains)* restos *mpl* mortales, despojos *mpl*.

relief [rɪ'li:f] *n* **1** alivio *m*; **to breathe sigh of r.,** dar un suspiro de alivio; **to bring r. from pain,** aliviar el dolor; **what a r.!,** ¡qué alivio! **2** *(aid)* auxilio *m*, ayuda *f*. ■ **r. fund,** fondo *m* de asistencia a los necesitados. **3** *(substitute)* relevo *m*. **4** *Art* relieve *m*; **in r.,** en relieve. **5** *Geog* relieve *m*. ■ **r. map,** mapa *m* en relieve. **6** *(of city)* liberación *f*.

relieve [rɪ'li:v] *vtr* **1** *(ease)* aliviar; *(pain)* mitigar; *(monotony)* romper; **to r. sb of an obligation,** librar a algn de una obligación. **2** *(substitute)* relevar, sustituir. **3** *(city)* liberar; *euph* **to r. oneself,** hacer sus necesidades; *euph* **to r. sb of sth,** coger algo a algn.

relieved [rɪ'li:vd] *adj* aliviado,-a, tranquilizado,-a; **I'm r. to hear it,** me tranquiliza oírlo.

religion [rɪ'lɪdʒən] *n* religión *f*.

religious [rɪ'lɪdʒəs] *adj* religioso,-a. ◆ **religiously** *adv* religiosamente; *fig* **to do sth r.,** hacer algo sin faltar nunca *or* religiosamente.

relinquish [rɪ'lɪŋkwɪʃ] *vtr fml* renunciar a; **to r. one's hold on sth,** soltar algo.

relish ['relɪʃ] **I** *n* **1** *fml (enjoyment)* gusto *m*, deleite *m*; **to do sth with great r.,** deleitarse haciendo algo. **2** *Culin* condimento *m*. **II** *vtr* agradar, gustar; **I don't r. the idea,** no me agrada la idea.

relocate [ri:ləʊ'keɪt] *vtr fml* trasladar.

relocation [ri:ləʊ'keɪʃən] *n fml* traslado *m*.

reluctance [rɪ'lʌktəns] *n* desgana *f*.

reluctant [rɪ'lʌktənt] *adj* reacio,-a; **to be r. to do sth,** no estar dispuesto,-a a hacer algo; **we were r. to explain,** nos resistíamos a dar explicaciones. ◆ **reluctantly** *adv* de mala gana, a regañadientes.

rely [rɪ'laɪ] *vi (pt & pp relied)* contar (**on,** con), confiar (**on,** en); **r. on me,** confía en mí; **they relied on the money he sent,** contaban con el dinero que les mandaba.

remain [rɪ'meɪn] *vi* **1** *(stay)* permanecer, quedarse; **he remained at home,** se quedó en casa; **they remained seated,** permanecieron sentados,-as; **to r. silent,** permanecer silencioso,-a. **2** *(be left)* quedar; **it remains to be seen,** está por ver; **only one remains,** sólo queda uno. **3** *(in letters)* **I r.,** yours faithfully, le saluda atentamente. **4 remains,** *(of building)* restos *mpl*; *(of earlier civilization)* vestigios *mpl*; **human r.,** restos mortales.

remainder [rɪ'meɪndəʳ] **I** *n* **1** *(rest)* resto *m*; **the r. of the year,** el resto del año. **2** *Math* resto *m*. **II** *vtr Com* saldar.

remaining [rɪ'meɪnɪŋ] *adj* restante.

remake ['ri:meɪk] **I** *n Cin* nueva versión *f*. **II** [ri:'meɪk] *vtr (pt & pp remade)* hacer de nuevo.

remand [rɪ'mɑ:nd] **I** *vtr Jur* remitir; **remanded in custody,** en prevención; **remanded on bail,** bajo fianza. **II** *n* detención *f*; **on r.,** detenido,-a.

remark [rɪ'mɑ:k] **I** *n* comentario *m*, observación *f*; **to pass a r. about sth,** hacer una observación sobre algo. **II** *vtr* comentar, observar.

remarkable [rɪ'mɑ:kəbəl] *adj* **1** *(extraordinary)* extraordinario,-a. **2** *(strange)* curioso,-a, singular. ◆ **remarkably** *adv* extraordinariamente.

remedial [rɪ'mi:dɪəl] *adj fml* reparador,-a; *Educ* **r. classes,** clases *fpl* para niños atrasados; **r. exercises,** ejercicios correctivos.

remedy ['remɪdɪ] **I** *n fml* remedio *m*; **household r.,** remedio casero; **r. for a cold,** remedio contra un catarro. **II** *vtr (pt & pp remedied)* remediar.

remember [rɪ'membəʳ] *vtr & vi* **1** *(recall)* acordarse, recordar; **as far as I r.,** que yo recuerde; **do you r. doing it?,** ¿recuerdas haberlo hecho?; **I can't r. his name,** no me acuerdo de su nombre. **2** *(commemorate)* conmemorar; *(dead)* recordar. **3** *(send good wishes)* dar recuerdos; **r. me to her,** dale recuerdos de mi parte.

remembrance [rɪ'membrəns] *n fml* **1** *(reminiscence)* recuerdo *m*. **2** *(act)* conmemoración *f*; **in r. of,** para conmemorar. ■ **R. Day,** día *m* en que se conmemora el armisticio de 1918.

remind [rɪ'maɪnd] *vtr* recordar; **r. me to do it,** recuérdame que lo haga; **she reminds me of your sister,** me recuerda a tu hermana; **that reminds me,** ahora que me acuerdo.

reminder [rɪ'maɪndə'] *n* recordatorio *m*, aviso *m*; **to act as a r.,** recordar, servir de recordatorio.

reminisce [remɪ'nɪs] *vtr & vi* rememorar; **to r. about the past,** rememorar el pasado.

reminiscence [remɪ'nɪsəns] *n fml* memorias *fpl*.

reminiscent [remɪ'nɪsənt] *adj fml* nostálgico,-a; **to be r. of,** recordar.

remiss [rɪ'mɪs] *adj* **1** *(lack of energy)* remiso,-a. **2** *(negligent)* negligente, descuidado,-a.

remission [rɪ'mɪʃən] *n* **1** remisión *f*; **without r.,** sin remisión. **2** *Jur* perdón *m*; **to give six months r. for good conduct,** descontar seis meses de pena por buena conducta.

remit [rɪ'mɪt] **I** *vtr (pt & pp remitted) fml* **1** *(pardon)* perdonar, remitir. **2** *(send)* enviar, remitir. **3** *Jur* referir a otro tribunal. **II** ['riːmɪt] *n* informe *m*, órdenes *fpl*.

remittance [rɪ'mɪtəns] *n* **1** *(sending)* envío *m*. **2** *(payment)* giro *m*, pago *m*.

remnant ['remnənt] *n* resto *m*; *fig (trace)* vestigio *m*; **remnants of cloth,** retales *mpl*.

remold ['riːməʊld] *n US see* **remould.**

remonstrance [rɪ'mɒnstrəns] *n fml (complaint)* queja *f*; *(protest)* protesta *f*.

remonstrate ['remənstreɪt] *vi fml* protestar *(about sth,* por algo*)*; **to r. with sb,** quejarse a algn.

remorse [rɪ'mɔːs] *n fml* remordimiento *m*; **to feel r. about sth,** sentir remordimientos por algo.

remorseful [rɪ'mɔːsfʊl] *adj fml* lleno,-a de remordimiento.

remorseless [rɪ'mɔːslɪs] *adj fml* despiadado,-a, implacable.

remote [rɪ'məʊt] *adj* **1** *(far away)* remoto,-a; **r. country,** país *m* remoto. ■ **r. control,** mando *m* a distancia. **2** *(isolated)* aislado,-a, apartado,-a, remoto,-a; **r. spot,** lugar apartado. **3** *(unlikely)* improbable; **not the remotest chance,** ni la más mínima posibilidad. **4** *(distant)* distante; **r. person,** persona *f* reservada. ◆ **remotely** *adv* **1** *(vaguely)* vagamente. **2** *(distantly)* aisladamente.

remote-controlled [rɪməʊtkən'trəʊld] *adj* teledirigido,-a, por control remoto.

remoteness [rɪ'məʊtnɪs] *n* **1** *(distance)* lejanía *f*. **2** *(improbability)* improbabilidad *f*.

remould, *US* **remold** ['riːməʊld] *n Aut* neumático *m* recauchutado.

remount [riː'maʊnt] *vtr & vi* **1** *(bicycle)* volver a subir. **2** *(photo)* volver a enmarcar.

removable [rɪ'muːvəbəl] *adj* **1** *(movable)* móvil, movible. **2** *(detachable)* que se puede quitar; **r. covers,** fundas *fpl* de quita y pon.

removal [rɪ'muːvəl] *n* **1** *(moving house)* mudanza *f*, traslado *m*; **r. expenses,** gastos *mpl* de traslado; **r. van,** camión *m* de mudanzas. **2** *(getting rid of)* eliminación *f*.

remove [rɪ'muːv] **I** *vtr* **1** *(move)* quitar; **to r. an obstacle,** eliminar un obstáculo; **to r. one's coat/hat,** quitarse el abrigo/el sombrero; **to r. one's make-up,** desmaquillarse; **to r. one's name from a list,** tachar su nombre de una lista. **2** *(dismiss)* despedir; **to r. sb from his or her post,** despedir a algn. **II** *adj fml* **at one r. from,** relacionado,-a con.

removed [rɪ'muːvd] *adj* **1** **far r. from,** muy diferente de, ajeno,-a a. **2 cousin once r.,** primo,-a *m*,*f* segundo,-a.

remover [rɪ'muːvə'] *n* **make-up r.,** desmaquillador *m*; **nail varnish r.,** quitaesmalte *m*; **paint r.,** quitapinturas *m inv*; **stain r.,** quitamanchas *m inv*.

remunerate [rɪ'mjuːnəreɪt] *vtr fml* remunerar.

remuneration [rɪmjuːnə'reɪʃən] *n fml* remuneración *f*.

remunerative [rɪ'mjuːnərətɪv] *adj fml* remunerativo,-a.

renaissance [rə'neɪsəns] **I** *n* renacimiento *m*; **the R.,** el Renacimiento. **II** *adj* renacentista.

renal ['riːnəl] *adj* renal.

rename [riː'neɪm] *vtr* renombrar.

rend [rend] *vtr (pt & pp rent) (tear)* desgarrar, rasgar; *(noise)* invadir, irrumpir.

render ['rendə'] *vtr* **1** *(give)* dar, prestar; **for services rendered,** por los servicios prestados; **to r. homage to sb,** rendir homenaje a algn. **2** *(make)* hacer. **3** *Com* presentar; **to r. an account,** presentar una factura. **4** *(translate)* traducir; **rendered into Spanish,** traducido,-a al castellano. **5** *(plaster)* enlucir.

rendering ['rendərɪŋ] *n* **1** *(performance)* interpretación *f*. **2** *(translation)* traducción *f*.

rendezvous ['rɒndɪvuː] *n (pl rendezvous* ['rɒndɪvuːz]*)* **1** *(meeting)* cita *f*; **to have a r. with sb,** tener una cita con algn. **2** *(place)* lugar *m* de reunión. **II** *vi* reunirse.

rendition [ren'dɪʃən] *n* interpretación *f*.

renegade ['renɪgeɪd] *n* renegado,-a *m*,*f*.

reneg(u)e [rɪ'niːg, rɪ'neɪg] *vi fml* **1** *(break)* faltar a; **he reneged on his promise,** faltó a su promesa. **2** *Cards* renunciar.

renew [rɪ'njuː] *vtr (passport, contract)* renovar; *(talks, activity)* reanudar; **to r. talks,** reanudar las conversaciones; **with renewed vigour,** con nuevas fuerzas.

renewable [rɪ'njuːəbəl] *adj* renovable.

renewal [rɪ'njuːəl] *n (of passport, contract)* renovación *f*; *(of talks, activity)* reanudación *f*.

rennet ['renɪt] *n* cuajo *m*.

renounce [rɪ'naʊns] *vtr fml* renunciar.

renouncement [rɪ'naʊnsmənt] *n fml* renuncia *f*.

renovate ['renəveɪt] *vtr* restaurar.

renovation [renə'veɪʃən] *n* restauración *f*.

renown [rɪ'naʊn] *n* renombre *m*, fama *f*.

renowned [rɪ'naʊnd] *adj* renombrado,-a, célebre, famoso,-a.

rent [rent] **I** *n* **1** *(of building, car, TV)* alquiler *m*; **flat for r.,** se alquila piso; **how much r. do you pay?,** ¿cuánto pagas de alquiler?; **r. rebate,** devolución *f* de alquiler. **2** *(of land)* arriendo *m*. **II** *pt & pp see* **rend. III** *vtr* **1** *(building, car, TV)* alquilar. **2** *(land)* arrendar, ◆ **rent out** *vtr* alquilar.

rentable ['rentəbəl] *adj* **1** *(house etc)* alquilable. **2** *(land)* arrendable.

rental ['rentəl] **I** *n* **1** *(of house etc)* alquiler *m*. **2** *(of land)* arriendo *m*. **II** *adj* de alquiler; **r. company,** compañía *f* de alquileres.

rented ['rentɪd] *adj* **1** *(house etc)* alquilado,-a, de alquiler. **2** *(land)* arrendado,-a.

rent-free [rent'friː] **I** *adj* exento,-a de alquiler, gratuito,-a. **II** *adv* sin pagar alquiler, gratis.

renunciation [rɪnʌnsɪ'eɪʃən] *n fml* renuncia *f*.

reorder [riː'ɔːdə'] *vtr Com* pedir de nuevo, hacer un nuevo pedido de.

reorganization [riːɔːgənaɪ'zeɪʃən] *n* reorganización *f*.

reorganize [riː'ɔːgənaɪz] *vtr* reorganizar; **to r. oneself,** reorganizarse.

reorient [riː'ɔːrɪent] *vtr* reorientar; **to r. oneself,** orientarse de nuevo.

rep [rep] *fam* **1** *Com* representante *mf*. **2** *Theat* teatro *m* de repertorio.

repair [rɪ'peə'] **I** *n* reparación *f*, arreglo *m*; **in good/bad r.,** en buen/mal estado; **to be beyond r.,** no tener arreglo; **to be under r.,** estar en reparación. **II** *vtr* **1** *(gen)* arreglar; *(car)* reparar; *(clothes)* remendar; **to take sth to be repaired,** llevar algo a arreglar. **2** *(make amends)* reparar.

repairable [rɪ'peərəbəl] *adj* reparable.

reparation [repəˈreɪʃən] *n* **I** *(amends)* reparación *f.* **2 reparations,** *(compensation)* indemnización *f sing.*

repartee [repɑːˈtiː] *n* respuesta *f* ingeniosa, réplica *f* aguda.

repatriate [riːˈpætrɪeɪt] *vtr* repatriar.

repatriation [riːpætrɪˈeɪʃən] *n* repatriación *f.*

repay [riːˈpeɪ] *vtr (pt & pp repaid)* devolver; **to r. a debt,** liquidar una deuda; **to r. a kindness,** devolver un favor.

repayable [riːˈpeɪəbəl] *adj* pagadero,-a, reembolsable.

repayment [riːˈpeɪmənt] *n* pago *m,* reembolso *m,* devolución *f.*

repeal [rɪˈpiːl] *Jur* **I** *n* revocación *f,* abrogación *f.* **II** *vtr* revocar, abrogar.

repeat [rɪˈpiːt] **I** *vtr* repetir; **don't r. this to anyone,** no se lo digas a nadie; *Com* **an offer that can't be repeated,** una oferta única; **to r. oneself,** repetirse. **II** *vi fam (food)* repetir. **III** *n (repetition)* repitición *f; TV* reposición *f; Cin* reestreno *m.*

repeated [rɪˈpiːtɪd] *adj* repetido,-a. ◆ **repeatedly** *adv* repetidas veces.

repeater [rɪˈpiːtə^r] *n (arms)* arma *f* de repetición.

repel [rɪˈpel] *vtr (pt & pp repelled)* **1** *(fight off)* repeler, rechazar. **2** *(disgust)* repugnar, repeler. **3** *Tech* repeler.

repellent [rɪˈpelənt] **I** *adj* repelente. **II** *n (insect)* **r.,** loción *f or* spray *m* anti-insectos; **water-r.,** impermeable *m.*

repent [rɪˈpent] *vtr & vi* arrepentirse (de).

repentance [rɪˈpentəns] *n* arrepentimiento *m.*

repentant [rɪˈpentənt] *adj* arrepentido,-a.

repercussion [riːpəˈkʌʃən] *n* repercusión *f.*

repertoire [ˈrepətwɑː^r] *n* repertorio *m;* **she has a great r. of songs,** tiene un extenso repertorio de canciones.

repertory [ˈrepətərɪ] *n Theat* teatro *m* de repertorio.

repetition [repɪˈtɪʃən] *n* repetición *f.*

repetitious [repɪˈtɪʃəs] *adj* repetitivo,-a.

repetitive [rɪˈpetɪtɪv] *adj* reiterativo,-a, lleno,-a de repeticiones; *(work)* monótono,-a; *(rhythm)* machacón,-ona.

rephrase [riːˈfreɪz] *vtr* decir de otra manera.

replace [rɪˈpleɪs] *vtr* **1** *(put back)* volver a poner en su sitio; *Tel* **r. the receiver,** cuelgue el teléfono. **2** *(substitute)* sustituir, reemplazar; **to r. a broken glass,** reemplazar un vaso roto; **to r. one thing for another,** sustituir una cosa por otra.

replacement [rɪˈpleɪsmənt] *n* **1** *(putting back)* sustitución *f,* substitución *f,* reemplazo *m.* **2** *(person)* sustituto,-a *m, f.* substituto,-a *m, f.* **3** *(part)* pieza *f* de recambio.

replay [ˈriːpleɪ] *n Sport* repetición *f; TV* **(action) r.,** repetición de una secuencia.

replenish [rɪˈplenɪʃ] *vtr* **1** *(fill up)* rellenar **(with,** con). **2** *(stock up)* abastecer **(with,** de); **to r. stocks,** reponer las existencias.

replete [rɪˈpliːt] *adj fml* repleto,-a.

replica [ˈreplɪkə] *n* réplica *f,* copia *f.*

reply [rɪˈplaɪ] **I** *n* respuesta *f,* contestación *f; Com* **in r. to your letter,** en respuesta a su carta; **what was his r.?,** ¿cuál fue su respuesta? **II** *vi (pt & pp replied)* responder, contestar; **to r. to a letter,** contestar una carta.

report [rɪˈpɔːt] **I** *n* **1** informe *m;* **medical r.,** parte *m* médico; **monthly r.,** informe mensual; *GB* **school r.,** informe escolar; **weather r.,** boletín *m* del tiempo. **2** *(piece of news)* noticia *f.* **3** *Press Rad TV* reportaje *m* **(on,** sobre). **4** *(rumour)* rumor *m,* voz *f;* **there are reports that ...,** corre el rumor de que ... . **5** *fml (of gun)* estampido *m,* detonación *f.* **II** *vtr* **1** *(record)* informar, comunicar; **it is reported that ...,** se dice que ...; **they reported that everything was going well,** informaron de que todo iba bien. **2** *(tell)* dar parte de, denunciar; **to r. an accident/a theft to the police,** dar parte a la policía

de un accidente/denunciar un robo a la policía. **3** *Press* hacer un reportaje sobre. **4** *(complain)* denunciar, acusar; **she reported him to her teacher,** se quejó de él a su profesor. **III** *vi* **1** hacer un informe. **2** *Press* hacer un reportaje. **3** *(present oneself)* presentarse; **to r. for work,** presentarse al trabajo; **to r. sick,** coger la baja por enfermedad.

reported [rɪˈpɔːtɪd] *adj Ling* **r. speech,** estilo *m* indirecto. ◆ **reportedly** *adv fml* según se dice.

reporter [rɪˈpɔːtə^r] *n* periodista *mf,* reportero,-a *m,f.*

repose [rɪˈpəʊz] **I** *n* reposo *m.* **II** *vtr & vi* reposar, descansar.

repository [rɪˈpɒzɪtərɪ] *n* **1** *(place)* depósito *m;* **furniture r.,** guardamuebles *m inv.* **2** *(person)* depositario,-a *m,f.* **3** *(source)* fuente *f,* mina *f.*

repossess [riːpəˈzes] *vtr* recuperar, volver a tomar posesión.

repossession [riːpəˈzeʃən] *n* recuperación *f.*

reprehensible [reprɪˈhensəbəl] *adj* reprensible, censurable.

represent [reprɪˈzent] *vtr* representar, **she represented France in the Olympic Games,** representó a Francia en los Juegos Olímpicos; **what does that symbol r.?,** ¿qué representa ese símbolo?

representation [reprɪzenˈteɪʃən] *n* **1** *(gen)* representación *f.* ■ *Pol* **proportional r.,** representación *f* proporcional. **2** *fml* **representations,** queja *f sing;* **to make r. to sb about sth,** protestar a algn por algo.

representative [reprɪˈzentətɪv] **I** *adj* representativo,-a, típico,-a, característico,-a; **to be r. of,** reflejar. **II** *n* **1** representante *mf.* **2** *US Pol* representante *mf,* diputado,-a *m, f;* **House of Representatives,** Cámara *f* de Representantes.

repress [rɪˈpres] *vtr* reprimir, contener.

repressed [rɪˈprest] *adj* reprimido,-a.

repression [rɪˈpreʃən] *n* represión *f.*

repressive [rɪˈpresɪv] *adj* represivo,-a; **r. measures,** medidas represivas.

reprieve [rɪˈpriːv] **I** *n* **1** *Jur* suspensión *f* de la ejecución de sentencia; *(pardon)* indulto *m.* **2** *fig* alivio *m,* respiro *m;* **I've been given a month's r.,** me lo han aplazado un mes. **II** *vtr* **1** *Jur* suspender la ejecución de sentencia; *(pardon)* indultar. **2** *(give temporary relief)* aliviar temporalmente. **3** *(postpone)* aplazar.

reprimand [ˈreprɪmɑːnd] **I** *n* reprimenda *f,* reprensión *f.* **II** *vtr* reprender.

reprint [ˈriːprɪnt] **I** *n* reimpresión *f,* reedición *f.* **II** [riːˈprɪnt] *vtr* reimprimir.

reprisal [rɪˈpraɪzəl] *n* represalia *f;* **there were no reprisals,** no hubo represalias.

reproach [rɪˈprəʊtʃ] **I** *n fml* reproche *m;* **a look of r.,** una mirada de reproche; **above** *or* **beyond r.,** sin tacha, intachable. **II** *vtr* reprochar; **to r. oneself for sth,** reprocharse algo.

reproachful [rɪˈprəʊtʃful] *adj* reprochador,-a, reprobador,-a.

reprobate [ˈreprəʊbeɪt] *adj & n* réprobo,-a *(m, f),* libertino,-a *(m,f).*

reproduce [riːprəˈdjuːs] **I** *vtr* reproducir. **II** *vi* reproducirse, multiplicarse.

reproduction [riːprəˈdʌkʃən] *n* reproducción *f.* ■ **r. furniture,** reproducciones *fpl* de muebles antiguos.

reproductive [riːprəˈdʌktɪv] *adj* reproductor,-a; **r. organs,** órganos reproductores.

reproof [rɪˈpruːf] *n fml* reprobación *f,* censura *f.*

reprove [rɪˈpruːv] *vtr fml* reprobar, censurar.

reproving [rɪˈpruːvɪŋ] *adj fml* reprobatorio,-a.

reptile [ˈreptaɪl] *n Zool* reptil *m.*

republic [rɪˈpʌblɪk] *n* república *f.*

republican [rɪ'pʌblɪkən] *adj* & *n* republicano,-a *(m, f)*; *US Pol* **R. Party,** Partido *m* Republicano.

repudiate [rɪ'pjuːdɪeɪt] *vtr fml* **1** *(reject)* rechazar. **2** *(disown)* repudiar. **3** *(refuse to acknowledge)* negarse a reconocer.

repudiation [rɪpjuːdɪ'eɪʃən] *n* **1** *(rejection)* rechazo *m*. **2** *(disowning)* repudio *m*, repudiación *f*. **3** *(refusal to acknowledge)* repudio *m*, repudiación *f*.

repugnance [rɪ'pʌgnəns] *n* repugnancia *f*, repulsión *f*, aversión *f*.

repugnant [rɪ'pʌgnənt] *adj* repugnante, repulsivo,-a.

repulse [rɪ'pʌls] *vtr* **1** *(repel)* rechazar. **2** *(cause to retreat)* hacer retroceder a.

repulsion [rɪ'pʌlʃən] *n* **1** *(revulsion)* repulsión *f*, repugnancia *f*. **2** *(rejection)* rechazo *m*.

repulsive [rɪ'pʌlsɪv] *adj* repulsivo,-a.

reputable ['repjʊtəbəl] *adj (company etc)* acreditado,-a; *(person, institution)* de buena reputación; *(person, products)* de toda confianza. ◆ **reputably** *adv* acreditadamente.

reputation [repjʊ'teɪʃən] *n* reputación *f*, fama *f*; **to have a good r.,** tener buena reputación; **to have a r. for being a heavy drinker,** tener fama de borracho,-a.

repute [rɪ'pjuːt] *n fml* reputación *f*, fama *f*, **a singer of r.,** un cantante famoso; **to hold in r.,** tener en gran estima.

reputed [rɪ'pjuːtɪd] *adj* **1** *(supposed)* supuesto,-a; **the r. offender,** el supuesto delincuente. **2** *(considered as)* considerado,-a como; **she is r. to be the best cook in the village,** se la considera la mejor cocinera del pueblo. ◆ **reputedly** *adv* según se dice, supuestamente.

request [rɪ'kwest] **I** *n* petición *f*, solicitud *f*; **at her r.,** a petición suya; **available on r.,** disponible a petición de los interesados; **to make a r. for sth,** solicitar algo. ■ *Aut* **r. stop,** parada *f* discrecional. **II** *vtr* pedir, solicitar; *fml* **Mr and Mrs Walton r. the pleasure of your company at their daughter's wedding,** los Señores Walton tienen el honor de invitarles a la boda de su hija; *fml* **you are requested not to smoke,** se ruega no fumar.

requiem ['rekwɪəm] *n Rel* réquiem *m*. ■ **r. mass,** misa *f* de réquiem.

require [rɪ'kwaɪəʳ] *vtr* **1** *(need)* necesitar, requerir; **what do you r.?,** ¿qué necesitas?; **when required,** cuando haga falta, en caso de necesidad. **2** *(demand)* requerir, exigir, pedir; **it's a job which requires great patience,** es un trabajo que exige mucha paciencia; **we are required by law to wear seat belts,** la ley nos obliga a llevar cinturones de seguridad.

required [rɪ'kwaɪəd] *adj* necesario,-a, requerido,-a; **the r. number of words,** el número prescrito de palabras.

requirement [rɪ'kwaɪəmənt] *n* **1** *(need)* necesidad *f*. **2** *(demand)* requisito *m*; **to meet all the requirements,** satisfacer todos los requisitos.

requisite ['rekwɪzɪt] *fml* **1** *adj* requerido,-a, indispensable; *(decided beforehand)* prescrito,-a. **II** *n* requisito *m*. ■ **sports requisites,** equipo *m sing* para deporte; **travel requisites,** artículos *mpl* de viaje.

requisition [rekwɪ'zɪʃən] **I** *n* requisición *f*, requisa *f*. **II** *vtr* requisar.

reran [riː'ræn] *pt see* **rerun.**

reredos ['rɪədɒs] *n* retablo *m*.

rerun [riː'rʌn] **I** *vtr (pt* **reran;** *pp* **rerun)** *Cin* reestrenar; *TV Theat* reponer. **II** ['riːrʌn] *n Cin* reestreno *m*; *TV Theat* reposición *f*.

resale ['riːseɪl, riː'seɪl] *n* reventa *f*.

resat [riː'sæt] *pt* & *pp see* **resit.**

rescind [rɪ'sɪnd] *vtr fml Jur (contract)* rescindir; *(law)* abrogar, revocar.

rescue ['reskjuː] **I** *n* rescate *m*; **to go to sb's r.,** acudir en auxilio de algn. ■ **r. team,** equipo *m* de rescate. **II** *vtr* rescatar, salvar.

rescuer ['reskjʊəʳ] *n* rescatador,-a *m, f*, salvador,-a *m, f*.

research [rɪ'sɜːtʃ] **I** *n* investigación *f*; **to do r. on a subject,** investigar un tema. ■ **r. work,** trabajo *m* de investigación. **II** *vtr* & *vi* investigar; **to r. a book.** documentarse para escribir un libro; **to r. into smoking habits,** investigar los hábitos de los fumadores; **well researched,** bien documentado,-a.

researcher [rɪ'sɜːtʃəʳ] *n* investigador,-a *m, f*.

resemblance [rɪ'zembləns] *n* parecido *m*, semejanza *f*; **it bears no r. to cheese,** no se parece en absoluto al queso.

resemble [rɪ'zembəl] *vtr* parecerse a; **she resembles her mother,** se parece a su madre.

resent [rɪ'zent] *vtr* resentirse, ofenderse por, tomar a mal; **he resented my being there,** mi presencia le molestó; **I r. your attitude,** tu actitud me ofende.

resentful [rɪ'zentfʊl] *adj* resentido,-a, ofendido,-a.

resentment [rɪ'zentmənt] *n* resentimiento *m*; **to feel r. towards sb,** guardar rencor a algn.

reservation [rezə'veɪʃən] *n* **1** *(booking)* reserva *f*; **to make a r.,** hacer la reserva. **2** *(misgiving)* reserva *f*; **with reservations,** con ciertas reservas. **3** *(reserve)* reserva *f*; **Indian r.,** reserva *f* india.

reserve [rɪ'zɜːv] **I** *n* **1** *(gen)* reserva *f*; **reserves of food,** reservas de alimentos; **to keep sth in r.,** guardar algo de reserva. ■ **game r.,** coto *m* de caza; **natural r.,** parque *m* natural. **2** *Sport* reserva *mf*, suplente *mf*. **3** *Mil* **reserves,** reservas *fpl*. **II** *vtr* reservar; **to r. one's judgement on sth,** reservarse la opinión sobre algo; **to r. one's strength,** ahorrar fuerzas; **to r. seats,** reservar plazas; **to r. sth for later,** guardar algo para después.

reserved [rɪ'zɜːvd] *adj* reservado,-a; **all rights r.,** reservados todos los derechos.

reservist [rɪ'zɜːvɪst] *n Mil* reservista *mf*.

reservoir ['rezəvwɑːʳ] *n* **1** *(artificial lake)* embalse *m*, pantano *m*. **2** *(large supply)* reserva *f*, acumulación *f*.

reshape [riː'ʃeɪp] *vtr* rehacer; *fig* reorganizar.

reshuffle [riː'ʃʌfəl] **I** *n Pol* reorganización *f*, remodelación *f*; **cabinet r.,** reorganización del gabinete. **II** *vtr* **1** *Pol* reorganizar. **2** *Cards* volver a barajar.

reside [rɪ'zaɪd] *vi fml* **1** *(live)* residir; **to r. in London,** residir en Londres. **2** *(be)* hallar; **power resides in the unions,** los sindicatos tienen mucho poder.

residence ['rezɪdəns] *n fml (home)* residencia *f*; *(address)* domicilio *m*; *(period of time)* permanencia *f*; **to take up r.,** fijar residencia. ■ *Univ* **hall of r.,** residencia *f*.

resident ['rezɪdənt] *adj* & *n* residente *(mf)*; **to be r. in a town,** residir en una ciudad. ■ **r. population,** población *f* fija.

residential [rezɪ'denʃəl] *adj* residencial; **r. area,** barrio residencial.

residual [rɪ'zɪdjʊəl] *adj* residual.

residue ['rezɪdjuː] *n* residuo *m*.

resign [rɪ'zaɪn] **I** *vtr* **1** *(give up)* dimitir; **he resigned from the committee,** dimitió de la comisión. **2** *(accept sth unpleasant)* resignarse a; **to r. oneself to sth,** resignarse a algo. **II** *vi* dimitir, presentar la dimisión.

resignation [rezɪg'neɪʃən] *n* **1** *(from a job)* dimisión *f*; **to hand in one's r.,** presentar la dimisión. **2** *(surrender)* resignación *f*.

resigned [rɪ'zaɪnd] *adj* resignado,-a; **he's r. to his fate,** está resignado con su suerte.

resilience [rɪ'zɪlɪəns] *n* **1** *(strength)* resistencia *f*. **2** *(flexibility)* elasticidad *f*.

resilient [rɪ'zɪlɪənt] *adj* **1** *(strong)* resistente, fuerte. **2** *(flexible)* elástico,-a.

resin ['rezɪn] *n* resina *f*.

resist [rɪ'zɪst] *vtr* **I** *(not yield to)* resistir; **I couldn't r. eating another chocolate,** no pude resistir a la tentación de comer otro bombón. **2** *(oppose)* oponerse a; **to r. change,** oponerse a los cambios.

resistance [rɪ'zɪstəns] n resistencia f; **he offered no r.,** no ofreció resistencia; **her r. to illness is low,** tiene poca resistencia a las enfermedades; **to take the line of least r.,** optar por la solución más fácil.

resistant [rɪ'zɪstənt] adj resistente.

resistor [rɪ'zɪstə^r] n Elec reóstato m.

resit [ri:'sɪt] vtr (pt & pp **resat**) (an exam) volver a presentarse a.

resolute ['rezəluːt] adj resuelto,-a, decidido,-a. ◆ **resolutely** adv resueltamente, con firmeza.

resolution [rezə'luːʃən] n resolución f, decisión f, determinación f; **she showed a great deal of r.,** se mostró muy decidida; **to make/pass a r.,** tomar/aprobar una resolución.

resolve [rɪ'zɒlv] I n resolución f. II vtr resolver. III vi resolverse; **to r. to do sth,** resolverse a hacer algo.

resonance ['rezənəns] n resonancia f.

resonant ['rezənənt] adj resonante.

resort [rɪ'zɔːt] I n 1 (place) lugar m de vacaciones. ■ **seaside r.,** lugar m de veraneo; **ski r.,** estación f de esquí; **tourist r.,** centro m turístico. 2 (recourse) recurso m; **as a last r.,** como último recurso. II vi recurrir; **to r. to violence,** recurrir a la violencia.

resound [rɪ'zaʊnd] vi resonar; fig tener resonancia.

resounding [rɪ'zaʊndɪŋ] adj (of sound) resonante; (very great) importante, resonante; **a r. failure,** un fracaso total; **a r. success,** un éxito rotundo.

resource [rɪ'sɔːs] n recurso m; **natural resources,** recursos naturales; **to be left to one's own resources,** tener que apañárselas por cuenta propia.

resourceful [rɪ'sɔːsful] adj ingenioso,-a, despabilado,-a.

respect [rɪ'spekt] I n 1 (deference) respeto m; **lack of r.,** falta f de respeto; **to pay one's respects to sb,** presentar sus respetos a algn; **to show r. for sb,** respetar a algn. 2 (relation, reference) respecto m; **in that r.,** a ese respecto; **with r. to,** con referencia a. II vtr respetar; **she was respected as a teacher,** estaba bien considerada como profesora; **to r. sb's opinion,** respetar la opinión de algn. ◆ **respectively** adv respectivamente.

respectability [rɪspektə'bɪlɪtɪ] n respetabilidad f.

respectable [rɪ'spektəbəl] adj respetable; **to put on some r. clothes,** ponerse ropa decente. ◆ **respectably** adv de forma respetable; **r. dressed,** vestido,-a con decoro.

respectful [rɪ'spektful] adj respetuoso,-a. ◆ **respectfully** adv respetuosamente, con respeto.

respective [rɪ'spektɪv] adj respectivo,-a. ◆ **respectively** adv respectivamente.

respiration [respə'reɪʃən] n respiración f.

respiratory ['respərətərɪ] adj respiratorio,-a.

respite ['respaɪt] n fml 1 (rest) respiro m, tregua f; **I haven't had a moment's r.,** no he tenido ni un momento de respiro. 2 (postponement) plazo m.

resplendent [rɪ'splendənt] adj resplandeciente; **to be r.,** resplandecer.

respond [rɪ'spɒnd] vi 1 (reply) responder, contestar. 2 (react favourably) responder; Med **to r. to treatment,** responder al tratamiento.

respondent [rɪ'spɒndənt] n 1 Jur demandado,-a m,f. 2 (of questionnaire) encuestado,-a m,f.

response [rɪ'spɒns] n 1 (reply) respuesta f, contestación f; **in r. to,** en respuesta a. 2 (reaction) reacción f.

responsibility [rɪspɒnsə'bɪlɪtɪ] n responsabilidad f; **opening the shop is your r.,** te corresponde a ti abrir la tienda; **to accept r.,** asumir la responsabilidad; **to hold a position of r.,** ocupar un puesto de responsabilidad.

responsible [rɪ'spɒnsəbəl] adj responsable; **to be r. for one's actions,** hacerse responsable de sus acciones; **to be r. to sb,** tener que dar cuentas a algn, estar bajo las ordenes de algn.

responsive [rɪ'spɒnsɪv] adj sensible (**to,** a); Med **he was r. to treatment,** respondió bien al tratamiento.

responsiveness [rɪ'spɒnsɪvnɪs] n sensibilidad f.

rest[1] [rest] I n 1 (break, repose) descanso m, reposo m; **I need a r.,** necesito descansar; **to have a good r.,** descansar bien; fml **to lay sb to r.,** enterrar a algn. ■ **r. cure,** cura f de reposo; **r. home,** Med casa f de reposo; (for old people) asilo m de ancianos; US **r. room,** aseos mpl, servicios mpl. 2 (peace) tranquilidad f, sosiego m; **at r.,** (person) tranquilo,-a; (object) inmóvil; **I shan't have any r. until they phone,** no me quedaré tranquilo hasta que no llamen; **to set sb's mind at r.,** tranquilizar a algn. 3 (support) apoyo m, soporte m. 4 Mus pausa f. II vtr 1 descansar; **to r. one's legs,** descansar las piernas. 2 (lean) apoyar; **to r. a ladder against a wall,** apoyar una escalera contra una pared. III vi 1 descansar, reposar; fml **may he r. in peace,** que descanse en paz; **she's resting,** está descansando; (actor) **to be resting,** estar sin trabajo. 2 (be calm) estar tranquilo,-a, quedarse tranquilo,-a; **I won't r. until I've finished it,** no me quedaré tranquilo hasta que no lo termine. 3 Jur **the case rests on ...,** el pleito se basa en ...

rest[2] [rest] I n (remainder) **the r.,** el resto, lo demás; **I'll tell you the r. tomorrow,** mañana te contaré el resto; **the r. of the day,** el resto del día; **the r. of the girls,** las demás chicas; **the r. of us,** los demás. II vi quedar; **it doesn't r. with me,** no depende de mí; **it rests with him to decide,** le corresponde a él decidir; **r. assured that,** tenga la seguridad de que; **there the matter rests,** allí queda el asunto.

restaurant ['restərɒnt] n restaurante m. ■ Rail **r. car,** coche m restaurante.

restaurateur [restərə'tɜː^r] n fml dueño,-a m,f de un restaurante.

restful ['restful] adj descansado,-a, tranquilo,-a; **a r. holiday,** unas vacaciones tranquilas.

restitution [restɪ'tjuːʃən] n fml restitución f; **to make r.,** restituir.

restive ['restɪv] adj inquieto,-a, nervioso,-a.

restless ['restlɪs] adj agitado,-a, inquieto,-a, intranquilo,-a; **to have a r. night,** pasar una noche agitada.

restlessness ['restlɪsnɪs] n agitación f, inquietud f.

restoration [restə'reɪʃən] n 1 (giving back) devolución f, restitución f. 2 Hist **the R.,** la Restauración. 3 (repairing) restauración f.

restorative [rɪ'stɒrətɪv] adj & n reconstituyente (m).

restore [rɪ'stɔː^r] vtr 1 (give back) devolver, restituir; **to r. sth to its owner,** devolver algo a su dueño. 2 (re-establish) restablecer; **to r. order,** restablecer el orden; **to r. the monarchy,** restaurar la monarquía. 3 (repair) restaurar.

restorer [rɪ'stɔːrə^r] n 1 Art restaurador,-a m,f. 2 Hairdr **hair r.,** tónico m capilar.

restrain [rɪ'streɪn] vtr contener, controlar; **to r. one's anger,** reprimir la cólera; **to r. oneself,** contenerse.

restrained [rɪ'streɪnd] adj (emotion) contenido,-a. 2 (person) sereno,-a, dueño,-a de sí mismo,-a.

restraint [rɪ'streɪnt] n 1 (restriction) restricción f; (hindrance) traba f. 2 (moderation) moderación f; **to act with r.,** actuar con moderación; **to show r./a lack of r.,** saber/no saber dominarse.

restrict [rɪ'strɪkt] vtr restringir, limitar; **to r. oneself to two glasses of wine a day,** limitarse a dos vasos de vino al día.

restricted [rɪ'strɪktɪd] adj restringido,-a, limitado,-a; Aut **r. area,** zona f de velocidad limitada; **r. document,** documento m reservado.

restriction [rɪ'strɪkʃən] n restricción f, limitación f.

restrictive [rɪ'strɪktɪv] adj restrictivo,-a; Ind **r. practices,** prácticas restrictivas de producción.

result [rɪ'zʌlt] I n 1 (outcome) resultado m; Pol **election results,** resultados mpl de las elecciones; **without r.,** (no result) sin resultado; (unsuccessful) sin éxito. 2

(consequence) consecuencia *f*; **as a r. of,** como consecuencia de; **with the r. that ...,** así es que ... . **II** *vi* 1 resultar; **to r. from,** resultar de. **2 to r. in,** causar; **it resulted in victory,** acabó siendo una victoria.

resultant [rɪ'sʌltənt] *adj* resultante.

resume [rɪ'zjuːm] **I** *vtr (journey, work, negotiations)* reanudar; *(control)* reasumir; *(conversation)* seguir; **to r. one's seat,** volver a sentarse. **II** *vi* recomenzar, comenzar de nuevo; continuar; **we will r. at ten o'clock,** seguiremos a las diez.

résumé ['rezjʊmeɪ] *n* resumen *m*.

resumption [rɪ'zʌmpʃən] *n* reanudación *f*; continuación *f*; **on r. of work,** al reanudarse el trabajo.

resurface [riː'sɜːfɪs] **I** *vtr (roads)* rehacer el firme de. **II** *vi* 1 *(submarine)* volver a salir a la superficie. 2 *fig* resurgir, surgir de nuevo.

resurgence [riː'sɜːdʒəns] *n* resurgimiento *m*.

resurgent [rɪ'sɜːdʒənt] *adj* renaciente.

resurrect [rezə'rekt] *vtr* resucitar; **to r. old customs,** resucitar las viejas costumbres.

resurrection [rezə'rekʃən] *n* resurrección *f*; *Rel* **the R.,** la Resurrección.

resuscitate [rɪ'sʌsɪteɪt] *vtr Med* reanimar, resucitar.

resuscitation [rɪsʌsɪ'teɪʃən] *n Med* reanimación *f*, resucitación *f*.

retail ['riːteɪl] *Com* **I** *n* venta *f* al por menor *or* al detalle. ■ **r. outlet,** punto *m* de venta; **r. price,** precio *m* de venta al público. **II** *vtr* vender al por menor *or* al detalle. **III** *vi* venderse al por menor *or* al detalle; **it retails at ten pounds,** se vende a diez libras. **IV** *adv* al por menor, al detalle.

retailer ['riːteɪlə'] *n Com* detallista *mf*.

retain [rɪ'teɪn] *vtr* 1 *(keep temperature)* conservar; *(personal effects)* guardar, quedarse con; **to r. control of sth,** mantener el control sobre algo. 2 *(hold) (water etc)* retener. 3 *(remember)* recordar, acordarse de, retener; **I can't r. names,** no se me quedan los nombres en la memoria. 4 *Jur* **to r. the services of a lawyer,** contratar a un abogado.

retainer [rɪ'teɪnə'] *n* 1 *(payment)* anticipo *m* sobre los honorarios. 2 *(servant)* criado,-a *m*,*f*.

retake ['riːteɪk] **I** *n Cin (of a scene)* nueva toma *f*. **II** [riː'teɪk] *vtr (pt retook; pp retaken* [riː'teɪkən]*)* 1 *Mil* volver a tomar *or* capturar. 2 *Cin* volver a rodar *or* tomar. 3 *(exam)* presentarse a examen de recuperación.

retaliate [rɪ'tælɪeɪt] *vi* tomar represalias **(against,** contra), vengarse **(against,** de).

retaliation [rɪtælɪ'eɪʃən] *n* represalias *fpl*, venganza *f*; **in r.,** como represalia, para vengarse.

retard [rɪ'tɑːd] *vtr* retardar, retrasar.

retarded [rɪ'tɑːdɪd] *adj* atrasado,-a; **the mentally r.,** atrasados mentales.

retch [retʃ] *vi* tener náuseas, vomitar.

retell [riː'tel] *vtr (pt & pp retold)* volver a contar.

retention [rɪ'tenʃən] *n* retención *f*.

retentive [rɪ'tentɪv] *adj* retentivo,-a; **to have a r. memory,** tener buena memoria.

rethink ['riːθɪŋk] **I** *n fam* **to have a r. about sth,** volver a reflexionar sobre algo. **II** [riː'θɪŋk] *vtr (pt & pp rethought* [riː'θɔːt]*)* volver a considerar, repensar.

reticence ['retɪsəns] *n* reticencia *f*, reserva *f*.

reticent ['retɪsənt] *adj* reticente, reservado,-a.

retina ['retɪnə] *n Anat* retina *f*.

retinue ['retɪnjuː] *n* séquito *m*.

retire [rɪ'taɪə'] **I** *vtr* jubilar. **II** *vi* 1 *(stop working)* jubilarse. 2 *fml (withdraw)* retirarse; **to r. for the night,** írse a la cama, acostarse; **to r. to one's room,** retirarse a su aposento.

retired [rɪ'taɪəd] *adj* jubilado,-a.

retirement [rɪ'taɪəmənt] *n* jubilación *f*. ■ **r. age,** edad *f* de jubilarse.

retiring [rɪ'taɪərɪŋ] *adj* 1 *(reserved)* reservado,-a. 2 *(leaving)* saliente; **the r. chairwoman,** la presidenta saliente.

retold [riː'təʊld] *pt & pp see* **retell.**

retook [riː'tʊk] *pt see* **retake II.**

retort¹ [rɪ'tɔːt] **I** *n (reply)* réplica *f*. **II** *vi* replicar.

retort² [rɪ'tɔːt] *n Chem* retorta *f*.

retouch [riː'tʌtʃ] *vtr Art Phot* retocar.

retrace [rɪ'treɪs] *vtr (go back over)* volver; *(recall)* reconstruir, reconstituir; **to r. one's steps,** volver sobre sus pasos.

retract [rɪ'trækt] **I** *vtr* 1 *(draw in)* retraer, encoger; *Av (landing gear)* replegar. 2 *fml (withdraw) (a promise)* retractar, retirar. **II** *vi* 1 *(draw in)* retraerse, encoger; *Av (landing gear)* replegarse. 2 *fml (withdraw)* retractarse.

retractable [rɪ'træktəbəl] *adj (gen)* retractable, retráctil; *Av (landing gear)* replegable.

retraction [rɪtræk'ʃən] *n (of a promise, statement, etc)* retractación *f*; *Av (landing gear)* retracción *f*.

retread ['riːtred] **I** *n Aut* neumático *m* recauchutado. **II** [riː'tred] *vtr* recauchutar.

retreat [rɪ'triːt] **I** *n* 1 *Mil* retirada *f*; **to beat a hasty r.,** irse corriendo. 2 *(shelter)* refugio *m*. 3 *Rel* retiro *m*. **II** *vi* retirarse; *(danger)* refugiarse **(from,** de); *(renege)* renegar; **they retreated to a warmer climate,** se refugiaron en un clima más cálido.

retrench [rɪ'trentʃ] *fml* **I** *vtr (expenses)* reducir. **II** *vi* economizar, hacer ahorros.

retrial [riː'traɪəl] *n Jur* nuevo juicio *m*, revisión *f* del caso.

retribution [retrɪ'bjuːʃən] *n* justo castigo *m*, merecido *m*.

retrieval [rɪ'triːvəl] *n* recuperación *f*; **beyond r.,** irreparable. ■ *Comput* **information r. system,** sistema *m* para la recuperación de datos.

retrieve [rɪ'triːv] *vtr* 1 *(recover)* recuperar, recobrar; *(hunting)* cobrar; *Comput (data)* recoger. 2 *(rescue)* salvar. 3 *Ten* devolver.

retriever [rɪ'triːvə'] *n Zool* perro *m* cazador.

retroactive [retrəʊ'æktɪv] *adj fml* retroactivo,-a; **r. pay rise,** aumento *m* de sueldo con efecto retroactivo.

retrograde ['retrəʊgreɪd] *adj* retrógrado,-a; **r. step,** paso *m* hacia atrás.

retrospect ['retrəʊspekt] *n* **in r.,** retrospectivamente.

retrospective [retrəʊ'spektɪv] **I** *adj* retrospectivo,-a. **II** *n Art* exposición *f* retrospectiva Phot. ◆ **retrospectively** *adv* retrospectivamente.

return [rɪ'tɜːn] **I** *n* 1 *(coming or going back)* regreso *m*, vuelta *f*; **by r. of post,** a vuelta de correo; **in r. for,** a cambio de; **many happy returns!,** ¡felicidades!, ¡feliz cumpleaños!; **on her r.,** a su regreso; *Pol* **r. to office,** reelección *f*; **the r. to school,** la vuelta al colegio; **to pay sb a r. visit,** devolver la visita a algn. ■ *Sport* **r. match,** partido *m* de vuelta; **r. ticket,** billete *m* de ida y vuelta. 2 *(giving back)* devolución *f*; *Com (goods)* **on sale or r.,** en depósito. ■ *Pol* **election returns,** resultados *mpl* de la elección; **income tax r.,** declaración *f* de impuestos. 3 *Com (profit)* beneficio *m*, ganancia *f*; **to bring a good r.,** dar mucho beneficio. 4 *Fin (interest)* interés *m*. **II** *vtr* 1 *(give back)* devolver; *(on letter)* **'r. to sender',** 'devuélvase al remitente'; **to r. a favour/sb's love,** corresponder a un favor/al amor de algn. 2 *Pol* reelegir; **to r. sb to office,** reelegir a algn. 3 *Jur* pronunciar; **to r. a verdict,** pronunciar un veredicto; **they returned a verdict of guilty,** le declararon culpable. **III** *vi* **I** *(come or go back)* volver, regresar; **they have returned,** están de vuelta; **to r. home,** volver a casa; **to r. to work,** reanudar el trabajo. 2 *(reappear)* reaparecer.

returnable [rɪ'tɜːnəbəl] *adj (bottle)* recuperable, retornable.

reunion [riːˈjuːnjən] *n* reencuentro *m*, reunión *m*.

reunite [riːjuːˈnaɪt] I *vtr* 1 reunir. 2 *(reconcile)* reconciliar; **they were reunited,** se reconciliaron. II *vi* 1 reunirse. 2 *(reconcile)* reconciliarse.

rev [rev] *fam* I *n* Aut revolución *f*. ■ **r. counter,** cuentarrevoluciones *m inv*. II *vtr (pt & pp revved)* **to r. (up),** acelerar el motor.

Rev, Revd [rev] *abbr of* **Reverend,** Reverendo *m*, R., Rev., Revdo.

revalue [riːˈvæljuː] *vtr, US* **revaluate** [riːˈvæljʊeɪt] *vtr* revalorizar.

revamp [riːˈvæmp] *vtr* modernizar, renovar.

reveal [rɪˈviːl] *vtr* 1 *(make known) (secret, emotions)* revelar. 2 *(show)* dejar ver.

revealing [rɪˈviːlɪŋ] *adj* revelador,-a.

reveille [rɪˈvælɪ] *n Mil* diana *f*; **to sound the r.,** tocar diana.

revel [ˈrevəl] *vi (pt & pp revelled, US reveled)* disfrutar **(in,** con); **to r. in doing sth,** gozar muchísimo haciendo algo.

revelation [revəˈleɪʃən] *n* revelación *f*; **it came as a r. to me,** me sorprendió muchísimo; *Rel* **the book of Revelations,** el Apocalipsis.

reveller, *US* **reveler** [ˈrevələ*ʳ*] *n* juerguista *mf*.

revelry [ˈrevəlrɪ] *n* jarana *f*, juerga *f*.

revenge [rɪˈvendʒ] I *n* venganza *f*; **he did it in r.,** lo hizo para vengarse; **to take r. on sb for sth,** vengarse de algo en algn. II *vtr* vengar; **to be revenged,** vengarse.

revengeful [rɪˈvendʒfʊl] *adj* vengativo,-a.

revenue [ˈrevinjuː] *n* renta *f*. ■ **Inland R.,** Hacienda *f*; **public r.,** rentas públicas.

reverberate [rɪˈvɜːbəreɪt] *vi* 1 *(sound)* reverberar, resonar. 2 *(ideas, news, etc)* resonar, repercutir.

reverberation [rɪvɜːbəˈreɪʃən] *n* 1 *(sound)* resonancia *f*, reverberación *f*. 2 *(ideas, news, etc)* resonancia *f*, repercusión *f*.

revere [rɪˈvɪə*ʳ*] *vtr fml* reverenciar.

reverence [ˈrevərəns] *n* reverencia *f*.

reverend [ˈrevərənd] *Rel* I *adj* reverendo,-a. ■ **R. Mother,** reverenda madre *m*. II *n C of E* pastor *m*; *RC* padre *m*.

reverent [ˈrevərənt] *adj* reverente. ◆ **reverently** *adv* con reverencia.

reverie [ˈrevərɪ] *n* ensueño *m*.

reversal [rɪˈvɜːsəl] *n* 1 *(of an order)* inversión *f*. 2 *(change)* cambio *m* total; **r. of fortune,** revés *m* de fortuna. 3 *Jur (of a sentence)* revocación *f*.

reverse [rɪˈvɜːs] I *adj* inverso,-a; **in r. order,** en orden inverso; **the r. side,** el revés. II *n* 1 *(opposite)* **the r.,** lo contrario; **quite the r.,** todo lo contrario. 2 *(other side) (of cloth)* revés *m*; *(of coin)* cruz *f*; *(of medal)* reverso *m*; *(of page)* dorso *m*. 3 *Aut* **r. gear,** marcha *f* atrás; **to go into r.,** poner marcha atrás. III *vtr* 1 *(invert) (order)* invertir. 2 *(turn round)* volver al revés; *(picture)* dar la vuelta a. 3 *(change)* cambiar totalmente; **to r. one's policy,** cambiar radicalmente de política. 4 *Jur (a sentence)* revocar, anular. 5 *Tel* **to r. the charges,** poner una conferencia a cobro revertido. IV *vi Aut* dar marcha atrás; **to r. into a parking space,** dar marcha atrás para aparcar.

reversible [rɪˈvɜːsəbəl] *adj* 1 *(garment, cloth)* reversible. 2 *Jur (decision)* revocable.

reversion [rɪˈvɜːʃən] *n* reversión *f*.

revert [rɪˈvɜːt] 1 *fml* volver **(to,** a); **they reverted to the original agreement,** volvieron al primer acuerdo. 2 *Jur (property)* revertir.

review [rɪˈvjuː] I *n* 1 *(examination)* examen *m*, análisis *m*; **to come under r.,** ser examinado,-a. 2 *Mil* revista *f*. 3 *Press (article)* crítica *f*, reseña *f*. ■ **r. copy,** ejemplar *m* para la prensa. 4 *Press (magazine)* revista *f*. II *vtr* 1 *(examine)* examinar, analizar. 2 *Mil* **to r. the troops,** pasar revista a las tropas. 3 *Press (of book etc)* hacer una crítica de.

reviewer [rɪˈvjuːə*ʳ*] *n* crítico,-a *m*,*f*.

revile [rɪˈvaɪl] *vtr fml* injuriar, insultar.

revise [rɪˈvaɪz] *vtr (look over)* revisar; *(a text)* repasar. 2 *(change)* modificar; **to r. one's opinion,** modificar su opinión. 3 *Print (proofs)* corregir; *(text)* refundir.

revision [rɪˈvɪʒən] *n* 1 *(study)* revisión *f*. 2 *(opinion)* modificación *f*. 3 *Print (proofs)* corrección *f*; *(text)* refundición *f*.

revisionism [rɪˈvɪʒənɪzəm] *n Pol* revisionismo *m*.

revisionist [rɪˈvɪʒənɪst] *n* revisionista *mf*.

revitalize [riːˈvaɪtəlaɪz] *vtr* revivificar.

revival [rɪˈvaɪvəl] *n* 1 *(of interest)* renacimiento *m*; *(of old customs)* restablecimiento *m*; *(of a fashion)* reaparición *f*; *(of the economy)* reactivación *f*; *(of a country)* resurgimiento *m*. ■ **religious r.,** despertar *m* religioso. 2 *Theat* reestreno *m*, reposición *f*. 3 *Med* reanimación *f*, resucitación *f*.

revive [rɪˈvaɪv] I *vtr* 1 *(interest)* renovar; *(a law)* restablecer; *(a fashion)* resucitar; *(the economy)* reactivar; *(conversation)* reanimar; *(hopes)* despertar. 2 *Theat (a play)* reestrenar, reponer. 3 *Med* reanimar, resucitar. II *vi* 1 *(interest, hopes)* renacer; *(feelings)* resucitar. 2 *Med* volver en sí.

revoke [rɪˈvəʊk] I *vtr (a law)* revocar; *(permission)* suspender. II *vi Cards* renunciar.

revolt [rɪˈvəʊlt] I *n* rebelión *f*, sublevación *f*; **to rise in r.,** sublevarse, levantarse. II *vi* rebelarse, sublevarse **(against,** contra). III *vtr* repugnar, dar asco a; **tripe revolts me,** comer callos me da asco.

revolting [rɪˈvəʊltɪŋ] *adj* 1 *(in revolt)* rebelde. 2 *(disgusting)* repugnante, asqueroso,-a.

revolution [revəˈluːʃən] *n* 1 *(uprising)* revolución *f*. 2 *Tech (of wheel)* revolución *f*; *(of planet)* rotación *f*; **40 revolutions per minute,** 40 revoluciones por minuto.

revolutionary [revəˈluːʃənərɪ] *adj & n* revolucionario,-a *(m,f)*.

revolutionize [revəˈluːʃənaɪz] *vtr* revolucionar.

revolve [rɪˈvɒlv] I *vi* girar; **to r. around a planet,** girar alrededor de un planeta; *fig* **to r. around,** girar en torno a, centrarse en. II *vtr* hacer girar.

revolver [rɪˈvɒlvə*ʳ*] *n* revólver *m*.

revolving [rɪˈvɒlvɪŋ] *adj* giratorio,-a. ■ **r. door,** puerta *f* giratoria.

revue [rɪˈvjuː] *n Theat* revista *f*.

revulsion [rɪˈvʌlʃən] *n* repulsión *f*, repugnancia *f*.

reward [rɪˈwɔːd] I *n* recompensa *f*; **as a r. for,** en recompensa a *or* por. II *vtr* recompensar, premiar.

rewarding [rɪˈwɔːdɪŋ] *adj* provechoso,-a, gratificador,-a.

rewire [riːˈwaɪə*ʳ*] *vtr* **to r. a house,** poner nueva instalación eléctrica a una casa.

reword [riːˈwɜːd] *vtr* expresar con otras palabras.

rewrite [riːˈraɪt] *vtr (pt rewrote* [riːˈrəʊt]; *pp rewritten* [riːˈrɪtən]) volver a escribir, escribir de nuevo.

Reykjavik [ˈreɪkjəviːk] *n* Reikiavik.

rh [ɑːˈreɪtʃ] 1 *abbr of* **right hand,** mano *f* derecha 2 *Med abbr of* **rhesus,** rhesus *m*.

rhapsodize [ˈræpsədaɪz] *vi fml* entusiasmar; **to r. over** *or* **about,** hablar con entusiasmo de.

rhapsody [ˈræpsədɪ] *n Mus* rapsodia *f*; *fig* **to go into rhapsodies over sth,** entusiasmarse con algo.

rheostat [ˈrɪəstæt] *n Elec* reóstato *m*.

rhesus [ˈriːsəs] *n* 1 *Biol* rhesus *m*. ■ **r. factor,** factor *m* Rhesus; **R. positive/negative,** Rhesus positivo/negativo. 2 *Zool* **r. monkey,** macaco *m* de la India.

rhetoric [ˈretərɪk] *n* retórica *f*.

rhetorical [rɪˈtɒrɪkəl] *adj* retórico,-a; **r. question,** pregunta *f* sin respuesta.

rheumatism [ˈruːmətɪzəm] *n Med* reuma *m*, reumatismo *m*.

rheumatic [ruːˈmætɪk] *adj* & *n* reumático,-a *(m, f)*. ■ **r. fever,** fiebre *f* reumática.

rheumatoid [ˈruːmətɔɪd] *adj* **r. arthritis,** reuma *m* articular.

Rhine [raɪn] *n* the **R.**, el Rin.

rhinestone [ˈraɪnstəʊn] *n* piedra *f* falsa, diamante *m* de imitación.

rhinoceros [raɪˈnɒsərəs] *n (pl **rhinoceroses**)* Zool rinoceronte *m*.

rhizome [ˈraɪzəʊm] *n* Bot rizoma *m*.

Rhodes [rəʊdz] *n* Rodas.

rhododendron [rəʊdəˈdendrən] *n* Bot rododendro *m*.

rhombus [ˈrɒmbəs] *n (pl **rhombuses** or **rhombi** [ˈrɒmbaɪ])* Geom rombo *m*.

Rhone [rəʊn] *n* the **R.**, el Ródano.

rhubarb [ˈruːbɑːb] *n* Bot ruibarbo *m*.

rhyme [raɪm] *n* **1** rima *f*, *fig* **without r. or reason,** sin ton ni son. **2** *(poetry)* poesía *f*, versos *mpl*. ■ **nursery r.**, poesía *f* or canción *f* infantil. **II** *vtr* & *vi* rimar.

rhythm [ˈrɪðəm] *n* ritmo *m*. ■ *Med* **r. method,** método *m* Ogino.

rhythmic [ˈrɪðmɪk] *adj* rítmico,-a.

rib¹ [rɪb] *n* **1** Anat costilla *f*. ■ **r. cage,** caja *f* torácica. **2** Knit canalé *m*. **3** *(of umbrella)* varilla *f*. **4** Bot nervio *m*.

rib² [rɪb] *vtr fam* burlarse de; **to r. sb,** tomar el pelo a algn, burlarse de algn.

ribbed [rɪbd] *adj* Knit de canalé, acanalado,-a.

ribald [ˈrɪbəld] *adj (humour, joke)* verde, obsceno,-a; *(language)* procaz.

ribbon [ˈrɪbən] *n* cinta *f*; *(in hair, clothes, etc)* lazo *m*; **torn to ribbons,** hecho,-a jirones. ■ *Arch* **r. development,** urbanización *f* lineal.

riboflavin [raɪbəʊˈfleɪvɪn] *n* riboflavina *f*.

rice [raɪs] *n* arroz *m*. ■ **brown r.,** arroz *m* integral; **r. field,** arrozal *m*; **r. grower,** arrocero,-a *m, f*; **r. paper,** papel *m* de arroz; *Culin* **r. pudding,** arroz *m* con leche.

rich [rɪtʃ] **I** *adj (wealthy)* rico,-a; *(sumptuous)* suntuoso,-a; *(food)* rico,-a; *(heavy)* fuerte, pesado,-a; *(wine)* generoso,-a; *(soil)* fértil; *(harvest)* abundante; *(voice)* sonoro,-a; *(colour)* vivo,-a; *(perfume)* fuerte; **a r. family,** una familia adinerada; **r. in minerals,** rico,-a en minerales; **to grow r.,** hacerse rico,-a, enriquecerse. **II** **the r.** *npl* los ricos. ◆ **richly** *adv (wealthily)* ricamente; *(sumptuously)* suntuosamente; **r. deserved,** bien merecido,-a.

riches [ˈrɪtʃɪz] *npl* riquezas *fpl*.

richness [ˈrɪtʃnɪs] *n* riqueza *f*; *(sumptuousness)* suntuosidad *f*; *(of soil)* fertilidad *f*; *(abundance)* abundancia *f*; *(of voice)* sonoridad *f*; *(of colour)* viveza *f*.

rick¹ [rɪk] *n* Agr *(hay)* **r.,** almiar *m*.

rick² [rɪk] *vtr fam* torcer.

rickets [ˈrɪkɪts] *n* Med raquitismo *m*.

rickety [ˈrɪkətɪ] *adj (chair etc)* cojo,-a; *(car)* desvencijado,-a.

ricochet [ˈrɪkəʃeɪ, ˈrɪkəʃet] **I** *n* rebote *m*. **II** *vi (pt & pp **ricoche(t)ted** [ˈrɪkəʃeɪd, ˈrɪkəʃetɪd])* rebotar.

rid [rɪd] *vtr (pt & pp **rid**)* librar; **to get r. of sth,** deshacerse de algo; **to r. oneself of,** librarse de.

riddance [ˈrɪdəns] *n* liberación *f*; *fam (when sb has left)* **good r. (to bad rubbish)!,** ¡ya era hora!

ridden [ˈrɪdən] *pp see* **ride.**

riddle¹ [ˈrɪdəl] *n* **1** *(puzzle)* acertijo *m*, adivinanza *f*. **2** *(mystery)* enigma *m*.

riddle² [ˈrɪdəl] **I** *vtr* **1** acribillar; **riddled with bullets,** acribillado,-a a balazos. **2** *(sieve)* cribar. **II** *n (sieve)* criba *f*.

ride [raɪd] **I** *n* paseo *m*, vuelta *f*; **a short bus r.,** un corto trayecto en autobús; **to give a child a r. on one's back,** llevar a un niño a cuestas; **to go for a r. in the car,** dar una vuelta en el coche; *fam* **to take sb for a r.,** tomar el pelo a algn. ■ **horse r.,** paseo *m* a caballo; **train r.,** excursión *f* en tren. **II** *vtr (pt **rode**; pp **ridden**)* **1** *(bicycle)* montar; *(horse)* montar; **can you r. a bike?,** ¿sabes montar en bici?; **he rode his horse into town,** fue al pueblo a caballo. **2** *(travel over)* US recorrer, cruzar, atravesar. **III** *vi* **1** *(a horse)* montar a caballo; **can you r.?,** ¿sabes montar a caballo? **2** *(travel) (in bus, train, etc)* viajar; *fig* **our whole future is riding on it,** nuestro futuro depende de ello. **3** *Naut* flotar; **to r. at anchor,** estar anclado,-a or fondeado,-a; *fam* **let it r.,** déjalo correr. ◆ **ride out** *vtr* sobrevivir; **to r. out the storm,** capear el temporal. ◆ **ride up** *vi (sweater etc)* subirse.

rider [ˈraɪdə] *n* **1** *(of horse)* jinete *m*, amazona *f*; *(of bicycle)* ciclista *mf*; *(of moped, motorbike)* motociclista *mf*, motorista *mf*. **2** Jur cláusula *f* adicional.

ridge [rɪdʒ] *n (crest of a hill)* cresta *f*; *(hillock)* loma *f*; Agr *(between furrows)* caballón *m*; *(of roof)* caballete *m*; Anat *(of nose)* caballete *m*; Meteor **r. of high pressure,** línea *f* de alta presión.

ridicule [ˈrɪdɪkjuːl] **I** *n* burla *f*; **to expose sb to r.,** poner a algn en ridículo. **II** *vtr* burlarse de, poner en ridículo, ridiculizar.

ridiculous [rɪˈdɪkjʊləs] *adj* ridículo,-a; **to look r.,** parecer ridículo,-a. ◆ **ridiculously** *adv* **1** *(stupidly)* ridículamente; **he was r. dressed,** iba vestido de forma ridícula. **2** *fam (very)* muy; **it was r. cheap,** era baratísimo.

ridiculousness [rɪˈdɪkjʊləsnɪs] *n* ridiculez *f*, lo ridículo.

riding [ˈraɪdɪŋ] *n* equitación *f*. ■ **r. breeches/habit,** arch pantalones *mpl*/traje *m* de montar; **r. school,** escuela *f* hípica; **r. stables,** picadero *m*.

rife [raɪf] *adj fml* abundante; **rumour is r. that ...,** corre la voz de que ...; **to be r. with,** abundar en, estar lleno,-a de.

riffraff [ˈrɪfræf] *n fam* chusma *f*, gentuza *f*.

rifle¹ [ˈraɪfəl] *n* fusil *m*, rifle *m*. ■ **r. range,** campo *m* de tiro.

rifle² [ˈraɪfəl] **I** *vtr* saquear, desvalijar; *(pockets)* vaciar. **II** *vi (search)* echar un vistazo **(through,** a).

rift [rɪft] *n* **1** *(crack)* grieta *f*, fisura *f*; Geol *(fault)* falla *f*. **2** *fig (in friendship)* ruptura *f*; Pol *(in party)* escisión *f*; *(quarrel)* desavenencia *f*.

rig [rɪg] **I** *n* **1** Naut aparejo *m*. **2** Petrol *(oil)* **r.,** *(onshore)* torre *f* de perforación; *(offshore)* plataforma *f* petrolífera. **3** *(dress)* atuendo *m*. **II** *vtr (pt & pp **rigged**)* **1** Naut *(a boat)* aparejar. **2** *(manipulate)* amañar; **to r. an election,** amañar unas elecciones; Box **the fight was rigged,** hubo tongo en el combate. ◆ **rig out** *vtr fam* vestir, ataviar. ◆ **rig up** *vtr* improvisar; **they rigged up a shelter,** improvisaron un refugio.

rigging [ˈrɪgɪŋ] *n* Naut aparejo *m*, jarcia *f*.

right [raɪt] **I** *adj* **1** *(not left)* derecho,-a; **I'd give my r. arm to do that,** daría una mano por hacerlo; **the r. hand,** la mano derecha. **2** *(correct)* correcto,-a, bueno,-a; **all r.,** de acuerdo; **r.?,** ¿vale?; **that's r.,** eso es; **the r. answer,** la respuesta correcta; **the r. word,** la palabra justa; **to stay on the r. side of sb,** no llevarle la contraria a algn; *fam* **she's not r. in the head,** no está bien de la cabeza. **3** *(true)* cierto,-a, verdad; **is that r.?,** ¿es cierto?; **to be r.,** tener razón. **4** *(suitable)* adecuado,-a; **the r. time,** el momento oportuno. **5** *(proper)* apropiado,-a. **6** *fam (healthy)* bien; **I don't feel r.,** no me encuentro bien; **to feel as r. as rain,** encontrarse la mar de bien. **7** *(exact)* exacto,-a; **have you got the r. time?,** ¿tiene la hora exacta? **8** *fam (complete)* auténtico,-a, verdadero,-a, completo,-a; **it's a r. muddle,** es un auténtico lío. **9** *(in order)* en orden, ordenado,-a. **10** Geom **r. angle,** ángulo recto. **II** *n* **1** *(right side)* derecha *f*; Aut **keep to the r.,** circulen por la derecha. **2** *(right hand)* mano *f* derecha. **3** Pol **the R.,** la derecha. **4** *(lawful claim)* derecho *m*; **in one's own r.,** por derecho propio; **r. of way,** *(across land)* derecho *m* de paso; *(on roads)* prioridad *f*; **to be within one's rights,** estar en su derecho; **what r. have you to do that?,** ¿con qué derecho haces eso? ■ **civil**

rights, derechos *mpl* civiles; **women's rights,** derechos de la mujer. **5 r. and wrong,** el bien y el mal. III *adv* **1** *(correctly)* bien; **do it r.,** hazlo bien; **if I remember r.,** si mal no recuerdo; **it's just r.,** es justo lo que hace falta; **it serves you r.,** lo tienes bien merecido; **nothing is going r.,** todo sale mal; **to treat sb r.,** tratar bien a algn. **2** *(immediately)* inmediatamente; **I'll be r. back,** en seguida vuelvo; **I'll be r. over,** en seguida estoy ahí; **r. after lunch,** justo después de comer; **r. away,** en seguida. **3** *(to the right)* a la derecha; *Mil* **eyes r.!,** ¡vista a la derecha!; **r. and left,** a diestro y siniestro; **to turn r.,** girar a la derecha. **4** *(precisely)* directamente, derecho; **go r. on,** sigue recto; **r. at the front,** delante de todo; **r. at the top,** en todo lo alto; **r. in the middle,** en pleno centro; **r. to the end,** hasta el final. **5** *Rel* **the R. Reverend,** el reverendísimo. IV *vtr* **1** *(correct)* corregir; **to r. a wrong,** enmendar un error. **2** *Naut (put straight)* enderezar; **it righted itself,** se enderezó.

righteous ['raɪtʃəs] *adj (upright)* recto,-a; *(honest)* honrado,-a.

righteousness ['raɪtʃəsnɪs] *n* rectitud *f*, honradez *f*.

rightful ['raɪtful] *adj* legítimo,-a.

right-hand ['raɪthænd] *adj* derecho,-a; *Aut* **r.-h. drive,** conducción por la derecha; **r.-h. side,** lado derecho; *fam* **r.-h. man,** brazo derecho.

right-handed [raɪt'hændɪd] *adj (person)* que usa la mano derecha; *(tool)* para la mano derecha.

rightist ['raɪtɪst] *Pol* I *adj* de derechas, derechista. II *n* derechista *mf*.

rightly ['raɪtlɪ] *adv* debidamente; **and r. so,** y con razón; **r. or wrongly,** con razón o sin ella.

right-minded [raɪt'maɪndɪd] *adj* recto,-a y honrado,-a.

rightness ['raɪtnɪs] *n* **1** *(accuracy)* exactitud *f*. **2** *(honesty)* rectitud *f*, honradez *f*. **3** *(fairness)* justicia *f*.

right-wing ['raɪtwɪŋ] *adj Pol* de derechas, derechista.

right-winger [raɪt'wɪŋə'] *n Pol* derechista *mf*.

rigid ['rɪdʒɪd] *adj* rígido,-a, inflexible; **r. discipline,** disciplina rigurosa; **to have r. ideas,** tener unas ideas muy fijas. ◆ **rigidly** *adv* rígidamente.

rigidity [rɪ'dʒɪdɪtɪ] *n* rigidez *f*, inflexibilidad *f*.

rigmarole ['rɪgmərəʊl] *n fam* galimatías *m inv*; *form* **filling is a r.,** rellenar formularios es un rollo.

rigorous ['rɪgərəs] *adj* riguroso,-a. ◆ **rigorously** *adv* rigurosamente, severamente.

rigour, *US* **rigor** ['rɪgə'] *n* rigor *m*, severidad *f*.

rig-out ['rɪgaʊt] *n fam* atuendo *m*.

rile [raɪl] *vtr fam* irritar, sacar de quicio, poner nervioso,-a; **her shouting riles me,** sus gritos me ponen nervioso,-a.

rim [rɪm] *n (edge)* borde *m*; *(of wheel)* llanta *f*; *(of spectacles)* montura *f*.

rime¹ [raɪm] *n Lit* escarcha *f*.

rime² [raɪm] *n see* **rhyme.**

rind [raɪnd] *n (de fruta, queso)* corteza *f*.

ring¹ [rɪŋ] I *n* **1** *(sound of bell)* toque *m*, repique *m*, tañido *m*; *(of doorbell)* timbre *m*; *(of alarm clock)* timbre *m*; **there was a r. at the door,** llamaron a la puerta; *fig* **it has a nice r. about it,** suena bien. **2** *Tel (call)* llamada *f*; **to give sb a r.,** llamar por teléfono a algn. II *vtr (pt rang; pp rung)* **1** *(bell)* tocar; *fig* **it rings a bell,** me suena; *fig* **to r. true,** parecer verdad. **2** *Tel* llamar por teléfono, telefonear. III *vi* **1** *(bell etc)* sonar; **the telephone rang,** sonó el teléfono. **2** *(ears)* zumbar. **3** *(call)* llamar; **to r. for sb,** llamar a algn; **to r. for the lift,** llamar el ascensor. ◆ **ring back** *vtr Tel* volver a llamar. ◆ **ring in** *vi Tel* llamar (al lugar de trabajo). ◆ **ring off** *vi Tel* colgar. ◆ **ring out** *vi* resonar. ◆ **ring up** *vtr* **1** *fam Tel* llamar por teléfono a. **2** *(on a cash register)* teclear las cifras.

ring² [rɪŋ] I *n* **1** *(metal hoop)* aro *m*. ◆ **curtain r.,** anilla *f*; **key r.,** llavero *m*; **napkin r.,** servilletero *m*; **r. binder,** carpeta *f* de anillas. **2** *(for finger)* anillo *m*, sortija *f*. ▪

diamond r., sortija *f* de diamantes; **r. finger,** dedo *m* anular. **3** *(circle)* círculo *m*; **dark rings under the eyes,** ojeras *fpl*; *fig* **to run rings round sb,** dar cien vueltas a algn. ▪ *Aut* **r. road,** carretera *f* de circunvalación, ronda *f*. **4** *Gymn* **rings,** anillas *fpl*. **5** *(group of people)* corro *m*, grupo *m*; *(of spies)* red *f*; *(of thieves)* banda *f*; **to stand in a r.,** hacer un corro. **6** *(arena etc)* pista *f*; *Box* ring *m*, cuadrilátero *m*; *(for bullfights)* ruedo *m*. ▪ **circus r.,** pista *f* del circo. II *vtr (pt & pp ringed)* **1** *(bird, animal)* anillar. **2** *(surround)* rodear.

ringing ['rɪŋɪŋ] *n (of bell)* toque *m*, repique *m*, tañido *m*; *(of doorbell)* toque *m* de timbre; *(in ears)* zumbido *m*; *Tel* **r. tone,** señal *f* de llamada.

ringleader ['rɪŋliːdə'] *n* cabecilla *mf*.

ringlet ['rɪŋlɪt] *n* tirabuzón *m*, rizo *m*.

ringmaster ['rɪŋmɑːstə'] *n* maestro *m* de ceremonias.

ringside ['rɪŋsaɪd] I *n* primera fila *f*. II *adj* de primera fila.

ringworm ['rɪŋwɜːm] *n Med* tiña *f*.

rink [rɪŋk] *n Sport* pista *f*. ▪ **ice (skating) r.,** pista *f* de hielo; **roller skating r.,** pista *f* de patinaje.

rinse [rɪns] I *n* **1** *(of clothes, hair)* aclarado *m*; *(of dishes)* enjuague *m*. **2** *Hairdr (tint)* reflejo *m*; **blue r.,** reflejos *mpl* azules. II *vtr* **1** *gen* aclarar *(out, -)*; *(the dishes)* enjuagar; **to r. out one's mouth,** enjuagarse la boca. **2** *Hairdr (tint)* **to r. one's hair,** dar reflejos a su pelo.

riot ['raɪət] I *n* **1** disturbio *m*, motín *m*; **to run r.,** desmandarse; *fam* **to read the r. act to sb,** echar un rapapolvo a algn. ▪ **race riots,** disturbios *mpl* raciales; **r. police,** policía *f* antidisturbios. **2** *fig* profusión *f*; **a r. of colour,** una profusión de colores. II *vi* amotinarse.

rioter ['raɪətə'] *n* amotinado,-a *m,f*.

riotous ['raɪətəs] *adj* **1** amotinado,-a. **2** *(noisy)* ruidoso,-a, bullicioso,-a. **3** *(unrestrained)* desenfrenado,-a; **a r. success,** un éxito clamoroso; **r. living,** vida desenfrenada.

rip [rɪp] I *n (tear)* rasgón *m*, desgarrón *m*. II *vtr (pt & pp ripped)* rasgar, desgarrar; **to r. a letter open,** abrir un sobre desgarrándolo; **to r. one's trousers,** hacerse un siete en el pantalón. III *vi* **1** rasgarse, desgarrarse. **2** *fam* **to let r.,** reventar de cólera; **let it r.!,** ¡dale al gas! ◆ **rip off** *vtr* **1** *(buttons etc)* arrancar. **2** *fam* **to r. sb off,** timar a algn. ◆ **rip up** *vtr* hacer pedazos de.

RIP [ɑːraɪ'piː] *abbr of* **requiescat** *or* **requiescant in pace** *(rest in peace),* en paz descanse, E.P.D.

ripcord ['rɪpkɔːd] *n (of parachute)* cuerda *f* de apertura.

ripe [raɪp] *adj* **1** maduro,-a; *fam (language)* verde; **a r. old age,** una edad avanzada. **2** *(ready)* preparado,-a, listo,-a; **the time is r.,** es el momento oportuno.

ripen ['raɪpən] *vtr & vi* madurar.

ripeness ['raɪpnɪs] *n* madurez *f*.

rip-off ['rɪpɒf] *n fam* timo *m*; **it's been a real r.-o.,** nos han clavado de verdad.

riposte ['rɪpɒst] I *n lit* **1** respuesta *f* aguda. **2** *Fenc* respuesta *f*. II *vi* lit responder, replicar.

ripper ['rɪpə'] *n fam* destripador,-a *m,f*; **Jack the R.,** Jack el Destripador.

ripple ['rɪpəl] I *n* **1** *(on water)* onda *f*; *(fabric etc)* onda *f*, ondulación *f*. **2** *(sound)* murmullo *m*. **3** *(bodily sensation)* estremecimiento *m*. II *vtr* **1** *(water)* ondular, rizar. III *vi* **1** *(water)* ondularse, rizarse. **2** *(stream)* murmurar. **3** *(applause)* extenderse.

rise [raɪz] I *n* **1** *(of slope, hill)* cuesta *f*, subida *f*. **2** *(of waters)* crecida *f*. **3** *(in status)* subida *f*; **his r. to fame was sudden,** se hizo famoso en un abrir y cerrar de ojos; **the r. to power,** el ascenso al poder. **4** *(in prices, temperature)* subida *f*; *(of wages)* aumento *m*; **to be on the r.,** estar subiendo. **6** *(in sound)* aumento *m*. **6** **to give r. to,** ocasionar, provocar, dar lugar a. II *vi (pt rose; pp risen* ['rɪzən]*)* **1** *(mountain, land)* elevarse. **2** *(waters)* crecer; *(in level)* subir; *(river)* nacer; *(tide)* subir; *(wind)* levantarse. **3** *(sun, moon)* salir. **4** *(from death)* resucitar. **5** *(voice)* alzarse, levantarse. **6** *(in rank)* ascender. **7** *(prices, temperature)* subir; *(wages)* aumentar. **8** *Theat (curtain)* subir. **9** *Culin (dough)* leudarse, fermentar; *(in oven)* subir. **10** *(from bed)* levantarse. **11** *(stand up)* levantarse, ponerse de pie; *fig (city, building)* erguirse, levantarse. **12** *(meeting, court)* levantarse; **the court rises at three,** la sesión se levanta a las tres. **13** *(feelings, emotions)* crecer, aumentar. **14 to r. to a challenge,** aceptar un reto; **to r. to the occasion,** ponerse a la altura de las circunstancias. ◆ **rise above** *vi (be unaffected by)* estar por encima de. ◆ **rise up** *vi* **1** *(feelings)* crecer, aumentar. **2** *(rebel)* rebelarse, sublevarse.

riser ['raɪzə^r] *n* **1 early r.,** madrugador,-a *m, f.* **2** *Tech (chair)* contrahuella *f.*

risible ['rɪzɪbəl] *adj fml* ridículo,-a.

rising ['raɪzɪŋ] **I** *adj* **1** *(sun)* naciente. **2** *(tide)* creciente. **3** *(prices)* creciente, en aumento. **4** *(generation)* nuevo,-a. **5** *(age)* cercano,-a; **John is r. five,** John va para los cinco años. **II** *n* **1** *(of sun)* salida *f.* ■ *Constr* **r. damp,** humedad *f.* **2** *(rebellion)* levantamiento *m.*

risk [rɪsk] **I** *n* riesgo *m*; **at r.,** en peligro; **at your own r.,** por su cuenta y riesgo; **it's not worth the r.,** no merece la pena arriesgarse; **to take risks,** arriesgarse. **II** *vtr* arriesgar, arriesgarse; **I'll r. it,** correré el riesgo; **to r. everything,** jugarse el todo por el todo; **to r. failure,** exponerse al fracaso; *fam* **to r. one's neck,** jugarse el tipo.

risky ['rɪskɪ] *adj (riskier, riskiest)* arriesgado,-a, peligroso,-a.

risotto [rɪs'zɒtəʊ] *n Culin* risotto *m.*

risqué ['rɪskeɪ] *adj* atrevido,-a; *(joke)* picante.

rite [raɪt] *n* rito *m*; *Rel* **the last rites,** los últimos sacramentos, la extremaunción.

ritual ['rɪtjʊəl] *adj & n* ritual *(m).*

ritzy ['rɪtsɪ] *adj (ritzier, ritziest) fam* lujoso,-a, de película.

rival ['raɪvəl] **I** *adj & n* rival *(m, f)*, competidor,-a *(m, f).* **II** *vtr (pt & pp rivalled, US rivaled) (compete with)* rivalizar con, competir con; *(match)* alcanzar.

rivalry ['raɪvəlrɪ] *n* rivalidad *f*, competencia *f.*

river ['rɪvə^r] *n* río *m*; **down/up r.,** río abajo/arriba; **r. traffic,** navegación *f* fluvial; *fig* **rivers of blood,** ríos de sangre.

river-bank ['rɪvəbæŋk] *n* orilla *f*, ribera *f.*

river-bed ['rɪvəbed] *n* lecho *m.*

riverside ['rɪvəsaɪd] *n* orilla *f*, ribera *f*; **r. restaurant,** restaurante *m* al lado del río.

rivet ['rɪvɪt] **I** *n Tech* remache *m*, roblón *m.* **II** *vtr Tech* remachar, roblonar; *fig* fascinar, cautivar.

riveting ['rɪvɪtɪŋ] *adj fig* fascinante.

rly *abbr of* **railway,** ferrocarril *m*, FC.

RM [ɑː'em] *GB Naut abbr of* **Royal Marines,** Infantería *f sing* Real de Marina.

rm *abbr of* **room,** habitación *f*, Hab.

RN [ɑː'en] **1** *US abbr of* **registered nurse,** enfermera *f* diplomada. **2** *GB Mil abbr of* **Royal Navy,** Armada *f* Real.

RNIB [ɑːrenaɪ'biː] *GB abbr of* **Royal National Institute for the Blind,** ≈ Organización *f* Nacional de Ciegos Españoles, ONCE *f.*

roach[1] [rəʊtʃ] *n (fish)* pardilla *f.*

roach[2] [rəʊtʃ] *n* **1** *fam Ent* cucaracha *f.* **2** *sl (drugs) (filter)* colilla *f* de un porro.

road [rəʊd] **I** *n* **1** carretera *f*; **A r.,** carretera nacional; **B r.,** carretera secundaria; **main r.,** carretera principal; **r. accident,** accidente *m* de tráfico; **'r. up',** 'obras' *fpl*; *fam* **my car is off the r.,** tengo el coche averiado; *fam fig* **to have one for the r.,** tomar la espuela *or* la última copa. ■ **r. haulage,** transporte *m* por carretera; **r. safety,** seguridad *f* vial *or* en carretera; **r. sign,** señal *f* de tráfico; **r. works,** obras *fpl.* **2** *(street)* calle *f*; **Peterloo R.,** la calle Peterloo; **to cross the r.,** cruzar la calle. **3** *(way)* camino *m*; *fig* **on the r. to recovery,** en vías de recuperación; *fam* **get out of my r.!,** ¡quítate de en medio!

roadblock ['rəʊdblɒk] *n* control *m* policial.

roadhog ['rəʊdhɒg] *n Aut fam* dominguero,-a *m, f.*

roadhouse ['rəʊdhaʊs] *n dated* bar *m* de carretera.

roadroller ['rəʊdrəʊlə^r] *n* apisonadora *f.*

roadside ['rəʊdsaɪd] *n* borde *m* de la carretera; **r. restaurant/café,** restaurante *m*/cafetería *m* de carretera.

roadway ['rəʊdweɪ] *n* calzada *f.*

roadworthy ['rəʊdwɜːðɪ] *adj Aut (vehicle)* en buen estado.

roam [rəʊm] **I** *vtr* vagar por, rondar. **II** *vi* vagar, errar.

roaming ['rəʊmɪŋ] *adj* vagabundo,-a, errante.

roan [rəʊn] *n Zool* caballo *m* ruano.

roar [rɔː^r] **I** *n (of lion)* rugido *m*; *(of bull, sea, wind)* bramido *m*; *(of crowd)* clamor *m.* **II** *vi (lion, crowd)* rugir; *(bull, sea, wind)* bramar; *(crowd)* clamar; *fig* **to r. with laughter,** reírse a carcajadas.

roaring ['rɔːrɪŋ] *adj (lion)* rugiente; *(fire)* espectacular; *fam* **a r. success,** un éxito clamoroso; *fam fig* **to do a r. trade,** hacer un negocio redondo.

roast [rəʊst] **I** *adj (meat)* asado,-a; **r. beef,** rosbif *m.* **II** *n Culin* asado *m.* **III** *vtr (meat)* asar; *(coffee)* tostar, torrefactar; *(nuts, beans, fruits)* tostar. **IV** *vi* asarse; *fam fig* **I'm roasting,** me aso de calor.

roasted ['rəʊstɪd] *adj Culin (coffee)* tostado,-a, torrefacto,-a; *(nuts, beans, fruit)* tostado,-a.

roasting ['rəʊstɪŋ] **I** *adj* abrasador,-a. **II** *n* **1** *(of meat)* asado *m*; *(of coffee)* tostado *m*, torrefacción *f*; *(nuts, beans, fruit)* tostada *m.* **2** *fam fig* bronca *f*; **to give sb a r.,** echar un rapapolvo *or* una bronca a algn.

rob [rɒb] *vtr & vi (pt & pp robbed)* robar; **to r. a bank,** atracar un banco; *fam* **we were robbed!,** ¡nos robaron el partido!

robber ['rɒbə^r] *n* ladrón,-a *m, f*; **bank r.,** atracador,-a *m, f.*

robbery ['rɒbərɪ] *n* robo *m*; **to commit a r.,** cometer un robo. ■ **armed r.,** robo *m* a mano armada.

robe [rəʊb] **I** *n* **1** *(ceremonial)* toga *f.* **2** *(dressing gown)* bata *f.* ■ **bath r.,** albornoz *m.* **II** *vi fml* llevar, ir vestido,-a. **III** *vtr fml* vestir(se).

robin ['rɒbɪn] *n Orn* petirrojo *m*; **R. Hood,** Robín *m* de los bosques.

robinia [rə'bɪnɪə] *n Bot* acacia *f* falsa, robinia *f.*

robot ['rəʊbɒt] *n* robot *m.*

robotic [rəʊ'bɒtɪk] *adj* robótico,-a.

robotics [rəʊ'bɒtɪks] *n sing* robótica *f.*

robust [rəʊ'bʌst] *adj (strong, sturdy)* robusto,-a; *(strong, energetic)* fuerte.

rock [rɒk] **I** *n* **1** roca *f*; **the R. (of Gibraltar),** el Peñón (de Gibraltar); *fig* **r. solid,** sólido como una roca; *fig (marriage etc)* **to be on the rocks,** estar a punto de fracasar; *fam fig* **whisky on the rocks,** whisky *m* con hielo. ■ **r. face,** vertiente *f* rocosa; **r. garden,** jardín *m* de rocas; *(fish)* **r. salmon,** lija *f.* **2** *US (stone)* piedra *f.* **3** *(sweet)* **stick of r.,** barra *f* de caramelo. ■ **r. candy,** azúcar *m* candi. **4** *Mus* rock *m*, música *f* rock; **r. and roll,** rock and roll *m.* **II** *vtr* **1** *(chair)* mecer; *(baby)* acunar. **2** *(shake)* sacudir, hacer temblar; *fig* **to r. the boat,** crear problemas. **III** *vi* **1** *(move to and fro)* mecerse, balancearse. **2** *(shake)* temblar, vibrar.

rock-bottom [rɒk'bɒtəm] *adj* bajísimo,-a; **r.-b. prices,** precios *mpl* regalados.

rock-climber ['rɒkklaɪmə^r] *n* escalador,-a *m, f*, alpinista *mf.*

rock-climbing ['rɒkklaɪmɪŋ] *n* escalada *f*, alpinismo *m.*

rocker ['rɒkə^r] *n* **1** *Mech* balancín *m.* **2** *(rocking-chair)* mecedora *f.* **3** *Mus* roquero,-a *m, f.* **4** *fam* **to be off one's r.,** estar mal de la cabeza, estar chalado,-a.

rockery ['rɒkərɪ] *n* jardín *m* de rocas.

rocket ['rɒkɪt] **I** *n* cohete *m*; *fam fig* **to give sb a r.,** echar una bronca a algn. ■ **r. launcher,** lanzacohetes *m inv.* **II** *vi fam (prices)* aumentar enormemente; *fig* **to r. to fame,** hacerse famoso,-a de la noche a la mañana.

rock-hard ['rɒkhɑːd] *adj* (muy) duro,-a.

Rockies ['rɒkɪz] *n* (Montañas *fpl*) Rocosas *fpl*.

rocking-chair ['rɒkɪŋtʃeəʳ] *n* mecedora *f*.

rocking-horse ['rɒkɪŋhɔːs] *n* caballito *m* de balancín.

rock'n'roll [rɒkən'rəʊl] *n Mus* rock and roll *m*.

rocky ['rɒkɪ] *adj* (*rockier, rockiest*) rocoso,-a; *fam fig* (*unsteady*) bamboleante; **the R. Mountains**, las Montañas Rocosas; *fam fig* **a r. government**, un gobierno débil.

rod [rɒd] *n* **1** (*of metal*) barra *f*; (*stick*) vara *f*. ■ **fishing r.**, caña *f* de pescar. **2** (*symbol of authority*) vara *f*; *fig* **to rule with a r. of iron**, mandar con mano de hierro.

rode [rəʊd] *pt see* **ride**.

rodent ['rəʊdənt] *n Zool* roedor *m*.

rodeo ['rəʊdɪəʊ] *n* rodeo *m*.

roe[1] [rəʊ] *n* (*pl* **roe** *or* **roes**) *Zool* **r.** (**deer**), corzo,-a *m,f*.

roe[2] [rəʊ] *n* (*pl* **roe**) (*fish eggs*) hueva *f*.

roebuck ['rəʊbʌk] *n Zool* corzo *m*.

roger ['rɒdʒəʳ] *interj Rad* ¡recibido!

rogue [rəʊg] *n pej* **1** granuja *m*, pícaro *m*; (*criminal*) delincuente *mf*. **2** (*loner*) solitario,-a *m,f*. ■ **r. elephant**, elefante *m* solitario.

roguish ['rəʊgɪʃ] *adj pej* pícaro,-a, pillo,-a.

role *n*, **rôle** [rəʊl] *n* **1** *Cin Theat* papel *m*; **leading r.**, papel principal; **supporting r.**, papel secundario. **2** (*in life*) papel *m*, función *f*; **to play a r.**, desempeñar un papel.

role-playing ['rəʊlpleɪɪŋ] *n* imitación *f*.

roll [rəʊl] **I** *n* **1** rollo *m*; **r. of banknotes**, fajo *m* de billetes; **toilet r.**, rollo de papel higiénico; *fam fig* **rolls of fat**, michelines *mpl*. **2** *Culin* (**bread**) **r.**, bollo *m*. ■ **ham r.**, bocadillo *m* de jamón; **sausage r.**, salchicha *f* empanada; **swiss r.**, brazo *m* de gitano. **3** (*list of names*) lista *f*, nómina *f*; (*register*) registro *m*; **to call the r.**, pasar lista. ■ **electoral r.**, censo *m*; **r. of honour**, lista *f* de honor; *Jur* **to strike sb off the rolls**, tachar a algn de la lista. **4** (*ship etc*) balanceo *m*. **5** (*of drum*) redoble *m*; (*of thunder*) fragor *m*. **II** *vtr* **1** (*ball*) hacer rodar; **to r. one's eyes**, poner los ojos en blanco; **to r. one's r's**, pronunciar fuerte las erres. **2** (*cigarette*) liar. **3** (*move*) mover. **4** (*push*) empujar. **5** (*flatten*) allanar. **III** *vi* **1** (*ball, marble*) rodar; *fig* **to keep the ball rolling**, mantener la conversación; *fam* **they were rolling in the aisles**, se tronchaban de risa; *fam* **to be rolling in money**, estar forrado,-a. **2** (*animal*) revolcarse. **3** *Naut* (*ship*) balancearse. **4** (*drum*) redoblar; (*thunder*) retumbar; (*cannon*) tronar. ◆ **roll about, roll around** *vi* ir de acá para allá. ◆ **roll along** *i vtr* hacer rodar por. **II** *vi* hacer rodar; **things are rolling along nicely**, todo anda muy bien. ◆ **roll back** *vtr* **1** hacer retroceder. **2** *US* (*prices*) bajar, reducir. ◆ **roll by** *vi* (*years, months*) pasar. ◆ **roll down** *vtr* (*blinds etc*) bajar; (*sleeves*) bajarse. ◆ **roll in** *vi fam* **1** (*arrive*) llegar, presentarse. **2** (*money*) llegar a raudales. ◆ **roll on** *vi* **1** (*gen*) seguir rodando. **2** *fam* (*time*) pasar; **r. on the holidays!**, ¡que vengan las vacaciones! ◆ **roll over** **I** *vtr* derribar. **II** *vi* dar una vuelta; **she rolled over on her side**, se puso de costado. ◆ **roll up** **I** *vtr* enrollar; (*blinds*) subir; **to r. up one's sleeves**, (ar)remangarse. **II** *vi* **1** enrollarse. **2** *fam* (*arrive*) llegar, presentarse.

roll-call ['rəʊlkɔːl] *n* el acto de pasar lista.

rolled-up ['rəʊldʌp] *adj* (*umbrella, newspaper*) arrollado,-a; (*clothes*) (ar)remangado,-a.

roller ['rəʊləʳ] *n* **1** *Tech* rodillo *m*. ■ **r. blind**, persiana *f* enrollable; **r. coaster**, montaña *f* rusa; **r. skate**, patín *m* de ruedas; **r. skating**, patinaje *m* sobre ruedas; **r. towel**, toalla *f* de rodillo; (*large wave*) ola *f* grande. **3** *usu pl* (*for hair*) rulo *m*. **4** *Orn* carraca *f*.

roller-skate ['rəʊləskeɪt] *vi* patinar sobre ruedas.

rolling ['rəʊlɪŋ] **I** *adj* **1** (*stone*) rodante, que rueda; *fig* **a r. stone**, un,-a vagabundo,-a; *prov* **a r. stone gathers no moss**, piedra movidiza nunca moho la cobija. ■ *Rail* **r.**

stock, material *m* rodante. **2** *fam fig* rico,-a; **he's rolling in money** *or* **in it**, está forrado. **2** (*countryside*) ondulado,-a. **II** *n* rodamiento *m*; (*of ground*) apisonamiento *m*. ■ **r. pin**, rodillo *m* (de cocina).

roll-neck(ed) ['rəʊlnek(t)] *adj* **r.-n. sweater**, jersey con cuello cisne.

roll-on ['rəʊlɒn] *n* faja *f* elástica.

rolltop ['rəʊltɒp] *adj* (*desk*) de tapa corrediza.

roly-poly ['rəʊlɪ'pəʊlɪ] *n* **1** *Culin* ≈ brazo *m* de gitano. **2** *fam* gordiflón,-ona *m,f*.

ROM [rɒm] *Comput abbr of* **read only memory**, memoria *f* sólo de lectura, ROM *f*.

Roman ['rəʊmən] *adj* & *n* romano,-a (*m, f*). ■ **R. alphabet**, alfabeto *m* romano; **R. Catholic**, católico,-a *m,f* (romano,-a); **R. Catholicism**, catolicismo *m*; **R. law**, ley romana; **R. numerals**, números romanos; **R. nose**, nariz aguileña.

Romance [rəʊ'mæns] *adj Ling* románico,-a, romance; **R. languages**, lenguas románicas.

romance [rəʊ'mæns] **I** *n* **1** (*tale*) novela *f* romántica; (*medieval*) libro *m* de caballerías, romance *m*. **2** *Mus* romanza *f*. **3** (*love affair*) idilio *m*, aventura *f* amorosa, romance *m*. **4** (*romantic quality*) lo romántico. **II** *vi* fantasear.

Romanesque [rəʊmə'nesk] *Archit* **I** *adj* románico,-a. **II** *n* románico *m*, arte *m* románico.

Romania [rəʊ'meɪnɪə] *n see* **Rumania**.

romantic [rəʊ'mæntɪk] *adj* & *n* romántico,-a (*m,f*).

romanticism [rəʊ'mæntɪsɪzəm] *n* romanticismo *m*.

romanticize [rəʊ'mæntɪsaɪz] *vi* fantasear.

Romany ['rɒmənɪ, 'rəʊmənɪ] **I** *adj* & *n* gitano,-a *m,f*). **II** *n* (*language*) lengua *f* de los gitanos; (*in Spain*) caló *m*.

Rom Cath *Rel abbr of* **Roman Catholic**, católico,-a *m,f* (romano,-a), Cat.

Rome [rəʊm] *n* Roma *f*; *prov* **all roads lead to R.**, todos los caminos llevan a Roma; *prov* **R. was not built in a day**, no se ganó Zamora en una hora; *prov* **when in R. do as the Romans do**, cuando a Roma fueres, haz lo que vieres.

romp [rɒmp] **I** *n* jugueteo *m*. **II** *vi* juguetear; *fam* retozar; *fam* **to r. home**, ganar con facilidad. ◆ **romp through** *vtr* hacer con facilidad.

rompers ['rɒmpəz] *npl* pelele *m sing*.

roof [ruːf] **I** *n* (*pl* **roofs** [ruːfs, 'ruːvz]) **1** *Archit* tejado *m*; **flat r.**, azotea *f*; **tiled r.**, tejado *m*; *fig* **to have a r. over one's head**, tener donde cobijarse; *fam fig* **they can't live under the same r.**, no pueden vivir bajo el mismo techo; *fam fig* **to go through the r.**, (*prices*) estar por las nubes; (*with anger*) subirse por las paredes; *fam fig* **to hit the r.**, enfadarse. **2 r. garden**, jardín *m* en la azotea. **2** *Aut* techo *m*. ■ **r. rack**, baca *f*. **3** (*of mouth*) cielo *m*. **II** *vtr* techar.

roofing ['ruːfɪŋ] *n Constr* materiales *mpl* usados para techar.

roofless ['ruːflɪs] *adj* sin tejado.

rooftop ['ruːftɒp] *n* tejado *m*; *fig* **to shout from the rooftops**, divulgar a los cuatro vientos.

rook [rʊk] **I** *n* **1** *Orn* grajo *m*. **2** *Chess* torre *f*. **II** *vtr fam* (*swindle*) estafar, timar.

rookery ['rʊkərɪ] *n Orn* colonia *f* de grajos.

rookie ['rʊkɪ] *n US fam* **1** *Mil* recluta *m*, quinto *m*. **2** (*novice*) novato,-a *m,f*.

room [ruːm] *n* **1** habitación *f*, cuarto *m*; **r. and board**, pensión *f* completa; **single r.**, habitación individual. ■ **r. service**, servicio *m* de habitación. **2** (*space*) sitio *m*, espacio *m*; **make r. for me**, hazme sitio; *fig* **r. for improvement**, posibilidades *fpl* de mejora. **II** *vi US* alojarse; **to r. with sb**, compartir la habitación *or* piso *or* casa con algn.

roomful ['ruːmfʊl] *n* **a r. of people**, una habitación llena de gente.

rooming-house ['ruːmɪŋhaʊs] *n US* casa *f* de huéspedes, pensión *f*.

roommate ['ruːmmeɪt] *n* compañero,-a *m, f* de habitación.

roomy ['ruːmɪ] *adj (roomier, roomiest)* amplio,-a, espacioso,-a.

roost [ruːst] **I** *n* palo *m*, percha *f*; **(hen) r.,** gallinero *m; fig* **to come home to r.,** volverse en contra de uno; *fig* **to rule the r.,** llevar la batuta. **II** *vi* posarse.

rooster ['ruːstər] *n Orn esp US* gallo *m*.

root¹ [ruːt] *n* **1** *(plant, teeth, hair)* raíz *f; Bot* **r. crops,** tubérculos *mpl;* **to take r.,** echar raíces; **to pull up by the roots,** arrancar de raíz; *fig* **to put down roots in a country,** establecerse en un país. **2** *Math* raíz *f;* **square r.,** raíz *f* cuadrada. **3** *fig* raíz *f,* origen *m*. **II** *vtr* arraigar; *fig* **rooted to the spot,** paralizado,-a. **III** *vi Bot* echar raíces, arraigar. ◆ **root out, root up** *vtr (plant)* desarraigar, arrancar de raíz.

root² [ruːt] *vi (search)* buscar; **to r. about** *or* **around for sth,** hurgar en busca de algo.

root³ [ruːt] *vi fam* animar; **to r. for a team,** animar a un equipo.

rope [rəʊp] **I** *n* **1** *(small)* cuerda *f; (big)* soga *f; Naut* cabo *m;* **to give sb enough** *or* **plenty of r.,** dar rienda suelta a algn. **2 ropes,** *Box* cuerdas *fpl; (way)* truco *m sing; fig* **to have sb on the r.,** tener a algn contra las cuerdas; *fam fig* **to know the r.,** estar al tanto; *fam fig* **to learn the r.,** ponerse al tanto; *fam fig* **to show sb the r.,** poner a algn al tanto. **II** *vtr (package)* atar; *(climbers)* encordar. ◆ **rope in** *vtr fam (press-gang)* hacer participar; **we were roped in to going to the communion,** no pudimos escaparnos de ir a la comunión. ◆ **rope off** *vtr (cordon off)* acordonar.

rop(e)y ['rəʊpɪ] *adj (ropier, ropiest) fam* **1** *(bad quality)* de mala calidad, de pacotilla. **2** *(ill)* enfermo,-a.

rosary ['rəʊzərɪ] *n Rel* rosario *m;* **to say the r.,** rezar el rosario.

rose¹ [rəʊz] *pt see* **rise.**

rose² [rəʊz] *n* **1** *Bot* rosa *f, fam fig* **life is no bed of roses,** la vida no es un camino de rosas; *prov* **there is no r. without a thorn,** no hay rosa sin espina. ■ **dog r.,** gavanza *f;* **r. bed,** rosaleda *f;* **r. bush,** rosal *m; Archit* **r. window,** rosetón *m*. **2** *(colour)* rosa *m; fig* **to put the roses back into sb's cheeks,** sentar (algo) como agua bendita. **3** *(of watering can)* al cachofa *f*.

rosé ['rəʊzeɪ] *n (vino)* rosado *m*.

rosebud ['rəʊzbʌd] *n Bot* capullo *m* de rosa.

rose-coloured, *US* **rose-colored** ['rəʊzkʌləd] *adj* rosa; *fam fig* **to see everything through r.-c. spectacles,** verlo todo de color rosa.

rosemary ['rəʊsmərɪ] *n Bot* romero *m*.

rosette [rəʊ'zet] *n* **1** *(of ribbons)* escarapela *f*. **2** *Archit* florón *m*.

rose-water ['rəʊzwɔːtər] *n* agua *f* de rosas.

rosewood ['rəʊzwʊd] *n Bot* palisandro *m*.

roster ['rɒstər] *n* lista *f*.

rostrum ['rɒstrəm] *n (pl* **rostrums** *or* **rostra** ['rɒstrə]*)* tribuna *f*.

rosy ['rəʊzɪ] *adj (rosier, rosiest)* **1** *(complexion)* sonrosado,-a. **2** *fig (future)* prometedor,-a, optimista.

rot [rɒt] **I** *n* **1** *(decay)* putrefacción *f; fig* **when the r. sets in,** cuando las cosas empiezan a decaer. ■ **dry r.,** putrefacción *f* de la madera. **2** *fam (nonsense)* tonterías *fpl*. **II** *vtr (pt & pp* **rotted)** pudrir. ◆ **rot away** *vi* pudrirse, descomponerse.

rota ['rəʊtə] *n usu GB* lista *f*.

rotary ['rəʊtərɪ] *adj* rotatorio,-a, giratorio,-a. ■ *Print* **r. press,** rotativa *f*.

rotate [rəʊ'teɪt] **I** *vtr* **1** *(revolve)* hacer girar, hacer *or* dar vueltas a. **2** *(jobs, crops)* alternarse. **II** *vi* **1** *(revolve)* girar, dar vueltas. **2** *(jobs, crops)* alternarse.

rotating [rəʊ'teɪtɪŋ] *adj* **I** rotativo,-a, giratorio,-a. **2** *Agr* alternativo,-a.

rotation [rəʊ'teɪʃən] *n* **1** rotación *f,* giro *m*. **2** *Agr* **crop r.,** rotación *f* de cultivos; *(to work)* **in r.,** por turno *or* turnos.

rote [rəʊt] *n* rutina *f;* **to learn sth by r.,** aprender algo de memoria.

rotor ['rəʊtər] *n Tech* rotor *m*.

rotten ['rɒtən] *adj* **1** *(decayed)* podrido,-a; *(tooth)* cariado,-a, picado,-a; *(eggs)* podrido,-a. **2** *fam (quality, situation, luck)* malísimo,-a, pésimo,-a; *(health)* enfermo,-a; *fam* **I feel r.,** me encuentro fatal; *fam* **I feel r. about it,** me sabe muy mal.

rotter ['rɒtər] *n fam dated* sinvergüenza *mf*.

rotund [rəʊ'tʌnd] *adj lit* **1** *(rounded)* redondo,-a. **2** *(plump)* regordete, corpulento,-a. **3** *(bombastic)* rimbombante.

rotunda [rəʊ'tʌndə] *n Archit* rotonda *f*.

rouble ['ruːbəl] *n Fin* rublo *m*.

rouge [ruːʒ] **I** *n* colorete *m*. **II** *vtr* poner colorete a, pintar.

rough [rʌf] **I** *adj* **1** *(surface, skin)* áspero,-a; *(terrain)* accidentado,-a; *(road)* desigual; *(sea)* agitado,-a; *(weather)* tempestuoso,-a, borrascoso,-a. **2** *(rude, ill-mannered)* tosco,-a, rudo,-a, grosero,-a; *(violent)* violento,-a. **3** *(voice)* bronco,-a. **4** *(wine)* áspero,-a, agrio,-a. **5** *(bad)* malo,-a; **to have a r. time of it,** pasarlo mal; *fam* **to feel r.,** encontrarse fatal. **6** *(approximate)* aproximado,-a; **a r. guess/idea,** un cálculo aproximado/ una idea aproximada. **7** *(plan etc)* preliminar. ■ **r. draft,** borrador *m;* **r. sketch,** esbozo *m,* boceto *m*. **8** *(hard severe)* duro,-a, severo,-a; **r. justice,** justicia *f* sumaria. **II** *adv* duramente; **to play r.,** jugar duro; *fam fig* **to sleep r.,** dormir al raso. **III** *n* **1** *fam (person)* matón *m,* duro *m*. **2** *Golf* la hierba alta, rough *m*. **3** *fig (bad times)* lo malo; **to take the r. with the smooth,** estar a las duras y a las maduras. **IV** *vtr fam* **to r. it,** vivir sin comodidades. ◆ **rough out** *vtr* esbozar. ◆ **rough up** *vtr fam* **to r. sb up,** darle una paliza a algn. ◆ **roughly** *adv* **1** *(crudely)* toscamente. **2** *(clumsily)* torpemente. **3** *(not gently)* bruscamente; **to treat sb r.,** maltratar a algn. **4** *(approximately)* aproximadamente, más o menos.

roughage ['rʌfɪdʒ] *n (substance)* fibra *f; (food)* alimentos *mpl* ricos en fibra.

rough-and-ready [rʌfən'redɪ] *adj (makeshift)* improvisado,-a; *(person)* campechano,-a.

rough-and-tumble [rʌfən'tʌmbəl] *n (fight)* pelea *f, fig* **the r.-a.-t. of life,** los altibajos de la vida.

roughcast ['rʌfkɑːst] *n Constr* mortero *m* grueso.

roughen ['rʌfən] *vtr* poner áspero,-a.

roughhewn ['rʌfhjuːn] *adj (stone, wood)* desbastado,-a.

roughneck ['rʌfnek] *n fam* **1** matón *m,* duro *m*. **2** *Ind* trabajador *m* en un pozo petrolífero.

roughness ['rʌfnɪs] *n* **1** *(of surface, skin)* aspereza *f; (of terrain, road)* desigualdad *f; (of sea)* agitación *f*. **2** *(of weather)* inclemencia *f*. **3** *(of manner)* brusquedad *f; (impoliteness)* falta *f* de educación. **4** *(violence)* violencia *f*.

roughshod ['rʌfʃɒd] *adv* **to ride i. over sb's feelings,** ignorar las opiniones de algn.

rough-spoken [rʌf'spəʊkən] *adj (rude)* malhablado,-a.

roulette [ruː'let] *n* ruleta *f*. ■ **Russian r.,** ruleta *f* rusa.

Roumania [ruː'meɪnɪə] *n see* **Rumania.**

Roumanian [ruː'meɪnɪən] *adj & n see* **Rumanian.**

round [raʊnd] **I** *adj* redondo,-a; **in r. figures,** en números redondos; **to have r. shoulders,** tener las espaldas cargadas. ■ **r. table,** mesa *m* redonda; **r. trip,** viaje *m* de ida y vuelta. **II** *n* **1** *(circle)* círculo *m*. **2** *(series)* serie *f,* sucesión *f,* tanda *f; (session)* ronda *f;* **r. of talks,** ronda de negociaciones. **3** *Mil (ammunition)* cartucho *m; (salvo)* salva *f*. **4** *(slice)* rebanada *f* (de pan); **a r. of toast,** unas tostadas. **5** *(of drinks)* ronda *f*. **6** *(delivery)* reparto *m*. **7** *(routine)* rutina *f;* **the daily r.,** la rutina cotidiana. **8** *(game)*

Golf partido *m*; *Cards* partida *f*. **9** *Box* round *m*. **10** *(stage in a competition)* vuelta *f*, eliminatoria *f*. **11 rounds,** *(doctor's)* visita *f sing*; *(of salesman)* recorrido *m sing*. **III** *adv* a la redonda; **all year r.,** durante todo el año; **to invite sb r.,** invitar a algn a casa. **IV** *prep* alrededor de; **r. here,** por aquí; **r. the clock,** día y noche; **r. the corner,** a la vuelta de la esquina; **r. the garden,** alrededor del jardín. **V** *vtr (turn)* dar la vuelta a; **to r. a corner,** dar la vuelta a una esquina. ◆ **round off** *vtr* acabar, concluir. ◆ **round on** *vtr (attack)* atacar. ◆ **round up** *vtr (cattle)* acorralar, rodear; *(people)* reunir. ◆ **roundly** *adv* completamente, totalmente.

roundabout ['raʊndəbaʊt] **I** *n* **1** *(merry-go-round)* tiovivo *m*. **2** *GB Aut* plaza *f* circular, glorieta *f*. **II** *adj* indirecto,-a; **r. phrase,** rodeo *m*, circunloquio *m*; **could you explain it in a less r. way?,** ¿podría explicarlo sin tantos rodeos?

rounded ['raʊndɪd] *adj* redondeado,-a.

rounders ['raʊndəz] *n GB Sport* juego *m* parecido al béisbol.

round-shouldered [raʊnd'ʃəʊldəd] *adj* cargado,-a de espaldas.

roundsman ['raʊndzmən] *n (pl* **roundsmen)** repartidor *m*.

round-the-clock [raʊndðə'klɒk] *adj* (servicio) de veinticuatro horas.

round-up ['raʊndʌp] *n* **1** *(of cattle)* rodeo *m*; *(of suspects)* redada *f*. **2** *(summary)* resumen *m*.

rouse [raʊz] *vtr* **1** despertar; **to r. sb,** *(from sleep)* despertar a algn; *(from torpor)* animar a algn. **2** *(stir up)* suscitar, provocar.

rousing ['raʊzɪŋ] *adj (cheer)* entusiasta; *(applause)* caluroso,-a; *(speech, song)* conmovedor,-a.

rout¹ [raʊt] **I** *n* **1** *(defeat)* derrota *f* completa. **2** *(flight)* desbandada *f*. **II** *vtr* **1** *(defeat)* derrotar. **2** *(put to flight)* poner en fuga.

rout² [raʊt] *vtr* **1** *(person)* hacer salir; *(burrow)* escarbar. **2** *(locate)* localizar.

route [ruːt] **I** *n* **1** ruta *f*; *(of bus)* línea *f*, recorrido *m*; *Av* ruta (aérea); *Naut* rumbo *m*, derrota *f*; *fig* camino *m*. ■ **r. map,** mapa *m* de carreteras; *Mil* **r. march,** marcha *f* de entrenamiento. **2** *US* **R.,** ≈ carretera *f* nacional. **II** *vtr* encaminar, mandar.

routine [ruː'tiːn] **I** *n* **1** rutina *f*. **2** *Theat* número *m*; **to go through a r.,** ensayar un número; *fam* **don't give me that oppressed female r.!,** ¡no me vengas con eso de las mujeres oprimidas! **II** *adj* **1** rutinario,-a, habitual. **2** *(dull)* rutinario,-a, aburrido,-a.

rove [rəʊv] *vtr & vi lit* errar.

roving ['rəʊvɪŋ] *adj* errante; **r. reporter,** enviado,-a *m, f* especial; *fam* **to have a r. eye,** ser un ligón *or* una ligona.

row¹ [rəʊ] *n* fila *f*, hilera *f*; *fig* **three times in a r.,** tres veces seguidas.

row² [rəʊ] **I** *n (trip in a rowing boat)* paseo *m* en bote. **II** *vtr & vi* remar.

row³ [raʊ] **I** *n* **1** *(quarrel)* pelea *f*, bronca *f*, riña *f*; *(industrial)* disputa *f*. **2** *(noise, disturbance)* jaleo *m*; *(protest)* escándalo *m*. **II** *vi* pelearse, reñir.

rowan ['rəʊən, 'raʊən] *n Bot* **r. tree,** serbal *m* silvestre.

rowboat ['rəʊbəʊt] *n US* bote *m* de remos.

rowdiness ['raʊdɪnɪs] *n (noise)* ruido *m*; *(disorder)* alboroto *m*.

rowdy ['raʊdɪ] **I** *adj (rowdier, rowdiest)* **1** *(noisy)* ruidoso,-a; *(disorderly)* alborotador,-a. **2** *(quarrelsome)* camorrista, pendenciero,-a. **II** *n* camorrista *mf*, pendenciero,-a *m, f*.

rower ['rəʊəʳ] *n* remero,-a *m, f*.

rowing ['rəʊɪŋ] *n Sport* remo *m*. ■ **r. boat,** barco *m* a remo.

rowlock ['rəʊlɒk] *n Naut* tolete *m*, escálamo *m*.

royal ['rɔɪəl] **I** *adj* real; **r. welcome,** una acogida muy calurosa; **r. blue,** azul marino; **the R. Family,** la Familia Real. ■ *Cards* **r. flush,** escalera *f* real. **II the Royals** *npl*

los miembros de la Familia Real. ◆ **royalty** *adv fig* magníficamente; *fam fig* **they get on r.,** se llevan estupendamente bien.

royalist ['rɔɪəlɪst] *adj & n* monárquico,-a *(m, f)*.

royalty ['rɔɪəltɪ] *n* **1** *(rank)* realeza *f*. **2** *(royal persons)* miembro(s) *m(pl)* de la Familia Real. **3 royalties,** derechos *mpl* de autor, royalties *mpl*.

rpm [ɑːpiː'em] *abbr* **revolutions per minute,** revoluciones *fpl* por minuto, r.p.m.

RRP [ɑːrɑː'piː] *Com abbr of* **recommended retail price,** precio *m* recomendado de venta al público.

RSA [ɑːres'eɪ] *GB Theat abbr of* **Royal Society of Arts,** ≈ Real Academia *f* de Bellas Artes, RABA.

RSC [ɑːres'siː] *GB Theat abbr of* **Royal Shakespeare Company.**

RSPB [ɑːrespiː'biː] *GB abbr of* **Royal Society for the Protection of Birds.**

RSPCA [ɑːrespiːsiː'eɪ] *GB abbr of* **Royal Society for the Prevention of Cruelty to Animals,** ≈ Sociedad *f* Protectora de Animales, SPA.

RSPCC [ɑːrespiːsiː'siː] *GB abbr of* **Royal Society for the Prevention of Cruelty to Children.**

RSVP [ɑːresviː'piː] *abbr of* **répondez s'll vous plaît** (please reply), se ruega contestación, S. R. C.

Rt Hon *GB Pol abbr of* **(the) Right Honourable,** su Señoría.

Rt Rev(d) *Rel abbr of* **Right Reverend,** muy Reverendo,-a.

RU *GB Sport abbr of* **Rugby Union,** ≈ Federación *f* de Rugby.

rub [rʌb] **I** *n* frotamiento *m*, fricción *f*; *(touch)* roce *m*; **give it a r.,** frótalo un poco; *fig* **there's the r.,** ahí está el quid *or* el problema; *fig* **to r. shoulders with sb,** codearse con algn. **II** *vtr (pt & pp* **rubbed)** **1** frotar; *(hard)* restregar; **to r. one's hands together,** frotarse las manos. **2** *(massage)* friccionar. **III** *vi* rozar **(against,** contra). ◆ **rub along** *vi fam* **1** *(manage)* ir tirando. **2** *(get on well)* llevarse bien. ◆ **rub away** *vtr* quitar frotando; *(erase)* borrar. ◆ **rub down** *vtr* frotar, friccionar; *(horse)* almohazar; *(surface)* raspar. ◆ **rub in** *vtr* **1** *(cream etc)* frotar con; *fig* **to r. sb's nose in it,** echar en cara a algn algo. **2** *fam* insistir. ◆ **rub off** **I** *vtr* quitar frotando; *(erase)* borrar. **II** *vi (stain)* quitarse frotando, borrarse; *fig* **to r. off on sb,** influir en algn. ◆ **rub on** *vtr (cream etc)* frotar con. ◆ **rub out** *vtr* borrar. ◆ **rub up** *vtr* limpiar, sacar brillo a; *fam fig* **to r. sb up the wrong way,** fastidiar a algn.

rubber¹ ['rʌbəʳ] *n* **1** *(substance)* caucho *m*, goma *f*. ■ **r. band,** goma *f*; *fam* **r. cheque,** cheque *m* sin fondos; **r. industry,** industria *f* del caucho; **r. plant,** gomero *m*; **r. stamp,** tampón *m*. **2** *(eraser)* goma *f* de borrar; **blackboard r.,** borrador *m*. **3** *sl (contraceptive)* goma *f*.

rubber² ['rʌbəʳ] *n* **1** *Bridge* rubber *m*. **2** *Sport* serie *f* de juegos o partidos en cualquier deporte.

rubberized ['rʌbəraɪzd] *adj* cauchutado,-a.

rubbery ['rʌbərɪ] *adj* **1** parecido,-a a la goma. **2** *(elastic)* elástico,-a.

rubbing ['rʌbɪŋ] *n (scrubbing etc)* frotamiento *m*; *(friction)* fricción *f*.

rubbish ['rʌbɪʃ] *n* **1** *(refuse)* basura *f*. ■ **r. bin,** cubo *m* de la basura; **r. collection,** recogida *f* de la basura; **r. dump,** vertedero *m*. **2** *fam (worthless thing)* birria *f*, porquería *f*; **the film was r.,** la película fue una birria. **3** *fam (nonsense)* tonterías *fpl*; **don't talk r.!,** ¡no digas tonterías!

rubbishy ['rʌbɪʃɪ] *adj fam* sin valor, de pacotilla.

rubble ['rʌbəl] *n* escombros *mpl*.

rubella [ruː'belə] *n Med* rubéola *f*.

rubicund ['ruːbɪkənd] *adj* rubicundo,-a.

ruble ['ruːbəl] *n Fin see* **rouble.**

rubric ['ruːbrɪk] *n* rúbrica *f*.

ruby ['ruːbɪ] *n* rubí *m*. ■ **r. ring,** sortija *f* de rubíes.

ruck¹ [rʌk] *n (rugby)* melé *f* espontánea; *fig* canalla *f*.

ruck² [rʌk] **I** n (clothing, material) arruga f. **II** vi to r. up, arrugarse.

ruck³ [rʌk] n sl pelea f.

rucksack ['rʌksæk] n mochila f.

ructions ['rʌkʃənz] npl fam jaleo m sing, follón m sing; **there will be r.**, se armará la gorda.

rudder ['rʌdəʳ] n Av Naut timón m.

rudderless ['rʌdəlɪs] adj sin timón.

ruddy ['rʌdɪ] adj (ruddier, ruddiest) 1 (complexion) rojizo,-a, colorado,-a. 2 GB fam (damned) maldito,-a, condenado,-a.

rude [ruːd] adj 1 (impolite) maleducado,-a, descortés; (foul-mouthed) grosero,-a; **don't be r. to your mother**, no le faltes al respeto a tu madre. 2 lit (primitive) tosco,-a. 3 lit (sudden) brusco,-a; **a r. awakening**, un despertar repentino.

rudeness ['ruːdnɪs] n 1 (impoliteness) falta f de educación, descortesía f; (offensiveness) grosería f. 2 (roughness) tosquedad f. 3 (suddenness) brusquedad f.

rudimentary [ruːdɪ'mentərɪ] adj fml rudimentario,-a.

rudiments ['ruːdɪmənts] npl rudimentos mpl.

rue¹ [ruː] n Bot ruda f.

rue² [ruː] vtr arrepentirse de, lamentar.

rueful ['ruːfʊl] adj 1 (regretful) arrepentido,-a. 2 (sad) triste.

ruff¹ [rʌf] n 1 (on animal, bird) collarín m. 2 (starched collar) gorguera f. 3 Orn combatiente m.

ruff² [rʌf] n Cards fallo m.

ruffian ['rʌfɪən] n dated rufián m.

ruffle ['rʌfəl] **I** n usu pl (on blouse, shirt) chorrera f; (on cuffs) volante m. **II** vtr 1 (disturb) agitar; (by wind) levantar. 2 (feathers) erizar; (hair) despeinar. 3 fig (annoy) hacer perder la calma a.

ruffled ['rʌfəld] adj 1 (hair) alborotado,-a; (clothes) en desorden. 2 (perturbed) perturbado,-a; **she never gets r.**, nunca se altera. 3 (with a ruff) (blouse, shirt) con chorrera; (on cuffs) con volante.

rug [rʌg] n alfombra f, alfombrilla f. ■ **travelling r.**, manta f de viaje.

rugby ['rʌgbɪ] n Sport rugby m; **r. league**, rugby a trece; **r. union**, rugby a quince.

rugged ['rʌgɪd] adj 1 (terrain) accidentado,-a, desigual. 2 (features) duro,-a. 3 (character) robusto,-a, fuerte; (manner) tosco,-a.

rugger ['rʌgəʳ] n fam rugby m.

ruin ['ruːɪn] **I** n 1 ruina f; **to fall into r.**, caer en la ruina. 2 **ruins** ruinas fpl, restos mpl; **in r.**, en ruinas. **II** vtr arruinar; (spoil) estropear.

ruination [ruːɪ'neɪʃən] n ruina f, perdición f.

ruined ['ruːɪnd] adj 1 arruinado,-a; (spoiled) estropeado,-a. 2 (building) en ruinas.

ruinous ['ruːɪnəs] adj ruinoso,-a. ◆ **ruinously** adv r. **expensive**, carísimo,-a.

rule [ruːl] **I** n 1 (law) regla f, norma f; **rules and regulations**, reglamento m; Ind **to work to r.**, hacer una huelga de celo; fig **by r. of thumb**, a ojo de buen cubero. 2 (government) dominio m, mando m; (of monarch) reinado m; **majority r.**, gobierno m de la mayoría; **r. of law**, imperio m de la ley. 3 (ruler) regla f (graduada). **II** vtr & vi 1 (govern) mandar, gobernar; (monarch) reinar. 2 (decide) decidir; (decree) decretar. 3 (draw) tirar, trazar. ◆ **rule out** vtr descartar, excluir.

ruled [ruːld] adj rayado,-a.

ruler ['ruːləʳ] n 1 dirigente mf; (monarch) soberano,-a m,f. 2 (for measuring) regla f.

ruling ['ruːlɪŋ] **I** adj 1 (in charge) dirigente; fig (predominant) predominante, principal; **the r. party**, el partido en el poder. **II** n Jur fallo m; **to give a r. on**, pronunciar un fallo sobre.

rum [rʌm] **I** n (drink) ron m. **II** adj GB dated (odd) extraño,-a.

Rumania [ruː'meɪnɪə] n Rumania.

Rumanian [ruː'meɪnɪən] **I** adj rumano,-a. **II** n (person) rumano,-a m,f; (language) rumano m.

rumble ['rʌmbəl] **I** n 1 ruido m sordo; (of thunder) estruendo m. 2 (of stomach) borborigmo m. **II** vi 1 hacer un ruido sordo; (thunder) retumbar; (vehicle) **to r. past**, pasar ruidosamente. 2 (stomach) hacer ruidos. 3 (drone) perorar; **the lecturer rumbled on**, el conferenciante siguió con el rollo. **III** vtr fam (catch on) calar; **we've been rumbled**, nos han pillado or pescado or calado.

rumbling ['rʌmblɪŋ] n 1 ruido m sordo; (of thunder) estruendo m. 2 (of stomach) borborigmo m. 3 **rumblings**, (of danger, dissatisfaction) señales mpl, signos mpl; **there were r. about a strike**, se mascaba una huelga.

rumbustious [rʌm'bʌstjəs] adj bullicioso,-a.

ruminant ['ruːmɪnənt] **I** n Zool rumiante m. **II** adj 1 Zool rumiante. 2 fml (thoughtful) rumiante.

ruminate ['ruːmɪneɪt] vi 1 Zool (chew) rumiar. 2 fig (ponder) rumiar; **to r. on a matter**, meditar sobre un asunto.

rumination [ruːmɪ'neɪʃən] n reflexión f, meditación f.

ruminative ['ruːmɪnətɪv] adj lit pensativo,-a; **it was a r. period in his life**, fue un período de reflexión en su vida.

rummage ['rʌmɪdʒ] **I** n búsqueda f; **to have a r. about**, rebuscar. ■ US **r. sale**, venta f de artículos usados. **II** vi revolver; **to r. through a drawer**, revolver en un cajón.

rummy ['rʌmɪ] n Cards rummy m.

rumour, US **rumor** ['ruːməʳ] **I** n rumor m; **r. has it that ...**, se dice que ..., corre el rumor de que ... . **II** vtr rumorear.

rump [rʌmp] n 1 (of animal) ancas fpl; (quadruped) grupa f; fam hum (of person) trasero m. ■ **r. steak**, filete m de lomo. 2 **rumps**, (die-hards) incondicionales mpl, irreductibles mpl.

rumple ['rʌmpəl] vtr fam (crease) arrugar; **to r. sb's hair**, despeinar a algn.

rumpus ['rʌmpəs] n fam jaleo m; **to kick up a r.**, armar jaleo; US Canada NZ **r. room**, cuarto m de juegos.

run [rʌn] **I** n 1 carrera f; (fugitive) **to be on the r.**, haberse fugado; **to break into a r.**, echar a correr; **to go for a r.**, hacer footing; **to make a r. for it**, escaparse; Crick **to score a r.**, marcar una carrera; fig **in the long r.**, a largo plazo; fig **to have a good r. for one's money**, sacarle jugo al dinero. ■ **trial r.**, prueba f. 2 (trip) paseo m, vuelta f; **a ten minute r.**, un viajecito de diez minutos. 3 (sequence) serie f; **to have a r. of bad luck**, tener una mala racha. 4 (track) pista f. ■ **ski r.**, pista f de esquí. 5 (demand) gran demanda f. 6 (use) uso m; **to give sb the r. of a house**, poner una casa a disposición de algn. 7 Print tirada f. 8 Cards escalera f. 9 (in stocking) carrera f. **II** vtr (pt ran; pp run) 1 (gen) correr, recorrer; **to r. a race**, correr or participar en una carrera; **to r. errands**, hacer recados. 2 (drive) llevar; **to r. sb to the airport**, llevar a algn (en coche) al aeropuerto. 3 (house, business, etc) llevar; (company) dirigir; (organize) organizar, montar; **to r. one's own life**, ser dueño de sí mismo. 4 (pass) pasar; **to r. one's fingers through ones' hair**, pasarse la mano por el pelo. 5 (operate) circular; **it's a cheap car to r.**, es un coche económico; **they r. trains every hour**, hay un servicio de trenes cada hora; Comput **to r. a program**, pasar un programa. 6 Press publicar; **to r. articles on drug addiction**, publicar artículos sobre la drogadicción. 7 (temperature) tener. **III** vi 1 correr; **to r. for a train**, correr para coger un tren; fam **r. for it!**, ¡corre! 2 (colour) desteñirse. 3 (flow) (water, river) correr; (drip) gotear; **to leave the tap running**, dejar el grifo abierto; **to r. dry**, secarse; fam **your nose is running**, tienes mocos. 4 (operate) funcionar; **to leave an engine running**, dejar un motor en marcha; **trains r. every two hours**, hay trenes cada dos horas. 5 Naut navegar; **to r. aground/ashore**, encallar/embarrancar. 6 Pol participar, presentarse; **to r. for president**, presentarse como candidato a la presidencia. **7** (*story*) decir; **so the story runs,** según lo que se dice. **8** (*range*) oscilar; **prices r. from ten to fifty pounds,** los precios oscilan entre las diez y las cincuenta libras. **9** (*quantity*) abastecer; **we're running low on** *or* **short of milk,** nos queda poca leche. **10** (*traits*) venir de; **shyness runs in the family,** la timidez le viene de familia. **11** *Cin Theat* estar en cartel. **12** (*last*) durar. **13** (*stocking*) hacerse una carrera. ◆ **run about** *vi* correr por todas partes. ◆ **run across** *vtr* **1** cruzar corriendo. **2** (*meet*) tropezar con. ◆ **run away** *vi* escaparse, fugarse; (*horse*) desbocarse; *fig* **don't r. away with the idea that,** no te vayas a creer que. ◆ **run down I** *vtr* **1** bajar corriendo. **2** (*knock down*) atropellar; (*hit*) pillar; **she was r. down by a car,** la atropelló *or* pilló un coche. **3** (*criticize*) criticar. **II** *vi* (*battery*) acabarse, agotarse; (*watch*) pararse. ◆ **run in** *vtr* **1** entrar corriendo. **2** (*arrest*) detener. **3** *Aut* rodar. ◆ **run into** *vtr* **1** entrar corriendo en. **2** (*river*) desembocar en. **3** (*people, problems*) tropezar con. **4** (*crash into*) chocar contra. **5** (*amount to*) sumar, alcanzar. ◆ **run off I** *vtr* **1** *Print* (*copies*) tirar. **2** (*radio etc*) **to r. off the mains/ batteries,** funcionar con electricidad/pilas. **II** *vi* escaparse; **to r. off with sth,** llevarse algo. ◆ **run on I** *vtr Typ* enlazar. **II** *vi* **1** (*function*) funcionar con. **2** (*continue*) continuar. **3** *fam* hablar sin parar. ◆ **run out** *vi* **1** (*exit*) salir corriendo. **2** (*finish*) acabarse, agotarse; (*stocks*) agotarse; (*contract*) vencer; **to r. out of,** quedarse sin. ◆ **run over I** *vtr* **1** (*knock down*) atropellar; (*hit*) pillar. **2** (*rehearse*) ensayar. **II** *vi* (*overflow*) rebosar; (*spill*) derramarse. ◆ **run through** *vtr* **1** (*cross*) atravesar corriendo; (*river*) pasar por. **2** (*read quickly*) echar un vistazo a. **3** (*rehearse*) ensayar. **4** (*fortune*) despilfarrar. ◆ **run up I** *vi* **1** (*ascend*) subir corriendo; (*arrive*) llegar corriendo. **2** (*difficulties*) tropezar con. **II** *vtr* **1** (*flag*) izar. **2** (*debts*) acumular. **3** *Sew* hacer rápidamente.

runabout ['rʌnəbaʊt] *n fam* coche *m* pequeño. ▪ *Rail* **r. (ticket),** billete *m* kilométrico.

runaway ['rʌnəweɪ] **I** *n* fugitivo,-a *m,f*. **II** *adj* (*person*) huido,-a, fugitivo,-a; (*horse*) desbocado,-a; (*vehicle*) incontrolado,-a; (*inflation*) galopante; (*success, victory*) aplastante; (*leader*) indiscutible.

rundown ['rʌndaʊn] *n fam* informe *m* detallado; **to give sb a r.,** poner a algn al corriente.

run-down [rʌn'daʊn] *adj* **1** (*exhausted*) agotado,-a. **2** (*dilapidated*) ruinoso,-a; (*inefficient*) de capa caída, en declive.

rung¹ [rʌŋ] *pp see* **ring**.

rung² [rʌŋ] *n* (*of ladder*) escalón *m*, peldaño *m*; *fig* escalón *m*.

runner ['rʌnəʳ] *n* **1** corredor,-a *m,f*. **2** (*horse*) caballo *m* de carreras. **3** (*messenger*) mensajero,-a *m,f*, recadero,-a *m, f*. **4** *Tech* carro *m*; (*of skate*) cuchilla *f*. **5** (*on table*) tapete *m*. **6** (*carpet*) alfombra *f* de escalera *or* pasillo. **7** *Bot* **r. bean,** judía *f* escarlata.

runner-up [rʌnər'ʌp] *n* (*pl* **runners-up**) *Sport* subcampeón,-ona *m, f*; (*in competition*) ganadores *mpl* del segundo premio.

running ['rʌnɪŋ] **I** *n* **1** *Sport* atletismo *m*; (*race*) carrera *f*; **long-distance r.,** carreras de fondo; *fig* **to be in the r. for sth,** tener posibilidades de ganar *or* conseguir algo. **2** (*management*) dirección *f*, organización *f*. **3** (*machine*) funcionamiento *m*. **II** *adj* **1** *Sport* de carreras. ▪ *Aut* **r. board,** estribo *m*; *Rad TV* **r. commentary,** comentario *m* en directo; **r. costs,** gastos *mpl* de mantenimiento; *Pol* **r. mate,** candidato *m* a la vicepresidencia; **r. track,** pista *f*; *Med* **r. sore,** llaga *f* supurante; **r. water,** agua *f* corriente. **2** (*consecutive*) seguido,-a; **three weeks r.,** tres semanas seguidas. **3** *Aut* funcionamiento *m*; **in good r. order,** en buen estado; **r. in,** en rodaje.

runny ['rʌnɪ] *adj* (**runnier, runniest**) **1** (*soft*) blando,-a; (*egg*) crudo,-a; (*liquid*) líquido,-a; (*melted*) derretido,-a. **2** (*nose*) que moquea.

run-off ['rʌnɒf] *n* (*pl* **run-offs**) (*contest*) partido *m* de desempate; (*race*) carrera *f* de desempate.

run-of-the-mill [rʌnəvðə'mɪl] *adj* corriente y moliente.

runproof ['rʌnpruːf] *adj* (*stockings*) indesmallable.

runt [rʌnt] *n fam* enano,-a *m,f*.

run-through ['rʌnθruː] *n* ensayo *m*.

run-up ['rʌnʌp] *n* **1** (*elections*) preliminares *mpl*. **2** *Sport* carrera *f*.

runway ['rʌnweɪ] *n* **1** *Av* pista *f* (de aterrizaje y despegue). **2** *Sport* recorrido *m* de una carrera.

rupee [ruː'piː] *n Fin* rupia *f*.

rupture ['rʌptʃəʳ] **I** *n* **1** *Med* hernia *f*. **2** *fig* ruptura *f*. **II** *vtr* **1** *Med* **to r. oneself,** hacerse una hernia, herniarse. **2** (*break*) romper.

rural ['rʊərəl] *adj* rural.

ruse [ruːz] *n* ardid *m*, astucia *f*.

rush¹ [rʌʃ] *n Bot* junco *m*. ▪ **r. matting,** estera *f* de juncos.

rush² [rʌʃ] **I** *n* **1** (*hurry*) prisa *f*, precipitación *f*; (*hustle and bustle*) ajetreo *m*; **it's a r. job,** es urgente; **there's no r.,** no corre prisa; **they made a r. for the exit,** se precipitaron hacia la salida. ▪ **r. hour,** hora *f* punta. **2** (*demand*) demanda *f*; **there's a r. on sugar,** hay una gran demanda de azúcar. **3** (*wind*) ráfaga *f*. **4** (*water*) torrente *m*. **5** *Mil* ataque *m*. **6** *Cin* **rushes,** primeras pruebas *fpl*. **II** *vtr* **1** (*do hastily*) (*thing*) hacer de prisa; (*person*) meter prisa, apresurar; **don't r. me!,** ¡no me metas prisa!; **to r. a meal,** comer de prisa; **to be rushed off one's feet,** tener un día muy ajetreado. **2** (*hasten*) darse prisa; **to r. sb to hospital,** llevar a algn urgentemente al hospital. **3** (*attack*) abalanzarse sobre; *Mil* tomar por asalto. **4** *fam* cobrar; **how much did they r. you for,** ¿cuánto te han cobrado? **III** *vi* **1** (*go quickly*) precipitarse. **2** abalanzarse (**at sb,** sobre algn); **don't r. at it,** no te precipites; *fig* **the blood rushed to her cheeks,** se puso colorada. ◆ **rush about** *vi* correr de un lado a otro. ◆ **rush in** *vi* entrar precipitadamente. ◆ **rush into** *vtr* entrar precipitadamente en; *fig* **to r. into sth,** hacer algo sin pensarlo bien. ◆ **rush off** *vi* irse corriendo. ◆ **rush out** *vtr* salir precipitadamente. ◆ **rush through** *vtr* hacer de prisa; (*piece of business*) despachar rápidamente.

rusk [rʌsk] *n* galleta *f* dura para niños.

russet ['rʌsɪt] **I** *adj* rojizo,-a. **II** *n* (*colour*) color *m* rojizo.

Russia ['rʌʃə] *n* Rusia.

Russian ['rʌʃən] **I** *adj* ruso,-a. **II** *n* **1** (*person*) ruso,-a *m,f*. **2** (*language*) ruso *m*.

rust [rʌst] **I** *n* **1** (*action*) oxidación *f*; (*substance*) orín *m*, herrumbre *f*. **2** (*colour*) color *m* de orín, pardo *m* rojizo. **3** *Bot* roya *f*. **II** *vtr* oxidar. **III** *vi* oxidarse.

rustic ['rʌstɪk] *adj* rústico,-a, campestre.

rusticate ['rʌstɪkeɪt] *vtr Univ* (*student*) expulsar temporalmente.

rustle ['rʌsəl] **I** *n* (*of paper, leaves*) crujido *m*. **II** *vtr* (*paper etc*) hacer crujir. **III** *vi US* (*steal cattle*) robar ganado. ◆ **rustle up** *vtr fam* (*food*) preparar en un momento.

rustler ['rʌsləʳ] *n US* (*cattle thief*) ladrón *m* de ganado, cuatrero *m*.

rustling ['rʌslɪŋ] *n* **1** (*of paper, leaves*) crujido *m*. **2** *US* (*cattle theft*) robo *m* de ganado.

rustproof ['rʌstpruːf] *adj* inoxidable.

rusty ['rʌstɪ] *adj* (**rustier, rustiest**) oxidado,-a; *fam fig* **my French is a bit r.,** tengo el francés un poco oxidado.

rut [rʌt] *n* **1** (*furrow*) surco *m*; (*groove*) ranura *f*. **2** *fig* **to be in a r.,** ser esclavo de la rutina; **to get out of a r.,** salir de la rutina. **3** *Zool* celo *m*.

ruthless ['ruːθlɪs] *adj* (*cruel*) cruel, despiadado,-a; (*merciless*) implacable.

ruthlessness ['ruːθlɪsnɪs] *n* crueldad *f*, implacabilidad *f*.

rutted ['rʌtɪd] *adj* (*surface*) surcado,-a, con ranuras.

Rwanda [rʊ'ændə] *n* **1** (*country*) Ruanda. **2** (*language*) ruandés *m*.

Rwandan [rʊ'ændən] *adj & n* ruandés,-esa (*m,f*).

rye [raɪ] *n Bot* centeno *m*. ▪ **r. bread,** pan *m* de centeno; **r. grass,** ballica *f*; *US* **r. (whiskey),** whisky *m* de centeno.

S

S, s [es] *n (the letter)* S, s *f.*

S 1 *abbr of* **Saint,** San *m*, Santo *m*, S., Sto.; Santa *f*, Sta. **2** *(on clothes etc) abbr of* **small (size),** (talla *f*) pequeña. **3** *abbr of* **South,** Sur, S.

s *abbr of* **single,** soltero,-a.

SA *abbr of* **South Africa,** Africa del Sur.

Sabbath ['sæbəθ] *n (Jewish)* sábado *m*; *(Christian)* domingo *m.*

sabbatical [sə'bætɪkəl] *adj* sabático,-a.

saber ['seɪbəʳ] *n US see* **sabre.**

sable ['seɪbəl] **I** *n (animal, fur)* marta *f* cebellina. **II** *adj (colour)* negro,-a.

sabotage ['sæbətɑːʒ] **I** *n* sabotaje *m.* **II** *vtr (machinery, plan)* sabotear.

saboteur [sæbə'tɜːʳ] *n* saboteador,-a *m,f.*

sabre ['seɪbəʳ] *n* sable *m.*

sac [sæk] *n Anat Biol* bolsa *f.*

saccharin ['sækərɪn] *n* sacarina *f.*

sachet ['sæʃeɪ] *n* bolsita *f*, sobrecito *m.*

sack [sæk] **I** *n* **1** *(bag)* saco *m.* **2** *fam* **to get the s.,** ser despedido,-a; *fam* **to give sb the s.,** despedir a algn, echar del trabajo a algn, poner de patitas en la calle a algn. **3** *fam (bed)* **to hit the s.,** irse al sobre. **II** *vtr* **1** *fam* despedir a, echar del trabajo a. **2** *Mil* saquear.

sackcloth ['sækklɒθ] *n Tex* arpillera *f*; *Rel* **in s. and ashes,** en túnica de penitente.

sacking ['sækɪŋ] *n* **1** *Tex* arpillera *f.* **2** *(dismissal)* despido *m.* **3** *(of city)* saqueo *m.*

sacrament ['sækrəmənt] *n Rel* sacramento *m*; **to receive the S.,** comulgar.

sacred ['seɪkrɪd] *adj* sagrado,-a, sacro,-a; **nothing is s. any more,** ya no se respeta nada; *fig* **s. to,** dedicado,-a a. ■ **s. cow,** vaca *f* sagrada; **s. music,** música *f* religiosa.

sacredness ['seɪkrɪdnɪs] *n* carácter *m* sagrado, santidad *f.*

sacrifice ['sækrɪfaɪs] **I** *n* **1** sacrificio *m.* **2** *(offering)* ofrenda *f.* **II** *vtr* sacrificar.

sacrificial [sækrɪ'fɪʃəl] *adj* de sacrificio. ■ **s. lamb,** chivo *m* expiatorio.

sacrilege ['sækrɪlɪdʒ] *n* sacrilegio *m.*

sacrilegious [sækrɪ'lɪdʒəs] *adj* sacrílego,-a.

sacristan ['sækrɪstən] *n* sacristán,-ana *m,f.*

sacristy ['sækrɪstɪ] *n Rel* sacristía *f.*

sacrosanct ['sækrəʊsæŋkt] *adj* sacrosanto,-a.

sacrum ['sækrəm] *n (pl sacra* ['sækrə]*) Anat* sacro *m.*

sad [sæd] *adj (sadder, saddest)* **1** *(unhappy)* triste; **how s.!,** ¡qué pena! **2** *(deplorable)* lamentable. **3** *(colour)* apagado,-a.

sadden ['sædən] *vtr* entristecer.

saddle ['sædəl] **I** *n (for horse)* silla *f* (de montar); *(of bicycle, motorbike)* sillín *m*; *fam* **to be in the s.,** llevar las riendas. **II** *vtr (horse)* ensillar.

saddlebag ['sædəlbæg] *n* alforja *f.*

saddler ['sædləʳ] *n* guarnicionero,-a *m,f.*

saddlery ['sædlərɪ] *n (equipment)* guarniciones *fpl*; *(workshop)* guarnicionería *f.*

sadism ['seɪdɪzəm] *n* sadismo *m.*

sadist ['seɪdɪst] *n* sádico,-a *m,f.*

sadistic [sə'dɪstɪk] *adj* sádico,-a.

sadness ['sædnɪs] *n* tristeza *f.*

sadomasochism [seɪdəʊ'mæsəkɪzəm] *n* sadomasoquismo *m.*

sae [eseɪ'iː] *abbr of* **stamped addressed envelope,** sobre *m* franqueado.

safari [sə'fɑːrɪ] *n* safari *m*; **on s.,** de safari. ■ **s. park,** safari *m*, reserva *f.*

safe [seɪf] **I** *adj* **1** *(unharmed)* ileso,-a; *(out of danger)* a salvo, fuera de peligro; **s. and sound,** sano,-a y salvo,-a; **s. from,** a salvo de. **2** *(not dangerous)* inofensivo,-a, inocuo,-a. **3** *(secure, sure)* seguro,-a; **it is s. to say that ...,** se puede decir con seguridad que ...; **to be on the s. side,** para mayor seguridad. ■ *fam* **s. house,** piso *m* franco; *Med* **s. period,** período *m* de seguridad. **4** *(cautious)* prudente. **II** *n (for money etc)* caja *f* fuerte *or* de caudales *or* de seguridad. ■ **meat s.,** fresquera *f.* ◆ **safely** *adv* **1** *(certainly)* con toda seguridad. **2** *(without mishap)* sin accidentes *or* contratiempos *or* percance; **to arrive s.,** llegar a buen puerto.

safe-breaker ['seɪfbreɪkəʳ] *n* ladrón,-ona *m*, *f* de cajas fuertes.

safe-conduct [seɪf'kɒndəkt] *n* salvoconducto *m.*

safe-deposit [seɪfdɪ'pɒzɪt] *n* **s.-d. (box),** cámara *f* blindada *or* acorazada.

safe-cracker ['seɪfkrækəʳ] *n see* **safe-breaker.**

safeguard ['seɪfgɑːd] **I** *n (protection)* salvaguarda *f*, protección *f*; *(guarantee)* garantía *f.* **II** *vtr* proteger, salvaguardar.

safekeeping [seɪf'kiːpɪŋ] *n* custodia *f*; **to be in s.,** estar a buen recaudo.

safety ['seɪftɪ] *n* seguridad *f*; **s. first!,** ¡seguridad ante todo! ■ **road s.,** seguridad *f* vial; *Aut Av* **s. belt,** cinturón *m* de seguridad; **s. catch,** seguro *m*; **s. device,** dispositivo *m* de seguridad; *US* **s. island,** isleta *f* para peatones; *Min* **s. lamp,** lámpara *f* de seguridad; **s. measures,** medidas *fpl* de seguridad; **s. net,** red *f* de protección *or* de seguridad; **s. pin,** imperdible *m*; **s. valve,** válvula *f* de seguridad.

saffron ['sæfrən] **I** *n Bot & Culin* azafrán *m.* **II** *adj (colour)* de color azafrán.

sag [sæg] *vi (pt & pp sagged)* **1** *(roof)* hundirse; *(wall)* pandear; *(wood, iron)* combarse; *(flesh)* colgar. **2** *fig (spirits)* flaquear.

saga ['sɑːgə] *n Lit* saga *f.*

sagacious [sə'geɪʃəs] *adj* sagaz, perspicaz.

sagacity [sə'gæsɪtɪ] *n* sagacidad *f.*

sage¹ [seɪdʒ] **I** *adj (wise)* sabio,-a. **II** *n (wise person)* sabio,-a *m,f.*

sage² [seɪdʒ] *n Bot* salvia *f*; **s. green,** verde salvia, verdigris.

sagging ['sægɪŋ] **I** *adj (roof)* hundido,-a; *(wall)* pandeado,-a; *(wood, iron)* combado,-a. **II** *n (of roof)* hundimiento *m*; *(of wall)* pandeo *m*; *(of wood, iron)* comba *f.*

Sagittarius [sædʒɪ'teərɪəs] *n Astrol Astron* Sagitario *m.*

sago ['seɪgəʊ] *n Bot* sagú *m.*

Sahara [sə'hɑːrə] *n* **the S.,** el Sahara.

Saharan [sə'hɑːrən] *adj* saharaui, sahariano,-a.

said [sed] **I** *pt & pp see* **say.** **II** *adj (aforementioned)* dicho,-a, antes citado,-a *or* mencionado,-a.

sail [seɪl] **I** *n* **1** *(canvas)* vela *f*; **to set s.,** zarpar; *fam* **to take the wind out of sb's sails,** bajarle los humos a algn. **2** *(trip)* paseo *m* en barco; *(journey)* viaje *m* en barco. **3** *(of windmill)* aspa *f.* **4** *(on boat)* velero *m.* **II** *vtr* navegar; *(ship)* gobernar; **to s. the Atlantic,** cruzar el Atlántico en barco. **III** *vi* **1** *(gen)* ir en barco. **2** *(set sail)* zarpar. ◆ **sail through** *vtr fam* **you'll s. through the exam,** te resultará muy fácil el examen.

sailcloth ['seɪlklɒθ] *n Tex* lona *f*.

sailing ['seɪlɪŋ] *n* navegación *f; (yachting)* vela *f; fam* **it's all plain s.,** es todo coser y cantar. ■ **s. boat** *or* **ship,** velero *m,* barco *m* de vela.

sailor ['seɪləʳ] *n* marinero *m; fam* **to be a bad s.,** marearse fácilmente.

saint [seɪnt] *n* santo,-a *m, f, (before all masculine names except those beginning Do or To)* San; *(before feminine names)* Santa; **S. Dominic,** Santo Domingo; **S. Helen,** Santa Elena; **S. John,** San Juan; **S. Thomas,** Santo Tomás. ■ **All Saints' Day,** Día *m* de Todos los Santos; **s.'s day,** santo *m,* onomástica *f*.

saintliness ['seɪntlɪnɪs] *n* santidad *f*.

saintly ['seɪntlɪ] *adj (saintlier, saintliest)* santo,-a.

sake [seɪk] *n* bien *m;* **for old times' sake,** por los viejos tiempos; **for the s. of,** por (el bien de); **for your own s.,** por tu propio bien; **to talk for the s. of talking,** hablar por hablar; *fam* **for goodness' s.!,** ¡por el amor de Dios!

salable ['seɪləbəl] *adj US see* **saleable.**

salacious [sə'leɪʃəs] *adj* salaz.

salad ['sæləd] *n Culin* ensalada *f*. ■ **fruit s.,** macedonia *f* de frutas; **potato s.,** ensaladilla *f* (rusa); **s. bowl,** ensaladera *f;* **s. cream,** salsa *f* tipo mahonesa; *fig* **s. days,** años *mpl* de juventud; **s. dressing,** vinagreta *f,* aliño *m,* aderezo *m*.

salamander ['sæləmændəʳ] *n* salamandra *f*.

salami [sə'lɑːmɪ] *n Culin* salchichón *m,* salami *m*.

salaried ['sælərɪd] *adj* asalariado,-a.

salary ['sælərɪ] *n* salario *m,* sueldo *m*.

sale [seɪl] *n* **1** *(gen)* venta *f;* **for** *or* **on s.,** en venta; **to put sth up for s.,** poner algo a la venta. ■ **sales department,** departamento *m* comercial *or* de ventas; **sales manager,** jefe,-a *m, f* de ventas, director,-a *m, f* comercial. **2** *(at bargain prices)* liquidación *f,* saldo *m,* rebajas *fpl*. **3** *(auction)* subasta *f*.

saleable ['seɪləbəl] *adj* vendible.

salesclerk ['seɪlzklɑːk] *n* dependiente,-a *m,f*.

salesgirl ['seɪlzgɜːl] *n* dependienta *f*.

salesman ['seɪlzmən] *n (pl salesmen)* **1** *(gen)* vendedor *m; (in shop)* dependiente *m*. **2** *(commercial traveller)* representante *m*.

salesroom ['seɪlzruːm] *n* **1** sala *f* de subastas. **2** *US (showroom)* exposición *f*.

saleswoman ['seɪlzwumən] *n (pl saleswomen* ['seɪlzwɪmɪn]*)* **1** *(gen)* vendedora *f; (in shop)* dependienta *f*. **2** *(commercial traveller)* representante *f*.

Salic ['sælɪk] *adj* sálico,-a.

salient ['seɪlɪənt] *adj* **1** *(angle etc)* saliente, saledizo,-a. **2** *fig (feature)* sobresaliente, destacado,-a.

saline ['seɪlaɪn] *adj* salino,-a.

saliva [sə'laɪvə] *n* saliva *f*.

salivary ['sælɪvərɪ] *adj* salival, salivar.

sallow ['sæləʊ] *adj* cetrino,-a.

sallowness ['sæləʊnɪs] *n* color *m* cetrino, palidez *f*.

sally ['sælɪ] **I** *n* **1** *Mil* salida *f*. **2** *(remark)* agudeza *f,* réplica *f*. **II** *vi* **1** *Mil (also s. forth)* hacer una salida. **2** *(gen)* salir a buen paso, emprender la marcha.

salmon ['sæmən] **I** *n* salmón *m*. ■ **s. trout,** trucha *f* asalmonada, reo *m*. **II** *adj* de color salmón.

salmonella [sælmə'nelə] *n Biol Med* salmonela *f; (food poisoning)* salmonelosis *f*.

salon ['sælɒn] *n* salón *m*. ■ **beauty s.,** salón *m or* instituto *m* de belleza; **hairdressing s.,** peluquería *f*.

saloon [sə'luːn] *n* **1** *(public room)* salón *m,* sala *f; (on ship)* cámara *f*. **2** *US (bar)* taberna *f,* bar *m; GB* **s. (bar),** bar *m* de lujo. **3** *(car)* turismo *m*.

saloonkeeper [sə'luːnkiːpəʳ] *n US* tabernero,-a *m,f*.

salopettes [sælə'pets] *npl Sport* pantalón *m sing* de esquí.

salsify ['sælsɪfɪ] *n Bot* salsifí *m*.

salt [sɔːlt] **I** *n* **1** sal *f; fig* **the s. of the earth,** la sal de la tierra; *fig* **to take sth with a pinch of s.,** creer algo con reservas; *fig* **to be worth one's s.,** merecer el pan que se come. ■ **s. industry,** industria *f* salinera; **s. mine,** mina *f* de sal, salina *f; US* **s. shaker,** salero *m*. **2 salts,** sales *fpl*. ■ **bath s.,** sales *fpl* de baño; **Epsom s., liver s.,** sal *f sing* de la Higuera, epsomita *f sing;* **smelling s.,** sales *fpl* aromáticas. **II** *adj (food, water)* salado,-a. ■ **s. beef,** cecina *f;* **s. pork,** tocino *m*. **III** *vtr* **1** *(cure)* salar, conservar en sal. **2** *(add salt to)* echar sal a, sazonar con sal. ◆ **salt away** *vtr fam (money)* ahorrar.

saltcellar ['sɔːltselə'] *n* salero *m*.

salt-free ['sɔːltfriː] *adj* sin sal.

saltiness ['sɔːltɪnɪs] *n (water)* salubridad *f; (sea)* salinidad *f; (food)* sabor *m* salado.

saltpetre, *US* **saltpeter** ['sɔːlt'piːtəʳ] *n* salitre *m*.

saltwater ['sɔːltwɔːtəʳ] *adj* de mar, de agua salada; **s. fish,** pez *m* de agua salada.

salty ['sɔːltɪ] *adj (saltier, saltiest)* salado,-a.

salubrious [sə'luːbrɪəs] *adj* salubre, sano,-a.

salutary ['sæljutərɪ] *adj* **1** *(climate etc)* saludable. **2** *(experience)* beneficioso,-a; *(warning)* útil.

salute [sə'luːt] **I** *n Mil (greeting)* saludo *m*. **II** *vtr* **1** *Mil* saludar; **to s. the flag,** jurar bandera. **2** *fig (applaud)* aplaudir, aclamar. **III** *vi Mil* saludar.

Salvador(i)an [sækvə'dɔːr(ɪ)ən] *adj & n* salvadoreño,-a *(m,f)*.

salvage ['sælvɪdʒ] **I** *n* **1** *(recovery)* salvamento *m,* rescate *m;* **s. team,** equipo *m* de rescate. **2** *(objects recovered)* objetos *mpl* recuperados, material *m* rescatado. **3** *Jur* derecho *m* de salvamento. **II** *vtr (from ship etc)* salvar, rescatar.

salvation [sæl'veɪʃən] *n* salvación *f*.

salve [sælv, *US* sæv] **I** *n* pomada *f,* ungüento *m,* bálsamo *m*. ■ **lip s.,** crema *f or* barra *f* protectora de labios. **II** *vtr* curar (con pomada); *fig* **to s. one's conscience,** aliviarse la conciencia.

salver ['sælvəʳ] *n (gen)* salvilla *f; (of silver)* bandeja *f* (de plata).

salvo ['sælvəʊ] *n (pl salvos* or *salvoes) (of guns, applause)* salva *f*.

SAM [sæm] *Mil abbr of* **surface-to-air missile,** misil *m* tierra-aire.

Samaritan [sə'mærɪtən] *n Rel* samaritano *a m, f,* **the Samaritans,** ≈ el teléfono de la Esperanza.

samba ['sæmbə] *n (dance)* samba *f*.

same [seɪm] **I** *adj* mismo,-a, igual, idéntico,-a; **at that very s. moment,** en ese mismísimo momento; **at the s. time,** *(simultaneously)* al mismo tiempo, a la vez; *(however)* sin embargo, aun así; **in the s. way,** del mismo modo; **it amounts to the s. thing,** viene a ser lo mismo; **it's the s. old story,** es la misma historia de siempre; **the two cars are the s.,** los dos coches son iguales. **II** *pron* **1** el mismo, la misma, lo mismo; *(on phone)* **is that Harry Browne? —the very s.!,** ¿es usted Harry Browne? —¡el mismísimo!; **I would do the s. again,** volvería a hacer lo mismo; *fam* **the s. here,** lo mismo digo yo; *fam* **the s. to you!,** ¡igualmente! **2** *Com (it)* lo; **we will ship s. tomorrow,** lo enviaremos mañana. **III** *adv* del mismo modo, igual; **all the s., just the s.,** sin embargo, aun así; **it's all the s. to me,** (a mí) me da igual *or* lo mismo.

sameness ['seɪmnɪs] *n* **1** *(identical nature)* identidad *f,* igualdad *f*. **2** *(monotony)* monotonía *f*.

sampan ['sæmpæn] *n Naut* sampán *m*.

sample ['sɑːmpəl] **I** *n* muestra *f*. ■ *Med* **blood s.,** muestra *f* de sangre; **s. copy,** ejemplar *m* de muestra. **II** *vtr (wines)* catar, probar; *(dish)* probar.

sampler ['sɑːmpləʳ] n **1** (person) catador,-a m, f, probador,-a m, f. **2** Sew dechado m.

sanatorium [sænə'tɔːrɪəm] n (pl **sanatoriums** or **sanatoria** [sænə'tɔːrɪə]) sanatorio m.

sanctify ['sæŋktɪfaɪ] vtr (pt & pp **sanctified**) santificar, consagrar.

sanctimonious [sæŋktɪ'məʊnɪəs] adj beato,-a, santurrón,-ona, mojigato,-a.

sanctimoniousness [sæŋktɪ'məʊnɪəsnɪs] n, **sanctimony** ['sæŋktɪməʊnɪ] n beatería f, santurronería f, mojigatería f.

sanction ['sæŋkʃən] I n **1** (authorization) autorización f, permiso m. **2** (penalty) sanción f. **3** Pol **sanctions**, sanciones fpl. II vtr (law etc) sancionar, autorizar.

sanctity ['sæŋktɪtɪ] n (sacredness) santidad f, carácter m sagrado; (of marriage) inviolabilidad f.

sanctuary ['sæŋktjʊərɪ] n **1** Rel santuario m. **2** Pol asilo m; **to take s.**, refugiarse. **3** (for birds, animals) reserva f.

sanctum ['sæŋktəm] n (pl **sanctums** or **sancta** ['sæŋktə]) fam **the inner s.**, el sanctasanctórum.

sand [sænd] I n **1** (gen) arena f. ■ **s. castle**, castillo m de arena; **s. dune**, duna f; **s. pie**, flan m de arena; Golf **s. trap**, búnker m. **2** **sands**, (beach) playa f sing. II vtr **to s. (down)**, lijar.

sandal ['sændəl] n sandalia f, abarca f.

sandalwood ['sændəlwʊd] n Bot sándalo m.

sandbag ['sændbæg] I n saco m terrero. II vtr (pt & pp **sandbagged**) proteger con sacos terreros.

sandbank ['sændbæŋk] n banco m de arena.

sandblast ['sændblɑːst] I n chorro m de arena. II vtr limpiar con chorro de arena.

sandboy ['sændbɔɪ] n **as happy as a s.**, como un niño con zapatos nuevos.

sander ['sændəʳ] n (tool) lijadora f.

sandman ['sændmæn] n (pl **sandmen** ['sændmen]) ser m imaginario que **trae** el sueño a los niños.

sandpaper ['sændpeɪpəʳ] I n papel m de lija. II vtr lijar.

sandpit ['sændpɪt] n **1** Min cantera f de arena. **2** (in playground etc) arenal m.

sandstone ['sændstəʊn] n Geol arenisca f.

sandstorm ['sændstɔːm] n tempestad f e arena.

sandwich ['sænwɪdʒ, 'sænwɪtʃ] I n (bread roll) bocadillo m; (sliced bread) sandwich m, emparedado m; **double-decker s.**, sandwich de dos pisos. ■ Educ **s. course**, curso m teórico-práctico. II vtr intercalar; **it was sandwiched between two lorries**, quedó encajonado entre dos camiones.

sandy ['sændɪ] adj (**sandier, sandiest**) **1** (earth, beach) arenoso,-a. **2** (hair) rubio rojizo.

sane [seɪn] adj (person) cuerdo,-a; (judgement) sensato,-a; (mind) sano,-a; **perfectly s.**, en su sano juicio.

sang [sæŋ] pt see **sing**.

sang-froid [sɒŋ'frwɑː] n sangre f fría.

sanguine ['sæŋgwɪn] I adj **1** (optimistic) optimista. **2** (colour) sanguino,-a. II n (pencil) sanguina f.

sanitarium [sænɪ'teərɪəm] n (pl **sanitariums** or **sanitaria** [sænɪ'teərɪə]) US sanatorio m.

sanitary ['sænɪtərɪ] adj sanitario,-a, de sanidad; (hygienic) higiénico,-a. ■ **s. inspector**, inspector,-a m, f de sanidad; **s. towel**, US **s. napkin**, compresa f.

sanitation [sænɪ'teɪʃən] n sanidad f (pública); (hygiene) higiene f; (plumbing) sistema m de saneamiento;

sanitize ['sænɪtaɪz] vtr US esterilizar.

sanity ['sænɪtɪ] n (judgement) cordura f, juicio m; (good sense) sensatez f.

sank [sæŋk] pt see **sink**.

Sanskrit ['sænskrɪt] I adj sánscrito,-a. II n (language) sánscrito m.

Santa Claus [sæntə'klɔːz] n Papá Noel m, San Nicolás m.

sap¹ [sæp] n Bot savia f.

sap² [sæp] I Mil zapa f. II vtr zapar; (undermine) minar; fig debilitar, agotar.

sapling ['sæplɪŋ] n **1** Bot árbol m joven. **2** fig (youth) jovenzuelo m, zagal m.

sapper ['sæpəʳ] n Mil zapador m.

sapphire ['sæfaɪəʳ] n Min zafiro m.

sarcasm ['sɑːkæzəm] n sarcasmo m, sorna f.

sarcastic [sɑː'kæstɪk] adj (person, remark) sarcástico,-a.

sarcophagus [sɑː'kɒfəgəs] n (pl **sarcophaguses** or **sarcophagi** [sɑː'kɒfəgaɪ]) sarcófago m.

sardine [sɑː'diːn] n (fish) sardina f; fig **packed in like sardines**, como sardinas en lata.

Sardinia [sɑː'dɪnɪə] n Cerdeña f.

Sardinian [sɑː'dɪnɪən] I adj sardo,-a. II n **1** (person) sardo,-a m, f. **2** (language) sardo m.

sardonic [sɑː'dɒnɪk] adj sardónico,-a.

sarge [sɑːdʒ] n Mil fam abbr of **sergeant**.

sari ['sɑːrɪ] n (garment) sari m.

sartorial [sɑː'tɔːrɪəl] adj **1** (dress) de sastre; **s. elegance**, elegancia f en el vestir. **2** Anat sartorio,-a.

sartorius [sɑː'tɔːrɪəs] n (pl **sartorii** [sɑː'tɔːrɪaɪ]) Anat sartorio m.

SAS [eseɪ'es] GB Mil abbr of **Special Air Service**, ≈ Grupos mpl Especiales de Operaciones, GEO.

sash¹ [sæʃ] n (waistband etc) faja f.

sash² [sæʃ] n marco m de ventana. ■ **s. window**, ventana f de guillotina.

Sassenach ['sæsənæx] n Scot pej inglés,-esa m, f.

sassy ['sæsɪ] adj (**sassier, sassiest**) US fam descarado,-a, fresco,-a.

Sat abbr of **Saturday**, sábado m, sáb.

sat [sæt] pt & pp see **sit**.

Satan ['seɪtən] n Satán m, Satanás m.

satanic [sə'tænɪk] adj satánico,-a.

satchel ['sætʃəl] n cartera f de colegial.

satellite ['sætəlaɪt] n satélite m. ■ TV **s. broad-casting**, transmisión f por satélite; TV **s. dish aerial**, antena f parabólica; Pol **s. state**, país m satélite.

satiate ['seɪʃɪeɪt] vtr saciar.

satiation [seɪʃɪ'eɪʃən] n saciedad f.

satin ['sætɪn] n Tex satén m; (paint) **s. finish**, acabado m satinado.

satire ['sætaɪəʳ] n sátira f.

satirical [sə'tɪrɪkəl] adj satírico,-a.

satirist ['sætərɪst] n escritor,-a m, f satírico,-a.

satisfaction [sætɪs'fækʃən] n satisfacción f; **to express one's s.**, expresar su satisfacción.

satisfactory [sætɪs'fæktərɪ] I adj satisfactorio,-a. II n Sch Univ suficiente m, aprobado m.

satisfied ['sætɪsfaɪd] adj satisfecho,-a.

satisfy ['sætɪsfaɪ] vtr (pt & pp **satisfied**) **1** (make happy) satisfacer. **2** (fulfil) cumplir con, satisfacer; **to s. the requirements**, cumplir los requisitos. **3** (convince) convencer. **4** (debt) liquidar.

satisfying ['sætɪsfaɪɪŋ] adj **1** (gen) satisfactorio,-a, substancioso,-a, sustancioso,-a; (pleasing) agradable. **2** (meal) completo,-a.

saturate ['sætʃəreɪt] vtr saturar; fam empapar (**with**, de).

saturation [sætʃə'reɪʃən] n saturación f.

Saturday ['sætədɪ] n sábado m; **every other S.**, un sábado sí y otro no, cada dos sábados; **every S.**, todos los sábados; **last S.**, el sábado pasado; **next S.**, el próximo sábado, el sábado que viene; **on S.**, el sábado; **on S. morning/afternoon** or **evening/night**, el sábado por la mañana/tarde *or* noche; **on Saturdays,** los sábados; **S.'s paper,** el periódico del sábado; **the following S.,** el sábado siguiente; **the S. after next, a week on S., S. week,** este sábado en ocho; **the S. before last,** el sábado anterior; *TV* **the S. film,** la película del sábado; **this S.,** este sábado.

Saturn ['sætɜːn] *n Astron* Saturno *m*.

satyr ['sætər] *n Myth* sátiro *m*.

sauce [sɔːs] *n* **1** *Culin* salsa *f*. ■ **s. boat,** *US* **s. dish,** salsera *f*; **white s.,** salsa *f* bechamel. **2** *fam (impudence)* descaro *m*, frescura *f*.

saucepan ['sɔːspən] *n* cazo *m*, cacerola *f*; *(large)* olla *f*.

saucer ['sɔːsər] *n* platillo *m*. ■ *fam* **flying s.,** platillo *m* volante.

saucy ['sɔːsɪ] *adj (saucier, sauciest) fam (impudent)* descarado,-a, fresco,-a.

Saudi Arabia [saʊdɪəˈreɪbɪə] *n* Arabia *f* Saudita *or* Saudí.

Saudi Arabian [saʊdɪəˈreɪbɪən] *adj & n* saudita *(mf)*, saudí *(mf)*.

sauna ['sɔːnə] *n* sauna *f*.

saunter ['sɔːntər] **I** *n* paseo *m*. **II** *vi* pasearse.

sausage ['sɒsɪdʒ] *n (uncooked)* salchicha *f*; *(cured)* salchichón *m*; *(spicy)* chorizo *m*, embutido *m*, salami *m*. ■ *US* **blood s.,** morcilla *f*; *fam* **s. dog,** perro *m* salchicha; **s. meat,** carne *f* de embutido; *GB* **s. roll,** empanada *f* de carne.

sauté ['səʊteɪ] *Culin* **I** *adj* salteado,-a. **II** *vtr (pt & pp sautéed)* saltear.

savage ['sævɪdʒ] **I** *adj* **1** *(ferocious)* feroz; *(cruel)* cruel; *(violent)* salvaje, violento,-a. **2** *(primitive)* salvaje, primitivo,-a. **II** *n (primitive person)* salvaje *mf*. **III** *vtr* **1** *(attack) (animal)* embestir; *fig (person)* atacar violentamente. **2** *(criticize)* desacreditar.

savageness ['sævɪdʒnɪs] *n*, **savagery** ['sævɪdʒrɪ] *n* **1** *(ferocity)* ferocidad *f*; *(cruelty)* crueldad *f*; *(violence)* violencia *f*; *(cruel act)* salvajada *f*. **2** *(primitive state)* salvajismo *m*.

savanna(h) [səˈvænə] *n Geol* sabana *f*.

save [seɪv] **I** *vtr* **1** *(rescue)* salvar, rescatar *(from,* de); *Rel* salvar; **God s. the Queen!,** ¡Dios guarde a la Reina!; *fig* **to s. face,** salvar las apariencias; *fig* **to s. the day,** salvar la situación. **2** *(gen) (put by)* guardar; *(money)* ahorrar; *(food)* almacenar; *(stamps)* coleccionar; **s. me a seat,** guárdame un asiento. **3** *(avoid spending) (money, energy)* ahorrar; *(time)* ahorrar, ahorrarse, ganar; **it saved him a lot of trouble,** le evitó muchos problemas; **that way we'll s. ourselves an hour/£5,** así nos ahorramos una hora/5 libras. **II** *vi* **1 to s. (up),** ahorrar. **2** *(economize)* **to s. on food/gas/paper,** ahorrar comida/gas/papel. **III** *n Ftb* parada *f*. **IV** *prep (old use)* salvo, excepto.

saver ['seɪvər] **I** *n* ahorrador,-a *m,f*.

saving ['seɪvɪŋ] **I** *n (of time, money)* ahorro *m*, economía *f*; **to make savings,** hacer economías, economizar. **2 savings,** ahorros *mpl*; **to live off one's s.,** vivir de sus ahorros. ■ **s. account,** cuenta *f* de ahorros; **s. bank,** caja *f* de ahorros. **II** *adj* **it's his only s. grace,** es el único mérito que tiene.

saviour, *US* **savior** ['seɪvjər] *n* salvador,-a *m,f*; *Rel* **Our S.,** El Salvador.

savoir-faire [sævwɑːˈfeər] *n* tacto *m*, don *m* de gentes.

savour, *US* **savor** ['seɪvər] **I** *n* sabor *m*, gusto *m*. **II** *vi* saborear.

savoury, *US* **savory** ['seɪvərɪ] **I** *adj (tasty)* sabroso,-a; *(salted)* salado,-a; *(spicy)* picante. **II** *n GB* entremés *m* salado, tapa *f*, canapé *m*.

savvy ['sævɪ] *fam* **I** *n (gen)* entendederas *fpl*, sentido *m* común; *(political)* habilidad *f*. **II** *vtr* comprender, entender; captar.

saw¹ [sɔː] **I** *n (tool)* sierra *f*, serrucho *m*. ■ **mechanical s.,** sierra *f* mecánica. **II** *vtr & vi (pt sawed; pp sawed or sawn)* serrar, aserrar. ◆ **saw up** *vtr* serrar *(into,* en), aserrar *(into,* en), cortar *(into,* en).

saw² [sɔː] *pt see* **see¹**.

sawdust ['sɔːdʌst] *n* serrín *m*, aserrín *m*.

sawhorse ['sɔːhɔːs] *n* burro *m*, caballete *m*.

sawmill ['sɔːmɪl] *n* aserradero *m*, serrería *f*.

sawn [sɔːn] *pp see* **saw¹**.

sawn-off ['sɔːnɒf] *adj* recortado,-a; **s.-o. shotgun,** escopeta *f* de cañones recortados.

sax [sæks] *n Mus fam* saxo *m*.

Saxon ['sæksən] *adj & n* sajón,-ona *(m,f)*.

saxophone ['sæksəfəʊn] *n Mus* saxofón *m*.

saxophonist [sækˈsɒfənɪst] *n* saxofonista *mf*, saxo *mf*.

say [seɪ] **I** *vtr (pt & pp said)* **1** *(gen)* decir; *(express)* expresar; *(affirm)* afirmar, declarar; **as they s.,** como se suele decir; **it goes without saying that ...,** por supuesto que ..., huelga decir que ...; **it is said that ..., that they s., dicen que ..., se dice que ...; **it's easier said than done,** es más fácil decirlo que hacerlo; **no sooner said than done,** dicho y hecho; **not to s.,** incluso; **that is to s.,** es decir; **there's no saying,** es imposible de decir; **to s. the least,** como mínimo; **to s. to oneself,** decir para sí; **to s. yes/no,** decir que sí/no; **to s. yes/no to an offer,** aceptar/rechazar una oferta; **when all is said and done,** al fin y al cabo; *fam* **I s.!,** ¡oiga!, ¡oye!; *fam* **you don't s.!,** ¡no me digas! **2** *(dictionary, notice, etc)* decir, rezar; *(clock, thermometer, etc)* decir, marcar; **what does the sign s.?,** ¿qué pone en el letrero? **3** *(think)* pensar, opinar; **what do you s. to that?,** ¿qué piensas de eso?, ¿qué te parece eso? **4** *(suppose)* suponer, poner; **(let's) s. it costs about £10,** pongamos *or* digamos que cuesta unas 10 libras; **shall we s. Friday then?,** ¿quedamos el viernes, pues? **II** *n (gen)* opinión *f*; **I have no s. in the matter,** no tengo ni voz ni voto en el asunto; **let him have his s.,** déjele hablar; **to have one's s.,** dar su opinión.

say-so ['seɪsəʊ] *n fam* **1** *(assertion)* afirmaciones *fpl*. **2** *(approval)* aprobación *f*, visto *m* bueno.

saying ['seɪɪŋ] *n* refrán *m*, dicho *m*, proverbio *m*; **as the s. goes,** como dice el refrán.

s/c *abbr* of **self-contained,** con acceso independiente.

scab [skæb] *n* **1** *Med* costra *f*, postilla *f*. **2** *fam pej (blackleg)* esquirol *mf*.

scabbard ['skæbəd] *n* vaina *f*. ■ **s. fish,** pez *m* cinto.

scabby ['skæbɪ] *adj (scabbier, scabbiest) Med* costroso,-a, lleno,-a de costras.

scabies ['skeɪbiːz] *n inv Med* sarna *f*.

scabrous ['skeɪbrəs] *adj* escabroso,-a.

scad [skæd] *n (fish)* jurel *m*.

scaffold ['skæfəld] *n* **1** *Constr* andamio *m*. **2** *(for execution)* patíbulo *m*, cadalso *m*.

scaffolding ['skæfəldɪŋ] *n Constr* andamio *n*, andamiaje *m*.

scald [skɔːld] **I** *n* escaldadura *f*. **II** *vtr* **1** *(skin etc)* escaldar. **2** *(liquid)* calentar. **3** *(sterilize)* esterilizar.

scale¹ [skeɪl] **I** *n* **1** *(of fish, reptile)* escama *f*. **2** *(on skin)* escama *f*; *(on teeth)* sarro *m*; *(on ship, boiler)* incrustaciones *fpl*. **II** *vtr* **1** *(fish)* escamar, quitar las escamas a. **2** *(teeth)* quitar el sarro a, limpiar; *(ship, boiler)* desincrustar, limpiar.

scale² [skeɪl] **I** *n* **1** *(gen)* escala *f*; **on a large s.,** a gran escala; **sliding s.,** escala móvil; **to s.,** a escala. ■ **s. drawing,** dibujo *m* (hecho) a escala; **s. model,** maqueta *f*. **2** *(of accident, disaster)* alcance *m*. **3** *Mus* escala *f*. **II** *vtr (mountain, wall)* escalar. ◆ **scale down** *vtr (gen)* reducir proporcionalmente; *(drawing, map)* reducir a escala; *(production)* reducir, bajar. ◆ **scale up** *vtr (gen)* aumentar proporcionalmente; *(drawing, map)* aumentar a escala; *(production)* aumentar.

scales [skeɪlz] *npl (pair or set of)* **s.,** *(shop, kitchen)* balanza *f sing*; *(bathroom)* báscula *f sing*; *Astrol* **the S.,** Libra *f sing*; *fig* **to tip the s. in sb's favour,** inclinar la balanza a favor de algn. ■ **letter s.,** pesacartas *m inv*.

scallion ['skæljən] *n* cebolleta *f*.

scallop ['skɒləp] **I** *n* **1** *(mollusc)* vieira *f*, concha *f* de peregrino. **2** *(shell)* concha *f* de peregrino, venera *f*. **3** *Sew* festón *m*. **II** *vtr* **1** *Culin* guisar al gratén. **2** *Sew* festonear.

scalp [skælp] **I** *n* Anat cuero *m* cabelludo; *fig* cabeza *f*. **II** *vtr* **1** arrancar el cuero cabelludo a. **2** *fam (tickets)* revender.

scalpel ['skælpəl] *n* Med bisturí *m*; *(dissection)* escalpelo *m*.

scaly ['skeɪlɪ] *adj (scalier, scaliest)* escamoso,-a.

scam [skæm] *n sl* timo *m*, estafa *f*.

scamp [skæmp] *n (child)* diablillo *m*, pilluelo,-a *m, f*; *(adult)* granuja *mf*, pícaro,-a *m, f*.

scamper ['skæmpə'] *vi* corretear.

scampi ['skæmpɪ] *n Culin* cigalas *fpl* empanadas *or* rebozadas.

scan [skæn] **I** *vtr (pt & pp scanned)* **1** *(scrutinize)* escrutar, escudriñar; *(horizon)* otear. **2** *(glance at)* ojear, echar un vistazo a. **3** *(radar)* explorar. **II** *vi (poetry)* estar bien medido. **III** *n Med (gen)* exploración *f* ultrasónica; *(gynaecology, etc)* ecografía *f*.

scandal ['skændəl] *n* **1** *(gen)* escándalo *m*; **political s.,** escándalo político; **what a s.!,** ¡qué vergüenza! **2** *(gossip)* chismes *mpl*.

scandalize ['skændəlaɪz] *vtr* escandalizar.

scandalous ['skændələs] *adj* escandaloso,-a, vergonzoso,-a.

Scandinavia [skændɪ'neɪvɪə] *n* Escandinavia.

Scandinavian [skændɪ'neɪvɪən] *adj & n* escandinavo,-a *(m, f)*.

scanner ['skænə'] *n* **1** *(radar)* antena *f* direccional. **2** Med escáner *m*.

scant [skænt] *adj* escaso,-a.

scanty ['skæntɪ] *adj (scantier, scantiest) (gen)* escaso,-a; *(meal)* parco,-a, insuficiente; *(clothes)* ligero,-a. ◆ **scantily** *adv* escasamente; **to be s. clad** *or* **dressed,** ir ligero,-a de ropa.

scapegoat ['skeɪpgəʊt] *n* cabeza *f* de turco, chivo *m* expiatorio.

scar [skɑːr] *n* **1** cicatriz *f*. **2** *fig* huella *f*. **II** *vtr (pt & pp scarred)* marcar con una cicatriz; *fig* **to s. sb for life,** marcar a algn para toda la vida. **III** *vi* dejar una cicatriz.

scarce [skeəs] *adj (in short supply)* escaso,-a; *(rare)* raro,-a; **to be s.,** faltar, escasear; *fam* **to make oneself s.,** esfumarse, largarse. ◆ **scarcely** *adv* apenas; **I can s. believe it,** me cuesta creerlo; **s. ever,** casi nunca; **she s. spoke,** apenas habló.

scarceness ['skeəsnɪs] *n,* **scarcity** ['skeəsɪtɪ] *n* escasez *f*; *(shortage)* escasez *f*, falta *f*; *(rarity)* rareza *f*.

scare [skeə'] **I** *n* **1** *(fright)* susto *m*; *(widespread alarm)* pánico *m*, alarma *f*; **to cause a s.,** sembrar el pánico; **what a s. you gave me!,** ¡qué susto me pegaste! ■ **bomb s.,** amenaza *f* de bomba; **polio s.,** temor *m* a una epidemia de polio. **II** *vtr* asustar, espantar; *fam* **to be scared out of one's wits,** sufrir un susto mortal; *fam* **to be scared stiff,** estar muerto,-a de miedo. **III** *vi* asustarse. ◆ **scare away, scare off** *vtr* ahuyentar, espantar.

scarecrow ['skeəkrəʊ] *n* espantapájaros *m inv*, espantajo *m*.

scaremonger ['skeəmʌŋgə'] *n* alarmista *mf*.

scarf [skɑːf] *n (pl scarfs or scarves* [skɑːvz]*) (long, woollen)* bufanda *f*; *(square)* pañuelo *m*; *(silk)* fular *m*.

scarlet ['skɑːlɪt] **I** *n* escarlata *f*. **II** *adj* escarlata. ■ Med **s. fever,** escarlatina *f*; *pej* **s. woman,** mujer *f* de la calle.

scarp [skɑːp] *n* escarpa *f*, pendiente *f*.

scarper ['skɑːpə'] *vi GB sl* largarse, abrirse.

scarves [skɑːvz] *npl* see **scarf.**

scary ['skeərɪ] *adj (scarier, scariest) fam* espantoso,-a, pavoroso,-a; *(film)* de miedo *or* terror.

scathing ['skeɪðɪŋ] *adj* mordaz, cáustico,-a; **to be s. about,** criticar duramente.

scatological [skætə'lɒdʒɪkəl] *adj* escatológico,-a.

scatter ['skætə'] **I** *vtr* **1** *(spread) (papers etc)* esparcir, desparramar; *(seeds)* sembrar a voleo. **2** *(disperse)* dispersar. **II** *vi (crowd, flock)* dispersarse.

scatterbrain ['skætəbreɪn] *n fam* cabeza *f* de chorlito.

scatterbrained ['skætəbreɪnd] *adj fam* ligero,-a de cascos; *(forgetful)* despistado,-a, olvidadizo,-a.

scattered ['skætəd] *adj* esparcido,-a, disperso,-a; **s. population,** población diseminada; Meteor **s. showers,** chubascos aislados; **s. villages,** pueblos dispersos.

scattering ['skætərɪŋ] *n* **a s. of,** unos,-as pocos,-as, unos,-as cuantos,-as.

scatty ['skætɪ] *adj (scattier, scattiest) fam* see **scatterbrained.**

scavenge ['skævɪndʒ] **I** *vi (search)* rebuscar; **to s. through the dustbin,** remover la basura en busca de algo. **II** *vtr (find among rubbish)* encontrar en la basura.

scavenger ['skævɪndʒə'] *n* **1** *(person)* rebuscador,-a *m, f*, trapero *m*. **2** *(animal)* animal *m* carroñero.

scenario [sɪ'nɑːrɪəʊ] *n* Theat argumento *m*; Cin guión *m*.

scene [siːn] *n* **1** Theat Cin TV escena *f*; **behind the scenes,** entre bastidores; **the current political s.,** el panorama político actual. **2** *(place)* lugar *m*, escenario *m*; **a change of s.,** un cambio de aires; **the s. of the crime,** el lugar del crimen; **to appear on the s.,** aparecer en escena; **to disappear from the s.,** desaparecer de escena; *fam* **it's not my s.,** no me va nada. ■ **s. shifter,** tramoyista *mf*. **3** *(view)* panorama *m*, vista *f*. **4** *(fuss)* escena *f*, escándalo *m*; *(quarrel)* riña *f*, pelea *f*; **to make a s.,** armar un escándalo.

scenery ['siːnərɪ] *n* **1** *(landscape)* paisaje *m*. **2** Theat *(on stage)* decorado *m*.

scenic ['siːnɪk] *adj (picturesque)* pintoresco,-a. ■ **s. railway,** *(miniature train)* tren *m* de recreo; *(roller coaster)* montaña *f* rusa; **s. route,** ruta *f* panorámica.

scent [sent] **I** *n* **1** *(smell)* olor *m*; *(of food)* aroma *m*. **2** *(perfume)* perfume *m*. **3** *(hunting)* rastro *m*, pista *f*, *fig* **to lose the s.,** perder la pista. **II** *vtr* **1** *(add perfume to)* perfumar. **2** *(smell)* olfatear; *fig* presentir.

scepter ['septə'] *n US* see **sceptre.**

sceptic ['skeptɪk] *n* escéptico,-a *m, f*.

sceptical ['skeptɪkəl] *adj* escéptico,-a.

scepticism ['skeptɪsɪzəm] *n* escepticismo *m*.

sceptre ['septə'] *n* cetro *m*.

sch *abbr of* **school,** escuela *f*, esc.

schedule ['ʃedjuːl, *US* 'skedʒʊəl] **I** *n* **1** *(plan, agenda)* programa *m*; *(timetable)* horario *m*; **according to s.,** según lo previsto; **on s., a la hora** prevista); **to be behind s.,** llevar retraso, ir atrasado,-a. **2** *(list)* lista *f*; *(inventory)* inventario *m*. **II** *vtr (plan)* programar, fijar.

scheduled ['ʃedjuːld, *US* 'skedʒʊəld] *adj* previsto,-a, fijo,-a; **at the s. time,** a la hora prevista; Av **s. flight,** vuelo regular.

schematic [skiː'mætɪk, skɪ'mætɪk] *adj* esquemático,-a.

scheme [skiːm] **I** *n* **1** *(plan)* plan *m*, programa *m*; *(project)* proyecto *m*; *(idea)* idea *f*. ■ **colour s.,** combinación *f* de colores. **2** *(plot)* intriga *f*, conspiración *f*; *(trick)* ardid *m*, estratagema *f*, truco *m*. **II** *vi (plot)* tramar, intrigar, conspirar *(against,* contra).

schemer ['skiːmə'] *n* intrigante *mf*, maquinador,-a *m, f*.

scheming ['skiːmɪŋ] **I** *adj* intrigante, maquinador,-a. **II** *n* intrigas *fpl*, maquinaciones *fpl*.

schism ['sɪzəm] *n* cisma *m*.

schizophrenia [skɪtsəʊ'friːnɪə] *n* esquizofrenia *f*.

schizophrenic [skɪtsəʊ'frenɪk] *adj & n* esquizofrénico,-a *(m, f)*.

schlep [ʃlep] *vtr (pt & pp schlepped) US sl (drag)* arrastrar.

schmaltz [ʃmælts] *n fam* sentimentalismo *m*.

schnapps [ʃnæps] *n* aguardiente *m* alemán.

scholar ['skɒləʳ] *n* **1** *(learned person)* erudito,-a *m, f*: *(specialist)* especialista *mf*, experto,-a *m, f*; **Greek s.**, helenista *mf*; **Latin s.**, latinista *mf*. **2** *(pupil)* alumno,-a *m, f*; *(scholarship holder)* becario,-a *m, f*.

scholarship ['skɒləʃɪp] *n* **1** *(learning)* erudición *f*. **2** *(award, grant)* beca *f*. ■**s. holder**, becario,-a *m, f*.

scholastic [skəˈlæstɪk] *adj* **1** *(year)* escolar; *(profession)* docente. **2** *Hist* escolástico,-a.

school [skuːl] I *n* **1** *(gen)* escuela *f*, colegio *m*; **to leave s.**, terminar *or* dejar la escuela. ■ **comprehensive s.**, **grammar s.**, **high s.**, instituto *m* (de enseñanza media *or* de educación secundaria); **convent s.**, colegio *m* de monjas; **drama s.**, academia *f* de arte dramático; **driving s.**, autoescuela *f*; **language s.**, academia *f* or escuela *f* de idiomas; **night s.**, escuela *f* nocturna; **nursery s.**, jardín *m* de infancia, parvulario *m*; **primary s.**, escuela *f* primaria; **public s.**, *GB* colegio *m* privado, *US* instituto *m*; **s. age**, edad *f* escolar; **s. holidays**, vacaciones *fpl* escolares; **s. year**, año *m* escolar; **secondary s.**, *(gen)* escuela *f* secundaria; *(private)* colegio *m*; *(state)* instituto *m* (de enseñanza media *or* de educación secundaria); **summer s.**, cursos *mpl* de verano. **2** *(pupils)* alumnado *m*, alumnos *mpl*. **3** *US (university)* universidad *f*. **4** *(university department)* facultad *f*; **law s.**, facultad de derecho; **s. of medicine**, facultad de medicina. **5** *(group of artists etc)* escuela *f*; **s. of thought**, corriente *f* de opinión *f*; **the Cubist s.**, la escuela cubista. II *vtr* **1** *(teach)* enseñar; *(train)* educar, formar; **to s. sb in sth**, enseñar algo a algn. **2** *(discipline)* disciplinar; **to s. one's temper**, controlar el mal genio *or* humor.

school² [skuːl] *n (of fish)* banco *m*.

schoolbook ['skuːlbʊk] *n* libro *m* de texto.

schoolboy ['skuːlbɔɪ] *n* alumno *m*, colegial *m*.

schoolchild ['skuːltʃaɪld] *n (pl **schoolchildren** ['skuːltʃɪldrən])* alumno,-a *m, f*.

schooldays ['skuːldeɪz] *npl* años *mpl* de colegio, tiempos *mpl* de colegio.

schoolfellow ['skuːlfeləʊ] *n* compañero,-a *m, f* de clase.

schoolgirl ['skuːlɡɜːl] *n* alumna *f*, colegiala *f*.

schooling ['skuːlɪŋ] *n* educación *f*, estudios *mpl*.

schoolmaster ['skuːlmɑːstəʳ] *n* profesor *m*; *(primary school)* maestro *m*.

schoolmate ['skuːlmeɪt] *n see* **schoolfellow**.

schoolmistress ['skuːlmɪstrɪs] *n* profesora *f*; *(primary school)* maestra *f*.

schoolroom ['skuːlruːm] *n* aula *f*, clase *f*.

schoolteacher ['skuːltiːtʃəʳ] *n* profesor,-a *m, f*; *(primary school)* maestro,-a *m, f*.

schoolyard ['skuːljɑːd] *n* patio *m* de recreo.

schooner ['skuːnəʳ] *n* **1** *Naut* goleta *f*. **2** *(for sherry)* copa *f*; *US & Austral (for beer)* jarra *f*.

sciatica [saɪˈætɪkə] *n Med* ciática *f*.

science ['saɪəns] *n* ciencia *f*; *(school subject)* ciencias *fpl*. ■ **natural s.**, ciencias *fpl* naturales; **s. fiction**, ciencia-ficción *f*.

scientific [saɪənˈtɪfɪk] *adj* científico,-a.

scientist ['saɪəntɪst] *n* científico,-a *m, f*.

sci-fi ['saɪfaɪ] *n fam abbr of* **science fiction**.

scintillate ['sɪntɪleɪt] *vi (sparkle)* centellear, destellar; *fig* brillar.

scintillating ['sɪntɪleɪtɪŋ] *adj* brillante.

scissors ['sɪzəz] *npl* **1** tijeras *fpl*; **a pair of s.**, unas tijeras. **2** *Wrest* tijera *f*.

sclerosis [sklɪəˈrəʊsɪs] *n Med* esclerosis *f*; **multiple s.**, esclerosis *f* en placas.

scoff¹ [skɒf] *vi (mock)* mofarse (**at**, de), burlarse (**at**, de).

scoff² [skɒf] *vtr fam (eat fast)* tragarse, zamparse.

scoffing ['skɒfɪŋ] *n* mofa *f*, burla *f*.

scold [skəʊld] *vtr* regañar, reñir.

scolding ['skəʊldɪŋ] *n* regañina *f*, reprimenda *f*.

scone [skəʊn, skɒn] *n Culin* bollo *m*, pastelito *m*.

scoop [skuːp] I *n* **1** *(for flour)* pala *f*; *(for ice cream)* cucharón *m*; *(amount)* palada *f*, cucharada *f*. **2** *Fin sl* golpe *m* financiero. **3** *Press* exclusiva *f*. II *vtr* **1** *Fin sl (benefit)* forrarse de. **2** *Press fam* **to s. the other newspapers**, pisar una noticia a los otros periódicos. ◆ **scoop out** *vtr (flour etc)* sacar con pala; *(water) (from boat)* achicar. ◆ **scoop up** *vtr* recoger.

scooter ['skuːtəʳ] *n (child's)* patinete *m*, patineta *f*; *(adult's)* escúter *m*, Vespa® *f*.

scope [skəʊp] *n* **1** *(range)* alcance *m*; *(of book, undertaking)* ámbito *m*; *(ability)* competencia *f*. **2** *(freedom)* libertad *f*; *(opportunity)* oportunidad *f*; **to give sb full s.**, dar campo libre *or* carta blanca a algn.

scorch [skɔːtʃ] I *n* quemadura *f*. II *vtr (burn)* quemar; *(singe)* chamuscar.

scorcher ['skɔːtʃəʳ] *n fam* día *m* abrasador.

scorching ['skɔːtʃɪŋ] *adj* abrasador,-a.

score [skɔːʳ] I *n* **1** *Sport* tanteo *m*; *Cards Golf* puntuación *f*; *(result)* resultado *m*, marcador *m*; **to keep the s.**, seguir el marcador; **what's the s.?**, ¿cómo van?; *fig* **to know the s.**, estar al tanto. **2** *(notch)* muesca *f*. **3** *(account)* cuenta *f*. **4** *(reason)* **on that s.**, por lo que se refiere a eso, a ese respecto. **5** *(twenty)* veintena *f*; *fam* **scores of**, montones de. **6** *Mus (of opera)* partitura *f*; *(of film)* música *f*. II *vtr* **1** *(goal)* marcar; *(points)* ganar; **to s. a victory**, conseguir una victoria. **2** *(notch) (wood)* hacer una muesca en; *(paper)* rayar. III *vi* **1** *Sport* marcar un tanto; *Ftb* marcar un gol; *(keep the score)* llevar el marcador. **2** *(have success)* tener éxito **(with**, con); *sl* ligar **(with**, con); *sl (obtain drugs)* ligar *or* pillar droga. ◆ **score out** *vtr (word etc)* tachar.

scoreboard ['skɔːbɔːd] *n* marcador *m*, tanteador *m*.

scorecard ['skɔːkɑːd] *n Golf* tarjeta *f*.

scorekeeper ['skɔːkiːpəʳ] *n* encargado,-a *m, f* del marcador.

scorer ['skɔːrəʳ] *n* **1** *(goal striker)* goleador *m*. **2** *(scorekeeper)* encargado,-a *m, f* del marcador.

scorn [skɔːn] I *n* desprecio *m*, desdén *m*. II *vtr* despreciar, desdeñar, menospreciar.

scornful ['skɔːnfʊl] *adj* desdeñoso,-a.

Scorpio ['skɔːpɪəʊ] *n Astrol Astron* Escorpión *m*.

scorpion ['skɔːpɪən] *n Zool* alacrán *m*, escorpión *m*. ■ **s. fish**, cabracho *m*.

Scot [skɒt] *n* escocés,-esa *m, f*.

Scotch [skɒtʃ] I *adj* escocés,-esa. ■ *Culin* **S. broth**, potaje *m* de cordero, cebada y verduras; **S. egg**, huevo *m* envuelto con carne de salchicha; **S. tape®**, cinta *f* adhesiva, celo® *m*. II *n (whisky)* whisky *m* escocés, scotch *m*.

scotch [skɒtʃ] *vtr (plot etc)* frustrar, hacer fracasar; *(rumour)* sofocar.

scot-free [skɒtˈfriː] *adj* impune.

Scotland ['skɒtlənd] *n* Escocia, **S. Yard**, sede *f* de la policía londinense.

Scots [skɒts] I *adj* escocés,-esa. II *n* **1** *(language)* escocés *m*. **2** *pl* **the S.**, los escoceses.

Scotsman ['skɒtsmən] *n (pl Scotsmen)* escocés *m*.

Scotswoman ['skɒtswʊmən] *n (pl Scotswomen* ['skɒtswɪmɪn]*)* escocesa *f*.

Scottish ['skɒtɪʃ] I *adj* escocés,-esa. II *n (language)* escocés *m*.

scoundrel ['skaʊndrəl] *n* sinvergüenza *mf*, canalla *m*.

scour¹ [skaʊəʳ] *vtr (clean) (pots etc)* fregar, restregar.

scour² [skaʊəʳ] *vtr (search) (countryside)* recorrer; *(building)* registrar.

scourer ['skaʊrəʳ] *n*, **scouring pad** ['skaʊrɪŋpæd] *n* estropajo *m*.

scourge [skɜːdʒ] *fig* I *n* azote *m*. II *vtr* azotar.

scout [skaʊt] I *n Mil* explorador,-a *m, f*; **boy s.,** boy *m* scout; *Mil* **s. plane,** avión *m* explorador; *Sport Cin* **talent s.,** cazatalentos *m inv*. II *vi Mil* reconocer el terreno; **to s. around for sth,** andar en busca de algo.

scouting ['skaʊtɪŋ] *n* 1 *(activities)* actividades *fpl* de los exploradores *or* los scouts. 2 *(boy scout movement)* escultismo *m*.

scoutmaster ['skaʊtmɑːstəʳ] *n* jefe *m* de los exploradores *or* los scouts.

scowl [skaʊl] I *vi* fruncir el ceño; **to s. at sb,** mirar a algn con ceño. II *n* ceño *m*.

scrabble ['skræbəl] I *vi* escarbar; *fig* **to s. around for sth,** revolver todo para encontrar algo. II *n (game)* S.®, Scrabble® *m*.

scrag [skræg] I *n* pescuezo *m*. II *vtr* retorcer el pescuezo.

scraggly ['skræglɪ] *adj (scragglier, scraggliest)* 1 *(beard etc)* descuidado,-a. 2 *(rock)* mellado,-a.

scraggy ['skrægɪ] *adj (scraggier, scraggiest)* delgado,-a, flacucho,-a.

scram [skræm] *vi fam* largarse.

scramble ['skræmbəl] I *vi* 1 trepar; **to s. for seats,** pelearse por encontrar asiento; **to s. into one's clothes,** vestirse rápidamente; **to s. up a tree,** trepar a un árbol. 2 *Sport* **to go scrambling,** hacer motocross. II *vtr* 1 *Culin* revolver; **scrambled eggs,** huevos revueltos. 2 *Rad Tel (message)* cifrar; *(broadcast)* interferir, perturbar. III *n* 1 *(climb)* subida *f*, trepa *f*; *(struggle)* lucha *f*, pelea *f*. 2 *Sport* carrera *f* de motocross.

scrambling ['skræmblɪŋ] *n Sport* **(motorcycle) s.,** motocross *m*.

scrap¹ [skræp] I *n* 1 *(small piece)* trozo *m*, trocito *m*, pedazo *m*; *(of conversation)* fragmento *m*; *(newspaper cutting)* recorte *m*; **s. (metal),** chatarra *f*; **there isn't a s. of truth in it,** no tiene ni un ápice de verdad. ◆ **s. dealer** *or* **merchant,** chatarrero,-a *m, f*; **s. paper,** papel *m* de borrador; **s. yard,** *(gen)* parque *m* de chatarra; *(for cars)* cementerio *m* de coches. 2 **scraps,** *(gen)* restos *mpl*; *(of food)* sobras *fpl*. II *vtr (pt & pp scrapped) (discard)* desechar; *(cars etc)* convertir en chatarra; *fig (idea)* descartar.

scrap² [skræp] *fam* I *n* pelea *f*. II *vi (pt & pp scrapped)* pelearse (**with,** con).

scrapbook ['skræpbʊk] *n* álbum *m* de recortes.

scrape [skreɪp] I *vtr (paint, wood)* raspar; *(vegetables)* rascar; *(graze) (knee etc)* arañarse, hacerse un rasguño; *fig* **to s. together,** reunir a duras penas; *fig* **to s. a living,** vivir muy apretado,-a, ganar lo justo para vivir; *fig* **to s. the bottom of the barrel,** tocar fondo. II *vi (make noise)* chirriar; *(rub)* rozar; **to s. against the wall,** pasar rozando la pared. III *n* 1 *(act)* raspado *m*; *(noise)* chirrido *m*; *(mark)* arañazo *m*, rasguño *m*. 2 *fam (trouble)* lío *m*, apuro *m*, aprieto *m*. ◆ **scrape along, scrape by** *vi fam* ir tirando. ◆ **scrap away, scrape off** *vtr* quitar raspando. ◆ **scrape through** *vi fam (exam)* aprobar por los pelos *or* de chiripa.

scraper ['skreɪpəʳ] *n* 1 *(tool)* rasqueta *f*, rascador *m*. 2 *(for shoes)* limpiabarros *m inv*.

scrapheap ['skræphiːp] *n (rubbish pile)* montón *m* de desechos; *(dump)* vertedero *m*.

scrappy ['skræpɪ] *adj (scrappier, scrappiest) (report, speech)* deshilvanado,-a; *(conversation)* fragmentario,-a; *(knowledge)* superficial; *(meal)* pobre, hecho,-a con sobras.

scratch [skrætʃ] I *n* 1 *(mark) (on skin)* arañazo *m*, rasguño *m*; *(on paintwork)* arañazo *m*; *(on record, photo)* raya *f*; **to escape without a s.,** salir ileso,-a. ◆ **s. pad,** bloc *m* de notas; *Med* **s. test,** cutirreacción *f*. 2 *(noise)* chirrido *m*. 3 *fig* **to be** *or* **come up to s.,** estar a la altura de las circunstancias,

dar la talla; *fig* **to start from s.,** partir de cero. II *adj* improvisado,-a; *Sport* **s. team,** equipo improvisado. III *vtr* 1 *(with fingernail, claw)* arañar, rasguñar; *(paintwork, furniture)* rayar; *(initials on a tree)* grabar; *fig* **to s. the surface of,** tocar por encima. 2 *(to relieve itching)* rascarse; *fam* **you s. my back and I'll s. yours,** hoy por ti y mañana por mí. 3 *Sport (cancel)* cancelar, suspender. IV *vi* 1 *(cat etc)* arañar, rasguñar; *(pen)* raspear. 2 *(to relieve itching)* rascarse. 3 *US fam* **to s. for oneself,** buscarse la vida. ◆ **scratch out** *vtr* tachar, borrar, retirar.

scratchy ['skrætʃɪ] *adj (scratchier, scratchiest) (pen)* que raspea; *(sound)* que chirria; *(fabric)* que pica; *(record)* rayado,-a.

scrawl [skrɔːl] I *n* garabatos *mpl*. II *vtr (message etc)* garabatear, garrapatear. III *vi* garabatear, hacer garabatos.

scrawny ['skrɔːnɪ] *adj (scrawnier, scrawniest)* flaco,-a, flacucho,-a.

scream [skriːm] I *n (of pain, fear)* grito *m*, chillido *m*, alarido *m*; **screams of laughter,** carcajadas *fpl*; **to let out a s.,** soltar un grito; *fam* **it was a s.,** fue la monda, fue para mondarse de risa; *fam* **she's a s.,** es divertidísima, es la monda. II *vtr (insults etc)* gritar, vociferar; *fam* **to s. the place down,** desgañitarse. III *vi* gritar, chillar; **to s. at sb,** pegar gritos a algn; **to s. for help,** pedir socorro a gritos; **to s. with laughter,** partirse *or* troncharse de risa.

scree [skriː] *n Geol* pedregal *m*.

screech [skriːtʃ] I *n (of person)* chillido *m*; *(of tyres, brakes)* chirrido *m*. II *vtr* gritar, decir a gritos, vocear. III *vi (person)* chillar; *(tyres, brakes)* chirriar.

screed [skriːd] *n fam (long speech etc)* rollo *m*; **to write screeds,** escribir mucho.

screen [skriːn] I *n* 1 *(movable partition)* biombo *m*. ◼ **fire s.,** pantalla *f*. 2 *fig* cortina *f*; **to act as a s.,** servir de tapadera. ◼ **smoke s.,** cortina *f* de humo. 3 *Cin TV Comput* pantalla *f*; **the small s.,** la pequeña pantalla. ◼ **s. test,** prueba *f*; **s. writer,** guionista *mf*. II *vtr* 1 *(protect)* proteger (**from,** de); *(conceal)* tapar, ocultar (**from,** de). 2 *(sieve) (coal etc)* cribar, tamizar; *fig (candidates for a job)* seleccionar; *(pass)* pasar por el tamiz. 3 *(show) (film)* proyectar; *(for first time)* estrenar. 4 *Med* examinar; **to s. sb for an illness,** hacer una exploración a algn.

screening ['skriːnɪŋ] *n* 1 *(of candidates)* selección *f*. 2 *(of flim)* proyección *f*; *(for first time)* estreno *m*. 3 *Med (of patient)* exploración *f*.

screenplay ['skriːnpleɪ] *n Cin* guión *m*.

screw [skruː] I *n* 1 tornillo *m*; *fam* **he has a s. loose,** le falta un tornillo. 2 *fam* **to put the screws on sb,** apretarle los tornillos a algn. 2 *Av Naut (propeller)* hélice *f*. 3 *sl (prison guard)* carcelero,-a *m, f*. II *vtr* 1 *(gen)* atornillar; **to s. sth down** *or* **in** *or* **on,** fijar algo con tornillos; *fam* **he's got his head screwed on (the right way),** tiene la cabeza bien sentada. 2 *sl* **to s. money out of sb,** sacarle dinero a algn. 3 *vulg (have sex with)* joder, follar. ◆ **screw up** *vtr* 1 *(piece of paper)* arrugar; *(one's face)* torcer; *fig* **to s. up one's courage,** armarse de valor. 2 *sl (spoil, ruin)* joder, jorobar, fastidiar; **now he's really screwed things up,** ahora lo ha jodido de verdad. 3 *fam* ponerse nervioso,-a; **she's all screwed up,** está muy nerviosa.

screwball ['skruːbɔːl] *adj & n US sl* chalado,-a *(m, f)*, excéntrico,-a *(m, f)*.

screwdriver ['skruːdraɪvəʳ] *n* 1 destornillador *m*. 2 *(cocktail)* destornillador *m*.

screw-top(ped) ['skruːtɒp(t)] *adj* de tapón a rosca.

screwy ['skruːɪ] *adj (screwier, screwiest) fam (thinking etc)* retorcido,-a.

scribble ['skrɪbəl] I *n* garabatos *mpl*. II *vtr (message etc)* garabatear, garrapatear. III *vi* garabatear, hacer garabatos.

scribbler ['skrɪbləʳ] *n pej (author)* escritorzuelo,-a *m, f*.

scribbling ['skrɪblɪŋ] *n* garabatos *mpl*. ◼ **s. pad,** bloc *m* de notas.

scribe [skraɪb] *n* escribiente *mf*, amanuense *mf*; *(in Bible)* escriba *m*.

scrimmage ['skrɪmɪdʒ] *n* escaramuza *f*, refriega *f*.

scrimp [skrɪmp] *vi* ahorrar, hacer economías; **to s. and save,** apretarse el cinturón.

script [skrɪpt] *n* 1 *(writing)* escritura *f*; *(handwriting)* letra *f*; *Typ* letra *f* cursiva. 2 *(in exam)* escrito *m*, examen *m*. 3 *Cin* guión *m*. ■ **s. girl,** scriptgirl *f*. 4 *Jur (document)* escritura *f*.

Scripture ['skrɪptʃər] *n Rel* **Holy S.,** Sagrada Escritura *f*.

scriptwriter ['skrɪptraɪtər] *n* guionista *mf*.

scroll [skrəʊl] *n* rollo *m* de pergamino.

scrooge [skruːdʒ] *n fam (miser)* tacaño,-a *m,f*, avaro,-a *m,f*, agarrado,-a *m,f*, roña *mf*.

scrotum ['skrəʊtəm] *n (pl **scrotums** or **scrota** ['skrəʊtə]) Anat* escroto *m*.

scrounge [skraʊndʒ] *fam* **I** *vi (gen)* gorrear, gorronear, vivir de gorra; *(for money)* dar sablazos, sablear; **to s. (around) for,** buscar; **to s. off sb,** vivir a costa de algn. **II** *vtr* gorrear **(from,** a); *(money)* sablear **(from,** a). **III** *n* **to be on the s.,** ir sacando cosas de gorra.

scrounger ['skraʊndʒər] *n fam* gorrón,-ona *m,f*, sablista *mf*.

scrub¹ [skrʌb] *n (undergrowth)* maleza *f*.

scrub² [skrʌb] **I** *vtr (pt & pp **scrubbed**)* 1 *(clean) (floor, dishes)* fregar; *(clothes)* lavar; **s. the tables clean,** limpia bien las mesas. 2 *fam (cancel)* cancelar. **II** *n (act of cleaning)* fregado *m*, lavado *m*; **to give sth a good s.,** limpiar algo a fondo. ◆ **scrub off** *vtr (dirt, stain)* quitar frotando. ◆ **scrub up** *vtr (surgeon)* lavarse (las manos).

scrubber ['skrʌbər] *n GB sl* fulana *f*, golfa *f*, furcia *f*.

scrubbing ['skrʌbɪŋ] *n* fregado *m*, lavado *m*. ■ **s. brush,** *(gen)* estregadera *f*; *(for horses)* bruza *f*.

scruff¹ [skrʌf] *n* pescuezo *m*, cogote *m*.

scruff² [skrʌf] *n fam (untidy person)* desaliñado,-a *m,f*, zarrapastroso,-a *m,f*, desaseado,-a *m,f*.

scruffy ['skrʌfɪ] *adj (scruffier, scruffiest) fam* desaliñado,-a, zarrapastroso,-a, desaseado,-a.

scrum [skrʌm] *n Rugby (abbr of scrummage)* melée *f*; **s. half,** medio *m* melée; *fam* **what a s. to get on the train!,** ¡vaya apretujones para subir al tren!

scrummage ['skrʌmɪdʒ] *Rugby* **I** *n* melée *f*. **II** *vi* formar una melée.

scrumptious ['skrʌmpʃəs] *adj fam* delicioso,-a, de rechupete.

scrunch [skrʌntʃ] *vtr (crush)* aplastar; *(crumple) (also s. up)* estrujar.

scruple ['skruːpəl] *n* escrúpulo *m*.

scrupulous ['skruːpjʊləs] *adj* escrupuloso,-a. ◆ **scrupulously** *adv* escrupulosamente; **s. clean,** de lo más limpio, impecable; **s. honest/careful,** sumamente honrado,-a/cuidadoso,-a.

scrupulousness ['skruːpjʊləsnɪs] *n* escrupulosidad *f*.

scrutineer [skruːtɪ'nɪər] *n (of votes)* escrutador,-a *m,f*.

scrutinize ['skruːtɪnaɪz] *vtr* 1 *(document etc)* escudriñar, examinar a fondo. 2 *(votes)* escrutar, hacer el escrutinio de; *(re-count)* hacer el recuento de.

scrutiny ['skruːtɪnɪ] *n* 1 *(of document)* examen *m* profundo, escrutinio *m*. 2 *(of votes)* escrutinio *m*; *(re-count)* recuento *m*.

scuba ['skjuːbə] *n* **s. diving,** buceo *m* con botellas de oxígeno.

scuff [skʌf] **I** *vtr (the floor)* rayar; *(one's feet)* arrastrar. **II** *n* **s. mark,** raya *f*.

scuffle ['skʌfəl] **I** *n* refriega *f*, riña *f*, pelea *f*. **II** *vi* reñirse, pelearse **(with,** con).

scull [skʌl] **I** *n* remo *m* corto. **II** *vi* remar.

scullery ['skʌlərɪ] *n* fregadero *m*, trascocina *f*; **s. maid,** fregona *f*.

sculpt [skʌlpt] *vtr & vi* esculpir.

sculptor ['skʌlptər] *n* escultor *m*.

sculptress ['skʌlptrɪs] *n* escultora *f*.

sculpture ['skʌlptʃər] **I** *n* escultura *f*. **II** *vtr* esculpir.

scum [skʌm] *n* 1 *(on liquid)* espuma *f*, telilla *f*; *(on pond)* verdín *m*. 2 *fig* escoria *f*.

scupper ['skʌpər] *vtr* **I** *(ship)* barrenar, hundir deliberadamente. **2** *GB fam (plan etc)* sabotear, desbaratar, frustrar.

scurf [skɜːf] *n (dandruff)* caspa *f*.

scurrilous ['skʌrɪləs] *adj (abusive)* difamatorio,-a, calumnioso,-a; *(coarse)* grosero,-a.

scurry ['skʌrɪ] *vi (pt & pp **scurried**) (run)* correr, corretear; *(hurry)* apresurarse; **to s. away or off,** escabullirse.

scurvy ['skɜːvɪ] *n Med* escorbuto *m*.

scuttle¹ ['skʌtəl] *n* 1 cubo *m*. ■ **coal s.,** cubo del carbón. 2 *Naut* escotilla *f*.

scuttle² ['skʌtəl] *vtr* 1 *(ship)* barrenar, hundir deliberadamente. **2** *fam (plan etc)* sabotear, desbaratar, frustrar.

scuttle³ ['skʌtəl] *vi (run)* corretear; **to s. away or off,** escabullirse.

scythe [saɪð] **I** *n* guadaña *f*. **II** *vtr* guadañar, segar (con guadaña).

SDP [esdiː'piː] *GB Pol abbr of* **Social Democratic Party.**

SDI [esdiː'aɪ] *Mil abbr of* **Strategic Defence Initiative,** Iniciativa *f* para la Defensa Estratégica.

SE *abbr of* **South-East,** sudeste, SE.

sea [siː] *n* mar *mf*; **at s.,** en el mar; **by the s.,** a orillas del mar; **choppy s.,** mar picado; **out at s.,** en alta mar; **rough s.,** marejada *f*; **stormy s.,** mar gruesa; **to go by s.,** ir en barco; *(person)* **to go to s.,** hacerse marinero; *(ship, crew)* **to put to s.,** zarpar; *fig* **a s. of faces,** un mar de caras; *fig* **to be all at s.,** estar totalmente desorientado,-a, estar perdido,-a. ■ **s. anemone,** anémona *f* de mar; **s. breeze,** brisa *f* marina; *fig* **s. change,** metamorfosis *f*; *Zool* **s. cow,** manatí *m*; *fig* **s. legs,** equilibrio *m*; *fam* **to find one's s. legs,** acostumbrarse al mar, no marearse; **s. level,** nivel *m* del mar; *Zool* **s. lion,** león *m* marino; **s. trout,** trucha *f* de mar, reo *m*; **s. water,** agua *f* de mar.

seabed ['siːbed] *n* fondo *m* del mar *or* marino.

seabird ['siːbɜːd] *n* ave *f* marina.

seaboard ['siːbɔːd] *n US* costa *f*, litoral *m*.

seafarer ['siːfeərər] *n* marinero *m*.

seafaring ['siːfeərɪŋ] *adj* marinero,-a.

seafood ['siːfuːd] *n* mariscos *mpl*; **s. restaurant,** marisquería *f*.

seafront ['siːfrʌnt] *n* paseo *m* marítimo.

seagoing ['siːgəʊɪŋ] *adj* de alta mar.

sea-green [siː'griːn] *adj* verdemar.

seagull ['siːgʌl] *n* gaviota *f*.

sea-horse ['siːhɔːs] *n* caballito *m* de mar, hipocampo *m*.

seal¹ [siːl] *n Zool* foca *f*.

seal² [siːl] *n* 1 *(official stamp) (on document)* sello *m*; **wax s.,** sello de lacre; *fig* **to give one's s. of approval to sth, to set one's s. to sth,** aprobar algo, dar el visto bueno a algo. 2 *(airtight closure)* cierre *m* hermético; *(on bottle)* precinto *m*. **II** *vtr* 1 *(document) (with official stamp)* sellar; *(with wax)* lacrar, sellar con lacre; *(bottle)* precintar. 2 *(close)* cerrar; *(make airtight)* cerrar herméticamente; *Culin (meat)* encerrar el sabor de; **my lips are sealed,** seré como una tumba. 3 *(determine)* decidir, determinar; **this sealed his fate,** esto decidió su destino. ◆ **seal in** *vtr (flavour etc)* cerrar. ◆ **seal off** *vtr (close) (pipe etc)* cerrar; *(block entry to) (street, area)* acordonar, cerrar el acceso a. ◆ **seal up** *vtr (parcel, letter)* precintar, cerrar con precinto; *(crack, window)* tapar (completamente); *(jar)* cerrar herméticamente.

sea-lane ['si:leɪn] n vía f or ruta f marítima.

sealing ['si:lɪŋ] n s. **wax,** lacre m.

sealskin ['si:lskɪn] n piel f de foca.

seam [si:m] n **1** Sew costura f; Tech juntura f, junta f; Med sutura f; **to come apart at the seams,** descoserse; **to let out a s.,** soltar una costura; fam **to be bursting at the seams,** (person) estar a punto de reventar; (room) rebosar de gente. **2** Geol Min veta f, filón m; **coal s.,** veta de carbón.

seaman ['si:mən] n (pl **seamen**) marinero m.

seamanship ['si:mənʃɪp] n náutica f.

seamless ['si:mlɪs] adj Sew sin costura; Tech sin soldadura.

seamstress ['semstrɪs] n Sew costurera f.

seamy ['si:mɪ] adj (**seamier, seamiest**) fig sórdido,-a.

séance ['seɪɑːns] n sesión f de espiritismo.

seaplane ['si:pleɪn] n hidroavión m.

seaport ['si:pɔːt] n puerto m marítimo or de mar.

seaquake ['si:kweɪk] n maremoto m.

search [sɜːtʃ] I vtr (records, files) buscar en; (building, suitcase, etc) registrar; (person) cachear; (one's conscience) examinar; fam **s. me!,** ¡yo qué sé! II vi buscar (**for, after, -**); **to s. through sb's pockets,** registrar los bolsillos a algn. III n (gen) búsqueda f; (of building etc) registro m; (of person) cacheo m; **in s. of,** en busca de. ■ **s. party,** equipo m de salvamento; **s. warrant,** orden f de registro.

searcher ['sɜːtʃəʳ] n buscador,-a m,f.

searching ['sɜːtʃɪŋ] adj (look) penetrante; (question) agudo,-a.

searchlight ['sɜːtʃlaɪt] n reflector m, proyector m.

seascape ['si:skeɪp] n marina f.

seashell ['si:ʃel] n concha f marina.

seashore ['si:ʃɔːʳ] n (shore) costa f, litoral m; (beach) playa f.

seasick ['si:sɪk] adj mareado,-a, **to get s.,** marearse.

seasickness ['si:sɪknɪs] n mareo m.

seaside ['si:saɪd] n playa f, costa f. ■ **s. resort,** lugar m or complejo m turístico de veraneo; **s. town,** pueblo m or ciudad f costero,-a.

season¹ ['si:zən] n (gen) época f, (spring, summer, etc) estación f; (for social activity, sport, etc) temporada f; **at the height of the s.,** en plena temporada; **'Season's Greetings',** 'Felices Pascuas'; **the busy s.,** la temporada alta; **the dry/rainy s.,** la estación seca/de lluvias; **the football s.,** la temporada de fútbol or futbolística; **the four seasons,** las cuatro estaciones; **the off s.,** la temporada baja; (hunting) **the open/close s.,** la temporada de caza or de pesca/la veda; **the tourist s.,** la temporada turística; **to be in s.,** (fruit) estar en sazón; (animal) estar en celo. ■ Rail Theat **s. ticket,** fam **s.,** abono m; **s. ticket holder,** abonado,-a m,f.

season² ['si:zən] vtr **1** Culin sazonar, condimentar. **2** (wood) secar; (wine) madurar. **3** (person) acostumbrar, avezar.

seasonable ['si:zənəbəl] adj (weather) propio,-a de la estación; (timely) oportuno,-a.

seasonal ['si:zənəl] adj (activity) estacional, temporal; **s. worker,** temporero,-a m,f.

seasoned ['si:zənd] adj **1** Culin (food) sazonado,-a, condimentado,-a; **a highly s. dish,** un plato muy picante. **2** (wood) seco,-a; (wine) maduro,-a. **3** fig (person) experimentado,-a, curtido,-a, avezado,-a.

seasoning ['si:zənɪŋ] n condimento m, aderezo m.

seat [si:t] I n **1** (gen) asiento m; (place) plaza f; Cin Theat localidad f; (ticket) entrada f; Cin Theat **to book seats,** reservar localidades; **to take a s.,** sentarse. ■ Aut Av **s. belt,** cinturón m de seguridad. **2** (of cycle) sillín m; (of toilet) asiento m; (of trousers) fondillos mpl; fam

(buttocks) trasero m, pompis m. **3** (centre) centro m, sede f; **s. of learning,** centro de estudios. **4** Parl escaño m. II vtr **1** (child, guests, etc) sentar; **please be seated,** siéntense por favor; **to remain seated,** quedarse sentado,-a. **2** (accommodate) tener sitio para; (theatre, hall, etc) tener cabida para; **it will s. five hundred,** tendrá un aforo para quinientas personas; **this table seats eight,** esta mesa es para ocho personas.

seater ['si:təʳ] n **a two-s. car,** un (coche) dos plazas; **a three-s. sofa,** un sofá tres plazas.

seating ['si:tɪŋ] n **1** (capacity) asientos mpl; **s. capacity,** cabida f, aforo m. **2** (distribution) distribución f de asientos.

sea-urchin ['si:ɜːtʃɪn] n erizo m de mar.

sea-wall ['si:wɔːl] n rompeolas m inv.

seaweed ['si:wi:d] n Bot alga f (marina).

seaworthy ['si:wɜːðɪ] adj (boat) en condiciones de navegar.

sebaceous [sɪ'beɪʃəs] adj sebáceo,-a.

seborrhoea [sebə'rɪə] n Med seborrea f.

sebum ['si:bəm] n Biol sebo m.

sec¹ [sek] n fam (abbr of **second¹**) segundo m.

sec² abbr of **secretary,** secretario,-a m,f.

secant ['si:kənt] n Geom secante f.

secateurs [sekə'tɜːz] npl podadera f sing.

secede [sɪ'si:d] vi Pol separarse (**from,** de), independizarse (**from,** de).

secession [sɪ'seʃən] n Pol secesión f.

secluded [sɪ'klu:dɪd] adj aislado,-a, retirado,-a, apartado,-a.

seclusion [sɪ'klu:ʒən] n aislamiento m, retiro m; **in s.,** aislado,-a.

second¹ ['sekənd] I adj segundo,-a; **every s. day,** cada dos días; **it's s. nature to him,** le viene de naturaleza; **it's the s. highest mountain in the world,** es la segunda montaña más alta en el mundo; **on s. thought(s) ...,** pensándolo bien ...; **s. teeth,** segunda dentición f; **he's a s. Dr Crippen,** parece otro Dr Crippen; **to be s. to none,** no tener igual; **to have s. helping of sth,** repetir algo; **to have s. thoughts about sth,** dudar de algo; **to marry for the s. time,** casarse en segundas nupcias; **to play s. fiddle,** ser segundón,-ona, desempeñar un papel secundario; **to settle for s. best,** conformarse con lo que hay; fig **to get one's s. wind,** despabilarse, espabilarse. ■ **s. class,** segunda clase f; **s. cousin,** primo,-a m,f segundo,-a; **s. floor,** GB segundo piso m, US primer piso m; Jur **s. offence,** reincidencia f; Ling **s. person,** segunda persona f; **s. sight,** clarividencia f. II n **1** (in series, rank, etc) segundo,-a m,f; **Charles the S.,** Carlos Segundo; Sport **he came in s.,** llegó segundo; (date) **the s. of October,** el dos de octubre. **2** GB Univ (degree) **to obtain a s.,** sacar un notable. **3** Aut (gear) segunda f; **in s.,** en segunda. **4** Com **seconds,** artículos mpl con tara or defectuosos. III vtr (motion, proposal) apoyar, secundar. IV adv (in race, exam, etc) segundo, en segundo lugar; **to come s.,** terminar en segundo lugar. ◆ **secondly** adv en segundo lugar.

second² ['sekənd] n (time) segundo m; **in a split s.,** en un abrir y cerrar de ojos; fam **I'll be back in a s.,** enseguida vuelvo; fam **just a s.!,** ¡un momentito! ■ **s. hand,** segundero m.

second³ [sɪ'kɒnd] vtr Mil trasladar temporalmente.

secondary ['sekəndərɪ] adj secundario,-a. ■ **s. education,** educación f secundaria; **s. school,** (gen) escuela f secundaria; (private) colegio m; (state) instituto m de enseñanza media or de educación secundaria.

second-best [sekənd'best] I adj segundo,-a, inferior. II adv **to come off s.-b.,** quedar en segundo lugar.

second-class [sekənd'klɑːs] **1** adj (ticket, hotel) de segunda (clase); (mail, citizen) de segunda clase; (goods) de segunda categoría, de calidad inferior. II adv **to travel s.-c.,** viajar en segunda.

second-degree ['sekəndıgri:] *adj Med* de segundo grado; **s.-d. burns,** quemaduras *fpl* de segundo grado.

second-hand ['sekəndhænd] **I** *adj (gen)* de segunda mano; *(car, clothes)* viejo,-a, usado,-a. ■ **s.-h. car,** coche *m* de segunda mano; **s.-h. dealer,** chamarilero,-a *m, f,* trapero,-a *m, f;* **s.-h. shop,** rastrillo *m,* bazar *m,* rastro *m.* **II** *adv* de segunda mano; **to buy sth s.-h.,** comprar algo de segunda mano.

second-in-command [sekəndınkə'mɑ:nd] *n Mil* segundo *m* en jefe.

secondment [sɪ'kɒndmənt] *n GB* traslado *m* temporal; **she's on s. to accounts,** la han trasladado a contabilidad.

second-rate ['sekəndreıt] *adj* de segunda *or* baja categoría, de calidad inferior.

secrecy ['si:krəsı] *n* **1** *(gen)* secreto *m;* **in s.,** en secreto. **2** *(ability to keep secrets)* discreción *f,* reserva *f.*

secret ['si:krıt] **I** *adj* secreto,-a; **to keep sth s.,** mantener algo en secreto; **s. ballot,** votación *f* secreta. ■ **s. agent,** agente *mf* secreto,-a, espía *mf;* **s. police,** policía *f* secreta; **s. service,** servicio *m* secreto. **II** *n* secreto *m; fig* clave *f;* **in s.,** en secreto; **open s.,** secreto a voces; **to be in on the s.,** estar al tanto, estar en el ajo; **to keep a s.,** guardar un secreto; **to let sb into a s.,** revelar un secreto a algn, compartir un secreto con algn; **theres no s. about it,** no tiene ningún misterio. ◆ **secretly** *adv* en secreto, a escondidas.

secretarial [sekrı'teərıəl] *adj* de secretarioa,-a. ■ **s. college,** escuela *f* de secretariado; **s. studies,** secretariado *m.*

secratariat [sekrı'teərıət] *n* secretaría *f,* secretariado *m.*

secretary ['sekrətrı] *n* secretario,-a *m, f;* **general s.,** secretario,-a *m, f* general; **private s.,** secretario,-a *m, f* particular; **S. of State,** *GB* ministro,-a *m, f* con cartera, *US* secretario,-a *m, f* de Estado, ministro,-a *f* de Asuntos Exteriores; *US* **S. of the Treasury,** ministro,-a *m, f* de Hacienda.

secretary-general [sekrətrı'dʒenərəl] *n (pl secretaries-general)* secretario *m* general.

secrete [sı'kri:t] *vtr* **1** *(emit liquid etc)* secretar, segregar. **2** *(hide)* ocultar, esconder.

secretion [sı'kri:ʃən] *n* **1** *(of liquid)* secreción *f.* **2** *(hiding)* ocultación *f.*

secretive ['si:krıtıv] *adj* sigiloso,-a; *(quiet)* reservado,-a, callado,-a.

sect [sekt] *n* secta *f.*

sectarian [sek'teərıən] *adj & n* sectario,-a *(m, f).*

sectarianism [sek'teərıənızəm] *n* sectarismo *m.*

section ['sekʃən] **I** *n* **1** *(part)* sección *f,* parte *f; (of road, track)* tramo *m; (of law)* artículo *m,* apartado *m; (of newspaper)* sección *f,* página *f; (of population, community)* sector *m; (of orchestra)* sección *f; (department)* sección *f.* **2** *(cut)* corte *m,* sección *f.* ■ *Med* **Caesarian s.,** *(operación f* de) cesárea *f;* **cross s.,** sección *f* transversal. **II** *vtr* cortar, seccionar.

sectional ['sekʃənəl] *adj* **1** *(furniture)* desmontable. **2** *(plan, diagram)* en corte. **3** *(interest)* particular.

sector ['sektə'] *n* sector *m;* **the public s.,** el sector público.

secular ['sekjolə'] *adj (school, teaching)* laico,-a *(music, art)* profano,-a; *(priest)* seglar, secular.

secularize ['sekjoləraız] *vtr* secularizar.

secure [sı'kjuə'] **I** *adj* **1** *(safe, confident, certain)* seguro,-a; **s. in the knowledge that,** con la certeza de que; **to feel s.,** sentirse seguro,-a; **to have a s. job/future,** tener un puesto seguro/el porvenir asegurado. **2** *(firmly fastened) (knot etc)* seguro,-a; *(window, door)* bien cerrado,-a; *(steady) (ladder etc)* firme. **II** *vtr* **1** *(make safe) (future)* asegurar; **to s. oneself against sth,** protegerse contra algo. **2** *(fasten, fix) (rope, knot)* sujetar, fijar; *(object to floor)* afianzar; *(window, door)* asegurar, cerrar bien; *(animal, prisoner)* atar firmemente. **3** *(obtain)* conseguir, obtener. **4** *Fin (guarantee)* garantizar, avalar.

security [sı'kjuərıtı] *n* **1** *(safety, confidence)* seguridad *f;* **emotional s.,** estabilidad *f* emocional; **job s.,** seguridad en el empleo; **national s.,** seguridad nacional; **social s.,** seguridad social. **2** *(physical attack, spying, etc)* seguridad *f;* **s. was tight,** se adoptaron fuertes medidas de seguridad. ■ **S. Council,** Consejo *m* de Seguridad; **s. leak,** fuga *f* (de información). **3** *Fin (guarantee)* fianza *f,* garantía *f,* aval *m; (guarantor)* fiador,-a *m, f;* **to lend money on s.,** prestar dinero sobre fianza; **to stand s. for sb,** salir fiador de algn, garantizar a algn. **4** *Fin* **securities,** valores *mpl,* títulos *mpl;* **Government s.,** valores del Estado.

sedan [sı'dæn] *n* **1** *(also s. chair)* silla *f* de manos. **2** *US Aut* turismo *m.*

sedate [sı'deıt] **I** *adj* sosegado,-a, sereno,-a, tranquilo,-a. **II** *vtr Med* administrar sedantes a, sedar.

sedation [sı'deıʃən] *n Med* sedación *f,* administración *f* de sedantes.

sedative ['sedətıv] *adj & n* sedativo,-a *(m),* sedante *(m),* calmante *(m).*

sedentary ['sedəntərı] *adj* sedentario,-a; **s. life,** vida sedentaria.

sediment ['sedımənt] *n (gen)* sedimento *m; (of wine)* poso *m,* hez *f.*

sedition [sı'dıʃən] *n* sedición *f.*

seditious [sı'dıʃəs] *adj* sedicioso,-a.

seduce [sı'dju:s] *vtr* seducir.

seducer [sı'dju:sə'] *n* seductor,-a *m, f.*

seduction [sı'dʌkʃən] *n* seducción *f.*

seductive [sı'dʌktıv] *adj (person, idea)* seductor,-a; *(smile, clothes)* provocativo,-a; *(offer)* tentador,-a.

see¹ [si:] *vtr & vi (pt saw; pp seen)* **1** *(gen)* ver; **go and s. if ...,** vete a ver si ...; **I don't know what he sees in her,** no sé qué ve en ella; **I'll s. what can be done,** veré lo que se puede hacer; **it is worth seeing,** merece la pena verlo; **let's s.,** a ver, vamos a ver; **that remains to be seen,** queda por ver; **this handbag has seen better days,** este bolso ha conocido mejores tiempos; **seeing is believing,** ver para creer; **s. page 10,** véase la página 10; **s. yon (later)/soon/Monday!,** ¡hasta luego/pronto/el lunes!; **we were glad to s. the back of him,** nos alegramos de perderlo de vista; *fig* **to s. the light,** ver la luz; *fam* **to s. red,** ponerse negro,-a (de ira). **2** *(meet with)* ver, tener cita con; **the manager will s. you in just a moment,** el jefe le verá en seguida; *(couple)* **they have been seeing each other for six months,** hace seis meses que salen juntos. **3** *(visit)* ver, visitar; **they s. a lot of each other,** se ven muy a menudo; **to s. the sights/the world,** recorrer la ciudad/el mundo. **4** *(understand)* comprender, entender, ver; **as far as I can s.,** por lo visto, por lo que veo; **I don't s. the joke,** no le veo la gracia; **I don't s. why he can't go,** no entiendo porqué no puede ir; **I s.,** ya veo; **you s., he hasn't got a car,** es que no tiene coche, ¿sabes? **5** *(imagine, visualize)* imaginarse, ver; **he sees himself as a second Caruso,** se cree otro Caruso; **I can't s. her living abroad,** no me la imagino viviendo en el extranjero; **you must be seeing things,** ves visiones. **6** *(ensure)* asegurarse de; procurar; **s. that the windows are securely fastened,** asegúrese de que todas las ventanas estén bien cerradas; **s. that yon arrive on time,** procura llegar a la hora. **7** *(accompany)* acompañar; **to s. sb home,** acompañar a algn a casa. ◆ **see about** *vtr* **1** *(deal with)* ocuparse de, encargarse de. **2** *(consider)* pensar. ◆ **see in** *vtr* celebrar; **to s. in the New Year,** celebrar el Año Nuevo. ◆ **see into** *vtr (investigate)* investigar. ◆ **see off** *vtr (say goodbye to)* despedirse de. ◆ **see out** *vtr* **1** *(show out)* acompañar hasta la puerta. **2** *(survive)* sobrevivir; **she will s. us all out,** nos enterrará a todos. ◆ **see over** *vtr (house etc)* visitar, recorrer. ◆ **see through** *vtr* **1** *fam (person)* calar a, verle el plumero a. **2** *(help)* ayudar a salir de un apuro; **I'll s. you through,** puedes contar con mi ayuda; **£20 should s. me through,** con 20 libras me las apaño. **3** *(carry out)* llevar a cabo. ◆ **see to** *vtr (deal with)* atender a, ocuparse de; **s. to it that** dinner is served on time, procura que la cena se sirva a la hora.

see² [si:] *n Rel* sede *f*. ■ the Holy S., la Santa Sede.

seed [si:d] **I** *n* **1** *Bot (gen)* semilla *f; (for sowing)* simiente *f*, semilla *f; (of fruit)* pepita *f; to go or* run to s., *(plant)* granar; *fig (person)* descuidarse, abandonarse, echarse a perder; *fig* to sow the seeds of discord, sembrar las semillas de la discordia. ■ s. pearl, aljófar *m*; s. potato, patata *f* de siembra. **2** *Ten (player)* cabeza *mf* de serie. **II** *vtr* **1** *(sow with seed) (lawn etc)* sembrar. **2** *(grapes, raisins)* despepitar. **3** *Ten (players)* preseleccionar; **seeded player,** cabeza *mf* de serie. **III** *vi (of plants)* granar.

seedbed ['si:dbed] *n* semillero *m*.

seedcake ['si:dkeɪk] *n Culin* torta *f* de semillas aromáticas.

seedless ['si:dlɪs] *adj* sin pepitas *or* semillas.

seedling ['si:dlɪŋ] *n* plantón *m*.

seedy ['si:dɪ] *adj (seedier, seediest) fam* **1** *(run-down) (district, bar)* sórdido,-a; *(shabby) (clothes)* raído,-a; *(appearance)* desaseado,-a. **2** *(unwell)* pachucho,-a; to look s., tener mala pinta.

seeing ['si:ɪŋ] **I** *adj* vidente, que ve. ■ *US* s. eye dog, perro *m* lazarillo *or* guía. **II** *n Astron* visibilidad *f*. **III** *conj* s. that, visto que, en vista de que, dado que.

seek [si:k] **I** *vtr (pt & pp sought)* **1** *(look for)* buscar; to s. employment/shelter, buscar empleo/cobijo; to s. one's fortune, probar fortuna. **2** *(ask for)* pedir, solicitar; *(post)* solicitar. **II** *vi* buscar; to s. to do sth, procurar hacer algo. ◆ **seek after** *vtr* buscar; much sought after, *(person)* muy solicitado,-a; *(thing)* muy cotizado,-a. ◆ **seek out** *vtr (person)* buscar.

seeker ['si:kəʳ] *n* buscador,-a *m,f*. ■ status s., trepa *mf*, arribista *mf*.

seem [si:m] *vi* parecer; he seems (to be) tired, parece cansado; I s. to remember his name was Colin, creo recordar que su nombre era Colin; it seems not, parece que no; it seems to me that, me parece que; she seems to have lost sth, parece que ha perdido algo; so it seems, eso parece; what seems to be the trouble?, ¿qué ocurre?, ¿qué pasa?

seeming ['si:mɪŋ] *adj* aparente, supuesto,-a. ◆ **seemingly** *adv* aparentemente, según parece, al parecer.

seemly ['si:mlɪ] *adj (seemlier, seemliest) (behaviour)* correcto,-a, decente.

seen [si:n] *pp see* see¹.

seep [si:p] *vi (ooze)* rezumarse; to s. through/into/out, filtrarse *or* calarse *or* colarse por/en/de.

seepage ['si:pɪdʒ] *n* filtración *f*.

seer [sɪəʳ] *n* vidente *mf*.

seersucker ['sɪəsʌkəʳ] *n Tex* vichy *m*.

seesaw ['si:sɔ:] **I** *n* balancín *m*, subibaja· *m*. ■ s. movement, balanceo *m*, vaivén *m*. **II** *vi* **1** columpiarse, balancearse. **2** *fig* vacilar, oscilar.

seethe [si:ð] *vi* bullir, hervir; *fig (person)* to s. with anger, estar furibundo,-a, rabiar; *(place)* to s. with people, estar a rebosar, ser (come) un hormiguero.

see-through ['si:θru:] *adj* transparente.

segment ['segmənt] *n (gen)* segmento *m*; *(of orange)* gajo *m*.

segregate ['segrɪgeɪt] *vtr* segregar (from, de).

segregation [segrɪ'geɪʃən] *n* segregación *f*.

Seine [seɪn, sen] *n* Sena *f*.

seismic ['saɪzmɪk] *adj* sísmico,-a. ■ s. wave, onda *f* sísmica.

seismograph ['saɪzməgræf, 'saɪzməgrɑ:f] *n* sismógrafo *m*.

seismologist [saɪz'mɒlədʒɪst] *n* sismólogo,-a *m,f*.

seismology [saɪz'mɒlədʒɪ] *n* sismología *f*.

seize [si:z] *vtr (grab)* agarrar, asir, coger; *Jur (property, drugs)* incautar, embargar; *(newspaper, magazine)* secuestrar; *Mil (territory)* tomar, apoderarse de; *(hostages)* secuestrar; *(arrest)* detener; to be seized with fear, estar sobrecogido,-a por el miedo; to s. an opportunity, aprovechar una ocasión; *Pol* to s. power, tomar el poder. ◆ **seize on** *vtr (chance, offer)* valerse de, aprovechar; *(idea)* aferrarse a. ◆ **seize up** *vi* agarrotarse.

seizure ['si:ʒəʳ] *n* **1** *Jur (of property, drugs)* incautación *f*, embargo *m*; *(of newspaper, magazine)* secuestro *m*; *Mil (of territory)* toma *f*; *(of hostages)* secuestro *m*; *(arrest)* detención *f*. **2** *Med* ataque *m* (de apoplejía).

seldom ['seldəm] *adv* rara vez, raramente; **I s. see you,** te veo muy poco.

select [sɪ'lekt] **I** *vtr (thing)* escoger, elegir; *(team, player)* seleccionar. **II** *adj (audience)* selecto,-a, escogido,-a; *(club, society)* selecto,-a, exclusivo,-a; *(fruit, wines)* selecto,-a, de primera calidad; **a s. few,** una minoría privilegiada. ■ *Parl* s. committee, comisión *f* especial de investigación.

selected [sɪ'lektɪd] *adj (gen)* selecto,-a, escogido,-a; *(team, player)* seleccionado,-a; *Lit* s. works, obras escogidas.

selection [sɪ'lekʃən] *n (choosing)* elección *f; (people or things chosen)* selección *f; (range)* surtido *m*. ■ *Biol* natural s., selección *f* natural.

selective [sɪ'lektɪv] *adj* selectivo,-a.

selectivity [sɪlek'tɪvɪtɪ] *n* selectividad *f*.

selector [sɪ'lektəʳ] *n* **1** *Sport* seleccionador,-a *m,f*. **2** *Tech* selector *m*.

selenium [sɪ'li:nɪəm] *n Chem* selenio *m*.

self [self] *n (pl selves* [selvz]*)* uno,-a mismo,-a, sí mismo,-a; his better s., su lado bueno; my other s., mi otro yo; she's her old s. again, es la misma de antes; *Psych* the s., el yo.

self- [self] *pref* auto-.

self-acting [self'æktɪŋ] *adj* automático,-a.

self-addressed [selfə'drest] *adj* s.-a. envelope, sobre *m* respuesta.

self-adhesive [selfəd'hi:sɪv] *adj (label, envelope)* autoadhesivo,-a, autoadherente.

self-appointed [selfə'pɔɪntɪd] *adj* que se elige a sí mismo,-a.

self-assurance [selfə'ʃuərəns] *n* seguridad *f or* confianza *f* en sí mismo,-a.

self-assured [selfə'ʃuəd] *adj* seguro,-a de sí mismo,-a.

self-catering [self'keɪtərɪŋ] *adj (holiday, flat)* sin servicio de comida.

self-centred, *US* **self-centered** [self'sentəd] *adj* egocéntrico,-a.

self-cleaning [self'kli:nɪŋ] *adj* auto limpiable.

self-closing [self'kləuzɪŋ] *adj* de cierre automático.

self-confessed [selfkən'fest] *adj* confeso,-a.

self-confidence [self'kɒnfɪdəns] *n* seguridad *f or* confianza *f* en sí mismo,-a.

self-confident [self'kɒnfɪdənt] *adj* seguro,-a de sí mismo,-a.

self-conscious [self'kɒnʃəs] *adj* cohibido,-a, tímido,-a.

self-contained [selfkən'teɪnd] *adj* **1** *(flat)* independiente, con entrada propia; *(person)* independiente. **2** *(reserved) (person)* reservado,-a, poco comunicativo,-a.

self-control [selfkən'trəul] *n* dominio *m* de sí mismo,-a, autocontrol *m*.

self-defence, *US* **self-defense** [selfdɪ'fens] *n* defensa *f* personal, autodefensa *f*.

self-denial [selfdɪ'naɪəl] *n* abnegación *f*.

self-determination [selfdɪtɜ:mɪ'neɪʃən] *n Pol* autodeterminación *f*, autonomía *f*.

self-discipline [self'dɪsɪplɪn] *n* autodisciplina *f*.

self-drive [self'draɪv] *adj* sin chófer.

self-educated [self'edjʊkeɪtɪd] *adj* autodidacta.

self-effacing [selfɪ'feɪsɪŋ] *adj* modesto,-a, humilde.

self-employed [selfɪm'plɔɪd] *adj (worker)* autónomo,-a, que trabaja por cuenta propia.

self-esteem [selfɪ'stiːm] *n* amor *m* propio.

self-evident [self'evɪdənt] *adj* evidente, patente.

self-explanatory [selfɪk'splænətərɪ] *adj* que se explica por sí mismo,-a, evidente.

self-governing [self'gʌvənɪŋ] *adj* autónomo,-a.

self-government [self'gʌvənmənt] *n* autonomía *f*, autogobierno *m*.

self-help [self'help] *n* autosuficiencia *f*.

self-importance [selfɪm'pɔːtəns] *n* engreimiento *m*, presunción *f*.

self-important [selfɪm'pɔːtənt] *adj* engreído,-a, presumido,-a.

self-indulgence [selfɪn'dʌldʒəns] *n* tendencia *f* a permitirse excesos, indulgencia *f* consigo mismo,-a.

self-indulgent [selfɪn'dʌldʒənt] *adj* que se permite excesos, inmoderado,-a.

self-interest [self'ɪntrɪst] *n* interés *m* propio, egoísmo *m*.

selfish ['selfɪʃ] *adj* egoísta.

selfishness ['selfɪʃnɪs] *n* egoísmo *m*.

selfless ['selflɪs] *adj* desinteresado,-a.

self-made ['selfmeɪd] *adj* **s.-m. man,** hombre *m* que ha triunfado por sus propios esfuerzos, hombre *m* que se ha hecho a sí mismo.

self-opinionated [selfə'pɪnjəneɪtɪd] *adj (stubborn)* testarudo,-a, terco,-a.

self-pity [self'pɪtɪ] *n* lástima *f* de sí mismo,-a.

self-portrait [self'pɔːtreɪt] *n* autorretrato *m*.

self-possessed [selfpə'zest] *adj* sereno,-a, dueño,-a de sí mismo,-a.

self-preservation [selfprezə'veɪʃən] *n* (instinct of) **s.-p.,** instinto *m* de conservación.

self-raising ['selfreɪzɪŋ] *adj* Culin **s.-r. flour,** harina *f* con levadura.

self-regulating [self'regjʊleɪtɪŋ] *adj* Tech autorregulador,-a.

self-reliance [selfrɪ'laɪəns] *n* independencia *f*, autosuficiencia *f*.

self-reliant [selfrɪ'laɪənt] *adj* independiente, autosuficiente.

self-respect [selfrɪ'spekt] *n* amor *m* propio, dignidad *f*.

self-respecting [selfrɪ'spektɪŋ] *adj* que tiene amor propio, que se respeta a sí mismo,-a.

self-restraint [selfrɪ'streɪnt] *n* dominio *m* de sí mismo,-a.

self-righteous [self'raɪtʃəs] *adj* farisaico,-a, santurrón,-ona, beato,-a.

self-righteousness [self'raɪtʃəsnɪs] *n* fariseísmo *m*, santurronería *f*, beatería *f*.

self-rising ['selfraɪzɪŋ] *adj* US *see* **self-raising.**

self-rule [self'ruːl] *n see* **self-government.**

selfsame ['selfseɪm] *adj* mismísimo,-a.

self-satisfied [self'sætɪsfaɪd] *adj* satisfecho,-a de sí mismo,-a, pagado,-a de sí.

self-service [self'sɜːvɪs] **1** *(in shop etc) n* autoservicio *m*. **II** *adj* de autoservicio.

self-sufficiency [selfsə'fɪʃənsɪ] *n* autosuficiencia *f*.

self-sufficient [selfsə'fɪʃənt] *adj*, **self-sufficing** [selfsə'faɪsɪŋ] *adj* autosuficiente.

self-supporting [selfsə'pɔːtɪŋ] *adj* económicamente independiente.

self-taught [self'tɔːt] *adj* autodidacta,-a.

sell [sel] **I** *vtr (pt & pp sold)* **1** *(gen)* vender; **to know how to s. oneself,** saber presentarse con ventaja; **to s. sth at a loss,** vender algo con pérdida; *fam* **to s. sb down the river,** traicionar a algn. **2** to be sold on sth, entusiasmarse por algo; **he's not sold on it,** no le convence. **II** *vi* vender; *fig* **to s. like hot cakes,** venderse como rosquillas. **III** *n* Com **hard/soft s.,** publicidad *f* agresiva/discreta. ◆ **sell off** *vtr (gen)* vender; *(stocks and shares)* vender, realizar; *(goods)* liquidar. ◆ **sell out I** *vi* **1** Com vender el negocio. **2** *(be disloyal)* **to s. out to the enemy,** venderse al enemigo, claudicar. **II** *vtr* Com agotarse; *Theat* **'sold out',** 'agotadas (todas) las localidades'; **we've sold out of milk,** se (nos) acabó la leche, ya no queda más leche. ◆ **sell up** *vi* vender el negocio.

seller ['selər] *n* **1** *(person)* vendedor,-a *m,f*. **2** *(product)* **to be a good s.,** tener demanda, venderse bien.

selling ['selɪŋ] *n* venta *f*. ■ **s. point,** atractivo *m* comercial; **s. price,** precio *m* de venta.

sellotape® ['seləteɪp] **I** *n* celo® *m*, cinta *f* adhesiva. **II** *vtr* pegar *or* fijar con celo®.

sell-out ['selaʊt] *n* **1** Theat éxito *m* taquillero *or* de taquilla. **2** *(act of disloyalty)* claudicación *f*, traición *f*.

selvage *n*, **selvedge** ['selvɪdʒ] *n* Sew orillo *m*.

semantic [sɪ'mæntɪk] *adj* semántico,-a.

semantics [sɪ'mæntɪks] *n* semántica *f*.

semaphore ['seməfɔːr] *n* Rail semáforo *m*.

semblance ['sembləns] *n* apariencia *f*; **there was some s. of truth in it,** había algo de verdad en ello.

semen ['siːmen] *n* semen *m*.

semester [sɪ'mestər] *n* semestre *m*.

semi ['semɪ] *n (abbr of semidetached) GB fam* chalet *m or* chalé *m* adosado, casa *f* adosada.

semi- ['semɪ] *pref* semi-.

semibreve ['semɪbriːv] *n* Mus semibreve *f*.

semicircle ['semɪsɜːkəl] *n* semicírculo *m*.

semicircular [semɪ'sɜːkjʊlər] *adj* semicircular.

semicolon [semɪ'kəʊlən] *n* punto y coma *m*.

semiconductor [semɪkən'dʌktər] *n* Elec semiconductor *m*.

semiconscious [semɪ'kɒnʃəs] *adj* semiconsciente.

semidetached [semɪdɪ'tætʃt] **I** *adj (building)* adosado,-a. **II** *n* chalet *m or* chalé *m* adosado, casa *f* adosada.

semifinal [semɪ'faɪnəl] *n* semifinal *f*.

semifinalist [semɪ'faɪnəlɪst] *n* Sport semifinalista *mf*.

seminar ['semɪnɑːr] *n* seminario *m*, clase *f*.

seminary ['semɪnərɪ] *n* Rel seminario *m*.

semiofficial [semɪə'fɪʃəl] *adj* semioficial.

semiotics [semɪ'ɒtɪks] *n* semiótica *f*.

semiprecious [semɪ'preʃəs] *adj* Min semiprecioso,-a.

semiquaver [semɪ'kweɪvər] *n* Mus semicorchea *f*.

Semite ['siːmaɪt] *n* semita *mf*.

Semitic [sɪ'mɪtɪk] *adj* semita, semítico,-a.

semolina [semə'liːnə] *n* sémola *f*.

SEN [esiː'en] *GB abbr of* State Enrolled Nurse, enfermera *f* diplomada.

Sen 1 *abbr of* Senator, senador,-a *m,f*. **2** *abbr see* Snr.

senate ['senɪt] *n* **1** Pol senado *m*. **2** Univ claustro *m*.

senator ['senətər] *n* senador,-a *m,f*.

send [send] **I** *vtr (pt & pp sent)* **1** *(letter etc)* enviar, mandar; *(telex etc)* mandar, poner; *(radio signal)* transmitir; *(rocket, ball)* lanzar; **he was sent to prison,** lo mandaron a la cárcel; **it sent a shiver down my spine,** me dio escalofríos; **s. her my regards,** dale recuerdos de mi parte; **to s. sb to Coventry,** hacerle el vacío a algn; **to s. sth flying,** tirar algo; **to s. word to sb,** avisar a algn; *fam* **to s. sb packing,** mandar a algn a paseo. **2** *(cause to* *become)* volver; **the noise sent her mad,** el ruido la volvió loca. **3** *sl (enrapture)* chiflar. **II** *vi* **to s. for sb,** mandar llamar a algn; **to s, for sth,** encargar *or* pedir algo. ◆ **send away I** *vtr (dismiss)* despedir, despachar. **II** *vi* **to s. away for sth,** escribir pidiendo algo. ◆ **send back** *vtr (goods, meal, etc)* devolver; *(person)* hacer volver *or* regresar. ◆ **send down** *vtr* **1** *(prices, temperature)* hacer bajar. **2** *GB Univ* expulsar. **3** *fam (imprison)* meter en chirona *or* el talego. ◆ **send in** *vtr (application form etc)* mandar, enviar; *(troops, supplies)* enviar; *(visitor)* hacer pasar. ◆ **send off** *vtr* **1** *(letter etc)* enviar (por correo); *(goods)* despachar, mandar. **2** *Ftb (player)* expulsar. **II** *vi* **to s. off for sth,** escribir pidiendo algo. ◆ **send on** *vtr* **1** *(letter)* reexpedir, hacer seguir; *(luggage)* *(ahead)* facturar; *(later)* enviar, mandar (más tarde). **2** *Ftb (substitute)* sustituir. ◆ **send out I** *vtr* **1** *(person)* mandar salir, echar. **2** *(leaflets, invitations)* enviar, mandar. **3** *(emit) (smoke, light, heat)* emitir; *(radio signals)* emitir, dar. **II** *vi* **to s. out for sth,** mandar traer algo. ◆ **send round** *vtr* **1** mandar a domicilio. **2** *(circulate)* hacer circular. ◆ **send up** *vtr* **1** *(person, luggage, meal)* hacer subir *or* montar; *(rocket etc)* lanzar; *(smoke, flames)* echar, arrojar; *(prices, temperature)* hacer subir. **2** *GB fam (make fun of) (person)* burlarse de; *(book etc)* satirizar. **3** *sl* meter en chirona *or* el talego.

sender ['sendə'] *n* remitente *mf.*

send-up ['sendʌp] *n GB fam* sátira *f,* paradio *m.*

sendoff ['sendɒf] *n fam* despedida *f.*

Senegal [senɪ'gɔːl] *n* Senegal.

Senegalese [senɪgə'liːz] *adj & n* senegalés,-esa *(m,f).*

senile ['siːnaɪl] *adj* senil.

senility [sɪ'nɪlɪtɪ] *n* senilidad *f.*

senior ['siːnjə'] **I** *adj* **1** *(in age)* mayor; **William Armstrong S.,** William Armstrong padre. ■ **s. citizen,** jubilado,-a *m,f,* persona *f* de la tercera edad; *US Sch* **s. high (school),** instituto *m* de enseñanza superior. **2** *(in position, rank)* superior; *(with longer service)* más antiguo,-a, de más antigüedad; *Mil* **s. officer,** oficial *mf* de alta graduación; **s. partner,** socio,-a *m,f* mayoritario,-a; *GB* **the s. service,** la marina. **II** *n* **1** *(in age)* mayor *mf;* **she's three years my s.,** me lleva tres años. **2** *GB Sch* mayor *mf; US Sch Univ* estudiante *mf* del último curso.

seniority [siːnɪ'ɒrɪtɪ] *n* antigüedad *f.*

sensation [sen'seɪʃən] *n* **1** *(feeling)* sensación *f.* **2** *(great success)* sensación *f,* éxito *m;* **to be a s.,** ser un éxito; **to cause a s.,** causar sensación.

sensational [sen'seɪʃənəl] *adj (marvellous)* sensacional; *(exaggerated) (headlines etc)* sensacionalista.

sensationalism [sen'seɪʃənəlɪzəm] *n* sensacionalismo *m.*

sense [sens] **I** *n* **1** *(faculty)* sentido *m;* **s. of hearing/smell,** sentido del oído/del olfato. ■ **s. organ,** órgano *m* sensorial; **sixth s.,** sexto sentido *m.* **2** *(feeling)* sensación *f;* **s. of direction/duty/humour,** sentido *m* de la orientación/ del deber/del humor; **to lose all s. of time,** perder toda noción del tiempo. **3** *(wisdom)* sentido *m* común, juicio *m,* sensatez *f;* **there's no s. in crying,** ¿de qué sirve llorar?; **to make sb see s., to talk some s. into sb,** hacer entrar en razón a algn. ■ **common s.,** sentido *m* común. **4** *(meaning) (gen)* sentido *m; (of word)* significado *m;* **I can't make (any) s. of it,** no llego a comprenderlo; **in a s.,** en cierto sentido, hasta cierto punto; **it doesn't make s.,** no tiene sentido. **5 senses,** juicio *m sing;* **to come to one's s.,** recobrar el juicio; **to take leave of one's s.,** perder el juicio. **II** *vtr* sentir, percibir, presentir.

senseless ['senslɪs] *adj* **1** *(absurd)* insensato,-a, absurdo,-a. **2** *(unconscious)* sin conocimiento, inconsciente.

sensibility [sensɪ'bɪlɪtɪ] *n* **1** sensibilidad *f.* **2** **sensibilities,** susceptibilidad *f sing,* sensibilidad *f sing.*

sensible ['sensɪbəl] *adj* **1** *(wise)* sensato,-a. **2** *(reasonable) (decision)* razonable, prudente; *(choice)* acertado,-a. **3** *(clothes, shoes)* práctico,-a, cómodo,-a. **4** *(difference)* apreciable, perceptible.

sensitive ['sensɪtɪv] *adj* **1** sensible; *(touchy)* susceptible. **2** *(skin, issue, etc)* delicado,-a, sensible; *(document)* confidencial.

sensitivity [sensɪ'tɪvɪtɪ] *n* **1** *(gen)* sensibilidad *f;* *(touchiness)* susceptibilidad *f.* **2** *(of skin, issue, etc)* delicadeza *f.*

sensitize ['sensɪtaɪz] *vtr* sensibilizar.

sensor ['sensə'] *n Tech* sensor *m,* detector *m.*

sensory ['sensərɪ] *adj* sensorial.

sensual ['sensjʊəl] *adj* sensual.

sensuality [sensjʊ'ælɪtɪ] *n* sensualidad *f.*

sensuous ['sensjʊəs] *adj* sensual.

sent [sent] *pt & pp see* **send.**

sentence ['sentəns] **I** *n* **1** frase *f; Ling* oración *f.* **2** *Jur* sentencia *f,* fallo *m,* condena *f;* **to pass s.,** dictar sentencia; **to pass s. on sb,** imponer una pena a algn. ■ **death s.,** pena *f* de muerte; **life s.,** cadena *f* perpetua. **II** *vtr Jur* condenar.

sententious [sen'tenʃəs] *adj* sentencioso,-a.

sentiment ['sentɪmənt] *n* **1** *(sentimentality)* sentimentalismo *m,* sensiblería *f.* **2** *(feeling)* sentimiento *m.* **3** *(opinion)* opinión *f,* parecer *m,* juicio *m.*

sentimental [sentɪ'mentəl] *adj* sentimental. ■ **s. value,** valor *m* sentimental.

sentimentality [sentɪmen'tælɪtɪ] *n* sentimentalismo *m,* sensiblería *f.*

sentry ['sentrɪ] *n Mil* centinela *m;* **to be on s. duty,** estar de guardia, hacer guardia. ■ **s. box,** garita *f* de centinela; **s. duty,** guardia *f.*

Seoul [səʊl] *n* Seúl.

sepal ['sepəl] *n Bot* sépalo *m.*

separable ['sepərəbəl] *adj* separable.

separate ['sepəreɪt] **I** *vtr (gen)* separar **(from,** de); *(divide)* dividir **(into,** en); *(distinguish)* distinguir; *Culin* **separated milk, she is separated from her husband,** está *or* vive separada de su marido. **II** *vi* separarse. **III** ['sepərɪt] *adj (gen)* separado,-a; *(apart)* apartado,-a; *(different)* distinto,-a, diferente; *(of organization)* independiente; *(of entrance)* particular; **to send sth under s. cover,** mandar algo por separado. **IV separates** *npl (clothes)* piezas *fpl.* ◆ **separately** *adv* por separado.

separation [sepə'reɪʃən] *n* separación *f.*

separatism ['sepərətɪzəm] *n* separatismo *m.*

separatist ['sepərətɪst] *n* separatista *mf.*

Sephardi [sɪ'fɑːdiː] *n (pl* **Sephardim** [sɪ'fɑːdɪm]*)* sefardí *mf,* sefardita *mf.*

Sephardic [sɪ'fɑːdɪk] *adj* sefardí, sefardita.

sepia ['siːpɪə] *adj & n* sepia *(f).*

sepsis ['sepsɪs] *n Med* sepsia *f.*

Sept *abbr of* **September,** setiembre *m,* septiembre *m,* sept, sep.

September [sep'tembə'] *n* septiembre *m,* setiembre *m;* **in S.,** en septiembre; **(on) the 7th of S.,** el 7 de septiembre; *see also* **May.**

septet [sep'tet] *n Mus* septeto *m.*

septic ['septɪk] *adj Med* séptico,-a; *(wound)* **to become s.,** infectarse. ■ **s. tank,** fosa *f* séptica.

septicaemia, *US* **septicemia** [septɪ'siːmɪə] *n Med* septicemia *f.*

sepulchre, *US* **sepulcher** ['sepəlkə'] *n* sepulcro *m.*

sequel ['siːkwəl] *n* secuela *f.*

sequence ['siːkwəns] *n* **1** *(order)* secuencia *f,* orden *m; Ling (of tenses)* concordancia *f.* **2** *(series)* secuencia *f,* serie *f,* sucesión *f; Cards* escala *f; dance* **s.,** número *m* (de baile); *Cin* **film s.,** secuencia.

sequester [sɪ'kwestə'] *vtr* **1** *Jur (seize)* embargar, secuestrar. **2** *(separate)* aislar.

sequestration [siːkweˈstreɪʃən] n Jur (seizure) embargo m, secuestro m.

sequin [ˈsiːkwɪn] n lentejuela f.

sequoia [sɪˈkwɔɪə] n Bot secoya f, secuoya f. ■ **giant s.**, secuoya f gigante.

serenade [serɪˈneɪd] Mus I n serenata f. II vtr dar una serenata a.

serene [sɪˈriːn] adj sereno-a, tranquilo,-a. ◆ **serenely** adv serenamente, con serenidad, con calma.

serenity [sɪˈrenɪtɪ] n serenidad f.

serf [sɜːf] n Hist siervo,-a m,f.

serge [sɜːdʒ] n Tex sarga f.

sergeant [ˈsɑːdʒənt] n Mil sargento m; (of police) cabo m. ■ **s. major**, sargento m mayor, brigada m.

serial [ˈsɪərɪəl] n 1 Rad TV (gen) serial m; (soap opera) radionovela f, telenovela f. 2 Press novela f por entregas. 3 **s. number**, número m de serie.

serialize [ˈsɪərɪəlaɪz] vtr seriar.

series [ˈsɪəriːz] n inv (gen) serie f; (of books) colección f; (of concerts, lectures) ciclo m.

serigraph [ˈserɪgræf] n serigrafía f.

serigraphy [səˈrɪgrəfɪ] n serigrafía f.

serin [ˈserɪn] n Orn verdecillo m.

serious [ˈsɪərɪəs] adj 1 (solemn) serio,-a; (earnest) serio,-a, formal; **I am s.**, hablo en serio; **he's s. about leaving the country**, está decidido a salir del país; **she's s. about your brother**, está enamorada de tu hermano; **you can't be s.!**, no lo dirás en serio, ¿verdad?, ¿es una broma, ¿no? 2 (causing concern) grave, serio,-a; **s. damage/losses**, daños/pérdidas importantes; **things are looking s.**, la situación se está poniendo grave or seria. ◆ **seriously** adv 1 (in earnest) en serio; **don't take things so s.**, no tome las cosas tan en serio; **s. though**, bromas aparte. 2 (dangerously, severely) gravemente, seriamente; **s. damaged**, seriamente dañado,-a; **s. wounded**, herido,-a de gravedad.

seriousness [ˈsɪərɪəsnɪs] n gravedad f, seriedad f; **in all s.**, hablando en serio.

sermon [ˈsɜːmən] n sermón m.

serous [ˈsɪərəs] adj Med seroso,-a.

serpent [ˈsɜːpənt] n Zool lit serpiente f.

serrated [sɪˈreɪtɪd] adj dentado,-a, serrado,-a; **a knife with a s. edge**, un cuchillo de sierra.

serum [ˈsɪərəm] n (pl serums or sera [ˈsɪərə]) Med suero m.

servant [ˈsɜːvənt] n (domestic) criado,-a m,f, sirviente,-a m,f; fig servidor,-a m,f. ■ **civil s., public s.**, funcionario,-a m,f del Estado.

serve [sɜːv] I vtr 1 (work for) servir. 2 (customer) servir, atender; (food, drink) servir; **are you being served?**, ¿le atienden?; **dinner is served**, la cena está servida; (on recipe) **'serves four'**, 'para cuatro personas'; Rel to **s. mass**, ayudar en misa. 3 Ten sacar, servir. 4 (be useful to) servir, ser útil; **if my memory serves me right**, si no me falla la memoria, si mal no recuerdo; **it serves him right**, bien merecido lo tiene. 5 (provide with) equipar; **the area is served by both bus and underground**, en la zona hay autobús y metro. 6 Jur to **s. a summons on sb**, entregar una citación a algn. 7 (complete, carry out) cumplir, hacer; to **s. a prison sentence**, fam to **s. time**, cumplir una condena; to **s. one's apprenticeship**, hacer el aprendizaje. II vi 1 (in household, army, etc) servir; to **s. at table**, servir la mesa; to **s. on a comittee/Jury**, ser miembro de una comisión/un jurado. 2 Ten sacar, servir. 3 (be useful) servir (as, de); to **s. as an example**, servir de ejemplo. III n Ten saque m. ◆ **serve out, serve up** vtr (food) servir.

server [ˈsɜːvəʳ] n 1 Rel (at mass) monaguillo m. 2 Ten saque mf. 3 (cutlery) cubierto m de servir. 4 (tray) bandeja f, salvilla f.

service [ˈsɜːvɪs] I n 1 (provided by hotel, etc) servicio m; **after-sales s.**, servicio postventa or posventa; **at your s.!**, ¡a sus órdenes!; **how can I be of s. to you?**, ¿en qué puedo servirle?; **military s.**, servicio militar; (on bill) **s. (charge) included**, servicio incluido; to **die in active s.**, morir en acto de servicio; to **do sb a s.**, hacerle un favor a algn; to **see s.**, prestar serivicio. ■ **s. area**, área f de servicio; **s. flat**, apartamento m con servicio; **s. Industry**, sector m de servicios; **s. road**, vía f de acceso or de salida; Aut **s. station**, estación f de servicio. 2 (department, system) servicio m; **medical/social s.**, servicios médicos/ sociales; **National Health S.**, Seguridad Social; **postal s.**, servicio de correos; Mil **the Services**, las Fuerzas Armadas; **the train/bus s. to Bristol**, la línea de trenes/ autobuses a Bristol. ■ **civil s.**, administración f pública. 3 (maintenance) revisión f, mantenimiento m; (of car) puesta f a punto. 4 Rel oficio m, servicios mpl; (mass) misa f; to **hold a s.**, celebrar un oficio; (say mass) celebrar misa. 5 Ten saque m, servicio m. ■ **s. line**, línea f de saque or de servicio. 6 (set of dishes) juego m, servicio m. ■ **dinner s.**, vajilla f; **ten s.**, juego m de té. II vtr (car, machine) revisar.

serviceable [ˈsɜːvɪsəbəl] adj 1 (fit for use) útil, utilizable, servible. 2 (practical) práctico,-a; (durable) duradero,-a.

serviceman [ˈsɜːvɪsmən] n (pl servicemen) Mil militar m.

servicewoman [ˈsɜːvɪswʊmən] n (pl servicewomen [ˈsɜːvɪswɪmɪn]) Mil militar f.

serviette [sɜːvɪˈet] n GB servilleta f. ■ **s. ring**, servilletero m.

servile [ˈsɜːvaɪl] adj servil.

servitude [ˈsɜːvɪtjuːd] n servidumbre f; **penal s.**, trabajos mpl forzados.

servo [ˈsɜːvəʊ] n (pl servos) fam (abbr of servo-mechanism) servosistema m, servomecanismo m. ■ **s. brakes**, servofrenos mpl.

servo-assisted [ˈsɜːvəʊəsɪstɪd] adj servoasistido,-a; **s. brakes**, servofrenos mpl.

servomechanism [ˈsɜːvəʊmekənɪzəm] n servosistema m, servomecanismo m.

sesame [ˈsesəmɪ] n Bot sésamo m, ajonjolí m; **open s.!**, ¡ábrete sésamo!

session [ˈseʃən] n 1 (meeting) sesión f, junta f, reunión f; (sitting) sesión f; to **be in s.**, (gen) estar reunido,-a; (Parliament, court) celebrar una sesión; **we're in for a long s.**, tenemos para rato. 2 Sch Univ (academic year) año m or curso m académico.

set¹ [set] I vtr (pt & pp set) I (put, place) poner, colocar; (dog) azuzar (on, contra); (trap) poner (for, para); **the novel is s. in Moscow**, la novela se desarrolla en Moscú; to **s. fire to sth**, prender fuego a algo; to **s. sb's mind at rest**, tranquilizar a algn. 2 (fix) (date, time) fijar, señalar; (price) fijar; (record) establecer; (fashion) imponer. 3 (adjust) (mechanism etc) ajustar; (bone) encajar, componer; (fix) (mechanism etc) componer, arreglar; **she s. her alarm for six**, puso el despertador para las seis; to **s. one's watch**, poner el reloj en hora. 4 (arrange) arreglar; **he s. the words to music**, puso música a la letra; **I had my hair s.**, me han peinado; to **s. the table**, poner la mesa. 5 (assign) (exam, homework) poner; (example) dar, poner; (precedent) sentar. 6 (cause to begin, do, etc) poner; **it s. him thinking**, le dio que pensar, le hizo reflexionar; Naut to **s. sail**, zarpar; to **s. sb free**, poner en libertad a algn; to **s. sth going**, poner algo en marcha. 7 (mount) (diamond etc) montar, engastar. 8 Print (text) componer. II vi 1 (sun, moon) ponerse. 2 (jelly, jam) cuajar; (glue) endurecerse; (cement) fraguarse, endurecerse; (bone) encajarse, componerse. 3 (begin) to **s. to**, ponerse a. III n 1 Hairdr marcado m; **shampoo and s.**, lavar y marcar. 2 (stage) Cin plató m; Theat escenario m; (scenery) decorado m. IV adj 1 (fixed) (task, idea, purpose) fijo,-a; (date, time) señalado,-a, determinado,-a; (opinion) inflexible; (smile) rígido,-a, forzado,-a; (gaze) fijo,-a; (speech)

375

preparado,-a; **s. lunch,** menú del día; **s. phrase,** frase hecha; **s. price,** precio fijo; **to be dead s. against sth,** oponerse rotundamente a algo; **to be s. in one's ways,** tener unas costumbres muy arraigadas, ser reacio,-a al cambio; **to be s. on doing sth,** estar empeñado,-a en hacer algo. ■ **s. square,** cartabón *m*, escuadra *f*. 2 *(ready)* listo,-a; **on your marks, get s., go!,** ¡preparados, listos, ya! ◆ **set about** *vi* 1 *(begin)* empezar; **I don't know how to s. about it,** no sé por dónde empezar. 2 *(attack)* atacar, agredir. ◆ **set against** *vtr* 1 **to s. one person against another,** enemistar a dos personas. 2 *(balance against)* comparar con. ◆ **set aside** *vtr* 1 *(time, money)* guardar, reservar; *(differences)* dejar de lado. 2 *(reject)* rechazar, desechar. ◆ **set back** *vtr* 1 *(place at a distance)* apartar; **s. back from the road,** apartado,-a de la carretera. 2 *(delay)* retrasar; *(hinder)* entorpecer. 3 *fam (cost)* costar. ◆ **set down** *vtr* 1 *(luggage etc)* poner, dejar (en el suelo); *GB (passengers)* dejar. 2 *(write down)* poner por escrito. ◆ **set forth** *vi arch* emprender marcha, partir. ◆ **set in** *vi (winter, rain)* comenzar; *(problems, complications)* aparecer, surgir; **panic s. in,** cundió el pánico. ◆ **set off** *vi (depart)* salir, marcharse, ponerse en camino. II *vtr* 1 *(bomb)* hacer estallar; *(burglar alarm)* hacer sonar or saltar; *(reaction)* desencadenar. 2 *(enhance)* hacer resaltar. ◆ **set out** I *vi* 1 *(depart)* salir, marcharse, ponerse en camino; **to s. out for ...,** partir hacia ... . 2 *(intend)* **to s. out to do sth,** intentar or proponerse hacer algo. II *vtr (arrange, display) (goods)* disponer; *(present) (work)* presentar. ◆ **set to** *vi* ponerse a trabajar. ◆ **set up** I *vtr* 1 *(position)* colocar; *(statue, barricades, camp)* levantar; *(assemble) (tent, stall, machinery)* montar. 2 *(establish) (school, business)* establecer, crear; *fam* montar; *(committee, inquiry)* constituir; **to s. oneself up as a photographer,** establecerse como fotógrafo; **to s. sb up in business,** ayudar a algn a establecerse; **to s. up house,** poner la casa, instalarse; **to s. up shop,** montar una tienda; *fam* **to be s. up for life,** tener el porvenir asegurado; *fam* **you've been s. up!,** ¡te han timado! II *vi* establecerse; **to s. up in business,** establecerse. ◆ **set upon** *vtr (attack)* abalanzarse sobre, atacar.

set² [set] I *n* 1 *(series)* serie *f*; *(of brushes, golf clubs)* juego *m*; *(of dishes)* juego *m*, servicio *m*; *(of tools)* estuche *m*; *(of turbines etc)* equipo *m*, grupo *m*; *(of books, poems)* colección *f*; *(of teeth)* dentadura *f*. ■ **chess s.,** juego *m* de ajedrez; **electric train s.,** tren *m* eléctrico; **manicure s.,** estuche *m* de manicura; **s. of cutlery,** cubertería *f*; **s. of kitchen utensils,** batería *f* de cocina; **s. of teeth,** dentadura *f*; **tea s.,** juego *m* de té. 2 *(of people)* grupo *m*; *pej (clique)* pandilla *f*, camarilla *f*; **the smart s.,** la gente bien. 3 *Math* conjunto *m*. 4 *Ten* set *m*. 5 *Elec* aparato *m*. ■ *TV* **s.,** televisor *m*. 6 **to make a dead s. at,** *(attack)* emprenderla con; *(seduce)* proponerse ligar con. II *vtr (pt & pp set) (divide up)* dividir en grupos.

setback ['setbæk] *n* revés *m*, contratiempo *m*.

settee [se'ti:] *n* sofá *m*.

setter ['setə'] *n (dog)* (perro *m*) setter *m*.

setting ['setɪŋ] *n* 1 *(background etc)* marco *m*; *(of novel, film)* escenario *m*. 2 *(of jewel)* engaste *m*, montura *f*. 3 *Tech (of controls, machine)* ajuste *m*. 4 *Print* composición *f*. 5 *Hairdr* **s. lotion,** fijador *m*.

setting-up [setɪŋ'ʌp] *n (creation)* creación *f*, fundación *f*.

settle¹ ['setəl] I *vtr* 1 *(place)* colocar, asentar. 2 *(decide on)* decidir, acordar; *(date, price)* fijar; *(sort out) (problem)* resolver, solucionar; *(differences)* resolver, arreglar; **that settles it,** queda decidido entonces; *Jur* **to s. a case out of court,** llegar a un acuerdo amistoso; **to s. one's affairs,** poner los asuntos en orden; *fam* **that settles it!,** ¡se acabó! 3 *(Pay) (debt)* pagar; *(account)* saldar, liquidar. 4 *(calm) (nerves)* calmar; *(stomach)* asentar. 5 *fam (put an end to)* terminar, acabar con; **I'll soon s. him!,** ¡ya me las pagará! 6 *(establish) (person)* instalar. 7 *(colonize) (land)* colonizar, poblar. II *vi* 1 *(bird, insect)* posarse; *(dust)* depositarse; *(snow)*

cuajar; *(sediment)* precipitarse; *(liquid)* asentarse, clarificarse; **a thick fog settled over the city,** una densa niebla cayó sobre la ciudad; **to s. into an armchair,** acomodarse en un sillón. 2 *(put down roots)* afincarse, domiciliarse. 3 *(weather)* serenarse, estabilizarse. 4 *(child, nerves)* calmarse; *(situation)* normalizarse. 5 *(pay)* pagar; *Jur* **to s. out of court,** llegar a un acuerdo amistoso. ◆ **settle down** *vi* 1 *(put down roots)* afincarse, domiciliarse, instalarse; *(marry)* casarse; *(become more responsible)* sentar la cabeza. 2 *(become accustomed)* acostumbrarse, adaptarse. 3 *(begin)* **to s. down to work,** ponerse a trabajar. 4 *(child)* calmarse; *(situation)* normalizarse, volver a la normalidad. ◆ **settle for** *vtr* conformarse con, contentarse con. ◆ **settle in** *vi (move in)* instalarse; *(become adapted)* acostumbrarse, adaptarse. ◆ **settle into** *vtr (get used to)* acostumbrarse a, adaptarse a, hacerse a. ◆ **settle on** *vtr (decide on)* decidirse por; *(choose)* escoger; *(agree on)* ponerse de acuerdo sobre. ◆ **settle with** *vtr (pay-debt to)* ajustar cuentas con.

settle² ['setəl] *n (wooden bench)* banco *m*.

settlement ['setəlmənt] *n* 1 *(agreement)* acuerdo *m*, solución *f*; **out-of-court s.,** acuerdo amistoso. 2 *(of debt)* pago *m*; *(of account)* liquidación *f*. 3 *(dowry)* dote *m*; *(pension)* pensión *f*, renta *f*. 4 *(colonization)* colonización *f*, población *f*. 5 *(colony)* colonia *f*; *(village)* pueblo *m*, poblado *m*.

settler ['setlə] *n* colono *m*, colonizador,-a *m,f*, poblador,-a *m,f*.

set-to [set'tu:] *n fam (quarrel, fight)* riña *f*, pelea *f*.

setup ['setəp] *n (system)* sistema *m*; *(situation)* situación *f*; *sl* montaje *m*.

seven ['sevən] I *adj* siete *inv*; **all s. of them left,** se marcharon todos siete; **chapter/page s.,** el capítulo/la página número siete; **it costs s. dollars,** cuesta siete dólares; **it's s. minutes to five,** son las cinco menos siete, faltan siete minutos para las cinco; **s. hundred,** setecientos,-as; **s. thousand,** siete mil; **she is s. years old,** tiene siete años; **they live at number s.,** viven en el número siete. II *n* siete *m inv*; **a boy of s.,** un niño de siete años; **come at s.,** ven a las siete; **it's s. o'clock,** son las siete; **s. and s. are fourteen,** siete más siete son catorce; **the clock struck s.,** dieron las siete; **the s. of hearts,** el siete de corazones; **there were s. of us,** éramos siete; **they are sold in sevens,** se venden de siete en siete; **three out of s.,** tres sobre siete; **we live at s. Carlton Street,** vivimos en la calle Carlton, número siete.

seventeen [sevən'ti:n] *adj & n* diecisiete *(m)*, diez y siete *(m); see also* **seven.**

seventeenth [sevən'ti:nθ] I *adj* decimoséptimo,-a; **the s. century,** el siglo diecisiete. II *n (in series)* decimoséptimo,-a *m, f; (fraction)* decimoséptima parte *f*; **the s. of May,** el diecisiete de mayo; *see also* **seventh.**

seventh ['sevənθ] I *adj* séptimo,-a; **Edward the s.,** Eduardo séptimo; **he was the s. to arrive,** fue el séptimo en llegar; **the s. century,** el siglo siete; **the s. of October, October the s.,** el siete de octubre; **to be in s. heaven,** estar en la gloria, estar en el séptimo cielo; **to come s.,** quedar en séptimo lugar; **we're leaving on the s.,** nos marchamos el día siete; **your letter of the s.,** su carta del día siete del corriente. II *n* 1 *(in series)* séptimo,-a *m, f*. 2 *(fraction)* séptimo *m*, séptima parte *f*; **three sevenths,** tres séptimos. 3 *Mus* séptima *f*.

seventieth ['sevəntɪθ] I *adj* septuagésimo,-a. II *n* 1 *(in series)* septuagésimo,-a *m, f*. 2 *(fraction)* septuagésimo *m*, septuagésima parte *f; see also* **seventh.**

seventy [sevəntɪ] I *adj* setenta *inv*; **about s. cars/passengers,** unos setenta coches/pasajeros; **he's about s. (years old),** anda por los setenta; **he will be s. (years old) tomorrow,** mañana cumplirá los setenta años; **s. per cent of the staff,** el setenta por ciento del personal. II *n* setenta *m inv*; **he must be in his seventies,** debe andar por los setenta; **in the seventies,** durante los (años) setenta; **the temperature was in the seventies,** hacía más de setenta grados; **to be in one's early/late seventies,** tener poco más de setenta/casi ochenta años; **to do s.,** ir a setenta millas la hora.

sever ['sevə'] vtr (cut) cortar; fig (relations, communications) romper.

several ['sevərəl] **I** adj **1** (more than a few) varios,-as. **2** (different) distintos,-as; (separate) respectivos,-as. **II** pron algunos,-as.

severance ['sevərəns] n (of relations etc) ruptura f. ■ Ind **s. pay,** indemnización f por despido.

severe [sɪ'vɪə'] adj (gen) severo,-a; (discipline, measures) severo,-a, riguroso,-a, estricto,-a; (climate) duro,-a, riguroso,-a; (criticism, punishment) severo,-a; (illness, loss) grave, serio,-a; (blow) duro,-a, fuerte; (pain) agudo,-a; (style, architecture) austero,-a; **to be s. on sb,** ser muy duro,-a con algn. ◆ **severely** adv (gen) severamente; (criticized, punished) severamente, rigurosamente; (ill) gravemente.

severeness [sɪ'vɪənɪs] n, **severity** [sɪ'verɪtɪ] n (of person, criticism, punishment) severidad f; (of climate) rigor m; (of illness) gravedad f, seriedad f; (of pain) agudeza f; (of style) austeridad f.

Seville [sə'vɪl] n Sevilla.

sew [səʊ] vtr & vi (pt sewed; pp sewed or sewn) coser (**on,** a). ◆ **sew up** vtr (stitch together) coser; (mend) remendar; fig **it's all sewn up,** ya está todo arreglado.

sewage ['suːɪdʒ] n aguas fpl residuales. ■ **s. disposal,** depuración f de aguas residuales; **s. farm** or **works,** estación f depuradora; **s. system,** alcantarillado m.

sewer ['suːə'] n alcantarilla f, cloaca f, albañal m; **main s.,** colector m.

sewerage ['suːərɪdʒ] n alcantarillado m.

sewing ['səʊɪŋ] n costura f. ■ **s. machine,** máquina f de coser.

sewn [səʊn] pp see **sew.**

sex [seks] n sexo m; **s. education,** educación f sexual; **s. maniac,** maníaco,-a m, f sexual; fam obseso,-a m, f; **the fair s.,** el bello sexo; **the opposite s.,** el sexo opuesto; **the weaker s.,** el sexo débil; **to have s. with sb,** tener relaciones sexuales con algn; fam hacer el amor or acostarse con algn. ■ **s. appeal,** sex-appeal m; fam gancho m; **s. shop,** sex-shop m; **s. symbol,** símbolo m sexual, sex-symbol m.

sexism ['seksɪzəm] n sexismo m.

sexist ['seksɪst] adj & n sexista (mf).

sexless ['seksĺɪs] adj asexual, asexuado,-a.

sexologist [sek'sɒlədʒɪst] n sexólogo,-a m, f.

sexology [sek'sɒlədʒɪ] n sexología f.

sextet [seks'tet] n Mus sexteto m.

sexton ['sekstən] n Rel sacristán m.

sexual ['seksjʊəl] adj sexual.

sexuality [seksjʊ'ælɪtɪ] n sexualidad f.

sexy ['seksɪ] adj (sexier, sexiest) fam sexi, erótico,-a.

Seychelles [seɪ'ʃel(z)] npl Seychelles fpl.

sgd abbr of **signed,** firmado,-a, Fdo.

Sgt abbr of **Sergeant,** Sargento m, Sarg.

shabbiness ['ʃæbɪnɪs] n **1** (of dress) pobreza f, aspecto m lastimoso or harapiento; (raggedness) aspecto m desharrapado or andrajoso; (of furniture etc) aspecto m descuidado, mal aspecto m. **2** (of treatment) mezquindad f.

shabby ['ʃæbɪ] adj (shabbier, shabbiest) **1** (garment) raído,-a, desharrapado,-a; (furniture) de aspecto lastimoso; (house) desvencijado,-a, destartalado,-a; (person) pobremente vestido,-a; (in rags) andrajoso,-a, harapiento,-a; (unkempt) desaseado,-a. **2** (treatment) mezquino,-a; **a s. trick,** una mala pasada.

shack [ʃæk] **I** n choza f. **II** vi fam **to s. up with sb,** juntarse con algn.

shackle ['ʃækəl] **I** vtr (prisoner) poner grilletes a; fig (plan etc) poner trabas a. **II** shackles npl grilletes mpl, grillos mpl; fig trabas fpl; **to cast** or **throw off one's s.,** librarse de las ataduras or las trabas.

shade [ʃeɪd] **I** n **1** (shadow) sombra f; **in the s.,** a la sombra; fig **to put sb in the s.,** dejar a algn en la sombra, hacer sombra a algn. **2** (eyeshade) visera f; (lampshade) pantalla f; US (blind) persiana f. **3** (of colour) tono m, matiz m; fig (of opinion, meaning) matiz m; **of every s. and hue,** de toda calaña. **4** (small amount) poquito m. **5** **shades,** sl gafas fpl de sol. **II** vtr (from sun) proteger contra el sol, resguardar. ◆ **shade in** vtr Art sombrear.

shading ['ʃeɪdɪŋ] n Art degradación f.

shadow ['ʃædəʊ] **I** n **1** (shade etc) sombra f; (darkness) oscuridad f; Art sombreado m; **to cast a s.,** hacer sombra, proyectar una sombra; fig ensombrecer (**over,** -); fig **she's a s. of her former self,** es sólo una sombra de lo que fue; fam **five o'clock s.,** barba f de un día; fig **without a s. of a doubt,** sin lugar a dudas. **2** GB Parl de la oposición; **the s. cabinet,** el gabinete de la oposición. ■ **eye s.,** sombra f de ojos; TV **s. mask,** máscara f perforada con ranuras; Theat **s. play,** sombras fpl chinescas. **II** vtr fig (follow) seguir la pista a.

shadow-box ['ʃædəʊbɒks] vi fig luchar contra molinos de viento.

shadowy ['ʃædəʊɪ] adj (dark) oscuro,-a; (hazy) vago,-a, impreciso,-a.

shady ['ʃeɪdɪ] adj (shadier, shadiest) **1** (place) a la sombra; (tree) que da sombra. **2** (suspicious) (person) sospechoso,-a; (deal) turbio,-a.

shaft [ʃɑːft] n **1** (of tool, golf club) mango m; (of lance) asta f; (of arrow) astil m; (of cart) vara f. **2** Tech eje m. ■ **drive s.,** árbol m motor. **3** (of mine) pozo m; (of lift, elevator) hueco m. **4** (beam of light) rayo m.

shag¹ [ʃæg] n (shredded tobacco) tabaco m picado.

shag² [ʃæg] n Orn cormorán m moñudo.

shag³ [ʃæg] vtr GB vulg follar, joder.

shaggy ['ʃægɪ] adj (shaggier, shaggiest) (hairy) peludo,-a; (long-haired) melenudo,-a; (hair, beard) desgreñado,-a, enmarañado,-a; fam **a s. dog story,** un cuento chino.

shah [ʃɑː] n cha m.

shake [ʃeɪk] **I** n **1** (gen) sacudida f; **he denied it with a s. of the head,** lo negó con un movimiento de la cabeza; fam **in two shakes, in half a s.,** en un santiamén. **2** fam **the shakes,** (trembling) tembleque ra f sing; (feverish) tiritera f sing; **it gives me the s.,** me hace temblar de miedo; fam **it's no great s.,** no es nada del otro jueves or mundo. **3** (milkshake) batido m. **II** vtr (pt **shook;** pp **shaken**) (carpet etc) sacudir; (bottle) agitar; (dice) mover; (building, table) hacer temblar; fig the news shook him, la noticia le conmocionó; **to s. hands with sb,** estrechar or dar la mano a algn; **to s. one's head,** negar con la cabeza; fam **to s. a leg,** darse prisa, apresurarse. **III** vi (person, building) temblar, estremecerse; **to s. with cold,** tiritar de frío; **to s. with fear,** temblar de miedo; **to s. with laughter,** troncharse de risa. ◆ **shake down** vtr **1** sacudir, hacer caer. **2** US sl (blackmail) chantajear. **3** US sl (search) cachear. ◆ **shake off** vtr **1** (dust etc) sacudirse. **2** fig (bad habit) librarse de; (cough, cold) quitarse de encima; (pursuer) deshacerse de, dar esquinazo a, despistar. ◆ **shake up** vtr **1** (liquid in bottle) agitar; (pillow) sacudir. **2** fig (shock, stun) conmocionar, trastornar. **3** fig (reorganize) reorganizar.

shake-up ['ʃeɪkʌp] n fig reorganización f.

shaken ['ʃeɪkən] pp see **shake.**

Shakespearian [ʃeɪk'spɪərɪən] adj shakesperiano,-a.

shaky ['ʃeɪkɪ] adj (shakier, shakiest) (hand, voice) tembloroso,-a; (step) inseguro,-a; (handwriting) temblón,-ona; (table, ladder) inestable; (health) débil; (memory) olvidadizo,-a; (argument) sin fundamento; **his French is s.,** su francés deja bastante que desear.

shale [ʃeɪl] n Geol esquisto m.

shall [ʃæl, *unstressed* ʃəl] *v aux* **1** *(used to form future tense)* *(first person only)* **I s.** *(or* **I'll) buy it tomorrow,** lo compraré mañana; **I s. not** *(or* **I shan't) say anything about it,** no diré nada al respecto; **we s.** *(or* **we'll) see them on Sunday,** los veremos el domingo. **2** *(used to form questions)* *(usu first person)* **s. I close the door?,** ¿cierro la puerta?; **s. I mend it for you,?** ¿quieres que te lo repare?; **s. we go?,** ¿nos vamos? **3** *(emphatic, command, threat)* *(all persons)* **we s. overcome,** venceremos; **you s. leave immediately,** te irás enseguida.

shallot [ʃəˈlɒt] *n Bot* chalote *m*.

shallow [ˈʃæləʊ] **I** *adj* *(gen)* poco profundo,-a; *fig* superficial; **s. dish,** plato llano. **II shallows** *npl* bajío *m sing*, bajos *mpl*.

shallowness [ˈʃæləʊnɪs] *n* *(gen)* poca profundidad *f*, falta *f* de profundidad; *fig* superficialidad *f*, falsa apariencia *f*.

sham [ʃæm] **I** *adj* *(gen)* falso,-a; *(illness etc)* fingido,-a; *(jewellery)* de bisutería. **II** *n* **1** *(pretence)* simulacro *m*, farsa *f*; **it's all a big s.,** es un timo como una catedral. **2** *(person)* fantasma *m*, fantoche *m*. **III** *vtr* *(pt & pp* **shammed)** fingir, simular. **IV** *vi* fingir, fingirse; *fam* hacer el paripé; **she's just shamming,** lo está fingiendo.

shamble [ˈʃæmbəl] *vi* **to s. along,** andar arrastrando los pies, andar con paso pesado.

shambles [ˈʃæmbəlz] *n* *(chaos, mess)* confusión *f*, desorden *m*; **the performance was a s.,** la función fue un desastre; *fam* **what a s.!,** ¡qué follón!

shame [ʃeɪm] **I** *n* **1** *(feeling of humiliation)* vergüenza *f*; **s. on you!,** ¡qué vergüenza!; **to bring s. on,** deshonrar a; **to put to s.,** *(disgrace)* deshonrar; *(surpass by far)* humillar, aplastar. **2** *(pity)* pena *f*, lástima *f*; **what a s.!,** ¡qué pena!, ¡qué lástima! **II** *vtr* avergonzar; *(disgrace)* deshonrar.

shamefaced [ʃeɪmˈfeɪst] *adj* avergonzado,-a.

shameful [ˈʃeɪmfʊl] *adj* vergonzoso,-a; **how s.!,** ¡qué vergüenza!

shameless [ˈʃeɪmlɪs] *adj* desvergonzado,-a, descarado,-a.

shamelessness [ˈʃeɪmlɪsnɪs] *adj* desvergüenza *f*, descaro *m*.

shammy [ˈʃæmɪ] *n* **s. (leather),** gamuza *f*.

shampoo [ʃæmˈpuː] **I** *n* champú *m*. **II** *vtr* lavar con champú; *(hair)* lavarse.

shamrock [ˈʃæmrɒk] *n Bot* trébol *m*.

shandy [ˈʃændɪ] *n GB* clara *f*, blanca *f*, cerveza *f* con gaseosa; *fam* champán *m* andaluz.

shanty¹ [ˈʃæntɪ] *n Mus* **(sea) s.,** saloma *f*.

shanty² [ˈʃæntɪ] *n* *(dwelling)* chabola *f*.

shantytown [ˈʃæntɪtaʊn] *n* (barrio *m* de) chabolas *fpl*.

shape [ʃeɪp] **I** *n* **1** *(form, outline)* forma *f*; *(shadow)* silueta *m*, figura *f*; **in the s. of,** en forma de; **to take s.,** tomar forma; **what is it?,** ¿qué forma tiene? **2** *(order, condition)* *(thing)* **in good/bad s.,** en buen/mal estado; **he was in no s. to work,** no estaba en condiciones de trabajar; **out of s.,** en baja forma; *(health)* *(person)* **to be in good s.,** estar en forma; **to get oneself into s.,** ponerse en forma. **II** *vtr* *(gen)* dar forma a; *(clay)* modelar; *(stone)* tallar; *(character)* formar; *(future, destiny)* decidir, determinar; **star-shaped,** con forma de estrella. **III** *vi* *(also s. up)* tomar forma; **how's it shaping up?,** ¿cómo evoluciona? **b** *(events)* tomar buen cariz; **to s. up well,** *(events)* tomar buen cariz, prometer; *(person)* hacer progresos, prometer.

shape-up [ˈʃeɪpʌp] *n* **s.-up classes,** clases *fpl* de gimnasia *or* de puesta a punto.

shapeless [ˈʃeɪplɪs] *adj* sin forma, informe.

shapelessness [ˈʃeɪplɪsnɪs] *n* falta *f* de forma.

shapely [ˈʃeɪplɪ] *adj* **(shapelier, shapeliest)** *(woman)* escultural.

share [ʃeəʳ] **I** *n* **1** *(portion)* parte *f*; **to do one's s.,** hacer su parte; *fig* **the lion's s.,** la parte del león; *fam* **to go shares,** compartir. **2** *Fin* acción *f*. ■ **s. certificate,** certificado *m* de acciones; **s. index,** índice *m* de la Bolsa; **s. prices,** cotizaciones *fpl*. **II** *vtr* **1** *(divide)* dividir. **2** *(have in common)* compartir. **III** *vi* compartir; **s. and s. alike,** a partes iguales; **I s. in your sorrow,** te acompaño en el sentimiento; **to s. in the profits,** participar en los beneficios. ◆ **share out** *vtr* repartir, distribuir.

share-out [ˈʃeəraʊt] *n* reparto *m*.

shareholder [ˈʃeəhəʊldəʳ] *n* accionista *mf*.

shark [ʃɑːk] *n* **1** *(fish)* tiburón *m*. ■ **blue s.,** tintorera *f*. **2** *fam* *(swindler)* estafador,-a *m,f*, timador,-a *m,f*. ■ **loan s.,** usurero,-a *m,f*.

sharp [ʃɑːp] *adj* **1** *(razor, knife)* afilado,-a; *(needle, pencil)* puntiagudo,-a. **2** *(angle)* agudo,-a; *(features)* anguloso,-a; *Aut* *(bend)* cerrado,-a; *(slope)* empinado,-a. **3** *(outline)* definido,-a; *(photograph)* nítido,-a; *(contrast)* marcado,-a. **4** *(observant)* perspicaz; *(clever)* listo,-a, inteligente; *(quick-witted)* (d)espabilado,-a, avispado,-a; *(cunning)* astuto,-a; **s. practice,** mañas *fpl*, tejemanejes *mpl*. **5** *(sudden)* brusco,-a, repentino,-a. **6** *(intense)* *(pain, cry)* agudo,-a; *(wind)* penetrante; *(frost)* fuerte. **7** *(taste)* *(sour)* acre; *(acidic)* ácido,-a. **8** *(criticism)* mordaz; *(reprimand)* severo,-a; *(temper)* arisco,-a, violento,-a; *(tone)* seco,-a; *(tongue)* viperina. **9** *Mus* sostenido,-a; **F s.,** fa sostenido; *(out of tune)* desafinado,-a. **II** *adv* **1** *(exactly)* **at 2 o'clock s.,** a las dos en punto. **2** *(quickly)* **look s.!,** ¡rápido!, ¡muévete!; **to stop s.,** pararse en seco. **III** *n Mus* sostenido *m*. ◆ **sharply** *adv* **1** *(abruptly)* bruscamente, repentinamente. **2** *(clearly)* claramente, marcadamente.

sharp-edged [ʃɑːpˈedʒd] *adj* afilado,-a.

sharpen [ˈʃɑːpən] *vtr* **1** *(knife)* afilar; *(pencil)* sacar punta a. **2** *fig* *(desire, intelligence)* agudizar; *(appetite)* abrir; **to s. one's wits,** (d)espabilarse.

sharpener [ˈʃɑːpənəʳ] *n* *(for knife)* afilador *m*; *(for pencil)* sacapuntas *m inv*.

sharp-eyed [ʃɑːpˈaɪd] *adj* con ojos de lince *or* de águila.

sharp-tongued [ʃɑːpˈtʌŋd] *adj* de lengua viperina.

sharp-witted [ʃɑːpˈwɪtɪd] *adj* listo,-a, avispado,-a, perspicaz.

sharpshooter [ˈʃɑːpʃuːtəʳ] *n Mil* tirador,-a *m, f* de primera *or* de élite.

shatter [ˈʃætəʳ] **I** *vtr* *(gen)* hacer añicos *or* pedazos, romper, despedazar; *(health)* destrozar, minar, quebrantar; *(nerves)* destrozar; *(hopes)* frustrar. **II** *vi* *(gen)* hacerse añicos *or* pedazos, romperse, despedazarse; *(esp glass)* astillarse.

shattered [ˈʃætəd] *adj fam* *(shocked)* trastornado,-a, pasmado,-a; *(tired)* reventado,-a.

shattering [ˈʃætərɪŋ] *adj* *(blow, defeat)* aplastante, contundente; *(news, experience)* terrible.

shatterproof [ˈʃætəpruːf] *adj* inastillable.

shave [ʃeɪv] **I** *n* afeitado *m*; **to have a s.,** afeitarse; *fig* **to have a close** *or* **narrow s.,** escaparse *or* salvarse por los pelos. **II** *vtr* *(pt* **shaved;** *pp* **shaved** *or* **shaven** [ˈʃeɪvən]) *(person)* afeitar; *(wood)* cepillar; **to s. off one's beard,** afeitarse la barba. **III** *vi* afeitarse.

shaver [ˈʃeɪvəʳ] *n* **(electric) s.,** máquina *f* de afeitar.

shaving [ˈʃeɪvɪŋ] *n* **1** *(thin stip of wood)* viruta *f*. **2** *(of the face)* afeitado *m*. ■ **s. brush,** brocha *f* de afeitar; **s. cream,** crema *f* de afeitar; **s. foam,** espuma *f* de afeitar.

shawl [ʃɔːl] *n* *(garment)* chal *m*.

she [ʃiː] *I pers pron* ella; **it was s. who did it,** fue ella quien lo hizo; **s. and I,** ella y yo. **II** *n* **is it a he or a s.?,** *(animal)* ¿es macho o hembra?; *(baby)* ¿es niño o niña?

she- [ʃi:] *pref* *(of animal)* hembra; **s.-bear,** osa *f*; **s.-cat,** gata *f*.

sheaf [ʃiːf] *n* *(pl* **sheaves** [ʃiːvz]) *Agr* gavilla *f*; *(of arrows)* haz *m*; *(of papers, banknotes)* fajo *m*.

shear [ʃɪəʳ] **I** *vtr* *(pt* **sheared;** *pp* **shorn** *or* **sheared)** *(sheep)* esquilar; **to s. off** *or* **through,** cortar; *fig* **to be shorn of sth,** verse despojado,-a de algo, quedarse sin algo. **II** *vi* esquilar ovejas.

shearer ['ʃɪərəˈ] n esquilador,-a m,f.

shearing ['ʃrɔrɪŋ] n esquileo m, esquila f.

shears [ʃɪəz] npl (gen) tijeras f (grandes); (for metal) cizalla f sing; **a pair of s.,** unas tijeras.

shearwater ['ʃrɔwɔːtəˈ] n Orn pardela f.

sheath [ʃiːθ] n 1 (for sword) vaina f; (for knife, scissors) funda f; (for cable) forro m, cubierta f. ■ **s. knife,** cuchillo m de monte. 2 (contraceptive) preservativo m, condón m.

sheaves [ʃiːvz] npl see **sheaf.**

shed¹ [ʃed] **I** n (in garden) cobertizo m, tinglado m; (workmen's hut) barraca f; (for cattle) establo m; (in factory) nave f.

shed² [ʃed] vtr (pt & pp **shed**) 1 (get rid of) (clothes, leaves) despojarse de; (unwanted thing) deshacerse de; **a lorry has s. its load on the motorway,** un camión ha perdido su carga en la autopista; **the snake s. its skin,** la serpiente mudó de piel; fam **to s. a few pounds,** perder unos kilos. 2 (pour forth) (blood, tears) derramar; fig **to s. light on,** aclarar.

sheen [ʃiːn] n brillo m, lustre m.

sheep [ʃiːp] n inv oveja f; fig **the black s. of the family,** la oveja negra de la familia. ■ **s. farming,** cría f de ovejas.

sheep-dip ['ʃiːpdɪp] n baño m desinfectante (para ovejas).

sheepdog ['ʃiːpdɒg] n perro m pastor.

sheepfold ['ʃiːpfəʊld] n redil m, aprisco m.

sheepish ['ʃiːpɪʃ] adj tímido,-a, avergonzado,-a.

sheepishness ['ʃiːpɪʃnɪs] n timidez f.

sheepskin ['ʃiːpskɪn] n piel f de carnero. ■ **s. jacket,** pelliza f, zamarra f.

sheer¹ [ʃɪəˈ] adj 1 (total, utter) total, absoluto,-a, puro,-a; **in s. desperation,** a la desesperada. 2 (cliff) escarpado,-a; (drop) vertical. 3 (transparent) (stockings, cloth) fino,-a.

sheer² [ʃɪəˈ] vi Naut **to s. off** or **away,** desviarse; fig apartarse.

sheet [ʃiːt] n 1 (on bed) sábana f; **bottom s.,** sábana bajera; **top s.,** encimera f; fig **as white as a s.,** blanco como el papel. 2 (of paper) hoja f; (of tin, glass, plastic) lámina f; (of water, ice) capa f; (of flames, rain) cortina f. ■ Com **balance s.,** balance m; Com **order s.,** hoja f de pedidos; **s. lightning,** relámpago m, fucilazo m; **s. metal,** chapa f de metal; **s. music,** hojas fpl de partitura, papel m pautado. **II** vi (rain) diluviar.

sheik(h) [ʃeɪk] n jeque m.

shelduck ['ʃeldʌk] n Orn tarro m.

shelf [ʃelf] n (pl **shelves** [ʃelvz]) 1 (bookcase) anaquel m, estante m; (in cupboard) tabla f, anaquel m; (on wall) estante m, repisa f; (in oven) parrilla f; (set of) **shelves,** estantería f; fam **to be left on the s.,** quedarse para vestir santos. ■ Com **s. life,** duración f. 2 (in rock) promontorio m; (underwater) plataforma f. ■ **continental s.,** plataforma f continental.

shell [ʃel] **I** n 1 (of egg, nut) cáscara f; (of pea) vaina f; (of tortoise, lobster, etc) caparazón m; (of snail, oyster, etc) concha f; fig **to come out of one's s.,** salir del cascarón. 2 (of building) armazón m, esqueleto m; (of ship) casco m. 3 Mil (mortar etc) obús m, proyectil m; (cartridge) cartucho m. ■ Med **s. shock,** neurosis f de guerra. **II** vtr 1 (peas) desvainar; (nuts) descascarar, pelar. 2 Mil bombardear. ◆ **shell out** vtr fam (money) soltar.

shell-shocked ['ʃelʃɒkt] adj Med que padece neurosis de guerra.

shellac [ʃəˈlæk, 'ʃelæk] n (resin) laca f; (varnish) barniz m.

shellfire ['ʃelfaɪəˈ] n Mil bombardeo m.

shellfish ['ʃelfɪʃ] n inv marisco m, mariscos mpl.

shelling ['ʃelɪŋ] n Mil bombardeo m.

shellproof ['ʃelpruːf] adj a prueba de bombas.

shelter ['ʃeltəˈ] **I** n 1 (protection) abrigo m, protección f, amparo m; **to take s.,** refugiarse (**from,** de). 2 (gen)

(place) refugio m, cobijo m; (for homeless etc) asilo m; (in mountain) albergue m. ■ **air-raid s.,** refugio m antiaéreo; **bus s.,** marquesina f; **fallout s.,** refugio m atomico. **II** vtr 1 (protect) abrigar, proteger, amparar. 2 (take into one's home) esconder, dar refugio a. **III** vi refugiarse, ponerse a cubierto; **to s. from the rain,** abrigarse de la lluvia.

sheltered ['ʃeltəd] adj (place) abrigado,-a, protegido,-a; **to lead a s. life,** vivir apartado,-a del mundo. ■ **s. housing** or **homes,** viviendas fpl de protección oficial para la tercera edad.

shelve [ʃelv] vtr 1 (place on shelf) poner or ordenar en la estantería. 2 fig (postpone) dar carpetazo a, arrinconar.

shelves [ʃelvz] npl see **shelf.**

shelving ['ʃelvɪŋ] n estanterías fpl.

shepherd ['ʃepəd] **I** n pastor m. ■ **s. boy,** zagal m; Culin **s.'s pie,** pastel m de carne picada con puré de patatas. **II** vtr fig **to s. sb in,** hacer entrar a algn; **to s. sb out,** acompañar a algn hasta la puerta.

shepherdess ['ʃepədɪs] n pastora f.

sherbet ['ʃɜːbət] n 1 GB (sweet powder) polvos mpl azucarados. 2 US (ice) sorbete m.

sheriff ['ʃerɪf] n GB gobernador m civil; Scot juez m presidente; US sheriff m, alguacil m mayor.

sherry ['ʃerɪ] n jerez m, vino m de jerez.

Shetland ['ʃetlənd] n the **S. Isles, S.,** las Islas Shetland. ■ **s. pony,** poney m Shetland; **S. wool,** lana f Shetland.

shield [ʃiːld] **I** n 1 Mil Herald escudo m; (of policeman) placa f. 2 Tech (on machinery) blindaje m, pantalla f protectora. **II** vtr proteger (**from,** de); **to s. one's eyes,** taparse los ojos.

shift [ʃɪft] **I** n 1 (change) cambio m; **a s. towards,** un movimiento hacia; **there has been a s. in policy,** ha habido un cambio de política. ■ US Aut (gear) **s.,** cambio m de velocidades; (on typewriter) **s. key,** tecla f de mayúsculas. 2 (period of work, group of workers) turno m, tanda f; **she's on the 4 to 10 s.,** está en el turno de 4 a 10; **to be on the day s.,** hacer el turno de día; **to work (in) shifts,** trabajar por turnos. 3 (expedient) expediente m, recurso m; **to make s. with/without sth,** conformarse con/arreglárselas sin algo. **II** vtr (change) cambiar; (move) cambiar de sitio, trasladar, desplazar; US Aut **to s. gears,** cambiar de velocidad; fig **to s. one's ground,** cambiar de táctica, adoptar una nueva postura. **III** vi 1 (move) mover; (change place) cambiar de sitio; (cargo) desplazarse; (wind, opinion) cambiar; US Aut cambiar de velocidad; **to s. over** or **up,** apartarse, correrse; fam **he won't s.,** no se quiere mover; fam **s.!,** ¡quítate de ahí en medio!, ¡apártate! 2 (manage) **to s. for oneself,** arreglárselas.

shiftless ['ʃɪftlɪs] n perezoso,-a, vago,-a.

shiftwork ['ʃɪftwɜːk] n trabajo m por turnos.

shifty ['ʃɪftɪ] adj (**shiftier, shiftiest**) furtivo,-a, disimulado,-a, sospechoso,-a; **s. look,** mirada f huidiza.

Shiite ['ʃiːaɪt] n Rel chuta mf.

shillelagh [ʃəˈleɪlɪ] n Ir cachiporra f.

shilling ['ʃɪlɪŋ] n Fin chelín m.

shillyshally ['ʃɪlɪʃælɪ] vi (pt & pp **shillyshallied**) fam vacilar, titubear.

shimmer ['ʃɪməˈ] **I** vi relucir, rielar; (shine) brillar. **II** n luz f trémula, reflejo m trémulo; (shining) brillo m.

shimmering ['ʃɪmərɪŋ] adj reluciente, brillante.

shin [ʃɪn] **I** n Anat espinilla f; Culin (of meat) jarrete m. ■ Sport **s. pad,** espinillera f. **II** vi **to s. up a tree,** trepar a un árbol.

shinbone ['ʃɪnbəʊn] n Anat tibia f.

shindy ['ʃɪndɪ] n fam jaleo m, escándalo m; **to kick up a s.,** armar (un) jaleo.

shine [ʃaɪn] **I** vi (pt & pp **shone**) 1 (sun, light) brillar; (polished metal) relucir; fig **his face shone with happiness,** su cara irradiaba felicidad. 2 fig (excel) sobresalir (**at, en**). **II** *vtr* **1** *(light, lamp)* dirigir; **s. the light over there,** dirige la luz hacia allá. **2** *(pt & pp* **shined***)* *(polish)* sacar brillo a; *(shoes)* limpiar, lustrar. **III** *n* brillo *m*, lustre *m*; **to give one's shoes a s.,** limpiarse *or* lustrarse los zapatos; **to give sth a s.,** sacar brillo a algo; *fig* **come rain or (come) s.,** pase lo que pase; *fam* **to take a s. to sb,** tomarle cariño a algn.

shiner ['ʃaɪnər] *n fam* ojo *m* a la funerala.

shingle ['ʃɪŋgəl] *n* **1** *(pebbles)* guijarros *mpl.* **2** *(roof tile)* tablilla *f.* **3** *US fam (name plate)* placa *f.*

shingles ['ʃɪŋgəlz] *npl Med* herpes *m.*

shining ['ʃaɪnɪŋ] *adj* **1** *(light, metal, eyes)* brillante, reluciente; *(face)* radiante; *(hair)* lustroso,-a. **2** *fig (outstanding)* destacado,-a, ilustre, magnífico,-a.

shinty ['ʃɪntɪ] *n Sport* hockey *m* (escocés) sobre hierba.

shiny ['ʃaɪnɪ] *adj (shinier, shiniest)* **1** *(bright)* brillante. **2** *(worn) (clothes)* sobado,-a.

ship [ʃɪp] **I** *n* barco *m*, buque *m*, navío *m*; **on board s.,** a bordo; **to abandon s.,** abandonar *or* evacuar el barco; **the s.'s company,** la tripulación; *fig* **when my s. comes in** *or* **home,** cuando lleguen las vacas gordas. ■ **hospital s.,** buque *m* hospital; **merchant s.,** buque *m* mercante; **passenger s.,** buque *m* de pasajeros. **II** *vtr (pt & pp* **shipped***)* **1** *(take on board)* embarcar, traer a bordo; **to s. oars,** desarmar los remos. **2** *(transport)* transportar (en barco); *(send) (gen)* enviar, mandar. ◆ **ship off** *vtr fam* despachar.

shipboard ['ʃɪpbɔːd] *n* **a s. encounter,** un encuentro a bordo; **on s.,** a bordo.

shipbuilder ['ʃɪpbɪldər] *n* constructor,-a *m, f* de buques.

shipbuilding ['ʃɪpbɪldɪŋ] *n* construcción *f* naval.

shipload ['ʃɪpləʊd] *n* cargamento *m*, carga *f.*

shipmate ['ʃɪpmeɪt] *n* compañero,-a *m, f* de tripulación.

shipment ['ʃɪpmənt] *n* **1** *(act)* embarque *m*, transporte *m.* **2** *(load)* consignación *f*, envío *m*, remesa *f.*

shipowner ['ʃɪpəʊnər] *n* armador,-a *m, f*, naviero,-a *m, f.*

shipper ['ʃɪpər] *n (person)* cargador,-a *m, f*; *(company)* compañía *f* naviera.

shipping ['ʃɪpɪŋ] *n* **1** *(ships)* barcos *mpl*, buques *mpl*; *(fleet)* flota *f.* ■ **s. lane,** vía *f* de navegación. **2** *(loading)* embarque *m*; *(transporting)* transporte *m* (en barco); *(sending)* envío *m.* ■ **s. agent,** agente *mf* marítimo,-a; **s. company** *or* **line,** compañía *f* naviera.

shipshape ['ʃɪpʃeɪp] *adj & adv* en perfecto orden.

shipwreck ['ʃɪprek] **I** *n* naufragio *m.* **II** *vtr* **to be shipwrecked,** naufragar.

shipyard ['ʃɪpjɑːd] *n* astillero *m.*

shire [ʃaɪər] *n GB* condado *m.* ■ **s. horse,** percherón,-a *m, f*, caballo *m* de tiro.

shirk [ʃɜːk] **I** *vtr (duty)* esquivar; *(problem)* eludir. **II** *vi* gandulear, hacer el vago.

shirker ['ʃɜːkər] *n* gandul,-a *m, f*, vago,-a *m, f.*

shirt [ʃɜːt] *n* camisa *f*; **in s. sleeves,** en mangas de camisa; *fig* **to put one's s. on a horse,** apostarse hasta el último real a un caballo; *fam* **a stuffed s.,** un pedante; *fam* **keep your s. on!,** ¡no te sulfures!

shirtwaister ['ʃɜːtweɪstər] *n*, *US* **shirtwaist** ['ʃɜːtweɪst] *n* vestido *m* camisero.

shirty ['ʃɜːtɪ] *adj (shirtier, shirtiest) GB sl* **to get s.,** enfadarse, ponerse de mal humor.

shit [ʃɪt] *vulg* **I** *n* mierda *f*; *sl* **in the s.,** jodido,-a. **II** *interj* ¡mierda! **III** *vi (pt & pp* **shitted** *or* **shit***)* cagar.

shitty ['ʃɪtɪ] *adj (shittier, shittiest) vulg* **a s. book,** una porquería de libro; **what a s. thing to do!,** qué putada!

shiver ['ʃɪvər] **I** *vi (with cold)* tiritar; *(with fear)* temblar, estremecerse. **II** *n (with cold)* escalofrío *m*, tiritón *m*; *(with fear)* escalofrío *m*; **it sent shivers down my spine,** me dio escalofríos; **that sort of talk gives me the shivers,** esa manera de hablar me da horror.

shivery ['ʃɪvərɪ] *adj (with cold)* estremecido,-a; *(feverish)* destemplado,-a; *(sensitive to the cold)* friolero,-a.

shoal [ʃəʊl] *n (of fish)* banco *m.*

shock [ʃɒk] **I** *n* **1** *(jolt)* choque *m*, sacudida *f*, golpe *m*; **electric s.,** descarga *f* eléctrica. ■ *Aut* **s. absorber,** amortiguador *m*; *Mil* **s. tactics,** táctica *f sing* de choque; *Mil* **s. troops,** tropas *fpl* de choque *or* de asalto; **s. wave,** onda *f* expansiva. **2** *(upset)* conmoción *f*, golpe *m*; *(scare)* susto *m*; **it was a great s. to us,** fue un golpe duro para nosotros; **the s. killed him,** murió del susto; **what a s. you gave me!,** ¡qué susto me has dado! **3** *Med* shock *m*, choque *m*; **in a state of s.,** en estado de shock. ■ **s. therapy,** tratamiento *m* de electrochoque. **II** *vtr (upset)* conmover, conmocionar; *(startle)* sobresaltar, asustar; *(scandalize)* escandalizar.

shockheaded ['ʃɒkhedɪd] *adj* greñudo,-a, melenudo,-a.

shocking ['ʃɒkɪŋ] *adj* **1** *(causing horror)* espantoso,-a, horroroso,-a; *fam (very bad)* malísimo,-a, horroroso,-a; **what s. weather!,** ¡qué tiempo más feo! **2** *(disgraceful)* escandaloso,-a, vergonzoso,-a, chocante. **3** *(colour)* chillón; **s. pink,** rosa chillón. ◆ **shockingly** *adv fam* la mar de, super; **s. expensive,** super caro,-a.

shockproof ['ʃɒkpruːf] *adj (watch etc)* a prueba de choques.

shod [ʃɒd] *pt & pp see* **shoe.**

shoddy ['ʃɒdɪ] *adj (shoddier, shoddiest) (goods)* de pacotilla; *(work)* chapucero,-a.

shoe [ʃuː] **I** *n* **1** *(gen)* zapato *m*; *(for horse)* herradura *f*; **to put on one's shoes,** ponerse los zapatos; *fig* **I wouldn't like to be in her shoes,** no me gustaría estar en su lugar. ■ *Aut* **brake s.,** zapata *f*, *Com* **s. industry,** industria *f* del calzado; **s. leather,** cuero *m* para zapatos; **s. polish,** betún *m*; **s. repair (shop),** remiendo *m* de zapatos, rápido *m*; **s. shop,** *US* **s. store,** zapatería *f*, tienda *f* de calzado. **2** *Com* **shoes,** calzado *m sing*. **II** *vtr (pt & pp* **shod***) (person)* calzar; *(horse)* herrar.

shoebrush ['ʃuːbrʌʃ] *n* cepillo *m* para los zapatos.

shoehorn ['ʃuːhɔːn] *n* calzador *m.*

shoelace ['ʃuːleɪs] *n* cordón *m* (de zapato).

shoemaker ['ʃuːmeɪkər] *n* zapatero,-a *m, f.*

shoeshine ['ʃuːʃaɪn] *n* limpieza *f* de zapatos. ■ **s. boy,** limpiabotas *m inv.*

shoestring ['ʃuːstrɪŋ] *n* cordón *m* (de zapato); *fig* **to do sth on a s.,** hacer algo con poquísimo dinero.

shoetree ['ʃuːtriː] *n* horma *f.*

shone [ʃɒn, *US* ʃəʊn] *pt & pp see* **shine I & II.**

shoo [ʃuː] **I** *interj* ¡fuera! ¡zape! **II** *vtr* **to s. (away),** *(birds, animals)* espantar, ahuyentar.

shook [ʃʊk] *pt see* **shake.**

shoot [ʃuːt] **I** *n* **1** *Bot* brote *m*, retoño *m*, renuevo *m*; *(of vine)* sarmiento *m*. **2** *GB (hunting party)* cacería *f*; *(shooting contest)* concurso *m* de tiro al blanco. **3** *(game preserve)* coto *m* de caza. **II** *vtr (pt & pp* **shot***) (fire on)* pegar un tiro a; *(wound)* herir (de bala); *(kill)* matar; *(execute)* fusilar; *(hunt)* cazar; **he was shot in the head,** una bala le alcanzó la cabeza; **to s. dead,** matar a tiros; *fam* **you'll get shot if you do that!,** ¡te matarán si haces eso! **2** *(missile)* lanzar; *(bullet, arrow)* disparar; *(glance)* lanzar; *(kick) (ball)* disparar; *Ftb (goal)* marcar; *US* **to s. craps,** jugar a los dados; **to s. questions at sb,** bombardear a algn a preguntas. **3** *(film)* rodar, filmar; *Phot (subject)* fotografiar, sacar una foto de; *(photograph)* sacar. **4** *(pass through) (rapids)* salvar; *(traffic lights)* saltarse. **5** *sl (heroin etc)* **to s. (up),** chutarse. **III** *vi* **1** *(with gun, bow)* disparar (**at sb,** sobre algn); **to s. at a target,** tirar al blanco; *Ftb* **to s. at the goal,** tirar a puerta, chutar. **2** *(move rapidly)* **to s. past** *or* **by,** pasar volando *or* como un rayo. **3** *Bot* brotar. ◆ **shoot down** *vtr (person)* matar de un tiro a *or* a tiros; *(aircraft)* derribar. ◆ **shoot off** *vi fam* salir disparado,-a. ◆ **shoot out I** *vi (rush out) (person)* salir disparado,-a; *(water)* brotar; *(flames)* salir. **II** *vtr* **to s. it out,** resolverlo a tiros.

◆ **shoot up** vi (flames) salir; (water) brotar; (prices) dispararse, subir de repente; (hands) alzarse rápidamente; (child, plant) crecer rápidamente; (new buildings) construirse de la noche a la mañana.

shoot-out ['ʃuːtaʊt] n tiroteo m.

shooting ['ʃuːtɪŋ] I n 1 (shots) disparos mpl, tiros mpl; (murder) asesinato m; (execution) fusilamiento m; (hunting) caza f; fam **the whole s. match**, todo el tinglado. ■ Aut GB (old use) **s. brake**, furgoneta f, camioneta f; **s. gallery**, barraca f or caseta f de tiro al blanco; **s. match**, tiroteo m; **s. star**, estrella f fugaz; **s. stick**, bastón m asiento. 2 (of film) rodaje m, filmación f; Phot foto f. II adj (pain) punzante.

shop [ʃɒp] I n 1 (gen) tienda f; (large store) almacén m; (business) comercio m, negocio m; **to keep s.**, tener una tienda; **to set up s.**, poner or abrir una tienda; **to talk s.**, hablar del trabajo; fam **all over the s.**, por todas partes. ■ **fish s.**, pescadería f; **grocer's s.**, tienda f de ultramarinos; **s. assistant**, dependiente,-a m, f; **s. window**, escaparate m. 2 (workshop) taller m; **assembly s.**, taller de montaje. ■ **s. floor**, (place) planta f; (workers) personal m obrero, obreros mpl, operarios mpl; **s. steward**, enlace mf sindical; **to work on the s. floor**, trabajar en producción. II vi (pt & pp **shopped**) hacer compras; **to go shopping**, ir de compras; **to s. for**, buscar. III vtr fam **to s. sb**, denunciar or delatar a algn. ◆ **shop around** vi comparar precios; **to s. around for bargains**, ir de tienda en tienda en busca de gangas.

shopgirl ['ʃɒpɡɜːl] n dependiente f.

shopkeeper ['ʃɒpkiːpəʳ] n tendero,-a m, f.

shoplifter ['ʃɒplɪftəʳ] n mechero,-a m, f, ratero,-a m, f.

shoplifting ['ʃɒplɪftɪŋ] n ratería f, hurto m.

shopper ['ʃɒpəʳ] n comprador,-a m, f.

shopping ['ʃɒpɪŋ] n compra f; (purchases) compras fpl; **to do the s.**, hacer la compra. ■ **s. bag/basket**, bolsa f/ cesta f de la compra; **s. centre** or **precinct**, centro m comercial; **s. trolley**, US **s. cart**, carrito m.

shopsoiled ['ʃɒpsɔɪld] and, US **shopworn** ['ʃɒpwɔːn] adj deteriorado,-a, desgastado,-a.

shore[1] [ʃɔːʳ] n (of sea, lake) orilla f; US (beach) playa f; (coast) costa f; **on s.**, en tierra; (passengers) **to go on s.**, desembarcar. ■ Naut **s. leave**, permiso m para bajar a tierra. 2 **shores**, fig país m sing; **his native s.**, su tierra natal.

shore[2] [ʃɔːʳ] vtr **to s. (up)**, (building, tunnel) apuntalar; fig (company, prices) apoyar, sostener, consolidar.

shorn [ʃɔːn] pp see **shear**.

short [ʃɔːt] I adj 1 (gen) corto,-a; (not tall) bajo,-a; **at s. notice**, con poca antelación; **in a s. while**, dentro de un rato; **in the s. term**, a corto plazo; fam **to make s. work of sth**, despachar algo rápidamente. ■ Elec **s. circuit**, cortocircuito m; **s. cut**, atajo m; GB **s. list**, lista f de seleccionados; US **s. order**, comida f rápida; **s. story**, cuento m; US Cin **s. subject**, cortometraje m; Ind **s. time**, jornada f reducida; Rad **s. wave**, onda f corta. 2 (brief) corto,-a, breve; **'Bob' is s. for 'Robert'**, 'Bob' es el diminutivo de 'Robert' for **s.**, para abreviar; **in s.**, en pocas palabras. 3 (insufficient) **she's a bit s. of cash**, anda bastante mal de dinero; **to be s. of breath**, faltarle a uno la respiración; **to be s. of food**, andar escaso,-a de comida; **to be s. on experience**, tener poca experiencia; **to give s. weight**, no dar el peso justo; **water is in s. supply**, hay escasez de agua. 4 (brusque, curt) brusco,-a, seco,-a, corto,-a; **to be s. with sb**, mostrarse seco,-a con algn; **to have a s. temper**, tener mal genio. II adv 1 (abruptly) **to pull up s.**, pararse en seco. 2 (less than expected) **to cut s.**, (holiday) interrumpir; (meeting) suspender; **to go s. of food**, pasarse sin comida, pasar hambre; **we're running s. of coffee**, se nos está acabando el café; fig **to sell sb s.**, engañar a algn. 3 (except) **s. of**, excepto, menos. III n 1 Cin cortometraje m. 2 Elec cortocircuito m. 3 fam (drink) bebida f corta, copa f. IV vtr Elec provocar un cortocircuito en. V vi **to s. (out)**, tener un cortocircuito. ◆ **shortly** adv (soon) dentro de poco; **s. after**, poco después.

shortage ['ʃɔːtɪdʒ] n falta f, escasez f, carencia f, carestia f; **manpower s.**, falta de mano de obra.

shortbread ['ʃɔːtbred] n Culin mantecada f.

shortcake ['ʃɔːtkeɪk] n Culin 1 GB mantecada f. 2 US torta f de frutas.

short-change [ʃɔːt'tʃeɪndʒ] vtr fam **to s.-c. sb**, no devolver el cambio completo a algn; sl timar a algn.

short-circuit [ʃɔːt'sɜːkɪt] Elec I vtr provocar un cortocircuito en. II vi tener un cortocircuito.

shortcomings ['ʃɔːtkʌmɪŋz] npl defectos mpl, puntos mpl flacos.

shortcrust ['ʃɔːtkrʌst] n Culin **s. pastry**, pasta f brisa, pasta f medio hojaldrada.

shorten ['ʃɔːtən] vtr (skirt, visit) acortar; (word) abreviar; (text) resumir; (rations) reducir.

shortening ['ʃɔːtənɪŋ] n Culin (butter) mantequilla f; (lard) manteca f.

shortfall ['ʃɔːtfɔːl] n Com déficit m.

short-haired [ʃɔːt'heəd] adj de pelo corto.

shorthand ['ʃɔːthænd] n taquigrafía f; **to take sth down in s.**, escribir algo taquigráficamente. ■ **s. typing**, taquimecanografia f; **s. typist**, taquimecanógrafo,-a m, f; fam taquígrafo m.

short-handed [ʃɔːt'hændɪd] adj falto,-a de mano de obra.

short-list ['ʃɔːtlɪst] vtr seleccionar, poner en la lista de seleccionados.

short-lived [ʃɔːt'lɪvd] adv efímero,-a.

short-range ['ʃɔːtreɪndʒ] adj Mil de corto alcance.

shorts [ʃɔːts] npl 1 pantalones mpl cortos, shorts mpl; **a pair of s.**, un pantalón corto. 2 US (underpants) calzoncillos mpl.

short-sighted [ʃɔːt'saɪtɪd] adj (person) miope, corto,-a de vista; fig (plan etc) corto,-a de vista.

short-sightedness [ʃɔːt'saɪtɪdnɪs] n miopía f; fig falta f de perspicacia.

short-sleeved ['ʃɔːtsliːvd] adj de manga corta.

short-staffed [ʃɔːt'stɑːft] adj escaso,-a de personal.

short-tempered [ʃɔːt'tempəd] adj de mal genio, de genio vivo.

short-term ['ʃɔːttɜːm] adj a corto plazo.

short-wave ['ʃɔːtweɪv] adj Rad de onda corta.

short-winded [ʃɔːt'wɪndɪd] adj corto,-a de resuello.

shot[1] [ʃɒt] I n 1 (act, sound) tiro m, disparo m, balazo m; **exchange of shots**, tiroteo m; **to fire a s. at sb**, disparar sobre algn; **warning s.**, disparo al aire; **without firing a s.**, sin pegar un tiro; fig **long s.**, posibilidad f remota; fig **not by a long s.**, ni mucho menos. 2 (projectile) bala f; (pellets) perdigones mpl; fig **he was off like a s.**, salió disparado. ■ Athlet **s. put**, lanzamiento m de peso. 3 (person) tirador,-a m, f. ■ fam **big s.**, pez m gordo; **crack s.**, tirador m de elite. 4 Ftb (kick) tiro m (a gol), chut m; Bill Crick Golf (stroke) golpe m. 5 (attempt) tentativa f, intento m; (in game) **it's your s.**, te toca a ti; **to have a s.**, probar; **to have a s. at sth**, intentar hacer algo; fig **a s. in the dark**, un intento a ciegas. 6 (injection) inyección f; fam pinchazo m. ■ **polio s.**, vacuna f contra la polio. 7 (drink) trago m. 8 Phot foto f; Cin toma f; **location shots**, exteriores mpl.

shot[2] [ʃɒt] I pt & pp see **shoot**. II adj fam **to get s. of sth/ sb**, quitarse algo/a algn de encima.

shotgun ['ʃɒtɡʌn] n escopeta f; fam **it was a s. wedding**, se casaron de penalty or a la fuerza.

should [ʃʊd, unstressed ʃəd] v aux 1 (duty, advisability) deber; **all employees s. wear helmets**, todos los empleados deben llevar casco; **he s. have been an architect**, debería haber sido arquitecto; **you s. see the dentist**, deberías ir (a ver) al dentista. 2 (probability) deber de; **he s. have finished work by now**, ya debe de haber acabado el trabajo; **it s. be fine tomorrow,** seguramente hará buen tiempo mañana; **this s. be interesting,** esto promete ser interesante. **3** *(conditional use)* **if anything strange s. happen,** si pasara algo raro; **s. you wish to attend,** si desea asistir. **4** *(tentative statement)* **I s. like to ask a question,** quisiera hacer una pregunta; **I s. like to have met your grandfather,** me hubiera gustado conocer a tu abuelo; **I s. think so,** me imagino que sí. **5** *(surprise)* **who s. I meet but Charlie!,** ¡imagínate mi sorpresa al encontrarme con Charlie!

shoulder [ˈʃəʊldəʳ] **I** *n* **1** *Anat* hombro *m*; *(of meat)* espalda *f*; **s. to s.,** hombro con hombro; **to carry sth on one's s.,** llevar algo a hombros; **to shrug one's shoulders,** encogerse de hombros; *fig* **to cry on sb's s.,** desahogarse con algn; *fig* **to give sb the cold s.,** volver la espalda *or* dar de lado a algn; *fig* **to look over sb's s.,** tener vigilado,-a a algn; *fig* **to rub shoulders with sb,** codearse con algn. ■ **s. bag,** bolso *m* (de bandolera); *Anat* **s. blade,** omóplato *m*; **s. pad,** hombrera *f*; *(of garment)* tirante *m*; *(of bag)* correa *f*. **2** *Culin (of lamb etc)* paletilla *f*. **3** *(of hill)* lomo *m*; *(of road)* andén *m*. ■ **hard s.,** arcén *m*; **soft s.,** escalón *m* lateral. **II** *vtr* **1** *fig (responsibilities)* cargar con. **2** *(push)* **to s. one's way through,** abrirse paso a codazos.

shoulder-high [ʃəʊldəˈhaɪ] *adj* a hombros.

shoulder-length [ˈʃəʊldəleŋθ] *adj* (que llega) hasta los hombros.

shout [ʃaʊt] **I** *n* grito *m*; **shouts of laughter,** carcajadas *fpl*; *fam* **give me a s. when you're ready,** avísame cuando estés listo. **II** *vtr* gritar. **III** *vi* gritar, chillar; **to s. at sb,** gritar a algn; **to s. for help,** pedir socorro a gritos. ◆ **shout down** *vtr (person)* abuchear.

shouting [ˈʃaʊtɪŋ] *n* gritos *mpl*, vocerío *m*.

shove [ʃʌv] **I** *n fam* empujón *m*; **to give sth a s.,** dar un empujón a *or* empujar algo. **II** *vtr* empujar; **to s. sth into one's pocket,** meterse algo en el bolsillo (a empellones). **III** *vi* empujar; *(jostle)* dar empellones. ◆ **shove off** *vi fam* largarse. ◆ **shove up** *vi fam* correrse.

shovel [ˈʃʌvəl] **I** *n* pala *f*; **mechanical s.,** pala mecánica, excavadora *f*. **II** *vtr (pt & pp shovelled)* mover *or* echar *or* quitar con pala *or* a paladas; *fam* **to s. food into one's mouth,** zamparse la comida.

shoveler [ˈʃʌvələʳ] *n Orn* pato *m* cuchara.

shovelful [ˈʃʌvəlful] *n* palada *f*, paletada *f*.

show [ʃəʊ] **I** *vtr (pt showed; pp shown or showed)* **1** *(exhibit)* mostrar, enseñar; *(ticket etc)* mostrar, enseñar; *(painting etc)* exponer; *(film, slides)* poner, pasar, proyectar; *(latest plans etc)* presentar. **2** *(display, reveal)* demostrar, mostrar; **to s. the dirt,** dejar ver la suciedad; **to s. kindness to sb,** mostrarse amable con algn; **to s. oneself to be a coward,** comportarse como un cobarde; **to s. signs of life,** dar señales de vida; *fam* **she'll never s. her face here again,** nunca más aparecerá por aquí. **3** *(teach)* enseñar, mostrar; *(explain)* explicar; **s. me how to do it,** enséñame cómo se hace; *fam* **I'll s. him!,** ¡se va a enterar! **4** *(indicate)* indicar; *(temperature etc)* marcar, indicar; *(profit etc)* registrar; *(way)* indicar, enseñar; **as shown below,** según se ve abajo; **the clock showed 4 o'clock,** el reloj marcaba las 4. **5** *(prove)* demostrar, probar; **it only goes to s. that ...,** demuestra claramente que ...; **time will s.,** el tiempo lo dirá; *fam* **it just goes to s.!,** ¡hay que ver! **6** *(conduct)* llevar, conducir; **she was shown round the factory,** la llevaron a visitar la fábrica; **to s. sb in,** hacer pasar a algn; **to s. sb to the door,** acompañar a algn hasta la puerta. **II** *vi* **1** *(be visible)* verse, notarse; **the stain doesn't s.,** no se nota *or* no se ve la mancha. **2** *(appear)* aparecer. **3** *Cin* dar, poner, proyectar; **what's showing at the Roxy?,** ¿qué ponen en el Roxy? **III** *n* **1** *(display)* demostración *f*; **s. of hands,** votación *f* a mano alzada. ■ **s. house,** casa *f* piloto. **2** *(outward appearance)* apariencia *f*; **for s.,** por pura comedia; **to make a s. of,** hacer gala *or* alarde de. **3** *(exhibition)* exposición *f*; **to be on s.,** estar expuesto,-a. ■ **agricultural s.,** feria *f* del campo; **boat s.,** salón *m* náutico; **fashion s.,** desfile *m* *or* pase *m* de

modelos; **flower s.,** exposición *f* de flores; **horse s.,** concurso *m* hípico; **motor s.,** salón *m* del automóvil. **4** *Theat (entertainment)* espectáculo *m*; *(performance)* función *f*; *Rad TV* programa *m*; *fig* **(jolly) good s.!,** ¡muy bien!, ¡bien hecho!; *fig* **to put up a good/poor s.,** hacer un buen/pobre papel; *fig* **to steal the s.,** llevarse la palma; *fam* **to give the s. away,** descubrir el pastel. ■ **s. business,** *fam* **s. biz,** el mundo del espectáculo; *fam* **s. stopper,** plato *m* fuerte. **5** *(organization)* negocio *m*, empresa *f*; *fam* tinglado *m*; **the grandfather runs the whole s.,** el abuelo es el que lo lleva todo. ◆ **show off** *vtr* **1** *(highlight)* hacer resaltar. **2** *fam (flaunt)* hacer alarde de. **II** *vi fam* fardar, farolear; *(child)* hacerse el gracioso *or* la graciosa. ◆ **show up** *vtr* **1** *(visitor etc)* hacer pasar. **2** *(reveal)* revelar, sacar a luz; *(highlight)* hacer resaltar *or* destacar. **3** *fam (embarrass)* avergonzar, hacer pasar vergüenza, dejar en ridículo. **II** *vi* **1** *(stand out)* resaltar, destacarse. **2** *fam (arrive, appear)* acudir, presentarse, aparecer.

showcase [ˈʃəʊkeɪs] *n* vitrina *f*.

showdown [ˈʃəʊdaʊn] *n* enfrentamiento *m*, confrontación *f*; **to have a s. with sb,** enfrentarse con algn.

shower [ˈʃaʊəʳ] **I** *n* **1** *(of rain)* chubasco *m*, chaparrón *m*, aguacero *m*; **scattered showers,** chubascos aislados. **2** *fig (of stones, blows, insults)* lluvia *f*. **3** *(bath)* ducha *f*; **to have** *or* **take a s.,** ducharse, tomar *or* darse una ducha. ■ **s. cap,** gorro *m* de baño. **4** *US fam* **s. (party),** fiesta *f* de obsequio. **II** *vtr* **1** *(sprinkle)* espolvorear; *(spray)* rociar. **2** *fig* colmar, inundar; **to s. gifts/praise on** *or* **upon sb,** colmar a algn de regalos/elogios; **we were showered with invitations,** nos llovieron invitaciones. **III** *vi* ducharse, tomar *or* darse una ducha.

showerproof [ˈʃaʊəpruːf] *adj* impermeable.

showery [ˈʃaʊərɪ] *adj* lluvioso,-a.

showgirl [ˈʃəʊɡɜːl] *n* corista *f*.

showground [ˈʃəʊɡraʊnd] *n* real *m*, recinto *m* ferial.

showing [ˈʃəʊɪŋ] *n (gen)* exposición *f*; *(of film)* proyección *f*.

showjumper [ˈʃəʊdʒʌmpəʳ] *n Equit* jinete *m*.

showjumping [ˈʃəʊdʒʌmpɪŋ] *n Equit (gen)* hípica *f*; *(event)* concurso *m* hípico.

showman [ˈʃəʊmən] *n (pl showmen)* **1** *(entertainment manager)* empresario *m* (de espectáculos). **2** *(skilled performer)* actor *m* de primera, showman *m*.

showmanship [ˈʃəʊmənʃɪp] *n* talento *m* para el teatro, teatralidad *f*.

shown [ʃəʊn] *pp see* **show.**

show-off [ˈʃəʊɒf] *n fam* fardón,-ona *m,f*.

showpiece [ˈʃəʊpiːs] *n (in exhibition etc)* obra *f* maestra; *fig (at school etc)* modelo *f*.

showplace [ˈʃəʊpleɪs] *n* lugar *m* de interés turístico.

showroom [ˈʃəʊruːm] *n Com* exposición *f*; *Art* galería *f*, sala *f* de exposiciones.

showy [ˈʃaʊɪ] *adj (showier, showiest) fam* llamativo,-a, chillón,-ona; *(person)* ostentoso,-a.

shrank [ʃræŋk] *pt see* **shrink.**

shrapnel [ˈʃræpnəl] *n Mil* metralla *f*.

shred [ʃred] **I** *n (gen)* triza *f*; *(of cloth)* jirón *m*; *(of paper)* tira *f*, *fig* chispa *f*; **in shreds,** hecho,-a trizas *or* jirones; **to tear sth to shreds,** hacer algo trizas; *fig* **without a s. of evidence,** sin la más mínima prueba. **II** *vtr (pt & pp shredded) (paper)* hacer trizas, triturar; *(vegetables)* rallar.

shredder [ˈʃredəʳ] *n (for waste paper)* trituradora *f*; *(for vegetables)* rallador *m*.

shrew [ʃruː] *n* **1** *Zool* musaraña *f*. **2** *fig (woman)* arpía *f*, bruja *f*, fiera *f*.

shrewd [ʃruːd] *adj (gen)* astuto,-a; *(clear-sighted)* perspicaz; *(wise)* sabio,-a; *(witty)* sagaz, astuto,-a; *(clever)* listo,-a; *(of decision)* acertado,-a; **to make a s. guess,** hacer una suposición razonable.

shrewdness [ˈʃruːdnɪs] *n (gen)* astucia *f; (clear-sightedness)* perspicacia *f; (wisdom)* juicio *m; (wit)* tino *m.*

shriek [ʃriːk] **I** *n* chillido *m,* grito *m* agudo; **shrieks of laughter,** carcajadas *fpl.* **II** *vi* chillar, gritar; **to s. with laughter,** reírse a mandíbula batiente.

shrift [ʃrɪft] *n fam* **to give sb short s.,** despachar a algn sin rodeos, mandar a algn a paseo.

shrike [ʃraɪk] *n Orn* alcaudón *m.*

shrill [ʃrɪl] *adj (voice)* chillón,-ona, agudo,-a; *(sound)* agudo,-a, estridente.

shrimp [ʃrɪmp] **I** *n* 1 *(fish)* camarón *m,* gamba *f* (pequeña). 2 *fam (person)* enano,-a *m, f,* renacuajo *m.* **II** *vi* pescar camarones.

shrine [ʃraɪn] *n Rel (tomb)* sepulcro *m; (relic case)* relicario *m; (chapel)* capilla *f; (in remote place)* ermita *f; (holy place)* lugar *m* santo *or* sagrado, santuario *m.*

shrink [ʃrɪŋk] **I** *vtr (pt shrank; pp shrunk) (material, clothes)* encoger. **II** *vi* 1 *(clothes)* encoger(se). 2 *(savings etc)* disminuir. 3 *fig* **to s. (back *or* away),** retroceder, echarse atrás; **to s. from doing sth,** no tener valor para hacer algo. **II** *n* 1 *(shrinkage)* encogimiento *m.* 2 *fam (psychiatrist)* loquero,-a *m, f.*

shrinkage [ˈʃrɪŋkɪdʒ] *n* 1 *(of cloth)* encogimiento *m; (of metal)* contracción *f.* 2 *(of savings etc)* disminución *f,* reducción *f.*

shrinking [ˈʃrɪŋkɪŋ] *adj fam* **s. violet,** persona *f* tímida.

shrink-wrapped [ˈʃrɪŋkræpt] *adj Com* envuelto,-a en plástico.

shrivel [ˈʃrɪvəl] **I** *vtr (pt & pp shrivelled)* **to s. (up),** encoger; *(plant)* marchitar, secar; *(skin)* arrugar. **II** *vi (gen)* encogerse; *(plant)* marchitarse, secarse; *(skin)* arrugarse.

shroud [ʃraʊd] **I** *n* 1 *Rel* mortaja *f,* sudario *m.* 2 *fig (of mist, secrecy)* velo *m.* **II** *vtr fig* envolver.

Shrove Tuesday [ʃrəʊvˈtjuːzdɪ] *n* martes *m* de carnaval.

shrub [ʃrʌb] *n* arbusto *m.*

shrubbery [ˈʃrʌbərɪ] *n* arbustos *mpl.*

shrug [ʃrʌg] **I** *vtr (pt & pp shrugged)* encoger; **to s. one's shoulders,** encogerse de hombros. **II** *vi* encogerse de hombros. **III** *n* encogimiento *m* de hombros. ◆ **shrug off** *vtr* no hacer caso de, quitar importancia a.

shrunk [ʃrʌŋk] *pp see* **shrink.**

shrunken [ˈʃrʌŋkən] *adj (body)* encogido,-a.

shudder [ˈʃʌdə'] **I** *n* 1 *(shiver)* escalofrío *m,* estremecimiento *m; fam* **it gives me the shudders,** me pone los pelos de punta. 2 *(of engine, machinery)* vibración *f,* sacudida *f.* **II** *vi* 1 *(person)* estremecerse, temblar **(with,** de); **I s. to think of it,** sólo pensarlo me dan escalofríos. 2 *(machinery)* vibrar, dar sacudidas.

shuffle [ˈʃʌfəl] **I** *vtr* 1 *(drag)* arrastrar. 2 *(papers etc)* revolver; *(cards)* barajar. **II** *vi* 1 *(walk)* andar arrastrando los pies. 2 *Cards* barajar. **III** *n* 1 *(dragging)* arrastre *m;* **to walk with a s.,** andar arrastrando los pies. 2 *Cards* **to give the cards a s.,** barajar las cartas.

shun [ʃʌn] *vtr (pt & pp shunned) (person)* evitar, esquivar; *(responsibility, publicity)* rehuir.

shunt [ʃʌnt] *vtr Rail* cambiar de vía; *Elec* derivar; *fig* desviar.

shunting [ˈʃʌntɪŋ] *n Rail* maniobras *fpl.* ◆ **s. yard,** estación *f* de maniobras.

shush [ʃʊʃ] **I** *interj* ¡chis!, ¡chitón! **II** *vtr* callar, hacer callar.

shut [ʃʌt] **I** *vtr (pt & pp shut)* cerrar; **to s. one's finger in the door,** pillarse el dedo en la puerta; *fig* **to s. the door on sb/sth,** negarse a pensar en algn/algo; *fam* **s. your mouth!,** ¡cierra el pico! **II** *vi* cerrarse. **III** *adj* cerrado,-a. ◆ **shut away** *vtr (imprison)* encerrar. ◆ **shut down I** *vtr (factory)* cerrar; *(machinery)* desconectar, apagar. **II** *vi (factory)* cerrarse. ◆ **shut in** *vtr* encerrar. ◆ **shut off** *vtr* 1 *(switch off) (gas, water, etc)* cortar, cerrar; *(machinery)* cerrar, desconectar, apagar. 2 *(street, area)* aislar **(from,** de). ◆ **shut out** *vtr* 1 *(leave outside)* dejar

fuera; *(put outside)* sacar, echar a la calle; *(lock out)* cerrar la puerta a. 2 *(exclude)* excluir. 3 *(light, view)* tapar. ◆ **shut up I** *vtr* 1 *(close)* cerrar. 1 *(enclose, imprison)* encerrar. 3 *fam (silence)* callar, hacer callar. **II** *vi fam (keep quiet)* callarse; **s.up!,** ¡cállate!

shutdown [ˈʃʌtdaʊn] *n* cierre *m.*

shuteye [ˈʃʌtaɪ] *n fam* cabezada *f,* siesta *f;* **to get some s.,** echar una cabezadilla.

shut-in [ʃʌtˈɪn] *adj* encerrado,-a.

shutout [ˈʃʌtaʊt] *n Ind* cierre *m* patronal, locaut *m,* lock-out *m.*

shutter [ˈʃʌtə'] *n* 1 *(on window)* contraventana *f,* postigo *m; fig* **to put up the shutters,** echar el cierre. 2 *Phot* obturador *m.*

shuttered [ˈʃʌtəd] *adj* con las contraventanas cerradas.

shuttle [ˈʃʌtəl] **I** *n* 1 *(in weaving)* lanzadera *f.* 2 *Av* puente *m* aéreo. ■ **s. service,** servicio *m* regular; *Astronaut* **(space) s.,** transbordador *m* espacial. **II** *vtr* trasladar, transportar; *fam* **to s. sb about,** mandar a algn de acá para allá. **III** *vi* ir y venir.

shuttlecock [ˈʃʌtəlkɒk] *n (badminton)* volante *m.*

shy[1] [ʃaɪ] **I** *adj (shyer, shyest *or* shier, shiest) (timid)* tímido,-a; *(reserved)* reservado,-a; *(cautious)* receloso,-a; **don't be s.,** no tengas vergüenza; **to be s. of doing sth,** no atreverse a hacer algo; **to fight s. of sth,** rehuir *or* esquivar algo. **II** *vi (pt & pp shied) (horse)* espantarse **(at,** de); *fig* **to s. away from sth,** huir de algo; *fig* **to s. away from doing sth,** negarse a hacer algo.

shy[2] [ʃaɪ] *vtr (pt & pp shied) (throw)* tirar, lanzar.

shyness [ˈʃaɪnɪs] *n* timidez *f,* vergüenza *f.*

shyster [ˈʃaɪstə'] *n US (gen)* estafado,-a *m, f,* timador,-a *m, f; fam (lawyer)* picapleitos *mf inv.*

Siamese [saɪəˈmiːz] *adj & n* 1 siamés,-esa *(m, f);* **S. cat,** gato siamés; **S. twins,** hermanos siameses. 2 *(Thai)* tailandés,-esa *(m, f).*

Siberia [saɪˈbɪərɪə] *n* Siberia.

Siberian [saɪˈbɪərɪən] *adj & n* siberiano,-a *(m, f).*

sibilant [ˈsɪbɪlənt] *adj & n Ling* sibilante *(f).*

sibling [ˈsɪblɪŋ] *n fml (brother)* hermano *m; (sister)* hermana *f.*

Sicilian [sɪˈsɪlɪən] *adj & n* siciliano,-a *(m, f).*

Sicily [ˈsɪsɪlɪ] *n* Sicilia.

sick [sɪk] **I** *adj* 1 *(ill)* enfermo,-a; **to be off s.,** estar ausente por enfermedad; **to go s.,** darse de baja por enfermedad. ■ **s. leave,** baja *f* por enfermedad; **s. list,** lista *f* de enfermos; **s. pay,** subsidio *m* de enfermedad. 2 *(about to vomit)* mareado,-a; **s. headache,** jaqueca *f,* migraña *f;* **to be s.,** vomitar, devolver; **to feel s.,** estar mareado,-a, tener náuseas. 3 *fam (fed up)* harto,-a; **it (really) makes me s.,** me revienta; **to be s. (and tired) of sth/sb,** estar (más que) harto,-a de algo/algn. 4 *fam (mind, joke)* morboso,-a; **s. humour,** humor negro. **II the s.** *npl* los enfermos. **III** *vi* **to s. up,** vomitar, devolver.

sickbay [ˈsɪkbeɪ] *n* enfermería *f.*

sickbed [ˈsɪkbed] *n* lecho *m* de enfermo.

sicken [ˈsɪkən] **I** *vtr (make ill)* poner enfermo; *(revolt, disgust)* dar asco; **his attitude sickens me,** su actitud me pone enfermo. **II** *vi* 1 *(fall ill)* caer *or* ponerse enfermo,-a, enfermar; **to be sickening for flu,** tener síntomas de gripe. 2 *(crave)* ansiar **(for,** -); **I'm sickening for an ice cream,** me muero por comerme un helado.

sickening [ˈsɪkənɪŋ] *adj* 1 *(nauseating)* nauseabundo,-a; *(revolting, disgusting)* repugnante, asqueroso,-a; *(horrifying)* escalofriante. 2 *(annoying)* irritante, exasperante.

sickle [ˈsɪkəl] *n Agr* hoz *f; Pol* **the hammer and s.,** la hoz y el martillo.

sickly [ˈsɪklɪ] *adj (sicklier, sickliest)* 1 *(person)* enfermizo,-a; *(pale)* pálido,-a, paliducho,-a. 2 *(smell, taste)* empalagoso,-a. 3 *(smile, affectation)* forzado,-a.

sickness ['sɪknɪs] n 1 (illness) enfermedad f. ■ GB s. benefit, subsidio m de enfermedad. 2 (nausea) náuseas fpl, ganas fpl de vomitar.

sickroom ['sɪkru:m] n enfermería f.

side [saɪd] I n 1 (gen) lado m; (of coin etc) cara f; (of mountain, hill) ladera f, falda f; by the s. of, junto a; on the heavy s., más bien pesado,-a; to put sth on one s. for sb, guardar algo para algn; fig (in order) to be on the safe s., para estar seguro,-a. para mayor seguridad; fig to keep on the right s. of sb, tratar de llevarse bien con algn; fig to make a bit of money on the s., ganar algún dinero extra; TV fam the other s., el otro canal. 2 (of body) lado m, costado m; (of animal) ijar m, ijada f; a s. of bacon, una lonja de tocino; by my s., a mi lado; s. by s., juntos, uno al lado de otro; fam to split one's sides laughing, troncharse de risa. 3 (edge) borde m; (of lake, river) orilla f. 4 fig (aspect) aspecto m, faceta f, lado m; to look on the bright s., ver el lado bueno de las cosas. 5 Sport (team) equipo m; Pol (party) partido m; on his mother's s., por parte de madre; she's on our s., está de nuestro lado; to take sides with sb, ponerse de parte de algn, unirse a algn. ■ s. dish, acompañamiento m, guarnición f; s. door, puerta f lateral; s. effect, efecto m secundario; s. entrance, entrada f lateral; s. street, calle f lateral; s. view, (vista f de) perfil m. III vi (in argument) to s. with sb, ponerse de parte de algn.

sideboard ['saɪdbɔ:d] n Furn aparador m.

sideboards ['saɪdbɔ:dz] npl, US **sideburns** ['saɪdbɜ:nz] npl patillas fpl.

sidecar ['saɪdkɑː'] n Aut sidecar m.

sidekick ['saɪdkɪk] n US fam compinche m, amigote m, colega mf.

sidelight ['saɪdlaɪt] n Aut luz f lateral, piloto m.

sideline ['saɪdlaɪn] n 1 Sport línea f de banda; fig to sit on the sidelines, quedarse en el banquillo. 2 Com (product) línea f suplementaria; (business) negocio m suplementario; (job) empleo m suplementario.

sidelong ['saɪdlɒŋ] I adj (glance etc) de reojo, de soslayo. II adv de lado.

sidereal [saɪ'dɪərɪəl] adj Astron sideral, sidéreo,-a.

side-saddle ['saɪdsædəl] I n silla f de amazona. II adv to ride s., montar a la amazona.

sideshow ['saɪdʃəʊ] n (at fairground) atracción f secundaria.

sidestep ['saɪdstep] I vtr (pt & pp sidestepped) (question, issue) eludir, esquivar. II vi Box dar un quiebro, fintar.

sidetrack ['saɪdtræk] vtr fig (person) despistar; (issue) dejar de lado.

sidewalk ['saɪdwɔ:k] n US acera f.

sideways ['saɪdweɪz] I adj (step, movement) lateral; (glance, look) de reojo, de soslayo. II adv (gen) de lado; to step s., dar un paso hacia un lado.

siding ['saɪdɪŋ] n 1 Rail apartadero m, vía f muerta. 2 US Constr tabiques mpl pluviales.

sidle ['saɪdəl] vi to s. up to sb, acercarse furtivamente or sigilosamente a algn.

siege [si:dʒ] n sitio m, cerco m; to lay s. to, sitiar, poner sitio a, cercar; to raise the s., levantar el sitio.

sienna [sɪ'enə] n Art (tierra f de) siena f.

Sierra Leone [sɪeərɑlɪ'əʊn(ɪ)] n Sierra Leona.

siesta [sɪ'estə] n siesta f; to have a s., echar or dormir la siesta.

sieve [sɪv] I n (fine) tamiz m; (coarse) criba f; fam to have a memory like a s., tener muy mala memoria. II vtr (fine) tamizar, pasar por el tamiz; (coarse) cribar.

sift [sɪft] vtr 1 (sieve) tamizar, cribar; fig to s. through, examinar cuidadosamente. 2 (sprinkle) espolvorear.

sifter ['sɪftə'] n 1 (sieve) tamiz m. 2 (sprinkler) espolvoreador m.

sigh [saɪ] I vi (person) suspirar; (wind) susurrar, gemir. II n (of person) suspiro m; (of wind) susurro m, gemido m; to breathe or heave a s. of relief, dar un suspiro de alivio.

sight [saɪt] I n 1 (faculty) vista f; at first s., a primera vista; he faints at the s. of blood, se desmaya cuando ve sangre; it was love at first s., fue un flechazo, fue amor a primera vista; to catch s. of sth/sb, divisar algo/a algn; to know sb by s., conocer a algn de vista; to lose s. of sth/sb, perder algo/a algn de vista; fig I hate the s. of him, no puedo ni verlo. ■ long s., presbicia f; second s., intuición f; short s., miopía f. 2 (range of vision) vista f; to be within s., estar a la vista; to come into s., aparecer; to keep out of s., no dejarse ver, esconderse; to shoot at or on s., disparar a matar; sl out of s., alucinante; prov out of s., out of mind, ojos que no ven, corazón que no siente. 3 (spectacle) espectáculo m; it's a s. for sore eyes, da gusto verlo; it was a sorry s., fue un triste espectáculo; fam what a s. you look!, ¡qué pinta tienes! 4 (on gun) mira f; to take s., apuntar; fig to set one's sights on sth, tener la mira puesta en algo; fig to set one's sights too high, apuntar demasiado alto, ser demasiado ambicioso,-a. 5 fam (a great deal) a s. more expensive, machísimo más caro,-a; not by a long s., ni mucho menos. 6 sights, (tourist attractions) monumentos mpl; to see the s. of the city, visitar la ciudad, hacer un recorrido turístico de la ciudad. II vtr (bird, animal) observar, ver; (person) ver; (land) divisar.

sighted ['saɪtɪd] adj vidente, de vista normal; the partially s., los que tienen problemas de vista.

sighting ['saɪtɪŋ] n observación f.

sightless ['saɪtlɪs] adj ciego,-a, invidente.

sightly ['saɪtlɪ] adj (sightlier, sightliest) atractivo,-a.

sight-read ['saɪtri:d] vtr Mus repentizar.

sight-reading ['saɪtri:dɪŋ] n Mus repentización f.

sightseeing ['saɪtsi:ɪŋ] n turismo m, visita f turística; to go s., hacer turismo, visitar la ciudad.

sightseer ['saɪtsɪə'] n turista mf.

sign [saɪn] I n 1 (symbol) signo m, símbolo m; Math plus/minus s., signo de más/de menos; Astrol the signs of the zodiac, los signos del zodíaco. 2 (gesture) gesto m, seña f; (signal) señal f; to make a s. to sb, hacer una señal a algn; to make the s. of the Cross, hacer la señal de la cruz. ■ s. language, lenguaje m por señas; to use s. language, hablar por señas. 3 (indication) señal f, muestra f; (proof) prueba f; (trace) rastro m, huella f, as a s. of, como muestra de; it's a sure s. of, es un claro indicio de; there was no s. of him anywhere, no se le veía por ninguna parte; to show signs of life, dar señales de vida. 4 (notice) anuncio m, aviso m; (board) letrero m; (over shop) letrero m, rótulo m; there's a s. which says 'keep out', hay un letrero que dice 'prohibida la entrada'. ■ neon s., rótulo m de neón; road s., (giving warnings etc) señal f de tráfico; (showing route) indicador m de carretera. II vtr 1 (letter, document) firmar; to s. one's name, firmar. 2 Ftb (player) fichar. III vi (with name) firmar. ◆ sign away vtr ceder. ◆ sign in vi firmar el registro, registrarse. ◆ sign off vi Rad TV despedirse, cerrar el programa. ◆ sign on I vtr (worker) contratar; Ftb (player) fichar. II vi (worker) firmar un contrato; Ftb (player) fichar (for, por); (student) matricularse; fam (unemployed person) apuntarse al paro. ◆ sign over vtr ceder. ◆ sign up I vtr (soldier) reclutar; (worker) contratar; Ftb (player) fichar. II vi (soldier) alistarse; (worker) firmar un contrato; Ftb (player) fichar (with, por).

signal ['sɪgnəl] I n (gen) señal f; Rad TV sintonía f; US Tel busy s., señal de ocupado; to give the alarm s., dar la señal de alarma. ■ Rail s. box, garita f de señales; Aut traffic signals, señales mpl de tráfico. II vtr (pt & pp signalled, US signaled) 1 (transmit) (message) transmitir or comunicar por señales. 2 (indicate) (direction etc) indicar. 3 (signify) señalar; it signalled the end of an era, señaló el fin de toda una época. III vi (with hands) hacer señales; (in car) señalar, poner el intermitente.

signalman ['sɪgnəlmən] *n (pl **signalmen**) Rail* guardavía *m*.

signatory ['sɪgnətərɪ] *n* firmante *mf*, signatario,-a *m*,*f*.

signature ['sɪgnɪtʃər] *n (name)* firma *f*; *Rad TV* **s. tune**, sintonía *f*.

signboard ['saɪnbɔːd] *n (sign)* letrero *m*; *(hoarding)* cartelera *f*; *(noticeboard)* tablón *m* de anuncios.

signet ['sɪgnɪt] *n* sello *m*. ■ **s. ring**, (anillo *m* de) sello *m*.

signficance [sɪg'nɪfɪkəns] *n (meaning)* significado *m*; *(importance)* importancia *f*; **it's of no s.**, carece de importancia.

significant [sɪg'nɪfɪkənt] *adj (meaningful)* significativo,-a; *(important)* importante, considerable. ◆ **significantly** *adv (markedly)* sensiblemente; **s. enough, they are both women**, es importante destacar que ambas son mujeres.

signify ['sɪgnɪfaɪ] *vtr (pt & pp **signified**)* **1** *(mean)* significar; *(denote)* señalar, indicar. **2** *(show, make known)* indicar, mostrar.

signpost ['saɪnpəʊst] *Aut* **1** *n* poste *m* indicador. **II** *vtr (route etc)* señalizar.

signwriter ['saɪnraɪtər] *n* rotulista *mf*.

Sikh [siːk] *adj & n* sij *(mf)*.

silage ['saɪlɪdʒ] *n Agr* ensilado *m*, ensilaje *m*.

silence ['saɪləns] **I** *n* silencio *m*; **deadly s.**, silencio sepulcral; **in s.**, en silencio; **to break s.**, romper el silencio; *prov* **s. is golden**, el silencio es oro. **II** *vtr (person)* acallar, hacer callar; *(protests)* apagar; *(engine)* silenciar.

silencer ['saɪlənsər] *n* silenciador *m*.

silent ['saɪlənt] *adj (gen)* silencioso,-a; *(not talkative)* callado,-a; *(film, letter)* mudo,-a; **the s. majority**, la mayoría silenciosa; **to be s.**, callarse; **to keep or remain s.**, guardar silencio. ◆ **silently** *adv* silenciosamente, en silencio.

silhouette [sɪluː'et] **I** *n* silueta *f*. **II** *vtr* **to be silhouetted against**, recortarse *or* perfilarse en *or* sobre.

silica ['sɪlɪkə] *n Chem* sílice *f*.

silicon ['sɪlɪkən] *n Chem* silicio *m*. ■ *Comput* **s. chip**, chip *m* (de silicio).

silicone ['sɪlɪkəʊn] *n Chem* silicona *f*.

silicosis [sɪlɪ'kəʊsɪs] *n Med* silicosis *f*.

silk [sɪlk] **I** *n* seda *f*; **raw s.**, seda cruda; *fig* **to be of the same s.**, ser del mismo paño. **II** *adj (shirt etc)* de seda; **the s. industry**, la industria sedera.

silken ['sɪlkən] *adj fig* sedoso,-a.

silk-screen ['sɪlkskriːn] *n* **s.-s. printing**, serigrafía *f*.

silkworm ['sɪlkwɜːm] *n Zool* gusano *m* de seda.

silky ['sɪlkɪ] *adj (silkier, silkiest) (cloth)* sedoso,-a; *(voice etc)* suave.

sill [sɪl] *n (of window)* alféizar *m*, antepecho *m*; *(of car)* faldón *m* trasero.

silliness ['sɪlɪnɪs] *n* **1** *(quality)* estupidez *f*, necedad *f*. **2** *(act)* tontería *f*, bobada *f*.

silly ['sɪlɪ] *adj (sillier, silliest) (stupid)* tonto,-a, bobo,-a, necio,-a; *(absurd)* absurdo,-a; *(ridiculous)* ridículo,-a; **to do sth s.**, hacer una tontería; **to make sb look s.**, poner a algn en ridículo; *fam* **to drink oneself s.**, agarrar una trompa de órdago.

silo ['saɪləʊ] *n (pl **silos**) Agr Mil* silo *m*.

silt [sɪlt] *n* cieno *m*, légamo *m*. ◆ **silt up** *vi* obstruirse con cieno *or* sedimentos.

silting ['sɪltɪŋ] *n* sedimentación *f*.

silver ['sɪlvər] **I** *n* **1** *(metal)* plata *f*; **sterling s.**, plata de ley. **2** *(coins)* monedas *fpl* (de plata). **3** *(tableware, articles)* plata *f*, vajilla *f* de plata; *prov* **every cloud has a s. lining**, no hay mal que por bien no venga. ■ **s. foil**, papel *m* de plata, *(tinfoil)* papel *m* de aluminio; **s. jubilee**, vigésimo quinto aniversario *m*, bodas *fpl* de plata; **s.**

medal, medalla *f* de plata; **s. paper**, papel *m* de plata; **s. plate**, *(coating)* plateado *m*; *(articles)* vajilla *f* plateada; **s. wedding**, bodas *fpl* de plata.

silver-plated [sɪlvə'pleɪtɪd] *adj* plateado,-a, con un baño de plata.

silversmith ['sɪlvəsmɪθ] *n* platero,-a *m*,*f*.

silverware ['sɪlvəweər] *n* plata *f*, vajilla *f* de plata.

silvery ['sɪlvərɪ] *adj* **1** *(colour, material)* plateado,-a. **2** *(sound)* argentino,-a.

similar ['sɪmɪlər] *adj* parecido,-a, semejante, similar **(to, a)**; **s. in size**, de tamaño parecido; **to be very s.**, parecerse mucho. ■ *Geom* **s. triangle**, triángulo *m* semejante. ◆ **similarly** *adv* **1** *(as well)* igualmente. **2** *(likewise)* del mismo modo, asimismo.

similarity [sɪmɪ'lærɪtɪ] *n* semejanza *f*, parecido *m*.

simile ['sɪmɪlɪ] *n Lit* símil *m*.

simmer ['sɪmər] **I** *vtr Culin* cocer *or* hervir a fuego lento. **II** *vi Culin* cocerse *or* hervir a fuego lento. ◆ **simmer down** *vi fam* calmarse, tranquilizarse.

simper ['sɪmpər] **I** *n* sonrisa *f* afectada. **II** *vi* sonreír con afectación.

simpering ['sɪmpərɪŋ] **I** *adj* afectado,-a, melindroso,-a. **II** *n* melindres *mpl*.

simple ['sɪmpəl] *adj* **1** *(easy, straight-foward)* fácil, sencillo,-a; *(not complicated)* sencillo,-a, simple; **it's a question of money pure and s.**, es pura y simplemente una cuestión de dinero. ■ *Fin* **s. interest**, interés *m* simple. **2** *(plain, unsophisticated)* sencillo,-a; *(natural)* natural; **to be a s. soul**, ser un alma de Dios. **3** *(foolish, backward)* simple, tonto,-a; *(naïve)* ingenuo,-a, inocente; *(dim)* corto,-a de alcances, de pocas luces. ◆ **simply** *adv* **1** *(plainly, modestly)* simplemente, sencillamente. **2** *(only)* simplemente, solamente, sólo; *(just, merely)* meramente. **3** *(really)* francamente, realmente.

simple-minded [sɪmpəl'maɪndɪd] *adj* simple, tonto,-a, necio,-a.

simpleton ['sɪmpəltən] *n arch* simplón,-ona *m*, *f*, inocentón,-ona *m*,*f*, papanatas *mf*.

simplicity [sɪm'plɪsɪtɪ] *n* **1** *(lack of sophistication)* sencillez *f*, naturalidad *f*. **2** *(foolishness)* simpleza *f*; *(naïveté)* ingenuidad *f*. **3** *(incomplexity)* sencillez *f*.

simplification [sɪmplɪfɪ'keɪʃən] *n* simplificación *f*.

simplify ['sɪmplɪfaɪ] *vtr (pt & pp **simplified**)* simplificar.

simplistic [sɪm'plɪstɪk] *adj* simplista.

simulate ['sɪmjʊleɪt] *vtr (gen)* simular; *(object, noise)* imitar.

simulated ['sɪmjʊleɪtɪd] *adj (flight)* simulado,-a; *(leather etc)* de imitación.

simulation [sɪmjʊ'leɪʃən] *n* simulación *f*, simulacro *m*.

simulator ['sɪmjʊleɪtər] *n* simulador *m*; *Av* **flight s.**, simulador de vuelo.

simultaneous [sɪməl'teɪnɪəs] *adj* simultáneo,-a; *Math* **s. equations**, sistema *m* de ecuaciones. ◆ **simultaneously** *adv* simultáneamente, a la vez.

sin¹ [sɪn] **I** *n* pecado *m*; **mortal s.**, pecado mortal; *fig* **it would be a s. to waste it**, sería un crimen desperdiciarlo; *fam* **as ugly as s.**, más feo que un pecado. **II** *vi* pecar.

sin² [saɪn] *Math abbr of* **sine**, seno *m*, sen.

since [sɪns] **I** *adv* desde entonces; **ever s.**, desde entonces; **I have not seen him s.**, no lo he vuelto a ver desde entonces; **long s.**, hace mucho tiempo; *(subsequently)* **it has s. come out that ...**, desde entonces se ha sabido que ... . **II** *prep* desde; **she has been living here s. 1975**, vive aquí desde 1975. **III** *conj* **1** *(time)* desde que; **he hasn't worked s. he left school**, está en paro desde que dejó el colegio; **how long is s. you last saw him?**, ¿cuánto tiempo hace desde que lo viste por última vez? **2** *(because, as)* ya que, puesto que; **s. he is unwell**, ya que está enfermo.

sincere [sɪn'sɪə^r] *adj* sincero,-a. ◆ **sincerely** *adv* sinceramente; *(in letter)* **Yours s.,** (le saluda) atentamente.

sincerity [sɪn'serɪtɪ] *n* sinceridad *f*; **in all s.,** con toda sinceridad.

sinecure ['saɪnɪkjʊə^r] *n* sinecura *f*.

sinew ['sɪnjuː] *n (tendon)* tendón *m*; *(in meat)* nervio *m*.

sinewy ['sɪnjʊɪ] *adj* nervudo,-a.

sinful ['sɪnfʊl] *adj (person)* pecador,-a; *(act, thought)* pecaminoso,-a; *fig (waste etc)* escandaloso,-a.

sing [sɪŋ] **I** *vtr (pt sang; pp sung)* cantar; **to s. a baby to sleep,** arrullar a un niño; *fig* **to s. the praises of sth/sb** alabar algo/a algn. **II** *vi (person, bird)* cantar; *(kettle, bullets)* silbar; *(insect, ears)* zumbar; **can you s.?,** ¿sabes cantar? ◆ **sing out** *vi* **1** *(sing loudly)* cantar fuerte. **2** *fam (shout)* gritar.

singe [sɪndʒ] *vtr* chamuscar.

singer ['sɪŋə^r] *n* cantante *mf*; *(in choir)* cantor,-a *m,f*.

singing ['sɪŋɪŋ] **I** *n (art)* canto *m*, cantar *m*; *(songs)* canciones *fpl*; *(of kettle)* silbido *m*; *(in ears)* zumbido *m*. **II** *adj* **s. lessons,** lecciones de canto; **he has a fine s. voice,** tiene buena voz.

single ['sɪŋgəl] **I** *adj* **1** *(solitary, individual)* solo,-a; **every s. day,** todos los días; **there wasn't a s. ticket left,** no quedó ni una sola entrada. **2** *(only one)* único,-a, sencillo,-a; **in s. figures,** por debajo del diez; **in s. file,** en fila india. **3** *(not double)* individual, sencillo,-a. ■ *GB Culin* **s. cream,** nata *f* líquida; **s. bed/room,** cama *f*/habitación *f* individual; *Rail* **s. (ticket),** billete *m* sencillo *or* de ida. **4** *(unmarried)* soltero,-a. **II** *n* **1** *Rail* billete *m* sencillo *or* de ida. **2** *(record)* disco *m* sencillo, single *m*. **3** *Sport* **singles,** barco *or* buque *m*. **3 singles,** *Sport* individuales *mpl*. **4 singles bar/holiday,** bar *m*/ vacaciones *fpl* para solteros. ◆ **single out** *vtr (choose)* escoger, seleccionar; *(distinguish)* distinguir, destacar, resaltar. ◆ **singly** *adv (individually)* por separado; *(one by one)* uno por uno.

single-breasted [sɪŋgəl'brestɪd] *adj (suit, jacket)* recto,-a, sin cruzar.

single-decker [sɪŋgəl'dekə^r] *n* autobús *m* de un solo piso.

single-handed [sɪŋgəl'hændɪd] *adj & adv* sin ayuda, solo,-a.

single-minded [sɪŋgəl'maɪndɪd] *adj* resuelto,-a.

singleness ['sɪŋgəlnɪs] *n* **s. of purpose,** resolución *f*, ahínco *m*.

singlet ['sɪŋglɪt] *n GB (vest)* camiseta *f*.

sing-song ['sɪŋsɒŋ] **I** *adj (voice, tone)* cantarín,-ina. **II** *n* **1** *(voice, tone)* sonsonete *m*. **2** *(singing session)* concierto *m* improvisado.

singular ['sɪŋgjʊlə^r] **I** *adj* **1** *Ling* singular. **2** *fml (outstanding)* extraordinario,-a, excepcional; **a woman of s. beauty,** una mujer de excepcional belleza. **3** *fml (unique, unusual)* único,-a, extraño,-a, particular. **II** *n Ling* singular *m*; **in the s.,** en singular. ◆ **singularly** *adv* extraordinariamente, excepcionalmente.

sinister ['sɪnɪstə^r] *adj* siniestro,-a.

sink¹ [sɪŋk] *n (in kitchen)* fregadero *m*.

sink² [sɪŋk] **I** *vtr (pt sank; pp sunk)* **1** *(ship)* hundir, echar a pique; *fig (hopes, plans)* acabar con; **we sank our differences,** hicimos las paces. **2** *(shaft, hole)* cavar, excavar; *(well)* abrir; *(post, pipe)* hincar; *(knife)* clavar, hundir; *(teeth)* hincar **(into,** en). **3** *(invest)* invertir **(into,** en). **4** *GB fam (drink)* soplar. **5** *Sport sl (golf, snooker)* meter. **II** *vi* **1** *(ship, etc)* hundirse, irse a pique; *fig* **to be sunk in thought,** estar sumido,-a en el pensamiento; *fig* **to leave sb to s. or swim,** abandonar a algn a su suerte; *fig* **to s. into oblivion,** caer en el olvido; *fam* **we're sunk!,** ¡estamos perdidos! **2** *(land, building) (subside)* hundirse; **Venice is slowly sinking,** Venecia se hunde lentamente; *fig* **his hopes sank,** sus esperanzas se vinieron abajo; *fig* **my heart sank,** se me cayó el alma a los pies. **3** *(sun)* ponerse, bajar. **4** *(figures, prices)* bajar. **5** *(slump)* dejarse caer; **to s. back into an armchair,**

arrellanarse en un sillón; **to s. to one's knees,** hincarse de rodillas. ◆ **sink in** *vi (penetrate)* penetrar; *fig (words)* causar impresión; **it hasn't sunk in yet,** todavía no ha hecho impacto.

sinker ['sɪŋkə^r] *n Fishing* plomo *m*.

sinking ['sɪŋkɪŋ] *n (of ship)* hundimiento *m*.

sinner ['sɪnə^r] *n* pecador,-a *m,f*.

sinuous ['sɪnjʊəs] *adj Lit* sinuoso,-a, tortuoso,-a, zigzagueante.

sinus ['saɪnəs] *n Anat* seno *m*.

sip [sɪp] **I** *n* sorbo *m*. **II** *vtr (pt & pp sipped)* sorber, beber a sorbos.

siphon ['saɪfən] *n* sifón *m*. ◆ **siphon off** *vtr (liquid)* sacar con sifón; *fig (funds, traffic)* desviar.

sir [sɜː^r] *n fml* señor *m*; **yes, s.,** sí, señor; *Mil* **s.!,** ¡a sus órdenes!; *(in letter)* **Dear Sir,** muy señor mío, estimado señor; *(title)* sir; **S. Walter Raleigh,** Sir Walter Raleigh.

sire [saɪə^r] **I** *vtr (beget)* ser padre de, engendrar. **II** *n (animals)* macho *m*.

siren ['saɪərən] *n Myth* sirena *f*.

sirloin ['sɜːlɔɪn] *n Culin* solomillo *m*.

sissy ['sɪsɪ] *n fam (coward)* miedica *mf*.

sister ['sɪstə^r] **I** *n* **1** *(relation)* hermana *f*. **2** *GB Med* enfermera *f* jefe. **3** *Rel* hermana *f*, monja *f*; *(before name)* sor; **s. Maria,** Sor María. **II** *adj* **s. nation,** nación *f* hermana; **s. ship,** barco *or* gemelo.

sister-in-law ['sɪstərɪnlɔː] *n (pl sisters-in-law)* cuñada *f*.

sisterhood ['sɪstəhʊd] *n* hermandad *f*.

sisterly ['sɪstəlɪ] *adj* de hermana.

sit [sɪt] **I** *vtr (pt & pp sat)* **1** *(child etc)* sentar **(in, on,** en). **2** *(hall etc)* tener cabida para. **3** *GB (exam)* presentarse a. **II** *vi* **1** *(action)* sentarse; *(to dog)* **s.!,** ¡siéntate! **2** *(be seated)* estar sentado,-a; **to be sitting at table,** estar sentado,-a a la mesa; *fig* **to be sitting pretty,** tenerlo todo resuelto; *fig* **to s. tight,** mantenerse en sus trece. **3** *(object) (lie, rest)* yacer; *(be situated)* ubicarse, estar, hallarse; *(person) (remain)* quedarse; **he sits there all day,** se pasa todo el día allí sentado. **4** *(pose)* posar. **5** *(be a member)* ser miembro; **to s. on a jury,** ser miembro de un jurado. **6** *Pol (represent)* representar. **7** *(assembly)* reunirse, estar reunido,-a. **8** *fam (babysit)* cuidar niños, hacer de canguro. ◆ **sit about, sit around** *vi* holgazanear, hacer el vago. ◆ **sit back** *vi* recostarse; *fig* **he just sat back and did nothing,** no levantó ni un dedo para ayudar. ◆ **sit down** *I* *vtr* sentar; **he sat himself down,** se sentó. **II** *vi* sentarse; **please s. down,** siéntese por favor. ◆ **sit in on** *vtr* asistir sin participar. ◆ **sit on** *vtr fam* **1** *(keep secret)* ocultar, callar; *(delay dealing with)* dejar dormir, aplazar. **2** *(person) (silence)* hacer callar; *(repress)* hacer la vida difícil a. ◆ **sit out** *vtr (endure)* quedarse *or* aguantar hasta el final. ◆ **sit through** *vi (as a spectator etc)* aguantar. ◆ **sit up** I *vtr (baby etc)* sentar. **II** *vi* **1** *(straight)* ponerse derecho; *(in bed)* incorporarse; *fig* **to s. up and take notice,** prestar atención. **2** *(stay up late)* quedarse levantado,-a; **no acostarse; to s. up waiting for sb,** quedarse esperando a algn.

sit-down ['sɪtdʊn] *adj* **s.-d. meal,** comida *f* servida en la mesa. **I** *n* **1** *(protest)* entada *f*. **2** *fam* breve reposo *m*.

site [saɪt] **I** *n* **1** *(area)* terreno *m*, lugar *m*. ■ **building s.,** solar *m*; *(under construction)* obra *f*; **camp s.,** camping *m*; **caravan s.,** camping *m* de caravanas. **2** *(location)* situación *f*, emplazamiento *m*; **nuclear testing s.,** zona *f* de pruebas nucleares. **II** *vtr (building etc)* situar, ubicar.

sit-in ['sɪtɪn] *n fam (demonstration)* sentada *f*; *(strike)* huelga *f* de brazos caídos.

siting ['saɪtɪŋ] *n* emplazamiento *m*, ubicación *f*.

sitter ['sɪtə^r] *n* **1** *Art* modelo *mf*. **2** *(baby)* **s.,** canguro *mf*. **3** *Sport* gol *m* cantado.

sitting ['sɪtɪŋ] **I** *n (of committee, for portrait)* sesión *f*; *(in canteen)* turno *m*. **II** *adj* **1** sentado,-a. ■ *Pol* **s. member,** miembro *m* activo; **s. room,** sala *f* de estar, salón *m*, living *m*; **s. tenant** inquilino,-a *m*,*f* con derecho a propiedad. **2** *fam fig* **s. duck,** blanco *m* facilísimo; **s. pretty,** aventajado,-a.

situate ['sɪtjueɪt] *vtr fml* situar, ubicar.

situated ['sɪtjueɪtɪd] *adj (building etc)* situado,-a, ubicado,-a; *fam* **how are you s. for money?,** ¿cómo andas de dinero?

situation [sɪtjuˈeɪʃən] *n* **1** *(location)* situación *f*, ubicación *f*. **2** *(circumstances etc)* situación *f*; **the current economic s.,** la situación económica actual. **3** *(job, position)* empleo *m*, puesto *m*; *(in newspaper)* **'situations vacant',** 'ofertas de trabajo', 'bolsa de trabajo'.

sit-up ['sɪtʌp] *n Gymn* abdominal *m*.

six [sɪks] **I** *adj* seis *inv*. **II** *n* seis *m inv*; *fam fig* **it's s. of one and half a dozen of the other,** viene a ser lo mismo, da lo mismo, da igual; *fam fig* **to be at sixes and sevens,** estar confuso,-a, estar hecho un lío; *see also* **seven.**

six-pack ['sɪkspæk] *n Com (of beer etc)* caja *f* de seis botellas *or* latas.

sixpence ['sɪkspəns] *n Hist (coin)* moneda *f* de seis peniques.

sixteen [sɪks'tiːn] *adj & n* dieciséis *(m) inv*, diez y seis *(m) inv*; *see also* **seven.**

sixteenth [sɪks'tiːnθ] **I** *adj*; decimosexto,-a. **II** *n* **1** *(in series)* decimosexto,-a *m*,*f*. **2** *(fraction)* dieciseisavo *m*, diecisexta parte *f*; *see also* **seventh.**

sixth [sɪksθ] **I** *adj* sexto,-a; **s. sense,** sexto sentido; *Educ* **s. form,** ≈ COU; **s. former,** ≈ estudiante de COU. **II** *n* **1** *(in series)* sexto,-a *m*,*f*. **2** *(fraction)* sexto *m*, sexta parte *f*; *see also* **seventh.**

sixtieth ['sɪkstɪəθ] **I** *adj* sexagésimo,-a. **II** *n* **1** *(in series)* sexagésimo,-a *m*,*f*. **2** *(fraction)* sesentavo *m*, sexagésima parte *f*; *see also* **seventh.**

sixty ['sɪkstɪ] **I** *adj* sesenta *inv*. **II** *n* sesenta *m inv*; *see also* **seventy** and **seven.**

size¹ [saɪz] *n (gen)* tamaño *m*; *(of garment)* talla *f*; *(of shoes)* número *m*; *(of person)* talla *f*, estatura *f*, *(scope)* alcance *m*; *(magnitude)* magnitud *f*; **life s.,** tamaño natural; **she's a size ten,** gasta la talla diez; **try it on for s.,** pruébatelo para ver la talla que necesitas; **what s. do you take?,** *(garment)* ¿qué talla tienes?; *(shoes)* ¿qué número calzas?; **what s. is the kitchen?,** ¿de qué tamaño es la cocina?; **to cut sth to s.,** cortar algo al tamaño que se necesita; *fig* **to cut sb down to s.,** bajar los humos a algn; *fig* **that's about the s. of it,** es más o menos así. ◆ **size up** *vtr (person)* juzgar; *(situation, problem)* evaluar.

size² [saɪz] **I** *n (for paper, textiles)* cola *f*, apresto *m*. **II** *vtr (paper, textiles)* encolar, aprestar.

siz(e)able ['saɪzəbəl] *adj (estate, building, etc)* (bastante) grande; *(sum)* considerable; *(problem)* importante.

sizzle ['sɪzəl] **I** *n* chisporroteo *m*. **II** *vi* chisporrotear.

skate¹ [skeɪt] **I** *n* patín *m*; *fam* **get your skates on!,** ¡date prisa! **II** *vtr* patinar; *fig* **to s. on thin ice,** pisar un terreno peligroso. ◆ **skate over, skate around** *vtr fig (problem, difficulty)* evitar.

skate² [skeɪt] *n (fish)* raya *f*.

skateboard ['skeɪtbɔːd] *n* monopatín *m*.

skater ['skeɪtər] *n* patinador,-a *m*,*f*.

skating ['skeɪtɪŋ] *n* patinaje *m*; **ice/roller s.,** patinaje sobre hielo/sobre ruedas. ■ **s. rink,** pista *f* de patinaje.

skedaddle [skɪ'dædəl] *vi fam* largarse, pirarse.

skeletal ['skelɪtəl] *adj fml* esquelético,-a.

skeleton ['skelɪtən] **I** *n* **1** *(of person, animal)* esqueleto *m*. **2** *(of building, ship)* armazón *m*, estructura *f*. **3** *(outline, plan)* esquema *m*, bosquejo *m*. **II** *adj (staff, service)* reducido,-a, limitado,-a. ■ **s. key,** llave *f* maestra.

skeptic ['skeptɪk] *US see* **sceptic.**

skeptical ['skeptɪkəl] *US see* **sceptical.**

sketch [sketʃ] **I** *n* **1** *(rough drawing)* croquis *m*; *(preliminary drawing)* bosquejo *m*, esbozo *m*; *(drawing)* dibujo *m*; *(outline)* esquema *m*; *(rough draft)* boceto *m*, borrador *m*; *Lit* **character s.,** breve descripción *f* de un personaje. **2** *Theat TV* sketch *m*. **II** *vtr (draw)* dibujar; *(rough drawing)* hacer un croquis de; *(preliminary drawing)* bosquejar, esbozar. **III** *vi (draw)* dibujar. ◆ **sketch in** *vtr (details)* dibujar; *fig* dar un resumen de.

sketch-book ['sketʃbuk] *n*, **sketch-pad** ['sketʃpæd] *n* bloc *m* de dibujo.

sketchy ['sketʃɪ] *adj (sketchier, sketchiest) (incomplete)* incompleto,-a; *(not detailed)* sin detalles; *(vague)* vago,-a, impreciso,-a.

skewer ['skjuər] **I** *n Culin* pincho *m*, broqueta *f*, brocheta *f*. **II** *vtr (pieces of meat etc)* ensartar (en un pincho).

ski [skiː] **I** *n (equipment)* esquí *m*. **II** *adj* de esquí, de esquiar. ■ **s. boots,** botas *fpl* de esquiar; **s. instructor,** monitor,-a *m*,*f* de esquí; **s. jump,** *(action)* salto *m* con esquís; *(course)* pista *f* de salto; **s. lift,** telesquí *m*; *(with seats)* telesilla *f*; **s. pants,** pantalón *m sing* de esquiar; **s. resort,** estación *f* de esquí *or* esquiar; **s. run,** pista *f* de esquí; **s. stick,** palo *m* de esquiar. **III** *vi* esquiar; **to go skiing,** ir a esquiar, bajar esquiando.

skid [skɪd] **I** *n* **1** *Aut* patinazo *m*, derrapaje *m*, resbalón *m*. **2 s. row,** *US fam* barrio *m* bajo. **II** *vi (pt & pp skidded) Aut* patinar, derrapar; **to s. to a halt,** frenar patinando.

skier ['skiːər] *n* esquiador,-a *m*,*f*.

skiff [skɪf] *n Naut* esquife *m*.

skiing ['skiːɪŋ] *n* esquí *m*; **s. holiday,** vacaciones de esquí.

skilful, *US* **skillful** ['skɪlful] *adj* hábil, diestro,-a; *fam* mañoso,-a. ◆ **skilfully,** *US* **skillfully** *adv* hábilmente, con destreza.

skill [skɪl] *n* **1** *(ability)* habilidad *f*, destreza *f*; *(talent)* talento *m*, don *m*. **2** *(technique)* técnica *f*, arte *m*, especialidad *f*.

skilled [skɪld] *adj* **1** *(able, dextrous)* hábil, diestro,-a; *(expert)* experto,-a. **2** *(specialized) (worker)* cualificado,-a, especializado,-a; *(work)* especializado,-a, de especialista.

skim [skɪm] **I** *vtr (pt & pp skimmed)* **1** *(milk)* desnatar, descremar; *(soup)* espumar; **to s. the cream off the milk,** quitar la nata a la leche. ■ **skimmed milk,** leche *f* descremada *or* desnatada. **2** *(brush against)* rozar; **to s. the ground,** rozar el suelo; *(bird, plane)* volar a ras de suelo; **to s. stones,** hacer cabrillas con piedrecitas. **II** *vi* **to s. across the water/ground,** pasar rozando el agua/suelo; *fig* **to s. through a book,** hojear un libro.

skimp [skɪmp] *vtr & vi (food, material)* escatimar; *(work)* chapucear; **to s. on food/material,** escatimar comida/tela.

skimpy ['skɪmpɪ] *adj (skimpier, skimpiest) (dress)* ligero,-a; *(meal)* escaso,-a, pobre. ◆ **skimpily** *adv* **s. dressed,** ligeramente vestido,-a.

skin [skɪn] **I** *n* **1** *(of person)* piel *f*; *(of face)* cutis *m*; *(complexion)* tez *f*; *fig* **to be all s. and bone,** estar en los huesos; *fig* **to escape by the s. of one's teeth,** librarse por los pelos; *fig* **to get under one's s.,** irritar a uno; *fig* **to have a thick/thin s.,** ser poco sensible/muy susceptible; *fam* **it's no s. off my nose,** a mí me da lo mismo, a mí me trae sin cuidado; *fam* **to save one's own s.,** salvar el pellejo. ■ **s. cream,** crema *f* de belleza; *Med* **s. disease,** enfermedad *f* de la piel, dermatosis *f*; *Med* **s. graft,** injerto *m* cutáneo *or* de piel; *Med* **s. test,** prueba *f* cutánea, cutirreacción *f*. **2** *(of animal)* piel *f*, pellejo *m*; *(pelt)* piel *f*; *(hide)* cuero *m* (curtido). **3** *Bot (of fruit)* piel *f*; *(hard)* cáscara *f*, corteza *f*; *(soft)* piel *f*; *(peeling)* monda *f*, mondadura *f*. **4** *(of sausage)* pellejo *m*. **5** *(on paint)* telilla *f*, capa *f* fina; *(on milk, custard)* nata *f*. **II** *vtr (pt & pp skinned)* **1** *(animal, fruit)* despellejar, desollar; *(fruit, vegetable)* pelar. **2** *(graze)* arañar, rascar; **to s. one's elbow/knee,** hacerse un rasguño en el codo/la rodilla.

skin-deep [skɪn'diːp] *adj* superficial.

skin-diver ['skɪndaɪvər] *n* buceador,-a *m*,*f*, submarinista *mf*.

skin-diving ['skɪndaɪvɪŋ] *n* buceo *m*, submarinismo *m*.

skinflint ['skɪnflɪnt] *n arch fam* tacaño,-a *m,f*.

skinful ['skɪnfʊl] *n fam* **to have had a s.**, estar como una cuba.

skinhead ['skɪnhed] *n fam* cabeza *mf* rapada.

skinny ['skɪnɪ] *adj (skinnier, skinniest) fam* flaco,-a, enjuto,-a, delgaducho,-a.

skint [skɪnt] *adj fam* **to be s.**, estar sin blanca *or* sin un duro.

skin-tight ['skɪntaɪt] *adj (clothing)* muy ajustado,-a.

skip¹ [skɪp] **I** *n (jump)* salto *m*, brinco *m*. **II** *vi (pt & pp skipped) (jump)* saltar, brincar; *(with rope)* saltar a la comba; *fig* saltar; *fig* **to s. over sth**, saltarse algo. **III** *vtr fig (page, meal, class)* saltarse; *fam* **s. it!**, ¡déjalo!

skip² [skɪp] *n Constr (container)* contenedor *m*, container *m*.

skipper ['skɪpəʳ] **I** *n Naut fam* patrón *m*, capitán,-ana *m,f*; *Sport fam* capitán,-ana *m,f*. **II** *vtr* capitanear.

skipping ['skɪpɪŋ] *n* comba *f*. ■ **s. rope**, comba *f*, cuerda *f* de saltar.

skirmish ['skɜːmɪʃ] *n Mil* escaramuza *f*; *(fight)* pelea *f*, refriega *f*, trifulca *f*; *(argument)* escaramuza *f*, discusión *f*.

skirt [skɜːt] **I** *n* **1** *(garment)* falda; **straight/pleated s.**, falda recta/plisada. **2** *(machinery guard)* cubierta *f*. **II** *vtr (town, hill, etc)* rodear; *(lake, coast)* bordear; *fig (problem, difficulty)* esquivar, eludir.

skirting ['skɜːtɪŋ] *GB n* **s. (board)**, zócalo *m*, rodapié *m*.

skit [skɪt] *n Lit* sátira *f*, parodia *f*; *Theat* sketch *m* satírico.

skittish ['skɪtɪʃ] *adj (capricious)* caprichoso,-a, frívolo,-a; *(animal)* excitable.

skittle ['skɪtəl] *n* **1** *(pin)* bolo *m*. **2** **skittles**, *(game)* (juego *m* de) bolos *mpl*, boliche *m*. ■ **s. alley**, bolera *f*, boliche *m*.

skive [skaɪv] *GB vi fam* escaquearse, escurrir el bulto.

skiver ['skaɪvəʳ] *GB n fam* frescales *mf inv*, irresponsable *mf*.

skulduggery, *US* **skullduggery** [skʌl'dʌgərɪ] *n* tejemaneje *m*.

skulk [skʌlk] *vi (hide)* esconderse; *(prowl)* merodear; *(lie in wait)* estar al acecho.

skull [skʌl] *n* **1** *Anat* cráneo *m*, *fam* calavera *f*, *(picture, sign)* **s. and crossbones**, calavera *f* **2** *fam* coco *m*

skullcap ['skʌlkæp] *n* casquete *m*, *(of priest)* solideo *m*

skunk [skʌŋk] *n Zool* mofeta *f*

sky [skaɪ] *n* cielo *m*, firmamento *m*; **in the s.**, en el cielo, *fam fig* **the s.'s the limit!**, ¡todo es posible! ■ **s. blue**, azul *m* celeste

sky-blue ['skaɪblu:] *adj (colour)* celeste

sky-diver ['skaɪdaɪvəʳ] *n* paracaidista *mf*

sky-diving ['skaɪdaɪvɪŋ] *n* paracaidismo *m*

sky-high [skaɪ'haɪ] *adv* por las nubes, **to blow sth s.-h.**, hacer volar algo por los aires

skylark ['skaɪlɑːk] *n Orn* alondra *f*

skylight ['skaɪlaɪt] *n* tragaluz *m*, claraboya *f*

skyline ['skaɪlaɪn] *n (horizon)* horizonte *m*, *(of city)* perfil *m*.

skyscraper ['skaɪskreɪpəʳ] *n* rascacielos *m inv*.

slab [slæb] *n (of stone)* losa *f*, *(of chocolate)* tableta *f*, *(of cake)* trozo *m*.

slack [slæk] **I** *adj* **1** *(not taut)* flojo,-a **2** *(lax, careless)* descuidado,-a, negligente, *(lazy)* perezoso,-a, vago,-a. **3** *(market)* flojo,-a; **the s. season**, la temporada baja, **business is s.**, hay poco trabajo **II** *n* **1** *(in rope)* parte *f* floja; **to take up the s.**, tensar una cuerda. **2** *Min* cisco *m* **III** *vi fam* gandulear, holgazanear

slacken ['slækən] **I** *vtr* **1** *(rope)* aflojar, *(reins)* soltar. **2** *(speed)* reducir, disminuir, *(one's pace)* reducir, aminorar. **II** *vi* **1** *(rope)* aflojarse, *(wind)* amainar. **2** *(trade)* aflojar, flaquear. ◆ **slacken off** *vi (speed, untensity)* reducirse, disminuirse.

slackcer ['slækəʳ] *n fam* gandul,-a *m,f*, holgazán,-ana *m,f*, vago,-a *m,f*

slackness ['slæknɪs] *n* **1** *(of rope)* flojedad *f*. **2** *(laxness, careless)* descuido *m*, negligencia *f*, *(laziness)* pereza *f*, gandulería *f*. **3** *(of trade)* inactividad *f*, estancamiento *m*

slacks [slæks] *npl dated (trousers)* pantalones *mpl*, pantalón *m*

slag [slæg] *n* **1** *Min* escoria *f*. ■ **s. heap**, escorial *m*. **2** *sl (woman)* puta *f*, fulana *f*. ◆ **slag off** *vtr (pt & pp slagged)* poner verde a, hablar mal de

slain [sleɪn] **I** *pp see* **slay. II the s.** *npl* los caídos.

slake [sleɪk] *vtr (one's thirst)* apagar, aplacar; **slaked lime**, cal *f* apagada *or* muerta

slalom ['slɑːləm] *n Sport* slalom *m*

slam [slæm] *n* **1** *(of lid etc)* golpe *m*; *(of door)* portazo *m*. **2** *Bridge* **slam** *m*; **grand s.**, gran slam. **II** *vtr (pt & pp slammed)* **1** *(bang)* cerrar de golpe, *Aut* **to s. on the brakes**, dar un frenazo; **to s. sth down on the table**, arrojar algo sobre la mesa, **to s. the door**, dar un portazo; **to s. the door in sb's face**, dar con la puerta en las narices de algn. **2** *fig (criticize, slate)* criticar duramente. **III** *vi (lid, door, etc)* cerrarse de golpe

slander ['slɑːndəʳ] **I** *n (smear)* difamación *f*; *Jur (defamation)* calumnia *f*. **II** *vtr* difamar; *Jur* calummar

slanderer ['slɑːndərəʳ] *n* difamador,-a *m, f*, *Jur* calumniador,-a *m,f*

slanderous ['slɑːndərəs] *adj* difamatorio,-a, *Jur* calumnioso,-a

slang [slæŋ] **I** *n* argot *m*, jerga *f*; **'fag' is s. for cigarette**, en argot 'pitillo' quiere decir cigarrillo. **II** *vtr* **insultar**, *fam* **slanging match**, intercambio *m* de insultos

slangy ['slæŋɪ] *adj (slangier, slangiest)* muy coloquial, con mucho argot

slant [slɑːnt] **I** *n* **1** *(gen)* inclinación *f*, *(slope)* pendiente *f*, declive *m*. **2** *fig (turn)* giro *m*, *(point of view)* punto *m* de vista. **II** *vtr* **1** *(gen)* inclinar. **2** *fig (problem etc)* enfocar subjectivamente. **III** *vi* inclinarse

slanting ['slɑːntɪŋ] *adj* inclinado,-a

slap ['slæp] **I** *n (gen)* palmada *f*, *(smack)* cachete *m*; *(in face)* bofetada *f*, bofetón *m*, *fig* desaire *m*; **s. on the wrist**, tirón *m* de orejas. **II** *adv fam* de lleno; **he ran s. into the fence**, dio de lleno contra la valla; **s. in the middle of ...**, justo en medio de .... **III** *vtr (pt & pp slapped) (gen)* pegar con la mano, *(hit in face)* abofetear, dar una bofetada a, **to s. sb on the back**, dar a algn una palmada en la espalda, **to s. sth down on the table**, arrojar algo sobre la mesa, *fam* **to s. paint on a wall**, dar un poco de pintura a la pared. ◆ **slap around** *vtr* pegar

slap-bang ['slæpbæŋ] *adv fam* **1** *(violently)* violentamente, con fuerza. **2** *(exactly)* justo, exactamente, **s.-b. in the middle**, justo en medio

slapdash [slæp'dæʃ] *adj fam (careless)* descuidado,-a, *(work)* chapucero,-a

slap-happy [slæp'hæpɪ] *adv fam (carefree)* despreocupado,-a

slapstick ['slæpstɪk] *n* bufonadas *fpl*, payasadas *fpl*

slap-up ['slæpʌp] *adj fam* **s.-up meal**, comilona *f*, banquete *m*

slash [slæʃ] **I** *n* **1** *(with sword)* tajo *m*, *(with knife)* cuchillada *f*, *(with razor)* navajazo *m*, *(with whip)* latigazo *m*. **2** *vulg* meada *f*, **to have** *or* **go for a s.**, mear. **3** *Typ fam* barra *f* oblicua. **II** *vtr* **1** *(with knife)* acuchillar; *(with sword etc)* dar un tajo a; *(with whip)* azotar. **2** *fig (prices, wages)* rebajar, reducir; *Com* **'prices slashed'**, 'precios de remate'

slat [slæt] *n* tablilla *f*, listón *m*

slate [sleɪt] **I** *n* **1** pizarra *f*. **s. quarry**, pizarral *m*; *fig* **to wipe the s. clean**, hacer borrón y cuenta nueva. **2** *GB fam* cuenta *f*. **II** *vtr* **1** *(roof)* empizarrar. **2** *GB fam fig (criticize)* criticar duramente

slaughter ['slɔːtəʳ] **I** n *(animals)* matanza f, *(people)* carnicería f, matanza f. **II** vtr *(animals)* matar, sacrificar, *(people)* matar brutalmente, *(in large numbers)* masacrar, exterminar; *fam fig (thrash, defeat)* dar una paliza a; **United got slaughtered,** le dieron una paliza al United

slaughterhouse ['slɔːtəhaʊs] n matadero m.

Slav [slɑːv] adj & n eslavo,-a *(m,f)*

slave [sleɪv] **I** n esclavo,-a m,f; *fig* **s. to fashion,** esclavo,-a de la moda ◆ *fam* **s. driver,** negrero,-a m,f, tirano,-a m,f, **s. labour,** US **s. labor,** *(work)* trabajo m de negros; *(people)* esclavos mpl, **s. trade,** trata f de esclavos. **II** vi *(slog)* **to s. (away) at sth,** trabajar como un negro en algo.

slaver ['slævəʳ] vi babear

slavery ['sleɪvərɪ] n esclavitud f.

slavish ['sleɪvɪʃ] adj *(servile)* esclavo,-a, servil; *fig* ciego,-a ◆ **slavishly** adv *(with obedience)* servilmente, *(blindly)* ciegamente

Slavonic [slə'vɒnɪk] adj eslavo,-a

slay [sleɪ] vtr *(pt* **slew,** *pp* **slain)** *Lit (kill)* matar, asesinar.

sleazy ['sliːzɪ] adj *(sleazier, sleaziest)* sórdido,-a

sled [sled] **I** n US trineo m. **II** vi ir en trineo

sledge [sledʒ] **I** n **1** GB trineo m. **2** *fam (tool)* almádana f. **II** vi ir en trineo

sledgehammer ['sledʒhæməʳ] n *(tool)* almádana f

sleek [sliːk] adj *(hair)* liso,-a, lustroso,-a; *(appearance)* impecable, elegante; *(manner)* meloso,-a.

sleep [sliːp] **I** n sueño m; **to have a short s.,** echar una siesta; *fig* **she didn't lose any s. over it,** no perdió el sueño por ello. **II** vtr *(pt & pp* **slept)** **1** *(gen)* dormir; **I haven't slept a wink all night,** no he pegado ojo en toda la noche; **to s. the hours away,** pasar las horas durmiendo. **2** *(accommodate)* caber en una vivienda; **the cottage sleeps six,** el chalet tiene camas para seis personas. **III** vi **1** *(gen)* dormir; **to get off to s.,** conciliar el sueño; **to go to s.,** dormirse; **to s. soundly,** dormir profundamente; *euph* **to put an animal to s.,** sacrificar un animal; *fig* **to send sb to s.,** hacer dormir a algn; *fig* **to s. on sth,** consultar algo con la almohada; *fam* **to drop off to s.,** quedarse dormido,-a; *fam* **to put a patient to s.,** dormir a un paciente; *fam* **to s. like a log** *or* **top,** dormir como un lirón *or* como un tronco; *fam* **to s. rough,** dormir al aire libre. **2** *(go numb)* entumecerse; *fam* **my foot has gone to s.,** se me ha dormido el pie. ◆ **sleep around** vi *fam* acostarse con cualquiera. ◆ **sleep in** vi GB *(oversleep)* quedarse dormido,-a, no levantarse a tiempo; *(have a lie-in)* quedarse en la cama. ◆ **sleep off** vtr dormir la s. it off, dormir la mona. ◆ **sleep out** vi dormir al aire libre; **it was so warm we decided to s. out,** hacía tan buen tiempo que decidimos dormir al raso. ◆ **sleep through** vtr **to s. through the alarm,** no oír el despertador. ◆ **sleep together** vi *(couple)* dormir juntos. ◆ **sleep with** vtr *fam* **to s. with sb,** acostarse con algn.

sleeper ['sliːpəʳ] n **1** *(person)* durmiente mf; **to be a heavy/light s.,** tener el sueño pesado/ligero. **2** GB Rail *(on track)* traviesa f. **3** Rail *(coach)* coche-cama m; *(berth)* litera f.

sleeping ['sliːpɪŋ] adj durmiente, dormido,-a. ■ **s. bag,** saco m de dormir; **S. Beauty,** la Bella durmiente; Rail **s. car,** coche-cama m; GB Com **s. partner,** socio,-a m,f comanditario,-a; ■ **s. pill,** somnífero m; **s. quarters,** dormitorio m; Med **s. sickness,** encefalitis f letárgica, enfermedad f del sueño.

sleepless ['sliːplɪs] adj **to have a s. night,** pasar la noche en blanco.

sleeplessness ['sliːplɪsnɪs] n insomnio m.

sleepwalker ['sliːpwɔːkəʳ] n sonámbulo,-a m,f.

sleepwalking ['sliːpwɔːkɪŋ] n sonambulismo m.

sleepy ['sliːpɪ] adj *(sleepier, sleepiest)* soñoliento,-a; **to be** *or* **feel s.,** tener sueño; **to make s.,** dar sueño; **it makes me s.,** me da sueño. ◆ **sleepily** adv soñolientamente; **'yes,' he replied s.,** 'sí,' contestó medio dormido.

sleepyhead ['sliːpɪhed] n *fam* dormilón,-ona m,f.

sleet [sliːt] **I** n aguanieve f, cellisca f. **II** vi **it's sleeting,** cae aguanieve.

sleeve [sliːv] n *(of garment)* manga f; *(of record)* funda f; *fig* **to have something up one's s.,** guardar una carta en la manga.

sleeveless ['sliːvlɪs] adj *(garment)* sin mangas.

sleigh [sleɪ] n trineo m. ■ **s. bell,** cascabel m.

sleight [slaɪt] n **s. of hand,** prestidigitación f, juego m de manos.

slender ['slendəʳ] adj **1** *(thin, slim) (person)* delgado,-a, esbelto,-a; *(wineglass)* delgado,-a, fino,-a. **2** *fig (slight, poor) (hope, chance)* ligero,-a; *(income)* escaso,-a; **by a s. majority,** por una escasa mayoría; **of s. means,** de recursos escasos.

slept [slept] pt & pp see **sleep.**

sleuth [sluːθ] n *arch fam* detective m, sabueso m.

slew [sluː] pt & pp see **slay.**

slice [slaɪs] **I** n **1** *(of bread)* rebanada f; *(of ham)* lonja f, loncha f; *(of beef etc)* tajada f; *(of salami, cucumber, lemon)* rodaja f; *(of melon)* raja f; *(of cake)* porción f, trozo m; *fig (of population etc)* parte f; *(proportion)* proporción f. **2** *(utensil)* pala f, paleta f. **II** vtr *(food)* cortar a rebanadas *or* tajos *or* rodajas; *(divide)* partir; **sliced bread,** pan de molde. **III** vi Sport dar efecto a la pelota. ◆ **slice off** vtr cortar. ◆ **slice through** vtr cortar, partir. ◆ **slice up** vtr cortar a rebanadas *or* tajos *or* rodajas.

slick [slɪk] **I** adj **1** *(programme, show)* ingenioso,-a, logrado,-a. **2** *(skilful)* hábil, mañoso,-a; **a s. answer,** una respuesta fácil. **3** *pej (glib)* despabilado,-a; **to be a s. operator,** ser un listillo *or* un tipo despabilado; **he's a very s. dresser,** siempre va hecho un maniquí. **II** n *(oil)* **s.,** marea f negra. ◆ **slick back, slick down** vtr alisar; **to s. back** *or* **down one's hair,** alisarse el pelo.

slicker ['slɪkəʳ] n *fam pej (city)* **s.,** tío,-a m,f, chulo,-a m,f.

slide [slaɪd] **I** n **1** *(act)* deslizamiento m, desliz m; *(slip)* resbalón m. **2** Fin *(drop)* baja f; **a s. in share prices,** una baja en las cotizaciones. **3** *(in playground)* tobogán m. **4** Phot diapositiva f. ■ **s. projector,** proyector m de diapositivas; **s. show,** exposición f de diapositivas. **5** *(of microscope)* platina f, portaobjetos m inv. **6** Math **s. rule,** regla f de cálculo. **7** Mus *(on instrument)* vara f, corredera f. **8** GB Hairdr pasador m. **II** vtr *(pt & pp* **slid)** deslizar; *(furniture)* correr. **III** vi *(gen)* deslizarse; *(slip)* resbalar; **to s. down a drainpipe,** deslizarse por un tubo de desagüe; *fig* **to let things s.,** no ocuparse de algo, abandonar algo a su suerte.

sliding ['slaɪdɪŋ] adj *(door, window)* corredizo,-a. ■ Fin **s. scale,** escala f móvil.

slight [slaɪt] **I** adj **1** *(small)* pequeño,-a, ligero,-a; **I haven't got the slightest idea,** no tengo la menor idea; **not in the slightest,** en absoluto; **to a s. extent,** hasta cierto punto; **to take offence at the slightest thing,** ofenderse por nada. **2** *(person, build) (small)* menudo,-a; *(slim)* delgado,-a; *(weak-looking)* delicado,-a. **3** *(trivial)* leve, insignificante; **a s. wound,** una herida leve. **II** n *(affront)* desaire m. **III** vtr **1** *(scorn)* despreciar, menospreciar. **2** *(snub, insult)* desairar, ofender, insultar. ◆ **slightly** adv **1** *(a little)* un poco, ligeramente, algo. **2** *(person)* **s. built,** *(small)* menudo,-a; *(slim)* delgado,-a.

slighting ['slaɪtɪŋ] adj **1** *(scornful)* despreciativo,-a, menospreciativo,-a. **2.** *(offensive)* ofensivo,-a.

slim [slɪm] **I** adj *(slimmer, slimmest)* **1** *(person, build)* delgado,-a; *(slender)* esbelto,-a. **2** *fig (resources, profits)* escaso,-a; *(hopes, chances)* remoto,-a; *(evidence)* insuficiente. **II** vi *(pt & pp* **slimmed)** adelgazar, hacer régimen. ◆ **slim down** vtr *fig* reducir.

slime [slaɪm] n *(mud etc)* lodo m, cieno m; *(of snail)* baba f.

slimmer ['slɪməʳ] n persona f a régimen.

slimming ['slɪmɪŋ] **I** adj *(diet, pills)* para adelgazar; *(food)* que no engorda. **II** n *(process)* adelgazamiento m.

slimy ['slaɪmɪ] *adj* (*slimier, slimiest*) **1** (*muddy*) lodoso,-a; (*snail*) baboso,-a; (*sticky*) viscoso,-a. **2** *fig* (*person*) falso,-a, zamalero,-a.

sling [slɪŋ] **I** *n* **1** (*catapult*) honda *f*; (*child's*) tirador *m*. **2** *Med* cabestrillo *m*. **II** *vtr* (*pt & pp* **slung**) **1** (*throw*) lanzar, arrojar, tirar; *fam* **to s. one's book**, largarse. **2** *fam* (*throw away*) botar, tirar ◆ **sling out** *vtr fam* echar, botar, tirar.

slink [slɪŋk] *vi* (*pt & pp* **slunk**) desplazarse siglosamente, **to s. away** *or* **off**, escabullirse

slinky ['slɪŋkɪ] *adj* (*slinkier, slinkiest*) *fam* **1** (*garment*) ceñido,-a, muy ajustado,-a al cuerpo **2** (*movement*) sensual, provocativo,-a

slip [slɪp] **I** *n* **1** (*slide*) resbalón *m*, (*fall*) caída *f*; (*trip*) traspiés *m inv*, tropezón *m*, paso *m* en falso, *fam fig* **to give sb the s.**, dar esquinazo a algn. **2** (*mistake*) error *m*, equivocación *f*, (*moral*) desliz *m*, **a s. of the pen** *or* **tongue**, un lapsus, *prov* **there's many a s. between cup and lip**, del dicho al hecho hay mucho trecho **3** (*underskirt*) combinación *f*; (*petticoat*) enaguas *fpl*. ■ (**pillow**) **s.**, funda *f*. **4** (*of paper*) papelito *m*, trocito *m* del papel. ■ **sales s.**, resguardo *m*. **5** *fam* menudencia *f*, **a s. of a boy/girl**, un chiquillo/una chiquilla. **II** *vi* (*pt & pp* **slipped**) **1** (*slide*) resbalar, *Aut* (*clutch*) patinar, **it slipped from his hand**, se le fue de la mano; **my foot slipped**, me resbaló el pie; *fig* **then everything slipped into place**, entonces todo quedó claro, *fig* **to let an opportunity s.**, dejar escapar una oportunidad. **2** *Med* dislocarse, **to have a slipped disc**, tener una vértebra dislocada. **3** (*move quickly*) ir de prisa, escabullirse, **to s. round to the baker's**, ir un momento a la panadería. **4** (*decline*) (*standards etc*) empeorar, *fam* **you're slipping**, estás perdiendo facultades. **III** *vtr* **1** (*slide*) pasar, dar a escondidas, *fam* **he slipped me a fiver**, me puso en la mano un billete de cinco libras. **2** (*miss*) escapar; *Knit* **to s. a stitch**, dejar escapar un punto. **3** (*overlook, forget*) pasar por alto, **it must have slipped his notice**, le habrá pasado desapercibido; **it slipped my memory**, se me fue de la memoria. **4** (*escape from*) soltar; **the dog slipped its leash**, el perro se soltó de la correa. ◆ **slip away** *vi* **1** (*time, years*) pasar volando. **2** (*person*) escabullirse. ◆ **slip by** *vi* (*time, years*) pasar volando. ◆ **slip off** *vtr* (*clothes*) quitarse rápidamente. ◆ **slip on** *vtr* (*clothes*) ponerse rápidamente. ◆ **slip out** *vi* **1** (*leave*) salir, escabullirse. **2** *fig* **the secret slipped out**, se le escapó el secreto. ◆ **slip up** *vi fam* (*make a mistake*) equivocarse; (*blunder*) cometer un desliz, meter la pata.

slipknot ['slɪpnɒt] *n* nudo *m* corredizo

slip-on ['slɪpɒn] *adj* (*shoes*) sin cordones

slipper ['slɪpər] *n* **1** (*shoe*) zapatilla *f*. **2** *Tech* (*of brake*) zapata *f*, patín *m*.

slippery ['slɪpərɪ] *adj* **1** (*surface*) resbaladizo,-a; (*viscous*) escurridizo,-a, *fig* **to be on a s. slope**, estar en un callejón sin salida. **2** *fig* (*person*) astuto,-a, que no es de fiar.

slip-road ['slɪprəʊd] *n GB* (*on motorway*) vía *f* de acceso

slipshod ['slɪpʃɒd] *adj* (*careless*) descuidado,-a, (*work*) chapucero,-a.

slipstream ['slɪpstriːm] *n* estela *f*

slip-up ['slɪpʌp] *n fam* (*mistake*) error *m*; (*blunder*) desliz *m*, metedura *f* de pata

slipway ['slɪpweɪ] *n Naut* grada *f*.

slit [slɪt] **I** *n* (*opening*) abertura *f*, hendidura *f*; (*cut*) corte *m*, raja *f*. **II** *vtr* (*pt & pp* **slit**) cortar, hender, rajar, **to s. open an envelope**, abrir un sobre.

slither ['slɪðər] *vi* (*snake etc*) deslizarse

slithery ['slɪðərɪ] *adj* (*surface*) resbaladizo,-a

sliver ['slɪvər] *n* (*of wood, glass*) astilla *f*; (*of ham*) loncha *f or* tajada *f* fina

slob [slɒb] *n fam* (*untidy person*) dejado,-a *m, f*, (*boor*) palurdo,-a *m, f*

slobber ['slɒbər] *vi* (*dribble*) babear, *fig* **to s. over sb**, hacerle la pamema a algn

sloe [sləʊ] *n Bot* **1** (*shrub*) endrino *m*. **2** (*fruit*) endrina *f*. ■ **s. gin**, ginebra *f* de endrinas

slog [slɒg] **I** *n fam* paliza *f*, **it was a hard s. back to base camp**, les costó un montón volver al campamento base. **II** *vi* (*pt & pp* **slogged**) **1** *fam* (*work*) currar, **to s. away**, trabajar como un negro, sudar tinta, **to s. away at sth**, trabajar con empeño en algo. **2** (*walk*) caminar *or* avanzar trabajosamente, **to s. up a hill**, subir una cuesta a duras penas. **III** *vtr* (*hit*) (*ball, opponent*) golpear fuerte

slogan ['sləʊgən] *n* slogan *m*, eslogan *m*, lema *m*

slogger ['slɒgər] *n fam* (*hard worker*) currante *mf*, trabajador,-a *m, f*

sloop [sluːp] *n Naut* balandro *m*

slop [slɒp] **I** *vi* (*pt & pp* **slopped**) **to s. (over)**, derramarse, verterse; **to s. about**, chapotear. **II** *vtr* derramar, verter. **III** *n* **1** **slops**, (*liquid food*) gachas *fpl*, aguachirle *m sing*; (*left-over food*) bazofia *f*, (*dirty water*) lavazas *fpl*, agua *f sing* sucia, (*dregs of tea*) posos *mpl* de té. **2** *Lit Cin* (*slush*) novela *f or* película *f* sentimentaloide

slope [sləʊp] **I** *n* (*incline*) cuesta *f*, pendiente *f*, (*up*) subida *f*, (*down*) bajada *f*, declive *m*, (*of mountain*) ladera *f*, falda *f*, vertiente *f*, (*of roof*) vertiente *f*, **steep s.**, cuesta empinada, **the southern slopes**, la vertiente sur. **II** *vi* inclinarse, **to s. up/down**, subir/bajar en pendiente, **the gardens s. down to the sea**, los jardines bajan hasta el mar. ◆ **slope off** *vi fam* largarse

sloping ['sləʊpɪŋ] *adj* (*ground*) en pendiente, inclinado,-a; (*roof, handwriting*) inclinado,-a, **s. shoulders**, hombros caídos

sloppy ['slɒpɪ] *adj* (*sloppier, sloppiest*) *fam* **1** (*careless*) descuidado,-a, (*slipshod*) chapucero,-a; (*appearance, dress*) desaliñado,-a, dejado,-a. **2** (*slushy*) empalagoso,-a, sentimentaloide. **3** (*loose*) (*garment*) muy ancho,-a, *fam* **s. joe**, jersey muy ancho. ◆ **sloppily** *adv* **1** (*carelessly*) de modo descuidado; **s. done**, hecho,-a a la ligera *or* a la buena de Dios, **s. dressed**, vestido,-a de cualquier manera. **2** (*slushy*) de modo empalagoso *or* sentimentaloide

slosh [slɒʃ] *vtr fam* (*splash*) echar; **to s. paint on a wall.**, dar pintura a una pared a brochazos. ◆ **slosh about** *vi* chapotear

sloshed [slɒʃt] *adj fam* borracho,-a, **to get s.**, pillar una trompa, coger una tajada

slot [slɒt] **I** *n* **1** (*for coin*) ranura *f*, (*groove*) muesca *f*, (*opening*) abertura *f*, rendija *f*. ■ **s. machine**, (*for gambling*) (máquina *f*) tragaperras *m inv*; (*vending machine*) distribuidor *m* automático, **s. meter**, contador *m*. **2** *fig* (*in timetable*) hueco *m*, *Rad TV* espacio *m*. **II** *vtr* (*pt & pp* **slotted**) (*place*) meter, colocar, (*put in*) introducir, **s. piece X into piece Y**, encaja la pieza X con la pieza Y, *fig* **to s. a new song into the programme**, incluir una nueva canción en el programa. **III** *vi* **to s. in** *or* **together**, encajar.

sloth [sləʊθ] *n* **1** *fml* (*laziness, idleness*) pereza *f*, indolencia *f*. **2** *Zool* (oso *m*) perezoso *m*

slothful ['sləʊθfʊl] *adj* (*indolent*) perezoso,-a

slouch [slaʊtʃ] **I** *vi* andar *or* sentarse con los hombros caídos, **don't s.!**, ¡ponte derecho!, **to s. in an armchair**, repantigarse en un sillón. **II** *n fam* vago,-a, **he's no s. when it comes to doing the housework**, no tienes que decirle dos veces que haga la limpieza

slovenly ['slʌvənlɪ] *adj* (*careless*) descuidado,-a, dejado,-a; (*scruffy*) desaliñado,-a, desaseado,-a; (*inefficient*) chapucero,-a.

slow [sləʊ] **I** *adj* **1** (*gen*) lento,-a; *Culin* **in a s. oven**, a fuego lento; *Cin* **in s. motion**, a cámara lenta, al ralentí; **it's s. going**, avanzamos muy lentamente; **s. recovery**, recuperación lenta; **to be s. to do sth**, tardar en hacer algo. **2** (*clock*) atrasado,-a; **my watch is 10 minutes s.**, mi reloj está retrasado 10 minutos. **3** (*performance etc*) aburrido,-a, pesado,-a. **4** (*person*) (*stupid*) lento,-a, torpe, corto,-a de alcances; **he's a s. learner**, le cuesta aprender; *fig* **he's a bit s. on the uptake** *or* **off the mark**, le cuesta entender las cosas, es un poco lento de reflejos. **II** *adv* despacio, lentamente; *Ind* **to go s.,** trabajar a ritmo lento, hacer una huelga de celo. **III** *vtr (car, machine)* reducir la marcha de; *(progress, production)* retrasar, retardar. **IV** *vi* **to s. down** *or* **up,** *(gen)* ir más despacio; *(in car)* reducir la velocidad; *(when walking)* aminorar el paso. ◆ **slowly** *adv* despacio, lentamente; **s. but surely,** lento pero seguro.

slowcoach ['sləʊkəʊtʃ] *n fam, US* **slowpoke** ['sləʊpəʊk] *n fam* tortuga *f*.

slowish ['sləʊɪʃ] *adj* algo lento,-a.

slowness ['sləʊnɪs] *n* **1** *(gen)* lentitud *f*. **2** *(stupidity)* torpeza *f*. **3** *(dullness)* pesadez *f*.

slow-witted [sləʊ'wɪtɪd] *adj* lento,-a, torpe, corto,-a de alcances.

slowworm ['sləʊwɜːm] *n Zool* lución *m*.

sludge [slʌdʒ] *n* **1** *(mud)* fango *m*, cieno *m*, lodo *m*; *(sediment)* sedimento *m*, residuos *mpl*. **2** *(sewage)* aguas *fpl* residuales.

slug [slʌg] **I** *n* **1** *Zool* babosa *f*. **2** *US fam (bullet)* posta *f*. **3** *fam (blow)* porrazo *m*. **4** *US fam (shot)* traguito *m*; **a s. of whisky,** un traguito de whisky. **II** *vtr (pt & pp slugged) fam (hit)* aporrear, pegar un porrazo a.

sluggish ['slʌgɪʃ] *adj* **1** *(slow-moving) (river, engine)* lento,-a; *Com (market, trade)* flojo,-a, inactivo,-a. **2** *(lazy)* perezoso,-a, holgazán,-ana; *Med (liver)* perezoso,-a.

sluggishness ['slʌgɪʃnɪs] *n* **1** *(slowness)* lentitud *f*; *Com* inactividad *f*. **2** *(laziness)* pereza *f*.

sluice [sluːs] **I** *n* *(waterway)* canal *m*; *(valve)* compuerta *f*. **II** *vtr* **to s. sth down,** lavar algo a chorro, regar algo.

sluicegate ['sluːsgeɪt] *n* esclusa *f*.

slum [slʌm] **I** *n* *(room, house)* chabola *f*. **2** **slums,** *(area)* barrios *mpl* bajos, barrio *m sing* de chabolas; **s. clearance programme,** programa para la erradicación del chabolismo. **II** *vi (pt & pp slummed) fam* **to s. (it),** vivir con muy poco dinero; *(in squalor)* vivir en la miseria.

slumber ['slʌmbəʳ] *Lit* **I** *n* *(sleep)* sueño *m*; *(deep sleep)* sopor *m*. ■ *US Canada* **s. party,** fiesta *f* nocturna de chicas. **II** *vi* dormir.

slummy ['slʌmi] *adj fam (run-down)* sórdido,-a.

slump [slʌmp] **I** *n* **1** *(drop in production, sales, etc)* baja *f* or caída *f* repentina, bajón *m*. **2** *(economic depression)* crisis *f* económica, depresión *f* económica; **the 1929 s.,** el crac de 1929; *fig* **there was a s. in staff morale,** se hundió la moral del personal. **II** *vi* **1** *(production, sales, demand)* bajar *or* caer de repente; *(prices)* desplomarse, hundirse; *(the economy)* hundirse; *fig (morale)* desplomarse. **2** *(fall into)* caer; **to s. into an armchair,** derrumbarse en un sillón; **he slumped to the floor,** se desplomó en el suelo, cayó desmayado al suelo; **she was slumped over the steering wheel,** su cuerpo yacía encima del volante.

slung [slʌŋ] *pt & pp see* **sling.**

slunk [slʌŋk] *pt & pp see* **slink.**

slur [slɜːʳ] **I** *n* **1** *(stigma)* mancha *f*; *(slanderous remark)* calumnia *f*, difamación *f*; *(insult)* afrenta *f*; **to cast a s. on sb's reputation,** manchar la reputación de algn. **2** *Mus (symbol)* ligado *m*. **II** *vtr (pt & pp slurred)* **1** *(word)* pronunciar mal, comerse, tragarse. **2** *Mus (note)* ligar.

slurp [slɜːp] **I** *vtr & vi fam (beer, soup, etc)* sorber *or* beber ruidosamente. **II** *n* *(drinking noise)* ruido que se hace al beber.

slush [slʌʃ] *n* **1** *(melting snow)* aguanieve *f*, nieve *f* derretida; *(mud)* lodo *m*, fango *m*. **2** *fam (over sentimental novel, film, etc)* sentimentalismo *m*, sensiblería *f*. **3** *US fam* **s. fund,** fondos *mpl* para sobornos.

slushy ['slʌʃi] *adj (slushier, slushiest)* **1** *(snow)* medio derretido,-a; *(muddy)* lodoso,-a, fangoso,-a. **2** *fam (novel, film, etc)* sentimentaloide, sensiblero,-a.

slut [slʌt] *n offens* **1** *(dirty, untidy woman)* marrana *f*, guarra *f*. **2** *(whore)* ramera *f*, fulana *f*.

sly [slaɪ] **I** *adj (slyer, slyest or slier, sliest)* **1** *(cunning)* astuto,-a, ladino,-a, taimado,-a. **2** *(secretive)* furtivo,-a. **3** *(mischievous)* travieso,-a. **4** *(underhand)* malicioso,-a; **he's a s. old devil,** es muy zorro. **II** *n* **to do sth on the s.,** hacer algo a hurtadillas *or* a escondidas. ◆ **slyly, slily** *adv* **1** *(cunningly)* con astucia, astutamente. **2** *(secretively)* furtivamente. **3** *(underhandedly)* con malicia, maliciosamente.

slyboots ['slaɪbuːts] *n inv fam* zorro,-a *m,f*.

smack¹ [smæk] **I** *n* **1** *(slap)* bofetada *f*, tortazo *m*, cachete *m*; **to give a child a s.,** dar una bofetada a un niño. **2** *(sharp sound)* ruido *m* sonoro. **II** *vtr* **1** *(kiss)* besazo *m*, a bofetear; **I'll s. your bottom!,** ¡te pegaré en el trasero! **2** *(hit)* golpear; *fig* **to s. one's lips,** relamerse. **III** *adv fam* directamente; **he ran s. into the wall,** dio de lleno contra la pared; **s. (bang) in the middle,** justo en medio.

smack² [smæk] *vi fig (be reminiscent of)* oler; **to s. of,** oler a.

smack³ [smæk] *n Naut* barca *f* de pesca.

smack⁴ [smæk] *n sl (drug)* heroína *f*, caballo *m*.

smacker ['smækəʳ] *n fam* **1** *(kiss)* besazo *m*, besuqueo *m*. **2** *GB (pound)* libra *f*; *US (dollar)* dólar *m*.

small [smɔːl] **I** *adj* **1** *(gen)* pequeño,-a, chico,-a; **a s. table,** una mesita; **a s. present,** un regalito; **very s.,** pequeñito,-a; **in s. letters,** en minúsculas; **in the s. hours,** a altas horas de la noche; **in a s. voice,** con la boca pequeña; **this skirt is too s.,** esta falda es pequeña; **to cut sth up s.,** cortar algo en trocitos; **to have a s. appetite,** no ser de mucho comer; *fig* **it's a s. world,** el mundo es un pañuelo; *fig* **it's s. wonder that ...,** no me sorprende nada que ... . ■ **s. ads,** pequeños anuncios *mpl*, anuncios *mpl* por palabras; **s. arms,** armas *fpl* portátiles; *fig* **s. print,** letra *f* pequeña; *fig* **s. screen,** pequeña pantalla *f*. **2** *(in height)* bajo,-a, pequeño,-a. **3** *(young)* joven, pequeño,-a. **4** *(scant)* escaso,-a; *(meal)* ligero,-a; *(sum)* pequeño,-a, modesto,-a. ■ **s. change,** cambio *m*, suelto *m*. **5** *(unimportant, minor)* sin importancia, insignificante; **s. businessmen,** pequeños comerciantes; *fig* **to feel** *or* **look s.,** sentirse humillado,-a. ■ *fig* **s. fry,** gente *f* de poca monta; **s. talk,** charla *f*, charloteo *m*. **6** *(increase, improvement)* ligero,-a, mínimo,-a. **II** *n* **1** **s. of the back,** región *f* lumbar. **2** **smalls,** *GB fam (underwear)* paños *mpl* menores, ropa *f sing* interior.

smallholder ['smɔːlhəʊldəʳ] *n* minifundista *mf*.

smallholding ['smɔːlhəʊldɪŋ] *n* parcela *f*, granja *f* pequeña, minifundio *m*.

smallish ['smɔːlɪʃ] *adj* más bien pequeño,-a.

small-minded [smɔːl'maɪndɪd] *adj (narrow-minded)* de miras estrechas; *(petty)* mezquino,-a.

smallness ['smɔːlnɪs] *n (size)* pequeñez *f*; *(scantiness)* escasez *f*.

smallpox ['smɔːlpɒks] *n Med* viruela *f*.

small-scale ['smɔːlskeɪl] *adj* en pequeña escala.

small-time ['smɔːltaɪm] *adj fam* de poca categoría *or* monta; **a s.-t. crook,** un delincuente menor.

small-town ['smɔːltaʊn] *adj* provinciano,-a, pueblerino,-a.

smarmy ['smɑːmi] *adj (smarmier, smarmiest) fam* zalamero,-a, cobista.

smart [smɑːt] *adj* **1** *(elegant)* elegante; *(chic)* fino,-a, de buen tono; **the s. set,** la gente bien; **how s. you look!,** ¡cuán elegante vas! **2** *(clever, bright)* listo,-a, inteligente; *(sharp)* listo,-a, espabilado,-a, despabilado,-a; **he thinks he's very s.,** se las da de listo; *fam* **s. alec(k),** listillo, sabelotodo. **3** *(quick) (action)* rápido,-a; *(pace)* ligero,-a; *fam* **look s. about it!,** ¡date prisa! **II** *vi* **1** *(sting) (eyes, graze)* picar, escocer; *(wound)* dar punzadas. **2** *fig* sufrir, dolerse; **he smarted from the injustice of her remarks,** la injusticia de sus comentarios le hirió en lo más vivo. ◆ **smartly** *adv* **1** *(elegantly)* elegantemente, con elegancia. **2** *(cleverly)* inteligentemente. **3** *(quickly)* rápidamente.

smarten ['smɑːtən] **I** *vtr* **to s. (up),** *(person, house)* arreglar; *fam* **to s. up one's ideas,** espabilarse. **II** *vi* **to s. oneself (up),** arreglarse.

smartness ['smɑːtnɪs] *n* **1** *(elegance)* elegancia *f*, buen tono *m*. **2** *(cleverness)* inteligencia *f*.

smarty-pants ['smɑːtɪpænts] *n inv fam* listillo *m*, sabelotodo *m*.

smash [smæʃ] **I** *n* **1** *(breaking)* rotura *f*; *(loud noise)* estrépito *m*, estruendo *m*; *Aut (collision)* choque *m* violento, colisión *f*. ■ *fig* **s. hit,** exitazo *m*. **2** *Fin* quiebra *f*. **3** *Ten* smash *m*, mate *m*. **II** *vtr* **1** *(break)* romper; *(shatter)* hacer pedazos *or* añicos; *(crush)* aplastar; *(car)* estrellar **(into,** contra). **2** *(ruin)* arruinar; *(destroy)* destrozar; *(defeat)* vencer a, derrotar a; **a drugs ring has been smashed,** se ha desarticulado una red de narcotraficantes. **3** *Sport (record)* batir, superar. **4** *Ten* hacer un mate; **to s. the ball,** dar un mate. **III** *vi* **1** *(break)* romperse; *(shatter)* hacerse pedazos *or* añicos; *(crash)* estrellar **(into,** contra). ◆ **smash down** *vtr (knock down)* tirar abajo, derribar. ◆ **smash in** *vtr (door)* forzar; *GB fam* **to s. sb's face in,** romperle *or* partirle la cara a algn. ◆ **smash up** *vtr fam (car)* hacer pedazos; *(place)* destrozar, destruir.

smash-and-grab [smæʃən'græb] *n* **s.-a.-g. raid,** robo *m* relámpago.

smashed [smæʃt] *adj fam (stoned, wrecked)* borracho,-a.

smasher ['smæʃər] *n fam* tío,-a *m,f* bueno,-a; **to be a s.,** estar como un tren.

smashing ['smæʃɪŋ] *adj fam* estupendo,-a, bárbaro,-a; **to have a s. time,** pasarlo bomba *or* fenomenal.

smash-up ['smæʃʌp] *n Aut (collision)* choque *m* violento, colisión *f*; *(accident)* accidente *m*.

smattering ['smætərɪŋ] *n* nociones *fpl*; **Brian had a s. of French,** Brian hablaba un poquito de francés.

smear [smɪər] **I** *n* **1** *(stain, smudge)* mancha *f*. ■ *Med* **s. (test),** frotis *f* del cuello del útero. **2** *fig (defamation)* calumnia *f*. ■ **s. campaign,** campaña *f* de difamación. **II** *vtr* **1** *(spread) (butter, ointment)* untar; *(grease, paint)* embadurnar. **2** *(make dirty)* manchar; *(writing, ink)* borrar. **3** *fig (defame)* calumniar, difamar. **III** *vi (ink, paint)* correrse.

smell [smel] **I** *n* **1** *(sense)* olfato *m*. **2** *(odour) m*; *(perfume)* perfume *m*, aroma *m*; **it has a funny s.,** huele raro; **there was a s. of burning,** olía a quemado. **3** *(action)* olfateo *m*; **have a s. of this flower,** huele esta flor. **II** *vtr (pt & pp* **smelled** *or* **smelt)** oler; *fig* olfatear; *fig* **I can s. a rat,** aquí hay gato encerrado; *fig* **to s. danger,** olfatear el peligro. **III** *vi* oler (a); *(stink)* apestar; **it smells good/bad/stuffy/like lavender,** huele bien/mal/a cerrado/a lavanda; **his breath smelt of whisky,** su aliento olía a whisky. ◆ **smell out** *vtr (dog etc)* husmear; *fam* apestar; **that cheese is smelling the house out,** aquel queso está apestando la casa.

smelling salts ['smelɪŋsɒlts] *npl* sales *fpl* aromáticas.

smelly ['smelɪ] *adj (smellier, smelliest) fam* maloliente, apestoso,-a; *(stinking)* hediondo,-a.

smelt¹ [smelt] *pt & pp see* **smell.**

smelt² [smelt] *vtr (ore)* fundir.

smelting ['smeltɪŋ] *adj* **s. works,** fundición *f*.

smile [smaɪl] **I** *n* sonrisa *f*; **he was all smiles,** no paraba de sonreír; **'hello,' she said with a s.,** 'hola,' dijo sonriente; **to give sb a s.,** sonreír a algn; **to wipe the s. off sb's face,** quitarle a algn las ganas de sonreír. **II** *vi* sonreír; **to s. at sb,** sonreír a algn; **to s. at sth,** reírse de algo; *fig* **fortune smiled on them,** la fortuna les sonrió; *fam* **keep smiling!,** ¡ánimo!

smiling ['smaɪlɪŋ] *adj* sonriente, risueño,-a.

smirk [smɜːk] **I** *n (conceited)* sonrisa *f* satisfecha; *(foolish)* sonrisa *f* boba. **II** *vi (conceitedly)* sonreír con satisfacción; *(foolishly)* sonreír bobamente.

smite [smaɪt] *vtr (pt* **smote;** *pp* **smitten)** *arch* **1** *(hit)* golpear, pegar. **2** *(punish)* castigar.

smith [smɪθ] *n* herrero *m*.

smithereens [smɪðə'riːnz] *npl fam* añicos *mpl*; **to smash sth to s.,** hacer algo añicos *or* trizas.

smithy ['smɪðɪ] *n (forge)* herrería *f*.

smitten ['smɪtən] **I** *pp see* **smite. II** *adj* **to be s., with flu,** estar aquejado,-a de gripe; **to be s. with fear,** estar lleno,-a de miedo; **to be s. with remorse,** remorderle a uno la conciencia; *fam (besotted)* **to be s. with sb,** estar enamorado,-a de algn.

smock [smɒk] *n (blouse)* camisa *f*, blusón *m*; *(worn in pregnancy)* blusón *m* de premamá; *(overall)* bata *f*, guardapolvo *m*.

smocking ['smɒkɪŋ] *n Sew (gen)* adorno *m* con frunces.

smog [smɒg] *n Meteor* niebla *f* tóxica, smog *m*.

smoke [sməʊk] **I** *n* **1** humo *m*; **to go up in s.,** quemarse, ser destruido,-a por un incendio; *fig* irse en humo, quedar en agua de borrajas; *prov* **there's no s. without fire,** cuando el río suena, agua lleva. ■ **s. bomb,** bomba *f* fumígena *or* de humo; **s. screen,** cortina *f* de humo; **s. signal,** señal *f* de humo. **2** *fam (cigarette)* cigarrillo *m*, cigarro *m*, pitillo *m*; *fam (gen)* tabaco *m*; **to have a s.,** fumarse un pitillo. **3** *sl* **the S.,** Londres. **II** *vi* **1** *(chimney, fire, etc)* humear, echar humo. **2** *(tobacco)* fumar; **do you s.?,** ¿fumas?; **do you mind if I s.?,** ¿le molesta que fume? **III** *vtr* **1** *(tobacco)* fumar; **to s. a pipe,** fumar en pipa. **2** *(fish, meat)* ahumar. ◆ **smoke out** *vtr (insects)* ahuyentar con humo; *(people)* desalojar con bombas fumígenas.

smoked [sməʊkt] *adj* ahumado,-a.

smokeless ['sməʊklɪs] *adj* sin humo; **s. fuel,** combustible sin humo; **s. zone,** zona libre de humos.

smoker ['sməʊkər] *n* **1** *(person)* fumador,-a *m,f*; **s.'s cough,** tos *f* de fumador; **to be a heavy s.,** fumar mucho, fumar como un carretero. **2** *Rail (carriage)* vagón *m* de fumadores.

smokestack ['sməʊkstæk] *n* chimenea *f*.

smoking ['sməʊkɪŋ] **I** *adj* humeante, que echa humo. **II** *n* fumar; **'no s.',** 'prohibido fumar'. ■ *Rail* **s. compartment,** *US* **s. car,** vagón *m* de fumadores; **s. jacket,** batín *m*.

smoky ['sməʊkɪ] *adj (smokier, smokiest)* **1** *(chimney, fire)* humeante, que echa humo; *(room)* lleno,-a de humo; *(atmosphere)* cargado,-a de humo; *(food)* ahumado,-a. **2** *(colour)* ahumado,-a; **s. blue,** azul ahumado.

smolder ['sməʊldər] *vi US see* **smoulder.**

smooch [smuːtʃ] *vi fam* **1** *(kiss, cuddle)* besuquearse. **2** *(dance)* bailar a lo agarrado.

smooth [smuːð] **I** *adj* **1** *(texture, surface)* liso,-a; *(skin)* suave; *(road)* llano,-a, uniforme; *(sea)* tranquilo,-a, en calma. **2** *(without lumps)* sin grumos. **3** *(beer, wine)* suave. **4** *(flowing)* fluido,-a. **5** *(troublefree) (journey, flight)* tranquilo,-a; *(take-off, landing)* suave; *(take-over, transition)* sin problemas. **6** *pej (slick, ingratiating)* zalamero,-a, meloso,-a; **he's a s. operator,** *(in business)* es un tipo muy hábil; *(in love)* es un ligón de profesión; **to be a s. talker,** tener un pico de oro. **II** *vtr* **1** *(hair)* alisar; *(surface)* alisar, igualar; *fig* **to s. the path** *or* **way for sb,** preparar el terreno para algn. **2** *(plane down)* limar. **3** *(polish)* pulir. ◆ **smooth away** *vtr (wrinkles)* quitar, hacer desaparecer; *fig (doubts, fears)* calmar. ◆ **smooth back** *vtr (hair)* alisar. ◆ **smooth down** *vtr (hair)* alisar; *(surface)* alisar, igualar. ◆ **smooth out** *vtr (creases)* alisar; *fig (difficulties)* allanar; *(problems)* resolver. ◆ **smooth over** *vtr fig* limar; **to s. things over,** limar asperezas. ◆ **smoothly** *adv* tranquilamente, correctamente; **everything is running s.,** todo va sobre ruedas.

smooth-running [smuːð'rʌnɪŋ] *adj (engine, machine)* suave; *(business, organization)* que funciona bien.

smoothie ['smuːðɪ] *n fam* tipo *m* zalamero, pelota *mf*.

smoothness ['smuːðnɪs] *n* **1** *(softness)* suavidad *f*; *(flatness)* llaneza *f*, lisura *f*, uniformidad *f*. **2** *(peacefulness)* tranquilidad *f*. **3** *(flattery etc)* zalamería *f*.

smooth-talking ['smu:ðɔ:kɪŋ] *adj* zalamero,-a.

smote [sməʊt] *pt see* **smite.**

smother ['smʌðəʳ] **I** *vtr* **1** *(asphyxiate)* asfixiar; *(suffocate)* sofocar. **2** *(cover)* cubrir **(with,** de); **to s. sb with kisses,** colmar a algn de besos. **II** *vi (asphyxiate)* asifixiarse, ahogarse.

smoulder ['sməʊldəʳ] *vi (fire)* arder sin llama; *fig (passions)* arder; **smouldering hatred,** odio latente.

smudge [smʌdʒ] **I** *n (stain)* mancha *f; (of ink)* borrón *m.* **II** *vtr* manchar; *(piece of writing)* emborronar. **III** *vi (ink, paint)* correrse.

smudgy ['smʌdʒɪ] *adj (smudgier, smudgiest) (stain)* manchado,-a; *(piece of writing)* emborronado,-a.

smug [smʌg] *adj (smugger, smuggest) (self-satisfied)* engreído,-a, satisfecho,-a. ◆ **smugly** *adv* con engreimiento.

smuggle ['smʌgəl] *vtr (goods)* pasar de contrabando; **to s. sth in/out,** pasar/sacar algo de contrabando; **to s. sth through customs,** pasar algo de contrabando por la aduana.

smuggler ['smʌgələʳ] *n* contrabandista *mf.*

smuggling ['smʌgəlɪŋ] *n* contrabando *m.*

smugness ['smʌgnɪs] *n* engreimiento *m.*

smut [smʌt] *n* **1** *(flake of soot)* hollín *m,* carbonilla *f; (stain)* mancha *f* de hollín, tizón *m.* **2** *fam (crude talk)* obscenidades *fpl; (dirty jokes)* chistes *mpl* verdes; *(pornography)* pornografía *f.*

smutty ['smʌtɪ] *adj (smuttier, smuttiest)* **1** *(dirty)* manchado,-a, sucio,-a; *(of smut)* tiznado,-a. **2** *fam (crude)* obsceno,-a; *(joke)* verde; *(book, film, etc)* pornográfico,-a.

snack [snæk] *n* bocado *m,* piscolabis *m,* tentempié *m,* refrigerio *m,* merienda *f.* ■ **cocktail s.,** tapa *f;* **s. bar,** cafetería *f,* bar *m.*

snag [snæg] **I** *n* **1** *(of tree)* tocón *m,* gancho *m; (of tooth)* raigón *m.* **2** *(pulled thread)* enganchón *m,* desgarrón *m,* rasgón *m,* siete *m.* **3** *(difficulty)* pega *f,* problema *m,* dificultad *f;* **that's the s.,** ahí esta la pega; **to come up against a s.,** encontrarse con una pega. **II** *vtr (pt & pp snagged) (catch clothing)* enganchar.

snail [sneɪl] *n Zool* caracol *m;* **at a s.'s pace,** a paso de tortuga.

snake [sneɪk] *n Zool (big)* serpiente *f; (small)* culebra *f; (game)* **snakes and ladders,** (el juego de) la oca; *fig* **a s. in the grass,** un traidor. ■ **s. charmer,** encantador,-a *m,f* de serpientes. **II** *vi fig* serpentear.

snakebite ['sneɪkbaɪt] *n* **1** mordedura *f* de serpiente. **2** *GB fam (cocktail)* cóctel *m* preparado con sidra y cerveza.

snakeskin ['sneɪkskɪn] *n* piel *f* de serpiente.

snaky ['sneɪkɪ] *adj (snakier, snakiest) (winding)* tortuoso,-a, sinuoso,-a.

snap [snæp] **I** *n* **1** *(sharp noise)* ruido *m* seco; *(of branch, fingers)* chasquido *m.* **2** *(bite)* mordisco *m.* **3** *Phot* (foto *f)* instantánea *f.* **4** *Cards* = guerra *f.* **II** *adj (sudden)* repentino,-a; *(unexpected)* inesperado,-a; **a s. decision,** una decisión instantánea. **III** *vtr (pt & pp snapped)* **1** *(break) (branch etc)* partir (en dos), romper. **2** *(make sharp noise)* hacer un ruido seco; **to s. one's fingers,** chasquear los dedos; **to s. sth shut,** cerrar algo de golpe; *fig* **to s. one's fingers at sb,** burlarse de algn. **3** *Phot* sacar una foto de. **IV** *vi* **1** *(break)* romperse. **2** *(whip)* chasquear; *(lid etc)* to s. shut, cerrarse de golpe. **3** *(dog)* amenazar; *fig* ladrar; **to s. at sb,** intentar morder a algn; *fam (person)* regañar a algn; **fam there's no need to s.!,** ¡no hace falta morder! **V** *GB interj (on seeing two identical things)* ¡toma! ◆ **snap off I** *vtr (branch etc)* separar; *fam* **to s. sb's head off,** echarle un rapapolvo a algn. **II** *vi (branch etc)* separarse, desprenderse. ◆ **snap out I** *vtr (order etc)* gritar, decir con brusquedad. **II** *vi fam* **s. out of it!,** *(forget it)* ¡olvídalo!; *(cheer up)* ¡anímate! ◆ **snap up** *vtr fam* **to s. up a bargain,** conseguir *or* llevarse una ganga.

snapdragon ['snæpdrægən] *n Bot* dragón *m.*

snappy ['snæpɪ] *adj (snappier, snappiest) fam* **1** *(quick)* rápido,-a; **look s.!, make it s.!,** ¡date prisa! **2** *(stylish)* elegante; **to be a s. dresser,** vestirse con elegancia. **3** *(short-tempered)* irritable, irascible.

snapshot ['snæpʃɒt] *n Phot* (foto *f)* instantánea *f.*

snare [sneəʳ] **I** *n (hunting)* lazo *m,* trampa *f,* cepo *m; fig* trampa *f.* **II** *vtr (animal)* coger con lazo, cazar con trampa; *fig (person)* hacer caer en la trampa, engañar.

snarl¹ [snɑ:l] **I** *n (growl)* gruñido *m.* **II** *vi (dog, person)* gruñir; **to s. at sb,** decirle algo a algn gruñendo.

snarl² [snɑ:l] **I** *n (in wool)* maraña *f,* enredo *m;* **traffic s.,** atasco *m,* embotellamiento *m.* **II** *vtr* **to s. (up),** *(wool)* enmarañar; *(traffic)* atascar; *(plans)* enredar. **III** *vi (traffic)* atascarse.

snarl-up ['snɑ:lʌp] *n (gen)* enredo *m,* maraña *f; (in traffic)* atasco *m.*

snatch [snætʃ] **I** *n* **1** *(grabbing)* arrebatamiento *m;* **to make a s. at sth,** intentar arrebatar *or* agarrar algo. **2** *fam (theft)* robo *m,* hurto *m.* ■ **bag s.,** tirón *m;* **wages s.,** robo *m* de la nómina de una empresa. **3** *(fragment)* trocito *m,* fragmentos *mpl.* **II** *vtr* **1** *(grab)* arrebatar; *fig* **to s. an opportunity,** aprovechar una ocasión; *fig* **to s. a meal,** comer sobre la marcha; *fig* **to s. same sleep,** echar una cabecita. **2** *fam (steal) (kidnap)* secuestrar. **III** *vi* **don't s.!,** ¡no me lo quites así!; **to s. at sth,** intentar agarrar algo. ◆ **snatch out** *vtr* agarrar rápidamente.

snazzy ['snæzɪ] *adj (snazzier, snazziest) fam (trendy, stylish)* elegante; *(flashy)* vistoso,-a, llamativo,-a.

sneak [sni:k] **I** *n fam (split)* chivato,-a *m,f,* soplón,-ona *m,f.* ■ **s. preview,** estreno *m* preliminar; **s. thief,** ladronzuelo,-a *m,f,* ratero,-a *m,f.* **II** *vtr* sacar; **to s. sth out of a place,** sacar algo de un lugar a escondidas; **to s. a look at sth,** mirar algo furtivamente *or* de reojo. **III** *vi* **1** *(gen)* moverse, ir; **to s. about,** moverse sigilosamente; **to s. away** *or* **off,** escabullirse; **to s. in/out,** entrar/salir a hurtadillas; **to s. off with sth,** llevarse algo furtivamente; **to s. past sb,** pasar desapercibido,-a delante de algn; **to s. up on sb,** sorprender a algn. **2** *(tell tales)* chivarse; **to s. on sb,** chivarse de algn, denunciar a algn.

sneakers ['sni:kəz] *npl US* zapatos *mpl* de lona, zapatillas *fpl* de tenis *or* de deporte, playeras *fpl.*

sneaking ['sni:kɪŋ] *adj* **1** *(secret)* secreto,-a; **I have a s. admiration for him,** en el fondo le admiro. **2** *(slight)* ligero,-a; **to have a s. feeling that ...,** tener la sensación de que ... .

sneaky ['sni:kɪ] *adj (sneakier, sneakiest) (sly)* solapado,-a; *(splitter)* soplón,-ona.

sneer [snɪəʳ] **I** *n* **1** *(expression)* cara *f* de desprecio; *(smirk)* risa *f* burlona. **2** *(remark)* comentario *m* desdeñoso *or* sarcástico. **II** *vi* **to s. at sth/sb,** *(mock)* burlarse *or* mofarse de algo/algn; *(scorn)* desdeñar *or* despreciar algo a algn.

sneering ['snɪərɪŋ] *adj (mocking)* burlón,-ona; *(scornful)* desdeñoso,-a, despreciativo,-a; *(sarcastic)* sarcástico,-a, socarrón,-ona.

sneeze [sni:z] **I** *n* estornudo *m.* **II** *vi* estornudar; *fam fig* **it's not to be sneezed at,** no es de despreciar.

snide [snaɪd] *adj fam (trick etc)* bajo,-a, vil; *(remark)* sarcástico,-a.

sniff [snɪf] **I** *n* **1** *(act of inhaling)* aspiración *f,* inhalación *f; (by dog)* husmeo *m,* olfateo *m.* **2** *(amount sniffed)* cantidad *f* inhalada. **3** *(faint smell)* olorcito *m.* **II** *vtr (flower etc)* oler; *(suspiciously)* husmear, olfatear; *(snuff, smelling salts)* aspirar, inhalar; *(glue)* esnifar. **III** *vi* aspirar por la nariz, sorber; **to. s. at sth,** *(person)* oler algo; *(dog)* husmear *or* olfatear algo; *GB fam fig* **it's not to be sniffed at,** no es de despreciar. ◆ **sniff out** *vtr fig (secret, plot)* descubrir husmeando.

sniffer dog ['snɪfədɒg] *n* perro *m* antidroga.

sniffle ['snɪfəl] **I** *n* resfriado *m;* **to have the sniffles,** estar resfriado,-a. **II** *vi (due to head cold)* sorberse los mocos; *(on weeping)* lloriquear, gimotear.

snifter ['snɪftə^r] n 1 fam copa f, trago m; **to have a s.,** echarse un trago. 2 US (brandy glass) copa f de coñac.

snigger ['snɪgə^r] I n (snicker) risa f disimulada, risilla f. II vi reír disimuladamente; **to s. at sth,** burlarse or mofarse de algo.

sniggering ['snɪgərɪŋ] n risas fpl disimuladas, risillas fpl.

snip [snɪp] I n 1 (cut) tijeretada f, tijeretazo m; (action, noise) tijereteo m; (small piece) recorte m. 2 GB fam (bargain) ganga f, chollo m; **we got the car for a s.,** el coche nos salió tirado de precio. II vtr (pt & pp snipped) tijeretear; **to s. sth off,** cortar algo con tijeras.

snipe [snaɪp] I n Orn agachadiza f. II vi 1 (sneer, dig) criticar. 2 (shoot at) disparar (at, sobre); **to s. at sb,** disparar sobre algn desde un escondite.

sniper ['snaɪpə^r] n Mil francotirador,-a m,f.

snippet ['snɪpɪt] n (of cloth, paper) trocito m, recorte m; (of conversation, information) fragmento m; **snippets of news,** noticias fpl breves.

snitch [snɪtʃ] vtr fam 1 (steal) birlar, afanar. 2 (tell tales) **to s. on sb,** chivarse de algn, delatar a algn.

snivel ['snɪvəl] vi (pt & pp snivelled) lloriquear.

snivelling ['snɪvəlɪŋ] I adj llorón,-ona. II n lloriqueo m.

snob [snɒb] n esnob mf, snob mf.

snobbery ['snɒbərɪ] n esnobismo m, snobismo m.

snobbish ['snɒbɪʃ] adj esnob, snob.

snobby ['snɒbɪ] adj (snobbier, snobbiest) esnob, snob.

snog [snɒg] fam I vi (pt & pp snogged) besuquearse. II n besuqueo m; **to have a s.,** besuquearse.

snooker ['snu:kə^r] I n snooker m, billar m ruso. II vtr GB fam poner en aprietos; **to be snookered,** estar con el agua al cuello.

snoop [snu:p] I n (nosey person) fisgón,-ona m, f; (meddler) entrometido,-a m, f; **to have a s. around,** fisgar, fisgonear. II vi fisgar, fisgonear; (meddle) entrometerse.

snooper ['snu:pə^r] n (nosy person) fisgón,-ona m, f; (meddler) entrometido,-a m,f.

snooty ['snu:tɪ] adj (snootier, snootiest) fam altivo,-a, presumido,-a, esnob, snob.

snooze [snu:z] I n fam cabezada f, siesta f; **to have a s.,** echar una cabezada or una siestecilla. II vi dormitar, echar una cabezada.

snore [snɔ:^r] I n ronquido m. II vi roncar.

snoring ['snɔ:rɪŋ] n ronquidos mpl.

snorkel ['snɔ:kəl] I n (of swimmer) tubo m de respiración; (of submarine) esnórquel m. II vi (pt & pp snorkelled, US snorkeled) bucear con tubo de respiración.

snorkelling, US **snorkeling** ['snɔ:kəlɪŋ] n **to go s.,** bucear con tubo de respiración.

snort [snɔ:t] I n (horse) resoplido m; (person) resoplido m, bufido m. II vi (horse) resoplar; (person) (with rage etc) resoplar, bufar.

snorter ['snɔ:tə^r] n fam (drink) trago m, copa f, chupito m; fig **a s. of a problem,** un problema de órdago.

snot [snɒt] n fam mocos mpl.

snotty ['snɒtɪ] adj (snottier, snottiest) fam 1 (nose) mocoso,-a. 2 (snooty) altivo,-a, presumido,-a, esnob, snob.

snout [snaʊt] n 1 (animal) morro m, hocico m; fam fig (person's nose) morro m, napias fpl. 2 (gun, bottle, etc) morro m.

snow [snəʊ] I n 1 Meteor nieve f. ■ **s. line,** límite m de las nieves perpetuas; **s. report,** informe m sobre el estado de la nieve; **s. shower,** nevada f. 2 (on TV screen) nieve f, lluvia f. 3 sl (cocaine) cocaína f, nieve f. II vi nevar; **it's snowing,** está nevando. III vtr **to be snowed in** or **up,** quedar aislado,-a or bloqueado,-a por la nieve; fig **to be snowed under with work,** estar agobiado,-a de trabajo.

snowball ['snəʊbɔ:l] I n bola f de nieve. II vi fig aumentar rápidamente.

snow-blind ['snəʊblaɪnd] adj cegado,-a por la nieve.

snow-blindness ['snəʊblaɪndnɪs] n ceguera f de la nieve.

snowbound ['snəʊbaʊnd] adj aislado,-a or bloqueado,-a por la nieve.

snow-covered ['snəʊkʌvəd] adj cubierto,-a de nieve, nevado,-a.

snowdrift ['snəʊdrɪft] n ventisquero m.

snowdrop ['snəʊdrɒp] n Bot campanilla f de invierno.

snowfall ['snəʊfɔ:l] n nevada f.

snowflake ['snəʊfleɪk] n copo m de nieve.

snowman ['snəʊmæn] n (pl snowmen ['snəʊmen]) figura f or muñeco m de nieve; **the abominable s.,** el abominable hombre de las nieves.

snowmobile ['snəʊməbi:l] n moto f para la nieve.

snowplough, US **snowplow** ['snəʊplaʊ] n quitanieves m inv.

snowshoe ['snəʊʃu:] n raqueta f (de nieve).

snowstorm ['snəʊstɔ:m] n (blizzard) nevasca f, ventisca f, tormenta f de nieve.

snowsuit ['snəʊsu:t] n traje m de esquiar.

Snow White [snəʊ'waɪt] n Blancanieves f.

snow-white ['snəʊ'waɪt] adj blanco,-a como la nieve, níveo,-a.

snowy ['snəʊɪ] adj (snowier, snowiest) 1 (mountain) nevado,-a; (region, climate) de mucha nieve, nevoso,-a; (day) de nieve; (season) de nieves; **it was very s. yesterday,** ayer nevó mucho. 2 (white) blanco,-a como la nieve, níveo,-a.

Snr, snr esp US abbr of **senior.**

snub [snʌb] I n (of person) desaire m; (of offer) rechazo m. II vtr (pt & pp snubbed) (person) desairar; (offer) rechazar; **to be snubbed,** sufrir un desaire. III adj respingón,-ona; **s. nose,** nariz chata or respingona.

snub-nosed ['snʌbnəʊzd] adj de nariz chata or respingona.

snuff¹ [snʌf] n rapé m; **a pinch of s.,** un pellizco de rapé; **to take s.,** tomar rapé.

snuff² [snʌf] vtr apagar; GB fam **to s. it,** estirar la pata, liar el petate. ◆ **snuff out** vtr (rebellion) sofocar.

snuffbox ['snʌfbɒks] n caja f de rapé, tabaquera f.

snuffle ['snʌfəl] I n cajaro m; **to have the snuffles,** estar resfriado,-a or acatarrado,-a. II vi (due to head cold) sorberse los mocos; (when weeping) gimotear.

snug [snʌg] I adj (snugger, snuggest) 1 (cosy) cómodo,-a; (cosy and warm) calentito,-a. 2 (tight-fitting) ajustado,-a, ceñido,-a. II n GB (in pub) saloncito m. ◆ **snugly** adv cómodamente; **to fit s.,** (clothes) quedar ajustado,-a; (object in box etc) caber perfectamente, encajar.

snuggle ['snʌgəl] vi **to s. down** or **up in bed,** acurrucarse en la cama; **to s. up to sb,** arrimarse a algn.

so [səʊ] I adv 1 (to such an extent) tanto; **he was so tired that ...,** estaba tan cansado que ...; **it's so long since ...,** hace tanto tiempo que ...; **please be so kind as to ...,** tenga la bondad de ...; **she isn't so clever as her sister,** no es tan lista como su hermana; **I'm so long!,** ¡hasta luego!, ¡hasta pronto! 2 (degree) tanto; **a week or so,** una semana más o menos; **he earns so much per hour,** gana tanto por hora; **I haven't so much as a farthing,** no tengo ni un real; **so many books,** tantos libros; **so much money,** tanto dinero; **twenty or so,** una veintena; **we didn't get so much as a reply,** ni siquiera nos contestaron; **we loved her so (much),** la queríamos tanto; fam **he's ever so handsome,** ¡es tan guapo!; fam **what's so funny?,** ¿qué pasa?, ¿de qué te ríes?; iron **so much for his promises then!,** ¡eso valen sus promesas!; iron **so much for that,** ¿qué le vamos a hacer? 3 (thus, in this way) así, de esta manera, de este modo; **and so on, and so forth,** y así sucesivamente, etcétera; **he is right and so are you,** él tiene razón y tú también; **how so?,** ¿cómo es eso?; **if so,**

en este caso, de ser así; **I'm afraid so,** me temo que sí; **I suppose so,** me imagino que sí; **I think/hope so,** creo/ espero que sí; **I told you so,** ya te lo dije; **it so happens that ...,** da la casualidad de que ...; **press the button so,** aprieta el botón así; **she likes everything to be just so,** le gusta tener todo en orden; **so be it!,** ¡así sea!; **so for,** hasta aquí *or* allí *or* ahora; **so far as I know,** que yo sepa; **so it is!,** ¡así es!; **so it seems,** según parece; **so they say,** según dicen; **stand just so,** ponte así; **you're late! —so I am!** ¡llegas tarde! — ¡tienes razón! **II** *conj* **1** *(expresses result)* así que, por lo tanto; **so you like England, do you?,** ¿así que te gusta Inglaterra, pues?; **the child was feverish, so she called the doctor,** el niño tenía fiebre, así que llamó al médico; *fam* **so what?,** ¿y qué? **2** *(expresses purpose)* para que; **he left his job so (that) he could concentrate on his studies,** dejó el trabajo para dedicarse plenamente a los estudios; **I'll put the key here so (that) everyone can see it,** pongo la llave aquí para que todos la vean; **they left early so as to arrive on time/so as not to miss the meeting,** se marcharon antes para llegar a tiempo/ para no perderse la reunión.

so-and-so ['səʊənsəʊ] *n fam* fulano,-a *m,f;* **Mr So-a.-so,** Don Fulano (de tal); *pej* **an old so-a.-so,** un viejo imbécil, un tío cabrón.

so-called ['səʊkɔ:ld] *adj* supuesto,-a, llamado,-a; **all these so-c. experts,** estos así llamados expertos.

soak [səʊk] **I** *vtr (washing, food)* poner en remojo, remojar; *(cotton, wool)* empapar **(in,** en), mojar **(in,** en). **II** *vi (washing, food)* estar en remojo; **to leave sth to s.,** dejar algo en remojo; **to s. through,** penetrar. **III** *n fam (drunkard)* **an old s.,** un borracho perdido. ◆ **soak in** *vtr & vi* penetrar; *fig* **it hasn't soaked in yet,** todavía no lo creo. ◆ **soak up** *vtr* absorber.

soaked [səʊkt] *adj* **1** *(person)* empapado,-a, calado,-a; **s. to the skin,** calado,-a hasta los huesos; **we got s.,** nos quedamos empapados. **2** *(food)* macerado,-a; **a cake s. in sherry,** un pastel emborrachado con jerez.

soaking ['səʊkɪŋ] **I** *n* remojo *m;* **to give sth a s.,** poner algo en remojo; **to get a s.,** empaparse. **II** *adj (object)* completamente mojado,-a; *(person)* empapado,-a, calado,-a hasta los huesos.

soap [səʊp] **I** *n* **1** jabón *m.* ■ **bar of s.,** pastilla *f* de jabón; **s. dish,** jabonera *f;* **s. falkes,** jabón *m* en escamas; **s. powder,** jabón *m* en polvo. **2 s. opera,** *TV* telenovela *f; Rad* radionovela *f.* **II** *vtr* enjabonar, jabonar.

soapbox ['səʊpbɒks] *n* tribuna *f* improvisada.

soapsuds ['səʊpsʌdz] *npl* jabonaduras *fpl,* espuma *f sing.*

soapy ['səʊpɪ] *adj (soapier, soapiest) (water)* jabonoso,-a; *(hands)* cubierto,-a de jabón; *(taste, smell)* jabonoso,-a, parecido,-a al jabón.

soar [sɔːr] *vi* **1** *(bird, plane)* remontar el vuelo; *(hover, glide)* planear. **2** *fig (skyscraper)* elevarse, encumbrarse; *(hopes, prices)* aumentar, crecer; *(music)* subir.

soaring ['sɔːrɪŋ] *adj* **1** *(bird, plane)* que planea. **2** *fig (skyscraper)* altísimo,-a; *(prices)* en alza; *(hopes, prices)* en aumento.

sob [sɒb] **I** *n* sollozo *m; fam iron* **s. story,** tragedia, drama. **II** *vi (pt & pp sobbed)* sollozar; *fig* **to s. one's heart out,** llorar a lágrima viva.

sobbing ['sɒbɪŋ] *n* sollozos *mpl.*

sober ['səʊbər] *adj* **1** *(not drunk)* sobrio,-a. **2** *(moderate)* moderado,-a sobrio,-a. **3** *(sensible)* sensato,-a; *(serious)* serio,-a. **4** *(colour)* discreto,-a. ◆ **sober up** *vi* pasarse la borrachera, despejarse. **II** *vtr* hacer que le pase la borrachera, despejar. ◆ **soberly** *adv* con moderación; con sobriedad.

sober-minded [səʊbə'maɪndɪd] *adj* sensato,-a.

sobering ['səʊbərɪŋ] *adj* moderador,-a; **it had a s. effect on him,** lo hizo entrar en razón, le dio que pensar.

sobriety [səʊ'braɪətɪ] *n fml* **1** *(being sober)* sobriedad *f.* **2** *(moderation)* moderación *f.* **3** *(good sense)* sensatez *f;* *(seriousness)* seriedad *f.*

Soc [sɒk] *abbr of* **society** sociedad *f,* S.

soccer ['sɒkər] *n* fútbol *m.* ■ **s. match,** partido *m* de fútbol; **s. player,** futbolista *mf,* jugador,-a *m,f* de fútbol.

sociable ['səʊʃəbəl] *adj (gregarious)* sociable, tratable; *(friendly)* amistoso,-a, simpático,-a.

social ['səʊʃəl] **I** *adj* **1** *(gen)* social; **to have a good s. life,** hacer buena vida social. ■ **s. class,** clase *f* social; **s. climber,** arribista *mf; Journ* **s. column,** ecos *mpl* de sociedad; *Pol* **S. Democrat,** socialdemócrata *mf; Pol* **S. Democratic,** socialdemócrata; *US* **s. insurance,** seguro *m* social; **s. outcast,** marginado,-a *m,f;* **s. sciences,** ciencias *fpl* sociales; **s. security,** seguro *m or* seguridad *f* social; **the s. services,** los servicios sociales; **s. welfare,** asistencia *f* social; **s. work,** asistencia *f or* trabajo *m* social; **s. worker,** asistente,-a *m,f* social, trabajador,-a *m,f* social. **2** *(gregarious)* sociable. **II** *n (do)* acto *m* social, reunion *f.* ◆ **socially** *adv* socialmente; **s. deprived,** marginado,-a; **we don't see each other s.,** no hacemos vida social en común.

socialist ['səʊʃəlɪst] *adj & n Pol* socialista *(mf).*

socialistic [səʊʃə'lɪstɪk] *adj Pol* socialista.

socialite ['səʊʃəlaɪt] *n* vividor,-a *m,f,* mundano,-a *m,f.*

socialization [səʊʃəlaɪ'zeɪʃən] *n* socialización *f.*

socialize ['səʊʃəlaɪz] **I** *vi (at party etc)* circular, alternar, mezclarse con la gente; **he's good at socializing,** tiene mucho don de gentes. **II** *vtr* socializar.

society [sə'saɪətɪ] **I** *n* **1** *(social community)* sociedad *f;* **the consumer s.,** la sociedad de consumo; **to be a danger to s.,** ser un peligro para la sociedad. **2** *(upper social circle)* **(high) s.,** la alta sociedad. **3** *(organization, club)* sociedad *f,* asociación *f.* ■ **building s.,** ≈ banco *m* hipotecario; **film s.,** club *m* de cine, cineclub *m.* **4** *(company, companionship)* compañía *f.* **II** *adj* de sociedad. ■ **s. column,** ecos *mpl* de sociedad; **s. wedding,** boda *f* de sociedad.

socio- ['səʊsɪəʊ, 'səʊʃɪəʊ] *pref* socio-; **sociobiology,** sociobiología *f.*

socioeconomic [səʊsɪəʊiːkə'nɒmɪk] *adj* socioeconómico,-a.

sociological [səʊsɪə'lɒdʒɪkəl] *adj* sociológico,-a.

sociologist [səʊsɪ'ɒlədʒɪst] *n* sociólogo,-a *m,f.*

sociology [səʊsɪ'ɒlədʒɪ] *n* sociología *f.*

sociopolitical [səʊsɪəʊpə'lɪtɪkəl] *adj* sociopolítico,-a.

sock[1] [sɒk] *n* calcetín *m; GB fam* **put a s. in it!,** ¡cierra el pico!; *GB fam fig* **to pull one's socks up,** hacer un esfuerzo.

sock[2] [sɒk] *fam* **I** *n (blow)* puñetazo *m,* tortazo *m.* **II** *vtr* pegar, zurrar; **she socked him one,** le pegó un tortazo; *fam fig* **s. it to them!,** ¡a por ellos!, ¡dales caña!

socket ['sɒkɪt] *n* **1** *(of eye)* cuenca *f; (of joint)* glena *f.* **2** *Elec (power point)* enchufe *m,* toma *f* de corriente. **3** *Tech* **s. wrench,** llave *f* de tubo.

sod[1] [sɒd] *n fml (piece of turf)* tepe *m,* terrón *m; fam* **the old s.,** su tierra natal, el terruño.

sod[2] [sɒd] *offens* **I** *n* **1** *(bastard)* cabrón,-ona *m,f;* **the lazy s.!,** ¡qué tío más vago! **2** *vulg (wretch)* desgraciado,-a *m,f;* **the poor s. has got no family,** el pobre no tiene familia. **3** *vulg (nothing)* ni leches; **I've done s. all today,** hoy no he pegado ni golpe. **4** *fam (pain, fag)* rollo *m,* putada *f,* coñazo *m.* **II** *vtr vulg* **s. it!,** ¡maldito sea!; **s. the TV and listen to me,** ¡a la mierda tele, escúchame!

soda ['səʊdə] *n* **1** *Chem* sosa *f;* **baking s.,** bicarbonato *m* sódico *or* de sosa; **causic s.,** sosa cáustica. **2** *(drink)* **s. water,** soda *f,* sifón *m;* **a whisky and s.,** un whisky con sifón *or* soda. ■ **s. syphon,** sifón *m.* **3** *US (sweet fizzy drink)* gaseosa *f.*

sodden ['sɒdən] *adj* empapado,-a.

sodding ['sɒdɪŋ] *adj vulg* maldito,-a, puñetero,-a.

sodium ['səʊdɪəm] *n Chem* sodio *m.* ■ **s. bicarbonate,** bicarbonato *m* sódico *or* de sosa.

sodomy ['sɒdəmɪ] n sodomía f.

sofa ['səʊfə] n sofá m; **s. bed,** sofá cama.

soft [sɒft] adj 1 (not hard) blando,-a; (spongy) esponjoso,-a; (bed) mullido,-a; (flabby) fofo,-a. ■ **s. currency,** moneda f débil; **s. furnishings,** tejidos mpl para cortinas, fundas fpl de sofá; **s. goods,** tejidos mpl; **s. toy,** muñeco m or animal m de peluche. 2 (smooth) (skin, colour, etc) suave; (hair) suave, liso,-a. 3 (not harsh) (light, music, etc) suave; (breeze, steps) ligero,-a. ■ **s. focus,** difuminado m; Mus **s. pedal,** sordina f. 4 (weak) débil; (lenient) poco severo,-a. ■ **s. sell,** venta f basada en la persuasión. 5 (consonant, sound) suave; (voice) bajo,-a. ■ **s. palate,** velo m del paladar. 6 (foolish) tonto,-a, lelo,-a; **to be a s. touch,** ser fácil de engañar; **to be s. in the head,** ser tonto,-a del culo. 7 (sentimental) sensiblero,-a, sentimentaloide; **to have a s. spot for sb,** tener debilidad por algn. 8 (easy) (life etc) fácil. ■ **s. drinks,** refrescos mpl. 9 (drink) no alcohólico,-a. ■ **s. drinks,** refrescos mpl. 10 (less harmful) blando,-a. ■ **s. drugs,** drogas fpl blandas; **s. porn,** pornografía f blanda. ◆ **softly** adv (gently) suavemente; (quietly) silenciosamente, suavemente; **to tread s.,** pisar con cuidado.

soft-boiled ['sɒftbɔɪld] adj (egg) pasado,-a por agua.

soften ['sɒfən] I vtr (leather, heart) ablandar; (skin) suavizar; (light) atenuar; (voice) bajar; fig (blow) amortiguar. II vi (leather, heart) ablandarse; (skin) suavizarse; (light) atenuarse. ◆ **soften up** vtr fam (person) ablandar.

softener ['sɒfənəʳ] n (for water) suavizador m. ■ **fabric s.,** suavizante m.

soft-hearted [sɒft'hɑːtɪd] adj tierno,-a, compasivo,-a, bondadoso,-a.

softie ['sɒftɪ] n fam blandengue mf.

softly-softly [sɒftlɪ'sɒftlɪ] adj (manner, approach) cauteloso,-a.

softness ['sɒftnɪs] n 1 (gen) blandura f. 2 (of hair, colours) suavidad f. 3 (weakness) debilidad f. 4 (foolishness) estupidez f.

soft-pedal [sɒft'pedəl] vtr (pt & pp soft-pedalled) US fig minimizar la importancia de.

soft-soap [sɒft'səʊp] vtr fam dar jabón a, dar coba a.

soft-spoken [sɒft'spəʊkən] adj de voz dulce or baja.

software ['sɒftweəʳ] n Comput software m.

softy ['sɒftɪ] n fam see softle.

soggy ['sɒgɪ] adj (soggier, soggiest) (gen) empapado,-a, saturado,-a; (bread) pastoso,-a, gomoso,-a.

soil [sɔɪl] I n (earth) tierra f, fig (land) tierra; **on British s.,** en suelo británico; **my native s.,** mi tierra or país natal. II vtr (dirty) ensuciar; (stain) manchar; fig (reputation) manchar.

soiled [sɔɪld] adj (dirty) sucio,-a; (stained) manchado,-a; **s. linen,** ropa sucia.

soirée ['swɑːreɪ] n fml sarao m, velada f.

solace ['sɒlɪs] n fml consuelo m.

solar ['səʊləʳ] adj solar. ■ **s. energy,** energía f solar; Anat **s. plexus,** plexo m solar.

solarium [səʊ'leərɪəm] n (pl solariums or solaria [səʊ'leərɪə]) solario m, solarium m.

sold [səʊld] pt & pp see sell.

solder ['sɒldəʳ] I n soldadura f. II vtr soldar.

soldering ['sɒldərɪŋ] adj s. iron, soldador m.

soldier ['səʊldʒəʳ] I n soldado m; (military man) militar m; old s., veterano m, excombatiente m; toy s., soldadito de plomo. II vi servir como soldado. ◆ **soldier on** vi fig seguir adelante a pesar de todo, continuar contra viento y marea.

sole¹ [səʊl] I n (foot) planta f; (shoe, sock) suela f; half s., media suela. II vtr (shoes) poner suela a.

sole² [səʊl] n (fish) lenguado m.

sole³ [səʊl] adj 1 (only, single) único,-a. 2 (exclusive) exclusivo,-a. ◆ **solely** adv 1 (only) únicamente, solamente. 2 (exclusively) exclusivamente.

solecism ['sɒləsɪzəm] n fml solecismo m.

solemn ['sɒləm] adj (ceremony) solemne; (expression) serio,-a.

solemnity [sə'lemnɪtɪ] n solemnidad f.

solemnize ['sɒləmnaɪz] vtr solemnizar; (marriage) celebrar.

solfa ['sɒl'fɑː] n Mus método m de enseñanza del solfeo.

solicit [sə'lɪsɪt] I vtr (request) solicitar, pedir. II vi (prostitute) buscar clientes, abordar a los clientes.

solicitor [sə'lɪsɪtəʳ] n Jur procurador,-a m, f, abogado,-a m, f; (for wills) notario,-a m, f. ■ **S. General, GB** procurador,-a m, f de la Corona, US subsecretario,-a m, f de Justicia.

solicitous [sə'lɪsɪtəs] adj fml 1 (attentive) solícito,-a (towards, con), atento,-a (about, for, a). 2 (eager) deseoso,-a (to, de).

solicitude [sə'lɪsɪtjuːd] n 1 (attention) solicitud f, atención f. 2 (concern) preocupación f. 3 (anxiety) ansiedad f.

solid ['sɒlɪd] I adj 1 (not liquid) sólido,-a; (firm) firme; **s. food,** alimentos sólidos; **s. fuel,** combustible sólido. 2 (not hollow) macizo,-a. 3 (pure) (metal) puro,-a, macizo,-a. 4 (dense) (fog, jungle) denso,-a, espeso,-a; (of strong material) (building etc) fuerte, resistente; **a man of s. build,** un hombre fornido or bien plantado; **a s. mass,** una masa compacta; **the streets were packed s.,** las calles estaban abarrotadas de gente; fig **we waited for two s. hours,** esperamos (durante) dos horas enteras. 4 (reliable) sólido,-a, consistente; **he's a good s. worker,** es un trabajador serio or de fiar. 5 (unanimous) unánime; **s. support,** apoyo unánime; **we're s. in our resolve,** nos mantenemos firmes en nuestra resolución. 6 Geom **s. angle,** ángulo m sólido; **s. geometry,** geometría f del espacio. II n 1 Chem sólido m. 2 (usu pl) (food) (alimento m) sólido m. 3 Geom sólido m. ◆ **solidly** adv (gen) sólidamente; (house etc) s. built, de construcción sólida; **to work s.,** trabajar sin descanso; **they voted s. in favour of the agreement,** votaron unánimes a favor del acuerdo.

solidarity [sɒlɪ'dærɪtɪ] n solidaridad f.

solidify [sə'lɪdɪfaɪ] vi (pt & pp solidified) solidificarse.

solidity [sɒ'lɪdɪtɪ] n solidez f.

solid-state [sɒlɪd'steɪt] adj Elec de estado sólido, transistorizado,-a.

soliloquy [sə'lɪləkwɪ] n soliloquio m.

solitaire ['sɒlɪteəʳ] n solitario m.

solitary ['sɒlɪtərɪ] adj 1 (alone) solitario,-a; (secluded) retirado,-a, apartado,-a; **to be in s. confinement,** estar incomunicado,-a. 2 (sole, only) solo,-a, único,-a; **not a s. soul,** ni un alma.

solitude ['sɒlɪtjuːd] n soledad f.

solo ['səʊləʊ] I n (pl solos) 1 Mus solo m; **a violin s.,** un solo para violín. 2 Cards solitario m. II adj 1 Mus **for s. violin,** para violín solo. 2 Av **s. flight,** vuelo m en solitario. III adv solo,-a solas; **to fly s.,** volar en solitario.

soloist ['səʊləʊɪst] n Mus solista mf.

solstice ['sɒlstɪs] n solsticio m.

soluble ['sɒljubəl] adj soluble.

solution [sə'luːʃən] n solución f.

solve [sɒlv] vtr resolver, solucionar.

solvent ['sɒlvənt] adj & n solvente (m).

sombre, US **somber** ['sɒmbəʳ] adj (dark) sombrío,-a; (gloomy) umbrío,-a, lúgubre; (pessimistic) pesimista; (melancholy) melancólico,-a; **a s. prospect,** una perspectiva sombría.

sombrero [sɒm'breərəʊ] n sombrero m de ala ancha.

some [sʌm] **I** adj **1** (with plural nouns) unos,-as, algunos,-as; (several) varios,-as; (a few); unos,-as cuantos,-as or pocos,-as; **did she bring s. flowers?**, ¿trajo flores?; **there were s. roses**, había unas or algunas rosas; **who wants s. more peas?**, ¿quién quiere más guisantes? **2** (with singular nouns) algún, alguna; (a little) algo de, un poco de; **if you need s. help**, si necesitas (alguna) ayuda; **there's s. wine left**, queda un poco de vino; **try to get s. rest**, intenta descansar un poco; **would you like s. coffee?**, ¿quiere café? **3** (certain, but not all) cierto,-a, alguno,-a; **in s. ways**, en cierto modo o sentido; **s. days I stay at home**, hay días que me quedo en casa; **to s. extent**, hasta cierto punto; **s. people say that ...**, algunos dicen que ..., hay quien dice que ... . **4** (unknown, unspecified) algún, alguna; **for s. reason or other**, por una razón o por otra; **in s. book or other**, en algún libro que otro; **s. day**, algún día, un día de éstos; **s. day next week**, algún día de la semana que viene; **s. other time**, otra vez, otro día. **5** (quite a lot of) bastante; **after s. time**, pasado algún tiempo; **it's s. distance away**, queda bastante lejos; **s. years ago**, hace algunos años; US (quite a) **that was s. film!**, esto sí que fue una buena película; **the wound will take s. time to heal**, la herida tardará bastante en cicatrizarse; iron **s. friend you are!**, ¡valiente amigo eres tú! **II** pron **1** (people) algunos,-as, unos,-as; (certain, but not all) algunos, algunas personas; **s. go by bus and s. by train**, unos van en autobús y otros en tren; **s. of my friends**, algunos de mis amigos. **2** (objects) algunos,-as; (a few) unos,-as cuantos,-as; (a little) algo, un poco; (certain ones) ciertos,-as, algunos,-as; **have s.!**, ¡toma!; **I agree with s. of what you say**, estoy de acuerdo en parte con lo que dices; **s. more wine?** — No thanks, **I've got s.**, ¿quiere más vino? — gracias, ya tengo; **would you like to take s. with you?**, (a few) ¿quieres llevarte unos cuantos?; (a little) ¿quieres llevarte un poco? **III** adv (approximately, about) aproximadamente; **s. fifty people**, unas cincuenta personas; **s. seventy miles away**, a unas setenta millas de aquí.

somebody ['sʌmbədɪ] **1** pron alguien; **s. is knocking at the door**, alguien está llamando a la puerta; **s. else**, otro,-a, otra persona; **s. or other**, alguien, no sé quién. **II** n **to be a s.**, ser todo un personaje; **he thinks he's a s.**, se cree alguien.

somehow ['sʌmhaʊ] adv **1** (in some way) de algún modo, de una u otra manera; **I'll manage s.**, me las apañaré como sea. **2** (for some reason) por alguna razón; **I never liked her s.**, no sé por qué, pero nunca me cayó bien.

someone ['sʌmwʌn] pron & n see **somebody**.

someplace ['sʌmpleɪs] adv US see **somewhere**.

somersault ['sʌməsɔːlt] **I** n (by acrobat etc) salto m mortal; (by child) voltereta f; (by car) vuelta f de campana, vuelco m. **II** vi (acrobat etc) dar un salto mortal; (child) dar volteretas; (car) dar una vuelta de campana.

something ['sʌmθɪŋ] **I** pron & n **1** (a bit, a bit of) algo; **has it s. to do with the hold-up?**, ¿tiene algo que ver con el atraco?; **it came as s. of a surprise to us**, nos pilló un poco por sorpresa; **she's s. of an artist**, tiene algo de artista; **s. to eat/drink**, algo de comer/beber; **would you like s. to drink?**, ¿quieres tomar algo? **2** (unidentified) algo; **are you drunk or s.?**, ¿estás borracho o qué?; **s. must be done**, hay que hacer algo; **s. or other**, algo, alguna cosa; **s. tells me he's lying**, no sé por qué, pero me parece que miente; **s. went wrong**, algo falló; **she has a certain s.**, tiene un no sé qué; **there's s. in what you say**, hay algo de verdad en lo que dices; **you've got s. there**, eso puede ser interesante. **3** (ill-defined) algo; **is s. the matter?**, ¿le pasa algo?; **she's called Jane s. or other**, se llama Jane no sé qué más; **s. else**, otra cosa; **s. nice**, algo bonito; **s. of the kind**, algo por el estilo. **4** (impressive) algo; **it was really s.!**, US **it was s. else!**, ¡fue algo extraordinario! **II** adv **it cost s. like £10**, costó unas diez libras; **now that's s. like it!**, ¡eso sí que es!; fam **the pain is s. shocking**, duele una barbaridad.

sometime ['sʌmtaɪm] **I** adv algún día; **s. last week**, un día de la semana pasada; **s. next year**, durante el año que viene; **s. or other**, tarde o temprano; **s. soon**, un día de éstos. **II** adj (former) antiguo,-a, ex.

sometimes ['sʌmtaɪmz] adv a veces, de vez en cuando.

somewhat ['sʌmwɒt] adv fml algo, un tanto.

somewhere ['sʌmweəᵣ] adv **1** (in some place) en alguna parte; (to some place) a alguna parte; **s. else**, (in some other place) en otra parte; (to some other place) a alguna parte; **s. in Australia**, en algún lugar de Australia; **I read s. that ...**, leí en alguna parte que ...; **s. near Oxford**, cerca de Oxford; **s. or other**, no sé dónde; fam **now we're getting s.**, ya empezamos a hacer progresos, ya empieza a marchar la cosa. **2** (approximately) más o menos, alrededor; **it cost s. in the region of £70**, costó unas 70 libras más o menos; **she's s. in her forties**, tendrá unos cuarenta y pico años.

somnambulism [sɒm'næmbjʊlɪzəm] n sonambulismo m.

somnambulist [sɒm'næmbjʊlɪst] n sonámbulo,-a m,f.

somnolence ['sɒmnələns] n somnolencia f.

somnolent ['sɒmnələnt] adj somnoliento,-a, soñoliento,-a.

son [sʌn] n hijo m; **eldest/youngest s.**, hijo mayor/menor; offens **s. of a bitch**, hijo de puta.

sonar ['səʊnɑːᵣ] n Tech sonar m.

sonata [sə'nɑːtə] n Mus sonata f.

son et lumière [sɒneɪ'luːmɪeəᵣ] n espectáculo m de luz y sonido.

song [sɒŋ] n (gen) canción f; (of bird) canto m; **give us a s.!**, ¡cántanos algo!; **to burst into s.**, ponerse a cantar; GB fam **there's no need to make a s. and dance about it**, no es para tanto; fam **we bought it for a s.**, lo compramos regalado.

songbird ['sɒŋbɜːd] n pájaro m cantor.

songbook ['sɒŋbʊk] n cancionero m.

songwriter ['sɒŋraɪtəᵣ] n compositor,-a m, f (de canciones).

sonic ['sɒnɪk] adj sónico,-a. ■ **s. boom**, estampido m sónico; **s. depth finder**, sonda f acústica.

son-in-law ['sʌnɪnlɔː] n (pl sons-in-law) yerno m, hijo m político.

sonnet ['sɒnɪt] n soneto m.

sonny ['sʌnɪ] n fam hijo m, hijito m.

sonorous ['sɒnərəs] adj sonoro,-a.

soon [suːn] adv **1** (within a short time) pronto, dentro de poco; (quickly) rápidamente; **it will s. be Friday**, falta poco para el viernes; **see you s.?**, ¡hasta pronto!; **she's changed her mind**, cambió rápidamente de idea; **s. after midnight**, poco después de medianoche; **s. afterwards**, poco después; **write to me s.**, escríbeme pronto; **as s. as**, en cuanto; **as s. as possible**, cuanto antes, lo más pronto posible. **3** (early) temprano, pronto; **are you leaving so s.?**, ¿ya os marcháis?; **it's still too s. to tell**, todavía es demasiado pronto para saber; **how s. will it be ready?**, ¿cuándo estará listo or a punto?; **we arrived too s.**, llegamos demasiado temprano; fig **don't speak too s.**, no cantes victoria. **4** (expresses preference) **I would just as s. stay at home**, prefiero or preferiría quedarme en casa; **I would as s. not see him now**, prefiero or preferiría no verlo ahora mismo. **5** (expresses indifference) **I would (just) as s. read as watch TV**, tanto me da leer como mirar la tele.

sooner ['suːnəᵣ] adv **1** (earlier) más temprano; **s. or later**, tarde o temprano; **the s. the better**, cuanto antes mejor. **2** (immediately after) **no s. had he finished than he fainted**, nada más acabar se desmayó; **no s. had she left than the telephone began to ring**, apenas se había ido cuando empezó a sonar el teléfono; **no s. said than done**, dicho y hecho. **3** (rather) **I would s. do it alone**, prefiero or preferiría hacerlo yo solo; **I would s. not go by train**, prefiero or preferiría no ir en tren; fam **I'd s. die!**, ¡antes morir!, ¡antes la muerte!; fam **s. you than me!**, ¡no me das ninguna envidia!

soot [sʊt] n hollín m.

soothe [suːð] vtr (calm) calmar, tranquilizar; (quieten) acallar; (anger) aplacar; (pain) aliviar, calmar.

soother ['suːðə'] n chupete m.

soothing ['suːðɪŋ] adj (ointment, medicine) calmante, sedante; (bath) relajante; (tone, words) calmante, tranquilizador,-a.

sooty ['sʊtɪ] adj (sootier, sootiest) (dirty) cubierto,-a de hollín; (black) negro,-a como el hollín.

sop [sɒp] n 1 fig (concession) concesión f, favor m; (bribe) soborno m; **the bonus was intended as a s. to the workers**, la prima fue ideada para apaciguar a los obreros. 2 sops, (food) sopa f sing. ◆ **sop up** vtr absorber.

sophism ['sɒfɪzəm] n sofisma m.

sophisticated [sə'fɪstɪkeɪtɪd] adj sofisticado,-a.

sophistication [səfɪstɪ'keɪʃən] n sofisticación f.

sophistry ['sɒfɪstrɪ] n (art) sofistería f; (argument) sofisma m.

sophomore ['sɒfəmɔː'] n US estudiante mf de segundo año.

soporific [sɒpə'rɪfɪk] I adj soporífero,-a, soporífico,-a. II n soporífero m.

sopping ['sɒpɪŋ] adj fam **s. (wet)**, como una sopa.

soppy ['sɒpɪ] adj (soppier, soppiest) fam sentimentaloide.

soprano [sə'prɑːnəʊ] n (pl sopranos) Mus soprano mf, triple mf. ■ **s. clef**, clave f de do; **s. voice**, voz f de soprano.

sorbet ['sɔːbɪt] n Culin sorbete m.

sorcerer ['sɔːsərə'] n brujo m, hechicero m.

sorceress ['sɔːsəris] n bruja f, hechicera f.

sorcery ['sɔːsəri] n brujería f, hechicería f.

sordid ['sɔːdɪd] adj sórdido,-a.

sordidness ['sɔːdɪdnɪs] n sordidez f.

sore [sɔː'] I adj 1 Med (aching) dolorido,-a; (painful) doloroso,-a; (inflamed) inflamado,-a; **my eyes are s.**, me pican los ojos; **to have a s. throat**, tener dolor de garganta; **to have s. feet**, tener los pies doloridos; fig **it's a s. point**, es un asunto delicado or espinoso. 2 fam (angry) enfadado,-a (at, con); **to feel s. about sth**, estar resentido,-a por algo. II n Med llaga f, úlcera f. ■ **cold s.**, herpes m labial. ◆ **sorely** adv (very) muy; (a lot) mucho; (deeply) profundamente; (seriously) gravemente, fuertemente; **he will be s. missed**, le echaremos mucho de menos.

soreness ['sɔːnɪs] n dolor m.

sorrel[1] ['sɒrəl] n Zool alazán m.

sorrel[2] ['sɒrəl] n Bot acedera f.

sorrow ['sɒrəʊ] n pena f, pesar m, dolor m, tristeza f; **much to my s.**, con gran pesar mío; fam **to drown one's sorrows**, ahogar las penas.

sorrowful ['sɒrəʊfʊl] adj afligido,-a, apenado,-a, triste.

sorry ['sɒrɪ] I adj (sorrier, sorriest) 1 (pity) lleno,-a de lástima; **to feel s. for sb**, compadecer a algn; **I feel very s. for her**, me da mucha pena; **to feel s. for oneself**, compadecerse de uno mismo. 2 (pitiful, wretched) triste, lamentable; **a s. sight**, un triste espectáculo; **in a s. state**, en un estado lamentable. 3 (regretful) **to be s. (about sth)**, sentir or lamentar (algo); **I'm s. I'm late**, siento haber llegado tarde; **I'm very s. you couldn't come**, siento de verdad que no hayas podido venir; **you'll be s.!**, ¡te arrepentirás! II interj 1 (apology) ¡perdón!, ¡perdone!, ¡disculpe! 2 GB (for repetition) ¿perdón?, ¿cómo?

sort [sɔːt] I n 1 (kind) clase f, género m, tipo m, suerte f; (make, brand) marca f; **all sorts of cakes**, toda clase de pasteles; **it's a s. of teapot**, es una especie de tetera; **nothing of the s.!**, ¡en absoluto!, ¡ni pensarlo!; **something of the s.**, algo por el estilo. 2 fam (person) tipo m; **he's a strange s.**, es un tipo raro; **I know his s.**, conozco el paño; **it takes all sorts to make a world**, s.,

todo hay en la viña del Señor. 3 **of a s.**, **of sorts**, de alguna clase; **he is a musician of a s.**, tiene algo de músico; **there's an office of sorts**, hay una especie de despacho. 4 **s. of**, un poco, en cierto modo; **did you like the film? —s. of**, ¿te gustó la película? —en cierto modo; **it's s. of blue**, es azulado; **it's s. of round**, es más bien redondo; **I'm s. of lost**, estoy como perdido,-a; **I s. of expected it**, en cierto modo me lo esperaba. 5 **out of sorts**, (unwell) pachucho,-a; (moody) de mal humor. II vtr (classify) clasificar. ◆ **sort out** vtr 1 (classify) clasificar; (put in order) ordenar; **to s. out the good from the bad**, separar lo bueno de lo malo. 2 (problem, difficulty) arreglar, solucionar. 3 fam **to s. sb out**, ajustar cuentas con algn.

sortie ['sɔːtɪ] n Av Mil salida f.

sorting ['sɔːtɪŋ] n clasificación f. ■ (in post office) **s. office**, sala f de batalla.

SOS [esəʊ'es] abbr of **save our souls**, llamada f de socorro, S.O.S. m.

so-so ['səʊsəʊ] adv fam así así, de aquella manera, regular.

soufflé ['suːfleɪ] n Culin soufflé m.

sought [sɔːt] pt & pp see **seek**.

sought-after ['sɔːtɑːftə'] adj (person) solicitado,-a; (object) codiciado,-a.

soul [səʊl] n 1 (inner being) alma f, espíritu m, ánimo m; **it lacks s.**, le falta ánimo; **the life and s. of the party**, el alma de la fiesta. ■ **s. mate**, compañero,-a m, f del alma. 2 Rel alma f; **All Souls' Day**, día de los Difuntos; **bless my s.!**, ¡Dios mío!; **God rest his s.**, que Dios le tenga en su gloria. 3 (person) alma f, persona f; **not a s.**, ni un alma; **he's a good s.**, es muy buena persona; **poor s.!**, ¡pobrecito,-a! 4 (personification) ejemplo m; **she's the s. of discretion**, es la discreción personificada. 5 Mus música f soul.

soul-destroying ['səʊldɪstrɔɪɪŋ] adj (boring) tedioso,-a, monótono,-a; (demoralizing) desmoralizador,-a, degradante.

soulful ['səʊlfʊl] adj conmovedor,-a, emotivo,-a.

soul-searching ['səʊlsɜːtʃɪŋ] n examen m de conciencia.

soul-stirring ['səʊlstɜːrɪŋ] adj conmovedor,-a.

sound[1] [saʊnd] I n (gen) sonido m; (noise) ruido m; **stereophonic s.**, sonido estereofónico; **to the s. of the accordion**, al son del acordeón; fig **I don't like the s. of it**, no me gusta nada la idea. ■ **s. archives**, fonoteca f sing; **s. barrier**, barrera f del sonido; **s. effects**, efectos mpl sonoros; **s. engineer**, ingeniero,-a m, f del sonido; **s. wave**, onda f sonora. II vtr 1 (trumpet, bell, alarm) tocar, hacer sonar; **to s. the alarm**, dar la señal de alarma; **to s. the retreat**, tocar a retirada. 2 (pronounce) pronunciar. 3 Med (chest etc) auscultar. III vi 1 (trumpet, bell, alarm) sonar, resonar. 2 (give an impression) sonar, parecer; **he sounds German to me**, yo diría que es alemán; **how does it s. to you?**, ¿qué te parece?; **it sounds as if the match will be postponed**, parece que el partido será aplazado; **it sounds empty**, suena a vacío; **it sounds interesting**, parece interesante; **it sounds like an ambulance**, suena como una ambulancia; **it sounds like Mozart**, me suena a Mozart; **she sounded upset**, parecía trastornada. ◆ **sound off** vi fam hablar a gritos; **to s. off about**, (boast) jactarse de; (complain) quejarse de.

sound[2] [saʊnd] I adj 1 (healthy) sano,-a; (in good condition) en buen estado; **of s. mind**, en su sano juicio; **safe and s.**, sano y salvo. 2 (safe, dependable) seguro,-a; (correct) acertado,-a; (logical) lógico,-a, razonable; **a s. investment**, una inversión segura; **a s. piece of advice**, un buen consejo. 3 (basis etc) sólido,-a, fuerte, robusto,-a. 4 (thorough) (defeat etc) rotundo,-a; (examination etc) a fondo. 5 (sleep) profundo,-a. II adv **to be s. asleep**, estar profundamente dormido,-a.

sound[3] [saʊnd] vtr Naut Med sondar. ◆ **sound out** vtr (person) sondear.

sound[4] [saʊnd] n Geog estrecho m, brazo m de mar.

sounding¹ ['saʊndɪŋ] *adj (resonant)* resonante. ■ **s. board,** caja *f* de resonancia.

sounding² ['saʊndɪŋ] *n Naut* sondeo *m.* ■ **s. balloon,** globo *m* sonda.

soundless ['saʊndlɪs] *adj* silencioso,-a.

soundproof ['saʊndpruːf] **I** *adj* insonorizado,-a, a prueba de sonidos. **II** *vtr* insonorizar.

soundproofing ['saʊndpruːfɪŋ] *n* **1** *(action)* insonorización *f.* **2** *(material)* aislante *m* acústico.

soundtrack ['saʊndtræk] *n* banda *f* sonora.

soup [suːp] *n Culin* sopa *f; (thin, clear)* caldo *m*, consomé *m; fam* **in the s.,** en un apuro *or* aprieto. ■ **s. dish,** plato *m* sopero; **s. kitchen,** comedor *m* popular, olla *f* común; **s. spoon,** cuchara *f* sopera.

souped-up ['suːptʌp] *adj Aut* al trucado,-a.

sour [saʊə ʳ] *adj* **1** *(fruit)* agrio,-a, ácido,-a; *(milk)* cortado,-a; *(butter)* rancio,-a; *(wine)* agrio,-a; **to go** *or* **turn s.,** *(milk)* cortarse; *(wine)* agriarse; *fig (situation)* empeorar; *fam* **fig s. grapes!,** ¡te aguantas! ■ **s. cream,** nata *f* agria. **2** *fig (person)* amargado,-a. ◆ **sourly** *adv* agriamente, con amargura.

source [sɔːs] *n (of river)* fuente *f*, nacimiento *m; fig (origin)* fuente *f*, origen *m; (of information)* fuente *f; Med (of infection)* foco *m;* **according to reliable sources,** según fuentes fidedignas; **what was the s. of the information?,** ¿de dónde procedía la información?

sourness ['saʊənɪs] *n* **1** *(of fruit)* acidez *f*, agrura *f; (of milk)* agrura *f.* **2** *fig (of person)* amargura *f*, acritud *f.*

sourpuss ['saʊəpʊs] *n fam* amargado,-a *m,f.*

souse [saʊs] *vtr* **1** *Culin (fish)* escabechar; *(meat)* adobar. **2** *(soak)* empapar, mojar; *(plunge)* sumergir; **to s. oneself with water,** empaparse de agua. **3** *sl (make drunk)* **to get soused,** coger una trompa.

south [saʊθ] **I** *n* sur *m;* **in the s. of England,** en el sur de Inglaterra; **to the s. of York,** al sur de York. **II** *adj* del sur; **s. wind,** viento del sur. ■ **S. Africa,** Sudáfrica; **S. African,** sudafricano,-a *(m, f);* **S. China Sea,** Mar *m* de la China Meridional; **S. Dakota,** Dakota del Sur; **S. Pole,** Polo *m* Sur; **S. Seas,** los mares del Sur; **S. West Africa,** Namibia. **III** *adv (location)* al sur; *(direction)* hacia el sur; **s. of the border,** al sur de la frontera; **to travel s.,** viajar hacia el sur.

southeast [saʊθ'iːst] **I** *n* sudeste *m.* **II** *adj* (del) sudeste. **III** *adv (location)* al sudeste; *(direction)* hacia el sudeste.

southeasterly [saʊθ'iːstəlɪ] *adj (wind)* del sudeste.

southerly ['sʌðəlɪ] *adj (direction)* hacia el sur; *(point, aspect)* al sur; *(wind)* del sur.

southern ['sʌðən] *adj* del sur, meridional, austral; **in s. Spain,** en el sur de España; **s. accent,** acento del sur; **S. Europe,** Europa del Sur; **the s. hemisphere,** el hemisferio sur *or* meridional.

southerner ['sʌðənə ʳ] *n* habitante *mf* del sur, sureño,-a *m,f.*

southward ['saʊθwəd] *adj & adv Naut* hacia el sur, en dirección sur.

southwest [saʊθ'west] **I** *n* suroeste *m.* **II** *adj* suroeste. **III** *adv (location)* al suroeste; *(direction) hacia* el suroeste.

southwestern [saʊθ'westən] *adj* del suroeste.

souvenir [suːvə'nɪə ʳ] *n* recuerdo *m.*

sou'wester [saʊ'westə ʳ] *n* sueste *m.*

sovereign ['sɒvrɪn] **I** *n* **1** *(monarch)* soberano,-a *m,f.* **2** *(coin)* soberano *m.* **II** *adj* **1** *(self-governing)* soberano,-a. **2** *(supreme)* soberano,-a, supremo,-a.

sovereignty ['sɒvrəntɪ] *n* soberanía *f.*

soviet ['saʊvɪət] **I** *n* **1** *(government council)* soviet *m.* **2** **the Soviets,** los soviéticos. **II** *adj* soviético,-a. ■ **S. Russia,** Rusia Soviética; **S. Union,** Unión Soviética.

sow¹ [saʊ] *vtr (pt sowed; pp sowed or sown) (seeds)* sembrar.

sow² [saʊ] *n Zool* cerda *f*, puerca *f.*

sower ['saʊə ʳ] *n (person)* sembrador,-a *m, f; (machine)* sembradora *f.*

sowing ['saʊɪŋ] *n* siembra *f.*

sown [saʊn] *pp see* **sow¹.**

soy [sɔɪ] *n US* soja *f.* ■ **s. sauce,** salsa *f* de soja.

soya ['sɔɪə] *n GB* soja *f.*

sozzled ['sɒzəld] *adj fam* **to be s.,** estar trompa; **to get s.,** pillarse una trompa.

spa [spɑː] *n* balneario *m.* ■ **s. resort,** estación *f* balnearia.

space [speɪs] **I** *n* **1** *(gen)* espacio *m;* **the conquest of s.,** la conquista del espacio; **to gaze** *or* **stare into s.,** mirar al vacío, tener la mirada perdida; **to travel through s.,** viajar por el espacio; **to vanish into s.,** desaparecer en el espacio. ■ **outer s.,** el espacio exterior; **s. age,** era *f* espacial; **s. agency,** agencia *f* espacial; **s. capsule,** cápsula *f* espacial; **s. flight,** vuelo *m* espacial; **s. lab,** laboratorio *m* espacial; **s. probe,** sonda *f* espacial; **s. program(me),** programa *m* de vuelos espaciales; **s. shuttle,** transbordador *m* espacial; **s. station,** estación *f* espacial; **s. travel,** viajes *mpl* por el espacio. **2** *(room)* sitio *m*, lugar *m*, espacio *m;* **there isn't enough s. for all of them,** no caben todos; **to clear a s. for sth,** hacer sitio para algo; **to take up a lot of s.,** ocupar mucho sitio; **in a confined s.,** en un espacio cerrado; **they sell newspaper advertising s.,** venden espacio publicitario en los periódicos. **3** *(gap, empty place)* espacio *m*, hueco *m;* **blank s.,** espacio en blanco; **he loves the wide open spaces,** le encanta el campo abierto; **I'm looking for a parking s.,** estoy buscando un lugar donde aparcar. **4** *(in time)* espacio *m;* **in a short s. of time,** en un corto espacio; **in the s. of half an hour,** en el espacio de media hora. **II** *vtr (also s. out)* espaciar, separar.

space-age ['speɪseɪdʒ] *adj* de la era espacial.

spacecraft ['speɪskrɑːft] *n inv* nave *f* espacial, astronave *f.*

spaced out [speɪst'aʊt] *adj sl* colocado,-a, flipado,-a.

spaceman ['speɪsmən] *n (pl spacemen)* astronauta *m*, cosmonauta *m.*

spacing ['speɪsɪŋ] *n Typ* espacio *m;* **double s.,** doble espacio.

spacious ['speɪʃəs] *adj* espacioso,-a, amplio,-a, de gran extensión.

spade¹ [speɪd] *n (for digging)* pala *f; fig* **to call a s. a s.,** llamar al pan pan y al vino vino.

spade² [speɪd] *n Cards (international pack)* pica *f, (Spanish pack)* espada *f;* **the ace of spades,** el as de picas *or* de espadas.

spaghetti [spə'getɪ] *n Culin (gen)* espaguetis *mpl; (vermicelli)* fideos *mpl.*

Spain [speɪn] *n* España.

span [spæn] **I** *n* **1** *(of wing)* envergadura *f; (of hand)* palmo *m; (of arch, bridge)* luz *f*, ojo *m; (of road)* tramo *m.* **2** *(of time)* lapso *m*, espacio *m;* **life s.,** duración de vida. **II** *vtr (pt & pp spanned)* **1** *(bridge etc)* extenderse sobre, atravesar, cruzar. **2** *(life etc)* abarcar.

spangle ['spæŋgəl] *n* lentejuela *f.*

Spaniard ['spænjəd] *n* español,-a *m,f.*

spaniel ['spænjəl] *n (dog)* perro *m* de aguas. ■ **cocker s.,** cócker *m.*

Spanish ['spænɪʃ] **I** *adj* español,-a; **the S. Armada,** la Armada Invencible; **the S. Embassy,** la Embajada de España. ■ **S. America,** Hispanoamérica; **S. fly,** cantárida *f;* **S. guitar,** guitarra *f* clásica. **II** *n* **1** *(person)* español,-a *m,f;* **the S.,** los españoles. **2** *(language)* español *m*, castellano *m.*

Spanish-American [spænɪʃə'merɪkən] *adj* hispanoamericano,-a; **the S.-A. War,** la Guerra de Cuba.

Spanish-speaking ['spænɪʃspiːkɪŋ] *adj* de habla española, hispanohablante.

spank [spæŋk] *vtr* zurrar *f*, pegar, dar azotes a.

spanking[1] ['spæŋkɪŋ] *n* zurra *f*, azotaina *f*.

spanking[2] ['spæŋkɪŋ] **I** *adj fam (lively)* vivaz. **II** *adv fam* **s. clean**, limpísimo,-a; **s. new**, completamente nuevo,-a, flamante.

spanner ['spænə[r]] *n* llave *f* de tuercas; *GB fam* **to put** *or* **throw a s. in the works**, meter un palo en la rueda, sabotear. ■ **box s.**, llave *f* de tubo.

spar[1] [spɑː[r]] *n Naut* palo *m*, verga *f*.

spar[2] [spɑː[r]] *vi (pt & pp sparred)* **1** *Box* entrenarse. **2** *(argue)* discutir.

spar[3] [spɑː[r]] *n Min* esparto *m*.

spare [speə[r]] **I** *vtr* **1** *(do without)* prescindir de, pasar sin; **can you s. five minutes?**, ¿tienes cinco minutos?; **can you s. me 10?**, ¿me puedes dejar 10?; **I can't s. the time**, no tengo tiempo; **there's none to s.**, no sobra nada; **we can't s. her today**, hoy no podemos prescindir de ella. **2** *(begrudge)* escatimar; **they spared no efforts**, no escatimaron esfuerzos; **to s. no expense**, no reparar en gastos; *prov* **s. the rod and spoil the child**, escatima la vara y malcriarás al niño. **3** *(show mercy to)* perdonar; **to s. sb's feelings**, procurar no herir los sentimientos de algn. **4** *(save)* ahorrar; **s. me the details**, ahórrate los detalles. **II** *adj* **1** *(left over)* sobrante, que sobra; *(surplus)* de sobra, de más; *(available)* disponible; **a s. moment**, un momento libre; **have you got any s. leaflets?**, ¿te sobra algún folleto?; **there's some fish going s.**, queda algo de pescado. ■ **s. bed**, cama *f* supletoria; *Fin* **s. capital**, fondos *mpl* disponibles; *Aut* **s. part**, (pieza *f* de) recambio *m or* repuesto *m*; **s. room**, cuarto *m* de los invitados; **s. tyre**, *Aut* neumático *m* de recambio; *GB fam (on body)* michelines *mpl*; *Aut* **s. wheel**, rueda *f* de recambio. **2** *(thin, emaciated)* enjuto,-a; *GB sl* **to go s.**, cabrearse. **III** *n Aut* (pieza *f* de) recambio *m or* repuesto *m*.

sparerib [speə'rɪb] *n Culin* costilla *f* de cerdo.

sparing ['speərɪŋ] *adj (frugal)* frugal; *(economical)* económico,-a; **to be s. with food**, racionar la comida; **to be s. with praise**, escatimar elogios; **to be s. with words**, ser parco,-a en palabras. ◆ **sparingly** *adv* en poca cantidad.

spark [spɑːk] **I** *n* **1** *(electrical from fire)* chispa *f*; *GB fam* **bright s.**, listillo,-a *m, f*. ■ *Aut* **s. plug**, bujía *f*. **2** *fig (glimmer, trace)* chispa *f*, pizca *f*. **II** *vi* echar chispas. ◆ **spark off** *vtr* provocar, desatar.

sparking ['spɑːkɪŋ] *adj Aut* **s. plug**, bujía *f*.

sparkle ['spɑːkəl] **I** *vi* **1** *(diamond, glass)* centellear, destellar, brillar; *(eyes)* brillar, chispear; *(firework)* echar chispas, chispear. **2** *fig (person)* brillar, lucirse; *(conversation)* brillar. **II** *n* **1** *(of diamond, glass)* centelleo *m*, destello *m*, brillo *m*; *(of eyes)* brillo *m*. **2** *fig (liveliness)* viveza *f*; *(wit)* brillo *m*; **she lacks s.**, le falta brillo.

sparkler ['spɑːklə[r]] *n* **1** *(firework)* bengala *f*. **2** *fam (gem)* brillante *m*.

sparkling ['spɑːklɪŋ] *adj* **1** *(diamond, glass)* centelleante, brillante; *(eyes)* brillante, chispeante; **s. clean**, limpio,-a como un espejo. ■ **s. wine**, vino *m* espumoso. **2** *fig (person, conversation)* brillante, chispeante.

sparring ['spɑːrɪŋ] *n Box* **s. partner**, sparring *m*, compañero *m* de entrenamiento.

sparrow ['spærəʊ] *n Orn* gorrión *m*. ■ **house s.**, gorrión *m* común; **rock s.**, gorrión *m* chillón; **Spanish s.**, gorrión *m* moruno.

sparrowhawk ['spærəʊhɔːk] *n Orn* gavilán *m*.

sparse [spɑːs] *adj (thin)* escaso,-a; *(scattered)* espaciado,-a, disperso,-a; *(hair)* ralo,-a; **s. vegetation**, vegetación escasa.

Spartan ['spɑːtən] *adj & n* espartano,-a *(m, f)*.

spasm ['spæzəm] *n* **1** *Med* espasmo *m*; *(of coughing)* acceso *m*. **2** *(of anger, activity)* arrebato *m*, acceso *m*; **in spasms**, a rachas.

spasmodic [spæz'mɒdɪk] *adj* **1** *Med* espasmódico,-a. **2** *(irregular)* irregular, intermitente. ◆ **spasmodically** *adv fig* de forma irregular, a rachas, de vez en cuando.

spastic ['spæstɪk] *adj & n* **1** *Med* espástico,-a *(m, f)*. **2** *sl pej* inútil *(mf)*, patoso,-a *(m, f)*.

spat[1] [spæt] *pt & pp see* **spit**[1].

spat[2] [spæt] *n* polaina *f*.

spate [speɪt] *n* **1** *(of letters)* avalancha *f*; *(of words)* torrente *m*; *(of accidents)* racha *f*. **2** *GB (river)* desbordamiento *m*; **to be in full s.**, estar crecido,-a.

spatial ['speɪʃəl] *adj* espacial, del espacio.

spatter ['spætə[r]] *vtr (splash)* salpicar (**with**, de); *(sprinkle)* rociar (**with**, de).

spatula ['spætjʊlə] *n* espátula *f*.

spawn [spɔːn] **I** *n* **1** *(of fish, frogs)* huevas *fpl*, freza *f*. **2** *Bot* **mushroom s.**, micelio *m* del hongo. **II** *vi (fish, frogs)* frezar. **III** *vtr fig pej* engendrar, producir.

speak [spiːk] **I** *vtr (pt spoke; pp spoken)* **1** *(utter)* decir; **to s. one's mind**, hablar claro *or* sin rodeos; **to s. the truth**, decir la verdad. **2** *(language)* hablar; **'English spoken'**, 'se habla inglés'. **II** *vi* **1** *(gen)* hablar; **generally speaking**, en términos generales; **I don't know him to s. to**, sólo lo conozco de vista; **I'll s. to my boss about it**, *(discuss)* lo hablaré con el jefe; *(mention)* se lo diré al jefe; **legally speaking**, desde el punto de vista legal; **roughly speaking**, a grandes rasgos; **she has no savings to s. of**, no tiene ahorros que digamos; **so to s.**, por así decirlo; **speaking of ...**, a propósito de ...; **to be nothing to s. of**, no ser nada especial; **to s. to sb**, hablar con algn. **2** *(make a speech)* pronunciar un discurso; *(take the floor)* tomar la palabra; **she spoke on cookery**, habló de cocina. **3** *Tel* hablar; **Browne speaking!**, Browne al habla; **I'd like to s. to Mr Bow**, póngame con el Sr. Bow, por favor; **speaking!**, ¡al habla!; **who's speaking, please?**, ¿de parte de quién? ◆ **speak for** *vtr (person, group)* hablar en nombre de; *(motion)* hablar en favor de; **it speaks for itself**, es evidente, habla por sí solo; *fam* **s. for yourself!**, ¡eso lo dirás tú! ◆ **speak out** *vi (give opinion)* hablar claro *or* sin rodeos; **to s. out against sth**, denunciar algo. ◆ **speak up** *vi* hablar más fuerte; *fig* **to s. up for sb**, intervenir a favor de algn.

speakeasy ['spiːkiːzɪ] *n US fam* taberna *f* clandestina.

speaker ['spiːkə[r]] *n* **1** *(gen)* persona *f* que habla, el *or* la que habla; *(in dialogue)* interlocutor,-a *m, f*; **he's a good s.**, es buen orador; *(public)* s., orador,-a *m, f*; *(lecturer)* conferenciante *mf*. **2** *(of language)* hablante *mf*; **Spanish s.**, hispanohablante *mf*. **3** *GB Parl* **the S.**, el Presidente de la Cámara de los Comunes; *US* **the S. of the House**, el Presidente de la Cámara de los Representantes; *(form of address)* **Mr S.**, Señor Presidente. **4** *(loudspeaker)* altavoz *m*.

speaking ['spiːkɪŋ] **I** *adj* hablante; *Theat* **a s. part**, un papel hablante; **we are not on s. terms**, no nos hablamos. ■ *GB Tel* **s. clock**, información *f* horaria. **II** *n (skill, art)* oratoria *f*; **plain s.**, franqueza *f*.

spear [spɪə[r]] *n (gen)* lanza *f*; *(javelin)* jabalina *f*; *(harpoon)* arpón *m*.

spearhead ['spɪəhed] **I** *n* punta *f* de lanza. **II** *vtr (attack etc)* encabezar.

spearmint ['spɪəmɪnt] *n Bot* menta *f* verde.

spec [spek] *n fam* **on s.**, sin garantías; **we went to the cinema on s.**, fuimos al cine sin saber si quedarían entradas.

special ['speʃəl] **I** *adj (gen)* especial; *(specific)* específico,-a, particular; *(exceptional)* extraordinario,-a; **nothing s.**, nada del otro mundo; **what's so s. about him?**, ¿qué tiene él de particular? ■ **s. agent**, agente *mf* secreto,-a; *GB* **the S. Branch**, el Servicio de Seguridad del Estado; **s. delivery**, *(letter)* express; *(parcel)* de entrega inmediata; **s. edition**, edición *f or* número *m* especial; *Cin* **s. effects**, efectos *mpl* especiales; *Com* **s. offer**, oferta *f* (especial); *Pol* **s. powers**, poderes *mpl* extraordinarios. **II** *n* **1** *(train)* tren *m* especial. **2** *Rad TV* programa *m* especial; *Journ (newspaper edition)* número *m* especial; *(on menu)* **today's s.,** plato *m* del día. ◆ **specially** *adv (specifically)* especialmente; *(on purpose)* expresamente, a propósito.

specialist ['speʃəlɪst] *n* especialista *mf*; **to become an electronics s.,** especializarse en la electrónica.

speciality [speʃɪ'ælɪtɪ] *n* especialidad *f*.

specialization [speʃəlaɪ'zeɪʃən] *n (of study)* especialidad *f*; *(act)* especialización *f*.

specialize ['speʃəlaɪz] *vi* especializarse (**in**, en).

specialty ['speʃəltɪ] *n US see* **speciality.**

species ['spiːʃiːz] *n (pl* **species)** *Biol* especie *f*.

specific [spɪ'sɪfɪk] **I** *adj (gen)* específico,-a; *(definite)* concreto,-a; *(precise, exact)* preciso,-a; *(clear in meaning)* explícito,-a; **for a s. reason,** por una razón concreta; **to be s.,** concretar. ▪ **s. gravity,** peso *m* específico. **II** *n* **1** *Med (drug)* específico *m*. **2 specifics,** datos *mpl* (concretos). ◆ **specifically** *adv* **1** *(exactly)* específicamente, concretamente; *(expressly)* expresamente. **2** *(namely)* en concreto.

specification [spesɪfɪ'keɪʃən] *n* **1** *(gen)* especificación *f*. **2** *(plan)* plan *m* detallado; *(proposal)* propuesta *f* detallada. **3 specifications,** datos *mpl* específicos.

specify ['spesɪfaɪ] *vtr (pt & pp* **specified)** especificar, precisar, concretar.

specimen ['spesɪmɪn] *n (sample)* muestra *f*, espécimen *m*; *(example)* ejemplar *m*; **blood s.,** muestra de sangre; **s. copy,** ejemplar de muestra; **s. signature,** muestra de firma; **urine/tissue s.,** espécimen de orina/tejido; *fam* **he's a strange s.,** es un bicho raro.

specious ['spiːʃəs] *adj* engañoso,-a, especioso,-a.

speck [spek] *n (of dust, soot)* mota *f*; *(stain)* manchita *f*; *(small trace)* pizca *f*; *(dot)* punto *m* negro.

speckled ['spekəld] *adj* moteado,-a, con puntitos.

specs [speks] *npl fam abbr of* **spectacles.**

spectacle ['spektəkəl] *n* **1** *(display)* espectáculo *m*; **to make a s. of oneself,** hacer el ridículo, ponerse en ridículo. **2 spectacles,** *(glasses)* gafas *fpl*; *fig* **to see everything through rose-tinted s.,** verlo todo de color rosa. ▪ **s. case,** estuche *m* de gafas.

spectacular [spek'tækjʊləʳ] **I** *adj* espectacular, impresionante. **II** *n Cin TV* (gran) espectáculo *m*, superproducción *f*.

spectator [spek'teɪtəʳ] *n* espectador,-a *m, f*; **the spectators,** el público. ▪ **s. sport,** deporte *m* espectáculo, deporte *m* de masas.

spectre, *US* **specter** ['spektəʳ] *n* espectro *m*, fantasma *m*.

spectrum ['spektrəm] *n (pl* **spectra** ['spektrə]) **1** *Phys* espectro *m*. **2** *(range)* espectro *m*, gama *f*.

speculate ['spekjʊleɪt] *vi (gen)* especular (**on** *or* **about**, sobre).

speculation [spekjʊ'leɪʃən] *n* especulación *f*.

speculator ['spekjʊleɪtəʳ] *n Fin* especulador,-a *m, f*.

sped [sped] *pt & pp see* **speed.**

speech [spiːtʃ] *n* **1** *(faculty)* habla *f*; *(pronunciation)* pronunciación *f*; **freedom of s.,** libertad de expresión; **s. defect,** defecto del habla. ▪ **s. therapist,** foniatra *mf*, logopeda *mf*; **s. therapy,** terapia *f* de la palabra. **2** *(address)* discurso *m*; *(talk)* charla *f*; *(lecture)* conferencia *f*; **to give** *or* **make a s.,** pronunciar un discurso (**on**, sobre); *GB Sch* **s. day,** día *m* del reparto de premios. **3** *Ling* oración *f*; **direct/indirect s.,** oración directa/ indirecta; **part of s.,** parte *f* de la oración.

speechless ['spiːtʃlɪs] *adj* mudo,-a, boquiabierto,-a.

speed [spiːd] **I** *n* **1** *(rate of movement)* velocidad *f*; *(quickness, rapidity)* rapidez *f*; *(haste)* prisa *f*; **at a s. of ...,** a una velocidad de ...; **at top s.,** a toda velocidad, a toda marcha; **to pick up** *or* **gain s.,** coger velocidad. ▪ *fam* **s. cop,** motoricón *m*; **s. limit,** velocidad *f* máxima; **s. trap,**

control *m* policial de velocidad, foto-radar *f*. **2** *Cycl* velocidad *f*. **3** *Phot (of film)* velocidad *f*; *(aperture)* abertura *f*. **4** *(drug) sl* anfeta *f*. **II** *vi* **1** *(pt & pp* **sped)** *(person) (go fast)* ir corriendo, ir a toda prisa; *(hurry)* apresurarse, darse prisa; *(car etc)* ir a toda velocidad; **to s. along,** ir a toda velocidad; **to s. past,** pasar volando. **2** *(pt & pp* **speeded)** *Jur (exceed speed limit)* conducir con exceso de velocidad. ◆ **speed up I** *vtr (pt & pp* **speeded up)** *(process, matter)* acelerar; *(person)* apresurar. **II** *vi (of person)* darse prisa, apresurarse.

speedboat ['spiːdbəʊt] *n* lancha *f* rápida.

speeding ['spiːdɪŋ] *n Aut* exceso *m* de velocidad.

speedometer [spɪ'dɒmɪtəʳ] *n Aut* velocímetro *m*.

speedway ['spiːdweɪ] *n Sport* **1** *(racing)* carreras *fpl* de moto. **2** *(track)* pista *f* de carreras.

speedwell ['spiːdwel] *n Bot* verónica *f*.

speedy ['spiːdɪ] *adj (speedier, speediest) (quick)* veloz, rápido,-a; *(prompt)* pronto,-a. ◆ **speedily** *adv (quickly)* rápidamente, con toda prisa; *(promptly)* con la mayor prontitud.

spell[1] [spel] **I** *vtr (pt & pp* **spelt** *or* **spelled)** **1** *(write)* escribir correctamente; *(letter by letter)* deletrear; **b-o-x spells 'box',** 'box' se deletrea b-o-x; **how do you s. it?,** ¿cómo se escribe *or* deletrea? **2** *fig (denote)* significar, representar; *(foretell)* presagiar; **this news spells disaster for the country,** esta noticia representa un desastre para el país. **II** *vi* saber escribir correctamente; **she can't s.,** (siempre) hace faltas de ortografía. ◆ **spell out** *vtr fig* explicar con detalle.

spell[2] [spel] *n (magical)* hechizo *m*, encanto *m*; **to cast a s. on sb,** hechizar a algn.

spell[3] [spel] *n* **1** *(period)* temporada *f*, período *m*; *(short period)* rato *m*, racha *f*; *(rest)* descanso *m*; *Meteor* **cold s.,** ola *f* *or* racha de frío; **he's going through a good/bad s.,** está pasando una buena/mala época *or* racha. **2** *(shift)* turno *m*, tanda *f*.

spellbound ['spelbaʊnd] *adj* hechizado,-a, embelesado,-a.

spelling ['spelɪŋ] *n* ortografía *f*; **s. mistake,** falta de ortografía.

spelt [spelt] *pt & pp see* **spell**[1].

spend [spend] *vtr (pt & pp* **spent) 1** *(money)* gastar (**on**, en); *GB fam* **to s. a penny,** hacer pipí. **2** *(time)* pasar; **we spent Christmas in Scotland,** pasamos las Navidades en Escocia. **3** *(devote) (time)* dedicar; **s. more time on your homework,** dedica más tiempo a tus deberes.

spending ['spendɪŋ] *n* gasto *m*, gastos *mpl*; **public s.,** gasto público. ▪ **s. cuts,** recortes *mpl* en el presupuesto; **s. money,** dinero *m* de bolsillo; **s. power,** poder *m* adquisitivo.

spendthrift ['spendθrɪft] *adj & n* derrochador,-a *(m, f)*, despilfarrador,-a *(m, f)*, manirroto,-a *(m, f)*.

spent [spent] **I** *pt & pp see* **spend. II** *adj* gastado,-a; **s. bullet,** bala muerta; *(person)* **to be a s. force,** estar quemado,-a.

sperm [spɜːm] *n (pl* **sperms** *or* **sperm)** *Biol* esperma *mf*. ◆ **sperm s. bank,** banco *m* de esperma; *Zool* **s. whale,** cachalote *m*.

spermicide ['spɜːmɪsaɪd] *n Med* espermicida *m*.

spew [spjuː] **I** *vtr* **1 to s. (up),** vomitar, devolver. **2 to s. (out),** *(flames etc)* vomitar, arrojar. **II** *vi* vomitar, devolver.

sphere [sfɪəʳ] *n (gen)* esfera *f*; **in the s. of politics,** en el mundo de la política; **it's outside my s.,** no es de mi competencia; **s. of activity/influence,** esfera de actividad/influencia.

spheric(al) ['sferɪk(əl)] *adj* esférico,-a.

sphincter ['sfɪŋktəʳ] *n Anat* esfínter *m*.

sphinx [sfɪŋks] *n (pl* **sphinxes** *or* **sphinges** ['sfɪndʒiːz]) esfinge *f*.

spice [spaɪs] **I** n **1** Culin especia f; **mixed spice(s),** especias mixtas. **2** fig sazón m, sal f; prov **variety is the s. of life,** en la variedad está el gusto. **II** vtr **1** Culin sazonar, condimentar. **2** (story etc) **to s. (up),** echar salsa a, cargar las tintas.

spic(k)-and-span [spɪkən'spæn] adj (very clean) limpísimo,-a; (like new) flamante; (neat) pulcro,-a; (well-groomed) acicalado,-a.

spicy ['spaɪsɪ] adj (spicier, spiciest) **1** Culin sazonado,-a, condimentado,-a; (hot) picante. **2** fig (story etc) picante.

spider ['spaɪdəʳ] n araña f. ■ **s.'s web,** telaraña f; **s. plant,** cinta f.

spiel [ʃpiːl] n fam rollo m.

spigot ['spɪgət] n **1** (stopper) espita f, bitoque m. **2** US (tap) grifo m.

spike[1] [spaɪk] n **1** (sharp point) punta f; (metal rod) pincho m; (stake) estaca f; (on railing) barrote m; Sport (on shoes) clavo m. **2** Sport **spikes,** zapatillas fpl con clavos.

spike[2] [spaɪk] n Bot espiga f.

spiky ['spaɪkɪ] adj (spikier, spikiest) (gen) puntiagudo,-a; (hedgehog) erizado,-a; (hairstyle) de punta.

spill [spɪl] **I** vtr (pt & pp **spilled** or **spilt**) (liquid) derramar; (pour) verter; (knock over) volcar; fam **to s. the beans,** descubrir el pastel. **II** vi (liquid) derramarse, verterse. **III** n (spilling) derrame m; fam **to take a s.,** caerse, medir el suelo. ◆ **spill out** vi (crowd) salir en tropel. ◆ **spill over** vi salirse, desbordarse.

spillage ['spɪlɪdʒ] n derrame m.

spilt [spɪlt] pt & pp see **spill.**

spin [spɪn] **I** vtr (pt & pp **spun**) **1** (turn) (wheel etc) hacer girar, dar vueltas a; (washing) centrifugar; **to s. a coin for sth,** echar algo a cara o cruz. **II** vtr **1** (cotton, wool, etc) hilar; (spider's web) tejer; fam **to s. sb a yarn,** pegarle un rollo a algn. **II** vi **1** (wheel etc) girar, dar vueltas; Av (dive) caer en barrena; Aut (slide) patinar; **my head was spinning,** la cabeza me daba vueltas; **to send sth spinning,** echar algo a rodar; **to s. round and round,** dar vueltas y más vueltas. **2** (cotton, wool, etc) hilar. **III** n **1** (turn) vuelta f, giro m, revolución f; (of spin-dryer) **long/short s.,** centrifugado m largo/corto; **to give sth a s.,** hacer girar algo; GB fam **to be in a flat s.,** estar hecho un lío. **2** Sport efecto m; **to put s. on the ball,** dar efecto a la pelota. **3** Av barrena f; Aut patinazo m; **to go into a s.,** Av caer en barrena; Aut patinar. **4** (ride) vuelta f, paseo m (en coche or en moto); **to go for a s.,** dar una vuelta. ◆ **spin out** vtr fam (holiday, speech) alargar, prolongar; (time, money) estirar.

spinach ['spɪnɪtʃ] n espinacas fpl

spinal ['spaɪnəl] adj Anat espinal, vertebral. ■ **s. column,** columna f vertebral, **s. cord,** médula f espinal

spindle ['spɪndəl] n **1** (for spinning) huso m. **2** Tech (axle) eje m, (of lathe) mandril m

spindly ['spɪndlɪ] adj (spindlier, spindliest) fam (long-bodied) larguirucho,-a, (long-legged) zanquilargo,-a, zanquivano,-a

spin-dry [spɪn'draɪ] vtr centrifugar

spin-dryer [spɪn'draɪəʳ] n secador m centrífugo

spine [spaɪn] n **1** Anat columna f vertebral, espina f dorsal, espinazo m, (of book) lomo m. **2** Zool (of hedgehog etc) púa f, Bot espina f

spine-chilling ['spaɪntʃɪlɪŋ] adj horripilante, escalofriante

spineless ['spaɪnlɪs] adj **1** (invertebrate) invertebrado,-a. **2** fig (weak) débil, sin carácter

spinet ['spɪnɪt] n Mus espineta f

spinner ['spɪnəʳ] n **1** (of cotton, wool, etc) hilandero,-a m, f. **2** Fishing cuchara f

spinney ['spɪnɪ] n bosquecillo m, soto m

spinning ['spɪnɪŋ] n **1** (of cotton, wool, etc) (act) hilado m, (art) hilandería f. ■ **s. machine,** máquina f de hilar, **s. wheel,** rueca f, torno m de hilar. **2** (toy) **s. top,** peonza f, trompo m

spin-off ['spɪnɒf] n (by-product) derivado m, producto m secundario, fig efecto m secundario

spinster ['spɪnstəʳ] n soltera f, pej **she's an old s.,** es una vieja solterona

spiny ['spaɪnɪ] adj (spinier, spiniest) espinoso,-a

spiral ['spaɪərəl] **I** n Geom espiral f. **II** adj espiral, en espiral. ■ **s. staircase,** escalera f de caracol. **III** vi (pt & pp **spiralled,** US **spiraled**) moverse en espiral, **spiralling prices,** precios en alza vertiginosa, **to s. up/down,** subir/bajar en espiral

spire [spaɪəʳ] n Archit aguja f

spirit[1] ['spɪrɪt] n **1** (soul) espíritu m, alma f, (ghost) fantasma m, **evil s.,** espíritu maligno. ■ Rel **the Holy S.,** el Espíritu Santo. **2** (person) ser m, alma f. **3** (attitude) espíritu m, (mood) humor m, **community s.,** civismo m, **team s.,** espíritu de equipo, **to enter into the s. of sth,** meterse en el ambiente de algo, fam **that's the s.!** ¡eso es!, ¡así me gusta! **4** (courage) valor m, (liveliness) ánimo m, energía f, (vitality) vitalidad f, vigor m, (strength) fuerza f, **she lacks s.,** le falta carácter, **to break sb's s.,** quebrar la voluntad de algn, **to show s.,** dar muestras de valor. **5** (intention) espíritu m, sentido m, **to take sth in the right s.,** tomar algo a bien. **6 spirits,** (mood) humor m sing, moral f sing, **to be in good s.,** estar de buen humor, **to be in high/low s.,** estar muy animado/desanimado, **to raise sb's s.,** subirle la moral a algn. ◆ **spirit away, spirit off** vtr llevarse como por arte de magia

spirit[2] ['spɪrɪt] n **I** Chem alcohol m. ■ **s. lamp,** lámpara f de alcohol, Constr **s. level,** nivel m de aire. **2 spirits,** (alcoholic drink) licores m, alcohol m sing

spirited ['spɪrɪtɪd] adj (person) animado,-a, (horse) fogoso,-a, (attack, reply) enérgico,-a, vigoroso,-a, (person, attempt) valiente, Mus **to give a s. performance,** tocar con brío

spiritual ['spɪrɪtjʊəl] **I** adj espiritual. **II** n Mus (Negro) **s.,** espiritual m negro

spiritualism ['spɪrɪtjʊəlɪzəm] n espiritismo m

spiritualist ['spɪrɪtjʊəlɪst] adj & n espiritista (mf)

spit[1] [spɪt] **I** vtr (pt & pp **spat**) escupir. **II** vi escupir (**at, in** or **on, en**), (fire) chisporrotear, **it's spitting (with rain),** chispea, caen gotas, fam **he's the spitting image of his father,** es el vivo retrato de su padre, es clavado a su padre. **III** n (saliva) saliva f, esputo m, fam **s. and polish,** pulcritud f, limpieza f. ◆ **spit out** vtr escupir, GB fam **s. it out!,** suéltalo ya!

spit[2] [spɪt] n **1** Culin asador m, espetón m. **2** Geog (of sand) banco m, (of land) punta f, lengua f

spite [spaɪt] n **I** n **1** (ill will) rencor m, ojeriza f, **out of s.,** por despecho. **2** (despite) **in s. of,** a pesar de, pese a, **in s. of being shy,** a pesar de ser tímido,-a, **in s. of everything,** a pesar de todo, **in s. of the fact that,** a pesar de que, pese a que. **II** vtr (annoy) fastidiar

spiteful ['spaɪtfʊl] adj (person) rencoroso,-a, (remark) malévolo,-a, (tongue) viperino,-a ◆ **spitefully** adv con rencor, por despecho

spitefulness ['spaɪtfʊlnɪs] n rencor m, despecho m

spittle ['spɪtəl] n saliva f, baba f

spittoon [spɪ'tuːn] n escupidera f.

spiv [spɪv] n GB sl chanchullero m, (black marketeer) chalán m

splash [splæʃ] **I** vtr **1** (make noise) chapotear, chapalear. **2** (spray) salpicar, rociar (**with,** de), **he splashed coffee on his suit,** se manchó el traje de café, **to s. sb with water,** salpicar a algn de agua, fig **the news was splashed across the front page,** la noticia salió en grandes titulares de primera plana. **II** vi **1** (move) chapotear, **to s. (about),** chapotear. **2** (of water, mud, etc) esparcirse, rociarse. **III** n **1** (noise) chapoteo m, chapaleo m. **2** (spray) salpicadura f, rociada f, fig (of colour, light) mancha f, fam **to make a s.,** causar sensación. **IV** interj ¡plaf! ◆ **splash down** vi Astronaut amerizar. ◆ **splash out** vi fam derrochar dinero (**on,** en), tirar la casa por la ventana

splashdown ['splæʃdaʊn] *n Astronaut* amerizaje *m*, amaraje *m*

spleen [spli:n] *n* 1 *Anat* bazo *m*. 2 *fml fig (anger)* cólera *f*, ira *f*, **to vent one's s.**, descargar cólera (**on**, en)

splendid ['splendɪd] *adj (excellent)* estupendo,-a, maravilloso,-a, *(magnificent)* espléndido,-a, magnífico,-a

splendour, *US* **splendor** ['splendə^r] *n* esplendor *m*

splice [splaɪs] *vtr (rope)* empalmar, *Cin* montar, *GB fam* **to get spliced**, pasar por la vicaría, casarse

splicer ['splaɪsə^r] *n Cin* máquina *f* de montaje, montadora *f*

splint [splɪnt] *n Med* tablilla *f*, **to be in splints**, estar entablillado,-a

splinter ['splɪntə^r] I *n (wood)* astilla *f*, *(bone, stone, metal)* esquirla *f*, *(glass)* fragmento *m*. ▪ *Pol* **s. group**, grupo *m* disidente, facción *f*. II *vi* 1 *(wood, metal, etc)* astillarse, hacerse astillas. 2 *Pol (party)* escindirse. III *vtr (wood, metal, etc)* astillar, hacer astillas

split [splɪt] I *n* 1 *(crack)* grieta *f*, hendidura *f*; *(tear)* desgarrón *m*, rasgón *m*, *fig (division)* división *f*, ruptura *f*, cisma *m*, *Pol* escisión *f*. 2 *Gymn* **splits**, **to do the s.**, abrir las piernas en cruz, despatarrarse. 3 *Culin* **banana s.**, postre *m* de plátano con helado, banana split *m*, **cream/ jam s.**, pastelito *m* con relleno de nata/mermelada. II *adj (gen)* partido,-a, hendido,-a, *(party)* escindido,-a, **in a s. second**, en una fracción de segundo. ◆ *Hairdr* **s. ends**, puntas *fpl* rotas; *Culin* **s. peas**, guisantes *mpl* secos; *Psych* **s. personality**, desdoblamiento *m* de personalidad. III *vtr (pt & pp* **split**) 1 *(crack, break)* agrietar, hender; *(cut)* partir; *(tear)* rajar, desgarrar; *Phys (atom)* desintegrar; **to s. one's head open**, romperse *or* partirse la crisma; *fig* **to s. hairs**, rizar el rizo, buscarle tres pies al gato; *fig* **to s. one's sides laughing**, partirse *or* troncharse de risa. 2 *(divide)* dividir. 3 *(share out)* repartir, dividir; *fam* **to s. the difference**, partir la diferencia. 4 *Pol (party)* escindir. IV *vi* 1 *(crack, break)* agrietarse, henderse; *(into two parts)* partirse; *(garment)* rajarse, desgarrarse. 2 *(divide)* dividirse. 3 *Pol (party)* escindirse. 4 *fam (tell tales)* soplar, chivarse; **to s. on sb**, chivarse de algn. 5 *sl (leave)* pirárselas, largarse. ◆ **split off** I *vtr* separar. II *vi* separarse, desprenderse. ◆ **split up** I *vtr (break up)* partir; *(separate, divide up)* dividir; *(share out)* repartir. II *vi (crowd, meeting)* dispersarse; *(couple)* separarse.

splitting ['splɪtɪŋ] *adj (headache)* terrible, muy fuerte.

splodge [splɒdʒ] *n fam*, **splotch** [splɒtʃ] *n fam* mancha *f*, borrón *m*.

splurge [splɜːdʒ] *vtr fam* despilfarrar el dinero (**on**, en).

splutter ['splʌtə^r] *vi* 1 *(person)* balbucear, farfullar. 2 *(candle, fat)* chisporrotear; *(engine)* petardear, renquear.

spoil [spɔɪl] I *vtr (pt & pp* **spoiled** *or* **spoilt**) 1 *(ruin)* estropear, echar a perder; **it will s. your appetite**, te quitará el apetito; **to s. sb's fun**, aguarle la fiesta a algn. 2 *(allow everything)* mimar, consentir; *(treat generously)* mimar; **to be spoilt for choice**, tener demasiadas cosas para elegir. II *vi (food)* estropearse, echarse a perder. III **spoils** *npl fml* botín *m sing*. ◆ **spoil for** *vtr* buscar; **to be spoiling for a fight**, buscar camorra.

spoilsport ['spɔɪlspɔːt] *n fam* aguafiestas *mf inv*.

spoilt [spɔɪlt] I *vtr pt & pp see* **spoil.** II *adj* 1 *(food, merchandise)* estropeado,-a. 2 *(child)* mimado,-a, consentido,-a.

spoke¹ [spəʊk] *pt see* **speak.**

spoke² [spəʊk] *n (of wheel)* radio *m*, rayo *m*; *fam* **to put a s. in sb's wheel**, poner trabas a algn.

spoken ['spəʊkən] *pp see* **speak.**

spokesman ['spəʊksmən] *n (pl* **spokesmen**) portavoz *m*.

spokeswoman ['spəʊkswʊmən] *n (pl* **spokeswomen** ['spəʊkswɪmɪn]) *n* portavoz *f*.

sponge [spʌndʒ] I *n (gen)* esponja *f*, *fig* **to throw in the s.**, arrojar la toalla. ▪ *GB* **s. bag**, bolsa *f* de aseo, neceser *m*; *GB Culin* **s. cake**, bizcocho *m*. II *vtr (wash)* limpiar *or* lavar *or* fregar con esponja; **to s. a stain off** *or* **out**, quitar una mancha con una esponja. III *vi fam (scrounge)* vivir de gorra, gorrear, dar sablazos. ◆ **sponge down** *vtr* limpiar *or* lavar *or* fregar con esponja. ◆ **sponge off**, **sponge on** *vtr* vivir a costa de.

sponger ['spʌndʒə^r] *n fam* gorrón,-ona *m,f*, sablista *mf*.

spongy ['spʌndʒɪ] *adj (spongier, spongiest)* esponjoso,-a.

sponsor ['spɒnsə^r] I *vtr (gen)* patrocinar; *Fin* avalar, garantizar; *Rel* apadrinar; *(support)* respaldar, apoyar. II *n (gen)* patrocinador,-a *m,f*; *Fin* avalador,-a *m,f*, garante *mf*; *Rel* padrino,-a *m,f*.

sponsorship ['spɒnsəʃɪp] *n (gen)* patrocinio *m*; *Fin* aval *m*, garantía *f*; *(support)* respaldo *m*, apoyo *m*.

spontaneity [spɒntə'neɪtɪ] *n* espontaneidad *f*.

spontaneous [spɒn'teɪnɪəs] *adj* espontáneo,-a.

spoof [spu:f] *n fam* 1 *(parody)* parodia *f*, burla *f*. 2 *(hoax)* engaño *m*, broma *f*.

spooky ['spu:kɪ] *adj (spookier, spookiest)* *fam* espeluznante, horripilante, escalofriante.

spool [spu:l] *n Phot Sew* bobina *f*, carrete *m*.

spoon [spu:n] I *n (gen)* cuchara *f*; *(small)* cucharilla *f*, cucharita *f*; **coffee s.**, cucharilla de café; **dessert s.**, cuchara de postre; **soup s.**, cuchara sopera; *fig* **to be born with a silver s. in one's mouth**, nacer con un pan bajo el brazo. II *vtr (gen)* sacar con cuchara; *(serve)* servir con cuchara.

spoon-feed ['spu:nfi:d] *vtr (pt & pp* **spoon-fed**) *(baby)* dar de comer con cuchara a; *fig (pupil)* dar la lección masticada a; *(spoil)* mimar.

spoonerism ['spu:nərɪzəm] *n* trastocamiento *m* de letras, juego *m* de palabras.

spoonful ['spu:nfʊl] *(pl* **spoonfuls** *or* **spoonsful**) *n* cucharada *f*.

sporadic [spə'rædɪk] *adj* esporádico,-a, intermitente.

spore [spɔː^r] *n Biol* espora *f*.

sporran ['spɒrən] *n Scot* escarcela *f* que se lleva encima de la falda escocesa.

sport [spɔːt] I *n* 1 *(gen)* deporte *m*; **to be good at s.**, ser buen deportista. 2 *(amusement)* diversión *f*; *fml* **to say sth in s.**, decir algo en broma; *fam* **he's a good s.**, es buena persona; **be a s.!**, ¡sé amable! II *vtr (display)* lucir.

sporting ['spɔːtɪŋ] *adj* 1 *(of sport)* deportivo,-a; **s. event**, acontecimiento deportivo. 2 *(generous)* caballeroso,-a, justo,-a, deportivo,-a.

sports [spɔːts] I *npl* deportes *mpl*, deporte *m sing*; **winter s.**, deportes de invierno. II *adj* deportivo,-a, de sport. ▪ **s. car**, coche *m* deportivo; **s. day**, día *m* dedicado a los deportes; **s. ground**, terreno *m* de deportes; **s. jacket**, chaqueta *f* (de) sport.

sportsman ['spɔːtsmən] *n (pl* **sportsmen**) deportista *m*.

sportsmanlike ['spɔːtsmənlaɪk] *adj (attitude, gesture)* caballeroso,-a, deportivo,-a.

sportsmanship ['spɔːtsmənʃɪp] *n* espíritu *m* deportivo, deportividad *f*.

sportswear ['spɔːtsweə^r] *n (for sport)* ropa *f* de deporte; *(casual clothes)* ropa *f* (de) sport.

sportswoman ['spɔːtswʊmən] *n (pl* **sportswomen** ['spɔːtswɪmɪn]) deportista *f*.

sporty ['spɔːtɪ] *adj (sportier, sportiest)* *fam* deportivo,-a, aficionado,-a a los deportes.

spot [spɒt] *n* 1 *(dot)* punto *m*; *(on fabric)* lunar *m*; **to have spots before one's eyes**, ver manchas; *fam* **to knock spots off sb**, *(defeat)* vencer fácilmente a algn; *(surpass)* dejar atrás a algn. 2 *(mark, stain)* mancha *f*. 3 *Med* grano *m*. 4 *(place)* sitio *m*, lugar *m*; **a quiet s.**, un lugar tranquilo. ▪ **accident black s.**, punto *m* negro; **night s.**, centro *m* de vida nocturna; 5 *(there)* **on the s.**, allí, presente; **to decide sth on the s.**, decidir algo en el acto. ▪ **s. check**, comprobación *f* al instante, chequeo *m or* reconocimiento *m* rápido. 6 *(point on the body)* punto *m*;

tender s., punto sensible; *fig* weak s., punto débil *or* flaco; *fig* to have a soft s. for sb, tener una debilidad por algn. 7 *(trouble)* lío *m*, apuro *m*, aprieto *m*; to be in a tight s., estar en un apuro *or* aprieto; to put sb on the s., poner a algn en un aprieto. 8 *fam (small amount)* poquito *m*, poquitín *m*; a s. of bother, unos problemillas, un pequeño disgusto. 9 *Rad TV Theat (in show)* espacio *m*; *(advertisement)* spot *m* (publicitario), anuncio *m*. 10 *fam (spotlight)* foco *m*. II *vtr (pt & pp* spotted) *(notice)* darse cuenta de, notar; *(see)* ver; *(recognize)* reconocer; *(find)* encontrar; *(catch out)* pillar; to s. the winner, elegir el ganador.

spotless ['spɒtlɪs] *adj (very clean)* limpísimo,-a; *(well-groomed)* impecable; *fig (reputation, character)* intachable.

spotlight ['spɒtlaɪt] *n (beam)* foco *m*; *Theat* proyector *m*, foco *m*; *(light)* luz *f* de foco; *Aut* faro *m* auxiliar; *fig* to be in the s., ser objeto de la atención pública, ser el blanco de las miradas.

spot-on [spɒt'ɒn] *adj fam* perfecto,-a, exacto,-a.

spotted ['spɒtɪd] *adj (with dots)* con puntos; *(fabric)* con lunares; *(speckled)* moteado,-a; *(stained)* manchado,-a.

spotter ['spɒtər] *n* observador,-a *m*, *f*. ■ train s., aficionado,-a *m*, *f* a trenes; *Av Mil* s. plane, avión *m* de reconocimiento.

spotty ['spɒtɪ] *adj (spottier, spottiest) pej* con granos.

spot-welding ['spɒtweldɪŋ] *n* soldadura *f* por puntos.

spouse [spauz] *n* cónyuge *mf*.

spout [spaut] I *n (of jug)* pico *m*; *(of teapot)* pitorro *m*; *(of roof gutter)* canalón *m*; *(of fountain)* surtidor *m*; *(jet of water)* chorro *m*; *fam* our plans are up the s., se han fastidiado nuestros planes; *fam* Richard's really up the s. now, Richard se ha metido en un buen apuro. II *vtr* 1 *(liquid)* echar, arrojar. 2 *fam (verse)* declamar; *(nonsense)* soltar. III *vi* 1 *(liquid)* brotar, salir a chorros. 2 *fam (verse etc)* declamar.

sprain [spreɪn] *Med* I *n* torcedura *f*. II *vtr* torcer; to s. one's ankle/wrist, torcerse el tobillo/la muñeca.

sprang [spræŋ] *pt see* spring².

sprat [spræt] *n (fish)* espadín *m*.

sprawl [sprɔːl] I *vi* 1 *(sit, lie)* tumbarse, echarse, repantigarse, repanchingarse. 2 *(city, plant) (stretch out)* extenderse. II *n (of city)* extensión *f*; the urban s., el crecimiento urbano descontrolado.

sprawling ['sprɔːlɪŋ] *adj* 1 *(person)* tumbado,-a. 2 *(city)* de crecimiento descontrolado.

spray¹ [spreɪ] I *n* 1 *(of water)* rociada *f*; *(from sea)* espuma *f*; *(from aerosol, atomizer)* pulverización *f*. 2 *(aerosol)* spray *m*; *(atomizer)* atomizador *m*, vaporizador *m*; *(for garden)* pulverizador *m*. ■ s. can, aerosol *m*; s.gun, pistola *f* pulverizadora, pulverizador *m*; s. paint, pintura *f* spray. II *vtr (water)* rociar, regar; *(perfume)* atomizar, vaporizar; *(insecticide)* pulverizar; *(crops)* fumigar; *fig* to s. sb with bullets, rociar a algn de balas.

spray² [spreɪ] *n (of flowers)* ramita *f*.

sprayer ['spreɪər] *n* pulverizador *m*.

spread [spred] I *n* 1 *(gen)* extensión *f*; *(of ideas)* difusión *f*, diseminación *f*; *(of disease, fire)* propagación *f*; *(of nuclear weapons)* proliferación *f*; *(of terrorism)* aumento *m*. 2 *(scope)* extensión *f*, envergadura *f*; *(range)* gama *f*. 3 *(of wings, sails)* envergadura *f*; *fam* middle-age s., la curva de la felicidad. 4 *Culin (for bread)* pasta *f*; *(cheese)* s., queso para untar. 5 *fam (large meal)* banquetazo *m*, comilona *f*. 6 *Press* full-page s., plana *f* entera; two-page s., doble página *f*. II *vtr (pt & pp* spread) 1 *(unfold)* desplegar; *(lay out)* extender, tender; *fig* to s. one's wings, desplegar las alas. 2 *(butter etc)* untar, extender. 3 *(paint, glue)* extender, repartir. 4 *(news, ideas)* difundir; *(rumour)* hacer correr; *(disease, fire)* propagar; *(panic, terror)* sembrar. III *vi* 1 *(stretch out)* extenderse *(open out, unfold)* desplegarse. 2 *(paint, glue)* extenderse. 3 *(news, ideas)* difundirse, diseminarse, propalarse;

(rumour) correr; *(disease, fire)* propagarse; the news s. like wildfire, la noticia corrió como la pólvora. ◆ spread out I *vtr* 1 *(unfold)* desplegar; *(lay out)* extender, tender; *(scatter)* esparcir. 2 *(payments, visits, etc)* repartir, distribuir. II *vi (stretch out)* extenderse; *(widen)* ensancharse.

spread-eagled [spred'iːɡəld] *adj* con los brazos y piernas abiertos, despatarrado,-a.

spree [spriː] *n* juerga *f*, jarana *f*, parranda *f*; to go on a s., ir de juerga; to go on a shoppbing s., ir a la compra loca.

sprig [sprɪɡ] *n* ramita *f*, ramito *m*.

sprightly ['spraɪtlɪ] *adj (sprightlier, sprightliest) (nimble)* ágil; *(energetic)* enérgico,-a; *(lively)* animado,-a.

spring¹ [sprɪŋ] I *n (season)* primavera *f*; in s., en la primavera. II *adj* primaveral. ■ *Hortic* s. cabbage, col *f* rizada; *Hortic* s. onion, cebolleta *f*; *Culin* s. roll, rollo *m* de primavera; s. tide, marea *f* viva.

spring² [sprɪŋ] I *n* 1 *(of water)* manantial *m*, fuente *f*; hot springs, aguas *fpl* termales. 2 *Tech (watch, lock, etc)* resorte *m*; *(of mattress, seat)* muelle *m*; *Aut* ballesta *f*. II *vi (pt* sprang; *pp* sprung) 1 *(jump)* saltar; he sprang to his feet, se levantó de un salto; nothing springs to mind, no se me ocurre nada; the lid sprang open, la tapa se abrió de golpe. 2 *(appear)* aparecer (de repente); where did you s. from?, ¿de dónde has salido tú? II *vtr* 1 *(boat, pipe)* to s. a leak, hacer agua. 2 *fam (set free)* soltar. 3 *fig (news, surprise)* espetar; he sprang the news on me, me espetó la noticia. ◆ spring up *vi* aparecer; *(plants)* brotar; *(buildings)* elevarse, levantarse; *(friendship)* nacer; *(problems)* surgir.

springboard ['sprɪŋbɔːd] *n* trampolín *m*.

spring-clean [sprɪŋ'kliːn] *vtr* limpiar a fondo, hacer una limpieza general de.

spring-cleaning [sprɪŋ'kliːnɪŋ] *n* limpieza *f* a fondo, limpieza *f* general.

spring-like ['sprɪŋlaɪk] *adj* primaveral.

springtime ['sprɪŋtaɪm] *n* primavera *f*.

springy ['sprɪŋɪ] *adj (springier, springiest) (bouncy)* elástico,-a; *fig (step)* ligero,-a.

sprinkle ['sprɪŋkəl] *vtr (with water)* rociar, salpicar (with, de); *(with sugar, flour)* espolvorear (with, de).

sprinkler ['sprɪŋklər] *n* 1 *(water)* aspersor *m*. 2 *(for sugar)* espolvoreador *m* de azúcar.

sprinkling ['sprɪŋklɪŋ] *n fig* pizca *f*; there was a s. of rain, cayeron unas gotas.

sprint [sprɪnt] I *n Sport* sprint *m*, esprint *m*; *(dash)* carrera *f* corta. II *vi Sport* sprintar, esprintar; *(dash)* correr a toda velocidad.

sprinter ['sprɪntər] *n Sport* sprínter *mf*, esprínter *mf*. ■

sprocket ['sprɒkɪt] *n Tech* diente *m* de engranaje. ■ s. wheel, rueda *f* dentada.

sprout [spraut] I *vtr* echar; he's sprouting a beard, le está saliendo barba. II *vi (bud)* brotar; *(branch)* echar brotes; *fig* crecer rápidamente. III *n Bot (shoot)* brote *m*, retoño *m*. ■ (Brussels) sprouts, coles *fpl* de Bruselas.

spruce¹ [spruːs] *n inv Bot* picea *f*. ■ Norway s., picea *f* de Noruega, abeto *m* rojo.

spruce² [spruːs] *adj (neat)* pulcro,-a, acicalado,-a; *(smart)* apuesto,-a. ◆ spruce up *vtr* arreglar, acicalar.

sprung [sprʌŋ] I *pp see* spring². II *adj* de muelles.

spry [spraɪ] *adj (sprier, spriest) (nimble)* ágil; *(active)* activo,-a; *(energetic)* enérgico,-a; *(lively)* vivaz, animado,-a.

spud [spʌd] *n fam* patata *f*.

spun [spʌn] I *pt & pp see* spin. II *adj* s. silk, seda *f* hilada.

spunk [spʌŋk] *n* 1 *fam (courage)* valor *m*. 2 *sl vulg (semen)* leche *f*.

spunky ['spʌŋkɪ] *adj (spunkier, spunkiest) fam* valiente.

spur [spɜːʳ] **I** n **1** (of horserider) espuela f; Zool (of cock) espolón m. **2** fig (stimulus) aguijón m, espuela f; **on the s. of the moment,** sin pensarlo; fig **to win one's spurs,** dar pruebas de su valor. **2** Geog espolón m, estribación f. **II** vtr (pt & pp **spurred**) **1** (horse) espolear, picar con las espuelas. **2** fig (stimulate) estimular, incitar, aguijonear.

spurious ['spjʊərɪəs] adj falso,-a, espurio,-a.

spurn [spɜːn] vtr fml (disdain) desdeñar, despreciar; (reject) rechazar.

spurt [spɜːt] **I** n **1** (of liquid) chorro m. **2** fig (of activity, effort, emotion) racha f, ataque m; (effort) esfuerzo m; Sport **final s.,** esfuerzo final. **II** vi **1** (liquid) chorrear, salir a chorro. **2** (make an effort) hacer un último esfuerzo, esforzarse; (accelerate) acelerar; Sport **to s. ahead,** acelerar, esprintar.

sputter ['spʌtəʳ] vi (candle, fat, fire) chisporrotear; (engine) petardear, renquear.

sputum ['spjuːtəm] n (pl **sputa** ['spjuːtə]) Med esputo m.

spy [spaɪ] **I** n espía mf. ■ **police s.,** confidente mf, soplón,-ona m, f, chivato,-a m, f; **s. ring,** red f de espionaje. **II** vtr (pt & pp **spied**) fml (see) divisar. **III** vi espiar (on, a). ◆
spy out vtr **1** (investigate) espiar, investigar. **2** (land) reconocer, explorar.

spyglass ['spaɪglɑːs] n catalejo m.

spyhole ['spaɪhəʊl] n mirilla f.

spying ['spaɪɪŋ] n espionaje m.

Sq abbr of **Square,** Plaza f, Pza., Plza.

sq abbr of **square,** cuadrado,-a.

Sqn Ldr Mil abbr of **Squadron Leader,** Comandante m (de escuadrilla), Cte.

squabble ['skwɒbəl] **I** n riña f, disputa f, pelea f. **II** vi reñir, disputar, pelearse (over, por; about, sobre).

squabbling ['skwɒbəlɪŋ] n riñas fpl, disputas fpl, peleas fpl.

squad [skwɒd] n Mil pelotón m; (of police) brigada f; Sport equipo m. ■ **drugs s.,** brigada f antidroga; **firing s.,** pelotón m de fusilamiento or ejecución; **flying s.,** brigada f móvil; **s. car,** coche m patrulla.

squadron ['skwɒdrən] n Mil escuadrón m; Av escuadrilla f; Naut escuadra f; **s. leader,** comandante de escuadrilla.

squalid ['skwɒlɪd] adj (very dirty) sucio,-a, mugriento,-a, asqueroso,-a; (poor) miserable; (sordid) sórdido,-a; (motive) vil.

squall¹ [skwɔːl] n (wind) ráfaga f; (storm) chubasco m, tormenta f.

squall² [skwɔːl] vi chillar, berrear.

squalor ['skwɒləʳ] n (dirtiness) suciedad f, mugre f, (poverty) miseria f.

squander ['skwɒndəʳ] vtr (money) malgastar, derrochar, despilfarrar; (inheritance) dilapidar; (time) desperdiciar.

square [skweəʳ] **I** n **1** (shape) cuadrado m, cuadro m; (on fabric) cuadro m; (on chessboard, crossword, graph paper) casilla f; fig **we're back to s. one!,** ¡volvemos a partir desde cero! **2** (in town) plaza f; (in barracks) patio m; US (block of houses) manzana f. **3** Math cuadrado m; **9 is the s. of 3,** 9 es el cuadrado de 3. **4** fam (old-fashioned person) carroza mf; (conservative) carca mf. **II** adj **1** (in shape) cuadrado,-a; (forming right angle) en ángulo recto; fam **a s. peg in a round hole,** gallina en corral ajeno. ■ Typ **s. brackets,** corchetes mpl; **s. dance,** baile m de figuras. **2** Math cuadrado,-a. ■ **s. metre,** metro m cuadrado; **s. root,** raíz f cuadrada. **3** fam (fair) justo,-a, equitativo,-a; (honest) honesto,-a; **to be s. with sb,** ser franco,-a con algn; **to get a s. deal,** recibir un trato justo; **to get s. with sb,** ajustar cuentas con algn. **4** a **s. meal,** una buena comida, una comida decente. **5** fam (old-fashioned) carroza; (conservative) carca. **III** adv (straight) justamente, exactamente; **s. in the middle of,** justo en medio de; **s. on the chin,** de lleno en la barbilla. **IV** vtr **1** (make square) cuadrar; **to s. one's shoulders,** ponerse derecho, sacar el pecho. **2** Math

cuadrar, elevar al cuadrado; **3 squared is 9,** 3 al cuadrado es 9. **3** (settle) arreglar, ajustar; **to s. matters,** arreglar las cosas. **V** vi (agree) cuadrar, concordar (with, con). ◆
square up vi **1** (fighters) ponerse en guardia; fig **to s. up to a problem,** hacer frente a un problema. **2** fam (settle) ajustar saldar cuentas con algn. ◆ **squarely** adv (directly, straight) directamente, de lleno.

squared ['skweəd] adj (paper) cuadriculado,-a.

squash¹ [skwɒʃ] **I** n **1** (crush) aplastamiento m; (in crowd) apiñamiento m, agolpamiento m, apretujón m. **2** GB Culin (drink) zumo m, jugo m. ■ **orange s.,** naranjada f, zumo m de naranja. **II** vtr **1** (crush, flatten) aplastar, esparruchar, chafar. **2** fig (argument, objection) echar por tierra, dar al traste con; (person) apabullar, callar. **III** vi (crush) aplastarse, espachurrarse, chafarse.

squash² [skwɒʃ] n Sport squash m. ■ **s. court,** pista f de squash.

squash³ [skwɒʃ] n Bot calabaza f.

squashy ['skwɒʃɪ] adj (squashier, squashiest) blando,-a, fofo,-a, esponjoso,-a.

squat [skwɒt] **I** adj **1** (person) rechoncho,-a, achaparrado,-a. **2** (building) ocupado,-a ilegalmente. **II** vi (pt & pp **squatted**) **1** (crouch) agacharse, sentarse en cuclillas. **2** (in building) ocupar ilegalmente. **III** n GB (action) ocupación f ilegal; (building) edificio m ocupado ilegalmente.

squatter ['skwɒtəʳ] n ocupante mf ilegal.

squaw [skwɔː] n india f norteamericana, piel roja f.

squawk [skwɔːk] **I** n graznido m, chillido m. **II** vi graznar, chillar.

squeak [skwiːk] **I** n (of mouse) chillido m; (of hinge, wheel) chirrido m, rechinamiento m; (of shoes) crujido m; fam **there wasn't a s. out of him,** no dijo ni pío. **II** vi (mouse) chillar; (hinge, wheel) chirriar, rechinar; (shoes) crujir.

squeaky ['skwiːkɪ] adj (squeakier, squeakiest) (gen) chirriante; (voice) chillón,-ona; (shoes) que crujen.

squeal [skwiːl] **I** n (gen) chirrido m; (of animal, person) chillido m. **II** vi **1** (gen) chirriar; (animal, person) chillar. **2** fam (inform) cantar, chivarse; **to s. on sb,** delatar a algn. **III** vtr decir chillando.

squeamish ['skwiːmɪʃ] adj muy sensible, remilgado,-a, delicado,-a; **to be s. about sth,** tener horror a algo.

squeeze [skwiːz] **I** vtr (gen) apretar, (lemon, orange) exprimir; (sponge) estrujar; **he squeezed her hand,** le apretó la mano; **to s. paste out of a tube,** sacar pasta de un tubo; **to s. sth into one's pocket,** meter algo atropelladamente en el bolsillo; **can you s. me in before midday?,** ¿me podrá ver antes del mediodía? **II** vi **to s. in/out,** meterse/salir apenas or con dificultad; **to s. through a crowd,** abrirse paso entre una muchedumbre con dificultad; fam **s. up a bit!,** ¡hazme sitio!, ¡córrete un poco! **III** n **1** (pressure) estrujón m, presión f; **a s. of lemon,** unas gotas de limón. **2** (of hand) apretón m; (hug) abrazo m; (crowd, crush) apiñamiento m, agolpamiento m, apretujón m; **a s. a tight s. for us,** íbamos como sardinas en lata. ■ Fin **credit s.,** reducción f de créditos.

squeezer ['skwiːzəʳ] n exprimidor m; **lemon s.,** exprimelimones m inv.

squelch [skweltʃ] chapotear; **to s. through the mud,** ir chapoteando por el lodo.

squib [skwɪb] n petardo m; fam **it was a damp s.,** fue un chasco.

squid [skwɪd] n Zool calamar m; (small) chipirón m.

squiffy ['skwɪfɪ] adj (squiffier, squiffiest) fam achispado,-a, piripi.

squiggle ['skwɪgəl] **I** n garabato m. **II** vi garabatear, hacer garabatos.

squint [skwɪnt] **I** n **1** Med bizquera f; **to have a s.,** ser bizco,-a. **2** fig (quick look) vistazo m, ojeada f; fam **let's have a s.,** déjame echarle un vistazo. **II** vi Med bizquear, ser bizco,-a. **2** *(in sunlight etc)* entrecerrar los ojos; **to s. at sth,** *(glance)* echar un vistazo a algo; *(with eyes half-closed)* mirar algo con los ojos entrecerrados.

squire [skwaɪəʳ] *n (landowner)* terrateniente *m*, hacendado *m*.

squirm [skwɜːm] *vi* retorcerse; *fig (feel embarrassed)* sentirse incómodo,-a.

squirrel ['skwɪrəl] *n Zool* ardilla *f*.

squirt [skwɜːt] **I** *n* **1** *(of liquid)* chorro *m*. **2** *offens (person)* mequetrefe *mf*. **II** *vtr (liquid)* lanzar a chorro. **III** *vi (liquid)* **to s. out,** salir a chorros.

Sr 1 *abbr see* **Snr. 2** *Rel abbr of* **Sister,** Hermana *f*, Hna.

Sri Lanka [sriːˈlæŋkə] *n* Sri Lanka.

SRN [esɑːrˈen] *GB abbr of* **State Registered Nurse,** enfermera *f* titulada.

SS *abbr of* **1 Saints,** Santos *mpl*, Santas *fpl*, Stos, Stas. **2** [esˈes] **steamship,** buque *m* de vapor, vapor *m*.

St 1 *abbr of* **Saint,** San *m*, Santo *m*, Santa *f*, Sto., Sta. **2** *abbr of* **Street,** calle *f*, c/.

st *GB abbr of* **stone,** peso que equivale a 6,350 kilogramos.

Sta *abbr of* **Station,** Estación *f*.

stab [stæb] **I** *n (with knife)* puñalada *f*, navajazo *m*; *(of pain)* punzada *f*; *fam fig* **to have a s. at doing sth,** intentar hacer algo. **II** *vtr (pt & pp stabbed)* apuñalar, acuchillar; *fig* **to s. sb in the back,** apuñalar a algn por la espalda.

stabbing ['stæbɪŋ] **I** *adj (pain)* punzante. **II** *n* puñaladas *fpl*.

stability [stəˈbɪlɪtɪ] *n* estabilidad *f*.

stabilize ['steɪbɪlaɪz] **I** *vtr* estabilizar. **II** *vi* estabilizarse.

stabilizer ['steɪbɪlaɪzəʳ] *n Tech* estabilizador *m*.

stable¹ ['steɪbəl] *adj (unchanging)* estable, constante; *(secure)* fijo,-a, sujeto,-a, estable.

stable² ['steɪbəl] **I** *n (building)* cuadra *f*, caballeriza *f*, establo *m*; *fig* **to close the s. door after the horse has bolted,** a buenas horas, mangas verdes. **II** *vtr (put in stable)* encerrar en una cuadra; *(keep in stable)* guardar en una cuadra.

stack [stæk] **I** *n* **1** *(pile)* montón *m*; *fam* **he's got stacks of money,** está forrado. **2** *(haystack)* almiar *m*. **3** *(chimneystack)* (cañon *m* de) chimenea *f*. **II** *vtr (pile up)* amontonar, apilar; *fig* **stacked with books,** lleno,-a de libros; *fig* **the cards** *or* **odds are stacked against us,** todo está en contra nuestra.

stadium ['steɪdɪəm] *n (pl stadiums or stadia* ['steɪdɪə])* estadio *m*.

staff [stɑːf] *n* **1** *(personnel)* personal *m*, empleados *mpl*; *Mil* estado *m* mayor; **on the s.,** en plantilla. ■ **editorial s.,** redactores *mpl*, redacción *f*; **s. entrance,** entrada *f* del personal; **s. meeting,** reunión *f* de profesores, claustro *m*; **s. nurse,** enfermera *f* cualificada; **teaching s.,** cuerpo *m* docente, profesorado *m*. **2** *(stick)* bastón *m*; *(of shepherd)* cayado *m*; *Rel* báculo *m*; *(flagpole)* asta *f*; *fig* **the s. of life,** el báculo de la vida. **3** *Mus (pl staves)* pentagrama *m*. **II** *vtr* proveer de personal.

staffroom [stɑːfruːm] *n* sala *f* de profesores.

stag [stæg] *n Zool* ciervo *m*, venado *m*. ■ *Ent* **s. beetle,** ciervo *m* volante; *fam* **s. party** *or* **night,** despedida *f* de soltero.

stage [steɪdʒ] *n* **1** *(platform)* plataforma *f*, estrado *m*, tablado *m*. **2** *(in theatre)* escenario *m*, escena *f*; *(theatre)* teatro *m*; **to go on s.,** salir al escenario; **to go on the s.,** hacerse actor *or* actriz. ■ **s. directions,** acotaciones *fpl*; **s. door,** entrada *f* de artistas; **s. fright,** miedo *m* escénico; **s. manager,** director,-a *m, f* de escena; **s. name,** nombre *m* artístico; **s. whisper,** aparte *m*. **3** *(section, period, phase) (of development)* etapa *f*, fase *f*; *(of journey)* etapa *f*, jornada *f*; *(of road, pipeline)* tramo *m*; *(of rocket)* piso *m*, etapa *f*; **at this s. of the negotiations,** a estas alturas de las negociaciones; **by** *or* **in stages,** por etapas; **it's in its early stages,** está aún en pañales. **4** *fam (stagecoach)*

diligencia *f*. **II** *vtr* **1** *Theat (play)* poner en escena, montar, representar. **2** *(demonstration, welcome) (arrange)* organizar; *(carry out)* llevar a cabo, efectuar.

stagecoach ['steɪdʒkəʊtʃ] *n* diligencia *f*.

stagehand ['steɪdʒhænd] *n* tramoyista *mf*.

stage-struck ['steɪdʒstrʌk] *adj* apasionado,-a por el teatro.

stag(e)y ['steɪdʒɪ] *adj (stagier, stagiest) pej* teatral, histriónico,-a.

stagger ['stægəʳ] **I** *vi* tambalearse; **to s. along,** ir tambaleándose, ir dando tumbos; **to s. to one's feet,** levantarse tambaleante. **II** *vtr* **1** *(amaze)* asombrar. **2** *(hours, work)* escalonar.

staggering ['stægərɪŋ] *adj* asombroso,-a, pasmoso,-a.

stagnant ['stægnənt] *adj (water)* estancado,-a; *fig* paralizado,-a, inactivo,-a, anquilosado,-a.

stagnate [stæg'neɪt] *vi* estancarse, quedarse *or* estar estancado,-a.

stagnation [stæg'neɪʃən] *n* estancamiento *m*; *fig* estancamiento *m*, paralización *f*.

staid [steɪd] *adj (person)* conservador,-a, tradicionalista; *(manner, clothes)* serio,-a, formal.

stain [steɪn] **I** *n* **1** *(gen)* mancha *f*; **blood s.,** mancha de sangre. ■ **s. remover,** quitamanchas *m inv*. **2** *(dye)* tinte *m*, tintura *f*. **II** *vtr* **1** *(gen)* manchar. **2** *(dye)* teñir. **III** *vi* mancharse.

stained [steɪnd] *adj* manchado,-a. ■ **s. glass,** vidrio *m* de colores; **s. glass window,** vidriera *f* de colores.

stainless ['steɪnlɪs] *adj (gen)* inmaculado,-a; *(steel)* inoxidable.

stair [steəʳ] *n* **1** *(single step)* escalón *m*, peldaño *m*. **2** **stairs,** escalera *f sing*.

staircase ['steəkeɪs] *n* escalera *f*; **spiral s.,** escalera de caracol.

stake¹ [steɪk] **I** *n (stick)* estaca *f*, palo *m*; *(for plant)* rodrigón *m*; *(post)* poste *m*; *Hist* **to be burnt at the s.,** morir en la hoguera. **II** *vtr* **to s. (out),** cercar *or* señalar con estacas.

stake² [steɪk] **I** *n* **1** *(bet)* puesta *f*, apuesta *f*; **the issue at s.,** el tema en cuestión; **to be at s.,** *(at risk)* estar en juego; *(in danger)* estar en peligro. **2** *(investment)* interés *m*; **he has a s. in the company** tiene intereses en la compañía. **II** *vtr (bet)* apostar; *(invest)* invertir; **to s. a claim to sth,** reivindicar algo; **to s. one's life on sth,** jugarse la vida en algo.

stalactite ['stæləktaɪt] *n* estalactita *f*.

stalagmite ['stæləgmaɪt] *n* estalagmita *f*.

stale [steɪl] *adj* **1** *(food)* pasado,-a; *(bread)* duro,-a. **2** *(air)* viciado,-a; **to s. smell,** olor a cerrado. **3** *(person)* agotado,-a, gastado,-a, quemado,-a.

stalemate ['steɪlmeɪt] *n Chess* tablas *fpl*; *fig* punto *m* muerto; **to reach s.,** llegar a un punto muerto, estancarse.

staleness ['steɪlnɪs] *n* **1** *(of food)* rancidez *f*; *(of bread)* dureza *f*. **2** *(of air)* lo viciado. **3** *(of person)* agotamiento *m*.

stalk¹ [stɔːk] *n Bot (of plant)* tallo *m*; *(of fruit)* rabo *m*; *(of cabbage)* troncho *m*.

stalk² [stɔːk] **I** *vtr (hunter)* cazar al acecho; *(animal)* acechar; *(detective etc)* seguir los pasos de. **II** *vi (walk)* andar con paso majestuoso; **he stalked out of the room,** salió airado de la habitación.

stall¹ [stɔːl] *n* **1** *(in market)* puesto *m*, tenderete *m*; *(at fair)* caseta *f*. ■ **newspaper s.,** quiosco *m* de periódicos. **2** *Agr (stable)* establo *m*; *(stable compartment)* casilla *f* de establo; *(manger)* pesebre *m*. **3** *(in church)* coro *m*. **4** *Theat* **stalls,** platea *f sing*. **II** *vtr Aut (engine)* calar, parar. **III** *vi Aut (engine)* calarse, pararse; *Av (plane)* perder velocidad.

stall² [stɔːl] *vi* andar con rodeos, dar largas a un asunto, contestar con evasivas.

stallholder ['stɔ:lhəʊldəʳ] *n* dueño,-a *m, f* de un puesto (de mercado).

stallion ['stæljən] *n Zool* semental *m*, garañón *m*.

stalwart ['stɔ:lwət] **I** *adj* **1** *(sturdy)* fuerte, robusto,-a, fornido,-a. **2** *(loyal)* leal, fiel. **II** *n* partidario,-a *m, f* incondicional *or* leal.

stamén ['steɪmen] *n Bot* estambre *m*.

stamina ['stæmɪnə] *n (energy)* energía *f*, vigor *m*; *(endurance)* aguante *m*, resistencia *f*.

stammer ['stæməʳ] **I** *n* tartamudeo *m*; **she has a s.**, tartamudea. **II** *vi* tartamudear. **III** *vtr* decir tartamudeando.

stammering ['stæmərɪŋ] **I** *adj* tartamudeante. **II** *n* tartamudez *f*.

stamp [stæmp] **I** *n* **1** *(postage stamp)* sello *m*; *(fiscal)* timbre *m*. ■ **s. album**, álbum *m* de sellos; **s. collector**, coleccionista *mf* de sellos, filatelista *mf*; **s. duty**, impuesto *m* del timbre, póliza *f*; **s. machine**, distribuidora *f* automática de sellos; **trading s.**, cupón *m*. **2** *(rubber stamp)* sello *m* de goma, tampón *m*; *(mark, seal)* sello *m*, tampón *m*; *(for metals)* cuño *m*. **3** *(with foot)* patada *f*; *(in dancing)* zapateo *m*. **II** *vtr* **1** *(letter) (with postage stamp)* sellar, poner el sello a; **stamped addressed envelope**, sobre franqueado. **2** *(passport, document) (with rubber stamp)* sellar, marcar con sello; *(money)* acuñar. **3 to s. one's feet**, patear, patalear; *(in dancing)* zapatear. **III** *vi* patear, patalear; **to s. on sb's foot**, pisarle *or* pisotearle el pie a algn. ◆ **stamp out** *vtr* **1** *(fire)* apagar con los pies. **2** *fig (racism, violence)* acabar con; *(rebellion, epidemic)* sofocar.

stampede [stæm'pi:d] **I** *n* estampida *f*, desbandada *f*, espantada *f*; *fig (rush)* desbandada *f*; **there was a sudden s. for the door**, todos se precipitaron hacia la puerta. **II** *vi* huir *or* salir en estampida, desbandarse; *fig (rush)* precipitarse. **III** *vtr* provocar una estampida en.

stance [stæns] *n* postura *f*; *fig* postura *f*, actitud *f*.

stand [stænd] **I** *n* **1** *(position)* posición *f*, postura *f*; *Mil* **to make a s. against the enemy**, resistir al enemigo; *fig* **to take a s. on a matter**, adoptar una postura hacia una cuestión. **2** *(of lamp, sculpture)* pie *m*, pedestal *m*. ■ **coat s.**, perchero *m*; **music s.**, atril *m*. **3** *(market stall)* puesto *m*, tenderete *m*; *(at fair)* caseta *f*; *(at exhibition)* stand *m*, pabellón *m*. ■ **newspaper s.**, quiosco *m*. **4** *(platform)* plataforma *f*; *(in sports stadium)* tribuna *f*; *US Jur (witness box)* estrado *m*; **to take the s.**, subir al estrado. **II** *vtr (pt & pp stood)* **1** *(place)* poner, colocar. **2** *(withstand, tolerate)* aguantar, soportar; **to s. one's ground**, mantenerse firme, seguir en sus trece; *fam* **I can't s. him**, no lo aguanto, no lo puedo tragar, no lo puedo ver. **3** *fam (invite)* invitar; **to s. sb a drink**, invitar a algn a una copa. **III** *vi* **1** *(be upright)* estar de pie; *(get up)* ponerse de pie, levantarse; *(remain upright)* quedarse de pie; **she could scarcely s.**, apenas se tenía de pie; *fig* **to s. fast**, mantenerse firme; *fig* **to s. on one's own two feet**, apañárselas sólo; *fam* **she just stood there**, se quedó allí mirando; *fam* **s. still!**, ¡estáte quieto,-a!, ¡no te muevas! **2** *(measure)* medir; **the tower stands 70 feet high**, la torre tiene 70 pies de alto; **the thermometer stood at 40 degrees**, el termómetro marcaba 40 grados. **3** *(be situated) (castle, village, etc)* estar, encontrarse. **4** *(remain unchanged)* permanecer; **leave the dough to s. for half an hour**, deja reposar la masa una media hora. **5** *(remain valid) (decision, arrangement)* seguir en pie, seguir vigente. **6** *(be, be placed)* estar; **as things s.**, tal como están las cosas; **he stands to lose a lot of money**, puede que pierda mucho dinero; **it stands to reason**, es lógico; **we would like to know where we s.**, nos gustaría saber a qué atenernos. **7** *Pol* presentarse. ◆ **stand back** *vi (set back)* estar apartado,-a; *(allowing sb to pass)* abrir paso. ◆ **stand by I** *vi* **1** *(do nothing)* quedarse sin hacer nada. **2** *(be ready for action)* estar preparado,-a *or* listo,-a; *Av* **s. by for take-off!**, ¡listos para el despegue! **II** *vtr (person)* apoyar a, respaldar a; *(promise)* cumplir con; *(decision)* atenerse a; **I s. by what I said**, me atengo a lo

dicho. ◆ **stand down** *vi fig (withdraw)* retirarse. ◆ **stand for** *vtr* **1** *(mean)* significar; **BR stands for British Rail**, BR son las siglas de la British Rail. **2** *(represent)* representar; *Pol* **we have always stood for freedom**, nosotros siempre hemos defendido la libertad. **4** *(tolerate)* tolerar, aguantar. ◆ **stand in** *vi (substitute)* sustituir **(for, -)**. ◆ **stand out** *vi (building, mountain, etc)* destacarse *fig (person, qualities)* destacar, sobresalir; *fam* **it stands out a mile!**, ¡salta a la vista! ◆ **stand to** *vi Mil* estar en estado de alerta. ◆ **stand up I** *vi (get up)* ponerse de pie, levantarse; *(be standing)* estar de pie; *fig* **it will s. up to wear and tear**, es muy resistente; *fig* **this will not s. up in court**, esto no convencerá a ningún tribunal; *fig* **to s. up for oneself**, defenderse solo; *fig* **to s. up for sb**, defender algn; *fig* **to s. up to sb**, hacer frente a algn. **II** *vtr fam* **to s. sb up**, dejar plantado,-a a algn.

standard ['stændəd] **I** *n* **1** *(level, degree)* nivel *m*; **of a high/low s.**, de alto/bajo nivel; **s. of living**, nivel de vida. **2** *(criterion, principle)* criterio *m*, valor *m*. **3** *(norm)* norma *f*, regla *f*, estándar *m*; **to be up to/below s.**, satisfacer/no satisfacer los requisitos. **4** *(flag)* estandarte *m*, bandera *f*; *Naut* pabellón *m*. **5** *(measure)* patrón *m*; *Fin* **the gold s.**, el patrón oro. **II** *adj* normal, estándar, corriente, común; **it is now s. practice**, se ha impuesto ya como norma; **s. English**, inglés normativo; **s. lamp**, lámpara de pie; **s. model**, modelo estándar; **s. size**, tamaño normal; **s. time**, hora oficial.

standard-bearer ['stændəbeərəʳ] *n Mil* abanderado *m*.

standardization [stændədar'zeɪʃən] *n* normalización *f*, estandarización *f*.

standardize ['stændədaɪz] *vtr* normalizar, estandarizar, estandardizar.

standby ['stændbaɪ] *n* **1** *(thing)* recurso *m*. **2** *(person)* suplente *mf*, sustituto,-a *m, f*; **to be on s.**, *Mil (troops)* estar de retén; *Av (passenger)* estar en la lista de espera. ■ *Av* **s. ticket**, billete *m* standby.

stand-in ['stændɪn] *n* suplente *mf*, sustituto,-a *m, f* **(for, de)**; *Cin* doble *mf*.

standing ['stændɪŋ] **I** *adj* **1** *(not sitting)* de pie; *(upright)* derecho,-a, recto,-a, vertical; **s. ovation**, ovación calurosa; **there was s. room only**, no quedaban asientos; *fig* **he left everyone else s.**, dejó atrás a los demás. **2** *Sport* **s. start**, salida *f* parada. **3** *(committee, body)* permanente; *(rule)* fijo,-a; *(invitation)* abierto,-a; *Fin* **s. order**, pago fijo. **II** *n* **1** *(social position)* rango *m*, categoría *f*, estatus *m*, standing *m*; *(importance)* importancia *f*; *(reputation)* reputación *f*, fama *f*; **of high s.**, de mucha categoría, de alto standing. **2** *(duration)* duración *f*; *(in job)* antigüedad *f*.

stand-offish [stænd'ɒfɪʃ] *adj fam* estirado,-a, altivo,-a.

stand-offishness [stænd'ɒfɪʃnɪs] *n fam* altivez *f*, distancia *f*, reserva *f*.

standpipe ['stændpaɪp] *n* tubo *m* vertical.

standpoint ['stændpɔɪnt] *n* punto *m* de vista; **from our s.**, desde nuestro punto de vista.

standstill ['stændstɪl] *n* **at a s.**, *(car, traffic)* parado,-a; *(industry, business)* paralizado,-a; **to come to a s.**, *(car, traffic)* pararse; *(industry, business)* paralizarse.

stank [stæŋk] *pt see* **stink.**

stanza ['stænzə] *n* estrofa *f*.

staple[1] ['steɪpəl] **I** *n (fastener)* grapa *f*. **II** *vtr* grapar.

staple[2] ['steɪpəl] **I** *adj (food, diet)* básico,-a; *(product)* de primera necesidad. **II** *n (food)* alimento *m* básico; *(product)* artículo *m* de primera necesidad.

stapler ['steɪpələʳ] *n* grapadora *f*.

star ['stɑːʳ] **I** *n* **1** *Astrol Astron* estrella *f*; **shooting s.**, estrella fugaz; **5-s. hotel**, hotel *m* de 5 estrellas; **4-s. petrol**, (gasolina *f*) súper *f*; *fig* **to thank one's lucky stars**, dar gracias al cielo; *fig* **to see stars**, ver estrellas; *fam* **what do the slars say?**, ¿qué dice el horóscopo? ■ *US* **the Stars and Stripes**, la bandera de las barras y estrellas. **2** *(person)* estrella *f*, astro *m*. ■ **film s.**, estrella *f* de cine. **II** *adj* estelar. ■ **s. attraction, s. turn**, atracción *f* estelar; **s. part**, papel *m* estelar. **III** *vtr Cin* presentar como estrella a, tener como protagonista. **IV** *vi Cin* actuar en papel principal, protagonizar.

starboard ['stɑːbəd] *n Naut* estribor *m*.

starch ['stɑːtʃ] **I** *n (for laundry)* almidón *m*; *(in rice)* almidón *m*; *(in potatoes etc)* fécula *f*. **II** *vtr (laundry)* almidonar.

starchy ['stɑːtʃɪ] *adj (starchier, starchiest) (food)* feculento,-a; *fig (person)* rígido,-a, estirado,-a.

stardom ['stɑːdəm] *n* estrellato *m*; **to rise to s.**, convertirse en estrella, alcanzar el estrellato.

stare [steəʳ] **I** *n* mirada *f* fija. **II** *vi* mirar fijamente **(at**, a), mirar de hito en hito **(at**, a), clavar los ojos *or* la vista **(at**, en); **to s. into space**, mirar al vacío; **to s. one in the face**, salta a la vista.

starfish ['stɑːfɪʃ] *n Zool* estrella *f* de mar.

stark [stɑːk] **I** *adj (landscape)* desolado,-a, desierto,-a; *(décor, colour)* austero,-a; *(realism, truth)* escueto,-a, sin adornos, desnudo,-a; **s. poverty**, la miseria. **II** *adv* completamente; *fam* **s. raving** *or* **staring mad**, loco,-a de remate *or* de atar.

starkers ['stɑːkəz] *adj fam*, **stark-naked** ['stɑːkneɪkɪd] *adj fam* en cueros *or* pelotas, desnudo,-a.

starlight ['stɑːlaɪt] *n* luz *f* de las estrellas.

starling ['stɑːlɪŋ] *n Orn* estornino *m*.

starlit ['stɑːlɪt] *adj* iluminado,-a por las estrellas.

starry ['stɑːrɪ] *adj (starrier, starriest)* estrellado,-a, sembrado,-a de estrellas.

starry-eyed ['stɑːrɪˈaɪd] *adj (idealistic)* idealista, ilusionado,-a; *(in love)* enamorado,-a.

START [stɑːt] *abbr of* **Strategic Arms Reduction Talks**, conversaciones *fpl* sobre la reducción de las armas estratégicas.

start [stɑːt] **I** *n* **1** *(beginning)* principio *m*, comienzo *m*, inicio *m*; *(of race)* salida *f*; **at the s.**, al principio; **false s.**, salida nula; **for a s.**, para empezar; **from the s.**, desde el principio; **to get off to a good s.**, empezar con buen pie; **to give sb a s. in life**, ayudar a algn a establecerse; **to make an early s.**, ponerse en camino *or* marcha a primera hora; **to make a fresh s. in life**, comenzar una nueva vida, volver a empezar. **2** *(advantage)* ventaja *f*, **I'll give you a 5 minute s.**, te daré 5 minutos de ventaja. **3** *(fright, jump)* susto *m*, sobresalto *m*; **to give sb a s.**, dar un susto a algn; **to wake up with a s.**, despertarse sobresaltado; **to work by fits and starts**, trabajar a trompicones. **II** *vtr* **1** *(begin)* empezar, comenzar; *(conversation)* entablar; **s. doing** *or* **to do sth**, empezar a hacer algo; **to s. negotiations**, iniciar negociaciones. **2** *(cause, give rise to)* causar, provocar; **to s. a fashion**, lanzar una moda. **3** *(found)* fundar, establecer; **to s. a business**, montar un negocio. **4** *(set in motion)* arrancar, poner en marcha. **III** *vi* **1** *(begin)* empezar, comenzar; *(on journey)* ponerse en camino; *(car, engine)* arrancar, ponerse en marcha; **he started by welcoming everyone**, empezó por dar la bienvenida a todos; **starting from Monday**, a partir del lunes; **to s. at the beginning**, empezar desde el principio; **to s. with ...**, *(firstly)* para empezar ..., en primer lugar ...; *(at the beginning)* al principio ... . **2** *(in fright)* asustarse, sobresaltarse. ◆ **start back** *vi* emprender el viaje de regreso. ◆ **start off** *vi* **1** *(begin)* empezar, comenzar; **his father started him off in the shoe business**, su padre le dio el primer empujón en el comercio del calzado; **to s. off by/with**, empezar por/con. **2** *(leave)* salir, partir, ponerse en camino. **II** *vtr (cause) (dispute, war, etc)* causar, provocar; **don't s. her off!**, ¡no le des cuerda! ◆ **start out** *vi (begin)* empezar, comenzar; *(on journey)* salir, partir, ponerse en camino. ◆ **start over** *vi US* volver a empezar. ◆ **start up I** *vtr (car, engine)* arrancar. **II** *vi (car)* arrancar; *(orchestra etc)* empezar a tocar.

starter ['stɑːtəʳ] *n* **1** *Sport (official)* juez *mf* de salida; *(competitor)* competidor,-a *m*, *f*, participante *mf*; *fam (child)* **to be a late s.**, ser tardío en el desarrollo. **2** *Aut (motor)* motor *m* de arranque. **3** *Culin fam* primer plato *m*, entrada *f*; **fig for starters**, para empezar.

starting ['stɑːtɪŋ] *n* comienzo *m*, inicio *m*. ■ **s. block**, taco *m* de salida; *Aut* **s. handle**, manivela *f* de arranque; **s. point**, punto *m* de partida; *Sport* **s. post**, línea *f* de salida; *Fin* **s. price**, precio *m* inicial.

startle ['stɑːtəl] *vtr* asustar, sobresaltar.

startling ['stɑːtlɪŋ] *adj* **1** *(frightening)* alarmante, sobrecogedor,-a. **2** *(astonishing) (news, discovery)* asombroso,-a, sorprendente; *(coincidence)* extraordinario,-a. **3** *(eye-catching)* llamativo,-a.

start-up ['stɑːtʌp] *n* puesta *f* en marcha.

starvation [stɑːˈveɪʃən] *n* hambre *f*, inanición *f*; **to die of s.**, morir de inanición. ■ **s. diet**, régimen *m* de hambre; **s. wages**, sueldos *mpl* miserables.

starve [stɑːv] **I** *vtr* privar de comida, hacer pasar hambre a; **to s. sb to death**, hacer morir de hambre a algn, matar de hambre a algn; *fig* **he was starved of affection**, fue privado de cariño. **II** *vi (suffer from hunger)* pasar hambre; **to s. to death**, morirse de hambre.

starving ['stɑːvɪŋ] *adj* hambriento,-a, muerto,-a de hambre; *fam* **I'm s.!**, estoy muerto,-a de hambre, tengo un hambre que no veo.

stash [stæʃ] *vtr fam* **to s. sth away**, esconder algo, guardar algo en un lugar seguro.

state [steɪt] **I** *n* **1** *(gen)* estado *m*; **s. of emergency**, estado de emergencia; **s. of mind**, estado de ánimo; **the s. of the nation**, el estado de la nación; **to be in no fit s. to do sth.**, no estar en condiciones de hacer algo; **what a s. of affairs!**, ¡qué lío!; *fam* **to get into a s. about sth**, afligirse por algo. **2** *Pol* estado *m*; *US* **Secretary of S.**, ministro,-a *m*, *f* de Asuntos Exteriores; *GB* **Secretary of S. for Education**, ministro,-a *m*, *f* de Educación; *US* **The States**, los Estados Unidos; *US* **the S. Department**, el Ministerio de Asuntos Exteriores. **3** *(of deceased)* **to lie in s.**, estar de cuerpo presente. **II** *adj* **1** *Pol* estatal, del Estado. ■ **s. capitalism**, capitalismo *m* de Estado; **s. education**, enseñanza *f* pública; **s. ownership**, propiedad *f* del Estado; **s. secret**, secreto *m* de Estado; **s. sector**, sector *m* estatal *or* público. **2** *(ceremonial) (apartment, banquet, coach)* de gala; **s. occasion**, ocasión *f* solemne; **s. visit**, visita *f* oficial. **III** *vtr* declarar, afirmar; *(case, claim)* exponer; *(problem)* plantear; *(time, place)* fijar; **as stated above**, como queda indicado arriba; **to s. one's opinion**, dar su opinión.

stated ['steɪtɪd] *adj* indicado,-a, señalado,-a; **at the s. time**, a la hora indicada *or* señalada.

stateless ['steɪtlɪs] *adj* apátrida.

stately ['steɪtlɪ] *adj (statelier, stateliest)* majestuoso,-a, imponente. ■ **s. home**, casa *f* solariega.

statement ['steɪtmənt] *n* **1** *(gen)* declaración *f*, afirmación *f*; **official s.**, comunicado *m*; *Jur* **to make a s.**, prestar declaración. **2** *Fin* estado de cuenta; **monthly s.**, balance *m* mensual.

stateroom ['steɪtruːm] *n Naut* camarote *m*.

statesman ['steɪtsmən] *n (pl statesmen)* estadista *m*, hombre *m* de Estado.

statesman-like ['steɪtsmənlaɪk] *adj* propio,-a de un estadista.

statesmanship ['steɪtsmənʃɪp] *n (skill)* habilidad *f* política; *(activity)* arte *m* de gobernar.

static ['stætɪk] *adj* **1** *(gen)* estático,-a. ■ **s. electricity**, electricidad estática. **II statics** *npl Rad* parásitos *mpl*, interferencias *fpl*.

station ['steɪʃən] **I** *n* **1** *Rail* estación *f* de ferrocarril; *Rel* **the Stations of the Cross**, el Viacrucis. ■ **bus s.**, estación *f or* terminal *f* de autobuses; **fire s.**, cuartel *m* de bomberos; **petrol** *or* **filling s.**, gasolinera *f*, estación *f* de servicio; **police s.**, comisaría *f*; **power s.**, central *f*; **radio**

s., emisora *f*; **service s.,** área *f* de servicio; *Aust* **sheep s.,** granja *f* de ovejas; *Aut* **s. wagon,** break *m*, rubia *f*, camioneta *f*; **weather s.,** estación *f* meteorológica. **2** *(position)* puesto *m*, lugar *m*; *Mil* **action stations!,** ¡zafarrancho de combate! **3** *(social standing)* rango *m*; **to have ideas above one's s.,** dárselas de importante. **II** *vtr* *(place)* colocar; *Mil (troops)* apostar, estacionar.

stationary ['steɪʃənərɪ] *adj (not moving)* inmóvil, parado,-a; *(unchanging)* estacionario,-a, fijo,-a.

stationer ['steɪʃənər'] *n* papelero,-a *m*, *f*; **s.'s (shop),** papelería *f*.

stationery ['steɪsənərɪ] *n (paper)* papel *m* de escribir; *(pens, ink, etc)* artículos *mpl* de escritorio.

stationmaster ['steɪʃənmɑːstər'] *n* *Rail* jefe *m* de estación.

statistic [stə'tɪstɪk] *n* estadística *f*.

statistical [stə'tɪstɪkəl] *adj* estadístico,-a.

statistician [stætɪ'stɪʃən] *n* estadístico,-a *m*, *f*.

statistics [stə'tɪstɪks] *npl (science)* estadística *f sing*; *(data)* estadísticas *fpl*.

statue ['stætjuː] *n* estatua *f*.

statuesque [stætjʊ'esk] *adj* escultural.

statuette [stætjʊ'et] *n* figurilla *f*.

stature ['stætʃər'] *n (size)* estatura *f*, talla *f*; *fig* estatus *m*, rango *m*, categoría *f*.

status ['steɪtəs] *n* estado *m*, condición *f*. ■ **legal s.,** validez *f*; **marital s.,** estado *m* civil; **social s.,** posición *f* social, estatus *m*; **s. symbol,** signo *m* de prestigio; **s. quo,** status quo *m*.

statute ['stætjuːt] *n* estatuto *m*, decreto *m*, ley *f*; **in accordance with the statutes,** según los estatutos. ■ **s. book,** código *m* de leyes.

statutory ['stætjʊtərɪ] *adj (gen)* reglamentario,-a; *(offence)* establecido,-a por la ley; *(right)* legal; *(holiday)* oficial.

staunch[1] [stɔːntʃ] *adj* fiel, leal; **s. supporter,** partidario acérrimo.

staunch[2] [stɔːntʃ] *vtr (blood)* restañar.

stave [steɪv] **I** *n* **1** *(of barrel)* duela *f*. **2** *Mus* pentagrama *m*. **II** *vtr (pt & pp stove)* desfondar *(in, -)*. ◆ **stave off** *vtr (pt & pp staved off) (repel) (attack, crisis)* rechazar; *(avoid)* evitar; *(delay)* aplazar, diferir.

staves [steɪvz] *npl see* **staff.**

stay[1] [steɪ] **I** *n* estancia *f*; permanencia *f*; **a three-week s.,** una estancia de tres semanas; *Jur* **s. of execution,** aplazamiento *m* de sentencia. **II** *vi* **1** *(remain)* quedarse, permanecer; **if it stays sunny,** si el tiempo sigue soleado; **s. away from the river,** no te acerques al río; **it's here to s.,** ya forma parte de nuestras vidas; **to s. at home,** quedarse en casa; **why don't you s. to dinner?,** ¿por qué no te quedas a cenar?; **you s. out of this,** ¡tú no te metas en esto! **2** *(reside temporarily)* alojarse, hospedarse; **she's staying with us for a few days,** ha venido a pasar unos días con nosotros. **III** *vtr* resistir; **to s. the course,** terminar la carrera; *fig* aguantar hasta el final. ■ **staying power,** resistencia *f*, aguante *m*. ◆ **stay in** *vi* quedarse en casa, no salir. ◆ **stay on** *vi* quedarse, permanecer. ◆ **stay out** *vi* quedarse fuera; **to s. out all night,** no volver a casa en toda la noche; **the strikers have decided to s. out,** los huelguistas han decidido no volver al trabajo. ◆ **stay up** *vi* no acostarse; **to s. up late,** acostarse tarde.

stay[2] [steɪ] *n Naut (guy rape)* estay *m*, viento *m*.

stay[3] [steɪ] *n* **1** *Archit (prop)* sostén *m*, soporte *m*. **2** *(in corset)* ballena *f*.

stay-at-home ['steɪəθhəʊm] **I** *adj* casero,-a, hogareño,-a. **II** *n* persona *f* casera *or* hogareña.

stayer ['steɪər'] *n Sport* caballo *m* *or* yegua *f* de fondo; *fig* persona *f* de mucha resistencia.

stead [sted] *n* **in sb's s.,** en lugar de algn; **to stand sb in good s.,** resultar muy útil a algn.

steadfast ['stedfəst, 'stedfɑːst] *adj* firme, resuelto,-a.

steadfastness ['stedfəstnɪs] *n* firmeza *f*, resolución *f*.

steadiness ['stedɪnɪs] *n (of gait, hand)* firmeza *f*; *(of prices)* estabilidad *f*; *(of demand)* constancia *f*; *(of character)* formalidad *f*.

steady ['stedɪ] **I** *adj (steadier, steadiest) (gen)* firme, seguro,-a; *(gaze)* fijo,-a; *(table)* estable, equilibrado,-a; *(prices)* estable; *(demand, speed)* constante; *(heartbeat, pace)* regular; *(worker, student)* aplicado,-a; **she is making s. progress,** hace progresos continuos; **s downpour,** lluvia continua; **s. boyfriend,** novio; **s. job,** empleo fijo. **II** *adv* **s. (on)!,** ¡despacio!, ¡quieto!; *fam* **go s. on the brandy,** cuidado con el coñac; *fam* **they're going s.,** son novios. **III** *n fam* novio,-a *m*, *f*. **IV** *vtr (table etc)* estabilizar, equilibrar; *(nervous person)* calmar, tranquilizar; **this herb tea will s. your nerves,** esta infusión de hierbas te calmará los nervios. **V** *vi (market, prices)* estabilizarse. ◆ **steadily** *adv (grow, improve)* constantemente; *(walk)* con paso seguro, decididamente; *(gaze)* fijamente; *(rain, work)* sin parar; **the situation is getting s. worse,** la situación se vuelve cada vez peor.

steak [steɪk] *n* bistec *m*, filete *m* de buey. ■ **rump s.,** filete *m* de cadera; **s. and kidney pie,** empanada *f* de carne con riñones; **s. house,** restaurante *m* especializado en bistecs; **stewing s.,** carne *f* de vaca para estofar, *Am* carne *f* de res para estofar.

steal [stiːl] *(pt stole; pp stolen)* **I** *vtr* robar, hurtar; **to s. a glance at sth,** echar una mirada furtiva a algo; **to s. a kiss,** robar un beso; **to s. a march on sb,** anticiparse a algn; **to s. the show,** acaparar la atención de todos, llevarse todos los aplausos. **II** *vi* **1** *(rob)* robar, hurtar; **children often s.,** los niños roban a menudo. **2** *(move quietly)* moverse con sigilo; **to s. away,** escabullirse, marcharse a hurtadillas; **to s. into a room,** colarse en una habitación; **to s. up on sb,** acercarse sigilosamente a algn, sorprender a algn.

stealing ['stiːlɪŋ] *n* robo *m*.

stealth [stelθ] *n* cautela *f*, sigilo *m*.

stealthy ['stelθɪ] *adj (stealthier, stealthiest)* sigiloso,-a, furtivo,-a. ◆ **stealthily** *adv* a hurtadillas, furtivamente.

steam [stiːm] **I** *n* vapor *m*; *Naut* **full s. ahead!,** ¡avante toda!; **to get up s.,** dar presión; *fam* **to let off s.,** desfogarse, desahogarse; *fam* **to run out of s.,** quedar agotado,-a, quemarse; *fam* **under one's own s.,** por sus propios medios. ■ **s. bath,** baño *m* de vapor; **s. engine,** máquina *f* de vapor; **s. iron,** plancha *f* de vapor. **II** *vtr* *Culin* cocer al vapor; **to s. open a letter,** abrir una carta al vapor. **III** *vi (give off steam)* echar vapor; *(bowl of soup etc)* humear; **the ship steamed into port,** el buque entró en el puerto echando vapor. ◆ **steam up** *vi (window, spectacles)* empañarse; *fam* **to get steamed up about sth,** sulfurarse *or* enfadarse por algo.

steamer ['stiːmər'] *n* **1** *Naut* vapor *m*, buque *m* de vapor. **2** *Culin* olla *f* a vapor.

steamroller ['stiːmrəʊlər'] **I** *n* apisonadora *f*. **II** *vtr fig* forzar; **to s. sb into doing sth,** forzar *or* obligar a algn a hacer algo.

steamship ['stiːmʃɪp] *n Naut* vapor *m*, buque *m* de vapor.

steamy ['stiːmɪ] *adj (steamier, steamiest)* lleno,-a de vapor.

steel [stiːl] **I** *n* acero *m*. ■ **stainless s.,** acero *m* inoxidable; *Mus* **s. band,** conjunto *m* de percusión del Caribe; **s. industry,** industria *f* siderúrgica; **s. mill,** fundición *f* de acero, altos hornos *mpl*, acería *f*, acerería *f*; **s. wool,** estropajo *m* de acero. **II** *vtr fig* endurecer; **to s. one's heart,** endurecerse; **to s. oneself to do sth,** armarse de valor para hacer algo; **to s. oneself against sth,** hacer frente a algo.

steelworks ['stiːlwɜːks] *npl* fundición *f sing* de acero, acería *f sing*, acerería *f sing*.

steep[1] [stiːp] *adj (hill, slope, climb)* empinado,-a, escarpado,-a, abrupto,-a; *fig (price)* excesivo,-a, exorbitante, desmedido,-a; *(increase)* excesivo,-a; *fam* **that's a bit s.!,** ¡eso es demasiado!

steep² [stiːp] *vtr (washing)* remojar; *(comida)* poner en remojo; *fig* **a city steeped in history,** una ciudad empapada de historia.

steeple ['stiːpəl] *n (spire)* aguja *f*, chapitel *m*.

steeplechase ['stiːpəltʃeɪs] *n Sport* carrera *f* de obstáculos.

steeplejack ['stiːpəldʒæk] *n* reparador,-a *m*, *f* de chimeneas *or* torres *or* campanarios.

steer¹ [stɪəʳ] **I** *vtr (gen)* dirigir, guiar; *(car)* conducir; *(ship)* gobernar; *(conversation etc)* llevar. **II** *vi (car)* conducir; **to s. for sth,** dirigirse hacia algo; *fig* **to s. clear of sth,** evitar algo.

steer² [stɪəʳ] *n* buey *m*.

steering ['stɪərɪŋ] *n. Aut* dirección *f*. ■ *Aut* **assisted s.,** dirección *f* asistida; *Aut* **s. column,** columna *f or* árbol *m* de dirección; *Pol* **s. committee,** comité *m* directivo, comisión *f* directiva; *Aut* **s. wheel,** volante *m*.

stem [stem] **I** *n* **1** *(of plants)* tallo *m*; *(of glass)* pie *m*; *(of pipe)* tubo *m*, cañón *m*. **2** *Ling (of word)* raíz *f*, lema *m*. **II** *vi* **to s. from,** ser el resultado de, derivarse de. **III** *vtr (blood)* restañar; *(flood, attack)* contener, detener; **to s. the tide of inflation,** poner freno a la inflación.

stench [stentʃ] *n* hedor *m*, peste *f*.

stencil ['stensəl] *n* **1** *(for artwork etc)* plantilla *f*. **2** *(for typing)* cliché *m*.

stenography [ste'nɒgrəfɪ] *n* taquigrafía *f*.

step [step] **I** *n* **1** *(gen)* paso *m*; *(sound)* paso *m*, pisada *f*; **It's quite a s. to the station,** hay una buena caminata desde aquí hasta la estación; **s. by s.,** paso a paso, poco a poco; **to keep in s.,** *(walking)* llevar el paso; *(dancing)* llevar el compás *or* ritmo; *fig* **to watch one's s.,** ir con cuidado. **2** *(measure)* medida *f*, paso *m*; *(formality)* gestión *f*, trámite *m*; **it was a s. in the right direction,** fue un paso acertado; **to take steps to control sth,** tomar medidas para controlar algo. **3** *(stair)* peldaño *m*, escalón *m*; *(of vehicle)* estribo *m*. **4 steps,** *(outdoor)* escalinata *f*; *(indoor)* escalera *f*; *(in stadium)* gradas *fpl*, graderío *m*, tribunas *fpl*; *(of plane)* escalerilla *f*. ■ **folding s., pair of s.,** escalera *f* sing de tijera. **II** *vi (pt & pp stepped)* dar un paso; **s. this way, please,** haga el favor de pasar por aquí; **to s. aside,** hacerse a un lado, apartarse; **to s. on sb's foot,** pisar *or* pisotear el pie a algn; **to s. over sth,** pasar por encima de algo; *fam* **s. on it!,** ¡date prisa!; *US Aut fam* **s. on the gas!,** ¡dale al gas!, ¡pisa a fondo! ◆ **step back** *vi* **to s. back from a situation,** enfocar una situación con más objetividad. ◆ **step down** *vi* renunciar; **to s. down from office,** renunciar a un cargo. ◆ **step forward** *vi* ofrecerse. ◆ **step in** *vi* intervenir. ◆ **step out** *vi* apretar el paso. ◆ **step up** *vtr (production, efforts)* aumentar.

stepbrother ['stepbrʌðəʳ] *n* hermanastro *m*, medio hermano *m*.

stepchild ['steptʃaɪld] *n (pl stepchildren* ['steptʃɪldrən]*)* hijastro,-a *m*, *f*.

stepdaughter ['stepdɔːtəʳ] *n* hijastra *f*.

stepfather ['stepfɑːðəʳ] *n* padrastro *m*.

stepladder ['steplædəʳ] *n* escalera *f* de tijera.

stepmother ['stepmʌðəʳ] *n* madrastra *f*.

steppe [step] *n Geog* estepa *f*.

stepping-stone ['stepɪŋstəʊn] *n* pasadera *f*; *fig* trampolín *m*.

stepsister ['stepsɪstəʳ] *n* hermanastra *f*, media hermana *f*.

stepson ['stepsʌn] *n* hijastro *m*.

stereo ['sterɪəʊ] **I** *n (system)* equipo *m* estereofónico; *(sound)* sonido *m*, en estéreo. **II** *adj* estereofónico,-a.

stereophonic [sterɪə'fɒnɪk] *adj* estereofónico,-a.

stereotype ['sterɪətaɪp] *n* estereotipo *m*.

stereotyped ['sterɪətaɪpt] *adj* estereotipado,-a.

sterile ['steraɪl] *adj* **1** *(barren)* estéril. **2** *(germ-free)* esterilizado,-a.

sterility [ste'rɪlɪtɪ] *n* esterilidad *f*.

sterilization [sterɪlaɪ'zeɪʃən] *n* esterilización *f*.

sterilize ['sterɪlaɪz] *vtr* esterilizar.

sterilizer ['sterɪlaɪzəʳ] *n* esterilizador *m*.

sterling ['stɜːlɪŋ] **I** *n* libra *f* esterlina, libras *fpl* esterlinas. ■ **s. silver,** plata *f* de ley; **the pound s.,** la libra esterlina. **II** *adj (person, quality)* excelente, de buena calidad.

stern¹ [stɜːn] *adj (severe)* severo,-a, austero,-a; *(hard)* duro,-a; **s. resolve,** resolución firme.

stern² [stɜːn] *n Naut* popa *f*.

sternum ['stɜːnəm] *n (pl sternums or sterna* ['stɜːnəl]*)* *Anat* esternón *m*.

steroid ['sterɔɪd] *n* esteroide *m*.

stethoscope ['steθəskəʊp] *n Med* estetoscopio *m*.

stetson ['stetsən] *n* sombrero *m* tejano.

stevedore ['stiːvɪdɔːʳ] *n* estibador *m*.

stew [stjuː] **I** *n Culin* guisado *m*, estofado *m*, cocido *m*; *fig* **to be in a s.,** estar hecho un lío. **II** *vtr (meat)* guisar, estofar; *(fruit)* cocer, hacer una compota de; **stewed apple,** manzana en compota; *fam* **I let her s. in her own juice before helping her to sort it out,** la dejé sufrir un poco antes de acudir en su ayuda.

steward ['stjʊəd] *n (on estate)* administrador *m*; *(on ship)* camarero *m*; *(on plane)* auxiliar *m* de vuelo; *(butler)* mayordomo *m*. ■ *Ind* **shop s.,** enlace *mf* sindical.

stewardess ['stjʊədɪs] *n (on ship)* camarera *f*; *(on plane)* azafata *f*.

Sth *abbr of* **South,** Sur, S.

stick¹ [stɪk] *n* **1** *(piece of wood)* trozo *m* de madera, madera *f*; *(twig)* ramita *f*; *(for hitting)* palo *m*; *(walking stick)* bastón *m*; *(for plants)* rodrigón *m*, tutor *m*; *Mus (conductor's baton)* batuta *f*; *(of rhubarb)* tallo *m*; *(of celery)* rama *f*; *(of dynamite)* cartucho *m*; *Pol fig* **big s. policy,** política del palo y tente tieso; *fig* **to be in a cleft s.,** estar entre la espada y la pared; *fig* **to get hold of the wrong end of the s.,** coger el rábano por las hojas; *fam* **to give sb s.,** dar caña a algn. ■ *Ent* **s. insect,** fasmo *m*, insecto *m* palo. **2 sticks,** *(for fire)* astillas *fpl*, leña *f* sing; *fam* **a few s. of furniture,** unos cuantos muebles; *fam* **to live in the s.,** vivir en el quinto pino.

stick² [stɪk] **I** *vtr (pt & pp stuck)* **1** *(push)* meter; *(knife, bayonet)* clavar, hincar; **I've stuck the needle in my finger,** me he pinchado el dedo con la aguja; **he stuck his head out of the window,** asomó la cabeza por la ventana. **2** *fam (put)* poner, meter; *(place)* colocar; *fam* **she's always sticking her nose into other people's business,** siempre anda metiendo la nariz en asuntos ajenos; *fam* **s. it in your pocket,** métalo en el bolsillo; *fam* **to get stuck into sth,** meterse de lleno *or* de cabeza en algo. **3** *(attach with glue etc)* pegar; **to s. photos in an album,** pegar fotos en un álbum. **4** *fam (tolerate)* soportar, aguantar; **I can't s. her,** no la puedo tragar. **II** *vi* **1** *(fix, become attached)* pegarse; **the rice has stuck to the pan,** el arroz se ha quedado pegado a la cacerola; **these labels don't s. very well,** estas etiquetas no pegan muy bien; **they can't make the charges s.,** no pueden acusarle de nada. **2** *(become fixed) (window, drawer)* estar atrancado,-a, atrancarse; *(machine part)* encasquillarse; *(car in mud)* estar atascado,-a, atascarse; **the phrase stuck in my mind,** la frase se me quedó grabada en la memoria; *fam* **she's stuck at home all day,** está metida en casa todo el día. ◆ **stick around** *vi fam* quedarse. ◆ **stick at** *vtr* perseverar en, seguir con; **he will s. at nothing to get his own way,** no se para en barras *or* ante nada para salirse con la suya. ◆ **stick by** *vtr (friend)* apoyar, ser fiel a; *(promise)* cumplir con. ◆ **stick out I** *vi* **1** *(project, protude)* salir, sobresalir; *(be noticeable)* resaltar, destacarse. **2** *(be very obvious)* ser obvio *or* evidente; *fam* **it sticks out a mile** *or* **like a sore thumb,** salta a la vista. **II** *vtr* **1** *(tongue, hand)* sacar; *fig* **to s. one's neck out,** jugarse el tipo. **2** *(difficult situation)* aguantar hasta el final. ◆ **stick out for** *vtr* empeñarse en conseguir. ◆ **stick to** *vtr (principles)* atenerse a;

(promise) cumplir con; *(plans)* seguir con; **to s. to one's guns,** mantenerse en sus trece. ◆ **stick together** *vi* mantenerse unidos, no separarse. ◆ **stick up I** *vi* *(project, protrude)* salir, sobresalir; *(hair)* ponerse de punta, erizarse. **II** *vtr* **1** *(poster)* fijar. **2** *(raise) (hand etc)* levantar; *fam* **s. 'em up!,** ¡arriba las manos! **3** *US fam (rob) (bank etc)* atracar. ◆ **stick up for** *vtr (person, rights)* defender. ◆ **stick with** *vtr (activity, idea)* seguir con.

sticker ['stɪkəʳ] *n* **1** *(label)* etiqueta *f* adhesiva; *(with slogan, for charity, etc)* pegatina *f*. **2** *fam (determined person)* persona *f* tenaz.

stickiness ['stɪkɪnɪs] *n* pegajosidad *f*, lo pegajoso; *fam (of situation)* dificultad *f*.

stick-in-the-mud ['stɪkɪndəmʌd] *n* *fam* persona *f* chapada a la antigua, carroza *mf*.

stickleback ['stɪkəlbæk] *n (fish)* espinoso *m*, espinosillo *m*.

stickler ['stɪkləʳ] *n* persona *f* quisquillosa; **to be a s. for detail,** ser muy detallista, dar mucha importancia a los detalles.

stick-on ['stɪkɒn] *adj* adhesivo,-a.

stick-up ['stɪkʌp] *n US fam* atraco *m*, asalto *m*, robo *m* a mano armada.

sticky ['stɪkɪ] *adj (stickier, stickiest) (gen)* pegajoso,-a; *(label)* engomado,-a; *(weather)* bochornoso,-a; *fam (situation)* difícil, violento,-a; *fam* **to be on a s. wicket,** estar en un aprieto; *fam* **to come to a s. end,** acabar mal; *fam* **to have s. fingers,** tener los dedos largos.

stiff [stɪf] **I** *adj* **1** *(gen)* rígido,-a, tieso,-a; *(card, collar, lock)* duro,-a; *(paste)* espeso,-a; *(joint)* entumecido,-a; *(machine part)* encasquillado,-a, atascado,-a; **to feel s.,** tener agujetas; **to have a s. neck,** tener tortícolis; *fig* **to be as s. as a board,** estar más tieso,-a que un palo or una tabla. **2** *fig (climb, test)* difícil, duro,-a; *(breeze)* fuerte; *(punishment, sentence)* severo,-a; *(resistance)* tenaz; *(price)* excesivo,-a; *(drink)* fuerte, cargado,-a; *(person, manner) (unnatural)* estirado,-a; *(unyielding)* inflexible; *fig* **to keep a s. upper lip,** poner a mal tiempo buena cara; *fam* **that's a bit s.!,** ¡eso es demasiado! **II** *adv* *fam* **to be bored s.,** aburrirse como una ostra; *fam* **to be scared s.,** estar muerto,-a de miedo. **III** *n US fam (corpse)* fiambre *m*. ◆ **stiffly** *adv (move, turn)* rígidamente; *(smile, greet, bow)* fríamente, con frialdad.

stiffen ['stɪfən] **I** *vtr (card, fabric)* reforzar; *(collar)* almidonar; *(paste)* endurecer; *fig (resistance, morale)* fortalecer. **II** *vi (person)* ponerse rígido,-a or tieso,-a; *(joints)* entumecerse; *fig (resistance, morale)* fortalecerse.

stiff-necked ['stɪfnekt] *adj (stubborn)* terco,-a, testarudo,-a.

stiffness ['stɪfnɪs] *n* rigidez *f*.

stifle ['staɪfəl] **I** *vtr (gen)* ahogar, sofocar; *(rebellion, opposition)* reprimir, sofocar; *(sound)* amortiguar, sofocar, *(yawn)* reprimir. **II** *vi* ahogarse, sofocarse.

stifling ['staɪflɪŋ] *adj* sofocante, agobiante.

stigma ['stɪgmə] *n* estigma *m*.

stigmatize ['stɪgmətaɪz] *vtr* estigmatizar.

stile [staɪl] *n* escalones *mpl* para pasar por encima de una valla.

stiletto [stɪ'letəʊ] *n (dagger)* estilete *m*; *(shoe)* zapato *m* con tacón fino or de aguja. ■ **s. heel,** tacón *m* fino or de aguja.

still¹ [stɪl] **I** *adv* **1** *(up to this time)* todavía, aún; **I can s. remember it,** todavía lo recuerdo, aún lo recuerdo; **they're s. discussing the weather,** siguen hablando del tiempo. **2** *(with comp adj & adv) (even)* aún; **s. colder,** aún más frío, más frío todavía. **3** *(nonetheless)* no obstante, con todo, a pesar de todo; **he is s. your son,** a pesar de todo, sigue siendo tu hijo. **4** *(however)* sin embargo; **s., there's nothing we can do,** en fin, nada podemos hacer. **5** *(motionless)* quieto; **keep s.!,** ¡estáte quieto!; **to stand s.,** no moverse. **II** *adj (quiet, calm)* tranquilo,-a; *(peaceful)*

sosegado,-a; *(silent)* silencioso,-a; *(motionless)* inmóvil; *(wine)* no espumoso,-a; *(orange juice)* sin gas; *prov* **s. waters run deep,** del agua mansa me guarde Dios, (que de la brava me guardaré yo). **III** *n* **1** *lit* tranquilidad *f*, silencio *m*. **2** *Cin* vista *f* fija, fotograma *m*. ■ *Arts.* **s. life,** bodegón *fm*, naturaleza *f* muerta. **IV** *vtr (fears etc)* calmar, acallar.

still² [stɪl] *n (apparatus)* alambique *m*; *(place)* destilería *f*.

stillbirth ['stɪlbɜːθ] *n* mortinato,-a *m,f*.

stillborn ['stɪlbɔːn] *adj* mortinato,-a, nacido,-a muerto,-a.

stillness ['stɪlnɪs] *n* calma *f*, quietud *f*, tranquilidad *f*; *(silence)* silencio *m*.

stilt [stɪlt] *n* zanco *m*.

stilted ['stɪltɪd] *adj* afectado,-a.

stimulant ['stɪmjʊlənt] *n* estimulante *m*.

stimulate ['stɪmjʊleɪt] *vtr* estimular; **to s. sb to do sth,** animar or alentar a algn para que haga algo.

stimulating ['stɪmjʊleɪtɪŋ] *adj* estimulante.

stimulation [stɪmjʊ'leɪʃən] *n (stimulus)* estímulo *m*; *(act)* estimulación *f*; *(state)* excitación *f*.

stimulus ['stɪmjʊləs] *n (pl stimuli* ['stɪmjʊlaɪ]*)* estímulo *m*; *fig* incentivo *m*.

sting [stɪŋ] **I** *n (of bee, wasp) (organ)* aguijón *m*; *(wound)* picadura *f*; *(burning sensation)* escozor *m*, picazón *m*; *fig (of remorse)* punzada *f*; *fig (of remark)* sarcasmo *m*; *fig* **the proposal had a s. in its tail,** la propuesta traía cola; *fig* **to take the s. out of sth,** quitar el hierro a algo. **II** *vtr (pt & pp stung) (insect, nettle)* picar; *fig (conscience)* remorder; *fig (remark)* herir en lo vivo or lo más hondo; *fam (overcharge etc)* **they stung him for £10,** le clavaron 10 libras. **III** *vi* picar.

stinginess ['stɪndʒɪnɪs] *n* tacañería *f*.

stingy ['stɪndʒɪ] *adj (stingier, stingiest) (person)* tacaño,-a, roñoso,-a; *(amount, meal)* escaso,-a; **to be s. with food,** escatimar la comida.

stink [stɪŋk] **I** *n* peste *f*, hedor *m*; *fam* **to kick up a s. about sth,** armar un escándalo por algo. ■ **s. bomb,** bomba *f* fétida. **II** *vi (pt stank; pp stunk)* apestar, heder (**of,** a); **he stinks of garlic,** apesta a ajo; *fam* **to s. to high heaven,** oler a tigre; *fam fig* **the whole idea stinks to me,** a mí me parece una pésima idea.

stinker ['stɪŋkəʳ] *n fam (person)* canalla *mf*; *(difficult task)* **this problem is a real s.,** este problema es un verdadero quebradero de cabeza.

stinking ['stɪŋkɪŋ] **I** *adj (smelly)* apestoso,-a; *(unpleasant)* asqueroso,-a; *fam* **to have a s. cold,** tener un catarro asqueroso. **II** *adv fam* **he's s. rich,** está podrido de dinero.

stint [stɪnt] **I** *n (period of work etc)* período *m*, temporada *f*; *(shift)* turno *m*, tanda *f*; **he did a two-year s. in the navy,** sirvió durante dos años en la Marina. **II** *vtr* escatimar; **don't s. on the cheese!,** ¡no escatimes el queso!; **to s. oneself,** privarse (**of,** de).

stipend ['staɪpend] *n* estipendio *m*, remuneración *f*, salario *m*.

stipple ['stɪpəl] *vtr* puntear.

stipulate ['stɪpjʊleɪt] *vtr* estipular.

stipulation [stɪpjʊ'leɪʃən] *n* estipulación *f*, condición *f*.

stir [stɜːʳ] **I** *n* **1** acción *f* de agitar; **to give sth a s.,** remover algo. **2** *fig* escándalo *m*, revuelo *m*, conmoción *f*; **it caused a great s.,** causó un gran revuelo. **II** *vtr (pt & pp stirred)* **1** *(liquid, mixture)* remover, revolver. **2** *(move)* mover, agitar; **the wind stirred the leaves,** el viento movía las hojas. **3** *fig (curiosity, interest)* despertar, excitar; *(anger)* provocar; *(imagination)* avivar, estimular; **to s. sb to do sth,** incitar a algn a hacer algo; *fam* **come on, s. yourself!,** ¡anda, muévete!, ¡mueve el trasero! **III** *vi (move)* moverse; **she didn't s. from her seat,** no dejó su asiento ni un momento. ◆ **stir up** *vtr* **1** *(dust, mud, etc)* remover. **2** *fig (memories, curiosity)* despertar; *(passions)* excitar; *(anger)* provocar; *(revolt)* fomentar; **to s. up trouble,** provocar un escándalo; *fam* **she's always trying to s. things up,** siempre anda con ganas de liar las cosas.

stirrer ['stɜːrəʳ] *n fam* liante *mf*, follonero,-a *m*, *f*.

stirring ['stɜːrɪŋ] *adj* conmovedor,-a.

stirrup ['stɪrəp] *n* estribo *m*.

stitch [stɪtʃ] **I** *n* **1** *Sew* puntada *f*; *Knit* punto *m*; *Med* punto *m* de sutura; *fam* **he hadn't a s. on,** estaba en cueros *or* en pelotas; *fam* **we were in stitches,** nos tronchábamos de risa; *prov* **a s. in time saves nine,** un remiendo a tiempo ahorra ciento. **2** *(sharp pain)* punzada *f*. **II** *vtr Sew* coser **(on,** a); *Med* suturar.

stoat [stəʊt] *n Zool* armiño *m*.

stock [stɒk] **I** *n* **1** *(supply)* reserva *f*; *Com (goods)* existencias *fpl*, stock *m*; *(selection)* surtido *m*; **surplus s.,** excedentes *mpl*; **it's out of s.,** está agotado,-a; **to have sth in s.,** tener existencias de algo, tener algo en stock; *fig* **to take s. of the situation,** evaluar la situación. **2** *Fin (company's capital)* capital *m* social; **stocks and shares,** acciones *fpl*, valores *mpl*. ■ **Government s.,** papel *m* del Estado; **S. Exchange,** Bolsa *f* de valores; **s. market,** bolsa *f*, mercado *m* bursátil. **3** *Agr (livestock)* ganado *m*. ■ **s. farming,** ganadería *f*. **4** *Culin* caldo *m*. ■ **s. cube,** cubito *m* *or* pastilla *f* de caldo. **5** *(descent, family)* linaje *m*, estirpe *f*; **to be of good s.,** ser de buena cepa *or* familia. **6** *Bot* alhelí *m*. **II** *adj* **1** *(goods, size)* corriente, normal, de serie. **2** *(argument, excuse, response)* de siempre; *(greeting, speech)* consabido,-a; *(phrase, theme)* trillado,-a gastado,-a, muy visto,-a. **III** *vtr* **1** *(shop) (have in stock)* tener existencias de, tener en el almacén; **we don't s. wine,** no tenemos *or* no tocamos vino. **2** *(shop, library) (provide)* abastecer, surtir **(with,** de); *(cupboard)* **(fill up** llenar **(with,** de); *(river, pond)* repoblar, poblar **(with,** de).
 ♦ **stock up** *vi* abastecerse **(on, with,** de).

stockade [stɒ'keɪd] *n* empalizada *f*, estacada *f*.

stockbreeder ['stɒkbriːdəʳ] *n* ganadero,-a *m*, *f*.

stockbreeding ['stɒkbriːdɪŋ] *n* ganadería *f*, cría *f* del ganado.

stockbroker ['stɒkbrəʊkəʳ] *n* corredor,-a *m*, *f* de Bolsa, bolsista *mf*.

stockholder ['stɒkhəʊldəʳ] *n US* accionista *mf*.

Stockholm ['stɒkhəʊm] *n* Estocolmo.

stocking ['stɒkɪŋ] *n* media *f*; **a pair of stockings,** unas medias, un par de medias. ■ **body s.,** malla *f*; *Knit* **s. stitch,** punto *m* de media.

stockist ['stɒkɪst] *n* almacenista *mf*, proveedor,-a *m*, *f*, distribuidor,-a *m*, *f*.

stockman ['stɒkmən] *n (pl* **stockmen)** *Agr* ganadero *m*.

stockpile ['stɒkpaɪl] **I** *n* reservas *fpl*. **II** *vtr (gen)* almacenar; *(accumulate)* acumular.

stockpot ['stɒkpɒt] *n* olla *f*, marmita *f*.

stockroom ['stɒkruːm] *n* almacén *m*, deposito *m*.

stocks [stɒks] *npl* **1** *Hist (as punishment)* cepo *m sing.* **2** *Naut* grada *f sing* de construcción, astillero *m sing*; **to be on the stocks,** estar en construcción *or* astilleros.

stock-still [stɒk'stɪl] *adv* inmovil.

stocktaking ['stɒkteɪkɪŋ] *n Com* inventario *m*, balance *m*.

stocky ['stɒkɪ] *adj* **(stockier, stockiest)** *(squat)* chaparro,-a; *(heavily built)* robusto,-a, fornido,-a.

stockyard ['stɒkjɑːd] *n Agr* corral *m* de ganado.

stodge [stɒdʒ] *n fam* comida *f* indigesta, mazacote *m*.

stodgy ['stɒdʒɪ] *adj* **(stodgier, stodgiest)** *(food)* indigesto,-a; *fig (book, person)* pesado,-a.

stoical ['stəʊɪkəl] *adj* estoico,-a.

stoicism ['stəʊɪsɪzəm] *n* estoicismo *m*.

stoke [stəʊk] *vtr* **1** *(poke)* atizar, avivar. **2** **to s. (up),** *(feed)* alimentar.

stoker ['stəʊkəʳ] *n Naut* fogonero *m*.

stole[1] [stəʊl] *pt see* **steal.**

stole[2] [stəʊl] *n* estola *f*.

stolen ['stəʊlən] *pp see* **steal.**

stolid ['stɒlɪd] *adj* imperturbable, impasible.

stomach ['stʌmək] **I** *n Anat* estómago *m*; **on an empty s.,** en ayunas; *fig* **it turns my s.,** me revuelve el estómago. ■ **s. ache,** dolor *m* de estómago; *Med* **s. pump,** bomba *f* estomacal; **s. upset,** trastorno *m* gástrico. **II** *vtr fig* aguantar, soportar, tragar.

stomp [stɒmp] *vi* **to s. about,** pisar muy fuerte.

stone [stəʊn] **I** *n* **1** piedra *f*; *(on grave)* lápida *f*; *fig* **at a s.'s throw,** a tiro de piedra; *fig* **to leave no s. unturned,** no dejar piedra por mover, revolver Roma con Santiago. **2** *Med* cálculo *m*, piedra *f*. **3** *(of fruit)* hueso *m*. **4** *(weight) =* 6.348 kg; **she weighs 9 s.,** pesa 57 kilos. **II** *adj* de piedra, pétreo,-a; **the S. Age,** la Edad de Piedra. **III** *vtr* **1** *(person)* apedrear. **2** *(fruit)* deshuesar.

stonechat ['stəʊntʃæt] *n Orn* tarabilla *f*.

stone-cold [stəʊn'kəʊld] *adj* helado,-a.

stoned [stəʊnd] *adj sl (drugged)* colocado,-a, flipado,-a, puesto,-a; *(drunk)* trompa.

stone-dead [stəʊn'ded] *adj fam* tieso,-a, muerto,-a.

stone-deaf [stəʊn'def] *adj* sordo,-a como una tapia.

stonemason ['stəʊnmeɪsən] *n* albañil *m*.

stonewall [stəʊn'wɔːl] *vi (gen)* andarse con evasivas; *Sport* jugar a la defensiva; *Parl* practicar el obstruccionismo.

stoneware ['stəʊnweəʳ] *n (cerámica f* de) gres *m*.

stonework ['stəʊnwɜːk] *n* manposteria *f*.

stony ['stəʊnɪ] *adj* **(stonier, stoniest)** *(ground, beach)* pedregoso,-a; *fig (look, silence)* frío,-a, glacial; *fig* **s. heart,** corazón de piedra.

stony-broke ['stəʊnɪ'brəʊk] *adj fam* **to be s.-b.,** estar sin blanca.

stood [stʊd] *pt & pp see* **stand.**

stooge [stuːdʒ] *n Theat* comparsa *mf*; *fam* títere *m*, pelele *m*.

stool [stuːl] *n* **1** *(seat)* taburete *m*, banqueta *f*, banquillo *m*; *fig* **to fall between two stools,** quedarse entre dos aguas. ■ *fam* **s. pigeon,** chivato,-a *m*, *f*, soplón,-ona *m*, *f*. **2** *Med (faeces)* deposición *f*, heces *fpl*.

stoop [stuːp] *n* **1** espaldas *fpl* encorvadas; **to walk with a s.,** andar encorvado,-a. **II** *vi* **1** *(have a stoop)* andar encorvado,-a, ser cargado,-a de espaldas. **2** *(bend)* inclinarse, agacharse **(down,** -). **3** *fig* **to s. to,** rebajarse a; **to s. to sth/to doing sth,** rebajarse a algo/a hacer algo; **he wouldn't s. so low,** a ese punto no llegaría.

stop [stɒp] **I** *n* **1** *(halt)* parada *f*, alto *m*; **to come to a s.,** pararse, hacer un alto; **to put a s. to sth,** poner fin *or* término a algo. ■ *Aut* **s. sign,** stop *m*. **2** *(break)* pausa *f*, descanso *m*; *Av (for refuelling etc)* escala *f*; *(overnight stay)* estancia *f*. **3** *(stopping place) (for bus, tram)* parada *f*. ■ **request s.,** parada *f* discrecional. **4** *(punctuation mark)* punto *m*; *(in telegram)* stop *m*. **5** *Mus (on organ)* registro *m*; *fig* **to pull out all the stops,** tocar todos los registros. **II** *vtr (pt & pp* **stopped) 1** *(gen)* parar; *(moving vehicle)* parar, detener; *(production)* parar, paralizar; *(gas, water supply)* cortar; *(conversation)* interrumpir; *(pain, abuse, etc)* poner fin *or* término a, acabar con; **s. thief!,** ¡al ladrón!; *fam* **he stopped a bullet,** recibió un balazo. **2** *(suspend) (payments, holidays)* suspender; *(cheque)* anular, cancelar, invalidar; **they stopped £20 from his wages,** le retuvieron 20 libras del sueldo. **3** *(cease)* dejar de; **she stopped smoking,** dejó de fumar; **s. it!,** ¡basta ya! **4** *(prevent)* evitar; **to s. sb from doing sth,** impedir a algn hacer algo; **to s. sth from happening,** evitar que algo ocurra; **what's stopping you?,** ¿por qué no lo haces?, ¿qué te retiene? **5** *(block) (hole)* tapar, taponar **(up,-)**; *(gap)* rellenar; *(tooth)* empastar; *(flow of blood)* restañar. **III** *vi* **1** *(person, moving vehicle)* pararse, detenerse; **he stopped to clean his shoe,** se detuvo para limpiarse el zapato; **my watch has stopped,** se me ha parado el reloj; **s.!,** ¡pare!, ¡alto!; **to s. at nothing to do**

sth, no pararse en barras para hacer algo, no tener miramientos para hacer algo; **to s. dead** *or* **short,** pararse en seco. **2** *(cease)* acabarse, terminar; **the rain has stopped,** ha dejado de llover; **without stopping,** sin parar, sin cesar. **3** *fam (stay)* quedarse; **he's stopping at his aunt's,** se aloja en casa de su tía; **why don't you s. for dinner?,** ¿por qué no te quedas a cenar? ◆ **stop by** *vi fam* visitar; **I'll s. by this evening,** pasaré esta tarde. ◆ **stop in** *vi fam* quedarse en casa, no salir. ◆ **stop off** *vi* pararse un rato; **we stopped off in Rome on our way home,** pasamos por Roma en el viaje de casa. ◆ **stop over** *vi (spend the night)* pasar la noche; *Av (for refuelling etc)* hacer escala. ◆ **stop up I** *vtr (block up) (hole)* tapar, taponar. **II** *vi (stay awake)* no acostarse.

stopcock ['stɒpkɒk] *n* llave *f* de paso.

stopgap ['stɒpgæp] *n (thing)* recurso *m*, medida *f* provisional; *(person)* sustituto,-a *m,f*.

stopover ['stɒpəʊvə'] *n (gen)* parada *f*; *Av* escala *f*.

stoppage ['stɒpɪdʒ] *n* **1** *(of game)* suspensión *f*; *(of work)* paro *m*, suspensión *f*; *(strike)* huelga *f*; *(of payments, leave)* suspensión *f*; *(deduction)* deducción *f*. **2** *(blockage) (of pipe etc)* obstrucción *f*.

stopper ['stɒpə'] *n* tapón *m*.

stop-press [stɒp'pres] *n Journ* noticias *fpl* de última hora.

stopwatch ['stɒpwɒtʃ] *n* cronómetro *m*.

storage ['stɔ:rɪdʒ] *n* almacenaje *m*, almacenamiento *m*; **to put sth into s.,** poner algo en almacén *or* en depósito. ■ **s. battery,** acumulador *m*; **s. charges,** (gastos *mpl* de) almacenaje *m*; **s. heater,** placa *f* acumuladora; **s. space,** sitio *m* para guardar los trastos; **s. unit,** armario *m*.

store [stɔ:'] **I** *n* **1** *(stock)* provisión *f*, reserva *f*; *fig (of wisdom, knowledge)* reserva *f*; **there's a big surprise in s. for them,** les aguarda una gran sorpresa; **to set great s. by sth,** valorar algo mucho. **2 stores,** *(provisions)* provisiones *fpl*, víveres *mpl*; *Mil* pertrechos *mpl*. **3** *(warehouse)* almacén *m*, depósito *m*. **4** *US (shop)* tienda *f*. ■ **department s.,** gran almacén *m*. **II** *vtr* **1** *(put in storage etc) (furniture, computer data)* almacenar; *(keep)* guardar. **2 to s. (up),** *(amass, keep in reserve)* acumular.

storehouse ['stɔ:haʊs] *n* almacén *m*, depósito *m*; *fig (of information)* mina *f*.

storekeeper ['stɔ:ki:pə'] *n US (shopkeeper)* tendero,-a *m,f*.

storeroom ['stɔ:ru:m] *n* despensa *f*.

storey ['stɔ:rɪ] *n* piso *m*; **a ten-s. building,** un edificio de 10 pisos; **multi-s. carpark,** parking de varios pisos.

stork [stɔ:k] *n Orn* cigüeña *f*.

storm [stɔ:m] **I** *n* **1** *(thunderstorm)* tormenta *f*; *(at sea)* tempestad *f*, temporal *m*; *(with wind)* borrasca *f*; *fig (uproar)* escándalo *m*, revuelo *m*; *fig* **a s. in a teacup,** una tempestad en un vaso de agua. ■ **s. cloud,** nubarrón *m*. **2** *fig (of missiles)* lluvia *f*; *(of insults, protests)* torrente *m*, lluvia *f*; **a s. of applause,** una salva de aplausos; *fig* **she has taken New York by s.** ha cautivado a todo Nueva York; *Mil* **to take a city by s.,** tomar una ciudad por asalto. ■ *Mil* **s. troops,** tropas *fpl* de asalto. **II** *vtr Mil* asaltar, tomar por asalto. **III** *vi (with rage)* echar pestes, vociferar; **she stormed out,** salió echando pestes.

stormy ['stɔ:mɪ] *adj (stormier, stormiest) (weather)* tormentoso,-a; *fig (meeting, discussion)* acalorado,-a; *fig (relationship)* borrascoso,-a, de muchos altibajos, tempestuoso,-a.

story¹ ['stɔ:rɪ] *n (gen)* historia *f*; *(tale)* cuento *m*, relato *m*; *(account)* relato *m*, relación *f*; *Journ (article)* artículo *m*; *(plot)* argumento *m*, trama *f*; *(joke)* chiste *m*; *(rumour)* rumor *m*; *(lie)* mentira *f*, cuento *m*; **but that's another s.,** pero eso es otro cantar; **it's a long s.,** sería largo de contar; **it's always the same old s.,** es la historia de siempre; **so the s. goes,** según cuenta la historia; **to cut a long s. short,** en resumidas cuentas, en pocas palabras. ■ **love s.,** historia *f* de amor; *Lit* **short s.,** novela *f* corta; **tall s.,** cuento *m* chino.

story² ['stɔ:rɪ] *n US see* **storey.**

storybook ['stɔ:rɪbʊk] *n* libro *m* de cuentos.

storyteller ['stɔ:rɪtelə'] *n* cuentista *mf*.

stout [staʊt] **I** *adj* **1** *(fat) (person)* gordo,-a, corpulento,-a, robusto,-a. **2** *(strong) (shoes, walking stick, etc)* fuerte, sólido,-a. **3** *(brave) (person, resistance)* valiente; *(determined)* firme, resuelto,-a; **with a s. heart,** valientemente, resueltamente. **II** *n (beer)* cerveza *f* negra. ◆ **stoutly** *adv* resueltamente.

stout-hearted [staʊt'hɑ:tɪd] *adj* valiente, resuelto,-a.

stove¹ [stəʊv] *n* **1** *(for heating)* estufa *f*. ■ **oil s.,** estufa *f* de petróleo. **2** *(cooker)* cocina *f*; *(cooking ring)* hornillo *m*; *(oven)* horno *m*.

stove² [stəʊv] *pt & pp see* **stave.**

stow [stəʊ] *vtr* **1** *Naut (cargo)* estibar, arrumar. **2** *(put away)* guardar. ◆ **stow away** *vi (on ship, plane)* viajar de polizón.

stowaway ['stəʊəweɪ] *n* polizón *mf*.

straddle ['strædəl] *vtr* **1** *(horse etc)* sentarse a horcajadas sobre. **2** abarcar.

strafe [streɪf, strɑ:f] *vtr* bombardear.

straggle ['strægəl] *vi* **1** *(lag behind)* rezagarse. **2** *(spread untidily)* desparramarse.

straggler ['stræglə'] *n* rezagado,-a *m,f*.

straggling ['stræglɪŋ] *adj* **1** *(of town, houses)* disperso,-a, esparcido,-a; *(of plant)* desparramado,-a. **2** *(of hair)* desordenado,-a.

straggly ['strægli] *adj (stragglier, straggliest)* desordenado,-a.

straight [streɪt] **I** *adj* **1** *(not bent)* recto,-a, derecho,-a; *(of line, skirt)* recto,-a; *(of hair)* liso,-a; **as s. as a die,** derecho,-a como una vela. ■ **s. angle,** ángulo *m* recto; *Sew* **s. edge,** recta *f*. ■ **s. face,** cara *f* seria; **to keep a s. face,** contener la risa. **2** *(successive)* seguido,-a; **I work eight hours s.,** trabajo ocho horas seguidas. **3** *(honest) (person)* honrado,-a, de confianza; *(answer)* sincero,-a, claro,-a; *(refusal, rejection)* categórico,-a, rotundo,-a; **let's get things s.,** hablemos claro. **4** *Theat (part, play)* serio,-a. **5** *(alcoholic drink)* solo,-a, sin mezcla. **6** *(tidy)* arreglado,-a, en orden; **to be all s.,** estar en orden; **to put things s.,** poner las cosas en orden. **7** *sl (conventional)* carca. **8** *sl (heterosexual)* heterosexual. **II** *adv* **1** *(in a straight line)* en línea recta; **sit up s.!,** ¡ponte derecho!; *fam (criminal)* **to go s.,** dejar el oficio. **2** *(directly)* directamente, derecho; **keep s. ahead,** sigue todo recto; **she walked s. in,** entró sin llamar. **3** *(immediately)* en seguida; **I'll come s. back,** en seguida vuelvo; **s. away,** en seguida; **s. off,** en el acto, sin pensarlo. **4** *(frankly)* francamente, con franqueza; **tell him s.,** díselo sin rodeos. **III** *n* **1** *(straight line)* línea *f* recta; *fig* **to keep to the s. and narrow,** ir por el buen camino. **2** *GB Sport* **the s.,** la recta final. **3** *Cards* escalera *f*, escalerilla *f*.

straightaway [streɪtə'weɪ] *adv* en seguida, inmediatamente.

straighten ['streɪtən] *vtr* **1** *(sth bent)* enderezar, poner derecho,-a; *(tie, picture)* poner bien; *(hair)* estirar; **s. your shoulders,** ponte derecho *or* recto. **2 to s. (up),** *(tidy)* ordenar, arreglar. ◆ **straighten out I** *vtr (problem)* resolver; *(one's affairs)* arreglar. **II** *vi* resolverse, arreglarse. ◆ **straighten up I** *vtr* **1** *(make erect)* enderezar, poner derecho,-a. **2** *(tidy)* ordenar, arreglar. **II** *vi* ponerse derecho.

straightforward [streɪt'fɔ:wəd] *adj* **1** *(honest)* honrado,-a; *(sincere)* sincero,-a, franco,-a. **2** *GB (simple)* sencillo,-a, simple.

strain¹ [streɪn] **I** *vtr* **1** *(stretch) (rope etc)* estirar, tensar; *fig* crear tensiones *or* tirantez en. **2** *Med (muscle, back)* torcer(se); *(eyes, voice)* forzar; *(heart)* cansar; **to s. one's ears,** aguzar el oído. **3** *(filter) (liquid)* filtrar; *(vegetables, tea)* colar, pasar por (un) colador. **II** *vi (pull)* tirar (**at, de**); *fig (strive)* **to s. to do sth,** esforzarse por hacer algo.

III *n* **1** *(on rope etc)* tensión *f*; *Phys (on metal etc)* deformación *f*. **2** *fig (gen)* tensión *f*; *(of atmosphere)* tensión *f*, tirantez *f*; *(effort)* esfuerzo *m*; *(exhaustion)* agotamiento *m*; **mental s.,** tensión nerviosa; **to be under a lot of s.,** estar sometido,-a a muchas tensiones; **it put a great s. on her,** le exigió un gran esfuerzo. **3** *Med (to muscle)* torcedura *f*, torsión *f*. **4** *Mus* **strains,** son *m sing*, compás *m sing*.

strain² [streɪn] *n* **1** *(race, breed)* raza *f*; *(descent)* linaje *m*, cepa *f*. **2** *(streak)* vena *f*; **a s. of madness,** una vena de loco.

strained ['streɪnd] **I** *pt & pp see* **strain¹**. **II** *adj* **1** *(muscle)* torcido,-a; *(eyes)* cansado,-a; *(voice, performance)* forzado,-a. **2** *(atmosphere, relationship)* tenso,-a, tirante.

strainer ['streɪnəʳ] *n Culin* colador *m*.

strait [streɪt] *n* **1** *(gen pl) Geog* estrecho *m*; **the S. of Gibraltar,** el estrecho de Gibraltar. **2** *(gen pl) (difficulty)* aprieto *m*; **in dire** *or* **desperate straits,** en un gran aprieto.

straitjacket ['streɪtdʒækɪt] *n* camisa *f* de fuerza.

strait-laced [streɪt'leɪst] *adj* puritano,-a, remilgado,-a, mojigato,-a.

strand¹ [strænd] *vtr* **1** *Naut (ship)* varar; **to be stranded,** quedar varado,-a *or* encallado,-a. **2** *fig (person)* abandonar; *(without money, friends, transport)* **to leave stranded,** dejar en la estacada, dejar plantado,-a.

strand² [strænd] *n (of thread)* hebra *f*, hilo *m*; *(of rope)* ramal *m*; *(of hair)* pelo *m*; *(of pearls)* sarta *f*.

strange [streɪndʒ] *adj* **1** *(unknown)* desconocido,-a; *(unfamiliar)* nuevo,-a; **s. to the job,** nuevo,-a en el oficio. **2** *(odd, bizarre)* raro,-a, extraño,-a; **she felt a bit s. at first,** al principio se sentía un poco desplazada; **s. to say,** aunque parezca extraño. ◆ **strangely** *adv* extrañamente, de forma extraña; **s. enough,** aunque parezca extraño.

strangeness ['streɪndʒnɪs] *n (oddness)* rareza *f*, extrañeza *f*.

stranger ['streɪndʒəʳ] *n (unknown person)* extraño,-a *m*, *f*, desconocido,-a *m,f*; *(outsider)* forastero,-a *m,f*.

strangle ['stræŋgəl] *vtr* **estrangular.**

strangler ['stræŋgləʳ] *n* estrangulador,-a *m,f*.

stranglehold ['stræŋgəlhəʊld] *n Wrest* collar *m* de fuerza; **to have a s. on sb,** tener a algn por el cuello; *fig* tener a algn entre la espada y la pared.

strangulation [stræŋgjʊ'leɪʃən] *n* estrangulación *f*.

strap ['stræp] **I** *n (of leather)* correa *f*, tira *f*; *(on shoulder bag)* bandolera *f*; *(on dress)* tirante *m*; *(as punishment)* **to give sb the s.,** azotar a algn con una correa. **II** *vtr (pt & pp strapped)* atar *or* sujetar con correa; *(in car, plane)* **to s. oneself in,** ponerse el cinturón de seguridad.

straphanger ['stræphæŋəʳ] *n fam* pasajero,-a *m,f* que va de pie.

strapless ['stræplɪs] *adj* sin tirantes.

strapping ['stræpɪŋ] *adj fam* fornido,-a, robusto,-a.

Strasbourg ['stræzbɜːg] *n* Estrasburgo.

strata ['strɑːtə] *npl see* **stratum.**

strategic [strə'tiːdʒɪk] **I** *adj* estratégico,-a. **II strategics** *n Mil* estrategia *f*.

strategist ['strætɪdʒɪst] *n* estratega *mf*.

strategy ['strætɪdʒɪ] *n* estrategia *f*.

stratification [strætɪfɪ'keɪʃən] *n* estratificación *f*.

stratify ['strætɪfaɪ] *vtr (pt & pp stratified)* estratificar.

stratosphere ['strætəsfɪəʳ] *n* estratosfera *f*.

stratum ['strɑːtəm] *n (pl stratums or strata) Geol* estrato *m*; *fig* estrato *m*, nivel *m*.

straw [strɔː] *n* **1** *Agr* paja *f*; **s. hat,** sombrero de paja; *fig* **to clutch** *or* **grasp at straws,** agarrarse a un clavo ardiente; *fam* **that's the last s.!,** ¡eso ya es el colmo!, ¡lo que faltaba para el duro! ■ **s. man,** hombre *m* de paja. **2** *(for drinking)* paja *f*, pajita *f*.

strawberry ['strɔːbərɪ] *n* fresa *f*; *(large)* fresón *m*. ■ **s. jam,** mermelada *f* de fresa; **s. mark,** antojo *m*; **s. tree,** madroño *m*.

straw-coloured, *US* **straw-colored** ['strɔːkʌləd] *adj* pajizo,-a, de color de paja.

stray [streɪ] **I** *vi (from path etc)* desviarse; *(get lost)* extraviarse, perderse; **to let one's thoughts s.,** dejar correr los pensamientos; **to s. from the point,** divagar. **II** *n (gen)* animal *m* extraviado. **III** *adj (haphazard)* perdido,-a, extraviado,-a; *(bullet)* perdido,-a; *(animal)* callejero,-a.

streak [striːk] **I** *n* **1** *(line)* raya *f*, lista *f*; *(in minerals)* veta *f*. ■ **s. of lightning,** rayo *m*. **2** *Hairdr* mecha *f*, mechón *m*, reflejo *m*. **3** *fig (of genius, madness)* vena *f*; *fig (of luck)* racha *f*; **he has a mean s. in him,** tiene un lado mezquino. **II** *vtr* rayar *(with, de)*; **his hair is streaked with grey,** tiene mechones grises. **III** *vi* **1 to s. past,** pasar como un rayo. **2** *fam (run naked)* correr desnudo,-a por un lugar público.

streaker ['striːkəʳ] *n fam* persona *f* que corre desnuda por un lugar público.

streaky ['striːkɪ] *adj (streakier, streakiest)* **1** *(hair)* con mechas *or* mechones. **2** *(bacon)* entreverado,-a.

stream [striːm] **I** *n* **1** *(brook)* arroyo *m*, riachuelo *m*; *(river)* río *m*. **2** *(current)* corriente *f*; **to go with/against the s.,** ir con la corriente/a contracorriente. **3** *(of water, air)* flujo *m*; *(of lava, tears)* torrente *m*; *(of blood)* chorro *m*; *(of light)* raudal *m*; *Tech* **to come on s.,** entrar en servicio. **4** *fig (of abuse, excuses)* torrente *m*, sarta *f*; *(of tourists, immigrants)* oleada *f*; *(of cars, lorries)* desfile *m* continuo, caravana *f*. ◆ *Lit* **s. of consciousness,** monólogo *m* interior. **3** *GB Sch* clase *f*, grupo *m*. **II** *vtr* **1** *(liquid)* derramar, hacer correr. **2** *Sch (pupils)* poner en grupos. **III** *vi* **1** *(liquid)* correr, manar, chorrear; **her eyes were streaming with tears,** lloraba a lágrima viva. **2** *fig (people, vehicles)* desfilar; **to s. in/out/past,** entrar/salir/pasar a raudales *or* en tropel. **3** *(wave) (hair, banner)* ondear, flotar.

streamer ['striːməʳ] *n (paper ribbon)* serpentina *f*.

streaming ['striːmɪŋ] **I** *adj fam* **a s. cold,** un catarro muy fuerte. **II** *n Sch (of pupils)* clasificación *f* por niveles *or* grupos.

streamline ['striːmlaɪn] **I** *n (contour)* línea *f* aerodinámica. **II** *vtr* **1** *(car)* aerodinamizar. **2** *(system, method)* racionalizar.

street [striːt] *n* calle *f*; **one-way s.,** calle de sentido único; *Mil* **s. fighting,** combates callejeros; **s. lighting,** alumbrado público; **the back streets,** las callejuelas; *fig* los barrios bajos; **the man in the s.,** el hombre de la calle; **to be on the streets,** estar sin vivienda; **to walk the streets,** *(person in gen)* callejear; *(prostitute)* hacer la carrera, trabajar las calles; *fam* **it's right up my s.!,** ¡me viene de perlas! ■ **s. map, s. plan,** (plano *m*) callejero *m*; **s. sweeper,** *(person)* barrendero,-a *m*, *f*; *(machine)* barredora *f*; **s. theatre,** teatro *m* callejero *or* ambulante.

streetcar ['striːtkɑːʳ] *n US* tranvía *m*.

streetlamp ['striːtlæmp] *n*, **streetlight** ['striːtlaɪt] *n* farol *m*.

streetwalker ['striːtwɔːkəʳ] *n* prostituta *f* callejera.

streetwise ['striːtwaɪz] *adj* espabilado,-a, despabilado,-a.

strength [streŋθ] *n* **1** *(gen)* fuerza *f*; *(of nail, rope, etc)* resistencia *f*; *(of currency)* valor *m*, poder *m*; *(of argument, evidence)* fuerza *f*, validez *f*; *(of emotion, conviction, colour)* intensidad *f*; *(of alcohol)* graduación *f*; *(light, sound)* potencia *f*; **by sheer s.,** a viva fuerza. **2** *(power)* poder *m*, potencia *f*; **on the s. of,** a base de, en base a, fundándose en; **to go from s. to s.,** ir ganando fuerzas. **3** *(ability)* punto *m* fuerte. **4** *(of character, mind)* entereza *f*, fuerza *f*; **to recover one's s.,** recobrar las fuerzas, reponerse. **5** *(workers, soldiers)* fuerza *f* numérica, número *m*; **in s.,** en gran número; **to be at full s./below full s.,** tener/no tener completo el cupo.

strengthen ['streŋθən] **I** *vtr* **1** *(gen)* reforzar; *(muscle, character)* fortalecer; *(economy etc)* reforzar, fortalecer; *(friendship)* consolidar. **2** *(intensify)* intensificar. **II** *vi* **1** *(gen) (economy etc)* reforzarse, fortalecerse; *(friendship)* consolidarse, reforzarse. **2** *(intensify)* intensificarse.

strenuous ['strenjʊəs] *adj* **1** *(energetic) (gen)* enérgico,-a; *(effort, life)* intenso,-a; *(opposition)* firme, tenaz. **2** *(exhausting) (occupation, game)* cansado,-a, fatigoso,-a. ◆ **strenuously** *adv* enérgicamente.

stress [stres] **I** *n* **1** *Tech* tensión *f.* **2** *Med* tensión *f* (nerviosa), estrés *m.* **2** *(emphasis)* hincapié *m*, énfasis *m*; **to lay great s. on sth,** hacer hincapié en algo. **3** *(on word)* acento *m.* **II** *vtr* **1** *(emphasize)* recalcar, subrayar. **2** *(word)* acentuar.

stressful ['stresfʊl] *adj* estresante.

stretch [stretʃ] **I** *vtr* **1** *(extend) (elastic)* estirar; *(shoes)* ensanchar; *(arm, hand)* alargar; *(wings)* desplegar, extender; **to s. one's legs,** estirar las piernas. **2** *fig (elaborate, expand)* forzar. **II** *vi (elastic)* estirarse; *(fabric)* dar de sí; *(shoes)* ensancharse, dar de sí; *fig (money)* llegar. **III** *n* **1** *(elasticity)* elasticidad *f*; **by no s. of the imagination,** de ningún modo; *fig* **to go at full s.,** ir a todo gas *or* a toda mecha. **2** *(length)* trecho *m*, tramo *m*. **3** *(expanse) (of land)* extensión *f*; *(of time)* período *m*, tiempo *m*, intervalo *m*. ■ *Sport* **home s.,** recta *f* final. **4** *fig (extent)* **at a s.,** de un tirón. ◆ **stretch out I** *vtr* **1** *(extend) (arm, hand)* alargar; *(legs)* estirar. **2** *fig (make long)* alargar, estirar. **II** *vi* **1** *(person)* estirarse; *(lie down)* tumbarse. **2** *(countryside, years, etc)* extenderse.

stretcher ['stretʃəʳ] *n* camilla *f.*

stretcher-bearer ['stretʃəbeərəʳ] *n* camillero,-a *m,f.*

stretchmarks ['stretʃmɑːks] *npl* estrías *fpl.*

stretchsuit ['stretʃsuːt] *n (for baby)* pijama *m.*

stretchy ['stretʃi] *adj* **(stretchier, stretchiest)** elástico,-a.

strew [struː] *vtr (pt* **strewed;** *pp* **strewed** *or* **strewn** [struːn]) esparcir, desparramar.

stricken ['strikən] *adj (with grief)* afligido,-a acongojado,-a; *(with illness)* aquejado,-a; *(by disaster etc)* afectado,-a, damnificado,-a; *(damaged)* dañado,-a, destrozado,-a; **to be s. with remorse,** remorderle a uno la conciencia.

strict [strikt] *adj* **1** *(severe)* severo,-a, estricto,-a; *(discipline)* riguroso,-a. **2** *(precise)* estricto,-a exacto,-a, preciso,-a. **3** *(absolute)* absoluto,-a; **in the strictest confidence,** en el más absoluto secreto. ◆ **strictly** *adv* **1** *(severely)* severamente, estrictamente. **2** *(categorically)* terminantemente. **3** *(precisely)* estrictamente, exactamente; **s. speaking,** en sentido estricto. **4** *(exclusively)* exclusivamente, sólo.

strictness ['striktnis] *n* **1** *(severity)* severidad *f.* **2** *(precision)* exactitud *f*, precisión *f.*

stride [straid] **I** *n* zancada *f*, trancada *f*, tranco *m*; *fig (progress)* progresos *mpl*; *fig* **to get into one's s.,** coger el ritmo; *fig* **to take sth in one's s.,** tomarse las cosas con calma. **II** *vi (pt* **strode;** *pp* **stridden** ['stridən]) **to s. (along),** andar a zancadas. **III** *vtr* cruzar de una zancada.

strident ['straidənt] *adj (voice, sound)* estridente; *(protest etc)* fuerte.

strife [straif] *n* conflictos *mpl*, luchas *fpl*; **industrial s.,** conflictos laborales.

strike [straik] **I** *vtr (pt & pp* **struck) 1** *(hit)* pegar, golpear; **to s. a blow,** pegar un golpe **(at,** a); *fig* **to s. a blow for sth,** romper una lanza en defensa de algo; *prov* **s. while the iron is hot,** al hierro caliente batir de repente. **2** *(knock against, collide with)* dar *or* chocar contra; *(car)* atropellar; *(bullet, lightning)* alcanzar; **she struck her head against the door,** dio con la cabeza contra la puerta; **the church tower was struck by lightning,** cayó un rayo en el campanario; **then disaster struck,** entonces sobrevino el desastre; *fig* **to s. the eye,** saltar a la vista. **3** *(coin, medal)* acuñar. **4** *(match)* encender. **5** *(pose, attitude)* adoptar. **6** *(bargain, deal)* cerrar; *(balance)* encontrar. **7** *(of clock)* dar, tocar;

the clock struck three, el reloj dio las tres. **8** *(oil, gold)* descubrir, encontrar; *fam* **to s. it lucky/rich,** tener suerte/ hacerse rico,-a. **9** *(impress)* impresionar; **it strikes me ...,** me parece ...; *fam* **I'm not struck with the idea,** esta idea no me va. **10** *(pp* **struck** *or* **stricken)** *(render)* **to be struck dumb,** quedarse mudo,-a; **to s. sb dead,** matar a algn. **II** *vi (pt & pp* **struck) 1** *Mil (attack)* atacar; *(disaster, misfortune)* sobrevenir; *(disease)* atacar, golpear; **to s. home,** dar en el blanco. **2** *(clock)* dar la hora; **midnight struck,** dieron las doce. **3** *(workers)* declararse en *or* hacer huelga; **to s. for higher wages,** ir a la huelga para conseguir un aumento de sueldo. **III** *n* **1** *(by workers, students)* huelga *f*; **to be on s.,** estar en huelga; **to call a s.,** convocar una huelga. ■ **hunger s.,** huelga *f* de hambre; **lightning s.,** huelga *f* salvaje; **sit-down s.,** sentada *f*; **s. fund,** caja *f* de resistencia; **s. pay,** subsidio *m* de huelga. **2** *(of oil, gold)* hallazgo *m*, descubrimiento *m*. **3** *(blow)* golpe *m*; Crick golpe *m*; Bowling bolada *f*; *fig* **lucky s.,** golpe de suerte. **4** *Baseb (miss)* strike *m*. **5** *Mil* ataque *m*; **air s.,** ataque aéreo. ◆ **strike back** *vi (gen)* devolver el golpe; *Mil* contraatacar. ◆ **strike down** *vtr (disease)* fulminar, abatir; **she was struck down in her prime,** murió en la flor de la vida. ◆ **strike off** *vtr (name from list)* tachar; *(doctor, lawyer)* suspender, no permitir que ejerza. ◆ **strike out I** *vtr (cross out)* tachar. **II** *vi* **1** *(hit out)* **to s. out at sb,** arremeter a *or* contra algn. **2** *(set off)* ponerse en camino *or* dirigirse **(for,** hacia); *(in business)* **to s. out on one's own,** volar con sus propias alas. ◆ **strike up** *vtr* **1** *(friendship)* trabar, entablar; *(conversation)* entablar, iniciar. **2** *(tune)* empezar a tocar. **II** *vi (band)* empezar a tocar.

strikebound ['straikbaʊnd] *adj* paralizado,-a por la huelga.

strikebreaker ['straikbreikəʳ] *n* esquirol *mf*, rompehuelgas *mf inv.*

striker ['straikəʳ] *n* **1** *(worker)* huelguista *mf*. **2** *fam Ftb* marcador,-a *m,f*; Crick bateador,-a *m,f.*

striking ['straikiŋ] *adj* **1** *(eye-catching)* llamativo,-a; *(noticeable)* notable, sorprendente; *(impressive)* impresionante. **2** *(on strike)* en huelga.

string [striŋ] **I** *n* **1** *(cord)* cuerda *f*, cordel *m*; *(lace)* cordón *m*; *(of puppet)* hilo *m*; *fig* **to pull strings for sb,** enchufar a algn; *fig* **with no strings attached,** sin (ningún) compromiso. **2** *(of garlic, onions)* ristra *f*; *(of cars)* fila *f*, hilera *f*; *(of hotels)* cadena *f*; *(of events)* cadena *f*, sucesión *f*; *(of lies)* sarta *f*; *(of insults)* retahíla *f*. ■ **s. bean,** judía *f* verde. **3** *(of racket, guitar)* cuerda *f*; Mus **the strings,** los instrumentos de cuerda. ■ Mus **s. orchestra,** *fam* **s. band,** orquesta *f* de cuerdas; Mus **s. quartet,** cuarteto *m* de cuerdas. **II** *vtr (pt & pp* **strung) 1** *(beads)* ensartar, enhebrar. **2** *(racket, guitar)* encordar. **3** *(beans)* quitar la hebra a. ◆ **string along** *fam* **I** *vi (agree)* seguir la corriente **(with,** a). **II** *vtr* tomar el pelo a.

stringed [striŋd] *adj (instrument)* de cuerda.

stringent ['strindʒənt] *adj* severo,-a, estricto,-a, riguroso,-a.

string-pulling ['striŋpʊliŋ] *n fam* enchufismo *m.*

stringy ['striŋi] *adj* **(stringier, stringiest)** fibroso,-a, hebroso,-a.

strip¹ [strip] **I** *vtr (pt & pp* **stripped) 1** *(person)* desnudar; *(bed)* quitar la ropa de; *(room)* vaciar; *(wallpaper, paint)* quitar; **to s. sb of sth,** despojar a algn de algo. **2** *Tech* **to s. (down),** *(engine)* desmontar; *(ship)* desaparejar. **II** *vi (undress)* desnudarse; *(perform striptease)* hacer un striptease. **III** *n* striptease *m*; **s. club,** club de striptease. ◆ **strip off** *vtr* quitar, sacar. **II** *vi (undress)* desnudarse.

strip² [strip] **I** *n (of paper, leather)* tira *f*; *(of land)* franja *f*; *(of metal)* fleje *m*; *fam* **to tear sb off a s.,** echar una bronca a algn. ■ *Av* **landing s.,** pista *f* de aterrizaje; **s. cartoon,** historieta *f*; **s. lighting,** alumbrado *m* fluorescente. **II** *vtr (pt & pp* **stripped)** hacer tiras *or* pedazos.

stripe [straip] **I** *n (gen)* raya *f*, lista *f*; Mil galón *m.* **II** *vtr* pintar *or* dibujar a rayas.

striped ['straɪpt] *adj* rayado,-a, a rayas.

stripper ['straɪpəʳ] *n* **1** persona *f* que hace striptease. **2** *(for paint)* quitapinturas *m inv*.

striptease ['strɪptiːz] *n* striptease *m*.

strive [straɪv] *vi (pt strove; pp striven* ['strɪvən]*)* esforzarse, procurar; **to s. for** *or* **after sth**, esforzarse por conseguir algo.

strobe [strəʊb] *n* estroboscopio *m*. ◼ **s. lighting**, luces *fpl* estroboscópicas.

strode [strəʊd] *pt see* **stride**.

stroke [strəʊk] **I** *n* **1** *(blow)* golpe *m*; *fig (feat)* **a s. of genius**, una genialidad; **a s. of luck**, un golpe de suerte. **2** *Crick Golf* golpe *m*, jugada *f*; *Bill* tacada *f*; *(rowing)* remada *f*; *Swimming* brazada *f*; *(style)* estilo *m*; **butterfly s.**, estilo mariposa; *fig* **to put sb off his s.**, distraer a algn. **3** *(of bell)* campanada *f*. **4** *(of piston)* carrera *f*; *(of engine)* tiempo *m*. **5** *(of pen)* trazo *m*; *(of brush)* pincelada *f*. **6** *(caress)* caricia *f*. **7** *Med* apoplejía *f*, derrame *m* cerebral; **to have a s.**, tener una apoplejía. **8** *fam (bit)* **I haven't done a s.**, no he dado golpe. **II** *vtr* acariciar.

stroll [strəʊl] **I** *vi* dar un paseo *or* una vuelta, pasear. **II** *n* paseo *m*, vuelta *f*.

stroller ['strəʊləʳ] *n US* cochecito *m*.

strong [strɒŋ] **I** *adj* **1** *(gen)* fuerte; *(person)* fuerte, fornido,-a; *(robust)* robusto,-a; **to be as s. as an ox**, ser fuerte como un toro. ◼ **s. point**, punto *m* fuerte. **2** *(durable)* sólido,-a, resistente. **3** *(firm, resolute)* firme, profundo,-a; *(of supporter)* acérrimo,-a; *(protest)* fuerte, enérgico,-a. **4** *(intense) (colour)* fuerte, intenso,-a, vivo,-a; *(smell, food, drink)* fuerte; *(light)* brillante; *(resemblance, accent)* fuerte, marcado,-a; *fam* **that scene was really s. meat**, esa escena era muy fuerte. **5** *(incontestable)* poderoso,-a, convincente. **6** *(team etc)* **to be 20 s.**, contar con 20 miembros. **7** *(severe)* severo,-a; *(drastic)* drástico,-a. **8** *Fin Com (of currency etc)* fuerte, en alza. **II** *adv* fuerte; **to be going s.**, *(business)* ir fuerte *or* en auge; *(elderly person)* conservarse bien. ◆ **strongly** *adv (gen)* fuertemente; **a s. worded letter**, una carta en tono fuerte; **he feels very s. about it**, sus opiniones al respecto son muy contundentes.

strong-arm ['strɒŋɑːm] *adj* de mano dura.

strongbox ['strɒŋbɒks] *n* caja *f* fuerte.

stronghold ['strɒŋhəʊld] *n Mil* fortaleza *f*; *fig* baluarte *m*.

strong-minded [strɒŋ'maɪndɪd] *adj* resuelto,-a, decidido,-a.

strongroom ['strɒŋruːm] *n* cámara *f* acorazada.

strong-willed [strɒŋ'wɪld] *adj* decidido,-a, obstinado,-a.

strontium ['strɒntɪəm] *n Chem* estroncio *m*.

stroppy ['strɒpɪ] *adj (stroppier, stroppiest) GB fam* negro,-a, de mala uva.

strove [strəʊv] *pt see* **strive**.

struck [strʌk] *pt & pp see* **strike**.

structural ['strʌktʃərəl] *adj (gen)* estructural; **s. engineer**, ingeniero,-a *m*, *f* de estructuras; *(in building)* **s. fault**, fallo *m* de armazón.

structuralist ['strʌktʃərəlɪst] *adj & n* estructuralista *(mf)*.

structure ['strʌktʃəʳ] **I** *n* **1** *(organization, composition)* estructura *f* **2** *(constructed thing)* construcción *f*; *(building)* edificio *m*. **II** *vtr (argument, novel)* estructurar.

struggle ['strʌgəl] **I** *vi (gen)* luchar, *(physically)* forcejear; **to s. to achieve sth**, esforzarse por conseguir algo; **to s. to one's feet**, levantarse con dificultad **II** *n (gen)* lucha *f*; *(physical fight)* pelea *f*, forcejeo *m*, forcejeo *m*, **it's a real s. to make ends meet**, nos cuesta Dios y ayuda llegar a fin de mes, **without a s.**, sin oponer resistencia

strum [strʌm] *vtr (pt & pp strummed)* (guitar) rasguear

strung [strʌŋ] *pt & pp see* **string**.

strut [strʌt] **I** *vi (pt & pp strutted)* pavonearse; **to s. about the room**, andar pavoneándose por la habitación **II** *n Archit* puntal *m*, riostra *f*

strychnine ['strɪkniːn] *n Chem* estricnina *f*.

stub [stʌb] **I** *n* **1** *(of cigarette)* colilla *f* **2** *(of pencil, candle)* cabo *m*. **3** *(of cheque)* matriz *f*. **II** *vtr (pt & pp stubbed)* **1** *(strike)* golpear **2** *(cigarette)* **to s. (out)**, apagar.

stubble ['stʌbəl] *n (in field)* rastrojo *m*, *(on chin)* barba *f* incipiente *or* mal afeitada.

stubborn ['stʌbən] *adj* **1** *(person, animal)* terco,-a testarudo,-a, obstinado,-a. **2** *(stain)* difícil **3** *(illness)* rebelde. **4** *(refusal)* rotundo,-a

stubbornnes ['stʌbənnɪs] *n (gen)* terquedad *f*, testarudez *f*.

stubby ['stʌbɪ] *adj (stubbier, stubbiest)* rechoncho,-a.

stucco ['stʌkəʊ] *n (pl stuccos or stuccoes)* estuco *m*

stuck [stʌk] *pt & pp see* **stick²**.

stuck-up [stʌk'ʌp] *adj fam* creído,-a, orgulloso,-a

stud¹ [stʌd] **I** *n (on clothing)* tachón *m*; *(on furniture)* tachuela *f*; *(in road)* clavo *m*, *(on football boots)* taco *m*, *(on shirt)* botonadura *f* ◼ *GB* **press s.**, *(cierre m)* automático *m* **II** *vtr (pt & pp studded) (decorate)* tachonar **(with**, de); *fig (dot, cover)* salpicar **(with**, de).

stud² [stʌd] *n* semental *m*. ◼ **s. (farm)**, cuadra *f*, caballeriza *f*

student ['stjuːdənt] *n Univ* estudiante *mf*, universitario,-a *m*, *f*; *Sch* alumno,-a *m*, *f*, *(researcher)* investigador,-a *m*, *f*; **part-time s.**, estudiante a tiempo parcial. ◼ **s. teacher**, profesor,-a *m*, *f* en prácticas.

studied ['stʌdɪd] *adj (gen)* pensado,-a, estudiado,-a, *(insult, indifference)* premeditado,-a, calculado,-a, *(style etc)* afectado,-a

studio ['stjuːdɪəʊ] *n (pl studios) TV Cin* estudio *m*; *(artist's)* estudio *m*, taller *m* ◼ **s. apartment, s. flat**, estudio *m*; *TV* **s. audience**, público *m* (invitado), **s. couch**, sofa cama *m*.

studious ['stjuːdɪəs] *adj* **1** *(devoted to study)* estudioso,-a, aplicado,-a **2** *(thoughtful)* atento,-a, solícito,-a ◆ **studiously** *adv* cuidadosamente, deliberadamente

study ['stʌdɪ] **I** *vtr (pt & pp studied) (gen)* estudiar, *(university subject)* estudiar, cursar; *(facts etc)* examinar, investigar; *(behaviour, the stars)* observar **II** *vi* estudiar, *fml* cursar estudios, **to s. for a exam**, preparar un examen, **to s. hard**, estudiar mucho, **to s. to be a doctor**, estudiar para médico **III** *n* **1** *(gen)* estudio *m*; *(of facts, text, etc)* investigación *f*, estudio *m*, **s. group**, grupo de trabajo, **to make a s. of sth**, investigar algo **2** *(room)* despacho *m*, estudio *m*

stuff [stʌf] **I** *vtr* **1** *(-ful) (container)* llenar **(with**, de), *(cushion, doll)* rellenar **(with**, con *or* de); *Culin* rellenar **(with**, con *or* de), *(animal for display)* disecar **2** *(cram)* meter a la fuerza, atiborrar **(with**, de), *fam* **to s. oneself**, hartarse de comida, *sl offens* **he can s. his money!**, ¡que se meta el dinero por el culo! **3** *offens (have sex)* joder, **get stuffed!**, ¡vete a hacer puñetas!, **s. him!**, ¡que se joda! **4** *sl (thrash)* dar una paliza **a II** *n* **1** *fam (material, substance)* materia *f*, material *m*; **he certainly knows his s.**, sabe lo que se hace, **that's the s.!**, ¡así es!, ¡así me gusta!; **to be hot s.**, *(sexy)* estar bueno,-a; **to do one's s.**, hacer lo suyo **2** *fam (things, possessions, equipment)* cosas *fpl*, *fam* trastos *mpl*, cachivaches *mpl*, **put all your s. away**, guarda tus cosas **3** *(cloth, fabric)* tela *f*, paño *m*, género *m*.

stuffed [stʌft] *adj* **1** relleno,-a; *Culin* **s. tomatoes**, tomates rellenos ◼ *Sew* **s. toy**, muñeco *m* de peluche, *fam* **s. shirt**, persona *f* envarada *or* estirada **2** *(nose)* **s. (up)**, tapado,-a

stuffing ['stʌfɪŋ] *n* relleno *m*

stuffy ['stʌfɪ] *adj (stuffier, stuffiest)* **1** *(room)* mal ventilado,-a, *(atmosphere)* cargado,-a, **it's s. in here**, aquí dentro huele a cerrado **2** *(pompous)* pomposo,-a, estirado,-a, *(narrow-minded)* de miras estrechas; *(strait-laced)* remilgado,-a **3** *(nose)* tapado,-a

stultify ['stʌltɪfaɪ] *vtr (pt & pp stultified)* anular; aniquilar

stumble ['stʌmbəl] **I** *vi* tropezar, dar un traspié; *fig* **to s. across** *or* **on** *or* **upon**, tropezar *or* dar con **II** *n (trip, blunder)* tropezón *m*, traspié *m*

stumbling ['stʌmblɪŋ] *n* **s. block,** escollo *m*, tropiezo *m*

stump [stʌmp] **I** *n* **1** *(of pencil, candle)* cabo *m* **2** *(of tree)* tocón *m*; *(of arm, leg)* muñón *m*, chueca *f* **3** *Crick* estaca *f*, palo *m* **4** *US* **to go on the s.,** hacer una campaña electoral. **II** *vtr* **1** *(puzzle)* confundir, **to be stumped,** estar perplejo,-a *or* confuso,-a. **2** *Crick (dismiss)* poner fuera de juego **III** *vi (walk heavily)* pisar fuerte ◆ **stump up** *vi* *GB fam* pagar, soltar la pasta

stumpy ['stʌmpɪ] *adj* **(stumpier, stumpiest)** rechoncho,-a, achaparrado,-a

stun [stʌn] *vtr (pt & pp* **stunned)** *(blow)* aturdir, atontar, *fig (news etc)* sorprender

stung [stʌŋ] *pt & pp see* **sting.**

stunk [stʌŋk] *pt & pp see* **stink.**

stunner ['stʌnə^r] *n fam (woman)* mujer *f* fenomenal, *(thing)* cosa *f* alucinante

stunning ['stʌnɪŋ] *adj (blow)* aturdidor,-a, *(news)* alucinante, *fam (woman, outfit)* imponente, fenomenal

stunt¹ [stʌnt] *vtr (growth)* atrofiar

stunt² [stʌnt] *n* **1** *Av* acrobacia *f* peligrosa **2** *(trick)* truco *m* ■ **publicity s.,** truco *m* publicitario **3** *Cin* escena *f* peligrosa ■ **s. man,** doble *m*

stunted ['stʌntɪd] *adj (tree etc)* enano,-a, mal desarrollado,-a ■ **s. growth,** atrofia *f*

stupefaction [stjuːpɪ'fækʃən] *n* estupefacción *f*

stupefy ['stjuːpɪfaɪ] *vtr (pt &pp* **stupefied)** *(alcohol, drugs)* atontar, aletargar, *fig (news etc)* dejar estupefacto,-a *or* pasmado,-a

stupendous [stjuː'pendəs] *adj (wonderful)* estupendo,-a, fabuloso,-a; *(enormous)* tremendo,-a, formidable; *(unusual)* extraordinario,-a.

stupid ['stjuːpɪd] **I** *adj* tonto,-a, imbécil; **how s. of me!,** ¡mira que soy tonto,-a!; **don't be s.!,** ¡no seas tonto,-a! **II** *n (person)* imbécil *m*, tonto,-a *m,f.*

stupidity [stjuː'pɪdɪtɪ] *n* estupidez *f.*

stupor ['stjuːpə^r] *n* estupor *m.*

sturdiness ['stɜːdɪnɪs] *n* robustez *f,* fuerza *f; fig* energía *f,* vigor *m.*

sturdy ['stɜːdɪ] *adj* **(sturdier, sturdiest)** *(child, table, material)* robusto,-a, fuerte; *(opposition, resistance)* enérgico,-a, vigoroso,-a.

sturgeon ['stɜːdʒən] *n (fish)* esturión *m.*

stutter ['stʌtə^r] **I** *vi* tartamudear. **II** *vtr* decir tartamudeando. **III** *n* tartamudeo *m.*

stutterer ['stʌtərə^r] *n* tartamudo,-a *m,f.*

sty [staɪ] *n (pen)* pocilga *f.*

sty(e) [staɪ] *n (pl* **sties** *or* **styes)** *Med* orzuelo *m.*

style [staɪl] **I** *n* **1** *(gen)* estilo *m*; *(of dress, suit)* modelo *m*; *(hairstyle)* peinado *m*; **in the s. of,** al estilo de. **2** *(fashion)* moda *f*; **in s.,** de moda; **it's the latest s.,** es lo que se lleva. **3** *(elegance)* estilo *m,* elegancia *f,* clase *f*; **to live in s.,** vivir a lo grande. **II** *vtr Hairdr* marcar.

styli ['staɪlaɪ] *npl see* **stylus.**

stylish ['staɪlɪʃ] *adj (elegant)* fino,-a, elegante; *(fashionable)* a la moda, de última moda.

stylist ['staɪlɪst] *n Hairdr* estilista *mf*, peluquero,-a *m,f.*

stylistic [staɪ'lɪstɪk] *adj (device)* estilístico,-a.

stylized ['staɪlaɪzd] *adj* estilizado,-a.

stylus ['staɪləs] *n (pl* **styluses** *or* **styli) 1** *(of record player)* aguja *f.* **2** *(writing instrument)* estilo *m.*

stymie ['staɪmɪ] *vtr fam* frustrar; *Golf* interferir.

styptic ['stɪptɪk] *adj* astringente. ■ **s. pencil,** barra *f* astringente.

suave [swɑːv] *adj* amable, afable; *pej* zalamero,-a.

sub [sʌb] **I** *n fam* **1** *(abbr of* **submarine)** submarino *m.* **2** *Sport (abbr of* **substitute)** sustituto,-a *m,f.* **3** *Journ (abbr of* **subeditor)** redactor,-a *m,f.* **4** *(abbr of* **subscription)** subscripción *f,* suscripción *f.* **5** *GB fam (advance*

payment) anticipo *m.* **II** *vtr (pt & pp* **subbed)** *Journ* corregir. **III** *vi (in job)* hacer una suplencia; **to s. for sb,** sustituir a algn.

sub- [sʌb] *pref* sub-.

subaltern ['sʌbəltən] *n Mil* alférez *m.*

subcommittee ['sʌbkəmɪtɪ] *n* subcomisión *f,* subcomité *m.*

subconscious [sʌb'kɒnʃəs] **I** *adj* subconsciente. **II the s.** *n,* el subconsciente.

subcontinent [sʌb'kɒntɪnənt] *n* subcontinente *m.*

subcontract [sʌb'kɒntrækt] **I** *n* subcontrato *m.* **II** [sʌbkən'trækt] *vtr* subcontratar.

subcontrator [sʌbkən'træktə^r] *n* subcontratista *mf.*

subdivide [sʌbdɪ'vaɪd] *vtr* subdividir **(into,** en).

subdue [səb'djuː] *vtr* **1** *(nation, people)* someter, sojuzgar. **2** *(feelings, passions)* dominar, contener. **3** *(sound, colour, light)* atenuar, suavizar.

subdued [səb'djuːd] *adj* **1** *(person, emotion)* callado,-a, apagado,-a. **2** *(voice, tone)* bajo,-a. **3** *(light)* tenue; *(colour)* apagado,-a.

subedit [sʌb'edɪt] *vtr (article, story)* corregir.

subeditor [sʌb'edɪtə^r] *n* redactor,-a *m,f.*

subhead(ing) ['sʌbhed(ɪŋ)] *n* subtítulo *m.*

subhuman [sʌb'hjuːmən] *adj* infrabumano,-a.

subject ['sʌbdʒɪkt] **I** *n* **1** *(citizen)* súbdito *m.* **2** *(theme, topic)* tema *m*; **to change the s.,** cambiar de tema; **while we are on the s. of holidays ...,** ya que hablamos de vacaciones ... . ■ **s. matter,** tema *m*, materia *f*; *(contents)* contenido *m.* **3** *Sch Univ* asignatura *f.* **4** *Ling* sujeto *m.* **II** *adj* **s. to,** *(law, tax)* sujeto,-a a; *(charge, fine)* expuesto,-a a; *(changes, delays)* susceptible de; *(illness)* propenso,-a a; *(conditional upon)* previo,-a; **s. to government approval,** previa aprobación gubernamental. **III** [səb'dʒekt] *vtr* someter; **to s. to torture,** someter a tortura, torturar.

subjective [səb'dʒektɪv] *adj* subjecivo,-a.

sub judice [sʌb'dʒuːdɪsɪ] *adj Jur* pendiente de resolución.

subjugate ['sʌbdʒugeɪt] *vtr* sojuzgar, subyugar.

subjunctive [səb'dʒʌŋktɪv] *Ling* **I** *adj* subjuntivo,-a. **II** *n* subjuntivo *m.*

sublet [sʌb'let] *vtr & vi (pt & pp* **sublet)** realkilar, subaquilar, subarrendar.

sublieutenant [sʌblə'tenənt] *n Naut* alférez *m* de navío; *Mil* subteniente *m.*

sublimate ['sʌblɪmeɪt] *vtr* sublimar.

sublime [sə'blaɪm] **I** *adj* **1** *(beauty etc)* sublime. **2** *iron (indifference, ignorance)* sumo,-a, total. **II** **the s.,** la sublimación.

subliminal [sʌb'lɪmɪnəl] *adj* subliminal.

sub-machine-gun [sʌbmə'ʃiːngʌn] *n* ametralladora *f,* metralleta *f.*

submarine ['sʌbməriːn] *n Naut* submarino *m.*

submerge [səb'mɜːdʒ] **I** *vtr (plunge)* sumergir, hundir **(in,** en); *(flood)* inundar; *fig* **submerged in ...,** sumido,-a en ... . **II** *vi (submarine, diver)* sumergirse.

submersion [səb'mɜːʃən] *n* sumersión *f.*

submission [səb'mɪʃən] *n* **1** *(yielding)* sumisión *f*; **to starve into s.,** reducir por hambre. **2** *(of documents)* presentación *f.* **3** *(report)* ponencia *f,* informe *m.*

submissive [səb'mɪsɪv] *adj* sumiso,-a, resignado,-a.

submit [səb'mɪt] **I** *vtr (pt &pp* **submitted)** **1** *(present)* *(application, proposal, claim)* presentar. **2** *(subject)* *(person)* someter **(to,** a). **3** *Jur* alegar, **II** *vi (surrender)* rendirse, ceder.

subnormal [sʌb'nɔːməl] *adj* subnormal.

subordinate [sʌbɔːdɪnɪt] **1** *adj* subordinado,-a; *Gram* **s. clause,** oración subordinada. **II** *n* subordinado,-a *m,f.* **III** [sə'bɔːdɪneɪt] *vtr* subordinar **(to,** a).

subordination [səbɔːdɪ'neɪʃən] **I** *n* subordinación *f.*

subplot ['sʌbplɒt] n Lit argumento m secundario.

subpoena [səb'piːnə] Jur I n citación f. II vtr citar.

subscribe [səb'skraɪb] vi (newspaper, magazine) subscribirse, suscribirse, abonarse (to, a); (opinion, theory) estar de acuerdo (to, con).

subscriber [səb'skraɪbər] n (to newspaper, magazine) subscriptor,-a m,f, suscriptor,-a m,f, abonado,-a m,f; Tel abonado,-a m,f.

subscription [səb'skrɪpʃən] n (to newspaper, magazine) subscripción f, suscripción f, abono m; (to club) cuota f; (to opinion, theory) adhesión f; **to take out a s.,** suscribirse (to, a).

subsequent ['sʌbsɪkwənt] adj subsiguiente; **s. to,** posterior a. ◆ **subsequently** adv posteriormente.

subservient [səb'sɜːvɪənt] adj servil.

subside [səb'saɪd] vi (land, building) hundirse; (floodwater) bajar, descender; (storm, wind) amainar; fig (anger) calmarse, amainar.

subsidence [səb'saɪdəns] n (of land, building) hundimiento m; (of floodwater) bajada f, descenso m; (of storm, wind) amaine m; fig (of anger) apaciguamiento m.

subsidiary [sʌb'sɪdɪərɪ] I adj (role, interest) secundario,-a; (troops) subsidiario,-a. II n Com sucursal f, filial f.

subsidize ['sʌbsɪdaɪz] vtr (gen) subvencionar; (exports) primar.

subsidy ['sʌbsɪdɪ] n subvención f, subsidio m. ■ **export s.,** prima f; **housing s.,** subsidio m de vivienda.

subsist [səb'sɪst] vi subsistir; **to s. on ...,** subsistir a base de ... .

subsistence [səb'sɪstəns] n (existence) subsistencia f, existencia f; (sustenance) sustento m, subsistencia f. ■ GB s. allowance, (advance payment) anticipo m; (for expenses) dietas mpl; s. wage, sueldo m miserable or muy bajo.

subsoil ['sʌbsɔɪl] n subsuelo m.

substance ['sʌbstəns] n 1 (material) substancia f, sustancia f, materia f. 2 (solid worth) substancia f, solidez f; (essence, gist) esencia f; **an argument of little s.,** un argumento que carece de substancia. 3 (wealth) riqueza f; **a woman of s.,** una mujer acaudalada.

substandard [sʌb'stædəd] adj inferior (a la media).

substantial [səb'stænʃəl] adj 1 (solid) sólido,-a. 2 (considerable) (sum, loss, etc) importante; (difference, improvement) substancial, notable; (meal) abundante. ◆ **substantially** adv 1 (solidly) sólidamente; **a s. built house,** una casa muy sólida. 2 (considerably) notablemente. 3 (essentially) esencialmente; (to a large extent) en gran parte.

substantiate [səb'stænʃɪeɪt] vtr (claim) justificar.

substantive ['sʌbstəntɪv] n Ling substantivo m, sustantivo m.

substitute ['sʌbstɪtjuːt] I vtr substituir, sustituir; **to s. X for Y,** sustituir X por Y. II vi sustituir, suplir (for, a). III n (person) sustituto,-a m,f, suplente mf; (thing) sucedáneo m; **a coffee s.,** un sucedáneo del café.

substitution [sʌbstɪ'tjuːʃən] n 1 (gen) substitución f, sustitución f. 2 (in job) suplencia f.

substratum [sʌb'strɑːtəm] n (pl **substrata** [sʌb'strɑːtə]) substrato m, subsuelo m.

subterfuge ['sʌbtəfjuːdʒ] n subterfugio m.

subterranean [sʌbtə'reɪnɪən] adj subterráneo,-a.

subtitle ['sʌbtaɪtəl] Cin I n subtítulo m. II vtr subtitular, poner subtítulos a.

subtle ['sʌbtəl] adj (colour, difference) sutil; (perfume, taste) delicado,-a; (remark, analysis) ingenioso,-a, agudo,-a; (irony, joke) fino,-a. ◆ **subtly** adv sútilmente, con sutileza.

subtlety ['sʌtəltɪ] n (of colour, difference) sutileza f; (of perfume, taste) delicadeza f; (of remark, analysis) ingeniosidad f, agudeza f; (of irony, joke) finura f.

subtotal [sʌb'təutəl] n subtotal m.

subtract [səb'trækt] vtr Math restar; **to s. 3 from 10,** restar 3 de 10.

subtraction [sʌb'trækʃən] n Math resta f.

suburb ['sʌbɜːb] n barrio m periférico or residencial; **the suburbs,** las afueras.

suburban ['səbɜːbən] adj suburbano,-a. ■ **s. train,** tren m de cercanías.

suburbia [sə'bɜːbɪə] n barrios mpl periféricos or satélites.

subversion [səb'vɜːʃən] n subversión f.

subversive [səb'vɜːsɪv] adj & n subversivo,-a (m,f).

subvert [səb'vɜːt] vtr (values) subvertir; (government) derribar, derrocar.

subway ['sʌbweɪ] n 1 GB (underpass) paso m subterráneo. 2 US (underground railway) metro m.

succeed [sək'siːd] I vi 1 (be successful) (person) tener éxito; (plan, attempt) salir bien; **to s. in doing sth,** conseguir or lograr hacer algo; **to s. in life,** triunfar en la vida. 2 (follow after) suceder; **to s. to,** (throne, fortune) suceder a, heredar. II vtr (monarch, son) suceder a.

succeeding [sək'siːdɪŋ] adj subsiguiente, sucesivo,-a.

sucess [sək'ses] n éxito m; **he had no s.,** no le salió bien; **it was a great s.,** fue todo un éxito; **to make a s. of sth,** triunfar en algo; **to meet with s.,** tener éxito.

successful [sək'sesfʊl] adj (gen) que tiene éxito, de éxito; (application, plan) logrado,-a, acertado,-a; (business, businessman) próspero,-a; (marriage) feliz; **s. candidate,** Pol candidato,-a elegido,-a; Sch alumno,-a aprobado,-a; **to be s. in doing sth,** conseguir or lograr hacer algo. ◆ **successfully** adv con éxito.

succession [sək'seʃən] n 1 (series) sucesión f, serie f; **for three years in s.,** durante tres años consecutivos; **in s.,** sucesivamente. 2 (to post, throne) sucesión f.

successive [sək'sesɪv] adj sucesivo,-a, consecutivo,-a; **for five s. months,** durante cinco meses seguidos.

successor [sək'sesər] n sucesor,-a m,f.

succinct [sək'sɪŋkt] adj sucinto,-a.

succulent ['sʌkjʊlənt] I adj (juicy, tasty) suculento,-a. II n Bot planta f carnosa.

succumb [sə'kʌm] vi sucumbir (to, a).

such [sʌtʃ] I adj 1 (of that sort) tal, semejante, parecido,-a; **artists s. as Monet and Renoir,** artistas como Monet y Renoir; **at s. and s. a time,** a tal hora; **in s. a case,** en tal caso; **in s. a way that,** de tal manera que; **I said no s. thing,** no dije nada por el estilo; **s. is life!,** ¡así es la vida!; **there's no s. thing,** no existe tal cosa; **he comes from Salford or some s. place,** es de Salford o de un sitio parecido or así. 2 (so much, so great) tanto,-a; **he's always in s. a hurry ...,** siempre anda con tanta prisa ...; **she was in s. pain,** sufría tanto; **s. a lot of books,** tantos libros; **with s. courage,** con tanto valor. II adv (so very) tan; **it's s. a long time,** hace tanto tiempo; **she's s. a clever woman,** es una mujer tan inteligente; **we had s. good weather,** hizo un tiempo tan bueno.

suchlike ['sʌtʃlaɪk] I adj tal, semejante; **football, rugby and s. sports,** fútbol, rugby y otros deportes por el estilo. II n (things) cosas fpl por el estilo; (people) gente f por el estilo.

suck [sʌk] I vtr (vacuum cleaner, pump) aspirar; (person) (liquid) sorber; (lollipop, blood, etc) chupar; (baby) (at breast) mamar; **to s. one's thumb,** chuparse el dedo. II vi (person) chupar, dar chupadas; (baby) mamar. III n (on lollipop, thumb, etc) chupada f. ◆ **suck down** vtr (whirlpool, mud) tragar. ◆ **suck in** vtr (whirlpool, mud) tragar; (vacuum cleaner, pump) aspirar. ◆ **suck up** I vtr (dust etc) aspirar. II vi fam **to s. up to sb,** hacerle la pelota a algn, dar coba a algn.

sucker ['sʌkər] n 1 Zool ventosa f; Bot chupón m. 2 fam (mug, pushover) primo,-a m,f, bobo,-a m,f; **he's a s. for blondes,** no puede resistir a las rubias.

suckle ['sʌkəl] **I** *vtr (mother)* amamantar, dar el pecho a. **II** *vi (child)* mamar.

suckling ['sʌklɪŋ] *adj (child)* lactante.

sucrose ['sjuːkrəʊz] *n* sacarosa *f*.

suction ['sʌkʃən] *n (stick together)* succión *f*; *(water, air, etc)* aspiración *f*. ■ **s. pump**, bomba *f* de aspiración.

Sudan [suːˈdɑːn, suːˈdæn] *n* the S., (el) Sudán.

Sudanese [suːdəˈniːz] **I** *adj* sudanés,-esa. **II** *n inv* **1** *(person)* sudanés,-esa *m, f*; the S., los sudaneses. **2** *(language)* sudanés *m*.

sudden ['sʌdən] *adj* **1** *(hurried)* súbito,-a, repentino,-a. **2** *(unexpected)* imprevisto,-a, inesperado,-a. **3** *(abrupt)* brusco,-a; **all of a s.**, de repente, de pronto, de golpe. ■ **s. bend**, viraje *m*. ◆ **suddenly** *adv* de repente, de pronto.

suddenness ['sʌdənnɪs] *n (rapidity)* lo súbito, lo repentino; *(unexpectedness)* lo imprevisto, lo inesperado; *(abruptness)* brusquedad *f*.

suds [sʌdz] *npl* espuma *f* de jabón, jabonaduras *fpl*.

sue [suː, sjuː] **I** *vtr Jur (person, organization)* demandar, presentar una demanda contra, llevar a juicio; **to s. sb for damages**, demandar a algn por daños y perjuicios. **II** *vi* presentar una demanda, entablar acción judicial; **to s. for divorce**, solicitar el divorcio.

suede [sweɪd] **I** *n* ante *m*, gamuza *f*, *(for gloves)* cabritilla *f*. **II** *adj* de ante *or* gamuza; *(gloves)* de cabritilla.

suet ['suːɪt] *n Culin* sebo *m*.

suffer ['sʌfəʳ] **I** *vtr* **1** *(pain, injury)* sufrir. **2** *(hardship, defeat, setback)* sufrir, padecer, experimentar. **3** *(bear, tolerate)* aguantar, soportar; **he doesn't s. fools gladly**, no aguanta a los imbéciles. **II** *vi* sufrir; **to s. from**, sufrir de, padecer de, adolecer de; **she was suffering from shock**, sufría los efectos de un shock; **they were suffering from the effects of the smoke**, se resentían del humo; **your health/work will s.**, perjudicara a tu salud/trabajo.

sufferance ['sʌfərəns] *n* tolerancia *f*; *(forbearance)* resistencia *f*; **on s.**, por tolerancia.

sufferer ['sʌfərəʳ] *n Med* enfermo,-a *m, f*; **arthritis sufferers**, los artríticos.

suffering ['sʌfərɪŋ] *n (affliction)* sufrimiento *m*; *(pain, torment)* dolor *m*.

suffice [səˈfaɪs] *vtr & vi fml* bastar, ser suficiente (para).

sufficient [səˈfɪʃənt] *adj* suficiente, bastante; **2 kilos will be s.**, con 2 kilos basta. ◆ **sufficiently** *adv* suficientemente, bastante; **the food isn't s. hot**, la comida no está lo suficientemente caliente.

suffix ['sʌfɪks] *n Ling* sufijo *m*.

suffocate ['sʌfəkeɪt] **1** *vtr* asfixiar, ahogar. **2** *vi* asfixiarse, ahogarse.

suffocating ['sʌfəkeɪtɪŋ] *adj (heat)* sofocante, agobiante; *(atmosphere)* bochornoso,-a.

suffocation [sʌfəˈkeɪʃən] *n* asfixia *f*, ahogo *m*.

suffrage ['sʌfrɪdʒ] *n* sufragio *m*.

suffragette [sʌfrəˈdʒet] *n Hist* sufragista *mf*.

suffuse [səˈfjuːz] *vtr Lit* bañar, cubrir; **suffused with light**, bañado,-a de luz.

sugar ['ʃʊgəʳ] **I** *n* **1** azúcar *m & f*. ■ **brown s.**, azúcar *f* morena; **caster s.**, azúcar *m* extrafino; *Bot* **s. beet**, remolacha *f* (azucarera); **s. bowl**, azucarero *m*; **s. candy**, azúcar *m* cande; **s. cane**, caña *f* de azúcar; *fam* **s. daddy**, amante *m* viejo y rico; **s. loaf**, pan *m* de azúcar; **s. lump**, terrón *m* de azúcar; **s. plantation**, plantación *f* de azúcar; **s. refinery**, refinería *f* de azúcar; **s, tongs**, tenacillas *fpl* para el azúcar. **2** *fam (darling)* querido,-a *m,f*, cariño *m*. **II** *interj* ¡ostras! **III** *vtr* azucarar, echar azúcar a; *fig* **to s. the pill**, dorar la píldora.

sugar-coated [ʃʊgəˈkəʊtɪd] *adj* azucarado,-a.

sugary ['ʃʊgərɪ] *adj* **1** *(like sugar)* azucarado,-a; *(sweet)* dulce. **2** *fig (insincere)* meloso,-a, almibarado,-a; *(oversentimental)* sentimentaloide.

suggest [səˈdʒest] *vtr* **1** *(propose)* sugerir, proponer; **I s. that we leave at once**, sugiero que nos vayamos en seguida. **2** *(advise, recommend)* aconsejar; **he suggested we looked** *or* **should look for alternative accommodation**, nos aconsejó que buscáramos otro alojamiento. **3** *(evoke)* evocar, sugerir; **what does the poem s. to you?**, ¿qué te sugiere el poema? **4** *(indicate, imply)* indicar; **this suggests that he came alone**, esto hace pensar que vino solo; **what are you trying to s.?**, ¿qué insinúas?

suggestible [səˈdʒestɪbəl] *adj* sugestionable.

suggestion [seˈdʒestʃən] *n* **1** *(proposal)* sugerencia *f*; *(insinuation)* insinuación *f*; **his s. was that ...**, él proponía que ...; **to make a s.**, hacer una sugerencia. **2** *(hint, trace)* sombra *f*, traza *f*; *(small amount)* pizca *f*.

suggestive [səˈdʒestɪv] *adj* **1** *(gen)* sugestivo,-a; **to be s. of sth**, evocar algo. **2** *(indecent, remark)* indecente, subido,-a de tono; *(gesture, look)* provocativo,-a, provocador,-a.

suicidal [sjuːɪˈsaɪdəl] *adj* suicida; **s. tendencies**, tendencias suicidas.

suicide ['sjuːɪsaɪd] *n* suicidio *m*; **to commit s.**, suicidarse; *fam* **it would be s. to do that**, sería una locura hacer eso.

suit [suːt, sjuːt] *n* **1** *(man's)* traje *m*; *(woman's)* traje *m* de chaqueta. ■ **bathing s.**, bañador *m*, traje *m* de baño; **s. of armour**, armadura *f*. **2** *Jur (lawsuit)* pleito *m*; **to bring** *or* **file a s. against sb**, entablar un pleito contra algn. **3** *Cards* palo *m*; **to follow s.**, arrastrar; *fig (copy)* seguir el ejemplo. **II** *vtr* **1** *(be convenient, acceptable)* convenir a, venir bien a; *fam* **that suits me fine**, me viene de perlas. **2** *(be right, appropriate)* ir bien a, sentar bien a; **red really suits you**, el rojo te favorece mucho; **they are well suited to each other**, están hechos el uno para el otro. **3** *(adapt)* adaptar a, ajustar a; **she suited her speech to her audience**, ajustó su discurso al público. **4** *(please)* agradar, satisfacer; **s. yourself!**, ¡como quieras!; **you can't s. everybody**, es imposible satisfacer a todos.

suitability [sjuːtəˈbɪlɪtɪ] *n (convenience)* conveniencia *f*; *(aptness)* idoneidad *f*.

suitable ['sjuːtəbəl] *adj (convenient)* conveniente; *(appropriate)* apropiado,-a, adecuado,-a; *(apt)* apto,-a; **the most s. woman for the job**, la mujer más indicada para el puesto; *TV* **this programme is not s. for children**, este programa no es apto para niños. ◆ **suitably** *adv (correctly)* correctamente, como es debido; *(properly)* apropiadamente, adecuadamente.

suitcase ['suːtkeɪs] *n* maleta *f*.

suite [swiːt] *n* **1** *(of furniture)* juego *m*, mobiliario *m*. ■ **dining-room s.**, (juego *m* de) comedor *m*; **three-piece s.**, tresillo *m*. **2** *(of hotel rooms)* suite *f*. **3** *Mus* suit *f*.

suitor ['sjuːtəʳ] *n* **1** *(wooer)* pretendiente *m*. **2** *Jur* demandante *mf*.

sulfate ['sʌlfeɪt] *n US see* **sulphate.**

sulfide ['sʌlfaɪd] *n US see* **sulphide.**

sulfur ['sʌlfəʳ] *n US see* **sulphur.**

sulfuric [sʌlˈfjʊərɪk] *adj US see* **sulphuric.**

sulk [sʌlk] **I** *vi* enfurruñarse, tener murria, estar de mal humor. **II** *n* mal humor *m*, murria *f*; **to have the sulks**, enfurruñarse, poner morros.

sulky ['sʌlkɪ] *adj (sulkier, sulkiest)* malhumorado,-a, resentido,-a.

sullen ['sʌlən] *adj (moody, surly)* hosco,-a, arisco,-a, huraño,-a; *(sky)* plomizo,-a.

sullenness ['sʌlənnɪs] *n* malhumor *m*, murria *f*.

sully ['sʌlɪ] *vtr (pt & pp sullied)* ensuciar; *fig* manchar, mancillar.

sulphate ['sʌlfeɪt] *n* sulfato *m*. ■ **copper s.**, sulfato *m* de cobre.

sulphide [sʌlfaɪd] *n* sulfuro *m*.

sulphur ['sʌlfəʳ] *n* azufre *m*.

sulphuric [sʌl'fjʊərɪk] *adj* sulfúrico,-a. ■ **s. acid,** ácido *m* sulfúrico.

sultan ['sʌltən] *n* sultán *m*.

sultana [sʌl'tɑːnə] *n* 1 *(wife of sultan)* sultana *f*. 2 *(raisin)* pasa *f* de Esmirna.

sultanate ['sʌltəneɪt] *n* sultanato *m*.

sultry ['sʌltrɪ] *adj (sultrier, sultriest)* 1 *(muggy)* bochornoso,-a, sofocante. 2 *(seductive)* sensual.

sum [sʌm] *n* 1 *(arithmetic problem)* suma *f*, adición *f*; **sums,** aritmética *f*, cálculo *m*; *fam* **to be good at sums,** estar fuerte en aritmética. 2 *(amount of money)* suma *f*, cantidad *f*; **lump s.,** suma *f* global, cantidad *f* global; *(total amount)* suma *f*, total *m*; *(of money, invoice)* importe *m*, monto *m*; **s. total,** suma *f* total, total *m*; *fig* **in s.,** en suma, en resumen. ♦ **sum up I** *vtr (pt & pp summed)* 1 *(summarize, encapsulate)* resumir, hacer un resumen de. 2 *(size up)* evaluar (en el acto). **II** *vi* resumir; **to s. up ...,** en resumidas cuentas *or* en resumen, ...

summarily ['sʌmerɪlɪ] *adv* sumariamente.

summarize ['sʌməraɪz] *vtr* resumir.

summary ['sʌmərɪ] **I** *n* resumen *m*. ■ *Rad TV* **news s.,** resumen *m* de las noticias. **II** *adj (trial, dismissal, etc)* sumario,-a.

summer ['sʌməʳ] **I** *n* verano *m*; **in s.,** en verano. ■ **Indian s.,** veranillo *m* de San Martín. **II** *adj (holiday, clothes)* de verano; *(weather, atmosphere)* veraniego,-a; *(resort)* de, veraneo. ■ **s. camp,** colonia *f* de vacaciones; **s. school,** escuela *f* de verano; **S. Time,** hora *f* de verano.

summerhouse ['sʌməhaʊs] *n* cenador *m*, glorieta *f*.

summertime ['sʌmətaɪm] *n* verano *m*.

summery ['sʌmərɪ] *adj* veraniego,-a.

summing-up [sʌmɪŋ'ʌp] *n* Jur resumen *m*.

summit ['sʌmɪt] *n* 1 *(of mountain)* cima *f*, cumbre *f*. 2 *Pol* cumbre *f*.

summon ['sʌmən] *vtr* 1 *(meeting)* convocar. 2 *(servant)* llamar; *(doctor, police)* llamar; *(aid, reinforcements)* pedir. 3 *Jur (person)* citar, emplazar. ♦ **summon up** *vtr (resources, help)* reunir, conseguir; **to s. up one's courage** *or* **strength,** armarse de valor.

summons ['sʌmənz] **I** *n* 1 *(call)* llamada *f*, llamamiento *m*. 2 *Jur* citación *f* judicial, emplazamiento *m*. **II** *vtr* Jur citar, emplazar.

sump [sʌmp] *n* 1 *Aut* cárter *m*. 2 *Min* sumidero *m*; *(cesspool)* letrina *f*.

sumptuous ['sʌmptjʊəs] *adj* suntuoso,-a.

sumptuousness ['sʌmptjʊəsnɪs] *n* suntuosidad *f*.

Sun *abbr of* **Sunday,** domingo *m*, dom°.

sun [sʌn] **I** *n* sol *m*; **in the s.,** al sol; **you've caught the s.,** te ha cogido el sol. ■ **s. blind,** *(awning)* toldo *m*; *(Venetian blind)* persiana *f*; **s. deck,** cubierta *f* superior; **s. lounge,** *US* **s. parlor,** solana *f*. **II** *vtr (pt & pp sunned)* **to s. oneself,** tomar el sol.

sun-baked ['sʌnbeɪkt] *adj (parched)* quemado,-a por el sol; *(brick)* secado,-a al sol.

sunbathe ['sʌnbeɪð] *vi* tomar el sol.

sunbathing ['sʌnbeɪðɪŋ] *n* baños *mpl* de sol.

sunbeam ['sʌnbiːm] *n* rayo *m* de sol.

sunbed ['sʌnbed] *n* tumbona *f*.

sunburn ['sʌnbɜːn] *n (burn)* quemadura *f* de sol; *(tan)* bronceado *m*.

sunburnt ['sʌnbɜːnt] *adj (burnt)* quemado,-a por el sol; *(tanned)* bronceado,-a.

sundae ['sʌndeɪ, 'sʌndɪ] *n Culin* helado *m* con fruta y nueces.

Sunday ['sʌndɪ] *n* domingo *m inv*; **Easter S.,** Domingo de Resurrección; **Palm S.,** Domingo de Ramos; **S. newspaper,** periódico del domingo; **S. school,** catequesis; *fig* **to be dressed in one's S. best,** llevar el traje de los domingos, ir endomingado,-a; *see also* **Saturday.**

sundial ['sʌndaɪəl] *n* reloj *m* de sol.

sundown ['sʌndaʊn] *n US* anochecer *m*; **at s.,** al anochecer.

sun-drenched ['sʌndrentʃt] *adj* bañado,-a por el sol.

sundry ['sʌndrɪ] **I** *adj (various)* diversos,-as, varios,-as; *fam* **all and s.,** todos sin excepción, todo quisque. **II sundries** *npl Com (miscellaneous goods)* artículos *mpl* diversos; *(expenses)* gastos *mpl* diversos.

sunflower ['sʌnflaʊəʳ] *n Bot* girasol *m*.

sung [sʌŋ] *pp see* **sing.**

sunglasses ['sʌnɡlɑːsɪz] *npl* gafas *fpl* de sol.

sunhat ['sʌnhæt] pamela *f*, sombrero *m* de ala ancha.

sunk [sʌŋk] *pp see* **sink.**

sunken ['sʌŋkən] *adj* hundido,-a.

sunlamp ['sʌnlæmp] *n* lámpara *f* solar, lámpara *f* de rayos ultravioletas.

sunlight ['sʌnlaɪt] *n (sunshine)* sol *m*, luz *f* del sol; **in the s.,** al sol.

sunlit ['sʌnlɪt] *adj* iluminado,-a por el sol.

sunny ['sʌnɪ] *adj (sunnier, sunniest)* 1 *(day)* de sol; *(place, room)* soleado,-a; **it is s.,** hace sol. 2 *fig (smile, disposition)* alegre; *(future)* risueño,-a.

sunray ['sʌnreɪ] *n* rayo *m* de sol.

sunrise ['sʌnraɪz] *n (sun-up)* salida *f* del sol; *(dawn)* alba *m*, amanecer *m*.

sunroof ['sʌnruːf] *n* 1 *Aut* techo *m* solar. 2 *(on building)* azotea *f*.

sunset ['sʌnset] *n (sundown)* puesta *f* del sol; *(twilight)* crepúsculo *m*, anochecer *m*.

sunshade ['sʌnʃeɪd] *n (parasol)* sombrilla *f*; *(awning)* toldo *m*.

sunshine ['sʌnʃaɪn] *n* sol *m*, luz *f* del sol; *Meteor* **hours of s.,** horas *fpl* de sol or de insolación.

sunspot ['sʌnspɒt] *n* 1 *Astron* mancha *f* solar. 2 *fam* lugar *m* de veraneo con mucho sol.

sunstroke ['sʌnstrəʊk] *n* insolación *f*.

suntan ['sʌntæn] *n* bronceado *m*. ■ **s. oil** or **lotion,** (aceite *m*) bronceador *m*.

sun-tanned ['sʌntænd] *adj* bronceado,a.

suntrap ['sʌntræp] *n* lugar *m* muy soleado.

sun-up ['sʌnʌp] *n US (sunrise)* salida *f* de sol; *(dawn)* alba *m*, amanecer *m*.

sup [sʌp] *vtr (pt & pp supped)* beber a sorbos; *fam* **s. up!,** bébetelo de una vez.

super ['suːpəʳ] **I** *adj fam* tremendo,-a, bárbaro,-a, fenomenal, de primera. **II** *n (petrol)* (gasolina *f*) súper *f*.

super- ['suːpəʳ] *pref* super-, sobre-.

superabundant [suːpərə'bʌndənt] *adj* superabundante.

superannuated [suːpər'ænjʊeɪtɪd] *adj fml* antiquado,-a.

superannuation [suːpərænjʊ'eɪʃən] *n GB* jubilación *f*, pensión *f*.

superb [sʊ'pɜːb] *adj* espléndido,-a, estupendo,-a, magnífico,-a.

supercharged ['suːpətʃɑːdʒd] *adj Aut* sobrealimentado,-a.

supercharger ['suːpətʃɑːdʒəʳ] *n Aut* sobrealimentador *m*, compresor *m* de sobrealimentación.

supercilious [suːpə'sɪlɪəs] *adj (condescending)* altanero,-a; *(disdainful)* desdeñoso,-a.

superciliousness [suːpə'sɪlɪəsnɪs] *n (condescending)* altanería *f*; *(disdain)* desdén *m*.

superficial [suːpə'fɪʃəl] *adj* superficial.

superficiality [suːpəfɪʃɪ'ælɪtɪ] *n* superficialidad *f*.

superfluous [suː'pɜːflʊəs] *adj* superfluo,-a, sobrante; **to be s.,** sobrar.

superhuman [suːpə'hjuːmən] *adj* sobrehumano,-a.

superimpose [su:pərɪm'pəʊz] *vtr* sobreponer, superponer (**on**, en).

superintendent [su:pərɪn'tendənt] *n* director,-a *m, f*; **police s.**, subjefe,-a *m, f* de policía.

superior [su:'pɪərɪəʳ] **I** *adj* **1** *(gen)* superior (**to**, a). **2** *(haughty)* presumido,-a, altanero,-a. **II** *n* *(senior)* superior,-a *m, f*; *Rel* **Mother S.**, madre *f* superiora.

superiority [su:pɪərɪ'ɒrɪtɪ] *n* superioridad *f*; **s. complex**, complejo *m* de superioridad.

superlative [su:'pɜ:lətɪv] **I** *adj* *(superb, excellent, outstanding)* superlativo,-a, supremo,-a, sumo,-a. **II** *n* *Ling* superlativo *m*; *fig* **to speak in superlatives**, deshacerse en elogios.

superman ['su:pəmæn] *n* (*pl* **supermen** ['su:pəmen]) superhombre *m*.

supermarket ['su:pəmɑ:kɪt] *n* supermercado *m*.

supernatural [su:pə'nætʃərəl] **I** *adj* sobrenatural. **II the s.** *n*, lo sobrenatural.

superpower ['su:pəpaʊəʳ] *n* *Pol* superpotencia *f*.

supersede [su:pə'si:d] *vtr fml* suplantar.

supersonic [su:pə'sɒnɪk] *adj* supersónico,-a.

superstar ['su:pəstɑ:ʳ] *n* superestrella *f*.

superstition [su:pə'stɪʃən] *n* superstición *f*.

superstitious [su:pə'stɪʃəs] *adj* supersticioso,-a.

superstructure ['su:pəstrʌktʃəʳ] *n* superestructura *f*.

supertanker ['su:pətæŋkəʳ] *n* superpetrolero *m*.

supertax ['su:pətæks] *n* impuesto *m* adicional.

supervise ['su:pəvaɪz] *vtr* **1** *(watch over)* vigilar. **2** *(superintend)* inspeccionar. **3** *(run)* supervisar.

supervision [su:pə'vɪʒən] *n* supervisión *f*; **under s.**, bajo la supervisión.

supervisor ['su:pəvaɪzəʳ] *n* supervisor,-a *m, f*.

supervisory [su:pə'vaɪzərɪ] *adj* de supervisión.

superwoman ['su:pəwʊmən] *n* (*pl* **superwomen** ['su:pəwɪmɪn]) supermujer *f*.

supine ['su:paɪn] *adj* supino,-a.

supper ['sʌpəʳ] *n* cena *f*; **to have s.**, cenar; **we had fish for s.**, cenamos pescado.

supper-time ['sʌpətaɪm] *n* hora *f* de cenar.

supplant [sə'plɑ:nt] *vtr* suplantar, reemplazar.

supple ['sʌpəl] *adj* flexible.

suppleness ['sʌpəlnɪs] *n* flexibilidad *f*.

supplement ['sʌplɪmənt] **I** *n* *(gen)* suplemeno *m*. **II** *vtr* ['sʌplɪmənt] complementar.

supplementary [sʌplɪ'mentərɪ] *adj* suplementario,-a, adicional.

supplicant ['sʌplɪkənt] *n fml* suplicante *mf*.

supplication [sʌplɪ'keɪʃən] *n* súplica *f*.

supplier [sə'plaɪəʳ] *n* *(gen)* suministrador,-a *m, f*; *Com* proveedor,-a *m, f*, abastecedor,-a *m, f*.

supply [sə'plaɪ] **I** *n* **1** *(provision)* suministro *m*; *Com* provisión *f*, abastecimiento *m*; *(stock)* surtido *m*, existencias *fpl*; **salt is in short s.**, hay escasez de sal; **s. and demand**, oferta *f* y demanda. ■ **s. ship**, buque *m* de abastecimiento; **s. teacher**, profesor,-a *m, f* suplente. **2 supplies**, *(food)* provisiones *fpl*, víveres *mpl*; *Mil* pertrechos *mpl*; **office s.**, material *m sing* para oficina. **II** *vtr* (*pt & pp* **supplied**) **1** *(provide)* suministrar, proveer, abastecer; *(electricity, water, arms)* suministrar. **2** *Mil* *(with provisions)* aprovisionar. **3** *(information, proof)* facilitar, provisionar. **4** *Com* surtir.

support [sə'pɔ:t] **I** *n* **1** *Constr Tech* soporte *m*, apoyo *m*. **2** *fig (moral)* apoyo *m*, respaldo *m*; *(allegiance, backing)* **to give** *or* **lend one's s. to sth**, apoyar *or* respaldar a algo. **3** *(sustenance)* sustento *m*; **fishing is their sole means of s.**, se sustentan únicamente con la pesca; *Jur* **without visible means of s.**, sin oficio ni beneficio. **4** *(financial assistance, funding)* ayuda *f* económica. **5** *Sport* afición *f*.

II *vtr* **1** *Constr Tech (weight, roof, etc)* sostener. **2** *(physical)* sostener; **her legs can't s. the weight**, no le sostienen las piernas. **3** *fig (back)* apoyar, respaldar; *(proposal, plan)* apoyar, estar de acuerdo con; *(corroborate, substantiate) (theory, evidence)* confirmar, respaldar. **4** *Sport (team)* seguir. **5** *(sustain, keep)* mantener; *(feed)* alimentar; **to s. oneself**, ganarse la vida.

supporter [sə'pɔ:təʳ] *n* *Pol* partidario,-a *m, f*; *Sport* seguidor,-a *m, f*; *(fan)* hincha *mf*, forofo,-a *m, f*; **supporters**, la afición; **supporters' club**, peña *f* deportiva.

supporting [sə'pɔ:tɪŋ] *adj* *Cin Theat* secundario,-a.

supportive [sə'pɔ:tɪv] *adj* *(helpful)* que ayuda; *(understanding)* comprensivo,-a.

suppose [sə'pəʊz] *vtr* **1** *(gen)* suponer; **let us s. that ...**, supongamos que ...; **s. she's right**, ¿y si tiene razón? **2** *(presume, guess)* suponer, creer; **I don't s. she'll phone now**, no creo que llame ahora; **I don't s. you know where she is?**, ¿no sabrías por casualidad dónde se encuentra?; **I s. he's very tired**, supongo que estará muy cansado; **I s. not/so**, supongo que no/sí; **it's supposed to be the best restaurant in town**, dicen que es el mejor restaurante de la ciudad; **she is supposed to be an expert on the subject**, se supone que es una experta en el tema; **what do you s. it means?**, ¿qué significado tendrá?; **you're not supposed to smoke in here**, no está permitido fumar aquí dentro; **you're supposed to be in bed**, deberías estar acostado,-a *or* en la cama ya. **3** *(when making a suggestion or proposal)* **s. we change the subject?**, ¿qué tal si cambiamos de tema?; **s. we leave now?**, ¿y si nos fuéramos ya?.

supposed [sə'pəʊzd] *adj* supuesto,-a. ◆ **supposedly** *adv* según cabe suponer, aparentemente.

supposition [sʌpə'zɪʃən] *n* suposición *f*.

suppository [sə'pɒzɪtərɪ] *n* *Med* supositorio *m*.

suppress [sə'pres] *vtr* *(gen)* suprimir; *(feelings, laugh, etc)* contener, reprimir; *(news, truth)* callar, ocultar; *(revolt)* sofocar, reprimir.

suppression [sə'preʃən] *n* *(gen)* supresión *f*; *(of feelings, revolt)* represión *f*; *(of facts, truth)* ocultación *f*.

suppressor [sə'presəʳ] *n* *Elec* supresor *m*; *Rad* antiparásito *m*.

suppurate ['sʌpjʊreɪt] *vi* *Med* supurar.

suppuration [sʌpjʊ'reɪʃən] *n* *Med* supuración *f*.

supra- [su:prə] *pref* supra; **suprarenal**, suprarrenal.

supranational [su:prə'næʃənəl] *adj* supranacional.

supremacy [su'preməsɪ] *n* supremacía *f*.

supreme [su'pri:m] *adj* *(gen)* supremo,-a; **with s. indifference**, con suma indiferencia. ■ *Mil* **s. commander**, jefe *m* supremo; *Jur* **s. court**, tribunal *m* supremo. ◆ **supremely** *adv* sumamente, totalmente.

supremo [su'pri:məʊ] *n* (*pl* **supremos**) *GB fam* gran jefe *m*.

Supt *abbr* of **Superintendent**, Subjefe,-a *m, f* de Policía.

surcharge [sə:'tʃɑ:dʒ] *n* recargo *m*.

sure [ʃʊəʳ] **I** *adj* **1** *(positive, certain)* seguro,-a, cierto,-a; **be s. not to ...**, ten cuidado de no ...; **be s. to ...**, no te olvides de ...; **I'm not s. why ...**, no sé muy bien por qué ...; **I'am s. (that) ...**, estoy seguro,-a de que ...; **it's almost s. to be fine**, seguramente hará buen tiempo; **make s. that it's ready**, asegúrate de que esté listo; **to be s. of sth**, asegurarse de algo. **2** *(safe, reliable)* seguro,-a; **it's the surest way of winning**, es la manera más segura de ganar. **3** *(confident)* seguro,-a; **to be s. of oneself**, estar seguro,-a de sí mismo,-a. **4** *US fam (of course)* **s. thing!**, ¡claro!, ¡por supuesto! **II** *adv* **1** *(of course)* claro; **will you come with me?** —s.!, ¿me acompañarás?—¡claro que sí! **2** *US (really)* **he s. is handsome!**, ¡qué guapo es!; **it s. was cold**, ¡vaya frío que hacía! **3** *(for certain, certainly)* seguro; **as s. as fate**, tan cierto como dos y dos son cuatro; **as s. as I'm standing here**, palabra de honor; **tomorrow for s.**, mañana sin falta. **4** *(in agreement)* claro; **s. enough**, efectivamente. ◆ **surely** *adv* **1** *(without a doubt)* seguramente, sin duda; **s.**

not!, ¡no puede ser!; **s. you don't mean it!,** ¡no lo dices en serio! **2** *(in a sure manner)* con seguridad; **slowly but s.,** lentamente pero con seguridad.

sure-fire [ˈʃʊəfaɪəʳ] *adj US fam* seguro,-a, de éxito seguro.

sure-footed [ʃʊəˈfʊtɪd] *adj* de pie firme.

surety [ˈʃʊərɪtɪ] *n Jur* **1** *(sum)* fianza *f*, garantía *f*. **2** *(guarantor)* fiador,-a *m,f*, garante *mf*; **to stand s. for sb,** ser fiador de algn.

surf [sɜːf] **I** *n (waves)* oleaje *m*; *(foam)* espuma *f*. **II** *vi Sport* hacer surf.

surface [ˈsɜːfɪs] **I** *n (gen)* superficie *f*; *(of road)* firme *m*; *fig* **on the s. it seems a good idea,** a primera vista parece una buena idea. **II** *adj* superficial; **s. area,** área *f* de la superficie; **s. route/transport,** ruta *f*/transporte *m* de superficie; **by s. mail,** por vía terrestre *or* marítima. **III** *vtr (road)* revestir. **IV** *vi (submarine etc)* salir a la superficie, emerger; *fig (person)* asomarse, dejarse ver.

surface-to-air [sɜːfɪstʊˈeəʳ] *adj* **s.-to-a. missile,** misil *m* tierra-aire.

surfboard [ˈsɜːfbɔːd] *n Sport* plancha *f or* tabla *f* de surf.

surfeit [ˈsɜːfɪt] *n fml* exceso *m*.

surfer [ˈsɜːfəʳ] *n Sport* surfista *mf*.

surfing [ˈsɜːfɪŋ] *n Sport* hacer surf *m*.

surge [sɜːdʒ] **I** *n* **1** *(growth)* alza *f*, aumento *m*. **2** *(of sea)* oleada *f*, oleaje *m* marejada *f*; *fig (of sympathy)* oleada *f*; *fig (of anger, energy)* arranque *m*; **a s. of people,** una oleada de gente. **II** *vi (sea)* levantarse, encresparse; *(people)* avanzar a manadas.

surgeon [ˈsɜːdʒən] *n* cirujano,-a *m, f*. ■ **dental s.,** odontólogo,-a *m, f*, dentista *mf*; **veterinary s.,** veterinario,-a *m,f*.

surgery [ˈsɜːdʒərɪ] *n* **1** *(operation)* cirujía *f*. ■ **plastic s.,** cirugía *f* estética. **2** *GB (consulting room)* consultorio *m*. ■ **s. hours,** horas *fpl* de consulta. **3** *US (operating theatre)* quirófano *m*, sala *f* de operaciones.

surgical [ˈsɜːdʒɪkəl] *adj* quirúrgico,-a. ■ **s. spirit,** alcohol *m* de 90°; **s. stockings,** medias *fpl* elasticas.

surly [ˈsɜːlɪ] *adj (surlier, surliest) (bad-tempered)* hosco,-a, malhumorado,-a, arisco,-a; *(rude)* maleducado,-a.

surmise [sɜːˈmaɪz] **I** *n* conjetura *f*, suposición *f*. **II** *vtr* conjeturar, suponer.

surmount [sɜːˈmaʊnt] *vtr* superar, vencer.

surmountable [sɜːˈmaʊntəbəl] *adj* superable.

surname [ˈsɜːneɪm] *n* apellido *m*.

surpass [sɜːˈpɑːs] *vtr* superar, sobrepasar.

surplice [ˈsɜːplɪs] *n Rel* sobrepelliz *f*.

surplus [ˈsɜːpləs] **I** *n (of goods)* excedente *m*, sobrante *m*; *(of budget)* superávit *m*. **II** *adj* excedente, sobrante; **sale of s. stock,** liquidación de saldos.

surprise [səˈpraɪz] **I** *n* sorpresa *f*; **what a s.!,** ¡vaya sorpresa!; **much to my s.,** con gran sorpresa por mi parte; **to take sb by s.,** coger desprevenido,-a a algn. **II** *adj (visit, result)* inesperado,-a; **s. attack,** ataque sorpresa; **s. party,** fiesta sorpresa. **III** *vtr* **1** *(astonish)* sorprender, extrañar; **I should not be surprised if it rained,** no me extrañaría que lloviese. **2** *(catch unawares)* sorprender; *Mil (enemy)* coger por sorpresa.

surprising [səˈpraɪzɪŋ] *adj* sorprendente. ♦ **surprisingly** *adv* sorprendentemente, de modo sorprendente; **s. enough, she stayed,** para sorpresa de todos, se quedó.

surreal [səˈrɪəl] *adj* surrealista.

surrealism [səˈrɪəlɪzəm] *n Art* surrealismo *m*.

surrealist [səˈrɪəlɪst] *adj & n Art* surrealista *(mf)*.

surrealistic [sərɪəˈlɪstɪk] *adj* surrealista.

surrender [səˈrendəʳ] **I** *n Mil (capitulate)* rendición *f*; *(of weapons)* entrega *f*, *Ins* rescate *m*; **s. value,** valor de rescate. **II** *vtr Mil (weapons, town)* rendir, entregar **(to,** a); *(right, privilege)* ceder, renunciar a. **III** *vi (give in)* rendirse, entregarse.

surreptitious [sʌrəpˈtɪʃəs] *adj* subrepticio,-a, furtivo,-a.

surrogate [ˈsʌrəgɪt] *n fml* sustituto,-a *m,f*. ■ **s. mother,** madre *f* alquilada *or* de alquiler.

surround [səˈraʊnd] **I** *n* marco *m*, borde *m*. **II** *vtr* rodear; **surrounded by trees,** rodeado,-a de árboles.

surrounding [səˈraʊndɪŋ] **I** *adj* circundante; **in the s. countryside,** en el campo alrededor. **II** **surroundings,** *npl (of place)* alrededores *mpl*, cercanías *fpl*; *(environment)* entorno *m sing*.

surtax [ˈsɜːtæks] *n* recargo *m*.

surveillance [sɜːˈveɪləns] *n* vigilancia *f*; **under s.,** bajo vigilancia.

survey [ˈsɜːveɪ] **I** *n* **1** *(of building, land)* inspección *f*, reconocimiento *m*; *(in topography)* medición *f*. **2** *(of prices, trends, etc)* estudio *m*, encuesta *f*; *(report)* informe *m*; **to carry out a s.,** hacer una encuesta; **a s. of public opinion,** un sondeo de la opinión pública. **3** *(overall view)* vista *f* de conjunto, panorama *m*. **II** [sɜːˈveɪ] *vtr* **1** *(building)* inspeccionar; *(land)* hacer un reconocimiento de; *(in topography)* medir. **2** *(prices, trends, etc)* estudiar, hacer una encuesta sobre. **3** *(look at)* contemplar; *(give overall view of)* repasar.

surveying [sɜːˈveɪɪŋ] *n* agrimensura *f*, topografía *f*.

surveyor [sɜːˈveɪəʳ] *n* agrimensor,-a *m, f*, topógrafo,-a *m,f*. ■ **quantity s.,** aparejador,-a *m,f*.

survival [səˈvaɪvəl] *n* **1** supervivencia *f*. ■ **s. kit,** equipo *m* para emergencias. **2** *(relic)* reliquia *f*, vestigio *m*.

survive [səˈvaɪv] **I** *vi (gen)* sobrevivir; *(remain)* perdurar, quedar; **my pay is barely enough to s. on,** mi salario apenas me llega para ir tirando; **only two paintings survived,** sólo quedaron dos cuadros. **II** *vtr* sobrevivir a.

survivor [səˈvaɪvəʳ] *n* superviviente *mf*, sobreviviente *mf*.

susceptibility [səseptəˈbɪlɪtɪ] *n* **1** *(to attack)* susceptibilidad *f*; *(to illness)* propensión *f*; *(to beauty, flattery)* sensibilidad *f*. **2** **susceptibilities,** *(sensibilities)* sentimientos *mpl*, susceptibilidad *f sing*.

susceptible [səˈseptəbəl] *adj (to attack)* susceptible **(to,** a); *(to illness)* propenso,-a a; *(to beauty, flattery)* sensible a; *(impressionable)* **s. to suggestion,** sugestionable.

suspect [ˈsʌspekt] **I** *adj (dubious)* sospechoso,-a. **II** *n* sospechoso,-a *m, f*. **III** [səˈspekt] *vtr* **1** *(person)* sospechar **(of,** de); *(plot, motives)* recelar de; **he is suspected of being a terrorist,** es sospechoso de terrorismo. **2** *(think likely)* imaginar, creer; **a suspected case of typhoid,** un caso no confirmado de la fiebre tifoidea; **I suspected as much,** me lo imaginaba.

suspend [səˈspend] *vtr* suspender; *(pupil)* expulsar.

suspended [səˈspendɪd] *adj* **1** *(gen)* suspendido,-a. ■ **s. animation,** muerte *f* aparente; *Jur* **s. sentence,** condena *f* condicional. **2** *Sport (player)* sancionado,-a. **3** *(pupil)* expulsado,-a.

suspender [səˈspendəʳ] *n* **1** *(for stocking)* liga *f*. ■ **s. belt,** liguero *m*. **2** **suspenders,** *US* tirantes *mpl*.

suspense [səˈspens] *n (anticipation)* incertidumbre *f*; *Cin Theat* suspense *m*, intriga *f*; **to keep sb in s.,** mantener a algn en la incertidumbre; *fam* **the s. is killing me,** la duda *or* la incertidumbre no me deja vivir.

suspension [səˈspenʃən] *n* **1** *(postponement)* suspensión *f*. **2** *Sport (player)* sanción *f*. **3** *(pupil, employee)* expulsión *f*. **4** *(car)* suspensión *f*. **5** *Tech* **s. bridge,** puente *m* colgante.

suspicion [səˈspɪʃən] *n* **1** *(gen)* sospecha *f*; *(mistrust)* recelo *m*, desconfianza *f*; *(doubt)* duda *f*; **I have my suspicions about his loyalty,** dudo de su lealtad; **to arouse s.,** despertar sospechas; **to arrest sb on s.,** detener a algn como sospechoso; **to be above s.,** estar por encima de toda sospecha; **to be under s.,** estar bajo sospecha. **2** *(slight trace)* pizca *f*, poco *m*; **a s. of garlic,** una pizca de ajo.

suspicious [səˈspɪʃəs] *adj* **1** *(arousing suspicion)* sospechoso,-a; *fam* **he's a s. looking customer,** es un tipo sospechoso; **it looks s. to me,** me da mala espina. **2**

(distrustful, wary) receloso,-a, desconfiado,-a; **to be s. of sb,** desconfiar de algn. ◆ **suspiciously** *adv* 1 *(behave)* de modo sospechoso; **it sounds s. like a case of murder,** tiene todo el aspecto de ser un caso de asesinato. 2 *(glance etc)* con recelo.

suss [sʌs] *vtr fam* **to s. out,** calar; **I can't s. out how it works,** no llego a averiguar cómo funciona; **I sussed him out straight away,** le calé en seguida.

sustain [səˈsteɪn] *vtr* 1 *(weight)* sostener. 2 *(nourish)* sustentar. 3 *(pretence, conversation, etc)* sostener, mantener. 4 *Mus (note)* sostener. 5 *Jur* admitir; **objection sustained,** se admite la protesta. 6 *(injury, loss, etc)* sufrir; *(wound)* recibir.

sustained [səˈsteɪnd] *adj (effort)* sostenido,-a; *(applause)* prolongado,-a; *Mus (note)* sostenido,-a.

sustenance [ˈsʌstənəns] *n* sustento *m*. ■ **means of s.,** medios *mpl* de subsistencia.

suture [ˈsuːtʃəʳ] *n Med* sutura *f.*

svelte [svelt] *adj* esbelto,-a.

SW 1 *abbr of* **short wave,** onda *f* corta, OC *f.* 2 *abbr of* **South-West,** Sudoeste, SO.

swab [swɒb] I *n Med (cotton wool)* algodón *m*, tapón *m*; *(for specimen)* frotis *m*. II *vtr (pt & pp swabbed)* 1 *Med (wound)* limpiar. 2 *Naut (deck)* limpiar, fregar.

swag [swæg] *n fam* botín *m.*

swagger [ˈswægəʳ] I *n* contoneo *m*, pavoneo *m*. II *vi* contonearse, pavonearse.

swaggering [ˈswægərɪŋ] *adj* fachendoso,-a, farolero,-a.

swallow¹ [ˈswɒləʊ] I *n (of drink, food)* trago *m*. II *vtr* 1 *(gulp drink, food)* tragar. 2 *fig (believe)* tragarse; **to s. the bait,** tragar el anzuelo; *(choke back)* **to s. one's pride,** tragarse el orgullo; **to one's words,** desdecirse de sus palabras. III *vi* tragar; *fig* **to s. hard,** tragar saliva. ◆ **swallow up** *vtr fig* 1 *(of sea, darkness, crowd)* tragar, engullir. 2 *(eat up)* consumir, absorber.

swallow² [ˈswɒləʊ] *n Orn* golondrina *f.* ■ *Swimming* **s. dive,** salto *m* del ángel.

swam [swæm] *pt see* **swim.**

swamp [swɒmp] I *n* pantano *m*, ciénaga *f*. ■ *Med* **s. fever,** paludismo *m*. II *vtr* 1 *(land)* inundar, anegar; *(boat)* hundir. 2 *fig* inundar **(with, by,** de); **we were swamped by letters,** recibimos una avalancha de cartas. 3 *fig* agobiar, abrumar **(with, by,** de).

swampy [ˈswɒmpɪ] *adj (swampier, swampiest)* pantanoso,-a.

swan [swɒn] I *n Orn* cisne *m*. ■ **Bewick's s.,** cisne *m* chico *or* de Bewick; **mute s.,** cisne *m* vulgar; **whooper s.,** cisne *m* cantor. II *vi fam* **to s. around,** pavonearse; **to s. around doing nothing,** hacer el vago; **we s. off to Grimsby every weekend,** nos escapamos a Grimsby todos los fines de semana.

swank [swæŋk] *fam* I *n* 1 *(arrogance, ostentation)* fanfarronada *f*, farol *m*. 2 *(person)* fanfarrón-ona *m*, *f*, fardón,-ona *m*, *f*. II *adj (swish)* de lujo. III *vi (show off)* fanfarronear; *(posturing)* farolear, fardar, darse tono.

swanky [ˈswæŋkɪ] *adj (swankier, swankiest) fam (person)* fanfarrón,-ona, fardón,-ona; *(restaurant, car, etc)* de lujo.

swan-song [ˈswɒnsɒŋ] *n fig* canto *m* del cisne.

swap [swɒp] I *n fam (exchange)* canje *m*, trueque *m*, cambalache *m*; **to do a s.,** hacer un intercambio. II *vtr (pt & pp swapped) (exchange, substitute)* canjear, cambiar. 2 *(exchange)* cambiar; **to s. places with sb,** cambiarse de sitio con algn. III *vi* hacer un intercambio. ◆ **swap round, swap over** *vtr (switch)* cambiar; **I swapped them round when he wasn't looking,** los cambié de sitio cuando no miraba.

swarm [swɔːm] I *n (of bees)* enjambre *m*; *(of people)* enjambre *m*, multitud *f*. II *vi (bees)* enjambrar; **Neath was swarming with tourists,** Neath estaba lleno de turistas.

swarthy [ˈswɔːðɪ] *adj (swarthier, swarthiest)* moreno,-a, atezado,-a.

swashbuckling [ˈswɒʃbʌklɪŋ] *adj* bravucón,-ona.

swastika [ˈswɒstɪkə] *n* esvástica *f*, cruz *f* gamada.

swat [swɒt] I *vtr (pt & pp swatted) (flies)* aplastar. II *n* **to take a s. at sth,** aplastar algo.

swatter [ˈswɒtəʳ] *n* matamoscas *m inv.*

swath(e)¹ [sweɪð] *n Agr* ringlera *f.*

swathe² [sweɪð] *vtr (bind up)* envolver, vendar.

sway [sweɪ] I *n* 1 *(movement)* balanceo *m*, vaivén *m*, movimiento *m*. 2 *(power, influence)* dominio *m*, influencia *f* **(over,** sobre); **to bold s. over sb,** dominar a algn. II *vi* 1 *(swing)* balancearse, mecerse. 2 *(totter)* tambalearse. III *vtr fig (influence, persuade)* convencer.

swear [sweəʳ] I *vtr (pt swore; pp sworn) (vow)* jurar; **I s. (that) I did not do it,** juro que no lo hice; **to s. an oath,** prestar juramento, jurar; **to s. sb to secrecy,** hacer que algn jure guardar un secreto; **to s. to do sth,** jurar hacer algo; *fig* **I could have sworn I heard footsteps,** juraría que oí pasos. II *vi* 1 *(formally, solemnly)* jurar, prestar juramento; **to s. on the Bible,** jurar sobre la Biblia; **I couldn't s. to it,** no lo juraría. 2 *(curse)* soltar tacos, decir palabrotas; *(blaspheme)* jurar, blasfemar; **to s. at sb,** echar pestes contra algn; **to s. like a trooper,** jurar como un carretero. ◆ **swear by** *vtr fam (rely on)* tener una fe absoluta en. ◆ **swear in** *vtr Jur (witness)* tomar juramento a; **to be sworn in,** *(witness)* prestar juramento; *(official)* jurar el cargo.

swear-word [ˈsweəwɜːd] *n* palabrota *f*, taco *m.*

sweat [swet] I *n (perspiration)* sudor *m*; *fam (hard work)* trabajo *m* pesado; **to be dripping with s.,** estar empapado,-a en sudor; *fig* **by the s. of one's brow,** con el sudor de su frente; *fam* **no s.!,** ¡no hay problema!; *fam* **to be in a cold s.,** tener canguelo; *fam* **to get into a s. about sth,** apurarse por algo; *fam fig* **this job's a real s.,** este trabajo es una auténtica paliza. ■ **s. gland,** glándula *f* sudorípara. II *vi (perspire)* sudar; *fig (work hard)* sudar la gota gorda. III *vtr fig* sudar; **to s. blood,** sudar sangre *or* tinta, sudar la gota gorda; *fam* **to s. it out,** aguantar.

sweatband [ˈswetbænd] *n Sport* 1 *(around forehead)* venda *f*, banda *f*. 2 *(around wrist)* muñequera *f.*

sweated [ˈswetɪd] *adj* **s. labour,** trabajo *m* mal pagado.

sweater [ˈswetəʳ] *n* suéter *m*, jersey *m.*

sweatshirt [ˈswetʃɜːt] *n* camiseta *f.*

sweatshop [ˈswetʃɒp] *n* fábrica *f or* taller *m* donde se explota al obrero.

sweaty [ˈswetɪ] *adj (sweatier, sweatiest)* sudoroso,-a, sudado,-a; **s. smell,** olor *m* a sudor.

Swede [swiːd] *n (person)* sueco,-a *m*, *f.*

swede [swiːd] *n Bot* nabo *m* sueco.

Sweden [ˈswiːdən] *n* Suecia *f.*

Swedish [ˈswiːdɪʃ] I *adj* sueco,-a. II *n* 1 *(language)* sueco *m*. 2 *pl* **the S.,** los suecos.

sweep [swiːp] I *n* 1 *(with broom)* barrido *m*; **it needs a s.,** hay que barrerlo; *fig* **to make a clean s. of things,** barrer con todo, hacer tabla rasa; *fig* **to s. the board,** llevarse todos los premios. 2 *(movement of arm)* movimiento *m or* gesto *m* amplio. 3 *(range)* abanico *m*. 4 *(of river, road)* curva *f*. 5 *(stretch, extent)* extensión *f*. 5 *(person)* **(chimney) s.,** deshollinador,-a *m*, *f*. 6 *(police)* redada *f*. II *vtr (pt & pp swept)* 1 *(floor etc)* barrer; *(chimney)* deshollinar; *fig* **to s. sth under the carpet,** ocultar algo. 2 *(searchlight, telescope)* recorrer; *(minefield)* rastrear; *(wind, waves)* barrer, azotar. 3 *(spread throughout)* extenderse, recorrer; **there's a craze which is sweeping the country,** es una moda que hace furor en todo el país. 4 *(remove at a stroke)* arrastrar, llevarse; **he was swept overboard,** fue arrastrado al mar; *fig* **she swept him off his feet,** le hizo perder la cabeza. III *vi* 1 *(with broom)* barrer. 2 *(move quickly)* desplazarse rápidamente; **to s. in/ out/past,** entrar/salir/pasar rápidamente. 3 *(road, river,* *etc)* extenderse. ◆ **sweep aside** *vtr* apartar bruscamente; *fig (suggestion)* descartar; *(objections)* rechazar. ◆ **sweep away** *vtr* 1 *(dust, rubbish)* barrer. 2 *(storm)* arrastrar, llevarse. ◆ **sweep up I** *vi* barrer, limpiar. **II** *vtr (room)* barrer; *(dust, rubbish)* recoger.

sweeper ['swiːpəʳ] *n* 1 *(person)* barrendero,-a *m, f; (machine)* barredora *f.* 2 *Ftb* defensa *m* escoba, líbero *m.*

sweeping ['swiːpɪŋ] *adj* 1 *(broad, huge)* amplio,-a; **a s. statement,** una declaración demasiado general. 2 *(victory)* aplastante, arrollador,-a. 3 *(far-reaching) (reforms, changes, etc)* radical.

sweepstake ['swiːpsteɪk] *n* lotería *f.*

sweet [swiːt] **I** *adj* 1 *(taste)* dulce; *(containing sugar)* azucurado,-a; *(wine, cider)* dulce; **as a. as honey,** dulce como la miel; **to have a s. tooth,** ser goloso,-a. ■ *Bot* **s. basil,** albahaca *f; Bot* **s. chestnut,** castaño *m* dulce; *Bot* **s. corn,** maíz *m* tierno; *Bot* **s. pea,** guisante *m* de olor; *Bot* **s. pepper,** pimiento *m* morrón; *Bot* **s. potato,** batata *f,* boniato *m;* **s. shop,** confitería *f,* bombonería *f; Bot* **s. william,** minutisa *f.* 2 *(pleasant)* agradable; *(smell)* fragante; *(sound)* melodioso,-a, suave; **s. nothings,** susurros *mpl* amorosos; **'home s. home',** 'hogar, dulce hogar'. 3 *(person, animal)* encantador,-a, simpático,-a; **what a s. little girl!,** ¡qué monada!; **to go one's own s. way,** actuar a su antojo. **II** *n* 1 *(candy)* caramelo *m,* golosina *f; (chocolate)* bombón *m.* 2 *(dessert)* postre *m.* 3 *fam (darling etc)* cariño *m,* cielo *m,* amor *m.* ◆ **sweetly** *adv* dulcemente, con dulzura.

sweet-and-sour ['swiːtənsaʊəʳ] *adj Culin* agridulce.

sweetbreads ['swiːtbredz] *npl* mollejas *fpl,* lechecillas *fpl.*

sweeten ['swiːtən] *vtr* 1 *(tea, coffee)* azucarar. 2 *fig (temper)* aplacar, calmar; **to s. the pill,** dorar la píldora. ◆ **sweeten up** *vtr (person)* ablandar.

sweetener ['swiːtənəʳ] *n* dulcificante *m,* edulcorante *m.*

sweetheart ['swiːthɑːt] *n* 1 *(boyfriend)* novio *m; (girlfriend)* novia *f.* 2 *(dear, love)* cariño *m,* amor *m.*

sweetie ['swiːtɪ] *n* 1 *(baby-talk)* caramelo *m,* golosina *f.* 2 *fam (darling)* cariño,-a *m, f;* **isn't she a s.!,** ¡es un ángel!

sweetness ['swiːtnɪs] *n (gen)* dulzura *f; (of smell)* fragancia *f; (of sound)* suavidad *f; (of character)* dulzura *f,* simpatía *f;* **now it's all s. and light between them,** ahora hay perfecta armonía entre ellos.

sweet-tempered [swiːt'tempəd] *adj* amable, simpático,-a.

sweet-toothed [swiːt'tuːθt] *adj* goloso,-a.

swell [swel] **I** *n (of sea)* marejada *f,* oleaje *m.* **II** *adj US fam* fenomenal, bárbaro,-a; **he's a s. guy,** es un tipo estupendo. **III** *vi (pt swelled; pp swollen) (part of body)* hincharse; *(river)* subir, crecer; *(sea)* levantarse; *(sales)* crecer, aumentar; *fig* **to s. with pride,** hincharse de orgullo. **IV** *vtr (sales etc)* aumentar. ◆ **swell up** *vi* hincharse.

swelling ['swelɪŋ] *n (gen)* bulto *m,* hinchazón *f; Med* tumefacción *f.*

swelter ['sweltəʳ] *vi* ahogarse de calor.

sweltering ['sweltərɪŋ] *adj* agobiante, sofocante.

swept [swept] *pt & pp see* **sweep.**

sweptback ['sweptbæk] *adj (wing)* en flecha.

swerve [swɜːv] **I** *n* 1 *(by car)* viraje *m or* desvío *m* brusco. 2 *Sport (by player)* regate *m; (ball)* efecto *m.* **II** *vi* 1 *(car)* dar un viraje brusco, desviarse bruscamente; **the taxi swerved to the right,** el taxi viró bruscamente a la derecha. 2 *Sport (player)* dar un regate, regatear; *(ball)* llevar efecto. **III** *vtr Sport (ball)* tirar *or* lanzar con efecto.

swift [swɪft] **I** *adj* 1 *(runner, horse)* rápido,-a, veloz. 2 *(reaction, reply)* pronto,-a, rápido,-a. **II** *n Orn* vencejo *m* común; **alpine s.,** vencejo *m* real. ◆ **swiftly** *adv (speedily)* rápidamente, velozmente; *(promptly)* pronto, rápidamente.

swift-footed [swɪft'fʊtɪd] *adj* rápido,-a.

swiftness ['swɪftnɪs] *n* 1 *(speed)* rapidez *f,* velocidad *f.* 2 *(promptness)* prontitud *f,* rapidez *f.*

swig [swɪg] *fam* **I** *n* trago *m.* **II** *vtr (pt & pp swigged)* beber a tragos.

swill [swɪl] **I** *n* 1 *(pig's food)* bazofia *f; (rubbish)* basura *f.* 2 *(rinse)* enjuage *m;* **to give sth a quick s.,** lavar algo a toda prisa. **II** *vi* 1 *(rinse)* enjuagar. 2 *(drink)* beber a tragos, pimplar. ◆ **swill out** *vi (rinse)* enjuagar.

swim [swɪm] **I** *vi (pt swam; pp swum)* nadar; **to go swimming,** ir a nadar, ir a bañarse; *fig* **to s. with the tide,** seguir la corriente; *fam* **my head is swimming,** la cabeza me da vueltas. **II** *vtr (river, the Channel)* pasar *or* cruzar a nado; **he can't s. a stroke,** no sabe nadar en absoluto; **to s. the butterfly,** nadar estilo mariposa. **III** *n* baño *m;* **to go for a or have a s.,** ir a nadar *or* bañarse; *fam* **to be in the s.,** estar al tanto *or* al corriente.

swimmer ['swɪməʳ] *n* nadador,-a *m, f.*

swimming ['swɪmɪŋ] *n* natación *f.* ■ **s. baths,** piscina *f sing;* **s. cap,** gorro *m* de baño; **s. costume,** traje *m* de baño, bañador *m;* **s. pool,** piscina *f;* **s. trunks,** bañador *m.* ◆ **swimmingly** *adv* a las mil maravillas.

swimsuit ['swɪmsuːt] *n* traje *m* de baño, bañador *m.*

swindle ['swɪndəl] **I** *n (fiddle)* estafa *f; (con)* timo *m;* **what a s.!,** ¡vaya timo! **II** *vtr* estafar, timar; **to s. sb out of sth,** estafar algo a algn.

swindler ['swɪndələʳ] *n* estafador,-a *m, f,* timador,-a *m, f.*

swine [swaɪn] *n* 1 *(pl swine) (pig)* cerdo *m,* puerco *m,* cochino *m; Vet* **s. fever,** peste *f* porcina. 2 *(pl swines) fam (person)* canalla *mf,* cochino,-a *m, f,* marrano,-a *m, f;* **you s.!,** ¡canalla!

swing [swɪŋ] **I** *n* 1 *(movement)* balanceo *m,* vaivén *m; (of pendulum)* oscilación *f, fig (shift in votes etc)* cambio *m* brusco, giro *m,* viraje *m.* ■ **s. bridge,** puente *m* giratorio; **s. door,** puerta *f* giratoria. 2 *Box Golf (swipe)* swing *m;* **to take a s. at sb,** asestar un golpe a algn. 3 *(plaything)* columpio *m; fig* **it's a case of swings and roundabouts,** lo que se pierde acá se gana allá. 4 *(rhythm)* ritmo *m; (jazz style)* swing *m;* **to be in full s.,** estar en plena marcha; **to go with a s.,** ir sobre ruedas; *fig* **to get into the s. of things,** coger el ritmo de las cosas. **II** *vi (pt & pp swung)* 1 *(move to and fro)* balancearse; *(pendulum, hanging object)* oscilar; *(arms, legs)* menearse; *(child on swing)* columpiarse; *(door)* **to s. open/shut,** abrirse/cerrarse de golpe; *fam* **he'll s. for this,** le ahorcarán por eso. 2 *(turn, change direction)* girar, cambiar de dirección *or* sentido; **he swung round,** dio media vuelta; *Pol* **the country has swung to the left,** el país ha virado a la izquierda; **to s. into action,** ponerse en marcha. 3 *(aim at, try to hit)* intentar golpear. **III** *vtr* 1 *(cause to move to and fro)* balancear; *(arms, legs)* menear; *(child on swing)* columpiar, balancear; **he swung his racket at the ball,** intentó golpear la pelota con su raqueta; **she swung an axe at the tree,** asestó un hachazo al árbol; *fam* **to s. the lead,** no dar golpe. 2 *(turn)* hacer girar; **she swung the sack onto her back,** se echó el saco a los hombros; *fig* **they are hoping to s. the voters in their favour,** esperan atraer el favor de los votantes; *fam fig* **there isn't room to s. a cat in here,** aquí no hay sitio para nada; **to s. a deal,** hacer un buen negocio; *fam* **he swung it so that we could have a day off,** lo arregló para que nos diesen un día de fiesta.

swingeing ['swɪndʒɪŋ] *adj* aplastante, abrumador,-a.

swipe [swaɪp] **I** *n* golpe *m;* **to take a s. at sb,** asestar un golpe a algn. **II** *vtr* 1 *(hit)* golpear, pegar, dar un tortazo a. 2 *fam (pinch, whip)* birlar, mangar, robar. **III** *vi (swipe, lunge)* **to s. at sb,** asestar un golpe a algn.

swirl [swɜːl] **I** *n (gen)* remolino *m; (of cream, smoke)* voluta *f; (of skirts)* vuelo *m.* **II** *vi (whirl)* arremolinarse; *(person)* girar, dar vueltas.

swish [swɪʃ] **I** *n (of water)* susurro *m; (of whip, cane)* silbido *m,* chasquido *m; (of skirt, silk)* frufrú *m,* crujido *m.* **II** *adj fam (smart)* muy elegante, elegantón,-ona. **III** *vtr* *(whip, cane)* chasquear; *(skirt)* hacer crujir; *(tail)* menear, sacudir. **IV** *vi (water)* susurrar, *(whip, cane)* dar un chasquido; *(skirt)* crujir.

Swiss [swɪs] **I** *adj* suizo,-a; **the S. Guard,** la Guardia Suiza. ■ *Culin* **s. roll,** brazo *m* de gitano con relleno de mermelada y nata. **II** *n inv (person)* suizo,-a *m, f*; **the S.,** los suizos.

switch [swɪtʃ] **I** *n* **1** *Elec* interruptor *m*, botón *m*, llave *f*. **2** *(changeover)* cambio *m* repentino; *(exchange, swap)* canje *m*, trueque *m*. **3** *(stick)* vara *f*; *(whip)* látigo *m*; *(riding whip)* fusta *f*. **4** *(hairpiece)* trenza *f* postiza. **5** *US Canada Rail* (points) agujas *fpl*. **II** *vtr* **1** *(plans, jobs, direction)* cambiar de. **2** *(allegiance, support)* cambiar **(to,** por); *(attention, conversation)* desviar **(to,** hacia); **they've switched production to their Glasgow plant,** han trasladado la producción a la fábrica de Glasgow. **3** *Elec* poner; **s. the heater to 'low',** pon la estufa al mínimo. **4** *Rail (train)* desviar, cambiar de vía. ◆ **switch off I** *vtr (light, radio, TV, etc)* apagar; *(electrical current)* cortar; *Aut (engine)* parar. **II** *vi (light, radio, TV)* apagar; *Aut (engine)* parar; *fam (person)* distraerse. ◆ **switch on** *vtr (light)* encender; *(radio, TV)* encender, poner; *Aut (engine)* encender. ◆ **switch over** *vi* cambiar; **s. over to BBC1,** cambiar a la BBC 1; **they switched over to gas last year,** to cambiaron todo a gas el año pasado.

switchback [ˈswɪtʃbæk] *n* carretera *f* con muchos cambios de rasante.

switchboard [ˈswɪtʃbɔːd] *n Tel* centralita *f*. ■ **s. operator,** telefonista *mf*.

Switzerland [ˈswɪtsələnd] *n* Suiza.

swivel [ˈswɪvəl] **I** *n Tech* eslabón *m* giratorio. ■ **s. chair,** silla *f* giratoria. **II** *vi (pt & pp* **swivelled,** *US* **swiveled)** girarse. **III** *vtr (head)* girar.

swizz [swɪz] *n fam* timo *m*, estafa *f*.

swollen [ˈswəʊlən] **I** *pp see* **swell.** **II** *adj (ankle, face)* hinchado,-a; *(river, lake)* crecido,-a; **he's got such a s. head,** es tan engreído; **to have s. glands,** tener los ganglios inflamados.

swoon [swuːn] *arc* **I** *n* desmayo *m*. **II** *vi* desmayarse.

swoop [swuːp] **I** *n* **1** *(of bird)* calada *f*; *(of plane)* descenso *m* en picado; *fig* **at one fell s.,** de un golpe. **2** *(by police)* redada *f*. **II** *vi* **1 to s. down,** *(bird)* abalanzarse **(on,** sobre); *(plane)* bajar en picado. **2** *(police)* hacer una redada.

swop [swɒp] *vtr see* **swap.**

sword [sɔːd] *n* espada *f*; *fig* **to cross swords with sb,** reñirse con algn, habérselas con algn. ■ *Mus* **s. dance,** danza *f* de las espadas.

swordfish [ˈsɔːdfɪʃ] *n* pez *m* espada.

swore [swɔːʳ] *pt see* **swear.**

sworn [swɔːn] **I** *pp see* **swear.** **II** *adj* jurado,-a.

swot [swɒt] *fam* **I** *n* empollón,-a *m, f*. **II** *vi (pt & pp* **swotted)** empollar; **to s. up on sth,** empollar algo.

swum [swʌm] *pp see* **swim.**

swung [swʌŋ] *pt & pp see* **swing.**

sybaritic [sɪbəˈrɪtɪk] *adj* sibarita, sibarítico,-a.

sycamore [ˈsɪkəmɔːʳ] *n Bot* plátano *m* falso, sicómoro *m*.

sycophant [ˈsɪkəfənt] *n* adulador,-a *m, f*, pelota *mf*.

syllabic [sɪˈlæbɪk] *adj* silábico,-a.

syllable [ˈsɪləbl] *n Ling* sílaba *f*.

syllabus [ˈsɪləbəs] *n (pl* **syllabuses** *or* **syllabi** [ˈsɪləbaɪ]) *Sch Univ* programa *m* de estudios.

syllogism [ˈsɪlədʒɪzəm] *n* silogismo *m*.

sylph [sɪlf] *n* sílfide *f*.

sylphlike [ˈsɪlflaɪk] *adj* de sílfide.

symbiosis [sɪmbɪˈəʊsɪs] *n* simbiosis *f*.

symbiotic [sɪmbɪˈɒtɪk] *adj* simbiótico,-a.

symbol [ˈsɪmbəl] *n* símbolo *m*.

symbolic [sɪmˈbɒlɪk] *adj* simbólico,-a.

symbolism [ˈsɪmbəlɪzem] *n* simbolismo *m*.

symbolize [ˈsɪmbəlaɪz] *vtr* simbolizar.

symmetrical [sɪˈmetrɪkəl] *adj* simétrico,-a.

symmetry [ˈsɪmɪtrɪ] *n* simetría *f*.

sympathetic [sɪmpəˈθetɪk] *adj* **1** *(showing pity, compassion)* compasivo,-a. **2** *(understanding)* comprensivo,-a; *(kind)* amable; **to be s. to a cause,** simpatizar con una causa. ◆ **s. strike,** huelga *f* por solidaridad. ◆ **sympathetically** *adv* **1** *(showing pity)* compasivamente. **2** *(understanding)* comprensivamente; *(kindly)* amablemente.

sympathize [ˈsɪmpəθaɪz] *vi* **1** *(show pity, compassion)* compadecerse **(with,** de); *(express condolences)* dar el pésame. **2** *(understand)* comprender; **I s. with your point of view,** comprendo tu punto de vista.

sympathizer [ˈsɪmpəθaɪzəʳ] *n Pol* simpatizante *mf*.

sympathy [ˈsɪmpəθɪ] *n* **1** *(pity, compassion)* compasión *f*, lástima *f*. **2** *(condolences)* condolencia *f*, pésame *m*; **letter** *or* **message of s.,** pésame *m*; **she has my deepest s.,** le compadezco; **to express one's s.,** dar el pésame; **you won't get any s. from him,** él no mostrará ninguna compasión por ti. **3** *(understanding)* comprensión *f*; **to strike in s.,** declararse en huelga por solidaridad.

symphonic [sɪmˈfɒnɪk] *adj* sinfónico,-a.

symphony [ˈsɪmfənɪ] *n* sinfonía *f*. ■ **s. orchestra,** orquesta *f* sinfónica.

symposium [sɪmˈpəʊzɪəm] *n (pl* **symposiums** *or* **simposia** [sɪmˈpəʊzɪə]) simposio *m*, conferencia *f*, coloquio *m*.

symptom [ˈsɪmptəm] *n* síntoma *m*; *fig* síntoma *m*, señal *f*, indicio *m*; **to show symptoms of,** dar señales de.

symptomatic [sɪmptəˈmætɪk] *adj* sintomático,-a **(of,** de).

synagogue [ˈsɪnəɡɒɡ] *n Rel* sinagoga *f*.

synchromesh [ˈsɪŋkrəʊmeʃ] *n Aut* sincronizador *m*, cambio *m* sincronizado de velocidades.

synchronization [sɪŋkrənaɪˈzeɪʃən] *n* sincronización *f*.

synchronize [ˈsɪŋkrənaɪz] *vtr* sincronizar.

synchronizer [ˈsɪŋkrənaɪzəʳ] *n* sincronizador *m*.

syncopated [ˈsɪŋkəpeɪtɪd] *adj Mus* sincopado,-a.

syncopation [sɪŋkəˈpeɪʃən] *n Mus* síncopa *f*.

syndicate [ˈsɪndɪkɪt] **I** *n (gen)* corporación *f*, empresa *f*. ■ **crime s.,** sindicato *m* del crimen; **newspaper s.,** sindicato *m* periodístico. **II** [ˈsɪndɪkeɪt] *vtr (workers, newspaper article)* sindicar.

syndrome [ˈsɪndrəʊm] *n Med* síndrome *m*.

synod [ˈsɪnəd] *n Rel* sínodo *m*.

synonym [ˈsɪnənɪm] *n Ling* sinónimo *m*.

synonymous [sɪˈnɒnɪməs] *adj* sinónimo,-a **(with,** de).

synopsis [sɪˈnɒpsɪs] *n (pl* **synopses** [sɪˈnɒpsiːz]) sinopsis *f inv*, resumen *m*.

synoptic [sɪˈnɒptɪk] *adj* sinóptico,-a.

syntax [ˈsɪntæks] *n Ling* sintaxis *f inv*.

synthesis [ˈsɪnθɪsɪs] *n (pl* **syntheses** [ˈsɪnθɪsiːz]) síntesis *f inv*.

synthesize [ˈsɪnθɪsaɪz] *vtr* sintetizar.

synthesizer [ˈsɪnθɪsaɪzəʳ] *n Mus* sintetizador *m*.

synthetic [sɪnˈθetɪk] **I** *adj* sintético,-a. **II** *n* sintético *m*.

syphilis [ˈsɪfɪlɪs] *n Med* sífilis *f*.

syphon [ˈsaɪfən] *n see* **siphon.**

Syria [ˈsɪrɪə] *n* Siria.

Syrian [ˈsɪrɪən] *adj & n* sirio,-a *(m, f)*.

syringe [sɪˈrɪndʒ] **I** *n* jeringa *f*, jeringuilla *f*. **II** *vtr Med* jeringar, inyectar.

syrup [ˈsɪrəp] *n* jarabe *m*, almíbar *m*. ■ **cough s.,** jarabe *m* para la tos; **golden s.,** melaza *f*.

syrupy [ˈsɪrəpɪ] *adj* almibarado,-a.

system ['sɪstəm] n sistema m; fig **it was a shock to her s.**, fue un golpe muy duro para ella; fig **to get sth out of one's s.**, desahogarse de algo; fam **the s.**, el sistema, el orden establecido. ■ **digestive s.**, aparato m digestivo; **metric s.**, sistema m métrico; **nervous s.**, sistema m nervioso; **solar s.**, sistema m solar; Comput **systems analysis,**

análisis m de sistema; **systems analyst,** analista mf de sistemas.

systematic [sɪstɪ'mætɪk] adj sistemático,-a, metódico,-a.

systematize ['sɪstɪmətaɪz] vtr, **systemize** ['sɪstəmaɪz] vtr sistematizar.

systolic [sɪ'stɒlɪk] adj Biol sistólico,-a.

T

T, t [tiː] n (the letter) T, t f; fig **it suits me to a T,** me viene de perlas, me sienta como anillo al dedo.

t abbr of **ton(s), tonne(s),** tonelada(s) f(pl) (métrica(s), t.

TA GB abbr of **Territorial Army,** voluntarios mpl de la segunda reserva.

ta [tɑː] interj fam gracias.

tab¹ [tæb] n **1** (of garment) presilla f; (flap) lengüeta f; (label) etiqueta f; fam **to keep tabs on sb,** vigilar a algn. **2** US fam (bill) cuenta f.

tab² [tæb] n fam tabulador m.

tabby ['tæbɪ] n **t. (cat),** gato,-a m, f, atigrado,-a.

tabernacle ['tæbənækəl] n Rel tabernáculo m.

table ['teɪbəl] **I** n **1** Furn mesa f; **at t.,** en la mesa; **to clear the t.,** quitar la mesa; **to lay** or **set the t.,** poner la mesa; fig **to turn the tables on sb,** volverle las tornas a algn. ■ **t. lamp,** lámpara f de mesa; **t. linen,** mantelería f; **t. mat,** salvamanteles m inv; Sport **t. tennis,** ping-pong® m, tenis m de mesa; **t. wine,** vino m de mesa. **2** (of figures) tabla f, cuadro m. ■ Math **multiplication t.,** tabla f de multiplicar; **t. of contents,** índice m de materias. **II** vtr presentar; **to t. a motion,** presentar una moción.

tableau ['tæbləʊ] n (pl **tableaux**) cuadro m viviente.

tablecloth ['teɪbəlklɒθ] n mantel m.

tableland ['teɪbəllænd] n Geog meseta f.

tablespoon ['teɪbəlspuːn] n cucharón m.

tablespoonful ['teɪbəlspuːnfʊl] n cucharada f grande.

tablet ['tæblɪt] n **1** Med tableta f, comprimido m. pastilla f. **2** (of stone) lápida f. **3** (of soap) pastilla f; (of chocolate) tableta f. **4** US (of writing paper) bloc m.

tableware ['teɪbəlweəʳ] n vajilla f.

tabloid ['tæblɔɪd] n Press periódico m de pequeño formato; pej periódico m de poca categoría. ■ **t. press,** prensa f sensacionalista.

taboo [tə'buː] adj & n tabú (m).

tabular ['tæbjʊləʳ] adj tabular.

tabulate ['tæbjʊleɪt] vtr (figures) disponer en listas or tablas; (results) clasificar.

tabulator ['tæbjʊleɪtəʳ] n tabulador m.

tachometer [tæ'kɒmɪtəʳ] n tacómetro m.

tacit ['tæsɪt] adj tácito,-a; **a t. understanding,** un acuerdo tácito.

taciturn ['tæsɪtɜːn] adj taciturno,-a.

taciturnity [tæsɪ'tɜːnɪtɪ] n taciturnidad f.

tack [tæk] **I** n **1** (small nail) tachuela f; fig **to get down to brass tacks,** ir al grano. **2** Sew hilván m. **3** Naut amura f; (distance) bordada f; **to make a t.,** dar una bordada; fig **on the right/wrong t.,** encaminado,-a/desencaminado,-a; fig **to change t.,** cambiar de rumbo. **II** vtr **1** (to nail) clavar; **to t. sth down,** clavar algo con tachuelas. **2** Sew hilvanar. **3** (add) añadir; **t. this on to the end of the letter,** adjunta esto al final de la carta. **III** vi Naut virar de bordo.

tacking ['tækɪŋ] n Sew hilvanado m; **to take out the t.,** quitar los hilvanes.

tackle ['tækəl] **I** n **1** (equipment) aparejos mpl, trastos mpl. ■ **fishing t.,** aparejos mpl de pescar. **2** Naut aparejo m. **3** Sport carga f, placaje m; Ftb entrada f. **II** vtr (task) emprender; (problem) abordar; (grapple with) agarrar; Sport placar; Ftb entrar a.

tacky¹ ['tækɪ] adj (tackier, tackiest) pegajoso,-a.

tacky² ['tækɪ] adj fam (shoddy) cutre; (badly made) mal hecho,-a.

tact [tækt] n tacto m, diplomacia f.

tactful ['tæktfʊl] adj diplomático,-a, discreto,-a.

tactical ['tæktɪkəl] adj táctico,-a; **a person of great t. skill,** un,-a gran estratega.

tactician [tæk'tɪʃən] n táctico,-a m, f.

tactic ['tæktɪk] n **1** táctica f. **2 tactics,** táctica f sing.

tactile ['tæktaɪl] adj táctil.

tactless ['tæktlɪs] adj (person) falto de tacto, poco diplomático,-a; (question) indiscreto,-a. ◆ **tactlessly** adv sin tacto.

tadpole ['tædpəʊl] n Zool renacuajo m.

taffeta ['tæfɪtə] n Tex tafetán m.

tag¹ [tæg] **I** n **1** (label) etiqueta f. **2** (saying) coletilla f. **II** vtr (pt & pp **tagged**) **1** (label) etiquetar. **2** (attach) añadir, incluir; **you could t. this sentence on to the first paragraph,** podrías añadir esta frase al final del primer párrafo. ◆ **tag along** vi fam pegarse; **to t. along** or **on behind,** ir a la zaga.

tag² [tæg] n (game) marro m.

Tagus ['teɪgəs] n **the T.,** el Tajo.

tail [teɪl] **I** n **1** (of animal) cola f, rabo m; fig **to turn t.,** huir; fig **with his t. between his legs,** con el rabo entre las piernas. **2** (last or rear part) cola f; fig **there's a car on my t.,** un coche me está pisando los talones. ■ **t. end,** cola f; Av **t. unit,** plano m de cola. **3** (of shirt) faldón m; **to wear tails,** ir de frac. ■ **t. coat,** frac m. **4** sl (spy) detective. **5 tails,** (of coin) cruz f sing. **II** vtr **1** sl (follow) perseguir, seguir de cerca. **2** Culin (fruit) quitar los rabos a. ◆ **tail away, tail off** vi (sound) desvanecerse.

tailback ['teɪlbæk] n Aut caravana f.

tail-gate ['teɪlgeɪt] n puerta f trasera.

tailless ['teɪllɪs] adj rabón,-ona.

taillight ['teɪllaɪt] n Aut faro m or piloto m trasero.

tailor ['teɪləʳ] **I** n sastre m; **t.'s (shop),** sastrería f. ■ **t.'s chalk,** jaboncillo m de sastre. **II** vtr (suit) confeccionar; fig adaptar.

tailor-made [teɪlə'meɪd] adj hecho,-a a medida; **it was t.-m. for her,** estaba hecho,-a a su medida; **t.-m. suit,** traje sastre or a medida.

tailplane ['teɪlpleɪn] n Av plano m de cola.

tailwind ['teɪlwɪnd] n Av Naut viento m de cola.

taint [teɪnt] vtr contaminar; fig corromper.

tainted ['teɪntɪd] adj contaminado,-a; (reputation) manchado,-a.

Taiwan [teɪ'wɑːn] n Taiwán.

take [teɪk] **I** *vtr* (*Pt* **took**; *pp* **taken**) **1** (*gen*) tomar, coger; **t. it or leave it**, cógelo o déjalo; *Mil* **to t. a city**, tomar una ciudad; **to t. an opportunity**, aprovechar una oportunidad; *Chess* **to t. a piece**, comer una pieza; **to t. hold of sth**, coger *or* agarrar algo; **to t. sb by the hand**, coger a algn de la mano; **to t. sb in one's arms**, abrazar a algn; **to t. sth from one's pocket**, sacarse algo del bolsillo. **2** (*accept, receive*) tomar, aceptar; **not to t. no for an answer**, no estar dispuesto,-a a aceptar una negativa; **she took the news very well/badly**, se tomó la noticia muy bien/mal; **to t. all the responsibility**, aceptar *or* asumir toda la responsabilidad; **to t. legal advice**, consultar a un abogado; (*earn*) **how much per week**, recaudar tanto por semana; **what will you t. for it?**, ¿cuánto pide por ello? **3** (*have*) darse; **t. your time!**, ¡tómate tu tiempo!; **to t. a bath**, bañarse; **to t. a holiday**, tomarse unas vacaciones; **to t. a walk**, dar un paseo; **to t. care**, cuidar, **to t. fright**, asustarse; **to t. it easy**, tomárselo con calma. **4** (*contain, hold*) caber, **his car takes six people**, caben seis personas en su coche. **5** (*win*) ganar; (*prize*) llevarse; **Cards to t. a trick**, ganar una baza. **6** (*occupy*) ocupar; **is this seat taken?**, ¿está ocupado este asiento? **7** (*subtract*) quitar; **t. six from ten**, resta seis a diez. **8** (*make, produce, develop*) tomar; **to t. a decision**, tomar una decisión; **to t. a liking/dislike to sb**, tomar cariño/antipatía a algn; **to t. a photograph**, hacer *or* sacar una fotografía; **to t. effect**, surtir efecto; (*eat, drink*) tomar; **to t. notes**, tomar notas. **9** (*eat, drink*) tomar; **to t. drugs**, drogarse. **10** (*in school, university, etc*) **she's taking** (a degree in) law, estudia derecho; **she's taking us for geography**, ella nos da clase de geografía; **to t. an examination** (**in** ...), examinarse (de ...). **11** (*accompany*) llevar; **t. us to the station**, llévanos a la estación; **they took me home**, me acompañaron a casa. **12** (*travel by*) coger; **he took the corner too quickly**, tomó la curva demasiado rápido; **t. the first road on the left**, coja la primera a la izquierda; **to t. the bus/the train**, tomar *or* coger el autobús/el tren. **13** (*rent*) alquilar. **14** (*endure*) soportar, aguantar; **I can't t. any more**, no aguanto más. **15** (*consider*) considerar; **he takes it all very seriously**, se lo toma muy en serio; **t. the Basque country for example**, tomemos por ejemplo el País Vasco. **16** (*assume*) **I t. it that** ..., supongo que ...; **I took him for an Englishman**, le tomé por un inglés; **what do you t. me for?**, ¿por quién me tomas? **17** (*require*) requerir; **that will t. some explaining**, costará trabajo explicar eso; **it takes an hour to walk there**, se tarda una hora en ir andando hasta allí; **it took four men to hold him**, hicieron falta cuatro hombres para sujetarle; **the journey takes five days**, el viaje dura cinco días; **what size do you t.?**, (*in clothes*) ¿cuál es tu talla?; (*in shoes*) ¿qué número calza? **18** (*passive*) **to be taken ill**, enfermar, ponerse enfermo,-a. **19** *Ling* (*preposition*) regir. **II** *vi* prender; **the fire has taken**, ha prendido fuego. **III** *n Cin* toma *f*. ◆ **take after** *vtr* parecerse a; **she doesn't t. after her father**, no se parece en nada a su padre. ◆ **take apart** *vtr* (*machine*) desmontar; *fig* (*criticize*) poner a la altura del betún. ◆ **take away** *vtr* **1** (*carry off*) llevarse consigo; **food to t. away**, comida para llevar (a casa). **2** (*remove*) quitar, **to t. sth away from sb**, quitarle algo a algn. **3** *Math* restar; **to t. three away from five**, restar tres de cinco. ◆ **take back** *vtr* **1** (*give back*) devolver; (*receive back*) recuperar; *fig* **that takes me back!**, ¡esto me recuerda los viejos tiempos! **2** (*withdraw*) retractarse. **3** (*re-employ*) readmitir. ◆ **take down** *vtr* **1** (*lower*) bajar. **2** (*demolish*) derribar, demoler, desmontar. **3** (*write*) apuntar; **to t. down notes**, tomar apuntes *or* notas. ◆ **take in** *vtr* **1** (*lodge*) alojar, recibir en casa; **to t. in lodgers**, tener una casa de huéspedes. **2** *Sew* meter; **to t. in a dress at the waist**, meter la cintura a un vestido. **3** (*include*) abarcar, comprender, incluir. **4** (*understand*) entender; **to t. in the situation**, comprender la situación. **5** (*deceive*) engañar, embaucar. **6** (*boat*) **to t. in water**, hacer agua. ◆ **take off** *vtr* **1** (*gen*) quitar, quitarse; **he took off his jacket**, se quitó la chaqueta; **not to t. one's eyes off sth**, no apartar la vista de algo; *Med* **they took his leg off**, le amputaron la pierna; **to t. off one's clothes**, desnudarse. **2** (*lead or carry away*) llevarse; **to t. oneself off**, marcharse, irse. **3** (*deduct*) descontar; **they took off 10% of the price**,

rebajaron el precio en un 10%. **4** (*imitate*) hacer burla de, remedar, imitar. **II** *vi Av* despegar. ◆ **take on** *vtr* **1** (*undertake*) coger, encargarse de; **she took on the responsibility**, asumió la responsabilidad. **2** (*acquire*) tomar. **3** (*employ*) contratar. **4** (*compete with, challenge*) competir con, aceptar el reto de. ◆ **take out** *vtr* **1** sacar, quitar; **he's taking me out to dinner**, me ha invitado a cenar (en un restaurante); **to t. a child out for a walk**, sacar a pasear a un niño; **to t. out a tooth**, quitar un diente. **2.** (*obtain*) obtener; **to t. out an insurance policy**, hacerse un seguro. **3** **the heat takes it out of me**, el calor me agota; **to t. it out on sb**, desquitarse con algn. ◆ **take over I** *vtr* **1** *Com Pol* tomar posesión de; (*responsibility*) encargarse de; **the rebels took over the country**, los rebeldes se apoderaron del país. **2** (*convey*) transportar. **II** *vi* **to t. over from sb**, relevar a algn. ◆ **take to** *vtr* (*become fond of*) coger cariño a; *fig* **to t. to drink/drugs**, darse a la bebida/a las drogas; *fig* **to t. to one's heels**, huir, fugarse. ◆ **take up I** *vtr* **1** **to t. sth up**, (*from ground*) levantar algo; (*upstairs*) subir algo. **2** *Sew* acortar. **3** (*accept*) aceptar; (*adopt*) adoptar. **4** (*start doing*) dedicarse a; (*sport*) empezar a practicar. **5** (*occupy*) ocupar; **he's very taken up with her**, no piensa más que en ella; **to t. up all one's attention**, absorber la atención de algn; **to t. up too much room**, ocupar demasiado sitio. **II** *vi* **to t. up with sb**, trabar amistad con algn.

takeaway ['teɪkəweɪ] *GB & NZ* **I** *n* (*food*) comida *f* para llevar; (*restaurant*) restaurante *m* que vende comidas para llevar. **II** *adj* (*food*) para llevar (a casa).

take-home pay ['teɪkhəʊmpeɪ] *n Fin* sueldo *m* neto.

taken ['teɪkən] **I** *pp see* **take**. **II** *adj fam* cogido,-a; **we're very t. with the idea**, nos atrae mucho la idea.

takeoff ['teɪkɒf] *n* **1** *Av* despegue *m*. **2** (*imitation*) burla *f*, remedo *m*, imitación *f*.

takeover ['teɪkəʊvəʳ] *n* toma *f* de posesión; *Com* (*of company*) absorción *f*, adquisición *f*. ■ **military t.**, golpe *m* de estado; *Fin* **t. bid**, oferta *f* pública de adquisición, OPA *f*.

taker ['teɪkəʳ] *n* (*purchaser*) comprador,-a *m,f*; (*of lease*) arrendatario,-a *m,f*.

takings ['teɪkɪŋz] *npl Com* caja *f sing*, recaudación *f sing*.

talc [tælk] *n* talco *m*.

talcum powder ['tælkəmpaʊdəʳ] *n* polvos *mpl* de talco.

tale [teɪl] *n* cuento *m*; **old wives' tales**, cuentos de viejas; **to tell tales**, contar chismes *or* cuentos.

talent ['tælənt] *n* (*ability*) talento *m*, dotes *mpl*; *Art* **exhibiton of local t.**, exposición *f* de las obras de artistas locales; **to have a t. for sth**, tener talento para algo. ■ *Cin* **t. scout**, cazador,-a *m*, *f* de talentos.

talented ['tæləntɪd] *adj* dotado,-a, con talento.

talisman ['tælɪzmən] *n* (*pl* **talismans**) talismán *m*.

talk [tɔːk] **I** *vi* **1** hablar; **talking of that** ..., a propósito de eso ...; **to learn to t.**, aprender a hablar; **to t. big**, fanfarronear, farolear; *fig* **to t. through one's hat**, decir tonterías; *fam* **now you're talking!**, ¡eso sí que me interesa!; *fam* **t. about luck!**, ¡vaya suerte! **2** (*converse*) hablar, conversar; (*chat*) charlar; (*gossip*) chismorrear; **people will t.**, la gente hablará; **to be talked about**, ser algn la comidilla de todos; **to t. about the weather**, hablar del tiempo. **II** *vtr* hablar; **to t. business**, hablar de negocios; **to t. nonsense**, decir tonterías; **to t. sense**, hablar con sentido común; **to t. shop**, hablar del trabajo. **III** *n* **1** (*conversation*) conversación *f*; *Rad TV* coloquio *m*, entrevista *f*; **to have a t. with sb**, tener una conversación con algn. **2** (*words*) palabras *fpl*; **he's all t.**, no hace más que hablar. **3** (*rumour*) rumor *m*, voz *f*; (*gossip*) chismes *mpl*, habladurías *fpl*; **it's the t. of the town**, es la comidilla de la ciudad; **there's some t. of his returning**, corre la voz de que va a regresar. **4** (*lecture*) conferencia *f*, charla *f*; **to give a t. on sth**, dar una charla sobre algo. ◆ **talk down I** *vtr Av* **to t. a plane down**, dirigir un aterrizaje por radio. **II** *vi* **to t. down to sb**, hablar a algn con desprecio. ◆ **talk into** *vtr* **to t. sb into sth**, convencer a algn para hacer algo. ◆ **talk out of** *vtr* **to t. sb out of sth,** disuadir a algn de hacer algo. ◆ **talk over** *vtr* discutir; **I have to t. it over with my friend,** tengo que discutirlo con mi amigo. ◆ **talk round** *vtr* **1 to t. sb round,** convencer a algn. **2 to t. round a subject,** no ir al grano, andarse con rodeos.

talkative ['tɔːkətɪv] *adj* hablador,-a, locuaz; *pej* charlatán,-ana, parlanchín,-ina.

talkativeness ['tɔːkətɪvnɪs] *n* locuacidad *f*.

talker ['tɔːkəʳ] *n* hablador,-a *m,f*; *pej* parlanchín,-ina *m,f*, charlatán,-ana *m,f*.

talking ['tɔːkɪŋ] *n (conversation)* conversación *f*; *(chatter)* cháchara *f*; **no t. please!,** ¡silencio, por favor!; **to do all the t.,** ser el único que habla. ■ **t. point,** tema *m* de conversación.

talking-to ['tɔːkɪŋtuː] *n (pl talking-tos) fam* bronca *f*; **to give sb a t.-to,** cantar las cuarenta a algn.

tall [tɔːl] *adj* alto,-a; **a tree ten metres t.,** un árbol de diez metros (de alto); **how t. are you?,** ¿cuánto mides?; **she's getting t.,** está creciendo; *fig* **that's a t. order,** eso es mucho pedir; *fig* **that's a t. story,** ¡vaya cuento!

tallboy ['tɔːlbɔɪ] *n Furn* cómoda *f* alta.

tally ['tælɪ] **I** *vi (pt & pp tallied) (correspond)* **they don't t.,** no concuerdan; **to t. with sth,** corresponder *or* concordar con algo. **II** *n Com* anotación *f*, apunte *m*; **to keep a t. of goods,** llevar la cuenta de las mercancías.

talon ['tælən] *n* garra *f*.

tambourine [tæmbə'riːn] *n Mus* pandereta *f*.

tame [teɪm] **I** *adj* **1** *(animal)* domado,-a, domesticado,-a; *(by nature)* manso,-a; *(person)* dócil, sumiso,-a. **2** *(style)* insípido,-a, soso,-a. **II** *vtr* domesticar, domar.

tamer ['teɪməʳ] *n* domador,-a *m,f*.

tamper ['tæmpəʳ] *vi* **to t. with,** *(machinery)* estropear; *(text)* adulterar; *(records, an entry)* falsificar; *(lock)* intentar forzar.

tampon ['tæmpɒn] *n* tampón *m*.

tan¹ [tæn] **I** *n (colour)* marrón *m* rojizo; *(of skin)* bronceado *m*; **to get a t.,** ponerse moreno,-a, broncearse. **II** *adj (colour)* de color marrón rojizo; *(sunburn)* bronceado,-a. **III** *vtr (pt & pp tanned)* **1** *(leather)* curtir; *fam fig* **to t. sb's hide,** dar una paliza a algn. **2** *(skin)* broncear, tostar. **IV** *vi* broncearse, ponerse moreno,-a.

tan² *abbr* of **tangent,** tangente *f*, tang.

tandem ['tændəm] *n* tándem *m*.

tang [tæŋ] *n (taste)* sabor *m* fuerte; *(smell)* olor *m* fuerte.

tangent ['tændʒənt] *n* tangente *f*; *fig* **to go** *or* **fly off at a t.,** salirse por la tangente.

tangerine [tændʒə'riːn] *n Bot* clementina *f*.

tangible ['tændʒəbəl] *adj* tangible; **t. assets,** bienes *mpl* materiales. ◆ **tangibly** *adv* de manera tangible *or* palpable.

Tangier [tæn'dʒɪəʳ] *n* Tánger.

tangle ['tæŋgəl] **I** *n (of thread)* maraña *f*, enredo *m*; *fig* embrollo *m*, lío *m*; *fig* **to be in a t.,** estar hecho,-a un lío; *fig* **to get into a t.,** enredarse. **II** *vtr (threads)* enmarañar, enredar; *fig* embrollar; **to get tangled up,** enredarse, liarse. ◆ **tangle with** *vtr* **to t. with sb,** meterse con algn.

tank [tæŋk] *n* **1** *(container)* depósito *m*, tanque *m*; **to fill (up) the t.,** llenar el depósito. ■ **petrol t.,** depósito *m* de gasolina. **2** *Mil* tanque *m*, carro *m* de combate. ◆ **tank up I** *vi Aut* llenar el depósito. **II** *vtr fam* **to get tanked up,** emborracharse.

tankard ['tæŋkəd] *n* bock *m*.

tanker ['tæŋkəʳ] *n Naut* tanque *m*, barco *m* cisterna; *(for oil)* petrolero *m*; *Aut* camión *m* cisterna.

tanned [tænd] *pt & pp* see **tan.**

tanner ['tænəʳ] *n* curtidor,-a *m,f*.

tannery ['tænərɪ] *n* curtiduría *f*, tenería *f*.

tannin ['tænɪn] *n Chem* tanino *m*.

tanning ['tænɪŋ] *n* **1** *(of hide)* curtido *m*. **2** *(of skin)* bronceado *m*. **3** *fig (thrashing)* paliza *f*, zurra *f*.

Tannoy® ['tænɔɪ] *n* sistema *m* de megafonía; **over the T.,** por los altavoces.

tantalize ['tæntəlaɪz] *vtr* atormentar (con una esperanza falsa).

tantalizing ['tæntəlaɪzɪŋ] *adj* atormentador,-a.

tantamount ['tæntəmaʊnt] *adj* **t. to,** equivalente a; **that's t. to a refusal,** eso equivale a una negativa.

tantrum ['tæntrəm] *n* rabieta *f*; **to fly into a t.,** coger una rabieta.

Tanzania [tænzə'nɪə] *n* Tanzania.

Tanzanian [tænzə'nɪən] *adj & n* tanzano,-a *(m,f)*.

tap¹ [tæp] **I** *vtr (pt & pp tapped) (knock)* golpear ligeramente; *(with hand)* dar una palmadita a. **II** *vi* **to t. at** *or* **on the door,** llamar suavemente a la puerta. **III** *n* golpecito *m*; **there was a t. at the door,** llamaron suavemente a la puerta. ■ **t. dancing,** claqué *m*.

tap² [tæp] **I** *n (for water)* grifo *m*; *(of barrel)* espita *f*; **to turn on/off the t.,** abrir/cerrar el grifo; *fig Fin* **funds on t.,** fondos *mpl* disponibles. ■ **t. water,** agua *f* del grifo. **II** *vtr (pt & pp tapped)* **1** *(barrel)* agujerear; *(tree)* sangrar; *(wine, beer)* tirar, sacar del barril; *fig Com* **to t. new markets,** explotar nuevos mercados; *fam* **to t. sb for a loan,** sablear a algn. **2** *Tel (phone)* interceptar.

tape [teɪp] **I** *n* **1** *(gen)* cinta *f*. ■ *Sport* **(finishing) t.,** cinta *f* de llegada; **insulating t.,** cinta *f* aislante; *fam* **red t.,** papeleo *m*; **sticky t.,** cinta *f* adhesiva; **t. measure,** cinta *f* métrica. **2** *(for recording)* cinta *f* magnetofónica. ■ **t. recorder,** magnetofón *m*, magnetófono *m*; **t. recording,** grabación *f*. **II** *vtr* **1** pegar con cinta adhesiva; *fig* **I've got him taped,** le tengo calado. **2** *(record)* grabar en cinta.

taper ['teɪpəʳ] **I** *vtr (make narrow)* estrechar; *(to a point)* afilar. **II** *vi* estrecharse; *(to a point)* afilarse. **III** *n* vela *f*. ◆ **taper off** *vi* ir disminuyendo.

tapestry ['tæpɪstrɪ] *n* tapiz *m*.

tapeworm ['teɪpwɜːm] *n Ent* tenia *f*, solitaria *f*.

tapioca [tæpɪ'əʊkə] *n* tapioca *f*.

tapped [tæpt] *pt & pp* see **tap¹** & **tap².**

tapping¹ ['tæpɪŋ] *n (knocking)* golpecitos *mpl*.

tappting² ['tæpɪŋ] *n* **1** *(of barrel)* apertura *f*; *(of tree)* sangría *f*; *(of resources)* explotación *f*. **2** *Tel* interceptación *f* de un teléfono.

tar [tɑːʳ] **I** *n* alquitrán *m*, brea *f*. **II** *vtr (pt & pp tarred) (road)* alquitranar; *(boa)* embrear; *fig* **they are tarred with the same brush,** están cortados por el mismo patrón.

tarantula [tə'ræntjʊlə] *n* tarántula *f*.

tardy ['tɑːdɪ] *adj (tardier, tardiest) fml* tardío,-a.

target ['tɑːgɪt] *n* **1** *(object, aimed at)* blanco *m*; **he was a t. for blackmailers,** fue el blanco de los chantajistas; **to hit the t.,** dar en el blanco. ■ **t. practice,** tiro *m* al blanco. **2** *(purpose)* fin *m*, meta *f*; **his t. was to raise £1,000,** su objetivo era reunir 1,000 libras.

tariff ['tærɪf] *n* tarifa *f*, arancel *m*; *(in hotel etc)* lista *f* de precios.

Tarmac® ['tɑːmæk] **I** *n* **1** *(substance)* alquitrán *m*. **2** *Av* pista *f* de aterrizaje *or* despegue. **II** *vtr* alquitranar.

tarnish ['tɑːnɪʃ] **I** *vtr* empañar; *fig (sb's honour)* manchar, empañar. **II** *vi* empañarse, perder brillo.

tarot ['tærəʊ] *n* tarot *m*.

tarpaulin [tɑː'pɔːlɪn] *n Tex* lona *f*.

tarragon ['tærəgən] *n Bot* estragón *m*.

tarred [tɑːd] *pt & pp* see **tar.**

tart¹ [tɑːt] *n GB Culin* tarta *f*.

tart² [tɑːt] *adj (taste)* ácido,-a, agrio,-a; *fig (answer)* acre, mordaz.

tart³ [tɑːt] *fam* **I** *n* fulana *f*, furcia *f*. **II** *vtr GB* **to t. oneself up,** emperifollarse.

tartan ['tɑːtən] *n* tartán *m*.

Tartar ['tɑːtə^r] **I** *adj* tártaro,-a. **II** *n* tártaro,-a *m*, *f*, *fig* persona *f* intratable; **he's a t.**, es una fiera.

tartar ['tɑːtə^r] *n* **1** *Chem* tártaro *m*. **2** *Culin* **t. sauce**, salsa *f* tártara.

tartaric [tɑːˈtærɪk] *adj Chem* tártrico,-a, tartárico,-a.

tartness ['tɑːtnes] *n* (*of taste*) acidez *f*; *fig* (*of remark*) acritud *f*.

task [tɑːsk] *n* tarea *f*, labor *f*; **to carry out a t.**, llevar a cabo una tarea; **to take sb to t.**, reprender a algn. ■ *Mil* **t. force**, destacamento *m* de fuerzas.

taskmaster ['tɑːskmɑːstə^r] *n* **a hard t.**, un auténtico tirano.

Tasmania [tæzˈmeɪnɪə] *n* Tasmania.

Tasmanian [tæzˈmeɪnɪən] *adj & n* tasmanio,-a (*m*, *f*).

Tasman Sea [tæzmənˈsiː] *n* **the T. S.**, el Mar de Tasmania.

tassel ['tæsəl] *n* borla *f*.

taste [teɪst] **I** *n* **1** (*sense*) gusto *m*; (*flavour*) sabor *m*, gusto *m*; **it has a burnt t.**, sabe a quemado; **it has no t.**, no tiene sabor. **2** (*sample*) (*of food*) bocado *m*; (*of drink*) trago *m*, sorbo *m*; **to give sb a t. of his own medicine**, pagar a algn con la misma moneda. **3** (*liking*) afición *f*; **everyone to his t.**, sobre gustos no hay nada escrito; **to have a t. for sth**, gustarle a uno algo. **4** (*choice*) gusto *m*; **it's in bad t.**, es de mal gusto; **to have (good) t.**, tener (buen) gusto. **II** *vtr* **1** (*sample*) probar, catar; **t. this wine**, prueba este vino. **2** (*experience*) experimentar, conocer. **III** *vi* **to t. of sth**, saber a algo; **what does it t. like?**, ¿a qué sabe?

tasteful ['teɪstful] *adj* de buen gasto. ◆ **tastefully** *adv* con buen gusto.

tasteless ['teɪstlɪs] *adj* **1** (*food*) insípido,-a, soso,-a. **2** (*in bad taste*) de mal gusto.

taster ['teɪstə^r] *n* catador,-a *m*, *f*.

tastiness ['teɪstɪnɪs] *n* buen sabor *m*.

tasting ['teɪstɪŋ] *n* degustación *f*.

tasty ['teɪstɪ] *adj* (*tastier, tastiest*) sabroso,-a.

tat [tæt] *n fam* porquería *f*.

ta-ta [tæˈtɑː] *interj GB fam* ¡hasta lueguito!

tattered ['tætəd] *adj* hecho,-a jirones, andrajoso,-a.

tatters ['tætəz] *npl* andrajos *mpl*, jirones *mpl*; **in t.**, hecho,-a jirones.

tattle ['tætəl] **I** *vi* parlotear; (*gossip*) chismorrear, chismear. **II** *n* (*empty talk*) parloteo *m*, cháchara *f*; (*gossip*) chismes *mpl*, habladurías *fpl*.

tattoo¹ [tæˈtuː] *n Mil* retreta *f*.

tattoo² [tæˈtuː] **I** *vtr* tatuar. **II** *n* (*pl tattoos*) (*mark*) tatuaje *m*.

tatty ['tætɪ] *adj* (*tattier, tattiest*) *GB* en mal estado; (*material, clothing*) raído,-a; (*décor*) deslustrado,-a.

taught [tɔːt] *pt & pp see* **teach**.

taunt [tɔːnt] **I** *vtr* **to t. sb with sth**, echar algo en cara a algn. **II** *n* pulla *f*, puyazo *m*.

taunting ['tɔːntɪŋ] **I** *adj* (*tone*) sarcástico,-a, burlón,-ona. **II** *n* sarcasmo *m*.

Taurus ['tɔːrəs] *n Astrol Astron* Tauro *m*.

taut [tɔːt] *adj* tenso,-a, tirante; **to make sth t.**, tensar algo.

tautness ['tɔːtnɪs] *n* tensión *f*.

tavern ['tævən] *n* taberna *f*.

tawdry ['tɔːdrɪ] *adj* (*tawdrier, tawdriest*) hortera, de oropel; (*motive*) indigno,-a.

tawn(e)y ['tɔːnɪ] *adj* leonado,-a, rojizo,-a.

tax [tæks] **I** *n* contribución *f*, impuesto *m*, tasa *f*; **how much t. do you pay?**, ¿cuánto pagas de impuestos?; **t. free**, exento,-a de contribución *or* de impuestos. ■ **t. collector**, recaudador,-a *m*, *f* (de impuestos); **t. evasion**, evasión *f* fiscal; **t. return**, declaración *f* de renta. **II** *vtr* **1** (*person*) imponer contribución a; (*thing*) gravar. **2** (*patience etc*) poner a prueba. **3** **to t. sb about sth**, acusar a algn acerca de algo.

taxable ['tæksəbəl] *adj* imponible.

taxation [tækˈseɪʃən] *n* **1** (*taxes*) impuestos *mpl*, cargas *fpl* fiscales. **2** (*act of taxing*) imposición *f* de contribuciones.

taxi ['tæksɪ] **I** *n* (*pl taxis or taxies*) taxi *m*. ■ **t. driver**, taxista *mf*; **t. rank**, parade *f* de taxis. **II** *vi* (*pt & pp taxied*) (*aircraft*) rodar por la pista.

taxidermist ['tæksɪdɜːmɪst] *n* taxidermista *mf*.

taxidermy ['tæksɪdɜːmɪ] *n* taxidermia *f*.

taximeter ['tæksɪmiːtə^r] *n* taxímetro *m*.

taxing ['tæksɪŋ] *adj* exigente.

taxpayer ['tækspeɪə^r] *n* contribuyente *mf*.

TB, tb [tiːˈbiː] *abbr of* **tuberculosis**, tuberculosis *f*.

tbsp *abbr of* **tablespoonful**, cucharada *f* grande.

tea [tiː] *n* **1** (*plant, drink*) té *m*; **t. bag**, bolsita *f* de té; **t. break**, descanso *m*; **t. caddy**, cajita *f* para el té; **t. cosy**, cubretetera *f*; **t. leaf**, hoja *f* de té; *Bot* **t. rose**, rosa *f* de té; **t. service** *or* **set**, juego *m* de té; **t. towel**, paño *m* (de cocina). **2** (*snack*) merienda *f*; **to give a t. party**, dar una merienda. ■ **(high) t.**, (*meal*) merienda-cena *f*.

teach [tiːtʃ] **I** *vtr* (*pt & pp taught*) enseñar; (*subject*) dar clases de; **she teaches French**, da clases de francés; *US* **she teaches school**, se dedica a la enseñanza; **to t. sb (how) to do sth**, enseñar a algn a hacer algo; *fam* **that will t. him**, eso le servirá de lección; *fam* **to t. sb a thing or two**, despabilar a algn. **II** *vi* dedicarse a la enseñanza, dar clases.

teacher ['tiːtʃə^r] *n* profesor,-a *m*, *f*, (*in primary school*) maestro,-a *m*, *f*; **the teachers**, el profesorado.

teaching ['tiːtʃɪŋ] *n* **1** enseñanza *f*; **t. profession**, la enseñanza; **t. staff**, profesorado *m*; **to go in for t.**, dedicarse a la enseñanza. **2** **teachings**, enseñanzas *fpl*, doctrina *f sing*; **the teachings of the Church**, la doctrina de la Iglesia.

tea-cloth ['tiːklɒθ] *n* paño *m or* trapo *m* (de cocina).

teacup ['tiːkʌp] *n* taza *f* de té.

teak [tiːk] *n Bot* teca *f*.

teal [tiːl] *n* (*pl teals or teal*) *Orn* cerceta *f* común.

team [tiːm] **I** *n* equipo *m*; (*of oxen*) yunta *f*. **II** *vi* **to t. up with sb**, juntarse con algn.

team-mate ['tiːmmeɪt] *n* compañero,-a *m*, *f* de equipo.

teamster ['tiːmstə^r] *n US* camionero,-a *m*, *f*.

teamwork ['tiːmwɜːk] *n* trabajo *m* en equipo.

teapot ['tiːpɒt] *n* tetera *f*.

tear¹ [tɪə^r] *n* lágrima *f*; **to be in tears**, estar llorando; **to burst into tears**, ponerse a llorar. ■ **t. gas**, gas *m* lacrimógeno.

tear² [teə^r] **I** *vtr* (*pt tore*; *pp torn*) **1** rasgar, desgarrar; **to t. a hole in sth**, hacer un agujero *or* un desgarrón en algo; *fig* **to be torn between two courses of action**, vacilar entre dos maneras de actuar. **2** (*snatch*) **to t. sth out of sb's hands**, arrancarle algo de las manos a algn. **II** *vi* **1** (*cloth*) rasgarse. **2** *Aut* **to t. along**, ir a toda velocidad. **III** *n* desgarrón *m*, rasgón *m*; **wear and t.**, desgaste *m*. ◆ **tear away** *vtr* **to t. sb away from his work**, arrancar a algn de su trabajo. ◆ **tear down** *vtr* (*pull down*) derribar, arrancar; (*demolish*) derribar, demoler. ◆ **tear off** **I** *vtr* arrancar. **II** *vi* irse a toda prisa. ◆ **tear out** *vtr* arrancar. ◆ **tear up** *vtr* **1** romper, hacer pedazos. **2** (*uproot*) arrancar, desarraigar.

tearaway ['teərəweɪ] *n GB* pillo,-a *m*, *f*, pillastre *m*.

teardrop ['tɪədrɒp] *n* lágrima *f*.

tearful ['tɪəful] *adj* lloroso,-a, lacrimoso,-a. ◆ **tearfully** *adv* llorando, con lágrimas en los ojos.

tearing ['teərɪŋ] **I** *n* **t. off** *or* **out**, arranque *m*. **II** *adj* **to be in a t. hurry**, tener muchísima prisa.

tearoom ['tiːruːm] *n GB see* **teashop**.

tear-stained ['tɪəsteɪnd] *adj* manchado,-a de lágrimas.

tease [tiːz] **I** *vtr* tomar el pelo a, burlarse de. **II** *n* (*person*) bromista *mf*.

teaser ['tiːzə^r] *n* (*puzzle*) rompecabezas *m inv*.

teashop ['ti:ʃɒp] *n GB* salón *m* de té.

teasing ['ti:zɪŋ] I *adj (person)* burlón,-ona. II *n* burlas *fpl*; **she was tired of his t.,** estaba cansada de que le tomara el pelo.

teaspoon ['ti:spu:n] *n* cucharilla *f*.

teaspoonful ['ti:spu:nfʊl] *n* cucharadita *f*.

teat [ti:t] *n (of animal)* teta *f*; *(of bottle)* tetina *f*.

teatime ['ti:taɪm] *n* hora *f* del té.

technical ['teknɪkəl] *adj* técnico,-a. ■ *Educ* **t. college,** instituto *m* de formación profesional; **t. term,** tecnicismo *m*. ♦ **technically** *adv* **1** técnicamente. **2** *(theoretically)* en teoría.

technicality [teknɪ'kælɪtɪ] *n* detalle *m* técnico.

technician [tek'nɪʃən] *n* técnico,-a *m,f*.

technique [tek'ni:k] *n* técnica *f*.

technological [teknə'lɒdʒɪkəl] *adj* tecnológico,-a.

technologist [tek'nɒlədʒɪst] *n* tecnólogo,-a *m,f*.

technology [tek'nɒlədʒɪ] *n* tecnología *f*.

teddy bear ['tedɪbeəʳ] *n* oso *m* de felpa *or* de peluche.

tedious ['ti:dɪəs] *adj* tedioso,-a, aburrido,-a, pesado,-a.

tedium ['ti:dɪəm] *n* tedio *m*, aburrimiento *m*, pesadez *f*.

tee [ti:] I *n Golf* tee *m*. II *vi* **to t. off,** dar el primer golpe.

teem [ti:m] *vi* abundar, rebosar; **teeming with wildlife,** rebosante de vida salvaje; *fam* **it was teeming down,** llovía a cántaros.

teenage ['ti:neɪdʒ] *adj* adolescente.

teenager ['ti:neɪdʒəʳ] *n* adolescente *mf*.

teens [ti:nz] *npl* adolescencia *f sing*; **she's in her early t.,** tendrá trece o catorce años.

teeny(-weeny) ['ti:nɪ('wi:nɪ] *adj (teenier, teeniest) fam* pequeñito,-a, chiquitín,-ina.

tee-shirt ['ti:ʃɜ:t] *n* camiseta *f*.

teeter ['ti:təʳ] *vi* balancearse.

teeth [ti:θ] *npl see* **tooth.**

teethe [ti:ð] *vi* echar los dientes.

teething ['ti:ðɪŋ] *n* dentición *f*. ■ **t. ring,** chupador *m*; *fig* **t. troubles,** dificultades *fpl* iniciales.

teetotal [ti:'təʊtəl] *adj* abstemio,-a.

teetotalism [ti:'təʊtəlɪzəm] *n* abstinencia, *f* de bebidas alcohólicas.

teetotaller [ti:'təʊtələʳ] *n* abstemio,-a *m,f*.

TEFL [ti:i:ef'el, 'tefəl] *abbr of* **Teaching (of) English as a Foreign Language,** enseñanza *f* del inglés como idioma extranjero.

The(e)ran [teə'rɑ:n] *n* Teherán.

tel *abbr of* **telephone (number),** (número *m* de) teléfono *m*, tel.

telecommunications ['telɪkəmju:nɪ'keɪʃənz] *n* telecomunicación *f*.

telegram ['telɪgræm] *n* telegrama *m*.

telegraph ['telɪgræf, 'telɪgrɑ:f] I *n* telégrafo *m*. ■ **t. operator,** telegrafista *mf*; **t. pole,** poste *m* telegráfico. II *vtr & vi* telegrafiar.

telegraphic [telɪ'græfɪk] *adj* telegráfico,-a.

telegraphist [tɪ'legrəfɪst] *n* telegrafista *mf*.

telegraphy [tɪ'legrəfɪ] *n* telegrafía *f*.

telepathic [telɪ'pæθɪk] *adj Psych* telepático,-a.

telepathy [tɪ'lepəθɪ] *n Psych* telepatía *f*.

telephone ['telɪfəʊn] I *n* teléfono *m*; **are you on the t.?,** ¿tiene teléfono?; *(speaking)* **he's on the t.,** está al aparato; **you're wanted on the t.,** le llaman por teléfono. ■ **t. booth, t. box,** cabina *f* (telefónica); **t. call,** llamada *f* telefónica; **t. directory,** guía *f* telefónica; **t. exchange,** central *f* telefónica; **t. number,** número *m* de teléfono; *US* **t. operator,** telefonista *mf*. II *vtr* telefonear, llamar por teléfono. III *vi* telefonear, hacer una llamada telefónica.

telephonist [tɪ'lefənɪst] *n GB* telefonista *mf*.

telephoto ['telɪfəʊtəʊ] *adj Phot* **t. lens,** teleobjetivo *m*.

teleprinter ['telɪprɪntəʳ] *n* teletipo *m*.

telescope ['telɪskəʊp] I *n Astron* telescopio *m*. II *vi* plegarse (como un catalejo). III *vtr* plegar; **to t. two things together,** empotrar una cosa en otra.

telescopic [telɪ'skɒpɪk] *adj* telescópico,-a; *(umbrella)* plegable.

televise ['telɪvaɪz] *vtr* televisar.

television ['telɪvɪʒən] *n* televisión *f*; **colour t.,** televisión en color; **it's on (the) t.,** lo van a poner en la televisión mañana. ■ **t. play,** obra *f* televisada; **t. programme,** programa *m* de televisión; **t. screen,** pantalla *f* de televisión; **t. (set),** televisor *m*, aparato *m* de televisión.

telex ['teleks] I *n* télex *m*. II *vtr* enviar por télex.

tell [tel] I *vtr (pt & pp* **told) 1** *(say)* decir; *(relate)* contar, relatar, narrar, *(inform)* comunicar, informar; **can you t. me the way to the hospital?,** puede indicarme como se va al hospital; **I have been told that ...,** me han dicho que ...; **I'll t. you what happened,** le contaré lo que sucedió; **I shall t. him the truth,** le diré la verdad; **I told you so!,** ¡ya te lo dije!; **t. me when they arrive,** avísame cuando lleguen; **to t. lies,** mentir; **to t. sb about sth,** contarle algo a algn; *fam* **t. you what ...,** mira pues ...; *fam* **t. me another!,** ¡cuéntaselo a tu abue a!; *fam* **you're telling me!,** ¡a mi me lo vas a contar! **2** *(assure)* asegurar; **he'll be furious, I (can) t. you!,** ¡se va a poner furioso, te lo garantizo!; **it's not so easy, let me t. you,** le aseguro que no es tan fácil. **3** *(order)* ordenar, mandar; **do as you're told,** haz lo que te dicen; **to t. sb to do sth,** decir *or* mandar a algn que haga algo. **4** *(distinguish)* distinguir; **I can't t. them apart,** no puedo distinguirlos; **to know how to t. the time,** saber decir la hora; **to t. right from wrong,** discernir lo que está bien de lo que está mal; **you can t. him by his voice,** se le reconoce por la voz; **you can't t. she is intelligent,** se nota que es inteligente; **you can't t. her from her sister,** es imposible distinguirla de su hermana. **5** *(count)* contar; **all told,** en total, todo incluido. II *vi* **1** *(reveal)* reflejar, notarse; **his face told of suffering,** su rostro reflejaba el sufrimiento. **2** *(know)* **who can t.?,** ¿quién sabe?; **you never can t.,** nunca se sabe. **3** *(have effect)* notarse; **it's beginning to t.,** su empieza a notar; **these drugs t.** on one, el efecto de estas drogas se hace sentir. ♦ **tell off** *vtr fam* regañar, reprender, reñir. ♦ **tell on** *vtr fam* acusar.

teller ['teləʳ] *n* **1** *(cashier)* cajero,-a *m,f*. **2** *Pol* escrutador,-a *m,f*. **3** *(of story)* narrador,-a *m,f*.

telling ['telɪŋ] I *adj (action)* eficaz; *(blow, argument)* contundente. II *n* **1** *(of story)* narración *f*, relato *m*; *(of secret)* divulgación *f*. **2** *(knowing)* **there's no t.,** no se sabe.

telling-off [telɪŋ'ɒf] *n fam* bronca; **to give sb a t.-o.,** echar *or* propinar una bronca a algn.

telltale ['telteɪl] *n* chivato,-a *m,f*, acusica *mf*. ■ **t. signs,** señales *fpl* reveladoras.

telly ['telɪ] *n GB fam* **the t.,** la tele.

temerity [tɪ'merɪtɪ] *n* temeridad *f*, audacia *f*.

temp¹ [temp] *n (abbr of* **temporary)** *fam* trabajador,-a *m,f* temporal.

temp² *abbr of* **temperature,** temperatura *f*, temp.

temper ['tempəʳ] I *n* **1** *(mood)* humor *m*; **to be in a foul t.,** estar muy enfadado,-a; **to keep one's t.,** no perder la calma; **to lose one's t.,** perder los estribos. **2** *(temperament)* temperamento *m*, carácter *m*; **to have a bad t.,** tener (mal) genio *or* carácter. **3** *Metal* temple *m*. II *vtr Metal* templar; *fig* suavizar.

temperament ['tempərəmənt] *n* temperamento *m*.

temperamental [tempərə'mentəl] *adj* temperamental.

temperance ['tempərəns] *n (restraint)* moderación *f*; *(from alcohol)* abstinencia *f*.

temperate ['tempərɪt] *adj* **1** mesurado,-a, sbbrio,-a. **2** *(climate)* templado,-a.

temperature ['temprɪtʃəʳ] *n* temperatura *f*; **to have a t.,** tener fiebre.

tempest ['tempɪst] *n* tempestad *f*.

tempestuous [tem'pestjuəs] *adj* tempestuoso,-a.

temple¹ ['tempəl] *n Archit* templo *m*.

temple² ['tempəl] *n Anat* sien *f*.

tempo ['tempəu] *n (pl tempos or tempi* ['tempi:]) *Mus* tempo *m*.

temporal ['tempərəl] *adj* **1** *Rel* temporal, seglar. **2** *Anat Gram* temporal.

temporary ['tempərəri] *adj* temporal, provisional; *(setback, improvement)* momentáneo,-a, pasajero,-a; *(teacher)* suplente.

temporize ['tempəraɪz] *vi* contemporizar, intentar ganar tiempo.

tempt [tempt] *vtr* tentar; **I am tempted to accept,** estoy tentado,-a de acepta; **to t.** providence, tentar la suerte; **to t. sb to do sth,** incitar a algn a hacer algo.

temptation [temp'teɪʃən] *n* tentación *f*.

tempter ['temptəʳ] *n* tentador,-a *m,f*.

tempting ['temptɪŋ] *adj (offer)* tentador,-a, apetecible; *(food)* apetitoso,-a.

ten [ten] **I** *adj* diez *inv*; **t. workers,** una decena de trabajadores. **II** *n* diez *m inv*; *fam* **t. to one he finds out!,** ¡a que se entera!; *see also* **seven.**

tenable ['tenəbəl] *adj (opinion)* sostenible.

tenacious [tɪ'neɪʃəs] *adj* tenaz, firme.

tenacity [tɪ'næsɪtɪ] *n* tenacidad *f*.

tenancy ['tenənsɪ] *n (of house)* alquiler *m*; *(of land)* arrendamiento *m*.

tenant ['tenənt] *n (of house)* inquilino,-a *m, f*, *(of farm)* arrendatario,-a *m,f*.

tench [tentʃ] *n (fish)* tenca *f*.

tend¹ [tend] *vi (be inclined)* tender, tener tendencia (**to,** a); **I t. to agree with you,** me inclino a compartir tu opinión; **wool tends to shrink,** la lana suele encoger.

tend² [tend] *vtr (care for)* cuidar, ocuparse de.

tendency ['tendənsɪ] *n* tendencia *f*.

tendentious [ten'denʃəs] *adj* tendencioso,-a.

tender¹ ['tendəʳ] *adj (affectionate)* cariñoso,-a; *(sensitive, compassionate)* compasivo,-a; *(fragile)* frágil, delicado,-a; *(meat)* tierno,-a; **t. to the touch,** suave al tacto; *fig* **of t. years,** de tierna edad.

tender² ['tendəʳ] **I** *vtr (offer)* ofrecer; *(in payment)* **please t. the exact fare,** por favor, tenga preparado el precio exacto; **to t. one's resignation,** presentar la dimisión. **II** *vi Com* **to t. for,** sacar a concurso. **III** *n* **1** *Com* oferta *f*, propuesta *f*, licitación *f*; **to invite tenders for a piece of work,** sacar un trabajo *or* una obra a concurso. **2** *(money)* **legal t.,** moneda *f* de curso legal.

tender³ ['tendəʳ] *n Naut* barco *m* avituallador; *Rail* ténder *m*.

tenderhearted [tendə'hɑ:tɪd] *adj (compassionate)* compasivo,-a; *(gentle)* bondadoso,-a.

tenderloin ['tendələɪn] *n Culin* filete *m*.

tenderness ['tendənɪs] *n* ternura *f*.

tendon ['tendən] *n Anat* tendón *m*.

tendril ['tendrɪl] *n Bot* zarcillo *m*.

tenement ['tenɪmənt] *n* casa *f* de vecindad.

tenet ['tenɪt] *n* principio *m*, dogma *m*.

tennis ['tenɪs] *n* tenis *m*; **to play t.,** jugar al tenis. ▪ **t. ball,** pelota *f* de tenis; **t. court,** pista *f* de tenis; *Med* **t. elbow,** codo *m* de tenista; **t. player,** jugador,-a *m, f* de tenis, tenista *mf*; **t. racket** *or* **racquet,** raqueta *f* de tenis; **t. shoe,** zapatilla *f* de tenis.

tenor ['tenəʳ] *n* **1** *Mus* tenor *m*. **2** *(content, sense)* contenido *m*, sentido *m* general. **3** *(of events)* curso *m*, marcha *f*.

tense¹ [tens] **I** *adj* tenso,-a. **II** *vtr* **to t. (up),** poner en tensión.

tense² [tens] *n Gram* tiempo *m*.

tension ['tenʃən] *n* tensión *f*; *Elec* **high t.** circuit, circuito *m* de alta tensión.

tent [tent] *n* tienda *f* de campaña; **to pitch a t.,** armar *or* montar una tienda de campaña. ▪ **t. peg,** estaca *f*.

tentacle ['tentəkəl] *n* tentáculo *m*.

tentative ['tentətɪv] *adj* **1** *(not definite)* de prueba, provisional; **a t. scheme,** un plan experimental. **2** *(hesitant)* indeciso,-a. ◆ **tentatively** *adv* a modo de prueba, provisionalmente; *(hesitantly)* con reservas, con indecisión.

tenterhooks ['tentəhʊks] *npl fig* ascuas *fpl*; **to be on t.,** estar sobre ascuas; **to keep sb on t.,** tener a algn sobre ascuas.

tenth [tenθ] **I** *adj* décimo,-a. **II** *n* **1** *(in series)* décimo,-a *m, f*. **2** *(fraction)* décimo *m*; *see also* **seventh.**

tenuous ['tenjuəs] *adj* **1** tenue, ligero,-a, sutil. **2** *(argument)* poco convincente, flojo,-a.

tenure ['tenjuəʳ] *n* **1** *(of office)* ocupación *f*, ejercicio *m*. **2** *Jur* tenencia *f*. **3** *(of property)* arrendamiento *m*.

tepid ['tepɪd] *adj* tibio,-a.

term [tɜ:m] **I** *n* **1** *(limit)* término *m*, límite *m*; *(for payment)* plazo *m*. **2** *(period)* período *m*, duración *f*; *Educ* trimestre *m*; *Jur* período *m* de sesiones; **during his t. of office,** durante su mandato; **in the long/short t.,** a largo/corto plazo. **3** *(word, expression)* término *m*, expresión *f*; **legal t.** término jurídico; **that is a contradiction in terms,** esos son términos contradictorios. **4** *Math* término *m*; *fig* **in terms of money,** en cuanto al dinero. **5** **terms,** *(conditions)* condiciones *fpl*, términos *mpl*; *Com* **easy t.,** facilidades *fpl* de pago; *Com* **inclusive t.,** precio *m* todo incluido; *Com* **t. of payment,** condiciones de pago; **to come to t. with sth,** aceptar algo; **to dictate t.,** imponer condiciones. **6 terms,** *(relationship)* relaciones *fpl*; **to be on good/bad t. with sb,** mantener buenas/malas relaciones con algn; **we are on the best of t.,** somos muy amigos. **II** *vtr (call)* calificar de.

terminal ['tɜ:mɪnəl] **I** *adj Med* terminal; **t. cancer,** cáncer incurable. **II** *n* terminal *f*.

terminate ['tɜ:mɪneɪt] **I** *vtr* terminar, poner fin a; *Med* **to t. a pregnancy,** abortar, interrumpir el embarazo. **II** *vi* terminarse, concluirse.

termination [tɜ:mɪ'neɪʃən] *n* **1** *(end)* terminación *f*, fin *m*; *Med* **t. of pregnancy,** aborto *m* provocado, interrupción *f* del embarazo. **2** *Ling* terminación *f*, desinencia *f*.

terminology [tɜ:mɪ'nɒlədʒɪ] *n* terminología *f*.

terminus ['tɜ:mɪnəs] *n (pl* **terminuses** *or* **termini** ['tɜ:mɪnaɪ]*)* término *m*.

termite ['tɜ:maɪt] *n* termita *f*, termes *m inv*.

tern [tɜ:n] *n Orn* **black t.,** fumarel *m* común; **common t.,** charrán *m* común; **little t.,** charrancito *m*; **whiskered t.,** fumarel *m* cariblanco.

terrace ['terəs] **I** *n* **1** *Agr* bancal *m*. **2** *(of houses)* hilera *f* de casas (de estilo uniforme). **3** *(patio)* terraza *f*. **4** *Ftb* **the terraces,** las gradas. **II** *vtr Agr (hillside)* disponer en bancales.

terraced ['terəst] *adj GB* **t. houses,** casas *fpl* (de estilo uniforme) en hilera.

terracotta [terə'kɒtə] *n* terracota *f*.

terrain [tə'reɪn] *n* terreno *m*.

terrapin ['terəpɪn] *n Zool* tortuga *f* acuática.

terrestrial [tə'restrɪəl] *adj* terrestre.

terrible ['terəbəl] *adj* terrible, espantoso,-a; *fig* **I feel t.,** me encuentro fatal; *fam* **a t. meal,** una comida horrible. ◆ **terribly** *adv* terriblemente; *fam* **I am t. grateful to you,** te estoy muy agradecido,-a.

terrier ['terɪəʳ] *n Zool* terrier *m*.

terrific [tə'rɪfɪk] *adj* **1** *(excellent)* fabuloso,-a, bárbaro,-a; **to have a t. time,** pasarlo en grande. **2** *(extreme)* tremendo,-a; **a t. heat,** un calor insoportable; **at a t. speed,** a una velocidad vertiginosa. ◆ **terrifically** *adv fam (very)* **she's t. clever,** es un genio.

terrify ['terɪfaɪ] *vtr (pt & pp **terrified**)* aterrar, aterrorizar; **to be terrified of sth,** tener pánico a algo; **to t. sb out of their wits,** darle un susto de mil demonios a algn.

terrifying ['terɪfaɪɪŋ] *adj* aterrador,-a, espantoso,-a.

territorial [terɪ'tɔːrɪəl] *adj* territorial.

territory ['terɪtərɪ] *n* territorio *m*.

terror ['terəʳ] *n (fear)* terror *m*, espanto *m*; **to be in t. of one's life,** temer por la vida; *fam (person)* **that child is a t.,** es un niño terrible.

terrorism ['terərɪzəm] *n* terrorismo *m*.

terrorist ['terərɪst] *adj & n* terrorista *(mf).*

terrorize ['terəraɪz] *vtr* aterrorizar.

terror-stricken ['terəstrɪkən] *adj* **terror-struck** ['terəstrʌk] *adj* muerto,-a de miedo.

terry ['terɪ] *n Tex* **t. towel,** toalla *f* de rizo.

terse [tɜːs] *adj (curt)* lacónico,-a.

terseness ['tɜːsnɪs] *n (curtness)* laconismo *m*.

Tertiary ['tɜːʃərɪ] *adj* **1** *(era)* terciario,-a. **2** *GB* **t. education,** enseñanza *f* superior.

TESL [tiːiːes'el, 'tesəl] *abbr of* **Teaching (of) English as a Second Language,** enseñanza *f* del inglés como segunda lengua.

test [test] **I** *vtr (gen)* probar, someter a una prueba; *(analyze)* analizar; *Med (blood, urine)* hacer un análisis de; *(new drug)* experimentar; **to t. sb in algebra,** examinar a algn de álgebra; **to t. sb's ability,** comprobar la capacidad de algn. **II** *n* prueba *f*, examen *m*, test *m*; **to do tests,** hacer pruebas; **to put to the t.,** poner a prueba; **to stand the t.,** pasar la prueba; *fig* **acid t.,** la prueba del fuego; *fig* **it was a t. of her patience,** puso a prueba su paciencia. ■ *Med* **blood t.,** análisis *m inv* de sangre; *Aut* **driving t.,** examen *m* de conducir; *Jur* **t. case,** juicio *m* que hace jurisprudencia; *Sport* **t. match,** partido *m* internacional; *Av* **t. pilot,** piloto *m* de pruebas; **t. tube,** probeta *f*, tubo *m* de ensayo; **t.-tube baby,** niño *m* probeta.

testament ['testəmənt] *n* testamento *m*. ■ **Old/New T.,** Antiguo/Nuevo Testamento.

testicle ['testɪkəl] *n* testículo *m*.

testify ['testɪfaɪ] **I** *vtr (pt & pp **testified**)* *Jur* atestiguar, declarar; **to t. sth under oath,** declarar algo bajo juramento; **to t. that ...,** declarar que ... . **II** *vi* **to t. in sb's favour/against sb,** declarar a favor/en contra de algn; *fig* **to t. to sth,** atestiguar algo.

testimonial [testɪ'məʊnɪəl] *n* (carta *f* de) recomendación *f*.

testimony ['testɪmənɪ] *n Jur* testimonio *m*, declaración *f*; **to bear t. to sth,** atestiguar algo.

testing ['testɪŋ] *adj* **a t. time,** una época difícil. ■ **t. ground,** zona *f* de pruebas.

testis ['testɪs] *n (pl **testes** ['testiːz])* testículo *m*.

testy ['testɪ] *adj (testier, testiest)* irritable; **he's very t.,** es un cascarrabias. ◆ **testily** *adv* en tono irritado.

tetanus ['tetənəs] *n Med* tétanos *m inv*.

tetchy ['tetʃɪ] *adj (tetchier, tetchiest)* *fam* irritable, susceptible.

tête-à-tête [teɪtə'teɪt] *n* conversación *f* confidencial, tête-à-tête *m*.

tether ['teðəʳ] **I** *n* ronzal *m*; *fig* **to be at the end of one's t.,** estar hasta la coronilla, estar harto,-a. **II** *vtr (animal)* atar.

Texan ['teksən] *adj & n* tejano,-a *(m,f).*

Texas ['teksəs] *n* Tejas.

text [tekst] *n* texto *m*.

textbook ['tekstbʊk] *n* libro *m* de texto; *fig* **a t. example,** un ejemplo típico.

textile ['tekstaɪl] **I** *n* tejido *m*, téxtil *m*. **II** *adj* téxtil.

textual ['tekstjʊəl] *adj* textual.

texture ['tekstʃəʳ] *n* textura *f*.

Thai [taɪ] *adj & n* tailandés,-esa *(m,f).*

Thailand ['taɪlænd] *n* Tailandia.

Thames [temz] *n* **the T.,** el Támesis.

than [ðæn, *unstressed* ðən] *conj* que; *(with numbers)* de; **he's older t. me,** es mayor que yo; **I have more/less t. you,** tengo más/menos que tú; **it was more interesting t. we thought,** fue más interesante de lo que creíamos; **more t. once,** más de una vez; **no sooner had we arrived t. the music began,** nada más llegar nosotros comenzó la música; **rather t. going to the cinema, let's go dancing,** vayamos a bailar en vez de ir al cine.

thank [θæŋk] *vtr* dar las gracias a, agradecer a; **I don't know how to t. you for your kindness,** no sé cómo agradecerle su amabilidad; **no t. you,** no gracias; **t. goodness!,** ¡gracias a Dios!; **t. you,** gracias; **t. you very much for your interest,** le agradezco mucho su interés; *iron* **you have only yourself to t.,** la culpa la tienes tú.

thankful ['θæŋkfʊl] *adj* agradecido,-a; **to be t. for sth,** agradecer algo. ◆ **thankfully** *adv* con agradecimiento.

thankless ['θæŋklɪs] *adj (task)* ingrato,-a.

thanks [θæŋks] *npl* gracias *fpl*; **give him my t.,** dele las gracias de mi parte; **many t.,** muchas gracias; **t. for your visit/for phoning,** gracias por su visita/por llamar; **t. to your help,** gracias a tu ayuda; *fam* **that's all the t. I get!,** ¡vaya manera de agradecérmelo!

thanksgiving [θæŋks'gɪvɪŋ] *n US* **T. Day,** Día *m* de Acción de Gracias.

that [ðæt, *unstressed* ðət] **I** *dem pron (pl **those**)* **1** ése *m*, ésa *f*; *(remote)* aquél *m*, aquella *f*; **this one is new but t. is old,** éste es nuevo pero ése es viejo. **2** *(indefinite)* eso; *(remote)* aquello; **after t.,** después de eso; **all t. came to an end,** todo aquello se acabó; **don't talk like t.,** no hables así; **give me t.,** dame eso; **have things come to t.?,** ¿hasta ahí han llegado las cosas?; **like t.,** así; **t.'s all,** eso es todo; **t.'s right,** eso es; **t.'s where I live,** allí vivo yo; **what's t.?,** ¿qué es eso?; **who's t.?,** ¿quién es? **3** *(with relative)* el, la; **all those I saw,** todos los que vi; **there are those who say that ...,** hay quien dice que ... . **II** *dem adj (pl **those**) (masculine)* ese; *(feminine)* esa; *(remote) (masculine)* aquel; *(feminine)* aquella; **at t. time,** en aquella época; **I saw him just t. once,** no le vi más que aquella vez; **t. book,** ese *or* aquel libro; *fam* **well, how's t. leg of yours?,** bueno, ¿cómo va esa pierna? **III** *rel pron* **1** *(subject, direct object)* que; **all t. you said,** todo lo que dijiste; **the letter t. I sent you,** la carta que te envié. **2** *(governed by preposition)* que, el que, la que, los que, las que, el cual, la cual, los cuales, las cuales; **nobody has come, t. I know of,** no ha venido nadie, que yo sepa; **the envelope t. I put it in,** el sobre en que lo puse. **3** *(when)* que, en que; **the moment t. you arrived,** el momento en que llegaste; **the night t. we went to the theatre,** la noche que fuimos al teatro. **IV** *conj* que; **come here so t. I can see you,** ven aquí para que te vea; **he said (t.) he would come,** dijo que vendría; **I'm telling you so t. you'll know,** se lo digo para que lo sepa; **not t. I admire him,** no es que le admire. **V** *adv* así de, tanto, tan; **cut off t. much (for me),** córteme un trozo así de grande; **I don't think it can be t. old,** no creo que sea tan viejo como dicen; **we haven't got t. much money,** no tenemos tanto dinero.

thatch [θætʃ] **I** *n* paja *f*; *fam* **a good t. of hair,** una buena mata de pelo. **II** *vtr* cubrir con paja.

thatched [θætʃed] *adj* cubierto,-a con paja; **t. cottage,** casita con techo de paja; **t. roof,** techo de paja.

thaw [θɔː] **I** *vtr (snow)* derretir; *(food, freezer)* descongelar. **II** *vi* descongelarse, deshelarse; *(snow)* derretirse; *fig (person)* ablandarse. **III** *n* deshielo *m*.

the [ðə, *before vowel* ðɪ, *emphatic* ðiː] **I** *def art* **1** el, la; *pl* los, las; **at** *or* **to t.,** al, a la; *pl* a los, a las; **of** *or* **from t.,** del, de la; *pl* de los, de las; **t. Alps,** los Alpes; **t. right time,** la hora exacta; **t. voice of t. people**, la voz del pueblo; **translated from t. Russian**, traducido,-a del ruso. **2** *(omitted)* **Cardiff, t. capital of Wales,** Cardiff, capital de Gales; **George t. Sixth,** Jorge Sexto. **3** *(in exclamations)* **t. impudence of it!,** ¡qué caradura! **4** *(with measurements)* **by t. day/month,** al día/mes; **by t. dozen,** a docenas. **5** *(with adjectives used as nouns)* **t. poor,** los pobres. **6** *(specifying)* **how's t. arm?,** ¿cómo va ese brazo?; **I was away at t. time,** yo estaba entonces fuera. **7** *(indicating kind)* **he's not t. person to do that,** no es de los que hacen tales cosas. **8** *(sufficient)* **he hasn't t. patience to wait,** no tiene suficiente paciencia para esperar. **9** *(stressed)* [ðiː] **el** *or* **la** *or* **lo mejor; he is t. surgeon here,** él es el cirujano que más fama tiene aquí; **it is t. restaurant for fish,** es el mejor restaurante para comer buen pescado. **II** *adv* **t. more t. merrier,** cuanto más mejor; **t. sooner t. better,** cuanto antes mejor.

theatre, *US* **theater** ['θɪətər] *n* **1** *Theat* teatro *m*. **2** *Med* quirófano *m*.

theatre-goer, *US* **theater-goer** ['θɪətəgəʊər] *n* aficionado,-a *m, f* al teatro.

theatrical [θɪ'ætrɪkəl] *adj* teatral; **t. company,** compañía teatral.

theatricals [θɪ'ætrɪkəlz] *npl* funciones *fpl*; **amateur t.,** teatro *m sing* de aficionados.

theft [θeft] *n* robo *m*. ■ **petty t.,** hurto *m*.

their [ðeər] *poss adj (one thing)* su; *(various things)* sus; **t. children and grandchildren,** sus hijos sus nietos; **t. home,** su hogar.

theirs [ðeəz] *poss pron* (el) suyo, (la) suya; *pl* (los) suyos, (las) suyas; de ellos, de ellas; **he's a friend of t.,** es un amigo suyo *or* de ellos; **this house is t.,** esta casa es suya *or* de ellos; *pej* **those dogs of t.!,** ¡sus malditos perros!

them [ðem] *pers pron pl* **1** *(direct object)* los, las; *(indirect object)* les; **I know t.,** los *or* las conozco; **I shall tell t. so,** se lo diré (a ellos *or* ellas); **speak to t.,** hábleles. **2** *(with preposition)* ellos, ellas; **lay the tables and put some flowers on t.,** ponga las mesas y coloque unas flores en cada una de ellas; **walk in front of t.,** camine delante de ellos. **3** *(reflexive)* **they took the keys away with t.,** se llevaron las llaves. **4** *(stressed)* **it's t.!,** ¡son ellos!; **tell t.,** dígaselo a ellos. **5** *(with numbers etc)* **both of t., the two of t.,** los dos; **neither of t.,** ninguno de los dos; **none of t.,** ninguno de ellos.

theme [θiːm] *n* tema *m*; *Mus* **t. and variations,** tema y variaciones *fpl*. ■ *Mus* **t. song,** tema *m* central; *Rad* **t. tune,** sintonía *f*.

themselves [ðəm'selvz] *pers pron pl (as subject)* ellos mismos, ellas mismas; *(as direct or indirect object)* se; *(after a preposition)* sí mismos, sí mismas; **they did it by t.,** lo hicieron ellos solos; **they whispered among t.,** intercambiaron comentarios en voz baja.

then [ðen] **I** *adv* **1** *(at that time)* entonces; **before t.,** antes de aquel momento; **now and t.,** de vez en cuando; **since t.,** desde entonces; **there and t.,** en el acto, acto seguido; **till t.,** hasta entonces; **what t.?,** ¿y entonces? **3** *(anyway)* de todas formas; **I wasn't invited, but t. I don't know them,** no me invitaron, pero claro, yo no los conozco. **4** *(in that case)* entonces, en este caso; **go t.,** pues vete; **but t., pues bien,** vamos a ver; **you knew all the time,** así que tú ya lo sabías; **what t.?,** ¿y entonces qué? **II** *conj* entonces; **they ate and t. they went out,** comieron y luego se marcharon. **III** *adj* (de) entonces; **the t. president,** el entonces presidente, el presidente de entonces.

theodolite [θɪ'ɒdəlaɪt] *n* teodolito *m*.

theologian [θɪə'ləʊdʒɪən] *n* teólogo,-a *m, f*.

theological [θɪə'lɒdʒɪkəl] *adj* teológico,-a.

theology [θɪ'ɒlədʒɪ] *n* teología *f*.

theorem ['θɪərəm] *n Math* teorema *m*.

theoretic(al) [θɪə'retɪk(əl)] *adj* teórico,-a. ◆ **theoretically** *adv* teóricamente.

theoretician [θɪərɪ'tɪʃən] *n*, **theorist** ['θɪərɪst] *n* teórico,-a *m, f*.

theorize ['θɪəraɪz] *vi* teorizar.

theory ['θɪərɪ] *n* teoría *f*.

therapeutic [θerə'pjuːtɪk] *adj* terapéutico,-a.

therapist ['θerəpɪst] *n* terapeuta *mf*.

therapy ['θerəpɪ] *n* terapia *f*, terapéutica *f*. ■ **occupational t.,** terapia *f* ocupacional.

there [ðeər] **I** *adv* **1** *(indicating place)* allí, allá; *(near speaker or hearer)* ahí; **a hundred kilometres t. and back,** cien kilómetros ida y vuelta; **here and t.,** acá y allá; **here, t. and everywhere,** en todas partes; **in t.,** ahí dentro; *Tel* **is Peter t.?,** ¿está Peter?; **we're t.,** hemos llegado; *fam* **he's not all t.,** está chalado. **2** *(emphatic)* **that man t.,** aquel hombre; **hurry up t.!,** ¡venga!, ¡dese prisa! **3** *(unstressed)* **t. is ...,** **t. are ...,** hay...; **t.'s a page missing,** falta una página; **t. were many cars,** había muchos coches; **t. were six of us,** éramos seis. **4** *(in respect)* **t.'s the difficulty,** ahí está la dificultad; **t. you have me,** de eso sí que no tengo ni idea. **II** *interj* **I shall do as I like, so t.!,** haré lo que me da la gana, ¡ea!; **t., t.,** bien, bien; **t., this is for you,** ten, esto es para ti.

thereabouts ['ðeərəbaʊts] *adv,* *US* **thereabout** ['ðeərəbaʊt] *adv* **1** *(place)* allí cerca, por ahí; **he lives in Cambridge or t.,** vive en Cambridge o por allí cerca. **2** *(approximately)* por ahí, más o menos; **four o'clock or t.,** a eso de las cuatro; **he must be forty or t.,** debe de tener cuarenta años más o menos.

thereafter [ðeər'ɑːftər] *adv fml* a partir de entonces.

thereby ['ðeəbaɪ] *adv fml* por eso *o* ello; **t. hangs a tale,** eso es una larga historia.

therefore ['ðeəfɔːr] *adv* por lo tanto, por eso; **I think, t. I am,** pienso, luego existo.

therein [ðeər'ɪn] *adv fml* ahí, aquí, en eso.

thereupon [ðeərə'pɒn] *adv fml* **t., he left us,** llegados a este punto se marchó.

therm [θɜːm] *n GB Phys* termia *f*.

thermal ['θɜːməl] **I** *adj (spring)* termal; *Phys* térmico,-a. ■ **t. baths,** termas *fpl*; **t. current,** corriente *f* térmica; **t. efficiency,** rendimiento *m* térmico. **II** *n Meteor (current)* corriente *f* térmica.

thermodynamics [θɜːməʊdaɪ'næmɪks] *n* termodinámica *f*.

thermometer [θə'mɒmɪtər] *n* termómetro *m*.

thermonuclear [θɜːməʊ'njuːklɪər] *adj* termonuclear.

Thermos® ['θɜːməs] *n* **T. (flask),** termo *m*.

thermostat ['θɜːməstæt] *n* termostato *m*.

thesaurus [θɪ'sɔːrəs] *n (pl thesauruses or thesauri* [θɪ'sɔːraɪ]*)* diccionario *m* de sinónimos, tesoro *m*, tesauro *m*.

these [ðiːz] **I** *dem adj pl* estos,-as. **II** *dem pron pl* éstos,-as; *see* **this.**

thesis ['θiːsɪs] *n (pl theses* ['θiːsiːz]*)* tesis *f inv*.

they [ðeɪ] *pron pl* **1** ellos, ellas; **here t. come,** aquí vienen; **t. are dancing,** están bailando; **t. are rich people,** son ricos. **2** *(stressed)* **t. alone,** ellos solos; **t. told me themselves,** me lo dijeron ellos mismos. **3** *(with relative)* los, las; **t. who say such things,** los que dicen tales cosas. **4** *(indefinite)* **that's what t. say,** eso es lo que se dice; **t. say that ...,** dicen que ..., se dice que ...

thick [θɪk] **I** *adj* **1** *(book etc)* grueso,-a; **a wall two metres t.,** un muro de dos metros de espesor. **2** *(liquid, soup, etc)* espeso,-a. **3** *(vegetation)* espeso,-a. **4** *fam (stupid)* simple, corto,-a de alcances; **that's a hit t.,** no hay derecho; *(very friendly)* **they're as t. as thieves,** están a partir un piñón. **II** *adv* con espesor, densamente; **to cut the bread t.,** cortar el pan en rebanadas gruesas; *fig* **to lay it on t.,** *(exaggerate)* exagerar; *(flatter)* dar coba. **III** *n* **to be in the t. of it,** estar metido,-a de lleno; **through t. and thin,** para lo bueno y para lo malo. ◆ **thickly** *adv* espesamente; **snow fell t.,** nevaba copiosamente; **to cover sth t. with sth,** cubrir algo con una capa gruesa de algo.

thicken [ˈθɪkən] I *vtr* espesar. II *vi* espesarse; *fig (plot)* complicarse.

thicket [ˈθɪkɪt] *n* matorral *m*, espesura *f.*

thickness [ˈθɪknɪs] *n (of wall, with measurement)* espesor *m; (of wire, lips)* grosor *m*, grueso *m; (of liquid, woodland)* espesura *f.*

thickset [θɪkˈset] *adj (person)* rechoncho,-a.

thick-skinned [θɪkˈskɪnd] *adj fig* poco sensible.

thief [θiːf] *n (pl **thieves** [θiːvz])* ladrón,-ona *m, f*; **stop t.!,** ¡al ladrón!; *prov* **set a t. to catch a t.,** al ladrón, ladrón y medio.

thieve [θiːv] *vtr & vi* robar, hurtar, ratear.

thieving [ˈθiːvɪŋ] I *adj* ladrón,-ona. II *n* robos *mpl*, hurtos *mpl.*

thigh [θaɪ] *n* muslo *m.*

thighbone [ˈθaɪbəʊn] *n Anat* fémur *m.*

thimble [ˈθɪmbəl] *n* dedal *m.*

thimbleful [ˈθɪmbəlfʊl] *n (of cognac etc)* dedo *m.*

thin [θɪn] I *adj (**thinner, thinnest**)* **1** delgado,-a, fino, a; *(person)* delgado,-a, flaco,-a; **a t. slice,** una loncha fina; **t.-lipped,** de labios finos; **to get thinner,** adelgazar. **2** *(not thick or dense) (hair, vegetation)* ralo,-a; *(liquid)* claro,-a, poco denso,-a; *(population)* escaso,-a. **3** *fig (voice)* endeble, débil; **a t. excuse,** un pobre pretexto; **to have a t. time of it,** pasarlo mal. II *adv* **to cut t.,** cortar en rebanadas finas; **to spread the paint t.,** pintar con capas finas. III *vtr (pt & pp **thinned**)* **to t. (down),** *(person)* adelgazar; *(paint)* diluir; **to t. (out),** *(wood)* aclarar; *(plants)* entresacar. IV *vi* adelgazar; *(diminish)* disminuir (en espesor); **his hair is thinning,** está perdiendo pelo. ◆ **thinly** *adv* poco, ligeramente; *(spread)* con capas finas; **t. populated,** poco poblado,-a.

thing [θɪŋ] *n* **1** *(object)* cosa *f*, objeto *m*; **that's the very t. for me,** eso es exactamente lo que (me) hace falta; **what's that t.?,** ¿qué es eso? **2** *fam (person)* tío,-a *m, f*; **poor little t.!,** ¡pobrecito,-a!; **you lucky t.!,** ¡vaya suerte que tienes! **3** *(situation, fashion, progress, etc)* cosas *fpl*; **as things are,** tal como están las cosas; **first t. to the morning,** a primera hora de la mañana; **for another t.,** por otra parte; **for one t.,** en primer lugar; **he expects great things of the new treatmeat,** espera mucho del nuevo tratamiento; **I'd like to go, but the t. is ...,** me gustaría ir, pero resulta que ...; **it's just one of those things,** son cosas que pasan; **it's not the (done) t.,** eso no se hace; **the latest t. in hats,** lo último en sombreros; **things are going badly,** las cosas van mal; **what with one t. and another,** entre unas cosas y otras; *fig* **to know a t. or two,** conocer el percal. **4** **things,** *fam (clothing)* ropa *f sing*; *(possessions)* cosas *fpl*; **to pack up one's t.,** hacer las maletas; **to put one's t. away,** ordenar las cosas; **to wash up the tea** *or* **dinner t.,** fregar los platos.

thingamajig [ˈθɪŋəmədʒɪg] *n fam*, **thingumabob** [ˈθɪŋəməbɒb] *n fam*, **thingummy** [ˈθɪŋəmɪ] *n fam* chisme *m.*

think [θɪŋk] I *vtr (pt & pp **thought**)* **1** *(believe, consider)* pensar, creer; **I hardly t. it likely,** me parece poco probable; **I t. so/not,** creo que sí/no; **they are thought to be rich,** pasan por ricos. **2** *(imagine)* imaginar; **I thought as much,** yo me lo imaginaba; **to t. that it cost only a pound,** y pensar que costó solo una libra; **who would have thought it?,** ¿quién lo hubiera dicho *o* imaginado? II *vi* **1** pensar **(of, about,** en); **give me time to t.,** dame tiempo para reflexionar; **his name was ...,** let me t.,** se llamaba ..., vamos a ver; **I didn't t. of telling her,** no se me ocurrió decírselo; **she thinks of everything,** piensa en todo; **to t. ahead,** prevenir; *fam* **to t. big,** tener grandes proyectos (para el futuro). **2** *(have as opinion)* opinar, pensar; **I don't t. much of the idea,** no me hace mucha gracia la idea; **she thought nothing**

of getting up at six a.m.,** se levantaba a las seis de la madrugada y tan tranquila; **t. nothing of it,** no tiene importancia; **to t. well *or* highly of sb,** apreciar a algn; **what do you t.?,** ¿a ti qué te parece?; **what do you t. of the house?,** ¿qué opinas de la casa? **3** *(imagine)* imaginar; **just t.!,** ¡imagínate!; **t. of what could happen,** imagina lo que podría pasar. **4** *(remember)* **I can't t. of her name,** no recuerdo su nombre. III *n* **to have a quiet t. about sth,** pensar algo con calma; *fam* **you've got another t. coming!,** ¡no te hagas ilusiones! ◆ **think back** *vi* **to t. back to when ...,** recordar cuando ..., acordarse de cuando ... . ◆ **think out** *vtr (matter)* examinar, meditar; *(plan)* elaborar; **a carefully thought-out answer,** una respuesta razonada; **to t. things out for oneself,** juzgar las cosas por uno mismo. ◆ **think over** *vtr* reflexionar, pensar (detenidamente); **we'll have to t. it over,** lo tendremos que pensar. ◆ **think up** *vtr* imaginar, idear; *fam* **what have you been thinking up?,** ¿qué estás tramando?

thinker [ˈθɪŋkəʳ] *n* pensador,-a *m, f.*

thinking [ˈθɪŋkɪŋ] I *n* pensamiento *m*; **I'll have to do some t.,** lo tendré que pensar; **to my way of t.,** a mi parecer. II *adj* racional; **to put on one's t. cap,** reflexionar.

think-tank [ˈθɪŋktæŋk] *n fam* grupo *m* de expertos.

thinned [θɪnd] *pt & pp see* **thin.**

thinner [ˈθɪnəʳ] *n* disolvente *m.*

thinness [ˈθɪnnɪs] *n (of person)* delgadez *f*, flaqueza *f*; *(of liquid)* fluidez *f.*

third [θɜːd] I *adj* tercero,-a; *(before masculine singular noun)* tercer; **George the t.,** Jorge III, Jorge Tercero; **(on) the t. of March,** el tres de marzo. ■ **the T. World,** el Tercer Mundo; *Ins* **t. party insurance,** seguro *m* a terceros; *Jur* **t. person,** tercero,-a *m, f.* II *n* **1** *(in series)* tercero,-a *m, f.* **2** *(fraction)* tercio *m*, tercera parte *f*; **a t. of the inhabitants,** la tercera parte de los habitantes; *see also* **seventh. 3** *Mus* tercera *f.* **4** *Aut* tercera (velocidad) *f.* ◆ **thirdly** *adv* en tercer lugar.

third-class [ˈθɜːdklɑːs] *adj* de tercera clase.

third-rate [ˈθɜːdreɪt] *adj* de calidad inferior.

thirst [θɜːst] *n* sed *f. fig* afán *m*; **to quench one's t.,** apagar la sed; *fig* **the t. for knowledge,** la sed de saber.

thirsting [ˈθɜːstɪŋ] *adj fig* sediento,-a **(for,** de).

thirsty [ˈθɜːstɪ] *adj (**thirstier, thirstiest**)* sediento,-a; **to be t.,** tener sed.

thirteen [θɜːˈtiːn] *adj & n* trece *(m)*; *see also* **seven.**

thirteenth [θɜːˈtiːnθ] I *adj* decimotercero,-a; **(on) the t. of May,** el trece de mayo. II *n* **1** *(in series)* decimotercero,-a *m, f.* **2** *(fraction)* decimotercera parte *f*; *see also* **seventh.**

thirtieth [ˈθɜːtɪɪθ] I *adj* trigésimo,-a; **(on) the t. of June,** el treinta de junio. II *n* **1** *(in series)* trigésimo,-a *m, f.* **2** *(fraction)* trigésima parte *f*; *see also* **seventh.**

thirty [ˈθɜːtɪ] *adj & n* treinta *(m)*; **t.-one,** treinta y uno; **about t. people,** una treintena de personas; *see also* **seven.**

this [ðɪs] I *(pl **these**)* dem pron **1** *(indefinite)* esto; **do you want t. or that?,** ¿quieres esto o aquello?; **it was like t.,** fue así; **the thing is t.,** lo que pasa es esto; **what good is t.?,** ¿para qué sirve esto? **2** *(place)* **t. is where we met,** fue aquí donde nos conocimos. **3** *(time)* **it should have come before t.,** debería haber llegado ya. **4** *(specific person or thing)* éste *m*, ésta *f*; **I prefer these to those,** me gustan más éstos que aquéllos; *(introduction)* **t. is Mr Alvarez,** le presento al Sr. Alvarez; *Tel* **t. is Julia (speaking),** soy Julia. II *dem adj (pl **these**) (masculine)* este; *(feminine)* esta; **t. book/these books,** este libro/estos libros. III *adv* **he got t. far,** llegó hasta aquí; **t. high,** así de alto.

thistle [ˈθɪsəl] *n Bot* cardo *m.*

thistledown [ˈθɪsəldaʊn] *n* vilano *m* de cardo.

thither [ˈðɪðəʳ] *adv* **to run hither and t.,** correr de un lado para otro.

thong [θɒŋ] *n* tira *f* de cuero, correa *f*.

thorax ['θɔːræks] *n* (*pl* **thoraxes** *or* **thoraces** ['θɔːrəsiːz]) *Anat* tórax *m*.

thorn [θɔːn] *n* espina *f*; *fig* **to be a t. in sb's flesh**, ser una espina clavada.

thorny ['θɔːnɪ] *adj* (**thornier, thorniest**) espinoso,-a.

thorough ['θʌrə] *adj* **1** (*careful*) minucioso,-a; (*work*) concienzudo,-a; (*knowledge*) profundo,-a; **to carry out a t. enquiry into a matter**, investigar a fondo un asunto; **to give a room a t. cleaning**, limpiar una habitación a fondo. **2** (*utter*) total; *fam* **a t. scoundrel**, un sinvergüenza redomado. ◆ **thoroughly** *adv* **1** (*carefully*) a fondo. **2** (*wholly*) completamente; **I t. enjoyed myself**, me lo pasé en grande.

thoroughbred ['θʌrəbred] **I** *adj* (*horse*) de pura sangre; (*dog*) de raza. **II** *n* (*horse*) pura sangre *mf*; (*dog*) perro,-a *m, f* de raza.

thoroughfare ['θʌrəfeəʳ] *n* (*road*) carretera *f*; (*street*) calle *f*; **public t.**, vía *f* pública.

thoroughgoing ['θʌrəgəʊɪŋ] *adj* **1** (*careful*) minucioso,-a. **2** (*absolute*) completo,-a, total; (*stupidity*) profundo,-a. **3** (*firm*) (*supporter*) acérrimo,-a.

thoroughness ['θʌrənɪs] *n* minuciosidad *f*, perfección *f*.

those [ðəʊz] **I** *dem pron pl* ésos,-as; (*remote*) aquéllos,-as; (*with rel*) los, las. **II** *dem adj pl* esos,-as; (*remote*) aquellos,-as; *see* **that I & II**.

though [ðəʊ] **I** *conj* **1** aunque; **strange t. it may seem**, por (muy) extraño que parezca; **we shall have to do it, even t. it's going to be difficult**, tendremos que hacerlo, aunque resulte difícil. **2 as t.**, como si; **he spoke as t. we were right**, hablaba como si tuviéramos razón; **it looks as t. he's gone**, parece que se ha ido. **II** *adv* a pesar de todo, sin embargo; **we had a good time, t.**, sin embargo, lo pasamos bien.

thought [θɔːt] **I** *pt & pp see* **think**. **II** *n* **1** (*act of thinking*) pensamiento *m*; **gloomy thoughts**, pensamientos sombríos; **I don't give it another t.**, no volví a pensar en ello; **the mere t. of it**, nada más pensarlo; **what a tempting t.!**, *fam* ¡qué idea más tentadora!; **what a t.!**, ¡qué horror!; **a penny for your thoughts**, ¿en qué estás pensando? **2** (*reflection*) reflexión *f*, consideración *f*; **after much t.**, después de pensarlo mucho; **lack of t.**, irreflexión *f*; **lost in t.**, ensimismado,-a; **on second thoughts**, si bien se mira. **3** (*intention*) intención *f*, propósito *m*; **it's the t. that counts**, lo que cuenta es la intención; **with the t. of talking to him**, con la intención de hablar con él.

thoughtful ['θɔːtfʊl] *adj* (*pensive*) pensativo,-a, meditabundo,-a; (*careful*) sensato,-a, prudente; (*considerate*) atento,-a; **he was t. enough to let me know**, tuvo la amabilidad de avisarme. ◆ **thoughtfully** *adv* pensativamente; (*carefully*) prudentemente; (*considerately*) con consideración, atentamente.

thoughtfulness ['θɔːtfʊlnɪs] *n* meditación *f*; (*carefulness*) prudencia *f*; (*consideration*) consideración *f*.

thoughtless ['θɔːtlɪs] *adj* (*person*) desconsiderado,-a, poco atento,-a; (*action*) irreflexivo,-a.

thoughtlessness ['θɔːtlɪsnɪs] *n* (*of person*) falta *f* de consideración; (*in action*) irreflexión *f*.

thousand ['θaʊzənd] **I** *adj* mil; **a t. men**, mil hombres; **about a t. men**, un millar de hombres; **a t. years**, un milenio. **II** *n* mil *m*, millar *m*; **he's one in a t.**, es un hombre entre mil; **thousands of people**, miles *or* millares de personas.

thousandth ['θaʊzənθ] **I** *adj* milésimo,-a. **II** *n* **1** (*in series*) milésimo,-a *m, f*. **2** (*fraction*) milésima parte *f*.

Thrace [θreɪs] *n* Tracia.

Thracian ['θreɪʃən] *adj & n* tracio,-a (*m, f*).

thrash [θræʃ] **I** *vtr* dar una paliza a. **II** *vi* **to t. about** *or* **around**, agitarse, revolverse. ◆ **thrash out** *vtr* (*matter*) discutir a fondo.

thread [θred] **I** *n* **1** hilo *m*; **length of t.**, hebra *f*; *fig* **to hang by a t.**, pender de un hilo. **2** *fig* (*of argument etc*) hilo *m*; **to lose the t.** (*of the story*), perder el hilo (de la historia). **3** (*of screw*) rosca *f*, filete *m*. **II** *vtr* **1** (*needle*) enhebrar; (*beads*) ensartar. **2 to t. one's way**, abrirse, paso, colarse (**through,** por).

threadbare ['θredbeəʳ] *adj* (*clothes etc*) raído,-a; (*argument*) trillado,-a.

threat [θret] *n* amenaza *f*; **to be under the t. of sth**, estar amenazado,-a de algo; *fig* **there is a t. of rain**, amenaza lluvia.

threaten ['θretən] **I** *vtr* amenazar; **to t. to do sth**, amenazar con hacer algo. **II** *vi* **a storm is threatening**, amenaza tormenta.

threatening ['θretənɪŋ] *adj* amenazador,-a. ◆ **threateningly** *adv* (*act*) de modo amenazador; (*speak*) en tono amenazador.

three [θriː] *adj & n* tres (*m*); **to come in t. by t.** *or* **t. at a time**, entrar de tres en tres; *see also* **seven**.

three-act ['θriːækt] *adj* (*play*) en tres actos.

three-cornered ['θriːkɔːnəd] *adj* triangular. ■ **t.-c. hat**, sombrero *m* de tres picos, tricornio *m*.

three-dimensional [θriːdɪ'menʃənəl] *adj* tridimensional.

threefold ['θriːfəʊld] **I** *adj* triple. **II** *adv* tres veces; **the population has increased t.**, la población se ha triplicado.

three-four ['θriːfɔːʳ] *adj Mus* **t.-f. time**, compás *m* de tres por cuatro.

three-legged ['θriːlegɪd] *adj* de tres patas.

three-piece ['θriːpiːs] *adj* **t.-p. suit**, traje *m* de tres piezas; **t.-p. suite**, tresillo *m*.

three-ply ['θriːplaɪ] *adj Tex* de tres hebras.

three-point ['θriːpɔɪnt] *adj Aut* **t.-p. turn**, cambio *m* de sentido.

three-quarter [θriːkwɔːtəʳ] *adj* (de) tres cuartos; **t.-q. length coat**, abrigo *m* tres cuartos.

threesome ['θriːsəm] *n* grupo *m* de tres personas; **we went in a t.**, fuimos los tres juntos.

three-wheeler [θriː'wiːləʳ] *n Aut* coche *m* de tres ruedas; (*bicycle*) triciclo *m*.

thresh [θreʃ] *vtr Agr* trillar.

thresher ['θreʃəʳ] *n* (*implement*) trillo *m*; (*machine*) trilladora *f*.

threshold ['θreʃəʊld] *n* umbral *m*; *fig* **to be on the t. of a new discovery**, estar a las puertas de un nuevo descubrimiento.

threw [θruː] *pt see* **throw**.

thrift [θrɪft] *n*, **thriftiness** ['θrɪftɪnɪs] *n* economía *f*, frugalidad *f*.

thrifty ['θrɪftɪ] *adj* (**thriftier, thriftiest**) económico,-a, aborrador,-a.

thrill [θrɪl] **I** *n* **1** (*excitement*) emoción *f*, ilusión *f*; **what a t.!**, ¡qué emoción! **2** (*quiver*) estremecimiento *m*. **II** *vtr* **1** (*excite*) emocionar; (*audience*) electrizar; **I am thrilled about the trip**, estoy muy ilusionado,-a con el viaje. **2** (*make tremble*) estremecer. **III** *vi* (*be excited*) emocionarse; (*tremble*) estremecerse.

thriller ['θrɪləʳ] *n Lit* novela *f* de suspense; (*detective story*) novela *f* policíaca; *Cin* película *f* de suspense; *Theat* obra *f* de teatro de suspense.

thrilling ['θrɪlɪŋ] *adj* emocionante, apasionante; **how t.!**, ¡qué emocionante!

thrive [θraɪv] *vi* (*pt* **thrived** *or* **throve;** *pp* **thrived** *or* **thriven** ['θrɪvən]) **1** (*person*) rebosar de salud; (*plant*) crecer bien; **2** *fig* (*business*) prosperar, medrar; **he thrives on it**, le viene de maravilla; **to t. on other people's misfortunes**, sacar provecho de las desgracias de otros.

thriving ['θraɪvɪŋ] *adj* **1** (*plant*) lozano,-a. **2** *fig* (*person, business*) próspero,-a, floreciente.

throat [θrəʊt] *n* garganta *f*; **to clear one's t.,** aclararse la voz; **to have a lump in one's t.,** tener un nudo en la garganta; **to have a sore t.,** tener dolor de garganta; *fig* **to jump down sb's t.,** echar una bronca a algn.

throaty ['θrəʊtɪ] *adj* (**throatier, throatiest**) gutural.

throb [θrɒb] **I** *n* (*of heart*) latido *m*, pulsación *f*; (*of machine*) zumbido *m*. **II** *vi* (*pt & pp* **throbbed**) (*heart*) latir, palpitar; (*machine*) zumbar; **my head is throbbing,** me va a estallar la cabeza.

throbbing ['θrɒbɪŋ] *n* (*of heart*) latido *m*, palpitación *f*; (*of motor*) zumbido *m*; (*of wound*) punzada *f*.

throes [θrəʊz] *npl* **to be in one's death t.,** estar agonizando; *fig* **we're in the t. of a resolution,** estamos en plena revolución.

thrombosis [θrɒm'bəʊsɪs] *npl Med* trombosis *f sing*. ▪ **coronary t.,** infarto *m sing* de miocardio.

throne [θrəʊn] *n* trono *m*; **to come to the t.,** subir al trono.

throng [θrɒŋ] **I** *n* multitud *f*, gentío *m*. **II** *vi* (*pack together*) apiñarse; **people thronged into the house,** la gente entraba en tropel en la casa. **III** *vtr* atestar; **a street thronged with people,** una calle llena de gente.

throttle ['θrɒtəl] **I** *n* (*of engine*) **t.** (**valve**), válvula *f* reguladora; **to open (up) the t.,** acelerar. **II** *vtr* (*person*) estrangular, ahogar. ◆ **throttle back** *vtr* (*engine*) desacelerar.

throttling ['θrɒtəlɪŋ] *n* (*of person*) estrangulación *f*, estrangulamiento *m*.

through [θruː] **I** *prep* **1** (*place*) a través de, por; **to look t. the window,** mirar por la ventana; **to pass t. a city,** pasar por una ciudad; **to talk t. one's nose,** hablar con la nariz; *fig* **to go t. sb's pockets,** registrar los bolsillos de algn; *fam* **he's been t. it,** ha pasado lo suyo. **2** (*time*) a lo largo de; **all t. his life,** durante toda su vida; *US* **Monday t. Friday,** de lunes a viernes. **3** (*expressing progress*) **he's t. his examination,** ha aprobado el examen; **I'm half-way t. this book,** he leído la mitad de este libro. **4** (*by means of*) por, mediante; **I learnt of it t. Jack,** me enteré por Jack; **to send sth t. the post,** enviar algo por correo. **5** (*because of*) a *o* por causa de; **absent t. illness,** ausente por enfermedad; **t. fear/ignorance,** por miedo/ ignorancia; **t. your stupidity, we got lost,** por tu estupidez, nos perdimos. **II** *adj* **a t. train,** un tren directo; **t. traffic,** tránsito *m*. **III** *adv* **1** (*from one side to the other*) de un lado a otro; **the water poured t.,** el agua entraba *or* salía a raudales; **to let sb t.,** dejar pasar a algn; **wet t.,** calado,-a hasta los huesos; *fig* **socialist t. and t.,** socialista a ultranza. **2** (*to or at an end*) **I'm t. with him,** he terminado con él; **to see sth t.,** llevar algo a cabo. **3** (*directly*) **the train runs t. to Paris,** el tren va directo hasta París. **4** *Tel* **to get t. to sb,** comunicar con algn; **you're t.,** ¡hablen!

throughout [θruː'aʊt] **I** *prep* (por) todo,-a; **t. the country,** por todo el país; **t. the year,** durante todo el año. **II** *adv* (*place*) en todas partes; (*time*) todo el tiempo; **central heating t.,** calefacción central en todas las habitaciones.

throughput ['θruːpʊt] *n* rendimiento *m*.

throughway ['θruːweɪ] *n US* autopista *f*.

throve [θrəʊv] *pt see* **thrive**.

throw [θrəʊ] **I** *vtr* (*pt* **threw**; *pp* **thrown**) **1** (*gen*) tirar, arrojar; (*to the ground*) derribar, tumbar; (*rider*) desmontar; **to t. a sheet over sth,** cubrir algo con una sábana; *fig* **he threw a fit,** le dio un ataque; *fig* **to t. a party,** organizar una fiesta; *fig* **to t. open the door,** abrir la puerta de par en par. **2** *fig* proyectar; **to t. some light on a question,** arrojar luz sobre un asunto; **to t. the blame on sb,** echar la culpa a algn. **3** (*disconcert*) desconcertar. **II** *n* tiro *m*, lanzamiento *m*; (*of dice*) tirada *f*; (*in wrestling*) derribo *m*; **within a stone's t. of ...,** a tiro de piedra de ... . ◆ **throw about** *vtr* (*things*) esparcir; (*money*) derrochar; **to be thrown about,** ser sacudido,-a; **to t. one's arms about,** agitar los brazos. ◆ **throw away** *vtr* (*rubbish*) tirar; (*time, money*) malgastar; (*opportunity*) perder, desaprovechar. ◆ **throw down** *vtr* tirar (hacia abajo *or* al

suelo); **to t. down a challenge,** lanzar un desafío. ◆ **throw in** *vtr* **1** tirar; *Sport* sacar de banda; **he threw it in the river,** lo tiró al río; *Cards* **to t. in one's hand,** abandonar la partida; *fig* **to t. in the towel,** arrojar la toalla. **2** (*include*) añadir; (*in deal*) incluir (gratis); *fig* **to t. in one's lot with sb,** compartir la suerte de algn. ◆ **throw off** *vtr* (*person, thing*) deshacerse de; (*clothes*) quitarse; **to t. off a cold,** curarse de un resfriado; **to t. the dogs off the scent,** despistar a los perros. ◆ **throw out** *vtr* **1** (*rubbish*) tirar; (*person*) echar, expulsar; (*legislation*) rechazar. **2 to t. out one's chest,** sacar pecho. **3** (*heat*) despedir, arrojar. ◆ **throw up I** *vtr* **1** lanzar al aire. **2** *Constr* construir rápidamente. **3 to t. up one's job,** dejar el trabajo. **II** *vi* vomitar, devolver.

throwaway ['θrəʊəweɪ] *adj* desechable; **t. cups/plates,** tazas/platos desechables.

throwback ['θrəʊbæk] *n* retroceso *m*.

thrower ['θrəʊə'] *n Sport* lanzador,-a *m,f*.

throw-in ['θrəʊɪn] *n Sport* saque *m* de banda.

thrown [θrəʊn] *pp see* **throw**.

thru [θruː] *prep US see* **through**.

thrush [θrʌʃ] *n Orn* tordo *m*, zorzal *m*. ▪ **blue rock t.,** roquero *m* solitario; **mistle t.,** zorzal *m* charlo; **rock t.,** roquero *m* rojo; **song t.,** zorzal *m* común.

thrust [θrʌst] **I** *vtr* (*pt & pp* **thrust**) (*push*) empujar con fuerza; **he t. a letter into my hand,** me puso una carta violentamente en la mano; **to t. oneself upon sb,** pegarse a algn; **to t. one's way through the crowd,** abrirse paso entre la multitud. **II** *n* (*push*) empujón *m*; (*with sword*) estocada *f*; *Av Phys* empuje *m*; *Mil* ofensiva *f*.

thud [θʌd] **I** *n* ruido *m* sordo. **II** *vi* (*pt & pp* **thudded**) emitir un ruido sordo; **it thudded to the ground,** cayó a tierra.

thug [θʌg] *n* (*lout*) gamberro *m*, matón *m*; (*criminal*) gángster *m*.

thumb [θʌm] **I** *n* pulgar *m*; **he's under his brother's t.,** su hermano lo tiene metido en un puño; **to give sth the thumbs up/down,** aprobar/desaprobar algo; *fig* **to be all thumbs,** ser un manazas. ▪ *Print* **t. index,** uñeros *mpl*. **II** *vtr* **1** manosear; **a well-thumbed book,** un libro manoseado. **2 to t. a lift,** hacer autostop. ◆ **thumb through** *vtr* (*book*) hojear.

thumb-index ['θʌmɪndeks] *vtr* (*book*) poner uñeros a.

thumbnail ['θʌmneɪl] *n* uña *f* del pulgar. ▪ **t. sketch,** *Art* croquis *m* en miniatura; (*description*) retrato *m* breve.

thumbprint ['θʌmprɪnt] *n* huella *f* del pulgar.

thumbtack ['θʌmtæk] *n US* chincheta *f*.

thump [θʌmp] **I** *n* **1** (*sound*) ruido *m* sordo. **2** (*blow*) golpazo *m*; (*with fist*) puñetazo *m*; *fam* tortazo *m*, torta *f*. **II** *vtr* golpear; *fam* dar un tortazo a. **III** *vi* **1 to t. on the table,** golpear la mesa. **2** (*heart*) latir ruidosamente.

thumping ['θʌmpɪŋ] *adj sl* **a t. great lorry,** un enorme camionazo.

thunder ['θʌndə'] **I** *n* trueno *m*; **peals of t.,** truenos *mpl*; **there's t. in the air,** hace tiempo de tormenta; **t. of applause,** estruendo *m* de aplausos. **II** *vi* tronar; *fig* **to t. out threats,** fulminar con amenazas.

thunderbolt ['θʌndəbəʊlt] *n* (*lighting*) rayo *m*; *fig* (*news*) bomba *f*.

thunderclap ['θʌndəklæp] *n* trueno *m*.

thundercloud ['θʌndəklaʊd] *n* nube *f* de tormenta; *fig* nube negra.

thundering ['θʌndərɪŋ] *adj* **1** (*sound*) atronador,-a. **2** *fig* (*success etc*) inmenso,-a, fulminante; **to be in a t. rage,** estar de un humor de perros.

thunderous ['θʌndərəs] *adj fig* ensordecedor,-a; **t. applause,** aplausos ensordecedores.

thunderstorm ['θʌndəstɔːm] *n* tormenta *f*.

thundery ['θʌndərɪ] *adj* (*weather*) tormentoso,-a, de tormenta.

Thur, Thurs *abbr of* **Thursday,** jueves *m*, juev.

Thursday ['θɜːzdɪ] n jueves m; see also **Saturday**.

thus [ðʌs] adv así, de esta manera; **and t. ...,** así que ...; **you do it t.,** lo haces así.

thwart [θwɔːt] vtr frustrar, desbaratar.

thyme [taɪm] n Bot tomillo m.

thyroid ['θaɪrɔɪd] I adj tiroideo,-a. II n t. **(gland),** (glándula f) tiroides f inv.

tiara [tɪ'ɑːrə] n Rel tiara f; (diadem) diadema f.

Tiber ['taɪbə'] n the T., el Tíber.

Tibet [tɪ'bet] n Tibet.

Tibetan [tɪ'betən] adj & n tibetano,-a (m,f).

tibia ['tɪbɪə] n (pl tibios or tibiae ['tɪbiiː]) Anat tibia f.

tic [tɪk] n tic m.

tick[1] [tɪk] I n 1 (sound) tic-tac m. 2 fam (moment) momento m, instante m; **half a t.!,** ¡un momentito!; **I'll do it in a t.,** ahora mismo lo hago. 3 (mark) marca f, señal f; **to put a t. against a name,** hacer una marca al lado del un nombre. II vi hacer tic-tac. III vtr marcar, señalar; **to t. an answer,** señalar la respuesta correcta. ◆ **tick off** vtr 1 (mark) marcar. 2 fam (reprimand) regañar, echar un rapapolvo a. ◆ **tick over** vi Aut (engine) funcionar al ralentí.

tick[2] [tɪk] n Ent garrapata f.

tick[3] [tɪk] n GB fam (credit) crédito m; **to buy sth on t.,** comprar algo a crédito.

ticker ['tɪkə'] n 1 sl (heart) corazón m. 2 (stock exchange) **t. tape,** cinta f de teletipo.

ticket ['tɪkɪt] n 1 (for bus, train) billete m; Theat entrada f, localidad f; (for lottery) décimo m; **t. collector,** revisor,-a m,f; **t. office,** taquilla f. 2 (receipt) recibo m. 3 (label) etiqueta f, rótulo m. 4 Aut multa f; **he got a t. for speeding,** le pusieron una multa por exceso de velocidad. 5 fam **that's the t.,** justo lo que necesitaba.

ticking[1] ['tɪkɪŋ] n (of clock) tic-tac m.

ticking[2] ['tɪkɪŋ] n Tex terliz m.

ticking-off [tɪkɪŋ'ɒf] n fam **to give sb a t.-o.,** echar un rapapolvo a algn.

tickle ['tɪkəl] I vtr hacer cosquillas a; fam **she was tickled pink with her new car,** estaba feliz como unas pascuas con el coche nuevo; fam **to t. sb's fancy,** caer en gracia a algn. II vi hacer cosquillas, picar; **this scarf tickles,** esta bufanda pica. III n cosquillas fpl; **to have a t. in one's throat,** tener la garganta irritada.

tickling ['tɪklɪŋ] n cosquilleo m.

ticklish ['tɪklɪʃ] adj 1 **to be t.,** tener cosquillas. 2 fig (situation) delicado,-a, peliagudo,-a.

tick-tock ['tɪktɒk] n tic-tac m.

tic-tac-toe [tɪktæk'təʊ] n US tres en raya m.

tidal ['taɪdəl] adj de la marea; **the river is t. as far as the lock,** los efectos de la marea llegan hasta la esclusa. ■ **t. wave,** ola f gigante.

tidbit ['tɪdbɪt] n US see **titbit.**

tiddler ['tɪdlə'] n GB fam (fish) pececito m; (child) renacuajo m.

tiddly ['tɪdlɪ] adj GB fam trompa.

tiddlywinks ['tɪdlɪwɪŋks] n (game) pulga f.

tide [taɪd] I n 1 marea f; **high/low t.,** marea alta/baja. 2 fig (of events) marcha f, curso m; **the t. has turned,** han cambiado las cosas; **the t. of opinion,** la corriente de opinión; **to go against the t.,** ir contra corriente. II vtr **to t. over,** echar un capote a algn; **ten pounds will t. me over till the weekend,** con diez libras me las arreglaré hasta el fin de semana.

tidemark ['taɪdmɑːk] n línea f de la marea alta.

tideway ['taɪdweɪ] n canal m de marea.

tidied ['taɪdɪd] pt & pp see **tidy.**

tidiness ['taɪdɪnɪs] n (in good order) orden m; (of appearance) pulcritud f, limpieza f.

tidings ['taɪdɪŋz] npl fml noticias fpl.

tidy ['taɪdɪ] I adj (tidier, tidiest) 1 (room) ordenado,-a, arreglado,-a. 2 (appearance) arreglado,-a, aseado,-a; (habits) ordenado,-a, metódico,-a. 3 fam **it cost him a t. sum,** le salió bastante caro. II vtr (pt & pp tidied) arreglar, poner en orden; **to t. away,** poner en su sitio; **to t. oneself (up),** arreglarse. III vi **to t. (up),** ordenar las cosas.

tie [taɪ] I vtr (pt & pp tied) 1 (shoelaces etc) atar; **to t. a knot,** hacer un nudo; fig **to be tied to one's family,** estar muy atado,-a a la familia; fig **to have one's hands tied,** tener atadas las manos. 2 Mus ligar. II vi Sport empatar (**with,** con). II n 1 (bond) lazo m, vínculo m; **blood ties,** vínculos de sangre. 2 fig (hindrance) atadura f, traba f; **children can be a t.,** los niños pueden ser una atadura. 3 (clothing) corbata f; (on invitation) **black t.,** de etiqueta. ◆ **bow t.,** pajarita f. 4 Mus ligado m. 5 Sport (match) partido m; (draw) empate m; GB Ftb **cup t.,** partido m de copa. ◆ **tie back** vtr (hair) recoger. ◆ **tie down** vtr sujetar; fig **to be tied down,** no tener tiempo libre; fig **to t. sb down to a promise,** obligar a algn a cumplir una promesa. ◆ **tie up** vtr 1 (parcel, dog) atar. 2 (wound) vendar. 3 (deal) concluir. 4 (bind up) (capital) inmovilizar; **my money is tied up in shares,** mi dinero está invertido en acciones; Com **we are tied up with another firm,** estamos vinculados a otra empresa; fig **just now I'm tied up,** de momento estoy muy ocupado,-a; fig **to get tied up (in sth),** embrollarse (en algo).

tiebreaker ['taɪbreɪkə'] n Tennis tie-break m, muerte f súbita.

tiepin ['taɪpɪn] n alfiler m de corbata.

tier [tɪə'] n (of seats) fila f, hilera f; (in stadium) grada f; **four-t. cake,** pastel m de cuatro pisos.

tie-up ['taɪʌp] n enlace m, vínculo m.

tiff [tɪf] n fam riña f, desavenencia f.

tiger ['taɪgə'] n Zool tigre m.

tight [taɪt] I adj 1 (gen) apretado,-a, ajustado,-a; (clothing) ajustado,-a, ceñido,-a; (seal) hermético,-a; **my shoes are too t.,** me aprietan los zapatos; **to keep a t. hold over sb,** tener a algn muy controlado; fig **to be in a t. corner,** estar en un apuro. 2 (scarce) escaso,-a; **money is a bit t.,** andamos escasos de dinero. 3 (mean) agarrado,-a, tacaño,-a. 4 fam (drunk) borracho,-a; **to get t.,** coger una borrachera. II adv estrechamente, firmemente; (seal) herméticamente; **hold t.,** agárrate fuerte; **shut t.,** bien cerrado,-a; **to fit t.,** ser muy ceñido,-a; **to pull a rope t.,** tensar or estirar una cuerda; **to screw a nut t.,** apretar una tuerca lo más posible; **to sit t.,** no moverse de su sitio.

tighten ['taɪtən] I vtr (screw) apretar, ajustar; (rope) tensar; fig **to t. one's belt,** apretarse el cinturón; fig **to t. (up) restrictions,** intensificar las restricciones. II vi (gen) apretarse; (cable) tensarse.

tightfisted [taɪt'fɪstɪd] adj tacaño,-a.

tight-fitting [taɪt'fɪtɪŋ] adj (garment) ceñido,-a; (lid, cap) hermético,-a.

tight-lipped [taɪt'lɪpt] adj (secretive) hermético,-a, reservado,-a; (with anger) con los labios apretados.

tightness ['taɪtnɪs] n (of cable) tensión f, tirantez f; (of clothes) estrechez f.

tightrope ['taɪtrəʊp] n cuerda f floja. ■ **t. walker,** funámbulo,-a m,f.

tights [taɪts] npl (thin) medias fpl, panties mpl; (thick) leotardos mpl; (of dancer) mallas fpl.

tigress ['taɪgrɪs] n Zool tigresa f.

tilde ['tɪldə] n tilde f.

tile [taɪl] I n (of roof) teja f; (glazed) azulejo m; (for paving, floor) baldosa f. II vtr (roof) tejar; (wall) alicatar, azulejar, revestir de azulejos; (floor) embaldosar.

tiled [taɪld] adj (roof) de or con tejas; (wall) revestido,-a de azulejos; (floor) embaldosado,-a.

tiling ['taɪlɪŋ] n (of roof) tejas fpl; (on wall) azulejos mpl; (on floor) embaldosado m, baldosas fpl.

till¹ [tɪl] *n (for cash)* caja *f; fig* **caught with one's hands in the t.,** cogido,-a con las manos en la masa.

till² [tɪl] *vtr (field)* labrar, cultivar.

till³ [tɪl] **I** *prep* hasta; **from morning t. night,** de la mañana a la noche; **t. then,** hasta entonces. **II** *conj* hasta que; **I laughed t. I cried,** reí hasta llorar; **I stayed t. it ended,** me quedé hasta que terminó; **wait t. he comes,** espera a que venga.

tiller ['tɪləʳ] *n Naut* caña *f* del timón.

tilt [tɪlt] **I** *n* **1** *(sloping position)* ladeo *m,* inclinación *f;* **to be at a t.,** estar inclinado,-a. **2** *(speed)* **(at) full t.,** a toda velocidad. **II** *vi* **to t. over,** volcarse; **to t. (up),** inclinarse, ladearse. **III** *vtr* inclinar, ladear; **to t. one's chair back,** balancearse sobre la silla.

timber ['tɪmbəʳ] *n (wood)* madera *f* de construcción; *(trees)* árboles *mpl,* bosque *m;* **(piece of) t.,** viga *f,* madero *m.*

timbered ['tɪmbəd] *adj (house)* enmaderado,-a.

timberyard ['tɪmbəjɑːd] *n* depósito *m* or almacén *m* de madera.

time [taɪm] **I** *n* **1** *(gen)* tiempo *m;* **all the t.,** todo el tiempo; **as t. goes on,** con el tiempo; **for a long t.** to come, de aquí a mucho tiempo; **for some t.** *(past),* desde hace algún tiempo; **I haven't seen him for a long t.,** hace mucho (tiempo) que no lo veo; **in a short t.,** en poco tiempo; **in no t.,** en un abrir y cerrar de ojos; **in t.,** a tiempo; **in three weeks' t.,** dentro de tres semanas; **it will take all your t. to ...,** te costará trabajo ...; **I've no t. for him,** no tengo tiempo para él; **t.'s up!,** ¡ya es la hora!; **to kill t.,** matar el tiempo; **to lose** *or* **waste t.,** perder el tiempo; **to make up for lost t.,** recuperar el tiempo perdido; **to take one's t. over sth,** hacer algo con calma; *fig* **t. will tell,** el tiempo dirá; *fam* **to do t.,** cumplir una condena. ■ **t. bomb,** bomba *f* de relojería; *Ind* **t. clock,** reloj *m* registrador; **t. limit,** límite *m* de tiempo; *(for payment, completion of task)* plazo *m; Rad* **t. signal,** señal *f* horaria; **t. switch,** interruptor *m* electrónico automático; **t. zone,** huso *m* horario. **2** *(period, age, era)* época *f,* tiempos *mpl;* **a sign of the times,** un signo de los tiempos; **in our t.,** en los tiempos en que vivimos; **in time(s) to come,** en el futuro; **to be behind the times,** tener ideas anticuadas. **3** *(point in time)* momento *m;* **at a given t.,** en un momento dado or determinado; **(at) any t.** *(you like),* cuando quiera; **at no t.,** nunca; **at one t.,** en otros tiempos; **at that t.,** (en aquel) entonces; **at the present t.,** actualmente, en la actualidad; **at the same t.,** al mismo tiempo, a la vez; **at times,** a veces; **by the t. that I got there it was over,** cuando llegué ya se había acabado; **from t. to t.,** de vez en cuando; **he may turn up at any t.,** puede llegar en cualquier momento; **I was away at the t.,** estaba ausente en aquel momento; **now's the t. to ...,** ahora es el momento de ...; *fig* **to die before one's t.,** morir prematuramente. **4** *(time of day)* hora *f;* **and about t. too!,** ¡ya era hora!; **at dinner t.,** a la hora de la cena; **a watch that keeps good t.,** un reloj exacto; **Greenwich Mean T.,** la hora de Greenwich; **in good t.,** con anticipación, temprano; **to arrive ahead of t./on t.,** llegar con anticipación/puntualmente; **what's the t.?,** ¿qué hora es?; **what t. do you make it?,** ¿qué hora tiene? **5** *(season)* **t. of the year,** época *f* del año. **6** *(age)* **at my t. of life,** a mi edad. **7** *(experience)* **to have a good/bad t.,** pasarlo bien/mal; **to have a rough t. (of it),** pasarlo mal; **we had a marvellous t.,** lo pasamos en grande. **8** *(occasion)* vez *f;* **for weeks at a t.,** durante semanas enteras; **four at a t.,** cuatro a la vez; **four times as big,** cuatro veces más grande; **next t.,** la próxima vez; **several times over,** varias veces; **three times running,** tres veces seguidas; **t. and t. again,** una y otra vez. **9** *(in multiplication)* (multiplicado) por; **three times four is twelve,** tres (multiplicado) por cuatro es igual a doce. **10** *Mus (rhythm)* compás *m;* **in (strict) t.,** a compás; **to beat t.,** llevar el compás. **II** *vtr* **1** *(speech, programme)* calcular la duración; *Sport (race)* cronometrar. **2** *(choose the time of)* escoger *or* calcular el momento oportuno para; *(meeting)* fijar la hora de; **it is timed for three o'clock,** debe

comenzar a las tres; **to t. a blow,** calcular un golpe; **you timed your arrival badly,** escogiste mal momento para llegar.

time-consuming ['taɪmkənsjuːmɪŋ] *adj* que ocupa *or* requiere mucho tiempo.

time-honoured, *US* **time-honored** ['taɪmɒnəd] *adj* consagrado,-a.

timekeeper ['taɪmkiːpəʳ] *n Sport (person)* cronometrador,-a *m,f; (watch)* cronómetro *m.*

time-lag ['taɪmlæg] *n* intervalo *m.*

timeless ['taɪmlɪs] *adj* eterno,-a.

timely ['taɪmlɪ] *adj (timelier, timeliest)* oportuno,-a.

timepiece ['taɪmpiːs] *n* reloj *m.*

timer ['taɪməʳ] *n (device)* temporizador *m.*

timeserver ['taɪmsɜːvəʳ] *n pej* oportunista *mf,* chaquetero,-a *m,f.*

timetable ['taɪmteɪbl] *n Educ Rail* horario *m.*

timework ['taɪmwɜːk] *n Ind* trabajo *m* por horas.

timid ['tɪmɪd] *adj* tímido,-a. ◆ **timidly** *adv* con timidez.

timidity [tɪ'mɪdɪtɪ] *n* timidez *f.*

timing ['taɪmɪŋ] *n* **1** *(timeliness)* oportunidad *f; (coordination)* coordinación *f;* **your t. was wrong,** no calculaste bien. **2** *Sport* cronometraje *m.* **3** *Tech* regulación *f.*

timorous ['tɪmərəs] *adj* asustadizo,-a, miedoso,-a timorato,-a.

tin [tɪn] **I** *n* **1** *(metal)* estaño *m.* sing ■ **t. plate,** hojalata *f; Mus* **t. whistle,** flautín *m.* **2** *(container)* lata *f,* bote *m;* **baking t.,** molde *m* (para pasteles); **biscuit t.,** caja *f* para galletas. **II** *adj (made of tin)* de estaño; *(of tinplate)* de hojalata; **t. soldiers,** soldaditos *mpl* de plomo. **III** *vtr (pt & pp tinned) (preserve in tins)* enlatar, conservar en lata; **tinned food,** alimentos *mpl* enlatados, conservas *fpl.*

tinder ['tɪndəʳ] *n* yesca *f.*

tinfoil ['tɪnfɔɪl] *n* papel *m* de estaño.

ting-a-ling [tɪŋə'lɪŋ] *n (sound)* tilín *m.*

tinge [tɪndʒ] **I** *n* tinte *m,* matiz *m.* **II** *vtr* teñir; **to t. sth with red,** teñir algo de rojo; *fig* **words tinged with sadness,** palabras teñidas de tristeza.

tingle ['tɪŋgl] *vi (with emotion)* estremecerse; **her cheeks tingled,** le ardían las mejillas; **my feet are tingling,** siento un hormigueo en los pies.

tingling ['tɪŋglɪŋ] *n* estremecimiento *m; (in feet etc)* hormigueo *m.*

tinker ['tɪŋkəʳ] **I** *n pej* quinqui *mf,* gitano,-a *m,f.* **II** *vi* **to t. about with sth,** enredar con algo; **to t. with,** *(mend)* arreglar; *(ruin)* estropear.

tinkle ['tɪŋkl] **I** *vi* tintinear. **II** *vtr* hacer tintinear. **III** *n* tintineo *m; fam* **to give sb a t.,** llamar a algn por teléfono.

tinkling ['tɪŋklɪŋ] *n* tintineo *m,* tilín *m.*

tinned [tɪnd] *pt & pp see* **tin.**

tinny ['tɪnɪ] *adj (tinnier, tinniest) (sound)* metálico,-a.

tin-opener ['tɪnəʊpənəʳ] *n* abrelatas *m inv.*

tinsel ['tɪnsəl] *n* oropel *m.*

tint [tɪnt] **I** *n* tinte *m,* matiz *m.* **II** *vtr* teñir; **to t. one's hair,** teñirse el pelo.

tiny ['taɪnɪ] *adj (tinier, tiniest)* minúsculo,-a, pequeñito,-a; **a t. bit,** un poquitín.

tip¹ [tɪp] **I** *n (end)* punta *f,* extremidad *f; (of cigarette)* filtro *m;* **filter-t. cigarette,** cigarrillo con filtro; **on the tips of one's toes,** sobre las puntas de los pies; *fig* **to have sth on the t. of one's tongue,** tener algo en la punta de la lengua. **II** *vtr (pt & pp tipped)* poner regatón *or* cantera a; **tipped cigarettes,** cigarrillos *mpl* con filtro; **tipped with steel,** con punta de acero.

tip² [tɪp] **I** *n* **1** *(gratuity)* propina *f.* **2** *(advice)* consejo *m;* **to take a t. from sb,** seguir el consejo de algn. **3** *Sport (racing)* pronóstico *m.* **II** *vtr (pt & pp tipped)* **1** dar una propina a. **2** *Sport* pronosticar; **to t. a horse,** pronosticar que un caballo ganará una carrera. ◆ **tip off** *vtr (police)* pasar información a.

tip³ [tɪp] I *n* **rubbish t.,** basurero *m*, vertedero *m*. II *vtr (pt & pp **tipped**)* ladear, inclinar; *(rubbish)* verter, **to t; sth onto the floor,** tirar algo al suelo. III *vi* **to t. (up),** ladearse; *(cart)* bascular. ◆ **tip over** I *vtr* volcar. II *vi* volcarse; *(boat)* zozobrar.

tipper lorry ['tɪpəlɒrɪ] *n Aut* volquete *m*.

tipped [tɪpt] *pt & pp see* **tip.**

tipping ['tɪpɪŋ] *n* vertido *m*; **'t. (of rubbish) prohibzited',** 'prohibido verter basura'.

tipple ['tɪpəl] *fam* I *vi* empinar el codo. II *n* bebida *f* alcohólica; **what's your t.?,** ¿qué te gusta beber?

tippler ['tɪplə'] *n fam* bebedor,-a *m,f*, borrachín,-ina *m,f*.

tipster ['tɪpstə'] *n Sport* pronosticador,-a *m,f*.

tipsy ['tɪpsɪ] *adj (**tipsier, tipsiest**)* achispado,-a, piripi; **to get t.,** achisparse.

tiptoe ['tɪptəʊ] I *vi (pt & pp **tiptoed**)* andar de puntillas; **to t. in/out,** entrar/salir de puntillas. II *n* **on t.,** de puntillas.

tiptop ['tɪptɒp] *adj fam* excelente, de primera.

tip-up ['tɪpʌp] *adj (cart, lorry)* basculante; *(seat)* abatible.

TIR [tiːɑːr'ɑːr'] *abbr of* **international road transport,** transporte *m* internacional por carretera, TIR.

tirade [taɪ'reɪd] *n* diatriba *f*, invectiva *f*.

Tirana [tɪ'rɑːnə] *n* Tirana.

tire¹ [taɪə'] *n US see* **tyre.**

tire² [taɪə'] I *vtr* cansar; **to t. sb out,** agotar a algn. II *vi* cansarse, fatigarse; **to t. of doing sth,** cansarse de hacer algo.

tired ['taɪəd] *adj* cansado,-a; **t. out,** rendido,-a; **to be t.,** estar cansado,-a; **to be t. of sth,** estar harto,-a de algo.

tiredness ['taɪədnɪs] *n* cansancio *m*, fatiga *f*.

tireless ['taɪəlɪs] *adj* incansable, infatigable.

tiresome ['taɪəsəm] *adj* pesado,-a, aburrido,-a.

tiring ['taɪərɪŋ] *adj* fatigoso,-a, agotador,-a.

tiro ['taɪərəʊ] *n (pl **tiros**)* see **tyro.**

tissue ['tɪʃuː, 'tɪsjuː] *n* **1** *Biol* tejido *m*. **2** *Tex* tisú *m*. ■ **t. paper,** papel *m* de seda. **3** *(handkerchief)* pañuelo *m* de papel, kleenex® *m*; *fig* **a t. of lies,** una sarta de mentiras.

tit¹ [tɪt] *n Orn* coal t., carbonero *m* garrapinos; **crested t.,** herrerillo *m* capuchino; **great t.,** carbonero *m* común; **long-tailed t.,** mito *m*; **marsh t.,** carbonero *m* palustre; **willow t.,** carbonero *m* sibilino.

tit² [tɪt] *n* **t. for tat,** donde las dan las toman; **to give t. for tat,** devolver la pelota.

tit³ [tɪt] *n sl (breast)* teta *f*.

titanic [taɪ'tænɪk] *adj* titánico,-a.

titbit ['tɪtbɪt] *n* golosina *f*.

titillate ['tɪtɪleɪt] *vtr* excitar.

titillation [tɪtɪ'leɪʃən] *n* excitación *f*.

tit(t)ivato ['tɪtɪveɪt] *vtr* emperifollar; **to t. oneself,** emperifollarse.

title ['taɪtəl] *n* **1** *(gen)* título *n*. ■ *Cin* **credit titles,** créditos *mpl*, ficha técnica; **t. page,** portada *f*; *Theat* **t. role,** papel *m* principal (que da el título a la obra). **2** *Jur* título *m*, derecho *m*. ■ **t. deed,** título *m* or escritura *f* de propiedad.

titled ['taɪtəld] *adj (person)* con título de nobleza, noble.

titter ['tɪtə'] I *vi* reírse nerviosamente; *(foolishly)* reírse tontamente. II *n* risa *f* ahogada; *(foolish)* risilla *f* tonta.

tittle-tattle ['tɪtəltætəl] *n* chismes *mpl*.

titular ['tɪtjʊlə'] *adj* titular.

tizz [tɪz] *n fam*, **tizzy** ['tɪzɪ] *n fam* **to get into a t.,** ponerse nervioso,-a.

TM *abbr of* **trademark,** marca *f* (de fábrica).

tn *US abbr see* **t.**

TNT [tiːen'tiː] *abbr of* **trinitrotoluene,** trinitrotolueno *m*, TNT.

to [tuː; *unstressed before vowels* tʊ, *before consonants* tə] **I** *prep* **1** *(with place)* a; *(expressing direction)* hacia; **airlines to America,** líneas aéreas con destino a América; **from town to town,** de ciudad en ciudad; **he went to France/Japan,** fue a Francia/al Japón; **I'm going to Mary's,** voy a casa de Mary; **I am on my way to his house,** voy hacia su casa; **it is thirty miles to London,** está a treinta millas de Londres; **the road to London,** la carretera de Londres; **to the east,** hacia el este; **to the right,** a la derecha; **what school do you go to?,** ¿a qué escuela vas?; *fig* **the road to ruin,** el camino de la ruina. **2** *(time)* a; **from day to day,** de día en día; **from morning to night,** de la mañana a la noche; **from two to four,** de dos a cuatro; **ten (minutes) to six,** las seis menos diez; *fam* **it's ten to,** son menos diez. **3** *(as far as, until, down to)* hasta; **accurate to a millimetre,** exacto,-a hasta el milímetro; **a year ago to the day,** hace un año exactamente; **soaked to the skin,** calado,-a hasta los huesos. **4** *(with indirect object)* **he gave it to his cousin,** se lo dio a su primo; **to drink to sb,** brindar por algn; **what's that to you?,** ¿qué te importa a ti? **5** *(towards a person)* con, para con; **he was very kind to me,** se portó muy bien conmigo. **6** *(of)* de; **heir to an estate,** heredero *m* de una propiedad; **secretary to the manager,** secretaria *f* del director. **7** *(purpose, result)* **to come to sb's aid,** acudir en auxilio de algn; **to everyone's surprise,** para sorpresa de todos; **to this end,** con este fin. **8** *(according to)* **to all appearances,** según todos los indicios; **to the best of my knowledge,** que yo sepa. **9** *(compared to)* **that's nothing to what I've seen,** eso no es nada en comparación con lo que he visto yo. **10** *(in proportion)* **one house to the square kilometre,** una casa por kilómetro cuadrado; **six votes to four,** seis votos contra cuatro; **to bet ten to one,** apostar diez contra uno. **11** *(about)* **that's all there is to it,** no hay nada más que decir; **there's nothing to it,** es facilísimo; **what did he say to my suggestion?,** ¿qué contestó a mi sugerencia?; **what do you say to a holiday?,** ¿qué te parece ir de vacaciones? **II** *with infin* **1** *with simple infinitives to is not translated but is shown by the verb endings;* **to buy,** comprar; **to come,** venir; **to sell,** vender. **2** *(in order to)* para; *(with verbs of motion or purpose)* a, por; **he did it to help me,** lo hizo para ayudarme; **he stopped to talk,** se detuvo a hablar; **he strove to obtain it,** se esforzó por conseguirlo; **he went to visit him,** fue a visitarle. **3** *various verbs followed by dependent infinitives take particular prepositions* (a, de, en, por, con, para, etc) *and others take no preposition; see the entry of the verb in question.* **4** *(with adj and infin)* a, de; **difficult to do,** difícil de hacer; **ready to listen,** dispuesto,-a a escuchar; **to be good to eat,** tener buen sabor; **too hot to drink,** demasiado caliente para bebérselo. **5** *(with infin used as noun)* **to lie is unwise,** es imprudente mentir. **6** *(with noun and infin)* **the first to complain,** el primero en quejarse; **the only one to do it,** el único en hacerlo; **this is the time to do it,** éste es el momento de hacerlo; **to have a great deal to do,** tener mucho que hacer. **7** *(on doing sth)* **to look at her you wouldn't imagine that ...,** al verla no te imaginarías que ... . **8** *(expressing following action)* **he awoke to find the light still on,** al despertarse encontró la lámpara todavía encendida. **9** *(with verbs of ordering, wishing, etc)* **he asked me to do it,** me pidió que lo hiciera; **I want him to do it,** quiero que lo haga. **10** *(expressing obligation)* **fifty employes are to go,** cincuenta empleados deben ser despedidos; **these are still to be done,** éstos quedan por hacer; **to have to do sth,** tener que hacer algo. **11** *(replacing infin)* **go if you want to,** váyase si quiere; **I didn't want to go, but I had to,** no quería ir, pero no me quedaba más remedio. **III** *adv* **movement to and fro,** vaivén *m*; **to come to,** volver en sí; **to go to and fro,** ir y venir; **to push the door to,** ajustar la puerta.

toad [təʊd] *n Zool* sapo *m*.

toadstool ['təʊdstuːl] *n* hongo *m* (venenoso).

toady ['təʊdɪ] *I n* cobista *mf.* **II** *vtr* dar coba a.

toast¹ [təʊst] **I** *n* *Culin* pan *m* tostado; **a slice** *or* **piece of t.,** una tostada. **II** *vtr* tostar.

toast² [təʊst] **I** *n* (*drink*) brindis *m inv*; **to drink** *or* **give a t. to,** brindar por. **II** *vtr* brindar por.

toaster ['təʊstəʳ] *n* tostador *m* (de pan).

tobacco [tə'bækəʊ] *n* (*pl* **tobaccos** *or* **tobaccoes**) tabaco *m.* ■ **t. pouch,** petaca *f.*

tobacconist [tə'bækənɪst] *n* GB estanquero,-a *m, f*; **t.'s (shop),** estanco *m.*

Tobago [tə'beɪɡəʊ] *n* Tobago.

-to-be [tə'biː] *adj* futuro,-a; **bride-to-be,** novia *f*; **mother-to-be,** futura madre.

toboggan [tə'bɒɡən] **I** *n* tobogán *m.* ■ **t. run, pista** *f* de tobogán. **II** *vi* deslizarse en tobogán.

today [tə'deɪ] **I** *n* hoy *m*; **t.'s paper,** el periódico de hoy. **II** *adv* hoy; (*nowadays*) hoy en día, actualmente; **t. week, a week t.,** de hoy en ocho (días).

toddle ['tɒdəl] **I** *vi* (*child*) dar los primeros pasos; *fam* **I must t. off,** tengo que irme. **II** *n fam* paseíto *m.*

toddler ['tɒdləʳ] *n* niño,-a *m, f* que empieza a andar; **the toddlers,** los pequeñitos.

toddy ['tɒdɪ] *n* (*drink*) ponche *m.*

to-do [tə'duː] *n* (*pl* **to-dos**) lío *m,* jaleo *m*; **what a t.!,** ¡menudo lío!

toe [təʊ] **I** *n* *Anat* dedo *m* del pie; **big t.,** dedo gordo (del pie); *fig* **to be on one's toes,** estar alerta. **II** *vtr* (*pt & pp* **toed**) **to t. the line,** conformarse, obedecer las órdenes.

toecap ['təʊkæp] *n* puntera *f.*

toenail ['təʊneɪl] *n* uña *f* del dedo del pie.

toffee ['tɒfɪ] *n* caramelo *m*; *fam* **he can't sing for t.,** no tiene n idea de cantar.

toffee-nosed ['tɒfɪnəʊzd] *adj* GB *sl* engreído,-a.

together [tə'ɡeðəʳ] *adv* junto, juntos,-as; **all t.,** todos juntos; **the letter arrived t. with the book,** la carta llegó junto con el libro; **to bring t.,** reunir, juntar; **to go** *or* **belong t.,** ir juntos.

togged up [tɒɡd'ʌp] *adj fam* **to get t. up,** emperifollarse.

toggle ['tɒɡəl] *n* botón *m* de una trenca. ■ *Elec* **t. switch** conmutador *m* de palanca.

Togo ['təʊɡəʊ] *n* Togo.

Togolese [təʊɡə'liːz] *adj & n* togolés,-esa (*m, f*).

togs [tɒɡz] *npl fam* ropa *f sing.*

toil [tɔɪl] **I** *n* trabajo *m* duro, esfuerzo *m.* **II** *vi* afanarse, trabajar (duro); **to t. up a hill,** subir penosamente una cuesta.

toilet ['tɔɪlɪt] *n* **1** (*lavatory*) wáter *m,* retrete *m*; (*for public*) servicios *mpl,* lavabos *mpl.* ■ **t. paper** *or* **tissue,** papel *m* higiénico; **t. roll,** rollo *m* de papel higiénico. **2** (*washing etc*) aseo *m* (personal). ■ **t. bag** *or* **case,** neceser *m*; **t. soap,** jabón *m* de tocador.

toiletries ['tɔɪlɪtrɪz] *npl* artículos *mpl* de aseo.

token ['təʊkən] **I** *n* **1** (*sign*) señal *f*, prueba *f*; **as a t. of respect,** en señal de respeto; **t. of friendship,** prueba de amistad. **2** *Tel* ficha *f*; *Com* vale *m.* ■ **book/record t.,** vale *m* para comprar libros/discos. **II** *adj* (*payment, strike*) simbólico,-a.

told [təʊld] *pt & pp see* **tell.**

tolerable ['tɒlərəbəl] *adj* (*pain*) tolerable, soportable; (*performance, effort*) regular, tolerable.

tolerance ['tɒlərəns] *n* tolerancia *f.*

tolerant ['tɒlərənt] *adj* tolerante.

tolerate ['tɒləreɪt] *vtr* tolerar, soportar; **I can't t. noise,** no aguanto *or* soporto el ruido.

toleration [tɒlə'reɪʃən] *n* tolerancia *f.*

toll¹ [təʊl] *vtr & vi* (*bell*) tañir, doblar; **to t. for the dead,** doblar las campanas, tocar a muertos.

toll² [təʊl] *n* **1** *Aut* peaje *m*; **t. at 200 metres,** peaje a 200 metros; **t. bridge/motorway,** puente *m*/autopista *f* de peaje. **2** (*loss*) pérdidas *fpl*; **rent takes a heavy t. of one's income,** el alquiler supone una gran parte de los ingresos; **the death t. on the roads,** el número de víctimas mortales en las carreteras.

tolling ['təʊlɪŋ] *n* (*of bell*) doblar *m,* tañido *m* (de una campana).

Toltec ['tɒltek] *adj & n* *Hist* tolteca (*mf*).

Tom [tɒm] *prn* Tomás; *fam* **any T., Disk or Harry,** todo hijo de vecino; *fam* **Peeping T.,** mirón *m.*

tomahawk ['tɒməhɔːk] *n* tomahawk *m,* hacha *f* de guerra.

tomato [tə'mɑːtəʊ, US tə'meɪtəʊ] *n* (*pl* **tomatoes**) *Bot* tomate *m.* ■ *Culin* **t. ketchup,** ketchup *m*; **t. plant,** tomatera *f*; **t. sauce,** salsa *f* de tomate.

tomb [tuːm] *n* tumba *f,* sepulcro *m.*

tombola [tɒm'bəʊlə] *n* GB tómbola *f.*

tomboy ['tɒmbɔɪ] *n* chica *f* poco femenina.

tombstone ['tuːmstəʊm] *n* lápida *f* sepulcral.

tomcat ['tɒmkæt] *n* *Zool* gato *m* (macho).

tome [təʊm] *n* tomo *m.*

tomfool [tɒm'fuːl] *adj* (*plan etc*) absurdo,-a, ridículo,-a.

tomfoolery [tɒm'fuːlərɪ] *n* tonterías *fpl.*

Tommy gun ['tɒmɪɡʌn] *n fam* metralleta *f.*

tomorrow [tə'mɒrəʊ] **I** *n* mañana *m*; **the day after t.,** pasado mañana; **t. night,** mañana por la noche. **II** *adv* mañana; **see you t.!,** ¡hasta mañana!; **t. week,** mañana en ocho (días).

tom-tom ['tɒmtɒm] *n* tam-tam *m.*

ton [tʌn] *n* tonelada *f*; **t. ship,** un barco de 500 toneladas; *fam* **we have tons of it,** tenemos montones.

tone [təʊn] **I** *n* **1** tono *m*; **in a gentle t.,** en tono dulce; **to change one's t.,** cambiar de tono; **t. of voice,** tono de voz. **2** (*of colour*) tono *m,* matiz *m.* **3** (*quality, class*) clase *f*; **he's lowering the t. of the place,** su presencia hace bajar el nivel del lugar. **4** *Fin* tendencia *f*; **the t. of the market,** la tendencia del mercado. **5** *Med* tono *m* (muscular). **II** *vi* **to t. with sth,** armonizar con algo. ◆ **tone down** *vtr* atenuar, suavizar.

tone-deaf ['təʊndef] *adj* **to be t.-d.,** no tener oído.

toneless ['təʊnlɪs] *adj* (*voice*) monótono,-a.

Tonga ['tɒŋɡə, 'tɒŋə] *n* Tonga.

Tongan ['tɒŋən] *adj & n* tongano,-a (*m, f*).

tongs [tɒŋz] *npl* (*for sugar*) tenacillas *fpl*; (*fire*) tenazas *fpl*; *Hairdr* **curling t.,** tenacillas (de rizar).

tongue [tʌŋ] *n* **1** *Anat* lengua *f*; **to stick one's t. out at sb,** sacar la lengua a algn; *fig* **to hold one's t.,** morderse la lengua; *fig* **to say sth t. in cheek,** decir algo con la boca pequeña. ■ *fig* **t. twister,** trabalenguas *m inv.* **2** (*language*) lengua *f,* idioma *m*; **mother/native t.,** lengua materna/nativa. **3** (*of shoe*) lengüeta *f*; (*of bell*) badajo *m.*

tongue-tied ['tʌŋtaɪd] *adj* mudo,-a (por la timidez); **she gets t.,** se le traba la lengua.

tonic ['tɒnɪk] **I** *n* **1** *Med* tónico *m.* **2** (*drink*) tónica *f*; **a gin and t.,** un gintonic. **II** *adj* tónico,-a. ■ *Mus* **t. sol-fa,** solfeo *m.*

tonight [tə'naɪt] *adv & n* esta noche.

tonnage ['tʌnɪdʒ] *n* (*of ship*) tonelaje *m.*

tonne [tʌn] *n see* **ton.**

tonsil ['tɒnsəl] *n* *Anat* amígdala *f*; **to have one's tonsils out,** ser operado,-a de las amígdalas.

tonsillectomy [tɒnsɪ'lektəmɪ] *n* *Med* amigdalotomía *f.*

tonsilitis [tɒnsɪ'laɪtɪs] *n* *Med* amigdalitis *f.*

too [tuː] *adv* **1** (*besides*) además, también; **it was very expensive t.,** y además era muy caro,-a. **2** (*also*) también; **I shall go t.,** yo iré también. **3** (*excessively*) demasiado; **I know him all t. well,** le conozco de sobra; **ten pounds t.**

much, diez libras de más; **the work is t. much for me,** es demasiado trabajo para mí; **t. frequently,** con demasiada frecuencia; **t. much money,** demasiado dinero; **t. old,** demasiado viejo; *fam* **he's not t. well,** está pachucho.

took [tʊk] *pt see* **take.**

tool [tuːl] **I** *n* **1** *(utensil)* herramienta *f*, utensilio *m*; **farming/gardening tools,** útiles *mpl or* herramientas de labranza/jardinería. ■ **t. shed,** cobertizo *m* (para herramientas). **2** *(person)* instrumento *m*; **to make a t. of sb,** servise de algn. **II** *vtr (metal, leather)* labrar; *(cover of book)* estampar.

toolbag ['tuːlbæg] *n* bolsa *f* de herramientas.

toolbox ['tuːlbɒks] *n* caja *f* de herramientas.

tooling ['tuːlɪŋ] *n (of metal)* labrado *m; (of cover, of book)* estampación *f*.

toolkit ['tuːlkɪt] *n* juego *m* de herramientas

toot [tuːt] **I** *vtr* tocar **II** *vt Aut* tocar la bocina **III** *n Aut* bocinazo *m. Mus* toque *m* (de trompeta)

tooth [tuːθ] *n (pl* **teeth** [tiːθ]*)* **1** *Anat* diente *m (molar)* muela *f*. **I had a t. out,** me sacaron *or* extrajeron un diente *or* una muela, **(set of) false teeth,** dentadura *f* postiza, *(child)* **to cut one's teeth,** echar los dientes, *fig* **to be sick to the teeth of sth,** estar hasta la coronilla de algo, *fig* **to fight t. and nail,** luchar a brazo partido, *fig* **to have a sweet t.,** ser goloso,-a, *fam* **long in the t.,** en rado,-a en años **2** *(of saw)* diente *m, (of comb)* púa *f*

toothache ['tuːθeɪk] *n* dolor *m* de muelas

toothbrush ['tuːθbrʌʃ] *n* cepillo *m* de dientes

toothless ['tuːθlɪs] *adj* sin dientes, desdentado,-a

toothpaste ['tuːθpeɪst] *n* pasta *f* dentífrica *or* de dientes, dentífrico *m*

toothpick ['tuːθpɪk] *n* mondadientes *m inv*

toothy ['tuːθɪ] *adj (toothier, toothiest)* **to give a t. smile,** sonreír enseñando los dientes

top¹ [tɒp] **I** *n* **1** *(upper part)* parte *f* superior, parte de arriba parta alta, *(of hill)* cumbre *f*, cima *f, (of tree)* copa *f*, **from t. to bottom,** de arriba a abajo, **on t. of the tower,** encima de la torre, **put them on t.,** ponlos encima, *fig* **from t. to toe,** de pies a cabeza, *fig* **on t. of it all he wanted ...,** para colmo quería ..., *fig* **to come out on t.,** salir ganando ■ **t. hat,** sombrero *m* de copa **2** *(surface)* superficie *f*, **to come to the t.,** salir a la superficie **3** *(head)* cabeza *f*, **at the t. of the list,** a la cabeza de la lista, *fig* **to blow one's t.,** salirse de sus casillas **4** *(of bottle, container)* tapa *f*, tapón *m* **5** *(garment)* blusa *f*, camiseta *f* **6** *(best)* lo mejor, **this one is the t. of the range,** este es el mejor de su categoría **7** *Aut* directa *f* **8** *fig* **at the t. of one's voice,** a voz en cuello *or* en grito **II** *adj* **1** *(part)* superior, de arriba ■ **t. drawer,** el cajón de arriba, **the t. floor,** el último piso, **t. coat,** *(of paint)* última mano *f*, *(overcoat)* abrigo *m* **2** *(highest)* extremo,-a, máximo,-a, *Mus* **the t. notes,** las notas más altas ■ *Aut* **t. gear,** directa *f* **3** *(best)* primero,-a, principal, **the t. people,** la élite, *Educ* **to be t.,** ser el primero de la clase, *fam* **the t. dog,** ser un gallito **III** *vtr (pt & pp* **topped)** **1** *(cover)* coronar, rematar, **to t. a cake with ...,** cubrir una tarta con ..., *fam* **and to t. it all ...,** y para colmo ... **2** *(tree)* desmochar, **to t. and tall gooseberries,** quitar los rabillos a las grosellas **3** *(lead)* encabezar, *Theat* **to t. the bill,** encabezar el reparto. ◆ **top up** *vtr* llenar hasta el tope, *Aut* **to t. up the petrol tank,** llenar el depósito (de gasolina)

top² [tɒp] *n* peonza *f*

topaz ['təʊpæz] *n Min* topacio *m*

top-heavy [tɒp'hevɪ] *adj* demasiado pesado,-a en la parte superior, *fig* poco estable

topic ['tɒpɪk] *n* tema *m*

topical ['tɒpɪkəl] *adj* de actualidad, **t. conversation,** conversación *f* sobre temas de actualidad

topless ['tɒplɪs] *adj* desnudo,-a de cintura para arriba, *(bar)* topless, **t swimsuit,** monobikini *m*, topless *m*

top-level ['tɒplevəl] *adj* de alto nivel

topmost ['tɒpməʊst] *adj* (el) más alto, (la) más alta

topography [tə'pɒgrəfɪ] *n* topografía *f*

topped [tɒpt] *pt & pp see* **top¹.**

topple ['tɒpəl] **I** *vi (building)* derribarse, venirse abajo, **to t. (over),** volcarse **II** *vtr* volcar, *fig (government)* derribar, derrocar

top-secret [tɒp'siːkrɪt] *adj* sumamente secreto,-a

topside ['tɒpsaɪd] *n Culin (beef)* redondo *m*

topsoil ['tɒpsɔɪl] *n* superficie *f* del suelo

topsy-turvy [tɒpsɪ'tɜːvɪ] *adj & adv* al revés, *(in confusion)* en desorden, patas arriba, **a t. world,** un mundo al revés

torch [tɔːtʃ] *n (burning)* antorcha *f*, tea *f*, *(electric)* linterna *f*

torchlight ['tɔːtʃlaɪt] *n* luz *f* de antorchas. ■ **t. procession,** procesión *f* con antorchas

tore [tɔːʳ] *pt see* **tear².**

toreador ['tɒrɪədɔːʳ] *n* torero *m*

torment [tɔː'ment] **I** *vtr* atormentar, torturar, *fig* **tormented by hunger,** atormentado,-a por el hambre **II** *n* ['tɔːment] tormento *m*, suplicio *m*

tormentor [tɔː'mentəʳ] *n* atormentador,-a *m, f*

torn [tɔːn] *pp see* **tear².**

tornado [tɔː'neɪdəʊ] *n (pl* **tornados** *or* **tornadoes)** tornado *m*

torpedo [tɔː'piːdəʊ] **I** *n (pl* **torpedoes)** torpedo *m*, **t. boat,** torpedero,-a *m, f* **II** *vtr (pt & pp* **torpedoed)** torpedear

torpid ['tɔːpɪd] *adj (sleepy)* letárgico,-a, somnoliento,-a, aletargado,-a, *(sluggish)* torpe

torpor ['tɔːpəʳ] *n* letargo *m*, *(sluggishness)* torpeza *f*

torrent ['tɒrənt] *n* torrente *m*, **to rain in torrents,** llover a cántaros, *fig* **t. of abuse,** torrente de in sultos

torrential [tɒ'renʃəl] *adj* torrencial

torrid ['tɒrɪd] *adj* tórrido,-a

torso ['tɔːsəʊ] *n (pl* **torsos)** torso *m*

tortoise ['tɔːtəs] *n* tortuga *f* de tierra

tortoiseshell ['tɔːtəsʃel] **I** *n* carey *n*, concha *f* **II** *adj* de carey

tortuous ['tɔːtjʊəs] *adj* tortuoso,-a

torture ['tɔːtʃəʳ] **I** *n* vtr torturar, atormentar **II** *n* tortura *f*, tormento *m*, *fig* **it was sheer t.,** fue un auténtico suplicio

Tory ['tɔːrɪ] *adj & n Pol* conservador,-a *(m, f)*, **the T. Party,** el Partido Conservador

toss [tɒs] **I** *vtr* **1** *(ball)* lanzar, tirar, *(rider)* derribar, desmontar, **he was tossed by a bull,** fue embestido por un toro, **to t. (up) a coin,** jugar a cara o cruz **2** *(throw about)* sacudir, agitar, **tossed by the waves,** sacudido,-a por las olas, **to t. one's head,** sacudir la cabeza **II** *vi* **1** *(move)* **to t. about,** agitarse **2** *(coin)* **to t. and turn,** dar vueltas en la cama **2** *Sport* **to t. (up),** sortear **III** *n* **1** *(of ball)* lanzamiento *m*, *(of coin)* sorteo *m* (a cara o cruz) **2** *(of head)* sacudida *f*, movimiento *m* brusco (de la cabeza). ◆ **toss off** *vtr* **1** *(drink)* beber de un trago **2** *(write)* escribir rápidamente

toss-up ['tɒsʌp] *n* **it's a t.-up whether we do it or not,** quizá lo hagamos, quizá no, **to settle sth by a t.-up,** echar algo a cara o cruz

tot¹ [tɒt] *n* **1** *(child)* **(tiny) t.,** nene,-a *m, f*, peque *mf* **2** *(of whisky etc)* trago *m*

tot² [tɒt] *GB* **I** *vtr (pt & pp* **totted) to t. up,** sumar **II** *vt* **to t. up to,** ascender a

total ['təʊtəl] **I** *n* total *m*, *(in bill)* importe *m* total, **grand t.,** suma *f* total **II** *adj* total, global, **a t. failure,** un fracaso total, **they were in t. ignorance of it,** lo ignoraban totalmente *or* por completo **III** *vtr (pt & pp* **totalled,** *US* **totaled)** sumar, hacer el total. **IV** *vi* **to t. up to,** ascender a, sumar. ◆ **totally** *adv* totalmente, completamente.

totalitarian [təʊtælɪ'teərɪən] *adj* totalitario,-a.

totalitarianism [təʊtælɪ'teərɪənɪzəm] *n* totalitarismo *m*.

totality [təʊ'tælɪtɪ] n totalidad f.

totalizator ['təʊtəlaɪzeɪtə'] n totalizador m.

totalled ['təʊtəld] pt & pp see **total.**

tote[1] [təʊt] I vtr fam acarrear. II n US **t. bag,** petate m.

tote[2] [təʊt] n fam totalizador m.

totem ['təʊtəm] n tótem m.

totted ['tɒtɪd] pt & pp see **tot**[2].

totter ['tɒtə'] vi tambalearse; **to t. in,** entrar tambaleándose.

tottering ['tɒtərɪŋ] adj tambaleante; **a t. empire,** un imperio a punto de caer; **t. steps,** pasos titubeantes.

toucan ['tuːkən] n tucán m.

touch [tʌtʃ] I vtr 1 (gen) tocar; (lightly) rozar; **to t. sb on the shoulder,** tocar a algn en el hombro; fig the law can't t. him, la ley no puede hacer nada contra él; fig to t. on a subject, tocar un tema; fam t. wood!, ¡toca madera! 2 (consume) tocar; I never t. wine, nunca bebo vino. 3 (equal) igualar; nobody can t. Frank as a comedian, Frank no tiene rival como cómico. 4 (move) conmover, afectar; I was touched by their kindness, me llegó al alma su amabilidad. 5 fam to t. sb for a loan, dar un sablazo a algn. II vi tocarse; (lightly) rozarse; (properties) ser contiguos,-as, tocar; fig it was t. and go whether we caught the train, estuvimos a punto de perder el tren. III n 1 (gen) toque m; (light contact) roce m; (of typist) pulsación f; Mus ejecución f; I felt a t. on the arm, sentí que me tocaban en el brazo. 2 (sense of touch) tacto m; rough to the t., áspero,-a al tacto. 3 (detail) detalle m; it was a nice t. of his, fue un detalle de su parte; to add a few touches to a picture, retocar un cuadro; to put the finishing t. to sth, dar el último toque a algo. 4 (ability) he's losing his t., está perdiendo su habilidad. 5 (contact) contacto m; the personal t., el contacto personal; to be/get/keep on t. with sb, estar/ponerse/mantenerse en contacto con algn; to be out of t. with sth, no estar al tanto de algo; to get in t. with the police, avisar a la policía. 6 (small amount) pizca f; a t. of salt/garlic, una pizca de sal/ajo; to have a t. of flu, estar ligeramente griposo,-a; with a t. of bitterness, con una nota de amargura. 7 Sport in t. fuera de juego. ◆ **touch down** vi 1 (plane) aterrizar, tomar tierra. 2 Rugby hacer un ensayo m. ◆ **touch off** vtr desencadenar, provocar. ◆ **touch up** vtr (picture) retocar.

touchdown ['tʌtʃdaʊn] n 1 (of plane) aterrizaje m; (of space capsule) amerizaje m. 2 Rugby ensayo m.

touched [tʌtʃt] adj 1 (moved) emocionado,-a, conmovido,-a. 2 fam (crazy) tocado,-a, chiflado,-a.

touchiness ['tʌtʃɪnɪs] n susceptibilidad f.

touching ['tʌtʃɪŋ] I adj conmovedor,-a, enternecedor,-a. II prep tocante a, respecto a.

touchline ['tʌtʃlaɪn] n Rugby línea f de banda.

touch-type ['tʌtʃtaɪp] vi mecanografiar (sin mirar el teclado).

touchy ['tʌtʃɪ] adj (touchier, touchiest) fam (person) susceptible; (subject) delicado,-a.

tough [tʌf] I adj (material) fuerte, resistente; (test) duro,-a, difícil; (competitor etc) fuerte, resistente; (criminal, meat) duro,-a; (judgement, punishment) severo,-a; (problem) difícil; fam t. luck!, ¡mala suerte! II n (person) matón m.

toughen ['tʌfən] I vtr endurecer. II vi endurecerse.

toughness ['tʌfnɪs] n (of material etc) resistencia f; (of test) dureza f; (of judgement, punishment) severidad f; (of problem, job) dificultad f.

Toulouse [tuː'luːz] n Tolosa.

toupee ['tuːpeɪ] n tupé m.

tour[2] [tʊə'] I n 1 (journey, holiday) viaje m; **package t.,** viaje organizado; **to do a t. of Europe,** hacer un viaje por Europa. ■ **walking t.,** excursión f a pie. 2 (of building, monument) visita f; (of city) recorrido m turístico; Ind t. **of inspection,** recorrido de inspección. 3 Sport Theat gira f; **on t.,** de gira. II vtr 1 (country) recorrer, viajar por. 2

(building) visitar. 3 Theat estar de gira; **to t. the province** recorrer las provincias. ■ **t. comany,** compañía f que está de gira. III vi estar de viaje.

tour de force [tʊədə'fɔːs] n hazaña f, proeza f.

tourism ['tʊərɪzəm] n turismo m.

tourist ['tʊərɪst] n turista mf; **the t. trade,** la industria del turismo. ■ **t. agency,** agencia f de viajes; **t. centre,** centro m turístico; **t. class,** clase f turista; **t. menu,** menú m turístico.

touristy ['tʊərɪstɪ] adj pej demasiado turístico,-a.

tournament ['tʊənəmənt] n Sport torneo m.

tourniquet ['tʊənɪkeɪ] n Med torniquete m.

tousle ['taʊzəl] vtr despeinar.

tousled ['taʊzəld] adj (hair) despeinado,-a.

tout [taʊt] I vtr Com tratar de vender; (tickets) revender. II vi salir a la caza y captura de compradores or clientes. III n 1 Com gancho m. ■ **ticket t.,** revendedor m de entradas. 2 Sport (in racing) pronosticador m.

tow [təʊ] I n 1 (pull) **to take a ship/car in t.,** remolcar un barco/un coche; **we can give you a t.,** podemos remolcar su coche; fam he always has his family in t., siempre va acompañado de su familia. 2 (vehicle towed) vehículo m remolcado; Naut a t. of barges, un convoy de barcazas. II vtr remolcar; his car was towed away by the police, la grúa se llevó su coche.

towards [tə'wɔːdz, tɔːdz] prep 1 (direction) hacia; **t. me,** hacia mí. 2 (of time) hacia, alrededor de; **t. noon,** hacia mediodía; **t. the end of his life,** hacia el fin de su vida. 3 (for) hacia, (para) con; he feels a great affection t. her, siente gran afecto hacia ella; our duty t. others, nuestro deber para con los demás; **to save t. sth,** ahorrar para algo; **what is your attitude t. religion?,** ¿cuál es su actitud respecto a la religión?

towbar ['təʊbɑː'] n Aut barra f de remolque.

towboat ['təʊbəʊt] n Naut remolcador m.

towel ['taʊəl] I n toalla f. ■ **hand t.,** toallita f; **t. rail,** toallero m. II vtr **to t. dry,** secar con una toalla.

towelling ['taʊəlɪŋ] n Tex felpa f.

tower ['taʊə'] I n torre f; (bell) t., campanario m; fig he's a t. of strength, es un poderoso apoyo. II vi encumbrarse; **to t. over** or **above sth,** dominar algo.

towering ['taʊərɪŋ] adj grande, sobresaliente, altísimo,-a.

towing ['təʊɪŋ] n (act) remolque m.

towline ['təʊlaɪn] n see **towrope.**

town [taʊn] n ciudad f; (small town) pueblo m, población f; **to go into t.,** ir al centro; fam **to go out on the t., to paint the t. red,** ir de juerga; fam **to go to t. over sth,** gastar dinero a manos llenas en algo. ■ **t. council,** ayuntamiento m; **t. councillor,** concejal,-a m, f; edil,-a m, f; **t. hall,** ayuntamiento m; **t. planning,** urbanismo m.

townsfolk ['taʊnzfəʊk] npl see **townspeople.**

township ['taʊnʃɪp] n municipio m.

townsman ['taʊnzmən] n (pl townsmen) ciudadano m.

townspeople ['taʊnzpiːpəl] npl ciudadanos mpl, conciudadanos mpl.

townswoman ['taʊnzwʊmən] n (pl townswomen ['taʊnzwɪmɪn]) ciudadana f.

towpath ['təʊpɑːθ] n camino m de sirga.

towrope ['təʊrəʊp] n cable m de remolque.

toxaemia, US **toxemia** [tɒk'siːmɪə] n Med toxemia f.

toxic ['tɒksɪk] adj Med tóxico,-a.

toxicologist [tɒksɪ'kɒlədʒɪst] n Med toxicólogo,-a m, f.

toxicology [tɒksɪ'kɒlədʒɪ] n Med toxicología f.

toxin ['tɒksɪn] n Med toxina f.

toy [tɔɪ] I n juguete m. ■ **t. car,** coche m de juguete; **t. trumpet,** trompeta f de niño. II vi jugar; **to t. with an idea,** acariciar una idea; **to t. with one's food,** comer sin gana, juguetear con la comida; **to t. with sb's feelings,** jugar con los sentimientos de algn.

toyshop ['tɔɪʃɒp] *n* juguetería *f*.

trace [treɪs] **I** *n* **1** *(sign)* indicio *m*, vestigio *m*, señal *f*; **there's no t. of it**, no queda ningún vestigio de ello; **to disappear without a t.**, desaparecer sin dejar huella. ■ *Chem* **t. element**, oligoelemento *m*. **2** *(tracks)* huella(s) *f(pl)*, rastro *m*. **II** *vtr* **1** *(drawing)* calcar. **2** *(plan)* trazar, bosquejar. **3** *(track down, locate)* seguir la pista de; **he has been traced to Paris**, le han seguido la pista hasta París; **he traced his family (back) to the Crusades**, el origen de su familia se remonta a las Cruzadas; **I can't t. any reference to the accident**, no encuentro ninguna mención del accidente; **to t. lost goods**, encontrar *or* recobrar unos objetos perdidos.

tracer ['treɪsəʳ] *adj Mil* **t. bullet**, bala *f* trazadora.

tracery ['treɪsərɪ] *n* (*pl* **traceries**) *Archit* **(window) t.**, tracería *f*.

trachea [trə'kiːə] *n* (*pl* **tracheae** [trə'kiːiː]) *Anat* tráquea *f*.

tracheotomy [trækɪ'ɒtəmɪ] *n Med* traqueotomía *f*.

tracing ['treɪsɪŋ] *n* calco *m*. ■ **t. paper**, papel *m* de calco.

track [træk] **I** *n* *(mark, trail)* huellas *fpl*, pista *f*; **to follow in sb's tracks**, seguir la pista a algn; **to keep/lose t. of sb**, no perder/perder de vista a algn; **to throw sb off the t.**, despistar a algn; *fig* **to make tracks**, largarse, marcharse. **2** *(pathway)* camino *m*; **off the beaten t.**, lugar *m* apartado *or* perdido; **to be on the right/wrong t.**, ir por el buen/mal camino; **to put sb on the right t.**, encaminar a algn. **3** *Sport* pista *f*; *(for motor racing)* autódromo *m*, circuito *m*. ■ **t. events**, atletismo *m sing* en pista; **t. racing**, carreras *fpl* en pista; **t. shoes**, zapatillas *mpl* de atletismo; *fig* **t. record**, historial *m*. **4** *Rail* vía *f*; **single t.**, vía única; *fig* **he has a one-t. mind**, no piensa más que en eso. **5** *(on record)* canción *f*. **6** *(of tractor)* oruga *f*. **II** *vtr* *(follow, hunt)* rastrear, seguir la pista de; *(with radar)* seguir la trayectoria de. ◆ **track down** *vtr (locate)* localizar, encontrar; *(investigate)* averiguar.

tracked [trækt] *adj Aut* con orugas.

tracker ['trækəʳ] *n* **t. dog**, perro *m* rastreador.

tracksuit ['træksuːt] *n* chandal *m*, chándal *m*.

tract¹ [trækt] *n (expanse)* extensión *f*.

tract² [trækt] *n (treatise)* tratado *m*; *(pamphlet)* folleto *m*.

tractability [træktə'bɪlɪtɪ] *n* docilidad *f*.

tractable ['træktəbəl] *adj* dócil, tratable.

traction ['trækʃən] *n* tracción *f*. ■ *Rail* **t. engine**, locomotora *f* de tracción; *Rail* **t. wheels**, ruedas *fpl* tractoras *or* de tracción.

tractor ['træktəʳ] *n* tractor *m*.

trade [treɪd] **I** *n* **1** *(job)* oficio *m*; **he's a carpenter by t.**, es carpintero de oficio; **to carry on a t.**, ejercer un oficio. **2** *(business)* industria *f*; **the building t.**, (la industria de) la construcción. **3** *Com* comercio *m*, negocios *mpl*; *GB* **Board of T.**, *US* **Department of T.**, Ministerio *m* de Comercio; **foreign t.**, comercio exterior; **it's good for t.**, es bueno para los negocios; **the t. in diamonds**, el comercio de diamantes; *fam* **to do a roaring t.**, vender muchísimo. ■ **t. name**, nombre *m* comercial; **t. union**, sindicato *m*; **t. unionism**, sindicalismo *m*; **t. unionist**, sindicalista *mf*. **4** **t. winds**, vientos *mpl* alisios. **II** *vi* comerciar **(in**, en); *fig* **to t. on sb's ignorance**, aprovecharse de la ignorancia de algn. **III** *vtr* **to t. sth for sth**, cambiar *or* trocar algo por algo. ◆ **trade in** *vtr* dar como entrada; **I'm trading in my old car for a new one**, el coche viejo me sirve de entrada para el nuevo.

trademark ['treɪdmɑːk] *n* marca *f* (de fábrica); **registered t.**, marca registrada.

trader ['treɪdəʳ] *n* comerciante *mf*.

tradesman ['treɪdzmən] *n* (*pl* **tradesmen**) comerciante *m*; *(shopkeeper)* tendero *m*.

trading ['treɪdɪŋ] *n* comercio *m*. ■ *GB* **t. estate**, zona *f* industrial.

tradition [trə'dɪʃən] *n* tradición *f*.

traditional [trə'dɪʃənəl] *adj* tradicional.

traffic ['træfɪk] **I** *n* **1** *Aut* tráfico *m*, circulación *f*; **heavy t.**, circulación densa. ■ **t. island**, refugio *m*; **t. jam**, atasco *m*, embotellamiento *m*; **t. lights**, semáforos *mpl*; **t. warden**, ≈ guardia *mf* urbano,-a. **2** *(trade)* tráfico *m*, comercio *m*; **t. in arms/drugs**, tráfico de armas/ narcóticos. ■ **white slave t.**, trata *f* de blancas. **II** *vi (pt & pp trafficked)* traficar; **to t. in drugs**, traficar con droga.

trafficator ['træfɪkeɪtəʳ] *n Aut* intermitente *m*.

trafficked ['træfɪkt] *pt & pp see* **traffic.**

trafficker ['træfɪkəʳ] *n* traficante *mf*.

tragedy ['trædʒɪdɪ] *n* tragedia *f*; **the t. of it was ...**, lo trágico fue que ... .

tragic ['trædʒɪk] *adj* trágico,-a. ■ *Theat* **t. actor**, actor *m* dramático.

trail [treɪl] **I** *vtr* **1** *(drag)* **to t. sth (along)**, arrastrar algo. **2** *(follow)* rastrear. **II** *vi* **1** *(drag)* arrastrarse; **to have sth trailing behind you**, llevar algo arrastrando. **2** *(linger)* **to t. (along)**, rezagarse. **3** *(of plant)* trepar. **III** *n* **1** *(track)* pista *f*, rastro *m*; **to pick up the t.**, encontrar la pista. **2** *(path)* senda *f*, camino *m*. **3** *(of smoke)* estela *f*; *fig* **to leave a t. of destruction**, arrasar todo al pasar. ◆ **trail away**, **trail off** *vi (voice)* esfumarse, apagarse.

trailer ['treɪləʳ] *n* **1** *Aut* remolque *m*. **2** *US Aut (caravan)* caravana *f*. **3** *Cin* trailer *m*, avance *m*.

trailing ['treɪlɪŋ] *adj (plant)* trepador,-a.

train [treɪn] **I** *n* **1** *Rail* tren *m*; **to board the t.**, subir al tren; **to change trains**, cambiar de tren, hacer transbordo; **to travel by t.**, viajar en tren. ■ **goods t.**, mercancías *m inv*; **passenger t.**, tren *m* de pasajeros. **2** *(of vehicle)* convoy *m*; *(of mules)* recua *f*; *(of followers)* séquito *m*; *(of animals)* serie *f*, sucesión *f*. **3** *(of dress)* cola *f*. **4** *Tech* **t. of gears**, tren *m* de engranajes. **II** *vtr* **1** *(teach)* formar, capacitar, preparar; *Sport* entrenar; *(animal)* amaestrar; *(voice etc)* educar. **2** *(plant)* guiar; **to t. a plant along a wall**, hacer trepar una planta por una pared. **3** *(gun)* apuntar **(on**, a); *(camera)* enfocar **(on**, a). **III** *vi (be taught)* formarse prepararse; *(practise)* ejercitarse; *Sport* entrenarse; **he is training as a teacher/lawyer**, está estudiando magisterio/derecho.

trainee [treɪ'niː] *n* persona *f* que sigue un curso de formación profesional; *(apprentice)* aprendiz,-a *m,f*.

trainer ['treɪnəʳ] *n* **1** *Sport* entrenador,-a *m, f*; *(of dogs)* amaestrador,-a *m, f*; *(of lions, horses)* domador,-a *m, f*. **2** **trainers**, *(shoes)* zapatillas *mpl* de deporte.

training ['treɪnɪŋ] *n (instruction)* formación *f*, capacitación *f*; *Sport* entrenamiento *m*; *(of animals)* amaestramiento *m*; *(of lions, horses)* doma *f*; **to go into t.**, entrenarse; **vocational t.**, formación profesional.

traipse [treɪps] *vi fam* andar, vagar; **to t. round the shops**, ir de tienda en tienda.

trait [treɪt] *n* rasgo *m*.

traitor ['treɪtəʳ] *n* traidor,-a *m, f*; **to turn t.**, pasarse al enemigo.

trajectory [trə'dʒektərɪ] *n* trayectoria *f*.

tram [træm] *n*, **tramcar** ['træmkɑːʳ] *n* tranvía *m*.

tramp [træmp] **I** *vi* **1** *(travel on foot)* caminar, viajar a pie. **2** *(walk heavily)* andar *or* caminar con pasos pesados. **II** *n* **1** *(person)* vagabundo,-a *m, f*, *pej* **she's a t.**, es una fulana. **2** *(hike)* caminata *f*. **3** *(sound)* ruido *m* de pasos pesados. **4** *Naut* **t. (steamer)**, vapor *m* volandero.

trample ['træmpəl] **I** *vtr* **to t. down the grass**, hollar la hierba; **to t. sth, underfoot**, pisotear algo. **II** *vi* **to t. on sth**, pisotear *or* pisar algo; *fig* **to t. on sb's feelings**, herir los sentimientos de algn.

trampoline ['træmpəliːn] *n Sport* trampolín *m*.

trance [trɑːns] *n* trance *m*; **to go into a t.**, entrar en trance.

tranquil ['træŋkwɪl] *adj* tranquilo,-a, sereno,-a.

tranquillity, *US* **tranquility** [træŋ'kwɪlɪtɪ] *n* tranquilidad *f*, serenidad *f*.

tranquillize, *US* **tranquilize** ['træŋkwɪlaɪz] *vtr* tranquilizar, calmar.

tranquillizer, *US* **tranquilizer** ['træŋkwɪlaɪzə'] *n* tranquilizante *m*, calmante *m*.

trans *abbr of* **translated,** traducido,-a (por), trad.

transact [træn'zækt] *vtr* negociar; **to t. business with sb,** hacer un negocio con algn.

transaction [træn'zækʃən] *n (procedure)* tramitación *f*; *(deal)* transacción *f*, operación *f* (comercial).

transalpine [trænz'ælpaɪn] *adj* transalpino,-a transalpino,-a.

transatlantic [trænzət'læntɪk] *adj* transatlántico,-a trasatlántico,-a.

transcend [træn'send] *vtr* estar por encima de, sobrepasar, rebasar; *Philos Rel* trascender, trascender.

transcendental [trænsen'dentəl] *adj* trascendental, trascendental. ■ **t. meditation,** meditación *f* trascendental.

transcontinental [trænzkɒntɪ'nentəl] *adj* transcontinental, trascontinental.

transcribe [træn'skraɪb] *vtr* transcribir trascribir.

transcript ['trænskrɪpt] *n*, transcripción *f*, trascripción *f*.

transcription [træn'skrɪpʃən] *n* transcripción *f*, trascripción *f*.

transept ['trænsept] *n Archit* crucero *m*.

transfar [træns'fɜːʳ] **I** *vtr (pt & pp transferred)* **1** trasladar; *(funds)* transferir, trasferir, girar; *Jur* ceder, transferir; *Rail* transbordar, trasbordar; *Ftb* traspasar; *Tel* **a transferred charge call,** una conferencia a cobro revertido. **2** *(design)* calcar. **II** ['trænsfɜːʳ] *n* **1** traslado *m*; *(of funds)* transferencia *f*, trasferencia *f*; *Jur (of goods, rights)* cesión *f*, transferencia *f*; *Ftb* traspaso *m*. **2** *(picture, design)* calcomanía *f*.

transferable [træns'fɜːrəbəl] *adj* transferible trasferible; **not t.,** intransferible, intrasferible.

transferred [træns'fɜːd] *pt & pp see* **transfer.**

transfigure [træns'fɪgə'] *vtr* transfigurar, trasfigurar.

transfix [træns'fɪks] *vtr (usu pass)* transfigurar, trasfigurar; **she was transfixed,** se quedó traspuesta; **transfixed with horror,** horrorizado,-a.

transform [træns'fɔːm] *vtr* transformar, trasformar.

transformation [trænsfə'meɪʃən] *n* transformación *f*, trasformación *f*.

transformar [træns'fɔːmə'] *n Elec* transformador *m*, trasformador *m*.

transfuse [træns'fjuːz] *vtr* trasvasar; *Med* **to t. blood,** hacer una transfusión de sangre.

transfusion [træns'fjuːʒən] *n Med* transfusión *f* (de sangre).

transgress [trænz'gres] *vi* transgredir, trasgredir, infringir.

transgressor [trænz'gresə'] *n* transgresor,-a *m*, *f*, transgresor,-a *m*, *f*.

transient ['trænzɪənt] **I** *adj* transitorio,-a, pasajero,-a. **II** **transients** *npl US (in hotel)* transeúntes *mpl*.

transistor [træn'zɪstə'] *n* transistor *m*.

transit ['trænzɪt] *n* tránsito *m*; **in t.,** de tránsito; **it was damaged in t.,** ha sufrido daño durante el viaje.

transition [træn'zɪʃən] *n* transición *f*. ■ **t. period,** período *m* transitorio *or* de transición.

transitive ['trænzɪtɪv] *adj* transitivo,-a.

transitory ['trænzɪtɔrɪ] *adj* transitorio,-a, pasajero,-a.

translate [træns'leɪt] *vtr* traducir; **it can't really be translated,** no tiene traducción exacta; **it's translated as ...,** se traduce por ...; **translated from/into English** traducido,-a del/al inglés.

translation [træns'leɪʃən] *n* traducción *f*.

translator [træns'leɪtə'] *n* traductor,-a *m*, *f*.

transliteration [trænzlɪtə'reɪʃən] *n* transcripción *f*, trascripción *f*.

translucent [trænz'luːsənt] *adj* translúcido,-a, traslúcido,-a.

transmissible [trænz'mɪsəbəl] *adj* transmisible, trasmisible.

transmission [trænz'mɪʃən] *n* transmisión *f*, trasmisión *f*.

transmit [trænz'mɪt] *vtr (pt & pp transmitted)* transmitir, trasmitir.

transmitter [trænz'mɪtə'] *n Rad (set)* transmisor *m*; *Rad TV (station)* emisora *f*.

transom ['trænsəm] *n Constr* travesaño *m*, dintel *m*.

transparency [træns'pærənsɪ] *n* **1** *(quality)* transparencia *f*, trasparencia *f*. **2** *phot* diapositiva *f*.

transparent [træns'pærənt] *adj* transparente, trasparente.

transpiration [trænspə'reɪʃən] *n* transpiración *f*, traspiración *f*.

transpire [træn'spaɪə'] *vi* **1** *Bot* transpirar, traspirar. **2** *fam (happen)* ocurrir; **his version of what transpired,** su versión de lo que ocurrió; **it transpired that ...,** ocurrió que ... .

transplant [træns'pɔːnt] **I** *vtr Hortic Med* transplantar, trasplantar. **II** ['trænspɑːnt] *n Med* transplante *m*, trasplante *m*. ■ **heart t.,** transplante *m* de corazón.

transport [træns'pɔːt] **I** *vtr* transportar, trasportar. **II** ['trænspɔːt] *n* transporte *m*, trasporte *m*; **have you got t.?,** ¿tienes coche? ■ **Ministry of T.,** Ministerio *m* de Transportes; **t. aircraft/ship,** avión *m*/buque *m* de transporte; *GB* **t. café,** bar *m* de carretera.

transportation [trænspɔː'teɪʃən] *n* transporte *m*, trasporte *m*.

transporter [træns'pɔːtə'] *n* transportador *m*, trasportador *m*.

transpose [træns'pəʊz] *vtr (gen)* transponer; *Mus* trasportar.

transposition [trænspə'zɪʃən] *n* transposición *f*; *Mus* transporte *m*.

tran(s)ship [træn(s)'ʃɪp] *vtr (pt & pp tran(s)shipped)* transbordar.

transversal [trænz'vɜːsəl] *adj* **transverse** [trænz'vɜːs] *adj* transversal, trasversal.

transvestism [trænz'vestɪzəm] *n* travestismo *m*.

transvestite [trænz'vestaɪt] *n* travestido,-a *m*, *f*; *fam* travestí *mf*.

trap [træp] **I** *n* trampa *f*; **to set a t.,** poner una trampa; *fig* **to fall into the t.,** caer en la trampa; *Aut fig* **speed t.,** control *m* de velocidad. ■ **t. door,** *(gen)* trampilla *f*; *Theat* escotillón *m*. **II** *vtr (pt & pp trapped)* coger en una trampa, atrapar, **trapped by flames,** cercado,-a por las llamas; *fig* **to t. sb,** entrampar a algn.

trapeze [trə'piːz] *n* trapecio *m*. ■ **t. artist,** trapecista *mf*.

trapped [træpt] *pt & pp see* **trap.**

trapper ['træpə'] *n* trampero,-a *m*, *f*.

trappings ['træpɪŋz] *npl* parafernalia *f sing*.

Trappist ['træpɪst] *n & adj Rel* trapense *(m)*.

trash [træʃ] *n (inferior goods)* pacotilla *f*; *US (rubbish)* basura *f*; *fig* basura *f*; *fig* **to talk a lot of t.,** decir tonterías. ■ *US* **t. can,** cubo *m* de la basura.

trashy ['træʃɪ] *adj (trashier, trashiest) (goods)* de pacotilla; *(literature)* de ínfima calidad.

trauma ['trɔːmə] *n (pl traumas or traumata* ['trɔːmətə]) *Med Psych* trauma *m*.

traumatic [trɔː'mætɪk] *adj* traumático,-a.

travel ['trævəl] **I** *vi (pt & travelled, US traveled)* **1** viajar; **he is travelling,** está de viaje; **to t. through,** viajar por, recorrer. **2** *(vehicle, electric current)* ir, correr; *fig (news)* propagarse. **II** *vtr* viajar por, recorrer; **distance travelled,** distancia recorrida. **III** *n* viajes *mpl*; **I am fond of t.,** me gusta viajar; **is he still on his travels?,** ¿todavía está de viaje? ■ **t. agency, t. bureau,** agencia *f* de viajes.

traveller, *US* **traveler** ['trævələʳ] *n* **1** (*gen*) viajero,-a *m*,*f*. ■ **t.'s cheque**, cheque *m* de viaje. **2** (**commercial**) **t.**, viajante *mf* (de comercio).

travelling, *US* **traveling** ['trævəlɪŋ] **I** *adj* (*salesman, performer*) ambulante. ■ **t. crane**, grúa *f* móvil. **II** *n* viajes *mpl*, viajar *m*; **I'm fond of t.**, me gusta viajar. ■ **t. bag**, bolsa *f* de viaje; **t. expenses**, gastos *mpl* de viaje.

travelogue ['trævəlɒg] *n* (*film*) documental *m*; (*talk*) conferencia *f* sobre un viaje.

travel-sick ['trævəlsɪk] *adj* **to be t.**, marearse.

travel-sickness ['trævəlsɪknɪs] *n* mareo *m*.

traverse ['trævɜːs, trəˈvɜːs] **I** *vtr* atravesar, cruzar. **II** *n* travesía *f*.

travesty ['trævɪstɪ] **I** *n* (*also pej*) parodia *f*. **II** *vtr* (*pt & pp* **travestied**) parodiar.

trawl [trɔːl] **I** *n* **t.** (**net**), red *f* barredera. **II** *vtr & vi* pescar con red barredera.

trawling ['trɔːlɪŋ] *n* pesca *f* con red barredera.

tray [treɪ] *n* **1** (*for food*) bandeja *f*. ■ **t. cloth**, cubrebandeja *f*. **2** (*for letters*) caja *f*, cesta *f* (para correspondencia); *Phot* cubeta *f*.

treacherous ['tretʃərəs] *adj* **1** (*betraying*) (*person*) traidor,-a; (*action*) traicionero,-a. **2** (*dangerous*) peligroso,-a. ◆ **treacherously** *adv* **1** (*betrayingly*) a traición. **2** (*dangerously*) peligrosamente.

treachery ['tretʃərɪ] *n* traición *f*.

treacle ['triːkəl] *n GB* melaza *f*.

tread [tred] **I** *vi* (*pt* **trod**; *pp* **trod** *or* **trodden**) pisar; **to t. in sth**, meter el pie en algo; **to t. on sth**, pisar algo; **you're treading on my foot**, me estás pisando; *fig* **to t. warily**, andar con pies de plomo. **II** *vtr* **1** (*step on*) pisar; **to t. sth in** *or* **down** *or* **underfoot**, pisotear algo. **2** **to t. water**, mantenerse a flote verticalmente. **III** *n* **1** (*step*) paso *m*; (*sound*) ruido *m* de pasos. **2** (*of stair*) escalón *m*. **3** (*of tyre*) banda *f* de rodadura.

treadle ['tredəl] *n* pedal *m*. ■ **t. sewing machine**, máquina *f* de coser a pedales.

treadmill ['tredmɪl] *n* rueda *f* de ardilla; *fig* rutina *f*.

treas *abbr of* **treasurer**, tesorero,-a *m*,*f*.

treason ['triːzən] *n* traición *f*; **high t.**, alta traición.

treasonable ['triːzənəbəl] *adj* traicionero,-a.

treasure ['treʒəʳ] **I** *n* tesoro *m*; *fig* (*child etc*) **she's a t.**, es un cielo *or* un tesoro. ■ **t. hunt**, caza *f* del tesoro. **II** *vtr* (*keep*) guardar como oro en paño; (*value*) apreciar muchísimo.

treasurer ['treʒərəʳ] *n* tesorero,-a *m*,*f*.

treasure-trove ['treʒətrəʊv] *n Jur* tesoro *m* encontrado.

treasury ['treʒərɪ] *n* tesoro *m*, tesorería *f*; *Pol* **the T.**, ≈ Ministerio *m* de Hacienda. ■ **T. bill**, bono *m* del Tesoro.

treat [triːt] **I** *n* **1** (*present*) regalo *m*; (*meal*) festín *m*, convite *m*; **it's my t.**, invito yo. **2** (*pleasure*) placer *m*; **to give oneself a t.**, permitirse un lujo especial. **II** *vtr* **1** (*gen*) tratar; **to t. badly**, maltratar. **2** (*regard*) tomarse; **he treats it very seriously**, se lo toma muy en serio; **to t. sth as a joke**, tomar algo a broma. **3** (*invite*) invitar; **he treated them to dinner**, les invitó a cenar. **4** *Med* tratar. **5** (*subject*) tratar.

treatise ['triːtɪz] *n* tratado *m*.

treatment ['triːtmənt] *n* **1** (*of person*) trato *m*; **his t. of his friends**, su forma de portarse con los amigos; **preferential t.**, trato preferencial. **2** *Med* tratamiento *m*; **patient undergoing t.**, enfermo sometido a tratamiento; *fam* **to give sb the t.**, dar una paliza a algn. **3** (*interpretation, handling*) tratamiento *m*; **the t. of this subject**, el tratamiento de este tema.

treaty ['triːtɪ] *n* **1** (*between nations*) tratado *m*. **2** (*between persons*) acuerdo *m*, contrato *m*.

treble ['trebəl] **I** *adj* **1** (*triple*) triple. **2** *Mus* de tiple *or* soprano. ■ **t. clef**, clave *f* de sol; **t. voice**, voz *f* tiple *or* de soprano. **II** *vtr* triplicar. **III** *vi* triplicarse.

tree [triː] *n* árbol *m*; **apple/cherry t.**, manzano *m*/ cerezo *m*; **to climb a t.**, subirse a un árbol; *fig* **at the top of the t.**, en la cúspide. ■ *Orn* **t. creeper**, agateador *m* norteño; *Bot* **t. of heaven**, ailanto *m*, árbol *m* del cielo.

treeless ['triːlɪs] *adj* sin árboles.

treetop ['triːtɒp] *n* copa *f*.

trefoil ['trefɔɪl] *n Bot* trébol *m*.

trek [trek] **I** *n* **1** (*journey*) viaje *m* (largo y difícil); *fam* (*walk*) caminata *f*; *fam* **it's quite a t.**, queda bien lejos. **II** *vi* (*pt & pp* **trekked**) hacer un viaje largo y difícil; *fam* (*walk*) ir caminando.

trelliswork ['trelɪswɜːk] *n* enrejado *m*.

tremble ['trembəl] **I** *vi* temblar, estremecerse. **II** *n* temblor *m*; (*shiver*) estremecimiento *m*; **to be all of a t.**, temblequear.

trembling ['tremblɪŋ] **I** *adj* tembloroso,-a; **t. all over**, todo tembloroso,-a. **II** *n* temblor *m*.

tremendous [trɪˈmendəs] *adj* (*huge*) inmenso,-a, enorme; (*success*) arrollador,-a; (*shock, blow, mistake*) tremendo,-a; *fam* (*marvellous*) estupendo,-a, fabuloso,-a; *fam* **to have a t. time**, pasarlo bomba. ◆ **tremendously** *adv* inmensamente, enormemente; *fam* **she does it t. well**, lo hace a las mil maravillas.

tremor ['treməʳ] *n* temblor *m*.

tremulous ['tremjʊləs] *adj* **1** (*timid*) tímido,-a. **2** (*trembling*) tembloroso,-a.

trench [trentʃ] *n* **1** (*ditch*) zanja *f*; *Mil* trinchera *f*. **2 t. coat**, trinchera *f*.

trenchant ['trentʃənt] *adj* (*tone*) cáustico,-a, mordaz.

trend [trend] **I** *n* (*tendency*) tendencia *f*; (*fashion*) moda *f*. **II** *vi* tender (**to**, **towards**), hacia.

trendy ['trendɪ] *adj* (**trendier, trendiest**) *fam* (*person*) moderno,-a; (*clothes*) a la última.

trepidation [trepɪˈdeɪʃən] *n* (*anxiety*) turbación *f*, agitación *f*; (*trembling*) trepidación *f*.

trepass ['trespəs] *vi* entrar sin autorización (en la propiedad de algn).

trespasser ['trespəsəʳ] *n* intruso,-a *m*, *f*, 'trespassers will be prosecuted', 'prohibida la entrada'.

trestle ['tresəl] *n* caballete *m*.

trial ['traɪəl] *n* **1** *Jur* proceso *m*, juicio *m*; **on t.**, procesado,-a; **to bring sb to t.**, procesar a algn; **to stand t.**, ser procesado,-a. **2** (*test*) prueba *f*, ensayo *m*; **on t.**, a prueba; **to do sth by t. and error**, encontrar la forma de hacer algo probando diferentes posibilidades. ■ *Sport* **t.** (**game**), partido *m* de selección; *Com* **t. order**, pedido *m* de prueba; **t. run**, ensayo *m*. **3** *trials*, (*competition*) concurso *m sing*. **4** *trials*, (*suffering*) aflicción *f sing*, sufrimiento *m sing*; (*nuisance*) molestia *f sing*; **t. and tribulations**, tribulaciones *fpl*.

triangle ['traɪæŋgəl] *n Geom* triángulo *m*.

triangular [traɪˈæŋgjʊləʳ] *adj Geom* triangular.

tribal ['traɪbəl] *adj* tribal.

tribe [traɪb] *n* tribu *f*; *fig* multitud *f*.

tribesman ['traɪbzmən] *n* (*pl* **tribesmen**) miembro *m* de una tribu.

tribunal [traɪˈbjuːnəl] *n* tribunal *m*.

tributary ['trɪbjʊtərɪ] **I** *n* (*river*) afluente *m*. **II** *adj* tributario,-a.

tribute ['trɪbjuːt] *n* **1** (*payment*) tributo *m*. **2** (*mark of respect*) homenaje *m*; **floral tributes**, (*to actress*) ramos *mpl* de flores; (*at funeral*) ramos *mpl* y coronas; **to pay t. to**, rendir homenaje a.

trice [traɪs] *n fam* **in a t.**, en un dos por tres, en un abrir y cerrar de ojos.

trick [trɪk] **I** *n* **1** (*ruse*) ardid *m*, artificio *m*; (*dishonest*) engaño *m*, estafa *f*; (*in question*) trampa *f*; **there's a t. in it**, hay trampa. **2** (*practical joke*) broma *f*; **dirty t.**, faena *f*, trastada *f*, mala pasada *f*; **to play a t. on sb**, gastarle una broma a algn; *(malicious)* jugar una mala pasada a algn; **you've been up to your old tricks,** ya has vuelto a hacer de las tuyas. **3** *(skill, knack)* truco *m*; **he knows all the tricks,** conoce todas las triquiñuelas; **that'll do the t.!,** ¡eso es exactamente lo que hace falta!; **the whole bag of tricks,** todo el tinglado; **to get the t. of sth,** cogerle el tranquillo a algo. **4** *Cards* baza *f*; **to take a t.,** ganar una baza. *f* **II** *vtr* engañar, burlar; **to t. sb into doing sth,** engañar a algn para que haga algo; **to t. sb out of sth,** estafar algo a algn; **we've been tricked!,** ¡nos han timado!

trickery ['trɪkərɪ] *n* engaños *mpl*, trampas *fpl*; **piece of t.,** trampa *f*, superchería *f*; **they got it by t.,** lo consiguieron con trampas.

trickle ['trɪkəl] **I** *vi* correr, discurrir; *(water)* gotear; *fig (resources)* **to t. away,** consumirse poco a poco. **II** *n* hilo *m*, hilillo *m*. ■ *Elec* **t. charger,** cargador *m* de régimen lento.

trickster ['trɪkstə'] *n (gen)* tramposo,-a *m, f; (swindler)* estafador,-a *m, f.*

tricky ['trɪkɪ] *adj (trickier, trickiest) (person)* astuto,-a, tramposo,-a; *(situation, mechanism)* delicado,-a.

tricolour, *US* **tricolor** ['trɪkələ', traɪkʌlə'] *n* tricolor *f*; **the T.,** la bandera tricolor.

tricycle ['traɪsɪkəl] *n* triciclo *m.*

trident ['traɪdənt] *n* tridente *m.*

tried [traɪd] *pt & pp see* **try.**

trier ['traɪə'] *n fam* **he's a t.,** se esfuerza al máximo.

trifle ['traɪfəl] **I** *n* **1** *(insignificant thing)* bagatela *f*, fruslería *f*; **he's a t. optimistic,** es ligeramente optimista; **she worries over trifles,** se preocupa por tonterías. **2** *GB Culin* postre *m* (de bizcocho, jerez, gelatina, frutas y nata). **II** *vi* **to t. with,** tomar a la ligera; **to t. with sb's affections,** jugar con los sentimientos de algn.

trifling ['traɪflɪŋ] *adj* insignificante, trivial; **of t. value,** de un valor mínimo.

trigger ['trɪgə'] **I** *n (of gun)* gatillo *m*; *(of mechanism)* disparador *m*; *fam* **to be t.-happy,** estar siempre con el dedo en el gatillo. **II** *vtr* **to t. (off),** *(reaction)* desencadenar.

trigonometry [trɪgə'nɒmɪtrɪ] *n Math* trigonometría *f.*

trill [trɪl] **I** *n* **1** *Mus* trino *m*. **2** *Ling* vibración *f*. **3** *(of bird)* trino *m*, gorjeo *m*. **II** *vi Mus* trinar. **III** *vtr* **1** *Mus* trinar. **2** *Ling* vibrar.

trillion ['trɪljən] *n* **1** *GB* trillón *m*. **2** *US* billón *m.*

trilogy ['trɪlədʒɪ] *n* trilogía *f*

trim [trɪm] **I** *adj (trimmer, trimmest) (neat)* aseado,-a, arreglado,-a; **to have a t. figure,** tener buen tipo. **II** *vtr (pt & pp trimmed)* **1** *(cut)* recortar; *(hedge)* podar; *fig (expenses)* disminuir. **2** *(decorate)* adornar, guarnecer **(with,** de); **trimmed with lace,** adornado,-a con encajes. **III** *n* **1** *(state)* orden *m*, estado *m*; *Naut* asiento *m*, estiba *f*; **to be in good t.,** *(ship)* estar bien estibado,-a. **2** *(cut)* recorte *m*; **to give sth a t.,** recortar algo; **your hair needs a t.,** tienes que cortarte las puntas.

trimming ['trɪmɪŋ] *n* **1** *(cut)* recorte *m*; *(of hedge)* poda *f*; *(of wood)* desbaste *m*. **2** *(on clothes)* adorno *m*. **3** *Culin* **trimmings,** guarnición *f sing*; **dish with (the usual) t.,** plato *m* guarnecido,-a (de la manera **habitual).**

Trinidad ['trɪnɪdæd] *n* Trinidad. ■ **T. and Tobago,** Trinidad y Tobago.

Trinity ['trɪnɪtɪ] *n* La (Santísima) Trinidad. ■ **T. Sunday** fiesta *f* de la Trinidad.

trinket ['trɪŋkɪt] *n* baratija *f*, abalorio *m.*

trio ['triːəʊ] *n (pl* **trios)** trío *m.*

trip [trɪp] **I** *n* **1** *(journey)* viaje *m*; *(excursion)* excursión *f*; **to go on a t.,** ir de excursión. **2** *sl (on drugs)* viaje *m*; **to be on a t.,** estar colocado,-a; **to have a bad t.,** reaccionar mal a una droga. **II** *vi (pt & pp* **tripped) 1 to t. (up),** *(stumble)* tropezar **(over,** con); *fig (err)* equivocarse, cometer un error. **2 to t. along,** ir con paso ligero. **III** *vtr*

to t. sb (up), *(make stumble)* zancadillear a algn; *fig (catch)* coger *or* pillar a algn.

tripe [traɪp] *n* **1** *Culin* callos *mpl*. **2** *fam* bobadas *fpl*; *fam* **it's a load of t.,** son tonterías.

triple ['trɪpəl] **I** *adj* triple. ■ *Mus* **t. time,** compás *m* ternario. **II** *vtr* triplicar. **III** *vi* triplicarse.

triplet ['trɪplɪt] *n* trillizo,-a *m, f.*

triplicate ['trɪplɪkɪt] **I** *adj* triplicado,-a; **in t.,** por triplicado. **II** *n* triplicado *m*. **III** ['trɪplɪkeɪt] *vtr* redactar por triplicado.

tripod ['traɪpɒd] *n* trípode *m.*

Tripoli ['trɪpəlɪ] *n* Trípoli.

tripped [trɪpt] *pt & pp see* **trip.**

tripper ['trɪpə'] *n* excursionista *mf*, turista *mf.*

triptych ['trɪptɪk] *n Art* tríptico *m.*

tripwire ['trɪpwaɪə'] *n* cable *m* trampa.

trite [traɪt] *adj (sentiment)* banal; *(subject)* trillado,-a.

triteness ['traɪtnɪs] *n* banalidad *f.*

triumph ['traɪəmf] **I** *n (success)* triunfo *m*; *(joy)* júbilo *m*, alegría *f.* ■ **II** *vi* triunfar.

triumphal [traɪʌmfəl] *adj* triunfal. ■ **t. arch,** arco *m* de triunfo.

triumphant [traɪʌmfənt] *adj* triunfante. ◆ **triumphantly** *adv (gen)* triunfalmente; *(speak)* en tono triunfal.

trivia ['trɪvɪə] *npl* futilidades *fpl*, trivialidades *fpl.*

trivial ['trɪvɪəl] *adj* trivial, banal.

triviality [trɪvɪ'ælɪtɪ] *n* trivialidad *f*; **to talk of trivialities,** hablar de cosas triviales.

trod [trɒd] *pt & pp see* **tread.**

trodden ['trɒdən] *pp see* **tread.**

Trojan ['trəʊdʒən] *adj* troyano,-a. ■ **T. Horse,** caballo *m* de Troya.

trolley ['trɒlɪ] *n GB (for shopping, luggage)* carro *m*; *(for serving food, drinks)* carro, mesita *f* de ruedas. ■ **t. bus,** trolebús *m*; *US* **t. car,** tranvía *m.*

trombone [trɒm'bəʊn] *n Mus* trombón *m.*

troop [truːp] **I** *n* **1** *(of people)* grupo *m*. **2** *Mil (unit)* escuadrón *m* (de caballería); **troops,** tropas *fpl*. ■ **t. train,** tren *m* militar. **II** *vi* **to t. in/out/off,** entrar/salir/marcharse en tropel.

trooper ['truːpə'] *n Mil* soldado *m* de caballería; *fig* **to swear like a t.,** hablar como un carretero.

trooping ['truːpɪŋ] *n GB Mil* **t. the colour,** ceremonia *f* en la que se rinde honores a la bandera de un regimiento.

trophy ['trəʊfɪ] *n* trofeo *m.*

tropic ['trɒpɪk] *n* trópico *m*; **the T. of Capricorn/Cancer,** el Trópico de Capricornio/Cáncer.

tropical ['trɒpɪkəl] *adj* tropical.

trot [trɒt] **I** *vi (pt & pp* **trotted)** trotar, ir al trote; *fam* **I'll just t. round to the shop,** voy a salir un momento a la tienda. **II** *n* trote *m*; **to break into a t.,** empezar a trotar; **to go at a t.,** ir al trote; *fam* **they won six times on the t.,** ganaron seis veces seguidas; *fam* **to keep sb on the t.,** no dejar a algn tranquilo ni un momento. ◆ **trot out** *vtr (names, list)* recitar de memoria; *(excuses)* sacar a relucir; *(for show)* hacer alarde de.

trotter ['trɒtə'] *n* **1** *(horse)* trotón *m*. **2** *Culin* **trotters,** manos *fpl*; **sheep's/pig's t.,** manos de oveja/cerdo.

trouble ['trʌbəl] **I** *n* **1** *(affliction)* pena *f*, aflicción *f*; *(misfortune)* desgracia *f.* **2** *(problems)* problemas *mpl*, dificultades *fpl*; **he's asking for t.,** se está buscando problemas; **his troubles are over,** ya se acabaron sus problemas; **money troubles,** problemas económicos; **the t. is that ...,** lo que pasa es que ...; **there was t. between his wife and his mother,** entre su mujer y su madre había problemas; **to be in t.,** estar en un lío *or* en un apuro; **to cause sb a lot of t.,** dar mucha guerra a algn; **to get into t.,**

meterse en un lío; **to get sb out of t.**, sacar a algn de un apuro; **to make t.**, armar jaleo; *fam* **fig to get a girl into t.**, dejar embarazada a una chica. 3 *(effort)* esfuerzo *m*; **it's no t.**, no es ninguna molestia; **it's not worth the t.**, no merece la pena; **nothing is too much t. for him**, no escatima esfuerzos; **to take the t. to do sth**, molestarse en hacer algo. 4 *Pol Ind (unrest, conflict)* conflicto *m*; **labour troubles**, conflictos *mpl* laborales. ■ **t. spot**, lugar *m* conflictivo. 5 *Med* enfermedad *f*, mal *m*; **heart t.**, enfermedad cardíaca; **to have eye/liver t.**, padecer de los ojos/del hígado. 6 *Aut* **engine t.**, avería *f* del motor. II *vtr* 1 *(affect)* afligir, afectar; *(worry)* preocupar; **that doesn't t. him at all**, eso le tiene sin cuidado; **to be troubled**, estar muy preocupado,-a; **to t. oneself about sth**, preocuparse por algo. 2 *(bother, disturb)* molestar, incomodar; **I'm sorry to t. you**, perdone que le moleste; **I won't t. you with the details**, no le cansaré con más detalles. III *vi* molestarse; **don't t. to write**, no se moleste en escribir.

troubled ['trʌbəld] *adj (agitated)* agitado,-a, inquieto,-a; *(liquid)* turbio,-a, revuelto,-a.

trouble-free ['trʌbəlfriː] *adj* sin problemas.

troublemaker ['trʌbəlmeɪkəʳ] *n* alborotador,-a *m*, *f*, provocador,-a *m*,*f*.

troubleshooter ['trʌbəlʃuːtəʳ] *n Ind* conciliador,-a *m*,*f*, mediador,-a *m*, *f*; *(mechanic)* especialista *mf* en diagnóstico de averías.

troublesome ['trʌbəlsəm] *adj* molesto,-a, fastidioso,-a, pesado,-a.

trough [trɒf] *n* 1 *(container)* **(drinking) t.**, abrevadero *m*; **(feeding) t.**, pesebre *m*; **(kneading) t.**, artesa *f*. 2 *Phys (of wave)* seno *m*. 3 *Geog* depresión *f*. 4 *Meteor* isobara *f* de mínima presión; *(area of low pressure)* zona *f* de baja presión, depresión *f*.

trounce [trauns] *vtr* dar una paliza a.

trouncing ['traunsɪŋ] *n* paliza *f*.

troupe [truːp] *n Theat* compañía *f*.

trousers ['trauzəz] *npl* pantalón *m sing*, pantalones *mpl*; **a pair of t.**, un par de pantalones; *fig* **who wears the t. in their house?**, ¿quién lleva los pantalones en su casa?

trousseau ['truːsəʊ] *n* ajuar *m*.

trout [traut] *n (pl* **trout** *or* **trouts***)* trucha *f*. ■ **t. fishing**, pesca *f* de truchas; **t. stream**, río *m* truchero.

trowel ['trauəl] *n* 1 *(builder's)* palustre *m*; *fig* **to lay it on with a t.**, *(exaggerate)* recargar las tintas; *(flatter excessively)* dar coba. 2 *Hortic* desplantador *m*.

truancy ['truːənsɪ] *n* el hacer novillos.

truant ['truːənt] I *n* niño,-a *m*,*f* que hace novillos; **to play t.**, hacer novillos. II *adj (pupil)* que hace novillos.

truce [truːs] *n* tregua *f*; **to call a t.**, acordar una tregua.

truck[1] [trʌk] *n* 1 *GB Rail* vagón *m*. 2 *Aut* camión *m*. ■ **t. driver**, camionero,-a *m*, *f*. 3 *(handcart)* carretilla *f*; *(in mines)* vagoneta *f*.

truck[2] [trʌk] *n* 1 *(dealings)* tratos *mpl*; **he'll have no t. with such schemes**, no quiere tener nada que ver con tales proyectos; **to have no t. with sb**, no tratar con algn. 2 *US Hortic* productos *mpl* de la huerta, verduras *fpl*. ■ **t. farmer**, hortelano,-a *m*, *f*; **t. farming**, cultivo *m* de productos hortenses.

trucker ['trʌkəʳ] *n US* camionero,-a *m*,*f*.

trucking ['trʌkɪŋ] *n US* camionaje *m*.

truculence ['trʌkjʊləns] *n* violencia *f*, agresividad *f*, truculencia *f*.

truculent ['trʌkjʊlənt] *adj* truculento,-a, agresivo,-a, violento,-a.

trudge [trʌdʒ] *vi* caminar con dificultad; **we trudged up the hill**, nos costó subir la colina.

true [truː] I *adj (truer, truest)* 1 *(factual)* verdadero,-a; **it's t. that ...**, es verdad *or* cierto que ...; **to come t.**, cumplirse, realizarse. 2 *(genuine)* verdadero,-a, auténtico,-a; **a t.**

friend, un amigo de verdad; **a t. Spaniard**, un español auténtico. 3 *(faithful)* fiel, leal; **to be t. to one's convictions/a promise**, ser fiel a las propias convicciones/a una promesa; **to be** *or* **run t. to form**, ser fiel a sí mismo. 4 *(accurate) (aim)* acertado,-a; *(mechanism)* exacto,-a. 5 *(level)* nivelado,-a. II *n* **to be out of t.**, *(wall)* no estar a plomo; *(surface)* no estar a nivel; *(beam)* estar aldeado,-a; *(wheel)* estar descentrado,-a. III *adv (of wheel)* **to run t.**, estar bien centrado,-a. ◆ **truly** *adv* 1 verdaderamente, de verdad; **I am t. grateful**, se lo agradezco de verdad; **really and t.?**, ¿de veras? 2 *(faithfully)* fielmente, lealmente; *(in letters)* **yours t.**, atentamente.

true-blue ['truːbluː] *adj* fiel, leal.

true-life ['truːlaɪf] *adj* verdadero,-a, cierto,-a.

truffle ['trʌfəl] *n* 1 *Bot* trufa *f*. 2 *GB Culin* **(chocolate) t.**, trufa *f* de chocolate.

truism ['truːɪzəm] *n* truismo *m*.

trump [trʌmp] I *n Cards* triunfo *m*; **what's trumps?**, ¿qué pinta?; *fig* **she always turns up trumps**, siempre le favorece la suerte; *fig* **to play one's t. card**, jugar su carta maestra. II *vtr Cards* fallar. ◆ **trump up** *vtr* **to t. up an excuse**, inventar una excusa.

trumped-up ['trʌmptʌp] *adj* inventado,-a.

trumpet ['trʌmpɪt] I *n Mus* trompeta *f*; **to blow one's own t.**, cantar sus propias alabanzas. II *vi* 1 *Mus* tocar la trompeta. 2 *(elephant)* berrear, bramar, barritar.

trumpeter ['trʌmpɪtəʳ] *n Mus* trompetista *mf*, trompeta *mf*.

trumpeting ['trʌmpɪtɪŋ] *n (of elephant)* berrido *m*, bramido *m*.

truncate [trʌŋ'keɪt] *vtr* truncar.

truncheon ['trʌntʃən] *n GB* porra *f* (de policía).

trundle ['trʌndəl] I *vtr (cart)* empujar. II *vi* rodar.

trunk [trʌŋk] *n* 1 *(of tree, body)* tronco *m*. 2 *(of elepant)* trompa *f*. 3 *(case)* baúl *m*. 4 *Tel* **t. call**, conferencia *f* interurbana; *Aut* **t. road**, carretera *f* principal.

trunks [trʌŋks] *npl* **(bathing) t.**, bañador *m sing*, traje *m sing* de baño.

truss [trʌs] I *vtr (tie)* atar. II *n* 1 *(of hay, straw)* haz *m*, lío *m*. 2 *Constr* cuchillo *m* de armadura. 3 *Med* braguero *m*. 4 *(on plant)* racimo *m*.

trust [trʌst] I *n* 1 *(belief, confidence)* confianza *f*; **breach of t.**, abuso *m* de confianza; **position of t.**, puesto *m* de responsabilidad; **to take sth on t.**, creer algo a ojos cerrados. 2 *Jur* fideicomiso *m*. ■ **t. deed**, acta *f* de fideicomiso. 3 *Com* **on t.**, a crédito. 4 *Fin* trust *m*. II *vtr* 1 *(hope)* esperar; **I t. he will come**, confío en que vendrá. 2 *(rely upon)* confiar en, fiarse de; **he's not to be trusted**, no es de fiar; **to t. sb with sth**, confiar algo a algn. 3 *Com (client)* dar crédito a. III *vi* confiar (**in**, de); **to t. in God**, confiar en Dios; **to t. to luck**, abandonarse al azar.

trusted ['trʌstɪd] *adj (trustworthy)* de fiar, digno,-a de confianza; *(remedy)* probado,-a.

trustee [trʌ'stiː] *n Jur* fideicomisario,-a *m*, *f*; *(in bankruptcy)* síndico *m*.

trusteeship [trʌ'stiːʃɪp] *n Jur* cargo *m* de fideicomisario.

trustful ['trʌstfʊl] *adj*, **trusting** ['trʌstɪŋ] *adj* confiado,-a.

trustworthiness ['trʌstwɜːðɪnɪs] *n (of person)* honradez *f*, formalidad *f*; *(of information)* veracidad *f*, exactitud *f*.

trustworthy ['trʌstwɜːðɪ] *adj (person)* honrado,-a, de confianza; *(information)* fidedigno,-a.

trusty ['trʌstɪ] *adj (trustier, trustiest)* fiel, leal.

truth [truːθ] *n* verdad *f*; **the honest t.**, la pura verdad; **the t. is that ...**, la verdad es que ...; **to tell the t.**, decir la verdad; *fam* **to tell sb a few home truths**, decirle a algn cuatro verdades.

truthful ['truːθfʊl] *adj (person)* veraz; *(testimony)* verídico,-a. ◆ **truthfully** *adv* sinceramente, sin mentir; **tell me t.**, dígame la verdad.

truthfulness ['truːθfʊlnɪs] *n* veracidad *f*.

try [traɪ] **I** *vtr (pt & pp* **tried)** **1** *(attempt)* intentar; **to t. one's hand at (doing) sth,** intentar (hacer) algo. **2** *(test)* probar, ensayar, poner *or* someter a prueba; **to t. sb's patience,** poner a prueba la paciencia de algn. **3** *(taste)* probar; **have you tried alcohol-free beer?,** ¿has probado la cerveza sin alcohol? **4** *Jur* juzgar; **his case is being tried at the High Court,** el Tribunal Supremo está juzgando el caso. **II** *vi* intentar; **he tried his hardest to save then,** hizo todo lo posible para salvarles; **I shall t. again,** volveré a intentarlo; **to t. for sth,** intentar conseguir algo; **to t. to do sth,** and do sth, tratar de *or* intentar hacer algo. **III** *n* **1** *(attempt)* tentativa *f*, intento *m*; **it's worth a t.,** vale la pena intentarlo; **to have a t. at doing sth,** intentar hacer algo. **2** *Sport* ensayo *m*. ◆ **try on** *vtr* **1** *(dress)* probarse. **2** *fam* **to t. it on with sb,** intentar engañar a algn. ◆ **try out** *vtr* probar, ensayar; **t. it out on us first,** pruébalo primero con nosotros, a ver qué pasa.

trying ['traɪɪŋ] *adj (person)* molesto,-a, pesado,-a; **he's very t.,** es pesadísimo; **to have a t. time,** pasar un mal rato.

tsar [zɑːʳ] *n* zar *m*.

tsarina [zɑːˈriːnə] *n* zarina *f*.

tsetse fly ['tsetsɪflaɪ] *n Ent* mosca *f* tsetsé.

T-shirt ['tiːʃɜːt] *n* camiseta *f*.

tsp *abbr of* **teaspoonful,** cucharadita *f*.

tub [tʌb] *n* **1** *(container)* tina *f*, cuba *f*. **2** *(bath)* bañera *f*.

tuba ['tjuːbə] *n Mus* tuba *f*.

tubby ['tʌbɪ] *adj (tubbier, tubbiest)* rechoncho,-a.

tube [tjuːb] *n* **1** *(gen)* tubo *m; Anat* conducto *m*, trompa *f; (of bicycle)* **(inner) t.,** cámara *f* (de aire). **2** *GB fam (underground)* **the t.,** el metro.

tubeless ['tjuːblɪs] *adj* sin cámara.

tuber ['tjuːbəʳ] *n Bot* tubérculo *m*.

tubercle ['tjuːbəkəl] *n* tubérculo *m*.

tubercular [tjʊˈbɜːkjʊləʳ] *adj* tuberculoso,-a.

tuberculin [tjʊˈbɜːkjʊlɪn] *n Med* tuberculina *f*.

tuberculosis [tjʊbɜːkjʊˈləʊsɪs] *n* tuberculosis *f*.

tuberous ['tjuːbərəs] *adj Bot* tuberoso,-a.

tubing ['tjuːbɪŋ] *n* tubería *f*; **(piece of) t.,** (trozo *m* de) tubo *m*.

tubular ['tjuːbjʊləʳ] *adj* tubular.

tuck [tʌk] **I** *vtr* **to t. in the bedclothes,** remeter la ropa de la cama; **to t. one's shirt into one's trousers,** meter la camisa por dentro (de los pantalones); **to t. sb up in bed,** tapar a algn en la cama; **to t. sth away,** esconder algo. **II** *n* **1** *Sew* pliegue *m*; **to make** *or* **take a t. in a skirt,** poner un pliegue a una falda. **2** *GB fam (food)* golosinas *fpl*. ■ **t. shop,** tienda *f* que vende caramelos y patatas fritas (cerca de un colegio). ◆ **tuck in** *vi fam* devorar; **t. in!,** ¡adentro!, ¡come! ◆ **tuck into** *vtr* **to t. into a good meal,** comer a dos carrillos.

tuck-in ['tʌkɪn] *n GB fam* comilona *f*.

Tudor ['tjuːdəʳ] *adj Hist* Tudor.

Tue(s) *abbr of* **Tuesday,** martes *m*, mart.

Tuesday ['tjuːzdɪ] *n* martes *m; see also* **Saturday.**

tuft [tʌft] *n (of hair)* mechón *m; (of feathers)* copete *m; (of wool)* copo *m*, manojo *m*.

tufted ['tʌftɪd] *adj Orn* copetudo,-a.

tug [tʌg] **I** *vtr (pt & pp* **tugged)** *(pull at)* tirar de; *(haul along)* arrastrar; *Naut* remolcar. **II** *vi* **to t. at sth,** tirar de algo. **III** *n* **1** *(pull)* tirón *m*, estirón *m*; **to give a good t.,** tirar fuerte; **t. of war,** *(game)* lucha *f* de la cuerda; *fig* lucha encarnizada y prolongada. **2** *Naut* remolcador *m*.

tugboat ['tʌgbəʊt] *n* remolcador *m*.

tugged [tʌgd] *pt & pp see* **tug.**

tuition [tjuːˈɪʃən] *n* instrucción *f*, enseñanza *f*; **private t.,** clases *fpl* particulares. ■ **t. fees,** honorarios *mpl*.

tulip ['tjuːlɪp] *n Bot* tulipán *m*. ■ **t. tree,** tulipero *m* de Virginia.

tulle [tjuːl] *n Tex* tul *m*.

tumble ['tʌmbəl] **I** *vi (person)* caerse; *(acrobat)* dar volteretas; *(building)* hundirse, venirse abajo; **to t. downstairs,** caer escaleras abajo; *fig* **to t. into bed,** echarse en la cama; *fig* **to t. out of a car,** bajar precipitadamente de un coche. **II** *vtr* volcar. **III** *n* **1** *(fall)* caída *f*, tumbo *m*; **to take** *or* **have a t.,** caerse. **2 t. dryer,** secadora *f*.

tumbledown ['tʌmbəldaʊn] *adj (house)* en ruinas, ruinoso,-a.

tumbler ['tʌmbləʳ] *n* vaso *m*.

tummy ['tʌmɪ] *n fam* estómago *m*, barriga *f*; **he has a t. ache,** le duele el estómago.

tumour, *US* **tumor** ['tjuːməʳ] *n Med* tumor *m*; ■ **brain t.,** tumor *m* cerebral.

tumult ['tjuːmʌlt] *n* tumulto *m*.

tumultuous [tjuːˈmʌltjʊəs] *adj* tumultuoso,-a.

tumulus ['tjuːmjʊləs] *n (pl* **tumuli** ['tjuːmjʊliː]) *Archeol* túmulo *m*.

tuna ['tjuːnə] *n (pl* **tuna** *or* **tunas)** atún *m*, bonito *m*.

tundra ['tʌndrə] *n* tundra *f*.

tune [tjuːn] **I** *n* **1** *(melody)* melodía *f*; **to play a t.,** tocar una melodía; *fig* **to call the t.,** imponer condiciones; *fig* **to change one's t.,** cambiar de tono; *fam fig* **expenses to the t. of £100,** gastos por la friolera de cien libras. **2** *Mus* tono *m*; **the piano is in/out of t.,** el piano está afinado/ desafinado; **to sing out of t.,** desafinar; *fig (harmony)* **to be in/out of t. with one's surroundings,** entonar/ desentonar con el ambiente. **II** *vtr* **1** *Mus (instrument)* afinar. **2** *Aut* **to t. (up) the engine,** poner a punto *or* regular el motor. **III** *vi Rad TV* **to t. in to a station/channel,** sintonizar una emisora/cadena. ◆ **tune up** *vi (orchestra)* afinar los instrumentos.

tuneful ['tjuːnfʊl] *adj* melodioso,-a, armonioso,-a.

tuneless ['tjuːnlɪs] *adj* disonante, poco melodioso,-a.

tuner ['tjuːnəʳ] *n (of pianos)* afinador,-a *m, f*. **2** *Rad TV (knob)* sintonizador *m*.

tune-up ['tjuːnʌp] *n Aut (of engine)* puesta *f* a punto, reglaje *m*.

tungsten ['tʌŋstən] *n Chem* tungsteno *m*. ■ **t. steel,** acero *m* al tungsteno.

tunic ['tjuːnɪk] *n* túnica *f*.

tuning ['tjuːnɪŋ] *n* **1** *Mus* afinación *f*. ■ **t. fork,** diapasón *m*. **2** *Rad TV* **t. in,** sintonización *f*.

Tunis ['tjuːnɪs] *n* Túnez.

Tunisia [tjuːˈnɪzɪə] *n* Túnez.

Tunisian [tjuːˈnɪzɪən] *adj & n* tunecino,-a *(m,f)*.

tunnel ['tʌnəl] **1** *n* túnel *m; Min* galería *f*; **to dig a t.,** construir un túnel. **II** *vi (pt & pp* **tunnelled,** *US* **tunneled)** **to t. through a mountain,** abrir un túnel a través de una montaña.

tunnelling, *US* **tunneling** ['tʌnəlɪŋ] *n* construcción *f* de un túnel *or* de túneles.

tunny ['tʌnɪ] *n (fish)* atún *m*, bonito *m*.

tupelo ['tjuːpɪləʊ] *n (pl* **tupelos)** *Bot* tupelo *m* negro.

tuppence ['tʌpəns] *n see* **twopence.**

Tupperware® ['tʌpəweəʳ] *n* táper *m*, recipiente *m* hermético de plástico.

turban ['tɜːbən] *n* turbante *m*.

turbid ['tɜːbɪd] *adj (liquid)* turbio,-a.

turbine ['tɜːbaɪn] *n* turbina *f*.

turbojet [tɜːbəʊˈdʒet] *n Tech* turborreactor *m; Av* avión *m* turborreactor.

turboprop [tɜːbəʊˈprɒp] *n Tech* turbopropulsor *m*.

turbot ['tɜːbət] *n (pl* **turbot** *or* **turbots)** *(fish)* rodaballo *m*.

turbulence ['tɜːbjʊləns] *n* turbulencia *f*.

turbulent ['tɜ:bjʊlənt] *adj* turbulento,-a.

tureen [təˈriːn] *n* sopera *f*.

turf [tɜːf] **I** *n* (*pl* **turfs** *or* **turves** [tɜːvz]) **1** (*grass*) césped *m*; (*peat*) turba *f*. **2** *Sport* (*horse racing*) the T., el Turf. **t. accountant**, corredor,-a *m*, *f* de apuestas. **II** *vtr* cubrir con césped. ◆ **turf out** *vtr* GB *fam* **to t. sb out**, poner a algn de patitas en la calle.

Turk [tɜːk] *n* turco,-a *m*, *f*.

Turkey ['tɜːkɪ] *n* Turquía.

turkey ['tɜːkɪ] *n* (*pl* **turkey** *or* **turkeys**) *Orn* pavo *m*. ■ **t. cock**, pavo *m*; **t. hen**, pava *f*.

Turkish ['tɜːkɪʃ] **I** *adj* turco,-a. ■ **T. bath**, baño *m* turco. **II** *n* (*language*) turco *m*.

turmeric ['tɜːmərɪk] *n* *Bot* cúrcuma *f*.

turmoil ['tɜːmɔɪl] *n* confusión *f*, alboroto *m*; **mental t.**, trastorno *m* mental; **to be in a t.**, estar alborotado,-a.

turn [tɜːn] **I** *vtr* **1** (*revolve*) girar, hacer girar; **to t. a key in a lock**, dar la vuelta a una llave. **2** (*turn over*) **to t. a garment inside out**, volver una prenda del revés; **to t. a page**, volver *or* pasar una hoja. **3** (*change direction of*) **to t. one's head/gaze**, volver la cabeza/mirada (**towards**, hacia); *fig* **success has turned his head**, el éxito se le ha subido a la cabeza; *fig* **without turning a hair**, sin inmutarse. **4** (*deflect*) desviar; **we couldn't t. him from his plan**, no pudimos convencerle de que abandonara su plan. **5** (*pass*) volver; **to t. the corner**, doblar la esquina; *fig* **he's turned forty**, ha cumplido los cuarenta (años). **6** (*change*) cambiar, transformar (**into**, en); **to t. a book into a film**, adaptar un libro al cine; **to t. a house into flats**, convertir una casa en pisos; **to t. a text into English**, traducir un texto al inglés. **7** (*on lathe*) tornear; *fig* **a well-turned sentence**, una frase elegante. **II** *vi* **1** (*revolve*) girar, dar vueltas; *fig* **everything turns on your answer**, todo depende de tu respuesta; *fig* **the talk turned on sport**, la conversación giró en torno al deporte. **2** (*change direction*) torcer, girar; (*turn round*) volverse, dar la vuelta; *fig* (*for help*) acudir a; *Mil* **right t.!**, ¡derecha!; **to t. to sb**, volverse hacia algn; **to t. to the left**, torcer a la izquierda; **to t. upside down**, volcarse; *fig* **I don't know which way to t.**, no sé a quién acudir; *fig* **to t. against sb**, coger *or* tomar antipatía a algn; *fig* **to t. on sb**, volverse contra algn. **3** (*become*) ponerse, volverse; **the milk has turned sour**, la leche se ha cortado; **the situation is turning nasty**, la situación se está poniendo fea; **to t. awkward**, ponerse difícil; **to t. socialist**, hacerse socialista; *fig* **everything he touches turns to gold**, convierte en oro todo lo que toca. **III** *n* **1** (*of wheel*) vuelta *f*, revolución *f*; *Culin* **meat done to a t.**, carne en su punto. **2** (*change of direction*) cambio *m* de dirección; (*in road*) curva *f*, vuelta *f*; **sudden/sharp t.**, curva brusca/cerrada; **to take a new t.**, tomar otro sesgo; **to take a t. for the better**, empezar a mejorar; *fig* **at every t.**, a cada paso. **3** (*deed, action*) **to do sb a good t.**, hacer un favor a algn. **4** *Med* (*fit*) ataque *m*; *fig* **you gave me quite a t.!**, ¡vaya susto que me diste! **5** (*in game, queue*) turno *m*, vez *f*; **it's your t.**, te toca a ti; **to take it in turns to do sth**, turnarse para hacer algo; **whose t. is it?**, ¿a quién le toca? **6** *Theat* número *m*; **to do a t.**, hacer un número. **7** (*form*) **t. of phrase**, giro *m*. **8** (*inclination*) **t. of mind**, disposición *f*. ◆ **turn aside** **I** *vtr* desviar, apartar. **II** *vi* desviarse. ◆ **turn away** **I** *vtr* (*person*) rechazar. **II** *vi* (*look aside*) volver la cabeza. ◆ **turn back** **I** *vtr* (*person*) hacer retroceder; (*clock*) retrasar; (*corner of page*) doblar. **II** *vi* retroceder, volver(se) atrás. ◆ **turn down** *vtr* **1** (*gas, radio, etc*) bajar. **2** (*reject*) rechazar. **3** (*fold*) doblar; **to t. down the bedclothes**, abrir la cama. ◆ **turn in** **I** *vtr* **1** (*person*) entregar a la policía. **2** (*entregar*); **to t. in an essay**, entregar una redacción *or* un trabajo (escrito). **II** *vi* *fam* acostarse. ◆ **turn off** **I** *vtr* (*electricity*) desconectar; (*gas, light*) apagar; (*water*) cerrar, parar. **II** *vi* desviarse (de la carretera). ◆ **turn on** *vtr* (*electricity*) conectar, encender; (*tap, gas*) abrir; (*machine*) poner en marcha; *fam* **it turns me on**, me chifla. ◆ **turn out** *vtr* **1**

(*extinguish*) apagar, cerrar. **2** (*eject*) echar, expulsar; (*empty*) vaciar; (*room*) limpiar, arreglar; *Culin* sacar del molde. **3** (*produce*) producir, fabricar. **4** (*person*) **well turned-out**, elegante, bien vestido,-a. **5** *Mil* **to t. out the guard**, formar la guardia. **II** *vi* **1** (*attend*) asistir, aparecer; **very few people turned out for the meeting**, muy pocas personas asistieron a la reunión. **2** (*result*) salir; **it turns out that ...**, resulta que ...; **the weather has turned out fine**, el tiempo ha mejorado; **things have turned out well**, las cosas han salido bien. ◆ **turn over** **I** *vtr* **1** (*turn upside down*) poner al revés; (*page*) dar la vuelta a; *fig* **to t. over an idea in one's mind**, darle vueltas a una idea. **2** *Com* hacer caja; **he turns over £5,000 a week**, hace 5.000 libras a la semana de caja. **3** (*transfer*) **to t. sth over to sb**, entregar algo a algn. **II** *vi* (*animal, page*) volverse; **to t. (right) over**, volcarse, dar una vuelta de campana; *fig* **my stomach turned over**, se me revolvió el estómago. ◆ **turn round** **I** *vtr* volver, dar la vuelta a. **II** *vi* (*rotate*) girar, dar vueltas; (*about face*) darse la vuelta, volverse; **to t. round and round**, dar muchas vueltas. ◆ **turn up** **I** *vtr* **1** (*collar*) levantar, alzar; (*skirt*) hacer un dobladillo a; **to t. up one's shirt sleeves**, arremangarse, remangarse; **turned-up nose**, nariz *f* respingona; *fig* **to t. up one's nose at sth**, despreciar *or* desdeñar algo. **2** *Elec Rad TV* subir, poner más fuerte; **t. the radio up**, sube la radio. **3** *Cards* (*ace, king*) sacar. **II** *vi* **1** (*appear*) aparecer; **he turned up in Spain**, apareció en España; *fig* **something is sure to t. up**, algo pasará. **2** (*arrive*) llegar, presentarse; **he turned up too late for the meeting**, llegó demasiado tarde para la reunión. **3** (*attend*) asistir, acudir; **very few people turned up**, asistieron muy pocas personas. **4** *Cards* salir.

turncoat ['tɜːnkəʊt] *n* renegado,-a *m*, *f*.

turning ['tɜːnɪŋ] **I** *adj* que da vueltas, giratorio,-a. **II** *n* **1** (*turnabout*) cambio *m* de dirección. ■ *fig* **t. point**, punto *m* decisivo, momento *m* crítico. **2** (*in road*) vuelta *f*, recodo *m*; (*in town*) **take the first t. on the right**, toma la primera bocacalle a mano derecha.

turnip ['tɜːnɪp] *n* *Bot* nabo *m*.

turnout ['tɜːnaʊt] *n* asistencia *f*; **there was a good/poor t.**, asistió mucha/poca gente.

turnover ['tɜːnəʊvə^r] *n* **1** *Com* facturación *f*, volumen *m* de negocios; (*movement*) movimiento *m*; **quick t. of goods**, movimiento *m* rápido de mercancías. **2** *Culin* **apple t.**, empanada *f* de manzana.

turnpike ['tɜːnpaɪk] *n* US autopista *f* de peaje.

turnstile ['tɜːnstaɪl] *n* torniquete *m*.

turnstone ['tɜːnstəʊn] *n* *Orn* vuelvepiedras *m inv*.

turntable ['tɜːnteɪbəl] *n* **1** *Rail* placa *f* or plataforma *f* giratoria. **2** (*for record*) plato *m* giratorio.

turn-up ['tɜːnʌp] *n* GB (*of trousers*) vuelta *f*; *fam fig* **what a t. for the books!**, ¡vaya sorpresa!

turpentine ['tɜːpəntaɪn] *n* (esencia *f* de) trementina *f*, aguarrás *m*.

turquoise ['tɜːkwɔɪz] **I** *n* (*colour, stone*) turquesa *f*. **II** *adj* **t.** (**blue**), de color azul turquesa.

turret ['tʌrɪt] *n* **1** *Archit* torrecilla *f*. **2** *Mil* (*of tank*) torreta *f*.

turtle ['tɜːtəl] *n* *Zool* tortuga *f*; *Naut fig* **to turn t.**, zozobrar. ■ **t. soup**, consomé *m* de tortuga.

turtledove ['tɜːtəldʌv] *n* *Orn* tórtola *f*.

turtleneck ['tɜːtəlnek] *n* cuello *m* alto; **a t. sweater**, un jersey de cuello alto.

tusk [tʌsk] *n* colmillo *m*.

tussle ['tʌsəl] **I** *vi* pelearse, luchar. **II** *n* (*fight*) pelea *f*, lucha *f*; (*commotion*) follón *m*; **to have a t.**, pelearse.

tussock ['tʌsək] *n* mata *f* de hierba.

tutor ['tjuːtə^r] **I** *n* *Univ* tutor,-a *m*, *f*; **private t.**, profesor,-a *m*, *f* particular. **II** *vtr* **to t. sb in English**, dar clases particulares de inglés a algn.

tutorial [tjuːˈtɔːrɪəl] *n* *Univ* (*clase f*) tutorial *f*.

tutu ['tuːtuː] *n* tutú *m*.

Tuvalu [tuːvəˈluː] *n* Tuvalu.

tuxedo [tʌkˈsiːdəʊ] *n (pl tuxedos) US* smoking *m*.

TV [tiːˈviː] *abbr of* **television**, televisión *f*, TV.

twaddle [ˈtwɒdəl] *n fam* tonterías *fpl*, bobadas *fpl*; **stop talking t.!**, ¡déjate de tonterías!

twang [twæŋ] **I** *n* **1** *(of instrument)* sonido *m* vibrante. **2** *(quality)* nasal t., gangueo *m*, voz *f* gangosa; **to speak with a t.**, ganguear. **II** *vtr* **to t. a guitar**, puntear una guitarra. **III** *vi Mus (string)* vibrar.

tweak [twiːk] *vtr* pellizcar; **to t. sb's ears**, tirar de las orejas a algn.

twee [twiː] *adj GB* cursi; **it's rather t.**, es un poco cursi.

tweed [twiːd] *n Tex* cheviot *m*.

tweet [twiːt] **I** *n* pío *m*, gorjeo *m*. **II** *vi* piar, gorjear.

tweeter [ˈtwiːtə^r] *n (loudspeaker)* altavoz *m* para los sonidos agudos.

tweezers [ˈtwiːzəz] *npl* pinzas *fpl*.

twelfth [twelfθ] **I** *adj* duodécimo,-a; **(on) the t. of March**, el doce de Marzo. ■ **T. Night**, Noche *f* de Reyes. **II** *n* **1** *(in series)* duodécimo,-a *m*, *f*. **2** *(fraction)* duodécimo *m*; *see also* **seventh**.

twelve [twelv] **I** *adj* doce; **t. o'clock**, las doce. **II** *n* doce *m*; *see also* **seven**.

twentieth [ˈtwentɪθ] **I** *adj* vigésimo,-a; **(on) the t. of June**, el veinte de Junio. **II** *n* **1** *(in series)* vigésimo,-a *m*, *f*. **2** *(fraction)* vigésimo *m*; *see also* **seventh**.

twenty [ˈtwentɪ] **I** *adj* veinte; **about t. people**, una veintena de personas; **the t.-first of May**, el veintiuno de mayo; **t.-one**, veintiuno; *Med* **t.-t. vision**, visión *f* normal; **t.-two**, veintidós. **II** *n* veinte *m*; **he's in his late twenties**, tiene veintimuchos años; **in the early twenties**, a principios de los años veinte; *see also* **seven**.

twerp [twɜːp] *n fam* jilipollas *mf inv*, imbécil *mf*.

twice [twaɪs] *adv* dos veces; **he's t. as old as I am**, tiene el doble de años que yo; **in England it would cost t. as much**, en Inglaterra costaría el doble; **to be t. as big as sth**, ser el doble de grande que algo; **to do sth t. (over)**, hacer algo dos veces; *fam* **he did't have to be asked t.**, no se hizo de rogar.

twiddle [ˈtwɪdəl] **I** *vtr* dar vueltas a, girar; **to t. one's moustache**, mesarse el bigote; **to t. one's thumbs**, estar mano sobre mano. **II** *vi* **to t. with sth**, juguetear con algo.

twig¹ [twɪg] *n* ramilla *f*, ramita *f*.

twig² [twɪg] **I** *vtr (pt & pp twigged) GB fam* comprender, caer en la cuenta de. **II** *vi* comprender, caer en la cuenta.

twilight [ˈtwaɪlaɪt] *n* crepúsculo *m*; **in the t.**, a media luz.

twin [twɪn] **I** *n* gemelo,-a *m*, *f*, mellizo,-a *m*, *f*; **identical twins**, gemelos idénticos. ■ **t. beds**, camas *f* gemelas; **t. brother/sister**, hermano gemelo/hermana gemela; **t.-engined aircraft**, bimotor *m*. **II** *vtr (pt & pp twinned)* hermanar; **our town is twinned with one in Germany**, nuestra ciudad está hermanada con una alemana.

twine [twaɪn] **I** *n* bramante *m*. **II** *vtr* entretejer; **to t. sth round sth**, enrollar algo en algo. **III** *vi* **to t. round sth**, enroscarse alrededor de algo.

twinge [twɪndʒ] *n (of pain)* punzada *f*; *fig* **t. of conscience**, remordimiento *m*.

twinkle [ˈtwɪŋkəl] **I** *vi (stars)* centellear, parpadear; *(eyes)* brillar. **II** *n (of stars)* centelleo *m*, parpadeo *m*; *(of eyes)* brillo *m*.

twinkling [ˈtwɪŋklɪŋ] *n (of stars)* centelleo *m*, parpadeo *m*; *fig* **in the t. of an eye**, en un abrir y cerrar de ojos.

twinned [twɪnd] *pt & pp see* **twin**.

twinset [ˈtwɪnset] *n GB (matching garments)* conjunto *m*.

twirl [twɜːl] **I** *vtr* **1** *(whirl)* girar rápidamente, hacer molinetes con. **2** *(twist)* **to t. one's moustache**, mesarse el bigote. **II** *vi (spin)* girar rápidamente; *(dancer)* piruetear. **III** *n* **1** *(movement)* giro *m* rápido; *(of dancer)* pirueta *f*. **2** *(of smoke)* voluta *f*, espiral *f*.

twist [twɪst] **I** *vtr* **1** torcer; *(sense of something)* retorcer, tergiversar; **to t. off a lid**, desenroscar una tapa; *Med* **to t. one's ankle**, torcerse el tobillo; **to t. sb's arm**, retorcerle el brazo a algn; **to t. sth round sth**, enrollar algo alrededor de algo; **to t. together**, entrelazar; *fig* **she can t. him round her little finger**, hace con él todo lo que quiere. **2** *GB fam (cheat)* estafar, timar. **II** *vi (smoke)* formar volutas; *(path)* serpentear; *(worm)* retorcerse. **III** *n* **1** *(of yarn)* torzal *m*; **t. of hair**, trenza *f*; **t. of paper**, cucurucho *m* de papel. **2** *(movement)* torsión *f*; *Med* torcedura *f*, esguince *m*; **to give sth a t.**, torcer algo; *fig* **to give a new t. to sth**, dar un nuevo enfoque a algo. **3** *(in road)* vuelta *f*, recodo *m*; **twists and turns**, vueltas y más vueltas; *fam* **to be round the t.**, estar chiflado,-a. **4** *(dance)* twist *m*.

twisted [ˈtwɪstɪd] *adj* torcido,-a, retorcido,-a.

twister [ˈtwɪstə^r] *n GB fam (person)* estafador,-a *m*, *f*.

twisting [ˈtwɪstɪŋ] **I** *adj (road, path)* que serpentea, que da vueltas. **II** *n* tercedura *f*; *fig (of facts)* deformación *f*.

twit [twɪt] *n fam* jilipollas *mf inv*.

twitch [twɪtʃ] **I** *vtr* **1** dar un tirón a. **2** *(hands)* crispar; *(animal)* **to t. its ears**, mover nerviosamente las orejas. **II** *vi* crisparse; **his face twitches**, tiene un tic. **III** *n* **1** *(movement)* tirón *m*. **2** *(nervous)* tic *m* nervioso.

twitter [ˈtwɪtə^r] **I** *vi (bird)* gorjear. **II** *n (of bird)* gorjeo *m*; *fam* **to be in a t.** *or* **all of a t.**, estar muy nervioso,-a.

twittering [ˈtwɪtərɪŋ] *n* gorjeo *m*.

two [tuː] **I** *adj* dos *inv*; *fig* **to be in** *or* **of t. minds about sth**, estar indeciso,-a respecto a algo. **II** *n (pl twos)* dos *m inv*; **the t. of us, we t.**, nosotros dos; *fig* **he and his brother are t. of a kind**, él y su hermano son tal para cual; *fig* **to put t. and t. together**, atar *or* juntar cabos; *see also* **seven**.

two-edged [ˈtuːedʒd] *adj* de doble filo.

two-faced [ˈtuːfeɪst] *adj* hipócrita.

two-legged [ˈtuːlegɪd] *adj* bípedo,-a.

two-party [ˈtuːpɑːtɪ] *adj Pol* bipartidista.

twopence [ˈtʌpəns] *n GB* dos peniques; *fig* **I don't care t.**, (no) me importa un bledo.

two-piece [ˈtuːpiːs] **I** *adj* de dos piezas. **II** *n (suit)* traje *m* de dos piezas.

two-ply [ˈtuːplaɪ] *adj (wool)* de dos hilos.

two-seater [ˈtuːsiːtə^r] *adj & n Aut* biplaza (*f*).

twosome [ˈtuːsəm] *n* pareja *f*; **we went in a t.**, fuimos los dos juntos.

two-storey [ˈtuːstɔːrɪ] *adj* de dos pisos.

two-stroke [ˈtuːstrəʊk] *adj (engine)* de dos tiempos. ■ **t. mixture**, carburante *m* para un motor de dos tiempos.

two-time [ˈtuːtaɪm] *vtr fam* engañar en el amor.

two-tone [ˈtuːtəʊn] *adj* de dos colores.

two-way [ˈtuːweɪ] *adj* **1** *(street)* de dos direcciones. **2** *Rad* **t. radio**, aparato *m* emisor y receptor; *Elec* **t. switch**, conmutador *m* bidireccional.

two-wheeler [ˈtuːwiːlə^r] *n fam* bicicleta *f*.

tycoon [taɪˈkuːn] *n* magnate *m*.

type [taɪp] **I** *n* **1** *(kind)* tipo *m*, clase *f*; *(brand)* marca *f*; *(of car)* modelo *m*; **Gruyère-t. cheese**, queso *m* tipo Gruyère; **he's a nasty t.**, es un tipo antipático; **she's not my t.**, no es mi tipo; **what t. of person is she?**, ¿qué clase de persona es? **2** *Typ* carácter *m*, tipo *m*; *(print)* caracteres *mpl*, tipos *mpl* **in bold t.**, en negrita; **in large/small t.**, en caracteres grandes/pequeños. **II** *vtr* escribir a máquina, mecanografiar; **to t. out a piece of work**, pasar un trabajo a máquina. **III** *vi* escribir a máquina.

typecast [ˈtaɪpkɑːst] *vtr (pt & pp typecast)* encasillar.

typescript [ˈtaɪpskrɪpt] *n* texto *m* escrito a máquina *or* mecanografiado.

typeset [ˈtaɪpset] *vtr (pt & pp typeset) Print* componer.

typesetter [ˈtaɪpsetə^r] *n Print* **1** *(person)* cajista *mf*. **2** *(machine)* máquina *f* para componer tipos.

typewriter ['taɪpraɪtəʳ] *n* máquina *f* de escribir.

typewritten ['taɪprɪtən] *adj* escrito,-a a máquina, mecanografiado,-a.

typhoid ['taɪfɔɪd] *n Med* **t. (fever),** fiebre *f* tifoidea.

typhoon [taɪ'fuːn] *n* tifón *m*.

typhus ['taɪfəs] *n Med* tifus *m*.

typical ['tɪpɪkəl] *adj* típico,-a; **that's t. of him,** es muy típico de él.

typify ['tɪpɪfaɪ] *vtr (pt & pp **typified**)* tipificar, ser característico,-a de.

typing ['taɪpɪŋ] *n* mecanografía *f*. **t. paper,** papel *m* para escribir a máquina.

typist ['taɪpɪst] *n* mecanógrafo,-a *m,f*.

typography [taɪ'pɒɡrəfɪ] *n* tipografía *f*.

tyrannical [tɪ'rænɪkəl] *adj* tiránico,-a.

tyrannize ['tɪrənaɪz] *vtr* tiranizar.

tyrannous ['tɪrənəs] *adj see* **tyrannical.**

tyranny ['tɪrənɪ] *n* tiranía *f*.

tyrant ['taɪrənt] *n* tirano,-a *m,f*.

tyre [taɪəʳ] *n* neumático *m*. ■ **t. pressure,** presión *f* de los neumáticos.

tyro ['taɪrəʊ] *n (pl **tyros**)* aprendiz,-a *m,f*, principjiante *mf*.

Tyrol [tɪ'rəʊl] *n* Tirol.

Tyrolean [tɪrə'lɪən] *adj & n* tirolés,-esa *(m,f)*.

Tyrrhenian Sea [tɪriː'nɪən'siː] *n* **the T. S.,** el Mar Tirreno.

U

U, u [juː] *n (the letter)* U, u *f*.

UAE [juːeɪ'iː] *abbr of* **United Arab Emirates,** Emiratos *mpl* Arabes Unidos, EAU *mpl*.

ubiquity [juː'bɪkwɪtɪ] *n (gen)* ubicuidad *f*; *(of God)* omnipresencia *f*.

udder ['ʌdəʳ] *n* ubre *f*.

UDR [juːdiː'ɑːʳ] *abbr of* **Ulster Defence Regiment.**

UEFA [juː'eɪfə, juː'iːfə] *Sport abbr of* **Union of European Football Associations,** Unión *f* de Asociaciones Europeas de Fútbol, UEFA *f*.

UFO, ufo ['juːef'əʊ, 'juːfəʊ] *(pl **UFOs, ufos**) abbr of* **unidentified flying object,** objeto *m* volador no identificado, OVNI *m*, ovni *m*.

Uganda [juː'ɡændə] *n* Uganda.

Ugandan [juː'ɡændən] *adj & n* ugandés,-esa *(m,f)*.

ugh [ʊx, ʊh, ʌh] *interj* ¡uf!, ¡puf!

ugliness ['ʌɡlɪnɪs] *n* fealdad *f*.

ugly ['ʌɡlɪ] *adj (**uglier, ugliest**) (gen)* feo,-a; *(incident, situation)* desagradable; **as u. as sin,** más feo que un pecado; **to grow u.,** afearse; **to have an u. temper,** tener mal genio; *fig* **u. ducking,** patito feo.

UHF [juːeɪtʃ'ef] *Rad TV abbr of* **ultra high frequency,** frecuencia *f* ultraaita, UHF *f*.

UK [juːkeɪ] *abbr of* **United Kingdom,** Reino *m* Unido, R.U. *m*.

Ukraine ['juːkreɪn] *n* **the U.,** Ucrania.

Ukranian [juː'kreɪnɪən] **I** *adj* ucraniano,-a, ucranio,-a. **II** *n* **1** *(people)* ucraniano,-a *(m,f)*. **2** *(language)* ucranio *m*.

ulcer ['ʌlsəʳ] *n (outer)* llaga *f*; *(inner)* úlcera *f*. **stomach u.,** úlcera *f* de estómago.

ulcerate ['ʌlsəreɪt] **I** *vtr* ulcerar. **II** *vi* ulcerarse.

ulterior [ʌl'tɪərɪəʳ] *adj* **1** *(hidden)* oculto,-a. **2** *(further)* ulterior.

ultimate ['ʌltɪmɪt] **I** *adj* **1** *(final)* último,-a; *(of aim)* final; *(of decision)* definitivo,-a. **2** *(basic)* esencial, fundamental. **II the u.** *n* el no va más. ◆ **ultimately** *adv* **1** *(finally)* finalmente. **2** *(basically)* en el fondo.

ultimatum [ʌltɪ'meɪtəm] *n (pl **ultimatums** or **ultimata** [ʌltɪ'meɪtəl])* ultimátum *m*.

ultra- ['ʌltrə] *pref* ultra-.

ultrafashionable [ʌltrə'fæʃənəbəl] *adj* a la última moda, muy de moda.

ultramarine [ʌltrəmə'riːn] **I** *n* azul *m* ultramarino *or* de ultramar. **II** *adj (from overseas)* ultramarino,-a.

ultrasound [ʌltrə'saʊnd] *n* ultrasonido *m*.

urtraviolet [ʌltrə'vaɪələt] *adj* ultravioleta.

umbilical [ʌm'bɪlɪkəl, ʌmbɪ'laɪkəl] *adj* umbilical; **u. cord,** cordón umbilical.

umbrage ['ʌmbrɪdʒ] *n* resentimiento *m*; **to take u. at sth,** sentirse ofendido,-a por algo.

umbrella [ʌm'brelə] *n* **1** *(device)* paraguas *m inv*. ■ **beach u.,** quitasol *m*, parasol *m*, sombrilla *f*; **u. stand,** paragüero *m*. **2** *Av Mil* cobertura *f* aérea. **3** *fig (protection)* manto *m*, protección *f*; *(patronage)* patrocinio *m*. ■ **u. organization,** organismo *m* madre.

umpire ['ʌmpaɪəʳ] **I** *n* árbitro *m*. **II** *vtr* arbitrar.

umpteen [ʌmp'tiːn] *adj fam* muchísimos,-as, la tira de; **u. guests,** un montón de invitados.

umpteenth [ʌmp'tiːnθ] *adj* enésimo,-a.

UN [juː'en] *abbr of* **United Nations (Organization),** (Organización *f* de las) Naciones *fpl* Unidas, ONU *f sing*.

un- [ʌn] *pref* in-, des-, poco ..., sin ...; **unadvisable,** desaconsejable, poco aconsejable; **unanswered.** sin contestar.

'un [ʌn] *pron fam* **he's a bad 'un,** es un tipo de mucho cuidado; **the little 'uns,** los chiquitines, los peques.

unabashed [ʌnə'bæʃt] *adj* **1** *(unperturbed)* inmutable, imperturbable. **2** *(shameless)* desvergonzado,-a, descarado,-a.

unable [ʌn'eɪbəl] *adj* incapaz; **I'm u. to attend the meeting,** me es imposible asistir a la reunión; **to be u. to do sth/anything,** no poder hacer algo/nada.

unabridged [ʌnə'brɪdʒd] *adj* íntegro,-a; **u. edition,** edición íntegra.

unacceptable [ʌnək'septəbəl] *adj* inaceptable.

unaccommodating [ʌnə'kɒmədeɪtɪŋ] *adj (person)* poco sociable.

unaccompanied [ʌnə'kʌmpənɪd] *adj* **1** *(person)* solo,-a, sin compañía. **2** *Mus* sin acompañamiento.

unaccomplished [ʌnə'kʌmplɪʃt] *adj* **1** *(unfinished)* incompleto,-a, sin acabar. **2** *(mediocre)* mediocre.

unaccountable [ʌnə'kaʊntəbəl] *adj* inexplicable.

unaccounted-for [ʌnə'kaʊntɪdfɔːʳ] *adj* **to be u.-f.,** faltar; **five passengers are still u.-f.,** se desconoce aún el paradero de cinco pasajeros.

unaccustomed [ʌnə'kʌstəmd] *adj* desacostumbrado,-a **(to,** a); **he's u. to this climate,** no está muy acostumbrado a este clima.

unacquainted [ʌnə'kweɪntɪd] *adj* **to be u. with,** no conocer, ignorar; **I'm u. with Shaw's plays,** no conozco las obras de Shaw.

unadventurous [ʌnəd'ventʃərəs] *adj* poco atrevido,-a *or* arriesgado,-a.

unadvisable [ʌnəd'vaɪzəbəl] *adj* desaconsejable, poco aconsejable.

unaffected [ʌnə'fektɪd] *adj* **1** *(unchanged)* no afectado,-a (**by**, por). **2** *(indifferent)* indiferente (**by**, a); **u. by his insults,** inmutable ante sus insultos. **3** *(natural) (person)* natural, afable, campechano,-a; *(style)* llano,-a, sin afectación.

unafraid [ʌnə'freɪd] *adj* sin miedo (**of**, a); **to be u. of sb/ sth,** no tenerle miedo a algn/algo.

unaided [ʌn'eɪdɪd] *adj* sin ayuda, solo,-a.

unalterable [ʌn'ɔːltərəbəl] *adj* inalterable.

unambiguous [ʌnæm'bɪgjʊəs] *adj* nequívoco,-a.

unambitious [ʌnæm'bɪʃəs] *adj* **1** *(person)* poco ambicioso,-a, sin ambición. **2** *(idea, project)* poco ambicioso,-a, de corto alcance.

unanimous [juː'nænɪməs] *adj* unánime.

unannounced [ʌnə'naʊnst] *adj* sin avisar; **she came in u.,** *(without knocking)* entró sin llamar; *(without announcement)* entró sin ser anunciada.

unanswerable [ʌn'ɑːnsərəbəl] *adj* **1** *(argument etc)* irrefutable. **2** *(question)* sin respuesta (posible), que no tiene respuesta.

unanswered [ʌn'ɑːnsəd] *adj* sin contestar.

unappreciated [ʌnə'priːʃieɪtɪd] *adj* poco apreciado,-a *or* valorado,-a.

unappreciative [ʌnə'priːʃiətɪv] *adj* desagradecido,-a; **to be u. of,** no apreciar, no valorar.

unapproachable [ʌnə'prəʊtʃəbəl] *adj* inabordable, inaccesible.

unarmed [ʌn'ɑːmd] *adj* desarmado,-a; **u. combat,** lucha a cuerpo limpio.

unashamed [ʌnə'ʃeɪmd] *adj* desvergonzado,-a, descarado,-a.

unasked [ʌn'ɑːskt] *adv* **1** **u. (for),** *(unrequested)* no solicitado,-a; *(spontaneous)* espontáneo,-a. **2** *(not invited)* sin ser invitado,-a; **she often helps quite u.,** muchas veces ayuda sin que se lo pidan.

unassuming [ʌnə'sjuːmɪŋ] *adj* modesto,-a, sin pretensiones.

unattached [ʌnə'tætʃt] *adj* **1** *(independent)* libre, independiente; *(loose)* suelto,-a. **2** *(not engaged or married)* soltero-a y sin compromiso. **3** *Jur (of property etc)* no embargado,-a.

unattainable [ʌnə'teɪnəbəl] *adj* inalcanzable.

unattended [ʌnə'tendɪd] *adj* **1** *(not looked after) (counter, desk)* desatendido,-a; **to leave a child u.,** dejar a un niño sin nadie que le vigile. **2** *(alone)* solo,-a.

unattractive [ʌnə'træktɪv] *adj* poco atractivo,-a, feo,-a.

unauthorized [ʌn'ɔːθəraɪzd] *adj* **1** *(person)* no autorizado,-a; **'no entry to u. persons',** 'prohibido el paso a toda persona ajena a la empresa *or* a la obra'. **2** *(trade etc)* ilícito,-a, ilegal.

unavailable [ʌnə'veɪləbəl] *adj* no disponible; **Mr X is u. today,** el Sr. X no le puede atender hoy; **that brand is u. in supermarkets,** esa marca no se vende en los supermercados.

unavoidable [ʌnə'vɔɪdəbəl] *adj* *(gen)* inevitable; *(accident)* fortuito,-a.

unaware [ʌnə'weər] *adj* ignorante, inconsciente (**of**, de); **to be u. of danger,** ser inconsciente del peligro; **to be u. of sth,** ignorar algo.

unawares [ʌnə'weəz] *adv* **1** *(unexpectedly)* desprevenido,-a; **he caught me u.,** me cogió desprevenido. **2** *(without knowing)* inconscientemente, sin darse cuenta; **she dropped it u.,** se le cayó sin darse cuenta.

unbalanced [ʌn'bælənst] *adj* desequilibrado,-a.

unbearable [ʌn'beərəbəl] *adj* insoportable, inaguantable, intolerable.

unbeatable [ʌn'biːtəbəl] *adj* *(team)* invencible, sin rival; *(price, quality)* inmejorable, inigualable.

unbecoming [ʌnbɪ'kʌmɪŋ] *adj* *(unsuitable)* poco apropiado,-a, impropio,-a (**de**, of); **u. of a gentleman,** impropio de un caballero. **2** *(unflattering)* poco favorecedor,-a.

unbelievable [ʌnbɪ'liːvəbəl] *adj* increíble.

unbend [ʌn'bend] **I** *vtr (pt & pp unbent* [ʌn'bent]*) fig* hacerse más amable. **II** *vi fam fig* relajarse.

unbia(s)sed [ʌn'baɪəst] *adj* imparcial.

unblinking [ʌn'blɪŋkɪŋ] *adj* sin pestañear; *fig* imperturbable.

unborn [ʌn'bɔːn] *adj* sin nacer, aún no nacido,-a, nonato,-a.

unbounded [ʌn'baʊndɪd] *adj* ilimitado,-a; *fig* desmedido,-a.

unbreakable [ʌn'breɪkəbəl] *adj* irrompible; *fig* inquebrantable.

unbridled [ʌn'braɪdəld] *adj fig* desenfrenado,-a.

unbroken [ʌn'brəʊkən] *adj* **1** *(whole)* intacto,-a, sin romper. **2** *(uninterrupted)* ininterrumpido,-a, continuo,-a; **six hours of u. sleep,** seis horas de sueño continuo. **3** *(untamed)* sin domar. **4** *(record)* sin batir *or* igualar.

unburden [ʌn'bɜːdən] *vtr descargar; fig* **to u. one's heart to sb,** desahogarse con algn, confiarse a algn.

unbusinesslike [ʌn'bɪznɪslaɪk] *adj* *(lacking in method)* poco metódico,-a, desorganizado,-a; *(informal)* informal.

unbutton [ʌn'bʌtən] *vtr* **1** *(undo)* desabrochar. **2** *fam* **to u. oneself,** relajarse.

uncalled-for [ʌn'kɔːldfɔːr] *adj* **1** *(inappropriate)* inapropiado,-a, insensato,-a, fuera de lugar. **2** *(unjustified)* inmerecido,-a, injustificado,-a. **2** *(unnecessary)* innecesario,-a, superfluo,-a.

uncanny [ʌn'kænɪ] *adj* misterioso,-a, extraño,-a.

uncaring [ʌn'keərɪŋ] *adj* indiferente.

unceasing [ʌn'siːsɪŋ] *adj* incesante, continuo,-a.

uncertain [ʌn'sɜːtən] *adj* **1** *(not certain)* incierto,-a; *(doubtful)* dudoso,-a; *(unspecified)* indeterminado,-a; **I'm still u. (as to) whether or not she is coming,** aún no sé con toda seguridad si viene ella o no; **in no u. terms,** claramente, sin rodeos. **2** *(not reliable)* inseguro,-a. **3** *(changeable) (weather etc)* variable. **4** *(hesitant)* indeciso,-a.

uncertainty [ʌn'sɜːtəntɪ] *n* incertidumbre *f*, duda *f*.

unchallenged [ʌn'tʃælɪndʒd] *adj* *(right etc)* indiscutido,-a, incontestado,-a.

unchangeable [ʌn'tʃeɪndʒəbəl] *adj* inmutable, inalterable.

unchanged [ʌn'tʃeɪndʒd] *adj* igual, sin alteración; **it has remained u.,** ha quedado igual.

unchecked [ʌn'tʃekt] *adj* **1** *(not restrained)* desenfrenado,-a; **u. advance,** avance sin obstáculos. **2** *(not examined)* no comprobado,-a, sin comprobar.

uncivil [ʌn'sɪvəl] *adj* *(impolite)* descortés.

uncivilized [ʌn'sɪvɪlaɪzd] *adj* *(tribe)* incivilizado,-a, salvaje; *(not cultured)* inculto,-a; *fig* **u. hour,** hora intempestiva.

unclaimed [ʌn'kleɪmd] *adj* sin reclamar.

uncle ['ʌŋkəl] *n* tío *m*. ▪ *fam* **U. Sam,** el Tío Sam.

unclean [ʌn'kliːn] *adj* sucio,-a; *Rel* impuro,-a.

unclear [ʌn'klɪər] *adj* poco claro,-a, confuso,-a.

uncoil [ʌn'kɔɪl] **I** *vtr* desenrollar. **II** *vi* desenrollarse.

uncombed [ʌn'kəʊmd] *adj (hair)* despeinado,-a.

uncomfortable [ʌn'kʌmftəbəl] *adj* **1** *(physically)* incómodo,-a, poco confortable. **2** *(awkward)* incómodo,-a, molesto,-a; **to feel u.,** no estar a gusto, sentirse incómodo,-a. **3** *(unpleasant)* desagradable; **to make things u. for sb,** complicarle la vida a algn.

uncommitted [ʌnkə'mɪtɪd] *adj* no comprometido,-a.

uncommon [ʌn'kɒmən] *adj* **1** *(rare)* poco común *or* corriente, insólito,-a; *(unusual)* extraordinario,-a. **2** *(excessive)* excesivo,-a, desmesurado,-a. ◆ **uncommonly** *adv* extraordinariamente; **not u.,** con cierta frecuencia.

uncommunicative [ʌnkə'mjuːnɪkətɪv] *adj* poco comunicativo,-a, reservado,-a, cerrado,-a.

uncompromising [ʌn'kɒmprəmaɪzɪŋ] *adj* intransigente, inflexible; **u. honesty,** sinceridad absoluta.

unconcealed [ʌnkən'siːld] *adj* no dismulado,-a, evidente.

unconcerned [ʌnkən'sɜːnd] *adj* indiferente **(about,** a).

unconditional [ʌnkən'dɪʃənəl] *adj* incondicional; **u. refusal,** negativa rotunda.

unconditioned [ʌnkən'dɪʃənd] *adj* **1** *Psych* no condicionado,-a; **u. reflex,** reflejo espontáneo. **2** *(unconditional)* incondicional.

unconfirmed [ʌnkən'fɜːmd] *adj* no confirmado,-a, sin confirmar.

uncongenial [ʌnkən'dʒiːnɪəl] *adj (person)* antipático,-a; *(work)* desagradable.

unconnected [ʌnkə'nektɪd] *adj* no relacionado,-a; **the two events are quite u.,** los dos sucesos no guardan relación entre sí.

unconscionable [ʌn'kɒnʃənəbəl] *adj* **1** *(unscrupulous)* sin escrúpulos. **2** *(excessive)* excesivo,-a, desmesurado,-a.

unconscious [ʌn'kɒnʃəs] *adj* **1** *Med* inconsciente; **she was u. for two hours,** estuvo dos horas sin conocimiento; **to become u.,** perder el conocimiento. **2** *(unaware)* inconsciente **(of,** de). **3** *(unintentional)* involuntario,-a. **II the u.** *n Psych* el inconsciente.

unconsciousness [ʌn'kɒnʃəsnɪs] *n Med* pérdida *f* del conocimiento, inconsciencia *f*.

unconsidered [ʌnkən'sɪdəd] *adj (rash)* irreflexivo,-a.

unconstitutional [ʌnkɒnstɪ'tjuːʃənəl] *adj* anticonstitucional, inconstitucional.

uncontested [ʌnkən'testɪd] *adj* incontestado,-a. ▦ *Pol* **u. seat,** escaño *m* ganado sin oposición.

uncontrollable [ʌnkən'trəʊləbəl] *adj (gen)* incontrolable; *(people)* ingobernable; *(desire)* irresistible; **u. laughter,** ataque de risa.

unconventional [ʌnkən'venʃənəl] *adj* poco convencional, original.

unconvinced [ʌnkən'vɪnst] *adj* poco convencido,-a, escéptico,-a.

uncooperative [ʌnkəʊ'ɒpərətɪv] *adj* poco cooperativo,-a.

uncoordinated [ʌnkəʊ'ɔːdɪneɪtɪd] *adj* no coordinado,-a, sin coordinar.

uncork [ʌn'kɔːk] *vtr* descorchar; *fig* soltar, dar rienda suelta a.

uncorrected [ʌnkə'rektɪd] *adj* sin corregir.

uncouple [ʌn'kʌpəl] *vtr Rail* desenganchar, desacoplar, desconectar.

uncouth [ʌn'kuːθ] *adj (rude)* grosero,-a; *(rough)* tosco,-a.

uncover [ʌn'kʌvəʳ] *vtr* **1** destapar. **2** *fig (plot etc)* revelar, descubrir.

uncovered [ʌn'kʌvəd] *adj* **1** destapado,-a, al descubierto. **2** *Fin* **u. cheque,** cheque *m* sin fondos.

uncrossed [ʌn'krɒst] *adj GB (cheque)* sin barrar *or* cruzar.

unction [ʌnkʃən] *n* **1** *Rel* unción *f*; **extreme u.,** extremaunción *f*. **2** *(suavity)* zalamería *f*, fervor *m* fingido. **3** *(ointment)* ungüento *m*.

uncultivated [ʌn'kʌltɪveɪtɪd] *adj* **1** *(person)* inculto,-a. **2** *Agr (land)* sin cultivar, baldío,-a, yermo,-a.

uncurbed [ʌn'kɜːbd] *adj (unchecked)* desenfrenado,-a.

uncut [ʌn'kʌt] *adj* **1** *(of grass etc)* sin cortar; *Print (of book)* intonso,-a. **2** *(of gemstone)* sin tallar.

undamaged [ʌn'dæmɪdʒd] *adj* **1** *(article etc)* sin desperfectos, en buen estado; *(person)* indemne, ileso,-a. **2** *fig (reputation etc)* intacto,-a.

undated [ʌn'deɪtɪd] *adj* sin fecha.

undaunted [ʌn'dɔːntɪd] *adj* firme, impávido,-a **(by,** ante); **to be u. in one's resolve,** ser firme en sus propósitos.

undeceive [ʌndɪ'siːv] *vtr fml* desengañar.

undecided [ʌndɪ'saɪdɪd] *adj* **1** *(person)* indeciso,-a; **he is u. whether to go,** no sabe si ir o no. **2** *(issue)* pendiente; **that's still u.,** eso está aún por decidir.

undecipherable [ʌndɪ'saɪfərəbəl] *adj* indescifrable.

undefeated [ʌndɪ'fiːtɪd] *adj* invicto,-a.

undefended [ʌndɪ'fendɪd] *adj* indefenso,-a; *Jur* **u. suit,** pleito *m* sin defensa.

undefined [ʌndɪ'faɪnd] *adj* indefinido,-a, indeterminado,-a.

undelivered [ʌndɪ'lɪvəd] *adj* sin entregar; **if u. please return to sender,** en caso de ausencia devuélvase al remitente; **u. letter,** carta devuelta.

undeniable [ʌndɪ'naɪəbəl] *adj* innegable, irrefutable.

under ['ʌndəʳ] **I** *prep* **1** *(below, beneath)* debajo de, bajo; **u. the table,** debajo de la mesa; **from u.,** de debajo de; **u. the sun,** bajo el sol. **2** *(less than)* menos de; **he ran a mile in u. four minutes,** corrió una milla en menos de cuatro minutos; **incomes u. £1,000,** ingresos inferiores a 1,000 libras; **u. age,** menor de edad. **3** *Mil (lower than)* de rango inferior a; **no one u. a captain,** nadie de rango inferior a capitán. **4** *(in the power of)* bajo; **u. Caesar,** bajo César;. **u. the doctor,** en manos del médico. **5** *(subject to, in)* bajo; **u. arrest,** bajo arresto, detenido,-a; **u. cover,** a cubierto; **u. lock and key,** bajo llave; **u. obligation to,** en la obligación de; **u. repair,** en reparación; **u. the circumstances,** dadas las circunstancias; *fig* **I was u. the impression that ...,** tenía la impresión de que ... . **6** *(according to)* según, conforme a; **u. his father's will,** según el testamento de su padre; **u. the terms of the contract,** según los términos del contrato. **7** *(known by)* bajo; **he worked there u. a false name,** trabajó allí bajo un nombre falso. **8** *Astrol* bajo; **born u. Aries,** nacido bajo el signo de Aries. **II** *adv* abajo, debajo; **to go u.,** ir a pique; *fam* **down u.,** a *or* en Australia; *fam* **he's one degree u. today,** hoy no anda muy fino.

under- ['ʌndəʳ] *pref (below)* sub-, infra-; *(insufficiently)* insuficientemente.

underarm ['ʌndərɑːm] **I** *adj* **1** *Sport (throw)* por debajo del hombro. **2** *(below the arm)* axilar; **u. deodorant,** desodorante para las axilas. **II** *adv Sport* por debajo del hombro; *Cricket* **to bowl u.,** lanzar la pelota por debajo.

undercarriage [ʌndə'kærɪdʒ] *n Av* tren *m* de aterrizaje.

undercharge [ʌndə'tʃɑːdʒ] *vtr* cobrar menos de lo debido.

underclothes ['ʌndəkləʊðz] *npl*, **underclothing** ['ʌndəkləʊðɪŋ] *n* ropa *f sing* interior.

undercoat ['ʌndəkəʊt] *n (of paint)* primera mano *f*.

undercover [ʌndə'kʌvəʳ] **I** *adj* secreto,-a, clandestino,-a. **II** *adv* en la clandestinidad; **to go u.,** pasar a la clandestinidad.

undercurrent ['ʌndəkʌrənt] *n* **1** *(in sea)* corriente *f* submarina. **2** *fig* tendencia *f* oculta.

undercut [ʌndə'kʌt] **I** *vtr (pt & pp* **undercut)** *Com (competitor)* vender más barato que. **II** ['ʌndəkʌt] *n Culin* filete *m* de solomillo.

underdeveloped [ʌndədɪ'veləpt] *adj* **1** subdesarrollado,-a. **2** *Phot* insuficientemente revelado,-a.

underdevelopment [ʌndədɪ'veləpmənt] *n* subdesarrollo *m*.

underdog ['ʌndədɒg] *n* desvalido,-a *m,f*, perdedor,-a *m,f*.

underestimate [ʌndər'estɪmeɪt] **I** *vtr* subestimar, infravalorar. **II** [ʌndər'estɪmɪt] *n* infravaloración *f*, menosprecio *m*.

underexposure [ˌʌndərɪk'spəʊʒəʳ] *n Phot* subexposición *f*.

underfed [ˌʌndə'fed] *adj* subalimentado,-a, desnutrido,-a.

underfoot [ˌʌndə'fʊt] *adv* debajo de los pies, en el suelo; **to trample sth u.**, pisotear algo.

undergo [ˌʌndə'gəʊ] *vtr (pt underwent; pp undergone* [ˌʌndə'gɒn]) *(gen)* experimentar; *(change)* sufrir; *(test etc)* pasar por; **to u. an operation**, someterse a una intervención quirúrgica.

undergraduate [ˌʌndə'grædjʊɪt] *n* estudiante *mf* universitario,-a.

underground ['ʌndəgraʊnd] **I** *adj* subterráneo,-a; *fig* clandestino,-a; *fig Cin Mus* underground; **the u. press**, la prensa clandestina. **II** [ˌʌndə'graʊnd] *adv* bajo tierra; *fig* clandestinamente; *fig* **to go u.**, pasar a la clandestinidad; *fig* **we had to work u.**, tuvimos que trabajar en la clandestinidad. **III** ['ʌndəgraʊnd] *n* **1** *(area, region)* subterráneo *m*. **2** *Pol (gen)* movimiento *m* clandestino; *(during World War II)* resistencia *f*. **3** *(transport)* **the u.**, el metro, *SAm* el subterráneo.

undergrowth ['ʌndəgrəʊθ] maleza *f*.

underhand ['ʌndəhænd] **I** *adj (method)* ilícito,-a, poco limpio,-a; *(person)* solapado,-a, ladino,-a; **u. affair**, asunto turbio. **II** *adv* bajo cuerda, ilícitamente.

underline [ˌʌndə'laɪn] *vtr* subrayar.

underling ['ʌndəlɪŋ] *n pej* mandado,-a *m, f*, subordinado,-a *m,f*.

underlying [ˌʌndə'laɪɪŋ] *adj* **1** *(concealed)* subyacente. **2** *(basic)* esencial, fundamental.

undermanned [ˌʌndə'mænd] *adj* escaso,-a de personal; *Naut* con una tripulación insuficiente.

undermentioned ['ʌndəmenʃənd] *adj* abajo citado,-a *or* mencionado,-a.

undermine [ˌʌndə'maɪn] *vtr* socavar, minar.

underneath [ˌʌndə'niːθ] **I** *prep* debajo de, bajo. **II** *adv* abajo, debajo. **III** *adj* de abajo, inferior. **IV** *n* parte *f* inferior, fondo *m*.

undernourished [ˌʌndə'nʌrɪʃt] *adj* desnutrido,-a, subalimentado,-a.

underpaid [ˌʌndə'peɪd] *adj* mal pagado,-a; **we're u. and overworked**, nos pagan mal y encima nos matan a trabajar.

underpass ['ʌndəpaːs] *n* paso *m* subterráneo.

underprivileged [ˌʌndə'prɪvɪlɪdʒd] **I** *adj* desvalido,-a, marginado,-a. **II the u.** *npl* los desvalidos.

underrate [ˌʌndə'reɪt] *vtr see* **undervalue**.

undersell [ˌʌndə'sel] *vtr (pt & pp undersold)* **1** *(sell at low price)* malvender. **2** *(undercut)* vender a menor precio que.

undershirt ['ʌndəʃɜːt] *n US* camiseta *f*.

undersigned ['ʌndəsaɪnd] *adj & n* abajo firmante *(mf)*.

undersized [ˌʌndə'saɪzd] *adj (thing)* demasiado pequeño,-a, diminuto,-a; *(person)* diminuto,-a.

underskirt ['ʌndəskɜːt] *n* **1** *(petticoat)* enaguas *fpl*; *(modern use)* combinación *f*. **2** *(lining)* forro *m*.

undersold [ˌʌndə'səʊld] *pt & pp see* **undersell**.

understaffed [ˌʌndə'staːft] *adj* falto,-a de personal.

understand [ˌʌndə'stænd] *vtr & vi (pt & pp understood)* **1** *(comprehend)* entender, comprender; **I can't u. it**, no logro entenderlo; **I u. French perfectly**, entiendo perfectamente el francés; **that's easily understood**, eso se comprende fácilmente; **to u. business**, entender de negocios; *fam* **do I make myself understood?**, ¿me explico? **2** *(assume, believe)* entender; **am I to u. that ...?**, ¿quiere eso decir que ...?; **she gave me to u. that ...**, me dio a entender que ... . **3** *(hear)* tener entendido; **I u. he'll give his consent**, tengo entendido que dará su aprobación. **4** *(be compatible with)* **to u. one another**, entenderse. **5** *(take for granted) (word, meaning)* sobreentender.

understandable [ˌʌndə'stændəbəl] *adj* comprensible.

understanding [ˌʌndə'stændɪŋ] **I** *n* **1** *(intellectual grasp)* entendimiento *m*, comprensión *f*; **it's beyond u.**, no hay forma de entenderlo. **2** *(interpretation)* intepretación *f*; **it was my u. that he would pay the expenses**, yo tenía entendido que los gastos correrían a su cargo. **3** *(agreement)* acuerdo *m*; **to come to** *or* **reach an u.**, llegar a un acuerdo. **4** *(condition)* condición *f*; **on the u. that ...**, a condición de que ... . **II** *adj* comprensivo,-a, compasivo,-a.

understatement [ˌʌndə'steɪtmənt] *n* atenuación *f*, eufemismo *m*; **to say that the boy is rather clever is an u.**, decir que el chico es bastante listo es quedarse corto.

understood [ˌʌndə'stʊd] **I** *pt & pp see* **understand**. **II** *adj* **1** *(assumed)* entendido,-a; **I wish it to be u. that ...**, (quiero) que conste que ... . **2** *(agreed on)* convenido,-a. **3** *(implied)* sobreentendido,-a, implícito,-a.

understudy ['ʌndəstʌdɪ] *n Theat* suplente *mf*.

undertake [ˌʌndə'teɪk] *vtr (pt undertook; pp undertaken* [ˌʌndə'teɪkən]) **1** *(take on) (responsibility)* asumir; *(task, job)* encargarse de. **2** *(promise)* comprometerse a.

undertaker ['ʌndəteɪkəʳ] *n* empresario,-a *m, f* de pompas fúnebres; **u.'s**, funeraria *f*, pompas *fpl* fúnebres.

undertaking [ˌʌndə'teɪkɪŋ] *n* **1** *(responsibility)* responsabilidad *f*, carga *f*; *(task)* tarea *f*, empresa *f*; **large-scale u.**, empresa a gran escala. **2** *(guarantee)* garantía *f*; **I can give you no such u.**, no puedo garantizárselo.

undertone ['ʌndətəʊn] *n* **1** *(low voice)* voz *f* baja; **in an u.**, en voz baja. **2** *fig (suggestion)* fondo *m*, matiz *m*.

undertook [ˌʌndə'tʊk] *pp see* **undertake**.

undervalue [ˌʌndə'vælju:] *vtr* subestimar, infravalorar.

underwater [ˌʌndə'wɔːtəʳ] **I** *adj* submarino,-a. **II** *adv* bajo el agua.

underwear ['ʌndəweəʳ] *n inv* ropa *f* interior.

underweight [ˌʌndə'weɪt] *adj* de peso insuficiente; **to be u.**, *(gen)* pesar menos de lo debido; *(boxer, jockey)* no dar el peso.

underwent [ˌʌndə'went] *pt see* **undergo**.

underworld ['ʌndəwɜːld] *n* **1** *(of criminals)* hampa *f*, bajos fondos *mpl*. **2** *Myth* **the u.**, el averno, el Hades.

underwrite [ˌʌndə'raɪt] *vtr (pt underwrote; pp underwritten)* **1** *Fin* suscribir. **2** *(guarantee)* garantizar, avalar. **3** *(insure)* asegurar.

underwriter ['ʌndəraɪtəʳ] *n* **1** *Fin* suscriptor,-a *m, f*. **2** *(insurer)* asegurador,-a *m,f*.

underwritten [ˌʌndə'rɪtən] *pp see* **underwrite**.

underwrote [ˌʌndə'rəʊt] *pt see* **underwrite**.

undeserved [ˌʌndɪ'zɜːd] *adj* inmerecido,-a.

undeserving [ˌʌndɪ'zɜːvɪŋ] *adj (case etc)* de poco mérito, que no merece atención; **u. of**, indigno,-a de.

undesirable [ˌʌndɪ'zaɪrəbəl] *adj & n* indeseable *(mf)*.

undetected [ˌʌndɪ'tektɪd] *adj (mistake etc)* pasado,-a por alto, no detectado,-a; **to pass u.**, pasar desapercibido.

undetermined [ˌʌndɪ'tɜːmɪnd] *adj* indeterminado,-a, indefinido,-a.

undeterred [ˌʌndɪ'tɜːd] *adj* sin inmutarse; **u. by**, sin arredrarse ante.

undeveloped [ˌʌndɪ'veləpt] *adj (gen)* sin desarrollar; *(land)* sin explotar.

undid [ʌn'dɪd] *pt see* **undo**.

undies ['ʌndɪz] *npl fam* bragas *fpl*.

undigested [ˌʌndɪ'dʒestɪd] *adj* **1** indigesto,-a. **2** *fig* mal digerido,-a *or* asimilado,-a; **u. knowledge**, conocimientos mal asimilados.

undignified [ʌn'dɪgnɪfaɪd] *adj (person)* poco digno,-a; *(attitude etc)* indecoroso,-a, indigno,-a.

undiluted [ˌʌndaɪ'lu:tɪd] *adj* no diluido,-a, sin diluir; *fig* **to talk u. nonsense**, decir disparates *or* chorradas.

undiplomatic [ʌndɪpləˈmætɪk] *adj* poco diplomático,-a.

undiscerning [ʌndɪˈsɜːnɪŋ] *adj* sin discernimiento.

undischarged [ʌndɪsˈtʃɑːdʒd] *adj* **1** *(bankrupt)* no rehabilitado,-a. **2** *(debt)* sin liquidar. **3** *(duty)* no cumplido,-a.

undisciplined [ʌnˈdɪsɪplɪnd] *adj* indisciplinado,-a.

undisclosed [ʌndɪsˈkləʊzd] *adj* sin revelar.

undiscovered [ʌndɪsˈkʌvəd] *adj* sin descubrir, desconocido,-a.

undiscriminating [ʌndɪsˈkrɪmɪneɪtɪŋ] *adj* indiscriminado,-a, sin discriminación.

undisguised [ʌndɪsˈgaɪzd] *adj (person)* sin disfraz; *fig* franco,-a, no disimulado,-a.

undisputed [ʌndɪˈspjuːtɪd] *adj (unchallenged)* incontestable; *(unquestionable)* indiscutible, incuestionable.

undisturbed [ʌndɪsˈtɜːbd] *adj* **1** *(person)* tranquilo,-a; **I wish to be left u.**, que no me molesten. **2** *(things)* sin tocar; **we left everything u.**, dejamos las cosas tal como estaban.

undivided [ʌndɪˈvaɪdɪd] *adj* **1** *(complete)* entero,-a. **2** *(unanimous)* unánime; **to give one's u. attention**, prestar toda la atención.

undo [ʌnˈduː] *vtr (pt* **undid**; *pp* **undone**) **1** *(unfasten) (knot)* desatar, deshacer; *(button)* desabrochar. **2** *(destroy)* deshacer, destruir; *prov* **what is done cannot be undone**, a lo hecho pecho. **3** *(put right)* enmendar; **to u. the damage**, reparar el daño.

undone[1] [ʌnˈdʌn] *adj (unfinished)* inacabado,-a; **to leave some work u.**, dejar trabajo sin hacer *or* acabar.

undone[2] [ʌnˈdʌn] **I** *pp see* **undo**. **II** *adj (unfastened) (knot etc)* deshecho,-a; **to come u.**, *(shoelace)* desatarse; *(button, blouse)* desabrocharse; *(necklace etc)* soltarse.

undoubted [ʌnˈdaʊtɪd] *adj* indudable.

undreamed [ʌnˈdriːmd] *adj*, **undreamt** [ʌnˈdremt] *adj* **u. (of)**, nunca soñado,-a, inimaginable.

undress [ʌnˈdres] **I** *vtr* desnudar. **II** *vi* desnudarse.

undressed [ʌnˈdrest] *adj (naked)* desnudo,-a; *(partially dressed)* medio vestido,-a; **to get u.**, desnudarse.

undue [ʌnˈdjuː] **1** *adj (excessive)* excesivo,-a; **with u. haste**, con demasiada premura. **2** *(improper)* indebido,-a; **u. optimism**, optimismo injustificado.

undulate [ˈʌndjʊleɪt] **I** *vtr* hacer ondear. **II** *vi* ondular, ondear.

undulation [ʌndjʊˈleɪʃən] *n* ondulación *f*.

unearned [ʌnˈɜːnd] *adj* **1** *(undeserved)* inmerecido,-a. **2** *(wages etc)* no ganado,-a. ■ *Fin* **u. income**, renta *f*; *Fin* **u. increment**, plusvalía *f*.

unearth [ʌnˈɜːθ] *vtr* desenterrar; *fig (information etc)* desenterrar, sacar a luz; *fig (plot etc)* descubrir.

unearthly [ʌnˈɜːθlɪ] *adj* **1** *(supernatural)* sobrenatural, de otro mundo; *(mysterious)* misterioso,-a. **2** *(heavenly)* celestial. **3** *fam (outlandish)* espantoso,-a; **u. din**, ruido de mil demonios; **why do we have to get up at this u. hour?**, ¿por qué nos tenemos que levantar a esta hora tan intempestiva?

uneasiness [ʌnˈiːzɪnɪs] *n* **1** *(of person)* inquietud *f*, desasosiego *m*. **2** *(of situation)* incomodidad *f*.

uneasy [ʌnˈiːzɪ] *adj* **1** *(troubled, worried)* inquieto,-a, preocupado,-a; *(disturbing)* inquietante; **to be u. about sth**, inquietarse *or* preocuparse por algo; **u. sleep**, sueño agitado. **2** *(uncomfortable)* incómodo,-a, molesto,-a.

uneconomic(al) [ʌniːkəˈnɒmɪk(əl)] *adj* poco económico,-a *or* rentable.

uneducated [ʌnˈedjʊkeɪtɪd] *adj* inculto,-a, ignorante; **u. speech**, habla popular.

unemployed [ʌnɪmˈplɔɪd] **I** *adj* sin trabajo, en paro, parado,-a; **to be u.**, estar en paro. **II the u.** *npl* los parados.

unemployment [ʌnɪmˈplɔɪmənt] *n* **1** *(condition)* paro *m*, desempleo *m*; **to be on u. benefit**, cobrar el paro. ■ *Admin* **u. benefit**, *US* **u. compensation**, subsidio *m* de desempleo. **2** *(number, percentage)* número *m* de parados, paro *m*.

unending [ʌnˈendɪŋ] *adj* interminable, inacabable.

unenthusiastic [ʌnɪnθjuːzɪˈæstɪk] *adj* poco entusiasta.

unenviable [ʌnˈenvɪəbəl] *adj* poco *or* nada envidiable.

unequal [ʌnˈiːkwəl] *adj* **1** *(not equal)* desigual; *(pulse)* irregular. **2** *(inadequate)* poco apto,-a; **to be u. to a task**, no estar a la altura de una tarea.

unequalled, *US* **unequaled** [ʌnˈiːkwəld] *adj* sin igual *or* par; **u. strength**, fuerza inigualable.

unequivocal [ʌnɪˈkwɪvəkəl] *adj* inequívoco,-a, claro,-a.

UNESCO, Unesco [juːˈneskəʊ] *abbr of* **United Nations Educational, Scientific and Cultural Organization**, Organización *f* de las Naciones Unidas para la Educación, la Ciencia y la Cultura, UNESCO *f*.

unethical [ʌnˈeθɪkəl] *adj* poco ético,-a.

uneven [ʌnˈiːvən] *adj* **1** *(not level)* desigual; *(jagged, bumpy)* accidentado,-a; **an u. road**, una carretera con baches. **2** *(variable)* variable, irregular. **3** *(not fairly matched)* desigual.

unevenness [ʌnˈiːvənnɪs] *n* **1** *(of surface, distribution)* desigualdad *f*. **2** *(of progress etc)* irregularidad *f*.

uneventful [ʌnɪˈventfʊl] *adj* sin acontecimientos; **an u. life**, *(quiet)* una vida tranquila; *(routine)* una vida monótona *or* rutinaria.

unexceptionable [ʌnɪkˈsepʃənəbəl] *adj* irreprochable, intachable.

unexceptional [ʌnɪkˈsepʃənəl] *adj* ordinario,-a, corriente.

unexciting [ʌnɪkˈsaɪtɪŋ] *adj (monotonous)* monótono,-a; *(uninteresting)* sin interés.

unexpected [ʌnɪkˈspektɪd] *adj (unhoped for)* inesperado,-a; *(event)* imprevisto,-a.

unexplained [ʌnɪkˈspleɪnd] *adj* inexplicado,-a; **his disappearance ramains u.**, su desaparición sigue siendo un enigma.

unexplored [ʌnɪkˈsplɔːd] *adj* inexplorado,-a.

unexposed [ʌnɪkˈspəʊzd] *adj* **1** *Phot (film)* virgen. **2** *(crime)* no descubierto,-a.

unexpurgated [ʌnˈekspəgeɪtɪd] *adj* no expurgado,-a, íntegro,-a.

unfailing [ʌnˈfeɪlɪŋ] *adj (gen)* indefectible; *(incessant)* constante; *(patience)* inagotable; *(humour)* inalterable; *(memory)* infalible.

unfair [ʌnˈfeəʳ] *adj* injusto,-a; *Sport* sucio,-a. ◆ **unfairly** *adv* injustamente.

unfairness [ʌnˈfeənɪs] *n* injusticia *f*.

unfaithful [ʌnˈfeɪθfʊl] *adj (friend)* desleal; *(husband, wife)* infiel.

unfaithfulness [ʌnˈfeɪθfʊlnɪs] *n (of friend)* deslealtad *f*; *(of husband, wife)* infidelidad *f*.

unfamiliar [ʌnfəˈmɪljəʳ] *adj* **1** *(unknown)* desconocido,-a. **2** *(not conversant)* no familiarizado,-a *(with*, con).

unfashionable [ʌnˈfæʃənəbəl] *adj (fashion etc)* pasado,-a de moda; *(ideas etc)* poco popular.

unfasten [ʌnˈfɑːsən] *vtr (knot)* desatar; *(clothing, belt)* desabrochar; *(door, window)* abrir.

unfathomable [ʌnˈfæðəməbəl] *adj fml* insondable.

unfavourable, US unfavorable [ʌnˈfeɪvərəbəl] *adj (gen)* desfavorable; *(criticism)* adverso,-a; *(winds)* contrario,-a. ◆ **unfavourably** *adv* desfavorablemente.

unfeeling [ʌnˈfiːlɪŋ] *adj (insensitive)* insensible; *(not sympathetic)* sin compasión.

unfettered [ʌnˈfetəd] *adj* sin trabas.

unfinished [ʌnˈfɪnɪʃt] *adj* inacabado,-a, sin acabar, incompleto,-a; **u. business**, un asunto pendiente.

unfit [ʌn'fɪt] *adj* **1** *(not suitable) (thing)* inadecuado,-a. impropio,-a; *(person)* no apto,-a **(for,** para), incapaz **(to,** de). **2** *(incompetent)* incompetente. **3** *(physically)* incapacitado,-a, inútil; **to be u.,** no estar en forma.

unflagging [ʌn'flægɪŋ] *adj (courage)* infatigable, incansable; *(interest)* constante.

unflappable [ʌn'flæpəbəl] *adj fam* imperturbable, flemático,-a.

unflattering [ʌn'flætərɪŋ] *adj* poco halagüeño,-a *or* halagador,-a.

unflinching [ʌn'flɪntʃɪŋ] *adj* **1** *(determined)* resuelto,-a. **2** *(fearless)* impávido,-a.

unfold [ʌn'fəʊld] **I** *vtr* **1** *(paper etc)* desplegar; *(sheet)* desdoblar; *(newspaper)* abrir; *(map)* extender. **2** *(outline)* exponer. **3** *(reveal)* revelar; *(secret)* descubrir. **II** *vi* **1** *(open up)* desplegarse, desdoblarse, abrirse; *(landscape)* extenderse. **2** *(thoughts, plot)* desarrollarse. **3** *(secret)* revelarse, descubrirse.

unforeseeable [ʌnfɔː'siːəbəl] *adj* imprevisible.

unforeseen [ʌnfɔː'siːn] *adj* imprevisto,-a.

unforgettable [ʌnfə'getəbəl] *adj* inolvidable.

unforgivable [ʌnfə'gɪvəbəl] *adj* imperdonable.

unforgiving [ʌnfə'gɪvɪŋ] *adj* que no perdona, implacable.

unfortunate [ʌn'fɔːtʃənɪt] *adj (person)* desgraciado,-a, desafortunado,-a; *(event)* desgraciado,-a; *(remark)* desafortunado,-a; **how u.!,** ¡qué mala suerte!, ¡qué pena! ◆ **unfortunately** *adv* desgraciadamente, por desgracia.

unfounded [ʌn'faʊndɪd] *adj (rumour)* infundado,-a, sin fundamento; *(complaint)* injustificado,-a.

unfreeze [ʌn'friːz] *vtr (pt* unfroze; *pp* unfrozen) **1** *(thaw)* descongelar. **2** *Fin Com' (prices, wages)* descongelar; *(credit, account)* desbloquear.

unfrequented [ʌnfrɪ'kwentɪd] *adj* poco frecuentado,-a.

unfriendly [ʌn'frendlɪ] *adj (unfriendlier, unfriendliest)* antipático,-a, poco amistoso,-a, hostil.

unfroze [ʌn'frəʊz] *pt;* **unfrozen** [ʌn'frəʊzən] *pp see* **unfreeze.**

unfruitful [ʌn'fruːtfʊl] *adj fig* infructuoso,-a.

unfulfilled [ʌnfʊl'fɪld] *adj* **1** *(not carried out)* incumplido,-a, frustrado,-a. **2** *(not satisfied)* no satisfecho,-a, insatisfecho,-a; *(ambition)* frustrado,-a; *(dream)* irrealizado,-a.

unfurl [ʌn'fɜːl] **I** *vtr (flag, sails)* desplegar. **II** *vi* desplegarse.

unfurnished [ʌn'fɜːnɪʃt] *adj* sin amueblar.

ungainly [ʌn'geɪnlɪ] *adj (clumsy)* torpe; *(gait)* desgarbado,-a.

ungodly [ʌn'gɒdlɪ] *adj (ungodlier, ungodliest) (behaviour, language)* impío,-a; *fam fig* **at an u. hour,** a una hora intempestiva, a las tantas de la noche.

ungovernable [ʌn'gʌvənəbəl] *adj* **1** *Pol (people)* ingobernable. **2** *(feelings)* incontrolable, incontenible, irreprimible.

ungracious [ʌn'greɪʃəs] *adj* descortés, poco amable.

ungrateful [ʌn'greɪtfʊl] *adj (unthankful)* desagradecido,-a; *(thankless)* ingrato,-a.

ungrudging [ʌn'grʌdʒɪŋ] *adj (liberal)* generoso,-a; *(of support)* incondicional. ◆ **ungrudgingly** *adv* de buena gana.

unguarded [ʌn'gɑːdɪd] *adj* **1** *(unprotected)* indefenso,-a, sin protección. **2** *(imprudent)* desprevenido,-a, descuidado,-a, imprudente. **3** *(frank)* franco,-a.

unhampered [ʌn'hæmpəd] *adj* libre **(by,** de), sin estorbos.

unhappy [ʌn'hæpɪ] *adj (unhappier, unhappiest)* **1** *(sad)* triste. **2** *(wretched)* desdichado,-a, desgraciado,-a, infeliz; *(unfortunate)* desafortunado,-a, poco afortunado,-a. ◆ **unhappily** *adv (unfortunately)* desgraciadamente; *(sadly)* tristemente.

unhappiness [ʌn'hæpɪnɪs] *n* **1** *(sadness)* tristeza *f.* **2** *(wretchedness)* desdicha *f,* infelicidad *f.*

unharmed [ʌn'hɑːmd] *adj* ileso,-a, indemne.

unhealthy [ʌn'helθɪ] *adj (unhealthier, unhealthiest)* **1** *(ill)* enfermo,-a, enfermizo,-a. **2** *(unwholesome)* malsano,-a, insalubre. **3** *fig* morboso,-a, malsano,-a.

unheard [ʌn'hɜːd] *adj* **1** no oído,-a; **her request went u.,** su petición no fue atendida, **2 u. of,** *(outrageous)* inaudito,-a; *(without precedent)* sin precedente; *(unknown)* desconocido,-a.

unheard-of [ʌn'hɜːdɒv] *adj (before noun)* inaudito,-a.

unheeded [ʌn'hiːdɪd] *adj* desatendido,-a; **the warning went u.,** la advertencia no se tuvo en cuenta.

unhelpful [ʌn'helpfʊl] *adj (advice)* inútil; *(person)* poco servicial.

unhesitating [ʌn'hezɪteɪtɪŋ] *adj* **1** *(person)* resuelto,-a, decidido,-a. **2** *(reply)* inmediato,-a. ◆ **unhesitatingly** *adv* sin vacilar.

unhinged [ʌn'hɪndʒd] *adj* **1** *(door)* desquiciado,-a. **2** *fig (mind)* trastornado,-a, desquiciado,-a.

unholy [ʌn'həʊlɪ] *adj (unholier, unholiest)* **1** *(place, subject)* profano,-a; *(person)* impío,-a. **2** *fam* terrible; **an u. muddle,** un lío enorme; **an u. row,** un escándalo de órdago.

unhook [ʌn'hʊk] *vtr (from hook, nail, etc)* descolgar; *(clothing)* desabrochar.

unhoped [ʌn'həʊpt] *adj* **u. for,** inesperado,-a.

unhurt [ʌn'hɜːt] *adj* ileso,-a, indemne.

unhygienic [ʌnhaɪ'dʒiːnɪk] *adj* antihigiénico,-a.

UNICEF ['juːnɪsef] *abbr of* **United Nations Children's Fund,** Fondo *m* de las Naciones Unidas para la Ayuda a la Infancia, UNICEF *f.*

unicorn ['juːnɪkɔːn] *n Myth* unicornio *m.*

unidentified [ʌnaɪ'dentɪfaɪd] *adj* no identificado,-a, sin identificar. ■ **u. flying object,** objeto *m* volador no identificado, ovni *m.*

unification [juːnɪfɪ'keɪʃən] *n* unificación *f.*

uniform ['juːnɪfɔːm] **I** *adj* uniforme; *(temperature)* constante. **II** *n* uniforme *m;* **in u.,** de uniforme, uniformado,-a.

uniformed ['juːnɪfɔːmd] *adj* uniformado,-a.

uniformity [juːnɪ'fɔːmɪtɪ] *n* uniformidad *f.*

unify ['juːnɪfaɪ] *vtr (pt & pp unified)* unificar.

unilateral [juːnɪ'lætərəl] *adj* unilateral.

unimaginable [ʌnɪ'mædʒɪnəbəl] *adj* inimaginable.

unimaginative [ʌnɪ'mædʒɪnɪtɪv] *adj* poco imaginativo,-a, falto,-a de imaginación.

unimpaired [ʌnɪm'peəd] *adj (unharmed)* intacto,-a; *(health)* inalterado,-a; *(strength)* no disminuido,-a.

unimportant [ʌnɪm'pɔːtənt] *adj* sin importancia, poco importante, insignificante.

unimpressed [ʌnɪm'prest] *adj* no impresionado,-a.

unimpressive [ʌnɪm'presɪv] *adj* poco impresionante, mediocre.

uninformed [ʌnɪn'fɔːmd] *adj* mal informado,-a, ignorante; *(opinion)* sin fundamento.

uninhabitable [ʌnɪn'hæbɪtəbəl] *adj* inhabitable.

uninhabited [ʌnɪn'hæbɪtɪd] *adj (uninhabited)* deshabitado,-a; *(deserted)* despoblado,-a.

uninhibited [ʌnɪn'hɪbɪtɪd] *adj* sin inhibición.

uninitiated [ʌnɪ'nɪʃɪeɪtɪd] *adj* lego,-a, no iniciado,-a, ignorante.

uninspired [ʌnɪn'spaɪəd] *adj (person)* falto,-a de inspiración; *(performance)* insulso,-a, aburrido,-a, poco inspirado,-a.

uninspiring [ʌnɪn'spaɪərɪŋ] *adj* que no inspira.

unintelligent [ʌnɪn'telɪdʒənt] *adj* poco inteligente.

unintelligible [ʌnɪn'telɪdʒəbəl] *adj* ininteligible, incomprensible.

unintentional [ʌnɪn'tenʃənəl] *adj* involuntario,-a. ◆ **unintentionally** *adv* involuntariamente, sin querer; **I did it u.**, lo hice sin querer.

uninterested [ʌn'ɪntrɪstɪd] *adj* no interesado,-a, indiferente.

uninteresting [ʌn'ɪntrɪstɪŋ] *adj* poco interesante, sin interés.

uninterrupted [ʌnɪntə'rʊptɪd] *adj* ininterrumpido,-a.

uninvited [ʌnɪn'vaɪtɪd] *adj* **1** *(guest)* no invitado,-a. **2** *(comment)* gratuito,-a, no solicitado,-a.

uninviting [ʌnɪn'vaɪtɪŋ] *adj (offer, appearance)* poco atractivo,-a; *(food)* poco apetecible *or* apetitoso,-a.

union ['juːnjən] **I** *n* unión *f*; *fig (marriage)* enlace *m*; **to live in perfect u.**, vivir en perfecta armonía. **2** *(organization)* sindicato *m*; **the students' u.**, el sindicato estudiantil; *Ind* (**trade**) **U.**, sindicato *m*. **3** *Mech* unión *f*. **4** *US* **the U.**, los Estados Unidos. ■ **U. Jack,** bandera *f* del Reino Unido, bandera *f* británica. **II** *adj* sindical, del sindicato.

unionization [juːnjənaɪ'zeɪʃən] *n* sindicación *f*, sindicalización *f*.

unionize ['juːnjənaɪz] **I** *vtr* sindicalizar. **II** *vi* sindicalizarse.

unique [juː'niːk] *adj (singular, peculiar)* único,-a; *(extraordinary)* extraordinario,-a.

unisex ['juːnɪseks] *adj* unisex.

unison ['juːnɪsən] *n Mus* unisonancia *f*; *fig (harmony)* armonía *f*; **in u.**, al unísono.

unit ['juːnɪt] *n* **1** unidad *f*. ■ **monetary u.**, unidad *f* monetaria; **u. price**, precio *m* por unidad; *Fin* **u. trust**, sociedad *f* de inversiones. **2** *Furn* módulo *m*, elemento *m*. ■ **kitchen u.**, mueble *m* de cocina. **3** *Math* unidad *f*. **4** *Mil* unidad *f*. **5** *Tech* grupo *m*. ■ *Comput* **central processing u.**, procesador *m* central; **generator u.**, grupo *m* electrógeno; **stereo u.**, equipo *m* estereofónico; *Comput* **visual display u.**, pantalla *f*. **6** *(centre)* centro *m*; *(department)* servicio *m*. ■ *Med* **intensive care u.**, unidad *f* de cuidados intensivos, unidad *f* de vigilancia intensiva; **research u.**, centro *m* de investigaciones. **7** *(team)* equipo *m*; *Cin TV* **film u.**, equipo *m* de rodaje.

unite [juː'naɪt] **I** *vtr* **1** *(join)* unir. **2** *(assemble)* reunir. **II** *vi* unirse, juntarse.

united [juː'naɪtɪd] *adj* unido,-a. ■ **United Arab Emirates**, Emiratos *mpl* Árabes Unidos; **U. Kingdom**, Reino *m* Unido; **U. States (of America)**, Estados *mpl* Unidos (de América); **U. Nations**, Naciones *fpl* Unidas.

unity ['juːnɪtɪ] *n (union)* unidad *f*; *(harmony)* armonía *f*.

Univ *abbr of* **University**, Universidad *f*, Univ *f*.

universal [juːnɪ'vɜːsəl] *adj* universal; **u. remedy**, panacea *f*.

universe ['juːnɪvɜːs] *n* universo *m*.

university [juːnɪ'vɜːsɪtɪ] **I** *n* universidad *f*. **II** *adj* universitario, a.

unjust [ʌn'dʒʌst] *adj (unfair)* injusto,-a; *(unfounded)* sin fundamento, infundado,-a.

unjustifiable [ʌndʒʌstɪ'faɪəbəl] *adj* injustificable.

unjustified [ʌn'dʒʌstɪfaɪd] *adj* injustificado,-a.

unkempt [ʌn'kempt] *adj (gen)* descuidado,-a; *(hair)* despeinado,-a; *(appearance)* desaliñado,-a.

unkind [ʌn'kaɪnd] *adj (not nice)* poco amable, desconsiderado,-a; *(cruel)* cruel; *(criticism)* despiadado,-a. ◆ **unkindly** *adv* con poca amabilidad, desconsideradamente.

unkindness [ʌn'kaɪndnɪs] *n* falta *f* de amabilidad *or* consideración.

unknowing [ʌn'nəʊɪŋ] *adj* **1** *(unaware)* inconsciente. **2** *(ignorant)* ignorante. ◆ **unknowingly** *adv* inconscientemente, sin darse cuenta.

unknown [ʌn'nəʊn] **I** *adj* desconocido,-a; **the u. soldier**, el soldado desconocido. ■ *Math* **u. quantity**, incógnita *f*. **II** **the u.** *n* lo desconocido.

unlabelled [ʌn'leɪbəld] *adj* sin etiqueta.

unlawful [ʌn'lɔːfʊl] *adj (not legal)* ilegal; *(not legitimate)* ilegítimo,-a.

unleash [ʌn'liːʃ] *vtr* **1** *(dog)* soltar. **2** *fig (release)* liberar, dar rienda suelta a; *(provoke)* provocar, desencadenar.

unleavened [ʌn'levənd] *adj* ácimo, sin levadura. ■ **u. bread,** pan *m* ácimo.

unless [ʌn'les] *conj* a menos que, a no ser que.

unlike [ʌn'laɪk] **I** *adj* diferente (a), distinto,-a (de); **she is not u. her sister**, se parece bastante a su hermana; **that was very u. her**, eso no es lo normal en ella. **II** *adv* a diferencia de; **he, u. his father, ...,** a diferencia de su padre, él ... .

unlikely [ʌn'laɪklɪ] *adj* **1** *(improbable)* poco probable **it's not at all u. that ...,** bien pudiera ser que ... . **2** *(unusual, unexpected)* inverosímil; **in the u. event that she should want to come**, suponiendo que quisiera venir, lo cual es mucho suponer.

unlimited [ʌn'lɪmɪtɪd] *adj* ilimitado,-a; **there were u. supplies of beer**, había cerveza a granel.

unlit [ʌn'lɪt] *adj (fire, cigarette, etc)* sin encender, no encendido,-a; *(place)* sin luz, no iluminado,-a.

unload [ʌn'ləʊd] *vtr & vi (gen)* descargar; *fig (get rid of)* deshacerse de; *(problems)* descargar **(on,** en).

unloading [ʌn'ləʊdɪŋ] *n* descarga *f*. ■ **u. bay,** descargadero *m*.

unlock [ʌn'lɒk] *vtr* **1** *(door)* abrir (con llave). **2** *fig (mystery)* resolver, revelar.

unlooked-for [ʌn'lʊktfɔː'] *adj* inesperado,-a.

unloved [ʌn'lʌvd] *adj* no amado,-a.

unloving [ʌn'lʌvɪŋ] *adj* poco cariñoso,-a.

unlucky [ʌn'lʌkɪ] *adj (unluckier, unluckiest) (unfortunate)* desafortunado,-a, desgraciado,-a; **to be u.,** *(person)* tener mala suerte; *(thing)* traer mala suerte. ◆ **unluckily** *adv* desafortunadamente, desgraciadamente, por desgracia.

unmade [ʌn'meɪd] *adj (bed)* sin hacer.

unmanageable [ʌn'mænɪdʒəbəl] *adj (people)* ingobernable; *(child, hair)* indomable; *(machine)* difícil de manejar, poco manejable.

unmanly [ʌn'mænlɪ] *adj* poco viril, afeminado,-a.

unmanned [ʌn'mænd] *adj (spacecraft etc)* no tripulado,-a.

unmarked [ʌn'mɑːkt] *adj* **1** *(spotless)* en perfecto estado, como nuevo,-a. **2** *(street)* sin letrero. **3** *Ftb (player)* desmarcado,-a.

unmarried [ʌn'mærɪd] *adj* soltero,-a.

unmask [ʌn'mɑːsk] *vtr* desenmascarar; *fig (plot)* descubrir.

unmatched [ʌn'mætʃt] *adj (unique)* sin par, incomparable.

unmentionable [ʌn'menʃənəbəl] *adj* que no se debe mencionar, tabú.

unmerciful [ʌn'mɜːsɪfʊl] *adj* despiadado,-a, sin piedad.

unmethodical [ʌnmɪ'θɒdɪkəl] *adj* poco metódico,-a.

unmistak(e)able [ʌnmɪs'teɪkəbəl] *adj* inconfundible. ◆ **unmistak(e)ably** *adv* sin lugar a dudas.

unmitigated [ʌn'mɪtɪgeɪtɪd] *adj* **1** *(absolute)* absoluto,-a, total; *(liar)* rematado,-a. **2** *(grief)* profundo,-a.

unmolested [ʌnmə'lestɪd] *adv* tranquilamente, sin problemas.

unmoved [ʌn'muːvd] *adj* impasible, indiferente; *(to pleas etc)* insensible **(by,** a).

unmusical [ʌn'mjuːzɪkəl] *adj* **1** *(sound)* poco armonioso,-a. **2** *(person) (untalented)* sin dotes para la música; *(unenthusiastic)* poco aficionado,-a a la música.

unnamed [ʌn'neɪmd] *adj* **1** sin nombre. **2** *(anonymous)* anónimo,-a.

unnatural [ʌn'nætʃərəl] *adj* **1** *(against nature)* antinatural; *(abnormal)* anormal. **2** *(affected)* afectado,-a, poco natural.

unnecessary [ʌn'nesɪsərɪ] *adj* innecesario,-a, inútil; **it's u. to add that ...,** sobra añadir que ... .

unnerve [ʌn'nɜːv] *vtr (disconcert)* desconcertar, turbar; *(frighten)* acobardar.

unnerving [ʌn'nɜːvɪŋ] *adj* desconcertante.

unnoticed [ʌn'nəʊtɪst] *adj* inadvertido,-a, desapercibido,-a; **to let sth pass u.,** pasar algo por alto, no reparar en algo.

unnumbered [ʌn'nʌmbəd] *adj* sin numerar.

UNO ['juːnəʊ] *abbr of* **United Nations Organization,** Organización *f* de las Naciones Unidas, ONU *f*.

unobserved [ʌnɒb'zɜːvd] *adj* inadvertido,-a, desapercibido,-a.

unobtainable [ʌnəb'teɪnəbəl] *adj* inasequible, inalcanzable.

unobtrusive [ʌnəb'truːsɪv] *adj* discreto,-a. ◆ **unobtrusively** *adv* con discreción.

unoccupied [ʌn'ɒkjʊpaɪd] *adj* **1** *(person)* desocupado,-a. **2** *(house)* desocupado,-a; *(region)* despoblado,-a; *(seat)* libre; *Mil (territory)* no ocupado,-a.

unofficial [ʌnə'fɪʃəl] *adj* extraoficial, no oficial. ◆ **unofficially** *adv* extraoficialmente.

unopened [ʌn'əʊpənd] *adj* sin abrir.

unorthodox [ʌn'ɔːθədɒks] *adj* **1** *(behaviour, technique, etc)* poco ortodoxo,-a. **2** *Rel* heterodoxo,-a.

unpack [ʌn'pæk] **I** *vtr (boxes)* desembalar; *(suitcase)* deshacer; *(objects)* desempaquetar, desenvolver. **II** *vi* deshacer la(s) maleta(s).

unpaid [ʌn'peɪd] *adj* **1** *(bill, debt)* sin pagar, impagado,-a. **2** *(work)* no retribuido,-a, sin renumeración.

unpalatable [ʌn'pælətəbəl] *adj (taste)* desagradable (al gusto); *fig* desagradable, difícil de aceptar.

unparalleled [ʌn'pærəleld] *adj* **1** *(in quality)* sin par, incomparable. **2** *(without precedent)* sin precedente.

unpardonable [ʌn'pɑːdənəbəl] *adj* imperdonable.

unpatriotic [ʌnpætrɪ'ɒtɪk] *adj (person)* poco patriota; *(action)* antipatriótico,-a.

unperturbed [ʌnpə'tɜːbd] *adj* impasible; **she carried on u.,** continuó sin inmutarse; **u. by,** no perturbado,-a por.

unpick [ʌn'pɪk] *vtr Sew* descoser.

unplanned [ʌn'plænd] *adj* imprevisto,-a, inesperado,-a.

unplayable [ʌn'pleɪəbəl] *adj Sport (ball)* imposible de jugar.

unpleasant [ʌn'plezənt] *adj* **1** *(nasty, not nice)* desagradable, molesto,-a. **2** *(unfriendly)* antipático,-a **(to, con)**.

unpleasantness [ʌn'plezəntnɪs] *n* **1** *(nastiness)* carácter *m* desagradable, lo desagradable. **2** *(illfeeling)* disgusto *m*.

unplug [ʌn'plʌg] *vtr (pt & pp unplugged)* desenchufar.

unpolished [ʌn'pɒlɪʃt] *adj* **1** *(gen)* sin brillo; *(shoes)* sin lustrar; *(diamond)* en broto. **2** *fig (manner, style)* poco pulido,-a.

unpolluted [ʌnpə'luːtɪd] *adj* no contaminado,-a.

unpopular [ʌn'pɒpjʊləʳ] *adj* impopular; **to make oneself u.,** ganarse la antipatía de todos.

unpopularity [ʌnpɒpjʊ'lærɪtɪ] *n* impopularidad *f*.

unprecedented [ʌn'presɪdəntɪd] *adj (without precedent)* sin precedente; *(unheard of)* inaudito,-a.

unpredictable [ʌnprɪ'dɪktəbəl] *adj* imprevisible; **she's very u.,** no se sabe nunca cómo reaccionará *or* cómo actuará.

unprepared [ʌnprɪ'peəd] *adj* **1** *(speech etc)* improvisado,-a; *(person)* desprevenido,-a. **2** *(not ready) no* preparado,-a; **I was u. for what happened,** no esperaba lo que ocurrió; **she went into marriage u.,** se casó sin saber en lo que se metía.

unprepossessing [ʌnpriːpə'zesɪŋ] *adj* poco atractivo,-a.

unpresentable [ʌnprɪ'zentəbəl] *adj* impresentable.

unpretentious [ʌnprɪ'tenʃəs] *adj (simple)* modesto,-a, sencillo,-a; *(humble)* sin pretensiones.

unprincipled [ʌn'prɪnsɪpəld] *adj* sin principios *or* escrúpulos.

unprintable [ʌn'prɪntəbəl] *adj (book)*, impublicable; *(word, comment)* que no se puede repetir.

unproductive [ʌnprə'dʌktɪv] *adj (inefficient)* improductivo,-a; *(fruitless)* infructuoso,-a.

unprofessional [ʌnprə'feʃənəl] *adj (ethical)* poco profesional, no ético,-a; *(substandard)* de aficionado,-a.

unprofitable [ʌn'prɒfɪtəbəl] *adj (inefficient)* poco rentable; *(fruitless)* poco provechoso,-a.

unpronounceable [ʌnprə'naʊnsəbəl] *adj* impronunciable.

unprotected [ʌnprə'tektɪd] *adj* indefenso,-a, sin protección.

unprovoked [ʌnprə'vəʊkt] *adj* no provocado,-a; *(attack)* gratuito,-a.

unpublishable [ʌn'pʌblɪʃəbəl] *adj* impublicable.

unpublished [ʌn'pʌblɪʃt] *adj* inédito,-a no publicado,-a.

unpunished [ʌn'pʌnɪʃt] *adj* sin castigar; *(crime)* impune; **to go u.,** *(person)* no ser castigado,-a; *(deed)* quedar impune.

unqualified [ʌn'kwɒlɪfaɪd] *adj* **1** *(without qualification)* sin título; *(incompetent)* incompetent; **I am u. to speak on the subject,** no soy quién para hablar sobre este tema; **u. to vote,** sin derecho a voto. **2** *(unconditional)* incondicional; *(denial)* rotundo,-a; *(endorsement)* sin reserva; *(success)* total.

unquenchable [ʌn'kwentʃəbəl] *adj (thirst)* insaciable.

unquestionable [ʌn'kwestʃənəbəl] *adj* indiscutible, incuestionable.

unquestioned [ʌn'kwestʃənd] *adj (right etc)* indiscutido,-a, incontrovertido,-a; *(undoubted)* indudable.

unquestioning [ʌn'kwestʃənɪŋ] *adj (gen)* incondicional; *(obedience)* ciego,-a.

unquote [ʌn'kwəʊt] *vi* **quote ... unquote,** se abren comillas ... se cierran comillas.

unravel [ʌn'rævəl] **I** *vtr (pt & pp unravelled, US unraveled)* **1** *(untangle)* desenredar, desenmarañar. **2** *fig (mystery)* desenmarañar, desembrollar. **II** *vi* **1** *(become untangled)* desenredarse, desenmarañarse. **2** *fig (mystery)* desenmarañarse.

unread [ʌn'red] *adj (book)* sin leer, no leído,-a.

unreadable [ʌn'riːdəbəl] *adj* **1** *(handwriting)* ilegible. **2** *(book)* imposible de leer.

unreal [ʌn'rɪəl] *adj* irreal.

uneralistic [ʌnrɪə'lɪstɪk] *adj* poco realista.

unreasonable [ʌn'riːzənəbəl] *adj* poco razonable; *(demands)* desmedido,-a; *(prices)* exorbitante; *(hour)* inoportuno,-a.

unreasoning [ʌn'riːzənɪŋ] *adj* irracional.

unrecognizable [ʌnrekəg'naɪzəbəl] *adj* irreconocible.

unrecognized [ʌn'rekəgnaɪzd] *adj (talent, government, etc)* no reconocido,-a; **to go u.,** pasar sin ser reconocido.

unrecorded [ʌnrɪ'kɔːdɪd] *adj* **1** *(music)* no grabado,-a, sin grabar. **2** *(fact, comment)* no mencionado,-a; *(not taken down)* no registrado,-a, sin registrar.

unrefined [ʌnrɪ'faɪnd] *adj* **1** *Ind* no refinado,-a, sin refinar. ■ **u. sugar,** azúcar *m* sin refinar. **2** *(person)* tosco,-a, poco fino,-a, basto,-a.

unrehearsed [ʌnrɪˈhɜːst] *adj (unprepared)* improvisado,-a; *Theat (play)* sin ensayar.

unrelated [ʌnrɪˈleɪtɪd] *adj* **1** *(not connected)* no relacionado,-a, inconexo,-a. **2** *(family)* sin parentesco; **Mr Hardy and Miss Miller are u.,** entre el Sr. Hardy y la Srta. Miller no hay parentesco alguno.

unrelenting [ʌnrɪˈlentɪŋ] *adj (behaviour)* implacable; *(struggle)* encarnizado,-a.

unreliable [ʌnrɪˈlaɪəbəl] *adj* **1** *(person)* que no es de fiar, de poca confianza; **my daily help is very u.,** no se puede contar con mi asistenta. **2** *(information)* que no es de fiar; *(machine)* poco seguro,-a *or* fiable; **their washing machine is u.,** su lavadora es poco fiable.

unreliability [ʌnrɪlaɪəˈbɪlɪtɪ] *n* **1** *(of person)* poca formalidad *f*. **2** *(of information)* poca seguridad *f; (of weather)* inestabilidad *f; (of machine)* tendencia *f* a averiarse.

unrelieved [ʌnrɪˈliːvd] *adj* **1** *(pain)* no aliviado,-a. **2** *(monotonous)* monótono,-a; *(boredom)* total.

unremitting [ʌnrɪˈmɪtɪŋ] *adj* **1** *(efforts etc)* incesante, continuo,-a. **2** *(person)* incansable.

unrepentant [ʌnrɪˈpentənt] *adj* impenitente.

unrequited [ʌnrɪˈkwaɪtɪd] *adj* **u. love,** amor no correspondido.

unrepresented [ʌnreprɪˈsentɪd] *adj* no representado,-a, sin representación.

unreserved [ʌnrɪˈzɜːvd] *adj* **1** *(praise, support)* sin reserva, incondicional. **2** *(person, nature)* abierto,-a. **3** *(seats)* libre, sin reservar. ◆ **unreservedly** *adv* sin reserva.

unresolved [ʌnrɪˈzɒlvd] *adj see* **unsolved.**

unresponsive [ʌnrɪˈspɒnsɪv] *adj* insensible.

unrest [ʌnˈrest] *n (social etc)* malestar *m;* **political u.,** desasosiego *m* de raíz política.

unrewarded [ʌnrɪˈwɔːdɪd] *adj* sin recompensa; **my efforts were u.,** mis esfuerzos no se vieron premiados.

unrivalled, *US* **unrivaled** [ʌnˈraɪvəld] *adj* único,-a, sin par, sin rival.

unroll [ʌnˈrəʊl] **I** *vtr* desenrollar. **II** *vi* desenrollarse.

unruffled [ʌnˈrʌfəld] *adj fig* tranquilo,-a, sereno,-a.

unruly [ʌnˈruːlɪ] *adj (unrulier, unruliest)* **1** *(child)* revoltoso,-a, indisciplinado,-a. **2** *(hair)* rebelde.

unsaddle [ʌnˈsædəl] *vtr* desensillar.

unsafe [ʌnˈseɪf] *adj (dangerous)* peligroso,-a; *(risky)* inseguro,-a, arriesgado,-a; **to feel u.,** sentirse inseguro.

unsaid [ʌnˈsed] *adj* sin decir; **it's better left u.,** más vale no decir nada; **much was left u.,** quedó mucho por decir.

unsalaried [ʌnˈsælərɪd] *adj* no remunerado,-a.

unsalted [ʌnˈsɔːltɪd] *adj* sin sal.

unsanitary [ʌnˈsænɪtərɪ] *adj* antihigiénico,-a.

unsatisfactory [ʌnsætɪsˈfæktərɪ] *adj* insatisfactorio,-a; **it's most u.,** deja mucho que desear.

unsatisfied [ʌnˈsætɪsfaɪd] *adj* insatisfecho,-a.

unsatisfying [ʌnˈsætɪsfaɪɪŋ] *adj* **1** *(job etc)* poco satisfactorio,-a. **2** *(meal)* insuficiente.

unsavoury, *US* **unsavory** [ʌnˈseɪvərɪ] *adj* desagradable.

unscathed [ʌnˈskeɪðd] *adj* ileso,-a, indemne.

unscented [ʌnˈsentɪd] *adj* sin perfume.

unscientific [ʌnsaɪənˈtɪfɪk] *adj* poco científico,-a.

unscrew [ʌnˈskruː] *vtr* destornillar, desatornillar.

unscrupulous [ʌnˈskruːpjʊləs] *adj* sin escrúpulos.

unseasonable [ʌnˈsiːzənəbəl] *adj (weather)* atípico,-a, anormal.

unseasoned [ʌnˈsiːzənd] *adj* **1** *(inexperienced)* inexperto,-a, poco avezado,-a. **2** *(green)* verde. **3** *Culin* sin sazonar *or* aderezar.

unseat [ʌnˈsiːt] *vtr* **I** *Equit* derribar. **2** *Parl (deputy etc)* quitarle el escaño a; *Pol (government)* derribar, derrocar.

unseconded [ʌnˈsekəndɪd] *adj (motion)* no apoyado,-a.

unseemly [ʌnˈsiːmlɪ] *adj* impropio,-a; **in an u. manner,** sin decoro.

unseen [ʌnˈsiːn] **I** *adj (invisible)* no visto,-a, invisible; *(unnoticed)* inadvertido,-a. **II** *n* **1** *GB Educ* texto *m* no trabajado en clase. **2 the u.,** lo invisible.

unselfish [ʌnˈselfɪʃ] *adj* desinteresado,-a, generoso,-a.

unserviceable [ʌnˈsɜːvɪsəbəl] *adj* inservible, inútil.

unsettle [ʌnˈsetəl] *vtr* perturbar, inquietar.

unsettled [ʌnˈsetəld] *adj* **1** *(person)* nervioso,-a, intranquilo,-a; *(situation)* inestable. **2** *(weather)* variable, inestable. ⸍3 *(lifestyle etc)* agitado,-a. **4** *(matter, question)* pendiente. **5** *(debt)* pendiente. **6** *(land)* sin colonizar.

unshak(e)able [ʌnˈʃeɪkəbəl] *adj* firme, inquebrantable.

unshaven [ʌnˈʃeɪvən] *adj* sin afeitar.

unshrinkable [ʌnˈʃrɪŋkəbəl] *adj Tex* que no encoge.

unsightly [ʌnˈsaɪtlɪ] *adj* feo,-a, desagradable.

unsigned [ʌnˈsaɪnd] *adj* sin firmar.

unskilful, *US* **unskillful** [ʌnˈskɪlfʊl] *adj* torpe, desmañado,-a.

unskilled [ʌnˈskɪld] *adj* **1** *(without skill) (worker)* no cualificado,-a; *(work)* no especializado,-a. **2** *(untalented)* inexperto,-a; **he is quite u. at drawing,** se le da bastante mal el dibujo.

unsociable [ʌnˈsəʊʃəbəl] *adj* insociable, huraño,-a.

unsold [ʌnˈsəʊld] *adj* no vendido,-a, sin vender.

unsolicited [ʌnsəˈlɪsɪtɪd] *adj* no solicitado,-a, voluntario,-a; **he did it u.,** lo hizo espontáneamente.

unsolved [ʌnˈsɒlvd] *adj* no resuelto,-a, sin resolver.

unsophisticated [ʌnsəˈfɪstɪkeɪtɪd] *adj* **1** *(naïve)* ingenuo,-a. **2** *(simple)* poco sofisticado,-a, sencillo,-a.

unsound [ʌnˈsaʊnd] *adj* **1** *(unstable)* inestable, débil; *Jur* **of u. mind,** demente. **2** *(fallacious)* falso,-a, erróneo,-a. **3** *(defective)* defectuoso,-a; *(not firm)* poco sólido,-a. **4** *Fin (investment)* poco seguro,-a, especulativo,-a.

unsparing [ʌnˈspeərɪŋ] *adj* pródigo,-a; **u. in one's efforts,** sin escatimar esfuerzos; **u. of praise,** pródigo en alabanzas.

unspeakable [ʌnˈspiːkəbəl] *adj* **1** indecible. **2** *fig (evil)* infando,-a, atroz.

unspecified [ʌnˈspesɪfaɪd] *adj* indeterminado,-a, sin especificar.

unspoiled [ʌnˈspɔɪld] *adj,* **unspoilt** [ʌnˈspɔɪlt] *adj (unaltered)* intacto,-a, conservado,-a; *(not developed)* sin explotar.

unspoken [ʌnˈspəʊkən] *adj* **1** *(tacit)* tácito,-a, implícito,-a. **2** *(unuttered) (word)* sin pronunciar; *(feeling)* no expresado,-a.

unstable [ʌnˈsteɪbəl] *adj (thing)* inestable, movedizo,-a; *(person)* inestable, voluble, tornadizo,-a.

unsteady [ʌnˈstedɪ] *adj* **1** *(not firm)* inestable; *(table, chair)* cojo,-a; *(hand, voice)* tembloroso,-a; **to be u. on one's feet,** tambalearse. **2** *(varying)* variable; *(pulse)* irregular.

unstinting [ʌnˈstɪntɪŋ] *adj* pródigo,-a **(in,** en, de); **to be u. in one's praise,** no escatimar elogios.

unstitch [ʌnˈstɪtʃ] *vtr* descoser; **to come unstitched,** descoserse.

unstressed [ʌnˈstrest] *adj Ling* átono,-a.

unstuck [ʌnˈstʌk] *adj* desoegado,-a; **to come u.,** despegarse, desengancharse; *fig* venirse abajo, fracasar.

unsubstantiated [ʌnsəbˈstænʃɪeɪtɪd] *adj (accusation)* no probado,-a, no demostrado,-a; *(rumour)* infundado,-a.

unsuccessful [ʌnsəkˈsesfʊl] *adj (fruitless)* fracasado,-a, fallido,-a; *(useless)* vano,-a, inútil. **2** *(businessman etc)* fracasado,-a; *(candidate)* derrotado,-a, vencido,-a; *(in exam)* suspendido,-a; **to be u. at sth,** no tener éxito con algo, fracasar en algo. ◆ **unsuccessfully** *adv* sin éxito, infructuosamente, en vano.

unsuitable [ʌn'suːtəbəl] *adj* **1** *(person)* no apto,-a; **he's quite u. for the post,** es la persona menos indicada para el puesto. **2** *(thing)* impropio,-a, inadecuado,-a; *(remark)* inoportuno,-a; *(time)* inconveniente, intempestivo,-a; *Cin* **'u. for children',** 'no apto para menores'; **u. for the occasion,** impropio para la ocasión.

unsuited [ʌn'suːtɪd] *adj* **1** *(inappropiate) (person)* no apto,-a; *(thing)* impropio,-a (**to,** para). **2** *(incompatible)* incompatible.

unsupported [ʌnsə'pɔːtɪd] *adj* **1** *(statement)* infundado,-a. **2** *(person)* sin apoyo, sin respaldo; **u. financially,** sin apoyo financiero.

unsure [ʌn'ʃʊəʳ] *adj* poco seguro,-a; **to be u. about sth,** dudar de algo; **to be u. of oneself,** carecer de confianza en sí mismo.

unsurpassed [ʌnsɜː'pɑːst] *adj* no superado,-a.

unsuspected [ʌnsə'spektɪd] *adj* **1** *(not suspected)* insospechado,-a. **2** *(unknown)* desconocido,-a.

unsuspecting [ʌnsə'spektɪŋ] *adj* confiado,-a; **he went in u.,** entró sin sospechar nada.

unsweetened [ʌn'swiːtənd] *adj* sin azúcar; *Ind* sin edulcorar.

unswerving [ʌn'swɜːvɪŋ] *adj* firme, constante (**in,** en).

unsympathetic [ʌnsɪmpə'θetɪk] *adj* *(unfeeling)* impasible, sin compasión; *(not understanding)* poco comprensivo,-a; **she was totally u.,** no fue nada comprensiva; **they were u. to my request,** se mostraron indiferentes a mi petición.

unsystematic [ʌnsɪstɪ'mætɪk] *adj* poco sistemático,-a, poco metódico,-a.

untainted [ʌn'teɪntɪd] *adj* **1** *(water etc)* no contaminado,-a. **2** *fig (reputation)* sin mancha; **u. by scandal,** limpio,-a de escándalos.

untapped [ʌn'tæpt] *adj* *(mine etc)* sin explotar.

untarnished [ʌn'tɑːnɪʃt] *adj* *(metal)* sin oxidar; *fig* sin mancha.

untaxed [ʌn'tækst] *adj* libre de impuestos.

untempered [ʌn'tempəd] *adj Metal* sin templar.

untenable [ʌn'tenəbəl] *adj* insostenible, indefendible.

untested [ʌn'testɪd] *adj* **1** *(not tested)* no probado,-a. **2** *(not proved)* sin comprobar.

unthinkable [ʌn'θɪŋkəbəl] *adj* impensable,- inconcebible; **it's u. that ...,** es impensable que (+ *subj*).

untidiness [ʌn'taɪdɪnɪs] *n* *(gen)* desorden *m*; *(of appearance)* desaseo *m*, desaliño *m*.

untidy [ʌn'taɪdɪ] *adj* **(untidier, untidiest)** *(room, person)* desordenado,-a; *(hair)* despeinado,-a; *(appearance)* desaseado,-a, desaliñado,-a.

untie [ʌn'taɪ] *vtr* **1** *(unfasten)* desatar. **2** *(set free)* soltar, desligar.

until [ʌn'tɪl] **I** *conj* hasta que; **he won't come u. you invite him,** no vendrá hasta que no le invites; **she worked u. she collapsed,** trabajó hasta caerse; **u. she gets back,** hasta que vuelva; **u. you told me,** hasta que me lo dijiste. **II** *prep* hasta; **u. after dinner,** hasta después de cenar; **u. now,** hasta ahora; **u. ten o'clock,** hasta las diez; **not u. Monday,** hasta el lunes no.

untimely [ʌn'taɪmlɪ] **I** *adj* **1** *(premature)* prematuro,-a; **to come to an u. end,** morir antes de tiempo. **2** *(inopportune) (intervention); (hour)* intempestivo,-a. **II** *adv* **1** *(early)* prematuramente. **2** *(inopportunely)* inoportunamente, a deshora.

untiring [ʌn'taɪərɪŋ] *adj* incansable, infatigable.

untold [ʌn'təʊld] *adj* **1** *(undescribable)* indecible, inefable. **2** *fig (incalculable) (loss)* incalculable; *(wealth)* fabuloso,-a. **3** *(not told)* no contar, nunca contado,-a.

untouchable [ʌn'tʌtʃəbəl] *adj* & *n* intocable *(mf)*.

untouched [ʌn'tʌtʃt] *adj* **1** *(not touched)* intacto,-a. **2** *(unharmed)* ileso,-a, indemne; *(not damaged)* intacto,-a. **3** *(unaffected)* insensible (**by,** a).

untoward [ʌntə'wɔːd, ʌn'təʊəd] *adj* **1** *(unfortunate)* desafortunado,-a; **I hope nothing u. has happened,** espero que no hayan tenido ningún contratiempo. **2** *(adverse)* adverso,-a.

untrained [ʌn'treɪnd] *adj* **1** *(unskilled)* sin preparación profesional; *(teacher)* sin título. **2** *(inexpert)* inexperto,-a. **2** *Sport* sin entrenar, desentrenado,-a. **2** *(animal)* no amaestrado,-a.

untransferable [ʌntræns'fɜːrəbəl] *adj* intransferible.

untried [ʌn'traɪd] *adj* **1** *(not attempted)* no probado,-a; **to leave nothing u.,** intentarlo *or* probarlo todo. **2** *Jur (person)* no juzgado,-a, sin juicio; *(case)* no visto,-a.

untrue [ʌn'truː] *adj* **1** *(false)* falso,-a. **2** *(unfaithful)* infiel, desleal. **3** *(inexact)* inexacto,-a.

untrustworthy [ʌn'trʌstwɜːðɪ] *adj* **1** *(person)* de poca confianza; **he's quite u.,** no es de fiar en absoluto. **2** *(source)* dudoso,-a, no fidedigno,-a.

untruth [ʌn'truːθ] *n* mentira *f*.

untruthful [ʌn'truːθʊl] *adj* **1** *(person)* mentiroso,-a; **she was u. about her past,** mintió sobre su pasado. **2** *(report)* falso,-a.

untuned [ʌn'tjuːnd] *adj Mus* desafinado,-a.

unusable [ʌn'juːzəbəl] *adj* inservible, inutilizable.

unused [ʌn'juːzd] *adj* **1** *(not used) (car)* sin usar, nuevo,-a; *(flat etc)* sin estrenar; *(stamp)* sin matar. **2** *(not in use)* que no se utiliza. **3** [ʌn'juːst] *(unaccustomed)* desacostumbrado,-a (**to,** a); **I'm u. to this kind of life,** no estoy acostumbrado a este tipo de vida.

unusual [ʌn'juːʒʊəl] *adj* *(rare)* insólito,-a, raro,-a, poco común; *(original)* original; *(exceptional)* excepcional; **it's u. for her to be so late,** es raro que llegue tan tarde; **of u. interest,** de excepcional interés; **that's u.!,** ¡qué raro! ◆ **unusually** *adv* excepcionalmente. **u. attentive,** más atento que de costumbre.

unutterable [ʌn'ʌtərəbəl] *adj* indecible, inefable.

unvarying [ʌn'veərɪŋ] *adj* invariable, constante.

unveil [ʌn'veɪl] *vtr* **1** *(uncover)* descubrir. **2** *fig (reveal) (plot)* descubrir, desvelar; *(secret)* revelar.

unventilated [ʌn'ventɪleɪtɪd] *adj* sin ventilación.

unverifiable [ʌn'verɪfaɪəbəl] *adj* que no puede verificarse.

unvoiced [ʌn'vɔɪst] *adj* **1** *(untold)* no expresado,-a. **2** *Ling* sordo,-a.

unwaged [ʌn'weɪdʒd] **I** *adj (not paid)* no remunerado,-a. **II** *n* *npl (not paid)* los no asalariados; *(unemployed)* los parados.

unwanted [ʌn'wɒntɪd] *adj* **1** *(gen)* indeseado,-a; *(child)* no deseado,-a. **2** *(superfluous)* superfluo,-a; **u. hair,** vello *m*.

unwarranted [ʌn'wɒrəntɪd] *adj* **1** *(gen)* injustificado,-a; *(remark)* gratuito,-a. **2** *(interference)* indebido,-a. **2** *(unauthorized)* no autorizado,-a.

unwary [ʌn'weərɪ] *adj* imprudente, incauto,-a.

unwashed [ʌn'wɒʃt] *adj* sucio,-a, sin lavar.

unwavering [ʌn'weɪvərɪŋ] *adj* **1** *(undaunted) (loyalty)* constante, firme; *(courage)* inquebrantable; **u. in one's resolve,** firme en sus propósitos. **2** *(fixed)* fijo,-a.

unwelcome [ʌn'welkəm] *adj* **1** *(visitor)* molesto,-a; **to make sb feel u.,** hacer que algn se sienta incómodo,-a. **2** *(visit)* inoportuno,-a; *fig (news etc)* desagradable.

unwell [ʌn'wel] *adj* malo,-a, indispuesto,-a.

unwholesome [ʌn'həʊlsəm] *adj* **1** *(climate etc)* insalubre. **2** *fig (practice etc)* depravado,-a.

unwieldy(ly) [ʌn'wiːld(l)ɪ] *adj* **1** *(heavy)* pesado,-a; *(cumbersome)* abultado,-a. **2** *(difficult to handle)* poco manejable, de difícil manejo. **3** *(clumsy)* torpe, patoso,-a.

unwilling [ʌn'wɪlɪŋ] *adj* no dispuesto,-a; **to be u. to do sth,** no estar dispuesto a hacer algo. ◆ **unwillingly** *adv* de mala gana.

unwillingness [ʌn'wɪlɪŋnɪs] n desgana f.

unwind [ʌn'waɪnd] (pt & pp **unwound**) **I** vtr desenrollar. **II** vi **1** desenrollarse. **2** (relax) relajarse.

unwise [ʌn'waɪz] adj imprudente, desaconsejable.

unwitting [ʌn'wɪtɪŋ] adj involuntario,-a.

unworkable [ʌn'wɜːkəbəl] adj **1** (not feasible) impracticable; (suggestion) irrealizable. **2** (mine) inexplotable.

unworldly [ʌn'wɜːldlɪ] adj poco mundano,-a, espiritual.

unworthy [ʌn'wɜːðɪ] adj no digno,-a, indigno,-a (**of**, de); **he is u. of my confidence**, no merece mi confianza; **u. conduct**, conducta reprobable; **u. of notice**, que no merece atención.

unwound [ʌn'waʊnd] pt & pp see **unwind.**

unwrap [ʌn'ræp] vtr (pt & pp **unwrapped**) (gift) desenvolver; (package) deshacer, abrir.

unwritten [ʌn'rɪtən] adj (gen) no escrito,-a; (agreement) verbal. ■ Jur **u. law**, derecho m consuetudinario.

unyielding [ʌn'jiːldɪŋ] adj inflexible, rígido,-a.

unzip [ʌn'zɪp] vtr (pt & pp **unzipped**) bajar la cremallera de.

up [ʌp] **I** prep **1** (movement) **to climb** or **go up the mountain**, escalar la montaña; **to walk up and down the room**, ir de un lado a otro de la habitación; **to walk up the street**, ir calle arriba. **2** (position) en lo alto de; **further up the street**, más adelante (en la misma calle); **halfway up the ladder**, a mitad de la escalera; **up a tree**, en lo alto de un árbol. **II** adv **1** (upwards) arriba, hacia arriba; **from ten pounds up**, de diez libras para arriba; **halfway up**, a medio camino; **hands up!**, ¡arriba las manos!; **right up (to the top)**, hasta arriba (del todo); **to go** or **come up**, subir; **to look up**, mirar hacia arriba; **to stand up**, ponerse en pie, levantarse; **to throw sth up into the air**, lanzar algo al aire; **to walk up and down**, ir de un lado para otro. **2** (stationary) arriba; **face up**, boca arriba; (on parcel) **'this side up'**, 'este lado hacia arriba'. **3** (in the sky) **the moon is up**, ha salido la luna. **4** (torn apart) **'road up,'** 'carretera en obras'; fig **his blood was up**, le hervía la sangre; fig **to be up in arms**, poner el grito en el cielo. **5** (towards) hacia; **to come** or **go up to sb**, acercarse a algn. **6** (in, to) **he's up in Yorkshire**, está en Yorkshire; **to go up north**, ir al norte. **7** (out of bed) **to get up**, levantarse; **to stay up all night**, no acostarse. **8** (increased) **bread is up again**, el pan ha subido otra vez; **he put up his offer**, aumentó su oferta; **prices have gone up**, los precios han subido. **9** Jur (in court) **he was up before the magistrate**, compareció ante el juez; **she was up for speeding**, le inculparon por exceso de velocidad. **10** (exposed) **it's up for discussion**, se está discutiendo; **up for sale**, en venta. **11** (taught) **she's well up in Latin**, sabe mucho latín. **12** fam (happening) **something's up**, pasa algo; **what's up (with you)?**, ¿qué pasa (contigo)? **13 up with ...!**, ¡viva ...! **14 to be up against sth**, enfrentarse con algo. **15 up to**, (as far as, until) hasta; **I can spend up to £5**, puedo gastar un máximo de cinco libras; **up to here**, hasta aquí; **up to now**, hasta ahora, hasta la fecha. **16 to be up to**, (depend on) depender de; **it's up to him to do it**, le toca a él hacerlo; **it's up to you**, depende de ti, la decisión está en tus manos. **17 to be ap to**, (be capable of) estar a la altura de; **I don't feel up to doing it today**, hoy no me encuentro con fuerzas para hacerlo; **it's not up to much**, no vale gran cosa; **she isn't up to the journey**, no está en condiciones de hacer el viaje. **18 to be up to**, (devise) traerse entre manos; **he's up to sth**, está tramando algo; **she's up to no good**, no puede estar haciendo nada bueno; **what are you up to?**, ¿qué te traes entre manos? **19** sl offens **up yours**, ¡métetelo por el culo! **III** adj **1** (out of bed) **up (and about)**, levantado,-a. **2** (finished) terminado,-a; **his leave's up**, se le ha acabado el permiso; **time's up**, (ya) es la hora; fam **the game's up**, se acabó (la broma)! **3** Rail (line) de ascenso; (train) ascendente. **4** (escalator etc) de subida. **IV** vtr (pt & pp **upped**) fam aumentar. **V** vi fam **to up and ...**, coger y ...; **she upped and went**, cogió y se fue, de pronto se fue. **VI** n GB fig **on the up and up**, en alza; fig **ups and downs**, altibajos mpl, vicisitudes fpl.

up-and-coming [ʌpən'kʌmɪŋ] adj que promete mucho; **an up-a.-c. lawyer**, un abogado con futuro.

upbringing ['ʌpbrɪŋɪŋ] n educación f.

update [ʌp'deɪt] **I** vtr actualizar, poner al día. **II** ['ʌpdeɪt] n puesta f al día.

upfront ['ʌpfrʌnt] adj fam franco,-a, sincero,-a.

upgrade [ʌp'ɡreɪd] **I** vtr **1** (promote) ascender, subir de categoría. **2** (improve) mejorar la calidad de. **II** ['ʌpɡreɪd] n **to be on the u.**, ir a más.

upheaval [ʌp'hiːvəl] n trastorno m, agitación f.

upheld [ʌp'held] pt & pp see **uphold.**

uphill ['ʌphɪl] **I** adj ascendente; fig arduo,-a, duro,-a. **II** adv cuesta arriba.

uphold [ʌp'həʊld] vtr (pt & pp **upheld**) **1** (maintain) sostener, mantener; **to u. the law**, hacer respetar las leyes. **2** (support) apoyar.

upholster [ʌp'həʊlstər] vtr tapizar.

upholstery [ʌp'həʊlstərɪ] n **1** (covering) tapizado m, tapicería f. **2** (padding) relleno m. **3** (trade) tapicería f.

upkeep ['ʌpkiːp] n **1** (maintenance) mantenimiento m, conservación f. **2** (costs) gastos mpl de mantenimiento.

uplift [ʌp'lɪft] **I** vtr elevar; fig inspirar. **II** ['ʌplɪft] n fig edificación f.

uplifting [ʌp'lɪftɪŋ] adj fig edificante.

up-market ['ʌpmɑːkɪt] adj de calidad superior, de categoría.

upon [ə'pɒn] prep fml en, sobre; **once u. a time ...**, érase una vez ...; **u. my word**, (mi) palabra de honor.

upper ['ʌpər] **I** adj **1** (position) superior; **the u. jaw**, la mandíbula superior; **u. storey**, piso de arriba; fig **to get** or **have the u. hand**, llevar ventaja, llevar la delantera. ■ Typ **u. case**, mayúscula f; U. **Volta**, Alto Volta. **2** (in rank) alto,-a; **the u. class**, la clase alta; Pol **the U. House**, la Cámara Alta; fam **the u. crust**, la flor y nata. **II** n **1** (of shoe) pala f. **2** fam **to be on one's uppers**, estar sin blanca or un céntimo. **3** sl (drugs) anfeta f.

upper-class ['ʌpəklɑːs] adj de la clase alta.

uppermost ['ʌpəməʊst] adj más alto,-a; fig predominante; fig **it was u. in my mind**, era lo que me preocupaba más.

uppish ['ʌpɪʃ] adj GB fam presumido,-a; **don't get so u.!**, ¡baja esos humos!

upright ['ʌpraɪt] **I** adj **1** (vertical) vertical; **u. piano**, piano vertical. **2** (honest) honrado,-a, de honor. **II** adv derecho, en posición vertical. **III** n **1** (stake) montante m; Ftb (post) poste m. **2** (piano) piano m vertical.

uprising ['ʌpraɪzɪŋ, ʌp'raɪzɪŋ] n sublevación f, alzamiento m.

uproar ['ʌprɔːr] n tumulto m, alboroto m; **the town is in an u.**, la ciudad está alborotada.

uproot [ʌp'ruːt] vtr desarraigar.

upset [ʌp'set] **I** vtr (pt & pp **upset**) **1** (overturn) volcar; (capsize) hacer zozobrar; (spill) derramar. **2** (shock) trastornar; (worry) preocupar; (displease) disgustar; **he is easily u.**, se disgusta por nada. **3** (spoil) desbaratar. **4** (make ill) sentar mal; **spicy food upsets my stomach**, las comidas picantes me sientan mal. **II** ['ʌpset] n **1** (reversal) revés m, contratiempo m. **2** Sport (win) victoria f inesperada. **3** (disorder etc) trastorno m, disgusto m; **we had a bit of an u.**, sufrimos un ligero contratiempo. **III** [ʌp'set] adj **1** (overturned) volcado,-a. **2** (shocked) trastornado,-a, alterado,-a; (displeased) disgustado,-a. **3 to have an u. stomach**, sentirse mal del estómago. **4** (spoiled) desbaratado,-a.

upsetting [ʌp'setɪŋ] adj preocupante, desconcertante.

upshot ['ʌpʃɒt] n resultado m; **what will be the u. of it all?**, ¿cómo acabará todo?

upside ['ʌpsaɪd] n **1** (top) parte f superior. **2 u. down**, al revés; **to turn sth u. down**, poner algo al revés; fam **the house was u. down**, la casa estaba patas arriba.

upstage [ʌp'steɪdʒ] **I** *adv & adj Theat* en el fondo del escenario. **II** *vtr fam* eclipsar.

upstairs [ʌp'steəz] **I** *adv* al piso de arriba; **she lives u.,** vive en el piso de arriba; **to go u.,** subir. **II** *n* piso *m* de arriba *or* superior.

upstanding [ʌp'stændɪŋ] *adj fig* recto,-a, honrado,-a, ejemplar.

upstart ['ʌpstɑːt] *n* 1 *(newly risen)* advenedizo,-a *m,f*. 2 *(arrogant)* impertinente *mf*.

upstream [ʌp'striːm] *adv* río arriba, contra la corriente.

upsurge ['ʌpsɜːdʒ] *n* aumento *m*, subida *f*.

uptake ['ʌpteɪk] *n fam* **to be quick on the u.,** cogerlas al vuelo.

uptight [ʌp'taɪt] *adj fam* nervioso,-a; **to get u.,** agobiarse.

up to date [ʌptə'deɪt] *adj* 1 *(current)* al día; **to be up to d. on sth,** estar al tanto *or* al corriente de algo. 2 *(modern)* moderno,-a, a la moda.

upturn ['ʌptɜːn] *n (improvement)* mejora *f*.

upturned [ʌp'tɜːnd] *adj* **u. nose,** nariz respingona.

upward ['ʌpwəd] *adj* ascendente, hacia arriba; *Fin* **u. tendency,** tendencia al alza.

upward(s) ['ʌpwəd(z)] *adv* 1 hacia arriba; **face u.,** boca arriba; **from ten (years) u.,** a partir de los diez años; **from twenty pounds u.,** de veinte libras para arriba; *fam* **u. of,** algo más de.

Urals ['jʊərəlz] *n pl* **the U.,** los (Montes) Urales.

uranium [jʊ'reɪnɪəm] *n Chem* uranio *m*.

Uranus [jʊ'reɪnəs] *n Astron* Urano *m*.

urban ['ɜːbən] *adj* urbano,-a.

urbane [ɜː'beɪn] *adj* urbano,-a, cortés.

urbanize ['ɜːbənaɪz] *vtr* urbanizar.

urchin ['ɜːtʃɪn] *n* 1 *(child)* pilluelo,-a *m,f*, golfillo,-a *m,f*. 2 *Zool* **sea u.,** erizo *m* de mar.

urea ['jʊərɪə] *n* urea *f*.

urethra [jʊ'riːθrə] *n (pl* **uretras** *or* **urethrae** [jʊ'riːθriː]) *Anat* uretra *f*.

urge [ɜːdʒ] **I** *vtr* 1 *(incite)* incitar; *(press)* instar; *(plead)* exhortar; **she urged the soldiers to put down their arms,** exhortó a los soldados a que dejaran las armas. 2 *(advocate)* preconizar; *(insist on)* instar; **to u. that sth should be done,** insistir en que se haga algo. 3 **to u. sb on,** *(incite)* darle cuerda a algn; *(encourage)* animar a algn. **II** *n* impulso *m*; **to feel an u. to do sth,** sentir un vivo deseo de hacer algo.

urgency ['ɜːdʒənsɪ] *n* urgencia *f*; **of great u.,** muy urgente.

urgent ['ɜːdʒənt] *adj (gen)* urgente; *(need, tone)* apremiante; **it is u. that I speak to her,** me urge hablar con ella.

urinal [jʊ'raɪnəl, 'jʊərɪnəl] *n* 1 *(toilet)* urinario *m*. 2 *(bowl)* orinal *m*.

urinate ['jʊərɪneɪt] *vi* orinar.

urine ['jʊərɪn] *n* orina *f*.

urn [ɜːn] *n* 1 urna *f*; **burial u.,** urna cineraria. 2 **tea u.,** tetera *f* grande.

urology [jʊ'rɒlədʒɪ] *n Med* urología *f*.

Ursa ['ɜːsə] *n Astron* Osa *f*. ■ **U. Major,** Osa *f* Mayor; **U. Minor,** Osa *f* Menor.

Uruguay ['jʊərəgwaɪ] *n* Uruguay.

Uruguayan [jʊərə'gwaɪən] *adj & n* uruguayo,-a *(m,f)*.

us [ʌs] *pers pron* 1 *(as object)* nos; **give us some,** danos algo; **he sees us,** nos ve; **let's forget it,** olvidémoslo; **let us in,** déjanos entrar. 2 *(after prep)* nosotras,-as; **among us,** entre nosotros; **both of us,** nosotros dos; **come with us,** ven con nosotros; **four of us,** cuatro de nosotros; **he's one of us,** es de los nuestros; **there are three of us,** somos tres; **they are luckier than us,** tienen más suerte que nosotros. 3 *(after v* to be) nosotros,-as; **she wouldn't believe it was us,** no creía que fuéramos nosotros. 4 *fam* me; **give us a kiss!,** ¡dame un beso!; **let's have a look,** déjame ver.

US [juː'es] *abbr of* **United States,** Estados *mpl* Unidos, EE.UU. *mpl*.

USA [juːes'eɪ] 1 *US abbr of* **United States Army,** Ejército *m* de los Estados Unidos. 2 *abbr of* **United States of America,** Estados *mpl* Unidos de América, EE.UU. *mpl*.

usable ['juːzəbəl] *adj* utilizable.

USAF [juːeser'ef] *US Mil abbr of* **United States Air Force,** Fuerzas *fpl* Aéreas de los Estados Unidos, USAF.

usage ['juːsɪdʒ] *n* 1 *(use)* uso *m*, empleo *m*. 2 *(habit, custom)* costumbre *f*. 3 *Ling* uso *m*.

use [juːz] **I** *vtr* 1 *(gen)* emplear, utilizar, usar; **he used a pair of pliers to remove the nails,** utilizó unos alicates para sacar los clavos; **I u. it as a hammer,** me sirve de martillo; **you can u. my name as a reference,** puedes dar mi nombre si te piden referencias; **what is it used for?,** ¿para qué sirve?; *fam* **u. your head!,** ¡piensa un poco!, ¡utiliza la cabeza! 2 *(apply)* emplear; **to u. every means,** emplear todos los medios; **to u. force,** hacer uso de la fuerza; **to u. one's influence,** valerse de su influencia. 3 *(consume)* consumir, gastar; **how much coffee have you used so far?,** ¿cuánto café llevas gastado? 4 **to u. up,** acabar; **it's all used up,** está agotado, no queda nada; **to u. up the scraps,** aprovechar los restos. 5 *(take unfair advantage of)* aprovecharse de; **they are (just) using you,** se aprovechan de ti. 6 *fam (need)* **I could u. a drink,** no me vendría mal un trago. **II** *v aux (past tense only)* soler, acostumbrar; **I used to live in Scotland as a child,** de pequeño viví en Escocia; **they didn't u. to play together,** no solían jugar juntos; **things aren't what they used to be,** las cosas han cambiado, ya no es como antes; **where did you u. to live?,** ¿dónde vivías (antes)? **III** [juːs] *n* 1 *(gen)* uso *m*, empleo *m*, utilización *f*; *(handling)* manejo *m*; **directions for u.,** modo de empleo, instrucciones para el uso; **fit for u.,** en buen estado; **for emergency u. only,** *Pharm* **'for external u.',** 'para uso externo'; **in everyday u.,** de uso corriente; **in u.,** en uso; *(on lift)* **'not in u.',** 'no funciona'; **ready for u.,** listo para usar; **room with u. of kitchen,** habitación con derecho a cocina; **to come into u.,** empezar a utilizarse; **to make (good) u. of sth,** aprovechar algo; **to put sth to good u.,** sacar partido de algo. 2 *(application)* aplicación *f*. 3 *(usefulness)* utilidad *f*; **I have no further u. for it,** ya no me sirve para nada; **it's no u.,** es inútil, no vale la pena; **what's the u.?,** ¿para qué?; **what the u. of writing to her?,** ¿de qué sirve escribirle?; *fam* **it's no u. crying,** no sirve de nada llorar. 4 *of u.,* útil; **to be of u.,** servir; **can I be of any u. to you?,** ¿puedo serle útil en algo?

used [juːzd] *adj* 1 *(second-hand)* usado,-a, de segunda mano. 2 [juːst] *(accustomed)* **to be u. to,** estar acostumbrado,-a a a; **to get u. to,** acostumbrarse a.

useful ['juːsfʊl] *adj (gen)* útil; *(practical)* práctico,-a; **this is u. for storing things,** esto va bien para guardar cosas; **to come in u.,** venir bien; **to make oneself u.,** ser útil, ayudar.

usefulness ['juːsfʊlnɪs] *n* utilidad *f*.

useless ['juːslɪs] *adj* 1 inútil; **it's u.,** es inútil. 2 *fam (person)* inútil (**at,** para); **I'm u. at that sort of thing,** soy un negado para ese tipo de cosas; **she's quite u.,** es un cero a la izquierda.

user ['juːzər] *n* usuario,-a *m, f*; **telephone users,** los usuarios de teléfono. 2 *fam (of drugs)* drogadicto,-a *m,f*.

usher ['ʌʃər] **I** *n* 1 *Cin Theat* acomodador,-a *m, f*. 2 *(in court etc)* ujier *m*. **II** *vtr* **to u. in,** *Cin Theat* acomodar; *(at home)* hacer pasar; **to u. out,** acompañar hasta la puerta.

USN [juːes'en] *US Mil abbr of* **United States Navy,** Armada *f* de los Estados Unidos, USN.

USS [juːes'es] *US Naut abbr of* **United States Ship,** barco *m* de los Estados Unidos.

USSR [juːeses'ɑːr] *abbr of* **Union of Soviet Socialist Republics,** Unión *f* de Repúblicas Socialistas Soviéticas, URSS *f*.

usual ['juːʒʊəl] **I** *adj* corriente, normal; **as u.,** como siempre, como de costumbre; **at the u. hour,** a la hora habitual; **earlier than u.,** más pronto que de costumbre;

it's not u. for her to be late, no suele llegar tarde; it's the u. practice es lo normal; the u. problems, los problemas de siempre; the u. thing, lo de siempre. II *n* 1 lo habitual, lo usual; out of the u., fuera de lo común. 2 *fam (drink etc)* the u., lo de siempre. ◆ usually *adv* normalmente; she was more than u. polite, estuvo más amable de lo habitual; what do you u. do on Sundays?, ¿qué sueles hacer los domingos?

usurer ['juːʒərəʳ] *n* usurero,-a *m,f*.

usurpation [juːzɜː'peɪʃən] *n* usurpación *f*.

utensil [juː'tensəl] *n* utensilio *m*. ■ kitchen utensils, batería *f sing or* utensilios *mpl* de cocina.

uterus ['juːtərəs] *n (pl* uteri ['juːtəraɪ]) *Anat* útero *m*, matriz *f*.

utilitarian [juːtɪlɪ'teərɪən] I *adj* 1 *Philos* utilitarista. 2 *(useful)* utilitario,-a. II *n Philos* utilitarista *mf*.

utility [juː'tɪlɪtɪ] *n* 1 utilidad *f*. ■ u. goods, artículos *mpl* utilitarios; u. room, *(for storage)* trascocina *f*; *(for ironing)* cuarto *m* de planchar; u. vehicle, utilitario *m*. 2 (public) u., empresa *f* de servicio público.

utilize ['juːtɪlaɪz] *vtr* utilizar, servirse de.

utmost ['ʌtməʊst] I *adj* sumo,-a, extremo,-a; it is of the u. importance that ..., es de suma importancia que ... *(+ subj)*; the u. ends of the earth, los confines más remotos de la tierra; with the u. ease, con suma facilidad. II *n* máximo *m*; to do *or* try one's u., hacer todo lo posible; to the u., al máximo, a más no poder.

utopia [juː'təʊpɪə] *n* utopía *f*.

utopian [juː'təʊpɪən] I *adj* utópico,-a. II *n* utopista *mf*.

utter¹ ['ʌtəʳ] *vtr (words)* pronunciar; *(threat)* proferir; *(sigh)* dar; *(cry)* lanzar; she didn't u. a word, no pronunció palabra, no dijo ni pío.

utter² ['ʌtəʳ] *adj* total, completo,-a, absoluto,-a; he's an u. fool, es tonto de remate; she's an u. stranger to me, no le conozco de nada; that's. u. nonsense!, ¡es pura tontería!; u. bliss, la más complete felicidad.

utterance ['ʌtərəns] *n* declaración *f*.

U-turn ['juːtɜːn] *n* cambio *m* de sentido.

uvula ['juːvjʊlə] *n (pl* uvulas *or* uvulae ['juːvjʊliː]) *Anat* úvula *f*, campanilla *f*.

uvular ['juːvjʊləʳ] *adj* uvular.

V

V, v [viː] *n (the letter)* V, v *f*.

V *Elec abbr of* volt(s), voltio(s) *m(pl)*, V.

v 1 *(pl* vv) *abbr of* verse, verso *m*, v. 2 *(also vs) Jur Sport abbr of* versus, contra. 3 *fam abbr of* very, muy. 4 *abbr of* vide (see), véase, vid.

vac [væk] *n (abbr of vacation) GB Sch Univ fam* vacaciones *fpl*.

vacancy ['veɪkənsɪ] *n* 1 *(job, post)* vacante *f*, puesto *m* vacante; to fill a v., ocupar un puesto; 'v. for a waiter', 'se necesita camarero'. 2 *(room in hotel)* habitación *f* libre; 'no vacancies', 'completo'.

vacant ['veɪkənt] *adj* 1 *(empty)* vacío,-a. 2 *(job, post)* vacante; 'situations v.', 'ofertas de trabajo'. 2 *(room, seat, hour)* libre. 3 *(mind, expression)* vacío,-a; with a v. stare, con la mirada perdida. ◆ vacantly *adv (absent-mindedly)* distraídamente.

vacate [və'keɪt] *vtr* 1 *(post)* dejar, dejar vacante. 2 *(flat etc)* desalojar, desocupar.

vacation [və'keɪʃən] I *n* 1 *GB Sch Univ* vacaciones *fpl*; the long v., las vacaciones de verano. 2 *US* vacaciones *fpl*; to be on v., estar de vacaciones; to take a v., tomarse unas vacaciones. II *vi US* pasar las vacaciones (in, at, en).

vacationer [və'keɪʃənəʳ] *n*, vacationist [və'keɪʃənɪst] *n US* summer v., veraneante *mf*.

vaccinate ['væksɪneɪt] *vtr Med* vacunar.

vaccine ['væksiːn] *n Med* vacuna *f*.

vacillate ['væsɪleɪt] *vi* 1 *(hesitate)* vacilar, dudar. 2 *(sway)* oscilar.

vacillating ['væsɪleɪtɪŋ] *adj* 1 *(hesitating)* vacilante, indeciso,-a. 2 *(swaying)* oscilante.

vacuous ['vækjʊəs] *adj* 1 *(empty)* vacío,-a, vacuo,-a. 2 *(mindless)* necio,-a, tonto,-a.

vacuum ['vækjʊəm] *n (pl* vacuums *or* vacua ['vækjʊə]) *Phys* vacío *m*; *fig* to leave a v., dejar un vacío. ■ v. brake, freno *m* de vacío; v. cleaner, aspiradora *f*; v. flask, termo *m*. II *vtr* limpiar con aspiradora; to v. the living room, pasar la aspiradora por el salón.

vacuum-packed ['vækjʊəmpækt] *adj* envasado,-a al vacío.

vade mecum [vɑːdɪ'meɪkʊm] *n* vademécum *m*.

vagabond ['vægəbɒnd] *adj & n* vagabundo,-a *(m,f)*.

vagary ['veɪgərɪ, və'geərɪ] *n fml* capricho *m*.

vagina [və'dʒaɪnə] *n (pl* vaginas *or* vaginae [və'dʒaɪniː]) *Anat* vagina *f*.

vaginal [və'dʒaɪnəl] *adj* vaginal.

vagrancy [və'veɪgrənsɪ] *n* vagabundeo *m*, vagabundería *f*.

vagrant ['veɪgrənt] *adj & n* vagabundo,-a *(m,f)*.

vague [veɪg] *adj* 1 *(imprecise)* vago,-a, impreciso,-a; *(indistinct)* borroso,-a; I haven't the vaguest idea, no tengo la más mínima idea; she was v. about it, no dio detalles.

vagueness ['veɪgnɪs] *n (gen)* vaguedad *f*, imprecisión *f*; *(of outline)* lo borroso.

vain [veɪn] *adj* 1 *(proud)* vanidoso,-a, presumido,-a. 2 *(hopeless)* vano,-a; in v., en vano.

valance ['væləns] *n (of bed)* cenefa *f*, doselera *f*.

vale [veɪl] *n lit* valle *m*; *fig* v. of tears, valle de lágrimas.

valence ['veɪləns] *n US Chem see* valency.

Valencian [və'lensɪən] *adj & n* valenciano,-a *(m,f)*.

valency ['veɪlənsɪ] *n Chem* valencia *f*.

valentine ['væləntaɪn] *n* 1 *(card)* tarjeta *f* que se manda el Día de los Enamorados (14 de febrero). 2 *(sweetheart)* novio,-a *m,f*.

valerian [və'leərɪən] *n Bot* valeriana *f*.

valet ['vælɪt, 'væleɪ] *n* ayuda *m* de cámara.

valiant ['væljənt] *adj* valiente.

valid ['vælɪd] *adj (gen)* válido,-a; *(ticket)* valedero,-a; no longer v., caducado,-a; *(ticket)* v. for six months, valedero para seis meses.

validate ['vælɪdeɪt] *vtr* validar.

validity [və'lɪdtɪ] *n* validez *f*.

Valletta [və'letə] *n* (La) Valeta.

valley ['vælɪ] *n* valle *m*.

valour, *US* valor ['væləʳ] *n* valor *m*, valentía *f*.

valuable ['væljʊəbəl] I *adj* valioso,-a, de valor. II valuables *npl* objetos *mpl* de valor.

valuation [væljʊ'eɪʃən] *n* 1 *(act)* valoración *f*, valuación *f*. 2 *(price)* valor *m*.

value ['vælju:] **I** *n* (*gen*) valor *m*; **50 pence is good v.,** 50 peniques es un buen precio; **of great/little v.,** de gran/poco valor; **of no v.,** sin valor; **to get good v. for money,** sacarle jugo al dinero; **to increase in v.,** aumentar en valor; **to the v. of,** por el valor de; **traditional values,** valores tradicionales. ■ **v. added tax,** impuesto *m* sobre el valor añadido. **II** *vtr* **1** (*estimate value of*) valorar, tasar. **2** (*appreciate*) valorar, estimar, apreciar.

valueless ['væljʊlɪs] *adj* sin valor.

valuer ['væljʊə^r] *n* tasador,-a *m,f*.

valve [vælv] *n* **1** *Anat Tech* válvula *f*. ■ **safety v.,** válvula *f* de seguridad. **2** *Rad* lámpara *f*. **3** *Bot Zool* valva *f*. **4** *Mus* llave *f*.

valvular ['vælvjʊlə^r] *adj* valvular.

vamp¹ [væmp] *n fam* vampiresa *f*.

vamp² [væmp] *n* pala *f*, empella *f*.

vampire ['væmpaɪə^r] *n* vampiro *m*. ■ *Zool* **v. bat,** vampiro *m*.

van¹ [væn] *n* **1** *Aut* furgoneta *f*, camioneta *f*. ■ *GB* **breakdown v.,** grúa *f*; **delivery v.,** furgoneta *f* de reparto; **prison v.,** coche *m* celular; **removal v.,** camión *m* de mudanza. **2** *GB Rail* furgón *m*.

van² [væn] *n fam abbr of* **vanguard.**

vandal ['vændəl] *n* **1** vándalo,-a *m,f*. **2** *Hist* **V.,** vándalo,-a *m,f*.

vandalism ['vændəlɪzəm] *n* vandalismo *m*.

vandalize ['vændəlaɪz] *vtr* destruir, destrozar, hacer estragos en.

vane [veɪn] *n* (**weather** *or* **wind**) **v.,** veleta *f*.

vanguard ['vænɡɑːd] *n* vanguardia *f*; **to be in the v. of,** estar en la vanguardia de.

vanilla [vəˈnɪlə] *n* vainilla *f*.

vanish ['vænɪʃ] *vi* desaparecer, esfumarse; **to v. from sight,** desaparecer de la vista; *fig* **to v. into thin air,** desaparecer sin dejar rastro.

vanishing point ['vænɪʃɪŋpɔɪnt] *n* punto *m* de fuga.

vanity ['vænɪtɪ] *n* vanidad *f*; **out of sheer v.,** por pura vanidad. ■ **v. bag, v. case,** neceser *m*.

vanquish ['væŋkwɪʃ] *vtr lit* vencer.

vantage ['vɑːntɪdʒ] *n* ventaja *f*; **v. point,** posición *f* ventajosa *or* estratégica.

Vanuatu ['vænuːæːtuː] *n* Vanuatu.

vapid ['væpɪd] *adj* insípido,-a, soso,-a.

vaporize ['veɪpəraɪz] **I** *vtr* vaporizar. **II** *vi* vaporizarse.

vaporizer ['veɪpəraɪzə^r] *n* (*device*) vaporizador *m*; (*spray*) pulverizador *m*, atomizador *m*.

vaporous ['veɪpərəs] *adj* vaporoso,-a.

vapour, *US* **vapor** ['veɪpə^r] *n* (*gen*) vapor *m*; (*on windowpane*) vaho *m*. ■ **v. trail,** estela *f* de humo.

variability [veərɪəˈbɪlɪtɪ] *n* variabilidad *f*.

variable ['veərɪəbəl] *adj & n* variable (*f*).

variance ['veərɪəns] *n fml* discrepancia *f*; **to be at v.,** no concordar; **to be at v. with sb,** estar en desacuerdo con algn.

variant ['veərɪənt] *adj & n* variante (*f*).

variation [veərɪˈeɪʃən] *n* variación *f*.

varicose ['værɪkəʊs] *adj Med* varicoso,-a. ■ **v. veins** varices *fpl*.

varied ['veərɪd] *adj* variado,-a, diverso,-a.

variegated ['veərɪɡeɪtɪd] *adj* abigarrado,-a.

variety [vəˈraɪtɪ] *n* **1** (*diversity*) variedad *f*, diversidad *f*; (*assortment*) surtido *m*; **for a v. of reasons,** por razones diversas; **there is a wide v. of opinions,** hay gran diversidad de opiniones; *prov* **v. is the spice of life,** en la variedad está el gusto. **2** *Theat* variedades *fpl*. ■ **v. show,** espectáculo *m* de variedades.

various ['veərɪəs] *adj* **1** (*different*) diverso,-a, vario,-a; **the v. authorities on the subject,** las distintas autoridades en el tema. **2** (*several*) varios,-as.

varnish ['vɑːnɪʃ] **I** *n* barniz *m*. ■ *GB* **nail v.,** esmalte *m* de uñas. **II** *vtr* barnizar.

vary ['veərɪ] *vi* (*pt & pp* **varied**) variar; **opinions v.,** las opiniones varían; **prices v. from £2 to £4,** los precios oscilan entre 2 y 4 libras; **to v. in size,** variar de tamaño.

varying *adj* diverso,-a; **with v. degrees of success,** con más o menos éxito.

vascular ['væskjʊlə^r] *adj Anat Biol* vascular.

vase [vɑːz] *n* florero *m*, jarrón *m*.

vasectomy [væˈsektəmɪ] *n Med* vasectomía *f*.

Vaseline® ['væsɪliːn] *n* vaselina *f*.

vassal ['væsəl] *n Hist* vasallo,-a *m,f*.

vast [vɑːst] *adj* (*area etc*) vasto,-a, inmenso,-a, enorme; (*majority*) abrumador,-a; **v. sums of money,** grandes cantidades de dinero.

vastness ['vɑːstnɪs] *n* vastedad *f*, inmensidad *f*.

VAT, Vat [viːeɪˈtiː, væt] *Econ abbr of* **value added tax,** impuesto *m* sobre el valor añadido, IVA *m*.

vat [væt] *n* cuba *f*; tina *f*.

Vatican ['vætɪkən] *n* **the V.,** el Vaticano. ■ **V.City,** Ciudad *f* del Vaticano.

vaudeville ['vəʊdəvɪl, 'vɔːdəvɪl] *n Theat* vodevil *m*.

vault¹ [vɔːlt] *n* **1** *Archit* bóveda *f*. **2** (*cellar*) sótano *m*; (*for wine*) bodega *f*. **3** (*tomb*) tumba *f*. **4** (*of bank*) cámara *f* acorazada.

vault² [vɔːlt] **I** *vtr & vi* saltar. **II** *n Gymn* salto *m*. ■ **pole v.,** salto *m* de pértiga.

vaulting ['vɔːltɪŋ] *adj Gymn* **v. horse,** potro *m*; *Sport* **v. pole,** pértiga *f*.

vaunt [vɔːnt] *vtr fml* jactarse de, hacer alarde de.

VC [viːˈsiː] **1** *Com abbr of* **Vice-Chairman,** Vicepresidente *m*. **2** *Univ abbr of* **Vice Chancellor,** Rector *m*. **3** *Pol abbr of* **Vice-Consul,** Vicecónsul *m*. **4** *GB Mil abbr of* **Victoria Cross,** Cruz *f* de (la Reina) Victoria.

VCR [viːsiːˈɑː^r] *abbr of* **video cassette recorder,** (grabador *m* de) video *m*.

VD [viːˈdiː] *Med abbr of* **venereal disease,** enfermedad *f* venérea.

VDU [viːdiːˈjuː] *Comput abbr of* **visual display unit,** pantalla *f*.

veal [viːl] *n Culin* ternera *f*.

vector ['vektə^r] *n Math* vector *m*.

veer¹ [vɪə^r] *vi* (*ship*) virar; (*car*) cambiar de dirección, girar; (*road*) torcer; *fig* **to v. from one's course,** desviarse de su camino; *fig* **to v. round,** cambiar de opinión.

veg [vedʒ] *n* (*abbr of* **vegetable** *or* **vegetables**) *fam* verdura(s) *f(pl)*, hortaliza(s) *f(pl)*.

vegetable ['vedʒtəbəl] *n* (*gen*) vegetal *m*; (*food*) verdura *f*, hortaliza *f*, legumbre *f*; **early vegetables,** verduras tempranas. ■ **the v. kingdom,** el reino vegetal; **v. garden,** huerta *f*, huerto *m*.

vegetarian [vedʒɪˈteərɪən] *adj & n* vegetariano,-a (*m,f*).

vegetarianism [vedʒɪˈteərɪənɪzəm] *n* vegetarianismo *m*.

vegetate ['vedʒɪteɪt] *vi* vegetar.

vegetation [vedʒɪˈteɪʃən] *n* vegetación *f*.

vehemence ['viːɪməns] *n* vehemencia *f*.

vehement ['viːɪmənt] *adj* vehemente.

vehicle ['viːɪkəl] *n* **1** *Tech* vehículo *m*. ■ **armoured v.,** vehículo *m*, blindado; **motor v.,** automóvil *m*. **2** *fig* vehículo *m*, medio *m*.

vehicular [vɪˈhɪkjʊlə^r] *adj* de vehículos; **v. traffic,** tránsito rodado.

veil [veɪl] **I** *n* velo *m*; *Rel f* **to take the v.,** tomar el velo; *fig* **to draw a v. over sth,** correr un tupido velo sobre algo. **II** *vtr* **1** velar, cubrir con velo. **2** *fig* velar, disimular; **veiled reference,** alusión velada.

vein [veɪn] *n* **1** *Anat* vena *f*. **2** *Bot* vena *f*, nervio *m*. **3** *Geol Min* vena *f*, veta *f*. **4** *(in wood, marble)* vena *f*, filón *m*. **5** *fig (mood)* vena *f*, humor *m*; **to be in v.,** estar en vena.

veined [veɪnd] *adj* veteado,-a.

veiny ['veɪnɪ] *adj (veinier, veiniest)* venoso,-a.

vela ['viːlə] *npl see* **velum.**

velar ['viːlə^r] *adj & n Ling* velar *(f).*

vellum ['veləm] *n* vitela *f*. ◆ **v. paper,** papel *m* vitela.

velocity [vɪ'lɒsɪtɪ] *n* velocidad *f*.

velodrome ['viːlədrəʊm, 'velədrəʊm] *n* velódromo *m*.

velour(s) [ve'lʊə^r] *n Tex* veludillo *m*.

velum ['viːləm] *n Anat* velo *m* (del paladar).

velvet ['velvɪt] *n Tex* terciopelo *m*; **an iron hand in a v. glove,** mano de hierro en guante de terciopelo.

velveteen [velvɪ'tiːn] *n Tex* pana *f*.

velvety ['velvɪtɪ] *adj* aterciopelado,-a.

venal ['viːnəl] *adj* venal, sobornable.

venality [vɪ'nælɪtɪ] *n* venalidad *f*.

vend [vend] *vtr Jur* vender.

vendetta [ven'detə] *n* enemistad *f*, odio *m*.

vending ['vendɪŋ] *n* **v. machina,** máquina *f* expendedora.

vendor ['vendɔː^r] *n Jur* vendedor,-a *m,f*.

veneer [vɪ'nɪə^r] **I** *n* **1** *(covering)* chapa *f*. **2** *fig* apariencia *f*. **II** *vtr* chapar, chapear.

venerable ['venərəbəl] *adj* venerable.

venerate ['venəreɪt] *vtr* venerar.

venereal [vɪ'nɪərɪəl] *adj Med* venéreo,-a.

Venetian [vɪ'niːʃən] *adj & n* veneciano,-a *(m, f).* ◼ **v. blind,** persiana *f* graduable.

Venezuela [venɪ'zweɪlə] *n* Venezuela.

Venezuelan [venɪ'zweɪlən] *adj & n* venezolano,-a *(m,f).*

vengeance ['vendʒəns] *n* venganza *f*; **to take v. on sb,** vengarse de algn; *fam* **it was raining with a v.,** llovía con ganas.

vengeful ['vendʒfʊl] *adj* vengativo,-a.

venial ['viːnɪəl] *adj* venial; **v. sin,** pecado venial.

Venice ['venɪs] *n* Venecia.

venison ['venzən, 'venɪsən] *n Culin* carne *f* de venado.

venom ['venəm] *n* veneno *m*.

venomous ['venəməs] *adj* venenoso,-a; *fig* **v. tongue,** lengua viperina.

venous ['viːnəs] *adj Anat* venoso,-a.

vent [vent] **I** *n* **1** *(opening)* abertura *f*, orificio *m*; *(grille)* rejilla *f* de ventilación; *fig* **to give v. to one's feelings,** desahogarse. ◼ **air v.,** respiradero *m*. **2** *(of volcano)* chimenea *f*. **II** *vtr fig (feelings)* descargar; **to v. one's anger on sb,** desahogarse con algn.

ventilate ['ventɪleɪt] *vtr* ventilar, airear.

ventilation [ventɪ'leɪʃən] *n* ventilación *f*. ◼ *Min* **v. shaft,** pozo *m* de ventilación.

ventilator ['ventɪleɪtə^r] *n* ventilador *m*.

ventricle ['ventrɪkəl] *n Anat* ventrículo *m*.

ventriloquist [ven'trɪləkwɪst] *n* ventrílocuo,-a *m,f*.

ventriloquism [ven'trɪləkwɪzəm] *n*, **ventriloquy** [ven'trɪləkwɪ] *n* ventriloquia *f*.

venture ['ventʃə^r] **I** *vtr* arriesgar, aventurar; **to v. an opinion,** aventurar una opinión; **he didn't v. to ask,** no se atrevió a preguntarlo; *prov* **nothing ventured, nothing gained,** quien no arriesga no cruza la mar. **II** *vi* arriesgarse; **to v. out of doors,** atreverse a salir. **III** *n* empresa *f* arriesgada, aventura *f*; **business/joint v.,** empresa comercial/colectiva; **it's a completely new v.,** es algo completamente nuevo.

venue ['venjuː] *n* **1** *Jur* jurisdicción *f*. **2** *(meeting place)* lugar *m* de reunión. **3** *(for concert etc)* local *m*.

Venus ['viːnəs] *n* **1** *Myth* Venus *f*. **2** *Astron* Venus *m*.

veracious [ve'reɪʃəs] *adj* veraz, sincero,-a.

veracity [ve'ræsɪtɪ] *n* veracidad *f*.

veranda(h) [ve'rændə] *n* veranda *f*, terraza *f*.

verb [vɜːb] *n Ling* verbo *m*.

verbal ['vɜːbəl] *adj* verbal. ◆ **verbally** *adv* verbalmente, de palabra.

verbalize ['vɜːbəlaɪz] *vtr* verbalizar.

verbatim [vɜː'beɪtɪm] **I** *adj* textual. **II** *adv* palabra por palabra, textualmente.

verbena [vɜː'biːnə] *n Bot* verbena *f*.

verbiage ['vɜːbɪɪdʒ] *n* verborrea *f*, verbosidad *f*.

verbose [vɜː'bəʊs] *adj* verboso,-a, locuaz.

verbosity [vɜː'bɒsɪtɪ] *n* verbosidad *f*.

verdant ['vɜːdənt] *adj lit* verde.

verdict ['vɜːdɪkt] *n* **1** *Jur* veredicto *m*, fallo *m*; **to return a v. of guilty/not guilty,** pronunciar un veredicto de culpabilidad/inocencia. **2** *(opinion)* opinión *f*, juicio *m*; **give me your v. on it,** dime lo que opinas de ello.

verge [vɜːdʒ] **I** *n* **1** *(margin)* borde *m*, margen *m*; *fig* **on the v. of,** al borde de, a dos dedos de; *fig* **to be on the v. of doing sth,** estar a punto de hacer algo. **2** *GB (of road)* arcén *m*. **II** *vi* rayar **(on, en); it verges on madness,** raya en la locura; **she's verging on fifty,** ronda los cincuenta años.

verger ['vɜːdʒə^r] *n C of E* sacristán *m*.

verifiable ['verɪfaɪəbəl] *adj* verificable.

verification [verɪfɪ'keɪʃən] *n* verificación *f*, comprobación *f*.

verify ['verɪfaɪ] *vtr (pt & pp verified)* verificar, comprobar.

verisimilitude [verɪsɪ'mɪlɪtjuːd] *n* verosimilitud *f*.

veritable ['verɪtəbəl] *adj* verdadero,-a, auténtico,-a.

verity ['verɪtɪ] *n* verdad *f*.

vermicelli [vɜːmɪ'selɪ] *npl Culin* fideos *mpl*.

vermil(l)ion [və'mɪljən] **I** *n* bermellón *m*. **II** *adj* bermejo,-a.

vermin ['vɜːmɪn] *npl* **1** *(animals)* bichos *mpl*, sabandijas *fpl*. **2** *fig* gentuza *f sing*, chusma *f sing*.

verminous ['vɜːmɪnəs] *adj* lleno,-a de bichos.

vermouth ['vɜːməθ] *n* vermú *m*, vermut *m*.

vernacular [və'nækjʊlə^r] **I** *n* lengua *f* vernácula. **II** *adj* vernáculo,-a.

veronica [və'rɒnɪkə] *n Bot* verónica *f*.

verruca [və'ruːkə] *n (pl verruccas or verruccae* [və'ruːsiː]*) Med* verruga *f*.

Versailles [veə'saɪ] *n* Versalles.

versatile ['vɜːsətaɪl] *adj* **1** *(person)* polifacético,-a; *(object)* dúctil, de múltiples aplicaciones. **2** *Zool* versátil.

versatility [vɜːsə'tɪlɪtɪ] *n* **1** *(of person)* carácter *m* polifacético; *(of object)* ductilidad *f*, variedad *f* de aplicaciones. **2** *Zool* versatilidad *f*.

verse [vɜːs] *n* **1** *(stanza)* estrofa *f*. **2** *(poetry)* versos *mpl*, poesía *f*; **blank v.,** verso blanco; **free v.,** verso libre; **in v.,** en verso. **3** *(of song)* copla *f*. **4** *(of Bible)* versículo *m*.

versed [vɜːst] *adj* versado,-a; **to be (well) v. in,** ser (muy) versado en.

versification [vɜːsɪfɪ'keɪʃən] *n* versificación *f*.

versify ['vɜːsɪfaɪ] *vi (pt & pp versified)* versificar.

version ['vɜːʃən, 'vɜːʒən] *n* **1** *(gen)* versión *f*; **the uncut v. of the film,** la versión íntegra de la película. ◼ *Theat* **stage v.,** adaptación *f* teatral. **2** *Mus* interpretación *f*. **3** *Aut* modelo *m*; **the economy v.,** el modelo económico.

verso ['vɜːsəʊ] *n (pl versos)* Print reverso *m*.

versus ['vɜːsəs] *prep Jur Sport* contra.

vertebra ['vɜːtɪbrə] *n (pl vertebras or vertebrae* ['vɜːtɪbriː]*) Anat* vértebra *f*.

vertebral ['vɜ:tɪbrəl] *adj* vertebral.

vertebrate ['vɜ:tɪbreɪt, 'vɜ:tɪbrɪt] *adj & n* vertebrado,-a *(m).*

vertex ['vɜ:teks] *n (pl vertexes or vertices)* **1** *Anat Geom* vértice *m.* **2** *fig* cumbre *f,* cima *f.*

vertical ['vɜ:tɪkəl] *adj & n* vertical *(f).*

vertices ['vɜ:tɪsi:z] *npl see* **vertex.**

vertigo ['vɜ:tɪgəʊ] *n (pl vertigoes or vertigines* [vɜ:'tɪdʒɪni:z]) *Med* vértigo *m.*

vervain ['vɜ:veɪn] *n Bot* verbena *f.*

verve [vɜ:v] *n* vigor *m,* brío *m,* energía *f.*

very ['verɪ] **I** *adv* **1** *(extremely)* muy; **it's v. kind of you,** es muy amable de tu parte; **to be v. hungry,** tener mucha hambre; **v. few,** muy pocos,-as, poquísimos,-as; **v. little,** muy poco; **v. much,** mucho, muchísimo; **v. tall,** muy alto,-a, altísimo,-a; **v. well,** muy bien. **2** *(emphatic)* **at the v. latest,** a más tardar, como máximo; **at the v. least,** como mínimo, por lo menos; **the v. best,** el mejor de todos; **the v. first/last,** el primero/último de todos; **the v. same day,** el mismo día. **II** *adj* **1** *(extreme)* de todo; **at the v. end,** al final de todo. **2** *(precise)* exacto,-a, mismo,-a; **at this v. moment,** en este mismo momento; **her v. words,** sus palabras exactas; **in the v. middle,** justo en medio; *fam* **it's the v. thing,** es justo lo que hacía falta. **3** *(mere)* **the v. thought of it!,** ¡sólo con pensarlo!

vesicle ['vesɪkəl] *n Anat* vesícula *f.*

vesicular [ve'sɪkjulə'] *adj Anat* vesicular.

vespers ['vespəz] *npl Rel* vísperas *fpl.*

vessel ['vesəl] *n* **1** *(container)* vasija *f,* recipiente *m.* **2** *Naut* buque *m,* nave *f,* navío *m.* ■ **cargo v.,** buque *m* de carga. **3** *Anat Bot* vaso *m.* ■ **blood v.,** vaso *m* sanguíneo.

vest [vest] **I** *n* **1** *(undershirt)* camiseta *f.* **2** *US* chaleco *m.* **II** *vtr Jur* dar posesión a **(with,** de), conferir a **(with,** -); **to v. sb with rights,** conferir derechos a algn.

vestal ['vestəl] *adj* vestal. ■ **v. virgin,** vestal *f.*

vested ['vestɪd] *adj Jur Fin* absoluto,-a, efectivo,-a; **v. interests,** derechos adquiridos; *fig* intereses creados *or* personales; **to have a v. interest in a matter,** tener intereses personales en un asunto.

vestibule ['vestɪbju:l] *n* **1** *(entrance hall)* vestíbulo *m,* entrada *f.* **2** *Anat* vestíbulo *m.*

vestige ['vestɪdʒ] *n* vestigio *m,* rastro *m.*

vestigial [ves'tɪdʒɪəl] *adj* vestigial.

vestment ['vestmənt] *n Rel* vestidura *f* sacerdotal.

vestry ['vestrɪ] *n Rel* sacristía *f.*

Vesuvius [vɪ'su:vɪəs] *n* Vesubio *m.*

vet¹ [vet] **I** *n fam abbr of* **veterinary surgeon.** **II** *vtr (pt & pp vetted) GB* someter a investigación, examinar.

vet² [vet] *n (abbr of veteran) US Mil* excombatiente *mf.*

vetch [vetʃ] *n Bot* arveja *f.*

veteran ['vetərən] *n* **1** *(gen)* veterano,-a *m,f, fig* **he's a v. photographer,** es un fotógrafo experimentado. ■ *GB* **v. car,** coche *m* de época (construido antes de 1919); **v. soldier,** soldado *m* veterano. **2** *US Mil* **(war)** *m,* ex combatiente *mf.*

veterinarian [vetərɪ'neərɪən] *n US* veterinario,-a *m,f.*

veterinary ['vetərɪnərɪ] *adj* veterinario,-a. ■ **v. medicine,** veterinaria *f; GB* **v. surgeon,** veterinario,-a *m,f.*

veto ['vi:təʊ] **I** *n (pt vetoes)* veto *m;* **power** *or* **right of v.,** derecho de veto; **to impose a v. over sth,** poner el veto a algo. **II** *vtr (pt & pp vetoed)* vetar; *(forbid)* vedar, prohibir.

vetting ['vetɪŋ] *n GB* investigación *f,* examen *m.*

vexation [vek'seɪʃən] *n* **1** *(annoyance)* disgusto *m,* vejación *f.* **2** *(worry)* preocupación *f.*

vexatious [vek'seɪʃəs] *adj* molesto,-a.

vexed [vekst] *adj* **1** *(annoyed)* disgustado,-a, molesto,-a; **she was v. at the delay,** le disgustó el retraso. **2** *(worried)* inquieto,-a. **3** *(debated)* controvertido,-a.

VHF [vi:eɪtʃ'ef] *Rad abbr of* **very high frequency,** frecuencia *f* muy alta, VHF.

via ['vaɪə] *prep* por, vía; **they travelled v. Paris,** viajaron vía París.

viability [vaɪə'bɪlɪtɪ] *n* viabilidad *f.*

viable ['vaɪəbəl] *adj* viable, factible, practicable.

viaduct ['vaɪədʌkt] *n* viaducto *m.*

viand ['vaɪənd] *n (gen pl)* vianda *f.*

viaticum [vaɪ'ætɪkəm] *n (pl viaticums or viatica* [vaɪ'ætɪkə]) *Rel* viático *m.*

vibes [vaɪbz] *npl (abbr of vibrations) fam* vibraciones *fpl.*

vibrant ['vaɪbrənt] *adj* **1** *(sound)* vibrante. **2** *fig (personality)* vital, fuerte; *(city)* animado,-a.

vibraphone ['vaɪbrəfəʊn] *n Mus* vibráfono *m.*

vibrate [vaɪ'breɪt] *vi* vibrar **(with,** de).

vibration [vaɪ'breɪʃən] *n* vibración *f.*

vibrator [vaɪ'breɪtə'] *n* vibrador *m.*

vibratory ['vaɪbrətərɪ] *adj* vibratorio,-a.

viburnum [vaɪ'bɜ:nəm] *n Bot* viburno *m.*

vicar ['vɪkə'] *n* **1** *C of E* párroco *m.* **2** *RC* vicario *m;* **the V. of Christ,** el Vicario de Cristo. ■ **v. general,** vicario *m* general.

vicarage ['vɪkərɪdʒ] *n* casa *f* del párroco, vicaría *f.*

vicarious [vɪ'keərɪəs] *adj (gen)* experimentado,-a por otro; *(punishment)* sufrido,-a por otro; **v. pleasure,** placer indirecto.

vice¹ [vaɪs] *n* vicio *m.* ■ **v. squad,** brigada *f* contra el vicio.

vice² [vaɪs] *n (tool)* torno *m or* tornillo *m* de banco.

vice³ [vaɪs] *pref* vice-. ■ *Mil* **v. admiral,** vicealmirante *m; Univ* **v. chancellor,** rector,-a *m, f;* **v.- presidency,** vicepresidencia *f;* **v. president,** vicepresidente,-a *m,f.*

vice-chairman [vaɪs'tʃeəmən] *n (pl vice-chairmen)* vicepresidente *m.*

viceroy ['vaɪsrɔɪ] *n* virrey *m.*

viceroyalty [vaɪs'rɔɪəltɪ] *n* virreinato *m.*

vice versa [vaɪsɪ'vɜ:sə] *adv* viceversa.

vicinity [vɪ'sɪnɪtɪ] *n* **1** *(area)* vecindad *f,* inmediaciones *fpl;* **in the v. of,** cerca de, en las inmediaciones de. **2** *(nearness)* proximidad *f.*

vicious ['vɪʃəs] *adj (violent)* virulento,-a, violento,-a; *(malicious)* malintencionado,-a; *(cruel)* cruel, depravado,-a, perverso,-a; **to have a v. tongue,** tener una lengua viperina. ■ **v. circle,** círculo *m* vicioso.

viciousness ['vɪʃəsnɪs] *n (violence)* virulencia *f,* violencia *f; (malice)* maldad *f,* mala intención *f; (cruelty)* crueldad *f,* depravación *f,* perversidad *f.*

vicissitude [vɪ'sɪsɪtju:d] *n* vicisitud *f.*

victim ['vɪktɪm] *n* víctima *f;* **to be the v. of,** ser víctima de; *fig* **to fall v. to sb's charms,** sucumbir ante los encantos de algn.

victimize ['vɪktɪmaɪz] *vtr (punish)* perseguir, tomar como víctima; *(retaliate against)* tomar represalias contra.

victor ['vɪktə'] *n* vencedor,-a *m,f,* triunfador,-a *m,f.*

Victorian [vɪk'tɔ:rɪən] *adj* victoriano,-a.

Victoriana [vɪktɔ:rɪ'ɑ:nə] *npl* antigüedades *fpl* victorianas.

victorious [vɪk'tɔ:rɪəs] *adj* victorioso,-a, vencedor,-a; *Sport* **v. team,** el equipo ganador.

victory ['vɪktərɪ] *n* victoria *f,* triunfo *m;* **a sweeping v.,** una victoria aplastante; *fam* **to pull off a v.,** conseguir una victoria.

victualler ['vɪtələ'] *n GB* **licensed v.,** *(gen)* vendedor *m* autorizado de bebidas alcohólicas; *(pub owner)* dueño *m* de un bar.

victuals ['vɪtəlz] *npl (food)* víveres *mpl,* vituallas *fpl; (provisions)* provisiones *fpl.*

video ['vɪdɪəʊ] n vídeo m. ■ **v. camera,** videocámara f; **v. cassette,** videocasete f; **v. club,** videclub m; **v. frequency,** videofrecuencia f; **v. game,** videojuego m; **v. (cassette) recorder,** vídeo m; **v. tape,** videocinta f, cinta f de vídeo.

videodisc ['vɪdɪəʊdɪsk] n videodisco m.

videophone ['vɪdɪəfəʊn] n videoteléfono m.

video-tape ['vɪdɪəʊteɪp] vtr grabar (en vídeo).

vie [vaɪ] vi (pt &pp vied) competir, rivalizar (**against, with,** con).

Vienna [vɪ'enə] n Viena.

Viennese [vɪə'ni:z] adj & n vienés,-esa (m,f).

Viet Nam, Vietnam [vjet'næm] n Vietnam.

Vietnamese [vjetnə'mi:z] I adj vietnamita. II n 1 (person) vietnamita mf; **the v.,** los vietnamitas. 2 (language) vietnamita m.

view [vju:] I n 1 (sight) vista f, panorama m; **a lovely v.,** una vista preciosa; **in full v. of,** a plena vista de; **to be on v.,** estar a la vista; **to come into v.,** aparecer; fig **in v. of,** en vista de; fig **in v. of the fact that ...,** dado que ... . 2 (opinion) opinión f, parecer m; **in my v.,** en mi opinión; **point of v.,** punto de vista; **to take a dim** or **poor v. of sth,** ver algo con malos ojos. 3 (survey) visión f de conjunto, panorama m. 4 (aim) fin m; **with a v. to doing sth,** con la intención de hacer algo; **with this in v.,** con este fin. II vtr 1 (look at) mirar; (house etc) visitar. 2 (look on) contemplar, ver; (topic, problem) enfocar; **they v. his policies as a potential threat,** consideran que su política es amenazadora.

viewer ['vju:əʳ] n 1 TV telespectador,-a m,f, televidente mf. 2 Phot visionador m.

viewfinder ['vju:faɪndəʳ] n Phot visor m.

viewpoint ['vju:pɔɪnt] n punto m de vista.

vigil ['vɪdʒɪl] n 1 (watch) vigilia f, vela f; **all-night v.,** vela nocturna; **to keep v.,** velar. 2 Rel vigilia f.

vigilance ['vɪdʒɪləns] n vigilancia f.

vigilante [vɪdʒɪ'læntɪ] n vigilante mf.

vignette [vɪ'njet] n Print viñeta f.

vigorous ['vɪgərəs] adj vigoroso,-a, enérgico,-a.

vigour, US **vigor** ['vɪgəʳ] n vigor m, fuerza f.

Viking ['vaɪkɪŋ] adj & n vikingo (m).

vile [vaɪl] adj 1 (evil) vil, infame, despreciable. 2 (disgusting) repugnante. 3 fam (awful) malísimo,-a, horrible; **to be in a v. temper,** estar de un humor de perros.

vileness ['vaɪlnɪs] n vileza f.

vilify ['vɪlɪfaɪ] vtr (pt & pp vilified) denigrar, difamar.

villa ['vɪlə] n 1 (country house) villa f, quinta f, casa f de campo. 2 GB chalet m.

village ['vɪlɪdʒ] n (small) pueblecito m, aldea f; (larger) pueblo m.

villager ['vɪlɪdʒəʳ] n aldeano,-a m,f.

villain ['vɪlən] n (gen) villano,-a m,f, canalla m; Cin Theat malo,-a m,f.

villainous ['vɪlənəs] adj 1 (evil) vil, infame. 2 fam (very bad) malísimo,-a, horrible.

villainy ['vɪlənɪ] n villanía f, vileza f, bajeza f.

vim [vɪm] n sl marcha f.

vinaigrette [vɪneɪ'gret] n Culin **v. (sauce),** (salsa f) vinagreta f.

vindicate ['vɪndɪkeɪt] vtr 1 (actions etc) justificar, vindicar. 2 (rights) reivindicar.

vindication [vɪndɪ'keɪʃən] n 1 (justification) justificación f, vindicación f, **in v. of sth,** para justificar algo. 2 (claim) reivindicación f.

vindicatory ['vɪndɪkeɪtərɪ] adj vindicatorio,-a, vindicativo,-a.

vindictive [vɪn'dɪktɪv] adj vindicativo,-a, vengativo,-a; **to feel v. towards sb,** guardar rencor a algn. ◆ **vindictively** adv con venganza, con rencor.

vine [vaɪn] n Bot (along ground) vid f; (climbing) parra f. ■ **v. grower,** viticultor,-a m,f, viñador,-a m,f; **v. growing,** viticultura f; **v. leaf,** hoja f de parra or de vid; **v. shoot,** sarmiento m.

vinegar ['vɪnɪgəʳ] n vinagre m. ■ **v. bottle,** vinagrera f; **wine v.,** vinagre m.

vine-growing ['vaɪngrəʊɪŋ] adj vitícola.

vineyard ['vɪnjəd] n viña f, viñedo m.

vintage ['vɪntɪdʒ] n 1 (crop, year) cosecha f; **what v. is it?,** ¿de qué cosecha es? 2 (season) vendimia f. 3 (era) era f, **of Victorian v.,** de la era victoriana. II adj 1 (wine) añejo,-a. 2 (classic) clásico,-a; Aut **v. car,** coche m de época (construido entre 1919 y 1930).

vinyl ['vaɪnɪl] Chem n vinilo m.

viola¹ [vɪ'əʊlə] n Mus viola f.

viola² [vɪ'əʊlə] n Bot viola f, violeta f.

violate ['vaɪəleɪt] vtr 1 (rape) violar. 2 (break) infringir.

violation [vaɪə'leɪʃən] n 1 (rape) violación f. 2 (of law etc) infracción f.

violator ['vaɪəleɪtəʳ] n Jur violador,-a m,f.

violence ['vaɪələns] n violencia f; **to resort to v.,** recurrir a la violencia; fig **to do v. to sth,** perjudicar algo.

violent ['vaɪələnt] adj 1 violento,-a; **to have a v. temper,** ser de temperamento violento. 2 (intense) intenso,-a; profundo,-a; **to take a v. dislike for sth,** sentir una fuerte aversión por algo. ◆ **violently** adv 1 (with violence) violentamente; **to behave v.,** mostrarse violento. 2 (intensely) terriblemente; **to be v. ill,** vomitar mucho.

violet ['vaɪəlɪt] I n 1 Bot violeta f. ■ fam **shrinking v.,** persona f tímida. 2 (colour) violeta m, violado m. II adj violeta, violado,-a.

violin [vaɪə'lɪn] n Mus violín m.

violinist [vaɪə'lɪnɪst] n violinista mf, violín mf.

VIP [vi:aɪ'pi:] fam abbr of **very important person,** personaje m muy importante; **VIP lounge,** (at airport etc) sala f de personalidades; **VIP treatment,** privilegios mpl especiales.

viper ['vaɪpəʳ] n Zool víbora f.

viperine ['vaɪpəraɪn] adj, **viperous** ['vaɪpərəs] adj viperino,-a.

virago [vɪ'rɑ:gəʊ] n (pl viragoes or viragos) arpía f.

viral ['vaɪrəl] adj Med viral, vírico,-a.

virgin ['vɜ:dʒɪn] I n virgen f; **the V. Mary,** la Virgen María; **to be a v.,** ser virgen. II adj virgen. ■ **V. Islands,** Islas fpl Vírgenes.

virginal¹ ['vɜ:dʒɪnəl] adj virginal.

virginal² ['vɜ:dʒɪnəl] n Mus virginal m.

virginity [və'dʒɪnɪtɪ] n virginidad f.

Virgo ['vɜ:gəʊ] n Astrol Astron Virgo m.

virile ['vɪraɪl] adj viril, varonil.

virility [vɪ'rɪlɪtɪ] n virilidad f.

virtual ['vɜ:tʃʊəl] adj virtual. ◆ **virtually** adv (in effect) virtualmente, en la práctica; (almost) casi; **it's v. impossible,** es prácticamente imposible.

virtue ['vɜ:tju:, 'vɜ:tʃu:] n 1 (gen) virtud f; **by v. of,** en virtud de; prov **to make a v. of necessity,** poner a mal tiempo buena cara. 2 (advantage) ventaja f.

virtuoso [vɜ:tjʊ'əʊzəʊ] n (pl virtuosos or virtuosi [vɜ:tjʊ'əʊsi:]) Mus virtuoso,-a m,f.

virtuous ['vɜ:tʃʊəs] adj virtuoso,-a.

virulence ['vɪrʊləns] n virulencia f.

virulent ['vɪrʊlənt] adj virulento,-a.

virus ['vaɪrəs] n (pl viruses) Med virus m inv. ■ **v. infection,** infección f viral or vírica.

Vis, Visc 1 abbr of **Viscount,** Vizconde m. 2 abbr of **Viscountess,** Vizcondesa f.

visa ['vi:zə] n visado m, Am visa f.

vis-à-vis [viːzɑːˈviː] *prep* **1** *(regarding)* respecto a. **2** *(opposite)* frente a, enfrente de.

viscera [ˈvɪsərə] *npl Anat* vísceras *fpl*.

visceral [ˈvɪsərəl] *adj* visceral.

viscose [ˈvɪskəʊs] *n Tex* viscosa *f*.

viscosity [vɪsˈkɒsɪtɪ] *n* viscosidad *f*.

viscount [ˈvaɪkaʊnt] *n* vizconde *m*.

viscountess [ˈvaɪkaʊntɪs] *n* vizcondesa *f*.

viscous [ˈvɪskəs] *adj* viscoso,-a.

vise [vaɪs] *n US see* **vice**[2].

visibility [vɪzɪˈbɪlɪtɪ] *n* visibilidad *f*; **poor v.,** escasa visibilidad.

visible [ˈvɪzɪbəl] *adj* visible.

Visigoth [ˈvɪzɪgɒθ] *n Hist* visigodo,-a *m,f*.

Visigothic [vɪzɪˈgɒθɪk] *adj* visigodo,-a, visigótico,-a.

vision [ˈvɪʒən] *n* **1** *(faculty)* visión *f*. **2** *(eyesight)* vista *f*; **to have good v.,** tener buena vista. ■ *fig* **tunnel v.,** estrechez *f* de miras. **3** *(apparition)* visión *f*; **to see visions,** ver visiones; *fam* **I had visions of being left homeless,** ya me veía sin casa. **4** *(foresight)* visión *f*, clarividencia *f*; **a man of v.,** un hombre con visión de futuro.

visionary [ˈvɪʒənərɪ] *n* visionario,-a *m,f*.

visit [ˈvɪzɪt] **I** *vtr* **1** *(person)* visitar, hacer una visita a. **2** *(place)* visitar, ir a; **we are visiting the town,** estamos de visita en la ciudad, **II** *n* visita *f*; **he's on a v. to France,** se ha ido de viaje a Francia; **official v.,** visita oficial; **to pay sb a v.,** ir a ver a algn; *fam* **flying v.,** visita relámpago.

visitation [vɪzɪˈteɪʃən] *n* **1** *(visit)* visita *f* oficial. **2** *Rel* **the V.,** la Visitación.

visiting [ˈvɪzɪtɪŋ] *adj* **1** *(for visiting)* de visita; *GB* **v. card,** tarjeta de visita; *Med* **v. hours,** horas de visita. **2** *(guest)* visitante; *Sport* **v. team,** equipo visitante; *Univ* **v. lecturer,** profesor invitado.

visitor [ˈvɪzɪtə⁂] *n* **1** *(guest)* invitado,-a *m,f*; **we've got visitors,** tenemos visita. **2** *(in hotel)* cliente,-a *m,f*. **3** *(tourist)* turista *mf*, visitante *mf*; **visitors to our city,** los visitantes de nuestra ciudad. **4** *GB Med* **health v.,** enfermera *f* visitante.

visor [ˈvaɪzə⁂] *n* visera *f*.

vista [ˈvɪstə] *n* vista *f*, panorama *m*; *fig* perspectiva *f*, horizonte *m*.

visual [ˈvɪʒʊəl, ˈvɪzjʊəl] *adj* **1** *(gen)* visual. ■ *Educ* **v. aids,** medios *mpl* visuales; **v. arts,** artes *mpl* visuales. **2** *(optical)* ocular.

visualize [ˈvɪʒʊəlaɪz, ˈvɪzjʊəlaɪz] *vtr* **1** *(imagine)* imaginar, imaginarse, plantearse. **2** *(foresee)* prever.

vital [ˈvaɪtəl] *adj* **1** *(gen)* vital; *Med* **v. function,** función vital. **2** *(lively)* vital, vivo,-a, enérgico,-a. **3** *(essential)* fundamental, indispensable; **of v. importance,** de suma importancia. **4** *(decisive)* decisivo,-a, clave. ■ **v. statistics,** *(data)* datos *mpl* demográficos; *fam* medidas *fpl* del cuerpo de la mujer. ◆ **vitally** *adv* sumamente; **it's v. important,** es de suma importancia.

vitalist [ˈvaɪtəlɪst] *adj & n* vitalista *(mf)*.

vitality [vaɪˈtælɪtɪ] *n* vitalidad *f*.

vitalize [ˈvaɪtəlaɪz] *vtr* vitalizar.

vitamin [ˈvɪtəmɪn, *US* ˈvaɪtəmɪn] *n* vitamina *f*; **with added vitamins,** vitaminado,-a. ■ **v. B,** vitamina *f* B; **v. content,** contenido *m* vitamínico; **v. deficiency,** avitaminosis *f inv*.

vitiate [ˈvɪʃɪeɪt] *vtr* viciar.

vitreous [ˈvɪtrɪəs] *adj* vítreo,-a.

vitriol [ˈvɪtrɪɒl] *n Chem* vitriolo *m*.

vitriolic [vɪtrɪˈɒlɪk] *adj* **1** *Chem* vitriólico,-a. **2** *fig* virulento,-a, mordaz.

vituperation [vɪtjuːpəˈreɪʃən] *n* vituperación *f*.

viva [ˈvaɪvə] *n (abbr of viva voce) GB Univ* examen *m* oral.

vivacious [vɪˈveɪʃəs] *adj* vivaz, animado,-a.

vivaciousness [vɪˈveɪʃəsnɪs] *n*, **vivacity** [vɪˈvæsɪtɪ] *n* viveza *f*, vivacidad *f*.

vivid [ˈvɪvɪd] *adj* **1** *(bright, lively)* vivo,-a, intenso,-a. **2** *(graphic)* gráfico,-a, realista.

vividness [ˈvɪvɪdnɪs] *n* viveza *f*.

viviparous [vɪˈvɪpərəs] *adj Biol* vivíparo,-a.

vivisection [vɪvɪˈsekʃən] *n* vivisección *f*.

vixen [ˈvɪksən] *n* **1** *Zool* zorra *f*. **2** *fig* arpía *f*.

viz [vɪz] *abbr of* **videlicet** (namely), a saber, es decir.

V-neck(ed) [ˈviːnek(t)] *adj* con el cuello en pico.

vocabulary [vəˈkæbjʊlərɪ] *n* vocabulario *m*, léxico *m*.

vocal [ˈvəʊkəl] *adj* **1** *(gen)* vocal. ■ *Anat* **v. cords,** cuerdas *fpl* vocales. **2** *(noisy)* ruidoso,-a, chillón,-ona.

vocalist [ˈvəʊkəlɪst] *n* cantante *mf*, vocalista *mf*.

vocalize [ˈvəʊkəlaɪz] **I** *vtr* vocalizar. **II** *vi Ling* vocalizarse.

vocation [vəʊˈkeɪʃən] *n* vocación *f*; **to miss one's v.,** errar la vocación.

vocational [vəʊˈkeɪʃənəl] *adj* profesional; **v. guidance,** orientación profesional.

vocative [ˈvɒkətɪv] *adj & n Ling* vocativo,-a *(m)*.

vociferate [vəʊˈsɪfəreɪt] *vi* vociferar.

vociferous [vəʊˈsɪfərəs] *adj* **1** *(vehement)* vociferador,-a, vociferante. **2** *(noisy)* ruidoso,-a, clamoroso,-a. ◆ **vociferously** *adv* a gritos, a voces.

vodka [ˈvɒdkə] *n* vodka *m & f*.

vogue [vəʊg] *n* boga *f*, moda *f*; **to be in v.,** estar de moda, estar en boga.

voice [vɔɪs] **I** *n* **1** voz *f*; **in a loud/low v.,** en voz alta/baja; **to lose one's v.,** quedarse afónico; **to raise one's v.,** levantar la voz; *fig* **at the top of one's v.,** a voz en grito; *fig* **to give v. to an opinion,** expresar una opinión. **2** *Ling* voz *f*. **II** *vtr* **1** *(express)* expresar. **2** *Ling* sonorizar.

voiced [vɔɪst] *adj Ling* sonoro,-a.

voiceless [ˈvɔɪslɪs] *adj* **1** *(hoarse)* afónico,-a. **2** *Ling* sordo,-a.

voice-over [vɔɪsˈəʊvə⁂] *n Cin TV* voz *f* en off.

void [vɔɪd] **I** *adj* **1** *(empty)* vacío,-a; *(post)* vacante. **2** *jur* nulo,-a, inválido,-a; **to make a contract v.,** anular un contrato. **II** *n* vacío *m*.

vol 1 *(pl vols) abbr of* **volume,** tomo *m*, t.; **a 3 v. edition,** una edición en tres tomos. **2** *abbr of* **volume,** volumen *m*, cantidad *f*, vol.

volatile [ˈvɒlətaɪl] *adj* volátil.

volcanic [vɒlˈkænɪk] *adj* volcánico,-a.

volcano [vɒlˈkeɪnəʊ] *n (pl* **volcanos** *or* **volcanoes)** volcán *m*.

volcanology [vɒlkəˈnɒlədʒɪ] *n* vulcanología *f*.

vole [vəʊl] *n Zool* campañol *m*, ratón *m* campestre.

volition [vəˈlɪʃən] *n fml* volición *f*; **of** *or* **on one's own v.,** por voluntad propia.

volley [ˈvɒlɪ] **I** *n* **1** *(of shots)* descarga *f*. **2** *fig (of stones, insults)* lluvia *f*. **3** *Ten* volea *f*. **II** *vi Mil* lanzar una descarga. **III** *vtr Ten* volear.

volleyball [ˈvɒlɪbɔːl] *n sport* balonvolea *m*, voleibol *m*.

volt [vəʊlt] *n Elec* voltio *m*.

Volta [ˈvɒltə] *n* **Upper V.,** Alto Volta.

voltage [ˈvəʊltɪdʒ] *n Elec* voltaje *m*.

volte-face [vɒltˈfɑːs] *n inv* cambio *m* de opinión.

voltmeter [ˈvəʊltmiːtə⁂] *n* voltímetro *m*.

volubility [vɒljuˈbɪlɪtɪ] *n* locuacidad *f*.

voluble [ˈvɒljubəl] *adj* locuaz, hablador,-a.

volume [ˈvɒljuːm] *n* **1** *Phys* volumen *m*. **2** *(amount)* volumen *m*, cantidad *f*. **3** *Rad TV* volumen *m*; **to turn up/down the v.,** subir/bajar el volumen. **4** *(book)* volumen *m*, tomo *m*; *fig* **to speak volumes,** decirlo todo.

voluminous [vəˈluːmɪnəs] *adj* voluminoso,-a.

voluntary ['vɒləntərɪ] *adj* voluntario,-a. ■ **v. organization,** organización *f* benéfica; **v. work,** obras *fpl* benéficas; **v. worker,** voluntario,-a *m,f*.

volunteer [vɒlən'tɪəʳ] **I** *n* voluntario,-a *m, f*. ■ *Mil* **v. army,** ejército *m* de voluntarios. **II** *vtr (help etc)* ofrecer; **to v. information,** facilitar datos. **III** *vi* **1** ofrecerse **(for,** para); **she volunteered to do the washing up,** se ofreció para lavar los platos. **2** *Mil* alistarse como voluntario.

voluptuous [və'lʌptjuəs] *adj* voluptuoso,-a.

voluptuousness [və'lʌptjuəsnɪs] *n* voluptuosidad *f*.

vomit ['vɒmɪt] **I** *vtr & vi* vomitar, devolver. **II** *n* vómito *m*.

voodoo ['vuːduː] *n (pl voodoos)* vudú *m*.

voracious [vɒ'reɪʃəs] *adj* voraz.

voraciousness [vɒ'reɪʃəsnɪs] *n,* **voracity** [vɒ'ræsɪtɪ] *n* voracidad *f*.

vortex ['vɔːteks] *n (pl vortexes or vortices* ['vɔːtɪsiːz]) vórtice *m; fig* vorágine *f*.

votary ['vəʊtərɪ] *n* **1** *Rel* devoto,-a *m, f*. **2** *(adherent)* partidario,-a *m,f*.

vote [vəʊt] **I** *n* **1** *(choice)* voto *m*; **by a majority v.,** por mayoría de votos. **2** *(voting)* votación *f*; **to take a v. on sth,** someter algo a votación; **v. of censure,** voto *m* de censura; **v. of confidence,** voto de confianza; **write-in v.,** votación por escrito. **3** *(right to vote)* derecho *m* al voto *or* de votar. **II** *vtr* **1** votar; **they voted to adjourn the meeting,** votaron que sesuspendiera la reunión; **to v. sb into office,** elegir a algn para un cargo. **2** *(elect)* elegir; **she was voted president,** fue elegida presidenta. **3** *fam* proponer. **II** *vi (gen)* votar; **to-v. by a show of hands,** votar a mano alzada; **to v. Communist,** votar comunista; **to v. for sb,** votar por algn; **to v. on sth,** someter algo a votación.

voter ['vəʊtəʳ] *n* votante *mf*.

voting ['vəʊtɪŋ] *n* votación *f*. ■ **v. paper,** papeleta *f*; **v. pattern,** tendencia *f* del voto.

votive ['vəʊtɪv] *adj Rel* votivo,-a.

vouch [vaʊtʃ] **I** *vi* **to v. for sth/sb,** responder de algo/por algn. **II** *vtr* asegurar, garantizar.

voucher ['vaʊtʃəʳ] *n* **1** *(document)* comprobante *m*. **2** *GB* vale *m*. ■ **luncheon v.,** vale *m* de comida.

vow [vaʊ] **I** *n Rel* voto *m*; **v. of chasity,** voto de castidad; **v. of poverty,** voto de pobreza; **to take one's vows,** pronunciar sus votos. **II** *vtr* jurar; **to v. obedience,** jurar obediencia; **to v. that ...,** jurar que ... .

vowel ['vaʊəl] *n Gram* vocal *f*.

voyage ['vɔɪɪdʒ] *n (gen)* viaje *m; (by sea)* viaje en barco; *(crossing)* travesía *f*; **maiden v.,** viaje inaugural; **to go on a v.,** hacer un viaje en barco.

voyager ['vɔɪɪdʒəʳ] *n* viajero,-a *m,f*.

VP *abbr of* **Vice President,** Vicepresidente *m*.

V-sign ['viːsaɪn] *n* **1** *(of victory)* señal *f* de la victoria. **2** *GB (as insult)* ≈ corte *m* de mangas.

VSO [viːesˈəʊ] *GB abbr of* **Voluntary Service Overseas.**

VTOL [viːtiːəʊˈel] *Av abbr of* **vertical take-off and landing (aircraft),** avión *m* de despegue y aterrizaje vertical; **VTOL fighters,** aviones *mpl* de combate, VTOL.

VTR [viːtiːˈɑːʳ] *abbr of* **video tape racorder, grabador** *m* de videocinta.

vulcanite ['vʌlkənaɪt] *n Min* vulcanita *f*.

vulcanize ['vʌlkənaɪz] *vtr Tech* vulcanizar.

vulcanology [vʌlkəˈnɒlədʒɪ] *n see* **volcanology.**

vulgar ['vʌlgəʳ] *adj* **1** *(coarse)* vulgar, ordinario,-a, grosero,-a; *(in poor taste)* de mal gusto; **don't be v.!,** ¡no seas grosero! **2** *Ling* vulgar; **v. Latin,** latín vulgar. **3** *Math* **v. fraction,** fracción *f* común.

vulgarism ['vʌlgərɪzəm] *n Ling* vulgarismo *m*.

vulgarity [vʌl'gærɪtɪ] *n (coarseness)* vulgaridad *f*, ordinariez *f*, grosería *f*; *(poor taste)* mal gusto *m*.

vulgarize ['vʌlgəraɪz] *vtr* **1** *(debase)* degradar. **2** *(popularize)* vulgarizar.

vulnerability [vʌlnərə'bɪlɪtɪ] *n* vulnerabilidad *f*.

vulnerable ['vʌlnərəbəl] *adj* vulnerable.

vulture ['vʌltʃəʳ] *n Orn* buitre *m*. ■ **bearded v.,** quebrantahuesos *m inv*.

vulva ['vʌlvə] *n (pl vulvas or vulvae* ['vʌlviː]*) Anat* vulva *f*.

W

W, w ['dʌbəljuː] *n (the letter)* W, w *f*.

W 1 *abbr of* **West,** Oeste, O. **2** *Elec abbr of* **Watt(s),** vatio(s) *m(pl)*, W.

wacky ['wækɪ] *adj (wackier, wackiest) US fam (person)* chiflado,-a, chalado,-a; *(thing)* absurdo,-a.

wad [wɒd] **I** *n (of paper)* taco *m; (of cotton wool)* bolita *f*; *Med* tapón *m; (of banknotes)* fajo *m*. **II** *vtr (pt & pp wadded)* rellenar, acolchar.

wadding ['wɒdɪŋ] *n* relleno *m*.

waddle ['wɒdəl] **I** *n* forma *f* de andar de los patos. **II** *vi* andar como los patos.

wade [weɪd] *vi* caminar por el agua; **to w. across a river,** vadear un río. ◆ **wade through** *vi* hacer con dificultad; **I'm wading through the book,** me cuesta mucho terminar el libro.

wader ['weɪdəʳ] *n* **1** *Orn* ave *f* zancuda. **2 waders,** botas *fpl* de pescador.

wafer ['weɪfəʳ] *n Culin* barquillo *m; Rel* hostia *f; (for sealing)* oblea *f*.

wafer-thin ['weɪfəθɪn] *adj* **1** muy fino,-a; **to cut sth w.-t.,** cortar algo en lonchas muy finas. **2** *fig (majority)* escasísimo,-a.

waffle¹ ['wɒfəl] *n Culin* (tipo *m* de) barquillo *m*.

waffle² ['wɒfəl] *GB fam* **I** *vi* meter mucha paja; **to w. on,** parlotear. **II** *n* paja *f*.

waft [wɑːft, wɒft] **I** *vtr (sound, smell)* llevar por el aire. **II** *vi (sound, scent)* flotar (por *or* en el aire).

wag¹ [wæg] **I** *vtr (pt & pp wagged) (tail, finger)* menear. **II** *vi (tail)* menearse; **fam tongues will w.,** van a chismorrear. **III** *n* meneo *m*; **with a w. of its tail,** meneando la cola.

wag² [wæg] *n fam (wit)* bromista *mf*, guasón,-ona *m,f*.

wage [weɪdʒ] **I** *n (also wages)* salario *m*, sueldo *m*; **basic/ minimum w.,** salario base/mínimo; **w. claim,** reivindicación *f* salarial; **w. earner,** asalariado,-a *m,f*. **II** *vtr (campaign)* realizar **(against,** contra); **to w. war,** hacer la guerra **(on,** a).

wage-packet ['weɪdʒpækɪt] *n* sueldo *m*.

wager ['weɪdʒəʳ] *lit* **I** *n* apuesta *f*. **II** *vtr lit* apostar.

waggish ['wægɪʃ] *adj* burlón,-ona, bromista.

waggle ['wægəl] **I** *vtr (ears etc)* menear. **II** *vi* menearse.

wa(g)gon ['wægən] *n (horse-drawn)* carro *m; (lorry)* camión *m; GB Rail* vagón *m*; **covered w.,** carromato *m*; **goods w.,** vagón de mercancías; *fam* **to go on the w.,** dejar la bebida.

wagtail ['wægteɪl] n Orn lavandera f. ■ **grey w.,** lavandera f cascadeña; **white w.,** lavandera f blanca.

waif [weɪf] n niño,-a m, f desamparado,-a.

wail [weɪl] **I** n **1** (of sorrow) lamento m, gemido m, plañido m. **2** (of siren) aullido m. **II** vi **1** (person) lamentar, gemir, plañir. **2** (siren) aullar, ulular.

wailing ['weɪlɪŋ] **I** adj gemidor,-a. **II** n lamentaciones fpl, gemidos mpl. ■ **W. Wall,** Muro m de las Lamentaciones.

waist [weɪst] n Anat cintura f; Sew talle m.

waistband ['weɪstbænd] n cinturilla f.

waistcoat ['weɪstkəʊt] n GB chaleco m.

waistline ['weɪstlaɪn] n Anat cintura; Sew talle m.

wait [weɪt] **I** n espera f; (delay) demora f; **to lie in w.,** estar al acecho; **we had a long w.,** tuvimos que esperar mucho tiempo. **II** vtr esperar; **to wait one's turn,** esperar su turno. **III** vi **1** esperar, aguardar; **I can't w. to see her,** me muero de ganas de verla; **let's w. and see,** esperemos a ver qué pasa; **repairs while you w.,** reparaciones en el acto; **to keep sb waiting,** hacer esperar a algn; **to w. for sth,** esperar algo, aguardar algo; **w. a moment!,** ¡un momento! **2** (serve) **to w. at table,** servir la mesa. ◆ **wait about, wait around** vi esperar, perder el tiempo. ◆ **wait on** vtr servir; **to w. on sb hand and foot,** tratar a algn a cuerpo de rey. ◆ **wait up** vi **to w. up for sb,** esperar a algn levantado,-a.

waiter ['weɪtəʳ] n camarero m.

waiting ['weɪtɪŋ] n espera f; **'No W.',** 'Prohibido Aparcar'; **to play a w. game,** esperar el momento oportuno. ■ **w. list,** lista f de espera; **w. room,** sala f de espera.

waitress ['weɪtrɪs] n camarera f.

waive [weɪv] vtr fml (demand, rights) abdicar, renunciar a; (rule) no aplicar.

wake[1] [weɪk] **1** vtr (pt **woke**; pp **woken**) **to w. sb (up),** despertar a algn. **II** vi **to w. (up),** despertar(se); fig **to w. up to the truth,** darse cuenta de la verdad; fig **w. up!,** ¡despierta!, ¡despabílate! **III** n Ir (for dead) velatorio m.

wake[2] [weɪk] n (in water) estela f; fig **in the w. of the storm,** tras la tormenta; fig **to leave chaos in one's w.,** dejar una estela de caos.

wakeful ['weɪkfʊl] adj **1** (sleepless) desvelado,-a; **to have a w. night,** pasar la noche en blanco. **2** fml (alert) vigilante, alerta.

waken ['weɪkən] vtr lit despertar.

wakey ['weɪkɪ] interj fam **w.!, w.!,** ¡despierta!, ¡arriba!

Wales [weɪlz] n (el país de) Gales; **the Prince of W.,** el príncipe de Gales.

walk [wɔːk] **I** n **1** (long) caminata m; (short) paseo m; **it's an hour's w.,** está a una hora de camino; **to go for a w.,** dar un paseo, pasear; **to slow down to a w.,** aflojar el paso; **to take the dog for a w.,** sacar a pasear al perro. **2** (fait) modo m de andar, andares mpl. **3** (avenue) paseo m. **4** (sphere) **people from all walks of life,** gente f de toda condición. **II** vi **1** andar; **to w. it,** ir a pie; fam ganar fácil; **to w. the streets,** callejear; euph (prostitute) hacer la carrera; **we walked her home,** la acompañamos a casa. **2** (dog) pasear; (horse) llevar al paso; **he walked me off my feet,** me agotó a fuerza de pasear. **III** vi **1** andar; **can the child w.?,** ¿sabe andar el niño?; US **'W.!',** 'Pasen'. **2** (go on foot) ir andando, ir a pie; **I had to w. home,** tuve que volver a casa a pie. ◆ **walk about** vi ir y venir, pasear. ◆ **walk across I** vtr atravesar. **II** vi acercarse; **to w. across to sb,** abordar a algn. ◆ **walk away** vi acercarse; fig **she walked away from the crash,** salió ilesa del choque; fig **to w. away with a prize,** llevarse un premio. ◆ **walk down** vtr (stairs) bajar; (street) bajar por. ◆ **walk into** vtr **1** (place) entrar en; fig (trap) caer en. **2** (bump into) tropezar con. **3** fig **to w. into a job,** encontrar un trabajo sin esfuerzo alguno. ◆ **walk off** vi (steal, win easily) **to w. off with sth,** llevarse algo. ◆ **walk on** vi **1** seguir su camino. **2** Theat salir a escena. ◆ **walk out** vi salir; Ind declararse en huelga; **to w. out of a meeting,**

abandonar una reunión en señal de protesta; **to w. out on sb,** abandonar a algn. ◆ **walk over** vtr fam **to w. all over sb,** tratar a algn a patadas. **II** vi acercarse; **to w. over to sb,** abordar a algn. ◆ **walk up I** vtr (stairs) subir; (street) subir por. **II** vi acercarse; **to w. up to sb,** abordar a algn; **to w. up and down,** andar or pasear de un lado para otro.

walkabout ['wɔːkəbaʊt] n (by Queen, President, etc) paseo m informal entre la gente.

walker ['wɔːkəʳ] n paseante mf; Sport marchador,-a m, f; **he's a fast w.,** anda deprisa.

walkie-talkie [wɔːkɪ'tɔːkɪ] n Rad walkie-talkie m.

walking ['wɔːkɪŋ] **I** n (gen) andar m, pasear m; (hiking) excursionismo m. **II** adj **at w. pace,** a paso de marcha; fam fig **he's a w. encyclopaedia,** es una enciclopedia ambulante. ■ **w. shoes,** zapatos mpl de andar; **w. stick,** bastón m; **w. tour,** excursión f a pie.

Walkman® ['wɔːkmən] n (pl **Walkmans**) walkman® m.

walk-on ['wɔːkɒn] adj Theat **w.-o. part,** papel m de figurante or comparsa.

walkout ['wɔːkaʊt] n Ind huelga f.

walkover ['wɔːkəʊvəʳ] n triunfo m fácil; **it was a w.,** fue un paseo or pan comido.

walk-up ['wɔːkʌp] n US casa m sin ascensor.

walkway ['wɔːkweɪ] n esp US paso m de peatones.

wall [wɔːl] **I** n **1** (freestanding, exterior) muro m; **the Berlin W.,** el muro de Berlín; fig **a w. of flame,** una cortina de llamas; fig **a w. of silence,** un muro de silencio; fig **to form a human w.,** formar una pared humana; fig **to go to the w.,** arruinarse; Com quebrar; fig **to have one's back to the w.,** estar entre la espada y la pared; fam fig **it's driving me up the w.,** me está volviendo loca,-a. ■ **cavity w.,** muro m doble; **city w.,** muralla f; **garden w.,** tapia f; **sea w.,** dique m. **2** (interior) pared f; **partition w.,** tabique m; **party w.,** pared medianera; fam fig **I'm banging my head against a brick w.,** es para darse contra las paredes. ■ **w. lamp,** aplique m; **w. map,** mapa m mural; **w. unit,** módulo m de estantería. **3** (of cave, rock) pared f. **4** Anat abdominal w., pared f abdominal. **5** Ftb barrera f. ◆ **wall in** vtr tapiar, cercar con tapia. ◆ **wall off** vtr amurallar, aislar o separar con pared. ◆ **wall up** vtr tapiar; (door, fireplace) condenar.

wallaby ['wɒləbɪ] n (pl **wallaby** or **wallabies**) Austral Zool ualabí m.

walled [wɔːld] adj (city) amurallado,-a; (garden) cercado,-a con tapia.

wallet ['wɒlɪt] n cartera f.

wallflower ['wɔːlflaʊəʳ] n **1** Bot alhelí m. **2** (person) fam **to be a w.,** ser un invitado de piedra.

Walloon [wɒ'luːn] **I** adj valón,-ona. **II** n (person) valón,-ona m, f; (language) valón m.

wallop ['wɒləp] fam **I** n golpazo m. **II** vtr **1** (hit) pegar fuerte. **2** (defeat) dar una paliza a.

walloping ['wɒləpɪŋ] n fam (beating, defeat) paliza f.

wallow ['wɒləʊ] vi (animal) revolcarse (en, in); **to w. in the mud,** revolcarse en el lodo; fig **to w. in self-pity,** sumirse en la lástima de sí mismo.

wallpaper ['wɔːlpeɪpəʳ] **I** n papel m pintado. **II** vtr (decorate) empapelar.

wall-to-wall [wɔːltə'wɔːl] adj **w.-to-w. carpeting,** moqueta f.

wally ['wɒlɪ] n fam idiota mf, inútil mf.

walnut ['wɔːlnʌt] n Bot (fruit) nuez f, (tree, wood) nogal m. ■ **black walnut,** nogal m negro; **common w.,** nogal m.

walrus ['wɔːlrəs] n Zool morsa f.

waltz [wɔːls] Mus **I** n vals m. **II** vi valsar; fam fig **to w. in/out,** entrar/salir con desenvoltura; fam fig **to w. off with sth,** llevarse algo como si tal cosa.

wan [wɒn] adj (**wanner, wannest**) (face) pálido,-a; (look, smile) apagado,-a; (light) macilento,-a.

wand [wɒnd] *n* (**magic**) **w.**, varita *f* (mágica).

wander ['wɒndə^r] **I** *n* paseo *m*, vuelta *f*; **to go for a w.**, dar una vuelta. **II** *vtr* **to w. the streets**, vagar por las calles. **III** *vi* **1** *(aimlessly)* vagar, errar; **to w. about,** deambular; **to w. in/out,** entrar/salir sin prisas; **to w. off on one's own,** apartarse para estar solo,-a. **2** *(stray)* desviarse, apartarse; *(mind)* divagar; **his glance wandered round the room,** recorrió el cuarto con la mirada; **to let one's thoughts w.,** dejar vagar la imaginación.

wanderer ['wɒndərə^r] *n* andariego,-a, *m, f; (traveller)* viajero,-a *m, f; (nomad)* nómada *mf.*

wandering ['wɒndərɪŋ] **I** *adj* errante, errabundo,-a; *(tribe)* nómada; *(minstrel)* ambulante; *(speech)* divagador,-a. ■ *Bot* **w. Jew,** tradescantia *f.* **II wanderings** *npl* **1** andanzas *fpl,* viajes *mpl.* **2** *(of mind, speech)* divagaciones *fpl.*

wane [weɪn] **I** *vi (moon)* menguar; *fig (strength, influence)* menguar, decrecer; *(interest)* decaer, decrecer; *(light)* mermar. **II** *n* **to be on the w.,** *(moon, strength)* estar menguando; *(power)* estar en decadencia.

waning ['weɪnɪŋ] *adj (moon)* menguante; *fig* decadente, decreciente.

wangle ['wæŋgəl] *vtr fam* agenciarse; **she'll w. it somehow,** se las amañará de algún modo; **to w. a free ticket,** pillar una invitación.

wank [wæŋk] *sl* **I** *n* paja *f.* **II** *vi* hacerse una paja.

wanker ['wæŋkə^r] *n sl* gilipollas *mf inv;* mamón,-ona *m, f.*

want [wɒnt] **I** *n* **1** *(lack)* falta *f,* carencia *f;* **for w. of anything better to do,** a falta de algo mejor que hacer; **it wasn't for w. of trying,** no fue por falta de esfuerzos. **2** *(poverty)* indigencia *f,* miseria *f.* **II** *vtr* **1** *(desire)* querer, desear; **do you w. a cigarette?,** ¿quieres un pitillo?; **I know when I'm not wanted,** sé cuando estoy de más; **it's just what I w.,** es exactamente lo que quiero; **she wants a bike for her birthday,** pide *or* quiere una bicicleta para so cumpleaños; **what more do you w.?,** ¿qué más quieres? **2** *(wish)* **I don't w. to,** no quiero; **I don't w. you making a noise,** no quiero que hagas ruido; **to w. to do sth,** querer/ desear hacer algo; **you can say what you w.,** puedes decir lo que quieras. **3** *fam (need)* necesitar; **he wants a good talking-to,** no le vendría mal un fuerte rapapolvo; **the grass wants cutting,** hace falta cortar el césped. **4** *(seek)* buscar; **'cook wanted',** 'se necesita cocinero,-a'; **he is wanted by the police,** le busca la policía; **you're wanted on the phone,** te llaman al teléfono. ◆ **want for** *vtr* carecer de algo; **they w. for nothing,** lo tienen todo. ◆ **want out** *vi fam* dejarlo; **he'd had enough and wanted out,** estaba harto y quería dejarlo.

wanted ['wɒntɪd] *adj* **1** *(necessary)* necesario,-a. **2** *(by police)* buscado,-a.

wanting ['wɒntɪŋ] *adj* **1** *(have missing)* **to be w.,** faltar; **she is w. in tact,** le falta tacto. **2** *(deficient, short)* deficiente (**in,** en); **he was found w.,** no daba la talla.

wanton ['wɒntən] *adj* **1** *(motiveless)* sin motivo, sin sentido; **w. cruelty,** crueldad *f* inmotivada *or* gratuita. **2** *(person) (unrestrained)* desenfrenado,-a; *(licentious)* lascivo,-a.

war [wɔː^r] *n* guerra *f;* **between the wars,** en el período de entreguerras; **to be at w.,** estar en guerra (**with,** con); **to go to w.,** emprender la guerra (**over,** por); *fig* **to declare/ wage w.,** declarar/hacer la guerra; *hum* **you seem to have been in the wars,** te noto bastante maltrecho,-a. ■ **cold w.,** guerra *f* fría; **w. games,** *Mil* ejercicios *mpl* de simulacro de combate; *(games)* juegos *mpl* de estrategia militar; **w. memorial,** monumento *m* a los caídos; **w. of nerves,** guerra *f* de nervios.

warble ['wɔːbəl] **I** *n* gorjeo *m.* **II** *vi* gorjear.

warbler ['wɔːblə^r] *n Orn* pájaro *m* cantor, ave *f* cantora. ■ **Cetti's w.,** ruiseñor *m* bastardo; **Dartford w.,** curruca *f* cabilarga; **garden w.,** curruca *f* mosquitera; **melodious w.,** zarcero *m* común; **Orphean w.,** curruca *f* mirlona; **reed w.,** carricero *m* común; **willow w.,** mosquitero *m* musical; **wood w.,** mosquitero *m* silbador.

warbling ['wɔːblɪŋ] *n* gorjeo *m,* trinos *mpl.*

ward [wɔːd] **I** *n* **1** *(of hospital)* sala *f.* **2** *Jur* pupilo,-a *m, f.* ■ **w. of court,** pupilo,-a *m, f* bajo tutela judicial. **3** *GB Pol* distrito *m* electoral. ◆ **ward off** *vtr (blow)* parar, desviar; *(attack)* rechazar; *(danger)* evitar; *(illness)* prevenir.

warden ['wɔːdən] *n (of residence)* guardián,-ana *m, f,* encargado,-a *m, f.* ■ **game w.,** guardia *m* de coto; **traffic w.,** ≈ guardia *m* urbano.

warder ['wɔːdə^r] *n GB* carcelero,-a *m, f.*

wardrobe ['wɔːdrəʊb] *n* **1** *Furn* armario *m,* ropero *m.* **2** *(clothes)* guardarropa *m;* **she has a large w.,** tiene un vestuario muy amplio. **3** *Theat* vestuario *m.*

wardroom ['wɔːdruːm] *n Naut* cámara *f* de oficiales.

wardship ['wɔːdʃɪp] *n Jur* tutela *f.*

warehouse ['weəhaʊs] *n* almacén *m,* depósito *m.*

wares [weəz] *npl* mercancías *fpl.*

warfare ['wɔːfeə^r] *n* guerra *f;* **germ w.,** guerra bacteriológica; *fig* **class w.,** lucha *f* de clases.

warhead ['wɔːhed] *n* **(nuclear) w.,** cabeza *f or* ojiva *f* nuclear.

warhorse ['wɔːhɔːs] *n fig* **an old w.,** un,-a veterano,-a.

warlike ['wɔːlaɪk] *adj* belicoso,-a, guerrero,-a.

warm [wɔːm] **I** *adj* **1** *(water)* tibio,-a, templado,-a; *(hands)* caliente; *(wind, climate)* cálido,-a; **a w. day,** un día caluroso *or* de calor; **I am w.,** *(disagreeably)* tengo calor; *(rather than old)* ya he entrado en calor; **it is (very) w. today,** hoy hace (mucho) calor; **keep w.,** abrígate; **this coffee is only w.,** este café está templado; **to get w.,** calentarse; **to keep sth w.,** mantener algo caliente; **w. clothing,** ropa de abrigo; *fig (riddles)* **you're getting w.,** ¡caliente, caliente! **2** *(welcome, applause)* cálido,-a. **II** *n fam* **to sit in the w.,** sentarse al calor. **III** *vtr* calentar; *fig* **to w. one's hands,** calentarse las manos. **IV** *vi* calentarse; *fig* **to w. to an idea,** (empezar a) entusiasmarse con una idea; **to w. to sb,** cogerle simpatía a algn. ◆ **warm up** **I** *vtr* **1** *(room, engine)* calentar; *(soup)* (re)calentar; *(person)* hacer entrar en calor. **2** *fig (audience etc)* animar. **II** *vi* **1** *(room, engine)* calentarse; *(food)* (re)calentarse; *(person)* entrar en calor. **2** *(athlete)* hacer ejercicios de calentamiento; *(performer)* ambientarse. **3** *fig (audience, party)* animarse. ◆ **warmly** *adv fig* calurosamente; *(thank)* con efusión; *(recommend)* con entusiasmo.

warm-blooded [wɔːm'blʌdɪd] *adj* de sangre caliente.

warm-hearted [wɔːm'hɑːtɪd] *adj* afectuoso,-a, bondadoso,-a.

warmonger ['wɔːmʌŋgə^r] *n* belicista *mf.*

warmth [wɔːmθ] *n (heat)* calor *m; fig* cordialidad *f.*

warm-up ['wɔːmʌp] *n Sport* (ejercicios *mpl* de) calentamiento *m;* **a w.-up match,** un partido de preparación.

warn [wɔːn] *vtr* avisar (**of,** de), advertir, prevenir (**about,** sobre; **against,** contra); **he warned me not to go** *or* **against going,** me advirtió que no fuera; **the policeman warned me for speeding,** el policía me amonestó por exceso de velocidad; **to w. sb that,** advertir a algn que, prevenir a algn de que; **you've been warned!,** ¡estás avisado,-a! ◆ **warn away, warn off** *vtr* avisar.

warning ['wɔːnɪŋ] **I** *adj (glance, shot)* de advertencia, de aviso; *(letter)* admonitorio,-a. ■ *Aut* **w. light,** piloto *m;* **w. sign,** *(of illness)* síntoma *m; Traffic* señal *f* de aviso. **II** *n* **1** *(of danger)* advertencia *f,* aviso *m; Meteor* **gale w.,** aviso de vientos fuertes; **let this be a w. to you,** que esto te sirva de escarmiento. **2** *(replacing punishment)* amonestación *f.* **3** *(notice)* aviso *m;* **to give sb fair w.,** avisar a algn debidamente; **without w.,** sin previo aviso.

warp [wɔːp] *n* **1** *(also* **warping)** *(of wood)* alabeo *m.* **2** *Tex* urdimbre *f.* **II** *vtr* **1** *(wood)* alabear, combar. **2** *fig (mind)* pervertir, torcer. **III** *vi* **1** alabearse, combarse.

war-paint ['wɔːpeɪnt] *n* pintura *f* de guerra.

warpath ['wɔːpɑːθ] *n fam* **to be on the w.,** estar buscando follón.

warped [wɔːpt] *adj* **1** *(wood)* alabeado,-a, combado,-a. **2** *(mind, sense of humour)* retorcido,-a.

warplane [ˈwɔːpleɪn] *n* avión *m* de combate.

warrant [ˈwɒrənt] **I** *n* **1** *Jur* mandamiento *m or* orden *f* judicial; **there is a w. out for his arrest,** se ha ordenado su detención. ■ **death w.,** sentencia *f* de muerte; **search w.,** mandamiento *m or* orden *f* de registro; *Mil* **w. officer,** suboficial *m*. **2** *(authorization note)* cédula *f*; *Com* bono *m*, vale *m*; **w. for payment,** libramiento *m*, orden *f* de pago. ■ **travel w.,** vale *m* de viaje. **II** *vtr* **1** *(justify)* justificar. **2** *(guarantee)* garantizar; **I w. you,** se lo aseguro.

warranty [ˈwɒrəntɪ] *n Com* garantía *f*.

warren [ˈwɒrən] *n* zona *f* de conejeras; *fig* laberinto *m*.

warring [ˈwɔːrɪŋ] *adj (nations)* en guerra; **the w. factions,** las facciones opuestas.

warrior [ˈwɒrɪəˀ] *n* guerrero,-a *m,f*; **the Unknown W.,** el Soldado Desconocido.

Warsaw [ˈwɔːsɔː] *n* Varsovia.

warship [ˈwɔːʃɪp] *n* buque *m or* barco *m* de guerra.

wart [wɔːt] *n Med* verruga *f*; *fam* **warts and all,** con todas sus imperfecciones.

wart-hog [ˈwɔːthɒg] *n* jabalí *m* verrugoso.

wartime [ˈwɔːtaɪm] **I** *n* tiempos *mpl* de guerra. **II** *adj* **w. economy,** economía de guerra.

wary [ˈweərɪ] *adj (warier, wariest)* cauteloso,-a, precavido,-a, prudente; **to be w. of doing sth,** temer *or* dudar en hacer algo; **to be w. of sb/sth,** tener cuidado con algn/algo, recelar de algn/algo.

was [wɒz] *pt see* **be.**

wash [wɒʃ] **I** *n* **1** *(person)* lavado *m*; *(of clothes)* lavado *m*, colada *f*; **to give sth a w.,** lavar algo; **to have a w.,** lavarse; *fig* **it will all come out in the w.,** todo saldrá bien. **2** *(of ship)* estela *f*; *(of water)* remolinos *mpl*; *(sound)* chapoteo *m*. **3** *(of paint)* capa *f*. **II** *vtr* **1** *(gen)* lavar; *(dishes)* fregar; **to w. oneself,** lavarse; **to w. one's hair,** lavarse la cabeza. **2** *(sea, river)* llevar; **to w. sth ashore,** echar algo a la playa; **he was washed overboard,** un golpe de mar le arrojó por la borda. **III** *vi* **1** *(person)* lavarse; *(do the laundry)* hacer la colada; **this material doesn't w. well,** esta tela no se lava bien; *fam* **that (story) won't wash,** eso no colará. **2** *(lap)* batir; **the waves washed against the ship,** las olas bañaban el navío. ◆ **wash away** *vtr (of sea)* llevarse; *(traces)* borrar; **he was washed away by the current,** fue arrastrado por la corriente. ◆ **wash down** *vtr (wall etc)* lavar; *(food)* rociar. ◆ **wash off** *vi* quitarse lavando. ◆ **wash out I** *vtr* **1** *(stain)* quitar lavando. **2** *(bottle)* enjuagar; *(shirt)* dar un lavado rápido a. **II** *vi* quitarse lavando. ◆ **wash up I** *vtr GB (washing-up)* fregar. **2** *(of sea)* arrojar a la playa. **3** *fam* **to be (all) washed up,** estar acabado,-a. **II** *vi* **1** *GB* fregar los platos. **2** *US* lavarse rápidamente.

washable [ˈwɒʃəbəl] *adj* lavable.

washbasin [ˈwɒʃbeɪsən] *n*, **washbowl** [ˈwɒʃbəʊl] *n* jofaina *f*, palangana *f*, lavamanos *m inv*.

washcloth [ˈwɒʃklɒθ] *n US* manopla *f*.

washed-out [wɒʃtˈaʊt] **1** *(colours)* descolorido,-a, desteñido,-a. **2** *fig (tired)* sin energías, agotado,-a; *(complexion)* pálido,-a.

washer [ˈwɒʃəˀ] *n* **1** *(machine)* lavadora *f*. **2** *Tech (bolt)* arandela *f*; *(on tap)* junta *f*.

washer-up [wɒʃərˈʌp] *n (pl washers-up)* *fam* friegaplatos *mf inv*.

washing [ˈwɒʃɪŋ] *n* **1** *(action)* lavado *m*; *(of clothes)* lavado *m*, colada *f*; **are there w. facilities?,** *(personal)* ¿hay lavabos?; *(for clothes)* ¿hay lavadero?; **bring in the w.,** recoge la ropa tendida; **(dirty) w.,** ropa *f* sucia *or* para lavar, la ropa sucia; **to do the w.,** hacer la colada. ■ **w. line,** tendedero *m*; **w. machine,** lavadora *f*; **w. powder,** detergente *m*; **w. soda,** sosa *f*.

washing-up [wɒʃɪŋˈʌp] *n GB* **1** *(action)* fregado *m*; **to do the w.-up,** fregar los platos. ■ **w.-up bowl,** barreño *m*; **w.-up liquid,** detergente *m* para vajillas. **2** *(dishes)* platos *mpl* (para fregar).

wash-leather [ˈwɒʃleðəˀ] *n* gamuza *f*.

washout [ˈwɒʃaʊt] *n fam* fracaso *m*.

washroom [ˈwɒʃruːm] *n US euph* servicios *mpl*.

washstand [ˈwɒʃstænd] *n* lavabo *m*.

wasp [wɒsp] *n Ent* avispa *f*. ■ **wasps' nest,** avispero *m*.

waspish [ˈwɒspɪʃ] *adj (temperament)* irritable, enojadizo,-a, irascible; *(comment)* punzante.

wastage [ˈweɪstɪdʒ] *n* pérdidas *fpl*, merma *f*.

waste [weɪst] **I** *n* **1** *(unwanted)* desechado,-a; **w.food,** restos *mpl* de comida; *Ind* **w. products,** productos *mpl* de desecho. **2** *(ground)* baldío,-a, yermo,-a; **w. ground,** terreno baldío. **II** *n* **1** *(unnecessary use)* desperdicio *m*; *(of resources, effort)* derroche *m*; *(of money)* despilfarro *m*, derroche *m*; *(of time)* pérdida *f*; **it's a w. of money,** es tirar el dinero; **to go to w.,** desperdiciarse, echarse a perder. **2** *(left-overs)* desperdicios *mpl*, desechos *mpl*; *(rubbish)* basura *f*. ■ **radio-active w.,** desechos radioactivos; **w. disposal unit,** trituradora *f* (de desperdicios); **w. pipe,** tubo *m* de desagüe. **3** *(usu pl)* yermo *m*; **the Arctic wastes,** los desiertos árticos. **III** *vtr (squander)* desperdiciar, malgastar; *(resources)* derrochar; *(money)* despilfarrar; *(time, chance)* desperdiciar, perder; *fig* **kindness is wasted on her,** ser amable con ella es una pérdida de tiempo; *prov* **w. not, want not,** quien guarda halla. ◆ **waste away** *vi* consumirse, demacrarse.

wasted [ˈweɪstɪd] *adj (life)* desperdiciado,-a; *(body)* atrofiado,-a.

wasteful [ˈweɪstful] *adj (person)* despilfarrador,-a, pródigo,-a; *(habits, use)* pródigo,-a.

wastefulness [ˈweɪstfulnɪs] *n* despilfarro *m*, prodigalidad *f*.

wasteland [ˈweɪstlænd] *n* baldío *m*, yermo *m*.

wastepaper [weɪstˈpeɪpəˀ] *n* papeles *mpl* usados *or* viejos. ■ **w. basket,** papelera *f*.

waster [ˈweɪstəˀ] *n fam* vago,-a *m,f*.

wasting [ˈweɪstɪŋ] *adj Med* **w. disease,** enfermedad *f* que debilita.

wastrel [ˈweɪstrəl] *n (spendthrift)* manirroto,-a *m, f*; *(good-for-nothing)* perdido *m*.

watch [wɒtʃ] **I** *n* **1** *(look-out)* vigilancia *f*; **to be on the w.,** estar al acecho **(for,** de); **to keep a close w. on sth/sb,** vigilar algo/a algn muy atentamente; **to keep w.,** vigilar **(over,** a). **2** *Mil (period, body)* guardia *f*; *(individual)* centinela *m*; *Naut (period, body)* guardia *f*; *(individual)* vigía *m*; **to be on w., keep w.,** estar de guardia. **3** *Hist* **(night) w.,** ronda *f*. **4** *(timepiece)* reloj *m*; **digital/wrist w.,** reloj digital/de pulsera. ■ **w. chain,** leontina *f*. **II** *vtr* **1** *(observe)* mirar, observar; **to w. sb do sth,** mirar a algn hacer algo; **to w. television/a match,** mirar la televisión/ un partido. **2** *(keep an eye on)* vigilar, observar; *(with suspicion)* acechar; **w. the noticeboard/the time,** estén atentos al tablón de anuncios/al reloj. **3** *(be careful of)* tener cuidado con; **w. it!,** ¡ojo!, ¡cuidado!; **w. what you say,** fíjate en *or* ten cuidado con lo que dices; **w. you don't fall,** ten cuidado de no caerte; **w. your head!,** ¡cuidado con la cabeza!; *fig* **to w.one's step,** ir con pies de plomo. **III** *vi (look)* mirar, observar. ◆ **watch out for** *vtr* tener cuidado con; **w. out!,** ¡ojo!; **w. out for the traps,** cuidado *or* ojo con las trampas. ◆ **watch over** *vtr* vigilar; **to w. over sb's interesta,** velar por los intereses de algn.

watchband [ˈwɒtʃbænd] *n US see* **watchstrap.**

watchdog [ˈwɒtʃdɒg] *n* perro *m* guardián; *f* guardián,-ana *m, f*.

watcher [ˈwɒtʃəˀ] *n* observador,-a *m, f*, espectador,-a *m, f*.

watchful [ˈwɒtʃful] *adj* vigilante, atento,-a.

watchfulness [ˈwɒtʃfulnɪs] *n* vigilancia *f*.

watchmaker [ˈwɒtʃmeɪkəˀ] *n* relojero,-a *m, f*.

watchman [ˈwɒtʃmən] *n (pl watchmen)* vigilante *m*; **night w.,** *(of factory, site)* vigilante nocturno; *(on Spanish street)* sereno *m*.

watchstrap ['wɒtʃstræp] *n* correa *f* (de reloj).

watchtower ['wɒtʃtauə'] *n* atalaya *f*.

watchword ['wɒtʃwɜːd] *n* 1 *(password)* contraseña *f*. 2 *(motto)* lema *m*.

water ['wɔːtə'] I *n* 1 agua *f*; **drinking/running w.**, agua potable/corriente; **hard/soft w.**, agua dura/blanda; **salt/fresh w.**, agua salada/dulce; **the road is under w.**, la carretera está inundada; *fig* **the theory doesn't hold w.**, la teoría cae por su base; *fig* **to get into hot w.**, meterse en un buen lío; *fig* **to spend money like w.**, gastar dinero como agua. ■ **hot w. bottle**, bolsa *f* de agua caliente; **w. bottle**, cantimplora *f*; **w. closet**, wáter *m*, retrete *m*; **w. jump**, ría *f*; *Bot* **w. lily**, nenúfar *m*; **w. main**, conducción *f* de aguas; **w. pipe**, cañería *f*; **w. pistol**, pistola *f* de agua; **w. polo**, water polo *m*; **w. power**, fuerza *f* hidráulica; **w. rate**, tarifa *f* del agua; **w. softener**, acondicionador *m* de agua; **w. tank**, depósito *m* de agua; **w. wings**, flotadores *mpl*. 2 *(of river, sea)* agua *f*; **coastal/territorial waters**, aguas costeras/jurisdiccionales; *Naut* **high/low w.**, marea *f* alta/baja; *fig* **it's all w. under the bridge**, ha llovido mucho desde entonces; *fig* **to get into deep w.**, meterse en camisa de once varas; *fig* **to keep one's head above w.**, mantenerse a flote. ■ **w. rat**, rata *f* de agua; **w. sports**, deportes *mpl* acuáticos. 3 *(urine)* **to pass w.**, orinar; *Med* **difficulty in passing w.**, retención *f* de orina. 4 *Med* **w. on the brain**, hidrocefalia *f*; **w. on the knee**, derrame *m* sinovial. II *vtr* 1 *(plants, river)* regar. 2 *(horses)* abrevar. ◆ **water down** *(drink)* aguar; *(water)* bautizar; *fig* **a watered-down version**, una versión atenuada. III *vi* *(eyes)* lagrimear, llorar; **my mouth watered**, se me hizo la boca agua.

water-bed ['wɔːtəbed] *n* colchón *m* de agua

watercolour, *US* **watercolor** ['wɔːtəkʌlə] *n* *Art* acuarela *f*.

water-cooled ['wɔːtəkuːld] *adj Tech* refrigerado,-a por agua.

watercourse ['wɔːtəkɔːs] *n* lecho *m*, cauce *m*, canal *m*.

watercress ['wɔːtəkres] *n Bot* berro *m*.

waterfall ['wɔːtəfɔːl] *n* cascada *f*, salto *m* de agua, catarata *f*.

waterfowl ['wɔːtəfaul] *n Orn* ave *f* acuática.

waterfront ['wɔːtəfrʌnt] *n* *(shore)* orilla *f* del agua; *(promenade)* paseo *m* marítimo; *(harbour)* puerto *m*.

waterhole ['wɔːtəhəul] *n* charca *f*.

watering ['wɔːtərɪŋ] *n* 1 *(of plants)* riego *m*; **w. can**, regadera *f*. 2 *(of drink)* **w. (down)**, dilución *f*; *fig* atenuación *f*. ■ *(for cattle)* **w. place**, abrevadero *m*.

waterline ['wɔːtəlaɪn] *n Naut* línea *f* de flotación.

waterlogged ['wɔːtəlɒgd] *adj* *(land, wood)* empapado,-a, anegado,-a.

watermark ['wɔːtəmɑːk] *n* filigrana *f*.

watermelon ['wɔːtəmelən] *n Bot* sandía *f*.

watermill ['wɔːtəmɪl] *n* molino *m* de agua.

waterproof ['wɔːtəpruːf] I *adj* *(material)* impermeable; *(watch)* sumergible. II *n* *(coat)* impermeable *m*. III *vtr* impermeabilizar.

watershed ['wɔːtəʃed] *n Geog* línea *f* divisoria de aguas; *fig* coyuntura *f* crítica, punto *m* decisivo.

waterside ['wɔːtəsaɪd] *n* ribera *f*.

water-ski ['wɔːtəskiː] *Sport* I *n* esquí *m* acuático, II *vi* *(pt & pp* **water-skied** *or* **water-ski'd)** hacer esquí acuático.

water-skiing ['wɔːtəskiːɪŋ] *n Sport* esquí *m* acuático.

watertight ['wɔːtətaɪt] *adj* *(waterproof)* estanco,-a, hermético,-a; *fig* irrefutable.

waterway ['wɔːtəweɪ] *n* vía *f* fluvial; **inland w.**, canal *m* (navegable).

water-wheel ['wɔːtəwiːl] *n Ind* rueda *f* hidráulica; *(mill)* molino *m*.

waterworks ['wɔːtəwɜːks] *npl* 1 central *f* *sing* de abastecimiento de agua. 2 *Med fam euph* aparato *m* *sing* urinario. 3 *fam fig* **to turn on the w.**, empezar a llorar.

watery ['wɔːtərɪ] *adj* 1 *(like water)* acuoso,-a; *(soup)* aguado,-a; *(coffee)* flojo,-a. 2 *(eyes)* lacrimoso,-a. 3 *(pale)* pálido,-a.

watt [wɒt] *n Elec* vatio *m*.

wattage ['wɒtɪdʒ] *n* potencia *f* en vatios.

wave [weɪv] I *n* 1 *(at sea)* onda *f*. 2 *(in hair)* onda *f*. 3 *Rad Phys* onda *f*. ■ **medium/short w.**, onda *f* media/corta; **shock waves**, *(of explosion)* onda *f* sing expansiva; *fig* conmoción *f* sing, repercusión *f* sing. 4 *fig* *(of anger, strikes, attackers)* oleada *f*; *(of protest, crime)* ola *f*, oleada *f*. 5 *(fashion)* **the new w.**, la nueva ola. 6 *(gesture)* saludo *m* con la mano. II *vtr* I *(shake)* agitar; *(brandish)* blandir; *(help, objection)* **to w. aside**, rechazar, desechar; **to w. goodbye to sb**, despedirse de algn con la mano; **to w. one's arms (about)**, agitar los brazos. 2 *Hairdr* ondular, marcar. III *vi* 1 *(shake arm)* agitar el brazo; **she waved (to me)**, *(greeting)* me saludó con la mano; *(goodbye)* se despidió (de mí) con la mano; *(signal)* me hizo señas *or* señales con la mano. 2 *(flag)* ondear; *(corn)* ondular. 3 *(shake)* agitarse. 4 *(hair)* ondular.

waveband ['weɪvbænd] *n Rad* banda *f* (sonora).

wavelength ['weɪvleŋθ] *n Rad* longitud *f* de onda; *fam* **we're not on the same w.**, no estamos en la misma onda.

waver ['weɪvə'] I *vi* *(hesitate)* vacilar, oscilar *(between, entre)*; *(voice)* temblar; *(courage)* flaquear, vacilar.

wavering ['weɪvərɪŋ] *adj* *(person)* indeciso,-a, vacilante; *(voice)* tembloroso,-a.

wavy ['weɪvɪ] *adj* *(wavier, waviest)* *(hair, line)* ondulado,-a.

wax[1] [wæks] I *n* cera *f*; *(in ear)* cerumen *m*. II *vtr* 1 *(polish)* encerar. 2 *fam (record)* grabar.

wax[2] [wæks] *vi* 1 *(moon)* crecer. 2 *fml* ponerse; **to w. lyrical**, entusiasmarse, exaltarse.

waxen ['wæksən] *adj* de cera; *fig* *(complexion)* céreo,-a.

waxwing ['wækswɪŋ] *n Orn* ampelis *m* europeo.

waxwork ['wækswɜːk] *n* 1 figura *f* de cera. 2 **waxworks**, museo *m* de cera.

waxy ['wæksɪ] *adj* *(waxier, waxiest)* céreo,-a.

way [weɪ] I *n* 1 *(route)* camino *m*; **a letter/another baby is on the w.**, una carta/otro niño está en camino; **he made his own w. back (home)**, volvió solo (a casa); **I know my w. about**, conozco estos parajes; **I must be on my w.**, es hora de irme; **on the w.**, en el camino, de paso; **on the w. here**, de camino para aquí; **out of the w.**, apartado,-a, remoto,-a; **the bank is on your w.**, el banco te pilla de camino; **the river wound its w. along the valley**, el río serpenteaba *or* el valle; **to ask the w.**, preguntar el camino; **to force one's w. in**, entrar a la fuerza; **to go by w. of Burgos**, ir vía Burgos; **to go the long w. round**, ir por el camino más largo; **to go the wrong w.**, errar el camino; **to lose one's w.**, perderse; **to make one's w. through the crowd**, abrirse camino entre la multitud; **to push one's w. through**, abrise paso a empujones; **which is the w. to the station?**, ¿por dónde se va a la estación?; *fig* **is there a w. round the problem?**, ¿hay un modo de soslayar el problema?; *fig* **reforms are on the w.**, se avecinan reformas; *fig* **she went out of her w. to help**, se desvivió para ayudar; *fig* **to go one's own w.**, ir a lo suyo; *fig* **to make one's w. (in the world)**, abrirse camino (en el mundo); *fig* **to see one's w. (clear) to doing sth**, ver la forma *or* la manera de hacer algo; *fig* **to work one's w. up**, ascender a fuerza de trabajo; *fig* **we went our separate ways**, seguimos cada cual por nuestro camino; *fam fig* **to talk one's w. out of trouble**, salir del apuro a base de labia; *fam fig* **to pay one's w.**, *(person)* pagar su parte; *(firm)* ser solvente; *fam fig* **we drank our w. through three bottles**, nos liquidamos tres botellas. 2 *(with adv)* **I can't find my w. out**, no me encuentro la salida; **I stopped off on the w. back**, hice escala en el viaje de regreso; **I stopped on the w. out**, me detuve al salir; **on the w. up/down**, en la subida/bajada; **she's on the w. back**, está regresando; **there's no w. through**, el paso está cerrado; **to be on the w. up**, ir subiendo; **w. in**, entrada *f*; **w. out**, salida *f*; *fig* **the easy w. out**, la solución fácil; *fig* **to look for a w. out,** buscar una salida; *fig* **waistcoats are on the w. out,** los chalecos van camino de desaparecer. **3** *(road)* vía *f*, camino *m*; **across** *or* **over the w.,** enfrente (**from,** de); **the Appian W.,** la Vía Apia; *Rel* **the W. of the Cross,** el viacrucis; *fig* **the parting of the ways,** el momento de separarse. **4** *(space, path)* paso *m*; **(get) out of the** *or* **my w.!,** ¡quítate de en medio!; **I kept out of the w.,** me mantuve a distancia; **right of w.,** derecho *m* de paso; *Jur* servidumbre *f* de paso; *Aut* prioridad *f*; **there's a wall in the w.,** hay un muro de por medio; **to get out of the w. of sth,** dejarle paso a algo, apartarse de algo; **to give w.,** *(collapse)* ceder, hundirse; *(yield)* ceder (**to,** a); *Aut* ceder el paso; **to keep out of sb's w.,** evitar encontrarse con algn; **to push sb out of the w.,** apartar a algn a empujones; **to put obstacles in sb's w.,** ponerle obstáculos en el camino a algn; **you're in the w.,** estás estorbando; *fig* **as soon as the elections are out of the w.,** en cuanto terminen las elecciones; *fig* **to get sb/sth out of the w.,** desembarazarse de algn/algo; *fig* **to stand in the w.,** ser un obstáculo. **5** *(direction)* dirección *f*; **a three-w. discussion,** una discusión trilateral; **come this w.,** venga por aquí; **I'll be down your w. tomorrow,** estaré en su barrio mañana; **if the opportunity comes my w.,** si se me presenta la oportunidad; **which w. did he go?,** ¿por dónde se fue?; **that w.,** por allá; **the other w. round,** al revés; **to be the right/wrong w. up,** estar cabeza arriba/abajo; **to split sth three ways,** dividir algo en tres partes iguales; *fig* **it's the other w. round,** es el contrario; *fig* **to look the other w.,** hacer la vista gorda. ■ **one-w. street,** calle *f* de sentido único. **6** *(distance)* distancia *f*; **a long w. off,** lejos; **it's long w.,** es un largo camino; **we've a long w. to go,** nos queda un gran trecho por recorrer; *fig* **he'll go a long w.,** llegará lejos; *fig* **I'm with you all the w.,** estoy totalmente de acuerdo contigo; *fig* **that went a long w. towards reassuring her,** eso contribuyó en gran medida a tranquilizarla; *fig* **the soup went a long w.,** la sopa cundió mucho; *fig* **we've come a long w.,** hemos hecho grandes progresos; *fig fam* **you're w. out,** andas muy desacertado,-a. **7** *(motion, progress)* **to be under w.,** *Naut* estar en marcha; *(work)* estar en marcha, avanzar; *(meeting, match)* haber empezado, **the building is well under w.,** la construcción ya está bastante avanzada; **to get under w.,** *Naut* zarpar; *(travellers, work)* ponerse en marcha; *(meeting, match)* empezar. **8** *(means, method)* método *m*, manera *f*, camino *m*; **do it any w. you like,** hazlo del modo que quieras; **have it your own w.,** como tú quieras, **I'll do it my w.,** lo haré a mi manera; **there are many ways of doing it,** hay muchas maneras de hacerlo; **ways and means,** medios *mpl*; **to get one's own w.,** salirse con la suya. **9** *(manner)* modo *m*, manera *f*, forma *f*; **can I help in any w.?,** ¿puedo ayudar de alguna manera?; **I feel the same w.,** yo opino lo mismo; **in a friendly w.,** de modo amistoso; **in a small w.,** en plan modesto; **one w. or another,** de un modo o de otro; **strikes have become a w. of life,** las huelgas son ya una costumbre; **that's the w. it is,** asi es; **that's the w.!,** ¡eso es!; **the French w. of life,** el estilo de vida francés; **the w. he spoke,** el modo en que habló; **the w. things are going,** tal como van las cosas; **there's no w. I can accept it,** me es imposible aceptarlo, **to do things in a big w.,** hacer las cosas a lo grande; **to my w. of thinking,** a mi modo de ver; **you're goiog about it the wrong w.,** vas por camino equivocado; *fam* **no w.!,** ¡ni hablar!, ¡de ninguna manera! **10** *(talent)* don *m*; **she has a w. with children,** tiene un don para los niños. **11** *(respect)* aspecto *m*; **by w. of introduction/of an experiment,** a modo de introducción/de experimento; **either w. you lose,** en cualquier caso pierdes; **in a w.,** en cierto sentido *or* modo; **in many ways,** desde muchos puntos de vista; **in some ways,** en algunos aspectos; **it doesn't matter to me one w. or the other,** me da exactamente igual; **she is in no w. to blame,** no es culpable de ninguna manera; **there are no two ways about it,** no tiene vuelta de hoja; **what is there in the w. of refreshment?,** ¿qué hay como refrigerio?; **you can't have it both ways,** no se puede repicar e ir en la procesión. ■ *(racing)* **each w. bet,** apuesta *f* a colocado. **12** *(custom)* hábito *m*, costumbre *f*; **it's always the w.,**

siempre es así; **to be set in one's ways,** tener costumbres arraigadas; **to get out of the w. of doing sth,** perder la costumbre de hacer algo; **to mend one's ways,** enmendarse. **13** *(state)* estado *m*; **leave it the w. it is,** déjalo tal como está, **the car is in a bad w.,** el coche está en mal estado; **the patient is in a bad w.,** el enfermo está bastante mal; *euph* **to be in the family w.,** estar en estado. **14** *(course)* **by the w.,** a propósito, por cierto, dicho sea de paso; **in the w. of business,** en el curso de los negocios; **that is by the w.,** eso no viene *or* no hace al caso. II *adv fam* mucho; muy; **I'm w. behind with my work,** estoy atrasadísimo,-a en mi trabajo; **it was w. off target,** no alcanzó ni con mucho el blanco; **w. back in 1940,** allá en 1940; **w. past the church,** mucho más allá de la iglesia.

wayfarer ['weɪfeərər] *n* caminante *mf*, viajero,-a *m*,*f*.

waylay [weɪ'leɪ] *vtr* (*pt & pp* **waylaid**) **1** *(attack)* atacar por sorpresa. **2** *fig (intercept)* salirle al paso a algn, abordar.

wayout [weɪ'aʊt] *adj fam* estrafalario,-a, exagerado,-a, supermoderno,-a.

wayside ['weɪsaɪd] *n* borde *or* lado *m* del camino; **s w. inn,** una posada de camino; *fig* **to fall by w.,** quedarse en el camino.

wayward ['weɪwəd] *adj (non-conformist)* rebelde; *(capricious)* caprichoso,-a;*(shot, aim)* desviado,-a.

WC, wc [dʌblju:'si:] *abbr of* **water closet,** wáter *m*, WC.

we [wi:] *pers pron* nosotros,-as; **we went in,** (nosotros,-as) entramos; **here we are,** aquí estamos; **we English,** nosotros los ingleses.

WEA [dʌblju:i:'eɪ] *GB abbr of* **Workers' Educational Association.**

weak [wi:k] *adj (structure, body)* débil, endeble; *(character, government)* débil; *(argument, excuse)* pobre, poco convincente; *(tea, team, piece of work)* flojo,-a; *(tea)* flojo,-a; **I know your w. spot,** conozco tu punto flaco; **to be w. at French,** estar flojo,-a en francés; **to grow w.,** debilitarse, desfallecer. ● **weakly** *adv* débilmente.

weaken ['wi:kən] I *vtr* debilitar; *(argument)* quitar fuerza. II *vi* **1** *(person)* debilitarse, desfallecer; *(structure, resistance, opponent)* flaquear. **2** *(concede ground)* ceder, aflojar.

weak-kneed [wi:k'ni:d] *adj fig* medroso,-a, pusilánime.

weakling ['wi:klɪŋ] *n (physical, moral)* débil *mf*; *(physical)* debilucho *m*, alfeñique *m*.

weak-minded [wi:k'maɪndɪd] *adj (indecisive)* indeciso,-a; *(weak-willed)* de poca voluntad.

weakness ['wi:knɪs] *n* **1** *(in strength)* debilidad *f*, flaqueza *f*. **2** *(character flaw)* flaqueza *f*, punto *m* flaco; **to have a w. for sb/sth,** tener una debilidad por algn/algo.

weak-willed [wi:k'wɪld] *adj* de poca voluntad.

weal [wi:l] *n Med* cardenal *m*, equimosis *f inv*.

wealth [welθ] *n* riqueza *f*; *fig* abundancia *f*; **a w. of detail,** una profusión de detalles.

wealthy ['welθɪ] *adj* (**wealthier, wealthiest**) rico,-a, adinerado,-a, acaudalado,-a; **the w.,** los ricos.

wean [wi:n] *vtr (child)* destetar; *fig* **to w. sb from the habit,** desacostumbrar (gradualmente) a algn de un hábito.

weapon ['wepən] *n* arma *f*.

wear [weə^r] I *vtr* (*pt* **wore**; *pp* **worn**) **1** *(clothes)* llevar (puesto,-a), vestir; *(shoes)* calzar; **he usually wears a suit,** suele usar traje; **he wears glasses,** lleva gafas; **he wears his hair long,** lleva el pelo largo; **to w. black,** vestirse de negro; *(mourning)* ir de luto; **what shall I w.?,** ¿qué me voy a poner? **2** *(erode)* desgastar; **he walked so far that he wore a hole in his shoes,** caminó tanto que se le agujerearon los zapatos. **3** *fam (tolerate)* tolerar, aceptar; **he won't w. it,** no lo soportará. II *vi (gen)* llevarse, aguantar; **these shoes are wearing well,** estos zapatos están dando buen resultado; *(garment)* **to w. into holes,** agujerearse con el uso; **to w. (thin/smooth),**

desgastarse (con el roce); *fig* **my patience is wearing thin,** se me está acabando la paciencia; *fig* **she is wearing well,** se conserva bien. **III** *n* 1 ropa *f*. ■ **evening w.,** traje *m* de noche; **leisure w.,** ropa *f* de sport. **2** *(use) (clothes)* uso *m*; **for everyday w.,** para todos los días; **I got a lot of w. out of it,** me duró mucho; **it will stand hard w.,** es muy resistente. **3** *(deterioration)* desgaste *m*; **normal w. and tear,** desgaste *m* or deterioro *m* natural; **to be the worse for w.,** *(object)* estar deteriorado,-a; *fig (person)* estar desmejorado,-a; **I feel the worse for w.,** me siento maltrecho,-a. ◆ **wear away** I *vtr (stone etc)* erosionar, desgastar; *(inscription)* borrar. II *vi (stone etc)* erosionarse, desgastarse; *(inscription)* borrarse. ◆ **wear down** I *vtr (heels)* desgastar; *fig* **to w. sb down,** vencer la resistencia de algn. II *vi* desgastarse. ◆ **wear off** *vi (effect, pain)* pasar, desaparecer; **the novelty has worn off,** ha dejado de ser una novedad. ◆ **wear on** *vi (time)* transcurrir, pasar; **the day wore on,** avanzaba el día. ◆ **wear out** I *vtr* gastar, desgastar; *fig* agotar, rendir; **to w. oneself out,** agotarse. II *vi* gastarse, desgastarse.

wearable ['weərəbəl] *adj (clothes, shoes)* llevable.

wearing ['weərɪŋ] *adj 1 (tiring)* cansado,-a, agotador,-a. **2** *fig (tiresome)* pesado,-a.

weary ['wɪərɪ] I *adj (wearier, weariest)* 1 *(tired)* cansado,-a, fatigado,-a. 2 *(fed up)* cansado,-a, harto,-a; **to grow w. of doing sth,** cansarse de hacer algo. II *vtr (pt & pp wearied)* cansar. III *vi* cansarse **(of,** de). ◆ **wearily** *adv* con cansancio, cansadamente.

weariness ['wɪərɪnɪs] *n* cansancio *m*, fatiga *f*.

wearisome ['wɪərɪsəm] *adj* 1 *(tiring)* cansado,-a, fatigoso,-a. 2 *(tedious)* pesado,-a, fatigoso,-a.

weasel ['wiːzəl] *n (pl weasels or weasel) Zool* comadreja *f*.

weather ['weðə'] I *n* tiempo *m*; **bad w.,** mal tiempo; **in hot w.,** en tiempo caluroso; **in this w.,** con el tiempo que hace; **the w. is fine,** hace buen tiempo; **w. permitting,** si el tiempo no lo impide; **what's the w. like?,** ¿qué tiempo hace?; *fig* **he made heavy w. of it,** le costó mucho trabajo hacerlo; *fig* **to feel, under the w.,** no encontrarse bien. ■ **w. centre,** servicio *m* meteorológico; **w. chart, w. map,** mapa *m* meteorológico; **w. forecast, w. report,** parte *m* meteorológico; **w. vane,** veleta *f*. II *vtr* 1 *(wood)* curar; *Geol* **weathered rocks,** rocas erosionadas. 2 *fig (crisis)* aguantar; *Naut fig* **to w. the storm,** capear el temporal. II *vi (rock)* desgastarse; *(building)* adquirir la pátina del tiempo.

weather-beaten ['weðəbiːtən] *adj (person)* curtido,-a; *(building)* deteriorado,-a por los agentes naturales.

weathercock ['weðəkɒk] *n* veleta *f*.

weatherfish ['weðəfɪʃ] *n (fish)* lomo *m* de lago.

weatherproof ['weðəpruːf] *adj (house)* impermeabilizado,-a; *(clothing)* impermeable.

weave [wiːv] I *n* tejido *m*. II *vtr (pt wove; pp woven)* 1 *Tex* tejer. 2 *(interwine)* entretejer, tejer; *(wicker)* trenzar. 3 *(intrigues)* tramar, urdir, tejer; **to w. a spell,** echar un conjuro **(on,** a). III *vi* 1 *(person, road)* zigzaguear; **the car wove in and out of the traffic,** el coche se abría paso por entre el tráfico. 2 *fam* **get weaving!,** ¡espabílate!

weaver ['wiːvə'] *n* tejedor,-a *m,f*.

weaving ['wiːvɪŋ] *n* tejido *m*.

web [web] *n* 1 *(spider's)* **w.,** telaraña *f*. 2 *fig (intrigue)* red *f*, organización *f*; *(tangle)* embrollo *m*. 3 *(lies)* sarta *f*. 4 *Orn (of foot)* membrana *f*, interdigital *m*.

webbed [webd] *adj Orn* palmeado,-a; **w. foot,** pata *f* palmeada.

webbing ['webɪŋ] *n Furn (entramado m)* de tiras *fpl* de cáñamo.

web-footed [web'fʊtɪd] *adj Orn* palmípedo,-a.

Wed *abbr of* **Wednesday,** miercolés *m*, miérc.

wed [wed] *vtr arch (pt & pp wed or wedded)* casarse con.

wedded ['wedɪd] *adj* 1 *(married)* casado,-a; **w. bliss,** felicidad *f* conyugal. 2 *fig* **to be w. to an idea,** aferrarse *or* estar aferrado,-a a una idea.

wedding ['wedɪŋ] *n* boda *f*, casamiento *m*; **to have a church w.,** casarse por la iglesia. ■ **w. breakfast,** banquete *m* nupcial; **w. cake,** tarta *f* nupcial; **w. day,** día *m* de la boda; **w. dress,** traje *m or* vestido *m* de novia; **w. present,** regalo *m* de boda; **w. ring,** alianza *f*, anillo *m* de boda.

wedge [wedʒ] I *n* 1 *(for door, wheel)* cuña *f*, calzo *m*; *(for table leg)* calce *m*; *(for splitting)* cuña; *fig* **it's the thin end of the w.,** éste es sólo el primer paso. 2 *(of cake, cheese)* trozo *m* grande. II *vtr (wheel, leg of chair, etc)* calzar; *(object)* **to be wedged tight,** estar atrancado,-a *or* atascado,-a; **to wedge a door open,** mantener abierta una puerta mediante una cuña.

Wednesday ['wenzdɪ] *n* miércoles *m*; *see also* **Saturday.**

wee[1] [wiː] I *adj esp Scot* pequeñito,-a, chiquito,-a; **a w. bit,** un poquitín; **a w. bit heavy,** un poco pesado,-a.

wee[2] [wiː] *fam* I *n* pipí *m*; **to go for a w.,** (ir a) hacer pipí. II *vi* hacer pipí.

weed [wiːd] *n* 1 *Bot* mala hierba *f*. 2 *sl (marijuana)* hierba *f*, hachís *m*. 3 *pej (person)* debilucho,-a *m,f*, canijo,-a *m,f*. II *vtr* 1 *(garden)* desherbar, escardar. 2 *fig* **to w. out,** eliminar, suprimir, III *vi* escardar.

weeding ['wiːdɪŋ] *n* escarda *f*.

weedkiller ['wiːkɪlə'] *n* herbicida *m*.

weedy ['wiːdɪ] *adj (weeedier, weediest) pej* debilucho,-a, desmirriado,-a.

week [wiːk] *n* semana *f*; **a w. (ago) today/yesterday,** hoy hace/ayer hizo una semana; **a w. today,** de hoy en ocho días; **in a w.'s time,** dentro de una semana; **in/during the w.,** entre semana; **last/next w.,** la semana pasada/que viene; **once a w.,** una vez a la/por semana; **the w. after next,** no la semana que viene sino la otra; **w. in, w. out,** semana tras semana. ■ *Rel* **Holy W.,** Semana *f* Santa.

weekday ['wiːkdeɪ] *n* día *m* laborable; **on a w.,** entre semana.

weekend [wiːk'end] *n* fin *m* de semana; **at the w.,** *(once)* (durante) el fin de semana; *(regularly)* los fines de semana.

weekly ['wiːklɪ] I *adj* semanal. II *adv* semanalmente; **twice w.,** dos veces por semana. III *Press* semanario *m*.

weep [wiːp] I *vi (pt & pp wept)* llorar; **to w. for sb,** llorar a algn; **to w. with joy,** llorar de alegría. II *vtr (tears)* derramar. III *n* **to have a good w.,** llorar a lágrima viva; **to have a little w.,** llorar un poco.

weeping ['wiːpɪŋ] I *adj* lloroso,-a; *Bot* **w. willow,** sauce *m* llorón. II *n* llanto *m*.

weepy ['wiːpɪ] *adj (weepier, weepiest) fam* lloroso,-a llorón,-ona.

weevil ['wiːvɪl] *n Ent* gorgojo *m*.

wee-wee ['wiːwiː] *n & vi see* **wee**[2].

weft [weft] *n Tex* trama *f*.

weigh [weɪ] *vtr* 1 *(gen)* pesar. 2 *fig (consider)* ponderar, sopesar; **he weighs his words,** pondera sus palabras; **to w. one thing against another,** contraponer una cosa a otra. 3 *Naut* **to w. anchor,** levar anclas. II *vi* 1 *(gen)* pesar; *(responsibilities)* pesar **(upon,** sobre); **it doesn't w. anything,** no pesa; **it weighs three kilos,** pesa tres kilos; *fig* **it is weighing on his conscience,** pesa sobre su conciencia; *fig* **time weighs heavily on his hands,** se le hace largo el tiempo; *fam* **it weighs a ton,** pesa una tonelada. 2 *fig (influence)* influir; **his age weighed heavily in his favour,** su edad influyó mucho a favor suyo. ◆ **weigh down** *vtr* sobrecargar **(with,** de); **she was weighed down with parcels,** iba muy cargada de paquetes. ◆ **weigh in** *vi* 1 *Sport* pesarse. 2 *fam (join in)* intervenir. ◆ **weigh out** *vtr (food etc)* pesar. ◆ **weigh up** *vtr (consider) (thing, matter)* evaluar, ponderar; *(person)* formar una opinión sobre; **she soon had him weighed up,** no tardó en calarle; **to w. up the pros and cons,** sopesar los pros y los contras.

weighbridge ['weɪbrɪdʒ] *n* báscula *f* de puente.

weigh-in ['weɪɪn] n Sport pesaje m.

weight [weɪt] I n 1 peso m; **feel the w.of this,** sopesa esto; **to lose w.,** perder peso, adelgazar; **to put on w.,** ganar peso, engordar; **to sell sth by w.,** vender algo a peso; **weights and measures,** pesos y medidas; fig **it's worth its w. in gold,** vale su peso en oro; fam fig **to pull one's w.,** poner de su parte; fam fig **to throw one's w. about,** hacer sentir su autoridad or su fuerza. **2** (of clock, scales) pesa f. **3** fig (influence) peso m; **this adds w. to the case,** esto le da peso al argumento; **to carry w.,** (opinion, argument) tener peso; (person) pesar, tener influencia. **4** fig (burden) peso m, carga f; **that's a w. off my mind,** eso me quita un peso de encima. **II** vtr poner peso en; (net) lastrar; **to w. sth down,** sujetar algo con pesos.

weighting ['weɪtɪŋ] n (on salary) suplemento m de salario.

weightless ['weɪtlɪs] adj ingrávido,-a.

weightlessness ['weɪtlɪsnɪs] n ingravidez f.

weightlifter ['weɪtlɪftəʳ] n Sport levantador,-a m, f de pesos, halterófilo,-a m, f.

weightlifting ['weɪtlɪftɪŋ] n Sport halterofilia f, levantamiento m de pesos.

weighty ['weɪtɪ] adj (weightier, weightiest) pesado,-a; fig (problem, matter) importante, grave; (argument) de peso.

weir [wɪəʳ] n presa f.

weird [wɪəd] adj raro,-a, extraño,-a.

weirdness ['wɪədnɪs] n rareza f.

weirdo ['wɪədəʊ] n fam tipo m raro.

welcome ['welkəm] I adj (person) bienvenido,-a; (news) grato,-a; (change) oportuno,-a; **the money would be most w.,** el dinero nos vendría muy bien; **to make sb w.,** acoger a algn calurosamente; **w. home!,** ¡bienvenido,-a a casa!; **you're w.!,** ¡no hay de qué!; **you're w. to stay,** puede quedarse con toda confianza. **II** n (greeting) bienvenida f, acogida f. **III** vtr (gen) acoger, recibir; (more formally) darle la bienvenida a; (news) acoger con agrado; (decision) aplaudir; **I would w. the opportunity,** agradecería la oportunidad.

welcoming ['welkəmɪŋ] adj (speech) de bienvenido; (smile) acogedor,-a.

weld [weld] vtr soldar.

welder ['weldəʳ] n soldador m.

welding ['weldɪŋ] n soldadura f. ■ **spot w.,** soldadura f por puntos.

welfare ['welfeəʳ] n 1 (well-being) bienestar m; (public) salud f. ■ **animal/child w.,** protección f de animales/de menores; **w. work,** (trabajos mpl de) asistencia f social; **w. worker,** asistente mf social. **2** US (social security) **w. (payments),** (prestaciones fpl de) seguridad f social.

well¹ [wel] n 1 pozo m, manantial m. ■ **oil w.,** pozo m de petróleo. **2** (of staircase) caja f; (of lift) hueco m. **3** (of court, hall) hemiciclo m. ◆ **well up** vi brotar; **tears welled up in his eyes,** se le llenaron los ojos de lágrimas.

well² [wel] I adj 1 (healthy) bien; **are you keeping w.?,** estás bien de salud?; **he's not w.,** no se encuentra bien; **(I'm) very w., thank you,** (estoy) muy bien, gracias; **I don't feel w.,** no me siento bien; **to get w.,** reponerse; **you look w.,** tienes buena cara. **2** (satisfactory, fortunate) bien; **all is w.,** todo va bien; **if that's the case, w. and good,** si es así, bien está; **it's just as w.,** menos mal; **just as w. you stayed,** menos mal que te quedaste; **that's all very w. but ...,** todo eso está muy bien, pero ...; **you're w. rid of him,** menos mal que te has librado de él; prov **all's w. that ends w.,** bien está lo que bien acaba. **3** (advisable) recomendable; **it is as w. to remember that,** conviene recordar que; **it might/would be as w. to consult him,** quizás convenga/estaría bien consultarle. **II** adv (better, best) **1** (properly, successfully) bien; **he has done w. (for himself),** ha prosperado; **the business is doing or going w.,** el negocio marcha bien; **they get on very w. (together),** se entienden muy bien; **to do sth w.,** hacer algo bien; **she did w. in the exam,** el examen le fue bien; **w. done!,** ¡bien hecho!, ¡muy bien!, ¡bravo! **2** (favourably),

kindly) bien; **he speaks w. of you,** habla bien de ti; **it was in bad taste but he took it w.,** fue de mal gusto pero lo tomó a bien. **3** (thoroughly) bien; **I know him w.,** le conozco bien; **I know it only too w.,** lo sé de sobra; Culin **w. done,** muy hecho,-a. **4** (much, by a big margin) bien; **he's w. over thirty,** tiene treinta años bien cumplidos; **it's pretty w. finished,** está casi terminado,-a; **it's w. worth a visit,** vale la pena visitarlo; **w. after six o'clock,** mucho después de las seis; **w. in advance,** muy por adelantado; **w. over a hundred,** mucho más de cien; fam **he'll damn or jolly w. have to go!,** ¡mal que bien tendrá que ir! **5** (easily, with good reason) bien; **he couldn't very w. say no,** difícilmente podía decir que no; **I may w. do that,** bien puedo hacer eso; **it may w. rain,** es muy posible que llueva; **you might as w. admit it,** más vale que lo confieses. **6 as w.,** también; **as w. as,** así como, lo mismo que; **bring the baby as w.,** traiga al niño también; **children as w. as adults,** tanto niños como adultos; **he is clever as w. as good-looking,** además de guapo es inteligente. **III** interj **1** (surprise) ¡bueno!, ¡vaya!; **w. I never!,** ¡no me digas!; **w., w.!,** ¡vaya, vaya! **2** (agreement, interrogation, resignation) bueno; **very w.,** bueno, muy bien; **w.?,** ¿y bien?, ¿qué?; **w., all right,** bueno, está bien; **w., what now?,** ¿bueno, y ahora qué? **3** (doubt) bueno; **w., I don't know,** bueno, pues. **4** (resumption) bueno, pues (bien); **w., as I was saying,** bueno or pues (bien), como iba diciendo. **5** (consequence) (bueno) pues; **I'm tired –w., go to bed,** estoy cansando – (bueno) pues, acuéstate.

well-balanced ['welbælənst] adj (diet, person) equilibrado,-a.

well-behaved ['welbeheɪvd] adj (child) formal, educado,-a.

well-being ['welbi:ɪŋ] n bienestar m.

well-bred ['welbred] adj (person) (bien) educado,-a.

well-built ['welbɪlt] adj (building etc) de construcción sólida; (person) fornido,-a.

well-chosen [wel'tʃəʊzən] adj (remarks) acertado,-a.

well-disposed [weldɪ'spəʊzd] adj bien dispuesto,-a (**towards,** hacia).

well-done [wel'dʌn] adj bien hecho,-a; (steak etc) bien pasado,-a.

well-earned [wel'ɜ:nd] adj (bien) merecido,-a.

well-educated [wel'edʊkeɪtɪd] adj culto,-a, instruido,-a.

well-founded ['welfaʊndɪd] adj (suspicion) bien fundado,-a.

well-heeled [wel'hi:ld] adj fam adinerado,-a.

wellies ['weliz] npl GB fam, **wellingtons** ['welɪŋtənz] npl, botas fpl de goma.

well-informed [welɪnfə'mɔ:d] adj bien informado,-a (**on,** acerca de).

well-judged ['weldʒʌdʒd] adj bien calculado,-a.

well-known ['welnəʊn] adj (bien) conocido,-a.

well-made ['welmeɪd] adj bien hecho,-a.

well-mannered ['welmænəd] adj educado,-a, cortés, formal.

well-meaning [wel'mi:nɪŋ] adj bien intencionado,-a.

well-meant ['welment] adj bienintencionado,-a.

well-nigh ['welnaɪ] adv casi.

well-off [wel'ɒf] adj 1 (rich) acomodado,-a, rico,-a, pudiente. **2** fam fig (fortunate) **you don't know when you're w. o.,** no te das cuenta de la suerte que tienes.

well-spoken [wel'spəʊkən] adj con acento culto.

well-timed [wel'taɪmd] adj oportuno,-a.

well-to-do [weltə'du:] adj acomodado,-a; **the w.-to-do,** la gente pudiente.

well-wisher ['welwɪʃəʳ] n admirador,-a m, f, partidario,-a m, f.

well-worn ['welwɔ:n] adj (clothes etc) gastado,-a, raído,-a; (path) trillado,-a; fig (theme, phrase) gastado,-a, trillado,-a.

Welsh [welʃ] **I** *adj* galés,-esa. ■ *Furn* **W. dresser,** aparador *m*; *Culin* **W. rarebit,** tostada *f* con queso fundido. **II** *n* **1** *(language)* galés *m*. **2** *pl* the **W.,** los galeses.

Welshman ['welʃmən] *n* (*pl* **Welshmen**) galés *m*.

Welshwoman ['welʃwʊmən] *n* (*pl* **Welshwomen** ['welʃwɪmɪn]) galesa *f*.

welt [welt] **I** *n* **1** *(of shoe)* vira *f*. **2** *Sew* ribete *m*. **3** *(weal)* cardenal *m*, verdugón *m*. **II** *vtr* *(shoe)* poner una vira a; *fam fig* pegar, dar una hostia a.

welter ['weltə'] *n fml* mezcla *f* confusa, mescolanza *f*.

welterweight ['weltəweɪt] *n* *Box* *(category, boxer)* (peso *m*) wélter *m*.

wench [wentʃ] *n dated pej* moza *f*, mozuela *f*.

wend [wend] *vtr fml lit* **to w. one's way,** dirigir sus pasos (**towards,** hacia).

went [went] *pt see* **go.**

wept [wept] *pt & pp see* **weep.**

were [wɜːr, *unstressed* wər] *pt see* **be.**

werewolf ['wɪəwʊlf] *n* (*pl* **werewolves** ['wɪəwʊlvz]) hombre *m* lobo.

west [west] **I** *n* oeste *m*, occidente *m*; **in** *or* **to the w.,** al oeste; **the Far W.,** el Lejano Oeste; *Pol* the **W.,** los países occidentales. **II** *adj* del oeste, occidental; **the w. coast,** la costa occidental; **the W. Indies,** las Antillas; **w. wind,** viento del oeste; **W. Indian,** antillano,-a. **III** *adv* al oeste, hacia el oeste; **it faces w.,** da al oeste; *fam fig* (*be ruined*) **to go w.,** desgraciarse, estropearse.

westbound ['westbaʊnd] *adj (traffic etc)* en dirección al oeste.

westerly ['westəlɪ] *adj (wind)* del oeste; **in a w. position,** orientado,-a hacia el oeste; **in a w. direction,** en dirección al oeste.

western ['westən] **I** *adj* del oeste, occidental; **W. Europe,** Europa Occidental; **in W. France,** en el oeste de Francia. **II** *n Cin* western *m*.

westward ['westwəd] *adj* **in a w. direction,** hacia el oeste.

westwards ['westwəds] *adv* hacia el oeste.

wet [wet] **I** *adj* (**wetter, wettest**) **1** mojado,-a; *(slightly)* húmedo,-a; *(paint, ink)* fresco,-a; **I got (my feet) w.,** me mojé (los pies); **'w. paint',** 'recién pintado'; **w. through, soaking w.,** *(person)* calado,-a hasta los huesos; *(thing)* empapado,-a. ■ **w. suit,** traje *m* isotérmico. **2** *(rainy)* lluvioso,-a; **it has been very w.,** ha llovido mucho; **the w. season,** la época de las lluvias. **3** *fam (person)* apocado,-a, soso,-a. ■ **w. blanket,** aguafiestas *mf inv.***II** *n* **1** *(rain)* lluvia *f*; *(damp)* humedad *f*. **2** *fam* apocado,-a *m*, *f*. **III** *vtr* *(pt & pp* **wet**) mojar, humedecer; **to w. oneself,** orinarse; **to w. the bed,** mojar, orinarse en la cama.

wetness ['wetnɪs] *n* humedad *f*.

whack [wæk] **I** *vtr* **1** *(hit hard)* pegar, zurrar; *(ball)* golpear fuertemente. **2** *fam (defeat)* dar una paliza a. **II** *n* **1** *(blow)* porrazo *m*. **2** *fam (share)* parte *f*, porción *f*.

whacked [wækt] *adj fam* agotado,-a.

whacking ['wækɪŋ] *adj fam* **w. great car,** un coche grandísimo.

whale [weɪl] *n* (*pl* **whale** *or* **whales**) *Zool* ballena *f*; *fam* **we had a w. of a time,** nos lo pasamos pipa/en grande.

whalebone ['weɪlbəʊn] *n* (barba *f* de) ballena *f*.

whaler ['weɪlə'] *n* *(person)* ballenero *m*, *f*; *(ship)* ballenero *m*.

whaling ['weɪlɪŋ] *n* caza *f* de ballenas; **the w. industry,** la industria ballenera.

wharf [wɔːf] *n* (*pl* **wharfs** *or* **wharves** [wɔːvz]) muelle *m*, embarcadero *m*.

wharfage ['wɔːfɪdʒ] *n* muellaje *m*.

what [wɒt, *unstressed* wət] **I** *adj* **1** *(direct question)* qué; **w. (sort of) bird is that?,** ¿qué tipo de ave es ésa?; **w. good is that?,** ¿para qué sirve eso?; **w. time is it?,** ¿qué

hora es? **2** *(indirect question)* qué; **ask him w. size he takes,** pregúntale qué talla usa. **3** *(all the)* **he gave me w. money he had,** me dio (todo) el dinero que tenía; **she lost w. little she had,** perdió lo poco que tenía. **II** *pron* **1** *(direct question)* qué; **w. are you talking about?,** ¿de qué estás hablando?; **w. about me?,** ¿y yo?; **w. about going tomorrow?,** ¿qué te parece si vamos mañana?; **w. about the money you owe me?,** ¿qué hay del dinero que me debes?; **w. can I do for you?,** ¿en qué puedo servirle?; **w. did it cost?,** ¿cuánto costó?; **w. did you do that for?,** ¿por qué hiciste eso?; **w. about me?,** *(did you say)?,* ¿cómo?; **w. does he look like?,** ¿qué aspecto tiene?; **w. does it sound like?,** ¿cómo suena?; **w. do you take me for?,** ¿por quién me tomas?; **w. if it rains?,** ¿y si llueve?; **w. is happening?,** ¿qué pasa?; **w. is it?,** *(definition)* ¿qué es?; *(what's the matter)* ¿qué hay?; **w. is your surname?,** ¿cuál es su apellido?; **w.'s it called?,** ¿cómo se llama?; **w.'s the French for 'cat'?,** ¿cómo se dice 'cat' en francés?; **w.'s she's true esto?,** **w. was the film like?,** ¿qué tal la película?; *fam* **so w.?,** **w. about it?, w. of it?,** ¿y qué?; *fam* **w. d'you know!,** ¡mira por dónde! **2** *(indirect question)* qué, lo que; **he asked me w. I thought,** me preguntó lo que pensaba; **I didn't know w. to say,** no sabía qué decir; **I wonder w. will happen,** me pregunto qué va a pasar; *fam* **books, journals and w. have you,** libros, revistas y tal; *fam* **he knows w.'s w.,** sabe lo que se hace, 3 lo que; **(and) w.'s more, y** además; **come w. may,** pase lo que pase; **guess w.!,** ¿sabes qué?; **it's just w. I need,** es exactamente lo que necesito; **w. with the heat and the noise, I couldn't sleep,** entre el calor y el ruido no pude dormir; *fam* **I'll tell you w.,** pues, mira; *fam* **to give sb w. for,** darle a algn su merecido. **4** *exclam (surprise, indignation)* ¡cómo!; **w., no coffee!,** ¡cómo que no hay café! **III** *interj* **w. a goal!,** ¡qué *or* vaya golazo!; **w. a lovely picture!,** ¡qué cuadro más bonito!; **w. weather!,** ¡qué tiempo!

what-d'you-call-it ['wɒtdʒʊkɔːlɪt] *n fam* chisme *m* este *or* ese.

whatever [wɒt'evə', *unstressed* wət'evə'] **I** *adj* **1** *(any)* cualquiera que; **at w. time you like,** a la hora que quieras; **of w. colour,** no importa de qué color. **2** *(with negative)* **nothing w.,** nada en absoluto; **with no interest w.,** sin interés alguno. **II** *pron* **1** *(anything, all that)* (todo) lo que; **do w. you like,** haz lo que quieras; **w. I have is yours,** todo lo que tengo es tuyo. **2** *(no matter what)* **don't tell him w. you do,** no se te ocurra decírselo bajo ningún concepto; **w. (else) you find,** cualquier (otra) cosa que encuentres; **he goes out w. the weather,** sale haga el tiempo que haga. **III** *interr* **w. happened?,** ¿qué (diablos) pasó?

whatnot ['wɒtnɒt] *n fam* **1** *(what-d'you-call-it)* chisme *m*. **2** *Furn* estantería *f*.

whatsoever [wɒtsəʊ'evə'] *adj* en absoluto; **nothing w.,** nada en absoluto.

wheat [wiːt] *n Bot* trigo *m*. ■ **w. germ,** germen *m* de trigo.

wheatear ['wiːtɪə'] *n Orn* collalba *f* gris.

wheedle ['wiːdəl] *vtr* engatusar; **to w. sb into doing sth,** engatusar a algn para que haga algo; **to w. sth out of sb,** sonsacar algo a algn halagándole.

wheel [wiːl] **I** *n* rueda *f*; **the big w.,** la noria; *Aut* **the front wheels,** las ruedas delanteras; **to be at the w.,** *Aut* ir al volante; *Naut* llevar el timón; *fig* **the wheels of government,** la maquinaria del gobierno; *fig* **there are wheels within wheels,** es más complicado de lo que parece. **II** *vtr (bicycle)* empujar. **III** *vi* **1** *(bird)* revolotear. **2** *(person)* **to w. round,** girar sobre los talones. **3** *Mil* dar la vuelta; **right w.!,** ¡vuelta a la derecha!

wheelbarrow ['wiːlbærəʊ] *n* carretilla *f*.

wheelbase ['wiːlbeɪs] *n Aut* distancia *f* entre ejes.

wheelchair ['wiːltʃeə'] *n* silla *f* de ruedas.

wheeler ['wiːlə'] *n Aut* **three-w.,** vehículo *m* de tres ruedas.

wheeling ['wiːlɪŋ] *n* **w. and dealing,** negocios *mpl* sucios, maquinaciones *fpl*.

wheeze [wiːz] I *vi* respirar con dificultad, resollar. II *n* respiración *f* dificultosa *or* sibilante, resuello *m*.

wheezy ['wiːzɪ] *adj* (*wheezier, wheeziest*) (*person*) asmático,-a; (*breathing*) sibilante.

whelk [welk] *n Zool* buccino *m*.

when [wen] I *adv* 1 (*direct question*) cuándo; **from** *or* **since w.?**, ¿desde cuándo?; **w. did he arrive?**, ¿cuándo llegó? 2 (*indirect question*) cuándo; **tell me w. to go**, dime cuándo he de irme; (*while pouring*) **say w.**, me dirás basta. 3 (*on which*) cuando, en que; **one day w. I'm passing through**, un día cuando esté de paso; **the days w. I work**, los días en que trabajo. II *conj* 1 cuando; **I'll tell you w. she comes**, se lo diré cuando llegue; **it will look good w. painted**, tendrá buen aspecto cuando esté pintado,-a; **it was raining w. I got up**, llovía cuando me levanté; **w. he saw her he stopped**, al verla se detuvo; **w. he was a boy ...**, de niño ..., cuando era pequeño ... . 2 (*whenever*) cuando; **we have fun w. he comes**, nos divertimos mucho cuando viene. 3 (*given that, if*) cuando, si; **you should stay in bed w. you've got the flu**, deberías quedarte en la cama cuando tienes la gripe. 4 (*although*) aunque; **he withdrew w. he might have won**, se retiró aunque podía haber ganado.

whence [wens] *adv fml lit* 1 (*from where*) de dónde. 2 *fig* por lo cual.

whenever [wen'evə^r] I *conj* (*when*) cuando; (*every time*) siempre que; **come w. you like**, venga cuando quiera; **w. I see I think of you**, siempre que lo veo, pienso en ti. II *adv* **Monday, Tuesday or w.**, lunes, martes o cuando sea; **w. that might be**, sea cuando sea.

where [weə^r] I *adv* 1 (*direct question*) dónde; (*direction*) adónde; **w. are you going?**, ¿adónde vas?; **w. did we go wrong?**, ¿en qué nos equivocamos?; **w. do we begin?**, ¿por dónde empezamos?; **w. do you come from?**, ¿de dónde es usted?; **w. is the exit?**, ¿dónde está la salida?; **w. to?**, ¿adónde? 2 (*indirect question*) dónde; (*direction*) adónde; **tell me w. you went**, dime adónde fuiste. 3 (*at, in which*) donde, en que; (*direction*) adonde, a donde; **I'll stay w. I am**, me quedaré donde estoy; **that's** (*just*) **w. you're wrong**, en eso se equivoca usted; **the house w. I was born**, la casa donde *or* en que nací; **go w. you like**, ve donde quieras. 4 (*when*) cuando; **w. safety is involved**, cuando se trata de seguridad.

whereabouts [weərə'baʊts] I *adv* (por) dónde; **w. do you live?**, ¿por dónde vives? II ['weərəbaʊts] *n* paradero *m*; **his w. are unknown**, se desconoce su paradero.

whereas [weər'æz] *conj* 1 (*but, while*) mientras que; **she is tall w. her sister is short**, ella es alta mientras que su hermana es baja. 2 *Jur* considerando que.

whereby [weə'baɪ] *adv* por el *or* la *or* lo cual; **the means w.**, el medio por el cual.

wherefore ['weəfɔː^r] *n see* **why**.

whereupon [weərə'pɒn] *conj fml* con lo cual, después de lo cual.

wherever [weər'evə^r] I *conj* dondequiera que; **I'll find him w. he is**, le encontraré dondequiera que esté; **I try to help w. possible**, procuro ayudar donde sea posible; **sit w. you like**, siéntate donde quieras; **Zafra, w. that might be**, Zafra, quién sabe dónde está. II *adv* 1 (*direct question*) adónde; (*emphatic*) **w. did you go?**, ¿adónde diablos fuiste? 2 (*somewhere*) **Burgos, Avila or w.**, Burgos, Avila o donde sea.

wherewithal ['weəwɪðɔːl] *n fam* pelas *fpl*; **we don't have the w. to go on holiday this year**, no tenemos dinero para ir de vacaciones este año.

whet [wet] *vtr* (*pt & pp* **whetted**) 1 **to w. sb's appetite**, despertar *or* abrir el apetito a algn. 2 *dated* (*tool*) afilar.

whether ['weðə^r] *conj* 1 (*if*) si; **I don't know w. it is true**, no sé si es verdad; **I doubt w. he'll win**, dudo que gane; **it depends on w. he comes** (**or not**), depende de si viene (o no). 2 (*in comparison*) **w. by accident or design**, fuera por accidente o a propósito; **w. be comes or not**, venga o no.

whey [weɪ] *n* suero *m*.

which [wɪtʃ] I *adj* 1 (*direct question*) qué; **w. colour do yon prefer?**, ¿qué color prefieres?; **w. one?**, ¿cuál?; **w. ones?**, ¿cuáles?; **w. shop did you go to?**, ¿a qué tiendas fuiste?; **w. way?**, ¿por dónde? 2 (*indirect question*) qué; **tell me w. dress you like**, dime qué vestido te gusta. 3 **el** *or* **la cual, los** *or* **las cuales; by w. time**, y para entonces; **in w. case**, en cuyo caso. II *pron* 1 (*direct question*) cuál, cuáles; **w. is the faster road?**, ¿cuál es la carretera más rápida?; **w. of the cars did you buy?**, ¿qué coche compraste?; **w. of you did it?**, ¿quién de vosotros lo hizo? 2 (*indirect question*) cuál, cuáles; **I can't tell w. is w.**, no distingo cuál es cuál; **I don't know w.** (**one**) **I'd rather have**, no sé cuál prefiero. 3 (*defining relative*) que; (*after preposition*) que, el *or* la cual, los *or* las cuales, el *or* la que, los *or* las que; **here are the books w. I have read**, aquí están los libros que he leído; **the accident w. I told you about**, el accidente de que te hablé; **the car in w. he was travelling**, el coche en (el) que viajaba; **the countries through w. we passed**, los países por donde pasamos; **the match w. we went to**, el partido a que asistimos; **this is the one** (**w.**) **I like**, éste es el que me gusta, ésta es la que me gusta. 4 (*non-defining relative*) el *or* la cual, los *or* las cuales; **I played three sets, all of w. I lost**, jugué tres sets, todos los cuales perdí; **six pears, half of w. are ripe**, seis peras, de las cuales la mitad están maduras. 5 (*referring to a clause*) lo cual, lo que; **he won, w. made me very happy**, ganó, lo cual *or* lo que me alegró mucho.

whichever [wɪtʃ'evə^r] I *adj* el/la que, cualquiera que; **I'll take w. books you don't want**, tomaré los libros que no quieras; **w. system you choose**, cualquiera que sea el sistema que elijas; **w. way you go**, por dondequiera que vayas. II *pron* el que, la que; **take w. suits you best**, tome el que le convenga más.

whiff [wɪf] *n* 1 (*quick smell*) olor *m* pasajero, vaharada *f*; (*of air, smoke*) bocanada *f*; **I caught a w. of gas**, percibí de repente un olor de gas. 2 *fam* (*bad smell*) tufo *m*.

while [waɪl] I *n* 1 (*length of time*) rato *m*, tiempo *m*; **after a w.**, al rato, al poco tiempo; **all the w.**, (*constantly*) a cada rato; (*without stopping*) todo el tiempo; **I'll be a good w.**, tardaré un buen rato; **in a little w.**, dentro de poco; **once in a w.**, de vez en cuando; **stay a little w.**, quédate un ratito. 2 (*compensation*) pena *f*, recompensa *f*; **it's not worth your w. staying**, no merece la pena que te quedes; **it's worth w. going**, vale la pena ir; *fam* **I'll make it worth your w.**, te recompensaré bien. II *vtr* (*spend*) **to w. away the time** (**doing sth**), pasar el rato (haciendo algo). III *conj* 1 (*time*) mientras; **he fell asleep w. driving**, se durmió mientras conducía; **w. he was here**, mientras estuvo aquí. 2 (*although*) aunque; **w. I understand your fears, I don't share them**, aunque comprendo tus temores, no los comparto. 3 (*whereas*) mientras que; **I like football, w. he prefers tennis**, a mí me gusta el fútbol mientras que él prefiere el tenis.

whilst [waɪlst] *conj see* **while** III.

whim [wɪm] *n* capricho *m*, antojo *m*; **as the w. takes him**, según se le antoja.

whimsical ['wɪmsɪkəl] *adj* (*person, idea*) caprichoso,-a; (*smile*) enigmático,-a.

whimper ['wɪmpə^r] I *n* gimoteo *m*, quejido *m*; (*of dog*) gemido *m*. II *vi* gimotear, lloriquear; (*dog*) gemir.

whinchat ['wɪntʃæt] *n Orn* tarabilla *f* norteña.

whine [waɪn] I *n* 1 (*of pain*) quejido *m*; (*of dog*) gemido *m*. 2 (*of engine*) rechinamiento *m*. II *vi* 1 (*child*) gimotear, lloriquear; (*dog*) gemir, (*with pain*) dar quejidos. 2 (*complain*) gimotear, quejarse. 3 (*engine*) rechinar.

whining ['waɪnɪŋ] I *adj* (*child*) quejica. II *n* (*of child*) gimoteo *m*; (*of dog*) gemidos *mpl*.

whinny ['wɪnɪ] I *vi* relinchar. II *n* relincho *m*.

whip [wɪp] I *n* 1 (*for punishment*) azote *m*; (*for riding*) fusta *f*; *GB fam fig* **to get a fair crack of the w.**, tener la misma oportunidad. 2 *Parl* *(person)* oficial *mf* encargado,-a de la disciplina de un partido. **II** *vtr (pt & pp whipped)* **1** *(as punishment)* azotar, fustigar; *(horse)* dar latigazos a. **2** *Culin* batir; **whipped cream,** nata *f* montada. **3** *fam fig (beat easily)* dar una paliza a. **4** *fam (steal)* mangar. ◆ **whip away** *vtr* arrebatar, coger bruscamente. ◆ **whip off** *vtr (clothes etc)* quitarse bruscamente. ◆ **whip out** *vtr* sacar de repente. ◆ **whip up** *vtr (passions, enthusiasm)* avivar, excitar; *(help)* activar, fomentar.

whiplash ['wɪplæʃ] *n* **1** *(thong)* tralla *f*. **2** *(stroke)* latigazo *m*.

whippet ['wɪpɪt] *n Zool* galgo *m* pequeño.

whipping ['wɪpɪŋ] *n* **1** azotamiento *m*; **to give sb a w.,** azotar a algn. **2** *(beating)* azotaina *f*, zurra *f*; *fig (defeat)* paliza *f*. ■ *Culin* **w. cream,** nata *f* para batir; *fig* **w. boy,** cabeza *f* de turco.

whip-round ['wɪpraʊnd] *n fam* colecta *f*; **to have a w.-r.,** hacer una colecta.

whirl [wɜːl] **I** *n* giro *m*, vuelta *f*; *fig* torbellino *m*; *fig* **my thoughts/senses are in a w.,** tengo los pensamientos/los sentidos trastornados; *fig* **the social w.,** la vida mundana; *fam* **let's give it a w.,** probemos suerte. **II** *vtr* **to w. sth round,** dar vueltas a *or* hacer girar algo. **III** *vi* **to w. along/past,** ir/pasar como un relámpago; **to w. round,** girar con rapidez; *(of dust, leaves)* arremolinarse; **my head's whirling,** me está dando vueltas la cabeza.

whirlpool ['wɜːlpuːl] *n* remolino *m*, vorágine *f*.

whirlwind ['wɜːlwɪnd] *n* torbellino *m*, remolino *m*.

whir(r) [wɜːr] **I** *n* zumbido *m*, runrún *m*. **II** *vi* zumbar, runrunear.

whisk [wɪsk] **I** *n* **1** *(movement)* movimiento *m* brusco; **a w. of the tail,** un coletazo. **2** *Culin* batidor *m*; *(electric)* batidora *f*. **II** *vtr* **1** *(animal)* sacudir (la cola); **using its tail to w. away the flies,** sacudiéndose las moscas con la cola. **2** *Culin (eggs etc)* batir. **III** *vi* **to w. past,** pasar a toda velocidad. ◆ **whisk away, whisk off** *vtr* quitar bruscamente, llevarse de repente; **he was whisked (off) to hospital,** lo llevaron a toda prisa al hospital.

whisker ['wɪskər] *n* **1** pelo *m* (de la barba); *fig* **to win by a w.,** ganar por un pelo. **2 whiskers,** *(of person)* barbas *fpl*, patillas *fpl*; *(of cat)* bigotes *mpl*.

whisky, *Ir US* **whiskey** ['wɪskɪ] *n* whisky *m*, güisqui *m*.

whisper ['wɪspər] **I** *n* **1** *(of person, leaves)* susurro *m*; **to speak in a w.,** hablar en voz baja. **2** *(rumour)* rumor *m*. **II** *vtr* decir en voz baja; **a whispered conversation,** una conversación en voz baja. **III** *vi* cuchichear, susurrar, hablar en voz baja; *fig (leaves)* susurrar.

whispering ['wɪspərɪŋ] *n* **1** cuchicheo *m*; *(of leaves)* murmullo *m*. **2** *(rumours)* murmuración *f*. **2 whisperings,** rumores *mpl*, chismes *mpl*, murmuraciones *fpl*.

whist [wɪst] *n Cards* whist *m*.

whistle ['wɪsəl] **I** *n* **1** *(instrument)* pito *m*, silbato *m*; **to blow a** *or* **the w.,** pitar; *fig* **it broke as clean as a w.,** se rompió limpiamente. **2** *(sound)* silbido *m*, pitido *m*; **blast on a w.,** pitido *m*, silbido *m*. **II** *vtr (tune)* silbar. **III** *vi* **1** *(person, kettle, wind)* silbar; *(train)* pitar; **to w. (to) sb/a dog,** llamar a algn/a un perro con un silbido. **2** *(in protest)* silbar pitar. **3** *fig (missile, train)* **to w. past,** pasar silbando. **4** *fam* **he can w. for his money,** en lo que se refiere a su dinero, ya puede esperar sentado.

whistle-stop tour [wɪsəlstɒp'tʊər] *n Pol* serie *f* de visitas breves durante una campaña electoral.

whistling ['wɪsəlɪŋ] *n* silbido(s) *m(pl)*.

Whit [wɪt] **I** *adj* **W. Sunday/Monday,** domingo *m*/lunes *m* de pentecostés. **II** *n fam* pentecostés *m*; **at W.,** en pentecostés.

whit [wɪt] *n fam* pizca *f*; **not a w.,** ni un ápice, ni pizca.

white [waɪt] **I** *adj* blanco,-a; **a w. man,** un hombre blanco; **to go w.,** *(face)* palidecer, ponerse pálido,-a; *(hair)* encanecer; **w. bread,** pan blanco; **w. coffee,** café *m* con leche; **w. hair,** pelo *m* blanco *or* cano; *fig* **a w. Christmas,** una Navidad con nieve; *fig* **a w. lie,** una mentira piadosa;

fig **as w. as a sheet,** pálido,-a como la muerte; **as w. as snow,** más blanco,-a que la nieve; *fig* **to have a w. wedding,** casarse por la iglesia. ■ *US* **the W. House,** la Casa Blanca; **w. elephant,** elefante *m* blanco; **w. heat,** incandescencia *f*; *(sea)* **w. horses,** palomas *fpl*; *Admin* **w. paper,** libro *m* blanco; *Bot* **w. poplar,** álamo *m* blanco, chopo *m* blanco; *Cook* **w. sauce,** bechamel *m*. **II** *n* **1** *(colour)* blanco *m*; **dressed in w.,** vestido,-a de blanco. **2** *(person)* blanco,-a *m*, *f*. **3** *(of egg)* clara *f*. **4** *Anat (of eye)* blanco *m*. **5 whites,** ropa *f* sing blanca.

whitebait ['waɪtbeɪt] *n* pescaditos *mpl* fritos.

whitebeam ['waɪtbiːm] *n Bot* **common w.,** mostajo *m*, mostellar *m*.

white-collar ['waɪtkɒlər] *adj* **w.-c. worker,** empleado *m* administrativo *or* de oficina.

white-hot [waɪt'hɒt] *adj* candente, incandescente.

whiten ['waɪtən] *vtr* blanquear, blanquecer.

whiteness ['waɪtnɪs] *n* blancura *f*.

whitening ['waɪtənɪŋ] *n (for walls, shoes)* blanco *m* de España.

whitethroat ['waɪtθrəʊt] *n Orn* curruca *f* zarcera.

whitewash ['waɪtwɒʃ] **I** *n* **1** lechada *f*, cal *f*. **2** *fig (cover-up)* encubrimiento *m*. **3** *fig (defeat)* paliza *f*. **II** *vtr* **1** *(wall)* enjalbegar, encalar, blanquear. **2** *fig (matter)* encubrir.

whither ['wɪðər] *adv arch* ¿adónde?

whiting ['waɪtɪŋ] *n inv (fish)* pescadilla *f*.

whitish ['waɪtɪʃ] *adj* blanquecino,-a.

Whitsun(tide) ['wɪtsən(taɪd)] *n Rel* pentecostés *m*.

whittle ['wɪtəl] *vtr* cortar en pedazos; **to w. away at,** roer; *fig* **to w. down,** cercenar; *(expenses, list)* reducir poco a poco.

whiz(z) [wɪz] *vi (pt & pp whizzed)* **1** *(sound)* silbar, zumbar. **2** *(speed)* pasar zumbando; *(arrow)* rehilar; **to w. past,** pasar silbando *or* zumbando. ■ *fam* **w. kid,** joven *mf* dinámico,-a y emprendedor,-a.

WHO [dʌbəljuːeɪtʃ'əʊ] *abbr of* **World Health Organization,** Organización *f* Mundial de la Salud, OMS.

who [huː] *pron* **1** *(direct question)* quién, quiénes; **w. are they?,** ¿quiénes son?; **w. is it?,** ¿quién es?; *fam* **w. did you meet?,** ¿a quién encontraste?; *fam* **w. is the book for?,** ¿para quién es el libro? **2** *(indirect question)* quién; **I don't know w. did it,** no sé quién lo hizo; **to know w.'s w.,** saber quién es quién; **w. should it be but Maria!,** no podía ser otra (más) que María. **3** *rel (defining)* que; **those w. don't know,** los que no saben; *fam* **the man w. I saw,** el hombre que *or* a quien vi. **4** *rel (non-defining)* quien, quienes, el *or* la cual, tos *or* las cuales; **Elena's mother, w. is very rich ...,** la madre de Elena, la cual es muy rica ... . **5** 'Who's W.', 'Quién es Quién'.

whoa [wəʊ] *interj* ¡so!

whodun(n)it [huː'dʌnɪt] *n fam* novela *f or* obra *f* de teatro *or* película *f* de suspenso.

whoever [huː'evər] *pron* **1** quien, quienquiera que, el que; **give it to w. you like,** dáselo a quien quieras; **w. said that is a fool,** el que dijo eso es un tonto; **w. you are,** quienquiera que seas. **2** *(direct question)* **w. told you that?,** *(surprised)* ¿pero quién te dijo eso?; *(annoyed)* ¿quién (diablos) te dijo eso?

whole [həʊl] **I** *adj* **1** *(entire)* entero,-a, íntegro,-a; **a w. week,** una semana entera; **he took the w. lot,** se los llevó todos; **the w. truth,** toda la verdad; **the w. world,** el mundo entero; *fig* **a w. lot of things,** muchas *or* muchísimas cosas. **2** *(in one piece)* intacto,-a, sano,-a; **there was not a glass left w.,** no quedó un vaso sano. **3** *Math* entero,-a; **a w. number,** un número entero. **II** *n* **1** *(single unit)* todo *m*, conjunto *m*; **as a w.,** en su totalidad, en conjunto; **the parts form a w.,** las partes forman un conjunto. **2** *(all)* totalidad *f*; **the w. of London,** todo Londres; **the w. of the school,** la escuela entera. **3 on the w.,** en general, en conjunto.

wholefood ['həʊlfuːd] n alimento(s) m(pl) integral(es). ∎ **w. shop,** tienda f de dietética.

wholehearted [həʊl'hɑːtɪd] adj (enthusiastic) entusiasta; (sincere) sincero,-a; (unreserved) incondicional; **my w. support,** mi apoyo absoluto. ◆ **wholeheartedly** adv con entusiasmo, sinceramente de todo corazón, sin reserva; **I agree w.,** estoy completamente de acuerdo.

wholemeal ['həʊlmiːl] adj integral. ∎ **w. bread,** pan m integral.

wholesale ['həʊlseɪl] Com I n venta f al por mayor. II adj al por mayor; fig total, general; fig **the w. destruction of plant life in the region,** la destrucción absoluta de la vida vegetal de la región. III adv al por mayor; fig de modo general, en su totalidad; **the prisoners were massacred w.,** los prisioneros fueron aniquilados por completo.

wholesaler ['həʊlseɪlə'] n mayorista mf.

wholesome ['həʊlsəm] adj (food) sano,-a; fig sano,-a saludable.

wholly ['həʊllɪ] adv enteramente, completamente.

whom [huːm] pron fml 1 (direct question) (accusative) a quién; **w. did you see?,** ¿a quién viste?; (after preposition) of or from w.?, ¿de quién?; **to w. are you referring?,** ¿a quién te refieres? 2 rel (accusative) que, a quien, a quienes; **those w. I have seen,** los que he visto. 3 rel (after preposition) quien, quienes, el or la cual, los or las cuales; **my brothers, both of w. are miners,** mis hermanos, que son mineros los dos.

whoop [wuːp] I n grito m de alegría. II vi gritar de alegría; fam **to w. it up,** pasárselo en grande.

whoopee [wʊ'piː] interj ¡hurra!

whooping cough ['huːpɪŋkɒf] n Med tos f ferina.

whoops [wʊps] interj ¡ay!, ¡up lá!

whopper ['wɒpə'] n fam 1 (big things) cosa f descomunal; (of fish) **what a w.!,** ¡qué pez más gigante! 2 (lie) trola f, bola f.

whopping ['wɒpɪŋ] adj fam enorme, descomunal; **a w. great dinner,** una cena impresionante.

whore [hɔːʳ] n offens puta f.

whose [huːz] pron 1 (direct question) de quién, de quiénes; **w. are these gloves?,** ¿de quién son estos guantes?; **w. car should we go in?,** ¿en qué coche vamos a ir?; **w. daughter are you?,** ¿de quién es usted hija?; **w. is this?,** ¿a quién pertenece esto? 2 (indirect question) de quién, de quiénes; **I don't know w. these coats are,** no sé de quién son estos abrigos. 3 rel cuyo(s), cuya(s); **the man w. children we saw,** el hombre a cuyos hijos vimos.

why [waɪ] I adv por qué; (for what purpose) para qué; **I don't know w. he did it,** no sé por qué lo hizo; **that is w. I didn't come,** por eso no vine; **there's no reason w. you shouldn't go,** no hay motivo para que no vayas; **w. not go to bed?,** ¿por qué no te acuestas?; **w. (on earth) did you do that?,** ¿por qué (demonios) hiciste eso?; **w. worry?,** ¿por qué preocuparse? II n fam porqué m; **the whys and wherefores,** el porqué y el cómo. III interj 1 (fancy that!) ¡toma!, ¡vaya!; **w., it's David!,** ¡sí es David! 2 (protest, assertion) ¡sí, vamos; **w. its quite simple!,** ¡si es muy sencillo!; **w., of course!,** ¡vaya que sí!, ¡por supuesto que sí!

wick [wɪk] n mecha f; GB fam fig **to get on sb's w.,** tocarle las narices a algn.

wicked ['wɪkɪd] adj 1 (person) malvado,-a malo,-a; (action) malo,-a, perverso,-a; **a w. grin,** una sonrisa traviesa. 2 fam malísimo,-a; (temper) terrible; (waste) vergonzoso,-a; (weather) feo,-a, horrible. ◆ **wickedly** adv 1 (behave) malvadamente, perversamente. 2 fam **w. expensive,** terriblemente caro,-a.

wickedness ['wɪkɪdnɪs] n maldad f.

wicker ['wɪkəʳ] I n mimbre f. II adj de mimbre; **w. chair,** silla f de mimbre.

wickerwork ['wɪkəwɜːk] n (material) mimbre m; (art) cestería f; (articles) artículos mpl de mimbre.

wicket ['wɪkɪt] n 1 Cricket (stumps) palos mpl; (pitch) terreno m; fig **to be on a sticky w.,** encontrarse en apuros. 2 **w. gate,** postigo m, portillo m.

wicketkeeper ['wɪkɪtkiːpəʳ] n Cricket cátcher m.

wide [waɪd] I adj 1 (road, trousers) ancho,-a; (eyes) muy abiertos; (gap, interval) grande; (measure) **it is ten metres w.,** tiene diez metros de ancho; **the curtain is too w. for the window,** la cortina es demasiado ancha para la ventana. 2 (area) amplio,-o extenso,-a; (knowledge, experience, repercussions) amplio,-a; (coverage, range, support) extenso,-a; **a w. variety,** una gran variedad; **to win by a w. margin,** ganar por un amplio margen; **w. interests,** intereses muy diversos. 3 (off target) desviado,-a; Ftb **the shot was w.,** el tiro salió desviado; **to be w. of the mark,** no dar en el blanco; fig no acertar. II adv **from far and w.,** de todas partes; (at dentist) open w.!, ¡abra bien la boca!; **to open one's eyes w.,** abrir los ojos de par en par; Ftb **to shoot w.,** chutar el balón muy desviado; Aut **to take the bend w.,** tomar la curva abierta; **w. apart,** muy separados,-as; **w. awake,** completamente despierto,-a; fig despabilado,-a; **w. open,** (door, eyes, mouth) abierto,-a de par en par; (spaces) muy abiertos,-as; **with mouth w. open,** boquiabierto,-a. ◆ **widely** adv (travel, scatter) extensamente; (believed, available) generalmente; **he is w. known,** es muy conocido; **her books are w. read,** su obra es muy leída.

wide-angle ['waɪdæŋgəl] adj Phot **w.-a. lens,** objetivo m gran angular.

wide-eyed [waɪd'aɪd] adj con los ojos muy abiertos.

widen ['waɪdən] I vtr (road, hole, etc) ensanchar; (interests) ampliar, extender. II vi ensancharse; fig **the gap has widened,** las diferencias han aumentado.

wide-ranging ['waɪdreɪndʒɪŋ] adj (interests) múltiples, muy diversos,-as; (discussion) amplio,-a; (survey, study) de gran alcance.

widespread ['waɪdspred] adj (unrest, belief) general; (damage) extenso,-a; **to become w.,** generalizarse.

widow ['wɪdəʊ] n viuda f.

widowed ['wɪdəʊd] adj enviudado,-a; **to be w.,** enviudar.

widower ['wɪdəʊəʳ] n viudo m.

widowhood ['wɪdəʊhʊd] n viudez f.

width [wɪdθ] n 1 (gen) extensión f, anchura f. 2 (of material) ancho m.

wield [wiːld] vtr (weapon, pen) manejar; (weapon) blandir; fig (power) ejercer.

wife [waɪf] n (pl wives) mujer f, esposa f. ∎ fig **old wives' tale,** cuento m de viejas.

wig [wɪg] n peluca f.

wigeon ['wɪdʒən] n Orn ánade m silbón.

wigging ['wɪgɪŋ] n fam **to give sb a w.,** echar un rapapolvo a algn.

wiggle ['wɪgəl] I vtr (finger etc) menear; **to w. (one's hips),** contonearse. II vi menearse.

wiggly ['wɪglɪ] adj ondulado,-a.

Wight [waɪt] n Isle of W., Isla f de Wight.

wigwam ['wɪgwæm] n US tienda f india, tepe m.

wild [waɪld] I adj 1 (animal, tribe) salvaje; (bull) bravo,-a; **w. beast,** fiera f; **w. goose,** ganso m salvaje; fig **w. horses wouldn't drag me there,** no iría ni por todo el oro del mundo. ∎ fig **w. goose chase,** búsqueda f inútil. 2 (plant) silvestre, salvaje. 3 (landscape) agreste, salvaje; (wind) furioso,-a, borrascoso,-a; **a w. night,** una noche tormentosa; **the W. West,** el Salvaje Oeste. 4 (temperament, behaviour) alocado,-a, desordenado,-a; (appearance) desordenado,-a; (passions, imagination, dance) desenfrenado,-a; (laughter, enthusiasm) loco,-a; (applause) fervoroso,-a; (thoughts) extravagante, loco,-a; (exaggeration) enorme; **a w. party,** una fiesta bárbara; Sport **a w. shot,** un tiro incontrolado; **to make a w. guess,** adivinar al azar; **w. with joy/jealousy,** loco,-a de alegría/ celos; fam fig **she is w. about him/about tennis,** está loca por él/por el tenis. **5** *GB fam fig (angry)* enfadado,-a; **it makes me w.**, me exaspera; **to be w.**, estar furioso,-a (**with**, contra). **6** *Cards* **w. card**, comodín *m*. **II** *adv (garden)* **to grow w.**, ser silvestre; **to run w.**, *(animal)* vivir en su estado natural; *(garden)* volver al estado silvestre; *fig (children)* desmandarse; *fig (hooligans)* portarse como salvajes. **III** *n (animals)* **in the w.**, en el estado salvaje *or* natural; **the wild (of Africa)**, las regiones salvajes (de Africa); *fig* **to live out in the wilds**, vivir en el quinto pino. ◆ **wildly** *adv* **1** *(rush round, gesticulate)* como un,-a loco,-a. frenéticamente; *(applaud)* fervorosamente; *(shoot)* sin apuntar; *(hit out)* a tontas y a locas. **2 w. enthusiastic**, loco,-a de entusiasmo; **w. exaggerated**, exageradísimo,-a; **w. inaccurate**, sumamente inexacto,-a.

wildcat ['waɪldkæt] *n (pl* **wildcat** *or* **wildcats**) *Zool* gato,- a m, f montes. ■ *Ind* **w. strike**, huelga f salvaje.

wildebeest ['wɪldɪbiːst, 'vɪldɪbiːst] *n Zool* ñu *m*.

wilderness ['wɪldənɪs] *n* desierto *m*, yermo *m*.

wildfire ['waɪldfaɪə'] *n* **to spread like w.**, correr como la pólvora.

wildfowl ['waɪldfaʊl] *npl Orn* aves *fpl* de caza.

wildlife ['waɪldlaɪf] *n* fauna *f*. ■ **w. park**, safari *m*.

wildness ['waɪldnɪs] *n* **1** *(of animal)* estado *m* salvaje; *(plants)* estado *m* silvestre. **2** *(of landscape)* aspecto *m* agreste *or* salvaje. **3** *(of wind)* furia f. **4** *(of temperament, passions)* locura *f*, desenfreno *m*; *(of behaviour)* desórdenes *mpl*; *(of appearance)* desorden *m*; *(of ideas)* extravagancia f.

wiles [waɪlz] *npl (tricks)* artimañas *fpl*, artificios *mpl*; *(cunning)* astucia f.

wilful, *US* **willful** ['wɪlful] *adj* **1** *(stubborn)* voluntarioso,- a; **a w. child**, un niño terco. **2** *Jur* premeditado,-a. ◆ **wilfully** *adv* **1** *(stubbornly)* voluntariosamente, tercamente. **2** *esp Jur (deliberately)* premeditadamente; **on the day in question, you did w. and maliciously plan the bombing**, en el día de la fecha, planeó con premeditación y alevosía la colocación de la bomba.

will¹ [wɪl] **I** *n* **1** voluntad *f*; **against my w.**, contra mi voluntad, a pesar mío; **an iron w.**, una voluntad de hierro; **good/Ill w.**, buena/mala voluntad; **of my own free w.**, por mi propia voluntad; **the w. to live**, la voluntad de vivir; **with the best w. in the world**, con la mejor voluntad del mundo; *prov* **where there's a w. there's a way**, querer es poder. **2** *Jur (testament)* testamento *m*, últimas *fpl* voluntades; **he left me the house in his w.**, me *or* legó la casa; **last w. and testament**, última disposición *f or* voluntad *f*; **to make one's w.**, hacer testamento. **II** *vtr* desear; **fate willed that ...**, el destino quiso que ... .

will² [wɪl] *v aux (pt* **would**) **1** *(future) (esp 2nd & 3rd person)* **don't forget, w. you!**, ¡que no se te olvide, eh!; **I'll starve — no, you won't!**, voy a morir de hambre — ¡qué va!; **she w. not** *or* **she won't do it**, no lo hará; **they w. come, they'll come**, vendrán; **w. he be there?** — yes, he w., ¿estará allí? —sí, (estará); **you'll tell him, won't you?**, se lo dirás, ¿verdad? **2** *(command)* **you w. be here at eleven!**, ¡estarás aquí a las once! **3** *(future perfect)* **they w.** *or* **they'll have finished by tomorrow**, habrán terminado para mañana. **4** *(willingness)* **be quiet, w. you! - no, I won't!**, ¿quiere callarse? — no quiero; *(marriage ceremony)* **I w.**, sí, quiero; **I won't have it!**, ¡no lo permito!; **the car won't start**, no arranca el coche; **w. you have a drink? - yes, I w.**, ¿quiere tomar algo? —sí, por favor; **won't you sit down?**, ¿quiere sentarse? **5** *(custom)* **accidents w. happen**, siempre habrá accidentes; **he w. play for hours**, suele jugar durante horas y horas. **6** *(persistence)* **he w. have it that ...**, se obstina en creer que ...; **if you w. go out without a coat ...**, si te empeñas en salir sin abrigo ... . **7** *(probability)* **he'll be on holiday now**, ahora estará de vacaciones. **8** *(ability)* **the car w. do 100 miles per hour**, el coche puede alcanzar 100 millas por hora; **the lift w. hold ten people**, en el ascensor caben diez personas.

willie ['wɪlɪ] *fam* pitilín *m*.

willies ['wɪlɪz] *npl fam* susto *m sing*; **that man gives me the w.**, ese hombre me pone la piel de gallina; **to put the w. up sb**, poner los pelos de punta a algn.

willing ['wɪlɪŋ] *adj (obliging)* servicial, complaciente; **God w.**, si Dios quiere; **I'm quite w. to do it**, lo haré con mucho gusto; **there were plenty of w. hands**, no faltaban personas dispuestas a ayudar; **to be w. to do sth**, estar dispuesto,-a a hacer algo; **to show w.**, dar pruebas de buena voluntad. ◆ **willingly** *adv* de buena gana, de (buen) grado; **I would w. pay but ...**, pagaría de buena gana pero ... .

willingness ['wɪlɪŋnɪs] *n* buena voluntad *f*; **his w. to help**, su buena disposición para ayudar.

will-o'-the-wisp [wɪlədə'wɪsp] *n* fuego *m* fatuo.

willow ['wɪləʊ] *n Bot* **w. (tree)**, sauce *m*. ■ **crack w.**, mimbrera *f*; **goat w.**, sauce *m* cabruno; **white w.**, sauce *m* blanco.

willowy ['wɪləʊɪ] *adj* esbelto,-a.

willpower ['wɪlpaʊə'] *n* (fuerza f de) voluntad *f*; **she lacks w.**, tiene poca voluntad.

willy-nilly [wɪlɪ'nɪlɪ] *adv* de grado o por fuerza.

wilt [wɪlt] *vi (plant)* marchitarse.

wily ['waɪlɪ] *adj (wilier, wiliest)* astuto,-a, zorro,-a.

win [wɪn] **I** *n* victoria *f*; **to have a w. (on the pools)**, ganar (en las quinielas). **II** *vtr (pt & pp* **won**) **1** *(gen)* ganar; *(prize)* ganar, llevarse; *(victory)* conseguir, ganar; **to w. a place in the team**, conseguir, un puesto en el equipo; **to w. sth from sb**, ganarle algo a algn; **to w. the pools**, ganar en las quinielas. **2** *fig (sympathy)* ganarse, granjearse; *(friendship)* granjearse; *(praise)* cosechar, atraerse; **to w. friends**, granjearse amistades; **to w. sb's love** *or* **heart**, conquistar a algn. **III** *vi* ganar; *fam* **you can't w.!**, ¡no hay manera de hacerlo bien! ◆ **win back** *vtr (land etc)* reconquistar; *(money)* recuperar. ◆ **win over** *vtr* ganar; *(cause, idea)* atraer (**to**, a, hacia); *(voters)* ganarse, arrastrar; *(sympathy, support)* ganarse, conquistar. ◆ **win through** *vi* conseguir triunfar.

winner ['wɪnə'] *n* ganador,-a *m*, *f*, vencedor,-a *m*, *f*; *fam fig* **this product is a w.**, este producto será un gran éxito.

winning ['wɪnɪŋ] *adj (person, team)* ganador,-a, vencedor,-a; *(number, ticket)* premiado,-a; *(stroke, goal)* decisivo,-a; *(ways, smile)* atractivo,-a. ■ **w. post**, meta *f*.

winnings ['wɪnɪŋz] *npl* ganancias *fpl*.

wince [wɪns] **I** *vi* tener un rictus de dolor. **II** *n* mueca *f or* rictus *m* de dolor.

winch [wɪntʃ] **I** *n* cigüeña *f*, torno *m*, cabrestante *m*. **II** *vtr* **to w. sth up**, levantar algo con un torno.

wind¹ [wɪnd] **I** *n* **1** viento *m*; **high winds**, vientos fuertes; **into the w.**, contra el viento; **north w.**, viento del norte; **to sail close to the w.**, *Naut* navegar de bolina; *fig* jugar con una situación peligrosa; *Naut* **to sail/run before the w.**, navegar viento en popa; *fig* **there's something in the w.**, algo flota en el aire; *fig* **to get w. of sth**, olerse algo; *fig (curb)* **to take the w. out of sb's sails**, pararle los pies a algn; *fig* **to throw caution to the w.**, dejar de lado la prudencia; *fam fig* **to get the w. up**, ponerse nervioso,-a; *prov* **it's an ill w. (that blows nobody any good)**, no hay mal que por bien no venga. ■ **w. tunnel**, túnel *m* aerodinámico. **2** *(breath)* aliento *m*; **to get one's second w.**, recobrar el aliento. **3** *Med* flato *m*, flatulencia *f*; **to have w.**, tener gases; *euph* **to break w.**, ventosear. **4** *Mus* **w. instrument**, instrumento *m* de viento. **II** *vtr* cortar la respiración a; **to be winded**, quedarse sin aliento.

wind² [waɪnd] **I** *vtr (pt & pp* **wound**) **1** *(onto a red)* arrollar, devanar; **to w. a bandage round one's finger**, envolverse el dedo con una venda; **to w. wool (up) into a ball**, ovillar lana. **2** *(film, tape)* **to w. on/back**, avanzar/rebobinar. **3** *(in fishing)* **to w. in the line**, cobrar el sedal. **4** *(clock)* dar cuerda a. **5** *(handle, winch)* dar vueltas a. **II** *vi (road, river)* serpentear; *(snake)* enroscarse (**around**, alrededor de). **III** *n (of road, river)* recodo *m*, vuelta *f*. ◆ **wind down** *I vtr Aut (window)* bajar. **II** *vi* **1** *(clock)* quedarse sin cuerda. **2** *fam (relax)* relajarse. ◆ **wind up I** *vtr* **1** *(roll up)* devanar, enrollar. **2** *(close business etc)* cerrar, liquidar; *(session, debate)* clausurar. **3** *(clock)* dar cuerda a. **4** *fam* **to be all wound up**, estar nerviosísimo,-a. **II** *vi* **1** *(meeting)* terminar; *(speaker)* acabar el discurso. **2** *fam* acabar; **you'll w. up in hospital**, acabarás en el hospital.

windbag ['wɪndbæg] *n fam* charlatán,-ana *m,f*.

windbreak ['wɪndbreɪk] *n* abrigo *m*, abrigadero *m*.

winder ['waɪndər] *n (of watch)* corona *f*.

windfall ['wɪndfɔːl] *n (fruit)* fruta *f* caída; *fig* ganancia *f* inesperada *or* caída del cielo.

winding ['waɪndɪŋ] *adj (road, river)* sinuoso,-a, tortuoso,-a; *(staircase)* de caracol.

windlass ['wɪndləs] *n Tech* torno *m*.

windmill ['wɪndmɪl] *n* molino *m* (de viento).

window ['wɪndəʊ] *n* ventana *f*; *(of vehicle, of ticket office, in post office)* ventanilla *f*; *Rail* **a w. seat**, un asiento junto a la ventanilla; *(shop)* **w.**, escaparate *m*; **to clean the windows**, limpiar los cristales; **to lean out of the window**, asomarse a la ventana. ■ *Arch* **stained-glass w.**, vidriera *f*; **w. box**, jardinera *f*; **w. cleaner**, limpiacristales *mf inv*; **w. dresser**, escaparatista *mf*; **w. dressing**, decoración *f* de escaparates; *fig* fachada *f*, apariencias *fpl*; **w. frame**, marco *m* de ventana.

windowpane ['wɪndəʊpeɪn] *n* cristal *m*.

window-shopping ['wɪndəʊʃɒpɪŋ] *n* **to go w.-s.**, ir a mirar escaparates.

windowsill ['wɪndəʊsɪl] *n* alféizar *m*, antepecho *m*.

windpipe ['wɪndpaɪp] *n Anat* tráquea *f*.

windscreen ['wɪndskriːn] *n*, *US* **windshield** ['wɪndfiːld] *n Aut* parabrisas *m inv*. ■ **w. washer**, lavaparabrisas *m inv*; **w. wiper**, limpiaparabrisas *m inv*.

windsock ['wɪndsɒk] *n Av* manga *f*, catavientos *m*.

windswept ['wɪndswept] *adj (landscape)* azotado,-a por el viento; *(person, hair)* despeinado,-a (por el viento).

windward ['wɪndwəd] *I adj Naut* de barlovento; **the W. Islands**, las Islas de Barlovento. **II** *n* barlovento *m*; **to w.**, a barlovento.

windy ['wɪndɪ] *adj (windier, windiest)* **1** *(day, weather)* ventoso,-a; *(place)* expuesto,-a al viento; **it is very w. today**, hoy hace mucho viento. **2** *fam fig* miedoso,-a, cagón,-ona; **he got w.**, le entró canguelo *or* mieditis.

wine [waɪn] *I n* vino *m*; **red w.**, vino tinto; **table w.**, vino de mesa; **w.-producing region**, región *f* vitícola. ■ **w. cellar**, bodega *f*; **w. list**, lista *f* de vinos; **w. merchant**, vinatero,-a *m, f*; **w. tasting**, cata *f* de vinos; **w. vinegar**, vinagre *m* de vino. **II** *vtr fam fig* **to w. and dine sb**, agasajar a algn, tratar a algn por todo lo alto.

wineglass ['waɪnglɑːs] *n* copa *f* (para vino).

wineskin ['waɪnskɪn] *n* odre *m*.

wing [wɪŋ] *I n* **1** *Orn Av* ala *f*; **to take w.**, alzar el vuelo; *fig* **to clip sb's wings**, cortarle las alas a algn; *fig* **to take sb under one's w.**, tomar a algn bajo su protección. ■ *GB Av* **w. commander**, teniente *m* coronel; **w. tip**, punta *f* del ala. **2** *(of building)* ala *f*. **3** *Aut* aleta *f*. ■ **w. mirror**, retrovisor *m* externo. **4** *(of armchair)* oreja *f*. **5 wings**, *Theat* **(in the) w.**, (entre) bastidores *mpl*; *fig* **to wait in the w.**, esperar la entrada en escena. **6** *Ftb* banda *f*; **to dribble down the right w.**, driblar por la banda derecha. **7** *Pol* ala *f*; **the left w.**, el ala izquierda, la izquierda. **8** *Mech* **w. nut**, tuerca *f* mariposa. **II** *vtr* **to w. its way**, ir volando.

winger ['wɪŋər] *n Ftb* extremo *m*.

wingspan ['wɪŋspæn] *n (of bird, plane)* envergadura *f*.

wink [wɪŋk] *I n* guiño *m*; **to give sb a w.**, hacerle un guiño a algn; *fig* **as quick as a w.**, en un abrir y cerrar de ojos; *fig* **to tip sb the w.**, darle el soplo a algn; *fam fig* **a nod is as good as a w.**, a buen entendedor con pocas palabras basta; *fam fig* **I didn't get a w. (of sleep)**, no pegué ojo; *fam fig* **to have forty winks**, echar una siestecita *or* una cabezada. **II** *vi* **1** *(person)* guiñar el ojo. **2** *(light)* titil(e)ar, parpadear.

winker ['wɪŋkər] *n GB Aut* intermitente *m*.

winking ['wɪŋkɪŋ] *adj* pestañeante.

winkle ['wɪŋkəl] *I n Zool* bígaro *m*, bígarro *m*. **II** *vtr GB fam* **to w. sth out of sb**, sacar *or* sonsacar algo a algn.

winnow ['wɪnəʊ] *vtr Agr* aventar.

winsome ['wɪnsəm] *adj* encantador,-a, atractivo,-a.

winter ['wɪntər] *I n* invierno *m*; **in w.** *(time)*, en invierno. **II** *adj* de invierno, invernal; **w. clothes**, ropa *f* de invierno. ■ **w. sports**, deportes *mpl* de invierno. **III** *vi* pasar el invierno, invernar.

wintry ['wɪntrɪ] *adj (wintrier, wintriest) (scene, weather)* invernal, de invierno.

wipe [waɪp] *I vtr* limpiar, enjugar; **to w. one's brow**, enjugarse la frente; **to w. one's feet/nose**, limpiarse los pies/las narices; **to w. sth** *(dry/clean)*, enjugar/limpiar algo; **to w. the dishes**, enjugar los platos; *fam fig (defeat)* **to w. the floor with sb**, cascarle una paliza a algn. **II** *n* limpión *m*; **to give sth a w.**, darle un limpión a algo. ◆ **wipe away** *vtr (tear)* enjugar. ◆ **wipe down** *vtr (walls)* rascar. ◆ **wipe off** *vtr* quitar frotando; **to w. sth off the blackboard/the tape**, borrar algo de la pizarra/de la cinta; *fam fig* **to w. the smile off sb's face**, quitarle a algn las ganas de reír. ◆ **wipe out** *vtr* **1** *(erase)* borrar; *fig* **to w. out the memory of sth**, borrar algo de la memoria. **2** *(illness)* erradicar, extirpar. **3** *(destroy) (army)* aniquilar; *(species, population)* exterminar. ◆ **wipe up** *vtr* limpiar.

wiper ['waɪpər] *n Aut* limpiaparabrisas *m inv*; **w. blade**, goma *f* del limpiaparabrisas.

wire [waɪər] *I n* **1** alambre *m*; *Elec* cable *m*, hilo *m*; *Tel* hilo; *fig* **she's a live w.**, tiene muchísima energía. ■ **barbed w.**, alambre *m* de espino; *Mil* **barbed w. entanglement** *or* **fence**, alambrada *f*; **w. brush**, cepillo *m* metálico; **w. cutters**, cortaalambres *m inv*, cizalla *f sing*; **w. netting**, red *f* de alambre, tela *f* metálica; *(on window)* alambrera *f*; **w. wool**, estropajo *m* metálico. **2** *(telegram)* telegrama *m*, cable(grama) *m*. **II** *vtr* **1** *(tie)* atar con alambre. **2** *Elec* **to w. (up) a house**, poner *or* instalar el cableado de una casa; **to w. (up) an appliance to the mains**, conectar un aparato a la toma eléctrica; **wired for sound**, sonorizado,-a. **3** *(telegram etc)* poner un telegrama a, enviar por telegrama.

wireless ['waɪəlɪs] *n dated* **1** *(system)* radiofonía *f*, radio *f*. ■ **w. message**, radiograma *m*; *Av* **w. operator**, radiotelegrafista *mf*. **2 w. (set)**, *(aparato m de)* radio *f*; **I heard it on the w.**, lo oí por la radio.

wiretapping ['waɪətæpɪŋ] *n* intervención *f* de teléfonos.

wiring ['waɪərɪŋ] *n Elec (network)* cableado *m*; *(action)* instalación *f* del cableado. ■ **w. diagram**, esquema *m* del cableado.

wiry ['waɪərɪ] *adj (wirier, wiriest) (hair)* estropajoso,-a; *(person)* nervudo,-a.

wisdom ['wɪzdəm] *n* **1** *(learning)* sabiduría *f*, saber *m*. **2** *(good sense) (of person)* cordura *f*, (buen) juicio *m*; *(of action)* prudencia *f*, lo prudente. **3** *Dent* **w. tooth**, muela *f* del juicio.

wise [waɪz] *adj* **1** *(learned)* sabio,-a; **a w. man**, un sabio; *(Bible)* **the Three W. Men**, los Reyes Magos. ■ *US fam* **w. guy**, sabelotodo *mf*. **2** *(knowledgeable)* sabio,-a, entendido,-a; *fig* **it's easy to be w. after the event**, todo el mundo es listo después de visto; *fam fig* **I'm none the wiser**, sigo sin entender; *fam fig* **I've got w. to him**, ya le he calado; *fam fig* **nobody will be any the wiser**, nadie se dará cuenta; *fam fig* **to put sb w.**, poner a algn al tanto (**to**, **about**, de). **3** *(sensible) (advice)* sabio,-a, cuerdo,-a; *(remark)* juicioso,-a; *(decision, move)* atinado,-a, acertado,-a; **it would be w. to keep quiet**, sería prudente callarse; **you were very w.**, obraste con acierto *or* con mucho tino. ◆ **wise up** *vi fam* **1** *(realise)* darse cuenta. **2** *(accept)* aceptar; **w. up!**, ¡para uno lo sepas!, ¡a ver si te enteras! ◆ **wisely** *adv* **1** *(with wisdom)* sabiamente. **2** *(with prudence)* juiciosamente, prudentemente.

wisecrack ['waɪzkræk] *fam* I *n* salida *f*, chiste *m*. II *vi* chancear, bromear.

wish [wɪʃ] I *n* 1 *(desire)* deseo *m* (for, de); **according to/against his wishes,** según/contra sus deseos; **I haven't the slightest w. to go,** no tengo el menor deseo de ir; **to make a w.,** pedir un deseo. 2 **wishes,** deseos *mpl*; *(greeting)* **best w.,** felicitaciones *fpl*; **give your mother my best w.,** salude a su madre de mi parte; **with best w. for the future,** con mis mejores deseos para el futuro; *(end of letter)* **with best w.,** Peter, saludos (cordiales) de Peter. II *vtr* 1 *(want)* querer, desear; **I w. he would hurry up,** estoy deseando que se dé prisa; **I w. I could stay longer,** me gustaría poder quedarme más tiempo; **I w. that I were in your place,** quisiera estar en tu lugar; **I w. you had told me!,** ¡ojalá me lo hubieras dicho!; **to w. to do sth,** querer *or* desear hacer algo. 2 *(foist)* desear; **to w. sth onto sb,** endosarle algo a algn; **I wouldn't w. it on anyone,** no desearía que lo sufriera nadie. 3 *(desire)* desear; **to w. sb goodnight,** darle las buenas noches a algn; **to w. sb well** *or* **luck** *or* **all the best,** desearle a algn mucha suerte. III *vi* 1 *(with wishbone etc)* pedir un deseo. 2 *(want)* desear; **as you w.,** como quieras; **do as you w.,** haga lo que quiera; **I have everything I could w. for,** tengo todo cuanto pudiera desear; **to w. for sth,** desear algo.

wishbone ['wɪʃbəʊn] *n* Anat Orn espoleta *f*.

wishful ['wɪʃful] *adj* **it's w. thinking,** es hacerse ilusiones.

wishy-washy ['wɪʃɪwɒʃɪ] *adj fam (person)* soso,-a, insípido,-a, sin carácter; *(ideas)* borroso,-a.

wisp [wɪsp] *n (of straw)* brizna *f*; *(of wool, hair)* mechón *m*; *(of smoke)* voluta *f*; *fig* **a mere w. of a girl,** una chica menudita.

wispy ['wɪspɪ] *adj (wispier, wispiest)* tenue, delgado,-a.

wistful ['wɪstful] *adj* melancólico,-a, nostálgico,-a, pensativo,-a.

wit [wɪt] *n* 1 *(intelligence) (often pl)* inteligencia *f*; *(ingenuity)* ingenio *m*; **a battle of wits,** una pugna de inteligencias; **she didn't have the w. to say no,** no tuvo suficiente inteligencia *or* presencia de ánimo para decir que no; *fig* **to be at one's wits' end,** estar para volverse loco,-a; *fam fig* **to have one's wits about one,** ser *or* estar despabilado,-a. 2 *(humour)* ingenio *m*, agudeza *f*, chispa *f*. 3 *(person)* chistoso,-a *m,f*, persona *f* salada.

witch [wɪtʃ] *n* bruja *f*. ■ **w. doctor,** hechicero *m*; *fig* **w. hunt,** caza *f* de brujas.

witchcraft ['wɪtʃkrɑːft] *n* brujería *f*, hechicería *f*.

with [wɪð, wɪθ] *prep* 1 *(in possession of)* con; **a room w. bath/w. no bath,** un cuarto con baño/sin baño; **do you have any money w. you?,** ¿traes dinero?; **the man w. the glasses,** el hombre de las gafas. 2 *(accompanying)* con; **he went w. me/you,** fue conmigo/contigo; **to leave a child w. sb,** dejar a un niño al cuidado de algn; *Naut* **to sail w. the wind,** navegar con el viento; *fam* **w. (sugar) or without (sugar)?,** ¿azúcar? 3 *(including)* con; **I have six w. this one,** con éste tengo seis; **it cost 2,000 pesetas w. wine,** costó 2,000 pesetas vino incluido. 4 *(despite)* con; **w. all his faults, I admire him,** le admiro con todos sus defectos. 5 *(given)* con; **w. your help/permission,** con su ayuda/permiso;. **w. your intelligence it will be easy,** dada su inteligencia será fácil. 6 *fig (on the side of)* con; **we're all w. you,** todos estamos contigo. 7 *(contact, relationship)* con; **he's w. Lloyd's,** trabaja para Lloyd's; **it has nothing to do w. politics,** no tiene nada que ver con la política; **she is popular w. her colleagues,** es popular entre sus colegas; **to deal/mix w. sb,** tratar/asociarse con algn. 8 *(against)* con; **at war w. France,** en guerra con Francia; **to fight/compete w. sb,** pelearse/competir con algn. 9 *(regarding)* con; **I had trouble w. the clutch,** tuve problemas con el embrague; **w. him, money is everything,** para él todo es cuestión de dinero. 10 *(manner)* con, de; **to fill a vase w. water,** llenar un jarrón de agua; **w. difficulty,** con dificultad; **w. one gulp,** de un trago; **w. tears in her eyes,** con los ojos llenos de lágrimas. 11 *(instrument)* con; **it is made w. butter,** está hecho con mantequilla; **they cut the bread w. a knife,** cortaron el pan con un cuchillo. 12 *(circumstances)* con; **I can't phone w. my boss here,** no puedo telefonear estando mi jefe aquí; **to sleep w. the window open,** dormir con la ventana abierta. 13 *(because of)* de; **she put on weight w. so much eating,** engordó de tanto comer; **to be paralysed w. fear,** estar paralizado,-a de miedo. 14 *(after)* con; **w. experience,** con la experiencia; **w. that, he went out,** con lo cual salió; **w. these words he left,** dicho esto, se marchó. 15 *(from)* de, con; **to break w. sb,** romper con algn; **to part company w. sb,** separarse de algn. 16 *(according to)* con, según; **it varies w. the season,** varía con la temporada. 17 *(expressions)* **down w. the president!,** ¡abajo el presidente!; **on w. the show!,** ¡que siga el espectáculo!; **to hell w. the neighbours!,** ¡al diablo con los vecinos!

withdraw [wɪð'drɔː] I *vtr (pt* **withdrew;** *pp* **withdrawn)** 1 *(gen)* retirar, sacar; **to w. money from the bank,** retirar *or* sacar dinero del banco. 2 *(go back on)* retirar; *(statement, accusation)* retractarse de; *(plan)* renunciar a; *Jur (demand)* renunciar a, apartarse de. II *vi* 1 *(move back)* retirarse, apartarse; *(from room)* retirarse; *Mil* replegarse, retirarse. 2 *(drop out)* renunciar; *Sport* **to w. from a competition,** retirarse de un concurso.

withdrawal [wɪð'drɔːəl] *n* retirada *f*; *(of statement, accusation)* retractación *f*; *(of complaint, plan, candidate)* renuncia *f*; *Sport* retirada *f*. ■ **w. method,** *fam* marcha *f* atrás; *Med* **w. symptoms,** síndrome *m* de abstinencia.

withdrawn [wɪð'drɔːn] I *pp see* **withdraw.** II *adj (person)* introvertido,-a, cerrado,-a.

withdrew [wɪð'druː] *pt see* **withdraw.**

wither ['wɪðə'] I *vtr (plant)* marchitar. II *vi* marchitarse.

withered ['wɪðəd] *adj (plant)* marchito,-a; *fig (person)* **old and w.,** viejo,-a y ajado,-a.

withering ['wɪðərɪŋ] *adj (look)* fulminante; *(criticism)* mordaz.

withhold [wɪð'həʊld] *vtr (pt & pp* **withheld** [wɪð'held]*) (money)* retener; *(decision)* aplazar; *(consent)* negar; *(information)* ocultar.

within [wɪ'ðɪn] I *prep* 1 *(inside)* dentro de; **w. the city limits,** dento de los límites de la ciudad. 2 *(distance, range)* **accurate to w. a centimetre,** exacto,-a con una diferencia de un centímetro; **it is w. walking distance,** queda bastante cerca para ir andando; **situated w. five kilometres of the town,** situado,-a a menos de cinco kilómetros de la ciudad; **w. a radius of ten miles,** en un radio de diez millas; **w. sight of the sea,** con vistas al mar; *fig* **w. an inch of death;** a dos dedos de la muerte. 3 *(time)* **they arrived w. a few days of each other,** llegaron con pocos días de diferencia; **w. the hour,** dentro de una hora; **w. the next five years,** durante los cinco años que vienen. II *adv* dentro; **enquire w.,** razón aquí; **from w.,** desde dentro.

with-it ['wɪðɪt] *adj fam* **a w.-it hairstyle,** un peinado a la última moda; **she is very w. it,** tiene ideas muy modernas; **to get w. it,** ponerse de moda.

without [wɪ'ðaʊt] *prep* sin; **he did it w. my knowing,** lo hizo sin que lo supiera yo *or* sin saberlo yo; **the house is not w. charm,** la casa no deja de tener su encanto; **to go out w. a coat,** salir sin abrigo; **w. money or luggage,** sin dinero ni equipaje; *fig* **to do** *or* **go w. sth,** *(voluntarily)* prescindir de algo; *(forcibly)* pasarse sin algo, arreglárselas sin algo. II *adv lit arch* fuera, desde fuera; **w. the city walls,** extramuros.

withstand [wɪð'stænd] *vtr (pt & pp* **withstood)** *(gen)* resistir a; *(pain)* aguantar, soportar.

witness ['wɪtnɪs] I *n* 1 *(person)* testigo *mf*; **John will be my w.,** pongo por testigo a John; **to call sb as a w.,** citar a algn como testigo; *Jur* **w. for the prosecution/for the defence,** testigo de cargo/de descargo. ■ *Jur* **w. box,** *US*

w. stand, barra *f* de los testigos. **2** *(evidence)* testimonio *m*; **to bear w. to sth,** dar fe de *or* atestiguar algo. **3** *Rel* **Jehovah's W.,** testigo *mf* de Jehová. **II** *vtr* **1** *(see)* presenciar; **was the crash witnessed by anybody?,** ¿hay testigos del accidente? **2** *fig (notice)* notar. **3** *Jur* **to w. a document,** firmar un documento como testigo.

witter ['wɪtəʳ] *vi* parlotear; **to w. on about sth,** insistir en un tema.

witty ['wɪtɪ] *adj (wittier, wittiest) (person)* ingenioso,-a, salado,-a; *(remark)* agudo,-a; *(speech)* gracioso,-a.

witticism ['wɪtɪsɪzəm] *n* agudeza *f*, ocurrencia *f*, salida *f*.
◆ **wittily** *adv* ingeniosamente, con gracia.

wittiness ['wɪtɪnɪs] *n* agudeza *f*, ingenio *m*.

wives [waɪvz] *npl see* **wife.**

wizard ['wɪzəd] *n* hechicero *m*, mago *m*; *fam* **a financial w.,** un lince de los negocios.

wizardry ['wɪzədrɪ] *n* hechicería *f*, magia *f*; *fam* genio *m*.

wizened ['wɪzənd] *adj (face)* arrugado,-a; *(withered)* marchito,-a.

wk *abbr of* **week,** semana, sem.

wobble ['wɒbəl] **I** *vi (table)* cojear, tambalearse; *(ladder, bicycle)* titubear; *(jelly)* temblar; *(needle)* oscilar; *(wheel)* trepidar. **2** *(sway)* bambolearse, tambalearse. **II** *n* **1** *(table)* tambaleo *m*; *(ladder, bicycle)* titubeo *m*; *(jelly)* temblor *m*; *(needle)* oscilación *f*; *Aut* **wheel w.,** trepidación *f* de las ruedas. **2** *(swaying)* bamboleo *m*.

wobbly ['wɒblɪ] *adj (table)* tambaleante, cojo,-a; *(ladder, bicycle)* titubeante, poco firme; *(jelly)* temblón,-ona; **my legs feel w.,** tengo las piernas débiles.

woe [wəʊ] *n lit* infortunio *m*, mal *m*; **a tale of w.,** una retahíla de desgracias; **w. betide you if I catch you!,** ¡ay de ti si te cojo! **2 woes,** penas *fpl*, desgracias *f*.

woebegone ['wəʊbɪgɒn] *adj* desconsolado,-a, cariacontecido,-a.

woeful ['wəʊful] *adj* **1** *(person)* afligido,-a, apenado,-a. **2** *(sight)* triste, penoso,-a; **w. ignorance,** una ignorancia lamentable. ◆ **woefully** *adv* tristemente, lamentablemente.

woke [wəʊk] *pt see* **wake**[1].

woken ['wəʊkən] *pp see* **wake**[1].

wolf [wʊlf] **I** *n (pl* **wolves)** **1** *Zool* lobo *m*; *fig* **a w. in sheep's clothing,** un lobo con piel de cordero; *fig* **to cry w.,** gritar '¡al lobo!'; *fig* **to keep the w. from the door,** no pasar hambre. ■ **lone w.,** lobo *m* solitario; **w. cub,** lobato *m*, lobezno *m*. **2** *fam* seductor *m*, tenorio *m*. ■ **w. whistle,** silbido *m* de admiración. **II** *vtr* **to w. (down) one's food,** zampar(se) la comida.

wolfhound ['wʊlfhaʊnd] *n* perro *m* lobo.

wolfish ['wʊlfɪʃ] *adj* lobuno,-a.

wolves [wʊlvz] *npl see* **wolf.**

woman ['wʊmən] *n (pl* **women)** mujer *f*; **old w.,** vieja *f*, anciana *f*; **women's magazine,** revista *f* femenina; **women's libber,** feminista *mf*; **women's liberation movement,** *fam* **women's lib,** movimiento *m* feminista; **women's rights,** derechos *mpl* de la mujer; **young w.,** joven *f*.

womanhood ['wʊmənhʊd] *n (adulto)* edad *f* de mujer; **to reach w.,** hacerse mujer.

womanizer ['wʊmənaɪzəʳ] *n* mujeriego *m*.

womanly ['wʊmənlɪ] *adj* femenino,-a.

women ['wɪmɪn] *npl see* **woman.**

womb [wu:m] *n Anat* matriz *f*, útero *m*.

won [wʌn] *pt & pp see* **win.**

wonder ['wʌndəʳ] **I** *n* **1** *(miracle)* maravilla *f*, milagro *m*; **a nine-day w.,** un prodigio efímero; **no w. he hasn't come,** no es de extrañar que no haya venido; *fig* **to da** *or* **work wonders,** hacer maravillas; *fam* **it's a w. he hasn't lost it,** es un milagro que no lo haya perdido. **2** *(amazement)* admiración *f*, asombro *m*; **they gazed at it in w.,** lo contemplaban asombrados. **II** *adj* **w. drug,** remedio *m* milagroso, panacea *f*. **III** *vtr* **1** *(be surprised)* sorprenderse; **I don't w. that he is angry,** no me extraña que esté enfadado. **2** *(ask oneself)* preguntarse; **I w. why,** ¿por qué será? **IV** *vi* **1** *(marvel)* maravillarse; **to w. at sth,** admirarse de algo; *fam* **he'll be in the bar I shouldn't w.,** me imagino que estará en el bar. **2** *(reflect)* pensar; **it makes you w.,** te da en qué pensar; **I was wondering about going to Spain,** pensaba en la posibilidad de ir a España; **why do you ask? —just wondered,** ¿por qué preguntaste? —por pura curiosidad.

wonderful ['wʌndəful] *adj* maravilloso,-a, estupendo,-a; **we had a w. time,** lo pasamos de maravilla *or* en grande. ◆ **wonderfully** *adv* maravillosamente, de maravilla.

wonderland ['wʌndəlænd] *n* mundo *m* maravilloso; *Lit* **Alice in W.,** Alicia en el País de las Maravillas.

wonderment ['wʌndəmənt] *n* admiración *f*.

wonky ['wɒŋkɪ] *adj (wonkier, wonkiest) fam GB (unstable)* cojo,-a, poco firme; *(not straight)* torcido,-a.

wont [wəʊnt] **I** *adj fml* acostumbrado,-a; **to be w. to,** soler. **II** *n* costumbre; **it is his wont to ...,** tiene la costumbre de ... .

woo [wu:] *vtr (pt & pp* **wooed)** *lit (court)* cortejar; *fig* buscar el favor de; *(voters)* solicitar el apoyo de.

wood [wʊd] *n* **1** *(forest) (often pl)* bosque *m*; *fig* **we're not out of the w. yet,** todavía no estamos a salvo; *fig* **you can't see the w. for the trees,** los árboles no dejan ver el bosque. **2** *(material)* madera *f*; *(for fire)* leña *f*; **sherry from the w.,** jerez *m* de barril; *fig fam* **touch w.!,** ¡toca madera! ■ **w. pulp,** pulpa *f* de madera; **w. shavings,** virutas *fpl*. **3** *Golf* palo *m* de madera. **4** *Sport (bowling)* bola *f*.

woodcarver ['wʊdkɑ:vəʳ] *n* tallista *mf*.

woodcarving ['wʊdkɑ:vɪŋ] *n* **1** *(craft)* tallado *m* en madera. **2** *(object)* talla *f* en madera.

woodcock ['wʊdkɒk] *n Orn* becada *f*, chochaperdiz *f*.

woodcut ['wʊdkʌt] *n* grabado *m* en madera.

woodcutter ['wʊdkʌtəʳ] *n* leñador,-a *m*, *f*.

wooded ['wʊdɪd] *adj* arbolado,-a.

wooden ['wʊdən] *adj* **1** *(of wood)* de madera; **w. spoon/ leg,** cuchara *f*/pata *f* de palo; *GB Sport fam* **to win the w. spoon,** ser el colista. **2** *fig (expression, style)* rígido,-a; *(movement)* tieso,-a; *(acting)* sin expresión.

woodland ['wʊdlənd] *n* bosque *m*, monte *m*, arbolado *m*.

woodlouse ['wʊdlaʊs] *n (pl* **woodlice** ['wʊdlaɪs]*) Ent* cochinilla *f*.

woodpecker ['wʊdpekəʳ] *n Orn* pico *m*, pájaro *m* carpintero. ■ **great spotted w.,** pico *m* picapinos; **green w.,** pito *m* real; **lesser-spotted w.,** pico *m* menor.

wood-pigeon ['wʊdpɪdʒən] *n Orn* paloma *f* torcaz.

woodpile ['wʊdpaɪl] *n* montón *m* de leña.

woodshed ['wʊdʃed] *n* leñera *f*.

woodwind ['wʊdwɪnd] *n Mus* **w. (instruments),** instrumentos *mpl* de viento de madera.

woodwork ['wʊdwɜ:k] *n* **1** *(craft)* carpintería *f*. **2** *(of building)* maderaje *m*, maderamen *m*.

woodworm ['wʊdwɜ:m] *n* carcoma *f*; **it has w.,** está carcomido,-a.

woody ['wʊdɪ] *adj (woodier, woodiest)* **1** *(area)* arbolado,-a. **2** *(texture)* leñoso,-a.

woof [wʊf] *interj (of dog)* ¡guau!

wool [wʊl] **I** *n Tex* lana *f*; **ball of w.,** ovillo *m* de lana; *fig* **to pull the w. over sb's eyes,** engañar a algn, dar gato por liebre a algn; *fam fig* **dyed-in-the-w. communist,** comunista fanático *or* acérrimo. ■ **steel w.,** fibra *f* metálica. **II** *adj* de lana.

woollen, *US* **woolen** ['wʊlən] **I** *adj* **1** *(cloth, dress)* de lana. **2** *Com* lanero,-a. **II** **woollens** *npl* géneros *mpl* de lana *or* de punto.

woolly, *US* **wooly** ['wʊlɪ] **I** *adj* (**woollier, woolliest**, *US* **woolier, wooliest**) **1** (*made of wool*) de lana, lanudo,-a. **2** *fig* (*unclear*) confuso,-a; (*outline*) borroso,-a; (*sound*) impreciso,-a. **II woollies** *npl fam* ropa *f sing* de lana.

word [wɜːd] **I** *n* **1** (*spoken*) palabra *f*; **in other words ...**, es decir ..., o sea ...; **she didn't say a w.**, no dijo ni una palabra *or* ni pío; **without a w.**, sin decir palabra, sin chistar; **words failed me**, me quedé sin habla; *fig* **a w. of advice**, un consejo; *fig* **a w. of warning**, una advertencia; *fig* **don't put words in my mouth**, no me atribuyas cosas que no he dicho; *fig* **he's too stupid for words**, es de lo más estúpido que hay; *fig* **I'd like a w. with you**, quiero hablar contigo un momento; *fig* **it's the last w. in cameras**, el grito en cámaras; *fig* **she didn't have a good w. (to say) for him**, no dijo absolutamente nada en su favor; *fig* **she didn't say it in so many words**, no lo dijo de modo explícito; *fig* **to get a w. in (edgeways)**, meter baza; *fig* **to have words with sb**, tener unas palabras con algn; *fam fig* **to put in a good w. for sb**, interceder por algn. **2** (*written*) palabra *f*, vocablo *m*, voz *f*; **in the words of the poet ...**, como dice el poeta ...; **the words of a song**, la letra de una canción; *fig* **w. for w.**, palabra por palabra. ■ **w. processing**, procesamiento *m* de textos; **w. processor**, procesador *m* de textos. **3** (*message*) mensaje *m*, recado *m*; **by w. of mouth**, de palabra; **is there any w. from him?**, ¿hay noticias de él?; **he left w. that he was going away**, dejó dicho que se marchaba; **to send w.**, mandar recado; **w. came that ...**, llegó noticia de que ... **4** *fig* (*rumour*) voz *f*, rumor *m*; **w. is going round that ...**, corre la voz de que ... **5** *fig* (*promise, assurance*) palabra *f*; **he's a man of his w.**, es hombre de palabra; **I give my w. that...**, doy mi palabra que...; **to keep** *or* **be as good as one's w.**, cumplir su palabra; **w. of honour!**, ¡palabra de honor! **6** *fig* (*command*) orden *f*; **just say the w.**, sus deseos son órdenes. **II** *vtr* (*express*) expresar, formular; **a badly worded letter**, una carta mal redactada.

wording ['wɜːdɪŋ] *n* términos *mpl*, expresión *f*; **I changed the w. slightly**, cambié algunas palabras.

word-perfect [wɜːd'pɜːfekt] *adj* **to be w.-p.**, (*actor*) saber su papel; (*text, speech*) ser correcto,-a hasta la última palabra.

wordplay ['wɜːdpleɪ] *n* juego *m* de palabras.

wordy ['wɜːdɪ] *adj* (**wordier, wordiest**) prolijo,-a, verboso,-a.

wore [wɔː*r*] *pt see* **wear**.

work [wɜːk] **I** *n* **1** (*gen*) trabajo *m*; **a day's w.**, el trabajo de un día; **he was hard at w.**, trabajaba con ahínco; **his w. in the field of physics**, su labor en el campo de la física; **it's hard w.**, cuesta trabajo; **'Men at W.'**; 'Obras'; **to be at w.**, estar trabajando; **to set to w.**, ponerse a trabajar; **we have our w. cut out to finish it**, nos va a costar trabajo terminarlo; *fam* **to make short w. of sth**, despachar algo deprisa. **2** (*employment*) trabajo *m*, empleo *m*; **a day off w.**, un día de asueto; **to be off w.**, estar ausente en el trabajo; **to be out of w.**, estar parado,-a *or* desempleado,-a; **to go to w.**, ir al trabajo. **3** (*action*) obra *f*; **keep up the good w.!**, ¡que siga así!; *fig* **the forces at w.**, los elementos en juego; **just nice w.!**, ¡muy bien!, ¡bravo! **4** (*product*) trabajo *m*, obra *f*; **a piece of w.**, un trabajo, una labor; **a w. of art/action**, una obra de arte/de ficción; **crochet w.**, labor *f* de ganchillo; **it's all my own w.**, es obra de mi propia mano. **5 works**, obras *fpl*; **public w.**, obras (públicas); **road w.**, obras (de carretera). **6 works**, (*machinery*) mecanismo *m sing*; *fam fig* **to give sb the (full) w.**, (*treat well*) tratar a algn a lo grande; (*beat, scold*) sacudirle el polvo a algn. **7 works**, (*factory*) fábrica *f*. **II** *vtr* **1** (*drive*) hacer trabajar; **he works his men very hard**, hace trabajar muchísimo a sus empleados; **to w. oneself to death**, matarse trabajando; **to w. one's way through college**, costearse los estudios trabajando; **to w. one's way up/down**, subir/bajar a duras penas; *fig* **to w. one's way up in a firm**, lograr ascender en una empresa. **2** (*machine*) manejar; (*mechanism*) accionar; (*plan*) realizar; **how do you w. this lighter?** ¿cómo haces funcionar este mechero?; **it is**

worked by electricity, funciona con electricidad. **3** (*miracles, changes*) operar, hacer; *fam* **how can we w. it** (**so that we don't pay**), ¿cómo podemos arreglárnoslas (para no pagar)? **4** *Agr* (*land*) trabajar, cultivar; *Min* (*mine*) explotar. **5** (*wood, metal, etc*) trabajar, labrar; *Culin* **w. the butter into the flour**, mézclese la mantequilla con la harina. **III** *vi* **1** (*gen*) trabajar (**on, at, en**); **down to w.!**, ¡a trabajar!, ¡manos a la obra!; **he's working on the car**, está reparando el coche; **my wife goes out to w.**, mi mujer trabaja fuera de casa; **to w. as a gardener**, trabajar de jardinero; **to w. hard/harder**, trabajar mucho/más; *fam fig* **to w. like a Trojan**, trabajar como un negro; **to w. on a case**, investigar un caso; *Ind* **to w. to rule**, estar en huelga de celo; *fam* **I'm working on it**, estoy en ello. **2** (*machine*) funcionar, marchar; **it works on gas**, funciona con gas; **the light isn't working**, la luz no funciona. **3** (*drug*) surtir efecto; (*system*) funcionar bien; (*plan, trick*) tener éxito, salir bien; **that idea won't w.**, esa idea no es factible. **4** (*operate*) obrar; **it will w. against you**, redundará en contra de ti; **to w. loose**, soltarse, aflojarse; **to w. through**, penetrar (**to**, hasta); **we have no data to w. on**, no tenemos datos en que basarnos; **we w. on the principle that ...**, nos guiamos guiados por el principio de que ...; **we're working towards a solution**, nos vamos aproximando poco a poco a una solución; *fig* **it works both ways**, es un arma de dos filos. ◆ **work off** *vtr* (*fat*) quitarse trabajando; (*energy*) consumir trabajando; (*anger*) desahogar. ◆ **work out I** *vtr* **1** (*plan*) idear, elaborar; (*itinerary*) planear; (*details*) desarrollar; **I've got it all worked out**, lo tengo todo perfectamente planeado. **2** (*problem*) resolver, solucionar; (*solution*) encontrar; (*amount*) calcular; **I can't w. out how he did it**, no me explico cómo lo hizo; **w. out how much I owe you**, calcule cuánto le debo. **II** *vi* **1** (*problem*) resolverse; **things didn't w. out for her**, las cosas no le salieron bien. **2** (*calculation*) salir; **it works out at 5 each**, sale a 5 cada uno. **3** *Sport* hacer ejercicio. ◆ **work up I** *vtr* **1** (*develop*) desarrollar; **I'm working up an appetite**, se me está abriendo el apetito. **2** (*excite*) exaltar, acalorar; **to get worked up**, excitarse, exaltarse; **to w. up enthusiasm**, entusiasmarse (**for**, con, por). **II** *vi* **to w. up to sth**, preparar el terreno para algo.

workable ['wɜːkəbəl] *adj* factible, viable.

workaday ['wɜːkədeɪ] *adj* rutinario,-a.

workaholic [wɜːkə'hɒlɪk] *n fam* adicto,-a *m*, *f* al trabajo.

work-basket ['wɜːkbɑːskɪt] *n Sew* costurero *m*.

workbench ['wɜːkbentʃ] *n* banco *m* de trabajo.

worker ['wɜːkə*r*] *n* **1** (*gen*) trabajador,-a *m*, *f*; (*manual*) obrero,-a *m*, *f*; **he's a good/fast w.**, trabaja bien/con rapidez; *Pol* **the workers**, los obreros, los trabajadores. ■ *Ent* **w. bee**, (abeja) obrera *f*.

workforce ['wɜːkfɔːs] *n* mano *f* de obra.

work-in ['wɜːkɪn] *n* encierro *m* en la fábrica.

working ['wɜːkɪŋ] **I** *adj* **1** (*population, partner, capital*) activo,-a. ■ **w. class**, clase *f* obrera; **w. man**, obrero *m*; **w. party**, grupo *m* de trabajo. **2** (*clothes, surface, conditions*) de trabajo; (*week, hours*) laborable. ■ **w. day**, (*not rest day*) día *m* laborable; (*number of hours*) jornada *f* laboral; **w. lunch**, comida *m* de negocios. **3** (*machine*) **it is in w. order**, funciona; **the w. parts of a machine**, las piezas móviles de una maquina. ■ **w. model**, modelo *m* que funciona. **4** (*majority, knowledge*) suficiente; **w. knoledge**, conocimientos *mlp* básicos. ■ **w. agreement**, acuerdo *m* provisional. **II** *n* **1** (*of machine*) funcionamiento *m*. **2 workings**, (*mechanics*) funcionamiento *m sing*; *Min* (*of pit*) explotación *f sing*.

workload ['wɜːkləʊd] *n* cantidad *f* de trabajo.

workman ['wɜːkmən] *n* (*pl* **workmen**) (*gen*) trabajador *m*; (*manual*) obrero *m*.

workmanlike ['wɜːkmənlaɪk] *adj* hábil, concienzudo,-a, bien hecho,-a.

workmanship ['wɜːkmənʃɪp] *n* (*appearance*) ejecución *f*, hechura *f*; (*skill*) habilidad *f*, arte *m*, **a fine piece of w.**, un trabajo primoroso.

workmate ['wɜːkmeɪt] n compañero,-a m,f de trabajo.

work-out ['wɜːkaʊt] n Sport entrenamiento m; **to have a w.-o.,** hacer ejercicio.

workroom ['wɜːkruːm] n sala f de trabajo.

work-sharing ['wɜːkʃeərɪŋ] n repartición f del trabajo.

worksheet ['wɜːkʃiːt] n Ind plan m de trabajo.

workshop ['wɜːkʃɒp] n taller m.

workshy ['wɜːkʃaɪ] adj gandul,-a, holgazán,-ana.

worktop ['wɜːktɒp] n encimera f.

work-to-rule ['wɜːktə'ruːl] n Ind huelga f de celo.

world [wɜːld] n 1 (gen) mundo m; **all over the w.,** en todo el mundo; **the best in the w.,** el mejor del mundo; **to see the w.,** ver mundo; fig **he would give the w. to know,** daría lo que fuera por saberlo; fig **it will do you the w. of good,** te hará un provecho enorme; fig **there is a w. of difference between A and B, A and B are worlds apart,** hay un mundo de diferencia entre A y B; fig **to come down in the w.,** venir a menos; fig **to come up in the w.,** prosperar, medrar; fig **to feel on top of the w.,** (health) estar como una rosa; (morale) sentirse fenomenal; fig **to think the w. of sb,** querer mucho or adorar a algn; fam fig **his house is out of this w.,** tiene una casa que es un sueño or una maravilla; fam fig **I wouldn't hurt her for the w.,** no la heriría por nada del mundo; fam fig **it's a small w.,** el mundo es un pañuelo; fam fig **it's not the end of the w.,** el mundo no va a hundirse por esto. ■ **the Third W.,** el Tercer Mundo; Fin **the W. Bank,** el Banco Mundial; Ftb **the W. Cup,** el Mundial; **w. power,** potencia f mundial; **w. record,** récord m mundial; **w. war,** guerra f mundial. 2 (life) mundo m, vida f; fig **in this w.,** en esta vida; fig **the next w.,** el otro mundo; fig **to be dead to the w.,** estar profundamente dormido,-a. 3 (sphere) mundo m; **the animal w.,** el reino animal; **the business/theatre w.,** el mundo comercial/del teatro; fam fig **he is** or **lives in a w. of his own,** vive ajeno a las cosas de este mundo.

world-class ['wɜːldklɑːs] adj de categoría mundial.

world-famous ['wɜːldfeɪməs] adj de fama mundial.

worldliness ['wɜːldlɪnɪs] n mundanería f.

worldly ['wɜːldlɪ] adj mundano,-a; **w. goods,** bienes mpl materiales.

world-weary ['wɜːldwɪːrɪ] adj hastiado,-a del mundo.

worldwide ['wɜːldwaɪd] adj mundial, universal.

worm [wɜːm] n 1 Zool gusano m; fig **w.'s eye view,** vista f a ras de tierra; fam fig **the w. has turned,** se me or le ha agotado la paciencia; fam fig **you w.!,** ¡vil gusano! ■ **(earth) w.,** lombriz f. 2 Med worms, lombrices fpl. 3 Mech (of screw) tornillo m sin fin. ■ **w. gear,** engranaje m de tornillo sin fin. II vtr sacar; **to w. a secret out of sb,** sonsacarle un secreto a algn; fam fig **to w. one's way into a group,** colarse en un grupo.

worm-eaten ['wɜːmiːtən] adj (wood) carcomido,-a; (fruit) agusanado,-a.

wormwood ['wɜːmwʊd] n Bot ajenjo m.

worn [wɔːn] I pp of **wear.** II adj gastado,-a, usado,-a.

worn-out ['wɔːnaʊt] adj (thing) gastado,-a, estropeado,-a, (person) rendido,-a, agotado,-a.

worried ['wʌrɪd] adj inquieto,-a, preocupado,-a; **to get w.,** inquietarse.

worrier ['wʌrɪəʳ] n **to be a w.,** ser propenso,-a a preocuparse.

worry ['wʌrɪ] I vtr (pt & pp **worried**) 1 (make anxious) preocupar, inquietar; **it doesn't w. me,** me tiene sin cuidado; fam **don't w. your head about it,** no te preocupes en absoluto por eso. 2 (pester) molestar. 3 (dog) perseguir, atacar. II vi preocuparse, inquietarse (about, over, por); **don't w.,** no te preocupes, no importa; **there's no need to w.,** no hay por qué inquietarse. III n (state) inquietud f, intranquilidad f; (cause) preocupación f; **financial worries,** problemas mpl económicos; **that's the least of my worries,** eso es lo que menos me preocupa.

worrying ['wʌrɪŋ] adj inquietante, preocupante; fam **he's the w. sort,** es de los que se inquietan por nada.

worse [wɜːs] I adj (comp of **bad**) peor; **I have seen w.,** he visto casos peores; **in a w. condition than before,** en peor condición que antes; **it** or **he gets w. and w.,** va de mal en peor; **to get w.,** empeorar; **to make matters w.,** para colmo de desgracias; fig **he's none the w. for the experience,** la experiencia no le ha perjudicado; fam **so much** or **all the w. for him,** tanto peor para él; fam **w. luck!,** mala suerte; fam fig **to be the w. for drink,** estar bebido,-a or borracho,-a. II **the w.** n lo peor; **a change for the w.,** un empeoramiento; fig **to take a turn for the w.,** empeorar. III adv (comp of **badly**) peor; **he is behaving w. than ever/w. and w.,** se está portando peor que nunca/ cada vez peor; **I am w. off than before,** (in health) me encuentro peor que antes; (financially) ando peor de dinero que antes; **I don't think any the w. of her for that,** no la estimo en menos por eso.

worship ['wɜːʃɪp] I vtr (pt & pp **worshipped**) Rel adorar, venerar; fig **he worships money,** rinde culto al dinero. II n 1 Rel adoración f, culto m; fig adoración f, veneración f. 2 Rel (ceremony) culto m. ■ **place of w.,** templo m. 3 GB (address) **his W. the Mayor,** el señor alcalde; Jur **yes, your W.,** sí, su señoría.

worshipper ['wɜːʃɪpəʳ] n adorador,-a m,f, devoto,-a m,f.

worst [wɜːst] I adj (superl of **bad**) peor; **his w. mistake,** su error más grave; **the w. part about it is that ...,** lo peor es que ...; **the w. two pupils in the class,** los dos peores alumnos de la clase. II n 1 (person) el or la peor, los or las peores. 2 (impersonal) lo peor; **the w. of the storm is over,** ya ha pasado lo peor de la tormenta; fig **let him do his w.,** que haga todo lo que quiera. III adv (superl of **badly**) peor; **the w. dressed man,** el hombre peor vestido; **the w. off,** (gen) los más perjudicados; (financially) los más pobres; fig **to come off w.,** llevarse la peor parte.

worsted ['wʊstɪd] n Tex estambre m.

worth [wɜːθ] I adj 1 (of the value of) que vale, con un valor de; **a house w. £50,000,** una casa que vale 50.000 libras; **it's w. the money,** (before buying) vale lo que piden; (after buying) vale lo que costó; fam fig **it's more than my job is w.,** me jugaría or arriesgaría mi empleo; fam fig **she's w. a fortune,** está forrada. 2 (deserving of) lo que merece, merecedor,-a de; **a book w. reading,** un libro que merece la pena leer; **for what it's w.,** por si sirve de algo; **it's w. a visit,** vale la pena visitarlo; **it's w. the trouble** or **it's w. your while** or **it's w. it,** vale or merece la pena; **it's w. thinking about/mentioning,** es digno de consideración/mención. II n 1 (in money) valor m; **five pounds' w. of petrol,** gasolina por valor de 5 libras, 5 libras de gasolina; fam fig **to get one's money's w.,** sacarle jugo a su dinero. 2 (of person) valía f.

worthless ['wɜːθlɪs] adj (gen) sin valor; (effort) inútil; (person) despreciable.

worthlessness ['wɜːθlɪsnɪs] n falta f de valor.

worthwhile [wɜːθ'waɪl] adj valioso,-a, útil, que vale la pena; **the journey was w.,** el viaje merecía la pena.

worthy ['wɜːðɪ] I adj (**worthier, worthiest**) 1 (deserving) digno,-a (**of,** de), merecedor,-a (**of,** de); (winner, cause) justo,-a; **it is w. of attention,** es digno,-a de atención; **there is no musem w. of the name,** no hay museo que merezca ese nombre; **w. opponent,** un adversario digno de respeto. 2 (distinguished) benemérito,-a; (citizen) respetable, honorable; (effort, motives) loable; (action) meritorio,-a. II n hum prócer m.

worthiness ['wɜːðɪnɪs] n mérito m.

would [wʊd, unstressed wəd] v aux 1 (conditional) **I w.** or **I'd go if I had time,** iría si tuviera tiempo; **he w.** or **he'd have won but for that,** habría ganado si no hubiera sido por eso; **we w. if we could,** lo haríamos si pudiéramos. 2 (reported speech) **he said that he w.** or **he'd come,** dijo que vendría. 3 (willingness) **the car wouldn't start,** el coche no arrancaba; **they asked him to come but he wouldn't,** le invitaron a venir pero no quiso; **w. you do me a favour?,** ¿quiere hacerme un favor? **4** *(wishing)* **he w.** *or* **he'd like to know why,** quisiera saber por qué; **I'd rather go home,** preferiría ir a casa; **w. you like a cigarette?,** ¿quiere un pitillo?; *arch* **w. that I could,** ojalá que pudiera. **5** *(custom)* **we w.** *or* **we'd go for walks,** solíamos dar un paseo. **6** *(persistence)* **try as I w.,** por mucho que lo intentara; **well, if you w. eat so many apples ...,** pues si te empeñaste en comer tantas manzanas ... . **7** *(conjecture)* **it w. have been about three weeks ago,** debe haber sido hace unas tres semanas; **w. this be your cousin?,** ¿será éste su primo? **8** *(expectation)* **so it w. appear,** según parece.

would-be ['wʊdbiː] *adj* en potencia; **a w.-be politician,** un aspirante a político; **the w.-be assassin,** el asesino fracasado; *pej* **a w.-be poet,** un supuesto poeta.

wound¹ [waʊnd] *pt & pp see* **wind².**

wound² [wuːnd] **I** *n* herida *f*; *fig* **he left licking his wounds,** se fue con el rabo entre las piernas; *fig* **to rub salt into the w., he said ...,** para hacer más daño todavía, dijo ... . **II** *vtr* herir.

wounded ['wuːndɪd] *adj* herido,-a.

wounding ['wuːndɪŋ] *adj* hiriente.

wove [wəʊv] *pt see* **weave.**

woven ['wəʊvən] *pp see* **weave.**

wow [waʊ] *fam* **I** *n* éxito *m* sensacional; **it was a w.,** fue sensacional. **II** *vtr (spectators etc)* encandilar. **III** *interj* ¡caramba!

WP [dʌbəljuː'piː] **1** *abbr of* **word processing,** procesamiento *m* de textos. **2** *abbr of* **word processor,** procesador *m* de textos.

WPC [dʌbəljuːpiː'siː] *GB abbr of* **Woman Police Constable.**

wpm [dʌbəljuːpiː'em] *Com abbr of* **words per minute,** pulsaciones *fpl* por minuto, p.p.m.

WRAC [dʌbəljuːɑːreɪ'siː, *fam* ræk] *fam GB Mil abbr of* **Women's Royal Army Corps.**

WRAF [dʌbəljuːɑːreɪ'ef, *fam* ræf] *GB Mil abbr of* **Women's Royal Air Force.**

wrangle ['ræŋgəl] **I** *n* disputa *f*, altercado *m*. **II** *vi* disputar (**over,** acerca de, por), reñir (**over,** acerca de, por).

wrap [ræp] **I** *vtr (pt & pp wrapped)* **1** *(parcel etc)* **to w.** (**up**), envolver; **he wrapped his arms around her,** la estrechó entre sus brazos; **he wrapped his scarf round his neck,** se abrigó con la bufanda; *fig* **wrapped in mystery,** rodeado,-a en el misterio; *fig* **wrapped up in one's work/one's thoughts/oneself,** absorto,-a en su trabajo/en sus pensamientos/en sí mismo,-a; *fam* **we soon wrapped up the deal,** no tardamos nada en concluir el negocio. **II** *vi* **1** *(snake, rope)* **to w. round sth,** enrollarse *or* enroscarse en algo; *fam* **w. up well,** abrígate. **2** *(be quiet)* callarse; *fam* **w. up!,** ¡cierra el pico! **III** *n (shawl)* chal *m*; *(cape)* capa *f*; *(housecoat)* bata *f*; *fam fig* **to keep sth under wraps,** mantener algo secreto.

wrapper ['ræpər] *n (of sweet)* envoltorio *m*; *(of book)* sobrecubierta *f*.

wrapping ['ræpɪŋ] *n* envoltura *f*, envoltorio *m*. ■ **w. paper,** papel *m* de envolver.

wreath [riːθ] *n (pl wreaths* [riːðz, riːθs]*) (of flowers)* corona *f*. ■ **laurel w.,** corona *f* de laurel.

wreathe [riːð] *vtr* enguirnaldar, coronar; *fig* **wreathed in mist,** envuelto,-a en niebla.

wreck [rek] **I** *n* **1** *Naut* naufragio *m*; *(ship)* barco *m* naufragado *or* hundido. **2** *(of car, plane)* restos *mpl*; *(of building)* ruinas *fpl*; **the car was a complete w.,** el coche quedó completamente destrozado; *fam* **he drives an old w.,** conduce un cacharro. **3** *fig (person)* ruina *f*; **I'm a nervous w.,** tengo los nervios destrozados. **II** *vtr* **1** *Naut (ship)* hacer naufragar. **2** *(car, plane)* destrozar, estropear; *(machine)* desbaratar. **3** *fig (health, career)* arruinar; *(life, marriage)* destrozar; *(hopes)* destruir; *(plans)* estropear, desbaratar; *(chances)* echar a perder.

wreckage ['rekɪdʒ] *n (of ship, car, plane)* restos *mpl*; *(of building)* ruinas *fpl*.

wrecked ['rekt] *adj* **1** *(ship)* naufragado,-a; *(sailor)* náufrago,-a. **2** *(car, plane)* destrozado,-a; *(building)* destruido,-a. **3** *fig (life, career)* arruinado,-a; *(hopes)* arruinado,-a; *(plans)* estropeado,-a.

wrecker ['rekər] *n US* **1** *(of building)* demoledor,-a *m,f*. **2** *Aut* **w. (truck),** grúa *f*.

wren [ren] *n Orn* chochín *m*.

wrench [rentʃ] **I** *n* **1** *(pull)* tirón *m*, arranque *m*; **to give sth a w.,** darle un tirón brusco a algo. **2** *Med* torcedura *f*. **3** *fig* separación *f* dolorosa; **it will be a w. for me to leave,** me costará trabajo irme. **4** *(tool)* **(monkey) w.,** *GB* llave *f* inglesa; *US* llave *f*. **II** *vtr (pull)* **to w. oneself free,** soltarse de un tirón; **to w. sth off sb/out of sb's hands,** arrebatarle algo a algn/de las manos de algn; **to w. sth off/out/open,** quitar/arrancar/abrir algo de un tirón.

wrest [rest] *vtr* **to w. sth from sb,** arrebatarle *or* arrancarle algo a algn.

wrestle ['resəl] *vi Sport* luchar.

wrestler ['reslər] *n Sport* luchador,-a *m,f*.

wrestling ['reslɪŋ] *n Sport* lucha *f*. ■ **all-in w.,** lucha libre; **w. match,** combate *m* de lucha.

wretch [retʃ] **I** *n* **1** **(poor) w.,** pobre diablo *m*, desgraciado,-a *m,f*. **2** *(child)* pillo,-a *m,f*, pícaro,-a *m,f*; **you little w.!,** ¡granuja!, ¡tunante!

wretched ['retʃɪd] *adj* **1** *(unhappy)* desdichado,-a, abatido,-a; **I felt w. about it,** me dio mucha pena. **2** *(pitiful, unfortunate)* desgraciado,-a, desdichado,-a; *(conditions)* miserable, lamentable; *fam (bad, poor)* horrible, malísimo; **what w. weather!,** ¡qué tiempo más feo *or* espantoso! **3** *(ill)* indispuesto,-a; **I feel w.,** me encuentro fatal. **4** *(contemptible)* miserable, despreciable. **5** *fam (damned)* maldito,-a, condenado,-a; **that w. boy,** ese maldito chiquillo.

wretchedness ['retʃɪdnɪs] *n* **1** *(unhappiness, misfortune)* desdicha *f*, desgracia *f*. **2** *(of conditions)* miseria *f*.

wriggle ['rɪgəl] **I** *vtr (gen)* menear; *fam fig* **how did he w. his way in?,** ¿cómo logró introducirse? **II** *vi* **to w.** (**about**), *(worm)* serpentear, retorcerse; *(restless child)* moverse *or* revolverse nerviosamente; **to w. free,** escapar deslizándose; *fam fig* **to w. out of tight spot/obligation,** librarse habilmente de un apuro/una obligación.

wriggly ['rɪglɪ] *adj* sinuoso,-a.

wring [rɪŋ] *vtr (pt & pp wrung)* **1** *(clothes)* escurrir; *(hands)* retorcer; **to w. the neck of a chicken,** retorcerle el pescuezo a un pollo; *fam* **I'll w. his neck if I catch him,** si lo pillo lo mato *or* le retuerzo el pescuezo. **2** *fig (extract)* arrancar, sacar; **to w. money/a secret out of sb,** arrancarle dinero/un secreto a algn.

wringer ['rɪŋər] *n* escurridor *m*; *fam* **to put sb through the w.,** hacer pasar un mal trago a algn.

wringing ['rɪŋɪŋ] *adj* **to be w. wet,** *(garment)* estar empapado,-a; *(person)* estar calado,-a hasta los huesos.

wrinkle ['rɪŋkəl] **I** *n* arruga *f*. **II** *vtr* arrugar. **III** *vi* arrugarse.

wrinkled ['rɪŋkəld] *adj* arrugado,-a.

wrist [rɪst] *n Anat* muñeca *f*.

wristwatch ['rɪstwɒtʃ] *n* reloj *m* de pulsera.

writ [rɪt] *n Jur* mandamiento *m or* orden *f* judicial, auto *m*; **to issue a w. against sb,** llevar a algn a juicio; **to serve a w. on sb,** entregar una orden a algn.

write [raɪt] **I** *vtr (pt wrote; pp written) (gen)* escribir; *(article)* redactar; *(cheque)* extender; *US* **to w. sb,** escribir a algn; *fig* **his guilt is written all over his face,** lleva la culpabilidad escrita *or* impresa en la cara. **II** *vi* escribir (**about,** sobre); **he writes,** es escritor; *Press* **to w. for a paper,** colaborar en un periódico; **to w. (in) for sth,** escribir pidiendo algo; **we w. (to each other) regularly,** nos escribimos *or* nos carteamos con regularidad; **w. to this address,** diríjase a la dirección siguiente; *fam fig* **it's**

nothing to w. home about, no es nada del otro mundo. ◆ **write away** *vi* to **w. away for sth,** pedir algo por escrito. ◆ **write back** *vi* contestar. ◆ **write down** *vtr (gen)* poner por escrito; *(note)* apuntar, anotar. ◆ **write in I** *vtr* insertar (en un escrito). **II** *vi* escribir; **many listeners wrote in to complain,** muchos oyentes escribieron quejándose. ◆ **write off I** *vtr Fin* dar por perdido; *(car)* destrozar, *(person)* dar por acabado,-a. **II** *vi* escribir; **to w. off for sth,** pedir algo por escrito. ◆ **write out** *vtr (cheque, recipe)* extender; **to w. sth out neatly,** pasar algo a limpio; **w. up your name out in full,** escríbase su nombre completo. ◆ **write up** *vtr (notes, theis)* redactar; *(diary, journal)* poner al día.

write-off ['raɪtɒf] *n* ruina *f*; **the car's a w.-o.,** el coche está hecho una ruina.

writer ['raɪtə'] *n* **1** *(by profession)* escritor,-a *m,f*; *(of book, letter)* autor,-a *m,f*. **2** *(of handwriting)* **to be a good/bad w.,** tener buena/mala letra.

write-up ['raɪtʌp] *n* reportaje *m*; *Cin Theat* crítica *f*, reseña *f*.

writhe [raɪð] *vi* retorcerse.

writing ['raɪtɪŋ] *n* **1** *(script)* escritura *f*; *(handwriting)* letra *f*; **I can't read his w.,** no entiendo su letra; **(to put sth) in w.,** (poner algo) por escrito; *fig* **the w. on the wall,** los malos presagios. **2 writings,** escritos *mpl*. **3** *(action)* escritura *f*. ■ **w. desk,** escritorio *m*. **4** *(profession)* profesión *f* de escritor, trabajo *m* literario.

written ['rɪtən] **I** *pp see* **write. II** *adj* escrito,-a; **w. consent,** consentimiento por escrito; **w. exam,** examen escrito.

WRNS [dʌbəljuːɑːren'es, *fam* renz] *GB Mil abbr of* **Women's Royal Naval Service.**

wrong [rɒŋ] **I** *adj* **1** *(erroneous)* incorrecto,-a, erróneo,-a, equivocado,-a; *Mus* **a w. note,** una nota falsa; **I got the w. train,** me equivoqué de tren; **my watch is I w.,** mi reloj anda mal; *Tel* **sorry, I've got the w. number,** lo siento, me he confundido de número; **the lamp is in the w. place,** la lámpara está mal colocada; **to drive on the w. side of the road,** conducir por el lado contrario de la carretera; **to go the w. way,** equivocarse de camino; *fam* **the cake has gone down the w. way,** se me ha atragantado el pastel; *fam fig* **you're going the w. way about it,** lo estás haciendo mal. **2** *(unsuitable)* impropio,-a inadecuado,-a; *(time)* inoportuno,-a; **he's the w. man for the job,** no es la persona apropiada para el puesto; **to say the w. thing,** decir algo inoportuno; *fig* **to be on the w. side of forty,** tener cuarenta años bien cumplidos; *fam fig* **to get out of bed on the w. side,** levantarse con el pie izquierdo. **3** *(not right) (person)* equivocado,-a; **I was w. about that boy,** me equivoqué con ese chico; **to be w.,** no tener razón, estar equivocado,-a; **you're not all w.,** no andas muy descaminado,-a; **you're w. in thinking that ...,** te equivocas si piensas que ... . **4** *(immoral etc)* malo,-a; **it is w. to steal,** robar está mal; **it was w. of him to say that,** hizo mal en decir eso; **there's nothing w. in that,** no hay nada malo en eso; **what's w. with smoking?,** ¿qué tiene de malo fumar? **5** *(amiss)* **is anything w.?,** ¿pasa algo?; **something's w. (somewhere),** hay algo que no está bien; **there's something w. with the car,** se ha averiado el coche; **what's w.?,** ¿qué hay?; **what's w. with you?,** ¿qué te pasa?, ¿qué tienes? **II** *adv* mal, incorrectamente; **everything has gone w.,** todo ha salido mal; **to get it w.,** equivocarse, no acertar; **to get the answer w.,** contestar mal; *Math* equivocarse en el cálculo; **you can't go w.,** no tiene pérdida; **you won't go far w. if ...,** no andarás muy descaminado,-a si ...; *fam fig* **don't get me w.,** no me comprendas mal; *fam* **to go w.,** *(mistake)* equivocarse; *(on road)* equivocarse de camino; *(machinery, watch)* estropearse; *(plan)* fallar, fracasar; *fam fig* **you've got it w.,** te equivocas lo entiendes mal; *fam* **you're doing it (all) w.,** lo estás haciendo (muy) mal. **III** *n* **1** *(evil, bad action)* mal *m*; **to know right from w.,** saber distinguir entre el bien y el mal; **you did w. to hit him,** hiciste mal en pegarle; *fam fig* **two wrongs do not make a right,** no se subsana un error cometiendo otro. **2** *(injustice)* injusticia *f*; *(offence)* agravio *m*; **the rights and wrongs of a matter,** lo justo y lo injusto de un asunto; **to right a w.,** deshacer un entuerto. **3** **to be in the w.,** *(to blame)* tener la culpa; *(mistaken)* no tener razón. **IV** *vtr (treat unfairly)* ser injusto,-a con; *(judge unfairly)* juzgar mal; *(offend)* agraviar. ◆ **wrongly** *adv* **1** *(incorrectly)* incorrectamente, mal; **w. worded,** mal expresado,-a. **2** *(mistakenly)* equivocadamente, erróneamente, sin razón; **rightly or w.,** por fas o por nefas. **3** *(unjustly)* injustamente.

wrongdoer ['rɒŋduːə'] *n* malhechor,-a *m,f*.

wrongdoing ['rɒŋduːɪŋ] *n* maldad *f*.

wrongful ['rɒŋfʊl] *adj* injusto,-a, ilegal; **w. dismissal,** despido *m* improcedente.

wrote [rəʊt] *pt see* **write.**

wrung [rʌŋ] *pt & pp see* **wring.**

wry [raɪ] *adj (wrier, wriest or wryer, wryest)* sardónico,-a, irónico,-a.

wryneck ['raɪnek] *n Orn* torcecuello *m*.

WWF [dʌbəljuːdʌbəljuː'ef] *abbr of* **World Wildlife Fund,** Fondo *m* mundial para la naturaleza.

X

X, x [eks] *n (the letter)* X, x *f*; **Mr X,** el Sr. X; *Cin* **X certificate,** para mayores de 18 años.

xenon ['zenɒn] *n Chem* xenón *m*.

xenophobia [zanə'fəʊbɪə] *adj* xenofobia *f*.

xenophobic [zanə'fəʊbɪk] *adj* xenófobo,-a.

xerography [zɪ'rɒgrəfɪ] *n* xerografía *f*.

Xerox® ['zɪərɒks] **I** *n* xerocopia *f*. **II** *vtr* xerocopiar.

XL [eks'el] *abbr of* **extra large (size),** (talla *f*) muy grande.

Xmas [eksməs, 'krɪsməs] *n abbr of* **Christmas,** Navidad *f*.

X-ray [eks'reɪ] **I** *n* **1** *(beam)* rayo *m* X; **X-r. therapy,** radioterapia *f*. **2** *(picture)* radiografía *f*; **to have an X-r.,** hacerse una radiografía. **II** *vtr* radiografiar.

xylene ['zaɪliːn] *n Chem* xileno *m*.

xylograph ['zaɪləgrɑːf] *n* xilografía *f*.

xylography [zaɪ'lɒgrəfɪ] *n* xilografía *f*.

xylophone ['zaɪləfəʊn] *n* xilófono *m*.

xylophonist [zaɪ'lɒfənɪst] *n* xilofonista *mf*.

Y

Y, y [waɪ] *n (the letter)* Y, y *f*.

yacht [jɒt] I *n* yate *m*; **y. club,** club *m* náutico; **y. race,** regata *f*. II *vi* **1** ir en yate, dar un paseo en yate. **2** *Sport* participar en una regata.

yachting ['jɒtɪŋ] *n Sport* navegación *f* a vela; *(competition)* regatas *fpl*.

yachtsman ['jɒtsmən] *n (pl yachtsmen)* tripulante *m* de yates, deportista *m* de vela, balandrista *m*.

yachtswoman ['jɒtswʊmən] *n (pl yatchtswomen* ['jɒtswɪmɪn]*)* tripulante *f* de yates, deportista *f* de vela, balandrista *f*.

yak [jæk] *n Zool* yac *m*, yak *m*.

yam [jæm] *n Bol* **1** ñame *m*. **2** *US (sweet potato)* boniato *m*.

Yank [jæŋk] *n GB pej* yanqui *mf*.

yank [jæŋk] *fam* I *vtr* tirar; *(tooth)* arrancar. II *n* tirón *m*; **give it a y.,** dale un tirón.

Yankee ['jæŋkɪ] *adj & n pej* yanqui *mf*.

yap [jæp] I *vi (pt & pp yapped)* **1** *(of dog)* aullar. **2** *fam (of person)* darle al pico *or* a la sinhueso. II *n* aullido *m*.

yard¹ [jɑ:d] *n* **1** *(measure)* yarda *f* (=0.914 metros). **2** *Naut* verga *f*.

yard² [jɑ:d] *n* patio *m*; *US* jardín *m*; *(of school)* patio de recreo; **back y.,** patio *m*; **builder's y.,** depósito *m* de materiales; *Rail* **goods y.,** depósito *m* de mercancías.

yardage ['jɑ:dɪdʒ] *n* medida *f* en yardas.

yardarm ['jɑ:dɑ:m] *n Naut* penol *m*.

yardstick ['jɑ:dstɪk] *n* vara *f* que mide una yarda; *fig* criterio *m*, norma *f*.

yarn [jɑ:n] *n* **1** *Sew* hilo *m*, hilado *m*. **2** *(story)* historia *f*, cuento *m*; *(lie)* **to spin a y.,** inventarse *or* contar una historia.

yawl [jɔ:l] *n Naut* yola *f*.

yawn [jɔ:n] I *vi* bostezar. II *n* bostezo *m*; *fig* aburrimiento *m*.

yawning ['jɔ:nɪŋ] *adj (of gap)* profundo,-a.

yaws [jɔ:z] *n Med* pián *m*, frambesia *f*.

yd *(pl yds)* abbr of **yard,** yarda *f*.

ye [ji:, *unstressed* jɪ] *pers pron arch* vos.

yea [jeɪ] *adv & n arch* sí *m*.

yeah [jeə] *adv fam* sí.

year [jɪəʳ] *n* **1** *(period of time)* año *m*; **all y. round,** durante todo el año; **a y. ago last March,** en marzo hizo un año; **I haven't seen you for (donkey's) years,** hace siglos que no te veo; **last y.,** el año pasado; **next y.,** el próximo año, el año que viene; **the New Y.,** el Año nuevo; **y. in, y. out, y. after y.,** año tras año. ■ **calendar y.,** año *m* civil; **financial y.,** año *m* económico; **leap y.,** año *m* bisiesto; **light y.,** año *m* luz; **New Y.'s Day,** el día de Año nuevo; **New Y.'s Eve,** Noche *f* vieja; **school y.,** año *m* escolar. **2** *(age)* año *m*; **he's getting on in years,** va para viejo; **I'm ten years old,** tengo diez años; *fam fig* **to put years on sb,** echarle años a algn. **3** *Educ* curso *m*; **first-y-student,** estudiante de primero; **she's in my y.,** es de mi curso.

yearbook ['jɪəbʊk] *n* boletín *m* or revista *f* anual, anuario *m*.

yearling ['jɪəlɪŋ] *adj & n* primal,-a *m, f*. ■ **y. (colt),** potro *m* de un año.

yearly ['jɪəlɪ] I *adj* anual. II *adv* anualmente, cada año.

yearn [jɜ:n] *vi* anhelar, añorar; **to y. for sth,** anhelar algo.

yearning ['jɜ:nɪŋ] *n* anhelo *m*, ansia *f* (**for,** de).

yeast [ji:st] *n Culin* levadura *f*.

yell [jel] I *vi* gritar, aullar. II *vtr (insults etc)* gritar. III *n* grito *m*, alarido *m*.

yellow ['jeləʊ] I *adj* amarillo,-a; *Press (press)* sensacionalista; *fam fig (cowardly)* cobarde. ■ **y. fever,** fiebre *f* amarilla; **y. pages,** páginas *fpl* amarillas. II *n* amarillo *m*. III *vi* volverse amarillo,-a.

yellowhammer ['jeləʊhæməʳ] *n Orn* escribano *m* cerillo.

yellowish ['jeləʊɪʃ] *adj* amarillento,-a.

yelp [jelp] I *vi* gañir, aullar. II *n* gañido *m*, aullido *m*.

Yemen ['jemən] *n (the)* Y., (el) Yemen.

Yemeni ['jemənɪ] *adj & n* yemení *(mf)*, yemenita *(mf)*.

Yen [jen] *n inv Fin* yen *m*.

yen [jen] *n (desire)* deseo *m*, ganas *fpl*.

yeoman ['jəʊmən] *n (pl yeomen)* GB Mil **Y. of the Guard,** alabardero *m* de la Casa Real británica.

yes [jes] I *adv* **1** *(affirmation)* sí; **to answer y. or no,** responder sí o no; **you said y.,** dijiste que sí. **2** *(interrogation) (answering knock at the door)* ¿quién es?; *(answering person in same room)* ¿dime?; *Tel* ¿dígame?; *(in surprise)* ¿de verdad? **3** *(answering a summons)* **y.!,** ¡voy! II *n (affirmation)* sí *m*.

yes-man ['jesmæn] *n (pl yes-men* ['jesmen]*)* cobista *m*, pelota *m*.

yesterday ['jestədeɪ] *adv & n* ayer *m*; **the day before y.,** anteayer; **y. morning,** ayer por la mañana; **y. week,** ayer hizo una semana.

yesteryear ['jestəjɪəʳ] *adv lit (of)* **y.,** (de) antaño.

yet [jet] I *adv* **1** *(so far)* aún no, todavía no; **as y.,** hasta ahora; **I haven't decided y.,** aún no lo he decidido; *(in a question)* **has he arrived y.?,** ¿ha venido ya? **2** *(even)* más; **y. again,** otra vez; **y. more,** todavía más, más aún; **y. more flowers,** más flores aún. **3** *(eventually)* todavía, aún; **he'll win y.,** todavía puede ganar. II *conj* sin embargo; **y. I like him,** sin embargo, me gusta.

yeti ['jetɪ] *n* yeti *m*.

yew [ju:] *n Bot* tejo *m*.

Yiddish ['jɪdɪʃ] I *adj* judeoalemán,-a. II *n (language)* dialecto *m* judeoalemán, yiddish *m*.

yield [ji:ld] I *n* **1** *(gen)* rendimiento *m*, producción *f*. **2** *Agr* cosecha *f*. **3** *Fin* beneficio *m*, rédito *m*. ■ **net y.,** rédito *m*. II *vtr (results, interest)* producir; *Agr* dar buena cosecha; *(money)* rendir. III *vi* **1** *(surrender)* rendirse, ceder. **2** *(break)* hundirse, ceder; *Traffic* ceder el paso.

yielding ['ji:ldɪŋ] *adj* **1** *(flexible)* blando,-a, flexible. **2** *(person)* complaciente.

yippee [jɪ'pi:] *interj fam* ¡yupi!

YMCA [waɪemsɪ'eɪ] *abbr of* **Young Men's Christian Association,** albergue *m* para jóvenes hombres.

yob(bo) [jɒb(əʊ)] *n fam* gamberro,-a *m, f*, macarra *mf*.

yod [jɒd] *n Ling* yod *f*.

yodel ['jəʊdəl] *vi (pt & pp yodelled, US yodeled)* cantar a la tirolesa *or* al estilo tirolés.

yoga ['jəʊgə] *n* yoga *m*.

yog(h)urt ['jɒgət] *n* yogur *m*.

yoke [jəʊk] I *n* **1** *(cross-piece)* yugo *m*; *fig* yugo *m*. **2** *(pair of oxen)* yunta *f*. **3** *Sew* canesú *m*. II *vtr (oxen)* uncir; *fig* unir.

yokel ['jəʊkəl] *n pej* paleto,-a *m, f*, patán *m*.

yolk [jəʊk] *n* yema *f*.

yon [jɒn] *adj arch (sing)* aquel, aquella; *(pl)* aquellos,-as.

yonder ['jɒndəʳ] I *adj arch (sing)* aquel, aquella; *(pl)* aquellos,-as. II *adv* más allá.

yonks [jɒŋks] *n pl fam* tira *f*; **y. ago,** hace la tira.

you [juː, *unstressed* jʊ] *pers pron* **1** *(subject) (familiar use) (sing)* tú; *(pl)* vosotros,-as; **how are y?,** ¿cómo estás?, ¿cómo estáis? **2** *(subject) (polite use) (sing)* usted; *(pl)* ustedes; **how are y.?,** ¿cómo está?, ¿cómo están? **3** *(subject) (impers use)* se; **y. never know,** nunca se sabe. **4** *(object) (familiar use) (sing) (before verb)* te; *(after preposition)* ti; *(pl) (before verb)* os; *(after preposition)* vosotros,-as; **I saw y.,** te vi, os vi; **it's for y.,** es para ti, es para vosotros,-as; **with you,** contigo, con vosotros,-as. **5** *(object) (polite use) (sing) (before verb)* le; *(after preposition)* usted; *(pl) (before verb)* les; *(after preposition)* ustedes; **I saw y.,** le vi, les vi; **it's for y.,** es para usted, es para ustedes; **with you,** con usted, con ustedes. **6** *(object) (impers use)* **alcohol makes you drunk,** el alcohol emborracha.

young [jʌŋ] **I** *adj (age)* joven; *(sister, brother, etc)* pequeño,-a; *fig* **the night is still y.,** la noche es joven; *fam* **I'm not as y. as I was,** los años no pasan en balde; *fam* **you are only y. once,** sólo se vive una vez. ■ **y. lady,** señorita *f; (fiancée)* prometida *f;* **y. man,** joven *m; (fiancé)* prometido *m.* **II** *n* **1** *(people)* **the y.,** los jóvenes, la juventud. **2** *(animals)* crías *fpl.*

youngster ['jʌŋstə'] *n* muchacho,-a *m,f,* joven *mf;* **the youngsters,** los chicos.

your [jɔː, *unstressed* jə] *poss adj* **1** *(familiar use) (sing)* tu, tus; *(pl)* vuestro,-a, vuestros,-as; **y. car,** tu coche, vuestro coche; **y. books,** tus libros, vuestros libros. **2** *(polite use)* su, sus; **y. car,** su coche; **y. books,** sus libros. **3** *(impers use)* el, la, los, las; **the house is on y. right,** la casa queda a la derecha; **they clean y. shoes for you,** te limpian los zapatos; **you get y. ticket first,** primero se compra el billete. **4** *(formal address)* Su; **Y. Excellency,** Su Excelencia; **Y. Highness,** Su Alteza; **Y. Majesty,** Su Majestad. **5** *fam (emphatic use)* el, la, los, las; **y. average Spaniard,** el español medio; **y. tipical feminist,** la típica feminista.

yours [jɔːz] *poss pron* **1** *(familiar use) (sing)* el tuyo, la tuya, los tuyos, las tuyas; *(pl)* el vuestro, la vuestra, los vuestros, las vuestras; **the cup is y.,** la taza es tuya, la taza es vuestra; **the cups are y.,** las tazas son tuyas, las tazas son vuestras; **is this y.?,** ¿es el tuyo?, ¿es la tuya?, ¿es el vuestro?, ¿es la vuestra? **2** *(polite use) (sing)* el suyo, la suya; *(pl)* los suyos, las suyas; **the cup is y.,** la taza es suya; **the cups are y.,** las tazas son suyas; **is this y.?,** ¿es

el suyo?, ¿es la suya? **3** *(in letters)* **y. faithfully,** le(s) saluda atentamente; **y. sincerely,** reciba un cordial saludo de.

yourself [jɔː'self, *unstressed* jə'self] *(pl* **yourselves** [jɔː'selvz]*)* **I** *pers pron* **1** *(familiar use) (sing)* tú mismo,-a; *(pl)* vosotros,-as mismos,-as; **by y.,** (tú) solo; **by yourselves,** vosotros,-as solos,-as; **do it y.,** hazlo tú; **do it yourselves,** hacedlo vosotros,-as. **2** *(polite use) (sing)* usted mismo,-a; *(pl)* ustedes mismos,-as; **by y.,** (usted) solo,-a; **by yourselves,** (ustedes) solos,-as; **do it y.,** hágalo usted; **do it yourselves,** háganlo ustedes. **II** *reflexive pron* **1** *(familiar use) (sing)* te; *pl (familiar use)* os; **enjoy y.!,** ¡diviértete!, ¡que te diviertas!; **enjoy yourselves,** ¡divertíos!, ¡que os divertáis!; **have you hurt y.,** ¿te has hecho daño?; **have you hurt yourselves?,** ¿os habéis hecho daño? **2** *(polite use)* se; **enjoy y.,** ¡diviértase!, ¡que se divierta!; **enjoy yourselves,** ¡diviértanse!, ¡que se diviertan!; **have you hurt y.?,** ¿se ha hecho daño?; **have you hurt yourselves?,** ¿se han hecho daño?

youth [juːθ] *n* **1** *(period of life)* juventud *f.* **2** *(young man)* joven *m.* **3** *(young people)* juventud *f.* ■ **y. club,** club *m* juvenil; **y. hostal,** albergue *m* juvenil.

youthful ['juːθfʊl] *adj* juvenil, joven.

youthfulness ['juːθfʊlnɪs] *n* juventud *f.*

yowl [jaʊl] **I** *n* aullido *m.* **II** *vi* aullar.

yo-yo ['jəʊjəʊ] *n* yoyo *m,* yoyó *m.*

yr *(pl yrs)* **1** *abbr of* **year,** año *m,* A. **2** *abbr of* **your,** tu, su.

Yucatan ['juːkətən] *n* Yucatán *m.*

Yucatecan ['juːkə'tekən] *adj* yucateco,-a.

yucca ['jʌkə] *n Bot* yuca *f.*

yucky ['jʌkɪ] *adj (yuckier, yuckiest) fam* asqueroso,-a.

Yugoslav ['juːgəʊslɑːv] **I** *adj* yugoslavo,-a. **II** *n* yugoslavo,-a *m,f.*

Yugoslavia [juːgəʊ'slɑːvɪə] *n* Yugoslavia.

Yugoslavian [juːgəʊ'slɑːvɪən] **I** *adj* yugoslavo,-a. **II** *n (person)* yugoslavo,-a *m,f.*

Yuletide ['juːltaɪd] *n fml* Navidades *fpl.*

yummy ['jʌmɪ] *adj (yummier, yummiest) fam* riquísimo,-a, de rechupete, de chuparse los dedos.

YWCA [waɪdʌbəljuːsiː'eɪ] *abbr of* **Young Women's Christian Association,** albergue *m* para jóvenes mujeres.

Z

Z, z [zed, *US* ziː] *n (the letter)* Z, z *f.*

Zaire [zɑːˈɪə'] *n* Zaire.

Zairean [zɑːˈɪərɪən] *adj & n* zaireño,-a *(mf).*

Zambezi [zæm'biːzɪ] a Zambeze.

Zambia ['zæmbɪə] *n* Zambia.

Zambian ['zæmbɪən] *adj & n* zambiano,-a *(m,f).*

zany ['zeɪnɪ] *(zanier, zaniest) fam* **1** *(mad)* loco,-a, chiflado,-a. **2** *(eccentric)* estrafalario,-a, extravagante.

zap [zæp] **I** *interj* zas; **II** *vtr sl (pt & pp* **zapped***)* **1** *(hit)* pegar. **2** *fam (kill)* cargarse. **3** *(do sth quickly)* hacer rápidamente.

zeal [ziːl] *n (fantical)* celo *m,* excesivo,-a; *(enthusiam)* entusiasmo *m.*

zealot ['zelət] *n* fanático,-a *m,f.*

zealous ['zeləs] *adj (fanatical)* celoso,-a; *(enthusiastic)* entusiasta.

zebra ['ziːbrə, 'zebrə] *n Zool* cebra *f.* ■ *GB* **z. crossing,** paso *m* cebra *or* de peatones.

zebu ['ziːbuː] *n Zool* cebú *m.*

zed [zed] *n, US* **zee** [ziː] *n* zeta *f.*

Zen [zen] *n* Zen *m.*

zenith ['zenɪθ] *n Astron* cenit *m; fig* apogeo *m.*

zephyr ['zefə'] *n* céfiro *m.*

zeppelin ['zepəlɪn] *n Av* zepelín *m.*

zero ['zɪərəʊ] **I** *n (pl* **zeros** *or* **zeroes***)* cero *m;* **two degrees below z.,** dos grados bajo cero. ■ **z. hour,** hora *f* cero. **II** *vi (pt & pp* **zeroed***) Mil* **to z. in on,** apuntar hacia; *fig (problem)* centrarse en.

zest [zest] *n* **1** *(eagerness)* brío *m,* entusiasmo *m.* **2** *(wit)* gracia *f.* **3** *Culin* cáscara *f,* corteza *f.*

zigzag ['zɪgzæg] **I** *n* zigzag *m.* **II** *vi (pt & pp* **zigzagged***)* zigzaguear.

zilch [zɪltʃ] *n US sl* nada, nada de nada.

Zimbabwe [zɪm'bɑːbweɪ] *n* Zimbabue.

Zimbabwean [zɪm'bɑːbweɪən] *adj & n* zimbabuense *(mf),* zimbabuoa,-a *(m,f).*

zinc [zɪŋk] *n Chem* cinc *m,* zinc *m.*

Zion ['zaɪən] *n* Sión *m.*

Zionism ['zaɪənɪzəm] *n* sionismo *m*.

Zionist ['zaɪənɪst] *adj & n* sionista *(mf)*.

zip [zɪp] **I** *n* **1** *Sew* **z. (fastener),** cremallera *f*. **2** *fam* brío *m*, energía *f*. ■ *US* **z. code,** código *m* postal. **II** *vi (pt & pp zipped)* cerrar *or* unir *or* subir la cremallera. ◆ **zip by** *vi* pasar como un rayo. ◆ **zip up** *vtr* cerrar con cremallera; **z. me up, please,** súbeme la cremallera, por favor.

zipper ['zɪpə'] *n US* cremallera *f*.

zippy ['zɪpɪ] *adj (zippier, zippiest) fam* brioso,-a, vivaz.

zircon ['zɜːkɒn] *n Min* circón *m*.

zirconium [zɜː'kəʊnɪəm] *n Chem* circonio *m*.

zither ['zɪðə'] *n Mus* cítara *f*.

zodiac ['zəʊdɪæk] *n Astrol* zodiaco *m*, zodíaco *m*.

zombie ['zɒmbɪ] *n* zombie *f*.

zone [zəʊn] **I** *n* zona *f* ■ *US* **postal z.,** distrito *m* postal; **time z.,** huso *m* horario. **II** *vtr* dividir en zonas.

zoning ['zəʊnɪŋ] *n* división *f* en zonas.

zonked [zɒnkt] *adj fam* **1** *(exhausted)* reventado,-a, molido,-a. **2** *(drunk)* ciego,-a, colocado,-a. **3** *(drugged)* colocado,-a, flipado,-a.

zoo [zuː] *n* zoo *m*.

zoology [zəʊ'ɒlədʒɪ] *n* zoología *f*.

zoological [zəʊə'lɒdʒɪkəl] *adj* zoológico,-a; **z. garden,** parque *m* zoológico.

zoologist [zəʊ'ɒlədʒɪst] *n* zoólogo,-a *m,f*.

zoom [zuːm] **I** *n* **1** *(buzz)* zumbido *m*. **2** *Phot* **z. lens,** zoom *m*, teleobjetivo *m*. **II** *vi* **1** *(buzz)* zumbar. **2** *(rush)* **to z. past,** pasar volando. ◆ **zoom in** *vi (camera)* acercarse rápidamente. ◆ **zoom out** *vi (camera)* alejarse rápidamente.

zucchini [zuː'kiːnɪ] *n (pl zucchini or zucchinis) US* calabacín *m*.

Zulu ['zuːluː] *adj & n* zulú *(mf)*.

Zululand ['zuːluːlænd] *n* Zululandia.

Spanish–English

Dictionary

Abreviaturas usadas en este diccionario

abr	abreviatura	Cuba	Cuba
adj	adjetivo	Culin	cocina
Admin	administración	Damas	damas
adv	adverbio	def	definido
Agr	agricultura	defect	defectivo
Ajedrez	ajedrez	dem	demostrativo
algn	alguien	Dep	deporte
algo	algo	desus	desusado
Alpin	alpinismo	dimin	diminutivo
Am	Hispano América	Ecol	ecología
Anat	anatomía	Econ	economía
Antill	Antillas	Ecuad	Ecuador
aprox	aproximadamente	Educ	educación
arc	arcaico	Elec	electricidad
arg	argot	Ent	entomología
Arg	Argentina	Equit	equitación
Arqueol	arqueología	Esc	escuela
Arquit	arquitectura	Esgr	esgrima
art	artículo	esp	especialmente
Arte	bellas artes	Esp	España, español
Astrol	astrología	Esquí	esquí
Astron	astronomía	etc	etcétera
Astronáut	astronáutica	euf	eufemismo
Atlet	atletismo	exclam	exclamativo
Austral	Australia	f	femenino
Aut	autmóviles, circulación rodada	fam	familiar, coloquial
aux	auxiliar	Farm	farmacia
Av	aviación	Ferroc	ferrocarriles
Béisb	béisbol	fig	uso figurado
Bill	billar	Filat	filatelia
Biol	biología	Filip	Filipinas
Bol	Bolivia	Filos	filosofía
Bolos	bolos	Fin	finanazas
Bot	botánica	Fisiol	fisiología
Box	boxeo	Fis	física
Bridge	bridge	fml	uso formal
CAm	América Central	Fot	fotografia
Can	Canarias	Ftb	fútbol
Carp	carpintería	fut	futuro
Cat	Cataluña	Gal	Galicia
Caza	caza	GB	británico, Gran Bretaña
Chi	Chile	Geog	geografía
Cicl	ciclismo, bicicletas	Geol	geología
Cin	cine, películas	Geom	geometría
Col	Colombia	ger	gerundio
Com	comercio	Gimn	gimnasia
comp	comparativo	Golf	golf
cond	condicional	Guat	Guatemala
conj	conjuncíon	Herald	heráldica
Constr	construcción	Hist	historia
Cost	costura	Hond	Honduras
CR	Costa Rica	Hortic	horticultura
Crick	cricket	hum	humorístico

Abreviaturas usadas en este diccionario

IgAng	Iglesia Anglicana	Pesca	pesca
IgCat	Iglesia Católica	Petról	industria petrolera
imperat	imperativo	pey	peyorativo
imperf	imperfecto	pl	plural
impers	impersonal	Pol	política
Impr	imprenta	pos	posesivo
Ind	industria	pp	participio pasado
indef	indefinido	PR	Puerto Rico
indet	indeterminado	pref	prefijo
indic	indicativo	Prensa	prensa
infin	infinitivo	prep	preposicíon
Inform	informática, ordenadores	pres	presente
interj	interjección	pron	pronombre
interr	interrogativo	prov	proverbio, refrán
inv	invariable	Psic	psicología, psiquiatría
Ir	Irlanda	pt	pretérito
irón	irónico	Quím	química
irreg	irregular	®	marca registrada
Jur	derecho, jurídico	Rad	radio
Ling	lingüistica	RD	República Dominicana
lit	literario	rel	relativo
Lit	literatura	Rel	religión
loc	locución	RPl	Río de la Plata
loc adj	locución adjetiva	Rugby	rugby
loc adv	locución adverbial	Salv	El Salvador
Lucha	lucha libre	SAm	América del Sur
m	masculino	Seg	seguros
Mat	matemáticas	sing	singular
Med	medicina	subj	subjuntivo
Metal	metalurgia	suf	sufijo
Meteor	meteorología	superl	superlativo
Méx	México	tamb	también
Mil	militar	Taur	tauromaquia
Min	minas, mineralogía	Teat	teatro
Mit	mitología	Téc	técnica
Mueb	muebles	Tel	teléfonos
Mús	música	Telec	telecomunicaciones
n	nombre	Ten	tenis
Naipes	naipes	Tex	textiles
Natacíon	natacíon	Tip	tipografía
Náut	náutica, naval	Tricot	tricotar, punto
neg	negativo	TV	televisión
neut	neutro	Univ	universidad
Nic	Nicaragua	Urug	Uruguay
nf	nombre femenino	US	Estados Unidos
nfpl	nombre femenino plural	usu	usualmente
nm	nombre masculino	v	verbo
nmf / nm,f	nombre masculino y femenino	Val	Valencia
nmpl	nombre masculino plural	Vasc	Vascongadas
npl	nombre plural	v aux	verbo auxiliar
Numis	numismática	véase, véanse	véase, véanse
ofens	ofensivo	Ven	Venezuela
Odont	odontología	Vet	veterinaria
Opt	óptica	vi	verbo intransitivo
Orn	ornitología	v impers	verbo impersonal
Pan	Panamá	vr	verbo reflexivo
Par	Paraguay	vtr	verbo transitivo
Parl	parlamento	v unipers	verbo unipersonal
pas	voz pasiva	Zool	zoología
p ej	por ejemplo		
Peluq	peluquería	■	nombres en construcciones fijas
Per	Perú	◆	adverbios de manera como
pers	personal		subentradas

Phonetics

It is virtually impossible to provide in a book an accurate description of how a foreign language is pronounced. The following table is based on IPA with certain modifications and attempts to give an approximate idea of the Spanish sound system as compared with the British English one.

Letter	Phonetic symbol	Examples	Approximate British English equivalent
Vowels			
a	[a]	gato, amar, mesa	first element of the diphthongs [aɪ] as in m*i*ght, or [aʊ] as in h*o*w
e	[e]	estrella, vez, firme	first element of the diphthong [eɪ] in p*a*y
i	[i]	inicuo, iris, pitiminí	[iː] as in s*ee*, but shorter
o	[o]	bolo, cómodo, oso	somewhere between [ʊ] as in l*o*t and [ɔː] as in t*au*ght
u	[u]	turuta, puro, tribu	[uː] as in f*oo*d, but shorter
y	[i]	rey, buey, y	[iː] as in s*ee*, but shorter

Diphthongs

The pronunciation of the Spanish diphthongs as in baile, hay, fauna, peine, ley, feudo, boina, bocoy and bou presents no difficulties since these are merely combinations of the pure vowels above.

Semi-consonants

u	[w]	buey, cuando, fuiste	[w] as in *w*ait
i	[j]	viernes, vicio, ciudad, ciar	[j] as in *y*es
y	[j]	yermo, ayer, yate	[j] as in *y*es

Consonants

b	[b]	boda, burro, ambos	[b] as in b*e*
	[β]	haba, traba	This voiced bilabial fricative does not exist in English. It is similar to a [b] but is continuous rather than explosive.
c	[k]	cabeza, cuco, acoso, frac	[k] as in *c*ar, *k*eep, *q*ueen
	[θ]	cecina, cielo	[θ] as in *th*ing
ch	[tʃ]	chepa, ocho	[tʃ] as in *ch*amber
d	[d]	dedo, andar	[d] as in *d*ay
	[ð]	dedo, ánade, abad	[ð] as in *th*is
f	[f]	fiesta, afición	[f] as in *f*or
g	[g]	gas, rango, gula	[g] as in *g*et
	[ɣ]	agua, agosto, lagar	This velar fricative dos not exist in English. It is similar to the noise made when gargling.
	[x]	genio, legión	similar to Scottish [x] in lo*ch*
h	—	hambre, ahíto	The Spanish h is silent.
j	[x]	jabón, ajo, carcaj	similar to Scottish [x] in lo*ch*
k	[k]	kilo, kimono	[k] as in *c*ar, *k*eep, *q*ueen
l	[l]	labio, hábil, elegante	[l] as in law
ll	[ʎ]	lluvia, calle	similar to the sound [lj] in mi*lli*on
m	[m]	mano, amigo, hambre, pum	[m] as in *m*an
n	[n]	nata, ratón, antes, enemigo	[n] as in *n*ight
ñ	[ɲ]	año, ñoño	similar to the sound [nj] in o*ni*on
p	[p]	pipa, pelo	[p] as in *p*oint
q	[k]	quiosco. querer, alambique	[k] as in *c*ar, *k*eep, *q*ueen
r(r)	[r]	pero, correr, padre	This single vibrant [r] does not exist in English.
	[rr]	reír, honrado, perro	This multiple vibrant [r] does not exist in English.

s	[s]	sauna, asado, cortés	similar to the [s] in hissing but articulated with the tip of the tongue rather than the blade
t	[t]	teja, estén, atraco, tarot	[t] as in *t*ime
v	[b]	verbena, vena	See **b** above
	[β]	ave, vivo	See **b** above
w	[b]	wagón, waterpolo	[b] as in *b*e
x	[ks]	éxito, examen, extensión	[ks] as in e*x*ercise
z	[θ]	zorro, azul, caza, soez	[θ] as in *th*ing

A

A, a *nf (la letra)* A, a.

A *abr de* **amperio,** ampère, amp, A.

a *abr de* **área,** are.

(a) *abr de* **alias,** alias.

a *prep véase tamb* **al. 1** *(dirección)* to; **caer al suelo,** to fall to *or* onto the floor; **girar a la izquierda,** to turn (to the) left; **ir a Colombia,** to go to Colombia; **ir al cine,** to go to the cinema; **llegar a Valencia,** to arrive in *or* reach Valencia; **subir a un tren/al autobús,** to get on a train/the bus; **vete a casa,** go home. **2** *(distancia)* away; **a cien kilómetros de aquí,** a hundred kilometres (away) from here. **3** *(posición)* at, on; **a la derecha,** on the right; **a la entrada,** at the entrance; **a la orilla del mar,** by the sea; **a lo lejos,** in the distance; **a mi lado,** at *or* by my side, next to me; **a orillas del Támesis,** on the banks of the Thames; **al lado de,** at the side of, next to, beside; **al norte/sur de,** to the north/south of; **al sol,** in the sun; **sentarse a la mesa,** to sit down at (the) table. **4** *(tiempo)* at; **a la mañana,** (on) the following, morning; **a la semana,** per week; **a los sesenta años,** at the age of sixty; **a los tres meses/la media hora,** three months/half an hour later; **a los tres meses de su llegada,** three months after his arrival; **a tiempo,** in time; **al final,** in the end; **al principio,** at first. **5** *(manera)* **a ciegas,** blindly; **a la carta,** à la carte; **a la francesa,** (in the) French fashion *or* manner *or* style; **a lápiz,** in pencil; **a mano,** by hand; **escrito a mano/máquina,** handwritten/typewritten; **hecho a mano/máquina,** hand-made/machine-made; **a oscuras,** in the dark; **a pie,** on foot; **a su manera,** in his *or* her own way; **olla a presión,** pressure cooker. **6** *(cantidad)* **a cientos,** in hundreds, by the hundreds; *(medida)* **a 90 kilómetros por hora,** at 90 kilometres an hour; *(precio)* **¿a cuánto están las cerezas? —a 300 pesetas el kilo,** how much are the cherries?—three hundred pesetas a kilo; **ganar cuatro a dos,** to win four to two. **7** *(complemento directo) (no se traduce)* **saludé a tu tía,** I said hello to your aunt; **vi a tu madre/al rey,** I saw your mother/the king. **8** *(complemento indirecto) (destinatario)* to; **díselo a Javier,** tell Javier; **te lo di a ti,** I gave it to you; **se lo compré al representante,** I bought it from the sales representative. **9** *(finalidad)* **fueron a ayudarle,** they went to help him; **vino a vernos,** he came to see us; **fam ir a por vino,** to go and fetch some wine. **10** *(verbo + a + infin)* to; **aprender a nadar,** to learn (how) to swim; **negarse a salir,** to refuse to come out. **11** *(nombre + a + infin)* **sueldo a convenir,** salary to be agreed; **total a pagar,** total amount payable. **12** *(condicional)* **a decir verdad,** to tell (you) the truth; **a no ser por ...,** if it were not for ... . **13** *(desafío)* **¿a que no lo haces?,** I bet you don't do it! **14** *(exclamaciones imperativas)* **¡a comer!,** lunch/dinner etc. is ready!; **¡a dormir!,** bedtime!; **a ver,** let's see; **¡a ver!,** **¿qué pasa aquí?,** all right, what's going on here?

abacería *nf* grocer's (shop).

abacero,-a *nm, f* grocer.

ábaco *nm* abacus.

abacorar *vtr Ant Can Ven* **1** *(acosar)* to hound, harass; *(acometer)* to attack. **2** *(sujetar)* to hold (down).

abad *nm Rel* abbot.

abadejo *nm (pez)* pollack.

abadesa *nf Rel* abbess.

abadía *nf Rel* **1** *(edificio)* abbey. **2** *(dignidad)* abbacy.

abajeño,-a *Am* **I** *adj* lowland, coastal. **II** *nm, f* lowlander, coastal dweller.

abajo I *adv* **1** *(posición)* below, down; *(en una casa)* downstairs; **ahí a.,** down there; **aquí a.,** down here; **a. del todo,** right at the bottom; **el piso de a.,** *(apartamento)* the flat downstairs; *(planta)* the floor below; **¿la de arriba o la de a.?,** the top one or the bottom one?; **la parte de a.,** the bottom (part); **más a.,** further down. **2** *(dirección)* down, downward; **calle a.,** down the street; **cuesta a.,** downhill; **echar algo a.,** to knock sth down; **hacia a.,** down, downwards; **ven aquí a.,** come down here; *(en una casa)* come downstairs; **venirse a.,** *(caer)* to fall down; *fig (proyecto)* to fall through. **II** *interj* **¡a. la censura!,** down with censorship!

abalanzarse *vr* to rush forward, spring forward; **a. hacia,** to rush towards; **a. sobre,** to rush at, pounce on, swoop down on.

abalear *vtr Am* to shoot *or* fire at.

abalorio *nm* **1** *(cuenta de vidrio)* glass bead. **2** *(adorno de poco valor)* trinket.

abanderado,-a I *pp de* **abanderar. II** *nm, f* **1** *(portaestandarte)* standard bearer. **2** *fig* leader, champion.

abanderar *vtr Náut* to register.

abandonado,-a I *pp de* **abandonar. II** *adj* **1** abandoned, deserted; **sentirse a.,** to feel deserted. **2** *(descuidado)* neglected; **el jardín está a.,** the garden hasn't been looked after. **3** *(desaseado)* untidy, unkempt.

abandonar I *vtr* **1** *(lugar)* to leave, quit; *(persona)* to abandon; *(actividad)* to give up, withdraw from; *(traicionar)* to desert; **a. el barco,** to abandon ship; **a. la carrera,** to drop out; **me ha abandonado la suerte,** luck has forsaken me. **2** *(renunciar)* to relinquish, renounce. **3** *(descuidar)* to neglect; **abandomó sus obligaciones,** he neglected his duties. **4** *Dep* to withdraw from. **II abandonarse** *vr* **1** *(ceder)* to give way, give in; **a. a la bebida,** to overindulge in drinking. **2** *(descuidarse)* to neglect one's appearance, let oneself go.

abandono *nm* **1** *(acción)* abandoning, desertion. **2** *(actividad, idea)* giving up. **3** *(descuido)* neglect, lack of care; **estado de a.,** abandoned state. **4** *(dejadez)* apathy, carelessness, laziness. **5** *Dep* withdrawal; **ganar por a.,** to win by default. **6** *Náut* abandonment.

abanicar I *vtr* to fan. **II abanicarse** *vr* to fan oneself.

abanico *nm* **1** fan; **en (forma de) a.,** fan-shaped. ■ *Inform* **a. de salida,** fan out. **2** *fig (gama)* range; **un amplio a. de posibilidades,** a wide range of possibilities.

abaniqueo *nm* fanning.

abarajar *vtr* **1** *Arg Par Urug (cuchillazos)* to fend off. **2** *(tomar en el aire)* to catch.

abaratamiento *nm* reduction in price.

abaratar I *vtr* to cut *or* reduce the price of. **II abaratarse** *vr (artículos)* to become cheaper, come down in price; *(precios)* to come down.

abarca *nf (prenda)* sandal.

abarcar *vtr* **1** *(con los brazos)* to get one's arms round. **2** *(englobar)* to cover, embrace; **el libro abarca varios temas,** the book covers several topics; *prov* **quien mucho abarca poco aprieta,** do not bite off more than you can chew. **3** *(trabajo)* to undertake, take on. **4** *Am (acaparar)* to monopolize.

abaritonado,-a *adj Mús* baritone.

abarquillamiento *nm (madera)* warping; *(cartón)* curling up.

abarquillar *vtr,* **abarquillarse** *vr (madera)* to warp; *(cartón)* to curl up.

abarrajado,-a *adj Am (desvergonzado)* shameless; *(descarado)* insolent.

abarrancarse *vr fig* to get bogged down, get stuck (**en,** in).

abarrotado,-a I *pp de* **abarrotar** II *adj* packed (**de**, with), crammed (**de**, with); **a. de gente,** (jam-) packed, very crowded.

abarrotar I *vtr* 1 (*llenar*) to pack, cram, fill up (**de**, with); **el público abarrotaba la sala,** the room was packed (with people). 2 *Am* (*acaparar*) to buy up. II **abarrotarse** *vr Am* (*abaratarse*) to go down in price.

abarrotería *nf* 1 *Am* (*tienda de comestibles*) grocer's shop, grocery store. 2 *CAm* (*ferretería*) ironmonger's (shop).

abarrotero,-a *nm, f Am* grocer.

abarrotes *nmpl Am* groceries.

abastecedor,-a I *adj* supplying, providing. II *nm, f* supplier, purveyor.

abastecer I *vtr* to supply, provide. II **abastecerse** *vr* to stock up (**de** *or* **con**, with) lay in supplies (**de** *or* **con**, **of**); **a. de víveres,** to get in supplies.

abastecimiento *nm* (*acción*) supplying, provision; **a. de agua,** water supply.

abasto *nm* 1 (*provisión*) supplying, provisioning; *fam* **es que no doy a.,** I just can't cope, I can't keep up. 2 **abastos,** (*víveres*) provisions, supplies. ■ **mercado de a.,** wholesale food market.

abatanar *vtr* 1 *Tex* (*paño*) to full. 2 *fig* (*golpear*) to beat.

abate *nm Rel* father, abbé.

abatible *adj* folding, collapsible; **asiento a.,** folding seat.

abatido,-a I *pp de* **abatir** II *adj* 1 (*deprimido*) depressed, downhearted. 2 (*caído*) fallen, drooping. 3 (*despreciable*) despicable, low.

abatimiento *nm* depression, dejection.

abatir I *vtr* 1 (*derribar*) to knock down, pull down; (*árbol*) to cut down. 2 (*matar*) to kill; (*herir*) to wound; (*a tiros*) to shoot down. 3 (*desanimar*) to depress, dishearten. 4 *fml* (*bajar*) to lower, take down. II **abatirse** *vr* 1 (*ave, avión*) to swoop (**sobre,** down on), dive (**sobre,** down on); *fig* **la desgracia se abatió sobre la familia,** misfortune fell upon the family. 2 (*desanimarse*) to lose heart, become depressed.

abdicación *nf* abdication.

abdicar *vtr & vi to* abdícate; **abdicó (la corona) en su hijo,** she abdicated (from the throne) in favour of her son; *fig* **a. de una ideología,** to give up an ideology.

abdomen *nm Anat* abdomen.

abdominal I *adj Anat* abdominal. II **abdominales** *nmpl Gimn* sit-ups.

abecé *nm* 1 (*alfabeto*) ABC, alphabet. 2 *fig* (*principio*) basics *pl*, rudiments *pl*.

abecedario *nm* 1 (*alfabeto*) alphabet. 2 (*libro*) spelling book.

abedul *nm Bot* birch. ■ **a. pubescente,** downy birch.

abeja *nf* 1 *Ent* bec. ■ **a. reina,** queen bee. 2 *fig* (*persona*) busy bee.

abejaruco *nm Orn* bee-eater.

abejón *nm Ent* 1 (*zángano*) drone. 2 (*abejorro*) bumblebee.

abejorreo *nm* buzzing.

abejorro *nm* 1 *Ent* (*abeja*) bumblebee; (*coleóptero*) cockchafer. 2 *fig* (*persona*) bore, nuisance.

aberración *nf* aberration.

aberrante *adj* aberrant.

aberrar *vi* to be mistaken.

abertura *nf* 1 (*hueco*) opening, gap; (*grieta*) crack, slit. 2 *Geog* (*entre montañas*) pass; (*ensenada*) cove, creek. 3 *Cost* vent. 4 *Fot* aperture.

abetal *nm* fir plantation.

abeto *nm Bot* fir (tree). ■ **a. rojo,** spruce.

abicharse *vr Arg Urug* to go maggoty.

abierto,-a I *pp de* **abrir** II *adj* I open, unlocked; **a campe a.,** open country; **a. de par en par,** wide open; **cindad**

abierta al mar, a seaward-looking city; **guerra abierta,** open war; **herida abierta,** open *or* gaping wound; *fig* **con los brazos abiertos,** with open arms; *fig* **quedarse con la boca abierta,** to be left speechless; *fig* **ver el cielo a.,** to see a way out. 2 (*grifo*) (turned) on; **dejar el grifo a.,** to leave the tap running. 3 *fig* (*persona*) (*sincero*) open, frank; (*comprensivo*) open-minded. 4 *Ling* (*vocal*) open.

abigarrado,-a *adj* I (*multicolor*) gaudy. 2 (*mezclado*) jumbled, mixed up; **un discurso a.,** a disjointed speech.

Abisinia *n* Abyssinia.

abisinio,-a *adj & nm, f* Abyssinian.

abismal *adj* abysmal; *fig* **una diferencia a.,** a world of a difference.

abismar I *vtr* (*confundir*) to confuse, bewilder. II **abismarse** *vr* 1 to be engrossed (**en**, in), become absorbed (**en**, in). 2 *Am* (*asombrarse*) to be amazed.

abismo *nm* abyss; *fig* **al borde del a.,** on the brink of ruin; *fig* **entre ellos media un a.,** they are worlds apart.

abjuración *nf* abjuration.

abjurar *vtr & vi* to abjure, forswear.

ablandamiento *nm* softening.

ablandar I *vtr* 1 (*gen*) to soften. 2 *fig* (*calmar*) to soothe, appease; *fig* **a. a algn,** to soften sb up; *fig* **la música ablanda a las fieras,** music soothes the savage breast. II *vi* (*tiempo*) to get warmer *or* milder; (*nieve, hielo*) to melt. III **ablandarse** *vr* 1 (*gen*) to soften (up), go soft *or* softer. 2 (*tiempo*) to get warmer *or* milder; (*nieve, hielo*) to melt. 3 *fig* (*persona*) to mellow.

ablativo *nm Ling* ablative (case).

ablución *nf Rel* 1 ablution. 2 **abluciones,** water and wine *sing*.

abnegación *nf* abnegation, self-denial.

abnegado,-a *adj* selfless, self-sacrificing.

abobado,-a *adj* 1 (*tonto*) stupid, silly. 2 (*pasmado*) bewildered.

abocado,-a *adj* 1 **estar** *or* **verse a. a,** to be heading for; **está a. al fracaso,** it is doomed to failure. 2 (*vino*) medium dry.

abochornado,-a I *pp de* **abochornar.** II *adj fig* ashamed, embarrassed.

abochornar I *vtr* 1 (*avergonzar*) to shame, embarrass. 2 (*acalorar*) to make flushed. II **abochornarse** *vr* 1 (*avergonzarse*) to become embarrassed; (*estar avergonzado*) to be ashamed. 2 (*planta*) to wilt.

abocinado,-a *adj* (*gen*) trumpet-shaped; *Arquit* splayed.

abofetear *vtr* to slap.

abogacía *nf* legal profession.

abogadillo,-a *nm, f pey* second-rate lawyer, pettifogger.

abogado,-a *nm, f* 1 lawyer, solicitor; (*en tribunal supremo*) barrister; **ejercer de a.,** to practise law, be a lawyer. ■ **a. de oficio,** legal aid lawyer; **a. defensor,** counsel for the defense; **a. del diablo,** devil's advocate; **a. del Estado,** public prosecutor, *US* attorney general; **a. laboralista,** union lawyer. 2 *fig* (*defensor*) advocate, champion.

abogar *vtr* to plead; **a. a favor de,** to plead for, defend; **a. por algo,** to advocate *or* champion sth.

abolengo *nm* ancestry, lineage; **de rancio a.,** of ancient lineage.

abolición *nf* abolition.

abolicionismo *nm* abolítionism.

abolicionista *adj & nmf* abolitionist.

abolir *vtr* defect to abolish.

abollado,-a I *pp de* **abollar.** II *adj* dented.

abolladura *nf* (*hundimiento*) dent; (*bollo*) bump.

abollar I *vtr* 1 to dent. 2 *Arte* to emboss. II **abollarse** *vr* to get dented.

abombado,-a I *pp de* **abombar.** II *adj* convex.

abombar I *vtr* to make convex. **II abombarse** *vr* **1** (*pudrirse*) to rot. **2** *fam* (*achisparse*) to get tipsy.

abominable *adj* abominable; **el a. hombre de las nieves,** the abominable snowman.

abominación *nf* abomination.

abominar *vtr* & *vi* **a.** (**de**), to abominate, loathe.

abonable *adj Fin* payable.

abonado,-a I *pp* **de abonar. II** *adj* **1** *Fin* (*pagado*) paid; **a. en cuenta,** credited. **2** *Agr* (*tierra*) fertilized, manured. **III** *nm,f* **1** *Ferroc Teat* season ticket holder. **2** (*al teléfono, a revista*) subscriber.

abonanzar *vi* (*tiempo*) to become settled, grow calm; (*tormenta*) to clear up.

abonar I *vtr* **1** *fml* (*pagar*) to pay (for); **a. al centado,** to pay cash. **2** (*avalar*) to vouch for, guarantee; **le abona su reputación,** his reputation speaks for itself. **3** (*subscribir*) to subscribe. **4** *Agr* (*tierra*) to manure, fertilize. **II abonarse** *vr* **1** (*a una revista*) to subscribe (**a,** to). **2** *Ferroc Teat* to buy a season ticket.

abonaré *nm* promissory *or* credit note, IOU.

abono *nm* **1** (*pago*) payment; (*depósito*) deposit. **2** *Agr* (*producto*) fertilizer; (*estiércol*) manure; (*acción*) fertilizing. **3** (*a revista etc*) subscription; *Ferroc Teat* season ticket.

abordable *adj* (*persona*) approachable; (*lugar*) accessible; (*asunto*) manageable.

abordaje *nm Náut* (*choque*) collision, fouling; (*ataque*) boarding; **¡al a.!,** stand by to board!

abordar I *vtr* **1** *Náut* (*chocar*) to run foul of, collide with; (*atacar*) to board. **2** *fig* to approach; **a. a algn,** to approach sb; **a. un asunto,** to tackle a subject.

aborigen (*pl* **aborígenes**) **I** *adj* native, indigenous; *esp Austral* aboriginal. **II** *nmf* native; *esp Austral* aborigine.

aborrecer *vtr* **1** (*odiar*) to detest, hate, loathe. **2** (*las crías*) to abandon.

aborrecible *adj* detestable, loathesome.

aborrecimiento *nm* hate, hatred, loathing.

aborregado,-a I *pp* **de aborregarse. II** *adj* **1** (*cielo*) covered with fleecy clouds. **2** *fam* (*persona*) mindless, sheeplike.

aborregarse *vr* **1** (*cielo*) to become covered with fleecy clouds. **2** *fam* (*persona*) to become sheeplike, follow the crowd.

abortar I *vi* **1** (*involuntariamente*) to miscarry, have a miscarriage; (*intencionadamente*) to abort, have an abortion. **2** *fig* (*fracasar*) to fail, miscarry. **II** *vtr* **1** (*feto*) *Med* to abort. **2** *Av* (*despegue*) to abort.

abortista *nmf* abortionist.

abortivo,-a I *adj* abortive. **II** *nm* abortifacient.

aborto *nm* **I** (*espontáneo*) miscarriage; (*provocado*) abortion. **2** *ofens* (*persona*) freak, ugly person; (*cosa*) abortion.

abotargado,-a I *pp* **de abotargarsa. II** *adj* swollen.

abotargamiento *nm* swelling.

abotargarse *vr* to swell up.

abotinado,-a *adj* **zapato a.,** ankle boot.

abotonar I *vtr* (*ropa*) to button (up). **II aotonarse** *vr* **1** (*persona*) to do one's buttons up. **2** (*ropa*) to button (up).

abovedado,-a I *pp* **de abovadar. II** *adj Arquit* vaulted, arched.

abovedar *vtr Arquit* to vault, arch.

abra *nf* **1** *Geog* (**bahía**) cove, inlet; (*desfiladero*) gorge, mountain pass. **2** *Geol* (*grieta*) fissure. **3** *Am* (*en bosque*) clearing.

abracadabra *nm* abracadabra.

abracar *vtr Am* to include, embrace, cover.

abrasado,-a I *pp* **de abrasar. II** *adj* burnt; **morir a.,** to be burnt to death.

abrasador,-a *adj* burning, scorching; *fig* **pasión abrasadora,** consuming passion.

abrasar I *vtr* & *vi* to burn, scorch; **este café abrasa,** this coffee is scalding hot. **II abrasarse** *vr* to burn; *fig* **a. de calor,** to be sweltering; *fig* **a. de sed,** to be parched.

abrasión *nf* abrasion.

abrasivo,-a *adj* & *nm* abrasive.

abrazadera *nf Téc* clamp, brace.

abrazar 1 *vtr* to embrace, hug; *fig* (*doctrina, causa*) to embrace. **II abrazarse** *vr* **a.** *or* **con algn,** to embrace sb; **se abrazaron,** they embraced each other.

abrazo *nm* embrace, hug; **dar un a. a algn,** to embrace sb; (*en carta*) **un a.** *or* **abrazos,** with best wishes from; (*más íntimo*) love.

abrecartas *nm inv* letter-opener, paperknife.

abrelatas *nm inv* tin-opener, *US* can opener.

abrevadero *nm* drinking trough.

abrevar *vtr* (*animales*) to water, give water to.

abreviado,-a I *pp* **de abreviar. II** *adj* shortened; (*texto*) abridged; (*palabra*) abbreviated; (*explicación*) brief.

abreviar I *vtr* to shorten; (*texto*) to abridge; (*palabra*) to abbreviate; (*discurso, estancia*) to cut short; **a. los trámites,** to speed up the formalities. **II** *vi* to be quick *or* brief; **para a.,** to cut a long story short.

abreviatura *nf* abbreviation.

abridor *nm* **1** (*de latas, botellas*) opener. **2** (*pendiente*) sleeper.

abrigadero *nm* shelter, sheltered place.

abrigado,-a I *pp* **de abrigar. II** *adj* **1** (*lugar*) sheltered, protected. **2** (*persona*) wrapped up; **ir muy a.,** to be well wrapped up.

abrigar I *vtr* **1** (*contra el frío*) to wrap up; keep warm; **abriga al niño,** wrap the child up well; **esta chaqueta abriga mucho,** this cardigan is very warm. **2** (*proteger*) to protect, shelter. **3** *fig* (*esperanza*) to foster, cherish. **4** (*duda, sospecha*) to have, harbour, *US* harbor. **II abrigarse** *vr* **1** (*protegerse*) to shelter, take shelter. **2** to wrap oneself up.

abrigo *nm* **1** (*prenda*) coat, overcoat; **ropa de a.,** warm clothes *pl*. **2** (*refugio*) shelter; **al a. de,** protected *or* sheltered from; **al a. de la ley,** under the protection of the law. **3** *fam* (*de cuidado*) **es un tipo de a.,** he's an ugly character, (*tremendo*) **hace un sol de a.,** it's roasting hot.

abril *nm April*; *fig* **una muchacha de quince abriles,** a girl of fifteen summers; *prov* **en a., aguas mil,** (March winds and) April showers bring forth May flowers; *véase tamb* **noviembre.**

abrileño,-a *adj* April; **tiempo a.,** April weather.

abrillantador,-a I *nm* **1** (*producto*) polish. **2** (*instrumento*) polishing tool. **II** *nm,f* (*persona*) polisher.

abrillantar *vtr* **1** (*pulir*) to polish, burnish, make shine. **2** *fig* (*embellecer*) to embellish.

abrir (*pp* **abierto**) **I** *vtr* **1** to open; **¡abrid paso!,** make way!; **a. un agujero,** to make a hole; **a. un túnel,** to dig a tunnel; **a. una cremallera,** to undo a zip; *fig* **a. la mano,** to relax standards; *fig* **en un a. y cerrar de ojos,** in the twinkling of an eye; *fam* **abrirle la cabeza a algn,** to smash sb's head in; *fam* **no abrió la boca,** he didn't say a word. **2** (*gas, luz*) to switch on, turn on; **abre el grifo,** turn the tap on. **3** (*empezar*) (*campaña*) to head; (*manifestación*) to lead; (*baile*) to open; (*negocio*) to open, set up, start up; *Jur* **a. un expediente,** to start proceedings; *Mil* **a. fuego,** to open fire. **II abrirse** *vr* **1** (*gen*) to open; (*apetito*) to whet; (*extenderse*) to spread out, unfold; *fig* **a. paso en la vida,** to make one's way in life. **2** (*dar*) to open (**a,** onto); **look** (**a,** onto). **3** (*ligamentos*) to sprain. **4** (*sincerarse*) to open out; **a. a algn,** to confide in sb. **5** *arg* (*largarse*) to clear off, be off; **¡me abro!,** I'm off!

abrochar *vtr*, **abrocharse** *vr* (*botones*) to do up; (*camisa*) to button (up); (*cierre*) to fasten; (*zapatos*) to tie up, do up; (*cremallera*) to do up.

abrogación *nf Jur* abrogation, repeal.
abrogar *vtr Jur* to abrogate.
abrojal *nm* thistle patch.
abrojo *nm* **1** *Bot* thistle. **2** *Náut* **abrojos,** reef *sing*.
abroncar *vtr fam* **1** *(reñir)* to tear a strip off, give a dressing-down to. **2** *(abuchear)* to boo, heckle.
abrótano *nm Bot* southernwood.
abrumado,-a I *pp de* **abrumar. II** *adj* overwhelmed; **a. de trabajo,** snowed under with work.
abrumador,-a *adj* overwhelming, crushing; **mayoría abrumadora,** overwhelming majority.
abrumar I *vtr* to overwhelm, crush; **tantos problemas me abruman,** all these problems are getting on top of me; *fig* **le abrumó con sus atenciones,** his attentions made her feel uncomfortable. **II abrumarse** *vr Meteor* to become misty.
abrupto,-a *adj* **1** *(montaña, pendiente)* steep, abrupt; *(terreno)* rugged. **2** *fig (brusco)* abrupt, sudden.
absceso *nm Med* abscess.
absentismo *nm (de trabajadores)* absenteeism; *(de terrateniente)* absentee landlordism.
ábside *nm Arquit* apse.
absolución *nf* **1** *Rel* absolution. **2** *Jur* acquittal.
absolutismo *nm* absolutism.
absolutista *adj & nmf* absolutist.
absoluto,-a *adj* absolute; **en a.,** not at all, by no means; **nada en a.,** nothing at all; **lo a.,** the absolute. ◆ **absolutamente** *adv* absolutely, completely; **a. nada,** nothing at all.
absolutorio,-a *adj Jur* **sentencia absolutoria,** verdict of not guilty.
absolver [32] *(pp* **absuelto)** *vtr* **1** *Rel* to absolve. **2** *Jur* to acquit.
absorbencia *nf* absorbency.
absorbente I *adj* **1** *(papel)* absorbent. **2** *fig (trabajo)* absorbing, engrossing; *(exigente)* demanding; *(persona)* domineering. **II** *nm* absorbent.
absorber *vtr* **1** *(líquidos)* to absorb, soak up. **2** *fig (conocimientos)* to absorb; *(consumir)* to use up; *(cautivar)* to captivate; **la lectura le absorbe por completo,** he gets completely absorbed in his reading.
absorción *nf* absorption.
absorto,-a *adj* **1** *(ensimismado)* absorbed, engrossed **(en,** in); **estar a. en sus pensamientos,** to be lost in thought. **2** *(pasmado)* amazed, bewildered.
abstemio,-a I *adj* teetotal, abstemious; **es a.,** he's a teetotaller. **II** *nm,f* teetotaller.
abstención *nf* abstention.
abstencionismo *nm* abstentionism.
abstencionista *adj & nmf* abstentionist.
abstenerse *vr* to abstain **(de,** from), refrain **(de,** from); **a. de votar,** to abstain (from voting); **en la duda a.,** when in doubt, don't.
abstinencia *nf* abstinence; *(de drogas)* withdrawal; **síndrome de a.,** withdrawal symptoms *pl*.
abstracción *nf* **1** *(gen)* abstraction. **2** *(concentración mental)* concentration; **tiene gran capacidad de a.,** he has great powers of concentration.
abstracto,-a *adj* abstract; **en a.,** in the abstract.
abstraer I *vtr* to abstract. **II** *vi* to think in the abstract. **III abstraerse** *vr* **1** *(ensimismarse)* to become lost in thought; *(concentrarse)* to engross oneself **(en,** in). **2** *(prescindir)* **a. de,** to leave aside.
abstraído,-a I *pp de* **abstraer. II** *adj* **1** *(ensimismado)* absorbed, engrossed. **2** *(distraído)* absentminded.
abstruso,-a *adj* abstruse.
abstuve *pt indef véase* **abstenerse.**

absuelto,-a I *pp de* **absolver. II** *adj* **1** *Rel* absolved. **2** *Jur* acquitted.
absurdidad *nf* absurdity.
absurdo,-a I *adj* absurd; **lo a. sería irse ahora,** it would be crazy for us to leave now; **¡no seas a.!,** don't be ridiculous!; **¡qué a.!,** how absurd! **II** *nm* absurdity, absurd thing; **eso es un a.,** that's an absurdity.
abubilla *nf Orn* hoopoe.
abuchear *vt* to boo, jeer at.
abucheo *nm* booing, jeering.
abuela *nf* **1** grandmother; *fam* grandma, granny; *fam* **¡cuéntaselo a tu a.!** pull the other one!; *fam* **éramos pocos y parió la a.,** as if that wasn't enough, that was all we needed; *fam* **no tiene a.,** he is not afraid of blowing his own trumpet; *fam* **¡tu a.!,** rubbish! **2** *fig* old woman.
abuelo *nm* **1** grandfather; *fam* grandad, grandpa. **2 abuelos,** grandparents; *fig (antepasados)* ancestors. **3** *fig* old man.
abuhardillado,-a *adj* **techo a.,** sloping *or* slanted roof.
abulense I *adj* of *or* from Avila. **II** *nmf* native *or* inhabitant of Avila.
abulia *nf* apathy, lack of willpower.
abúlico,-a *adj* apathetic, lacking in willpower.
abultado,-a I *pp de* **abultar. II** *adj (paquete, bulto)* bulky, big.
abultamiento *nm* **1** *(bulto)* bulkiness. **2** *(agrandamiento)* increase (in size). **3** *(hinchazón)* swelling.
abultar I *vtr* **1** *(agrandar)* to enlarge, increase. **2** *fig* to exaggerate. **II** *vi* to be bulky; **abulta mucho,** it takes up a lot of space.
abundamiento *nm fml* **a mayor a.,** furthermore.
abundancia *nf* abundance, plenty; **en a.,** in abundance; *fig* **nadar en la a.,** to be rolling in money.
abundante *adj* abundant, plentiful.
abundar *vi* **1** to abound, be plentiful; **abundan las ciruelas,** there are plenty of plums; **a. en,** to abound in, be full of; **en Noruega abunda la madera,** Norway is rich in timber. **2** *fig* **a. en,** *(idea)* to share, support.
abur *interj fam* cheerio!, see you!
aburguesado,-a I *pp de* **aburguesarse. II** *adj* bourgeois.
aburguesamiento *nm* process of becoming bourgeois.
aburguesarse *vr* to become bourgeois.
aburrición *nf Am (antipatía)* dislike; *(odio)* hate, loathing.
aburrido,-a I *adj* **1** boring, tedious; *(monótono)* dull, dreary; **¡qué a.!,** how boring!; **ser a.,** to be boring. **2** *(persona)* bored; **a. de,** *(cansado)* tired of; *(harto)* fed up with; **a. de esperar,** tired of waiting; **estar a.,** to be bored.
aburrimiento *nm* boredom; **¡qué a.!,** how boring!, what a bore!; *(cosa, persona)* **ser un a.,** to be a bore.
aburrir I *vtr* to bore; *(cansar)* to tire. **II aburrirse** *vr* to get bored; **a. como una ostra,** to be bored stiff.
abusar *vi* **1** *(propasarse)* to go too far; **a. de,** *(situación, persona)* to take (unfair) advantage of; *(poder)* to abuse, misuse; *(salud, amabilidad)* to abuse; *Jur* **a. de un niño/una mujer,** to molest a child/woman; **¡sin a.!,** don't push it too far! **2** *(usar demasiado)* to overindulge **(de,** in), overuse; **a. de la bebida,** to drink too much *or* to excess.
abusivo,-a *adj* excessive, exorbitant; **precio a.,** exorbitant price; **trato a.,** ill-treatment.
abuso *nm* **1** abuse, misuse; **a. de confianza,** betrayal of trust, breach of faith. ■ *Jur* **abusos deshonestos,** indecent assault *sing*. **2** *(injusticia)* injustice; **¡es un a.!,** this is most unfair!
abusón,-ona *adj fam* **1** *(fresco)* shameless; *(gorrón)* sponging, scrounging; *(injusto)* unfair, abusive. **II** *nm,f* *(gorrón)* sponger, scrounger; *(injusto)* unfair person.
abyección *nf* abjection, wretchedness.

abyecto,-a *adj* abject, wretched.

a. C. *abr de* **antes de Cristo,** before Christ, BC.

a/c *Com abr de* **a cuenta,** on account.

acá *adv* **1** *(lugar)* here, over here; **a. y allá,** here and there; **de a. para allá,** to and fro, up and down; **más a.,** nearer; **¡ven a.!,** come here! **2** *(tiempo)* **de entonces a.,** since then; **de un tiempo a.,** lately.

acabado,-a I *pp de* **acabar. II** *adj* **1** *(terminado)* finished, complete. **2** *fig (gastado)* worn-out, spent; **a. como político,** a burnt-out politician; **una persona acabada,** a has-been. **III** *nm Téc* finish.

acabamiento *nm (terminación)* completion; *(fin)* end; *euf (muerte)* end.

acabar I *vtr* to finish (off); *(completar)* to complete. **II** *vi* **1** to finish, end; **acaba en punta,** it has a pointed end; **a. bien,** to have a happy ending; **a. con algo,** *(terminarlo)* to finish sth; *(romperlo)* to break sth; **acabarás conmiga,** you'll be the end of me; **a. de ...,** to have just ...; **no acaba de convencerme,** I'm not quite convinced; **a. mal,** to end badly; *fam* **¡acabáramos!,** now I get it!, you could have said so before!; *fam* **para a. de arreglarlo,** to cap it all. **2** (**a. + ger, a. + por + inf**) to end up; **acabaron casándose** *or* **por casarse,** they ended up getting married. **III acabarse** *vr* **1** to finish, end, come to an end, stop; **acábate la leche,** drink up your milk; **se (nos) acabó la gasolina,** we ran out of petrol; *fam* **¡se acabó!** that's that!; *fam* **se acabó lo que se daba,** that's it! **2** *(morir)* to die.

acabóse *nm fam* **eres el a.,** you're the limit; **esto es el a.,** this is the end.

acacia *nf Bot* acacia.

academia *nf* **1** *(sociedad)* academy; **A. de Bellas Artes,** Royal Academy of Arts; **La Real A. Española,** the Spanish Academy. **2** *(centro de enseñanza)* school, academy. ■ **a. de idiomas,** language school; **a. militar,** military academy.

academicismo *nm* academicism.

académico,-a I *adj* academic; *Univ* **estudios académicos,** university studies. **II** *nm, f* academician, member of an academy.

acaecer *v unipers* to happen, occur.

acallar *vtr* **1** to silence, quieten. **2** *fig (persona)* to pacify; *(protestas)* to silence.

acalorado,-a I *pp de* **acalorar. II** *adj* **1** hot; *(cara)* flushed. **2** *fig (excitado)* worked up, excited; *(debate etc)* heated, angry.

acaloramiento *nm* **1** heat. **2** *fig* heat, passion.

acalorar I *vtr* **1** to warm up, heat up. **2** *fig* to excite; *(pasiones)* to arouse, inflame. **II acalorarse** *vr* **1** to get warm *or* hot. **2** *fig (persona)* to get excited *or* worked up; *(debate etc)* to become heated.

acampada *nf* camping. ■ **zona de a.,** camp site.

acampanado,-a *adj* bell-shaped; *(prendas)* flared.

acampar *vi* to camp.

acanalado,-a *adj (gen)* grooved; *Arquit* fluted; *Tricot* ribbed.

acanaladura *nf (gen)* groove; *Arquit* fluting.

acantilado,-a I *adj (costa)* steep, sheer; *(fondo del mar)* shelving; *(rocoso)* rocky, craggy. **II** *nm* cliff.

acantonar *vtr Mil (tropas)* to billet, quarter (**en,** in).

acaparador,-a I *adj* **1** hoarding. **2** *fig (instinto)* acquisitive; *(tendencia)* monopolizing. **II** *nm, f* hoarder; *(monopolizador)* monopolizer.

acaparamiento *nm* hoarding; *fig* monopolizing.

acaparar *vtr* **1** *(productos)* to hoard; *(el mercado)* to corner. **2** *fig* to monopolize, keep for oneself; **acaparó la atención de todos,** he commanded the attention of everyone.

acaracolado,-a *adj* spiral-shaped; *(pelo)* very curly.

acaramelado,-a I *pp de* **acaramelar. II** *adj* **1** *(color)* caramel-coloured, *US* caramel-colored. **2** *fig (pareja)* lovey-dovey, starry-eyed; *(voz)* syrupy, sugary.

acaramelar I *vtr* to coat with caramel. **II acaramelarse** *vr fig* to become lovey-dovey *or* starryeyed.

acariciador,-a *adj* caressing; *fig* **una voz acariciadora,** a sensuous voice.

acariciar I *vtr* **1** to caress, fondle; *(pelo, animal)* to stroke. **2** *fig (esperanza, sueño)* to cherish; *(idea)* to have in mind. **II acariciarse** *vr* to caress each other; **a. el bigote,** to stroke one's moustache.

acariñar *vtr Am* to caress, fondle.

acarrear *vtr* **1** *(transportar)* to carry, transport. **2** *fig (conllevar)* to cause, bring, give rise to.

acarreo *nm* transport, carriage; **gastos de a.,** transport costs, haulage.

acartonado,-a I *pp de* **acartonarse. II** *adj* **1** cardboard-like. **2** *(piel)* wizened, shrivelled up.

acartonarse *vr* **1** to go stiff *or* hard. **2** *fig (piel)* to become wizened, shrivel up. **3** *Am* to look consumptive.

acaso *adv* perhaps, maybe; **¿a. no te lo dijo?,** didn't she tell you?; **a. podamos verlo,** perhaps we will see him; **no es torpe, si a. inseguro,** he's not dull, if anything insecure; **por si a.,** just in case; **si a. viene ...,** if he should come ... .

acatamiento *nm (de la ley)* observance; *(persona)* respect.

acatar *vtr* **1** *(leyes, normas)* to observe, comply with; *(persona)* to respect. **2** *Am (notar)* to notice.

acatarrado,-a I *pp de* **acatarrarse. II** *adj* **estar a.,** to have a cold.

acatarrarse *vr* to catch a cold.

acato *nm véase* **acatamiento.**

acaudalado,-a I *pp de* **acaudalar. II** *adj* rich, wealthy, well-off.

acaudalar *vtr* to accumulate, amass.

acaudillar *vtr* to lead.

acceder *vi* **1** *(consentir)* **a. a,** to agree to, accede to, consent to. **2** *(tener acceso)* **a. a la universidad,** to gain admittance to *or* enter university; **a. al poder,** to accede to power, take office; **a. al trono,** to accede *or* succeed to the throne.

accesibilidad *nf* accessibility.

accesible *adj* accessible; *(persona)* approachable.

accésit *nm (pl* **accésits** *or* **accésis) (mención)** honourable mention; *(premio)* consolation prize.

acceso *nm* **1** *(entrada)* access, entry; **'prohibido el a.',** 'no admittance'. ■ *Inform* **a. al azar, a. directo,** random access; *Univ* **prueba de a.,** entrance examination. **2** *(paso)* approach, access; **los accesos a Barcelona,** the approaches to Barcelona. ■ **carretera de a.,** approach road; **vía de a.,** slip road. **3** *Med (de tos)* fit; *(de fiebre)* attack, bout; *fig* fit, outburst.

accesorio,-a I *adj* accessory; *(gastos)* incidental. **II** *nm* accesory, extra.

accidentado,-a I *pp de* **accidentarse. II** *adj* **1** *(persona)* injured. **2** *(lleno de incidentes)* eventful; *(vida)* troubled, stormy. **3** *(terreno)* uneven, bumpy, hilly. **III** *nm, f* casualty, accident victim.

accidental *adj* accidental; **un encuentro a.,** a chance meeting.

accidentarse *vr* to have an accident.

accidente *nm* **I** accident; **por a.,** by accident, accidentally; **sufrir un a.,** to have an accident. ■ **a. de trabajo,** industrial accident; **a. ferroviario/de carretera,** rail/road accident. **2** *Geog (del terreno)* unevenness, irregularity. ■ **accidentes geográficos,** geographical features.

acción *nf* **1** *(gen)* action; *(acto)* act, deed; **poner en a.,** to put in action; **ponerse en a.,** to start doing sth. ■ *Rel* **a. de**

gracias, thanksgiving; *Mil* **a. de guerra,** act of war; **buena a.,** good deed; **campo de a.,** field of action; **hombre de a.,** man of action; **película de a.,** adventure film; *Téc* **radio de a.,** operating range. **2** *Jur* action, lawsuit; **ejercitar una a. contra algn,** to bring an action against sb. **3** *Com Fin (bolsa)* share; **acciones amortizadas,** redeemed shares; **acciones en cartera,** shares in portfolio.

accionamiento *nm* starting, activation.

accionar I *vtr (máquina)* to drive, activate, work. **II** *vi* to gesticulate.

accionista *nmf Com Fin* shareholder, stockholder.

acebo *nm Bot (hoja)* holly; *(árbol)* holly tree.

acechanza *nf véase* **acecho.**

acechar I *vtr* **1** *(vigilar)* to watch, spy on; *(esperar)* to lie in wait for; *(animal)* to stalk. **2** *(amenazar)* to threaten, lurk; **un grave peligro nos acecha,** great danger is looming (up).

acecho *nm* watching; **estar al a. de,** *(vigilar)* to be on the watch for; *(esperar)* to lie in wait for.

acecinar I *vtr (carne)* to cure, salt. **II acecinarse** *vr fig (persona)* to become thin and wizened.

acedera *nf Bot* sorrel.

acedía¹ *nf* **1** *(acidez)* sourness, acidity. **2** *Med* heartburn. **3** *fig (desabrimiento)* sourness, unpleasantness.

acedía² *nf (pez)* dab.

acéfalo,-a *adj Zool* acephalous; *fig (sociedad, partido)* leaderless.

aceitar *vtr* to oil.

aceite *nm* oil. ■ **a. de girasol/maíz/oliva,** sunflower/corn/olive oil; *(en el mar)* **mancha de a.,** oil slick; *fig* **balsa de a.,** millpond.

aceitera *nf* **1** *Culin* oil bottle; **aceiteras,** oil and vinegar set *sing*. **2** *Aut* oil can.

aceitero,-a I *adj* oil; **la industria aceitera,** the oil industry. **II** *nm, f* oil merchant.

aceitillo *nm SAm* scented oil.

aceitoso,-a *adj* oily; *(grasiento)* greasy.

aceituna *nf* olive. ■ **a. rellena,** stuffed olive.

aceitunado,-a *adj* olive, olive-coloured; **de tez aceitunada,** olive-skinned.

aceitunero,-a *nm, f* **1** *(recolector)* olive picker *or* harvester. **2** *(vendedor)* olive seller.

aceituno,-a I *nm Bot* olive tree. **II** *adj Ám* olive, olive-coloured.

aceleración *nf Fís* acceleration. ■ *Aut* **poder de a.,** speeding up, acceleration; *fig* hastening.

acelerada *nf* acceleration.

acelerado,-a I *pp de* **acelerar. II** *adj* accelerated, fast, quick; *Fís* **movimiento a.,** accelerated motion. **III** *nf* acceleration.

acelerador,-a I *adj* accelerating. **II** *nm Aut* accelerator; **pisar el a.,** to step on the accelerator.

aceleramiento *nm* réase **aceleración.**

acelerar I *vtr* to accelerate; *fig* to speed up; **a. el paso,** to quicken one's pace. **II acelerarse** *vr fig (apresurarse)* to hasten, hurry up.

acelerón *nm* sudden acceleration; *Aut* **dar un a.,** to step on the accelerator, put one's foot down.

acelga *nf Bot* chard.

acémila *nf* **1** *Zool (mula)* mule; *(bestia carga)* pack horse. **2** *fig (persona torpe)* clumsy idiot.

acendrado,-a I *pp de* **acendrar. II** *adj* pure, unblemished.

acendrar *vtr* to purify.

acento *nm* **1** *Ling (gráfico)* accent; *(tónico)* stress. ■ **a. ortográfico,** (written) accent. **2** *fig (énfasis)* stress, emphasis; **poner el a. en algo,** to stress *or* emphasise sth. **3** *(tono)* accent; **a. vasco,** Basque accent.

acentor *nm Orn* hedge sparrow, dunnock.

acentuación *nf* accentuation.

acentuado,-a I *pp de* **acentuar. II** *adj* **1** *Ling (con acento gráfico)* accentuated; *(con acento tónico)* stressed. **2** *fig (marcado)* strong, marked.

acentuar I *vtr* **1** to stress, accentuate. **2** *fig* to emphasize, stress, accentuate. **II acentuarse** *vr fig* to become more pronounced *or* noticeable *or* marked.

aceña *nf* watermill.

acepción *nf* **1** *(de palabra)* meaning, sense; **en su más amplia a.,** in the broadest sense of the word. **2** *(preferencia)* preference; **sin a. de personas,** without respect of persons.

acepilladora *nf* planer, planing machine.

aceptabilidad *nf* acceptability.

aceptable *adj* acceptable.

aceptación *nf* **1** acceptance. **2** *(éxito)* success; **tener poca a.,** to have little success, not to be popular.

aceptar *vtr* to accept.

acequia *nf* **1** *(zanja)* irrigation ditch *or* channel. **2** *Am (arroyo)* stream.

acera *nf* pavement, *US* sidewalk; *fam pey* **ser de la a. de enfrente,** to be gay *or* queer.

acerado,-a I *pp de* **acerar. II** *adj* **1** *Metal* steel, steely. **2** *fig (mordaz)* cutting, sharp.

acerar *vtr* **1** *(recubrir de acero)* to steel. **2** *(convertir en acero)* to turn into steel. **3** *fig (fortalecer)* to strengthen.

acerbo,-a *adj* **1** *(sabor)* sour, bitter. **2** *fig (tono)* harsh, bitter; *(dolor)* cruel, harsh.

acerca *adv* **a. de,** about, on.

acercamiento *nm* **1** *(acción)* bringing together, coming together. **2** *fig (de enemigos)* bringing together, reconciliation; *Pol (entre naciones, partidos)* rapprochement; **se produjo un a. entre los dos,** the two of them came closer together.

acercar I *vtr* to bring near *or* nearer, bring (over), draw up; *fig* to bring together; **acerca un poco la tele,** could you move the TV a bit closer?; **¿me acercas la sal?,** can you pass me the salt?; **¿te acerco a casa?,** can I give you a lift home? **II acercarse** *vr* **1** to come closer *or* up, move closer, approach; **a. a algn,** to go up to sb, come up to sb. **2** *(ir)* to go; **acércate a la farmacia,** go to the chemist's; *(venir)* **Pilar se acercó a vernos,** Pilar dropped in to see us.

acería *nf* steelworks *sing*, steel mill.

acerico *nm Cost* pincushion.

acero *nm* **1** steel; *fig* **tener nervios de a.,** to have nerves of steel. ■ **a. inoxidable,** stainless steel. **2** *fig (espada)* sword, steel.

acérrimo,-a *adj (partidario)* staunch, steadfast, earnest; *(enemigo)* bitter.

acertado,-a I *pp de* **acertar. II** *adj* **1** *(opinión, solución)* right, correct; *(comentario)* fitting; *(idea, decisión)* clever; *(color)* well-chosen; **la palabra acertada,** the exact word. **2** *(conveniente)* suitable, wise; **no estuviste muy a. al decir eso,** it wasn't very wise of you to say that.

acertante I *adj* winning. **II** *nmf (ganador)* winner; *(de problemas)* solver.

acertar I *vtr* to get right; *(adivinar)* to guess correctly; **a. el tiro,** to hit the mark; **a. las quinielas,** to win the pools; **acertó tres preguntas,** she got three questions right. **II** *vi* **1** to guess correctly, be right; **acertó con la calle que buscaba,** she found the street she was looking for; **has acertado,** you are right. **2** *(suceder)* **a. a,** to happen to; **acertó a pasar por allí un hombre,** a man happened to pass nearby.

acertijo *nm* riddle.

acervo *nm Jur* common property. ■ **a. cultural,** cultural tradition *or* heritage; **a. familiar,** family property.

acetato *nm Quím* acetate.

acético,-a *adj Quím* acetic.

acetileno *nm Quím* acetylene.

acetona *nf Quím* acetone.

achacar *vtr (atribuir)* to attribute.

achacoso,-a *adj* ailing, unwell.

achampañado,-a *adj (vino)* champagne-style.

achantar I *vi fam* to scare, frighten. **II achantarse** *vr* **1** *(acobardarse)* to lose one's nerve, get frightened. **2** *fam (esconderse)* to hide. **3** *fam (callarse)* to shut up. **4** *Am (detenerse)* to stop.

achaparrado,-a *adj* squat, stocky.

achaque *nm* ailment, complaint; **achaques propios de la vejez,** old age complaints.

achará *interj CAm* oh dear!, what a pity!

acharolado,-a *adj* varnished.

achatado,-a *pp de* achatar. **II** *adj* flattened.

achatamiento *nm* flattening.

achatar *vtr* to flatten.

achicado,-a *adj* childish.

achicar I *vtr* **1** *(amilanar)* to intimidate. **2** *(encoger)* to reduce, make smaller. **3** *(mina)* to drain; *(barco)* to bale out. **4** *CAm* to fasten, tie up. **II achicarse** *vr* **1** *(amilanarse)* to lose heart. **2** *(encogerse)* to get smaller.

achicharradero *nm fam* oven, furnace; **esta habitación es un a.,** this room is like an oven.

achicharrante *adj* burning, scorching, searing, sweltering.

achicharrar I *vtr* **1** *(quemar)* to burn, scorch; *fam* **hace un sol que achicharra,** it's roasting. **2** *(importunar)* to bother, pester; **a. a preguntas,** to plague with questions. **3** *Am* to crush. **II achicharrarse** *vr (quemarse)* to roast.

achicharronar *vtr CAm véase* **achicharrar**.

achicoria *nf Bot* chicory.

achinado,-a *adj* **1** *(gen)* oriental-looking; *(ojos)* slanting. **2** *Am (aplebeyado)* common, coarse, vulgar. **3** *Am (tez)* yellow-skinned.

achingar *vtr CAm (acortar)* to shorten; *(achicar)* to take in.

achira *nf Bot* **1** *Am* arrowhead. **2** *SAm* canna.

achispar I *vtr (emborrachar)* to make tipsy. **II achisparse** *vr (emborracharse)* to get tipsy *or* tight.

acholado,-a *adj Am* **1** half-caste. **2** *(avergonzado)* ashamed; *(amilanado)* scared.

acholar *Am* **I** *vtr (avergonzar)* to shame; *(amilanar)* to scare. **II acholarse** *vr* **1** to adopt half-caste ways. **2** *(avergonzarse)* to be ashamed; *(amilanarse)* to become scared.

achuchado,-a I *pp de* achuchar. **II** *adj hum* tough, difficult.

achuchar *vtr* **1** *(en ataque)* to set on; *(atosigar)* to set against. **2** *(estrujar)* to crush, squeeze.

achucharrar *vtr Am* to crush, squash.

achuchón *nm* **1** *(empujón)* push, shove. **2** *(indisposición)* indisposition. **3** *fam (pareja)* **darse achuchones,** to pet.

achucutar *vtr (humillar)* to shame, humiliate; *(abatir)* to depress, discourage. **II achucutarse** *vr (humillarse)* to be ashamed; *(abatirse)* to become depressed *or* discouraged.

achulado,-a *adj fam* **1** *(grosero)* vulgar, common, crude. **2** *(presumido)* cocky.

achunchar *SAm* **I** *vtr (asustar)* to frighten, scare; *(avergonzar)* to shame. **II achuncharse** *vr (asustarse)* to become scared; *(avergonzarse)* to feel ashamed.

achurruscar I *vtr Am* to squash. **II achurruscarse** *vr* **1** *Am* to get squashed. **2** *Col Ecuad Guat (ensortijarse)* to curl up.

aciago,-a *adj* ill-fated, fateful; **un día a.,** a fateful day.

acíbar *nm (planta)* aloe; *(jugo)* aloes *pl; fig* bitterness, sorrow.

acibarar *vtr fig* to embitter.

acicalado,-a I *pp de* acicalar. **II** *adj* well-dressed, smart.

acicalamiento *nm* smartening up.

acicalar I *vtr (persona, habitación)* to smarten up. **II acicalarse** *vr* to dress up, smarten up.

acicate *nm* **1** *(espuela)* spur. **2** *fig (aliciente)* spur, incentive, stimulus.

acidez *nf* **1** *(de sabor)* sharpness, sourness. **2** *Quím* acidity. ■ *Med* **a. de estómago,** heartburn.

acidia *nf* idleness, indolence.

acidificar *vtr* to acidify.

ácido,-a I *adj (sabor)* sharp, tart, acidic; *Quím* acidic; *fig (tono)* harsh. **II** *nm Quím* acid. ■ **a. acético/clorhídrico/ sulfúrico,** acetic/hydrochloric/sulphuric acid.

acierto *nm* **1** correct guess, right answer; *(idea, decisión)* good choice *or* idea. **2** *(tino)* wisdom, good judgement; **con gran a.,** very wisely. **3** *(éxito)* success.

ácimo,-a *adj* unleavened; **pan á.,** unleavened bread.

aclamación *nf* acclamation, acclaim.

aclamar *vtr* to acclaim.

aclaración *nf* explanation; **exijo una a.,** I demand an explanation.

aclarado *nm* rinsing, rinse.

aclarar I *vtr* **1** *(color, pelo)* to lighten, make lighter. **2** *(líquido)* to thin (down). **3** *(enjuagar)* to rinse. **4** *(explicar)* to clarify, explain; **quiero a. una cosa,** I'd like to make something clear. **II** *v impers (el tiempo)* to clear (up). **III aclararse** *vr* **1** *(entender)* to understand; **es que no me aclaro,** I don't really know what's going on; *fam* **ja ver si te aclaras!,** *(explícate)* explain yourself!; *(decídete)* make up your mind! **2** *(el tiempo)* to clear (up); *fig* **a. la voz,** to clear one's throat.

aclaratorio,-a *adj* explanatory.

aclimatable *adj* able to become acclimatized *or US* acclimated.

aclimatación *nf* acclimatization, *US* acclimation.

aclimatar I *vtr* to acclimatize, *US* acclimate **(a,** to). **II aclimatarse** *vr* to become acclimatized *or US* acclimated **(a,** to); *fig* **a. a algo,** to get used to sth.

acné *nf Med* acne.

acobardar I *vtr* to frighten, unnerve. **II acobardarse** *vr* to become frightened, lose one's nerve, shrink back **(ante,** from).

acochambrar *vtr Am fam (ensuciar)* to dirty, soil; *(manchar)* to stain.

acocuyado,-a *adj SAm fam* merry, tipsy.

acodado,-a *adj* **1** *(cañería)* elbowed. **2** *(apoyado)* leaning (on one's elbows).

acodalar *vtr Arquit* to prop *or* shore up.

acodar I *vtr* **1** *(doblar)* to bend. **2** *Bot* to layer. **II acodarse** *vr* to lean on one's elbows.

acodo *nm* **1** *Bot* layering. **2** *Constr (moldura)* frame.

acogedor,-a *adj (persona)* friendly, welcoming; *(lugar)* cosy, warm.

acoger I *vtr* **1** *(recibir)* to receive; *(a invitado)* to welcome; **le acogieron con los brazos abiertos,** they welcomed him with open arms. **2** *(admitir)* to admit, accept; **a. a un huérfano/refugiado,** to take in an orphan/refugee. **3** *(guarecer)* to shelter, protect. **II acogerse** *vr* **1** *(protegerse)* to take refuge; *fig* **a. a,** to take refuge in. **2** *(promesa, amnistía)* to avail oneself of; **a. a la ley,** to have recourse to the law.

acogida *nf* reception, welcome; **dar a. a algn,** to welcome sb.

acogido,-a I *pp de* acoger. **II** *nm,f (en asilo, orfanato)* inmate, resident.

acogotar *vtr* **I** *(matar)* to kill (with a blow on the neck). **2** *(derribar)* to knock down. **3** *fig (acobardar)* to frighten, intimidate.

acojonado,-a *vulg* **I** *pp de* **acojonar. II** *adj* **1** *(asustado)* shit-scared. **2** *(asombrado)* amazed; **estaban acojonados,** they were bloody amazed.

acojonamiento *nm vulg* funk, jitters *pl.*

acojonante *adj vulg (impresionante)* bloody great *or* terrific.

acojonar I *vtr vulg* **1** *(atemorizar)* to scare, put the wind up. **2** *(impresionar)* to impress; *(pasmar)* to amaze, stun; **acojonó al personal con su voz,** everyone was bloody amazed by ·her voice. **II acojonarse** *vr vulg (acobardarse)* to get the wind up, shit oneself, be shit-scared.

acojone *nm,* **acojono** *nm vulg* funk, jitters·*pl.*

acolchado,-a I *pp de* **acolchar. II** *adj* **1** *(pared, puerta)* padded; *(prenda)* quilted. **III** *nm* **1** padding, quilting. **2** *Arg (edredón)* eiderdown.

acolchar *vtr (rellenar)* to pad; *(prenda)* to quilt.

acólito *nm* **I** *Rel* acolyte; *(monaguillo)* altar boy. **2** *fig (ayudante)* acolyte; *irón* minion.

acollarar I *vtr* **1** *(perro)* to put a collar on; *(bueyes)* to yoke. **2** *Am (unir)* to couple. **II acollararse** *vr Am* **1** *(unirse)* to get together. **2** *(confabularse)* to plot. **3** *(casarse)* to get married.

acomedido,-a *adj* helpful.

acomedirse *vr Am* to offer, volunteer.

acometedor,-a *adj* **1** *(emprendedor)* enterprising. **2** *(que ataca)* aggressive.

acometer *vtr* **1** *(emprender)* to undertake; **a. una tarea,** to undertake a task. **2** *(atacar)* to attack. **3** *(afectar súbitamente)* to be seized by; **le acometió la tos,** he had a coughing fit; **le acometió la risa,** she burst out laughing.

acometida *nf* **1** *(ataque)* attack. **2** *Elec (conexión)* connection.

acometividad *nf* **1** *(dinamismo)* enterprise. **2** *(agresividad)* aggression, aggressiveness.

acomodación *nf* **1** *(colocación conveniente)* arrangement; **la a. de los invitados al banquete,** the seating arrangements for the banquet. **2** *(vivienda)* preparation. **3** *(adaptación)* adaptation; **la a. de los hechos a la realidad,** the adaptation of theory to practice.

acomodadizo,-a *adj* accommodating, easy-going.

acomodado,-a I *pp de* **acomodar. II** *adj* **1** *(ordenado, colocado)* arranged. **2** *(adaptado)* applied, adapted. **3** *(rico)* well-off, well-to-do. **4** *(comodón)* comfort-loving. **5** *(precio)* moderate, reasonable. **6** *(conveniente)* suitable.

acomodador,-a *nm,f (hombre)* usher; *(mujer)* usherette.

acomodar I *vtr* **1** *(colocar)* to arrange; **a. los paquetes en el maletero,** to fit the parcels into the boot. **2** *(aplicar)* to apply, adapt; **se podría a. este ejemplo a otros casos,** this example is applicable in other cases. **3** *(alojar)* to lodge, accommodate. **4** *(proporcionar empleo a)* to provide with a job, find a job for. **5** *(en un cine, teatro)* to find a place for; **nos acomodó en la segunda fila,** he found us a seat in the second row. **6** *(conciliar)* to reconcile. **II acomodarse** *vr* **1** *(instalarse)* to make oneself comfortable; **se acomodó en el sillón,** he settled down in the armchair. **2** *(adaptarse)* to adapt oneself; **se acomoda a todo,** he adapts to everything.

acomodaticio,-a *adj* **1** accommodating, easygoing. **2** *pey* pliable.

acomodo *nm* **1** *(trabajo)* job. **2** *(alojamiento)* accommodation.

acompañado,-a I *pp de* **acompañar. II** *adj* accompanied; **bien/mal a.,** in good/bad company.

acompañamiento *nm* **1** *(gen)* accompaniment. **2** *(comitiva)* retinue, escort. **3** *Mús* accompaniment.

acompañanta *nf* **1** *(female)* companion, chaperon, chaperone. **2** *Mús* (female) accompanist.

acompañante I *adj* accompanying. **II** *nmf* **1** companion, escort. **2** *Mús* accompanist.

acompañar I *vtr* **1** to accompany, go with; **le acompañó hasta la puerta,** she saw him to the door; **me acompañó al médico,** he came with me to see the doctor, **¿te acompaño a casa?,** can I walk you home?; *fml* **le acompaño en el sentimiento,** my condolences. **2** *Mús* to accompany. **3** *(adjuntar)* to enclose, attach. **II acompañarse** *vr Mús* to accompany oneself (a, on).

acompaño *nm CAm* meeting.

acompasado,-a I *pp de* **acompasar. II** *adj* **1** *(ruido, movimiento)* rhythmic. **2** *(paso)* slow, measured; *(habla)* slow, deliberate.

acompasar *vtr* **1** *Mús* to mark the time of, mark the rhythm of. **2** *fig (ajustar)* to keep in time, adjust.

acomplejado,-a I *pp de* **acomplejar. II** *adj* **1** with a complex; **estar a.,** to have a complex (**por,** about). **2** *(tímido)* shy. **III** *nm,f* person with a complex; **es un a.,** he has a complex.

acomplejar I *vtr* to give a complex; *fam* **me acomplejas con tantos conocimientos,** I feel so ignorant in your company. **II acomplejarse** *vr* **a. por,** to develop a complex about.

acondicionado,-a I *pp de* **acondicionar. II** *adj* *(preparado)* equipped, fitted-out; **el piso no está a.,** the flat is not fit to be lived in.

acondicionador *nm* conditioner; **a. de aire,** air conditioner.

acondicionamiento *nm* conditioning, setting up, fitting up; *(mejoramiento)* improvement.

acondicionar *vtr* to prepare, set up, fit up; *(mejorar)* to improve; **a. la red ferroviaria/viaria,** to improve the railway/road network.

acongojado,-a I *pp de* **acongojar. II** *adj* distressed, afflicted, anguished.

acongojar I *vtr* to grieve, make suffer. **II acongojarse** *vr* to be grieved, be distressed.

aconsejable *adj* advisable.

aconsejar I *vtr* to advise; **necesito que me aconsejes,** I need your advice. **II aconsejarse** *vr* to seek advice.

acontecer *v unipers* to happen, take place.

acontecimiento *nm* event, happening.

acopiar *vtr* to gather, collect.

acopio *nm* **1** *(acción)* storing. **2** *(cosa)* store, stock; **hacer a. de,** to store up.

acoplable *adj* adjustable, **adaptable.**

acoplado *nm SAm* trailer.

acoplador *nm* coupler, adapter.

acopladura *nf,* **acoplamiento** *nm* **1** fitting, adaptation. **2** *Téc (acción)* coupling connection; *(junta)* joint. **3** *Astronáut* docking. **4** *Inform* handshaking.

acoplar I *vtr* **1** *(juntar)* to fit (together), to join, adjust. **2** *Téc (conectar)* to couple, connect, join. **3** *(animales)* to mate, pair. **II acoplarse** *vr* **1** to fit, join. **2** *(animales)* to mate, pair. **3** *Astronáut* to dock.

acoquinamiento *nm fam* fear, loss of nerve.

acoquinar *fam* **I** *vtr* to frighten, intimidate. **II acoquinarse** *vr* to become frightened, lose one's nerve.

acorazado,-a I *pp de* **acorazar. II** *adj (blindado)* armoured, *US* armored, armour-plated, *US* armor-plated. **III** *nm Náut (barco)* battleship.

acorazar I *vtr (blindar)* to armour. *US* armor, armour-plate, *US* armor-plate. **II acorazarse** *vr (endurecerse)* to steel oneself, harden oneself (**contra,** against).

acorazonado,-a *adj* heart-shaped.

acorchado,-a I *pp de* **acorchar. II** *adj* **1** cork-like. **2** *(miembro)* numb.

acorchar I *vtr* to cover with cork. **II acorcharse** *vr* **1** to become cork-like. **2** *(miembro)* to go numb.

acordado,-a I *pp de* **acordar**. II *adj* agreed; **en el plazo a.,** within the agreed period; **según lo a.,** as agreed.

acordar I *vtr* 1 to agree; *(decidir)* to decide; **acordaron no ir a la huelga,** they decided not to go on strike. 2 *Am (otorgar)* to award. II **acordarse** *vr* to remember; **no me acuerdo,** I can't remember; **¿te acuerdas de Iñaki?,** do you remember Iñaki?

acorde I *adj* in agreement. II *nm Mús* chord; **a los acordes del himno nacional,** to the tune of the National Anthem.

acordeón *nm Mús* accordion.

acordeonista *nmf* accordionist.

acordonado,-a I *pp de* **acordonar**. II *adj* cordoned off, sealed off.

acordonar *vtr* 1 *(zona)* to cordon off, seal off. 2 *(atar con cordones)* to lace up.

acorralado,-a I *pp de* **acorralar**. II *adj* cornered; *(animal)* at bay.

acorralar *vtr* to corner; **a. a un animal,** to put an animal at bay.

acortar I *vtr* to shorten, make shorter; **a. distancias,** to cut down the distance. II **acortarse** *vr fig* to be shy.

acosar *vtr* to chase, pursue; *fig* **a. a algn a preguntas,** to bombard sb with questions.

acoso *nm* chase, pursuit; *fig* hounding. ■ **a. sexual,** sexual harassment.

acostar *vtr* to put to bed; **está acostado,** he's gone to bed, he's sleeping. II **acostarse** *vr* 1 to go to bed; **hora de a.,** bedtime; **voy a acostarme un ratito,** I'm going to lie down for a while. 2 *fam* **a. con algn,** to sleep with sb, go to bed with sb.

acostillar *vi Am* to fall over (sideways).

acostumbrado,-a I *pp de* **acostumbrar**. II *adj* 1 *(habitual)* usual, customary; **es lo a.,** it is the custom. 2 *(habituado)* used, accustomed; **a. al frío,** used to the cold.

acostumbrar I *vtr* 1 *(habituar)* to accustom to; **hay que acostumbrarlos desde el principio,** you must get them used to it from the start. 2 *(soler)* to be in the habit of; **acostumbra salir por las tardes,** she usually goes out in the evenings. II **acostumbrarse** *vr* 1 *(habituarse)* to become accustomed **(a,** to), get used **(a,** to); **pronto te acostumbrarás,** you'll soon get used to it. 2 *(uso impers)* to be usual; **ya no se acostumbra,** it is no longer usual.

acotación *nf* 1 *(en un escrito)* (marginal) note; *Teat* stage direction. 2 *(en un mapa)* elevation mark.

acotado,-a I *pp de* **acotar**. II *adj* 1 *(terreno)* enclosed. 2 *(escrito)* annotated.

acotamiento *nm* enclosing, demarcation.

acotar *vtr* 1 *(área)* to enclose, demarcate; *fig (tema)* to delimit. 2 *(poner notas)* to add notes to; *(texto)* to annotate. 3 *Geog (mapa)* to mark with elevations.

acotejar *Am* I *vtr (arreglar)* to arrange. II *vr (ponerse cómodo)* to make oneself comfortable.

ácrata *adj & nmf* anarchist.

acre¹ *adj* 1 *(sabor)* sour, bitter; *(olor)* acrid. 2 *fig (palabras)* bitter, harsh; *(crítica)* biting.

acre² *nm (medida)* acre.

acrecentamiento *nm* increase, growth.

acrecentar *vtr* to increase. II **acrecentarse** *vr* to increase, grow.

acreditación *nf* accreditation.

acreditado,-a I *pp de* **acreditar**. II *adj* 1 reputable, prestigious. 2 *(embajador, representante)* accredited.

acreditar I *vtr* 1 to give credit to, be a credit to, add to the reputation of. 2 *(probar)* to prove; **este documento le acredita como único heredero,** this document proves him to be the only heir. 3 *(embajador)* to accredit. 4 *Fin (abonar en cuenta)* to credit. II **acreditarse** *vr* to make one's name, gain a reputation.

acreditativo,-a *adj* which proves, which gives proof.

acreedor,-a I *adj* deserving; **a. a un premio,** worthy of a prize. II *nm,f Com* creditor.

acribillar *vtr* 1 to riddle, pepper; **a. a algn a balazos,** to riddle sb with bullets. 2 *fig* to pester, harass; **a. a algn a preguntas,** to bombard sb with questions.

acrílico,-a *adj* acrylic.

acrimonia *nf véase* **acritud**.

acriollarse *vr Am* to adopt local customs.

acrisolar *vtr* 1 *Metal* to purify; *fig* to perfect. 2 *fig (probar)* to prove, show.

acritud *nf* 1 *(al gusto)* sourness, bitterness; *(al olfato)* acridness. 2 *(de dolor)* intensity, sharpness. 3 *fig (mordacidad)* acrimony.

acrobacia *nf* 1 acrobatics *sing*. 2 *fig* manoeuvre, *US* maneuver.

acróbata *nmf* acrobat.

acrobático,-a *adj* acrobatic.

acrobatismo *nm véase* **acrobacia**.

acromático,-a *adj* achromatic.

acromatismo *nm* achromatism.

acrónimo *nm Ling* acronym.

acrópolis *nf inv* acropolis.

acta *nf* 1 *(de junta, reunión)* minutes *pl*, record; *(publicadas)* transactions *pl*; **levantar a.,** to draw up the minutes. 2 *(certificado)* certificate, official document. ■ **a. notarial,** affidavit. 3 **actas,** minutes, record *sing*; *(publicadas)* transactions.

actitud *nf (disposición)* attitude; *(postura)* position; **en a. de ataque,** ready to attack.

activación *nf* 1 *Téc* activation. 2 *fig (avivamiento)* livening up, quickening.

activar *vtr* 1 *Téc* to activate. 2 *Inform* to enable. 3 *fig (avivar)* to liven up, quicken.

actividad *nf* activity.

activismo *nm Pol* activism.

activista *nmf Pol* activist.

activo,-a I *adj* 1 active; **volcán a.,** active volcano; **en a.,** on active service. 2 *Ling* active. II *nm Fin* asset, assets *pl*; **a. disponible,** liquid assets *pl*; **a. y pasivo,** assets and liabilities.

acto *nm* 1 act, action; **a. seguido,** immediately afterwards; **en a. de servicio,** in action; **en el a.,** at once; **hacer a. de presencia,** to put in an appearance; **'se hacen llaves en el a.',** 'keys cut while you wait'. ■ **a. reflejo,** reflex action; **a. sexual,** sexual intercourse. 2 *(ceremonia)* ceremony; **a. de inauguración,** opening ceremony. ■ **salón de actos,** assembly hall. 3 *Teat* act; **comedia en tres actos,** three-act play. 4 *Rel* Act; **Actos de los Apóstoles,** Acts of the Apostles.

actor,-a I *adj Jur* **parte actora,** prosecution. II *nm Cin Teat* actor.

actriz *nf Cin Teat* actress.

actuación *nf* 1 *Cin Teat Dep* performance. 2 *(intervención)* intervention, action.

actual I *adj* current, present; *(al día)* up-to-date; **en las circunstancias actuales,** under the present circumstances; **un tema muy a.,** a very topical subject. II *nm fml* this month; **el 28 del a.,** the 28th of this month. ◆ **actualmente** *adv (hoy en día)* nowadays, these days; *(ahora)* at the moment, at present.

actualidad *nf* 1 present time; **en la a.,** at present; **estar de a.,** to be fashionable; **temas de a.,** topical subjects. 2 *(hechos)* current affairs *pl*; **la a. deportiva,** *(estado)* the current state of things in the sports world; *(noticias)* sports newsreel.

actualización *nf* 1 *(puesta al día)* updating, bringing up to date. 2 *Filos* actualization.

actualizar *vtr* 1 *(poner al día)* to update, bring up to date. 2 *Filos* to actualize.

actuar I *vtr* to actuate, work. **II** *vi* **1** to act; **a. como** *or* **de,** to act as; **actuó como debía,** he did what he had to do. **2** *Cin Teat* to perform, act.

actuario *nm Jur* clerk (of the court); *Fin* actuary.

acuarela *nf Art* watercolour, *US* watercolor.

acuarelista *nmf* watercolourist, *US* watercolorist.

Acuario *nm Astrol Astron* Aquarius.

acuario *nm (de peces)* aquarium.

acuartelamiento *nm Mil* **1** *(alojamiento)* quartering. **2** *(retención)* confinement to barracks. **3** *(lugar)* barracks (for confinement).

acuartelar *vtr Mil* **1** *(alojar)* to quarter, billet. **2** *(retener)* to confine to barracks.

acuático,-a *adj* aquatic, water; **ave acuática,** aquatic bird.

acuatinta *nf Arte* aquatint.

acuchillar *vtr* **1** *(herir, matar)* to knife, stab. **2** *Cost (hacer aberturas)* to slash. **3** *Corp* to plane (down).

acuciante *adj* urgent, pressing; **necesidad a.,** urgent need.

acuciar *vtr* **1** to urge on; **acuciado por la necesidad,** urged on by necessity. **2** *(dar prisa)* to hurry up. **3** *(desear)* to long *or* yearn for.

acudir *vi* **1** *(ir)* to go; *(venir)* to come, arrive; **acudió puntualmente a la cita,** he arrived punctually for the meeting. **2** *(sobrevenir)* to come back; **aquellos recuerdos acudían a su memoria,** those memories kept coming back to him. **3** *(ir en ayuda)* to help, come forward; **pidió ayuda pero nadie acudió,** she asked for help, but nobody came forward. **4** *(recurrir)* to resort; **acudiré al gobernador,** I'll see the governor (about it), I'll take this matter to the governor; **no sé dónde a.,** I don't know where to turn.

acueducto *nm* aqueduct.

acuerdo *nm* agreement; **¡de a.!,** all right!, O.K.!; **de a. con,** in accordance with; **de común a.,** by common consent; **estar de a. en algo/en hacer algo,** to agree on sth/to do sth; **llegar a un a.,** to come to an agreement; **ponerse de a.,** to agree. ■ **a. comercial,** commercial agreement; **a. marco,** framework agreement.

acuerpar *vtr CAm* to support, defend.

acuidad *nf fml* acuity, sharpness.

acuilmarse *vr CAm* to become depressed, lose heart.

acullá *adv fml* far away; **a. de los mares,** far beyond the sea.

acullicar *vi SAm* to chew coca.

acumulable *adj* accumulable; *Com* **intereses acumulables,** accumulable interest *sing*.

acumulación *nf* accumulation.

acumulador,-a I *adj* accumulative. **II** *nm Elec* accumulator, storage battery.

acumular I *vtr* to accumulate; **a. datos,** to gather data; **a. dinero,** to amass money. **II acumularse** *vr* **1** to accumulate, pile up, build up. **2** *(gente)* to gather.

acumulativo,-a *adj* accumulative.

acunar *vtr* to rock.

acuñación *nf* striking, minting.

acuñar *vtr* **1** *(monedas)* to strike, mint, coin; *fig* **a. una frase,** to coin a phrase. **2** *(poner cuñas)* to wedge.

acuosidad *nf* **1** *(gen)* wateriness. **2** *(jugosidad)* juiciness.

acuoso,-a *adj* **1** *(gen)* watery. **2** *(jugoso)* juicy; **un buen melocotón a.,** a nice juicy peach.

acupuntura *nf Med* acupuncture.

acurrucarse *vr* to curl up, snuggle up.

acusación *nf* **1** accusation. **2** *Jur* charge; **la a. particular,** the private prosecutor. ■ **acta de a.,** indictment.

acusado,-a I *pp de* **acusar. II** *adj* **1** accused; **a. de asesinato,** charged with murder. **2** *fig (marcado)* marked, noticeable. **III** *nm,f* accused, defendant.

acusador,-a I *adj* accusing. **II** *nm,f* accuser.

acusar I *vtr* **1** to accuse **(de,** of); *Jur* to charge **(de,** with). **2** *(delatar)* **todo parece acusarla,** all evidence seems to point to her; *fig* **esta máquina acusa cualquier cambio de temperatura,** this machine is susceptible to any slight change in temperature; *fig* **se acusa la falta de organización,** the lack of organization is evident; *fig* **su cara acusaba el cansancio,** his face showed his exhaustion. **3** *(recibir)* to take; **a. los golpes,** to take the blows. **4** *Com* **a. recibo,** to acknowledge receipt. **II acusarse** *vr* **1** *(confesar)* to confess. **2** *(acentuarse)* to become more pronounced.

acusativo *nm Ling* accusative.

acusatorio,-a *adj* accusatory.

acuse *nm Com* **a. de recibo,** acknowledgment of receipt.

acusetas *nm inv Am,* **acusete** *nm Am* telltale.

acusica *adj & nmf,* **acusón,-ona** *adj & nm,f fam* telltale.

acústica *nf* acoustics *sing*.

acústico,-a *adj* acoustic.

adagio *nm* **1** *(proverbio)* proverb. **2** *Mús* adagio.

adalid *nm* **1** *(caudillo)* leader. **2** *(guía)* champion.

adamascado,-a *adj* damask.

Adán *nm* Adam. ■ *Anat* **nuez de A.,** Adam's apple.

adán *nm fam* untidy *or* slovenly person.

adaptable *adj* adaptable.

adaptación *nf* adaptation.

adaptado,-a I *pp de* **adaptar. II** *adj* adapted.

adaptador *nm Elec* adapter.

adaptar I *vtr* **1** to adapt. **2** *(ajustar)* to adjust, fit. **II adaptarse** *vr* to adapt oneself **(a,** to).

adarga *nf* shield.

adarme *nm* jot, whit, scrap; **por adarmes,** in dribs and drabs.

adecentar I *vtr* to tidy (up), clean (up). **II adecentarse** *vr* to tidy oneself up.

adecuación *nf* adaptation.

adecuado,-a I *pp de* **adecuar. II** *adj* appropriate, suitable, fitting.

adecuar *vtr* to adapt, make suitable.

adefesiero,-a *adj Am* nonsensical.

adefesio *nm* **1** *(persona)* freak. **2** *(cosa)* monstrosity. **3** *fam (disparate)* nonsense.

a. de J.C. *abr de* **antes de Jesucristo,** before Christ, BC.

Adelaida *n* Adelaide.

adelantado,-a I *pp de* **adelantar. II** *adj* **1** *(aventajado)* advanced; *(desarrollado)* developed; *(precoz)* precocious. **2** *(antes de tiempo)* early; **pagar por a.,** to pay in advance. **3** *(reloj)* fast. **4** *(atrevido)* bold, forward.

adelantamiento *nm Aut* overtaking; **hacer un a.,** to overtake.

adelantar I *vtr* **1** to move *or* bring forward; *fig* to advance; *Dep (pelota)* to pass forward; **a. tres puestos,** to go up three places. **2** *(reloj)* to put forward. **3** *(pasar delante)* to pass; *Aut* to overtake; **adelantó un coche rojo,** he overtook a red car. **4** *(acelerar)* to speed up, accelerate; *fig* **no nos adelantemos los acontecimientos,** let's not jump the gun, we'll cross that bridge when we come to it. **5** *(dinero)* to pay in advance, advance; **a. a algn el sueldo,** to advance sb's pay. **6** *fig (aventajar)* to overtake; **le adelantó en matemáticas,** he overtook him in maths. **II** *vi* **1** to advance; **así adelantamos más,** it's quicker this way. **2** *(progresar)* to make progress; **ha adelantado bastante,** she's been doing very well. **3** *(ganar)* to gain, get; **con eso no adelantas nada,** that's a waste of time. **4** *(reloj)* to be fast. **III adelantarse** *vr* **1** *(ir delante)* to go ahead; **adelántate y compra las entradas,** go ahead and get the tickets; **se adelantó a su tiempo,** he was ahead of his time. **2** *(llegar temprano)* to be early; **el verano se ha adelantado,** we are having an early summer. **3** *(anticiparse)* to get ahead **(a,** of); **se me adelantó a**

pagar, I was going to pay, but he beat me to it. **4** *(aproximarse)* to go *or* come forward; **se me adelantó a saludarla,** he went forward to greet her. **5** *(reloj)* to gain, be fast.

adelante I *adv* further, forward; **de ahora en a.,** from now on; **de aquí en a.,** from here on; **llevar a. un plan,** to carry out a plan; **más a.,** *(lugar)* further on; *(tiempo)* later; **sacó a sus hijos a.,** he gave his children all they needed; **seguir a.,** to keep going, carry on; *fig* **van saliendo a.,** they're managing. **II** *interj (pase)* come in!; *(siga)* go ahead!, carry on!

adelanto *nm* **1** advance; **los adelantos de la ciencia,** the progress of science. **2** *(tiempo)* **este reloj lleva diez minutos de a.,** this watch is ten minutes fast; **le lleva media hora de a.,** he has half an hour's lead over her. **3** *Com (de dinero)* advance payment.

adelfa *nf Bot* oleander, rosebay.

adelgazador,-a *adj* slimming, weight-reducing.

adelgazamiento *nm* slimming. ■ **cura de a.,** slimming cure *or* diet.

adelgazar I *vtr (persona)* to make thin, slim; *(cosa)* to make slim. **II** *vi (enflaquecer)* to slim, lose weight; **ha adelgazado mucho,** he's lost a lot of weight.

ademán *nm* **1** *(movimiento)* movement; *(gesto)* gesture; **en a. de,** with the intention of, as if about to; **hacer a. de,** to look as if one is about to. **2** **ademanes,** manners.

además *adv* besides, in addition; **a. de él,** besides him; *(también)* also, as well; **a., no lo he visto nunca,** furthermore, I've never seen him; **llegó cansado, y a., enfermo,** he arrived tired and ill to boot.

Adén *n* Aden.

ADENA *nf Ecol abr de* Asociación para la Defensa de la Naturaleza.

adentrarse *vr* **1** *(penetrar)* to penetrate deep, enter deep **(en,** into). **2** *fig (profundizar)* to go deeply into, study thoroughly.

adentro I *adv* **1** *(dentro)* inside; **venid a.,** come inside. **2** *(hacia or en el interior)* **mar a.,** out to sea; **no os vayáis muy a.,** don't go too far in; **tierra a.,** inland. **II adentros** *nmpl* **decir algo para sus a.,** to say sth to oneself.

adepto,-a I *adj* who follows, who supports. **II** *nm, f* follower, supporter.

aderezar I *vtr* **1** *Culin (comida)* to season; *(ensalada)* to dress; *(bebidas)* to mix. **2** *(preparar)* to get ready, prepare. **3** *fig (adornar) (persona)* to make beautiful; *(cosa)* to embellish. **II aderezarse** *vr (arreglarse)* to dress up, get ready.

aderezo *nm* **1** *Culin (de comida)* seasoning; *(de ensalada)* dressing. **2** *(preparación)* preparation, disposition. **3** *(joyas)* set of jewellery. **4** *(arreos)* harness, trappings *pl.*

adeudar I *vtr* **1** *(deber)* to owe, have a debt of. **2** *Com (en cuenta)* to charge, debit; **a. una cuenta,** to charge an account. **II adeudarse** *vr (contraer deudas)* to get into debt.

adeudo *nm* **1** *(deuda)* debt. **2** *Com* debit, charge.

a D. g. *abr de* **a Dios gracias,** thanks be to God.

adherencia *nf* **1** *(adhesión)* adherence; *(pegajosidad)* adhesion, sticking. **2** *Aut* roadholding.

adherente I *adj* adherent. **II** *nm* **1** *(requisito)* requisite. **2** *(adhesivo)* adhesive.

adherir I *vtr* to stick on. **II** *vi* to stick **(a,** to). **III adherirse** *vr fig* **a. a,** to adhere to, follow.

adhesión *nf* adhesion, adherence; *fig (apoyo)* support; *fig (afiliación)* **a. a una doctrina,** adherence to a doctrine; *fig* **contaba con la a. de todos,** he had everyone's support.

adhesivo,-a *adj* & *nm* adhesive.

adicción *nf* addiction; **crear a.,** to be addictive.

adición *nf* addition.

adicional *adj* additional.

adicionar *vtr* to add; *Mat* to add up.

adicto,-a I *adj* **1** fond **(a,** of), keen **(a,** on); *(drogas)* addicted **(a,** to). **2** *(partidario)* supporting. **II** *nm, f* **1** supporter, follower. **2** *(drogas)* addict.

adiestrado,-a I *pp de* **adiestrar. II** *adj* **1** trained, instructed. **2** *Herald* dexterwise.

adiestramiento *nm* training, instruction.

adiestrar I *vtr* to train, instruct. **II adiestrarse** *vr* to train oneself.

adinerado,-a I *pp de* **adinerarse. II** *adj* wealthy, rich. **III** *nm, f* rich person.

adinerarse *vr fam* to get rich.

adiós *(pl* **adioses) I** *interj* goodbye; *fam* bye-bye; *(al cruzarse con algn)* hello; *fam* **¡a. a las vacaciones!,** that's my holidays finished! **II** *nm* goodbye; **decir a. con la mano,** to wave goodbye; *fam fig* **decir a. a algo,** to say goodbye to sth.

adiposidad *nf* adiposity; *(obesidad)* obesity.

adiposo,-a *adj Anat* adipose.

aditamento *nm* *(añadidura)* added piece, addition; *(complemento)* accessory.

aditivo,-a *adj* & *nm* additive.

adivinación *nf* **1** guessing; **a. del pensamiento,** mind-reading. **2** *(predicción)* divination, forecast.

adivinador,-a *nm, f* fortune-teller.

adivinanza *nf* riddle, puzzle.

adivinar *vtr* **1** to guess; **a. el pensamiento,** to read sb's mind. **2** *(presagiar)* to foretell, forecast. **3** *(enigma)* to solve.

adivinatorio,-a *adj* divinatory.

adivino,-a *nm, f* fortune-teller.

adjetivación *nf Ling* adjectival use.

adjetival *adj Ling* adjectival.

adjetivar *vtr* **1** *Ling* to use adjectivally *or* as an adjective. **2** *fig (calificar)* to label, describe.

adjetivo,-a I *adj* adjectival, adjective. **II** *nm* adjective.

adjudicación *nf* **1** *(concesión)* award, awarding. **2** *(en subasta)* sale.

adjudicar I *vtr* **1** *(premio)* to award. **2** *(vender)* to sell, knock down; **¡adjudicado!,** sold! **II adjudicarse** *vr (apropiarse)* to appropriate, take over.

adjudicatario,-a *nm, f* **1** *(premiado)* awardee. **2** *(comprador)* buyer, successful bidder.

adjuntar *vtr* to enclose, attach; *(en carta)* **adjunto una muestra,** please find enclosed sample.

adjunto,-a I *pp de* **adjuntar. II** *adj* **1** enclosed, attached; **rellenar el cupón a.,** fill in the enclosed form. **2** *Educ* assistant; **profesor a.,** assistant teacher. **III** *nm, f Educ* assistant teacher.

adlátere *nm* henchman, follower.

adm., admón., *abr de* **administración,** administration.

administración *nf* **1** *(gobierno)* administration, authorities *pl.* ■ *Pol* **a. central,** central government; **a. pública,** public administration. **2** *(de empresa)* administration, management. ■ **consejo de a.,** board of directors. **3** *(cargo)* post of administrator; post of manager. **4** *(despacho)* administrator's office, manager's office. **5** *(oficina)* (branch) office. ■ **A. de Hacienda,** (local) tax office; **a. de lotería,** lottery office.

administrador,-a I *adj* administrating. **II** *nm, f* **1** administrator; *(ama de casa)* **es muy buena administradora,** she knows how to stretch money. **2** manager; *(de bienes, fincas)* administrator.

administrar I *vtr* **1** to administer; **a. justicia,** to administer justice. **2** *(dirigir)* to run, manage. **3** *fml (dar)* to give; **le administró un antibiótico,** he gave him an antibiotic. **II administrarse** *vr* to manage one's own money.

administrativo,-a I *adj* administrative. **II** *nm, f* **1** (*funcionario*) official. **2** (*de empresa, banco*) office worker.

admirable *adj* admirable.

admiración *nf* admiration; **causar a.,** to impress; **sentir a.,** to admire.

admirador,-a I *adj* admiring. **II** *nm, f* admirer.

admirar I *vtr* **1** to admire. **2** (*sorprender*) to amaze, surprise, astound, astonish; **me admira su valor,** I am amazed by his courage; **quedarse admirado,** to be astonished. **II admirarse** *vr* to be amazed, be astonished.

admirativo,-a *adj* admiring.

admisibilidad *nf* admissibility.

admisible *adj* admissible, acceptable.

admisión *nf* **1** admission; 'reservado el derecho de a.', 'the management reserves the right to refuse admission'. **2** (*aceptación*) acceptance. **3** *Téc* inlet, intake.

admitir *vtr* **1** to admit, let in. **2** (*aceptar*) to admit, accept; **'no se admiten cheques',** 'no cheques accepted'. **3** (*permitir*) to allow; **no admito este tipo de conversación,** I will not tolerate this type of conversation; *fig* **este libro admite varias lecturas,** this book is open to various interpretations. **4** (*reconocer*) to admit, acknowledge; **admito que fui demasiado lejos,** I admit that I took things too far. **5** (*haber lugar*) to hold; **admite hasta cien personas,** there is room for up to a hundred people.

admonición *nf* warning, reproof.

admonitorio,-a *adj* warning.

ADN *nm abr de* **ácido desoxirribonucleico,** desoxyribonucleic acid, DNA.

adobado,-a I *pp de* **adobar. II** *adj Culin* marinated.

adobar *vtr* **1** *Culin* (*carne, pescado*) to marinate. **2** (*pieles*) to tan.

adobe *nm* **1** *Constr* adobe. **2** *SAm fig* big foot.

adobo *nm Culin* **1** (*acción*) marinating. **2** (*salsa*) marinade.

adocenado,-a I *pp de* **adocenarse. II** *adj* common or garden, ordinary.

adocenarse *vr* to become commonplace.

adoctrinamiento *nm* indoctrination.

adoctrinar *vtr* to indoctrinate.

adolecer *vi* **1** (*sufrir*) to be ill; **adolecía de asma,** he suffered from asthma; *fig fml* **adolece de excesivo barroquismo,** it is far too baroque. **2** (*carecer*) to lack; **adolece de interés,** he lacks enthusiasm.

adolescencia *nf* adolescence.

adolescente *adj & nmf* adolescent.

adónde *adv interr* where (to)?

adonde *adv* where.

adondequiera *adv* wherever.

adopción *nf* adoption; **país de a.,** country of adoption.

adoptar *vtr* to adopt.

adoptivo,-a *adj* (*hijo*) adopted, adoptive; (*padres*) adoptive; *fig* **hijo a. de la cindad,** honorary citizen; *fig* **país a.,** country of adoption.

adoquin *nm* cobble, paving stone.

adoquinado,-a I *pp de* **adoquinar. II** *adj* cobbled. **III** *nm* cobbling, paving.

adoquinar *vtr* to cobble, pave.

adorable *adj* adorable.

adoración *nf* **1** *Rel* worship, adoration. **2** *fig* adoration, worshipping.

adorador,-a I *adj* **1** *Rel* worshipping. **2** *fig* adoring. **II** *nm, f* **1** *Rel* worshipper. **2** *fig* adorer, worshipper.

adorar *vtr* **1** *Rel* to worship. **2** *fig* to adore.

adormecedor,-a *adj* sleep-inducing, soporific.

adormecer I *vtr* **1** to send to sleep, make sleepy. **2** *fig* (*acallar*) to quieten; (*calmar*) to soothe. **II adormecerse** *vr* **1** (*dormirse*) to doze off. **2** (*miembro*) to go to sleep, go numb.

adormecido,-a I *pp de* **adormecer. II** *adj* sleepy, drowsy.

adormecimiento *nm* **1** (*sueño*) drowsiness, sleepiness. **2** (*de miembro*) numbness.

adormidera *nf Bot* poppy.

adormilarse *vr* to doze, drowse.

adornamiento *nm* adornment, decoration.

adornar *vtr* to adorn, decorate; *fig* to embellish.

adorno *nm* (*gen*) decoration, adornment; *Cost* trimming; **de a.,** decorative.

adorote *nm SAm* handbarrow.

adosado,-a I *pp de* **adosar. II** *adj Constr* semi-detached.

adosar *vtr* to lean (**a,** against).

adquirido,-a I *pp de* **adquirir. II** *adj* acquired.

adquirir *vtr* to acquire.

adquisición *nf* (*gen*) acquisition; (*compra*) buy, purchase.

adquisitivo,-a *adj* acquisitive.

adrede *adv* deliberately, on purpose, purposely.

adrenalina *nf* adrenalin.

adriático,-a I *adj* Adriatic. **II** *nm* **el (Mar) A.,** the Adriatic (Sea).

adscribir (*pp adscrito*) **I** *vtr* **1** (*atribuir*) to ascribe to. **2** (*a un trabajo*) to appoint to. **II adscribirse** *vr* (*afiliarse*) to affiliate (**a,** to).

adscripción *nf* **1** (*atribución*) ascription. **2** (*a un trabajo*) appointment.

adscrito,-a I *pp de* **adscribir. II** *adj* **1** (*atribuido*) ascribed. **2** (*a un trabajo*) appointed.

adsorbente *adj & nm Fís* adsorbent.

adsorber *vtr* to adsorb.

adsorción *nf Fís* adsorption.

aduana *nf* **1** customs *pl*; **el tabaco no paga a.,** there's no duty on tobacco; **pasar por la a.,** to go through customs. ■ **oficial de a.,** customs officer. **2** (*oficinas*) customs building.

aduanero,-a I *adj* customs. **II** *nm, f* customs officer.

aducir *vtr* to adduce, allege.

adueñarse *vr* **a. de,** to appropriate, seize; *fig* **el terror se adueñó de ella,** she was seized by terror.

aduje *pt indef véase* **aducir.**

adulación *nf* adulation, flattery.

adulador,-a I *adj* adulating, flattering. **II** *nm, f* adulator, flatterer.

adular *vtr* to adulate, flatter, soft-soap.

adulón,-ona I *adj* fawning, grovelling, *US* groveling. **II** *nm, f* crawler, groveller, *US* groveler.

adulteración *nf* adulteration.

adulterado,-a I *pp de* **adulterar. II** *adj* adulterated.

adulterar *vtr* to adulterate.

adulterio *nm* adultery.

adúltero,-a I *adj* adulterous. **II** *nm, f* (*hombre*) adulterer; (*mujer*) adulteress.

adultez *nf* **1** adulthood. **2** *CAm* (*virilidad*) virility.

adulto,-a *adj & nm, f* adult; **los adultos,** grown-ups; **una persona adulta,** an adult.

adustez *nf fig* harshness, severity.

adusto,-a *adj* **1** scorched, charred, burnt. **2** *fig* (*austero*) harsh, stern, austere, severe.

aduzco *indic pres véase* **aducir.**

advenedizo,-a *adj & nm, f* parvenu, parvenue, upstart.

advenimiento *nm* (*gen*) advent, coming; (*al trono*) accession.

adventicio,-a *adj* accidental; *Biol* adventitious.
adventismo *nm Rel* Adventism.
adventista *adj & nmf Rel* Adventist.
adverbial *adj Ling* adverbial.
adverbio *nm Ling* adverb.
adversario,-a I *adj* opposing; **el equipo a.,** the opposing team. **II** *nm,f* adversary, opponent.
adversidad *nf* adversity, misfortune, setback.
adverso,-a *adj* **1** adverse, unfavourable; **en condiciones adversas,** in adverse conditions. **2** *(opuesto)* opposed. **3** *(adversario)* opposing.
advertencia *nf* warning; *(consejo)* piece of advice; **te voy a hacer una a.,** mark my words.
advertido,-a I *pp de* **advertir. II** *adj* warned; *(informado)* informed; **estás** *or* **quedas a.,** you've been warned.
advertir *vtr* **1** to warn; *(informar)* to inform, advise; **te lo había advertido,** I told you; *fam* **te advierto que él tampoco lo vio,** mind you, he didn't see it either. **2** *(darse cuenta)* to realize, notice; **no advirtió su presencia,** he didn't notice he was there.
adviento *nm Rel* Advent.
advocación *nf Rel* invocation; **bajo la a. de,** under the protection of.
adyacente *adj* adjacent.
aéreo,-a *adj* **1** aerial; **vista aérea,** aerial view. **2** *Av* air; **líneas aéreas,** airlines; **tráfico a.,** air traffic.
aero- *pref* aero-; *Av* **aerobús,** airbus.
aeróbica *nf* aerobics *sing*.
aerobio,-a *Biol* **I** *adj* aerobic. **II** *nm* aerobe.
aeroclub *nm Av* flying club.
aerodeslizador *nm* hovercraft.
aerodinámica *nf Fís* aerodynamics *sing*.
aerodinámico,-a *adj Fís* aerodynamic; **de línea aero dinámica,** streamlined.
aeródromo *nm Av* aerodrome.
aerofagia *nf Med* aerophagia.
aerofaro *nm* beacon.
aerógrafo *nm Arte* airbrush.
aerograma *nm* aerogram, aerogramme.
aeromodelismo *nm* aeroplane modelling *or US* modeling.
aeromodelista I *adj* aeroplane modelling *or US* modeling. **II** *nmf* aeroplane modeller *or US* modeler.
aeromodelo *nm* model aeroplane.
aeromoza *nf Am* air hostess.
aeronáutica *nf Av Náut* aeronautics *sing*.
aeronáutico,-a *adj Av Náut* aeronautic, aeronautical.
aeronaval *adj Av Náut* air-sea.
aeronave *nf Av* airship. ■ **a. espacial,** spaceship.
aeroplano *nm Av* aeroplane.
aeropuerto *nm Av* airport.
aerosol *nm Quím* aerosol.
aerostática *nf Fís* aerostatics *sing*.
aerostático,-a *adj Fís* aerostatic; **globo a.,** hot-air balloon.
aerostato *nm Fís* hot-air balloon.
a/f *abr de* **a favor,** in favour *or US* favor.
afabilidad *nf* affability.
afable *adj* affable.
afamado,-a I *pp de* **afamar. II** *adj* famous, well-known.
afamar I *vtr* to make famous. **II afamarse** *vr* to become famous.
afán *nm (pl afanes)* **1** *(esfuerzo)* effort. **2** *(celo)* zeal; *(interés)* keenness, eagerness; **con a.,** keenly.
afanador,-a I *adj* zealous, eager. **II** *nm,f* **1** zealous *or* eager person. **2** *(ratero)* thief.

afanar I *vtr* **1** *fam (robar)* to nick, pinch, swipe. **2** *Am (dinero)* to carn. **II afanarse** *vr* **1** to work with zeal; **a. por conseguir algo,** to do one's best to achieve *or* obtain sth. **2** *fam (robar)* to nick, pinch, swipe.
afanoso,-a *adj* **1** *(persona)* keen, zealous, eager. **2** *(tarea)* hard, tough, laborious.
afarolarse *vr Am (emocionarse)* to get worked up, get excited; *(enfadarse)* to get angry.
afasia *nf Med* aphasia.
afásico,-a *adj & nm,f Med* aphasic.
afear *vtr* **1** to make ugly. **2** *fig (reprochar)* to reproach; **afearle a algn la conducta,** to censure sb's behaviour.
afección *nf* **1** *(enfermedad)* affection, disease; **una a. de garganta,** a throat complaint. **2** *(afición)* fondness.
afeccionarse *vr* to take a liking (**a**, to), become fond (**a**, of).
afectación *nf* affectation.
afectado,-a I *pp de* **afectar. II** *adj* **1** *(gen)* affected; **la región afectada por la sequía,** the area affected by (the) drought. **2** *(fingido)* pretended, affected. **3** *(emocionado)* affected, upset; **está muy a.,** he's very upset. **4** *(involucrado)* involved; **las personas afectadas,** the people involved. **5** *Med* **a. de hepatitis,** suffering from hepatitis.
afectar *vtr* **1** *(gen)* to affect; **a. la voz,** to talk in an affected way; **afectó indiferencia,** she affected indifference; **le afectó mucho,** she was deeply affected; **nos afecta a todos,** it concerns all of us. **2** *(dañar)* to damage; **le afectó a los ojos,** it damaged his eyes.
afectísimo,-a *adj fml superl de* **afecto,-a;** *(en una carta)* **suyo a.,** yours faithfully.
afectividad *nf* affectivity.
afectivo,-a *adj* **1** *(sensibilidad)* sensitive. **2** *Psic* affective.
afecto,-a I *adj* **1** *(aficionado)* fond (**a**, of). **2** *Med* suffering (**de**, from). **II** *nm* affection; *(en carta)* **con todo mi a.,** with all my love; **tomarle a. a algn,** to become fond of sb.
afectuosidad *nf* affection.
afectuoso,-a *adj* affectionate.
afeitado *nm* shave, shaving. **2** *Taur (cuernos)* blunting.
afeitadora *nf* razor, shaver.
afeitar I *vtr* **1** to shave. **2** *Taur (de toro)* to blunt the horns of. **II afeitarse** *vr* to shave.
afeite *nm arc* make-up.
afelpado,-a *adj Tex* velvety.
afeminación *nf* effeminacy.
afeminado,-a I *pp de* **afeminar. II** *adj* effeminate. **III** *nm* effeminate man; *fam* sissy.
afeminamiento *nm* effeminacy.
afeminar I *vtr* to make effeminate. **II afeminarse** *vr* to become effeminate.
aferrado,-a I *pp de* **aferrar. II** *adj* clinging to, clutching, holding on to; *fig* **a. a sus ideas,** sticking to his guns.
aferramiento *nm* **1** clutching, clinging. **2** *fig (obstinación)* stubbornness.
aferrar I *vtr* **1** to clutch, cling, grasp. **2** *Náut (anclar)* to anchor, moor; **a. las velas,** to furl the sails. **II aferrarse** *vr* to clutch, cling; **aférrate bien,** hold (on) tight; *fig* **a. a una creencia,** to cling to a belief.
Afganistán *n* Afghanistan.
afgano,-a *adj & nm,f* Afghan.
AFI *nm Ling abr de* **Asociación Fonética Internacional,** International Phonetic Association, IPA.
afianzamiento *nm* strengthening, reinforcement; *(definitivo)* consolidation.
afianzar I *vtr* **1** to strengthen, reinforce, consolidate. **2** *Jur (pagar fianza)* to stand bail for. **II afianzarse** *vr* to steady oneself; *(agarrarse)* to cling; *fig* **su fama se afianzó,** he became a man of well-established reputation.

afición *nf* 1 *(inclinación)* penchant, liking; **tiene a. por la música**, he is fond of music. 2 *(ahínco)* interest, zeal; **con a.**, keenly. 3 *Dep* **la a.**, the fans *pl*.

aficionado,-a I *pp de* **aficionar.** II *adj* 1 keen, fond; **ser a. a viajar**, to be fond of travelling. 2 *(no profesional)* amateur. III *nm,f* 1 enthusiast; **un a. a la música**, a music lover. 2 amateur.

aficionar I *vtr (interesar)* to interest, make fond of. II **aficionarse** *vr (interesarse)* to become fond (**a**, of), take a liking (**a**, to); **se aficionó al teatro**, she became a theatre lover.

afijo,-a *Ling* I *adj* affixed. II *nm* affix.

afilado,-a I *pp de* **afilar.** II *adj (con filo)* sharp; *(con punta)* pointed; *fig* **cara afilada**, long, thin face. III *nm* sharpening.

afilador,-a I *adj* sharpening. II *nm (persona)* knife-grinder. III *nf (máquina)* sharpener.

afilalápices *nm inv* pencil sharpener.

afilamiento *nm fig (de cara, nariz)* sharpness.

afilar I *vtr* 1 *(cuchillo, lápiz)* to sharpen. 2 *Arg Par Urug (cortejar)* to court; *(requebrar)* to flatter. II **afilarse** *vr* to grow pointed *or* sharp.

afiliación *nf* affiliation.

afiliado, -a I *pp de* **afiliac.** II *adj* affiliated, member. III *nm,f* affiliate, member.

afiliar I *vtr* to affiliate, make a member. II **afiliarse** *vr* to affiliate, become a member.

afiligranado,-a *adj Arte* filigreed; *fig* delicate, dainty, fine.

afín *adj* 1 *(semejante)* kindred, similar; *(relacionado)* related; **el alcohol y los productos afines**, alcohol and related products; **gustos afines**, similar tastes. 2 *(próximo)* adjacent, next.

afinación *nf* 1 *(gen)* polishing, refining. 2 *(música, máquina)* tuning.

afinado,-a I *pp de* **afinar.** II *adj* 1 *(gen)* polished, refined. 2 *(música)* in tune, tuned.

afinador,-a *Mús* I *nm,f (persona)* tuner. II *nm* tuning key.

afinar *vtr* 1 *(gen)* to polish, perfect; *(puntería)* to sharpen. 2 *(instrumento)* to tune. 3 *(metales)* to refine.

afincar *vtr*, **afincarse** *vr* to settle down, establish oneself.

afinidad *nf* affinity; *Quím* similarity.

afirmación *nf* 1 *(aseveración)* statement, assertion. 2 *(afianzamiento)* strengthening.

afirmado *nm (de carretera)* road surface.

afirmar I *vtr* 1 *(aseverar)* to state, declare; **afirmó no saber nada**, he said he knew nothing (about it). 2 *(afianzar)* to strengthen, reinforce. II **afirmarse** *vr (opinión)* to maintain; **se afirmó en su negativa**, he insisted on refusing.

afirmativo,-a I *adj* affirmative; **en caso a. ...,** if the answer is yes ... . II *nf* affirmative answer.

aflautado,-a *adj* flute-like.

aflicción *nf* affliction, suffering, grief.

afligido,-a I *pp de* **afligir.** II *adj* afflicted, grieved, troubled.

afligir I *vtr* to afflict, grieve, trouble. II **afligirse** *vr* to grieve, be distressed.

aflojamiento *nm* loosening; *fig* relaxation.

aflojar I *vtr (soltar)* to loosen; *fig (esfuerzo)* to relax; *fam* **a. la mosca**, to fork out. II *vi (disminuir)* to weaken, grow weak; **el calor ha aflojado un poco**, the heat has let up a bit. III **aflojarse** *vr (soltarse)* to come *or* work loose; **se aflojó el tornillo**, the screw came loose.

afloramiento *nm Min* outcrop.

aflorar *vi* 1 *Min* to crop out, outcrop. 2 *fig (asomar)* to come to the surface, appear.

afluencia *nf* inflow, influx; **la a. de público**, the flow of people.

afluente I *adj (caudaloso)* flowing, inflowing; *(persona)* verbose, wordy. II *nm Geog* tributary.

afluir *vi* to flow (**a**, into).

aflujo *nm* afflux.

afluxionarse *vr CAm* to swell up.

afonía *nf Med* loss of voice, hoarseness.

afónico,-a *adj* voiceless, hoarse; **estar a.**, to have lost one's voice.

aforismo *nm* aphorism.

aforístico,-a *adj* aphoristic.

aforo *nm* 1 *(capacidad)* seating capacity. 2 *(evaluación)* valuation, assessment.

afortunado,-a *adj* fortunate, lucky; *(dichoso)* happy; *fig* **una respuesta poco afortunada**, a rather inappropriate answer; *prov* **a. en el juego, desgraciado en amores**, lucky at cards, unlucky in love.

afrancesado,-a I *adj* 1 *(galicista)* pro-French, who has gone French. 2 *Hist* supporting Napoleon. II *nm,f Hist* (Spanish) supporter of Napoleon.

afrancesamiento *nm* pro-French attitude, Frenchification.

afrecha *nf* bran.

afrenta *nf fml* affront, offense; **hacerle una a. a algn**, to affront sb.

afrentar *fml* I *vtr* to affront, offend. II **afrentarse** *vr* to be ashamed (**de**, of).

afrentoso,-a *adj fml* 1 *(que ofende)* offending, offensive. 2 *(que avergüenza)* shameful, disgraceful.

Africa *n* Africa.

africado,-a *Ling* I *adj* affricative. II *nf* affricate.

africano,-a *adj & nm,f* African.

afrikaans *nm (idioma)* Afrikaans.

afro *adj fam* afro.

afroamericano,-a *adj & nm,f* Afro-American.

afroasiático,-a *adj & nm,f* Afro-Asian.

afrodisíaco,-a *adj & nm* aphrodisiac.

afrontamiento *nm* confrontation.

afrontar *vtr* 1 *(hacer frente)* to confront, face; **a. las consecuencias**, to face up to the consequences; **a. una situación**, to face a situation. 2 *Jur (carear)* to confront, bring face to face. 3 *(poner enfrente)* to face.

afta *nf Med* aphtha.

aftoso,-a *adj Med* **fiebre aftosa**, foot-and-mouth disease.

afuera I *adv* outside; **la parte de a.**, the outside; **más a.**, further out; **salir a.**, to come *or* go out. II **afueras** *nfpl* outskirts; **vivían en las a. de Pamplona**, they lived on the outskirts of Pamplona.

afystreño,-a *adj Am* strange; *(extranjero)* foreign.

agachada *nf (acción)* squatting; *(ardid)* trick, ruse.

agachadiza *nf Orn* snipe. ■ **a. común**, snipe; **a. real**, great snipe.

agachado,-a *adj CAm* sly, furtive.

agachar I *vtr* to lower, bow. II **agacharse** *vr* 1 *(encogerse)* to cower; *(agazaparse)* to crouch (down), squat; *(protegerse)* to duck (down). 2 *fam (aguantarse)* to put up with. 3 *Am (someterse)* to give in (**a**, to); to submit (**a**, to).

agalla *nf* 1 *(de pez)* gill. 2 *Orn* temple. 3 *Bot* gall, gallnut. 4 **agallas**, *(angina)* sore throat *sing*; *fig (valor)* guts, pluck *sing*; **tiene a.**, she's got guts. 5 *Am (codicia)* greed; **tener agallas**, to be greedy.

agallado,-a *adj Arg Chi PR* graceful, debonair.

ágape *nm* 1 feast, banquet. 2 *Hist* agape.

agareno,-a *adj & nm,f Rel* Muslim, Moslem; **un perfil a.**, an Arab-like profile.

agarrada *nf fam* quarrel; **tener una a. con algn**, to have a row with sb.

agarraderas *nfpl fam* **tener buenas a.**, to be well connected, have the right friends.

agarradero *nm* **1** (*asa*) handle. **2** *fam* (*excusa*) excuse.

agarrado,-a I *pp de* **agarrar. II** *adj fam* stingy, tight; **baile a.**, cheek-to-cheek dancing.

agarrador,-a *adj Am* (*licor*) strong.

agarrar I *vtr* **1** (*asir con las manos*) to grasp, clutch, seize; **agárralo fuerte**, hold it tight. **2** (*conseguir*) to take advantage of; **agarré la oferta que me brindaban, I** jumped at the offer which they made me. **3** *fam* (*pillar*) to catch; **agarrarla, a. una borrachera**, to get drunk *or* pissed; **agarró un cabreo**, he flew off the handle. **II agarrarse** *vr* **1** to hold on to, cling to, clutch; **agarraos bien**, hold tight; *fig* **a. a un clavo ardiendo**, to clutch at a straw; *fam* **se agarra a lo que sea para no trabajar**, he seizes on any excuse to avoid work. **2** *Culin* (*pegarse*) to stick. **3** *fam* (*pelearse*) to quarrel, fight.

agarrón *nm fam* **1** (*tirón*) pull, tug. **2** (*agarrada*) fight, quarrel.

agarroso,-a *adj CAm* sour, tart.

agarrotado,-a I *pp de* **agarrotar. II** *adj* **1** (*apretado*) tight. **2** (*músculo*) stiff. **3** (*motor*) seized up.

agarrotamiento *nm* **1** (*atadura*) tightening. **2** (*rigidez*) stiffening. **3** (*de máquina*) seizing up.

agarrotar I *vtr* **1** (*atar*) to tighten, tie up tightly. **2** (*músculos*) to stiffen. **3** (*estrangular*) to strangle; (*dar garrote*) to garotte. **II agarrotarse** *vr* **1** (*entumecerse músculos*) to stiffen; (*perder sensibilidad*) to go numb. **2** (*máquina*) to seize up.

agasajado,-a I *pp de* **agasajar. II** *nm,f* guest of honour *or* US honor.

agasajar *vtr* (*obsequiar*) to smother with attentions, treat well; (*dar agasajo*) to wine and dine.

agasajo *nm* **1** (*acogida*) royal welcome; (*trato*) kindness. **2** (*comida*) reception, banquet. **3** (*regalo*) gift.

ágata *nf Min* agate.

agatas *adv SAm* (*apenas*) hardly; (*con dificultad*) with great difficulty.

agateador *nm Orn* tree creeper.

agaucharse *vr SAm* to adopt **gaucho** ways.

agave *nf Bot* agave.

agavilladora *nf Agr* binder.

agavillar I *vtr Agr* to bind, sheave. **II agavillarse** *vr fig* to get together, form groups.

agazapar I *vtr* to grab (hold of). **II agazaparse** *vr* (*agacharse*) to crouch (down), squat; (*esconderse*) to hide.

agencia *nf* agency; (*sucursal*) branch. ■ **a. bancaria**, bank; **a. de viajes**, travel agency.

agenciarse *vr* **1** (*apañarse*) to manage, look after oneself; **agenciárselas**, to manage; **ya me las agenciaré como pueda**, I'll manage. **2** (*proporcionarse*) to get oneself; **se ha agenciado un cochazo increíble**, he's got himself a fantastic car.

agenda *nf* diary; **a. del día**, agenda.

agente I *adj Ling* **complemento a.**, agent. **II** *nmf* agent. ■ **a. de policía**, (*hombre*) policeman; (*mujer*) police-woman; **a. de tráfico**, (*hombre*) traffic policeman; (*mujer*) traffic policewoman; **a. secreto**, secret agent. **III** *nm* agent. ■ **a. provocador**, agent provocateur; **agentes naturales**, natural agents.

agigantado,-a I *pp de* **agigantar. II** *adj* massive, huge; **a pasos agigantados**, by leaps and bounds.

agigantar I *vtr* to enlarge; *fig* to exaggerate. **II agigantarse** *vr* to become huge.

ágil *adj* agile.

agilidad *nf* agility; **con a.**, swiftly.

agilipollado,-a *adj vulg* stupid, daft.

agilización *nf* speeding up.

agilizar *vtr* to make agile; *fig* to speed up; **a. los trámites**, to speed up the paperwork.

agiotaje *nm Com* speculation.

agiotista *nmf Com* speculator.

agitación *nf* agitation; *fig* (*inquietud*) excitement, restlessness; **a. política**, political agitation.

agitado,-a I *pp de* **agitar. II** *adj* **1** agitated, shaken; *fig* anxious. **2** (*ajetreado*) hectic; **una vida muy agitada**, a very hectic life. **3** (*mar*) rough.

agitador,-a I *nm,f* (*persona*) agitator. **II** *nm Quím* agitator.

agitanado,-a *adj* gypsy-like.

agitar I *vtr* (*botella*) to shake; (*pañuelo*) to wave; *fig* (*multitudes*) to agitate; **'agítese antes de usarlo'**, 'shake before use'. **II agitarse** *vr* **1** to move restlessly; *fig* (*inquietarse*) to become agitated. **2** (*mar*) to become rough.

aglomeración *nf* **1** (*gen*) agglomeration. **2** (*degente*) crowd.

aglomerado *nm* **1** *Constr* agglomerate. **2** (*combustible*) briquette.

aglomerante *nm* binding material.

aglomerar I *vtr* (*agrupar*) to agglomerate, amass. **II aglomerarse** *vr* **1** (*agruparse*) to agglomerate, amass; **los coches se aglomeraban en la plaza**, cars piled up in the square. **2** (*gente*) to crowd, form a crowd.

aglutinación *nf* agglutination.

aglutinante I *adj* agglutinant, binding; *Ling* **lengua a.**, agglutinative language. **II** *nm* agglutinant.

aglutinar I *vtr* to agglutinate, bind; *fig* to bring together. **II aglutinarse** *vr* to agglutinate; *fig* to come together.

agnosticismo *nm* agnosticism.

agnóstico,-a *adj & nm,f* agnostic.

agobiado,-a I *pp de* **agobiar. II** *adj* (*doblado*) bent down, weighed down; *fig* **a. de problemas**, snowed under with problems; *fig* **a. de trabajo**, up to one's eyes in work.

agobiador,-a *adj*, **agobiante** *adj* (*cansado*) back-breaking, exhausting; (*carga*) overwhelming; (*lugar*) claustrophobic; (*calor*) oppressive; (*persona*) tiresome, tiring.

agobiar I *vtr* (*doblar*) to bend down, weigh down; *fig* (*abrumar*) to overwhelm, overburden; **me agobia la gran ciudad**, the big city is too much for me. **II agobiarse** *vr* (*angustiarse*) to worry too much; **enseguida se agobia por todo**, he worries about everything.

agobio *nm* burden, suffocation, oppression.

agolpamiento *nm* crowd, crush.

agolparse *vr* to crowd, throng; *fig* **las lágrimas se agolpaban en sus ojos**, tears welled up in his eyes.

agonía *nf* **1** dying breath, last gasp; **en su a.**, on his deathbed; **tener una larga a.**, to die after a long illness. **2** *fig* (*sufrimiento*) agony, grief, sorrow.

agónico,-a *adj* dying, death; **estertores agónicos**, death rattle; **estar en estado a.**, to be about to die.

agonizante I *adj* dying. **II** *nmf* dying person.

agonizar *vi* **1** to be dying; **está agonizando**, he could die any moment now. **2** *fig* (*extinguirse*) to fail, fade away.

ágora *nm Hist* agora.

agorafobia *nf Psic* agoraphobia.

agorero,-a I *adj* ominous; *fig* **ave agorera**, bird of ill omen; *fam* **¡qué a. eres!**, what a jinx you are! **II** *nm,f* fortune-teller.

agostar *vtr*, **agostarse** *vr* (*marchitarse*) to wither, wilt; *fig* to extinguish, kill.

agosto *nm* August; *fam* **hacer su a.**, to make a packet *or* pile; *véase tamb* **noviembre.**

agotado,-a I *pp de* **agotar. II** *adj* **1** (*cansado*) exhausted, worn out. **2** *Com* sold out; (*existencias*) exhausted; (*libro*) out of print.

agotador,-a *adj* exhausting.

agotamiento *nm* exhaustion. ■ **a. físico,** physical strain.

agotar I *vtr* **1** *(cansar)* to exhaust, tire out, wear out. **2** *(acabar)* to exhaust, use up (completely). **II agotarse** *vr* **1** *(acabarse)* to run out, be used up; *Com* to be sold out. **2** *(persona)* to become exhausted *or* tired out.

agrá *nm CAm fig* disappointment, sorrow, grief.

agraciado,-a I *pp de* **agraciar. II** *adj* **1** *(hermoso)* beautiful, pretty; **poco a.,** unattractive, plain. **2** *(ganador)* winning. **III** *nm,f* lucky winner.

agraciar *vtr* **1** *(embellecer)* to beautify, make more attractive. **2** *fml (conceder una gracia)* to reward with a favour.

agradable *adj* pleasant, agreeable; **de sabor a.,** pleasant tasting; **poco a.,** unpleasant.

agradar *vi* to please; **no me agrada,** I don't like it.

agradecer *vtr* **1** to thank, be grateful to; **te lo agradezco mucho,** I am very grateful to you. **2** *(uso impers)* to be welcome; **siempre se agradece un descanso,** a rest is always welcome.

agradecido,-a I *pp de* **agradecer. II** *adj* grateful; **le estoy muy a.,** I am very grateful to you; **le quedaría muy a. si ...,** I should be very much obliged if ... .

agradecimiento *nm* gratefulness, gratitude.

agrado *nm* pleasure; **con a.,** with pleasure; **no es de su a.,** he doesn't like it, it isn't to his liking.

agrandar I *vtr* **1** *(ampliar)* to enlarge, make larger. **2** *fig (exagerar)* to exaggerate. **II agrandarse** *vr* **1** *(ampliarse)* to enlarge, become larger. **2** *(acentuarse)* to become more intense.

agrario,-a *adj* agrarian, land; **política agraria,** agricultural policy.

agrarismo *nm* agrarianism.

agravamiento *nm* aggravation, worsening.

agravante I *adj Jur* aggravating. **II** *nm & f* added difficulty; *Jur* aggravating circumstance. ■ **robo con a.,** aggravated theft.

agravar I *vtr* to aggravate, worsen. **II agravarse** *vr* to worsen, get worse.

agraviante I *adj* offending, insulting. **II** *nmf* offender.

agraviar *vtr* to offend, insult.

agravio *nm* offense, insult.

agraz *nm* **1** *(uva)* unripe *or* sour grape; *(zumo)* sour grape juice; *fig* **en a.,** prematurely, before its time. **2** *fig (amargura)* bitterness; *(sinsabor)* unpleasantness.

agredir *vtr* defect to attack.

agregación *nf* **1** *(añadidura)* aggregation. **2** *Educ* post of teacher. **3** *Pol* post of attaché; *(oficina)* office of the attaché.

agregado,-a I *pp de* **agregar. II** *adj Educ* **profesor a.,** *(escuela)* secondary school teacher; *Univ* assistant teacher. **II** *nm,f* **1** *Pol* attaché; **a. cultural,** cultural attaché. **2** *Arg Par Urug* tenant who pays rent in kind.

agregaduría *nf véase* **agregación** 2 & 3.

agregar I *vtr* **1** *(añadir)* to add; **a. un poco de agua,** add a small amount of water. **2** *(destinar)* to appoint. **II agregarse** *vr* *(añadirse a)* to join; **se agregó al grupo,** she joined the group.

agresión *nf* aggression, attack.

agresividad *nf* aggressiveness.

agresivo,-a *adj* aggressive.

agresor,-a I *adj* attacking. **II** *nm,f* aggressor, attacker.

agreste *adj* **1** *(campesino)* country, rural. **2** *(sin cultivar)* uncultivated, wild. **3** *fig (grosero)* coarse, uncouth.

agriado,-a I *pp de* **agriar. II** *adj* **1** *(agrio)* sour. **2** *fig (persona)* sour, embittered.

agriar I *vtr* **1** *(vino)* to turn sour. **2** *(persona)* to embitter. **II agriarse** *vr* to turn sour.

agrícola *adj* agricultural.

agricultor,-a *nm,f* farmer.

agricultura *nf* agriculture; **dedicarse a la a.,** to be a farmer, farm.

agridulce *adj* bittersweet; *Culin* **cerdo a.,** sweet and sour pork.

agriera *nf Am* heartburn.

agrietamiento *nm* cracking.

agrietar I *vtr* *(resquebrajar)* to crack; *(piel, labios)* to chap. **II agrietarse** *vr* *(resquebrajarse)* to crack; *(manos)* to get chapped.

agrimensor,-a *nm,f* surveyor.

agrimensura *nf* surveying.

agringarse *vr Am* to behave like a gringo.

agrio,-a I *adj* sour. **II agrios** *nmpl* citrus fruits.

agrisado,-a *adj* greyish.

agro *nm* agriculture.

agronomía *nf* agronomy.

agronómico,-a *adj* agronomical, agronomic.

agrónomo,-a I *adj* farming. **II** *nm, f* **(ingeníero) a.,** agronomist.

agropecuario,-a *adj* farming, agricultural.

agrupación *nf,* **agrupamiento** *nm* **1** grouping, group. **2** *(asociación)* association.

agrupar I *vtr* *(congregar)* to group; put into groups. **II agruparse** *vr* **1** *(congregarse)* to group together, form a group. **2** *(asociarse)* to associate.

agrura *nf* sourness, tartness.

agua *nf* water; **aguas arriba,** upstream; *Med (parturienta)* **romper aguas,** to break one's water bag; *fig* **ahogarse en un vaso de a.,** to make a mountain out of a molehill; *fig* **está más claro que el a.,** it's as clear as crystal; *fig* **estar con el a. al cuello,** to be up to one's neck in it; *fig* **nos vino como a. de mayo,** it was a godsend; *fam* **nunca digas de este a. no beheré,** never say never; *fam* **se me hace la boca a.,** it makes my mouth water; *fam* **parecerse como dos gotas de a.,** to be as like as two peas in a pod. ■ **a. bendita,** holy water; **a. corriente,** running water; **a. de colonia,** (eau de) cologne; **a. de lluvia,** rainwater; **a. de mar,** seawater; **a. del grifo,** tap water; **a. dulce,** fresh water; **a. mineral sin gas,** still mineral water; **a. mineral con gas,** fizzy *or* sparkling mineral water; **a. potable,** drinking water; **a. salada,** salt water; **aguas jurisdiccionales,** territorial waters; *fam* **aguas menores,** *pee sing;* **aguas residuales,** sewage *sing;* **aguas termales,** thermal springs.

aguacatal *nm* avocado plantation.

aguacate *nm Bot (árbol)* avocado; *(fruto)* avocado (pear).

aguacero *nm* shower, downpour.

aguachirle *nm* dishwater.

aguada *nf* **1** fresh water supply; **hacer a.,** to take on water. **2** *Arte* gouache.

aguado,-a I *pp de* **aguar. II** *adj* wishy-washy, watered down; **leche aguada,** watered-down milk.

aguador,-a *nm,f* water carrier.

aguafiestas *nmf inv* spoilsport, killjoy, wet blanket.

aguafuerte *nm* **1** *Arte* etching; **grabar al a.,** to etch. **2** *Quím* nitric acid.

aguamanil *nm (jarro)* water jug; *(palangana)* water bowl.

aguamar *nm (pez)* jellyfish.

aguamarina *nf Min* aquamarine.

aguamiel *nm* **1** *(bebida)* hydromel. **2** *Méx* agave juice.

aguanieve *nf Meteor* sleet.

aguanoso,-a *adj* **1** *(fruto)* watery. **2** *(lugar)* waterlogged.

aguantable *adj* bearable, tolerable.

aguantaderas *nfpl fam* patience *sing.*

aguantar I *vtr* **1** *(retener)* to hold, hold back; **aguanta la respiración,** hold your breath. **2** *(soportar)* to tolerate; **no**

lo aguanto más, I can't stand it any longer. **3** *(sostener)* to support, hold; **aguanta esto,** hold this. **II aguantarse** *vr* **1** *(contenerse)* to keep back; *(risa, lágrimas)* to hold back. **2** *(resignarse)* to resign oneself; *fam* **¡que se aguante!,** that's his *or* her tough luck!

aguante *nm* patience, endurance; **tener mucho a.,** *(ser paciente)* to be very patient; *(tener resistencia)* to be strong, have a lot of stamina.

aguar I *vtr* to water down, add water to; *fig* **a. la fiesta a algn,** to spoil sb's fun. **II aguarse** *vr* to be flooded.

aguardar I *vtr* to wait for, await; **no sabía lo que le aguardaba,** he didn't know what was in store for him. **II** *vi* to wait.

aguardentoso,-a *adj* which contains liquor.

aguardiente *nm* liquor, brandy. ■ **a. de caña,** rum.

aguarrás *nm* turpentine.

aguatero,-a *nm,f Am* water carrier *or* seller.

aguazal *nm* puddle.

agudeza *nf* **1** sharpness, keenness; *(del dolor)* acuteness. **2** *fig (viveza)* wit, wittiness. **3** *fig (ingenio)* witticism, witty saying.

agudización *nf,* **agudizamiento** *nm* **1** sharpening. **2** *(empeoramiento)* worsening.

agudizar I *vtr* **1** *(afilar)* to sharpen (up). **2** *(empeorar)* to intensify, worsen, make more acute. **II agudizarse** *vr* **1** *(afilarse)* to sharpen. **2** *(empeorar)* to intensify, worsen, become more acute.

agudo,-a *adj* **1** *(afilado)* sharp; *(dolor)* acute. **2** *fig (sentido)* sharp, keen. **3** *fig (ingenioso)* witty; *(mordaz)* sharp. **4** *Ling* oxytone. **5** *Mat* acute. **6** *(sonido)* treble, high; *(voz)* high-pitched. **7** *Med* acute.

agüero *nm* omen, presage; *fig* **pájaro de mal a.,** bird of ill omen.

aguerrido,-a *adj* hardened; **a. en la lucha,** battle-hardened.

aguijón *nm* **1** *Zool* sting. **2** *Bot* thorn, prickle. **3** *fig (estímulo)* sting, spur. **4** *(espuela)* spur.

aguijonazo *nm (punzada)* sting; *fig* goad.

aguijonear *vtr* **1** *(punzar)* to goad. **2** *fig (estimular)* to spur on.

águila *nf Orn* eagle; *fig* **tener vista de á,** to be eagle-eyed. ■ **á. imperial,** Imperial eagle; **á. pescadora,** osprey; **á. real,** golden eagle.

aguileño,-a *adj* aquiline; **nariz aguileña,** aquiline nose.

aguilera *nf* eyrie.

aguililla *Am* **I** *adj (caballo)* fast, swift. **II** *nmf (estafador)* swindler.

aguilucho *nm Orn* **1** *(águila joven)* eaglet. **2** harrier.

aguinaldo *nm* **1** *(de navidad)* Christmas box. **2** *(retribución)* bonus. **3** *(villancico)* Christmas carol.

aguja *nf* **1** needle; *Tricot* knitting needle; *(de reloj)* hand; *(de tocadiscos)* stylus; *(de arma de fuego)* firing pin; *fig* **buscar una a. en un pajar,** to look for a needle in a haystack. **2** *(pez)* garfish. **3** *Orn* godwit. **4** *Arquit (obelisco)* obelisk; *(capitel)* spire, steeple. **5** *Culin (dulce)* sweet pastry; *(de carne)* meat pastry. **6** *Culin* **carne de agujas,** shoulder. **7** *Ferroc* point, *US* switch.

agujereado,-a I *pp* de **agujerear. II** *adj* with holes, perforated.

agujerear *vtr* to make holes in, perforate.

agujero *nm* hole; **lleno de agujeros,** riddled with holes; *fig* **la empresa tiene un a. de seis millones de pesetas,** six million pesetas are missing from the company's books.

agujetas *nfpl* stiffness *sing*; **tener a.,** to be stiff.

agujetero,-a I *nm,f (fabricante)* needle maker; *(vendedor)* needle seller. **II** *Am (alfiletero)* pin-cushion.

agur *interj fam* bye!, see you!

agusanado,-a I *pp de* **agusanarse. II** *adj* maggoty, wormy.

agusanarse *vr* to get maggoty *or* wormy.

agustino,-a I *adj & nm,f Rel* Augustinian.

agutí *nm Zool* agouti.

aguzanieves *nf inv Orn* pied wagtail.

aguzar *vtr* **1** *(afilar)* to sharpen. **2** *fig (estimular)* to spur on, prick; **a. el oído,** to prick up one's ears; **a. la vista,** to look attentively; **la necesidad aguza el ingenio,** necessity is the mother of invention.

ah *interj* oh!

aherrojar *vtr* **1** *(encadenar)* to chain, put in irons. **2** *fig (oprimir)* to oppress.

aherrumbrarse *vr* **1** *(oxidarse)* to rust, go rusty. **2** *(saber a hierro)* to taste of rust.

ahí *adv* **1** *(lugar determinado)* there; **a. está,** there he *or* she *or* it is; **vete por a.,** go that way; *fig* **a. está el problema,** that's the problem; *fam* **a. es nada,** not bad eh?; *fam* **¡a. le duele!,** you've hit the nail on the head; *fam* **¡a. va!,** my goodness! **2** *(lugar indeterminado)* **por a.,** there, round there; out; **luego nos vamos por a.,** then we can go out. **3** *(aproximadamente)* **por a., por a.,** more or less; **por a. va la cosa,** that's not a bad guess. **4** *(consecuencia)* **de a. se deduce que no es verdad,** from which we deduce that it is not true.

ahijado,-a I *pp de* **ahijar. II** *nm, f* **1** godchild; *(hombre)* godson; *(mujer)* goddaughter; **ahijados,** godchildren. **2** *(hijo adoptivo)* adopted child.

ahijar I *vtr* **1** *(niño)* to adopt. **2** *fig* to attribute, impute. **II ahijarse** *vr (niño)* to adopt.

ahínco *nm* keenness, enthusiasm, eagerness; **con a.,** enthusiastically, eagerly.

ahíto,-a I *adj* **1** *(de comida)* full, stuffed. **2** *fig (harto)* fed up. **II** *nm* indigestion.

ahogado,-a I *pp de* **ahogar. II** *adj* **1** *(en líquido)* drowned; **morir a.,** to drown. **2** *(asfixiado)* asphyxiated, suffocated; *fig* **a. de tiempo,** pushed for time; *fig* **estar a. de dinero,** to find it difficult to make ends meet; *fig* **un grito a.,** a muffled cry. **3** *(lugar)* stuffy, close. **III** *nm, f* drowned person.

ahogar I *vtr* **1** *(en líquido)* to drown. **2** *(asfixiar)* to asphyxiate, suffocate. **3** *fig (reprimir)* to stifle; **a. las lágrimas,** to hold back one's tears; **a. las penas,** to drown one's sorrows. **4** *fig (oprimir)* to oppress, afflict; **el trabajo nos ahoga,** we're snowed under with work. **5** *Aut (motor)* to flood. **6** *Am Culin (rehogar)* to brown. **II ahogarse** *vr* **1** *(en líquido)* to drown, be drowned; *fig* **a. en un vaso de agua,** to make a mountain out of a molehill. **2** *(asfixiarse)* to suffocate; *fig* **me ahogo de calor,** I'm suffocating with this heat. **3** *Aut (motor)* to be flooded.

ahogo *nm* **1** *(al respirar)* breathing trouble, tightness of the chest. **2** *fig (congoja)* grief, sorrow, distress. **3** *fig (penuria)* financial difficulty.

ahondar I *vtr (profundizar)* to deepen, make deeper. **II** *vi* to go deep; *fig* **a. en un problema,** to examine a problem in depth.

ahora I *adv* **1** *(en este momento)* now; **a. mismo,** right now; **a.** *or* **nunca,** it's now or never; **a. que lo pienso,** now that I come to think of it; **de a. en adelante,** from now on; **por a.,** for the time being. **2** *(hace poco tiempo)* a while ago; **a. mismo acabo de enterarme,** I've just heard about it. **3** *(dentro de poco tiempo)* shortly; **a. voy,** I'm coming; **a. vuelvo,** I'll be back in a minute; **hasta a.,** *(hasta el momento)* until now, so far; *(hasta luego)* see you later. **II** *conj* **a. bien** *or* **que,** but, however; **a. bien, ¿tú estás de acuerdo?,** now then, do you agree?; **a. bien, ¿le gustará a ella?,** I like it, but will she like it?

ahorcado,-a I *pp de* **ahorcar. II** *adj* hanged. **III** *nm, f* hanged person.

ahorcadora *nf CAm Zool* large wasp.

ahorcajarse *vr* to sit astride.

ahorcamiento *nm* hanging.

ahorcar I *vtr* to hang. **II ahorcarse** *vr* to hang oneself.

ahorita *adv Am véase* **ahora.**

ahormar *vtr* **1** *(zapatos, ropa)* to shape, form. **2** *fig (carácter)* to mould, *US* mold.

ahorquillado,-a *adj* forked.

ahorrador,-a I *adj* thrifty. **II** *nm, f* thrifty person.

ahorrar I *vtr (dinero)* to save, put aside; *fig* **eso me ahorra tener que ir al centro,** it'll save me going into town. **II ahorrarse** *vr* **1** to save oneself; **a. trabajo,** to save oneself work, **ahórrate los comentarios,** keep your comments to yourself. **2** *Am (malograrse)* to come to nothing, fall through.

ahorrativo,-a *adj* thrifty.

ahorro *nm* saving; **tener unos ahorros,** to have a few savings; **un a. de energía,** an energy saving. ■ *Fin* **caja de ahorros,** savings bank.

ahuate *nm CAm Méx Bot* needle.

ahuecamiento *nm* **1** hollowing out. **2** *(de colchón)* fluffing up; *(de tierra)* loosening. **3** *(de voz)* deepening.

ahuecar I *vtr* **1** to hollow out; **a. las manos,** to cup one's hands; *fam* **a. el ala,** to clear off, beat it. **2** *(almohada, cabello)* to fluff up; *(tierra)* to loosen. **3** *(voz)* to deepen. **II ahuecarse** *vr fam (engreírse)* to become conceited, give oneself airs.

ahuevar I *vi Méx* to lay eggs. **II** *vtr Col Nic Per (atontar)* to stun; *(azorar)* to embarrass; *(acobardar)* to frighten, scare.

ahulado *nm* **1** *Am (hule)* oilskin, oilcloth. **2** *CAm (chanclo)* overshoe.

ahumado,-a I *pp de* **ahumar. II** *adj* **1** *(pescado, jamón)* smoked; *(bacon)* smoky; **salmón a.,** smoked salmon. **2** *(cristal)* smoked. **III** *nm (proceso)* smoking.

ahumar I *vtr* **1** *(carne, pescado)* to smoke; **a. un cristal,** to smoke a pane of glass. **2** *(lugar)* to fill with smoke, smoke out. **II** *vi (echar humo)* to smoke, give off smoke. **III ahumarse** *vr* **1** to be blackened by smoke. **2** *Culin* to acquire a smoky taste. **3** *fam (emborracharse)* to get drunk.

ahusado,-a *adj* tapered, tapering.

ahuyentar *vtr* to scare away, drive away; *fig* **a. los malos pensamientos,** to dismiss bad thoughts.

ailanto *nm Bot* tree of heaven.

aimará *adj & nmf* Aymara.

aindiado,-a *adj Am* Indian-like.

airado,-a I *pp de* **airar. II** *adj* angry, irritated, furious.

airar I *vtr (irritar)* to anger, irritate, make furious. **II airarse** *vr (irritarse)* to get angry.

aire *nm* **1** air; **al a.,** *(hacia arriba)* into the air; *(al descubierto)* uncovered; **al a. libre,** in the open air; **cambiar de aires,** to change one's surroundings; **en el a.,** *(pendiente)* in the air; *Rad (en antena)* on the air; **hacerse a.,** to fan oneself; **saltar por los aires,** to blow up; **tomar el a.,** to take the air, get some fresh air; **vivir del a.,** to live on air. ■ **a. acondicionado,** air conditioning. **2** *(viento)* wind; *(corriente)* draught; **hace a.,** it's windy. **3** *fig (aspecto)* air, appearance; **con a. cansado,** looking tired. **4** *fig (parecido)* likeness; **a. de familia,** family likeness. **5** *fig (gracia)* gracefulness. **6** *(estilo)* style, manner, way; **dejar a algn a su a.,** to let sb do what he *or* she wants. **7** *Mús (canción)* air, tune. **8** **aires,** *fig (vanidad)* conceit *sing;* **darse a.,** to put on airs.

aireación *nf* ventilation.

airear I *vtr (ropa, habitación)* to air; *fig (asunto)* to publicize. **II airearse** *vr* **1** *(pillar un resfriado)* to catch a cold. **2** *(tomar el aire)* to get some fresh air.

aireo *nm* airing; *fig* publicizing.

airón *nm* **1** *Orn (garza)* heron. **2** *(penacho)* crest, tuft.

airoso,-a *adj* graceful, elegant; *fig* **salir a. de una situación,** to come out of a situation with flying colours.

aisa *nf Arg Bol Per* rockfall.

aislacionismo *nm* isolationism.

aislacionista *adj & nmf* isolationist.

aislado,-a I *pp de* **aislar. II** *adj* **1** isolated. **2** *Téc* insulated.

aislador,-a *Téc* **I** *adj* insulating. **II** *nm* insulator.

aislamiento *nm* **1** isolation. **2** *Téc* insulation.

aislante *Téc* **I** *adj* insulating. **II** *nm* insulator.

aislar I *vtr* **1** to isolate. **2** *Téc* to insulate. **II aislarse** *vr* to isolate oneself **(de,** from).

ajá *interj* good!

ajado,-a I *pp de* **ajar. II** *adj* **1** *(ropa)* shabby. **2** *(piel)* wizened.

ajambado,-a *adj CAm* greedy, piggish.

ajamonarse *vr fam (mujer)* to get plump.

ajar I *vtr* to wear out, spoil. **II ajarse** *vr (piel)* to become wizened, wrinkle.

ajardinar *vtr* to landscape, lay out with gardens.

ajedrecista *nmf* chess player.

ajedrez *nm* **1** *(juego)* chess. **2** *(piezas y tablero)* chess set.

ajedrezado,-a *adj* chequered, *US* checkered.

ajenjo *nm* **1** *Bot* wormwood, absinth, absinthe. **2** *(licor)* absinth, absinthe.

ajeno,-a *adj* **1** belonging to other people; *Dep* **jugar en campo a.,** to play away from home; **por causas ajenas a nuestra voluntad,** for reasons beyond our control; **vivir a costa ajena,** to live off other people. **2** *(distante)* detached; **a. a lo que estaba ocurriendo,** unaware of what was happening; **a. al tema,** outside the subject. **3** *(impropio)* **a. a su manera de ser,** unlike him. **4** *(extraño)* **'prohibido el paso a toda persona ajena a la obra',** 'workers only'.

ajetreado,-a *adj* (very) busy, hectic.

ajetreo *nm* activity, hard work, bustle.

ajigolones *nmpl Guat Méx Salv* difficulties.

ajillo *nm dimin Culin* **al a.,** fried with garlic.

ajo *nm* garlic; *fam* **estar en el a.,** to be in on it. ■ **cabeza de a.,** head of garlic; **diente de a.,** clove of garlic.

ajolote *nm Zool* axolotl.

ajonjolí *nm Bot* sesame.

ajorca *nf* bracelet; *(en el tobillo)* anklet.

ajotar *vtr CAm PR* to urge on, incite.

ajuar *nm (de novia)* trousseau; *(de niño)* layette; *(moblaje)* household furnishings *pl; (bienes)* property, goods *pl.*

ajumarse *vr fam* to get drunk.

ajuntar I *vtr fam* to be friends with; **¿me ajuntas?,** will you be my friend?; **ya no te ajunto,** I am not friends with you any more. **II ajuntarse** *vr fam (una pareja)* to live together, cohabit.

ajustado,-a I *pp de* **ajustar. II** *adj* **1** *(justo)* right, correct; **un precio a.,** a reasonable price. **2** *(ropa)* tight, clinging; **bien a.,** well-fitting.

ajustador,-a I *adj* adjusting, fitting. **II** *nm, f* fitter.

ajustar I *vtr* **1** to adjust, fit; **a. dos piezas,** to make two pieces fit. **2** *(ceñir)* to tighten. **3** *(encajar)* to insert, fit into *or* together. **4** *(concertar)* to settle, fix; *fig* **ajustarle las cuentas a algn,** to settle a score with sb. **5** *(acordar)* to agree, arrange. **6** *Impr* to make up. **7** *Com Fin (cuenta) (saldar)* to balance; *(liquidar)* to settle. **8** *Am (enfermedad)* to attack. **9** *CAm (cumplir)* to be. **10** *CAm Col (contratar)* to take on. **II ajustarse** *vr* to fit; **a. el cinturón,** to tighten one's belt; *fig (adaptarse)* **ajústate a lo que te han dicho,** just do as you have been told.

ajuste *nm* **1** adjustment, fitting; *Téc* assembly. ■ *TV* **carta de a.,** test card. **2** *(de precio, cuenta)* settlement, fixing. ■ *fig* **a. de cuentas,** settling of scores. **3** *Impr* make-up, composition.

ajusticiado,-a I *pp de* **ajusticiar. II** *adj* **morir a.,** to be executed. **III** *nm, f* executed person.

ajusticiamiento *nm* execution.

ajusticiar *vtr* to execute.

ajustón *nm Ecuad Guat Hond (castigo)* punishment; *(mal trato)* ill-treatment.

al *(contracción de a & el)* **1** *véase* **a.** **2** *(al + infin)* **al parecer,** apparently; **al salir,** on leaving; **está al caer,** it's about to happen.

ala *nf* **1** wing; *fig* **cortarle las alas a algn,** to clip sb's wings; *fig* **dar alas a,** to egg on, encourage; *fig* **volar uno con sus propias alas,** to stand on one's own two feet. **2** *(de sombrero)* brim. **3** *(de hélice)* blade. **4** *Dep (jugador)* winger. **5** *fam* peseta; **me costó cinco mil del a.,** it cost me all of five thousand pesetas.

alabanza *nf* **1** *(elogio)* praise. **2** *(jactancia)* boasting, bragging.

alabar **I** *vtr (elogiar)* to praise. **II alabarse** *vr (jactarse)* to boast, brag.

alabastrino,-a **I** *adj* alabastrine. **II** *nf* thin sheet of alabaster.

alabastro *nm* alabaster.

álabe *nm* **1** *Téc (de rueda hidráulica)* paddle; *(de rueda dentada)* tooth. **2** *(rama caída)* drooping branch.

alabear *vtr,* **alabearse** *vr* to warp.

alabeo *nm* warp, warping.

alacena *nf* (food) cupboard.

alaco *nm CAm* **1** *(persona)* good-for-nothing. **2** *(harapo)* rag, tatter. **3** *(trasto)* piece of junk.

alacrán *nm Zool* scorpion.

alado,-a *adj* **1** *(con alas)* winged. **2** *fig (veloz)* fast, quick.

alagartado,-a *adj* **1** *(parecido al lagarto)* motley. **2** *CAm (tacaño)* stingy, mean, tight.

alagartarse *vr CAm* to become stingy.

alalau *interj Bol Ecuad Per* brrrrrr!

alambicado,-a **I** *pp de* **alambicar.** **II** *adj* **1** *fig (escaso)* given sparingly. **2** *fig (rebuscado)* overcomplicated.

alambicamiento *nm* **1** *(destilación)* distilling, distillation. **2** *(sutileza)* affectation.

alambicar *vtr* **1** *(líquidos)* to distil, *US* distill. **2** *(examinar)* to scrutinize. **3** *fig (estilo, lenguaje)* to subtilize, overcomplicate. **4** *fig (ganancias)* to reduce to a minimum.

alambique *nm* still.

alambrada *nf* wire fence.

alambrado *nm* **1** *véase* **alambrada.** **2** *véase* **alambrera.**

alambrar *vtr* to fence with wire.

alambre *nm* wire; *fig* **estar como un a.,** to be as thin as a rake. ■ **a. de púas,** barbed wire.

alambrera *nf (de ventana)* wire netting; *(para comida)* food safe.

alambrista *nmf* tightrope walker.

alameda *nf* **1** poplar grove. **2** *(paseo)* promenade, avenue, boulevard.

álamo *nm Bot* poplar.

alancear *vtr* to spear.

alano,-a *adj & nm,f* **1** *Hist* Alan. **2** *Zool* **(perro) a.,** mastiff.

alar *nm* eaves *pl.*

alarde *nm (ostentación)* bragging, boasting, (vain) display; **hacer a. de,** to flaunt, parade, show off.

alardear *vi* to brag, boast, show off; **a. de rico** *or* **de riqueza,** to flaunt one's wealth.

alardeo *nm véase* **alarde.**

alargado,-a **I** *pp de* **alargar.** **II** *adj* elongated, long.

alargamiento *nm* **1** lengthening; *(estirado)* stretching. **2** *(prolongación)* prolongation, extension.

alargar *vtr* **1** to lengthen; *(estirar)* to stretch; **ella alargó la mano para cogerlo,** she stretched out her hand to get it. **2** *(prolongar)* to prolong, extend; **alargaron su estancia**

en Madrid, they extended their stay in Madrid. **3** *(dar)* to pass, hand over; **alárgame ese jersey,** can you pass me that jumper? **II alargarse** *vr* **1** to lengthen, get longer; **en verano los días se alargan,** in summer the days get longer; **la reunión se alargó hasta las dos,** the meeting went on until two. **2** *(excederse)* to be long-winded, go on (too long).

alargo *nm Elec* extension (lead).

alarido *nm* screech, shriek, yell; **dar un a.,** to howl.

alarma *nf* **1** alarm; **dar la a.,** to give the alarm; **entonces sonó la a.,** then the alarm went off. ■ **falsa a.,** false alarm; **señal de a.,** (signal); **voz de a.,** alarm (call). **2** *(dispositivo)* alarm.

alarmado,-a **I** *pp de* **alarmar.** **II** *adj* alarmed.

alarmante *adj* alarming.

alarmar **I** *vtr* to alarm. **II alarmarse** *vr* to be alarmed; to alarm oneself.

alarmismo *nm* alarmism.

alarmista *nmf* alarmist.

alavense *adj & nm,f* **alavés,-esa** *adj & nm,f* **I** *adj* of or from Alava. **II** *nmf & nm,f* native *or* inhabitant of Alava.

alazán,-ana *adj & nm,f* **(caballo) a.,** chestnut.

alba *nf* **1** dawn, daybreak; **al (rayar el) a.,** at daybreak, at dawn. **2** *Rel (prenda)* alb.

albacea *nmf (hombre)* executor; *(mujer)* executrix.

albacetense *adj & nmf,* **albaceteño,-a** *adj & nm,f* **I** *adj* of *or* from Albacete. **II** *nmf & nm,f* native *or* inhabitant of Albacete.

albacora *nf (pez)* albacore, long-fin tunny.

albahaca *nf Bot* basil.

albanés,-esa *adj & nm,f* Albanian.

Albania *n* Albania.

albano,-a *adj & nm,f véase* **albanés,-esa.**

albañal *nm* **1** sewer, drain. **2** *fig* mess.

albañil *nm* bricklayer; *(obrero)* building worker. ■ **peón de a.,** labourer, *US* laborer.

albañilería *nf* **1** bricklaying. **2** *(obra)* **pared de a.,** brick wall.

albar *adj* white.

albarán *nm Com* delivery note, despatch note.

albarda *nf* **1** packsaddle. **2** *CAm* saddle.

albardear *vtr* **1** *CAm (fastidiar)* to annoy, bother. **2** *CAm & Méx (domar)* to break in.

albardón *nm* **I** *Am* raised land between lakes *or* beaches. **II** *Méx* type of saddle.

albaricoque *nm Bot* **1** *(fruta)* apricot. **2** *(árbol)* apricot tree.

albaricoquero *nm Bot* apricot tree.

albarrana *adj* **torre a.,** watchtower.

albatros *nm inv Orn* albatross.

albayalde *nm* white lead.

albazo *nm* **1** *Am Mil (ataque)* dawn raid *or* attack; *(toque)* reveille. **2** *Arg (madrugón)* early rising. **3** *Méx* early morning theft.

albedrío *nm* will. ■ **libre a.,** free will.

albéitar *nm* veterinary surgeon.

alberca *nf* **1** *(poza)* (small) reservoir. **2** *Méx (piscina)* swimming pool.

albergar **I** *vtr (alojar)* to house, accommodate; *fig (sentimientos)* to cherish, harbour, *US* harbor. **II albergarse** *vr (alojarse)* to stay.

albergue *nm* **1** *(lugar)* hostel. ■ **a. juvenil,** youth hostel. **2** *(refugio)* shelter, refuge; **dar a.,** to take in, put up.

albero,-a **I** *adj (blanco)* white. **II** *nm (paño)* dishcloth.

albilla *nf* uva a., white grape.

albinismo *nm* albinism.

albino,-a *adj & nm,f* albino.

Albión n Albion.

albis (in) loc adv left in the dark; **estar in a.,** not to have the faintest idea; **me quedé in a.,** my mind went blank.

albo,-a adj lit white.

albóndiga nf, **albondiguilla** nf Culin meatball.

albor nm 1 (blancura) whiteness. **2 albores,** beginning sing; **en los a. de ...,** at the dawn of ..., at the beginning of ... .

alborada nf 1 (alba) dawn, daybreak. 2 Mús dawn song. 3 Mil (diana) reveille.

alborear v impers to dawn.

albornoz nm (prenda) bathrobe.

alborotadizo,-a adj excitable.

alborotado,-a I pp de **alborotar.** II adj 1 worked up, agitated, excited. 2 (desordenado) untidy, messy. 3 (irreflexivo) reckless, rash.

alborotador,-a I adj 1 (rebelde) rebellious, turbulent; (ruidoso) noisy, rowdy. 2 (mar) rough, tempestuous. II nm, f troublemaker, agitator.

alborotar I vtr 1 (agitar) to stir up, agitate, work up. 2 (desordenar) to make untidy, turn upside down. 3 (sublevar) to incite to rebel. II vi 1 (hacer jaleo) to kick up a racket. 2 (causar desorden) to cause disorder; **no alborotéis más,** stop it, behave yourselves. III **alborotarse** vr 1 to get excited or worked up. 2 (mar) to get rough.

alboroto nm 1 (jaleo) din, racket, row. 2 (desorden) disturbance, uproar. 3 (susto) shock, alarm. **4 alborotos,** CAm Culin popcorn sing.

alborozar I vtr to fill with joy, delight. II **alborozarse** vr to be overjoyed.

alborozo nm merriment, gaiety, joy.

albricias I nfpl (regalo) present sing, gift sing. II interj great!, smashing!

albufera nf Geog lagoon, pool.

álbum nm album

albumen nm Bot albumen.

albúmina nf Biol albumin.

albur nm chance; **los albures de la vida,** the ups and downs of life.

albura nf fml whiteness.

alca nf Orn razorbill.

alcachofa nf 1 Bot artichoke. 2 (de tubo, regadera) rose, sprinkler.

alcahuete,-a nm, f 1 (celestino) (hombre) procurer, pimp; (mujer) procuress. 2 fig (chismoso) gossipmonger.

alcahuetería nf 1 (tercería) procuring. 2 (chismes) gossiping.

alcaldada nf abuse of authority.

alcalde nm mayor.

alcaldesa nf (que ejerce) lady mayor, mayoress; (mujer del alcalde) mayoress.

alcaldía nf 1 (cargo) mayorship; **fue durante la a. del Sr Reyes,** it was when Sr Reyes was mayor. 2 (oficina) mayoralty, mayor's office. 3 (territorio) land under the jurisdiction of a mayor.

álcali nm Quím alkali.

alcalinidad nf Quím alkalinity.

alcalino,-a adj Quím alkaline.

alcaloide nm Quím alkaloid.

alcance nm 1 reach; **al a. de cualquiera,** within everybody's reach; **al a. de la vista,** in sight; **dar a. a,** to catch up with; **fuera del a. de los niños,** out of the reach of children; **no está a mi a.,** I can't afford it. 2 (de arma, radio) range. 3 fig scope, importance, significance; **de gran a.,** far-reaching. **4 alcances,** (inteligencia) intelligence sing; **persona de pocos a.,** unintelligent person.

alcancía nf 1 (hucha) money box. 2 Am (para limosnas) collecting box.

alcanfor nm camphor.

alcanforado,-a I pp de **alcanforar.** II adj camphorated.

alcanforar I vtr to camphorate. II **alcanforarse** vr Am (desaparecer) to vanish, disappear.

alcanforero nm Bot camphor tree.

alcantarilla nf sewer; (boca) drain.

alcantarillado nm sewer system.

alcantarillar vtr to lay sewers in.

alcanzable adj within reach, attainable.

alcanzar I vtr 1 (gen) to reach; (tren, autobús) to catch; (persona) to catch up with; **la piedra le alcanzó en la cabeza,** the stone hit him on the head; **la producción alcanza dos mil unidades diarias,** production is up to two thousand units a day. 2 (pasar) to pass, hand over; **alcánzame el pan,** pass me the bread. 3 (llegar a tener) to attain, achieve, obtain; **alcanzó lo que tanto deseaba,** he got what he was longing for. 4 (afectar) to affect; **las consecuencias nos alcanzan a todos,** its consequences affect us all. 5 (conseguir) to manage; **a. a ver/ comprender,** to be able to see/understand. II vi 1 (ser suficiente) to be sufficient; **con un kilo no alcanza para todos,** one kilo won't be enough for all of us; **me alcanzó para un mes,** it lasted me a month. 2 (ser capaz) to manage; **él alcanza a todo,** he manages to do everything.

alcaparra nf Bot 1 (fruto) caper. 2 (planta) caper bush.

alcaraván nm Orn stone curlew.

alcaravea nf caraway.

alcarraza nf clay jar.

alcatraz nm Orn gannet.

alcaudón nm Orn shrike.

alcayata nf hook.

alcazaba nf Mil fortress, citadel.

alcázar nm 1 (fortaleza) fortress, citadel. 2 (castillo) castle, palace.

alce nm Zool elk, moose.

alción nm Orn kingfisher; Mit halcyon.

alcista I adj (bolsa) rising, bullish; **tendencia a.,** upward tendency. II nmf (bolsa) bull.

alcoba nf bedroom. ■ fig **secretos de a.,** intimacies.

alcohol nm 1 Quím alcohol. ■ **a. metílico** or **desnaturalizado,** methylated spirit. 2 (bebida) alcohol, spirits pl.

alcohólico,-a adj & nm, f alcoholic. ■ **Alcohólicos Anónimos,** Alcoholics Anonymous.

alcoholímetro nm Breathalyzer®.

alcoholismo nm alcoholism.

alcoholización nf alcoholization.

alcoholizado,-a I pp de **alcoholizar.** II adj & nm, f alcoholic.

alcoholizar I vtr to alcoholize. II **alcoholizarse** vr to become an alcoholic.

alcohómetro nm Breathalyzer®.

alcor nm Geog hill.

alcornocal nm cork oak grove.

alcornoque nm 1 Bot cork oak. 2 fig (persona) idiot, dimwit.

alcotán nm Orn hobby.

alcotana nf pickaxe, US pickax.

alcurnia nf lineage, ancestry; **de alta a.,** of noble lineage.

alcuza nf 1 oil bottle. 2 Am (vinagreras) cruet.

alcuzcúz nm Culin couscous.

aldaba nf 1 (llamador) door knocker. 2 (pestillo) latch, bar, bolt. 3 fig **tener buenas aldabas,** to know the right people.

aldabilla nf latch, hook.

aldabón *nm* large door knocker.

aldabonazo *nm* **1** loud knock; *fig* shock. **2** *(advertencia)* warning.

aldea *nf* small village, hamlet.

aldeano,-a I *adj* **1** *(de aldea)* village. **2** *fig* rustic. II *nm,f* villager.

aleación *nf* alloy.

alear *vtr (metales)* to alloy.

aleatorio,-a *adj* fortuitous, chance, accidental.

alebrestado,-a I *pp de* **alebrestarse**. II *adj* **1** CAm Col *(mujeriego)* fond of women *or* girls. **2** *Méx (irritable)* irascible, touchy.

alebrestarse *vr* **1** to lie down flat. **2** *fig (acobardarse)* to cower, shrink back. **3** *(alarmarse)* to be *or* get alarmed. **4** *(caballo)* to rear up.

aleccionador,-a *adj (instructivo)* instructive; *(ejemplar)* exemplary.

aleccionamiento *nm (instrucción)* instruction; *(adiestramiento)* training.

aleccionar *vtr (instruir)* to teach, instruct; *(adiestrar)* to train.

aledaño,-a I *adj* adjoining, adjacent. II **aledaños** *nmpl* outskirts.

alegación *nf* claim, plea, allegation.

alegador,-a *adj Am* argumentative.

alegar *vtr* **1** *(aducir)* to claim, allege, plea. **2** *Am (discutir)* to argue.

alegato *nm* **1** *(argumento)* claim, plea. **2** *(razonamiento)* forceful statement. **3** *Am (disputa)* dispute, argument.

alegoría *nf* allegory.

alegórico,-a *adj* allegorical, allegoric.

alegrar I *vtr* **1** *(complacer)* to make happy *or* glad; **me alegra que se lo hayas dicho,** I am glad you told her. **2** *fig (avivar)* to enliven, brighten up. **3** *fig euf (achispar)* to make tipsy. II **alegrarse** *vr* **1** *(estar contento)* to be glad, be happy, be pleased; **me alegro de verte,** I am pleased to see you; **me alegro por ti,** I am happy for you. **2** *fig euf (achisparse)* to get merry.

alegre *adj* **1** *(contento)* happy, glad, joyful; **es muy a.,** she is a very happy person. **2** *(color)* bright; *(música)* lively; *(habitación)* pleasant, cheerful. **3** *fig euf (achispado)* tipsy, merry. **4** *fig pey* **mujer de vida a.,** loose woman. **5** *fig pey (irreflexivo)* thoughtless, irresponsible, rash.

alegría *nf* **1** *(felicidad)* joy, happiness; **saltar de a.,** to jump with joy; *fig* **¡qué a.!,** that's wonderful! **2** *pey (irresponsabilidad)* thoughtlessness, irresponsibility, rashness. **3** **alegrías,** *Mús* song *or* dance from Cádiz.

alegrón *nm fam* pleasant surprise.

alegrona *nf Am* prostitute.

alejado,-a I *adj pp de* **alejar**. II *adj* **1** *(lejano)* far away, remote. **2** *(separado)* aloof, apart; **a. de su familia,** aloof from his family.

alejamiento *nm* **1** *(separación)* spacing out, separation. **2** *(persona)* estrangement.

Alejandría *n* Alexandria.

alejandrino,-a¹ I *adj* **1** of *or* from Alexandria. II *nm,f* native *or* inhabitant of Alexandria.

alejandrino² *adj & nm Lit* Alexandrine.

alejar I *vtr* to move further away, remove; *(separar)* to separate; *fig* **aleja esos pensamientos,** stop thinking like that; *fig* **a. las dudas,** to avert doubts. II **alejarse** *vr* **1** to go away, move away; **el coche se alejó,** the car drove off into the distance; **no te alejes de mí,** keep close to me.

alela *nf CAm* big foot.

alelado,-a I *pp de* **alelar**. II *adj* **1** *(tonto)* stupid, foolish. **2** *(atontado)* stupefied, bewildered.

alelar I *vtr* to bewilder. II **alelarse** *vr* **1** to become stupid *or* foolish. **2** to be bewildered.

aleluya I *nm & f* hallelujah, alleluia. II *interj* hallelujah! III *nm* Easter time. IV *nf* **1** *Lit fam (pareado)* couplet. **2** *Am (excusa)* frivolous excuse.

alemán,-ana I *adj* German. II *nm,f (persona)* German. III *nm (idioma)* German.

Alemania *n* Germany. ■ **A. del Este,** East Germany; **A. Occidental/Oriental,** West/East Germany.

alentado,-a I *pp de* **alentar**. II *adj* **1** *(valiente)* brave, daring. **2** *(altanero)* haughty, arrogant. **3** *Am (sano)* healthy, strong.

alentador,-a *adj* encouraging; **un panorama poco a.,** a rather black future.

alentar I *vtr fig (animar)* to encourage. II *vi* **1** *desus* to breathe. **2** *fig (albergar)* to harbour; **su corazón alienta los más bellos sentimientos,** the most noble sentiments burn within his heart. III **alentarse** *vr CAm Col (dar a luz)* to give birth (**de,** to).

alerce *nm Bot* larch.

alérgeno *nm* allergen.

alergia *nf* allergy.

alérgico,-a *adj* allergic.

alero *nm* **1** *Arquit* eaves *pl.* **2** *Aut (guardabarros)* wing.

alerón *nm Av* aileron.

alerta I *adv (vigilante)* alert. II *nf (atención)* alert; **dar la (voz de) a.,** to give the alert; **en estado de a.,** to be (on the) alert. III *adj* alert. IV *interj* look out!, watch out!

alertar I *vtr* to alert (**de,** to); **nos alertó del peligro,** he alerted us to the danger. II *vi* to be alert.

aleta *nf* **1** *(de pez)* fin; *(de foca, de nadador)* flipper. **2** *Av (alerón)* aileron. **3** *Aut (guardabarros)* wing. **4** *(de nariz)* ala, wing.

aletargado,-a I *pp de* **aletargar**. II *adj* lethargic; *(amodorrado)* drowsy.

aletargamiento *nm* **1** *(letargo)* lethargy. **2** *fig (modorra)* drowsiness, sleepiness.

aletargar I *vtr (amodorrar)* to make drowsy *or* sleepy. II **aletargarse** *vr (amodorrarse)* to become drowsy *or* sleepy.

aletear *vi* **1** *(aves)* to flutter *or* flap its wings. **2** *(con los brazos)* to wave *or* flap one's arms about.

aleteo *nm* **1** *(de alas)* fluttering *or* flapping of wings. **2** *(de brazos)* waving *or* flapping of the arms. **3** *fig (palpitación)* palpitation.

aleutiano,-a *adj* Aleutian; **las Islas Aleutianas,** the Aleutian Islands.

alevín *nm* **1** *(pescadito)* fry, young fish. **2** *fig (principiante)* beginner.

alevosía *nf (traición)* treachery; *(premeditación)* premeditation; **con a., (a traición)** treacherously; *(premeditadamente)* deliberately.

alevoso,-a *adj (traidor)* treacherous; *(premeditado)* premeditated.

alfa *nf (letra)* alpha; *fig* **a. y omega,** beginning and end, alpha and omega.

alfabético,-a *adj* alphabetical, alphabetic.

alfabetización *nf* teaching to read and write; **campaña de a.,** literacy campaign.

alfabetizar *vtr* **1** *(ordenar)* to alphabetize, arrange in alphabetical order. **2** *(enseñar)* to teach to read and write.

alfabeto *nm* **1** *(abecedario)* alphabet. **2** *(código)* code; **a. telegráfico,** telegraphic code.

alfaguara *nf* abundant spring.

alfajor *nm* **1** *Am (golosina)* sweet, *US* candy. **2** *SAm (daga)* dagger knife.

alfalfa *nf Bot* lucerne, alfalfa.

alfalfal *nm,* **alfalfar** *nm* lucerne *or* alfalfa field.

alfalque *nm Geog* sandbank.

alfanje *nm* **1** *(sable)* cutlass. **2** *(pez)* swordfish.

alfar *nm* **1** *(taller)* pottery, potter's workshop. **2** *(arcilla)* clay.

alfarería *nf* **1** *(arte)* pottery. **2** *(taller)* potter's workshop; *(tienda)* pottery shop.

alfarero,-a *nm,f* potter.

alféizar *nm Arquit* sill, windowsill.

alfeñique *nm* **1** *(dulce)* almond flavoured sugar pastry. **2** *fig (persona)* weakling. **3** *(remilgo)* primness, affectation.

alférez *nm* **1** *Mil* second lieutenant. **2** *SAm* person who pays for a party.

alfil *nm (pl alfiles) Ajedrez* bishop.

alfiler *nm* **1** *Cost* pin; **sujetar con alfileres,** to pin up; *fam* **no cabe ni un a.,** it's crammed full. **2** *(broche)* pin, brooch; *(del pelo)* clip; *(de corbata)* tiepin; *(de tender ropa)* peg.

alfilerazo *nm* **1** *(punzada)* pinprick. **2** *fig (pulla)* taunt.

alfiletero *nm* pin box, pin case.

alfombra *nf* **1** carpet. **2** *(del baño)* bathmat; *(alfombrilla)* rug, mat.

alfombrado,-a I *pp de* **alfombrar. II** *adj* carpeted. **III** *nm* carpeting.

alfombrar *vtr* to carpet.

alfombrilla *nf* rug, mat.

alforja *nf* **1** *(para caballerías)* saddlebag; *(al hombro)* knapsack. **2 alforjas,** *fig* provisions.

alga *nf Bot* alga; *(marina)* seaweed.

algalia *nf Zool* civet.

algarabía *nf* hubbub, hullabaloo.

algarada *nf* **1** *(alboroto)* din, row, racket. **2** *Mil (correría)* raid.

algarroba *nf Bot* **1** *(planta)* vetch. **2** *(fruto)* carob bean.

algarrobal *nm* **1** *(de algarrobas)* vetch plantation. **2** *(de algarrobos)* carob tree plantation.

algarrobo *nm* carob tree.

algazara *nf* din, row, racket.

álgebra *nf Mat* algebra.

algebraico,-a *adj* algebraic, algebraical.

álgido,-a *adj* **1** *fig (culminante)* culminating, critical; **el punto a.,** the height. **2** *fml (muy frío)* very cold, icy.

algo I *pron indef* **1** something; **a. así,** something like that; **a. así como veinte,** round about twenty; **de hacer a. te llamaría,** if I decided to do anything, I'd give you a ring; **di a.,** say something; **por a. será,** there must be a reason for it; **¿te pasa a.?,** is there something wrong?; **toma a.,** have something to drink or eat; *fam* **a es a.,** it's better than nothing, isn't it?; *fam* **me va a dar a.,** I'm going to go round the bend. **2** *(cantidad indeterminada)* some; **¿queda a. de pastel?,** is there any cake left? **II** *adv (un poco)* quite, somewhat; **está a. mejor,** she's feeling a bit better; **te queda a. grande,** it's a bit too big for you. **III** *nm fam* **ella tiene a.,** she has a certain something about her.

algodón *nm Bot Text* cotton; *fam* **criado entre algodones,** pampered. ▪ *Farm* **a. (hidrófilo),** cotton wool.

algodonal *nm* cotton plantation or field.

algodonero,-a I *adj* cotton; **la industria algodonera,** the cotton industry. **II** *nm Bot* cotton plant. **III** *nm,f* cotton grower.

algodonoso,-a *adj* cottony.

algoritmo *nm Inform Mat* algorithm.

alguacil *nm* **1** *(esbirro)* bailiff. **2** *Zool (araña)* zebra spider; *Arg Urug (libélula)* dragonfly.

alguien *pron indef* **1** *(afirmativo)* somebody, someone; **a. ha robado mi paraguas,** someone has stolen my umbrella; *fig* **creerse a.,** to think one is somebody; *fig* **ser a.,** to be somebody or important. **2** *(interrogativo)* anybody, anyone; **¿has visto a a.?,** have you seen anybody?

algún *adj (delante de nombres masculinos) véase* **alguno,-a.**

alguno,-a I *adj* **1** *(delante del nombre) (afirmativo)* some; **alguna que otra vez,** now and then; **algunos días,** some days; **salgo alguna (que otra) tarde,** I go out the odd evening; *(interrogativo)* any; **¿has to mado alguna medicina?,** have you taken any medicine?; **¿le has visto alguna vez?,** have you ever seen him? **2** *(después del nombre) (negativo)* not at all; **no vino persona alguna,** nobody came. **II** *pron indef* **1** someone, somebody; **a. dirá que ...,** someone might say that ...; **a. que otro,** someone. **2 algunos,-as,** some (people); **a. de** or **entre ellos,** some of them.

alhaja *nf* **1** *(joya)* jewel, gem. **2** *fig (objeto, persona)* gem, treasure; *irón (persona)* **¡menuda a.!,** he's a fine one!

alharaca *nf* fuss; **hacer alharacas,** to make a lot of fuss and bother.

alhelí *nm (pl alhelíes) Bot* wallfower, stock.

alheña *nf* **I** *Bot (planta)* privet; *(flor)* privet blossom. **2** *(polvo)* henna.

alhucema *nf Bot* lavender.

aliado,-a I *pp de* **aliar. II** *adj* allied. **III** *nm,f* ally; *Hist* **los Aliados,** the Allies.

alianza *nf* **1** *(pacto)* alliance. **2** *(anillo)* wedding ring.

aliar [13] **I** *vtr* **1** to ally. **2** *(combinar)* to combine. **II aliarse** *vr* to become allies, form an alliance.

alias *adv & nm inv* alias.

alicaído,-a *adj* **1** *fig (débil)* weak, feeble. **2** *fig (deprimido)* down, depressed.

alicantino,-a I *adj* of or from Alicante. **II** *nm,f* native or inhabitant of Alicante.

alicatado,-a I *pp de* **alicatar. II** *nm* glazed tiling.

alicatar *vtr* **1** to tile. **2** *(azulejos)* to cut.

alicates *nmpl* pliers *pl.*

aliciente *nm* **1** *(atractivo)* lure, charm. **2** *(incentivo)* incentive, encouragement.

alicorear *vtr CAm* to decorate.

alicorto,-a *adj* **1** *(de alas cortas)* with clipped wings. **2** *fig (sin aspiraciones)* without ambition.

alicrejo *nm CAm* **1** *(caballo)* old nag, hack. **2** *(feo)* ugly person or thing.

alícuota *adj* aliquot.

alienación *nf Psic* alienation, derangement.

alienado,-a I *pp de* **alienar. II** *adj (loco)* insane, deranged. **III** *nm,f (lunático)* lunatic.

alienar I *vtr* to alienate. **II alienarse** *vr* to become alienated.

alienígeno,-a *adj & nm,f* alien.

alienista *nmf* alienist, psychiatrist.

aliento *nm* **1** *(respiración)* breath; **cobrar a.,** to get one's breath back; **sin a.,** breathless. **2** *fig (ánimo)* encouragement, boost; **dar a. a,** to encourage to.

alifafe *nm* (minor) ailment, complaint.

aligeramiento *nm* **1** *(carga)* lightening. **2** *(paso)* quickening. **3** *(dolor)* easing, soothing.

aligerar *vtr* **1** *(descargar)* to make lighter. **2** *(acelerar)* to speed up; **a. el paso,** to quicken one's pace; *fam* **¡aligera!,** hurry up! **3** *fig (atenuar)* to relieve, soothe.

alijo *nm* contraband; **un a. de drogas,** a consignment of drugs.

alimaña *nf Zool* vermin, pest.

alimentación *nf* **1** *(acción)* feeding; *Téc* feed. **2** *(comida)* food; **una a. basada en cereales,** a diet based on cereals.

alimentador,-a I *adj Téc* feeding. **II** *nm* feeder.

alimentar I *vtr* **1** *(dar alimento)* to feed; *(server de alimento)* to nourish; **el pescado alimenta mucho,** fish is very nutritious; **la madre alimenta a su hijo,** the mother feeds her son; **la fábrica alimenta a toda la comarca,** the whole area owes its living to the factory. **2** *fig (alentar)* to encourage, foster; **a. pasiones,** to feed passions. **3** *Inform* to feed. **II alimentarse** *vr* **a. con** or **de,** to live on.

alimentario,-a *adj* food.

alimenticio,-a *adj* nutritious; **productos alimenticios,** food products, foodstuffs; **valor a.,** nutritional value.

alimento *nm* **1** *(comida)* food; *fig* **el odio es el a. de las guerras,** hate fuels war. **2** *(valor nutritivo)* nutritional value; **tiene poco a.,** it is not very nourishing.

alimón *adv* **al a.,** together, in collaboration.

alinderar *vtr Am* to mark the boundaries of.

alineación *nf* **1** alignment, lining up; *Pol* **política de no a.,** non-alignment policy. **2** *Dep (equipo)* lineup.

alineado,-a I *pp de* **alinear. II** *adj* aligned, linedup; *Pol* **países no alineados,** non-aligned countries.

alineamiento *nm* alignment.

alinear I *vtr* **1** to align, line up. **2** *Dep (formar equipo)* to line up. **3** *Mil (formar)* to form up. **II alinearse** *vr* **1** to line up. **2** *Mil (formar)* to fall in. **3** *Pol* to become aligned.

aliñar *vtr Culin* to season, flavour, *US* flavor; *(ensalada)* to dress.

aliño *nm Culin* seasoning, dressing.

alioli *nm Culin* garlic mayonnaise.

alipegarse *vr CAm* to stick (**a,** to).

alipego *nm CAm* bonus, extra.

alisador,-a I *adj* smoothing. **II** *nm* smoothing tool.

alisar *vtr,* **alisarse** *vr* to smooth.

alisios *adj & nmpl* **(vientos) alisios,** trade winds.

aliso *nm Bot* alder.

alistado,-a I *pp de* **alistar. II** *adj Mil* enlisted, enrolled.

alistamiento *nm Mil* recruitment, enlistment.

alistar I *vtr Mil* to recruit, enlist. **II alistarse** *vr Mil* to enlist, enrol, *US* enroll; **¡alístate!,** join the army!

aliteración *nf Lit* alliteration.

aliviadero *nm* spillway.

aliviador,-a *adj* comforting, consoling.

alivianar *vtr Am véase* **aliviar.**

aliviar I *vtr* **1** *(aligerar)* to lighten, make lighter. **2** *(calmar)* to soothe, relieve. **3** *(consolar)* to comfort, console. **4** *fam (darse prisa)* to hurry. **II aliviarse** *vr (dolor)* to diminish, get better.

alivio *nm* **1** *(mejoría)* relief. **2** *(consuelo)* comfort, consolation. **3** *fam* **es un tipo de a.,** a fine one, he is!; **un calor de a.,** stifling heat.

aljaba *nf* **1** *(para flechas)* quiver. **2** *Am Bot* fuchsia.

aljama *nf* **1** *(junta)* assembly. **2** *Rel (sinagoga)* synagogue; *(mezquita)* masque.

aljamía *nf Ling* Spanish language written in Arabic characters.

aljibe *nm* cistern, tank.

aljófar *nm (perla)* pearl; *(rocío)* dewdrop.

aljofifa *nf* floorcloth.

allá *adv* **1** *(lugar alejado)* there, over there; **a. abajo/ arriba,** down/up there; **¡a. voy!,** here I go!; **más a.,** further on; **más a. de,** beyond; **no tan a.,** not that far. ■ **el más a.,** the beyond. **2** *(tiempo)* back; **a. por los años veinte,** back in the twenties. **3** *(locuciones)* **a cada uno,** you have to decide for yourself; **a. se las componga,** that's his problem, that's his tough luck; **a. tú, a. vosotros,** that's your problem; *fam* **no muy a.,** nothing special.

allanamiento *nm* **1** *(aplanamiento)* levelling, flattening. **2** *fig (de dificultades)* smoothing-out. **3** *Jur* **a. de morada,** unlawful entry; *(robo)* house-breaking, breaking and entering.

allanar I *vtr* **1** *(aplanar)* to level, flatten. **2** *fig (dificultades)* to smooth out; **a. el terreno,** to clear the way. **3** *Jur* to break into. **II allanarse** *vr (acceder)* to agree, conform.

allegado,-a I *pp de* **allegar. II** *adj* close, related; **personas allegadas,** close friends. **III** *nm, f* close friend.

allegar I *vtr* **1** *(reunir)* to gather, collect. **2** *(acercar)* to bring closer. **II allegarse** *vr (acceder)* to agree, conform.

allende *adv fml* beyond; **a. los mares,** overseas.

allí *adv (lugar)* there, over there; *(tiempo)* then; **a. abajo/ arriba,** down/up there; **de a. para acá,** back and forth; **hasta a. no tuvimos problemas,** up until then we had no problems.

alma *nf* soul; **como a. que lleva el diablo,** in a flash; **con el a. destrozada,** broken-hearted; **con toda el a.,** wholeheartedly; **en cuerpo y a.,** body and mind; **llegar al a. de algn,** to touch or move sb; **no había ni un a.,** there was not a soul; **no poder algn con su a.,** to be absolutely exhausted; **parecer un a. en pena,** to look like a ghost; **se le cayó el a. a los pies,** her heart sank; **sentir algo en el a.,** to be deeply sorry about or for sth; **ser el a. de la fiesta,** to be the life and soul of the party; *fig* **a. de Dios,** good soul; *fam* **almas gemelas,** kindred spirits.

almacén *nm* **1** *(local)* warehouse, storehouse; *(habitación)* storeroom. **2** **(grandes) almacenes,** *Com* department store *sing.* **3** *Arg Par Urug (colmado)* grocer's shop.

almacenaje *nm* **1** *(almacenamiento)* storage, warehousing. **2** *Com (coste)* storage charge.

almacenamiento *nm* **1** *(gen)* storage, warehousing. **2** *(cosas almacenadas)* stock. **3** *Inform* storage.

almacenar *vtr* **1** to store, warehouse. **2** *(acumular)* to store up, keep; **a. trastos,** to keep junk.

almacenero *nm* warehouseman, storekeeper.

almacenista *nmf (vendedor)* wholesaler; *(propietario)* warehouse owner.

almáciga *nf* **1** *(semillero)* seedbed. **2** *(resina)* mastic.

almácigo *nm* **1** *(semillero)* seedbed. **2** *Bot* mastic tree.

almadena *nf Téc* sledgehammer.

almadraba *nf* **1** *(pesca)* tunny fishing. **2** *(lugar)* tunny-fishing ground. **3** *(red)* tunny net.

almadreña *nf* clog.

almagre *nm* red ochre.

almanaque *nm* almanac, calendar.

almario *nm* wardrobe, cupboard.

almazara *nf Ind* oilmill.

almeja *nf Zool* clam.

almena *nf* merlon; **almenas,** battlements; **con almenas,** castellated, battlemented.

almenar *vtr* to build battlements on. **II** *nm (para fuego)* torch holder.

almenara *nf* **1** *(fuego)* beacon. **2** *(candelabro)* can delabrum. **3** *(para fuego)* torch holder, cresset.

almendra *nf* **1** *Bot* almond. ■ **a. garapiñada,** sugared almond. **2** *(piedra)* pebble.

almendrado,-a I *adj* almond-shaped. **II** *nm* almond paste.

almendral *nm Bot* almond grove.

almendro *nm Bot* almond tree.

almendruco *nm* unripe almond.

almeriense I *adj* of or from Almería. **II** *nmf* native or inhabitant of Almería.

almiar *nm Agr* haystack.

almíbar *nm* syrup.

almibarado,-a I *pp de* **almibarar. II** *adj* **1** *(dulce)* syrupy. **2** *fig (meloso)* sugary, sweet.

almibarar *vtr (cubrir con almíbar)* to cover in syrup; *fig* **a. las palabras,** to use honeyed words.

almidón *nm* starch.

almidonar *vtr* to starch.

almilla *nf* **1** *(jubón)* jerkin. **2** *Téc* tenon. **3** *Culin* breast of pork.

alminar *nm Arquit* minaret.

almirantazgo *nm Mil* admiralty.

almirante *nm Mil* admiral.

almirez *nm* mortar.

almizcle *nm* musk.

almizcleña *nf Bot* grape hyacinth.

almizcleño,-a *adj* musky.

almizclero,-a I *adj* musky. **II** *nm Zool* musk deer.

almofrej *nm*, **almofrez** *nm Am* sleeping bag.

almohada *nf* pillow; *fam* **consultarlo con la a.,** to sleep on it.

almohade *adj & nmf Hist* Almohade.

almohadilla *nf* 1 (small) cushion. 2 *(tampón)* inkpad.

almohadillado,-a I *pp de* **almohadillar. II** *adj* 1 *(forrado)* padded. 2 *Arquit* bossed. **III** *nm* 1 padding. 2 bossing.

almohadillar *vtr* 1 *(forrar)* to pad. 2 *Arquit* to boss.

almohadón *nm* large pillow, cushion.

almoneda *nf* 1 *(subasta)* auction. 2 *(venta a bajo precio)* clearance.

almorávide *adj & nmf* Almoràvid.

almorrana *nf Med fam* pile.

almorzar I *vi (al mediodía)* to have lunch; *(desayunar)* to have breakfast. **II** *vtr (al mediodía)* to have for lunch; *(desayunar)* to have for breakfast.

Almte. *abr de* **almirante,** admiral, Adm.

almuecín *nm*, **almuédano** *nm Rel* muezzin.

almuerzo *nm* 1 *(al mediodía)* lunch. 2 *(desayuno)* breakfast. 3 *(a media mañana)* mid-morning snack.

alocado,-a *adj (distraído)* scatterbrained; *(irreflexivo)* thoughtless, rash.

alocución *nf* speech, address.

aloe *nm*, **áloe** *nm* 1 *Bot* aloe: 2 *Med* aloes *sing.*

alojamiento *nm* accommodation, lodging; **dar a.,** to accommodate.

alojar I *vtr* 1 *(hospedar)* to accommodate, house, lodge. 2 *(balsa)* to lodge. **II alojarse** *vr (hospedarse)* to be lodge, stay.

alón[1] *nm* plucked wing.

alón,-ona[2] *adj CR Cub Chi* large-winged.

alondra *nf Orn* lark. ■ **a. común,** skylark.

alopatia *nf Med* allopathy.

alopecia *nf Med* alopecia.

alotropía *nf Quím* allotropy.

alpaca[1] *nf Zool Tex* alpaca.

alpaca[2] *nf Metal* alpaca, German silver.

alpargata *nf* canvas sandal, espadrille.

alpargatería *nf* 1 *(tienda)* espadrille shop. 2 *(taller)* espadrille factory.

Alpes *npl* **los A.,** the Alps.

alpestre *adj* Alpine; *fig* mountainous, rough.

alpinismo *nm Dep* mountaineering, climbing.

alpinista *nmf Dep* mountaineer, climber.

alpino,-a *adj* Alpine.

alpiste *nm* 1 *Bot* birdseed, canary grass. 2 *fam (bebida)* booze; *(comida)* food.

alquería *nf* 1 *(casa)* farmstead. 2 *(conjunto de casas)* hamlet.

alquilar *vtr* to hire; *(pisos, casas)* to rent; **'se alquila',** 'to let'.

alquiler *nm* 1 *(acción)* hiring; *(de pisos, casas)* renting, letting; **a. de coches,** car hire; **de a.,** *(pisos, casas)* to let, rented; *(coche)* for hire; *(televisión)* for rent. 2 *(precio)* hire, rental; *(de pisos, casas)* rent.

alquimia *nf* alchemy.

alquimista *nmf* alchemist.

alquitrán *nm* tar. ■ **a. de hulla,** coal tar.

alquitranado,-a I *pp de* **alquitranar. II** *adj* tarred, tarry. **III** *nm* 1 *(acción)* tarring. 2 *(pavimento)* tarmac.

alquitranar *vtr* to tar.

alrededor I *adv (lugar)* round, around; **a. de la mesa,** round the table; *(aproximadamente)* **a. de las dos,** around two o'clock; **a. de quince,** about fifteen; **mira a.,** look around. **II alrededores** *nmpl* surrounding area *sing*; **en los a. de Barcelona,** in the area round Barcelona, just outside Barcelona.

Alsacia *n* Alsace.

alsaciano,-a *adj & nm,f* Alsatian.

alt. *abr de* **altitud,** altitude, alt.

alta *nf (ingreso)* admission; **dar de** *or* **el a.,** *(a un empleado)* to register in the National Health System; *(a un enfermo)* to discharge from hospital; *Mil* to pass as fit; **darse de a.,** *(socio)* to join; *(enfermo)* to discharge oneself; **solicitar el a.,** to apply to be a member.

altanería *nf* arrogance, haughtiness, conceit.

altanero,-a *adj* arrogant, haughty, conceited.

altar *nm Rel* altar; *fig* **llevar al a.,** to lead to the altar; *fig* **poner en un a.,** to put on a pedestal.

altavoz *nm* loudspeaker.

alterabilidad *nf* changeability.

alterable *adj* changeable.

alteración *nf* 1 *(cambio)* alteration. 2 *(alboroto)* quarrel, row; **a. del orden público,** disturbance of the peace. 3 *(excitación)* uneasiness, agitation, restlessness.

alterar I *vtr* 1 *(cambiar)* to alter, change. 2 *(deteriorar)* to worsen, deteriorate; *(dañar)* to spoil, make go bad. 3 *(enfadar)* to upset, annoy; *(poner nervioso)* to agitate, make feel restless. **II alterarse** *vr* 1 *(cambiar)* to change. 2 *(deteriorarse)* to spoil, go bad *or* off. 3 *(enfadarse)* to be upset, lose one's temper; **no se altera por nada,** he never loses his temper.

altercado *nm* quarrel, argument.

alternador *nm Elec* alternator.

alternancia *nf* alternation.

alternante *adj* alternating.

alternar I *vtr (sucederse)* to alternate. **II** *vi* 1 *(relacionarse)* to meet people, socialize; **le gusta a.,** he's very sociable. 2 *(con hombres)* to entertain; **(ella) alterna con hombres,** she entertains men. **III alternarse** *vr* to alternate.

alternativa *nf* alternative, option, choice; **tomar una a.,** to decide, choose.

alternativo,-a *adj* alternative.

alterne *nm fam* 1 **bar de a.,** bar (with hostesses); **chica de a.,** hostess. 2 *euf (prostitución)* prostitution.

alterno,-a *adj* alternate, alternating; **días alternos,** alternate days.

alteza *nf* Highness; **Su A. Real,** His *or* Her Royal Highness.

altibajos *nmpl fig* **los a. de la vida,** the ups and downs of life.

altillo *nm* 1 *Arquit* attic. 2 *Geog* hillock.

altilocuente *adj* grandiloquent.

altímetro *nm* altimeter.

altiplanicie *nf*, **altiplano** *nm Geog* high plateau.

altísimo,-a I *superl de* **alto. II el A.** *nm Rel* the Almighty.

altisonancia *nf* grandiloquence.

altisonante *adj* grandiloquent, pompous.

altitud *nf* altitude, height.

altivez *nf*, **altiveza** *nf* arrogance, haughtiness, conceit.

altivo,-a *adj* arrogant, haughty, conceited.

alto[1] *nm* 1 *(interrupción)* stop, break; **hacer un a. en el trabajo,** to take a short break from work. 2 *Mil* halt; **¡a.!,** halt; **¡a. el fuego!,** cease fire!; **dar el a.,** to order to halt; **un a. el fuego,** a cease-fire.

alto,-a[2] **I** *adj* 1 *(persona, árbol, edificio)* tall; *(montaña, techo, presión)* high; **mi hija Ana es muy alta,** my daughter Ana is very tall; **tiene una casa de techos altos,**

she has a house with high ceilings; **un barco en alta mar,** a ship on the high seas; *fig* **pasar por a.,** to overlook. **2** *(elevado)* top, upper; **el A. Aragón,** Upper Aragon; **en lo a.,** at the top; **los pisos altos,** the top floors. **3** *(superior, avanzado)* **a altas horas de la noche,** late at night; **alta sociedad,** high society; **alta tecnología,** high technology; **clase alta,** upper class; **precio a.,** high price. **4** *(sonido) (fuerte)* loud; *(agudo)* high, sharp; **en voz alta,** aloud, in a loud voice; **una nota alta,** a high note. **II** *adv* **1** high, high up; **no subas tan a.,** don't go so far up; **sal con las manos en a.,** come out with your hands up. **2** *(fuerte)* loud, loudly; **pon la radio más alta,** turn the radio up. **III** *nm* **1** *(altura)* height; **¿cuánto mide de a.?,** *(persona)* how tall is he?; *(cosa)* how high is it?; *fig* **por todo lo a.,** in a grand way; *fig* **tirando por lo a.,** at the most, at the outside. **2** *(elevación)* hill. **3** *Am (montón)* pile, heap. **4 altos,** *Am* upstairs *sing.* ◆ **altamente** *adv* highly, extremely.

altoparlante *nm Am* loudspeaker.

altozano *nm* **1** *(elevación)* hillock, hill; *(de una ciudad)* upper part. **2** *Am (de iglesia)* atrium.

altramuz *nm Bot* lupin.

altruismo *nm* altruism.

altruista I *adj* altruistic. II *nmf* altruist.

altura *nf* **1** height; **a. del agua,** depth of the water; **de diez metros de a.,** ten metres high; **de poca a.,** not very high. **2** *(nivel)* level; **a la a. de la calle Ancha,** at the junction with Calle Ancha; **a la a. del cine,** by the cinema; **a la misma a.,** on the same level; *Geog* on the same latitude; *fig* **estar a la a. de las circunstancias,** to rise to the occasion; *fig* **no está a su a.,** he does not measure up to him; *fam* **quedar a la a. del betún,** to make a very poor showing. **3** *fig (de sentimientos)* loftiness, nobleness. **4 alturas,** *(cumbres)* heights; *Rel* heaven *sing*; *fig* **a estas a.,** by now; *fig* **a estas a. ya no se puede cambiar nada,** it's too late to change anything.

alubia *nf Culin* bean.

alucinación *nf* hallucination.

alucinado,-a I *pp de* **alucinar.** II *adj arg* amazed, spaced out.

alucinador,-a *adj* hallucinatory.

alucinamiento *nm* hallucination.

alucinante *adj* **1** hallucinatory. **2** *arg (extraordinario)* brilliant, mind-blowing.

alucinar I *vtr* **1** to hallucinate. **2** *fig (cautivar)* to fascinate. II *vi arg* to be amazed, be spaced out.

alucinógeno,-a I *adj* hallucinogenic. II *nm* hallucinogen.

alud *nm* avalanche.

aludido,-a I *pp de* **aludir.** II *adj* above-mentioned, in question; *fig* **darse por a.,** to take the hint.

aludir *vi* to allude to, mention.

alujar *vtr CAm* to polish, shine.

alumbrado,-a I *pp de* **alumbrar.** II *adj* **1** *(iluminado)* lit, lighted. **2** *fam (alegre)* merry, tipsy. III *nm* **1** *Elec* lighting. ■ **a. público,** street lighting. **2** *Aut* lights *pl.*

alumbramiento *nm* **1** *Elec* lighting. **2** *Med* childbirth.

alumbrar I *vtr* **1** *(iluminar)* to light, give light to, illuminate; **el sol nos alumbra,** the sun gives us light. **2** *fig (instruir)* to enlighten. **3** *Am (examinar al trasluz)* to hold up to the light. II *vi Med (parir)* to give birth. III **alumbrarse** *vr fam* to get tipsy.

alumbre *nm Quím* alum.

alúmina *nf Quím* alumina.

aluminio *nm Metal* aluminium, *US* aluminum.

alumnado *nm Educ* **1** *(de colegio)* pupils *pl.* **2** *Univ* student body.

alumno,-a *nm,f* **1** *(de colegio)* pupil; **a. externo,** day pupil; **a. interno,** boarder. **2** *Univ* student.

alunizaje *nm* moon landing.

alunizar *vi* to land on the moon.

alusión *nf* allusion, mention.

alusivo,-a *adj* allusive (**a,** to).

aluvial *adj* alluvial.

aluvión *nm* alluvion, flood; *fig* **un a. de preguntas,** a barrage of questions.

aluzar *vtr Am* to light, lighten.

álveo *nm* river-bed, bed.

alveolar *adj Anat Ling* alveolar.

alveolo *nm*, **alvéolo** *nm* **1** *Anat* alveolus. **2** *(de panal)* cell.

alverja *nf*, **alverjana** *nf Am* pea.

alza *nf* **1** *(de tiempo, temperatura)* rise; **en a.,** rising; *(bolsa)* **jugar al a.,** to bull the market; *fig* **estar en a.,** to be coming up. **2** *Impr* underlay. **3** *Mil* sight.

alzacuello *nm* clerical collar.

alzada *nf* **1** *(de un caballo)* height at the withers. **2** *Jur (apelación)* appeal.

alzado,-a I *pp de* **alzar.** II *adj* **1** raised, lifted; **votación a mano alzada,** vote by a show of hands. **2** *(persona)* fraudulently bankrupt. **3** *Am (animal)* runaway. **4** *Am (persona)* insolent, impudent. **5** *SAm (animal) (hembra)* on heat; *(macho)* in rut. III *nm* **1** *Arquit* elevation. **2** *Impr* gathering. **3** *(robo)* theft.

alzamiento *nm* **1** *(aumento)* raising, increase. **2** *(rebelión)* uprising.

alzaprima *nf* **1** *(palanca)* crowbar, lever. **2** *(cuña)* wedge. **3** *Mús* bridge.

alzaprimar *vtr* to lever up.

alzar I *vtr* **1** *(levantar)* to raise, lift; **a. el telón,** to raise the curtain; **a. el vuelo,** to take off; **a. la voz,** to raise one's voice; **a. los ojos,** to look up; **a. un edificio,** to raise a building; *Náut* **a. velas,** to hoist sail. **2** *(quitar)* to remove, take off. **3** *Impr* to gather. **4** *(cosecha)* to get in, gather in. II **alzarse** *vr* **1** *(levantarse)* to get up, rise. **2** *(sobresalir)* to stand out. **3** *Pol (rebelarse)* to rise, rebel; **a. en armas,** to rise. **4** *(conseguir)* to obtain, achieve; **a. con la victoria,** to win, be victorious. **5** *Am (animal)* to go back to the wild.

alzo *nm CAm* theft.

ama *nf (señora)* lady of the house; *(dueña)* owner. ■ **a. de casa,** housewife; **a. de cría,** wet nurse; **a. de llaves,** housekeeper; *CAm Col PR* **a. de brazos,** nanny, nurse.

amabilidad *nf* kindness; *fml* **tenga la a. de esperar,** would you be so kind as to wait.

amable *adj* kind, nice; *fml* **¿sería usted tan a. de seguirme?,** would you be so kind as to follow me?

amacayo *nm Am Bot* amaryllis.

amacizar *vtr* **1** *CAm Col (abarrotar)* to cram, stuff, pack. **2** *Col Méx (afianzar)* to strengthen, secure.

amachimbrarse *vr Am,* **amachinarse** *vr Am* to live together.

amacho,-a *adj CAm* outstanding.

amachorrarse *vr Am (hembra)* to go sterile.

amado,-a I *pp de* **amar.** II *adj* loved, beloved. III *nm,f* sweetheart.

amadrinar *vtr* to be the godmother of.

amaestrado,-a I *pp de* **amaestrar.** II *adj* trained; *(domado)* tamed; **ratón a.,** performing mouse.

amaestrador,-a I *adj* training; *(domador)* taming. II *nm,f (entrenador)* trainer; *(domador)* tamer.

amaestramiento *nm* training; *(doma)* taming.

amaestrar *vtr (animal)* to train; *(domar)* to tame; **amaestró a su perro,** he trained his dog.

amagamiento *nm Am* ravine.

amagar I *vtr* **1** *(dar indicios de)* to show signs of; **amagaba una sonrisa,** there was the hint of a smile on his lips. **2** *(amenazar)* to threaten; **a. y no dar,** to make threats but not carry them out; **le amaga un gran peligro,**

he is threatened by great danger. **3** *(fingir)* to dissemble, simulate; **a. una retirada,** to simulate a retreat. **II** *vi* **1** *(ser inminente)* to threaten, be imminent; **amagaba tormenta,** a storm was threatening. **2** *(enfermedad)* to show the first signs; **a. un ataque al corazón,** to show symptoms of the onset of a heart attack.

amago *nm* first sign, indication; **a. de infarto,** onset of a heart attack.

amainar *vi* **1***(viento, tormenta)* to drop, die down. **2** *fig (apaciguarse)* to calm down.

amalgama *nf* amalgam.

amalgamación *nf* amalgamation.

amalgamar *vtr* to amalgamate.

amalhayar *vtr CAm Col* to desire, covet, long for.

amamantamiento *nm* breast-feeding, suckling.

amamantar *vtr* to breast-feed, suckle.

amancay *nm Am* amaryllis.

amancebamiento *nm* cohabitation.

amancebarse *vr* to cohabit.

amanecer I *v impers* to dawn; **amanece temprano,** day breaks early. **II** *vi* to be somewhere at daybreak; **amanecimos en Finlandia,** we were in Finland at daybreak. **III** *nm* dawn, daybreak; **al a.,** at dawn.

amanerado,-a I *pp de* **amanerar II** *adj* mannered, affected.

amaneramiento *nm* affectation.

amanerar I *vtr (maneras)* to affect. **II amanerarse** *vr* to become affected.

amansador *nm Am* horsebreaker.

amansar I *vtr* **1** to tame; **a. un caballo,** to break in a horse. **2** *fig (apaciguar)* to tame, calm. **II amansarse** *vr* to become tame.

amante I *adj* loving, fond (**de,** of); **a. del arte,** fond of art. **II** *nmf* lover.

amanuense *nmf* scribe.

amañado,-a I *pp de* **amañar. II** *adj* **1** *(hábil)* clever, skilful, *US* skillful. **2** *(falso)* faked.

amañar I *vtr (falsear)* to fix, fiddle; **a. las cuentas,** to cook the books; **a. las elecciones,** to rig the elections; **a. una historia,** to fabricate a story. **II amañarse** *vr fam (apañárselas)* **amañárselas,** to manage; **siempre se las amaña para conseguir lo que quiere,** he always manages to get his way.

amaño *nm* trick, fiddle, scheme.

amapola *nf Bot* poppy.

amar I *vtr* to love. **II amarse** *vr* to love each other, be in love (with each other).

amaraje *nm* **1** *Náut* landing at sea. **2** *Astronáut* splashdown.

amaranto *nm Bot* amaranth.

amarar *vi* **1** *Náut* to land at sea. **2** *Astronáut* to splash down.

amarchantarse *vr Am* to become a regular customer (**en,** of).

amargado,-a I *pp de* **amargar. II** *adj fig* embittered, bitter; *(resentida)* resentful; **ella está amargada,** she feels very bitter; **una sonrisa amargada,** a sour smile. **III** *nm,f* bitter person.

amargar I *vtr* to make bitter; *fig* to embitter, sour; **amargarle la existencia a algn,** to make sb's life a misery; **aquello nos amargó la tarde,** that ruined the whole evening. **II** *vi* to taste bitter. **III amargarse** *vr fig* to become embittered *or* bitter; **no te amargues por eso,** don't let that make you bitter.

amargo,-a I *adj* bitter. **II** *nm* bitterness.

amargor *nm* bitterness.

amargura *nf* bitterness, grief, sorrow, sadness.

amariconado,-a *adj vulg* queer.

amarillear *vi* **1** *(volverse amarillo)* to yellow, go yellow. **2** *(tirar a amarillo)* to be yellowish.

amarillento,-a *adj* yellowish.

amarillez *nf* yellowness.

amarillismo *nm Prensa* sensationalism.

amarillista *adj Prensa* sensationalist.

amarillo,-a *adj & nm* yellow.

amarilloso,-a *adj Am* yellowish.

amaro *nm Bot* clary sage.

amarra *nf* **1** *Náut* mooring rope; **soltar amarras,** to cast off, let go. **2** *fig (lazo)* tie, binding; **soltarse las amarras,** to break loose. **3** **amarras,** *fam* connections.

amarradero *nm Náut (argolla)* mooring ring; *(lugar)* mooring.

amarraje *nm Náut* mooring charges *pl.*

amarrar I *vtr* **1** *Náut* to moor, tie up. **2** *(atar)* to tie (up), bind. **II amarrarse** *vr CAm Col (emborracharse)* to get drunk.

amarre *nm Náut* mooring.

amarrete *adj Am* mean, stingy, tight.

amartelado,-a I *pp de* **amartelarse. II** *adj* starryeyed.

amartelarse *vr* to become very loving.

amartillar *vtr* **1** *(martillear)* to hammer. **2** *(escopeta)* to cock.

amasadera *nf* kneading trough.

amasandería *nf Am* baker's shop, bakery.

amasar *vtr* **1** *Culin (masa)* to knead. **2** *Constr (yeso, cemento)* to mix. **3** *fig (dinero)* to amass. **4** *fam (urdir)* to cook up.

amasijo *nm* **1** *Culin (masa)* dough. **2** *Constr (de yeso, cemento)* mixture. **3** *fam (mezcolanza)* hotchpotch, jumble.

amateur *adj & nmf* amateur.

amatista *nf Min* amethyst.

amatorio,-a *adj* love; **poesía amatoria,** love poetry.

amazacotado,-a *adj* **1** *(duro)* hard, tough; **arroz a.,** stodgy rice. **2** *(apretado)* crammed.

amazona *nf* **1** *(jinete)* horsewoman. **2** *Mit* Amazon.

Amazonas *n* **el A.,** the Amazon.

amazónico,-a *adj* Amazonian.

ambages *nmpl* **hablar sin a.,** to go straight to the point; **ir** *or* **andarse con a.,** to beat around the bush.

ámbar *nm* amber.

ambarino,-a I *adj* amber. **II** *nf Am Bot* scabious.

Amberes *n* Antwerp.

ambición *nf* ambition.

ambicionar *vtr* to have as an ambition; **siempre ambicionó ser rico,** he always wanted to be rich.

ambicioso,-a I *adj* ambitious. **II** *nm,f* ambitious person.

ambidextro,-a I *adj* ambidextrous. **II** *nm,f* ambidextrous person.

ambientación *nf Lit Teat* setting.

ambiental *adj* environmental.

ambientar I *vtr* **1** *(dar ambiente)* to give atmosphere to; **este café está muy bien ambientado,** this cafe has a very nice atmosphere. **2** *Lit Teat (situar)* to set; **la obra está ambientada en la Edad Media,** the play *or* the book is set in the Middle Ages. **II ambientarse** *vr (adaptarse)* to get used to.

ambiente I *adj* environmental; **temperatura a.,** room temperature. **II** *nm* environment; *fig (medio)* atmosphere, environment, milieu; **cambiar de a.,** to change one's surroundings; **el a, familiar,** the family environment; **en este a. no hay quien trabaje,** it is impossible to work in these conditions; **en este pueblo no hay a.,** there is not much going on in this village.

ambigú *nm (pl* **ambigúes)** buffet, buffet supper.

ambigüedad *nf* ambiguity.

ambíguo,-a *adj* ambiguous.

ámbito *nm* **1** *(espacio)* space, sphere; **de a. local**, local; **empresa de a. nacional**, nationwide company; **en el a. de**, within; **en el a. de esta provincia**, within this county. **2** *(ambiente)* atmosphere, environment.

ambivalencia *nf* ambivalence.

ambivalente *adj* ambivalent.

ambos,-as *adj pl fml* both; **por a. lados**, on both sides.

ambrosía *nf* ambrosia.

ambulancia *nf* ambulance.

ambulante *adj* travelling, *US* traveling, mobile; **biblioteca a.**, mobile library.

ambulatorio,-a I *adj* ambulatory. **II** *nm* surgery, clinic.

ameba *nf* amoeba, *US* ameba.

amedrantar I *vtr fml* *(asustar)* to frighten, scare. **II amedrantarse** *vr* *(asustarse)* to be frightened, scared; *(acobardarse)* to become intimidated.

amelcochar *Am* I *vtr* *(espesar)* to thicken. **II amelcocharse** I *vtr* *(espesarse)* to thicken. **2** *(reblandecerse)* to soften, go soft.

amelonado,-a *adj* **1** melon-shaped. **2** *fam* *(enamorado)* lovesick.

amén¹ *nm Rel* amen; *fam* **decir a. a todo**, to agree with everything; *fam* **en un decir a.**, in the twinkling of an eye.

amén² *adv* **a. de**, *(excepto)* except for; *(además de)* in addition to.

amenaza *nf* threat, menace.

amenazador,-a *adj*, **amenazante** *adj* threatening, menacing.

amenazar *vtr* to threaten; **a. de muerte a algn**, to threaten to kill sb; *fig* **amenaza lluvia**, it is threatening to rain.

amenguar *vtr* **1** *(disminuir)* to lessen, reduce. **2** *(deshonrar)* to defame, belittle.

amenidad *nf* pleasantness, agreeableness.

amenizar *vtr* to make (more) entertaining; **para a. la velada**, to liven up the party.

ameno,-a *adj* pleasant, enjoyable, entertaining.

América *n* America. ■ **A. Central**, Central America; **A. del Norte**, North America; **A. del Sur**, South America.

americana *nf* *(prenda)* jacket.

americanismo *nm Ling* Americanism.

americanista *nmf* Americanist.

americanización *nf* Americanization.

americanizar I *vtr* to Americanize. **II americanizarse** *vr* to become Americanized, go American.

americano,-a *adj & nm,f* American.

amerindio,-a *adj & nm,f* Amerindian, American Indian.

ameritado,-a I *pp de* **ameritar**. **II** *adj Am* worthy.

ameritar *vtr* **1** *(merecer)* to deserve. **2** *Am* *(otorgar méritos)* to recognize the worth *or* merit of.

amerizaje *nm véase* **amaraje**.

amerizar *vi véase* **amarar**.

amestizado,-a *adj* like a half-breed.

ametrallador,-a *adj* **fusil a.**, automatic rifle.

ametralladora *nf* machine-gun.

ametrallar *vtr* to machine-gun.

amianto *nm Min* asbestos *sing*.

amiba *nf véase* **ameba**.

amigable *adj* amicable, friendly.

amigacho,-a *nm,f fam* mate, friend.

amígdala *nf Anat* tonsil.

amigdalitis *nf Med* tonsillitis.

amigo,-a I *adj* **1** friendly; **una mano amiga**, a friendly hand; **son muy amigos**, they are very good friends. **2** *(aficionado)* fond *(de*, of); **a. del buen vino**, fond of good wine. **II** *nm,f* **1** friend; **hacerse a. de**, to make friends

with; **hacerse amigos**, to become friends; **un a. mío**, a friend of mine. **2** *(novio)* boyfriend; *(novia)* girlfriend; *(amante)* lover.

amigote *nm fam* pal, mate, chum.

amiguero,-a *adj Am* who makes friends easily.

amiguete *nm fam véase* **amigote**.

amilanamiento *nm* **1** *(miedo)* fear. **2** *(desánimo)* discouragement; *(abatimiento)* depression.

amilanar I *vtr* **1** *(asustar)* to frighten, scare. **2** *(desanimar)* to discourage, depress. **II amilanarse** *vr* **1** *(asustarse)* to be frightened. **2** *(desanimarse)* to be discouraged, become depressed.

aminoácido *nm Quím* amino acid.

aminoración *nf* reduction, decrease, cut; **a. de la velocidad**, slowing down.

aminorar *vtr* to reduce, decrease, cut; **a. el paso**, to slow down.

amistad *nf* **1** friendship; **trabar a. con**, to make friends with. **2 amistades**, friends; **hacer nuevas a.**, to make new friends.

amistoso,-a *adj* friendly; **en plan a.**, in a friendly way; *Dep* **partido a.**, friendly match.

amnesia *nf Med* amnesia, loss of memory.

amnésico,-a I *adj* amnesic. **II** *nm,f* amnesiac.

amnistía *nf* amnesty.

amnistiar *vtr* to amnesty, grant an amnesty to.

amo *nm* **1** *(señor)* master; *fig* **ser el a.**, to be the boss; *fam* **ser el a. del cotarro**, to rule the roost. **2** *(dueño)* owner.

amoblar *vtr* to furnish.

amodorrado,-a I *pp de* **amodorrarse**. **II** *adj* sleepy, drowsy.

amodorramiento *nm* sleepiness, drowsiness.

amodorrarse *vr* *(adormecerse)* to become sleepy *or* drowsy; *(dormirse)* to fall into a stupor.

amohosarse *vr Am* to go mouldy *or US* moldy.

amojamado,-a *adj* wizened, wrinkled.

amojonamiento *nm* marking out.

amojonar *vtr* to mark out.

amojosarse *vr SAm* to go mouldy *or US* moldy.

amolado,-a I *pp de* **amolar**. **II** *adj* sharpened, ground. **III** *nm* sharpening, grinding.

amolar *vtr* **1** to sharpen, grind. **2** *fam* *(fastidiar)* to annoy, pester.

amoldable *adj* adaptable; *fig* **Juan es muy a.**, Juan adapts to everything.

amoldamiento *nm* **1** adapting, adjusting. **2** *fig* *(persona)* adaptation.

amoldar I *vtr* to adapt, adjust. **II amoldarse** *vr* to adapt oneself; **ella no pudo a. a la nueva vida**, she couldn't get used to the new lifestyle.

amollar I *vi* *(ceder)* to yield, give in. **II** *vtr & vi Náut* *(cabos)* to pay out.

amonestación *nf* **1** *(advertencia)* rebuke, reprimand, reprehension; *Dep* *(tarjeta)* warning. **2 amonestaciones**, *Rel* banns.

amonestar *vtr* **1** *(advertir)* to rebuke, reprimand; *Dep* to warn. **2** *Rel* to publish the banns of.

amoniacal *adj Quím* ammoniacal.

amoniaco *nm*, **amoníaco** *nm* ammonia.

amontillado,-a *adj* *(vino)* pale dry, amontillado.

amontonado,-a *adj* heaped up, piled up.

amontonamiento *nm* **1** *(acción)* piling, heaping. **2** *(montón)* pile, heap.

amontonar I *vtr* **1** to pile up, heap up. **2** *(juntar)* to collect, gather; **a. trastos**, to keep junk. **II amontonarse** *vr* to pile up, heap up; *(gente)* to crowd together.

amor *nm* **1** love; *(con esmero)* loving care; **ella fue su gran a.,** she was his great love; **hacer el a.,** to make love; **por el a. de Dios,** for God's sake; *fig* **en cada puerto, un a.,** a girl in every port; *fam* **con** *or* **de mil amores,** with pleasure; *fam* **por a. al arte,** for the sake of it; *prov* **a. con a. se paga,** one good turn deserves another. ■ *Lit* **a. cortés,** courtly love; **a. propio,** self-esteem. **2 amores,** *(persona)* loves; *(asuntos)* love affairs.

amoral *adj* amoral.

amoralidad *nf* amorality.

amoratado,-a I *pp de* **amoratarse. II** *adj* **1** *(de frío)* blue with cold. **2** *(de un golpe)* black and blue; **con un ojo a.,** with a black eye.

amoratarse *vr* **1** *(de frío)* to turn blue. **2** *(de un golpe)* to turn black and blue.

amorcillo *nm* Cupid.

amordazar *vtr (perro)* to muzzle; *(persona)* to gag.

amorfo,-a *adj* amorphous.

amorío *nm* love affair, flirtation.

amoroso,-a *adj* loving, affectionate.

amortajamiento *nm* shrouding.

amortajar *vtr* to shroud, wrap in a shroud.

amortiguación *nf (de un dolor)* alleviation, mitigation; *(de un golpe)* damping; *(de un ruido)* muffling; *(de una luz)* subduing.

amortiguador,-a I *adj (de dolor)* alleviating, mitigating; *(de golpe)* damping, cushioning; *(de ruido)* muffling; *(de luz)* subduing. **II** *nm Aut* shock absorber; *Téc* damper.

amortiguamiento *nm véase* **amortiguación.**

amortiguar *vtr (dolor)* to alleviate, mitigate; *(golpe)* to damp, cushion; *(ruido)* to muffle; *(luz)* to subdue.

amortizable *adj Fin* redeemable.

amortización *nf Fin* **1** *(reembolso)* redemption. **2** *(depreciación)* amortization, depreciation, writing off.

amortizar *vtr Fin* **1** *(reembolsar)* to redeem. **2** *(depreciar)* to amortize, depreciate, write off; *fam* **me costó caro, pero lo he amortizado,** it was expensive, but I've got my money's worth out of it.

amoscarse *vr fam* to get angry.

amostazar *vtr fam* to make angry, annoy.

amotinado,-a I *pp de* **amotinar. II** *adj (insurrecto)* riotous, insurgent; *Mil* mutinous. **III** *nm,f (insurrecto)* rioter, insurgent; *Mil* mutineer.

amotinamiento *nm* riot, rioting; *(insurrección)* insurrection; *Mil* mutiny.

amotinar I *vtr* to incite to riot; *Mil* to incite to mutiny. **II amotinarse** *vr* to rise up, riot; *Mil* to mutiny.

amovible *adj* detachable, removable.

amovilidad *nf* detachability, removability.

amparar I *vtr* to protect; *(ayudar)* to help; *(favorecer)* to favour, *US* favor. **II ampararse** *vr* to use as protection; *(defenderse)* to take shelter; **se amparó en sus amigos,** he sought the help of his friends.

amparo *nm* protection, shelter; **al a. de,** under the protection of.

ampelis *nm inv Orn* waxwing.

amperímetro *nm Elec* ammeter.

amperio *nm Elec* ampère, amp.

ampliable *adj* enlargeable.

ampliación *nf* enlargement, extension; *Constr* extension; *Fot* enlargement; *Fin* **a. de capital,** increase in capital; **a. de estudios,** furthering of studies.

ampliado,-a I *pp de* **ampliar. II** *adj* enlarged, extended.

ampliadora *nf Fot* enlarger.

ampliar *vtr* to enlarge extend; *Constr (casa, edificio)* to build an extension to; *Fot (fotografía)* to enlarge; *Fin (capital)* to increase; **a. una idea,** to develop an idea.

amplificación *nf* amplification.

amplificador,-a I *adj* amplifying. **II** *nm* amplifier.

amplificar *vtr* to amplify.

amplio,-a *adj* large, roomy, spacious; *(ancho)* wide, broad; **en el sentido más a. de la palabra,** in the broadest sense of the word.

amplitud *nf* **1** spaciousness, expanse, extent; *fig* **de gran a.,** far-reaching. ■ **a. de miras,** broad-mindedness. **2** *(espacio)* room, space. **3** *Fís* amplitude.

ampolla *nf* **1** *Med* blister. **2** *(vasija)* flask, bottle. **3** *(burbuja)* bubble.

ampulosidad *nf* pomposity, bombast.

ampuloso,-a *adj* pompous, bombastic.

amputación *nf* **1** *Med* amputation. **2** *fig (supresión)* cutting out.

amputar *vtr* **1** *Med* to amputate. **2** *fig (suprimir)* to cut out.

Amsterdam *n* Amsterdam.

amuchar *vtr Am* to increase, multiply.

amueblar *vtr* to furnish.

amuermado,-a *adj fam* **1** *(atontado)* dopy, dopey, groggy. **2** *(deprimido)* down, depressed. **3** *(aburrido)* bored.

amuermar *vtr fam* **1** *(atontar)* to make feel dopy *or* dopey *or* groggy. **2** *(deprimir)* to depress. **3** *(aburrir)* to bore.

amujerado,-a *adj* effeminate.

amulatado,-a *adj* like a mulatto.

amuleto *nm* amulet. ■ **a. de la suerte,** lucky charm.

amura *nf Náut* **1** *(proa)* bow. **2** *(cabo)* tack.

amurallado,-a I *pp de* **amurallar. II** *adj* walled.

amurallar *vtr* to wall, fortify.

anabaptismo *nm Rel* Anabaptism.

anabaptista *adj & nmf Rel* Anabaptist.

anabolismo *nm Biol* anabolism.

anacarado,-a *adj* pearly.

anacardo *nm Bot (árbol)* cashew tree; *(fruto)* cashew nut.

anacoluto *nm Ling* anacoluthon.

anaconda *nf Zool* anaconda.

anacoreta *nmf* anchorite, anchoret.

anacrónico,-a *adj* anachronistic, anachronic.

anacronismo *nm* anachronism.

ánade *nm Orn* duck. ■ **á. friso,** gadwall; **á. rabudo,** pintail; **á. real,** mallard; **á. silbón,** wigeon.

anaerobio,-a *Biol* **I** *adj* anaerobic. **II** *nm* anaerobe.

anafe *nm* portable stove *or* cooker.

anagrama *nm* anagram.

anal *adj Anat* anal.

anales *nmpl* annals.

analfabetismo *nm* illiteracy.

analfabeto,-a *nm,f* illiterate; *fig* **es un a.,** he is stupid.

analgesia *nf Med* analgesia.

analgésico,-a *adj & nm Med* analgesic.

análisis *nm inv* analysis. ■ **a. de orina,** urine analysis; **a. de sangre,** blood test.

analista *nmf* analyst.

analítico,-a *adj* analytical, analytic.

analizable *adj* analyzable.

analizador,-a I *adj* analyzing. **II** *nm Fís* analyzer.

analizar *vtr* to analyze.

analogía *nf* analogy.

analógico,-a *adj* analogical.

analogismo *nm* analogism.

análogo,-a *adj* analogous, similar.

ananá *nm (pl ananaes)*, **ananás** *nm (pl ananases) Bot* pineapple.

anaquel *nm* shelf.

anaranjado,-a *adj & nm (color)* orange.

anarco *nmf fam* anarchist.

anarquía *nf* anarchy.

anárquico,-a *adj* anarchical, anarchic.

anarquismo *nm* anarchism.

anarquista *adj & nmf* anarchist.

anarquizante *adj* anarchist.

anatema *nm* anathema; **lanzar anatemas,** to curse.

anatematizar *vtr* to anathematize; *fig* to curse.

anatomía *nf* anatomy.

anatómico,-a *adj* anatomical, anatomic.

anca *nf* haunch. ■ **ancas de rana,** frogs' legs.

ancestral *adj* ancestral.

ancestro *nm* ancestor.

ancho,-a I *adj* wide, broad; **a lo a.,** breadthwise; **te está muy a.,** it's too big for you; *fam* **quedarse tan a.,** to behave as if nothing had happened. **II** *nm* **1** *(anchura)* width, breadth; **dos metros de a.,** two metres wide; **¿qué a. tiene?,** how wide is it? **2** *Cost* width. **III anchas** *nfpl fam* **a mis** *or* **tus a.,** at ease, comfortable; **me sentí a mis a.,** I felt comfortable *or* at home.

anchoa *nf (pez)* anchovy.

anchura *nf (ancho)* width, breadth; *Cost* **a. de cintura,** waist measurement.

anchuroso,-a *adj* wide, broad; *(espacioso)* spacious.

ancianidad *nf* old age.

anciano,-a I *adj* very old. **II** *nm,f* old person; **los ancianos,** old people. ■ **residencia de ancianos,** old people's home.

ancla *nf Náut* anchor; **echar anclas,** to drop anchor; **levar anclas,** to weigh anchor.

anclaje *nm* **1** *Náut* anchorage. **2** *Constr Téc* anchor.

anclar *vtr & vi Náut Téc* to anchor.

áncora *nf Náut Téc* anchor.

ancorar *vtr & vi véase* **anclar.**

andadas *nfpl fam* old ways; **volver a las a.,** to go back to one's old tricks.

andaderas *nfpl* baby-walker *sing.*

andado,-a I *pp de* **andar. II** *adj* **1** *(común)* common. **2** *(gastado)* worn out. **III** *nm CAm (modo de andar)* way of walking, gait.

andador,-a I *adj (aficionado a andar)* fond of walking; *(rápido)* fast-walking. **II** *nm, f (bueno)* good walker; *(rápido)* fast walker. **III** *nm* baby-walker.

andadura *nf* walking.

andalón,-ona *adj CAm* fond of walking.

Andalucía *n* Andalusia.

andalucismo *nm* **1** *Ling* Andalusian word *or* expression. **2** *Pol* Andalusian nationalism.

andaluz,-a *adj & nm,f* Andalusian.

andamiaje *nm Constr* scaffolding.

andamio *nm Constr* scaffold.

andana *nf* row, line.

andanada *nf* **1** *(represión)* reprimand, rebuke. **2** *Taur* covered stand. **3** *Mil (descarga)* broadside. **4** *(andana)* row, line.

andancia *nf* **1** *Am (andanza)* adventure. **2** *CAm (éxito)* success.

andante I *adj* **caballero a.,** knight errant. **II** *nm Mús* andante.

andanza *nf* adventure, happening.

andares *nmpl* walk *sing,* gait *sing.*

andar I *vi* **1** to walk; *(venir)* to come; *(ir)* to go; **a. de puntillas,** to tiptoe; *fam (sorpresa)* **¡anda!,** come off it!, get away!; *fam* **¡andando!,** let's go!, let's get a move on! **2** *(trasladarse algo)* to move; **este coche anda despacio,**

this car goes very slowly. **3** *(funcionar)* to work, go, function; **este ascensor no anda,** this lift is out of order; **esto no anda,** this doesn't work. **4** *fam (estar)* to be; **anda por los cuarenta,** he's about forty; **anda preocupada estos días,** she's been rather worried lately; **anda siempre diciendo que ...,** he's always saying that ...; **¿qué tal andamos de tiempo?,** how are we off for time?; **tus calcetines deben a. por ahí,** your socks must be there somewhere. **5** *(obrar)* **anda con cuidado,** take care, be careful; *prov* **dime con quién andas y te diré quién eres,** birds of a feather flock together; *prov* **quien mal anda mal acaba,** those who live by the sword die by the sword. **II** *vtr (recorrer)* to walk; **a. diez kilómetros,** to walk ten kilometres. **III andarse** *vr* **ándate con cuidado,** mind what you do, take good care of yourself; *fig* **a.con rodeos, a. por las ramas,** to beat about the bush.

andariego,-a I *adj* **1** *(que anda)* fond of walking. **2** *(que viaja)* fond of travelling. **II** *nm, f* **1** *(andador)* good walker. **2** *(viajero)* person who likes travelling.

andarín,-ina I *adj* good at walking. **II** *nm,f* good walker.

andas *nfpl* portable platform *sing;* *Rel* **llevaban el santo en a.,** they carried the saint on a float; *fig* **llevar a algn en a.,** to pamper sb.

andén *nm Ferroc* platform.

Andes *npl* Andes.

andinismo *nm Am* mountaineering.

andino,-a *adj & nm,f* Andean.

andoba *nmf (hombre)* guy; *(mujer)* bird.

Andorra *n* Andorra.

andorrano,-a *adj & nm,f* Andorran.

andrajo *nm* rag, tatter; **hecho un a.,** in rags.

andrajoso,-a *adj* ragged, tattered.

androceo *nm Bot* androecium.

andrógeno *nm Biol* androgen.

andrógino,-a *Biol* **I** *adj* androgynous, androgyne. **II** *nm* androgyne.

androide *nm* android.

andullo *nm* **1** *(rollo)* rolled tobacco leaf. **2** *(manojo)* bunch of tobacco leaves. **3** *SAm (hoja grande)* large leaf for wrapping.

andurriales *nmpl fam* out-of-the way place *sing.*

anea *nf Bot* bulrush, reed mace.

anécdota *nf* anecdote.

anecdotario *nm* collection of anecdotes.

anecdótico,-a *adj* anecdotic, anecdotal.

anegación *nf* flooding.

anegadizo,-a *adj* subject to flooding.

anegamiento *nm véase* **anegación.**

anegar I *vtr* to flood. **II anegarse** *vr* to flood; *fig* **a. en lágrimas,** to fill with tears.

anejo,-a I *adj* attached, joined (**a,** to). **II** *nm* annexe, *US* annex.

anemia *nf Med* anaemia, *US* anemia.

anémico,-a I *adj Med* anaemic *US* anemic. **II** *nm, f Med* anemia *or US* anemia sufferer.

anemómetro *nm Fís* anemometer.

anémona *nf,* **anemona** *nf,* **anemone** *nf* **1** *Bot* anemone. **2** *Zool* **a. de mar,** sea anemone.

anestesia *nf Med* anaesthesia, *US* anesthesia.

anestesiar [12] *vtr Med* to anaesthetize, *US* anesthetize.

anestésico,-a *adj & nm Med* anaesthetic, *US* anesthetic.

anestesista *nmf Med* anaesthetist, *US* anesthesiologist.

aneurisma *nm Med* anaeurysm.

anexar *vtr* to annex.

anexión *nf* annexation.

anexionar *vtr véase* **anexar.**

anexionismo *nm Pol* annexationism, annexionism.

anexionista *adj & nmf Pol* annexationist, annexionist.

anexo,-a I *adj* attached, joined (**a,** to). **II** *nm* annexe, *US* annex.

anfeta *nf arg* amphetamine.

anfetamina *nf Farm* amphetamine.

anfibio,-a I *adj* amphibious. **II** *nm Zool* amphibian; los **anfibios,** amphibia *pl.*

anfibología *nf Ling* amphibology.

anfiteatro *nm* 1 amphitheatre, *US* amphitheater. 2 *Univ* lecture theatre *or US* theater. 2 *Cin Teat* gallery.

anfitrión,-ona I *nm* host. **II** *nf* hostess.

ánfora *nf* amphora.

anfractuosidad *nf* roughness, cragginess; *(camino)* twisting, winding.

angarillas *nfpl (carretilla)* handbarrow *sing; (camilla)* stretcher *sing.*

ángel *nm* 1 *Rel* angel; *fig* es **un á.,** he behaves beautifully; *fig* **tener á.,** to have a something about one. ■ *Rel* **á. de la guarda,** guardian angel; *Dep* **salto del á.,** swallow dive. 2 *Am (micrófono)* hand microphone.

angélica *nf Bot* angelica.

angelical *adj,* **angélico,-a** *adj* angelical, angelic.

angelito *nm dimin fam* little angel; *irón* **menudo a. estás tú hecho,** you are a fine one!

angelote *nm* 1 *(niño)* chubby child. 2 *(adulto)* good person.

ángelus *nm inv Rel* Angelus.

angina *nf Med* angina; **estar con anginas,** to have a sore throat. ■ *Med* **á. de pecho,** angina pectoris.

anglicanismo *nm Rel* Anglicanism.

anglicano,-a *adj & nm, f Rel* Anglican; **la Iglesia Anglicana,** the Anglican Church, the Church of England.

anglicismo *nm* Anglicism.

anglo,-a I *adj* Anglian. **II** *nm,f* Angle, Anglian.

angloamericano,-a *adj & nm,f* Anglo-American.

anglófilo,-a *adj & nm,f* Anglophile.

anglófobo,-a *adj & nm,f* Anglophobe.

anglófono,-a I *adj* English-speaking. **II** *nm, f* English speaker.

anglosajón,-ona *adj & nm,f* Anglo-Saxon.

Anglonormando,-a *adj* **las Islas Anglonormandas,** the Channel Islands.

Angola *n* Angola.

angoleño,-a *adj & nm,f* Angolan, Angolese.

angora *nf* angora; **gato de a.,** Angora cat; **lana de a.,** angora wool.

angosto,-a *adj fml* narrow.

angostura *nf* 1 *(estrechez)* narrowness. 2 *Bot* angostura.

angra *nf Geog* cove, inlet, creek.

anguila *nf (pez)* eel. ■ **a. de mar,** conger eel.

anguilla *nf Am* eel.

angula *nf (pez)* elver.

angular *adj* angular; *Fot* **(objetivo) gran a.,** wideangle lens; *Arquit* **piedra a.,** cornerstone.

ángulo *nm* 1 *Geom* angle; **en á. con,** at an angle to. ■ **á. recto,** right angle; *Mil* **á. de tiro,** elevation. 2 *(esquina, rincón)* corner.

anguloso,-a *adj* angular.

angustia *nf* 1 anguish; **¡qué a.!,** how distressing! 2 *(malestar físico)* sickness, nausea.

angustiado,-a I *pp de* **angustiar. II** *adj (afligido)* distressed; *(preocupado)* worried.

angustiar I *vtr (afligir)* to distress; *(preocupar)* to worry. **II angustiarse** *vr (afligirse)* to become distressed; *(preocuparse)* to worry.

angustioso,-a *adj (acongojante)* distressing; *(preocupado)* worrying.

anhelante *adj* longing, yearning.

anhelar *vtr* to long for, yearn for; **anhelaba encontrarse con ella,** he was longing to meet her.

anhelo *nm* longing, yearning.

anhídrido *nm Quím* anhydride.

anidar I *vi Orn* to nest, make one's nest; *fig* **la esperanza anidó en su corazón,** hope filled his heart. **II** *vtr fig* to shelter.

anilina *nf Quím* aniline, anilin.

anilla *nf (aro)* ring. 2 **anillas,** *Dep* rings.

anillado,-a I *pp de* **anillar. II** *adj* 1 ringed. 2 *(en forma de anillo)* annular, ring-like. **III** *nm Orn* ringing.

anillar *vtr* 1 *(dar forma de anillo)* to make into a ring. 2 *(sujetar con anillos)* to ring. 3 *Orn (marcar)* to ring.

anillo *nm* 1 ring; *fig* **me viene como a. al dedo,** it's just what I needed; *fig irón* **no se te van a caer los anillos por eso,** doing that wouldn't be beneath you. ■ **a. de boda,** wedding ring; **a. de prometida,** engagement ring. 2 *Astron* ring. 3 *Arquit* annulet. 4 *(de gusano)* annulus; *(de culebra)* coil.

ánima *nf* 1 *Rel* soul. ■ **á. bendita,** soul in Purgatory. 2 *(de arma)* bore 3 **ánimas,** *Rel* evening bell *sing.*

animación *nf* 1 movement, activity; **hay gran a. en la plaza,** there is a lot of bustle in the square. 2 *(diversión)* entertainment; **dar a. a una fiesta,** to liven a party up.

animado,-a I *pp de* **animar. II** *adj* 1 *(movido)* lively, entertaining, jolly; **una película muy animada,** a very entertaining film. 2 *(alegre)* cheerful, in high spirits. ◆ **animadamente** *adv* cheerfully.

animador,-a I *adj* cheering, encouraging. **II** *nm, f (en baile)* entertainer; *Dep* cheerleader.

animadversión *nf* ill feeling, animosity.

animal I *adj* 1 animal; **el reino a.,** the animal kingdom. 2 *fam (persona) (basto)* rough; *(necio)* ignorant; *(grosero)* rude, coarse. **II** *nm* 1 animal. ■ **a. de bellota,** pig; **a. de carga,** beast of burden. 2 *fam (persona) (basto)* rough person, brute; *(necio)* dunce; *(grosero)* rude person.

animalada *nf fam* stupid thing to do *or* say; **es una a. que conduzcas sin carné,** it's incredibly stupid of you to drive without a licence!

animalidad *nf* animality.

animar I *vtr* 1 *(alentar)* to encourage. 2 *(alegrar) (persona)* to cheer up; *(local, fiesta, reunión)* to liven up, brighten up. **II animarse** *vr* 1 *(persona)* to cheer up; *(cosas)* to brighten up. 2 *(decidirse)* to make up one's mind; **¿te animas a venir?,** do you feel like coming along, then?; **¡venga, anímate!,** come on, say that you will!

anímico,-a estado a., frame *or* state of mind.

animismo *nm Rel* animism.

animista I *Rel adj* animistic. **II** *Rel nmf* animist.

ánimo *nm* 1 *(espíritu)* spirit; *(mente)* mind; *(alma)* soul; **no tenía en el á. sino una idea,** he had only one idea in his mind. ■ **estado de á.,** frame *or* state of mind. 2 *(intención)* intention; **con á. de,** with the intention of; **no eataba en mí á. ofenderle,** it wasn't my intention to offend him; **sin á. de ofenderte,** no offence intended. 3 *(valor, coraje)* courage; **dar ánimos a,** to encourage; **¡levanta ese á.!,** cheer up!; **no tiene ánimos para nada,** he's really in low spirits.

animosidad *nf* animosity, ill feeling.

animoso,-a *adj* cheerful, encouraged.

aniñado,-a I *pp de* **aniñarse. II** *adj* childlike; *pey* childish.

aniñarse *vr to* grow *or* become childish.

anión *nm Fís* anion.

aniquilación *nf* annihilation, destruction.

aniquilador,-a *adj* annihilating, destructive.

aniquilamiento *nm véase* **aniquilación.**

aniquilar *vtr* to annihilate, destroy; **a. al enemigo,** to wipe out the enemy.

anís *nm* **1** *Bot (planta)* anise; *(grano)* aniseed; *fam* **no ser grano de a.,** to be no trifle. **2** *(bebida)* anisette. **3** *Culin (confite)* aniseed ball.

anisado,-a I *pp de* **anisar.** II *adj* flavoured with aniseed.

anisar *vtr* to flavour with aniseed.

anisete *nm* anisette.

aniversario *nm* anniversary.

Ankara *n* Ankara.

ano *nm Anat* anus.

anoche *adv (late)* last night; *(early)* yesterday evening; **antes de a.,** the night before last.

anochecer I *v impers* to get dark; **cuando anochece,** at nightfall, at dusk. II *vi* to be somewhere at dusk; **anochecimos en Cuenca,** we were in Cuenca at dusk. III *nm* nightfall, dusk.

anochecido,-a I *pp de* **anochecer.** II *adv* night, dark. III *nf* nightfall, dusk.

anodino,-a *adj* **1** *Med* anodyne. **2** *fig (ineficaz)* inefficient; *(insubstancial)* insubstantial. **3** *fig (soso)* insipid, dull.

ánodo *nm Fís* anode.

anomalía *nf* anomaly.

anómalo,-a *adj* anomalous.

anona I *nf* **1** *Bot* soursop. **2** *CAm (estupidez)* stupidity. II *adj CAm (estúpido)* stupid.

anonadación *nf,* **anonadamiento** *nm* **1** *(destruir)* annihilation, destruction. **2** *(abatimiento)* discouragement. **3** *(humillación)* humiliation. **4** *(estupefacción)* amazement, astonishment.

anonadar *vtr* **1** *(aniquilar)* to annihilate, destroy; *fig* to crush. **2** *(abatir)* to dishearten, dismay, dispirit. **3** *(humillar)* to humiliate. **4** *(maravillar)* to amaze, astonish, astound.

anonimato *nm* anonimity; **permanecer en el a.,** to remain anonymous or nameless.

anonimista *nmf Am* anonymous author.

anónimo,-a I *adj* **1** *(desconocido)* anonymous. **2** *Com (sociedad)* limited, *US* incorporated. II *nm* **1** *(carta)* anonymous letter; *(obra)* anonymous work. **2** *(anonimato)* anonimity.

anorak *nm (pl* **anoraks)** *(prenda)* anorak.

anorexia *nf Med* anorexia.

anormal I *adj* **1** abnormal. **2** *(inhabitual)* unusual; **una situación a.,** an irregular situation. **3** *Med* subnormal. II *nmf Med* subnormal person.

anormalidad *nf* abnormality.

anotación *nf* **1** *(acotación)* annotation. **2** *(apunte)* noting. **3** *(nota)* note.

anotar *vtr* **1** *(acotar)* to annotate, add notes to. **2** *(apuntar)* to take down, make a note of.

anovulación *nf Med* anovulation.

anovulatorio *nm Farm* anovulatory.

anquilosado,-a I *pp de* **anquilosar.** II *adj* anchylosed, ankylosed; *fig* paralysed; **costumbres anquilosadas** stagnated customs.

anquilosamiento *nm* anchylosis, ankylosis; *fig* stagnation, paralysis.

anquilosar I *vtr* to anchylose, ankylose. II **anquilosarse** *vr* to anchylose, ankylose; *fig* to stagnate, be paralysed.

anquilosis *nf* anchylosis, ankylosis.

anquilostoma *nf* hookworm.

ánsar *nm Orn* goose. ■ **á. común,** greylag goose.

ansia *nf* **1** *(deseo)* longing, yearning; **a. de poder,** longing for power. **2** *(ansiedad)* anxiety; *(angustia)* anguish. **3** *Med* sick feeling.

ansiado,-a I *pp de* **ansiar.** II *adj* longed-for.

ansiar *vtr* to long for, yearn for; **ansiaba volver a casa,** he was longing to go back home.

ansiedad *nf* anxiety; **con a.,** anxiously; *Med* nervous tension.

ansioso,-a *adj* **1** *(deseoso)* eager, longing **2** *(desasosegado)* anxious, worried. **3** *(codicioso)* greedy, covetous.

anta¹ *nf Zool* elk, moose.

anta² *nf* **1** menhir. **2** *Arquit* anta.

antagónico,-a *adj* antagonistic.

antagonismo *nm* antagonism.

antagonista I *adj* antagonistic. II *nmf* antagonist.

antaño *adv* in the past, formerly.

antañón,-ona *adj fam* very old.

antártico,-a I *adj* Antarctic. II **el A.** *nm* the Antarctic Ocean.

Antártida *n* Antarctica.

ante¹ *nm* **1** *Zool* elk, moose. **2** *(piel)* suede.

ante² *prep* **1** before, in the presence of; *Jur* **a. notario,** in the presence of a notary; **a. todo,** first of all. **2** *(en comparación con)* compared with, next to. **3** *(delante de)* in the face of; **a. las circunstancias,** under the circumstances; **a. tanta amabilidad,** seeing how very kind he was.

anteanoche *adv* the night before last.

anteayer *adv* the day before yesterday.

antebrazo *nm Anat* forearm.

antecámara *nf* antechamber, anteroom.

antecedente I *adj* antecedent, previous. II *nm* antecedent; **¿hay algún a. de esta enfermedad en su familia?,** is there any history of this illness in your family? III **antecedentes** *nmpl* **1** *(historial)* record *sing;* **tener malos a.,** to have a bad record. ■ *Jur* **a. penales,** criminal record *sing.* **2** *fig (persona)* **estar en a.,** to be in the picture; **poner en a.,** to put in the picture.

anteceder *vtr* to precede, go before.

antecesor,-a *nm, f* **1** *(en un cargo)* predecessor. **2** *(antepasado)* ancestor.

antedata *nf* antedate.

antedatar *vtr* to antedate.

antedicho,-a I *adj* aforementioned, aforesaid. II *nm, f* person mentioned before.

antediluviano,-a *adj* antediluvian; *fig* as old as the hills.

antefirma *nf fml* title of the signatory.

antelación *nf* precedence; **con a. a estos hechos,** before these things happened; **con poca a.,** at short notice; **con un mes de a.,** a month beforehand, with a month's notice; *fml* **con la debida a.,** well in advance, in good time.

antemano *adv* **de a.,** beforehand, in advance.

antena *nf* **1** *Rad TV* aerial, antenna. **2** *Zool Ent* antenna, feeler.

anteojeras *nfpl* blinkers, *US* blinders.

anteojo *nm* **1** telescope. **2** **anteojos,** *(gafas)* glasses, spectacles; *(binoculares)* binoculars, field glasses.

antepalco *nm Teat* anteroom to a box.

antepasado,-a I *adj* previous, prior. II *nm, f* ancestor.

antepatio *nm* forecourt.

antepecho *nm* **1** *(de ventana)* sill. **2** *(pretil)* parapet, guardrail.

antepenúltimo,-a *adj* antepenultimate; **el capítulo a.,** the last chapter but two.

anteponer *(pp* **antepuesto)** *vtr* to put *or* place in front.

anteproyecto *nm* **1** *(gen)* preliminary plan, draft. **2** *Jur* first draft, discussion document; **a. de ley,** draft bill.

antepuesto,-a I *pp de* **anteponer.** II *adj* placed in front.

antepuse *pt indef véase* **anteponer.**

anterior I *adj* **1** previous, before; **el día a.,** the day before. **2** *(delantero)* anterior, fore, front; **parte a.,** front part. **II el a., la a.** *nmf* the previous one. ◆ **anteriormente** *adv* previously, before.

anterioridad *nf* **con a.,** before; **con a. a,** prior to, before.

antes I *adv* **1** *(tiempo)* before, earlier; **'a. de entrar dejen salir',** 'let people off *or* out before boarding'; **cuanto a., lo a. posible,** as soon as possible; **él llegó a.,** he arrived first; **mucho a.,** long before. **2** *(antaño)* in the past; **'a. llovía más,** it used to rain more in the past. **3** *(lugar)* in front, before; **a. de mí en la cola,** in front of me in the quene; **a. del semáforo,** before the traffic lights. **4** *(preferencia)* **a. prefiero hacerlo yo,** I'd rather do it myself. **II** *conj* **a. (bien),** on the contrary. **III** *adj* before; **la noche a.,** the night before.

antesala *nf* antechamber, anteroom; **hacer a.,** to wait; *fig* **en la a. de,** on the verge of.

antevíspera *nf* two days before.

anti- *pref* anti-; **antimilitarismo,** antimilitarism.

antiácido,-a *adj & nm Med* antacid.

antiadherente *adj* nonstick.

antiaéreo,-a *adj Mil* anti-aircraft.

antialcohólico,-a I *adj* teetotal. **II** *nm,f* teetotaller.

antiatómico,-a *adj* **refugio a.,** fall-out shelter.

antibiótico,-a *adj & nm Med* antibiotic.

anticiclón *nm Meteor* anticyclone, high pressure area.

anticipación *nf* bringing forward; **con a.,** in advance; **con suficiente a.,** in good time, enough in advance.

anticipado,-a I *pp de* **anticipar. II** *adj* brought forward; *(temprano)* early; **elecciones anticipadas,** early elections; **gracias anticipadas,** thanks in advance; *Com* **por a.,** in advance. ◆ **anticipadamente** *adv* in advance.

anticipar I *vtr (acontecimiento)* to bring forward; *(dinero)* to pay in advance; **no anticipemos acontecimientos,** we'll cross that bridge when we come to it. **II anticiparse** *vr* **1** *(adelantarse)* to beat to it; **iba a decírtelo, pero él se me anticipó,** I was going to tell you, but he beat me to it. **2** *(llegar antes)* to arrive early; **las lluvias se han anticipado este año,** the rain has come earlier than expected this year; *fig* **a. a su tiempo,** to be ahead of one's time.

anticipo *nm* **1** foretaste. **2** *Fin (adelanto)* advance; **pedir un a.,** to ask for an advance (on one's wages). **3** *Fin (préstamo)* prepayment.

anticlerical *adj & nmf* anticlerical.

anticlericalismo *nm* anticlericalism.

anticlinal *nm Geol* anticline.

anticoagulante *adj & nm* anticoagulant.

anticomunista *adj & nmf* anti-communist.

anticoncepción *nf* contraception.

anticonceptivo,-a *adj & nm* contraceptive.

anticongelante *adj & nm (de radiador)* anti-freeze; *(de parabrisas)* de-icer.

anticonstitucional *adj* unconstitutional.

anticorrosiva,-a *adj & nm* anticorrosive.

anticristo *nm Rel* Antichrist.

anticuado,-a *adj* antiquated, old-fashioned, out-of-date.

anticuario,-a *nm, f (conocedor)* antiquarian, antiquary; *(comerciante)* antique dealer.

anticuerpo *nm Biol* antibody.

antidemocrático,-a *adj Pol* undemocratic.

antideportivo,-a *adj Dep* unsportsmanlike, unsporting.

antideslizante I *adj (neumático)* anti-skid; *(suelo)* nonslip. **II** *nm* anti-skid device.

antideslumbrante *adj* anti-glare, anti-dazzle.

antidetonante *adj* antiknock.

antídoto *nm Farm* antidote.

antiestético,-a *adj* ugly, unsightly.

antifascismo *nm Pol* anti-fascism.

antifascista *nmf Pol* anti-fascist.

antifaz *nm (prenda)* mask.

antigás *adj* **careta a.,** gas mask.

antígeno,-a *Med* **I** *adj* antigenic. **II** *nm* antigen.

antigualla *nf (cosa)* old-fashioned thing; *(persona)* has-been.

antigüedad *nf* **1** *(período histórico)* antiquity, age; **en la a.,** in olden days, in former times. **2** *(en un empleo, cargo)* seniority. **3** *(objeto)* antique; **tienda de antigüedades,** antique shop.

antiguo,-a I *adj* **1** old, ancient; **de a.,** since ancient times; **un coche a.,** an old car. **2** *(pasado de moda)* old-fashioned; **a la antigua,** in an old-fashioned way; **estar chapado a la antigua,** to be an old fogey. **3** *(en un empleo, cargo)* senior; **los socios más antiguos,** the most senior members. **4** *(anterior)* former; **antiguos alumnos,** former pupils *or* students. **II los antiguos** *nmpl* the ancients.

antihéroe *nm* antihero.

antihigiénico,-a *adj* unhygienic, unhealthy.

antihistamínico,-a *adj & nm Med* antihistamine.

antiinflacionista *adj Econ* anti-inflationary.

antillano,-a *adj & nm,f* West Indian.

Antillas *npl* **las A.,** the West Indies, the Antilles.

antílope *nm Zool* antelope.

antimateria *nf Fís* antimatter.

antimísil *adj* antimissile.

antimonio *nm Quím* antimony.

antinatural *adj* unnatural, contrary to nature.

antiniebla *adj inv* **luces a.,** foglamps, *US* foglights.

antinomia *nf* antinomy.

antinómico,-a *adj* antinomic.

antioxidante *Quím* **I** *adj (para alimentos)* antioxidant; *(para metales)* antirust. **II** *nm (para alimentos)* antioxidant; *(para metales)* antirust substance.

antipapa *nm Rel* antipope.

antiparras *nfpl fam* specs, glasses.

antipatía *nf* antipathy, dislike; **coger a. a,** to take a dislike to; **tener a. a,** to dislike.

antipático,-a *adj* unfriendly, unkind, unpleasant, not nice; **Julio me es a.,** I don't like Julio; **ser a.,** to be unfriendly; **una persona antipática,** an unpleasant person.

antipatizar *vi Am* not to get on (**con,** with).

antipatriótico,-a *adj* unpatriotic.

antipirético,-a *adj & nm Med* antipyretic.

antípoda I *adj* antipodean, antipodal. **II** *nmf (persona)* antipodean. **III** *nm* **1** *(punto)* antipode. **2 antípodas,** Antipodes.

antiqueño,-a *adj & nm,f* Antiguan.

antiquísimo,-a I *superl de* **antiguo. II** *adj* very old, ancient.

antirrábico,-a *adj Farm* anti-rabies, anti-rabic.

antirreglamentario,-a *adj* against the rules.

antirrobo I *adj inv* antitheft; **alarma a.,** burglar alarm. **II** *nm (para coche)* antitheft device; *(para casa)* burglar alarm.

antisemita I *adj* anti-Semitic. **II** *nmf* anti-Semite.

antisemítico,-a *adj* anti-Semitic.

antisemitismo *nm* anti-Semitism.

antiséptico,-a *adj & nm Farm* antiseptic.

antisocial *adj* antisocial.

antitanque *adj inv* antitank.

antítesis *nf inv* antithesis.

antitetánico,-a *adj Farm* anti-tetanus.

antitético,-a *adj* antithetic, antithetical.

antitóxico,-a *adj Farm* antitoxic.

antitoxina *nf* antitoxin.

antojadizo,-a *adj* capricious, fanciful, unpredictable.

antojarse *vr* **1** *(encapricharse)* to feel like, fancy; **cuando se me antoje**, when I feel like it; **se le antojó un helado**, he fancied an ice cream. **2** *(suponer)* to suppose; **se me antoja que no lo sabe**, I have the feeling that he doesn't know.

antojo *nm* **1** *(capricho)* whim, fancy, caprice; *(de embarazada)* craving; **a su a.**, in one's own way, as one pleases. **2** *Anat* birthmark.

antología *nf* anthology; *fig* **de a.**, remarkable, outstanding.

antológico,-a *adj* anthological.

antónimo,-a *Ling* **I** *adj* antonymous. **II** *nm* antonym.

antonomasia *nf* antonomasia; **por a.**, par excellence.

antorcha *nf* **1** *(tea)* torch. **2** *fig (guía)* guiding light.

antracita *nf Min* anthracite.

ántrax *nm inv Med* anthrax.

antro *nm (tugurio)* dump, hole; *fig* **a. de perdición,** den of vice.

antropocéntrico,-a *adj* anthropocentric.

antropofagia *nf* anthropophagy.

antropófago,-a I *adj* anthropophagic, anthropophagous. **II** *nm, f* anthrophagite.

antropoide I *adj* anthropoid, anthropoidal. **II** *nmf* anthropoid.

antropología *nf* anthropology.

antropológico,-a *adj* anthropological.

antropólogo,-a *nm, f* anthropologist.

antropomorfismo *nm* anthropomorphism.

antropomofo,-a I *adj* anthropomorphic. **II** *nm, f* anthropomorphist.

anual *adj* annual; **ingresos anuales,** yearly income.

anualidad *nf* annual payment, annuity.

anuario *nm* yearbook.

anudadura *nf*, **anudamiento** *nm* **1** *(acción)* knotting, tying, fastening. **2** *(nudo)* knot.

anudar I *vtr* **1** *(atar)* to knot, tie, fasten. **2** *fig (unir)* to join, bring together. **II anudarse** *vr* to get into a knot; *fig* **se le anudó la lengua,** he became tongue-tied.

anuencia *nf* consent, approval.

anuente *adj* consenting, consentient.

anulable *adj* cancellable.

anulación *nf* annulment, cancellation; *(de ley)* repeal; **a. de matrimonio,** annulment of marriage.

anular¹ I *adj* annular, ring-shaped; **dedo a.,** ring finger. **II** *nm* ring finger.

anular² I *vtr* **1** *(matrimonio)* to annul; *Com (pedido)* to cancel; *Dep (gol)* to disallow; *Jur (ley)* to repeal; *(sentencia)* to quash; **a. un efecto,** to cancel out the effect of sth. **2** *fig (persona)* to deprive of authority. **3** *Inform* to delete. **II anularse** *vr (persona)* to lose one's authority.

anunciación *nf Rel* **la a. de la Virgen,** the Annunciation.

anunciador,-a *adj & nm,f*, **anunciante** *adj & nmf* **I** *adj* **1** announcing, who announces. **2** *(publicidad)* advertising, who advertises; **empresa anunciadora,** advertising agency. **II** *nm, f & nmf* **1** announcer. **2** *(publicista)* advertiser.

anunciar I *vtr* **1** *(avisar)* to announce. **2** *(dar publicidad)* to advertise. **II anunciarse** *vr (darse publicidad)* to advertise oneself; **a. en un periódico,** to put an advert in a newspaper.

anuncio *nm* **1** *(aviso)* announcement; **son un a. de primavera,** they are a sign of spring. **2** *(comercial)* advertisment, advert, ad; *(valla publicitaria)* hoarding,

US billboard. **3** *(cartel)* notice, poster; **pon un a. en la escuela,** put a notice up in the school; **tablón de anuncios,** noticeboard.

anverso *nm* **1** *(de moneda)* obverse. **2** *(de página)* recto.

anzuelo *nm Pesca* (fish) hook; *fig* **echar el a. a,** to try to hook; *fig* **morder** *or* **picar el a.,** to swallow the bait, take the hook.

añadido,-a I *pp de* **añadir. II** *adj* added. **III** *nm* **1** *(postizo)* switch, hairpiece. **2** *(cosa añadida)* addition, piece added on.

añadidura *nf* addition, piece added on; **por a.,** besides, on top of everything else.

añadir *vtr* to add **(a, to).**

añagaza *nf* **1** *Caza* decoy, stool pigeon, lure. **2** *fig (artificio)* lure, trick.

añal I *adj* **1** *(anual)* annual. **2** *(animal)* year-old. **II** *nmf (animal)* yearling.

añejar I *vr (envejecer)* to age; *(vino, queso)* to mature; *(jamón)* to cure. **II añejarse** *vr* **1** *(mejorar)* to improve with age, mature. **2** *(estropearse)* to deteriorate.

añejo,-a *adj* **1** *(vino, queso)* mature; *(jamón)* cured. **2** *(viejo)* old. **3** *(estropeado)* stale.

añicos *nmpl* bits; **hacer a.,** to smash to pieces.

añil I *adj* indigo, blue. **II** *nm* **1** *Bot* indigo plant. **2** *(color)* indigo. **3** *(para lavar)* blue.

año *nm* **1** year; **el a. pasado,** last year; **hace años,** a long time ago, years ago; **los años cincuenta,** the fifties; **todo el a.,** all the year (round); **una vez al a.,** once a year; *fig* **estar a años luz de,** to be miles away from. ■ **a. bisiesto,** leap year; *Educ* **a. escolar,** school year; **a. luz,** light year. **2 años,** age *sing*; **¿cuántos a. tienes?,** how old are you?; **cumplió 18 a.,** she was 18, she celebrated her 18th birthday; **en sus a. mozos,** in his youth; **entrado en a.,** getting on; **tiene nueve a.,** he's nine years old.

añojo *nm (becerro)* yearling calf; *(cordero)* yearling lamb.

añoranza *nf* longing, yearning, nostalgia; **sentir a. de su país,** to be homesick.

añorar I *vtr* **1** *(pasado)* to long for, yearn for, miss. **2** *(país)* to feel homesick for, miss. **3** *(persona fallecida)* to mourn. **II** *vi* to pine.

añoso,-a *adj* very old.

aojar *vtr* to cast the evil eye on.

aorta *nf Anat* aorta.

aovar *vi* to lay eggs.

apabullamiento *nm* bewilderment, perplexity, confusion.

apabullar *vtr* **1** *fam (aplastar)* to crush, flatten. **2** *(dejar confuso)* to bewilder, perplex, confuse.

apacentadero *nm* pasture.

apacentamiento *nm* pasturing, grazing.

apacentar I *vtr* **1** *(ganado)* to put out to pasture, graze. **2** *fig (cuidar)* to take care of; *(alimentar)* to feed. **II apacentarse** *vr (ganado)* to pasture, graze.

apache *adj & nmf* Apache.

apacheta *nf SAm* cairn, shrine.

apachico *nm Am* bundle, package.

apachurrar *vtr* **I** *(despachurrar)* to squash, flatten. **II apachurrarse** *vr Am (achaparrar)* to get stocky.

apacibilidad *nf* gentleness, mildness, calmness.

apacible *adj* gentle, mild, calm.

apaciguador,-a I *adj* pacifying. **II** *nm,f* pacifier.

apaciguamiento *nm* pacifying, appeasement.

apaciguar I *vtr (calmar)* to pacify, appease. **II apaciguarse** *vr (calmarse)* to calm down; *(tormenta)* to abate.

apadrinamiento *nm* **1** *(de bautizo)* function of godfather. **2** *(de boda)* function of best man. **3** *(de duelo)* function of second. **4** *(mecenazgo)* sponsoring, patronage.

apadrinar *vtr* **1** *(bautizo)* to act as godfather to. **2** *(boda)* to be best man for. **3** *(duelo)* to act as second to. **4** *(artista)* to sponsor.

apagadizo,-a *adj* slow to burn.

apagado,-a I *pp de* **apagar. II** *adj* **1** *(luz etc)* out; **este cigarrillo está a.**, this cigarette is out. **2** *(color)* dull. **3** *(voz)* sad; *(mirada)* expressionless, lifeless; *(carácter, persona)* spiritless.

apagar I *vtr* **1** *(fuego)* to extinguish, put out. **2** *(luz)* to turn out *or* off, put out; **apaga esa luz**, turn off that light. **3** *(desconectar)* to turn off, switch off; **apaga la tele**, switch the telly off. **4** *(color)* to soften. **5** *fig (dolor)* to soothe; **a. la sed**, to quench one's thirst. **5** *fam* **apaga y vámonos**, let's call it a day. **II apagarse** *vr* **1** *(luz)* to go out; *(televisión)* to go off. **2** *(morir)* to pass away.

apagavelas *nm inv* candle snuffer.

apagón *nm* power cut, blackout.

apainelado,-a *adj Arquit* basket-handle.

apaisado,-a *adj* **1** oblong. **2** *Inform* landscape.

apalabrar *vtr* **1** *(concertar)* to make a verbal agreement on; **apalabraron el precio por teléfono**, they agreed the price over the phone. **2** *(contratar)* to engage verbally.

Apalaches *npl* los **(Montes) A.**, the Appalachians.

apalancado,-a I *pp de* **apalancar. II** *adj* **1** *(escondido)* hidden. **2** *arg (perezoso)* ensconced.

apalancar I *vtr* **1** to lever up; **a. una puerta**, to lever a door open. **2** *(esconder)* to hide. **II apalancarse** *vr arg* to ensconce oneself, settle down; **se apalancaron delante de la tele**, they settled down in front of the telly.

apalancamiento *nm* **1** leverage. **2** *arg (pereza)* laziness.

apalanque *nm arg* laziness.

apaleado,-a I *pp de* **apalear. II** *adj* beaten.

apaleamiento *nm* beating, hitting, thrashing.

apalear[1] *vtr* **1** *(pegar)* to beat, hit, thrash. **2** *Agr (varear)* to thresh.

apalear[2] *vtr Agr (grano)* to winnow.

apaleo *nm Agr* **1** *(acción)* winnowing. **2** *(tiempo)* winnowing time.

apangado,-a *CAm* **I** *pp de* **apangarse II** *adj (zopenco)* silly, stupid.

apangarse *vr CAm* to crouch, squat.

apaniguarse *vr Am* to gang up.

apañado,-a I *pp de* **apañar II** *adj* **1** *(ordenado)* tidy; *(limpio)* clean; *(arreglado)* well-dressed, smart. **2** *(hábil)* clever, skilful, *US* skillful; *(mañoso)* handy. **3** *(adecuado)* smart and practical; **va un vestido muy a.**, it's a very smart dress and you can wear it anywhere. **4** *fam* **estar a.**, to be in for a surprise; *fam* **pues sí que estamos apañados**, now we're really done for, now we've had it.

apañar I *vtr* **1** *(ordenar)* to tidy; *(limpiar)* to clean; *(ataviar)* to smarten up. **2** *(comprender, remendar)* to mend, fix. **3** *(recoger)* to collect; *fig (robar)* to clean out. **4** *Am (proteger)* to shelter, conceal, protect. **II apañarse** *vr fam* **apañárselas**, to manage; **ya me las apañaré solo**, I'll manage on my own.

apaño *nm* **1** *(arreglo)* tidying; *(limpieza)* cleaning; *(atavío)* smartening up. **2** *(componenda, remiendo)* mend, repair; **no tiene a.**, nothing can be done about it. **3** *(habilidad)* skill. **4** *fam (lío amoroso)* (love) affair; *(persona)* lover; **tener un a.**, to have a bit on the side.

aparador *nm* **1** *(mueble)* sideboard, cupboard. **2** *(escaparate)* shop window.

aparato *nm* **1** *(pieza de)* apparatus, set; *(dispositivo)* device; *(instrumento)* instrument; **a. para destilar el agua**, water-distilling device. ■ **a. de radio**, radio set; **a. de televisión**, television set; *Anat* **a. digestivo**, digestive system; **a. ortopédico**, orthopaedic aid; **aparatos eléctricos**, domestic appliances; *Pol* **el a. del estado**, the State apparatus. **2** *Tel* telephone; **¿quién está al a.?**, who's speaking? **3** *Av* plane. **4** *(ostentación)* display;

pomposity, splendour; **con mucho a.**, very pompously; **una tormenta con gran a. eléctrico**, a storm with tremendous flashes of lightning.

aparatosidad *nf* **1** *(pomposidad)* pomposity, ostentation, showiness, show. **2** *(espectacularidad)* spectacularity.

aparatoso,-a *adj* **1** *(pomposo)* pompous, ostentatious, showy. **2** *(espectacular)* spectacular; **un accidente a.**, a spectacular accident.

aparcamiento *nm* **1** *(acción)* parking; **maniobra de a.**, parking manoeuvre. **2** *(en la calle)* place to park, parking place. **3** *(parking)* car park, *US* parking lot.

aparcar *vtr* **1** to park; **'prohibido a.'**, 'no parking'. **2** *fig (tema, cuestión)* to put on one side.

aparcería *nf Agr* sharecropping.

aparcero,-a *nm,f Agr* sharecropper.

apareamiento *nm* **1** *(de cosas)* pairing off, matching up. **2** *(de animales)* mating.

aparear I *vtr* **1** *(cosas)* to pair off, match up. **2** *(animales)* to mate. **II aparearse** *vr (animales)* to mate.

aparecer I *vi* **1** *(gen)* to appear; **no aparece en mi lista**, he is not on my list. **2** *(en el mercado)* to come out **(en**, onto). **3** to turn up, show up; **¿apareció por fin el dinero?**, did the money turn up in the end?; **rara vez aparece por aquí**, he seldom shows his face round here. **II aparecerse** *vr* to appear; **se le apareció un ángel**, an angel appeared to him.

aparecido,-a I *pp de* **aparecer. II** *nm,f* ghost.

aparejado,-a I *pp de* **aparejar. II** *adj* **1** *(adecuado)* suitable, fit. **2** **ir a. con**, to go along with; **llevar** *or* **traer a.**, to entail.

aparejador,-a *nm,f* **1** *Arquit* quantity surveyor; clerk of works. **2** *Náut* rigger.

aparejar I *vtr* **1** *(caballo)* to harness. **2** *(aparear)* to pair off, match up. **3** *Náut* to rig out. **4** *(preparar)* to get ready, prepare. **II aparejarse** *vr CAm (emparejarse)* to pair, mate.

aparejo *nm* **1** *(equipo)* equipment, gear. ■ **a. de pesca**, fishing tackle. **2** *(arreos)* harness. **3** *Náut* rigging. **4** *Arquit* bond. **5** *Téc (poleas)* block and tackle.

aparentar I *vtr* **1** *(simular)* to pretend, affect; **a. indiferencia**, to pretend to be indifferent, affect indifference. **2** *(tener aspecto)* to look; **no aparenta esa edad**, she doesn't look that age. **II** *vi* to show off.

aparente *adj* **1** apparent; **sin motivo a.**, for no apparent reason. **2** *(conveniente)* suitable. **3** *(vistoso)* showy.

aparición *nf* **1** appearance, appearing. **2** *(visión)* apparition.

apariencia *nf* appearance; **en a.**, apparently; **según todas las apariencias**, to all appearances; **tiene a. de bueno**, he looks like a good person; *fig* **guardar las apariencias**, to keep up appearances.

aparragarse *vr Am (achapararrarse)* to get stocky.

apartado,-a I *pp de* **apartar. II** *adj (distante)* remote, isolated; **a. de la vida política**, retired from political life; **mantente a. de él**, keep away from him; **un lugar a.**, a remote place. **III** *nm* **1** *(párrafo)* section, paragraph. **2 a. de correos**, Post Office Box.

apartamento *nm* (small) flat, apartment.

apartamiento *nm* **1** *(separación)* separation, putting aside. **2** *(habitación)* room, lodging.

apartar I *vtr* **1** *(alejar)* to move away, remove; **aparta**, move out of the way; **aparta eso de mi vista**, take that away immediately; **a. (a algn) de un empujón**, to push (sb) aside; **a. (algo) de una patada**, to kick (sth) aside; **a. la mirada**, to look away. **2** *(separar)* to separate, put aside; **apártame la comida**, keep my lunch for me; **apartó sus libros**, she put her books aside. **II apartarse** *vr* **1** *(alejarse)* to move over, move away; **apártate de en medio**, move out of the away; **apártate el pelo de la cara**, move your hair out of your face. **2** *(separarse)* to separate, withdraw; **no nos apartemos del tema**, let's not get off the subject; **se apartó de todos,** she cut herself off from everybody.

aparte I *adv* **1** aside, apart, separately; **envíalo a.,** send it under separate cover; **eso hay que pagarlo a.,** you have to pay for that separately. **2** *(además)* besides; **a. de eso,** besides that; *(con omisión de)* apart from; **eso a.,** apart from that. **3** *(por separado)* separately; **vino a.,** it didn't come with the rest. **II** *adj (especial)* special; *(diferente)* different, separate; **ella es algo a.,** she is something special; **eso es capítulo a., eso es caso a.,** that's completely different, that's another kettle of fish altogether. **III** *nm* **1** *Teat* aside; *fig* **ella se lo comentó en un a.,** she called him aside and told him. **2** *Ling* new paragraph; **punto y a.,** full stop, new paragraph.

apasionado,-a I *pp de* **apasionar. II** *adj* passionate, fervent, enthusiastic; **a. por la música,** very fond of music.

apasionamiento *nm* passion, enthusiasm; **hablar con a.,** to speak passionately *or* with passion.

apasionante *adj* exciting, fascinating.

apasionar I *vtr* to excite, thrill, fascinate; **le apasiona el jazz,** he is mad about jazz. **II apasionarse** *vr* **1** to get excited, become enthusiastic **(por, de,** about); **se apasionó por ese trabajo,** she got really involved in that job. **2** *(enamorarse)* to fall head over heels in love **(por, de,** with).

apaste *nm CAm Méx* earthenware bowl.

apatía *nf* apathy.

apático,-a I *adj* apathetic. **II** *nm,f* apathetic person.

apátrida I *adj* stateless. **II** *nmf* stateless person.

apdo. *abr de* **apartado,** Post Office Box, P.O.B.

apeadero *nm Ferroc* halt.

apear I *vtr* **1** *(desmontar)* to take down; *(del caballo)* to help down **(de,** from); *fig* **a. el tratamiento,** to drop sb's formal title. **2** *(árbol)* to fell. **3** *(caballo)* to hobble. **4.** *(finca)* to survey. **5** *(vehículo)* to wedge, scotch. **6** *Constr (apuntalar)* to prop up. **7** *fam (disuadir)* to convince, dissuade. **8** *CAm (reprender)* to tell off. **II apearse** *vi (de un autobús, tren)* to alight, get off; *(de un coche)* to get out; **se apeó en Jerez,** he got off in Jerez; *fig* **a. de sus ideas,** to give up one's ideas; *fam* **a. del burro,** to back down.

apechugar *vi* **1** *fam (aguantar)* to put up with; **a. con todo el trabajo,** to shoulder all the work. **2** *Am (robar)* to steal.

apedrear I *vtr* **1** *(tirar piedras a)* to throw stones at. **2** *(matar a pedradas)* to stone (to death). **II** *v impers Meteor (granizar)* to hail. **III apedrearse** *vr Agr* to be damaged by hail.

apegado I *pp de* **apegarse. II** *adj* devoted, attached **(a,** to).

apegarse *vr* to become devoted *or* attached **(a,** to).

apego *nm* love, affection; **tomar a. a,** to become attached to.

apelable *adj Jur* appealable.

apelación *nf* **1** *Jur* appeal; **interponer a.,** to appeal; **recurso de a.,** appeal. **2** *fig* help; **no tener a.,** to be helpless.

apelar *vi* **1** *Jur* to appeal; **a. de una sentencia,** to appeal against a sentence. **2** *fig (recurrir)* to resort to; **a. a la buena voluntad de algn,** to appeal to sb's goodwill.

apelativo,-a I *adj & nm* appellative. **II** *nm Am (apellido)* surname, family name.

apellidar I *vtr* to call. **II apellidarse** *vr* to have as a surname, be called.

apellido *nm* surname, family name; **a. de soltera,** maiden name; *fig* **con nombre y apellidos,** with all the details.

apelmazado,-a *adj* heavy, stodgy.

apelmazar I *vtr (amazacotar)* to compress, squeeze together. **II apelmazarse** *vr (amazacotarse)* to cake, go lumpy.

apelotonar I *vtr* **1** *(amontonar)* to pile up, put into a pile. **2** *(hacer una pelota)* to roll into a ball. **II apelotonarse** *vr (gente)* to crowd together.

apenar I *vtr (entristecer)* to grieve, make sad. **II apenarse** *vr* **1** *(entristecerse)* to be grieved. **2** *Am (avergonzarse)* to be ashamed; *(ruborizarse)* to blush.

apenas *adv* **1** *(casi no)* hardly, scarcely; **a. come,** he hardly eats anything; **a si hay nieve,** there is hardly any snow. **2** *(tan pronto como)* as soon as; **a. llegó, sonó el teléfono,** just as he arrived the phone rang, no sooner had he arrived than the phone rang.

apencar *vi fam véase* **apechugar.**

apendectomía *nf Med* apendectomy.

apéndice *nm* **1** *Anat* appendix **2** *fig (persona)* lapdog.

apendicitis *nf Med* appendicitis.

Apeninos *nmpl* **los (Montes) A.,** the Apennines.

apensionarse *vr Am* to get sad *or* depressed.

apeo *nm* **1** *(de un árbol)* felling. **2** *(de una finca)* surveying.

aperar *vtr Am* **1** *(caballo)* to harness; to saddle. **2** *(abastecer)* to supply.

apercibimiento *nm* **1** *(preparación)* preparation. **2** *Jur (advertencia)* warning.

apercibir I *vtr* **1** *(preparar)* to get ready, prepare. **2** *(avisar)* to warn. **II apercibirse** *vr* **1** *(prepararse)* to get ready. **2** *(percatarse)* to notice.

apercollar *vtr Arg* to corner, trap.

apergaminado,-a I *pp de* **apergaminarse. II** *adj* **1** parchment-like; **papel a.,** parchment paper. **2** *fig (piel)* wrinkled; *(cara)* wizened.

apergaminarse *vr fig* to wrinkle, become wizened.

aperitivo,-a I *adj* appetizing. **II** *nm (bebida)* apéritif; *(comida)* appetizer.

apero *nm (gen pl)* equipment, tools *pl*. ■ **aperos de labranza,** farming implements.

aperreado,-a I *pp de* **aperrear. II** *adj fam* lousy, wretched; **una vida aperreada,** a dog's life.

aperrear I *vtr (cansar)* to wear out, exhaust. **II aperrearse** *vr fig (emperrarse)* to insist.

apertura *nf* **1** *(comienzo)* opening, beginning; **a. delcurso,** beginning of the academic year; **sesión de a.,** opening session. **2** *Pol (liberalización)* liberalization.

apesadumbrado,-a I *pp de* **apesadumbrar. II** *adj* sad, distressed.

apesadumbrar *vtr* to sadden, distress, pain.

apestado,-a I *pp de* **apestar. II** *adj* **1** *Med* plague-ridden. **2** *(olor)* foul, pestilential. **3** *fig* infested **(de,** with).

apestar I *vi* **1** to stink; **esta habitación apesta,** this room stinks. **2** *fam (estar lleno)* to be teeming with. **II** *vtr* to infect with the plague.

apestoso,-a *adj* stinking; **olor a.,** foul smell.

apetecer *vi* to feel like, fancy; **¿qué te apetece para cenar?,** what would you like for supper?; **¿te apetece ir al cine?,** do you fancy going to the cinema?

apetecible *adj* tempting, inviting.

apetencia *nf* **1** *(apetito)* hunger, appetite. **2** *fig (deseo)* longing, craving, desire.

apetito *nm* appetite; **abrir el a.,** to whet one's appetite; **a. carnal,** sexual appetite, desire.

apetitoso,-a *adj* appetizing, tempting; *(comida)* delicious, tasty.

api *nm Am* boiled maize *or* wheat *or* rice.

apiadar I *vtr* to move to pity. **II apiadarse** *vr (compadecerse)* to take pity **(de,** on).

ápice *nm* **1** *(punta)* apex. **2** *fig (parte pequeña)* tiny piece; **ni un á.,** not a bit; **no me gusta ni un á.,** I don't like it at all.

apicultor,-a *nm,f* beekeeper, apiculturist, apiarist.

apicultura *nf* beekeeping, apiculture.

apilamiento *nm* piling up, heaping up.

apilar *vtr*, **apilarse** *vr* to pile up, heap up.

apilonar *vtr Am* to pile up, heap up.

apiñado,-a I *pp de* **apiñar.** II *adj* 1 *(apretado)* crammed, packed. 2 cone-shaped.

apiñamiento *nm* cramming, packing.

apiñar I *vtr (apretar)* to cram, pack. II **apiñarse** *vr (arremolinarse)* to crowd together.

apio *nm Bot* celery.

apiolar *vtr* to catch.

apiri *nm SAm* 1 *(peón)* mineworker. 2 *(mozo)* porter.

apisonadora *nf* roadroller, steamroller.

apisonar *vtr (carretera)* to roll.

aplacamiento *nm* placation, calming.

aplacar I *vtr* to placate, calm; **a. el hambre,** to satisfy one's hunger. II **aplacarse** *vr* to calm down.

aplanacalles *nmf inv Am* loafer, idler.

aplanador,-a I *adj* levelling, *US* leveling, smoothing. II *nf Am* steamroller.

aplanamiento *nm* levelling, *US* leveling, smoothing.

aplanar I *vtr* 1 *(igualar)* to level, smooth, flatten. 2 *fig (deprimir)* to dishearten, depress. II **aplanarse** *vr* 1 *(edificio)* to fall down. 2 *fig (persona)* to become disheartened *or* depressed.

aplastamiento *nm* 1 flattening, squashing. 2 *fig* crushing.

aplastante *adj* crushing, overwhelming; *fig (en elecciones)* **triunfo a.,** landslide victory.

aplastar I *vtr* 1 to flatten, squash; **el árbol aplastó el coche,** the tree crushed the car. 2 *fig (vencer)* to crush, destroy. II **aplastarse** *vr* to be crushed; **se aplastó contra la pared,** it got smashed against the wall.

aplatanado,-a I *pp de* **aplatanarse.** II *adj fam* apathetic, lazy.

aplatanarse *vr fam* to become apathetic.

aplaudir *vtr* 1 to clap, applaud. 2 *fig (aprobar)* to applaud, approve.

aplauso *nm* 1 applause. 2 *fig (aprobación)* applause, praise.

aplazamiento *nm* postponement, adjournment; *Fin (de un pago)* deferment.

aplazar *vtr* 1 to postpone, adjourn; *Fin (pago)* to defer. 2 *Am (examen)* to fail.

aplicable *adj* applicable.

aplicación *nf* 1 application. 2 *(adorno)* appliqué.

aplicado,-a I *pp de* **aplicar.** II *adj* 1 *(diligente)* studious, diligent, hard-working; **un alumno a.,** a hard-working pupil. 2 *(práctico)* applied; **ciencias aplicadas,** applied sciences.

aplicar I *vtr* 1 to apply. 2 *(destinar)* to assign. II **aplicarse** *vr* 1 *(esforzarse)* to apply oneself, work hard. 2 *(usar)* to apply, be applicable; **puede a. en todos los casos,** it can be applied in all cases.

aplique *nm* 1 *(adorno)* appliqué. 2 *(lámpara)* wall light, wall lamp.

aplomar *vtr* to plumb.

aplomo *nm* aplomb, composure, self-assurance.

apocado,-a I *pp de* **apocar.** II *adj* 1 *(intimidado)* intimidated, frightened. 2 *(tímido)* shy, timid.

apocalipsis *nm inv* apocalypse.

apocalíptico,-a *adj* apocalyptic.

apocamiento *nm* timidity, lack of self-confidence.

apocar *vtr* 1 *(intimidar)* to intimidate, frighten. 2 *(humillar)* to humilate, belittle.

apocopar *vtr Ling* to apocopate.

apócope *nm Ling* apocope, apocopation.

apócrifo,-a *adj* apocryphal.

apodar *vtr* to nickname.

apoderado,-a I *pp de* **apoderar.** II *adj* authorized; *Jur* with power of attorney to. III *nm, f* 1 agent, representative. 2 *(de torero, deportista)* manager.

apoderar I *vtr* to authorize, empower; *Jur* to grant power of attorney. II **apoderarse** *vr* to take possession **(de,** of), seize; *fig* **el miedo se apoderó de ella,** she was seized by fear.

apodo *nm* nickname.

apófisis *nf Anat* apophysis.

apogeo *nm* 1 *Astron* apogee. 2 *fig (punto culminante)* height, climax; **en pleno a. de,** at the height of.

apolillado,-a I *pp de* **apolillar.** II *adj* moth-eaten.

apolilladura *nf* moth hole.

apolillar I *vtr* to eat, make holes in. II **apolillarse** *vr* to get moth-eaten.

apolíneo,-a *adj* Apollonian.

apolismar I *vtr Am (estropear)* to make a mess of, spoil, ruin. II **apolismarse** *vr CAm (quedarse raquítico)* to waste (away), wither, become debilitated.

apoliticismo *nm* apoliticism.

apolítico,-a *adj* apolitical.

apologético,-a I *adj* apologetic. II *nf* apologetics *sing.*

apología *nf* apology, defence, *US* defense.

apologista *nmf* apologist.

apólogo *nm* apologue.

apoltronado,-a I *pp de* **apoltronarse.** II *adj* lazy, idle.

apoltronamiento *nm* laziness, idleness.

apoltronarse *vr* 1 *(vegetar)* to get lazy, get idle. 2 *(sentarse)* to sit back, lounge.

apoplejía *nf Med* apoplexy.

apoplético,-a *adj & nm, f* apoplectic.

apoquinar *vtr fam* to cough up, fork out.

aporcar *vtr Agr* to earth up.

aporreado,-a I *pp de* **aporrear.** II *adj* beaten; *fig* **una vida aporreada,** a dog's life.

aporrear *vtr* to beat, hit, thrash; **a. la puerta,** to bang the door; *fam* **a. el piano,** to bang (away) on the piano.

aporreo *nm* beating, thrashing; *(de puerta)* banging; *fam (de piano)* thumping.

aportación *nf* contribution.

aportar I *vtr* 1 to contribute; *fig* **a. su granito de arena,** to chip in one's small contribution. 2 *(proporcionar)* to give, provide; **a. ideas,** to offer some ideas. II *vi Náut* to reach port.

aporte *nm* 1 supply. 2 *fig (contribución)* contribution.

aportillar *vtr* to breach, make a breach in.

aposentamiento *nm* 1 *(acción)* housing, lodging. 2 *(habitación)* room. 3 *(hospedaje)* lodgings.

aposentar I *vtr (alojar)* to house, lodge. II **aposentarse** *vr (alojarse)* to stay, lodge.

aposento *nm* 1 *(cuarto)* room. 2 *(hospedaje)* lodgings *pl*; **tomar a. en,** to put up at.

aposición *nf Ling* apposition.

apósito *nm Med* dressing.

aposta *adv* on purpose, intentionally.

apostadero *nm Mil* post, station; *Naút* naval station.

apostador,-a *adj & nm, f*, **apostante** *adj & nmf* I *adj* betting. II *nm, f & nmf* better, bettor.

apostar[1] I *vtr* to bet, stake; **a. a los caballos,** to bet on horses; **te apuesto una cena a que no viene,** I bet you a dinner that he won't come. II *vi* to bet; **aposté por tu caballo,** I bet on your horse; **apuesto a que sí viene,** I bet she will come. III **apostarse** *vr* to bet; **me apuesto lo que quieras,** I bet you anything.

apostar[2] I *vtr (situar)* to post, station. II **apostarse** *vr (situarse)* to post oneself, station oneself.

apostasía *nf Rel* apostasy.

apóstata *nmf* apostate.

apostatar *vi* to apostatize.

apostilla *nf* note; *Jur* apostille.

apostillar *vtr* to add notes to, annotate.

apóstol *nm* **1** *Rel* apostle. **2** *fig (defensor)* apostle, champion.

apostolado *nm* apostolate.

apostólico,-a *adj* **1** *(de los apóstoles)* apostolic. **2** *(del papa)* apostolic, papal; **bendición apostólica,** papal blessing.

apostrofar *vtr* **1** to apostrophize. **2** *fig (reprender)* to reprimand, tell off.

apóstrofe *nm & f* **1** apostrophe. **2** *fig (reprimenda)* insult, offence.

apóstrofo *nm Ling* apostrophe.

apostura *nf* **1** *(garbo)* good bearing. **2** *(apariencia)* appearance, look.

apoteósico,-a *adj* enormous, tremendous; **un recibimiento a.,** a mass welcome.

apoteosis *nf inv* apotheosis; *(de un espectáculo)* **a. final,** grand finale.

apoyar I *vtr* **1** to lean; **apoya la cabeza en la pared,** rest your head against the wall. **2** *(basar)* to base, found. **3** *(defender) (una causa)* to support; *(persona)* to back, second. **II apoyarse** *vr* **1** to lean; **apóyate en mi brazo,** hold my arm. **2** *fig (basarse)* to be based, rest; **su teoría se apoya en la investigación,** his theory is based on research.

apoyo *nm* **1** support. ■ **punto de a.,** *Fís* fulcrum; *fig (fundamento)* base. **2** *fig* support, backing, help.

apreciable *adj* **1** appreciable, noticeable. **2** *(estimable)* valuable, precious.

apreciación *nf* appreciation.

apreciar I *vtr* **1** *(sentir aprecio)* to regard highly, hold in high esteem; **le aprecia mucho,** she is very fond of him. **2** *(reconocer el valor)* to appreciate; **a. el buen vino,** to appreciate good wine. **3** *(formar juicio)* to appraise, value. **4** *(percibir)* to notice, see; **no puedo a. la diferencia,** I can't really tell the difference. **II apreciarse** *vr* to be noticeable; **se aprecia un cambio notable,** a remarkable change can be seen.

apreciativo,-a *adj* appreciative.

aprecio *nm* regard, esteem; **sentir a. por algn,** to be fond of sb.

aprehender *vtr* **1** *(coger)* to apprehend, seize. **2** *(entender)* to understand.

aprehensión *nf* **1** apprehension, capture, seizure. **2** *(entendimiento)* comprehension, understanding.

apremiador,-a *adj*, **apremiante** *adj* urgent, pressing.

apremiar I *vtr* **1** *(compeler)* to compel, urge, press. **2** *(dar prisa)* to hurry (along). **3** *(oprimir)* to oppress. **II** *vi* to be urgent; **el tiempo apremia,** we are running short of time.

apremio *nm* **1** urgency, **por a. de trabajo,** because of pressure of work. **2** *Jur* writ.

aprender *vtr* to learn; **así aprenderás,** that'll teach you.

aprendiz,-a *nm, f* apprentice, trainee.

aprendizaje *nm* **1** apprenticeship, traineeship. **2** *Psic* learning; **técnicas de a.,** learning techniques.

aprensión *nf* apprehension; **sentir a.,** to feel apprehensive.

aprensivo,-a *adj & nm, f* apprehensive.

apresamiento *nm* seizure, capture.

apresar *vtr* to seize, capture.

aprestar I *vtr* **1** *(preparar)* to prepare, get ready. **2** *Tex* to size. **II aprestarse** *vr (prepararse)* to get ready.

apresto *nm* **1** *(preparación)* preparation. **2** *(acción)* sizing; *(material)* size.

apresuración *nf* haste, hurry.

apresurado,-a *adj* **I** *pp* de **apresurarse.** **II** *adj* **1** *(persona)* in a hurry. **2** *(cosa)* hurried.

apresuramiento *nm véase* **apresuración.**

apresurar I *vtr* to accelerate, hurry up, speed up. **II apresurarse** *vr* to hurry up; **se apresuró a salir,** he hurried towards the door.

apretado,-a I *pp* de **apretar.** **II** *adj* **1** tight; **íbamos todos apretados en el coche,** we were all squashed together in the car. **2** *fig (difícil)* tight, difficult; **una situación apretada,** a tight spot. **3** *(ocupado)* busy; **una jornada apretada,** a busy day.

apretar I *vtr* **1** *(nudo, tornillo)* to tighten; *(botón)* to press; **a. el gatillo,** to pull the trigger; **a. el paso,** to quicken one's pace; **me aprietan las botas,** these boots are too tight for me. **2** *(estrechar)* to squeeze, hug; **a. la mano a algn,** to shake sb's hand; **la apretó contra sí,** he hugged her. **3** *fig (acosar)* to pester; *(presionar)* to put pressure on. **4** *(aumentar)* to get worse, get stronger; **apretaba el calor,** it got hotter and hotter. **5** *(esforzarse)* to work hard; **tienes que a. más si quieres aprobar,** you'll have to pull your socks up if you want to pass. **II apretarse** *vr* **1** to narrow; *fig* **a. el cinturón,** to tighten one's belt. **2** *(agolparse)* to crowd together.

apretón *nm* **1** squeeze. ■ **a. de manos,** handshake. **2 apretones,** crush *sing*; **los a del metro,** the crush of the tube.

apretujar I *vtr* to squeeze, crush. **II apretujarse** *vr* to squeeze together, cram together.

apretujón *nm fam* squeeze, crowding, crush.

apretura *nf* **1** *(gen pl) (apretón)* crush. **2** *fig (aprieto)* tight spot, fix. **3** *(escasez)* scarcity; **pasar apreturas,** to suffer hardship.

aprevenir *vtr Am véase* **prevenir.**

aprieto *nm* tight spot, fix, jam; **poner a algn en un a.,** to put sb in an awkward situation; **salir del a.,** to get out of trouble.

apriorismo *nm Filos* apriorism.

apriorístico,-a *adj Filos* aprioristic.

aprisa *adv* quickly.

aprisco *nm* (sheep) fold.

aprisionar *vtr* **1** *(encarcelar)* to put in prison, imprison. **2** *fig (atrapar)* to trap.

aprobación *nf* approval; **le dio su a.,** he gave his consent, he approved it.

aprobado,-a I *pp* de **aprobar.** **II** *adj* approved. **III** *nm Educ* pass, passing grade; **sacar un a.,** to get a pass.

aprobar *vtr* **1** to approve. **2** *(estar de acuerdo)* to approve of; **no apruebo su conducta,** I do not approve of his behaviour. **3** *Educ (examen)* to pass; *(estudiante)* to pass, give a pass to; **todos aprobaron el examen de francés,** they all passed the French exam. **4** *Pol (ley)* to pass. **5** *Am (ir bien)* to suit; **le aprobaron las vacaciones,** the holidays did him good.

aprobatorio,-a *adj* approving, approbatory.

apropiación *nf* **1** *(adecuación)* adaptation. **2** *(robo)* appropriation. ■ *Jur* **a. indebida,** theft.

apropiado,-a I *pp* de **apropiar.** **II** *adj* suitable, appropriate.

apropiar I *vtr* to adapt, make suitable. **II apropiarse** *vr* to appropriate, steal.

aprovechable *adj* that can be used, usable, serviceable.

aprovechado,-a I *pp* de **aprovechar.** **II** *adj* **1** well used *or* spent; **mal a.** wasted. **2** *(espacio)* well-planned. **3** *(alumno)* diligent, studious. **4** *fam pey (egoísta)* selfish; *(sinvergüenza)* who sponges *or* scrounges; **es un tipo muy a.,** he's a sponger *or* scrounger.

aprovechamiento *nm* **1** *(uso)* use, exploitation; **a. de aguas residuales,** use of sewage. **2** *Educ* progress, improvement.

aprovechar I *vtr* **1** to make good use of, make the most of; **Ana aprovechó el tiempo,** Ana made good use of her time. **2** *(sacar provecho)* to take advantage of, benefit from; **a. la ocasión,** to seize the opportunity; *pey* **aprovechó que era un pobre diablo para engañarlo,** seeing that he was a poor devil he cheated him; *fam* **¡que aproveche!,** enjoy your meal!, bon appétit! **II** *vi* to be useful; **aprovechamos mucho la tarde,** we've done lots of things this afternoon. **III aprovecharse** *vr* to use to one's advantage, take advantage; **a. de algn,** to take advantage of sb; **a. de algo,** to make the most of sth.

aprovisionamiento *nm* supply, suplying, provision.

aprovisionar *vtr* to supply, provide; **a. las tropas,** to give supplies to the troops.

aproximación *nf* **1** approximation; **por a.,** by approximation; *fam* **ni por a.,** far from it. **2** *(acercamiento)* bringing together; *(de países)* rapprochement. **3** *(lotería)* consolation prize.

aproximado,-a I *pp de* **aproximar. II** *adj* approximate; **un cálcule a.,** a rough estimate.

aproximar I *vtr* to bring *or* put nearer; **aproxima la silla un poco,** draw your chair up a bit; **aquello las aproximó más,** that made them feel closer together. **II aproximarse** *vr* **1** to move nearer; **aproxímate más,** come closer. **2** *(estar cerca)* to be near, be close; **se aproximan los exámenes,** the exams are getting nearer.

aproximativo,-a *adj* approximate, rough.

aprudenciarse *vr Am* to control oneself, be careful.

áptero,-a *adj Eni* apterous.

aptitud *nf* **1** aptitude; **a. para la pintura,** aptitude for painting; **prueba de a.,** aptitude test. **2** *(idoneidad)* suitability, aptness.

apto,-a *adj* **1** *(apropiado)* suitable, appropriate; *Cin* **a. para todos los públicos,** U-certificate film, *US* rated 'G'; *Cin* **no a.,** for adults only. **2** *(capaz)* capable, able; **un trabajador a.,** a capable worker. **3** *(físicamente)* fit; **a. para el servicio,** fit for *(military)* service.

apuesta *nf bet,* wager.

apuesto,-a *adj* good-looking; *(hombre)* handsome.

apulismarse *vr CAm* to waste (away), wither.

apunarse *vr SAm* to get mountain sickness.

apuntado,-a I *pp de* **apuntar. II** *adj* **1** *(anotado)* written down, taken down. **2** *(terminado en punta)* pointed, sharp.

apuntador,-a *nm, f Teat* prompter.

apuntalamiento *nm* propping-up, shoring-up, underpinning.

apuntalar *vtr* to prop up, shore up, underpin.

apuntar I *vtr* **1** *(señalar)* to point at; **no apuntes con el dedo,** don't point at people *or* things with your finger; **quisiera a. que ...,** I'd like to point out that .... **2** *(arma)* to aim, point; *Mil* **¡apunten!,** take aim! **3** *(anotar)* to note down, make a note of; **apúntalo en mi cuenta,** put it on my account; **a. a algn en una lista,** to put sb on a list. **4** *(estar encaminado)* to be aimed at, be designed to; **estas medidas apuntan a mejorar la situación,** these measures are aimed at improving the situation. **5** *(indicar)* to indicate, suggest; **todo parece a. a ...,** everything seems to point to .... **6** *Teat* to prompt; *Educ fam* to whisper the answer (a, to). **7** *Cost* to tack. **II** *vi* **1** *(empezar a manifestarse)* to (begin to) show; **cuando apunta el día,** when day breaks. **2** *Teat* to prompt. **III apuntarse** *vr* **1** *(en una lista)* to put one's name down. **2** *(matricularse)* to enrol, *US* enroll. **3** *fam (participar)* to take part (a, in); **¿te apuntas?,** are you game?

apunte *nm* **1** *(gen pl)* note; **tomar apuntes,** to take notes. **2** *(dibujo)* sketch; **sacar un a.,** to do a sketch. **3** *Teat (apuntador)* prompter; *(voz de apuntador)* prompt; *(impreso)* prompt book. **4** *Naipes* stake.

apuntillar *vtr Taur* to finish off.

apuñalar *vtr* to stab.

apurado,-a I *pp de* **apurar. II** *adj* **1** *(terminado)* finished. **2** *(preocupado)* worried; *(avergonzado)* embarrassed. **3** *(necesitado)* in need; **a. de dinero,** hard up for money; **a. de tiempo,** in a hurry. **4** *(difícil)* awkward, difficult; **una situación apurada,** a tight spot, a jam.

apurar I *vtr* **1** *(terminar)* to finish off, end; *(agotar)* to wear out, exhaust; **a. una copa,** to drain a glass; *fig* **apurarle la paciencia a algn,** to exhaust sb's patience; *fig* **si me apuras,** if you insist; *fam* if you twist my arm; **2** *(preocupar)* to worry. **3** *(apremiar)* to rush, hurry, pester; **no me apures,** don't rush me, don't pester me. **II apurarse** *vr (preocuparse)* to worry, get worried; **no te apures,** don't worry.

apuro *nm* **1** *(situación difícil)* tight spot, fix, jam; **estar** *or* **encontrarse en un a.,** to be in a tight spot. **2** *(escasez de dinero)* hardship; **pasar apuros,** to be hard up. **3** *(vergüenza)* embarrassment; **¡qué a.!,** how embarrassing!

apurruñar *vtr Am (manosear)* to handle roughly. **2** *SAm Cub (apiñar)* to cram, pack, stuff.

apusurarse *vr CAm* to get moth-eaten.

aquejado,-a I *pp de* **aquejar. II** *adj* suffering **(de,** from).

aquejar *vtr* to afflict, affect; **le aqueja una grave enfermedad,** he suffering from a serious illness.

aquel,-ella *adj dem* **1** that; **a. niño,** that boy. **2 aquellos,-as,** those; **aquellas niñas,** those girls.

aquél,-élla I *pron dem m, f* **1** that one; *(el anterior)* the former; coge a., take that one; **vinieron Pedro y Manuel, a. disfrazado de Tarzán,** Pedro and Manuel came, the former dressed up as Tarzan. **2 todo a. que,** anyone who, whoever; **a. que hable,** he who speaks. **3 aquéllos,-as,** those; *(los anteriores)* the former; **llévate a.,** take those. **II** *nm fam* something; **ella tiene un a.,** she's got something about her.

aquelarre *nm* witches' sabbath.

aquella *adj dem f* véase **aquel.**

aquélla *pron dem f* véase **aquél.**

aquello *pron dem neut* that, it; **a. parecía una casa de locos,** it was sheer bedlam in that place; **¿le has hablado de a.?,** have you spoken to him about it?; *fig* **a. de que no hacían falta entradas era verdad,** it was true that we didn't need (to get) tickets; *fam* **por a. de que no se molestara,** so that he wouldn't feel put out.

aquellos,-as *adj dem pl* véase **aquel,-ella.**

aquéllos,-as *pron dem m,fpl* véase **aquél,-élla.**

aquerenciarse *vr (a un lugar)* to become fond of.

aquí *adv* **1** *(lugar)* here; **a. arriba,** up here; **a. está,** here it is; **a. fuera,** out here; **a. mismo,** right here; **a. y allá,** here and there; **de a. para allá,** up and down, to and fro; **hasta a.,** this far; **por a. por favor,** this way please; **tiene que estar por a.,** it must be around here somewhere; *fig* **hasta a. podíamos llegar,** that's the end of it; *fam* **a. un amigo,** this is a friend. **2** *(tiempo)* now; then; **a. empieza lo peor,** here begins the worst; **de a. a poco,** soon; **de a. en adelante,** from now on; **hasta a.,** up till now. **3** *(consecuencia)* **de a. (que),** hence; **de a. que no te lo dijera,** which was why I didn't tell you.

aquiescencia *nf* acquiescence.

aquietar I *vtr* to pacify, calm down. **II aquietarse** *vr* to calm down.

aquilatamiento *nm* **1** *(de oro, piedra preciosa)* assay. **2** *fig (evaluación)* assessment, evaluation.

aquilatar *vtr* **1** *(metales, piedras preciosas)* to assay. **2** *fig (evaluar)* to assess, evaluate.

aquileño,-a *adj,* **aquilino,-a** *adj* véase **aguileño,-a.**

Aquiles *nm* Achilles. ■ **talón de A.,** Achilles heel.

ara *nf* altar; *(piedra)* altar stone; *fml* **en aras de,** for the sake of; **en aras de la paz,** so as to keep the peace.

árabe I *adj (de Arabia)* Arab, Arabian; Arabic; **literatura a.,** Arabic literature. **II** *nmf (persona)* Arab. **III** *nm (idioma)* Arabic.

arabesco *nm* arabesque.

Arabia *n* Arabia, **A. Saudita,** Saudi Arabia.

arábigo,-a I *adj* Arabic, Arabian; **goma arábiga,** gum arabic; **números arábigos,** Arabic numerals. **II** *nm (idioma)* Arabic.

arabismo *nm* Arabic expression.

arabista *nmf* Arabist.

arácnido *nm Zool* arachnid.

arada *nf* 1 *(acción)* ploughing, *US* plowing. 2 *(tierra)* ploughed *or US* plowed land.

arado *nm* plough, *US* plow.

arador *nm* ploughman, *US* plowman.

Aragón *n* Aragon.

aragonés,-esa *adj & nm,f* Aragonese.

arameo,-a I *adj* Aramaean, Aramean. **II** *nm, f (persona)* Aramaean, Aramean. **III** *nm (idioma)* Aramaic.

arancel *nm* tariff, customs duty.

arancelar *vtr CAm* to pay.

arancelario,-a *adj* tariff, duty; **derechos arancelarios,** duties.

arándano *nm Bot* bilberry.

arandela *nf* 1 *Téc* washer. 2 *SAm Cost* frill.

araña *nf* 1 *Zool* spider. ■ **tela de a.,** spider's web. 2 *(cangrejo)* **a. de mar,** spider crab. 3 *(pez)* weever. 4 *Bot* love-in-a-mist. 5 *(lámpara)* chandelier.

arañar I *vtr* 1 *(raspar)* to scratch. 2 *fig (reunir)* to scrape together. **II arañarse** *vr* to scratch oneself.

arañazo *nm* scratch.

arao *nm Orn* guillemot.

arar *vtr Agr* to plough, *US* plow.

arasá *nm Am* guava.

araucano,-a *adj & nm,f* Araucanian.

araucaria *nf Bot* araucaria, monkey puzzle tree.

arbitraje *nm* 1 *(desacuerdo)* arbitration. 2 *Dep* refereeing; *Cricket Ten* umpiring.

arbitral *adj* of the referee; **sentencia a.,** judgement by arbitration.

arbitrar *vtr* 1 to arbitrate. 2 *(obtener)* to contrive; *(reunir)* to collect; **a. fondos,** to raise funds. 3 *Dep* to referee, umpire.

arbitrariedad *nf* 1 arbitrariness. 2 *(acción)* arbitrary action.

arbitrario,-a *adj* arbitrary.

arbitrio *nm* 1 *(voluntad)* will; *(juicio)* judgement; **lo dejo a tu a.,** I leave it to your discretion. 2 *(medio)* mean. 3 **arbitrios,** taxes.

árbitro,-a *nm, f* 1 arbiter, arbitrator; *(mujer)* arbitress. 2 *Dep* referee, umpire.

árbol *nm* 1 *Bot* tree; *fig* **los árboles no dejan ver el bosque,** you can't see the wood for the trees. ■ **á. del amor,** Judas tree; **á. del cielo,** tree of Heaven; **á. frutal,** fruit tree. 2 *Téc* shaft. 3 *Náut* mast. 4 *(gráfico)* tree (diagram). ■ **á. genealógico,** family *or* genealogical tree.

arbolado,-a I *pp de* **arbolar. II** *adj* I *(con árboles)* wooded, with trees. 2 *(mar)* very high. **III** *nm* woodland.

arboladura *nf Náut* masts and spars *pl*.

arbolar I *vtr* 1 *Náut* to mast. 2 *(enarbolar)* to hoist; *(esgrimir)* to brandish. **II arbolarse** *vr (las olas)* to rear up.

arboleda *nf* wood, copse, spinney, grove.

arboreo,-a *adj* arboreal; **vegetación arbórea,** trees *pl*.

arborescente *adj* arborescent.

arboricultor,-a *nm, f* arboriculturist.

arboricultura *nf* arboriculture.

arbotante *nm Arquit* flying buttress.

arbustivo,-a *adj* bushlike.

arbusto *nm Bot* bush, shrub.

arca *nf* 1 chest. 2 *(caja de caudales)* strongbox, safe. ■ **arcas públicas,** Treasury *sing*. 3 *Rel* **el A. de Noé,** Noah's Ark.

arcabucero *nm Hist* arquebusier.

arcabuz *nm Hist* arquebus.

arcada *nf* 1 *(conjunto de arcos)* arcade. 2 *(de puente)* arch. 3 *(náusea)* retching.

arcaico,-a *adj* archaic.

arcaísmo *nm* archaism.

arcaizante *adj* archaistic.

arcángel *nm* archangel.

arcano,-a I *adj* arcane. **II** *nm* mystery.

arce *nm Bot* maple (tree). ■ **a. menor,** common *or* field maple; **a. real,** Norway maple; **a. rojo,** red maple.

arcediano *nm* archdeacon.

arcén *nm* side of the road, verge; *(de autopista)* hard shoulder.

archi- *pref* super-; **archiconocido,** super-famous; **archisabido,** extremely well-known.

archibebe *nm Orn* redshank.

archidiácono *nm* archdeacon.

archidiócesis *nf inv* archdiocese.

archiduque,-esa *nm, f (hombre)* archduke; *(mujer)* archduchess.

archimandrita *nm* archimandrite.

archipiélago *nm Geog* archipelago.

archivador,-a I *nm, f* archivist. **II** *nm* filing cabinet.

archivar *vtr* 1 *(ordenar)* to file (away). 2 *(arrinconar)* to shelve. 3 *Inform* to save. 4 *fam (guardar)* to put (away).

archivero,-a *nm, f* archivist.

archivo *nm* 1 *(gen)* file. 2 *Inform* file. 3 *(conjunto de documentos)* files *pl*, archives *pl*. 4 *(archivador)* filing cabinet. 5 *fig (modelo)* model, example.

archivolta *nf Arquit* archivolt.

arcilla *nf* clay; **a. cocida,** baked clay.

arcilloso,-a *adj* clayey, clayish.

arcipreste *nm Rel* archpriest.

arco *nm* 1 *Mat* arc. 2 *Arquit* arch. ■ **a. apuntado,** lancet *or* pointed arch; **a. carpanel,** three-centred arch; **a. de herradura,** horseshoe arch; **a. de medio punto,** semicircular arch; **a. de triunfo,** triumphal arch; **a. tutor,** four-ecntred *or* Tudor arch. 3 *Mús (de violín)* bow. 4 *Elec* arc. ■ **a. voltaico,** electric arc. 5 *Dep* bow. ■ **tiro con a.,** archery. 6 *Meteor* **a. iris,** rainbow.

arcón *nm Mueb* large chest.

arder *vi* to burn; **a. completamente,** to burn down; **la casa estaba ardiendo,** the house was in flames; *fig* **ardiendo de fiebre,** burning with fever; *fig* **a. de pasión,** to burn with passion; *fig* **a. en guerras,** to be lashed by war; *fam* **la cosa está que arde,** things are getting pretty hot.

ardid *nm* scheme, trick, plot.

ardiente *adj* 1 *(encendido)* burning, scalding, boiling hot; **capilla a.,** funeral *or* mortuary chapel. 2 *fig (intenso)* ardent, passionate; *(fervoroso, activo)* eager.

ardilla *nf Zool* squirrel.

ardite *nm* **me importa un a.,** I couldn't give a damn.

ardor *nm* 1 burning sensation, burn; *(calor)* heat. ■ *Med* **a. de estómago,** heartburn. 2 *fig (ansia)* ardour, *US* ardor, fervour, *US* fervor; **con a.,** passionately.

ardoroso,-a *adj* 1 burning, boiling hot. 2 *fig* ardent, passionate.

arduo,-a *adj* arduous, very difficult, awkward.

área *nf* 1 *(zona)* area, zone; **en esta á. de la ciudad,** in this part of (the) town. ■ *Dep* **á. de castigo,** penalty area; *Aut* **á. de servicio,** service área. 2 *(superficie)* área. 3 *(medida)* are (100 square metres).

arena *nf* **1** sand; **playa de a.,** sandy beach. ■ **arenas movedizas,** quicksand *sing.* **2** *(de circo romano)* arena. **3** *Taur (plaza)* bullring.

arenal *nm* large extension of sand.

arenga *nf* harangue; **pronunciar una a.,** to harangue.

arengar *vtr* to harangue.

arenilla *nf* **1** fine sand. **2 arenillas,** *Med (del riñón)* stones.

arenisca *nf* sandstone.

arenoso,-a *adj* sandy.

arenque *nm (pez)* herring. ■ *Culin* **a. ahumado,** kipper, kippered herring.

arete *nm* **1** *(anillo)* small ring. **2** *(pendiente)* earring. **3** *(pez)* red gurnard.

argamasa *nf Constr* mortar.

Argel *n* Algiers.

Argelia *n* Algeria.

argelino,-a *adj & nm,f* Algerian.

argentado,-a *adj* **1** *(bañado de plata)* silver-plated. **2** *lit* silvery.

argentífero,-a *adj* argentiferous.

Argentina *n* Argentina.

argentinismo *nm Ling* Argentinean expression.

argentino,-a *adj & nm,f* Argentinean, Argentine.

argolla *nf* **1** *(aro)* (large) ring. **2** *fig* shackles *pl.* **3** *Am (alianza)* wedding ring.

argón *nm Quím* argon.

argonauta *nm Mit* argonaut.

argot *nm (popular)* slang; *(técnico)* jargon.

argucia *nf* sophism, fallacy.

argüir *vtr* **1** *(deducir)* to deduce, conclude. **2** *(argumentar)* to argue. **3** *(probar)* to prove, show.

argumenista *nmf* scriptwriter.

argumentación *nf* **1** arguing, argument; **mediante a.,** by argument. **2** *(argumento)* argument.

argumentar *vtr véase* **argüir.**

argumento *nm* **1** *(razonamiento)* argument. **2** *Lit Teat (trama)* plot.

arguyo *indic pres véase* **argüir.**

aria *nf Mús* aria.

aridecer I *vtr & vi* to dry up. **II aridecerse** *vr* to dry up.

aridez *nf* **1** aridity. **2** *fig (monotonía)* dryness.

árido,-a I *adj* arid; *fig* dry. **II áridos** *nmpl Com* dry goods.

Aries *nm Astron Astral* Aries.

ariete *nm* **1** *Mil Hist* battering ram. **2** *Ftb* centre for ward.

ario,-a *adj & nm,f* Aryan.

arisco,-a 1 *(persona)* unfriendly, stand-offish; *(áspera)* surly, gruff; *(huidiza)* shy. **2** *(animal)* unfriendly.

arista *nf* edge.

aristocracia *nf* aristocracy.

aristócrata *nmf* aristocrat.

aristocrático,-a *adj* aristocratic.

aristotélico,-a *adj Filos* Aristotelian.

aritmética *nf Mat* arithmetic.

aritmético,-a *adj Mat* arithmetical, arithmetic.

arito *nm Col Guat Hond* earring.

arlequín *Lit* Harlequin.

arlequinada *nf* (piece of) clowning *or* buffoonery.

arma *nf* **1** weapon, arm; **alzarse en armas,** to rise up in arms; **pasar las armas,** to execute; **presentar armas,** to present arms; **rendir armas,** to surrender; **tomar las armas,** to take up arms; *fig* **a. de doble filo,** double-edged sword; *fam* **ser de armas tomar,** to be formidable *or* frightening. ■ **a. blanca,** knife, blade, steel; **a. corta,** small arm; **a. de artillería,** artillery; **a. de**
fuego,** firearm; **a. homicida,** murder weapon; **a. nuclear,** nuclear weapon; **licencia de armas,** firearms licence. **2 armas,** *Mil (profesión militar)* army *sing; (fuerzas militares)* military forces; *(empresa militar)* military combat *sing;* **hecho de a.,** fact of arms.

armada *nf* navy, naval forces *pl; Hist* **la A. Invencible,** the Spanish Armada.

armadía *nf* raft.

armadijo *nm Caza* snare, trap.

armadillo *nm Zool* armadillo.

armado,-a I *pp de* **armar. II** *adj* armed; **ir a.,** to be armed.

armador,-a *nm,f Náut* shipowner.

armadura *nf* **1** *Hist* suit of armour *or US* armor. **2** *(armazón)* frame; **a. de las gafas,** spectacle frame. **3** *Arquit* framework.

armamentista I *adj* **1** arms; **la carrera a.,** the arms race. **2** *CAm (militarista)* militarist. **II** *nmf Am (militarista)* militarist. **III** *nm (fabricante)* arms manufacturer.

armamento *nm* **1** *(acción)* armament, arming. **2 armamentos,** *(armas)* armaments, arms.

armar I *vtr* **1** *(tropas, personas)* to arm. **2** *(cargar) (arma de fuego)* to load; *(bayoneta)* to fix. **3** *(montar)* to fit *or* put together, assemble; *(tienda)* to pitch; **está sin a.,** it hasn't been put up yet. **4** *(disponer, preparar)* to arrange, prepare. **5** *fam (organizar)* **¡ahora sí que la has armado!,** you've really done it now!; **armaron un escándalo,** they created a scandal. **II armarse** *vr* to arm oneself; **todos los habitantes se armaron,** everybody prepared for war; *fig* **a. de paciencia,** to summon up one's patience; *fig* **a. de valor,** to pluck up courage; *fig* **a. de papel y lápiz,** to provide oneself with paper and pencil; *fam* **se va a a. te de Dios es Cristo, se va a a. la gorda,** there's going to be real trouble.

armario *nm (para ropa)* wardrobe; *(de cocina)* cupboard. ■ **a. empotrado,** built-in wardrobe *or* cupboard.

armatoste *nm (cosa)* monstrosity; *(máquina)* useless contraption; *(persona)* useless great oaf.

armazón I *nf* frame, framework; *(de madera)* timberwork; *Arquit* shell; *(de una escultura)* armature. **II** *nm Am (estantería)* shelf, shelving.

Armenia *n* Armenia.

armenio,-a I *adj & nm, f* Armenian. **II** *nm (idioma)* Armenian.

armería *nf* **1** *(tienda)* gunsmith's (shop). **2** *(oficio)* gunsmith's craft. **3** *(museo)* armoury, *US* armory, museum of arms.

armero,-a *nm, f* armourer, *US* armorer; *(de armas de fuego)* gunsmith; *Mil* **(maestro) a.,** armourer, *US* armorer.

armiño *nm Zool* ermine.

armisticio *nm Mil* armistice.

armonía *nf* harmony.

armónico,-a I *adj* harmonic. **II** *nm Mús* harmonic. **III** *nf Mús* harmonica, mouth organ. ◆ **armónicamente** *adv* in harmony, harmoniously.

armonio *nm Mús* harmonium.

armonioso,-a *adj* harmonious.

armonización *nf* harmonizing.

armonizar *vtr & vi* to harmonize.

arnés *nm* **1** *(armadura)* armour, *US* armor. **2 arneses,** *(arreos)* harness *sing,* trappings.

árnica *nf Bot* arnica; **tintura de á.,** (tincture of) arnica.

aro *nm* **1** hoop, iron ring; *(servilletero)* serviette ring; *fam* **entrar** *or* **pasar por el a.,** to knuckle under. **2** *(juego)* hoop. **3** *Bot* cuckoopint. **4** *(sortija)* ring.

aroma *nm* aroma, fragrance; *(de vino)* bouquet.

aromático,-a *adj* aromatic, fragrant.

aromatización *nf* scenting, perfuming.

aromatizador *nm* air freshener.

aromatizar *vtr* to scent, perfume.

arpa *nf Mús* harp.

arpado,-a *adj* serrated.

arpegio *nm Mús* arpeggio.

arpía *nf* **1** *Mit* harpy. **2** *fig (mujer)* harpy, old witch.

arpillera *nf Tex* sackcloth, burlap.

arpista *nmf Mús* harpist.

arpón *nm* harpoon.

arponar *vtr*, **arponear** *vtr* to harpoon.

arponero,-a *nm,f* harpooner.

arqueado,-a I *pp de* **arquear. II** *adj* bowed, bent, curved; **piernas arqueadas,** bow legs.

arquear *vtr*, **arquearse** *vr* to bend, curve.

arqueo *nm* **1** bending, curving. **2** *Com* checking, cashing up; **hacer el a.,** to cash up. **3** *Náut* gauging.

arqueolítico,-a *adj* Stone-Age.

arqueología *nf* archaeology, *US* archeology.

arqueológico,-a *adj* archaeological, *US* archeological.

arqueólogo,-a *nm,f* archaeologist, *US* archeologist.

arquería *nf Arquit* arcade.

arquero,-a *nm,f* archer; *(hombre)* bowman.

arqueta *nf* small chest.

arquetípico,-a *adj* archetypal.

arquetipo *nm* archetype.

arquitecto,-a *nm,f* architect.

arquitectónico,-a *adj* architectural, architectonic.

arquitectura *nf* architecture.

arquitrabe *nm Arquit* architrave.

arquivolta *nf Arquit* archivolt.

arrabal *nm* **1** *(suburbio)* suburb. **2 arrabales,** *(afueras)* outskirts.

arrabalero,-a I *adj pey* ill-bred. **II** *nm,f* ill-bred person.

arrabiatar *Am* **I** *vtr (dos animales)* to tie by the tail to. **II arrabiatarse** *vr* to submit slavishly **(a,** to), bow down **(a,** to).

arrabio *nm Metal* cast iron.

arracada *nf* pendant, earring.

arracimarse *vr* to bunch *or* cluster together.

arraigado,-a I *pp de* **arraigar. II** *adj* deeply rooted.

arraigar I *vi* to take root. **II arraigarse** *vr* to settle down.

arraigo *nm (acción)* the act of taking root; *fig (raíces)* roots *pl;* **una tradición con mucho a.,** a deeply-rooted tradition.

arramblar I *vtr* to cover with sand. **II** *vi fam* **a. con algo,** to make off with sth.

arrancaclavos *nm inv* claw hammer, nail extractor.

arranoada *nf* jerk, jolt.

arrancar I *vtr* **1** to uproot, pull up; **a. de raíz,** *(árbol)* to uproot; *fig (eliminar una costumbre)* to wipe out. **2** *(separar con fuerza)* to pull *or* tear off *or* out; **a. un diente/el pelo,** to pull out a tooth/one's hair; **a. una etiqueta,** to tear off a label; **me arrancó el libro de las manos,** he wrenched the book from my hands; *fig* **le arrancaron la confesión con torturas,** they extracted the information from him by torture. **3** *Aut (coche)* to start. **II** *vi* **1** *Aut Téc* to start; **el coche no arranca,** the car won't start. **2** *(partir)* to set off, start out; *(barco)* to set sail. **3** *(empezar)* to begin; **a. a correr,** to break into a run; **a. a llorar/reír,** to burst out crying/laughing; *fig* **el problema arranca de años atrás,** the problem goes back several years. **III arrancarse** *vr* to do something unexpected; *fam* **¿y ahora te arrancas con eso?,** why on earth didn't you tell me before?

arranchar *vtr* **1** *Náut* to skirt. **2** *Am* to grab, snatch.

arranque *nm* **1** *Aut Téc* starting. ■ **motor de a.,** starting motor. **2** *(comienzo)* start. ■ **punto de a.,** beginning. **3** *Arquit* foot. **4** *fam (arrebato)* outburst, fit. **5** *CAm (pobreza)* poverty.

arranquera *nf Am* poverty.

arrapiezo *nm* **1** *(andrajo)* rag, tatter. **2** *(niño)* whippersnapper, urchin.

arrasado,-a I *pp de* **arrasar. II** *adj* **1** devastated, destroyed; *fig* **ojos arrasados en lágrimas,** eyes brimming with tears. **2** *(allanado)* levelled, *US* leveled, smooth.

arrasar *vtr* **1** to devastate, destroy. **2** *(terreno)* to level, smooth.

arrastradizo,-a *adj* trailing, dragging.

arrastrado,-a I *pp de* **arrastrar. II** *adj* **1** *fam (miserable)* miserable, wretched. **2** *Naipes* in which one must follow suit.

arrastrar I *vtr* to pull (along), drag (along), haul; **arrástralo,** pull it along; **a. los pies,** to drag one's feet; **la corriente lo arrastró,** the current swept him away; *fig* **a. a las masas,** to sway the crowds; *fig* **dejarse a.,** to get carried away. **II** *vi* **1** *(por el suelo)* to trail (on the ground). **2** *Naipes* to lead. **III arrastrarse** *vr* to drag oneself, crawl; *fig (humillarse)* to creep, crawl.

arrastre *nm* **1** pulling, dragging; *fam* **para el a.,** *(persona)* on one's last legs; *(cosa)* done for. ■ *Pesca* **(pesca de) a.,** trawling. **2** *Naipes* lead. **3** *(telesquí)* drag lift.

arrayán *nm Bot* myrtle.

arre *interj* gee up!, giddy up!

arrea *interj* goodness me!

arreada *nf Am* cattle rustling.

arrear *fam* **I** *vtr* **1** to spur on; *(caballos)* to urge on; *(ganado)* to drive. **2** *(apresurar)* to hurry up. **3** *fam (asestar)* to give; **a. una bofetada a algn,** to slap sb in the face, give sb a slap in the face. **4** *Am (ganado)* to rustle. **II** *vi fam* **salir arreando,** to rush off.

arrebatado,-a I *pp de* **arrebatar. II** *adj* **1** *(precipitado)* rash, hasty. **2** *(iracundo)* furious, enraged. **3** *(impulsivo)* impulsive. **4** *(ruborizado)* blushing, flushed. **5** *Culin fam (quemado)* burnt.

arrebatador,-a *adj fig* captivating, fascinating.

arrebatar I *vtr* **1** *(coger)* to snatch, seize; *fig (cautivar)* to captivate, fascinate. **2** *Am (atropellar)* to run over, knock down. **II arrebatarse** *vr* **1** *(enfurecerse)* to become furious; *(exaltarse)* to get carried away. **2** *Culin fam (quemarse)* to burn.

arrebato *nm*, **arrebatamiento** *nm* **I** *(arranque)* outburst, fit; **le dio un a. y dejó el trabajo,** he suddenly upped and left his job. **2** *(furor)* anger, fury, rage.

arrebol *nm* **1** *(de las nubes)* red glow; *(de las mejillas)* ruddiness, redness. **2 arreboles,** red clouds.

arrebolar I *vtr* **1** *(enrojecer)* to give a red glow to. **2** *(persona)* to make ruddy. **II arrebolarse** *vr* **1** *(enrojecer)* to glow red. **2** *(persona)* to blush.

arrebujar I *vtr* **1** *(arrugar)* to crumple up. **2** *(envolver)* to wrap up. **II arrebujarse** *vr (envolverse)* to wrap oneself up.

arrechucho *nm fam* **1** *Med* temporary ailment. **2** *(arranque)* sudden impulse, outburst, fit.

arreciar *vi (empeorar)* to get worse; *(aumentar)* to get heavier *or* stronger.

arrecife *nm Náut* reef.

arrecloques *nmpl CAm* **1** *(perifollos)* frills, trimmings. **2** *(rodeos)* evasiveness *sing,* circumlocution *sing.*

arredrar I *vtr (asustar)* to frighten. **II arredrarse** *vr (asustarse)* to be frightened.

arreglado,-a I *pp de* **arreglar. II** *adj* **1** *(solucionado)* settled, fixed, sorted out; **lo de tu billete ya está a.,** your ticket is all sorted out now. **2** *(reparado)* repaired, fixed. **3** *(ordenado)* tidy, arranged, neat. **4** *(persona)* well-dressed, smart. **5** *fam* **¡estamos arreglados!,** we're really done for!; *irón* **¡vas a. si crees que él lo va a hacer!,** you're in for a shock if you think he's going to do it!

arreglar I *vtr* **1** *(gen)* to settle, fix up, sort out, arrange; **arreglaron los papeles para casarse,** they got their papers in order so that they could get married; **yo lo arreglaré,** I'll see to it. **2** *(componer)* to repair, fix, mend; *(cabello)* to do; *(habitación)* to decorate; *(escrito)* to rearrange; *Mús (composición)* to arrange; *Cost (vestido)* to alter; **lo llevé a a.,** I had it repaired; *fig* **el tiempo lo arregla todo,** time heals all wounds. **3** *(ordenar)* to tidy up, put in order; **a. la casa,** to do the housework. **4** *(niño)* to dress and smarten up, get ready. **5** *fam* to sort out; **yo le arreglaré,** I'll teach him! **6** *Am (capar)* to castrate, geld. **II arreglarse** *vr* **1** *(acicalarse)* to get ready, dress up; *fam* **a. de punta en blanco,** to dress up to the nines. **2** *fam (apañarse)* to manage; **arréglatelas como puedas,** *(haz lo que puedas)* do as best you can; *(allá tú)* that's your problem, not mine; **con este trozo me arreglo,** this piece will do (for) me, I'll make do with this piece; **él siempre se las arregla para hacer lo que quiere,** he always manages to get his way; **tendrás que arreglarte sin el coche,** you'll have to get by without the car. **3** *(resolverse)* to be solved; **todo se arreglará,** things will be all right (in the end). **4** *(pactar)* to reach an agreement.

arreglista *nmf Mús* arranger.

arreglo *nm* **1** *(de una disputa)* settlement, arrangement. **2** *(reparación)* repair, mend; *(modificación)* change, alteration; *(de una casa)* conversion, redecoration; **no tiene a.,** it is beyond repair; *fam* **¡tú no tienes a.!,** you're hopeless! **3** *(limpieza)* cleaning, tidying. **4** *fml* **con a. a,** in accordance with.

arrejuntarse *vr fam* to cohabit, live together.

arrellanarse *vr* to sit back; **se arrellanó en el sillón,** he settled back in the armchair.

arremangar I *vtr (mangas etc)* to roll up. **II arremangarse** *vr* to roll one's sleeves *or* trousers up.

arremansar *vi CAm* to hold up *or* back.

arremeter *vi* to attack; **el toro arremetió contra él,** the bull charged at him; *fig* **arremetió contra la ley,** he attacked the law.

arremetida *nf* attack, assault.

arremolinarse *vr* to whirl about; *fig (gente)* to crowd together, cram together.

arrendable *adj (piso)* rentable; *Jur* leasable.

arrendador,-a I *adj* renting, leasing. **II** *nm, f* lessor; *(hombre)* landlord; *(mujer)* landlady.

arrendajo *nm Orn* jay; *fam* mimic.

arrendamiento *nm* **1** *(alquiler)* renting, leasing. **2** *(precio)* rent, lease.

arrendar *vtr (piso)* to rent, lease; *(dar en arriendo)* to let on lease; *(tomar en arriendo)* to take on lease.

arrendatario,-a I *adj* renting, leasing. **II** *nm, f* leaseholder, lessee; *(inquilino)* tenant.

arrenquín *nm Am* **1** *(bestia)* leading animal. **2** *(persona)* follower.

arreo I *nm Am* mule train. **II arreos** *nmpl* **1** *(de caballería)* harness *sing*, trappings. **2** *(adornos)* adornments; *(cosas, bultos)* stuff *sing*, trappings.

arrepanchingarse *vtr fam* to lounge, nestle.

arrepentido,-a I *pp de* **arrepentirse**. **II** *adj* regretful, repentant; **está a.,** he's regretful (of having done it), he regrets it. **II** *nf euf* reformed prostitute.

arrepentimiento *nm* regret, repentance.

arrepentirse *vr* to regret; **te arrepentirás** you'll regret it; *Rel* **a. de sus pecados,** to repent one's sins.

arrepollar *vi CAm* to squat, crouch.

arrequintar *vtr Am* to tie *or* bind tightly.

arrestado,-a I *pp de* **arrestar**. **II** *adj* arrested, detained imprisoned.

arrestar *vtr* to arrest, detain; *(encarcelar)* to put in prison.

arresto *nm* **1** arrest. ■ *Jur* **a. domiciliario,** under house arrest; **a. mayor,** close arrest; **a. menor,** open arrest. **2** **arrestos,** *(determinación)* daring *sing*; *fam* guts.

arriar *vtr (bandera)* to strike; *(velas)* to lower.

arriate *nm* flower bed.

arriba I *adv* up; *(encima)* on the top; **ahí a.,** up there; **a. del todo,** right on the top; **cuesta a.,** uphill; **de a. abajo,** from top to toe, from top to bottom; **desde a.,** from above; **hacia a.,** upwards; **la parte de a.,** the top (part); **más a.,** higher up, further up; **patas a.,** upside down; **sueldos de un millón para a.,** salaries from one million upwards; **ven aquí a.,** come up here; **vive a.,** he lives upstairs; *fml* **véase más a.,** see above; *fig* **los de a.,** the upper classes; *fam* **mirar a uno de a. abajo,** to look sb up and down. **II** *interj* get up!, up you get!; **¡a. la República!,** long live the Republic!; **¡a. las manos!,** hands up!

arribada *nf Náut* arrival.

arribar *vi Náut* to reach port, arrive.

arribeño,-a *Am* I *adj* highland. **II** *nm, f* highlander.

arribismo *nm* arrivisme, social climbing.

arribista I *adj* ambitious, self-seeking. **II** *nm f* arriviste, parvenu, parvenue, social climbing.

arribo *nm Náut* arrival.

arriendo *nm* lease; *(de un piso)* renting; **dar en a.,** to let out on lease; **tomar en a.,** to take on lease.

arriero,-a *nm, f* muleteer.

arriesgado,-a I *pp de* **arriesgar**. **II** *adj* **1** *(peligroso)* risky, dangerous. **2** *(persona)* fearless, daring.

arriesgar I *vtr* to risk, endanger; **a. todo lo que uno tiene,** to stake all one has got; **a. una hipótesis,** to venture a theory; *fam* **a. el pellejo,** to risk one's skin. **II arriesgarse** *vr* to risk; **a. a fracasar,** to risk failure; **se arriesga demasiado,** he's taking too many risks.

arrimadero *nm* **1** *(estribo)* support. **2** *(de pared)* wainscot.

arrimadizo,-a *fig* I *adj* parasitic. **II** *nm, f (oportunista)* parasite.

arrimado,-a I *pp de* **arrimar**. **II** *nm, f Am* **1** guest, lodger. **2** *(concubino)* lover.

arrimar I *vtr* **1** *(acercar)* to move closer, bring near *or* nearer; **arrímalo a la pared,** move it up to the wall; *fam* **a. el hombro,** to lend a hand. **2** *(arrinconar)* to put away. **II arrimarse** *vr* to move *or* get close, come near *or* nearer; **no te arrimes a la pared,** keep away from the wall, don't lean against the wall; *fig* **a. a algn,** to seek sb's protection; *fam* **a. al sol que más calienta,** to get on the winning side.

arrimo *nm (apoyo)* support, protection; *(ayuda)* help; **al a. de,** under the protection of.

arrinconado,-a I *pp de* **arrinconar**. **II** *adj* put away, laid aside, forgotten; *(persona)* forsaken.

arrinconar I *vtr* **1** *(poner en un rincón)* to put in a corner. **2** *(retirar del uso)* to put away, lay aside. **3** *(acorralar)* to corner. **II arrinconarse** *vr (aislarse)* to isolate oneself.

arriscado,-a *adj* **1** *(arriesgado)* risky, dangerous. **2** *(con riscos)* craggy, cliffy.

arroba *nf (medida)* arroba; *(de peso)* 11.5 kg; *(de volumen)* variable liquid measure; *fig* **por arrobas,** by the score.

arrobamiento *nm véase* **arrobo.**

arrobar I *vtr (embelesar)* to rapture, enthral, *US* enthrall, fascinate. **II arrobarse** *vr (embelesarse)* to go into raptures, be enthralled, be fascinated.

arrobo *nm* rapture, enthralment, *US* enthrallment, fascination.

arrocero,-a I *adj* rice; **la industria arrocera,** the rice industry. **II** *nm, f* rice grower.

arrodajarse *vr CAm* to sit down cross-legged.

arrodillado,-a I *pp de* **arrodillar**. **II** *adj* kneeling down, on one's knees; **estar a.,** to be kneeling down.

arrodillar I *vtr* to make sb kneel down. **II arrodillarse** *vr* to kneel down.

arrogación *nf Jur* arrogation.

arrogancia *nf* 1 *(orgullo)* arrogance. 2 *(gallardía)* gallantry, valour, *US* valor, bravery.

arrogante *adj* 1 *(orgulloso)* arrogant. 2 *(gallardo)* gallant, valiant, brave.

arrogarse *vr* to arrogate.

arrojadizo,-a *adj* for throwing; **arma arrojadiza,** projectile, missile.

arrojado,-a I *pp de* **arrojar. II** *adj* 1 thrown (out); *fig* **el saldo a.,** the resulting balance. 2 *(osado)* fearless, bold, daring.

arrojar I *vtr* 1 *(tirar)* to throw, fling, hurl; **'prohibido a. basuras',** 'no dumping'. 2 *(echar)* to throw out; **los arrojó de su casa,** he threw them out of the house. 3 *(humo)* to kick *or* belch out; *(lava)* to spew out; *fig* **a. luz sobre,** to shed light on. 4 *Com* to produce; **a. un saldo positivo,** to give a favourable balance. **II** *vi fam (vomitar)* to throw up, be sick. **III arrojarse** *vr (tirarse)* to throw oneself, fling oneself; **a. por la ventana,** to throw oneself out of the window; **se arrojó sobre él,** he jumped on him.

arrojo *nm* fearlessness, daring, courage.

arrollable *adj* rollable.

arrollador,-a *adj fig* irresistible, overwhelming; **un éxito a.,** a resounding success; **una personalidad arrolladora,** a captivating personality.

arrollamiento *nm* 1 *(acción)* rolling, rolling up. 2 *(atropello)* running over, knocking down. 3 *fig (aplastamiento)* crushing, routing. 4 *(por agua, viento)* sweeping away, carrying off. 5 *Elec* winding.

arrollar *vtr* 1 *(enrollar)* to roll, roll up. 2 *(atropellar)* to run over, knock down. 3 *fig (aplastar)* to crush, rout. 4 *(agua, viento)* to sweep away, carry off. **II arrollarse** *vr CAm Per (mangas)* to roll up one's sleeves; *(faldas)* to gather one's skirts up.

arropamiento *nm* wrapping up.

arropar I *vtr* to wrap up; **elia lo arropó en la cama,** she tucked him up in bed. **II arroparse** *vr* to wrap oneself up.

arrope *nm Culin* boiled must, grape syrup.

arrostrar *vtr (las consecuencias)* to face; *(peligro)* to brave.

arroyo *nm* 1 *(corriente)* brook, stream. 2 *(de calle)* gutter; *fig* **sacar (a algn) del a.,** to drag (sb) from the gutter; *fig* **poner (a algn) en el a.,** to chuck (sb) out. 3 *SAm (río)* river.

arroyuelo *nm* (small) stream, brook.

arroz *nm* rice. ■ **a. blanco,** boiled rice; **a. con leche,** rice pudding; **a. integral,** brown rice.

arrozal *nm* rice field, rice plantation.

arruga *nf* 1 *(piel)* wrinkle. 2 *(ropa)* crease.

arrugamiento *nm (piel)* wrinkling; *(ropa)* creasing.

arrugar I *vtr (piel)* to wrinkle; *(ropa)* to crease; *(papel)* to crumple (up); *fig* **a. el ceño,** to frown. **II arrugarse** *vr* 1 *(piel)* to wrinkle; *(ropa)* to crease. 2 *fam (acobardarse)* to get the wind up.

arruinado,-a I *pp de* **arruinar. II** *adj* 1 bankrupt, ruined. 2 *(inservible)* ruined.

arruinar I *vtr* to bankrupt, ruin. **II arruinarse** *vr* to be bankrupt, be ruined.

arrullador,-a *adj* 1 *Orn (paloma)* cooing. 2 *(sonido, voz)* lulling.

arrullar I *vtr* 1 *Orn (paloma)* to coo at. 2 *(bebé)* to lull. **II arrullarse** *vr* to bill and coo.

arrullo *nm* 1 *Orn (de paloma)* cooing. 2 *(nana)* lullaby. 3 *(de enamorados)* billing and cooing.

arrumaco *nm fam* kissing, hugging, **hacerse arrumacos,** to pet; **ir con arrumacos a algn,** to flatter sb.

arrumar I *vtr Náut* to stow. **II arrumarse** *vr Náut* to cloud over.

arrumbar I *vtr* 1 *(deshechar)* to put away, lay aside. 2 *fig (persona)* to neglect, ignore. **II** *vi Náut* to set course (hacia, for).

arrurrú *nm Am* lullaby.

arsenal *nm* 1 *Náut* shipyard. 2 *(de armas)* arsenal. 3 *fig (cúmulo)* store, storehouse; *(conjunto)* array.

arsénico *nm Quim* arsenic.

art. *abr de* **artículo,** article, art.

arte *nm & f* 1 art; **el a. bizantino,** Byzantine art; *fig* **no tener ni a. ni parte en algo,** to have nothing to do with sth; *fam* **hacer algo por amor al a.,** to do sth for the love of it; *(sin cobrar)* to do sth for free; *fam* **por a. de birlibirloque,** as if by magic. ■ **artes plásticas,** plastic arts; **bellas artes,** fine arts. 2 *(habilidad)* workmanship, skill. ■ **malas artes,** deceit *sing.* 3 *Pesca* a. **(de pesca),** fishing gear.

artefacto *nm* 1 appliance, device. ■ **a. explosivo,** explosive device, bomb. 2 *Arqueol* artefact.

artejo *nm* I *Anat (nudillo)* knuckle. 2 *Zool (de artrópodos)* article, segment.

artemisa *nf Bot* artemisia.

artería *nf* craftiness, artfulness.

arteria *nf Anat* artery. ■ **a. carótida,** carotid artery; **a. coronaria,** coronary artery.

arterial *adj Anat* arterial.

arterio(e)sclerosis *nf Med* arteriosclerosis.

artero,-a *adj* crafty, artful.

artesa *nf* trough.

artesanado *nm* craftsmen *pl.*

artesanal *adj* handmade; **actividades artesanales,** arts and crafts.

artesanía *nf* 1 *(cualidad)* craftsmanship. 2 *(obra)* crafts *pl,* handicrafts *pl.* ■ **objeto de a.,** handmade object.

artesano,-a I *adj* handmade. **II** *nm,f (hombre)* craftsman; *(mujer)* craftswoman.

artesiano,-a *adj* artesian; **pozo a.,** artesian well.

artesón *nm Arquit* 1 coffer. 2 *(artesonado)* coffered ceiling.

artesonado,-a *Arquit* **I** *adj* coffered. **II** *nm* coffered ceiling.

ártico,-a I *adj* arctic; **el océano a.,** the Arctic Ocean. **II el Á.** *nm* the Arctic.

articulación *nf* 1 *Ling* articulation. 2 *Anat* joint, articulation. 3 *Téc* joint.

articulado,-a I *pp de* **articular. II** *adj* 1 *(lenguaje)* articulate. 2 *(tren, muñeco)* articulated. **III** *nm (de una ley, un reglamento)* articles *pl.*

articular I *adj* articulated. **II** *vtr* to articulate.

articulatorio,-a *adj* articulatory.

articulista *nmf Prensa* writer of articles.

artículo *nm* 1 *Ling* article. ■ **a. definido,** definite article; **a. indefinido,** indefinite article. 2 *Prensa* article. ■ **a. de fondo,** leading article. 3 *(mercancía)* article, product; **artículos alimenticios,** foodstuffs; **artículos de limpieza,** cleaning products. ■ **a. de primera necesidad,** basic commodity; *fam* **hacer el a.,** to plug sth. 4 *Rel* article; **a. de fe,** article of faith; *fam* **como a. de fe,** as if it were gospel truth.

artífice *nmf* 1 *(artista)* artist. 2 *(autor)* author; *fig* **ella ha sido el a. del acuerdo,** she is the architect of the agreement.

artificial *adj* artificial; *Tex* **fibras artificiales,** man made *or* synthetic fibres; **una sonrisa a.,** an artificial smile.

artificiero,-a *nm,f* artificier, armourer, *US* armorer.

artificio *nm* 1 *(mecanismo)* artifice. ■ **a. pirotécnico, fuego de a.,** firework. 2 *(habilidad, arte)* skill, dexterity. 3 *(astucia)* artifice.

artificioso,-a *adj* **1** *(habilidoso)* skilful, *US* skillful, dexterous. **2** *(astuto)* crafty, artful.

artillería *nf Mil* artillery. ■ **a. antiaérea,** anti-aircraft guns *pl*.

artillero *nm Mil* artilleryman.

artilugio *nm* **1** *(aparato)* gadget, device. **2** *(ardid)* trick, scheme.

artimaña *nf* artifice, trick, ruse.

artista *nmf* artist; **a. de cine,** film star.

artístico,-a *adj* artistic.

artrítico,-a *adj* arthritic.

artritis *nf Med* arthritis.

artrópodo *nm Zool* arthropod.

artrosis *nf Med* arthrosis.

aruñón *nm Am* threat.

arveja *nf* **1** *Bot* vetch, tare. **2 arvejas,** *Am (guisantes)* peas.

Arz., Arzpo. *abr de* **Arzobispo,** Archbishop, Abp.

arzobispal *adj* of *or* relating to the archbishop.

arzobispo *nm* archbishop.

as *nm* **1** *(cartas)* ace; **a. de picas/tréboles,** ace of spades/clubs. **2** *fig* ace, star, wizard; **a. del volante,** ace driver.

asa *nf* handle.

asadero,-a I *adj* (for) roasting. **II** *nm fig* oven.

asado,-a I *pp de* **asar. II** *adj Culin* roast, roasted; **pollo a.,** roast chicken; *fig* **a. de calor,** roasting, boiling hot. **III** *nm Culin* roast.

asador *nm* **1** roaster. **2** restaurant serving roast meat (and fish).

asaduras *nfpl Culin* offal *sing*; *(de ave)* giblets.

asaetar *vtr* to shoot arrows at; *(herir)* to wound with arrows; *(matar)* to kill with arrows; *fig* **a. a preguntas,** to bombard with questions.

asalariado,-a I *pp de* **asalariar. II** *adj* salaried; **trabajador a.,** wage earner, salaried worker. **III** *nm, f* wage earner, salaried worker.

asalariar *vtr* to employ.

asaltador,-a I *adj* assaulting, attacking. **II** *nm, f* attacker; *(en un robo)* raider, robber.

asaltante I *adj* assaulting, attacking. **II** *nmf* attacker; *(en un robo)* raider, robber.

asaltar *vtr* to assault, attack; *(para robar)* to raid, rob; *fig* **le asaltaron las dudas,** he was filled with doubts.

asalto *nm* **1** assault, attack; *(con robo)* raid, robbery; **tomar por a.,** to take by storm. **2** *Box* round.

asamblea *nf* assembly, meeting. ■ **a. general,** general meeting.

asambleísta *nmf* member of an assembly *or* meeting.

asar I *vtr* **1** *Culin* to roast; **a. a la parrilla,** to grill. **2** *fig (molestar)* to annoy, pester. **II asarse** *vr fig* to be roasting, be boiling hot.

asaz *adj lit* **1** *(muy)* very. **2** *(bastante)* rather, quite.

asbesto *nm Min* asbestos *sing*.

ascendencia *nf* **1** ancestry, ancestors *pl*; **de a. judía,** of Jewish descent. **2** *(influencia)* ascendancy.

ascendente I *adj* ascendant, ascending. **II** *nm* ascendant.

ascender I *vtr* to promote; **le han ascendido a capitán,** he's been promoted to captain. **II** *vi* **1** to ascend, move upward; *(temperatura, nivel)* to rise; **la cuenta asciende a diez mill pesetas,** the bill adds up to ten thousand pesetas. **2** *(aumentar)* to increase. **3** *(al trono)* to ascend; *(de categoría)* to be promoted; **a. a primera división,** to be promoted to the first division.

ascendiente I *nm* ascendancy, power. **II** *nmf (persona)* ancestor.

ascensión *nf* **1** climb, climbing. ■ *Rel* **día de la A.,** Ascension Day. **2** *(al trono)* accoession.

ascensional *adj* ascendant, upward.

ascensionista *nmf (en globo)* balloonist; *(alpinista)* mountaineer.

ascenso *nm* promotion.

ascensor *nm* lift, *US* elevator.

ascensorista *nmf* lift attendant.

asceta *nmf* ascetic.

ascético,-a I *adj* asectic. **II** *nf* asceticism.

ascetismo *nm* asceticism.

asco *nm* disgust, repugnance; **está hecho un a.,** *(cosa)* it's filthy, it's a mess; *(persona)* he's very much under the weather; **me da a.,** it makes me (feel) sick; **¡qué a.!,** how disgusting *or* revolting!

ascua *nf* live coal; *fig* **en** *or* **sobre ascuas,** on tenterhooks; *fam* **arrimar el a. a su sardina,** to look after number one.

aseado,-a I *pp de* **asear. II** *adj* clean, tidy, neat.

asear I *vtr* to clean, tidy up. **II asearse** *vr* to wash, get washed.

asechanza *nf (conspiración)* scheme; *(trampa)* trap.

asediar *vtr to* besiege, lay siege to; *fig* **a. con preguntas,** to besiege with questions.

asedio *nm* siege; *fig* **el a. de los periodistas,** the harassment by journalists.

asegurado,-a I *pp de* **asegurar. II** *adj* **1** *Seg* insured. **2** *(indudable)* secure; **el éxito está a.,** it's bound to be a success.

asegurador,-a *Seg* **I** *adj* insuring, insurance. **II** *nm, f* insurer.

asegurar I *vtr* **1** *Seg* to insure. **2** *(garantizar)* to assure, guarantee; **le aseguro que ...,** I can assure you that ...; **me han asegurado que llega hoy,** I've been promised that it'll arrive today. **3** *(sujetar)* *(puerta)* to secure; *(cerrar)* to close tightly. **II asegurarse** *vr* to make sure; **a. de cerrar d gas,** to make sure that the gas is turned off.

asemejar I *vtr to* make alike, make similar. **II asemejarse** *vr* to look like, be like.

asenso *nm* assent, consent; **dar a.,** to believe.

asentaderas *nfpl fam* bottom *sing*, buttocks.

asentado,-a I *pp de* **asentar. II** *adj* **1** *(situado)* placed, situated. **2** *(firme)* firm, secure; **un edificiomal a.,** a building with bad foundations. **3** *(establecido)* established, settled.

asentamiento *nm* **1** *Mil* emplacement. **2** *(poblado)* settlement.

asentar I *vtr* **1** *(situar)* to place, situate, site; **a. un campamento,** to set up camp; **a. los cimientos,** to lay the foundations. **2** *(asegurar)* to secure, make firm; **no está bien asentado,** it's not steady. **II asentarse** *vr* **1** *(situarse)* to be situated. **2** *(persona)* to settle down, establish oneself. **3** *(tierra)* to sink.

asentimiento *nm* assent, consent.

asentir *vi* to assent, agree; **a. con la cabeza,** to nod.

aseo *nm* **1** *(accion)* cleaning, tidying up. **2** *(limpieza)* cleanliness, tidiness. ■ **a. personal,** personal cleanliness. **3** **(cuarto de) a.,** bathroom; *(retrete)* toilet.

asepsia *nf* **1** *Med* asepsis. **2** *fig (frialdad)* coldness, coolness.

aséptico,-a *adj* **1** *Med* aseptic. **2** *fig (frío)* cold, cool.

asequible *adj* obtainable, accessible; **a. a todos,** *(de comprar)* within everybody's reach; *(de entender)* easy to understand.

aserción *nf* assertion, statement.

aserradero *nm* sawmill.

aserrado,-a I *pp de* **aserrar. II** *adj* serrated. **III** *nm* sawing.

aserrador,-a I *adj* sawing. **II** *nm* sawyer. **III** *nf (máquina)* power saw.

aserradura *nf* **1** *(acción)* sawing. **2** *(corte)* saw cut. **3 aserraduras,** sawdust *sing*.

aserrar *vtr* to saw (up).

aserrín *nm* sawdust.

aserruchar *vtr Am* to saw (up).

aserto *nm* assertion, statement.

asesinar *vtr* to murder, kill; *Pol (cometer magnicidio)* to assassinate.

asesinato *nm* murder, killing; *(magnicidio)* assassination.

asesino,-a I *adj* murderous; **el arma asesina,** the murder weapon; *fig* **una mirada asesina,** a murderous look. **II** *nm,f* killer; *(hombre)* murderer; *(mujer)* murderess.

asesor,-a I *adj* advisory. **II** *nm, f* adviser, advisor, consultant. ■ **a. fiscal,** tax advisor.

asesoramiento *nm* **1** *(acción)* advising. **2** *(consejo)* advice.

asesorar I *vtr* **1** *(gen)* to advise, give (professional) advice to. **2** *Com* to act as consultant to. **II asesorarse** *vr* to consult; **asesórate bien antes de actuar,** take good advice before you do anything.

asesoría *nf* **1** *(cargo)* consultancy, consultantship. **2** *(oficina)* consultant's office.

asestar *vtr* to deal; **a. un golpe a algn,** to hit sb; **a. un puñetaze,** to punch; **a. una patada,** to kick; **a. una puñalada,** to stab.

aseveración *nf* asseveration, assertion.

aseverar *vtr* to asseverate, assert.

asexuado,-a *adj*, **asexual** *adj* asexual.

asfaltado,-a I *pp de* **asfaltar. II** *adj* asphalted. **III** *nm* **1** *(acción)* asphalting. **2** *(pavimento)* asphalted (road) surface, Tarmac.

asfaltar *vtr* to asphalt.

asfáltico,-a *adj* containing asphalt.

asfalto *nm* asphalt.

asfixia *nf Med* asphyxia, asphyxiation, suffocation.

asfixiado,-a I *pp de* **asfixiar. II** *adj fam* broke; **estar a.,** to be broke.

asfixiador,-a *adj*, **asfixiante** *adj* asphyxiating, suffocating; *fam* **hace un calor a.,** it's stifling.

asfixiar *vtr*, **asfixiarse** *vr* to asphyxiate, suffocate.

asgo *indic véase* **asir.**

así I *adv* **1** *(de esta manera)* thus, like this *or* that, this way, so; **a las seis** *or* **a.,** around six o'clock; **algo a.,** something like this *or* that, something along these *or* those lines; **a. a.,** so-so; **a. de grande/alto,** this big/tall; **a. es,** that's right; **a. es la vida,** such is life; **a. fue,** that's how it was; **a. se lo dije,** I told him so; **¿cómo a.?,** how come?; **diez años** *or* **a.,** ten years more or less; **¿no es a.?,** isn't that so *or* right?; **ponlo a.,** put in this way; **y a. todo,** and the same applies to all the rest; *fam* **lo mismo le da a. que asá,** she couldn't care less. **2** *(tanto como)* as; **a. en casa como en la oficina,** the same at home as in the office; **no puedo decidirlo a. como a.,** I can't decide just like that. **3** *(aunque)* **a. tenga que hacerlo yo mismo,** even if I have to do it myself. **4** *(a pesar de todo)* **y aun a.,** and despite that; **y a. y todo no lo entiendo,** even now I can't understand it. **5** *(por lo tanto, de modo que)* **a. pues,** therefore; **a. que no pude ir,** that's why I couldn't go; *fam* **¿a. que te has casado?,** so you've got married, have you? **6** *(tan pronto como)* **a. que lo sepas llámame,** as soon as you know give me a ring. **II** *adj* **un marido a. es una joya,** a husband like that is a gem.

Asia *n* Asia. ■ **A. Menor,** Asia Minor.

asiático,-a *adj & nm,f* Asian.

asidero *nm* **1** *(asa)* handle. **2** *fig (pretexto)* pretext, excuse.

asiduidad *nf* assiduity; **con a.,** frequently, regularly.

asiduo,-a *adj* assiduous, regular.

asiento *nm* **1** seat; **a. trasero,** rear *or* back seat; **tome a.,** take a seat. **2** *(de vasija)* bottom. **3** *(poso)* sediment. **4** *Fin* entry, registry. **5** *Com (contrato)* trading contract. **6** *Arquit* settling.

asignación *nf* **1** assignment, allocation. **2** *(nombramiento)* appointment, assignment. **3** *(paga)* allocation, allowance; *(sueldo)* wage, salary.

asignar *vtr* **1** to assign, allot, allocate. **2** *(nombrar)* to assign, appoint.

asignatario,-a *nm, f Am Jur* beneficiary.

asignatura *nf Educ* subject; **a. pendiente,** failed subject.

asilado,-a *nm, f* **1** *(pobre)* person who lives in a charity home. **2** *Pol (refugiado)* refugee.

asilar *vtr* **1** *(recoger)* to take in, give shelter to. **2** *Pol (dar refugio)* to grant *or* give political asylum to.

asilo *nm* **1** asylum. ■ **a. de ancianos,** old people's home; *Pol* **a. político,** political asylum. **2** *fig (protección)* protection, help, assistance; **dar a.,** to shelter.

asimetría *nf* asymmetry.

asimétrico,-a *adj* asymmetrical, asymmetric.

asimiento *nm* **1** *(acción)* grasping, seizing, holding. **2** *(efecto)* attachment.

asimilable *adj* assimilable.

asimilación *nf* assimilation.

asimilar I *vtr* to assimilate **II asimilarse** *vr* to asimílate, be assimilated.

asimilativo,-a *adj* assimilative, assimilating.

asimismo *adv* **1** *(también)* also, as well. **2** *(de esta manera)* likewise; *(además)* moreover.

asir I *vtr (agrarrar)* to take, grasp, seize, take hold of. **II** *vi Bot (echar raíces)* to take root. **III asirse** *vr (agrarrarse)* to get hold of one another; *fig* **a. a una idea,** to cling to an idea.

asirio,-a *adj & nm,f Hist* Assyrian.

asistencia *nf* **1** *(presencia)* attendance; **con la a. de,** in the presence of; **falta de a. al trabajo,** absence from work. **2** *(público)* audience, public; **hubo mucha a.,** there was a large audience **3** *(ayuda)* assistance, help, aid; **a. médica/técnica,** medical/ technical assistance; **con la a. de,** with the help of.

asistenta *nf* charlady, cleaning lady.

asistente I *adj* attending; **el público a.,** the audience. **II** *nmf* **1 a. social,** social worker. **2 asistentes,** public *sing*; **los a. al acto,** the audience, the public. **III** *nm* assistant.

asistido,-a I *pp de* **asistir, II** *adj* assisted; **a. por ordenador,** computer-assisted. **III** *nm SAm* temporary labourer *or US* laborer.

asistir I *vtr* to assist, help; **le asistió el médico de cabecera,** he was treated *or* attended by his general practitioner; *fml* **le asiste la razón,** he's right. **II** *vi* **1** to attend, be present; **lleva un mes sin a. a clase,** he hasn't been to school for a month. **2** *(servir)* to work as a servant.

asma *nf Med* asthma.

asmático,-a *adj Med* **I** *adj* asthmatic. **II** *nm, f* asthmatic person, person suffering from asthma.

asnal *adj* asinine, of a donkey, of an ass.

asno *nm* **1** *Zool* donkey, ass. **2** *fam (persona)* ass, idiot.

asociación *nf* association. ■ **a. de ideas,** association of ideas; **a. de vecinos,** neighbours' association.

associacionismo *nm* associationism.

asociado,-a I *pp de* **asociar. II** *adj* associated, associate. **III** *nm,f* associate, partner.

asociamiento *nm* association.

asociar I *vtr* **1** to associate, link, connect; **a. ideas,** to associate ideas. **2** *Com* to take into partnership. **II asociarse** *vr* **1** to be associated; **se asocia con el alcohol,** it is associated with alcohol. **2** *Com* to become partners; **a. con algn,** to become sb's partner.

asociativo,-a *adj* associative.

asocio *nm Am* association.

asolación *nf* devastation, destruction, razing.

asolador,-a *adj* devastating, destructive.

asolamiento *nf* devastation, destruction, razing.

asolar *vtr* to devastate, destroy, raze.

asoleada *nf Am* sunstroke.

asolear I *vtr* to put in the sun. **II asolearse** *vr* to sunbathe.

asomar I *vtr* to show, put out, stick out; **asoma la cabeza por la ventana,** put your head out of the window. **II** *vi (empezar)* to appear; **ya asoma el día,** day is breaking. **III asomarse** *vr* to lean out; *(balcón)* to come out; **a. a la ventana,** to lean out of the window.

asombrado,-a I *pp de* **asombrar. II** *adj* surprised; amazed, astonished; **me dejó a.,** I was amazed.

asombrar I *vtr (sorprender)* to surprise, amaze, astonish. **II asombrarse** *vr (sorprenderse)* to be astonished; **a. de algo,** to be amazed at sth.

asombro *nm* surprise, amazement, astonishment.

asombroso,-a *adj* surprising, amazing, astonishing.

asomo *nm* sign, trace, hint; **sin el menor a. de interés,** without any interest at all.

asonada *nf Mil* putsch.

asonancia *nf Lit* assonance.

asonante *adj* assonant.

asordar *vtr* to deafen.

asorocharse *vr SAm* 1 to suffer from mountain sickness. 2 *fig (ruborizarse)* to blush; *(avergonzarse)* to feel ashamed.

aspa *nf* 1 *(de molino)* arm; *(de ventilador)* blade; *(armazón)* arms *pl*. 2 *(cruz)* X-shaped cross; **en forma de a.,** X-shaped. 3 *SAm (asta)* horn.

aspar *vtr* 1 to crucify. 2 *fig (fastidiar)* to annoy, pester. 3 *fam* **¡que me aspen si ...!,** I'll be damned if ...!

aspaventoso,-a *adj* fussy, theatrical, exaggerated.

aspaventarse *vr CAm* to become frightened.

aspaviento *nm* fuss; **hacer aspavientos,** to gesticulate and wave one's arms about.

aspecto *nm* 1 look, appearance; **¿qué a. tenía?,** what did he look like?; **tener a. de,** to look like; **tiene muy buen a.,** *(persona)* he's looking very well; *(cosa)* it looks very good. 2 *(de un asunto)* aspect, side; **bajo este a.,** from this angle; **en todos los aspectos,** in every respect.

aspereza *nf* roughness, coarseness, asperity; *fig* **limar asperezas,** to smooth things over.

asperezar *vtr CAm* to roughen.

asperges *nm inv* 1 sprinkling. 2 *Rel* aspergillum.

asperjar *vtr* to sprinkle; *Rel* to sprinkle with holy water.

áspero,-a *adj* rough, coarse, asperous; *fig (carácter)* surly.

asperón *nm* sandstone.

aspersión *nf* sprinkling. ■ **riego por a.,** spraying.

aspersor *nm* sprinkler.

aspersorio *nm Rel* aspergillum.

áspid *nm Zool* asp.

aspidistra *nf Bot* aspidistra.

aspillera *nf Mil* loophole.

aspiración *nf* 1 inhalation, breathing in; **a. de aire,** intake of air. 2 *Ling* aspiration. 3 *Téc* sucking in. 4 **aspiraciones,** *(pretensión)* aspiration *sing*, strong desire *sing*; **tiene pocas a. profesionales,** he has few professional ambitions.

aspirado,-a I *pp de* **aspirar. II** *adj Ling* aspirated. **III** *n Ling* aspirate.

aspirador,-a I *adj* sucking; **bomba aspiradora,** suction pump. **II** *nm,f* vacuum cleaner.

aspirante I *adj* **bomba a.,** suction pump. **II** *nmf (para puesto de trabajo)* candidate, applicant.

aspirar I *vtr* 1 *(respirar)* to inhale, breath in. 2 *Ling (sonido)* to aspirate. 3 *Téc (absorber)* to suck in, draw in. **II** *vi fig (desear)* to aspire; **a. a ser famoso,** to aspire after fame.

aspirina *nf Farm* aspirin.

asquear I *vtr* to disgust, revolt, make sick. **II asquearse** *vr* to be disgusted *or* revolted.

asquerosidad *nf* filthy *or* revolting thing; **¡que a.!,** how revolting!

asqueroso,-a I *adj (sucio)* filthy; *(desagradable)* revolting, disgusting, foul. **II** *nm,f* 1 filthy *or* revolting person. 2 *(cerdo)* swine.

asta *nf* 1 *(de bandera)* staff, pole; **a media a.,** at half-mast. 2 *Zool (cuerno)* horn. 3 *Mil (palo de la lanza)* haft; *(pica)* lance, pike.

astado,-a I *adj Zool* horned. **II** *nm Taur* bull.

astenia *nf Med* asthenia.

asténico,-a *adj & nm,f Med* asthenic.

asterisco *nm* asterisk.

asteroide *adj & nm Astron* asteroid.

astifino,-a *adj Taur* narrow-horned.

astigmático,-a *Med* **I** *adj* astigmatic. **II** *nm, f* astigmat, astigmatic.

astigmatismo *nm Med* astigmatism.

astil *nm* 1 *(mango)* handle. 2 *(de flecha)* shaft. 3 *(de balanza)* arm, beam.

astilla *nf* splinter, chip; *fig* **hacer astillas,** to smash to smithereens; *prov* **de tal palo, tal a.** like father, like son.

astillar *vtr* to splinter.

astillero *nm* shipyard, dockyard.

astilloso,-a *adj* brittle, easily splintered.

astracán *nm* astrakhan.

astrágalo *nm* 1 *Anat* astragalus. 2 *Arquit* astragal.

astral *adj* astral; *Astrol* **carta a.,** birth chart, individual horoscope.

astringencia *nf* astringency.

astringente *adj & nm* astringent.

astringir *vtr* to astringe, constrict.

astro *nm* star. ■ *lit* **el a. rey,** the sun; *fig* **a. de la pantalla,** film star.

astrofísica *nf* astrophysics *sing*.

astrolabio *nm Astron* astrolabe.

astrología *nf* astrology.

astrológico,-a *adj* astrological.

astrólogo,-a *nm, f* astrologer.

astronauta *nmf* astronaut.

astronáutica *nf* astronautics *sing*.

astronave *nf Astronáut* spacecraft, spaceship.

astronomía *nf* astronomy.

astronómico,-a *adj* 1 *(de los astros)* astronomical, astronomic. 2 *fig (elevado)* astronomical.

astrónomo,-a *nm, f* astronomer.

astroso,-a *adj* 1 *(andrajoso)* shabby, ragged, untidy. 2 *(desdichado)* unfortunate.

astucia *nf* astuteness, cunning, shrewdness.

astur *adj & nmf*, **asturiano,-a** *adj & nm,f* Asturian.

Asturias *n* Asturias; **Príncipe de A.,** ≈ Prince of Wales.

astuto,-a *adj* astute, cunning, shrewd.

asueto *nm* short holiday.

asumir *vtr* to assume, take upon oneself; **a. el poder,** to assume control.

asunceno,-a I *adj* of *or* from Asunción. **II** *nm, f* native *or* inhabitant of Asunción.

asunción *nf* assumption, taking on.

asunto *nm* **I** subject, topic, matter, issue, affair; **a. de faldas,** affair with a woman; **el a. es que ...,** the thing is that ...; **no es a. mío,** it is nothing to do with me; **no es a. tuyo,** mind your own business; **y a. concluido,** and let that be the end of the matter. 2 **asuntos,** *Pol* affairs; **A. Exteriores,** Foreign Affairs.

asustadizo,-a *adj* easily frightened *or* scared.

asustar I *vtr* to frighten, scare. **II asustarse** *vr* to be frightened, be scared; **ella se asusta por todo,** she's frightened of everything.

asustón,-ona *adj Am* frightening.

atacante I *adj* attacking, assailing. **II** *nmf* attacker, assailant.

atacar *vtr* 1 to attack, assault, assail. 2 *(dañar)* to attack, affect, damage; **atacó la cosecha,** it attacked the crops; **le atacó a los pulmones,** it attacked his lungs; *fig* **a. los nervios,** to get on someone's nerves. 3 *(combatir)* **todos atacaron sus ideas,** everyone attacked his ideas.

atadero *nm* 1 *(cuerda)* cord, rope; *(cadena)* chain. 2 *(anilla)* halter ring, hitching hook.

atadijo *nm fam* bundle.

atado,-a I *pp de* **atar. II** *adj* 1 *(ligado)* tied, bound; **a. a un árbol,** tied to a tree. 2 *fig (tímido)* timid, shy. **III** *nm (legajo)* bundle. **IV** *nf Arg* packet of cigarettes.

atadura *nf* 1 *(acción)* tying, binding, fastening. 2 *(cuerda)* binding, string, cord. 3 *fig (impedimento)* tie hindrance.

atajar I *vi* to take a shortcut **(por,** across *or* through). **II** *vtr* 1 *(entorpecer el paso)* to halt, stop; **a. un incendio,** to check the spread of a fire; **a. un mal de raíz,** to kill sth at the root; **a. una manifestación,** to check a demonstration; **Eva me atajó cuando salía,** Eva stopped me as I was leaving. 2 *(interrumpir)* to interrupt, cut short; **atajaron al orador,** they interrupted the speaker.

atajo *nm* 1 shortcut; *fig* **echar por un a.,** to take a shortcut, take the easiest way out. 2 *(grupo)* bunch; **sois un a. de sinvergüenzas,** you're a bunch of rotters.

atalaya I *nf (torre)* watchtower, lookout; *(mirador)* vantage point. **II** *nm (persona)* watcher, lookout.

atalayar *vtr* 1 *(vigilar)* to walch (over), observe. 2 *fig (espiar)* to spy on.

atañer *v unipers* to concern, have to do with; **en lo que atañe a este asunto,** as far as this subject is concerned, with regard to this subject; **eso a ti no te atañe,** that has nothing to do with you.

ataque *nm* 1 attack; assault. ■ **a. aéreo,** air raid. 2 *Med* fit; *fig* **a. de celos/ odio,** a fit of jealousy/ hatred. ■ **a. al corazón,** heart attack; **a. de nervios,** fit of hysterics; **a. de tos,** fit of coughing.

atar I *vtr;* 1 *(ligar)* to tie, bind; **átale tos zapatos,** do his shoes up; **átalo bien,** fasten it tight; **a. de pies y manos,** to bind hand and foot; *fig* **a. cabos,** to put two and two together; *fam* **estar loco da a.,** to be as mad as a hatter. 2 *fig* to bind, tie down; **a. corto a algn,** to keep a tight rein on sb; **una profesión que ata mucho,** a profession that ties one down a lot. **II atarse** *vr fig* to get tied up.

atarazana nf shipyard, dockyard.

atardecer I *v impers* to get *or* grow dark. **II** *nm* evening, dusk.

ataredo,-a *pp de* **atarear. II** *adj* busy, occupied.

atarear I *vtr* to keep busy, assign a task to. **II atarearse** *vtr* to be busy, work hard.

atarugar I *vtr fam (llenar)* to stuff, pack, cram; **a. a algn con comida,** to stuff sb with food. 2 *fig (hacer callar)* to shut up. **II atarugarse** *vrI* 1 *fig (avergonzarse)* to feel confused *or* embarrassed; *(cortarse)* to stop short, become tongue-tied. 2 *fig (atragantarse)* to choke.

atascadero *nm fig* stumbling block, obstacle.

atascar I *vtr* 1 *(bloquear)* to block up, obstruct; **a. una cañería,** to clog up a pipe. 2 *fig (obstaculizar)* to hamper, hinder. **II atascarse** *vr* 1 *(bloquearse)* to become obstructed, become blocked; **se ha atascado el fregadero,** the sink is blocked. 2 *(coche, motor)* to get jammed, get stuck. 3 *fig (estancarse)* to get tangled up, get bogged down.

atasco *nm* 1 *(acción)* obstruction, blockage. 2 *(de tráfico)* traffic jam.

ataúd *nm* coffin.

ataviar I *vtr* 1 *(adornar)* to deck, adorn. 2 *(arreglar)* to dress up. **II ataviarse** *vr (arreglarse)* to dress oneself up, attire oneself.

atávico,-a *adj* atavistic.

atavío *nm* 1 *(adorno)* adornment. 2 *(vestido)* dress, attire.

atavismo *nm* atavism.

ateísmo *nm* atheism.

ateláje *nm* 1 *(caballos)* team of horses. 2 *(guarnición)* harness.

atemorizar I *vtr* to frighten, scare. **II atemorizarse** *vr* to be frightened, be scared.

atemperación *nf* 1 *(moderación)* moderation, restraint, tempering. 2 *(acomodación)* adjustment, accommodation.

atemperar I *vtr* 1 *(moderar)* to moderate, temper. 2 *(adaptar)* to adjust, accommodate **(a,** to). **II atemperarse** *vr* 1 *(moderarse)* to moderate oneself, restrain oneself. 2 *(ajustarse)* to adjust oneself, accommodate oneself.

Atenas *n* Athens.

atenazado,-a I *pp de* **atenazar. II** *adj* 1 gnashed, clenched. 2 *fig* gripped, tormented; **a. por el miedo,** seized by fear.

atenazar *vtr* 1 to gnash, clench. 2 *fig* to torture, torment; **el remordimiento lo atenazaba,** remorse tormented him.

atención I *nf* 1 attention; **al principio no me llamó la a.,** at first I didn't notice anything unusual; **'a., carretera en obras',** 'danger, roadworks ahead'; **llamar la a.,** to attract attention; **llamar la a. a algn,** to tell sb off; **prestar a.,** to pay attention **(a,** to). 2 *(detalle)* nice thought; **en a. a,** as a sign of respect for; **ha sido una a. por su parte,** it was terribly kind of him. 3 **atenciones,** attentions; **tener muchas a. con algn,** to smother sb with attentions. **II** *interj (cuidado)* watch out!

atender I *vtr* 1 *(cliente)* to attend to; *(consejo, advertencia)* to heed, listen to; *(máquina)* to service; *(niño, inválido)* to look after, care for. 2 *(escuchar)* to attend to, pay attention to. **II** *vi* 1 **a. a,** to attend to, pay attention to. 2 **a. por,** to answer to the name of.

atendible *adj* worthy of attention *or* consideration.

atendido,-a I *pp de* **atender. II** *adj SAm Méx* considerate, helpful.

ateneo *nm* athenaeum, *US* atheneum.

atenerse *vr* 1 **a. a,** *(regla)* to abide by; *(promesa)* to stand by. 2 to rely on; **atente a las consecuencias,** bear the consequecnces in mind; **no sabe a que a.,** he doesn't know where he stands.

ateniense *adj & nmf* Athenian.

atentado *nm* attack, assault; **a. contra la vida de algn,** attempt on sb's life. ■ **a. terrorista,** terrorist attack.

atentar I *vi.* **a** *or* **contra,** to commit a crime against; **a. contra la vida de algn,** to make an attempt on sb's life. **II** *vtr (delito)* to attempt, commit.

atento,-a I *pp de* **atender II** *adj* 1 attentive, observant; **estar a. a los riesgos,** to be mindful *or* aware of the risks. 2 *(amable)* polite, thoughful, considerate; **es muy a.,** he is very considerate; *(en carta)* **su atenta (carta),** your esteemed letter. 3 *fml* **a. a,** in view of, considering. ◆ **atentamente** *adv* 1 attentively. 2 *(amablemente)* politely, kindly, thoughtfully; *(en carta)* **le saluda a.,** yours sincerely *or* faithfully.

atenuación *nf* attenuation, lessening; *Jur* extenuation.

atenuante I *adj* attenuating; *Jur (circunstancias)* extenuating. **II** *nm Jur* extenuating circumstance.

atenuar *vtr* 1 to attenuate; *Jur* to extenuate. 2 *(importancia)* to lessen, diminish.

ateo,-a I *adj* atheistic. **II** *nm,f* atheist.

ateperetarse *vr CAm* to get confused, lose one's head.

aterciopeiado,-a *adj* velvet, velvety; *fig* **voz aterciopelada,** sweet voice.

aterido,-a I *pp de* **aterirse II** *adj* stiff with cold, numb.

aterimiento *nm* stiffness with cold, numbness.

aterirse *vr defect* to be stiff with cold, be numb.

aterrada *nf Náut* landfall.

aterrador,-a terrfying, frightful.

aterraje *nm* **1** *Av* landing. **2** *Náut* landfall.

aterramiento *nm* fear, terror.

aterrar[1] **I** *vtr* to terrify, frighten. **II aterrarse** *vr* to be terrified *or* frightened, panic.

aterrar[2] **I** *vtr* **I** (*derribar*) to pull down, demolish. **2** to cover with earth. **II** *vi Av* to land; *Náut* to stand inshore.

aterrizaje *nm Av* landing. ■ **a. forzoso,** forced landing; **a. violento,** crash landing.

aterrizar *vi* **I** *Av* to land. **2** *fig* to show up, arrive.

aterronar I *vtr* to cake, barden. **II aterronarse** *vr* to go lumpy, cake, harden.

aterrorizar *vtr* to terrify; *Mil Pol* to terrorize. **II aterrorizarse** *vr* to be terrified.

atesoramiento *nm* hoarding, accumulation, storing up.

atesorar *vtr* **I** (*acumular*) to hoard, accumulate, store up. **2** *fig* (*cualidades, defectos*) to possess.

atestación *nf* attestation, testimony.

atestado,-a[1] *Jur* affidavit, statement; **atestados,** testimonials.

atestado,-a[2] **I** *pp de* **atestar II** *adj* (*abarrotar*) packed, crammed; **estaba a. gente,** it was full of people.

atestar[1] *vtr Jur* (*testificar*) to testify.

atestar[2] **I** *vtr* (*abarrotar*) to pack, cram, stuff (**de,** with). **II atestarse** *vr* (*de comida*) to stuff oneself.

atestiguación *nf* attestation, testimony.

atestiguar *vtr Jur* (*testificar*) to testify to, bear witness to, give evidence of. **2** *fig* to vouch for.

atetar *vtr* (*animal*) to suckle; (*niño*) to feed.

atezado,-a I *pp de* **atezar. II** *adj* **I** (*por el sol*) tanned. **2** (*negro*) black, blackened.

atezar I *vtr a* (*al sol*) to tan, burn. **2** (*ennegrecer*) to blacken, turn black. **II atezarse** *vr* (*ennegrecerse*) to go black.

atiborrado,-a *adj* **a. de,** full of, stuffed with, packed with.

atiborrar I *vtr* (*abarrotar*) to fill, pack, stuff (**de,** with). **II atiborrarse** *vr fam* (*de comida*) to stuff oneself.

atiburnar *vtr CAm,* **atiburrar** *vtr CAm Col véase* **atiborrar**

ático *nm Arquit* attic; (*vivienda*) attic flat, penthouse.

atiesar *vtr* to stiffen, tighten, stretch taut.

atigrado,-a *adj* (*tigre*) striped; (*gato*) tabby.

atildado,-a I *pp de* **atildar II** *adj*(*elegante*) smart, neat, spruce.

atildamiento *nm* **I** (*esmero*) elegance, tidiness. **2** *fig* (*censura*) censure.

atildar I *vtr* **1** *Tip* to mark with a tilde. **2** *fig* (*asear*) to tidy, clean up. **3** *fig* (*censurar*) to criticize, censure, find fault with. **II atildarse** *vr* (*asearse*) to titivate oneself, spruce oneself up.

atilintar *vtr CAm* to tense, tauten.

atinado,-a I *pp de* **atinar II** *adj* (*corecto*) accurate, correct; (*pertinente*) pertinent; (*persona*) sensible; **una decisión a.,** a wise decisión. ◆ **atinadamente** *adv* correctly, sensibly; **según dijo a.,** as he rightly said.

atinar *vi* (*acertar*) to guess right, be right, do the right thing; **a. a hacer algo,** to succeed in doing sth; **a. al blanco,** to hit the target; **atinó con la solución,** he found the solution.

atingencia *nf Am* connection, relation.

atiparse *vr fam* (*de comida*) to stuff oneself, guzzle.

atípico,-a *adj* atypical.

atiplado,-a I *pp de* **atipiar II** *adj* high-pitched.

atiplar I *vtr* (*agudizar*) to raise the pitch of. **II atiplarse** *vr* (*voz*) to go squeaky.

atipujarse *vr CAm Méx* to stuff oneslf (**de,** with).

atiriciarse *vr Med* to contract jaundice.

atisbadero *nm* peephole; (*atalaya*) lookout.

atisbador,-a I *adj* prying, nosy. **II** *nm,f* observer, snooper, spy.

atisbar I (*observar*) to spy on, observe, watch. **2** *fig* (*vislumbrar*) to make out.

atisbo *nm* **I** (*acción*) spying, watching. **2** *fig* (*indicios*) slight sign, inkling; **no hay el menor a. de esperanza,** there's not the slightest hope.

atizadero *nm* **1** poker. **2** *fig* (*estímulo*) spark, stimulus.

atizador *nm* poker.

atizar I *vtr* (*fuego*) to poke, stoke; (*vela*) to snuff. **II** *fig* (*rebelión*) to stir up; (*pasiones*) to rouse, excite. **III atizarse** *vr fam* (*comer, beber*) to knock back; **se atizó toda una botella de vino,** he knocked back a whole bottle of wine.

atizonar *vtr Bot* to blight.

atlántico,-a I *adj* Atlantic. **II** *nm* **el (océano) A.** the Atlantic (Ocean).

atlas I *adj* **los (montes) A.,** the Atlas Mountains. **II** *nm inv* atlas.

atleta *nmf* athlete.

atlético,-a *adj* athletic.

atletismo *nm* athletics *sing*.

atmósfera *nf* **1** atmosphere. **2** *fig* atmosphere, sphere of influence.

atmosférico,-a *adj* atmospheric, atmospherical.

atoar *vtr* to tow.

atocha *nf Bot* esparto.

atochal *nm Bot* esparto field.

atocinar I *vtr* **1** (*cerdo*) to slice up, make into bacon. **2** *fam fig* (*asesinar*) to do in, carve up. **II atocinarse** *vr fam* **1** (*enfadarse*) to get het up. **2** (*enamorarse*) to fall madly in love.

atol *nm CAm Ven* drink made from maize flour.

atolería *nf Am* atol shop *or* stall.

atolladero *nm* **1** (*lugar fangoso*) morass, quagmire. **2** *fig* (*aprieto*) fix, jam, scrape; **estar en un a.,** to be in a jam; **sacar a algn de un a.,** to get sb out of a fix; **salir del a.,** to get out of a jam.

atollar *vi,* **atollarse** *vr* **1** (*atascarse*) to get stuck in the mud, get bogged down. **2** *fig* (*atrancarse*) to get into a fix *or* scrape.

atolón *nm Geog* atoll.

atolondrado,-a I *pp de* **atolondrar. II** *adj* **1** (*desatinado*) scatterbrained, reckless, silly. **2** (*aturdido*) stunned, bewildered.

atolondramiento *nm* **1** (*desatino*) recklessness, silliness. **2** (*aturdimiento*) confusion, bewilderment.

atolondrar I *vtr* to confuse, stun, bewilder. **II atolondrarse** *vr* to be confused, stunned, bewildered.

atómico,-a *adj* atomic.

atomización *nf* atomization, spraying.

atomizador *nm* atomizer, spray, scent spray.

atomizar *vtr* to atomize, spray.

átomo *nm* **1** *Quím* atom. **2** *fig* (*pizca*) atom, particle, speck; **ni un a. de,** not a trace of.

atonal *adj* atonal.

atónito,-a *adf* amazed, astonished, nonplussed.

átono,-a *adj* atonic, unstressed.

atontado,-a I *pp de* **atontar. II** *adj* **1** (*tonto*) silly, foolish. **2** (*aturdido*) stunned, bewildered, amazed. ◆ **atontadamente** *adv* **1** (*tontamente*) foolishly, recklessly. **2** (*de manera confusa*) in a stunned *or* bewildered way.

atontamiento *nm* bewilderment.

atontar I *vtr (aturdir)* to stun, confuse, bewilder, **II atontarse** *vr (aturdirse)* to be *or* get confused, mixed-up, bewildered.

atorar I *vtr (embarrancar)* to obstruct, block, choke. **II atorarse** *vr (embarrancarse)* to get stuck in the mud.

atormentador,-a I *adj* tormenting. **II** *nm, f (hombre)* tormentor; *(mujer)* tormentress.

atormentar I *vtr* 1 *(torturar)* to torture. 2 *fig (importunar)* to torment, harass; *(tentar) (tentar)* to tantalize. **II atormentarse** *vr (sufrir)* to torment oneself, suffer agonies.

atornillar *vtr* 1 *(enroscar)* to screw on *or* up *or* down *or* together. 2 *Am* to pester, annoy.

atorradero *nm SAm* tramp's resting place.

atorrante *nmf SAm* tramp, *US* bum, *US* hobo.

atortojar *vfr Am véase* **atortolar.**

atortolar I *vtr fam* 1 *(acobardar)* to intimidate, scare. 2 *(aturdir)* to confuse. **II atsortolarse** *vr (enamorarse)* to bill and coo.

atortujar *vtr* to squash, flatten.

atosigador,-a I *adj* 1 *(venenoso)* poisonous. 2 *fig (apremio)* harassing, pressing. **II** *nm, f* 1 *(envenenador)* poisoner. 2 *fig (opresor)* oppressor, tormentor.

atosigamiento *nm* 1 *(envenenamiento)* poisoning. 2 *fig (apremio)* harassment.

atosigar *vtr* 1 *(envenenar)* to poison. 2 *(preocupar)* to worry. 3 *fig (apremiar)* to harass, pester.

atrabancar I *vtr* to rush *or* hurry over. **II atrabancarse** *vr* to get into a jam.

atrabiliario,-a I *adj* bad-tempered, moody. **II** *nm, f* bad-tempered person, moody person.

atrabilis *nf inv fig* bad temper, moodiness.

atracadero *nf Náut* landing place, wharf, berth.

atracador,-a *nm, f (de banco)* (bank) robber; *(en la calle)* attacker, mugger.

atracar I *vtr* 1 *(robar)* to hold up, rob. 2 *fam (de comida)* to stuff, gorge. **II** *vi Náut* to come alongside, tie up. **III atracarse** *vr (de comida)* to stuff oneself, gorge oneself (**de**, on).

atracción *nf* 1 attraction. 2 **atracciones**, attractions, show *sing.* ◼ **parque de a.,** funfair.

atraco *nm* hold-up, robbery. ◼ *Jur* **a. a mano armada,** armed robbery.

atracón *nm* 1 *fam (de comida)* binge, blowout; **pegarse un a.,** to make a pig of oneself. 2 *Am (pelea)* fight, brawl.

atractivo,-a I *adj* attractive, charming, appealing. **II** *nm* attraction, charm, appeal. ◆ **atractivamente** *adv* attractively.

atraer *vtr* 1 *(gen)* to attract; *(imaginación)* to appeal to; *(adhesión)* to win. 2 *(cautivar)* to charm, captivate.

atrafagar *vi*, **atrafagarse** *vr* to bustle about, be busy.

atragantarse *vr* to choke (**con**, on), swallow the wrong way; **a. con un cacahuete,** to choke on a peanut; *fig* **ese chico se me atraganta,** I can't stand that boy.

atraígo *indic pres véase* **atraer.**

atraillar *vtr* 1 *(perro)* to put on a leash. 2 *fig (dominar)* to control.

atraje *pt indef véase* **atraer.**

atramparse *vr* 1 *(caer en la trampa)* to be trapped, fall into a trap. 2 *(conducto)* to get clogged *or* blocked up. 3 *fig (persona)* to get into a fix, be in a scrape.

atrancar I *vtr (puerta)* to bar, bolt. **II** *vi fam (persona)* to stride along; *(en la lectura)* to read hastily. **III atrancarse** *vr (encerrarse)* to lock oneself in.

atrapar *vtr* to seize, capture, catch.

atraque *nm Náut* mooring place, berth; *(de, nave espacial)* link-up.

atrás I *adv* I *(lugar)* at the back, behind; **cuenta a.,** countdown; **estar a.,** to be behind *or* at the back; **ir hacia a.,** to go backwards; **puerta de a.,** back *or* rear door; *fig* **volverse a.,** to change one's mind. 2 *(tiempo)* previously, in the past, ago; **un año a.,** a year ago; **venir de muy a.,** to go *or* date back a long time. **II** *interj* get back!

atrasado,-a I *pp de* **atrasar.** **II** *adj* 1 late, slow; *(pago)* overdue; *(reloj)* slow; **andar a.,** to be slow; *Prensa* **número a.,** back number. 2 *(país)* backward, underdeveloped; *(alumno)* backward, retarded.

atrasar I *vtr* to delay; *(reloj)* to put back. **II** *vi (reloj)* to lose, be slow. **III atrasarse** *vr* 1 to remain *or* stay behind, lag behind; *fig* **a. con un pago,** to get into debt, be in arrears. 2 *(tren)* to be late.

atraso *nm* 1 delay; *(de reloj)* slowness; **llegar con media hora de a.,** to arrive half an hour late. 2 *(de país)* backwardness 3 **atrasos,** *Fin* arrears.

atravesado,-a I *pp de* **atravesar.** **II** *adj* 1 *(persona)* cross-eyed, squinting. 2 *(animal)* mongrel, crossbred. 3 *fig (mal intencionado)* wicked, difficult, bloody-minded; **me tiene a.,** he can't stand me.

atravesar I *vtr* 1 *(cruzar)* to cross, cross over, go across, go over, pass through; *fig* **a. una mala racha,** to go through a bad patch. 2 *(bala, navaja)* to pierce, go through. 3 *(puente)* to cross, span, bridge. 4 *(objeto)* to lay across, put across, put crosswise. **II atravesarse** *vr* 1 *(estar atravesado)* to be across, be in the way. 2 *fig* to interrupt, butt in. 3 *fig (inmiscuirse)* to interfere, meddle. 4 *fig* **a. algn a uno,** not to be able to bear *or* stand sb.

atrayente *adj* attractive.

atreguar *vtr* to agree to a truce (with).

atrenzo *nm Am* difficulty, trouble, conflict.

atreverse *vr* to dare, venture; **a. a hacer algo,** to dare to do sth; **a. con algn,** to be cheeky *or* insolent to sb; **a. con algo,** to take sth on; **¿te atreves?,** are you game?

atrevido,-a I *pp de* **atreverse.** **II** *adj* 1 *(osado)* daring, bold. 2 *(insolente)* insolent, impudent. 3 *(indecoroso)* daring, risqué.

atrevimiento *nm* 1 *(actitud)* daring, audacity. 2 *(insolencia)* insolence, impudence, effrontery.

atribución *nf* 1 *(acción)* attribution. 2 *(poder)* power, authority.

atribuible *adj* attributable.

atribuir *vtr* to attribute, ascribe. **II atribuirse** *vr* to assume.

atribular I *vtr* to afflict, distress, grieve. **II atribularse** *vr* to suffer, be distressed, be grieved.

atributivo,-a *adj* attributive.

atributo *nm* attribute.

atrición *nf Rel* attrition, sorrow.

atril *nm* lectern, bookrest; *Mús* music stand.

atrincheramiento *nm* entrenchment.

atrincherar I *vtr* to entrench, dig a trench. **II atrincherarse** *vr* to entrench.

atrio *nm Hist* atrium, portico; *Arquit* entrance hall, porch.

atrito,-a *adj* contrite.

atrochar *vi* to take a short cut.

atrocidad *nf* 1 *(barbaridad)* atrocity, outrage. 2 *(disparate)* silly remark, foolish thing.

atrofia *nf Med* atrophy.

atrofiar *vtr*, **atrofiarse** *vr* to atrophy.

atronado,-a I *pp de* **atronar.** **II** *adj* rash, thoughtless, reckless.

atronador,-a *adj* thundering, deafening.

atronamiento *nm* 1 *(ruido)* thundering. 2 *(aturdimiento)* daze, stunned state. 3 *fig (confusión)* bewilderment, confusion.

atronar *vtr* 1 *(ensordecer)* to deafen. 2 *(aturdir)* to stun, daze. 3 *fig (confundir)* to bewilder, confuse.

atropar *vtr*, **atroparse** *vr* to group together.

atropellado,-a I *pp de* **atropellar. II** *adj* **1** *(persona)* hasty, impetuous, rash. **2** *(comportamiento)* abrupt, brusque.

atropellador,-a I *adj* rough, inconsiderate. **II** *nm, f* lout.

atropellar I *vtr* **1** to trample underfoot; *Aut* to knock down, run over. **2** *fig* to rush through, hurry over; *(sentimientos)* to outrage, hurt; *(derechos)* to disregard; *(inferior)* to bully, oppress. **II** *vi* **a. por,** *(abrirse camino)* to push one's way through; *fig (abusar)* to ride roughshod over. **III atropellarse** *vr fig* to speak *or* act hastily, rush in.

atropello *nm* **1** accident, collision; *Aut* knocking down, running over. **2** *fig (abuso)* abuse, outrage.

atroz *adj* **1** *(bárbaro)* atrocious, outrageous. **2** *fam (enorme)* enormous, huge, tremendous. ◆ **atrozmente** *adv* **1** atrociously, outrageously. **2** *fam* dreadfully, tremendously.

ATS *nmf Med abr de* **ayudante técnico sanitario.**

atta. *abr de* **atenta.**

atto. *abr de* **atento.**

atuendo *nm* dress, attire.

atufar I *vtr fig (irritar)* to vex, irritate. **II** *vi (oler mal)* to stink. **III atufarse** *vr* **1** to be overcome; **se atufó por los gases,** he was overcome by the fumes. **2** *(vino)* to turn sour. **3** *fig (enfadarse)* to get angry *or* annoyed.

atufo *nm* anger, annoyance.

atujar *vtr*, **atular** *vtr CAm (perros)* to set **(a,** on).

atún *nm (pez)* tunny, tuna.

atunero,-a I *adj* tuna. **II** *nm* tuna *or* tunny fisherman.

aturdido,-a I *pp de* **aturdir. II** *adj* **1** *(confundido)* stunned, dazed. **2** *(atolondrado)* harebrained, reckless.

aturdimiento *nm* **1** *(confusión)* confusion, bewilderment. **2** *(atolondramiento)* thoughtlessness, recklessness.

aturdir I *vtr* **1** *(por un golpe)* to stun, daze; *(por un ruido)* to deafen; *(por una droga)* to stupefy. **2** *fig (atolondrar)* to stun, dumbfound; *(confundir)* to be wilder, confuse. **II aturdirse** *vr* **1** to be stunned. **2** *fig (atolondrarse)* to become confused *or* bewildered.

aturrado,-a *adj CAm* **1** *(tullido)* crippled; *(entumido)* numb, stiff. **2** *(arrugado)* creased; wrinkled.

aturrullar I *vtr (aturdir)* to confuse, bewilder. **II aturrullarse** *(aturdirse)* to get confused *or* bewildered.

atusar I *vtr (pelo) (cortar)* to trim; *(peinar)* to comb, smooth down. **II atusarse** *vr* to overdress.

atuve *pt indef véase* **atenerse.**

auca *nf Orn* wild goose.

audacia *nf* audacity, boldness, daring.

audaz *adj* audacious, bold, daring.

audible *adj* audible.

audición *nf* **1** *(acción)* hearing; *Rad TV* reception. **2** *Teat (prueba)* audition; **le hicieron una a.,** they gave him an audition. **3** *Mús (concierto)* concert.

audiencia *nf* **1** *(recepción)* audience, hearing; *(entrevista)* formal interview. **2** *Jur (tribunal)* high court. **3** *(público)* audience.

audífono *nm* hearing aid, deaf aid.

audiovisual *adj* audio-visual.

auditar *vtr* to audit.

auditivo,-a I *adj* auditory; ear. **II** *nm (auricular)* earpiece, receiver.

auditor *nm* **1** *Fin* auditor. **2** *Mil* legal adviser.

auditoría *nf* **1** *(proceso)* audit, auditing. **2** *(empleo)* auditorship.

auditorio *nm* **1** *(público)* audience. **2** *(sala)* auditorium, hall.

auge *nm* **1** *(punto culminante)* peak, summit; *Com* boom, upsurge, upturn; *fig* **estar en a.,** to be thriving *or* booming. **2** *Astron* apogee.

auguración *nf* augury.

augural *adj* augural.

augurar *vtr* to augur.

augusto,-a *adj* august, magnificent, majestic.

aula *nf Educ* classroom; *Univ* lecture room.

aulaga *nf Bot* gorse, furze.

aullador,-a *adj* howling, yelling.

aullar *vtr* to howl, yell.

aullido *nm*, **aúllo** *nm* howl, yell.

aumentador,-a I *adj* augmenting, increasing. **II** *nm Elec* booster.

aumentar I *vtr* to augment, increase, add to; *(precios)* to put up; *(producción)* to step up; *Fot* to enlarge; *Opt* to magnify; *Rad (sanido)* to amplify. **II aumentarse** *vr* to increase, be on the increase; *(precios)* to go up, rise; *(valor)* to appreciate.

aumentativo,-a *adj* augmentative.

aumento *nm* increase, growth; *Fot* enlargement; *Ópt* magnification; *Rad* amplification; **a. de precios,** rise in prices; **ir en a.,** to be on the increase.

aun *adv* **1** even; **a. así,** even so, even then; **a. cuando,** even though; **a. más,** even more.

aún *adv* still, yet; **a. está aquí,** he's still here; **ella no ha venido a.,** she hasn't come yet.

aunar I *vtr* to unite, join, combine. **II aunarse** *vr* to unite, combine.

aunque *conj* although, though; *(enfático)* even if, even though; **a. no vengas,** even if you don't come; **es severo a. justo,** he's strict but fair.

aúpa *interj* up!, get up!

aupar *vtr* **1** *(levantar)* to help up. **2** *fig (alabar)* to praise.

aura *nf* **1** *lit (brisa)* gentle breeze. **2** *fig (aplauso)* applause, acclamation. **3** *(halo)* aura.

áureo,-a *adj* golden.

aureola *nf* aureole, halo.

aurícula *nf* auricle.

auricular I *adj* auricular, of the ear. **II** *nm* **1** *(dedo)* little finger. **2** *Tel* earpiece, receiver. **3** **auriculares,** earphones, headphones.

auriense I *adj* of *or* from Orense. **II** *nmf* native *or* inhabitant of Orense.

aurora *nf* daybreak, dawn. ■ **a. borealis,** aurora borealis, northern lights.

auscultación *nf Med* sounding, auscultation.

auscultar *vtr Med* to sound (with a stethoscope).

ausencia *nf* absence.

ausentarse *vr* **1** *(faltar)* to absent oneself. **2** *(irse)* to disappear, go missing.

ausente I *adj* **1** absent. **2** *(distraído)* lost in thought. **II** *nmf* **1** absentee. **2** *Jur* missing person.

ausentismo *nm* absenteeism.

auspicio *nm* auspice.

austeridad *nf* **1** *(sobriedad)* austerity. **2** *(severidad)* severity.

austero,-a *adj* **1** *(sobrio)* austere. **2** *(severo)* severe, stern.

austral *adj* south, southern.

Australia *n* Australia.

australiano,-a *adj & nm, f* Australian.

Austria *n* Austria.

austríaco,-a *adj & nm, f* Austrian.

austro *nm Meteor* south wind.

autarquía *nf Econ* autarky.

autenticación *nf* authentication; *(legalización)* legalization.

autenticar *vtr* to authenticate; (*legalizar*) to authorize, legalize.

autenticidad *nf* authenticity.

auténtico,-a I *adj* authentic, genuine. **II** *nf* (*certificado*) certificate; (*copia legalizada*) certified copy.

autentificar *vtr* to authenticate.

autillo *nm Orn* scops owl.

autismo *nm* autism.

autista *nmf* autistic person.

autístico,-a *adj* autistic.

auto¹ *nm Aut* car.

auto² *nm Jur* decree, writ; (*pleito*) **autos,** papers, documents; *fam* **estar en autos,** to be in the know.

autoadhesivo,-a *adj* self-adhesive.

autoanálisis *nm* self-analysis.

autobiografía *nf* autobiography.

autobiográfico,-a *adj* autobiographical.

autobomba *nf* fire engine.

autobombearse *vr fam* to blow one's own trumpet.

autobombo *nm fam* self-praise, blowing one's own trumpet.

autobús *nm* bus.

autocamión *nm Aut* lorry.

autocar *nm Aut* coach.

autociclo *nm Aut* motorcycle.

autoclave *nf* **1** *Med* autoclave, sterilizer. **2** *Culin* pressure cooker.

autocopista *nf* stencilling machine.

autocracia *nf Pol* autocracy.

autocrático,-a *adj Pol* autocratic.

autocrítica *nf* self-criticism.

autóctono,-a *adj* indigenous, autochthonous.

autodefensa *nf* self-defence, *US* self-defense.

autodidacto,-a I *adj* self-taught. **II** *nm, f* self-taught person.

autodisciplina *nf* self-discipline.

autódromo *nm* motor racing track.

autoescuela *nf Aut Educ* driving school, school of motoring.

autogiro *nm Av* autogyro, helicopter.

autogobierno *nm Pol* self-government.

autógrafo,-a I *adj* autographic. **II** *nm* **autograph.**

autohipnosis *nf* self-hypnosis.

autómata *nm* automaton.

automaticidad *nf* automaticity.

automático,-a *adj* automatic.

automatismo *nm* automatism.

automatización *nf* automation.

automatizar *vtr* to automate.

automotor,-a I *adj* self-propelled. **II** *nm Ferroc* diesel train.

automóvil *nm Aut* car.

automovilismo *nm Aut* motoring.

automovilista *nmf Aut* motorist.

automovilístico,-a *adj Aut* car; **accidente a.,** car accident.

autonomía *nf* autonomy, home rule.

autonómico,-a *adj* autonomous, self-governing.

autónomo,-a *adj* autonomous, free.

autopista *nf Aut* motorway.

autopsia *nf* **1** *Med* autopsy, post mortem. **2** *fig* critical dissection.

autor,-a *nm, f* (*gen*) writer; (*hombre*) author; (*mujer*) authoress; *Teat* manager; (*de crimen*) perpetrator.

autoridad *nf* authority.

autoritario,-a *adj* authoritarian.

autoritarismo *nm* authoritarianism.

autoritativo,-a *adj* authoritative.

autorizable *adj* authorizable.

autorización *nf* authorization.

autorizado,-a I *pp de* **autorizar. II** *adj* authoritative, official.

autorizar *vtr* **1** to authorize; *Jur* to legaliza. **2** (*aprobar*) to approve, give authority to.

autorretrato *nm* self-portrait.

autoservicio *nm* **1** (*restaurante*) self-service restaurant. **2** (*tienda*) supermarket.

autostop *nm* hitch-hiking; **hacer a.,** to hitch-hike.

autostopista *nmf* hitch-hiker.

autosuficiencia *nf* self-sufficiency.

autosuficiente *adj* self-sufficient.

autosugestión *nf* autosuggestion.

auxiliador,-a I *adj* helping. **II** *nm, f* helper.

auxiliar I *adj & nmf* auxiliary, assistant. **II** *vtr* to help, assist; (*país*) to bring aid to; (*moribundo*) to attend.

auxilio *nm* help, aid, assistance, relief. ▪ **primeros auxilios,** first aid *sing*.

Av., Avda. *abr de* **Avenida,** Avenue, Ave.

a/v *abr de* **a vista,** at *or* on sight.

aval *nm Com Fin* endorsement, guarantee.

avalancha *nf* avalanche.

avalar *vtr Com* to guarantee, endorse.

avalista *nmf Com* guarantor.

avalorar *vtr* **1** (*evaluar*) to value, assess, estimate. **2** (*animar*) to encourage.

avaluación *nf* valuation.

avaluar *vtr* to value, assess.

avance *nm* **1** (*acción*) advance. **2** *Fin* advance payment; *Com* (*balance*) balancing; (*presupuesto*) estimate. **3** *Cin* trailer. ▪ *TV* **a. informativo,** news preview, *US* news brief.

avante *adv Naút* ahead, forward.

avanzada *nf Mil* advance guard.

avanzado,-a I *pp de* **avanzar. II** *adj* advanced; **de avanzada edad,** advanced in years.

avanzar I *vtr* to advance, move forward; *Fin* (*dinero*) to advance; *Mil etc* to promote; (*propuesta*) to put forward. **II** *vi & avanzarse vr* **1** to advance, go forward. **2** (*noche, invierno*) to draw in.

avanzo *nm Fin Com* (*cómputos*) balancing; (*presupuesto*) estimate.

avaricia *nf* avarice, meanness, miserliness; *fam* **con a.,** extremely; **es pelma con a.,** he's terribly boring.

avariento,-a *adj* avaricious, mean, miserly.

avaro,-a I *adj* avaricious, mean, miserly. **II** *nm, f* miser.

avasallador,-a *adj* overwhelming.

avasallamiento *nm* subjection, subjugation, domination.

avasallar I *vtr* to subdue, subject. **II** **avasallarse** *vr* to yield, accept domination.

avatar *nm* **1** change, transformation. **2** **avatares,** ups and downs.

ave *nf* bird; *fig* **es un a. nocturna,** he's a night-bird. ▪ **a. de rapiña,** bird of prey; **aves de corral,** poultry.

avecinar I *vtr* to bring close *or* up to. **II** **avecinarse** *vr* to approach, come near.

avecindarse *vr* to settle, take up residence.

avefría *nf Orn* lapwing, common plover.

avejentarse *vr* to age (prematurely).

avejigar *vi*, **avejigarse** *vr* to blister.

avellana *nf Bot* hazelnut.

avellanal *nm,* **avellanedo** *nm* hazel wood, hazel plantation.

avellano *nm Bot* hazelnut tree; *(madera)* hazel wood.

avemaría *nf Rel* Ave Maria, Hail Mary; *fam* **en un a.,** in a jiffy; *fam* **saber algo como el a.,** to know sth backwards.

avena *nf Agr Bot* oats *pl.*

avenado,-a I *pp de* **avenar. II** *adj* half-crazy, with a streak of madness.

avenal *nm Agr* oatfield.

avenamiento *nm Agr* draining, drainage.

avenar *vtr Agr* to drain.

avendré *indic fut de* **avenir.**

avenencia *nf* agreement, compromise; *Com* deal.

avengo *indic pres de* **avenir.**

avenida *nf* 1 *(calle)* avenue. 2 *(de río)* flood, spate. 3 *(reunión)* gathering, meeting.

avenido,-a I *pp de* **avenir. II** *adj* **bien a.,** in agreement, on good terms; **mal a.,** in disagreement, on bad terms.

avenimiento *nm* agreement, compromise; *(concilio)* harmony, understanding.

avenir I *vtr* to reconcile, harmonize. **II** *vi* to happen. **III avenirse** *vr* to agree, be in agreement; to harmonize, be on good terms; **a. a hacer algo,** to agree to do sth; **a. con algo,** to come to terms with sth.

aventador,-a I *adj* winnowing. **II** *nm,f* winnower. **III** *nf* winnowing machine.

aventajado,-a I *pp de* **aventajar. II** *adj* 1 *(ventajoso)* advantageous, favourable, *US* favorable. 2 *(sobresaliente)* outstanding, exceptional; *(en cabeza)* in the lead.

aventajar *vtr* 1 to lead, be ahead *or* in front of; *(llegar aventajado)* to come first, come ahead of. 2 *(superar)* to surpass, outdo; **nadie le aventaja en compañerismo,** nobody beats him for team spirit.

aventamiento *nm Agr* winnowing.

aventar *vtr* 1 *Agr* to winnow. 2 *(el viento)* to blow away; *(el fuego)* to blow (on), fan; **a. las cenizas,** to cast ashes to the wind.

aventura *nf* 1 adventure; **novela de aventuras,** adventure novel. 2 *(riesgo)* risk, danger. 3 *(relación amorosa)* (love) affair.

aventurado,-a I *pp de* **aventurar. II** *adj* *(arriesgado)* risky, dangerous; **no sería demasiado a. afirmar que ...,** it would not be going too far to state that ... .

aventurar I *vtr* 1 to risk, put in danger. 2 **a. una opinión,** to hazard an opinion. **II aventurarse** *vr* to venture, dare.

aventurero,-a I *adj* adventurous; **de espíritu a.,** venturesome. **II** *nm,* *f (hombre)* adventurer; *(mujer)* adventuress.

avergonzado,-a I *pp de* **avergonzar. II** *adj* ashamed, embarrassed.

avergonzar I *vtr* to shame, put to shame; *(turbar)* to embarrass. **II avergonzarse** *vr* to be ashamed (**de**, of), be embarrassed.

avería *nf* 1 *Com Náut (daño)* damage. 2 *Téc (desperfecto)* failure; malfunction; **el viento ocasionó una a. en el transformador,** the wind damaged the transformer; **en caso de a.,** in case of breakdown. 3 *Aut* breakdown; **tuvimos una a.,** we had a breakdown in the car.

averiado,-a I *pp de* **averiar. II** *adj* 1 faulty; **está a.,** it's out of order, it's not working, something is wrong with it. 2 *Aut* broken down.

averiar I *vtr* 1 *(dañar)* to damage, spoil. 2 *Téc (estropear)* to cause to malfunction. 3 *Aut* to cause a breakdown. **II averiarse** *vr* 1 *(dañarse)* to get damaged. 2 *(estropearse)* to malfunction, go wrong, fail. 3 *Aut* to break down.

averiguable *adj* verifiable.

averiguación *nf* investigation, inquiry.

averiguar I *vtr* to investigate, inquire into, find out about, ascertain; **averigua su número de teléfono,** find out his phone number. **II** *vi CAm Méx (discutir)* to argue.

averno *nm Lit* Hades, the nether regions *pl.*

averroísmo *nm Fil* Averroism.

aversión *nf* aversion, loathing; **sentir a. por,** to loath.

avestruz *nm Orn* ostrich.

avetorillo *nm Orn* little bittern.

avetoro *nm Orn* bittern.

avezado,-a I *pp de* **avezar. II** *adj (acostumbrado)* used.

avezar I *vtr (acostumbrar)* to accustom, get used. **II avezarse** *vr (acostumbrarse)* to become accustomed, get used (**a**, to).

aviación *nf* 1 aviation. ■ **accidente de a.,** air crash; **a. civil,** civil aviation. 2 *Mil* air force.

aviado,-a I *pp de* **aviar. II** *adj* 1 *(preparado)* ready. 2 *fam* **¡pues sí que estamos aviados!,** that's all we needed!

aviador,-a[1] *nm,f* aviator, flier; *Mil (piloto)* air force pilot.

aviador,-a[2] *nm,f Am* 1 financier of mining enterprises. 2 one who lends money or equipment to cattlemen, miners or farmers.

aviar *vtr* 1 *(preparar)* to prepare, get ready. 2 *(arreglar)* to tidy; *(ordenar)* to put in order. 3 *(proveer)* to supply, equip. 4 *(apresurar)* to hurry up; **¡avía!,** hurry up! 5 *Am (dinero)* to lend money to; *(efectos)* to provide with equipment.

avícola *adj* poultry.

avicultor,-a *nm,f* poultry keeper.

avicultura *nf* aviculture; *(de aves de corral)* poultry keeping.

avidez *nf* avidity, eagerness.

ávido,-a *adj* avid, eager; **á. de aventuras,** thirsty for adventures.

avieso,-a *adj* evil, wicked, depraved.

avilés,-esa I *adj* of *or* from Avila. **II** *nm, f* native *or* inhabitant of Avila.

avinagrado,-a I *pp de* **avinagrar. II** *adj* vinegary, sour; *fig* sour; **carácter a.,** sour character.

avinagrar I *vtr* to turn sour, embitter. **II avinagrarse** *vr* to turn sour; *fig (carácter)* to become sour *or* bitter.

avío *nm* 1 preparation, tidying; **el a. de la casa,** household chores. 2 *(de labrador, de pastor)* provisions. 3 **avíos,** *(utensilios)* gear *sing,* tackle *sing,* equipment *sing.* 4 *Am (préstamo)* loan of money or equipment.

avión[1] *nm Orn* martin.

avión[2] *nm Av* I aeroplane, *US* airplane, plane, aircraft; *(en carta)* **por a.,** airmail; **viajar en a.,** to fly, go by plane. ■ **a, a reacción,** jet (plane). 2 *Am (cometa)* kite.

avioneta *nf Av* light aircraft *or* plane.

avisado,-a I *pp de* **avisar. II** *adj* 1 warned; **estás a.,** you've been warned. 2 *(sagaz)* shrewd; *(prudente)* wise, prudent.

avisador,-a I *adj* warning. **II** *nm* 1 *Téc (alarma)* warning device, bell. 2 *(persona)* messenger.

avisar *vtr* 1 *(informar)* to inform, notify, announce; **avísame cuando hayas acabado,** let me know when you finish; **a. con un mes de antelación,** to give a month's notice. 2 *(advertir)* to warn; **avisamos a los conductores que ...,** we warn motorists that ...; **ya te avisé,** I warned you. 3 *(mandar llamar)* to notify; **'avisamos grúa',** 'cars will be towed away'; **a. a la policía,** to notify the police; **a. al médico,** to send for the doctor.

aviso *nm* 1 notice; *(advertencia)* warning; *(nota)* note; **hasta nuevo a.,** until further notice; **mandar a. de que,** to inform that; **sin previo a.,** without notice. 2 **andar** *or* **estar sobre a.,** to be on the alert, keep one's eyes open; **estar sobre a.,** *(estar enterado)* to know what's going on, be in it; *(ya haber avisado)* to have been warned; **poner sobre**

a., to forewarn; **ya ma han paesto sobre a.**, I've been told (about it). **3** *Am (anuncio)* advertisement, advert.

avispa *nf Ent* wasp.

avispado,-a I *pp de* **avispar. II** *adj fam* quickwitted, quick on the uptake.

avispar *vtr*, **avisparse** *vr fam* to quicken *or* smarten up.

avispero *nm* **1** *Ent (conjunto de avispas)* swarm of wasps. **2** *Ent (nido)* wasps' nest. **3** *fig (atolladero)* tight spot, mess. **4** *Med* carbuncle.

avistar *vtr* to see, sight.

avitaminosis *nf Med* avitaminosis, vitamin deficiency.

avituallamiento *nm* provisioning.

avituallar *vtr* to provision, supply with food.

avivado,-a I *pp de* **avivar. II** *adj fig* enlivened, quickened; *(pasión, enfado)* stirred, aroused.

avivar I *vtr* **1** *(fuego)* to stoke (up); *(color, luz)* to brighten; *(pasión, dolor)* to intensify. **2** *fig (anhelos, deseos)* to enliven; *(paso)* to quicken. **II** *vi fam* **¡aviva!**, hurry up!, move on! **III** **avivarse** *vr* to become brighter *or* livelier.

avizor,-a *adj* **estar ojo a.**, to be on the alert *or* on the lookout.

avizorar *vtr* to spy on, watch.

avocatero *nm Am* avocado pear tree.

avutarda *nf Orn* great bustard.

axial *adj*, **axil** *adj* axial.

axila *nf* **1** *Anat* armpit, axilla. **2** *Bot* axil.

axilar *adj* axillar, axillary.

axioma *nm* axiom.

axiomático,-a *adj* axiomatic.

ay I *interj (dolor)* ouch!; *(queja)* **¡ay de mí!**, poor me!; *(amenaza)* **¡ay de ti como te coja!**, I'll give it to you if I catch you!; *(sobresalto)* **¡ay! ¡qué susto!**, God! what a fright! **II** *nm (suspiro, queja)* aah!

aya *nf arc* **1** *(ama de cría)* wet nurse. **2** *(niñera)* nanny. **3** *(institutriz)* governess.

ayayay *nm Am* peasant song.

ayer I *adv* **1** yesterday; **antes de a.**, the day before yesterday; **a. por la mañana/por la tarde**, yesterday morning/afternoon; **a. por la noche**, last night; **parece que fue a.**, apparently it was yesterday. **2** *(en tiempo pasado)* before, formerly. **II** *nm* past; **los recuerdos del a.**, memories from the past.

ayo *nm arc* private tutor.

ayocote *nm Am* kidney bean.

ayote *nm Bot CAm (fruto)* gourd, pumpkin.

ayotera *nf Bot (planta)* gourd, pumpkin.

ayuda *nf* **1** help, assistance; **con la a. de un bastón**, with the aid of a walking stick; **ir en a. de algn**, to come to sb's assistance; **prestar a.**, to help. ■ **a. de cámara**, valet. **2** *Med (lavativa)* enema.

ayudante *nmf* assistant. ■ *Cin Teat* **a. de dirección**, production assistant; *Med* **a. técnico-sanitario**, nurse; *Mil* adjutant.

ayudantía *nf* assistantship; *Mil* adjutancy.

ayudar I *vtr* to help, assist, aid; **¿en qué puedo ayudarle?**, (how) can I help you? **II** **ayudarse** *vr (hacer uso de, apoyarse)* to use, make use of; *(unos a otros)* to help.

ayunar *vi* to fast.

ayunas *nfpl* **1** *(sin comer)* **en a.**, without having eaten breakfast; **hay que tomarlo en a.**, you have to take it on an empty stomach. **2** *fig* in the dark; **quedarse en a.**, not to understand a thing.

ayuno *nm* fasting, fast; **guardar a.**, to fast.

ayuntamiento *nm* **1** *(corporación)* town council, city council. **2** *(edificio)* town hall, city hall. **3** *fml* **a. carnal**, sexual intercourse.

azabache *nm Min* jet; *fig* **pelo negro como el a.**, jet black hair, raven hair.

azada *nf Agr* hoe.

azadón *nm Agr* (wide) hoe.

azafata *nf* **1** *(de avión)* air hostess *or* stewardess. **2** *(de congresos, exposiciones)* hostess, stewardess.

azafrán *nm Bot Culin* saffron.

azafranado,-a *adj* saffron-coloured, *US* saffron-colored.

azahar *nm Bot. (del naranjo)* orange blossom; *(del limonero)* lemon blossom. ■ **auga de a.**, orange-flower water.

azalea *nf Bot* azalea.

azar *nm* **1** chance; **al a.**, at random; **por puro a.**, by pure chance. ■ **juegos de a.**, games of chance. **2** *(desgracia)* misfortune, accident; **los azares de la vida**, the ups and downs of life.

azarado,-a I *pp de* **azarar. II** *adj* embarrassed.

azaramiento *nm* embarrassment.

azarar I *vtr* to embarrass. **II** **azararse** *vr* to be embarrassed.

azarearse *vr Am véase* **azararse.**

azaroso,-a *adj* hazardous, dangerous, risky.

ázimo,-a *adj* **pan á.**, unleavened bread.

ázoe *nm arc Quím* nitrogen.

azogado,-a I *pp de* **azogar. II** *adj* **1** silvered, quicksilvered. **2** *Med* suffering from mercurialism. **3** *fig (inquieto)* restless.

azogar *vtr* to (coat with) quicksilver; *(espejos)* to silver.

azogue *nm* mercury, quicksilver.

azor *nm Orn* goshawk.

azorado,-a I *pp de* **azorar. II** *adj* embarrassed.

azoramiento *nm* embarrassment.

azorar I *vtr* to embarrass. **II** **azorarse** *vr* to be embarrassed.

azorencarse *vr CAm* to get confused *or* mixedup.

Azores *nfpl* **las (Islas) A.**, the Azores.

azoro *nm* **1** *Am (azoramiento)* embarrassment. **2** *CAm (fantasma)* ghost, spirit.

azotado,-a I *pp de* **azotar. II** *adj (con látigo)* whipped, flogged. **2** *fig* whipped, lashed.

azotaina *nf fam* spanking, smacking; **darle una a. a un niño**, to spank a child.

azotar I *vtr* **1** *(con látigo)* to whip, flog. **2** *(golpear)* to beat, beat down on. **3** *fig (peste, hambre)* to scourge. **II** **azotarse** *vr Am (vagabundear)* to loaf around.

azotazo *nm fam* smack.

azote *nm* **1** *(vara)* whip, scourge. **2** *(golpe)* lash, stroke (of the whip); **diez azotes**, ten lashes. **3** *fam* smacking, spanking. **4** *fig* scourge.

azotea *nf* flat roof; *fam* **estar mal de la a.**, to have a screw loose, not be right in the head.

azotera *nf SAm* ≈ cat-o'nine-tails *sing.*

azteca *adj & nmf* Aztec.

azúcar *nm & f* sugar. ■ **a. blanco**, refined sugar; **a. cande**, **a. candi**, sugar candy; **a. de caña**, cane sugar; **a. de lustre**, icing sugar; **a. moreno**, **a. negro**, brown sugar; **terrón de a.**, lump of sugar.

azucarado,-a I *pp de* **azucarar. II** *adj* **1** *(con azúcar)* sugared, sweetened. **2** *(como el azúcar)* sugar-like; *(dulce)* sweet. **3** *fig* sugary.

azucarar I *vtr* to sugar, put sugar in, sweeten. **II** **azucararse** *vr Am* to crystallize.

azucarero,-a I *adj* sugar; **la industria azucarera**, the sugar industry. **II** *nm & f* sugar bowl. **III** *nf* sugar factory.

azucarillo *nm Culin* lemon candy.

azucena *nf Bot* white lily.

azuela *nf* adze.

azufaifa *nf Bot (fruto)* jujube.

azufaifo *nm Bot (árbol)* jujube tree.

azufrado,-a I *pp de* **azufrar. II** *adj* sulphured, *US* sulfured, sulphurated, *US* sulfurated.

azufrar *vtr Quím* to sulphur, *US* sulfur, sulphurate, *US* sulfurate.

azufre *nm Quím* sulphur, *US* sulfur.

azufroso,-a *adj Quím* sulphurous, *US* sulfurous.

azul *adj & nm* blue. ■ **a. celeste**, light blue; **a. eléctrico**, electric blue; **a. marino**, navy blue; **a. turquesa**, turquoise; **príncipe a.**, Prince Charming; **sangre a.**, blue blood.

azulado,-a I *pp de* **azular II** *adj* blue,bluish.

azular *vtr* to blue.

azulejo¹ *nm Orn* bluebird.

azulejo² *nm (baldosín)* (glazed) tile.

azulete *nm (para la ropa)* blue; **dar a.**, to blue.

azulgrana *adj inv 1 (colores)* blue and scarlet. **2** *Dep* related to Barcelona Football Club.

azulino,-a *adj* bluish.

azuzar *vtr* **1 a. los perros a algn,** to set the dogs on sb. **2** *fam* to egg on, urge.

B

B, b *nf (la letra)* B, b.

baba *nf (de niño)* dribble; *(de adulto)* saliva, spittle; *(de animal)* saliva; *(de caracol)* slime; *fig* **caérsele a uno la b.,** to be delighted; *fig* **se le cae la b. con su nieto,** he dotes on his grandson; *fam* **tener muy mala b.,** to have a nasty streak.

babear *vi* **1** *(niño)* to dribble; *(adulto, animal)* to slobber. **2** *fig* to drool.

babel *nm & f* bedlam; **la casa está hecha una b.,** the house is upside down; **la reunión se convirtió en un verdadero b.,** the meeting became sheer bedlam.

babero *nm* bib.

Babja *n fig* **estar en B.,** to be daydreaming, have one's head in the clouds.

babieca I *adj* silly, simple-minded. **II** *nmf* fool, simpleton.

babilla *nf Zool* stifle.

babilonio,-a *adj & nm, Hist* Babylonian.

bable *nm Ling* Asturian dialect.

babor *nm Náut* port, port side, larboard; **a b.,** to port, on the port side; **¡tierra a b.!,** land to port!

babosa *nf Zool* slug.

babosear *vtr* to slobber over, drool over.

baboseo *nm* slobbering, drooling.

baboso,-a *adj* **1** *(niño)* dribbly; *(adulto)* slobbery. **2** *fam fig* sloppy.

babucha *nf* slipper.

babuino *nm Zool* baboon.

baca *nf Aut* roof rack.

bacalao *nm (pez)* cod; *fam* **cortar el b.,** to be the boss; *fam* **¡te conozco b.!,** you can't fool me.

bacanal *nf* bacchanalia, orgy.

bacará *nm,* **bacarrá** *nm Naipes* baccarat.

bache *nm* **1** *(en la carretera)* pot hole. **2** *Av* air pocket. **3** *fig* bad patch; **pasar un b.,** to go through a bad patch; **salir del b.,** to recover from a bad patch. **4** *Econ* slump, depression.

bachiller I *nmf* pupil who has obtained the **bachillerato. II** *nm fam* ≈ General Certificate of Education *OR* level, *US* high school degree.

bachillerato *nm* General Certificate of Education *OR* level, *US* high school degree.

bacía *nf* basin; *(de afeitar)* shaving bowl.

bacilar *adj Biol* bacillary.

bacilo *nm Biol* bacillus, germ.

bacón bacon *nm* bacon.

bacteria *nf Biol* bacterium, germ; **bacterias**, bacteria.

bactericida *Biol* **I** *adj* bactericidal, germ-killing. **II** *nm* bactericide, germicide.

bacteriología *nf Biol* bacteriology.

bacteriológico,-a *adj Biol* bacteriological.

bacteriólogo,-a *nm, f Biol* bacteriologist.

báculo *nm* **1** *(bastón)* walking stick. **2** *(de obispo)* crosier. **3** *fig* support, comfort; **ella fue el b. de su vejez,** she was the staff of his old age.

badajo *nm* clapper.

badajocense I *adj* of or from Badajoz. **II** *nmf* native or inhabitant of Badajoz.

badajoceño,-a *adj & nm, f véase* **badajocense**

badana *nf* sheepskin; *fig* **zurrarle la b. a algn,** to give sb a good hiding.

badén *nm* **1** *(cauce)* paved ford. **2** *(zanja)* gully; *Aut* uneven road.

badil *nm,* **badila** *nf (pala)* fire shovel; *(atizador)* poker.

bádminton *nm Dep* badminton.

baf(f)le *nm* loudspeaker.

bagaje *nm* **1** *Mil* baggage. **2** *fig* experience, background; **b. intelectual,** intellectual background.

bagatela *nf (baratija)* knick-knack; *fig* trifle; **no te enlades por una b.,** don't get worked up over nothing.

Bagdad *n* Baghdad.

bagre *nm (pez)* catfish.

bah *interj* bah!

Bahamas *npl* **las (Islas) B.,** the Bahamas.

bahameño,-a *adj & nm, f* Bahamian.

bahía *nf Geog* bay; **B. de Hudson,** Hudson Bay.

Bahrein *n* Bahrain.

bailable *adj* dance, for dancing; **música b.,** dance music, music that one can dance to.

bailador,-a *nm, f (bailarín)* dancer; *(de flamenco)* Spanish folk dancer.

bailar I *vtr* to dance; **b. la polca,** to dance the polka. **II** *vi* I to dance; **nadie la saca a b.,** no one asks her to dance; **no me gusta b. agarrado,** I don't like dancing cheek to cheek; *fig* **b. al son que le tocan,** to toe the line; *fig* **le bailaban los ojos de alegría,** her eyes sparkled with joy; *fam* **otro que tal baila,** they're two of a kind; *fam* **¡que me quiten lo baila(d)o!,** but at least I had a good time!; *fam* **siempre me toca b. con la más fea,** I always get the short end of the stick. **2** *(quedar grande)* to be too big; **esta falda me b.,** this skirt is loose on me. **3** *(moverse)* to wobble; **esta mesa b.,** this table's wobbly.

bailarín-ina I *adj* dancing. **II** *nm, f* dancer; *(clásico)* ballet dancer.

baile *nm* **1** *(danza)* dance; **la sardana es un b. catalán,** the sardana is a Catalan dance; **¿me concede usted este b.?,** may I have the pleasure of this dance? ■ **b. clásico,** ballet. **2** *(fiesta popular)* dance, *(de etiqueta)* ball; **b. de disfraces,** masked ball, fancy dress ball; **b. de gala,** gala ball. **3** *Med* **b. de San Vito,** Saint Vitus's dance.

bailón,-ona *fam* **I** *adj* fond of dancing. **II** *nm, f* bopper.

bailongo *nm fam* low-class dance, hop.

bailotear *vi fam* to dance, jig about.

bailoteo *nm fam* dancing, jigging about.

baja *nf* **11** *(disminución)* drop, fall; **estar en b.,** to be dropping *or* falling; *Fin* **jugar a la b.,** to bear. **2** *Mil* loss, casualty; **bajas de guerra,** war losses; **dar a un soldado de b.,** to discharge a soldier; **ser b.,** to be reported missing. **3** *(cese)* **estar dado de b.,** to be on sick leave; **dar de b. a algn,** *(despedir) (de una empresa)* to lay sb off; *(de un club, de una sociedad)* to take away sb's membership; *(de un colegio profesional)* to strike sb off; **darse de b.,** *(por enfermedad)* to take sick leave; *(de un club)* to resign (**de,** from), drop out (**de,** of); *(en una suscripción)* to cancel.

bajada *nf* **1** *(descenso)* descent; *(disminución)* decrease, diminish, reduction. **2** *(camino por donde se baja)* way down, slope. **3** *(taxi)* **b. de bandera,** minimum fare.

bajamar *nf* low tide; ebb-tide.

bajante *nf Am* low tide.

bajar I *vtr* **1** *(descender)* to bring *or* get *or* take down; **baja la maleta del armario,** take the suitcase down from the cupboard; *Teat* **b. el telón,** to lower the curtain; **b. la categoría a algn,** to demote sb; **b. las persianas,** to let down the blinds; *fig* **b. los humos a algn,** to take sb down a peg or two. **2** *(recorrer de arriba abajo)* to come *or* go down; **b. la escalera,** to come *or* go downstairs. **3** *(inclinar)* to lower; **b. la cabeza,** to bow *or* lower one's head. **4** *(disminuir) (volumen)* to turn down; *(voz)* to lower; *(precios etc)* to reduce, lower, cut; **¡baja esa maldita música!,** turn that bloody music down!; **los mayoristas han bajado los precios,** the wholesalers have cut prices. **II** *vi* **1** *(ir de un lugar a otro más bajo)* to go *or* come down; **bajo en seguida,** I'll be down in a minute. **2** *(apearse) (de un tren, autobús, avión)* to get off; *(de un coche, bicicleta)* to get off; *(de un coche)* to get out (**de,** of); **bajó del coche,** he got out of the car. **3** *(disminuir)* to fall, drop; **ha bajado el azúcar,** sugar has come down in price; **han bajado las ventas,** sales are down; **no bajará de tres horas,** it will take at least three hours; **¡ojalá baje la temperatura!,** let's hope the temperature drops! **III bajarse** *vr* **1** to come *or* go down; **bájate de ahí,** get down. **2** *(apearse) (de un tren, autobús, avión)* to get off; *(de una moto, bicicleta)* to get off; *(de un coche)* to get out (**de,** of); **se bajó de la bici,** she got off the bike; **se bajó del coche,** he got out of the car. **3** *(inclinarse)* to bend over *or* down.

bajareque *nm Am* fence made of cane and mud.

bajel *nm lit Náut* vessel, ship.

bajera *nf* **1** *Am* low quality tobacco leaves. **2** *Arg (gualdrapa)* saddlecloth.

bajero,-a *adj* lower.

bajetón,-ona *adj Antill Col Ecuad (persona)* short, small.

bajeza *nf* **1** *(acción vil)* vile deed, base action. **2** *(condición)* lowliness; **b. intelectual,** lack of intelligence.

bejines (por lo) *loc adv*, **bajinis (por io)** *loc adv fam* on the sly; **hablar por lo b.,** to speak quietly.

bajío *nm* **1** *Mar (banco de arena)* sandbank. **2** *Am (terreno bajo)* lowland.

bajista *Fin* **I** *adj* bearish; **tendencia b.,** tendency to lower prices. **II** *nmf* bear.

bajo,-a I *adj* **1** *(cosa, precio)* low; *(persona)* short; *(sonido)* faint, soft; *(voz)* low; **en voz baja,** in a low voice; **un techo muy b.,** a very low ceiling; **una mujer baja,** a short *or* small woman. **2** *(en lugar inferior)* **un piso b.,** a lower floor flat; *(en nivel inferior)* **de baja calidad,** of poor quality; **la clase baja,** the lower class; *fig* **tirando por lo b.,** at a conservative guess. **3** *(inclinado)* low; **con la cabeza baja,** with bowed head. **4** *(territorio, río)* lower; **el B. Aragón,** lower Aragon. **5** *fig (vil)* base, contemptible. **II** *nm* **1** *Geog* lowland, depression. **2** *Náut* sandbank. **3** *Mús (cantante, voz, instrumento)* bass. **4 bajos,** *(planta baja)* ground floor *sing*; *(sótano)*

basement *sing*. **5 bajos,** *(de pantalones)* bottoms, *US* cuffs; *(de falda)* hem *sing*. **III** *adv* **1** *(en lugar inferior)* **volar b.,** to fly low. **2** *(en voz baja)* quietly, softly; **hablar b.,** to speak quietly, whisper; *fig* **por lo b.,** in secret, on the sly. **IV** *prep* **1** *(lugar)* under, underneath; **b. la lluvia,** in the rain; **b. tierra,** underground, buried. **2** *Pol Hist* under; **b. Nerón/la República,** under Nero/the Republic. **3** *(temperatura)* below; **cinco grados b. cero,** five degrees below zero. **4** *(garantía, condición)* under; **b. fianza,** on bail; **b. juramento,** under oath; **b. pena de muerte,** under sentence of death.

bajón *nm* **1** *Mús (instrumento)* bassoon; *(músico)* bassoonist. **2** *(bajada)* sharp fall, decline. **3** *Com Fin* slump. **4** *(de salud)* relapse, deterioration; **ha sufrido un b.,** she has taken a turn for the worse.

bajorrelieve *nm Arte* bas-relief.

bajura *nf* pesca **de b.,** coastal fishing.

bakelita *nf Quím véase* **baquelita.**

bala I *nf* **1** *Mil* bullet; *fig* **como una b.,** like a shot. ■ **b. de cañón,** cannonball; **b. de goma,** rubber bullet; **b. perdida,** stray bullet. **2** *(de lana, algodón)* bale. **3** *Am* **ni a b.,** by no means. **II** *nmf fam (persona)* **b. perdida,** oddball.

balaca *nf,* **balacada** *nf CAm Ecuad (fanfarronada)* bragging.

balacera *nf Am (tiroteo)* shooting.

balada *nf Lit Mús* ballad.

baladí *adj (pl* baladíes*)* trivial; **asunto b.,** secondary matter, triviality.

balalaika *nf Mús* balalaika.

balance *nm* **1** *(vaivén)* to-and-fro, rocking. **2** *Fin (operación contable)* balance; *(declaración)* balance sheet. **3** *(cálculo)* estimate; **el b. provisional de heridos,** the provisional estimate of casualties; **hacer b. de una situación,** to take stock of a situation.

balancear **I** *vtr* **1** *(poner en equilibrio)* to balance. **2** *(mecer)* to rock. **II balancearse** *vr* **1** *(en una mecedora)* to rock; *(en un columpio)* to swing. **2** *(barco)* to roll.

balanceo *nm* rocking, swinging, rolling.

balancín *nm* **1** *(mecedora)* rocking-chair. **2** *(de balanza)* balancing beam. **3** *Téc Aut* rocker arm. **4** *(circo)* balancing pole.

balandra *nf Náut* sloop.

balandro *nm Náut* yacht.

balanza *nf* **1** *(aparato)* scales *pl*; *fig* **estar en la b.,** to be in the balance *o.* in danger; **b. de precisión,** precision balance. **2** *Com Fin Pol* balance. ■ **b. comercial,** balance of trade; **b. de pagos,** balance of payments; **b. de poderes,** balance of power. **3** *Astrol* **B.,** Libra, the Scales *pl*.

balar *vi* to bleat, baa.

balarrasa *nm fam* **1** *(aguardiente)* strong brandy. **2** *(persona)* madcap.

balasto *nm* ballast.

balaustrada *nf* balustrade, railing.

balaustre *nm,* **baloústro** *nm* **1** baluster. **2** *Am (paleta de albañil)* trowel.

balay *nm Am (cesta)* wicker basket.

balazo *nm* **1** *(disparo)* shot; **matar a algn de un b.,** to shoot sb dead. **2** *(herida)* bullet wound; **murió de un b.,** she died of a bullet wound.

balboa *nm Fin* standard monetary unit of Panama.

balbucear *vi* **1** *(adulto)* to stutter, stammer. **2** *(niño)* to babble.

balbuceo *nm* **1** *(adulto)* stuttering, stammering. **2** *(niño)* babbling.

balbuciente *adj* **1** *(adulto)* stuttering, stammering. **2** *(niño)* babbling.

balbucir *vi defect véase* **balbucear.**

Balcanes *npl* **los B.,** the Balkans.

balcánico,-a *adj* Balkan; **la Península balcánica**, the Balkan Peninsula.

balcón *nm* 1 balcony; **asomarse al b.,** *(mirar a la calle)* to look over the balcony; *(salir)* to go out onto the balcony. ■ **b. corrido,** row of balconies. 2 *fig (miranda)* vantage point.

balda *nf* shelf.

baldado,-a I *pp de* **baldar. II** *adj* 1 *(impedido)* crippled. 2 *fam (cansado)* shattered.

baldaquín *nm*, **baldaquino** *nm* canopy, baldachin.

baldar I *vtr* 1 *(lisiar)* to cripple, maim; **b. a algn a palos,** to give sb a thorough beating. 2 *fam (cansar)* to wear out. **II baldarse** *vr fam (cansarse)* to wear oneself out.

balde[1] *nm* pail, bucket.

balde[2] *loc adv* 1 *(gratis)* **de b.,** free; **viajar de b.,** to travel without paying; **trabajar de b.,** to work without getting paid. 2 *(en vano)* **en b.,** in vain; **he venido en b.,** I have come for nothing.

baldear *vtr Náut* 1 *(regar)* to wash, swill down. 2 *(achicar)* to bale out.

baldeo *nm* wash, washing, swilling down.

baldío,-a I *adj* 1 *(tierra)* uncultivated, waste. 2 *(vano)* vain, useless. **II** *nm* 1 *(erial)* wasteland. 2 *Am (solar)* plot for building.

baldón *nm (deshonra)* shame; *(injuria)* insult, offence; **tu conducta es un b. para la familia,** your behaviour is a disgrace to the family.

baldosa *nf* (ceramic) floor tile; *(para pavimentar)* flagstone, paving stone.

baldosín *nm* small tile.

balear I *adj* Balearic. **II** *nm f* native *or* inhabitant of the Balearic Islands.

Baleares *npl* **las (Islas) B.,** the Balearic Islands.

baleárico,-a *adj & nm, f véase* **balear.**

balido *nm* bleating, bleat.

balín *nm* small bullet.

balística *nf* ballistic sing.

balístico,-a *adj* ballistic.

balita *nf Am (canica)* marble.

baliza *nf* 1 *Náut* buoy. 2 *Av* beacon.

ballena *nf* 1 *Zool* whale. 2 *(de corsé)* whalebone, stay. 3 *fam* fat person, fatso.

ballenero,-a I *adj* whaling; **industria ballenera,** whaling industry. **II** *nm* 1 *(persona)* whaler. 2 *(barco)* whaler, whaling boat.

ballesta *nf* 1 *Hist* crossbow. 2 *Aut* spring.

ballet *nm* ballet.

balneario,-a I *adj* health, thermal. **II** *nm* spa, health resort.

balompié *nm* football.

balón *nm* 1 *Dep* ball, football. 2 *(recipiente)* cylinder; *(gases)* bag. ■ **b. de oxígeno,** oxygen cylinder; *fig* godsend, boost, shot in the arm.

baloncesto *nm Dep* basketball.

balonmano *nm Dep* handball.

balonvolea *nm Dep* volleyball.

balsa *nf* 1 *(estanque, charca)* pond, pool; **como una b. de aceite,** *(mar)* as calm as a millpond; *fig* very quiet. 2 *Náut* raft; **b. salvavidas,** life raft.

balsámico,-a *adj* balsamic; *fig* soothing.

bálsamo *nm* balsam, balm.

Báltico *nm* **el (Mar) B.,** the Baltic (Sea).

baluarte *nm* 1 *(fortificación)* bulwark, bastion. 2 *fig* stronghold, bastion; **un b. de la democracia,** a bastion of democracy. 3 *Am Pesca* funnel-shaped fish trap.

bamba *nf* 1 *(baile)* Cuban dance. 2 *CAm (moneda)* one peso coin.

bambalina *nf Teat* fly, flies *pl.*

bambalúa *nm Am* untidy *or* scruffy person.

bambolear *vi*, **bambolearse** *vr (gen)* to swing; *(persona, árbol)* to sway; *(mesa, silla)* to wobble; *(barco)* to rock, roll.

bamboleo *nm (gen)* swinging; *(persona, árbol)* swaying; *(mesa, silla)* wobbling, wobble; *(barco)* rocking, rolling.

bambolla *nf Am* talk, chat.

bambú *nm (pl bambúes) Bot* bamboo.

banal *adj* banal, trivial.

banalidad *nf* triviality, banality.

banana *nf véase* **banano.**

bananero,-a I *adj* 1 banana. 2 *Am Pol fig pey* **república bananera,** banana republic. **II** *nm (plantación)* banana plantation.

banano *nm* 1 *(fruto)* banana. 2 *(árbol)* banana tree.

banca *nf* 1 *(asiento)* bench. 2 *Com Fin (conjunto de bancos)* (the) banks; *(actividad)* banking; **el sector de la b.,** the banking sector; **nacionalización de la b.,** nationalization of the banks. 3 *(en juegos)* bank; **hacer saltar la b.,** to break the bank.

bancada *nf Arg Par* members of the legislative body in the same political party.

bancario,-a *adj Com Fin* banking; **sistema b.,** banking system.

bancarrota *nf Fin* bankruptcy; **estar en b.,** to be bankrupt.

banco *nm* 1 *(asiento)* bench; *(de iglesia)* pew. 2 *Téc* bench. 3 *Com Fin* bank; ■ **B. Mundial,** World Bank. ■ **b. de datos,** data bank; **b. de ojos,** eye bank; **b. de sangre,** blood bank. 4 *Náut* bank; **b. de arena,** sandbank. 5 *(de peces)* shoal, school. 6 *Geol (estrato)* layer.

banda *nf* 1 *(faja, condecoración)* sash, band, ribbon; *Herald* band. 2 *Ind* belt; **b. transportadora,** conveyor belt. 3 *Mús* band. 4 *Cin* **b. sonora,** sound track. 5 *(personas)* gang; *(de pájaros)* flock. 6 *(lado)* side; **a la otra b. del río,** on the other side of the river. ■ *Ftb* **línea de b.,** touchline; **saque de b.,** throw-in. 7 *Náut* side. 8 *(en billar)* cushion.

bandada *nf (pájaros)* flock.

bandazo *nm* lurch; **dar bandazos,** to lurch.

bandear[1] **I** *vtr* 1 to rock, move from side to side. 2 *Am (taladrar)* to bore, drill. 3 *Am (cruzar un río)* to cross. **II bandearse** *vr* to manage, cope; **sabe bandeárselas bien,** he knows how to look after himself.

bandear[2] *vtr CAm* 1 *(perseguir)* to pursue, chase. 2 *(herir)* to wound severely.

bandeja *nf* tray; *fig* **servir algo a algn en b.,** to hand sth to sb on a plate.

bandera *nf* flag; *Mil* **jurar b.,** to swear allegiance to the flag; **la b. española,** the Spanish flag; *fam* **de b.,** fantastic, terrific; *fam* **lleno hasta la b.,** packed full; *fam* **una chica de b.,** a real cracker.

bandería *nf* party, faction.

banderilla *nf* 1 *Taur* banderilla; *fig* **clavar** *or* **plantar banderillas a algn,** to slight *or* taunt sb. 2 *Culin* savoury snack on a cocktail stick. 3 *Am (sablazo)* sponging, scrounging.

banderillear *vtr Taur* to thrust banderillas into the bull's neck.

banderillero *nm Taur* banderillero.

banderín *nf* 1 *(bandera pequeña)* pennant, small flag. 2 *Mil (soldado)* pennant bearer.

banderita *nf* little flag; **el día de la b.,** flag day.

banderola *nf* banderole.

bandidaje *nm* banditry.

bandido *nm* bandit, outlaw; *fam* crook.

bando[1] *nm* 1 *Jur (edicto)* edict, proclamation. **2 bandos,** banns.

bando² *nm* **1** *(facción)* faction, side; **pasarse al otro b.,** to go over to the other side, change allegiances; *fam* **ser del b. contrario,** to be gay. **2** *(de peces)* shoal, school; *(de aves)* flock.

bandolera¹ *nf (mujer)* woman bandit.

bandolera² *nf (correa)* bandoleer, bandolier; **en b.,** over one's shoulder.

bandolerismo *nm* banditry.

bandolero *nm* bandit, outlaw.

bandurria *nf Mús* bandurria.

Bangladesh *n* Bangladesh.

banjo *nm Mús* banjo.

banquero,-a *nm,f* banker.

banqueta *nf* **1** *(banco)* bench, form. **2** *(taburete)* stool.

banquete *nm* banquet, feast; **b. de bodas,** wedding reception *or* feast.

banquetear *vtr & vi* to banquet.

banquillo *nm* **1** *Jur* dock; *fig* **sentar a algn en el b. de los acusados,** to have sb on the carpet. **2** *Dep* bench.

banquisa *nf* floe, ice field.

bañadero *nm* water hole used by animals.

bañado,-a I *pp de* **bañar. II** *adj fig* bathed; **b. en lágrimas/ sangre/sudor,** bathed in tears/blood/sweat. **III** *nm Am* marshland, swamp.

bañador *nm (de mujer)* bathing *or* swimming costume; *(de hombre)* swimming trunks *pl.*

bañar I *vtr* **1** *(lavar)* to bath. **2** *(cubrir)* to coat, cover; *Téc* to dip; **b. de oro,** to gild; **b. un pastel en chocolate,** to cover a cake in chocolate. **3** *fml (dar el sol, la luz)* to bathe; **la luz de la luna bañaba la habitación,** the room was bathed in moonlight. **II bañarse** *vr (limpiarse)* to have *or* take a bath; *(mar, piscina)* to go swimming, go for a swim, have a swim *or* a dip.

bañera *nf (baño)* bath, bathtub.

bañero,-a *nm,f* lifeguard.

bañista *nmf* bather, swimmer.

baño *nm* **1** *(gen)* bath; **tomar un b.,** to have *or* take a bath; *fig* **b. de sangre,** bloodbath; *fig* **b. de sol,** sun-bath; *fig* **dar un b. a algn,** to beat *or* outshine sb. ■ *For* **b. fijador,** fixing bath; *Culin* **b. María,** bain-marie; **b. turco,** Turkish bath; **traje de b.,** swimming costume. **2** *(capa) (de pintura)* coat; *(de chocolate, almíbar)* coating, covering. **3** *(cuarto de baño)* bathroom; *(lavabo)* toilet. **4 baños,** *(balneario)* spa *sing; (aguas)* waters; **tomar los b.,** to take the waters. ■ **b. medicinales,** medicinal waters; **b. romanos,** Roman baths.

baptisterio *nm* **1** *(edificio)* baptistry. **2** *(pila)* font.

baquelita *nf Quím* Bakelite.

baqueta *nf* **1** *(de fusil)* ramrod; *fig* **tratar a algn a (la) b.,** to treat sb badly, push sb around. **2 baquetas,** *Mús* drumsticks.

baqueteado,-a I *pp de* **baquetear. II** *adj* hardened.

baquetear *vtr (tratar mal)* to treat harshly *or* roughly; *(curtir)* to toughen, harden.

baqueteo *nm* rough treatment.

baquía *nf Am (destreza)* knack, skill; **hombre de b.,** old hand.

báquico,-a *adj* bacchic, bacchanalian.

bar *nm* **1** *(lugar)* bar, snack bar, café. **2** *Fís* bar.

barahúnda *nf (ruido)* din, uproar; *(confusión)* chaos.

baraja *nf Naipes* **1** pack, deck; *fig* **jugar con dos barajas,** to doubledeal. **2** *Am* playing card.

barajar *vtr* **1** *Naipes* to shuffle; *(papeles)* to mix, jumble up; *fig (nombres)* to juggle, play with; **b. nombres de posibles candidatos,** to consider names of possible candidates. **2** *Arg Chi Urug (detener) (golpe)* to fend off; *(intento)* to thwart. **3** *Arg (agarrar al vuelo)* to grab.

barajustar *vi Am (escapar)* to go *or* run away.

baranda *nf* **1** *(de escalera)* handrail, banister; *(de balcón)* handrail. **2** *Bill* cushion.

barandal *nm (listón)* base; *(barandilla)* banister; *Fin* **b. imponible** *or* **impositiva,** tax assessment basis.

barandilla *nf* **1** *(escalera)* handrail, banister; *(balcón)* handrail. **2** *Am (adral de carro)* cart rail.

baratija *nf* **1** trinket, knick-knack. **2 baratijas,** junk *sing.*

baratillo *nm* **1** *(cosas)* junk, second-hand goods *pl.* **2** *(tienda)* junk shop, second-hand dealer's; *(mercadillo)* flea market.

barato,-a I *adj* cheap; sale **más b. en tren,** it's cheaper by train. **II** *adv* cheaply; **allí se come muy b.,** yon can eat very cheaply there.

baratura *nf* cheapness, low price.

baraúnda *nf véase* **barahúnda.**

barba I *nf* **1** *Anat* chin. **2** *(pelo)* beard; **b. cerrada,** thick beard; **barbas de chivo,** goatee (beard); *fig* **cien pesetas por b.,** a hundred pesetas a head; *fig* **es un tipo con toda la b.,** he's every inch a man; *fig* **se rió en mis barbas,** he laughed in my face. ■ *Impr* **papel con barbas,** deckle-edged paper. **3** *Orn* wattle. **II** *nm Teat* old man's part.

barbacana *nf* barbican.

barbacoa *nf,* **barbacuá** *nf* **1** barbecue. **2** *Am (camastro)* makeshift wattle bed. **3** *Am Agr (andamio)* watchtower over maize fields. **4** *Am (cabaña)* tree house, but on stilts. **5** *Am (granero)* loft.

barbado,-a I *adj* bearded. **II** *nm Bot (renuevo)* shoot.

Barbados *n* Barbados.

barbaridad *nf* **1** *(crueldad)* cruelty, atrocity, outrage; *fam* **¡qué b.!,** how terrible!, how awful! **2** *(disparate)* piece of nonsense; **no digas barbaridades,** don't talk nonsense. **3** *fig* a lot; **beber una b.,** to drink like a fish; **costar una b.,** to cost a fortune.

barbarie *nf* **1** *(crueldad)* savagery, cruelty. **2** *(falta de cultura)* ignorance.

barbarismo *nm Ling* barbarism.

bárbaro,-a I *adj* **1** *Hist* barbarian. **2** *(cruel)* barbaric, barbarous. **3** *(inculto, tosco)* rough, uncouth. **4** *(temerario)* daring, bold. **5** *fam (enorme)* massive; **tener un hambre bárbara,** to be ravenous *or* starving. **6** *fam (estupendo)* tremendous, terrific; **una cosa bárbara,** something fantastic. **II** *nm, f Hist* barbarian. **III** *interj* **¡b.!,** *fam* great!, fantastic! ◆ **bárbaramente** *adv* **1** savagely, barbarously. **2** *fam* fantastically.

barbechar *vtr Agr* to leave fallow.

barbechera *nf,* **barbecho** *nm Agr* fallow land; **dejar una tierra en b.,** to leave a piece of land fallow.

barbería *nf* barber's (shop).

barbero *nm* barber.

barbián,-ana I *adj* self-assured, carefree. **II** *nm, f* self-assured *or* carefree person.

barbicano *adj* grey-bearded.

barbicastaño *adj* brown-bearded.

barbilampiño I *adj* beardless, smooth-faced. **II** *nm* greenhorn, novice, inexperienced youth.

barbilindo I *adj* dandified. **II** *nm* dandy.

barbilla *nf Anat* chin.

barbiquejo *nm Am (type of)* bandage.

barbiquiú *nm Am (fiesta campestre)* barbecue.

barbitúrico *nm Farm* barbiturate.

barbo *nm (pez)* barbel. ■ **b. de mar,** red mullet.

barbudo,-a *adj* bearded.

barca *nf* small boat.

barcarola *nf Mús* barcarole.

barcaza *nf Náut* lighter.

barcelonés,-esa I *adj* of *or* from Barcelona. **II** *nm, f* native *or* inhabitant of Barcelona.

barco *nm* boat, ship, vessel. ■ **b. cisterna,** tanker; **b. de pasajeros,** liner; **b. de vapor,** steamer.

bardana *nf Bot* burdock.

bardo *nm* bard, poet, minstrel.

baremo *nm* **1** *Mat* ready reckoner. **2** *(tarifas)* scale, table, list.

bario *nm Quím* barium.

barítono *nm Mús* baritone.

barloventear *vi Náut* to ply windward, sail to windward.

barlovento *nm Náut* windward; **Islas de B.,** Windward Islands.

barman *nm (pl bármanes)* barman.

barnacla *nf Orn* goose. ■ **b. canadiense,** Canada goose; **b. cariblanca,** barnacle goose.

barniz *nm* **1** *(en madera)* varnish; *(en cerámica)* glaze. **2** *fig* smattering; **tener un b. de cultura,** to have a veneer of culture.

barnizado,-a I *pp de* **barnizar. II** *adj (madera)* varnished; *(cerámica)* glazed. **III** *nm (madera)* coat of varnish, varnishing; *(cerámica)* glaze, glazing.

barnizar *vtr (madera)* to varnish; *(cerámica)* to glaze.

barométrico,-a *adj* barometric.

barómetro *nm* barometer.

barón *nm* **1** *(noble)* baron. **2** *Pol fam* top man, mandarin.

baronesa *nf* baroness.

baronía *nf* barony.

barquero,-a *nm, f (hombre)* boatman; *(mujer)* boatwoman.

barquilla *nf Av* gondola.

barquillero,-a *nm, f* wafer seller.

barquillo *nm* wafer.

barquinazo *nm (vuelco)* overturning; *(tumbo)* jolt.

barra *nf* **1** *(gen)* bar; *fig* **no pararse en barras,** to stop at nothing. ■ **b. de bicicleta,** crossbar; **b. de hierro,** iron bar; **b. de labios,** lipstick; **b. de pan,** French loaf, baguette. **2** *Jur (del acusado)* dock; *(de testigo)* witness box; *(barandilla)* bar. **3** *(mostrador)* bar. ■ **b. americana,** bar with hostesses. **4** *Dep* **b. fija,** horizontal bar. **5** *Am Dep* supporters *pl.* **6** *Am Jur (público)* members of the public. **7** *Arg fam (amigos)* gang, group of friends.

barrabás *nm* scamp, rascal.

barrabasada *nf fam (travesura)* piece of mischief; *(mala pasada)* mean *or* low trick; **decir barrabasadas,** to talk nonsense.

barraca *nf* **1** *(caseta)* shack, hut. **2** *(en Valencia y Murcia)* thatched farmhouse. **3** *(puesto de feria)* stall, booth. **4** *Am (almacén)* warehouse, storehouse.

barracón *nm* prefab hut.

barracuda *nf (pez)* barracuda.

barranco *nm* **1** *(despeñadero)* cliff, precipice; *(torrentera)* gully, ravine. **2** *fig (obstáculo)* difficulty, obstacle.

barraquismo *nm* slums *pl*; **el ayuntamiento no ha podido erradicar el b. de la ciudad,** the council has not yet been able to eliminate slums from the town.

barreduras *nfpl* sweepings, robbish *sing.*

barreminas *nm inv* minesweeper.

barrena *nf* **1** *Téc (metal)* twist drill; *(madera)* bit; **b. de mano,** gimlet. **2** *Av* spin; **entrar en b.,** to go into a spin.

barrenar *vtr* **1** *Téc* to drill; *(agujeros)* to bore. **2** *Náut* to scuttle. **3** *(desbaratar)* to frustrate, foil. **4** *(infringir una ley)* to break, violate.

barrendero,-a *nm, f* sweeper, street sweeper.

barreno *nm* **1** *(taladro)* large drill. **2** *(agujero)* bore, borehole; *Min* blasthole. **3** *Min (carga explosiva)* charge.

barreño *nm* ceramic bowl.

barrer *vtr* **1** *(limpiar con escoba)* to sweep. **2** *fig (el viento)* to sweep away; *fig* **b. con todo,** to take everything away; *fig* **b. para adentro,** to look after number one.

barrera *nf* **1** barrier, fence; **b. del sonido,** sound barrier; *fig* barrier, obstacle; **poner barreras,** to hinder **(a, -),** impede **(a, -)**. **2** *Taur (valla)* fence; *(localidad)* first row of seats; *fig* **ver los toros desde la b.,** to sit on the fence.

barretina *nf* Catalan cap.

barrica *nf* (medium-sized) barrel.

barricada *nf* barricade; **levantar barricadas,** to erect barricades.

barriga *nf* **1** *(vientre)* belly; *fam* tummy; *fam* **echar b.,** to get a paunch, get fat; *fam* **llenarse la b.,** to gorge *or* stuff oneself; *fam* **rascarse** *or* **tocarse la b.,** to laze around, lounge about. **2** *(de una vasija)* belly, bulge. **3** *(comba de una pared)* bulge.

barrigón,-ona *adj*, **barrigudo,-a** *adj* big-bellied, potbellied.

barril *nm* barrel, keg; **cerveza de b.,** draught beer.

barrilete *nm* **1** small barrel. **2** *(de revólver)* chamber. **3** *Carp* clamp.

barrillo *nm* pimple, spot.

barrio *nm* area, district; **del b.,** local; **el B. Gótico,** the Gothic Quarter; *fam* **irse al otro b.,** to kick the bucket; *fam* **mandar a algn al otro b.,** to do sb in. ■ **b. chino,** red-light district; **barrios bajos,** slums.

barriobajero,-a *adj* slummy, slum.

barritar *vi (elefante)* to trumpet.

barrizal *nm* mire, quagmire.

barro¹ *nm* **1** *(lodo)* mud. **2** *(arcilla)* clay; **b. cocido,** baked clay; **objetos de b.,** earthenware *sing*; **un cacharro de b.,** an earthenware pot, a ceramic pot. **3** *Arg Par Urug (desacierto)* blunder.

barro² *nm Med* pimple, spot.

barroco,-a *adj* **1** *Arte* baroque. **2** *fig* ornate, extravagant.

barroquismo *nm* **1** baroque style. **2** *fig* extravagance.

barroso,-a¹ *adj (con barro)* muddy.

barroso,-a² *adj Med (con granos)* spotty.

barrote *nm* bar; *(de silla, mesa)* crosspiece.

barrumbada *nf Am (insensatez)* piece of nonsense.

barruntar *vtr (sospechar)* to suspect; *(presentir)* to have a feeling; **barruntaba un desenlace trágico,** I suspected a tragic outcome.

barrunto *nm* **1** *(presentimiento)* feeling, presentiment; *(sospecha)* suspicion. **2** *(señal, indicio)* sign, indication.

bartola (a la) *loc adv fam* carelessly; **tenderse** *or* **tumbarse a la b.,** to laze around, idle away one's time.

bártulos *nmpl Am* things, stuff *sing*, bits and pieces; **liar los b.,** to pack up one's things, pack one's bags *or* stuff.

barullo *nm (alboroto)* row, din; *(confusión)* confusion, mess; **armar b.,** to raise hell; **armarse un b.,** to get into a muddle; **a b.,** lots of, loads of, tons of; **bombones a b.,** chocolates galore; **había niños a b.,** there were loads of children.

basa *nf* base.

basáltico,-a *adj* basaltic.

basalto *nm* basalt.

basamento *nm (de una columna)* base, plinth.

basar I *vtr* **1** to put on a base. **2** *fig (argumentos)* to base **(en,** on). **II basarse** *vr* **1** to base oneself **(en,** on); **¿en qué te basas para decir eso?,** what grounds do you have for saying that?; **me baso en lo que he visto,** I'm going by what I have seen. **2** *(una teoría)* to be based **(en,** on).

basca *nf* **1** *(náusea)* nausea; **le produce bascas,** it makes him feel sick; *fam* **si me da la b.,** if I feel like it. **2** *arg* people, crowd.

báscula *nf* scales *pl*; *(para camiones)* weighbridge, platform scale.

basculante *adj* tilting; *(camión)* tip-up.

bascular *vi (oscilar)* to tilt.

base *nf* **1** *(gen)* base; *fig* basis; **el arroz es la b. de su alimentación,** rice forms the basis of their diet; **la b. de una estatua,** the base of a statue; *Pol fig* **la b. del partido,** the rank and file of the party; *fig* **su argumento carece de b.,** her argument has no foundation. ■ **alimento b.,** staple food *or* diet; **sueldo b.,** minimum wage. **2** *(principio, conocimiento)* basis, grounding; **este libro te dará una buena b. en astronomía,** this book will give you a good grounding in astronomy; **si partimos de la b. de que ...,** if we start from the premise that ... . **3** *Mil* base. ■ **b. aérea,** air base; **b. naval,** naval base; **b. de operaciones,** field headquarters. **4 a b. de,** by; **a b. de bien,** extremely well; **a b. de no hacer nada,** by doing nothing; **comida a b. de verduras,** vegetarian meal.

básico,-a *adj* **1** basic, essential. **2** *Quím* basic.

Basilea *n* Basel.

basílica *nf* basilica.

basilisco *nm Mit* basilisk; *fig* **ponerse hecho un b.,** to become furious.

básquet *nm Dep véase* **baloncesto**

basset *nm* basset hound.

bastante I *adj* **1** *(suficiente)* enough; **hay b. comida para todos,** there's enough food for everyone; **no tengo b. dinero,** I haven't got enough money; **¿tenéis bastantes libros?,** have you got enough books?; **ya tenemos bastantes problemas,** we've got enough problems already. **2** *(abundante)* quite a lot of; **b. gente,** quite a lot of people; **b. tiempo,** quite some time; **hace b. calor/frío,** it's quite hot/cold; **tiene bastantes amigos,** she's got quite a lot of friends. **II** *adv* **1** *(suficiente)* enough; **con esto hay b.,** that is enough; **no soy lo b. rico para ...,** I am not rich enough to ... . **2** *(un poco)* fairly, quite; **b. alto,** quite tall; **b. bien,** quite well; **me gusta b.,** I quite like it; **vamos b. al cine,** we go to the cinema quite often.

bastar I *vi* to be sufficient *or* enough, suffice; **basta con tocarlo para que se abra,** you only have to touch it and it opens; **basta con tres,** three will be enough; **¡basta de tonterías!,** enough of this nonsense!; *fam* **me basta y me sobra,** that's more than enough for me. **II bastarse** *vr* **b. a sí mismo,** to be self-sufficient, rely only on oneself. **III** *interj* **¡basta (ya)!,** that's enough!, that will do!

bastardía *nf (calidad de bastardo)* bastardy; *fig (bajeza)* baseness, meanness.

bastardilla *nf Impr* **en b.,** in italics.

bastardillo,-a *adj Impr* italic.

bastardo,-a I *adj* bastard; *fig (despreciable)* base, mean. **II** *nm,f* bastard.

basteza *nf* coarseness.

bastidor *nm* **1** *Constr Cost* frame. **2 bastidores,** *Teat* wings; *fig* **entre b.,** behind the scenes.

bastilla *nf Cost* hem.

bastión *nm* bastion.

basto¹ *nm* **1** *Naipes (carta española)* club; **bastos,** *(palo de la baraja)* ≈ clubs. **2** *Am (gualdrapa)* saddlecloth.

basto,-a² *adj* (cosa) rough, coarse; *(persona)* rude, coarse, uncouth.

bastón *nm* **1** stick, walking stick. **2** *(insignia)* baton; *fig* **empuñar el b.,** to take charge *or* command.

bastonazo *nm* blow with a stick.

bastoncillo *nm Anat* rod.

bastonera *nf* umbrella stand.

basura *nf (desperdicios)* rubbish, *US* trash, garbage; **tirar algo a la b.,** to throw something away ■ **cubo de la b.,** dustbin, *US* trash can

basurero *nm* **1** *(persona)* dustman, refuse collector, *US* garbage collector **2** *(lugar)* rubbish dump, *US* garbage dump

bata *nf (para casa)* dressing gown; *(para el trabajo)* overall, *(de médico etc)* white coat, lab coat

batacazo *nm* **1** crash, bang, bump; *fig* **darse un b.,** to come a cropper **2** *Am (carreras de caballos)* unexpected *or* surprise win; *fig* fluke, stroke of luck.

batalla *nf* **1** battle; **librar b.,** to do *or* join battle; **presentar b.,** to draw up in battle array, *fam* **dar b.,** to be a lot of trouble, **este niño da mucha b.,** this child is a real handful ■ **b. campal,** pitched battle, **campo de b.,** battlefield. **2** *Arte* battle scene. **3** *fam* **de b.,** ordinary, everyday, **zapatos de b.,** everyday shoes

batallador,-a I *adj* fighting, struggling **II** *nm,f* fighter, struggler

batallar *vi* **1** *(reñir con armas)* to battle, wage war **2** *fig (disputar)* to fight, quarrel, **tendré que b. con el jefe para que me aumente el sueldo,** I'll have to battle with the boss to get him to give me a rise.

batallón¹ *nm* battalion; **b. de infantería,** infantry battalion, *fam fig* **un b. de niños,** a crowd of children.

batallón,-ona² *adj* quarrelsome, contentious.

batata *nf Bot* sweet potato.

batatazo *nm Am véase* **batacazo.**

bate *nm Béisb Crick* bat

batea *nf* tray.

bateador,-a *nm,f Béisb* batter, *Crick (hombre)* batsman, *(mujer)* batswoman

batear *Am* **I** *vi* to bat; **es su turno para b.,** it is his turn to bat. **II** *vtr* to hit, **b. la pelota,** to hit *or* bat the ball.

batel *nm Náut* small boat

batería I *nf* **1** *Mil* battery; *fig* **una b. de preguntas,** a barrage of questions. **2** *Aut Elec* battery **3** *Teat* footlights *pl.* **4** *Mús (de orquesta)* percussion; *(de conjunto)* drums *pl;* **toca la b.,** he plays the drums. **5** *(conjunto de cosas)* set. ■ **b. de cocina,** pots and pans, set of pans. **6 aparcar en b.,** to park at an angle to the kerb **II** *nmf* drummer; **el b. del conjunto es holandés,** the group's drummer is Dutch

batiborrillo *nm*, **batiburrillo** *nm* jumble, mess

batida *nf* **1** *Caza* beat. **2** *Mil* reconnaissance. **3** *(de la policía)* raid.

batido,-a I *pp de* **batir. II** *adj Culin* whipped. **III** *nm* milk shake.

batidor,-a I *adj* beating. **II** *nm,f* **1** *Culin (manual)* whisk; *(automático)* blender; *(robot de cocina)* mixer. **2** *Mil (explorador)* scout. **3** *Caza* beater.

batiente I *adj* banging; **reírse a mandíbula b.,** to laugh one's head off. **II** *nm* **1** *(jamba)* jamb **2** *(hoja de puerta)* leaf.

batín *nm* short dressing gown.

batintín *nm* gong

batir I *vtr* **1** *(gen)* to beat; *(metales)* to hammer; *(palmas)* to clap; *(alas)* to flap. **2** *Culin (huevos)* to beat; *(nata, claras)* to whip, whisk **3** *Dep (marca, récord)* to break; **batió el récord mundial de los 100 metros libres,** she broke the world 100 metres freestyle record **4** *(derribar)* to break down; **b. una puerta,** to break down a door **5** *(desmontar)* to take down. **6** *(reconocer) Mil* to reconnoitre **7** *Caza* to beat **II batirse** *vr* to fight; **b. en duelo,** to fight a duel, **b. en retirada,** to beat a retreat

batiscafo *nm* bathyscaphe

batista *nf Tex* cambric, batiste.

batracio,-a *adj* & *nm* batrachian.

batuecas *nfpl fam* **estar en las b.,** to be daydreaming, have one's head in the clouds

batuquear *vtr Am* to shake

baturrillo *nm fam* jumble, mess, mishmash

baturro,-a *nm,f fam* Aragonese peasant

batuta *nf Mús* baton, *fig* **llevar la b.,** to be in charge, be the boss.

baúl *nm* **1** trunk. ■ **b. mundo,** large trunk **2** *Am (maletero)* boot, *US* trunk

bauprés *nm Náut* bowsprit.

bausán,-ana *adj Am* idle, lazy.

bautismal *adj* baptismal

bautismo *nm* baptism, christening, *fig* **b. de fuego,** baptism of fire, *fig* **b. del aire,** first flight, maiden flight. ■ **fe de b.,** certificate of baptism

bautista *adj & nmf Rel* Baptist

bautisterio *nm* baptistry.

bautizar *vtr* **1** *Rel* to baptize, christen; **bautizaron al niño con el nombre de David,** the child was christened David **2** *(poner nombre a)* to name; **b. una calle/un barco,** to name a street/ship; **le bautizaron con el mote de 'El Alto',** he was nicknamed 'El Alto' **3** *fam (mezclar con agua)* to water down.

bautizo *nm Rel* baptism, christening; *(fiesta)* christening party

bauxita *nf Min* bauxite.

bávaro,-a *adj & nm,f* Bavarian

Baviera *n* Bavaria.

baya *nf Bot* berry.

bayeta *nf* **1** *Tex* flannel. **2** *(paño)* floorcloth

bayo,-a I *adj (color)* whitish yellow. **II** *nm* **1** *(caballo)* bay. **2** *Ent (mariposa)* silkworm moth.

bayoneta *nf Mil* bayonet, **ataque a la b.,** bayonet charge; **calar la b.,** to fix bayonets.

bayonetazo *nm (golpe)* bayonet thrust; *(herida)* bayonet wound.

bayunco,-a *adj CAm (huraño)* unsociable, rude.

bayunquear *vi CAm (tontear)* to flirt

baza *nf Naipes* trick; *fig* **meter b.,** to interfere, butt in; **no me dejaron meter b.,** they didn't let me get a word edgeways.

bazar *nm* bazaar.

bazo *nm Anat* spleen

bazofia *nf (comida)* left-overs *pl*, scraps *pl*, pigswill; *fig pey* pigswill, rubbish, filth

bazooka *nm Mil* bazooka.

Bco. *abr de* **banco,** bank

be *nf* name of the letter B in Spanish; *fig* **be por be,** down to the last detail.

beata *nf* **1** *Rel* lay sister. **2** *Rel (beatificada)* woman who has been beatified. **3** *(piadosa)* devout woman. **4** *fam pey* prude, sanctimonious woman.

beatería *nf* sanctimoniousness.

beatificación *nf* beatification.

beatificar *vtr* to beatify.

beatífico,-a *adj* beatific.

beatitud *nf* beatitude.

beatnik *nmf (pl beatniks)* beatnik.

beato,-a I *adj* **1** *Rel (beatificado)* beatified; *(piadoso)* devout. **2** *pey* prudish, sanctimonious. **3** *(feliz)* happy. **II** *nm* **1** *Rel* lay brother. **2** *(beatificado)* man who has been beatified; *(piadoso)* devout person.

bebé *nm* baby. ■ **b. probeta,** test-tube baby.

bebedero *nm* **1** *(abrevadero)* drinking trough, water trough. **2** *(vasija)* drinking dish. **3** *(lugar)* watering place.

bebedizo *nm Med* potion; *Lit* poisonous potion; *(de amor)* love potion.

bebedor,-a I *adj* (hard *or* heavy) drinking. **II** *nm,f* (hard *or* heavy) drinker.

beber I *vtr & vi (agua, vino)* to drink; **b. a grandes tragos,** to guip down; **b. algo de un trago,** to drink sth down in one go; *fig* **b. de** *or* **en buenas fuentes,** to have reliable sources of information; *fig* **b. los vientos por algo,** to

long for sth, be dying for sth. **II** *vi (brindar)* to toast, drink to sb's health; **bebamos a** *or* **por la felicidad de los novios,** let us drink to the happiness of the bride and groom.

bebercio *nm arg* **el b.,** drink, booze; **dedicarse al b.,** *(siempre)* to take to the bottle; *(alguna vez)* to drink, booze.

bebible *adj* drinkable.

bebido,-a I *pp de* **beber. II** *adj (borracho)* drunk; *(entonado)* tipsy. **III** *nf* drink, beverage; **bebidas alcohólicas,** alcoholic drinks; **darse a la b.,** to take to drink.

bebistrajo *nm fam* concoction, witch's brew.

beca *nf* grant, scholarship, award.

becada *nf Orn* woodcock.

becar *vtr* to award a grant *or* scholarship to.

becario,-a *nm,f* grant *or* scholarship holder.

becerrada *nf Taur* bullfight with young bulls.

becerro *nm* calf; *fig* **b. de oro,** golden calf.

bechamel *adj & nf Culin* bechamel; **salsa b.,** bechamel sauce, white sauce.

becuadro *nm Mús* natural sign.

bedel *nm Univ* beadle, head porter.

beduino,-a *adj & nm,f* Bedouin.

befo,-a *adj* thick-lipped.

begonia *nf Bot* begonia.

beige *adj & nm* beige.

béisbol *nm Dep* baseball; **jugador de b.,** baseball player.

beisbolero,-a *nm,f* baseball player.

bejuco *nm Bot* liana, reed.

beldad *nf arc (hermosura)* beauty; *(mujer bella)* beauty, belle; **su hija es una b.,** your daughter is a real beauty.

belduque *nm Am* large pointed knife.

Belén *n* Bethlehem; *fig* **estar en B.,** to have one's head in the clouds.

belén *nm* **1** *Rel* nativity scene, crib. **2** *fig* mess, chaos; **armar un b.,** to kick up a fuss *or* rumpus; **esta casa es un b.,** it's bedlam in this house; **meterse en belenes,** to get into difficulties.

belfo,-a I *adj* thick-lipped. **II** *nm* thick lip.

belga *adj & nmf* Belgian.

Bélgica *n* Belgium.

bélgico,-a *adj* Belgian.

Belgrado *n* Belgrade.

Belice *n* Belize.

belicense *adj & nmf,* **beliceño,-a** *adj & nm,f* Belizean.

belicismo *nm* warmongering, bellicosity.

belicista I *adj* belligerent, bellicose. **II** *nmf* warmonger.

bélico,-a *adj (de espíritu)* warlike, bellicose; *(preparativos etc)* war; **material b.,** armaments *pl.*

belicoso,-a *adj (de guerra)* warlike, bellicose; *(pendenciero)* aggressive.

beligerancia *nf* belligerency, belligerence; **política de no b.,** policy of non-aggression.

beligerante *adj* belligerent; **los países beligerantes,** the countries at war.

bellaco,-a I *adj* **1** wicked, roguish. **2** *Am (caballo)* vicious. **II** *nm,f* villain, scoundrel, rogue.

belladona *nf Bot* belladonna, deadly nightshade.

bellaquería *nf* wickedness, roguery.

belleza *nf (gen)* beauty; **crema de b.,** beauty cream; *(mujer)* **una b.,** a beauty.

bello,-a *adj* beautiful; *Educ* **bellas artes,** (fine) arts; **el b. sexo,** the fair sex; *Lit* **la bella durmiente,** Sleeping Beauty.

bellota *nf Bot* acora; *fam fig* **animal de b.,** blockhead.

bemba *nf Am* thick lips *pl.*

bemol I *adj Mús* flat; **si b.,** B flat. **II** *nm* **1** *Mús* flat. **2 bemoles,** *fam (difícil)* **esto tiene b.,** this is a tough one. **3 bemoles,** *arg (valor)* guts; **para eso se necesitan b.,** you've got to have guts to do that.

benceno *nm Quím* benzene.

bencina *nf* benzine.

bendecir *vtr* to bless; **b. la mesa,** to say grace; **¡Dios te bendiga!,** God bless you!

bendición *nf* **1** *(acción)* blessing; *(ceremonia)* Benediction; **es una b. de Dios,** it's a godsend; **es una b. oírle,** he's a joy to listen to; **¡qué b.!,** how marvellous!; *fam* **echar la b. a algn,** to have done with sb. ■ **b. de la mesa,** grace. **2 bendiciones,** wedding *sing*; **echar las b. a los novios,** to join in marriage.

bendito,-a I *adj* **1** blessed; **¡b. sea Dios!,** *(liturgia)* thanks be to God!; *fam* thank goodness!; *fam* **esa bendita costumbre de fumar en la mesa,** this damned habit of smoking at table. **2** *(de pocos alcances)* simple, simpleminded. **II** *nm,f* **1** *(santo)* saint; **dormir como un b.,** to sleep like a baby. **2** *(bonachón)* good sort, kind soul; *(tontorrón)* simple soul.

benedictino,-a *adj & nm* Benedictine.

benefactor,-a I *adj* beneficent. **II** *nm,f* benefactor.

beneficencia *nf* beneficence, charity; **una organización de b.,** charity organization, welfare organization.

beneficiado,-a I *pp de* **beneficiar. II** *adj* favoured, *US* favored; **salir b. de algo,** to do well out of sth, profit from sth. **III** *nm Rel* beneficiary.

beneficiar I *vtr* **1** *(hacer bien)* to benefit, favour, *US* favor; **esa decisión no beneficia a nadie,** that decision benefits nobody. **2** *Fin (acciones)* to sell below par. **3** *Am (ganado)* to slaughter. **II beneficiarse** *vr* **1** to benefit. **2** *Com Fin* to profit; **b. de** *or* **con algo,** to profit from *or* by sth. **3** *vulg* to get one's oats.

beneficiario,-a *nm,f* beneficiary.

beneficio *nm* **1** *Com Fin* profit; **b. neto,** net profit. **2** *(bien)* benefit; **en b. de todos,** in everyone's interest; **en b. propio,** in one's own interest; **en b. tuyo/suyo,** for your/ his own good. **3** *Teat* charity performance; **un concierto a b. del asilo de ancianos,** a concert in aid of old people's home. **4** *Am (ganado)* slaughter. **5** *CAm (ingenio)* sugar refinery, coffee plantation.

beneficioso,-a *adj* beneficial, useful, good.

benéfico,-a *adj* charitable; **función benéfica,** charity performance; **institución benéfica,** charitable body, charity.

benemérito,-a I *adj fml* worthy, meritous. **II la Benemérita** *nf* the Spanish Civil Guard.

beneplácito *nm fml* approval, consent.

benevolencia *nf* benevolence, kindness.

benevolente *adj,* **benévolo,-a** *adj* benevolent, kind.

Bengala *n* Bengal.

bengala *nf* flare.

bengalí I *adj* Bengali. **II** *nmf (pl* **bengalíes)** *(persona)* Bengali. **III** *(idioma)* Bengali.

benigno,-a *adj (persona)* gentle, benign, affable; *(clima)* mild.

benimeño,-a *adj & nm,f* Beninese.

Benín *n* Benin.

benjamín,-ina *nm, f* youngest child; **Rosa es la benjamina de la familia,** Rosa is the baby of the family.

beodo,-a *adj & nm,f* drunk.

berberecho *nm Zool* (common) cockle.

berberisco,-a *adj & nm,f* Berber.

berbiquí *nm Téc* **b. y barrena,** brace and bit.

beréber *nmf,* **berebere** *nmf* Berber.

berenjena *nf Bot* aubergine, *US* eggplant.

berenjenal *nm Bot* aubergine *or US* eggplant bed; *fam* **te has metido en un b.,** you've got yourself into a fine mess.

bergamota *nf Bot* bergamot.

bergante *nm* scoundrel, ruffian.

bergantín *nm Náut* brig, brigantine.

beriberi *nm Med* beriberi.

berilo *nm Min* beryl.

Berlín *n* Berlin; **B. Este/Oeste,** East/West Berlin.

berlina *nf* **1** *(carruaje)* berlin. ■ **b. inglesa,** mailcoach. **2** *Aut* saloon.

berlinés,-esa I *adj* of *or* from Berlin. **II** *nm,f* Berliner.

bermejo,-a *adj* reddish, red.

bermellón *nm* vermilion.

Bermudas I *nfpl* **las (Islas) B.,** Bermuda *sing.* **II b.** *nmpl (prenda)* Bermuda shorts.

Berna *n* Bern.

bernés,-esa *adj & nm,f* Bernese.

berrear *vi* **1** *(becerro)* to bellow, low. **2** *fam (gritar)* to howl, bawl. **3** *Mús fam* to sing off key, sing out of tune.

berrido *nm* **1** bellowing, lowing. **2** *fam (grito)* howl, shriek; **dar berridos,** to howl, shriek. **3** *Mús fam* note which is off key, screech.

berrinche *nm fam* rage, tantrum; **coger** *or* **agarrar un b.,** to throw a tantrum.

berro *nm Bot* cress, watercress.

berrocal *nm* rocky place.

berza *nf Bot* cabbage; *arg* **estar con la b.,** to be an idiot.

berzal *nm* cabbage patch.

berzas *nmf inv,* **berzotas** *nmf inv fam* idiot, **halfwit.**

besamanos *nm inv* **1** *(recepción oficial)* royal audience. **2** *(modo de saludar)* hand kissing.

besamel *nf,* **besamela** *nf véase* **bechamel.**

besar I *vtr* to kiss; *fig* **b. el suelo,** to fall flat on one's face; *fig* **fue llegar y b. el santo,** it was as easy as pie, it was a piece of cake, it was a walkover. **II besarse** *vr* **1** to kiss; **se besaron al despedirse,** they kissed each other goodbye. **2** *fam (tropezar)* to bump heads; **se besaron al doblar la esquina,** they bumped into each other as they turned the corner.

besito *nm Am (panecillo)* coconut bun.

beso *nm* **1** kiss; *fam* **comerse a algn a besos,** to kiss sb passionately. **2** *fig* bump, collision; **darse un b.,** to bump into each other.

best-seller *nm* best-seller.

bestia I *nf* beast, animal; **b. de carga,** beast of burden. **II** *nmf fam fig* brute, beast; **estar hecho un b.,** to be as strong as a horse; **ser una mala b.,** to be a nasty piece of work. **III** *adj fig* brutish, boorish; **a lo b.,** rudely, inconsiderately; **aquí te tratan a lo b.,** they are really rude to you in here, they treat you like animals in here; **eso es muy b.,** *(malo)* that's really unpleasant; *(demasiado)* that's going too far; **¡no seas b.!,** *(grosero)* don't be rude!; *(exagerado)* don't exaggerate!

bestial *adj* **1** animal, bestial. **2** *fam (enorme)* huge, tremendous; *(extraordinario)* fantastic, terrific, great; **esa película es b.,** that film's brilliant; **una comida b.,** a huge meal. ◆ **bestialmente** *adv* fantastically; **lo pasamos b.,** we had a fantastic time.

bestialidad *nf* **1** bestiality, savagery. **2** *fam (estupidez)* stupidity; **decir bestialidades,** to say horrible things. **3** *fam (cantidad grande)* **una b. de,** tons of, stacks of.

bestiario *nm Lit* bestiary.

besucón,-ona I *adj* fond of kissing. **II** *nm,f* person who is fond of kissing.

besugo *nm* **1** *(pez)* sea bream. **2** *pey (persona)* idiot, halfwit; **mantener** *or* **sostener un diálogo de besugos,** to talk at cross purposes.

besuguera *nf* shallow oval fish pan.

besuquear *fam* **I** *vtr* to kiss, cover with kisses. **II besuquearse** *vtr* to smooch.

besuqueo *nm fam* smooching.

beta *nf (letra griega)* beta; **rayos b.,** beta rays.

bético,-a *adj Hist* Andalusian.

betún *nm* **1** *Quím* bitumen, asphalt. **2** *(para el calzado)* shoe polish; *fam* **quedar a la altura del b.,** to give a poor show.

bezo *nm* thick lip.

bezudo,-a *adj* thick-lipped.

Bhutan *n* Bhutan.

biberón *nm* baby's bottle, feeding bottle.

Biblia *nf* **1** *Rel* Bible; **la (Santa) B.,** the (Holy) Bible; *fam* **saber la B. en verso,** to know everything, be very knowledgeable. **2 b.,** *arg (drogas)* book of cigarette papers.

biblia *nf CAm fig (astucia, maña)* cunning, skill.

bíblico,-a *adj Rel* biblical.

bibliófilo,-a *nm,f* bibliophile, booklover.

bibliografía *nf* bibliography.

bibliográfico,-a *adj* bibliographic, bibliographical.

bibliógrafo,-a *nm,f* bibliographer.

biblioteca *nf* **1** library; **b. ambulante,** mobile library. **2** *Mueb* bookcase, bookshelves *pl*.

bibliotecario,-a *nm,f* librarian.

BIC *nf abr de* **Brigada de Investigación Criminal,** ≈ Criminal Investigation Department, CID.

bicameral *adj Pol* bicameral, two-chamber.

bicarbonato *nm Quím* bicarbonate. ■ **b. sódico,** bicarbonate of soda.

bicéfalo,-a *adj* bicephalous, two-headed.

bicentenario *nm* bicentenary, *US* bicentennial.

bíceps *nm inv Anat* biceps.

bicha *nf* snake.

biche *adj* **1** *Col (fruta)* green, unripe; *(persona)* weak, frail. **2** *Méx (vacío)* empty; *fam (fofo)* flabby.

bichero *nm Náut* boathook.

bicho *nm* **1** *(insecto)* bug, insect; *fig* **¿qué b. te ha picado?,** what's the matter with you?, what's got into you?, *US* what's bugging you? **2** *(animal)* beast, animal; *Taur* bull. **3** *fam (persona)* odd character; **mal b.,** nasty piece of work; **todo b. viviente,** every living soul; **um b. raro,** a weird person, an oddball.

bichoco,-a *adj Arg Chi Urug fig (persona)* over the hill, past it; **caballo b.,** nag.

bici *nf fam* bike.

bicicleta *nf* bicycle; **ir en b.,** to ride a bicycle; **¿sabes montar en b.?,** can you ride a bicycle?

bicoca *nf fam fig* bargain; **es ana bicoca,** it's a bargain.

bicolor *adj* two-colour, two-tone; *Pol* **gobierno b.,** two-party government.

bicoque *nm Am* rap on the head.

bicornio *nm* two-cornered hat.

bidé *nm* bidet.

bidón *nm* large can, drum; **b. de gasolina,** oil drum.

biela *nf Aut* connecting rod.

bielda *nf Agr* winnowing.

bieldo *nm Agr* winnowing fork.

bien[1] *adv* **1** *(tal como es debido)* well, properly; **habla b. el italiano,** she speaks Italian well; **hay que escribirlo b.,** it must be written correctly; **hiciste b. en decírmelo,** you were right to tell me; **las cosas le van b.,** things are going well for him; **oler b.,** to smell nice *or* lovely; *(comida)* to smell good; **poratarse b.,** to behave well; *prov* **quien b. te quiere te hará llorar,** you have to be cruel to be kind. **2** *(excelente)* all right, O.K.; **¡b.!,** good!, great!; **¡muy b.!,** excellent, first class!; **pasarlo b.,** to have a good time; **¡qué b.!,** great!, fantastic! **3** *(con buena salud)* well; **¿no te encuentras b.?,** aren't you feeling well? **4** *(cómodamente)* well, comfortably; **viven b.,** they're comfortably off. **5** *(fácilmente)* easily; **b. podía haberme avisado,** she might have let me know; **b. puede acabarlo en un día,** he can easily finish it off in a day; **b. puedes permitirte el lujo de fumar puros,** if anybody can afford to treat himself to cigars, you can; **b. puedo creer que ...,** I can well believe that ... . **6** *(con gusto)* really; *(de buena gana)* willingly, gladly; **b. lo pagaría si tuviera bastante dinero,** I'd gladly pay for it if I had enough money; **b. me tomaría ahora una sopita de cebolla,** I'd really love a bowl of onion soup right now. **7** *(seguramente)* **b. se gastaron la mitad de la herencia en aquella casa,** they must have spent half the inheritance on that house. **8** *(muy, bastante)* very, quite; **b. es verdad que ...,** it's quite clear that ...; **b. temprano,** very early, nice and early; **dame un té b. caliente,** I'd like a nice hot cup of tea; **la casa está b. lejos del pueblo,** the house is a long way from the village. **9** *(mucho)* lot, many; **b. de veces,** lots of times. **10** *(en interrogativas)* **¿y b.?,** and so?, what then? **11** *(estar + bien) (de dinero)* well-off; *(de salud)* well; **la abuela está muy b. de salud,** grandmother is in really good health; *(cómodamente)* **aquí dentro se está muy b.,** it's nice and cosy in here; *(de buena)* **esta comida está b.,** this meal is fine; *(prenda)* **esta falda te está b.,** this skirt suits you; *(merecer)* **le está b. empleado que se le haya escapado el avión,** I'm glad he missed the plane, it serves him right; **¡está b.!,** *(¡de acuerdo!)* fine!, all right!; *(¡basta!)* that's enough!; **¡ya está b.!,** that's (quite) enough!; *(un bonito, interesante)* **esa película francesa está muy b.,** that French film is very good; *fam* **su novia está muy b.,** his girlfriend is very nice; *(en apuros)* **sí que estamos b.!,** (well), we are in a fine mess! **12** **sentar b.,** agree with; **no me ha sentado b. la fruta,** the fruit has disagreed with me; **sus comentarios no se me sentaron b.,** I didn't like his remarks. **13** *fml* **tener a b. de,** to be so kind as to; **rogamos tenga a bien de ...,** would you please ...?, we should be grateful if you would ... . **14** **más b.,** rather, a little; **es más b. tímida,** she's on the shy side, she's a little shy. **II** *conj* **ahora b.,** now, now then; *or* **o b.,** or, or else; **b. ... or b. ...,** either ... or ...; **b. en metro** *or* **b. en coche,** either by tube or by car; **no b.,** as soon as; **no b. llegó el policía, empezó el tiroteo,** no sooner had the policeman arrived than the shooting began; **si b.,** while, although, even if. **III** *adj* well-to-do, well-off; **la gente b.,** the wealthy, the upper classes.

bien[2] *nm* **1** *(bondad)* good, good thing; **el b. y el mal,** good and evil; **un hombre de b.,** a upright *or* upstanding man; *prov* **haz b. y no mires a quien,** do well and dread no shame. **2** *(bienestar, provecho)* benefit, advantage; **dedicó su vida al bien de los demás,** she devoted her life to others; **por el b. de,** for the good of, in the interest of; **lo hace por el b. de sus hijos,** he does it for the sake of his children; **lo hicieron por tu b.,** they did it for your own good. **3** **bienes,** goods. ■ **b. de equipo,** *(maquinaria, instalaciones)* capital goods; *Jur* property; **b. gananciales,** communal property, property acquired during marriage; **b. inmuebles,** real estate; **b. muebles,** movables, personal property; **b. públicos,** public property.

bienal **I** *adj* biennial. **II** *nf* biennial (exhibition).

bienaventurado,-a **I** *adj* **1** *Rel* blessed. **2** *(afortunado)* fortunate, happy. **II** *nm,f* naïve person.

bienaventuranza *nf* **1** happiness, bliss. **2** *Rel* **las bienaventuranzas,** the Beatitudes.

bienestar *nm (personal)* well-being, contentment; *(comodidad)* ease, comfort.

bienhechor,-a **I** *adj* beneficent, beneficial. **II** *nm, f (hombre)* benefactor; *(mujer)* benefactress.

bienintencionado,-a *adj* well-meaning, well-in-tentioned.

bienio *nm* biennium, two-year period.

bienvenida *nf* welcome; **dar la b. a algn,** to welcome sb.

bienvenido,-a adj welcome.

bies nm inv Cost bias; **al b.,** on the bias.

bifásico,-a adj Elec two-phase.

bife nm Am **1** Culin steak; **b. a caballo,** steak with two fried eggs. **2** (bofetada) slap.

bífido,-a adj Anat Bot bifid.

bifocal adj bifocal; **gafas bifocales,** bifocals.

bifurcación nf bifurcation; (de la carretera) fork.

bifurcado,-a adj forked.

bifurcarse vr to fork, branch off.

bigamia nf bigamy.

bígamo,-a I adj bigamous. **II** nm,f bigamist.

bígaro nm Zool winkle.

bigote nm **1** (de persona) moustache, US mustache; (de gato) whiskers pl. **2** fam **de b.,** (enorme) huge; (sensacional) tremendous, great, terrific; **una comida de b.,** a fantastic meal.

bigotera nf (compás) bow compass.

bigotudo,-a adj with a large moustache, moustachioed.

biguán nm CAm large bundle.

bigudí nm hair-curler, roller.

bilateral adj bilateral; **acuerdo b.,** bilateral agreement.

bilbaíno,-a I adj of or from Bilbao. **II** nm, f native or inhabitant of Bilbao.

biliar adj biliary; Med **cálculo b.,** bile stone.

bilingüe adj bilingual.

bilingüismo nm bilingualism.

bilioso,-a adj bilious.

bilis nf **1** Med bile. **2** fig bile, spleen; fig **descargar la b. contra algn,** to vent one's spleen on sb; **esa actitud me exalta la b.,** that attitude makes my blood boil.

billar nm **1** (juego) billiards sing; **jugar al b.,** to play billiards. ■ **b. americano,** pool; **b. romano,** pinball; **b. ruso,** snooker. **2** (mesa) billiard table. **3** billares, billiard room sing, pool room sing.

billetaje nm tickets pl.

billete nm **1** (de sorteo, bus, avión, etc) ticket; **sacar un b.,** to buy a ticket. ■ **b. de ida y vuelta,** return (ticket), US round-trip ticket; **b. sencillo** or **de ida,** single (ticket); Ferroc **b. kilométrico,** ≈ Rail Rover. **2** (de banco) note, US bill; **un b. de mil,** a thousand peseta note.

billetera nf, **billetero** nm wallet, US billfold.

billón nm billion, US trillion.

bimensual adj twice-monthly, bi-monthly, fort-nightly.

bimestral adj every two months.

bimestre I adj véase **bimestral. II** nm period of two months.

bimotor I adj twin-engine, twin-engined. **II** nm twin-engined plane.

binario,-a adj **1** binary; Mat **sistema b.,** binary system. **2** Mús two beats to the bar, two-four measure.

bincha nf Am (pañuelo) kerchief.

bingo nm **1** (juego) bingo. **2** (sala) bingo hall.

binoculares nmpl field glasses, binoculars.

binóculo nm pince-nez.

binomio nm Mat binomial.

biodegradable adj biodegradable.

biofísica nf biophysics.

biografía nf biography.

biográfico,-a adj biographic, biographical.

biógrafo,-a nm,f biographer.

biología nf biology.

biológico,-a adj biological.

biólogo,-a nm,f biologist.

biombo nm (folding) screen.

biopsia nf Med biopsy.

bioquímica nf biochemistry.

bioquímico,-a I adj biochemical. **II** nm,f biochemist.

bióxido nm Quím dioxide. ■ **b. de carbono,** carbon dioxide.

bipartidismo nm Pol two-party system, bipartisanship.

bípedo,-a adj & nm,f biped.

biplano nm Av biplane.

biquini nm (prenda) bikini.

birlar vtr fam to pinch, nick, swipe; **me han birlado la cartera,** my wallet's been pinched.

birlibirloque loc adv **por arte de b.,** as if by magic.

Birmania n Burma.

birmano,-a adj & nm,f Burmese.

birreactor Av I adj twin-jet. **II** nm twin-jet plane.

birreta nf Rel biretta.

birrete nm cap, beret; Rel biretta; Univ mortar-board, academic cap.

birria nf fam monstrosity; **esa película es una b.,** that film is rubbish.

biruji nm fam chilly wind.

bis I adv twice; **viven en el 34 b.,** they live at 34 A. **II** nm encore.

bisabuela nf great-grandmother.

bisabuelo nm great-grandfather; **bisabuelos,** great-grandparents.

bisagra nf hinge.

bisar vtr to give an encore, repeat.

bisbisar vtr, **bisbisear** vtr to mutter, mumble.

bisbiseo nm muttering, mumbling.

bisbita nf Orn pipit. ■ **b. arbórea/campestre/común,** tree/tawny/meadow pipit.

bisección nf bisection.

bisector adj Geom bisecting.

bisectriz I adj Geom bisecting. **II** nf Geom bisector, bisectrix.

bisel nm bevel edge, bevel.

biselar vtr to bevel.

bisemanal adj twice-weekly.

bisexual adj & nmf bisexual.

bisiesto adj **año b.,** leap year.

bisílabo,-a adj two-syllabled, disyllabic.

bismuto nm Quím bismuth.

bisnieto,-a nm, f (niño) great-grandson; (niña) great-granddaughter; **mis bisnietos,** my great-grandchildren.

bisojo,-a adj cross-eyed.

bisonte nm Zool bison, American buffalo.

bisoñé nm toupee.

bisoño,-a I adj Mil raw; fig inexperienced, green. **II** nm,f Mil raw recruit, US rookie; fig greenhorn, novice.

bisté nm, **bistec** nm steak.

bisturí nm Med scalpel, surgical knife.

bisutería nf imitation jewellery or US jewelry.

bitácora nf Náut binnacle. ■ **cuaderno de b.,** log-book.

biter nm bitters pl.

bitoque nm **1** (tapón) spigot. **2** Am Med cannula. **3** CAm (sumidero) drain, sewer.

bituminoso,-a adj bituminous.

bivalente adj Quím bivalent.

bivalvo,-a adj bivalve.

bizantino,-a I adj **1** Byzantine. **2** fig pointless; **discusiones bizantinas,** hair-splitting arguments. **II** nm,f Byzantine.

bizarría nf 1 (valor) gallantry, bravery. 2 (generosidad) generosity.

bizarro,-a adj 1 (valiente) gallant, brave. 2 (generoso) generous.

bizco,-a I adj cross-eyed; fig **quedarse b.,** to be dumbfounded or flabbergasted. II nm,f cross-eyed person.

bizcocho nm Culin sponge cake or finger.

biznieto,-a nm,f véase **bisnieto,-a.**

bizquear vi to go cross-eyed.

blanca nf 1 fam estar or quedarse sin b., to be flat broke. 2 Mús minim.

Blancanieves nf Lit Snow White.

blanco,-a[1] I adj white; **más b. que la nieve,** as white as snow; **dar carta blanca,** to give sb a free rein; **tez blanca,** fair complexion. II nm, f (hombre) white man; (mujer) white woman; **los blancos,** whites.

blanco[2] nm 1 (color) white; **en b. y negro,** in black and white. ■ Constr b. de España, whiting; Anat b. de la uña, half-moon; Anat b. del ojo, white of the eye. 2 (vacío) blank; **dejó la hoja en b.,** he left the page blank; **votos en b.,** blank votes; fig **pasar la noche en b.,** to have a sleepless night; **quedarse en b.,** to fail to understand. 3 (diana) target; **dar en el b.,** to hit the target or the bull's eye; **tirar al b.,** to shoot at a target; **tiro al b.,** target shooting; fig **ser el b. de todas las miradas,** to be the centre of attention.

blancor nm, **blancura** nf whiteness.

blancuzco,-a adj pey whitish.

blandengue adj pey weak, soft, feeble.

blandir vtr defect to brandish.

blando,-a adj 1 (maleable) soft; **un colchón b.,** a soft mattress; **tiene las carnes muy blandas,** he is flabby. 2 fig (suave) soft, gentle; **clima b.,** mild climate; **es demasiado b. con sus hijos,** he's too soft with the children; **una mirada blanda,** a tender look.

blanducho,-a adj, **blandujo,-a** adj fam softish; pey (cuerpo) flabby.

blandura nf 1 (calidad) softness. 2 fig (dulzura) gentleness, tenderness; (debilidad) mildness, weakness.

blanduzco,-a adj pey softish.

blanqueador,-a I adj (que pone blanco) whitening; (con lejía) whitewashing; **un producto b.,** a whitening or bleaching agent. II nm,f whitewasher.

blanquear I vtr 1 (poner blanco) to whiten; (con lejía) to bleach. 2 (encalar) to whitewash. II vi to turn white, be whitish.

blanquecino,-a adj whitish.

blanqueo nm 1 whitening; (con lejía) bleaching. 2 (encalado) whitewashing; Téc blanching.

blasfemar vi Rel to blaspheme (contra, against); (decir palabrotas) to curse, swear.

blasfemia nf Rel blasphemy; (palabrota) curse.

blasfemo,-a I adj blasphemous. II nm,f blasphemer.

blasón nm 1 (escudo) coat of arms. 2 (heráldica) heraldry. 3 (divisa) device. 4 fig (gloria, honor) glory, honour, US honor; **hacer b. de algo,** to boast about sth.

blasonar I vtr to emblazon. II vi fig boast (de, about).

blástula nf Biol blastula.

bledo nm Bot blite; fam **me importa un b.,** I couldn't give a damn, I couldn't care less.

blenorragia nf Med blennorrhagia.

blenorrea nf Med blennorrhea, US blennorrhoea.

blindado,-a adj 1 Mil armoured, US armored, armour-plated, US armor-plated; (antibalas) bullet-proof; **coche b.,** bullet-proof car; (furgoneta) security van; **puerta blindada,** reinforced door, security door. 2 Téc shielded.

blindaje nm 1 armour, US armor; (vehículo) armour or US armor plating. 2 Téc shield.

blindar vtr 1 (vehículo) to armour, US armor. 2 Téc to shield.

bloc nm pad. ■ **b. de notas,** notepad.

blocar vtr Ftb to block.

blonda nf blond lace.

blondo,-a adj lit blond, fair.

bloque nm 1 (gen) block; **un b. de cemento,** a concrete block; **en b.,** en bloc. ■ **b. de pisos,** block, block of flats. 2 (manzana de casas) block. 3 Pol bloc; **el b. de países comunistas,** the Communist Bloc countries.

bloquear vtr 1 Mil to blockade. 2 Com Fin (precios) to freeze. 3 Téc to jam, block. 4 Ftb (pelota) to block. 5 Parl (ley, decreto) to block. 6 (obstruir) to block, obstruct; **la nieve bloqueó todas las vías de acceso al pueblo,** the village was cut off by snow.

bloqueo nm 1 Mil blockade; **forzar el b.,** to run the blockade; **levantar un b.,** to raise a blockade. 2 Com Fin (precios) freeze, freezing.

blues nm Mús blues pl.

bluff nm bluff.

blusa nf blouse.

blusón nm loose blouse, smock.

boa I nf Zool boa. II nm (prenda) (feather) boa.

boato nm show, ostentation.

bobada nf (acción) silliness, fooling about; (comentarios) nonsense, rubbish; **decir bobadas,** to talk nonsense; **¡no hagas bobadas!,** don't be silly!

bobalicón,-ona fam I adj simple, stupid. II nm, f simpleton, idiot.

bobear vi (decir bobadas) to talk nonsense; (hacer bobadas) to do silly things, fool about.

bobería nf véase **bobada.**

bóbilis bóbilis (de) loc adv fam 1 (de balde) free, for nothing. 2 (sin esfuerzo) without lifting a finger.

bobina nf 1 (de película) reel, spool; (de hilo) bobbin, reel, spool; (de cinta magnética) reel. 2 Elec coil. ■ **b. de encendido,** ignition coil.

bobinado nm Elec winding, coiling.

bobinar vtr to wind.

bobo,-a I adj (tonto) stupid, silly; (ingenuo) naïve, simple. II nm, f fool, simpleton, dunce; **entre bobos anda el juego,** they are all the same, they are all as bad as each other. III nm Teat buffoon, jester.

boca nf 1 Anat mouth, **b. abajo,** face downward, **b. arriba,** face upward; fig **a b. llena,** openly, straight out; fig **a pedir de b.,** in accordance with one's wishes; fig **todo le salió a pedir de b.,** everything turned out exactly as he had wished; fig **andar de b. en b.,** to be the talk of the town; fig **b. de escorpión,** evil tongue; fig **decir algo con la b. chica,** to say one thing and mean another, fig **hacer b.,** to whet one's appetite; fig **írsele la b. a algn,** to be unable to keep one's mouth shut, to let the cat out of the bag; fig **meterse en la b. del lobo,** to put one's head into the lion's mouth; fig **quitarle a algn las palabras de la b.,** to take the words right out of sb's mouth; fig **tengo cinco bocas que mantener,** I've got five mouths to feed; fam **cerrarle la b. a algn,** to shut sb up; fam **con la b. abierta,** open-mouthed, agape; fam **no abrir la b., no decir esta b. es mía,** not to open one's mouth, not to say a word; fam **quedarse con la b. abierta,** to be astounded or amazed; fam **se le hizo la b. agua,** his mouth watered; fam **taparle la b. a algn,** to shut sb up, keep sb quiet; vulg **¡cállate la b.!,** shut up!; prov **en b. cerrada no entran moscas,** silence is golden; prov **por la b. muere el pez,** the least said the better. ■ **b. a b.,** kiss of life, mouth-to-mouth respiration; **b. de riego,** hydrant. 2 (entrada) entrance; Téc opening, aperture; **b. del estómago,** pit of the stomach; **la b. de un túnel,** the mouth of a tunnel; **la b. del metro,** the entrance to the tube or underground station. 3 (vino) bouquet, aroma.

bocacalle *nf (calle secundaria)* side street; *(entrada)* entrance to a street, intersection.

bocadillo *nm* 1 sandwich; **tomar un b.,** to have a snack; **un b. de jamón/tortilla,** a ham/omelette sandwich. 2 *(de cómic, chiste)* balloon.

bocado *nm* 1 *(mordisco)* mouthful; *(piscolabis)* bite to eat, snack, tidbit; **con el b. en la boca,** having scarcely finished eating; **no he probado b. en todo el día,** I haven't had a bite to eat all day; *fam* **b. sin hueso,** soft job, cushy number. ■ *Anat* **b. de Adán,** Adam's apple. 2 *(mordedura)* bite. 3 *(freno del caballo)* bit.

bocajarro (a) *loc adv* point-blank.

bocamanga *nf* cuff, wristband.

bocanada *nf* 1 *(de vino)* mouthful. 2 *(de humo)* whiff, puff; **una b. de viento,** a gust of wind.

bocata *nm arg* sandwich, sarnie, buttie.

bocazas *nmf inv fam* bigmouth, blabbermouth.

bocel *nm Arquit* torus.

bocera *nf* 1 food left around the mouth after eating or drinking, moustache. 2 *Med* lip sore.

boceras *nmf inv fam* bigmouth, blabbermouth.

boceto *nm Arte* sketch, outline; *(de un trabajo escrito)* outline, plan.

bocha *nf* 1 *(bola)* bowl. 2 **bochas,** *(juego)* bowls.

bochar *vtr* 1 *(bocha)* to take out. 2 *Am (suspender)* to fail. 3 *Méx Ven (rechazar)* to reject.

bochinche *nm fam* uproar, din, riot; **armar un b.,** to kick up a row.

bochorno *nm* 1 *(tiempo)* sultry *or* close weather; *(calor sofocante)* stifling heat; **hacer b.,** to be sultry *or* close *or* muggy. 2 *fig (vergüenza)* shame, embarrassment. 3 *(rubor)* blush, flush.

bochornoso,-a *adj* 1 *(tiempo)* sultry, close, muggy, oppressive; *(calor)* stifling. 2 *fig (vergüenza)* shameful, embarrassing.

bocina *nf* 1 *Aut* horn; **tocar la b.,** to blow *or* sound one's horn. 2 *Mús* horn, trumpet. 3 *(de gramófono)* horn.

bocinazo *nm Aut* hoot, honk, toot.

bocio *nm Med* goitre.

bocón,-ona *fam* I *adj* big-mouthed. II *nm, f* big-mouth, braggart.

bocoy *nm (pl bocoyes)* large cask.

boda *nf* wedding, marriage. ■ **bodas de diamante/oro/plata,** diamond/gold/silver wedding *sing*; **lista de bodas,** wedding list.

bodega *nf* 1 wine cellar; *(tienda)* wine shop. 2 *Náut* hold. 3 *(almacén)* warehouse. 4 *Am (tienda de comestibles)* grocery store, grocer's.

bodegón *nm* 1 *(restaurante)* cheap restaurant. 2 *(taberna)* tavern. 3 *Arte* still-life painting.

bodeguero,-a *nm, f (propietario)* owner of a wine cellar; *(encargado)* cellarman.

bodoque I *nm* 1 *(bola de barro)* pellet. 2 *Cost* raised embroidery stitch. 3 *Méx (chichón)* bump, lump, swelling. 4 *CAm (pelota informe)* lump; *(de papel)* ball. II *nmf fam* dimwit, dunce.

bodorrio *nm pey* wedding.

bodrio *nm* 1 *(comida)* mishmash, hotchpotch. 2 *fam* rubbish, trash; **su última novela es un b.,** his latest novel is rubbish; **¡vaya b. de película!,** what a useless film!

body *nm* bodystocking, leotard.

BOE *nm abr de* **Boletín Oficial del Estado,** Official Gazette.

bóer *adj & nmf (pl bóers)* Boer.

bofe I *nm Zool (pulmón)* lung, lights *pl*; *fam fig (trabajar mucho)* **echar el b.** *or* **los bofes,** to work flat out, slog one's guts out; *(esforzarse mucho)* to go all out. II *adj CAm (antipático)* disagreeable, unpleasant.

bofetada *nf* slap round the face; *fig* blow; **dar una b. a algn,** to slap sb's face; *fig* **darse de bofetadas por algo,** to come to blows over sth; *fig* **esos colores se dan de bofetadas,** those colours really clash; *fig* **no tener (ni) media b.,** to be a weakling, be weedy; *fig* **¡qué b. le has dado al decir eso!,** what you said was a real blow to him!

bofetón *nm* hard slap round the face.

bofia *nf arg* **la b.,** the fuzz *pl*, the cops *pl*, the law; **tiene jaleos con la b.,** he's in trouble with the law.

boga¹ *nf (pez) (de agua dulce)* bream; *(de mar)* bogue.

boga² I *nf* 1 *Náut* rowing. 2 *fig* **estar en b.,** to be in fashion. II *nmf* rower.

bogada *nf (palada)* stroke.

bogador,-a *nm, f* rower.

bogar *vi* 1 *(remar)* to row. 2 *(navegar)* to sail.

bogavante *nm (pez)* lobster.

bogotano,-a I *adj* of *or* from Bogotá. II *nm, f* native of Bogotá.

bohardilla *nf véase* **buhardilla.**

bohemia *nf* Bohemia, Bohemian life.

bohemio,-a *adj & nm, f* Bohemian.

bohío *nm Am* hut, cabin.

boicot *nm (pl boicots)* boycott.

boicotear *vtr* to boycott.

boicoteo *nm* boycott, boycotting.

boina *nf* beret.

boîte *nf* **boite** *nf* nightclub, discotheque.

boj *nm Bot* 1 S *(árbol)* box. 2 *(madera)* boxwood.

bojar I *vtr (medir)* to measure; **b. una isla,** to measure the perimeter of an island. II *vi (medir)* to measure; **la isla boja cuarenta kilómetros,** the island has a perimeter of forty kilometres.

bojear *vi (navegar)* to coast.

bojote *nm Am* bundle, package.

bol *nm* bowl.

bola *nf* 1 *(cuerpo esférico)* ball, sphere; *(canica)* marble; *Dep fam* ball; *fig* **dejar que ruede la b.,** to let things take their course; **no dar pie con b.,** to be unable to do anything right. ■ **b. de billar,** billard ball; **b. de cristal,** crystal ball; **b. de nieve,** snowball; *Téc* **cojinete de bolas,** ball bearing; **queso de b.,** Edam cheese. 2 *fam fig (mentira)* fib, lie; **meter bolas,** to tell fibs. 3 *Bridge* slam. 4 **bolas,** *SAm* bolas. 5 **bolas,** *vulg (cojones)* balls.

bolacha *nf Am (masa de caucho)* lump of rubber.

bolada *nf (lanzamiento)* throw; *(en billar)* stroke.

bolado *nm* 1 *(azucarillo)* sweet. 2 *Am* business. 3 *Méx* love affair.

bolardo *nm Náut* bollard.

bolchevique *adj & nmf* Bolshevik.

bolcheviquismo *nm,* **bolchevismo** *nm* Bolshevism.

boldo *nm Bot* boldo.

boleada *nf Arg Urg* hunt using bolas

boleadoras *nfpl Arg Urug* bolas.

bolear¹ I *vtr* 1 *SAm* to catch with bolas. 2 *Arg fig (jugar una mala pasada)* to play a dirty trick on. 3 *Méx (embetunar)* to polish. II **bolearse** *vr Arg* 1 *(caballo)* to rear. 2 *(tropezar)* to trip **(con,** over), stumble **(con,** over). 3 *(equivocarse)* to make a mistake. 4 *(avergonzarse)* to become embarrassed; *(ruborizarse)* to blush.

bolear² *vtr (arrojar)* to throw.

bolera *nf* bowling alley, skittle alley.

bolero,-a¹ I *adj (mentiroso)* lying, fibbing. II *nm, f* liar, fibber.

bolero,-a² I *nm, f Mús* bolero dancer. II *nm* 1 *Mús* bolero. 2 *(chaquetilla)* bolero. 3 *CAm (sombrero de copa)* top hat. 4 *Méx (limpiabotas)* shoeblack.

boleta *nf* **1** *(permiso)* pass, permit. **2** *(vale)* voucher, slip. **3** *Am* ballot.

boletería *nf Am Dep Ferroc* ticket office, *GB* booking office; *Teat* ticket office, box office.

boletero,-a *nm, f Am* ticket seller.

boletín *nm* **1** *(publicación)* journal, bulletin; **B. Oficial del Estado,** Official Gazette. **2** *(de suscripción)* form.

boleto *nm* *(de rifa, lotería)* ticket; *(de quinielas)* coupon.

boli *nm fam* ballpen, biro®.

boliche *nm* **1** *(juego de bolos)* bowling, skittles. **2** *(en la petanca)* jack. **3** *(lugar)* bowling alley. **4** *(juguete)* cup-and-ball game. **5** *Am (tenducho)* small grocery store; *(taberna)* tavern; *(figón)* cheap restaurant. **6** *Chi (casa de juego)* gaming *or* gambling house.

bólido *nm* **1** *Astron* meteor, meteorite; *fam* **ir como un b.,** to be in a terrible rush; **siempre vas como un b.,** you're always in a mad rush. **2** *Aut* racing car.

bolígrafo *nm* ballpoint (pen), biro®.

bolilla *nf Arg Par Urug* **1** *(bolita de sorteos)* numbered ball. **2** *Educ (tema)* topic.

bolillero *nm Arg Par Urug* *(bombo de sorteos)* drum.

bolillo *nm Cost* bobbin; **encaje de bolillos,** bobbin lace.

bolívar *nm Fin* standard monetary unit of Venezuela.

bolivia *n* Bolivia.

boliviano,-a I *adj* Bolivian. **II** *nm, f (persona)* Bolivian. **III** *nm Fin* boliviano.

bollar *vtr* **1** *Tex* to stamp. **2** *(metal)* to dent, bump; **me han bollado el coche,** somebody's dented my car.

bollería *nf* bakery, baker's.

bollo *nm* **1** *Culin* bun, bread roll; *fig* **no está el horno para bollos,** it's not the right time. **2** *(abolladura)* dent. **3** *(chichón)* bump, swelling. **4** *(alboroto)* fuss, confusion.

bollón *nm* stud.

bolo I *nm* **1** skittle, ninepin. ■ **b. alimenticio,** bolus. **2** *(bolera)* bowling alley. **3 bolos,** *(juego)* skittles; *fig* **echar a rodar los b.,** to stir up trouble. **II** *adj CAm fam* drunk.

bolsa¹ *nf* **1** *(gen)* bag. ■ **b. de agua caliente,** hotwater bottle; **b. de aire,** air pocket; **b. de deportes,** sports bag; **b. de la compra,** shopping bag; **b. de papel,** paper bag; **b. de viaje,** travel bag. **2** *(de dinero)* purse; **¡la b. o la vida!,** your money or your life! **3** *Anat (lacrimal)* sac; *(bajo los ojos)* bag. **4** *Min* pocket. **5** *(en prenda)* bag, pucker.

bolsa² *nf Fin* Stock Exchange; **jugar a la b.,** to play the market. ■ **agente de b.,** stockbroker; **b. de trabajo,** employment exchange, job centre.

bolsear *vtr CAm Méx (robar)* to pick sb's pocket.

bolsero,-a *nm, f* **1** *(fabricante)* maker *or* seller of bags *or* purses. **2** *Méx (carterista)* pickpocket.

bolsillo *nm* **1** *(en prenda)* pocket; **de b.,** pocket, pocket-size; **diccionario de b.,** pocket dictionary; **edición de b.,** pocket edition; **libro de b.,** paperback; *fig* **meterse a algn en el b.,** to win sb over; *fig* **tener a algn en el b.,** to have sb in one's pocket *or* under one's control. **2** *(monedero)* purse, *US* pocketbook; **consultar con el b.,** to check the state of one's finances; **lo pagó de su b.,** he paid for it himself, he paid for it out of his own pocket; *fam* **rascarse el b.,** to give money.

bolsín *nm Fin* kerb *or* outside market.

bolso *nm* handbag, bag, *US* purse.

bomba¹ *nf* **1** *Téc* pump. ■ **b. aspirante,** suction pump; **b. de aire,** air pump; **b. de incendios,** fire engine; *Med* **b. gástrica,** stomach pump. **2** *Mús* slide.

bomba² **I** *nf* **1** *Mil* bomb; *fig* **a prueba de bombas,** bombproof, shellproof; *fig* **estar *or* ir echando bombas,** to be furious; *fig* **la noticia cayó como una b.,** the news burst like a bombshell. ■ **b. atómica,** atomic bomb; **b. de hidrógeno,** hydrogen bomb; **mano, b. de** hand grenade; **b. de neutrones,** neutron bomb; **b. de relojería,** time bomb; **b. fétida,** stink bomb; **b. incendiaria,** incendiary

bomb. **2** *(de lámpara)* glass lampshade, globe. **II** *adj fam* fantastic; **éxito b.,** tremendous success; **noticia b.,** shattering piece of news. **III** *adv fam* **pasarlo b.,** to have a great time *or* a whale of a time.

bombacho,-a *adj* baggy, loose-fitting; **pantalón b.,** knickerbockers *pl.*

bombachos *nmpl* knickerbockers.

bombardear *vtr Mil* to bomb, shell, bombard; *Fís (átomo)* to bombard; *fig* **b. a algn a preguntas,** to bombard sb with questions.

bombardeo *nm* **1** *Mil* bombing, bombardment. **2** *Fís* bombardment.

bombardero,-a I *adj* bombing, bomber; **avión b.,** bomber (plane); **lancha bombardera,** gunboat. **II** *nm* **1** *Av* bomber. **2** *Hist (soldado)* bombardier.

bombazo *nm* bomb explosion *or* blast; *fig* **menudo b. cuando se enteren,** there'll be hell to pay when they find out.

bombear *vtr* to pump.

bombeo *nm* **1** *(de líquido)* pumping; **estación de b.,** pumping station. **2** *(curvatura)* camber.

bombero,-a *nm, f (hombre)* fireman; *(mujer)* firewoman; *US (ambos sexos)* firefighter. ■ **cuerpo de bomberos,** fire brigade; **parque de bomberos,** fire station.

bombilla *nf Elec* (light) bulb.

bombín *nm* **1** *(sombrero)* bowler hat. **2** *(para hinchar)* pump. **3** *(de cerradura)* cylinder.

bombo *nm* **1** *Mús* bass drum; *fig* **a b. y platillo(s),** with a great song and dance; **anunciar algo a b. y platillo(s),** to announce sth with much ballyhoo; *fam* **dar b. a algn,** to praise sb excessively, *fam* **darse b.,** to blow one's own trumpet; *fam* **dejar a una chica con b.,** to get a girl into trouble. **2** *(de sorteo)* lottery drum. **3** *(de lavadora)* drum.

bombón *nm* **1** *(de chocolate)* chocolate; **de b.,** chocolate-coated; **una caja de bombones,** a box of chocolates. **2** *fam (mujer)* pretty girl, cracker; **es un b.,** she's a real dish.

bombona *nf* **1** *(garrafa)* carafe; *Quím* carboy; **una b. de vino,** a carafe of wine. **2** *(recipiente metálico)* cylinder. ■ **b. de butano,** butane gas cylinder.

bombonera *nf* **1** *(caja)* chocolate box. **2** *fig (lugar)* small, cosy place *or* room *or* house.

bombonería *nf* sweetshop, confectioner's.

bombote *nm CAm Ven* small boat.

bonachón,-ona I *adj* good-natured, easy-going. **II** *nm, f* kind *or* good-natured soul, easy-going person.

bonaerense I *adj* of *or* from Buenos Aires. **II** *nmf* native *or* inhabitant of Buenos Aires.

bonancible *adj* **1** *(tiempo)* fair; *(mar)* calm. **2** *(persona)* kind.

bonanza *nf* **1** *Náut (tiempo)* fair weather; *(mar)* calm at sea. **2** *fig (prosperidad)* prosperity. **3** *Min* bonanza.

bondad *nf (calidad de bueno)* goodness; *(amabilidad)* kindness, generosity; *fml* **tenga la b. de esperar,** please be so kind as to wait.

bondadoso,-a *adj* kind, good, good-natured.

bonete *nm Rel* cap, biretta; *Univ* cap, mortar-board.

bongó *nm Mús* bongo, bongo drum.

boniato *nm Bot* sweet potato.

bonificación *nf* **1** *(mejora)* improvement. **2** *Com (descuento)* discount, allowance, rebate; *Fin* **b. fiscal,** tax rebate.

bonificar *vtr Com* to discount, allow.

bonísimo,-a *adj superl de* **bueno.**

bonito,-a¹ *adj* pretty, nice.

bonito² *nm (pez)* (Atlantic) bonito.

Bonn *n* Bonn.

bono nm 1 *(vale)* voucher. 2 *Fin* bond, deventure; **bonos del tesoro** or **del Estado,** Treasury bonds.

bono-bus nm bus pass.

bonzo nm *Rel* bonze.

boñiga nf, **boñigo** nm cow dung.

boom nm boom; **el b. turístico,** the tourist boom.

boomerang nm boomerang.

boqueada nf last breath; **dar la última b.,** to breathe one's last.

boquear vi to gasp; *(en agonía)* to breathe one's last; *fam fig* to be on one's last legs.

boquera nf 1 *Med (pupa)* crack, lip sore. 2 *Agr* sluice.

boquerón nm *(pez)* anchovy.

boquete nm *(paso angosto)* narrow opening, small gap; *(brecha)* breach.

boquiabierto,-a adj open-mouthed; **se quedó b. al oír la noticia,** he was flabbergasted when he heard the news, he was stunned by the news.

boquilla nf 1 *(para fumar)* cigarette or cigar holder; *(de cigarrillo)* tip; *(de pipa)* mouthpiece; **decir algo de b.,** to pay lip service to sth. 2 *Mús* mouthpiece. 3 *(orificio)* opening. 4 *(de un bolso)* clasp. 5 *(de manguera)* nozzle; *(de lámpara)* burner. 6 *Agr* sluice.

bórax nm inv *Quím* borax.

Borbón n *Hist* Bourbon.

borbónico,-a adj Bourbon.

borborigmo nm *Med* rumbling.

borbotar vi, **borbotear** vi to bubble.

borboteo nm bubbling.

borbotón nm bubbling; *fig* **hablar a borbotones,** to gabble; *fig* **salir a borbotones,** to gush forth.

borceguí nm *(pl borceguíes)* half boot, ankle boot.

borda nf 1 *Náut (de barco)* gunwale; **arrojar** or **echar por la b.,** to throw overboard; *fig* to renounce. ■ **(motor de) fuera b.,** outboard motor. 2 *Náut (de galera)* mainsail.

bordada nf *Náut* tack, board.

bordado,-a I pp de **bordar. II** adj *Cost* embroidered. **III** nm embroidery.

bordador,-a nm,f embroiderer.

bordadura nf embroidery.

bordar vtr 1 *Cost* to embroider. 2 *fig (ejecutar perfectamente)* to do excellently; **el actor ha bordado su papel,** the actor gave an excellent performance.

borde[1] nm *(de mesa, camino)* edge; *Cost* hem, edge; *(de vasija)* rim, brim; **al b. de,** on the brink of, on the verge of; **al b. del mar,** at the seaside. ■ *Av* **b. de ataque/salida,** leading/trailing edge.

borde[2] I adj 1 *Bot (planta)* wild. 2 *fam (torpe)* clumsy; *(tonto)* daft, stupid. II nmf *fam (torpe)* clumsy person; *(tonto)* idiot.

bordear vtr 1 *(ir por el borde)* to go round the edge of, skirt. 2 *fig (aproximarse)* to border on, verge on; **bordeaba los cuarenta años,** he was pushing forty. 3 *Náut* to tack.

bordelés,-esa I adj of or from Bordeaux. **II** nm,f native or inhabitant of Bordeaux.

bordillo nm kerb, *US* curb.

bordín nm *Am* boarding house.

bordo nm *Náut* board; **a b.,** on board; **subir a b.,** to go on board; **de alto b.,** seagoing.

bordón nm 1 *(bastón)* staff. 2 *(muletilla)* pet phrase. 3 *Mús (cuerda)* bass string. 4 *Impr* omission.

bordonear vi *Mús (guitarra)* to strum.

boreal adj northern, boreal.

bóreas nm inv Boreas, north wind.

Borgoña n Burgundy.

borgoña nm *(vino)* Burgundy.

borgoñés,-esa adj & nm,f, **borgoñón,-ona** adj & nm,f Burgundian.

bórico,-a adj *Quím* boric. ■ **ácido b.,** boric acid.

borla nf 1 *Cost* tassel. 2 *(para polvos)* powder puff.

borne nm *Elec* terminal.

boro nm *Quím* boron.

borona nf 1 *(maíz)* maize, *US* corn. 2 *(mijo)* millet.

borra nf 1 *(para colchones)* flock; *fig* **meter b.,** to pad (out). 2 *(pelusa)* fluff. 3 *(poso)* sediment, dregs pl.

borrachera nf 1 *(embriaguez)* drunkenness; **agarrar** or **coger** or **pillar una b.,** to get drunk; *fam* **se pilló una b. de órdago,** he got drunk out of his skull. 2 *fig (exaltación)* ecstasy, rapture, enthusiasm.

borrachín nm *fam* soak, boozer.

borracho,-a I adj 1 *(bebido)* drunk; **b. como una cuba, b. perdido,** blind drunk; **estar b.,** to be drunk; *fig* **b. de poder/de felicidad,** drunk with power/happiness. 2 *Culin (bizcocho)* rum baba. **II** nm,f drunkard, drunk; **ser un b.,** to be a drunkard.

borrador nm 1 *(escrito)* rough copy, *US* first draft. 2 *(croquis)* rough or preliminary sketch. 3 *(goma de borrar)* rubber, eraser; *(de la pizarra)* board rubber or duster.

borradura nf crossing out, erasure.

borraja nf *Bot* borage; *fam fig* **quedar en agua de borrajas,** to come to nothing, fizzle or peter out.

borrajear vtr *(palabras)* to scribble; *(papel)* to doodle or scribble on.

borrar I vtr 1 *(con goma)* to erase, rub out; *(tachar)* to cross out or off; **b. la pizarra,** to clean the blackboard. 2 *Inform* to erase, delete; **b. un archivo/documento,** to erase a file/document. 3 *fig* to erase, wipe away. **II borrarse** vr 1 *(ovidarse)* to be erased; **se me borró de la memoria,** I forgot all about it. 2 *(darse de baja)* to drop out, withdraw; **me he borrado del club,** I'm not a member of the club any more.

borrasca nf 1 *Meteor (tormenta)* storm; *(chubasco)* squall; *(nieve)* flurry. 2 *fig (contratiempo)* hitch.

borrascoso,-a adj 1 *Meteor (tormentoso)* stormy; *(viento)* gusty, squally. 2 *fig* stormy, tempestuous.

borrego,-a nm,f 1 *Zool (corderillo)* yearling lamb. 2 *fam fig (persona)* ass, dimwit. 3 *fam (pelliza)* sheepskin coat.

borrico nm 1 *Zool* ass, donkey. 2 *fam fig* ass, dimwit.

borro nm *Zool* yearling lamb.

borrón nm 1 *(mancha de tinta)* blot, smudge; *fig* **b. y cuenta nueva,** let's wipe the slate clean, let's start afresh. 2 *(escrito)* rough copy, *US* rough draft. 3 *(croquis)* rough or preliminary sketch. 4 *fig (imperfección, deshonor)* blemish.

borronear vtr *(palabras)* to scribble; *(en papel)* to doodle or scribble on.

borroso,-a adj *(confuso, impreciso)* blurred, hazy, indistinct; **escritura borrosa,** smudgy or illegible handwriting; **ideas borrosas,** vague or hazy ideas; **veo b.,** I can't see clearly, everything's blurred.

boscaje nm 1 *(bosque pequeño)* thicket, grove, copse. 2 *Arte (paisaje)* woodland scene.

boscoso,-a adj wooded.

bosque nm wood, forest.

bosquejar vtr *(dibujo)* to sketch, outline; *fig (plan)* to draft, outline.

bosquejo nm *(dibujo)* sketch, study; *fig (plan)* draft, outline.

bosquimán nm Bushman.

bostezar vi to yawn.

bostezo nm yawn.

bota nf 1 boot; *fig* **morir con las botas puestas,** to die with one's boots on; *fam* **ponerse las botas,** to strike it rich, make a killing, feather one's nest; *fam* **ponerse las botas comiendo,** to stuff oneself. ■ **botas camperas,** cowboy boots; **botas de montar,** riding boots. 2 *(de vino)* wineskin.

botadero *nm Am* ford.

botador,-a *nm* 1 *Náut* boatpole. 2 *Carp* nail puller, claw hammer. 3 *Odont* forceps. 4 *Impr* shooting stick.

botadura *nf Náut* launching (of a boat).

botafumeiro *nm Rel* incense burner, thurible, censer.

botalón *nm Náut* boom.

botana *nf Am* snack.

botánica *nf* botany.

botánico,-a I *adj* botanical, botanic. **II** *nm,f* botanist.

botanista *nmf* botanist.

botar I *vi* 1 (*saltar*) to jump; (*caballo*) to buck; *fam* **está que bota**, she's hopping mad. 2 (*pelota*) to bounce, rebound. **II** *vtr* 1 *Náut* (*barco*) to launch. 2 (*arrojar*) to throw *or* chuck out; *Ftb* **b. un córner**, to take a corner. 3 (*despedir*) to fire. 4 (*pelota*) to bounce. 5 *Am* (*despilfarrar*) to squander.

botarate I *adj* foolish. **II** *nmf* 1 madcap, fool. 2 *Am* (*despilfarrador*) spendthrift, squanderer.

botarel *nm Arquit* flying buttress.

bote[1] *nm* (*acción de botar*) jump, bound; **dar botes**, to jump up and down; **de un b.**, with one leap. 2 (*de pelota*) bounce, rebound. 3 (*de caballo*) buck.

bote[2] *nm* 1 (*lata*) can, tin; (*de cristal*) jar; (*para propinas*) jar *or* box for tips; **leche de b.**, tinned milk; *fam* **chupar del b.**, to scrounge; **sólo quiere chupar del b.**, he's just a hanger-on; *fam* **tener a algn metido en el b.**, to have sb under one's thumb, have sb in the palm of one's hand. ■ **b. de humo**, smoke bomb.

bote[3] *nm* (*lancha*) boat. ■ **b. salvavidas**, lifeboat.

bote[4] *nm* **de b. en b.**, packed, full to bursting.

botella *nf* bottle.

botellazo *nm* blow with a bottle.

botellín *nm* small bottle.

botepronto *nm* (*rugby*) dropkick; (*football, tennis*) half volley; *fam* **a b.**, all of a sudden.

botica *nf* (*farmacia*) chemist's (shop), pharmacy, *US* drugstore; *fam* **hay de todo como en b.**, there's everything under the sun. 2 (*medicamentos*) medicines *pl.* 3 (*tienda*) shop.

boticario,-a *nm,f* chemist, pharmacist, *US* druggist.

botija *nf* 1 (*vasija*) earthenware pitcher. 2 *Am* (*tesorro enterrado*) buried treasure.

botijo *nm* earthenware pitcher (with spout and handle); *fam fig* **estar hecho un b.**, to be like a barrel.

botín[1] *nm* (*de un robo*) loot, booty.

botín[2] *nm* (*calzado*) ankle boot, spat, legging.

botiquín *nm* medicine chest *or* cabinet, first aid kit.

boto *nm* boot.

botón *nm* 1 *Cost* button; *fig* **b. de muestra**, sample. 2 *Bot* (*capullo*) bud. ■ **b. de oro**, buttercup. 3 *Téc* button; **pulsar el b.**, to press the button. 4 (*tirador*) knob.

botonadura *nf* buttons *pl*, set of buttons.

botones *nm inv* (*en un hotel*) buttons *sing*, bellboy, *US* bellhop; (*chico de recados*) messenger, errand boy.

bototo *nm Am* (*calabaza*) gourd *or* calabash (for carrying water).

Botswana *n* Botswana.

botswanés,-esa *adj & nm,f* Botswanan.

botulismo *nm Med* botulism.

boutique *nf* boutique.

bóveda *nf* 1 *Arquit* vault, crypt. ■ *fig* **b. celeste**, vault of heaven; *Anat* **b. craneana**, cranial cavity; *Arquit* **b. de cañón**, barrel vault. 2 (*cripta*) crypt.

bóvido,-a *Zool* **I** *adj* bovid. **II bóvidos** *nmpl* bovidae *pl*, bovines.

bovino,-a I *adj* bovine. **II bóvinos** *nmpl* bovines.

boxcalf *nm* box calf.

boxeador *nm* boxer.

boxear *vi* to box.

boxeo *nm* boxing.

bóxer *nm* (*pl* **bóxers**) *Hist* Boxer.

boya *nf* 1 *Náut* buoy. 2 *Pesca* (*corcha*) float.

boyante *adj* 1 Náut buoyant. 2 (*próspero*) prosperous, thriving. 3 (*feliz*) buoyant, happy. 4 *Taur* (*toro*) easy to fight.

boyar *vi* to float.

boyero,-a *nm,f* ox driver, cowherd.

boy-scout *nm* boy scout.

bozal *nm* muzzle.

bozo *nm* 1 (*vello*) down, fuzz; (*moustache*) youthful moustache, fine hairs. 2 (*parte exterior de la boca*) mouth, lips.

bracear *vi* 1 (*mover los brazos*) to swing *or* wave one's arms about. 2 (*nadar*) to swim. 3 (*forcejear*) to struggle, wrestle.

bracero *nm* (day) labourer.

bracete (de) *loc adv* arm-in-arm.

braco,-a I *adj* snub-nosed. **II** *nm* (*perro*) pointer, setter.

braga *nf* 1 (*cuerda*) (guy) rope. 2 (*pañal*) nappy, *US* diaper. 3 (*usu pl*) panties *pl*, knickers *pl*; *vulg* **estar en bragas**, to be flat broke; *vulg* **estar hecho una b.**, to be shattered *or* worn out; *vulg* **pillar a algn en bragas**, to catch sb with his trousers down.

bragadura *nf Anat Cost* crotch, crutch.

bragazas *nm inv fam* henpecked husband.

braguero *nm* truss.

bragueta *nf* fly, flies *pl*.

braguetazo *nm vulg* marriage of convenience; **dar el b.**, to marry (into) money.

braguetero *nm vulg* lecher.

brahmán *nm Rel* Brahman, Brahmin.

brahmánico,-a *adj Rel* Brahmanic, Brahminic.

brahmanismo *nm Rel* Brahmanism, Brahminism.

braille *nm* braille.

bramante *nm* hemp string *or* cord.

bramar *vi* 1 (*toro, vaca*) to low, bellow; (*elefante*) to trumpet. 2 (*persona*) (*de dolor*) to bawl, howl; (*de ira*) to roar, thunder. 3 (*viento*) to howl, roar; (*mar*) to roar, thunder; (*trueno*) to rumble, roll.

bramido *nm* 1 (*toro, vaca*) lowing, bellowing; (*elefante*) trumpeting. 2 (*de dolor*) bawling, howling; (*de ira*) roaring, thundering. 3 (*viento*) howling, roaring; (*mar*) roaring, thundering; (*trueno*) rumbling, rolling.

brandy *nm* brandy.

branquia *nf* gill, branchia.

branquial *adj* branchial.

brasa *nf* ember, red-hot coal; **chuletas a la b.**, barbecued chops.

brasero *nm* brazier.

Brasil *n* Brazil.

brasileño,-a *adj & nm,f*, **brasilero,-a** *adj & nm,f* Brazilian.

bravata *nf* 1 (*amenaza*) piece *or* act of bravado. 2 (*fanfarronada*) boasting, bragging, showing off; **decir bravatas**, to brag, boast, show off.

braveza *nf* 1 (*bravura*) courage, bravery. 2 (*de los elementos*) inclemency; **la b. del mar**, the fury of the sea.

bravío,-a I *adj* 1 (*salvaje*) wild, untamed; (*silvestre*) wild. 2 *fig* (*rústico*) uncouth, uneducated. **II** *nm* (*bravura*) wildness, ferocity.

bravo,-a I *adj* 1 (*valiente*) brave, courageous. 2 (*feroz*) fierce, ferocious; **un toro b.**, a fighting bull. 3 (*mar*) rough, stormy; (*terreno*) rugged; (*paisaje*) wild 4 (*carácter*) churlish, bad-tempered. **II** *interj* **¡b.!** well done!, bravo!

bravuconada *nf* boast, brag.

bravucón,-ona I *adj* boastful, boasting. **II** *nm, f* boaster, braggart.

bravura *nf* 1 *(de los animales)* ferocity, fierceness. 2 *(de las personas)* courage, bravery. 3 *(de toro)* fighting spirit. 4 *(balandronada)* boasting, bragging.

braza *nf* 1 *Náut (medida)* fathom. 2 *Natación* breast stroke; **nadar a b.**, to swim breast stroke.

brazada *nf* I *Natación* stroke. 2 *(cantidad)* armful.

brazado *nm* armful

brazal *nm* 1 *(insignia)* armband; **el b. de la Cruz Roja,** the Red Cross armband. 2 *Hist* brassard. 3 *(de un río)* irrigation ditch.

brazalete *nm* 1 *(insignia)* armband. 2 *(pulsera)* bracelet.

brazo *nm* 1 *Anat* arm; *Zool* foreleg; *(de sillón, tocadiscos, balanza)* arm; *(de río, candelabro)* branch; *(de árbol)* branch; *(de grúa)* boom, jib; *(de micrófono)* boom; *(de molino)* sail arm; **a b. partido,** with bare fists; *fig* tooth and nail; **en brazos,** in one's arms; **ir del b.**, to walk arm in arm; *fig* **con los brazos abiertos,** with open arms; *fig* **con los brazos cruzados,** lazily, doing nothing; *fig* **no dar su b. a torcer,** not to give in, stand firm; *fig* **serel b. derecho de algn,** to be sb's right-hand man; *fam* **estar hecho un b. de mar,** to be dressed to kill. ■ *Cat Culin* **b. de gitano,** type of Swiss roll containing cream; *Geog* **b. de mar,** inlet; **huelga de brazos caídos,** go slow. 2 *fig (poder, esfuerzo)* power strength; **el b. de la ley,** the arm of the law. 3 **brazos,** *(trabajadores, ayuda)* hands; **slempre faltan b.,** more hands are always needed.

brea *nf* 1 tar, pitch. 2 *(tela)* tarpaulin.

brebaje *nm* concoction, brew.

breca *nf (pez)* pandora.

brecha I *(en muro, pared)* opening, break, gap; **Mil** breach; *fig* **estar siempre en la b.**, to be always at it. 2 *(en la cabeza, en una ceja)* gash. 3 *fig* breach; **nada hace b. en él,** nothing affects him.

brécol *nm Bot* brocoli, broccoli.

brega *nf* 1 *(lucha)* struggle, fight. 2 *(riña)* row, quarrel. 3 *(trabajo duro)* hard work, toil; **andar a la b.**, to slog away, toil away.

bregar I *vtr (amasar)* to knead. **II** *vi* 1 *(luchar)* to struggle, fight. 2 *(reñir)* to row, quarrel. 3 *(trabajar con afán)* to slog away, toil away.

brema *nf (pez)* bream.

breña *nf*, **breñal** *nm* scrub.

breque *nm Ferroc* 1 *Am (freno)* brake. 2 *SAm (vagón de equipajes)* luggage van, *US* baggage car.

Bretaña *nf* 1 Brittany. 2 **Gran B.**, Great Britain.

brete *nm* shackles *pl*, fetters *pl*; *fig* **poner a algn en un b.**, to put sb in a tight spot.

bretón,-ona I *adj* Breton. **II** *nm, f (persona)* Breton. **III** *nm (idioma)* Breton.

breva *nf (higo)* early fig; *fam fig* **de higos a brevas,** once in a blue moon. 2 *(puro)* flat cigar. 3 *fig (suerte)* stroke of luck; *(chollo)* cushy job, cushy number; **¡no caerá esa b.!**, no such luck!

breve I *adj* brief, short; **en b.**, shortly, soon; **en breves palabras,** in short, **hicieron una b. pausa,** they paused briefly; **seré b.**, I shall be brief. **II** *nm Rel* (papal) brief. **III** *nf Mús Gram* breve.

brevedad *nf* briefness, brevity, shortness; **con b.**, concisely, briefly; **con la mayor b. posible,** as soon as possible.

breviario *nm* 1 *Rel* breviary. 2 *(compendio)* compendium, summary.

brezal *nm* heath, moor.

brezo *nm Bot* heather.

bribonada *nf* piece of mischief, rascally trick.

bribón,-ona I *adj* roguish, dishonest. **II** *nm, f* rogue, rascal.

bricolaje *nm* do-it-yourself, DIY; **le encanta el b.**, she's really keen on do-it-yourself; **la sección de b.**, the DIY department.

brida *nf* 1 *(rienda)* rein, bridle; **a toda b.**, at full gallop. 2 *Med* adhesion. 3 *Téc* flange.

bridge *nm Naipes* bridge; **jugar al b.**, to play bridge.

brigada I *nf* 1 *Mil* brigade. ■ **general de b.**, brigadier, *US* brigadier general. 2 *(de policías)* squad. ■ **b. antiterrorista,** anti-terrorist squad; **b. móvil,** flying squad. 3 *(de trabajadores)* gang. **II** *nm Mil* sergeant major.

brigadier *nm* brigadier.

brillante I *adj* 1 *(reluciente)* brilliant, sparkling. 2 *fig (excelente)* bright, brilliant; **un escritor b.**, an outstanding writer. **II** *nm* diamond; **un collar de brillantes,** a diamond necklace.

brillantez *nf* 1 *(resplandor)* brilliance, brightness. 2 *fig (excelencia)* brilliance.

brillantina *nf* brilliantine.

brillar *vi* 1 *(resplandecer)* to shine; *(piedra preciosa, ojos, etc)* to sparkle; *(estrella)* to twinkle, shine; *(sol, luna)* to shine; *(lentejuelas etc)* to glitter; *(metal pulido)* to gleam; *(seda)* to shimmer; *(luz muy fuerte)* to glare, sparkle; *(ascuas etc)* to glow. 2 *fig (destacar)* to stand out; **b. por su ausencia,** to be conspicuous by one's absence.

brillo *nm* 1 *(resplandor)* shine; *(de las estrellas)* twinkling; *(del sol, de la luna)* brightness; *(de lentejuelas etc)* glittering; *(de los metales)* shine; *(de una superficie)* gloss, shine; *(del cabello, de una tela)* sheen; *(de un color)* brilliance; *(de una pantalla)* brightness; *(de los zapatos)* shine; **sacar b. a,** to shine, polish. 2 *fig* brilliance, splendour.

brincar *vi* 1 *(dar saltos)* to jump, hop, skip, frolic; *(cordero)* to gambol. 2 *(enfadarse)* to fly into a rage, fly off the handle.

brinco *nm* jump, hop, skip; **de un b.**, with a jump.

brindar I *vi* to drink, toast, drink a toast; **brindemos por tu salud,** let us drink to your health. **II** *vtr* 1 *(ofrecer)* to offer, provide; **le agradezco la oportunidad que me brinda,** I thank you for giving me this opportunity. 2 *Taur* to dedicate the bull **(a,** to). **III brindarse** *vr* to offer **(a,** to), volunteer **(a,** to); **se brindó a invitarnos,** he offered to pay for the meal.

brindis *nm* 1 toast. 2 *Taur* dedication (of the bull).

brío *nm* 1 *(pujanza)* energy, force; **lleno de b.**, full of go. 2 *(resolución)* determination. 3 *(garbo, gallardía)* dash, spirit.

brioso,-a *adj* 1 *(enérgico)* energetic, vigorous. 2 *(decidido)* determined, resolute. 3 *(con garbo, gallardía)* dashing, spirited. 4 *(caballo)* fiery, spirited.

briqueta *nf* briquette, briquet.

brisa *nf* breeze; **b. marina,** sea breeze.

brisca *nf Naipes* Spanish card game.

británico,-a I *adj* British; **las Islas Británicas,** the British Isles. **II** *nm, f* British person, Briton; **los británicos,** the British.

brizna *nf* 1 *(de hierba)* blade; *(de hilo)* strand, thread. 2 *(trozo)* bit.

broca *nf* 1 *Téc (taladro)* drill, bit. 2 *(clavo)* tack. 3 *Cost* bobbin.

brocado *nm Tex* brocade.

brocal *nm* curb (of a well).

brocearse *vr SAm Min* to become mined out.

brocha I *adj Cam fam (entremetido)* meddlesome; *(adulador)* flattering. **II** *nf Arte Constr* paintbrush, brush; *(de afeitar)* shaving brush; *Constr* **pintor de b. gorda,** painter and decorator; **bromas de b. gorda,** crude *or* tasteless jokes.

brochada *nf*, **brochazo** *nm* brush stroke; *fig* **de un b.**, at one stroke.

broche *nm* **1** *(de prenda)* fastener, clasp, clip. **2** *(joya)* brooch; *fig* **cerrar con b. de oro,** to finish with a flourish.

brocheta *nf Culin* skewer.

bróculi *nf* brocoli, broccoli.

broma[1] *nf (chiste)* joke; *(chanza)* trick, prank, lark; **bromas aparte,** seriously (though); **¡déjate de bromas!,** stop mucking around!, let's talk seriously now!; **echar** *or* **tomar algo a b.,** not to take sth seriously, treat sth as a joke; **en b.,** as a joke; **estar de b.,** to be in a joking mood; **gastar bromas/una b. a algn,** to play jokes/a joke on sb; **medio en b. medio en serio, entre bromas y veras,** half jokingly; **¡ni en b.!,** not on your life!; **¡quince mil pesetas me costó la b.!,** fifteen thousand pesetas it cost me! ■ **b. pesada,** practical joke.

broma[2] *nf Zool* shipwonn.

bromato *nm Quím* bromate.

bromear *vi* to joke.

bromista **I** *adj* fond of joking *or* playing jokes. **II** *nmf* joker, prankster.

bromo *nm Quím* bromine.

bromuro *nm Quím* bromide.

bronca *nf* **1** *(riña)* quarrel, row; **se armó una b. de miedo,** an almighty row broke out. **2** *(pelea)* scuffle, brawl, fight. **3** *(reprensión)* telling off, ticking off, dressing down; **el jefe le echó una b.,** the boss told him off; **llevarse una b.,** to get a ticking *or* telling off. **4** *(abucheo)* jeering, booing, boos *pl.* **5** *Arg Chi Urug (rabia)* rage, anger.

bronce *nm* bronze; *fig* **ser de b.,** to be as hard as nails, have a heart of stone; *fam* **ligar b.,** to sunbathe.

bronceado,-a **I** *pp de* **broncear.** **II** *adj* **1** bronze, bronze coloured *or US* colored. **2** *(por el sol)* suntanned, tanned, sunburnt. **III** *nm* **1** bronzing. **2** *(por el sol)* suntan, tan.

bronceador,-a **I** *adj* tanning, suntan; **leche bronceadora,** suntan cream. **II** *nm (crema)* suntan cream *or* lotion; *(aceite)* suntan oil.

broncear *vtr (metal, estatua)* to bronze. **II broncearse** *vr* to get a tan *or* a suntan.

bronco,-a *adj* **1** *(superficie)* rough, coarse; *(metales)* brittle. **2** *(sonido, voz)* harsh, raucous. **3** *fig (carácter)* rough, rude, surly.

bronconeumonía *nf Med* bronchopneumonia.

broncoscopio *nm* bronchoscope.

bronquial *adj Anat* bronchial.

bronquio *nm Anat* bronchus.

bronquítico,-a *adj Med* bronchitic.

bronquitis *nf inv Med* bronchitis.

broqueta *nf véase* **brochota.**

brotar *vtr* **1** *Bot (planta)* to sprout, *(sacar capullos)* to come into bud, *(sacar hojas)* to sprout, come into leaf **2** *(manar)* to spring, gush forth, *(río)* to rise **3** *(lágrimas)* to well up **4** *Med (erupción)* to break out **5** *fig (nacer, manifestarse)* to appear, spring up

brote *nm* **1** *Bot (renuevo)* bud, shoot, *(acción de brotar)* budding **2** *(de agua)* gushing **3** *(de lágrimas)* welling up **4** *Med (de erupción)* outbreak, appearance **5** *fig (epidémico, violento)* outbreak

broza *nf* **1** *(despojo de las plantas)* dead leaves *or* wood **2** *(desechos)* rubbish, *US* trash **3** *(maleza)* undergrowth, thicket **4** *fig (paja)* pudding

brucelosis *nf Med* brucellosis

bruces (de) *loc adv* face downwards; **se cayó de b.,** he fell flat on his face

bruja *nf* **1** *(hechicera)* witch, sorceress **2** *fam (mujer fea)* old hag *or* crone, *(arpía)* witch

brujería *nf* witchcraft, sorcery

brujo *nm* wizard, sorcerer; *(en una tribu primitiva)* witch doctor, medicine man

brújula *nf* compass, *fig* **perder la b.,** to lose one's bearings.

---

bruma *nf (niebla)* mist, *(de calor)* (heat) haze

brumoso,-a *adj* misty, hazy

Brunei *n* Brunei

bruno[1] *nm Bot (árbol y fruta)* black plum

bruno,-a[2] *adj* dark brown

bruñido *nm* **1** *(acción)* polishing, burnishing **2** *(efecto)* polish, burnish

bruñir *vtr* **1** to polish, burnish **2** *Arg CR Guat fam (molestar)* to pester, annoy

brusco,-a **I** *adj* **1** *(persona)* brusque, abrupt **2** *(repentino)* sudden, sharp; **un descenso b. de temperatura,** a sharp drop in temperature **II** *nm Bot* butcher's broom

Bruselas *n* Brussels, **coles de B.,** Brussels sprouts

bruselense **I** *adj* of *or* from Brussels **II** *nmf* native *or* inhabitant of Brussels

brusquedad *nf* **1** *(de carácter)* brusqueness, abruptness **2** *(de superficies etc)* suddenness, abruptness

brutal *adj* **1** *(violento, cruel)* brutal, rough. **2** *fam (enorme)* huge, colossal, gigantic, **hubo una subida b. de precios,** there was a tremendous rise in prices **3** *fam (magnífico)* great, terrific, fantastic, **es una película b.,** it's a terrific film

brutalidad *nf* **1** *(crueldad)* brutality, savagery **2** *(acción cruel)* brutal *or* savage act.

bruto,-a **I** *adj* **1** *(necio, incapaz)* stupid, thick **2** *(inculto)* ignorant, uneducated **3** *(tosco)* rough, coarse, uncouth **4** *(piedra preciosa)* rough, uncut, **un diamante en b.,** an uncut diamond **5** *(sin refinar)* crude, **petróleo b.,** crude oil **6** *Fin* gross, **noventa mil pesetas brutas,** ninety thousand pesetas before tax **7** *(peso)* gross. **II** *nm, f* **1** *(estúpido)* blockhead, brute **2** *(inculto)* ignoramus **III** *nm Zool* brute, beast

bruza *nf* **1** *(para caballos)* horse brush **2** *Impr* printer's brush

bubónico,-a *adj Med* bubonic, **peste bubónica,** bubonic plague

bucal *adj Anat* buccal, oral, of the mouth

bucanero *nm Hist* buccaneer

Bucarest *n* Bucharest

búcaro *nm* vase *or* jar made of clay

buceador,-a *nm, f* diver

bucear *vi* **1** to dive, swim under water. **2** *fig* to investigate, explore, sound (out)

buche *nm* **1** *Zool (de ave)* crop, craw, *(de animales)* maw; *fig* **guardar algo en el b.,** to keep quiet about sth **2** *fam (estómago)* belly, stomach **3** *(de líquido)* mouthful

bucle *nm* curl, ringlet

bucólico,-a **I** *adj* bucolic, pastoral. **II** *nf* bucolic, pastoral poem

Buda *nm Rel* Buddha

Budapest *n* Budapest

budín *nm Culin* pudding

budismo *nm Rel* Buddhism

budista *adj* Buddhist

buen *adj (delante de un nombre)* **¡b. viaje!,** have a good trip[1]; **un b. trabajo,** a good job, *fig* **un b. día,** all of a sudden; *véase tamb* **bueno,-a.**

buenaventura *nf* good fortune, good luck; **echar la b. a algn,** to tell sb's fortune

buenazo,-a **I** *adj* good-natured **II** *nm, f* goodnatured person

bueno,-a I *adj* **1** *(gen)* good, **lo b.,** the good thing, *irón* **lo b. es que ...,** the funny thing (about it) is that ..., **ser de buena familia,** to be of a good family, **un buen alumno,** a good pupil, **una buena madre,** a good mother; **una buena película,** a good film **2** *(agradable)* nice, pleasant **3** *(amable) (con ser)* good, kind, good-natured; **el b. de Carlos,** good old Carlos, **es muy buena persona,** she's a very kind soul, **ser más b. que el pan,** to be as good as gold **4** *(sano) (con estar)* well, in good health **5** *(tiempo)* good, **hoy hace buen tiempo,** the weather is good today, **mañana hará un día b.,** it will be a nice day tomorrow **6** *(útil)* useful. **7** *(conveniente)* good, **no es b. comer tanto,** it's not good for you to eat so much, **sería b. que cambiáramos de coche este verano,** it would be a good idea if we changed our car this summer **8** *(todavía servible)* usable, **esos zapatos son buenos aún,** those shoes are still wearable. **9** *(considerable)* considerable, **un buen número de,** a good number of, **una buena cantidad,** a considerable amount. **10** *irón* fine, real, proper, **¡en buen lío te has metido, chico!,** that's a fine mess you've got yourself into, my boy! **11** *(grande)* good, big, **un buen trozo de pastel,** a nice big piece of cake, **una buena paliza,** a good hiding **12** *fam (de gran atractivo físico)* gorgeous, sexy, **¡qué b. está!, ¡tío b.!,** he's a bit of all right!, **¡tía buena!,** she's a bit of all right! **13** **¡buenas!,** *(saludos)* hello!, **buenas noches,** good evening, **buenas tardes,** good afternoon, good evening; **buenos días,** good morning **14** *(locuciones)* **de buena gana,** willingly, **de buenas a primeras,** suddenly, all at once, **estar de buenas,** to be in a good mood, **los buenos tiempos,** the good old days, **por las buenas,** willingly, **por las buenas** *or* **por las malas,** willy-nilly, *fam* **tirarse una buena vida,** to lead a cushy life, *irón* **¡bueno la has hecho!,** that's done it!, *irón* **de los buenos,** lovely, grand, **un susto de los buenos,** a real fright, *irón* **¡ésta sí que es buena!,** that's a good one, *irón* **¡estamos buenos!,** what a fine mess we're in!, *irón* **¡estaría b.!,** I should jolly well hope not!, *irón* **librarse de una buena,** to get away with sth, *irón* **poner b. a algn,** to criticize sb, *GB* slate sb **II** *interj* **¡b.! 1** *(sorpresa)* well! **2** *(bien, de acuerdo)* all right, OK ◆ **buenamente** *adv* **1** *(fácilmente)* easily, **haz lo que b. puedas,** *just do what you can,* **si b. puedes,** if you possibly can **2** *(voluntariamente)* readily, willingly

buey *nm Zool* ox, bullock ■ **b. marino,** sea cow

búfalo,-a *nm, f Zool* buffalo.

bufanda *nf* scarf, muffler.

bufar I *vi* **1** *(toro)* to snort; *(gato)* to spit; *(caballo)* to neigh. **2** *fig (persona)* to be fuming; **el jefe está que bufa,** the boss is hopping mad. **3** *Méx (emborracharse)* to get drunk. **II bufarse** *vr Méx (superficie)* to blister.

bufé *nm* **1** *Culin* buffet. ■ **b. libre,** self-service buffet meal. **2** *(mueble)* sideboard.

bufete *nm* **1** *(mesa de escribir)* desk, writing table. **2** *(despacho)* lawyer's office. **3** *(clientela del abogado)* practice.

buffet *nm (pl buffets) véase* **bufé.**

bufido *nm* **1** *(de toro)* snort; *(de gato)* spit; *(de caballo)* neigh. **2** *fig* outburst.

bufo,-a *adj* comic, clownish; **ópera bufa,** comic opera. **II** *nm, f* clown, buffoon.

bufonada *nf* jest, piece of buffoonery; **bufonadas,** clowning *sing,* buffoonery *sing.*

bufonesco,-a *adj* comical, farcical.

bufón,-ona I *adj* comical, farcical. **II** *nm, f* clown, buffoon, jester.

buganvilla *nf Bot* bougainvillea.

buhardilla *nf* **1** *(desván)* attic, garret. **2** *(ventana)* dormer window.

búho *nm Orn* owl. ■ **b. real,** eagle owl.

buhonería *nf* *(baratijas)* pedlar's *or* hawker's wares *pl;* *(oficio)* peddling, hawking.

buhonero,-a *nm, f* pedlar, hawker.

buitre *nm* **1** *Orn* vulture. **2** *fig (persona)* opportunist.

buje *nm Téc* axle box, bushing.

bujía *nf* **1** *(vela)* candle. **2** *Aut* sparking plug, spark plug. **3** *Fís* candlepower.

bula *nf* **1** *Rel (documento)* papal bull. **2** *Hist (sello de plomo)* bulla.

bulbo *nm Anat Bot* bulb.

bulboso,-a *adj* bulbous.

buldog *nm Zool* bulldog.

bulerías *nfpl* Andalusian song and dance, accompanied by clapping.

bulevar *nm* boulevard.

Bulgaria *n* Bulgaria.

búlgaro,-a I *adj* Bulgarian. **II** *nm, f (persona)* Bulgarian. **III** *nm (idioma)* Bulgarian.

bulla *nf* **1** *(griterío)* racket, row, uproar. **2** *(muchedumbre)* crowd, mob.

bullanga *nf* tumult, racket.

bullanguero,-a I *adj* noisy, riotous. **II** *nm, f* noisy person, troublemaker.

bullicio *nm* **1** *(ruido)* din, hubbub, noise. **2** *(movimiento y ruido)* bustle, hustle and bustle. **3** *(tumulto)* uproar.

bullicioso,-a *adj* **1** *(ruidoso)* noisy, rowdy. **2** *(animado)* bustling, busy.

bullir I *vi* **1** *(hervir)* to boil, bubble (up). **2** *fig (sangre)* to boil. **3** *fig (de ira)* to seethe. **4** *(pulular)* to swarm, teem. **5** *(tener gran actividad)* to bustle about. **6** *(moverse)* to move, stir. **II bullirse** *vr (moverse)* to move, stir, budge.

bulo *nm* hoax, rumour, *US* rumor, false report.

bulto *nm* **1** *(volumen, tamaño)*, size, volume, bulk; **hacer mucho b.,** to be very bulky, take up a lot of space; *fig* **a b.,** roughly, broadly; **escoger a b.,** to choose at random; *fig* **de b.,** important, obvious; **un error de b.,** a serious mistake; *fam* **escurrir el b.,** to dodge, pass the buck. **2** *(cuerpo que se distingue mal)* shape, form. **3** *(fardo, maleta, caja)* bundle, piece of luggage, box. **4** *Med (chichón)* bump, swelling. **5** *Med (protuberancia)* lump. **6** *Am (carpatocio)* satchel, briefcase.

bumeran *nm,* **bumerang** *nm* boomerang.

bungalow *nm* bungalow.

búnker *nm* **1** *(refugio)* bunker. **2** *fam Pol* **el b.,** reactionaries *pl,* reactionary forces *pl.*

bunkeriano,-a *adj fam Pol* reactionary, extreme right-wing.

buñuelo *nm* **1** *Culin* doughnut. **2** *fam (cosa mal hecha)* botch up, bungle, mess.

BUP *nm abr de* **Bachillerato Unificado Polivalente,** ≈ GCSE studies.

buqué *nm* bouquet.

buque *nm* ship. ■ **b. de desembarco,** landing craft; **b. de guerra,** warship; **b. de pasajeros,** liner, passenger ship; **b. escuela,** training ship; **b. insignia,** flagship.

burbuja *nf* bubble; **hacer burbujas,** to bubble, make bubbles.

burbujear *vi* to bubble.

burbujero *nm* bubbling.

burdégano *nm Zool* hinny.

burdel *nm* brothel.

Burdeos *n* Bordeaux.

burdo,-a *adj* **1** *(tosco)* coarse, rough; **paño b.,** coarse cloth. **2** *(grosero)* rude, rough. **3** *(torpe)* clumsy.

bure *nm fam* amusement, pastime; **darse un b.,** to go for a stroll; **irse de b.,** to go on a binge *or* a spree.

bureta *nf Quím* burette.

burgalés,-a I *adj* of *or* from Burgos. **II** *nm, f* native *or* inhabitant of Burgos.

burgo *nm* hamlet.

burgomaestre *nm* burgomaster, mayor.

burgués,-a I *adj* bourgeois, middle-class. **II** *nm, f* bourgeois *or* middle-class person.

burguesía *nf* bourgeoisie, middle class, middle classes *pl.*

buril *nm* burin, engraver's chisel.

burilar *vtr* to engrave with a burin.

Burkina Faso *n* Burkina-Faso.

burla *nf* **1** *(mofa)* gibe, jeer, taunt; **hacer b. de algo** *or* **algn,** to mock *or* make fun of sth *or* sb; *fig* **b. burlando,** quietly, on the quiet, without anyone noticing. **2** *(broma)* joke; **en son de b.,** in fun; **no te lo digo en son de b.,** I'm not joking; **entre burlas y veras,** half jokingly. **3** *(engaño)* trick, hoax, deception.

burladero *nm* **1** *Taur* refuge in bullring. **2** *Aut* (traffic) island, *US* safety island.

burlador *nm* Casanova, Don Juan, seducer.

burlar I *vtr* **1** *(engañar)* to deceive, trick, outwit. **2** *(eludir)* to dodge, evade; **b. las leyes,** to flout the law. **II burlarse** *vr* to make fun **(de,** of), mock **(de,** -), ridicule (de, -), laugh **(de,** at).

burlesco,-a *adj* burlesque, comic, funny.

burlete *nm Téc* draught *or US* draft excluder.

burlón,-ona I *adj* mocking. **II** *nm,f* joker, wag.

buró *nm* **1** *(escritorio)* bureau, desk. **2** *pol* executive committee. **3** *Mex (mesa de noche)* bedside table.

burocracia *nf* bureaucracy.

burócrata *nmf* bureaucrat.

burocrático,-a *adj* bureaucratic.

burrada *nf* **1** *(dicho necio)* stupid *or* foolish remark; **decir burradas,** to talk nonsense. **2** *(hecho necio)* stupid *or* foolish act. **3** *fam* loads *pl,* lots *pl;* **¿cuánto trabajo tienes?—una b.,** how much work have you got?—loads; **la película me gustó una b.,** I really liked the film; **una b. de gente,** loads of people, tons of people; **vale una b.,** it costs a fortune.

burrajo *nm* horse dung.

burro,-a I *adj* **1** *fam (de pocos alcances)* stupid, dumb; **tu hermano es muy b.,** your brother's a real dimwit. **2** *fam (tozudo)* stubborn; **ponerse b.,** to dig one's heels in. **II** *nm,f* **1** *Zool* donkey, ass; *fam fig* **apearse** *or* **bajarse del b.,** to climb *or* back down; *fam fig* **no ver tres en un b.,** to be as blind as a bat. **2** *fam (estúpido)* ass, dunce, dimwit, blockhead. **3** *fam (persona laboriosa)* drudge, plodder; **b. de carga,** dogsbody, drudge. **III** *nm Carp* sawhorse.

bursátil *adj* stock-exchange, stock-market; **precios bursátiles,** stock-exchange quotations.

burudanga *nf Am* worthless object, piece of junk.

burundés,-esa *adj* & *nm,f* Burundian.

Burundi *n* Burundi.

bus *nm* bus.

busca *nf* **1** search, hunt; **ir en b. de,** to go in search of. **2** *Caza* party of hunters, beating party. **3** *Cub Méx PR (provecho)* perks *pl,* fringe benefits *pl.*

buscapié *nm fig* hint, feeler.

buscapiés *nm inv* firecracker, jumping jack.

buscapleitos *nmf inv* troublemaker.

buscar I *vtr* **1** *(gen)* to look *or* search for; **b. una llave perdida,** to search for a lost key; **b. una palabra en el diccionario,** to look up a word in the dictionary; **buscó su nombre en la lista,** he looked for her name on the list; **está buscando empleo,** she's looking for work *or* a job; **ir a b. algo,** to go and get sth, fetch sth; **fue a buscarme a la estación,** she picked me up at the station; *fig* **b. ayuda,** to seek *or* fetch help; *fig* **b. camorra,** to be looking for trouble *or* a fight; *fig* **b. una aguja en un pajar,** to look for a needle in a haystack; *fig* **buscarle tres pies al gato,** to split hairs, complicate matters; *fam fig* **buscarle las cosquillas a algn,** to annoy sb, rub sb up the wrong way. **II buscarse** *vr fam* **b. la vida,** to try and earn one's living, try and make one's way in life; *fam* **buscársela,** to ask for it, be looking for trouble; *fam* **tú te lo has buscado,** you asked for it.

buscavidas *nmf inv fam* **1** *(entrometido)* snooper, busybody, meddler. **2** *(ambicioso, despabilado)* hustler, go-getter.

buscón,-ona I *nm, f (ladrón)* petty thief; *(estafador)* crook, swindler. **II** *nf (prostituta)* whore, streetwalker.

búsqueda *nf* search, quest; *Inform* search.

busto *nm* **1** *Anat (de mujer)* bust; *(de hombre)* chest. **2** *Arte* bust.

butaca *nf* **1** *(sillón)* armchair, easy chair. **2** *Cin Teat* seat; **b. de platea** *or* **patio,** seat in the stalls; **patio de butacas,** stalls *pl, US* orchestra.

butano *nm Quím* butane; **(gas) b.,** butane gas; **bombona de (gas) b.,** cylinder of butane gas.

butaque *nm Am* small armchair.

buten (de) *loc adv arg* first rate, excellent, terrific.

butifarra *nf Culin* Catalan sausage.

buzo *nm* diver. ◼ **campana de b.,** diving bell.

buzón *nm* **1** letter box, *US* mailbox; **echar una carta al b.,** to post a letter. **2** *fig (boca grande)* big mouth.

byte *nm Inform* byte.

C

C, c [θe] *nf (la letra)* C, c.

C 1 *abr de* **Celsius,** Celsius, C. **2** *abr de* **centígrado,** centigrade, C.

C., C/ *abr de* **calle,** Street, St; Road, Rd.

C. *abr de* **capítulo,** chapter, ch.

C/1 *abr de* **calle,** Street, St; Road, Rd. **2** *abr de* **cargo, cargo** *or* freight. **3** *abr de* **cuenta,** account, a/c.

C., C² *abr de* **compañía,** Company, Co.

ca *interj* not at all!, not a bit of it!

Cabal I *adj* **1** *(exacto)* exact, precise; **dos mil pesetas cabales,** two thousand pesetas exactly. **2** *(completo)* complete. **3** *fig* honest, upright; **un hombre c.,** an upright man. **II cabales** *nmpl fam* **no estar algn en sus c.,** to have a screw loose. ◆ **cabalmente** *adv* exactly.

cábala *nf* **I** cabala, cabbala. **2** *fig (suposición)* supposition; **hacer cábalas sobre algo,** to speculate about sth. **3** *fig (conjura)* plot.

cabalgada *nf Hist (tropa)* troop of riders; *(correría)* cavalry raid.

cabalgadura *nf* **1** *(montura)* mount. **2** *(de carga)* beast of burden.

cabalgar I *vtr* **1** to ride. **2** *(aparejar)* to cover. **II** *vi* to ride, go riding.

cabalgata *nf* cavalcade. ◼ **la c. de los Reyes Magos,** the procession of the Three Wise Men.

cabalista *nmf* cabalist, cabbalist; *fig (intrigante)* intriguer.

cabalístico,-a *adj* cabalistic, cabbalistic; *fig (oculto)* hidden.

caballa *nf (pez)* mackerel.

caballar *adj* horse; **ganado c.,** horses *pl.*

caballeresco,-a *adj* chivalric, chivalrous, knightly.

caballería *nf* **1** *(cabalgadura)* mount, steed. **2** *Mil* cavalry; **c. ligera,** light cavalry. **3** *Hist* chivalry, knighthood; *Lit* **libros de caballerías,** novels of chivalry.

caballeriza *nf* **1** (*cuadra*) stable. **2** (*conjunto de caballos*) stud. **3** (*personal*) grooms *pl*, stable hands *pl*.

caballerizo *nm* groom, stableboy, stableman; *Hist* **c. mayor del rey**, Master of the King's Horse.

caballero *nm* **1** (*señor*) gentleman, sir; ¿**qué desea, c.?**, can I help you, sir?; **ropa de c.**, menswear. **2** *Hist* knight, cavalier; **armar c. a algn**, to knight sb.

caballerosidad *nf* gentlemanliness, chivalry.

caballeroso,-a *adj* gentlemanly, chivalrous; **una actitud poco caballerosa**, an ungentlemanly attitude.

caballete *nm* **1** *Téc* (*soporte*) trestle. **2** *Anat* (*de la nariz*) bridge. **3** *Arquit* (*de tejado*) ridge. **4** (*de pintor*) easel.

caballista *nmf* **1** (*jinete*) good rider. **2** (*experto*) horse expert.

caballito *nm* **1** *Zool* **c. de mar**, sea-horse. **2** *Ent* **c. del diablo**, dragonfly. **3 caballitos**, merry-go-round *sing*, *US* carousel *sing*.

caballo *nm* **1** *Zool* horse; **a c.**, on horseback; **montar a c.**, to ride; *fig* **a c. entre ...**, halfway between ...; *prov* **a c. regalado no le mires el dentado**, don't look a gift horse in the mouth. ■ **c. de carreras**, racehorse. **2** *Téc* horsepower; **un (coche) dos caballos**, a 2 CV (car). **3** *Ajedrez* knight **4** *Naipes* queen. **5** *arg* (*heroína*) junk, horse, scag, smack.

caballuno,-a *adj* horsey, horse-like.

cabaña *nf* **I** (*choza*) hut, shack. **2** (*ganado*) livestock.

cabaret *nm* (*pl* **cabarets**) cabaret, nightclub.

cabarga *nf SAm* leather horseshoe.

cabe[1] *prep tit* next to.

cabe[2] *nm fam Ftb* header.

cabecear **I** *vi* **1** (*negar*) to shake one's head. **2** (*dormirse*) to nod. **3** (*inclinarse*) to bend, sway. **4** *Náut* to pitch. **II** *vtr Ftb* to head.

cabeceo *nm* **1** (*negación*) shake of the head. **2** (*al dormirse*) nodding, nod. **3** (*inclinación*) bending, swaying. **4** *Náut* pitching.

cabecera *nf* **1** top, head; **la c. de la mesa**, the head of the table. **2** (*de la cama*) bedhead. ■ **médico de c.**, family doctor, GP. **3** (*de un río*) source, headwaters. **4** *Tip* headline.

cabecilla *nmf* leader.

cabellera *nf* **1** (*pelo*) (long) hair. **2** (*de cometa*) tail.

cabello *nm* **1** hair. **2** *Culin* **c. de ángel**, sweet made of gourd and syrup. **3 cabellos**, (*de maíz*) corn silk *sing*.

cabelludo,-a *adj* hairy; **cuero c.**, scalp.

caber *vi* **1** to fit, be (able to be) contained; **cabe en el rincón**, it fits in the corner; ¿**cabemos todos?**, is there room for all of us?; ¿**cuántas personas caben en este teatro?**, what's the capacity of this theatre?; **en esta jarra caben tres litros**, this jar holds three litres; **no cabe por la puerta**, it won't go through the door; *fig* **no cabe (la menor) duda de que ...**, there is no doubt that ...; *fig* **no c. en sí de gozo**, to be beside oneself with joy; *fig* **no cabe ni un alfiler**, it is packed; *fig* **no me cabe en la cabeza**, I can't understand it. **2** (*ser posible*) to be possible; **cabe la posibilidad de que ...**, there is a possibility *or* chance that ...; **no está mal dentro de lo que cabe**, it isn't bad, considering the circumstances. **3** *fml* (*corresponder*) **me cabe la satisfacción de anunciar ...**, it gives me great pleasure to announce ...; **me cupo el honor de ...**, I had the honour to *or* of ... . **4** *Mat* to go; **doce entre cuatro caben a tres**, four into twelve goes three (times).

cabestrear *Am vi* **1** *fam fig* (*obedecer*) to follow blindly. **2** (*llevar del cabestro*) to lead by the halter.

cabestrillo *nm* sling; **con el brazo en c.**, with her arm in a sling.

cabestro *nm* **1** (*dogal*) halter. **2** *Zool* (*buey manso*) leading ox (for bulls).

cabeza *nf* **1** head; **c. abajo**, upside down; **c. arriba**, the right way up; **de c.**, (*directamente*) headfirst; (*abrumado*)

overwhelmed; (*de memoria*) by heart; **de pies a c.**, from top to toe; **lavarse la c.**, to wash one's hair; **volver la c.**, to look round; *fam* **c. cuadrada**, bigot; *fam* **c. de chorlito** *or* **loca**, scatterbrain; *fam* **calentarse la c. por**, to get worked up about; *fig* **a la c. de**, (*guiando*) at the head of; (*en primer lugar*) at the front *or* top of; *fig* **estar mal de la c.**, to be a mental case; *fig* **irse la c.**, to get dizzy; *fig* **no tener ni pies ni c.**, to be absurd *or* pointless; *fig* **pasarle a algn por la c.**, to occur to sb; *fig* (*sensatez*) **perder la c.**, to lose one's head; *fig* **quitarle a algn una idea de la c.**, to talk sb out of an idea; *fig* **subirse algo a la c.**, to go to one's head; *fig* **tener mucha c.**, to be very bright; *fam fig* **meterse algo en la c.**, to get sth into one's head; *fam fig* **no levantar c.**, not to recover, not get back to normal; *fam fig* **romperse la c.**, (*golpearse*) to smash one's head; (*devanarse los sesos*) to rack one's brains; *fam fig* **tengo la c. como un bombo**, my head's splitting. ■ **c. de puente**, bridgehead; **dolor de c.**, headache. **2** (*persona*) head; **veinte mil por c.**, twenty thousand a head *or* per person. ■ **c. de turco**, scapegoat; **el** *or* **la c. de familia**, the head of the family. **3** (*res*) head *inv*; **un rebaño de mil cabezas**, a thousand head of sheep. **4** *Inform* **c. fija**, fixed head.

cabezada *nf* **1** (*golpe*) butt, blow on the head. **2** (*gesto*) nod; *fam* **echar una c.**, to have a snooze. **3** (*correaje*) cavesson. **4** *Náut* pitch, pitching. **5** *Am* saddlebow.

cabezal *nm* **1** *Téc* head, headstock; (*de tocadiscos*) pick-up. **2** (*almohada*) bolster. **3** (*vendaje*) compress. **4** *Chi Méx* (*travesaño*) crossbeam.

cabezazo *nm* **1** (*golpe dado*) butt. **2** (*golpe recibido*) blow on the head. **3** *Ftb* header.

cabezón,-ona *adj fam* **1** (*presuntuoso*) bigheaded. **2** (*terco*) pigheaded.

cabezonada *nf fam* pigheaded action.

cabezonería *nf fam* **1** (*obstinación*) pigheadedness. **2** (*cabezonada*) pigheaded action.

cabezota *fam* **I** *adj* **1** bigheaded. **2** (*terco*) pigheaded. **II** *nmf* **1** bighead. **2** (*terco*) pigheaded person.

cabezudo,-a **I** *adj* **1** bigheaded. **2** *fig* (*terco*) pigheaded. **3** (*vino*) heady. **II** *nm* **1** carnival figure with a huge head. **2** (*pez*) bullhead, miller's thumb.

cabezuela *nf* **1** (*harina*) second grade flour. **2** *Bot* flower head.

cabida *nf* **1** capacity; **dar c. a**, to leave room for. **2** (*extensión*) area, extension.

cabildada *nf* abuse of authority.

cabildear *vi* to intrigue, scheme.

cabildeo *nm* intriguing, scheming.

cabildo *nm* **1** (*ayuntamiento*) towm council **2** *Rel* chapter.

cabina *nf* cabin, booth ■ *cin* **c. de proyección**, projection room; *Tel* **c. telefónica**, telephone box, *US* telephone booth.

cabizbajo,-a *adj* crestfallen.

cable[1] *nm* (*cuerda, maroma*) cable; *arg* **echarle un c. a algn**, to give sb a hand.

cable[2] *nm* (*cablegrama*) cablegram.

cablegrafiar *vtr* to send a cable, cable.

cablegrama *nm* cablegram, cable.

Cabo *n* **1** **Ciudad del C.**, Cape Town. **2 C. Verde**, Cape Verde.

cabo *nm* **1** (*extremo*) end, stub. **2** *fig* (*fin*) **al c.**, finally; **al c. de dos horas/tres días**, after two hours/three days; **al fin y al c.**, after all; **de c. a rabo**, from start to finish. **3** *Náut* rope, line, cable; *fig* **atar** *or* **juntar cabos**, to put two and two together; *fig* **no dejar ningún c. suelto**, to leave no loose ends. **4** *Mil* (*policía*) sergeant. **5** *Geog* cape. **6 cabos**, (*de caballo*) tail and mane *sing*.

cabotaje *nm* *Náut* coastal traffic, cabotage; **barco de c.**, coaster.

cabra *nf* **1** *Zool* goat; *fam* **estar como una c.**, to be off one's head. **2** *Am* (*trampa*) trick.

cabracho *nm (pez)* scorpion fish.

cabrahigar *vtr* to hang skewered figs on figtrees for superstitious reasons.

cabrales *nm inv Culin* type of blue cheese from Asturias.

cabré *indic fut véase* **caber.**

cabrear I *vtr vulg* to make angry; **estar cabreado,- a,** to be pissed off. **II cabrearse** *vr* to get worked up; **ella se cabrea por cualquier cosa,** she blows her top over everything.

cabreo *nm vulg* anger; **agarrar(se)** *or* **coger** *or* **pillar un c.,** to fly off the handle; **¡tengo** *or* **llevo un c. encima!,** I'm really pissed off!

cabrero,-a *nm,f* goatherd.

cabrestante *nm Náut* capstan.

cabria *nf Téc* gin.

cabrilla *nf* 1 *(trípode)* sawhorse. 2 **cabrillas,** *(espuma)* white horses, whitecaps.

cabrillear *vi* 1 *(olas)* to break into white horses. 2 *(rielar)* to glisten.

cabrillona *nf Arg Urug Zool* young goat.

cabrío,-a *adj* caprine, goat-like, goatish.

cabriola *nf (de caballo)* capriole; *(de niño)* caper, skip.

cabriolé *nm arc* cabriolet.

cabritilla *nf* kid, kidskin.

cabrito,-a I *nm* 1 *Zool* kid. 2 *desus (hombre)* cuckold. **II** *nm,f vulg* bugger, snot.

cabrón,-ona I *nm* 1 *Zool* he-goat, billy goat. 2 *desus* cuckold. **II** *nm, f ofens* 1 *(hombre)* bastard; *(woman)* bitch. 2 *SAm (chulo)* pimp.

cabronada *nf vulg* dirty trick; **hacer una c. a algn,** to do the dirty on sb, play a dirty trick on sb.

cabronazo *nm ofens* bastard, fucker.

cabujón *nm Min* cabochon.

cábula *nf Am* 1 *(ardid)* trick, stratagem. 2 *(cébala)* cabala, cabbala.

cabuya *nf Bot* agave, pita.

caca *nf fam* 1 *(excremento)* feces pl; **el niño (se) ha hecho c.,** the baby did it in his pants; *fig* **este libro es una c,** this book is shitty. 2 *(en lenguaje infantil)* poopoo; **no toques eso que es c.,** don't touch that, it's dirty or nasty.

cacahuate *nm Bot véase* **cacahuete.**

cacahuero *nm Am* owner of cacao plantations.

cacahuete *nm Bot (fruto)* peanut; *(planta)* groundnut.

cacalote *nm* 1 *Méx Orn* crow. 2 *CAm* popcorn.

cacao *nm* 1 *Bot* cacao. 2 *(polvo, bebida)* cocoa. 3 *fam (lío)* mess, cockup; **tener un c. mental,** to be confused or US screwed up. 4 *Am (chocolate)* chocolate.

cacaotal *nm* cacao plantation.

cacaraña *adj CAm (letra)* badly written.

cacarear I *vi (gallo or gallina)* to cluck. **II** *vtr fig* to strut about; **su tan cacareado éxito,** his much talkcd of success.

cacareo *nm* 1 *(de gallo or gallina)* clucking. 2 *fig* boasting, bragging.

cacarico,-a *adj Am* disabled, handicapped.

cacatúa *nf* **I** *Orn* cockatoo. 2 *fig pey (mujer)* ugly old woman.

cacaxtle *nm CAm (esqueleto)* skeleton.

cacereño,-a I *adj* of or from Cáceres. **II** *nm,f* native or inhabitant of Cáceres.

cacería *nf* hunting, shooting, hunt, shoot.

cacerola *nf Culin* saucepan, casserole.

cacha¹ *nf* 1 *fam Anat (muslo)* thigh; **estar cachas,** to be hunky, be a hunk. 2 *(de un arma)* butt.

cacha² *nf* 1 *Am (engaño)* trick, swindle. 2 *CAm (abuso)* abuse.

cachaco *nm Am (lechuguino)* fop, dandy.

cachada *nf* **I** *Am (cornada)* goring. 2 *Arg Par Urug (burla)* taunt, jeer.

cachafaz,-a *adj Arg Chi (sinvergüenza)* mischievous, cheeky.

cachafo *nm Méx (de cigarrillo)* end, *US* butt.

cachalote *nm Zool* cachalot, sperm whale.

cachar¹ *vsr* **I** *Am (burlar)* to deceive, fool. 2 *Am (cornear)* to gore. 3 *CAm (conseguir)* to get, obtain. 4 *CAm Urug (robar)* to steal. 5 *Arg (tomar)* to teke, hold, grab.

cachar² *vtrAm (pelota)* to catch.

cacharpas *nfpl Am* junk *sing*, useless obejcts.

cacharrazo *nm* 1 *fam* blow, punch. 2 *Am (trago)* a sip of a strong drink.

cacharreria *nf* pottery shop.

cacharrero,-a *nm,f* pottery maker or dealer.

cacharro *nm* 1 crock, earthenware pot or jar. 2 *fam (cosa)* thing, piece of junk. 3 *fam (coche)* banger. 4 *CAm (cárcel)* prison. 5 **cacharros,** *fam (de cocina)* pots and pans.

cachaza *nf* sluggishness, phlegm; **¡qué co. tienes!,** how slow you are!

cachazudo,-a *adj* sluggish, phlegmatic.

cache *adj Arg* sloppy, slovenly.

cachear *vtr* to frisk, search.

cachemir *nm,* **cachemira** *nf Tex* cashmere.

cacheo *nm* frisk, frisking.

cachería *nf* 1 *Am* small sbop. 2 *Alg* sloppiness.

cachetada *nf* slap.

cachete *nm* 1 *(puñetazo)* punch. 2 *desus (mejilla)* cheek.

cachetón,-ona *adj* 1 *Am (carrilludo)* fat-faced, chubby cheeked. 2 *Méx (descarado)* impudent, cheeky.

cachimbazo *nm CAm* 1 *(balazo)* shot. 2 *(bofetada)* slap. 3 *(trago)* shot.

cachipolla *nf Ent* mayfly.

cachiporra *nf* club, truncheon.

cachiporrazo *nm* clubbing, blow with a club.

cachirulos *nmpl fam* thingamabob *sing*, thingummy *sing*.

cachivache *nm fam* thing, knick-knack, piece of junk.

cacho¹ *nm* 1 *fam (pedazo)* bit, piece; *fig* **¡qué c. de animal!,** what a nasty piece of work! 2 *Méx PR (lotería)* part of lottery ticket.

cacho² *nm* 1 *Am (cuerno)* hora. 2 *Am (vasija)* vessel (made of horn). 3 *Am (anécdota)* story, tale, anecdote. 4 *Arg Chi (cubilete)* box for dice. 5 *Arg Par Urug* bunch of bananas.

cachón-ona I *adj* big-homed. **II** *nm,f* big-horned animal.

cachondearse *vr fam* **c. de,** to take the mickey out of; **se cachondea de todo,** he takes everything as a joke.

cachondeo *nm fam* laugh; **¡vaya c.!,** what a laugh!

cachondo-a *adj fam* 1 *(excitado sexualmente)* hot, randy, horny. 2 *(divertido)* funny.

cachorro,-a I *adj Cuba PR Ven (terco)* obstinate, stubborn; *(malcriado)* bad-mannered. **II** *nm, f* 1 *(de perro)* pup, puppy. 2 *(de gato)* kitten. 3 *(de otros animales)* cub, baby.

cachúa *nf SAm* Indian dance.

cachupín,-ina *nm, f CAm Méx* Spanish settler in Latín America.

cacique *nm* 1 *(jefe indio)* cacique. 2 *(déspota)* despot, tyrant.

caciquil *adj pey* despotic.

caciquismo *nm* 1 *pol* caciquism. 2 *pey* despotism.

caco *nm fam* thief.

cacofonía *nf* cacophony, dissonance.

cacofónico,-a *adj* cacophonous, cacophonic

cacreco,-a *adj CAm (vagabundo)* wandering, vagrant.

cacto *nm*, **cactus** *nm inv Bot* cactus *inv*.

cacumen *nm fam fig* brains *pl*.

cada *adj (de dos)* each; *(de varios)* each, every; **a c. cual lo suyo,** each to his own; **a c. paso,** at every step; **¿c. cuánto?,** how often?; **c. día,** every day; **c. dos por tres,** every other minute; **c. vez lo entiendo menos,** it becomes harder and harder for me) to understand; **c. vez más,** more, and more; **c. vez más tarde,** later; and later; **cuatro de c. diez,** four out of (every) ten; **nos deben mil a c. uno,** they owe each of us a thousand; **que c. cual se las apañe como pueda,** it's every man for himself; **¡te inventas c. historia!,** you come up with some fine stories!

cadalso *nm (patíbulo)* scaffold; *(plataforma)* platform.

cadáver *nm* **1** *(de persona)* corpse, (dead) body; **ingresar c.,** to be dead on arrival. **2** *(de animal)* body, carcass.

cadavérico,-a *adj* cadaverous; **con palidez c.,** deathly pale.

cadena *nf* **1** chain; *(correa de perro)* lead, leash; **tirar de la c. (del water),** to flush the toilet. **2** *(grupo de empresas)* chain; **una c. de cines/supermercados,** a chain of cinemas/supermarkets. **3** *Rad* chain of stations; *TV* channel. **4** *Ind* line. ■ **c. de fabricación,** production line; **c. de montaje,** assembly line; **trabajo en c.,** assembly line work. **5** *Geog* range. ■ **c. montañosa,** mountain range. **6** *Jur* **c. perpetua,** life imprisonment. **7** *fig (serie)* series, sequence. ■ **reacción en c.,** chain reaction. **8 cadenas,** *Aut* tyre *or US* tire chains.

cadencia *nf* cadence, rhythm; *Mús* cadenza.

cadencioso,-a *adj* **1** rhythmic, rhythmical. **2** *fig (ritmo adecuado)* measured, even.

cadeneta *nf* **1** *Tricot* chain stitch. **2** *(de papel)* paper chain.

cadera *nf Anat* hip; **con las manos en las caderas,** hands on hips.

cadete *nm* **1** *Mil* cadet. **2** *Arg Bol Par (aprendiz)* apprentice.

Cádiz *n* Cadiz.

cadmio *nm Quím* cadmium.

caducar *vi* to expire, lose validity.

caducidad *nf* expiration, loss of validity, lapse; **fecha de c.,** *(en alimentos)* ≈ sell-by date; *(en medicinas)* to be used before.

caduco,-a *adj* **1** expired, out-of-date, invalid. **2** *Bot* deciduous. **3** *(senil)* senile; *pey* decrepit.

caedizo *nm Am* sloping roof.

caer *vi* **1** to fall; **c. de bruces,** to fall flat on one's face; **c. de cabeza/de espaldas,** to fall on one's head/back; **dejar c.,** to drop; **la falda te cae por un lado,** your skirt dips at one side; *fig* **c. enfermo** *or* **en cama,** to fall ill; *fig* **c. en la tentación,** to give in *or* yield to temptation; *fig* **c. en manos de,** to fall into the hands of; *fig* **c. en un error,** to make a mistake; *fig* **está al c.,** *(llegar)* he'll arrive any minute now; *(ocurrir)* it's on the way; *fig* **¡qué bajo has caído!,** how low you have fallen!; *fam* **déjate c. alguna vez por casa,** come round and see us sometime. **2** *(coincidir fechas)* to be; **su cumpleaños cae en sábado,** his birthday falls on a Saturday. **3** *(premio, lotería)* *(tocar)* to go; **el primer premio cayó en Granada,** the first prize went to Granada; *fig* **¡la que nos ha caído encima!,** what a lovely situation to be in! **4** *(entender)* to understand, see; **no caigo en lo que me quieres decir,** I don't quite understand what you're getting at; **ya caigo,** I get it. **5** *(hallarse)* to be; **cae por Salamanca,** it is somewhere near Salamanca. **6** *(sentar)* to agree with; *(prenda)* to suit; **el pescado no me ha caído bien,** the fish didn't agree with me; **esa chaqueta te cae bien,** that jacket suits you; *(persona)* **me cae bien/gorda** *or* **mal,** I like/don't like her. **7** *(perder)* *(en combate)* to surrender; *(cargo, posición)* to fall; **el gobierno ha caído,** the government has fallen. **8** *(abalanzarse)* to throw oneself (sobre, on). **9** *(finalizar)* **al c. el día,** in the evening; **al c. la noche,** at nightfall. **II caerse** *vr* to fall (down); **me caí de la escalera,** I fell off the ladder; **se te ha caído el pañuelo,**

you've dropped your handkerchief; *fam* **no tener dónde c. muerto,** to have nothing to one's ñame; *fam fig* **caérsele a uno la cara de vergüenza,** to die of shame.

café *nm* **1** *Bot* coffee; **un grano de c.,** a coffee bean. **2** *(bebida)* (cup of) coffee; **c. Solo/con leche,** black/white coffee. **3** *(lugar)* café, coffee bar *or* shop.

cafeína *nf* caffeine.

cafetal *nf* coffee plantation.

cafetería *nf* snack bar, coffee bar; *Ferroc* buffet car.

cafetero,-a I *adj* coffee; **la producción cafetera,** coffee production. **2** *fam (persona)* coffee-loving; **es muy c.,** he loves coffee. **II** *nf* **1** *(para hacer café)* coffee-maker. ■ **cafetera exprés,** expresso-coffee machine. **2** *(para servir café)* coffeepot. **3** *fam (coche viejo)* old banger *or* crock; *(persona)* **estar como una cafetera,** to be barmy *or* nuts.

cafeto *nm Bot* coffee.

cafre I *adj (persona)* brutal, barbarous. **II** *nm,f (persona)* savage, beast.

cagada *nf vulg* **1** *(mierda)* shit. **2** *fig (error)* fuckup, cockup.

cagado,-a I *pp de* **cagar. II** *adj* **1** *fam* **lleva los pantalones cagados,** he's shit his pants. **2** *vulg (cobarde)* coward; **estar c.,** to be shit-scared. **III** *nm,f vulg (cobarde)* shit, yellow belly.

cagalera *nf vulg* the runs *pl*; **darle a algn la** *or* **una c.,** to be shit-scared.

cagar *vulg* **I** *vi* **1** to (have a) shit. **2** *(estropear)* to ruin, spoil; **la has cagado comprándote este coche,** you fucked up buying this car. **II cagarse** *vr* to shit oneself; **c. de miedo,** to be shit-scared; **¡me cago en ...!,** bloody ...!; **¡me cago en diez** *or* **la mar!,** damn it!; **¡me cago en la leche!,** fuck!

cagarruta *nf* **1** sheep *or* goat dirt. **2** *fig vulg (hombre insignificante)* little shit.

cagon,-ona *vulg* **I** *adj* **1** *fam* loose-bowelled. **2** *vulg (cobarde)* yellow. **II** *nm,f vulg* chicken.

cagueta *vulg* **I** *adj* yellow. **II** *nmf* coward, chicken.

caída *nf* **1** fall, falling; *(de pelo, de un diente)* loss; *(de una tela)* body, hang; **c. de ojos,** demure look. **2** *(del terreno)* slope. **3** *(de precios)* drop. **4** *Cost (ancho)* width; *(largo)* length. **5** *fig* downfall, collapse; *Hist* **la c. del Imperio Romano,** the fall of the Roman Empire.

caido,-a I *pp de* **caer. II** *adj* **1** fallen; *fig* **c. del cielo,** *(inesperado)* out of the blue; *(oportuno)* heavensent. **2** *(hombros)* drooping. **3** *fig (alicaído)* crestfallen. **III los caidos** *nmpl* the fallen *pl*.

caigo *indic pres véase* **caer.**

caima *adj Am* dull, flat.

caimán *nm* **1** *Zool* caiman, cayman, alligator. **2** *Am fig (persona astuta)* fox.

Caín I *adj* evil. **II** *nm* Cain; *fig* evil person; *fam* **pasar las de C.,** to go through hell.

Cairo *n* **El C.,** Cairo.

caito *nm SAm* wool thread.

caja *nf* **1** *(gen)* box; *fam fig* **echar a algn con cajas destempladas,** to send sb packing. ■ **c. de caudales,** safe, strongbox; **c. de colores,** paintbox; *Elec* **c. de empalmes,** junction box; **c. fuerte,** strongroom; **c. de música,** music *or* musical box; *Av* **c. negra,** black box; *fam TV* **la c. tonta,** the idiot box. **2** *(de embalaje)* crate, case; **una c. de cerveza,** a crate of beer. **3** *(féretro)* coffin, casket. **4** *Fin (en una tienda)* cash desk; *(en un banco)* cashier's desk; **ayer robaron la c.,** they robbed the till yesterday; **hacer mucha c.,** to take a lot; **pague en c.,** pay at the cash desk. **5** *Impr* case. **6** *Aut (carrocería)* body. ■ **c. de cambios,** gearbox. **7** *Com (banco)* bank; **c. de ahorros** *or* **de pensiones,** savings bank; **C. Postal de Ahorros,** Post Office Savings Bank. **8** *Anat* **c. craneana,** cranium, skull. **9** *Téc* housing, casing. **10** *Mús (de piano)* case; *(de violín)* body. **11** *Mil* **entrar en c.,** to enlist, join up.

cajear I *vtr CAm (zurrar)* to beat up. **II cajearse** *vr Guat Méx (en el juego)* to contract debts.

cajero,-a *nm, f* cashier. ■ **c. automático,** cash point, dispenser.

cajeta *CAm nf* **1** sweet *or* biscuit box. **2** *Méx Culin* (fruit) custard. **3 de c.,** excellent.

cajete *nm Guat Méx Salv* pan *or* bowl with glasscoated interior.

cajetero,-a I *adj CAm (ridículo)* ridiculous. **II** *nm Méx* matches maker *or* dealer.

cajetilla *nf (de cigarrillos)* packet, *US* pack.

cajista *nmf Impr* typesetter.

cajón *nm* **1** *(caja grande)* crate, chest. **2** *(en un mueble)* drawer; *fig* **c. de sastre,** jumble; *fam* **de c.,** obvious, self-evident. **3** *(caseta)* stall. **4** *Am (ataúd)* coffin. **5** *Méx (abacería)* grocer's (shop).

cal¹ *nf* lime; *fig* **a c. y canto,** hermetically; *fig* **de c. y canto,** strong, tough; *fam* **una c. y otra de arena,** six of one and half a dozen of the other. ■ **c. apagada** *or* **muerta,** slaked lime; **c. viva,** quicklime.

cal² *abr de* **caloría(s),** calorie(s), cal.

cala¹ *nf* **1** *(pedazo de fruta)* slice, sample. **2** *fam* peseta.

cala² *nf* **1** *Geog (ensenada)* creek, cove, inlet. **2** *Náut* hold.

cala³ *nf Bot* arum.

calabacín *nm Bol* **1** *(pequeño)* courgette, *US* zucchini. **2** *(grande)* marrow, *US* squash.

calabaza *nf* **1** *Bot* pumpkin, gourd. **2** *fam (persona)* dolt. **3** *fam fig* **dar calabazas a algn,** *(suspender)* to fail sb; *(a un pretendiente)* to turn sb down.

calabazada *nf fam véase* **cabezada 1.**

calabazar *nm* gourd *or* pumpkin field.

calabobos *nm inv Meteor* drizzle.

calabozo *nm* **1** *(prisión)* jail, prison. **2** *(celda)* cell.

calada *nf fam (de cigarrillo)* drag, puff; *arg (de porro)* hit, toke.

calado,-a I *pp de* **calar. II** *adj* soaked; **vengo calado,** I'm soaked (to the skin). **III** *nm* **1** *Cost* openwork, embroidery. **2** *Náut* draught, *US* draft. **3** *(profundidad del mar)* depth.

calador *nm Am* borer, probe.

calafate *nm* caulker.

calafatear *vtr Náut* to caulk.

calamar *nm Zool* squid *inv*; *Culin* **calamares a la romana,** squid fried in batter.

calambre *nm* **1** *Elec (descarga)* electric shock; **ese cable da c.,** that wire is live. **2** *(espasmo)* cramp; **me dio un c. en la pierna,** I got a cramp in my leg.

calamidad *nf* **1** calamity, disaster; *fam* **¡estás hecho una c.!,** what a sorry sight you are! **2** *(persona)* dead loss, good-for-nothing.

calamitoso,-a *adj* calamitous, disastrous.

calandraco *nm Am* **1** *(andrajo)* rag. **2** *(casquivano)* scatterbrain.

calandrado *nm Téc* calendering.

calandrar *vtr Téc* to calender.

calandria¹ *nf Orn* calandra lark.

calandria² *nf Téc (de lustrar)* calender; *(torno)* treadmill.

calaña *nf pey* **1** *(carácter)* nature, disposition; **una persona de mala c.,** a bad sort. **2** *(clase)* kind, stock; **no me gusta la gente de esa c.,** I don't like that kind of people.

calapé *nm Am Culin* roast tortoise *or* turtle.

calar I *vtr* **1** *(mojar)* to soak, drench. **2** *(agujerear)* to pierce, penetrate. **3** *(sombrero)* to jam on. **4** *Téc* to do fretwork on. **5** *Cost* to do openwork on. **6** *Mil (bayoneta)* to fix. **7** *fig (penetrar)* to have an effect on; **tus consejos han calado hondo en ella,** she has taken your advice to heart. **8** *fam (persona)* to rumble; **¡te tengo calado!,** I've

got your number! **II** *vi Náut* to draw. **III calarse** *vr* **1** *(mojarse)* to get soaked. **2** *(el sombrero)* to pull down. **3** *Aut (el motor)* to stop, stall.

calavera I *nf* **1** skull. **2** *Méx Aut* rear light. **II** *nm (hombre)* tearaway, madcap.

calaverada *nf* madcap escapade.

calcado,-a I *pp de* **calcar. II** *adj* traced, copied; *fig* **es c. a su padre,** he's the spitting image of his father. **III** *nm* tracing.

calcar *vtr* **1** *(un dibujo)* to trace. **2** *fig (imitar)* to copy, imitate.

calcáreo,-a *adj Geol* calcareous.

calce *nm* **1** *(llanta)* rim. **2** *(cuña)* wedge. **3** *CAm Méx (de un documento)* lower margin.

calceta *nf* **1** *(prenda)* stocking. **2** *Tricot* knitting; **hacer c.,** to knit.

calcetín *nm* sock.

cálcico,-a *adj* calcium, calcic.

calcificación *nf* calcification.

calcificar *vtr;* **calcificarse** *vr* to calcify.

calcinación *nf* calcination.

calcinar *vtr* to calcine; *fig* to burn.

calcio *nm Quím* calcium.

calco *nm* **1** *(de un dibujo)* tracing. **2** *(copia)* (carbon) copy. **3** *fig (imitación)* imitation, copy.

calcomanía *nf* transfer.

calcopirita *nf Min* chalcopyrite.

calculable *adj* calculable.

calculador,-a I *adj* calculating. **II** *nm & f* calculator.

calcular *vtr* **1** to calculate, work out, figure. **2** *(evaluar)* to (make an) estimate; **calcula lo que necesitas,** figure out how much you need; **calculando por lo bajo,** at the lowest estimate. **3** *(suponer)* to think, suppose, figure, guess; **calculo que llegará tarde,** I don't expect him until late.

cálculo *nm* **1** calculation, estimate, figures *pl*; **según mis cálculos,** by my reckoning; **si mis cálculos no fallan,** if I am right. ■ **c. mental,** mental arithmetic. **2** *Med* stone, gallstone. **3** *Mat* calculus. ■ **regla de c.,** slide rule.

caldas *nfpl Geol* thermal springs.

caldeamiento *nm* heating, warming.

caldear *vtr* **1** *(una habitación)* to heat, warm. **2** *fig (excitar)* to heat *or* warm up; **sus palabras caldearon el ambiente,** his words stirred up those present.

caldera *nf* boiler; *(caldero)* cauldron; *fam* **las calderas de Pedro Botero,** Hell.

calderada *nf* boilerful, cauldronful.

calderería *nf* **1** *(oficio)* boilermaking. **2** *(lugar)* boilermaker's shop.

calderero,-a *nm, f* boilermaker.

caldereta *nf Culin (de cordero)* lamb stew; *(de pescado)* fish stew.

calderilla *nf Fin* small change.

caldero *nm* **1** *(caldera)* small cauldron. **2** *(contenido)* cauldronful.

calderón *nm Mús* pause.

caldillo *nm Méx Culin* spicy minced meat stew.

caldo *nm* **1** *Culin* stock, broth. **2** *Biol* **c. de cultivo,** *Quím* culture medium; *fig (terreno abonado)* breeding ground. **3** **caldos,** *(vino)* wines.

caldoso,-a *adj* with a lot of stock.

calé *adj & nm* gypsy.

calefacción *nf* heating. ■ **c. central,** central heating.

calefactor,-a *nm* **1** *(persona)* heating engineer. **2** *(máquina)* heater.

caleidoscópico,-a *adj* kaleidoscopic.

caleidoscopio *nm* kaleidoscope.

calendario *nm* calendar; **c. académico,** school year.

calendas *nfpl* calends; *lit* **c. griegas,** never.

caléndula *nf Bot* calendula.

calentador,-a I *adj* heating. **II** *nm* heater; **c. de agua,** water heater.

calentamiento *nm* heating; **ejercicios de c.,** warming-up exercises.

calentar I *vtr* **1** *(agua, horno)* to heat; *(comida, habitación)* to warm up; *Dep* **c. los músculos,** to tone up one's muscles; *fig (no trabajar)* **c. el asiento,** to warm the chair; *fig (importunar)* **c. los sesos** *or* **los cascos,** to get hot under the collar. **2** *fig (exaltar)* to heat up, inflame. **3** *fig (irritar)* to annoy. **4** *fam (pegar)* to tan, warm. **5** *fam (excitar)* to arouse (sexually), turn on. **II calentarse** *vr* **1** to get hot *or* warm, heat up. **2** *fig (exaltarse)* to get excited; **se calentaron los ánimos,** people became very excited. **3** *fig (enfadarse)* to get heated *or* annoyed. **4** *fam (excitarse)* to get randy *or* horny.

calentón,-ona *adj*, **calentorro,-a** *adj fam* horny, randy.

calentura *nf Med* fever, temperature.

calenturiento,-a *adj* feverish; **mente calenturienta,** *(exaltada)* hothead; *(excitada)* dirty mind.

calesa *nf arc* calash, calèche.

calesera *nf* **1** *(prenda)* type of bolero jacket. **2** *Mús* Andalusian song.

calibrado *nm* boring, gauging.

calibrador *nm* borer, gauge, callipers *pl*, *US* calipers *pl*. ▪ **c. micrométrico,** vernier calliper, calliper rule.

calibrar *vtr* **1** *Téc* to gauge, bore. **2** *fig (juzgar)* to judge, size up.

calibre *nm* **1** *Téc* bore, gauge. **2** *(de arma)* calibre. **3** *fig (importancia)* size, importance.

caliche *nm* **1** *(partícula)* flake (of paint), chip (of plaster). **2** *fam (proyectil)* pellet. **3** *Am (mineral)* saltpetre, *US* saltpeter. **4** *SAm Quím* Chile saltpetre *or* nitre.

calidad *nf* **1** quality; **muebles de primera c.,** firstclass furniture; **un vino de c.,** good-quality wine. **2** *(condición)* capacity; **en c. de profesor,** as a teacher. **3** *(clase)* kind, type; **las distintas calidades de tomates,** the various types of tomatoes.

cálido,-a *adj* warm; **una cálida acogida,** a warm welcome.

calidoscópico,-a *adj véase* **caleidoscópico,-a.**

calidoscopio *nm véase* **caleidoscopio.**

calientabraguetas *nf inv vulg* prick teaser.

calientaplatos *nm inv* hotplate.

caliente *adj* **1** hot, warm; **un baño/café c.,** a hot bath/cup of coffee. **2** *fig (acalorado)* heated, spirited; **en c.,** in the heat of the moment. **3** *fam (excitado)* hot, randy.

califa *nm* caliph.

califato *nm* caliphate.

calificable *adj* qualifiable.

calificacion *nf* **1** qualification. **2** *Educ (nota)* mark; **libro de calificaciones,** school report.

calificado,-a I *pp de* **calificar II** *adj* **1** *(prestigioso)* eminent, well-known. **2** *(apto)* apt, suitable.

calificador,-a *adj* examining.

calificar *vtr* **1** to describe, consider; **calificaron sus ideas de progresistas,** they labelled *or* marked his ideas progressive; **le calificó de inmoral,** he called him immoral. **2** *Educ (examen, ejercicio)* to mark, grade. **3** *Ling (palabra)* to qualify.

calificativo,-a I *adj* qualifying; **adjetivo c.,** qualifying adjective. **II** *nm* **1** epithet; **no encuentro calificativos,** words fail me. **2** *Ling* qualifier.

californiano,-a,-a *adj & nm,f* Californian.

caligrafía *nf* calligraphy; **ejercicios de c.,** handwriting exercises; **tiene una c. infantil,** his handwriting looks childish.

caligráfico,-a *adj* calligraphic.

caligrafo,-a *nm,f* calligrapher.

calima *nf* haze, mist.

calimocho *nm* drínk made with wine and CocaCola.

calina *nf Meteor véase* **calima.**

caliqueño *nm fam* cheap cigar.

cáliz *nm* **1** *Rel* chalice. **2** *Bot* calyx. **3** *lit (copa)* cup.

caliza *nf Geol* limestone.

calizo,-a *adj Geol* lime.

calla *nf SAm* (garden) pick.

callada *nf* silence; **dar la c. por respuesta,** to ignore the other person's question *or* request.

callado,-a I *pp de* **callar, II** *adj* quiet, silent; **una persona muy callada,** a very quiet *or* reserved person; *fam* **más c. que un muerto,** as quiet as a mouse; *fam* **¡qué c. te lo tenías!,** how quiet you've kept it!

callampa *nf SAm (seta)* mushroom.

callana *nf SAm* flat earthenware pan.

callandito *adv fam*, **callando** *adv fam* **(a la chita) c.,** on the quiet or sly.

callar I *vi* **1** *(en silencio)* to be quiet, keep quiet, say nothing; **los que deberían hablar callan,** those who ought to speak remain silent. **2** *(dejar de hablar)* to stop talking, shut up; **¡callad!,** be quiet!; *fam* **¡calla! ¿de verdad?,** don't tell me!, is that true? **II** *vtr (esconder)* not to mention, keep to oneself; **ella calló su nombre,** she kept quiet about his name. **III callarse** *vr* **1** to be quiet, say nothing; **se calló cuando le preguntaron,** he didn't answer when (he was) asked. **2** *(dejar de hablar)* to stop talking, be quiet; *fam* **c. la boca,** to clam up, shut up.

calle *nf* **1** street, road; **c. de dirección única,** one-way street; **doblar la c.,** to turn the corner; *fig* **dejar a algn en la c.,** *(sin trabajo)* to fire sb; *(sin casa)* to leave sb homeless; *fig* **echar** *or* **poner a algn (de patitas) en la c.,** to throw *or* kick sb out; *fig* **el hombre de la c.,** the man in the street; *fig (prostitutas)* **hacer la c.,** to walk the streets, solicit; *fig* **llevar** *or* **traer a algn por la c. de la amargura,** to give sb a tough time; *fig* **quedarse en la c.,** to be left jobless *or* homeless. ▪ **c. mayor,** high street, *US* main street. **2** *Atlet Natación* lane.

calleja *nf* narrow street.

callejear *vi* to wander (about) the streets.

callejeo *nm* wandering about.

callejero,-a I *adj* **1** (in the) street; **celebración callejera,** celebration in the street; **gato c.,** street cat. **2** *(persona)* fond of going out. **II** *nm (mapa)* street directory.

callejón *nm* back alley *or* street. ▪ **c. sin salida,** culde-sac, dead end; *fig* **ea un c. sin salida,** at an impasse.

callejuela *nf* narrow street, lane.

callicida *nm* corn remover.

callista *nmf* chiropodist.

callo *nm* **1** *Med* callus, corn; *fam* **darle al c.,** to slog. **2** *fam (persona fea)* (ugly) sight. **3** *Culin* **callos,** tripe *sing.*

callosidad *nf* callosity, callus.

calloso,-a *adj* callous.

calma *nf* **1** calmness, tranquillity, *US* tranquility; **perder la c.,** to lose one's patience; **todo está en c.,** all is calm; **tómatelo con c.,** take it easy. **2** *(negocio)* slack period, lull. **3** *(cachaza)* phlegm, slowness; **¡qué c. tienes!,** how calm you are! **4** *Meteor* calm **weather.** ▪ **c. chicha,** dead calm.

calmante I *adj* sedative, soothing. **II** *nm Farm* painkiller, sedative, tranquillizer, *US* tranquilizer.

calmar I *vtr (persona)* to calm (down); *(dolor)* to soothe, relieve. **II** *vi (estado)* to fall calm. **III calmarse** *vr* **1** *(persona)* to calm down. **2** *(dolor, viento)* to abate, ease off.

calmoso,-a *adj* **1** calm, serene. **2** *(flemático)* phlegmatic, sluggish.

caló *nm (idioma)* gypsy dialect.

calor *nm* **1** heat, warmth; **al c. de,** *(calentado por)* in the heat of; *fig (amparado por)* under the wing of; **entrar en c.,** to warm up; **hacer c.,** to be hot; *(persona)* **tener c.,** to be *hot; fig* **el c. del hogar,** the warmth of home. **2** *fig (afecto)* warmth, love; *(entusiamo)* ardour, *US* ardor, passion.

caloría *nf* calorie, calory.

calórico,-a *adj,* **calorífico,-a** *adj* caloric, calorific.

calostro *nm Biol* colostrum.

calote *nm Arg* swindle, fraud.

calumnia *nf* **1** calumny. **2** *Jur* slander.

calumniador,-a I *adj* **1** calumnious, calumniatory. **2** *Jur* slanderous. **II** *nm,f* **1** calumniator. **2** *Jur* slanderer.

calumniar *vtr* **1** to calumniate, libel. **2** *Jur* to slander.

caluroso,-a *adj* warm, hot; *fig* **una calurosa acogida,** a warm reception.

calva *nf* **1** *(de la cabeza)* bald patch. **2** *(claro)* clearing.

calvario *nm* **1** *Rel* Calvary; *(Vía Crucis)* stations *pl* of the Cross. **2** *fig (sufrimiento)* ordeal, calvary.

calvero *nm (claro)* clearing.

calvicie *nf* baldness.

calvinismo *nm Rel* Calvinism.

calvinista *Rel* **I** *adj* Calvinist. **II** *nmf* Calvinist.

calvo,-a I *adj* **1** *(persona)* bald; **ni tanto ni tan c.,** neither one extreme nor the other. **2** *(terreno)* barren, bare. **II** *nm* bald man.

calza *nf* **1** *(cuña)* wedge, scotch. **2** *desus* stocking.

calzada *nf* road, roadway, *US* pavement.

calzado,-a I *pp de* calzar. **II** *adj* **1** wearing shoes; **c. por el mejor zapatero,** shod by the best shoemaker. **2** *Rel* calced, shod. **III** *nm* shoes *pl,* footwear; **un buen c.,** a good pair of shoes.

calzador *nm* shoehorn.

calzar I *vtr* **1** *(poner calzado)* to put shoes on; **viste y calza al niño,** dress the child and put his shoes on. **2** *(llevar calzado)* to wear (shoes); **¿qué número calza?,** what size do you take?; *fig* **el mismo que viste y calza,** in person. **3** *(hacer zapatos)* to make shoes; **le calza el mejor zapatero,** he has his shoes made by the best shoemaker. **4** *(poner una cuña)* to wedge, scotch. **II calzarse** *vr* **c. los zapatos,** to put on one's shoes.

calzo *nm* **1** *(cuña)* wedge, scotch. **2** calzos, *(de caballo)* stockings.

calzón *nm desus* trousers *pl.*

calzonazos *nm inv fam* henpecked husband.

calzoncillos *nmpl* underpants, pants.

calzonudo,-a *adj* **1** *Am (tonto)* stupid. **2** *Méx (valiente)* brave; *(enérgico)* energetic. **3** *Méx* native Indian.

cama *nf* bed; **estar en** *or* **guardar c.,** to be confined to bed; *(indefinidamente)* to be bedridden; **hacer la c.,** to make the bed; **irse a la c.,** to go to bed; **meterse en la c.,** *(para dormir)* to go to bed; *(meterse dentro)* to get into bed; *fam* **llevarse a algn a la c.,** to get off with sb. ■ **c. doble/ sencilla,** double/single bed; **c. turca,** couch.

camachuelo *nm Orn* bullfinch.

camada *nf* **1** *(de pájaros)* brood; *(de animal)* litter. **2** *(capa)* layer. **3** *fig (banda)* gang, band.

camafeo *nm* cameo.

camagua *adj CAm Méx (maíz)* ripening.

camaleón *nm Zool* chameleon.

camalote *nm Am Bot* water hyacinth.

camanance *nm CAm* dimple.

cámara I *nf* **1** *(de un palacio, castillo)* room, chamber. ■ **c. acorazada,** strongroom; **c. nupcial,** bridal suite. **2** *(persona)* **ayuda de c.,** valet; **médico de c.,** royal doctor.

3 *(institución)* chamber. ■ **c. de comercio,** chamber of commerce; **C. de los Diputados,** ≈ House of Commons, *US* House of Representatives. **4** *Cin Fot TV* camera; **a c. lenta,** in slow motion. **5** *Téc* chamber. ■ **c. de gas,** gas chamber; **c. frigorífica,** cold-storage room. **6** *Aut* inner tube. **7** *Mús* chamber; **música de c.,** chamber music. **II** *nm,f (hombre)* cameraman; *(mujer)* camerawoman.

camarada *nmf* **1** *(de trabajo)* colleague, fellow worker; *(de colegio)* schoolmate, schoolfellow. **2** *Pol* comrade.

camaradería *nf* **1** companionship, friendship. **2** *Pol* comradeship.

camarera *nf* **1** *(de hotel)* chambermaid. **2** *(sirvienta)* maid. **3** *Hist (de una reina)* lady-in-waiting.

camarero,-a *nm,f* **1** *(de bar, restaurante) (hombre)* waiter; *(mujer)* waitress; *(detrás de la barra) (hombre)* barman; *(mujer)* barmaid. **2** *(de barco, avión) (hombre)* steward; *(mujer)* stewardess.

camarilla *nf* clique; *Pol* pressure group, lobby.

camarín *nm Rel* small chapel.

camarlengo *nm Rel* camerlengo, camerlingo.

camarón *nm Zool* (common) prawn.

camarote *nm Náut* cabin.

camastro *nm* rickety old bed.

cambado,-a *adj Am* bow-legged.

cambalache *nm pey (de fruslerías)* swap, exchange.

cambalachear *vtr (fruslerías)* to swap, exchange.

cambiante I *adj* **1** changing. **2** *(carácter)* changeable. **II cambiantes** *nmpl* changing colours *or US* colors.

cambiar I *vtr* **1** to change; **eso no cambia nada,** that doesn't make any difference; **han cambiado el horario de los trenes,** the train schedules have been changed. **2** *(cambiar de sitio)* to shift, move; **no cambies esos libros (de sitio),** leave those books where they are. **3** *(intercambiar)* to swap exchange; **c. impresiones,** to exchange views. **4** *(dinero)* to change; **¿me puede c. mil pesetas?,** can you change a thousand pesetas for me? **5** *(moneda extranjera)* to change, exchange. **II** *vi* to change; **c. de casa,** to move (house); **c. de idea,** to change one's mind; **c. de táctica,** to shift one's ground; **c. de trabajo,** to get another job; *Aut* **c. de velocidad,** to change gear. **III cambiarse** *vr* **1** *(de ropa)* to change *(clothes).* **2** *(de casa)* to move (house).

cambiazo *nm fam* switch; **dar el c. (a algn),** to do a switch (on sb).

cambio *nm* **1** *(gen)* change, changing; **c. de planes/política,** change of plans/policy; **un c. en la opinión pública,** a shift in public opinion. ■ **c. de impresiones,** exchange of views; **c. de la guardia,** changing of the guard. **2** *(dinero)* change; **me han dado mal el c.,** they gave me the wrong change; **¿tienes c. de mil pesetas?,** have you got change for a thousand pesetas? **3** *Fin (de acciones)* price, quotation; *(de divisas)* exchange. ■ **letra de c.** bill of exchange; **libre c.,** free trade. **4** *Aut* gear change. ■ **caja de cambios,** gearbox; **c. automático,** automatic transmission. **5** *fig* **a c. de,** in exchange for, instead of. **6 en c.,** however; **para él significa mucho, en c. para mí no significa nada,** it means a lot to him but nothing to me.

cambista *nmf Fin* moneychanger.

Camboya *n* Cambodia.

camboyano,-a *adj & nm,f* Cambodian.

cambullón *nm* **1** *Am (enredo)* swindle; *(confabulación)* plot, intrigue. **2** *Col Méx (cambalache)* swap, exchange.

camelar *vtr fam,* **camelarse** *vr fam* **1** to cajole, blarney. **2** *(galantear)* to flirt (with).

camelia *nf Bot* camellia.

camello,-a I *nm, f Zool* camel. **II** *nm arg (traficante de drogas)* (drug) pusher, dope dealer.

camelo *nm fam* **1** *(engaño)* hoax; **¡vaya un c.!,** what a sham! **2** *(bulo)* cock-and-bull story.

camerino *nm Teat* dressing room.

camero,-a *adj* **cama camera,** small double bed.

Camerún *n* Cameroon.

camerunés,-esa *adj* & *nm,f* Cameroonian.

camilla *nf* 1 *(para enfermos)* stretcher. 2 *(mesa)* **(mesa) c.,** small round table under which a heater is placed.

camillero,-a *nm,f* stretcher-bearer.

camilucho,-a *adj* & *nm,f Am* Indian (day) labourer *or US* laborer.

caminante *nmf* walker.

caminar I *vi* to walk. II *vtr* to cover, travel; **caminaron diez kilómetros,** they walked for ten kilometres; **caminamos horas y horas,** we walked for hours.

caminata *nf* (tiring) long walk.

caminero,-a *adj* **peón c.,** roadman.

camino *nm* 1 *(vía)* path, track; **ir c. de,** to be going to; **ponerse en c.,** to set *off; fig* **c. de rasas,** bed of roses; *fig* **el c. del éxito,** the road to success; *fig* **ir por buen/mal c.,** to be on the right/wrong track. ■ **c. de herradura,** bridle path; *Astron* **el C. de Santiago,** the Milky Way. 2 *(ruta)* route, way; **a medio c.,** half-way; **en el c. de casa al trabajo,** on the way to work; **estar en c.,** to be on the way; **nos coge** *or* **pilla de c.,** it is on the way. 3 *(medio, modo)* way; **abrir c.,** to clear the way; **abrirse c.,** to break through; *fig* **ha abierto el c. para nuevas investigaciones,** he's paved the way for new research; *fig* **no es el c. para convencerla,** that's not the (best) way to bring her over. 4 *SAm* table runner.

camión *nm* lorry, *US* truck; *fam* **estar como un c.,** to be gorgeous *or* a knockout. ■ **c. cisterna,** tanker; **c. de la basura,** refuse lorry, *US* garbage truck; **c. frigorífico,** refrigerator lorry.

camionaje *nm* haulage, cartage.

camionero,-a *nm,f* lorry *or US* truck driver.

camioneta *nf* van.

camisa *nf* 1 *(prenda)* shirt; **en mangas de c.,** in one's shirtsleeves; *fig* **cambiar de c.,** to change sides; *fig* **dejar a algn sin c.,** to leave sb penniless; *fig* **jugarse hasta la c.,** to put one's shirt on sth; *fam* **meterse en c. de once varas,** *(inmiscuirse)* to poke one's nose into other people's business; *fig* to bite off more than one can chew; *fam* **no llegarte a algn la c. al cuerpo,** to be terrified. ■ **c. de dormir,** nightdress, nightgown; **c. de fuerza,** straightjacket. 2 *Téc (de horno)* lining; *(de cilindro)* sleeve. 3 *Zool (de serpiente)* slough. 4 *(carpeta)* folder.

camisería *nf* outfitter's (shop), shirt shop.

camisero,-a I *adj* **blusa camisera,** shirt blouse; **vestido c.,** shirtwaister. II *nm,f* outfitter, shirt maker.

camiseta *nf* 1 *(de uso interior)* vest, *US* undershirt. 2 *(de uso exterior)* T-shirt. 3 *Dep* shirt; **sudar la c.,** to sweat (for it).

camisola *nf arc* camisole.

camisón *nm* 1 *(para dormir)* nightdress, nightgown, nightie. 2 *Am (vestido)* dress.

camomila *nf Bot* camomile.

camorra *nf fam* trouble; *(riña)* fight; **buscar c.,** to look for trouble.

camorrista I *adj* quarrelsome, rowdy. II *nmf* troublemaker.

camote *nm* 1 *Am Bot (batata)* sweet potato. 2 *Am Bot (bulbo)* bulb. 3 *Am (mentira)* lie. 4 *Am fig (enamoramiento)* love, crush. 5 *Am fig (amante)* lover. 6 *Méx (bribón)* rascal.

campal *adj* **batalla c.,** pitched battle.

campamento *nm* camp. ■ **c. de trabajo,** work camp; **c. de verano,** summer camp.

campana *nf* 1 bell; **c. de buzo,** diving bell; **c. de cristal,** bell jar *or* glass; **dar la** *or* **una vuelta de c.,** to overturn; *fig* **a toque de c.,** to the sound of bells; *fam* **tú has oído campanas y no sabes dónde,** you haven't got a clue. 2 *CAm (floripondio)* large white flower.

campanada *nf* peal *or* ring of a bell; *fig* **dar la c.,** to cause a sensation *or* a scandal.

campanario *nm Arquit* belfry, bell tower.

campanear I *vi* to ring the bells. II **campanearse** *vr* to sway, swagger.

campaneo *nm* 1 peal *or* pealing of bells. 2 *(contoneo)* sway, swagger.

campanero,-a *nm, f* 1 bell-ringer. 2 *(constructor)* bell founder.

campanilla *nf* 1 small bell; **tocar la c.,** to ring the handbell; *fam* **de campanillas,** de luxe, topnotch. 2 *Anat* uvula. 3 *Bot* bell flower.

campanillear *vi* to ring the bells.

campanilleo *nm* ringing (of bells).

campante *adj fam* 1 *(despreocupado)* cool, unconcerned; **se quedó tan c.,** he didn't bat an eyelid. 2 *(ufano)* proud, self-satisfied.

campaña *nf* 1 *(actividad, empresa)* campaign. ■ *Pol* **c. electoral,** election campaign; **c. publicitaria,** advertising campaign. 2 *Mil (expedición)* expedition; **de c.,** field. ■ **misa de c.,** open-air mass. 3 *(campo)* country, countryside. ■ **tienda de c.,** tent.

campar *vi* to wander, roam; *fam* **c. por sus respetos,** to do as one pleases.

campear *vi* 1 *(dejarse ver)* to be visible; **en lo alto campeaba una bandera,** a flag could be seen at the top. 2 *Am Agr* to watch over cattle in fields.

campechanería *nf,* **campechanía** *nf* openness, informality.

campechano,-a I *adj (alegre)* open, good-natured. II *nf Cuba Méx (bebida)* mixture of spirits.

campeón,-ona *nm,f* champion.

campeonato *nm* championship; *fam* **de c.,** great, brilliant; **un tonto de c.,** an utter idiot.

campero,-a *adj* 1 *(de campo)* country, rural; **(botas) camperas,** Spanish leather boots. 2 *Arg Par Urug (persona)* expert in agricultural matters.

campesinado *nm* peasantry, peasants *pl.*

campesino,-a I *adj* country, rural. II *nm, f (hombre)* countryman; *(mujer)* countrywoman.

campestre *adj* country, rural.

camping *nm* camping site; **hacer** *or* **ir de c.,** to go camping.

campiña *nf* 1 *(campo)* countryside. 2 *Agr (cultivo)* stretch of cultivated land.

campista *nmf* camper.

campo *nm* 1 *(campiña)* country, countryside; **a c. raso,** in the open air; **a c. traviesa** *or* **través,** cross-country. ■ **casa de c.,** country house. 2 *Agr* field; **las faenas del c.,** agricultural work; **trabaja (en) el c.,** he works (on) the land. 3 *Mil* field. ■ **c. de batalla,** battlefield; **c. de concentración,** concentration camp; **c. de tiro,** shooting range. 4 *Dep* field. ■ **c. deportivo,** playing field; **c. de fútbol,** football pitch; **c. de golf,** golf links, golf course; **c. de tenis,** tennis court. 5 *(espacio)* space; *fig* **dejarle a algn el c. libre,** to leave the field open for sb; **c. visual,** visual field. 6 *(ámbito)* field, scope; **en el c. de la psicología,** in the field of psychology. ■ **trabajo de c.,** fieldwork. 7 *Elec Fís* field. ■ **c. magnético,** magnetic field; *Fot* **profundidad de c.,** depth of field.

camposanto *nm* cemetery.

camuesa *nf Bot* pippin.

camueso *nm Bot* pippin tree.

camuflaje *nm* camouflage, disguise.

camuflar *vtr* to camouflage, disguise.

can *nm lit Zool* dog.

cana *nf* grey hair, white hair; *fam* **echar una c.** *or* **una canita al aire,** to let one's hair down.

Canadá *n* Canada.

canadiense *adj & nmf* Canadian.

canal *nf* **1** *(artificial)* canal. ■ **c. de riego,** irrigation canal. **2** *(natural)* channel. ■ **C. de la Mancha,** English Channel. **3** *Elec Inform TV* channel. **4** *(de tejado)* gutter. **5** *Anat* canal. **6** *(res)* open carcass; **abrir (un animal) en c.,** to slit (an animal) open. **7** *fig (vía)* channel; **por otros canales,** through other channels.

canaleta *nf* **1** *Arg Náut* loading channel. **2** *SAm (canalón)* roof gutter.

canalización *nf* **1** *(acción)* canalization. **2** *(tubería)* piping. **3** *Am (alcantarillado)* sewage *or* sewerage system.

canalizar *vtr* **1** *(agua)* to canalize; *(riego)* to channel. **2** *(area)* to canalize. **3** *fig (dirigir) (opiniones etc)* to direct; *(dinero)* to channel.

canalla *pey* **I** *nm (bribón)* swine, rotter. **II** *nf (chusma)* riffraff, mob.

canallesco,-a *adj pey* rotten, despicable.

canalón *nm* gutter.

canalones *nmpl Culin* cannelloni.

canapé *nm* **1** *(sofá)* couch, sofa. **2** *Culin* canapé.

canario,-a **I** *adj & nm, f* Canarian. ■ **Islas Canarias,** Canary Islands, Canaries. **II** *nm Orn* canary.

canasta *nf* **1** *(cesto)* basket. **2** *Naipes* canasta. **3** *(en baloncesto)* basket.

canastilla *nf (cestito)* small basket. **2** *(de un bebé)* layette.

canastillo *nm Am (de niño)* layette; *(ajuar)* trousseau.

canasto *nm* **1** *(cesto)* big basket, hamper. **II canastos** *interj* good heavens!

cancán *nm* **1** *Mús* cancan. **2** *(prenda)* frilly petticoat.

cancanear *vi fam* **1** *Am (expresarse mal)* to stumble in one's speech. **2** *Arg Urug (bailar)* to dance the cancan. **3** *Arg Urug Pol* to be corrupt. **4** *CAm Col (tartamudear)* to stammer.

cancel *nm* **1** *(contrapuerta)* storm door. **2** *Arg (verja)* gate. **3** *Méx (biombo)* folding screen.

cancela *nf* wrought-iron gate.

cancelación *nf* cancellation.

cancelar *vtr* to cancel.

cáncer *nm* **1** *Med* cancer; **c. de pulmón/mama,** lung/breast cancer. **2** *Astrol Astron* Cancer. ■ **Trópico de C.,** Tropic of Cancer.

cancerbero,-a **I** *nm Mit* Cerberus. **II** *nm,f Ftb* goalkeeper.

cancerígeno,-a *Med* **I** *adj* carcinogenic. **II** *nm* substance that can produce cancer.

canceroso,-a *Med* **I** *adj* cancerous. **II** *nm* patient suffering from cancer.

cancha¹ **I** *nf* **1** *(gen)* ground. **2** *Tenis* court. **3** *(de peleas de gallos)* cockpit. **4** *Am (hipódromo)* racecourse. **5** *Am (terreno)* plot of land. **6** *Arg CR Chi fig* **abrir** *or* **dar c. (a algn),** to give sb an advantage. **7** *Arg Chi fig* **estar uno en su c.,** to be in one's element. **8** *Arg fig* **tener c.,** to have experience. **II** *interj Arg (abrir paso)* out of the way!

cancha² *nf SAm* toasted maize.

canche *adj CAm* blonde.

canciller *nm* chancellor.

cancillería *nf* chancellery, chancellory.

canción *nf* song; *fam* **ya estás otra vez con la misma c.,** you're harping on the same old story again.

cancionero *nm* **1** *Lit* collection of songs *or* poems. **2** *Mús* songbook.

candado *nm* padlock.

candanga *adj Am* the Devil.

candeal **I** *adj* **pan/trigo c.,** white bread/wheat. **II** *nm Am (bebida)* drink made of milk, eggs and brandy.

candela *nf* candle.

candelabro *nm* candelabrum, candlestick.

candelero *nm* candlestick; *fig* **en el c.,** at the top.

candente *adj* candescent, red-hot, white-hot; *fig* **tema c.,** pressing issue.

candidato,-a *nm,f* candidate.

candidatura *nf* **1** *(opción)* candidature, candidacy; **presentar su c.,** to put forward one's candidature. **2** *(lista)* list of candidates.

candidez *nf* candour, *US* candor, ingenuousness.

cándido,-a *adj* candid, ingenuous.

candil *nm* oil lamp.

candilejas *nfpl Teat* footlights.

candor *nm* candour, innocence, pureness.

candoroso,-a *adj* innocent, pure.

canela *nf* cinnamon; *fam* **ser c. fina,** to be exquisite *or* excellent.

canelo,-a **I** *adj* cinnamon. **II** *nm Bot* cinnamon tree.

caneo *nm Am* hut, shack.

canesú *nm Cost* bodice.

cangilón *nm* **1** *(jarro)* pitcher; *(de molino)* bucket. **2** *Am* cart track.

cangrejo *nm (de mar)* crab; *(de río)* freshwater crayfish; *fam* **avanzar como los cangrejos,** to take one step forward and two backwards; *fam* **rojo como un c.,** as red as a lobster.

canguelo *nm arg* funk.

canguro **I** *nm Zool* kangaroo. **II** *nmf fam* baby-sitter.

caníbal *adj & nmf* cannibal.

canibalismo *nm* cannibalism.

canica *nf* marble; **jugar a las canicas,** to play marbles.

canícula *nf* dog days, midsummer heat.

caniche *nm Zool* poodle.

canijo,-a *adj fam* puny, weak.

canilla *nf* **1** *Anat* long bone; *(de ave)* wing bone. **2** *(carrete)* bobbin, reel.

canillera *nf Am (cobardía)* cowardice; *(miedo)* fear.

canillita *nm SAm* newspaper boy.

canino,-a **I** *adj Zool* canine; *fam* **tener un hambre canina,** to be starving. **II** *nm (colmillo)* canine.

canje *nm* exchange.

canjeable *adj* exchangeable.

canjear *vtr* to exchange.

cano,-a *adj* white, grey; **de pelo c.,** with white *or* grey hair.

canoa *nf* **1** *Náut* canoe, small boat. **2** *Am (cajón)* oblong shaped box; *(canal)* wooden *or* metal pipe.

canódromo *nm* dog *or* greyhound track.

canon *nm* **1** *(gen)* canon, norm; **como mandan los cánones,** in accordance with the rules. **2** *Mús Rel* canon. **3** *Com* royalty.

canónico,-a *adj* canonical; *Rel* **derecho c.,** canon law.

canónigo *nm (persona)* canon.

canonización *nf* canonization.

canonizar *vtr* to canonize.

canoso,-a *adj* white-haired, grey-haired; **pelo c.,** white *or* grey hair.

cansado,-a **I** *pp de* **cansar.** **II** *adj* **1** *(gen)* tired, weary; **estar c.,** to be tired; **tiene la vista cansada,** his eyes are tired. **2** *(pesado)* boring, tiring; **un viaje c.,** a tiring journey.

cansancio *nm* tiredness, weariness; *fam* **estoy muerto de c.,** I'm on my last legs.

cansar **I** *vtr* to tire, weary; **me cansa subir corriendo,** running upstairs tires me out. **II** *vi* to be tiring; **después de un rato acaba por c.,** after a while it gets boring; **siempre el mismo trabajo cansa,** one gets tired of always doing the same job. **III cansarse** *vr* to get tired; **c. enseguida,** to get tired easily; **se cansó de esperar y se fue,** he got fed up (with) waiting and left.

cansino,-a *adj* weary, slow.

cantábrico,-a *adj* Cantabrian; **Mar C.,** Bay of Biscay.

cántabro,-a *adj & nm, f* Cantabrian.

cantada *nf fam* blunder.

cantaleta *nf Am* harping on, nagging.

cantamañanas *nm inv fam* bullshitter.

cantante I *adj* singing; **llevar la voz c.,** to rule the roost. **II** *nmf* singer.

cantaor,-a *nm, f* flamenco singer.

cantar[1] *vtr & vi* 1 *Mus* to sing; **c. a dos voces,** to sing a duet; *fig* **c. las excelencias de,** to sing the praises of; *fig* **cantarle a algn las verdades** *or* **las cuarenta,** to give sb a piece of one's mind; *fig* **en menos que canta un gallo,** in a flash; *fam* **c. como una almeja,** to stick out like a sore thumb; *fam* **cantarlas claras,** to give a piece of one's mind. 2 *arg (confesar)* to sing, spill the beans. 3 *arg (oler mal)* to stink, whiff.

cantar[2] *nm lit* song; *fam* **¡eso es otro c.!,** that's a totally different thing! ■ *Lit* **c. de gesta,** chanson de geste; *Rel* **C. de los Cantares,** Song of Songs, Song of Solomon.

cantárida *nf Ent* Spanish fly.

cantarín,-ina *adj* 1 *(persona)* fond of singing. 2 *(voz)* sing-song.

cántaro *nm (recipiente)* pitcher; *(contenido)* pitcherful; *fig* **a cántaros,** plenty, in buckets; *fig* **llover a cántaros,** to rain cats and dogs.

cantata *nf Mús* cantata.

cante *nm* 1 *(canto)* singing. ■ *Esp* **c. hondo, c. jondo,** flamenco. 2 *arg (error)* blunder; **¡vaya c.!,** what a clanger! 3 *fam (regañina)* scolding.

cantera *nf* 1 *(de piedra)* quarry. 2 *fig Ftb* young players.

cantería *nf* stone cutting; **puente de c.,** bridge made of hewn stone.

cantero *nm* stonemason.

cántico *nm Rel* canticle.

cantidad I *nf* quantity, amount, sum; **en c.,** a lot; **pagaron una c. astronómica por el rescate,** they paid an astronomical amount for his release; *fam* **había c. de gente,** there were thousands of people; *fam* **cantidades industriales,** tons, loads. **II** *adv fam* a lot; **me gusta c.,** I love it.

cántiga *nf,* **cantiga** *nf Lit Mús* song, ballad.

cantil *nm Am* edge of a cliff.

cantilena *nf Lit Mús* cantilena, song; *fam* **siempre estás con la misma c.,** you're always going on about the same old story.

cantimplora *nf* water bottle.

cantina *nf* canteen, buffet.

cantinela *nf véase* **cantilena.**

cantinero,-a *nm, f* bar attendant.

canto[1] *nm* 1 *Mús (arte)* singing; **estudia c.,** he is studying singing. 2 *(canción)* song; *fig* **c. del cisne,** swan-song. 3 *Lit* canto.

canto[2] *nm* 1 *(borde)* edge; **de c.,** on its side; **ponlo de c.,** put it sideways; **tiene cinco centímetros de c.,** it is five centimetres thick; *fam* **no me caí por el c. de un duro,** I missed falling by the skin of my teeth. 2 *(guijarro)* pebble, stone. ■ **c. rodado,** *(grande)* boulder; *(pequeño)* pebble. 3 *fam* **al c.,** for sure, straight away; **cada vez que nos vemos, bronca al c.,** every time we meet we have a row.

cantón *nm* canton.

cantonera *nf* corner piece.

cantor,-a I *adj* singing; **los niños cantores de Viena,** the Vienna Boys' Choir; **pájaro c.,** songbird. **II** *nm, f* singer.

canturrear *vi* to hum, croon.

canturreo *nm* humming, crooning.

cánula *nf Téc* cannula.

canutas *nfpl fam* **pasarlas c.,** to have a hard time.

canutero *nm Am (de bolígrafo)* barrel (of pen).

canuto *nm* 1 *(tubo)* tube. 2 *Bot* internode. 3 *arg (porro)* joint. 4 *CAm Méx (de bolígrafo)* barrel (of pen). 5 *Méx Culin (sorbete)* tube-shaped sorbet.

caña *nf* 1 *Bot (planta)* reed; *(tallo)* cane, stem. ■ **c. de azúcar,** sugar cane. 2 *(vaso)* tall slender glass. 3 *Anat* bone marrow. 4 *(de una bota)* leg; **botas de media c.,** calf-length boots. 5 *(de pescar)* rod. 6 *fam (cerveza)* glass of draught *or* US draft beer. 7 *fam* **dar** *or* **meter c.,** *(persona)* to do sb over; *(coche)* to go at full speed.

cañada *nf* 1 *Geog (barranco)* gully, ravine. 2 *(camino)* cattle track. 3 *Am (arroyo)* stream.

cañadón *nm Cuba SAm* narrow deep stream.

cañamazo *nm* burlap.

cáñamo *nm Bot* hemp; *(tela)* hempen cloth. ■ **c. indio,** cannabis.

cañamón *nm Bot* hemp seed.

cañaveral *nm* cane plantation.

cañería *nf* (piece of) piping.

cañí *adj & nmf (pl cañís) fam* gypsy.

cañizal *nm,* **cañizar** *nm véase* **cañaveral.**

cañizo *nm* cane wattle.

caño *nm* 1 *(tubo)* tube. 2 *(chorro)* spout. 3 *Min (galería)* gallery. 4 *Náut (canal)* navigation channel. 5 *Arg (tubería)* pipe, piping.

cañón *nm* 1 *(arma)* gun. ■ **c. antiaéreo,** anti-aircraft gun. 2 *Hist* cannon; *fig* **al pie del c.,** without yielding; *fam* **estar c.,** to be *or* look terrific. 3 *(de fusil)* barrel; **escopeta de doble c.,** double-barrelled rifle. 4 *(tubo)* tube, pipe; **c. de estufa,** stove flue. 5 *Geog* canyon. 6 *Teat TV* spotlight. 7 *(de pluma)* barrel.

cañonazo *nm* 1 *(disparo)* gunshot; **salva de 21 cañonazos,** 21-gun salute. 2 *Ftb* strong shot.

cañonear *vtr* to shell.

cañonero,-a *adj* armed; **(lancha) cañonera,** gun-boat.

caoba *nf Bot* mahogany.

caolín *nm Min* kaolin.

caos *nm* chaos.

caótico,-a *adj* chaotic.

Cap. *abr de* **capitán,** Captain, Capt.

cap. *abr de* **capítulo,** chapter, ch.

capa *nf* 1 *(prenda)* cloak, cape; *fig* **de c. caída,** low-spirited; **andar de c. caída,** to have seen better days; *fig* **defender a c. y espada,** to fight tooth and nail; *fam* **hacer de su c. un sayo,** to do as one feels like. 2 *(pretexto)* excuse; **so c. de,** with the excuse that, under the pretext of. 3 *(mano)* layer, coat; **una c. de pintura,** a coat of paint; **una c. de polvo,** a film of dust; *Culin* **una c. de chocolate,** a coating of chocolate. 4 *Geol (estrato)* stratum, layer. 5 *fig (clase social)* class, stratum.

capacidad *nf* 1 *(cabida)* capacity; **con c. para 100 personas,** with room for 100 people; **un depósito de 50 litros de c.,** a fifty-litre tank. 2 *(aptitud)* capacity, ability; **no tiene c. para la música,** he hasn't got an ear for music; **tiene una gran c. de trabajo,** he's a very hard worker.

capacitación *nf* training.

capacitar *vtr* 1 *(instruir)* to train; **estar capacitado para ...,** to be trained *or* qualified to ... . 2 *(autorizar)* to authorize, license, make able; **no estoy capacitado para responder,** I'm not able to answer.

capacho *nm* 1 *(cesto grande)* big basket. 2 *SAm (sombrero viejo)* old hat.

capar *vtr* 1 *(castrar)* to castrate. 2 *Am (podar)* to prune.

caparazón *nm* 1 *(concha)* shell. 2 *fig (refugio)* cover, protection.

capataz *nm, f (hombre)* foreman; *(mujer)* forewoman.

capaz *adj* **1** *(con capacidad)* capable, able; **Pedro no sería c. de una cosa así,** Pedro wouldn't do something like that; **¿serías c.?** *(podrías)* could you?; *(te atreverías)* would you dare?; **si se entera es c. de despedirle,** if he finds out he could quite easily sack him. **2** *(eficiente)* efficient. **3** *(con espacio)* with room **(para,** for); **un teatro c. para mil personas,** a theatre which holds a thousand people.

capazo *nm* **1** *(cesto)* basket. **2** *(de bebé)* carrycot.

capcioso,-a *adj pey* captious, artful; **pregunta c.,** catch question.

capea *nf Taur* amateur bullfight.

capear *vtr* **1** *(dificultad etc)* to dodge, shirk; *fig* **c. el temporal,** to weather the storm. **2** *Taur* to make passes with the cape. **3** *Náut* to ride out.

capellán *nm Rel* chaplain.

capellanía *nf Rel* chaplaincy.

capelo *nm* **1** *(sombrero)* cardinal's hat. **2** *(cargo)* cardinalship. **3** *Am (campana de cristal)* bell glass.

caperuza *nf* **1** *(prenda)* hood. **2** *(tapa)* cap; **la c. de la pluma,** the cap of a pen.

capia *nf Am Culin* maize, *US* corn.

capicúa I *adj* número c., reversible number; **palabra c.,** palindrome. II *nm* palindrome.

capilar I *adj* **1** hair; **loción c.,** hair lotion. **2** *Fís* capillary. II *nm* capillary.

capilaridad *nf* capillarity.

capilla *nf* **1** *(oratorio)* chapel; **estar en c.,** *(condenado a muerte)* to be awaiting execution; *fig (en ascuas)* to be like a cat on hot bricks. ■ **c. ardiente,** funeral chapel. **2** *Mús* choir.

capirotada *nf* **1** *Am Culin* criollo dish with meat, vegetables, cheese etc. **2** *Méx fam (cementerio)* common grave.

capirotazo *nm* flip, flick.

capirote *nm* **1** *(prenda)* hood. ■ *fam* **tonto de c.,** silly idiot. **2** *(capirotazo)* flip, flick.

capital I *adj* **1** *(primordial)* capital, main, chief; **de importancia c.,** of capital importance; **pena c.,** capital punishment. **2** *(ciudad)* capital. II *nf* capital. ■ **c. de provincia,** county town, *US* county seat. III *nm Com Fin* capital. ■ **c. activo** *or* **social,** working *or* share capital; **c. inicial,** capital.

capitalismo *nm Econ* capitalism.

capitalista *Econ* I *adj* capitalist, capitalistic. II *nmf* capitalist.

capitalización *nf Econ Fin* capitalization.

capitalizar *vtr Econ Fin* to capitalize.

capitán,-ana I *nm* **1** *Mil* captain. ■ **c. general,** field marshal, *US* general of the army. **2** *Náut* captain, skipper. ■ **c. de corbeta,** lieutenant-commander; **c. de fragata,** commander; **c. general de la Armada,** Admiral of the Fleet. II *nm,f* **1** *(jefe)* leader; **la capitana del grupo,** the leader of the group. **2** *Dep* captain. III *nf Náut* flagship.

capitanear *vtr* **1** *Mil Náut* to captain, command. **2** *(dirigir)* to lead. **3** *Dep (equipo)* to captain.

capitanía *nf Mil* captaincy, captainship. ■ **c. general,** *(cargo)* rank of field marshal; *(edificio)* military headquarters.

capitel *nm Arquit* capital, chapiter.

capitolio *nm* Capitol.

capitoste *nm pey* bigwig.

capitulación *nf* agreement; *Mil* capitulation. ■ *Jur* **capitulaciones matrimoniales,** marriage settlement.

capitular[1] *adj* capitular; **sala c.,** chapterhouse.

capitular[2] *vi Mil* to capitulate, surrender; *(llegar a un acuerdo)* to reach an agreement.

capítulo *nm* **1** *(de libro)* chapter. **2** *fig (tema)* subject; **dentro del c. de las innovaciones,** among the innovations; *fig* **eso ya es c. aparte,** that's another story; *fig* **llamar a algn a c.,** to call sb to account.

capó *nm Aut* bonnet, *US* hood.

capón *nm* **1** *(pollo)* capon. **2** *(golpe)* rap on the head with the knuckles.

caporal *nm* **1** *Mil (cabo)* corporal. **2** *Agr (capataz)* farm manager.

capota *nf Aut* folding hood *or* top.

capote *nm* **1** *(prenda)* cape, cloak with sleeves; *Mil* greatcoat; *fig* **pensar** *or* **decir algo para su c.,** to think *or* tell oneself. **2** *Taur* cape; *fig* **echarle un c. a algn,** to give sb a hand.

capotera *nf Am* clothes hanger, clothes hook.

capricho *nm* **1** *(antojo)* whim, caprice; **hacer algo por puro c.,** to do sth because it takes one's fancy. **2** *Mús* caprice, capriccio.

caprichoso,-a I *adj* whimsical, fanciful; **formas caprichosas,** fanciful forms. II *nm,f* whimsical person.

Capricornio *nm Astrol Astron* Capricorn.

caprino,-a *adj* goat; **ganado c.,** goats.

cápsula *nf* **1** *(gen)* capsule. **2** *(de botella)* top, cap.

capsular *adj* capsular.

Capt. *abr de* **Capitán,** Captain, Capt.

captación *nf* **1** *(de ondas, de agua)* reception. **2** *(comprensión)* understanding, comprehension. **3** *(atracción)* fascination, captivation; *Pol* **c. de votos,** winning of votes.

captar *vtr* **1** *(ondas, agua)* to receive, pick up. **2** *(comprender)* to understand, grasp. **3** *(atraer)* to attract *or* hold sb's attention *or* interest.

captura *nf* capture.

capturar *vtr (criminal)* to capture; *(cazar, pescar)* to catch; *Mil* to seize.

capucha *nf (prenda)* hood.

capuchino,-a I *adj Rel* Capuchin. II *nm* **1** *Rel (monje)* Capuchin monk. **2** *(café)* capuccino, white coffee. III *nf Rel (monja)* Capuchin nun.

capuera *nf Arg Pan Par* **1** *(en la selva)* clearing, deforested land. **2** *(huerta)* vegetable garden.

capullo *nm* **1** *Ent* cocoon. **2** *Bot* bud; **en c.,** budding. **3** *vulg Anat (prepucio)* foreskin. **4** *ofens (persona) (estúpido)* silly bugger.

caqui I *adj (color)* khaki. II *nm Bot* persimmon.

cara *nf* **1** *(gen)* face; **c. a c.,** face to face; **c. a la pared,** facing the wall; **con c. de felicidad,** with a happy expression; **poner buena c.,** to look pleased; **poner c. de asco,** to look disgusted; **poner mala c.,** to pull a long face; **tener buena/mala c.,** to look good/bad; **tener c. de,** to look; **tenía c. de no haber dormido,** he looked as if he hadn't had any sleep; **ella tiene c. de no estar a gusto,** she looks unhappy; **tienes mala c. hoy,** you look a bit off-colour today; **volver la c.,** to look the other way; *fig* **c. de circunstancias,** serious look; *fig* **dar la c.,** to face the consequences (of one's acts); *fig* **dar la c. por algn,** to stand up for sb; *fig* **(de) c. a las próximas elecciones,** with a view to the next elections; *fig* **echarle a algn algo en c.,** to reproach sb for sth; *fig* **plantar c. a algn,** to face up to sb; *fig* **verse las caras,** to come face to face; *fam* **c. de pocos amigos,** unfriendly face; *fam* **romperle la c. a algn,** to smash sb's face in. **2** *(lado)* side; *(de medalla, moneda)* right side; **¿c.** *or* **cruz?,** heads or tails?; **echar** *or* **jugar algo a c.** *or* **cruz,** to toss (a coin) for sth; **la c. oculta de la luna,** the dark side of the moon. **3** *(de un edificio)* face. **4** *fam (desfachatez)* cheek, nerve; **¡qué c. (más dura) tienes!,** what a cheek you've got!; **tener más c. que espalda,** to have a lot of cheek. II *nm fam (desvergonzado)* cheeky person.

carabela *nf Náut* caravel.

carabina *nf* **1** *(arma)* carbine, rifle. **2** *(persona)* chaperon; **ir de c.,** to be chaperon.

carabinero *nm* customs officer.

cárabo *nm Orn* tawny owl.

caracense I *adj* of *or* from Guadalajara. **II** *nmf* native *or* inhabitant of Guadalajara.

caracol I *nm* **1** *Zool* (*de tierra*) snail; (*de mar*) winkle. **2** *Anat* (*del oído*) cochlea. **3** (*rizo de pelo*) kiss-curl. **4** *Equit* caracole; **hacer caracoles,** to caracole. **II ¡caracoles!** *interj* good heavens!

caracola *nf Zool* conch.

carácter *nm* (*pl* **caracteres**) **1** (*temperamento*) character; **de gran** *or* **mucho c.,** with a strong character; **tener buen/ mal c.,** to be good-natured/bad-tempered. **2** *fig* (*índole*) nature; **con c. de invitado,** as a guest; **por razones de c. privado,** for private reasons. **3** *Impr* (*signo*) letter. ▪ **caracteres góticos,** Gothic type; **c. de imprenta,** type, typeface.

característico,-a I *adj & nf* characteristic. **II** *nm, f Teat* (*hombre*) character actor; (*mujer*) character actress.

caracterización *nf* characterization.

caracterizado,-a I *pp de* **caracterizar. II** *adj* **1** (*gen*) characterized, portrayed; **la figura del padre está muy bien caracterizada,** the character of the father is very well portrayed. **2** (*disfrazado*) disguised; **c. de Papá Noel,** dressed up as Father Christmas.

caracterizar I *vtr* to characterize, portray. **II caracterizarse** *vr* **1** (*distinguirse*) to be characterized. **2** *Teat* to portray.

caracterología *nf* study of character *or* character type.

caracterológico,-a *adj* character type.

caracú *nm* **1** *Bol Chi RPl* (*ganado vacuno*) type of cattle. **2** *Am Zool* bone marrow.

caradura *nmf fam* cheeky devil; **¡qué c. eres!,** you're so cheeky!

carajillo *nm fam* coffee with a dash of brandy.

carajo *vulg* **I** *nm* (*pene*) prick. **II** *interj* shit!; **la fiesta se fue al c.,** the party fell through; **¡vete al c.!,** go to hell!

caramanchel *nm Arg Chi* snack bar.

caramba¹ *interj fam* **1** (*sorpresa*) good grief! **2** (*enfado*) damn it!

caramba² *nf* **1** *CAm Mús* traditional musical instrument. **2** *Arg Méx* old traditional song.

carámbano *nm* icicle.

carambola *nf Bill* cannon, *US* carom; *fam* **por c.,** by a fluke.

caramelo *nm* **1** (*dulce*) sweet, *US* candy. **2** (*azúcar quemado*) caramel; *Culin* **a punto de c.,** syrupy.

carantoña *nf* **1** (*máscara*) ugly mask. **2** *pey* (*mujer*) mutton dressed as lamb. **3 carantoñas,** caresses; **hacerle c. a algn,** (*acariciar*) to fondle sb; *fig* (*adular*) to butter sb up.

carapacho *nm* **1** (*caparazón*) carapace. **2** *Am Culin* seafood dish cooked in the shell.

caraqueño,-a I *adj* of *or* from Caracas. **II** *nm, f* native *or* inhabitant of Caracas.

carátula *nf* **1** (*máscara*) mask; *fig* **el mundo de la c.,** theatre. **2** (*cubierta*) cover.

caravana *nf* **1** (*expedición*) caravan. **2** *Aut* (*vehículo*) caravan. **3** *Aut* (*atasco*) traffic jam; **había mucha c.,** there was a long tailback.

caray *interj* God!, good heavens!; **¡este c. de chico me tiene harta!,** this damned boy is trying my patience!

carbón *nm* **1** (*gen*) coal; *fam* **¡se acabó el c.!,** that's that! ▪ **c. de leña, c. vegetal,** charcoal; **c. mineral, c. de piedra,** coal; **mina de c.,** coal mine; **papel c.,** carbon paper. **2** (*para dibujar*) charcoal.

carbonada *nf Am Culin* meat vegetable and rice stew.

carboncillo *nm* charcoal.

carbonera *nf* coal cellar.

carbonería *nf* coal merchant's.

carbonero,-a I *adj* coal. **II** *nm* **1** (*persona*) coal merchant. **2** *Orn* tit. ▪ **c. común,** great tit.

carbónico,-a *adj* carbonic; *Quím* **anhídrido c.,** carbon dioxide; **agua carbónica,** mineral water.

carbonífero,-a *adj* carboniferous; *Geol Hist* **el periodo c.,** the Carboniferous period.

carbonilla *nf* **1** (*dibujo*) charcoal. **2** (*ceniza*) coal dust; **c. de locomotora,** locomotive soot.

carbonización *nf* carbonization; (*combustión*) burning, charring.

carbonizar I *vtr* to carbonize, burn, char; **morir carbonizado,** to be burnt to death. **II carbonizarse** *vr* (*gen*) to carbonize, burn, char.

carbono *nm Quím* carbon. ▪ **dióxido de c.,** carbon dioxide.

carbunco *nm Med* anthrax.

carburación *nf* carburation.

carburador *nm Aut Elec* carburettor, *US* carburetor.

carburante *nm Aut Elec* fuel.

carburar *vi* **1** (*quemar*) to carburet. **2** *fam* (*funcionar*) to work properly; **hoy no carburo,** I just can't do anything right today.

carburo *nm* carbide.

carca *adj & nmf fam* square, straight; *Pol* reactionary.

carcaj *nm* **1** (*de flechas*) quiver. **2** *Am* (*de arma*) rifle case, pistol holster.

carcajada *nf* guffaw; **reírse a carcajadas,** to laugh one's head off; **soltar una c.,** to burst out laughing.

carcajearse *vr* to laugh heartily; **me carcajeo yo de sus amenazas,** his threats make me laugh.

carcamal *nm fam* old fogey.

cárcava *nf Geol* gully.

cárcel *nf* **1** (*prisión*) prison, gaol, jail. **2** *Téc* clamp.

carcelario,-a *adj* **1** (*de cárcel*) prison, gaol, jail. **2** *Téc* clamping.

carcelero,-a *nm, f* gaoler, jailer, warder, *US* warden.

carcinoma *nm Med* carcinoma, cancer.

carcoma *nf* **1** *Ent* woodworm. **2** *fig* (*preocupación*) anguish, anxiety.

carcomer I *vtr* (*madera*) to eat away; *fig* (*salud*) to undermine, eat away. **II carcomerse** *vr* to be consumed (**de,** with).

carda *nf* **1** (*máquina*) card, carding machine, teasel. **2** (*cardado*) carding.

cardado *nm* **1** *Ind* carding. **2** *Peluq* backcombing.

cardar *vtr* **1** (*lana, algodón*) to card. **2** *Peluq* to backcomb.

cardenal *nm* **1** *Rel* cardinal. **2** *Med* (*hematoma*) bruise.

cardenalato *nm Rel* cardinalship.

cardenalicio,-a *adj Rel* of *or* related to a cardinal; **colegio c.,** college of cardinals.

cárdeno,-a *adj* purple, violet.

cardiaco,-a *adj & nm, f,* **cardíaco,-a** *adj & nm, f* **I** *adj* cardiac, heart; **ataque c.,** heart attack. **II** *nm, f* person with a heart condition.

cardinal *adj* cardinal; **punto/número c.,** cardinal point/ number.

cardiología *nf Med* cardiology.

cardiólogo,-a *nm, f Med* cardiologist.

cardiopatía *nf Med* heart condition *or* disease.

cardo *nm* **1** *Bot* (*comestible*) cardoon; (*con espinas*) thistle; **c. borriquero,** cotton thistle. (*persona*) *fam* **ser un c. (borriquero),** to be an unsociable *or* harsh person; **ser un c.,** to be very ugly.

carear *vtr* **1** *Jur* (*encarar*) to bring two people face to face. **2** (*comparar*) to compare.

carecer *vi* to lack; **carezco de experiencia,** I lack experience.

carena *nf,* **carenado** *nm* **1** *Náut* careening. **2** *Aut* streamlining.

carenar *vtr* **1** *Náut (un barco)* to careen. **2** *Aut (un coche)* to streamline.

carencia *nf* lack (**de,** of).

carente *adj* lacking; **c. de interés,** lacking interest.

careo *nm* Jur confrontation.

carero,-a *adj fam* expensive, overpriced.

carestía *nf* **1** *(falta)* lack, shortage. **2** *Fin* high price *or* cost; **la c. de la vida,** the high cost of living.

careta *nf* mask; *fig* **quitarle la c. a algn,** to unmask sb. ■ **c. antigas,** gas mask.

carey *nm* **1** *Zool* sea turtle. **2** *(concha)* tortoiseshell; **una montura de c.,** a tortoiseshell frame.

carezco *indic pres véase* **carecer.**

carga *nf* **1** *(acción)* loading; *fig* **c. afectiva,** emotional content; *fig* **ser un burro de c.,** to be a dogsbody; *fig* **volver a la c.,** to go on and on about sth. ■ *Ferroc* **andén de c.,** loading platform; *Náut* **buque de c.,** freighter; *Aut* **zona de c. y descarga,** loading and unloading bay. **2** *(cosa cargada)* load. ■ **animal de c.,** beast of burden; **c. máxima,** maximum load; *Av Náut (de avión, barco)* cargo, freight. **3** *Fin (gasto)* debit; *(peso)* burden, load. ■ **c. fiscal,** tax charge. **4** *(repuesto)* refill. **5** *Mil* charge; **a paso de c.,** at the double. ■ **c. explosiva,** explosive charge. **6** *Elec (de condensador)* charge; *(en circuito)* load. **7** *fig (obligación)* burden; **las cargas de un trabajo,** the duties *or* responsibilities of a job.

cargado,-a I *pp de* **cargar. II** *adj* **1** *(gen)* loaded; **una pistola cargada,** a loaded gun. **2** *fig* burdened; **c. de deudas,** up to one's eyes in debt; **c. de razón,** strongly convinced that one is right. **3** *Elec* charged. **4** *(bebida)* strong; **un café c.,** a strong coffee. **5** *(espeso)* dense, heavy; **atmósfera cargada,** stuffy atmosphere.

cargador,-a I *adj* loading. **II** *nm,f* **1** loader. **2** *(de muelle)* docker, stevedore. **3** *(de alto horno)* stocker. **III** *nm* **1** *(dispositivo)* charger. **2** *(de bolígrafo)* filler. **3** *Am* porter.

cargamento *nm* **1** *(carga)* load. **2** *(de avión, barco)* cargo, freight.

cargante *adj fam* annoying.

cargar I *vtr* **1** *(gen)* to load; **c. un mechero** *or* **una pluma,** to fill a lighter *or* a pen; **le cargó el saco a la espalda,** he put the sack on his back; *fig* **c. las culpas a algn,** to put the blame on sb; *fam* **c. la mano** *or* **las tintas,** to overdo it. **2** *fig (achacar)* to burden. **3** *Com (cobrar)* to charge; **cárguelo a mi cuenta,** charge it to my account. **4** *(recargar)* to put too much; **ha cargado la habitación de cuadros,** she's put too many paintings in the room. **5** *Fot Mil* to load. **6** *Elec (batería)* to charge. **7** *Naipes* to trump. **8** *fam (fastidiar)* to annoy; **su conversación me carga,** I find her conversation very boring. **II** *vi* **1** to load. **2** *Arquit (apoyarse)* to rest. **3** *(recaer)* to fall upon. **4** *(llevar)* to carry; **c. con la responsabilidad/con la culpa,** to take the responsibility/the blame; **yo cargaré con la mochila,** I'll carry the ruck-sack; *fig* **c. con las consecuencias,** to suffer the consequences. **5** *Mil (contra el enemigo etc)* to charge. **III cargarse** *vr* **1** *(gen)* to load oneself with; **c. de paciencia,** to display as much patience as one has got; **c. de pastillas,** to stuff oneself with pills; *fam* **cargársela,** to get into hot water; *fam* **te le vas a cargar,** you're asking for trouble and you're going to get it. **2** *Meteor* to become overcast. **3** *fam Educ* to fail. **4** *fam (estropear, destrozar)* to smash, ruin; **me he cargado la radio,** I've broken the radio. **5** *fam (matar)* to kill; **se cargaron a cuatro,** they bumped off four.

cargazón *nf* **1** *Med (estómago, ojos)* heavy feeling. **2** *Meteor* heavy cloud.

cargo *nm* **1** *(puesto)* post, position; **alto c.,** top job, high ranking position; **desempeñar** *or* **ocupar el c. de,** to have a post as; **jurar el c.,** to take an oath. **2** *(dirección, custodia)* charge; **correr** *or* **estar al c. de,** to be in charge of; **hacerse c. de,** to take charge of; **tener a su c.,** to have in one's charge. **3** *Fin (débito)* charge, debit; **con c. a mi**

cuenta, charged to my account. **4** *Jur* charge, accusation. ■ **testigo de c.,** witness for the prosecution. **5** *(carga)* load, weight; *fig* **hazte c. de mi situación,** please try to understand my situation. ■ *fig* **c. de conciencia,** weight on one's conscience.

cargosear *vtr* Arg Chi Urug to pester.

carguero,-a *nm* **1** *(avión)* transport plane, freighter. **2** *(barco)* freighter.

cariacontecido,-a *adj hum* down in the mouth, crestfallen.

cariar I *vtr (dientes, huesos)* to cause to decay. **II cariarse** *vr* to decay.

cariátide *nf Arquit* caryatid.

caribe I *adj* Caribbean. **II** *nm,f (persona)* Caribbean. **III** *nm (idioma)* Carib.

caricato *nm Teat* comedian who imitates famous people.

caricatura *nf* **1** *(dibujo)* caricature. **2** *Am (dibujos animados)* cartoon film.

caricaturista *nmf* caricaturist.

caricaturizar *vtr* to caricature.

caricia *nf* caress, stroke.

caridad *nf* charity. ■ **obra de c.,** charitable deed.

caries *nf inv Med* decay, caries.

carilla *nf Impr* page, side of a piece of paper.

carillón *nm Mús* carillon.

carimbo *nm Am* branding iron.

cariñena *nm (vino)* sweet wine from Cariñena (Zaragoza).

cariño *nm* **1** *(amor)* affection, love; **coger** *or* **tomar c. a algo/algn,** to grow fond of sth/sb; **con todo c.,** lots of love; **ella la tiene mucho c.,** she's very fond of him; **lo ha hecho con todo el c.,** he made it with loving care. *(querido)* darling; **ven c.,** come here darling *or* dear. **3** *CAm Col Chi (regalo)* gift, present.

cariñoso,-a *adj* loving, affectionate.

carioca *adj & nm,f* Brazilian.

carisma *nm* charisma, charism.

carismático,-a *adj* charismatic.

caritativo,-a *adj* charitable.

cariz *nm* aspect, look.

carlinga *nf Av* **1** *(para piloto)* cockpit. **2** *(para pasajeros)* cabin.

carlismo *nm Hist* Carlism.

carlista *adj & nmf Hist* Carlist.

carmelita *adj & nmf Rel* Carmelite.

carmesí *adj & nm lit* crimson.

carmín I *adj & nm* **(de color) c.,** carmine. **II** *nm* **c. (de labios),** lipstick.

carnada *nf* bait.

carnal *adj* **1** *(de carne)* fleshy, carnal. **2** *(pariente)* first; **primo/tía c.,** first cousin/aunt.

carnaval *nm* carnival. ■ **martes de c.,** Shrove Tuesday.

carnaza *nf véase* **carnada.**

carne *nf* **1** *Anat* flesh; *fig* **en c. y hueso,** in person; *fig* **poner la c. de gallina (a algn),** to give (sb) the creeps; *fam* **de pocas carnes,** thin; *fam* **metido en carnes,** plump; *fam* **uno es de c. y hueso,** one is only human. ■ *fig* **c. dé cañón,** cannon fodder; **c. de gallina,** goosepimples; **c. viva,** raw flesh. **2** *(alimento)* meat; **no come c.,** he doesn't eat meat; *fig* **echar toda la c. en el asador,** to go in for everything. ■ **c. de cerdo,** pork; **c. de cordero,** lamb; **c. de ternera,** veal; **c. de vaca,** beef; **c. picada,** mince (meat). **3** *(de fruta)* pulp. **4** *Filos Rel* **la c. y el espíritu,** flesh and spirit.

carné *nm,* **carnet** *nm* card. ■ **c. de conducir,** driving licence; **c. de identidad,** identity card.

carnear *vtr* **1** *Am (animal)* to slaughter. **2** *Arg Méx (matar)* to murder; *(herir)* to injure.

carnero *nm* **1** *Zool* ram. **2** *Culin (carne)* mutton.

carnicería *nf* **1** *(tienda)* butcher's (shop). **2** *fig (masacre)* slaughter, bloodshed.

carnicero,-a I *adj* **1** *(carnívoro)* carnivorous. **2** *fig (cruel)* bloodthirsty. **II** *nm,f* **1** butcher. **2** *fam (médico)* sawbones.

cárnico,-a *adj* meat; **productos cárnicos,** meat products.

carnívoro,-a *Zool* **I** *adj* carnivorous. **II** *nm,f* carnivore.

carnoso,-a *adj* fleshy.

caro,-a I *adj* **1** *(costoso)* expensive, dear. **2** *lit (querido)* dear. **II** *adv* **costar** *or* **salir c.,** to cost a lot; **pagar c.,** to pay a high price; **vender c.,** to sell at a high price.

carolingio,-a *adj Hist* Carolingian, Carlovingian.

carota *nmf fam* cheeky person.

carótida *nf Anat* carotid.

carpa *nf* **1** *(pez)* carp. ■ *Dep* **salto de la c.,** jack-knife. **2** *(de circo)* big top, marquee, big tent.

carpe *nm Bot* hornbeam.

carpeta *nf* folder, file.

carpetazo *nm* termination; **dar c. a un asunto,** to shelve a matter.

Cárpatos *npl* Carpathians.

carpetovetónico,-a I *adj* Spanish through and through. **II** *nm,f* Spanish chauvinist.

carpintería *nf* **1** *(oficio)* carpentry. ■ **c. metálica,** metalwork. **2** *(taller)* carpenter's (shop).

carpintero,-a *nm,f* carpenter.

carpir *vtr Am* to weed, hoe.

carraca *nf* **1** *(instrumento)* rattle. **2** *Orn* roller. **3** *fam (coche viejo)* banger; *(persona)* decrepit old person.

carrasca¹ *nf Bot* kermes oak.

carrasca² *nf Am Mús* scraper.

carrasco *nm Am* large forest, forest land.

carraspear *vi* to clear one's throat.

carraspeo *nm* clearing of the throat.

carraspera *nf* hoarseness.

carrera *nf* **1** *(acción)* run; **a la c.,** in a hurry; **darse una c.,** to hurry; **tomar c.,** to take a run. **2** *(trayecto)* route, ride. **3** *Dep* race. ■ **c. contra reloj,** race against the clock; **c. de caballos,** horse race; **coche de carreras,** racing car; **c. de coches,** rally, meeting; **c. de relevos/de vallas,** relay/hurdle race. **4** *(estudios)* university education *or* training; **Claudia estudió** *or* **hizo la c. de abogado,** Claudia studied law; **dar c. a algn,** to pay for sb's studies. **5** *(profesión)* career, profession, **hacer c. de,** to succeed as; **hacer c. en la vida,** to succeed in life; **c. diplomática,** diplomatic career. ■ *euf (prostitución)* prostitution; **hacer la c.,** to walk the streets. **7** *(calle)* street, avenue. **8** *(de media)* ladder. **9** *Mil* **c. de armamentos,** arms race.

carrerilla *nf* run; **de c.,** parrot fashion; **tomar c.,** to take a run.

carreta *nf* cart.

carretada *nf* **1** *(carga)* cartload. **2** *fam (montón)* heaps, loads.

carrete *nm (de hilo)* bobbin, reel; *(de película)* spool; *(de cable)* coil.

carretera *nf* road. ■ **c. comarcal,** B road; **c. de circunvalación,** ring road; **c. nacional,** A *or* main road; **mapa** *or* **red de carreteras,** road map *or* network.

carretería *nf* **1** *(oficio)* cartwright's work. **2** *(taller)* cartwright's shop.

carretero *nm* **1** *(constructor)* cartwright. **2** *(conductor)* carter, cart driver; *fam* **blasfemar** *or* **jurar como un c.,** to swear like a trooper.

carretilla *nf* wheelbarrow; *fam* **saber algo de c.,** to know sth parrot fashion.

carretón *nm* **1** *(carrito)* small cart. **2** *CAm (de hilo)* bobbin.

carricero *nm Orn* teal.

carricoche *nm* **1** *(carromato)* caravan. **2** *fam Aut (coche)* old crock, banger.

carril *nm* **1** *Ferroc* rail. **2** *Aut* lane. **3** *(surco)* furrow.

carrillo *nm Anat* cheek; *fam* **comer a dos carrillos,** to devour, gobble up.

carro *nm* **1** *(carreta)* cart; *fam* **¡alto** *or* **para el c.!,** hold your horses!; *fam* **apearse del c.,** to give up *or* way. **2** *Mil* tank. ■ **c. de combate,** tank. **3** *(de máquina de escribir)* carriage. **4** *fam (coche)* wheels, motor, car.

carrocería *nf Aut* body, bodywork.

carromato *nm* caravan, covered cart.

carroña *nf* carrion.

carroza I *nf* **1** *(coche de caballos)* coach, carriage. **2** *(de carnaval)* float. **II** *nmf fam* out-of-date person; **tu eres ya un c.,** you're not that young any more. **III** *adj fam* old-fashioned, out-of-date.

carruaje *nm* carriage, coach.

carta *nf* **1** *(gen)* letter; **echar una c.,** to post a letter; *fig* **a c. cabal,** through and through; *fig* **tomar cartas en un asunto,** to take part in an affair. ■ **c. abierta,** open letter, **c. certificada/urgente,** registered/express letter; **c. de presentación/recomendación,** letter of introduction/recommendation. **2** *(minuta)* menu; **a la c.,** á la carte. ■ **c. de vinos,** wine list. **3** *Naipes* card; **echar las cartas a algn,** to tell sb's fortune; *fig* **jugárselo todo a una c.,** to put all one's eggs in one basket; *fig* **no saber a qué c. quedarse,** not to know what to do *or* think; *fig* **poner las cartas sobre la mesa,** to put *or* lay one's cards on the table, come clean. **4** *Geog (mapa)* chart. ■ **c. de navegación,** navigation chart. **5** *Jur (documento)* chart. ■ **c. blanca,** carte blanche; **c. de naturaleza, c. de ciudadanía,** naturalization papers. **6** *TV* **c. de ajuste,** test card.

cartabón *nm* **1** *(regla)* set square, triangle. **2** *Am (talla)* size.

cartagenero,-a *I adj of or* from Cartagena. **II** *nm,f* native *or* inhabitant of Cartagena.

cartaginés,-esa *adj & nm,f Hist* Carthaginian.

cartapacio *nm* **1** *(cuaderno)* writing pad, notebook. **2** *(carpeta)* folder, file.

cartearse *vr* to correspond (with), exchange letters (with).

cartel *nm* poster, bill; **esta obra lleva tres años en c.,** this play's been running for three years; **pegar carteles,** to put *or* stick up bills; **prohibido fijar carteles,** post no bills; *fig* **de c.,** reputed; *fig* **tener buen c.,** to be popular.

cartelera *nf* hoarding, *US* billboard. ■ *Prensa* **c. de espectáculos,** entertainments section *or* page.

carteo *nm* correspondence, exchange of letters.

cárter *nm* **1** *Téc* housing. **2** *Aut* crankcase.

cartera *nf* **1** *(de bolsillo)* wallet. **2** *(de mano)* handbag; *(para documentos etc)* briefcase; *(de colegial)* satchel, schoolbag; *fig* **tener algo en c.,** to be planning sth. **3** *Pol (ministerio)* portfolio; **ministro sin c.,** minister without portfolio. **4** *Com* portfolio. ■ **c. de pedidos,** order book. **5** *Am (bolso)* handbag, *US* purse.

carterista *nm* pickpocket.

cartero,-a *nm,f (hombre)* postman; *(mujer)* postwoman.

cartesianismo *nm Filos* Cartesianism.

cartesiano,-a *adj & nm,f Filos* Cartesian.

cartilaginoso,-a *adj* cartilaginous.

cartílago *nm* cartilage.

cartilla *nf* **1** *(libreta)* book. ■ **c. de ahorros,** savings book; **c. militar,** military record. **2** *(libro)* first reader; *fam* **cantarle** *or* **leerle la c. a algn,** to tell sb off.

cartografía *nf* cartography.

cartográfico,-a *adj* cartographic, cartographical.

cartógrafo,-a *nm,f* cartographer.

cartomancia *nf* cartomancy.

cartón *nm* **1** *(material)* card, cardboard. ■ **caja de c.,** cardboard box; *Arte* **c. piedra,** papier mâché. **2** *(de cigarrillos)* carton. **3** *Arte (dibujo)* sketch.

cartuchera *nf* cartridge holder *or* belt.

cartucho *nm* **1** *(de arma)* cartridge; *fig* **quemar el último c.,** to play one's last card. ■ **c. de fogueo,** blank cartridge. **2** *(de papel)* paper bag, paper cone.

cartujo,-a **I** *nm,f* Carthusian; *fam* **vivir como un c.,** to live like a hermit. **II** *nf* Charterhouse.

cartulina *nf* card.

casa *nf* **1** *(edificio)* house; **buscar c.,** to look for a place to live; **c. de pisos,** block of flats *or* apartments; **en c. de un amigo,** at a friend's house; **fuimos a c. de Daniel,** we went to Daniel's; *fig* **echar** *or* **tirar la c. por la ventana,** to go all out, spare no expense; *fig* **empezar la c. por el tejado,** to put the cart before the horse; *fam* **hacer la c.,** to do the housework. **2** *(hogar)* home; **de andar por c.,** run-of-the-mill, ordinary; **vestido de andar por c.,** dressed casually; **no paro en c.,** I'm never at home; **no sale de c.,** she never goes out; **pásate por c.,** come round *or* over; **vete a c.,** go home; *fig* **como Pedro por su c.,** as if he owned the place; *fig* **llevar la c.,** to run the household; *fig* **ser muy de c.,** to be home-loving; *fam* **se me cae la c. encima,** I can't stand being in the house; *prov* **en c. del herrero cuchara de palo,** the shoemaker's wife is always the worst shod. **3** *(familia)* family; **un amigo de la c.,** a friend of the family. **4** *(linaje)* house; **la C. de los Austrias,** the House of Hapsburg. **5** *Com (empresa)* company, firm; **la política de esta c.,** the company's policy. ■ **c. matriz/principal,** head/central office. **6 c. de huéspedes,** boarding house; **c. de juego,** gambling house; **c. de modas,** fashion shop; **c. de socorro,** first aid post; *euf* **c. de citas,** brothel, house of ill repute.

casaca *nf* **1** *Hist* long coat. **2** *(chaqueta)* short coat.

casación *nf Jur* cassation, annulment.

casadero,-a *adj* of marrying age.

casado,-a I *pp de* **casar. II** *adj* married; **está c. con Adela,** he's married to Adela. **III** *nm,f* married person; **los recién casados,** the newlyweds.

casal *nm Arg Urug Zool* pair.

casamata *nf Mil* casemate.

casamentero,-a I *adj* matchmaking. **II** *nm,f* matchmaker.

casamiento *nm* **1** *(matrimonio)* marriage. **2** *(boda)* wedding.

casanova *nm desus* Casanova, ladies' man, rake.

casar I *vtr* **1** to marry; **ya ha casado a sus dos hijas,** he's already married off his two daughters. **2** *(encajar)* to join, fit. **3** *Jur (derogar)* to annul, quash. **II** *vi* to match, go *or* fit together. **III** **casarse** *vr* to marry, get married; **c. en segundas nupcias,** to get married again; **c. por la iglesia/por lo civil,** to get married in church/in a registry office; *fam* **se casaron de penalty,** it was a shotgun wedding.

cascabel *nm* **1** bell. ■ *Zool* **serpiente de c.,** rattle-snake. **2** *fig (persona)* happy person.

cascabelear I *vi* **1** *(zascandilear)* to act recklessly. **2** *Am (cascabeles)* to jingle. **II** *vtr fig (infundir ilusiones)* to beguile, raise the hopes of.

cascada *nf* waterfall, cascade.

cascado,-a I *pp de* **cascar. II** *adj fig* **1** *(persona)* worn-out, aged. **2** *(voz)* harsh, hoarse.

cascajo *nm* **1** gravel, rubble. **2** *(trozo)* fragment, shred. **3** *fig (persona)* **estar hecho un c.,** to be a wreck.

cascanueces *nm inv* nutcracker.

cascar I *vtr* **1** to crack. **2** *fam (pegar)* to belt, thump; **te voy a c. como no vuelvas a hacer,** I'll belt you one if you do it again. **3** *fam (dañar)* to harm; **el tabaco casca mucho,** smoking does you a lot of harm; *fam* **cascarla,** to kick the bucket, snuff it. **II** *vi* **1** *fam (charlar)* to chat away. **2** *fam (morir)* to peg out; **se puso enfermo y cascó,** he fell ill and died. **III** **cascarse** *vr* **1** *(romperse)* to crack. **2** *(voz)* to become harsh *or* hoarse. **3** *vulg (masturbarse)* **cascársela,** to wank, *US* jerk off.

cáscara I *nf* **1** *(de huevo, de nuez)* shell. **2** *(de fruta)* skin, peel. **3** *(de grano)* husk. **4** *fig Pol* **ser de (la) c. amarga,** to be progressive. **II** *interj* **¡cáscaras!,** well, I never!

cascarilla *nf* husk.

cascarón *nf* eggshell; *fig* **recién salido del c.,** wet behind the ears.

cascarrabias *nmf inv fam* short-tempered person.

casco *nm* **1** helmet; **c. protector** *or* **de motorista,** crash helmet. **2** *(de caballería)* hoof. **3** *Náut* hull. **4** *(de ciudad)* **c. urbano,** city centre, central area. **5** *(trozo)* broken piece, fragment. **6** *(de metralla)* piece of shrapnel. **7** *(envase)* empty bottle. **8** *(de sombrero)* crown. **9 cascos,** *(auriculares)* head-phones; *(cabeza)* brains, head *sing*; **calentarse** *or* **romperse los c.,** to rack one's brains; **ser alegre de c.,** to be a scatterbrain. **10** *Am (gajo de fruta)* segment, piece.

cascote *nm* **1** piece of rubble *or* debris; **cascotes,** rubble *sing*. **2** *(de metralla)* piece of shrapnel.

casería *nf Am* customers *pl*.

caserío *nm* **1** *(pueblo)* hamlet, small village. **2** *(casa)* country house.

casero,-a I *adj* **1** *(hecho en casa)* home-made; **comida casera,** home-made food. **2** *(familiar)* family; **una velada casera,** a family get-together. **3** *(persona)* home-loving. **4** *Dep fam (árbitro)* favouring *or US* favoring the home team. **II** *nm,f* **1** *(dueño) (hombre)* landlord; *(mujer)* landlady. **2** *(guarda)* keeper. **3** *Am (parroquiano)* customer, client.

caserón *nm* big rambling house.

caseta *nf* **1** *(barraca)* hut, booth. **2** *(de feria, exposición)* stand, stall; *(de balneario, de playa)* bathing hut, *US* bath house. **3** *Dep* changing room.

casete I *nm (magnetófono)* cassette player *or* recorder. **II** *nf (cinta)* cassette (tape).

casi *adv* almost, nearly; **c. mil personas,** almost one thousand people; **c. ni me acuerdo,** I can hardly remember it; **c. nunca,** hardly ever; **me fui c. sin comer,** I left having eaten hardly anything; *fam* **c., c.,** just about; *fam* **c. que,** sort of, nearly; *fam* **diez millones, ¡c. nada!,** ten million, peanuts!

casilla *nf* **1** *(de casillero)* pigeonhole. **2** *(cuadro, cuarícula)* square. **3** *fig* **sacar a algn de sus casillas,** to drive sb mad.

casillero *nm* **1** *(de cartas etc)* pigeonholes *pl*. **2** *Dep (marcador)* scoreboard.

casimba *nf Am* **1** *(pozo)* well; *(manantial)* spring, fountain. **2** *(vasija)* pan for collecting rainwater.

casino *nm* casino.

casis *nf inv Bot* blackcurrant bush.

caso *nm* **1** *(ocasión, evento)* case; **cuando llegue el c.,** in due course; **el c. es que ...,** the fact *or* thing is that ...; **el c. Mattei,** the Mattei affair; **en c. contrario,** otherwise; **en c. de necesidad,** if need be; **en cualquier c.,** in any case; **en el mejor/peor de los casos,** at best/worst; **en este c.,** in such a case; **en todo c.,** in any case *or* instance; **en un c. extremo, en último c.,** as a last resort; **hacer c. a** *or* **de algn,** to pay attention to sb; **hacer c. omiso de,** to take no notice of; **no venir al c.,** to be beside the point; **para el c. tanto da,** it doesn't make any difference; **pongamos por c.,** let's say; **se daba el c. de que ...,** it so happened that ...; *Med* **un c. de apendicitis,** an appendicitis case. ■ **c. de conciencia,** a case of conscience; **c. de fuerza mayor,** dire necessity. **2** *(suceso)* event, happening; **dado el c. de que,** in the event of; *fam* **¡eres un c.!,** you're a case! **3** *Ling* case.

casona *nf* large house.

casorio *nm fam* wedding.

caspa *nf* dandruff.

Caspio *n* Caspian Sea.

cáspita *interj* dear me!, goodness gracious!

casquete *nm* **1** (*prenda*) skullcap. **2** *Geom* **c. esférico,** fragment of a sphere. **3** *Geog* **c. polar,** polar cap. **4** *vulg* (*polvo*) bang, screw; **echar un c.,** to have a bang *or* a screw.

casquillo *nm* **1** (*de cartucho*) case. **2** *Téc* ferrule, tip. **3** *Am* (*herradura*) horseshoe.

casquivano,-a *adj fam* scatterbrained.

cassette *nm* & *f véase* **casete.**

casta *nf* **1** (*linaje*) lineage, descent; **de c.,** of breeding, of good stock; *prov* **de c. le viene al galgo,** it runs in the family. **2** (*animales*) breed; **de c.,** thoroughbred, purebred **3** (*división social*) caste.

castaña *nf* **1** *Bot* chestnut; *fig* **sacarle a algn las castañas del fuego,** to pull sb's chestnuts out of the fire for them. ■ **c. pilonga,** dried chestnut. **2** (*moño*) bun. **3** (*vasija*) demijohn. **4** *fam* (*bofetada*) slap; (*golpe*) blow, punch; **se pegó una c. con el coche,** he had a car crash; *fam* **¡toma c.!,** what do you think of that, then! **5** *fam* (*borrachera*) binge, skinful.

castañar *nm* chestnut grove.

castañazo *nm fam* **1** *Aut* crash. **2** (*golpe*) thump, whack.

castañero,-a *nm, f* chestnut seller.

castañeta *nf* snap of the fingers.

castañetear I *vtr* (*castañuelas*) to play castanets. **II** *vi* (*dientes*) to chatter.

castañeteo *nm* **1** *Bot* sound of castanets. **2** (*de dientes*) chattering.

castaño,-a I *adj* chestnut-brown; (*pelo*) brown, dark; **ojos castaños,** brown *or* chestnut eyes. **II** *nm* **1** *Bot* chestnut; *fam* **eso pasa de c. oscuro,** this is going a bit too far. **2** (*madera*) chestnut.

castañuela *nf* castanet; *fam* **más contento que unas castañuelas,** as happy as a sandboy.

castellanismo *nm* *Ling* word *or* expression common to the Castilian spoken in Castile.

castellanizar *vtr Ling* to Hispanicize.

castellano,-a I *adj* Castilian. **II** *nm, f* (*persona*) Castilian. **III** *nm* (*idioma*) Spanish, Castilian.

castellonense I *adj* of *or* from Castellón de la Plana. **II** *nmf* native *or* inhabitant of Castellón de la Plana.

casticismo *nm* love of tradition.

castidad *nf* chastity.

castigador,-a *fam nm, f* (*hombre*) ladies' man; (*mujer*) man-eater.

castigar *vtr* **1** to punish, chastise. **2** (*dañar*) to harm, ruin; **el viento castigó los árboles,** the wind whipped the trees. **3** (*afligir*) to afflict. **4** *Jur* to penalize. **5** *Dep* to punish, penalize. **6** *fam* (*enamorar*) to seduce.

castigo *nm* **1** punishment, chastisement; **c. ejemplar,** exemplary punishment; **levantar un c.,** to withdraw a punishment. **2** (*daño*) torture, suffering. **3** *Jur* penalty. **4** *Dep* **área de c.,** penalty area; **c. máximo,** penalty.

Castilla *n* Castile; **C. la Nueva/la Vieja,** New/Old Castile; *fig* **¡ancha es C.!,** it's a free world!

castillo *nm* castle; *fig* **hacer** *or* **levantar castillos en el aire,** to build castles in the sky. ■ **c. de fuegos artificiales,** firework display.

castizo,-a *adj* pure, authentic; **madrileño c.,** Madrilenian to the core.

casto,-a *adj* chaste.

castor *nm Zool* beaver.

castración *nf* castration, gelding.

castrado,-a I *pp de* **castras. II** *adj* castrated, gelded. **III** *nm* eunuch.

castrar *vtr* to castrate, geld; *fig* (*debilitar*) to mutilate.

castrense *adj* military; **vida c.,** military life.

castrismo *nm Pol* Castroism.

castrista *adj* & *nmf Pol* Castroist.

casual I *adj* accidental, chance; **fue un encuentro c.,** we met by chance. **II** *nm fam* chance; **por un c.,** by any chance. ◆ **casualmente** *adv* by chance.

casualidad *nf* chance, coincidence; **de** *or* **por c.,** by chance; **dió la c. que ...,** it so happened that ...; **¿tienes un lápiz, por c.?,** do you happen to have a pencil?; **una c. increíble,** an amazing coincidence.

casuca *nf*, **casucha** *nf pey* hovel.

casuístico,-a I *adj* casuistic, casuistical. **II** *nf* casuistry.

casulla *nf Rel* chasuble.

cata *nf* **1** (*acción*) tasting. **2** (*muestra*) taste, sample.

cataclismo *nm Geol* catastrophe; *fig* cataclysm.

catacumbas *nfpl Hist* catacombs.

catador,-a *nm, f* taster; **c. de vinos,** wine taster.

catadura *nf pey* looks *pl*.

catafalco *nm* catafalque.

catalán,-ana I *adj* Catalan, Catalonian. **II** *nm, f* Catalan, Catalonian. **III** *nm* (*idioma*) Catalan.

catalanismo *nm* **1** *Ling* Catalanism, Catalan word *or* expression used in Spanish. **2** *Pol* Catalan nationalism.

catalanista *Pol* **I** *adj* of *or* relating to Catalan nationalism. **II** *nmf* Catalan nationalist.

catalejo *nm* telescope.

catalepsia *nf* catalepsy.

cataléptico,-a *adj* & *nm, f* cataleptic.

catalizador,-a I *adj* catalytic. **II** *nm* catalyst.

catalizar *vtr* **I** *Quím* to catalyse. **2** *fig* (*atraer*) to act as a catalyst for.

catalogación *nf* cataloguing.

catalogar *vtr* **1** to catalogue, *US* catalog. **2** (*clasificar*) to classify.

catálogo *nm* catalogue, *US* catalog.

catalpa *nf Bot* catalpa, Indian bean tree.

Cataluña *n* Catalonia.

cataplasma *nf* **1** *Farm* cataplasm, poultice. **2** *fam* (*pelmazo*) bore; **que c. eres,** what a pain in the neck you are.

cataplines *nmpl fam* (*testículos*) nuts.

catapulta *nf* catapult.

catapultar *vtr* to catapult.

catar *vtr* (*vino, comida*) to taste.

catarata *nf* **1** waterfall; **las cataratas del Niágara,** the Niagara Falls. **2** *Med* cataract; **operar (a algn) de cataratas,** to perform a cataract operation (on sb).

catarral *adj* catarrhal, cold.

catarro *nm* (common) cold, catarrh.

catarsis *nf* catharsis, katharsis.

catártico,-a *adj* cathartic.

catastral *adj* cadastral.

catastro *nm* cadastre, cadaster.

catástrofe *nf* catastrophe.

catastrófico,-a *adj* catastrophic.

catavino *nm* (*recipiente*) wine taster.

catavinos *nm inv* (*persona*) wine taster.

cate *nm fam* **1** (*golpe*) thump, whack. **2** *Educ* failed subject, fail; **¿cuántos cates has sacado?,** how many subjects did you fail?

catear *vtr fam Educ* to fail, *US* flunk.

catecismo *nm Rel* catechism.

cátedra *nf* **1** *Univ* professorship; (*de instituto*) post of head of a department. ■ **ex c.,** ex cathedra; **sentar c.,** to master a science or an art. **2** *Univ* (*departamento*) department; **la c. de historia,** the history department.

catedral *nf* cathedral; *fam* **como una c.,** huge.

catedralicio,-a *adj* cathedral.

catedrático,-a *nm,f Educ* **1** *Univ* professor. **2** *(de instituto)* head of department.

cátedro,-a *nm,f fam véase* **catedrático,-a**

categoría *nf* category, class; **con/sin c.,** with/without class; **una persona de c.,** an important person.

categórico,-a *adj* categoric; **un no c.,** a flat refusal.

catenario,-a *adj & nf Téc* catenary.

catequesis *nf Rel* catechesis.

catequista *nmf Rel* catechist, catechizer.

catequizar *vtr Rel* to catechize.

cateto¹ *nm Geom* cathetus, short side of a right-angled triangle.

cateto,-a² *nm,f pey* yokel, bumpkin.

catinga *nf* **1** *Am (olor) (persona)* body odour *or US* odor; *(animales or plantas)* stench, strong smell. **2** *Arg (suciedad)* dirtiness, filthiness.

catión *nm Fís* cation.

cátodo *nm Elec* cathode.

catolicismo *nm Rel* Catholicism.

católico,-a *adj & nm,f Rel* Catholic; *fam* **no estar muy c.,** *(persona)* not to feel well.

catón¹ *nm fig* harsh critie.

catón² *nm (libro)* primer, first reading book.

catorce *inv* I *adj (cardinal)* fourteen; *(ordinal)* fourteenth. II *nm* **1** fourteen, fourteenth. **2** *fam (quiniela)* jackpot; *véase tamb* **ocho**

catorceavo,-a I *adj* fourteenth. II *nm,f* fourteenth (part); *véase tamb* **octavo,-a**

catre *nm fam* bed; *vulg* **llevarse algn al c.,** to lay sb.

caucásico,-a *adj & nm,f* Caucasian.

Cáucaso *n* Caucasus.

cauce *nm* **1** *(de un río)* bed. **2** *fig (canal)* channel; **cauces oficiales,** official channels.

caucho *nm Am* rubber.

caución *nf Jur* bail, guarantee.

caudal¹ *nm* **1** *(de un río)* flow. **2** *(riqueza)* wealth, riches *pl.* **3** *fig (abundancia)* plenty, abundance; **c. de conocimientos,** wealth of (intellectual) knowledge.

caudal² *adj* caudal; *(de pez)* **aleta c.,** caudal fin.

caudaloso,-a *adj* copious, heavy, abundant; **un río muy c.,** a large plentiful river.

caudillaje *nm* **1** leadership. **2** *Am (caciquiso)* tyranny, despotism. **3** *Arg Chi* tyrants *pl.* **4** *Arg* period of tyrannical rule.

caudillo *nm* leader, head.

causa *nf* **1** cause, motive; **a** *or* **por c. de,** because of; **c. común,** common cause; **con conocimiento de c.,** with full knowledge of the facts; **por tu c.,** for your sake. **2** *(ideal)* cause; **morir por una c.,** to die for a cause. **3** *Jur (caso)* case; *(juicio)* trial; **instruir una c.,** to take legal proceedings.

causal *adj* causal.

causalidad *nf* causality.

causante I *adj* causal, causing, **el hecho c. de la protesta,** what caused the protest II *nm,f* person who causes; **el c. del malentendido,** the one to blame for the misunderstanding.

causar *vtr* **1** *(gen)* to cause, bring about *or* on. **2** *(hacer, dar)* to make, give, **me causa un gran placer,** it gives me great pleasure; **me causó muy buena impresión,** he made a good impression on me

causticidad *nf* causticity

cáustico,-a *adj* caustic

cautela *nf* caution, cautiousness.

cauterización *nf Med* cauterization

cauterizador,-a *Med* I *adj* cauterizing, cauterant II *nm* cautery, cauterant.

cauterizante *adj Med* cauterizing.

cauterizar *vtr Med* to cauterize, fire, *fig* to apply drastic measures to

cautivador,-a *adj* captivating.

cautivar *vtr* **1** to capture, take prisoner **2** *fig (fascinar)* to captivate, capture.

cautiverio *nm*, **cautividad** *nf* captivity

cautivo,-a *adj & nm,f captive*.

cauto¹,-a *adj* cautious, wary.

cava¹ *nf (cavada)* digging.

cava² I *nf (bodega)* wine cellar. II *nm (vino espumoso)* cava, champagne.

cavar I *vtr* to dig, *fig* **c. uno su propia fosa,** to dig one's own grave. II *vi fig (meditar)* to meditate (**en,** on)

caverna *nf* **1** cave, cavern; **hombre de las cavernas,** caveman **2** *Anat* cavity

cavernícola I *adj* **1** cave dwelling, **hombre c.,** caveman. **2** *fam (carca)* reactionary II *nm, f* **1** cave dweller. **2** *fam* reactionary.

cavernoso,-a *adj* **1** cavernous. **2** *(voz, sonido)* deep, resounding; **voz cavernosa,** deep and hollow voice.

caviar *nf* caviar

cavidad *nf* cavity.

cavilación *nf* pondering, musing

cavilar *vtr* to ponder, brood over.

caviloso,-a *adj CAm* gossipy.

cayado *nm* **1** *(de pastor)* shepherd's crook. **2** *(de obispo)* crosier, crozier. **3** *Anat* **c. de la aorta,** arch of the aorta.

cayo *nm Geog* key

cayuco *nm Am* small flat-bottomed canoe.

caza I *nf* **1** hunting; **ir de c.,** to go hunting; **partida de c., hunt. 2** *(animales)* game. ■ **c. furtiva,** poaching; **c. mayor/menor,** big/small game. **3** *fig (persecución)* pursuit, chase; **andar a la c. de algo,** to hunt for sth; **levantar la c.,** to give the game away II *nm Av* fighter, fighter plane.

cazabombardero *nm Av* fighter bomber.

cazador,-a I *adj* hunting. II *nm, f* hunter; **c. furtivo,** poacher.

cazadora *nf* **1** *(prenda)* (waist-length) jacket. **2** *Am (camioneta)* van.

cazalla *nf* aniseed spirit.

cazar *vtr* **1** to hunt; **fue a c. elefantes,** he went elephant hunting. **2** *(cobrar)* to catch, bag; **han cazado diez faisanes,** they bagged ten pheasants; *fam* **cazarlas al vuelo,** to be quick on the uptake. **3** *fig (acosar)* to hunt *or* track down. **4** *fam (conseguir)* to catch, land; **c. un marido,** to trap a husband.

cazasubmarinos *nm inv Mil* submarine chaser.

cazatalentos *nmf inv* head-hunter.

cazatorpedero *nm Mil* (torpedo-boat) destroyer.

cazcarria *nf* splash of mud

cazo *nm* **1** *(cacerola)* saucepan. **2** *(cucharón)* ladle

cazón *nm (Pez)* dogfish

cazuela *nf* **1** casserole, saucepan **2** *Culin (guiso)* casserole, stew; **a la c.,** stewed

cazurrería *nf* sullenness, surliness

cazurro,-a *adj* sullen, surly

c/c *abr de* **cuenta corriente,** current account, c/a.

CCOO *nfpl abr de* **Comisiones Obreras.**

CDS *nm Pol abr de* **Centro Democrático y Social.**

ce *nf (la letra)* c; *fig* **ce por ce,** in great detail, with a fine-toothed comb; *fig* **por ce** *or* **por be,** for one reason or another

cebada *nf Bot* barley

cebador *nm Téc* primer

cebar I *vtr* **1** *(animal)* to fatten, *fam (persona)* **estar cebado,** to be as fat as a pig. **2** *(poner un cebo a)* to bait **3** *Téc (máquina, bomba)* to prime. **II cebarse** *vr* **1** *(ensañarse)* to make prey **(en,** on) **2** *(dedicarse)* to devote oneself to

cebo *nm* bait.

cebolla *nf Bot* **1** onion **2** *(bulbo)* bulb.

cebolleta *nf Bot* **1** *(especie)* chives *pl.* **2** *(cebolla tierna)* spring onion.

cebollino *nm* **1** *Bot (especie)* chives *pl.* **2** *Bot (cebolla)* spring onion **3** *fam (persona)* idiot, nitwit.

cebra *nf* **1** *Zool* zebra. **2** *Auf* **paso c.,** zebra crossing, *US* crosswalk

ceca *nf* **1** *Hist* Royal Mint **2** *fam fig* **de la C. a la Meca,** from pillar to post

cecear *vi* to lisp.

ceceo *nm* lisp.

cecina *nf Culin* cured beef.

cedazo *nm* sieve.

ceder I *vtr* **1** *(dar)* to cede, give, hand over; **c. una propiedad,** to cede a property. **2** *Aut* **c. el paso,** to give way; **señal de 'ceda el paso',** 'give way' sign, *US* 'yield way' sign **3** *Dep (pelota)* to pass (over). **II** *vi* **1** *(darse)* to yield, give way; **han cedido los cimientos,** the foundations have given way. **2** *(disminuir)* to diminish, slacken, go down. **3** *(rendirse)* to give up, yield; **hay que saber c.,** one has to make concessions at times.

cedilla *nf (la letra)* cedilla

cedro *nm Bot* cedar

cédula *nf* **1** document, certificate; **c. personal,** identity card. ■ *Arg Chi Urug* **c. de identidad,** identity card **2** *Com Fin* bond, certificate, warrant.

CEE *nf abr de* **Comunidad Económica Europea,** European Economic Community, EEC.

cefalalgia *nf Med* cephalalgia, headache.

cefalea *nf Med* severe cephalalgia, migraine.

céfiro *nm lit* zephyr.

cegador,-a *adj* blinding.

cegar I *vtr* **1** to blind; *fig* **cegado por la ira,** blind with rage. **2** *(tapar)* to blind, *(puerta, ventana)* to wall up **II cegarse** *vr fig* to become blinded.

cegato,-a *fam* **I** *adj* short-sighted. **II** *nm, f* shortsighted person.

ceguera *nf* **1** blindness. **2** *fig (ofuscación)* blindness, short-sightedness.

Ceilán *n* Ceylon.

ceilanés,-esa *adj & nm, f* Ceylonese.

ceja *nf* **1** *Anat* eyebrow; **fruncir las cejas,** to frown; *fig* **se le ha metido entre c. y c.,** she's got it into her head; *fam* **quemarse las cejas,** to burn the midnight oil. **2** *Mús (del violín etc)* bridge. **3** *SAm (sección de bosque)* forest with path.

cejar *vi* to yield, give way; **c. en el empeño,** to give up, slacken one's efforts.

cejijunto,-a *adj* **1** *(persona)* with bushy eyebrows too close together. **2** *(ceñudo)* frowning.

cejilla *nf* capo.

celada[1] *nf* trap, ambush.

celada[2] *nf Hist (de armadura)* sallet, helmet.

celador,-a *nm, f* attendant; *(de un colegio)* monitor; *(de una cárcel)* ward.

celar[1] *vtr* **1** *(la ley)* to observe closely, abide strictly by. **2** *(vigilar)* to watch over, spy on.

celar[2] *vtr* to hide, conceal.

celda *nf* **1** cell. ■ **c. de castigo,** punishment cell. **2** *Inform* cell.

celdilla *nf (beehive)* cell.

celebérrimo,-a *adj* most famous, well-known.

celebración *nf* **1** *(festejo)* celebration. **2** *(cumplimiento, realización)* holding; **la c. del juicio tendrá lugar hoy,** the trial will be held today.

celebrante I *adj* celebrating. **II** *nm Rel* celebrant *or* officiating priest.

celebrar I *vtr* **1** *(reunión)* to hold. **2** *(festejar)* to celebrate. **3** *(alabar)* to praise. **4** *Rel (misa)* to celebrate. **5** *(estar contento)* to be glad *or* happy; **celebro que todo saliera bien,** I'm glad everything went well. **II** *vi Rel (oficiar misa)* to celebrate mass. **III celebrarse** *vr* to take place, be held; **el partido se celebrará en Cádiz,** the match will be held in Cadiz; **su cumpleaños se celebra el ocho de abril,** his birthday falls on April 8th.

célebre *adj* **1** *(famoso)* famous, celebrated, well-known. **2** *Am (hermoso)* beautiful, pretty.

celebridad *nf* **1** celebrity, fame. **2** *(persona)* celebrity.

celeridad *nf* celerity, swiftness, speed.

celeste I *adj* **1** *(de cielo)* celestial. **2** *(color)* sky-blue. **II** *nm* sky blue.

celestial *adj* **1** celestial, heavenly; *fam* **ser algo música c.,** to be heavenly music. **2** *fig (delicioso)* heavenly, delightful.

celestina *nf* go-between.

celibato *nm* celibacy.

célibe *adj & nmf* celibate.

celo *nm* **1** zeal, conscientiousness. **2** *Biol (macho)* rut; *(hembra)* heat; **en c.,** *(macho)* in rut; *(hembra)* on *or* in heat. **3 celos,** jealousy *sing;* **tener c. (de algn/algo),** to be jealous (of sb/sth).

celo® *nm fam* sellotape®, *US* Scotch tape®.

celofán *nm* cellophane.

celosía *nf (reja)* lattice; *(ventana)* lattice window.

celoso,-a *adj* **1** *(cuidadoso)* zealous, conscientious; **c. de su vida privada,** protective of his private life. **2** *(envidioso)* jealous. **3** *Antill SAm (arma)* delicate. **4** *Am (mecanismo)* highly sensitive.

celta I *adj* Celtic, Keltic. **II** *nm, f* Celt, Kelt. **III** *nm (idioma)* Celtic, Keltic.

celtibérico,-a *adj & nm, f,* **celtíbero,-a** *adj & nm, f* Celtiberian.

céltico,-a *adj* Celtic, Keltic.

célula *nf* cell; *fig Pol* **c. comunista,** comunist cell.

celular *adj* **1** *Biol* cellular, cell. **2** *(penitenciario)* jail; **coche c.,** Black Maria.

celulitis *nf inv* cellulitis.

celuloide *nm* **1** *(material)* celluloid. **2** *fig (cine)* cinema; **estrella del c.,** film star.

celulosa *nf Quím* cellulose.

cembro *nm Bot* arolla pine.

cementación *nf* case-hardening.

cementar *vtr* to case-harden.

cementerio *nm* cemetery, graveyard. ■ **c. de coches,** scrapyard

cemento *nm* **1** *Constr* concrete, cement; **c. armado,** reinforced concrete. **2** *(de los dientes)* cement.

cena *nf* supper; *(completa or formal)* dinner.

cenáculo *nm* **1** *Hist* cenacle. **2** *fig (círculo social)* group.

cenacho *nm* basket.

cenador *nm* bower, arbour, US arbor.

cenagal *nm* **1** *(lugar cenagoso)* marsh, swamp. **2** *fig (apuro)* jam, tight spot.

cenagoso,-a *adj* muddy, marshlike.

cenar I *vi* to have supper *or* dinner. **II** *vtr* to have for supper *or* dinner; **¿qué cenamos hoy?,** what is there for supper tonight?

cenceño,-a *adj* thin, lean.

cencerrada *nf fam* tin-pan serenade (given to a widow *or* widower who remarries).

cencerro *nm* cowbell; *fam* **estar como un c.,** to be nuts *or* crackers.

cendal *nm Tex* silk stuff.

cenefa *nf* 1 *(de ropa)* edging, trimming. 2 *(de suelo, techo)* ornamental border, frieze.

cenetista *Pol* I *adj* of *or* related to the CNT (Confederación Nacional del Trabajo). II *nmf* member of the CNT.

cenicero *nm* ashtray.

Cenicienta *nf* la C., Cinderella.

ceniciento,-a *adj* ashy, ashen.

cenit *nm* zenith.

cenital *adj* zenithal.

ceniza *nf* 1 ash. ■ **Miércoles de C.,** Ash Wednesday. 2 **cenizas,** *(restos mortales)* ashes.

cenizo *nm fam* 1 *(aguafiestas)* wet blanket, killjoy. 2 *(gafe)* jinx.

cenobio *nm* monastery.

cenobita *nmf* coenobite.

censar I *vtr (incluir en el censo)* to register (in a census). II *vi (hacer un censo)* to take a census.

censo *nm* 1 census; **hacer un c.,** to take a census. ■ **c. electoral,** electoral roll. 2 *(tributo)* tax.

censor *nm* 1 censor; *Fin* **c. jurado de cuentas,** auditor. 2 *(crítico)* critic.

censura *nf* 1 censorship; **pasar por la c.,** to be censured. 2 *(crítica)* censure, criticism; **digno de c.,** censurable. ■ *Com Fin* **c. de cuentas,** audit, auditing; *Pol* **moción de c.,** motion of censure.

censurable *adj* censurable.

censurar *vtr* 1 *(libro, película)* to censor. 2 *(condenar)* to censure, criticize.

centauro *nm Mit* centaur.

centavo,-a I *adj* hundredth. II *nm* 1 hundredth (part). 2 *Am Fin (moneda)* cent, centavo; *véase tamb* **octavo,-a.**

centella *nf* 1 *(chispa)* spark; *(luz intermitente)* flash; *fig* **rápido como una c.,** (as) quick as a flash. 2 *(rayo)* lightning.

centelleante *adj* flashing, sparkling.

centellear *vi* to flash, sparkle; **las estrellas centelleaban en el cielo,** the stars twinkled in the sky.

centelleo *nm* flashing, sparkling.

centena *nf,* **centenar** *nm* hundred; **a centenares,** in hundreds.

centenario,-a I *adj* hundred-year-old, more than a hundred years old; **una cifra centenaria,** a threefigure sum. II *nm,f* centenarian. III *nm (aniversario)* centenary, hundredth anniversary.

centeno *nm Bot* rye.

centesimal *adj* centesimal.

centésimo,-a I *adj* hundredth; **centésima parte,** one hundredth. II *nm, f (de una serie)* hundredth. III *nm* 1 *(parte)* hundredth. 2 *(moneda)* cent, centesimo; *véase tamb* **octavo,-a.**

centígrado,-a *adj* centigrade.

centigramo *nm* centigram, centigramme.

centilitro *nm* centilitre, *US* centiliter.

centímetro *nm* centimetre, *US* centimeter.

céntimo *nm* cent, centime; *fam* **estar sin un c.,** to be penniless.

centinela *nm* 1 *Mil* sentry; **estar de c.,** to stand sentry 2 *fig (vigilante)* lookout, watch.

centolla *nf,* **centollo** *nm Zool* spider crab.

centrado,-a I *pp de* **centrar.** II *adj* 1 centred, *US* centered. 2 *(equilibrado)* balanced; *(dedicado)* devoted **(en,** to).

central I *adj* central. II *nf* 1 *Elec* power station ■ **c. nuclear/térmica,** nuclear/thermal power station. 2 *(oficina principal)* head office; **c. de correos,** central *or* main post office; **c. telefónica,** tetephone exchange. III *nm Am (hacienda)* sugar mill.

centralismo *nm* centralism.

centralista *adj & nmf* centralist, centralistic.

centralita *nf Tel* switchboard.

centralización *nf* centralization.

centralizador,-a *adj* centralizing.

centralizar I *vtr* to centralize. II **centralizarse** *vr* to become centralized.

centrar I *vtr* 1 to centre, *US* center; **c. un cuadro,** to centre a picture; *fig* **c. un tema,** to define a subject. 2 *(esfuerzos, atención)* to concentrate, centre, *US* center; **centra su vida en la política,** she dedicates herself to politics. 3 *(basar)* to centre *or US* center around, base. 4 *Dep* **c. el balón,** to centre *or US* center the ball. II *vi Dep* to centre, *US* center. III **centrarse** *vr* 1 to be centred *or US* centered *or* based; **la novela se centra en la vida del niño,** the novel revolves around the child's life. 2 *(concentrarse)* to concentrate **(en,** on).

céntrico,-a *adj* centrally situated; *(de ciudad)* **zona céntrica,** town *or* city centre, *US* downtown.

centrifugador,-a I *adj* centrifugal. II *nf* 1 centrifugal machine, spinning machine. 2 *(de ropa)* spin-dryer.

centrifugar *vtr* to centrifuge; *(ropa)* to spin-dry.

centrifugo,-a *adj* centrifugal.

centrípeto,-a *adj* centripetal.

centrista *Pol* I *adj* centre, *US* center; **partido c.,** centre party. II *nmf* centrist.

centro *nm* 1 middle, centre, *US* center; **c. de la ciudad,** town *or* city centre; **el c. de la Tierra,** the centre of the Earth. 2 *(establecimiento)* institution, centre, *US* center. ■ **c. benéfico,** charitable organization; **c. comercial,** shopping centre; **c. cultural,** cultural centre; **c. docente** *or* **de enseñanza,** educational institution; **c. sanitario,** hospital, clinic. 3 *Mat* centre, *US* center. 4 *Dep* centre, *US* center. ■ **delantero c.,** centre forward; **medio c.,** centre half. 5 *Pol* centre, *US* center; **partido de c.,** centre party.

centroafricano,-a *adj* of *or* from Central Africa; **República Centroafricana,** Central African Republic.

Centroamérica *n* Central America.

centroamericano,-a *adj & nm,f* Central American.

centrocampista *nmf Ftb* midfield player.

centuplicar I *vtr* to centuplicate, multiply a hundredfold. II **centuplicarse** *vr* to be multiplied a hundredfold.

céntuplo,-a *adj & nm* hundredfold, centuple.

centuria *nf* century.

centurión *nm* centurion.

ceñido,-a I *pp de* **ceñir.** II *adj* tight-fitting, clinging.

ceñir I *vsr* 1 to cling to, be tight on; **esa falda te ciñe demasiado,** that skirt is too tight on you. 2 *(rodear)* to surround, encircle; **la ciñó con sus brazos,** he embraced her tightly. 3 *lit (llevar ceñido)* to wear; **c. la espada,** to gird the sword. II **ceñirse** *vr* 1 *(atenerse, limitarse)* to limit oneself, stick **(a,** to); **c. al tema,** to keep to the subject; **ciñéndonos a este caso en concreto,** coming down to this particular case. 2 *(prenda)* to cling **(a,** to).

ceño *nm* scowl, frown; **con el c. fruncido,** frowning.

ceñudo,-a *adj* frowning.

CEOE *nf abr de* **Confederación Española de Organizaciones Empresariales,** ≈ Confederation of British Industry, CBI.

cepa *nf* 1 *Bot (de vid)* vine; *(tronco)* stump. 2 *fig (origen)* origin; **de pura c.,** authentic, true; **vasco de pura c.,** Basque through and through.

cepillado,-a I *pp de* **cepillar.** II *adj* 1 brushed. 2 *Carp* planed. III *nm* 1 brushing. 2 *Carp* planing.

cepillar I *vtr* 1 to brush. 2 *Carp* to plane (down). 3 *fam (adular)* to butter up. 4 *fam (desplumar)* to fleece. II **cepillarse** *vr* 1 *(con cepillo)* to brush. 2 *fam (matar)* to do in; *Educ* to plough; *(acabar)* to finish; **se cepilló la tarta él solito,** he gobbled up the whole cake himself. 3 *vulg (mujer)* to lay.

cepillo *nm* 1 brush. ■ **c. de dientes,** toothbrush; **c. del pelo,** hairbrush; **c. de uñas,** nailbrush. 2 *Carp* plane. 3 *(para limosnas)* alms box.

cepo *nm* 1 *(rama)* branch. 2 *Caza* trap 3 *Aut* clamp. 4 *Hist (tortura)* stocks *pl.* 5 *(para limosnas)* alms box.

ceporro *nm* 1 *(cepa)* log. 2 *fam* dimwit, blockhead; **dormir como un c.,** to sleep like a log.

cera *nf* 1 wax; *(de abeja)* beeswax; **blanco como la c.,** as white as snow. 2 *(del oído)* earwax, cerumen. 3 *(para suelos, muebles)* wax, polish.

cerámica *nf* 1 *(arte)* ceramics *sing*, pottery. 2 *(objeto)* piece of pottery.

cerámico,-a *adj* ceramic.

ceramista *nmf* ceramist, potter.

cerbatana *nf* blowpipe.

cerca¹ *nf* fence, wall.

cerca² *adv* 1 near, close; **ven más c,** come closer; **ya estamos c.,** we are almost there. 2 **c. de,** *(casi)* nearly, around; **c. de cien personas,** about one hundred people. 3 **c. de,** *(poco distante)* near, close; **el colegio está c. de mi casa,** the school is near my house, **4 de c.,** closely; **lo vi muy de c.,** I saw it close up.

cercado *nm* 1 *(lugar cerrado)* enclosure. 2 *(cerca)* fence, wall.

cercanía *nf* 1 proximity, nearness. 2 **cercanías,** outskirts, suburbs; ■ **tren de c.,** suburban train.

cercano,-a *adj* near, nearby, close; **de un pueblo c.,** from a neighbouring town *or* village. ■ **el C. Oriente,** the Near East.

cercar *vtr* 1 *(poner una cerca)* to fence, enclose. 2 *(rodear)* to fence in, wall in, encircle. 3 *Mil (sitiar)* to besiege, surround.

cercenar *vtr* 1 *(cortar)* to cut off, amputate. 2 *fig (disminuir)* to diminish, reduce, slash.

cerceta *nf Orn* teal.

cerciorar I *vtr* to assure. II **cerciorarse** *vr* to make sure; **se cercioró de que no había nadie en la casa,** he checked that the house was empty.

cerco *nm* 1 circle, ring; **c. luminoso** circle of light. 2 *Mil (sitio)* siege; **c. policíaco,** police cordon; **poner c. (a una ciudad),** to besiege (a town). 3 *(marco)* frame.

cerda *nf* 1 *Zool* sow. 2 *(pelo) (de cerdo)* bristle; *(de caballo)* horsehair; **cepillo de c.,** bristle brush. 3 *vulg (mujer)* pig.

cerdada *nf fam* dirty trick; **hacerle una c. a algn,** to do the dirty on sb.

Cerdeña *n* Sardinia.

cerdo *nm* 1 *Zool* pig. 2 *(carne)* pork. 3 *fam pey (hombre)* pig, arsehole.

cereal 1 *adj* cereal. II *nm* cereal; **cereales,** breakfast cereal *sing.*

cerealista *adj* cereal, cereal-producing.

cerebelo *nm Anat* cerebellum.

cerebral *adj* 1 cerebral, brain. 2 *(frío, intelectual)* calculating.

cerebro *nm* 1 *Anat* brain. 2 *fig (inteligencia)* brains *pl*; **ella es el c. de la organización,** she's the brains of the organization. ■ **lavado de c.,** brainwashing.

ceremonia *nf* ceremony. ■ **maestro de ceremonias,** master of ceremonies. 2 *(cumplido)* deference, ceremony; **con gran c.,** with great pomp.

ceremonial *nm* ceremonial.

ceremonioso,-a *adj* ceremonious, formal; *pey* pompous, stiff.

céreo,-a *adj* wax, waxen.

cerería *nf* chandler's shop.

cereza *nf* 1 *Bot (fruto)* cherry. 2 *Am* husk of the coffee bean.

cerezo *nm Bot* cherry tree.

cerilla *nm* match; **una caja de cerillas,** a box of matches.

cerillero,-a *nm, f* match seller.

cerner I *vtr (harina)* to sift. II **cernerse** *vr* I *(pájaro, avión)* to hover. 2 *fig* to loom, threaten.

cernícalo *nm* 1 *Orn* kestrel. 2 *fig (persona)* block-head, dolt.

cernir *vtr & vr véase* **cerner.**

cero *nm* 1 *Mat* zero; **tres grados bajo c.,** three degrees below zero. 2 *(cifra)* nought, zero; **sacar un c. en literatura,** to get a nought in literature; *fig* **partir de c.,** to start from scratch; *fig* **ser un c. a la izquierda,** to be useless *or* a good-for-nothing. 3 *Dep* nil; **dos a c.,** two nil. 4 *(ninguno)* none; **sacó c. puntos,** he didn't get any points at all.

cerquillo *nm Arg Méx* fringe.

cerrado,-a I *pp de* **cerrar.** II *adj* 1 closed, shut; **a puerta cerrada,** in camera; *fig* **a ojos cerrados,** with one's eyes closed. 2 *Ling* **vocal cerrada,** close vowel. 3 *(marcado) (acento)* broad; *(curva)* tight, sharp; *(ovación)* thunderous. 4 *(barba)* bushy. 5 *fig (oculto)* hidden, obscure. 6 *(persona) (introvertida)* uncommunicative, reserved; *(intransigente)* intransigent, uncompromising, unyielding; *fam (torpe)* thick; **c. de mollera,** thickheaded.

cerradura *nf* lock; **c. antirrobo,** antitheft lock.

cerrajería *nf* 1 *(oficio)* locksmith's trade. 2 *(taller)* locksmith's shop.

cerrajero,-a *nm, f* locksmith.

cerrar I *vtr (ventana, libro, tienda, ojos)* to shut, close; *(grifo, gas)* to turn off; *(luz)* to turn off, switch off; *(cremallera)* to fasten, zip (up); *(negocio, oficina)* to close down; *(cuenta)* to close; *(discusión)* to end, finish; *(compra)* to close, conclude; *(sobre)* to seal; *(agujero)* to plug; *(grieta)* to fill; *(puños)* to clench; *(en dominó)* to block; **c. con llave,** to lock; **c. el paso a algn** to block sb's way; **c. la marcha,** to bring up the rear; *fam* **c. el pico,** to shut one's trap. II *vi* 1 to close, shut. 2 *Tricot* to cast off. III **cerrarse** *vr* 1 to close, shut; **la puerta se cerró de golpe,** the door slammed shut; *fam* **c. en banda,** to stick to one's guns. 2 *(obstinarse)* to stand fast, persist **(en,** in). 3 *Med (cicatrizar)* to close up, heal. 4 *Aut* to close in. 5 *Meteor* to cloud over.

cerrazón *nf* 1 *(obstinación)* obstinacy. 2 *(estupidez)* dimness, denseness; **c. mental,** narrow-mindedness. 3 *Meteor* stormy *or* black sky.

cerril *adj* 1 *(terreno)* rough. 2 *(animal)* wild, untamed. 3 *(persona) (tosca)* uncouth, coarse; *(obstinada)* pig-headed, headstrong.

cerro *nm* hill; *fig* **irse por los cerros de Ubeda,** to beat around the bush.

cerrojazo *nm* **dar c. (a algo/algn),** to cut (sth/sb) short.

cerrojo *nm* 1 bolt; **echar** *or* **correr el c. (de una puerta),** to bolt (a door). 2 *Ftb* blanket defence.

certamen *nm* competition, contest.

certero,-a *adj* 1 *(tiro, tirador)* accurate, good; **es un tirador muy c.,** he's a crack shot. 2 *(acertado)* accurate, certain.

certeza *nf*, **certidumbre** *nf* certainty; **saber (algo) con c.,** to be certain (of sth); **tener la c. de que ...,** to be sure *or* certain that ... .

certificación *nf* 1 *(confirmación)* certification. 2 *(de un envío)* registration. 3 *(documento)* certificate.

certificado,-a I *pp de* **certificar.** II *adj* 1 certified. 2 *(envío)* registered. III *nm* 1 *(gen)* certificate ■ **c. médico,** medical certificate. 2 *(carta)* registered letter; *(paquete)* registered package.

certificar *vtr* **1** *(gen)* to certify, guarantee. **2** *(carta, paquete)* to register.

cerúleo,-a *adj* cerulean, deep-blue.

cerumen *nm* cerumen, earwax.

cerval *adj* **miedo c.**, terror, funk.

cervantino,-a *adj* of *or* relating to Cervantes, Cervantine.

cervato *nm Zool* fawn.

cervecería *nf* **1** *(bar)* pub, bar. **2** *(fábrica)* brewery.

cervecero,-a I *adj* beer; **la producción cervecera**, beer production. **II** *nm* brewer.

cerveza *nf* beer, ale. ■ **c. de barril**, draught beer; **c. dorada** *or* **ligera**, lager; **c. negra**, stout.

cervical *adj Anat* cervical, neck.

cérvido,-a I *adj* cervid **II** *nm Zool* cervid

cerviz *nf* cervix, nape of the neck, *fig* **ser duro de c.**, to be pig-headed

cesación *nf* cessation, suspension

cesante I *adj* dismissed, *(ministro)* removed from office, *(embajador)* recalled **II** *nm, f (funcionario)* suspended official, *(parado)* unemployed worker

cesar *vi* **1** to stop, cease, **sin c.**, incessantly **2** *(dejar un empleo)* to leave, quit. **c. en el cargo**, to cease one's functions.

cesárea *nf Med* Caesarean (section), *US* Cesarean (section)

cese *nm* **1** cessation, suspension **2** *(despido)* dismissal, **dar el c. (a algn)**, to dismiss (sb)

CESID *nm Mil abr de* **Centro Superior de Información de la Defensa**

cesión *nf* cession; **c. de tierras**, assignment of land

cesionario,-a *nm, f* cessionary, assignee

cesionista *nmf* grantor, assignee

césped *nm* lawn, grass, **cortar el c.**, to mow the lawn

cesta *nf* **1** basket ■ **c. de la compra**, shopping basket, **c. de Navidad**, Christmas hamper **2** *Dep* pelota *or* jai-alai basket

cestería *nf* **1** *(material)* wickerwork, basketwork **2** *(fabricación)* basket making **3** *(tienda)* basket shop

cesto *nm* basket, **c. de los papeles**, wastepaper basket.

cesura *nf Lit* caesura

ceta *nf véase* **zeta**

cetáceo,-a *Zool* **I** *adj & nm* cetacean, whale **II cetáceos** *nmpl* cetaceans

cetrería *nf* falconry, hawking

cetrino,-a *adj* **1** *(cara)* sallow **2** *fig (melancólico)* melancholic.

cetro *nm* sceptre, *US* scepter, *lit* **empuñar el c.**, to ascend the throne, *fig* **ostentar el c.**, to hold the lead

ceutí I *adj* of *or* from Ceuta **II** *nmf* native *or* inhabitant of Ceuta

CF *nm Dep abr de* **Club de Fútbol**, Football Club, FC

CGPJ *nm Jur abr de* **Consejo General del Poder Judicial**.

Ch, ch [tʃe, θe'atʃe] *nf (el dígrafo)* formerly fourth letter of the Spanish alphabet

cha *nm Pol* shah

chabacanada *nf*, **chabacanería** *nf* **1** *(vulgaridad)* vulgarity, bad taste **2** *(grosería)* rude *or* coarse remark, **decir chabacanerías**, to make rude *or* obscene remarks

chabacano,-a *adj* **1** *(objeto)* cheap, tacky **2** *(chiste, persona)* rude, foul-mouthed **3** *(trabajo)* shoddy, slipshod

chabola *nf* shack, **las chabolas**, shanty town *sing*

chabolismo *nm* shanty towns, **quieren acabar con el c.**, they want to do away with shanty dwellings

chabolista *nmf* shanty dweller

chacal *nm Zool* jackal

chácara¹ *nf Am* **1** *(bolsa)* leather bag **2** ulcer, sore

chácara² *nf CAm véase* **chacra**

chacarera *nf Arg* folk dance

chacarero,-a *nm, f SAm* peasant farmer, farm labourer, *US* farm laborer

chacha *nf fam (niñera)* nanny, nursemaid, *(criada)* maid

cha-cha-chá *nm*, **chachachá** *nm Mús* cha-cha, cha-cha-cha

chachalaca *nf CAm Méx fig (charlatán)* chatterbox

cháchara *nf* **1** *fam (charla)* small talk, chinwag, **estar de c.**, to have a yap **2 chácharas**, *(baratijas)* trinkets, junk *sing*

chacharear I *vi* **1** *fam (charlar)* to chatter, gossip **2** *Méx (comerciar)* to deal in trinkets **II** *vtr Méx (comprar y vender)* to buy and sell

chachi *adj fam véase* **chanchi**

chacho,-a *nm, f* **1** *fam (muchacho)* boy, lad, *(muchacha)* girl, lass **2** *fam (tratamiento) (muchacho)* mate, buddy, *(muchacha)* love, dear **3** *CAm (mellizo)* twin **4** *Méx (sirviente)* servant

chacina *nf* **1** smoked meat **2** seasoned pork

chacinería *nf* pork bucher's shop

chacinero,-a *nm, f* pork butcher

chacolí *nm (pl* **chacolíes***)* dry wine from the Basque Country.

chacolotear *vi (herraduras)* to clatter

chacoloteo *nm* clattering

chacona *nf arc Mús (baile)* chaconne

chacota *nf* joking, banter, **hacer c. de algo**, to have a laugh about something, **tomar algo a c.**, to take sth as a joke

chacotear *vi*, **chacotearse** *vr* to joke, have a laugh, *(mockingly)* to poke fun **(de**, at)

chacra *nf Am* small farm *or* holding.

chacuaco,-a I *adj (chapucero)* shoddy, slapdash **II** *nm* **1** *(horno)* smelting furnace **2** *CAm (cigarro)* roughly made cigar **3** *Méx Salv (colilla)* cigar stub **III** *nm, f (persona)* bungler

chacuaquería *nf Am* shoddiness, roughness

chafallar *vtr fam* to botch (up)

chafallo *nm fam* **1** *(chapuza)* botched job, botch up **2** *(borrón)* crossing out

chafalote,-a I *adj Arg Urug (persona)* coarse, rude **II** *nm Am (espada)* sword

chafar I *vtr* **1** *(aplastar)* to squash, crush, flatten **2** *(arrugar)* to crease, crumple **3** *fam (interrumpir)* to butt in **4** *fam (plan, negocio)* to ruin, spoil **5** *fam (abatir)* to crush, *(desilusionar)* to disappoint **II chafarse** *vr* **1** *(aplastarse)* to be squashed *or* crushed *or* flattened **2** *(arrugarse)* to become creased *or* crumpled

chafarrinada *nf*, **chafarrinón** *nm* spot, stain

chafirete *nm Méx* lorry driver, *US* truck driver

chaflán *nm* chamfer, **la casa que hace c.**, the house on the corner

chagolla *nf Méx* **1** *(moneda) (falsa)* counterfeit coin, *(gastada)* worn-out coin **2** *fig (cosa despreciable)* useless thing

chagorra *nf Méx* woman of the lower classes

chaguar *vtr Arg (clothes, sponge)* to wring out, squeeze

chaguite *nm CAm* **1** *(charco)* puddle **2** *(sementera) (acto)* sowing, *(época)* sowing season

chaira *nf* **1** *(cuchilla de zapatero)* shoemaker's knife **2** *(acero de afilar)* (sharpening) steel **3** *(navaja)* jack-knife

chal *nm (prenda)* shawl

chala *nf* **1** *Am* maize leaf **2** *Arg Bol fig (dinero)* dough, money; **pelar la c. a algn**, to swindle sb, do sb out of money

chalado,-a *fam* **1** *pp de* **chalar. II** *adj (chiflado)* crazy, nuts, crackers; *(enamorado)* **estar c. por algo/algn,** to be crazy about sth/sb.

chaladura *nf fam (chifladura)* crazy idea; *(enamoramiento)* crazy love.

chalán,-ana I *adj & nm, f* **1** *(comerciante en caballos)* horse-dealer. **2** *(timador)* shady businessman, wheeler-dealer, shark. **II** *nm Am (domador)* horsebreaker, *US* broncobuster.

chalana *nf Náut* barge, lighter.

chalanear *vtr* **1** *pey* to wheel and deal. **2** *Am (caballos)* to break (in). **3** *CAm (bromear)* to joke. **4** *Arg (molestar)* to annoy, pester.

chalar I *vtr fam* to drive crazy *or* nuts *or* round the bend. **II chalarse** *vr fam* to go mad *or* nuts; **c. por algo/algn,** to be mad about sth/sb.

chalchíhuite *nm* **1** *CR Méx (esmeralda)* rough emerald. **2** *CAm (baratija)* trinket, trifle. **3** *CAm (sortilegio)* spell.

chalé *nm (pl chalés) véase* **chalet.**

chaleco *nm* waistcoat, *US* vest; *(de punto)* sleeveless pullover. ■ **c. antibalas,** bullet-proof vest; **c. salvavidas,** life jacket.

chalet *nm (pl chalets) (casa de campo)* country house *or* cottage; *(de lujo)* villa; *(en la montaña)* mountain chalet; *(en la ciudad)* house; *(individual)* detached house; *(adosado)* semi-detached house.

chalina *nf* **1** *(corbata)* cravat. **2** *Am (chal estrecho)* stole.

chalón *nm Am* black shawl.

chalote *nm Bot* shallot.

chalupa I *nf* **1** *Náut (lancha)* boat, launch. **2** *Méx (canoa)* canoe. **3** *Méx (torta de maíz)* oval-shaped corn cake. **II** *adj fam (chalado)* nuts; **estar c.,** to be bonkers.

chamaco,-a *nm,* *f Méx fam (muchacho)* boy, lad; *(muchacha)* girl, lass.

chamagoso,-a *adj Méx* **1** *(astroso)* grubby, sbabby. **2** *(cosa)* rough, cheap.

chamal *nm Am* cloak worn by Indians.

chamarilear *vtr* to swap *or* deal in second-hand goods.

chamarileo *nm* trading in second-hand goods.

chamarilero,-a *nm, f,* **chamarillero,-a** *nm, f* second-hand *or* junk dealer.

chamarra *nf* **1** *(zamarra)* sheepskin jacket. **2** *CAm fig (engaño)* confidence trick.

chamarro *nm CAm* coarse woollen blanket.

chamba¹ *nf* **1** *Arg Ecuad (césped)* turf. **2** *Guat Méx (trabajo)* low-paid job.

chamba² *nf fam* fluke, piece of luck, lucky break; **por c.,** by a fluke.

chambear *vi Méx* **1** *(feriar)* to swap, exchange, barter. **2** *(trabajar)* to work for a pittance.

chambelán *nm* chamberlain.

chambergo *nm Hist* broad-brimmed hat.

chambón,-ona *fam* **I** *adj* **1** *(torpe)* clumsy. **2** *(afortunado)* flukey, jammy. **II** *nm, f* **1** *(torpe)* clumsy person. **2** *(suertudo)* lucky *or* jammy person.

chambonada *nf fam* **1** *(torpeza)* clumsiness; *(patinazo)* blunder. **2** *(suerte)* fluke, piece of luck.

chambonear *vi* to botch (up), bungle.

chambra *nf* housecoat.

chamiza *nf* **1** *(planta)* chamiso. **2** *(leña)* brushwood.

chamizo *nm* **1** *(leño, árbol)* half-burnt log *or* tree. **2** *(choza)* thatched hut. **3** *pey (tugurio)* hovel, shack, shanty.

chamorro,-a *adj* shorn, close-cropped.

champa *nf* **1** *SAm (césped)* sod, turf. **2** *CAm* palm leaf shack. **3** *Am fig (cosa enmarañada)* tangled jumble.

champán *nm,* **champaña** *nf* champagne.

champiñón *nm Bot* mushroom.

champola *nf CAm Cuba RD* drink made from the guanábana fruit.

champú *nm* shampoo. ■ **c. anticaspa,** anti-dandruff shampoo.

champurrado *nm Méx* **1** *(bebida)* drink made from chocolate. **2** *fam (enredo)* hotch-potch, jumble, mess.

champurrar *vtr fam (bebidas)* to mix.

champurro *nm Méx* liquor cocktail.

chamuchina *nf Am* **1** *(populacho)* rabble, mob. **2** *(niños)* gang of kids.

chamullar *vi vulg* **1** *(hablar)* to speak, talk. **2** *(chapurrear)* to jabber; **sólo sé c. en francés,** I only have a smattering of French.

chamuscar I *vtr* **1** *(socarrar)* to singe, scorch. **2** *Méx (vender barato)* to sell cheaply. **II chamuscarse** *vr (socarrarse)* to singe, scorch, get scorched.

chamusquina *nf* singeing, scorching; *fam* **esto me huele a c.,** there's something fishy going on here.

chanada *nf fam* trick, ruse.

chancaca *nf* **1** *Am (masa)* syrup cake. **2** *CAm (torta)* maize cake with honey.

chancaquita *nf Am* syrup cake with nuts *or* coconut.

chancar *vtr Am* **1** *(triturar)* to crush, grind. **2** *(maltratar)* to treat badly; *(golpear)* to beat.

chancear I *vi (bromear)* to joke, horse around. **II chancearse** *vr (bromear)* to joke; **c. de,** to make fun of.

chancero,-a *adj* fond of joking.

chanchada *nf Am* dirty trick.

chanchería *nf Am* pork butcher's shop.

chanchi *adj fam* great! terrific! fantastic!; **lo pasamos c.,** we had a ball.

chancho,-a *Am* **I** *adj (sucio)* dirty, filthy. **II** *nm, f* **1** *Zool* pig, hog. ■ **c. salvaje,** boar. **2** *(carne)* pork.

chanchullero,-a *fam* **I** *adj* crooked, bent, underhand. **II** *nm, f* crook, racketeer.

chanchullo *nm fam* fiddle, wangle, racket; **meterse en chanchullos,** to be on the fiddle.

chancla *nf* old worn-out shoe.

chancleta *nf* **1** *(zapato viejo)* old shoe. **2** *(zapatilla)* slipper, mule. **3** *Am fam* baby girl.

chancletero,-a *adj,* **chancletudo,-a** *adj Am* low-class, common.

chanclo *nm (zueco)* clog; *(de goma)* overshoe, galosh.

chancro *nm Med* chancre.

chancua *nf Arg Urug* ground maize.

chándal *nm Dep* track *or* jogging suit.

chanfaina *nf Culin* offal stew; *(en Andalucía)* vegetable soup.

changador *nm Arg Bol* porter.

chango,-a I *adj Méx (listo)* sharp, clever, quick on the uptake. **II** *nm, f Méx (persona lista)* clever dick. **III** *nm* **1** *Zool* monkey. **2** *Arg Urug (criado)* young servant. **3** *Méx (muchacho)* boy.

changuear *Am* **I** *vi (bromear)* to joke, jest. **II changuearse** *vr (bromear)* to joke. jest; **c. de,** to make fun of.

changüí *nm fam* **1** *(engaño)* trick, hoax; **dar c. a algn,** *(engañar)* to play a trick on sb; *(tomar el pelo)* to tease sb. **2** *(novato)* novice, beginner.

chanquete *nm (pez)* transparent goby.

chantaje *nm* blackmail; **hacer c. a algn,** to blackmail sb.

chantajear *vtr* to blackmail.

chantajista *nmf* blackmailer.

chantre *nm Rel* precentor, cantor.

chanza *nf* joke; **de** *or* **en c.,** jokingly, in fun; **estar de c.,** to be joking.

chao *interj fam* so long!, bye-bye!, ciao!

chapa *nf* **1** *(de metal)* sheet, plate; **c. ondulada,** corrugated iron. **2** *(de madera)* panel-board, sheet; *(enchapado)* veneer; *(contrachapado)* plywood; **madera de 3 chapas,** 3-ply wood. **3** *(tapón)* bottle top, cap. **4** *(ficha metálica)* metal tag, tally, token; *(medalla)* badge, disc; *Mil* **c. de identificación,** identity disc; *fam* **estar sin c.,** to be penniless. **5** *fig (sentido común)* common sense; **hombre de c.,** sensible man. **6 chapas,** *(juego)* pitch-and-toss, *US* penny-pitching.

chapado,-a I *pp de* **chapar.** II *adj* **1** *(metal)* plated; **c. en oro,** gold-plated. **2** *(madera, mueble)* veneered, finished. **3** *fig* **c. a la antigua,** old-fashioned.

chapalear *vi* to splash about.

chapaleo *nm* splash, splashing.

chapaleta *nf Téc* flap valve.

chapandongo *nm CAm* tangle, entanglement.

chapar *vtr* **1** *(metal)* to plate. **2** *(madera, mueble)* to veneer, finish.

chaparrada *nf Meteor* downpour, heavy shower.

chaparral *nm* thicket of kermes oaks.

chaparrear *vi Meteor* to pour down, rain heavily.

chaparro *nm* **1** *(rechoncho)* short, stocky person. **2** *Méx fam (muchacho)* kid, child.

chaparrón *nm* **1** *Meteor* downpour, heavy shower; **ha caído un buen c.,** there's been a heck of a downpour. **2** *fig (de preguntas etc)* shower, bombardment.

chapear *vtr* **1** *(metal)* to plate. **2** *(madera, mueble)* to veneer, finish.

chapero *nm arg* arse peddlar.

chapetón,-ona *Am* I *adj (torpe)* clumsy, awkward. II *nm, f* **1** *(inmigrante)* recently-arrived European immigrant. **2** *(torpe)* clumsy *or* awkward person. III *nm (chaparrón)* downpour, heavy shower.

chapín I *adj* **1** *CAm (guatemalteco)* Guatemalan. **2** *Col Guat Hond (patizambo)* bow-legged, bandy-legged. II *nm* **1** *(chanclo)* clog. **2** *CAm (guatemalteco)* Guatemalan.

chapinismo *nm CAm* **1** *(de Guatemala)* of *or* from Guatemala. **2** *(vocablo, giro)* Guatemalan way of speaking.

chapinizarse *vr CAm* to assume a Guatemalan character.

chapiscar *vtr CAm* to harvest maize.

chapista *nm, f* sheet metal worker; *Aut* panel beater.

chapistería *nf* sheet metal work; *Aut* panel beating; **taller de c.,** body repair shop.

chapitel *nm Arquit* **1** *(de torre)* spire. **2** *(de columna)* capital.

chapó[1] *nm* type of billiards.

chapó[2] *interj fam* well done!, bravo!

chapodar *vtr (plantas)* to prune, trim.

chapotear I *vtr (humedecer)* to moisten, dampen; *(con esponja)* to sponge (down). II *vi (chapalear)* to splash about, paddle.

chapoteo *nm* **1** moistening; *(con esponja)* sponging. **2** *(chapaleo)* splashing (about), paddling

chapucear I *vtr (hacer aprisa y mal)* to botch, bungle, make a mess of. II *vi Méx (hacer trampas)* to trick, deceive, swindle.

chapucería *nf* **1** *(chapuza)* botched job, shoddy piece of work. **2** *(tosquedad)* shoddiness. **3** *(embuste)* lie.

chapucero,-a I *adj (trabajo)* slapdash, shoddy, sloppy; *(persona)* bungling, clumsy. II *nm, f* **1** *(frangollón)* botcher, bungler. **2** *(embustero)* liar.

chapulín *nm* **1** *Am Zool (langosta)* locust. **2** *CAm (niño)* kid, child.

chapurrar, **chapurrear** *vtr* **1** *(idioma)* to speak badly *or* with difficulty; **sólo chapurreaba el francés,** he spoke only a few words of French. **2** *fam (licores)* to mix.

chapurreo *nm* jabbering.

chapuz *nm* **1** *(chapuzón)* duck, ducking. **2** *(chapuza)* botched job, shoddy piece of work.

chapuza *nf* **1** *(trabajo ocasional)* odd job. **2** *(trabajo mal hecho)* botched job, shoddy piece of work.

chapuzar I *vtr (zambullir)* to duck. II **chapuzarse** *vr (zambullirse)* to dive in; *(bañarse)* to have a dip.

chapuzón *nm (zambullida)* duck, ducking, dive; *(baño corto)* dip; **darse un c.,** to have a dip.

chaqué *nm* morning coat.

chaqueta *nf* jacket; **hay que ir de c.,** suits must be worn; *fig Pol* **cambiar de c.,** to change sides; *fam* **ser más vago que la c. de un guardia,** to be bone idle. ■ **c. de punto,** knitted cardigan; **c. de smoking,** dinner jacket; **traje de c.,** suit.

chaquete *nm* type of backgammon.

chaquetear *vi fam Pol* to change sides, be a turncoat.

chaqueteo *nm fam Pol* changing sides, turncoat tactics.

chaquetero,-a *nm, f fam Pol* turncoat.

chaquetilla *nf* short jacket. ■ *Taur* **c. torera,** bull-fighter's jacket.

chaquetón *nm (de lana)* heavy woollen jacket; *(trenca)* duffel jacket. ■ **c. tres cuartos,** three-quarter length jacket.

chaquira *nf Hist SAm* glass bead.

charada *nf* charade.

charamusca[1] *nf Méx* candy twist.

charamuscas[2] *nfpl Am Bot* brushwood.

charanagua *nf Méx* drink made from bitter pulque, honey, and chili.

charanga *nf* **1** *Mús Mil* brass band. **2** *fam (alboroto)* din, racket, hullabaloo. **3** *Am (baile)* informal dance.

charape *nm Méx* fermented drink made from corn, honey, cloves and cinnamon.

charca *nf* pond, pool.

charco *nm* puddle, pool; *fam (ir a América)* **cruzar** *or* **pasar el c.,** to cross the pond.

charcón,-ona *Arg Bol* I *adj* thin, skinny. II *nm, f* emaciated animal *or* person.

charcutería *nf* pork butcher's shop, delicatessen.

charcutero,-a *nm, f* pork butcher.

charla *nf (conversación)* talk, chat; *(conferencia)* talk, informal lecture *or* address.

charlador,-a *fam* I *adj* talkative. II *nm, f* chatterbox.

charlar *vi* to talk, chat.

charlatán,-ana I *adj (parlanchín)* talkative; *(chismoso)* gossipy. II *nm, f* **1** *(parlanchín)* chatterbox; *(chismoso)* gossip; *(bocazas)* charlatan, bigmouth. **2** *(embaucador)* trickster, charmer.

charlatanería *nf* **1** *(palabrería)* talkativeness, verbosity. **2** *(de vendedor)* sales patter, spiel.

charlestón *nm Mús* charleston.

charlotada *nf* **1** *Taur* comic bullfight. **2** *fam (payasada)* clowning around, buffoonery.

charlotear *vi fam (parlotear)* to chatter, prattle natter; *(charlar)* to chat.

charloteo *nm fam (parloteo)* prattling, nattering; *(charla)* chat.

charnego,-a *nm, f Cat pey* Spanish immigrant worker, often from southern Spain, who has settled in Catalonia.

charnela *nf* hinge.

charol *nm* **1** *(barniz)* varnish; *fam* **darse c.,** to blow one's trumpet, brag. **2** *(piel)* patent leather. ■ **zapatos de c.,** patent leather shoes.

charolar *vtr* to varnish.

charquear I *vtr SAm* **1** *(carne)* to dry, cure. **2** *(herir)* to slash, cut up, severely wound. II **charquearse** *vr Arg (a la montura)* to hold on tight.

charqui *nm Am (carne)* dried beef, cured meat; *(fruta)* dried fruit.

charquicán *nm SAm* **1** *Culin (guiso)* dried meat and vegetable stew. **2** *fig (barullo)* jumble, confusion.

charrada *nf* tacky ornament, cheap trinket.

charrán¹ *nm* rascal, scoundrel, rogue.

charrán² *nm Orn* tern.

charranada *nf* dirty trick.

charrancito *nm Orn* little tern.

charrasquear *vtr* **1** *(apuñalar)* to stab. **2** *Ecuad Pan Ven (instrumento)* to strum.

charreada *nf Méx* festival.

charretera *nf Mil* epaulette.

charro,-a I *adj* **1** *fig (persona)* coarse, uncouth, boorish. **2** *fig (objeto)* cheap, kitsch, gaudy; *(vestido)* loud. **3** *Méx (pintoresco)* picturesque. **4** *(jinete)* skilled. II *nm Méx* **1** *(jinete)* horseman, cowboy (in traditional costume). **2** *(sombrero)* widebrimmed hat.

chárter *adj inv* (**vuelo**) **c.,** charter (flight).

chas *interj* crash!, wham!

chasca *nf* **1** *(leña menuda)* brushwood. **2** *Am (cabellera revuelta)* mop of hair, tangled hair; *(maraña)* tangle.

chascar I *vtr (lengua)* to click; *(dedos)* to snap; *(látigo)* to crack; *(chocolate etc)* to crunch. II *vi (ruido de madera etc)* to crack.

chascarrillo *nm (chiste)* joke, funny story; *(historieta)* witty anecdote.

chasco *nm* **1** *(broma)* trick, joke; **dar un c. a algn,** to play a trick on sb. **2** *(decepción)* disappointment; **llevarse un c.,** to be disappointed; **¡menudo c. me llevé!,** I was so disappointed!

chasis *nm inv Aut* chassis; *fam* **quedarse en el c.,** to be reduced to skin and bone. **2** *Fot* plate holder.

chasquear¹ *vtr* **1** *(gastar una broma)* to play a trick on. **2** *(decepcionar)* to disappoint, let down. **3** *(promesa)* to break, fail to keep.

chasquear² I *vtr (lengua)* to click; *(dedos)* to snap; *(látigo)* to crack; *(chocolate etc)* to crunch. II *vi (madera etc)* to crack, crackle.

chasqui *nm Am* messenger, courier.

chasquido *nm (de la lengua)* click; *(de los dedos)* snap; *(de látigo, madera)* crack; *(de chocolate etc)* crunch.

chata *nf* bedpan.

chatarra *nf* **1** *(escoria)* scrap (metal); scrap iron; *fam* **este coche es una c.,** this car is a heap of junk. ■ **parque de c.,** scrap yard. **2** *fam (monedas)* small change. **3** *fam pey (joyas)* gaudy jewelery.

chatarrero,-a *nm, f* scrap dealer *or* merchant.

chatear *vi fam* to go out for a few drinks.

chateo *nf fam* **ir de c.,** to go out for a few drinks.

chati *adj fam* duckie, love.

chato,-a I *adj* **1** *(nariz)* snub; *(persona)* snub-nosed. **2** *(objeto)* flat, flattened; *(barco)* flat, shallow; *(torre)* low, squat. **3** *Am (pobre)* mean, wretched; **dejar c. a algn,** *(vencer)* to crush *or* defeat sb; *(engañar)* to trick *or* deceive sb; *fig (chasquearse)* **quedarse c.,** to be left dumbfounded. II *nm* (small) glass of wine; **tomar unos chotas,** to have a few drinks. III *nm, f* **1** *(persona)* snub-nosed person. **2** *fam (apelativo cariñoso)* dear, duckie, love; **¡muchas gracias, c.!,** thanks a lot, love!

chaucha I *adj inv RPl* **1** *(de mala calidad)* poor, inferior. **2** *(insípido)* insipid, tasteless. II *nf Arg (judía verde)* green bean.

chauvinismo *nm* chauvinism.

chauvinista *adj & nm* chauvinist.

chaval,-a *nm, f fam (chico)* boy, lad; *(chica)* girl, lass; *(joven)* kid, youngster; *fam (apelativo)* mate.

chaveta *nf Téc (clavija)* key, cotter (pin); *fam* **estar mal de la c.,** to have a screw loose; *fam* **perder la c.,** to go off one's rocker; *fam* **perder la c. por,** to be crazy about.

chavo *nm* brass coin; *fam* **estar sin un c.,** to be penniless *or* flat broke.

chayote *nm Bot (fruto y planta)* chayote.

chayotera *nf Bot (planta)* chayote plant.

che *(pl **ches**)* I *nf (dígrafo)* name of the digraph **Ch** in Spanish. II *interj Arg Bol Urug fam* **1** *(para llamar la atención)* hey!, listen! **2** *fam (muletilla)* man, mate, you know, I mean; **no sabe lo que dice, c.,** he doesn't know what he's saying, man.

checa *nf* detention cell, cooler.

checo,-a I *adj* Czech. II *nm, f (persona)* Czech. III *nm (idioma)* Czech.

checoslovaco,-a I *adj* Czechoslovakian, Czech. II *nm, f (persona)* Czechoslovakian, Czechoslovak, Czech.

Checoslovaquia *n* Czechoslovakia.

chele *nm CAm* I *adj (peliblanco)* white-haired. II *(legaña)* rheum.

chelear *vtr CAm* to whiten.

cheli *nm arg* Spanish urban slang.

chelín *nm* shilling.

chenca *nf CAm* cigarette end, butt.

chepa *nf fam* hump.

cheque *nm* cheque, *US* check; **cobrar un c.,** to cash a cheque; **extender un c.,** to issue a cheque, **extender** *or* **hacer un c. a nombre de,** to make out a cheque to. ■ **c. abierto/cruzado/en blanco,** open/crossed/blank cheque; **c. al portador,** cheque payable to bearer; **c. de viaje** *or* **de viajero,** traveller's cheque, *US* traveler's check; **c. sin fondos,** dud *or* bouncing cheque; **talonario de cheques,** cheque book, *US* check book.

chequear *vtr* **1** *(controlar, examinar)* to check; *(comprobar)* to check up on; *Aut (coche)* to service; *Med* to give a checkup to.

chequeo *nm Med* checkup.

chequera *nf Am* cheque book, *US* check book.

chéster *nm (pl **chéster** or **chésteres**)* Cheshire cheese.

chévere I *adj* **1** *Col Méx Ven fam (magnífico)* great, terrific, fantastic. **2** *Ecuad PR Ven (bonito)* pretty. II *nm Cuba PR Ven (valentón)* braggart.

chevió *nm (pl **cheviots**)* Tex cheviot.

chibola *nf Am* bump, swelling.

chic *adj inv (elegante)* chic, elegant; *(de moda)* fashionable.

chicana *nf* chicanery, trickery.

chicanear *vi* to engage in chicanery *or* trickery.

chicanero,-a *adj* trickster.

chicano,-a *adj & nm, f* chicano.

chicar *vtr Arg Urug* to chew tobacco.

chicarrón,-ona *nm, f fam (chico)* strapping lad; *(chica)* strapping lass.

chicha¹ *nf fam (carne)* meat; *(persona)* **tener muchas chichas,** to be chubby.

chicha² *nf Am* **1** chicha, maize liquor; **c. de uva,** drink made from grape juice; *fam* **de c. y nabo,** insignificant; *fam* **no ser ni c. ni limonada,** to be a waste of space. **2** *fig (berrinche)* rage, bad temper.

chicha³ *adj inv Náut* **calma c.,** dead calm.

chícharo *nm Bot* **1** *(guisante)* pea. **2** *(garbanzo)* chickpea.

chicharra *nf* **1** *Ent* cicada; *fig* **cantaba la c.,** it was boiling hot. **2** *Elec* buzzer, bell. **3** *fam (parlanchín)* chatterbox.

chicharrero *fam* I *nm, f (tinerfeño)* native *or* inhabitant of Tenerife. II *nm fam (lugar)* oven, hothouse.

chicharro *nm* **1** *(de cerdo)* pork crackling, fried pork rind. **2** *(pez)* scad, horse mackerel.

chicharrón *nm* **1** *(de cerdo)* pork crackling, fried pork rind; *fam* **quedar hecho un c.,** to be burnt to a cinder. **2** *fig (persona)* sunburnt person.

chiche¹ I *nm Am (pecho)* breast. **II** *nf Méx (niñera)* nanny, nursemaid.

chiche² Am I *adj fam (fácil)* easy, piece of cake. **II** *nm fam* **1** *(joya)* jewel; *(juguete)* toy; *(chuchería)* trinket, knick-knack. **2** *(persona) (elegante)* elegant person; *(hábil)* skilful *or* nifty person.

chichear *vtr & vi* to hiss.

chicheme *nm CAm* cold drink made from corn, milk, and sugar.

chicheo *nm* hissing.

chichería *nf Am (bar)* chicha bar, tavern; *(tienda)* chicha shop.

chichero,-a *nm, f Am* **1** *(vendedor)* chicha seller. **2** *(fabricante)* chicha maker.

chichón¹ un bump, lump.

chichón,-ona² *adj CAm* easy.

chichonera *nf (gorro)* padded cap; *(casco)* helmet.

chichote *nm CAm Ven* bump, swelling.

chicle *nm* **1** chewing gum. **2** *Mex (suciedad)* dirt, filth.

chiclear *vi* to chew gum.

chico,-a I *adj* **1** *(pequeño)* small, little; **estos pantalones se me han quedado chicos,** I've grown out of these trousers; *fig* **dejar c. a algn,** to make sb look small. **2** *Méx irón (descomunal)* big, enormous. **II** *nm, f* **1** *(muchacho)* boy, lad; *(muchacha)* girl, lass; **el c. de los recados,** the office boy; **es buena chica,** she's a good girl; *fam* **como c. con zapatos nuevos,** like a kid with a new toy; *Cin fam* **el c. de la película,** the goody. **2** *(para dirigirse a algn)* **mira, c., yo de ti me iría,** listen mate, if I were you I'd go. **III** *nf* **1** *(criada)* maid. **2** *Am (tanda, partida)* game.

chicolear *vi* to pay compliments, say nice things.

chicoleo *nm* compliment, flirtatious remark.

chicoria *nf Bot* chicory.

chicote,-a I *nm, f fam (hombre)* fine lad; *(mujer)* fine lass. **II** *nm* **1** *fam (puro)* cigar. **2** *Am (látigo)* whip. **3** *CAm (serie, retahíla)* volley, stream.

chicuite *nm SAm Min* bucket.

chifla *nf (siseo)* hiss, hissing; *(silbido)* whistle, whistling.

chiflado,-a *fam* **I** *pp de* **chiflar. II** *adj (loco)* mad, crazy, barmy, nuts, round the twist *or* bend; **estar c. con *or* por,** to be mad *or* crazy about. **III** *nm, f* nut, loony, headcase.

chifladura *nf fam* **1** *(locura)* madness, craziness. **2** *(idea alocada)* barmy idea, madcap scheme. **3** *(afición)* craze, mania; **su c. es el fútbol,** he's mad on football.

chiflar I *vtr* **1** *(silbar)* to hiss (at), boo (at), whistle (at); *(pito)* to blow. **2** *fam (encantar, fascinar)* to enchant, entrance, fascinate, captivate; **esa canción me chifla,** that song's fantastic; **nos chiflan los coches antiguos,** we're mad on old cars. **II** *vi Guat Méx (pájaros)* to sing. **III chiflarse** *vr fam (volverse loco)* to go mad *or* round the bend; **c. por,** to fall head over heels in love with.

chifleta *nf CAm Méx* joke.

chiflido *nm* whistle, whistling.

chigua *nf Am* large basket, hamper.

chigüín *nm Hond Nic Salv* rachitic child.

chiíta *adj & nmf* Shiite.

chilaba *nf (prenda)* jellaba, jellabah.

chilapeño *nm Mex* straw hat.

chilar *nm Agr* chili plantation.

chilca *nf Am Bot* boneset.

chilchote *nm Mex* type of hot chili.

chile *nm* **1** *Bot Culin* chili (pepper). ■ **c. molido,** chili powder. **2** *CAm fam (mentira)* lie.

chileno,-a *adj & nm, f* Chilean.

chilillo *nm CAm* whip.

chilindrina *nf fam* **1** *(cosilla)* trifle. **2** *(anécdota)* anecdote, story; *(chiste)* joke; *(chanza)* joking, banter.

chilindrón *nm* **1** *Culin* sauce made from tomatoes and red peppers; **pollo al c.,** chicken in a tomato and red pepper sauce. **2** *Naipes* type of card game.

chilla *nf Caza* decoy, bird call.

chillar I *vi* **1** *(persona)* to scream, shriek, shout, cry; *(cerdo)* to squeal; *(ratón)* to squeak; *(pájaro)* to squawk, screech; *(radio)* to blare; *(frenos)* to screech, squeal; *(puerta, ventana)* to creak, squeak; *fam* **chillarle a algn,** to give sb a dressing-down. **2** *fig (protestar)* to protest, complain; **¡no chilles!,** stop moaning! **3** *(colores)* to be loud *or* gaudy, clash. **II chillarse** *vr* **1** *Am (enojarse)* to become annoyed; *fam* to get cross; *(ofenderse)* to take offence. **2** *CAm (avergonzarse)* to become embarrassed.

chillería *nf* **1** *(griterío)* screaming, shrieking, yelling, howling. **2** *(regaño)* dressing-down, telling-off, reprimand.

chillido *nm (de persona)* scream, shriek, shout, cry; *(de cerdo)* squeal; *(de ratón)* squeak; *(de pájaro)* squawk, screech; *(de frenos)* screech, squeal; *(puerta, ventana)* creaking, sweaking.

chillón,-ona I *adj* **1** *(voz)* shrill, high-pitched; *(sonido)* harsh, strident, screechy. **2** *(color)* loud, gaudy, shocking. **II** *nm, f* loud person.

chilmole *nm Méx Culin* tomato, onion, and pepper sauce.

chimal *nm Mex* dishevelled hair.

chimar *vtr Méx* to annoy, bother, vex.

chimbo *nm Am* sweet made from egg yolk, syrup and almonds.

chimenea *nf* **1** *(conducto, tubo)* chimney; *(de barco)* funnel, stack. ■ **c. de ventilación,** air shaft. **2** *(hogar abierto)* fireplace, hearth. ■ **c. (francesa),** fireplace with a mantlepiece. **3** *fam (cabeza)* nut, block; **no andar bien de la c.,** to be off one's rocker. **4** *Am Min (pique)* shaft.

chimiscolear *vi Méx* **1** *(chismear)* to gossip. **2** *(beber)* to swig.

chimpancé *nm Zool* chimpanzee.

China *n* China.

china¹ *nf* **1** pebble, small stone; *fam* **tocarle a uno la c.,** to have bad luck, be left carrying the can. **2** *arg (droga)* deal.

china² *nf (porcelana)* china; *(vajilla)* china, chinaware.

chinampear *vi Mex* **1** *(huir)* to escape, flee. **2** *(evitar)* to avoid. **3** *(tener miedo)* to be afraid *or* scared. **4** *(compromiso)* to break.

chinaste *nm CAm* **1** prolific germ. **2** *(raza)* pedigree.

chinastear *vtr CAm (aves de corral)* to fertilize.

chinazo *nm* **1** *(piedra)* large pebble, stone. **2** *(golpe)* blow with a stone.

chinchar I *vtr (fastidiar)* to annoy, pester, bug; **eso es lo que más me chincha,** that's what bugs me most of all. **II chincharse** *vr (fastidiarse)* to grin and bear it, get on with it; **¡chínchate!, ¡para que te chinches!,** so there!; **no me hizo caso, pues ahora, que se chinche,** he didn't listen to me, so now he'll have to lump it.

chincharrero *nm* flea pit, bug-infested place.

chinche I *nf Ent* bug, bedbug; *fam* **caer *or* morir como chinches,** to fall like flies. **II** *nm, f fam (persona)* nuisance, pest, bore, drag.

chincheta *nf* drawing pin, *US* thumbtack.

chinchilla *nf* chinchilla.

chinchín *nm* **1** *(ruido)* chink, clash and tinkle; *Mús (orquesta)* tinny music; *(brindis)* toast, chin-chin, **¡c.!,** cheers!, (to) your (good) health!; **hacer c. con las copas,** to clink glasses. **2** *CAm RPl (sonajero)* baby's rattle. **3** *Cuba PR Ven (llovizna)* drizzle.

chinchinear *vtr CAm* to caress, pamper.

chinchón® *nm* aniseed liquor.

chinchona *nf Quím* quinine.

chinchorrería *nf* **1** *(impertinencia)* insolence, disrespect; *(pesadez)* tediousness. **2** *(chisme)* piece of gossip.

chinchorrero,-a *adj* **1** *(chinchoso)* insolent, cheeky; *(pesado)* tedious. **2** *(chismoso)* gossipy.

chinchorro *nm* **1** *(red)* dragnet. **2** *(bote)* dinghy.

chinchoso,-a *adj fam fig* wearisome, tiresome.

chinchulín *nm Am* cow's tripe.

chinear *vtr CAm* **1** *(niño)* to carry in one's arms *or* piggyback. **2** *(mimar)* to pamper, spoil.

chinela *nf (zapatilla)* slipper, mule; *(chanclo)* clog.

chinero *nm Mueb* china cupboard *or* cabinet; *(alacena)* dresser.

chinesco,-a *adj* Chinese; **sombras chinescas,** shadow theatre *sing.*

chingada *nf Méx vulg ofens* **hijo de la c.,** son of a bitch; **¡vete a la c.!,** bugger off!

chingana *nf Am* **1** *(taberna)* tavern, bar, saloon; dance hall. **2** *(fiesta)* wild party, rowdy celebration.

chingar I *vtr* **1** *fam (beber mucho)* to put away, knock back, drink a lot of. **2** *(fastidiar)* to annoy, pester. **3** *vulg (estropear)* to fuck up, ruin. **4** *vulg (joder)* to fuck, screw; *ofens* **¡chinga a tu madre!,** fuck off! **5** *Am (cortar el rabo)* to dock, cut the tail off. **II** *vi CAm fam (bromear)* to joke. **III chingarse** *vr fam* **1** *(emborracharse)* to get sloshed *or* sozzled *or* pissed. **2** *CAm (fracasar)* to go down the drain, fall through.

chingaste *nm CAm* residue, dregs *pl.*

chingo,-a I *adj CAm* **1** *(cuchillo)* blunt; *(animal)* tailless; *(vestido)* short. **2** *Ven (nariz)* snub. **II chingos** *nmpl (ropa interior)* underwear *sing.*

chino¹ *nm (piedrecita)* pebble, stone; **juego de los chinos,** guessing game in which pebbles *or* coins are hidden in clenched fists.

chino,-a²I *adj (de la China)* Chinese; **tinta china,** Indian ink; *fam* **barrio c.,** red-light district; *fam* **cuento c.,** tall story. **II** *nm, f (persona)* Chinese, Chinaman; *fam* **un trabajo de chinos,** a fiddly task *or* piece of work; *fam* **engañar a algn como a un c.,** to take sb for a ride. **III** *nm* **1** *(idioma)* Chinese; *fam* **eso me suena c.,** it's all Greek to me. **2** *(colador)* sieve.

chino³ I *adj* bald. **II** *nm, f* **1** *CAm vulg (mestizo)* mestizo, half-caste. **2** *SAm (criado)* servant; **trabajar como un c.,** to work like a slave. **3** *Am (hombre del pueblo)* country person. **4** *Am (cariño)* darling, sweetheart. **5** *Méx* **chinos,** *(rizos)* curls. **III** *nm Arg (enojo)* anger. **IV** *nf arg (droga)* (piece of) hash.

chip *nm (pl* chips*)* **1** *Inform* chip. **2 chips,** *fam* crisps.

chipa *nf SAm* straw fruit basket.

chipe *nm CAm* **1** *(encanijado)* skinny man *or* boy. **2** *(quejica)* moaner, grumbler.

chipén *adj fam* **de c.,** great, terrific, fantastic.

chipilingo *nm Co Méx* baby, young child.

chipirón *nm (pez)* baby squid.

chipolo *nm Am Naipes* card game.

Chipre *n* Cyprus.

chipriota *adj & nmf* Cypriot.

chiqueadores *nmpl Méx* poultice for headaches.

chiquear I *vtr Cuba Méx* **1** *(mimar)* to pamper, spoil. **2** *(adular)* to flatter. **II chiquearse** *vr* **1** *CAm (pavonearse)* to seek flattery. **2** *CAm (contonearse)* to swagger along.

chiquero *nm (corral)* stockyard; *(pocilga)* pigsty.

chiquigüite I *adj; Méx (abobado)* dim-witted, dumb. **II** *nm CAm (cesto)* basket without handles.

chiquillada *nf (travesura)* childish prank; *(niñería)* childish thing; **hacer chiquilladas,** to behave childishly.

chiquillería *nf fam* crowd of noisy kids *or* youngsters.

chiquillo,-a *nm, f* kid, youngster; **portarse como un c.,** to behave like a child.

chiquitín,-ina I *adj (pequeño)* tiny, weeny. **II** *nm, f (niño)* tiny tot.

chiquito,-a I *adj (pequeño)* tiny. weeny, very small. **II** *nm, f (niño)* tiny tot, kid; *fam* **no andarse con chiquitas,** not to beat about the bush.

chiquitura *nf* **1** *CAm RPl (pequeñez)* tiny thing. **2** *CAm (niñería)* childish thing to do.

chirajo *nm* **1** *CAm (trastos)* junk. **2** *Am (andrajos)* rag, tatter.

chiribita *nf* **1** *(chispa)* spark; *fam* **echar chiribitas,** to be furious *or* hopping mad. **2 chiribitas,** *fam* spots before the eyes. **3** *Bot* daisy.

chiribitil *nm (desván)* attic, loft, garret; *(cuchitril)* tiny room, cubbyhole.

chirigota *nf fam* joke; **estar de c.,** to be joking; **tomarse algo a c.,** to take sth as a joke.

chirigotero,-a *adj fam* fond of joking.

chirimbolo *nm fam* thing, thingummyjig, whatsit.

chirimía *nf Mús* type of hornpipe.

chirimiri *nm* drizzle, fine misty rain.

chirimoya *nf Bot (fruto)* custard apple.

chirimoyo *nm Bot (árbol)* custard apple tree.

chiringo *nm Méx* small piece of sth.

chiringuito *nm (en playa etc)* refreshment stall *or* stand; *(en carretera)* roadside *or* seaside snack bar; **montarse un c.,** to set up a small business.

chirinola *nf* **1** *(debate)* heated discussion; *(discusión)* quarrel, row. **2** *(fruslería)* trifle; **estar de c.,** to be in a good mood. **3** *(juego)* skittles *pl.* **4** *(conversación)* lengthy conversation.

chiripa *nf* **1** *Bill* fluke, scratch, lucky stroke. **2** *fam fig* **de** *or* **por c.,** by a fluke, by chance; **cogió el tren por c.,** it was sheer luck that he caught the train.

chirivía *nf* **1** *Bot* parsnip. **2** *Orn* wagtail.

chirla *nf (pez)* small clam.

chirle *adj fam* insipid.

chirlo *nm (herida)* gash, slash; *(cicatriz)* scar.

chirola *nf* **1** *CAm arg (cárcel)* clink, nick. **2** *CAm (bolita)* little ball. **3** *Arg Bol (moneda)* coin of little value.

chirona *nf arg (cárcel)* clink, nick; **estar en c.,** to be in the clink *or* nick, be inside.

chirota *nf CAm* shameless woman.

chirrear *vi,* **chirriar** *vi* **1** *(gozne, puerta)* to creak; *(frenos)* to screech, squeal. **2** *(de pájaro)* to squawk, screech. **3** *fig (persona)* to sing badly.

chirrido *nm* **1** *(de gozne, puerta)* crack, cracking; *(de frenos)* screech, screeching, squeal, squealing. **2** *(de pájaro)* squawk, squawking, screech, screeching.

chirrión *nm* **1** *Am (látigo)* leather whip. **2** *CAm (sarta)* string.

chirrisco,-a *adj* **1** *CAm Ven (pequeñito)* small, tiny. **2** *Méx (enamoradizo)* amorous.

chirumen *nm fam* brains *pl,* grey matter.

chirusa *nf,* **chiruza** *nf Am fam* coarse *or* uncouth woman.

chis *interj (¡silencio!)* sh!, ssh!, hush!

chiscón *nm* hut, hovel.

chischás *nm (de espada)* clash, clashing.

chisgarabís *nm fam (entrometido)* busybody, meddler.

chisgo *nm Méx fam* charm, elegance.

chisme *nm* **1** *(habladuría)* piece of gossip; **chismes,** gossip, tittle-tattle; **siempre andan con chismes,** they're always gossiping. **2** *fam (trasto)* knick-knack; *(utensilio)* gadget; *(cosa)* thing, odds and ends; **tiene mil y un chismes eléctricos,** she's got tons of electrical gadgets; **coge tus chismes y vete,** pack your bags and go; *(dispositivo)* **hay que apretar este c.,** you have to press this thing here.

chismear *vi* to gossip.

chismería *nf* gossip, piece of gossip.

chismero,-a *adj* gossipy, gossiping.

chismografía *nf hum* gossip, gossiping.

chismorrear *vi fam* to gossip.

chismorreo *nm fam* gossip, gossiping.

chismoso,-a I *adj (murmurador)* gossipy, gossiping. **II** *nm,f (individuo)* gossip, gossipmonger.

chispa I *nf* **1** *(de la lumbre)* spark, flash; *Elec* spark, flash; *fig* sparkle, glitter; *fam* **echar chispas, estar uno que echa chispas,** to be very annoyed. **2** *fam (pedacito, un poco)* bit, tiny amount; **ni c.,** nothing at all; **una c. de coñac,** a drop of brandy; **una c. de sal,** a pinch of salt; *fig* **no tiene ni c. de gracia,** it's not a bit funny; *fig* **no tienen ni c. de inteligencia,** they haven't an ounce of intelligence. **3** *Meteor (gota de lluvia)* drop, droplet; **caen chispas,** it's spitting. **4** *fam (agudeza, gracia)* wit, sparkle; *(inteligencia)* intelligence; *(viveza)* liveliness; **ser una c.,** to be very bright; **tener c.,** to be witty *or* funny, be a real live wire; **una película con c.,** a brilliant film. **5** *fam (borrachera)* drunkenness; **coger** *or* **pillar una c.,** to get sloshed; **¡menuda c. llevabas anoche!,** you were well and truly canned last night! **6** *(mentira)* lie. **7** *Guat Méx (éxito)* success. **II** *adj Méx (gracioso)* amusing.

chisparse *vr fam* to get drunk *or* tipsy.

chispazo *nm* **1** *(de la lumbre)* spark; *fig (brote)* **aquello fue el c. que originó el incidente,** this sparked off the incident; *fig* **c. de ingenio,** flash of genius. **2** *fam (chisme, cotilleo)* piece of gossip.

chispeante *adj* sparkling; *fig* scintillating, brilliant.

chispear *vi* **1** *(echar chispas)* to spark, throw out sparks; *fig (relucir)* to sparkle. **2** *Meteor (lloviznar)* to spit. **II chispearse** *vr Arg RD (emborracharse)* to get tipsy.

chispo,-a *fam* **I** *adj* drunk, tipsy. **II** *nm* swig, quick drink.

chisporrotear *vi (fuego)* to spark, throw out sparks; *(leña)* to crackle; *(aceite)* to splutter, spit; *(carne)* to sizzle.

chisporroteo *nm (del fuego)* sparking; *(de la leña)* crackling; *(del aceite)* spluttering, spitting; *(de la carne)* sizzling.

chisquero *nm* pocket lighter.

chisquete *nm* **1** *(trago)* swig, drink; **echar un c.,** to have a quick one. **2** *(chorro)* jet, squirt.

chist *interj* **1** *(¡silencio!)* sh!, ssh!, hush! **2** *(para llamar la atención)* psst!

chistar *vi* to speak; **no c.,** not to say a word; **sin c.,** without saying a word.

chistate *nm CAm Med* dysuria.

chiste *nm* **1** *(cuento gracioso)* joke, funny story; **caer en el c.,** to get the joke; **contar un c.,** to tell a joke; *irón* **tener c.,** to be funny; **la cosa no tiene c.,** it's no joke; **tomar algo a c.,** to take sth as a joke. ■ **c. verde,** blue joke, dirty joke. **2** *(dibujo humorístico)* cartoon.

chistera *nf* **1** *(sombrero de copa)* top hat. **2** *Dep (guante de mimbre) (en pelota)* basketwork glove. **3** *(cesta de pescador)* fish basket, angler's basket.

chistoso,-a I *adj (persona)* funny, witty, fond of joking; *(anécdota, suceso)* funny, amusing. **II** *nm,f (bromista)* joker, comic, comedian.

chistu *nm Mús* Basque flute.

chistulari *nm* Basque flute player.

chita *nf* **1** *Anat* anklebone. **2** *(juego)* jacks, knucklebones, quoits; **dar en la c.,** to hit the nail on the head. **3** *loc adv* **a la c. callando,** *(en silencio)* quietly, unobtrusively; *(con disimulo)* secretly, stealthily.

chito[1] *nm Méx* **1** *Culin* fried goat. **2** *(grasa)* muck; *(suciedad)* filth.

chito[2] *interj fam*, **chitón** *interj fam (¡silencio!)* sh!, ssh!, hush!

chivar I *vtr* **1** *fam (molestar)* to annoy, pester. **2** *fam (acusar)* inform. **II chivarse** *vr* **1** *fam* to tell, split; **c. a la policía,** to inform the police. **2** *vulg (fastidiarse)* to get cross.

chivatazo *nm fam (soplo)* informing; *(advertencia)* tip-off; **dar el c.,** to inform, squeal, give a tip-off.

chivatear *vi fam (soplonear)* to inform, split, squeal.

chivato,-a I *nm,f fam (delator)* informer, squealer, grass; *(acusica)* telltale. **II** *nm* **1** *(dispositivo)* device, gadget. **2** *Zool* kid, young goat.

chiverrazo *nm CAm (ruido)* bump, thud; *(caída)* fall.

chivo,-a[1] *nm,f Zool* kid, young goat; *fig* **c. expiatorio,** scapegoat; *fam* **estar como un c.** *or* **una chiva,** to be mad.

chivo,-a[2] I *nm* **1** *Am (berrinche)* fit of anger. **2** *CAm hum* local M.P. **3** *Méx (salario)* day's wage. **II** *nf* **1** *Am (perilla)* goatee beard. **2** *CAm (manta)* woollen blanket. **3** *Am (mala mujer)* whore. **4 chivas,** *Méx (bártulos)* things, junk *sing*.

chivudo,-a *adj & nm,f Arg Cuba Ven (barbudo)* bearded.

choc *nm Med* shock; **c. nervioso,** nervous shock.

chocante *adj* **1** *(persona)* funny, witty. **2** *(cosa)* surprising, startling; *(raro)* strange; *(escandaloso)* shocking, offensive. **3** *Méx (pesado)* tiresome, irritating, annoying. **4** *Arg (indigno)* unworthy.

chocar I *vi* **1** *(topar)* to crash, collide; *Aut* **c. con** *or* **contra,** to crash into, run into, collide with; **chocaron dos autobuses,** two buses collided *or* crashed (into each other); *(pelota)* **c. contra,** to hit, strike. **2** *Mil* to clash, fight. **3** *fig (en discusión)* to clash, fall out. **4** *fig (sorprender)* to surprise, startle; *(extrañar)* to shock; *(causar enfado)* to annoy; **me chocó que no me contestara,** I was very surprised that he didn't reply. **II** *vtr (gen)* to clink; *(la mano)* to shake; **vamos a chocar las copas y brindaremos por Juan,** let's raise our glasses and toast Juan; *fam* **¡chócala!, ¡choca esos cinco!,** shake (on it)!, put it there!

chocarrería *nf (chiste grosero)* coarse *or* dirty joke.

chocarrero,-a *adj* coarse, vulgar.

chocha perdiz *nf Orn* woodcock.

chochear *vi* **1** *(de viejo)* to dodder, be senile. **2** *(de cariño)* to be soft.

chochera *nf*, **chochez** *nf* **1** *(vejez)* dotage, senility. **2** *(sentimentalismo)* silliness, sentimentality.

chochín *nm Orn* wren.

chocho[1] *nm* **1** *(altramuz)* lupin. **2** cinammon candy stick. **3 chochos,** sweets, *US* candies **4** *vulg* cunt.

chocho,-a[2] *adj* **1** *(senil)* doddering, senile; **viejo c.,** old dodderer. **2** *(sentimental)* soft, sentimental.

chochocol *nm Méx* pitcher, jug.

choclo[1] *nm (chanclo) (de madera)* clog; *(de goma)* overshoe, galosh.

choclo[2] *nm* **1** *SAm* car of maize, corn on the cob; *fam* **¡qué c.!,** what a drag! **2** *Culin* stew made with tender maize. **3** *Arg (percance)* mishap. **4** *Arg (molestia)* annoyance. **5** *Méx (zapato)* flat shoe worn by men; *fam* **meter el c.,** to put one's foot in it.

choco[1] *nm (pez)* small cuttlefish.

choco[2] *nm Am (perro de aguas)* water spaniel.

choco,-a[3] *adj Am* handicapped; *(con una pierna)* one-legged; *(manco)* one-armed; *(con una oreja)* one-eared; *(tuerto)* one-eyed.

chócola *nf Am* children's game.

chocolate *nm* **1** *Culin* chocolate; *(bebida)* drinking chocolate, cocoa; **c. con leche,** milk chocolate; **tableta de c.,** bar of chocolate; *fam* **las cosas claras y el c. espeso,** let's get things clear. **2** *arg (drogas)* dope, hashish.

chocolatera *nf* **1** *(recipiente)* chocolate pot. **2** *fam (trasto)* piece of junk; *(coche)* old banger.

chocolatería *nf* **1** *(fábrica)* chocolate factory; *(granja)* café serving drinking chocolate. **2** *Am Ecuad fig* head.

chocolatero,-a I *adj* fond of chocolate, chocolate-loving. **II** *(fabricante)* chocolate maker; *(vendedor)* chocolate vendor.

chocolatín *nm*, **chocolatina** *nf (tableta)* bar of chocolate, chocolate bar; *(bombón)* chocolate.

chófer *nm (pl chóferes) Am*, **Chofer** *nm (pl choferes) (gen)* driver, *(particular)* chauffeur; **coche de alquiler sin c.**, self-drive hire car.

cholla *nf* 1 *fam (cabeza)* nut, block, head; *(inteligencia)* brains, grey matter. 2 *CAm (llaga)* wound. 3 *Am (pereza)* laziness.

chollar *vtr CAm* 1 *(desollar)* to skin. 2 *(mortificar)* to reprehend.

chollo *nm fam* 1 *(sinecura)* cushy number, doddle. 2 *(ganga)* bargain, snip.

cholludo,-a *adj Am pey (haragán)* lazy, slow.

cholo,-a *adj & nm,f Am (mestizo)* half-breed, mestizo.

choloque *nm Am Bot* soapberry.

chompa *nf Am* jumper, pullover, jersey.

chongo *nm Méx* 1 *(moño)* bun. 2 **chongos**, *Culin* type of caramel custard.

chonta *nf SAm Bot* palm tree.

chontal *adj & nmf Am* 1 *(tribu)* Chontal tribe. 2 *(inculto)* bumkin, yokel, peasant.

chopera *nf Bot* poplar grove.

chopo¹ *nm Bot* poplar. ■ **c. blanco**, white poplar; **c. lombardo**, Lombardy poplar; **c. negro**, black poplar.

chopo² *Mil fam* gun; *fig* **cargar con el c.**, to join up.

choque *nm* 1 *(gen)* impact; *Aut Ferroc etc* crash, smash, collision; **c. de frente**, head-on collision; **c. múltiple**, pile-up. 2 *fig (contienda)* clash; *Mil* skirmish; **fuerzas de c.**, shock troops; **la policía de c.**, riot police. 3 *Med* shock.

choquezuela *nf Anat* kneecap.

chorcha *nf* 1 *CAm (cresta de ave)* crest. 2 *CAm (bocio)* goitre. 3 *Méx (grupo gente alegre)* band, gang. 4 *Méx pey* rowdy party.

choricero,-a *nm, f* 1 *(fabricante)* sausage maker; *(vendedor)* sausage vendor. 2 *fig hum (extremeño)* from or of Extremadura.

chorizar *vtr fam* to pinch.

chorizo I *nm* 1 *Culin* chorizo, salami, highly-seasoned pork sausage. 2 *fam (ratero)* thief, pickpocket. 3 *(en el circo)* balancing pole. 4 *SAm* **Constr** clay and straw used for plastering. 5 *Arg Par Urug (carne)* sirloin. 6 *Méx (moneda)* roll tube of coins. II *adj Méx (malvado)* evil, wicked.

chorlitejo *nm Orn* plover. ■ **c. chico**, little ringed plover; **c. grande**, ringed plover; **c. patingro**, Kentish plover.

chorlito *nm Orn* plover; *fam fig* **cabeza de c.**, scatterbrain.

chorra I *adj & nmf vulg (tonto)* idiot, fool; **hacer el c.**, to act the fool. II *nf* 1 *fam (suerte)* luck; **¡qué c. tiene el tío ese!**, how lucky can you get! 2 *vulg (pene)* prick.

chorrada *nf* 1 *(de líquido)* extra drop. 2 *fam (adorno superfluo)* frill; *(fruslería)* trinket, knick-knack; *(tontería)* bits and pieces *pl*, odds and ends *pl*; *(regalito)* small gift, little something. 3 *fam (estupidez)* piece of nonsense; **decir** or **parir chorradas**, to talk rubbish; **el examen fue una c.**, the exam was a walkover.

chorrear I *vi* 1 *(salir a chorros)* to gush, spurt, spout; *fam* **c. de sudor**, to pour with sweat; *fam* **tengo el abrigo que chorrea**, my coat is dripping wet. 2 *(gotear)* to drip, trickle. 3 *fam (suceder sin interrupción)* to flow. II *vtr fam (reprender)* to tick off, give a dressing-down to.

chorreo *nm* 1 *(en chorro)* gush, gushing, spurting, spouting. 2 *(goteo)* dripping, trickle. 3 *fam (reprimenda)* ticking-off, dressing-down. 4 *fam fig (gasto)* drain; **un c. de gastos**, a drain on resources.

chorrera *nf* 1 *(canalón)* gully, channel; *(señal de agua)* mark. 2 *Cost* shirt frill. 3 *Am (serie)* **una c. de**, a string or stream of.

chorretada *nf* 1 *(chorro)* gush, spurt, jet; *fig* **hablar a chorretadas**, to gabble. 2 *(porción extra)* extra drop.

chorrillo *nm fig* steady flow or trickle.

chorro *nm* 1 *(de agua etc)* jet, spurt; *(poca cantidad)* trickle; **salir a chorros**, to gush forth. 2 *Téc* jet, blast; **de propulsión a c.**, jet propelled. ■ **avión a c.**, jet plane; **c. de arena**, sandblast; **c. de vapor**, steam jet. 3 *fig* stream, flood, torrent; **a chorros**, in plenty, in abundance, copiously; **hablar a chorros**, *(atropelladamente)* to gabble; *(mucho)* to talk nineteen to the dozen; **llover a chorros**, to pour down. 4 *Am (grifo)* tap, *US* faucet.

chota *nf Zool (cabrita)* female kid; *(ternera)* sucking calf; *fam* **estar como una c.**, to be nuts.

chotacabras *nm inv Orn* nightjar.

chotear I *vtr fam* to make fun of. II **chotearse** *vr* 1 *fam* to joke; **c. de**, to make fun of, scoff at. 2 *Arg (sombrero)* to lift the brim of a hat.

choteo *nm fam* joking; **de c.**, in fun; **tomarse algo a c.**, to take sth as a joke.

chotis *nm* schottische, dance typical of Madrid.

choto,-a *nm,f* 1 *Zool (cabrito)* kid, young goat; *(ternero)* sucking calf; *fam* **estar como una chota**, to be nuts. 2 *Arg Urug (trapacero)* swindler.

chova *nf Orn* **c. piquirroja**, chough.

chovinismo *nm* chauvinism.

chovinista I *adj* chauvinistic. II *nmf* chauvinist.

choza *nf* hut, shack.

chozno,-a *nm,f* great-great-great-grandchild.

christmas *nm inv* Christmas card.

chubasco *nm* 1 *Meteor* heavy shower, downpour; **c. de nieve**, brief snowstorm. 2 *fig (contratiempo)* setback; **aguantar el c.**, to weather the storm.

chubasquero *nm* raincoat.

chúcaro,-a *adj Am* 1 *(ganado)* wild, untamed. 2 *(tímido)* shy.

chucear *vtr Am* to wound with a pike or lance.

chucha *nf* 1 *Zool* bitch. 2 *fam* dear. 3 *fam* peseta. 4 *Bol Chi Per vulg* cunt.

chuchada *nf CAm* fraud, swindle, trick.

chuchería *nf fam* 1 *(fruslería)* trinket, knick-knack. 2 *(bocado)* tidbit, snack; *(golosina)* sweet, *US* candy.

chucho¹ *nm Zool fam* dog, mongrel.

chucho² *nm Am* shiver.

chucho³ *interj (al perro)* shoo!, scat!

chucho,-a⁴ *adj CAm* mean, stingy.

chuchoca *nf SAm (para sazonar)* toasted maize.

chuchoco,-a *adj Arg* old, decrepit.

chuchumeco *nm Am* 1 *(hombre mezquino)* contemptible fellow, rat. 2 *(enano)* dwarf, runt.

chuco,-a *adj Am (carne)* high, off.

chucrut *nf*, **chucruta** *nf Culin* sauerkraut.

chueca *nf* 1 *(de árbol)* stump. 2 *Anat* ball of socket joint. 3 *Dep* game resembling hockey. 4 *fam fig (broma)* practical joke, prank.

chueco,-a *adj Am* 1 *(torcido)* crooked, bent, twisted. 2 *(patizambo)* bow-legged, bandy-legged.

chueta *nmf* Balearic Jew.

chufa *nf Bot* chufa, groundnut; **horchata de c.**, milky drink made from chufas.

chufla *nf*, **chufleta** *nf fam (broma)* joke; *(mofa)* taunt, jeer; **hacer c. de**, to mock.

chufletear *vi* to joke, jest, banter.

chulada *nf fam* 1 *(grosería)* coarse remark or act; *(desfachatez)* cheeky remark or act; *(mala jugada)* dirty trick. 2 *(bravuconada)* brag, boast, swagger.

chulanchar *vtr Arg* to swagger.

chulapo,-a *nm, f*, **chulapón,-ona** *nm, f fam* 1 *(hombre)* spiv, flash Harry, show-off; *(mujer)* flashy female. 2 *(castizo)* working-class Madrilenian.

chulear *fam* **I** *vtr* **1** *(burlarse de)* to make fun of. **2** *(robar)* to pinch, nick. **II** *vi (pavonearse)* to brag, swagger, throw one's weight about. **III chulearse** *vr fam* **1** *(burlarse)* **c. de,** to make fun of. **2** *(pavonearse)* to brag, swagger, throw one's weight about.

chulería *nf fam* **1** *(donaire)* charm, sparkle, wit. **2** *(valentonería)* bragging, swaggering, bravado. **3** *(vulgaridad)* coarseness, vulgarity. **4** *(grosería)* coarse remark *or* behaviour; *(desfachatez)* cheeky remark *or* behaviour.

chulesco,-a *adj fam* **1** *(descarado)* cheeky, cocky. **2** *(vulgar)* flashy, loud, brassy.

chuleta *nf* **1** *Culin* chop, cutlet; **c. de cerdo,** pork chop. **2** *fam (bofetada)* slap. **3** *Educ fam* crib (note), *US* trot. **4 chuletas,** *fam* whiskers, sideburns.

chulo,-a *fam* **I** *adj* **1** *(descarado)* cheeky, cocky; **ponerse c.,** to get cocky. **2** *(vistoso)* showy, flashy. **3** *(bonito)* nice, pretty, sweet; **¡qué c. vas!,** how smart you look! **II** *nm,f* **1** *(castizo)* working-class Madrilenian. **2** *(matón)* flash Harry; *(presuntuoso)* show-off, swank. **III** *nm (proxeneta)* pimp.

chulón,-ona *adj CAm* naked.

chumacera *nf Téc* bearing; *Náut* rowlock, *US* oar-lock.

chumbe *nm Am (faja)* sash.

chumero *nm CAm* apprentice.

chunga *nf fam* joke, fun; **estar de c.,** to be in a joking mood; **tomar algo a** *or* **en c.,** to treat sth as a joke.

chungar I *vi fam* to joke. **II chungarse** *vr fam* to joke; **c. de,** to make fun of.

chungo,-a *adj fam (malo)* naff; *(sin valor)* worthless; **es un tío muy c.,** he's a really nasty piece of work.

chungón,-ona *adj fam* fond of joking.

chunguear I *vi fam* to joke. **II chunguearse** *vr fam* to joke; **c. de,** *(broma)* to joke about; *(mofa)* to make fun of.

chunguero,-a *adj fam* fond of joking.

chupa *nf (prenda)* short jacket; *fam* **poner a algn como c. de dómine,** to give sb a dressing-down, haul sb over the coals.

chupacirios *nm pej fam (beato)* Holy Joe, Holy Willie.

chupachup® *nm* lollipop.

chupada *nf (a un pirulí etc)* suck; *(a un cigarro)* puff, drag; *(en pipa)* pull, puff; **dar chupadas a un cigarro,** to puff at a cigar.

chupadero *nm (para bebé)* teething ring.

chupado,-a I *pp de* **chupar. II** *adj* **1** *(flaco)* skinny, bony, thin; **de cara chupada,** gaunt, hollowcheeked. **2** *(estrecho) (falda etc)* tight. **3** *arg* **está c.,** it's dead easy.

chupador *nm (para bebé)* teething ring.

chupar I *vtr* **1** *(gen)* to suck; *(un cigarro)* to puff at; *(beber a sorbos)* to sip; *fam* **chuparle la sangre a algn,** to bleed sb dry. **2** *(lamer)* to lick. **3** *(absorber)* to suck up, soak up, absorb. **II** *vi* to suck. **III chuparse** *vr* **1 c. el dedo,** to suck one's thumb; **c. los dedos,** to lick one's fingers; *fam* **está para c. los dedos,** it's really mouthwatering; *fam* **¡chúpate eso!,** stick that in your pipe and smoke it! **2** *(consumirse)* to grow thin, waste away. **3** *fam (aguantar)* to put up with; **nos chupamos toda la película,** we sat through the whole film. **4** *Am (conversación)* to put up with; **me chupé todo su viaje,** I put up with all the details of his trip.

chupatintas *nm inv pey* penpusher, office drudge.

chupete *nm* **1** *(para bebé)* dummy, soother, *US* pacifier; *(de biberón)* teat. **2** *Am (caramelo)* lollipop.

chupetear *vi* to suck at.

chupeteo *nm* sucking.

chupi *adj fam* great, terrific, fantastic.

chupinazo *nm* **1** *(cañonazo)* loud bang. **2** *Ftb fam* hard kick.

chupino,-a *adj Arg* tailless.

chupón,-ona I *adj* **1** *(que chupa)* sucking. **2** *fam (gorrón)* sponging, scrounging. **II** *nm* **1** *Bot* sucker. **2** *(pirulí)* lollipop. **3** *Am* dummy, soother, *US* pacifier; *(de biberón)* teat. **4** *(desatrancador)* plunger **5** *Hon Méx Med* boil.

chupóptero,-a *nm,f irón fam* sponger, scrounger.

churdón *nm Bot* raspberry.

churrasco *nm* barbecued meat, barbecued steak.

churre *nm fam* filth, grease.

churrería *nf* fritter shop.

churrero,-a *nm,f* **1** fritter maker, fritter seller. **2** *arg (afortunado)* lucky person.

churrete *nm* dirty mark, grease spot.

churretear *vtr Am* to stain.

churretón *nm* dirty mark, grease spot.

churretoso,-a *adj* dirty, filthy.

churria *nf* **1** *Méx* stain. **2** *Am* **churrias,** diarrhoea *sing, US* diarrhea *sing.*

churriento,-a *adj véase* **churretoso,-a.**

churrigueresco,-a *adj* **1** *Arquit* churrigueresque; Spanish baroque. **2** *fig* excessively ornate, loud, flashy, tawdry.

churro *nm* **1** *Culin* fritter, *US* cruller. **2** *fam (chapuza)* botch, mess, slapdash job. **3** *fam (chiripa)* fluke, piece of good luck.

churrullero,-a I *adj (hablador)* talkative; *(chismoso)* gossipy. **II** *nm, f (hablador)* chatterbox; *(chismoso)* gossip.

churruscar *vtr & vi,* **churruscarse** *vr (pan etc)* to burn.

churrusco *nm* piece of burnt toast.

churumbel *nm fam* kid, child.

churumbela *nf* **1** *Mús* hornpipe. **2** *Am* cup with tube from which maté is drunk.

chus *interj (al perro)* here, boy!; *fam* **no decir ni c., ni mus,** not to say a word.

chuscada *nf* funny remark, joke.

chusco,-a¹ *adj (divertido)* funny, droll; *(gracioso)* witty.

chusco² *nm* **1** *(mendrugo)* chunk of stale bread. **2** *Mil fam* ration bread.

chusma *nf* **1** rabble, mob, riffraff. **2** *Arg* group of Indians.

chuso,-a *nm Arg (seco)* parchment-like, wrinkled.

chuspa *nf Am* bag, pouch.

chusquero *nm Mil fam* ranker.

chut *nm Dep* shot, kick.

chutar I *vi* **1** *Dep (a gol)* to shoot. **2** *fam* to go well; **va que chuta,** it's going really well; **¡y vas que chutas!,** and then you're well away! **II chutarse** *vr (drogas) arg* to fix, shoot up, mainline.

chute *nm arg (drogas)* fix.

chuza *nf Méx Bolos* strike.

chuzo *nm Am (pila)* pike; *(bastón)* metal-tipped stick; *fam fig* **caer chuzos de punta,** to rain cats and dogs, pour down.

chuzón-ona *adj* **1** *(astuto)* crafty, wily, sly. **2** *(ingenioso)* witty, sharp, clever.

chuzonada *nf* piece of clowning around *or* tomfoolery, prank.

CI *nm abr de* **coeficiente intelectual,** intelligence quotient, IQ.

Cía., cía *abr de* **compañía,** Company, Co.

cianuro *nm Quím* cyanide.

ciática *nf Med* sciatica.

cibernética *nf* cybernetics *sing.*

cibernético,-a *adj* cybernetic.

cicatería *nf* stinginess, meanness.

cicatero,-a I *adj* stingy, mean. **II** *nm,f* miser.

cicatriz *nf Med* scar.

cicatrización *nf Med* healing.

cicatrizar *vtr & vi Med* to heal.

cicerone *nmf* guide, cicerone.

ciclamen *nm Bot* cyclamen.

cíclico,-a *adj* cyclic, cyclical.

ciclismo *nm Dep* cycling.

ciclista *Dep* **I** *adj* cycle, cycling. **II** *nmf* cyclist.

ciclo *nm (gen)* cycle; *(de conferencias etc)* course, series.

ciclocróss *nm Dep* cyclo-cross.

ciclomotor *nm Aut* moped.

ciclón *nm Meteor* cyclone; *fig* **como un c.,** like a whirlwind.

ciclope *nm Mit* Cyclops

ciclopeo,-a *adj* gigantic, huge, massive

ciclostil *nm* cyclostyle mimeograph

cicíostilar *vtr* to cyclostyle mimeograph

cicuta *nf Bot* hemlock

cidra *nf Bot (fruta)* citron

cidro *nm Bot (árbol)* citron (tree)

ciego,-a I *adj* **1** *(persona)* blind, **a ciegas,** blindly *fig* without a clue, **quedarse c.,** to go blind *fig* **c. de cólera,** blind with anger *fam* **ponerse c.,** *(bebiendo)* to get blind drunk *(drogas)* to get very stoned **2** *Constr* blocked up **II** *nm,f* blind person, **los ciegos,** the blind *pl* **III** *nm Anat* caecum

cielo I *nm* **1** sky **a c. abierto,** opencast, *US* opencut, *fig* **venirse el c. abajo,** *(llover)* to pour down, *(des moralizarse)* to lose heart, *fig* **ver el c. abierto,** to see the way out (of a difficulty) **2** *Rel* heaven *fig* **bajado** *or* **caído del c.,** *(oportuno)* heaven sent *(inesperado)* out of the blue, *fig* **clamar al c.,** to cry out to heaven, *fig* **mover** *or* **remover c. y tierra,** to move heaven and earth *fig* **ser un c.,** to be an angel ■ *Arquit* **c. raso,** ceiling **3** *Anat (de la boca)* roof **II** *interj* **¡c. santo!,** good heavens!

ciempies *nm inv Zool* centipede

cien *adj & nm inv* hundred **c. libras,** a *or* one hundred pounds, **es c. por c. cierto,** it's one hundred per cent true **este es el que hace c.,** this is the hundredth, *fam* **ponerse a c.,** to get worked up be up to a hundred

cienaga *nf Geog* marsh bog

ciencia *nf* **1** *(disciplina)* science, **hombre de c.,** scientist *fig* **saber algo a c. cierta,** to know some thing for certain ■ *Lit Cin* **c. ficcion,** science fiction **c. infusa,** intuition, **ciencias empresariales,** business studies **ciencias exactas,** mathematics, **ciencias ocultas,** the occult *sing* **2** *(saber)* knowledge erudition

cienmilesimo,-a *adj & nm,f.* **cienmillonesimo,-a** *adj & nm,f* hundred millionth

cieno *nm* mud mire

cientifico,-a I *adj* scientific. **II** *nm,f* scientist

ciento *adj* hundred **c. doce,** one hundred and twelve **por c.,** per cent, **por cientos,** by the hundred, *fam* **c. y la madre,** a crowd, *fam* **dar c. y raya a algn,** to run rings round sb

cierne *nm* **1** *Bot* budding *fig* **en c.** *or* **ciernes** *(en potencia)* in embryo *or* potential **es un tenista en c.,** he's got potential as a tennis player

cierre *nm* **1** *(acción)* closing shutting *(de fabrica)* shutdown *Rad TV* close-down ■ **c. patronal,** lock out **2** *(mecanismo) (de bolso)* clasp *(de puerta ventana)* catch *(de una tienda)* shutter *(prenda)* fastener ■ **c. de seguridad,** safety lock

cierto,-a I *adj* **1** *(seguro)* sure, definite *(verdade ro)* right true **estar en lo c.,** to be right, **lo c. es que ...,** the fact is that ..., **por c.,** by the way **2** *(al gun)* certain, **ciertas personas,** some people **de cierta edad,** elderly, **en ciertos casos,** in certain *or* some cases **II** *adv* certainly

ciervo,-a *nm,f Zool* deer *(macho)* stag hart *(hembra)* aoe, hind

cierzo *nm Meteor* north wind

cifra *nf* **1** *Mat (numero)* figure number **2** *(suma)* amount, **c. global,** lump sum **3** *(código)* cipher code **en c.,** in code, *fig* mysteriously

cifrado,-a I *pp de* **cifrar II** *adj (en cifra)* coded in code **2** *fig (ilusión, esperanza)* placed

cifrar I *vtr* **1** *(mensaje)* to encode **2** *fig (ilusion es peranza)* to place **II cifrarse** *vr* to amount *or* come to

cigala *nf Zool* Dublin Bay prawn Norway lobster

cigarra *nf Ent* cicada

cigarral *nm (en Toledo)* country house

cigarrero,-a I *nm,f (persona)* street tobacco seller **II** *nf (estuche)* cigar case

cigarrillo *nm* cigarette ■ **c. con filtro,** filter(-tip) cigarette

cigarro *nm* **1** *(puro)* cigar **2** *(cigarrillo)* cigarette

cigüeña *nf* **1** *Orn* stork **2** *Téc* crank

cigüeñal *nm Tec* crankshaft

cilicio *nm Rel (prenda)* hair shirt

cilindrada *nf Aut Tec* cylinder capacity

cilindrico,-a *adj* cylindric cylindrical

cilindro *nm* cylinder

cima *nf* summit, *fml* **dar c. a algo,** to crown sth

cimarron,-a Am I *adj* **1** *Zool* wild animal **2** *Hist* **esclavo c.,** runaway slave **II** *nm,f Hist* runaway slave

cimbalo *nm Mus* cymbal

cimborio *nm* **cimborrio** *nm Arquit* dome

cimbra I *Arquit* soffit **2** *Constr* centring, *US* centering

cimbrar *vtr* **cimbrear I** *vtr* **1** *(gen)* to make quiver, *(cana)* to waggle **2** *Constr* to erect a centring for an arch **II cimbrearse** *vr* to sway

cimbreo *nm* **1** *(balanceo)* waggle quiver **2** *(al andar)* sway swaying

cimentacion *nf Constr* **1** *(accion)* laying of foundations **2** *(cimientos)* foundation foundations *pl*

cimentar *vtr Constr* to lay the foundations of, *fig (amistad, idea)* to strengthen, consolidate

cimientos *nmpl Constr* foundations, **echar** *or* **poner los c.,** to lay the foundations *fig* **desde los c.,** from the very start

cinamomo *nm Bot* cinnamon (tree)

cinc *nm Metal* zinc

cincel *nm* chisel

cincelado,-a I *pp de* **cincelar II** *adj* chiselled *US* chiseled **III** *nm* chiselling, *US* chiseling

cincelar *vtr* to chisel

cincha *nf Equit* girth, *US* cinch

cincho *nm* belt *Tec* hoop

cinco *inv* **I** *adj (cardinal)* five, *(ordinal)* fifth, **el te de las c.,** five o' clock tea **II** *nm* five, *fam* **¡choca** *or* **vengan esos c.!,** slap me five! *véase tamb* **ocho**

cincuenta *inv* **I** *adj (cardinal)* fifty, *(ordinal)* fiftieth **II** *nm* fifty *véase tamb* **ochenta** *y* **ocho**

cincuentavo,-a I *adj* fiftieth **cincuentava parte,** fiftieth **II** *nm,f* fiftieth, *vease tamb* **octavo a**

cincuentena *nf* fifty

cincuentenario *nm* fiftieth anniversary

cincuenton,-ona *adj & nm,f fam* fifty year old

cine *nm* **1** *(local)* cinema *US* movie theater **ir al c.,** to go to the cinema, *US* go to the movies ■ **c. de estreno,** first-run cinema **2** *(arte)* cinema **hacer c.,** to make films *US* make movies *fam* **ser de c.,** to be fabulous ■ **c. mudo/sonoro,** silent/talking films *pl* **estrella de c.,** film star

cineasta *nmf* film director, film maker

cineclub *nm (pl cineclubs)* small film society

cinefilo,-a *nm,f* film lover, *US* moviegoer

cinegetica *nf* hunting

cinegético,-a *adj* of *or* related to hunting.

cinema *nm véase* **cine**

cinemateca *nf véase* **filmoteca**

cinemática *nf* kinematics *sing.*

cinematografía *nf* film making, cinematography.

cinematográfico,-a *adj* cinematographic; **la industria cinematográfica,** the film *or* US movie industry.

cinematógrafo *nm* film projector, *US* movie projector.

cinerama *nf* cinerama.

cinética, *nf* kinetics *sing.*

cinético,-a *adj* kinetic.

cingalés,-esa *adj* & *nm,f* Singhalese.

cíngaro,-a *adj* & *nm,f* Tzigane, gypsy.

cínico,-a I *adj* cynical. II *nm,f* cynic.

cinismo *nm* cynicism.

cinta *nf* **1** *(tira)* band, strip; *(para adornar)* ribbon; *Cost* braid, edging; **c. para (sujetar) el pelo,** head-band. **2** *Téc* tape. ■ **c. adhesiva/aislante,** adhesive/insulating tape; **c. de ametralladora,** loading belt; *Téc Inform* **c. magnética,** magnctic tape; **c. magnetofónica,** recording tape; **c. métrica,** tape measure; **c. transportadora,** conveyor belt. **3** *Cin* film.

cinto *nm* *(cinturón)* belt; *(de sable)* swordbelt.

cintura *nf Anat* waist; *fam* **meter a algn en c,** to bring sb into line.

cinturón *nm* belt; *fig* **apretarse el c.,** to tighten one's belt. ■ **c. de castidad/ seguridad,** chastity/safety belt.

cipe *adj CAm* **niño c.,** sickly child.

cipote I *adj* stupid. II *nm* **1** *ofens (persona)* tit, cunt. **2** *vulg (pene)* prick, cock.

ciprés *nm Bot* cypress.

CIR *nm Mil abr de* **Centro de Instrucción de Reclutas,** ≈ Recruits Trainnig Unit.

circense *adj* circus.

circo *nm* **1** *(espectáculo)* circus. **2** *Geog* cirque.

circuito *nm Elec Dep* circuit. ■ *TV* **c. cerrado de televisión,** closed circuit television; *Téc* **corto c.,** short circuit.

circulación *nf* **1** *(gen)* circulation; **fuera de c.,** out of circulation; *Fin* **poner en/retirar de la c.,** to put into/ withdraw from circulation. ■ *Med* **c. de la sangre** *or* **sanguínea,** blood circulation. **2** *Aut (tráfico)* traffic; **una carretera de mucha c.,** a very busy road. ■ **c. rodada,** vehicular traffic; **código de la c.,** highway code.

circular I *adj* & *nf* circular. II *vi* **1** *(moverse)* to circulate, move, pass; *(líquido)* to flow; *(trenes, autobuses)* to run; **circulan muchos coches por esta calle,** there's a lot of traffic on this street; **¡circulen!,** move along, please!; **hacer c.** *(documento)* to circulate; *(líquido)* to make flow; *fig (rumor)* to spread; **hoy no circulan trenes,** there are no trains running today; *(en letrero)* **peatón circule por la** *or* **su izquierda,** pedestrians keep to the left. **2** *Aut (conducir)* to drive; **c. por la izquierda/derecha,** to drive on the left/right.

circulatorio,-a *adj* circulatory.

círculo *nm* **1** *(gen)* circle. ■ *fig* **c. vicioso,** vicious circle. **2** *(club)* circle, club.

circuncidar *vtr* to circumcise.

circuncisión *nf* circumcision.

circunciso,-a *adj* cricumcised.

circundante *adj* surrounding.

circundar *vtr* to surround, encircle.

circunferencia *nf Geom* circumference.

circunflejo *adj* & *nm Ling* circumflex.

circunloquio *nm* circumlocution; **déjate de circunloquios,** stop beating about *or* around the bush.

circunscribir *(pp* **circunscrito***)* I *vtr Geom* to circumscribe. II **circunscribirse** *vr fig* to confine *or* limit oneself.

circunscripción *nf* district. ■ **c. electoral,** constituency.

circunscrito,-a I *pp de* **circunscribir.** II *adj* circumscribed.

circunspección *nf* circumspection, seriousness.

circunspecto,-a *adj* circumspect, serious, grave.

circunstancia *nf* circumstance; **en estas circunstancias ...,** under the circumstances...; **estar a la altura de las circunstancias,** to rise to the occasion; *fam* **poner cara de circunstancias,** to look grave.

circunstancial *adj* circumstancial; *Ling* **complemento c.,** adverbial complement.

circunvalación *nf* **1** *Hist* circumvallation. **2** *Aut* **carretera de c.,** ring road, *US* belt, beltway; **línea de c.,** *(de tren)* circular line; *(de autobús)* circular route.

circunvalar *vtr* to circumvallate, surround.

cirílico,-a *adj Ling* Cyrillic.

cirio *nm* wax candle; *fam* **armar un c.,** to kick up a rumpus.

cirro *nm Meteor* cirrus.

cirrosis *nf Med* cirrhosis.

cirroso,-a *adj,* **cirrótico,-a** *adj* cirrhotic.

ciruela *nf Bot* plum. ■ **c. claudia,** greengage; **c. pasa,** prune.

ciruelo *nm Bot* plum tree.

cirugía *nf Med* surgery. ■ **c. estética** *or* **plástica,** plastic surgery.

cirujano,-a *nm,f Med* surgeon.

ciscarse *vr euf* to soil oneself; **¡me cisco en ...!,** damn ...!

cisco *nm* **1** *(carbón)* charcoal. **2** *fam (trifulca)* row, rumpus; *fam* **estoy hecho c.,** I'm done for; *fam* **hacer c. (algo),** to smash (sth) to pieces.

cisma *nm* **1** *Rel* schism **2** *Pol* split.

cismático,-a *adj* & *nm,f* schismatic.

cisne *nm Orn* swan.

cisterna *nf* cistern, tank. ■ **buque** *or* **camión c.,** tanker.

cistitis *nf inv Med* cystitis.

cita *nf* **1** *(convocatoria)* appointment; **en el congreso se dieron c. casi mil especialistas,** almost a thousand experts attended the conference; **tener una c. con algn,** to have arranged to meet sb. **2** *(amorosa)* date. ■ **casa de citas,** house of ill repute, brothel. **3** *(mención)* quotation.

citación *nf Jur* citation, summon's *sing.*

citado,-a I *pp de* **citar.** II *adj* aforementioned.

citar I *vtr* **1** *(dar cita)* to arrange to meet, make an appointment with. **2** *Jur* to summon; **c. a algn a juicio,** to call sb as a witness. **3** *(mencionar)* to quote; **cito de memoria,** I'm quoting from memory; **para c. sólo un ejemplo,** to give just one example. II **citarse** *vr* to arrange to meet, make a date (**con,** with).

citara *nf Mús* zither, sitar.

citología *nf Biol* cytology.

citoplasma *nm* cytoplasm.

cítrico,-a I *adj* curie, citrus II **cítricos** *nmpl* citrus fruits.

ciudad *nf* town, city; **ir a la c.,** to go to *or* into town, **la gran c.,** the big city. ■ **c. dormitorio,** dormitory suburb *or* town; **c. jardín,** garden city.

ciudadanía *nf* citizenship.

ciudadano,-a *adj* civic; **deberes ciudadanos,** civic duties II *nm,f* citizen

ciudadela *nf* citadel, fortress.

ciudarealeño,-a I *adj* of *or* from Ciudad Real. II *nm, f* native *or* inhabitant of Ciudad Real.

civet *nm Culin* stew, ragout.

civeta *nf Zool* civet.

cívico,-a *adj* civic.

civil I *adj* **1** civil; **matrimonio c.,** civil marriage; **casarse por lo c.,** to get married in a registry office. **2** *Mil* civilian. II *nm* member of the **Guardia Civil.**

civilista *nmf Am Pol* defender of civil government.

civilización *nf* civilization.

civilizado,-a I *pp de* **civilizar. II** *adj* civilized.

civilizador,-a I *adj* civilizing. **II** *nm,f* civilizer.

civilizar I *vtr* to civilize. **II civilizarse** *vr* to become civilized.

civismo *nm* good citizenship, civility

cizalla *nf*, **cizallas** *nfpl* **1** *(herramienta)* metal shears *pl*, wire cutters *pl*. **2** *Metal* metal clippings *pl or* cuttings *pl*.

cizaña *nf Bot* bearded darnel, *fig* **sembrar c.,** to sow discord.

cl *abr de* **centilitro(s),** centilitre(s), *US* centiliter(s), cl.

clamar *vtr* to cry out for, clamour *or US* clamor for; **c. venganza,** to cry out for revenge

clamor *nm* clamour, *US* clamor.

clamoroso,-a *adj* clamorous; **un éxito c.,** an overwhelming success.

clan *nm* clan.

clandestinidad *nf* secrecy; **en la c.,** underground, in secrecy.

clandestino,-a *adj* clandestine, underground, secret.

claque *nf fig Teat* claque.

claqué *nm Mús* tap dancing.

clara *nf* **1** *(de huevo)* white. **2** *fam (bebida)* shandy.

claraboya *nf Arquit* skylight.

clarear I *vtr* to light up; *(habitación)* to illuminate; *(color)* to make lighter. **II** *vi* **1** *(amanecer)* to dawn. **2** *Meteor (despejar)* to clear up. **3** *Tex (transparentar)* to wear thin, become transparent. **III clarearse** *vr* to let the light through; *fig (delatarse)* to give oneself away.

clarete *adj & nm (vino)* claret.

claridad *nf* **1** *(luz)* light, brightness **2** *(inteligibilidad)* clearness, clarity; **con c.,** clearly.

clarificación *nf* clarification.

clarificador,-a I *adj* clarifying. **II** *nm,f* clarifier.

clarificar *vtr* to clarify, clear up.

clarín *nm Mús* bugle; **toque de c.,** bugle call.

clarinete *nm Mús* **1** *(instrumento)* clarinet. **2** *(persona)* clarinettist.

clarinetista *nmf* clarinettist.

clarividencia *nf* **1** *(lucidez)* lucidity, clear thinking. **2** *(percepción)* clairvoyance, far-sightedness.

clarividente I *adj* **1** *(lúcido)* lucid. **2** *(perceptivo)* clairvoyant, far-sighted. **II** *nmf (persona)* clairvoyant

claro,-a I *adj* **1** *(gen)* clear; **dejar algo c.,** to make sth clear; **¿está c.?,** is that clear?; *fig* **más c. que el agua,** as clear as daylight; *fig* **mente clara,** clear mind; *fam* **a las claras,** openly; *fam* **¡lo llevas c.!,** you've got it coming to you! **2** *(bien iluminado)* bright, well-lit. **3** *(líquido, salsa)* thin. **4** *(color)* light. **II** *interj* of course!; **¡c. que no!,** of course not!; **¡c. que sí!,** certainly! **III** *nm* **1** *(espacio)* gap, space, *(en un bosque)* clearing; **c. de luna,** moonlight, **dejar un c.,** to leave a gap. **2** *Meteor* bright spell. **IV** *adv* clearly, **¡habla c.!,** make yourself clear!; *fig* **no lo veo (nada)** c., I can't see it working.

claroscuro *nm Art* chiaroscuro.

clase *nf* **1** *(grupo, distinción)* class; **tener c.,** to have class. ■ **c. alta/media,** upper/middle class; **c. obrera/ dirigente,** working/ruling class; **clases pasivas,** pensioners; **primera/segunda c.,** first/second class. **2** *Educ (curso)* class; **dar c. a algn,** to teach sb. ■ **c. de conducir,** driving lesson; **c. particular,** private class *or* lesson **3** *Educ (aula)* classroom; *Univ* lecture hall. **4** *(tipo)* kind, sort; **de buena c.,** good quality; **de toda(s) clase(s),** of all kinds *or* sorts; **toda c. de ...,** all kinds of ... .

clasicismo *nm* classicism.

clasicista I *adj* classicistic. **II** *nmf* classicist.

clásico,-a I *adj* **1** classical; **música clásica,** classical music. **2** *(típico)* classic, typical; **es el ejemplo c.,** that's the classic example **3** *(en el vestir)* classic. **II** *nm* classic **III clásicas** *nfpl Ling* the classics

clasificación *nf* **1** *(gen)* classification; *Dep* league, table; *(de discos)* ≈ top twenty **2** *(distribución)* sorting (out).

clasificador,-a I *adj* classifying. **II** *nm,f* classifier. **III** *nm Mueb* filing cabinet.

clasificar I *vtr* to classify, class; *(libros, cartas)* to sort (out). **II clasificarse** *vr* **1** *Dep* to qualify; **el equipo se clasificó para la final,** the team qualified for the final. **2** *Dep (llegar)* to come; **se clasificó segundo,** he came (in) second.

clasismo *nm* class-consciousness.

clasista I *adj* class-conscious. **II** *nmf* class-conscious person.

claudicación *nf* submission, yielding.

claudicar *vi* to yield, give in.

claustro *nm* **1** *Arquit* cloister. **2** *Rel fig* monastic life. **3** *Educ (profesores)* staff; *(junta)* staff meeting; *Univ* senate.

claustrofobia *nf Med* claustrophobia.

cláusula *nf* clause.

clausura *nf* **1** *(cierre)* closure, closing. ■ **ceremonia de c.,** closing ceremony. **2** *Rel* enclosure. ■ **monja de c.,** enclosed nun.

clausurar *vtr (curso, conferencia)* to close; *(debate)* to end, conclude; *Jur (bar, local)* to close (down).

clavado,-a I *pp de* **clavar. II** *adj* **1** *(con clavos)* nail-studded, nailed. **2** *(fijo)* firmly fixed; *fig* **con la mirada clavada en ...,** staring at ...; *fam* **dejar (a algn) c.,** to leave (sb) dumbfounded. **3** *fam (exacto)* **es c. a su padre,** he's the spitting image of his father; **son las diez clavadas,** it's ten o'clock sharp *or* on the dot.

clavar I *vtr* **1** *(gen)* to nail; *(clavo)* to bang *or* hammer in; *(estaca)* to drive; *fig* **c. los ojos en.,** to rivet one's eyes on ... . **2** *fam (cobrar caro)* to sting *or* fleece. **II clavarse** *vr (gen)* to get; **c. un cuchillo,** to thrust a knife in one's hand *or* body; **c. una astilla,** to get a splinter in one's finger; **c. una espina,** to prick oneself on a thorn.

clave I *nm Mús* harpsichord. **II** *nf* **1** *(de un enigma)* key, clue; **la c. de su actitud,** the key to her attitude. **2** *(código)* key, cipher; **en c.,** in code. **3** *Mús (tono)* key; *(signo)* clef. **4** *Arquit* keystone. **III** *adj (importante)* important; **la palabra c.,** the key word; **ocupa un puesto clave,** he holds a top position.

clavel *nm Bot* carnation.

clavellina *nf Bot* pink.

clavetear *vtr* to stud with nails.

clavicordio *nm Mús* clavichord.

clavícula *nf Anat* clavicle, collarbone.

clavija *nf* **1** *Téc* peg; *fig* **apretarle las clavijas a algn,** to tighten the screws on sb. **2** *Elec Tel* plug.

clavo *nm* **1** nail, stud; *fig* **agarrarse a un c. ardiendo,** to clutch at a straw; *fig* **dar en el c.,** to hit the nail on the head; *fig* **remachar el c.,** to make matters worse; *fam* **como un c.,** very punctual; *fam* **estar sin un c.,** to be dead broke. **2** *Bot* clove. **3** *vulg (pene)* prick, horn.

claxon *nm (pl cláxones) Aut* horn, hooter; **tocar el c.,** to sound the horn.

clemencia *nf* mercy, clemency.

clemente *adj* merciful, clement.

clementina *nf Bot* clementine.

cleptomanía *nf* kleptomania.

cleptómano,-a *adj & nm,f* kleptomaniac.

clerecía *nf* clergy.

clergyman *nm (prenda)* clericals *pl*, clergyman's suit.

clerical I *adj* clerical. **II** *nmf* clericalist.

clericalismo *nm* clericalism.

clérigo *nm* priest.

clero *nm* clergy.

cliché *nm* **1** *Fot* negative. **2** *Impr* plate. **3** *fig (lugar común)* cliché.

cliente *nmf* customer, client.

clientela *nf* customers *pl*, clients *pl*, clientele.

clima *nm* climate; *fig* atmosphere; **en un c. de cordialidad,** in a cordial atmosphere.

climaterio *nm* climacteric.

climático,-a *adj* climatic, climatical.

climatización *nf* air conditioning.

climatizado,-a **I** *pp de* **climatizar**. **II** *adj* air-conditioned.

climatizar *vtr* to air-condition.

climatología *nf* climatology.

climatológico,-a *adj* climatologic, climatological.

clímax *nm inv* climax.

clínica *nf* clinic.

clínico,-a **I** *adj* clinical. **II** *nm, f (persona)* clinician, physician.

clip *nm (para papel)* clip; *(para pelo)* hair-grip, *US* bobby pin.

clíper *nm (pl clíperes)* Náut clipper.

clítoris *nm inv* Anat clitoris.

cloaca *nf* sewer, drain.

cloquear *vi* to cluck.

cloqueo *nm* cluck, clucking.

clorado,-a **I** *pp de* **clorar**. **II** *adj* chlorinated. **III** *nm* chlorination.

clorhídrico,-a *adj* Quím hydrochloric.

cloro *nm* Quím chlorine.

clorofila *nf* Bot chlorophyll, *US* chlorophyl.

clorofílico,-a *adj* chlorophyllous.

cloroformo *nm* Farm chloroform.

cloruro *nm* Quím chloride. ■ **c. sódico,** sodium chloride.

club *nm (pl clubs or clubes)* club. ■ **c. náutico,** yacht club.

clueca **I** *adj* broody. **II** *nf* broody hen.

cm *abr de* **centímetro(s),** centimetre(s), *US* centimeter(s), cm.

Cnel. *abr. de* **Coronel,** Colonel, Col.

CNT *nf abr de* **Confederación Nacional de Trabajadores,** workers national confederation.

coacción *nf* coercion.

coaccionar *vtr* to coerce, compel.

coactivo,-a *adj* coercive, compelling.

coadjutor,-a I *adj & nm, f* coadjutant. **II** *nm* Rel coadjutor.

coadyuvante *adj & nmf fml* coadjutant.

coadyuvar *vtr fml* to contribute, help.

coagulación *nf* coagulation, clotting.

coagulante **I** *adj* coagulative. **II** *nm* coagulant, coagulator.

coagular **I** *vtr & vi (gen)* to coagulate; *(sangre)* to clot; *(leche)* to curdle. **II coagularse** *vr (gen)* to coagulate; *(sangre)* to clot; *(leche)* to curdle.

coágulo *nm* coagulum, clot.

coala *nm* Zool koala (bear).

coalición *nf* coalition.

coaligar *vtr,* **coaligarse** *vr* to ally (with).

coartada *nf* alibi.

coartar *vtr* to hinder; *fig* to restrict.

coautor,-a *nm, f* coauthor.

coba *nf fam* soft soap; **dar c. a algn,** to soft-soap sb.

cobalto *nm* cobalt. ■ **bomba de c.,** cobalt bomb.

cobarde **I** *adj* cowardly. **II** *nmf* coward.

cobardía *nf* cowardice.

cobaya *nf,* **cobayo** *nm* Zool guinea pig.

cobertizo *nm* shed, shack.

cobertor *nm* (colcha) bedspread. **2** *(manta)* blanket.

cobertura *nf* cover; Seg **c. de seguros,** insurance cover.

cobija *nf Am* blanket.

cobijar **I** *vtr (gen)* to shelter; *(fugitivo)* to harbour, *US* harbor. **II cobijarse** *vr* to take shelter.

cobijo *nm (techo)* shelter; *fig (protección)* protection, refuge.

cobista *fam* **I** *adj* soapy. **II** *nmf* crawler, toady.

cobla *nf* Cat Mús brass band.

cobra *nf* Zool cobra.

cobrador,-a *nm, f* **1** *(de autobús etc) (hombre)* conductor; *(mujer)* conductress. **2** *(de luz, agua, etc)* collector.

cobrar **I** *vtr* **1** *(dinero)* to charge; *(cheque)* to cash; *(salario)* to earn; **cóbralo todo junto,** put it all together; **¿cuánto cobras al mes?,** how much do you earn a month?; **han venido a c. el alquiler,** they've been to collect the rent; **me ha cobrado diez duros,** she charged me fifty pesetas; Com **por c.,** unpaid. **2** *irón* to get beaten *or* a slap; **¡vas a c.!,** you'll cop a clout!, you're in for it! **3** *Caza* to retrieve. **4** *fig (adquirir)* to gain, get; **c. aliento,** to get one's breath back; **c. ánimos,** to take courage *or* heart; **c. importancia,** to become important. **II cobrarse** *vr* **1** *(dinero)* to take, collect; **cóbrese de aquí,** take it out of this, please. **2** *desus (recuperarse)* to recover.

cobre *nm* **1** Metal copper; *fam* **batir el c.,** to go hard at it. **2** *Am (moneda)* copper cent.

cobrizo,-a *adj* copper, copper-coloured, *US* copper-colored, coppery.

cobro *nm* **1** *(pago)* collecting; *(de cheque)* cashing; **el c. del gas,** the gas payment; Com **presentar al c.,** to hand in for payment. ■ Tel **c. revertido,** reverse-charge. *US* collect. **2** *Caza* retrieval.

coca *nf* **1** Bot coca. **2** *arg (droga)* cocaine, coke. **3** *fam (bebida)* Coke®. **4** Cat Culin type of flat cake.

cocaína *nf* cocaine.

cocainómano,a *nm, f* cocaine addict, coke head.

cocción *nf* Culin cooking; *(en agua)* boiling; *(en horno)* baking.

cocear *vi* to kick.

cocer **I** *vtr* Culin *(comida)* to cook; *(hervir)* to boil; *(en horno)* to bake. **II** *vi (hervir)* to boil. **III cocerse** *vr* **1** Culin *(comida)* to cook; *(hervir)* to boil; *(en horno)* to bake. **2** *fam (de calor)* to roast, be boiling. **3** *(tramarse)* to be afoot *or* going on, be cooking.

cochambre *nf* filth, muck.

cochambroso,-a *adj* filthy.

coche *nm* **1** Aut car, automobile, motorcar; **fuimos en c.,** we went by car. ■ **c. blindado,** armoured car; **c. celular,** police van; **c. de alquiler,** hired car, *US* rented car; **c. de bomberos,** fire engine; **c. de carreras,** racing car; **c. de época,** vintage car; **c. familiar,** estate (car), *US* station wagon; **c. fúnebre,** hearse. **2** Ferroc carriage, coach. ■ **c. cama,** sleeping car, *US* sleeper. **3** *(de caballos)* carriage, coach. **4** *(de niño)* pram, *US* baby carriage.

cochera *nf Aut* **1** *desus* garage. **2** *(de autobuses, tranvías)* depot.

cochero *nm* Aut coachman.

cochinada *nf fam* filthy *or* dirty thing; *fam fig (obscenidad)* obscenity; **decir cochinadas,** to say foul *or* obscene things; **hacer una c. (a algn),** to play a dirty trick (on sb).

cochinería *nf* **1** *(suciedad)* filthiness. **2** *véase* **cochinada**.

cochinilla¹ *nf* Zool woodlouse.

cochinilla² *nf* Ent cochineal.

cochinillo *nm* Zool sucking pig.

cochino,-a **I** *adj* **1** *(sucio)* filthy, disgusting. **2** *fam* *(miserable)* lousy, bloody; **¡c. dinero!,** damn money! **II** *nm, f* 1 *Zool (macho)* pig, swine; *(hembra)* sow. **2** *fam (persona)* filthy person, pig.

cocido,-a I *pp de* **cocer. II** *adj* cooked, boiled; *fam* **estar c.,** to be sloshed. **III** *nm Culin* stew.

cociente *nm Mat* quotient.

cocina *nf* **1** *(arte)* cooking. ■ **c. casera,** home cooking; **c. de mercado,** food in season; **c. española,** Spanish cooking *or* cuisine; **libro de c.,** cookery book, *US* cookbook. **2** *(habitación)* kitchen. ■ **utensilios de c.,** kitchen utensils. **3** *(aparato)* cooker, *US* stove. ■ **c. económica,** stove; **c. eléctrica/de gas,** electric/gas cooker.

cocinar *vtr & vi* to cook.

cocinero,-a *nm, f* cook.

cocinilla *nf* (small portable) cooker *or US* stove.

cocker *nm Zool* cocker (spaniel).

coco¹ *nm Bot (árbol)* coconut palm; *(fruta)* coconut.

coco² *nm* **1** *fam (fantasma)* bogeyman; **ser un c.,** *(ser feo)* to be ugly; *(dar miedo)* to be frightening. **2** *arg (cabeza)* hard nut; **comer el c. algn,** to brainwash sb; **comerse el c.,** to get worked up, rack one's brains.

cocodrilo *nm Zool* crocodile.

cócora *nf Col Cuba PR (cólera)* anger, rage.

cocotal *nm* coconut grove.

cocotero *nm Bot* coconut palm.

cóctel *nm* cocktail. ■ **c. Molotov,** Molotov cocktail.

coctelera *nf* cocktail shaker.

codazo *nm* **1** *(señal)* nudge with one's elbow. **2** *(golpe)* blow with one's elbow; *fig* **abrirse paso** *or* **camino a codazos,** to elbow one's way through.

codear I *vi* **1** *(empujar)* to elbow. **2** *SAm (pedir con insistencia)* to keep on. **II codearse** *vr (relacionarse)* to rub shoulders (**con,** with), hobnob (**con,** with).

codeína *nf Farm* codeine.

codera *nf Cost* elbow patch.

códice *nm Lit* codex.

codicia *nf* greed, thirst.

codiciable *adj* desirable.

codiciado,-a I *pp de* **codiciar. II** *adj* much desired, coveted.

codiciar *vtr* to covet, crave for.

codicioso,-a I *adj* covetous, greedy. **II** *nm, f* greedy person.

codificación *nf* **1** *Jur* codification. **2** *(de mensajes)* encoding.

codificador,-a I *adj* **1** *Jur* codifying. **2** *(de mensajes)* encoding. **II** *nm,f Jur* codifier. **2** *(de mensajes)* encoder. **3** *Inform* encoder.

codificar *vtr (ley)* to codify; *(mensajes)* to encode.

código *nm* code.

codillo *nm* **1** *Anat Zool* elbow. **2** *Culin* shoulder. **3** *Téc (de tubería)* elbow.

codo *nm* **1** *Anat* elbow; **de codos,** on one's elbows; *fig* **c. a** *or* **con c.,** side by side; *fig* **desgastarse** *or* **romperse los codos,** to study a lot, swot, cram; *fam* **alzar** *or* **empinar el c.,** to knock them back; *fam* **hablar por los codos,** to talk nonstop. **2** *Téc (de tubería)* elbow.

codorniz *nf Orn* quail.

COE *nm Dep abr de* **Comité Olímpico Español,** Spanish Olympic Committee.

coeducación *nf* coeducation.

coeficiente *nm* **1** *Mat* coefficient. **2** *(grado)* degree, rate. ■ **c. de crecimiento,** growth rate; **c. de inteligencia,** intelligence quotient.

coercitivo,-a *adj* coercive.

coetáneo,-a *adj & nm, f* contemporary.

coexistencia *nf* coexistence.

coexistir *vi* to coexist.

cofa *nf Náut* top. ■ **c. mayor,** maintop.

cofia *nf (prenda)* bonnet.

cofrade *nm, f (gen)* member (of brotherhood); *(hombre)* brother (of brotherhood); *(mujer)* sister (of brotherhood).

cofradía *nf (hermandad)* brotherhood; *(asociación)* association.

cofre *nm* **1** *(arca, baúl)* trunk, chest. **2** *(para dinero, joyas)* box, casket.

coger I *vtr* **1** *(asir)* to seize, take hold of; **coge esto un momento,** hold this a second; *fig* **c. algo por los pelos,** to just make sth; *fam* **cogió la puerta y se marchó,** he upped and left; *fam* **no hay por donde cogerlo,** he hasn't got a leg to stand on. **2** *(tomar)* to take; **he cogido un buen sitio,** I've got a very good place; *fig* **no ha cogido un libro en su vida,** he hasn't read a book in his life. **3** *(tomar prestado)* to borrow; **te he cogido la pluma,** I've borrowed your pen. **4** *(pelota, ladrón, resfriado)* to catch; *fig* **me cogió desprevenido,** I was caught unawares. **5** *fig (entender)* to understand; **no cogí el chiste,** I didn't get the joke. **6** *(recoger)* to pick (up); *(fruta, flores)* to gather; *Tricot* **c. puntos,** to pick up stitches. **7** *(acento, costumbre)* to pick up; *(sentimiento)* to take; **coger miedo a,** to become afraid of; *fam* **c. una manía,** to get hooked on sth. **8** *(velocidad, fuerza)* to gather. **9** *(emisora, canal)* to pick up. **10** *(transporte)* to take, catch. **11** *(empleados, empleo)* to take on. **12** *(atropellar)* to run over, knock down. **13** *(espacio)* to take up. **14** *Am vulg* to fuck. **II** *vi* **1** *(plantas, colores)* to take. **2** *(ir)* to go; **coge por la calle de la iglesia,** take the church road. **3** *fam* **cogió y se fue,** he upped and left; **cogió y se puso a chillar,** he started to scream like mad. **III cogerse** *vr (pillarse)* to catch; *(agarrarse)* to hold, clutch; **cógete bien,** hold tight; **ella se cogió de su brazo,** she took his arm; *fam* **se cogió un cabreo,** he got very angry.

cogestión *nf* copartnership.

cogida *nf Taur* gore, goring.

cogido,-a I *pp de* **coger. II** *adj (sujeto)* fixed; *(atrapado)* trapped, caught. **III** *nm Cost* gather, pleat.

cognición *nf* cognition.

cognoscitivo,-a *adj* cognitive.

cogollo *nm* **1** *(de lechuga, col)* heart; *fam* **hasta el c.,** to the core. **2** *(brote)* shoot. **3** *fig (la flor y la nata)* **el c.,** the cream. **4** *Arg Zool (chicharra)* large cicada.

cogorza *nf fam* **agarrar** *or* **pillar una c.,** to get blotto *or* smashed.

cogotazo *nm fam* blow on the back of the neck.

cogote *nm* nape *or* back of the neck.

cogotudo,-a *nm, f SAm* upstart.

cohabitación *nf* cohabitation.

cohabitar *vi* to live together, cohabit.

cohecho *nm fml Jur* bribery.

coherencia *nf* coherence, cohereney.

coherente *adj* coherent.

cohesión *nf* cohesion.

cohete *nm* rocket; *fam* **como un c.,** like a rocket. ■ *Astronáut* **c. espacial,** space rocket.

cohibición *nf* inhibition, restraint.

cohibido,-a I *pp de* **cohibir. II** *adj* inhibited, restrained.

cohibir I *vtr* to inhibit, restrain. **II cohibirse** *vr* to feel inhibited *or* embarrassed.

COI *nm Dep abr de* **Comité Olímpico Internacional,** International Olympic Committee, IOC.

coima *nf Chi Per RP* bribe.

coincidencia *nf* coincidence; **dio la c. de que ...,** it just so happened that ...; **en c. con,** in agreement with.

coincidente *adj* coincident, coinciding.

coincidir *vi* **1** *(acordar)* to coincide; **nuestras ideas no coinciden,** our ideas don't coincide *or* agree. **2** *(encontrarse)* to meet; **coincidí con ella en Madrid,** I was in Madrid at the same time as her.

coito *nm* coitus, intercourse.

cojear *vi (persona)* to limp, hobble; *(mueble)* to wobble; *fig (ir mal)* to falter; *fam* **c. del mismo pie,** to have the same faults.

cojera *nf* limp, lameness.

cojín *nm* cushion.

cojinete nm *Téc* beaxing. ■ **c.de agujas/bolas,** needle/ ball bearing.

cojo,-a I *adj (persona)* lame, limping; *(mueble)* wobbly; *fig (defectuoso)* faulty, incomplete. **II** *nm,f* lame person.

cojón *vulg* **1** *nm Anat* ball; **de cojones,** *(estupendo)* fucking brilliant *or* good; *(pésimo)* fucking awful *or* bad; **ponérsele los cojones como corbata,** to shit bricks; **por cojones,** like it or not; **tener cojones,** to have guts *or* balls. **II** *interj* fuck it!

cojonudo,-a *adj vulg* fucking great.

col *nf Bot* cabbage. ■ **c. de Bruselas,** Brussels sprout; **c. lombarda,** red cabbage; **c. rizada,** kale, collard.

col. 1 *abr de* **columna,** column, col. **2** *abr de* **colección,** collection.

cola¹ *nf* **1** *Av Zool* tail; *(de vestido)* train; *(de chaqueta)* tail. ■ **c. de caballo,** *Bot* horsetail; *(peinado)* ponytail. **2** *fam (pene)* willie. **3** *(parte posterior)* **a la c.,** at the back *or* rear. ■ *Ferroc* **vagón de c.,** rear coach. **4** *(fila)* queue, *US line;* **hacer c.,** to queue (up), *US* stand in line; **ponerse en la c.,** to get into the queue; *fam* **traer c.,** to have consequences.

cola² *nf* glue; *fam* **no pega ni con c.,** it doesn't match at all.

colaboración *nf* **1** collaboration. **2** *Prensa* contribution.

colaboracionismo *nm pol* collaboration.

colaboracionista *Pol* **I** *adj* collaborating. **II** *nmf* collaborator.

colaborador,-a I *adj* collaborating. **II** *nm,f* **1** collaborator. **2** *Prensa* contributor.

colaborar *vi* **1** to collaborate, cooperate. **2** *Prensa* to contribute.

colación *nf* **1** *(refrigerio)* light meal, snack. **2** *(cotejo)* collation; **sacar** *or* **traer (algo) a c.,** to bring (sth) up. **3** *SAm Culin (grajea, confite)* sweet. **4** *Méx Culin* mixed sweets *pl.*

coladera *nf* **1** *Am (alcantarilla)* sewer. **2** *Méj (desagüe)* grate.

colada *nf* **1** *(lavado)* wash, laundry; **hacer la c.,** to do the washing *or* laundry. **2** *Metal* tapping. **3** *Geol (volcánica)* outflow.

colado,-a I *pp de* **colar. II** *adj* **1** *(líquido)* filtered,-strained. **2** *fam (enamorado)* madly in love, head over heels (in love).

colador *nm (de té, café)* strainer; *(para comida, caldo)* colander, sieve; *fig* **como un c.,** full of holes, like a sieve; *fam* **dejar como un c.,** to be riddled with bullets.

coladura *nf fam* clanger, slip-up.

colapsar I *vtr* to cause to collapse. **II colapsarse** *vr* to break down, collapse.

colapso *nm* **1** *Med* collapse. **2** *(de tráfico)* traffic jam, hold-up.

colar I *vtr* **1** *(líquido)* to strain, filter. **2** *fam (hacer pasar)* to pass, slip; *(moneda)* to pass off; *(hecho, historia)* to give. **II** *vi fam* to wash; **esto no colará,** this won't wash. **III colarse** *vr* **1** *(escabullirse)* to slip in, gatecrash; *(en una cola)* to jump the queue. **2** *fam (equivocarse)* to slip up, make a mistake; *(enamorarse)* to fall (for).

colateral *adj* collateral.

colcha *nf* bedspread.

colchón *nm* mattress. ■ *Téc* **c. de aire,** air cushion; **c. neumático,** air mattress.

colchonería *nf* mattress maker's (shop).

colchonero,-a *nm,f* mattress maker.

colchoneta *nf Dep* small mattress.

colear *vi* **1** *(perro)* to wag its tail; *(vaca)* to switch its tail; *fam* **vivito y coleando,** alive and kicking. **2** *.fam (seguir)* to drag on; *fam* **el asunto aún colea,** we haven't heard the last of it yet. **3** *Am (animal)* to tackle by the tail. **4** *CAm PR (edad)* to be close on an age.

colección *nf* collection.

coleccionar *vtr* to collect.

coleccionista *nmf* collector.

colecta *nf* collection.

colectivero *nm Arg* minibus driver.

colectividad community; **en c.,** communally.

colectivización *nf* collectivization.

colectivizar *vtr* to collectivize.

colectivo,-a I *adj* collective. **II** *nm* **1** *(asociación)* association, guild. **2** *Ling* collective noun. **3** *Arg Par* hired car.

colector *nm* **1** *(sumidero)* main sewer. **2** *Téc* **c. de admisión/escape,** inlet/exhaust manifold.

colega *nmf* **1** colleague. **2** *arg (amigo)* buddy, chum, mate.

colegiado,-a I *pp de* **colegiarse. II** *adj* **1** *(afiliado)* collegiate. **2** *(colectivo)* collective. **III** *nm* collegian; *Dep* referee.

colegial I *adj* **1** collegial collegiate. **2** *(escolar)* school; **vida c.,** school life. **II** *nm* **1** schoolboy; **los colegiales,** the schoolchildren. **2** *Méx (mal jinete)* bad horseman.

colegiala *nf* schoolgirl.

colegiarse *vr* to join a professional association.

colegiata *nf* collegiate church.

colegio, *nm* **1** *(escuela)* school; **de vuelta al c.,** back to school. ■ **c. privado** *or* **de pago,** GB public *or* independent school. **2** *(asociación profesional)* association, college: **c. de abogados,** the Bar. ■ *Pol* **c. electoral,** electoral college. **3** *Univ (residencia)* **c. mayor** *or* **universitario,** hall of residence.

colegir *vtr* to infer, deduce.

cólera¹ *nf* **1** *(ira)* anger, rage; **montar en c.,** to fly into a temper. **2** *(bilis)* bile.

cólera² *nm Med* cholera.

colérico,-a *adj* **I** *(encolerizado)* furious. **2** *(carácter)* bad-tempered.

colesterina *nf,* **colesterol** *nm Med* cholesterin, cholesterol.

coleta *nf* pigtail, ponytail; **cortarse la c.,** *Taur* to retire from bullfighting; *fig* to retire.

coletazo *nm* **1** *(golpe de cola)* wag *or* swish of the tail; *Aut* **dar coletazos,** to sway about. **2** *fig (manifestación última)* death throes *pl,* final tremor, stir.

coletilla *nf* postcript, addition.

coleto *nm (prenda)* doublet; *fig* **echarse algo al c.,** *(comer)* to eat sth right up; *(beber)* to drink sth down.

colgado,-a I *pp de* **colgar. II** *adj* **1** hanging; **un jamón c. del techo,** a leg of ham hanging from the ceiling. **2** *(ahorcado)* hung. **3** *fam Educ* **tener asignaturas colgadas,** to still have subjects to pass. **4** *arg* **dejar (a algn) c.,** to leave (sb) in the lurch. **5** *arg (drogado)* stoned, high.

colgador *nm* (coat) hanger.

colgadura *nf (gen pl)* hangings *pl, US* drapes *pl.*

colgajo *nm* **1** *(de ropa)* rag, torn piece. **2** *(de uva)* bunch. **3** *Med (de piel)* flap, graft.

colgante I *adj* hanging. **II** *nm* **1** *Arquit (festón)* festoon. **2** *(joya)* pendant.

colgar I *vtr* **1** *(gen)* to hang (up); *(colada)* to hang (out). **2** *(ahorcar)* to hang. **3** *fam (suspender)* to fail; **me han colgado en matemáticas,** I've failed maths. **4** *(abandonar)* **c. los libros,** to give up studying. **II** *vi* **1** to hang **(de,** from); **cuelga de un lado,** it dips on one side; *fig* **c. de un hilo,** to hang by a thread. **2** *Tel* to put down, hang up; **me han colgado,** they've hung up on me; **¡no cuelgue!,** hold on! **III colgarse** *vr (ahorcarse)* to hang oneself.

colibrí *nm Orn* humming bird.

cólico *nm Med* colic.

coliflor *nf Bot* cauliflower.

coligallero *nm CAm* miner who steals gold to sell.

colijo *indic pres véase* **colegir.**

colilla *nf* (cigarette) end *or* butt.

colimbo *nm Orn* diver.

colina *nf Geog* hill, slope.

colindante *adj* adjoining, adjacent.

colindar *vi* to be adjacent **(con,** to).

colirio *nm Farm* eyewash, collyrium.

colirrojo *nm Orn* redstart.

coliseo *nm Arquit* coliseum, colosseum.

colisión *nf* collision, crash, clash.

colisionar *vi* to collide, crash, clash.

colista *nmf Dep (persona, equipo)* last.

colitis *nf Med* colitis.

collado *nm* **1** *(colina)* hill. **2** *(paso entre montañas)* pass.

collage *nm Arte* collage.

collalba *nf Orn* wheatear.

collar *nm* **1** *(adorno)* necklace. **2** *(de perro)* collar. **3** *Téc (abrazadera)* collar, ring.

collera *nf* **1** *(de arreos)* collar. **2** *Am (pareja)* couple. **3** *Arg Chi (animales)* pair. **4** *SAm* **colleras,** *(gemelos)* cufflinks.

colmado,-a I *pp de* **colmar. II** *adj* full, filled; **una cucharada colmada,** a heaped teaspoonful. **III** *nm* grocer's (shop), *US* grocery store.

colmar *vtr* **1** to fill (right up); *(vaso, copa)* to fill to the brim. **2** *fig* to shower, overwhelm; **nos colmaron de regalos,** they showered us with gifts. **3** *fig (ambiciones)* to fulfil, satisfy.

colmena *nf* beehive; *fig* **c. humana,** humas hive.

colmenar *nm* apiary.

colmenero,-a *nm,* beekeeper.

colmillo *nm Anat* eye *or* canine tooth; *Zool (de carnívoro)* fang; *(de jabalí, elefante)* tusk; *fig* **enseñar los colmillos,** *(los animales)* to bare its teeth; *fig* to show one's teeth.

colmo *nm* height, summit; **el c. de la ineficacia,** the height of inefficiency; **¡eso es el c!,** that's the last straw!; **para c. (de desgracias),** to top it all.

colocación *nf* **1** *(acto)* positioning, collocation. **2** *(situación)* situation, place. **3** *Fin (de capital)* investment. **4** *(empleo)* job, employment.

colocado,-a I *pp de* **colocar. II** *adj* **I** *(empleado)* cmployed; **estar muy bien c.,** to have a very good job. **2** *arg (embriagado)* sozzled; *(drogado)* stoned, high.

colocar I *vtr* **1** *(gen)* to place, put; *(alfombra)* to lay; *(cuadro)* to hang; *Mil (tropas)* to position. **2** *Fin (invertir)* to invest. **3** *(emplear)* to give work to. **4** *fam (casar)* to marry off; **ha colocado a todas sus hijas,** he's married off all his daughters. **5** *fam (artículos defectuosos)* to fob off. **6** *arg (drogar)* to stone. **II colocarse** *vr* **1** *(situarse)* to put *or* install *or US* instal oneself **2** *(emplearse)* to take a job, **se ha colocado de secretaria,** she's got a job as a secretary **3** *Dep (clasificarse)* to be, **se colocó en tercer lugar,** he moved into third position *or* place **4** *arg (embriagarse)* to get sozzled, *(drogarse)* to get stoned *or* high

colocho *nm CAm* **1** *(viruta)* wood shaving **2** *(rizo)* curl, ringlet

colocón *nm arg* high

colofón *nm* **1** *(apéndice)* colophon **2** *fig (remate)* crowning, climax

coloidal *adj* colloidal.

coloide *nm* colloid

colombiano,-a *adj & nm,f* Colombian.

colombino,-a *adj* of *or* relating to Christopher Columbus

colombofilia *nf* pigeon breeding

colombófilo,-I *adj* pigeon-breeding. **II** *nm, f* pigeon breeder

colon *nm Anat* colon

colón *nm* **1** *Fin* standard monetary unit of Costa Rica and El Salvador **2** *nm* **Cristóbal C.,** Christopher Columbus

colonia¹ *nf* **1** *Biol Pol* colony, **c. de veraneantes,** colony *or* group of holiday-makers. **2** *(gen pl) (campamento)* summer camp

colonia² *nf (agua de colonia)* cologne

coloniaje *nm Am Hist (período)* colonial period

colonial I *adj* **1** *Pol* colonial **2** *Com* imported. **II coloniales** *nmpl* imported *or* overseas foodstuffs

colonialismo *nm* colonialism

colonialista *adj & nmf* colonialist

colonización *nf* colonization

colonizador,-a I *adj* colonizing **II** *nm, f* colonizer, colonist

colonizar *vtr* to colonize

colono *nm* **1** *Agr* tenant farmer **2** *(habitante)* colonist, colonial, settler

coloquial *adj* colloquial

coloquialismo *nm* colloquialism

coloquio *nm* discussion, colloquium

color *nm* **1** colour, *US* color, **c. rojo,** red, *Tex* **c. sólido,** fast colour, **dar c.,** *(colorear)* to colour, *fig (animar)* to liven up, **de c.,** *(en colores)* in colour, coloured, *euf (persona)* coloured, **de colores,** multicoloured, *Cin Fot* **en color(es),** in colour, *fig* **un discurso carece de c.,** a boring speech, *fig Pol* **sin distinción de credos ni colores,** without prejudice to race or creed, *fig (picante)* **subido de c.,** risqué, *fig* **verlo todo de c. de rosa,** to see life through rosecoloured spectacles **2** *(colorido)* colour, *US* color **3 colores,** *(bandera)* colours, *US* colors, flag *sing, Dep (equipo)* team *sing*

coloración *nf* coloration, colouring, *US* coloring

colorado,-a I *adj* red, **ponerse c.,** to blush **II** *nm* red

colorante I *adj* colouring, *US* coloring **II** *nm* colouring, *US* coloring, dye

colorear *vtr* to colour, *US* color

colorete *nm* rouge

colorido *nm* colour, *US* color

colorín *nm* **1** bright *or* vivid colour *or US* color, **y c. colorado, este cuento se ha acabado,** and that's the end of the story **2** *Orn* goldfinch

colorismo *nm Arte* predominant use of colour *or US* color

colorista I *adj* colouristic, *US* coloristic **II** *nmf* colourist, *US* colorist

colosal *adj* **1** colossal **2** *fig (extraordinario)* splendid, excellent

coloso *nm* colossus

coludo,-a *adj Am* absent-minded

columbario *nm* columbarium

columbrar *vtr* **1** *(vislumbrar)* to see, make out **2** *fig (conjeturar)* to guess

columna *nf* column ■ *Anat* **c. vertebral,** vertebral column, spinal column

columnata *nf* colonnade

columnista *nmf Prensa* columnist

columpiar I *vtr (mecerse)* to swing **II columpiarse** *vr* **1** *(mecerse)* to swing. **2** *fam (meter la pata)* to drop a clanger

columpio *nm* swing.

colza *nf* colza, **aceite de c.,** colza oil

coma[1] *nf* **1** *Ling Mús* comma, **sin faltar (ni) una c.,** down to the last detail ■ **punto y c.,** semicolon **2** *Mat* point

coma[2] *nm Med* coma, **entrar en c.,** to go into a coma

comadre *nf* **1** *(vecina)* neighbour, *(amiga)* friend. **2** *pey (chismosa)* old wife, gossip, gossipmonger **3** *(madrina)* godmother **4** *fam (alcahueta)* gobetween

comadrear *vi* to gossip

comadreja *nf Zool* weasel

comadreo *nm* gossip, gossiping, tittle-tattle

comadrería *nf* piece of gossip.

comadrona *nf* midwife

comandancia *nf* **1** *(distrito, graduación)* command **2** *(local, edificio)* commander's headquarters **3** *(zona)* area under a commander's jurisdiction

comandante *nm* **1** *Mil (oficial)* commander, commanding officer, *(graduación)* ≈ major **2** *Av* pilot

comandar *vtr Mil* to command

comandita *nf Com* **(sociedad en) c.,** limited *or US* silent partnership, *fam* **en en c.,** to go en masse

comanditar *vtr Com* to enter as a sleeping *or US* silent partner

comanditario,-a *adj* sleeping, *US* silent, **sociedad comanditaria,** limited *or* silent partnership

comando *nm* **1** *Mil* commando **2** *Inform* command

comarca *nf* region, area

comarcal *adj* regional, local

comatoso,-a *adj Med* comatose; **en estado c.,** in coma

comba *nf* **1** *(curvatura)* curve, bend. **2** *(juego)* skipping, *(cuerda)* skipping rope, **saltar a la c.,** to skip

combadura *nf (de cuerda, cable)* bend, curve, *(de viga, pared)* sag, bulge

combar I *vtr (curvar)* to bend **II combarse** *vr (curvarse)* to bend, curve, *(una pared)* to sag

combate *nm* **1** *(lucha)* combat, struggle, *Box* fight, *Mil* battle, **fuera de c.,** knockout, *(eliminado)* out of action, **librar c.,** to wage battle **2** *Méx (ayuda)* mutual help

combatiente I *adj* fighting **II** *nmf (persona)* fighter, combatant **III** *nm Orn* ruff

combatir I *vtr (luchar)* to fight, *fig (oponerse)* to combat **II** *vi* to fight, struggle *(contra,* against)

combatividad *nf* fighting spirit, aggressiveness.

combativo,-a *adj* spirited, aggressive.

combinación *nf* **1** combination. **2** *(prenda)* slip. **3** *fam* fiddle, wangle.

combinado,-a I *pp de* **combinar. II** *adj* combined, mixed. **III** *nm (mezcla)* mixture; *(cóctel)* cocktail.

combinar I *vtr* **1** *(ingredientes, esfuerzos)* to combine. **2** *(colores)* to go with, match. **II combinarse** *vr* to combine.

combo,-a *adj* bent, curved; *(pared)* sagging.

combustible I *adj* combustible. **II** *nm* fuel.

combustión *nf* combustion.

comecocos *nm inv arg (de tragaperras)* pac-man; *(asunto, libro, etc)* soul-destroyer.

comedero *nm* feeding trough, manger.

comedia *nf Teat* comedy; *fig (farsa)* sham, farce; **hacer c.,** to put on an act. ■ **c. de enredo,** farce.

comediante,-a *nm, f Teat (hombre)* actor; *(mujer)* actress; *fig (hipócrita)* hypocrite, comedian.

comedido,-a *pp de* **comedirse. II** *adj* **1** *(moderado)* self-restrained, moderate, reserved. **2** *Am (servicial)* helpful, obliging, pleasing.

comedimiento *nm* restraint, moderation.

comediógrafo,-a *nm, f Teat* playwright, dramatist.

comedirse *vr* **1** *(moderarse)* to restrain oneself. **2** *Arg Ecuad (entrometerse)* to meddle, interfere.

comedor,-a I *adj* big-eating; **es muy c.,** he's a big eater. **II** *nm* **1** *(sala)* dining room; *(de fábrica)* canteen; *(de universidad)* refectory. **2** *Mueb* dining-room suite.

comensal *nmf* companion at table.

comentar *vtr (escribir)* to comment on; *(hablar, discutir)* to discuss, talk about.

comentario *nm* **1** *(observación)* comment, remark; *Lit Rad TV (crítica)* commentary. **2 comentarios,** *(murmuración)* gossip; **sin c.,** no comment.

comentarista *nmf Prensa Rad TV* commentator.

comenzar *vtr & vi* to begin, start, commence; comenzó a llover, it started raining *or* to rain; **comenzó diciendo que ...,** he started by saying that ... .

comer I *vtr* **1** to eat; **c. paella,** to have paella; *fam* **sin comerlo ni beberlo,** without having had anything to do with it. **2** *(color)* to fade. **3** *(corroer)* to corrode; *fig* **me come la envidia,** I'm green with envy. **4** *Ajedrez* to take, capture. **5** *fig (gastar)* to eat away; *(combustible)* to use (up). **II** *vi* to eat; **dar de c. a algn,** to feed sb; **echar de c. (a los animales),** to feed (animals); **¿has comido?,** have you eaten yet?; **no tener qué c.,** not to have enough to live on; *fig* **c. a dos carrillos,** to gulp down one's food. **III comerse** *vr* **1** to eat; **c. las uñas,** to bite one's nails; **¡cómetelo!,** eat it up!; *fig* **c. a algn a besos,** to smother sb with kisses; *fig* **c. a algn con los ojos,** to look at sb lovingly; *fig* **c. algo con los ojos,** to devour sth with one's eyes; *fam* **¿eso con qué se come?,** what the heck is that?; *vulg* **esta tía está como para comérsela,** I could really give her one. **2** *fig (saltarse)* to omit; *(párrafo)* to skip; *(palabra)* to swallow; **se come las palabras,** he slurs (his words). **3** *(color)* to fade.

comercial *adj* commercial, sales; **banco/tratado c.,** commercial bank/treaty; **película c.,** commercial film *or US* movie.

comercialización *nf* commercialization, marketing.

comercializar *vtr* to commercialize, market.

comerciante I *adj* business-minded. **II** *nmf* merchant; *pey* **ser (un) c.,** to be a moneymaker.

comerciar *vi (comprar y vender)* to trade, buy and sell; *(hacer negocios)* to do business.

comercio *nm* **1** commerce, trade; **c. exterior,** foreign trade. ■ **Cámara de C.,** Chamber of Commerce; **libre c.,** free trade. **2** *(tienda)* shop.

comestible I *adj* edible, eatable. **II comestibles** *nmpl* food *sing*, foodstuff(s); **tienda de comestibles,** grocer's shop, *US* grocery store.

cometa I *nm Astron* comet. **II** *nf (juguete)* kite.

cometer *vtr (error, falta)* to make; *(delito, crimen)* to commit.

cometido *nm* **1** *(tarea)* task, assignment; **desempeñar su c.,** to carry out one's task. **2** *(deber)* duty; **cumplir su c.,** to do one's duty.

comezón *nm* itch, itching; **sentir c.,** to have an itch; *fig* **sentía c. por replicar,** I was itching to answer back.

cómic *nm Arte Lit* comic.

comicial *adj* of *or* relating to elections.

comicidad *nf* comicalness, funniness.

comicios *nmpl Pol* elections.

cómico,-a I *adj* **1** *(divertido)* comical, comic, funny. **2** *Teat* comedy; **actor c.,** comedian. **II** *nm, f* comic; *(hombre)* comedian; *(mujer)* comedienne.

comida *nf* **1** *(alimento)* food; **c. y casa,** food and accommodation. **2** *(acción)* meal; **tres comidas al día,** three meals a day; **c. campestre,** picnic. **3** *(almuerzo)* lunch.

comidilla *nf fam* talk; **esa pareja es la c. del barrio,** that couple are the talk of the street.

comido,-a I *pp de* **comer. II** *adj* eaten; **c. por la polilla,** motheaten; **se fueron comidos,** they went after having had lunch.

comience I *subj pres véase* **comenzar. II** *imperat véase* **comenzar.**

comienzo *nm* beginning, start; **a comienzos de,** at the beginning of; **dar c. (a algo),** to begin *or* start (sth); **en sus comienzos,** in its early stages.

comilón,-ona I *adj* greedy, gluttonous. **II** *nm,f* big eater, glutton.

comilona *nf fam* big meal, feast.

comillas *nfpl* inverted commas; **entre c.,** in inverted commas.

comino *nm Bot* cumin, cummin; *fam* **me importa un c.,** I don't give a damn (about it); *fam* **no valer un c.,** not to be worth tuppence.

comisaría *nf* police station.

comisario *nm* **1** (*de policía*) police inspector. **2** (*delegado*) commissioner, deputy, delegate.

comiscar *vtr & vi fam* to nibble.

comisión *nf* **1** *Com* (*retribución*) commission; **a** *or* **con c.,** on a commission basis; **cobrar (una) c.,** to get a commission (**por** *or* **sobre,** on). **2** (*comité*) committee; **c. permanente,** standing commission. **3** *Jur* (*perpetración*) perpetration, committing.

comisionado,-a I *pp de* **comisionar. II** *adj* commissioned. **III** *nm,f* commissioner.

comisionar *vtr* to commission.

comisura *nf Anat* corner, angle.

comité *nm* committee.

comitiva *nf* suite, retinue, procession.

como I *adv* **1** as; (*modo, manera*) **blanco c. el marmol,** as white as snow; **dilo c. quieras,** say it however you like; **estás c. ausente,** you are in another world; **habla c. su padre,** he talks like his father; **me gusta c. cantas,** I like the way you sing; **tanto c. eso no,** not as much as that. **2** (*en calidad de*) as; **c. presidente,** as president; **lo compré c. recuerdo,** I bought it as a souvenir. **3** about; (*aproximadamente*) **c. a la mitad de camino,** halfway; **c. unos diez,** about ten. **4** (*según, conforme*) as; **c. decíamos ayer,** anyway, as we were saying yesterday. **II** *conj* **1** *desus* (*así que*) as; **c. llegaban se sentaban,** they sat as they came in. **2** (*que*) **no vimos nada de tanta gente c. había,** there were so many people that we couldn't see a thing. **3** (*si*) if; **c. no estudies vas a suspender,** if you don't study hard, you'll fail. **4** (*porque*) as, since; **c. no venías me marché,** as you didn't come I left. **5** (*modo, comparación*) as; **c. si nada** *or* **tal cosa,** as if nothing had happened; *fam* **c. si lo viera,** I can imagine perfectly well. **6 c. quiera,** *véase* **comoquiera.**

cómo I *adv* **1** (*interrogativo*) how, what; **¿c. es de grande/ancho?,** how big/wide is it?; **¿c. estás?,** how are you?; **¿c. ha dicho?,** I beg your pardon?; **¿c. lo sabes?,** how do you know?; (*a cuanto*) **¿a c. están los tomates?,** how much are the tomatoes?; (*por qué*) **¿c. fue que no viniste a la fiesta?,** why didn't you come to the party?; *fam* **¿c?,** what?; *fam* **¿c. es eso?,** **¿c. así?,** how come? **2** (*exclamativo*) how; **¡c. corre el tiempo!,** how time flies!; **¡c. has crecido!,** you've really grown a lot!; **¡c. no!,** but of course! **II** *nm* **el c. y el porqué,** the whys and wherefores.

cómoda *nf Mueb* chest of drawers, commode.

comodidad *nf* comfort, convenience; **con c.,** comfortably.

comodín *nm Naipes* joker; *fig* excuse.

cómodo,-a *adj* **1** comfortable; **ponerse c.,** to make oneself comfortable. **2** (*útil*) handy, convenient.

comodón,-ona *fam* **I** *adj* comfort-loving. **II** *nm,f* comfort lover.

comodoro *nm Mil* commodore.

comoquiera *adv* **1** (*de cualquier manera*) anyway, anyhow; **c. que sea,** whatever way, one way or another. **2** (*puesto que*) **c. que no estaba enterado,** as he didn't know.

compactar *vtr* to compact, compress.

compacto,-a *adj* compact, dense.

compadecer I *vtr* to feel sorry for, pity. **II compadecerse** *vr* to have *or* take pity (**de,** on).

compadraje *nm* conspiracy, plot.

compadre *nm* **1** (*padrino*) godfather. **2** *Am fam* (*amigo, compañero*) friend, mate. **3** *Arg Par* (*matón*) smoothy, boaster.

compadrear *vi* **1** *Am* (*ser amigos*) to be friends. **2** *Arg Par Urug* (*jactarse*) to bluster, boast. **3** *Arg Par Urug* (*hacer ostentación*) to show off.

compaginar I *vtr* **1** (*combinar*) to combine, make compatible, reconcile. **2** *Impr* to make up. **II compaginarse** *vr* to be compatible, go together

compaña *nf fam* company, friends.

compañerismo *nm* companionship, comradeship, fellowship.

compañero,-a *nm,f* **1** companion, mate, friend; **c. de armas,** comrade-in-arms; **c. de colegio** *or* **escuela,** schoolmate; **c. de equipo,** team-mate; **c. de habitación,** roommate. **2** *fig* (*de zapato, guante, etc*) other one.

compañía *nf* **1** (*gen*) company; **malas compañías,** bad company; **señora de c.,** lady companion; **hacer c. (a algn),** to keep (sb) company; **en c. de,** in the company of. **2** (*empresa*) company. ▪ **c. de seguros/de teatro,** insurance/theatre company. **3** *Mil* company.

comparable *adj* comparable.

comparación *nf* comparison; **en c.,** comparatively; **en c. con,** compared to; **sin c.,** beyond compare.

comparado,-a I *pp de* **comparar. II** *adj* comparative.

comparar *vtr* to compare; *fam* **¡no compares!,** far from it!

comparativo,-a *adj & nm* comparative.

comparecencia *nf Jur* appearance; **no c.,** nonappearance.

comparecer *vi* **1** *Jur* to appear (**ante,** before). **2** (*presentarse*) to show up.

comparsa I *nf* **1** *Teat* extras *pl.* **2** (*de carnaval*) group of people in carnival dress, masquerade. **II** *nm,f* walk-on, extra.

compartimentado,-a *adj* partitioned.

compartimento *nm,* **compartimiento** *nm* compartment. ▪ *Téc* **c. estanco,** watertight compartment; *Ferroc Náut* **c. de primera/segunda clase,** first-/second-class compartment.

compartir *vtr* **1** (*dividir*) to divide (up), share (out). **2** (*piso, opinión*) to share.

compás *nm* **1** *Téc* (*instrumento*) (pair of) compasses. **2** *Náut* (*brújula*) compass. **3** *Mús* (*división*) time; (*intervalo*) beat; (*ritmo*) rhythm; **c. de espera,** *Mús* bar rest; *fig* (*pausa*) delay; **al c, (de una música),** in time (to music); **llevar el c.,** (*con la mano*) to beat time; (*bailando*) to keep time; **perder el c.,** to lose the beat.

compasión *nf* compassion, pity; **una persona sin c.,** a merciless person; **tener c. (de algn),** to feel sorry (for sb).

compasivo,-a *adj* compassionate, sympathetic.

compatibilidad *nf* compatibility.

compatible *adj* compatible.

compatriota *nmf* compatriot; (*hombre*) fellow countryman; (*mujer*) fellow countrywoman.

compeler *vtr fnl* to compel, force.

compendiar *vtr* to abridge, summarize.

compendio *nm* summary, résumé, synopsis.

compenetración *nf* **1** (*persona*) mutual understanding. **2** *Fís* interpenetration.

compenetrarse *vr* 1 *(persona)* to understand each other *or* one another; **ella se compenetra muy bien con su papel,** she identifies herself very well with her role. 2 *Fís* to interpenetrate.

compensación *nf* compensation, indemnity; **en c.,** *(en pago)* in payment, as compensation; *(a cambio)* in exchange. ■ *Fin* **c. bancaria,** clearing.

compensador,-a I *adj* compensating. II *nm* compensator.

compensar I *vtr (pérdida, error)* to make up for; *(indemnizar)* to compensate (for), indemnify (against, for); *Téc* to balance, compensate; **te compensaré con diez mil pesetas,** I'll give you ten thousand pesetas as *or* in compensation. II *vi* to be worthwhile; **este trabajo no me compensa,** this job's not worth my time.

competencia *nf* 1 *(rivalidad)* competition; *(a algn, producto)* **hacer la c.,** to compete with *or* against. 2 *(incumbencia)* field, scope, province; **eso no es de mi c.,** that is outside my scope *or* not in my field. 3 *(capacidad)* ability, competence, proficiency.

competente *adj* 1 *(adecuado)* appropriate. 2 *(capaz)* competent, proficient. 3 *Jur* competent.

competer *vtr (incumbir)* to come under the jurisdiction of; *(concerner)* to be in the field of; *(corresponder)* to be up to.

competición *nf* competition, contest.

competido,-a *pp de* **competir.** II *adj* hard-fought.

competidor,-a I *adj* competing. II *nm, f* 1 *Com Dep* competitor. 2 *(participante)* contestant, candidate. 3 *(rival)* rival, opponent.

competir *vi* 1 to compete (**con,** with *or* against; **en,** in; **por,** for). 2 *(rivalizar)* to rival.

competitivo,-a *adj* competitive.

compilación *nf* 1 *(acción)* compiling. 2 *(colección)* compilation.

compilador,-a *nm, f* compiler.

compilar *vtr* to compile.

compinche *nmf* 1 *fam (compañero)* chum, pal. 2 *pey (cómplice)* accomplice.

complacencia *nf* 1 *(satisfacción)* satisfaction. 2 *(indulgencia)* indulgence; **tener excesivas complacencias con** *or* **hacia algn,** to be overindulgent towards sb.

complacer I *vtr* 1 *(agradar)* to please; **¿en qué puedo complacerle?,** what can I do for you?; *fml* **me complace presentarles a ...,** it gives me great pleasure to introduce to you ... 2 *(satisfacer)* to satisfy, gratify; *fml* to oblige. II **complacerse** *vr* 1*(satisfacerse)* to delight (**en,** in), take pleasure (**en,** in). 2 *fml* to take pleasure in, be pleased to.

complacido,-a I *pp de* **complacer.** II *adj* pleased, satisfied.

complaciente *adj* 1 *(agradable)* obliging, helpful. 2 *Lit (marido)* complaisant.

complejidad *nf* complexity.

complejo,-a I *adj* complex. II *nm* *Ind Psic* complex.

complementar I *vtr* to complement. II **complementarse** *vr* to complement (each other), be complementary to (each other).

complementario,-a *adj* complementary.

complemento *nm* 1 *(gen)* complement. ■ *Mil* **oficial de c.,** reserve officer. 2 *Ling* complement, object; **c. directo,** direct object. 3 *(perfección)* culmination, perfection.

completar *vtr (gen)* to complete; *(perfeccionar)* to round off; *(acabar)* to finish.

completo,-a *adj* 1 *(terminado)* complete, completed; **por c.,** completely; *(perfecto)* round, perfect; *(terminado)* finished. 2 *(total)* full; **al c.,** full up, to capacity. ◆ **completamente** *adv* completely.

complexión *nf Anat* build; **de c. fuerte,** well-built.

complicación *nf* complication; **buscarse complicaciones,** to make life difficult for oneself.

complicado,-a I *pp de* **complicar.** II *adj* 1 *(complejo)* complicated, complex. 2 *(implicado)* involved. 3 *(persona)* complex.

complicar I *vtr* 1 *(gen)* to make complicated, complicate. 2 *(involucrar)* to involve (**en,** in). II **complicarse** *vr* *(gen)* to get complicated; **c. la vida,** to make life difficult for oneself.

cómplice *nmf* accomplice.

complicidad *nf* complicity.

complot *nm* (*pl* **complots**) conspiracy, plot.

componenda *nf* shady deal; **hacer componendas,** to scheme.

componente I *adj* component, constituent. II *nm* 1 *(parte, pieza)* component, constituent; *(ingrediente)* ingredient. 2 *(persona)* member. 3 *Meteor* **viento de c. norte/sur,** northerly/southerly wind.

componer *(pp* **compuesto)** I *vtr* 1 *(formar)* to compose, make up, form. 2 *(reparar)* to mend, fix, repair. 3 *(discusión etc)* to settle; *(ánimos etc)* to soothe. 4 *(música, versos)* to compose. 5 *Impr (texto, página)* to compose, set. 6 *(adornar)* to decorate, adorn. II **componerse** *vr* 1 *(consistir)* to be made up (**de,** of), consist (**de,** of). 2 *(engalanarse, arreglarse)* to dress up. 3 *fam* **componérselas,** to manage; **¿cómo te las compondrás para hacerlo?,** how will you manage to do it?

comportamiento *nm* behaviour, *US* behavior, conduct.

comportar I *vtr (implicar)* to entail, involve. II **comportarse** *vr (conducirse)* to behave; **c. mal,** to misbehave; **saber c.,** to know how to behave oneself.

composición *nf* 1 *(gen)* composition; **hacer(se) una c. de lugar,** *(decidirse)* to make a plan of action; *(formarse una idea)* to get a picture of a situation. 2 *(acuerdo)* settlement; *(reconciliación)* reconciliation. 3 *Impr* setting, composition.

compositor,-a *nm, f Mús* composer.

compostelano,-a I *adj of or* from Santiago de Compostela. II *nm, f* native *or* inhabitant of Santiago de Compostela.

compostura *nf* 1 *(composición)* composition, arrangement. 2 *(reparación)* mending, repair. 3 *(moderación)* restraint, moderation; *(dignidad)* composure; **nunca pierde la c.,** he never loses his composure. 4 *(convenio)* agreement.

compota *nf Culin* compote.

compra *nf* purchase, buy; **la c. de un piso,** the purchase of a flat; **ir de c.,** to go shopping. ■ **c. a crédito,** credit purchase; **c. a plazes,** hire purchase, *US* instalment buying.

comprador,-a *nm, f* purchaser, buyer, shopper.

comprar I *vtr* 1 to buy; **cómprame uno,** *(para mí)* buy me one, buy one for me; *(yo te lo vendo)* buy one from me. 2 *fig (sobornar)* to bribe, buy off. II **comprarse** *vr* to buy (for oneself); **me compré una bicicleta,** I bought myself a bicycle.

compraventa *nf Com* buying and selling, dealing; **contrato de c.,** contract of sale.

comprender I *vtr* 1 *(entender)* to understand; **¿comprendes?,** you see?; **c. mal,** to misunderstand; **hacerse c.,** to make oneself understood; **se comprende,** it's understandable. 2 *(contener)* to comprise, include; **viaje con todo comprendido,** all-in *or* inclusive trip. II **comprenderse** *vr* to understand each other *or* one another.

comprensible *adj* understandable.

comprensión *nf* understanding.

comprensivo,-a *adj* understanding.

compresa *nf* 1 *(higiénica)* sanitary towel. 2 *Med (vendaje)* compress.

compresibilidad *nf* compressibility.

compresible *adj* compressible.

compresión *nf* compression; **relación de c.,** compression ratio.

compresor,-a I *adj* compressing. **II** *nm* compressor.

comprimible *adj* compressible.

comprimido,-a I *pp de* **comprimir. II** *adj* compressed; **escopeta de aire c.,** air rifle. **III** *nm Farm* tablet.

comprimir I *vtr* to compress; *(gente)* to cram together. **II comprimirse** *vr* to get compressed; *(gente)* to squeeze.

comprobable *adj* verifiable, provable.

comprobación *nf* verification, check, checking.

comprobante *nm* 1 *Com (recibo, justificante)* voucher, receipt. 2 *Jur* document in proof.

comprobar *vtr* 1 *(verificar)* to verify, check; *(demostrar)* to prove. 2 *(confirmar)* to confirm; **compruébalo tú mismo,** see *or* look for yourself.

comprometedor,-a I *adj* *(cosa)* compromising. 2 *(persona)* troublemaking. **II** *nm,f* troublemaker.

comprometer *vtr* 1 *(arriesgar)* to endanger, risk, jeopardize; *(persona)* to compromise. 2 *(empeñar)* to commit; *(obligar)* to compel, oblige, force. 3 *(involucrar)* to involve. 4 *(poner en un aprieto)* to embarrass. **II comprometerse** *vr* 1 *(gen)* to compromise oneself. 2 *(obligarse)* to commit oneself; **c. a hacer algo,** to undertake to do sth. 3 *(involucrarse)* to involve oneself; **no te comprometas,** don't get involved.

comprometido,-a I *pp de* **comprometer, II** *adj* *(arriesgado)* in jeopardy; *(persona)* compromised. 2 *(obligado)* obliged, compelled. 3 *(involucrado)* involved. 4 *(para casarse)* engaged. 5 *(trabajo, situación)* delicate, difficult, awkward.

compromisario,-a *adj & nm,f* representative.

compromiso *nm* 1 *(obligación)* obligation, commitment; **libre de c.,** without obligation; **por c.,** out of a sense of duty; **ella siempre cumple sus compromisos,** she always meets her obligations. 2 *(acuerdo)* agreement. 3 *fml (cita)* appointment; *(amorosa)* date; **c. matrimonial,** engagement; **soltero y sin c.,** single and unattached. 4 *(situación difícil)* difficult situation; **poner (a algn) en un c.,** to put (sb) in a difficult *or* embarrassing situation. 5 *Méx* **compromisos,** *(rizos)* curls, ringlets.

compuerta *nf Téc* sluice, floodgate.

compuesto,-a I *pp de* **componer. II** *adj* 1 compound, composite; **palabra/sustancia compuesta,** compound word/substance. 2 *(elegante)* dressed up; *(arreglado)* tidy. 3 *(comedido)* composed, 4 *(reparado)* mended, repaired. **III** *nm* compound.

compulsa *nf* 1 *(cotejo)* collation, comparison. 2 *Jur (documento)* certified true copy.

compulsar *vtr* 1 *(cotejar)* to collate. 2 *Jur (hacer copia)* to make a certified true copy.

compulsión *nf* compulsion.

compulsivo,-a *adj* compulsory.

compunción *nf* *(arrepentimiento)* compunction; *(tristeza)* sorrow, sadness.

compungido,-a I *pp de* **compungir. II** *adj* *(arrepentido)* remorseful; *(triste)* sorrowful, sad.

compungir I *vtr* *(entristecer)* to make sorry *or* sad. **II compungirse** *vr* *(arrepentirse)* to feel remorseful; *(entristecerse)* to feel sorry *or* sad.

compuse *pt indef véase* **componer.**

computable *adj Inform* computable.

computación *nf Inform* computing.

computador,-a *nm,f Inform* computer.

computar *vtr* 1 *(calcular)* to compute, calculate. 2 *fml (conmutar)* to consider valid; **el primer año no se computa a efectos de antigüedad,** the first year doesn't count for seniority.

cómputo *nm* computation, calculation.

comulgante *nmf* communicant.

comulgar *vi* 1 *Rel* to receive Holy Communion. 2 *fig (compartir ideas, etc)* to share; **no comulgo con esas teorías,** I don't agree with these theories; *fam* **c. con ruedas de molino,** to be extremely gullible *or* credulous. **II** *vtr* to administer Holy Communion.

comulgatorio *nm Rel* communion rail.

común I *adj* 1 *(gen)* common; **bien c.,** common good; **de c. acuerdo,** by common consent; **hacer algo en c.,** to do sth jointly; **poco c.,** unusual; **por lo c.,** generally. 2 *(compartido)* shared, communal; **amigos comunes,** mutual friends; **dormitorio/televisión c.,** communal dormitory/television; **gastos comunes,** shared expenses. **II** *nm* 1 *(pueblo)* **el c.,** the community; *(mayoría)* **el c. de la gente,** the majority of people. 2 *GB Pol* **los Comunes,** the Commons.

comuna *nf* 1 *(comunidad)* commune. 2 *Am (municipio)* municipality; *(ayuntamiento)* town council.

comunal *adj* 1 *(común)* communal. 2 *Am (del municipio)* municipal.

comunicable *adj* 1 *(transmitible)* communicable. 2 *(comunicativo)* sociable.

comunicación *nf* 1 *(gen)* communication; **estar/ponerse en c. (con algn),** to be/get in touch (with sb); **vía de c.,** thoroughfare. 2 *(comunicado)* communication; *(oficial)* communiqué. 3 *Tel* connection. 4 *(unión)* link, connection. 5 **comunicaciones,** *(correos, transportes, etc)* communications.

comunicado,-a I *pp de* **comunicar. II** *adj* served; **una zona bien comunicada,** a well-served zone; **dos ciudades bien comunicadas,** two towns with good connections (between them). **III** *nm* *(parte)* communiqué; **c. a la prensa,** press release.

comunicante I *adj* *(que comunica)* communicating; **vasos comunicantes,** communicating vessels. **II** *nmf* *(informador)* informer.

comunicar I *vtr* 1 *(gen)* to communicate; **comuníquenoslo lo antes posible,** let us know as soon as possible. 2 *(transmitir)* to convey. 3 *(conectar)* to connect. **II** *vi* 1 *(estar, ponerse en comunicación)* to communicate; *(por carta)* to correspond **c. con algn,** to get in touch with sb. 2 *(estar conectado)* to be linked, be connected. 3 *Tel* to be engaged; **está comunicando,** the line is engaged. **III comunicarse** *vr* 1 *(gen)* to communicate. 2 *(transmitirse)* to be transmitted.

comunicativo,-a *adj* communicative, sociable.

comunidad *nf* community; **en c.,** together. ■ *Jur* **c. de bienes,** co-ownership; **c. de propietarios,** owners' association.

comunión *nf* 1 *(compenetración)* communion, fellowship. 2 *(comunidad)* community. 3 *Rel* Holy Communion.

comunismo *nm Pol* communism.

comunista *adj & nmf Pol* communist.

comunitario,-a *adj* 1 of *or* relating to the community; **centro c.,** community centre. 2 of *or* relating to the EEC, Community.

con *prep* 1 *(gen)* with; *(instrumento, medio, modo)* with; **¿c. qué lo cortarás?,** what will you cut it with?; **voy cómodo c. estas botas/este jersey,** I'm comfortable in these boots/this sweater. 2 *(en compañía, juntamente)* with; **c. buena salud,** in good health; **c. ese frío/niebla,** in that cold/fog; **estar c. (la) gripe/(un) resfriado,** to have the flu/a cold; **vine c. mi hermana,** I came with my sister. 3 *(contenido)* with; **una bolsa c. dinero,** a bag full of money. 4 *(relación)* to; **habló c. todos,** he spoke to everybody; **sé amable c. ella,** be nice to her. 5 *(con la condición)* as; **c. (sólo) que ...,** as long as ...; **c. tal (de) que ...,** provided that ...; **c. todo (y eso),** even so. 6 *(con infinitivo)* **c. llamar ya quedarás bien,** you'll make a good impression just by phoning. 7 *(a pesar de)* in spite of; **c. ser tan caro no funciona bien,** it doesn't work despite being expensive.

conato *nm* **1** (*intento*) attempt; **hizo un c. de irse,** he made an attempt to go. **2** (*principio*) beginnings *pl*, start. **3** (*tendencia*) tendency, inclination.

concadenar *vtr véase* **concatenar.**

concatenación *nf* concatenation, linking.

concatenar *vtr*, **concatenarse** *vr* to concatenate, link together.

concavidad *nf* concavity.

concebible *adj* conceivable, imaginable.

concebir I *vtr* **1** (*plan, hijo*) to conceive; **no concibo cómo pudo hacerlo,** I can't understand how he did it. **2** *fig* (*sentimiento*) to have, experienec; **c. esperanzas,** to build up one's hopes; **no le hagas c. esperanzas,** don't raise his hopes. **II** *vi* (*quedarse embarazada*) to become pregnant, conceive.

conceder *vtr* **1** (*gen*) to grant, concede; (*premio*) to award; **concédeme cinco minutos,** give me five minutes; **c. demasiado valor a algo,** to attach too much value to sth. **2** (*admitir*) to admit, concede.

concejal,-a *nm,f* town councillor.

concejalía *nf* councillorship.

concejo *nm* (town) council.

concelebrar *vtr* Rel to concelebrate.

concentración *nf* (*gen*) concentration; (*de manifestantes*) gathering, rally. ■ **campo de c.,** concentration camp; **c. parcelaria,** (land) consolidation.

concentrado,-a I *pp de* **concentrar. II** *adj* (*gen*) concentrated; (*gente*) gathered. **III** *nm* concentrate, extract.

concentrar I *vtr* to concentrate; **la manifestación concentró miles de personas,** thousands of people turned up at the rally. **II concentrarse** *vr* to concentrate; **concéntrate en lo que haces,** concentrate on what you're doing; **se concentraron más de un millón de personas,** over a million people turned up.

concéntrico,-a *adj* concentric.

concepción *nf* conception.

concepto *nm* **1** (*idea*) concept, conception, idea; **formarse un c. (de algo/de algn)** to form an opinion (of sth/sb). **2** (*opinión*) opinion, view; **tener un buen/mal c. de,** to have a good/a bad opinion of. **3** (*aspecto*) **bajo/por ningún c.,** under no circumstances. **4** (*en calidad de*) **en c. de,** by way of. **5** Fin (*apartado*) heading, section. **6** Arg Urug (*beneficio*) profit, benefit; (*gasto*) expense.

conceptual *adj* conceptual.

conceptuar *vtr* to deem, consider, think; **bien/mal conceptuado,** well/badly considered.

conceptuoso,-a *adj* high-sounding, sententious.

concerniente *adj* concerning, regarding; *fml* **en lo c. a,** with regard to.

concernir *v unipers* **1** (*afectar*) to concern, touch; **en lo que a mí/ti concierne,** as far as I am/you are concerned; **en lo que concierne a,** with regard/respect to. **2** (*corresponder*) to be up to; **a ti te concierne decidir,** it's up to you to decide.

concertado,-a I *pp de* **concertar. II** *adj* concerted.

concertar I *vtr* **1** (*actividad, acción*) to plan, co-ordinate; (*cita, entrevista*) to arrange; (*precio*) to agree on; (*acuerdo*) to reach; (*tratado*) to conclude. **2** Mús (*voces*) to harmonize. **II** *vi* **1** (*concordar*) to agree, tally. **2** Mús (*armonizar*) to harmonize, be in tune. **III concertarse** *vr* (*ponerse de acuerdo*) to get together, reach an agreement.

concertina *nf* Mús concertina.

concertino *nm* Mús first violin.

concertista *nmf* soloist.

concesión *nf* **1** (*gen*) concession, granting; **hacer concesiones,** to make concessions. **2** (*de un premio*) awarding.

concesionario,-a I *adj* concessionary. **II** *nm, f* Com concessionaire, concessioner, licence holder, licensee.

concha *nf* **1** Zool (*caparazón*) shell; (*carey*) tortoiseshell. **2** Teat (*del apuntador*) prompt box. **3** Am *vulg* cunt. **4** Am (*descaro*) cheek.

conchabar I *vtr* **1** (*unir*) to blend. **2** Am (*tomar sirviente*) to hire. **II conchabarse** *vr* **1** (*confabularse*) to gang up on, scheme. **2** (*emplearse como criado*) to offer one's services as a servant.

concho¹ *nm* Am (*residuos*) residue; (*sobras comida*) leftovers *pl*.

concho² *interj fam* fudge!, sugar!

conciencia *nf* **1** (*conocimiento*) consciousness, awareness; **a c.,** conscientiously; **en c.,** in truth; **tener/tomar c. (de algo),** to be/become aware (of sth). **2** (*moral*) conscience; **con la c. tranquila,** with a clear conscience; **remorder la c. a algn,** to weigh on sb's conscience.

concienciar I *vtr* to make aware (**de,** of). **II concienciarse** *vr* to become aware (**de,** of).

concienzudo,-a *adj* conscientious.

concierto *nm* **1** (*acuerdo*) agreement; *fig* concord, concert. **2** (*disposición*) order; **sin orden ni c.,** any old how. **3** Mús concert; (*composición*) concerto.

conciliábulo *nm* secret meeting.

conciliación *nf* conciliation, reconciliation.

conciliador,-a *adj* conciliating, conciliatory.

conciliar¹ *vtr* **1** (*ideas, grupos, etc*) to conciliate, bring together; (*enemigos*) to reconcile, placate. **2 c. el sueño,** to get to sleep.

conciliar² *adj* conciliar.

conciliatorio,-a *adj* conciliatory.

concilio *nm* Rel council; **el C. de Trento,** the Council of Trent.

concisión *nf* concision, conciseness.

conciso,-a *adj* concise, brief.

concitar *vtv* to stir up, incite; **concitó el odio del pueblo contra el gobierno,** he incited the people's hatred for the government.

conciudadano,-a *nm,f* fellow citizen.

cónclave *nm*, **conclave** *nm* **1** Rel conclave. **2** *fig* (*reunión*) private meeting; **tener un c.,** to sit in conclave.

concluir I *vtr* **1** (*terminar*) to finish; (*negocio*) to close. **2** (*deducir*) to conclude, infer. **II** *vi* to finish, come to an end. **III concluirse** *vr* to finish, end.

conclusión *nf* **1** (*final*) conclusion, end; (*resultado*) result; **en c.,** in conclusion. **2** (*deducción*) conclusion; **llegar a una c.,** to come to a conclusion.

concluso,-a *adj* Jur adjourned pending sentence.

concluyente *adj* conclusive, decisive.

concomerse *vr* to be consumed, itch; **c. de impaciencia,** to itch with impatience; **c. de envidia,** to be green with envy.

concomitancia *nf* concomitance.

concomitante *adj* concomitant.

concordancia *nf* concordance.

concordante *adj* concordant.

concordar I *vtr* (*concertar*) to bring into agreement; Ling (*palabras*) to make agree. **II** *vi* (*gen*) to agree; **esto no concuerda con lo que dijo ayer,** this doesn't fit in with what he said yesterday.

concordato *nm* concordat.

concorde *adj* in agreement.

concordia *nf* concord, harmony.

concreción *nf* **1** (*concisión*) concision, conciseness. **2** Geol Med concretion.

concretar I *vtr* **1** (*precisar*) to specify, state explicitly; (*fijar*) to fix; **c. una fecha/una hora,** to fix a date/a time. **2**

(limitar) to limit, direct; **concretemos nuestros esfuerzos en algo práctico,** let's direct our efforts to practical objectives. **3** *(resumir)* to sum up. **II concretarse** *vr* **I** *(limitarse)* to confine oneself *or* keep to. **2** *(materializarse)* to become established *or* definite; **mis ideas empiezan a c.,** my ideas are beginning to take shape.

concreto,-a *adj* **I** *(preciso, real)* concrete; **en c.,** *(definido)* definite; *(en resumen)* in brief, in short. **2** *(particular)* particular; **buscaba un tipo de vestido c.,** I was looking for a particular type of dress; **en el caso c. de ...,** in the particular case of ... . ◆ **concretamente** *adv* **1** *(exactamente)* exactly; **no sé qué quiere c.,** I don't know exactly what he wants. **2** *(en particular)* in particular, specifically; **quiero ése c.,** I want this one in particular.

concubina *nf* concubine.

concubinato *nm* concubinage.

conculcar *vtr* to infringe, break; **este acto conculca los princípios de la ley,** this act violates all principles of law.

concuñado,-a *nm,f (hombre)* husband of one's brother-in-law *or* sister-in-law; *(mujer)* sister *or* wife of one's brother-in-law *or* sister in law.

concupiscencia *nf* concupiscence, lustfulness.

concupiscente *adj* concupiscent, lustful.

concurrencia *nf* **1** *(conjunción)* concurrence, conjunction. **2** *(público)* attendance, audience; **divirtió a la c.,** he kept the audience amused.

concurrente I *adj* concurrent. **II** *nmf* person present; **los concurrentes,** those present; *(público)* members of the audience.

concurrido,-a I *pp de* **concurrir. II** *adj* **1** *(espectáculo)* well-attended, popular. **2** *(calle, lugar público)* crowded, busy.

concurrir *vi* **1** *(convergir) (gente)* to converge **(en,** on), meet **(en,** in); *Geom (líneas)* to cross, intersect; **todos concurrieron a la boda,** everybody attended the wedding. **2** *(coincidir)* to concur, coincide; **concurren unas circunstancias especiales,** under very special circumstances. **3** *(contribuir)* to contribute **(en,** to). **4** *(concursar) (en concurso)* to compete; *(en elecciones, examen)* to be a candidate.

concursante *nmf* **1** *(en un concurso)* contestant, competitor, participant. **2** *(para un empleo)* candidate.

concursar *vi* **1** *(competir)* to compete. **2** *(para un empleo)* to be a candidate; *(para proyecto de trabajo)* to tender.

concurso *nm* **1** *(competición)* competition; *(de belleza, deportiva)* contest; **fuera de c.,** out of the running. ■ **c. radiofónico,** radio quiz (programme). **2** *fml (concurrencia)* concourse, help, collaboration; **con el c. de todos,** with everyone's assistance. **3** *(llamamiento)* tender; **presentar (una obra) a c.,** to invite tenders (for a piece of work).

condado *nm* county.

condal *adj* of *or* relating to a count; *euf* **la Ciudad C.,** Barcelona.

conde *nm* count.

condecoración *nf* decoration, medal.

condecorar *vtr* to decorate.

condena *nf* **1** *(desaprobación)* condemnation, disapproval. **2** *Jur (sentencia)* sentence, conviction; **cumplir la c.,** to serve one's sentence.

condenable *adj* condemnable, blameworthy.

condenación *nf* condemnation; *Rel* damnation.

condenado,-a I *pp de* **condenar. II** *adj* **1** *Jur* convicted; **c. a muerte,** condemned to death. **2** *Rel* damned. **3** *Constr (cegado)* condemned. **4** *(sin arreglo)* hopeless, doomed; **un plan c. al fracaso,** a plan doomed to fail. **5** *fam (maldito)* damn. **II** *nm,f* **1** *Jur* convicted person; *(a muerte)* condemned person; *fam* **trabajar como un c.,** to work like a horse. **2** *Rel* damned. **3** *fam (miserable)* wretch. ◆ **condenadamente** *adv fam* darned.

condenar I *vtr* **1** *Jur* to convict, find guilty; **la condenaron a muerte,** she was condemned to death. **2** *(desaprobar)* to condemn. **3** *(fallar un plan)* to doom. **4** *Constr (puerta, ventana)* to block *or* wall off. **II condenarse** *vr Rel* to be damned.

condenatorio,-a *adj* condemnatory.

condensable *adj* condensable.

condensación *nf* **1** *(acción)* condensing. **2** *(efecto)* condensation.

condensado,-a I *pp de* **condensar. II** *adj* condensed; *Culin* **leche condensada,** condensed milk.

condensador *nm Elec* condenser.

condensar I *vtr* to condense. **II condensarse** *vr* to condense.

condesa *nf* countess.

condescendencia *nf* **1** *(deferencia)* condescension. **2** *(amabilidad)* affability.

condescender *vi* **1** *(dignarse)* to condescend. **2** *(ceder)* to comply (with), consent (to).

condescendiente *adj* **1** *(transigente)* condescending. **2** *(complaciente)* obliging, helpful.

condestable *nm Hist* High Constable.

condición *nf* **1** *(situación)* condition, state; **condiciones de salud,** state of health; **en buenas/malas condiciones,** in good/bad condition; **estar en condiciones de hacer algo,** *(físicas)* to be fit to do sth; *(morales)* to be in a position to do sth. **2** *(manera de ser)* nature, character; **de c. rebelde/bonachona,** of a rebellious/an easy-going nature. **3** *(índole)* status, position; **en su c. de director,** in his capacity as director. **4** *(circunstancia)* circumstance, condition; **condiciones de trabajo,** working conditions; **con la c. de que ...,** on the condition that ...; **poner condiciones,** to lay down conditions. **5** *(aptitud)* aptitude, talent; **tener condiciones para la música,** to have an aptitude *or* a talent for music.

condicionado,-a I *pp de* **condicionar. II** *adj* conditioned.

condicional I *adj* conditional. **II** *nm Ling* conditional.

condicionamiento *nm* conditioning.

condicionar *vtr* to condition; **una cosa condiciona la otra,** one thing determines the other.

cóndilo *nm Anat* condyle.

condimentación *nf Culin* seasoning, flavouring, *US* flavoring.

condimentar *vtr Culin* to season, flavour, *US* flavor.

condimento *nm Culin* seasoning, flavouring, *US* flavoring.

condiscípulo,-a *nm, f Educ* fellow pupil *or* student, schoolmate.

condolencia *nf* condolence, sympathy.

condolerse *vr* to sympathize (with), feel pity (for), feel sorry (for).

condominio *nm* **1** *Jur* joint ownership. **2** *Pol* condominium.

condón *nf* condom, rubber.

condonación *nf* condonation, remission.

condonar *vtr (ofensa)* to condone; *(deuda)* to cancel, remit.

cóndor *nm Orn* condor.

conducción *nf* **I** *Aut* driving. **2** *Fís* conduction. **3** *(transporte)* transportation; *(por tubería)* piping; *(por cable)* wiring. **4** *(cañería)* pipe, intake.

conducir I *vtr (coche, ganado)* to drive; *(líquido)* to convey; *(electricidad)* to carry, conduct; *(gente, ejército)* to lead; *(negocio)* to manage. **II** *vi* **1** *Aut* to drive; **permiso de c.,** driving licence, *US* driver's license. **2** *(llevar)* to lead; **eso no conduce a nada,** this leads nowhere. **III conducirse** *vr fml* to conduct oneself, behave.

conducta *nf* behaviour, *US* behavior, conduct; **mala c.,** misbehaviour, misconduct.

conductibilidad *nf,* **conductividad** *nf Elec* conductivity.

conducto *nm* 1 *(tubería)* pipe. 2 *Anat* duct, canal. 3 *fig (canal)* channel; **por conductos oficiales,** through official channels.

conductor,-a I *adj* conductive. II *nm,f Aut* driver. III *nm Elec* conductor; **no c.,** nonconductor.

condumio *nm fam* 1 *fam (comida)* grub, nosh. 2 *Méx Culin* sort of nougat.

conectar I *vtr* 1 to connect up. 2 *Elec* to plug in, switch on. II *vi* 1 *Rad TV* to tune into a station. 2 *(comunicar)* to enter into a relationship with. 3 *fam (enterarse)* to be tuned in, understand.

coneja *nf Zool* doe; *fam* **ser una c.,** to breed like rabbits.

conejar *nm Zool* rabbit hutch.

conejera *nf (doméstica)* rabbit hutch; *(en libertad)* rabbit warren *or* burrow; *fig* **viven en una c.,** they live in a right drive.

conejero-a I *adj* rabbit-hunting. II *nm* rabbit breeder.

conejillo *nm Zool* **c. de Indias,** guinea pig.

conejo *nm* 1 *Zool* rabbit. 2 *vulg (coño)* cunt, pussy.

conexión *nf* 1 *Téc* connection; **estar en c. con,** to be connected to. 2 *fig* relationship; **nuestra empresa tiene buenas conexiones,** our company has good connections.

conexo *adj* connected.

confabulación *nf* conspiracy, plot.

confabulador,-a *nm,f* conspirator, plotter.

confabular I *vi* to confabulate, discuss II **confabularse** *vr* to conspire, plot.

confección *nf* 1 *Cost* dressmaking, tailoring; *(ropa hecha)* off-the-peg clothes; **la industria de la c.,** the clothing industry. 2 *(realización)* making, making up.

confeccionador,-a *nm,f* 1 *Cost* outfitter. 2 *(reatizador)* maker, author.

confeccionar *vtr (vestido, lista)* to make (up); *Culin (plato)* to cook.

confeccionista *nmf Cost* outfitter.

confederación *nf* confederation, confederacy.

confederado,-a I *pp de* **confederar.** II *adj & nm, f* confederate.

confederal *adj* confederative.

confederar I *vtr* to confederate. II **confederarse** *vr* to confederate, become a confederation.

conferencia *nf* 1 *(charla)* lecture, talk; **dar una c. (sobre algo),** to lecture (on sth), give a lecture (on sth). 2 *Pol* conference, meeting. ■ **c. de prensa,** press conference. 3 *Tel (llamada)* long-distance call; **poner una c. con Toledo,** to make *or* place a call to Toledo.

conferenciante *nmf* lecturer.

conferenciar *vi* to confer (**sobre,** on; **con,** with).

conferir *vtr fml* 1 *(honor, privilegio)* to confer, bestow, award. 2 *(dar)* to give; **las canas le conferían un aire digno,** his white hair gave him an air of dignity.

confesar I *vtr* to confess, admit; *(crimen)* to own up to; *Rel (pecados)* to confess, hear the confession of; **¡confiésalo!,** own up! II *vi Jur (decir toda la verdad)* to own up; *fam* **c. de plano,** to admit everything. III **confesarse** *vr* to confess; *Rel* to go to confession, make one's confession; **c. culpable,** to admit one's guilt.

confesión *nf* confession, admission; *Rel* confession.

confesional *adj* denominational.

confesionario *nm Rel* confessional.

confeso,-a *adj* 1 *Jur* self-confessed. 2 *Hist* coverted Jew.

confesonario *nm Rel véase* **confesionario.**

confesor *nm* confessor.

confeti *nm (pl confetis)* confetti.

confiado,-a I *pp de* **confiar.** II *adj* 1 *(engreído)* self-satisfied; *(presumido)* conceited. 2 *(crédulo)* gullible, unsuspecting.

confianza *nf* 1 *(seguridad)* confidence; **con toda c.,** in all confidence; **en c.,** confidentially; **tener c. en uno mismo,** to be self-confident; *fml (cartas)* **en la c. de que ...,** trusting that ... . 2 *(fe)* trust; **de c.,** *(fiable)* reliable; *(de responsabilidad)* trustworthy. 3 *(presunción)* conceit. 4 *(franqueza)* familiarity, intimacy; **estar en c.,** to be among friends; **tener mucha c. con algn,** to be on intimate terms with sb; **tomarse (demasiadas) confianzas,** to take liberties.

confiar I *vtr (entregar)* to entrust; *(información, secreto)* to confide. II *vi (estar seguro de)* to be confident; *(tener fe)* to trust; **confío en ella,** I trust her; **no confíes en su ayuda,** don't count on his help. III **confiarse** *vr* to confide (**en** *or* **a,** in); **c. demasiado en algo,** to be over-confident about sth.

confidencia *nf* confidence, secret.

confidencial *adj* confidential.

confidente,-a *nm,* *f* 1 *(hombre)* confidant; *(mujer)* confidante. 2 *(de la policía)* informer.

configuración *nf* configuration, shape; **la c. del terreno,** the lie of the land.

configurar *vtr* to shape, form.

confín *nm* limit, boundary; **los confines del conocimiento,** the confines of knowledge.

confinación *nf,* **confinamiento** *nm* confinement.

confinar I *vtr Jur* to confine. II *vi (territorio)* to border (on). III **confinarse** *vr* to shut oneself away *or* up.

confirmación *nf* confirmation.

confirmar *vtr* to confirm; *prov* **la excepción confirma la regla,** the exception proves the rule.

confirmatorio,-a *adj* confirmatory.

confiscación *nf* confiscation.

confiscar *vtr* to confiscate.

confitado,-a I *pp de* **confitar.** II *adj* candied, glacé; **frutas confitadas,** comfits.

confitar *vtr (fruta)* to candy; *(carne)* to preserve.

confite *nm* sweet, *US* candy.

confitería *nf* 1 *(tienda)* sweet shop, confectioner's (shop), *US* candy store. 2 *Am (cafetería)* café.

confitero,-a *nm,f* confectioner.

confitura *nf* preserve, jam.

conflagración *nf fml* 1 *(fuego)* conflagration. 2 *(guerra)* outbreak.

conflictividad *nf* **c. laboral,** labour *or US* labor disputes *pl or* unrest.

conflictivo,-a *adj* delicate; **tiempos conflictivos,** times of conflict; **un tema c.,** a delicate *or* difficult subject.

conflicto *nm* conflict. ■ **c. laboral,** labour *or US* labor dispute.

confluencia *nf* confluence.

confluente *adj* confluent.

confluir *vi* to converge; *(ríos, caminos)* to meet, come together.

conformación *nf* structure, shape.

conformar I *vtr (configurar)* to shape. II *vi (concordar)* to agree (**con,** with); **de buen c.,** easy going. III **conformarse** *vr (contentarse)* to resign oneself, be content; **se conformó con una recompensa insignificante,** he agreed to a small compensation.

conforme I *adj* 1 *(satisfecho)* satisfied; **c., agreed,** all right; **no estoy c.,** I don't agree. 2 *(acorde)* in accordance *or* keeping with. **c. a la realidad/sus necesidades,** in accordance with reality/his needs. II *conj* 1 *(según, como)* as; **c. lo vi/lo of,** as I saw/heard it. 2 *(en cuanto)* as soon as; **ven c. te llame,** como as soon as I call you. 3 *(a* *medida que)* as; **la policía los detenía c. iban saliendo,** the police were arresting them as they came out. **III** *nm* approval, agreement.

conformidad *nf* 1 *(aprobación)* approval, consent. 2 *(resignación)* resignation. 3 *(afinidad)* conformity; **en c. (con algo),** in conformity (with sth); **no c.,** nonconformity.

conformismo *nm* conformity.

conformista *adj & nmf* conformist.

confort *nm* (*pl* **conforts**) comfort; *(en anuncio)* 'todo c.', 'all mod cons', 'luxurious'.

confortable *adj* comfortable.

confortador,-a *adj* **confortante** *adj* 1 *(que fortalece)* invigorating. 2 *fig (que consuela)* comforting; *(que anima)* cheering.

confortar *vt* 1 *(fortalecer)* to invigorate. 2 *fig (consolar)* to comfort; *(animar)* to cheer.

confraternar *vi* to fraternize.

confraternidad *nf* brotherliness.

confraternizar *vi* to fraternize.

confrontación *nf* 1 *(enfrentamiento)* confrontation. 2 *(comparación)* comparison, collation.

confrontar **I** *vtr* 1 to confront; *(carear)* to bring face to face. 2 *(cotejar)* to compare, collate. **II** *vi (lindar)* to border. **III confrontarse** *vr* to face, confront.

confundible *adj* **c. con,** easily confused (with) *or* mistaken (for).

confundir **I** *vtr* 1 *(equivocar)* to confuse (**con,** with), mistake (**con,** for); *(persona)* to mislead; **le confundió con su prima,** he mistook her for his cousin. 2 *(mezclar)* to mix. 3 *(turbar)* to confound, embarrass; **me ha confundido su amabilidad,** I'm overwhelmed by his kindness. **II confundirse** *vr* 1 *(equivocarse)* to be mistaken; *(teléfono)* **se ha confundido,** you've got the wrong number. 2 *(mezclarse)* to mingle; *(colores, formas)* to blend; **la casa se confunde con el paisaje,** the house blends into the landscape; **se confundió entre el gentío,** he disappeared into the crowd. 3 *(turbarse)* to be confused *or* embarrassed.

confusión *nf* 1 *(desorden)* confusion, chaos. 2 *(equivocación)* confusion, mistake. 3 *(turbación)* confusion; embarrassment.

confusionismo *nm* confusion.

confuso,-a *adj* 1 *(poco claro) (estilo)* confused, obscure; *(formas, recuerdos)* blurred, vague; *(ideas)* confused. 2 *(mezclado)* mixed up. 3 *(turbado)* confused, embarrassed.

conga *nf Mús* conga.

congelación *nf* 1 *(gen)* freezing. 2 *Fin (de salarios, precios)* freeze. 3 *Med* frostbite.

congelado,-a **I** *pp de* **congelar. II** *adj* frozen; *Med* frostbitten. **III congelados** *nmpl* frozen food *sing.*

congelador *nm* freezer.

congelar **I** *vtr (gen)* to freeze; *Fin* **c. precios,** to freeze prices; *Med* **un dedo congelado,** a frostbitten finger. **II congelarse** *vr* 1 to freeze; *fam* **me estoy congelando,** I'm freezing. 2 *Med* to get *or* become frostbitten.

congénere 1 *adj* congeneric, congenerous. **II** *nm,f* 1 *Bot Zool* congener. 2 *pey* sort, kind.

congeniar *vi* to get on (**con,** with); **no congenia con su familia,** he doesn't get on very well with his family.

congénito,-a *adj* congenital, innate.

congestión *nf* congestion. ■ *Med* **c. cerebral,** stroke.

congestionar **I** *vtr Aut Med* to congest. **II congestionarse** *vr* to become congested.

conglomeración *nf* conglomeration.

conglomerado,-a I *pp de* **conglomerar. II** *nm Geol Téc* conglomerate.

conglomerar *vtr*, **conglomerarse** *vr* to conglomerate.

congoja *nf* 1 *(angustia)* anguish, distress. 2 *(pena)* sorrow, grief.

congoleño,-a *adj & nm, f*, **congolés,-esa** *adj & nm, f* Congolese.

congraciar **I** *vtr* to win over. **II congraciarse** *vr* to ingratiate oneself (**con,** with).

congratulación *nf fml* congratulation.

congratular **I** *vtr* to congratulate (**por,** on). **II congratularse** *vr* to congratulate oneself (**por,** on).

congregación *nf (junta)* assembly; *Rel* congregation.

congregante *nmf* member of a congregation.

congregar *vtr*, **congregarse** *vr* to congregate, assemble.

congresista *nmf* member of a congress.

congreso *nmf* congress, conference. ■ *Pol* **c. de los Diputados,** Parliament, *US* Congress.

congrio *nm (pez)* conger (eel).

congruencia *nf* 1 *(coherencia)* congruity. 2 *Mat* congruence.

congruente *adj* **congruo,-a** *adj* 1 *(coherente)* coherent, suitable. 2 *Mat* congruent.

cónico,-a *adj* 1 *(en forma de cono)* conical. 2 *Geom* conic.

conífero,-a *Bot* **I** *adj* coniferous. **II** *nf* conifer.

conjetura *nf* conjecture; **por c.,** by guesswork.

conjeturar *vtr* to conjecture.

conjugable *adj* conjugable.

conjugación *nf* conjugation.

conjugar *vtr* to conjugate; *fig (planes, opiniones)* to join, bring together.

conjunción *nf Ling* conjunction

conjuntado,-a I *pp de* **conjuntar II** *adj* co-ordinated

conjuntar *vtr* to co-ordinate.

conjuntiva *nf Anat* conjunctiva.

conjuntivitis *nf Med* conjunctivitis.

conjuntivo,-a *adj* conjunctive.

conjunto,-a **I** *adj* 1 *(combinado)* combined. 2 *(compartido)* joint. ■ **base conjunta,** joint base. **II** *nm* 1 *(grupo)* collection, group; **un c. de poemas,** a collection of poems. 2 *(todo)* whole; **de c.,** overall; **en c.,** on the whole; **en su c.,** as a whole. 3 *(prenda)* outfit, ensemble. 4 *Mús (clásico)* ensemble; *(pop)* group, band. 5 *Mat* set. 6 *Dep* team.

conjura *nf* **conjuración** *nf* conspiracy, plot.

conjurado,-a I *pp de* **conjurar II** *adj* conspiring, plotting. **III** *nm,f* conspirator, plotter.

conjurar **I** *vtr* 1 *(demonio, mal pensamiento)* to exorcise; *(peligro)* to stave off, ward off. 2 *lit (rogar)* to beseech. **II** *vi* to conspire, plot. **III conjurarse** *vr* to conspire, plot.

conjuro *nm* 1 *(exorcismo)* exorcism.. 2 *(encantamiento)* spell, incantation.

conllevar *vtr (enfermedad)* to put up with; *(dolor)* to bear.

conmemoración *nf* commemoration.

conmemorar *vtr* to commemorate.

conmemorativo,-a *adj* commemorative.

conmensurable *adj* commensurable.

conmigo *pron pers* with me; **Clara hablaba c.,** Clara was talking to me.

conminación *nf* threat, commination

conminador,-a *adj* threatening, menacing.

conminar *vtr* to threaten, menace.

conminativo,-a *adj,* **conminatorio,-a** *adj* threatening, menacing.

conmiseración *nf fml* commiseration, pity.

conmoción *nf* commotion, shock. ■ *Med* **c. cerebral,** concussion.

conmocionar *vtr* to shock; *Med* to concuss.

conmovedor,-a *adj* touching; **una película conmovedora,** a moving film.

conmover I *vtr* (*persona*) to touch, move; (*objeto, casa*) to shake. II **conmoverse** *vr* 1 (*persona*) to be touched *or* moved. 2 (*cosas*) to be shaken.

conmutabilidad *nf* commutability.

conmutable *adj* commutable.

conmutación *nf* commutation.

conmutador *nm* 1 *Elec* switch. 2 *Am Tel* switchboard.

conmutar *vtr* to exchange; *Jur* (*castigo, sentencia*) to commute; *Elec* (*corriente*) to commutate.

conmutativo,-a *adj* commutative.

connatural *adj* connatural, inherent.

connivencia *nf* connivance, collusion.

connotación *nf* connotation.

connotar *vtr* to connote.

connubio *nm* lit matrimony, marriage.

cono *nm Geom* cone.

conocedor,-a *adj & nm,f* expert.

conocer I *vtr* 1 to know; **dar (algo/algn) a c.,** to make (sth/sb) known; **darse a c.,** to make oneself known; **no conozco bien este tema,** I am not very familiar with this subject; *fam* **c. algo al dedillo** *or* **palmo a palmo,** to know something off by heart. 2 (*identificar*) to recognize; **¿de qué** *or* **dónde me conoces?,** where do you know me from?; **te he conocido por la voz,** I recognized you by your voice. 3 (*a algn por primera vez*) to meet; **c. (a algn) de vista,** to know (sb) by sight; **¿conoces a Teresa?,** have you met Teresa? 4 (*visitar país, lugar*) to be in; **no conozco Rusia,** I haven't been to Russia yet. II *vi* **c. de,** (*ser conocedor*) to know about; *Jur* (*caso*) to hear. III **conocerse** *vr* 1 (*a sí mismo*) to know oneself. 2 (*dos personas*) to know each other; (*por primera vez*) to meet; **se conocieron en el metro,** they met on the tube. 3 (*uso impers*) **se le conoce la felicidad en la cara,** happiness shows in his face; *fam* **se conoce que se enfadó,** apparently he got angry.

conocido,-a I *pp de* **conocer** II *adj* known; (*famoso*) well-known; **esa cara me es conocida,** I've seen that face before; **me suena a,** it rings a bell. III *nm,f* acquaintance; **es un c. suyo,** he's an acquaintance of his.

conocimiento *nm* 1 (*saber*) knowledge; **con c. de causa,** with full knowledge of the facts; **tener conocimiento (de algo),** to know (about sth); **tiene pocos conocimientos de biología,** he knows little about biology. 2 (*madurez*) **tener c.,** to have an understanding of. 3 (*conciencia*) conciousness; **perder/recobrar el c.,** to lose/regain conciousness. III (*sentido común*) common sense.

conque *conj* so; **llegas tarde, c. date prisa,** you're late, so hurry up.

conquense *adj* of *or* from Cuenca. II *nmf* native *or* inhabitant of Cuenca.

conquián *nm Méx Naipes* concan.

conquista *nf* conquest; (*amorosa*) **hacer una c.,** to make a conquest.

conquistador,-a *adj* conquering. II *nm,f* conqueror. III *nm* (*galán*) lady-killer.

conquistar *vtr Mil* (*país, ciudad*) to conquer; *fig* (*puesto, título*) to win; (*a un hombre or una mujer*) to win over.

consabido,-a *adj* I (*bien conocido*) well-known. 2 (*usual*) familiar, usual.

consagración *nf* 1 *Rel* consecration. 2 (*de un artista, escritor*) recognition; (*de una costumbre*) establishment.

consagrado,-a I *pp de* **consagrar** II *adj* 1 consecrated. 2 recognized, time-honoured, *US* time-honored, established, hallowed.

consagrar I *vtr* 1 *Rel* (*iglesia, pan y vino*) to consecrate. 2 (*persona*) (*confirmar*) to confirm; (*palabra, expresión*)

to establish. 3 (*dedicar*) to devote, consecrate, II **consagrarse** *vr* 1 (*dedicarse*) to devote oneself (**a,** to), dedicate oneself (**a,** to). 2 (*lograr fama*) to establish oneself.

consanguíneo,-a I *adj* related by birth, consanguineous; **hermano c.,** half-brother. II *nm,f* blood relation.

consanguinidad *nf* blood relationship, consanguinity.

consciencia *nf véase* **conciencia**

consciente *adj* 1 conscious, aware; **ser c. de algo,** to be aware of sth. 2 *Med* conscious; **estar c.,** to be conscious. 3 (*responsable*) reliable.

consecución *nf* 1 (*de un objetivo*) achievement, attainment; (*de un deseo*) realization. 2 (*obtención*) obtaining, obtainment.

consecuencia *nf* 1 (*resultado*) consequence, result; **a** *or* **como c. de,** as a consequence *or* result of; **atenerse a las consecuencias,** to suffer the consequences; **en c.,** therefore; **tener** *or* **traer (malas) consecuencias,** to have (ill) effects. 2 (*coherencia*) consistency.

consecuente *adj* 1 (*coherente*) consistent; **c. con sus ideas,** consistent with one's ideas. 2 (*siguiente*) consequent. ◆ **consecuentemente** *adv* 1 consistently. 2 (*seguidamente*) consequently, therefore.

consecutivo,-a *adj* consecutive.

conseguir *vtr* 1 (*obtener*) (*cosa*) to get, obtain; (*objetivo*) to achieve, attain. 2 (*lograr*) to manage, succeed in; **conseguí terminar,** I managed to finish.

conseja *nf Lit* fable, legend.

consejero,-a *nm,f* 1 (*asesor*) adviser. 2 *Pol* councillor. 3 *Com* member (of a board of directors). ▪ **c. delegado,** managing director.

consejo *nm* 1 (*recomendación*) advice; **pedir c. (a algn),** to ask (sb) for advice; **te daré un c.,** I'll give you a piece of advice. 2 (*junta*) council; **celebrar c.,** to hold council. ▪ **c. de administración,** board of directors; **c. de guerra,** court martial; **c. de ministros,** cabinet; (*reunión*) cabinet meeting.

consenso *nm* 1 (*consentimiento*) assent, consent. 2 (*acuerdo*) consensus.

consensual *adj* consensual.

consentido,-a I *pp de* **consentir** II *adj* (*mimado*) spoiled, spoilt. III *nm,f* spoiled *or* spoilt child *or* person.

consentimiento *nm* consent.

consentir I *vtr* 1 (*tolerar*) to tolerate, allow, permit; **no consientas que haga eso,** don't allow him to do that. 2 (*mimar*) to spoil. 3 (*aguantar peso, esfuerzo*) to bear, admit. II *vi* 1 to consent, give way; **consiente en quedarse,** he agrees to stay. 2 (*ceder mueble, pieza*) to weaken. III **consentirse** *vr* (*debilitarse*) to be weakened.

conserje *nm* porter; (*encargado*) caretaker.

conserjería *nf* 1 (*lugar*) porter's lodge, caretaker's quarters, reception. 2 (*oficio*) job of porter, caretaker etc.

conserva *nf* 1 (*en lata*) tinned *or* canned food. 2 (*dulces*) preserves *pl*.

conservación *nf* 1 preservation. ▪ **instinto de c.,** self-preservation. 2 (*mantenimiento*) maintenance, upkeep.

conservador,-a I *adj & nm, f* conservative; *Pol* Conservative. II *nm* (*de museo*) curator.

conservadurismo *nm Pol* conservatism.

conservante *nm* preservative.

conservar I *vtr* to conserve, preserve; (*mantener*) to keep up, maintain; *Culin* to preserve; **c. la salud,** to keep healthy; **consérvalo,** keep it, hold on to it. II **conservarse** *vr* 1 (*mantener hábito, tradición*) to survive. 2 *fig* to age well; **Ana se conserva muy bien,** Ana looks well for her age.

conservatorio *nm* 1 *Mús* conservatory, conservatoire, school of music. 2 *Arg Educ* private school.

conservería *nf* canning industry.

conservero,-a I *adj* canning. **II** *nm,f* canner.

considerable *adj* considerable, substantial, large.

consideración *nf* **1** *(reflexión)* consideration, attention; **tomar algo en c.,** to take sth into account. **2** *(respeto)* regard; **con c.,** *(con respeto)* respectfully; *(con cuidado)* carefully; **en c.,** considering; **por c. a,** out of consideration for. **3 de c.,** important, considerable; **herido de c.,** seriously injured.

considerado,-a I *pp de* **considerar II** *adj* **1** *(apreciado)* highly regarded *or* thought of; **estar bien/mal c.,** to well/badly thought of. **2** *(atento)* considerate, thoughtful.

considerar *vtr* **1** *(meditar)* to consider, think over; **c. los pros y los contras,** to weigh up the pros and cons. **2** *(juzgar)* to judge, regard, deem; **lo considero imposible,** I think it's impossible. **3** to treat with consideration, respect.

consigna *nf* **1** *Mil* orders, instructions. **2** *(de estación, aeropuerto)* left-luggage office, *US* checkroom. **3** *(señal, lema)* watchword; **'por la igualdad', era su c.,** 'equality for all', was their watchword.

consignación *nf* **1** *(asignación)* allocation. **2** *Com (de mercancías)* consignment; *Naut* shipment.

consignar *vtr* **1** *(asignar)* to allocate; *(cantidad)* to assign. **2** *Com (mercancía)* to consign, ship, dispatch. **3** *(hacer constar)* to record; *(declaración)* to take down.

consignatario,-a *nm,f* **1** *Com* consignee. ■ **c. de buques,** shipbroker. **2** *Jur (depositario)* trustee, mortgagee.

consigo[1] *pron pers* **1** *(tercera persona)* with him *or* her; *(plural)* with them; **c. mismo,** with himself *or* herself; **c. mismos,** with themselves; *fam fig* **ella no las tenía todas c.,** she didn't rate her chances highly. **2** *(usted)* you; **c. mismo,** with yourself.

consigo[2] *indic pres véase* **conseguir**

consiguiente *adj* resulting, resultant, consequent; **por c.,** therefore, consequently.

consintiente *adj* consenting, agreeing.

consistencia *nf* **1** consistency, firmness, solidity; *Culin* **tomar c.,** to thicken. **2** *fig* solidity.

consistente *adj* **1** *(firme)* firm, solid. **2** *fig* sound. **3 c. en,** consisting of.

consistir *vi* to consist **(en,** in, of); **el secreto consiste en tener paciencia,** the secret lies in being patient.

consistorial *adj* **casa c.,** town hall.

consistorio *nm* **1** *Rel* consistory. **2** *(ayuntamiento)* town council.

consocio,-a *nm,f* partner, associate.

consola *nf* **1** *Mueb* console table. **2** *(tablero de instrumentos)* console.

consolación *nf* consolation, comfort. ■ **premio de c.,** consolation prize.

consolador,-a *adj* consoling, comforting.

consolar I *vtr* to console, comfort. **II consolarse** *vr* to console oneself, take comfort **(con,** from).

consólida *nm Bot* comfrey.

consolidación *nf* consolidation.

consolidar I *vtr* to consolidate; *(deuda)* to fund. **II consolidarse** *vr* to consolidate.

consolidativo,-a *adj* consolidating, consolidatory.

consomé *nm Culin* clear soup consommé.

consonancia *nf* **1** *Lit* consonance, rhyme. **2** *fig* harmony; **en c. con,** in keeping with.

consonante *adj & nf* consonant.

consonántico,-a *adj* consonantal.

consonar *vi* **1** *Mús Lit* to harmonize, rhyme. **2** *fig* to agree, fit, be in harmony.

consorcio *nm Com* consortium, association, partnership.

consorte I *adj* **príncipe c.,** prince consort. **II** *nmf* **1** *(cónyuge)* partner, spouse. **2** *Jur* **consortes,** accomplices, joint partners.

conspicuo,-a *adj* **1** *lit* conspicuous, obvious. **2** *(notable)* prominent, outstanding.

conspiración *nf* conspiracy, plot.

conspirador,-a *nm,f* conspirator, plotter.

conspirar *vi* *(confabularse)* to conspire, plot.

constancia *nf* **1** *(perseverancia)* constancy, perseverance; **hacer algo con c.,** to persevere at sth. **2** *(testimonio)* proof, evidence; **dejar c. de algo,** *(registrar)* to put sth on record; *(probar)* to prove sth.

constante I *adj* constant, steady; *(persona)* steadfast. **II** *nf* constant. constant feature. ◆ **constantemente** *adv* constantly.

constar *vi* **1** *(figurar)* to figure in, be included (in); **c. en acta,** to be on record; **hacer c.,** *(decir)* to express; *(escribir)* to put down; *fml* **para que así conste,** for the record. **2** *(ser evidente)* to be a fact; **me consta que ...,** I am absolutely certain that ...; **que conste que ...,** it's a fact that ... . **3** *(consistir)* **c. de,** to be made up of, consist of.

constatación *nf* verification; *(verificación)* checking.

constatar *vtr* to verify, confirm; *(comprobar)* to check.

constelación *nf Astron* constellation.

constelado,-a *adj fig* strewn **(de,** with).

consternación *nf* consternation, panic, dismay.

consternar I *vtr* to dismay, shatter, shock. **II consternarse** *vr* to be dismayed, shocked, aghast.

constipación *nf Med* cold, chill.

constipado,-a *Med* **I** *adj* **estar c.,** to have a cold *or* a chill. **II** *nm* cold, chill.

constiparse *vr* to catch a cold *or* a chill.

constitución *nf (composición)* constitution; *Pol* **la C. española,** the Spanish constitution.

constitucional I *adj* constitutional. **II** *nm Pol* constitutionalist.

constituir I *vtr* **1** *(formar)* to constitute, make up; **está constituido por cinco islas,** it consists of five islands. **2** *(ser)* to be, represent; **constituye un honor para mí,** it is a great honour for me. **3** *(fundar)* to constitute, set up. **4** *(nombrar)* to appoint. **II constituirse** *vr* to set oneself up **(en,** as).

constitutivo,-a *adj* constituent, component.

constituyente *adj & nmf Pol* constituent.

constreñimiento *nm* **1** *(obligación)* constraint, imposition. **2** *(opresión)* restriction.

constreñir *vtr* **1** *(forzar)* to compel, force. **2** *(oprimir)* to restrict. **3** *Med (arteria)* to constrict; *(estreñimiento)* to constipate.

constricción *nf* constriction.

construcción *nf* **1** construction; **la industria de la c.,** the building industry; **en (vías de) c.,** under construction. **2** *(edificio)* building.

constructivo,-a *adj* constructive.

constructor,-a I *adj* building, construction; **empresa constructora,** builders *pl*, construction company. **II** *nm,f* builder.

construir *vtr* to construct, build.

consuegra *nf* son-in-law's *or* daughter-in-law's mother.

consuegro *nm* son-in-law's *or* daughter-in-law's father.

consuelo *nm* consolation; **es un c.,** that's comforting; **sin c.,** inconsolably.

cónsul *nmf* consul.

consulado *nm* **1** *(oficina)* consulate. **2** *(cargo)* consulship.

consular *adj* consular.

consulta *nf* **1** consultation; **quería hacerte una c.,** I need your advice. ■ **obra de c.,** reference book. **2** *Med* surgery; **pasar c.,** to see patients; **horas de c.,** surgery hours. **3** *Med (despacho)* consulting room.

consultar *vtr* to consult, seek advice (**con,** from); *(en un libro)* to look up; *fig* **consultarlo con la almohada,** to sleep on it.

consultivo,-a *adj* consultative, advisory.

consultorio *nm* **1** *(asesoría)* office, information office; *(de médico)* consulting room; *(en hospital)* outpatients'. **2** *Prensa* problem page, advice column.

consumación *nf* consummation, completion; *(de un crimen)* perpetration.

consumado,-a I *pp de* **consumar** II *adj* **1** consummated; **hecho c.,** fait accompli, accomplished fact. **2** *fig (perfecto)* consummate; **un bobo c.,** a complete fool.

consumar *vtr* to complete, carry out; *(crimen)* to commit; *(matrimonio)* to consummate.

consumición *nf* **1** consumption. **2** *(bebida)* drink. ■ **c. mínima,** basic charge.

consumido,-a I *pp de* **consumir** II *adj* **1** *(gastado)* wasted, spent **2** *fig (devorado)* **c. por los celos,** consumed by jealousy.

consumidor,-a I *adj* consuming; **países consumidores de café,** coffee-drinking countries. II *nm,f* consumer.

consumir I *vtr* **1** *(gastar)* to consume; *fig* **me consumió esperar tanto,** it got on my nerves waiting so long. **2** *(destruir)* to destroy; **el fuego consumió el edificio,** the fire destroyed the building. II **consumirse** *vr* **1** *(extinguirse)* to burn out; *fig (persona)* to waste away. **2** *(secarse)* to boil away. **3** *fig (por la pasión)* to be consumed *or* devoured.

consumismo *nm* consumerism.

consumo *nm* consumption. ■ **bienes de c.,** consumer goods; **sociedad de c.,** consumer society.

consunción *nf Med* consumption.

consuno *adv* **de c.,** with one accord.

consustancial *adj* **ser c. con,** to be inseparable from.

contabilidad *nf Com* **1** *(profesión)* accountancy. **2** *(de empresa, sociedad)* accounting, book-keeping; **llevar la c.,** to keep the books.

contabilizar *vtr Com* to enter in the books.

contable I *adj* countable. II *nmf Com* accountant, book-keeper.

contactar *vtr* to contact, get in touch (**con,** with).

contacto *nm* contact; *Aut* ignition; **entrar en c.,** to make contact; **perder el c.,** to lose touch; **ponerse en c.,** to get in touch. ■ *Opt* **lentes de c.,** contact lenses.

contado,-a I *pp de* **contar.** II *adj* **1** *(sumado)* counted; **tiene los días contados,** his days are numbered. **2** *(raro)* scarce; *(poco)* little; *(pocos)* few and far between; **contadas veces,** very seldom. **3** *Com* **pagar al c.,** to pay cash.

contador,-a I *nm, f* **1** *(narrador)* teller. **2** *(contable)* accountant, book-keeper. II *nm* meter. ■ **c. de agua,** water meter.

contaduría *nf* **1** *(oficio)* accountancy. **2** *(oficina)* accountant's office.

contagiar I *vtr Med (enfermedad)* to transmit, pass on; *fig* **me contagió la risa,** their laughter was infectious. II **contagiarse** *vr* **1** *(enfermar)* to get infected, catch. **2** *(transmitirse)* to be contagious.

contagio *nm* **1** *Med* contagion, infection. **2** *fig* corruption, perversion.

contagioso,-a *adj* **1** *Med* contagious, infectious. **2** *fam* catching; **risa contagiosa,** infectious laugh.

contaminación *nf* contamination; *(de la atmósfera)* pollution.

contaminador,-a *adj* contaminating; *(de la atmósfera)* polluting.

contaminar I *vtr* **1** to contaminate; *(aire, agua)* to pollute. **2** *fig (pervertir)* to contaminate, corrupt. II **contaminarse** *vr* to become contaminated (**con, de,** with, by).

contante *adj* **dinero c. (y sonante),** hard *or* ready cash.

contar I *vtr* **1** *(sumar)* to count; **c. con los dedos,** to count one's fingers; **cuenta los puntos,** count how many points. **2** *(considerar)* to consider, reckon. **3** *(tener)* to have; **cuenta cincuenta años,** he's fifty years old. **4** *(narrar)* to relate, tell; **cuéntame un cuento,** tell me a story; **habría mucho que c.,** it's a long story; *fam* **¡cuéntamelo a mí!,** you're telling me!; *vulg* **¡cuéntaselo a tu abuela!,** come off it! **5** *(incluir)* to count (in), include; **te cuento entre mis amigos,** I consider you one of my friends. **6** *(suponer)* to count (on), expect; **ella cuenta llegar allí a las doce,** she expects to arrive there at twelve. II *vi* **1** *(tener importancia)* to count; **ese partido no cuenta,** that match doesn't count. **2** **c. con algn,** *(confiar en algn)* to rely on sb; *(incluir a algn)* to count sb in; **cuenta con ello,** you can count on it. **3** *(tener presente)* to take into account; **no había contado con eso,** I hadn't allowed for that. **4** *(tener)* to have, be provided with; **cuenta con un dispositivo especial,** it has got a special device. III **contarse** *vr* **1** to be counted; **se cuentan por miles,** there are thousands of them. **2** *(incluirse)* to include oneself. **3** *fam* **¿qué te cuentas?,** how's it going?

contemplación *nf* contemplation; *fam* **no andarse con contemplaciones,** to make no bones about it, come straight to the point.

contemporaneidad *nf* contemporaneousness.

contemporáneo,-a *adj & nm,f* contemporary.

contemporizador,-a I *adj* compliant, compromising. II *nm,f* conformist, middle-of-the-road person.

contemporizar *vi* to compromise, be complaint.

contención *nf* **1** *(moderación)* moderation, control. **2** *Constr* **muro de c.,** retaining wall. **3** *Jur* lawsuit.

contencioso,-a I *adj* contentious; *Jur* litigious; **asunto c.,** judicial matter. II *nm Jur* legal action, case.

contendedor,-a *nm,f* contender, antagonist.

contender *vi* **1** *(pelear)* to contend, fight. **2** *(competir)* to contest.

contendiente I *adj* contending, competing. II *nmf* contender, contestant.

contener I *vtr* **1** *(encerrar, llevar)* to contain, hold. **2** *(reprimir)* to restrain, hold back; **no pudo c. la risa,** he couldn't hold back his laughter. II **contenerse** *vr* to control oneself, hold (oneself) back.

contenido,-a I *pp de* **contener.** II *adj* **1** contained (**en,** in). **2** *(persona)* reserved, circumspect. III *nm* content, contents *pl.*

contenta *nf* **1** *(agasajo)* good treatment *or* welcome. **2** *Am Com* acknowledgment.

contentadizo,-a *adj* easy to please.

contentar I *vtr* **1** *(satisfacer)* to please. **2** *(alegrar)* to cheer up. II **contentarse** *vr* **1** *(conformarse)* to make do (**con,** with), be satisfied (**con,** with). **2** *(alegrarse)* to cheer up.

contento,-a I *adj* happy, pleased (**con,** with; **de,** about). II *nm* happiness, contentment, joy.

contera *nf* tip; *fig* **echar la c.,** to finish, end; *fig* **por c.,** to cap it all.

contertulio,-a *nm,f* member of a social group *or* gathering.

contestable *adj* debatable.

contestador *nm* **c. automático,** answering machine.

contestación *nf* **1** *(respuesta)* answer; **dar c.,** to answer. **2** *(oposición)* opposition. **3** *Jur* plea.

contestar I *vtr* **1** *(responder)* to answer; **c. bien/mal,** to give the right/wrong answer. **2** *Jur* to confirm. II *vi* **1** *(replicar)* to answer back. **2** *(oponer)* to contest, question.

contestatario,-a I *adj* argumentative; *fam* bolshie. II *nm,f* attacker, dissenter.

contexto *nm* context; *fig* environment.

contextura *nf* **1** *(disposición)* texture. **2** *(complexión de persona)* build.

contienda *nf* contest, struggle, dispute.

contigo *pron pers* with you; *prov* **c. pan y cebolla,** anything will do as long as we are together.

contigüidad *nf* contiguity, closeness, nearness.

contiguo,-a *adj* contiguous (**a,** to), adjoining, adjacent (**a,** to).

continencia *nf* (*en el sexo*) continence; (*en la gula*) moderation.

continental *adj* continental.

continente *nm* **1** *Geog* continent. **2** (*recipiente*) container. **3** (*compostura*) countenance; (*aspecto*) air.

contingencia *nf* **1** (*probabilidad*) contingency, eventuality. **2** (*riesgo*) risk, hazard.

contingente I *adj* (*posible*) contingent, accidental. **II** *nm* **1** (*grupo*) contingent. **2** *Mil* contingent. **3** *Com Fin* quota, share. **4** (*contingencia*) contingency.

continuación *nf* continuation, follow-up; **a c.,** next; **tener c.,** to be continued.

continuador,-a I *adj* continuing. **II** *nm,f* continuator.

continuar I *vtr & vi* to continue, carry on (with); **ella continúa durmiendo,** she's still asleep; **continúa en Francia,** he's still in France; **continuará,** to be continued; **continuaron su camino,** they went on their way. **II continuarse** *vr* to continue, go on; **la carretera se continúa hasta el mar,** the road runs all the way down to the sea.

continuidad *nf* continuity.

continuo,-a I *adj* **1** (*seguido*) continuous, endless. ▪ **línea continua,** (*en dibujo etc*) unbroken line; *Aut* solid white line. **2** (*reiterado*) continual, constant. **II** *nm* continuum; **un c. de gente,** a constant flow of people. ◆ **continuamente** *adv* continuously.

contonearse *vr* to swing one's hips.

contoneo *nm* swinging of the hips, hip-swinging.

contorno *nm* **1** (*perfil*) outline; (*perímetro*) perimeter; **el c. de la figura,** the shape of the figure. **2** *Numis* (*canto*) rim. edge. **3** (*alrededores*) surroundings *pl*, environment; (*territorio*) region, district.

contorsión *nf* contortion.

contorsionarse *vr* to contort *or* twist oneself, writhe.

contorsionista *nmf* contorsionist.

contra I *prep* against; **debemos luchar c. ellos,** we must fight them; **en c. de lo que se esperaba,** contrary to expectations; **hablar en c. de,** to criticize; **opinar en c.,** to disagree. **II** *nm* **los pros y los contras,** the pros and cons. **III** *nf fam* drawback, snag; **llevar la c. a algn,** to disagree with sb.

contraalmirante *nm* *Mil* rear admiral.

contraatacar *vtr* to counterattack.

contraataque *nm* counterattack.

contrabajo *nm* *Mús* (*instrumento*) double bass; (*voz*) low bass.

contrabandista *nmf* smuggler; **c. de armas,** gunrunner.

contrabando *nm* **1** (*acción*) smuggling; **c. de armas,** gunrunning; **pasar algo de c.,** to smuggle sth in. **2** (*mercancías*) smuggled goods *pl*; **un reloj de c.,** a contraband watch.

contracción *nf* contraction.

contracepción *nf* contraception.

contrachapado *nm* plywood.

contracorriente I *nf* crosscurrent; **c. submarina,** underset. **II** **ir c.,** to go against the tide.

contráctil *adj* contractile.

contractual *adj* contractual.

contracultura *nf* counterculture.

contradanza *nf* country dance.

contradecir (*pp* **contradicho**) **I** *vtr* **1** (*decir lo contrario*) to contradict; **siempre me contradices,** you're always contradicting me. **2** (*estar en oposición*) to run against,

disagree with; **sus actos contradicen sus palabras,** he says one thing and does another. **II contradecirse** *vr* to contradict oneself; (*decir cosas contradictorias*) to be inconsistent.

contradicción *nf* contradiction; **el espíritu de la c.,** contrariness.

contradictorio,-a *adj* contradictory.

contraer I *vtr* **1** (*encoger*) to contract, tighten (up). **2** (*enfermedad*) to catch. **3** (*deuda*) to contract; (*hábito*) to pick up; **c. matrimonio con algn,** to marry sb. **II contraerse** *vr* **1** (*encogerse*) to contract, tighten. **2** *Am* (*concentrarse*) to apply oneself (**a,** to).

contraespionaje *nm* counterespionage.

contrafuerte *nm* **1** *Arquit* buttress. **2** (*en calzado*) stiffener. **3** (*de montaña*) foothill.

contrahecho,-a *adj* hunchbacked, deformed.

contraigo *indic pres véase* **contraer.**

contraindicación *nf* *Med* contraindication; **'contraindicaciones, ninguna,'** 'it can be used safely by anyone'.

contraje *pt indef véase* **contraer.**

contralmirante *nm* *Mil véase* **contraalmirante.**

contralto *nmf* *Mús* contralto.

contraluz *nm* view against the light; **a c.,** against the light.

contramaestre *nm* **1** *Náut* warrant officer. **2** (*capataz*) foreman.

contramano (a) *loc adv* the wrong way *or* direction.

contraofensiva *nf* *Mil* counteroffensive.

contraorden *nf* countermand.

contrapartida *nf* **1** *Com Fin* balancing entry. **2** *fig* compensation.

contrapelo (a) *loc adv* the wrong way; *fig* the wrong way, against the grain; **acariciar un gato a c.,** to stroke a cat the wrong way.

contrapesar *vtr* **1** (*equilibrar*) to counterbalance, counterpoise. **2** *fig* (*compensar*) to offset, balance.

contrapeso *nm* counterweight.

contraponer (*pp* **contrapuesto**) **I** *vtr* **1** (*oponer*) to set in opposition (**a,** to), set up (**a,** against); (*encarar*) to set against. **2** *fig* (*contrastar*) to contrast. **II contraponerse** *vr* (*oponerse*) to be opposed.

contraportada *nf* back page.

contraposición *nf* (*oposición*) clash, conflict; (*contraste*) contrast; **estar en c.,** to clash.

contraproducente *adj* counterproductive; **tener un resultado c.,** to have a boomerang effect.

contrapuerta *nf* storm door, double door.

contrapuesto,-a I *pp de* **contraponer. II** *adj* (*en oposición*) clashing, conflicting; (*en contraste*) contrasting.

contrapuntear *vi* *Am* **1** (*versos*) to compete in poetry improvising contest. **2** (*rivalizar*) to compete, contend.

contrapunto *nm* **1** *Mús* counterpoint. **2** *Am* (*de versos*) poetry improvisation contest.

contrariar *vtr* **1** (*oponerse*) to oppose, go against; **lo dice por contrariarme,** he says that just to be awkward. **2** (*disgustar*) to upset; **por no contrariarte,** so as not to upset you. **3** (*obstaculizar*) to obstruct, hinder.

contrariedad *nf* **1** (*oposición*) opposition. **2** (*disgusto*) annoyance; **hacer un gesto de c.,** to look annoyed. **3** (*contratiempo*) obstacle, setback, hitch.

contrario,-a I *adj* **1** (*opuesto*) contrary, opposite; **al c.,** on the contrary; **de lo c.,** otherwise; **en dirección contraria,** in the wrong direction; **llevar la contraria,** to be contrary; **no llevarle la contraria a algn,** to humour sb; **por el c.,** on the contrary; **todo lo c.,** quite the opposite. **2** (*perjudicial*) contrary (**a,** to), harmful (**a,** to); **c. a nuestros intereses,** not in our interests. **II** *nm,f* opponent, rival. ◆ **contrariamente** *adv* **c. a ...,** contrary to ... .

contrarrestar *vtr* **1** *(hacer frente)* to resist, oppose; *(compensar)* to offset, counteract. **2** *(pelota)* to return.

contrarrevolución *nf* counter-revolution.

contrasentido *nm* **1** *(gen)* contradiction; *(disparate)* piece of nonsense. **2** *(mala interpretación)* misinterpretation.

contraseña *nf* *(consigna)* secret mark; *Mil* password, watchword.

contrastar **I** *vtr* **1** *(oponer)* to contrast (**con**, with). **2** *(pesos, medidas)* to check. **3** *(oro, plata)* to hallmark. **II** *vi* *(oponerse)* to contrast (**con**, with), be in contrast (**a**, to).

contraste *nm* **1** *(oposición)* contrast. **2** *(de pesos y medidas)* verification, inspection. **3** *(en oro, plata)* hallmark.

contrata *nf* contract.

contratación *nf* **1** *(pedidos)* total orders *pl*, volume of business. **2** *(contrato)* hiring.

contratar *vtr* *(servicio, mercancía)* to sign a contract for; *(empleado)* to hire, engage; *(deportista)* to sign up; *(arriendo)* to take on.

contratiempo *nm* **1** *(contrariedad)* setback, hitch; *(accidente)* mishap. **2** *Mús* **a c.,** offbeat; *fig* in the offbeat.

contratista *nmf* contractor. ■ *Constr* **c. de obras,** building contractor.

contrato *nm* contract. ■ **c. de alquiler,** lease, leasing agreement; **c. de trabajo,** work contract.

contravención *nf* *Jur* contravention, infringement, violation.

contravenir *vtr Jur* to contravene, infringe, violate.

contraventana *nf* shutter.

contrayente **I** *adj* contracting. **II** *nmf* *(en un matrimonio)* contracting party.

contribución *nf* **1** contribution; **poner a c.,** to use, draw on. **2** *Fin* *(impuesto)* tax, *rates pl*. ■ **c. territorial,** land tax; **c. urbana,** rates *pl*.

contribuir **I** *vtr* to contribute (**a**, to; **para**, towards). **II** *vi* **1** to contribute; *fig* **c. al éxito de algo,** to contribute to the success of sth. **2** *Fin* *(pagar impuestos)* to pay taxes.

contribuyente *Fin* **I** *adj* taxpaying. **II** *nmf* taxpayer.

contrición *nf* contrition; **hacer un acto de c.,** to repent.

contrincante *nmf* rival, opponent.

contristar **I** *vtr* *(afligir)* to make sad. **II contristarse** *vr* *(afligirse)* to become sad, grieve.

contrito,-a *adj* contrite.

control *nm* **1** control; **bajo c.,** under control; **bajo el c. de,** under the supervision of; **c. de (la) natalidad,** birth control; **ejercer** *or* **llevar el c.,** to be in control. ■ **c. a distancia,** remote control. **2** *(lugar)* checkpoint. ■ **c. de pasaportes,** passport inspection *or* check; *Aut* **c. policial,** roadblock.

controlador,-a **I** *adj* control; **ficha controladora,** control chart. **II** *nm,f Av* **c. (aéreo),** air traffic controller.

controlar **I** *vtr* **1** *(gen)* to control. **2** *(comprobar)* to check; *Com Fin* to audit. **II controlarse** *vr* *(moderarse)* to control oneself.

controversia *nf* controversy, argument.

controvertir **I** *vtr* to dispute, argue about. **II** *vi* to argue.

contubernio *nm pey* **1** *(cohabitación ilícita)* cohabitation. **2** *(confabulación)* conspiracy, clique.

contumacia *nf* **1** *(obstinación)* obstinacy; *(desobediencia)* insubordination. **2** *Jur* contumacy.

contumaz *adj* **1** *(obstinado)* obstinate; *(desobediente)* insubordinate. **2** *Jur* contumacious.

contundencia *nf* **1** *(fuerza)* force, energy. **2** *fig* *(convicción)* conviction, force; **me convenció con la c. de sus argumentos,** I was convinced by the weight of her argument.

contundente *adj* **1** *(arma)* blunt. **2** *fig* *(convincente)* forceful, convincing; **un argumento c.,** a weighty argument.

conturbación *nf* anxiety, dismay, perturbation.

conturbado,-a **I** *pp de* **conturbar.** **II** *adj* anxious, dismayed, perturbed.

conturbar **I** *vtr* to trouble, dismay, perturb. **II conturbarse** *vr* to be troubled, be dismayed become perturbed.

contusión *nf* contusion, bruise.

contusionar *vtr* to contuse, bruise.

conuco *nm Am* small farm.

convalecencia *nf* convalescence.

convalecer *vi* to convalesce (**de**, after), recover (**de**, from).

convaleciente *adj & nmf* convalescent.

convalidación *nf* *Educ* validation; *(documento)* ratification.

convalidar *vtr* to validate; *(documento)* to ratify.

convección *nf Fis* convection.

convecino,-a **I** *adj* neighbouring, *US* neighboring. **II** *nm, f* neighbour, *US* neighbor.

convector *nm* convector.

convencer **I** *vtr* to convince, persuade; **c. a algn de algo,** to convince sb about sth; **dejarse c.,** to let oneself be persuaded; **no me convence la idea,** I'm not sold on the idea. **II convencerse** *vr* to be convinced, become convinced; **me convencí de mi error,** I realized my mistake.

convencimiento *nm* conviction, certainty; **llegar al c. de que ...,** to be convinced that ... .

convención *nf* **1** *Pol* *(pacto)* convention, treaty. **2** *(asamblea)* convention, congress. **3** *(conformidad)* convention.

convencional *adj* conventional.

convencionalismo *nm* conventionalism, conventionality.

convenible *adj* **1** *(conveniente)* suitable, fitting; *(precio)* fair, reasonable. **2** *(persona)* accommodating.

convenido,-a **I** *pp de* **convenir.** **II** *adj* agreed, arranged, set.

conveniencia *nf* **1** *(utilidad)* usefulness; *(oportunidad)* suitability, advisability. **2** *(provecho)* convenience. **3** *(convenio)* agreement. ■ **conveniencias sociales,** proprieties.

conveniente *adj* **1** *(útil)* useful; *(oportuno)* suitable, convenient; *(aconsejable)* advisable; **creo c. avisarle,** I feel I should warn him; **en el momento c.,** at the right time. **2** *(precio)* good, fair.

convenio *nm* agreement, treaty, convenant. ■ **c. laboral,** labour agreement.

convenir **I** *vtr & vi* **1** *(acordar)* to agree; **c. en,** to agree on; **c. una fecha,** to agree on a date; **sueldo a c.,** salary negotiable. **2** *(ser oportuno)* to suit, be good for; **conviene recordar que ...,** it's as well to remember that ...; **te conviene descansar,** you need a rest.

conventillero,-a *nm, f Arg* *(persona)* gossip.

convento *nm Rel* *(de monjas)* convent; *(de monjes)* monastery.

conventual *adj Rel* conventual.

convergencia *nf* convergence.

convergente *adj* convergent, converging, concurring.

converger *vi*, **convergir** *vi* to converge, meet.

conversación *nf* conversation, talk; **dar c.,** to keep sb chatting; *fig* **dejar caer una cosa en la c.,** to bring sth up in conversation; *fig* **trabar c. con algn,** to get into conversation with sb.

conversador,-a **I** *adj* talkative. **II** *nm, f* **1** *(hablador)* conversationalist, talker. **2** *Am* *(charlatán)* gabber.

conversar *vi* to converse, talk.

conversión *nf* conversion.

converso,-a I *adj* converted. **II** *nm, f* convert.

conversón,-ona *adj CAm* talkative.

convertibilidad *nf* convertibility.

convertible I *adj* convertible. **II** *nm Am* convertible.

convertir I *vtr* **1** (*transformar*) to change, convert. **2** *Rel* to convert; **c. a algn al cristianismo**, to convert sb to Christianity. **II convertirse** *vr* **1** **c. en**, to turn into, become; **se convirtió en una escritora famosa**, she became a famous writer. **2** *Rel* to be converted (**a**, to).

convexidad *nf* convexity.

convexo,-a *adj* convex.

convicción *nf* conviction; **mis convicciones no me permiten hacer eso**, it's against my beliefs to do that; **tengo la c. de que ...**, I firmly believe that ... . **convicto,-a** *adj* guilty, convicted.

convidado,-a I *pp de* **convidar**. **II** *adj* invited. **III** *nm, f* guest; *fig* **como un c. de piedra**, silent as the grave.

convidar I *vtr* **1** to invite; **nos convidó a una copa**, he offered us a drink. **2** *fig* (*incitar*) to inspire, prompt. **II convidarse** *vr fam* to invite oneself; **se convidó por la cara**, he invited himself along.

convincente *adj* convincing.

convite *nm* **1** (*fiesta*) party; (*comida*) dinner, lunch. **2** (*invitación*) invitation. **3** *Am* (*mojiganga*) masquerade.

convivencia *nf* life together; *fig* coexistence; **la c. se hizo imposible**, living together became impossible.

convivir *vi* to live together; **saber c.**, to give and take; *fig* to coexist (**con**, with).

convocar *vtr* to convoke, call together, summon; **c. oposiciones**, to hold competitive examinations; **c. una reunión**, to call a meeting.

convocatoria *nf* **1** (*citación*) convocation, summons *sing*, call (to a meeting). **2** *Educ* examination; **c. de setiembre**, second sitting (in September).

convoy *nm* **1** *Aut Náut* (*escolta*) convoy. **2** *Ferroc* train.

convoyar *vtr* to convoy, guard, escort.

convulsión *nf Med* convulsion; *fig* upheaval.

convulsionar *vtr Med* to convulse.

convulsivo,-a *adj* convulsive.

convulso,-a *adj* convulsed (**de**, with).

conyugal *adj* conjugal. ■ **vida c.**, married life.

cónyuge *nmf* spouse, partner; (*marido*) husband; (*mujer*) wife; **cónyuges**, married couple *sing*, husband and wife.

coña *nf vulg* **1** (*guasa*) joking, larking about; **estar de c.**, to have a joke; **ser la c.**, to be the limit; **tomar algo a c.**, to take sth as a joke. **2** (*molestia*) nuisance.

coñac *nm* brandy, cognac.

coñazo *nm vulg* pain, drag; **dar el c.**, to be a real pain.

coñearse *vr vulg* to take the piss (**de**, out of).

coño I *nm Anat vulg* cunt; **estar en el quinto c.**, to be far or miles away. **II** *interj vulg* (*sorpresa*) well, fuck me!; (*disgusto, enfado*) for fuck's sake!; **¡qué c. quieres!**, what the hell do you want!

coop. *abr de* **cooperativa**, co-operative, co-op.

cooperación *nf* co-operation.

cooperador,-a I *adj* co-operative, collaborating, participating. **II** *nm, f* collaborator, co-operator.

cooperar *vi* to co-operate (**a, en**, in; **con**, with); **c. a un fin**, to have a common aim.

cooperativo,-a I *adj* co-operative. **II** *nf* **1** (*asociación, local*) co-operative. ■ **c. agrícola**, farmers' co-operative.

coordenado,-a I *pp de* **coordenar**. **II** *adj* co-ordinated. **III** *nf* co-ordinate.

coordinación *nf* co-ordination.

coordinador,-a I *adj* co-ordinating, organizing. **II** *nm, f* co-ordinator, organizer. **III** *nf* (*comité*) co-ordinating committee; **c. general**, joint committee.

coordinar *vtr* to co-ordinate; **c. los esfuerzos**, to combine forces.

copa *nf* **1** (*vaso*) glass; (*alcohol*) **irse de copas**, to go out drinking; **llevar una c. de más**, to have one too many; **tomar una c.**, to have a drink. ■ **sombrero de c.**, top hat. **2** (*del árbol*) top. **3** *Dep* (*campeonato, trofeo*) cup; **la c. mundial**, the world cup. **4 copas**, *Naipes* (*baraja española*) hearts.

copar *vtr* to take; **los puestos están todos copados**, the jobs are all taken up.

copartícipe *adj & nmf* (*socio*) partner; (*colaborador*) collaborator; (*copropietario*) joint owner, co-owner.

copear *vi* to drink; (*ir de copas*) to go drinking.

Copenhague *n* Copenhagen.

copeo *nm* drinking; **ir de c.**, to go out drinking.

copete *nm* **1** (*de pelo*) tuft; (*penacho*) crest; (*de caballo*) forelock; (*de helado*) top. **2** *fig* (*altanería*) pride, haughtiness. **3** *fig* **de alto c.**, high-class.

copia *nf* **1** copy; **sacar una c.**, to make a copy. ■ **papel de c.**, copy paper. **2** (*persona*) image. **3** *Cin* print; **c. diaria**, rushes *pl*. **4** *lit* (*abundancia*) abundance.

copiador,-a I *adj* copying. **II** *nf* photocopier.

copiar *vtr* **1** (*gen*) to copy. **2** (*escribir*) to copy, take down. **3** (*imitar*) to copy, imitate. **4** *Educ* to cheat; **la pillaron copiando**, she was caught cheating.

copiloto *nm Av* copilot; *Aut* co-driver.

copinar *vtr Méx* **1** (*desollar*) to skin. **2** (*desatar*) to let loose.

copión,-ona *nm, f fam* cheat, cheater; (*imitador*) copycat.

copiosidad *nf* abundance.

copioso,-a *adj* abundant, copious, plentiful; **copiosas lluvias**, heavy rain *sing*.

copista *nmf* copyist.

copita *nf* **1** (*small*) glass. **2** *Golf* tee.

copla *nf* **1** (*verso, estrofa*) verse, couplet; *fam* **andar en coplas**, to be the talk of the town; *fam* **la misma c.**, the same old story. **2 coplas**, (*canciones*) folk songs, popular songs. **3** *Am* (*caño*) pipe (joint).

copo¹ *nm* **1** (*gen*) flake; (*de nieve*) snowflake; (*de algodón*) ball (of cotton); **copos de avena**, rolled oats. **2** *Arg Ven* (*nubes*) bank of clouds.

copo² *nm* (*pesca*) catch (of fish).

copón *nm fam* **se armó un lío del c.**, there was a great mess.

coproducción *nf* co-production, joint production.

coproductor *nm* co-producer.

copropiedad *nf* joint ownership.

copropietario,-a *adj & nm, f* co-owner, joint owner.

copudo,-a *adj* bushy, thick.

cópula *nf* **1** (*coito*) copulation, intercourse. **2** *Ling* conjunction.

copular *vtr* to copulate (**con**, with).

copulativo,-a *adj* copulative.

COPYME *nm abr de* **Confederación de la Pequeña y Mediana Empresa.**

coque *nm Min* coke.

coquetear *vi* to flirt (**con**, with).

coquetería *nf* coquetry, flirtation.

coqueto,-a I *adj* flirtatious. **II** *nm, f* **1** (*mujer*) coquette, flirt; (*hombre*) flirt. **2** *Mueb* (*tocador*) dressing table.

coquetón,-ona *adj* (*mujer*) coquette, flirty; (*hombre*) flirtatious.

coraje *nm* **1** (*valor*) toughness, courage; **echar c.**, to take courage. **2** (*ira*) anger, annoyance; **dar c.**, to infuriate; **¡qué c.!**, how maddening!

corajudo,-a *adj* **1** *(valiente)* tough, brave. **2** *(irritable)* quick-tempered.

coral¹ *nm Zool* coral; **corales,** coral necklace *sing.*

coral² **I** *adj* choral. **II** *nm Mús* choral, chorale.

coralina *nf Bot* coralline.

coralino,-a *adj* coral.

corambre *nf Rel* hides *pl,* skins *pl.*

Corán *nf Rel* Koran.

coraza *nf* **1** *(armadura)* armour, *US* armor, cuirass; *fig* armour, protection. **2** *Zool (caparazón)* shell.

corazón *nm* **1** *Anat* heart; **estar enfermo** *or* **padecer del c.,** to have heart trouble; *fig* **abrir algn su c.,** to open one's heart out; *fig* **con el c. en un puño,** with one's heart in one's mouth; *fig* **de (todo) c.,** in all sincerity; *fig* **hablar con el c. en la mano,** to wear one's heart on one's sleeve; *fig* **romper el c. a algn,** to break sb's heart; *fig* **tener buen c.,** to be kindhearted. **2** *(parte central)* heart, core; *(de fruta)* core; **en el c. de la ciudad,** in the heart of the city. **3** *(apelativo cariñoso)* darling, sweetheart. **4** **corazones,** *Naipes* hearts.

corazonada *nf* **1** *(presentimiento)* hunch, feeling; **tuve la c. de que ...,** something told me that ... . **2** *(impulso)* impulse.

corbata *nf* **1** tie, *US* necktie; **con c.,** wearing a tie. **2** *(en bandera)* sash, tassel. **3** *Arg (pañuelo)* bandanna, bandana, scarf.

corbatín *nm* bow tie.

corbeta *nf Náut* corvette.

Córcega *n* Corsica.

corcel *nm lit* steed, charger.

corchea *nf Mús* quaver.

corchero,-a *adj* cork; **industria corchera,** cork industry.

corchete *nm* **1** *Cost (gafete)* hook and eye, snap fastener. **2** *Impr* square bracket.

corcho *nm* **1** *(gen)* cork; *(corteza)* cork bark. **2** *(tapón)* cork. **3** *(pesca)* float. **4** *(flotador)* float.

córcholis *interj (sorpresa)* goodness me!, *US* gee!

corcor *nm CAm* gulp, gulping noise.

corcova *nf* **1** *Anat (joroba)* hunchback, hump. **2** *Am* party lasting one or more days.

corcovado,-a **I** *adj* hunchbacked. **II** *nm,f* hunchback.

corcovear *vi* **1** *Am (refunfuñar)* to grumble; *(indignarse)* to get upset. **2** *Méx (tener miedo)* to be afraid.

corcovo *nm* prance.

cordaje *nm* **1** *(cuerdas)* ropes *pl,* cordage. **2** *Náut* rigging.

cordel *nm* rope, cord; **a c.,** in a straight line.

cordelería *nf* **1** *(oficio)* ropemaking. **2** *Náut* rigging.

cordelero,-a *nm,f* ropemaker.

cordero,-a **I** *nm,f* lamb; *fig* **ser un c.,** to be as meek as a lamb. **II** *nm* lambskin.

cordial **I** *adj* **1** *(afable)* cordial, warm, friendly. **2** *Farm (tonificante)* cordial, stimulating. **II** *nm Farm* cordial.

cordialidad *nf* cordiality, warmth, friendliness.

cordillera *nf Geog* mountain chain *or* range.

cordobán *nm* cordovan (leather).

Córdoba *n* Cordova.

cordobés,-esa *adj & nm,f* Cordovan.

cordón *nm* **1** *(gen)* rope, string; *(de zapatos)* shoelace, shoestring; *Elec* flex; *(hebra)* **lana de 3 cordones,** 3-ply wool. ■ *Anat* **c. umbilical,** umbilical cord. **2** *(cadena humana)* cordon. ■ **c. policial,** police cordon.

cordoncillo *nm (cordón pequeño)* cord; *Cost* braid, piping.

cordura *nf* sound judgement, good sense; **con c.,** sensibly, prudently, wisely.

Corea *n* Korea.

corea *nf Med* Saint Vitus's dance.

coreano,-a **I** *adj & nm,f* Korean. **II** *nm (idioma)* Korean.

corear *vtr* **1** *(cantar a coro)* to sing in chorus. **2** *fig (opinión)* to echo. **3** *(aclamar)* to applaud.

coreografía *nf* choreography.

coreográfico,-a *adj* choreographic.

coreógrafo,-a *nm,f* choreographer.

corista *nf Teat* chorus girl.

coriza *nf Med* coryza.

cormorán *nm Orn* **c. (grande),** cormorant; **c. moñudo,** shag.

cornada *nf Taur* goring; **dar cornadas a,** to gore.

cornamenta *nf* **1** *(gen)* horns *pl;* *(del ciervo)* antlers *pl.* **2** *fam ofens (del marido)* cuckold's horns *pl.*

córnea *nf Anat* cornea.

cornear *vtr* to gore.

corneja *nf Orn* crow.

cornejo *nm Bot* dogwood.

córneo,-a *adj* horn-like, corneous.

córner *nm Ftb* corner, corner (kick); **sacar un c.,** to take a corner.

corneta **I** *nf Mús (instrumento)* bugle; **c. de llaves,** cornet. **II** *nm Mil (persona)* bugler; cornet player.

cornetín *nm Mús* **1** *(instrumento)* cornet. **2** *(persona)* cornet player.

cornisa *nf* **1** *Arquit* cornice. **2** *Geog* **la C. Cantábrica,** the Cantabrian Coast.

corno *nm Mús* horn; **c. inglés,** cor anglais, English horn.

cornucopia *nf* cornucopia, horn of plenty.

cornudo,-a **I** *adj* **1** *(animal)* horned, antlered. **2** *fam ofens (marido)* cuckolded. **II** *nm (marido)* cuckold.

coro *nm* **1** *mús* choir. **2** *Teat* chorus; *fig* **a c.,** all together; *fig* **hacer c.,** to join in the chorus.

corola *nf Bot* corolla.

corolario *nm* corollary.

corona *nf* **1** crown; **mensaje de la c.,** King's *or* Queen's speech. **2** *(aureola)* halo. **3** *(de ramas, flores)* wreath, garland. ■ **c. funeraria,** funeral wreath. **4** *Anat* crown (of the head); *(del diente)* crown. **5** *(moneda)* crown.

coronación *nf* **1** *(acto)* coronation. **2** *fig (culminación)* crowning.

coronamiento *nm* **1** *(culminación)* crowning. **2** *Arquit* crown.

coronar **I** *vtr* **1** *(poner una corona a)* to crown; *lit* **la sierra está coronada de nieve,** the mountains are capped with snow. **2** *fig (culminar)* to culminate, crown; **c. la cima,** to reach the summit. **II** **coronarse** *vr (en el parto)* to crown; **el niño se corona,** the baby's head is showing.

coronario,-a *adj Med* coronary; **insuficiencia coronaria,** cardiac arrest.

coronel *nm Mil* colonel.

coronilla *nf Anat* crown of the head; *fam* **andar de c.,** to run around in circles; *fam* **estar hasta la c.,** to be fed up (**de,** with).

corpiño *nm (prenda)* bodice.

corporación *nf* corporation; **c. metropolitana,** city corporation; *Com Fin* company, association.

corporal **I** *adj* corporal, body; **castigo c.,** corporal punishment. **II** *nm (lienzo)* corporal, corporale.

corporativo,-a *adj* corporative; **asociación corporativa,** syndicate.

corpóreo,-a *adj* bodily, physical.

corpulencia *nf* corpulence, stoutness.

corpulento,-a *adj* corpulent, stocky, stout.

corpus *nm* **1** *(conjunto)* corpus. **2** *Rel* **C.,** Corpus Christi.

corpúsculo *nm Biol* corpuscle.

corral *nm* **1** *(gen)* yard; *(de granja)* farmyard, *US* corral; *(de casa)* courtyard. **2** *(para niños)* playpen.

correa *nf* **1** *(tira)* strap; *(de reloj)* watchstrap; *(de pantalón)* belt; *(de perro)* lead, *US* leash. **2** *Téc* belt; **c. sin fin,** conveyor belt. **3** *(elasticidad)* elasticity, stretch; *fig* **tiene mucha c.,** he can take a joke.

correaje *nm* belts *pl*, straps *pl*.

corrección *nf* **1** *(rectificación)* correction, adjustment. ■ *Tip* **c. de pruebas,** proofreading. **2** *(cortesía)* courtesy, correctness, politeness; **tratar a la gente con c.,** to be polite. **3** *(reprimenda)* rebuke; *(castigo)* punishment.

correccional *adj & nm* reformatory.

correctivo,-a *adj & nm* corrective.

correcto,-a *adj* **1** *(sin errores)* correct, accurate, good. **2** *(rasgos)* regular; **facciones correctas,** regular *or* even features. **3** *(cortés)* polite, courteous (**con,** to); *(conducta)* proper, *(ropa)* suitable. ◆ **correctamente** *adv* **1** *(sin errores)* correctly, accurately. **2** *(con educación)* correctly, politely, properly.

corrector,-a **I** *adj* corrective. **II** *nm,f Impr* **c. de pruebas,** proofreader.

corredera *nf Téc* track, rail, runner; **puerta/ventana de c.,** sliding door/window.

corredizo,-a *adj* sliding; **nudo c.,** slipknot.

corredor,-a **I** *adj* running. **II** *nm,f* **1** *Dep* runner. **2** *Fin* **c. de bolsa,** stockbroker; **c. de fincas,** estate agent. **III** *nf Orn* **(ave) corredora,** flightless bird.

corregible *adj* which can be corrected, rectifiable.

corregir **I** *vtr* **1** *(gen)* to correct, rectify. **2** *Impr (pruebas etc)* to read. **3** *(reprender)* to scold, reprimand, tell off. **4** *Educ (ejercicios)* to mark. **II** **corregirse** *vr (persona)* to mend one's ways; *(defecto)* to right itself.

correlación *nf* correlation.

correlativo,-a *adj & nm* correlative.

corremolinos *nm inv Orn* dunlin.

correntoso,-a *adj Am* fast-flowing, torrential.

correo *nm* **1** post, *US* mail; **a vuelta de c.,** by return (of post); **echar al c.,** to post; **por c.,** by post. ■ **c. aéreo,** airmail; **c. certificado,** registered post; *Inform* **c. electrónico,** electronic mail; **(tren) c.,** mail train. **2 correos,** *(edificio)* post office sing; **lista de c.,** poste restante. **3** *(persona)* courier; *Mil* dispatch rider.

correoso,-a *adj* **1** *(flexible)* flexible, leathery. **2** *fig (difícil de masticar)* tough, leathery.

correr **I** *vi* **1** *(gen)* to run; **echar a c.,** to start running; **se fue corriendo,** he ran off *or* away. **2** *(ir deprisa)* to rush, hurry; **no corras, habla más despacio,** don't rush yourself, speak slower. **3** *(coche)* to go fast; *(conductor)* to drive fast; *(caballo)* to race, run. **4** *(tiempo)* to pass, go by; **el mes/año que corre,** the current month/year. **5** *(noticia)* to circulate, spread; **la noticia corrió como la pólvora,** the news spread like wildfire. **6** *(río)* to run, flow; *(camino etc)* to run; **la carretera corre entre las montañas,** the road winds through the mountains. **7** *(viento)* to blow. **8** *(sueldo)* to be payable. **9** *(encargarse)* **c. con los gastos,** to foot the bill; **corre a mi cargo,** I'll take care of it. **10 c. prisa,** to be urgent. **II** *vtr* **1** *(distancia)* to cover; *(país etc)* to travel through; **c. mundo,** to globetrot. **2** *(echar)* to close; *(cortina)* to draw; *(cerrojo)* to lock (the door). **3** *(mover)* to pull up, draw up. **4** *(arriesgarse)* to run. **5** *(aventura etc)* to have; **corrimos un gran peligro,** we were in great danger. **6** *(noticia etc)* to spread; **la voz,** to pass it on. **7** *fam* **correrla,** to live it up. **8** *(dejar) c. algo,** to let sth pass. **9** *Am (echar)* to let off, fire. **10** *Arg (asustar)* to frighten, scare. **III** **correrse** *vr* **1** *(persona)* to move over; *(objeto)* to shift, slide. **2** *(color, tinta)* to run; **se corre al lavarlo,** it runs in the wash. **3** *(avergonzarse)* to blush, go red. **4** *fam (juerga)* to go on; **se corrieron una juerga monumental,** they went on a real bender. **5** *arg (tener orgasmo)* to come.

correría *nf* **1** *(incursión)* raid, foray. **2 correrías,** *(andanzas)* travels.

correspondencia *nf* **1** *(gen)* correspondence; **esta palabra no tiene c. en español,** there's no translation for this word in Spanish. **2** *(comunicación)* communication; *Ferroc (enlace)* connection. **3** *(cartas)* correspondence, mail; **mantener c. con algn,** to correspond with sb.

corresponder **I** *vi* **1** *(gen)* to correspond (**a,** to; **con,** with), tally (**con,** with). **2** *(ser apropiado)* to be suitable *or* be right; *(color, mueble)* to match, go (**con,** with); *fig* **no corresponde con lo que esperaba,** it doesn't come up to my expectations. **3** *(incumbir)* to concern, be incumbent upon; **esta tarea te corresponde a ti,** it's your job to do this. **4** *(tocar, pertenecer)* to be one's due; **me dieron lo que me correspondía,** they gave me my share. **5** *(devolver)* to return, reciprocate; *(favor)* to repay; **amor no correspondido,** unrequited love; **c. a la amabilidad de algn,** to repay sb's kindness. **6** *Ferroc* to connect (**con,** with). **II** **corresponderse** *vr* **1** *(ajustarse)* to correspond, agree; *(armonizar)* to be in harmony (**con,** with). **2** *(apreciarse)* to have mutual affection; *(amarse)* to love one another, love each other. **3** *(cifras)* to tally.

correspondiente *adj* **1** *(que corresponde)* corresponding (**a,** to). **2** *(apropiado)* appropriate; *(oportuno)* convenient. **3** *(respectivo)* own; **cada uno con su c. etiqueta,** each one with its own label.

corresponsal *nmf Prensa* correspondent.

corresponsalía *nf Prensa* post of correspondent.

corretaje *nm Fin* brokerage (fee).

corretear **I** *vi* **1** *(correr)* to run about. **2** *fam (vagar)* to hang about. **II** *vtr* **1** *Am (perseguir)* to chase. **2** *CAm (ahuyentar)* to scare *or* ward off.

correteo *nm* running about, hustle and bustle.

correveidile *nmf inv fig* **1** *(chismoso)* gossip. **2** *(alcahuete)* go-between.

corrida *nf* **1** *(paso rápido)* run, dash, race; **de c.,** *(rápidamente)* in a flash; *(de memoria)* from memory, by heart. **2** *Taur (fiesta)* **c. (de toros),** bullfight.

corrido,-a **I** *pp de* correr. **II** *adj* **1** *(peso)* heavy; **un kilo c.,** over a kilo, a good kilo. **2** *(continuo)* drawn. **3** *(continuo)* continuous; **balcón c.,** full balcony; **seto c.,** unbroken hedge. **4** *fig (avergonzado)* abashed; **dejar c.,** to embarrass; **quedarse c.,** to feel embarrassed. **5** *fam (experimentado)* **hombre/mujer c.,** man/woman of the world. **6 de c.,** without stopping; **recitar de c.,** to reel off; **traducir de c.,** to translate at *or* on sight. **7** *Am (completo)* full, complete. **III** *nm Méx* ballad.

corriente **I** *adj* **1** *(común)* ordinary, average, run-of-the-mill; **es c. ver ...,** you often see ...; **lo más c. es ...,** the usual thing is ...; **salirse de lo c.,** to be out of the ordinary; **un vestido c.,** an ordinary dress. **2** *(agua)* running. **3** *(mes, año)* current, present; **el diez del c.,** the tenth of this month. **4** *Fin (cuenta)* current; *(moneda)* valid. **5** *(al día)* **al c.,** up to date; **estar al c.,** to be in the know; **poner (algn) al c. (de algo),** to fill (sb) in (on sth); **ponerse al c.,** to get up to date; **tener al c.,** to keep informed. **II** *nf* **1** current, stream, flow; **c. abajo,** downstream; **c. arriba,** upstream; **ir** *or* **navegar contra c.,** to swim against the tide; *fig* **ir a go against the tide;** *fig* **dejarse llevar por la c.,** to follow the herd; *fig* **seguir la c.,** to follow the crowd; *fam* **seguirle** *or* **llevarle la c. a algn,** to humour sb. ■ *Elec* **c. alterna,** alternating current; *Elec* **c. eléctrica,** (electric) current; *Geog* **c. del Golfo,** Gulf Stream; **c. sanguínea,** blood-stream. **2** *(de aire)* draught, *US* draft. **3** *(tendencia)* trend, current; **corrientes del arte,** currents in art. ◆ **corrientemente** *adv* usually, normally.

corrijo *indic pres véase* **corregir.**

corrillo *nm* small group of people talking, clique.

corrimiento *nm Geol* slipping, sliding. ■ **c. de tierras,** landslide.

corro *nm* **1** *(de personas)* circle, ring; *fig* **hacer c. aparte,** to form a small circle; *fig* **hacerle c. a algn,** to gather round sb. **2** *(juego infantil)* ring-a-ring-a-roses.

corroboración *nf* corroboration.

corroborar *vtr* to corroborate.

corroborativo,-a *adj* corroborative.

corroer I *vtr* 1 (*degastar*) to corrode; *Geol* to erode. 2 *fig* (*minar*) to corrode, eat away *or* up; **la envidia le corroe el alma,** envy eats away at the soul. **II corroerse** *vr* 1 (*desgastarse*) to become corroded. 2 *fig* to be eaten up (**de,** with).

corromper I *vtr* 1 (*pudrir*) to turn bad, rot. 2 (*pervertir*) to corrupt, pervert. 3 (*sobornar*) to bribe. 4 (*estropear*) to spoil; **la falta de lectura corroe el lenguaje,** not reading enough can impoverish one's language. **II corromperse** *vr* 1 (*pudrirse*) to go bad, rot. 2 (*pervertirse*) to become corrupted.

corrosión *nf* corrosión, rust; *Geol* erosion.

corrosivo,-a *adj* 1 corrosive. 2 *fig* (*mordaz*) caustic.

corrupción *nf* 1 (*putrefacción*) rot, decay. 2 *fig* corruption, degradation; (*soborno*) bribe; (*perversión*) seduction. ■ *Jur* **c. de menores,** corruption of minors.

corruptela *nf* corruption, sharp practice.

corrupto,-a *adj* corrupt; **un juez c.,** a corrupt judge.

corruptor,-a I *adj* corrupting. **II** *nm,f* corrupter, perverter.

corrusco *nm fam* crust of stale bread.

corsario,-a I *adj* privateer. **II** *nm* corsair, privateer.

corsé *nf* (*prenda*) corset.

corsetería *nf* ladies' underwear shop.

corso,-a *adj & nm,f* Corsican.

corta *nf* tree felling.

cortacésped *nm & f* lawnmower.

cortacircuitos *nm inv Elec* circuit breaker.

cortado,-a I *pp de* cortar. **II** *adj* 1 (*troceado*) cut (up); (*en lonchas*) sliced. 2 (*leche*) sour. 3 (*labios*) chapped. 4 *fig* (*estilo*) concise, clipped. 5 *fam* (*aturdido*) dumbfounded; **quedarse c.,** to be speechless *or* lost for words. 6 *Am* (*cuerpo*) chilly. 7 *SAm* (*sin dinero*) penniless. **III** *nm* small coffee with a dash of milk.

cortador,-a I *adj* cutting. **II** *nm* cutter.

cortadura *nf* 1 (*corte*) cut. 2 *Geog* (*paso*) gorge. 3 **cortaduras,** (*recortes*) cuttings, clippings.

cortafuego *nm* 1 *Agr* (*zanja*) firebreak. 2 *Arquit* (*pared*) fire wall.

cortante *adj* cutting, sharp; *fig* (*viento*) biting, bitter; *fig* (*estilo*) incisive, acrid, cutting.

cortapapeles *nm inv* paperknife; *Téc* guillotine.

cortapisa *nf fig* restriction, limitation, condition; **sin cortapisas,** with no strings attached.

cortaplumas *nm inv* penknife.

cortar I *vtr* 1 (*gen*) to cut; (*pelo*) to cut, trim; (*pastel*) to cut up; (*carne*) to carve; (*árbol*) to cut down; *Cost* (*vestido*) to cut out; **c. por la mitad,** to split down the middle; *fam fig* **c. con un amigo,** to split up with a friend. 2 (*piel*) to chap, crack. 3 *Naipes* to cut. 4 (*detener, interrumpir*) to cut off, interrupt; **nos han cortado el teléfono,** our telephone has been disconnected; *fig* **c. algo de raíz,** to nip sth in the bud; *fam* **c. algo por lo sano,** to take drastic measures. 5 (*bloquear*) to block; **la nieve nos cortó el paso,** we were cut off by the snow. 6 (*suprimir*) to cut out; *Cin* (*película*) to cut. 7 (*viento frío*) to chill, bite; **un viento que corta,** a biting wind. 8 *fig* (*dividir*) to divide, split; **el río corta el valle en dos,** the river cuts through the valley. 9 *Culin* (*mayonesa etc*) to curdle. 10 *Arg PR Urug* to take a short cut through. **II** *vi* (*destacarse*) to stand out. **III cortarse** *vr* 1 (*herirse*) to cut oneself; **c. el pelo,** (*uno mismo*) to cut one's hair; (*por otro*) to have one's hair cut. 2 (*piel*) to become chapped. 3 (*leche*) to curdle; (*mayonesa*) to separate, curdle. 4 *Tel* to be cut off; **se cortó la comunicación,** we were cut off. 5 *fam* (*aturdirse*) to get confused *or* tongue-tied; **hablar en público me corta mucho,** I get tongue-tied speaking in public. 6 *vulg* **cortársela,** to cut one's dick off.

cortaúñas *nm inv* nail clippers *pl*.

---

corte¹ I *nm* 1 (*gen*) cut; **c. de pelo,** haircut; **me he hecho un c. en la mano,** I cut my hand. 2 (*filo*) edge. 3 (*sección*) section; **c. transversal,** cross section. 4 *Cost* cross section; **este vestido tiene un c. elegante,** this dress has an elegant cut. ■ **c. y confección,** dressmaking. 5 (*de libro*) edge. 6 (*tela para vestido*) length. 7 *fam* (*respuesta brusca*) rebuff; **dar un c. a algn,** to cut so dead; **¡jo, qué c.!,** what a blow! 8 *vulg* **c. de mangas,** ≈ V-sign. 9 *Arg* (*gallardía*) grace, gracefulness.

corte² *nf* 1 (*de reyes*) court; *fig hum* (*séquito*) retinue; **hacer la c. a,** to court. 2 **Cortes,** (Spanish) Parliament *sing.* 3 *Am Jur* (*tribunal*) court.

cortedad *nf* 1 (*pequeñez*) shortness, smallness. 2 *fig* (*timidez*) shyness, timidity. 3 *fig* (*falta*) lack; **c. de ánimo,** lack of courage.

cortejar *vtr* to court.

cortejo *nm* 1 (*galanteo*) courting. 2 (*comitiva*) entourage, retinue. ■ **c. fúnebre,** funeral cortège. 3 *fig* (*secuela*) sequel, aftermath.

cortés *adj* courteous, polite; *prov* **lo c. no quita lo valiente,** you can be polite but firm at the same time. ◆ **cortésmente** *adv* courteously, politely.

cortesía *nf* 1 (*educación*) courtesy, politeness; **acto de c.,** politeness; **la c. pide que ...,** etiquette demands that ... . ■ **visita de c.,** courtesy call. 2 (*en cartas*) formal ending. 3 (*reverencia*) bow, curtsy.

corteza *nf* 1 (*de árbol*) bark; (*de fruta*) peel, skin; (*de queso*) rind; (*de pan*) crust. 2 *fig* (*apariencia*) outside, outward appearance.

cortijero,-a *nm,f* Andalusian farmer.

cortijo *nm* Andalusian farm *or* farmhouse.

cortina *nf* curtain, screen; **c. de tienda,** tent flap; **correr las cortinas,** to draw the curtains. ■ *Mil fig* **c. de fuego,** barrage; *fig* **c. de humo,** smoke screen.

cortinaje *nm* drapery.

cortinilla *nf* small lace curtain.

cortisona *nf Med* cortisone.

corto,-a I *adj* 1 (*distancia*) short; **novela corto,** short story; *fam* **c. de alcances,** not very bright, dim; *fam* **c. de miras,** narrow-minded. ■ **c. de vista,** short-sighted; *Aut* **luz corta,** dipped headlights *pl.* 2 (*tiempo*) short, brief; **el viaje se hizo c.,** the journey went by quickly; *fig* **a la corta** *or* **a la larga,** sooner or later. 3 (*escaso*) scant, meagre; *fam* **quedarse c.,** (*calcular mal*) to underestimate; (*no decir todo*) to hold sth back. 4 *fam* (*tonto*) thick, dim. 5 (*apocado*) timid, shy. **II** *nm Cin* short (film).

cortocircuito *nm Elec* short circuit.

cortometraje *nm Cin* short (film).

coruñés,-esa I *adj* of or from La Coruña. **II** *nm,f* native or inhabitant of La Coruña.

corvadura *nf* curvature, curve.

corvejón *nm* 1 (*de caballo*) hock; (*de gallo*) spur. 2 *Orn* cormorant.

corvina *nf* (*pez*) meagre.

corvo,-a *adj* curved, bent; **nariz corva,** hooked nose.

corzo,-a *nm,f Zool* (*macho*) roe buck; (*hembra*) roe deer.

cosa¹ *nf* 1 (*gen*) thing; **mete tus cosas en el cajón,** put your things in the drawer; **tengo que decirte una c.,** I've got something to tell you; **tal como están las cosas,** as things stand. 2 (*asunto*) matter, business; **cosas de negocios,** business matters; **eso es c. tuya,** that's your business *or* affair; **eso es otra c.,** that's different. 3 (*frase negativa*) nothing, not anything; **no he visto c. igual,** I've never seen anything like it. 4 (*tiempo*) **c. de,** about; **es c. de unas horas,** it'll take a couple of hours. 5 (*manía*) hang-up; **cada uno tiene sus cosas,** we've all got our hang-ups. 6 (*locuciones*) **como si tal c.,** just like that; **cosas de la vida,** that's life; **decir cuatro cosas,** to tell a few home truths; **no sea c. que ...,** make sure that ...; **no ser gran c.,** not to be important, not be up to much; **no valer gran c.,**

not to be worth much; **ser c. hecha,** to be no sooner said than done; **ser poquita c.,** not to be much.

cosa² *conj Am* so that.

cosaco,-a *adj & nm* Cossack; *fam* **beber como un c.,** to drink like a fish.

coscorrón *nm* knock *or* blow on the head.

cosecha *nf* **1** *Agr* harvest, crop; **de c. propia,** home-grown; *fig* of one's own invention; **hacer la c.,** to harvest. **2** *(tiempo)* harvest time. **3** *(año del vino)* vintage.

cosechadora *nf Téc* combine harvester.

cosechar *vtr* **1** *Agr* to harvest, gather (in); **se cosecha en setiembre,** harvest time is in September. **2** *(cultivar)* to grow. **3** *fig (recoger)* to reap, harvest; **c. disgustos,** to build up trouble (for oneself).

cosechero,-a *nm,f* harvester, grower.

coser *vtr* **1** to sew; **te he cosido el botón,** I've sewn the button on for you; *fam* **es c. y cantar,** it's plain sailing, it's a piece of cake. **2** *Med* to stitch up. **3** *(grapar)* to staple (together). **4** *fig (atravesar)* **c. a balazos,** to riddle with bullets.

cosido,-a I *pp* de **coser.** II *adj* sewn-on. III *nm* **1** sewing. **2** *Med* stitching.

cosijoso,-a *adj* **1** *Am (molesto)* annoying. **2** *Guat Méx (quejica)* grumbling.

cosmético,-a I *adj & nm* cosmetic. II *nf* cosmetics *pl*.

cósmico,-a *adj* cosmic.

cosmografía *nf* cosmography.

cosmográfico,-a *adj* cosmographic, cosmographical.

cosmología *nf* cosmology.

cosmológico,-a *adj* cosmologic, cosmological.

cosmonauta *nmf* cosmonaut.

cosmopolita *adj & nmf* cosmopolitan.

cosmos *nm inv* cosmos.

coso *nm* **1** *(cercado)* arena, enclosure; *Taur lit* bullring. **2** *(carcoma)* woodworm.

cosquillas *nfpl* tickles, tickling *sing*; **hacer c. algn,** to tickle sb; **tener c.,** to be ticklish; *fam* **buscarle las c. a algn,** to annoy sb.

cosquillear *vtr* to tickle; **me cosquillea la idea de ...,** I've been toying with the idea of ... .

cosquilleo *nm* tickling.

costa¹ *nf Geog (litoral)* coast, coastline; *(playa)* beach, seaside, *US* shore; **veraneamos en la c.,** we spend our summer holidays at the seaside. ■ **C. de Marfil,** Ivory Coast.

costa² *nf* **1** *(coste)* *Fin* cost, price; **a c. de,** at the expense of; **a c. de muchos esfuerzos,** by dint of great effort; **a toda c.,** at all costs, at any price; **vive a c. mía,** he lives off me. **2** **costas,** *Jur (gastos)* costs; **condenar a c.,** to order to cover the costs; **pagar las c.,** to pay costs.

costado *nm* **1** *(lado)* side; **de c.,** sideways. **2** *Méx Ferroc (andén)* platform. **3 costados,** *(genealogía)* lineage *sing*; **por los cuatro c.,** on all sides; **es catalana por los cuatro c.,** she's Catalan through and through.

costal *nm* sack; *fig* **vaciar el c.,** to relieve oneself of the burden; *prov* **ser harina de otro c.,** that's another kettle of fish.

costalada *nf,* **costalazo** *nm* fall (on one's back); **darse una c.,** to fall on one's back.

costanero,-a *adj* **1** *(inclinado)* sloping. **2** *Náut (costero)* coastal.

costanilla *nf* steep street.

costar *vi* **1** *Fin Com* to cost; **c. barato,** to be cheap; **c. caro,** to be expensive, cost a lot; **¿cuánto cuesta?,** how much is it?; *fam* **cuesta un ojo de la cara,** it costs an arm and a leg. **2** *fig* **c. caro algo a algn,** to pay dearly for sth; **c. trabajo** *or* **mucho,** to be hard; **cueste lo que cueste,** at any cost; **le costó la vida,** it cost him his life; **me cuesta hablar francés,** I find it difficult to speak French.

costarricense *adj & nmf,* **costarriqueño,-a** *adj & nm,f* Costa Rican.

coste *nm* cost, price, expense; **a precio de c.,** (at) cost price; **c. de la vida,** cost of living.

costear¹ I *vtr (pagar)* to afford, pay for; **c. los gastos,** to foot the bill. II **costearse** *vr (pagarse)* to pay one's way.

costear² *vtr* **1** *Náut* to coast. **2** *Arg Chi (lugar)* to reach with great difficulty.

costero,-a I *adj* coastal, coast; **ciudad costera,** sea-side town. II *nm Náut* coasting vessel, coaster.

costilla *nf* **1** *Anat* rib. **2** *Culin* cutlet. **3** *fam (esposa)* wife, other half. **4 costillas,** *Anat fam* back *sing*; **medirle las c. a algn,** to give sb a good hiding.

costillar *nm Anat* ribs *pl*.

costo¹ *nm* cost, price.

costo² *nm arg (hachís)* dope, shit, stuff.

costoso,-a *adj* **1** *(caro)* costly, expensive. **2** *(difícil)* hard; **es un trabajo c.,** it's hard work.

costra *nf* crust; *Med* scab.

costumbre *nf* **1** *(hábito)* habit; **como de c.,** as usual; **la fuerza de la c.,** force of habit; **tenía la c. de madrugar,** he used to get up early. **2** *(tradición)* custom; **es una c. china,** it's a Chinese custom. **3 costumbres,** *(personales)* manner *sing*, ways; *(de pueblo)* customs.

costumbrismo *nm Art Lit* folk literature.

costumbrista I *adj (novela)* about local customs *or* traditions. II *nmf* writer of folk literature.

costura *nf* **1** *(cosido)* sewing; **cesto de la c.,** needlework basket. **2** *(confección)* dressmaking. ■ **alta c.,** haute couture. **3** *(línea de puntadas)* seam; **medias sin c.,** seamless stockings; *fig* **sentar las costuras a algn,** to tan sb.

costurera *nf* seamstress.

costurero *nm* sewing basket.

costurón *nm* **1** *(cosido)* untidy seam. **2** *Med (cicatriz)* noticeable scar.

cota¹ *nf Geog* height above sea level; *fig* **la delincuencia ha alcanzado cotas muy elevadas,** delinquency has increased alarmingly.

cota² *nf Hist* tabard. ■ **c. de malla,** coat of mail.

cotarro *nm fam* noisy gathering; **dirigir el c., ser el amo del c.,** to be (the) boss, run the show.

cotejable *adj* comparable.

cotejar *vtr* to check, compare.

cotejo *nm* check, comparison.

coterráneo,-a *adj & nm,f* compatriot, fellow countryman *or* countrywoman.

cotidiano,-a *adj* daily; **vida cotidiana,** everyday life.

cotilla I *nf (faja)* corset. II *nmf fam* busybody, gossip.

cotillear *vi fam* to gossip (**de,** about).

cotilleo *nm fam* gossip, gossiping.

cotizable *adj Fin* quotable; **acciones cotizables en bolsa,** stock market shares.

cotización *nf* **1** *Fin* (market) price, quotation. ■ **c. de cierre,** closing price; **c. del día,** current price; **c. máxima,** high. **2** *(cuota)* membership fees *pl*, subscription.

cotizar I *vtr* **1** *Fin* to quote, price. **2** *(pagar cuota)* to pay a subscription. II **cotizarse** *vr* **1** *Com Fin* **c. a,** to sell at; **¿a cuánto se cotizan las acciones?,** what are the shares selling at? **2** *fig* to be valued, be in demand.

coto *nm* **1** *(vedado)* enclosure, reserve. ■ **c. de caza,** game preserve. **2** *(límite)* **poner c. a,** to put a stop to.

cotón *nm Am (prenda)* work shirt.

cotona *nf (prenda)* **1** *Am* cotton shirt. **2** *Méx* chamois leather jacket.

cotorra *nf* **1** *Orn* parrot. **2** *fig (persona)* chatterbox; **hablar como una c.,** to be a chatterbox.

cotorrear *vi fig* to chatter, prattle.

cotorreo *nm fig* chatter, prattle.

COU *nm Educ abr de* **Curso de Orientacion Universitaria,** ≈ GCE A-level studies, sixth-form studies.

covacha *nf* **1** *(cueva)* cave. **2** *Am (trastero)* lumber room.

covachuela *nf* small cave *or* cellar.

coyote *nm Zool* coyote, prairie wolf.

coyuntura *nf* **1** *Anat (articulación)* articulation, joint. **2** *fig (circunstancia)* moment, juncture; **c. crítica,** turning point; *Econ* **la c. económica,** the economic situation.

coz *nf* kick; **dar una c.,** to kick; *fig* **tratar a algn a coces,** to treat sb like dirt.

C.P. *abr de* **código postal,** postcode.

crac *nm* **1** *(onomatopeya)* crack, snap; **la silla hizó crac y me quedé sentado en el suelo,** the chair went 'crack' and I ended up (sitting) on the floor. **2** *Fin* bankruptcy, crash; *Hist* **el c. de la bolsa neoyorquina,** the Wall Street crash.

craneal *adj,* **craneano,-a** *adj* cranial, skull.

cráneo *nm Anat* cranium, skull; *fam* **romperle el c. a algn,** to smash sb's head in.

crápula *lit* **I** *nf (vida licenciosa)* debauchery. **II** *nm (persona)* reprobate.

craso,-a *adj lit* **1** *(person)* fat, gross. **2** *fig (error)* gross, crass.

cráter *nm* crater.

creación *nf* creation.

creador,-a *I adj* creative. **II** *nm,f* creator.

crear I *vtr (gen)* to create, make; *(inventar)* to invent; *(gobierno)* to set up; *(escuela, institución)* to found; **c. amistades,** to make friends; **c. problemas,** to create problems. **II crearse** *vr* to make; **te creas muchos problemas,** you make life difficult for yourself.

creatividad *nf* creativity.

creativo,-a *adj* creative.

crecer I *vi* **1** *(persona, planta)* to grow; **¡cómo has crecido!,** how you've grown!; **dejar c. la barba,** to grow a beard. **2** *(incrementar)* to increase; **crecen los días,** the days are getting longer; **c. en importancia,** to become more important. **3** *Tricot (puntos)* to add. increase. **2** *(río, marea)* to rise; *(luna)* to wax. **3** *(aumentar)* to spread; **crece el malestar,** discontent is spreading. **II crecerse** *vr* to become conceited; **c. ante los problemas,** to thrive on problems.

creces *nfpl* increase (in volume) *sing; fig* **con c.,** fully, in full; **devolver con c.,** to return with interest; **lo pagarás con c.,** you'll more than pay for this.

crecida *nf* flood, spate.

crecido,-a *I pp de* **crecer.** **II** *adj* **1** *(persona)* grown, grown-up. **2** *(número)* big, large. **3** *(río)* in flood *or* spate. **4** *fig* vain, conceited.

creciente *I adj (interés)* growing, increasing; *(precios)* rising; *(luna)* crescent. **II** *nf (de río)* flood, spate.

crecimiento *nm (desarrollo)* growth, increase; *(subida)* rise.

credencial I *adj* credential; **cartas credenciales,** credentials. **II credenciales** *nfpl* credentials.

credibilidad *nf* credibility.

crediticio,-a *adj Fin* credit; **restricción crediticia,** credit squeeze.

crédito *nm* **1** *(confianza)* credit, belief, credence; **dar c. a,** to believe (in), credit. **2** *(fama)* reputation, standing; **persona digna de c.,** reliable person. **3** *Com Fin* credit; **a c.,** on credit.

credo *nm* **1** *Rel* Creed. **2** *Mús* Credo. **3** *fig (creencias)* creed; credo.

credulidad *nf* credulity, gullibility.

crédulo,-a *adj* credulous, gullible.

creencia *nf* belief; **creencias religiosas,** religious beliefs.

creer I *vtr* **1** *(admitir)* to believe; **hay que verlo para creerlo,** it has to be seen to be believed. **2** *(estimar, opinar)* to think; **creo que no,** I don't think so; **creo que sí,** I think so; **creo que te equivocas,** I think you are mistaken. **3** *(tener fe)* to believe; **c. en,** to believe in; **no creo en las brujas,** I don't believe in witches. **II** *vi Rel (ser creyente)* to profess; **no cree, es ateo,** he's not a believer, he's an atheist. **III creerse** *vr* **1** *(estar convencido)* to consider oneself to be; **¿qué te has creído?,** what *or* who do you think you are?; **se creen muy inteligentes,** they think they are very intelligent. **2** *(aceptar)* to believe; **todo te lo crees,** you'll swallow everything.

creíble *adj* credible, believable.

creído,-a I *pp de* **creer. II** *adj* arrogant, vain; *fam* **ser un c.,** to be full of oneself.

crema I *nf* **1** *Culin (de leche)* cream; *(natillas)* custard; **c. de champiñones,** cream of mushroom soup. **2** *(ungüento)* cream; *(betún)* shoe polish; **c. de afeitar/de broncear,** shaving/suntan cream. **3** *fig (lo mejor)* the cream; **ella se codea con la c. de la ciudad,** she rubs shoulders with the top people in the city. **II** *adj* cream, cream coloured *or US* colored.

cremación *nf* cremation.

cremallera *nf* **1** *(de vestido)* zipper, zip (fastener); *fam* **echar la c.,** to shut one's mouth. **2** *Téc* rack. ■ **ferrocarril de c.,** rack *or* cog railway.

crematorio,-a *nm* **(horno) c.,** crematorium.

cremoso,-a *adj* creamy; **queso c.,** full fat cheese.

crepé *nm* **1** *Tex* crepe. **2** *Peluq* hairpiece. **3** *(suela)* crêpe.

crepe *nf Culin* crêpe, pancake.

crepitar *vi* to crackle.

crepuscular *adj* twilight; **luz c.,** twilight.

crepúsculo *nm* twilight.

crecendo (in) *loc adv* crescendo; **ir en c.,** to be increasing.

crespo,-a *adj* **1** *(pelo)* frizzy. **2** *(irritado)* angry. **3** *(estilo)* obscure.

crespón *nm Tex* crepe.

cresta *nf* **1** *Orn* crest; *(de gollo)* comb; *fig* **dar a algn en la c.,** to deflate sb. **2** *Geog (de montaña)* crest, summit. **3** *(de ola)* crest. **4** *(cabello)* toupee.

Creta *n* Crete.

creta *nf* chalk, chalky lime.

cretino,-a I *adj* stupid, cretinous. **II** *nm,f* cretin.

cretona *nf Tex* cretonne.

creyente *nmf* believer.

crezco *indic pres véase* **crecer.**

cría *nf* **1** *(de animales)* breeding, raising. **c. de cerdos,** pig breeding. **2** *(cachorro)* young; **la gata tuvo siete crías,** the cat had seven kittens. **3** *(camada)* brood, litter. **4** *Am (estirpe)* stock.

criada *nf* maid, servant.

criadero *nm* **1** *(de plantas)* nursery. ■ *Zool* **c. de ostras,** oyster bed. **2** *Min* seam.

criadilla *nf* **1** *Culin* bull's testicle. **2** *Bot* potato, tuber. **3** *(trufa)* **c. de tierra,** truffle.

criado,-a I *pp de* **criar. II** *adj (animal)* reared, raised; *(persona)* bred, brought up; **niño mal criado,** spoilt child. **III** *nm,f* servant.

crianza *nf (de animales)* breeding; *(lactancia)* nursing. ■ *fig* **vinos de c.,** vintage wines.

criar I *vtr* **1** *(animales)* to breed, raise, rear; *(niños)* to bring up, rear, care for; **me crió mi abuela,** my grandmother brought me up; *prov* **Dios los cría y ellos se juntan,** birds of a feather flock together. **2** *(nutrir, amamantar)* to nurse; **crió a sus niños a pecho,** she breast-fed her children. **3** *(producir)* to have, grow; **esta tierra cría buenos melones,** this is good soil for melons; **los perros crían pulgas,** dogs have fleas. **4** *(vino)* to make, mature. **II** *vi* *(engendrar)* to give birth; **las ovejas crían en primavera,** sheeps lamb in spring. **III criarse** *vr* **1** *(crecer)* to grow; *(formarse)* to be brought up. **2** *(producirse)* to grow; **aquí no se cría trigo,** wheat isn't grown here.

criatura *nf* **1** *(ser)* (living) creature. **2** *(crío)* baby, child; **a sus veinte años aún se comporta como una c.,** even though he's twenty he still behaves like a child.

criba *nf* **1** *(tamiz)* sieve; *fig* **estar como una c.,** to be riddled with holes. **2** *fig (sistema de selección)* screening; **pasar por la c.,** to screen; *fam Educ* **hacer una c.,** to fail many students.

cribado *nm SAm* type of embroidery.

cribar *vtr* **1** *(colar)* to sieve, sift. **2** *fig (candidatos)* to screen.

cric *nm (pl crics) Aut* jack.

crimen *nm (pl crímenes) (asesinato)* murder; *(delito)* crime.

criminal I *adj* **1** *(gen)* criminal. **2** *fam (malísimo)* awful, appalling, criminal. **II** *nmf (malhechor)* criminal.

criminalidad *nf* criminality, guilt. ■ **índice de c.,** crime rate.

criminalista *nmf* **1** *Jur (abogado)* criminal lawyer. **2** *(estudioso)* criminologist.

criminología *nf* criminology.

crin *nf*, **crines** *nfpl* mane *sing.*

crío,-a I *adj* young, babyish. **II** *nm fam* kid.

criollo,-a *adj & nm, f* Creole.

cripta *nf* crypt.

críptico,-a *adj* cryptic.

criptografía *nf* cryptography, coding.

críquet *nm Dep* cricket.

crisálida *nf Ent* chrysalis.

crisantemo *nm Bot* chrysanthemum.

crisis *nf inv* **1** *(ataque)* fit, attack. ■ **c. de asma,** asthma attack; **c. de llanto,** fit of tears; **c. nerviosa,** nervous breakdown. **2** *(dificultad)* crisis. ■ **c. financiera,** financial crisis; *Pol* **c. de gobierno,** cabinet crisis. **3** *(escasez)* shortage.

crisma I *nm Rel* chrism, holy oil. **II** *nf fam* head, nut; **se rompió la c.,** he split his head open.

crisol *nm* crucible; *fig* melting pot.

crispación *nf* tenseness, contraction.

crispar *vtr (causar contracción)* to tense; *fig* **eso me crispa los nervios,** that sets my nerves on edge, that gets on my nerves; *fam* **c. a algn,** to annoy sb intensely.

cristal *nm* **1** crystal. ■ **c. de cuarzo,** quartz crystal; **c. de roca,** rock crystal. **2** *(vidrio)* glass. ■ **botella de c.,** glass bottle; **copa de c.,** wine glass; **vaso de c.,** drinking glass. **3** *(de gafas)* lense. **4** *(de ventana)* (window) pane. **5** **cristales,** piece of glass; **ella se cortó el pie con unos c.,** she cut her foot on some broken glass. **6** *Am (vaso)* glass.

cristalería *nf* **1** *(fábrica)* glassworks *sing.* **2** *(tienda)* glassware shop. **3** *(conjunto)* glassware; *(vasos)* glasses *pl.*

cristalero,-a *nm, f* glazier.

cristalino,-a I *adj* transparent, clear. **II** *nm Opt* crystalline lens.

cristalización *nf* **1** *Quím* crystallization. **2** *fig* consolidation.

cristalizar *vi* **1** *Quím* to crystallize. **2** *fig* to crystallize, take shape.

cristianar *vtr fam* to christen, baptize.

cristiandad *nf* Christendom.

cristianismo *nm* Christianity.

cristianizar *vtr* to convert to Christianity.

cristiano,-a I *adj* **1** *Rel* Christian. **2** *fam (vino)* watered. **II** *nm fam* **1** *(persona)* person; **cualquier c.,** anybody; **ni un c.,** not a soul. **2** *(lenguaje)* plain language; **hablar en c.,**

(hablar claro) to speak plainly; *(hablar español)* to speak Spanish. **3** *CAm (bonachón)* good-natured person. **III** *nm, f Rel* Christian.

Cristo *nm Rel* Christ; *fam* **armar un c.,** to kick up a big fuss; *fam* **donde C. dio las tres voces,** in the middle of nowhere; *fam* **ni C.,** nobody; *fam* **poner a algn hecho un C.,** to have a real go at sb.

criterio *nm* **1** *(pauta)* criterion, yardstick; **c. estrecho,** narrow viewpoint; **persona de amplios criterios,** broad-minded person. **2** *(discernimiento)* discernment, discrimination; **lo dejo a tu c.,** I leave it to your discretion; **tener buen c.,** to have sound judgement. **3** *(opinión)* opinion, point of view; **cambiar de c.,** to change one's mind.

crítica *nf* **1** *(juicio)* criticism. **2** *Prensa (reseña)* review, write-up; **escribir una c.,** to write a review; **tener buena c.,** to get good reviews. ■ **c. teatral,** theatre column. **3** *(conjunto de críticos)* critics. **4** *(censura)* criticism; **ser dado a las críticas,** to be very critical.

criticar *I vtr* to criticize. **II** *vi (murmurar)* to gossip.

crítico,-a I *adj* critical. **II** *nm, f* critic.

criticón,-ona *fam* **I** *adj* fault-finding, hypercritical. **II** *nm, f* fault-finder.

croar *vi* to croak.

crocante *nm Culin* almond brittle.

croché *nm Cost* crochet.

croissant *nm Culin* croissant.

crol *nm Natación* crawl.

cromado I *pp de* **cromar. II** *adj* chrome. **III** *nm* chroming.

cromar *vtr* to chrome.

cromático,-a *adj* chromatic.

cromo *nm* **1** *(metal)* chromium, chrome. **2** *(cromolitografía)* picture card, transfer; *fam* **ir hecho un c.,** to look a real sight.

cromosoma *nm Biol* chromosome.

crónica *nf* **1** *(gen)* account, chronicle. **2** *Hist* chronicle. **3** *Prensa* column, feature, article. ■ **c. de sucesos,** news page *or* column. **4** *Rad* programme, feature.

crónico,-a *adj* chronic; *fig* deeply rooted.

cronista *nmf Prensa* feature writer, columnist; *(periodista)* journalist. ■ **c. de radio,** radio commentator.

cronología *nf* chronology.

cronológico,-a *adj* chronological.

cronometraje *nm* timing.

cronometrar *vtr* to time.

cronómetro *nm Dep* stopwatch.

croquet *nm Dep* croquet.

croqueta *nf Culin* croquette. ■ **c. de carne,** meat rissole; **c. de pescado,** fishcake.

croquis *nm inv* sketch.

cruce *nm* **1** *(gen)* crossing; *Aut* crossroads. **2** *(mezcla)* cross; *(de razas)* crossbreeding. **3** *Tel* crossed line; **hay un c. de líneas,** the lines are crossed.

crucero *nm* **1** *Arquit* transept. **2** *Náut* cruise; *(barco)* cruiser.

crucial *adj* crucial, critical.

crucificado,-a I *pp de* **crucificar. II** *adj* crucified.

crucificar *vtr* to crucify; *fig* to torture.

crucifijo *nm* crucifix.

crucifixión *nf* crucifixion.

crucigrama *nm* crossword (puzzle).

cruda *nf Guat Méx* drunkenness.

crudeza *nf* **1** *(dureza)* harshness. **2** *(rudeza)* crudeness, coarseness. **3** *(de alimento)* rawness, unripeness. **4** **crudezas,** undigested food *sing.*

crudo,-a I *adj* **1** *(natural)* raw; **este pollo está c.,** the chicken is underdone; *Téc* **seda cruda,** raw silk; *fam*

lo veo muy c., it doesn't look too good, I don't hold out much hope. **2** *(clima)* harsh. **3** *fig (fuerte)* crude, coarse. **4** *(color)* natural, unbleached. **5** *Méx (resaca)* hangover. **II** *nm (petróleo)* oil.

cruel *adj (persona)* cruel; *(inclemente)* harsh, severe.

crueldad *nf* cruelty; *fig* **la c. del clima,** the severity of the climate.

cruento,-a *adj* bloody, gory.

crujido *nm (de puerta)* creak, creaking; *(de patatas fritas)* crunching; *(de hojas, papel)* rustle, rustling; *(de dientes)* grinding.

crujiente *adj (alimentos)* crunchy; *(seda)* rustling.

crujir *vi (puerta)* to creak; *(patatas fritas)* to crunch; *(hojas, papel)* to rustle; *(dientes)* to grind.

crupier *nm* croupier.

crustáceo *nm Zool* crustacean.

cruz *nf* **1** *(gen)* cross; **con los brazos en c.,** with outstretched arms; *fig* **hacer c. y raya,** to swear never again. ■ **c. gamada,** swastika; **C. Roja,** Red Cross. **2** *fig (carga)* burden, cross. **3** *(de moneda)* tails *pl.* **¿cara o c.?,** heads or tails?

cruzada *nf* **1** *Hist* crusade. **2** *(campaña)* campaign.

cruzado,-a I *pp de* **cruzar. II** *adj* **1** *(gen)* crossed; **con los brazos cruzados,** arms folded; *Com* **cheque c./no cruzado,** crossed/open cheque; *fig* **estar de brazos cruzados,** to be doing nothing. **2** *Cost (abrigo, chaqueta)* double-breasted. **3** *(atravesado)* across; **había un camión c. en la carretera,** a lorry was blocking the road. **4** *(animal, planta)* crossbred. **III** *nm Hist* crusader.

cruzadora *nf Méx* pickpocket's female accomplice.

cruzar I *vtr* **1** *(gen)* to cross; *Geom (línea)* to intersect; **c. a nado,** to swim across; **c. apuestas,** to make bets; **c. los brazos,** to fold one's arms; **c. un río,** to cross a river; **cruzarle la cara a algn,** to slap sb's face. **2** *(poner atravesado)* **c. algo con una raya,** to draw a line across *or* through sth. **3** *(palabra, mirada)* to exchange. **4** *(animal, planta)* to cross, crossbreed. **II** *vi (atravesar)* to cross; **los coches cruzaban en todas direcciones,** cars were crossing in all directions. **III cruzarse** *vr* **1** *(juntarse)* to meet; **c. con algn,** to pass sb; **c. de brazos,** to fold one's arms; *fig* to sit back and do nothing; **c. en el camino de algn,** to cross sb's path.

CSD *nm abr de* **Consejo Superior de Deportes,** ≈ Sports Council.

c.s.f. *abr de* **coste, seguro y flete,** cost, insurance and freight, c.i.f.

CSIC *nm abr de* **Consejo Superior de Investigaciones Científicas.**

cta. *Com abr de* **cuenta,** account, a/c.

cta. cte. *Com abr de* **cuenta corriente,** current account, c/a.

Cte. *Mil abr de* **comandante,** Major, Maj.

cte. *abr de* **corriente,** of the present month *or* year.

CTNE *nf abr de* **Compañía Telefónica Nacional de España,** ≈ British Telecom.

ctra. *abr de* **carretera,** road, rd.

cts. *abr de* **céntimos,** cents.

c/u *abr de* **cada uno,** each, ea.

cuaderna *nf Náut* frame.

cuadernillo *nm* booklet.

cuaderno *nm (libreta)* notebook; *Educ* exercise book. ■ *Náut* **c. de bitácora,** logbook.

cuadra *nf* **1** *Agr (establo)* stable. **2** *Am (manzana)* block (of houses).

cuadrado,-a I *pp de* **cuadrar. II** *adj* **1** *Geom* square. **2** *(complexión física)* broad, stocky; *vulg* **tenerlos cuadrados,** to have the balls to do sth. **3** *fig (mente)* rigid; **tener una mente cuadrada,** to have a one-track mind. **III** *nm* **1** *Geom* square. **2** *Mat* square; **elevar (un número) al c.,** to square (a number).

cuadragésimo,-a I *adj* fortieth. **II** *nm, f (de una serie)* fortieth. **III** *nm* fortieth; *véase tamb* **octavo,-a.**

cuadrante *nm* **1** *Náut Mat (instrumento)* quadrant. **2** *(reloj de sol)* sundial. **3** *(cojín)* square pillow.

cuadrar I *vtr Mat* to square. **II** *vi* **1** *(coincidir)* to square, agree **(con,** with); *(sumas, cifras)* to tally. **2** *fig (convenir)* to suit. **III cuadrarse** *vr* **1** *(soldado)* to stand to attention. **2** *fig (mantenerse firme)* to dig one's heels in.

cuadratura *nf Mat* quadrature; **la c. del círculo,** squaring the circle.

cuadrícula *nf* squares *pl,* crisscross pattern. ■ **papel de c.,** squared paper.

cuadricular¹ *adj* squared.

cuadricular² *vtr* to square, divide into squares.

cuadrilátero I *adj* quadrilateral, four-sided. **II** *nm Box* ring.

cuadriplicar *vtr* to quadruple.

cuadrilla *nf (equipo)* gang, team; *Mil* squad; *Taur* bullfighter's team.

cuadro *nm* **1** *Geom* square; **tela a cuadros,** checked cloth. **2** *Arquit Téc* frame. **3** *Arte* painting, picture; **c. falso,** a fake. **4** *Teat* scene. **5** *Lit* description, picture; **c. de la vida rural,** picture of country life. **6** *(bancal)* bed, patch, plot. **7** *Elec Téc* panel. ■ **c. de distribución,** switchboard; **c. de mandos,** control panel. **8** *(gráfico)* chart, graph. **9** *(personal)* staff; *Mil* cadre. ■ **c. de dirigentes,** leaders *pl;* **c. facultativo,** medical staff.

cuadrúpedo,-a *adj & nm* quadruped.

cuádruple *adj* quadruple, fourfold.

cuajada *nf Culin* curd.

cuajado,-a I *pp de* **cuajar. II** *adj* **1** *(leche)* curdled; *(sangre)* clotted; *(huevo)* set. **2** *(lleno)* full, filled; **c. de,** filled with; **c. de peligros,** fraught with danger.

cuajar I *vtr* **1** *(leche)* to curdle; *(sangre)* to clot; *(huevo)* to set. **2** *(llenar)* to fill **(de,** with). **II** *vi* **1** *(nieve)* to lie. **2** *fig (tener éxito)* to be a success, be well received; *(idea)* to catch on; **la idea no cuajó,** the idea didn't get off the ground; **su estilo no cuajó,** his style wasn't liked. **3** *Méx (mentir)* to lie. **4** *Méx (hablar)* to chatter.

cuajo *nm* **1** *(cuajadura)* rennet. **2** *fam (cachaza)* calmness, phlegm; **tener mucho c.,** to be phlegmatic. **3** **arrancar algo de c.,** to tear sth out by the roots.

cual I *pro rel (precedido de artículo)* **1** *(persona)* who, whom; **inventado por un español el c. se llamaba ...,** invented by a Spaniard who was called ... . **2** *(cosa)* which; **la casa, la c. se construyó el año pasado,** the house which was built last year; **me levanté tarde con lo c. perdí el tren,** I got up late which meant I missed the train; **tuvieron una avería, lo c. les retrasó mucho,** they broke down which meant they were delayed a long time. **II** *pron* **1** *(correlativo)* as; **hicimos tal c. nos dijo,** we did exactly as he said we should; **arc la vida, c. la conocemos, es un valle de lágrimas,** life as we know it is a sea of troubles. **2** *arc (valor adverbial)* such as, like; **el agua brillaba c. un espejo,** the water sparkled like a mirror; **c. si,** as if; **se portó c. si fuera mayor,** he behaved as if he were older.

cuál I *pron interr* which (one)?, what?; **¿c. es tu nombre?,** what's your name?; **¿c. quieres?,** which one do you want? **II** *pron indef (oraciones distributivas)* **c. más, c. menos, todos ayudaron,** everybody did what they could to help. **III** *adj interr* which. **IV** *loc adv* **a c más,** equally; **a c. más deprisa,** each as fast as the other.

cualidad *nf* **1** *(de persona)* quality, attribute, trait. **2** *(de cosa)* quality.

cualificado,-a I *pp de* **cualificar. II** *adj (obrero)* qualified, skilled.

cualificar I *vtr* to qualify. **II cualificarse** *vr* to become qualified, complete one's training.

cualitativo,-a *adj* qualitative.

cualquier *adj indef* any; **en c. momento,** at any moment *or* time; **c. cosa vale,** anything will do.

cualquiera *(pl cualesquiera)* **I** *adj indef* **1** *(indefinido)* any; **una dificultad c.,** any difficulty. **2** *(corriente)* ordinary; **no compres uno c.,** don't buy any old one; **no es un plato c.,** it's no ordinary dish. **II** *pron indef* **1** anybody; **c. te lo puede decir,** anybody can tell you; **¡c. lo sabe!,** who knows? **2** nobody; **¡c. lo come!,** nobody could eat that! **3 c. que sea,** whatever it is; **c. que sea la hora,** no matter what time it is. **III** *nmf fig pey* **ser un c.,** to be a nobody; **es una c.,** she's a hussy.

cuan *adv* as ... as; *arc* **c. pronto pudo,** as soon as he could; **tendido c. largo era,** lying flat out.

cuán *adv interr arc* how; **¡c. agradable sería!,** how lovely it would be!; **c. pronto ocurrió,** as soon as it happened.

cuando I *adv (de tiempo)* when; **c. más** *or* **mucho,** at the most; **c. menos,** at least; **de c. en c., de vez en c.,** from time to time; **el martes es c. surgirán los problemas,** the problems will start on Tuesday. **II** *conj* **1** *(temporal)* when; **c. quieras,** whenever you want; **c. vengas,** when you come. **2** *(condicional) (si)* since, if; **c. tú lo dices,** if you say so. **3** *(concesiva) (aunque)* **(aun) c.,** even if; **aun c. lo supiera no te lo diría,** even if I knew I wouldn't tell you. **4** *(causal) (puesto que)* **c. tú lo dices, será verdad,** if you say so, then it must be true. **III** *prep* during, at the time; **c. la guerra,** during the war; **c. niño,** as a child; *(yo)* when I was a child.

cuándo I *adv interr* when?; **¿de c. acá?,** since when?; **¿para c. lo quieres?,** when do you want it for? **II** *nm* when; **debes especificar el como y el cuando,** you must make clear how and when.

cuantía *nf (suma)* quantity, amount; *(dimensión)* extent; **de mayor c.,** important; **de menor c.,** insignificant.

cuantificar *vtr* to quantify, measure.

cuantioso,-a *adj (cantidad)* substantial, considerable; *(número)* numerous.

cuantitativo,-a *adj* quantitative.

cuanto[1] *nm Fís* quantum; **teoría de los cuantos,** quantum theory.

cuanto,-a[2] **I** *adj rel* all that, whatever, whoever; **gasta c. dinero gana,** he spends every penny he earns. **II** *pron rel* as much as; **coma c. quiera,** eat as much as you want; **regala todo c. tiene,** he gives away everthing he's got. **III** *pron indef pl* **unos cuantos,** a few. **IV** *adv* **1** *(tiempo)* **c. antes,** as soon as possible; **en c. a,** when; **en c. termine,** as soon as *or* when I finish. **2** *(cantidad)* **c. más ... más,** the more ... the more; **c. más lo miro, más me gusta,** the more I look at it the more I like it. **3** *(por lo que corresponde a)* **c. a, en c. a,** with respect to, regarding. **4** *(causal)* **por c.,** since, that.

cuánto,-a *adj & pron interr* how many?, how much?; **¿cuántas veces?,** how many times?; **¿c. es?,** how much is it?; **¿cuántos alumnos sois?,** how many are there in your class?; **¿cuántos sois?,** how many of you are there? **II** *adv* how, how much; **¡cuánta gente hay!,** what a lot of people there are!; **¡c. me gusta!,** I really like it!; **¡c. has escrito!,** what a lot you've written!

cuáquero,-a *adj & nm,f Rel* Quaker.

cuarenta I *adj inv (cardinal)* forty; *(ordinal)* fortieth. **II** *nm inv* forty; *fam* **cantarle a algn las c.,** to give sb a piece of one's mind; *véase tamb* **ochenta** y **ocho.**

cuarentavo,-a I *adj* fortieth; **cuarentava parte,** fortieth. **II** *nm (parte)* fortieth; *véase tamb* **octavo**

cuarentena *nf* **1** *(cuarenta unidades)* forty, about forty. **2** *Med* quarantine; *fig* **poner a algn en c.,** to send sb to Coventry.

cuarentón,-ona I *adj (persona)* forty-year-old. **II** *nm, f* person in his *or* her forties.

cuaresma *nf Rel* Lent.

cuartear I *vtr* **1** *(carne)* to quarter. **2** *(rajar)* to crack, split. **3** *Méx (pegar)* to whip. **II** **cuartearse** *vr* **1** *(rajarse)* to crack, split. **2** *Méx (acobardarse)* to chicken out; *(desdecirse)* to go back on one's word.

cuartel *nm Mil* barracks *pl*; **vida de c.,** army life; *fig* **no dar c.,** to show no mercy. ■ **c. general,** headquarters; **c. de invierno,** winter quarters *pl*.

cuartelada *nf*, **cuartelazo** *nm Mil* putsch, military uprising.

cuartelero,-a *adj* barrack, barracks.

cuartelillo *nm Mil* post, station.

cuartería *nf Cuba Chi RD* block (of houses).

cuarterón *nm* **1** *(medida)* quarter pound. **2** *(de puerta* o *ventana)* panel.

cuarteto *nm Mús* quartet.

cuartilla *nf* **1** *(hoja)* sheet of paper. **2** **cuartillas,** *Tip* copy.

cuartillo *nm (medida)* pint, just over half a litre.

cuarto,-a I *adj* fourth; **cuarta fila,** fourth row. **II** *nm,f (de una serie)* fourth. **III** *nm* **I** *(parte)* fourth; **abrigo tres cuartos,** three-quarter length coat; *fam* **de tres al c.,** worthless; *véase tamb* **octavo,-a 2** *(de hora)* quarter; **las tres y c.,** quarter past three; **he esperado tres cuartos de hora,** I've been waiting for three quarters of an hour. ■ **c. creciente,** first quarter; **c. menguante,** last quarter. **3** *(de carne)* joint. **c. trasero,** hindquarter; ■ **c. delantero,** shoulder. **4** *Dep* **cuartos de final,** quarter finals. **5** *(habitación)* room. ■ **c. de baño,** bathroom; **c. de estar,** living room; *Fot* **c. oscuro,** darkroom; **c. trasero,** junk room. **6 cuartos,** *fam* dough, money; **cuatro cuartos,** very little money; **estar sin un c.,** to be broke *or* skint. **7** *Méx Aut* sidelight.

cuartucho *nm fam* hovel, cramped room.

cuarzo *nm Min* quartz.

cuás *nm Méx* best friend.

cuate,-a *adj & nm,f* **1** *Méx (mellizo)* twin; *fig* very similar, alike. **2** *Guat Méx (compinche)* buddy, mate.

cuatezón,-ona *nm,f Méx* hornless bull *or* goat.

cuatí *nm CAm Zool* coati.

cuatrero,-a I *adj* **1** *CAm (traidor)* treacherous. **2** *Méx (que dice disparates)* preposterous. **II** *nm, f (ladrón de caballos)* rustler, horse thief.

cuatrillizo,-a *adj & nm,f* quadruplet.

cuatrimotor *nm Av* four-engined plane.

cuatro I *adj inv (cardinal)* fourth; *(ordinal)* fourth; **a las c.,** at four o'clock. **II** *nm inv* **1** four. **2** *fam (unos cuantos)* a few; **cayeron c. gotas,** it rained a little bit; **decir c. cosas,** to say a few things; **más de c.,** several; **a más de c. les gustaría estar en tu lugar,** I know quite a few people who'd like to be in your position; *véase tamb* **ocho**

cuatrocientos,-as *adj & nm* four hundred.

Cuba *n* Cuba.

cuba *nf* cask, barrel; *fam* **estar como una c.,** to be (as) drunk as a lord.

cubalibre *nm* rum *or* gin and coke.

cubano,-a *adj & nm,f* Cuban.

cubata *nm fam véase* **cubalibre.**

cubertería *nf* cutlery.

cubeta *nf* **1** *(cubo)* bucket, pail; *(en laboratorio)* tank, dish. **2** *(del barómetro)* bulb. **3** *Méx (sombrero)* top hat.

cúbico,-a *adj* cubic; *Mat* **raíz cúbica,** cube root.

cubículo *nm* cubicle.

cubierta *nf* **1** *(gen)* cover, covering. **2** *Aut (capó)* bonnet, *US* hood. **3** *(neumático)* tyre, *US* tire. **4** *Arquit* roof. ■ **c. de lona,** tarpaulin, canvas. **5** *Av Náut* deck.

cubierto,-a I *pp de* **cubrir II** *adj* **1** *(gen)* covered; *(cielo)* overcast; *fam* **tener las espaldas cubiertas,** to be well-heeled. **2** *(plaza, vacante)* filled. **II** *nm* **1** *(en la mesa)* place setting; **a mil pesetas el c.,** one thousand pesetas per head; **precio del c.,** cover charge. **2** *(techumbre etc)* cover; **estar a c.,** to be under cover; **ponerse a c.,** to take cover. **3 cubiertos,** cutlery *sing*.

cubil *nm* lair.

cubilete *nm* **1** *Culin (flanero)* mould, *US* mold; *(dados)* dicebox; *(juego)* cup. **2** *Am (sombrero)* top hat.

cubiletear *vtr* **1** *(dados)* to shake. **2** *fig* to cheat, fiddle.

cubismo *nm Art* cubism.

cubista *adj & nmf Art* cubist.

cubito *nm* little cube. ■ **c. de hielo,** ice cube.

cubo *nm* **1** bucket. ■ **c. de la basura,** rubbish bin. **2** *Geom Mat* cube; **elevar al c.,** to cube. **2** *Aut (de rueda)* hub.

cubrecama *nm* bedspread.

cubrepié *nm Am* bedspread.

cubrir *(pp cubierto)* **I** *vtr* **1** *(gen)* to cover; **el agua le cubría hasta la cíntura,** the water came up to his waist; **una fina capa de polvo cubría la mesa,** the table was covered in a thin layer of dust. **2** *Arquit (edificio)* to put a roof (on). **3** *(ocultar)* to hide; **la niebla cubría el valle,** the valley was veiled in mist. **4** *(sentimiento)* to hide. **5** *(llenar)* to fill, cover with; **c. de besos,** to smother with kisses; **c. una plaza** *or* **una vacante,** to fill a vacancy. **6** *(satisfacer)* to meet; **c. gastos,** to cover expenses; **c. las necesidades,** to cover one's needs; **c. una deuda,** to meet a debt. **7** *(recorrer)* to cover; *(distancia)* to travel. **8** *Prensa (suceso, noticia)* to cover. **9** *Zool (montar)* to pair. **II cubrirse** *vr (ponerse sombrero)* to put one's hat on; *(revestirse)* to cover oneself *(con,* with). **3** *fig (protegerse)* to cover oneself against. **4** *Meteor (cielo)* to become overcast. **5** *(vacante)* to be filled.

cuca *nf* **1** *vulg* penis. **2 cucas,** *(caramelos)* sweets; *arg (pasta)* pesetas. **3** *Am Culin* sweet made of flour.

cucaña *nf* **1** *(juego)* greasy pole. **2** *fam (bicoca)* easy-pickings *pl*.

cucaracha *nf* **1** *Ent* cockroach. **2** *Méx Ferroc* tramcar.

cuchara *nf* spoon; **c. de palo,** wooden spoon; *fig* **meter algo a algn con c.,** to drum sth into sb; *fam* **meter c.,** to butt in.

cucharada *nf* spoonful; **c. rasa/colmada,** level/heaped spoonful.

cuchareta *nmf Cuba Méx* busybody.

cucharilla *nf* teaspoon. ■ **c. de café,** coffee spoon.

cucharón *nm* ladle.

cuche *nm,* **cuchi** *nm Am* pig.

cuchichear *vi* to whisper.

cuchicheo *nm* whispering.

cuchilla *nf* **1** *(hoja)* blade. ■ **c. de afeitar,** razor blade. **2** *Am (cortaplumas)* penknife. **3** *Am (cumbre)* ridge, crest.

cuchillada *nf,* **cuchillazo** *nm* cut, stab, knife wound; **ayer hubo cuchilladas en el puerto,** there was a stabbing down at the port last night.

cuchillo *nm* **1** *(gen)* knife. ■ **c. de monte,** hunting knife; **c. de pan,** breadknife; **c. de trinchar,** carving knife. **2** *Arquit* support.

cuchipanda *nf fam* spree, meal; **salir de c.,** to go out on the town.

cuchitril *nm* **1** *(establo)* pigsty. **2** *fam (cuartucho)* hovel, hole.

cucho,-a *adj* **1** *CAm (jorobado)* hunchback. **2** *Méx (desnarigado)* small nosed.

cuchufleta *nf fam* joke.

cuchugo *nm SAm* saddlebag.

cuchumbo *nm CAm* **1** *(embudo)* funnel. **2** *(cubeta)* bucket.

cuclillas *loc adv* **en c.,** crouching; **ponerse en c.,** to crouch down.

cuclillo *nm Orn* cuckoo.

cuco,-a I *adj fam* **1** *(mono)* cute. **2** *(astuto)* shrewd, crafty. **II** *nm* **1** *Orn* cuckoo. **2** *(pesca)* red gurnard.

cucú *nm (pl cucúes)* **1** *(canto)* cuckoo. **2** *(reloj)* cuckoo clock.

cucurucho *nm* **1** *(envoltorio)* paper cone. **2** *(helado)* cornet. **3** *(capirote)* pointed hood. **4** *Am (prenda)* hooded garment. **5** *Am Geom* summit, apex.

cuello *nm* **1** *Anat (garganta)* neck; **cortar el c. a algn,** to slit sb's throat; *fig* **con el agua hasta el c.,** in a tight spot; *fig* **estar metido hasta el c.,** to be up to one's neck in it; *fam* **me apuesto el c.,** I'd put my shirt on it. **2** *(de ropa)* collar; **jersey de c. redondo,** crew-necked jumper; **c. de pajarita,** bow tie; *fam* **hablar para el c. de su camisa,** to mutter to oneself. **3** *(de botella)* neck.

cuenca *nf* **1** *Geog* basin; **la c. del río,** the river basin. **2** *Anat (de los ojos)* socket. **3** *Min* **c. minera,** coalfield.

cuenco *nm* **1** *(vasija)* earthenware bowl. **2** *(concavidad)* hollow; **c. de la mano,** hollow of the hand.

cuenta *nf* **I** *(cálculo)* count, counting; **hacer cuentas,** to do sums; **sacar cuentas,** to work out; *fam* **la c. de la vieja,** counting on one's fingers. ■ **c. atrás,** countdown. **2** *Com (factura)* bill; **la c. del teléfono,** the telephone bill; **pasar la c.,** to send the bill; **por c. de la casa,** on the house. **3** *Fin (en banco)* account. ■ **c. bancaria,** bank account; **c. corriente,** current account; **c. al descubierto,** overdrawn account. **4** *(de collar, rosario)* bead. **5** *(locuciones)* **ajustar cuentas,** to settle up; **caer en la c.,** to realize; **dar c.,** to report; **dar cuentas a,** to inform *or* answer to; **beber más de la c.,** to have one too many; **darse c.,** to realize; **en resumidas cuentas,** in short; **pedir cuentas,** to ask for an explanation; **tener en c.,** to take into account; **trabajar por c. propia,** to be self-employed; **traer c.,** to be worthwhile.

cuentagotas *nm inv Med* dropper.

cuentakilómetros *nm inv (distancia)* milometer; *(velocidad)* speedometer.

cuentarrevoluciones *nm inv* rev counter.

cuentista I *nmf* **1** *(narrador)* storyteller. **2** *(cotilla)* gossip. **II** *adj & nmf (exagerado)* overdramatic (person).

cuento *nm (gen)* story, tale; *Lit* short story; **contar un c.,** to tell a story; *fig* **el c. de la lechera,** counting one's chickens before they are hatched; *fig* **eso no viene a c.,** that's beside the point; *fig* **traer algo a c.,** to mention sth, bring sth up; *fam* **¡déjate de cuentos!,** get on with it!; *fam* **es el c. de nunca acabar,** it just drags on and on; *fam* **ir a algn con el c.,** to tell tales to sb; *fam* **tiene más c. que Calleja,** he's always making such a fuss; *fam* **vivir del c.,** to live by one's wits. ■ **c. chino,** tall story; **c. de hadas,** *(narración)* fairy story; *(sensacional)* cock-and-bull story.

cuereada *nf Am* beating.

cuerda *nf* **1** *(cordel)* string, rope; *fig* **bailar en la c. floja,** to be hanging by a thread; *fig* **aflojar la c.,** to ease up; *fig* **apretar la c.,** to tighten up; *fig* **bajo c.,** dishonestly. ■ **c. de la ropa,** clothes-line; **c. de presos,** chain gang; **c. floja,** tightrope. **2** *Mús* string, cord; *Mús (voz)* voice. ■ *Anat* **cuerdas vocales,** vocal chords. **3** *(del reloj)* spring; **dar c. al reloj,** to wind up a watch; *fig* **parece que le hayan dado c.,** he seems to have been encouraged to talk; *fam fig* **se me acabó la c.,** I've nothing left to say; *(estar cansado)* I'm exhausted. **4** *Geom* chord.

cuerdo,-a I *adj (acto)* prudent, sensible; *(persona)* sane; **no está c.,** he's not in his right mind. **II** *nm, f* sane person.

cuerna *nf* **1** *(cornamenta)* antlers *pl,* horns *pl.* **2** *(de caza)* hunting horn.

cuerno *nm* **1** *(gen)* horn; *(de ciervo)* antler, *fig* **me huele a c. quemado,** I think there is something fishy going on; *fam* **mandar a algn al c.,** to send sb packing; *fam* **mandar algo al c.,** to pack sth in; *fam* **romperse los cuernos,** to break one's back; *fam fig* **poner cuernos a algn,** to be unfaithful to sb; *vulg* **¡vete al c.!,** get lost! **2** *Mil* wing. **3** *Mús* horn.

cuero *nm* **1** *(pellejo de animal)* skin, hide; leather; **chaqueta de c.,** leather jacket. **2** *(persona)* skin; **fam en cueros (vivos),** (stark) naked; *fam* **quedarse en cueros,** to strip off. ■ *Anat* **c. cabelludo,** scalp. **3** *(odre)* wineskin. **4** *Ftb (balón)* ball. **5** *Am (correa)* whip.

cuerpo *nm* **1** *Anat (ser)* body; *(constitución)* build; *(figura)* figure; *(tronco)* trunk; **a c. descubierto,** defenceless; **de c. entero,** full-length; **echar el c. atrás,** to lean back; **lucha c. a c.,** hand-to-hand combat; *fig* **hombre de c. entero,**

man of integrity; *fig* **entregarse en c. y alma,** to give one's all; *fig* **tomar c.,** to take shape; *fig* **vivir a c. de rey,** to live like a king; *euf* **hacer de c.,** to relieve oneself. ■ *Jur* **c. del delito,** evidence; *Mat* **c. geométrico,** regular solid; **cuerpos celestes,** heavenly bodies. 2 *(cadáver)* corpse; **de c. presente,** lying in state. 3 *(parte)* section part; *(parte principal)* main part, main body; **armario de tres cuerpos,** wardrobe in three sections; **c. superior,** upper section; **el c. del libro,** the main body of the book. 4 *(grosor)* body, thickness. 5 *(grupo)* body, corps, force. ■ **c. de baile,** corps de ballet; **c. de bomberos,** fire brigade; **c. diplomático,** diplomatic corps; **c. de sanidad,** medical corps.

cuervo *nm* 1 *Orn* raven; *prov* **cría cuervos (y te sacarán los ojos),** biting the hand that feeds you. ■ **c. marino,** cormorant. 2 *ofens* priest.

cuestal *nf* slope; **c. abajo,** downhill; **c. arriba,** up-hill; *fig* **ir c. abajo,** to be declining; *fig* **se me hace c. arriba,** I find it an uphill struggle. ■ *fig* **la c. de enero,** the January squeeze. II *loc adv* **a cuestas,** on one's back *or* shoulders.

cuestación *nf* charity collection; **hacer una c.,** to raise money for charity.

cuestión *nf* 1 *(pregunta)* question. 2 *(asunto)* matter, question, problem; **c. candente,** burning question; **c. de vida** *or* **muerte,** it's a matter of life or death; **en c. de unas horas,** in just a few hours; **no es c. de enfadarse,** it's nothing to get angry about; **una c. jurídica,** a legal matter. 3 *(discusión)* quarrel, argument; **tener una c.,** to have a quarrel.

cuestionable *adj* questionable, debatable.

cuestionar *vtr* to question, debate.

cuestionario *nm* questionnaire.

cuete *nm Méx* slice of meat from the leg.

cueva *nf* cave; *fig* **c. de ladrones,** den of thieves.

cuévano *nm* pannier.

cuezo *indic pres véase* **cocer**

cuidado,-a I *pp de* **cuidar** II *adj* looked after; **un jardín muy c.,** a well cared for garden. III *nm* 1 *(esmero)* care; **con c.,** carefully; **de c.,** *(enfermo)* very ill; *(peligroso)* dangerous, suspicious; **estar al c. de,** *(cosa)* to be in charge of; *(persona)* to look after; **ir** *or* **andarse con c.,** to go carefully; **me trae sin c.,** I don't care; **tener c.,** to be careful. 2 *fam Med* **cuidados intensivos,** intensive care (unit) *sing*. 3 *(recelo)* worry; **siente c. por la herida,** he's concerned about the injury. IV **¡c.!** *interj* look out!, watch out!; **¡c. con el perro!,** beware of the dog!; **¡c. con lo que dices!,** watch what you say!; **¡c. con los niños!,** mind the children!

cuidador,-a I *nm Arg (enfermero)* male nurse. II *nf Méx (niñera)* nanny.

cuidadoso,-a *adj* 1 *(atento)* careful. 2 *(celoso)* cautious.

cuidar I *vtr* to care for, look after; **c. de que,** to make sure that; **c. de que todo salga bien,** to make sure that everything goes alright; **c. los detalles,** to pay attention to details; **c. una herida,** to dress a wound. II **cuidarse** *vr* 1 *(conservarse)* to look after oneself, take care of oneself; **cuídate,** look after yourself. 2 *(preocuparse)* **c. de,** to worry, mind; **no se cuida de la opinión de la gente,** he doesn't care what people think; **c. de que,** to make sure that, be careful to.

cuita¹ *nf* worry, trouble.

cuita² *nf CAm* excrement.

cuja *nf* 1 *Am (cama)* bed. 2 *Hond Méx (sobre)* envelope. 3 *Méx (envoltura)* flap.

culamen *nm vulg* fat arse.

culata *nf* 1 *(de arma)* butt. 2 *Aut* cylinder head. 3 *(de animales)* haunch, hindquarters *pl*. 4 *Arg (del carro)* back end.

culatazo *nf (de arma)* recoil, kick.

culebra *nf* 1 *Zool (serpiente)* snake. 2 *Am (cuenta)* debt, bill. 3 *Méx* downpour, heavy shower.

culebrear *vi (zigzaguear)* to zigzag; *(río)* to meander, wind.

culebrilla *nf* 1 *(de cometa)* zigzag. 2 *Med* ringworm.

culebrina *nf* forked lightning.

culebrón *nm Méx* television serial, soap.

culeco,-a *adj Am* 1 *(contento)* very happy. 2 *(enamorado)* in love.

culero *nm Arg* leather belt.

culimiche *adj Méx* worthless.

culimpinarse *vr Méx* to stoop, get down.

culinario,-a *adj* culinary, cooking; **arte c.,** cuisine.

culminación *nf* culmination.

culminante *adj (punto)* highest; *(momento)* culminating.

culminar I *vi* 1 *(perfeccionarse)* to reach a peak *or* its highest point. 2 *fig (acabar)* to end, culminate (**con, en, in).**

culo *nm* 1 *fam Anat (trasero)* bottom; *fam (ano)* bum, *US* fanny; *vulg* arse, *US* ass; **caer de c.,** to fall flat on one's bottom; *fig* **con el c. al aire,** in a fix, in a tight spot; *fig* **ir de c.,** to be rushed off one's feet; *fig* **mojarse el c.,** to come down off the fence; *fig* **ser c. de mal asiento,** to be a fidget; *vulg* **lamer el c. a algn,** to lick sb's arse; *ofens* **¡métetelo por el c.!,** stick it up your arse!; *ofens* **¡vete tomar por el c.!,** fuck off! 2 *fam (de recipiente)* bottom; **queda** *or* **hay un c.,** there is a little bit left in the bottom.

culón,-ona *adj fam* big-bottomed.

culpa *nf* 1 *(error)* fault; **fue c. mía,** it was my fault; **por tu c.,** because of you. 2 *(responsabilidad)* blame; **cargar a algn con la c.,** to give sb the blame; **echar la c. a algn,** to put the blame on sb; **sentimiento de c.,** guilty feeling.

culpabilidad *nf* guilty, culpability.

culpable I *adj* guilty; *Jur* **declararse c.,** to plead guilty. II *nmf* offender, culprit; **yo no soy el c.,** I'm not to blame.

culpar I *vtr* to blame; **c. a algn de un delito,** to accuse sb of an offence; **no se puede c. a nadie,** nobody is to blame. II **culparse** *vr* to blame oneself, take the blame.

cultivado,-a I *pp de* **cultivar.** II *adj* 1 *Agr* cultivated, tilled. 2 *(con cultura)* cultured, refined.

cultivar *vtr* 1 *Agr* to cultivate, farm. 2 *fig (amistad)* to cultivate. 3 *(ejercitar)* to work at, practise, improve; **c. la memoria,** to improve one's memory. 4 *Biol (producir)* to culture.

cultivo *nm* 1 *(labranza)* farming, cultivation; **dedicarse al c. de,** to grow; **poner en c.,** to cultivate. 2 *(cultivo)* crop; **c. de maíz,** crop of corn. 3 *Biol* culture; **c. de tejidos,** tissue culture. 4 *fig (desarrollo)* development, growth.

culto,a I *adj (persona)* cultured, educated; *(estilo)* refined. II *nm* 1 worship; **c. dominical,** Sunday worship. 2 cult. ◆ **cultamente** *adv* in a refined *or* elegant manner.

cultura *nf* culture; **la c. prerromana,** Pre-Roman culture; **una mujer de c.,** an educated woman.

cultural *adj* cultural.

cumbarí *adj & nm Arg Culin* very hot red pepper.

cumbia *nf* Columbian dance.

cumbre *nf* 1 *(de montaña)* summit. top; 2 *fig (culminación)* pinnacle; **alcanzar la c.,** to reach the top. ■ *Pol* **(conferencia) c.,** summit conference.

cumiche *nm CAm* baby of the family.

cumpleaños *nm inv* birthday; **¡feliz c.!,** happy birthday!; **fiesta de c.,** birthday party.

cumplido,-a I *pp de* **cumplir.** II *adj* 1 completed; **misión cumplida,** mission accomplished; **plazo c.,** expiry date; **trabajo c.,** finished work. 2 *(abundante)* large; **un almuerzo muy c.,** a big lunch. 3 *(perfecto)* accomplished; **un c. caballero,** a perfect gentleman. 4 *(cortés)* polite, well-bred. III *nm (cortesía)* compliment; **cambiar cumplidos con algn,** to exchange pleasantries with sb; **por c.,** out of courtesy.

cumplidor,-a *adj* reliable, dependable.

cumplimentar *vtr* **1** *(felicitar)* to congratulate. **2** *(cumplir)* to fulfil, *US* fulfill, carry out.

cumplimiento *nm* **1** *(observación)* fulfilment, *US* fulfillment; **c. de la ley,** observance of the law. **2** *(cumplido)* courtesy, politeness.

cumplir I *vtr* **1** *(realizar)* to carry out, fulfil, *US* fulfill; **c. un deseo,** to fulfil a wish; **c. una orden,** to carry out an order; *Jur* **c. una pena,** to serve a sentence; **c. una promesa,** to keep a promise. **2** *(respetar)* **c. con algn,** to keep one's promise to sb; **c. con el deber,** to do one's duty; **c. con la ley,** to abide by the law. **3** *(años)* to be; **al c. los sesenta,** when he *or* she turned sixty; **ayer cumplí veinte años,** I was twenty (years old) yesterday; **¡que cumplas muchos años!,** many happy returns! **II** *vi* **1** *(cumplimentar)* to be polite; **lo hice por c.,** I was just being polite. **2** *(plazo)* to expire, end. **3** *(satisfacer)* to do one's duty. **III cumplirse** *vr* **1** *(realizarse)* to be fulfilled, come true; **se cumplió su deseo,** his wish came true. **2** *(años)* to be; **hoy se cumple la fecha de...,** today is the anniversary of ... .

cúmulo *nm* **1** *(sinnúmero)* pile, load; **un c. de problemas,** a load of problems. **2** *fig (conjunto)* accumulation; **este chico es un c. de cualidades,** that boy's got it all. **3** *Meteor* cumulus.

cuna *nf* **1** *(camita)* cradle, cot. ■ **canción de c.,** lullaby. **2** *fig (origen)* cradle, beginning; **c. de la civilización,** cradle of civilization. **3** *(estirpe)* stock; **de humilde c.,** of humble birth. **4** *(lugar de nacimiento)* birthplace.

cunda *nm Cuba Méx* wag.

cundir *vi* **1** *(dar de sí)* to go far *or* a long way; **me cunde mucho el trabajo** *or* **el tiempo,** I seem to get a lot done. **2** *(extenderse)* to spread; **cundió el pánico,** panic spread; **cundió la voz de que ...,** rumour had it that ... .

cuneta *nf (zanja)* ditch; *(de la carretera)* verge.

cuña *nf* **1** *(taco)* wedge; **hacer c.,** to be wedged in; *fig* **meter c.,** to stir up trouble. **2** *(influencia)* influence; **tener c.,** to have influence. **3** *CAm Aut* two-seater (car).

cuñado,-a *nm, f (hombre)* brother-in-law; *(mujer)* sister-in-law.

cuño *nm* **1** *(troquel)* die, stamp. **2** *(sello)* stamp, mark; **tener el c.,** to bear the mark; *fig* **de nuevo c.,** newly-coined.

cuota *nf* **1** *(porción)* quota, share. **2** *(contribución)* membership fees *pl*, dues *pl*.

cuotidiano,-a *adj* daily.

cupe *pt indef véase* **caber.**

cupé *nm Aut* coupé.

cupiera *subj imperf véase* **caber.**

cuplé *nm Mús* popular lyric song.

cupletista *nf* music-hall singer.

cupo *nm* **1** *(cuota)* quota. **2** *Mil* contingent; **excedente de c.,** exempt from military service. **3** *Am Aut (plaza)* seat. **4** *Méx fam (cárcel)* prison.

cupón *nm Com (vale)* coupon, voucher; *Com* trading stamp; *fam* **c. de los ciegos,** lottery for the blind.

cúpula *nf Arquit* dome, cupola.

cuquería *nf* **1** *(astucia)* craftiness. **2** *fam (monada)* pretty little thing; **¡qué c. de vestido!,** what a pretty little dress!

cura I *nm Rel* priest. ■ **c. párroco,** parish priest. **II** *nf Med* cure, healing; **hacer las primeras curas,** to gjve first aid; *fig* **no tiene c.,** there's no remedy.

curaca *nm Am* petty tyrant.

curación *nf (cura)* cure, treatment; *(de herida)* healing; **c. milagrosa,** miracle cure; **pronta c.,** speedy recovery.

curado,-a I *pp de* **curar. II** *adj* **1** *(sanado)* cured; *(herida)* healed. **2** *(carne, pescado)* cured, salted; *(piel)* tanned. **3** *Am (borracho)* drunk.

curandero,-a *nm, f* quack.

curar I *vtr* **1** (sanar) to cure; *(herida)* to dress a wound; *(enfermedad)* to treat; **c. con medicamentos,** to treat with medication; *fig* **c. un mal,** to right a wrong. **2** *(piel)* to tan; *(carne, pescado)* to cure; *(madera)* to season. **II** *vi* **1** *(recuperarse)* to recover, get well. **2** *(herida)* to heal (up). **III curarse** *vr (sanar)* to recover, get well; *(herida)* to heal up.

curare *nm Am* curare, curari.

curasao *nm (vinos)* curaçao.

curativo,-a *adj* curative; **poder c.,** healing power.

curato *nm Rel* **1** *(cargo)* curacy. **2** *(parroquia)* parish.

curco,-a *Am* **I** *adj (jorobado)* hunchbacked. **II** *nf (joroba)* hump.

curda *nf fam* drunkenness; **agarrar una c.,** to get plastered.

curia *nf* **1** *Rel* curia. **2** *Jur* Bar.

curiosear I *vtr & vi (fisgar)* to pry into; *(visitar)* to look round. **II** *vi (en asuntos ajenos)* to pry.

curiosidad *nf* **1** *(indiscreción)* curiosity, inquisitiveness; **despertar la c. de algn,** to arouse sb's curiosity; **tener c. de,** to be curious about. **2** *(objeto raro)* curiosity. **3** *(aseo)* care, cleanliness.

curioso,-a I *adj* **1** *(indiscreto)* curious, inquisitive. **2** *(extraño)* strange, odd; **lo c. es que ...,** the strange thing is that ... . **3** *(ordenado)* neat, tidy. **II** *nm, f* **1** *(mirón)* onlooker. **2** *pey (chismoso)* nosey-parker, busybody. **3** *Am (curandero)* quack.

currante *nmf arg* worker.

currar *vi*, **currelar** *vi arg* to graft, grind, slave.

curre *nm arg* job, meal ticket.

currículum *nm (pl currícula)* **c. vitae,** curriculum vitae.

curro *nm arg* **dar un c. a algn,** to give sb a hammering.

currutaco,-a I *adj Am (rechoncho)* plump. **II currutacos** *nmpl CAm* diarrhoea *sing*, *US* diarrhea *sing*.

curry *nm Culin* curry.

cursado,-a I *pp de* **cursar. II** *adj* **1** *(cartas)* dispatch. **2** *(versado)* experienced.

cursante *nmf* student.

cursar *vtr* **1** *(enviar)* to send, dispatch; *(orden)* to give. **2** *(tramitar)* to make an application. **3** *(estudiar)* to study, attend.

cursi I *adj* affected, showy, pretentious. **II** *nmf* affected *or* showy *or* pretentious person.

cursilada *nf* **hizo la c. de ...,** he was so vulgar as to ... .

cursilería *nf* **1** *(cualidad)* vulgarity, bad taste. **2** *(cosa cursi)* vulgar *or* kitsch object.

cursillista *adj & nmf* participant, member of a course.

cursillo *nm* short course, training course. ■ **c. de conferencias,** course of lectures; **c. de reciclaje,** refresher course.

cursivo,-a *adj* **letra cursiva,** italics.

curso *nm* **1** *(dirección)* course; **el c. de los acontecimientos,** the course of events; *fig* **año** *or* **mes en c.,** current year *or* month; *fig* **dar c. a,** *(tramitar)* to deal with; *fig (dar libertad)* to give free rein to; *fig* **dejar que las cosas sigan su c.,** to let things take their course; *fig* **en el c. de ...,** during the course of ...; *fig* **estar en c.,** to be under way. **2** *(del río)* flow, current. **3** *Educ (académico)* academic *or* school year; **estamos en el mismo c.,** we are in the same year *or* class; **exámenes de fin de c.,** final exams, finals; **mis compañeros de c.,** my classmates. **4** *Educ (asignatura)* course, subject; **c. de filosofía,** philosophy course. **5** *Fin* **moneda de c. legal,** legal tender.

cursor *nm Téc* slide; *Inform* cursor.

curtido,-a I *pp de* **curtir. II** *adj* **1** *(rostro)* tanned, sunburnt; *(cuero)* tanned. **2** *fig (avezado)* hardened. **III** *nm (piel)* tanning

curtidor,-a *nm, f* tanner.

curtiduría *nf* tannery.

curtir I *vtr* **1** *(piel)* to tan; **el sol y el viento curten la piel,** sun and wind tan the skin. **2** *fig (avezar)* to harden, toughen. **3** *Arg RPI (azotar)* to whip. **II curtirse** *vr* **1** *(piel)* to get tanned. **2** *fig (avezarse)* to become hardened. **3** *SAm (emporcarse)* to get dirty.

curva *nf* **1** *(gen)* curve; **trazar una c.,** to draw a curve; *fam* **¡vaya curvas tiene esa mujer!,** what a body that woman's got! **2** *(en carretera)* bend. ■ **c. cerrada,** sharp bend. **3** *(gráfico)* curve, graph.

curvar *vtr (gen)* to curve; *(espalda)* to arch.

curvatura *nf* curvature.

curvilíneo,-a *adj* **1** *Geom* curvilinear, curvilineal. **2** *fam (cuerpo de mujer)* curvaceous, shapely.

curvo,-a *adj (objeto)* curved; *(doblado)* crooked, bent.

cusca *nf pey Méx* flirty tart.

cuscurro *nm Culin* crust of bread.

cuscús *nm Culin* couscous.

cúspide *nf* **1** *Geog* summit, peak. **2** *Geom* apex. **3** *fig (culminación)* peak.

custodia *nf* **1** *(vigilancia)* custody, care; **bajo c.,** in custody; **encargar a algn la c. de algo,** to give sb custody of sth. **2** *Rel* monstrance.

custodiar *vtr (proteger)* to keep, take care of, look after; *(vigilar)* to guard, watch over.

custodio *nm* custodian, guardian, keeper.

cususa *nf CAm* liquor made from sugar cane.

cutacha *nf CR Hond Nic* long knife.

cutáneo,-a *adj* cutaneous, skin; *Med* **enfermedad cutánea,** skin disease; *Med* **erupción cutánea,** rash.

cutara *nf CR Cuba Méx* sandal.

cutícula *nf* cuticle.

cutis *nm* complexion, skin.

cuy *nm SAm Zool* guinea pig.

cuyo,-a *pron rel & pos* whose, of which; **en c. caso,** in which case; **la familia en cuya casa nos quedamos,** the family in whose house we stayed; **la señora, c. hijo es tu amigo, vive aquí,** the lady whose son is your friend lives here.

cv *abr de* **caballos de vapor,** horse power, hp.

D

D, d *nf (la letra)* D, d.

D. *abr de* **don,** Mister, Mr.

Da., D.ª *abr de* **doña,** Mrs, Miss.

dable *adj* possible, feasible, practicable.

dabute(n) *adj arg* great, terrific.

dactilar *adj* digital; **huellas dactilares,** fingerprints.

dactilografía *nf* typing, typewriting.

dactilógrafo,-a *nm,f* typist.

dadaísmo *nm Arte Lit* Dadaism.

dadaísta *adj & nmf Arte Lit* Dadaist.

dádiva *nf (regalo)* gift, present; *(donativo)* donation; *(compensación)* sop.

dadivoso,-a I *adj* generous. **II** *nm,f* generous person.

dado,-a¹ I *pp de* **dar. II** *adj* given; **dada su edad,** in view of his age; **en un caso d.,** in a given case; **en un momento d.,** at a given moment, at a certain point. **2** *(aficionado a)* **ser d. a,** to be keen on, be fond of; **sus padres son muy dados a viajar,** his parents are very fond of travelling. **3** *(en vista de)* **d. que,** as, since, in view of, given that; **d. que tienes fiebre, mejor que te quedes en casa,** since you've got a temperature, you'd better stay at home. **4** *fam* **ir d.,** to be heading for trouble; **con el nuevo jefe vamos dados,** we're in for it with this new boss.

dado² nm **1** *(para juegos)* die, dice *pl*; **echar los dados,** to throw the dice; *fig* **cargar los dados,** to load the dice. **2** *Téc* block. **3** *Arquit* dado.

dador,-a *nm,f* **1** *(gen)* donor. **2** *(de carta)* bearer; *(de letra de cambio etc)* drawer.

daga *nf* dagger.

daguerrotipo *nm Fot* daguerreotype.

Dakota *n* Dakota; **D. del Norte,** North Dakota; **D. del Sur,** South Dakota.

dalia *nf Bot* dahlia.

dálmata I *adj* Dalmatian. **II** *nm* Dalmatian (dog).

daltoniano,-a I *adj* colour-blind, *US* color-blind. **II** *nm,f* person who is colour-blind *or US* color-blind.

daltonismo *nm* colour *or US* color blindness.

dama *nf* **1** *(señora)* lady. ■ **d. de honor,** *(de reina)* lady-in-waiting; *(de novia)* bridesmaid; **primera d.,** *Teat* leading lady; *Pol* first lady. **2** *Ajedrez Naipes* queen; *Damas* king.

3 damas, *(juego)* draughts, *US* checkers; **tablero de d.,** draughtboard, *US* checkerboard.

damajuana *nf* demijohn.

Damasco *n* Damascus.

damasco *nm* **1** *Tex* damask. **2** *Bot* damson.

damasquina *nf Bot* French marigold.

damasquinado *nm Téc* damascene.

damasquinar *vtr* to damascene, damask.

damisela *nf Hist & irón* damsel, young lady.

damnificado,-a I *pp de* **damnificar. II** *adj (person)* injured; *(cosa)* damaged. **III** *nm,f* victim, injured person; **los damnificados por el incendio,** the victims of the fire.

damnificar *vtr (person)* to injure, harm; *(cosa)* to damage.

Damocles *nm* Damocles; *fig* **la espada de D.,** the sword of Damocles.

danés,-esa I *adj* Danish. **II** *nm,f (persona)* Dane. **III** *nm,* **1** *(idioma)* Danish. **2** *(perro)* **gran d.,** Great Dane.

dantesco,-a *adj fig* Dantesque, horrific.

Danubio *nm* **el D.,** the Danube.

danza *nf* **I** *(gen)* dancing; *(baile)* dance; **d. guerrera,** war dance; **la d. de la muerte,** the dance of death; *fig* **está siempre en d.,** she's always on the go. **2** *fig (negocio sucio)* shady business *or* deal; *(lío)* mess. **3** *fam (jaleo)* rumpus, row; **armar una d.,** to make a scene.

danzante I *adj* dancing. **II** *nmf* **1** dancer. **2** *fam (persona vivaracha)* enterprising person; *(entrometido)* busybody, meddler; *(casquivano)* scatterbrain, featherbrain.

danzar I *vtr* to dance. **II** *vi* **1** to dance **(con,** with). **2** *fam (entrometerse)* to meddle, interfere **(en,** with, in).

danzarín,-ina *nm,f (profesional)* dancer.

dañado,-a I *pp de* **dañar. II** *adj* **1** *(estropeado)* damaged, spoiled. **2** *(malo)* wicked, evil.

dañar I *vtr* **1** *(cosa)* to damage; *(persona)* to hurt, harm; *(estropear)* to spoil; **dañará su reputación,** it will damage her reputation. **II dañarse** *vr* **1** *(cosa)* to get damaged; *(persona)* to get hurt, be harmed. **2** *(comestibles)* to rot, go bad *or* off.

dañino,-a *adj* harmful, damaging **(para,** to); **animales dañinos,** pests, vermin *sing*.

daño *nm* (*a cosa*) damage; (*a persona*) hurt, harm, injury; (*perjuicio*) wrong; **hacer d. a,** (*a cosa*) to damage; (*a persona*) to harm; **hacerse d.,** to hurt oneself; **se hizo d. en la pierna,** he hurt his leg; **los daños ocasionados por la inundación,** the damage caused by the flooding; **no hace d.,** (*indoloro*) it doesn't hurt, it isn't painful; (*inofensivo*) it's harmless, it does no harm. ■ *Jur* **daños y perjuicios,** (legal) damages.

dañoso,-a *adj* harmful.

dar I *vtr* **1** (*gen*) to give; (*entregar*) (*paquete, carta, etc*) to deliver, hand over; (*pan, sal, etc*) to pass, hand; (*recado, recuerdos*) to pass on, give; (*noticia*) to tell, announce, report; (*consejos*) to give; (*naipes*) to deal; (*pintura, cera*) to apply, put on; (*olor*) to give off; (*gas, luz*) to turn on; **d. brilo a unos zapatos,** to polish one's shoes; **d. clase,** to teach; (*universidad*) to lecture; **d. la enhorabuena,** to congratulate (**por,** on); **d. la mano a algn,** to shake hands with sb; **d. las gracias por algo,** to say thank you for sth; *fml* to give thanks for sth; **d. los buenos días/las buenas noches a algn,** to wish sb good morning/good evening, say hello to sb; **d. lugar a,** to give rise to; **d. muestras de alegría/tristeza,** to look happy/sad; **d. palmadas,** to clap; **d. parte de,** to report; **d. razón,** to give an account (**de,** of); **d. un grito,** to let out a cry; **d. un paseo,** to go for a walk *or* stroll; **d. un paso,** to take a step; **d. una puñalada a algn,** to stab sb; **d. voces,** (*gritar*) to shout; (*correr la voz*) to let it be known; **me da asco/miedo/ lástima** *or* **pena,** it makes me feel sick/afraid/sad, it disgusts/frightens/saddens me; **me da lo mismo, lo mismo da, me da igual,** it's all the same to me; **me da no sé qué,** it gives me a strange feeling; **no d. una,** not to get anything right; **nos da mucho gusto verlo/oírlo,** we are very pleased to see/hear it; **¿qué más da?,** what does it matter?, it makes no difference. **2** (*reloj*) to strike; **el reloj de la catedral dio las 4,** the cathedral clock struck 4; **ya han dado las 9,** it's gone 9 (o'clock). **3** (*película*) to show, screen; (*obra de teatro*) to perform, put on; (*obra musical*) to play, perform; (*concierto*) to hold, put on; (*fiesta*) to throw, give; **¿qué dan en el Roxy?,** what's on at the Roxy? **4** (*producir*) (*cosecha*) to produce, yield; (*fruto, flores*) to bear; (*beneficio, interés*) to give, yield. **5** (*pegar*) to hit; **¡dale fuerte!,** hit him hard!, let him have it! **6** (*seguir*) **¡dale!,** go on!; (*¡venga!*) come on!; **seguir dale que dale con algo, seguir dale que te pego con algo,** to keep on and on doing sth; **¡y dale!,** there he *or* she goes again! **7 d. a conocer,** (*persona*) to introduce, present; (*noticia*) to release; **d. a entender que ...,** to give to understand that ..., imply that ... . **8** *fam* (*tener el hábito*) **darle a la botella,** to be (too) fond of the bottle. **II** *vi* **1** (*ataque, risa*) **darle a algn un ataque de tos/risa,** to have a coughing fit/an attack of the giggles. **2 d. a,** (*ventana, habitación*) to look out onto, overlook; (*puerta*) to open onto, lead to. **3 d. con,** (*persona*) to meet, come across, bump into; (*cosa*) to find, discover; **d. con los huesos en la cárcel,** to end *or* land up in jail; **d. consigo en el suelo,** to collapse; **dio con la moto contra el muro,** he crashed the motorbike into the wall. **4** (*suministrar*) to give; **d. de beber/comer a algn,** to give sb sth to drink/eat; **d. de comer al bebé/gato/perro,** to feed the baby/cat/dog; **d. de espaldas a,** to turn one's back on; **d. de palos a algn,** to beat sb (up). **5** (*ropa*) **d. de sí,** to stretch, give. **6** (*pegar*) **d. a algn en la cabeza,** to hit sb on the head; **el sol me daba en la cara,** the sun was shining in my face. **7** (*acertar*) **d. con** *or* **en una solución,** to hit upon *or* find a solution; *fig* **d. en el clavo,** to hit the nail on the head. **8** (*ser suficiente*) **d. para,** to be enough *or* sufficient for; **el presupuesto no da para más,** the budget will not stretch any further. **9** (*empeñarse*) **darle a uno por hacer algo,** to take it into one's head to do sth; **ahora le ha dado por ahí,** that's his latest fad; **le dio por la pintura,** he took up painting. **10** (*considerar*) **d. por,** to assume, consider; **lo dieron por muerto,** he was assumed dead, he was given up for dead; **d. por hecho** *or* **concluido un asunto,** to consider a matter closed. **11 d. que hablar,** to get people talking; **d. que hacer,** to make work, give trouble; **el suceso dio que pensar,** the incident gave people food for thought. **III**

darse *vr* **1** (*entregarse*) to give in, surrender. **2** (*suceder*) to happen, occur; **luego se dio un caso extraño,** then something strange happened. **3** (*crecer*) (*planta etc*) to grow; (*hallarse*) to be found, exist; **las setas se dan muy bien en este bosque,** there are lots of mushrooms in this wood; **no se dan mucho los pinos en esta zona,** few pine trees are to be found (growing) in this region. **4** (*consagrarse*) **d. a,** to devote oneself *or* give oneself over to; *pey* to take to, abandon oneself in; **se dio a la bebida,** he took to drink; **d. a conocer,** to make oneself known. **5** (*golpearse*) **d. con** *or* **contra,** to bump *or* crash into. **6** (*considerarse*) **d. por,** to consider oneself; **d. por aludido,** to take the hint; (*sentirse ofendido*) to take sth personally; **d. por satisfecho,** to feel satisfied; **d. por vencido,** to give in, surrender. **7** (*resultar*) **se le da bien/ mal el francés,** she's good/bad at French; **se me dan fatal las matemáticas,** I'm hopeless at maths. **8** (*importar*) **tanto se da suspender,** he couldn't care less about failing (the exam); *fam* **¿qué se me da?,** why should I care? **9** (*presumir*) **dárselas de,** to pose as, fancy oneself as; **no te las des de inocente,** stop acting innocent; **se las da de experto en el tema,** he thinks he's an expert on the subject.

dardo *nm* (*flecha*) dart, arrow; *fig* caustic remark.

dársena *nf* Náut dock.

darvinismo *nm* Darwinism.

darvinista *adj & nmf* Darwinist.

data *nf* **1** (*fecha*) date. **2** *Com* item.

datar I *vtr* to date, put a date on. **II** *vi* **d. de,** to date back to *or* from; **esa costumbre data del siglo doce,** that custom dates back to the twelfth century.

dátil *nm* **1** *Bot* (*fruto*) date. ■ **d. de mar,** date shell. **2 dátiles,** *fam* (*dedos*) fingers.

datilera *nf* Bot (*árbol*) date palm.

dativo,-a *adj & nm* Ling dative; **en d.,** in the dative.

dato *nm* fact, datum, piece of information; **por falta de datos,** because of lack of information. ■ *Inform* **banco de datos,** data bank; *Inform* **base de datos,** data base; **datos estadísticos,** statistical data *usu sing*; **datos personales,** personal details; *Inform* **procesamiento** *or* **proceso de datos,** data processing.

dB *abr de* **decibelio,** decibel, dB.

d.C. *abr de* **después de Cristo,** Anno Domini, AD.

dcha. *abr de* **derecha,** right.

de¹ *nf* name of the letter D in Spanish.

de² *prep* **1** (*pertenencia*) of, 's, s'; **el coche/hermano de Elvira,** Elvira's car/brother; **el padre de la niña,** the girl's father; **el padre de las niñas,** the girls' father; **el título de la novela,** the title of the novel. **2** (*procedencia*) from; **de Lugo a Monforte,** from Lugo to Monforte; **esta carta viene de tu officina,** this letter is from your office; **soy de Almería,** I am from Almería. **3** (*descripción*) **el niño de ojos azules,** the boy with blue eyes; **la señora del vestido rojo,** the lady in the red dress; **un reloj de oro,** a gold watch; **un vaso de plástico,** a plastic cup. **4** (*contenido*) of; **un saco de patatas,** a saek of potatoes. **5** (*uso*) **gafas de sol,** sunglasses; **goma de borrar,** rubber, *US* eraser **6** (*oficio*) by, as; **es arquitecto de profesión,** he's an architect by profession; **hace de secretaria,** she's working as a secretary. **7** (*precio*) at; **la de cincuenta pesetas,** the one at fifty pesetas, the fifty peseta one; **patatas de quince peniques el kilo,** potatoes at fifteen pence a kilo. **8** (*medida*) **una avenida de quince kilómetros,** an avenue fifteen kimometres long; **una botella de litro,** a litre bottle. **9** (*con superlativo*) in; **el más largo de España,** the longest in Spain; **el mejor del mundo,** the best in the world. **10** (*tiempo*) **a las tres de la trade,** at three in the afternoon; **de día,** by day; **de lunes a jueves,** from Monday to Thursday; **de noche,** at night. **11** (*causa*) with, because of; **llorar de alegría,** to cry with joy; **morir de hambre,** to die of hunger. **12** (*condicional*) **de haber llegado antes,** if he had arrived before; **de no ser así,** if that wasn't *or* weren't so, if that wasn't *or* weren't the case; **de ser cierto**, if it was *or* were true. **13** *(en expresiones de queja, lástima, etc)* **¡ay de mí!**, poor me!; **¡el desagraciado de mi hijo!**, oh my poor son!;

deambular *vi* to saunter, stroll, wander.

deambulatorio *nm Arquit* ambulatory.

deán *nm* dean.

debacle *nf* disaster, downfall.

debajo *adv* underneath, below; **el mío es el de d.**, mine is the one below; **está d. de la mesa**, it's under the table; **por d. de lo normal**, below normal; **salió por d. del coche**, he came out from under the car.

debate *nm* debate, discussion. ■ **d. parlamentario**, parliamentary debate.

debatir I *vtr* to debate. **II debatirse** *vr* to struggle; **d. entre la vida y la muerte**, to fight for one's life.

debe *nm Com* debit, debit side.

deber¹ *nm* **1** duty, obligation; **cumplir con su d.**, to do one's duty. **2 deberes**, *Educ* homework *sing*; **hacer los d.**, to do one's homework.

deber² I *vtr* **1** *(adeudar)* to owe; **me debes cien pesetas**, you owe me a hundred pesetas. **2** *(d. + infinitivo) (en presente y futuro)* to have to, must; **debe comer**, he must eat; **debe irse ahora**, she has to leave now; **deberás estar allí a las ocho**, you have to be there at eight (o'clock); **no debes salir con este tiempo**, you mustn't go out in this weather. **2** *(d. + infinitivo) (en condicional)* should, ought to; **debería haber ido ayer**, I should have gone yesterday; **deberías visitar a tus padres**, you ought to visit your parents; **no deberías haber ido**, you shouldn't have gone. **3** *(d. + infinitivo) (en pretérito)* should have, ought to have; **debiste decírmelo**, you ought to have told me; **debía hacerlo pero no tuve tiempo**, I should have done it, but I didn't have time; **debía hacerlo porque así me lo ordenaron**, I had to do it because I was ordered to; **no debiste hacerlo**, you shouldn't have done it. **II** *v aux* *(probabilidad)* **d. de**, must; **deben de estar fuera**, they must be out; **ha debido de caerse**, he must have fallen over; **no deben de estar en casa**, they can't be at home; **no debió de encontrarlo**, he can't have found it. **III deberse** *vr* **1** *(ser consecuencia de)* to be due to; **¿a qué se debe esta actitud?**, what is the reason for this attitude?; **esto se debe a la falta de agua**, this is because of the water shortage. **2** *(dedicarse a)* **se debe a la patria**, he has an obligation to his country; **ella se debe a su trabajo**, she must put her work first.

debido,-a I *pp de* **deber**. **II** *adj* **1** due; **a su d. tiempo**, in due course; **con el d. respeto**, with due respect. **2** *(conveniente)* right; **a la temperatura debida**, at the right temperature. **3** *(adecuado)* proper; **más de lo d.**, too much; **tomaron las debidas precauciones**, they took the proper precautions. **4** *(requerido)* **como es. d.**, properly; **come como es d.**, eat properly; **espero que le reciban como es d.**, I hope they will welcome him as they ought to. **5** *(a causa de)* **d. a**, because of, owing to, due to; **d. a que**, because of the fact that; **d. al mal tiempo**, because of the bad weather. ◆ **debidamente** *adv* duly, properly.

débil I *adj* **1** *(flojo)* weak, feeble; **punto d.**, weak spot; **tiene el pulso d.**, his pulse is weak. **2** *(poco perceptible)* faint; **un ruido d.**, a faint noise; **una luz d.**, a dim light. **3** *(vocal, sílaba)* weak. **II** *nmf* weak person; **d. mental**, mentally retarded person; **los económicamente débiles**, the poor.

debilidad *nf* weakness, feebleness; *fig* **tener d. por**, *(persona)* to have a soft spot for; *(cosa)* to have a weakness for; *fig* **tiene d. por el teatro**, he is really keen on the theatre.

debilitación *nf* weakening.

debilitador,-a *adj* weakening, debilitating.

debilitamiento *nm véase* **debilitación**.

debilitar I *vtr* to weaken, debilitate. **II debilitarse** *vr* to weaken, grow weak.

debilucho,-a *pey* I *adj* weak, frail, delicate. **II** *nm, f* weakling.

débito *nm* **1** *(deuda)* debt. **2** *(debe)* debit.

debocar *vi Arg Bol* to vomit.

debut *nm* début, debut.

debutante I *nmf* *(actor, actriz)* person who gives his *or* her first public perfomance. **II** *nf (en sociedad)* debutante.

debutar *vi* to make one's début *or* debut.

década *nf* decade.

decadencia *nf* decadence, decline, decay.

decadente *adj & nmf* decadent.

decaedro *nm Mat* decahedron.

decaer *vi* to decay, decline, deteriorate; **está decayendo el comercio**, business is falling off; **su ánimo no decae a pesar de la enfermedad**, she doesn't lose heart in spite of her illness; **su entusiasmo no decae**, his enthusiasm never flags; **su salud ha decaído**, his health has deteriorated; **tarde** *or* **temprano todos los imperios decaen**, all empires decay sooner or later.

decaído,-a I *pp de* **decaer**. **II** *adj* **1** *(débil)* weak. **2** *(desmoralizado)* depressed, downhearted.

decaimiento *nm* **1** *(decadencia)* decline, decay. **2** *(debilidad)* weakness, weakening. **3** *(desaliento)* gloominess, low spirits *pl*.

decalitro *nm* decalitre, *US* decaliter.

decálogo *nm* decalogue.

decámetro *nm* decametre, *US* decameter.

decanato *nm* **1** *(cargo)* deanship. **2** *(despacho del decano)* deanery.

decano,-a *nm, f* **1** *Univ* dean. **2** *(miembro más antiguo)* senior member; *(hombre)* doyen; *(mujer)* doyenne.

decantación *nf* decanting.

decantar¹ I *vtr lit (alabar)* to praise, extol. **II decantarse** *vr (inclinarse por)* to lean towards; *fig* to show a preference for.

decantar² *vtr (verter)* to decant.

decapitación *nf* beheading, decapitation.

decapitar *vtr* to behead, decapitate.

decasílabo,-a I *adj* decasyllabic. **II** *nm* decasyllable.

deceleración *nf* deceleration.

decelerar *vi* to decelerate, slow down.

decena *nf* (about) ten; **una d. de veces**, (about) ten times; **por decenas**, in tens.

decencia *nf* **1** *(decoro)* decency; **con d.**, decently. **2** *(honradez)* honesty.

decenio *nm* decade.

decentar *vtr* to begin to use up; *fig* **d. la salud**, to begin to lose one's health.

decente *adj* **1** *(honrado)* honest, respectable; **un hombre d.**, a respectable man. **2** *(decoroso)* decent, modest. **3** *(limpio)* clean, tidy.

decepción *nf* disappointment, disenchantment.

decepcionante *adj* disappointing.

decepcionar *vtr* to disappoint.

deceso *nm fml* decease, passing.

dechado *nm* model, example; **ser un d. de virtudes**, to be a paragon of virtue.

decibel *nm*, **decibelio** *nm Fís* decibel.

decidido,-a I *pp de* **decidir**. **II** *adj* determined, resolute. ◆ **decididamente** *adv* **1** *(resueltamente)* resolutely. **2** *(definitivamente)* definitely.

decidir I *vtr* **1** *(determinar)* to decide; *(asunto)* to settle; **decidieron suspender la reunión**, they decided to cancel the meeting. **2** *(resolver)* to resolve. **3** *(convencer, persuadir)* to decide, persuade; **su madre le decidió a dejar de fumar**, his mother persuaded him to stop smoking. **II** *vi* to decide, choose; **d. entre dos cosas**, to choose between two things. **III decidirse** *vr* to make up one's mind; **d. a hacer algo**, to make up one's mind to do sth; **d. por algo**, to decide on sth.

decidor,-a *adj* **1** *(gracioso)* witty. **2** *(que habla con facilidad)* fluent, eloquent.

decilitro *nm* decilitre, *US* deciliter.

décima *nf* **1** *Mat* tenth, tenth part. **2** *(en un termómetro)* tenth of a degree; **tener décimas,** to have a slight temperature. **3** *Lit* ten-line stanza.

decimal I *adj* decimal, **el sistema métrico d.,** the metric system. **II** *nm* **1** *(número)* decimal. **2** decimales, *Méx* money *sing*.

decímetro *nm* decimetre, *US* decimeter.

décimo,-a I *adj* tenth; **décima parte,** tenth. **II** *nm,f (de una serie)* tenth. **III** *nm* **1** *(parte)* tenth. **2** *(billete de lotería)* tenth part of a lottery ticket; *véase tamb* **octavo,-a.**

decimoctavo,-a I *adj* eighteenth; **decimoctava parte,** eighteenth. **II** *nm, f (de una serie)* eighteenth. **III** *nm (parte)* eighteenth; *véase tamb* **octavo,-a.**

decimocuarto,-a I *adj* fourteenth; **decimocuarta parte,** fourteenth. **II** *nm, f (de una serie)* fourteenth. **III** *nm (parte)* fourteenth; *véase tamb* **octavo,-a.**

decimonónico,-a *adj* nineteenth-century.

decimonono,-a, decimonoveno,-a I *adj* nineteenth; **decimonovena parte,** nineteenth. **II** *nm,f (de una serie)* nineteenth. **III** *nm (parte)* nineteenth; *véase tamb* **octavo,-a.**

decimoquinto,-a I *adj* fifteenth; **decimoquinta parte,** fifteenth. **II** *nm,f (de una serie)* fifteenth. **III** *nm (parte)* fifteenth; *véase tamb* **octavo,-a.**

decimoséptimo,-a I *adj* seventeenth; **decimoséptima parte,** seventeenth. **II** *nm, f (de una serie)* seventeenth. **III** *nm (parte)* seventeenth; *véase tamb* **octavo,-a.**

decimosexto,-a I *adj* sixteenth; **decimosexta parte,** sixteenth. **II** *nm,f (de una serie)* sixteenth. **III** *nm (parte)* sixteenth; *véase tamb* **octavo,-a.**

decimotercero,-a, decimotercio,-a I *adj* thirteenth; **decimotercera parte,** thirteenth. **II** *nm, f (de una serie)* thirteenth. **III** *nm (parte)* thirteenth; *véase tamb* **octavo,-a.**

decir¹ *nm* saying; *fam* **es un d.,** it's just a saying.

decir² *(pp dicho)* **I** *vtr* **1** to say; **¿cómo se dice 'papaya' en inglés?,** how do you say 'papaya' in English?; **dice que no quiere venir,** he says he doesn't want to come; **se dice que ...,** they say that ...; **d. el padrenuestro,** to say the Lord's Prayer. **2** *(contar)* to tell; **d. una mentira/la verdad,** to tell a lie/the truth. **3** *(llamar)* to call; **le dicen la casa del diablo,** it's known as the devil's house; **se llama Enrique pero le dicen Quique,** his name's Enrique, but he's called Quique (for short). **4** *(opinar)* to think; **¿qué me dices del nueva jefe?,** what do you think of the new boss? **5** *(denotar)* to tell, show; **su actitud dice mal de su educación,** his behaviour doesn't say much for his upbringing; **su cara dice que está mintiendo,** you can tell from his face that he's lying. **6** *(sugerir)* to mean; **los juegos electrónicos no me dicen nada,** I'm not the least bit interested in electronic games; **¿qué te dice el cuadro?,** what does the picture mean to you?; **su última película no me dice nada,** I'm not too impressed by her latest film. **7 querer d.,** to mean; **no quise d. eso,** I didn't mean to say that; **¿qué quieres d.?,** what do you mean? **8** *(locuciones)* **¿cómo diría yo?,** how shall I put it?; **como quien dice, como si dijéramos,** as it were, so to speak; **d. por d.,** to speak for the sake of speaking; **dicho de otro modo,** in other words; **dicho y hecho,** no sooner said than done; **digamos,** lets say; **digo yo,** in my opinion; **dímelo a mí,** you're telling me!; **el qué dirán,** what people say; **es d.,** that is (to say); **Juan es lo que se dice un imbécil,** Juan is what you would call an idiot; **ni que d. tiene,** needless to say; **¡no me digas!,** really!; *or* **mejor dicho,** or rather; **por así decirlo,** so to speak; **¡y que lo digas!,** you bet! **II decirse** *vr* to tell oneself; **sé lo que me digo,** I know what I am saying.

decisión *nf* **1** *(resolución)* decisión; **tomar una d.,** to take *or* make a decision. **2** *(firmeza de carácter)* determination, resolution; **con d.,** decisively.

decisivo,-a *adj,* **decisorio,-a** *adj* decisive; **de forma decisiva,** definitely.

declamación *nf* **1** *(acción)* recitation. **2** *(arte)* declamation.

declamar *vtr & vi* to declaim, recite.

declamatorio,-a *adj* declamatory.

declaración *nf* **1** *(gen)* declaration; *(afirmación)* statement; **d. de amor,** declaration of love; **d. de quiebra,** declaration of bankruptcy; **d. de renta,** tax declaration *or* return; **hacer una d.,** to make a statement; **negarse a hacer declaraciones,** to refuse to comment. **2** *Jur* **prestar d.,** to give evidence. **3** *Bridge* bid.

declarado,-a I *pp de* **declarar. II** *adj* open, professed; **enemigo d.,** sworn enemy. ◆ **declaradamente** *adv* openly.

declarante I *adj* declaring, who declares. **II** *nmf Jur* witness.

declarar I *vtr* **1** *(gen)* to declare; *(afirmar)* to state; **el presidente declaró que ...,** the president stated that ...; **fue declarado vencedor,** he was declared (the) winner. **2** *Jur* **d. culpable/inocente a algn,** to find sb guilty/not guilty. **3** *Bridge* to bid. **II** *vi* **1** to declare. **2** *Jur* to testify. **III declararse** *vr* **1** to declare oneself; *(a un chico, una chica)* to declare one's love (**a,** for); **d. a favor/en contra de,** to declare oneself in favour of/against; **d. en huelga,** to go on strike; **d. en quiebra,** to go into bankruptcy, become bankrupt. **2** *(epidemia, guerra, incendio)* to start, break out. **3** *Jur* **d. culpable,** to plead guilty.

declaratorio,-a *adj* declaratory.

declinable *adj Ling* declinable.

declinación *nf* **1** *(caída)* decline, decay. **2** *Ling* declension. **3** *Astron* declination.

declinar I *vi* **1** *(decaer)* to decline, decay. **2** *(disminuir)* to diminish, lessen; *(fiebre)* to abate, diminish. **3** *(terminar)* **al d. el día,** when the day draws to a close. **II** *vtr* **1** *(rechazar)* to decline. **2** *Ling* to decline.

declive *nm* **1** *(del terreno)* incline, slope. **2** *(decadencia)* decline.

decoloración *nf* bleaching; fading.

decolorante *nm* bleaching agent.

decolorar I *vtr* to fade; to bleach; **d. el pelo,** to bleach one's hair. **II decolorarse** *vr* to fade; to be bleached.

decomisar *vtr* to confiscate, seize.

decomiso *nm* **1** *(artículos, bienes)* confiscated article *or* goods *pl*. **2** *(acción)* confiscation, seizure.

decoración *nf* **1** decoration; **d. de escaparates,** window dressing. **2** *Teat* scenery, set.

decorado *nm Teat* scenery, set.

decorador,-a I *adj* decorating. **II** *nm, f* **1** *(persona)* decorator; **d. de escaparates,** window dresser; **pintor d.,** painter and decorator, interior designer. **2** *Teat* set designer.

decorar *vtr* to decorate, adorn; **d. una casa,** to decorate a house.

decorativo,-a *adj* decorative, ornamental; **ser** *or* **estar de figura decorativa,** to be there for decorative purposes only.

decorazonar I *vtr* to dishearten, discourage. **II descorazonarse** *vr* to lose heart, become discouraged.

decoro *nm* **1** *(respeto)* dignity, decorum; **el d. de la profesión** the dignity of the profession. **2** *(dignidad)* decency; **vivir con d.,** to live decently. **3** *(pudor)* modesty, decency; **hablar con d.,** to speak decorously; **sin d.,** indecently.

decoroso,-a *adj* **1** *(correcto)* proper, seemly, decorous. **2** *(digno)* decent, respectable; **un trabajo d.,** a respectable job; **un sueldo d.,** a decent salary. **3** *(decente)* decent, modest; **un vestido d.,** a decent dress.

decrecer *vi* to decrease, diminish; **las aguas decrecieron,** the waters subsided; **los días decrecen,** the days are getting shorter; **decrece el interés por el fútbol,** interest in football is declining.

decreciente *adj* decreasing, diminishing, declining.

decrecimiento *nm* decrease.

decrépito,-a *adj* decrepit.

decrepitud *nf* decrepitude.

decretar *vtr* to decree, ordain.

decreto *nm* decree, order. ■ **d.-ley**, decree.

decúbito *nm* horizontal position; **estar en d. prono/ supino**, to be lying face down/up, be lying prone/supine.

decurso *nm fml* **en el d. de los años**, over the years.

dedada *nf* **1** *(cantidad)* thimbleful, small amount. **2** *(mancha)* fingerprint.

dedal *nm* thimble.

dédalo *nm* labyrinth.

dedicación *nf* **1** dedication, devotion; **su d. a la familia/al partido**, his devotion to his family/to the party. **2** *Rel (consagración)* dedication, consecration.

dedicar I *vtr (gen)* to dedicate; *(tiempo, esfuerzos)* to devote (**a**, to); **dedicó al público unas palabras de agradecimiento**, he addressed a few words of thanks to the audience. **II dedicarse** *vr (consagrarse)* to devote *or* dedicate oneself to; **¿a qué se dedica?**, what do you do for a living?; **los fines de semana ella se dedica a la pesca**, at weekends she spends her time fishing.

dedicatoria *nf* dedication, inscription.

dedicatorio,-a *adj* dedicatory.

dedil *nm* fingerstall.

dedillo *nm* **cumplir las instrucciones al d.**, to carry out instructions to the letter; **saber algo al d.**, to have sth at one's fingertips, know sth very well.

dedo *nm Anat (de la mano)* finger; *(del pie)* toe; **meterse los dedos en la nariz**, to pick one's nose; *fig* **a dos dedos de**, only an inch away from; *fig* **elegir a algn a d.**, to handpick sb; *fig* **no mover un d.**, not to lift a finger; *fig* **no tener dos dedos de frente**, to be as thick as two short planks; *fig* **poner el d. en la llaga**, to touch on a sore spot; *fam* **cogerse** *or* **pillarse los dedos**, to get caught in the act; *fam* **entrar a d.**, to get in by the back door *or* by pulling strings; *fam* **escoger a algn a d.**, to designate sb; *fam* **hacer d.**, to hitchhike; *fam fig* **está para chuparse los dedos**, it's delicious *or* mouthwatering; *fam fig* **no se chupa el d.**, he wasn't born yesterday. ■ **d. anular**, third finger, ring finger; **d. corazón**, middle finger; **d. del pie**, toe; **d. índice**, index finger; **d. meñique**, little finger; **d. pulgar**, **d. gordo**, thumb; **yema del d.**, fingertip.

deducción *nf* deduction.

deducible *adj* **1** deducible, inferable. **2** *Com* deductible.

deducir I *vtr* **1** to deduce, infer. **2** *Com* to deduct, subtract. **II deducirse** *vr* to follow; **de aquí se deduce que ...**, from this it follows that ... .

deductivo,-a *adj* deductive.

defecación *nf* defecation.

defecar *vtr* to defecate.

defección *nf* defection, desertion.

defectivo,-a *adj* defective; *Ling* **verbo d.**, defective verb.

defecto *nm* **1** *(físico)* defect, fault; **d. de pronunciación**, speech defect; **d. físico**, physical defect. **2** *(moral)* fault, shortcoming; **en d. de**, for lack of, for want of.

defectuoso,-a *adj* defective, faulty.

defender I *vtr* **1** to defend (**contra**, against; **de**, from). **2** *(proteger)* to protect; **d. del frío**, to protect from the cold. **3** *(opinión, afirmación)* to defend, uphold; *(persona)* to stand up for. **4** *(tema)* **d. una causa**, to argue a case. **II defenderse** *vr* **1** to defend oneself. **2** *fam (espabilarse)* to get by, manage; **se defiende bastante bien en francés**, he can get by quite well in French.

defendible *adj* defensible, justifiable.

defendido,-a I *pp de* **defender. II** *adj* **1** defended. **2** *Jur* defendant. **III** *nm,f Jur* defendant.

defenestración *nf* defenestration.

defenestrar *vtr* to throw out of a window.

defensa I *nf* **1** defence, *US* defense; **en d. propia, en legítima d.**, in self-defence; **salir en d. de algn**, to come out in defence of sb. **2** *Cuba Chi Méx Aut (parachoques)* bumper, *US* fender. **II** *nm Dep* defender, back.

defensiva *nf* defensive; **estar/ponerse a la d.**, to be/go on the defensive.

defensivo,-a *adj* defensive.

defensor,-a I *adj* defending; *Jur* **abogado d.**, counsel for the defence. **II** *nm,f* defender; *Jur* counsel for the defence.

deferencia *nf* deference; **en** *or* **por d. a**, in deference to.

deferente *adj* deferential.

deferir I *vi* to defer to. **II** *vtr Jur* to delegate (**a**, to), transfer (**a**, to).

deficiencia *nf* **1** *(defecto)* defect, deficiency, shortcoming; **las deficiencias del servicio**, the shortcomings of the service. **2** *(insuficiencia)* lack; **d. mental**, mental deficiency; **la d. de medios**, the lack of means.

deficiente I *adj* **1** *(defectuoso)* deficient, faulty; **un trabajo d.**, a shoddy piece of work. **2** *(insuficiente)* insufficient, lacking; **una iluminación d.**, poor lighting. **II** *nmf* **d. mental**, mentally retarded person.

déficit *nm (pl déficits)* **1** *Com Fin* deficit. **2** *fig* shortage.

deficitario,-a *adj* showing a deficit; **balance d.**, balance showing a deficit.

definible *adj* definable.

definición *nf* definition; **por d.**, by definition.

definido,-a I *pp de* **definir. II** *adj* definite, defined; *Ling* **artículo d.**, definite article.

definir I *vtr* to define. **II definirse** *vr* to make oneself clear.

definitivo,-a *adj* definitive, final; **en definitiva**, finally, in short; **en definitiva, no hay motivo de alarma**, in short, there is nothing to worry about. ◆ **definitivamente** *adv* **1** *(para siempre)* for good, once and for all. **2** *(finalmente)* finally; **la boda será d. el catorce**, the wedding will finally be held on the fourteenth.

deflación *nf Econ* deflation.

deflacionista *adj Econ* deflationary.

deflector *nm Téc* baffle, deflector.

deformación *nf* deformation.

deformar I *vtr (gen)* to deform, put out of shape; *(cara)* to disfigure; *fig* **d. la realidad/la verdad/una imagen**, to distort reality/the truth/a picture. **II deformarse** *vr* to go out of shape, become distorted.

deforme *adj (persona, miembro)* deformed; *(imagen)* distorted; *(objetos)* misshapen.

deformidad *nf* **1** deformity, malformation. **2** *(error)* fault, shortcoming.

defraudación *nf* **1** *(decepción)* disillusionment. **2** *(fraude)* fraud. ■ **d. fiscal**, tax evasion.

defraudado,-a I *pp de* **defraudar. II** *adj* disillusioned.

defraudador,-a I *adj* **1** *(decepcionante)* disillusioning. **2** *(engañoso)* deceiving, cheating. **II** *nm, f* person who commits fraud. ■ **d. fiscal**, tax evader.

defraudar *vtr* **1** *(decepcionar)* to disillusion; *(esperanzas)* to dash; **tu comportamiento me ha defraudado**, I am disappointed with your behaviour. **2** *(cometer fraude)* to defraud, cheat; **d. a Hacienda**, to evade taxes.

defunción *nf fml* decease, demise.

degeneración *nf* degeneration.

degenerado,-a I *pp de* **degenerar. II** *adj & nm, f* degenerate.

degenerar *vi* to degenerate.

degenerativo,-a *adj* degenerative.

deglución *nf* swallow, swallowing.

deglutir *vtr & vi* to swallow.

degollación *nf* **1** *(decapitación)* beheading, execution. **2** *(matanza)* slaughter, massacre.

degolladero *nm* slaughterhouse.

degolladura *nf* cut in the throat.

degollar *vtr* **1** *(cortar la garganta a)* to cut *or* slit the throat of; *(decapitar)* to behead. **2** *fig (arruinar)* to ruin, spoil.

degollina *nf fam* slaughter, massacre.

degradación *nf* **1** degradation. **2** *Mil* demotion.

degradante *adj* degrading, humilating.

degradar **I** *vtr* **1** *(humillar)* to degrade, humitiate. **2** *Mil* to demote. **II degradarse** *vr* to degrade *or* demean oneself.

degüello *nm* *(degolladura)* throat cutting; *(decapitación)* beheading.

degustación *nf* tasting; **d. de vinos,** wine tasting.

degustar *vtr* to taste, try, sample.

dehesa *nf* pasture, meadow.

deidad *nf* deity.

deificación *nf* deification.

deificar *vtr* to deify.

deísmo *nm* deism.

deísta **I** *adj* deistic. **II** *nmf* deist.

dejadez *nf* **1** *(abandono de sí mismo)* slovenliness, neglect. **2** *(descuido general)* negligence, carelessness. **3** *(pereza)* laziness, apathy.

dejado,-a **I** *pp de* **dejar**. **II** *adj* **1** *(descuidado)* untidy, slovenly. **2** *(negligente)* negligent, careless. **3** *(perezoso)* lazy, apathetic. **4** *fam* **d. de la mano de Dios,** godforsaken. **III** *nm,f* untidy *or* slovenly person.

dejante *adv Am* **1** *(además de)* in addition to. **2** *(no obstante)* nevertheless.

dejar **I** *vtr* **1** *(colocar)* to put, leave; **deja el vaso donde estaba,** put the glass back where it was; **dejó las llaves sobre la mesa,** he left the keys on the table. **2** *(abandonar)* to leave; **d. algo por imposible,** to give sth up; **d. plantado a algn,** to stand sb up; **dejé el tabaco y la bebida,** I gave up smoking and drinking; **dejó a su familia,** he abandoned his family; **dejó la casa a las diez,** he left home at ten. **3** *(omitir)* to leave out, omit; **déjalo,** forget it. **4** *(legar)* to leave; **su abuela le dejó una fortuna,** her grandmother left her a fortune. **5** *(ceder)* to give, leave, hand over; **me dejó su silla cuando se fue,** he gave me his seat when he left. **6** *(producir)* to produce, leave; **el fuego deja ceniza,** fire leaves ashes; **el negocio le deja grandes beneficios,** he gets good profits from his business. **7** *(causar un efecto)* to make; **déjame en paz** *or* **tranquilo,** leave me alone; **d. preocupado,** to worry; **d. sorprendido,** to surprise; **d. triste,** to make sad; *fig* **d. frío,** to leave cold. **8** *(permitir)* to let, allow; **d. caer,** to drop; **d. el paso libre,** to get out of the way; **d. entrar/ salir,** to let in/out; **me dejaron salir antes,** they let me leave early; **no dejan fumar aquí,** smoking is not allowed here. **9** *(prestar)* to lend; **me dejó el libro,** she lent me the book. **10** *(esperar)* to wait; **deja que se le pase el enfado,** wait until he's cooled down. **11** *(aplazar)* to put off; **dejaron el viaje para el verano,** they put the trip off until the summer. **12** *(cesar)* to stop **(de, -)**, give up **(de, -)**; **dejé de verle en verano,** I stopped seeing him in the summer; **dejó de fumar el año pasado,** he gave up smoking last year; **no puedo d. de extrañarme,** I can't get used to the idea. **II** *v aux* **1** *(no d.de* + *infinitivo)* not to fail to; **no deja de venir a clase ni un día,** he never misses a class; **no deja de llamarme,** she's always phoning me up; **no deja de ser extraño que ...,** it is still surprising that ...; **no dejaré de tenerlo en cuenta,** I'll keep it in mind. **2** *(d.* + *participio)* **d. dicho,** to leave word *or* a message; **d. algo escrito,** to put sth into writing; **dejó dicho que le despertaran,** he asked to be woken up. **III dejarse** *vr* **1** *(permitir)* to let *or* allow oneself; **d. engañar,** to let oneself be deceived; **no te dejes insultar así,** don't let yourself be insulted like that. **2** *(olvidar)* to forget; **me he dejado las llaves dentro,** I've left the keys inside; **te has** **dejado tres líneas sin copiar,** you've forgotten to copy three lines. **3** *(abandonarse)* to neglect oneself, let oneself go. **4** *(locuciones)* **d. barba,** to grow a beard; **d. caer en un sillón,** to flop into an armchair; **d. caer por casa de algn,** to drop in on sb; **d. llevar por algn,** to be influenced by sb; **d. llevar por algo,** to get carried away by sth; **d. ver,** to be seen; **se deja sentir el frío/verano,** one can feel the cold/that summer is here.

deje *nm* slight accent.

del *(contracción de **de** + **el**)* *véase* **de**.

delación *nf* denunciation, accusation, revelation.

delantal *nm* apron.

delante *adv* **1** in front; **el de d.,** the one in front; **la entrada de d.,** the front entrance; **mi hermana es la que esté d.,** my sister is the one in front. **2 d. de,** in front of, ahead of; **d. de mí,** in front of me; **d. de tus ojos,** before your eyes; **nos encontramos d. de la estación,** we met outside the station. **3 por d.,** in front; **se entra por d.,** the entrance is at the front; **se lo lleva todo por d.,** he destroys everything in his path; **tiene toda la vida por d.,** he has his whole life ahead of him.

delantera *nf* **1** front (part). **2** *(ventaja)* lead; **coger** *or* **tomar la d.,** to get ahead, take the lead; **llevar la d.,** to be in the lead. **3** *Ftb* forward line, the forwards *pl*. **4 delanteras,** *vulg (tetas)* tits.

delantero,-a **I** *adj* front; **parte delantera,** front part; **rueda d.,** front wheel. **II** *nm* **1** *Ftb (jugador)* forward. ■ **d. centro,** centre forward. **2** *Cost* front.

delatar *vtr* **1** *(denunciar)* to denounce, inform on *or* against. **2** *fig* to give away; **sus ojos lo delataron,** his eyes gave him away.

delator,-a **I** *adj* **1** *(denunciante)* who informs, who denounces. **2** *fig* which gives away, that reveals; **tenía una sonrisa delatora en sus labios,** his smile was a giveaway. **II** *nm,f (informador)* informer.

delco *nm* *Aut* distributor.

deleble *adj* which can be erased *or* rubbed out easily.

delectación *nf* delight, delectation.

delegación *nf* **1** *(acto, delegados)* delegation. **2** *(oficina)* local office, branch.

delegado,-a **I** *pp de* **delegar**. **II** *adj* delegated. **III** *nm,f* **1** delegate; **d. de Hacienda,** chief tax inspector. **2** *Com* representative.

delegar *vtr* to delegate; **d. poderes en algn,** to delegate powers to sb.

delegatorio,-a *adj* delegating, that delegates.

deleitar **I** *vtr* to delight. **II deleitarse** *vr* to delight in, take delight in.

deleite *nm* delight, pleasure.

deleitoso,-a *adj* delightful, enjoyable.

deletéreo,-a *adj* poisonous, deadly.

deletrear *vtr* to spell (out).

deletreo *nm* spelling (out).

deleznable *adj* **1** *(resbaladizo)* slippery. **2** *(que se rompe fácilmente)* fragile; **arcilla d.,** crumbly clay. **3** *(poco duradero)* ephemeral. **4** *(inconsistente)* weak.

delfín[1] *nm* *Zool* dolphin.

delfín[2] *nm* *Hist* dauphin.

delgadez *nf* **1** *(flacura)* thinness. **2** *(esbeltez)* slenderness.

delgado,-a *adj* **1** *(flaco)* thin. **2** *(esbelto)* slender, slim.

delgaducho,-a *adj pey* skinny.

deliberación *nf* deliberation.

deliberado,-a **I** *pp de* **deliberar**. **II** *adj* deliberate, intentional.

deliberar *vi* to deliberate (on), consider.

deliberativo,-a *adj* deliberative.

delicadeza *nf* **1** *(finura)* delicacy, daintiness. **2** *(tacto)* tactfulness; **falta de d.,** tactlessness, bad manners *pl*; **es**

una falta de d. no levantarse para saludar, it's bad manners not to stand up when greeting sb; tuvo la d. de no mencionar el tema, he was tactful enough not to mention the subject. 3 *(fragilidad)* fragility.

delicado,-a *adj* 1 *(fino)* delicate, dainty; *(exquisito)* exquisite; un gusto d., a refined taste. 2 *(difícil)* delicate, difficult; un trabajo d., a tricky job; una situación delicada, a delicate situation. 3 *(enfermizo)* delicate, frail. 4 *(difícil de contentar)* fussy, hard to please. 5 *(cortés)* refined, polite. 6 *(muy sensible)* hypersensitive. 7 *(frágil)* fragile.

delicaducho,-a *adj pey* frail, sickly.

delicia *nf* delight; esta tarta es una d., this pie is delightful; hacer las delicias de algn, to delight sb.

delicioso,-a *adj* delightful, charming; una comida deliciosa, a delicious meal.

delictivo,-a *adj* criminal, punishable; conducta delictiva, criminal conduct.

delicuescencia *nf* deliquescence.

delimitación *nf* delimitation, demarcation.

delimitar *vtr* to delimit, mark the boundaries of.

delincuencia *nf* delinquency.

delincuente *adj & nmf* delinquent. ◼ d. juvenil, juvenile delinquent.

delíneación *nf* delineation, outlining.

delineante *nmf (hombre)* draughtsman; *(mujer)* draughtswoman.

delinear *vtr* to delineate, outline.

delinquir *vi* to break the law, commit an offence *or US* offense.

delirante *adj* delirious, frenzied.

delirar *vi* to be delirious, rave; *fig* to talk nonsense.

delirio *nm* 1 delirium; delirios de grandeza, delusions of grandeur. 2 *fig* nonsense. 3 *fam* ¡fue el d.!, it was really great!

delirium tremens *nm Med* delirium tremens.

delito *nm* crime, offence, *US* offense; lo cogieron en flagrante d., he was caught red-handed *or* in the act.

delta I *nm Geog* delta. II *nf (letra griega)* delta.

demacrado,-a I *pp de* demacrarse. II *adj* emaciated.

demacrarse *vr* to become emaciated.

demagogia *nf* demagogy.

demagógico,-a *adj* demagogic, demagogical.

demagogo,-a *nm, f* demagogue.

demanda *nf* 1 *(petición)* request, demand. 2 *(pregunta)* inquiry. 3 *(búsqueda)* search; en d. de, asking for. 4 *Jur* lawsuit; presentar una d. contra algn, to take legal action against sb. 5 *Com* demand; la ley de la oferta y la d., the law of supply and demand.

demandado,-a *pp de* demandar. II *nm, f Jur* defendant.

demandante *nmf Jur* claimant.

demandar *vtr* 1 *Jur* to sue. 2 *(pedir, rogar)* to request.

demarcación *nf* 1 demarcation. 2 *(terreno)* district, zone.

demarcar *vtr* to demarcate.

demás I *adj & pron* the rest (of); la d. gente, the rest of the people; lo d., ya lo sabes, you already know the rest; los d. se fueron antes, the rest left earlier; per lo d., otherwise, apart from that; estoy cansado pero, por lo d., me encuentro bien, I am tired, but apart from that, I am all right; todo lo d., everything else. II *adv* 1 besides; *véase tamb* además. 2 por d., in vain, uselessly; es por d. difícil, it's much too difficult; está por d. que le llames, there's no point in calling her; y d., etcetera; me levanté, me lavé, me vestí y d., I got up, had a wash, got dressed, and so on.

demasía *nf* 1 *(exceso)* excess, surplus; en d., excessively; bebe en d., he drinks too much. 2 *(abuso)* offence, outrage. 3 *(descaro)* insolence; *(atrevimiento)* audacity.

demasiado,-a I *adj (singular)* too much; *(plural)* too many; hay demasiada comida, there is too much food; quieres demasiadas cosas, you want too many things. II *adv* too (much); es d. grande/caro, it is too big/dear; fumas/trabajas d., you smoke/work too much.

demencia *nf* dementia, insanity, madness.

demencial *adj fam* chaotic.

demente I *adj* insane, mad. II *mnf* mental patient: *ofens* lunatic.

demérito *nm* demerit, fault.

democracia *nf* democracy.

demócrata I *adj* democratic. II *mnf* democrat.

democrático,-a *adj* democratic.

democratización *nf* democratization.

democratizar *vtr* to democratize.

demografía *nf* demography.

demográfico,-a *adj* demographic; crecimiento d., population increase *or* growth; explosión demográfica, population explosion.

demoledor,-a *adj* 1 demolishing. 2 *fig* devastating.

demoler *vtr* to demolish, pull down.

demolición *nf* demolition.

demoniaco,-a *adj* demoniac, demoniacal.

demonio *nm* devil, demon; *fig* llevarse (a algn) el d. *or* todos los demonios, to get furious; *fig* ponerse como un d., to get really angry; *fig* ser un d., to be a real devil; *fam* ¿cómo demonios ...?, how the hell ...?; *fam* ¡demonio(s)!, hell!; damn!; *fam* ¡d. de niño!, you little devil!; *fam* ¿dónde demonios ...?, where the hell ...?; *fam* el d. de tu hermano, your devil of a brother; *fam* es un frío de mil demonios, it's perishing; *fam* ¡qué demonio(s)!, damn it!; *fam* ¿quién demonios ...?, who the hell ...?; *fam* saber/oler a demonios, to taste/smell horrible *or* foul.

demonología *nf* demonology.

demontre *interj* damn it!

demora *nf* delay; sin d., without delay.

demorar I *vtr (aplazar)* to delay, hold up; la tormenta demoró la llegada del avión, the plane was held up by the storm. II demorarse *vr* 1 *(retrasarse)* to be delayed, be held up; la conferencia se demoró más de lo previsto, the lecture started later than expected. 2 *(detenerse)* to stay, linger on.

demostrable *adj* demonstrable.

demostración *nf* 1 *(gen)* demonstration; hacer una d. de cómo funciona una máquina, to demonstrate how a machine works; una d. atlética, an athletic display; una d. de fuerza, a show of strength. 2 *Mat* proof.

demostrar *vtr* 1 *(mostrar)* to show, demonstrate; eso demuestra que no entiendas bien el inglés, that shows that you don't understand English very well. 2 *(probar)* to prove; ha demostrado su valor en tales circunstancias, he has proved his courage in these circumstances. 3 *Mat* to prove.

demostrativo,-a *adj & nm Ling* demonstrative.

demudado,-a I *pp de* demudar. II *adj (pálido)* pale; *(alterado)* upset.

demudar I *vtr (color de la cara)* to alter, change. II demudarse *vr* 1 to change one's expression *or* colour. 2 *(alterarse)* to look upset.

denario *nm Hist* denarius.

dendrita *nf Biol Min* dendrite.

denegación *nf (desestimación)* refusal, denial. ◼ *Jur* d. de demanda, dismissal.

denegar *vtr (desestimar)* to refuse; *(negar)* to deny; *Jur* d. una demanda, to dismiss a claim.

dengue *nm* fastidiousness, fussiness; hacer dengues, to be fussy *or* finicky.

denigración *nf* denigration, defamation.

denigrante *adj* denigrating, disparaging.

denigrar *vtr* to denigrate, disparage, run down.

denominación *nf* **1** denomination, naming. **2** *(nombre)* denomination, name; *(vinos)* '**d. de origen**', 'appellation d'origine'.

denominado,-a *adj* named, designated; **el candidato d.,** the candidate appointed.

denominador,-a I *adj* denominative. **II** *nm* Mat denominator. ■ **mínimo común d.,** lowest common denominator.

denominar *vtr* to name, designate.

denominativo,-a *adj* Ling denominative.

denonado,-a *adj* brave, courageous. ◆ **denonadamente** *adv* bravely, courageously.

denostar *vtr* to insult.

denotar *vtr* to denote, indicate.

densidad *nf* density, thickness; **d. de población,** population density.

densificar *vtr* to make dense, densify, thicken.

denso,-a *adj* dense, thick.

dentado,-a I *pp de* **dentar. II** *adj* toothed; **cochillo d.,** knife with a serrated edge; *Bot* **hoja dentada,** dentate leaf; **rueda dentada,** cog wheel.

dentadura *nf* teeth, set of teeth; **tiene una d. preciosa,** she has beautiful teeth. ■ **d. postiza,** false teeth *pl*, dentures *pl*.

dental *adj* dental.

dentar I *vi* to teethe, cut teeth. **II** *vtr* to serrate.

dentellada *nf* **1** *(mordisco)* bite. **2** *(señal)* toothmark.

dentellar *vi* to chatter, **dentellaba de frío,** his teeth were chattering with cold.

dentellear *vtr* to nibble at.

dentera *nf* **dar d. a algn,** to set sb's teeth on edge; *fig* to make sb green with envy.

dentífrico,-a I *adj* tooth; **pasta dentífrica,** toothpaste. **II** *nm* toothpaste.

dentista *nmf* dentist; **ir al d.,** to go to the dentist's.

dentón,-ona I *adj* toothy, buck-toothed **II** *nm,f* toothy *or* goofy person **III** *nm (pez)* dentex.

dentro *adv* **1** *(en el interior)* inside; **aquí d.,** in here; **el regalo está d.,** the present is inside; **muy d.,** deep inside; **por d.,** inside; **es verde por d.,** its green (on the) inside; **por d. está triste,** deep down (inside) he feels sad; **vamos d. (de la casa),** let's go indoors. **2** *(tiempo)* **d. de lo posible,** as far as possible; **d. de lo que cabe,** under the circumstances; **d. de poco,** shortly, soon; **d. de un mes,** in a month's time.

dentudo,-a *adj & nm,f véase* **dentón,-ona I & II.**

denuesto *nm* insult.

denuncia *nf* **1** accusation; *(condena)* denunciation. **2** *Jur (documento)* report; **presentar una d.,** to report, lodge a complaint, bring an action.

denunciable *adj* which may be reported.

denunciador,-a *nm,f* **denunciante** *nmf Jur* person who reports a crime.

denunciar *vtr* **1** *(delito)* to report **(a,** to). **2** *(condenar)* to denounce. **3** *fig (indicar)* to indicate; **el retraso denuncia la falta de planificación,** the delay points to a lack of planning.

deontología *nf* deontology.

deparar *vtr* to give, afford; **el viaje me deparó un placer inesperado,** the journey brought me unexpected pleasure; **nunca se sabe lo que nos depara el destino,** we never know what fate has in store for us.

departamental *adj* departmental.

departamento *nm* **1** *(división territorial)* province, district. **2** *(de un organismo)* department, section. **3** *Educ* department; **d. de lenguas extranjeras,** modern languages department. **4** *Ferroc* compartment. **5** *(de un objeto)* compartment, section. **6** *Arg Chi* apartment, flat.

departir *vi fml* to talk, converse.

depauperación *nf fml* **1** *(empobrecimiento)* impoverishment. **2** *Med (debilitación)* weakening.

depauperar *vtr fml* **1** *(empobrecer)* to impoverish. **2** *Med (debilitar)* to weaken.

dependencia *nf* **1** dependence, dependency. **2** *(sucursal)* branch; *(sección)* section, department. **3** *Com (conjunto de dependientes)* (sales) staff. **4** **dependencias,** rooms, outbuildings.

depender *vi* to depend **(de,** on); **depende de ti,** it is up to you; **depende del tiempo (que haga),** it depends on the weather; **dependo de mis padres,** I am dependent on my parents; **en lo que de mí depende,** as far as I am concerned.

dependienta *nf* shop assistant, salesgirl, saleswoman.

dependiente I *adj* dependent **(de,** on). **II** *nm* shop assistant, salesman.

depilación *nf* depilation; **d. a la cera,** waxing.

depilar I *vtr* to depilate, remove the hair from; *(cejas)* to pluck. **II depilarse** *vr* to depilate.

depilatorio,-a *adj & nm* depilatory; **crema depilatoria,** hair-remover, hair-removing cream.

deplorable *adj* deplorable, regrettable.

deplorar *vtr* to deplore, regret deeply, lament.

deponente I *adj* **1** *Ling* deponent. **2** *Jur* testifying. **II** *nm Ling* deponent verb. **III** *nmf Jur* deponent, witness.

deponer *vtr* **1** *(dejar)* to abandon; **al final depuso su actitud hostil,** in the end he set aside his hostility; **d. las armas,** to lay down one's arms. **2** *(destituir)* to remove from office; *(líder)* to depose. **3** *Jur* to testify about, give evidence about. **4** *(defecar)* to defecate.

deportación *nf* deportation.

deportado,-a I *pp de* **deportar. II** *adj* deported. **III** *nm,f* deportee, deported person.

deportar *vtr* to deport.

deporte *nm* sport; **campo de deportes,** sports ground; **hacer algo por d.,** to do sth as a hobby; **hacer d.,** to practise sports; **¿practicas algún d.?,** do you go in for any sport?, do you take part in sports? ■ **deportes de invierno,** winter sports.

deportista I *adj* sporty, keen on sport. **II** *nmf (hombre)* sportsman; *(mujer)* sportswoman.

deportividad *nf* sportsmanship.

deportivo,-a I *adj* **1** sports; **club d.,** sports club; **chaqueta deportiva,** sports jacket. **2** *(imparcial)* sporting, sportsmanlike. **II** *nm Aut* sports car.

deposición *nf* **1** *(de un oficial)* removal from office; *(líder)* deposition. **2** *Jur* testimony, deposition, evidence. **3** *fml (evacuación de vientre)* defecation.

depositador,-a *nm,f* **depositante** *nmf Fin* depositor.

depositar I *vtr* **1** *Fin* to deposit. **2** *(colocar)* to place, put; *fig* **ha depositado en mí toda su confianza,** she has placed all her trust in me. **3** *(almacenar)* to store. **II depositarse** *vr (posos, polvo)* to settle.

depositaría *nf* depository.

depositario,-a I *nm,f* **1** depositary, trustee. **2** *(tesorero)* treasurer. **3** *(de un secreto etc)* repository. **II** *nm (tesorero)* treasurer, cashier.

depósito *nm* **1** *Fin (bancario)* deposit. **2** *(lugar)* dump; *(almacén)* store, warehouse, depot. ■ **d. de basuras,** rubbish tip *or* dump; **d. de cadáveres,** mortuary, *US* morgue; **d. de chatarra,** scrapyard; **d. de objetos perdidos,** lost property office, *US* lost-and-found department. **3** *(contenedor)* tank; **d. de agua,** water tank. ■ **d. de gasolina,** petrol tank. **4** *(sedimento)* deposit, sediment. **5** *Mil* depot.

depravación *nf* depravity, depravation.

depravado,-a I *pp de* **depravar. II** *adj* depraved. **III** *nm,f* depraved person, degenerate.

depravar I *vtr* to deprave, corrupt. **II depravarse** *vr* to become depraved.

depre *nf arg* downer, depression; **¡vaya d.!,** what a downer!

depreciación *nf Fin* depreciation; **la d. de la peseta,** the depreciation of the peseta.

depreciar I *vtr* to decrease *or* reduce the value of. **II depreciarse** *vr* to depreciate, lose value.

depredación *nf* 1 pillaging, plundering. 2 *(malversión)* misappropiation (of funds), embezzlement.

depredador,-a I *adj* pillaging, plundering. **II** *nm, f* pillager, plunderer.

depredar *vtr* to pillage, plunder.

depresión *nf* depression; **d. económica,** economic depression; *Hist* **los años de la d.,** the years of the Depression. ■ *Meteor* **d. atmosférica,** atmospheric depression; *Med* **d. nerviosa,** nervous breakdown.

depresivo,-a *adj* depressing; *Med* depressive.

depresor,-a I *adj* depressing. **II** *nm Med* depressor.

deprimente *adj* depressing.

deprimido,-a I *pp de* **deprimir. II** *adj* depressed.

deprimir I *vtr* to depress. **II deprimirse** *vr* to get depressed.

deprisa *adv* quickly.

depuesto,-a *pp de* **deponer.**

depuración *nf* 1 *(del agua)* purification, depuration; *(de la sangre)* cleansing. 2 *fig* purge, purging.

depurador,-a I *adj* purifying; **planta depuradora,** purifying plant. **II** *nm (sustancia)* depurative; *(máquina, aparato)* purifier.

depurar *vtr* 1 *(purificar) (agua)* to purify, depurate; *(sangre)* to cleanse. 2 *Pol (partido)* to purge. 3 *fig (perfeccionar)* to perfect, refine; **estilo depurado,** pure style.

depurativo,-a *adj & nm Med* depurative.

derecha I *nf* 1 *(mano)* right hand. 2 *(lugar)* right, right-hand side; **a la d.,** to *or* on the right, on the right-hand side. 3 *Pol* **la d.,** the right, the right wing; **de derechas,** right-wing. **II** *interj Mil* **¡d.!,** right turn.

derechazo *nm Box* right.

derechista I *adj* right-wing, rightist. **II** *nmf* right-winger, rightist.

derecho,-a I *adj* 1 *(de la derecha)* right; **el ojo d.,** the right eye. 2 *(recto)* upright, straight; **ponte d.,** stand up straight; *fig* **no hacer nada a derechas,** to do nothing right; *fig* **un hombre hecho y d.,** a real man. **II** *nm* 1 *Jur (conjunto de leyes)* law; **d. penal/político,** criminal/constitutional law; **estudiar d.,** to study law. 2 *(privilegio)* right, claim; **con d. a,** with the right to; **dar d.,** to entitle; **de d.,** by right; **derechos civiles/humanos,** civil/human rights; **el d. al voto,** the right to vote; **estar en su d.,** to be within one's rights; **no hay d.,** it's not fair; **'reservados todos los derechos',** 'all rights reserved', 'copyright'; **tener d. a,** to be entitled to, have the right to. 3 *(de una tela)* right side; **¿cuál es el d. y cuál es el revés?,** which is the right side and which the wrong side? 4 *Com* **derechos,** duties, taxes. ■ **d. de admisión,** right *sing* to refuse admission; **d. de aduana,** customs duties; **d. de autor,** royalties; **d. de matrícula,** registration *or* enrolment fees; **d. de sucesión,** death duties. **III** *adv* straight, directly; **andar d.,** to walk straight; **fue d. a la puerta,** he went straight to the door; **siga todo d.,** to go straight on. ◆ **derechamente** *adv* 1 *(de forma directa)* directly, straight. 2 *(con discreción)* properly.

deriva *nf Náut* drift; **a la d.,** adrift; **ir a la d.,** to drift.

derivación *nf* 1 *Ling* derivation. 2 *(de una carretera)* turn-off, diversion. 3 *Elec* shunt.

derivada *nf Mat* derivative.

derivado,-a I *pp de* **derivar. II** *adj* derived, derivative. **III** *nm* 1 *Ling* derivative. 2 *Quím* derivative, by-product.

derivar I *vtr* 1 *(cambiar la dirección)* to direct, divert; **derivó la conversación hacia otro tema,** he steered the conversation on to a different subject. 2 *Elec* to shunt. **II** *vi* 1 *(cambiar de dirección)* to drift; **después, sus gustos derivaron hacia el cine,** later, his tastes inclined towards the cinema; **la reunión derivó hacia otros derroteros,** the meeting drifted on to other matters. 2 *(proceder)* to spring, arise; **su amistad deriva de intereses comunes,** their friendship stems from common interests. 3 *Náut* to drift. 4 *Ling* to be derived (**de,** from), derive (**de,** from); **'ventanal' deriva de 'ventana',** 'ventanal' is derived from 'ventana'. **III derivarse** *vr* 1 *(proceder)* to result *or* stem (**de,** from). 2 *Ling* to be derived (**de,** from).

derivativo,-a *adj & nm* derivative.

dermatitis *nm inv Med* dermatitis.

dermatología *nf Med* dermatology.

dermatólogo,-a *nm, f Med* dermatologist.

dermatosis *nf inv Med* dermatosis.

dérmico,-a *adj* dermal, dermic, skin.

dermis *nf inv* dermis, derm.

derogable *adj Jur* repealable.

derogación *nf* repeal, abolition.

derogar *vtr* 1 *Jur* to repeal, abolish annul. 2 *(contrato)* to rescind, cancel.

derogatorio,-a *adj* repealing, abolishing, annulling.

derramamiento *nm* 1 spilling, overflowing; **d. de sangre,** bloodshed. 2 *(dispersión)* scattering (of people).

derramar I *vtr* to spill, pour; **d. lágrimas/sangre,** to shed tears/blood. **II derramarse** *vr* 1 *(líquido)* to spill; **la leche se derramó sobre la mesa,** the milk spilt all over the table. 2 *(desparramarse)* to scatter; **los rebeldes se derramaron por la ciudad,** the rebels scattered throughout the city.

derrame *nm* 1 *(gen)* spilling; *(de sangre)* shedding. 2 *(pérdida)* leak, leakage. 3 *Med* discharge. ■ **d. cerebral,** brain haemorrhage. 4 *Arquit (de puerta, ventana)* splay.

derrapar *vi Aut* to skid.

derredor *nm* surroundings *pl*; **al** *or* **en d. de,** round, around.

derrengar I *vtr* 1 *(deslomar)* to break sb's back. 2 *fig (cansar)* to wear out; **estoy derrengado,** I'm shattered. **II derrengarse** *vr* to wear oneself out.

derretido,-a I *pp de* **derretir. II** *adj* 1 melted; **mantequilla derretida,** melted butter; **plomo d.,** molten lead. 2 *fam fig* **está d. por ella,** he's madly in love with her.

derretimiento *nm* 1 melting; *(de la nieve)* thawing. 2 *fam fig* intense love, burning passion.

derretir I *vtr* 1 *(gen)* to melt (down); *(hielo, nieve)* to thaw. 2 *(derrochar)* to squander, waste. **II derretirse** *vr* 1 *(metal)* to melt; *(hielo, nieve)* to thaw; *fam fig* **d. de amor,** to burn with love. 2 *(inquietarse)* to fret, worry.

derribar *vtr* 1 *(demoler)* to pull down, knock down; **d. una casa,** to demolish a house; **el viento derribó muchos árboles,** the wind blew down a lot of trees. 2 *(hacer caer) (persona)* to knock down *or* over; *(avión)* to shoot down; **derribó tres aviones enemigos,** he shot down three enemy planes. 3 *fig (destituir) (cargo)* to remove *or* oust from office; *(gobierno)* to overthrow, bring down.

derribo *nm* 1 demolition, pulling down; **materiales de d.,** rubble. 2 *(lugar)* demolition site.

derrocamiento *nm* 1 *Pol* overthrow, toppling. 2 *(edificio)* demolition.

derrocar *vtr* 1 to overthrow; *(gobierno)* to bring down; *(ministro)* to oust from office, topple. 2 *(edificio)* to demolish, pull down.

derrochador,-a I *adj* spendthrift, wasteful, squandering. **II** *nm, f* spendthrift, wasteful person, squanderer.

derrochar *vtr* 1 *(dinero)* to waste, squander. 2 *(rebosar)* to be full of; **d. salud/simpatía,** to be full of health/good humour.

derroche *nm* **1** *(gasto)* waste, squandering. **2** *(abundancia)* profusion, abundance. **3** *(energía)* burst.

derrota *nf* **1** defeat, failure, setback. **2** *Náut (rumbo)* (ship's) course.

derrotado,-a I *pp de* **derrotar.** II *adj* **1** defeated. **2** *(andrajoso)* in tatters, ragged. **3** *arg (acabado)* knackered.

derrotar *vtr* to defeat, beat; **nuestro equipo derrotó al equipo local,** our team beat the local team.

derrotero *nm* **1** *Náut* sailing directions *pl.* **2** *fig* path, course *or* plan of action. **3** *Náut (libro de navegación)* book of charts.

derrotismo *nm* defeatism.

derrotista *adj & nmf* defeatist.

derruido,-a I *pp de* **derruir.** II *adj* in ruins.

derruir *vtr* to demolish, knock down, pull down.

derrumbadero *nm* precipice, cliff.

derrumbamiento *nm* **1** *(demolición)* demolition. **2** *(caída)* collapse, falling down; *(techo)* caving in. **3** *fig (gobierno, civilización)* collapse.

derrumbar I *vtr* **1** *(edificio)* to demolish, knock down, pull down. **2** *(despeñar)* to throw, hurl down. **3** *(hundir)* to ruin, destroy. II **derrumbarse** *vr* **1** *(edificio)* to collapse, fall down; *(techo)* to fall in, cave in. **2** *(precipitarse)* to hurl *or* fling oneself headlong (**por,** down). **3** *fig* to collapse; **sus esperanzas se derrumbaron,** her hopes were shattered.

derrumbe *nm véase* **derrumbadero.**

derviche *nm Rel* dervish.

desabastecido,-a *adj* short of, out of.

desaborido,-a *adj* **1** *(comida)* tasteless, insipid. **2** *fig (persona)* dull. II *nm,f fig* dull person.

desabrido,-a *adj* **1** *(comida)* tasteless, insipid. **2** *(tiempo)* unpleasant. **3** *fig (tono)* harsh; *(persona)* moody, irritable.

desabrigado,-a I *pp de* **desabrigar.** II *adj* **1** *(lugar)* open, exposed. **2** *(persona)* **ir muy d.,** to be lightly clad. **3** *fig* unprotected, defenceless, *US* defenseless.

desabrigar I *vtr (ropa)* to take off *or* remove. II **desabrigarse** *vr (sacar ropa)* to take off some of one's clothes; *(en la cama)* to throw off one's bed-clothes.

desabrochar I *vtr* to undo, unfasten. II **desabrocharse** *vr* **1** *(persona)* to undo, unfasten; **desabróchate la camisa,** undo your shirt. **2** *(prenda)* to come undone *or* unfastened.

desacatar *vtr (falta de respeto)* to show no respect towards; *(orden)* to disobey, not observe.

desacato *nm* lack of respect, disrespect (**a,** for); *Jur* **d. al tribunal,** contempt of court.

desacertado,-a I *pp de* **desacertar.** II *adj (inadecuado)* inappropriate, unwise; *(inoportuno)* untimely; *(erróneo)* wrong, mistaken; **un regalo d.,** a badly chosen present; **una observación desacertada,** a tactless remark.

desacertar *vi* **1** *(fallar)* to be wrong, be mistaken. **2** *(falta de tacto)* to lack tact, be tactless.

desacierto *nm (error)* mistake, error; *(mala selección)* bad choice; **fue un d. hacer este comentario,** it was an unfortunate remark to make.

desacompañado,-a *adj* alone, lonely; **se sintió desacompañada,** she felt alone.

desaconsejado,-a I *pp de* **desaconsejar.** II *adj* ill-advised.

desaconsejar *vtr* to advise against; **le desaconsejaron los viajes largos,** they advised him against long journeys.

desacoplar *vtr Téc* to uncouple; *Elec* to disconnect.

desacorde *adj* **1** *Mús* discordant. **2** clashing; **opiniones desacordes,** conflicting opinions.

desacostumbrado,-a I *pp de* **desacostumbrar.** II *adj* unusual, uncommon.

desacostumbrar I *vtr* **d. a algn de hacer algo,** to break sb

---

from the habit of doing sth; **estoy desacostumbrado,** I've lost the habit. II **desacostumbrarse** *vr* to get out of the habit, give up.

desacreditar I *vtr* to discredit, bring into discredit, run down, disparage. II **desacreditarse** *vr* to become discredited.

desactivar *vtr (bomba)* to defuse, make safe.

desacuerdo *nm* disagreement; **estar en d. con,** to be in disagreement *or* at variance with.

desafecto,-a I *adj* disaffected, opposed. II *nm* lack of affection, coldness.

desafiante *adj* challenging, defiant.

desafiar *vtr* to challenge, defy; **te desafío, ¿a que no lo haces?,** I dare you to do it.

desafinado,-a I *pp de* **desafinar.** II *adj Mús* out of tune.

desafinar I *vi (gen)* to be out of tune; *(canción)* to sing out of tune; *(instrumento)* to play out of tune. II *vtr* to put out of tune. III **desafinarse** *vr* to go out of tune.

desafío *nm* **1** *(reto)* challenge. **2** *(duelo)* duel.

desaforado,-a *adj* **1** *(desmedido)* huge, enormous; **gritos desaforados,** terrible cries. **2** *(escandaloso)* outrageous; *(persona)* loud, rowdy. ◆ **desaforadamente** *adv* *(desmedidamente)* excessively; *(escandalosamente)* outrageously.

desafortunado,-a *adj* unlucky, unfortunate.

desafuero *nm* **1** *Jur* violation *or* infringement of the laws. **2** *(abuso)* outrage, excess.

desagradable *adj* unpleasant, disagreeable.

desagradar *vi* to displease; **me desagrada su conducta,** I don't like his behaviour.

desagradecer *vtr* to be ungrateful for, show ingratitude for.

desagradecido,-a I *pp de* **desagradecer.** II *adj* ungrateful. III *nm,f* ungrateful person.

desagradecimiento *nm* ingratitude, ungratefulness.

desagrado *nm* displeasure; **con d.,** reluctantly.

desagraviar *vtr* **1** *(excusarse)* to make amends for. **2** *(compensar)* to indemnify, compensate.

desaguar I *vtr (vaciar)* to drain. II *vi* **1** *(vaciarse)* to drain (off); *(el baño)* to empty. **2** *(desembocar)* to flow, drain (**en,** into); **el Ebro desagua en el Mediterráneo,** the Ebro flows into the Mediterranean.

desagüe *nm (vaciado)* drain, outlet; *(cañería)* waste pipe, drainpipe; *Aut* **d. del radiador,** radiator overflow pipe.

desaguisado,-a I *adj (contra ley)* illegal, unlawful; *(contra razón)* outrageous. II *nm* **1** *(delito)* offence, *US* offense; *(agravio)* outrage. **2** *fam (destrozo)* damage; *(fechoría)* mischief.

desahogado,-a I *pp de* **desahogar.** II *adj* **1** *(espacioso)* spacious, roomy. **2** *(acomodado)* well-off, well-to-do. **3** *fig (descarado)* cheeky, insolent.

desahogar I *vtr (dolor)* to relieve; *(desfogar)* to vent, pour out. II **desahogarse** *vr* **1** *(desfogarse)* to let off steam. **2** *(confiarse)* to open one's heart (**con,** to). **3** *(descargarse)* to get something off one's chest.

desahogo *nm* **1** *(alivio)* relief; **le sirve de d.,** it helps him let off steam. **2** *(descanso)* relaxation. **3** *(holgura económica)* comfort, ease; **vivir con d.,** to live comfortably.

desahuciado,-a *adj* **1** *(enfermo)* hopeless. **2** *(inquilino)* evicted.

desahuciar *vtr* **1** *(desalojar)* to evict. **2** *(quitar toda esperanza)* to deprive of all hope; **d. a un enfermo,** to give up all hope for a patient.

desahucio *nm* eviction.

desairado,-a I *pp de* **desairar.** II *adj* **1** *(sin éxito)* unsuccessful; *(sin gracia)* awkward; *(humillado)* spurned; **quedar d.,** to come off badly, create a bad impression, **una situación desairada,** an awkward situation. 2 *(desgarbado)* unattractive.

desairar *vtr* to slight, snub, spurn; **acepté su regalo para no desairarla,** I accepted her present so as not to offend her.

desaire *nm* slight, rebuff; **hacerle un d. a algn,** to snub sb

desajustar I *vtr* 1 to disarrange; *(máquinas)* to put out of order 2 *fig* **d. los planes de algn,** to upset sb's plans. **II desajustarse** *vr (máquinas)* to go wrong, break down, *(piezas)* to come apart; *(tornillos)* to come loose.

desajuste *nm* 1 *(máquinas) (mal funcionamiento)* maladjustment, *(avería)* breakdown. 2 *(desconcierto)* disorder, *(desequilibrio)* imbalance; **d. económico,** economic imbalance; **un d. de horarios,** clashing timetables

desalado,-a¹ I *pp de* **desalar¹ II** *adj Culin* desalted; **bacalao d.,** desalted cod

desalado,-a² I *pp de* **desalar². II** *(apresurado)* hasty, **fue d. a la comisaría,** he rushed to the police station

desalar¹ *vtr Culin* to remove the salt from, desalt

desalar² *I* *vtr (aves)* to clip the wings of **II desalarse** *vr (apresurarse)* to rush, *fig* **se desalaba por llegar,** be longed to arrive.

desalentador,-a *adj* discouraging, disheartening

desalentar I *vtr* to leave *or* put out of breath, *fig* to discourage, dishearten **II desalentarse** *vr* to get discouraged, lose heart

desaliento *nm (desánimo)* discouragement, *(abatimiento)* dismay.

desalinear I *vtr* to put out of line. **II desalinearse** *vr* to get *or* go out of line.

desaliñado,-a I *pp de* **desaliñar. II** *adj* scruffy, untidy, down-at-heel.

desaliñar *vtr* to make scruffy *or* untidy.

desaliño *nm* scruffiness, untidiness.

desalmado,-a I *adj* 1 *(malo)* wicked. 2 *(cruel)* cruel, heartless. **II** *nm,f (malo)* wicked person. 2 *(cruel)* cruel *or* heartless person.

desalojamiento *nm* 1 *(expulsión) (inquilino)* eviction; *(personas)* dislodging, removal; *(lugar)* evacuation, clearing, 2 *(abandono)* abandonment

desalojar I *vtr* 1 *(inquilino)* to evict; *(personas)* to remove, dislodge; *(lugar)* to clear, evacuate; **la policía desalojó el teatro,** the police cleared the theatre 2 *(abandonar)* to move out of, abandon; **d. una casa,** to vacate a house. **II** *vi* to move house, move out

desalojo *nm véase* **desalojamiento.**

desalquilado,-a I *pp de* **desalquilar. II** *adj* vacant, unrented

desalquilarse *vr (local, inmueble)* to become vacant.

desamarrar *vtr Náut (barco)* to unmoor, cast off; *(desatar)* to untie.

desambientado,-a *adj* 1 *(persona)* out of place; *(desorientado)* - disoriented. 2 *(lugar)* lacking in atmosphere.

desamor *nm (desafecto)* lack of affection, coldness; *(indiferencia)* indifference; *(antipatía)* dislike.

desamortizable *adj* alienable.

desamortización *nf* alienation, disentailment.

desamortizar *vtr* to alienate, disentail.

desamparado,-a I *pp de* **desamparar. II** *adj (persona)* helpless, unprotected, *(lugar)* abandoned, forsaken **III** *nm,f* helpless *or* abandoned person.

desamparar *vtr* 1 to abandon, desert. 2 *Jur* to renounce, relinquish

desamparo *nm* helplessness, **en d.,** deserted, abandoned

desamueblado,-a I *pp de* **desamueblar. II** *adj* unfurnished.

desamueblar *vtr* to remove *or* clear the furniture from.

desandar *vi* to go back over, retrace, **d. lo andado,** to retrace one's steps.

desangrado,-a I *pp de* **desangrar II** *adj* **morir d.,** to bleed to death

desangramiento *nm* bleeding.

desangrar I *vtr* 1 *(sangrar)* to bleed. 2 *(desaguar)* to drain. 3 *fig (empobrecer)* to bleed white **II desangrarse** *vr* to lose (a lot of) blood

desanidar *vi* to leave the nest **II** *vtr fig* to oust **(de,** from).

desanimado,-a I *pp de* **desanimar II** *adj* 1 *(persona)* downhearted, dejected, discouraged. 2 *(fiesta etc)* dull, lifeless

desanimar I *vtr* to discourage, dishearten, depress. **II desanimarse** *vr* to lose heart, get depressed *or* discouraged.

desánimo *nm (desaliento)* discouragement, dejection; *(depresión)* depression.

desanudar *vtr* I *(nudo)* to untie; *(paquete, corbata)* to undo. 2 *fig (desenmarañar)* to straighten *or* sort out

desapacible *adj (gen)* unpleasant, disagreeable; *(sonido)* harsh, discordant, jarring; *(tiempo)* nasty, unpleasasnt

desaparecer *vi* to disappear, **hacer d.,** to cause to disappear, hide; *fam fig* **d. del mapa,** to vanish off the face of the earth

desaparecido,-a I *pp de* **desaparecer. II** *adj* missing **III** *nm,f* missing person; **hay tres desaparecidos,** there are three people missing.

desaparición *nf* disappearance

desapasionado,-a *adj* dispassionate, objective, impartial. ◆ **desapasionadamente** *adv* dispassionately, objectively, impartially.

desapego *nm* indifference, lack of affection.

desapercibido,-a *adj* 1 *(inadvertido)* unnoticed; **pasar d.,** to go unnoticed. 2 *(desprevenido)* unprepared.

desaplicado,-a I *adj* slack, lazy. **II** *nm,f* lazy bones *sing,* slacker.

desapolillarse *vr fam fig* to shake off the cobwebs.

desaprensión *nf* unscrupulousnsess.

desaprensivo,-a I *adj* unscrupulous. **II** *nm, f* unscrupulous person.

desaprobación *nf* disapproval.

desaprobador,-a *adj* disapproving

desaprobar *vtr* 1 *(no aprobar)* to disapprove of. 2 *(rechazar)* to reject; *(censurar)* to oppose.

desapropiar *I vtr* to deprive **(de,** of). **II desapropiarse** *vr* to give up; surrender, cede.

desaprovechado,-a I *pp de* **desaprovechar II** *adj* 1 *(desperdiciado)* wasted. 2 *(persona) (lento)* slow; *(poco trabajador)* unproductive, **un estudiante d.,** a student who could do better

desaprovechar *vtr* 1 *(dinero, tiempo)* to waste. 2 **no** to take advantage of; **d. una ocasión,** to fail to make the most of an opportunity.

desarbolar *vtr (nave)* to dismast.

desarmable *adj* that can be taken to pieces, collapsible.

desarmar *vtr* 1 *(desmontar)* to dismantle, take to pieces; **d. un motor,** to strip down an engine. 2 *Mil Pol* to disarm. 3 *fig* to disarm.

desarme *nm* 1 *Mil Pol* disarmament. ■ **d. nuclear,** nuclear disarmament. 2 *(de una máquina)* dismantling.

desarraigado,-a I *pp de* **desarraigar. II** *adj* 1 *(árbol)* uprooted. 2 *fig (persona)* rootless, without roots, uprooted.

desarraigar I *vtr* 1 *(árbol, persona)* to uproot. 2 *fig (vicio)* to break the habit of. **II desarraigarse** *vr* 1 *(árbol etc)* to become uprooted. 2 *fig (persona)* to lift up one's roots.

desarraigo *nm* 1 (*árbol, persona*) uprooting. 2 *fig* (*vicio*) breaking of a habit.

desarrapado,-a *adj & nm, f véase* **desharrapado,-a.**

desarreglado,-a I *pp de* **desarreglar.** II *adj* 1 (*habitación*) untidy. 2 (*persona*) untidy, slovenly.

desarreglar *vtr* 1 (*desordenar*) to untidy, make untidy, mess up; **los niños han desarreglado las camas,** the children have untidied the beds; **te han desarreglado todo el peinado,** they've messed your hair up. 2 (*estropear*) to spoil, upset; **has desarreglado mis planes,** you've upset my plans.

desarreglo *nm* (*desorden*) disorder, mess; (*desorganización*) confusion.

desarrollado-a I *pp de* **desarrollar.** II *adj* developed; **país d.,** developed country.

desarrollar I *vtr* 1 (*gen*) to develop, evolve, expand; **d. el crecimiento,** to promote growth; **d. la industria de un país,** to develop a country's industry. 2 (*desplegar*) to show; **d. un mapa,** to unfold a map; *fig* **d. una gran inteligencia,** to show great intelligence. 3 *Mat* (*ecuación*) to expand; (*problema*) to work out. 4 (*explicar*) to expound; (*teoría*) to explain. II **desarrollarse** *vr* 1 (*crecer*) to develop; (*incrementar*) to grow. 2 (*tener lugar*) to take place; **el concierto se desarrolló sin incidencias,** the concert went off without incident; **la acción se desarrolla en la India,** the story is set in India.

desarrollo *nm* 1 (*desenvolvimiento, crecimiento*) development; (*incremento*) growth; **índice de d.,** growth rate; **industria en pleno d.,** flourishing industry; **países en vías de d.,** developing countries. 2 *Mat* (*ecuación*) expansion; (*problema*) working out.

desarropar I *vtr* (*prendas*) to take off *or* remove. II **desarroparse** *vr* 1 to take off some of one's clothes. 2 (*en la cama*) to throw off one's bed-clothes.

desarrugar *vtr* to smooth out; (*ropa*) to remove the creases from; **desarruga el entrecejo,** stop frowning.

desarticulación *nf* 1 *Med* dislocation. 2 *fig* (*descoyuntar*) breaking up; **la d. de un comando terrorista,** the smashing of a terrorist command group.

desarticulado,-a I *pp de* **desarticular.** II *adj* disjointed.

desarticular *vtr* 1 *Med* to dislocate. 2 (*piezas*) to take to pieces. 3 *fig* (*descoyuntar*) to break up; *Pol* to smash; **d. un complot,** to foil a plot.

desaseado,-a I *adj* untidy, scruffy, unkempt. II *nm, f* untidy person, scruff.

desaseo *nm* untidiness, scruffiness, dirtiness.

desasir I *vtr* to release, let go. II **desasirse** *vr* to get loose; **d. de,** to free *or* rid oneself of.

desasnar *vtr fam* to teach good manners to, civilize.

desasosegado,-a I *pp de* **desasosegar.** II *adj* restless, anxious.

desasosegar I *vtr* (*intranquilizar*) to make restless *or* uneasy; (*inquietar*) to disturb. II **desasosegarse** *vr* to become uneasy *or* restless.

desasosiego *nm* restlessness, anxiety, uneasiness.

desastrado,-a I *adj* 1 (*desaseado*) untidy, scruffy. 2 (*sucio*) dirty. II *nm, f* scruffy person.

desastre *nm* 1 (*hecho*) disaster; **la excursión fue un d.,** the outing was a disaster; **¡que d.!,** what a mess! 2 (*persona*) disaster; **tu hermano es un d.,** your brother's just hopeless; **un d. de persona,** a dead loss, a hopeless case.

desastroso,-a *adj* disastrous.

desatado,-a I *pp de* **desatar.** II *adj* 1 undone, loose. 2 *fig* (*temperamento*) wild; (*pasiones*) uncontrolled.

desatar I *vtr* 1 to untie, undo, unfasten. 2 *fig* (*la lengua*) to loosen; (*pasiones*) to unleash. II **desatarse** *vr* 1 to come undone; **d. los zapatos,** to undo one's shoes; **el perro se desató,** the dog broke loose; **por fin se le desató la**

lengua, he finally began to talk. 2 *fig* (*desencadenarse*) to break loose, explode; **se desató la tormenta,** the storm broke; **su cólera se desató,** she exploded with anger.

desatascar *vtr* (*tubería*) to unblock, clear.

desatención *nf* 1 (*falta de atención*) lack of attention; (*distracción*) neglect. 2 (*descortesía*) impoliteness, discourtesy.

desatender *vtr* to neglect, not pay attention to; **dejar a un cliente desatendido,** to leave a customer unattended.

desatento,-a *adj* 1 (*distraído*) inattentive; (*descuidado*) careless. 2 (*descortés*) impolite, discourteous.

desatinado,-a I *pp de* **desatinar.** II *adj* 1 (*tonto*) silly, foolish. 2 (*imprudente*) rash, reckless. III *nm, f* (*persona*) fool.

desatinar I *vi* (*acto*) to act foolishly; (*hablando*) to talk nonsense. II *vtr* to exasperate, bewilder.

desatino *nm* 1 (*disparate*) silly thing; (*hablando*) foolish remark; **cometer desatinos,** to act foolishly; **decir desatinos,** to talk nonsense. 2 (*equivocación*) blunder, mistake.

desatornillar *vtr* to unscrew.

desatracar *vi Náut* to cast off, unmoor.

desatrancar *vtr* 1 (*tubería*) to unblock, clear. 2 (*puerta*) to unbolt, unbar.

desautorización *nf* 1 (*gen*) refusal to give permission *or* authority. 2 (*de manifestación, huelga*) banning. 3 (*desmentir*) denial. 4 (*desacreditar*) discrediting.

desautorizado,-a I *pp de* **desautorizar.** II *adj* 1 (*gen*) unauthorized. 2 (*manifestación, huelga*) banned, forbidden. 3 (*desmentir*) denied. 4 (*desacreditar*) discredited.

desautorizar *vtr* 1 (*gen*) to disallow, declare unauthorized. 2 (*manifestación, huelga*) to ban, forbid. 3 (*desmentir*) to deny. 4 (*desacreditar*) to discredit.

desavenencia *nf* 1 (*desacuerdo*) disagreement, discord. 2 (*riña*) quarrel, row.

desavenido,-a I *pp de* **desavenir.** II *adj* 1 (*desunido*) in disagreement. 2 (*enemistado*) on bad terms.

desavenir I *vtr* to cause to quarrel. II **desavenirse** *vr* to quarrel; **d. con algn,** to fall out with sb, have a difference of opinion with sb.

desaventajado,-a *adj* 1 (*persona*) at a disadvantage. 2 (*situación*) disadvantageous, unfavourable.

desayunar I *vi* to have breakfast; *fml* to breakfast; **ya he desayunado,** I have already had breakfast. II *vtr* to have for breakfast; **ayer desayuné café y tostadas,** yesterday, I had coffee and toast for breakfast. III **desayunarse** *vr* 1 to have breakfast. 2 *fig* to hear about sth for the first time; **¿no sabías que Pepe se había casado? —ahora me desayuno,** didn't you know that Pepe had got married? —that's the first I've heard of it.

desayuno *nm* breakfast.

desazón *nf* 1 (*de gusto*) lack of flavour, tastelessness. 2 *Med* discomfort. 3 *fig* anxiety, uneasiness.

desazonado,-a I *pp de* **desazonar.** II *adj* 1 (*gusto*) without flavour, tasteless. 2 *Med* feeling unwell. 3 *fig* anxious, uneasy.

desazonar I *vtr* 1 (*gusto*) to make tasteless. 2 *fig* to cause anxiety to, worry. II **desazonarse** *vr Med* to feel unwell *or* off-colour.

desbancar *vtr* 1 (*en el juego*) to take the bank from. 2 *fig* (*suplantar*) to supplant, replace, oust.

desbandada *nf* scattering; **a la d.,** in great disorder; **hubo una d. general,** everyone scattered.

desbandarse *vr* to scatter, disperse; **todos sus hijos se desbandaron después de su divorcio,** all their children went their own way after their divorce.

desbarajustar *vtr* (*desordenar*) to throw into confusion *or* disorder; (*trastocar*) to upset.

desbarajuste *nm* confusion, disorder; **hay tal d. que no encuentro tu libro,** everything's in such a mess that I can't find your book.

desbaratado,-a I *pp de* **desbaratar. II** *adj* ruined, wrecked.

desbaratamiento *nm* spoiling, wrecking.

desbaratar *vtr* **1** to spoil, ruin, wreck; **su llegada desbarató mis planes,** his arrival messed up my plans. **2** *Mil* to rout, throw into confusion.

desbarrar *vi (hablar)* to talk nonsense; *(hacer)* to do silly things.

desbastar *vtr* **1** *Carp (madera)* to rough plane; *Min (piedra, mineral)* to smooth down. **2** *fig (educar)* to refine.

desbloquear *vtr* **1** *(un sitio)* to lift the blockade on. **2** *Econ (créditos, precios)* to unfreeze.

desbloqueo *nm* **1** *(de un sitio)* lifting of the blockade. **2** *Econ (créditos, precios)* unfreezing.

desbocado,-a I *pp de* **desbocar. II** *adj* **1** *(caballo)* runaway. **2** *Cost (de cuello d.,* with a loose-fitting neck. **3** *(mal hablado)* foul-mouthed. **4** *(arma)* wide-mouthed. **5** *(herramienta)* worn smooth. **III** *nm, f* foul-mouthed person.

desbocar I *vtr (cántaro)* to break the rim of. **II desbocarse** *vr* **1** *(caballo)* to bolt, run away. **2** *fig (perder mesura)* to blow up, explode.

desbordamiento *nm* **1** overflowing. **2** *fig (de rabia, alegría)* outburst, outbreak, explosion.

desbordante *adj* overflowing, bursting.

desbordar I *vtr* **1** to overflow; **el agua desbordó el cauce del río,** the water overflowed the banks of the river. **2** *(sobrepasar)* to go beyond, surpass; **su actitud desborda mi comprensión,** his attitude is beyond my comprehension. **II** *vi* to overflow **(de,** with), burst **(de,** with). **III desbordarse** *vr* **1** to overflow, flood; **el café se está desbordando de la cafetera,** the coffeepot is overflowing. **2** *fig* to burst; **su corazón se desborda de alegría,** her heart is bursting with joy.

desbravar I *vtr (animal)* to tame; *(caballo)* to break in. **II desbravarse** *vr* **1** *(animal)* to become tame; *(caballo)* to be broken in. **2** *(de vino)* to lose its strength. **3** *fig (persona)* to calm down.

desbrozar *vtr (área)* to clear of weeds *or* undergrowth; *(camino)* to clear.

desbrozo *nm* **1** *(acción)* clearing of weeds *or* undergrowth. **2** *(hojarasca)* twigs *pl,* dead leaves *pl.*

descabalar *vtr* to leave incomplete.

descabalgar *vi Equit* to dismount.

descabellado,-a I *pp de* **descabellar. II** *adj* crazy, wild; **una idea descabellada,** a crazy idea.

descabellar *vtr* **1** *(despeinar)* to dishevel, ruffle. **2** *Taur* to kill with a final thrust, administer the coup de grâce to.

descabello *nm Taur* final thrust, coup de grâce.

descabezar I *vtr* **1** to behead, decapitate. **2** *Agr (árbol)* to cut the top off; *(plantas)* to top. **3** *fam fig* **d. un sueño,** to take a nap. **II descabezarse** *vr fam* to rack one's brains.

descacharrante *adj fam* hilarious.

descacharrar *vtr fam (romper)* to break; *(estropear)* to ruin, mess up.

descafeinado,-a *adj* **1** decaffeinated; **café d.,** decaffeinated coffee. **2** *hum* watered-down, diluted.

descafeinar *vtr* to decaffeinate.

descalabazarse *vr fam* to rack one's brains.

descalabrado,-a I *pp de* **descalabrar. II** *adj* **1** *(herido en la cabeza)* with a head injury, wounded in the head. **2** *fig* damaged, injured.

descalabrar I *vtr* **1** *(herir en la cabeza)* to wound in the head. **2** *fig* to damage, harm.

descalabro *nm* setback, misfortune.

descalcificación *nf Med* decalcification.

descalcificar I *vtr* to decalcify. **II descalcificarse** *vr* to become decalcified.

descalificación *nf* disqualification.

descalificar *vtr* to disqualify.

descalzar I *vtr (zapatos)* to take off. **II descalzarse** *vr* to take one's shoes off.

descalzo,-a I *adj* barefoot, barefooted; **ir d.,** to go barefoot. **2** *Rel* barefoot. **II** *nm, f Rel (hombre)* barefoot monk; *(mujer)* barefoot nun.

descamación *nf Med* desquamation, flaking; *(pelarse)* peeling.

descamarse *vr Med* to desquamate, flake off; *(pelarse)* to peel off.

descambiar *vtr Com* to exchange.

descaminar I *vtr* **1** to mislead, send in the wrong direction; **ir descaminado,** to be on the wrong road; *fig* to be on the wrong track. **2** *fig (corromper)* to lead astray; **las malas compañías le descaminaron,** bad company led him astray. **II descaminarse** *vr* **1** to go the wrong way. **2** *fig* to go astray.

descamisado,-a I *adj* **1** without a shirt, shirtless. **2** *fig* wretched, poor. **II** *nm* **1** *(pobre)* wretch, poor person. **2 descamisados,** *Hist (en España)* liberals who participated in the 1820 revolution. **3 descamisados,** *(en Argentina)* supporters of Perón.

descampado,-a I *adj* open, without trees *or* buildings. **II** *nm* open space, open field; **al d.,** in the open country.

descansado,-a I *pp de* **descansar. II** *adj* **1** *(persona)* rested; **estar d.,** to be rested. **2** *(tranquilo)* restful; **una vida descansada,** a peaceful life.

descansar I *vi* **1** *(gen)* to rest, have a rest; *(corto tiempo)* to take a break; **necesito d. un rato,** I need to have a little rest. **2** *(dormir)* to sleep; **hasta mañana y que descanses,** good night and sleep well; *euf* **que en paz descanse,** may he *or* she rest in peace. **3** *(confiar)* to trust **(sobre,** in), confide **(sobre,** in). **4** *Arquit (apoyarse)* to rest **(sobre,** on), be supported **(sobre,** by); *(basarse)* to be based **(sobre,** on). **5** *Agr* to lie fallow. **II** *vtr* to rest; **descansa los pies sobre el cojín,** rest your feet on the cushion; *Mil* **¡descansen armas!,** order arms!

descansillo *nm Arquit* landing.

descanso *nm* **1** rest, break; **me voy a tomar un día de d.,** I'm going to take a day off; **sin d.,** without a break. **2** *Cin Teat* interval; *Dep* half-time. interval. **3** *(alivio)* relief; **¡qué d.!,** what a relief! **4** *(rellano)* landing. **5** *Mil* **¡d.!,** at ease!

descapotable *adj & nm Aut* convertible.

descapotar *vtr Aut* **d. el coche,** to put the car roof down.

descarado,-a I *adj (insolente)* cheeky, insolent; *(desvergonzado)* shameless; **es un robo d.,** it's an absolute rip-off. **II** *nm, f* cheeky person, scoundrel. ◆ **descaradamente** *adv* impudently, shamelessly.

descarga *nf* **1** unloading. **2** *Elec* discharge. **3** *(arma)* firing, discharge; **d. cerrada,** volley.

descargadero *nm* wharf, unloading dock.

descargador,-a *nm, f* **d. de muelle,** docker, stevedore.

descargar I *vtr* **1** *(mercancías, barco)* to unload. **2** *fig (aliviar)* to relieve **(de,** of). **3** *Elec* to discharge; **d. la batería,** to run down the battery. **4** *(arma) (disparar)* to fire; *(vaciar)* to unload; *(golpe)* to deal; **descargó un golpe sobre el árbitro,** he dealt the referee a blow. **5** *Jur (absolver)* to absolve **(de,** of), acquit **(de,** of). **II** *vi Meteor (nubes)* to burst. **III descargarse** *vr* **1** *(de responsabilidad)* to free oneself. **2** *Jur (excusa)* to clear oneself. **3** *Elec (of battery)* to go flat.

descargo *nm* **1** *(gen)* unloading. **2** *Com* credit. **3** *Jur* discharge, acquittal; **en su d.,** in his defence; **testigo de d.,** witness for the defence.

descarnado,-a I *pp de* **descarnar. II** *adj* **1** *(delgado)* lean. **2** *fig* harsh, unadorned; **hizo una descripción descarnada del accidente,** he gave a straightforward description of the accident.

descarnar *vtr* **1** *(hueso)* to strip the flesh from. **2** *fig* to lay bare.

descaro *nm* cheek, impudence, nerve; **tuvo el d. de llamarme por teléfono,** he had the nerve to phone me; **¡qué d.!,** what a cheek!

descarriar I *vtr* to lead astray, put on the wrong road; *fig* **ser la oveja descarriada,** to be the lost sheep. **II descarriarse** *vr* to go astray, lose one's way.

descarrilamiento *nm Ferroc* derailment.

descarrilar *vi Ferroc* to run off the rails, go off the rails, be derailed.

descartar I *vtr* to discard, reject, rule out; **esto queda descartado,** this is out. **II descartarse** *vr Naipes* to discard, throw away.

descarte *nm* rejection, casting aside; *Naipes* cards thrown away.

descasar *vtr* to separate; *(matrimonio)* to annul the marriage of.

descascarillarse *vr* to chip, peel, flake off.

descastado,-a I *adj* ungrateful, cold. **II** *nm,f* ungrateful person.

descendencia *nf* descendants *pl*, offspring; **morir sin d.,** to die without issue.

descendente *adj* descending, downward.

descender I *vtr* **1** to lower. **2** *(bajar)* to descend, come *or* go down. **II** *vi* **1** *(temperatura)* to fall, drop. **2** *fig* to stop **(a, to).**

descendiente *nmf* descendant, offspring.

descendimiento *nm* descent, taking down, lowering.

descenso *nm* **1** descent; *(en la temperatura)* fall,drop. **2** *fig* lowering, decline. **3** *Dep* relegation.

descentrado,-a I *pp de* **descentrar. II** *adj* **1** offcentre, off-beam. **2** *fig* all-at-sea, disorientated.

descentralización *nf* decentralization.

descentralizar *vtr* to decentralize.

descentrar *vtr* **1** to knock off centre. **2** *fam fig* to put (one) off one's stroke.

desceñir *vtr (cinturón)* to loosen.

descepar *vtr (cepa)* to uproot; *(plantas)* to pull up by the roots.

descerrajar *vtr* **1** *(la cerradura)* to force, break open. **2** *fam (tiro)* to fire.

descifrable *adj* decipherable; *(letra)* legible.

desciframiento *nm* deciphering, decoding.

descifrar *vtr* **1** *(mensaje)* to decipher, decode. **2** *(misterio)* to solve; *(motivos, causas)* to figure out.

desclavar *vtr* to remove the nails from; **d. un cuadro,** to take down a picture.

descoagulación *nf* decoagulation.

descoagulante *adj* decoagulating.

descoagularse *vr* to decoagulate.

descocado,-a I *pp de* **descocarse. II** *adj fam* brazen, cheeky.

descocarse *vr* to get brazen *or* cheeky.

descoco *nm fam* cheek, boldness.

descojonado,-a I *pp de* **descojonarse. II** *adj vulg* **1** *(de risa)* **estábamos descojonados de risa,** we pissed ourselves laughing. **2** *(cansado)* knackered.

descojonante *adj vulg* bloody funny; **una película d.,** a bloody funny film.

descojonarse *vr vulg* to piss oneself laughing.

descolgar I *vtr (cuadro, cortinas)* to take down; **d. el teléfono,** to pick up the telephone; **el teléfono está**

descolgado, the telephone is off the hook. **II descolgarse** *vr* **1** *(bajar)* to let oneself down, slide down. **2** *fam* to appear suddenly *or* unexpectedly, turn up. **3** *fam (decir)* to come out with.

descollante *adj* outstanding.

descollar *vi* to stand out; **la iglesia descuella sobre las casas del pueblo,** the church towers above the houses in the village; *fig* **descuella por su inteligencia,** her intelligence makes her stand out.

descolocar *vtr* **1** to put out of place; **no descoloques los papeles,** don't disturb the papers. **2** *Ind* to lay off.

descolonización *nf* decolonization.

descolonizar *vtr* to decolonize.

descoloramiento *nm (desteñir)* fading; *(perder color)* discolouration, *US* discoloration.

descolorar *vtr (desteñir)* to fade; *(perder color)* to discolour, *US* discolor.

descolorido,-a *adj (desteñido)* faded; *(que pierde color)* discoloured, *US* discolored.

descombrar *vtr* to clear of debris.

descomedido,-a I *pp de* **descomedirse. II** *adj* **1** *(descortés)* rude, insolent. **2** *(desproporcionado)* excessive, disproportionate.

descomedimiento *nm* rudeness, insolence.

descomedirse *vr* to be rude *or* disrespectful.

descomponer *(pp descompuesto)* **I** *vtr* **1** *(corromper)* to rot, decompose. **2** *(separar)* to break down; *Mat* to split up. **3** *Téc* to put out of order. **4** *(desordenar)* to disturb, unsettle, upset. **5** *Fís* to resolve; **d. una fuerza,** to resolve a force. **6** *Mat* to factorize. **II descomponerse** *vi (turbarse)* to become upset; *(perder la paciencia)* to lose one's temper, lose control.

descomposición *nf* **1** decomposition, rotting, decay. **2** *(separación)* separation, analysis; *Téc* breakdown. **3** *fam (diarrea)* looseness of bowels, diarrhoea, *US* diarrhea. **4** *Mat* factorizing.

descompostura *nf* **1** *(desaliño)* slovenliness, untidiness. **2** *(falta de pudor)* insolence, lack of respect, rudeness.

descompresión *nf* decompression.

descompresor *nm Téc* decompressor.

descomprimir *vtr* to decompress, depressurize.

descompuesto,-a I *pp de* **descomponer. II** *adj* **1** rotten, decomposed, decayed. **2** *(estropeado)* out of order, broken down. **3** *(encolerizado)* furious. **4 estar d.,** to have diarrhoea *or US* diarrhea. **5** *fig (inmodesto)* brazen. **6** *Am (borracho)* drunk.

descompuse *pt indef véase* **descomponer.**

descomunal *adj* huge, massive.

desconcertante *adj* disconcerting, disturbing, upsetting.

desconcertar I *vtr* **1** *(perturbar)* to disconcert, disturb, upset. **2** *(desorientar)* to confuse. **3** *Anat* to dislocate. **II desconcertarse** *vr (desorientarse)* to be bewildered, be puzzled.

desconchado,-a I *pp de* **desconchar. II** *adj (pintura, yeso)* peeling, flaking; *(loza)* chipped.

desconchar I *vtr* to strip off. **II desconcharse** *vr* to flake off, chip.

desconchón *nm (acción)* flaking, chipping, peeling; *(marca)* bare patch, chip.

desconcierto *nm* disorder, chaos, confusion, bewilderment; **sembrar el d.,** cause confusion.

desconcordia *nf* discord, disagreement.

desconectado,-a I *pp de* **desconectar. II** *adj* disconnected, cut off.

desconectar *vtr* to disconnect, cut off, switch off, unplug.

desconexión *nf* disconnection.

desconfiado,-a I *pp de* **desconfiar. II** *adj* distrustful, wary, suspicious. **III** *nm,f* suspicious *or* wary person.

desconfianza *nf* distrust, mistrust, suspicion.

desconfiar *vi* to distrust (**de, -**), mistrust (**de, -**), be suspicious (**de,** of).

descongelar *vtr* (*nevera*) to defrost; (*créditos*) to unfreeze; (*comida*) to thaw out.

descongestión *nf* (*gen*) relieving of congestion; (*de la nariz*) clearing.

descongestionar *vtr* (*gen*) to relieve of congestion; (*nariz*) to clear.

desconocer *vtr* **1** (*no saber*) not to know, be unaware of; **desconozco su paradero,** I don't know where he is. **2** (*no reconocer*) not to recognize; (*fingir*) to ignore, pretend not to know; **me desconoció,** he ignored me. **3** (*rechazar*) to disown.

desconocido,-a I *pp de* **desconocer.** II *adj* unknown, unfamiliar; *fig* (*irreconocible*) unrecognizable; **Alan estaba d.,** Alan was unrecognizable; **lo d.,** the unknown; **una persona desconocida,** a stranger. III *nm, f* stranger.

desconocimiento *nm* ignorance, lack of knowledge.

desconsideración *nf* lack of consideration, inconsideration, thoughtlessness.

desconsiderado,-a I *pp de* **desconsiderar.** II *adj* inconsiderate, thoughtless, rash. III *nm, f* inconsiderate *or* thoughtless *or* rash person.

desconsolado,-a I *pp de* **desconsolar.** II *adj* disconsolate, grief-stricken, dejected.

desconsolador,-a *adj* heartbreaking, distressing.

desconsolar I *vtr* to distress, grieve. II **desconsolarse** *vr* to be distressed *or* full of grief.

desconsuelo *nm* grief, sorrow.

descontado,-a I *pp de* **descontar.** II *adj fam* **dar por d.,** to take for granted; **por d.,** needless to say, of course.

descontaminación *nf* decontamination.

descontaminar *vtr* to decontaminate.

descontar *vtr* **1** (*rebajar*) to discount, deduct; (*no incluir*) to leave out, disregard; **descontando los gastos,** excluding expenses. **2** *Dep* (*añadir*) to add on; **el árbitro descontó las perdidas de tiempo,** the referee added on time for stoppages.

descontentadizo,-a *adj* hard to please, fussy.

descontentar *vtr* to make unhappy *or* dissatisfied.

descontento,-a I *adj* discontented, unhappy, dissatisfied. II *nm* (*una persona*) discontent, malcontent; (*población*) dissatisfaction, unrest.

descontrol *nm fam* lack of control; **había un d. total,** it was absolute chaos.

descontrolado,-a I *pp de* **descontrolarse.** II *adj* uncontrolled, haywire; **estar d.,** to be out of control.

descontrolarse *vr* to lose control.

desconvocar *vtr* to call off, cancel.

descorazonador,-a *adj* disheartening.

descorchador *nm* corkscrew.

descorchar *vtr* to uncork.

descorche *nm* uncorking.

descornar I *vtr* to remove the horns from. II **descornarse** *vr fam* **1** (*pensar*) to rack one's brains. **2** (*trabajar*) to slave (away), toil.

descorrer I *vtr* (*gen*) to draw back; (*cortina*) to open; **d. el cerrojo,** to unbolt the door. II *vi* (*escurrir*) to drip, trickle.

descorrimiento *nm* dripping, trickling.

descortés *adj* rude, impolite, discourteous.

descortesía *nf* discourtesy, rudeness, impoliteness.

descortezar *vtr* **1** to bark, remove the bark from. **2** *Culin* to peel, remove the crust from.

descoser I *vtr Cost* to unstitch, unpick. II **descoserse** *vr* **1** *Cost* to come unstitched; *fig* to start to speak. **2** *fam fig* to fart.

descosido *nm* **1** open seam: *fam* **como un d.,** like mad, wildly. **2** *fig* (*persona*) babbler.

descoyuntar *vtr Med* (*hueso*) to dislocate; *fam* **estoy descoyuntado,** I am dead beat.

descrédito *nm* disrepute, discredit; **caer en d.,** to fall into disrepute.

descreído,-a I *adj* disbelieving, unbelieving. II *nm, f* disbeliever, unbeliever.

descreimiento *nm* disbelief.

descremado,-a I *pp de* **descremar.** II *adj* skimmed; **leche descremada,** skim *or* skimmed milk; **yogur d.,** low-fat yoghurt.

descremar *vtr* (*leche*) to skim.

describir (*pp descrito*) *vtr* **1** to describe. **2** (*trazar*) to trace.

descripción *nf* description, describing, tracing.

descriptible *adj* describable.

descriptivo,-a *adj* descriptive.

descrito,-a I *pp de* **describir.** II *adj* described.

descruzar *vtr* (*piernas*) to uncross; (*brazos*) to unfold.

descuajaringar I *vtr fam* to pull *or* take to pieces; *fig* **estoy descuajaringado,** I am on my last legs. II **descuajaringarse** *vr fam* **d. de risa,** to crack up, fall about laughing.

descuajilotado,-a *adj CAm* (*cara*) distraught; (*tez*) palid, pale.

descuartizamiento *nm* (*persona*) quartering; (*cosas*) carving up, cutting into pieces.

descuartizar *vtr* (*persona*) to quarter; (*cosas*) to cut up, cut into pieces; *fam fig* (*personas, opiniones*) to pull to pieces, tear apart.

descubierta *nf Mil* reconnaissance, reconnoitring, scouting.

descubierto,-a I *pp de* **descubrir.** II *adj* **1** (*sin cubierta*) open, uncovered; **a cara** *o* **a cuerpo d.,** openly; **a cielo d.,** in the open; (*sin sombrero*) bareheaded. **2** (*encontrado*) discovered. III *nm* **1** *Fin* overdraft; **estar al d.,** to be overdrawn, be in the red. **2** **dormir al d.,** to sleep out in the open; **poner al d.,** to uncover, expose, bring out into the open; **quedar en d.,** to be exposed, come out into the open. .

descubridor,-a *nm, f* discoverer.

descubrimiento *nm* discovery.

descubrir (*pp descubierto*) I *vtr* **1** (*gen*) to discover; (*conspiración*) to uncover; (*petróleo*) to find; (*remedio*) to discover. **2** (*enterarse*) to find out about, discover. **3** (*delatar*) to give away; **no me descubras a la policía,** don't tell the police about me. **4** (*divisar*) to make out, see. **5** (*destapar*) to uncover; **el rey descubrió una placa conmemorativa,** the king unveiled a commemorative plaque. II **descubrirse** *vr* **1** (*quitarse el sombrero*) to take off one's hat. **2** *Box* to lower one's guard.

descuento *nm Com* discount, reduction, deduction; **con d.,** at a discount.

descuidado,-a I *pp de* **descuidar.** II *adj* **1** (*desaseado*) untidy, neglected. **2** (*negligente*) careless, negligent. **3** (*desprevenido*) off one's guard.

descuidar I *vtr* to neglect, overlook. II *vi* to be careless; **descuida, voy yo,** don't worry, I'll go; **descuide usted,** don't worry, have no fear. III **descuidarse** *vr* to be careless; **como te descuides, llegarás tarde,** if you don't watch out, you'll be late.

descuidero *nm* pickpocket.

descuido *nm* **1** (*falta de cuidado*) negligence, carelessness, neglect. **2** (*distracción*) oversight, slip, mistake. **3 al d.,** casually, nonchalantly; **por d.,** inadvertently, by mistake.

desde *adv* **1** (*tiempo*) since; **d. ahora,** from now on; **¿d. cuándo?,** since when?; **d. el lunes,** since Monday; **d. entonces,** since then, from then on; **d. hace un año,** for a year; **d. siempre,** always. **2** (*lugar*) from; **d. aquí,** from here; **d. arriba/abajo,** from above/below; **d. mi casa hasta la tuya hay una buena tirada,** it's a bit of a way from my house to yours. **3 d. luego,** *(como coletilla)* well, really!; **d. luego no se puede confiar en nadie hoy en día,** really, you can't trust anyone these days. **4 d. luego,** *(como respuesta)* of course; **¿me puedes prestar tu coche? —d. luego,** can you lend me your car? —yes, of course.

desdecir *(pp desdicho)* **I** *vi* **1** not to be equal **(de,** to), not live up **(de,** to). **2** *(no armonizar)* not to match **(de, -),** not go **(de,** with), clash **(de,** with). **II desdecirse** *vr* to go back on one's word.

desdén *nm* disdain, contempt, scorn.

desdentado,-a I *adj* toothless. **II** *nm Zool* eden-tate.

desdeñable *adj* **1** *(despreciable)* contemptible, despicable. **2** *(sin importancia)* negligible, insignificant; **su fortuna no es nada d.,** he has a considerable fortune.

desdeñar I *vtr (despreciar)* to disdain, scorn. **2** *(rechazar)* to turn down. **3** *(no tener en cuenta)* to ignore, **II desdeñarse** *vr* to disdain to, not deign to.

desdeñoso,-a *adj* disdainful, scornful, contemptuous.

desdibujado,-a I *pp de* **desdibujar. II** *adj* blurred, faint, shadowy.

desdibujar I *vtr* to blur. **II desdibujarse** *vr* to become blurred *or* faint.

desdicha *nf* misfortune, adversity, misery; **por d.,** unfortunately; **para colmo de desdichas,** to top it all.

desdichado,-a I *adj* unfortunate, unlucky, wretched. **II** *nm,f* poor devil, wretch; *fam* **es un d.,** he's a poor soul. ◆ **desdichadamente** *adv* unfortunately.

desdigo *indic pres véase* **desdecir.**

desdiré *indic fut véase* **desdecir.**

desdoblamiento *nm* **1** *(enderezamiento)* straightening, unfolding. **2** *(duplicación)* splitting; **d. de personalidad,** split personality.

desdoblar *vtr* **1** *(enderezar)* to straighten. **2** *(extender)* to unfold. **3** *(duplicar)* to split; **van a d. esta carretera,** they're going to turn this road into a dual-carriageway.

desdoro *nm* tarnishing; *fig* blot, stain, dishonour, *US* dishonor.

deseable *adj* desirable.

deseado,-a I *pp de* **desear. II** *adj* desired.

desear *vtr (con pasión)* to desire; *(querer)* to want; *(anhelar)* to wish (for); **deja mucho que d.,** it leaves a lot to be desired; **estoy deseando que vengas,** I'm looking forward to your coming; **¿qué desea?,** can I help you?; **te deseo lo mejor,** I wish you all the very best.

desecación *nf (gen)* drying; *Quím* desiccation; **la d. de un pantano,** the draining of a marsh.

desecar *vtr* to desiccate, dry up; **d. una laguna,** to drain a lagoon.

desechable *adj* disposable, throw-away.

desechar *vtr* **1** *(tirar)* to discard, throw out *or* away; **desechó todas las piezas defectuosas,** he threw away all the defectiva pieces; *prov* **lo que uno desecha, otro lo ruega,** one man's meat is another man's poison. **2** *(renunciar)* to turn down, refuse; *(idea, proyecto)* to drop, discard; **debería d. esas locas ideas que se le han metido en la cabeza,** he should forget all these madcap ideas, **desecha cualquier consejo que pueda darle yo,** he brushes aside any advice I give him, **d. esa oferta sería un error,** to turn down this offer would be a mistake; **tuvimos que d. el proyecto,** we had to drop the plan

desecho *nm* **1** *(gen)* reject, **ropa de d.,** castoff; *fig* **es un d. de la sociedad,** he's a social outcast **2 desechos,** *(basura, residuos)* dregs, rubbish *sing*, debris *sing*; **d. radioactivos,** radioacive waste *sing*. **3** *Am (atajo)* short cut

deselectrizar *vtr Elec* to discharge

desembalaje *nm* unpacking

desembalar *vtr* to unpack

---

desembarazado,-a I *pp de* **desembarazar II** *adj* free and easy, uninhibited, nonchalant

desembarazar I *vtr* **1** *(librar)* to free, disencumber, *(vaciar)* to empty **2** *Am (dar a luz a)* to give birth to **II desembarazarse** *vr (librarse de)* to get rid **(de,** of), rid oneself **(de,** of), **intentaré desembarazarme de él lo antes posible,** I'll try and get rid of him as soon as possible

desembarazo *nm* **1** *(desenvoltura)* ease, nonchalance, *(seguridad en sí mismo)* self-assurance, self-confidence. **2** *Am (parto)* birth

desembarcadero *nm Náut* landing stage, pier, wharf

desembarcar I *vtr (mercancías)* to unload, *(personas)* to disembark, put ashore **II** *vi* to disembark, land, go ashore **III desembarcarse** *vr* to disembark, land, go ashore

desembarco *nm (mercancías)* landing, unloading, *(personas)* disembarkation

desembargar [7] *vtr jur* to lift *or* raise an embargo.

desembargo *nm Jur* lifting *or* raising of an embargo.

desembarque *nm véase* **desembarco.**

desembarrancar *vtr Náut (un barco)* to refloat

desembocadura *nf* **1** *(de río)* mouth, outlet. **2** *(salida)* exit, way out

desembocar *vi (río)* to flow **(en,** into), *(calle)* to lead **(en,** into), end **(en,** at), *fig* to lead **(en,** to), end up **(en,** in); **el Ebro desemboca en el Mediterráneo,** the river Ebro flows into the Mediterranean, *fig* **las actuales tensiones internacionales pueden d. en un conflicto armado,** current international tension may lead to armed conflict

desembolsar *vtr* to pay out

desembolso *nm* expenditure, expense, outgoings *pl*, payment, **d. inicial,** down payment

desemborrachar *vtr* to sober up

desembozar *vtr* to unmask, uncover, *fig* to uncover, bring out into the open

desembragar I *vtr* **1** *Mec* to disengage **2** *Aut* to release *or* disengage the clutch, declutch

desembrague *nm Aut* declutching, *Téc* disengaging

desembriagar *vtr* to sober up

desembridar *vtr* to unbridle.

desembrollar *vtr fam* **1** *(aclarar)* to clarify, clear up **2** *(desenredar)* to disentangle

desembuchar *vtr* **1** *(aves)* to disgorge **2** *fig (decir)* to blurt out, *fam fig* **¡desembucha!,** come out with it

desemejante *adj* dissimilar, different

desemejanza *nf* dissimilarity, difference

desempacar *vtr* to unpack

desempachar *vtr* to relieve from indigestion

desempacho *nm* assurance, self-confidence

desempañar *vtr (un cristal)* to wipe the condensation from, *Aut* to demist

desempapelar *vtr* **1** *(un paquete)* to unwrap **2** *(una pared)* to strip

desempaquetar *vtr* to unpack, unwrap

desemparejado,-a I *pp de* **desemparejar II** *adj* without a partner, **un calcetín d.,** an odd sock

desemparejar *vtr* to unmatch, separate

desempatar *vtr Dep* to play a deciding match, play off a tie, *(superar)* to take the lead

desempate *nm Dep* breaking the tie, play-off, **el gol del d.,** the deciding goal, **partido de d.,** play-off, deciding match

desempedrar *vtr* to remove the paving (stones) from, unpave, *fig* **d. la calle,** to roam *or* walk the streets.

desempeñar I *vtr* **1** *(recuperar lo empeñado)* to take out of pawn, redeem, **d. a algn,** to pay sb's debts **2** *(cumplir) (obligación)* to discharge, fulfil, *US* fulfill, carry out, *(cargo)* to fill, hold, occupy, **d. un cargo,** to hold a post 3 *Teat* to play, **desempeña el papel del bufón,** he plays the part of the fool **II desempeñarse** *vr (cancelar las deudas)* to get out of debt

desempeño *nm 1 (de lo empeñado)* redeeming, *(deuda)* payment. 2 *(obligaciones)* carrying out, fulfilment, *US* fulfillment. 3 *Teat* performance, playing, acting

desempleado,-a I *adj* unemployed, out of work **II** *nm, f* unemployed person; **los desempleados,** the unemployed.

desempleo *nm* unemployment; **cobrar el d.,** to be on the dole

desempolvar *vtr* 1 to dust 2 *(volver a usar)* to unearth, dig up, *fig* **d. recuerdos,** to revive memories

desencadenamiento *nm* 1 unchaining 2 *fig* setting in motion, **d. de una revolución,** outbreak of a revolution

desencadenar I *vtr* 1 to unchain 2 *(producir)* to spark off, start 3 *(desatar)* to unleash. **II desencadenarse** *vr* 1 *(desatarse)* to break loose, *(viento, pasión)* to rage 2 *(producirse)* to start, break out.

desencajado,-a I *pp de* **desencajar II** *adj (descolocado)* out of place, out of joint, *fig* **rostro d. por la ira,** face distorted by anger

desencajar I *vtr* to take apart, remove **II desencajarse** *vr* 1 to come loose 2 *(persona)* to look wild, *(cara)* to become distorted

desencajonar *vtr* to take out of a box, unpack

desencallar *vtr* to refloat

desencaminar *vtr véase* **descaminar**

desencantamiento *nm* disenchantment.

desencantar *vtr* 1 *(desembrujar)* to disenchant 2 *(decepcionar)* to disappoint, disillusion

desencanto *nm* disappointment, disillusionment

desencapotarse *vr (cielo)* to clear

desencapricharse *vr* to go off **(de, -),** lose interest **(de, in)**

desencarcelar *vtr* to release (from prison), free

desenchufar *vtr* to unplug, disconnect

desencofrar *vtr Constr* to remove the shuttering from

desenconarse *vr fig* to cool off, calm down

desencuadernar I *vtr* to unbind. **II desencuadernarse** *vr* to come unbound.

desenfadado,-a I *pp de* **desenfadar. II** *adj* carefree, free and easy; **en un tono d.,** in a carefree way. ◆ **desenfadadamente** *adv* casually

desenfadar(se) *vtr & vr* to calm down.

desenfado *nm (seguridad en uno mismo)* assurance, self-confidence; *(desenvoltura)* ease, openness.

desenfocado,-a I *pp de* **desenfocar. II** *adj* 1 *Fot* out of focus. 2 *fig (problema, asunto)* wrongly approached.

desenfocar *vtr* 1 *Fot* to take out of focus. 2 *fig* to get the wrong approach.

desenfoque *nm* 1 incorrect focusing. 2 *fig (tema)* wrong approach.

desenfrenado,-a I *pp de* **desenfrenar. II** *adj* frantic, uncontrolled; *(vicios, pasiones)* unbridled; **apetito d.,** insatiable appetite.

desenfrenar I *vtr Equit* to unbridle. **II desenfrenarse** *vr (pasiones, vicios)* to let loose, go wild.

desenfreno *nm (vicio)* licentiousness, debauchery, unrestraint; *(pasiones)* unleashing.

desenfundar *vtr* 1 *(sacar)* to draw or pull out. 2 *(destapar)* to uncover.

desenganchar *vtr* 1 *(soltar)* to set loose, unhook. 2 *(desunir)* to uncouple.

desengañar I *vtr* 1 **d. a algn,** to open sb's eyes, put sb wise. 2 *(quitar ilusión)* to disappoint, disillusion; **está desengañado de la política,** he's disillusioned with politics. **II desengañarse** *vr* 1 *(ver el error)* to see, realize. 2 *(sufrir un desengaño)* to be disappointed. 3

(perder ilusión) to face the truth or the facts; **se desengañó de llegar a ser actor famoso,** he accepted that he would never be a famous actor; *fam* **¡desengáñate!,** (let's) face it!

desengaño *nm* 1 disappointment; **llevarse** or **sufrir un d. con algo,** to be disappointed in sth. 2 *(verdad desagradable)* eye-opener.

desengrasar *vtr* to degrease, remove the grease from.

desenhebrar *vtr (una aguja)* to unthread.

desenlace *nm* 1 *(resultado)* result, outcome; **un feliz d.,** a happy end. 2 *Cin Teat Lit* ending, dénouement.

desenlazar *vtr* to untie, undo; *fig* to unravel, solve.

desenmarañar *vtr (pelo)* to untangle; *(un problema)* to unravel, clear up; *(un asunto)* to sort out.

desenmascarar I *vtr* to unmask. **II desenmascararse** *vr* 1 to take off one's mask. 2 *fig (conocerse)* to be revealed, show up.

desenredar I *vtr* to untangle, disentangle. **II desenredarse** *vr* to get out of, extricate oneself from.

desenrollar *vtr* to unroll, unwind.

desenroscar *vtr* to unscrew, uncoil.

desensillar *vtr (un caballo)* to unsaddle.

desentenderse *vr* 1 *(afectar ignorancia)* to ignore **(de, -),** pretend not to hear or know **(de, about); se desentiende de nuestros problemas,** he ignores our problems. 2 *(no ocuparse)* to have nothing to do with; **se desentendió del asunto,** he wanted nothing to do with the matter.

desenterrar *vtr* 1 *(un cadáver)* to exhume, disinter; **d. un tesoro escondido,** to dig up a hidden treasure. 2 *fig (traer a la memoria)* to revive, recall.

desentoldarse *vr Méx (cielo)* to clear.

desentonar *vi* 1 *Mús* to be out of tune, be out of tune. 2 *(contrastar)* not to match; **las cortinas desentonan del resto,** the curtains don't match the rest. 3 *(estar fuera de lugar)* to be out of place, seem wrong; **sus modales desentonan en tan selecta compañía,** his manners seem out of place in such refined company.

desentramar *vtr Arg (un andamio)* to dismantle, take apart.

desentrañar *vtr (destripar)* to disembowel; *fig (un problema)* to unravel, get to the bottom of, figure out.

desentrenado,-a *adj* out of training or shape.

desentumecer *vtr* to put the feeling back into; **d. las piernas,** to stretch one's legs.

desenvainar *vtr (espada)* to draw.

desenvoltura *nf* 1 *(soltura)* grace, ease. 2 *(naturalidad)* confidence. 3 *(desvergüenza)* boldness, insolence.

desenvolver *(pp* **desenvuelto) I** *vtr* to unwrap. **II desenvolverse** *vr* 1 *(manejarse)* to manage, cope; **se desenvuelve muy bien,** he copes very well. 2 *(desarrollarse)* to go, develop; **la entrevista se desenvolvió con normalidad,** the interview went (off) smoothly.

desenvuelto,-a I *pp de* **desenvolver. II** *adj* 1 natural, confident; **actitud desenvuelta,** naturalness. 2 *(hábil)* resourceful, quick. 3 *(ágil)* graceful, deft.

deseo *nm* desire, wish; **buenos deseos,** good intentions; **formular un d.,** to make a wish; **se cumplieron sus deseos,** his wishes came true.

deseoso,-a *adj* eager, desirous, anxious; **estar d. de amistad,** to long or yearn for friendship; **estar d. de hacer algo,** to be eager to do sth.

desequilibrado,-a I *pp de* **desequilibrar. II** *adj* unbalanced, off balance. **II** *nm, f* unbalanced person.

desequilibrar I *vtr* to unbalance, throw off balance. **II desequilibrarse** *vr* to become mentally disturbed.

desequilibrio *nm* lack of balance, imbalance; **d. mental,** mental disorder.

deserción *nf* 1 *Mil* desertion. 2 *(abandono)* abandonment.

desertar *vi* 1 *Mil* to desert. 2 *(abandonar) (obligaciones)* to abandon; *(fiesta)* to leave.

desértico,-a *adj* desert; **terrenos desérticos,** desert lands.

desertización *nf* desertification.

desertor,-a *nm,f Mil & fig* deserter.

desesperación *nf* despair, desperation; **con total d.,** in total despair; **es una d. tener que esperar tanto,** it's exasperating *or* unbearable to have to wait so long.

desesperado,-a I *pp de* **desesperar. II** *adj* 1 *(sin esperanza)* desperate, hopeless; **en situación desesperada,** in a hopeless situation. 2 *(desazonado)* exasperated, infuriated. **III** *nm,f* desperate person; *fig* **a la desesperada,** as a last hope; *fig* **como un d.,** like a madman; *fig* **correr como un d.,** to run like mad.

desesperante *adj* exasperating.

desesperanza *nf* despair, hopelessness, desperation.

desesperanzar I *vtr* to make lose hope; **la falta de noticias lo desesperanzó totalmente,** the lack of news plunged him into total despair. **II desesperanzarse** *vr* to despair, to lose hope.

desesperar I *vtr* to exasperate. **II** *vi* to have lost (all) hope; **desespero ya de encontrarlo,** I've given up all hope of finding it. **III desesperarse** *vr* 1 to lose hope, despair. 2 *(irritarse)* to feel helpless. 3 *(lamentarse)* to regret.

desestabilización *nf* destabilization.

desestabilizar *vtr* to destabilize.

desestimación *nf* refusal, rejection.

desestimar *vtr (solicitud, recurso)* to refuse, reject.

desfachatez *nf* cheek, nerve.

desfalcar *vtr Fin* to misappropriate, embezzle.

desfalco *nm Fin* embezzlement, misappropriation.

desfallecer *vi* 1 to lose strength, faint; **estoy que desfallezco,** I feel faint. 2 *(desanimarse)* to lose heart.

desfallecido,-a I *pp de* **desfallecer. II** *adj* exhausted, very weak, faint.

desfallecimiento *nm* faintness.

desfasado,-a I *pp de* **desfasar. II** *adj* 1 outdated; **tu libro está d.,** your book is out of date. 2 *(persona)* old-fashioned, behind the times. 3 *Téc* out of phase

desfasar I *vtr Téc* to phase out. **II desfasarse** *vr* 1 *Téc* to change the phase. 2 *(persona)* to be out of synch; *arg* to be high.

desfase *nm* 1 *(diferencia)* gap, imbalance; **d. horario,** jet lag; **hay un gran d. entre lo que dice y lo que hace,** he says one thing and does something quite different. 2 *Elec* phase difference.

desfavorable *adj* unfavourable, *US* unfavorable.

desfavorecer *vtr* 1 *(perjudicar)* to disadvantage; **la nueva ley de renta desfavorece a los solteros,** the new tax law has disadvantages for unmarried people. 2 *(sentar mal)* not to flatter, not suit; **ese corte de pelo te desfavorece,** this haircut doesn't suit you.

desfibrar *vtr Téc* to shred.

desfigurado,-a I *pp de* **desfigurar. II** *adj (persona)* disfigured; *(estatua etc)* disfaced; *fig (hecho)* distorted.

desfigurar *vtr (cara)* to disfigure; *(estatua)* to disface; *fig (verdad)* to distort; *fig* **su versión de los hechos defiguraba la realidad,** his version of the events did not reflect the truth.

desfiladero *nm* defile, narrow pass.

desfilar *vi* 1 *(gen)* to march in single file, defile. 2 *Mil* to march, march past, parade. 3 *(acudir)* to come; **por su casa desfilan todo tipo de personas,** all kinds of people are always dropping in at her place. 4 *(irse)* to leave, file out.

desfile *nm Mil* parade, march past; **d. de carrozas,** procession of floats; *Mil* **d. de la victoria,** victory parade; **d. de modas,** fashion show.

desfloración *nf* deflowering.

desflorar *vtr* 1 *(estropear)* to spoil, ruin. 2 *(desvirgar)* to deflower. 3 *(tema)* to touch on, skim over.

desfogar I *vtr* to let out, give vent to; **desfogasus problemas en el trabajo con sus hijos,** he takes his problems at work out on his children. **II desfogarse** *vr* to let off steam; **se desfoga con la bebida,** he drowns his sorrows in drink.

desfondar I *vtr* 1 *(quitar el fondo)* to knock the bottom out of; *fig (quitar fuerza)* to whack, tire out. 2 *Agr (la tierra)* to plough deeply. **II desfondarse** *vr* to collapse; fig to flake out.

desfonde *nm* removal *or* knocking out of the bottom; *fig* exhaustion.

desgaire *nm* nonchalance, careless; **al d.,** nonchalantly, carelessly.

desgajar I *vtr* 1 *(una rama)* to tear off; *(una página)* to rip *or* tear out. 2 *(romper)* to break. **II desgajarse** *vr* 1 *(separarse)* to come off. 2 *(persona)* to leave, split away **(de,** from), break ties **(de,** with).

desgalichado,-a *adj fam* gawky, ungainly.

desgana *nf* 1 *(inapetencia)* lack of appetite. 2 *(apatía)* apathy, indifference; **con d.,** reluctantly, unwillingly.

desganado,-a I *pp de* **desganar. II** *adj* 1 *(inapetente)* not hungry; **estar d.,** to have no appetite. 2 *(apático)* apathetic, half-hearted.

desganar I *vtr* to spoil the appetite of. **II desganarse** *vr* 1 *(perder el apetito)* to lose one's appetite. 2 *(desinteresarse)* to lose interest **(de,** in), go off **(de,** -).

desgañitarse *vr fam* to shout oneself hoarse, shout one's head off.

desgarbado,-a *adj* ungraceful, ungainly.

desgarrador,-a *adj* heart-breaking, heart-rending; *(aterrador)* bloodcurdling

desgarramiento *nm* ripping, tearing.

desgarrar *vtr* 1 *(romper)* to tear, rip. 2 *fig (corazón)* to break.

desgarriate *nm Méx (desastre)* disaster; *(destrozo)* damage.

desgarro *nm* 1 tear, rip. 2 *Am (esputo)* spit, spittle.

desgarrón *nm* big tear, rip, slash.

desgastar I *vtr (consumir)* to wear out; *fig* **los diez primeros minutos de la batalla desgastaron nuestras fuerzas,** we used up all our strength in the first ten minutes of the battle. **II desgastarse** *vr (consumirse)* to wear out; *fig (persona)* to wear oneself out.

desgaste *nm* wear, wear and tear; *(metal)* corrosion; *(cuerdas)* fraying.

desglosar *vtr (escrito)* to detach; *(gastos)* to break down.

desglose *nm* breakdown, separation.

desgobierno *nm* misgovernment, mismanagement, mishandling

desgracia *nf* 1 *(contrariedad)* misfortune, mishap; **para colmo de desgracias** *or* **para mayor d.,** to top it all; **por d.,** unfortunately; **¡qué d.!,** how awful! 2 *(deshonor)* disfavour, *US* disfavor, disgrace; **caer en d.,** to lose favour, fall into disgrace.

desgraciado,-a I *pp de* **desgraciar. II** *adj* unfortunate, unlucky; **una infancia desgraciada,** an unhappy childhood. **III** *nm,f* unfortunate *or* unlucky person; **ser un pobre d.,** to be a poor devil. ◆ **desgraciadamente** *adv* unfortunately.

desgraciar I *vtr* 1 *(echar a perder)* to spoil. 2 *(herir gravemente)* to injure seriously. **II desgraciarse** *vr* 1 *(plan)* to fall through. 2 *(persona)* to be hurt.

desgranadora *nf Agr* threshing machine.

desgranamiento *nm* 1 *(guisantes)* shelling. 2 *(trigo)* threshing.

desgranar I *vtr* 1 *(guisantes)* to shell; *(trigo)* to thresh; **d. un racimo de uvas,** to pick grapes from a bunch. 2 *fig (analizar)* to spell out. **II desgranarse** *vr* to come loose.

desgrane *nm véase* **desgranamiento.**

desgravable *adj Fin* tax-deductible.

desgravación *nf Fin* deduction; **d. fiscal,** tax deduction.

desgravar *vtr Fin (impuestos)* to deduct.

desgravio *nm* 1 *(persona)* atonement, satisfaction; **en d. de,** in amends for. 2 *(compensación)* indemnification, compensation.

desgreñado,-a I *pp de* **desgreñar.** II *adj* 1 *(pelo)* ruffled, tousled, dishevelled. 2 *(persona)* dishevelled.

desgreñar I *vtr* to ruffle, dishevel, tousle. II **desgreñarse** *vr* to mess up or untidy one's hair.

desguace *nm (de barcos)* breaking up; *Aut* scrapping.

desguanzo *nm Méx* weakness.

desguañangar *vtr Am fam* to wreck.

desguardo *nm Arg (medallón)* locket; *(talismán)* talisman.

desguarnecer *vtr* 1 to take off, remove, strip off. 2 *Mil* to leave unprotected, remove the garrison from.

desguazar *vtr Náut (un barco)* to break up; *Aut* to scrap.

deshabillé *nm* negligé, *US* negligee.

deshabitado,-a I *pp de* **deshabitar.** II *adj* uninhabited, unoccupied.

deshabitar *vtr (lugar, casa)* to leave, abandon, vacate.

deshabituar I *vtr (perder la costumbre de)* to get out of the habit of; *(superar un hábito)* to break the habit of. II **deshabituarse** *vr (perder la costumbre)* to get out of the habit, lose the habit; *(superar un hábito)* to break the habit.

deshacer *(pp deshecho)* I *vtr* 1 *(un paquete)* to undo; *(una cama)* to unmake; *(una maleta)* to unpack; *(puntadas)* to unpick; *fig* **d. el camino,** to retrace one's steps; *fig* **ser el que hace y deshace,** to be the boss, rule the roost. 2 *(destruir)* to destroy, ruin; *fig* **d. a algn,** to be the ruin of sb. 3 *(romper un acuerdo)* to break off. 4 *(disolver) (un sólido)* to dissolve; *(helado, chocolate, cera, etc)* to melt. II **deshacerse** *vr* 1 *(gen)* to come undone or untied. 2 *(afligirse)* to go to pieces; **se deshizo al morir su madre,** he went to pieces when his mother died. 3 *(disolverse) (un sólido)* to dissolve; *(helado, chocolate, cera, etc)* to melt. 4 *(desvanecerse)* to fade away, disappear. 5 *(prodigar)* to be full *(en,* of); **d. en elogios,** to be full of praise; **d. en lágrimas,** to cry one's eyes out. 6 *(esforzarse)* to break one's back, bend over backwards; **d. en atenciones,** to be extremely kind; **d. trabajando,** to wear oneself out working; **se deshace por complacerme,** he would do anything to please me. 7 *(desembarazarse)* to get rid *(de,* of); **deshazte de él,** get rid of him. 8 *(chiflarse)* to be crazy or mad (about).

desharrapado,-a I *adj* ragged, shabby, tattered. II *nm,f* shabby person, tramp.

deshecho,-a I *pp de* **deshacer.** II *adj* 1 undone, untied; *(cama)* unmade; *(maleta)* unpacked; *(paquete)* unwrapped. 2 *(destrozado)* destroyed, disintegrated; **el coche quedó d.,** the car was a write-off. 3 *(roto)* broken, smashed. 4 *(disuelto)* dissolved; *(derretido)* melted. 5 *(abatido)* devastated, shattered; **está d. con la enfermedad de su hijo,** he's shattered by his son's illness. 6 *(agotado)* exhausted, tired out, shattered.

deshelar *vtr* to thaw, melt; *(congelador)* to defrost; *(parabrisas)* to de-ice.

desherbar *vtr* to weed.

desheredado,-a I *pp de* **desheredar.** II *adj* disinherited; *fig* deprived, underprivileged. III *nm, f* disinherited person; *fig* deprived or underprivileged person; **los desheredados,** the deprived.

desheredar *vtr* to disinherit.

deshidratación *nf* dehydration.

deshidratado,-a I *pp de* **deshidratar.** II *adj* dehydrated.

deshidratar I *vtr* to dehydrate. II **deshidratarse** *vr* to become dehydrated.

deshidrogenar *vtr* to dehydrogenate, dehydrogenize.

deshielo *nm* 1 *(gen)* thaw; *(congelador)* defrosting; *(parabrisas)* de-icing. 2 *fig (distensión)* thaw.

deshilachado,-a I *pp de* **deshilacliar.** II *adj* frayed.

deshilachar *vtr* to fray.

deshilado,-a I *pp de* **deshilar.** II *adj* frayed.

deshilar *vtr véase* **deshilachar.**

deshilvanado,-a I *pp de* **deshilvanar.** II *adj* 1 *Cost* untacked. 2 *fig (sin enlace)* disjointed.

deshilvanar *vtr Cost* to untack.

deshinchado,-a I *pp de* **deshinchar.** II *adj* flat, deflated.

deshinchar I *vtr* to deflate, let down. II **deshincharse** *vr* 1 to go down; **ya se me ha deshinchado el brazo,** the swelling in my arm has gone down. 2 *fig (persona)* to get off one's high horse.

deshojar *vtr (flor)* to remove or strip the petals of; *(árbol)* to remove or strip the leaves of; *(libro)* to tear the pages out of.

deshollinador,-a *nm,f* chimney sweep.

deshollinar *vtr (chimenea)* to sweep.

deshonestidad *nf* 1 *(sin honestidad)* dishonesty. 2 *(impudor)* immodesty, impropriety, indecent.

deshonesto,-a *adj* 1 *(sin honestidad)* dishonest. 2 *(inmoral)* immodest, indecent, improper.

deshonor *nm,* **deshonra** *nf* dishonour, *US* dishonor, disgrace.

deshonrar *vtr* 1 *(gen)* to dishonour, *US* dishonor. 2 *(ofender)* to insult. 3 *(ultrajar)* to slander, difame; *(desprestigiar)* to bring disgrace on.

deshonroso,-a *adj* dishonourable, *US* dishonorable, disgraceful, shameful.

deshora (a) *loc adv* at an unreasonable or inconvenient time; **comer a d.,** to eat at odd times.

deshuesadora *nf* stoning or boning machine.

deshuesar *vtr (carne)* to bone; *(fruta)* to stone.

deshumanización *nf* dehumanization.

deshumanizado,-a I *pp de* **deshumanizar.** II *adj* dehumanized.

deshumanizar *vtr* to dehumanize.

desiderata *nf* desiderata.

desiderativo,-a *adj* desiderative.

desidia *nf* apathy, negligence, slovenliness.

desidioso,-a *adj* apathetic, negligent, slovenly.

desierto,-a I *adj* 1 *(deshabitado)* uninhabited; **isla desierta,** desert island. 2 *(con poca or sin gente)* empty, deserted; **el teatro estaba d.,** the theatre was empty. 3 *(no adjudicado)* void; **el jurado declaró d. el premio,** the prize was declared void; **quedar d.,** to be declared void. II *nm* desert; **clamar en el d.,** to cry in the desert.

designación *nf* 1 *(nombre)* name, designation. 2 *(nombramiento)* appointment, designation.

designar *vtr* 1 *(denominar)* to call, designate. 2 *(asignar un cargo)* to appoint, assign. 3 *(fijar)* to assign, fix.

designio *nm* intention, plan; **los designios del Señor,** God's will.

desigual *adj* 1 *(gen)* uneven. 2 *(diferente)* unequal, different. 3 *(variable)* changeable; **tiempo/carácter d.,** changeable weather/temper. 4 *(no liso)* uneven, rough. 5 *(irregular)* uneven, irregular, inconsistent.

desigualar I *vtr* to make unequal or uneven. II **desigualarse** *vr* to become unequal or uneven.

desigualdad *nf* 1 *(gen)* inequality. 2 *(diferencia)* difference. 3 *(de carácter)* changeability. 4 *(en el terreno)* roughness. 5 *(en la escritura)* unevenness, inconsistency.

desilusión *nf* disappointment, disillusionment.

desilusionado,-a I *pp de* **desilusionar.** II *adj* disappointed, disillusioned, disheartened.

desilusionar I *vtr* to disappoint, disillusion, dishearten. **II desilusionarse** *vr* to be disappointed, become disillusioned.

desimanar *vtr*, **desimantar** *vtr* to demagnetize.

desinencia *nf Ling* desinence.

desinfección *nf* disinfection.

desinfectante *adj & nm* disinfectant.

desinfectar *vtr* to disinfect.

desinflamación *nf Med* reduction of inflammation.

desinflamar *Med* **I** *vtr* to reduce the swelling *or* inflammation in. **II desinflamarse** *vr* to go down, become less swollen *or* inflamed.

desinflar I *vtr* to deflate; *(una rueda)* to let down. **II desinflarse** *vr* 1 to go flat. 2 *fam fig (desanimarse)* to lose interest, cool off.

desinsectación *nf* fumigation.

desinsectar *vtr (fumigar)* to fumigate.

desintegración *nf* disintegration, break up; **d. atómica,** atomic disintegration; **d. nuclear,** nuclear fission.

desintegrar I *vtr* 1 to desintegrate, break up. 2 *Fís (un átomo)* to split. **II desintegrarse** *vr* 1 to disintegrate, break up. 2 *Fís* to split.

desinterés *nm* 1 *(generosidad)* unselfishness, generosity; **todo lo hace con d.,** his motives are completely unselfish. 2 *(falta de interés)* lack of interest, apathy; **su desinterés por el trabajo es preocupante,** his lack of interest in work is worrying.

desinteresado,-a I *pp de* **desinterarse. II** *adj* selfless, unselfish.

desinteresarse *vr* 1 *(desentenderse)* to have nothing to do (**de,** with). 2 *(perder interés)* to lose interest (**de,** in), go off (**de,** -).

desintoxicación *nf* detoxication, detoxification; **una cura de d. alcohólica,** a drying-out cure.

desintoxicar I *vtr* to detoxicate, detoxify; *(alcohol)* to dry out. **II desintoxicarse** *vr Med* to detoxicate oneself; *(alcohol)* to dry out.

desistir *vi* to desist, give up; *Jur* to waive.

deslavar *vtr* 1 *(lavar mal)* to half-wash. 2 *Méx (ribera de un río)* to wash away.

deslavazado,-a *adj* 1 *(sin firmeza)* limp. 2 *(deshilvanado)* disjointed.

desleal *adj* disloyal.

deslealtad *nf* disloyalty.

desleír I *vtr (sólido)* to dissolve; *(líquido)* to dilute. **II desleírse** *vr* to dissolve.

deslenguado,-a I *pp de* **deslenguarse. II** *adj (insolente)* insolent, cheeky; *(grosero)* coarse, foulmouthed.

deslenguarse *vr* to be rude.

desliar I *vtr (un paquete)* to unwrap. **II desliarse** *vr* to come unwrapped *or* undone, open.

desligar *vtr* 1 *(desatar)* to untie, unfasten. 2 *fig (independizar)* to separate; **d. a algn de un compromiso,** to free *or* release sb from an obligation; **d. el aspecto político y el económico,** to consider the political and economic aspects separately.

deslindar *vtr* 1 *(una propiedad)* to set out the boundaries of. 2 *fig (aclarar)* to define, outline.

deslinde *nm* setting out of boundaries.

deslío *indic pres véase* **desleír & desliar.**

desliz *nm* 1 *(resbalón)* slip, slide. 2 *fig (error)* mistake, error, slip; **cometer** *or* **tener un d.,** to slip up, make a slip.

deslizamiento *nm* slipping, slip; **un d. de tierra,** landslide.

deslizar I *vtr* 1 *(pasar)* to slide, slip. 2 *(decir, hacer)* to slip in; **ella deslizó algunas indirectas sobre su ineficacia,** she dropped a few hints about his inefficiency; **le deslizó una nota en el bolso,** he slipped a note into her handbag.

II *vi (resbalar)* to slide, slip. **III deslizarse** *vr* 1 *(patinar)* to slide; *(sobre agua)* to glide. 2 *(fluir)* to flow; **las aguas se deslizan plácidamente,** the waters flow peacefully by. 3 *(transcurrir)* to go by, fly; **la mañana se deslizó sin sobresaltos,** the morning passed by without incidents. 4 *(entrar)* to slip into; *(salir)* to slip out of; **se deslizó en los camerinos sin que nadie lo viera,** he slipped unseen into the dressing rooms.

deslomar I *vtr* to wear out, exhaust. **II deslomarse** *vr* to wear oneself out, break one's back.

deslucido,-a I *pp de* **deslucir. II** *adj* 1 *(sin brillo)* faded, dull, lacklustre, *US* lackluster. 2 *(sin brillantez)* unimpressive, unexciting.

deslucir *vtr* 1 to dull, fade. 2 *(quitar atractivo)* to spoil.

deslumbrador,-a *adj* 1 dazzling. 2 *(que asombra)* dazzling, impressive.

deslumbramiento *nm* dazzle, dazzling.

deslumbrante *adj véase* **deslumbrador,-a.**

deslumbrar *vtr* to dazzle.

deslustrar *vtr* 1 *(quitar brillo)* to take the shine off, dull. 2 *(desacreditar)* to stain, tarnish.

desluzco *indic pres véase* **deslucir.**

desmadejado *adj* tired out, exhausted.

desmadejamiento *nm* exhaustion.

desmadejar *vtr* to tire out, exhaust.

desmadrado,-a I *pp de* **desmadrarse. II** *adj fam* wild, unruly; **los niños están desmadrados hoy,** the children are wild today.

desmadrarse *vr fam* to go wild.

desmadre *nm fam* chaos, havoc, hullabaloo.

desmagnetizar *vtr* to demagnetize.

desmalezar *vtr Am* to weed.

desmán *nm* outrage, excess.

desmanchar *Am* **I** *vtr* to clean, remove spots from. **II desmancharse** *vr* 1 *(apartarse)* to move away. 2 *(salir a correr)* to go for a run.

desmandado,-a I *pp de* **desmandarse. II** *adj* 1 *(persona)* rebellious; **multitud desmandada,** unruly crowd. 2 *(animal)* stray; **un caballo d.,** a runaway horse.

desmandarse *vr* to rebel, get out of hand, run wild; *(animal)* to stray from the herd; *(caballo)* to bolt.

desmano (a) *loc adv* out of the way; **me coge a d.,** it is out of my way.

desmantelado,-a I *pp de* **desmantelar. II** *adj* 1 dismantled. 2 *Náut* dismasted, unrigged.

desmantelamiento *nm* 1 dismantling. 2 *Náut* dismasting, unrigging.

desmantelar *vtr* 1 to dismantle. 2 *Náut* to dismast, unrig.

desmaquillador,-a I *adj* **leche desmaquilladora,** cleansing cream *or* milk, make-up remover. **II** *nm* make-up remover.

desmaquillar(se) *vtr & vr* to remove one's makeup.

desmarcarse *vr Dep* to lose one's marker.

desmayado,-a I *pp de* **desmayarse. II** *adj* unconscious; **caer d.,** to faint.

desmayarse *vr* to faint, lose consciousness, swoon.

desmayo *nm* faint, fainting fit; **tener un d.,** to faint.

desmedido,-a *adj* disproportionate, out of all proportion; **ambición desmedida,** unbounded ambition.

desmedrado,-a *adj* tiny, puny, emaciated.

desmejorar(se) *vi & vr* to deteriorate, go downhill; **estar desmejorado,-a,** to look off-colour *or* unwell.

desmelenado,-a I *pp de* **desmelenarse. II** *adj* tousled, ruffled, dishevelled.

desmelenar I *vtr (despeinar)* to dishevel. **II desmelenarse** *vr fam (desmadrarse)* to let one's hair down.

desmembración *nf*, **desmembramiento** *nm* dismemberment; *fig* separation, division.

desmembrar *vtr* to dismember; *fig* to split or break up.

desmemoriado,-a *adj* forgetful, absent-minded.

desmentir *vtr* 1 *(gen)* to deny. 2 *(contradecir)* to belie, contradict. 3 *(desmerecer)* not to live up to.

demenuzar *vtr* 1 *(deshacer)* to break into little pieces, crumble; *(carne)* to chop up. 2 *fig (analizar)* to examine in detail; **d. un asunto,** to look into a subject carefully.

desmerecer *vi* 1 *(perder valor)* to lose value. 2 *(ser inferior)* to compare unfavourably (**de,** with), be inferior (**de,** to).

desmerecimiento *nm* demerit.

desmesura *nf* immoderation, disproportion.

desmesurado,-a *adj* disproportionate, excessive. ◆ **desmesuradamente** *adv* extremely, disproportionately, excessively.

desmigajar *vtr*, **desmigar** *vtr (pan)* to crumble.

desmilitarización *nf* demilitarization.

desmilitarizar *vtr* to demilitarize.

desmineralización *nf* demineralization.

desmineralizar *vtr* to demineralize.

desmirriado,-a *adj véase* **esmirriado,-a.**

desmontable *adj* that can be taken to pieces; **estantería d.,** shelf in kit form.

desmontar I *vtr* 1 *(desarmar)* to take to pieces, take down, dismantle. 2 *(derribar)* to knock down. 3 *(cortar árboles)* to clear of trees. 4 *(allanar)* to level. 5 *(armas)* to uncock. II *vi (apearse)* to dismount (**de,** -), get off (**de,** -).

desmoralización *nf* demoralization.

desmoralizador,-a *adj* demoralizing.

desmoralizar *vtr* to demoralize.

desmoronamiento *nm* disintegration, decay, crumbling; **el d. de un imperio,** the fall of an empire.

desmoronar I *vtr* to disintegrate, destroy; *(una roca)* to erode. II **desmoronarse** *vr* to crumble, fall to pieces; *fig* **al oír la noticia se desmoronó,** he was devastated by the news.

desmotar *vtr* 1 *(la lana)* to burl. 2 *Am (el algodón)* to gin.

desmovilización *nf Mil* demobilization.

desmovilizar *vtr Mil* to demobilize.

desnacionalización *nf Fin* denationalization, privatization.

desnacionalizar *vtr Fin* to denationalize, privatize.

desnatar *vtr (leche)* to skim.

desnaturalización *nf* 1 adulteration. 2 *(destierro)* banishment. 3 *Quím* denaturation.

desnaturalizado,-a I *adj pp de* **desnaturalizar.** II *adj* 1 adulterated, distorted. 2 *Quím* denatured; **alcohol d.,** denatured alcohol. 3 *(descastado)* unnatural, inhuman.

desnaturalizar *vtr* 1 *(alterar)* to adulterate, tamper with. 2 *Quím* to denature. 3 *(desterrar)* to banish.

desnivel *nm* 1 unevenness, difference of level; *fig* **el d. económico,** the economic gap. 2 *(en el terreno)* drop, difference in height.

desnivelación *nf* unevenness, unlevelling.

desnivelado,-a I *adj* 1 *(desigual)* not level, uneven, unequal. 2 *(desequilibrado)* out of balance.

desnivelar *vtr* 1 to make uneven, put on a different level. 2 *(desequilibrar)* to throw out of balance; *(balanza)* to tip.

desnucar I *vtr* to break the neck of. II **desnucarse** *vr* to break one's neck.

desnuclearizar *vtr* to denuclearize.

desnudar I *vtr* to undress. II **desnudarse** *vr* to get undressed.

desnudez *nf* nudity, nakedness.

desnudismo *nm* nudism.

desnudista *adj & nmf* nudist.

desnudo,-a I *adj* naked, nude; **con los hombros desnudos,** with bare shoulders; **la verdad desnuda,** the plain or naked truth. II *nm Arte* nude.

desnutrición *nf* undernourishment, malnutrition.

desnutrido,-a I *adj pp de* **desnutrirse.** II *adj* undernourished.

desnutrirse *vr* to become undernourished.

desobedecer *vtr* to disobey.

desobediencia *nf* disobedience.

desobediente I *adj* disobedient. II *nmf* disobedient person.

desocarse *vr SAm* 1 *(animales)* to be footsore. 2 *(dislocarse)* to sprain one's hand or foot.

desocupación *nf* 1 *(paro)* unemployment 2 *(octosidad)* leisure

desocupado,-a I *adj pp de* **desocupar** II *adj* 1 *(vacío)* empty, vacant, **¿está d. este asiento?,** is this seat free? 2 *(ocioso)* free, not busy, **si estás d.,** if you're not busy 3 *(sin empleo)* unemployed

desocupar I *vtr* to empty, vacate, *Mil* to evacuate II **desocuparse** *vr (de un trabajo)* to give up work

desodorante *adj & nm* deodorant

desodorar *vtr* to deodorize

desoír *vtr* to ignore, take no notice of, turn a deaf ear to

desojarse *vr* to strain one's eyes

desolación *nf (aflicción)* desolation, *(pena)* grief

desolado,-a I *adj pp de* **desolar** II *adj* 1 *(devastado)* devastated, desolated 2 *(desconsolado)* inconsolable, disconsolate

desolador,-a *adj* 1 *(devastador)* devastating 2 *(desconsolador)* desolating

desolar *vtr* 1 *(devastar)* to devastate 2 *(desconsolar)* to desolate, distress

desollar *vtr (un animal)* to skin, *fig* **d. vivo a algn,** to tear sb to pieces

desorbitado,-a I *adj pp de* **desorbitar.** II *adj* 1 *(excesivo)* disproportionate, *(exagerado)* exaggerated; **precios desorbitados,** exhorbitant prices 2 **con los ojos desorbitados,** pop-eyed

desorbitar *vtr (exagerar)* to get out of proportion, exaggerate, **d. una noticia,** to blow a piece of news up out of all proportion

desorden *nm* 1 *(desarreglo)* untidiness, disorder, mess, **en d.,** in a mess, **¡qué d.!,** what a mess! 2 *(desarreglo)* irregularity; **evite el d. en las comidas,** take meals at regular times ■ **desórdenes gástricos,** stomach disorders 3 **desordenes,** *(disturbio)* not *sing,* disorder *sing,* **d. públicos,** civil disorder *sing,* **los últimos d. han alterado la vida ciudadana,** the recent disturbances have shaken people's lives 4 **desordenes,** *(excesos)* excesses

desordenado,-a I *adj pp de* **desordenar** II *adj* 1 *(desarreglado)* messy, untidy, **la casa está toda desordenada,** the house is upside down, *fig* **ideas desordenadas,** jumbled (up) or confused ideas 2 *fig (vida)* irregular

desordenar I *vtr* to make untidy, mess up II **desordenarse** *vr* to get or become untidy or messed up.

desorejado,-a *adj Am* without handles

desorganización *nf* disorganization

desorganizar *vtr* to disorganize, disrupt

desorientación *nf* disorientation; *fig* confusion

desorientado,-a I *adj pp de* **desorientar** II *adj* disoriented; *fig* **tu reacción le dejó d.,** your reaction confused him

desorientar I *vtr* to disorientate, *fig* to confuse II **desorientarse** *vr* to lose one's sense of direction, lose one's bearings, be lost or disoriented; *fig* to get confused

desosar *vtr (carne)* to bone, *(fruta)* to stone

desovar *vi (insectos)* to lay eggs; *(peces)* to spawn

desove *nm (de insectos)* egg-laying, *(de peces)* spawning

desoxidación *nf* deoxidization

desoxidante I *adj* deoxidizing II *nm* deoxidizer

desoxidar *vtr* to deoxidize

desoxirribonucleico,-a *adj Quím* deoxyribonucleic

desoye *indic pres véase* **desoír**

despabilado,-a I *pp de* **despabilar** II *adj* 1 *(sin sueño)* wide awake 2 *(listo)* quick, smart, **ser muy d.,** to be quick on the uptake, have one's wits about one

despabilar I *vtr* 1 *(despertar)* to wake up 2 *(avivar el ingenio)* to smarten up, wise up 3 *(consumir)* to finish off, eat up II *vi (avivar el ingenio)* to get a move on, **como no despabiles te quedas sin el trabajo,** get your act together or you'll lose the job III **despabilarse** *vr* 1 *(despertar)* to wake up 2 *(darse prisa)* to hurry up

despachar I *vtr* 1 *(terminar)* to finish, *(resolver)* to get through 2 *(enviar)* to send, dispatch 3 *(tratar un asunto)* to deal with, **debo d. un negocio con el director,** I must settle a matter with the director, **d. la correspondencia,** to sort out the mail 4 *(en tienda)* to serve, *(entradas)* to issue, sell 5 *fam (comer)* to polish off, get through 6 *fam fig (despedir)* to send away *or* packing, sack 7 *fam fig (matar)* to kill II **despacharse** *vr (acabar)* to finish off, **d. de algo,** to get rid of sth; *fig* **d. a gusto con algn,** to give sb a piece of one's mind

despacho *nm* 1 *(acción)* dispatch, handling 2 *(comunicación)* dispatch ■ **d. diplomático,** diplomatic dispatch, **d. telefónico,** telephone call, **d. telegráfico,** telegram 2 *(oficina)* office, **el d. del jefe,** the boss's office ■ **mesa de d.,** desk 3 *(en casa)* study. 4 *(venta)* selling, sale 5 *(lugar de venta)* **d. de billetes,** ticket office; **d. de localidades,** box office, **d. de vino,** wine merchant's.

despachurrar *fam* I *vtr* to squash, crush, flatten II **despachurrarse** *vr* to get squashed *or* crushed

despacio I *adv* 1 *(lentamente)* slowly; **camina d.,** walk slowly 2 *Arg Chi (en voz baja)* quietly II *interj* take it easy!

despacioso,a *adj* slow, sluggish

despampanante *adj fam* stunning

despancar *vtr SAm (maíz)* to husk

despanzurrar *vtr fam* to squash, crush

desparejado,-a I *pp de* **desparejar** II *adj* without a partner, un **calcetín d.,** an odd sock

desparejar *vtr,* **desaparejarse** *vr* to separate

desparejo,-a *adj* 1 *(dispar)* unlike, different 2 *Arg Par Urug (desigual)* uneven, uncentred, *US* uncentered, unbalanced

desparpajo *nm* 1 *(desenvoltura)* self-assurance, ease, **con d.,** in a carefree way, confidently 2 *CAm (desorden)* disorder, confusion

desparramar *vtr,* **desparramarse** *vr* to spread, scatter, *(líquido)* to spill

despatarrado,-a I *pp de* **despatarrar** II *adj* with legs wide open

despatarrar I *vtr fig* to amaze II **despatarrarse** *vr (abrir las piernas)* to open one's legs wide, sprawl, *(al caer)* to go sprawling

despavorido,-a *adj* terrified

despechado,-a *adj* bearing a grudge, spiteful

despecho *nm* spite, **por d.,** out of spite.

despechugado,-a *fam* I *pp de* **despechugarse** II *adj* bare chested

despechugarse *vr fam* to show *or* bare one's chest

despectivo,-a *adj* 1 derogatory, contemptuous, disparaging, **de forma despectiva,** in a derogatory way, **en tono d.,** contemptuously 2 *Ling* pejorative

despedazar *vtr* to cut or tear to pieces.

despedida *nf* 1 farewell, goodbye. ■ **cena de d.,** farewell dinner; **d. de soltera,** hen party; **d. de soltero,** stag party. 2 *Mús* last verse (of a song).

despedir I *vtr* 1 *(del trabajo)* to sack, fire, dismiss; **¡está Vd. despedido!,** you're fired! 2 *(decir adiós)* to see off, say goodbye to; **fue al aeropuerto a despedirlo,** he went to see him off at the airport. 3 *(desprender)* to give off; **esta máquina despide un olor muy desagradable,** this machine gives off an awful smell. 4 *(lanzar)* to shoot; **salir d.,** to shoot off. 5 *(echar)* to chuck or throw out. II **despedirse** *vr* 1 *(decir adiós)* to say goodbye (**de,** to); **vino a d.,** he came to say goodbye. 2 *(irse)* to take one's leave, leave; *fam* **d. a la francesa,** to take French leave. 3 *fig* to forget, give up; **puedes despedirte de la idea de comprarte el coche,** you can forget the idea of buying the car.

despegado,-a I *pp de* **despegar.** II *adj* 1 unstuck; **la foto está despegada,** the photo has come unstuck. 2 *fig* cold, distant, detached.

despegar I *vtr* to unstick, take off, detach. II *vi Av* to take off. III **despegarse** *vr (separarse)* to come unstuck. 2 *fig (perder afecto)* to lose affection (**de,** for); *(separarse)* to alienate oneself (**de,** from), cut oneself off (**de,** from).

despego *nm* coldness, detachment; **con d.,** with indifference.

despegue *nm Av* takeoff. ■ **pista de d.,** runway.

despeinado,-a I *pp de* **despeinar.** II *adj* dishevelled, with untidy hair.

despeinar I *vtr* to ruffle; *(peinado)* to mess up. II **despeinarse** *vr* to ruffle one's hair, make one's hair untidy.

despejado,-a I *pp de* **despejar.** II *adj* 1 *(ancho)* wide, spacious; **una frente despejada,** a broad forehead. 2 *(cielo)* clear, cloudless. 3 *(listo)* clever, bright. 4 *(despierto)* wide awake.

despejar I *vtr* 1 *(desocupar)* to clear (away); **despeja la mesa de papeles,** clear those papers off the table; *Ftb* **d. el balón,** to clear the ball. 2 *(aclarar)* to disentangle; **d. la mente,** to clear one's head; **d. un enigma,** to clear up a mystery. 3 *(espabilar)* to keep awake; **el paseo te despejará,** the walk will wake you up. 4 *Mat* to find the unknown quantity. 5 *Inform* to clear. II **despejarse** *vr* 1 *(cielo)* to clear. 2 *(persona) (despertar)* to wake up; *(espabilarse)* to clear one's head.

despeje *nm Dep* clearance.

despellejar *vtr* 1 *(quitar el pellejo)* to skin. 2 *fig (criticar)* to criticize unmercifully, pull to pieces.

despelotado,-a *vulg* I *pp de* **despelotarse.** II *adj* naked, starkers.

despelotarse *vr vulg* 1 *(desnudarse)* to strip. 2 *(descojonarse)* to laugh one's head off, die laughing.

despelote *nm vulg* 1 *(desnudo)* strip. 2 *(descojone)* laugh.

despensa *nf* 1 *(fresquera)* pantry, larder. 2 *(víveres)* stock of food, provisions *pl.*

despeñadero *nm* cliff, precipice.

despeñar I *vtr* to throw over a cliff. II **despeñarse** *vr* to throw oneself over a cliff.

despercudir *vtr Am* to liven up, wake up.

desperdiciar *vtr (gen)* to waste; *(oportunidad)* to throw away.

desperdicio *nm* 1 *(acto)* waste, wasting; *fig* **esta película no tiene d.,** this film is excellent from start to finish. 2 **desperdicios,** *(basura)* rubbish *sing*; *(desechos)* scraps, leftovers; *(residuos)* waste *sing.*

desperdigar *vtr,* **desperdigarse** *vr* to scatter, separate.

desperezarse *vr* to stretch (oneself).

desperfecto *nm* 1 *(defecto)* flaw, imperfection. 2 *(daño)* damage; **la lluvia causó algunos desperfectos,** the rain caused some damage.

despersonalizar *vtr* to depersonalize, make impersonal.

despertador *nm* alarm clock. ■ **reloj d.,** alarm watch.

despertar I *vtr* to wake (up), awaken; *fig (esperanzas, sentimientos)* to raise, arouse. **II despertarse** *vr* to wake (up), awaken.

despezuñarse *vr Am* **1** *(caminar de prisa)* to walk very quickly, rush. **2** *(esforzarse)* to exert oneself, make an effort.

despiadado,-a *adj* merciless, heartless, cruel.

despido *nm* dismissal, sacking. ■ **d. improcedente,** wrongful dismissal.

despierto,-a *adj* **1** *(desvelado)* awake. **2** *(espabilado)* quick, sharp, bright.

despilarar *vtr Am* to remove the props from.

despilfarrador,-a *adj & nm,f* spendthrift, waster.

despilfarrar *vtr* to waste, squander.

despilfarro *nm* wasting, squandering.

despintar I *vtr* **1** *(arrancar la pintura)* to take *or* strip the paint off. **2** *Am (apartar la mirada)* to look away. **II despintarse** *vr (desteñirse)* to fade, lose colour *or US* color; *(por la lluvia)* to wash off.

despistado,-a I *pp de* **despistar.** **II** *adj* **1** *(olvidadizo)* absent-minded, scatterbrained. **2** *(confuso)* confused; **este asunto me tiene muy d.,** this business has got me all muddled up. **III** *nm, f* absent-minded person, scatterbrain; **hacerse el d.,** to pretend not to understand.

despistar I *vtr* **1** *(hacer perder la pista)* to lose, throw off one's scent. **2** *fig* to mislead, muddle. **II despistarse** *vr* **1** *(perderse)* to get lost, lose one's way. **2** *(distraerse)* to do absent-mindedly; **me despisté y cogí su bolso en vez del mío,** without thinking I took her bag instead of mine. **3** *(olvidarse)* to forget about; **no vine porque me despisté,** I didn't come because it completely slipped my mind.

despiste *nm* **1** *(error)* mistake, slip; **¡vaya d.!,** what a blunder! **2** *(cualidad)* absent-mindedness.

desplante *nm* outspoken *or* cutting remark.

desplazado,-a I *pp de* **desplazar.** **II** *adj* out of place, misplaced; **sentirse d.,** to feel out of place.

desplazamiento *nm* **1** *(viaje)* trip, journey. **2** *Náut* displacement. **3** *(traslado)* removal, movement.

desplazar I *vtr* **1** *(trasladar)* to displace, move. **2** *Náut* to displace. **3** *fig (suplantar)* to take the place of, supplant. **II desplazarse** *vr (ir)* to travel, go.

desplegar I *vtr* **1** *(abrir)* to unfold, open (out), spread (out). **2** *fig (energías etc)* to use, deploy. **II desplegarse** *vr* **1** *(abrirse)* to unfold, open (out), spread (out). **2** *Mil* to deploy.

despliegue *nm* **1** *Mil* deployment. **2** *fig (muestra)* display, show, manifestation.

desplomarse *vr (gen)* to collapse; *(caer)* to fall, topple over; *(precios)* to slump, fall sharply.

desplome *nm,* **desplomo** *nm Arquit* overhang.

desplumar *vtr* **1** *(ave)* to pluck. **2** *fam (estafar)* to fleece, swindle.

despoblación *nf* depopulation. ■ **d. forestal,** deforestation.

despoblar I *vtr* to depopulate; **d. de árboles,** to deforest. **II despoblarse** *vr* to become depopulated.

despojar I *vtr* **1** *(quitar)* to strip, clear (**de,** of). **2** *fig* to divest, deprive (**de,** of). **3** *Jur* to dispossess. **II despojarse** *vr* **1** *(ropa)* to take off. **2** *fig (sentimiento etc)* to free oneself (**de,** of).

despojo *nm* **1** *(desposeimiento)* deprivation, stripping. **2 despojos,** *(de animal)* offal *sing; (desperdicios)* leftovers, scraps; *Constr* rubble *sing; (cadáver)* remains.

desportillar *vtr,* **desportillarse** *vr* to chip (off).

desposado,-a I *pp de* **desposar.** **II** *adj fml* newly-wed.

desposar I *vtr fml* to marry. **II desposarse** *vr fml (casarse)* to get married (**con,** to); *(prometerse)* to become engaged (**con,** to).

desposeer *vtr* to dispossess (**de,** of); **d. a algn de su autoridad,** to remove sb from authority.

desposeído,-a I *pp de* **desposeer.** **II los desposeídos** *nmpl* the have-nots.

desposorios *nmpl fml (boda)* marriage *sing; (esponsales)* engagement *sing,* betrothal *sing.*

despostar *vtr Am* to cut up.

déspota *nmf* despot.

despótico,-a *adj* despotic.

despotismo *nm* despotism. ■ *Hist* **d. ilustrádo,** enlightened despotism.

despotizar *vtr Am* to tyrannize.

despotricar *vi* to rave (**contra,** about), rant (on).

despreciable *adj* despicable, contemptible; *(en cantidad)* negligible; *(en calidad)* worthless.

despreciar *vtr* **1** *(desdeñar)* to scorn, despise, look down on. **2** *(rechazar)* to reject, spurn. **3** *(menospreciar)* to deprecate, belittle.

despreciativo,-a *adj* scornful, contemptuous.

desprecio *nm* **1** *(desdén)* scorn, contempt, disdain. **2** *(desaire)* slight, snub.

desprejuiciarse *vr Am* to free oneself of prejudices, become more open-minded.

desprender I *vtr* **1** *(separar)* to remove, detach. **2** *(soltar)* to give off. **II desprenderse** *vr* **1** *(soltarse)* to come off *or* away; *fig* **de aquí se desprende que ...,** it can be deduced from this that ...; *fig* **el enojo se desprende de sus palabras,** you can tell she's angry by what she's saying. **2** *(renunciar)* to part with, give away; **se desprendió de todos sus bienes,** she gave away all her possessions. **3** *fig (liberarse)* to rid (**de,** of), free (**de,** from); **se desprendió de todas sus dudas,** he rid himself of his doubts.

desprendido,-a I *pp de* **desprender.** **II** *adj fig* generous, unselfish, disinterested.

desprendimiento *nm* **1** *(acción)* loosening, detachment. ■ *Med* **d. de retina,** detachment of the retina; **d. de tierras,** landslide. **2** *fig (generosidad)* generosity, unselfishness.

despreocupación *nf* **1** *(tranquilidad)* unconcern, nonchalance; *(indiferencia)* indifference. **2** *(descuido)* carelessness, negligence.

despreocupado,-a I *pp de* **despreocuparse.** **II** *adj* **1** *(tranquilo)* unconcerned, unworried; *(indiferente)* indifferent. **2** *(descuidado)* careless, negligent, sloppy; **tener un estilo d. en el vestir,** to dress sloppily *or* carelessly.

despreocuparse *vr* **1** *(tranquilizarse)* to stop worrying. **2** *(desentenderse)* to be unconcerned, be indifferent (**de,** to).

desprestigiar I *vtr (desacreditar)* to discredit, run down; **su conducta le ha desprestigiado,** his behaviour has ruined his reputation. **II desprestigiarse** *vr* to lose one's prestige, bring discredit on oneself.

desprestigio *nm* discredit, loss of reputation; **campaña de d.,** smear campaign.

desprevenido,-a *adj* unprepared, unready; **coger** *or* **pillar a algn d.,** to catch sb unawares, take sb by surprise.

desproporción *nf* disproportion, lack of proportion.

desproporcionado,-a *adj* disproportionate, disproportioned, out of proportion.

despropósito *nm* piece of nonsense, silly remark; **decir muchos despropósitos,** to talk a lot of nonsense.

desprovisto,-a *adj* lacking (**de,** -), without (**de,** -), devoid (**de,** of); **d. de interés,** devoid of interest, uninteresting; **estar d. de,** to be lacking in, lack.

después *adv* **1** *(gen) (tiempo)* afterwards, later; *(entonces)* then; *(luego)* next; **poco d.,** soon after; **¿qué pasó d.?,**

(entonces) what happened then?; *(luego)* what happened next?; **vendrá d.,** he'll come later. **2** *(orden)* next, after; **mi calle está d.,** my street is next. **3 d. de,** *(tiempo)* after; *(desde)* since; **d. de la guerra,** after the war; **d. de 1975,** since 1975. **4 d. de,** *(orden)* after; **el 2 está d. del 1,** 2 comes after 1; **mi calle está d. de la tuya,** my street is the one after yours. **5 d. (de) que,** after; **d. (de) que amanezca saldremos,** we'll go out when the sun is up; **d. (de) que lo hice, me arrepentí,** after doing it, I regretted it. **6** *(al fin y al cabo)* **d. de todo,** after all; **d. de todo es un buen chico,** when all is said and done, he's a nice guy.

despuntado,-a I *pp de* **despuntar. II** *adj* blunt.

despuntar I *vtr* **1** *(embotar)* to blunt, make blunt. **2** *Náut (cabo, punta)* to round. **II 1** *(planta)* to sprout; *(flor)* to bud. **2** *(alba)* to break; **al d. el alba,** at daybreak, at dawn. **3** *fig (destacar)* to excel, stand out; **despunta por su inteligencia,** her intelligence is outstanding.

desquiciar I *vtr* **1** *(puerta)* to unhinge, take off its hinges. **2** *fig (transtornar)* to upset, unsettle; *(volver loco)* to unhinge. **II desquiciarse** *vr* **1** *(puerta)* to come off its hinges. **2** *fig (volverse loco)* to go crazy.

desquitarse *vr* to get even, take revenge; **hoy he perdido pero mañana me desquitaré de esta derrota,** I've lost today but I'll make up for my defeat tomorrow.

desquite *nm* *(satisfacción)* satisfaction; *(venganza)* revenge, retaliation; **tomarse el d.,** to have one's revenge, get one's own back.

destacado,-a I *pp de* **destacar. II** *adj* outstanding, prominent, distinguished.

destacamento *nm* Mil detachment.

destacar I *vtr* **1** Mil to detach. **2** Arte to make stand out, highlight. **3** *fig* to emphasize, point out; **me gustaría d. que ...,** I would like to point out that ... **II** *vi (descollar)* to stand out; **destaca por su bondad,** his kindness is exceptional. **III destacarse** *vr* to stand out.

destajo *nm* piecework; **trabajar a d.,** to do piecework; *fig* **hablar a d.,** to talk nineteen to the dozen.

destapar I *vtr* **1** *(abrir)* to open; *(descubrir)* to uncover; *(botella)* to uncork; *(abrir la tapa)* to take the lid off. **2** *fig* to reveal, uncover. **II** *vi* Méx *(echar a correr)* to start running. **III destaparse** *vr* **1** to get uncovered; **durmiendo me destapé,** the sheets slipped off me while I was asleep. **2** *fig* to do unexpectedly; **se destapó diciendo que no quería ir,** all of a sudden he said he didn't want to go.

destape *nm fam* Cin Teat striptease; **una película de d.,** a blue movie.

destartalado,-a *adj* *(desproporcionado)* rambling; *(desvencijado)* tumbledown, ramshackle; *(coche)* rickety.

destellar *vi* to flash, sparkle, glitter.

destello *nm* *(resplandor)* flash, sparkle; *(brillo)* gleam, wink; *fig* glimmer; **a veces tiene destellos de inteligencia,** sometimes he shows a glimmer of intelligence.

destemplado,-a I *pp de* **destemplar. II** *adj* **1** Mús harsh, out of tune, discordant. **2** *(voz, gesto)* sharp, snappy; **con cajas destempladas,** rudely, brusquely. **3** *(carácter, actitud)* irritable, tetchy. **4** Meteor *(tiempo)* unpleasant. **5** *(enfermo)* indisposed, out of sorts.

destemplanza *nf* **1** Mús harshness. **2** *(irritabilidad)* irritability. **3** Meteor unpleasantness. **4** Med *(indisposición)* indisposition.

destemplar I *vtr* **1** Mús *(desafinar)* to put out of tune. **2** *fig (descomponer)* to disturb, upset. **II destemplarse** *vr* **1** Mús *(desafinarse)* to get out of tune. **2** Med to become indisposed *or* out of sorts.

desteñir I *vtr* to discolour, US discolor. **II** *vi* to lose colour *or* US color, fade; *(color)* to run; **esta tela destiñe,** this fabric is not colour fast. **III desteñirse** *vr* to lose colour *or* US color, fade; **los pantalones se destiñeron,** the trousers faded.

desternillarse *vi fam* **d. (de risa),** to split one's sides laughing.

desterrado,-a I *pp de* **desterrar, II** *nm,f* exile.

desterrar *vtr* to exile, banish; *fig* **d. la tristeza,** to banish sadness.

destetar *vtr* to wean.

destete *nm* weaning.

destiempo (a) *loc adv* at the wrong time *or* moment.

destierro *nm* **1** *(acción, pena)* exile. **2** *(lugar)* place of exile.

destilación *nf* distillation.

destilado,-a *pp de* **destilar. II** *adj* distilled; **agua destilada,** distilled water.

destilador,-a I *adj* distilling. **II** *nm,f* **1** *(persona)* distiller. **2** *(alambique)* still.

destilar *vtr* **1** *(filtrar)* to distil. **2** *(sangre, pus)* to exude, ooze. **3** *fig (revelar)* to exude, reveal; **sus ojos destilaban odio,** the look in her eyes was full of hatred.

destilería *nf* distillery.

destinado,-a I *pp de* **destinar. II** *adj* destined, bound; *fig* **estar d. al fracaso,** to be doomed to failure.

destinar *vtr* **1** *(asignar)* to set aside, assign; **d. una cantidad de dinero para gastos,** to allot some money for expenses, put aside some money for expenses. **2** *(nombrar)* to appoint; **le han destinado a la sucursal de Granada,** he has been appointed to the Granada branch. **3** Mil *(asignar a puesto)* to post.

destinatario,-a *nm, f* **1** *(de paquete, carta)* addressee. **2** *(de mercancías)* consignee.

destino *nm* **1** *(uso)* purpose, use; **una habitación sin d. fijo,** an all-purpose room. **2** *(rumbo)* destination; **el avión con d. a Santiago,** the plane to Santiago; **el barco con d. a Dublín,** the boat bound for Dublin; **salir con d. a Salamanca,** to leave for Salamanca. **3** *(puesto de trabajo)* position, post; **salió ayer para su d.,** he left yesterday to take up his post; **un d. de cartero,** a job as a postman. **4** *(sino)* fate, fortune; **el d. lo quiso así,** it was fate, it was fated to be; **la fuerza del d.,** the power of destiny.

destitución *nf* dismissal from office.

destituir *vtr* to dismiss *or* remove from office.

destornillador *nm* **1** *(herramienta)* screwdriver. **2** *fam (combinado)* screwdriver, vodka and orange.

destornillar *vtr* to unscrew.

destorrentado,-a I *pp de* **destorrentarse. II** *adj* CAm *(manirroto)* lavish, reckless.

destorrentarse *vr* **1** Hond Méx *(perder el tino)* to go off the rails. **2** Méx *fig (ir por mal camino)* to go astray.

destratar *vtr* Am *(trato)* to break off.

destrenzar *vtr* to unplait.

destreza *nf* skill, dexterity; **tener d.,** to be skilful.

destripar *vtr* **1** *(animal, persona)* to disembowel; *(pescado)* to gut. **2** *(despanzurrar)* to cut open; **destripé el cojín,** I tore the cushion open.

destronamiento *nm* *(de un monarca)* dethronement; *fig* overthrow.

destronar *vtr* *(monarca)* to dethrone; *fig* to overthrow.

destrozado,-a I *pp de* **destrozar. II** *adj* **1** torn-up, smashed; **estos zapatos están destrozados,** these shoes are ruined. **2** *(moralmente)* shattered, broken. **3** *(muy cansado)* done in, worn-out, exhausted.

destrozar *vtr* **1** *(romper)* to destroy, ruin, wreck; *(rasgar)* to tear to shreds *or* pieces; **el huracán destrozó los edificios,** the hurricane wrecked the buildings; **el perro me ha destrozado la chaqueta,** the dog has torn my jacket to shreds. **2** *fig (abatir moralmente)* to crush, shatter. **3** *fig (vida, persona)* to ruin; *(corazón)* to break.

destrozo *nm* **1** *(gen)* destruction. **2 destrozos,** damage *sing*; **los destrozos ocasionados por la tormenta,** the damage caused by the storm.

destrucción *nf* destruction.

destructivo,-a *adj* destructive.

destructor,-a I *adj* destructive. **II** *nm Náut* destroyer.

destruir *vtr (gen)* to destroy; *fig (persona, proyecto)* to ruin.

desunión *nf* **1** *(división)* separation, division. **2** *fig (discordia)* dissension, discord; **la d. entre los trabajadores,** the lack of solidarity among the workers.

desunir *vtr* **1** *(dividir)* to separate, pull apart. **2** *(enemistar)* to set at odds, split; **las diferencias políticas desunen a los países,** political differences set countries against each other.

desusado,-a *adj* **1** *(anticuado)* old-fashioned, out-dated. **2** *(musitado)* unusual, extraordinary.

desuso *nm* disuse; **caer en d.,** to fall into disuse; **en d.,** obsolete, outdated.

desvaído,-a *adj* **1** *(color)* faded, pale; *(contorno)* blurred. **2** *(persona)* drab, dull.

desvalido,-a I *adj* helpless, destitute. **II** *nm, f* destitute person; **los desvalidos,** the needy.

desvalijamiento *nm* theft, robbery.

desvalijar *vtr (robar)* to clean out, rob; *(casa, tienda)* to burgle; **me desvalijaron la casa,** my house was stripped bare.

desvalorización *nf* devaluation, depreciation.

desvalorizar *vtr* to devalue, depreciate.

desván *nm* attic, loft.

desvanecer I *vtr* **1** *(disipar)* to cause to vanish, disappear; *fig* to dispel; **d. dudas/temores,** to dispel doubts/fears. **2** *(color)* to fade; *(contorno)* to blur. **II desvanecerse** *vr* **1** *(disiparse)* to vanish, fade away. **2** *(desmayarse)* to faint.

desvanecimiento *nm* **1** *(desaparición)* disappearance, dispelling. **2** *(desmayo)* faint, fainting fit.

desvariar *vi* to talk nonsense, rave.

desvarío *nm* **1** *(delirio)* raving, delirium. **2** *(disparate)* incoherence, wanderings *pl* of the mind.

desvelado,-a I *pp de* **desvelar. II** *adj* awake, wide awake.

desvelar I *vtr (despabilar)* to keep awake, stop from sleeping; **el café me desvela,** coffee keeps me awake. **II desvelarse** *vr* **1** *(desvivirse)* to devote oneself (**por,** to); **ella se desvela por el bienestar de todos,** she does her utmost to see that everybody is happy. **2** *(despavilarse)* to stay awake; **si leo novelas me desvelo,** if I read novels I can't get to sleep.

desvelo *nm* **1** *(insomnio)* insomnia, sleeplessness. **2 desvelos,** *(esfuerzos)* efforts, pains; **su familia es el objeto de todos sus d.,** he devotes himself entirely to his family.

desvencijado I *pp de* **desvencijar. II** *adj (gen)* broken; *(máquina)* broken-down.

desvencijar I *vtr (romper)* to break; *(máquina)* to break down. **II desvencijarse** *vr (romperse)* to fall apart; *(aflojarse)* to become loose.

desventaja *nf* disadvantage, drawback; **estar en d.,** to be at a disadvantage; **las desventajas de una profesión,** the drawbacks of a profession.

desventajoso,-a *adj* disadvantageous, unfavourable, *US* unfavorable.

desventura *nf* misfortune, bad luck.

desventurado,-a I *adj* unfortunate, unlucky; **una vida desventurada,** an unhappy life. **II** *nm, f* unfortunate person, wretch; **los desventurados,** the unfortunate; **un pobre d.,** a poor wretch.

desvergonzado,-a I *adj* **1** *(sin decoro)* shameless, impudent. **2** *(descarado)* insolent. **II** *nm, f* **1** *(sinvergüenza)* shameless person. **2** *(fresco)* insolent *or* cheeky person.

desvergüenza *nf* **1** *(falta de decoro)* impudence, shamelessness. **2** *(atrevimiento)* cheek, nerve, insolence; **tuvo la d. de negarlo,** he had the cheek to deny it. **3** *(impertinencia)* insolent *or* rude remark.

desvestir I *vtr* to undress. **II desvestirse** *vr* to undress, get undressed.

desviación *nf* deviation; *Med* **d. de columna,** slipped disc; **d. de la norma,** deviation from the norm; **d. de una carretera,** diversion, detour.

desviacionismo *nm* deviationism.

desviacionista *adj & nmf* deviationist.

desviar I *vtr* **1** to change the course of; *(río, carretera)* to divert; *(golpe)* to deflect; *fig (tema)* to change; *fig (pregunta)* to parry, evade; **d. la mirada,** to look away. **2** *(descaminar)* to lead away from; **d. del buen camino,** to lead astray. **II desviarse** *vr* **1** *(avión, barco)* to go off course; *(coche)* to make a detour. **2** *(persona, camino)* to leave; **nos desviamos de la carretera principal,** we left the main road; *fig* **d. del objetivo,** to lose sight of one's purpose; *fig* **d. del tema,** to digress.

desvinculación *nf* releasing, freeing.

desvincular I *vtr* to separate, free. **II desvincularse** *vr* to separate, cut oneself off; **d. de la familia,** to break away from one's family.

desvío *nm* diversion, detour; **d. por obras,** diversion due to roadworks.

desvirgar *vtr* to deflower.

desvirtuar *vtr* **1** *(debilitar)* to impair, spoil. **2** *(anular)* to cancel out, invalidate.

desvivirse *vr* **1** *(gustar mucho)* to be mad about; **se desvive por el chocolate,** he is mad about chocolate. **2** *(esforzarse)* to do one's utmost; **se desvivieron por ayudarnos,** they bent over backwards to help us.

detallado,-a I *pp de* **detallar. II** *adj* detailed, thorough. ◆ **detalladamente** *adv* in (great) detail.

detallar *vtr* **1** *(narrar con detalle)* to relate in detail. **2** *(precisar)* to give the details of; **d. la hora y el día,** to give the exact hour and day. **3** *Com* to retail.

detalle *nm* **1** detail; **contar con d.,** to go into detail; **dar detalles,** to give details; **sin entrar en d.,** without going into details. **2** *(delicadeza)* nice thought, nicety; **¡qué d.!,** how nice!, how sweet!; **tiene muchos detalles,** he is very considerate. **3** *(toque decorativo)* touch, ornament. **4** *Am Com* retailing.

detallista I *adj* **1** *(perfeccionista)* perfectionist, discriminating. **2** *(delicado)* thoughtful, considerate. **II** *nmf Com* retailer, retail trader.

detección *nf* detection.

detectar *vtr* to detect.

detective *nmf* detective. ■ **d. privado,** private detective *or* eye.

detector,-a *nm, f* detector. ■ **d. de incendios,** fire detector; **d. de mentiras,** lie detector; **d. de un radar,** radar scanner.

detención *nf* **1** *(paro)* stopping, halting, hold-up; **con d.,** carefully, thoroughly. **2** *Jur (arresto)* detention, arrest.

detener I *vtr* **1** to stop, halt. **2** *(retener)* to delay; **no quiero detenerle más,** I won't keep you any longer. **3** *Jur (arrestar)* to arrest, detain. **II detenerse** *vr* **1** to stop; **se detuvo y la miró,** he stopped and looked at her. **2** *(entretenerse)* to hang about, linger.

detenido,-a I *pp de* **detener. II** *adj* **1** *(parado)* standing still, stopped. **2** *(detallado)* detailed, thorough; **después de un d. análisis,** after a careful analysis. **III** *nm, f* detainee, person under arrest. ◆ **detenidamente** *adv* carefully, thoroughly.

detenimiento *nm* **con d.,** carefully, thoroughly.

detentar *vtr* to hold unlawfully.

detergente *adj & nm* detergent.

deteriorado,-a I *pp de* **deteriorar. II** *adj* damaged, worn.

deteriorar I *vtr (estropear)* to spoil, damage. **II deteriorarse** *vr* **1** *(estropearse)* to get damaged, wear out. **2** *(empeorar)* to get worse.

deterioro *nm* 1 (*daño*) damage; **el d. de la ropa,** wear and tear of clothes; **ir en d. de,** to harm. 2 (*empeoramiento*) deterioration, worsening; **el d. de las relaciones internacionales,** the deterioration of international relations.

determinable *adj* determinable.

determinación *nf* 1 (*decisión*) decision; **tomar una d.,** to make a resolution *or* a decision. 2 (*valor*) determination, resolution; **con d.,** determinedly.

determinado,-a **I** *pp de* **determinar.** **II** *adj* 1 (*preciso*) definite, precise; **en el día d.,** on the appointed day; **en este caso d.,** in this particular case. 2 (*resuelto*) decisive, resolute. 3 *Ling* definite; **el artículo d.,** the definite article. 4 *Mat* determinate.

determinante **I** *adj* decisive, determinant. **II** *nm Mat* determinant.

determinar **I** *vtr* 1 (*decidir*) to decide on; **han determinado salir el lunes,** they have decided to leave on Monday. 2 (*indicar*) to detect, grasp; **podemos d. las razones de su conducta,** we can see the reasons for his behaviour. 3 (*disponer*) to stipulate. 4 (*fijar*) to fix, set; **determinaron la fecha de la boda,** they fixed the date of the wedding. 5 (*ocasionar*) to bring about; **la nieve determinó el accidente,** the accident was caused by the snow; **las grandes manifestaciones determinaron un cambio en la legislación,** the massive demonstrations brought about a change in the law. **II determinarse** *vr* to bring oneself to, make up one's mind to; **no se determinaba a irse,** he couldn't make up his mind to go.

determinativo,-a *adj* determinant; *Ling* determinative.

determinismo *nm Filos* determinism.

determinista *adj & nmf Filos* determinist.

detestable *adj* detestable, respulsive; **un olor d.,** an awful smell.

detestación *nf* detestation, hatred.

detestar *vtr* to detest, hate.

detonación *nf* detonation, explosion.

detonador *nm* detonator.

detonante **I** *adj* detonating, explosive. **II** *nm* detonator; *fig* trigger; **el golpe de estado fue el d. de la crisis,** the coup d'état triggered off the crisis.

detonar *vtr* to detonate, explode.

detractar *vtr* to detract, slander.

detractor,-a **I** *adj* slanderous. **II** *nm,f* detractor, slanderer.

detrás *adv* 1 (*parte posterior*) behind, on *or* at the back (**de,** of); **el índice está d.,** the index is at the back; **ponlo d. de la mesa,** put it behind the table; **salió de d.,** she came out from behind. 2 (*después*) then, afterwards; **los jugadores salen primero y d. los entrenadores,** the players appear first and after them the coaches. 3 *fig* **d. de,** behind; **me pregunto qué hay d. de tanta amabilidad,** I wonder what is behind all his kindness. 4 *fig* **por d.,** behind the back; **hablan de él por d.,** they are talking about him behind his back.

detrimento *nm* detriment, harm; **en d. de,** to the detriment of; **sin d. de,** without detriment to.

detrito *nm*, **detritus** *nm inv Geol* detritus.

detuve *pt indef véase* **detener.**

deuda *nf Fin* debt; **contraer una d.,** to get into debt; **estoy en d. contigo,** (*monetaria*) I am in debt to you, I owe you money; (*moral*) I am indebted to you; *fig* **lo prometido es d.,** a promise is a promise. ▪ **d. del Estado,** public debt, government stock; **d. pública,** government stock, national debt.

deudo,-a *nm,f* relative.

deudor,-a **I** *adj* indebted. **II** *nm,f* debtor.

devalimiento *nm* destitution.

devaluación *nf* devaluation.

devaluar *vtr* to devaluate.

devanador *nm Am* winder, reel.

devanar **I** *vtr* (*hilo*) to wind; (*alambre*) to coil. **II devanarse** *vr* 1 *fam fig* **d. los sesos,** to rack one's brains. 2 *Cuba Méx* to double up with pain *or* laughter.

devaneo *nm* 1 (*pérdida de tiempo*) waste of time, frivolity. 2 (*amorío*) flirting.

devastación *nf* devastation.

devastador,-a **I** *adj* devastating. **II** *nm,f* devastator.

devastar *vtr* to devastate, ravage.

devengado,-a **I** *pp de* **devengar.** **II** *adj* (*sueldo*) due; (*intereses*) accrued.

devengar *vtr* (*sueldo*) to earn; (*intereses*) to earn, accrue; **ese dinero no devenga intereses,** that money does not earn any interest.

devenir¹ *nm Filos* flow of life.

devenir² *vi* to become, turn into.

devisar *vtr Méx* to stop.

devoción *nf* 1 *Rel* devotion; devoutness; **con d.,** devoutly; *fam* **Mozart no es santo de mi d.,** Mozart isn't really my cup of tea. 2 (*dedicación, afición*) devotion; **siente una gran d. por su madre,** he is devoted to his mother.

devocionario *nm* prayer book.

devolución *nf* 1 (*restitución*) giving back, return; *Com* refund, repayment; **d. del importe,** refund of money; **no se admiten devoluciones,** purchases cannot be exchanged. 2 *Jur* devolution.

devolver (*pp* **devuelto**) **I** *vtr* 1 (*restituir*) to give back, return; *Com* to refund, return, repay; **d. la mesa a su lugar,** to put the table back in its place; **d. los libros a la biblioteca,** to return the books to the library; **d. una visita,** to return a visit. 2 (*restaurar*) to restore, give back; **d. la paz a un país,** to restore peace to a country. 3 (*vomitar*) to vomit, throw *or* bring up. **II devolverse** *vr Am* to go *or* come back, return.

devorador,-a *adj* devouring; **hambre devoradora,** ravenous hunger.

devorar *vtr* 1 (*comer*) to devour. 2 (*engullir*) to eat up, gobble up. 3 *fig* (*consumir*) to devour, consume; **d. un libro,** to devour a book; **el fuego devoró la casa,** the fire devoured the house; **los celos la devoraban,** she was eaten up with jealousy.

devoto,-a **I** *adj Rel* pious, devout; **promesa devota,** devotional promise; *fig* **d. de su familia,** devoted to his family. **II** *nm, f* 1 *Rel* pious person. 2 *fig* (*seguidor*) devotee.

devuelto,-a **I** *pp de* **devolver.** **II** *adj* returned, given back; **el dinero d.,** the refunded money.

dextrina *nf Quím* dextrin, dextrina.

deyección *nf* 1 (*de volcán*) ejecta *pl.* 2 *Med* dejecta *pl,* faeces *pl.*

DF *nm abr de* **Distrito Federal,** Federal District.

DGS *nf* 1 *abr de* **Dirección General de Seguridad,** government department responsible for National Security. 2 *abr de* **Dirección General de Sanidad,** government department responsible for Public Health.

DGT *nf* 1 *abr de* **Dirección General de Tráfico,** government department responsible for Traffic. 2 *abr de* **Dirección General de Turismo,** government department responsible for Tourism.

di 1 *pt indef véase* **dar.** 2 *imperat véase* **decir.**

día *nm* 1 day; **al d. siguiente/al otro d.,** the following day; **cada d.,** each *or* every day; **de un d. para otro,** any day now; **del d.,** fresh; **d. a d.,** day by day; **hoy (en) d.,** nowadays; **¿qué d. es hoy?,** what's the date today; **todos los días,** every day, daily; **un d. sí y otro no,** every other day; *fig* **el d. de mañana,** in the future; *fig* **el d. menos pensado, cualquier d.,** when you least expect it, one of these fine days; *fig* **en su d.,** in due course; *fig* **estar al d.,** to be up to date; *fig* **poner al d.,** to bring up to date; *fig* **un buen d.,** one fine day; *fig* **un d. señalado,** a red-letter day;

fig **vivir al d.**, to live from hand to mouth. ■ **d. de page**, payday; **d. festivo**, holiday; **d. laborable**, working day; **d. lectivo**, teaching day; **d. libre**, free day, day off. **2** *(luz solar)* daytime; **a la luz del d.**, in daylight; **al caer el d.**, at dusk; **al despuntar el d.**, at dawn, at daybreak; **de d.**, by day; **durante el d.**, during the daytime; **es de d.**, it is daylight. **3** *(tiempo atmosférico)* weather, day; **hace buen/ mal d.**, it's a nice/bad day, the weather is nice/bad today.

diabetes *nf Med* diabetes.

diabético,-a *adj & nm,f* diabetic.

diablesa *nf* she-devil.

diablillo *nm fam* imp.

diablo *nm* devil, demon; *fig* **un pobre d.**, a poor devil; *fam* **¡al d. con los prejuicios!**, to hell with prejudice; *fam* **¿cómo/dónde diablos ...?**, how/where on earth ...?; how/ where the hell ...?; *fam* **este niño es un d.**, he's a little devil; *fam* **le mandó al d.**, she told him to go to hell; *fam* **¿qué diablos ...?**, what the hell ...?; *fam* **un jaleo de (todos) los diablos**, an almighty racket.

diablura *nf* mischief, naughtiness, naughty behaviour.

diabólico,-a *adj* **1** *(relativo al diablo)* devilish, diabolic. **2** *(muy intrincado)* diabolical.

diábolo *nm* diabolo.

diaconato *nm* deaconry, deaconate.

diácono *nm* deacon; **ordenar de d.**, to ordain as a deacon.

diacrónico,-a *adj* diachronic; **lingüística diacrónica**, diachronic linguistics.

diadema *nf* diadem; *(joya)* tiara.

diafanidad *nf* diaphaneity, translucence; *(transparencia)* transparence.

diáfano,-a *adj* diaphanous, translucent; *(transparente)* transparent.

diafragma *nm (gen)* diaphragm; *Fot* aperture; *Med* cap.

diagnosis *nf inv Med* diagnosis.

diagnosticar *vtr* to diagnose.

diagnóstico,-a I *adj* diagnostic. **II** *nm Med* diagnosis.

diagonal *adj & nf* diagonal; **en d.**, diagonally.

diagrama *nm* diagram. ■ *Inform* **d. de flujo**, flowchart.

dial *nm* dial.

dialectal *adj* dialectal.

dialéctica *nf* dialectic, dialectica *sing*.

dialéctico,-a *adj* dialectical; *Filos* **materialismo d.**, dialectical materialism.

dialecto *nm* dialect.

dialectología *nf* dialectology.

diálisis *nf inv* dialysis.

dialogar I *vi* to have a conversation, talk. **II** *vtr* to write in dialogue form.

diálogo *nm* dialogue, conversation.

dialtiro *adv Guat Méx* entirely, completely.

diamante *nm* diamond; **d. en bruto**, uncut diamond. ■ *fig* **bodas de d.**, diamond wedding *sing*.

diamantino,-a *adj* diamond-like, diamantine.

diametral *adj* diametrical, diametral. ◆ **diametralmente** *adv* diametrically; **d. opuesto a**, diametrically opposed to.

diámetro *nm Mat* diameter.

diana *nf* **1** *Mil* reveille; **tocar d.**, to sound reveille. **2** *(blanco)* bull's eye; **hacer d.**, to hit the bull's eye.

diantre *nm euf* hell.

diapasón *nm Mús* **1** *(instrumento)* tuning fork, diapason. **2** *(escala)* diapason, scale, range; **subir/bajar el d.**, to raise/lower the tone of one's voice. **3** *(de instrumento de cuerda)* fingerboard.

diapositiva *nf Fot* slide.

diario,-a I *adj* daily; **a d.**, daily, every day; **ropa de d.**, everyday clothes. **II** *nm* **1** *Prensa* (daily) newspaper; **d.**

de la mañana/la tarde, morning/evening newspaper. **2** *(libro, narración)* diary, journal. ■ *Náut* **d. de a bordo, d. de navegación**, logbook. ◆ **diariamente** *adv* daily, every day.

diarrea *nf Med* diarrhoea, *US* diarrhea; *fam fig* **d. verbal**, verbal diarrhoea.

diáspora *nf* diaspora.

diástole *nf Anat* diastole.

diatriba *nf* diatribe; **lanzar una d.**, to launch an attack.

dibujante *nmf* **1** sketcher, drawer; **d. de dibujos animados**, cartoonist. **2** *Téc* draughtsperson; *(hombre)* draughtsman, *US* draftsman; *(mujer)* draughtswoman, *US* draftswoman.

dibujar I *vtr* **1** *(trazar)* to draw, sketch. **2** *fig (describir)* to describe. **II dibujarse** *vr* to be outlined *or* shown; **en su rostro se dibujó la alegría**, her face showed her happiness.

dibujo *nm* **1** *(arte)* drawing, sketching. ■ **d. artístico**, artistic drawing; **d. lineal**, draughtsmanship. **2** *(figura)* drawing, sketch. ■ **dibujos animados**, cartoons. **3** *(muestra)* pattern.

dicción *nf* diction.

diccionario *nm* dictionary.

diceres *nmpl Am (murmuraciones)* gossip *sing*; *(rumores)* rumour *sing*.

dicha *nf* **1** *(hecho afortunado, suerte)* good fortune; **nunca es tarde si la d. es buena**, better late than never. **2** *(alegría)* happiness.

dicharachero,-a *adj* talkative and witty *or* funny.

dicho,-a I *pp de* **decir**. **II** *adj* said; **dicha información**, this (piece of) information; **d. de otro modo**, to pul it another way; **d. hombre**, the said man; **d. sea de paso**, let it be said in passing; **d. y hecho**, no sooner said than done; **lo d.**, what we said; **mejor d.**, or rather; **propiamente d.**, strictly speaking. **III** *nm (refrán)* saying, proverb; *prov* **del d. al hecho hay mucho trecho**, there's many a slip twixt cup and lip, it is easier said than done.

dichoso,-a *adj* **1** *(feliz)* happy, fortunate. **2** *fam (molesto)* damned; **¡este d. trabajo!**, this damned job!

diciembre *nm* December; *véase tamb* **noviembre**.

dicotomía *nf* dichotomy.

dictado I *pp de* **dictar**. **II** *nm* **1** dictation; **escribir algo al d.**, to take sth down. **2** dictados, *fig* dictates; **los dictados de la conciencia**, the dictates of conscience.

dictador,-a *nm,f* dictator.

dictadura *nf* dictatorship.

dictáfono® *nm* Dictaphone®.

dictamen *nm* **1** *(informe)* report; **la junta directiva emitió su d. final**, the board of directors gave their final report. **2** *(opinión)* opinion.

dictaminar *vi* to pronounce *or* pass judgement, give an opinion *(sobre,* on).

dictar *vtr* **1** *(texto)* to dictate. **2** *(ley)* to enact, decree; *(sentencia)* to pass. **3** *(aconsejar)* to suggest, say; **haz lo que el sentido común te dicte**, do what common sense tells you. **4** *Am (conferencia, discurso)* to give, deliver.

dictatorial *adj* dictatorial.

didáctica *nf* didactics *sing*.

didáctico,-a *adj* didactic.

diecinueve I *adj (cardinal)* nineteen; *(ordinal)* nineteenth; **a las d. horas**, at nineteen hundred hours. **II** *nm inv* **1** nineteen. **2** *(fecha)* nineteenth; *véase tamb* **ocho**.

diecinueveavo,-a I *adj* nineteenth. **II** *nm,f (de una serie)* nineteenth. **III** *nm (parte)* nineteenth; *véase tamb* **octavo,-a**.

dieciochesco,-a *adj* eighteenth-century.

dieciocho I *adj (cardinal)* eighteen; *(ordinal)* eighteenth; **a las d. horas**, at eighteen hundred hours. **II** *nm* **1** eighteen. **2** *(fecha)* eighteenth; *véase tamb* **ocho**.

dieciséis I *adj (cardinal)* sixteen; *(ordinal)* sixteenth; **a las d. horas,** at sixteen hundred hours. **II** *nm inv* **1** sixteen. **2** *(fecha)* sixteenth; *véase tamb* **ocho.**

dieciseisavo,-a I *adj* sixteenth. **II** *nm, f (de una serie)* sixteenth. **III** *nm (parte)* sixteenth; *véase tamb* **octavo,-a.**

diecisiete I *adj (cardinal)* seventeen; *(cardinal)* seventeenth; **a las d. horas,** at seventeen hundred hours. **II** *nm inv* **1** seventeen. **2** *(fecha)* seventeenth; *véase tamb* **ocho.**

diecisieteavo,-a I *adj* seventeenth. **II** *nm, f (de una serie)* seventeenth. **III** *nm (parte)* seventeenth; *véase tamb* **octavo,-a.**

diente *nm* tooth; *Arquit* toothing brick; *Téc* cog; **echar los dientes,** to teethe; *fig* **de dientes afuera,** without meaning it, hypocritically; *fig* **hablar entre dientes,** to mumble; *fig* **poner los dientes largos a algn,** to make sb green with envy; *fam* **tener buen d.,** to be a good eater. ■ *fig* **d. de ajo,** clove of garlic; **d. de leche,** milk tooth; **d. picado,** decayed tooth; **dientes postizos,** false teeth.

diera *subj imperf véase* **dar.**

diéresis *nm inv Ling* diaeresis.

diesel I *adj* diesel. **II** *nm* diesel engine.

diestra *nf* right hand; **a la d.,** on the right.

diestro,-a I *adj* **1** *lit* on the right-hand side; **estuvo sentado en la parte diestra,** he sat on the right-hand side; *fig* **a d. y siniestro,** right, left and centre, wildly. **2** *(hábil)* skilful, *US* skillfull, clever. **II** *nm Taur* bullfighter, matador. ◆ **diestramente** *adv* skillfully, *US* skillfully.

dieta¹ *nf (régimen)* diet; **estar a d.,** to be on a diet.

dieta² *nf* **1** *Pol (asamblea)* diet, assembly. **2 dietas,** *Com* expenses *or* subsistence allowance.

dietética *nf* dietetics *sing.*

dietético,-a *adj* dietetic, dietary; **médico d.,** dietician.

dietista *nmf* dietician.

diez I *adj (cardinal)* ten; *(ordinal)* tenth; **a las d.,** at ten o'clock. **II** *nm inv* **1** ten. **2** *(fecha)* tenth; *véase tamb* **ocho.**

diezmar *vtr* to decimate.

difamación *nf* defamation, slander; *(escrita)* libel.

difamador,-a I *adj* defamatory, slanderous; *(escrito)* libellous. **II** *nm, f* defamer, slanderer.

difamar *vtr* to defame, slander; *(por escrito)* to libel.

difamatorio,-a *adj* defamatory, slanderous; *(escrito)* libellous.

diferencia *nf* difference; **a d. de,** unlike; **d. de opinión,** disagreement; **hacer d. entre,** to make a distinction between.

diferenciación *nf* differentiation.

diferencial I *adj* distinguishing. **II** *nm* differential.

diferenciar I *vtr* **1** *(distinguir)* to differentiate, distinguish **(entre,** between); **los daltónicos no diferencian entre el verde y el rojo,** colour-blind people cannot tell green from red. **2** *(hacer diferente)* to make different; **¿qué te diferencia de mí?** what makes you different from me? **II diferenciarse** *vr* **1** *(distinguirse)* to differ **(de,** from), be different **(de,** from). **2** *(destacar)* to distinguish oneself, stand out; **se diferencia de las demás por sus rasgos orientales,** she stands out from the rest because of her Eastern features.

diferente I *adj* different; **d. de los demás,** different from the rest. **II** *adv* differently; **pensamos d.,** we disagree.

diferido,-a I *pp de* **diferir. II** *adj Rad TV* **retransmisión en d.,** recorded transmission.

diferir I *vtr (aplazar)* to postpone, defer, pul off; **han diferido la boda,** the wedding has been put off. **II** *vi (distinguirse)* to be different, differ **(entre, de,** from).

difícil *adj* difficult, hard; **d. de complacer,** hard to please; **d. de creer/hacer,** difficult to believe/do; **es d. que llegue hoy,** it is unlikely that she'll arrive today; **tiene un carácter d.,** he has a difficult character.

dificultad *nf (gen)* difficulty; *(problema)* trouble, problem.

dificultar *vtr* to make difficult, hinder, restrict, obstruct; **la niebla dificulta la visibilidad,** fog reduces visibility.

dificultoso,-a *adj* difficult, hard.

difteria *nm Med* diphtheria.

diftérico,-a *adj Med* diphtheric.

difuminar *vtr Arte* to blur, soften.

difundir I *vtr (luz, calor)* to diffuse; *fig (noticia, enfermedad)* to spread. **II difundirse** *vr (luz, calor) to* become diffused; *fig (noticia, enfermedad)* to spread; **se difundió la noticia de su muerte,** the news spread that he had died.

difunto,-a I *adj* late, deceased; **su difunta madre,** her late mother. **II** *nm, f* deceased. ■ **Día de los Difuntos,** All Souls' *or* Saints' Day; **misa de difuntos,** Requiem Mass.

difusión *nf* **1** *(de noticia, enfermedad)* spreading; **tener gran d.,** to be widely known. **2** *(calor, luz)* diffusion. **3** *Rad* broadcast, broadcasting.

difuso,-a *adj* **1** *(luz)* diffuse. **2** *fig (estilo, discurso)* diffuse wordy.

difusor,-a *adj* spreading, propagating; **la agencia difusora de la noticia,** the agency which made the news known.

digerible *adj* digestible.

digerir *vtr (comida)* to digest; *(información, hecho) to* assimilate.

digestión *nf* digestion. ■ **corte de d.,** sudden indigestion.

digestivo,-a I *adj* digestive. **II** *nm* digestive drink.

digital *adj* digital; **huellas digitales,** fingerprints.

dígito *nm Mat* digit.

dignarse *vr* to deign **(a,** to), condescend **(a,** to).

dignatario,-a *nm, f* dignitary.

dignidad *nf* **1** *(cualidad)* dignity. **2** *(cargo)* office, post; *(rango)* rank.

dignificante *adj* dignifying.

dignificar *vtr* to dignify.

digno,-a *adj* **1** *(merecedor)* worthy, deserving; **d. de admiración,** worthy of admiration; **d. de mención/ verse,** worth mentioning/seeing. **2** *(apropiado)* fitting, appropriate. **3** *(decoroso)* decent, good. ◆ **dignamente** *adv* with dignity.

digo *indic pres véase* **decir.**

digresión *nf* digression.

dije¹ *pt indef véase* **decir.**

dije² *nm* charm, trinket.

dilación *nf* delay, hold-up; **sin d.,** without delay.

dilapidación *nf* wasting, squandering,

dilapidar *vtr* to waste, squander.

dilatación *nf* dilation, expansion.

dilatado,-a I *pp de* **dilatar. II** *adj* **1** *(agrandado)* dilated; **pupilas dilatadas,** dilated pupils. **2** *(vasto)* vast, extensive; **un hombre de dilatada experiencia,** a man of vast experience. ◆ **dilatadamente** *adv* extensively, at length.

dilatar I *vtr* **1** *(agrandar)* to expand; **el calor dilata los cuerpos,** heat expands bodies. **2** *Med* to dilate. **3** *(prolongar)* to prolong. **4** *(retrasar)* to delay. **II dilatarse** *vr* **1** *(agrandarse)* to expand. **2** *Med* to dilate.

dilatoria *nf* delay, procrastination.

dilatorio,-a *adj* delaying.

dilema *nm* dilemma.

dilentante *nmf* dilettante.

diligencia *nf* **1** *(esmero)* diligence, care; **con d,** diligently. **2** *(gestión)* business. **3 diligencias,** *Jur* formalities; **hacer unas d.,** to go through the formalities; **instruir d.,** to start proceedings. ■ **d. previas,** inquiries.

diligenciar *vtr* to make a formal application (for).

diligente *adj* diligent.

dilucidación *nf* elucidation.

dilucidar *vtr* to elucidate, throw light (on), clarify.

diluir I *vtr* to dilute, dissolve. II **diluirse** *vr* to dilute.

diluviar *v impers Meteor* to pour down, pour with rain.

diluvio *nm* food; **el D. (Universal)**, the Flood; *fig* **un d. de consejos**, a torrent of advice; *fig* **un d. de protestas**, a storm *or* flood of rain.

diluyo *indic pres véase* **diluir.**

dimanar *vi* to emanate (**de**, from).

dimensión *nf* 1 dimension, size; **de gran d.**, very large. 2 *fig (importancia)* importance.

dimensional *adj* dimensional.

dimes y diretes *nmpl fam* 1 *(habladurías)* gossip *sing*. 2 *(discusión)* quibbling *sing*; **andar en d. y d.**, to bicker, quibble.

diminutivo,-a *adj & nm* diminutive.

diminuto,-a *adj* minute, tiny.

dimisión *nm* resignation; **presentar la d.**, to hand in one's resignation.

dimisionario,-a *adj* outgoing; **el director d.**, the outgoing director.

dimitir *vi & vtr* to resign (**de**, from); **d. de un cargo**, to give in *or* tender one's resignation.

Dinamarca *n* Denmark.

dinamarqués,-esa *adj & nm & nm, f véase* **danés,-esa.**

dinámica *nf* dynamics *sing*.

dinámico,-a *adj* dynamic.

dinamismo *nm* dynamism.

dinamita *nf* dynamite; **volar con d.**, to dynamite.

dinamitar *vtr* to dynamite, blow up.

dinamitero,-a *nm, f* dynamiter.

dínamo *nf*, **dínamo** *nf Elec* dynamo.

dinamoeléctrico,-a *adj* dynamoelectric, dynamoelectrical.

dinamometría *nf* dynamometry.

dinamómetro *nm* dynamometer.

dinar *nm Fin* dinar.

dinastía *nf* dynasty.

dinástico,-a *adj* dynastic.

dineral *nm* fortune; **ella se gastó un d. en la boda**, she spent a fortune on the wedding.

dinerillo *nm fam* small amount of money.

dinero *nm* money; **andar bien de d.**, to have plenty of money; **andar mal** *or* **escaso de d.**, to be short of money; **gente de d.** *(y sonante)*, wealthy people. ■ **d. contante** *(y sonante)*, cash; **d. efectivo** *or* **en metálico**, cash; **d. falso**, counterfeit money; **d. para gastos**, pocket money; **d. suelto**, loose change.

dinosaurio *nm* dinosaur.

dintel *nm Arquit* lintel.

diñar *vtr fam* to die; **diñarla**, to snuff it, kick the bucket.

diocesano,-a *adj & nm, f Rel* diocesan.

diócesis *nf inv Rel* diocese.

dioptría *nf Med* dioptre, *US* diopter.

dios *nm Rel* god; **a D. rogando y con el mazo dando**, God helps those who help themselves; **a la buena de D.**, any old how; **costar algo D. y ayuda**, to be very difficult, be a real hassle; **D. los cría y ellos se juntan**, birds of a feather flock together; **¡D. mío!**, my God!; **¡D. nos coja confesados!**, God help us!; **hacer algo como D. manda**, to do sth properly; **lo hice como D.**, I did my very best, I did it as best as I could; **¡por D.!**, for goodness sake!; **¡válgame D.!**, **¡vaya por D.!**, good heavens!; *fam* **armar la de D. es Cristo**, to raise hell, make an almighty racket; *fam* **ni D.**, nobody; *fam* **todo D.**, everybody.

diosa *nf* goddess.

diploma *nm* diploma.

diplomacia *nf* diplomacy.

diplomado,-a I *pp de* **diplomarse.** II *adj* qualified, with a diploma.

diplomarse *vr* to graduate.

diplomático,-a I *adj* diplomatic; **cuerpo d.**, diplomatic corps; **valija diplomática**, diplomatic bag. II *nm, f* diplomat.

díptero,-a I *adj* 1 *Zool* dipterous. 2 *Arquit* dipteral. II *nm, f Zool* dipteran; **los dípteros**, Diptera *pl.*

díptico *nm* diptych.

diptongo *nm Ling* diphthong.

diputación *nf* **d. provincial**, ≈ county council.

diputado,-a *nm, f* ≈ Member of Parliament, M.P.; *US (hombre)* Congressman; *(mujer)* Congresswoman. ■ **Cámara de Diputados**, ≈ House of Commons, *US* Congress; **d. provincial**, ≈ county councillor.

dique *nm Náut* dike. ■ **d. seco**, dry dock.

diré *fut véase* **decir.**

dire *nmf fam* boss.

dirección *nf* 1 direction; **le dieron la d. del proyecto**, they put him in charge of the project; **llevar la d. de algo**, to run sth. 2 *Cin Teat* production. 3 *(dirigentes)* management; **por orden de la d.**, by order of the management. 4 *(cargo)* directorship; *(de un partido)* leadership; *(de un colegio)* headship. 5 *(destino)* destination; **salieron con d. a Soria**, they left for Soria. 6 *(sentido)* way; **calle de d. única**, oneway street. 7 *(señas)* address. 8 *Aut Téc* steering. ■ **d. asistida**, power assisted steering.

direccional *nm Am Aut* indicator.

directivo,-a I *adj* directive; **junta directiva**, board of directors. II *nm, f* director, manager, board member. III *nf* board of directors, management.

directo,-a I *adj* direct; **emisión en d.**, live broadcast. II *nm Box* straight hit. III *nf Aut* top gear. ◆ **directamente** *adv* directly, straight away.

director,-a *nm, f (gen)* director; *Cin* (film) director; *(de colegio) (hombre)* headmaster; *(mujer)* headmistress; *Univ* principal; *(de editorial)* editor; *(de prisión)* governor. ■ *Teat* **d. de escena**, stage manager; **d. de orquesta**, conductor; **d. espiritual**, father confessor; **d. gerente**, managing director.

directorio *nm* 1 *(gobierno)* governing body. 2 *(normas)* instructions *pl*, directive. 3 *(guía)* directory, guide. 4 *(junta)* board of directors. 5 *Inform* directory.

directriz I *adj* guiding; **líneas directrices**, guidelines. II *nf* 1 directive, instruction. 2 *Mat* directrix.

dirigente I *adj* leading; **clase d.**, ruling class. II *nmf* leader; **los dirigentes de la empresa**, the company management.

dirigible *adj & nm Náut Aeronáut* dirigible.

dirigir I *vtr* 1 *(gen)* to direct. 2 *(empresa)* to manage; *(negocio, colegio)* lo run. 3 *Cin (película)* to direct; *Teat (obra)* to direct, produce; *Mús (orquesta)* to conduct; **d. un partido**, to lead a party; **d. un periódico**, to edit a newspaper; **d. una expedición/revuelta**, to head an expedition/a revolt. 4 *(guiar)* to guide; *Aut Náut* to steer. 5 *(orientar)* to aim; *(acusación)* to level; *(carta, protesta)* to address; **consejos dirigidos a los jóvenes**, advice aimed at the young; **d. los ojos hacia abajo**, to look down; **estas palabras no van dirigidas a mí**, these words are not meant for me. 6 *(esfuerzos, atención)* to concentrate. 7 *(apuntar)* to aim, point. II **dirigirse** *vr (ir)* to go; **¿hacia dónde te diriges?**, where are you heading for?; **nos dirigimos hacia el río**, we made our way towards the river. 2 *(escribir)* to write; **diríjase al apartado de correos 42**, write to P.O. Box 42. 3 *(hablar)* to address, speak; **nunca se dirige a mí**, he never speaks to me; **se dirigió a mí al hablar**, she looked at me as she spoke.

dirigismo *nm Econ* state control.

dirimente *adj* **1** *(que anula)* nullifying. **2** *(que zanja)* decisive, final; **un argumento d.,** a decisive argument.

dirimir *vtr* **1** *(anular)* to nullify, declare void. **2** *(zanjar)* to solve, end.

discar *vtr Arg Per Urug Tel* to dial.

discente 1 *adj Educ* **cuerpo d.,** student body. **II** *nmf* student.

discernimiento *nm* discernment, judgement.

discernir *vtr* to discern, distinguish, tell; **d. el bien del mal,** to tell good from evil.

disciplina *nf* **1** discipline. **2** *(asignatura)* subject.

disciplinado,-a *adj* disciplined.

disciplinar *vtr* to discipline, instruct.

disciplinario,-a *adj* disciplinary.

discípulo,-a *nm,f* **1** *(alumno)* student, pupil. **2** *(seguidor)* disciple, follower.

disco *nm* **1** disc, *US* disk. **2** *Dep* discus. **3** *Mús* record; **grabar un d.,** to make a record. **4** *Tel* dial. **5** *(semáforo)* **d. rojo/verde,** red/green light. **6** *Inform* disk. ■ **d. duro** *or* **fijo,** hard disk; **d. flexible,** floppy disk. **7** *fam (conversación repetida)* same old story.

discóbolo *nm Dep* discus thrower.

discográfico,-a *adj* **casa discográfica,** record company; **el mundo d.,** the record world.

díscolo,-a *adj* rebellious, disobedient.

disconforme *adj* in disagreement; **estoy d. con tu opinión,** I don't agree with you.

disconformidad *nf* disagreement, disconformity.

discontinuidad *nf* discontinuity, lack of continuity.

discontinuo,-a *adj* discontinuous; *Aut* **línea discontinua,** broken line.

discordancia *nf* discord.

discordante *adj* discordant; **ser la nota d.,** to clash.

discordia *nf* discord; **la manzana de la d.,** the bone of contention; **sembrar d.,** to sow discord.

discoteca *nf* **1** discotheque, nightclub. **2** *(colección de discos)* record collection, record library.

discotequero,-a *nm,f fam* nightclubber.

discreción *nf* **1** *(sensatez)* discretion, tact **2** *(a voluntad)* **a d.,** freely; **beba agua a d.,** drink water at your own discretion.

discrecional *adj* not prescribed, optional; **parada d.,** request stop; **servicio d. de autobuses,** special bus service.

discrepancia *nf* *(desacuerdo)* disagreement; *(diferencia)* discrepancy.

discrepante *adj* discrepant, conflicting.

discrepar *vi* *(disentir)* to disagree **(de,** with; **en,** on); *(diferenciarse)* to be different **(de,** from).

discreto,-a **I** *adj* **1** *(prudente)* discreet, tactful. **2** *(moderado)* average, reasonable; **de dimensiones discretas,** rather small; **un sueldo d.,** a moderate salary. **3** *(color)* sober. **4** *(prenda)* modest, sober. **II** *nm,f* discreet person.

discriminación *nf* discrimination.

discriminar *vtr* **1** *(diferenciar)* to discriminate between, distinguish. **2** *(tratar como inferior)* to discriminate against.

discriminatorio,-a *adj* discriminatory.

disculpa *nf* excuse; **dar disculpas,** to make excuses; **pedir disculpas a algn,** to apologize to sb.

disculpable *adj* excusable, forgivable.

disculpar **I** *vtr* to excuse, forgive; **discúlpame ante tus padres,** make my apologies to your parents; **disculpe mi inexperiencia,** forgive my inexperience. **II disculparse** *vr* to apologize, excuse oneself; **se disculpó por haber llegado tarde,** he apologized for arriving late.

discurrir I *vi* **1** *(pensar)* to think, ponder. **2** *fig (transcurrir)* to pass, go by; **la conferencia discurrió sin interrupciones,** the lecture went off without interruptions. **3** *fml (andar)* to walk, wander; **la gente discurría por la plaza,** people walked about the square. **II** *vtr* to think up.

discursivo,-a *adj* discursive.

discurso *nm* **1** *(conferencia)* speech; **dar** *or* **pronunciar un d.,** to make a speech. **2** *(raciocinio)* **d. mental,** mental powers. **3** *(expresión de idea)* discourse; **perder el hilo del d.,** to lose the thread of one's argument. **4** *(transcurso)* course, passing; **el d. del tiempo,** the passage of time.

discusión *nf* **1** *(charla)* discussion. **2** *(disputa)* argument; **eso no admite d.,** that's undeniable.

discutible *adj* debatable, questionable.

discutir I *vtr* **1** *(hablar)* to discuss, talk about; *(en Parlamento)* **d. on proyecto de ley,** to discuss a bill; **un personaje muy discutido,** a very controversial character. **2** *(contradecir)* to question. **II** *vi* to argue **(de,** about); **están discutiendo de política,** they're arguing about politics.

disecación *nf* *(taxidermia)* stuffing.

disecar *vtr* **1** *Med (cortar)* to dissect. **2** *(taxidermia)* to stuff. **3** *(planta)* to dry.

disección *nf véase* **disecación.**

diseminación *nf* dissemination, spreading.

diseminar *vtr* to disseminate, spread.

disensión *nf* dissension, disagreement.

disentería *nf Med* dysentery.

disentimiento *nm* dissent, disagreement.

disentir *vi* *(discrepar)* to dissent, disagree **(de,** with); *(diferir)* to differ, be different; **las dos versiones disienten,** the two versions differ.

diseñador,-a *nm,f* designer.

diseñar *vtr* to design.

diseño *nm* design.

disertación *nf* dissertation, discourse.

disertar *vi* to discourse **(sobre,** on, upon), lecture.

disfraz *nm* disguise; *(prenda)* fancy dress; **baile de disfraces,** fancy dress ball; *fig* **bajo el d. de,** under the guise of.

disfrazar I *vtr* to disguise; *fig (ideas, sentimientos)* to disguise, cover up. **II disfrazarse** *vr* to disguise oneself; **d. de pirata,** to dress up as a pirate.

disfrutar I *vi* **1** *(gozar)* to enjoy oneself; **disfruta viéndoles felices,** she enjoys seeing them happy. **2** *(poseer)* to enjoy, have **(de, -);** **disfruta de una excelente salud,** he enjoys excellent health; **¡hay que d. de la vida!,** life is for living! **II** *vtr* to get, receive; **disfrutan la pensión,** they receive a pension.

disfrute *nm* *(goce)* enjoyment; *(aprovechamiento)* benefit.

disgregación *nf* disintegration, break-up.

disgregar *vtr* **1** to disintegrate, break up. **2** *(dispersar)* to disperse.

disgustado,-a I *pp de* **disgustar. II** *adj* upset, displeased; **está disgustada con la actitud de su padre,** she is upset about her father's reaction; **están muy disgustados con el coche,** they are very unhappy with the car.

disgustar I *vtr (molestar)* to upset, make unhappy; **le disgustó mucho que no le saludaras,** he was very upset because you didn't say hello to him; **me disgusta que hables así,** it upsets me to hear you talk like that. **II disgustarse** *vr* **1** *(sentir enfado)* to get upset, be annoyed; **se disgustó porque no se lo dijiste,** she was annoyed because you didn't tell her. **2** *(enemistarse)* to quarrel.

disgusto *nm* **1** *(enfado)* annoyance, displeasure; **dar un d.,** to upset; **llevarse un d.,** to get upset; **no sabes qué d. me llevé,** you don't know how upset I was. **2** *(problema,* *disgracia)* trouble, misfortune; **no gano para disgustos,** it's just one thing after another; **¡qué d.!,** what a pity!, how sad! **3 a d.,** unwillingly; **sentirse** *or* **estar a d.,** to feel ill at ease.

disidencia *nf* dissidence, disagreement.

disidente *adj & nmf* dissident.

disidir *vi* to dissent.

disimulación *nf* pretence, dissemblance.

disimulado,-a I *pp de* **disimular. II** *adj* 1 *(persona)* sly, crafty; **hacerse el d.,** to pretend not to see *or* notice. 2 *(oculto)* hidden, concealed. ◆ **disimuladamente** *adv* *(con astucia)* craftily; *(escondiéndose)* without being seen, surreptitiously, hiddenly.

disimular *vtr* to conceal, hide; **con la pintura se disimulan las manchas,** stains don't show under the paint; **ella disimuló su pena,** she hid her sorrow.

disimulo *nm véase* **disimulación.**

disipado,-a I *pp de* **disipar. II** *adj* dissipated, debauched, wasted; **una vida disipada,** a life of debauchery.

disipar *vtr* 1 *(humos, niebla)* to drive away; *fig* to dispel; **d. esperanza,** to shatter hopes; **d. temores/dudas,** to dispel fears/doubts. 2 *(derrochar)* to squander.

dislate *nm* absurdity, nonsense.

dislexia *nf Med* dyslexia.

disléxico,-a I *adj Med* dyslexic. **II** *nm, f Med* dyslexic person.

dislocar I *vtr* 1 *(hueso)* to dislocate. 2 *fig (hechos)* to distort. **II dislocarse** *vr* to dislocate, become dislocated; **d. la muñeca,** to dislocate one's wrist.

disloque *nm fam* bedlam, madness; **cuando apareció el ídolo, aquello fue el d.,** when the idol appeared, the crowds went wild.

disminución *nf* decrease, drop; **ir en d.,** to diminish.

disminuir I *vtr* to decrease, reduce, diminish; **d. el tamaño/la velocidad,** to reduce size/speed. **II** *vi* to diminish, drop, fall; **las temperaturas han disminuido,** temperatures have dropped.

disociable *adj* dissociable.

disociación *nf* dissociation.

disociar *vtr* to dissociate.

disolubilidad *nf* solubility.

disoluble *adj* soluble, dissoluble.

disolución *nf* 1 *(desleimiento)* dissolution, dissolving. 2 *fig (anulación)* invalidation, cancellation. 3 *fig (relajación)* looseness, dissoluteness; **d. de las costumbres,** decadence. 4 *Quím* solution.

disoluto,-a I *adj* dissolute. **II** *nm, f* libertine.

disolvente *adj & nm* solvent, dissolvent.

disolver *(pp* **disuelto)** **I** *vtr* 1 to dissolve; **d. un matrimonio/el Parlamento,** to dissolve a marriage/ Parliament. 2 *(anular)* to annul. **II disolverse** *vr* to be dissolved; **la manifestación se disolvió pacíficamente,** the demonstration broke up peacefully.

disonancia *nf Mús* dissonance; *fig* disharmony.

disonante *adj Mús* dissonant; *Mús & fig* discordant.

dispar *adj* unlike, disparate.

disparada *nf Am* sudden and wild rush, stampede.

disparadero *nm* 1 *(arma)* trigger. 2 *fam* **poner a algn en el d.,** to get sb's dander up.

disparador *nm* 1 *(de arma)* trigger. 2 *Fot* shutter release. 3 *(de reloj)* escapement.

disparar I *vtr* *(arma de fuego)* to fire; *(bala, flecha)* to shoot; *Ftb* **d. el balón,** to shoot the ball; **¡nos disparan!,** they are firing at us! **II** *vi (disparatar)* to talk nonsense. **III dispararse** *vr* 1 *(arma)* to go off, fire. 2 *(precios)* to shoot up. 3 *(salir corriendo)* to fly *or* rush off. 4 *(hablar con volubilidad)* to get carried away. 5 *Méx (dinero)* to squander.

disparatado,-a I *pp de* **disparatar. II** *adj* absurd, senseless.

disparatar *vi* to talk nonsense.

disparata *nm* 1 *(desatino)* blunder, nonsense, senseless talk; **no digas disparates,** don't talk nonsense. 2 *(tontería)* foolish act; **ha sido un d. contestar así,** you were a fool to answer like that. 3 *(barbaridad)* enormity; **lo que has hecho es un d.,** you've done something terrible; **piden un d.,** they are asking an awful lot.

disparejo,-a *adj* unequal, uneven.

disparidad *nf* disparity, difference.

disparo *nm* 1 shot; **se oían disparos,** firing *or* shots *or* shooting could be heard. 2 *Dep* shot; **d. a puerta,** shot.

dispendio *nm* splurge.

dispensa *nf* dispensation, exemption.

dispensar *vtr* 1 *(otorgar)* to give, grant; **dispensó una palabra de agradecimiento,** he said a few words of thanks. 2 *(disculpar)* to pardon, forgive; **dispense la molestia,** I'm sorry to bother you. 3 *(eximir)* to exempt, free from an obligation; **me dispensaron (de) la gimnasia,** I was exempted from gym class.

dispensario *nm Med* dispensary.

dispersar I *vtr* 1 *(separar)* to disperse; *(esparcir)* to scatter; **d. la atención/los esfuerzos,** to spread one's attention/efforts. 2 *Mil* to disperse, rout. **II dispersarse** *vr* to disperse, scatter.

dispersión *nf (separación)* dispersion; *(esparcimiento)* scattering.

disperso,-a *adj (separado)* dispersed; *(esparcido)* scattered.

displicencia *nf* indifference, apathy; **con d.,** half-heartedly.

displicente *adj* indifferent, uninterested; **con un tono d.,** showing no emotion, coldly.

disponer *(pp* **dispuesto)** **I** *vtr* 1 *(arreglar)* to arrange, set out; **dispon las sillas para que todos vean,** arrange the chairs so that everyone can see. 2 *(preparar)* to prepare, get ready. 3 *(ordenar)* to order; **el alcalde dispuso suspender las fiestas,** the Mayor ordered the suspension of the festivities; **la ley dispone que,** the law stipulates that. **II** *vi* 1 *(tener)* to have at one's disposal; **d. de dinero/ tiempo,** to have money/time available; **los medios de que dispone,** the means available to him. 2 *(usar)* to make use of, do as one wants with. **III disponerse** *vr* 1 *(prepararse)* to prepare, get ready; **se disponía a marcharse, cuando sonó el teléfono,** he was about to leave when the phone rang. 2 *(mentalmente)* to be prepared, expect; **no me dispongo a perder,** I'm not prepared to lose.

disponibilidad *nf* availability; *Fin* liquidity; *Com* available stock.

disponible *adj* available.

disposición *nf* 1 *(uso)* disposition, disposal; **a la d. de,** at the disposal of; **a su d.,** at your disposal *or* service; **tener la libre d. de algo,** to have sth entirely at one's disposal. 2 *(estado de ánimo)* disposition, frame of mind; *(colocación)* arrangement, layout; **este niño no está en d. de salir,** this child isn't up to going out. 3 *(orden)* order, law; **las disposiciones vigentes,** current legislation. 4 *(aptitud)* talent, gift; **nunca he tenido d. para el dibujo,** I have never been any good at drawing.

dispositivo *nm* device, gadget.

dispuesto,-a I *pp de* **disponer. II** *adj* 1 *(a punto)* ready; **¿estamos todos dispuestos para salir?,** are we all ready to go? 2 *(decidido)* determined; **está d. a hablar,** he is determined to talk. 3 *(hábil)* bright, clever, capable. 4 *(que se presta)* willing, prepared; **está poco d. a ayudar,** he is reluctant to help; **estoy d. a lo que sea para conseguirlo,** I'll do anything to get it; **la empresa no está dispuesta a ofrecer más dinero,** the company is not prepared to offer more money; **siempre está d. a**

hacer de secretaria, he is always willing to act as secretary. **5** *(establecido)* established, stipulated; **según lo d. por la ley,** in accordance with what the law stipulates.

disputa *nf* dispute, argument.

disputar 1 *vtr* **1** *(discutir)* to argue. **2** *(oponerse a)* to dispute. **3** *(pretender) (premio)* to contend for. **4** *Dep (partido)* to play. **II disputarse** *vr* **1** *(pretender)* to contend for; **cinco aspirantes se disputan el puesto,** there are five candidates contending for the position. **2** *Dep* to be played; **el partido se disputa el jueves,** the match will be played on Thursday.

disquete *nm Inform* diskette, floppy disk.

disquisición *nf* **1** disquisition. **2 disquisiciones,** digressions; *fam* **d. filosóficas,** rambling *sing.*

distancia *nf* **1** *(espacio)* distance; **a d.,** from a distance; **guardar las distancias,** to keep one's distance. **2** *fig (diferencia)* difference, gap; **acortar distancias,** to bridge the gap; **hay gran d. de una cosa a la otra,** the two things are quite different. **3** *Fot* **d. focal,** focal length.

distanciado,-a I *pp de* **distanciar.** II *adj* distant, separated; *fig* **me he distanciado mucho de mi familia,** I've distanced myself from my family.

distanciamiento *nm* distancing, distance.

distanciar I *vtr* **1** to separate, distance. **2** *(poner a distancia)* to set apart *or* at a distance, make a gap between. **II distanciarse** *vr* to become separated; *fig* **distaociarse de los amigos,** to distance oneself from one's friends.

distante *adj* distant, far-off.

distar *vi* **1** *(estar a)* to be distant *or* away; **dista sesenta kilómetros del centro,** it's sixty kilometres away from the centre. **2** *fig (ser diferente)* to be far from; **dista mucho de ser perfecto,** it's far from (being) perfect.

distender *vtr fig* to ease, relax; **d. las relaciones internacionales,** to ease international relations.

distensión *nf* **1** *Med (lesión)* strain. **2** *(calma)* easing, relaxation, *Pol* **d. de las relaciones,** détente.

distinción *nf* **1** distinction; **a d. de,** unlike; **sin d. de,** irrespective of. **2** *(honor)* distinction; **d. de honor,** honour; **de gran d.,** highly distinguished. **3** *(deferencia)* deference, respect; **hacer una d. con algn,** to treat sb with special deference. **4** *(elegancia)* refinement.

distinguido,-a I *pp de* **distinguir.** II *adj* **1** *(ilustre)* distinguished. **2** *(elegante)* elegant; *(culto)* cultured, of distinction.

distinguir I *vtr* **1** *(diferenciar)* to distinguish. **2** *(ver)* to see, make out; **pude distinguirlo entre la multitud,** I saw *or* distinguished him among the crowd. **3** *(caracterizar)* to mark, distinguish. **4** *(mostrar preferencia)* to single out. **5** *(honrar)* to honour, *US* honor. II *vi (diferenciar)* to discriminate. III **distinguirse** *vr* **1** *(sobresalir)* to distinguish oneself, stand out. **2** *(verse)* to be visible.

distintivo,-a I *adj* distinctive, distinguishing; **rasgo d.,** characteristic feature. II *nm* **1** *(señal)* distinctive sign *or* mark. **2** *(característica)* characteristic, emblem; **el d. de una profesión,** the emblem *or* symbol of a profession.

distinto,-a *adj (diferente)* different; *(varios)* various; **comimos distintos tipos de queso y patés,** we ate various sorts of cheese and pâté.

distorsión *nf* **1** *Med* sprain. **2** distortion; *fig* **la d. de la verdad,** distortion of the truth.

distracción *nf* **1** *(pasatiempo)* pastime, hobby; *(recreo)* recreation, entertainment, relaxation; **en Barcelona hay distracciones para todos los gustos,** Barcelona offers something for everyone; **mi d. favorita es la música,** music is my favourite pastime. **2** *(error)* slip, oversight; **fue una d. por mi parte,** it was an oversight on my part. **3** *(descuido)* distraction, absent-mindedness; **en un momento de d. cogitus llaves,** in a moment of absent-mindedness I took your keys.

distraer I *vtr* **1** *(atención)* to distract; **está prohibido d. al conductor,** do not distract the driver; **por lo menos, te distrae de tus preocupaciones,** at least it takes your mind off your worries. **2** *(divertir)* to entertain, amuse. **3** *fam fig (robar)* to embezzle. II **distraerse** *vr* **1** *(divertirse)* to amuse oneself. **2** *(entretenerse)* to relax, pass the time; **necesitas distraerte,** you need to relax. **3** *(abstraerse)* to let one's mind wander; **te distraes mucho,** you are so absent-minded.

distraído,-a I *pp de* **distraer.** II *adj* **1** *(divertido)* entertaining, fun. **2** *(inatento)* absent-minded. **3** *Chi Méx (desaseado)* slovenly, unkempt. III *nm, f* absent-minded person; **hacerse el d.,** to pretend not to notice *or* know.

distribución *nf* **1** distribution. **2** *(entrega)* delivery; **la d. del correo,** mail delivery. **3** *(de una casa, un jardín)* layout.

distribuidor,-a I *adj* distributing, distributive. II *nm, f* **1** distributor; **los distribuidores de películas,** the film distributors. **2** *Com* wholesaler.

distribuir *vtr* to distribute, deliver; **d. el agua y la electricidad,** to supply gas and electricity; **d. el trabajo entre los miembros del equipo,** to share the work among everybody in the team.

distributivo,-a *adj* distributive.

distrito *nm* district. ■ **d. postal,** postal district.

disturbar *vtr* to disturb.

disturbio *nm* riot, disturbance; **disturbios callejeros,** riots.

disuadir *vtr* to dissuade, deter.

disuasión *nf* dissuasion, deterrence.

disuasivo,-a *adj,* **disuasorio,-a** *adj* dissuasive, deterrent.

disuelto,-a *pp de* **disolver.**

disyuntiva *nf* alternative.

dita *nf Am* debt.

DIU *nm Med abr de* **dispositivo intrauterino,** intrauterine device, IUD.

diuresis *nf Med* diuresis.

diurético,-a *adj & nm Med* diuretic.

diurno,-a *adj* daytime, daily; *(planta)* diurnal.

divagación *nf* digression.

divagar *vi* to digress, wander.

diván *nm Mueb* divan, couch.

díver *adj inv fam* great fun.

divergencia *nf* divergence; **d. de opiniones,** diverging opinions.

divergente *adj* divergent, diverging.

divergir *vi* to diverge.

diversidad *nf* diversity, variety.

diversificación *nf* diversification.

diversificar I *vtr* to diversify, vary. II **diversificarse** *vr* to be diversified *or* varied.

diversión *nf* fun, amusement.

diverso,-a *adj (diferente)* different; *(varios)* several, various; **trajo diversos regalos para los niños,** he brought various presents for the children.

divertido,-a I *pp de* **divertir.** II *adj* **1** *(de risa)* amusing, funny; **una película divertida,** a funny film. **2** *(entretenido)* fun, entertaining; **un tipo muy divertido,** a very amusing chap. **3** *Am (ebrio)* tipsy.

divertir I *vtr* to amuse, entertain. II **divertirse** *vr* to enjoy oneself, have a good time; **por divertirme,** for fun; **¡que te diviertas!,** enjoy yourself!, have fun!

dividendo *nm Mat Com* dividend.

dividir *vtr* to divide, split (**en,** into); **la guerra dividió al país,** the war divided the country; **los Andes dividen Chile de Argentina,** the Andes separate Chile from Argentina; **15 dividido entre 3 son 5,** 15 divided by 3 is 5. **II dividirse** *vr* to divide, split up; **el partido se dividió en dos facciones,** the party split into two factions.

divieso *nm* boil, furuncle.

divinidad *nf* 1 *Filos* God, divinity. 2 *(dios pagano)* deity. 3 *fam* **¡qué d.!,** how gorgeous!

divinización *nf* deification.

divinizar *vtr* to deify.

divino,-a *adj* 1 divine. 2 *fam (bonito)* wonderful, fantastic, gorgeous; **tienen una casa divina,** they have a fantastic house.

divisa *nf* 1 *(emblema)* symbol, emblem. 2 *Taur* bull owner's emblem. 3 *Herald* device, motto. 4 **divisas,** *Com* foreign currency *sing.*

divisar *vtr* to make out, discern.

divisibilidad *nf* divisibility.

divisible *adj* dividable; *Mat* divisible.

división *nf* division; **hay d. de opiniones,** opinions are divided; *Ftb* **primera/segunda d.,** first/second division. ■ *Mil* **d. acorazada** *or* **blindada,** armoured division.

divisor,-a I *adj* dividing. II *nm* divider; *Mat* divisor. ■ **máximo común d.,** highest common factor, *US* highest common denominator.

divisorio,-a I *adj* dividing. II *nf Geog* divide.

divo,-a *nm,f* star; **es una diva (de ópera),** she is a prima donna.

divorciado,-a I *pp de* **divorciar.** II *adj* divorced. III *nm,f* *(hombre)* divorcé; *(mujer)* divorcée.

divorciar I *vtr* to divorce. II **divorciarse** *vr* to get divorced; **se divorció de él,** she divorced him, she got a divorce from him.

divorcio *nm* 1 divorce. 2 *fig (discrepancia)* discrepancy; **hay un d. entre lo que dice y lo que hace,** he says one thing and does another.

divulgación *nf* 1 *(difusión)* disclosure, spreading; **la d. de una noticia,** the publication of a news item. 2 *(de conocimientos)* popularization.

divulgador,-a *adj* 1 *(difusor)* broadcasting. 2 *(propagador)* popularizing.

divulgar *vtr* 1 *(difundir)* to disclose, reveal; *Rad* to broadcast; **las emisoras de radio divulgaron la noticia,** the radio stations broadcast the news. 2 *(propagar)* to popularize.

Djibouti *n* Djibouti, Jibouti.

D.L. *abr de* **depósito legal,** legal deposit, bond.

D.m. *abr de* **Dios mediante,** God willing.

DNI *nm abr de* **Documento Nacional de Identidad,** Identity Card, ID card.

do *nm Mús (de solfa)* doh, do; *(de escala diatónica)* C. ■ **do de pecho,** high C; *fam* **dar el do de pecho,** to surpass oneself.

doberman *nm Zool* Doberman (pinscher).

dobladillo *nm Cost* hem.

doblaje *nm Cin* dubbing.

doblar I *vtr* 1 *(duplicar)* to double; **me dobla la edad,** he is twice as old as I am. 2 *(plegar)* to fold *or* turn up. 3 *(torcer)* to bend. 4 *Cin Teat (actor, actriz)* to double (**a,** for); *(película)* to dub. 5 *(esquina)* to go round. 6 *Méx (matar a disparos)* to shoot. II *vi* 1 *(girar)* to turn; **dobla a la derecha/izquierda,** turn right/left. 2 *(campanas)* to toll. 3 *Cin Teat* to play two roles, double. III **doblarse** *vr* 1 *(plegarse)* to fold. 2 *(torcerse)* to bend. 3 *(someterse)* to yield, give in.

doble I *adj* double; **arma de d. filo,** double-edged weapon; **una frase de d. sentido,** a sentence with a double meaning. II *nm* 1 double; **gana el d. que tú,** she earns twice as much as you do. 2 *Cost (dobladillo)* hem. 3 *(toque de campana)* toll. III *nmf Cin* stunt man, double. III *nf Cin* stunt woman, double. IV *adv* double; **d. peor/mejor,** twice as bad/good; *fig* **túoyes d.,** you must be imagining things. ◆ **doblemente** *adv* 1 *(muy)* doubly. 2 *fig (con hipocresía)* insincerely, two-facedly.

doblegar I *vtr* 1 *(doblar)* to bend. 2 *fig (ceder)* to make give in. II **doblegarse** *vr* to give in.

dobles *nmpl Dep* doubles; **d. femeninos/masculinos,** ladies'/men's doubles.

doblez I *nm (pliegue)* fold. II *nm & f fig* two-facedness, deceitfulness; **ser una persona sin d.,** to be an honest *or* guileless person.

doc *abr de* **documento,** document, doc.

doce I *adj (cardinal)* twelve; *(ordinal)* twelfth; **d. casas,** twelve houses; **el siglo d./XII,** the twelfth/12th century. II *nm inv* 1 twelve. 2 *(fecha)* twelfth; *véase tamb* **ocho.**

doceavo,-a I *adj* twelfth. II *nm,f (de una serie)* twelfth. III *nm (parte)* twelfth; *véase tamb* **octavo,-a.**

docena *nf* dozen; **a docenas,** by the dozen; *fig* **d. de fraile,** baker's dozen.

docencia *nf* teaching; **siempre le ha gustado la d.,** he has always liked teaching.

docente I *adj* teaching; **centros docentes,** educational centres; **personal d.,** teaching staff. II *nmf* teacher.

dócil *adj* docile, obedient.

docilidad *nf* docility, obedience.

dock *nm* 1 dock. 2 **docks,** warehouse *sing.*

docto,-a I *adj* learned. II *nm, f* learned person, connoisseur. ◆ **doctamente** *adv* learnedly.

doctor,-a *nm, f* doctor; **d. en filosofía,** doctor in *or* of philosophy; **la doctora le recetó antibióticos,** the doctor prescribed antibiotics for him.

doctorado *nm Univ* doctorate, PhD.

doctoral *adj* doctoral; **un tono d.,** a pedantic way of speaking.

doctorarse *vr Univ* to take *or* receive one's doctorate.

doctrina *nf* doctrine, teachings *pl.*

doctrinal *adj* doctrinal.

doctrinario,-a *adj & nm,f* doctrinaire.

documentación *nf* documentation; **la d. del coche,** the car papers; **la policía le pidió la d.,** the police asked to see his papers.

documentado,-a I *pp de* **documentar.** II *adj* 1 documented, researched; **una película bien documentada,** a well-researched film. 2 *fam (enterado)* informed.

documental *adj & nm Cin TV* documentar.

documentar I *vtr* 1 *(libro, informe)* to document. 2 *(persona)* to give information. II **documentarse** *vr* to research (**sobre, -**), get information (**sobre,** about *or* on).

documento *nm* document. ■ **d. nacional de identidad,** identity card.

dodecafónico,-a *adj Mús* dodecaphonic.

dogal *nm* 1 *(de caballo)* halter. 2 *(soga de reo)* hangman's noose.

dogma *nm* dogma.

dogmático,-a *adj & nm,f* dogmatic.

dogmatismo *nm* dogmatism.

dogmatizar *vi* to dogmatize.

dogo *nm Zool* bulldog.

dólar *nm* dollar.

dolencia *nf* ailment; **achaques y dolencias,** aches and pains.

doler I *vi* 1 to hurt, ache; **me duele la muela/la cabeza,** I've got toothache/a headache; **me duelen los ojos,** my eyes hurt. 2 *(sentir pena)* to feel hurt; **estar dolido,** to be hurt; **le duele que no le hayas invitado,** he is hurt that you didn't invite him. 3 *(sentir pesar)* to be sorry *or* sad; **me duele tener que echarte,** I'm sorry to have to throw you out. II **dolerse** *vr* 1 *(quejarse)* to complain (**de,** about). 2 *(arrepentirse)* to regret (**de,** for). 3 *(sentir pena)* to suffer (**de,** for)

dolmen *nm* dolmen.

dolo *nm Jur* fraud.

Dolomitas *npl* Dolomites.

dolor *nm* 1 *Med* pain, ache. ■ **d. de cabeza,** headache; **d. de muelas,** toothache. 2 *(padecimiento moral)* grief, sorrow; *(pesar)* regret.

dolorido,-a *adj* 1 *(dañado)* sore, aching. 2 *(apenado)* sad, grieved, hurt.

dolorosa *nf* 1 *Rel* Our Lady of Sorrow. 2 *arg (en restaurante)* bill; **tráeme la d.,** what's the damage?

doloroso,-a *adj* painful.

doma *nf* taming; *(de coballos)* breaking in.

domador,-a *nm,f* tamer. ■ **d. de caballos,** horse breaker.

domar *vtr (animal)* to tame; *(caballo)* to break in; *fig* to break in.

domesticable *adj* trainable.

domesticación *nf* domestication, taming.

domesticar *vtr* to domesticate; *(animal)* to tame; **d. leones para un circo,** to train lions for a circus.

doméstico,-a I *adj* domestic; **animal d.,** pet; **servicio d.,** domestic help. II *nm,f* domestic, house-hold servant.

domiciliación *nf Fin* payment by standing order.

domiciliado,-a I *pp de* **domiciliar.** II *adj* residing, living.

domiciliar *vtr* 1 *Fin* to pay by standing order. 2 to house.

domiciliaro,-a *adj* house; *Jur* **arresto d.,** house arrest.

domicilio *nm* home, residence; **escriba el nombre y el d.,** write your name and address; **servicio a d.,** house deliveries; **sin d. fijo,** of no fixed abode *or* residence. ■ **d. fiscal,** registered office.

dominación *nf* domination, dominion.

dominante *adj* 1 *(que domina)* dominant, dominating. 2 *(déspota)* domineering.

dominar I *vtr* 1 *(tener bajo el poder)* to dominate, rule. 2 *fig (contener)* to control; **d. el fuego,** to contain the fire; **d. la ira/los nervios,** to control one's rage/nerves. 3 *fig (conocer a fondo)* to master; **d. el francés,** to have a good command of French; **d. la fotografía,** to be very good at photography; **los estudiantes tienen que d. el verbo 'to be',** students have to master the verb 'to be'. 4 *(ver)* to see; **desde el balcón se domina la llanura,** from the balcony one can see the plain. 5 *(tener bajo el control)* to overpower, overcome; **le dominó la rabia,** he was overcome by rage. II *vi* 1 *(imperar sobre personas o cosas)* to dominate. 2 *(resaltar)* to stand out. 3 *fig (abundar)* to predominate, dominate; **el azul era el color que dominaba,** blue was the predominant colour. III **dominarse** *vr* to control oneself; **tuve que dominarme para no contestarle mal,** I had to restrain myself from answering him angrily.

domingas *nfpl arg* boobs.

domingo *nm inv* Sunday; **el traje de los domingos,** one's Sunday best. ■ **D. de Resurrección** *or* **Pascua,** Easter Sunday; *véase tamb* **viernes.**

dominguejo *nm Am* poor devil, wretch.

dominguero,-a I *adj* Sunday. II *nm,f fam* weekend driver.

Dominica *n* Dominica.

dominical *adj* Sunday; **periódico d.,** Sunday newspaper.

dominicano,-a *adj & nm, f* Dominican; **República Dominicana,** Dominican Republic.

dominico,-a *adj Rel* Dominican.

dominio *nm* 1 dominion; *(poder)* control, power; **d. de sí mismo,** self-control; **d. de un idioma,** command of a language; **d. del mar,** command of the sea; **ejercer d.,** to exert control; **del d. público,** to be public knowledge. 2 *(condominio)* domain. 3 *(ámbito)* scope, sphere; **el d. de la ciencia,** the field *or* sphere of science. 4 **dominios,** dominions; **los d. de la Commonwealth,** the dominions of the Commonwealth.

dominó *nm,* **dómino** *nm* 1 *(juego)* dominoes *pl*; *(fichas)* set of dominoes. 2 *(disfraz)* domino.

Don Quijote *nm Lit* Don Quixote.

don[1] *nm* 1 *(regalo)* present, gift. 2 *(talento)* natural gift, talent; **tiene el d. de sacarme de quicio,** he has a knack for getting my goat up. ■ **d. de gentes,** gift of the gab.

don[2] *(tratamiento)* **Señor D. Jesús Ayerra,** Mr Jesús Ayerra; **buenos días D. Jesús,** good morning, Mr Ayerra; **D. Fulano de Tal,** Mr So-and-So; **d. nadie,** a nobody.

donación *nf* donation.

donaire *nm* 1 *(garbo)* grace, elegance. 2 *(ocurrencia graciosa)* wisecrack, witticism.

donante *nmf* donor; *Med* **d. de sangre,** blood donor.

donar *vtr fml* to donate, give; **d. sangre,** to give blood.

donativo *nm* donation.

doncella *nf lit arc* 1 *(mujer joven)* maid, maiden. 2 *(criada)* maid, housemaid.

doncellez *nf* maidenhood.

dónde *adv interr* where; **¿de d. eres?,** where are you from?; **no sé d. le vi,** I can't remember where I saw him; **¿por d. se va a la playa?,** which way is it to the beach?

donde *adv rel* where, in which; **a** *or* **en d.,** where; **de** *or* **desde d.,** from where, wherever you want; **está d. lo dejaste,** it is right where you left it; **la casa d. nací,** the town where *or* in which I was born; **la fiesta d. nos conocimos,** the party where we met; *fam* **d. las dan las toman,** tit for tat; *fam* **¡vaya por d.!,** what do you know?

dondequiera *adv* everywhere; **d. que vaya,** wherever I go.

dondiego *nm Bot* marvel-of-Peru, four-o'clock. ■ **d. de día,** morning glory; **d. de noche,** marvel-of-Peru, four-o'clock.

donjuán *nm* Don Juan, womanizer; **tiene fama de d.,** he has reputation for being a Don Juan *or* a Casanova.

donoso,-a *adj desus* 1 *(gracioso)* graceful, elegant. 2 *(ocurrente)* witty; *irón* **donosa ocurrencia,** what a bright idea.

donostiarra I *adj* of *or* from San Sebastián. II *nmf* native of San Sebastián.

doña *nf (tratamiento)* **Señora D. Mercedes Torres,** Mrs Mercedes Torres; **D. Mercedes ha llegado,** Mrs Torres has arrived.

dopar *vtr Dep* to dope, drug.

doping *nm Dep* doping.

doquier *adv,* **doquiera** *adv lit* **por d. que,** everywhere.

dorada *nf (pez)* gilthead bream.

dorado,-a I *pp de* **dorar.** II *adj* golden; **con la piel dorada por el sol,** suntanned; **los años dorados de la juventud,** the golden years of youth. III *nm* 1 *Téc* gilding. 2 *(pez)* dorado. 3 **dorados,** gilt objects; **crema para limpiar d.,** metal polish.

dorar *vtr* 1 *(cubrir con oro)* to gild; *fig* **d. la píldora,** to sugar the pill. 2 *(tostar)* to brown.

dórico,-a I *adj* Dorian; *Arquit* **orden d.,** Doric order. II *nm* Doric.

dormido,-a I *pp de* **dormir.** II *adj* asleep; *(soñoliento)* sleepy; **quedarse d.,** to fall asleep; **tengo la pierna dormida,** my leg has gone numb.

dormilón,-ona I *adj fam* sleepyheaded. II *nm, f* sleepyhead.

dormir I *vi* to sleep; **¿dormiste bien?,** did you sleep well?; **d. con algn,** to sleep with sb; **tener ganas de d.,** to feel sleepy; *fam* **d. como un lirón, d. a pierna suelta,** to sleep like a log; *fam fig* **no te duermas** *or* **te quitarán el puesto,** don't let the grass grow under your feet. II *vtr* to put to sleep; **d. la siesta,** to have an afternoon nap; *fam* **d. la mona,** to sleep off. III **dormirse** *vr* to fall asleep, nod off; **duérmete,** go to sleep; **se me ha dormido el brazo,** my arm has gone to sleep; *fig* **d. en los laureles,** to rest on one's laurels.

dormitar *vi* to doze, snooze.

dormitorio *nm* 1 (*de una casa*) bedroom. 2 (*de uncolegio, residencia*) dormitory.

dorsal I *adj* dorsal, spinal, back. **II** *nm Dep* number.

dorso *nm* back; **instrucciones al d.,** instructions over; **ponga la fecha en el d.,** write the date on the back; **véase al d.,** see overleaf. ■ **el d. de la mano,** the back of the hand.

dos I *adj* 1 (*cardinal*) two; **d. amigos,** two friends; (*ordinal*) second; **el capítulo d.,** the second chapter. **II** *nm inv* (*gen*) two; (*fecha*) second; **de d. en d.,** in twos; **el d. de octubre,** the second of October; **entre (los) d.,** between the two of us *or* you *or* them; **los d.,** both; **para nosotros/ vosotros d.,** for both of us/you; **¿qué número quieres?** **—el d.,** what number do you want? —number two; *fam* **cada d. por tres,** every other minute; *fam* **como d. y d. son cuatro,** without any doubt; *fam* **en un d. por tres,** in a flash; *véase tamb* **ocho.**

doscientos,-as *adj & nm, f* (*cardinal*) two hundred; (*ordinal*) two hundredth.

dosel *nm* canopy.

dosificación *nf* dosage.

dosificar *vtr* 1 (*gen*) to dose. 2 (*esfuerzos, energías*) to measure.

dosis *nf inv* dose; **en pequeñas d.,** in small doses.

dossier *nm* dossier.

dotación *nf* 1 (*acción*) endowment. 2 (*personal*) personnel, staff; **la d. del barco,** the crew of the ship.

dotado,-a I *pp de* **dotar.** **II** *adj* equipped; **d. de un moderno equipo,** provided with modern equipment; *fam* (*chico*) **bien d.,** good looking; *vulg* (*órganos genitales*) well-hung.

dotar *vtr* 1 (*dar dote*) to give a dowry. 2 (*proveer*) to endow, provide; **d. de,** to provide with; **está dotado de un gran oído musical,** he's got an excellent ear for music; **d. una oficina,** (*de personal*) to staff an office; (*de dinero*) to assign money to an office.

dote *nf* 1 (*bienes*) dowry. 2 **dotes,** gift *sing*, talent *sing*; **tiene d. para la danza,** he is a gifted dancer.

doy *indic prec véase* **dar.**

DP *nm abr de* **distrito postal,** postal district, PD.

dpt. *abr de* **departamento,** department, Dept.

Dr. *abr de* **doctor,** doctor, Dr.

Dra. *abr de* **doctora,** doctor, Dr.

dracma *nf Fin* drachma.

draconiano,-a *adj fig* Draconian, harsh.

draga *nf* 1 (*máquina*) dredge. 2 (*barco*) dredger.

dragado,-a I *pp de* **dragar.** **II** *nm* dredging.

dragar *vtr* to dredge.

drago *nm Bot* dragon tree.

dragón *nm* 1 (*fiera*) dragon. 2 *Hist* (*soldado*) dragoon.

dragonear *Am vi* 1 to pose (**de,** as). 2 to boast.

drama *nm* drama.

dramático, a *adj* dramatic; **autor d.,** playwright; *fam* **una situación dramática,** a dramatic situation.

dramatismo *nm* 1 drama. 2 (*exageración*) dramatization.

dramatizar *vtr Lit Teat* to dramatize.

dramaturgia *nf Teat* dramatics *sing*.

dramaturgo,-a *nm, f Teat* playwright, dramatist.

dramón *nm fam* melodrama.

draque *nm Am* drink made of water, liquor, sugar and nutmeg.

drástico,-a *adj* drastic.

drenaje *nm* drainage; **colector de d.,** main drain.

drenar *vtr* to drain.

Dresde *n* Dresden.

driblar *vi Dep* to dribble.

dril *nm* 1 (*tela*) drill, drilling. 2 (*mono*) drill.

drive *nm Dep* drive.

droga *nf* 1 (*limpieza*) household product; (*pintura*) paint. 2 (*narcótico*) drug. ■ **d. blanda,** soft drug; **d. dura,** hard drug. 3 *Am* (*deuda*) debt; (*trampa*) trap. 4 *Am* medicine, medication.

drogadicto,-a *adj & nm, f* drug addict.

drogado,-a I *pp de* **drogar.** **II** *adj* drugged (up). **III** *nm, f* drug addict.

drogar I *vtr* to drug. **II drogarse** *vr* to drug oneself, take drugs.

drogata *nmf arg*, **drogota** *nmf arg* junkie.

droguería *nf* 1 hardware and household goods shop. 2 *Am* (*farmacia*) chemist.

droguero,-a *nm, f Am* swindler.

dromedario *nm Zool* dromedary.

druida,-esa *nm, f* druid.

DSE *abr de* **Dirección de la Seguridad del Estado.**

dto. *abr de* **descuento,** discount.

dual *adj* dual; *TV* **sistema d.,** dual system.

dualidad *nf* duality.

dualismo *nm* dualism.

dualista *adj* dualistic.

dubitativo,-a *adj* doubtful.

Dublín *n* Dublin.

dublinés,-esa I *adj* of *or* from Dublin. **II** *nm, f* Dubliner.

ducado *nm* 1 *Hist* dukedom, duchy. 2 *arc* (*moneda*) ducat.

ducal *adj* duke's, ducal.

ducha *nf* shower; **darse/tomar una d.,** to take/have a shower; *fam fig* **una d. de agua fría,** a hard blow, a kick in the teeth.

duchar I *vtr* to shower, give a shower. **II ducharse** *vr* to shower, have *or* take a shower.

ducho,-a *adj* expert; **estar d. en la materia,** to be well versed in the subject.

duco *nm* lacquer; **pintar al d.,** to lacquer.

dúctil *adj* ductile.

ductilidad *nm* ductility.

duda *nf* doubt; **no cabe d., no hay d.,** (there is) no doubt; **poner algo en d.,** to question sth; **sacar a algn de dudas,** to dispel sb's doubts; **salir de dudas,** to shed one's doubts; **sin d.,** no doubt, without a doubt; **sin la menor d.,** without the slightest doubt.

dudar I *vi* 1 (*gen*) to doubt, have doubts. 2 (*vacilar*) to hesitate; **dudaba entre ir** *or* **quedarme,** I hesitated whether to go *or* to stay; **estoy dudando si ir** *or* **no,** I am not sure whether to go or not. 3 (*desconfiar*) **d. de algn,** to suspect sb; **¿dudas de mi palabra?,** don't you trust me? **II** *vtr* to doubt; **dudo que llegue a tiempo,** I doubt she can come on time; **dudo que sea verdad,** I doubt that's true; **lo dudo,** I doubt it; **no lo dudé ni un momento,** I didn't think twice (about it).

dudoso,-a *adj* 1 (*incierto*) uncertain, doubtful. 2 (*indeciso*) undecided, hesitant; **estoy d.,** I'm hesitant. 3 (*poco honrado*) dubious, suspect. 4 (*poco seguro*) questionable.

duela *nf* stave.

duelo[1] *nm* (*combate*) duel; **batirse en d.,** to fight a duel.

duelo[2] *nm* 1 (*dolor*) grief, affliction. 2 (*luto*) mourning.

duende *nm* 1 (*espíritu*) goblin, elf. 2 (*nomo*) gnome. 3 (*encanto misterioso*) magic, charm; **Granada es una ciudad con d.,** Granada is a magical city; **para cantar flamenco hay que tener d.,** a flamenco singer must have a certain magnetism.

dueña *nf* 1 (*gen*) owner; (*casa huéspedes*) landlady; *fig* **es muy dueña de hacer de su vida lo que quiera,** she can do as she pleases with her life. 2 *arc* (*tratamiento*) lady.

dueño *nm* owner; *(de casa etc)* landlord; **es el d. y señor,** he is lord and master; **¿quién es el d.?,** who owns this?; **se ha hecho el d.,** he is boss now; *fig* **hacerse d. de la situación,** to get the situation under control; *fig* **ser d. de sí mismo,** to be self-possessed.

Duero *n* **el D.,** the Douro.

dulce I *adj* **1** *(sabor)* sweet. **2** *(carácter, voz, música)* soft, sweet, gentle. **3** *(metal)* soft. **4** *(agua)* fresh; **peces de agua d.,** freshwater fish. **II** *nm* **1** *Culin (pastel)* cake; **fruta en d.,** *(escarchada)* glacé fruit; *(confitada)* fruit in heavy syrup; **me encantan los dulces,** I have a sweet tooth. ■ **d. de almíbar,** preserved fruit; **d. de membrillo,** quince jelly. **2** *(caramelo)* sweet, *US* candy. **3** *Am* brown sugar.

dulcería *nf* confectionery; *(tienda)* confectioner's.

dulcero,-a I *adj* sweet-toothed. **II** *nm,f* confectioner.

dulcificar *vtr* **1** to sweeten. **2** *fig* to soften.

dulzaina *nf Mús* old type of pipe, dulzaina.

dulzaino,-a *adj* sweetish, sugary; **sus canciones son muy dulzainas,** his songs are very soppy.

dulzarrón,-ona *adj*, **dulzón,-ona** *adj* sickly, oversweet.

dulzor *nm* **1** sweetness. **2** *fig* gentleness, sweetness, softness.

dulzura *nf* **1** sweetness. **2** *fig* gentleness, sweetness, softness; **es una d. de niño,** he is such a sweet baby *or* little boy.

dumping *nm Com* dumping.

duna *nf Geog* dune.

dúo *nm Mús* duet.

duodécimo,-a I *adj* twelfth; **duodécima parte,** twelfth. **II** *nm,f (de una serie)* twelfth. **III** *nm (parte)* twelfth; *véase tamb* **octavo,-a.**

duodenal *adj Anat Med* duodenal.

duodeno *nm Anat* duodenum.

dúplex I *adj* duplex. **II** *nm* **1** *Arquit* duplex, duplex apartment. **2** *Telec* linkup.

duplicación *nf* duplication, doubling.

duplicado,-a I *pp de* **duplicar. II** *a adj* **por d.,** in duplicate; **hay que presentar los impresos por d.,** all forms must be handed in in duplicate. **III** *nm* duplicate, copy.

duplicar I *vtr (gen)* to duplicate; *(cifras)* to double. **II duplicarse** *vr* to double; **el número de parados se ha duplicado,** the number of unemployed has doubled.

duplicidad *nm* **1** duplicity. **2** *fig (falsedad)* duplicity, falseness.

duplo,-a *adj & mn,f* double.

duque *nm* duke.

duquesa *nf* duchess.

durabilidad *nf* durability.

durable *adj* durable, lasting.

duración *nf* duration, length; **disco de larga d.,** long-playing record; *fig* LP.

duradero,-a *adj* durable, lasting.

durante *prep (por)* during, in; *(todo el período)* for; **duerme d. el día,** he sleeps during the day; **d. todo el día,** all day long; **ha llovido d. la noche,** it rained during the night; **la vi tan sólo d. tres** *or* **cuatro segundos,** I saw her for only three or four seconds; **la vi varias veces d. las vacaciones,** I saw her several times during the holidays; **viví en La Coruña d. un año,** I lived in La Coruña for a year.

durar *vi* **1** to last, go on for; *fig* **Helena no durará ni tres meses en el cargo,** Helena won't last more than three months in her job. **2** *(ropa, calzado)* to wear well, last.

durazno *nm Bot (fruto)* peach; *(árbol)* peach tree.

dureza *nf* **1** hardness, toughness; *(severidad)* harshness, severity; *fig* **d. de corazón,** hardheartedness. **2** *(callosidad)* corn.

durmiente I *adj* sleeping; **la bella d.,** sleeping beauty. **II** *nmf* sleeping person *or* animal. **III** *nm Am Ferroc* sleeper, *US* tie.

duro,-a I *adj* **1** hard; *(carne)* tough; *Dep* **juego d.,** rough play. **2** *(penoso)* hard, difficult. **3** *(áspero)* tough, harsh. **4** *(resistente)* tough, strong. **5** *(sin sentimientos)* hardhearted, tough. **II** *nm* **1** *(moneda)* five-peseta coin; *fam* **¡lo que faltaba para el d.!,** just what we *or* I needed! **2** *(persona)* tough guy. **III** *adv* hard; **le da d. al trabajo,** he works hard; **pégale d.,** hit him hard.

dux *nm Hist* doge.

d/v *abr de* **días vista; a diez d/v,** due within ten days.

E

E, e *nf (la letra)* E, e.

E *abr de* **Este,** East, E.

e *conj (delante de palabras que empiecen por i or hi)* and; **verano e invierno,** summer and winter.

ea *interj (para animar)* come on!; *(para indicar resolución)* so there!

easonense I *adj* of *or* from San Sebastián. **II** *nmf* native *or* inhabitant of San Sebastián.

ebanista *nm Carp* cabinet-maker.

ebanistería *nf Carp* **1** *(arte)* cabinet-making. **2** *(taller)* cabinet-maker's.

ébano *nm* ebony.

ebonita *nf* ebonite, vulcanite.

ebriedad *nf* inebriation, intoxication, drunkenness.

ebrio,-a *adj* inebriated, intoxicated, drunk; *fig* **e. de ira,** furious.

Ebro *n* **el E.,** the Ebro.

ebullición *nf* boiling; **entrar en e.,** to come to the boil, **estar a punto de e.,** to be at boiling point, *fig* **estar en e.,** to be boiling over. ■ **punto de e.,** boiling point.

eccehomo *nm Rel* Ecce Homo, *fam fig* **estar hecho un e.,** to be a wreck.

eccema *nm Med* eczema.

echado,-a I *pp de* **echar II** *adj* **1** *(tumbado)* **estar e.,** to be lying down **2** *(arrojado)* thrown, *(descartado)* thrown away; *fam* **e. pa'lante,** go-getter

echador,-a I *adj CAm Méx* bigheaded **II** *nf* **echadora de cartas,** fortune-teller

echar I *vtr* **1** *(lanzar)* to throw; *fig* **e. algo a suertes,** to draw lots for sth; *fig* **e. maldiciones,** to curse; *fig* **e. pelillos a la mar,** to bury the hatchet; *fig* **e. una mano,** to give a hand; *fig* **e. una mirada/una ojeada,** to have a look/a quick look *or* glance. **2** *(depositar)* to put, drop, **e. dinero en un saco,** to put money into a bag. **3** *(correo)* to post **4** *(expulsar)* to throw out **5** *(despedir)* to sack, dismiss, fire; **le echaron del colegio,** he was expelled from school **6** *(derribar)* **e. por tierra** *or* **abajo,** *(edificio)* to demolish; *fig (proyecto)* to ruin **7** *(brotar, salir)* to grow; **e. bigotes,** to grow a moustache, *fig* **e. raíces,** to put down roots **8** *(emanar)* to emit, give out *or* off, **la chimenea echa mucho humo,** a lot of smoke is coming out of the chimney. **9** *(poner)* *Culin* to put in, add, **e. el cerrojo,** to bolt the door, *Aut* **e. el freno,** to put the brake on. **10** *(decir)* **e. la buenaventura,** to tell sb's fortune; **e. una regañina** *or* **un sermón a algn,** to tell sb off. **11** *(calcular)* to guess, **e. cuentas,** to calculate; **le echó 37**

años, he thought she looked 37; *fam* **échale precio,** guess how much I paid **12** *(apartar)* to push aside; **echa eso a un lado,** push that to one side **13** *(servir)* to give, serve up; *(gasolina)* to put in, **me has echado mucho,** you've given me a lot **14** *fam (exhibir) Cin TV* to show, **esta noche echan 'Yo, Claudio',** 'I, Claudius' is on tonight **15** *(acusar)* **e. en cara,** to blame, **no me eches en cara tus errores,** don't blame me for your mistakes. **16 e. de menos** *or* **en falta,** to miss; **echa de menos a su amigo Pepe,** he misses his friend Pepe. **II** *vi* **1** *(e. + a + infin) (empezar)* to begin to; **echó a correr,** he ran off; *(deteriorar)* **e. a perder,** to spoil. **2** *(dar)* **e. de comer,** to feed. **3** *(ir)* **e. por un camino,** to follow a path; **e. por la derecha,** to go right. **III echarse** *vr* **1** *(lanzarse)* to throw oneself; *fig* **la noche se nos echó encima,** it was night before we knew it. **2** *(tumbarse)* to lie down, **e. al suelo,** to lie on the floor. **3** *(apartarse)* **e. a un lado,** to move oneself to one side, *fig* **e. atrás,** to have second thoughts, get cold feet. **4** *fam* **e. novio/novia,** to get a steady boyfriend/girlfriend **5** *(e. + a + infin) (empezar)* to begin to, **e. a llorar,** to burst into tears, **e. a perder,** *(comida)* to go bad, *(personas)* to go downhill **e. a reír,** to burst out laughing. **6** *fam* **echárselas de,** to claim to be; **se las echa de muy listo,** he thinks he's very smart

echarpe *nm* shawl, stole

echazón *nf Náut* jetsam.

echona *nf Arg Chi Per Agr* sickle

eclampsia *nf Med* eclampsia.

eclecticismo *nm* eclecticism.

ecléctico,-a adj & *nm,f* eclectic

eclesial *adj* ecclesiastic, ecclesiastical, church.

eclesiástico,-a *adj* ecclesiastic, ecclesiastical, church. **II** *nm* clergyman.

eclipsar I *vtr Astron* to eclipse **2** *fig* to eclipse, outshine **II eclipsarse** *vr* **1** *Astron* to be eclipsed **2** *fig (desaparecer)* to disappear, vanish.

eclipse *nm* eclipse.

eclíptico,-a *adj* & *nf* ecliptic

eclisa *nf Ferroc* fishplate

eclosión *nf* **1** *Zool* hatching, emergence; *Bot* blossoming **2** *fig* upsurge, flowering, emergence

eclosionar *vi* to break *or* burst out, emerge

eco *nm* **1** *Fís* echo **2** *fig* echo, response, **hacer e.,** to have an effect, make an impression; **tener e.,** to arouse interest ■ *Prensa* **ecos de sociedad,** gossip column *sing*

ecografía *nf Med* scan

ecología *nf* ecology

ecológico,-a *adj* ecological

ecologista I *adj* ecological; *Pol* **partido e.,** ecology party **II** *nmf* ecologist

ecólogo,-a *nm,f* ecologist.

economato *nm Com* company store.

econometría *nf* econometrics *sing*

economía *nf* **1** *(gen)* economy, **e. doméstica,** housekeeping; **la e. británica,** the British economy **2** *(ciencia)* economics **3** *(ahorro)* economy, saving; **hacer economías,** to economize. **4** *(cualidad)* economy, thrift, thriftiness

económico,-a *adj* **1** *(gen)* economic **2** *(barato)* cheap, economical, inexpensive, **resultar e.,** to be cheap **3** *(persona)* thrifty, careful with money. ◆ **económicamente** *adv* economically, **viajar e.,** to travel cheaply

economista *nmf* economist.

economizar *vtr (dinero, tiempo)* to economize, save, *(cosas)* to use springly.

ecónomo *nm* **1** *Fin* trustee **2** *Rel* acting parish priest.

ecosistema *nm* ecosystem

ectoplasma *nm* ectoplasm

ecuación *nf Mat* equation ■ **e. de segundo grado,** quadratic equation, **sistema de ecuaciones,** set of equations

Ecuador *n* Ecuador.

ecuador *nm* **1** *Geog* equator **2** *Educ fam* **paso del e.,** trip organised by students celebrating half-way stage in their degree

ecualizador *nm Fís* equalizer.

ecuánime *adj* **1** *(temperamento)* equable, even-tempered **2** *(juicio)* impartial, fair

ecuanimidad *nf* **1** *(temperamento)* equanimity **2** *(juicio)* impartiality fairness

ecuatoguineano,-a I *adj* of *or* from Equatorial Guinea **II** native *or* inhabitant of Equatorial Guinea

ecuatorial *adj* equatorial.

ecuatoriano,-a *adj* & *nm,f* Ecuadorian, Ecuadoran.

ecuestre *adj* equestrian.

ecuménico,-a *adj Rel* ecumenic, ecumenical, oecumenical.

ecumenismo *nm* ecumenicalism, ecumenicalism

eczema *nm Med* eczema.

ed 1 *abr de* **edición,** edition, ed **2** *abr de* **editorial,** editorial, ed. **3** *abr de* **editor,** editor, ed.

edad *nf* age, **los menores de e.,** minors, children under age; **¿qué e. tienes?,** how old are you?; **ya tienes e. para ...,** you are old enough to ..., *euf* **latercera e.,** senior citizens *pl*; *euf* **una persona de e.,** an elderly person. ■ **e. media,** Middle Ages *pl*.

edén *nm* **1** Eden. **2** *fig* paradise, heaven.

edénico,-a *adj* idyllic, heavenly.

edición *nf* **1** *Impr (publicación)* publication; *(de sellos)* issue; **Ediciones Sánchez,** Sanchez Publications. **2** *(conjunto de ejemplares)* edition; **agotada la e.,** out of stock. ■ **e. anotada,** annotated text; **e. pirata,** pirate edition.

edicto *nm* edict, proclamation.

edificable *adj Arquit* **suelo e.,** land with planning permission.

edificación *nf Arquit* building, construction.

edificador,-a *adj* **1** *Constr* building. **2** *(ejemplar)* edifying.

edificante *adj* edifying, uplifting.

edificar *vtr* **1** *(construir)* to build. **2** *fig (enseñar)* to edify, uplift; **e. con el ejemplo,** to teach by example.

edificio *nm* building; **E. Cisneros,** Cisneros House.

edil,-a I *nm,f* town councillor. **II** *nm Hist* aedile.

Edimburgo *n* Edinburgh.

Edipo *nm* Oedipus; *Psic* **complejo de E.,** Oedipus complex.

editar *vtr* **1** *(libros, periódicos)* to publish; *(discos)* to release. **2** *Inform* to edit.

editor,-a I *adj* publishing. **II** *nm,f* publisher.

editorial I *adj* publishing. **II** *nf* publishers, publishing house. **III** *nm Prensa* editorial, leader article.

editorialista *nmf Prensa* leader writer.

edredón *nm* eiderdown, continental quilt, duvet, *US* comforter.

educación *nf* **1** *(preparación)* education; **gastos de e.,** school *or* college fees. **2** *(urbanidad)* upbringing, breeding; **falta de e.,** rudeness, discourtesy; **nunca había visto tal falta de e. en la mesa,** I'd never seen such bad table manners; **¡qué falta de e.!,** how rude!

educado,-a *adj* polite.

educador,-a I *adj* educating. **II** *nm, f* educationalist, teacher.

educando,-a *nm,f* pupil, student.

educar *vtr (enseñar)* to educate, teach; *(entrenar)* to train.

educativo,-a *adj* educational; **método e.,** teaching method; **sistema e.,** education system.

edulcorante *nm* sweetener.

edulcorar *vtr* to add sweeteners to; *fig* **tener una visión edulcorada de la realidad,** to look at the world through rose-tinted glasses.

EE.UU. *abr de* **Estados Unidos,** United States of America, USA.

efe *nf* name of the letter F in Spanish.

efectismo *nm* showiness, theatricality.

efectista *adj* showy, stagy.

efectividad *nf* effectiveness; **con e. desde ...,** with effect from ..., as from ... .

efectivo,-a I *adj* 1 *(con resultado)* effective; **medidas efectivas,** effective measures; **hacer algo e.,** to carry sth out; *Fin* **hacer e. un cheque,** to cash a cheque; *Jur* **hacerse e.,** to come into effect. 2 *(real)* real, actual. II *nm* 1 *Fin* cash, funds *pl*; **en e.,** in cash; **e. en caja,** petty cash. 2 *(plantilla)* personnel. 3 **efectivos,** *Mil* forces. ◆ **efectivamente** *adv* quite!, yes indeed!

efecto *nm* 1 *(resultado)* effect, end result; **surtir e.,** to work, do the job, be effective; **tener e.,** to take place. 2 *(impresión)* impression; **causar** *or* **hacer e.,** to make an impression; **hace buen e.,** it looks good; **no produjo ningún e.,** it had no effect. 3 *(fin práctico)* aim, object; **a tal e.,** to that end; **a efectos de ...,** with the object of ... . 4 *(efectivamente)* **en e.,** quite!, yes indeed! 5 *Dep* spin; *Ftb* **chutar con e.,** to bend *or* swerve the ball; **dar e. a la pelota,** to put some spin on the ball. 6 *Fin* bill, draft. ■ **e. interbancario,** bank draft *or* bill; **efectos públicos,** public bonds. 7 *Cin Rad Teat TV* effect; **efectos especiales/sonoros,** special/sound effects. 8 **efectos,** *(artículos)* effects, things. ■ **e. de escritorio,** stationery *sing*; **e. personales,** personal belongings *or* effects.

efectuación *nf* accomplishment.

efectuar I *vtr* to carry out, make, do; **e. un pago,** to make a payment; *Com* **e. un pedido,** to place an order; **e. una suma,** to do a sum; **e. un viaje,** to make a journey. II **efectuarse** *vr* to take place.

efeméride *nf* 1 *(aniversario)* anniversary; *(acontecimiento)* event. 2 **efemérides,** *Prensa* list of the day's anniversaries.

efervescencia *nf* 1 *(gen)* effervescence; *(de bebida)* fizziness. 2 *fig* high spirits *pl*.

efervescente *adj* 1 *(gen)* effervescent; *(bebidas)* fizzy. 2 *fig* vivacious, high-spirited.

eficacia *nf* *(persona)* efficiency, effectiveness; *(cosas)* efficacy, effectiveness; *(rendimiento)* efficiency.

eficaz *adj* *(competente)* efficient; *(cosas)* efficacious, effective; *(rendimiento)* efficient. ◆ **eficazmente** *adv* effectively.

eficiencia *nf* efficiency; *Econ* **e. económica,** cost-effectiveness.

eficiente *adj* efficient. ◆ **eficientemente** *adv* efficiently.

efigie *nm* effigy, image.

efímero,-a *adj* ephemeral, short-lived, fleeting.

efluvio *nm* emanation, flow, effusion; *fig* **e. de alegría,** surge of happiness.

efusión *nf* 1 *(derramamiento)* effusion, pouring out. 2 *(manifestación de afecto)* effusiveness.

efusividad *nf* effusiveness.

efusivo,-a *adj* effusive, warm. ◆ **efusivamente** *adv* effusively, warmly.

EGB *nf Educ abr de* **Enseñanza General Básica,** ≈ Primary School Education.

Egeo *n* el **(Mar) E.,** the Aegean Sea.

égida *nf* 1 *Mit* aegis. 2 *fig* protection; **bajo la é. de ...,** under the aegis of ... .

egipcio,-a *adj & nm,f* Egyptian; **la frontera e.-israelí,** the Israeli-Egyptian border.

Egipto *n* Egypt.

egiptología *nf* Egyptology.

egiptólogo,-a *nm,f* Egyptologist.

eglefino *nm (pez)* haddock.

ego *nm* ego.

egocéntrico,-a *adj* egocentric, self-centred.

egocentrismo *nm* egocentricity.

egoísmo *nm* egoism, selfishness.

egoísta I *adj* egoistic, egoistical, selfish. II *nmf* egoist, selfish person.

ególatra I *adj* egomaniacal. II *nmf* egomaniac.

egolatría *nf* egomania, self-worship.

egotismo *nm* egotism.

egotista I *adj* egotistic, egotistical. II *nmf* egotist.

egregio,-a *adj* eminent, illustrious, renowned.

egresar *vi Am* to leave school, *US* graduate.

egreso *nm Arg Chi* graduation.

eh *interj* 1 hey (you)! 2 *fam (al final de frase)* OK?, right? 3 *fam (pregunta)* you what?

eider *nm Orn* eider duck.

Eire *n* Eire, Republic of Ireland.

ej. *abr de* **ejemplo,** example, e.g.

eje *nm* 1 *Téc (de ruedas)* axle; *(de máquinas)* shaft, spindle; *Aut* **e. trasero/delantero** rear/front axle; *fam fig* **partir por el e. a algn,** to kill sb; **nos han subido el alquiler y nos han partido por el e.,** they've put the rent up and it's just about killing us. 2 *Mat* axis. 3 *Pol* **E.,** Axis. 4 *fig* centre, *US* center, core.

ejecución *nf* 1 *(orden)* carrying out. 2 *(ajusticiamiento)* execution. 3 *Mús* performance. 4 *Jur* seizure.

ejecutante *nmf Mús* performer.

ejecutar *vtr* 1 *(orden)* to carry out. 2 *(ajusticiar)* to execute. 3 *Mús* to perform, play. 4 *Jur (reclamar)* to seize. 5 *Inform* to run.

ejecutivo,-a I *adj* executive; *Pol* **el poder e.,** the executive. II *nm* board member, executive. II *nf Com* the executive.

ejecutor,-a *nm, f* 1 *Jur* executor. 2 *(verdugo)* executioner.

ejecutoria *nf Jur* writ of execution.

ejecutorio,-a *adj Jur* executory, enforceable.

ejem *interj* ahem, hmm.

ejemplar I *adj* exemplary, model. II *nm* 1 *Impr* copy, number, issue; **e. duplicado,** duplicate copy. 2 *(especimen)* specimen.

ejemplaridad *nf* exemplariness.

ejemplarizar *vtr* to set an example to.

ejemplificación *nf* illustration, exemplification.

ejemplificar *vtr* to illustrate, exemplify.

ejemplo *nm* example; **dar e.,** to set an example; **poner de e.,** to give as an example; **por e.,** for example; **servir de e.,** to serve as an example.

ejercer I *vtr* 1 *(practicar)* to practise; **e. una profesión,** to follow *or* practise a profession. 2 *(usar)* to exercise; *(una influencia)* to exert; **e. el derecho de ...,** to exercise one's right to ... . II *vi* to work (**de,** as).

ejercicio *nm* 1 *(gen)* exercise; **e. de una profesión,** practice of a profession; **hacer e.,** to take *or* do exercise. 2 *Educ* exercise; *(en un examen)* question; **cuaderno de ejercios,** exercise book. 3 *Fin Pol* year; **e. económico,** financial *or* fiscal year.

ejercitar I *vtr (dedicarse)* to practise. II **ejercitarse** *vr (entrenarse)* to practise; *Mil* to exercise.

ejército *nm* army.

ejido *nm* common land.

ejote *nm CAm Méx Agr* string bean.

el *art def* 1 *(gen)* the; **el sol, el mar y el cielo,** the sun, the sea and the sky. 2 *(no se traduce)* **el Canadá,** Canada; **el Sr.**

García, Mr. García. **3** *(el + de)* the one; **el de las once,** the eleven o'clock one; **el de Madrid,** the one from Madrid. **4** *(el + de) (no se traduce)* **el de ayer,** yesterday's; **el de tu amigo,** your friend's. **5** *(el + que)* the one; **el que quieras,** whichever one you want; **el que tienes en la mano,** the one you've got in your hand; **el que vino ayer,** the one who came yesterday.

él *pron pers* **1** *(sujeto) (persona)* he; **él me quiere,** he loves me. **2** *(animal, cosa)* it; **él ladró con fuerza,** it barked loudly. **3** *(complemento) (persona)* him; **con/sin él,** with/without him; **¡es él!,** it's him!; **fui a donde él,** I went over to him; **hablábamos de él,** we were talking about him; **pídeselo a él,** ask him for it. **4** *(animal, cosa)* it; **pon el libro dentro él,** put the book in it. **5** *(posesivo)* **de él,** his; **no es mío, es de él,** it isn't mine, it's his.

elaboración *nf* **1** *(de un producto)* manufacture, production; **de e, casera,** home-made. **2** *(de una idea)* working out, development.

elaborar *vtr* **1** *(producto)* to make, manufacture, produce. **2** *(teoría)* to develop.

elasticidad *nf* elasticity, stretch; *fig* flexibility.

elástico,-a *adj* **1** elastic; **cama e.,** trampoline. **2** *fig* flexible; **eso es muy e.,** that depends on other factors. **II** *nm* **1** elastic. **2 elásticos,** braces.

ele¹ *interj* eh!

ele² *nf* name of the letter L in Spanish.

elección *nf* **1** *(opción)* choice; **lo dejo a tu e.,** I leave that up to you. **2** *(de un cargo)* election. **3 elecciones,** *Pol* elections; **convocar a e.,** to call an election; **e. generales,** general election *sing.*

electivo,-a *adj* elective; *Pol* **cargo e.,** elective office.

electo,-a *adj* elect; **el presidente e.,** the president elect.

elector,-a *nm,f Pol* voter, elector.

electorado *nm* electorate, voters *pl.*

electoral *adj* electoral; **campaña e.,** election campaign; **colegio e.,** polling station; **distrito e.,** ≈ constituency.

electoralismo *nm pey* electioneering.

electoralista *adj pey* electioneering.

electorero,-a *nm,f pey* electioneer.

electricidad *nf* electricity.

electricista *nmf* electrician; **ingeniero e.,** electrical engineer.

eléctrico,-a *adj* electric, electrical.

electrificación *nf* electrification.

electrificar *vtr* to electrify.

electrizante *adj fig* electrifying.

electrizar *vtr* to electrify; *fig* **la audiencia quedó electrizada con su actuación,** the audience was electrified by his performance.

electrocardiograma *nm Med* electrocardiogram.

electrochoque *nm Med* electric shock therapy.

electrocución *nf* electrocution.

electrocutar I *vtr* to electrocute. **II electrocutarse** *vr* to be electrocuted.

electrodo *nm* electrode.

electrodoméstico *nm* (home) electrical appliance.

electroimán *nm* electromagnet.

electrólisis *nf* electrolysis.

electrolito *nm* electrolyte.

electromagnético,-a *adj* electromagaetic.

electrón *nm* electron.

electrónico,-a I *adj* electronic. **II** *nf* electronics *sing.*

electrostático,-a I *adj* electrostatic. **II** *nf* electrostatics *sing.*

elefanta *nf Zool* cow or female elephant.

elefante *nm Zool* elephant.

elefantiasis *nf Med* elephantiasis.

elegancia *nf* elegance, stylishness, smartness.

elegante *adj* elegant. stylish, smart ♦ **elegantemente** *adv* elegantly, stylishly, smartly.

elegía *nf* elegy.

elegiaco,-a *adj,* **elegiaco,-a** *adj* **1** elegiac. **2** *fig (lastimero)* elegiac, plaintive, lamenting.

elegibilidad *nf* eligibility.

elegible *adj* eligible.

elegido,-a I *pp de* **elegir. II** *adj* **1** chosen. **2** *Pol* elected. **III el e.** *nm* the chosen one; **los elegidos,** the chosen few.

elegir *vtr* **1** *(optar)* to choose. **2** *Pol* to elect.

elemental *adj* **1** *(relativo al elemento)* elemental. **2** *(básico)* basic, fundamental. **3** *(muy fácil)* elementary.

elemento *nm* **1** *(gen)* element. **2** *(individuo)* type, individual; *fam* **es un buen e.,** he's a good sort. **3** *(ambiente)* **estar en su e.,** to be in one's element. **4** *(pieza, componente)* component, part. **5 elementos,** *(fundamentos)* rudiments; **e. de filosofía/geometría,** basic principles of philosophy/geometry. **6 elementos,** *(fuerzas naturales)* elements; **nada puede el hombre contra los e.,** man is helpless against the elements.

elenco *nm* **1** *(catálogo)* index, catalogue. **2** *Teat* cast. **3** *(personas)* group of people.

elepé *nm Mús* LP (record).

elevación *nf (gen)* elevation, rise; **e. del terreno,** rise in the ground, elevation; **la e. del nivel de vida,** the rise in standard of living.

elevado,-a I *pp de* **elevar. II** *adj* **1** *(alto)* elevated, raised, high; *(edificio)* tall. **2** *fig (pensamiento)* lofty, noble. **3** *(tono, voz)* angry. **4** *Mat* **e. al cuadrado,** squared; **e. a la cuarta potencia,** raised to the power of four.

elevador,-a I *adj* elevating, hoisting, lifting. **II** *nm Am* hoist, lift, *US* elevator.

elevalunas *nm inv Aut* window mechanism. ■ **e. eléctrico,** electric window.

elevar I *vtr* **1** *(alzar)* to elevate, raise, lift. **2** *Mat* to raise; **e. a la cuarta potencia,** to raise to the power of four. **3** *fig* to exalt. **II elevarse** *vr* **1** *(subir)* to rise; *(llegar a una altura)* to reach; *(erguirse)* to stand (above), tower above. **2** *(sumar)* to amount *or* come to; **¿a cuanto se elevan los daños?,** how much does the damage amount *or* come to?

elfo *nm Mit* elf.

elidir *Ling* **I** *vtr* to elide. **II elidirse** *vr* to elide, be elided.

elijo *indic pres véase* **elegir.**

eliminación *nf* eliminiation.

eliminador,-a I *adj* eliminating. **II** *nm,f* eliminator.

eliminar *vtr* **1** *(gen)* to eliminate; *(desecho)* to get rid of; *(un factor)* to rule out. **2** *fam (matar)* to eliminate, kill.

eliminatorio,-a I *adj* qualifying, eliminatory. **II** *nf Dep* heat, qualifying round.

elipse *nf Mat* ellipse.

elipsis *nf inv Ling* ellipsis.

elíptico,-a *adj* elliptic, elliptical.

elisión *nf Ling* elision.

elite *nf,* **élite** *nf* elite, élite.

elitismo *nm* elitism.

elitista *adj* elitist.

elixir *nm* elixir.

ella *pron pers f* **1** *(sujeto)* she; **e. y yo,** she and I. **2** *(animal, cosa)* it, she; **e. ladró con fuerza,** it *or* she barked loudly. **3** *(complemento)* her; *(animal, cosa)* it, her; **para/con e.,** for/with her; **¡es e.!,** it's her!; **pon el libro sobre e.,** put the book on it. **4** *(posesivo)* **de e.,** hers; **la casa es de e.,** the house is hers; **eso es asunto de e.,** that's her affair.

ellas *pron pers fpl véase* **ellos.**

elle *nf* name of the digraph Ll in Spanish.

ello *pron pers neut* it; **¡a e.!,** to work!; **e. es, que ...,** the fact is that ...; **¡no se hable más de e.!,** (and) that's final!

ellos *pron pers mpl* **1** *(sujeto)* they. **2** *(complemento)* them; **con/sin e.,** with/without them. **3** *(posesivo)* **de e.,** theirs; **eso es cosa de e.,** that's their affair.

elocución *nf* elocution.

elocuencia *nf* eloquence.

elocuente *adj* eloquent.

elogiable *adj* praiseworthy.

elogiar *vtr* to praise, eulogize.

elogio *nm* praise, eulogy.

elogioso,-a *adj* appreciative, complimentary, eulogistic.
◆ **elogiosamente** *adv* eulogistically. admiringly.

elongación *nf* **1** *Med* elongation. **2** *Astron* elongation.

elote *nm Am* tender corncob.

El Salvador *n* El Salvador.

elucidación *nf* clarification, elucidation.

elucidar *vtr* to elucidate, explain.

elucubración *nf* **1** *(trabajo)* lucubration. **2** *(divagación)* rambling.

elucubrar *vtr* **1** *(trabajar)* to lucubrate. **2** *(divagar)* to ramble

eludible *adj* avoidable.

eludir *vtr* *(responsabilidad, obligación)* to evade; *(la justicia)* to evade; *(perseguidores)* to escape, avoid; **e. una respuesta,** to avoid answering.

elusivo,-a *adj* evasive.

E.M. *abr de* **Edad Media,** Middle Ages.

Emª *abr de* **Eminencia,** Eminence, Eminency.

emanación *nf* emanation.

emanar *vi* **1** *(desprenderse)* to emanate. **2** *(derivar)* to derive *or* come *(de,* from).

emancipación *nf* emancipation.

emancipado,-a I *pp de* **emancipar.** II *adj* emancipated, free, liberated.

emancipador,-a *adj* emancipating, liberating.

emancipar I *vtr* to emancipate, free. II **emanciparse** *vr* to become emancipated *or* liberated *or* **free.**

emasculación *nf* castration, emasculation.

embabiamiento *nm fam* daydreaming, having one's head in the clouds.

embadurnar *vtr* to daub, smear **(de,** with).

embajada *nf* **1** *(oficina, residencia)* embassy. **2** *(cargo)* ambassadorship, post of ambassador. **3** *(comunicación)* message. **4** *fam* cheeky proposition *or* suggestion.

embajador,-a *nm, f* ambassador.

embalador,-a *nm, f* packer.

embalaje *nm* packing, packaging; **gastos de e.,** packing (costs); **papel de e.,** wrapping paper.

embalar[1] *vtr (mercancías)* to pack, wrap.

embalar[2] I *vi* to speed up. II **embalarse** *vr* **1** *(acelerar)* to speed up. **2** *fig (persona)* to get carried away.

embaldosado *nm* **1** *(trabajo)* tiling. **2** *(suelo)* tiled floor.

embaldosar *vtr* to tile.

embalsadero *nm* fen, marsh, swamp.

embalsamador,-a *nm, f* embalmer.

embalsamar *vtr* to embalm.

embalsar *vtr* **1** *(llenar de agua)* to dam up. **2** *Náut (izar a una persona)* to sling *or* lift.

embalse *nm* **1** *(presa)* dam, reservoir. **2** *(acción)* damming.

embanastar *vtr* to put into a basket.

embancarse *vtr Náut* to run aground.

embarazado,-a I *pp de* **embarazar.** II *adj* **1** *(preñada)* pregnant. **2** *(turbado)* embarrassed. III *nf* pregnant woman, expectant mother.

embarazar *vtr* **1** *(dejar preñada)* to make pregnant. **2** *(dificultar)* to hinder. **3** *(turbar)* to embarrass.

embarazo *nm* **1** *(preñez)* pregnancy. **2** *(obstáculo)* obstacle. **3** *(turbación)* embarrassment.

embarazoso,-a *adj* awkward, troublesome, embarrassing.

embarcación *nf* **1** *(nave)* boat, craft; **e. de desembarco,** landing craft. **2** *(embarco)* embarkation. **3** *(viaje)* voyage.

embarcadero *nm* pier, quay, jetty.

embarcador,-a *nm, f* docker.

embarcar I *vtr* **1** *(personas)* to embark; *(mercancías)* to ship. **2** *fig (embarco)* **e. a algn en un asunto,** to involve sb in an affair. II **embarcarse** *vr* **1** *(barco)* to embark, go on board; *(avión)* to board. **2** *fig* to embark.

embarco *nm* embarkation.

embardar *vtr* to thatch.

embargar *vtr* **1** *Jur* to seize, impound. **2** *fig* to overwhelm; **le embargaba la emoción,** he was overcome by emotion.

embargo *nm* **1** *Jur* seizure of property. **2** *Com* embargo. **3** *Náut* embargo. **4** **sin e.** *loc adv* nevertheless, however, nonetheless.

embarque *nm (persona)* boarding; *(mercancías)* loading; **tarjeta de e.,** boarding card.

embarrado,-a I *pp de* **embarrar.** II *adj* muddy.

embarrancar(se) *vi & vr Náut* to run aground. **2** *fig* to get bogged down.

embarrar I *vtr* **1** *(llenar de barro)* to cover with mud. **2** *Am (fastidiar)* to annoy. **3** *CAm Méx (implicar)* to implicate, involve. II **embarrarse** *vr* to get covered in mud.

embarrialarse *vr CAm* **1** *Ven (embarrarse)* to get covered with mud. **2** *(atascarse)* to become bogged down.

embarullador,-a I *adj* bungling, muddling. II *n* bungler, muddler.

embarullar *vtr* to bungle, mess up.

embate *nm* **1** *(de las olas)* pounding. **2** *fig* outburst.

embaucador,-a I *adj* deceitful; **palabras embaucadoras,** lies. II *nm, f* deceiver, swindler, cheat.

embaucar *vtr* to deceive, dupe, swindle, cheat.

embebecer I *vtr (entretener)* to delight, fascinate. II **embebecerse** *vr* to be captivated *or* fascinated.

embeber I *vtr* **1** *(absorber)* to soak up. **2** *Cost* to take in. II **embeberse** *vr* to become absorbed *or* engrossed **(en,** in).

embebido,-a I *pp de* **embeber.** II *adj* engrossed, absorbed.

embelecar *vtr* to deceive, cheat.

embeleco *nm* deception, cheating.

embelequería *nf Am* deception, deceit, cheating.

embelesado,-a I *pp de* **embelesar.** II *adj* delighted, fascinated.

embelesar *vtr* to delight, fascinate.

embeleso *nm* delight, fascination.

embellecedor,-a I *adj* beautifying; **crema e.,** beauty cream. II *nm Aut* hubcap.

embellecer *vtr (cosa, sitio)* to embellish, brighten up; *(persona)* to flatter.

embellecímiento *nm* embellishment, beautifying.

emberrincharse *vr,* **emberrinchinarse** *vr fam* to fly into tantrum.

embestida *nf* I onslaught. **2** *Taur* charge.

embestir *vtr* **1** *Taur* to charge. **2** *(lanzarse)* to assault; **e. contra,** to attack.

embetunar *vtr (zapatos)* to black.

embicar *vi Am Naut* to head the boat straight for the coast.

embijar *vtr Am* to soil, dirty.

emblandecer I *vtr* to soften. II **emblandecerse** *vr fig* to relent.

emblanquecer *vtr* to whiten, bleach.

emblema *nm* emblem, badge; *Com* logo.

emblemático,-a *adj* emblematic.

embobado,-a I *pp de* **embobar. II** *adj* fascinated.

embobamiento *nm* fascination, amazement.

embobar I *vtr* to fascinate, amaze. **II embobarse** *vr* to be fascinated *or* besotted (**con, de,** by).

embocadura *nf* 1 (*de un río*) mouth. 2 *Mús* mouthpiece. 3 (*bocado*) bit. 4 (*sabor del vino*) taste, flavour, *US* flavor.

embocar *vtr* 1 (*meter*) to introduce; (*en la boca*) to put into the mouth. 2 *Golf* to hole.

embochinchar *vtr Am* (*alborotar*) to kick up a racket.

embolado *nm* 1 *Teat* minor role. 2 *Taur* bull with wooden balls on its horns. 3 *fam* fib, lie.

embolar¹ *vtr Taur* to put wooden balls on the horns of.

embolar² *I vtr CAm* to get drunk. **II embolarse** *vr* to get drunk.

embolia *nf Med* embolism, clot.

émbolo *nm Téc* piston.

embolsar I *vtr* 1 (*dinero*) to pocket. 2 *fig* (*cobrar*) to collect. **II embolsarse** *vr* to pocket, earn.

embonar *vtr Am* 1 (*ensamblar*) to join. 2 (*favorecer*) to suit. 3 to manure.

emboquillado *adj* filter-tipped.

emborrachar I *vtr* to get drunk. **II emborracharse** *vr* to get drunk.

emborrascarse *vr Meteor* to become stormy *or* overcast.

emborronar I *vtr* 1 (*garrapatear*) to blot. 2 *fig* to scribble. **II emborronarse** *vr* to smudge.

emboscada *nf* ambush; **tender una e.,** to lay an ambush.

emboscar *vtr* to ambush.

embotado,-a I *pp de* **embotar. II** *adj* dull, blunt, blunted.

embotadura *nf* dulling.

embotar *vtr* to blunt; *fig* (*los sentidos*) to dull; (*lamente*) to fuddle.

embotellado,-a I *pp de* **embotellar. II** *adj* bottled. **III** *nm* bottling.

embotellador,-a I *nm,f* (*persona*) bottler. **II** *nf* (*máquina*) bottling machine.

embotellamiento *nm* 1 (*acción*) bottling. 2 *Aut fig* traffic jam.

embotellar *vtr* 1 (*meter en botella*) to bottle. 2 *Aut fig* to block. 3 *fam* to swot up on.

embozar I *vtr* 1 (*cubrir el rostro*) to muffle. 2 *fig* to play one's cards close to one's chest. **II embozarse** *vr* 1 to muffle oneself up. 2 *fig* to play one's cards close to one's chest.

embozo *nm* 1 (*prenda*) muffler, mask, covering of the face. 2 *fig* (*recato*) reserve.

embragar *vi Aut* to engage the clutch.

embrague *nm* clutch.

embravecer I *vtr* to enrage. **II embravecerse** *vr* 1 (*enfadarse*) to become enraged. 2 (*mar*) to become rough.

embrear *vtr* to tar, pitch.

embriagado,-a I *pp de* **embriagar. II** *adj* intoxicated, drunk, drunken.

embriagador,-a *adj* intoxicating.

embriagar I *vtr* to intoxicate, get drunk; *fig* to transport, enrapture. **II embriagarse** *vr* to get drunk; *fig* to be transported *or* enraptured.

embriaguez *nf* intoxication, drunkenness; *fig* intoxication, rapture.

embridar *vtr* (*un caballo*) to bridle.

embrión *nm* 1 *Biol* embryo. 2 *fig* (*de una idea, novela*) beginnings *pl*, embryo; (*de revolución*) seeds *pl*; **en e.,** in embryo.

embrionario,-a *adj* embryonic, embryonal; **en estado e.,** in *or* at the embryonic stage.

embrocar *vtr Méx* to pull on.

embrollado,-a I *pp de* **embrollar. II** *adj* confused, muddled. ◆ **embrolladamente** *adv* confusedly.

embrollador,-a I *adj* confusing, muddling. **II** *nm, f* (*persona*) troublemaker.

embrollar I *vtr* to confuse, muddle. **II embrollarse** *vr* to get muddled *or* confused.

embrollo *nm* 1 (*lío*) muddle, confusion. 2 (*mentiras*) pack of lies. 3 *fig* embarrassing situation.

embromar *vtr* 1 (*hacer broma*) to tease, play a trick *or* a joke on. 2 *Am* to annoy.

embrujado,-a I *pp de* **embrujar. II** *adj* (*persona*) bewitched; (*sitio*) haunted.

embrujar *vtr* 1 (*un lugar*) to haunt; (*persona*) to bewitch. 2 *fig* (*fascinar*) to cast a spell on, bewitch.

embrujo *nm* spell, charm; *fig* attraction, fascination.

embrutecer I *vtr* to make dull and stupid. **II embrutecerse** *vr* to become dull and stupid.

embuchacarse *vr CAm* to pocket.

embuchado,-a I *pp de* **embuchar. II** *adj* **carne e.,** processed cold meat *or* meats. **III** *nm* 1 *Culin* processed cold meat. 2 *fig* (*asunto engañoso*) cover-up. 3 *fig Pol* (*fraude*) rigging of elections.

embuchar I *vtr* 1 (*embutir*) to stuff. 2 (*aves*) to force-feed. 3 (*comer*) to stuff oneself with. **II embucharse** *vr Am* to get angry without reason.

embudo *nm* funnel; *fam* **eso funciona según la ley del e.,** there's one law for the rich and another for the poor.

embullar *vi Am* to make a din.

embuste *nm* lie, trick.

embustero,-a I *adj* deceitful, lying. **II** *nm,f* cheater, liar.

embutido *nm* 1 (*embuchado*) cold cut, processed cold meat. 2 (*incrustación*) inlay. 3 *Am Cost* strip of lace.

embutir I *vtr* 1 (*carne*) to stuff. 2 (*meter*) to stuff or cram *or* squeeze (**en,** into). 3 (*incrustar*) to inlay. 4 *fig* (*resumir*) to condense. **II embutirse** *vr fam* (*atiborrarse*) to stuff oneself (**de,** with).

eme *nf* 1 name of the letter M in Spanish. 2 *fam euf* sugar; **esto es una e.,** this is rubbish; **¡vete a la e.!,** eff off!

emergencia *nf* 1 (*salida*) emergence. 2 (*caso imprevisto*) emergency; **en caso de e.,** in an emergency.

emergente *adj* 1 (*saliente*) emergent. 2 (*resultante*) resulting, consequent.

emerger *vi* to emerge.

emérito,-a *adj Educ* emeritus.

emigración *nf* emigration, migration.

emigrado,-a I *pp de* **emigrar. II** *nm, f* emigrant; *Pol* émigré.

emigrante *adj & nmf* emigrant.

emigrar *vi* (*gen*) to emigrate; (*aves*) to migrate.

eminencia *nf* 1 *Geog* height, hill, elevation. 2 *fig* (*mérito*) prominence. 3 *fig* (*persona*) eminence, eminency; **Su E.,** His Eminence.

eminente *adj* 1 (*alto*) high. 2 *fig* (*renombrado*) eminent; **un e. psiquiatra,** a top *or* eminent psychiatrist. ◆ **eminentemente** *adv* eminently.

emir *nm* emir.

emirato *nm* emirate; **Emiratos Árabes Unidos,** United Arab Emirates.

emisario,-a *nm,f* emissary.

emisión *nf* 1 (*gen*) emission. 2 *Fin Filat* issue; **e. de bonos,** bond issue; **e. pública,** public issue. 3 *Rad TV* (*programa*) broadcast; (*transmisión*) broadcasting; **cierre de la e.,** close-down; **e. en directo,** live transmission.

emisor,-a I *adj* **1** *Rad TV* **centro e.,** transmitter, broadcasting station. **2** *Fin* **banco e.,** issuing bank. **II** *nm* **1** *Rad* radio transmitter. **2** *Fin* issuer. **III** *nf Rad TV* radio *or* television station.

emitir *vtr* **1** *(gen)* to emit; *(sonidos de los seres vivos)* to utter, emit; *(luz, calor)* to give off. **2** *(manifestar)* to express; *Jur* **e. el fallo** *or* **la sentencia,** to pronounce judgement, pass sentence; **e. un juicio,** to express an opinion. **3** *Rad TV* to transmit. **4** *Fin Filat (moneda, títulos, etc)* to issue.

Emmo. *abr de* **Eminentísimo,** Most Eminent.

emoción *nf* **1** emotion; **regirse por las emociones,** to be ruled by the heart. **2** *(excitación)* excitement; **la e. del momento,** the heat of the moment; **¡qué e.!,** how exciting!

emocionado,-a I *pp de* **emocionar. II** *adj* deeply moved *or* touched.

emocional *adj* emotional.

emocionante *adj* **1** *(conmovedor)* moving, touching. **2** *(agitado)* exciting, thrilling.

emocionar I *vtr* **1** *(conmover)* to move, touch; **me emocionó la película,** I found the film really moving. **2** *(excitar)* to thrill; **a los niños les emociona ir en barco,** the kids love going out in a boat. **II emocionarse** *vr* **1** *(conmoverse)* to be moved to tears. **2** *(excitarse)* to get excited.

emolumento *nm* emolument.

emotividad *nf* emotiveness.

emotivo,-a *adj (palabras)* emotive, stirring, rousing; *(persona)* emotional; *(escena)* moving, touching.

empacadora *nf Téc* packing machine.

empacar I *vtr* **1** *(mercancías)* to pack. **2** *Am* to annoy. **II empacarse** *vr* **1** to dig one's heels in. **2** *fig* to become shy *or* embarrassed. **3** *Am (animales)* to balk.

empachado,-a I *pp de* **empachar. II** *adj* **1** *(desmañado)* slow-witted. **2** *(ahíto)* bloated.

empachar I *vtr* **1** *(comer demasiado)* to give indigestion. **2** *fig (hartar)* to be fed up; **me empacha tanta televisión,** I'm sick of so much television. **II empacharse** *vr* **1** *(indigestión)* to stuff oneself. **2** *(avergonzarse)* to get embarrassed.

empacho *nm* **1** *(comida)* indigestion, upset stomach. **2** *fig* surfeit; **tener un e. de ...,** to have had one's fill of ... . **3** *(vergüenza)* embarrassment; **no tener e. en decir ...,** to have no qualms about saying ...; **sin e.,** unashamedly.

empachoso,-a *adj* **1** *(comida)* heavy, indigestible. **2** *(vergonzoso)* shameful.

empadrar *vtr Méx (animales)* to mate.

empadronamiento *nm* **1** *(acción)* census taking. **2** *(padrón)* census.

empadronar I *vtr* to take a census. **II empadronarse** *vr* to register.

empalagamiento *nm* **1** *(comida)* cloyingness. **2** *(fastidio)* bother.

empalagar *vi* **1** *(dulces)* to pall, cloy. **2** *fig (fastidiar)* to bother, pester.

empalago *nm véase* **empalagamiento.**

empalagoso,-a *adj* **1***(dulces)* sickly sweet, palling. **2** *fig (persona)* smarmy.

empalar *vtr* to impale.

empalizada *nf* fence.

empalmar I *vtr* **1** *(unir)* to join; *(cuerdas, cintas)* to splice. **2** *fig (planes, ideas)* to combine. **3** *Ftb* to volley. **II** *vi* **1** *Ferroc* to connect. **2** *(suceder a continuación)* to follow on from. **III empalmarse** *vr vulg* to get a hard-on.

empalme *nm* **1** *(gen)* connection; *Carp* joint. **2** *Ferroc* junction; *(en carretera)* intersection, T-junction. **3** *Cin* splice.

empanada *nf Culin* pie; *fam fig* **e. mental,** muddle.

empanadilla *nf Culin* pasty.

empanado,-a I *pp de* **empanar. II** *adj Culin* breaded, in breadcrumbs.

empanar *vtr* **1** *Culin (rebozar)* to coat in bread-crumbs. **2** *(empanada)* to fill.

empantanado,-a I *pp de* **empantanar. II** *adj* **1** *(inundado)* flooded. **2** *fig (atascado)* bogged down.

empantanar I *vtr* **1** *(inundar)* to flood. **2** *fig (detener)* to bring to a standstill. **II empantanarse** *vr* **1** *(inundarse)* to become flooded. **2** *fig (trabajo)* to come to a standstill; *(persona)* to be bogged down.

empañado,-a I *pp de* **empañar. II** *adj* **1** *(cristal)* misty, steamed up. **2** *(voz)* faint. **3** *fig (honor)* tainted, tarnished.

empañar I *vtr* **1** *(bebé)* to put a nappy on. **2** *(cristales)* to steam up. **3** *fig (reputación)* to taint, tarnish. **II empañarse** *vr* **1** *(cristal)* to steam up. **2** *fig (reputación)* to become tainted *or* tarnished.

empañetar *vtr Am (encalar)* to whitewash.

empapado,-a I *pp de* **empapar. II** *adj* soaked, drenched, saturated.

empapar I *vtr* **1** *(humedecer)* to soak. **2** *(absorber)* to soak up. **II empaparse** *vr* **1** *Culin (leche)* to be soaked (**de,** in). **2** *(persona)* to get soaked. **3** *fam fig* to swot up.

empapelado *nm* **1** *(papel)* wallpaper. **2** *(acción)* wallpapering.

empapelar *vtr* **1** *(una pared)* to wallpaper. **2** *(envolver)* to wrap in paper. **3** *Jur fam fig (acusar)* to have up; **lo empapelaron por estafador,** he was had up for fraud.

empapuzado,-a I *pp de* **empapuzar. II** *adj* full, bloated.

empapuzar *vtr fam (personas)* to stuff with food; *(animales)* to force-feed.

empaque[1] *nm* **1** *(acción)* packing. **2** *(materiales)* packaging.

empaque[2] *nm* **1** *(aspecto)* bearing, presence. **2** *Am (descaro)* cheek, impudence.

empaquetador,-a *nm,f* packer.

empaquetadura *nf* packing.

empaquetar *vtr* **1** *(mercancías)* to pack. **2** *fig (personas)* to pack *or* squeeze in. **3** *Mil fig (castigar)* to punish.

emparedado,-a I *pp de* **emparedar. II** *adj* confined, imprisoned. **III** *nm* sandwich.

emparedar *vtr* to immure.

emparejar I *vtr* **1** *(juntar) (cosas)* to match; *(personas)* to pair off. **2** *(nivelar)* to make level. **II** *vi* **1** *(ser igual)* to be even. **2** *(alcanzar)* to catch up. **III emparejarse** *vr Méx* to manage to get.

emparentado,-a I *pp de* **emparentar. II** *adj* related by marriage (**con,** to).

emparentar *vi* to become related by marriage; **e. con ana familia,** to marry into a family.

emparrado *nm Hortic* vine arbour.

emparrillar *vtr* to grill.

empastar *vtr Odont* to fill.

empaste *nm Odont* filling.

empatar *vtr* **1** *Dep* to tie, draw; *Ftb* to equalize, **estar empatados,** to be equal. **2** *Am (unir)* to join.

empate *nm Dep* draw, tie; *Ftb* **el gol del e.,** the equalizer; **e. a tres,** three-all draw, *US* tie three to three.

empavesado *nm* bunting.

empavesar *vtr* to deck, dress, decorate.

empavonarse *vr CAm* to get dolled up.

empecatado,-a *adj* wretched.

empecer *lit* **I** *vi* to be an obstacle. **II** *vtr* to damage, harm.

empecinado,-a I *pp de* **empecinarse. II** *adj (obstinado)* stubborn, pigheaded.

empecinarse *vr* to be stubborn *or* pigheaded, persist.

empedernido,-a *adj* confirmed, hardened, inveterate.

empedrado,-a I *pp de* **empedrar. II** *adj (calle)* cobbled.
III *nm* **1** *(adoquines)* cobblestones *pl*. **2** *(acción)* paving.

empedrar *vtr* to cobble, pave.

empeine *nm* **1** *Anat (pubis)* groin; *(pie)* instep. **2** *(zapato)*
instep.

empellar *vtr* to push, jostle, shove.

empellón *nm* push, shove; **abrirse paso a empellones,** to
push one's way through.

empelotarse *vr Am* to strip off.

empeñar I *vtr* **1** *(cosas)* to pawn, *US* hock; **estar
empeñado,** to be in debt, *US* be in hock. **2** *(palabra,
honor)* to pledge; **e. su palabra,** to pledge *or* give one's
word. **II empeñarse** *vr* **I** *(insistir)* to insist (**en,** on), be
determined (**en,** to). **2** *(endeudarse)* to get into debt.

empeño *nm* **1** *(insistencia)* determination; **poner e. en
ello,** to put one's mind to it; **!qué e. tiene!,** he's obsessed
with it! **2** *(deuda)* pledge. ■ **casa de empeños** pawnshop.

empeñoso,-a *adj* unfailing, unflagging.

empeoramiento *nm* deterioration, worsening.

empeorar I *vi* to deteriorate, worsen. **II** *vtr* to make worse.
III empeorarse *vr* to get worse.

empequeñecer *vtr (reducir)* to diminish, make smaller;
fig to put in the shade, belittle.

empequeñecimiento *nm (de tamaño)* diminution,
reduction; *fig* belittling.

emperador *nm* **1** *(monarca)* emperor. **2** *(pez espada)*
swordfish.

emperatriz *nf* empress.

emperejilarse *vr*, **emperifollarse** *vr fam* to get dolled
up.

empero *conj lit* however.

emperramiento *nm* stubbornness.

emperrarse *vr* to dig one's heels in, become stubborn.

empezar *vtr & vi (a hacer algo)* to begin; *(algo)* to start,
commence; **empezar a hablar,** to begin to speak;
empezaron diciendo que ..., they began by saying that ... .

empiece *nm fam* start, beginning.

empiezo *nm Am* start, beginning.

empinado,-a I *pp de* **empinar. II** *adj* **1** *(alto)* very high. **2**
fig (hacia arriba) steep; *(vertical)* upright. **3** *fig
(orgulloso)* upright, proud.

empinar I *vtr (cabeza, brazo)* to lift up; *(un vaso)* to raise;
fam **e. el codo,** to drink (heavily). **II empinarse** *vr* **1**
(persona) to stand on tiptoe; *(caballo)* to rear up. **2** *fig
(árbol, edificio)* to tower.

empingorotado,-a *adj* **I** *(clase alta)* upper-class. **2**
(engreído) stuck-up, posh.

empiparse *vr Am* to stuff oneself.

empírico,-a *adj* empiric, empirical, ◆ **empíricamente**
adv empirically.

empirismo *nm* empiricism.

empitonar *vtr Taur* to gore.

empizarrado *nm* slate roof.

empizarrar *vtr* to put a slate roof on, slate.

emplastar *vtr Med* to apply a poultice to, put a poultice on.

emplasto *nm* **1** *Med* poultice. **2** *fig (componenda)* bad job,
botched job; **hacer un e. en algo,** to make a poor job of
sth, botch sth, make a botch of sth. **3** *(persona)* sickly
person.

emplazamiento *nm* **I** *(colocación)* site, location. **2** *Jur*
summons sing; *Ind* **e. a la huelga,** strike call.

emplazar¹ *vtr* to locate, situate, place.

emplazar² *vtr* **1** *Jur* to summons. **2** *(llamar)* to call
together, convene; *Jur* to summons; *Ind* **e. a la huelga,** to
call out on strike.

empleado,-a *nm, f* employee, clerk; **e. de banca,** bank
clerk. ■ **empleada del hogar,** servant, maid.

emplear I *vtr* **1** *(dar empleo)* to employ. **2** *(usar)* to use,
employ. **3** *(gastar) (dinero)* to spend; *(tiempo)* to invest,
spend. **II emplearse** *vr (palabra)* to be used.

empleo *nm* **1** *(oficio)* job, occupation; *Pol* employment;
política de pleno e., full employment policy; **sin e.,**
unemployed, out of work, jobless. **2** *(uso)* use; **modo de
e.,** instructions for use.

emplomado *nm Constr (ventana)* leading; *(tejado)* lead
roof.

emplomadura *nf Arg Urug (empaste)* filling.

emplomar *vtr* **1** *(soldar)* to join *or* seal with lead. **2** *Am
Odont* to fill.

emplumar I *vtr (adornar)* to put feathers *or* a feather on.
2 *(castigar)* to tar and feather. **3** *fam (castigar)* to punish.
II *vi* **1** *(pájaro)* to grow feathers. **2** *SAm* to run away,
escape.

empobrecer I *vi* to impoverish. **II empobrecerse** *vr* to
become impoverished *or* poor.

empollar I *vtr (huevos)* to brood, hatch. **2** *fam (estudiar)* to
swot (up), *US* bone up on.

empollón,-ona *fam* **I** *adj* swotty. **II** *nm,f* swot.

empolvado,-a I *pp de* **empolvar. II** *adj* dusty.

empolvar I *vtr* to cover in dust. **II empolvarse** *vr* **1** to
powder; **e. la cara,** to powder one's face. **2** *Méx fig* to be
out of practice.

emponchado,-a *adj Am* **1** *(ropa)* wearing a poncho. **2**
(astuto) cunning. **3** *fig* suspicious.

emponzoñamiento *nm* poisoning.

emponzoñar *vtr* **1** to poison. **2** *fig* to corrupt.

emporcar *vtr* to foul, dirty.

emporio *nm* **1** *Com* emporium, trading *or* commercial
centre. **2** *fig* artistic *or* cultural centre. **3** *Am* department
store.

emporrade,-a I *pp de* **emporrarse. II** *adj arg (drogas)*
stoned, high.

emporrarse *vr arg* to get high.

empreñar I *vtr* **1** *(mujer)* to make pregnant; *(animal)* to
mate with. **2** *fam fig* to bother, annoy. **II empreñarse** *vr*
to become pregnant.

emprendedor,-a *adj* enterprising, resourceful.

emprender *vtr (misión)* to tackle; *(negocio)* to start;
(viaje) to set off on; *fam* **emprenderla con algn,** to pick
on sb.

empresa *nf* **1** *(acción ardua)* enterprise, venture. **2** *Com
Ind* firm, business, company, undertaking, enterprise; **e.
naviera,** shipping company; **la libre e.,** free enterprise.

empresariado *nm* employers *pl*.

empresarial *adj* managerial; **ciencias empresariales**,
business *or* management studies; **espíritu e.,**
entrepreneurial spirit.

empresario,-a *nm, f* employer, entrepreneur; *(hombre)*
businessman, manager; *(mujer)* business woman,
manager, manageress; **e. de pompas funebres,**
undertaker.

emprésito *nm Fin* debenture loan; **lanzar un e.,** to float a
loan.

emprobrecimiento *nm* impoverishment, poverty.

empujar *vtr* **1** to push, shove. **2** *fig* to force, press; **e. a algn
a hacer algo,** to push sb into doing sth.

empuje *nm* push, thrust, drive; *fig* **necesita un poco de e.,**
he needs encouragement; *fig* **una persona de e.,** a person
with a lot of go.

empujón *nm* push, shove; **abrirse paso a empujones,** to
push one's way through; **dar empujones,** to push and
shove; *fig* **a empujones,** in fits and starts; **trabajar a
empujones,** to work in fits and starts; *fig* **dar un e. a algo,**
to give sth a push forward.

empuñadura *nf* **1** *(de espada)* hilt; **hasta la e.,** up to the
hilt. **2** *Am (de bastón, paraguas)* handle, grip.

empuñar *vtr* **1** *(cuchillo, bastón)* to grasp, seize. **2** *fig* to take up.

emú *nm Orn* emu.

emulación *nf* emulation.

emulador,-a *adj* emulating.

emular *vtr* to emulate.

émulo,-a *nm,f* emulator, rival.

emulsión *nf* emulsion.

emulsionar *vtr* to emulsify.

emulsivo,-a *adj* emulsifying.

en *prep* **1** *(lugar)* in, on, at; **en casa,** at home; **en el trabajo,** at work; **en la mesa,** on the table; **en Madrid,** in Madrid. **2** *(tiempo)* in, on, at; **cae en martes,** it falls on a Tuesday; **en ese momento,** at that moment; **en 1940,** in 1940; **en verano,** in summer. **3** *(transporte)* by, in; **ir en coche/tren,** to go by car/train; **ir en avión,** to fly; **ir en bici,** to cycle. **4** *(tema, materia)* at, in; **bueno en deportes,** good at sports; **Doctor en Física,** Doctor of Physics; **experto en política,** expert in politics. **5 fuiste tonto en creerlo,** you were silly to believe it; *(con infinitivo)* **la conocí en el andar,** I recognized her by her walk. **6** *(modo, manera)* **en broma,** jokingly; **en camino,** on the way; **en francés,** in French; **en guerra,** at war; **¡en marcha!,** let's go!; **en serio,** seriously; **en voz baja,** softly.

enaceitar *vtr* to oil, make oily.

enaguas *nfpl (prenda)* underskirt *sing*, petticoat *sing*.

enajenación *nf* distraction, absent-mindedness. ■ **e. mental,** mental derangement, insanity.

enajenador,-a *adj* alienating.

enajenamiento *nm véase* **enajenación.**

enajenar I *vtr* **1** *Jur (propiedad)* to alienate, transfer. **2** *(turbar)* to drive mad. II **enajenarse** *vr* **1** *(de una amistad)* to become estranged *or* alienated, alienate. **2** *(enloquecer)* to go mad.

enaltecer *vtr* **1** *(alabar)* to praise, extol. **2** *(ennoblecer)* to do credit to.

enamoradizo,-a *adj* easy infatuated.

enamorado,-a I *adj* in love, lovesick. II *nm,f* lover, sweetheart; *fig* **soy un e. del golf,** I love golf, I'm a lover of golf.

enamoramiento *nm* infatuation, falling in love.

enamorar I *vtr* to win the heart of. II **enamorarse** *vr* to fall in love **(de,** with).

enancar I *vtr* **1** *Am (montar)* to put on a horse's haunches. **2** *Arg* to follow, be a consequence **(a,** of). II **enancarse** *vr* **1** *Am (montar)* to ride on a horse's haunches. **2** *Am fig (entremeterse)* to meddle, interfere.

enanismo *nm* dwarfism.

enano,-a I *adj* dwarf; *Bot* **frutal e.,** dwarf fruit tree. II *nm, f* dwarf; *fam* **divertirse como un e.,** to have a great time.

enarbolar I *vtr* **1** *(izar)* to hoist, fly. **2** *(blandir) (bandera)* to wave; *(estandarte)* to carry; *(espada)* to brandish. II **enarbolarse** *vr* **1** *(caballo)* to rear up. **2** *fig (persona)* to get angry.

enarcar *vtr (lomo)* to arch; *(cejas)* to raise.

enardecedor,-a *adj* rousing, exciting.

enardecer I *vtr (sentimiento)* to rouse, stir up; *(persona)* to fill with enthusiasm. II **enardecerse** *vr fig* to become aroused *or* excited.

enardecimiento *nm* excitement, enthusiasm.

enarenar I *vtr* to sand. II **enarenarse** *vr Náut* to run aground.

enastar *vtr (cuchillo)* to put a handle on.

encabestrar *vtr (caballo)* to put a halter on.

encabezamiento *nm (de carta)* heading; *(de periódico)* headline, title; *(préambulo)* foreword, preamble.

encabezar *vtr* **1** *(carta, lista)* to head; *(periódico)* to title, head, lead. **2** *(movimiento, rebelión)* to lead; *(carrera)* to lead.

encabritarse *vr* **1** *(caballo)* to rear (up); *(barco)* to rise; *(coche, avión)* to stall. **2** *fig (enfurecerse)* to get cross.

encadenado,-a I *pp de* **encadenar.** II *nm* **1** *Arquit* buttress. **2** *Cin* dissolve.

encadenamiento *nm* **1** *(unión)* connection, linking. **2** *Lit* concatenation. **3** *Quím* chaining.

encadenar *vtr* **1** *(poner cadenas)* to chain, shackle. **2** *fig (enlazar)* to link up, connect. **3** *fig (atar)* to tie down, chain down; **los niños la encadenan,** she's tied to her children.

encajar I *vtr* **1** *(ajustar)* to encase, fit in, insert; *Téc* to gear; **e. la puerta,** to push the door to. **2** *fam (golpe, disparo)* to take, stand; *(acontecimiento, situación)* to drop; *(indirecta, comentario)* to get in; **e. un golpe a algn,** to land sb a blow. II *vi* **1** *(caber)* to fit; **estas piezas no encajan,** these pieces don't fit. **2** *fig (casar)* to fit (in), correspond, square; **su declaración no encaja con los hechos,** his statement doesn't match the facts. III **encajarse** *vr* **1** *(encalarse)* to sink, get stuck. **2** *(prenda)* to slip on; *(sombrero)* to put on. **3** *Arg (coche)* to get stuck.

encaje *nm* **1** *(acto)* fit, fitting. **2** *Téc (hueco)* socket; *(caja)* housing. **3** *Cost (bordado)* lace.

encajonar I *vtr* **1** *(poner en cajas)* to encase, put in a box, pack. **2** *(meter en un sitio estrecho)* to squeeze in *or* through. **3** *Arquit (pared)* to buttress, coffer. II **encajonarse** *vr* **1** *(en sitio estrecho)* to squeeze in *or* through. **2** *(río)* to narrow.

encalabrinar I *vtr* **1** *(olor, vino)* to go to one's head. **2** *(irritar)* to irritate, annoy. II **encalabrinarse** *vr* **1** *(irritarse)* to get annoyed. **2** *(encapricharse)* to become obsessed *or* infatuated. **3** *(obstinarse)* to be stubborn.

encalado I *pp de* **encalar.** II *nm* whitewashing.

encalambrarse *vr Am* **1** *(aterirse)* to go numb; *(de frío)* to get stiff with cold. **2** *(tener calambre)* to get cramp.

encalamocar [1], **encalamucar** *Col Méx Ven* I *vtr* to confuse, bewilder, stun. II **encalamocarse, encalamucarse** *vr* to get confused *or* bewildered, be stunned.

encalar *vtr* to whitewash.

encalladero *nm Náut* sandbank, reef.

encallar *vi* **1** *Náut* to run aground. **2** *fig* to flounder, fail.

encallecer I *vi (piel)* to harden, become callous. II **encallecerse** *vr fig (persona)* to become hardened *or* callous.

encalmarse *vr* **1** *(viento)* to drop; *(mar)* to become calm. **2** *(caballo)* to be overheated.

encamar I *vtr (en el suelo)* to stretch out, lie down. II **encamarse** *vr* **1** *(enfermo)* to go to bed. **2** *vulg ofens* **se encama fácilmente,** she's an easy lay.

encaminar I *vtr* **1** *(guiar)* to direct, guide, set *or* put on the right road; **estar bien encaminado,** to be on the right track. **2** *(orientar)* to direct, guide. II **encaminarse** *vr (dirigirse)* to head **(a,** for; **hacia,** towards).

encampanado,-a *adj* bell-shaped.

encandecer I *vtr* to make white-hot. II **encandecerse** *vr* to get white-hot.

encandilado,-a I *pp de* **encandilar.** II *adj* **1** *(erguido)* erect. **2** *(deslumbrado)* starry-eyed.

encandilar I *vtr* **1** *(deslumbrar)* to dazzle. **2** *fig (cautivar)* to fascinate, daze. **3** *fig (deseo, ilusión)* to kindle. II **encandilarse** *vr* **1** *(ojos, rostro)* to light up. **2** *Am (asustarse)* to become frightened.

encanecer *vi*, **encanecerse** *vr* **1** *(pelo)* to go grey *or US* gray. **2** *(persona)* to grow old.

encanijarse *vr* to become weak *or* puny, grow weak *or* puny.

encantado,-a I *pp de* **encantar.** II *adj* **1** *(contento)* delighted, pleased, charmed; **e. de conocerle,** pleased to meet you. **2** *(distraído)* absent-minded. **3** *(embrujado)* enchanted, haunted; **casa encantada,** haunted house.

encantador,-a I *adj* charming, delightful. II *nm, f* magician, enchanter. ■ **e. de serpientes**, snake charmer.

encantamiento *nm* spell, charm, enchantment.

encantar *vtr* 1 *(hechizar)* to bewitch, cast a spell on. 2 *(gustar)* to delight, charm, love; **estoy encantado de haber venido**, I'm delighted I came; **me encanta el alpinismo**, I love mountaineering.

encante *nm (subasta)* auction; *(lugar)* auction room.

encanto *nm* 1 *(hechizo)* spell, charm; *fig* **como por e.**, as if by magic. 2 *(atractivo)* delight, charm; **esta casa es un e.**, this house is lovely; *(persona)* **ser un e.**, to be charming. 3 *(expresión cariñosa)* love, sweetheart; **como tu quieras, e.**, whatever you say, darling.

encañado¹ I *pp de* **encañar¹**. II *nm (conducción de agua)* piping, drainage system.

encañado² *vtr* I *pp de* **encañar²**. II *nm (para plantas)* trellis.

encañar¹ *vtr* 1 *(agua)* to pipe. 2 *(terreno)* to drain.

encañar² *vtr (planta)* to train.

encañonar I *vtr* 1 *(arma)* to aim *or* point at. 2 *(agua)* to pipe, channel. II *vi (aves)* to grow feathers.

encaperuzado,-a *adj*, **encapirotado,-a** *adj* hooded.

encapotado,-a *adj Meteor* overcast, cloudy.

encapotarse *vr Meteor* to become overcast *or* cloudy.

encaprichamiento *nm* infatuation.

encapricharse *vr* to set one's mind (**con**, on); *(encariñarse)* to take a fancy (**con**, to); *(enamorarse)* to get a crush (**con**, on).

encapuchado,-a *adj* hooded.

encarado,-a *adj* **bien e.**, nice-looking, good-looking; **mal e.**, plain.

encaramar I *vtr* 1 *(alzar)* to raise, lift up. 2 *fig (alabar)* to praise, extol. II **encaramarse** *vr* 1 *(subirse)* to climb up, get high up. 2 *fig (encumbrarse)* to reach a high (social) position.

encarar I *vtr* 1 *(poner de frente)* to bring face to face. 2 *fig* to face, confront; **no sabía cómo e. el problema**, he didn't know how to deal with the problem. 3 *(arma)* to point, aim. II **encararse** *vr* **e. con** *or* **a**, to face up to, bring oneself face to face with.

encarcelación *nf* imprisonment, incarceration.

encarcelar *vtr* to imprison, jail, incarcerate.

encarecer I *vtr* 1 *(aumentar precios)* to put up the price of. 2 *fig (alabar)* to praise. 3 *fig (insistir)* to urge, recommend; **e. a algn que haga algo**, to urge sb to do sth. II **encarecerse** *vr* to go up (in price).

encarecidamente *adv* earnestly, insistently.

encarecimiento *nm* 1 *(aumento de precios)* increase *or* rise in price; **el e. de la vida**, the rise in the cost of living. 2 *(insistencia)* insistence; **con e.**, earnestly, insistently. 3 *(alabanza)* extolling, praising.

encargado,-a I *pp de* **encargar**. II *adj* in charge; **la persona encargada de este asunto**, the person in charge of this matter. III *nm, f Com (hombre)* manager; *(mujer)* manager, manageress; *(responsable)* person in charge. ■ *Educ* **e. de curso**, tutor; *Pol* **e. de negocios**, chargé d'affaires.

encargar I *vtr* 1 *(encomendar)* to put in charge of, entrust. 2 *(recomendar)* to advise, recommend. 3 *Com (pedir)* to order, place an order for; *(libro, cuadro)* to commission; **e. un traje**, to have a suit made. II **encargarse** *vr* **e. de**, to take charge of, look after, see to, deal with; **yo me encargaré de ella**, I'll take care of her.

encargo *nm* 1 *(recado)* errand; **hacer encargos**, to run errands. 2 *(tarea)* job, assignment. 3 *(responsabilidad)* responsibility. 4 *Com* order, commission; **hecho de e.**, *(a petición)* made to order; *(a la medida)* tailor-made.

encariñado,-a 1 *pp de* **encariñarse**. II *adj* attached (**con**, to).

encariñarse *vr* to become fond (**con**, of), get attached (**con**, to).

encarnación *nf* incarnation, embodiment; *fig* **la e. de la bondad**, kindness itself *or* personified.

encarnado,-a *adj* 1 *(hecho carne)* incarnate. 2 *(rojo)* red; **ponerse e.**, to blush, go red.

encarnadura *nf* **buena/mala e.**, (skin with) good/poor healing qualities.

encarnar I *vtr* 1 *(gen)* to personify, embody. 2 *Teat (personaje, papel)* to play. II *vi* 1 *Rel* to become incarnate. 2 *Med* to heal. III **encarnarse** *vr Rel* to become incarnate.

encarnizado,-a I *pp de* **encarnizar**. II *adj* fierce, bloody. ◆ **encarnizadamente** *adv* fiercely, cruelly.

encarnizamiento *nm* fierceness, savagery.

encarnizar I *vtr (enfurecer)* to enrage. II **encarnizarse** *vr* to be brutal *or* cruel; **e. con algn**, to attack sb savagely.

encarpetar *vtr* to file (away).

encarrilar *vtr* 1 *(coche, tren)* to put on the road *or* rails. 2 *fig* to direct, guide, **e. bien/mal un asunto**, to get off to a good/bad start.

encarrujar I *vtr Am (tela)* to gather. II **encarrujarse** *vr (rizarse)* to curl up.

encartar I *vi Naipes* to lead. II *vtr* 1 *Jur (encausar)* to indict. 2 *(proscribir)* to outlaw, ban, proscribe. 3 *(implicar)* to implicate; **los encartados en el asunto**, those involved in the affair.

encarte *nm* 1 *Naipes* lead. 2 *(en una publicación)* free leaflet, booklet.

encartuchar *vtr Am* to roll up into a cone.

encasillado,-a I *pp de* **encasillar**. II *adj (actor, actriz)* typecast. III *nm (conjunto de casillas)* set of squares *or* pigeonholes.

encasillar *vtr* 1 *(poner en casillas)* to pigeonhole. 2 *(clasificar)* to class, classify; *Teat (actor, actriz)* to typecast.

encasquetar I *vtr (sombrero)* to pull down, put on; *fig* **e. una idea a algn**, to put an idea into sb's head. II **encasquetarse** *vr* 1 *(sombrero)* to pull down, put on. 2 *(empeñarse)* **se le encasquetó en la cabeza la idea de irse de viaje**, he got it into his head to go away on a trip.

encasquillamiento *nm (arma)* jamming.

encasquillar I *vtr Am (caballo)* to shoe. II **encasquillarse** *vr (arma)* to jam.

encausar *vtr Jur* to prosecute.

encauzamiento *nm* 1 *(de agua)* channelling. 2 *fig* guidance, orientation.

encauzar *vtr* 1 *(agua)* to channel. 2 *fig* to channel, direct, guide.

encebollado,-a *adj Culin* with onion; **hígado e.**, liver and onions.

encefalitis *nf Med* encephalitis.

encelar I *vtr* to make jealous. II **encelarse** *vr* 1 *(sentir celos)* to be jealous. 2 *Zool (estar en celo)* to be in rut *or* on heat.

encenagado,-a I *pp de* **encenagarse**. II *adj* 1 *(lleno de barro)* muddy, covered in mud; **lugar e.**, bog. 2 *fig (vicioso)* depraved.

encenagarse *vr* 1 *(cubrirse de barro)* to get covered in mud. 2 *fig (en el vicio)* to wallow.

encendedor *nm (mechero)* lighter.

encender I *vtr* 1 *(incendiar)* to light, set fire to, ignite; *(cerilla)* to strike, light; *(vela)* to light; *(luz)* to turn on, switch on, put on; *(gas)* to light, turn on; *(radio)* to switch on, turn on. 2 *fig* to inflame, stir up, provoke. II **encenderse** *vr* 1 *(incendiarse)* to catch fire, ignite; *(llama)* to flare up; *(luz)* to go *or* come on. 2 *fig* to flare up. 3 *(cara)* to blush, go red.

encendido,-a I *pp de* **encender. II** *adj* **1** *(ardiendo)* on fire, burning; *(cigarrillo)* lit; *(luz)* on; *(cable)* live. **2** *(color)* glowing, fiery; *(cara)* red. **III** *nm Aut* ignition. ◆ **encendidamente** *adv* passionately, ardently.

encerado,-a I *pp de* **encerar. II** *adj (suelo, mueble)* waxed, polished. **III** *nm* **1** *(pizarra)* blackboard. **2** *(barniz de cera)* waxing.

encerar *vtr* to wax, polish.

encerrar I *vtr* **1** *(gen)* to shut in *or* up; *(con llave)* to lock in *or* up, put under lock and key; *(vallar)* to enclose; *(confinar)* to confine. **2** *fig (contener)* to contain, include; *(implicar)* to involve; **la situación encierra grave peligro,** the situation carries a great risk. **II encerrarse** *vr* **1** *(gen)* to shut oneself up *or* in; *(con llave)* to lock oneself in. **2** *(recluirse)* to go into seclusion *or* retreat.

encerrona *nf* **1** *Taur (corrida privada)* private bullfight. **2** *fig (trampa)* trap; **preparar** *or* **tender una e. a algn,** to lay a trap for sb.

encestar *vi Dep (baloncesto)* to score (a basket).

enceste *nm Dep (baloncesto)* basket.

enchaquetarse *vr Am* to put one's jacket on.

encharcado,-a I *pp de* **encharcar. II** *adj* **1** *(terreno)* flooded, swamped. **2** *(agua)* stagnant.

encharcar I *vtr* *(terreno)* to flood, swamp. **II encharcarse** *vr* **1** *(terreno)* to swamp, get flooded. **2** *(agua) (formar charcos)* to form puddles; *(estancarse)* to become stagnant.

enchicharse *vr* **1** *Am (emborracharse)* to get drunk (on **chicha**). **2** *CAm (enfurruñarse)* to sulk.

enchilada *nf Guat Méx Nic Culin* stuffed corn pancake seasoned with chili.

enchilar I *vtr* **1** *CR Hond Méx* to season with chili. **2** *Méx fig (molestar)* to annoy. **II** *vi CR Méx Nic (chile)* to be hot.

enchiloso,-a *adj CAm Méx* hot, peppery, spicy.

enchironar *vtr arg (encarcelar)* to put away.

enchisparse *vr Am* to get drunk.

enchivarse *vr Am* to get angry.

enchufado,-a I *pp de* **enchufar. II** *adj fam* **estar e.,** to have good connections *or* contacts, be well in. **III** *nm, f fam (persona)* wirepuller; *(en la escuela)* teacher's pet; **ser un e.,** to have good contacts, have friends in the right places.

enchufar I *vtr* **1** *Elec* to plug in. **2** *(unir)* to fit, join, connect. **3** *fam* to pull strings for; **ha enchufado a su hermano en la oficina,** he got his brother a job in his office. **II enchufarse** *vr fam* to get in through the back door; **consiguió e. gracias a la influencia de su padre,** his father's influence got him in.

enchufe *nm* **1** *Elec (hembra)* socket, point; *(macho)* plug; **e. bipolar/tripolar,** two/three pin plug; **a pilas** *or* **e. a la red,** battery or mains. **2** *fam* contact; **se lo dieron por e.,** he had a friend who put in a good word for him.

enchufismo *nm fam* string-pulling; **el e. y el amiguismo,** the old boy or girl network.

enchutar *vtr CAm* to stuff, cram.

encía *nf Anat* gum.

encíclica *nf Rel* encyclical.

enciclopedia *nf* encyclopaedia, encyclopedia.

enciclopédico,-a *adj* encyclopaedic, encyclopedic.

encierro *nm* **1** *Pol (protesta)* sit-in. **2** *Rel (reclusión)* retreat. **3** *(prisión)* locking up, confinement. **4** *Taur* bullpen; *(recorrido)* bull running.

encima *adv* **1** *(sobre)* on top, above, over; **déjalo e.,** put it on top; **llevar algo e.,** to have sth on; **¿llevas cambio e.?,** do you have any change on you?; *fig* **quitarse algo de e.,** to get rid of sth. **2** *(además)* besides; **se equivocó y e. no quiso reconocerlo,** he was wrong and what was more he wouldn't admit it. **3 e. de,** *(sobre)* over; *fig (además)* besides; **deja la taza e. de la mesa,** leave the cup on the

table; **e. de que no me pagan me insultan,** not only do they not pay, but they insult me as well; *fam* **estar algn e. de otro,** to be on sb's back. **4 por e.,** *(a más altura)* above; *fig (más importante)* above; *fig (más allá de)* beyond; **aquello estaba por e. de sus posibilidades,** it was beyond his capabilities; **él está por e. de mí,** he is over me; **leyó el libro muy por e.,** he only skipped through the book. **5 de e.,** top; **el piso de e.,** the floor above.

encimar *vtr Am* to add to.

encimero,-a I *adj* top; **sábana encimera,** top sheet. **II** *nf (cocina)* hob.

encina *nf Bot* holm *or* evergreen oak, ilex.

encinta *adj* pregnant.

encintar *vtr* to adorn with ribbons.

encizañar *vtr & vi* to disrupt, cause trouble (among).

enclaustrar I *vtr* to cloister, shut up in a convent *or* monastery; *fig* to cloister, shut up. **II enclaustrarse** *vr* to shut oneself up.

enclavar *vtr* **1** *(clavar)* to nail; *(atravesar)* to pierce, transfix. **2** *(ubicar)* to locate, place.

enclave *nm* enclave.

enclenque I *adj (débil)* weak, puny; *(enfermizo)* sickly; *(delgaducho)* skinny. **II** *nm, f (débil)* weak *or* puny person; *(enfermizo)* sickly person; *(delgaducho)* skinny person.

enclítico,-a *adj & nm, f Ling* enclitic.

encocorar I *vtr fam* to annoy, get on the nerves of. **II encocorarse** *vr fam* to get annoyed, get one's back up.

encoger I *vi (contraerse)* to contract; *(prenda)* to shrink. **II** *vtr* **1** *(reducir)* to shrink, contract, shorten. **2** *fig (amilanar)* to intimidate, scare. **III encogerse** *vr* **1** *(contraerse)* to contract; *(prenda)* to shrink; **e. de hombros,** to shrug (one's shoulders); *fig* **se me encogió el corazón,** my heart sank. **2** *fig (amilanarse)* to cringe; **no se encoge ante nada,** she isn't afraid of anything, nothing daunts her.

encogido,-a I *pp de* **encoger. II** *adj* **1** *(contraído)* contracted; *(prenda)* shrunk, shrunken. **2** *fig (tímido)* diffident, shy, timid.

encogimiento *nm* **1** *(de tela)* shrinkage; **e. de hombros,** shrug of the shoulders. **2** *(timidez)* diffidence, shyness.

encolado,-a I *pp de* **encolar. II** *nm* **1** *Arte* sizing, pasting; *Carp* gluing. **2** *Cin* splicing. **3** *(de vinos)* clarification.

encolar I *vtr* **1** *Arte (lienzo, pared)* to size, paste; *Carp (madera)* to glue. **2** *Cin (película, cinta)* to splice. **3** *(vino)* to clarify.

encolerizar I *vtr* to infuriate, anger, exasperate. **II encolerizarse** *vr* to lose one's temper, get angry.

encomendar I *vtr (encargar)* to commend, entrust, put in charge; **le encomendaron una misión,** they entrusted him with a mission. **II encomendarse** *vr* to entrust oneself (**a,** to); **e. a Dios,** to put one's trust in God.

encomiar *vtr* to extol, laud.

encomiástico,-a *adj* eulogistic, laudatory.

encomienda *nf* **1** *(encargo)* assignment, mission. **2** *Am (paquete postal)* postal parcel.

encomio *nm* praise, tribute, eulogy; **digno de e.,** praiseworthy.

enconado,-a I *pp de* **enconar. II** *adj* **I** *Med* inflamed, sore. **2** *(discusión)* bitter, fierce.

enconar I *vtr* **1** *Med (herida)* to inflame. **2** *(exasperar)* to anger; **e. el ánimo de algn,** to make sb angry. **II enconarse** *vr* **1** *Med (herida)* to become inflamed *or* sore. **2** *(exasperarse)* to get angry *or* irritated.

encono *nm* spitefulness, ill feeling.

encontradizo,-a *adj* **hacerse el e. (con algn),** to bump into (sb) accidentally on purpose.

encontrado,-a I *pp de* **encontrar. II** *adj (contrario)* conflicting, contrary; **pareceres encontrados,** conflicting opinions.

encontrar I *vtr* **1** *(gen)* to find; **no lo encuentro,** I can't find it. **2** *(persona)* to bump into, come across. **3** *(dificultades)* to run into, come up against. **4** *(pensar)* to find, think; **encuentro que no es justo,** I don't think it's fair; *(percibir)* **te encuentro muy cambiado,** you've changed a lot. II **encontrarse** *vr* **1** *(cosas, personas)* to meet; **¿dónde nos encontramos?,** where shall we meet?; **me encontré con Pilar,** I bumped into *or* met Pilar; **nos encontramos con muchos problemas,** we ran into a lot of trouble. **2** *(sentirse)* to feel, be; **e. a gusto,** to be *or* feel comfortable; **e. con ganas de** *or* **fuerzas para hacer algo,** to feel like doing sth. **3** *(estar)* to be, find oneself; **me encontraba en París,** I was in Paris; **me encuentro en apuros,** I am in a bit of trouble.

encontronazo *nm* **1** *(choque)* collision, crash. **2** *fig (de personalidades, ideas)* clash.

encoñado,-a I *vulg* **1** *pp de* **encoñarse.** II *adj* **estar e.,** to be infatuated.

encoñarse *vr vulg* to become infatuated **(de,** with).

encopetado,-a *adj (de alto copete)* upper-class, grand; *(presumido)* haughty, conceited.

encorajar I *vtr (animar)* to encourage. II **encorajarse** *vtr (irritarse)* to get furious *or* angry.

encorajinarse *vr fam* to get angry, lose one's temper.

encorchar *vtr (botellas)* to cork.

encordonar *vtr* to tie up (with cord).

encorvado,-a I *pp de* **encorvar.** II *adj (cosa)* curved, bent; *(persona)* bent, stooping.

encorvadura *nf,* **encorvamiento** *nm (acción)* bending; *(de persona)* stoop, curvature.

encorvar I *vtr* to bend. II **encorvarse** *vr* to stoop *or* bend (over).

encrespado,-a I *pp de* **encrespar.** II *adj* **1** *(pelo)* curly. **2** *(mar)* rough, choppy.

encrespar I *vtr* **1** *(pelo)* to curl, frizz. **2** *(mar)* to make choppy *or* rough; **el viento encrespó las aguas,** the wind whipped up waves on the sea. **3** *fig (enfurecer)* to infuriate. II **encresparse** *vr* **1** *(pelo)* to stand on end. **2** *(mar)* to get rough. **3** *fig (enfurecerse)* to get cross *or* irritated.

encrucijada *nf* crossroads *pl,* intersection; *fig (apuro)* crossroads; **estar en la e.,** to be at crisis point, not know which way to turn.

encrudecer *vi,* **encrudecerse** *vr Meteor (tiempo)* to get colder *or* worse.

encuadernación *nf* **1** *(oficio)* bookbinding. **2** *(cubierta)* binding; **e. en rústica,** paperback; **e. en tela,** cloth binding. ■ **(taller de) e.,** bindery.

encuadernador,-a *nm,f* bookbinder.

encuadernar *vtr* to bind.

encuadramiento *nm* framing.

encuadrar I *vtr* **1** *(cuadro, imagen)* to frame. **2** *fig (encajar)* to fit, insert. **3** *fig* to contain, comprise. II **encuadrarse** *vr* **1** *fig (tener como marco)* **la historia se encuadraba en la Inglaterra victoriana,** the story was set in Victorian England. **2** *(incorporarse)* to become part of, join.

encuadre *nm Cin TV* framing.

encubar *vtr (vino)* to vat.

encubierta *nf* fraud.

encubierto,-a I *pp de* **encubrir.** II *adj (secreto)* concealed, hidden, secret; *(fraudulento)* fraudulent, underhand. ◆ **encubiertamente** *adv (secretamente)* secretly; *(fraudulentamente)* fraudulently.

encubridor,-a *nm,f Jur* accessory (after the fact), abettor.

encubrimiento *nm* concealment, hiding; *Jur* complicity, abetment.

encubrir *(pp* **encubierto)** *vtr* **1** *(ocultar)* to conceal, hide; *(criminal)* to shelter. **2** *Jur (ser cómplice en)* to be an accomplice in, abet.

encucurucharse *vr CAm Col* to get up on top, reach the top.

encuentro *nm* **1** encounter, meeting; **e. casual** *or* **fortuito,** chance meeting; **ir** *or* **salir al e. de algn,** to go out to meet sb. **2** *(choque)* collision; **e. de opiniones,** clash of opinion. **3** *Dep* meeting, match, clash; **e. amistoso,** friendly match. **4** *Mil* skirmish.

encuesta *nf* **1** *(sondeo)* (opinion) poll, survey; **hacer una e.,** to carry out an opinion poll. **2** *(investigación)* investigation, inquiry.

encuestador,-a *nm,f* pollster.

encuestar *vtr* to poll.

encumbrado,-a I *pp de* **encumbrar.** II *adj (eminente)* eminent, distinguished; *(socialmente)* upperclass.

encumbramiento *nm* **1** *(acción)* rise, raising. **2** *(posición)* high position, elevated status.

encumbrar I *vtr* to elevate, exalt. II **encumbrarse** *vr* to rise to a high (social) position.

encurtidos *nmpl Culin* pickles.

encurtir *vtr* to pickle.

ende (por) *loc adv* therefore.

endeble *adj* weak, puny, feeble.

endeblez *nf* weakness, fragility, feebleness.

endemia *nf Med* endemic disease.

endémico,-a *adj* **1** *Med* endemic. **2** *fig* chronic.

endemoniado,-a *adj* **1** *(poseso)* possessed. **2** *fig (diabólico)* diabolical; *(maldito)* wretched.

endentar *vtr & vi Téc* to enmesh, interlock.

enderezamiento *nm (poner derecho)* straightening out *or* up; *(poner vertical)* setting upright.

enderezar I *vtr* **1** *(poner derecho)* to straighten out; *(poner vertical)* to set upright. **2** *(guiar)* to direct; *fig* to guide. **3** *(enmendar)* to put in order, set to rights. II **enderezarse** *vr (ponerse recto)* to straighten up.

endeudamiento *nm* borrowing, state of indebtedness. ■ **e. exterior,** foreign debt.

endeudarse *vr* to get *or* fall into debt.

endiablado,-a *adj* **1** *(poseso)* possessed. **2** *(malo)* evil, wicked; *(travieso)* mischievous, devilish. **3** *(maldito)* wretched, cursed. **4** *(desenfrenado)* wild. ◆ **endiabladamente** *adv* diabolically; *fig* **e. difícil,** extremely difficult.

endibia *nf Bot* endive.

endilgar *vtr fam* **1** *(trabajo)* to palm off onto; **endilgaron el trabajo a Elvira,** they lumbered Elvira with the job. **2** *(golpe)* to land, deal. **3** *fig* **nos endilgó un largo discurso,** she made us sit through a long speech.

endiñar *vtr (golpe)* to land; *(tortazo)* to fetch.

endiosamiento *nm* conceit, vanity.

endiosar I *vtr* to deify. II **endiosarse** *vr* to become conceited *or* vain.

enditarse *vr Am* to get into debt.

endocrino,-a I *adj Biol* endocrine, endocrinal. II *nm,f fam* endocrinologist.

endocrinología *nf Med* endocrinology.

endocrinólogo,-a *nm,f Med* endocrinologist.

endomingarse *vr fam* to put on one's Sunday best.

endosar *vtr* **1** *Fin (cheque)* to endorse; **e. una letra de cambio,** to endorse a bill of exchange. **2** *fam* to lumber; **me han endosado el trabajo más pesado,** I've been lumbered with the most boring job.

endoso *nm* endorsement; **sin e.,** unendorsed.

endrina *nf Bot* sloe.

endrino,-a I *adj (color)* blue-black. II *nm Bot* sloe, blackthorn.

endrogarse *vr Am* **1** *(endeudarse)* to get into debt. **2** *(drogarse)* to take drugs, use drugs.

endulzar vtr (dulcificar) to sweeten; fig (mitigar) to alleviate, ease.

endurecer I vtr 1 (poner duro) to harden, make hard. 2 fig (fortalecer) to harden, toughen; **e. su postura,** to take a hard or tough line. II **endurecerse** vr 1 (ponerse duro) to harden, become hard. 2 fig (fortalecerse) to become hardened or tough.

endurecimiento nm hardening, toughening.

ene nf 1 (letra) name of the letter N in Spanish. 2 (cantidad indeterminada) x; **un número e. de veces,** x number of times.

enebro nm Bot juniper.

enema nm Med enema.

enemigo,-a I adj enemy, hostile; **barco e.,** enemy ship; **soy e. de la bebida,** I'm against drink. II nm,f enemy, foe; **somos enemigos declarados,** there's no love lost between us.

enemistad nf hostility, hatred, enmity.

enemistar I vtr to set at odds, cause a rift between. II **enemistarse** vr to become enemies; **e. con algn,** to fall out with sb, become sb's enemy.

energético,-a adj energy, power; **crisis energética,** energy crisis.

energía nf energy. ■ **e. hidráulica/nuclear,** water/nuclear power; fig **e. vital,** vitality.

enérgico,-a adj energetic; **decisión enérgica,** firm decision; **en tono e.,** emphatically.

energúmeno,-a nm, f fam (hombre) madman; (mujer) mad woman; **ponerse como un e.,** to go up the wall.

enero nm January; **la cuesta de e.,** the post-Christmas slump; véase tamb **noviembre.**

enervación nf 1 Med (debilidad) enervation. 2 fam (irritación) irritation, exasperation, annoyance.

enervante adj 1 Med (debilitante) enervating. 2 fam (irritante) irritating, exasperating, annoying.

enervar vtr 1 Med (debilitar) to enervate. 2 fam (irritar) to irritate, exasperate, annoy.

enésimo,-a adj 1 Mat n[th]; **elevado a la enésima potencia,** raised to the nth power. 2 fam umpteenth; **por enésima vez,** for the umpteenth time.

enfadadizo,-a adj touchy, irritable.

enfadado,-a I pp de **enfadar.** II adj angry, cross, annoyed, US mad; **estamos enfadados,** we're angry with each other; **estoy e. contigo,** I'm cross with you; **tener cara de e.,** to look angry.

enfadar I vtr to make angry or cross or annoyed. II **enfadarse** vr 1 to get angry or cross (**con,** with); **e. por nada,** to make a fuss about nothing. 2 (dos personas) to fall out.

enfado nm anger, irritation; **fue un e. tonto,** she got angry for nothing; **¿se te ha pasado el e.?,** have you calmed down?

enfadoso,-a adj annoying, irritating.

enfangar I vtr to cover with mud. II **enfangarse** vr 1 (hundirse en el fango) to stick in or sink into the mud. 2 (ensuciarse de fango) to get muddy, get covered in mud. 3 fig to get involved in dirty business; **e. en el vicio,** to wallow in vice.

énfasis nm inv 1 (fuerza) emphasis, stress; **poner e. en algo,** to lay stress on sth. 2 (afectación) **hablar con e.,** to talk in an affected way.

enfático,-a adj emphatic.

enfatizar vtr to emphasize, stress.

enfermar vi to become or fall ill, be taken ill; **e. de agotamiento,** to suffer from exhaustion; **e. del corazón,** to have heart trouble.

enfermedad nf 1 Med illness, disease, sickness; **ausentarse por e.,** to be away ill or sick. ■ **e. contagiosa,** contagious disease; **e. venérea,** venereal disease. 2 fig

(mal) malady, sickness.

enfermería nf sick bay, infirmary.

enfermero,-a nm,f (mujer) nurse; (hombre) male nurse.

enfermizo,-a adj unhealthy, sickly; fig **mente enfermiza,** morbid mind.

enfermo,-a I adj sick, ill; **caer e.,** to be taken ill; fam **esa gente me pone e.,** those people make me sick. II nm, f sick person; (paciente) patient; **e. grave,** seriously ill patient.

enfermucho,-a adj fam ailing, sickly; **débil y e.,** frail and weak.

enfervorizar vtr to arouse passions, arouse fervour in, enthuse; **sus palabras enfervorizaron a la muchedumbre,** his words aroused the passions of the crowd.

enfiestarse vr Am to enjoy oneself.

enfilar I vtr 1 (ir) to make for; (calle) to go along or down; (túnel) to go through. 2 (dirigir) to direct.

enflaquecer I vtr (adelgazar) to make thin; (debilitar) to weaken. II vi (adelgazar) to get thin, lose weight.

enflaquecido,-a adj (delgado) thin; (débil) weak, extenuated.

enflaquecimiento nm 1 (adelgazamiento) loss of weight. 2 fig (debilidad) weakening.

enflatarse vr 1 Am (apenarse) to sulk. 2 Méx (ponerse de mal humor) to get into a bad mood.

enfocar vtr 1 to focus, focus on, get into focus; Fot **bien/mal enfocado,** in/out of focus. 2 (iluminar) to shine a light on. 3 fig to approach, look at; **e. un tema desde otro punto de vista,** to look at a subject from another angle.

enfoque nm 1 (acción) focus, focusing. 2 fig approach, angle, point of view.

enfrascar I vtr to bottle. II **enfrascarse** vr (en una actividad) to become absorbed or engrossed (**en,** in); (en la lectura) to bury oneself (**en,** in); **e. en un problema,** to get tangled up or deeply involved in a problem.

enfrenar vtr (caballo) to bridle.

enfrentamiento nm confrontation.

enfrentar I vtr 1 (encarar) to bring face to face, confront. 2 (afrontar) to face, confront. II **enfrentarse** vr 1 (encararse) to face (**a, -**), face up (**a,** to), confront (**a, -**). 2 Dep (rival) to face (**a, -**), meet (**a, -**); Box to take (**a,** on). 3 (pelearse) to have an argument (**a,** with), fall out (**a,** with).

enfrente adv 1 opposite, facing; **la casa de e.,** the house opposite or across the road. 2 **e. de.,** opposite (to), facing; **la casa está e. del colegio,** the house is opposite the school. 3 fig opposed to, against; **estaban uno e. del otro,** they were opposed to each other.

enfriador I adj cooling. II nm cooler.

enfriamiento nm 1 (proceso) cooling. 2 Med (catarro) cold, chill; **pillar un e.,** to catch a cold or chill.

enfriar I vtr to cool (down), chill. II vi 1 Meteor to get cold or colder. 2 fig to cool down; **dejar e. algo,** to let sth cool down. III **enfriarse** vr 1 (tener frío) to get or go cold; (resfriarse) to get or catch a cold. 2 (lo que estaba demasiado caliente) to cool down; (ponerse demasiado frío) to go cold; **el agua se ha enfriado un poco, ahora puedes bañar el bebé,** the water has cooled down a little, now you can bath the baby; **bebe el café, se está enfriando,** drink your coffee, it's getting cold. 3 fig (pasión, ánimo) to cool off.

enfundar I vtr to put in its case; (mueble) to cover; (espada) to sheathe. II **enfundarse** vr (abrigarse) to wrap oneself up.

enfurecer I vtr to enrage, enfuriate. II **enfurecerse** vr 1 to get furious, lose one's temper. 2 (mar) to become rough.

enfurecimiento nm infuriation, temper, rage.

enfurruñamiento nm fam sulking.

enfurruñarse *vr fam* to sulk.

engaitar *vtr fam* to take in, trick.

engalanado,-a I *pp* de **engalanar. II** *adj* decked out, festooned.

engalanar I *vtr (calle, balcón)* to deck out, adorn. **II engalanarse** *vr (persona)* to dress up, get dressed up.

engallarse *vr fig* to be *or* get cocky.

enganchado,-a I *pp* de **enganchar. II** *adj arg (droga)* hooked; **estar e.,** to be hooked (on drugs).

enganchar I *vtr* **1** *(pez)* to hook; *(animales)* to hitch (up), harness; *Ferroc* to couple. **2** *fig (pillar)* to hook, rope in. **II engancharse** *vr* **1** to get caught *or* hooked up; *arg (drogas)* to get hooked. **2** *Mil* to join up.

enganche *nm* **1** *(gancho)* hook; *(animales)* hitching, harnessing; *Ferroc* coupling. **2** *Mil* enlistment, recruitment.

enganchón *nm (ropa, pelo)* snag.

engañabobos *nm inv (persona)* con man, confidence trickster; *(trampa)* con trick, trap.

engañadizo,-a *adj* gullible.

engañar I *vtr (gen)* to deceive; *(estafar)* to cheat, trick; *(mentir)* to lie, mislead; **las apariencias engañan,** appearances can deceive; **me estás engañando,** I don't believe you, you're not telling me the truth; *fig* **e. el hambre,** to stave off hunger; *fam* **engaña a su mujer,** he's unfaithful to his wife. **II engañarse** *vr (ilusionarse)* to deceive oneself; *(equivocarse)* to be wrong *or* mistaken; **no nos engañemos,** let's not kid ourselves.

engañifa *nf fam* trick; *(estafa)* swindle.

engaño *nm* **1** *(gen)* deceit; *(estafa)* fraud, trick, swindle; *(mentira)* lie; **aquí no hay e. alguno,** it's all above board. **2** *(error)* mistake, misunderstanding; **estar en un e.,** to be mistaken.

engañoso,-a *adj (palabras)* deceitful, dishonest; *(apariencias)* deceptive; *(consejo)* misleading.

engarce *nm* **1** *(de perlas)* threading, stringing. **2** *(engaste)* setting.

engarzar *vtr* **1** *(collar)* to thread; *(perlas)* to string. **2** *(engastar)* to mount, set. **3** *fig (palabras)* to string together.

engastar *vtr* to set, mount.

engaste *nm* setting, mount.

engatusar *vtr fam* to coax, wheedle, get round; **e. a algn para que haga algo,** to coax sb into doing sth.

engendrar *vtr* **1** *Biol* to engender, beget. **2** *fig* to give rise to, cause; **e. la duda en algn,** to plant the seeds of doubt in sb's mind.

engendro *nm* **1** *Biol (feto)* foetus, *US* fetus. **2** *(criatura deforme)* malformed child; *fam (persona fea)* freak. **3** *fig pey* monstrosity; **este cuadro es un e.,** this painting is a monstrosity.

englobar *vtr (incluir)* to include, comprise; *(reunir)* to lump together, put all together.

engolado,-a *adj (persona)* arrogant, pompous; *(estilo)* high-flown.

engolfarse *vr fig* to get absorbed **(en,** in).

engolosinar I *vtr (tentar)* to tempt, entice. **II engolosinarse** *vr* to become fond **(con,** of), develop a taste **(con,** for).

engomar *vtr* to gum, glue, stick.

engordar I *vtr* to fatten (up), make fat. **II** *vi* **1** to put on weight, get fat; **he engordado tres kilos,** I've put on three kilos. **2** *(comida, bebida)* to be fattening; **el pan engorda,** bread is fattening.

engorde *nm* fattening (up).

engorro *nm fam* bother, nuisance.

engorroso,-a *adj fam* awkward, bothersome, tiring; **ser e.,** to be a bother *or* a nuisance.

engranaje *nm* **1** *Téc* gear, gears *pl*, gearing; *(de un reloj)* cogwheel. **2** *fig* machinery; **metido en el e. de la política,** caught up in the wheels of politics.

engranar I *vtr* **1** *Téc* to gear, engage. **2** *fig (ideas)* to connect, link. **II** *vi (encajar)* to engage, mesh.

engrandecer *vtr* **1** *(aumentar)* to enlarge, magnify. **2** *fig (realzar)* to extol, magnify; **viajar engrandece el espíritu,** travel broadens the mind. **3** *fig (alabar)* to exalt, raise up.

engrandecimiento *nm* **1** *(aumento)* enlargement, increase. **2** *fig (realce)* enhancement. **3** *fig (alabanza)* praise.

engrasar *vtr* **1** *(lubricar)* to grease, lubricate, oil. **2** *(manchar)* to make greasy, stain with grease. **3** *fam (sobornar)* to bribe.

engrase *nm* **1** *(acción)* greasing, lubrication, oiling. **2** *(sustancia)* lubricant.

engreído,-a *adj* vain, conceited, stuck-up.

engreimiento *nm* vanity, conceit.

engreír I *vtr Am (mimar)* to spoil, pamper. **II engreírse** *vr* **1** *(envanecerse)* to become vain, conceited, full of oneself. **2** *Am (encariñarse)* to become fond **(de,** of).

engrosar I *vtr (incrementar)* to enlarge; *(cantidad)* to increase, swell. **II** *vi (engordar)* to get fat, put on weight.

engrudar *vtr* to paste.

engrudo *nm* paste.

enguantado,-a *adj* gloved.

enguaracarse *vr CAm* to hide oneself away.

enguatar *vtr* to pad.

engullir *vtr* to gobble up, gulp down.

enharinar *vtr Culin* to (sprinkle with) flour.

enhebrar *vtr Cost* to thread.

enhiesto,-a *adj* upright, erect.

enhorabuena *nf* congratulations *pl*; **dar la e. a algn,** to congratulate sb; **mi más cordial e.,** my warmest congratulations.

enhornar *vtr Culin* to put into the oven.

enigma *nm* enigma, mystery, puzzle.

enigmático,-a *adj* enigmatic, mysterious, puzzling.

enjabonar *vtr* **1** *(dar jabón a)* to soap. **2** *fig (dar coba a)* to butter up, soft-soap.

enjaezar *vtr Am* to harness, saddle up.

enjalbegar *vtr* to whitewash.

enjambrar I *vtr* to hive. **II** *vi* to swarm.

enjambre *nm* **1** *(de abejas)* swarm. **2** *fig* swarm, crowd, throng.

enjaretar *vtr fam* to reel off; **le enjaretó un rollo sobre política,** he went on and on about politics to him.

enjaular *vtr* **1** *(animal)* to cage. **2** *fam* to put inside, put in jail.

enjoyar I *vtr* to adorn with jewels. **II enjoyarse** *vr fam* to overdo one's jewellery.

enjuagar I *vtr* to rinse. **II enjuagarse** *vr* **e. la boca,** to rinse out one's mouth.

enjuague *nm* **1** *(acción)* rinse; *(líquido)* mouthwash. **2** *fig* plot, scheme.

enjugar *vtr*, **enjugarse** *vr* **1** *(secar)* to dry, wipe (away), mop up; **enjugarse la frente,** to mop one's brow. **2** *Fin (deuda, déficit)* to clear, wipe out.

enjuiciamiento *nm* **1** *(opinión)* judgement. **2** *Jur (civil)* lawsuit; *(criminal)* trial, prosecution.

enjuiciar *vtr* **1** *(juzgar)* to judge, examine. **2** *Jur (juicio civil)* to sue; *(criminal)* to indict, prosecute.

enjundia *nf* **1** *(grasa)* fat. **2** *fig (sustancia)* substance; *(importancia)* importance. **3** *fig (vigor)* force, vitality; *(persona)* character.

enjundioso,-a *adj* meaty, solid.

enjuto,-a *adj* lean, skinny.

enlace *nm* **1** *(unión)* link, connection; **servir de e.,** to establecer un e.,** to link. ■ **e. químico,** chemical bond. **2** *(casamiento)* marriage. **3** *Ferroc* connection. ■ **estación de e.,** junction; **vía de e.,** crossover. **4** *(persona)* liaison officer. ■ **e. sindical,** shop steward, *US* union delegate.

enladrillado,-a I *pp de* **enladrillar. II** *adj* brick; **suelo e.,** brick floor. **III** *nm* brick paving.

enladrillar *vtr* to pave with bricks.

enlatado,-a I *pp de* **enlatar. II** *adj* canned, tinned.

enlatar *vtr* **1** *(meter en latas)* to can, tin. **2** *Am (techo)* to roof with tin.

enlazar I *vtr (unir)* to link, connect, tie (together); **e. una idea con otra,** to link one idea with another. **II** *vi Ferroc* to connect (**con,** with). **III enlazarse** *vr* **1** *(unirse)* to be linked *or* connected, link. **2** *(familias)* to become linked by marriage.

enlodar I *vtr* **1** *(enfangar)* to muddy, cover with mud. **2** *fig (reputación)* to stain, besmirch. **II enlodarse** *vr* to get muddy.

enloquecedor,-a *adj* maddening.

enloquecer I *vi (volverse loco)* to go mad. **II** *vtr* **1** *(volver loco)* to drive mad. **2** *fam (gustar mucho)* to be mad *or* wild about; **la enloquece el cine,** she's mad on the cinema. **III enloquecerse** *vr (volverse loco)* to go mad, go out of one's mind.

enloquecimiento *nm* madness, insanity.

enlosado,-a I *pp de* **enlosar. II** *nm* floor tiling; *(losas)* paving.

enlosar *vtr* to tile, pave (with tiles).

enlozar *vtr Am* to cover *or* coat with enamel.

enlucido,-a I *pp de* **enlucir. II** *nm* plaster.

enlucir *vtr (pared)* to plaster; *(metal)* to polish.

enlutado,-a I *pp de* **enlutar. II** *adj* mourning, in mourning.

enlutar I *vtr* **1** *(poner de luto)* to cast *or* put into mourning. **2** *fig (ensombrecer)* to cast a shadow over. **II enlutarse** *vr (estar de luto)* to be in mourning; *(ponerse de luto)* to go into mourning.

enmaderar *vtr (pared)* to panel; *(suelo)* to lay down floorboards.

enmadrado,-a *pp de* **enmadrarse. II** *adj (niño)* **estar e.,** to be tied to one's mother's apron strings.

enmadrarse *vr (niño)* to be tied to one's mother's apron strings.

enmarañamiento *nm* **1** *(enredo)* entanglement, tangle. **2** *fig* confusion, muddle.

enmarañar I *vtr* **1** *(pelo)* to tangle. **2** *fig (complicar)* to complicate, confuse, muddle up. **II enmarañarse** *vr* **1** *(pelo)* to get tangled. **2** *fig (complicarse)* to get confused, get into a mess *or* a muddle.

enmarcar *vtr (gen)* to frame; *(rodear)* to surround.

enmascarado,-a I *pp de* **enmascarar. II** *adj* masked. **III** *nm,f* masked person.

enmascarar I *vtr* **1** *(poner una máscara)* to mask. **2** *fig (ocultar)* to conceal, mask, disguise. **II enmascararse** *vr (ponerse una máscara)* to put on a mask; *(disfrazarse)* to masquerade (**de,** as).

enmasillar *vtr* to putty.

enmendadura *nf* correction.

enmendar I *vtr (corregir)* to correct, put right; *(daño)* to repair, put right; *Jur* to amend. **II enmendarse** *vr (persona)* to reform, mend one's ways.

enmienda *nf (corrección)* correction; *(de daño)* repair, indemnity, compensation; *Jur Pol* amendment; **hacer propósito de e.,** to turn over a new leaf.

enmohecer I *vi (metal)* to rust; *Bot* to make mouldy *or US* moldy. **II enmohecerse** *vr (metal)* to rust, get rusty; *Bot* to go mouldy *or US* moldy; *fig* to go rusty.

enmontarse *vr CAm Col Agr* to turn into a wilderness.

enmoquetar *vtr* to carpet.

enmudecer I *vi (callar)* to become dumb, lose one's voice. **II enmudecerse** *vr* **1** *(estar callado)* to be silent, say nothing. **2** *(callar)* to become dumb, lose one's voice.

ennegrecer I *vtr* to blacken, turn black, darken. **II ennegrecerse** *vr* to turn *or* go black; *fig* to get dark, darken.

ennoblecer *vtr* **1** *(hacer noble)* to ennoble. **2** *fig (dar esplendor)* to do honour to, be a credit to; **este comportamiento te ennoblece,** your behaviour is to your credit.

enojadizo,-a *adj* irritable, touchy, quick-tempered.

enojado,-a I *pp de* **enojar. II** *adj* angry, cross.

enojar I *vtr* to anger, annoy, upset. **II enojarse** *vr* to get angry, lose one's temper, get annoyed *or* cross.

enojo *nm* anger, annoyance, irritation.

enojoso,-a *adj* annoying, irritating.

enorgullecer I *vtr* to fill with pride. **II enorgullecerse** *vr* to be *or* feel proud; **e. de algo,** to pride oneself on sth, be proud of sth.

enorgullecimiento *nm* pride.

enorme *adj* **1** *(grande)* enormous, huge, vast, tremendous. **2** *fig (desmedido)* monstrous. ◆ **enormemente** *adv* enormously, greatly, tremendously.

enormidad *nf* **1** *(grandeza)* enormity, hugeness. **2** *fig (desmesura)* enormity, monstrousness; *fam* **nos gustó una e.,** we loved it. **3** *(acto)* wicked *or* monstrous thing.

enrabiar I *vtr* to enrage, infuriate. **II enrabiarse** *vr* to become enraged *or* infuriated.

enraizado,-a I *pp de* **enraizar. II** *adj* rooted.

enraizar *vi,* **enraizarse** *vr* **1** *Bot (planta)* to take root. **2** *fig (persona)* to put down roots.

enramada *nf* **1** *(follaje)* foliage, leaves *pl.* **2** *(cobertizo)* covering of branches.

enranciar I *vtr* to make rancid *or* stale. **II enranciarse** *vr* to go rancid, become stale.

enrarecer I *vtr (aire)* to rarefy. **II enrarecerse** *vr* **1** *(aire)* to rarefy. **2** *(escasear)* to become scarce.

enrarecido,-a I *pp de* **enrarecer. II** *adj* rarefied; *fig* **un ambiente e.,** a tense atmosphere.

enrasar *vtr* to make level *or* even.

enredadera *nf Bot* climbing plant, creeper.

enredador,-a I *adj (entrometido)* troublemaking, interfering, meddlesome; *(chismoso)* gossip; **una persona e.,** a busybody. **II** *nm,f (entrometido)* troublemaker; *(chismoso)* busybody, gossip.

enredar I *vtr* **1** *(animal)* to net, catch in a net. **2** *(trampa)* to set. **3** *(enmarañar)* to entangle, tangle up. **4** *fig (asunto)* to confuse, complicate; *(trabajo)* to make a mess of. **5** *fig (persona)* to involve, implicate (**en,** in). **6** *fig (meter cizaña)* **e. a A con B,** to set A against B. **II enredarse** *vr* **1** *(enmarañarse)* to get entangled, get tangled (up) *or* in a tangle. **2** *fig (asunto)* to get complicated *or* confused; *(trabajo)* to get in a mess; **e. en una discusión,** to get caught up in a argument. **3** *fig (persona)* to get involved (**con,** with), have an affair (**con,** with).

enredo *nm* **1** *(maraña)* tangle. **2** *fig (lío)* muddle, mess, mix-up, confusion. **3** *(amoroso)* love affair. **4** *Teat* plot. **5 enredos,** *fam (trastos)* bits and pieces.

enrejado *nm* **1** *(reja)* grating, railings *pl;* *(de jaula, celda)* bars *pl;* *(de jardín)* trellis; *(de ventana)* lattice; **e. de alambre,** wire netting fence. **2** *Cost* openwork.

enrejar *vtr* **1** *(puerta, ventana)* to put a grating on; *(terreno, área)* to fence, put railings round. **2** *Méx Cost* to darn, mend, sew up.

enrevesado,-a *adj* complicated, difficult.

enriquecer I *vtr* **1** *(hacer rico)* to make rich. **2** *fig (mejorar)* to enrich. **II enriquecerse** *vr (hacerse rico)* to get *or* become rich, prosper.

enriquecimiento *nm* enrichment.

enristrar *vtr (ajos, cebollas)* to string together; *(lanza)* to couch.

enrocar *vi Ajedrez* to castle.

enrojecer I *vtr (volver rojo)* to redden, turn red; *(metal)* to make red-hot. **II** *vi (ruborizarse)* to blush. **III enrojecerse** *vr (ruborizarse)* to blush; *(volverse rojo)* to go red; *(metal)* to get red-hot.

enrojecimiento *nm (metal)* reddening, glowing; *(rubor)* blushing.

enrolar I *vtr* to enrol, *US* enroll, sign on, sign up; *Mil* to enlist. **II enrolarse** *vr* to enrol, *US* enroll, sign on; *Mil* to enlist, join up.

enrollable *adj* that rolls up, roll-up; **persiana e.,** roller blind.

enrollado,-a I *pp de* **enrollar. II** *adj* **1** rolled up. **2** *fam* **estar e. con algn,** *(conversando)* to be deep in conversation with sb; *(tener relaciones con)* to go out with sb, see sb. **3** *fam* great; **es un tío muy e.,** he's a great guy.

enrollar I *vtr (papel)* to roll up; *(hilo)* to wind up; *(cable)* to coil. **II enrollarse** *vr* **1** *fam (hablar)* to chatter, go on and on; **e. como una persiana,** to go on and on. **2** *fam (tener relaciones)* **e. con algn,** to have an affair with sb. **3** *fam* **e. bien,** to get on well with people; **e. mal,** to be difficult to get on with.

enronquecer *vi,* **enronquecerse** *vr* to become *or* go hoarse.

enronquecimiento *nm* hoarseness, huskiness.

enroque *nm Ajedrez* castling.

enroscar I *vtr* **1** to coil (round), wind; *(cable)* to twist. **2** *(tornillo)* to screw in *or* on. **II enroscarse** *vr* to coil, wind; *(cable)* to twist, roll up; *(serpiente)* to coil itself.

enrostrar *vt Am* to reproach.

ensacar *vtr* to pack in sacks *or* bags, bag.

ensaimada *nf Culin* kind of spiral pastry from Majorca.

ensalada *nf Culin* salad; **e. de fruta,** fruit salad.

ensaladera *nf* salad bowl.

ensaladilla *nf Culin* **e. rusa,** Russian salad.

ensalmo *nm* spell, incantation, charm; **como por e.,** as if by magic.

ensalzamiento *nm (enaltecimiento)* exaltation;*(elogio)* praise.

ensalzar *vtr (enaltecer)* to exalt; *(elogiar)* to praise, extol, *US* extoll.

ensamblador *nm* **1** *Inform* assembler. **2** *Carp* joiner.

ensambladura *nf Téc* joint.

ensamblaje *nm Téc* assembly, joining.

ensamblar *vtr* to join, assemble.

ensañamiento *nm* cruelty, brutality.

ensañarse *vr* to be brutal **(con,** with), delight in tormenting **(con,** -).

ensanchamiento *nm* widening, broadening.

ensanchar I *vtr (hacer más ancho)* to enlarge, widen, extend, stretch, expand; *Cost (prenda)* to let out. **II ensancharse** *vr* **1** *(hacerse más ancho)* to get wider, spread, stretch, expand. **2** *fig (persona)* to get a big head, become conceited.

ensanche *nm* enlargement, widening, extension; *(de ciudad)* urban development.

ensangrentado,-a I *pp de* **ensangrentar. II** *adj* bloodstained, bloody.

ensangrentar *vtr* to stain with blood, cover in blood.

ensartar *vtr* **1** to string together. **2** *fig* to reel off, rattle off; **ensartaba una mentira detrás de otra,** he reeled off one lie after another.

ensayar *vtr* **1** *Teat* to rehearse; *Mus* to practise. **2** to test, try out.

ensayismo *nm Filos Lit* essay writing.

ensayista *nmf Filos Lit* essayist.

ensayo *nm* **1** test, trial, experiment, attempt; **a modo de e.,** as an experiment. **2** *Teat* rehearsal. ■ **e. general,** dress rehearsal. **3** *Filos Lit* essay. **4** *Rugby* try.

---

enseguida *adv,* **en seguida** *adv (inmediatamente)* at once, straight away; *(poco después)* in a minute, soon; **e. voy,** I'll be right there.

ensenada *nf* **1** *Geog* inlet, cove. **2** *Arg (corral)* farmyard.

enseña *nf* ensign, standard.

enseñado,-a I *pp de* **enseñar. II** *adj (adiestrado)* trained; *(persona)* educated, instructed.

enseñanza *nf* **1** *(educación)* education, teaching, schooling; **dedicarse a la e.,** to be a teacher. ■ **e. laboral,** vocational training; **e. primaria/secundaria/superior,** primary/secondary/higher education. **2** *(doctrina)* teaching, doctrine.

enseñar *vtr* **1** *(instruir)* to teach, instruct, train; *(educar)* to educate; **e. a algn a hacer algo,** to teach sb how to do sth. **2** *(mostrar)* to show; *(señalar)* to point out; **enseña la combinación,** her petticoat is showing; **nos enseñó la casa,** he showed us over the house; *fig* **e. los dientes,** to bare one's teeth.

enseñorearse *vr* to take over **(de,** -), take possession **(de,** of).

enseres *nmpl (bártulos)* belongings, goods; *(material)* equipment *sing.*

enseriarse *vr Am* to become *or* look serious.

ensillar *vtr Equit* to saddle (up), put a saddle on.

ensimismado,-a I *pp de* **ensimismarse. II** *adj (absorbido)* engrossed; *(abstraído)* lost in thought.

ensimismamiento *nm* absorption.

ensimismarse *vr (absorberse)* to become engrossed; *(abstraerse)* to be lost in thought.

ensoberbecer I *vtr* to make arrogant *or* conceited; **el triunfo le ensoberbeció,** success went to his head. **II ensoberbecerse** *vr* **1** to become arrogant *or* conceited. **2** *fig (mar)* to get rough.

ensombrecer I *vtr* to cast a shadow over. **II ensombrecerse** *vr* to darken; *fig* to become gloomy.

ensoñación *nf* daydream, pipe dream.

ensoñador,-a I *adj* dreamy. **II** *nm,f* dreamer.

ensoñar *vtr* to daydream about.

ensopar *vtr Am* to soak.

ensordecedor,-a *adj* deafening.

ensordecer I *vtr* to deafen. **II** *vi* to go deaf.

ensordecimiento *nm* deafness.

ensortijado,-a I *pp de* **ensortijarse. II** *adj* curly.

ensortijarse *vr* to curl.

ensuciar I *vtr* **1** to dirty, *US* get dirty, mess up. **2** *fig (reputación)* to harm, damage. **II ensuciarse** *vr* to get dirty; **e. las manos,** to get one's hands dirty.

ensueño *nm* dream, fantasy; **unas vacaciones de e.,** a dream holiday.

entablado I *pp de* **entablar. II** *nm* **1** *(entarimado)* planking, planks *pl.* **2** *(suelo)* wooden floor.

entablar I *vtr* **1** *(conversación)* to open, begin; *(amistad)* to strike up; *(negocios)* to start. **2** *Ajedrez* to set up. **3** *Am Jur* **e. acción** *or* **demanda,** to take legal action. **II** *vi Am (empatar)* to draw. **III entablarse** *vr Guat Méx (establecerse)* to settle.

entablillado I *pp de* **entablillar. II** *nm Med* splint.

entablillar *vtr Med* to splint.

entalegar *vtr* **1** *(embolsar)* to put in sacks. **2** *(dinero)* to hoard. **3** *arg* to put inside, put in the nick.

entallar *vtr Cost* to take in at the waist; **un vestido muy entallado,** a close-fitting dress; **una camisa entallada,** a fitted shirt.

entarimado,-a I *pp de* **entarimar. II** *nm* parquet floor.

entarimar *vtr* to cover with parquet.

ente *nm* **1** being. **2** *(institución)* entity, organization, body. **3** *pey* oddball.

enteco,-a *adj* puny, weak, frail.

entelerido,-a *adj Am* thin, skinny.

entendederas *nfpl fam* brains; **ser duro de e.,** to be slow on the uptake; **tener buenas e.,** to be quickwitted.

entendedor,-a *adj* understanding; *prov* **a buen e. con pocas palabras bastan,** a nod's as good as a wink.

entender I *vtr* **1** (*comprender*) to understand; (*darse cuenta*) to realize; **a mi e.,** to my way of thinking; **dar a e. que ...,** to imply that ...; **hacerse e.,** to make oneself understood; **tengo entendido que ...,** I understand that ...; *fam* **no entiendo ni jota,** I don't understand a word. **2** (*discurrir*) to think, believe. **3** (*significar*) to mean, intend; **¿qué entiende con eso?,** what does he mean by that? **4** (*oír*) to hear. **II** *vi* **1** (*comprender*) to understand. **2** (*saber*) **e. de** *or* **en,** to know about, be an expert in; **entiende de vinos,** she knows a lot about wine. **3** *Jur* to have jurisdiction over. **III entenderse** *vr* **1** (*comprenderse*) to be understood, be meant; **¿qué se entiende por esa palabra?,** what does that word mean? **2** *fam* to know what one is doing; **yo me entiendo,** I have my reasons. **3** *fam* to get on (well) (**con,** with); **e. con un hombre,** to have an affair with a man.

entendido,-a *pp de* **entender. II** *nm,f* expert.

entendimiento *nm* **1** (*sentido común*) understanding, comprehension, grasp. **2** (*inteligencia*) mind, intellect, understanding.

entenebrecer I *vtr* to darken, obscure. **II entenebrecerse** *vr* to become *or* get dark.

entente *nf* agreement; *Pol* entente (cordiale).

enterado,-a I *pp de* **enterar. II** *adj* knowledgeable, well-informed; **estar e.,** to be in the know; **estar e. de ...,** to be aware of ... . **III** *nm,f fam* expert; **es un e. de la música,** he's a real expert on music.

enterar I *vtr* (*informar*) to inform (**de,** about, of); (*poner al corriente*) to acquaint (**de,** with), tell (**de,** about). **II enterarse** *vr* to find out; **me he enterado de que ...,** I hear that ...; **ni me enteré,** I didn't even realize it!; **¡toma, paro que te enteres!,** so now you know!

enterciar *vtr Am* to pack.

entereza *nf* **1** wholeness, entirety. **2** *fig* integrity, strength of character.

enterizo,-a *adj* in one piece, whole.

enternecedor,-a *adj* moving, touching. ◆ **enternecidamente** *adv* tenderly.

enternecer I *vtr* to move, touch. **II enternecerse** *vr* to be moved *or* touched.

enternecimiento *nm* **1** (*cariño*) tenderness. **2** (*compasión*) pity.

entero,-a I *adj* **1** (*completo*) entire, complete, whole; **por e.,** completely. **2** *fig* (*recto, justo*) honest, upright. **3** *fig* (*que tiene entereza*) firm, resolute, unshaken. **II** *nm* **1** *Mat* whole number. **2** *Fin* point; **subir/bajar enteros,** to go up/down points. **3** *Am* (*entrega*) payment. ◆ **enteramente** *adv* entirely, completely.

enterrador *nm* gravedigger.

enterramiento *nm* burial, interment.

enterrar I *vt* **1** to bury, inter. **2** *fig* to forget, give up. **II enterrarse** *vr fig* to bury oneself; **se enterró en vida,** he cut himself off from the world.

entibiar I *vtr* **1** (*enfriar*) to cool, take the chill off. **2** *fig* (*debilitar*) to cool down. **II entibiarse** *vr* **1** (*enfriarse*) to become lukewarm, cool (down). **2** *fig* (*debilitarse*) to cool off.

entidad *nf* **1** entity, organization; **e. comercial,** company, firm. **2 de e.,** of importance, important.

entierro *nm* **1** burial. **2** (*ceremonia*) funeral; **asistir a un e.,** to go to a funeral; *arg* **parecer un e. de tercera,** to be like a funeral

entintar *vtr* **1** *Impr* to ink. **2** (*manchar*) to stain with ink.

entizar *vtr Am Bill* (*taco*) to chalk.

entlo. *abr de* **entresuelo,** first *or US* second floor, mezzanine.

entoldado,-a I *pp de* **entoldar. II** *nm* **1** awning. **2** (*para fiesta, baile*) marquee.

entoldar I *vtr* (*toldo*) to put up. **2** (*para fiesta, baile*) to put up. **II entoldarse** *vr Meteor* to become overcast, cloud over.

entomología *nf* entomology.

entomológico,-a *adj* entomologic, entomological.

entomólogo,-a *nm,f* entomologist.

entonación *nf* intonation.

entonado,-a I *pp de* **entonar. II** *adj* arrogant.

entonar I *vtr* **1** (*nota*) to pitch; (*canción*) to sing; (*voz*) to modulate. **2** *Med* (*tonificar*) to tone up. **II** *vi* **1** to intone. **2** *fig* to be in harmony, be in tune (**con,** with); **no entona,** she is out of tune. **III entonarse** *vr* to give oneself airs.

entonces *adv* then; **por aquel e.,** at that time; **¿qué hiciste e.?,** what did you do then?

entono *nm* arrogance.

entontar *vtr Am* to make silly.

entontecer *vtr* (*enloquecer*) to drive mad; (*atontar*) to befuddle.

entorchado,-a I *pp de* **entorchar. II** *nm* braid.

entorchar *vtr* **1** (*velas*) to twist into a torch. **2** (*cuerda, hilo*) to cover with wire *or* silk.

entornado,-a I *pp de* **entornar. II** *adj* (*ojos etc*) half-closed; (*puerta*) ajar.

entornar *vtr* (*ojos etc*) to half-close; (*puerta*) to leave ajar.

entorno *nm* environment, surroundings *pl*.

entorpecer I *vtr* to make numb *or* dull *or* sluggish. **2** *fig* to obstruct, hinder, impede.

entorpecimiento *nm* **1** numbness, dullness, sluggishness. **2** *fig* obstruction, stumbling block.

entortadura *nf* crookedness.

entortar *vtr* to make crooked.

entosigar *vtr* to poison.

entrada *nf* **1** (*gen*) entrance, entry; (*puerta*) way in, doorway; **dar e. a,** to let *or* allow in. ■ **e. principal,** main entrance. **2** *Teat Cin* ticket, admission; (*público*) audience; (*recaudación*) takings *pl*. **3** *fig* beginning; (*libro, discurso*) opening; *fig* **de e.,** for a start. **4** *Culin* entrée. **5** *Com* (*en el libro de cuentas*) entry; (*pago inicial*) down payment, deposit; **e. de capital,** capital inflow; **derechos de e.,** import duty *sing*. **6 entradas,** *Com* (*ingresos*) receipts; takings. **7 tener entradas (en la frente),** to have a receding hairline.

entrador,-a I *adj Am* (*animado*) spirited; (*intrépido*) intrepid, daring. **II** *nf Guat Méx Venez pey* easy woman.

entramado *nm* (wooden) framework.

entrambos,-as *adj & pron fml* both.

entramparse *vr* **1** (*enredarse*) to get into a mess. **2** (*endeudarse*) to get into debt.

entrante I *adj* entering, coming, incoming; **el mes e.,** next month. **II** *nf Culin* starter.

entrañable *adj* **1** (*íntimo*) intimate, close. **2** (*afectuoso*) affectionate, warm-hearted. ◆ **entrañablemente** *adv* deeply, dearly.

entrañar I *vtr* **1** (*ocultar*) to hide. **2** (*conllevar*) to carry; (*implicar*) to entail. **II entrañarse** *vr* to get deeply attached (**con,** to).

entrañas *nfpl* **1** *Anat* entrails, bowels. **2** *fig* heart *sing*; core *sing*. **de buenas/malas e.,** good-/evil-hearted; **no tener e.,** to be heartless; **sacar las e. a algn,** to bleed sb dry; **sin e.,** heartless; *fam* **echar las e.,** to puke one's guts up.

entrar I *vi* **1** to come in, go in, enter; **hazle e.,** invite him in; *fig* **entrado en edad** *or* **en años,** well on in years; *fig* **no me entra en la cabeza que ...,** I can't believe that ...; *fam* **esa mujer no me entra,** I can't stand that woman; *fam* **no e. ni salir en algo,** to be indifferent to sth; *fam* **no me**

entran las matemáticas, I can't get the hang of maths. 2 *(encajar)* to fit; **no me entra el zapato,** that shoe doesn't fit me. 3 *(período, época)* to enter. 4 *fig (asociación)* to go into. 5 *Mús* to come in; **entró el piano,** the piano came in; *Teat* to enter; **entró Macbeth,** Macbeth entered. 6 *(caber)* **en una libra entran tres manzanas,** you get three apples to the pound. 7 *(año etc)* to begin; **el año que entra,** next year, the coming year; *fig* **hasta bien entrada la tarde,** well into the evening. 8 *(e. + a + infin)* to begin to do sth; **entra a trabajar en la Embajada,** he's starting a new job at the Embassy. 9 *(venir)* to come over; **me entró dolor de cabeza,** I got a headache; **me entraron ganas de reír,** I felt like laughing. II *vtr* 1 to introduce; **e. el coche en el garaje,** to put the car into the garage. 2 *Inform* to access. III **entrarse** *vr* to get in.

entre *prep* 1 *(de dos términos)* between; **e. tu y yo,** between the two of us; *fig* **nadar e. dos aguas,** to sit on the fence; *fig* **tener un asunto e. manos,** to be tied up with a matter. 2 *(de más de dos)* among, amongst; **estaba escondido e. los árboles,** it was hidden amongst the trees; **estoy e. los aprobados,** I've passed. 3 *(entremedio)* somewhere between; **e. frío y caliente,** warmish; **e. gris y azul,** greyish-blue. 4 *(sumando)* counting; **e. el cine y la cena gastamos cinco mil pesetas,** what with the cinema and dinner we spent five thousand pesetas; **e. hombres y mujeres somos veinte,** there are twenty of us all together.

entreabierto,-a I *pp de* **entreabrir.** II *adj (ojos etc)* half-open; *(puerta)* ajar.

entreabrir *vtr (pp entreabierto) (ojos)* to half open; *(puerta)* to leave ajar.

entreacto *nm Teat* interval, intermission.

entrecano,-a *adj* greying, greyish.

entrecejo *nm* space between the eyebrows: *(ceño)* frown; **fruncir el e.,** to frown, knit one's brow.

entrechocarse *vr* to collide, crash.

entrecomillado,-a *adj* in quotation marks *or* inverted commas.

entrecortado,-a *adj* 1 intermittent; *(voz)* faltering, hesitant; *(objeto)* partially cut. 2 *fig* to cut off, interrupt.

entrecot *nm,* **entrecó** *nm Culin* fillet steak.

entrecruzarse *vr* to interweave; **e. los dedos,** to clasp one's hands.

entrecubiertas *nfpl Náut* between-decks.

entredicho *nm* 1 *(prohibición)* prohibition, ban; *Jur* injunction. 2 **estar en e.,** to be suspect; **poner algo en e.,** to have one's doubts about sth.

entredós *nm* 1 *Cost* insertion, panel. 2 *Mueb* cabinet, dresser.

entrefilete *nm Prensa* little piece.

entrefino,-a *adj* medium quality.

entrega *nf* 1 *(gen)* handing over; *(de premios)* presentation; *Com* delivery; **hacer e. de algo,** to present *or* deliver *or* hand over sth. ■ **e. contrareembolso,** cash on delivery. 2 *(de posesiones)* surrender; **la e. de armas,** the surrender of arms. 3 *(fascículo)* part, instalment, *US* installment. 4 *(devoción)* selflessness.

entregar I *vtr* 1 *(deberes etc)* to give in, hand in; *(ceder)* to give up; *(dar)* to deliver; *Com* to deliver; **e. algo en mano,** to hand sth over. 2 *Mil (posesiones)* to surrender. II **entregarse** *vr* 1 *(dedicarse)* give oneself up; *(rendirse)* to give in, surrender, submit. 2 **e. a,** to devote oneself to; *pey* to indulge in.

entrelazar I *vtr to* entwine, interlace; **e. las manos,** to clasp one's hands. II **entrelazarse** *vr* to entwine, interlace.

entrelinear *vtr* to write between lines.

entrelistado,-a *adj* striped, variegated.

entrelucir *vi* 1 *(dejarse ver)* to show through. 2 *(lucir poco)* to shine dimly.

entremedias *adv* in between; *(mientras tanto)* meanwhile, in the meantime; **e. de,** between, among.

entremés *nm* 1 *Teat* interlude, short farce *or* play. 2 **entremeses,** *Culin* hors d'oeuvres.

entremeter I *vtr* to insert, place between. II **entremeterse** *véase* **entrometerse.**

entremezclar *vr* to intermingle, intermix, mix.

entrenador,-a *nm,f Dep* trainer, coach.

entrenamiento *nm* training.

entrenar I *vtr* to train, coach. II **entrenarse** *vr* 1 *Dep* to train. 2 *fig* to train, prepare oneself.

entrenzar *vtr* to plait, braid.

entrepaño *nm Arquit* alcove, bay; *(de puerta, ventana)* panel; *(de estantería)* shelf.

entrepierna *nf* crotch, crutch; *vulg (órganos)* genitals *pl*; *vulg* **se lo pasó por la e.,** he didn't give a shit about it.

entreponer *pp (entrepuesto) vtr desus* to interpose, place between.

entresacar *vtr* to pick out, select; *(pelo, plantas)* to thin out.

entresijo *nm* secret, mystery, hidden aspect; **esto tiene muchos entresijos,** this is very complicated.

entresuelo *nm* mezzanine, first *or US* second floor.

entretanto I *adv* meanwhile, for the time being. II *nm* **en el e.,** in the meantime.

entretecho *nm Am* attic, loft.

entretejer *vtr* to interweave, intertwine, entwine; **entretejido de seda,** interwoven with silk.

entretela *nf* 1 *Cost* interfacing, interlining. 2 **entretelas,** *fam* heart *sing*, heartstrings; *(entrañas)* entrails.

entretención *nf Am* amusement, entertainment.

entretenedor,-a *adj* entertaining.

entretener I *vtr* 1 *(divertir)* to entertain, amuse, distract. 2 *(retrasar)* to delay; *(detener)* to hold up, detain; **no te entretengo más,** I won't keep you any longer. 3 *(engañar) (hambre)* to kill, stave off; *(tiempo)* to while away. II **entretenerse** *vr* 1 *(distraerse)* to amuse oneself. while away the time; **me entretengo tocando el piano,** I enjoy playing the piano; **sólo para e.,** just for fun. 2 *(retrasarse)* to be delayed, be held up.

entretenida *nf* 1 mistress, kept woman. 2 **dar a algn la e.,** to try to put sb off.

entretenido,-a I *pp de* **entretener.** II *adj* enjoyable, entertaining.

entretenimiento *nm* 1 *(distracción)* entertainment, amusement, distraction. 2 *(mantenimiento)* upkeep, maintenance; **gastos de e.,** maintenance costs.

entretiempo (de) *adj* period between seasons; **un abrigo de e.,** a lightweight coat.

entrever *vtr* 1 *(vislumbrar)* to glimpse, catch sight of. 2 *fig (adivinar)* to guess, suspect; **dejó e. que ...,** she hinted that ... .

entreverado,-a I *pp de* **entreverar.** II *adj* mixed, patchy; *Culin* **tocino e.,** streaky bacon.

entreverar *vtr* to mix, mix up.

entrevés *indic pres véase* **entrever.**

entreví *pt indef véase* **entrever.**

entrevía *nf Ferroc* gauge.

entrevista *nf (encuentro)* meeting; *(entrevista)* interview; **hacer una e. a algn,** to interview sb.

entrevistador,-a *nm,f* interviewer.

entrevistar I *vtr* to interview. II **entrevistarse** *vr* **e. con algn,** to have an interview *or* a meeting with sb.

entristecedor,-a *adj* saddening.

entristecer I *vtr* to sadden, make sad. II **entristecerse** *vr* to be sad **(por,** about).

entrometerse *vr* to meddle, interfere **(en,** in), intrude.

entrometido,-a I *pp de* **entrometerse.** II *adj* interfering, nosy. III *nm,f* meddler, busybody, nosey-parker.

entromparse vr 1 fam to get sloshed. 2 Am to get cross.

entroncamiento nm 1 relationship by marriage. 2 Ferroc junction.

entroncar I vtr 1 to relate, link, connect. 2 Méx to mate animals of the same coat. **II** vi to be related to, be connected with; **e. con una familia,** to marry into a family.

entronización nf enthronement.

entronizar vtr 1 to enthrone, put on the throne. 2 fig to worship, put on a pedestal.

entronque nm véase **entroncamiento**.

entrucharse vr Méx to meddle, interfere.

entubar vtr arg to sanction.

entuerto nm 1 injustice, wrong, injury; **deshacer entuertos,** to right wrongs. 2 **entuertos,** Med afterpains.

entumecer I vtr 1 to numb, make numb. 2 (mar, río) to swell. **II entumecerse** vr 1 to go numb, go dead. 2 (mar, río) to swell.

entumecido,-a I pp de **entumecer. II** adj 1 (entorpecido) numb, dead. 2 (mar, río) swollen.

entumecimiento nm 1 (entorpecimiento) numbness, deadness. 2 (mar, río) high.

entumido,-a adj Col Méx shy.

enturbiar I vtr 1 to make cloudy or muddy or turbid. 2 fig to cloud, obscure, muddle. **II enturbiarse** vr 1 to get muddy, become cloudy. 2 fig to get confused or muddled.

entusiasmar I vtr to fill with enthusiasm; (gustar) to delight; **me entusiasma Grecia,** I love Greece. **II entusiasmarse** vr to get excited or enthusiastic (con, about).

entusiasmo nm enthusiasm; **con e.,** keenly, enthusiastically; **desbordar e.,** to be over the moon.

entusiasta I adj enthusiastic, keen (de, on). **II** nmf lover; Dep fan, follower, supporter.

entusiástico,-a adj enthusiastic.

enumeración nf enumeration, count, reckoning.

enumerar vtr to enumerate, count, reckon.

enunciación nf (teoría) enunciation; (palabras) statement, declaration.

enunciado,-a I pp de **enunciar. II** nm 1 (problema) wording. 2 enunciation.

enunciar vtr (teoría) to enunciate; (palabras) to state, declare.

envainar vtr to sheathe.

envalentonamiento nm arrogance, boldness.

envalentonarse vr (ser valiente) to become bold or daring; (insolentarse) to become arrogant or aggressive.

envanecer I vtr to make proud or vain. **II envanecerse** vr to become conceited or proud, give oneself airs.

envanecimiento nm conceit, vanity.

envarado,-a I pp de **envarar. II** adj numb, stiff.

envaramiento nm numbness, stiffness.

envarar vtr to stiffen, make stiff.

envasado,-a I pp de **envasar. II** adj (botella) bottled; (paquete) packed; (conservas) canned, tinned; **e. al vacío,** vacuum-packed. **III** nm (botella) bottling; (paquete) packing, (conservas) canning.

envasar vtr (paquetes) to pack; (botellas) to bottle; (enlatar) to can, tin.

envase nm 1 (acto) (gen) packing; (botella) bottling; (lata) canning. 2 (recipiente) container; (botella vacía) empty; **e. de cartón,** carton; **e. plástico,** plastic container; **e. sin retorno,** nonreturnable container.

envedijarse vr 1 (lana, pelo) to get tangled. 2 fig to quarrel.

envejecer I vi to grow old. **II** vtr to age, make look old.

envejecido,-a I pp de **envejecer. II** adj old, aged, old-looking; **está muy e.,** he looks very old.

envejecimiento nm ageing, growing old.

envenenamiento nm poisoning; **e. por la comida,** food poisoning.

envenenar vtr to poison; fig **la envidia envenenó su mente,** envy poisoned his mind.

enverdecer vi to become green.

envergadura nf 1 (de pájaro, avión) span, wingspan; Náut breadth (of sail). 2 fig importance, scope; **de gran e.,** consequential, far-reaching.

envergar vtr Náut (velas) to bend.

envés nm 1 (de tela) wrong side; (de página) back, reverse; Bot reverse. 2 (espalda) back.

envestidura nf investiture, inauguration.

enviado I pp de **enviar. II** nm, f messenger, envoy. ■ Prensa **e. especial,** special correspondent.

enviar vtr to send; Com to remit, dispatch; (por barco) to ship; **e. a algn a hacer algo,** to send sb to do sth; fam **e. a algn a paseo,** to send sb packing.

enviciar I vtr to corrupt, spoil. **II** vi Bot to produce too many leaves and not enough fruit. **III enviciarse** vr to become addicted.

envidar vi Naipes to bid, bet.

envidia nf envy; **morirse de e.,** to be green with envy; **tener e.,** to envy (**de, -**).

envidiable adj enviable.

envidiar vtr to envy; **no te envidio la suerte,** sooner you than me; **no tener nada que e.,** to compare favourably (a, with).

envidioso,-a adj envious. ◆ **envidiosamente** adv with envy, enviously.

envilecer I vtr to degrade, debase. **II** vi to lose value, be debased.

envilecimiento nm degradation, debasement.

envío nm dispatch, shipment; (remesa) consignment; (paquete) parcel; **gastos de e.,** postage and packing; **hacer un e.,** to dispatch an order. ■ **e. contra reembolso,** cash on delivery.

envite nm 1 Naipes stake, side bet. 2 offer, bid. 3 **al primer e.,** right away, straightaway.

enviudar vi (hombre) to become a widower, lose one's wife; (mujer) to become a widow, lose one's husband.

envoltorio nm 1 (cosas atadas) bundle. 2 (cubierta) wrapper, wrapping; **deshacer el e.,** to undo the wrapping; **hacer un e. con algo,** to wrap sth up.

envoltura nf wrapper, wrapping.

envolver (pp envuelto) **I** vtr 1 (cubrir) (con papel) to wrap, wrap up; (con ropa etc) to cover, cover up; fig **la niebla envolvía la ciudad,** fog enveloped the city. 2 fig to imply, involve, mean; (persona) to involve, implicate (**en,** in); **estaba envuelto en el asesinato,** he was involved in the murder. **II envolverse** vr 1 to wrap oneself up (**en,** in). 2 fig to become involved (**en,** in).

enyerbar I vtr Col Chi Méx (hechizar) lo cast a spell on. **II enyerbarse** vr 1 Am to become covered with grass, grass over. 2 Guat Méx (envenenarse) to poison oneself.

enyesado,-a I pp de **enyesar. II** nm plastering; Med plaster cast.

enyesar vtr to plaster; Med to put in plaster.

enzapatar vtr Am to put shoes on.

enzarzar I vtr 1 to cover with brambles. 2 fig to sow discord among, set at odds. **II enzarzarse** vr 1 to get entangled in brambles. 2 fig to squabble; **e. en una disputa,** to get into an argument.

enzima nf Biol enzyme.

eñe nf name of the letter Ñ in Spanish.

eoceno,-a nm Geol Eocene.

eón nm aeon, US eon.

epatar vtr arg to knock dead.

E.P.D. *abr de* **en paz descause,** rest in peace, R.I.P.

épica *nf Lit* epic poetry.

epicentro *nm* epicentre, *US* epicenter.

épico,-a *adj Lit* epic, heroic; **poema é.**, epic poem.

epicureísmo *nm* Epicureanism.

epicúreo,-a *adj* Epicurean.

epidemia *nf* epidemic.

epidémico,-a *adj* epidemic.

epidérmico,-a *adj* epidermic; **enfermedad e.**, skin disease.

epidermis *nf* epidermis, skin.

epifanía *nf Rel* Epiphany, Twelfth Night.

epiglotis *nf Anat* epiglottis.

epígrafe *nm* 1 *(cita)* epigraph, 2 *(título)* heading, title.

epigrama *nm Lit* epigram, satirical poem.

epilepsia *nf Med* epilepsy.

epiléptico,-a *(adj)* & *nm,f* epileptic; **ataque e.**, epileptic fit.

epílogo *nm* 1 epilogue, *US* epilog, final chapter. 2 *(conclusión)* summary.

episcopado *nm Rel* 1 *(lugar)* bishopric. 2 *(época)* episcopate. 3 *(conjunto de obispos)* episcopacy.

episcopal *adj Rel* episcopal.

episiotomia *nf Med* episiotomy.

episódico,-a *adj* episodic.

episodio *nm* 1 *Lit* episode. 2 *(suceso)* event.

epístola *nf fml Lit* epistle, letter.

epistolario *nm* collection of letters.

epitafio *nm* epitaph.

epíteto *nm Lit* epithet; *fam* **fuertes epitetos,** strong words of criticism.

epítome *nm* epitome, summary.

época *nf* time, age; *Hist* period, epoch; *Agr* season; **hacer é.**, to be a landmark; **la é. de las fresas,** the strawberry season; **muebles de é.**, period furniture; **por aquella é.**, about that time.

epopeya *nf* 1 *Lit* epic poem. 2 heroic action.

E. P. M. *abr de* **en propia mano,** in person, personally.

epsomita *nf* Epsom salts *pl.*

equidad *nf* 1 *Jur* equity. 2 *(templanza)* reasonableness, fairness.

equidistancia *nf* equidistance.

equidistante *adj* equidistant.

equidistar *vi* to be equidistant **(de,** from).

equilátero *nm Geom* equilateral.

equilibrado,-a I *pp de* **equilibrar.** II *adj* balanced; *(persona)* sensible; **una dieta equilibrada,** a balanced diet.

equilibrar I *vtr* 1 to balance, poise. 2 *fig* to balance, adjust. II **equilibrarse** *vr* to balance **(en,** on).

equilibrio *nm* 1 balance, equilibrium; *(en el circo)* **hacer equilibrios,** to do a balancing act; **perder el e.,** to lose one's balance. 2 *fig (de poder etc)* balance.

equilibrismo *nm* balancing act.

equilibrista *nmf* 1 tightrope walker, trapeze artist. 2 *Am Pol* opportunist.

equino¹ *nm Zool* sea urchin.

equino,-a² *adj* equine, horse.

equinoccio *nm* equinox.

equipaje *nm* 1 *(maletas etc)* luggage, baggage; **hacer el e.,** to pack, do the packing. 2 *Náut* crew.

equipar I *vtr* to equip, furnish; *Náut* to fit out. II **equiparse** *vr* to kit oneself out, equip oneself **(con, de,** with).

equiparable *adj* comparable **(a,** to; **con,** with), applicable **(a, con,** to).

equiparación *nf* comparison.

equiparar *vtr* to compare **(con,** with), liken **(con,** to).

equipo *nm* 1 *Ind* equipment; **gastos de e.,** capital expenditure *sing.* 2 *(ropas, útiles)* outfit, kit. ■ **e. de alta fidelidad,** hi-fi stereo system; **e. de novia,** trousseau. 3 *(personas)* team; *Dep* **e. de fútbol/baloncesto,** football/ basketball team. ■ **e. de salvamento,** rescue team.

equis *nf* 1 name of the letter X in Spanish. 2 *Mat* certain amount, x number.

equitación *nf* horsemanship, horse *or US* horseback riding.

equitador *nm Am* expert in horses, horseman.

equitativo,-a *adj* equitable, fair; **trato e.,** fair *or* square deal.

equivalencia *nf (igual)* equivalence; *(que sustituye)* compensation.

equivalente *adj (igual)* equivalent; *(que sustituye)* compensatory.

equivaler *vi* 1 *(ser igual)* to be equal, be equivalent, amount **(to,** a). 2 *(significar)* to be tantamount **(a,** to); **esta respuesta equivale a una negativa,** this answer is tantamount to a refusal.

equivocación *nf* error, mistake; **cometiste una e. marchándote,** you were wrong to leave.

equivocado,-a I *pp de* **equivocar.** II *adj* mistaken, wrong. ◆ **equivocadamente** *adv* by mistake.

equivocar I *vtr* to mistake, get wrong, confuse. II **equivocarse** *vr* to be mistaken *or* wrong; *(dirección)* to go wrong, get it wrong; **se equivocó de camino,** he went the wrong way; **te has equivocado,** you've made a mistake.

equívoco,-a I *adj* equivocal, misleading, ambiguous. II *nm* equivocation; ambiguity, double meaning; *(malentendido)* misunderstanding. ◆ **equívocamente** *adv* equivocally.

era¹ *nf* era, age; **e. Cristiana,** Christian era.

era² *nf* 1 *Agr* threshing floor. 2 *Hortic* bed, plot, patch.

era³ *pt indef véase* **ser.**

erario *nm Fin* exchequer, treasury.

eras *pt indef véase* **ser.**

erección *nf* 1 erection, raising; *(del pene)* erection. 2 *fig* foundation, establishment.

eréctil *adj* erectil.

erecto,-a *adj* upright; *(pene)* erect.

eremita *nm* hermit, recluse.

erensano,-a *adj of or* from Orense.

eres *indic pres véase* **ser.**

erguido,-a I *pp de* **erguir.** II *adj* 1 *(derecho)* erect, straight, upright. 2 *fig (orgulloso)* proud.

erguir I *vtr* to raise up straight, erect, lift up. II **erguirse** *vr* 1 *(levantarse)* to straighten up, stand *or* sit up straight. 2 *fig (engreírse)* to swell with pride.

erial I *adj (tierra)* uncultivated, untilled. II *nm* uncultivated land.

erica *nf Bot* heather.

erigir I *vtr* 1 *(elevar)* to erect, raise, build. 2 *fig (fundar)* to establish, found. II **erigirse** *vr* **e. en algo,** to set oneself up in sth.

erizado,-a I *pp de* **erizarse.** II *adj* bristly, prickly.

erizarse *vr* to bristle, stand on end.

erizo *nm* 1 *Zool* hedgehog. ■ **e. de mar** *or* **marino,** sea urchin. 2 *Bot* burr, prickly husk. 3 *fam (persona)* surly *or* grumpy person.

ermita *nf* hermitage, shrine.

ermitaño,-a I *nm,f* hermit, recluse. II *nm Zool* hermit crab.

erogación *nf* 1 distribution, division. 2 *Fin* **erogaciones,** expenses, outgoings.

erogar *vtr* 1 to distribute, divide, apportion. 2 *Arg Méx Par (deudas)* to pay.

erógeno,-a *adj* erogenous, crogenic.

erosión *nf* **1** *Geol* erosion, wearing away. **2** *fig (desgaste)* wear and tear.

erosionar *vtr* *Geol* to erode; *(gastar)* to wear away.

erótico,-a *adj* erotic.

erotismo *nm* eroticism.

errabundo,-a *adj* **1** wandering, vagrant. **2** *fig* aimless.

erradicación *nf* eradication, extirpation; *(enfermedad)* stamping out.

erradicar *vtr* to eradicate; *(enfermedad)* to stamp out.

errado,-a I *pp de* **errar. II** *adj* mistaken, wrong, erroneous. ◆ **erradamente** *adv* mistakenly.

errante *adj* **1** wandering, vagrant, nomadic. **2** *fig* errant.

errar I *vtr* **1** *(objetivo)* to miss, get wrong; **e. el camino,** to lose one's way. **2** *fig (persona)* to fail, fail in one's duties to. **II** *vi* **1** to wander, rove, roam. **2** to err; **e. y porfiar,** to persist in error.

errata *nf Impr* erratum, misprint; **fe de erratas,** errata.

errático,-a *adj* erratic, wandering.

erre *nf* name of the letter R in Spanish; **e. que e.,** stubbornly, pigheadedly.

erro *nm Am* error, mistake.

erróneo,-a *adj* erroneous, wrong, false; **juicio e.,** faulty judgement. ◆ **erróneamente** *adv* erroneously, wrongly, falsely.

error *nm* error, mistake; **caer en un e.,** to make a mistake; *Impr* **e. de imprenta,** misprint; **por e.,** by mistake, in error.

eructar *vi* to belch, burp.

eructo *nm* belch, burp.

erudición *nf* erudition, learning, scholarship.

erudito,-a I *adj* erudite, learned, intellectual. **II** *nm, f* scholar, intellectual, expert; **e. a la violeta,** pseudo-intellectual. ◆ **eruditamente** *adv* scholarly.

erupción *nf* **1** *(de un volcán)* eruption; **entrar en e.,** to erupt. **2** *(en la piel)* rash.

es *indic pres véase* **ser.**

esa *adj dem véase* **ese.**

ésa *adj dem véase* **ése.**

esbeltez *nf* slimness, slenderness; *(delicadeza)* gracefulness.

esbelto,-a *adj* slim, willowy, slender; *(delicado)* graceful.

esbirro *nm* **1** henchman. **2** *Hist* bailiff.

esbozar *vi* to sketch, outline; *fig* **e. una sonrisa,** to force a smile, smile wanly.

esbozo *nm* sketch, outline, rough draft.

escabechar *vtr* **1** *Culin* to pickle; *(pescado)* to souse. **2** *fam* to do in, bump off; *Educ* to fail.

escabeche *nm Culin (líquido)* brine, pickle, souse; **arenques en e.,** soused herrings.

escabechina *nf* massacre; *fam Educ* **hacer una e.,** to fail everybody.

escabel *nm* low stool, footstool.

escabrosidad *nf* **1** *(aspereza)* unevenness, roughness. **2** *fig (dificultad)* toughness, difficulty. **3** *fig (indecencia)* coarseness, crudeness.

escabroso,-a *adj* **1** *(áspero)* uneven, rough. **2** *fig (difícil)* tough, difficult. **3** *fig (indecente)* coarse, crude. ◆ **escabrosamente** *adv* **1** unevenly, roughly. **2** *fig* with difficulty. **3** coarsely, crudely.

escabullirse *vr* **1** *(entre los dedos)* to slip through. **2** *(persona)* to slip away, scuttle *or* scurry off.

escachalandrado,-a *adj CAm fam* slovenly.

escacharrar *vtr fam (plato)* to break; *(coche)* to smash up; *(plan)* to spoil, ruin.

escafandra *nf*, **escafandro** *nm* diving helmet or suit; **escafandra autónoma,** scuba.

escala *nf* **1** *(escalera)* ladder, stepladder; **e. de gato,** rope ladder. **2** *(graduación)* scale; *(de colores)* range. ◼ **e. móvil,** sliding scale; *Mús* **e. musical,** scale. **3** *(proporción)* scale; **en gran e.,** on a large scale. **4** *Náut* port of call; *Av* stopover; **hacer e. en,** to call in at, stop over in.

escalada *nf* **1** climb, climbing, scaling. **2** *fig* escalation, increase; *(precios)* rise; **la e. del terrorismo,** the rise in terrorism.

escalador,-a *nm,f* climber, mountaineer.

escalafón *nm (de personal)* roll, list of officials; *(graduación)* ladder; *(de salarios)* salary *or* wage scale.

escalar *vtr* **1** *(montaña)* to climb, scale. **2** *fig (posición social)* to climb. **3** *(asaltar)* to burgle.

escaldado,-a I *pp de* **escaldar. II** *adj* scalded; *fig* wary, cautious; **salir e.,** to get one's fingers burnt; *prov* **gato e. del agua fría huye,** once bitten, twice shy.

escaldadura *nf* scald, scalding.

escaldar *vtr* to scald.

escalera *nf* **1** staircase, stair, stairway. ◼ **e. de caracol,** spiral staircase; **e. de incendios,** fire escape; **e. mecánica,** escalator. **2** *(escala)* ladder. ◼ **e. doble** *or* **de tijera,** stepladder. **3** *Naipes* run, sequence.

escalerilla *nf Náut* gangway; *Av* (boarding) ramp.

escalfar *vtr* **1** *Culin* to poach. **2** *Méx* to shortchange.

escalinata *nf Arquit* stoop.

escalofriante *adj* hair-raising, bloodcurdling, chilling.

escalofriar *vtr* to give the shivers to.

escalofrío *nm* shiver, shudder; *(de fiebre)* chill; **me dió un e.,** *(de frío)* it made me shiver; *(de miedo, horror)* it gave me the creeps.

escalón *nm* **1** *(peldaño)* step; stepping stone; *(escala)* rung. **2** *fig* degree, level, grade; *Mil* echelon.

escalonado,-a I *pp de* **escalonar. II** *adj* at regular intervals, spaced out; *Peluq* in layers, layered.

escalonar *vtr* to place at intervals, space out; *Mil* to echelon.

escalope *nm Culin* escalope.

escalpelo *nm Med* scalpel.

escama *nf* **1** *Bot Zool* scale; *(de jabón)* flake; **jabón en escamas,** soap flakes. **2** *fig* resentment, grudge, suspicion.

escamado,-a I *pp de* **escamar. II** *adj* **1** scaly. **2** *fig* wary, suspicious.

escamar I *vtr* **1** to scale, remove the scales from. **2** *fig* to make wary *or* suspicious; **mucho me escama,** it smells fishy to me. **II escamarse** *vr* to smell a rat, become suspicious.

escamoso,-a *adj* scaly; *(piel)* dry, flaky.

escamotear *vtr* **1** *(truquear)* to whisk away, make vanish. **2** *fam fig (robar)* to lift, pinch; *(engañar)* to diddle out of, do out of. **3** *(ocultar)* to disregard, avoid.

escamoteo *nm* **1** *(prestidigitación)* sleight of hand, conjuring. **2** *(robar)* pilfering; *(mangar)* diddling.

escampar I *vtr* to clear out. **II** *vi* to stop raining, clear up.

escanciador *nm* wine waiter.

escanciar *vtr (vino)* to pour out, serve.

escandalera *nf* racket, din, fuss, uproar.

escandalizar I *vtr* to scandalize, shock. **II** *vi* to make a racket *or* a din *or* a fuss. **III escandalizarse** *vr* to be shocked *(de,* at, by).

escandallar *vtr* **1** *(fondo del mar)* to sound. **2** *Com* to fix the price of.

escandallo *nm* **1** *(mar)* sounding lead. **2** *Com* price fixing, cost accounting.

escándalo *nm* **1** *(alboroto)* racket, din, fuss, uproar; **armar un e.,** to kick up a fuss. **2** *(asombro)* shock, astonishment. **3** *(desvergüenza)* scandal, outrage.

escandaloso,-a *adj* **1** *(alborotado)* noisy, rowdy. **2** *(irritante)* scandalous, shocking, outrageous. ◆ **escandalosamente** *adv* scandalously, shockingly, outrageously.

Escandinavia *n* Scandinavia.

escandinavo,-a *adj & nm, f* Scandinavian.

escaño *nm* **1** bench; *Parl* seat. **2** *Am* park bench.

escapada *nf* **1** escape, flight; *Dep* breakaway; **en una e.,** in a jiffy. **2** flying visit, quick trip.

escapar I *vi* to escape, flee, run away; **dejar e. un suspiro,** to let out a sigh; **e. a algn,** to run away from sb; **escapó de mis manos,** it slipped out of my hands. **II escaparse** *vr* **1** to escape, run away, get away; **e. con algo,** to make off with sth; **e. por un pelo,** to have a narrow escape, have a close shave; *fig* **escapársele a uno algo,** to go unnoticed; **este detalle se me había escapado,** that detail had escaped my notice. **2** *(gas etc)* to leak, leak out, escape. **3** *(autobús, tren)* to miss; **se nos escapó el último autobús,** we missed the last bus.

escaparate *nm* **1** shop window. **2** *Am (armario)* wardrobe.

escaparatista *nmf* window dresser.

escapatoria *nf* **1** escape, flight; *fam* **hacer una e.,** to get away, skive off. **2** *(excusa)* way out, loophole.

escape *nm* **1** escape, flight, getaway; **salirse a e.,** to rush out. **2** *(de gas etc)* leak, escape, leakage. **3** *Téc* exhaust; **tubo de e.,** exhaust (pipe).

escaque *nm Ajedrez* square.

escaqueado,-a I *pp de* **escaquearse. II** *adj Ajedrez* chequered, *US* checkered.

escaquearse *vr fam* to shirk, skive off.

escarabajo *nm* **1** *Zool* beetle, scarab. **2** *fam (feo y bajo)* toad. **3 escarabajos,** scribble *sing*.

escaramujo *nm* **1** *Bot (rosal silvestre)* wild rose, dog rose; *(fruto)* rosehip. **2** *Zool* barnacle.

escaramuza *nf* **1** *Mil* skirmish. **2** *fig (riña)* squabble, brush.

escaramuzar *vi Mil* to skirmish.

escarapela *nf* cockade, rosette.

escarapelar I *vtr Am (descascarar)* to peel; *(desconchar)* to shell. **II** *vi Méx Per (atemorizarse)* to get goose flesh.

escarbar *vtr* **1** *(suelo)* to scratch. **2** *(dientes)* to pick. **3** *(fuego)* to poke. **4** *fig* to inquire into, investigate.

escarceo *nm* **1** small wave, ripple. **2** *(tentativa)* attempt. **3 escarceos,** *(del caballo)* prancing *sing*; **escarceos amorosos,** romantic adventures, flings.

escarcha *nf Meteor* hoarfrost, frost.

escarchado,-a I *pp de* **escarchar. II** *adj* **1** *Meteor* frosty, frost-covered. **2** *Culin (fruta)* crystallized, candied.

escarchar I *vi Meteor* to be frosty *or* freezing. **II** *vtr* **1** *Meteor* to cover in frost. **2** *Culin (pastel)* to ice; *(fruta)* to crystallize.

escarda *nf Hortic* weeding hoe.

escardar *vtr Hortic* **1** to weed. **2** *fig* to weed out.

escardilla *nf*, **escardillo** *nm Hortic* weeding hoe.

escarlata I *adj* scarlet. **II** *nf* **1** *(color)* scarlet. **2** *Med* scarlatina, scarlet fever.

escarlatina *nf Med* scarlatina, scarlet fever.

escarmentar I *vtr* to punish severely, teach a lesson to. **II** *vi* to learn one's lesson; **para que escarmientes,** that'll teach you (a lesson).

escarmiento *nm* punishment, lesson; **que esto te sirva de e.,** let that be a lesson to you.

escarnecer *vtr* to scoff at, mock, ridicule.

escarnio *nm* derision, mockery, ridicule.

escarola *nf Bot* curly endive, *US* escarole.

escarpa *nf* slope; *Geog Mil* scarp, escarpment.

escarpado,-a *adj (inclinado)* steep, sheer; *(abrupto)* craggy.

escarpadura *nf véase* **escarpa.**

escarpia *nf* spike, hook.

escasear I *vtr* to be sparing with, skimp on. **II** *vi* to be scarce, get scarce; **escasean las provisiones,** stores are running low.

escasez *nf* **1** *(carencia)* scarcity, shortage, lack. **2** *(mezquindad)* meanness, stinginess.

escaso,-a *adj* scarce, scant, limited; *(recursos)* slender; *(dinero)* tight; **andar e. de dinero,** to be short of money; **conocimientos escasos,** scant knowledge; **e. público,** small audience. ◆ **escasamente** *adv* **1** *(insuficientemente)* scantly, sparingly, meagrely, *US* meagerly. **2** *(raramente)* scarcely, hardly, barely.

escatimar *vtr (limitar)* to curtail, cut down; *(regatear)* to give sparingly, skimp on; **no escatimó esfuerzo para ...,** he spared no efforts to ... .

escatimoso,-a *adj* **1** *(mezquino)* sparing, mean, stingy. **2** *(malicioso)* malicious, sly, cunning.

escatología¹ *nf* scatology.

escatología² *nf Rel* eschatology.

escatológico,-a¹ *adj* scatological.

escatológico,-a² *adj Rel* eschatological.

escayola *nf* **1** plaster of Paris, stucco. **2** *Med* plaster.

escayolar *vtr Med* to put in plaster, plaster; **con el brazo escayolado,** with his arm in plaster.

escena *nf* **1** scene; **una e. conmovedora,** a touching scene; *fam* **desaparecer de e.,** to vanish; *fam* **hacer** *or* **montar una e.,** to make a scene. **2** *Teat* stage; **entrar en e.,** to go on stage; **la segunda e. del primer acto,** the second scene of the first act; **poner en e. una obra,** to stage a play.

escenario *nm* **1** *Teat* stage. **2** *Cin* scenario. **3** *fig* scene, setting; **el e. de la tragedia,** the scene of the tragedy.

escénico,-a *adj* scenic.

escenografía *nf Cin* set design; *Teat* stage design.

escenógrafo,-a *nm, f Cin* set designer; *Teat* stage designer.

escepticismo *nm* scepticism, *US* skepticism.

escéptico,-a *adj & nm, f* sceptic, *US* skeptic.

escindible *adj* divisible.

escindir I *vtr* to split, divide. **II escindirse** *vr* to split (off) (en, into).

escisión *nf* **1** split, fission; *Med* excision. **2** *fig* split, division.

esclarecer I *vtr* **1** to light up, illuminate. **2** *fig (explicar)* to clear up, shed light on. **3** *fig (entendimiento)* to enlighten. **4** *fig (afamar)* to ennoble. **II** *vi (amanecer)* to dawn.

esclarecido,-a I *pp de* **esclarecer. II** *adj* illustrious, distinguished.

esclarecimiento *nm* **1** *(luz)* illumination. **2** *(explicación)* explanation, clarification. **3** *(entendimiento)* enlightenment.

esclavitud *nf* slavery, servitude.

esclavizar *vtr* to enslave.

esclavo,-a I *adj & nm, f* slave; *fig* **ser e. de algo,** to be a slave to sth. **II** *nf (brazalete)* bangle.

esclerosis *nf Med* sclerosis.

esclusa *nf* lock, sluicegate, floodgate.

escoba *nf* brush, broom; **pasar la e.,** to sweep up; *fam* **estar como una e.,** to be as thin as a rake.

escobazo *nm* blow with a brush *or* broom; **echar a algn a escobazos,** to boot sb out.

escobilla *nf* small brush; *Aut* windscreen wiper blade.

escobón *nm* large brush *or* broom.

escocedura *nf* **1** *(herida)* sore. **2** *(dolor)* soreness, smarting.

escocer I *vi* to sting, smart; *fig* to hurt. **II escocerse** *vr* *(piel)* to be sore; *(persona)* to have a rash.

escocés,-a I *adj* Scottish, Scots; **falda escocesa,** kilt. **II** *nm, f (hombre)* Scotsman; *(mujer)* Scotswoman.

Escocia *n* Scotland.

escoger *vtr* to choose, select, pick out; *Pol* to elect; **e. del montón,** to choose from the pile; **no hay donde e.,** they are all just as bad; **tener donde e.,** to have a good choice.

escogido,-a I *pp de* **escoger. II** *adj* chosen, selected; *(en calidad)* choice, select; *Lit* **obras escogidas,** selected works. ◆ **escogidamente** *adv* discerningly.

escogimiento *nm* **1** choice, selection, pick. **2** *(acto)* choosing, selecting, picking.

escolanía *nf* (church) choir.

escolar I *adj* scholastic, school; **curso** *or* **año e.,** school year; **vacaciones escolares,** school holidays. **II** *nm, f (niño)* schoolboy; *(niña)* schoolgirl.

escolaridad *nf* schooling, education; **libro de e.,** school record book.

escolástico,-a *adj* scholastic.

escollera *nf* breakwater, jetty.

escollo *nm* reef, rock; *fig* pitfall, snag.

escolopendra *nf Zool* centipede.

escolta *nf* escort; *Náut* convoy; **dar e.,** to escort, accompany. ■ **e. personal,** bodyguard.

escoltar *vtr* to escort, accompany; *Náut* to convoy.

escombrera *nf* dump, rubbish heap, *GB* tip.

escombros *nmpl* rubbish *sing,* debris *sing.*

esconder I *vtr* to hide **(de,** from), conceal **(de,** from). **II esconderse** *vr* to hide **(de,** from), hide oneself.

escondidas *adv* **a e.,** secretly.

escondite *nm* **1** hiding place, hide-out. **2** hide-and-seek, **jugar al e.,** to play hide-and-seek.

escondrijo *nm* hiding place, hide-out.

escoñado,-a *adj vulg* knackered; **esta máquina está escoñada,** this machine's had it.

escopeta *nf* shotgun; **e. de aire comprimido,** air gun; **e. de cañones recortados,** sawn-off shotgun.

escopetazo 1 *(tiro)* gunshot. **2** *(herida)* gunshot wound. **3** *fig (malas noticias)* bombshell.

escopeteado,-a *adj fam* **ir** *or* **salirse e.,** to be off like a shot.

escoplo *nm* chisel.

escora *nf Náut* **1** *(línea de fuerte)* load line. **2** *(inclinación)* list.

escorar *vi Náut* to list, heel; **el barco va escorado,** the boat has a list; **e. a babor,** to list to port.

escorbuto *nm Med* scurvy.

escoria *nf* **1** *(metal)* dross; *(metal, carbón)* slag. **2** *fig* scum, dregs *pl.* **3 escorias,** volcanic ash *sing.*

escoriación *nf* scraping.

escorial *nm* slag heap.

escoriar *vtr* to scrape.

Escorpio *nm Astrol Astron* Scorpio.

escorpión *nm Zool* scorpion.

escórpora *nf (pez)* rascasse.

escorzar *vtr Arte* to foreshorten.

escorzo *nm* foreshortening.

escota *nf Náut* sheet; **escotas mayores,** main sheets.

escotado,-a I *pp de* **escotar**[1]. **II** *adj Cost* low-cut, low-necked; **ir muy e.,** to wear a low-necked dress. **III** *nm Cost* low neckline.

escotadura *nf Cost* low neckline.

escotar[1] *vtr* **1** *Cost* to cut a low neckline in, cut out the neck of. **2** *(un río)* to draw water from.

escotar[2] *vtr* to share the cost of; *(pareja)* to go Dutch on.

escote[1] *nm Cost* low neckline.

escote[2] *nm* **pagar a e.,** to share the cost of; *(pareja)* to go Dutch on.

escotilla *nf Náut* hatch, hatchway.

escotillón *nm* **1** *Náut* small hatch, scuttle. **2** *Teat* trap door.

escoto,-a *adj & nm, f* Scot.

escozor *nm* **1** *(dolor)* stinging, smarting. **2** *fig (sentimiento)* pain, grief.

escribanía *nf* **1** *(escritorio)* writing desk. **2** *(material)* writing set. **3** *(oficio)* clerkship. **4** *(oficina)* clerk's office. **5** notary's office.

escribano,-a *nm, f Jur* court clerk. **II** *nm Orn* bunting; **e. cerillero,** yellowhammer; **e. hortelano,** ortolan bunting; **e. montesino,** rock bunting; **e. palustre,** reed bunting; **e soteño,** cirl bunting.

escribiente *nmf* clerk.

escribir *(pp escrito)* **I** *vtr* **1** to write; **e. a mano,** to write in longhand; **e. a máquina,** to type. **2** to spell; **se escribe con g y b,** it is spelt with a g and a b. **II escribirse** *vr* to write to each other, correspond.

escrito,-a I *pp de* **escribir. II** *adj* written, stated; **declarar por e.,** to give a written statement; **e. a mano,** handwritten, in longhand; **por e.,** in writing, in black and white. **III** *nm* **1** *(documento)* writing, document, letter, text. **2 escritos,** *Lit (obras)* writings, works.

escritor,-a *nm, f* writer.

escritorio *nm (mueble)* writing desk, bureau; *(oficina)* office; **objetos de e.,** stationery.

escritura *nf* **1** *(de un idioma)* writing, script, alphabet; **e. fonética,** phonetic script; *(de persona)* writing, handwriting; **e. a máquina,** typing. **2** *Jur* deed, document; **e. de propiedad,** title deed. **3 Sagradas Escrituras,** *Rel* Holy Scriptures.

escriturar *vtr* to formalize legally; *(una propiedad)* to register.

escrotal *adj Anat* scrotal.

escroto *nm Anat* scrotum.

escrúpulo *nm* **1** *(recelo)* scruple, qualm, doubt; **no tuvo escrúpulos en hacerlo,** he had no scruples about doing it; **una persona sin escrúpulos,** an unscrupulous person. **2** *(aprensión)* fussiness; **tener escrúpulos,** to be finicky *or* fussy. **3** *(china)* pebble, stone.

escrupulosidad *nf* scrupulousness, extreme care.

escrupuloso,-a *adj* **1** scrupulous. **2** *(quisquilloso)* finicky, fussy. ◆ **escrupulosamente** *adv* scrupulously.

escrutador,-a *adj* scrutinizing, searching, penetrating.

escrutar *vtr* **1** *(examen)* to scrutinize, examine carefully. **2** *(votos)* to count.

escrutinio *nm* **1** *(examinar)* examination. **2** *(votos)* counting of votes.

escuadra *nf* **1** *(instrumento)* square; **corte a e.,** cut at right angles; **e. de dibujo,** set square. **2** *(grupo) Mil* squad; *Mil (Armada)* squadron; *(de coches)* fleet.

escuadrar *vtr* to square.

escuadrilla *nf Mil* squadron.

escuadrón *nm Mil Av* squadron.

escualidez *nf* **1** *(delgadez)* emaciation, extreme thinness. **2** *(suciedad)* squalor.

escuálido,-a *adj* **1** *(delgado)* emaciated, extremely thin. **2** *(sucio)* squalid.

escualo *nm (pez)* (spiny) shark.

escucha I *nf* listening, listening-in; **escuchas telefónicas,** phone tapping *sing;* **estar a la e., estar en e.,** to be listening out **(de,** for). **II** *nm Mil* scout.

escuchar I *vtr* **1** to hear. **2** to listen to, heed, pay attention to. **II escucharse** *vr* to declaim, speak in an affected way.

escuchimizado,-a *adj* puny, scrawny.

escudar I *vtr* **1** *(amamparar con el escudo)* to shield. **2** *fig (proteger)* to shield, protect, defend. **II escudarse** *vr* to protect *or* shield oneself; **e. con algo,** to hide behind sth, use sth as an excuse; **e. del peligro,** to protect oneself from danger.

escudería *nf Aut* racing team.

escudero *nm Hist* page; *(que llevaba escudo)* squire.

escudilla *nf* bowl.

escudo *nm* **1** shield. **2** *(blasón)* coat of arms. **3** *(moneda)* escudo.

escudriñar *vtr (inquirir)* to inquire into, investigate; *(examinar)* to examine, scrutinize.

escuela *nf* **1** school; **e. de artes y oficios,** Technical College; **e. de Bellas Artes,** Art School; **e. de conducir,** driving school; **e. de equitación,** riding school; **e. de idiomas,** language school; **e. privada,** private school; **e. pública,** state school. **2** *(doctrina)* school; **gente de la vieja e.,** people of the old school. **3** *(experiencia)* experience, instruction; **la e. de la vida,** the university of life.

escueto,-a *adj* plain, unadorned, bare. ◆ **escuetamente** *adv* simply, baldly.

escuezo *indic pres véase* **escocer.**

esculcar *vtr Am (registrar)* to search.

esculpir *vtr Arte (gen)* to sculpt, sculpture; *(en madera)* to carve; *(en metales)* to engrave.

escultismo *nm* scouting.

escultor,-a *nm, f (gen) (hombre)* sculptor; *(mujer)* sculptress; *(de madera)* woodcarver; *(de metales)* engraver.

escultórico,-a *adj* sculptural.

escultura *nf (gen)* sculpture; *(madera)* carving.

escultural *adj* sculptural; statuesque; **una mujer e.,** a statuesque woman.

escupidera *nf* **1** *(recipiente)* spittoon, *US* cuspidor. **2** *Am (orinal)* chamberpot. **3** *Am fig* **pedir la e.,** to get scared, get cold feet.

escupidor *nm* **1** *Am* chamber pot. **2** *CAm Méx* fireworks *pl.*

escupir I *vi* **1** *(gen)* to spit; **e. a algn,** to spit at sb. **2** *vulg (confesar)* to come clean, confess. **II** *vtr* **1** to spit out. **2** *fig (palabras, insultos)* to spit out; **e. a algn,** to scoff at sb.

escupitajo *nm vulg* gob, spit, phlegm.

escurreplatos *nm inv* dish rack.

escurridero *nm* draining board.

escurridizo,-a *adj* **1** *(resbaladizo)* slippery. **2** *fig (elusivo)* elusive, slippery.

escurrido,-a I *pp de* **escurrir.** **II** *adj* **1** *(ropa)* tightfitting. **2** *(mujer)* slim-hipped. **III** *nm (de lavadora)* spin-drying programme.

escurridor *nm* colander; *(escurreplatos)* dish rack, draining board.

escurrir I *vtr (gen)* to drain; *(ropa)* to wring out; *Culin* to drain. **II** *vi (líquido)* to drip, trickle; *(objeto)* to slip, slide; *fig* **e. el bulto,** to dodge the issue. **III escurrirse** *vr* **1** *(gen)* to drain. **2** *(líquido)* to drip, trickle; *(objeto)* to slip, slide. **3** *(escapar)* to run *or* slip away. **4** *(decir más de lo debido)* to let sth slip.

escúter *nm (motor)* scooter.

ése,-a *pron dem m, f* **1** that one; *(el anterior)* the former; **coge é. de ahí,** take that one there; **entraron Pilar y Elvira, ésa vestida de azul,** Pilar and Elvira came in, the former dressed in blue. **2** **ésos,-as,** those (ones); *(los anteriores)* the former (ones); *fam* **¡ni por ésas!,** no way!; *fam* **¡no me vengas con ésas!,** come off it!

ese¹ *nf* **1** name of the letter S in Spanish. **2** **eses,** zigzags; **hacer e.,** to zigzag; *(persona)* to stagger about.

ese,-a² *adj dem* **1** that; **esa casa,** that house; *pey* **el hombre e.,** that bloke. **2** **esos,-as,** those; **e. coches,** those cars.

esencia *nf* **1** essence; **eso dijo en e.,** that's briefly what he said; **quinta e.,** quintessence. **2** *(perfume)* essence, scent.

esencial I *adj* essential; **lo e.,** the main thing. **II** *nm* essential. ◆ **esencialmente** *adv* essentially.

esfera *nf* **1** sphere, globe; **en forma de e.,** spherical, globular. **2** dial; *(del reloj)* face. **3** *fig* sphere, plane, field; **eso está fuera de mi e.,** that isn't my province.

esférico,-a I *adj* spherical. **II** *nm Ftb* ball.

esferoide *nm* spheroid.

esfinge *nf* sphinx; *fig* **parecer una e.,** to be inscrutable *or* enigmatic.

esfínter *nm Anat* sphincter.

esforzado,-a I *pp de* **esforzar.** **II** *adj (arrojado)* energetic, vigorous; *(valiente)* bold.

esforzar I *vtr* **1** *to* strengthen, invigorate. **2** to encourage, raise the spirits of. **II esforzarse** *vr* to exert oneself, make an effort, try hard; **e. por hacer algo,** to strive to do sth.

esfuerzo *nm* **1** effort, endeavour, *US* endeavor, exertion; *(la imaginación)* stretch. **2** courage, spirit; **con e.,** with spirit; **sin e.,** effortlessly.

esfumar *vtr,* **esfuminar** I *vtr (el contorno)* to soften; *(los colores)* to tone down. **II esfumarse** *vr,* **esfuminarse** *vr* to fade away, melt away; *(persona)* to disappear, vanish.

esgrima *nf Dep* fencing.

esgrimidor,-a *nm,f* fencer.

esgrimir I *vtr* **1** *(una espada)* to wield, brandish. **2** *fig (un argumento)* to put forward. **II** *vi* to fence.

esguince *nm* **1** *Med* sprain; **me hice un e. en el tobillo,** I sprained my ankle. **2** *(ademán)* swerve, dodge; **dar un e.,** to swerve, dodge. **3** *(gesto de disgusto)* frown.

eslabón *nm* link; **el e. perdido,** the missing link.

eslabonamiento *nm* linking.

eslabonar *vtr* to link together, join; *fig* to link, connect.

eslalon *nm Dep* slalom.

eslavo,-a I *adj* Slav, Slavonic. **II** *nm,f (persona)* Slav. **III** *nm (idioma)* Slavonic, Slavic.

eslip *nm (pl* **eslips)** *(prenda)* men's briefs *pl,* underpants *pl.*

eslogan *nm (pl* **eslóganes)** slogan; **e. publicitario,** catchword.

eslora *nf Náut* length; **e. máxima,** overall length.

esmaltado,-a I *pp de* **esmaltar.** **II** *adj* enamelled, *US* enameled. **III** *nm* enamelling, *US* enameling.

esmaltar *vtr* **1** *(cubrir)* to enamel; *(las uñas)* to varnish. **2** *fig (adornar)* to embellish, adorn.

esmalte *nm* **1** *(barniz)* enamel; *(de uñas)* nail polish *or* varnish. **2** *fig (esplendor)* splendour, *US* splendor.

esmerado,-a I *pp de* **esmerar.** **II** *adj (trabajo)* neat, careful; *(persona)* conscientious, painstaking, careful. ◆ **esmeradamente** *adv* neatly, carefully.

esmeralda *nf* emerald.

esmerar I *vtr* to polish. **II esmerarse** *vr* to take great pains (over sth), do one's best.

esmerejón *nm Orn* merlin.

esmeril *nm* emery; **papel de e.,** emery paper.

esmerilar *vtr* to polish with emery paper.

esmero *nm* painstaking care, neatness.

esmirriado,-a *adj fam* puny, scraggy.

esmoquin *nm (pl* **esmóquines)** *(prenda)* dinner jacket, *US* tuxedo.

esnifar *vtr arg (drogas)* to sniff.

esnob *(pl* **esnobs)** I *adj (persona)* snobbish; *(restaurante etc)* posh. **II** *nmf* snob.

esnobismo *nm* snobbery, snobbishness.

eso *pron dem neut* that; **¿cómo es e.?,** how come?; **¡e. es!,** that's it!; **e. es un rollo,** that's a drag; **no es e.,** it's not that; **por e.,** that's why; **¿y e. qué?,** so what?; *fam* **a e. de las diez,** around ten; *fam* **e. de las Navidades sale muy caro,** the whole Christmas deal costs a fortune.

esofágico,-a *adj Anat* oesophageal, *US* esophageal.

esófago *nm* oesophagus, *US* esophagus, gullet.

esos,-as *adj dem pl véase* **ése,-a²**

ésos,-as *pron dem m,fpl véase* **ése,-a.**

esotérico,-a *adj* esoteric.

esoterismo *nm* esotericism.

espabilado,-a I *pp de* **espabilar. II** *adj* **1** *(despierto)* wide awake. **2** *fig (adulto)* smart, on the ball; *(niño)* bright, sharp, clever; **su hijo es muy e.,** her little boy is very bright.

espabilar I *vtr* **1** *(una vela)* to snuff out. **2** *fig* to wake up, wise up; *(un niño)* to bring forward. **II espabilarse** *vr* to wake up, waken up; *(darse prisa)* to look sharp, hurry up.

espachurrar *vtr* to squash.

espaciador *nm Tip* space-bar.

espacial *adj* spatial, spacial.

espaciar I *vtr* to space out. **II espaciarse** *vr* to spread oneself out, stretch out.

espacio *nm* **1** space; *(de tiempo)* length; **mecanografiado a doble e.,** double-spaced. **2** room, space; **nos falta e.,** we're short of space; **ocupa mucho e.,** it takes up a lot of room. **3** *Rad TV* programme, *US* program.

espacioso,-a *adj* spacious, roomy; *(movimiento)* slow.

espada I *nf* **1** *(arma)* sword; **desnudar la e.,** to draw one's sword; *fig* **entrar con e. en mano,** to come in looking for trouble; *fig* **e. de dos filos,** double-edged sword; **estar entre la e. y la pared,** to be between the devil and the deep blue sea. ■ **pez e.,** swordfish. **2** *Naipes* spade; **as de espadas,** ace of spades. **II** *nm Taur* matador.

espadachín *nm* **1** swordsman. **2** *pey* bully.

espadaña *nf* **1** *Arquit* exposed belfry. **2** *Bot* bulrush.

espadista *nm arg* burglar.

espaguetis *nmpl* spaghetti *sing.*

espalda *nf* **1** *Anat* back; **espaldas,** back *sing*, shoulders *pl*; **a espaldas de algn,** behind sb's back; **ancho de espaldas,** broad-shouldered; **cargado de espaldas,** round-shouldered, stooping; **por la e.,** from behind; **volver la e. a algn,** to turn one's back on sb; *fig (sorprender)* **caerse de espaldas,** to fall flat on one's back; *fig* **echarse algo a la e.,** to take sth on; *fig (tener protección)* **tener guardadas las espaldas,** to have good connections; *fig* **tener las espaldas anchas,** to have broad shoulders, be responsible; *fam* **tira de espaldas,** it knocks you out. ■ *fam* **e. mojada,** *US* wetback. **2** *Natación* backstroke.

espaldar *nm (de silla)* back.

espaldarazo *nm* **1** slap on the back. **2** *fig* accolade.

espaldilla *nf* **1** *Anat* shoulder blade. **2** *Culin (de ternera etc)* shoulder.

espantada *nf (de animales)* stampede; *(de personas)* bolt, stampede; **dar la e.,** to stampede, run away.

espantadizo,-a *adj* easily frightened.

espantajo *nm* **1** *(muñeco)* scarecrow. **2** *fig (cosas)* sight, fright. **3** *fig (persona)* bogeyman, fright, sight; **parecía un auténtico e. tras tres meses en el desierto,** he looked a real sight after having spent three months in the desert.

espantapájaros *nm inv* scarecrow.

espantar I *vtr* **1** *(asustar)* to frighten, scare, scare off. **2** *(ahuyentar)* to frighten away. **II espantarse** *vr* **1** to get or feel frightened (**de,** of), get *or* feel scared (**de,** of). **2** to be amazed (**de,** at), astonished (**de,** at).

espanto *nm* **1** *(miedo)* fright, terror. **2** *(asombro)* amazement, astonishment; *fam* **de e.,** dreadful, shocking; *fam* **hace un frío de e.,** it's freezing cold; *fam* **¡qué e.!,** how awful! **3** *Am (fantasma)* ghost.

espantoso,-a *adj* **1** *(horrible)* frightening, dreadful. **2** *(pasmoso)* amazing, astonishing.

España *n* Spain.

español,-a I *adj* Spanish. **II** *nm, f (gen)* Spaniard; *(hombre)* Spanish man; *(mujer)* Spanish woman; **los españoles,** the Spanish. **III** *nm (idioma)* Spanish.

españolada *nf pey* something pseudo-Spanish.

españolear *vi* to publicise Spain or Spanish things in an exaggerated way.

españolismo *nm* **1** Spanishness, Spanish quality. **2** love of Spain and Spanish things.

españolista I *adj* pro-Spanish, Hispanophile. **II** *nmf* Hispanophile.

españolizar I *vtr* to make Spanish, hispanicize. **II españolizarse** *vr* to adopt Spanish ways.

esparadrapo *nm* sticking plaster.

esparaván *nm Orn* sparrowhawk.

esparcido,-a I *pp de* **esparcir. II** *adj* **1** *(desparramado)* scattered; *(rumor)* widespread. **2** *(carácter)* frank, open; *(divertido)* cheerful.

esparcimiento *nm* **1** scattering, spreading. **2** *fig* relaxation, amusement, recreation.

esparcir I *vtr (papeles, semillas)* to scatter; *fig (un rumor)* to spread. **II esparcirse** *vr* **1** to spread out, scatter, be scattered. **2** to relax, amuse oneself.

espárrago *nm* **1** *Bot* asparagus; **e. triguero,** wild asparagus; *fam* **¡vete a freír espárragos!,** get lost! **2** *Téc* stud.

esparraguera *nf* **1** *Bot* asparagus plant. **2** *Culin* asparagus dish.

espartano,-a I *adj* Spartan; *fig* Spartan, austere. **II** *nm,f* Spartan.

espartero,-a *nm,f* esparto worker.

esparto *nm* esparto grass.

espasmo *nm* spasm.

espasmódico,-a *adj* spasmodic, jerky.

espástico,-a *adj Med* spastic.

espatarrarse *vr* to slip and fall with one's legs wide open, sprawl.

espátula *nf (gen)* spatula; *Art* palette knife; *Téc* stripping knife; *(cristalero)* putty knife.

especia *nf* spice.

especial *adj* **1** special; **en e.,** especially; **e. para ...,** suitable for ...; **sólo en un caso e.,** only in special cases; **tiene un sabor e.,** it has a distinctive taste. **2** *(persona)* fussy, finicky (**para,** about). ◆ **especialmente** *adv (exclusivamente)* specially; *(particularmente)* especially.

especialidad *nf* speciality, *US* specialty; *Educ* main subject, specialized field; **no es de mi e.,** it's not in my line.

especialista *nmf* **1** specialist. **2** *Cin* stand-in; *(hombre)* stuntman; *(mujer)* stuntwoman.

especialización *nf* specialization.

especializado,-a I *pp de* **especializarse. II** *adj* specialized; **estar e. en algo,** to be a specialist in sth, be specialized in sth.

especializarse *vr* to specialize (**en,** in).

especie *nf* **1** *Biol* species *inv.* **2** *(clase)* kind, sort; **me gusta esa e. de gente,** I like that kind of person; **una e. de sopa,** a kind of soup. **3** *(tema, noticia)* matter, idea, notion; **corría entre los refugiados una e. extraña,** there was a strange idea going about amongst the refugees. **4 en e.,** in kind; **pagar en e.,** to pay in kind.

especiero *nm* spice rack.

especificación *nf* specification; **sin e. de hora,** without specifying the time.

especificar *vtr* to specify.

especifico,-a I *adj* specific; **peso e.,** specific gravity. **II** *nm Med* **1** specific. **2** patent medicine; **laboratorio de especificos,** pharmaceutical lab. ◆ **específicamente** *adv* specifically.

espécimen *nm* (*pl* **especímenes**) specimen.

espectacular *adj* spectacular. ◆ **espectacularmente** *adv* spectacularly.

espectacularidad *nf* spectacular nature; **su nuevo número de acrobacia es de gran e.,** his latest acrobatic feat is really spectacular.

espectáculo *nm* 1 (*escena*) spectacle, sight; **dar un e.,** to make a scene, make a spectacle of oneself. 2 *Teat Cin TV* show, performance; **montar un e.,** to put on a show.

espectador,-a *nm,* *f Dep* spectator; (*accidente, espectáculo improvisado*) onlooker; *Teat Cin* member of the audience; **los espectadores,** the audience *sing*; *TV* viewers.

espectral *adj* spectral, ghostly.

espectro *nm* 1 *Fís* spectrum. 2 (*fantasma*) spectre, *US* specter, ghost, apparition. 3 *fig* (*persona*) ghost; **parece un e.,** he looks like a ghost. 4 (*gama*) range; **un amplio e. de ideologías,** a wide range of political opinions.

espectrografía *nf Fís* spectrography.

espectrógrafo *nm Fís* spectrograph.

espectroscopia *nf Fís* spectroscopy.

espectroscopio *nm Fís* spectroscope.

especulación *nf* speculation; **e. del suelo,** land speculation.

especulador,-a *nm, f Fin* speculator.

especular I *vtr* (*conjeturar*) to speculate about, reflect on. **II** *vi* 1 (*comerciar*) to speculate (**en,** on). 2 (*hacer cábalas*) to speculate, guess (**sobre,** about).

especulativo,-a *adj* speculative, theoretical.

espejear *vi* to shine like a mirror, gleam.

espejismo *nm* 1 mirage. 2 *fig* mirage, illusion.

espejo *nm* 1 mirror; *Aut* **e. retrovisor,** rear-view mirror. 2 *fig* mirror, reflection; **la cara es el e. del alma,** one's face is the window of one's soul.

espejuelos *nmpl* spectacles.

espeleología *nf Dep* potholing, speleology.

espeleólogo,-a *nm, f Dep* potholer, speleologist.

espeluznante *adj* hair-raising, horrifying.

espeluznar *vtr* to horrify, terrify, make one's hair stand on end.

espera *nf* 1 (*acción de esperar*) wait, waiting; **en e. de ...,** waiting for ...; **estar a la e.,** to be waiting *or* expecting; **sala de e.,** waiting room. 2 (*paciencia*) calm, patience; **tener e.,** to have patience.

esperanto *nm Ling* Esperanto.

esperanza *nf* hope, expectance; **dar esperanzas a algn,** to give sb hope; **e. de vida,** life expectancy; **estar en estado de buena e.,** to be expecting *or* pregnant; **tener la e. puesta en algo,** to have one's hopes pinned on sth.

esperanzador,-a *adj* encouraging.

esperanzar I *vtr* to give hope to. **II esperanzarse** *vr* to have hope.

esperar *vtr* 1 (*tener esperanza*) to hope for, expect; **e. la victoria,** to hope for victory; **quien espera desespera,** a watched pot never boils; **te esperábamos ayer,** we were expecting you yesterday. 2 (+ *que*) to hope (that); **espero que así sea,** I hope it's like that; **espero que sí,** I hope so; **espero que vengas,** I hope you'll come; **no se podía e. menos,** it was the least you could hope for. 3 (*aguardar*) to wait for, await; **espera un momento,** wait a moment, hold on; **espero a mi hermano,** I'm waiting for my brother; **ya puedes e. sentado,** you'll be waiting till the cows come home. 4 (*suponer*) to expect; **espero la visita de un amigo,** I'm expecting a friend to call. 5 (+ *infin*) to hope to; **espero ganar el concurso,** I hope to win the competition. 6 *fig* (*bebé*) to expect.

esperma *nm Biol* sperm. ■ **e. de ballena,** spermaceti.

espermaticida *adj Med* spermicide.

espermatozoide *nm Biol* spermatozoid.

esperpéntico,-a *adj* 1 *Lit* pertaining to the literary genre created by Don Ramón del Valle-Inclán. 2 (*grotesco*) *fam* grotesque, macabre. 3 (*sin sentido*) ridiculous, absurd.

esperpento *nm* 1 *Lit* genre created by Don Ramón del Valle-Inclán. 2 fright, sight; **va hecho un e.,** he looks a real sight. 3 (*sin sentido*) absurdity, piece of nonsense.

espesante *nm* thickener.

espesar I *vtr* to make denser *or* thicker; *Culin* (*una salsa*) to thicken. **II espesarse** *vr* to thicken, get thicker.

espeso,-a *adj* (*bosque, niebla, muchedumbre*) dense; (*líquido, pared, libro*) thick; (*masa*) stiff.

espesor *nm* denseness, thickness; **tres metros de e.,** three metres thick.

espesura *nf* 1 (*grosor*) denseness, density. 2 (*de un bosque*) thicket, overgrown place.

espetar *vtr* 1 *Culin* (*carne*) to skewer. 2 (*clavar*) to stab. 3 *fig* (*decir*) to blurt out; **le espetó la sorpresa,** he sprang the surprise on him.

espeto *nm,* **espetón** *nm* spit, skewer.

espía *nmf* spy.

espiar *vtr* to spy on, watch.

espichar I *vtr* (*pinchar*) to stab. **II** *vi* 1 *vulg* (*morir*) to snuff it; **espicharla,** to kick the bucket. 2 *Arg* (*líquido*) to run out. 3 *Cuba Méx Ven* to slim.

espiche *nm* speech.

espiga *nf* 1 (*de trigo*) ear. 2 *Téc* pin; (*de cuchillo*) tang; (*de tornillo*) bolt; (*de clavo*) shank. 3 (*de campana*) clapper. 4 *Astron* **E.,** Spica.

espigado,-a I *pp* de **espigar. II** *adj* 1 *Bot* ripe. 2 (*con forma de espiga*) ear-shaped. 3 *fig* (*alto y delgado*) tall, lanky.

espigar I *vtr* to glean; *fig* **e. datos/noticias,** to glean information/news. **II espigarse** *vr* (*persona*) to shoot up.

espigón *nm* 1 (*punta*) sharp point, spike. 2 (*mazorca*) ear of corn. 3 (*mar*) breakwater, groyne, spur.

espín *nm Fís* spin.

espina *nf* 1 *Bot* thorn; *fig* **no hay rosa sin espinas,** you've got to take the rough with the smooth. 2 (*del pez*) bone. 3 *Anat* **e. dorsal,** spinal column, spine, backbone. 4 *fig* doubt, worry, suspicion; **ése me da mala e.,** I'm suspicious about that one, there's something fishy about that one.

espinaca *nf* spinach; *Culin* **espinacas a la crema,** creamed spinach.

espinal *adj* spinal; **médula e.,** spinal marrow.

espinapez *nm* herringbone.

espinazo *nm Anat* spine, backbone; *fam* **doblar el e.,** to bow and scrape.

espinilla *nf* 1 *Anat* shin. 2 (*barro*) blackhead.

espinillera *nf Dep* shin pad.

espino *nm Bot* 1 hawthorn; **e. albar,** common hawthorn; **e. negro,** blackthorn. 2 (*alambrada*) barbed wire.

espinosillo *nm* (*pez*) stickleback.

espionaje *nm* spying, espionage; **e. industrial,** industrial espionage; **novela de e.,** spy story.

espira *nf* spire.

espiración *nf* breathing out, expiration, exhalation.

espiral I *adj* spiral; **escalera e.,** spiral staircase. **II** *nf* spiral; (*de reloj*) hairspring.

espirar I *vtr* (*respirar*) to breathe out, exhale. **II** *vi* to breathe.

espiritismo *nm* spiritualism.

espiritista I *adj* spiritualistic. **II** *nmf* spiritualist.

espíritu *nm* 1 (*principio de vida*) spirit; **exhalar el e.,** to give up the ghost. 2 (*licores*) spirits *pl*; **e. de vino,** spirits of wine, alcohol. 3 *Rel* soul; **el E. Santo,** the Holy Ghost; **espíritus malignos,** evil spirits. 4 (*fantasma*) ghost. 5 *fig* (*ánimo*) spirit; **e. de cuerpo,** esprit de corps, corporal spirit; **e. combativo,** fighting spirit; **e. deportivo,** sportsmanship. **6** *(idea central)* essence, spirit, soul; **el e. de la ley,** the spirit of the law.

espiritual *adj* spiritual. ◆ **espiritualmente** *adv* spiritually.

espiritualidad *nf* spirituality.

espiritualismo *nm* spiritualism.

espiritualista *adj* spiritualist.

espita *nf* tap, *US* spigot.

espléndido,-a *adj* **1** splendid, magnificent, grand. **2** *(generoso)* lavish, generous. ◆ **espléndidamente** *adv* **1** splendidly, magnificently, grandly. **2** *(generosamente)* lavishly, generously.

esplendor *nm* **1** *(resplandor)* brilliance. **2** *fig (lustre)* splendour, *US* splendor, magnificence, grandeur. **3** *(auge)* glory.

esplendoroso,-a *adj* **1** *(luz)* brilliant, radiant. **2** *(grandioso)* magnificent.

espliego *nm* Bot lavender.

esplín *nm* (*pl* **esplines**) melancholy, depression.

espolada *nf* **1** prick with a spur. **2** *(de vino)* swig.

espolear *vtr* **1** *(un caballo)* to spur on. **2** *fig (estimular)* to spur on, encourage.

espoleta[1] *nf Mil* fuse; **quitar la e. de,** to defuse.

espoleta[2] *nf Anat (de ave)* wishbone.

espolio *nm véase* **expolio.**

espolón *nm* **1** *(de gallináceas)* spur; *(de caballo)* fetlock. **2** *Geog* spur. **3** *(malecón)* sea-wall; *Arquit (tajamar)* buttress. **4** *Náut* ram; **embestir con el e.,** to ram.

espolvorear *vtr* to dust, powder, sprinkle **(de,** with).

esponja *nf* sponge; *fig* **beber como una e., ser una e.,** to drink like a fish; *fam* **pasar la e.,** to let it drop, forget about it.

esponjar I *vr* to make spongy; *(ahuecar)* to fluff up. **II esponjarse** *vr* **1** *fig (envanecerse)* to swell with pride. **2** *fig* to glow with health.

esponjoso,-a *adj* *(tejido)* spongy; *(bizcocho)* light.

esponsales *nmpl* betrothal *sing*, engagement *sing*.

espontanearse *vr* to confide **(con,** in).

espontaneidad *nf* spontaneity; **obrar/hablar con e.,** to act/speak naturally.

espontáneo,-a I *adj* spontaneous; *(persona)* natural, unaffected; *(discurso)* impromptu, unprepared. **II** *nm Taur* spectator who spontaneously joins in the bullfight. ◆ **espontáneamente** *adv* spontaneously.

espora *nf Biol* spore.

esporádico,-a *adj* sporadic.

esporrondingárse *vr* **1** *CAm Col* to spend *or* blow a lot of money. **2** *CAm (desvencijarse)* to come apart.

esposado,-a *adj* **1** newly married. **2** handcuffed.

esposar *vtr* to handcuff.

esposas *nfpl* handcuffs.

esposo,-a I *nm, f* spouse; *(hombre)* husband; *(mujer)* wife. **II** *nf* bishop's ring.

esprint *nm* sprint.

esprintar *vi* to sprint.

esprínter *nmf* sprinter.

espuela *nf* **1** spur; *fig (última copa)* one for the road; *fig* **poner espuelas a algn,** to spur sb on. **2** *Am (de aves)* spur.

espuerta *nf* basket; **dinero a espuertas,** bags *or* stacks of money.

espulgar *vtr* **1** to delouse, rid of fleas. **2** *fig (examinar)* to scrutinize.

espuma *nf* **1** *(gen)* foam; *(olas)* surf; *(de cerveza)* froth, head; *(de jabón)* lather; **echarse e.,** to foam, froth. ■ **e. de afeitar,** shaving foam. **2** *(impurezas)* scum.

espumadera *nf Culin* spoon for skimming.

espumante *nm* foaming agent.

espumar I *vtr* to skin. **II** *vi (mar)* to foam; *(jabón)* to lather; *(cerveza)* to froth; *(cava)* to sparkle.

espumarajo *nm (de la boca)* foam, froth; **echando espumarajos,** foaming at the mouth.

espumilla *nf Am* meringue.

espumosidad *nf* frothiness.

espumoso,-a *adj* frothy, foamy, foaming; *(jabón)* lathery; *(vino)* sparkling.

espúreo,-a *adj*, **espurio,-a** *adj* **1** *(niño)* illegitimate. **2** *(falso)* spurious, adulterated.

esputar *vtr* to spit (out).

esputo *nm* sputum, spit.

esqueje *nm* Bot cutting.

esquela *nf* **1** *(carta)* short letter. **2** *(comunicación)* notice, announcement; **e. mortuoria,** announcement of a death.

esquelético,-a *adj* **1** *Anat* skeletal; **estructura e.,** bone structure. **2** *(muy flaco)* skinny; **estar e.,** to be skin and bones.

esqueleto *nm* **1** skeleton; *fam* **mover el e.,** to shake it about. **2** *Constr* framework.

esquema *nm* **1** outline; **seguir un e. fijo,** to follow a set pattern. **2** *(diagrama)* diagram; **dibuja** *or* **trazar un e.,** to draw a diagram.

esquemático,-a *adj* schematic, diagrammatic; **corte e.,** cross section.

esquematizar *vtr* *(un plano)* to sketch; *(unas ideas)* to outline.

esquí *nm* **1** *(objeto)* ski. **2** *Dep* skiing; **hacer e.,** to go skiing. ■ **e. acuático,** water-skiing.

esquiador,-a *nm, f* skier.

esquiar *vi* to ski.

esquife *nm Náut* skiff.

esquila[1] *nf* small bell, handbell, sheep bell.

esquila[2] *nf Agr* sheep shearing.

esquilador,-a I *nm, f (persona)* sheepshearer. **II** *nf (herramienta)* shears *pl*.

esquilar *vtr (cortar el pelo)* to clip; *(ovejas)* to shear.

esquileo *nm* sheepshearing.

esquilmar *vtr* **1** to harvest. **2** *fig (recursos)* to exhaust.

esquilón *nm* large cowbell.

esquimal I *adj & nmf* Eskimo. **II** *nm (idioma)* Eskimo.

esquina *nf* **1** corner; **a la vuelta de la e.,** just round the corner; **doblar la e.,** to turn the corner; **hacer e. con,** to be on the corner of. **2** *Am* grocer's, corner shop.

esquinado,-a *adj* **1** *(con esquinas)* having corners, sharp-cornered. **2** *fig (difícil)* touchy, irritable.

esquinazo *nm* **dar e. a algn,** to give sb the slip.

esquinera *nf Am,* **esquinero** *nm Méx* corner piece of furniture.

esquirla *nf* splinter.

esquirol *nm Ind* blackleg, scab.

esquite *nm CAm* popcorn.

esquivar *vtr (a una persona)* to shun, avoid; *(un golpe)* to elude, dodge; **e. hacer algo,** to avoid doing sth; **e. un golpe,** to dodge a blow.

esquivez *nf* coldness, aloofness.

esquivo,-a *adj* cold, aloof.

esquizofrenia *nf* schizophrenia.

esquizofrénico,-a *adj & nm, f* schizophrenic.

esquizoide *adj & nmf* schizoid.

esta *adj dem véase* **este,-a.**

está *indic pres véase* **estar.**

ésta *pron dem f véase* **éste.**

estabilidad *nf* stability.

estabilización *nf* stabilization.

estabilizador,-a I *adj* stabilizing; **elemento e.,** stabilizing influence *or* factor. **II** *nm Av Quím* stabilizer.

estabilizar I *vtr* to stabilize, make stable *or* steady. **II estabilizarse** *vr* to become stable *or* stabilized.

estable *adj* stable, steady, balanced.

establecer I *vtr* 1 *(gen)* to establish; *(fundar)* to set up, found; *(gente)* to settle; *(récord)* to set. 2 *(decretar)* to establish, state; **la ley establece que ...,** the law states that ... . **II establecerse** *vr (instalarse)* to establish oneself, settle; *Com* to set up in business.

establecimiento *nm* 1 *(acto)* establishment, setting-up, founding; *(de gente)* settlement. 2 *(edificio)* establishment; **e. central,** head office. 3 *Jur* statute, ordinance.

establo *nm* cow shed, stall, stable.

estabulación *nf* rearing of livestock in stables.

estabular *vtr* to stable.

estaca *nf* 1 *(madero)* stake, post; *(de tienda de campaña)* peg. 2 *(garrote)* stick, cudgel. 3 *Am* mining concession *or* claim.

estacada *nf* 1 fence, fencing; *Mil* stockade; *fig* **dejar a algn en la e.,** to leave sb in the lurch; **estar en la e.,** to be in a fix. 2 *CAm* wound.

estacazo *nm* blow with a stick.

estación *nf* 1 *(del año)* season; **la e. de las lluvias,** the rainy season. 2 *Ferroc Rad* station; **e. balnearia,** spa; **e. de esquí,** ski resort; **e. metereológica,** weather station; **e. de servicio,** service station; **hacer e. en un viaje,** to make a stop on a journey. 3 *Rel (de la cruz)* station.

estacional *adj* seasonal.

estacionamiento *nm* stationing, placing; *Aut (acción)* parking; *(lugar)* car park, *US* parking lot; *fig* **e. del conflicto,** stalemate, impasse.

estacionar I *vtr* to station, place; *Aut* to park. **II estacionarse** *vr* 1 *Aut* to park. 2 *(estancarse)* to remain in the same place, be stationary.

estacionario,-a *adj* stationary, stable.

estadio *nm* 1 *Dep* stadium. 2 *(fase)* stage, phase; **hacer algo por estadios,** to do sth in stages. 3 *arc (medida)* furlong.

estadista *nmf* 1 *Pol (hombre)* statesman; *(mujer)* stateswoman. 2 *Mat* statistician.

estadística *nf (ciencia)* statistics *sing*; **una e.,** a figure, a statistic.

estadístico,-a I *adj* statistical. **II** *nm,f* statistician.

estado *nm* 1 *(situación)* state, condition; **en buen e.,** in good condition; **e. de ánimo,** state of mind; **e. de excepción,** state of emergency; **e. de salud,** condition, state of health; **e. sólido,** solid state; **mujer en e.,** pregnant woman; *Med* **su e. es grave,** his condition is serious. 2 *(relación)* return, summary; **e. de cuentas,** statement of accounts. 3 *(orden social)* status, rank; **e. civil,** marital status. 4 *(clase)* class, estate; **e. noble,** noble estate. 5 *Pol* state; **e. de previsión,** welfare state; **hombre de e.,** statesman. 6 *Mil* **e. mayor general,** general staff.

Estados Unidos *npl* The United States.

estadounidense I *adj* United States, American; **las universidades estadounidenses,** American universities. **II** *nmf* United States citizen.

estafa *nf* swindle, fraud.

estafador,-a *nm,f* racketeer, swindler, trickster.

estafar *vtr* to swindle, cheat, trick, defraud; *fam* **te han estafado,** you've been done or had.

estafeta *nf* **e. de Correos,** sub post office.

estafilococo *nm Biol* staphylococcus.

estalactita *nf Geol* stalactite.

estalagmita *nf Geol* stalagmite.

estalinismo *nm Pol* Stalinism.

estalinista *adj & nm* Stalinist.

estallar *vi* 1 *(reventar)* to blow up, explode; *(neumático)* to burst; *(bomba)* to explode, go off; *(volcán)* to erupt; *(cristal)* to shatter; **estalló en pedazos,** it shattered. 2 *(rebelión, epidemia)* to break out; **al e. la guerra,** when war broke out. 3 *(restallar)* to crack; **hacer e. el látigo,** to crack the whip. 4 *fig (sentimientos)* to explode; **e. en sollozos,** to burst into tears.

estallido *nm* 1 *(explosión)* explosion; *(trueno)* crash; *(chasquido)* crack. 2 *fig (de una guerra)* outbreak.

estambre *nm* 1 *Cost* worsted, woollen *or US* woolen yarn. 2 *Bot* stamen.

Estambul *n* Istanbul.

estamento *nm (social)* class, stratum.

estameña *nf Tex* serge.

estampa *nf* 1 *(dibujo)* picture. 2 *fig (aspecto)* appearance, look, aspect; **ser la viva e. de ...,** to be the spitting image of ... . 3 *(marca)* hallmark. 4 *Impr* print; *(proceso)* printing; **dar a la e.,** to publish.

estampación *nf* printing.

estampado,-a I *pp de* **estampar. II** *adj* stamped, printed; *(vestido)* print. **III** *nm* 1 *(tela)* print. 2 *(proceso)* printing; *Metal* stamping.

estampar *vtr* 1 *(imprimir, dibujar) (vestidos)* to print; *Metal* to stamp. 2 *(escribir)* **e. la firma,** to sign. 3 *(dejar impreso)* to engrave, imprint. 4 *fam (arrojar)* to hurl. 5 *fig (dar)* to plant, place; **le estampó un beso en la frente,** she planted a kiss on his forehead.

estampida *nf* 1 *(estampido)* bang. 2 *(ganado)* stampede; **de e.,** suddenly; **salir de e.,** to be *or* go off like a shot.

estampido *nm* bang; **dar un e.,** to go bang.

estampilla *nf* (rubber) stamp; *Am* (postage) stamp.

estampillado *nm* rubber stamping.

estampillar *vtr* to stamp, put a stamp on; *(un documento)* to rubber-stamp.

estampita *nf* religious print.

estancado,-a I *pp de* **estancar. II** *adj* 1 *(aguas)* stagnant. 2 *fig* static, at a standstill; *(persona)* **quedarse e.,** to get stuck *or* bogged down.

estancamiento *nm* 1 stagnancy, stagnation. 2 *fig* stagnation, standstill.

estancar I *vtr* 1 *(aguas)* to hold up, hold back; *(el flujo)* to check. 2 *fig (progreso)* to check, block, hold up; *(negociaciones)* to bring to a standstill. 3 *Com (el mercado)* to corner; *(monopolizar)* to have a state monopoly on. **II estancarse** *vr* 1 to stagnate, become stagnant. 2 *fig* to stagnate, get bogged down.

estancia¹ *nf* 1 *(permanencia)* stay. 2 *(aposento)* room. 3 *Am (hacienda)* ranch, farm.

estancia² *nf Lit* stanza.

estanciero *nm Am* rancher, farmer.

estanco I *adj* watertight; **compartimento e.,** watertight compartment. **II** *nm* state monopoly; *(de tabaco)* tobacconist's.

estándar *(pl estándares)* **I** *adj* standard, standardized; **normas e.,** set rules. **II** *nm* standard.

estandarización *nf* standardization.

estandarizar *vtr* to standardize.

estandarte *nm* standard, banner.

estanque *nm* pool, pond; *(depósito)* tank, reservoir; **e. para chapotear,** paddling pool.

estanquero,-a *nm,f* tobacconist.

estanquidad *nf* watertightness.

estante *nm* 1 shelf, rack, stand; **e. para libros,** bookcase. 2 *Am* post, pillar.

estantería *nf* shelves, shelving.

estañado,-a I *pp de* **estañar. II** *adj* soldered. **III** *nm* tin plating.

estañar *vtr* **1** *(bañar con estaño)* to tin-plate. **2** *(soldar)* to solder.

estaño *nm* tin.

estaquilla *nf* **1** *(clavo)* tack, spike; *(de tienda de campaña)* tent peg. **2** *Constr* peg.

estaquillar *vtr* to peg *or* tag down, fasten with tacks *or* pegs.

estar I *vi* **1** *(existir, hallarse)* to be, be found; *(persona)* to be in; *(en casa)* to be at home; **aquí no está,** it is not here; **Dios está en todas partes,** God is everywhere; **el mejor vino tinto está en La Rioja,** the best red wine is found in La Rioja; **está fuera,** she's out; **¿está Jorge?,** is Jorge in? **2** *(posición)* to be, stand; **estamos en Barcelona,** we are in Barcelona; **la casa está en medio de la calle,** the house is half-way down the street; *fig* **los precios están bajos,** prices are low. **3** *(e. + adj) (cualidades transitorias)* to be; **el papel está arrugado,** the paper is crumpled; **está enfermo,** he's ill; **está vacío,** it's empty. **4** *(e. + ger) (tiempo continuo)* to be; **está escribiendo,** she is writing; **estaba comiendo,** he was eating. **5** *(e. + adv)* to be; **en seguida está,** it'll be ready in a moment; **está bien,** it's all right; **está mal,** it's wrong; **ya está,** that's done. **6** *(e. + a) (fecha)* to be; *(precio)* to sell *or* be at; **¿a cuántos estamos?,** what's the date?; **estamos a 10 de Enero,** it is the 10th of January; **están a 15 pesetas la pieza,** they're 15 pesetas each; **e. al caer,** to be just round the corner; **las vacaciones están al caer,** the holidays will soon be here; *fam* **e. a la que salta,** to ready to seize any opportunity; *fam* **e. a matar,** to be at daggers drawn. **7** *(e. + de) (condiciones transitorias)* **e. de etiqueta,** to be in evening dress; *(sobrar)* **e. de más,** not to be needed; **e. de paseo,** to be out for a walk; **e. de vacaciones,** to be (away) on holiday; **e de viaje,** to be (away) on a trip; **estos comentarios están de más,** we could do without those comments; **estoy de jefe hoy,** I'm the boss today. **8** *(e. + en) (permanecer)* to be in; *(consistir)* to be; **el problema está en el dinero,** the problem is money; **e. en casa,** to be at home; *(saber)* **e. en lo cierto,** to be right; **e. en todo,** not to miss a trick. **9** *(e. + para)* **e. para algo,** to be in the mood for sth; **estará para las seis,** it will be finished by six; **hoy no estoy para bromas,** I'm in no mood for jokes today. **10** *(e. + por)* **está por hacer,** it is still to be done, it hasn't been done yet; **está por explicar,** it remains to be explained; **está por suceder,** it is going to happen soon; **e. por algo,** to be in favour of sth; **estoy por esperar,** I'm for waiting. **11** *(e. + con)* to have; **e. con la gripe,** to have the flu, be down with flu; *(de acuerdo)* **estoy con Jaime,** I agree with Jaime. **12** *(e. + que)* **está que se duerme,** he is nearly asleep; **estoy que no puedo más,** I can't take any more; *fam* **está que rabia,** he's hopping mad; *fam* **la cosa está que arde,** things are really hotting up. **II estarse** *vr* **1** *(énfasis)* **se estaba muriendo,** he was slowly dying; **¡estáte quieto!,** keep still!, stop fidgeting! **2** *(permanecer)* to spend, stay; **se estuvo toda la tarde viendo la TV,** he spent all afternoon watching TV.

estarcido *nm* stencil.

estarcir *vtr* to stencil.

estatal *adj* state; **enseñanza e.,** state education; **política e.,** government policy.

estático,-a I *adj* static. **II** *nf* statics *sing*.

estatua *nf* statue; **quedarse hecho una e.,** to be transfixed.

estatuario,-a I *adj* statuary; *fig* statuesque. **II** *nf* sculptor.

estatuilla *nf* statuette, figurine.

estatuir *vtr* to establish, enact, ordain.

estatura *nf* stature, height; **¿cuál es su e.?,** how tall is she?

estatutario *adj* statutory.

estatuto *nm* Jur statute; *(de ciudad)* by-law; *Pol* **e. de autonomía,** statute of autonomy.

este I *adj* east, eastern; *(dirección)* easterly; *(viento)* east, easterly. **II** *nm* **1** east; **al e. de Bilbao,** to the east of Bilbao. **2** *(viento)* east wind.

esté *subj pres véase* **estar.**

este,-a *adj dem* **1** this; **esta casa,** this house. **2** estos,-as. these; **estas mujeres,** these women.

éste,-a *pron dem m, f* **1** this one; *(el anterior)* the former; **coge é.,** take this one; **vio a María pero ésta no le dijo nada,** he saw María but she didn't say anything to him. **2 éstos,-as,** these (ones); *(loss anteriores)* the former (ones); *fam* **en éstas,** just then; **estábamos viendo la televisión y en éstas sonó el teléfono,** we were watching television when suddenly the phone rang.

estela¹ *nf* **1** *Náut* wake, wash; *Av* vapour trail; *(de cometa)* tail. **2** *fig* trail.

estela² *nf* *(lápida)* stele, stela.

estelar *adj* **1** *Astron* stellar; **poblaciones estelares,** star clusters; **luz e.,** starlight. **2** *fig* *Cin Teat* star; **la figura e.,** the star.

estenografía *nf* stenography.

estenografiar *vtr* to take down in shorthand, stenograph.

estenográfico,-a *adj* stenographic, (in) shorthand.

estenógrafo,-a *nm, f* stenographer, shorthand writer.

estenotipia *nf* **1** *(arte)* stenotypy. **2** *Téc* Stenotype®.

estenotipista *nmf* stenotypist.

estentóreo,-a *adj* stentorian, thundering, booming.

estepa¹ *nf* *Geog* steppe.

estepa² *nf* *Bot* rockrose.

estepario,-a *adj* pertaining to a steppe.

estera *nf* rush mat.

esterar *vtr* to cover with rush matting.

estercolero *nm* dunghill, manure heap; *fig* pigsty.

estéreo *nm*, **estereofonía** *nf* stereo.

estereofónico,-a *adj* stereophonic, stereo.

estereografía *nf* stereography.

estereográfico,-a *adj* stereographic.

estereógrafo,-a *nm, f* stereographer.

estereotipado,-a I *pp de* **estereotipar. II** *adj* *fig* stereotyped, set, standard; **frase estereotipada,** hackneyed phrase, cliché.

estereotipar *vtr* **1** *Impr* to stereotype. **2** *fig* to stereotype.

estereotipo *nm* stereotype.

estéril *adj* **1** sterile, barren. **2** *Med* sterile. **3** *fig* futile useless.

esterilete *nm* Med coil, IUD.

esterilidad *nf* **1** sterility, barrenness. **2** *Med* sterility. **3** *fig* futility, uselessness.

esterilización *nf* sterilization.

esterilizador,-a I *adj* sterilizing. **II** *nm, f* sterilizer.

esterilizar *vtr* to sterilize.

esterilla *nf* **1** small mat. **2** rush matting, wickerwork; *Arg* **silla de e.,** wickerwork chair. **3** *(galón)* gold *or* silver braid.

esterlina *adj & nf* sterling; **libra e.,** pound (sterling).

esternocleidomastoideo *adj & nm* Anat sternocleidomastoid.

esternón *nm* Anat sternum, breastbone.

estero *nm* estuary, inlet; *Am* marsh, swamp.

estertor *nm* death rattle.

esteta *nmf* aesthete, *US* esthete.

esteticismo *nm* aestheticism, *US* estheticism.

esteticista *nmf* beautician.

estético,-a I *adj* aesthetic, *US* esthetic; *Med* **cirugía estética,** plastic surgery. **II** *nf* *Filos* aesthetics *or US* esthetics *sing*.

estetoscopio *nm* Med stethoscope.

estevado,-a *adj* bow-legged, bandy-legged.

estiba *nf* Náut stowing, loading.

estibador *nm* docker, stevedore.

estibar *vtr* **1** *(cargar)* to stow, load. **2** *Am (mercancías)* to arrange, place.

estiércol *nm* manure, dung.

estigma *nm* **1** *(gen)* stigma; *(marca)* brand, mark; *(de nacimiento)* birthmark. **2** *Rel* stigmata.

estigmatizar *vtr* **1** to stigmatize; *(marcar)* to brand, mark. **2** *(infamar)* to stigmatize.

estilar I *vtr (documento)* to draw up. **II** *vi* to be in the habit of; **estila pasearse al anochecer,** he usually takes a walk at dusk. **III estilarse** *vr* to be in vogue, be fashionable; **se estilan las camisas huecas,** baggy shirts are in.

estilete *nm (punzón)* stylus; *(puñal)* stiletto; *Med* probe.

estilista *nmf* stylist.

estilístico,-a I *adj* stylistic. **II** *nf* stylistics *sing*.

estilización *nf* styling.

estilizar *vtr* to stylize.

estilo *nm* **1** *(gen)* style; *(modo)* manner, fashion; **algo por el e.,** something like that; **e. de vida,** way of life. **2** *Ling* speech; **e. directo/indirecto,** direct/indirect speech. **3** *Natación* stroke; **e. braza,** breaststroke; **e. mariposa,** butterfly stroke; **e. libre,** freestyle. **4** *(punzón)* stylus.

estilográfica *nf* fountain pen.

estima *nf* **1** esteem, respect. **2** *Náut* dead reckoning.

estimable *adj* **1** esteemed, reputable, worthy. **2** *(cantidad)* considerable.

estimación *nf* **1** *(estima)* esteem, respect; **e. propia,** self-esteem. **2** *(valoración)* estimation, evaluation; *(cálculo)* estimate.

estimado,-a I *pp de* **estimar. II** *adj* esteemed, respected; *(en carta)* **E. Señor,** Dear Sir; **Estimada Señora,** Dear Madam.

estimar I *vtr* **1** *(apreciar)* to esteem, respect, admire. **2** *(valorar)* to estimate; *(un objeto)* to value. **3** *(juzgar)* to consider, think, reckon; **estimo conveniente dar una explicación,** I think an explanation is due. **II estimarse** *vr* **1** to be estimated (**en,** at), be valued (**en,** at). **2** to think highly of oneself.

estimativo,-a *adj* approximate, estimated.

estimulante I *adj* stimulating, encouraging. **II** *nm* stimulant.

estimular *vtr* **1** to stimulate; **e. el apetito,** to whet one's appetite. **2** *fig* to encourage.

estímulo *nm* **1** *Biol Fís* stimulus, stimulation. **2** *fig* encouragement; *Com* incentive.

estío *nm* summer.

estipendio *nm* stipend, fee, remuneration.

estipulación *nf* **1** *Jur (cláusula)* stipulation, condition, proviso. **2** *(acuerdo)* agreement.

estipular *vtr* **1** *(disponer)* to stipulate, establish. **2** *(acordar)* to agree on.

estirado,-a I *pp de* **estirar. II** *adj* **1** *(brazos)* stretched out; *(piel)* taut. **2** *fig* stiff, excessively formal; *fam* mean.

estirar I *vtr* **1** to stretch, draw out, pull out; **e. el cuello,** to crane one's neck; **e. las piernas,** to stretch one's legs; *fig* **e. el dinero,** to spin one's money out, make one's money go further; *fam fig* **e. la pata,** to kick the bucket. **II estirarse** *vr (alargarse)* to stretch; *fig* to shoot up.

estirón *nm* pull, jerk, tug; *fam* **dar** *or* **pegar un e.,** to shoot up *or* grow quickly.

estirpe *nf* race, stock, pedigree.

estival *adj* summer; **época e.,** summertime.

esto *pron dem neut* this, this thing, this matter; **en e.,** just then; **en e. llegó Asunción,** at that moment Asunción arrived; **e. es,** that is, ie; **vendrá tarde, e. es, a las diez,** he'll be coming late, I mean, at ten; **e. no lo sabe nadie,** nobody knows that; *fam* **e. de la fiesta,** this business about the party.

estocada *nf Taur* thrust, stab; *fig* **la e. final,** the coup de grâce.

Estocolmo *n* Stockholm.

estofado,-a¹ *Culin* **I** *adj (carne)* stewed. **II** *nm* stew.

estofado,-a² *Cost* **I** *adj* quilted. **II** *nm* quilting.

estofar¹ *vtr Culin* to stew.

estofar² *vtr Cost* to quilt.

estoicismo *nm* stoicism.

estoico,-a I *adj* stoic, stoical. **II** *nm,f* stoic.

estola *nf* stole.

estolidez *nf fml* stupidity, denseness.

estólido,-a *adj* stupid, dense, thick.

estomacal I *adj* (of the) stomach; **bebida e.,** digestive liqueur; **trastorno e.,** stomach upset. **II** *nm* digestive liqueur.

estómago *nm* stomach; **tener buen e.,** to have a strong stomach; *fig* to be thick-skinned; *fam* **revolver algo el e. a algn,** to turn one's stomach (over). ■ **dolor de e.,** stomach ache.

estopa *nf (fibra)* tow; *(tela)* burlap. ■ **e. de acero,** steel wool.

estoperol *nm Am* tack, stud.

estopilla *nf Tex* cheesecloth.

estoque *nm Taur* sword.

estoquear *vtr Taur* to thrust at, stab.

estorbar I *vtr* **1** *(dificultar)* to hinder, get in the way; **las obras en la calle estorban la libre circulación de los coches,** the road works hold up traffic. **2** *(impedir)* to impede, obstruct. **3** *(molestar)* to disturb, bother, upset; **la música me estorba cuando quiero estudiar,** I can't study when there's music playing. **II** *vi* **1** *(obstaculizar)* to be in the way, block. **2** *(persona)* to be a nuisance; **tu hermano no hace más que estorbar,** your brother is always getting in the way.

estorbo *nm* **1** *(obstáculo)* obstruction, obstacle. **2** *(molestia)* hindrance, encumbrance. **3** *(persona)* nuisance.

estornino *nm Orn* starling.

estornudar *vi* to sneeze.

estornudo *nm* sneeze.

estos,-as *adj dem pl véase* **este,-a.**

éstos,-as *pron dem m,fpl véase* **éste,-a.**

estoy *indic pres véase* **estar.**

estrabismo *nm Med* strabismus, squint; **tener e.,** to have a squint.

estrado *nm* stage, platform; *Mus* bandstand; *Jur* **estrados,** courtrooms.

estrafalario,-a *adj fam (extraño)* eccentric, weird, outlandish; *(desaliñado)* slovenly.

estragar *vtr* to ruin, devastate, ravage; *fig* **e. el paladar,** to deaden one's taste buds.

estrago *nm* ruin, ravage, waste, havoc; **hacer estragos en,** to play havoc with *or* on.

estragón *nm Bot Culin* tarragon.

estrambótico,-a *adj fam* outlandish, weird, eccentric, way-out.

estrangulación *nf* strangling; *Med* strangulation.

estrangulador,-a I *adj* strangling; *Med* strangulating. **II** *nm,f (persona)* strangler. **III** *nm Aut* choke.

estrangular *vtr* to strangle; *Med* to strangulate; *Téc (coche)* to throttle.

estraperlear *vi* to deal in black market goods.

estraperlista *nmf* black marketeer.

estraperlo *nm* black market; **tabaco de e.,** black market cigarettes.

Estrasburgo *n* Strasbourg.

estratagema *nf Mil* stratagem; *fam* trick, ruse.

estratega *nmf* strategist.

estrategia *nf* strategy.

estratégico,-a *adj* strategic.

estratificación *nf* stratification.

estratificar I *vtr* to stratify. **II estratificarse** *vr* to be stratified.

estrato *nm* **1** *Geol* stratum. **2** *Meteor (nube)* stratus. **3** *fig (clase)* stratum, layer, class, level; **estratos sociales,** social strata *pl*.

estratosfera *nf* stratosphere.

estraza *nf* rag, piece of cloth. ◼ **papel de e.,** brown paper.

estrechamiento *nm* **1** *(de valle etc)* narrowing; *Cost (de prenda)* taking in; *Aut* **'e. de calzada',** 'road narrows'. **2** *(punto estrecho)* narrow point. **3** *fig* tightening; **el estrechamiento de los lazos económicos entre el este y el oeste,** the tightening of economic links between east and west.

estrechar I *vtr* **1** *(carretera, valle)* to narrow; *(vestido)* to take in; **e. una falda,** to take in a skirt. **2** *(abrazar)* to squeeze, hug; *(mano)* to shake; **me estrechó la mano con fuerza,** he shook my hand firmly. **3** *fig (obligar)* to compel, constrain. **4** *fig (unir)* to bring closer *or* together; *(lazos)* to tighten; **e. los lazos de amistad,** to tighten the bonds of friendship. **II estrecharse** *vr* **1** *(carretera, valle)* to narrow, become narrower; **el camino se estrecha al llegar al pueblo,** as it nears the village the road narrows. **2** *(apretarse)* to squeeze together *or* up. **3** *fig* to tighten, get tighter. **4** *(dos personas)* to embrace one another, hug; **e. la mano,** to shake hands. **5** *fig* to economize, tighten one's belt.

estrechez *nf* **1** *(angostura)* narrowness, tightness; *(falta de espacio)* lack of space. **2** *fig (dificultad económica)* want, need; **pasar estrecheces,** to be hard up; **vivir en la e.,** to live from hand to mouth. **3** *fig (amistad)* closeness, intimacy. **4** *fig (rigidez)* strictness. ◼ **e. de miras,** narrow-mindedness. **5** *fig (apuro)* tight spot.

estrecho,-a I *adj* **1** narrow; *(vestido)* tight; *(habitación)* cramped, pokey; *(zapatos)* tight, small. **2** *(de dinero)* tight, short. **3** *(sin espacio)* packed, jampacked. **4** *fig (relación)* close, intimate; *(lazo)* close. **5** *fig (actitud)* narrow, rigid; *(carácter)* mean; **e. de miras,** narrow-minded; *fam* strait-laced; **¡no te hagas la estrecha!,** don't be so coy! **II** *nm Geog* strait, straits *pl*; **el E. de Gibraltar,** the Straits of Gibraltar. ◆ **estrechamente** *adv* **1** *(con estrechez)* narrowly, tightly. **2** *fig (íntimamente)* closely, intimately; **e. unidos,** very close; **e. vinculados,** closely linked. **3** *fig (con rigidez)* strictly, rigidly.

estrechura *nf* **1** *(angostura)* narrowness, narrow point. **2** *fig (intimidad)* closeness, intimacy.

estregar I *vtr (con cepillo)* to scrub; *(con trapo etc)* to rub. **II estregarse** *vr* to rub oneself.

estrella *nf (gen)* star; *fig* **haber nacido con buena e.,** to be born under a lucky star; *fig* **nacer con e.,** to be born lucky; *fig* **tener buena/mala e.,** to be lucky/unlucky; *fig* **ver las estrellas,** to see stars. ◼ **e. de cine,** film star; *Zool* **e. de mar,** starfish; *Astron* **e. errante, e. fugaz,** shooting star.

estrellado,-a I *pp de* **estrellar. II** *adj* **1** *(en forma de estrella)* star-shaped. **2** *(cielo)* starry, full of stars, star-spangled. **3** *(hecho pedazos)* smashed, shattered.

estrellar I *vtr* **1** *(llenar de estrellas)* to star, cover with stars. **2** *fam (hacer pedazos)* to smash (to pieces), shatter. **II estrellarse** *vr (hacerse pedazos)* to smash, shatter, crash (**contra,** against); *Aut Av (chocar)* to crash (**contra,** into); *fig* **e. contra un problema,** to come up against *or* run into a problem.

estrellato *nm* stardom.

estrellón *nm Am* crash, collision.

estremecedor,-a *adj (que asusta)* startling; *(grito)* bloodcurdling.

estremecer I *vtr (gen)* to shake. **II estremecerse** *vr (temblar)* to shake, tremble, vibrate; *(persona)* to tremble (**ante,** at; **de,** with); *(de miedo)* to tremble, shudder; *(de frío)* to shiver, tremble.

estremecido,-a I *pp de* **estremecer. II** *adj* shaking (**de,** with), trembling (**de,** with).

estremecimiento *nm (de tierra, edificio)* tremor, vibration; *(de miedo)* trembling, shuddering; *(de frío)* shiver, trembling.

estrena *nf* present, gift.

estrenar I *vtr* **1** *(gen)* to use for the first time; *(ropa)* to wear for the first time; **e. piso,** to move into a new flat. **2** *Teat (obra)* to perform for the first time, give the first performance of; *Cin (película)* to release, put on release. **II estrenarse** *vr* to start, make one's debut.

estreno *nm (de persona)* debut, first appearance; *Teat* first performance; *Cin* premiere, new release; **riguroso e.,** world premiere.

estreñido,-a *Med* **I** *pp de* **estreñir. II** *adj* constipated.

estreñimiento *nm Med* constipation.

estreñir *Med* **I** *vtr* to make constipated, constipate. **II estreñirse** *vr* to become constipated.

estrépito *nm (estruendo)* din, racket, clatter; *fig (ostentación)* ostentation, fuss.

estrepitoso,-a *adj* noisy, clamorous; *(ruido)* deafening; *fig (éxito)* resounding; *fig (fracaso)* spectacular. ◆ **estrepitosamente** *adv* noisily.

estreptococo *nm Med* streptococcus.

estreptomicina *nf Med* streptomycin.

estrés *nm Med* stress.

estría *nf* **1** *(ranura)* groove; *Arquit* flute, fluting. **2** *fam (en la piel)* stretch mark.

estribación *nf Geog* spur; **estribaciones,** foothills.

estribar *vi* **1** *(apoyarse)* to rest (**en,** on). **2** *fig (basarse)* to lie in, be based on; **su éxito estriba en su capacidad de concentración,** her success lies in her powers of concentration.

estribillo *nm* **1** *(en poesía)* refrain; *(en canción)* chorus. **2** *(muletilla)* pet phrase *or* saying, catchphrase.

estribo *nm* **1** *(de jinete)* stirrup; *Aut* running board, footboard; *(en carruaje)* step; *fig* **perder los estribos,** to lose one's temper, lose one's head. **2** *Arquit* buttress; *(de puente)* pier, support. **3** *Geog* spur. **4** *Anat* stirrup bone.

estribor *nm Náut* starboard.

estrictez *nf Am* strictness.

estricto,-a *adj* strict, rigorous.

estridencia *nf* stridency, shrillness.

estridente *adj* strident, shrill.

estripazón *nf CAm (apretura)* crush; *(destrozo)* destruction.

estrofa *nf Lit* stanza, verse, strophe.

estrógeno *nm* oestrogen, *US* estrogen.

estroncio *nm Quím* strontium.

estropajo *nm* scourer; *fam fig* **poner a algn como un e.,** to pull sb to pieces.

estropajoso,-a *adj* **1** *(lengua)* furry. **2** *(habla)* stammering. **3** *(carne)* gristly, tough. **4** *(pelo)* strawlike. **5** *(persona) (andrajoso)* ragged; *(desaliñado)* slovenly.

estropear I *vtr (máquina, cosecha)* to damage; *(fiesta, plan)* to spoil, ruin; *(salud)* to be bad for; *(pelo, manos)* to ruin. **II estropearse** *vr (máquina)* to break down; *(cosecha)* to be *or* get damaged, be spoiled; *(plan, proyecto)* to fail.

estropicio *nm fam* **1** *(destrozo)* breakage, smashing, damage; *(ruido)* crash, clatter. **2** *fig (desorden)* mess; *(jaleo)* fuss, rumpus; **hacer un e.,** to make a right mess of sth.

estructura *nf (gen)* structure; *(armazón)* frame, framework.

estructuración *nf* structure, organization.

estructural *adj* structural.

estructurar *vtr* to structure, organize.

estruendo *nm* 1 *(ruido)* din, racket. 2 *(confusión)* uproar, tumult.

estruendoso,-a *adj (ruido)* noisy, deafening; *(aplauso)* thunderous.

estrujar I *vtr* 1 *(exprimir)* to squeeze; *(apretar)* to crush; *(ropa)* to wring. 2 *fam (explotar)* to drain, bleed dry. II **estrujarse** *vr fam* **e. los sesos** *or* **el cerebro,** to rack one's brains.

estrujón *nm* tight squeeze, big hug.

estuario *nm Geol* estuary.

estucado,-a I *pp de* **estucar.** II *nm* stucco (work).

estucar *vtr* to stucco.

estuche *nm (caja)* case, box; *(vaina)* sheath. ■ **e. de aseo,** toilet bag.

estuco *nm* stucco.

estudiado,-a I *pp de* **estudiar.** II *adj (muy pensado)* studied; *(falso)* affected, studied; *(rebuscado)* elaborate, recherché.

estudiantado *nm* students *pl*, student body.

estudiante *nmf* student.

estudiantil *adj* student, of students.

estudiantina *nf* student band.

estudiar I *vtr* 1 *(gen)* to study; *(en la universidad)* to read, study; **e. medicina,** to study medicine. 2 *(trabajar)* to study, work; **este año tiene que e. mucho,** he has to work a lot this year. 3 *(pensar)* to think about *or* over, ponder; **lo estudiaré,** I'll think about it. 4 *(observar)* to examine, observe; **he estudiado todos sus movimientos,** I've observed all his movements. II *vi* to study; **estudia para médico,** he's studying to be a doctor.

estudio *nm* 1 *(gen)* study; *(encuesta)* survey, research; **dedicarse al e. de algo,** to study sth; **estar en e.,** to be under consideration. ■ *Com* **e. de mercado,** market research; **e. de viabilidad,** feasibility study. 2 *(sala)* studio. ■ *Cin* **e. cinematográfico,** film studio; *Mús* **e. de grabación,** recording studio; *TV* **e. de televisión,** television studio. 3 *(apartamento)* studio (flat). 4 **estudios,** studies, education *sing*; **dar e. a algn,** to pay for sb's education; **hizo sus e. en Europa,** she studied in Europe; **tener e.,** to be well-educated.

estudioso,-a I *adj* studious. II *nm,f* student, scholar.

estufa *nf* 1 *(calentador)* heater, stove; *(de gas, eléctrica)* fire. 2 *(invernadero)* hothouse, greenhouse.

estufilla *nf* 1 *(brasero)* brazier, foot-warmer. 2 *(manguito)* muff.

estulticia *nf lit* stupidity, foolishness.

estulto,-a *adj lit* stupid, foolish.

estupa I *nf arg (grupo)* drug squad. II *nmf (persona)* drug squad officer.

estupefacción *nf* stupefaction; *(asombro)* astonishment, amazement.

estupefaciente *nm* drug, narcotic.

estupefacto,-a *adj* astounded, flabbergasted.

estupendo,-a *adj* super, marvellous, *US* marvelous, wonderful; **¡e.!,** great! ◆ **estupendamente** *adv* marvellously, *US* marvelously, wonderfully.

estupidez *nf* stupidity, stupid thing; **cometer una e.,** to do something silly; **¡qué e.!,** what a stupid thing to do *or* to say!

estúpido,-a I *adj* silly, stupid. II *nm,f* berk, idiot.

estupor *nm* stupor, amazement, astonishment; **causar e.,** to astonish.

estupro *nm Jur* rape (of a minor).

estuquista *nmf* stucco worker.

esturión *nm (pez)* sturgeon.

estuve *pt indef véase* **estar.**

esvástica *nf* swastika.

ETA *nf abr de* **Euzkadi Ta Askatasuna** *(Patria Vasca y Libertad).*

etapa *nf* 1 *(fase)* period, stage; **por etapas,** in stages; **quemar etapas,** to get on in leaps and bounds. 2 *Dep* leg, stage.

etarra *Pol* I *adj* (of) ETA. II *nmf* member of ETA.

etc. *abr de* **etcétera,** etcetera, etc.

etcétera I *adv* etcetera, and so on. II *nm* list; **y un largo e. de quejas,** and a long list of complaints.

éter *nm* 1 *Quím* ether. 2 *lit (espacio celeste)* ether, sky, heavens *pl.*

etéreo,-a *adj* ethereal.

eternidad *nf* eternity; *fam* age; **tardaste una e.,** you took ages.

eternizar I *vtr* to eternalize, eternize; *fam* to prolong endlessly, make everlasting. II **eternizarse** *vr fam* to be interminable *or* endless; *(persona)* to take ages (**en,** over); *(discusión)* to drag on.

eterno,-a *adj* eternal, everlasting, endless.

ética *nf* ethic, ethics *sing.*

ético,-a I *adj* ethical. II *nm,f* ethicist.

etílico,-a *adj* ethylic; **alcohol e.,** ethyl alcohol; **en estado e.,** intoxicated; **intoxicación etílica,** alcohol poisoning.

etilo *nm Quím* ethyl.

etimología *nf* etymology.

etimológico,-a *adj* etymological.

etíope *adj & nmf*, **etíope** *adj & nmf* Ethiopian.

Etiopía *nf* Ethiopia.

etiqueta *nf* 1 *(marbete)* label, tag; *fig* **poner etiquetas a la gente,** to label people. 2 *(ceremonia)* etiquette, formality, ceremony; **de e.,** formal; **traje de e.,** evening *or* formal dress.

etiquetar *vtr* to label, put a label on.

etiquetero,-a *adj* formal, punctilious, ceremonious.

étnico,-a *adj* ethnic.

etnografía *nf* ethnography.

etnográfico,-a *adj* ethnographic, ethnographical.

etnológico,-a *adj* ethnologic, ethnological.

etnólogo,-a *nm,f* ethnologist.

etrusco,-a I *adj* Etruscan. II *nm,f (persona)* Etruscan. III *nm (idioma)* Etruscan.

eucalipto *nm Bot* eucalyptus.

eucaristía *nf Rel* Eucharist.

eucarístico,-a *adj* eucharistic, eucharistical.

eufemismo *nm* euphemism.

eufemístico,-a *adj* euphemistic.

eufonía *nf* euphony.

eufónico,-a *adj* euphonic, euphonious.

euforia *nf* euphoria, elation.

eufórico,-a *adj* euphoric, elated.

Eufrates *n* **(el) E.,** the Euphrates.

eunuco *nm* eunuch.

eureka *interj* eureka!

euroasiático,-a *adj & nm,f* Eurasian.

eurocomunísmo *nm Pol* Eurocommunism.

eurocomunista *adj & nmf Pol* Eurocommunist.

euromisil *nm* Euromissile.

Europa *n* Europe.

europeísmo *nm* Europeanism.

europeísta *adj & nmf* pro-European.

europeización *nf* Europeanization.

europeizar *vtr* to europeanize.

europeo,-a *adj* & *nm,f* European.

euscalduna **I** *adj* Basque; *(que habla vasco)* Basque-speaking. **II** *nmf* Basque speaker.

euskera *adj* & *nm*, **eusquera** *adj* & *nm (idioma)* Basque.

Eustaquio *nm Anat* **trompa de E.,** Eustachian tube.

eutanasia *nf* euthanasia.

evacuación *nf* evacuation.

evacuado,-a **I** *pp de* **evacuar. II** *adj* evacuated. **III** *nm,f* evacuee.

evacuar *vtr* **1** *(lugar)* to evacuate. **2** *(llevar a cabo)* to carry out; *Jur* to issue. **3** *Anat* to empty; **e. el vientre,** to have a bowel movement.

evadido,-a **I** *pp de* **evadir. II** *adj* escaped. **III** *nm, f* fugitive, escapee.

evadir **I** *vtr (respuesta, peligro)* to avoid; *(responsabilidad)* to shirk; *(divisas, impuestos)* to evade. **II** **evadirse** *vr (escaparse)* to escape.

evaluación *nf* evaluation. ■ *Educ* **e. continuada,** continuous assessment.

evaluar *vtr* to evaluate, assess.

evanescente *adj* evanescent.

evangélico,-a *adj Rel* evangelic, evangelical.

evangelio *nm* gospel; **el E. según San Juan,** the Gospel according to Saint John.

evangelismo *nm* evangelism.

evangelista *nm* evangelist.

evangelización *nf* evangelization, evangelizing.

evangelizador,-a I *adj* evangelizing. **II** *nm,f* evangelist.

evangelizar *vtr* to evangelize, preach the gospel to.

evaporable *adj* evaporable.

evaporación *nf* evaporation.

evaporar **I** *vtr* to evaporate. **II** **evaporarse** *vr* to evaporate; *fig* to vanish.

evasión *nf (fuga)* escape, flight; *fig* evasion, dodge. ■ **e. fiscal** *or* **de impuestos,** tax evasion; **novela de e.,** escapist novel.

evasiva *nf* evasive answer; **contestar con evasivas,** not to give a straight answer, avoid the issue.

evasivo,-a *adj* evasive.

evento *nm* eventuality, contingency, unforeseen event; **a todo e.,** in any event.

eventual I *adj* **1** *(casual)* chance, possible; *(gastos)* incidental; **circunstancias eventuales,** chance circumstances. **2** *(trabajo, obrero)* casual, temporary, provisional. **II** *nm, f (obrero)* temporary worker. ◆ **eventualmente** *adv* by chance.

eventualidad *nf* eventuality, contingency, chance.

evicción *nf Jur* eviction.

evidencia *nf* **1** *(claridad)* obviousness, clearness; *(certidumbre)* certainty; **poner algo en e.,** to demonstrate sth; **poner a algn en e.,** to make a fool of sb, show sb up. **2** *SAm (prueba)* proof, evidence.

evidenciar *vtr* to prove, show, demonstrate, make evident *or* obvious.

evidente *adj* evident, obvious. ◆ **evidentemente** *adv* evidently, obviously.

evitable *adj* avoidable, preventable.

evitación *nf* avoidance, prevention.

evitar **I** *vtr (gen)* to avoid; *(prevenir, impedir)* to prevent; *(tentación)* to shun; *(desastre)* to avert; **esto nos evitará muchas molestias,** this'll save us a lot of trouble; **quiero e. que sufra,** I want to spare him any suffering. **II** **evitarse** *vr* to avoid one another.

evocación *nf* evocation, recollection, recalling.

evocador,-a *adj* evocative, evocatory.

evocar *vtr* **1** *(espíritu)* to invoke. **2** *(recuerdo)* to evoke; *(pasado)* to recall.

evolución *nf* **1** *(cambio)* evolution; *(desarrollo)* development. **2** *(vuelta)* turn; *Mil (movimiento)* manoeuvre, *US* maneuver.

evolucionar *vi* **1** *(cambiar)* to evolve, develop; **e. a pasos agigantados,** to take giant strides. **2** *(dar vueltas)* to turn; *Mil (moverse)* to manoeuvre, *US* maneuver.

evolucionismo *nm* evolutionism.

evolucionista *adj* & *nmf* evolutionist.

evolutivo,-a *adj* evolutionary, evolving.

ex *pref* former, ex-; **ex alumno,** former pupil, exstudent; **ex combatiente,** ex-serviceman, *US* veteran.

exabrupto *nm* sharp comment, sudden outburst; **contestar a algn con un e.,** to snap at sb.

exacción *nf (de impuestos)* exaction; *(extorsión)* extortion.

exacerbación *nf* **1** *(agravamiento)* exacerbation, aggravation. **2** *(irritación)* exasperation.

exacerbante *adj* **1** *(agravante)* aggravating. **2** *(irritante)* exasperating, irritating.

exacerbar **I** *vtr* **1** *(agravar)* to exacerbate, aggravate. **2** *(irritar)* to exasperate, irritate. **II** **exacerbarse** *vr* *(irritarse)* to feel exasperated.

exactitud *nf (fidelidad)* exactness; *(precisión)* accuracy; **con e.,** accurately.

exacto,-a *adj (fiel)* exact; *(preciso)* exact, accurate; **¡e.!,** precisely!; **para ser e.,** to be precise. ◆ **exactamente** *adv* exactly, precisely, just so.

exageración *nf* exaggeration; **¡qué e.!,** come off it!

exagerado,-a **I** *pp de* **exagerar. II** *adj* exaggerated; *(historia)* far-fetched; *(castigo)* excessive; **es un tipo e.,** he overdoes everything; **precios exagerados,** exorbitant prices; **un gesto e.,** a flamboyant gesture; **una historia e.,** a tall story. ◆ **exageradamente** *adv* excessively.

exagerar *vtr* to exaggerate; *pey* to overdo, go too far.

exaltación *nf* **1** *(alabanza)* exaltation, praise. **2** *(júbilo)* exaltation, elation. **3** *(enardecimiento)* overexcitement. **4** *fam Pol (fanatismo)* fanaticism.

exaltado,-a **I** *pp de* **exaltar. II** *adj (discusión)* impassioned, heated; *(persona)* excitable, hotheaded, **los ánimos estaban exaltados,** feelings were running high. **III** *nm,f fam* hothead; *Pol* fanatic, extremist.

exaltar **I** *vtr* **1** *(elevar)* to raise, promote. **2** *(ensalzar)* to exalt, praise, extol. **II** **exaltarse** *vr (enardecerse)* to get overexcited, get carried away, get worked up.

exalumno,-a *nm, f Univ* former student; *(de escuela, colegio) (alumno)* old boy; *(alumna)* old girl.

examen *nm (gen)* examination, exam; *(de problema)* consideration; **aprobar un e.,** to pass an exam; **hacer un e.,** to do an exam; **presentarse a un e.,** to take *or* sit an exam. ■ **e. de conducir,** driving test; *Educ* **e. de ingreso,** entrance examination; *Med* **e. médico,** checkup.

examinador,-a I *adj* examining. **II** *nm,f* examiner.

examinando,-a *nm, f* candidate, examinee.

examinar **I** *vtr (gen)* to examine; *(inspeccionar)* to go over, inspect, consider. **II** **examinarse** *vr* to take *or* sit an examination.

exangüe *adj* **1** *(desangrado)* bloodless. **2** *fig (débil)* weak, lifeless.

exánime *adj* **1** *(muerto)* dead. **2** *fig (desmayado)* lifeless; *(muy débil)* worn-out, exhausted.

exasperación *nf* exasperation.

exasperante *adj* exasperating.

exasperar **I** *vtr* to exasperate. **II** **exasperarse** *vr* to become exasperated.

Exc., Exca., Exc.ª *abr de* **Excelencia,** Excellency.

excarcelación *nf* release (from prison).

excarcelar *vtr* to release (from prison).

excavación *nf* excavation, digging; *Arqueol* dig.

excavadora *nf* digger.

excavador,-a *nm,f* excavator, digger.

excavar *vtr* to excavate, dig.

excedencia *nf* (*ausencia*) leave (of absence); (*sueldo*) leave pay; (*de profesor*) sabbatical.

excedente I *adj* 1 (*excesivo*) excessive; (*que sobra*) excess, surplus. 2 (*persona*) on leave; (*profesor*) on sabbatical. II *nm Com* surplus, excess.

exceder I *vtr* (*superar*) to exceed, surpass; (*sobrepasar*) to excel, outdo; **e. el presupuesto,** to overspend; **e. en mucho a ...,** to greatly exceed ... . II *vi* **e. de,** to exceed, surpass. III **excederse** *vr* to overdo it, go to extremes; **e. a sí mismo,** to surpass *or* excel oneself; **e. en sus funciones,** to exceed one's duty.

excelencia *nf* 1 excellence; **por e.,** par excellence. 2 (*título*) **Su E.,** His *or* Her Excellency.

excelente *adj* excellent, first-rate.

excelentísimo,-a *adj* (*alcalde*) Your Worship; (*embajador*) Your Excellency; (*juez*) Your Honour.

excelso,-a *adj* sublime, lofty.

excentricidad *nf* eccentricity.

excéntrico,-a *adj* eccentric.

excepción *nf* exception; **a** *or* **con e. de,** with the exception of, except for; **de e.,** exceptional; **la e. confirma la regla,** the exception proves the rule. ■ *Pol* **estado de e.,** state of emergency.

excepcional *adj* (*extraordinario*) exceptional, outstanding; (*raro*) exceptional, unusual.

excepto *adv* except (for), excepting, apart from.

exceptuación *nf* exception, exclusion.

exceptuar *vtr* to except, exclude, leave out.

excesivo,-a *adj* excessive.

exceso *nm* 1 excess, surplus; **con e.,** too much; **bebe con e.,** he drinks too much; **en e.,** in excess, excessively. ■ **e. de equipaje,** excess baggage; **e. de velocidad,** speeding. 2 **excesos,** excesses; **cometer excesos,** to overindulge.

excitabilidad *nf* excitability.

excitable *adj* excitable, easily worked up.

excitación *nf* (*sentimiento*) excitement; (*acción*) excitation.

excitante I *adj* exciting; *Med* stimulating. II *nm* stimulant.

excitar I *vtr* (*gen*) to excite; (*emociones*) to arouse, stir up. II **excitarse** *vr* to get excited, get carried away, get worked up.

exclamación *nf* exclamation; (*grito*) cry; **lanzar** *or* **exhalar una e.,** to cry out. ■ *Ling* **signo de e.,** exclamation mark.

exclamar *vtr* & *vi* to exclaim, cry out.

exclamativo,-a *adj*, **exclamatorio,-a** *adj* exclamatory.

exclaustrado,-a I *pp de* **exclaustrar.** II *nm,f Rel* (*monje*) secularized monk; (*monja*) secularized nun.

exclaustrar *vtr Rel* to secularize.

excluir *vtr* to exclude, shut out; (*rechazar*) to reject.

exclusión *nf* exclusion, shutting out; **a e. de,** with the exclusion of, excluding, not counting.

exclusiva *nf Com* sole right; *Prensa* exclusive.

exclusive *adv* exclusively, exclusive; **del ocho de marzo al siete de noviembre e.,** from the eighth of March to the seventh of November exclusive.

exclusividad *nf* exclusiveness.

exclusivismo *nm* exclusionism.

exclusivista I *adj* exclusive, select. II *nm,f* exclusivist.

exclusivo,-a *adj* exclusive.

Excma. *abr de* **Excelentísima,** Most Excellent.

Excmo. *abr de* **Excelentísimo,** Most Excellent.

excomulgar *vtr Rel* to excommunicate.

excomunión *nf* excommunication.

excoriación *nf* excoriation, chafing; (*desolladura*) graze.

excoriar I *vtr* to excoriate, chafe. II **excoriarse** *vr* to graze oneself.

excrecencia *nf* excrescence.

excreción *nf* excretion.

excremento *nm* excrement.

excretar *vi* to excrete.

excretor,-a *adj Anat* excretory; **aparato e.,** excretory organ.

exculpación *nf* exoneration; *Jur* acquittal.

exculpar *vtr* to exonerate; *Jur* to acquit.

excursión *nf* excursion, trip, outing; **hacer una e.,** to go on a trip.

excursionismo *nm Dep* hiking.

excursionista *nmf* tripper; (*a pie*) hiker.

excusa *nf* (*pretexto*) excuse; (*disculpa*) excuse, apology; **presentar** *or* **ofrecer sus excusas,** to apologize.

excusado,-a I *pp de* **excusar.** II *adj* 1 (*disculpado*) excused, pardoned, forgiven; (*exempt*) exento; **estar e. de,** to be exempt from. 2 (*innecesario*) unnecessary, needless; **e. es decir que ...,** needless to say that ... . III *nm* (*baño*) toilet.

excusar I *vtr* 1 (*justificar*) to excuse. 2 (*disculpar*) to pardon, forgive. 3 (*eximir*) exempt (**de,** from). 4 (*evitar*) to avoid, prevent; **así excusamos problemas,** this way we avoid problems; **excuso decirte,** I don't have to tell you, needless to say. II **excusarse** *vr* (*disculparse*) to apologize, excuse oneself.

execrable *adj* execrable, abominable.

execración *nf* execration.

execrar *vtr* to execrate, abhor, deplore.

exención *nf* exemption; **e. de impuestos,** tax exemption.

exento,-a *adj* exempt, free (**de,** from); **e. de preocupaciones,** carefree; **está e. del servicio militar,** he's exempt from military service; **no está e. de peligros,** it is not without danger.

exequias *nfpl* obsequies, funeral rites.

exfoliación *nf* exfoliation.

exfoliar *vtr* to exfoliate.

exhalación *nf* 1 (*emanación*) exhalation. 2 (*estrella*) shooting star; (*rayo*) flash of lightning; *fam fig* **pasar como una e.,** to flash past.

exhalar I *vtr* (*aire*) to exhale, breathe out; (*gas*) to give off, emit; (*suspiro*) to heave; (*queja*) to utter. II **exhalarse** *vr* (*persona*) to rush.

exhaustivo,-a *adj* exhaustive, thorough; **de modo e.,** thoroughly.

exhausto,-a *adj* exhausted.

exheredación *nf* disinheritance.

exheredar *vtr* to disinherit.

exhibición *nf* exhibition, show; *Cin* showing.

exhibicionismo *nm* exhibitionism.

exhibicionista *nmf* exhibitionist.

exhibir I *vtr* 1 (*mostrar*) to exhibit, display, show. 2 (*ostentar*) to show off. II **exhibirse** *vr* (*ostentar*) to show off, make an exhibition of oneself.

exhortación *nf* exhortation.

exhortar *vtr* to exhort.

exhuberancia *nf* (*gen*) exuberance; (*abundancia de vegetación*) lushness, luxuriance.

exhumación *nf* exhumation.

exhumar *vtr* to exhume.

exigencia *nf* exigency, demand; *(requisito)* requirement.

exigente *adj* demanding, exacting.

exigir *vtr (persona)* to demand, insist on; *(situación)* to require, call for; **este problema exige una solución rápida,** this problem requires a swift solution; **exige demasiado,** he's extremely demanding; **e. buena cualidad en el servicio,** to insist upon good service.

exigüidad *nf (pequeñez)* smallness; *(escasez)* scantiness, meagreness, scarcity; **e. de recursos,** lack of funds.

exiguo,-a *adj (pequeño)* small, tiny; *(escaso)* scanty, meagre, *US* meager.

exilado,-a I *pp de* **exilar. II** *adj* exiled, in exile. **III** *nm, f* exile.

exilar I *vtr* to exile, send into exile. **II exilarse** *vr* to go into exile.

exiliado,-a I *pp de* **exiliar. II** *véase* **exilado,-a.**

exiliar *vtr*, **exiliarse** *vr véase* **exilar.**

exilio *nm* **1** *(acción)* exile, banishment; **enviar al e.,** to send into exile. **2** *(lugar)* (place of) exile.

eximio,-a *adj* distinguished, renowned, eminent.

eximir I *vtr* to exempt, free, excuse **(de,** from). **II eximirse** *vr* to free oneself **(de,** from).

exinanido,-a *adj* debilitated, very weak.

existencia *nf* **1** *(vida)* existence, life. **2 existencias,** *Com* stock *sing*, stocks; **en existencia,** in stock; **renovar las e.,** to restock. ▪ **liquidación de e.,** clearance sale.

existencial *adj Filos* existential.

existencialismo *nm Filos* existentialism.

existencialista *adj Filos* existentialist.

existente *adj* existing, existent; *Com* in stock.

existir *vi* to exist, be (in existence); **existen aún muchas dificultades,** there are still many difficulties.

exitazo *nm fam* terrific success, smash hit.

éxito *nm* success; **con é.,** successfully; **no tener é.,** to fail, not succeed; **tener é.,** to be successful.

éxodo *nm* exodus.

exoneración *nf* exoneration.

exonerar *vtr* to exonerate.

exorable *adj* exorable.

exorbitancia *nf* exorbitance, excessiveness.

exorbitante *adj* exorbitant, excessive.

exorcismo *nm* exorcism.

exorcista *nmf* exorcist.

exorcizar *vtr* to exorcize.

exordio *nm* exordium, foreword.

exótico,-a *adj* exotic.

expandir I *vtr (dilatar)* to expand; *fig (divulgar)* to spread. **II expandirse** *vr (dilatarse)* to expand; *fig (divulgarse)* to spread.

expansión *nf* **1** *(de un gas)* expansion; *(crecimiento)* growth. **2** *fig (difusión)* spreading. **3** *fig (diversión)* relaxation, recreation.

expansionarse *vr* **1** *(gas)* to expand. **2** *fig (divertirse)* to relax, amuse oneself, let one's hair down.

expansionismo *nm* expansionism.

expansionista *adj* expansionist.

expansivo,-a *adj* **1** *(gas)* expansive. **2** *fig (persona)* open, frank.

expatriación *nf* expatriation.

expatriado,-a I *pp de* **expatriar. II** *adj & nm,f* expatriate.

expatriar I *vtr* to exile, banish. **II expatriarse** *vr* to leave one's country, emigrate, go into exile.

expectación *nf (esperanza)* expectation, expectancy, anticipation; *(emoción)* excitement.

expectante *adj* expectant.

expectativa *nf* **1** *(esperanza)* expectation, expectancy. **2** *(perspectiva)* prospect; **estar a la e. de,** to be on the lookout for, be on the watch for.

expectoración *nf* **1** *(acción)* expectoration. **2** *(esputo)* sputum, phlegm.

expectorante *nm Farm* expectorant.

expectorar *vtr & vi* to expectorate.

expedición *nf* **1** *(gen)* expedition; *(viaje)* expedition; *(personas)* party. **2** *(envío)* dispatch, shipping; *(conjunto de mercancías)* shipment.

expedicionario,-a I *adj* expeditionary; *Mil* **cuerpo** *or* **grupo e.,** expeditionary force. **II** *nm, f* member of an expedition.

expedidor,-a *nm,f Com* sender, dispatcher, shipper.

expedientar *vtr* to make a file on, place under enquiry.

expediente *nm* **1** *(informe)* dossier, record; *(ficha)* file; *fam* **cubrir el e.,** to keep up appearances. ▪ *Educ* **e. académico,** student's record. **2** *Jur* proceedings *pl*, action; **formar e. a,** to take proceedings against; **incoar e.,** to start proceedings. **3** *(recurso)* expedient; **recurrir al e. de,** to resort to.

expedienteo *nm pey* red tape.

expedir I *vtr* **1** *(despachar) (carta etc)* to send, dispatch; *(mercancías)* to send, dispatch, ship. **2** *(pasaporte, título)* to issue; *(contrato, documento)* to draw up. **II expedirse** *vr Arg Chi Urug (manejarse)* to manage.

expeditar *vtr Am* to solve.

expeditivo,-a *adj* expeditious.

expedito,-a *adj (presto)* expeditious, prompt, speedy; *(libre)* free, clear.

expelente *adj* expelling.

expeler *vtr* to expel, eject, throw out.

expendedor,-a I *adj* selling, retailing, retail. **II** *nm, f* *(vendedor)* dealer, seller, retailer; **e. de tabaco,** tobacconist. **III** *nm* **e. automático,** vending machine.

expendeduría *nf* tobacconist's.

expender *vtr (al por menor)* to retail, sell; *(gastar)* to spend.

expensas *nfpl* expenses *pl*, charges *pl*, costs *pl*; **a e. de,** at the expense of.

experiencia *nf* experience; *(experimento)* experiment; **por e.,** from experience.

experimentación *nf* experimentation, experimenting, testing.

experimentado,-a I *pp de* **experimentar. II** *adj (persona)* experienced; *(método)* tested, tried.

experimental *adj* experimental.

experimentar *vtr* **1** *(hacer experimentos)* to experiment, test. **2** *(sentir)* to experience, feel; *(pérdida)* to suffer; *(aumento)* to show; *(cambio)* to undergo; *Med* **e. una mejoría,** to improve, make progress. **3** *(probar)* to test, try out.

experimento *nm* experiment, test.

experto,-a I *adj* expert. **II** *nm,f* expert. ◆ **expertamente** *adv* expertly, skilfully, *US* skillfully.

expiación *nf* expiation, atonement.

expiar *vtr* to expiate, atone for.

expiración *nf* expiration, expiry; **fecha de e.,** expiry date.

expirar *vi* to expire.

explanada *nf* esplanade.

explanar *vtr* **1** *(allanar)* to level, grade. **2** *fig (explicar)* to explain, elucidate; *(aclarar)* to clear up.

explayar I *vtr (extender)* to extend, spread out. **II explayarse** *vr* **1** *(hablar)* to dwell (on), elaborate (on), talk at length (about). **2** *(divertirse)* to enjoy oneself. **3** *(confiarse)* to confide **(con,** in), open one's heart **(con,** to).

explicable *adj* explicable, explainable.

explicación *nf* explanation; *(motivo)* reason; **sin dar explicaciones,** without giving any reason.

explicaderas *nfpl fam* way *sing* of explaining; **tener buenas e.,** to be good at explaining things.

explicar I *vtr* to explain, expound. **II explicarse** *vr* **1** *(persona)* to explain (oneself); **¿me explico?,** do you understand?; **se explica muy bien,** he's very articulate. **2** *(algo)* to understand, make out; **no me lo explico,** I can't understand it.

explicativo,-a *adj* explanatory.

explicitar *vtr* to state explicitly.

explícito,-a *adj* explicit.

exploración *nf* exploration; *Téc* scanning; *Mil* reconnaissance.

explorador,-a I *adj* exploring, exploratory; *Mil* **avión e.,** reconnaissance aircraft. **II** *nm, f* **1** *(persona)* explorer; *(niño)* boy scout; *(niña)* girl guide, *US* girl scout. **2** *Med* probe; *Téc* scanner.

explorar *vtr* to explore; *Med* to probe; *Téc* to scan; *Min* to drill, prospect; *Mil* to reconnoitre; *fig* **e. el terreno,** to see how the land lies.

exploratorio,-a *adj* exploratory; *Med* probing.

explosión *nf* **1** *(estallido)* explosion, blast, blowing up; **hacer e.,** to explode; **se oyó una fuerte e.,** there was a loud explosion. ■ **motor de e.,** internal combustion engine. **2** *fig* outburst.

explosionar *vtr & vi* to explode, blast, blow up.

explosivo,-a I *adj* explosive; *Ling* plosive. **II** *nm* explosive.

explotable *adj* *(mina)* exploitable, workable; *(terreno)* which can be farmed *or* cultivated.

explotación *nf* **1** *(utilización)* exploitation, working; *Agr* cultivation (of land); **e. de recursos,** tapping of resources. ■ **e. agrícola,** farm; **e. forestal,** forestry; **e. minera,** mine; **gastos de e.,** running costs *or* expenses. **2** *pey (abuso)* exploitation.

explotador,-a *nm, f pey* exploiter.

explotar I *vtr* **1** *(gen) (aprovechar)* to exploit; *(mina)* to work; *(recursos)* to tap; *(fábrica)* to operate; *(tierra)* to cultivate. **2** *pey (personas, situación)* to exploit. **II** *vi (bomba)* to explode, go off.

expoliación *nf* plundering, pillaging, sacking.

expoliar *vtr* to plunder, pillage, sack.

expolio *nm* *(acción)* plundering, pillaging; *(botín)* plunder, booty.

exponente I *nmf (persona)* exponent. **II** *nm Mat* index, exponent.

exponer *(pp* **expuesto***)* **I** *vtr* **1** *(mostrar)* to expose, show, exhibit, display. **2** *(explicar)* to expound, explain, put forward; *(propuesta)* to set out. **3** *(arriesgar)* to expose, risk, endanger. **II exponerse** *vr (arriesgarse)* to run the risk (**a,** of), expose oneself (**a,** to); **no te expongas a tal peligro,** don't expose yourself to such a danger; **te expones a perder el trabajo,** you run the risk of losing your job.

exportable *adj* exportable, for exportation.

exportación *nf* exportation, export. ■ **derechos de e.,** export duties; **licencia de e.,** export licence.

exportador,-a I *adj* exporting; **países exportadores de petróleo,** petroleum exporting countries. **II** *nm, f* exporter.

exportar *vtr* to export.

exposición *nf* **1** *Arte* exhibition, show, display. ■ **e. universal,** world fair; **sala de exposiciones,** gallery. **2** *(explicación)* account, claim, explanation; *(de hechos, ideas)* exposé. **3** *Fot* exposure.

expositivo,-a *adj* explanatory.

expósito,-a *nm, f (niño)* e., foundling.

expositor,-a *nm, f (de teoría)* exponent; *Arte* exhibitor.

exprés *adj* express; **(olla)** e., pressure cooker; **(café) e.,** espresso (coffee).

expresado,-a I *pp de* **expresar. II** *adj* aforesaid, above-mentioned.

expresar I *vtr (gen)* to express; *(manifestar)* to state; *(indicar)* to convey. **II expresarse** *vr* to express oneself.

expresión *nf* **1** *(gen)* expression; **reducir algo a la mínima e.,** to reduce sth to the bare minimum. ■ **e. corporal,** free expression. **2** *(locución)* expression, phrase. **3 expresiones,** greetings, regards.

expresionismo *nm Arte* expressionism.

expresionista *adj & nmf* expressionist.

expresivo,-a *adj* **1** *(elocuente)* expressive; **mirada expresiva,** meaningful glance; **silencio e.,** eloquent silence. **2** *(cariñoso)* warm, affectionate; **es poco e.,** he doesn't show his feelings. ◆ **expresivamente** *adv* affectionately.

expreso,-a I *adj (especificado)* express; **con el fin e. de,** with the express purpose of. **II** *nm Ferroc* express (train). **III** *adv* on purpose, deliberately; **lo hizo e. para fastidiar,** he did it just to be awkward. ◆ **expresamente** *adv (especificamente)* specifically, expressly; *(deliberadamente)* on purpose, deliberately.

exprimidor *nm* squeezer, *US* juicer.

exprimir *vtr* **1** *(limón)* to squeeze; *(zumo)* to squeeze out. **2** *fig (persona)* to exploit, bleed dry.

expropiación *nf* expropriation.

expropiar *vtr* to expropriate.

expuesto,-a I *pp de* **exponer. II** *adj* **1** *(sin protección)* exposed. **2** *(peligroso)* risky, dangerous; **estar e. a,** to be exposed to. **3** *(manifestado)* expressed, stated. **4** *(exhibido)* on display, exhibited, on show.

expulsar *vtr* **1** *(echar)* to expel, eject, throw out; *Dep (jugador)* to send off; *(de alumno)* to expel; *(de universidad)* to send down, *US* expel. **2** *(humo etc)* to belch out.

expulsión *nf* expulsion, ejection; *Dep* sending off; *(de alumno)* expulsion; *(de universidad)* sending down, *US* expulsion.

expulsor,-a I *adj* ejecting; **mecanismo e.,** ejector mechanism. **II** *nm Téc* ejector.

expurgación *nf* expurgation; *fig* purges, purging.

expurgar *vtr* to expurgate; *fig* to purge.

expuse *pt indef véase* **exponer.**

exquisitez *nf* exquisiteness; *(manjar)* delicacy, refinement.

exquisito,-a *adj (bello)* exquisite; *(delicioso)* delicious; *(gusto)* refined.

extasiado,-a I *pp de* **extasiarse. II** *adj* ecstatic; **quedarse e.,** to go into ecstasies *or* raptures.

extasiarse *vtr* to go into ectasies *or* raptures.

éxtasis *nm inv* ecstasy, rapture.

extemporáneo,-a *adj* **1** *(lluvia etc)* unseasonable. **2** *(inoportuno)* untimely, inappropriate.

extender I *vtr* **1** *(gen)* to extend; *(agrandar)* to enlarge. **2** *(mapa, plano)* to spread (out), open (out); *(mano, brazo)* to stretch (out). **3** *(documento)* to draw up; *(cheque)* to make out; *(pasaporte, certificado)* to issue. **II extenderse** *vr* **1** *(en el tiempo)* to extend, last. **2** *(terreno)* to spread out, stretch; **sus propiedades se extienden hasta el río,** his property stretches down to the river. **3** *(difundirse)* to spread, extend; **el rumor se extendió rápidamente,** the rumour spread quickly. **4** *fig (hablar demasiado)* to enlarge upon, go on about; **siempre se extiende demasiado en sus clases,** she always goes on too much in her classes.

extendido,-a I *pp de* **extender. II** *adj* **1** *(gen)* extended; *(mapa, plano)* spread out, open; *(mano, brazo)* outstretched. **2** *(difundido)* widespread.

extensible *adj* extending.

extensión *nf* (*gen*) extension; (*dimensión*) extent, size; (*superficie*) area, expanse; *Mús* range; **de gran e.,** very extensive; **en toda la e. de la palabra,** in every sense of the word; **por e.,** by extension.

extensivo,-a *adj* extendable, extensive; **hacer extensiva una invitación a algn,** to extend an invitation to sb.

extenso,-a *adj* (*amplio*) extensive, long, vast; (*grande*) large; (*largo*) long. ◆ **extensamente** *adv* extensively, at length; (*ampliamente*) widely.

extensor,-a I *adj* extending; *Anat* **músculo e.,** extensor muscle. **II** *nm* (*aparato*) chest expander.

extenuación *nf* (*agotamiento*) exhaustion; (*debilidad*) weakening; (*enflaquecimiento*) emaciation.

extenuado,-a I *pp de* **extenuar. II** *adj* exhausted, worn-out.

extenuante *adj* exhausting.

extenuar I *vtr* (*agotar*) to exhaust; (*debilitar*) to weaken. **II extenuarse** *vr* to exhaust oneself.

exterior I *adj* **1** (*de fuera*) outer, exterior, external; (*puerta*) outside; (*pared*) outer; **aspecto e.,** outward appearance.. **2** (*política, deuda*) foreign. ■ *Pol* **Ministerio de Asuntos Exteriores,** Ministry of Foreign Affairs, *GB* Foreign Office, *US* State Department; **política e.,** foreign policy. **II** *nm* **1** (*parte de fuera*) exterior, outside. **2** (*extranjero*) abroad, overseas; **en el e.,** abroad, in foreign countries. **3** *Dep* (*jugador*) outside. **4 exteriores,** *Cin* location *sing*. ◆ **exteriormente** *adv* outwardly.

exterioridad *nf* outward *or* external appearance.

exteriorización *nf* manifestation, showing, externalization.

exteriorizar *vtr* to show, reveal, manifest.

exterminación *nf* extermination, wiping out, destruction.

exterminador,-a I *adj* exterminating. **II** *nm, f* exterminator.

exterminar *vtr* to exerminate, wipe out, destroy.

exterminio *nm* extermination, wiping out, destruction.

externo,-a I *adj* external, outward, exterior; **parte externa,** outside; *Farm* **de uso e.,** for external use only. **II** *nm, f Educ* day pupil. ◆ **externamente** *adv* externally, outwardly.

extinción *nf* (*gen*) extinction; **los bomberos lograron la e. del fuego,** the firemen managed to put out the fire.

extinguir I *vtr* (*fuego*) to exinguish, put out; (*deuda, raza*) to wipe out. **II extinguirse** *vr* (*fuego*) to go out; (*especie*) to become extinct, die out.

extinto,-a *adj* extinct.

extintor *nm* fire extinguisher.

extirpable *adj* **1** *Med* removable. **2** *fig* eradicable.

extirpación *nf* **1** *Med* removal, extraction. **2** *fig* eradication, stamping out, wiping out.

extirpar *vtr* **1** *Med* to remove, extract. **2** *fig* to eradicate, stamp out, wipe out.

extorsión *nf* **1** (*molestia*) inconvenience, trouble; **si no le causa e.,** if it won't put you out. **2** (*de dinero*) extortion, exaction.

extorsionar *vtr* **1** (*plan*) to mess up. **2** (*dinero*) to extort, exact.

extra¹ I *adj* **1** (*de más*) extra; **horas e.,** overtime; **paga e.,** bonus. **2** (*superior*) **e. especial,** top quality. **II** *nm* extra. **III** *nm, f Cin Teat* extra.

extra² *pref* extra.

extracción *nf* **1** (*gen*) extraction. **2** (*lotería*) draw.

extractar *vtr* to summarize.

extracto *nm* **1** (*trozo*) extract, excerpt; *Fin* **e. de cuenta,** ment of account. **2** (*resumen*) summary. **3** *Quím* extract.

extractor *nm* extractor.

extradición *nf* extradition; **otorgar la e. de algn,** to extadite sb.

extraer *vtr* to extract, take out.

extraescolar *adj* out of school; **actividad e.,** extracurricular activity.

extrafino,-a *adj* superfine, best quality; **azúcar e.,** castor sugar; **chocolate e.,** superfine chocolate.

extrajudicial *adj* extrajudicial.

extralimitación *nf* abuse.

extralimitarse *vr* to go too far, overstep the mark; **e. en sus funciones,** to exceed one's authority.

extramuros *adv* outside the city.

extranjería *nf* status of foreigners. ■ **ley de e.,** law on aliens.

extranjerismo *nm* foreign expression.

extranjero,-a I *adj* foreign, alien. **II** *nm, f* foreigner, alien. **III** *nm* foreign countries *pl*, abroad; **viajar al e.,** to travel *or* go abroad.

extranjis (de) *loc adv fam* secretly, in an underhand way, on the sly.

extrañamiento *nm* banishment, exile.

extrañar I *vtr* **1** (*desterrar*) to banish, exile. **2** (*sorprender*) to surprise; (*encontrar extraño*) to find strange; **no es de e.,** it's hardly surprising, it's no wonder. **3** *Am* (*echar de menos*) to miss; **extraño mi cama,** I miss my bed. **II extrañarse** *vr* (*sorprenderse*) **e. de,** to be surprised at, find surprising.

extrañeza *nf* wonder, surprise, astonishment, strangeness.

extraño,-a I *adj* strange, odd, queer, peculiar; *Med* **cuerpo e.,** foreign body. **II** *nm, f* stranger. ◆ **extrañamente** *adv* strangely, oddly.

extraoficial *adj* unofficial, informal; **declaraciones extraoficiales,** off-the-record statement.

extraordinario,-a I *adj* (*poco común*) extraordinary, unusual; (*raro*) queer; odd; (*sorprendente*) surprising; *Prensa* **edición extraordinaria,** special edition; **hizo un calor e.,** it was unusually hot; **no tiene nada de e.,** there's nothing special about it. **II** *nf Prensa* special issue. ◆ **extraordinariamente** *adv* extraordinarily, unusually.

extrarradio *nm* outskirts *pl*, suburbs *pl*.

extraterrestre I *adj* extraterrestrial. **II** *nmf* alien.

extraterritorial *adj* extraterritorial.

extrauterino,-a *adj Med* extrauterine; **embarazo e.,** ectopic pregnancy.

extravagancia *nf* extravagance, eccentricity.

extravagante *adj* odd, outlandish, strange.

extravertido,-a *adj véase* **extrovertido,-a.**

extraviado,-a I *pp de* **extraviar. II** *adj* (*perdido*) lost, missing; **perro e.,** stray dog.

extraviar I *vtr* **1** (*objeto*) to mislay, lose. **2** (*persona*) to mislead, lead astray. **II extraviarse** *vr* **1** (*objeto*) to be missing, get mislaid. **2** (*persona*) to get lost, lose one's way.

extravío *nm* (*pérdida*) loss, mislaying; *fig* deviation, leading astray.

extremado,-a I *pp de* **extremar. II** *adj* extreme. ◆ **extremadamente** *adv* extremely.

extremar I *vtr* to carry to extremes *or* to the limit, overdo; **e. la prudencia,** to be extremely careful. **II extremarse** *vr* to take great pains, do one's utmost.

extremaunción *nf Rel* extreme unction.

extremeño,-a I *adj of or* from Extremadura. **II** *nm, f* native *or* inhabitant of Extremadura.

extremidad *nf* **1** (*extremo*) end, tip. **2** *Anat* (*miembro*) limb, extremity.

extremis (in) *loc adv* as a last resort.

extremismo *nm* extremism.

extremista *adj & nmf* extremist.

extremo,-a I *adj* extreme, utmost. **II** *nm, f* **1** *(límite)* end, extreme, furthest point; **en e.,** very much; **en último e.,** as a last resort; **pasar de un e. a otro,** to go from one extreme to another. **2** *Dep (jugador)* wing; *Ftb* **e. derecha/izquierda,** outside-right/-left.

extremoso,-a *adj (persona)* effusive, demonstrative; *(vehemente)* extreme in one's attitudes.

extrínseco,-a *adj* extrinsic.

extroversión *nf* extroversion.

extrovertido,-a *adj & nm, f* extrovert.

exuberante *adj (gen)* exuberant; *(vegetación)* lush, abundant.

exudar *vtr & vi* to exude, ooze (out).

exultación *nf* exultation.

exultar *vi* to exult, rejoice; **e. de alegría,** to jump for joy.

eyaculación *nf* ejaculation; **e. precoz,** premature ejaculation.

eyacular *vi* to ejaculate.

eyección *nf* ejection.

eyectable *adj* **asiento e.,** ejector seat.

eyectar *vtr* to eject.

eyector *nm* ejector.

F

F, f [efe] *nf (la letra)* F, f.

F *abr de* **Fahrenheit,** Fahrenheit, F.

fa *nm Mús* F.

fa., fª *abr de* **franco a bordo,** free on board, F.O.B.

fabada *nf Culin* stew of beans, pork sausage and bacon.

fábrica *nf* **1** *(industria)* factory, plant. ■ **f. de cerveza,** brewery; **f. de conservas,** canning plant; **f. de gas,** gasworks *sing*; **f. de harina,** flour mill; **f. de montaje,** assembly plant; **f. de pap/el,** paper mill; **marca de f.,** trademark; **precio de f.,** factory *or* ex-works price. **2** *(fabricación)* manufacture. **3** *Arquit* masonry; **una pared de f.,** a stonework wall.

fabricación *nf* manufacture, production, making; **de f. casera,** home-made; **de f. propia,** our own make. ■ **defecto de f.,** manufacturing fault; **f. en cadena,** mass production; **productos de f. defectuosa,** seconds.

fabricante *nmf* manufacturer, maker.

fabricar *vtr* **1** *Ind* to manufacture, produce, make; **fabricado en España,** made in Spain; **f. algo en serie,** to mass-produce sth. **2** *fig (inventar)* **f. cuentos/mentiras,** to fabricate stories/lies.

febril *adj* manufacturing; **la industria f.,** manufacturing industry.

fábula *nf* **1** *Lit* fable; *fam* **de f.,** smashing, fabulous. **2** *(mito)* myth, legend. **3** *fig (mentira)* invention.

fabulismo *nm SAm* story telling.

fabulista *nmf Lit* writer of fables.

fabuloso,-a *adj* **1** *(extraordinario)* fabulous, fantastic. **2** *Lit* fabulous, mythical.

faca *nf* large curved knife.

facción *nf* **1** *Pol* faction. **2** **facciones,** *(rasgos)* (facial) features.

faccioso,-a I *adj* factious, seditious. **II** *nm, f* rebel.

facete *nf* facet; *fig* **este problema presenta muchas facetas,** this problem has many sides to it.

faceto,-a *adj Méx* finicky, fussy.

facha[1] *nf fam* **1** *(aspecto)* appearance, look; **no puedes ir con esa f.,** you can't go (looking) like that. **2** *(mamarracho)* mess, sight; **estar hecho una f.,** to look a mess *or* a sight.

facha[2] **I** *adj pey fam* fascist, extreme right-wing. **II** *nmf pey* fascist, extreme right-winger.

fachada *nf* **1** *Arquit* façade, front; **con f. a,** facing, overlooking. **2** *fam (apariencia)* outward show, façade, window dressing.

fachado,-a *adj fam* **bien f.,** good-looking; **mal f.,** ugly.

fachenda *fam* **I** *nf (condición)* swankiness, conceit. **II** *nmf (persona)* swank, show-off.

fachendear *vi fam* to swank, show off.

fachendoso,-a *adj fam* swanky.

fachoso,-a *adj fam* odd-looking.

facial *adj* facial.

fácil *adj* **1** easy; **es muy f. de decir, pero ...,** it's easily said, but ...; **f. de comprender/de leer,** easy to understand/to read. **2** *(probable)* likely, probable; **a estas horas no es f. que venga,** it's unlikely that he will come at this late hour; **es f. que ...,** it's (quite) likely that ... . **3** *(acomodaticio)* compliant, easy-going. **4** *pey (mujer)* easy, loose. ◆ **fácilmente** *adv* easily.

facilidad *nf* **1** *(simplicidad)* easiness, facility; **ahoratiene mayor f. para viajar,** it is easier for him to travel now; **con gran f.,** easily; **dar facilidades,** to give every facility, make things easy. ■ *Com* **facilidades de pago,** easy terms. **2** *(talento)* talent, gift; **tiene f. para los idiomas,** she has a gift for languages.

facilitación *nf* **1** *(simplificación)* facilitation. **2** *(abastecimiento)* provision, furnishing.

facilitar *vtr* **1** *(simplificar)* to make easy *or* easier, facilitate. **2** *(proporcionar)* to provide, supply; **nos facilitarán todo el equipo,** they'll provide us with all the equipment. **3** *(entrevista etc)* to arrange.

facilón,-ona *adj fam* **1** *(muy fácil)* dead easy. **2** *(trivial)* hackneyed, lacking originality; **una canción facilona,** a catchy tune.

facineroso,-a *nm, f* criminal.

facistol I *nm (atril)* lectern. **II** *adj Antill Ven (petulante)* vain, boastful.

facón *nm Arg Urug* gaucho knife.

facsímil *nm,* **facsímile** *nm* fecsimile.

factible *adj* feasible, practicable, workable.

facticio,-a *adj & nm, f* factitious, artificial.

fáctico,-a *adj* **poderes fácticos,** extraparliamentary political powers.

factor *nm* **1** *(condicionante)* factor. **2** *Mat* factor. **3** *Ferroc* luggage clerk.

factoría *nf* **1** *Com* trading post. **2** *(fábrica)* factory, mill.

factótum *nm* **1** *(empleado)* factotum. **2** *(persona entrometida)* busybody.

factura *nf* **1** *Com* bill, invoice; **pasar** *or* **presentar f. a,** to invoice, send a bill to; *fig* **to make (sb) pay; según f.,** as per invoice. ■ **f. pro forma,** pro forma invoice. **2** *Arg Uru Culin* bread and cakes *pl*.

facturación *nf* **1** *Com* invoicing. **2** *(de equipajes)* registration.

facturar *vtr* **1** *Com* to invoice, charge for. **2** *(equipaje)* to register, check in.

facultad *nf* **1** *(capacidad)* faculty, ability. ■ **facultades mentales,** mental powers. **2** *fml (poder)* faculty, power; **tener f. para hacer algo,** to be authorized to do sth. **3** *Univ* faculty, school; **f. de Derecho,** faculty of Law; **f. de Letras,** Arts faculty.

facultar *vtr* to authorize, empower.

facultativo,-a I *adj* **1** *(no obligatorio)* optional. **2** *(profesional)* professional; *Med* medical. **II** *nm,f* doctor, physician.

facundia *nf* verbosity, wordiness, long-windedness.

facundo,-a *adj (locuaz)* verbose, wordy, long-winded; *(parlanchín)* talkative.

faena *nf* **1** *(terea)* task, job; *fam* **estar metido en f.,** to be hard at work; **faenas de la casa,** housework *sing*, household chores. **2** *fam (mala pasada)* dirty trick. **3** *Taur* series of passes. **4** *Cuba Guat Méx (horas extras)* overtime.

faenar *vi* **1** *(reses)* to slaughter. **2** *Pesca* to fish.

fagot *Mús* **I** *nm (instrumento)* bassoon. **II** *nmf (musico)* bassoonist.

faisán *nm Orn* pheasant.

faja *nf* **1** *(cinturón)* band, belt. **2** *(de mujer)* girdle, corset. **3** *(banda)* sash. **4** *(correo)* **f.** *(postal)*, wrapper. **5** *(franja)* strip; **una f. de terreno sin labrar,** a strip of unploughed land.

fajar *vtr* **1** *(ceñir)* to bind, wrap. **2** *Am (pegar)* to beat.

fajilia *nf Am (en cartas)* wrapper.

fajín *nm Mil* sash.

fajina *nf* **1** *(leña)* brushwood, kindling. **2** *Mil* mess call.

fajo *nm* **1** bundle, **un f. de billetes,** a wad of notes. **2** *Am (trago de licor)* swig. **3** *Méx (cinturón)* belt. **4** *Méx (golpe)* blow.

falacia *nf* **1** *(error)* fallacy. **2** *(engaño)* deceit, trick. **3** *(hábito de engañar)* deceitfulness.

falange *nf* **1** *Anat* phalange, phalanx. **2** *Mil* phalanx. **3** *Hist Pol* **la F. (Española),** the Spanish Falangist Movement.

falangista *adj & nmf Hist Pol* Falangist.

falaz *adj* **1** *(erróneo)* fallacious. **2** *(engañoso)* deceitful; *(falso)* false.

falca *nf* **1** *(defecto)* warp. **2** *(cuña)* wedge.

falda *nf* **1** *(prenda)* skirt; *fig* **está pegado** *or* **cosido a las faldas de su madre,** he is tied to his mother's apron strings; *fam* **anda siempre entre faldas,** he's always with the girls. ■ **f. escocesa,** kilt; **f. pantalón,** culottes *pl*. **2** *(regazo)* lap; **tener un niño en la f.,** to have a child on one's lap. **3** *Geog (ladera)* slope, hillside. **4** *Culin (corte de carne)* brisket. **5** *(de mesa camilla)* cover.

faldero,-a *adj* **1** *(mujeriego)* fond of the girls. **2** *(perro)* lapdog.

faldillas *nfpl (de traje)* coat-tails; *(de camisa)* shirt-tails.

faldón *nm* **1** *(de ropa)* skirt, tail. **2** *Arquit* gable.

falibilidad *nf* fallibility.

falible *adj* fallible.

falico,-a *adj* phallic.

falla¹ *nf* **1** *(defecto)* defect, fault. **2** *Am* fault. **3** *Am (faltar a la palabra)* failure to keep one's promises.

falla² *nf Geol* fault.

falla³ *nf Esp* **I** cardboard figure burnt on Saint Joseph's Day in Valencia. **2** **las Fallas,** firework celebrations held in Valencia on Saint Joseph's Day.

fallar¹ I *vtr* **1** *Jur (sentencia)* to pass, pronounce. **2** *(premio)* to award. **II** *vi* **1** *Jur* to pass sentence, pronounce judgement. **2** *(premio)* to award a prize.

fallar² *I* *vtr Naipes* to trump, ruff. **II** *vi* **1** *(fracasar)* to fail; **he fallado como padre,** I have failed as a father; **le falló la puntería,** he missed his aim; **me falló el plan,** my plan went wrong; **nos falló en el último momento,** he let us down at the last minute; **nuestros cálculos**

fallaron, we were wrong, we miscalculated. **2** *(no funcionar)* to fail; **le falló el corazón,** he had a heart attack; **le fallaron los frenos,** the brakes failed. **3** *(ceder)* to give way, collapse.

falleba *nf* espagnolette.

fallecer *vi fml* to pass away, die.

fallecido,-a I *pp de* **fallecer. II** *adj* deceased.

fallecimiento *nm* decease, demise.

fallero,-a *Esp* **I** *adj of or* relating to **las Fallas. II** *nm,f* **1** *(constructor)* maker of **fallas. 2** *(organizador)* organizer of **las Fallas.**

fallido,-a *adj* unsuccessful, vain; *Com* **deuda fallida,** bad debt.

fallo *nm* **1** *(error)* mistake, blunder; *(fracaso)* failure. **2** *(defecto)* fault, defect. **3** *Jur (sentencia)* judgement, sentence. **4** *(premio)* awarding. **5** *Med Téc* failure. **6** *Naipes* void; **f. en corazones,** void in hearts.

falo *nm* phallus.

falocracia *nf* male chauvinism.

falócrata *nm* male chauvinist (pig).

falsario,-a *nm,f* **1** *(mentiroso)* liar. **2** *(falsificador)* forger, counterfeiter.

falsemiento *nm* falsification.

falsear I *vtr* **1** *(informe etc)* to falsify; *(hechos, la verdad)* to distort. **2** *(falsificar)* to counterfeit, forge. **3** *Constr* to bevel. **II** *vi* **1** *(flaquear)* to give way. **2** *Mús* to be out of tune.

falsedad *nf* **1** *(hipocresía)* falseness, hypocrisy; *(doblez)* duplicity. **2** *(mentira)* falsehood, lie.

falsete *nm Mús* falsetto; **voz de f.,** falsetto voice.

falsía *nf* *(hipocresía)* falseness, hypocrisy; *(doublez)* duplicity.

falsificación *nf* **1** *(gen)* falsification; *(de cuadro, firma)* forging, forgery; *(de moneda)* counterfeiting, forgery. **2** *(objeto)* forgery.

falsificador,-a *adj (de cuadro, firma)* forgoing; *(de dinero)* counterfeiting, forging. **II** *nm,f (de cuadro, firma)* forger; *(de dinero)* counterfeiter, forger.

falsificar *vtr (gen)* to falsify; *(cuadro, firma)* to forge; *(dinero)* to counterfeit, forge.

falso,-a *adj* **1** false, untrue; **dar un paso en f.,** *(tropezar)* to trip, stumble; *(cometer un error)* to make a blunder, make a wrong move; **jurar en f.,** to commit perjury. **2** *(persona)* insincere, treacherous.

falta *nf* **1** *(carencia)* lack; **por f. de algo,** for want *or* lack of sth; **no fui por f. de ganas,** I didn't go because I didn't feel like it; **sin f.,** without fail. ■ **f. de educación,** bad manners; **f. de pago,** nonpayment. **2** *(escasez)* shortage; **f. de agua,** water shortage. **3** *(ausencia)* absence; **echar algo/a algn en f.,** to miss sth/sb; **poner f. a algn,** to mark sb absent. **4** *(error)* mistake; **tu redacción está llena de faltas,** you've made a lot of mistakes in your composition. ■ **f. de ortografía,** spelling mistake. **5** *(defecto)* fault, defect; **sacar faltas a algo/a algn,** to find fault with sth/sb. **6** *(mala acción)* misdeed; **coger** *or* **pillar a algn en f.,** to catch sb at fault. **7** *Med* missed period. **8** *Jur (infracción)* misdemeanour. **9** *Dep (fútbol)* foul; *(tenis)* fault; **sacar una f.,** to take a free kick. **10** **hacer f.,** to be necessary; **ahora sólo hace f. que llueva,** all we need now is for it to rain; **¡f. hacía!,** and about time too!; **hace f. una escalera,** we need a ladder; **harán f. dos personas para mover el piano,** it'll take two people to move the piano; **me hacen f. más libros,** I need more books; **no hace f. que ...,** there is no need for ... .

faltar *vi* **1** *(no estar) (cosa)* to be missing; *(persona)* to be absent; **me falta un bolígrafo,** one of my pens is missing; **¿quién falta?,** who is missing? **2** *(haber poco)* to be lacking *or* needed, not be enough; **falta (más) agua,** we need (more) water, there isn't enough water. **3** *(no tener)* to lack, not have (enough); **le falta confianza en sí mismo,** he lacks confidence in himself; **le falta una**

mano, he has got only one hand. **4** *(no acudir)* not to go, miss; **no faltaremos a la fiesta**, we won't miss the party; **no faltes**, be sure to come. **5** *(incumplir)* **f. a la verdad**, not to tell the truth, lie; **f. a so deber**, to fail in one's duty; **f. a su palabra/promesa**, to break one's word/promise; **f. en los pagos**, not to keep up with one's payments. **6** *(no respetar)* **faltó a mi dignidad**, she slighted me. **7** *(quedar)* **aún falta mucho por hacer**, there is still a lot to be done; **¿cuánto te falta?**, how long will you be?, how much more do you have to do?; **¿cuántos kilómetros faltan para Olite?**, how many kilometres is it to Olite?, how far is it to Olite?; **falta por ver si lo quiere**, whether she wants it or not remains to be seen; **faltó poco para que se liaran a bofetadas**, they very nearly came to blows; **ya falta poco par las vacaciones**, the holidays will soon be here. **8** *(locuciones)* **¡lo que me faltaba!**, that's all I needed!; **¡no faltaría o faltaba más!**, *(por supuesto)* (but) of course!; *(por supuesto que no)* think nothing of it!; **¡sólo me faltaba eso!**, that's all I needed!, that crowns it all!

falto,-a *adj* lacking, without; **f. de dinero**, short of money; **f. de recursos**, without resources.

faltón,-ona *adj fam* **1** *(informal)* unreliable. **2** *(grosero)* disrespectful. **3** *Arg (simple)* naïve, simple.

faltriquera *nf* fob (pocket); *fam* **rascarse la f.**, to dig into one's pocket.

falúa *nf Náut* launch.

fama I *nf* **1** *(renombre)* fame, renown; **de f. mundial**, world-famous. **2** *(reputación)* reputation; **tiene buena/ mala f.**, it has a good bad name.

famélico,-a *adj* starving, famished.

familia *nf* **1** family; **de buena f.**, from a good family; **de f. humilde**, of humble origin; **viene de la f.**, it runs in the family; *fig* **ser como de la f.**, to be like one of the family; *fam* **estar en f.**, to be among friends; *ofens* **acordarse de la f. de algn**, to insult sb. ■ **f. numerosa**, large family; **f. política**, in-laws *pl*; *Rel* **la Sagrada F.**, the Holy Family. **2** *(prole)* children *pl*, offspring *pl*.

familiar I *adj* **1** *(de la familia)* family, of the family; **fiesta f.**, a family party *or* get-together. **2** *(conocido)* familiar, well-known; **estos problemas me son familiares**, I'm familiar with these problems. **3** *Ling (informal)* colloquial. II *nmf* relation, relative.

familiaridad *nf* familiarity.

familiarizar I *vtr* to familiarize (**con**, with). II **familiarizarse** *vr* to familiarize oneself (**con**, with).

famoso,-a I *adj* famous, well-known; **sus famosas ocurrencias**, her well-known witticisms. II **los famosos** *nmpl* the famous.

fan *nmf* fan, admirer; **soy un f. de las motos**, I'm mad on motorbikes.

fanal *nm* **1** *Náut* beacon. **2** *(campana)* bell glass.

fanático,-a I *adj* fanatic, fanatical. II *nm,f* fanatic.

fanatismo *nm* fanaticism.

fanatizar *vtr* to make a fanatic.

fandango *nm* **1** *Mús* fandango. **2** *fam (jaleo)* row, rumpus.

fandanguero,-a *nm,f fam* reveller, *US* reveler.

fanega *nf (medida)* **1** *(de capacidad)* = 55.5 litres in Castile, 22.4 litres in Aragon. **2** *(de superficie)* = 64 square metres in Castile.

fanfarria *nf* **1** *Mús* fanfare. **2** *fam (fanfarronería)* showing off, swanking.

fanfarrón,-ona *fam* I *adj* swanky, boastful. II *nm,f* show-off, swank, braggart.

fanfarronada *nf fam (chulería)* showing off, swanking; *(bravata)* brag, boast.

fanfarronear *vi fam (chulear)* to show off, swank; *(bravear)* to brag, boast.

fanfarronería *nf véase* **fanfarronada.**

fangal *nm* mire, quagmire, bog.

fango *nm* **1** *(barro)* mud, mire. **2** *fig* degradation.

fangoso,-a *adj* muddy, miry.

fantasear *vi* to daydream, dream.

fantasía *nf (imaginación)* fantasy; *(irrealidad)* fancy; **una joya de f.**, a piece of imitation jewellery; *irón* **tienes mucha f. tú**, you're too full of imagination.

fantasioso,-a *adj* **1** imaginative. **2** *Am (jactancioso)* boastful.

fantasma *nm* **1** *(espectro)* ghost, phantom. **2** *fam (fanfarrón)* braggart, show-off.

fantasmagoría *nf* phantasmagoria.

fantasmal *adj* ghostly.

fantástico,-a *adj* fantastic.

fantochada *nf fam* foolish act; *(tontería)* silly thing.

fantoche *nm* **1** *(títere)* puppet, marionette. **2** *pey (fanfarrón)* braggart, show-off. **3** *pey (mamarracho)* nincompoop, ninny.

fantochería *nf Am* foolish act; *(tontería)* silly thing.

faquir *nm* fakir.

faralá *nm (pl faralaes) Cost* flounce, frill.

farallón *nm Geog* crag, rock.

faramalla *nf* **1** *(charla)* blarney, patter. **2** *(farfolla)* bauble.

farándula *nf* **1** *Teat (compañía)* group of strolling players; *(profesión)* acting, the theatre. **2** *fam fig (faramalla)* blarney.

farandulero,-a *nm,f* **1** *Teat (comediante)* strolling player. **2** *fam (trapacero)* bamboozler, trickster.

faraón *nm* Pharaoh.

faraónico,-a *adj* Pharaonic.

fardada *nf arg* show, display; **¡vaya f. de coche!**, what a flash car!

fardar *vi arg* **1** *(presumir)* to show off, swank; **siempre está fardando de novia guapa**, he's always boasting about having a beautiful girlfriend. **2** *(lucir)* to be classy *or* flash.

fardo *nm* **1** *(paquete)* bundle, pack. **2** *fam (gordo)* **está hecho un f.**, he looks like a barrel.

fardón,-ona *adj arg* classy, flash.

farfolla *nf* **1** *Bot* husk. **2** *fig* worthless thing.

farfolla *nf Am* **1** *véase* **farfolla. 2** *(fanfarronería)* showing off, swanking.

farfullador,-a *nm,f* gabbler, jabberer.

farfullar *vtr* to gabble, jabber.

farfullero,-a *adj* **1** *(tartamudo)* gabbling, jabbering. **2** *(chapucero)* slapdash, shoddy.

farináceo,-a *adj* farinaceous.

faringe *nf Anat* pharynx.

faríngeo,-a *adj* pharyngeal.

faringitis *nf Med* pharyngitis.

farisaico,-a *adj* **1** *Hist* Pharisaic, Pharisaical. **2** *(falso)* hypocritical. ·

fariseísmo *nm* **1** *Hist* Phariseeism. **2** *(falsedad)* hypocrisy.

fariseo,-a *nm,f* **1** *Hist* Pharisee. **2** *(falso)* hypocrite.

farmaceuta *nmf Am véase* **farmacéutico,-a.**

farmacéutico,-a I *adj* pharmaceutical. II *nm, f* **1** *(licenciado)* pharmacist. **2** *(en una farmacia)* chemist, *US* pharmacist, druggist.

farmacia *nf* **1** *Univ* pharmacology. **2** *(tienda)* chemist's (shop), *US* pharmacy, drugstore.

fármaco *nm* medicine, medication.

farmacología *nf* pharmacology.

farmacológico,-a *adj* pharmacological.

farmacólogo,-a *nm,f* pharmacologist, pharmacist.

faro *nm* **1** *(torre)* lighthouse; *(señal)* beacon. **2** *Aut* headlight, headlamp. **3** *fig (guía)* guiding light, guide.

farol *nm* **1** *(luz)* lantern; *(farola)* streetlight, streetlamp. **2** *arg (fardada)* bragging, swank; *(engaño)* bluff; **¡adelante con los faroles!,** come on then!, keep it up!; **marcarse** *or* **tirarse un f.,** to brag, boast, swank.

farola *nf* streetlight, streetlamp; *(de gas)* gas lamp.

farolear *vi arg (presumir)* to brag, boast, swank.

farolero,-a I *adj arg* boastful. **II** *nm,f* show-off.

farolillo *nm* **1** *(de papel)* Chinese lantern. ■ *fig* **el f. rojo,** the last to finish. **2** *Bot* Canterbury bell.

farra *nf fam* binge, spree; **ir de f.,** to go on a spree.

fárrago *nm* hotch-potch, jumble.

farragoso,-a *adj* confused, rambling.

farrear *vi* **1** *Am (ir de juerga)* to go out on the town, go on a binge *or* a spree. **2** *Arg (malbaratar)* to spend money like water. **3** *Arg Urug (burlarse)* to gibe, jeer, scoff.

farruco,-a *adj fam* conceited, cocky.

farruto,-a *adj Chi* weak, sickly.

farsa *nf* **1** *Teat* farce. **2** *fig* sham, farce; **el referéndum no fue más que una f.,** the referendum was nothing but a farce.

farsante I *adj* lying, deceitful. **II** *nmf* fake, impostor.

fas (por f. o por nefas) *loc adv* by hook or by crook, by any means.

fascículo *nm Impr* fascicle, instalment, *US* installment; **en treinta fascículos semanales,** in thirty weekly parts.

fascinación *nf* fascination.

fascinador,-a *adj*, **fascinante** *adj* fascinating.

fascinar *vtr* to fascinate, captivate.

fascismo *nm Pol* fascism.

fascista *adj & nmf Pol* fascist.

fase *nf* **1** *(etapa)* phase, stage. **2** *Elec Fís* phase.

fastidiado,-a I *pp de* **fastidiar. II** *adj* **1** *(hastiado)* sickened, disgusted. **2** *(molestado)* annoyed; *(dañado)* damaged, in bad condition; *fam* **su padre está f.,** her father's in a bad way; *fam* **tiene el estómago f.,** he's got a bad stomach.

fastidiar I *vtr* **1** *(hastiar)* to sicken, disgust. **2** *(molestar)* to annoy, bother; *(partes del cuerpo)* to hurt; **me fastidia tener que irme ahora,** it's a nuisance to have to leave now; **últimamente me está fastidiando la espalda,** my back's been bad lately. **3** *fam (estropear)* to damage, ruin; *(planes)* to spoil, upset, mess up; *fam* **¡no fastidies!,** you're kidding! **II fastidiarse** *vr* **1** *(aguantarse)* to put up with it, resign oneself; **¡a f. tocan!,** we'll have to grin and bear it!; **y si no te gusta, te fastidias** and if you don't like it you can lump it!; *fam* **¡que se fastidie!,** that's his tough luck! **2** *fam (estropearse)* to get damaged, break down; **se ha fastidiado el tocadiscos,** the record player is bust. **3** *(lastimarse)* to hurt *or* injure oneself; **me he fastidiado la mano,** I've hurt my hand.

fastidio *nm* **1** *(molestia)* bother, nuisance; **¡qué f.!,** what a nuisance! **2** *(aburrimiento)* boredom. **3** *(asco)* repugnance, revulsion.

fastidioso,-a *adj* **1** *(molesto)* annoying, irksome. **2** *(aburrido)* boring, tedious.

fasto *nm* pomp, display.

fastos *nmpl arc* annals, archives.

fastuosidad *nf* pomp, lavishness.

fastuoso,-a *adj* **1** *(cosa)* splendid, lavish. **2** *(persona)* lavish, ostentatious.

fatal I *adj* **1** *(inexorable)* fateful, inevitable; **ha llegado la hora** *or* **el momento f.,** the time has come. **2** *(mortal)* deadly, fatal; **dosis f.,** lethal dose. **3** *fam (muy malo)* awful, horrible, terrible; **tengo una suerte f.,** I'm having rotten luck. **II** *adv fam* very badly, awfully, terribly; **comimos f.,** the meal was awful; **lo pasó f.,** he had a rotten time; **veo f.,** I can't see a thing. ◆ **fatalmente** *adv* **1** *(inevitablemente)* inevitably. **2** *(muy mal)* very badly awfully, terribly.

fatalidad *nf* **1** *(destino)* fate. **2** *(desgracia)* misfortune.

fatalismo *nm* fatalism.

fatalista I *adj* fatalistic. **II** *nmf* fatalist.

fatídico,-a *adj* **1** *(desastroso)* disastrous, calmitous. **2** *fml (profético)* fateful, ominous.

fatigo *nf* **1** *(cansancio)* fatigue. **2 fatigas,** *(esfuerzos)* troubles, difficulties.

fatigar I *vtr* **1** to tire, weary. **2** *fig (molestar)* to annoy. **II fatigarse** *vr* to tire, become tired.

fatigoso,-a *adj* **1** tiring, exhausting. **2** *(en respiración)* laboured, *US* labored. ◆ **fatigosamente** *adv* with (great) difficulty, painfully.

fatuidad *nf* fatuity, fatuousness.

fatuo,-a *adj* **1** *(necio)* fatuous, foolish. **2** *(envanecido)* vain, conceited.

fauces *nfpl* **1** *Anat Zool* fauces, gullet *sing*. **2** *fig* jaws.

fauna *nf* fauna.

fauno *nm Mit* faun.

fausto,-a *fml* **1** *adj Lit* fortunate, auspicious. **II** *nm* pomp, splendour, *US* splendor.

fauvismo *nm Art* fauvism.

fauvista *nmf Art* fauvist.

favela *nf Am* shanty.

favor *nm* **1** favour, *US* favor, good turn; **a f. de,** in favour of; **a mi/su f.,** in my/his favour; **estamos seis juegos a uno a f. mío,** I'm winning six games to one; **¿puedes hacerme un f.?,** can you do me a favour?; **tener algo a su f.,** to have sth in one's favour; *fam* **tiene al presidente a su favor,** he has the president on his side. **2** **por f.,** please; **haga el f. de sentarse,** please sit down; **¿me da fuego, por f.?,** can you give me a light, please?; **¿me harías el f. de correrte un poco?,** could you move over a little please?

favorable *adj* favourable, *US* favorable; *(condiciones)* suitable; **se mostró f. al proyecto,** he was in favour of the project.

favorecedor,-a *adj* favouring, *US* favoring, favourable, *US* favorable; *(retrato)* flattering; *(vestido)* becoming.

favorecer *vtr* **1** to favour, *US* favor, work in sb's favour; **la oscuridad les favorecía,** the darkness was in their favour; **para f. a los más débiles,** to help the weakest; **su altura le ha favorecido,** being tall has been to her advantage. **2** *(agraciar)* to flatter, suit; **el bigote le favorece mucho,** his moustache really suits him.

favorecido,-a I *pp de* **favorecer. II** *adj* favoured, *US* favored; **está muy f. con ese peinado,** that hair style really suits him.

favoritismo *nm* favouritism, *US* favoritism.

favorito,-a *adj & nm,f* favourite, *US* favorite.

faz *nf (pl faces)* **1** *lit (cara)* face; **desaparecer de la f. de la tierra,** to disappear off the face of the earth. **2** *(de moneda)* obverse, head. **3** ■ *Rel* **la Santa** *or* **Sacra F.,** the Holy Face.

fdo *abr de* **firmado,** signed.

fe *nf* **1** faith; **de buena/mala fe,** with good/dishonest intentions; **lo hizo de buena fe,** he did it in good faith; *Rel* **la fe cristiana,** the Christian faith; **tener una fe ciega en algo/algn,** to have blind faith in sth/sb. **2** *Jur (certificado)* certificate. ■ **fe de bautismo/matrimonio,** baptism/ marriage certificate; **fe de vida,** document proving that sb is still alive. **3** *Impr* **fe de erratas,** list of errata.

fealdad *nf* ugliness.

febrero *nm* February; *véase tamb* **noviembre.**

febrífugo,-a *adj & nm Farm* febrifuge.

febril *adj* **1** *Med* feverish. **2** *fig* hectic; **una mente f.,** a restless mind.

febrilidad *nf* feverishness.

fecal *adj Med* faecal.

fecha *nf* **1** date; *Com* **a tres días f.,** three days after sight; **con** *or* **de f. 2 de mayo,** dated May 2nd; **en f. próxima,** at an early date; **fijar la f.,** to fix a date; **hasta la f.,** so far; **poner la f. a una carta,** to date a letter; **sin f.,** undated. ■ **f. límite** *or* **tope,** deadline. **2** *(día)* day; **diez fechas después de su publicación,** ten days after its publication. **3 fechas,** *(época)* time *sing*; **en estas f.,** in those days; **nos vimos hace un año por estas f.,** we met this time last year.

fechador *nm* date stamp.

fechar *vtr* to date, put the date on.

fechoría *nf* misdeed, misdemeanour, *US* misdemeanor; *(de niños)* mischief; *fam* **le han hecho una f. en el pelo,** they've ruined her hair.

fécula *nf* starch.

feculento,-a *adj* starchy.

fecundable *adj* fertilizable.

fecundación *nf* fertilization. ■ **f. in vitro,** in vitro fertilization.

fecundar *vtr* to fertilize, make fertile.

fecundidad *nf* **1** *(fertilidad)* fertility. **2** *fig (productividad)* productivity, fruitfulness.

fecundizar *vtr* **1** to make fertile. **2** *fig* to make fruitful.

fecundo,-a *adj* fertile, fecund.

federación *nf* federation.

federado,-a I *pp de* **federar. II** *adj* federated.

federal *adj & nmf* federal.

federalismo *nm* federalism.

federalista *adj & nmf* federalist.

federar *vtr* to federate.

féferes *nmpl Am* junk *sing*.

fehaciente *adj* **1** *fml* authentic, reliable. **2** *Jur* irrefutable; **documento** *or* **prueba f.,** irrefutable proof.

feldespato *nm Min* feldspar, felspar.

felicidad *nf* happiness; **(muchas) felicidades,** *(éxitos)* congratulations; *(navidad)* Merry Christmas; *(cumpleaños)* happy birthday.

felicitación *nf* **1** *(tarjeta)* greetings card. **2 felicitaciones,** congratulations.

felicitar I *vtr* to congratulate **(por,** on); **f. a algn por su santo,** to wish sb a happy Saint's Day; **¡te felicito!,** congratulations! **II felicitarse** *vr* to congratulate oneself.

félido,-a *nm Zool* felid, cat.

feligrés,-a *nm,f* parishioner.

feligresía *nf* parish, parishioners *pl*.

felino,-a *adj & nm Zool* feline.

feliz *adj* **1** *(contento)* happy; **¡felices Navidades** *or* **Pascuas!,** Happy *or* Merry Christmas!; **final f.,** happy ending **2** *(acertado)* fortunate. ◆ **felizmente** *adv* fortunately, happily; **f. no hubo víctimas,** fortunately, there were no casualties.

felonía *nf* treachery, villainy.

felón,-ona I *adj* treacherous, villainous, wicked. **II** *nm,f* traitor, villain.

felpa *nf Tex* plush; **oso** *or* **osito de f.,** teddy bear.

felpudo,-a I *adj Tex* plushy, velvety. **II** *nm* mat, doormat.

femenino,-a *adj* feminine; **equipo f.,** women's team; **sexo f.,** female sex.

femineidad *nf* **feminidad** *nf* femininity.

feminismo *nm* feminism.

feminista *adj & nmf* feminist.

femoral *adj Anat* femoral.

fémur *nm Anat* femur.

fenecer *vi arc* **1** *(acabarse)* to come to an end. **2** *euf (morir)* to pass away, die.

fenecimiento *nm arc* **1** *(fin)* close, end. **2** *euf (muerte)* decease, death.

fenicio,-a *adj & nm,f* Phoenician.

fénix *nm inv* **1** *Mit* phoenix. **2** *fig (genio)* genius, prodigy.

fenol *nm Quím* phenol.

fenomenal I *adj* **1** phenomenal. **2** *fam (fantástico)* great, terrific; **es un tipo f.,** he's a fantastic guy. **3** *fam (enorme)* colossal, huge. **II** *adv fam* wonderfully, marvellously; **lo pasamos f.,** we had a fantastic time.

fenómeno I *nm* **1** phenomenon. ■ **fenómenos atmosféricos,** atmospheric phenomena. **2** *(prodigio)* genius. **3** *(monstruo)* freak. **II** *adj fam* fantastic, terrific, smashing. **III** *interj* fantastic!, terrific!

feo,-a I *adj* **1** *(malo)* ugly; **tuvimos un tiempo muy f.,** we had horrible weather. **2** *fig (alarmante)* nasty; **se está poniendo f.,** I don't like the look of this, I don't like the way this is going; **un asunto f.,** a nasty affair. **3** *(indigno)* improper, rude, not nice; **es f. decir palabrotas,** it's rude to swear. **II** *nm,f* ugly person. **III** *nm fam* slight, insult; **hacerle un f. a algn,** to offend sb. ◆ **feamente** *adv* in an ugly manner.

feracidad *nf (tierra)* fertility.

feraz *adj* fertile.

féretro *nm* coffin.

feria *nf* **1** *Com* fair. ■ **f. de muestras/del libro,** trade/book fair. **2** *(fiesta)* fair, festival; **la F. de Sevilla,** the Seville Festival.

feriado,-a *adj* **día f.,** holiday.

ferial *adj & nm* fair; **recinto f.,** fairground.

feriante *nmf (vendedor)* stallholder, trader; *(comprador)* fair-goer.

feriar *vtr Col Guat PR* to sell off cheap.

ferina *adj Med* **tos f.,** whooping cough.

fermentación *nf* fermentation.

fermentar *vi* to ferment.

fermento *nm* ferment.

ferocidad *nf* ferocity, fierceness.

ferodo® *nm* brake lining.

feroz *adj* fierce, ferocious; **el lobo f.,** the big bad wolf. ◆ **ferozmente** *adv* fiercely, ferociously.

férreo,-a *adj* **1** ferreous. **2** *fig* iron; **voluntad férrea,** iron will.

ferrería *nf* ironworks *sing*, foundry.

ferretería *nf* **1** *(tienda)* ironmonger's (shop), hardware store. **2** *(género)* ironmongery, hardware. **3** *(ferrería)* forge. **4** *Am (quincallería)* scrap metal dealer's.

ferretero,-a *nm,f* ironmonger, hardware dealer.

férrico,-a *adj* ferric.

ferrita *nf* ferrite.

ferrocarril *nm* railway, *US* railroad.

ferrohormigón *nm Arquit* ferroconcrete.

ferroso,-a *adj Quím* ferrous.

ferroviario,-a I *adj* railway, rail. **II** *nm,f* railway employee *or* worker.

ferruginoso,-a *adj Min* ferruginous.

ferry *nm* ferry.

fértil *adj* **1** fertile. **2** *fig* rich, fertile; **imaginación f.,** fertile imagination.

fertilidad *nf* fertility, fecundity.

fertilización *nf* fertilization.

fertilizante I *adj* fertilizing. **II** *nm* fertilizer.

fertilizar *vtr* to fertilize.

férula *nf* ferule, rod; *fig* **bajo la f. de,** under the rule of.

férvido,-a *adj* fervid, ardent.

ferviente *adj* fervent, passionate.

fervor *nm* fervour, *US* fervor.

fervoroso,-a *adj* fervent, passionate.

festejar vtr **1** (celebrar) to celebrate. **2** (agasajar) to wine and dine, entertain. **3** (cortejar) to court, woo.

festejo nm **1** entertainment, feast. **2 festejos,** festivities.

festín nm feast, banquet.

festinar[1] vtr (apresurar) to speed up.

festinar[2] vtr (agasajar) to wine and dine, entertain.

festival nm festival; **f. de cine,** film festival.

festividad nf festivity, celebration.

festivo,-a I adj **1** (alegre) festive, merry. **2** (de fiesta) **día f.,** holiday. II nm holiday.

festón nm Cost festoon; (de flores) garland.

festonear vtr to festoon.

fetal adj foetal, US fetal; **posición f.,** foetal position.

fetén fam I adj **1** (formidable) terrific, smashing, great. **2** (auténtico) hundred per cent, genuine. II **la f.** nf the truth.

fetiche nm fetish.

fetichismo nm fetishism.

fetichista adj & nmf fetishist.

fetidez nf stink, stench, fetidness.

fétido,-a adj stinking, fetid.

feto nm **1** foetus, US fetus. **2** fam (persona muy fea) monster, ugly sod.

feucho,-a adj fam plain, unattractive.

feudal adj Hist feudal; **señor f.,** feudal lord.

feudalismo nm Hist feudalism.

feudo nm fief, feud.

FEVE nmpl abr de **Ferrocarriles Españoles de Vía Estrecha**

FF.AA. nfpl abr de **Fuerzas Armadas,** Armed Forces.

FF.CC. nmpl abr de **ferrocarriles,** railways, rly.

fiabilidad nf reliability, trustworthiness.

fiable adj reliable, trustworthy.

fiado,-a I pp de **fiar.** II adj **1** Com on credit; **comprar al f.,** to buy on credit. **2** (confiado) trusting.

fiador,-a I nm,f guarantor; **salir** or **ser f. de algn,** (pagar fianza) to stand bail for sb; (avalar) to vouch for sb. II nm **1** (de escopeta) safety catch. **2** (cerrojo) bolt.

fiambre I adj **1** Culin (served) cold. **2** irón stale, old. II nm **1** Culin cold meat; **plato de fiambres,** dish of cold meats. **2** fam (cadáver) stiff, corpse; **dejar f. a algn,** to do sb in.

fiambrera nf lunch box.

fianza nf (depósito) deposit, security; Jur bail; **dejar en libertad bajo f.,** to release on bail.

fiar I vtr **1** to guarantee. **2** (vender) to sell on credit. **3** (confiar) to confide, entrust. II vi to trust; **de f.,** trustworthy. III **fiarse** vr to trust (de, -); (en letrero) **no se fía,** no credit given.

fiasco nm fiasco, failure.

fibra nf **1** (filamento) fibre, US fiber; (de madera) grain. ■ **f. de vidrio,** fibreglass. **2** fig (carácter) push, go; **es una chica con f.,** she's full of go.

fibroso,-a adj fibrous.

ficción nf fiction.

ficha nf **1** (tarjeta) index card, file card. ■ **f. policíaca,** police record; **f. técnica,** specifications pl, technical data; Cin credits pl. **2** Tel token. **3** (en juegos) counter; Naipes chip; Ajedrez piece, man; (de dominó) domino. **4** Am (bribón) vagrant.

fichaje nm Dep signing (up).

fichar I vtr **1** to put on an index card; to file; **está fichado por la policía,** his name is on police files, he has a police record; fam **lo tengo bien fichado,** I've got him sized up. **2** Dep to sign up. II vi (al entrar) to clock in; (al salir) to clock out.

fichero nm **1** (archivo) card index. **2** Mueb filing cabinet, file.

ficticio,-a adj fictitious.

fidedigno,-a adj reliable, trustworthy; **fuentes fidedignas,** reliable sources.

fideicomisario,-a nm,f Jur trustee.

fideicomiso nm Jur trusteeship; **bajo** or **en f.,** in trusteeship.

fidelidad nf **1** (lealtad) faithfulness, fidelity. **2** (exactitud) accuracy. ■ **Mús alta f.,** high fidelity, hi-fi.

fideo nm Culin noodle; fam fig **estar como un f.,** to be as thin as a rake.

Fidji n Fiji.

fiduciario,-a adj & nm,f Jur fiduciary.

fiebre nf **1** Med fever; **tener f.,** to have a temperature. **2** fig fever, excitement.

fiel I adj **1** (leal) faithful, loyal; **es f. a su mujer,** he is faithful to his wife. **2** (exacto) accurate, exact; **memoria f.,** reliable memory. II nm **1** (de balanza) needle, pointer. **2 los fieles,** Rel the faithful.

fieltro nm Tex felt.

fiera nf **1** wild animal or beast; **luchó como una f.,** she fought like a tiger; fam **estar hecho una f.,** to be in a rage. ■ **casa de fieras,** menagerie. **2** fig (persona de mal carácter) beast, brute. **3** fig (genio) wizard; **es una f. para los idiomas,** she's brilliant at languages. **4** Taur bull.

fiereza nf (ferocidad) ferocity, ferociousness; (crueldad) cruelty.

fiero,-a adj (salvaje) wild; (feroz) fierce, ferocious; fig (persona) cruel.

fierro nm Am iron.

fiesta nf **1** (vacaciones) holiday; **ayer fue f.,** yesterday was a holiday; **el viernes haré f.,** I'll take Friday off. ■ **f. nacional,** bullfighting; **F. de la Hispanidad,** Columbus Day; **F. del Trabajo,** Labour or US Labor Day. **2** Rel feast. ■ **f. fija/móvil,** immovable/movable feast; **f. de guardar** or **precepto,** day of obligation. **3** (reunión) party; **estar de f.,** to be in a festive mood; **no estar para fiestas,** to be in no mood for jokes; **¡tengamos la f. en paz!,** cut it out! ■ **sala de fiestas,** dance hall. **4** (festividad) celebration, festivity; **el pueblo está de fiestas,** the town is holding its local festivities; **las fiestas de Navidad,** Christmas; **las fiestas de San Fermín,** the festival of San Fermín.

fifiriche adj CAm Méx sickly, weak.

figón nm arc cheap restaurant.

figura nf **1** figure, shape; **f. de cerámica,** pottery figure; **f. decorativa,** figurehead; **tener buena f.,** to have a good figure; **una f. de hombre,** the shape or figure of a man. **2** (personaje) figure; **una f. de las letras,** an important literary figure. **3** Cin Teat character. **4** Geom figure, diagram. **5** Ling figure.

figuración nf imagination; **son figuraciones tuyas,** you're just imagining things.

figurado,-a I pp de **figurar.** II adj figurative; **en sentido f.,** figuratively.

figurante,-a nm,f **1** Teat Cin extra. **2** fig figurehead.

figurar I vtr **1** (representar) to represent; **¿qué figuran estas rayas rojas?,** what do these red lines represent? **2** (simular) to simulate, feign, pretend; **figuró estar muerto,** he pretended to be dead. II vi **1** (aparecer) to appear, figure; **su nombre no figura en el listín,** her name isn't in the telephone directory. **2** (destacar) to stand out, be important. III **figurarse** vr **1** to imagine, suppose; **nunca me lo hubiera figurado,** I would never have suspected it; **ya me lo figuraba,** I thought as much. **2** interj **¡figúrate!, ¡figúrese!,** just imagine!

figurativo,-a adj figurative.

figurín nm **1** (dibujo) sketch. **2** (revista) fashion magazine. **3** pey dandy, fop.

figurinista nmf Teat Cin costume designer.

figurón *nm* 1 *pey* show-off, swank. 2 *Náut* **f. de proa**, figurehead.

fija *nf Am fam* sure thing.

fijacarteles *nmf inv* billposter.

fijación *nf* setting, fixing. ■ *Fot* **baño de f.**, fixing bath; **f. de impuestos**, tax assessment. 2 *(amarre)* fastening. 3 **fijaciones**, *Esquí* bindings.

fijado *nm Fot* fixing.

fijador *nm* fixative.

fijapelo *nm Peluq* hair spray *or* gel.

fijar I *vtr* 1 *(sujetar)* to fix, fasten; *(establecer)* to determine; **f. residencia**, to take up residence; **f. un sello en**, to stick a stamp on; **f. una fecha/un precio**, to fix a date/price; *(en letrero)* **prohibido f. carteles**, post no bills. 2 *Carp (puerta)* to hang; *(ventana)* to put in. 3 *Fot Quím* to fix. II **fijarse** *vr* 1 *(darse cuenta)* to notice; **se fija en todo**, she's very observant; **¿te fijas cómo me contesta?**, did you see how he answers me? 2 *(poner atención)* to pay attention, watch; **es que no te fijas**, you just don't pay attention; **¡fíjate!, ¡fíjese!**, (just) fancy that!; **fíjate cómo lo hago yo**, watch how I do it; **fíjate en esta foto**, look at this photo.

fijasello *nm Filat* stamp hinge.

fijativo *nm Fot* fixative.

fijeza *nf* 1 *(insistencia)* insistence, firmness; **mirar algo con f.**, to stare at sth. 2 *(certeza)* certainly; **saber algo con f.**, to know sth for certain.

Fiji *n* Fiji.

fijiano,-a *adj & nm,f* Fijian.

fijo,-a *adj* 1 *(sujeto)* fixed, fastened; **f. a la pared**, fixed to the wall. 2 *(determinado)* **aún no hay fecha fija**, the exact date hasn't been fixed yet; **con la mirada fija**, staring; **de f.**, for certain, for sure. 3 *(firme)* steady, stable; **asegúrate de que esté bien f.**, make sure it is steady. 4 *(permanente)* permanent; **está f. en Madrid**, he's settled in Madrid; **no quiero un empleo f.**, I don't want a permanent job; **sin residencia fija**, of no fixed abode. 5 *Fot* fast. ◆ **fijamente** *adv* fixedly; **mirar f.**, to stare.

fila *nf* 1 file, line; **en f. de uno, en f. india**, in single file; **nos pusieron en f.**, we were lined up; **salirse de la f.**, to step out of line. 2 *(de cine, teatro)* row; **en primera f.**, in the front row. 3 **filas**, ranks; **cerrar f.**, to close ranks; **entrar a engrosar las f. de**, to join the ranks of; *Mil* **Juan está en f. ahora**, Juan's doing his military service at the moment; **llamar a algn a f.**, to call sb up; **romper f.**, to break ranks; **¡rompan f.!**, fall out!, dismiss!

Filadelfia *n* Philadelphia.

filamento *nm* filament.

filantropía *nf* philanthropy.

filantrópico,-a *adj* philanthropic.

filántropo,-a *nm,f* philanthropist.

filarmónico,-a *adj* philharmonic.

filatelia *nf* philately, stamp collecting.

filatélico,-a *adj* philatelic.

filatelista *nmf* philatelist, stamp collector.

filazo *nm CAm* wound, injury.

filete *nm* 1 *(de carne, pescado)* fillet; *(solomillo)* sirloin. 2 *Téc (de tornillo)* thread.

filfa *nf fam* hoax.

filiación *nf* 1 *(datos personales)* particulars *pl*. 2 *Pol* affiliation.

filial I *adj* 1 filial. 2 *Com* subsidiary; **empresa f.**, subsidiary. II *nf Com* subsidiary.

filibusterismo *nm fam* filibustering.

filibustero,-a *nm,f fam* filibuster.

filigrana *nf* 1 *(en orfebrería)* filigree. 2 *(en el papel)* watermark. 3 **filigranas**, *fig* intricacy *sing*, intricate work *sing*.

filípica *nf* philippic, tirade.

Filipinas *npl* **(las) F.**, (the) Philippines.

filipino,-a *adj & nm,f* Philippine, Filipino.

filisteo,-a *adj & nm,f* Philistine.

film *nm* film, picture, *US* movie.

filmación *nf* filming, shooting.

filmar *vtr* to film, shoot.

filme *nm* film.

fílmico,-a *adj* film, cinema.

filmografía *nf* filmography, films *pl*; **la f. de los años treinta**, the films of the thirties.

filmoteca *nf (archivo)* film library; *(sala de exhibición)* film institute.

filo *nm* 1 *(cutting)* edge; **sacar f. a algo**, to sharpen sth; *fig* **al f. de la medianoche**, on the stroke of midnight; *fig* **arma de doble f.**, double-edged argument. 2 *CAm Méx (hambre)* hunger.

filología *nf* philology.

filológico,-a *adj* philological.

filólogo,-a *nm,f* philologist.

filón *nm* 1 *Min* seam, vein. 2 *fig (buen negocio)* gold mine.

filoso,-a *adj Am* sharp-edged.

filosofal *adj* **piedra f.**, philosopher's stone.

filosofar *vi* to philosophize.

filosofía *nf* philosophy; *fig* **tomar algo con f.**, to take sth philosophically.

filosófico,-a *adj* philosophical.

filósofo,-a *nm,f* philosopher.

filtración *nf* 1 filtration. 2 *(de información)* leak.

filtrador,-a I *adj* filtering. II *nm* filter.

filtrar *vtr*, **filtrarse** *vr* 1 to filter. 2 *(información)* to leak (out).

filtro *nm* 1 filter. ■ **cigarrillo con f.**, filter *or* filter-tip cigarette; **f. de café**, coffee filter. 2 *Hist (poción)* philtre, love potion.

fimbria *nf Cost (borde)* hem; *(orla)* edging, border.

fin *nm* 1 *(final)* end; **a fines de mes**, at the end of the month; **al f. y al cabo**, when all's said and done, in the end; **cuentos sin f.**, endless lies; **dar** *or* **poner f. a**, to put an end to; **en f.**, anyway; **llegar** *or* **tocar a su f.**, to come to an end; **no tener f.**, to be endless; **noche de F. de Año**, New Year's Eve; **¡por** *or* **al f.!**, at last! ■ **f. de semana**, weekend; **f. de fiesta**, grand finale. 2 *(objetivo)* purpose, aim; **a f. de**, in order to, so as to; **a f. de que**, in order that, so that; **con buen f.**, with good intentions; **con el f. de**, with the intention of; **con este f.**, with this aim; *prov* **el f. justifica los medios**, the end justifies the means.

finado,-a I *pp de* **finar**. II *nm,f* deceased.

final I *adj* final, last. II *nm* 1 end; **al f.**, in the end; **al f. del día**, at the end of the day; **hasta el f.**, until the end. ■ **f. de línea**, terminal; **f. feliz**, happy ending. 3 *Mús* finale. III *nf Dep* final. ■ **cuartos de f.**, quarterfinals. ◆ **finalmente** *adv* finally, eventually.

finalidad *nf* purpose, aim.

finalista I *adj* in the final; **equipo f.**, team in the final. II *nmf* finalist.

finalizar *vtr & vi* to end, finish.

financiación *nf*, **financiamiento** *nm* financing.

financiar *vtr* to finance.

financiero,-a I *adj* financial. II *nm,f* financier.

finanzas *nfpl* finances.

finar *fml* I *vi* to pass away, die. II **finarse** *vr* to yearn (**por**, for).

finca *nf* property, estate. ■ *Am* **f. rústica**, country estate; **f. urbana**, building.

finés,-a *adj & nm,f véase* **finlandés,-esa**.

fineza *nf* **1** *véase* **finura. 2** *(cumplido)* courtesy, compliment.

fingido,-a I *pp de* **finger.** II *adj* feigned, false; **nombre f.,** assumed name.

fingimiento *nm* pretence, simulation.

fingir I *vtr* to feign, pretend. II **fingirse** *vr* to pretend to be.

finiquitar *vtr* Com **1** *(saldar) (cuenta)* to settle; *(deuda)* to discharge. **2** *(terminar)* to finish, end.

finiquito *nm* **1** Com *(acción)* settlement. **2** *(documento)* final discharge.

finito,-a *adj* finite.

finlandés,-a I *adj* Finnish. II *nm,f (persona)* Finn. III *nm (idioma)* Finnish.

Finlandia *n* Finland.

fino,-a I *adj* **1** fine, delicate; **oro f.,** pure gold. **2** *(alimentos, bebidas)* choice, select. **3** *(sentidos)* sharp, acute; **olfato f.,** keen sense of smell. **4** *(delgado)* thin. **5** *(educado)* refined, polite. **6** *(humor, ironía)* subtle. **7** *fam* **estar f.,** to be witty *or* shrewd; **ir f.,** to be plastered *or* stoned. II *nm (vino)* type of dry sherry.

finolis *adj inv fam* **1** *(remilgado)* fussy, finicky. **2** *(cursi)* affected.

finta *nf* feint.

fintar *vi* to feint.

finura *nf* **1** *(calidad)* fineness, excellence. **2** *(agudeza)* sharpness, acuteness. **3** *(refinamiento)* refinement, politeness. **4** *(sutileza)* subtlety.

fiordo *nm* Geog fiord, fjord.

fique *nm* Am Bot agave fibre.

firma *nf* **1** *(autógrafo)* signature; **ponga la f. aquí,** sign here. **2** *(empresa)* firm, company.

firmamento *nm* Astron firmament.

firmante *adj* & *nmf* signatory; *fml* **el** *or* **la abajo f.,** the undersigned.

firmar *vtr* to sign.

firme I *adj* **1** firm, steady; *fig* **mantenerse f.,** to hold one's ground. ■ **tierra f.,** terra firma. **2** *(color)* fast. **3** *Jur* **sentencia f.,** final judgement. **4** *Mil* **¡firmes!,** attention! II *nm* Constr road surface. III *adv* hard. ◆ **firmemente** *adv* **1** *(resistente)* firmly. **2** *(fuerte)* strongly.

firmeza *nf* firmness, steadiness.

firulete *nm* Am cheap ornament.

fiscal I *adj* fiscal, tax. II *nmf* **1** *Jur* public prosecutor, *US* district attorney. **2** *fig* snooper; informer.

fiscalía *nf* office of public prosecutor.

fiscalización *nf* supervision, inspection.

fiscalizar *vtr* to supervise, investigate.

fisco *nm* treasury, exchequer.

fisgar *vi fam* to snoop, pry.

fisgón,-ona *nm,f (espía)* snooper; *(curioso)* busybody.

fisgonear *vi* to snoop, pry.

física *nf* physics *sing.*

físico,-a I *adj* physical. II *nm,f (profesión)* physicist. III *nm (aspecto)* physique. ◆ **físicamento** *adv* physically.

fisiología *nf* physiology.

fisiológico,-a *adj* physiological.

fisiólogo,-a *nm,f* physiologist.

fisión *nf* Fís fission.

fisioterapeuta *nmf* Med physiotherapist.

fisioterapia *nf* Med physiotherapy.

fisonomía *nf* physiognomy.

fisonomista *nmf fam* **ser buen/mal f.,** to be good/no good at remembering faces.

fístula *nf* Med fistula.

fisura *nf* fissure.

FIV *nf* Med *abr de* **fecundación in vitro,** in vitro fertilization, IVF.

flaccidez *nf,* **flacidez** *nf* flaccidity, flaccidness, flabbiness.

fláccido,-a *adj* **flácido,-a** *adj* flaccid, flabby.

flaco,-a I *adj* **1** *(delgado)* thin, skinny. **2** *fig (débil)* weak; **los números son su punto f.,** numbers are his weak point. II *nm* weak point *or* spot, weakness.

flacucho,-a *adj pey* skinny.

flacura *nf* thinness, skinniness.

flagelación *nf* flagellation, whipping.

flagelar I *vtr* **1** to flagellate, whip, scourge. **2** *fig (criticar)* to flay. II **flagelarse** *vr* to flagellate oneself.

flagelo *nm* **1** *(látigo)* whip, scourge. **2** *fig (calamidad)* scourge, calamity.

flagrante *adj* flagrant; **en f. delito,** red-handed.

flamante *adj* **1** *(vistoso)* splendid, brilliant. **2** *(nuevo)* brand-new.

flameado,-a *pp de* **flamear.** II *adj* Culin flambé.

flameante *adj* flamboyant.

flamear I *vtr* Culin to flambé. II *vi* **1** *(llamear)* to flame, blaze. **2** *(ondear)* to flutter, flap.

flamenco,-a I *adj* **1** *(de Flandes)* Flemish. **2** *(gitano)* Andalusian gypsy; *fam* **ponerse f.,** to get cocky. **3** *Mús* flamenco. II *nm,f (gitano)* Andalusian gypsy. III *nm* **1** *(idioma)* Flemish. **2** *Mús* flamenco. **3** *Orn* flamingo.

flámula *nf* streamer, pennant.

flan *nm* Culin caramel custard; **f. de arena,** sand pie; *fig fam* **estar como un f.,** *(físicamente)* to feel tired and washed out; *(anímicamente)* to be easily upset.

flanco *nm* flank, side.

flanera *nf* Culin custard mould.

flanquear *vtr* to flank.

flaquear *vi* **1** *(ceder)* to weaken, give way; **me flaquearon las piernas,** my legs gave way. **2** *(fallar)* to fail; **le flaquea la memoria,** his memory is failing. **3** *(desalentarse)* to lose heart. **4** *(disminuir)* to decrease, diminish.

flaqueza *nf* weakness, frailty.

flash *nm* **1** Fot flash, flashlight. **2** *fig (noticia)* newsflash.

flato *nm* **1** wind, flatulence. **2** Am *(melancolía)* gloom, melancholy, sadness. **3** CAm *(aprensión)* apprehension, fear.

flatulencia *nf* flatulence.

flatulento,-a *adj* flatulent.

flauta Mús I *nf* flute. ■ **f. de Pan,** pipes *pl* of **Pan; f. dulce,** recorder; **f. travesera,** transverse *or* cross flute. II *nmf* flautist, *US* flutist, flute player.

flautín Mús I *nm (instrumento)* piccolo. II *nmf (músico)* piccolo player.

flautista *nmf* Mús flautist, *US* flutist, flute player; **el F. de Hamelín,** the Pied Piper (of Hamelin).

flebitis *nf* Med phlebitis.

flecha *nf* **1** *(arma)* arrow; *(dardo)* dart; *fig* **salir como una f.,** to go off like a shot. **2** Aut arrow; **siga la f.,** follow the arrow. **3** Arquit spire, flèche.

flechar *vtr fig* to inspire sudden love in.

flechazo *nm* **1** *fig (enamoramiento)* love at first sight. **2** *(disparo)* arrow shot. **3** *(herida)* arrow wound.

fleco *nm* **1** *(adorno)* fringe. **2** *fig (borde deshilachado)* frayed edge. **3** Peluq fringe, *US* bangs *pl*.

fleje *nm* **1** Téc metal strip *or* band. **2** *(de tonel)* (metal) hoop.

flema *nf* phlegm.

flemático,-a *adj* phlegmatic.

flemón *nm* Med gumboil, abscess.

flequillo *nm* fringe, *US* bangs.

fleta *nf Am* **1** *(friega)* rub, rubbing. **2** *(azotaina)* tanning, spanking.

fletador,-a *nm,f* charterer, freighter.

fletamiento *nm* chartering.

fletar I *vtr* **1** *(avión, barco)* to charter, freight. **2** *Am (carro, bestia)* to hire. **3** *Arg (mandar)* to send, order to go (**a**, to). **4** *Arg Chi (despedir)* to fire, sack. **II fletarse** *vr* **1** *CAm (fastidiarse)* to get cross. **2** *Arg (colarse)* to gatecrash.

flete *nm* **1** *(alquiler)* freightage. **2** *(carga de un buque)* cargo. **3** *Am (alquiler)* hiring fee. **4** *Am (carga)* freight, cargo. **5** *Arg (caballo)* fast horse.

fletero,-a I *adj* hire, for hire; **carro f.**, hire car. **II** *nm* **1** *Am (cobrador)* collector. **2** *Arg (propietario)* owner of vehicles.

flexibilidad *nf* flexibility.

flexible *adj* flexible.

flexión *nf* **1** *(doblegamiento)* flexion. **2** *Ling* inflection. **3** *Gimn* press-up, *US* push-up.

flexionar *vtr (músculo)* to flex; *(cuerpo)* to bend.

flexo *nm* adjustable table lamp, anglepoise lamp.

flipado,-a I *arg* **1** *pp de* **flipar. II** *adj (drogas)* stoned.

flipante *adj arg* great, cool.

flipar *arg* **I** *vtr* to fascinate, captivate; **le flipan las motos**, he's crazy about motorbikes. **II fliparse** *vr* to get stoned.

flipe *nm arg* trip.

flirtear *vi* to flirt.

flirteo *nm* flirtation, flirting.

flojear *vi* **1** *(disminuir)* to fall off, go down; **han flojeado las ventas,** sales have fallen off. **2** *(debilitarse)* to weaken, grow weak; **le flojea la memoria,** his memory is failing.

flojedad *nf* **1** *(debilidad)* weakness, slackness. **2** *(atonía)* flabbiness, limpness.

flojera *nf fam* weakness, faintness.

flojo,-a I *adj* **I** *(suelto)* loose, slack; *vulg* **me la trae floja,** I couldn't give a toss. **2** *(débil)* weak; **está f. en matemáticas,** he's weak at mathematics; **un viento muy f.,** a light wind. **3** *fig (perezoso)* lazy, idle; **una alumna muy floja,** a very weak pupil. **4** *(cobarde)* cowardly. **II** *nm,f* **1** lazy person, idler. **2** *Am* coward.

flor *nf* **1** flower; **en f.**, in blossom; *fig* **en la f. de la vida,** in the prime of life; *fig* **la f. y nata,** the cream (of society). ■ **f. de harina,** pure wheat flour; **f. de lis,** fleur-de-lis. **2** *fig (piropo)* compliment; **echar flores,** to pay compliments. **3** *(superficie)* **a f. de piel,** skin-deep; **a f. de tierra,** at ground level.

flora *nf* flora.

floración *nf (plantas)* flowering, blooming; *(árboles)* blossoming.

floral *adj* floral.

florar *vi (plantas)* to flower, bloom; *(árboles)* to blossom.

floreado,-a I *pp de* **florear. II** *adj* **1** flowered, flowery. **2** *Lit (estilo)* florid.

florear I *vtr* **1** *(adornar)* to adorn with flowers. **2** *fam fig* to pay compliments to. **II** *vi* **1** *Mús (guitarra)* to play in arpeggio. **2** *Esgr* to flourish. **3** *Am (florecer) (plantas)* to flower, bloom; *(árboles)* to blossom. **4** *Arg Urug* to show off.

florecer I *vi* **1** *Bot (plantas)* to flower, bloom; *(árboles)* to blossom. **2** *fig (prosperar)* to flourish, thrive. **II florecerse** *vr* to go mouldy *or* mouldy.

floreciente *adj fig* flourishing, prosperous.

florecimiento *nm* **1** *Bot (plantas)* flowering, blooming; *(árboles)* blossoming. **2** *fig (auge)* flourishing, prospering.

Florencia *n* Florence.

florentino,-a *adj & nm,f* Florentine.

floreo *nm* flourish.

florero *nm (jarrón)* vase.

florescencia *nf Bot* florescence.

floresta *nf (bosque)* wood, thicket.

florete *nm Esgr* foil.

florezco *indic pres véase* **florecer.**

floricultor,-a *nm,f* flower grower.

floricultura *nf* flower growing, floriculture.

florido,-a *adj* **1** *(con flores)* flowery. **2** *fig (selecto)* choice, select; **lo más f.**, the cream. **3** *Lit (estilo)* florid.

florilegio *nm Lit* anthology.

florin *nm (moneda)* florin.

floripondio *nm pey* **1** *(flor grande)* large flower, gaudy flower. **2** *(adorno excesivo)* heavy ornamentation.

florista *nmf* florist.

floristería *nf* florist's (shop).

florón *nm* **1** *Arquit* rosette. **2** *Herald* fleuron.

flota *nf* fleet. ■ **f. pesquera,** fishing fleet.

flotación *nf* flotation, floating.

flotador *nm* **1** float. **2** *(de niño)* rubber ring. **3** *(de cisterna)* ballcock.

flotante *adj* floating.

flotar *vi* **1** to float. **2** *(ondear)* to wave, flutter.

flote *nm* floating; **a f.,** afloat; **sacar a f. un negocio,** to put a business on a sound footing; *fig* **salir a f.,** to get back on one's feet, get out of difficulty.

flotilla *nf* flotilla.

fluctuación *nf* fluctuation.

fluctuante *adj* fluctuating, subject to fluctuation.

fluctuar *vi* to fluctuate; *(vacilar)* to hesitate.

fluente *adj* flowing, fluid.

fluidez *nf* **1** fluidity. **2** *fig* fluency.

fluido,-a I *nm pp de* **fluir. II** *adj* **1** fluid. **2** *fig* fluent. **III** *nm* **1** *Fís* fluid. **2** *Elec* current.

fluir *vi* to flow.

flujo *nm* **1** flow. **2** *Mar* rising tide; **f. y reflujo,** ebb and flow. **3** *Fís* flux. **4** *Med* discharge. **5** *Inform* stream.

fluminense I *adj* of *or* from Rio de Janeiro. **II** *nmf* native *or* inhabitant of Rio de Janeiro.

flúor *nm* fluorine.

fluorescencia *nf* fluorescence.

fluorescente *adj* fluorescent.

fluorización *nf* fluoridation.

fluoruro *nm Quím* fluoride.

fluvial *adj* fluvial, river.

flux *nm Naipes* flush.

fluyo *indic pres véase* **fluir.**

FM *nf Rad abr de* **Frecuencia Modulada,** frequency modulation, FM.

FMI *nm Econ abr de* **Fondo Monetario Internacional,** International Monetary Fund, IMF.

fo., fol., f.° *abr de* **folio,** folio, fo., fol.

fobia *nf* phobia.

foca *nf* **1** *Zool* seal. ■ **piel de f.**, sealskin. **2** *fam (persona)* fat lump.

focal *adj* focal; **distancia f.,** focal length.

focha *nf Orn* coot.

foco *nm* **1** centre, *US* center, focal point. **2** *Fís Mat* focus. **3** *(lámpara)* spotlight, floodlight. **4** *fig* centre. **5** *Am* (electric light) bulb.

fofo,-a *adj* **1** soft, spongy. **2** *(persona)* flabby.

fogaje *nm Arg Méx Med* rash.

fogata *nf* bonfire.

fogón nm 1 (cocina) kitchen range, stove. 2 (de máquina de vapor) firebox. 3 Am (fogata) bonfire, camp fire. 4 Arg group of people round a camp fire.

fogonazo nm flash.

fogonero nm stoker.

fogosidad nf 1 (persona) ardour, US ardor, fire. 2 (caballo) fieriness.

fogoso,-a adj fiery, spirited.

foguear vtr 1 (personas, caballos) to accustom to gunfire. 2 fig to harden.

fogueo nm **cartucho de f.,** blank cartridge.

foja nf Orn coot.

folía nf popular song and dance of the Canary Isles.

foliación nf Bot Impr foliation.

foliar vtr Impr to foliate, folio, number.

folicular adj follicular.

folículo nm Bot Anat follicle.

folio nm (hoja) folio, leaf; Impr **en f.,** folio, in folio.

folklore nm folklore.

folklórico,-a I adj folkloric, popular, traditional. 2 fam pey quaint. II nf (cantante) flamenco singer.

folklorista nmf folklorist.

folla nf vulg **tener mala f.,** (mala pata) to have bad luck, be unlucky; (mala idea) to be a nasty piece of work.

follada nf vulg screw, fuck.

follaje nm 1 Bot foliage, leaves. 2 (palabrería) verbiage, verbosity.

follar vulg I vi (copular) to fuck, screw. II vtr (suspender) to fail; **me han follado en mates,** I've failed maths. III **follarse** vr to fuck, screw; **se la folló,** he screwed her.

folletín nm 1 (relato) newspaper serial. 2 fig melodrama; **¡menudo f.!,** what a saga!

folletinesco,-a adj melodramatic.

folletinista nmf serial writer.

folleto nm (prospecto) pamphlet, leaflet, brochure; (explicativo) instruction leaflet; (turístico) brochure.

follisca nf Am fight, brawl.

follón nm fam 1 (alboroto) rumpus, shindy; **armar (un) f.,** to kick up a rumpus. 2 (enredo, confusión) mess, trouble; **meterse en un f.,** to get into a mess; **nos quedó un f. de platos sucios,** we were left with a whole load of dirty dishes.

follonero,-a adj & nm,f **es muy f.,** he's a real troublemaker.

fomentar vtr to promote, encourage, foster.

fomento nm 1 promotion, encouragement, fostering. 2 Med fomentation.

fonda nf 1 (mesón) inn. 2 small restaurant. 3 Chi Guat Salv (taberna) tavern.

fondeadero nm Náut anchorage.

fondeado,-a I pp de **fondear.** II adj 1 anchored. 2 (rico) well-off, wealthy.

fondear I vtr 1 (sondear) to sound. 2 (registrar) to search. 3 fig (examinar) to get to the bottom of. II vi (barco) to anchor. III **fondearse** vr Am to get rich.

fondeo nm 1 (sondeo) sounding. 2 (registro) search. 3 (anclar) anchoring.

fondillos nmpl seat sing (of trousers).

fondiludo,-a adj 1 CAm Per big-bottomed. 2 Arg (calzonazos) henpecked.

fondista nmf 1 (de mesón) innkeeper. 2 Dep longdistance runner.

fondo nm 1 (parte más baja) bottom; **a f.,** thoroughly; **al f. de la calle,** at the bottom of the street; **tocar f.,** Náut to touch bottom; fig to reach rock bottom; fig **en el f.,** deep down, at heart; fig **hay un f. de verdad en sus palabras,** there is some truth in what he says. ■ **bajos fondos,** dregs of society; **doble f.,** false bottom; **f. del mar,** seabed; **forma y f.,** form and substance; **mar de f.,** Náut ground

swell; fig undercurrent of tension. 2 (parte más lejana) end, back; **al f. del auditorio,** at the back of the auditorium; **al f. del pasillo,** at the end of the corridor. 3 (segundo término) background; **un estampado azul sobre un f. blanco,** a blue pattern on a white background. ■ **música de f.,** background music. 4 Prensa **artículo de f.,** leading articte. 5 Dep **corredor/carrera de f.,** long-distance runner/race; **esquiador/esquí de f.,** cross-country skier/skiing. 6 Fin fund; **cheque sin fondas,** bad cheque; **reunir fondos,** to raise funds. ■ **f. común,** kitty; **fondos bloqueados,** frozen assets; **fondos disponibles,** available or liquid funds; **fondos públicos,** public funds.

fondón,-ona adj fam big-bottomed, fat.

fonducha nf, **fonducho** nm pey cheap restaurant, cheap boarding house.

fonema nm Ling phoneme.

fonendoscopio nm Med stethoscope.

fonético,-a I adj phonetic. II nf phonetics sing.

fónico,-a adj Ling phonic.

fonocaptor nm pick-up.

fonógrafo nm gramophone, US phonograph.

fonología nf Ling phonology.

fonológico,-a adj Ling phonological.

fonoteca nf record library.

fontana nf lit fountain, spring.

fontanería nf plumbing.

fontanero,-a nm,f plumber.

footing nm jogging; **hacer f.,** to go jogging.

F.O.P. nfpl abr de **Fuerzas del Orden Público,** the Police Force.

foque nm Náut jib.

forajido,-a nm,f outlaw, desperado.

foral adj of or relating to the **fueros.**

foráneo,-a adj alien, foreign.

forastero,-a I adj foreign, alien. II nm,f outsider, stranger.

forcejear vi to wrestle, struggle.

forcejeo nm struggle, struggling.

fórceps nm inv Med forceps pl.

forense I adj forensic, legal. II nmf (médico) f., forensic surgeon.

forestal adj forest; **repoblación f.,** reafforestation.

forja nf 1 (fragua) forge. 2 (forjado) forging. 3 (ferrería) ironworks sing, foundry.

forjado,-a I pp de **forjar.** II adj wrought. III nm Arquit forging.

forjar I vtr 1 (metales) to forge. 2 fig to create, make; **ella sola forjó un imperio,** she created an empire single-handed. II **forjarse** vr 1 to forge for oneself; **se ha forjado un buen porvenir,** he has forged a fine future for himself; **f. ilusiones,** to build up false hopes. 2 CAm to feather one's nest.

forma nf, 1 form, shape; **en f. de L,** L-shaped; **¿qué f. tiene?,** what shape is it? 2 (manera) way; **de esta f.,** in this way; **de f. que,** so that; **de todas formas,** anyway, in any case; **no hubo f. de convencerla,** there was no way we could convince her. ■ **f. de pago,** method of payment. 3 Dep form; **estar en f.,** to be on form; **estar en baja f.,** to be off form; **ponerse en f.,** to get fit. 4 Rel Sagrada F., Host. 5 formas, (modales) manners, social conventions; **guardar las formas,** to keep up appearances. 6 formas, fam (de mujer) curves.

formación nf 1 formation. 2 (educación) upbringing. 3 (enseñanza) education, training. ■ **f. musical,** musical training; **f. profesional,** technical education; **f. universitaria,** university education.

formal adj 1 (serio) serious, serious-minded; **noviazgo f.,** formal engagement. 2 (cumplidor) reliable, dependable. 3 (cortés) polite; **sed formales,** behave yourselves.

formaldehido *nm Quím* formaldehyde.

formalidad *nf* **1** formality. **2** *(seriedad)* seriousness. **3** *(fiabilidad)* reliability. **4** *(trámite)* formality, requisite.

formalina *nf Quím* formalin.

formalismo *nm* formalism.

formalista I *adj* formalistic. **II** *nmf* formalist.

formalizar I *vtr* **1** *(hacer formal)* to formalize. **2** *Jur (contrato)* to legalize. **II formalizarse** *vr* to become or grow serious.

formar I *vtr* **1** to form; **formó un círculo con las sillas,** she placed the chairs in a circle. **2** *(integrar, constituir)* to form, constitute; **f. un comité,** to form a commitee; **f. parte de algo,** to be a part of sth. **3** *(educar)* to bring up; *(enseñar)* to educate, train. **II** *vi* to form up; *Mil* **¡a f.!,** fall in! **III formarse** *vr* **1** to be formed, form; **se formó un charco,** a puddle formed; **f. una impresión equivocada,** to get the wrong impression. **2** *(educarse)* to be educated or trained.

formativo,-a *adj* formative.

formato *nm Inform Tip* format; *(del papel)* size.

formica® *nf* Formica®.

fórmico,-a *adj Quím* formic.

formidable *adj* **1** *(tremendo)* tremendous, formidable. **2** *(maravilloso)* wonderful, terrific; **¡f.!,** great!

formol *nm Quím* formol.

formón *nm Carp* firmer chisel.

fórmula *nf* formula; **por pura f.,** for form's sake. ■ *Aut* **f. uno,** formula one.

formulación *nf* formulation.

formular *vtr* **1** *(una teoría)* to formulate. **2** *(quejas, peticiones)* to make; **f. un deseo,** to express a desire; **f. una pregunta,** to ask a question.

formulario,-a I *adj* routine; **una visita formularia,** a formal visit. **II** *nm* **1** *Farm* formulary, collection of formulas. **2** *(documento)* form; **rellenar un f. de solicitud,** to fill in an application (form).

formulismo *nm* formulism.

fornicación *nf fml* fornication.

fornicador,-a *fml* **I** *adj* fornicating. **II** *nm,f* fornicator.

fornicar *vi fml* to fornicate.

fornido,-a *adj* strapping, hefty.

fornitura *nf* **1** *Mil* cartridge belt. **2** *(accesorios)* accessories *pl.* **3** *(de un reloj)* spare parts *pl.*

foro *nm* **1** *Hist* forum. **2** *Jur (tribunal)* law court, court of justice; *(profesión)* bar, legal profession. **3** *Teat* back (of the stage). **4** *(reunión)* meeting.

forofo,-a *nm,f fam* fan, supporter.

forrado,-a I *pp de* **forrar. II** *adj* **1** *Cost* lined; *(tapizado)* upholstered. **2** *fam (rico)* well-heeled, well-off.

forraje *nm* **1** *Agr* fodder, forage. **2** *fig (mezcla)* hotch-potch. **3** *Am* cattle food.

forrajear *vtr & vi* **1** to get in the fodder. **2** *Mil* to forage.

forrajero,-a *adj Agr* fodder; **plantas forrajeras,** fodder crops.

forrar I *vtr* **1** *(por dentro)* to line. **2** *(por fuera)* to cover; *(tapizar)* to upholster. **II forrarse** *vr fam (de dinero)* to make a packet.

forro *nm* **1** *Cost* lining. **2** *(funda)* cover, case; *(tapizado)* upholstery. **3** *fam fig* **ni por el f.,** not in the slightest.

fortachón,-ona *adj fam* strong, strapping.

fortalecedor,-a *adj* fortifying.

fortalecer I *vtr* to fortify, strengthen. **II fortalecerse** *vr* to fortify oneself, become stronger.

fortalecimiento *nm* fortification, strengthening.

fortaleza *nf* **1** *(vigor)* strength, vigour. **2** *(de espíritu)* fortitude. **3** *Mil* fortress, stronghold.

fortificación I *nf* fortification, fortifying.

fortificante I *adj* fortifying. **II** *nm* fortifier, tonic.

fortificar *vtr* to fortify, strengthen.

fortín *nm* small fort, bunker.

fortísimo,-a *adj* **1** *(muy fuerte)* very strong. **2** *Mús* fortissimo.

fortuito,-a *adj* fortuitous; **encuentro f.,** chance meeting.

fortuna *nf* **1** *(destino)* fortune, fate. ■ **la rueda de la f.,** the wheel of fortune. **2** *(suerte)* luck; **buena f.,** good luck; **mala f.,** misfortune; **por f.,** fortunately; **probar f.,** to try one's luck. **3** *(capital)* fortune; **heredó una f.,** he inherited a fortune.

forúnculo *nm Med* boil, furuncle.

forzado,-a I *pp de* **forzar. II** *adj* **1** *(obligado)* forced; **a marchas forzadas,** at a brisk pace. ■ **trabajos forzados,** hard labour *sing.* **2** *(rebuscado)* forced, strained; **una risa forzada,** a forced laugh.

forzar *vtr* **1** to force, compel; **f. a algn a hacer algo,** to compel sb to do sth. **2** to force, break open; **forzaron la puerta del coche,** they broke the car door open. **3** *fml (violar)* to rape.

forzoso,-a *adj* **1** *(inevitable)* inevitable, unavoidable, inescapable. **2** *(obligatorio)* obligatory, compulsory; **la asistencia es forzosa,** attendance is obligatory. ■ *Av* **aterrizaje f.,** forced landing.

forzudo,-a *adj* strong brawny.

fosa *nf* **1** *(sepultura)* grave. ■ **f. común,** common grave. **2** *(hoyo)* pit; hollow. ■ **f. séptica,** septic tank. **3** *Anat* fossa. ■ **fosas nasales,** nostrils.

fosfato *nm* phosphate. ■ **f. de cal,** calcium phosphate.

fosforecer *vi* to phosphoresce, glow.

fosforero,-a I *nm,f* match seller. **II** *nf* **1** *(caja)* matchbox. **2** *(fábrica)* match factory.

fosforescencia *nf* phosphorescence.

fosforescente *adj* phosphorescent.

fosfórico,-a *adj Quím* phosphoric.

fósforo *nm* **1** *Quím* phosphorus. **2** *(cerilla)* match.

fósil *adj & nm* fossil.

fosilización *nf* fossilization.

fosilizarse *vr* to fossilize, become fossilized.

fosilizado,-a I *pp de* **fosilizarse. II** *adj* fossilized.

foso *nm* **1** *(hoyo)* hole, pit. **2** *(de fortificación)* moat. **3** *Teat* pit. ■ **f. de la orquesta,** orchestra pit. **4** *(engarage)* inspection pit.

fotingo *nm Am* battered old car.

foto *nf fam* photo; **sacar fotos,** to take photos.

fotocalco *nm* photoprint.

fotocomposición *nf Impr* typesetting, *US* photosetting.

fotocopia *nf* photocopy, Xerox®. **hacer** or **sacar un f. de algo,** to photocopy sth.

fotocopiadora *nf* photocopier.

fotocopiar *vtr* to photocopy.

fotoeléctrico,-a *adj* photoelectric.

fotogénico,-a *adj* photogenic.

fotograbado *nm* photogravure, photoengraving.

fotograbar *vtr* to photoengrave.

fotografía *nf* **1** *(proceso)* photography. **2** *(retrato)* photograph; **hacer** or **sacar fotografías,** to take photographs.

fotografiar *vtr* to photograph, take a photograph of.

fotográfico,-a *adj* photographic.

fotógrafo,-a *nm, f* photographer; **f. de prensa,** press photographer.

fotomatón *nm* automatic coin-operated photo machine.

fotómetro *nm* light meter, exposure meter.

fotomontaje *nm Fot* photomontage.

fotón *nm Fís* photon.

fotosíntesis *nf* photosynthesis.

fotostato *nm* photostat.

fototeca *nf Fot* photograph library.

fox-trot *nm Mús* foxtrot.

FP *nf Educ abr de* **Formación Profesional,** technical education.

frac *nm* (*pl fracs or fraques*) (*prenda*) dress coat, tails *pl.*

fracasado,-a I *pp de* **fracasar.** II *adj* unsuccessful. III *nm,f* (*persona*) failure.

fracasar *vi* to fail, be unsuccessful.

fracaso *nm* failure.

fracción *nf* 1 (*porción*) fraction, fragment. 2 *Mat* fraction. 3 *Pol* faction.

fraccionamiento *nm* breaking up, splitting up, division; *Petról* cracking.

fraccionar *vtr,* **fraccionarse** *vr* to break up, split up, divide into fractions.

fraccionario,-a *adj* fractional; **moneda fraccionaria,** small change.

fractura *nf* fracture.

fracturar *vtr,* **fracturarse** *vr* to fracture, break.

fragancia *nf* fragrance.

fragante *adj* fragrant, scented.

fragata *nf Náut* frigate.

frágil *adj* 1 (*quebradizo*) fragile, breakable. 2 (*débil*) frail, weak.

fragilidad *nf* 1 fragility. 2 (*debilidad*) frailty, weakness.

fragmentación *nf* fragmentation.

fragmentar I *vtr* (*partir*) to fragment; (*dividir*) to divide up. II **fragmentarse** *vr* to break up.

fragmentario,-a *adj* fragmentary.

fragmento *nm* 1 (*pedazo*) fragment, piece. 2 *Lit* passage.

fragor *nm* din, roar; (*de trueno*) crash.

fragoroso,-a *adj* thunderous, deafening.

fragosidad *nf* 1 (*terreno*) roughness, unevenness. 2 (*vegetación*) thickness, denseness.

fragoso,-a *adj* thunderous, deafening.

fragua *nf* forge.

fraguado I *pp de* **fraguar.** II *nm* setting, hardening.

fraguar I *vtr* 1 (*metal*) to forge. 2 *fig* to think up, fabricate; (*conspiración*) to hatch. II *vi* (*endurecerse*) to set, harden.

fraile *nm* friar, monk.

frailecillo *nm Orn* puffin.

frailesco,-a *adj,* **fraileuno,-a** *adj* monkish.

frambuesa *nf Bot* raspberry.

francachela *nf fam* (*comilona*) feast.

francés,-a I *adj* French; **despedirse a la francesa,** to take French leave. ▪ *Culin* **tortilla francesa,** plain omelette. II *nm,f* (*hombre*) Frenchman; (*mujer*) Frenchwoman. III *nm* 1 (*idioma*) French. 2 *vulg* blow job; **hacer un f. a algn,** to give sb a blow job.

francesilla *nf Bot* buttercup.

Francfort *n* Frankfurt.

franchute,-a *nm,f pey* Frog, Froggy, Frenchy.

Francia *n* France.

franciscano,-a I *adj* 1 *Rel* Franciscan. 2 *Am* (*pardo*) brown. II *nm,f Rel* Franciscan.

francmasón,-ona *nm,f* freemason.

francmasonería *nf* freemasonry.

franco,-a[1] *adj* 1 (*persona*) frank, open. 2 (*cosa*) clear, obvious. 3 *Com* free; **f. a bordo,** free on board; **f. de aduana,** duty-free; **f. de porte y embalaje,** post and packaging free; **f. fábrica,** ex-works; **puerto f.,** free port. ◆ **francamente** *adv* frankly.

franco[2] *nm Fin* (*moneda*) franc.

franco,-a[3] *Hist* I *adj* Frankish. II *nm,f* (*persona*) Frank. III *nn* (*idioma*) Frankish.

francófilo,-a *adj & nm,f* francophile.

francófono,-a I *adj* French-speaking. II *nm,f* French speaker.

francote,-a *adj fam* outspoken, forthright.

francotirador,-a *nm,f Mil* sniper.

franela *nf* 1 *Tex* flannel. 2 *Am* (*prenda*) (man's) T-shirt, undershirt.

frangollón,-ona *adj Am* (*persona*) bungling.

franja *nf* (*banda*) band, strip; (*faja*) fringe; *Cost* fringe, border; *Geog* **la f. de Gaza,** the Gaza strip.

franjolín,-ina *adj Am* tailless.

franqueable *adj* 1 crossable, which can be crossed. 2 (*obstáculo*) surmountable.

franquear I *vtr* 1 (*dejar libre*) to free, clear; **f. el paso,** to clear the way; **f. la entrada,** to allow to enter. 2 (*atravesar*) to cross; *fig* **f. una dificultad,** to overcome a difficulty. 3 (*carta*) to frank; **máquina de f.,** franking machine; (*en sobre*) **a f. en destino,** postage paid. II **franquearse** *vr* to unbosom oneself, open up one's heart.

franqueo *nm* postage.

franqueza *nf* 1 (*sinceridad*) frankness, openness. 2 (*confianza*) familiarity, intimacy.

franquicia *nf* exemption; *Com* franchise. ■ *Com* **f. arancelaria,** exemption from customs duty.

franquismo *nm Hist* 1 Francoism. 2 (*régimen*) the Franco regime.

franquista *Hist* I *adj* Francoist, pro-Franco. II *nmf* Francoist, Franco supporter.

frasco *nm* 1 small bottle, flask. 2 *RPl* (*medida*) = 2.37 litres.

frase *nf* 1 *Ling* (*oración*) sentence. 2 (*expresión*) phrase; **f. hecha,** set phrase *or* expression, idiom.

fraseología *nf* 1 *Ling* phraseology. 2 (*palabrería*) verbosity.

fraternal *adj* brotherly, fraternal.

fraternidad *nf* brotherhood, fraternity.

fraternización *nf* fraternization.

fraternizar *vi* to fraternize.

fraterno,-a *adj* fraternal, brotherly.

fratricida I *adj* fratricidal. II *nmf* fratricide.

fratricidio *nm* fratricide.

fraude *nm* fraud. ■ **f. fiscal,** tax evasion.

fraudulencia *nf* fraudulence.

fraudulento,-a *adj* fraudulent.

fray *nm Rel* brother; **F. David,** Brother David.

frecuencia *nf* 1 frequency; **con f.,** frequently, often. 2 *Rad* frequency. ■ **alta/baja f.,** high/low frequency.

frecuentado,-a I *pp de* **frecuentar.** II *adj* frequented; **un lugar poco f.,** a rarely frequented spot.

frecuentar *vtr* to frequent, visit.

frecuente *adj* 1 (*repetido*) frequent. 2 (*usual*) common. ◆ **frecuentemente** *adv* frequently, often.

fregadero *nm* (kitchen) sink.

fregado[1] I *pp de* **fregar.** II *nm* 1 (*lavado*) washing; (*frotar*) scrubbing. 2 *fam* (*riña*) fight, quarrel.

fregado,-a[2] *adj* 1 *Am* (*fastidioso*) tiresome, annoying. 2 *Méx* (*bellaco*) wicked.

fregar *vtr* 1 (*lavar*) to wash; (*frotar*) to scrub; **f. los platos,** to wash up, do the dishes; **f. el suelo,** to mop the floor. 2 *Am fig* to annoy, irritate.

fregona *nf* 1 *pey* (*sirvienta*) skivvy. 2 (*utensilio*) mop.

fregón,-ona *adj Am* (*majadero*) silly, stupid.

fregotear *vtr fam* to give a quick wipe to.

fregoteo *nm fam* quick wipe.

freidora *nf* (deep) fryer.

freiduría *nf* fried-fish shop.

freír (*pp* **frito**) **I** *vtr* **1** *Culin* to fry. **2** *fam fig* (*exasperar*) to exasperate; **le están friendo a preguntas,** they are bombarding him with questions; *fam fig* **la mandé a f. espárragos,** I told her to go to blazes. **II freírse** *vr* to fry; *fig* **nos freíamos,** it was baking hot.

frenado I *pp de* **frenar. II** *nm* braking.

frenar *vtr* **1** to brake. **2** *fig* (*contener*) to restrain, check.

frenazo *nm* sudden braking; **dar un f.,** to jam on the brakes.

frenesí *nm* frenzy.

frenético,-a *adj* **1** (*exaltado*) frenzied, frenetic. **2** (*colérico*) wild, mad.

frenillo *nm Anat* fraenum, *US* frenum.

freno *nm* **1** *Aut* brake; **poner/soltar el f.,** to put on/release the brake. ■ **f. de disco/tambor,** disc/drum brake; **f. de mano,** handbrake; **líquido de frenos,** brake fluid. **2** (*de caballería*) bit; *fig* **morder** *or* **tascar el f.,** to champ at the bit. **3** *fig* curb, check; **poner f. a algo,** to curb sth.

frente I *nm* **1** (*parte delantera*) front; *Arquit* front, façade; **al f. de,** at the head of; (*mando*) at the head of; **hacer f. a algo,** to face sth, stand up to sth. **2** *Mil* front, front line. **3** *Meteor* front. ■ **f. frío/cálido,** cold/warm front. **4** *Pol* front. ■ **f. popular,** popular front. **II** *nf Anat* forehead; **arrugar la f.,** to frown; **f. a f.,** face to face; **no tener dos dedos de f.,** to be as thick as two short planks; *vulg* **adornar la f.,** to cuckold, be unfaithful to. **III** *adv* **f. a,** in front of, opposite; **viven f. a la estación,** they live opposite the station.

fresa I *adj* red. **II** *nf* **1** *Bot* (*planta*) strawberry plant; (*fruto*) (wild) strawberry. **2** *Téc* milling cutter. **3** *Odont* drill.

fresado I *pp de* **fresar. II** *nm* **1** *Téc* milling. **2** *Odont* drilling.

fresadora *nf* **1** *Téc* milling machine. **2** *Odont* drill.

fresar *vtr Téc* to mill.

fresca *nf* **1** (*aire fresco*) fresh air, cool air; **tomar la f.,** to get some fresh air. **2** *fam* (*impertinencia*) cheeky remark; **decirle cuatro frescas a algn,** to tell sb a few home truths.

frescachón,-ona *adj fam* healthy, robust.

frescales *nmf inv fam* brazen person, cheeky devil.

fresco,-a I *adj* **1** cool, cold; **agua fresca,** cold water; **viento f.,** cool wind. **2** (*tela, vestido*) light, fresh; **esta blusa es muy fresca,** this blouse is nice and cool. **3** (*aspecto*) healthy, fresh. **4** (*comida*) fresh; **fruta fresca,** fresh fruit. **5** (*reciente*) new; **las noticias más frescas,** the latest news *sing*. **6** *fig* (*impasible*) cool, calm, unworried; **se quedó tan f.,** he didn't bat an eyelid. **7** (*desvergonzado*) cheeky, shameless; **la muy fresca se fue sin pagar,** she had the nerve to leave without paying; **¡qué f.!,** what a nerve!; **¡sí que estamos frescos!,** now we're in a fine mess! **II** *nm* **1** (*frescor*) fresh air, cool air; **al f.,** in the cool; **hacer f.,** to be chilly; *fam* **mandar a algn a tomar el f.,** to send sb packing. **2** *Arte* fresco.

frescor *nm* coolness, freshness.

frescura *nf* **1** (*desvergüenza*) cheek, nerve; **¡qué f.!,** what a nerve! **2** (*impertinencia*) impertinence. **3** (*calma*) coolness, calmness.

fresno *nm Bot* ash tree.

fresón *nm Bot* (*planta*) strawberry plant; (*fruto*) (large) strawberry.

fresquera *nf Culin* meat safe.

fresquería *nf Am* refreshment stall.

freudiano,-a *adj & nm,f Psic* Freudian.

frialdad *nf* **1** (*frío*) coldness. **2** *fig* coldness, indifference; **me recibieron con f.,** I was given a cool reception.

fricativo,-a *adj Ling* fricative.

fricción *nf* **1** *Fís* friction. **2** (*friega*) rub, rubbing; (*masaje*) massage. **3** *fig* friction, discord.

friccionar *vtr* to rub, massage.

friega *nf* **1** rub, rubbing. **2** *Am* (*molestia*) nuisance, annoyance. **3** *Am* (*zurra*) thrashing. **4** *Am* (*regaño*) scolding, rebuke.

friegaplatos *nmf inv* (*persona*) dishwasher.

frigidez *nf* frigidity.

frígido,-a *adj* frigid.

frigio,-a *adj & nm,f Hist* Phrygian.

frigorífico,-a I *adj* refrigerating. **II** *nm* **1** (*de uso doméstico*) refrigerator, fridge. **2** (*cámara*) coldstorage room.

frijol *nm*, **fríjol** *nm Bot* bean, kidney bean.

frío,-a I *adj* **1** cold. **2** *fig* cold, cool, indifferent; **su muerte me dejó f.,** (*dejar indiferente*) her death didn't affect me in the least; (*afectar*) I was stunned by her death. **II** *nm* cold; **hace mucho f. hoy,** it's very cold today; **pasar f.,** to be cold; **pillar** *or* **coger f.,** to catch (a) cold; **¡qué f.!,** isn't it cold!; *fam* **hace un f. que pela,** it's freezing cold. ◆ **fríamente** *adv* coldly, coolly.

friolera *nf* **1** trifle, trinket. **2** *fam* (*dinero*) **se gastó la f. de dos mil dólares en ello,** he spent a mere two thousand dollars on it.

friolero,-a *adj* sensitive to the cold; **soy muy f.,** I really feel the cold.

frisar *vi* **f. con,** to approach, border on; **Armando frisa con los cuarenta,** Armando is getting on for forty.

friso *nm* **1** *Arquit* frieze. **2** (*zócalo*) skirting board.

frisón,-ona I *adj* Friesian. **II** *nm,f* (*persona*) Friesian. **III** *nm* (*idioma*) Friesian.

fritada *nf* fry, fried dish; *Culin* **f. de pescado,** dish of fried fish.

fritanga *nf pey* greasy food, greasy dish.

fritar *vtr Arg Col Salv* to fry.

frito,-a I *pp véase* **freír. II** *adj* **1** *Culin* fried. ■ **patatas fritas,** chips, *US* French fries. **2** *fam* exasperated fed up; **me tienes f. con tantas preguntas,** I'm sick to death of all your questions. **3** *fam* **quedarse f.,** to fall asleep. **III** *nm* fry, piece of fried food; **fritos de calamar,** fried squid *sing*.

frivolidad *nf* frivolity.

frívolo,-a *adj* frivolous.

fronda *nf* **1** (*espesura*) foliage. **2** (*de helecho*) frond.

frondosidad *nf* foliage, luxuriance.

frondoso,-a *adj* leafy, luxuriant.

frontal *adj* frontal; *Anat* **hueso f.,** frontal bone.

frontera *nf* **1** frontier, border. **2** *fig* limit, bounds *pl*.

fronterizo,-a *adj* frontier, border; **pueblos fronterizos,** border towns.

frontero,-a *adj* opposite.

frontis *nm*, **frontispicio** *nm* **1** *Arquit* (*fachada*) facade, front; (*frontón*) pediment. **2** *Impr* frontispiece.

frontón *nm* **1** *Dep* (*juego*) pelota. **2** *Dep* (*edificio*) pelota court. **3** *Arquit* pediment.

frotación *nf*, **frotamiento** *nm* rubbing.

frotar I *vtr* to rub. **II frotarse** *vr* to rub; **f. las manos,** to rub one's hands together.

froto *nm* rubbing.

fructífero,-a *adj* **1** *Bot* fruit-bearing. **2** *fig* fruitful.

fructificar *vi* **1** *Bot* to bear fruit, produce a crop. **2** *fig* to be fruitful.

fructuoso,-a *adj* fruitful.

frugal *adj* frugal.

frugalidad *nf* frugality, frugalness.

fruición *nf* pleasure, delight, enjoyment.

frunce *nm Cost* shir, shirring; **con frunces,** shirred, gathered.

fruncido,-a I *pp de* **fruncir. II** *nm Cost* shirring.

fruncir *vtr* **1** *Cost* to gather. **2 f. el ceño,** to frown, knit one's brow. **3** *(labios)* to purse, pucker.

fruslería *nf* **1** trinket. **2** *fam fig* trifle.

frustración *nf* frustration.

frustrado,-a I *pp de* **frustrar. II** *adj* frustrated; **el f. golpe de estado,** the attempted coup; **intento f.,** unsuccessful attempt.

frustrar I *vtr* *(intentos, esperanzas)* to frustrate, thwart; *(persona)* to disappoint. **II frustrarse** *vr* **1** *(proyectos, planes)* to fail, go awry. **2** *(persona)* to be frustrated *or* disappointed.

frustre *nm fam* frustration.

fruta *nf* **1** fruit. ■ **f. del tiempo,** fresh fruit; **f. escarchada,** candied fruit; **f. prohibida,** forbidden fruit; **f. seca,** dried fruit. **2** *fig* fruit, product, result.

frutal I *adj* fruit; **árbol f.,** fruit tree. **II** *nm* fruit tree.

frutería *nf* fruit shop.

frutero,-a I *adj* fruit; **mercado f.,** fruit market. **II** *nm, f* fruiterer. **III** *nm* fruit dish *or* bowl.

frutilla *nf Am Bot* variety of strawberry.

fruto *nm* **1** *Bot* fruit; **dar f.,** to bear fruit. ■ **frutos secos,** *(nueces, almendras)* nuts; *(pasas, higo paso)* dried fruit *sing*. **2** *fig* fruit, product, result; **dar f.,** to be fruitful; **no dar f.,** to be fruitless; **sacar f. de algo,** to profit from sth.

fu *interj* **ni f. ni fa,** so-so, average.

fucsia *nf Bot* fuchsia.

fuego *nm* **1** fire; **apagar el f.,** to put out the fire; **atizar el f.,** to poke the fire; **encender un f.,** to light a fire; **prender f. a algo,** to set fire to sth; *fig* **jugar con f.,** to play with fire; *fig* **poner las manos en el f. por,** to stake one's life on. ■ **f. de Santelmo,** Saint Elmo's fire; **f. fatuo,** will-o'-the-wisp, jack-o'-lantern; **fuegos artificiales,** fireworks; *fig* **prueba de f.,** trial by fire. **2** *(lumbre)* light; **¿me da f., por favor?,** have you got a light, please? **3** *(cocina)* burner, ring; **a f. lento,** on a low flame; *(al horno)* in a slow oven. **4** *Mil* fire; **¡f.!, fire!;** **hacer** *or* **romper f.,** to open fire; *fig* **estar entre dos fuegos,** to be caught between two fires. ■ **f. cruzado,** crossfire; **f. graneado,** sustained fire; **f. nutrido,** heavy fire. **5** *(ardor)* ardour *US* ardor, zeal; **atizar el f. de la discordia,** to stir up discord.

fuel *nm,* **fuel-Oil** *nm* fuel oil.

fuelle *nm* **1** bellows. **2** *Mús (de gaita)* bag.

fuente *nf* **1** *(manantial)* spring. **2** *(artificial)* fountain. **3** *(recipiente)* dish, serving dish. **4** *fig* source; **de f. desconocida,** from an unknown source; **fuentes fidedignas** *or* **bien informadas,** reliable sources.

fuer *nm fml* **a f. de,** as a; **a f. de caballero,** as a gentleman.

fuera[1] *adv* **1** outside, out; **desde f.,** from (the) outside; **¡f.!,** get out!; *Box* **f. de combate,** knocked out; **f. de duda,** beyond doubt; **f. de lo normal,** extraordinary, very unusual; **f. de lugar,** out of place; **f. de peligro,** out of danger; **f. de serie,** extraordinary; **la puerta de f.,** the outer door; **por f.,** on the outside; **quédate f.,** stay outside; **sal f.,** come out, go out; *fig* **estar f. de sí,** to be beside oneself. **2** away; **estar f.,** to be away; *(en el extranjero)* to be abroad; *Dep* **el equipo de f.,** the away team; *Dep* **jugar f.,** to play away. **3** *(excepto)* except for, apart from; **f. de esto,** apart from this.

fuera[2] I *subj imperf véase* **ir. II** *subj imperf véase* **ser.**

fuerano,-a *adj Am* foreign, alien.

fuero *nm* **1** code of laws. **2** *(privilegio)* privilege; *(exención)* exemption; **los fueros,** rights and privileges enjoyed by certain Spanish provinces. **3** *(jurisdicción)* jurisdiction. **4** *fig* **en tu f. interno,** deep down, in your heart of hearts.

fuerte I *adj* **1** strong; *fig* **palabras fuertes,** strong words; *fig* **está muy f. en matemáticas,** he's very good at mathematics. **2** *(intenso)* severe; **hacía un frío muy f.,** it was extremely cold; **padece dolores muy fuertes,** he suffers severe pain. **3** *(sonido)* loud; **la música está demasiado f.,** the music is too loud. **4** *(grande)* **el plato f.,** the main course; *fam fig* the most important event; **una comida f.,** a heavy meal; **una f. suma,** a large amount of money. **5** *(sujeto)* stiff; **este tornillo está muy f.,** this screw is stiff. **II** *nm* **1** *(fortificación)* fort. **2** *(punto fuerte)* forte, strong point; **su f. es la física,** she's very good at physics, physics is her strong point. **III** *adv* strongly; hard; **¡abrázame f.!,** hold me tight!; **comer f.,** to eat a lot; **¡habla más f.!,** speak up!; **¡pégalo f.!,** hit it hard.

fuerza *nf* **1** strength, force; **no tengo fuerzas para andar más,** I haven't got the energy to walk any further; **sacar fuerzas de flaqueza,** to muster up one's courage; *fig* **a f. de,** by dint of, by force of; *fig* **las fuerzas vivas de la localidad,** the local authorities; *fig* **por la f. de la costumbre,** by force of habit. ■ **f. de voluntad,** willpower; **f. mayor,** force majeure. **2** *Fís* force. ■ **f. de gravedad,** force of gravity. **3** *Mil* force; ■ **Fuerzas Aéreas,** ≈ *GB* Royal Air Force; **Fuerzas Armadas,** Armed Forces. **4 a la f.,** *(obligación)* of necessity; *(violencia)* by force; **por f.,** of necessity.

fuese I *subj imperf véase* **ir. II** *subj imperf véase* **ser.**

fuete *nm Am* whip.

fuga *nf* **1** *(escapada)* flight, escape; **darse a la f.,** to take flight; **poner en f.,** to put to flight. ■ **f. de cerebros,** brain drain; **f. de divisas,** flight of capital. **2** *(pérdida)* leak. **3** *Mús* fugue.

fugacidad *nf* fleetingness.

fugarse *vr* to escape, flee; **f. de casa,** to run away from home; **se ha fugado con su amante,** she has eloped with her lover.

fugaz *adj* fleeting, brief.

fugitivo,-a I *adj* **1** *(en fuga)* fleeing. **2** *fig (efímero)* ephemeral, fleeting. **II** *nm, f* fugitive, runaway.

fui I *pt indef véase* **ir. II** *pt indef véase* **ser.**

ful I *adj fam (falso)* bogus, phoney; **policía f.,** bogus policeman. **II** *nf arg (mierda)* shit.

fulano,-a I *nm, f* so-and-so; *(hombre)* what's his name; *(mujer)* what's her name; **Doña Fulana de tal,** Mrs So-and-so; **f., mengano y zutano,** Tom, Dick and Harry. **2** *fam pey* fellow, guy. **II** *nf pey* whore, tart. ■ **casa de fulanas,** brothel.

fular *nm* foulard, scarf.

fulcro *nm Téc* fulcrum.

fulero,-a *fam* **I** *adj* cheating, crooked. **II** *nm, f* cheater.

fúlgido,-a *adj lit* shining, glowing, bright.

fulgor *nm lit* **1** *(resplandor)* brilliance, glow. **2** *(esplendor)* splendour, *US* splendor.

fulgurante *adj* **1** *(que brilla)* brilliant, shining. **2** *fig* magnificent, stunning.

fulgurar *vi* to shine, glow.

fullería *nf* cheating; *Naipes* cardsharping; **hacer fullerías,** to cheat.

fullero,-a I *adj* cheating. **II** *nm, f Naipes* cheat, card-sharper.

fulmar *nm Orn* fulmar.

fulminación *nf* fulmination.

fulminado,-a I *pp de* **fulminar. II** *adj* struck by lightning.

fulminante I *adj* **1** fulminating. **2** *fig* staggering; **mirada f.,** withering look. **II** *nm* fuse, detonator. ■ **cápsula f.,** percussion cap.

fulminar *vtr* **1** to strike with lightning. **2** *fig* to strike dead; **f. a algn con la mirada,** to look daggers at sb.

fumada *nf* puff (of smoke).

fumadero *nm pey* smoking den.

fumado,-a I *pp de* fumar. **II** *arg (drogas)* stoned.

fumador,-a I *adj* smoking. **II** *nm, f* smoker; **los no fumadores,** nonsmokers.

fumar I *vtr & vi* **1** to smoke; *(en letrero)* **no fumar,** no smoking. **2** *Am (dominar)* to outdo, swindle. **II fumarse** *vr* **1** to smoke; **f. un pitillo,** to smoke a cigarette. **2** *fam* **f. las clases,** to play truant *or US* hookie.

fumarel *nm Orn* tern. ■ **f. cariblanco,** whiskered tern; **f. común,** black tern.

fumeta *nmf arg (drogas)* dope fiend, pot-head.

fumigación *nf* fumigation.

fumigar *vtr* to fumigate.

fumista *nm* stove *or* heater repairman.

funámbulo,-a *nm, f* tightrope walker.

funche *nm Am Culin* maize porridge.

función *nf* **1** function; **en f. de,** according to. **2** *(cargo)* duties *pl*; **entrar en funciones,** to take up one's duties; **estar en funciones,** to be in office; **presidente en funciones,** acting president. **3** *Cin Teat* performance; **no hay f.,** no performance. ■ **f. benéfica,** charity performance; **f. de noche,** late performance; **f. de tarde,** matinée.

funcional *adj* functional.

funcionamiento *nm* functioning, working; **poner algo en f.,** to put sth into operation.

funcionar *vi* to function, work; **hacer f. una máquina,** to operate a machine; *(en letrero)* **no funciona,** out of order; *fam* **así no podemos f.,** we can't go on like that.

funcionario,-a *nm, f* civil servant, official; **f. público,** public official.

funda *nf* **1** *(flexible)* cover; **f. de almohada,** pillowcase. **2** *(rígida)* case. **3** *(de arma blanca)* sheath. **4** *arg (condón)* French letter.

fundación *nf* foundation.

fundado,-a I *pp de* fundar. **II** *adj* firm, well-founded, justified; **mal f.,** ill-founded.

fundador,-a *nm, f* founder.

fundamental *adj* fundamental.

fundamentar *vtr* **1** *fig* to base **(en,** on). **2** *Constr* to lay the foundations of.

fundamento *nm* **1** *(base)* basis, grounds; **sin f.,** unfounded. **2** *(seriedad)* seriousness; *(confianza)* reliability; **una persona de f.,** a reliable person. **3** **fundamentos,** *Constr* foundations.

fundar I *vtr* **1** *(crear)* to found; *(erigir)* to raise. **2** *(basar)* to base, found. **II fundarse** *vr* **1** to be founded; **la empresa se fundó en 1901,** the firm was founded in 1901. **2** *(teoría, afirmación)* to be based; *(persona)* to base oneself.

fundición *nf* **1** melting. **2** *(de metales)* smelting, casting. ■ **hierro de f.,** cast iron. **3** *(lugar)* foundry, smelting works *pl*. ■ **f. de acero,** steelworks *pl*.

fundido *nm Cin TV* fade-in, fade-out.

fundidor *nm* caster, smelter.

fundir I *vtr* **1** *(un sólido)* to melt. **2** *Metal* to found, cast; **f. hierro,** to smelt iron; **f. una estatua en bronce,** to cast a statue in bronze. **3** *Elec (bombilla)* to blow; *(plomos)* to blow. **4** *(unir)* to unite, join. **5** *Am (arruinar)* to ruin. **II fundirse** *vr* **1** *(derretirse)* to melt. **2** *Elec* to blow, burn out; **se han fundido los plomos,** the fuses have gone. **4** *(unirse)* to merge. **5** *Am (arruinarse)* to be ruined.

fúnebre *adj* **1** *(mortuorio)* funeral. **2** *(lúgubre)* mournful, lugubrious.

funeral I *adj* funeral. **II** *nm (tamb funerales)* **1** *(entierro)* funeral. **2** *(conmemoración)* memorial service.

funerala (a la) *loc adv* **1** *Mil* with reversed arms. **2** *fam* **ojo a la f.,** black eye.

funeraria *nf* undertaker's, *US* funeral parlor.

funerario,-a *adj* funerary, funeral.

funesto,-a *adj* ill-fated, fatal; **consecuencias funestas,** disastrous consequences.

fungicida I *adj* fungicidal. **II** *nm* fungicide.

fungir **1** *vi CAm Méx* to act **(de,** as). **2** *Cuba Méx PR (dárselas)* **f. de algo,** to pretend to be sth.

funicular *nm Ferroc* funicular (railway).

fuñir I *vtr PR RD Ven* to mess up. **II fuñirse** *vr Am (fastidiarse)* to get cross.

furcia *nf ofens* whore, tart.

furgón *nm* **1** *Aut* van, wagon, waggon. **2** *Ferroc* goods wagon, waggon, *US* boxcar. ■ **f. de cola,** guard's van.

furgoneta *nf* van.

furia *nf* fury, rage; **ponerse hecho una f.,** to become furious, fly into a rage.

furibundo,-a *adj* furious, enraged.

furioso,-a *adj* furious; **ponerse f.,** to get angry; **una furiosa tempestad,** a raging storm.

furor *nm* fury, rage; *fig* **hacer f.,** to be all the rage.

furriel *nm Mil* quartermaster.

furtivo,-a *adj* furtive, stealthy; **caza furtiva, pesca furtiva,** poaching; **cazador f., pescador f.,** poacher.

furúnculo *nm Med* boil.

fusa *nf Mús* demisemiquaver, *US* thirty-second note.

fuselaje *nm Av* fuselage.

fusible I *adj* fusible. **II** *nm* fuse.

fusil *nm* gun, rifle; **echarse el f. a la cara,** to aim one's rifle; **f. ametrallador,** automatic rifle.

fusilamiento *nm* shooting, execution.

fusilar *vtr* **1** *(ejecutar)* to shoot, execute. **2** *(plagiar)* to plagiarize.

fusilería *nf* **1** *(fusiles)* rifles *pl*; **descarga** *or* **fuego de f.,** fusillade. **2** *(fusileros)* fusiliers *pl*.

fusilero *nm* fusilier, rifleman.

fusión *nf* **1** *Fís (metales)* fusion, melting; *(hielo)* thawing, melting. ■ **punto de f.,** melting point. **2** *(de intereses, ideas)* fusion. **3** *Com* merger, amalgamation.

fusionar *vtr,* **fusionarse** *vr* **1** to fuse. **2** *Com* to merge.

fusta *nm* riding whip.

fustal *nm,* **fustán** *nm,* **fustaño** *nm Am* (cotton) petticoat *or* underskirt.

fuste *nm* **1** *Arquit* shaft. **2** *(importancia)* importance; **un hombre de f.,** a man of consequence.

fustigar *vtr* **1** *(caballo)* to whip, lash. **2** *fig* to reprimand sharply.

fútbol *nm Dep* football, soccer.

futbolero,-a *nm, f fam* football *or* soccer fan.

futbolín *nm* table football.

futbolista *nmf Dep* footballer, football *or* soccer player.

futbolístico,-a *adj* football, soccer; **encuentro f.,** football *or* soccer match.

futesa *nf fam* trifle.

fútil *adj* futile, trivial.

futilidad *nf* futility, triviality; **hablar de futilidades,** to talk about trivialities.

futriaco,-a *nm, f Col PR RD pey (hombre)* bloke, guy; *(mujer)* bird.

futurismo *nm* futurism.

futurista *I adj* futuristic. **II** *nmf* futurist.

futuro,-a I *adj* future. **II** *nm* **1** future; **en un f. próximo,** the near future. **2** *Ling* future. ■ **f. perfecto,** future perfect. **3** *(novio)* fiancé, intended. **III** *nf* fiancée, intended.

futurología *nf* futurology.

futurólogo,-a *nm, f* futurologist.

G

G, g *nf (la letra)* G, g.

g *abr de* **gramo(s)**, gram, gramme, grams, grammes, g.

g/ *Fin abr de* **giro,** giro.

gabacho,-a *pey* **I** *adj* French. **II** *nm, f* Frog, Froggy.

gabán *nm* overcoat.

gabardina *nf* **1** *(prenda)* raincoat. **2** *Tex* gabardine.

gabarra *nf Náut* barge, lighter.

gabela *nf* tax, duty.

Gaberones *n* Gaborone.

gabinete *nm* **1** *(despacho)* study; *Fís Quím* laboratory; *Med* **g. de consulta,** surgery; **g. de lectura,** reading-room. **2** *(en museo)* section, room; **el g. demonedas,** the coín section. **3** *Pol* cabinet; **g. fantasma,** shadow cabinet.

gablete *nm Arquit* gable, gable end.

Gabón *n* Gabon.

gabonés,-esa *adj & nm, f* Gabonese.

gacela *nf Zool* gazelle.

gaceta *nf* **1** *Prensa* gazette; *fam* **mentir más que la g.,** to lie like mad. **2** *(persona chismosa)* gossip, gossipmonger.

gacetilla *nf* **1** *Prensa* 'news in brief'. **2** *(persona chismosa)* gossip, gossipmonger.

gacetillero *nm Prensa* **1** editor of 'news in brief' column. **2** *fam* journalist.

gacha *nf* **1** *(masa blanda)* paste, mush. **2 gachas,** *Culin (papilla)* porridge *sing,* pap *sing;* **g. de avena,** oatmeal porridge *sing; fam fig* **hacerse unas g.,** to turn sentimental *or* mushy.

gachí *nf arg (mujer)* bird, chick.

gachó *nm arg* bloke, guy, geezer.

gacho,-a *adj* drooping, bent downward; **a gachas,** on all fours; **con la cabeza gacha,** with one's head bowed; *fig* **estar con las orejas gachas,** to have one's tail between one's legs.

gachón,-ona *adj fam* amusing, charming.

gachumbo *nm SAm* hard fruit shell used for making utensils, vessels, etc.

gaditano,-a **I** *adj of or* from Cadiz. **II** *nm, f* native *or* inhabitant of Cadiz.

gaélico,-a **I** *adj* Gaelic. **II** *nm (idioma)* Gaelic.

gafa *nf* **1** *(grapa)* clamp. **2 gafas,** glasses, spectacles. ■ **g. de sol,** sunglasses.

gafar *vtr* **1** *(agarrar)* to hook. **2** *fam* to put a jinx on, bring bad luck to.

gafe *adj & nm fam* **ser g.,** to be a jinx.

gafete *nm Cost* hook and eye.

gafudo,-a *fam* **I** *adj* four-eyed. **II** *nm, f* four-eyes.

gag *nm Cin Teat* gag, comic situation.

gaguear *vi Am* to stutter.

gaita *nf* **1** *Mús* bagpipe, bagpipes *pl; fam* **templar gaitas,** to smooth things out; *fam* **¡vaya una g.!,** what a drag! **2** *Méx fam fig (maula)* dead loss. **II** *nm, f Arg pey* Galician.

gaitero,-a **I** *nm, f Mús* piper. **II** *adj* **1** *(color)* gaudy, flashy. **2** *(persona)* buffoonish, clownish.

gajes *nmpl* **1** *(ingresos)* pay *sing,* perquisites. **2** *fam irón* **g. del oficio,** occupational hazards.

gajo *nm* **1** *(de uvas)* bunch; *(de frutas)* cluster. **2** *(de naranja, pomelo, etc)* segment. **3** *(rama desprendida)* torn-off branch. **4** *Am (barbilla)* chin. **5** *CAm (mechón)* lock of hair. **6** *Arg Bot (esqueje)* cutting.

gala *nf* **1** *(vestido)* full dress, best clothes, **de g.,** dressed up, *Mil* in full uniform, *(ciudad)* decked out **2** *(espectáculo)* gala. **3** *(lo más selecto)* cream, pride, **hacer g. de,** to glory in, **la g. de la sociedad,** the cream of society, **la g. del pueblo,** the pride of the village, **tener algo a g.,** to be proud of sth. **4** *Antill Méx (obsequio)* gift, tip **5 galas,** finery *sing,* **lucir sus mejores g.,** to be dressed in all one's finery

galáctico,-a *adj Astron* galactic

galaico,-a *adj lit* Galician

galán *nm* **1** handsome young man, *hum* ladies' man **2** *(pretendiente)* suitor **3** *Teat* leading man, **segundo g.,** second lead **4 g. de noche,** *Bot* night jasmine **5 g. de noche,** *Mueb* valet.

galán,-ana *adj véase* **galano,-a**

galancete *nm* **1** *pey* foppish young man. **2** *Teat* young male lead

galano,-a *adj* smart, elegant.

galante *adj* gallant, chivalrous ♦ **galantemente** *adv* gallantly, politely

galanteador,-a *adj* flirtatious, wooing.

galantear *vtr (mujer)* to court, woo.

galanteo *nm* flirtation, wooing

galantería *nf* **1** *(caballerosidad)* gallantry, chivalry. **2** *(piropo)* compliment.

galanura *nf* gracefulness, elegance.

galápago *nm* **1** *Zool* turtle **2** *(lingote)* ingot, pig **3** *(silla de montar)* light saddle

Galápagos *npl* **las Islas G.,** Galapagos Islands

galardón *nm* prize

galardonado,-a **I** *pp de* **galardonar. II** *adj* prize-winning; **el ensayo g.,** the (prize-)winning essay **III** *nm, f* prizewinner

galardonar *vtr* to award a prize to

galaxia *nf Astron* galaxy

galbana *nf fam* torpor, laziness, apathy; **tener g.,** to feel lazy

galena *nf Min* lead sulphide.

galeno *nm fam* doctor.

galeón *nm Náut* galleon

galeote *nm* galley slave.

galera *nf* **1** *Náut* galley; **condenar a galeras,** to send to the galleys. **2** *(carro)* covered wagon. **3** *Impr* galley proof. **4** *CAm Méx* hut. shack **5** *Am* top hat

galerada *nf* **1** *(carro)* wagonload. **2** *Impr* galley proof.

galería *nf* **1** *Arquit* covered balcony **2** *(pinacoteca)* art gallery. **3** *(paso subterráneo)* underground passage, gallery **4** *Teat* gallery, gods *pl;* **hablar para la g.,** to play to the gallery **5** *(para cortinas)* curtain rail

galerín *nm Impr* small galley

galerna *nf,* **galerno** *nm Meteor* strong north-west wind on northern coast of Spain

galerón *nm Méx* large room, hall

Gales *n* **el país de G.,** Wales

galés,-esa **I** *adj* Welsh **II** *nm, f (hombre)* Welshman; *(mujer)* Welshwoman, **los galeses,** the Welsh **III** *nm (idioma)* Welsh

galga *nf* boulder, large stone

galgo *nm Zool* greyhound, **¡échale un g.!,** you'll be lucky!

galguear *vtr Am* to crave; *(deseos)* to have a craving for

Galia *n Hist* Gaul

gálibo *nm Téc* gauge.

Galicia *n* Galicia

galicismo *nm Ling* gallicism

gálico,-a *adj* Gallic, French

Galilea *n* Galilee

galileo,-a *adj & nm,f* Galilean.

galimatías *nm inv fam* gibberish, rigmarole

gallardear *vi (pavoneo)* to strut, *(presumir)* to swagger

gallardete *nm* pennant

gallardía *nf* 1 *(gentileza)* gracefulness, poise 2 *(arresto)* gallantry, boldness, dash

gallardo,-a *adj* 1 *(apuesto)* smart, elegant. 2 *(valeroso)* gallant, brave

gallear *vi* to swank, show off.

gallego,-a I *adj* 1 Galician. 2 *Am pey* Spanish **II** *nm, f* Galician, native of Galicia. 2 *Am pey* Spaniard **III** *nm (idioma)* Galician

gallera *nf (de gallos)* coop

galleta¹ *nf* 1 *Culin* biscuit 2 *Arg Chi* type of coarse bread 3 *Min* type of anthracite 4 *fam (cachete)* slap, smack

galleta² *nf SAm* maté bowl.

galletear *vtr Arg Urug* to sack, fire

gallina I *nf Orn* hen, chicken, **acostarse con las gallinas,** to go to bed very early, **jugar a la g. ciega,** to play blind man's buff, *fig* **como g. en corral ajeno,** like a fish out of water, *fig* **matar la g. de los huevos de oro,** to kill the goose that lays the golden eggs ■ **g. clueca,** broody hen, **g. de agua,** coot, **g. de Guinea,** guinea fowl; **g. de mar,** gurnard **II** *nmf fam* coward, chicken

gallinero *nm* 1 henhouse, hen run 2 *Teat* **el g.,** the gods *pl* 3 *fam fig* bedlam, madhouse

gallineta *nf Orn* coot.

gallito *nm fam fig (presumido)* cock of the walk, *(peleón)* bully

gallo *nm* 1 *Orn* cock, rooster, *fig* **alzar el g.,** to be high and mighty; *fig* **otro g. me cantara,** things would have turned out differently; *fig* **tener mucho g.,** to be very cocky; *fam fig* **en menos que un canto de g.,** before you could say Jack Robinson. ■ **g. de pelea,** fighting cock, gamecock; **g. silvestre,** caper-caillie, woodgrouse 2 *(pez de San Pedro)* John Dory, *(pez plano)* megrim, sail-fluke 3 *fam (persona mandona)* bully 4 *Mús* off-key note, squeak. 5 *Am* brave fellow. 6 *Méx* second-hand item. 7 *Méx* street serenade. 8 *Box* **peso g.,** bantamweight

gallote,-a *adj CR Méx* cocky.

galo,-a I *Hist adj* Gallic. **II** *nm,f* Gaul

galocha *nf* type of clog

galón¹ *nm* 1 *(cinta)* braid 2 *Mil* stripe, chevron

galón² *nm (medida)* gallon, *GB* 4.55 litres, *US* 3.79 litres.

galopada *nf Equit* gallop

galopante *adj* 1 *Equit* galloping 2 *fig (inflación etc)* galloping, escalating; *Med* **tisis g.,** galloping consumption.

galopar *vi Equit* to gallop.

galope *nm Equit* gallop; **a g., de g.,** at a gallop, fig very quickly, **llegó a g.,** he galloped up, **a g. tendido,** at full gallop ■ **medio g.,** canter

golopin *nm* 1 *(golfillo)* urchin, ragamuffin 2 *(bribón)* rogue

galpón *nm SAm* large shack

galvánico,-a *adj Fís* galvanic

galvanismo *nm Fís* galvanism.

galvanizado,-a I *pp de* **galvanizar. II** *adj* 1 *Fís* galvanized, electroplated. 2 *fig* galvanized. **III** *nm Fís* electroplating

galvanizar *vtr* 1 *Fís* to galvanize, electroplate. 2 *fig* to galvanize.

galvanómetro *nm Fís* galvanometer.

gama¹ *nf* 1 *Mús (escala)* scale. 2 *fig (gradación)* range, gamut, scale; **toda la g. colores,** the whole range of colours.

gama² *nf Zool* doe.

gamba¹ *nf Zool* prawn.

gamba² *nf arg* 1 *(pierna)* leg. 2 *(cien pesetas)* hundred-peseta note.

gamberrada *nf* act of hooliganism, **hacer una g.,** to do some mischief.

gamberrismo *nm* hooliganism, vandalism.

gamberro,-a I *adj* loutish, ill-bred. **II** *nm,f* hooligan, lout.

gambeta *nf* 1 *(en danza)* cross step. 2 *Equit* curvet, prance. 3 *Am Ftb* dodge, dribble. 4 *Arg Bol Urug (esguince)* dodge. 5 *Arg Urug fig (evasiva)* excuse.

gambetear *vi* 1 *(danzar)* to cross-step. 2 *Equit* to curvet, prance.

gambeto,-a *adj CAm* with downward-pointing horns.

Gambia *n* (The) Gambia.

gambiano,-a *adj & nm,f* Gambian.

gambito *nm Ajedrez* gambit.

gamella *nf* feeding trough.

gameto *nm Biol* gamete.

gamma *nf (letra)* gamma; **rayos g.,** gamma rays.

gamo *nm Zool* fallow deer.

gamonal *nm Am* cacique.

gamonalismo *nm Am* caciquism.

gamuza *nf* 1 *Zool* chamois. 2 *(trapo)* chamois *or* shammy leather.

gana *nf* 1 *(deseo)* wish (**de,** for); **de buena g.,** willingly; **de mala g.,** reluctantly, begrudgingly; **lo que te venga en g.,** whatever you feel like; **tenerle ganas a algn,** to have it in for sb; *fam* **no me da la real g.,** I don't damned well feel like it. 2 **tener ganas de (hacer) algo,** to feel like (doing) sth; **tengo** *or* **siento ganas de llorar,** I feel like crying; *fam* **tener unas ganas locas de hacer algo,** to be longing to do sth. 3 **entrarle a uno ganas de hacer algo,** to feel an urge to do sth; **me entran ganas de pegarle,** I feel like hitting her. 4 **quedarse con las ganas,** not to manage; **se quedó con las ganas de ver el Museo del Prado,** he didn't manage to see the Prado Museum. 5 *(apetito)* appetite; *(hambre)* hunger; **comer con ganas,** to eat heartily.

ganadería *nf* 1 *(crianza de ganado)* stockbreeding. 2 *(rancho)* stock farm, cattle ranch. 3 *(conjunto de ganado)* cattle; **la g. extremeña,** the livestock of Extremadura. 4 *(raza)* breed *or* strain of cattle.

ganadero,-a I *adj* relating to livestock, cattle; **enfermedad ganadera,** cattle disease. **II** *nm, f* stockbreeder, cattle raiser.

ganado,-a I *pp de* **ganar. II** *nm* 1 stock, livestock; *(vacas)* cattle; *(ovejas)* flock. ■ **g. caballar,** horses *pl*; **g. de cerda,** pigs *pl*; **g mayor/menor,** large/small livestock; **g. vacuno,** cattle. 2 *fam fig (gente)* crowd.

ganador,-a I *adj* winning. **II** *nm,f* winner.

ganancia *nf* 1 profit, gain; *Com* **g. líquida,** net profit; *Com* **margen de g.,** profit margin. 2 *Chi Guat Méx (propina)* tip. 3 **ganancias,** earnings.

ganancial *adj Com* relating to profits or earnings; *Jur* **bienes gananciales,** joint property.

ganancioso,-a *adj* profitable, lucrative; **salir g.,** to come out on top.

ganapán *nm* 1 *(recadero)* messenger; *(factótum)* odd-jobber; *fam (burro de carga)* dogsbody. 2 *fig (hombre tosco)* lout.

ganar I *vtr* 1 *(sueldo)* to earn; **gana mil pesetas la hora,** he earns one thousand pesetas an hour; **g. peso,** to gain

weight; *fig* **no g. para disgustos,** to have fate against one.
2 *(victoria)* to win; **ganamos el concurso/partido,** we
won the contest/match. **3** *(conquistar)* to capture; **después
de una dura lucha ganaron la ciudad,** after a hard battle
they captured the city. **4** *(alcanzar)* to reach; **finalmente
ganó la frontera,** he finally got to the border. **5** *(aventajar)*
to beat; **le gana en bondad,** he's much kinder than her; **le
gana en inteligencia,** she's much more intelligent than
him. **II** *vi* **1** *(prosperar)* to thrive, do well; **ganamos con el
cambio,** we gained with the change; *fig* **llevar las de g.,** to
hold the winning cards. **2** *(mejorar)* to improve; **gana en
destreza cada día,** he gets more skilful every day; **has
ganado mucho con este corte de pelo,** you look much
better with this new hairstyle. **3 salir ganando (en algo),**
to come out on top (in sth). **III ganarse** *vr* **1** to earn; **g. el
pan** *or* **los garbanzos,** to earn one's daily bread. **2**
(merecer) to deserve; **se lo ha ganado,** he deserves it; *fam*
¡te la vas a ganar!, you're going to get it!

ganchillo *nm* **1** *(aguja)* crochet hook. **2** *(labor)* crochet
work; **hacer g.,** to crochet.

gancho *nm* **1** *(gen)* hook; *(para ropa)* peg; **g. de
carnicero,** butcher's hook; *fam fig* **echar el g. a algn,** to
hook sb. **2** *(cayado)* shepherd's crook. **3** *fam fig (gracia,
atractivo)* attractiveness, charm, sex appeal. **4** *fam fig
(cómplice de un timador)* enticer, decoy. **5** *Am (horquilla)*
hairpin. **6** *Arg Guat (protección)* protection, help.

ganchudo,-a *adj* hook-shaped.

gandul,-a **I** *adj* lazy, bone idle. **II** *nm, f* idler, good-for-
nothing.

gandulear *vi* to idle, slack, loaf around.

gandulería *nf* idling, slacking.

ganga[1] *nf* **1** *Orn* sandgrouse. **2** *(algo barato)* bargain, good
buy; **precios de g.,** bargain prices. **3** *(momio)* cinch, gift;
(empleo) cushy job.

ganga[2] *nf Min* gang, gangue.

Ganges *n* Ganges.

ganglio *nm Med* ganglion.

gangoso,-a *adj* nasal, twanging.

gangrena *nf Med* gangrene.

gangrenarse *vr Med* to become gangrenous.

gangrenoso,-a *adj Med* gangrenous.

gángster *nm (pl* **gángsters)** gangster.

ganguear *vi* to speak with a twang.

gangueo *nm* nasal accent, twang.

gansada *nf fam* silly thing to say *or* do; **hasta de tus
gansadas,** enough of your antics *or* nonsense.

gansear *vi* to do *or* say silly things.

ganso,-a **I** *nm,f* **1** *Orn* goose; *(macho)* gander; *Mil* **paso de
g.,** goose-step. ■ **g. bravo,** wild goose. **2** *fam* dolt, idiot;
hacer el g., to act the goat. **II** *adj* sluggish, lazy, indolent.

ganzúa *nf* **1** *(garfio)* picklock. **2** *(ladrón)* burglar. **3**
(sonsacador) prying person, wheedler.

gañón *nm* farmhand.

gañido,-a **I** *pp de* **gañir.** **II** *nm* yelp.

gañir *vi* to yelp.

gañote *nm fam* throat, gullet; **de g.,** free.

garabatear *vtr & vi* to scrawl, scribble.

garabato *nm* **1** *(gancho)* hook. **2** *Am Agr* pitchfork. **3**
garabatos, scrawl *sing.*

garaje *nm* garage.

garambaina *nf* **1** cheap finery, frippery. **2 garambainas,**
fam foolery *sing,* nonsense *sing.*

garandumba *nf SAm* **1** *Náut* large raft. **2** *(mujer)* large
heavy woman.

garante *Fin* **I** *adj* acting as guarantor. **II** *nmf* guarantor.

garantía *nf* **I** guarantee, warranty; **bajo g.,** under
guarantee; **certificado de g.,** guarantee. **2** *Jur (fianza)*
bond, security.

garantizado,-a **I** *pp de* **garantizar.** **II** *adj* guaranteed,
secured.

garantizar *vtr* **1** *(cosa)* to guarantee; *(a persona)* to assure.
2 *(responder de)* to vouch for.

garañón *nm Zool* **1** stud jackass. **2** *Am* stallion.

garapiña *nf* **1** *Culin* sugar coating, icing. **2** *Am* iced
pineapple drink.

garapiñar *vtr Culin* to coat with sugar; *(fruta)* to candy;
almendra garapiñada, sugared almond.

garbanzo *nm Bot* chickpea; *fam fig* **en toda tierra de
garbanzos,** everywhere; *fam fig* **ganarse los garbanzos,**
to earn one's bread and butter; *fam fig* **g. negro,** black
sheep.

garbearse *vr fam* to take a stroll.

garbeo *nm fam (paseo)* stroll; *(viaje)* trip; **darse un g.,** to
go for a stroll.

garbo *nm* **1** *(airosidad al andar)* poise, jauntiness. **2**
(gracia) grace, stylishness. **3** *fig (generosidad)*
generosity, unselfishness.

garboso,-a *adj* **1** graceful, stylish. **2** *fig* generous.

garceta *nf Orn* **g. común,** little egret.

gardenia *nf Bot* gardenia.

garduña *nf Zool* marten.

garduño,-a **I** *adj* thieving. **II** *nm, f* sneak thief.

garete *nm Náut & fig* **ir** *or* **irse al g.,** to go adrift.

garfio *nm* hook, grapple.

gargajear *vi* to clear one's throat noisily, hawk, spit.

gargajo *nm* spit, phlegm.

garganta *nf* **1** *Anat* throat; **dolor de g.,** sore throat; *fam fig*
le tengo atravesado en la g., he sticks in my gullet; *fig* **se
me hizo n nudo en la g.,** I got a lump in my throat. **2** *(voz)*
voice; **tener buena g.,** to have a good singing voice. **3**
Anat (del pie) instep. **4** *(desfiladero)* narrow pass, gorge.
5 *Arquit (de columna)* neck.

gargantilla *nf* short necklace.

gárgaras *nfpl* **1** gargles, gargling *sing;* **hacer g.,** to gargle;
fam **mandarle a algn a hacer g.,** to tell sb to get lost; *fam*
¡vete a hacer g.!, get lost! **2** *Am (licor)* gargling solution
sing.

gargarismo *nm* **1** *acción* gargle. **2** *(líquido)* gargling
solution.

gargarizar *vi* to gargle.

gárgola *nf Arquit* gargoyle.

garguero *nm,* **gargüero** *nm fam* throat.

garita *nf* **1** *(caseta)* box, cabin, hut; *Mil* **g. de centinela,**
sentry box. **2** *(portería)* porter's lodge.

garito *nm* gambling den, gaming house.

garlar *vi* to chatter, prattle.

garlito *nm* **1** *(red)* fish trap. **2** *fig (celada)* trap; **coger a algn
en el g.,** to catch sb in the act, catch sb red-handed.

garlopa *nf Carp* jack plane.

garnacha[1] *nf* **1** *(uva)* sweet reddish-black grape. **2** *(vino)*
wine made from this grape.

garnacha[2] *nf Méx* tortilla containing meat, beans and
chilli.

Garona *n* Garonne.

garra *nf* **1** *Zool* claw; *(de ave)* talon; *fam pey (de persona)*
hand, paw; *fig* **caer en las garras de algn,** to fall into sb's
clutches; *fig* **echar la g. a algn,** to lay (one's) hands on sb.
2 *fig (fuerza)* force, power; **tener g.,** to be compelling,
have character; **una comedia sin g.,** a play lacking bite. **3**
Téc claw, hook. **4** *Am* piece of old leather. **5 garras,**
(harapos) rags, tatters. **6 garras,** *Méx* muscular strength
sing.

garrafa *nf* **1** carafe. **2** *Arg (de gas)* cylinder.

garrafal *adj* monumental, colossal; **un error g.,** a terrible
blunder; **una mentira g.,** a whopping lie.

garrafón *nm* demijohn, large carafe.

garrapata *nf Ent* tick.

garrapatear *vi véase* **garabatear.**

garrapato *nm véase* **garabato.**

garrapatoso,-a *adj* scrawled, scribbled.

garrapiñar *vtr véase* **garapiñar.**

garrear *Arg* **I** *vi* to sponge. **II** *vtr (robar)* to steal.

garrido,-a *adj* **1** handsome; **una moza garrida,** a pretty young woman. **2** *(elegante)* smart.

garrocha *nf* goad stick; *Taur* pike, lance.

garrochazo *nm* jab from a goad stick, pike thurst.

garrotazo *nm* cudgel blow.

garrote *nm* **1** *(palo grueso)* club, cudgel. **2** *Jur* garrotte; **dar g. a algn,** to garrotte sb.

garrotillo *nm Med* croup.

garrucha *nf* pulley.

garrulería *nf* garrulity.

gárrulo,-a *adj* **1** *(ave)* twittering. **2** *fig (persona)* garrulous.

garza *nf Orn* heron. ■ **g. real,** grey heron.

garzo,-a *adj* blue.

gas *nm* **1** gas; **agua con g.,** carbonated *or* fizzy water; *fam* **a todo g.,** flat out. ■ **g. butano,** butane gas; **g. de escape,** exhaust fumes *pl*; **g hilarante,** laughing gas; **g. lacrimógeno,** tear gas; **g. mostaza;** mustard gas; **g. natural,** natural gases, **g. pobre,** producer gas. **2** gas; flatulence *sing*; *Med* **tener g. en el estómago,** to suffer from flatulence.

gasa *nf* **1** *Tex* gauze. ■ **g. hidrófila,** surgical gauze. **2** *(pañal)* gauze nappy, *US* gauze diaper.

gaseosa *nf* lemonade, carbonated water.

gaseoso,-a *adj* gaseous, gassy.

gasificar *vtr* to gasify.

gasoducto *nm* gas pipeline.

gasógeno *nm* gazogene.

gasoil *nm*, **gasóleo** *nm* diesel oil.

gasolina *nf Aut* petrol, *US* gasoline; **poner g.,** to put petrol in the tank; **surtidor de g.,** petrol station.

gasolinera *nf* **1** *Aut* petrol *or US* gas station. **2** *(lancha)* motorboat.

gasómetro *nm Téc* gasometer.

gasta *nf Méx (de jabón)* small piece; *(de queso, jamón)* thin slice.

gastado,-a I *pp de* **gastar. II** *adj* **1** *(zapatos etc)* worn-out; *fig (frase)* meaningless; **ese tema está muy g.,** that's a well-worn subject; **este gobierno está ya muy g.,** this government is finished. **2** *(persona)* worn-out, burnt-out.

gastador,-a I *adj* spendthrift. **II** *nm,f* spendthrift, spender. **III** *nm Mil* sapper.

gastar I *vtr* **1** *(consumir) (dinero, tiempo)* to spend; *(gasolina, electricidad)* to use up, consume; **lo gastó todo en ropa,** he spent it all on clothes; **nuestro coche gasta mucha gasolina,** our car uses a lot of petrol. **2** *fig (malgastar)* to waste; **gasta el tiempo,** he wastes his time. **3** *(usar) (perfume, jabón)* to use; *(ropa)* to wear; **g. unos zapatos,** to wear a pair of shoes out; **¿qué número gasta?,** what size do you take? **4** *(tener)* to have; **g. bigote,** to have a moustache; **g. mal genio,** to have a bad temper. **5 g. una broma a algn,** to play a practical joke on sb; **le gastaron una broma pesada,** they played a dirty trick on him. **6 gastarlas,** *fam* to behave; **ya sé cómo las gastas,** I know what you get up to. **II gastarse** *vr* **1** *(zapatos etc)* to wear out. **2** *(gasolina etc)* to run out.

gasto *nm* **1** expense; **cubrir gastos,** to cover costs; **dinero para gastos,** pocket money. ■ **gastos de mantenimiento,** running *or* maintenance costs; **gastos de representación,** entertainment allowance *sing*; **gastos diarios,** daily expenses.

gástrico,-a *adj Med* gastric.

gastritis *nf Med* gastritis.

gastroenteritis *nf Med* gastroenteritis.

gastronomía *nf* gastronomy.

gastronómico,-a *adj* gastronomic, gastronomical.

gastrónomo,-a *nm,f* gourmet, gastronome.

gata *nf Zool* she-cat, cat.

gatas (a) *loc adv* on all fours; **andar a g.,** to crawl.

gatear *vi* **1** to crawl. **2** *(trepar)* to climb. **3** *Am fam* to flirt with women.

gatera *nf* **1** cat door, cat flap, cat hole. **2** *Náut* cat hole.

gatillazo *nm arg ofens* **pegar g.,** to go limp; *(por haber bebido)* to have brewer's droop.

gatillo *nm (de armas)* trigger; **apretar el g.,** to pull the trigger.

gato *nm* **1** *Zool* cat, tomcat; *fam fig* **aquí hay g. encerrado,** there's something fishy going on here; *fam fig* **buscarle tres pies al g.,** to complicate things unnecessarily; *fam fig* **dar g. por liebre,** to take sb in, trick sb; *fam fig* **ser g. viejo,** to be an old hand; *fam fig (personas)* **son cuatro gatos,** there are only a few of them; *prov* **g. escaldado del agua fría huye,** once bitten, twice shy. ■ **g. de algalia,** civet cat; **g. de Angora,** Angora cat; **g. montés,** wildcat; **g. siamés,** Siamese (cat). **2** *Aut Téc* jack. **3** *fam fig* native *or* inhabitant of Madrid.

gatuno,-a *adj* catlike, feline.

gatuperio *nm* **1** *(mezcla)* hotch-potch, mess, jumble. **2** *fig* web of intrigue, tangle.

gauchada *nf SAm* **1** typical gaucho action. **2** *(favor)* favour, *US* favor. **3** *(chiste)* story, joke.

gauchear *vi SAm* **1** to live as a gaucho. **2** *(errar)* to roam about, drift.

gaucho,-a I *adj* **1** *SAm* gaucho; *fig* coarse, rough. **2** *Am (lindo)* pleasant, nice. **3** *Arg Chi (astuto)* cunning, sly. **II** *nm,f* **1** *SAm* gaucho. **2** *Am Equit* good rider. **III** *nf* **1** *Arg (mujer hombruna)* masculine *or* butch woman. **2** *Arg (mujer de mala conducta)* lout.

gaudeamus *nm inv fam* party.

gaveta *nf* **1** *(cajón)* drawer. **2** *Am Aut (guantera)* glove compartment.

gavilán *nm Orn* sparrowhawk.

gavilla *nf* **1** *(de ramillas etc)* sheaf. **2** *fig pey* gang of thugs.

gavillero *nm Am* bully, lout.

gaviota *nf Orn* seagull, gull. ■ **g. argéntea,** herring gull; **g. cana,** common gull; **g. enana,** little gull; **g. reidora,** black-headed gull; **g. tridáctila,** kittiwake.

gay *adj inv & nm (pl gays)* gay, homosexual; **el movimiento g.,** the Gay Liberation Movement.

gayo,-a *adj lit* cheerful; **la gaya ciencia,** poetry, the art of poetry.

gazapo *nm* **1** *Zool* young rabbit. **2** *(error)* error, blunder.

gazmoñada *nf*, **gazmoñería** *nf* prudishness.

gazmoñero,-a *adj*, **gazmoño,-a** *adj* prudish.

gaznate *nm* gullet.

gazpacho *nm Culin* gazpacho.

gazuza *nf fam* hunger; **tener g.,** to be starving.

ge *nf* name of the letter G in Spanish.

géiser *nm (pl géiseres)* geyser.

geisha *nf* geisha.

gel *nm* gel. ■ **g. de baño,** shower gel, bubble bath.

gelatina *nf (ingrediente)* gelatin, gelatine; *Culin* jelly.

gelatinoso,-a *adj* gelatinous, jelly-like.

gélido,-a *adj lit* icy, icy cold.

gema *nf* **1** *Bot* bud, gemma. **2** *Min* gem.

gemelo,-a I *adj* & *nm*, *f* twin; **hermanos gemelos,** twins; *fig* **almas gemelas,** kindred spirits. **II gemelos** *nmpl* **1** *(de camisa)* cufflinks. **2** *(anteojos)* binoculars.

gemido,-a I *pp de* **gemir. II** *nm (quejido)* moan, groan; *(gimoteo)* whimper.

geminado,-a *adj* geminate.

Géminis *nm Astrol Astron* Gemini.

gemir *vi* to moan, groan; *(gimotear)* to whimper.

genciana *nf Bot* gentian.

gendarme *nm* gendarme.

gendarmería *nf* gendarmerie.

gene *nm Biol* gene.

genealogía *nf* genealogy.

genealógico,-a *adj* genealogical; **árbol g.,** family tree.

genealogista *nmf* genealogist.

generación *nf* generation; *Inform* **g. de lenguaje natural,** natural language generation.

generacional *adj* generation, generational; **la barrera g.,** the generation gap.

generador,-a I *adj* generating. **II** *nm Téc* generator.

general I *adj* general; **en** *or* **por lo g.,** in general, generally; **es una costumbre muy g.,** it is a very common custom. **II** *nm Mil Rel* general. ◆ **generalmente** *adv* generally.

generala *nf Mil* **tocar a g.,** to call to arms; **toque a g.,** call to arms.

generalato *nm Mil* **1** *(grado)* generalship. **2** *(conjunto de generales)* generals *pl*.

generalidad *nf* **1** generality, general statement. **2** *(mayoría)* majority.

generalísimo *nm* generalissimo, supreme commander.

Generalitat *nf Cat Val Pol* autonomous government.

generalización *nf* **1** generalization. **2** *(extensión)* spread, spreading.

generalizado,-a I *pp de* **generalizar. II** *adj* widespread, common.

generalizador,-a *adj* generalizing.

generalizar I *vtr* **1** to generalize. **2** *(extender)* to spread. **II generalizarse** *vr* to become widespread *or* common.

generar *vtr* to generate.

generativo,-a *adj* generative.

generatriz *nf Mat* generatrix.

genérico,-a *adj* generic.

género *nm* **1** *(clase)* kind, sort; **el g. humano,** mankind; **ese g. de vida no es para mí,** that sort of life is not for me. **2** *Arte Lit* genre. ■ **g. chico,** light opera; **g. dramático,** dramatic genre; **g. lírico,** opera. **3** *(mercancía)* article, piece of merchandise; **géneros de punto,** knitwear *sing*; **géneros de primera calidad,** quality goods. **4** *Ling* gender. **5** *Biol* genus.

generosidad *n* generosity, unselfishness.

generoso,-a *adj* **1** generous **(con, para, to),** splendid. **2** *(vinos)* rich, full-bodied.

Génesis *nm Rel* Genesis.

génesis *nf inv* genesis.

genético,-a I *adj* genetic. **II** *nf* genetics *sing*.

genial *adj* brilliant, inspired, exceptional; *fam* terrific.

genialidad *nf* **1** *(idea)* brilliant idea, stroke of genius. **2** *(acción)* eccentricity. **3** *(cualidad)* genius.

genio *nm* **1** *(carácter)* temperament; *(mal carácter)* temper; **es una persona de mucho g.,** he has a quick temper; **estar de mal g.,** to be in a bad mood; **tener mal g.,** to have a bad temper. **2** *(facultad)* genius; **Mozart fue un g.,** Mozart was a genius; *fam* **eres un g.,** you are brilliant. **3** *(espíritu)* spirit; **el g. español,** the Spanish spirit. **4** *(ser fantástico)* genie.

genital I *adj* genital. **II genitales** *nmpl* genitals.

genitivo *nm Ling* genitive.

geniudo *adj fam* bad-tempered.

Genl. *Mil abr de* **General,** General, Gen.

genocidio *nm* genocide.

genotipo *nm Biol* genotype.

Génova *n* Genoa.

genovés,-esa *adj* & *nm*, *f* Genoese, Genovese.

gente *nf* **1** *(gen)* people *pl*; **¡cuánta g.!,** what a crowd!; **había mucha g.,** there were a lot of people; **¡qué g.!,** what awful people! ■ **la g. bien,** the well-to-do; **g. de bien,** honest people; *fam fig* **g. gorda,** bigwigs; *fam* **g. menuda,** nippers, kids. **2** *(familia)* folks, people *pl*; **tengo a mi g. aquí de vacaciones,** my folks are here on holiday. **3** *(personal)* staff. **4** *Mil* troops. **5** *Am* respectable people.

gentil I *adj* **1** *(pagano)* pagan, heathen; *(no judío)* gentile. **2** *(apuesto)* charming. **3** *(amable)* kind. **II** *nmf* Gentile.

gentileza *nf* kindness; **esto es una g. de la casa,** this is on the house; *fml* **por g. de,** by courtesy of.

gentilhombre *nm arc* gentleman.

gentilicio *adj* & *nm Ling* gentile.

gentilidad *nf*, **gentilismo** *nm Rel* pagans *pl*.

gentío *nm* crowd; **¡qué g.!,** what a crowd!

gentuza *nf pey* rabble, riffraff.

genuflexión *nf* genuflexion.

genuino,-a *adj (puro)* genuine; *(verdadero)* authentic.

GEO *nmpl abr de* **Grupos Especiales de Operaciones,** ≈ Special Air Service, SAS.

geocéntrico,-a *adj* geocentric.

geodesia *nf* geodesy.

geofísico,-a I *adj* geophysical. **II** *nm*, *f* geophysicist. **III** *nf* geophysics *sing*.

geografía *nf* geography. ■ **g. física,** physical geography; **g. política,** political geography; **g. social,** social geography.

geográfico,-a *adj* geographic, geographical.

geógrafo,-a *nm*, *f* geographer.

geología *nf* geology.

geológico,-a *adj* geologic, geological.

geólogo,-a *nm*, *f* geologist.

geomagnético,-a *adj* geomagnetic.

geómetra *nmf* geometer, geometrician.

geometría *nmf* geometry. ■ **g. del espacio,** solid geometry; **g. descriptiva,** descriptive geometry.

geométrico,-a *adj* geometric, geometrical.

geomorfología *nf* geomorphology.

geopolítica *nf* geopolitics *sing*.

Georgia *n* Georgia.

Georgia del Sur *n* South Georgia.

geórgica *nf Lit* georgic.

geranio *nm Bot* geranium.

gerencia *nf* **1** *(actividad, cargo)* management. **2** *(despacho)* manager's *or* director's office.

gerente *nmf* manager, director.

geriatra *nmf Med* geriatrician, geriatrist.

geriatría *nf Med* geriatrics *sing*.

gerifalte *nm* **1** *Orn* gerfalcon, gyrfalcon. **2** *fig* boss; **vivir como un g.,** to live like a king.

germanía *nf* thieves' cant.

germánico,-a *adj* & *nm Ling* Germanic.

germanismo *nm* Germanism.

germanista *nmf* German specialist.

germano,-a I *adj* German, Germanic. **II** *nm*, *f* German.

germanooccidental *adj* & *nmf* West German.

germanooriental *adj & nmf* East German.

gérmen *nm* 1 *Biol* germ. ■ **g. de trigo,** wheatgerm. 2 *fig* seed, germ, origin.

germicida I *adj* germicidal. II *nm* germicide.

germinación *nf* germination.

germinal *adj* germinal.

germinar *vi* to geminate.

gerontología *nf* gerontology.

gerontólogo,-a *nm,f* gerontologist.

gerundense I *adj* of *or* from Gerona. II *nmf* native *or* inhabitant of Gerona.

gerundio *nm Ling* gerund.

gesta *nf arc* heroic exploit, gest, geste; *Lit* **cantar de g.,** chanson de geste.

gestación *nf* 1 *Biol* gestation. 2 *fig* **en g.,** in preparation, in the pipeline.

gestar I *vtr* to gestate. II **gestarse** *vr fig (proyecto)* to be under way *or* in the pipetine; *(sentimientos)* to grow; *(idea)* to develop.

gestatorio,-a *adj* **silla gestatoria,** gestatorial chair.

gesticulación *nf* gesticulation, gestures *pl*.

gesticular *vi* to gesticulate.

gestión *nf* 1 *(diligencia)* enquiry, search. 2 *(administración)* administration, management. 3 **gestiones,** *(negociaciones)* negotiations; *(medidas)* steps, measures.

gestionar *vtr* 1 *Fin* to take steps to acquire *or* obtain, conduct. 2 to negotiate; **están gestionando la entrada del país en la OTAN,** they are negotiating the country's entry into NATO.

gesto *nm* 1 *(mueca)* grimace, face; **hacer gestos,** to pull faces; **torcer el g.,** to look disappointed; **un g. de tristeza,** a sad face. 2 *(señal)* sign; **hizo un g. afirmativo con la cabeza,** he nodded his head in agreement; **tuvo un g. de delicadeza,** he made a gesture of kindness.

gestor,-a I *adj* managing; **actividades gestoras,** negotiations. II *nm,f* 1 ≈ solicitor. 2 manager.

gestoría *nf* 1 ≈ solicitor's office. 2 agency.

Ghana *n* Ghana.

ghanés,-esa *adj & nm,f* Ghanian, Ghanaian.

Ghates *n* Ghats.

giba *nf* hump, hunch.

gibar *vtr fam* to annoy; **lo hace para g.,** he does it deliberately.

giboso,-a *nm,f* humpback, hunchback.

Gibraltar *n* Gibraltar; **el peñón de G.,** the Rock of Gibraltar.

gibraltareño,-a I *adj* of *or* from Gibraltar. II *nm, f* Gibraltarian.

giennense I *adj* of *or* from Jaén. II *nmf* native *or* inhabitant of Jaén.

gigante *adj* giant, gigantic.

gigante,-a *nm,f (hombre)* giant; *(mujer)* giantess.

gigantesco,-a *adj* giant, gigantic, gigantesque.

gigantismo *nm Med* gigantism, giantism.

gigoló *nm* gigolo.

gijonés,-esa I *adj* of *or* from Gijón. II *nm, f* native *or* inhabitant of Gijón.

gili *nm*, **gilí** *nm arg ofens véase* **gilipolla.**

giliflautas *nm arg ofens véase* **gilipolla.**

gilipolla *nmf*, **gilipollas** *nmf ofens* bloody fool *or* idiot.

gilipollada *nf*, **gilipollez** *nf ofens* 1 *(dicho)* bullshit, rubbish. 2 *(hecho)* bloody stupid thing to do.

gimiente *adj* whimpering.

gimnasia *nf* gymnastics *pl*; *fam* **eso sería confundir la g. con la magnesia,** it's like chalk and cheese.

gimnasio *nm* gymnasium

gimnasta *nmf* gymnast.

gimnástico,-a *adj* gymnastic.

gimotear *vi* to whine, whimper.

gimoteo *nm* whining, whimpering.

Ginebra *n* Geneva.

ginebra *nf (bebida)* gin.

ginebrés,-esa *adj & nm, f,* **ginebrino,-a** *adj & nm, f* Genevan, Genevese.

ginecología *nf Med* gynaecology. *US* gynecology.

ginecológico,-a *adj Med* gynaecologic, gynaecological, *US* gynecologic, gynecological.

ginecólogo,-a *nm, f Med* gynaecologist, *US* gynecologist.

gingivitis. *nf Med* gingivitis.

gingko *nm Bot* ginkgo, gingko, maidenhair tree.

gira *nf* excursion, tour; *Teat* tour.

girado,-a I *pp de* **girar.** II *nm,f Fin* drawee.

girador,-a *nm,f Fin* drawer.

giralda *nf* weathercock.

girar I *vi* 1 *(dar vueltas)* to rotate, spin; **el dinero hace g. al mundo,** money makes the world go round. 2 *(torcer)* to turn; **al llegar a la esquina, gira a la derecha,** turn right at the corner. 3 *fig (versar)* to deal with; **la conversación giraba en torno a ti,** the conversation evolved around you. 4 *Fin (expedir)* to draw. II *vtr* 1 *(cambio sentido)* to turn; **g. la cabeza,** to turn one's head. 2 *Fin (giro postal)* to send, remit. 3 *Fin (cheque)* to draw; **g. contra,** to draw on; **g. en descubierto,** to overdraw.

girasol *nm Bot* sunflower.

giratorio,-a *adj* rotating, gyratory; **silla giratoria,** swivel chair.

giro[1] *nm* 1 *(vuelta)* turn, turning. 2 *(cariz)* turn, direction; **dar un nuevo g. a,** to put in a new light; **tomar un nuevo g.,** to change. 3 *(frase)* turn of phrase. 4 *Fin (giro)* **g. en descubierto,** overdraft; **g. telegráfico,** giro *or* money order. ■ **g. postal,** postal *or* money order.

giro[2] I *adj* 1 *Am (gallo)* with speckled yellow plumage. 2 *Arg Col Chi (gallo)* with speckled black and white plumage. 3 *Méx (persona)* confident. II *nm (fanfarronada)* blusterer, boaster, swaggerer.

girola *nf Arquit* ambulatory.

gitanada *nf fig* wheedling, cajolement.

gitanería *nf* 1 *véase* **gitanada.** 2 *(conjunto de gitanos)* gypsies *pl*, gipsies *pl*.

gitanesco,-a *adj* gypsy-like, gipsy-like.

gitano,-a I *adj* 1 gypsy, gipsy. II *nm,f* 1 gypsy, gipsy. 2 *fig (zalamero)* flatterer; *pey* wheedling, cajolement. 3 *fam (estafador)* fiddler, swindler. 4 *fam* vagrant.

glaciación *nf* glaciation.

glacial *adj* 1 glacial. 2 *fig* glacial, hostile; **una despedida g.,** an icy farewell.

glaciar *nm* glacier.

gladiador *nm Hist* gladiator.

gladiolo *nm*, **gladíolo** *nm Bot* gladiolus.

glande *nm Anat* glans penis.

glándula *nf Anat* gland.

glandular *adj* glandular.

glaseado,-a I *pp de* **glasear.** II *nm* glacé.

glasear *vtr Culin (pastel)* to glaze.

glauco,-a *adj fml* bluish-green, glaucous.

glaucoma *nm Med* glaucoma.

gleba *nf Hist* land; **siervo de la g.,** serf.

glicerina *nf Quím* glycerin, glycerine.

global *adj* global, comprehensive. ◆ **globalmente** *adv* globally, as a whole.

globo *nm* **1** balloon. ■ **g. aerostático,** hot air *or* gas balloon; **g. dirigible,** airship. **2** *(esfera)* globe, sphere. ■ **g. celeste,** globe; **g. terrestre** *or* **terráqueo,** globe. **3** *Anat* **g. ocular,** eyeball. **4** *(pantalla lámpara)* globe, glass lampshade. **5** *arg (condón)* French letter.

globular *adj* globular.

globulina *nf Biol* globulin.

glóbulo *nm* globle. ■ *Anat* **g. blanco/rojo,** white/red corpuscle.

gloria *nf* **1** *(fama)* honour, *US* honor, glory; **hacer g. de algo,** to boast about sth; *irón* **cubrirse de g.,** to make a fool of oneself. **2** *(persona famosa)* hero. **3** *Rel (canto)* Gloria; *(cielo)* heaven; *fam fig* **estar en la g.,** to be in seventh heaven. **4** *fam (cosa placentera)* delight; **dar g.,** to be a delight; *fam* **saber/oler a g.,** to taste/smell divine.

gloriado *nm Am* punch made from very strong liquor.

gloriarse *vr* **1** *(jactarse)* to boast, show off. **2** *(complacerse)* to take pride (**de,** in).

glorieta *nf* **1** *(en un jardín)* bower, arbour, *US* arbor. **2** *(plazoleta)* small square. **3** *(encrucijada de calles)* roundabout, *US* traffic circle.

glorificación *nf* glorification.

glorificar I *vtr* to glorify, exalt. **II glorificarse** *vr véase* **gloriarse.**

glorioso,-a *adj* glorious.

glosa *nf* **1** gloss. **2** *Lit (comentario)* notes *pl*, commentary.

glosar *vtr* **1** *(explicar)* to gloss; *(texto)* to interpret. **2** *(comentar)* to comment on, speak about.

glosario *nm* glossary.

glotis *nf Anat* glottis.

glotón,-ona I *adj* greedy gluttonous. **II** *nm,f* glutton. **III** *nm Zool* glutton, wolverine.

glotonear *vi* to eat greedily.

glotonería *nf* gluttony, greed.

glucemia *nf Med* glycemia.

glucosa *nf Quím* glucose.

gluten *nm* gluten.

glúteo,-a I *adj Anat* gluteal. **II** *nm* gluteus.

gnomo *nm* gnome.

gobernable *adj* governable.

gobernación *nf* governing, government; *Pol Hist* **Ministerio de la Gobernación,** ≈ *GB* Home Office, *US* Department of the Interior.

gobernador,-a I *adj* governing; **la junta gobernadora,** the governing board. **II** *nm, f* governor; **g. civil,** provincial governor.

gobernanta *nf* **1** manageress; *fam* bossy woman. **2** *Arg* governess.

gobernante I *adj* ruling; **la clase g.,** the ruling class. **II** *nmf* ruler, leader.

gobernar I *vtr* **1** *(gen)*; to govern; *(un país)* to govern, rule; *(una familia)* to run; *(un negocio)* to handle, run. **2** *(guiar)* to guide; *Náut* to steer. **3** *(dominar)* to dominate, boss about. **4** *Arg (castigar)* to punish. **II** *vi Náut* to steer. **III gobernarse** *vr (guiarse)* to manage one's affairs.

gobierno *nm* **1** *Pol* government; *(edificio)* Government House *or* building. **2** *(mando)* command, running, handling; **el g. de la casa,** the running of the household; **el g. de los asuntos,** the handling of affairs. **3** *Náut* steering. **4** *Náut (timón)* rudder. **5** *(locuciones)* **para tu g.,** for your own information; **servir de g.,** to serve as a guideline.

gobio *nm (pez)* gudgeon.

goce *nm* pleasure, enjoyment.

godo,-a I *adj Hist* Gothic. **II** *nm,f* **1** *Hist* Goth. **2** *SAm pey* Spaniard.

gofio *nm Am Can* roasted maize meal.

gol *nm Dep* goal; **g. cantado,** open goal, sitter; **g. fantasma,** controversial goal; **tiro a g.,** shot; *fam fig* **meter un g. a algn,** to pull a fast one on sb.

goleada *nf* feast of goals; **ganar por g.,** to hammer the opposition.

goleador,-a *nm,f* scorer; **el máximo g.,** the top scorer.

golear *vtr Dep* to hammer; **el Torpedo goleó 6-1 al Olympic,** Torpedo hammered Olympic 6-1.

goleta *nf Náut* schooner.

golf *nm Dep (deporte)* golf; *(terreno)* golf course; **club de g.,** golf club; **palo de g.,** golf club.

golfante *adj fam* rascal.

golfear *vi* **1** *(vagabundear)* to loaf around. **2** *(hacer gamberradas)* to get up to no good.

golfillo,-a *nm,f* street urchin.

golfista *nmf* golfer.

golfo,-a¹ I *nm, f* good-for-nothing, scoundrel, street urchin. **II** *nf fam pey* slut, tart, hussy.

golfo² *nm Geog* gulf, large bay; **g. de Bengala,** Bay of Bengal; **g. de Botnia,** Gulf of Bothnia; **g. de Guinea,** Gulf of Guinea; **g. de León,** Gulf of Lions; **g. de Méjico,** Gulf of Mexico; **g. de Vizcaya,** Bay of Biscay; **g. Pérsico,** Persian Gulf.

gollete *nm* **1** *Anat* throat. **2** *(de botella)* neck.

golondrina *nf* **1** *Orn* swallow. **2** *Náut* motorboat.

golondrino *nm* **1** *Orn* young swallow. **2** *fig (vagabundo)* tramp. **3** *Med* boil in the armpit. **4** *Mil* deserter.

golosear *vi* to eat sweets *or US* candy.

golosina *nf* **1** *(caramelos)* sweet, *US* candy. **2** *fig (cosa agradable)* treat.

golosinear *vi* to eat sweets *or US* candy.

goloso,-a *adj* **1** ser (un) g., to have a sweet tooth; *pey* to be greedy. **2** *fig* mouthwatering, inviting.

golpazo *nm* heavy blow.

golpe *nm* **1** blow, knock; *(puñetazo)* punch; **a golpes,** by force; **le dio un g.,** he hit him. **2** *Aut* bump, bang, collision. **3** *(desgracia)* blow, misfortune; **perder el trabajo fue un duro g.,** losing his job was a great blow. **4** *(gracia)* witticism, sally; **la película tiene unos golpes muy buenos,** the film has some very good bits in it. **5** *fig (sorpresa)* shock. **6** *Box* punch; *Box & fig* **g. bajo,** punch below the belt; *Ftb* **g. franco,** free kick. **7** *(atraco)* hold-up, robbery; *fam* **dar un g.,** to do a job. **8** *(locuciones)* **de g., de g. y porrazo,** all of a sudden; **de un g.,** in one go; **errar el g.,** to miss; **g. de efecto,** coup de théatre; **g. de estado,** coup d'état; **g. de fortuna,** stroke of luck; **g. de gracia,** coup de grâce; **g. de mano,** surprise attack; **g. de vista,** quick glance; **no dar ni g.,** not to lift a finger; **parar el g.,** to soften the blow. **9** *Méx (martillo)* sledgehammer.

golpear *vtr (gen)* to hit; *(cosas)* to knock, beat; *(personas)* to thump, hit, punch; *(una puerta, cabeza)* to bang.

golpetear *vtr & vi* to bang; **la puerta golpeteaba con el viento,** the door was banging in the wind.

golpeteo *nm* banging, hammering.

golpismo *nm Pol* tendency to coups d'état.

golpista I *nmf* person involved in a coup d'état. **II** *adj* relating to coups d'état.

golpiza *nf Ecuad Méx* thrashing.

goma *nf* **1** rubber, gum; *(caucho)* rubber; **g. arábiga,** gum arabic; **g. de pegar,** glue, gum; **suelas de g.,** rabber soles. **2** *(banda elástica)* rubber band. **3** **g. de borrar,** rubber, *US* eraser; **g. de mascar,** chewing gum. **4** *arg (preservativo)* rubber. **5** *CAm* hangover

gomaespuma *nf* foam rubber.

gomal *nm Am Agr* rubber plantation.

gomero *nm* **1** *Am Bot* gum tree. **2** *Am (recolector)* rubber collector. **3** *chi Méx* pot of glue.

gomina *nf Peluq* hair cream.

gomoso,-a I *adj* sticky. **II** *nm pey* fop.

gónada *nf Anat* gonad.

góndola *nf* **1** gondola **2** *(carruaje)* carriage.

gondolero,-a *nm,f* gondolier.

gong *nm*, **gongo** *nm gong*.

gongorino,-a *adj Lit* Gongoristic.

gongorismo *nm Lit* Gongorism.

gongorista *nmf Lit* Gongorist.

gonococo *nm Biol* gonococcus.

gonorrea *nf Med* gonorrhoea, *US* gonorrhea.

gordiano,-a *adj* nudo g., Gordian knot.

gordinflón,-ona *fam* **I** *adj* chubby, fat. **II** *nm, f* chubby person, fatty.

gordo,-a I *adj* **1** *(carnoso)* fat; **ponerse g.,** to get fat. **2** *(volumen)* thick; **el dedo g.,** *(mano)* the thumb; *(pie)* the big toe. **3** *(importante)* big; **algo g.,** something serious *or* important; **¡qué mentira tan gorda!,** what a big lie!; *fig* **el premio g.,** the first prize; *fig* **pez g.,** big shot. **4** *(locuciones)* **estar** *or* **quedarse sin g.,** to be broke; **hacer la vista gorda,** to turn a blind eye; **me cae g.,** I can't stand him; **se armó la gorda,** trouble broke out. **II** *nm, f* fat person; *fam* fatty. **III** *nm* **1** *(tocino)* fat. **2** *(lotería)* **el g.,** first prize. **3** *Méx* maize tortilla.

gordura *nf* fatness.

gorgorito *nm* trill.

gorgotear *vi* to gurgle.

gorgoteo *nm* gurgle, gurgling.

gorguera *nf* ruff; *(de un armadura)* gorget.

gorigori *nm fam* dirge, funeral chant; *hum* **cantar el g. a algn,** to bury sb.

gorila *nm* **1** *Zool* gorilla. **2** *fam fig (guardaespaldas)* gorilla, henchman, bodyguard.

gorjear I *vi* to chirp, twitter. **II gorjearse** *vr* **1** *(bebé)* to crow, gurgle. **2** *Am (burlarse)* **g. de algn,** to laugh at sb's expense.

gorjeo *nm* **1** chirping, twittering. **2** *(bebé)* crowing, gurgling.

gorra *nf* cap; *(con visera)* peaked cap; *fam* **de g.,** free; **comer de g.,** to cadge a meal; **vivir de g.,** to sponge, cadge, be a sponger.

gorrear *vi véase* **gorronear.**

gorrero,-a *nm,f véase* **gorrón,-ona.**

gorrino,-a I *adj* dirty, piglike. **II** *nm,f* pig.

gorrión,-ona I *nm, f Orn* sparrow; **g. común,** house sparrow; **g. chillón,** rock sparrow; **g. molinero,** tree sparrow; **g. moruno,** Spanish sparrow. **II** *nm CAm* hummingbird.

gorro *nm* **1** cap; **g. de dormir,** nightcap; **g. frigio,** Phrygian cap. **2** *fam* **estar hasta el g.,** to have had enough, be up to here **(de,** with); **ponerle el g. a algn,** *(irritar)* to annoy sb, get on sb's nerves; *(ridiculizar)* to make fun of sb.

gorrón,-ona I *adj* **1** scrounging. **2** *CAm (egoísta)* egoist. **II** *nm,f* sponger, scrounger.

gorronear *vi* to scrounge, be a parasite.

gota *nf* **1** *(gen)* drop; *(de sudor)* bead; **caen cuatro** *or* **unas gotas,** it's spitting; **g. a g.,** drop by drop; **la g. que colma el vaso,** the straw that broke the camel's back; **ni g.,** not a bit, nothing at all; **no tengo ni g. de sueño,** I am not at all sleepy; **sudar la g. gorda,** to sweat blood, work hard; *Med* **(transfusión) g. a g.,** drip. **2** *Med* gout. **3** *Arquit* gutta.

gotear *v impers* to drip; *(lluvia)* to drizzle; **el techo gotea,** there's a leak in the ceiling.

goteo *nm* dripping.

gotera *nf* **1** *(agujero)* leak; *(agua)* drip. **2** *(mancha)* drip mark. **3 goteras,** *(achaques)* aches and pains.

goterón *nm* large drop.

gótico,-a I *adj Arte & Hist* Gothic. **II** *nm (estilo)* Gothic.

gourmet *nmf (pl* **gourmets)** gourmet.

goyesco,-a *adj Arte* in the style of Goya.

gozada *nf fam* sheer joy; **¡qué g. de tarde!,** what a marvellous evening!

gozar I *vtr* to enjoy; **goza de buena salud,** he enjoys good health. **II** *vi* **1** *(divertirse)* to enjoy oneself; **g. con algo,** to be delighted by sth. **2** *(disfrutar)* to enjoy **(de, -).** **III gozarse** *vr* to enjoy; **me gozo con tu presencia,** I'm delighted to be with you.

gozne *nm* hinge.

gozo *nm* **1** joy, pleasure; **dar g.,** to be a joy; **no caber en sí de g.,** to be beside oneself with joy; **saltar de g.,** to jump with joy; *hum* **todo mi g. en un pozo,** that's just my luck. **2 gozos,** *Mús Rel* chorus *sing* in honour of the Virgin.

gozoso,-a I *adj* **1** *(contento)* delighted. **2** *(que produce alegría)* joyful, happy.

g. p., g/p. *abr de* **giro postal,** postal order, p.o.

grabación *nf* recording.

grabado,-a I *pp de* **grabar. II** *nm* **1** *(arte)* engraving; **g. al agua fuerte,** etching. **2** *(dibujo)* picture, drawing; **una revista con grabados,** an illustrated magazine.

grabador,-a I *adj* recording. **II** *nm, f* engraver. **III** *nf* tape recorder.

grabar *vtr* **1** *Arte* to engrave. **2** *(registrar sonidos, imágenes)* to record. **3** *fig (fijar en el ánimo)* **g. en la mente,** to engrave in one's mind *or* memory; **se me quedó muy grabado,** it stuck in my mind. **4** *Inform* to save.

gracejada *nf CAm Méx* dirty trick.

gracejo,-a I *nm* charm, winsomeness; **con mucho g.,** most engagingly. **II** *nm,f Guat Méx* fool.

gracia *nf* **1** *Rel* grace; **estar en g.,** to be in a state of grace; **por la g. de Dios,** by the grace of God. **2** *(favor)* favour, *US* favor, grace; **disfrutaba de la g. del rey,** he enjoyed the king's favour. **3** *(indulto)* pardon; **petición de g.,** petition of pardon. **4** *(buen trato)* graciousness; **caer en g. a algn,** to make a good impression on sb. **5** *fml (nombre)* **dígame usted su g.,** could you give me your name, please? **6** *(atractivo)* grace, charm; **la g. de su figura,** the charm of her figure. **7** *(garbo)* grace. **8** *(chiste)* joke; **a mí no me hace ninguna g.,** I don't find it funny at all; **hacer** *or* **tener g.,** to be funny; **me hace g.,** marvellous, isn't it?; **¡qué g.!,** how funny!; **reírle las gracias a algn,** to laugh at sb's jokes; **tiene g. que nos encontremos aquí,** it's funny that we should meet here; *(enfado)* **¡vaya (una) g.!,** oh, no!; *(desprecio)* **me hace g.,** makes me laugh; *iron* **tú y tus gracias,** you and your funny *or* witty remarks. **9** *Mil & fig* **tiro de g.,** coup de grâce. **10 gracias,** *(agradecimiento)* thanks; *Rel* **acción de g.,** thanksgiving; **a Dios g., g. a Dios,** thank God, thank goodness; **consiguió el trabajo g. a un amigo,** he got the job through a friend; **dar g. a algn,** to thank sb; **g. a,** thanks to; **muchas** *or* **muchísimas g.,** thank you very much; *iron* **y g.,** I *or* you should be so lucky; **¿en taxi?, en autobús y g.,** by taxi? we are lucky enough we can go by bus! **11** *Mit* **las Tres Gracias,** the Three Graces.

grácil *adj* graceful; *(delicado)* delicate.

gracilidad *nf* gracefulness; *(delicadez)* delicateness.

gracioso,-a I *adj* **1** *(divertido)* funny, amusing; **es el chiste más gracioso que he oído,** that's the funniest joke I've ever heard. **2** *(atractivo)* graceful, charming; **sus graciosos ojos,** her charming eyes. **3** *(monarca británico)* Gracious; **Su Graciosa Majestad,** Her Gracious Majesty. **II** *nm, f Teat* comic character; *fam* **no te hagas el g.,** I suppose you think you're very funny.

grada *nf* **1** *(peldaño)* step, stair. **2** *(asiento colectivo)* tier. **3** *(tarima)* stand. **4** *Náut* slipway, building berth. **5 gradas,** flight *sing* of steps, *US* forecourt *sing*.

gradación *nf* **1** gradation. **2** *Mús* scale. **3** *(retórica)* climax.

gradería *nf*, **graderio** *nm* tiers *pl* of seats, *US* bleachers *pl*.

gradiente I *nm* gradient, *US* grade. **II** *nf Am* slope.

grado *nm* **1** *(gen)* degree; **el g. de humedad/intensidad,** degree of humidity/intensity; **en sumo g.,** to an extreme degree; **en tal g.,** so much so. **2** *(fase)* stage. **3** *Educ (curso)* year, form, *US* grade; *(título)* degree. **4** *Mil* rank. **5** *(peldaño)* step. **6** *Ling* degree. **7** *(locuciones)* **de buen g.,** willingly, with (a) grace; **de mal g.,** unwillingly, with (a) bad grace.

graduable *adj* adjustable.

graduación *nf* **1** gradation. **2** *Mil* rank.

graduado,-a I *pp de* **graduar. II** *adj* graduated; **gafas graduadas,** prescription glasses. **III** *nm* graduate; **el g. escolar,** ≈ elementary school studies.

gradual *adj* gradual.

graduar I *vtr* **1** *(gen)* to graduate. **2** *Educ Mil (título, graduación)* to confer a degree *or* a rank, *US* graduate. **3** *(medir)* to measure; **g. la vista,** to test sb's eyes. **4** *(regular)* to regulate. **II graduarse** *vr* **1** *Educ Mil* to graduate, receive an academic degree *or* a military rank. **2 g. la vista,** to have one's eyes tested.

grafía *nf* **1** *(signo)* graphic symbol; *(escritura)* writing. **2** *(ortografía)* spelling.

gráfico,-a I *adj* graphic. **II** *nm,f* graph, chart.

grafismo *nm* **1** *(diseño gráfico)* graphics *pl.* **2** *(grafía)* graphic symbol. **3** *fig (fuerza descriptiva)* vividness, graphicness.

grafista *nmf* graphic designer.

grafiti *nmpl* graffiti *pl.*

grafito *nm Min* graphite.

grafología *nf* graphology.

grafólogo,-a *nm,f* graphologist.

gragea *nf Med* pill, tablet.

grajilla *nf Orn* jackdaw.

grajo,-a I *nm,f Orn* rook. **II** *nm Am* body odour.

gral. *abr de* **General,** General, gen.

grama *nf Bot* Bermuda grass.

gramática *nf* grammar; **g. generativa,** transformational grammar; *fam fig* **g. parda,** cunning, astuteness.

gramatical *adj* grammatical.

gramático,-a I *adj* grammatical. **II** *nm,f* grammarian.

gramináceo,-a *adj Bot* gramineous.

gramo *nm* gram, gramme.

gramófono *nm* gramophone.

gramola *nf* gramophone.

gran *adj* **1** *(superior)* tremendous; **a g. altura,** very high; **g. velocidad,** high speed; **me diste una g. alegría,** you've made me very happy; **un g. susto,** a terrible fright. **2** *(excelente, famoso)* great; **una g. persona,** a great person; **un g. libro,** a great book; *véase* **grande.**

grana[1] *nf (semilla)* seed; *(crecimiento)* seeding.

grana[2] **I** *nf* **1** *Ent* cochineal. **2** *(substancia)* cochineal. **II** *adj* scarlet.

granada *nf* **1** *Bot* pomegranate. **2** *Mil* grenade.

Granada *n* **1** *(ciudad)* Granada. **2** *(país)* Grenada.

granadero *nm Mil* grenadier.

granadino,-a I *adj* of *or* from Granada *or* Grenada. **II** *nm, f* native *or* inhabitant of Granada *or* Grenada. **III** *nf* **1** *Mús* type of flamenco song from Granada. **2** *(bebida)* grenadine.

granado,-a I *pp de* **granar. II** *adj* **1** *(maduro)* ripened. **2** *fig (selecto)* **el** *or* **lo más g.,** the finest. **3** *fig (persona)* mature, of a certain age. **III** *nm Bot* pomegranate tree.

granar *vi Agr* to seed, ripen.

granate I *adj inv (color)* maroon, dark crimson. **II** *nm* **1** *Min* garnet. **2** *(color)* maroon, garnet.

granazón *nf* seeding, ripening.

Gran Bahía Australiana *n* Great Australian Bight.

Gran Bretaña *n* Great Britain.

Gran Canarias *n* Canary Islands, Canaries.

grancanario,-a I *adj* of *or* from the Canary Islands. **2** *nm, f* native *or* inhabitant of the Canary Islands.

grande I *adj (before noun gran is used)* **1** *(tamaño)* big, large; **esta chaqueta me está g.,** this jacket is too big for me; *fig* **¡qué g. eres!,** you are really fantastic! **2** *(cantidad)* large; **a lo g.,** on a grand scale, in a big way; *fig* **pasarlo en g.,** to have a great time; *fig* **vivir a lo g.,** to live in style. **II** *nmf* **1** *(persona)* grown-up, adult. **2** *(título)* **g. de España,** grandee. **3** *Pol* **los cuatro grandes,** the Big Four.

grandeza *nf* **1** *(tamaño)* size. **2** *(importancia)* greatness; **g. de ánimo,** moral courage. **3** *(generosidad)* generosity; **g. de alma,** magnanimity. **4** *(dignidad nobiliaria)* nobility.

grandilocuencia *nf* grandiloquence, pomp.

grandilocuente *adj* grandiloquent, pompous.

grandiosidad *nf* grandeur, splendour, *US* splendor; **gesto de g.,** grand gesture.

grandioso,-a *adj* grandiose, splendid.

grandote *adj,* **grandullón,-ona** *adj (hombre)* oversized man; *(mujer)* oversized woman.

granel (a) *loc adv* **1** *(sin medir exactamente)* loose, in bulk; **vino a g.,** wine in bulk. **2** *(en abundancia)* tons *or* lots of; *fam* **whisky a g.,** whisky galore.

granero *nm Agr* granary.

granítico,-a *adj* granitic, granite.

granito *nm* **1** *Min* granite. **2** small grain; **aportar su g. de arena,** to make one's small contribution, do one's bit.

granizada *nf* hailstorm; *fig* **una g. de insultos,** a shower of insults.

granizado *nm* iced drink; **g. de limón,** iced lemon (drink).

granizar *v impers* to hail.

granizo *nm* hail, hailstone.

granja *nf* farm.

granjear(se) *vtr & vr* to gain, earn; **su simpatía le granjeó la amistad de todos,** his kindness won him everyone's affection.

granjero,-a *nm, f* farmer.

grano *nm* **1** grain; **un g. de arena/sal/trigo,** a grain of sand/ salt/wheat; **un g. de café,** a coffee bean. **2** *Med* spot, pimple. **3** *(locuciones)* **ir al g.,** to get to the point; **ni un g.,** not a bit; **no es g. de anís,** it's not to be sniffed at. **4 granos,** cereals.

granuja I *nf* grapes *pl.* **II** *nm* **1** *(pilluelo)* ragamuffin, urchin. **2** *(estafador)* crook, trickster.

granujada *nf* foul play, nasty trick.

granujería *nf* gang of rogues *or* urchins.

granulación *nf* granulation.

granulado,-a I *pp de* **granular. II** *adj* granulated. **III** *nm Farm* preparation.

granular I *adj* granular. **II** *vtr* to granulate.

gránulo *nm* **1** granule. **2** *Farm* small pill.

granuloso,-a *adj* **1** *(superficie)* granular. **2** *(piel)* pimply.

granzas *nfpl* **1** *Agr* chaff *sing.* **2** *Min* dross *sing.*

grao *nm* landing beach, shore.

grapa *nf* **1** staple. **2** *Constr* cramp. **3** *(de uvas)* bunch (of grapes). **4** *Arg* type of aniseed liquor *or* gin.

grapadora *nf* stapler.

grapar *vtr* to staple.

grasa *nf* grease, fat.

grasiento,-a *adj* greasy, oily.

graso,-a *adj* fatty; **alimentos grasos,** fatty foods; **pelo g.,** greasy hair.

grasoso,-a *adj* greasy, oily.

gratén *nm Culin* **al g.,** au gratin.

gratificación *nf* **1** *(satisfacción)* gratification. **2** *(recompensa)* reward. **3** *(extra)* bonus.

gratificador,-a *adj*, **gratificante** *adj* gratifying, rewarding.

gratificar *vtr* **1** *(satisfacer)* to gratify. **2** *(recompensar)* to reward.

gratinar *vtr Culin* to roast.

gratis *adv* free, for nothing.

gratitud *nf* gratitude.

grato,-a *adj* *(agradable)* pleasant, pleasing; **me es g. anunciarle que ...,** I am pleased to inform you that ... .

gratuidad *nf* **1** *(ausencia de pago)* **la g. en la enseñanza,** free education. **2** *(arbitrariedad)* gratuitousness.

gratuito,-a *adj* **1** *(de balde)* free (of charge); **entrada gratuita,** free entrance. **2** *(arbitrario)* gratuitous, arbitrary; **afirmación gratuita,** unwarranted statement. ◆ **gratuitamente** *adv* **1** *(de balde)* free, for nothing. **2** *(sin fundamento)* unfoundedly.

grava *nf* *(guijas)* gravel; *(piedra)* crushed stone.

gravamen *nm Jur* **1** *(carga)* burden. **2** *(impuesto)* tax.

gravar I *vtr Jur* **1** *(cargar)* to burden. **2** *(impuestos)* to tax; **estar gravado,** to be mortgaged. II **gravarse** *vr Am (empeorar)* to get worse.

grave *adj* **1** *(pesado)* heavy. **2** *(importante)* grave, serious. **3** *(muy enfermo)* **estar g.,** to be seriously ill. **4** *(de estilo)* solemn. **5** *(voz, nota)* low. **6** *Ling* **acento g.,** grave accent; **palabra g.,** paroxytone.

gravedad *nf* **1** graveness, seriousness; **herido de g.,** seriously injured. **2** *Fís* gravity; **centro de g.,** centre of gravity; **fuerza de g.,** force of gravity.

gravidez *nf* pregnancy; **en estado de g.,** pregnant.

grávido,-a *adj* **1** *(lleno)* full. **2** *(embarazada)* pregnant, gravid.

gravilla *nf* fine gravel.

gravitación *nf Fís* gravitation.

gravitacional *adj Fís* gravitational.

gravitar *vi* **1** *Fís* to gravitate. **2** *(apoyarse en)* to rest on; **sobre él gravita el peso de las decisiones,** the onus of the decisions rests on him. **3** *(amenazar)* to loom; **el peligro gravitaba sobre nuestras cabezas,** danger loomed over our heads.

gravoso,-a *adj* **1** *(costoso)* costly, expensive. **2** *(molesto)* burdensome.

graznar *vi* *(gen)* to squawk; *(pato)* to quack; *(cuervo)* to caw.

graznido *nm* *(un sonido)* squawk; *(varios)* squawking; *(pato)* quack; *(cuervo)* caw; **el g. del pato,** the quacking of the duck; **el g. del cuervo,** the cawing of the crow.

greca *nf* **1** *Arquit* fret, fretwork. **2** *Am* filtre coffeemaker.

Grecia *n* Greece.

grecolatino,-a *adj* Graeco-Latin.

grecorromano,-a *adj* Graeco-Roman.

greda *nf Min* fuller's earth, clay.

gregario,-a *adj* gregarious; **instinto g.,** herd instinct.

gregoriano,-a *adj* Gregorian; *Mús* **canto g.,** Gregorian chant.

greguería *nf* **1** *(algarabía)* hubbub. **2** *Lit* type of aphorism created by Ramón Gómez de la Serna.

grelos *nmpl* turnip tops.

gremial *adj* union, related to trade unions; **convenio g.,** union agreement.

gremio *nm* **1** *Hist* guild. **2** *(sindicato)* union. **3** *(profesión)* profession.

greña *nf* lock of entangled hair; *fam* **andar a la g.,** to squabble.

greñudo,-a *adj* *(pelo)* tangled; *(persona)* unkempt, dishevelled, *US* disheveled.

gres *nm* stoneware; **g. flameado,** glazed earthenware.

gresca *nf* **1** *(bulla)* racket; **armar g.,** to kick up a racket. **2** *(riña)* row.

grey *nf* **1** *(rebaño)* flock, herd. **2** *(personas)* group, bunch; *Rel* flock.

grial *nm* grail; **el Santo G.,** the Holy Grail.

griego,-a I *adj* Greek. II *nm, f* Greek. III *nm* *(idioma)* Greek; *fam* **hablar en g.,** to talk gibberish, *GB* talk double Dutch.

grieta *nf* crack; *(en la piel)* chap, crack.

grifa *nf* *(droga)* marijuana.

grifería *nf* taps *pl*, *US* faucet, plumbing.

grifo,-a¹ I *nm* tap, *US* faucet. II *adj* **1** *Méx* drunk. **2** *Méx* angry.

grifo² *nm Mit* griffin, gryphon, griffon.

grilla *nf* **1** *Ent* female cricket. **2** *Am* *(contrariedad)* obstacle.

grillado,-a *adj fam fig* barmy.

grillete *nm* shackle.

grillo¹ *nm Ent* cricket.

grillo² *nm Bot* sprout.

grillo³ *nm* fetters *pl*, shackles *pl*.

grima *nf* annoyance, displeasure; **me da g. ...,** I can't bear ... .

grímpola *nf* pennant.

gringo,-a *pey* I *adj* foreign; *Am* yankee. II *nm, f* **1** foreigner; *Am* yankee, gringo. **2** *Arg* *(persona)* blond, blonde.

gripal *adj Med* related to flu; **una afección g.,** flu.

gripe *nf* flu; **coger la g.,** to catch flu; **estar con** *or* **tener la g.,** to have flu.

griposo,-a *adj* **estar g.,** to have flu.

gris I *adj* **1** *(color)* grey, *US* gray. **2** *fig (mediocre)* mediocre, third-rate. **3** *fig (triste)* grey, *US* gray, gloomy. II *nm, f* **1** *(color)* grey, *US* gray. **2** *arg Hist* cop; **los grises,** the fuzz *pl*.

grisáceo,-a *adj* greyish.

grisalla *nf Arte* chiaroscuro, grisaille.

grisma *nf Chi Guat Hond* shred, bit.

grisú *nm Min* firedamp.

gritar *vtr & vi* shout, yell; **el público gritó al cantante,** the singer was booed by the audience; **¡no me grites!,** don't shout at me!

griterío *nm* shouting, din.

grito *nm* shout, yell; **a voz en g., a g. limpio** *or* **pelado,** at the top of one's voice; **dar** *or* **pegar un g.,** to shout, scream; **le llamó con un g.,** he yelled at him; *fig* **pedir algo a gritos,** to be badly in need of sth; *fig* **el último g.,** the latest craze *or* fashion; *fig* **poner el g. en el cielo,** to raise an outcry, hit the ceiling.

gritón,-ona I *adj* noisy, loud-mouthed. II *nm, f* loudmouth, yeller.

Groenlandia *n* Greenland.

grog *nm* grog, punch.

grogui *adj* **1** *Box* punch-drunk, groggy. **2** *fig* groggy, dazed.

grosella *nf Bot* redcurrant; **g. negra,** blackcurrant; **g. silvestre,** gooseberry.

grosellero *nm* currant bush, redcurrant; **g. negro,** gooseberry bush.

grosería *nf* **1** *(ordinariez)* rude word *or* expression; **decir una g.,** to say something rude. **2** *(rusticidad)* rudeness.

grosero,-a I *adj* *(tosco)* rough, coarse; *(maleducado)* rude, vulgar. II *nm, f* lout, boor.

grosor *nm* thickness.

grosura *nf* fat, suet.

grotesco,-a *adj* grotesque, ludicrous.

grúa *nf* 1 *Constr* crane, derrick. 2 *Aut* breakdown van, *US* tow truck.

grueso,-a I *adj* thick, heavy; **unas uvas gruesas,** some large grapes; **un hombre g.,** a fat man; *Mar* **mar gruesa,** heavy sea; *Med* **intestino g.,** large intestine. II *nm* 1 (*grosor*) thickness. 2 (*parte principal*) bulk, main body; **el g. de la población,** the bulk of the population. III *nf* (*doce docenas*) gross.

grulla *nf* 1 *Orn* **g. común,** crane. 2 *Méx* bright person.

grullo,-a *adj* scrounging.

grumete *nm* cabin boy.

grumo *nm* hump; (*leche*) curd.

gruñido *nm* grunt.

gruñir *vi* to grunt.

gruñón,-ona I *adj* grumpy, grumbly, grouchy. II *nm, f* grumbler, grouch.

grupa *nf* croup, hindquarters *pl*; **montar a la g.,** to ride pillion; *fig* **volver grupas,** to go back, retrace one's steps.

grupo *nm* 1 (*gen*) group; **en g.,** together as a group. 2 *Téc* unit, set; **g. electrógeno,** power plant.

gruta *nf* grotto, cave.

gua[1] *interj* *Am* 1 (*temor*) agh! 2 (*admiración*) wow!

gua[2] *nm* 1 (*juego*) game of marbles. 2 (*hoyo*) hole for the marbles.

guaca *nf* *Am* 1 (*tesoro*) buried treasure. 2 (*hucha*) piggy bank.

guacal *nm* *CAm* 1 *Bot* calabash tree. 2 calabash basket.

guacamayo,-a *nm, f* *Orn* macaw.

guacamol *nm*, **guacamole** *nm* *Am Culin* guacamole, avocado sauce.

guachafita *nf* *Am* confusion, uproar.

guache *nm* *Arte* gouache.

guacho,-a *adj* & *nm, f* *Am* orphan.

guaco,-a *adj* *Méx* twin. II *nm* 1 *Orn* curassow. 2 *Am Bot* guaco.

guadalajareño,-a I *adj* of or from Guadalajara. II *nm, f* native or inhabitant of Guadalajara.

Guadalupe *n* Guadaloupe.

guadamecí *nm* (*pl* **guademecíes**), **guadamecil** *nm* embossed leather.

guadaña *nf* scythe.

guadañador,-a I *nm, f* (*persona*) mower. II *nf* mowing machine.

guadañar *vtr* to mow; (*hierba*) to scythe.

guadarnés,-a I *nm* tack room. II *nm, f* (*hombre*) stable boy; (*mujer*) stable girl.

guagua[1] *nf* 1 worthless thing. 2 *Can Cuba PR* bus.

guagua[2] *nf* *Am* baby, babe.

guaico *nm* *Am Geog* depression.

guaina I *nmf* *Am* youngster. II *nf* *Arg* young girl.

guajada *nf* *Méx* silly thing.

guajalote *nm* *Méx* idiot.

guaje *nm* 1 (*niño*) boy. 2 *fam* (*granuja*) urchin. 3 *Méx Bot* type of acacia. 4 *Hond Méx Bot* calabash. 5 *Hond Méx fig* idiot. 6 *CAm fig* (*cosa inútil*) trinket; (*persona inútil*) waste of space.

gualdo,-a *adj* yellow; **la bandera roja y gualda,** the Spanish flag.

gualdrapa *nf* caparison.

guanaco,-a *nm, f* 1 *Zool* guanaco. 2 *Am fig* pey (*rústico*) rustic, (country) bumpkin. 3 *Am fig* (*simple*) simple soul.

guanche I *adj* Guanche. II *nmf* Guanche, original inhabitant of the Canary Islands.

guandajo,-a *adj* *Méx* badly dressed.

guando *nm* *Am* stretcher.

guanear *vi* *Am* (*animales*) to defecate.

guano *nm* (*abono natural*) guano; (*artificial*) manure, fertilizer.

guantada *nf* slap.

guantazo *nm* slap.

guante *nm* glove; *fig* **arrojar el g. a algn,** to throw down the gauntlet; *fig* **más suave que un g.,** as meek as a lamb; *fig* **sentar como un g.,** to fit like a glove; *fam* **echar el g. a algo** *or* **algn,** to nick sth *or* catch sb; *Box* **colgar los guantes,** to give up boxing.

guantear *nf* *Am* to slap.

guantera *nf* *Aut* glove compartment.

guaperas *inv* *fam* I *adj* slick, good-looking, *US* cute. II *nmf* good-looker.

guapetón,-ona *adj* *fam* good-looking.

guapo,-a I *adj* 1 good-looking, *US* cute; (*mujer*) beautiful, pretty; (*hombre*) handsome; **es muy guapa,** she's very pretty; **estar g.,** to look smart; **¡hola guapa!,** hello darling! 2 *sl* (*bonito*) flash. II *nm, f* good-looking person, good-looker. III *nm* 1 (*pendenciero*) quarrelsome person. 2 (*galán*) ladies' man. 3 *Am* (*valiente*) daredevil, plucky fellow.

guapote,-a *adj fam* good-looking.

guapura *nf* good looks *pl*.

guaquear *vtr* *CAm Col Arqueol* to excavate, dig.

guaraca[1] *nf* *Am* sling.

guaraca[2] *nf* *Am Orn* chachalaca.

guarache *nm* *Mex* type of sandal.

guaragua *nf* *Am Mús* swinging.

guarango,-a *adj* *Am* rude, rough, ill-bred.

guaraní (*pl* **guaraníes**) I *adj* Guarani. II *nmf* Guarani. III *nm* (*idioma*) Guarani.

guarapo,-a *nm, f* 1 juice of sugar cane. 2 sugar-cane liquor.

guarda I *nmf* guard, keeper; **Ángel de la G.,** Guardian Angel; **g. forestal,** forester; **g. jurado,** security guard. II *nf Impr* endpaper. III *nm Arg* (*cobrador*) tram *or* bus conductor.

guardabarrera *nmf* *Ferroc* crossing keeper.

guardabarros *nm inv* *Aut* mudguard, *US* fender.

guardabosque *nmf* forester.

guardacoches *nmf inv* parking attendant.

guardacostas *nm inv* *Mar* coastguard vessel.

guardador,-a *adj* & *nm, f* ser **g.,** to like to keep things; **ser g. de la ley,** to be law-abiding.

guardaespaldas *nmf inv* bodyguard.

guardafrenos *nmf inv* (*hombre*) pointsman, *US* brakeman; (*mujer*) pointswoman, *US* brakewoman.

guardagujas *nmf inv* *Ferroc* (*hombre*) switchman; (*mujer*) switchwoman.

guardameta *nmf* *Dep* goalkeeper.

guardamuebles *nm inv* furniture warehouse.

guardapelo *nm* locket.

guardapolvo *nm* (*cubierta*) dust cover; (*mono*) overalls *pl*.

guardar I *vtr* 1 (*conservar*) to keep, hold; **g. un buen recuerdo de,** to have a pleasant memory of. 2 (*observar*) (*la ley*) to observe, abide by; (*un secreto*) to keep; **g. la derecha,** to keep to the right; **g. las distancias,** to keep one's distance; **g. silencio,** to remain silent. 3 (*poner en un sitio*) to put away; **guárdalo en el cajón,** put it in the drawer. 4 (*reservar*) to save; **guárdame un sitio,** keep a seat for me, please; **guárdame un trozo,** save a bit for me. 5 (*proteger*) to protect; **¡Dios guarde a la reina!,** God save the Queen! 6 (*cuidar*) to look after. 7 **g. cama,** to stay in bed; **g. las formas,** to be polite; **g. rencor,** to harbour resentment. 8 *Inform* to save. II *vi* *Arg* **¡guarda!,** watch out!, look out! III **guardarse** *vr* 1 (*no dar, retener*) to keep; **me lo guardé en el bolsillo,** I put it in my pocket; **puedes guardarte tus consejos,** you can keep your advice. **2** *(abstenerse)* **g. de hacer algo,** to avoid doing sth; **g. muy mucho de ...,** to take good care not to ...; **me guardé muy bien de hablar,** I made sure not to say a word; *fam* **guardársela a algn,** to have it in for sb.

guardarropa I *nm* **1** *(cuarto)* cloakroom. **2** *(armario)* wardrobe. **II** *nmf* cloakroom attendant.

guardarropía *nf Teat* wardrobe for props.

guardatren *nm Arg Ferroc* guard.

guardavía *nmf Ferroc (hombre)* linesman, *US* lineman; *(mujer)* lineswoman, *US* linewoman.

guardería *nf* **1 g. infantil,** nursery (school). **2** *(oficio de guarda)* keeping.

guardia I *nf* **1** *(vigilancia)* watch, lookout, guard; **estar en g.,** to be on guard; **mantener la g.,** to keep watch; **ponerse en g.,** to put oneself on one's guard. **2** *(tropa)* guard; **g. de asalto,** assault guard; **g. municipal** *or* **urbana,** traffic police; **la g. civil,** the civil guard. **3** *(turno de servicio)* duty; *Mil* guard duty; **estar de g.,** to be on duty; **médico de g.,** doctor on duty; **tiene g. de noche,** she's on night duty. **II** *nmf (hombre)* policeman; *(mujer)* policewoman; **g. civil,** civil guard; **g. de tráfico,** traffic policeman *or* policewoman.

guardián,-ana *nm,f* keeper, custodian watchman.

guardilla *nf* attic, garret.

guardón,-ona *nm,f Méx* thrifty person.

guarecer I *vtr* to shelter, protect. **II guarecerse** *vr* to take shelter *or* refuge **(de,** from).

guaricha *nf Am pey* female, bird.

guarida *nf* **1** *Zool* haunt, lair. **2** *(refugio de maleantes)* hideout.

guarismo *nm* digit, number.

guarnecer *vtr* **1** *(poner adornos a)* to decorate, trim; *Culin* to garnish. **2** *(dotar)* to provide **(de,** with). **3** *Mil* to garrison. **4** *Constr* to plaster.

guarnecido,-a I *pp de* **guarnecer.** **II** *adj* **1** decorated, trimmed; *Culin* garnished. **2** *(dotado)* equipped. **3** *Mil* garrisoned. **III** *nm Constr* to plaster.

guarnición *nf* **1** decoration, trimmings *pl*; *Culin* garnish. **2** *Mil* garrison. **3** *(en joyería)* setting. **4** *(pieza del sable y espada)* guard. **5 guarniciones,** *Equit* harness *sing*.

guarnicionería *nf* saddlery.

guarnicionero,-a *nm,f* saddler.

guaro *nm CAm* cane liquor.

guarrada *nf,* **guarrería** *nf fam* **1** sth dirty *or* disgusting; **decir guarradas** *or* **guarrerías,** to have a foul mouth. **2** *(acción desaprensiva)* dirty trick.

guarro,-a I *adj* dirty, filthy. **II** *nm,f* pig, dirty pig.

guasa *nf* mockery; **con g.,** jokingly; **estar de g.,** to be joking; **le dijo con g. que cantaba muy bien,** she told him tongue in cheek that he sang very well.

guasango,-a *nm,f Am* uproar.

guasearse *vr* to tease, make fun **(de,** of); **no te guasees de él que es muy tímido,** don't take the mickey out of him, he's very shy.

guaso,-a *adj Am* uncivil, rude.

guasón,-ona I *adj* joking, humorous. **II** *nm, f* joker, humorist.

guata *nf Am* belly, paunch; **echar g.,** to get fat.

guatacudo,-a *adj Cuba Méx* big-eared.

guatana *adj Arg* absent-minded.

Guatemala *n* Guatemala.

guatemalteco,-a *adj & nm,f* Guatemalan.

guateque *nm* party.

guayaba *nf* **1** *Bot (fruto)* guava. **2** *Am fig (chica bonita)* pretty young girl. **3** *Am fig (mentira)* lie.

guayabate *nm Méx Salv* guava sweet.

guayabear *vi* **1** to have affairs with young girls. **2** *Arg PR Urug* to lie.

guayabero,-a I *adj Am* lying. **II** *nm,f Am* liar. **III** *nf* short jacket.

guayabo *nm* guava tree.

guayaca *nf SAm (bolsa)* bag; *fig (amuleto)* amulet.

Guayana *n* Guyana.

guayanés,-esa *adj & nm,f* Guyanese, Guyanan.

gubernamental *adj,* **gubernativo,-a** *adj* government, governmental; **fuerzas gubernamentales,** government forces.

gubernista *adj Am* advocating government policy.

gubia *nf* gouge.

guedeja *nf (cabellera)* mane of hair; *(de león)* mane.

güegüecho,-a I *adj* **1** *CAm Méx* suffering from goitre *or US* goiter. **2** *CAm Col (tonto)* silly, stupid. **II** *nm CAm Med* goitre, *US* goiter.

güelfo,-a *nm,f Hist* Guelph, Guelf.

guepardo *nm Zool* cheetah.

güero,-a *adj Méx* fair-haired.

guerra *nf* war, warfare; **en g.,** at war; **g. bacteriológica,** germ warfare; **g. civil/mundial/nuclear,** civil/world/ nuclear war; **g. de nervios,** war of nerves; **g. de las galaxias,** Star Wars; **g. fría,** cold war; *fam* **dar g.,** to be a real nuisance; *fam* **tenerle la g. declarada a algn,** to be openly against sb.

guerrear *vi* to war.

guerrero,-a I *adj* **1** warlike, warring; **danza guerrera,** war dance. **2** *fam (niño)* difficult. **II** *nm,f* warrior. **III** *nf* army jacket, trench coat.

guerrilla *nf* **1** *(partida armada)* guerrilla force *or* band. **2** *(lucha)* guerrilla warfare.

guerrillero,-a *nm,f* guerrilla.

gueto *nm* ghetto.

guía I *nmf (persona)* guide; **el g. turístico,** the tour guide. **II** *nf* **1** *(norma)* guidance, guideline. **2** *(libro, lista)* directory, guide; **la g. de teléfonos,** the telephone directory. **3** *Téc* rail, guide. **4** *(de bicicleta)* handlebar. **5** *(de bigote)* end, tip. **6** *(documento)* customs permit. **7** *Bot* main stem.

guiar I *vtr* **1** *(indicar el camino)* to guide, lead. **2** *(conducir) Aut* to drive; *Náut* to steer; *Av* to pilot; *(caballo, bici)* to ride. **3** *Agr (plantas)* to train. **II guiarse** *vr* to be guided, to go **(por,** by).

guija *nf* **1** *(piedra)* pebble. **2** *Bot* vetch.

guijarral *nm* pebbly place.

guijarro *nm* pebble, stone.

guijo *nm* gravel.

guillado,-a I *pp de* **guillarse.** **II** *adj fam* nutty, loony.

guilladura *nf fam* madness, craziness.

guillarse *vr fam* **1** *(chiflarse)* to become a real loony, go bonkers. **2** *(escabullirse)* to escape; **guillárselas,** to clear out.

guillotina *nf* guillotine; **ventana de g.,** sash window.

guillotinar *vtr* to guillotine.

güinche *nm Am* hoist.

guinda *nf Bot* morello (cherry).

guindaleza *nf Náut* hawser.

guindar *vtr* **1** *(levantar)* to lift; *Náut* to sway. **2** *fam (colgar)* to hang. **3** *arg* to nick, lift.

guindilla *nf Bot* chilli.

guindo *nm Bot* morello (cherry) tree.

guindola *nf Náut* life buoy.

Guinea *n* Guinea; **G. Bissau,** Guinea-Bissau; **G. Ecuatorial,** Equatorial Guinea.

guinea *nf* guinea.

guineano,-a *adj & nm,f* Guinean.

guineo,-a I *adj & nm,f* Guinean. **II** *nm* banana.

guiñada *nf* 1 *(guiño)* wink. 2 *Náut* yaw, yawing.

guiñapo *nm* 1 *(andrajo)* tatter, rag. 2 *fig (persona)* wreck; **poner a algn como un g.,** to pull sb to pieces.

guiñar *vtr* 1 to wink; **me guiñó un ojo,** he winked at me. 2 *Náut* to yaw.

guiño *nm* wink.

guiñol *nm* puppet theatre.

guiñolesco,-a *adj* like a puppet show.

guión *nm* 1 *(esquema)* sketch, outline. 2 *Cin TV* script. 3 *Ling* hyphen, dash. 4 *(estandarte)* standard, banner. 5 *Orn* **g. de codornices,** corncrake.

guionista *nmf Cin TV* scriptwriter.

guipar *vtr fam* 1 *(ver)* to see. 2 *(descubrir)* to see through.

guipur *nm Tex* guipure.

guipuzcoano,-a I *adj* from *or* of Guipúzcoa. **II** *nm,f* native *or* inhabitant of Guipúzcoa.

guiri *nmf arg* foreigner, tourist.

guirigay *nm* 1 *(lenguaje confuso)* gibberish. 2 *(griterío)* hubbub, commotion.

guirlache *nm Culin* almond brittle.

guirnalda *nf* garland.

guiropa *nf Culin* meat and potato stew.

guisa *nf* way, manner; **a g. de,** as, for; **llevaba una sábana a g. de túnica,** she was wearing a sheet as a tunic.

guisado *nm Culin* stew.

guisante *nm Bot* pea.

guisar *vtr* to cook, stew; **tú te lo guisas, tú te lo comes,** as you make your bed so must you lie in it.

guiso *nm* dish; *(guisado)* stew; **un g. de carne con verduras,** a meat and vegetable stew.

güisqui *nm* whisky; **g. escocés,** Scotch.

guita *nf arg* dough, spondulix.

guitarra I *nf* guitar. **II** *nmf* guitarist.

guitarreo *nm* strumming on the guitar.

guitarrería *nf (tienda)* guitar shop; *(fábrica)* guitar factory.

guitarrero,-a *nm,f (vendedor)* guitar seller; *(fabricante)* guitar maker.

guitarrillo *nm* small four-string guitar.

guitarrista *nmf* guitarist.

guitarro *nm véase* **guitarrillo.**

güito *nm* 1 *(hueso)* stone. 2 **güitos,** game played with this stone.

gula *nf* gluttony.

gurí,-isa *nm, f Arg Urug* 1 *(muchacho mestizo)* half-blooded boy. 2 *(hijo)* young child.

guripa *nm fam* 1 *(soldado)* soldier. 2 *(pillo)* scoundrel. 3 *(policía)* cop.

gurmet *nmf* gourmet.

gurrumino,-a I *adj* weak. **II** *nm, f Salv Méx* kid, youngster.

gurú *nm* guru.

gusanillo *nm* 1 little worm. 2 *(locuciones)* **el g. de la conciencia,** one's conscience, feelings of guilt; **matar el g.,** to drink spirits first thing in the morning.

gusano *nm* 1 *Zool* worm, earthworm, maggot; *(oruga)* caterpillar; **g. de seda,** silkworm. 2 *fam (persona despreciable)* worm, despicable person; *(persona insignificante)* poor devil.

gusarapo *nm* tiny creature.

gusgo,-a *adj Méx* sweet-toothed.

gustar I *vtr* 1 *(agradar)* to like; **¡así me gusta!,** that's what I like!, well done!; **me gusta el champán,** I like champagne; *fig* **cuando Ud. guste,** as *or* whenever you wish. 2 *(probar)* to taste, try; **¿Vd. gusta?, ¿gustas?,** would you like some? **II** *vi* **g. de,** to enjoy; **gustaba de leer teatro,** he enjoyed reading plays.

gustativo,-a *adj* gustative; **papilas gustativas,** taste buds.

gustazo *nm fam* great pleasure; **darse el g.,** to treat oneself; **¡qué g. que mañana sea fiesta!,** how wonderful tomorrow is a Bank Holiday!

gustillo *nm (regusto)* aftertaste; **g. ácido,** bitter tang; *fam fig* **¡qué g. me dio!,** how glad I was!; *fam fig (satisfacción)* **sentir un g.,** to be happy.

gusto *nm* 1 *(sentido)* taste; **este guiso tiene poco g.,** this stew is tasteless. 2 *(afición, inclinación)* liking, taste; **g. por la música,** a taste for music; **gustos sencillos,** simple tastes. 3 *(en fórmulas de cortesía)* pleasure; **con (mucho) g.,** with (great) pleasure; **el g. es mío,** the pleasure is mine; **tendré mucho g. en acompañarle al aeropuerto,** I'd be delighted to take you to the airport; **tengo el g. de comunicarle que ...,** it gives me great pleasure to inform you that .... 4 *(locuciones)* **cogerle el g. a algo,** to take a liking to sth; **dar g. a algn,** to please sb; **da g. ver a tanta gente joven,** it's a pleasure to see so many young people; **darse el g.,** to treat oneself; **eso va a gustos,** it's matter of taste; **estar a g.,** to feel comfortable *or* at ease; **hacer algo a g.,** to enjoy (doing) sth; **hay para todos los gustos,** there is sth for everyone; **nunca llueve a g. de todos,** you can't please everyone; **por g.,** for the sake of it; **¡qué g.!,** how lovely!; **ser de buen/mal g.,** to be in good/bad taste; **tener buen/mal g.,** to have good/bad taste.

gutapercha *nf* gutta-percha.

gutural *adj* guttural.

Guyana *n* Guyana.

guyanés,-esa *adj & nm,f* Guyanese, Guyanan.

guzguear *vtr Méx (comida)* to hunt for.

H

H, h ['atʃe] *nf (la letra)* H, h; **homba H,** H-bomb, hydrogen bomb.

h *abr de* **hora(s),** hour, hours, h.

ha¹ *abr de* **hectárea(s),** hectare, hectares, h.

ha² *indic pres véase* **haber.**

haba *nf* broad bean; *fig* **en todas partes cuecen habas,** it's the same the whole world over; *fam* **son habas contadas,** *(cierto)* it's for sure; *(escaso)* they are few and far between. ■ **h. de las Indias,** sweet pea.

Habana (La) *n* Havana.

habanera *nf Mús* dance and music from Havana.

habanero,-a I *adj of or* from Havana. **II** *nm, f* native *or* inhabitant of Havana.

habano *nm* Havana cigar.

hábeas corpus *nm Jur* habeas corpus.

haber I *v aux* **1** *(en tiempos compuestos)* to have; **¡de haberlo sabido!,** if only I had known!; **¡haberlo dicho!,** why didn't you say so?; **¡he dicho!,** and that's that!; **lo había visto,** I had seen it; **lo he hecho,** I have done it; **me habría gustado.** I would have liked it. **2** *(h. de + infin)* *(obligación)* **has de saber que ...,** you should know that ...; **has de ser bueno,** you must be good; **¿por qué he de ser yo?,** why must it be me?; **¿quién había de ser?,** who else could it have been? **3** *(h. que + infin)* **hay que,** one must, you have to; **habrá que ir a verlo,** we have to go and see it; **hay que hacer deporte,** you've got to do some sport; **hay que hacer las cosas bien,** one has to do things well; **hay que trabajar,** you've got to work; **no hay que llorar,** you mustn't cry; **no hay que tomarlo en serio,** you mustn't take it seriously. **II** *v impers* **1** *(existir, estar)* there is *or* are *or* was *or* were; **¿cuántos hay?,** how many are there?; **habría unas cuarenta personas,** there must have been about forty people; **hay un gato en el tejado,** there is a cat on the roof; **no hay (nada) como ...,** there is nothing like ..., nothing beats ...; **no hay como ser rico,** there is nothing like being rich; **no hay nada como tener un buen coche,** nothing beats having a good car; **no hay quien lo entienda,** it's impossible to understand; **no hay quien te aguante hoy,** you're impossible today; **no hay quien trabaje con este ruido,** it's impossible for anyone to work with this noise. **2** *Prensa Rad (tener lugar)* **en el encuentro habido entre ...,** in today's game between ...; **habrá una fiesta,** there will be a party; **hubo un accidente,** there was an accident. **3** *lit* **diez años ha,** ten years ago. **4** *(locuciones)* **algo habrá,** there must be something in it; ... **como hay pocos, donde los haya,** few and far between; **había una vez ...,** there was once ...; **¡habráse visto!,** have you ever seen anything like it?, what a cheek!; **¡hay que ver!,** well I never!, well really!; **no hay de qué,** you're welcome, don't mention it; **no hay tal,** it isn't true; **¿qué hay?,** hello!, hi!, how are things?; *fam* **eres de lo que no hay,** you're impossible; *fam* **no hay por donde cogerle,** he's impossible. **III** *vtr (tener) fml* **los hijos habidos en el matrimonio,** the children of the marriage; *fam* **todos los habidos y por h.,** every single ... . **IV haberse** *vr fam* **habérselas con algn,** to have it out with sb, be up against sb. **V** *nm* **1** *(gen pl) (bienes)* assets *pl,* property; *(sueldo)* salary, pay, wages *pl*. **2** *(en balance)* credit; *fig* **tiene en su h. que ...,** it must be said to his credit that ... .

habichuela *nf* kidney bean.

hábil *adj* **1** *(diestro)* skilful, *US* skillful; **h. para la costura,** good at sewing. **2** *(astuto)* clever, smart; **maniobra h.,** clever move. **3** *(apto)* usable; **días hábiles,** working days; **los muebles dejan poco espacio h.,** the furniture leaves little usable space. ◆ **hábilmente** *adv* skilfully, *US* skillfully.

habilidad *nf* **1** *(destreza)* skill; **con gran h.,** very skilfully; **tener h. manual,** to be good with one's hands; **tener h. para ...,** to be good at ... . **2** *(astucia)* cleverness, smartness. **3 habilidades,** *(dotes)* skills.

habilidoso,-a *adj* clever, skilful, *US* skillful.

habilitación *nf* **1** *(de un espacio)* fitting out. **2** *(capacitación)* entitlement; *(autorización)* authorization. **3** *(oficina del habilitado)* paymaster's office.

habilitado,-a I *pp de* **habilitar. II** *nm, f (hombre)* paymaster; *(mujer)* paymistress.

habilitar *vtr* **1** *(espacio)* to fit out; **h. un garaje para sala de juegos,** to fit a garage out as a games room. **2** *(capacitar)* to entitle, enable; *(autorizar)* to empower, authorize; **h. horas para visitas,** to set aside time for visitors. **3** *Fin (financiar)* to finance.

habitable *adj* habitable, inhabitable.

habitación *nf* **1** *(cuarto)* room; *(dormitorio)* bedroom; **h. individual/doble,** single/double room. **2** *Biol (hábitat)* habitat.

habitáculo *nm* **1** *(vivienda)* dwelling. **2** *Biol (hábitat)* habitat.

habitante *nmf* inhabitant.

habitar I *vtr (lugar)* to live in, inhabit; **los pueblos primitivos que habitaron la península,** the primitive peoples who inhabited the Peninsula; **una casa sin h.,** an empty house. **II** *vi* to live.

hábitat *nm (pl* **hábitats)** habitat.

hábito *nm* **1** *(costumbre)* habit, custom; **adquirir el h. de ...,** to get into the habit of ...; **el fumar crea h.,** smoking is habit-forming; **la puntualidad es un h. en mí,** punctuality is second nature to me; **tener el h. de ...,** to be in the habit of ... . **2** *Rel* habit; **colgar los hábitos,** to leave the priesthood; **tomar el h.,** *(hombre)* to take holy orders; *(mujer)* to take the veil; **el h. no hace al monje,** fine clothes don't make a fair lady, clothes don't make the man.

habituación *nf* habituation.

habitual *adj* usual, customary, habitual; *(cliente, lector)* regular. ◆ **habitualmente** *adv (repetidamente)* usually; *(con regularidad)* regularly.

habituar I *vtr* to accustom **(a,** to). **II habituarse** *vr* to get used **(a,** to), become accustomed **(a,** to).

habla *nf* **1** *(idioma)* language; **h. regional,** regional dialect; **países de h. española,** Spanish-speaking countries. **2** *(facultad de hablar)* speech; **perder el h.,** to lose one's power of speech; **quedarse sin h.,** to be left speechless. **3** *Tel (comunicación)* **¡al h.!,** speaking!; **estar/ponerse al h. con algn,** to be/get in touch with sb.

habladas *nfpl Am* bragging *sing,* boasting *sing.*

hablado,-a I *pp de* **hablar. II** *adj* **1** spoken; **bien h.,** well-spoken, nicely spoken; **un chico muy bien h.,** a well-spoken young man; **el inglés h.,** spoken English; **mal h.,** coarse, foul-mouthed; **¡qué mal h. eres!,** what a wicked tongue (you've got)! **2** *(tratado, discutido)* dealt with; **eso ya está h.,** that's been dealt with; **fue un asunto muy h.,** it was a widely discussed subject.

hablador,-a *adj (parlanchín)* talkative; *pey (chismoso)* gossipy, given to gossip.

habladuría *nf (rumor)* rumour, *US* rumor; *(chisme)* piece of gossip; **son habladurías de la gente,** it's just idle gossip.

hablante *nmf* speaker; **hay millones de hablantes de español,** there are millions of Spanish speakers.

hablar I *vi* **1** *(gen)* to speak, talk; **h. bien/mal de algn,** to speak well/badly of sb; **h. claro,** to speak plainly; **h. con**

algn, to speak to sb; **h. en nombre de algn**, to speak on sb's behalf. **2** *(mentar, tratar)* to mention; **hablaron de ir a París**, they talked of going to Paris; **no se habló de ese tema**, that subject wasn't mentioned; **no me hablaste de eso**, you never mentioned that. **3** *(murmurar)* to talk; **a la gente le gusta h.**, people will talk; **estás dando que h.**, you are making people talk. **4** *(dar un tratamiento)* to call; **háblame de tú**, call me John, Mary, *etc*. **5** *(locuciones)* **h. en broma**, to be joking; **h. por h.**, to talk for the sake of talking; **eso es h. por h.**, take no notice; **¡ni h.!**, certainly not!; **de eso ni h.**, that's out of the question; **no se hable más de ello**, and that's that; *fig* **es como h. a la pared**, I might as well be talking to myself; *fam* **h. en cristiano** *or* **en plata**, to speak plainly; *fam* **h. por los codos**, to be a chatterbox; *fam* **¡quién fue a h.!**, look who's talking! **II** *vtr* **1** *(tratar un asunto)* to talk over, discuss; **tenemos que hablarlo con el jefe**, we'd better talk to the boss (about it). **2** *(idioma)* to speak; **habla dos idiomas con soltura**, she can speak two languages fluently. **III hablarse** *vr* **1** to speak *or* talk to one another; **llevamos meses sin hablarnos**, we haven't spoken for months; **no me hablo con el jefe**, I don't speak to the boss, I'm not on speaking terms with the boss. **2** *(correr el rumor)* **se habla de que ...**, it's said that ..., there is talk of ... . **3** *(en letrero)* **'se habla español'**, 'Spanish spoken here'.

hablilla *nf (rumor)* rumour, *US* rumor; *(chisme)* piece of gossip.

habón *nm* swelling *or* lump on the skin.

habré *indic fut véase* **haber**.

hacedero,-a *adj* feasible, practicable, possible.

hacedor,-a *nm,f* maker; *Rel* **el Sumo** *or* **Supremo H.**, the Maker.

hacendado,-a I *adj* landed. **II** *nm,f* landowner.

hacendista *nmf* financial expert, tax consultant.

hacendoso,-a *adj* house-proud, hardworking.

hacer I *vtr* **1** *(crear, producir, fabricar)* to make; **h. ruido**, to make noise; **h. sombra**, to give shade; **h. un esfuerzo**, to make an effort; **h. un poema**, to write a poem; **h. una casa**, to build a house. **2** *(arreglar)* *(uñas)* to do; *(barba)* to trim; *(cama)* to make. **3** *(obrar, ejecutar)* to do; **eso no se hace**, you mustn't do that; **hazme un favor**, do me a favour; **¿qué haces?**, *(en este momento)* what are you doing?; *(para vivir)* what do you do (for a living)?; **tengo mucho que h.**, I have a lot to do. **4** *(conseguir) (amigos, dinero)* to make. **5** *(obligar)* to make; **hazle callar/trabajar**, make him shut up/work; **no me hagas esperar**, don't keep me waiting. **6** *(creer, suponer)* to think; **le hacía en París**, I thought she was in Paris; **te hacía más joven**, I thought you were younger. **7** *(recorrer)* to do; **hice Madrid-París de un tirón**, I did Madrid to Paris without stopping; **h. un recorrido de cinco kilómetros**, to cover a distance of five kilometres. **8** *Mat (sumar)* to make; **y con éste hacen cien**, and that makes a hundred. **9** *(ocupar un puesto)* to make; **hago el número seis en la lista**, I'm number six on the list. **10** *(dar aspecto)* to make look; **el negro le hace más delgado**, black makes him look slimmer; **estos pantalones te hacen gorda**, these trousers make you look fat. **11** *(acostumbrar)* to accustom; *fig* **h. el cuerpo a**, to get used to. **12** *(sustituyendo a otro verbo)* to do; **se negó a ir y yo hice lo mismo**, she refused to go and I did the same; **ya no puedo leer como solía hacerlo**, I can't read as well as I used to. **13** *(representar)* to play; **h. el bueno**, to play the (part of the) goody. **14** *(practicar)* to practise; *(pianista)* **h. dedos**, to do finger exercises; *(deportista)* **h. piernas**, to limber up. **15** *(locuciones)* **a medio h.**, half-finished, half-done; **¡así se hace!**, that's it!; **¡bien hecho!**, well done!; **eso está hecho**, *(acabado)* that's finished; *(lleva poco tiempo)* that'll only take a minute, that won't take long; **h. burla de**, to make fun of; **h. el ridículo**, to act the fool; **h. gracia**, to amuse; **h. pedazos**, to ruin; **h. por h.**, to do for the sake of doing; **h. saber**, to make known; **h. tiempo**, to kill time; *fig* **ser el que hace y deshace**, to be the boss; *fam* **¡buena la has hecho!**, you've done it now!; **h. una de las suyas**, she's *or*

he's done it again, there she *or* he goes again. **II** *vi* **1** *(actuar)* to play; **hizo de Desdémona**, she played Desdémona; **hizo de padre y madre**, he acted as both father and mother. **2** *(h. por or para + infin) (procurar)* to try to; **haz por venir**, try and come. **3** *(comportarse)* to act; **h. el imbécil**, to act stupid; *fam* **h. el indio**, to fool around. **4** *(fingirse)* to pretend; **h. como**, to act as; **h. algn como que no quiere**, to act as though you're not interested; **haz como si no lo supieras**, pretend you don't know. **5 h. bien/mal**, to do the right/wrong thing; **haces mal en no hablar**, you're wrong not to talk; **hice bien en ir**, I was right to go. **6** *(servir)* **eso no hace al caso**, that has nothing to do with it; **Pepe hace a todo**, Pepe can turn his hand to anything. **7** *(convenir)* to be suitable; **a las ocho si te hace**, will eight o'clock be all right for you?; **¿hace?, O.K.? III** *v impers* **1** *(clima)* **hace bueno**, it's a fine day; **hace calor**, it's hot; **no ha hecho verano**, we haven't had any summer weather. **2** *(tiempo transcurrido)* ago; **¿cuánto hace de eso?**, how long ago was that?; **hace dos días que no le veo**, I haven't seen him for two days; **hace mucho/poco**, a long/short time ago; **ocurrió hace dos años**, it happened two years ago. **IV hacerse** *vr* **1** *(volverse)* to become; **h. sacerdote**, to become a priest; **h. viejo**, to grow old; **Paco se ha hecho a sí mismo**, Paco's a selfmade man; **poeta no nace, se hace**, poets aren't born, they are made. **2** *(crecer)* to grow; **¡qué grande te has hecho!**, haven't you grown! **3** *(resultar)* to become, get; **así se hace más fácil**, it's easier that way; **la vuelta se me hizo más corta**, the return journey felt quicker, **se me hizo imposible ayudarte**, I couldn't help you. **4** *(simular)* to pretend; **se hace el gracioso**, he thinks he's funny; *fig* **h. el sordo**, to turn a deaf ear. **5** *(apropiarse)* **h. con**, to get hold of; **me hice con unos patines**, I got myself a pair of skates. **6** *(habituarse)* to get used **(a, to)**; **enseguida me hago a todo**, I soon get used to anything. **7** *(figurarse)* to imagine; **h. una idea de algo**, to imagine sth; **no te hagas ilusiones**, don't expect too much; **se me hace que va a llover**, I think it's going to rain. **8** *Náut* **h. a la mar**, to put to sea. **9** *(fabricar)* to make oneself; **me hice un vestido**, I made myself a dress. **10** *(mandar hacer)* to have made *or* built. **11** *(arreglarse)* *(uñas)* to do; *(barba)* to have a trim; **h. una permanente**, to have a perm.

hacha *nf* **1** *(herramienta)* axe, *US* ax. **2** *fam* **ser un h. en algo**, to be an ace *or* a wizard at sth.

hachazo *nm* blow with an axe, hack; **lo partió de un h.**, he chopped it straight down the middle.

hache *nf* aitch; *fam* **¡llámalo h.!**, call it what you like, it's all the same; *fam* **por h. or por he**, for one reason or another.

hachís *nm* hashish.

hacia *prep* **1** *(dirección)* towards, to; **h. abajo**, down, downwards; **h. acá**, this way; **h. adelante**, forwards; **h. allá**, that way; **h. arriba**, up, upwards; **h. atrás**, back, backwards; **sentir algo h. algn**, to feel sth for *or* towards sb. **2** *(tiempo)* at about, at around; **h. las tres**, at about three o'clock.

hacienda *nf* **1** *(finca agrícola)* estate, property, *US* ranch. **2** *(bienes propios)* property, wealth. **3** *Fin* Treasury; **Delegación de H.**, ≈ local Inland Revenue office; **h. pública**, public funds *or* finances *pl*; **Ministerio de H.**, ≈ Exchequer, Treasury, Finance Ministry; **Ministro de H.**, ≈ *GB* Chancellor of the Exchequer, *US* Secretary of the Treasury.

hacinamiento *nm* **1** *Agr* stacking; *fig (montón)* piling. **2** *(de gente)* overcrowding.

hacinar I *vtr Agr* to stack; *fig (amontonar)* to pile up, heap up. **II hacinarse** *vr (gente)* to be packed **(en, into)**.

hada *nf* fairy. ■ **cuento de hadas**, fairy tale; **h. madrina**, fairy godmother.

hado *nm* destiny, fate.

hagiografía *nf* hagiography.

hagiógrafo,-a *nm,f* hagiographer, hagiographist.

hago *indic pres véase* **hacer**.

Haití *n* Haiti.

haitiano,-a *adj & nm,f* Haitian, Haytian.

hala *interj* **1** *(¡ánimo!)* come on! **2** *(¡vete!)* clear off!, get out! **3** *(¡deprisa!)* go on!, get moving! **4** *(¡qué exageración!)* come off it!

halagador,-a *adj* **1** *(lisonjero)* flattering. **2** *(agradable)* gratifying.

halagar *vtr* **1** *(lisonjear)* to flatter; **h. el amor propio,** to flatter one's ego. **2** *(agradar)* to please, gratify; **lo hizo para halagarte,** she did it to please you.

halago *nm* flattery, compliment.

halagüeño,-a *adj* **1** *(lisonjero)* flattering; **en tono h.,** flatteringly. **2** *(noticia, impresión)* promising.

halar *vtr Naút* to haul, pull.

halcón *nm Orn* falcon. ■ **h. común,** péregrine (falcon).

halconería *nf* falconry.

halconero,-a *nm,f* falconer.

halda *nf* **1** *(falda)* skirt. **2** *(arpillera)* sackcloth, sacking.

hale *interj* get going!, get a move on!

haleche *nm* anchovy.

hálito *nm* **1** *(aliento)* breath. **2** *(vapor)* vapour, *US* vapor. **3** *lit* gentle breeze.

halitosis *nf Med* halitosis.

hall *nm* (entrance) hall, foyer.

hallar I *vtr (encontrar)* to find; *(averiguar)* to find out; *(descubrir)* to discover. II **hallarse** *vr (estar)* to be, find oneself; **h. de viaje,** to be away (on a trip); **h. presente,** to be present.

hallazgo *nm* **1** *(descubrimiento)* discovery, finding; **h. de un cadáver,** body found; **sensacional h. de ...,** sensational find of ... . **2** *(cosa encontrada)* find.

halo *nm* halo, aura.

halógeno,-a *Quím* I *adj* halogenous. II *nm* halogen.

halterofilia *nf Dep* weightlifting.

hamaca *nf* hammock; *(mecedora)* rocking chair.

hamacar *vtr,* **hamacarse** *vr SAm* to swing, rock.

hamaquear *vtr Am* **1** *véase* **hamacar. 2** *fig* **h. a algn,** to keep sb waiting.

hambre *nf* hunger, starvation, famine; **huelga de h.,** hunger strike; **morirse de h.,** to be starving; **nos están matando de h.,** they are starving us to death; **pasar h.,** to be hungry, go hungry; **tener h.,** to be hungry; *fig* **entretener el h.,** to stave off hunger; *fig* **h. y sed de justicia,** hunger and thirst for justice; *fig* **matar el h.,** to kill (one's) hunger; *fig* **sueldos de h.,** starvation wages; *fam* **es más listo que el h.,** he's a cunning devil; *fam* **pey un muerto de h.,** a good-for-nothing.

hambriento,-a I *adj* *(con hambre)* hungry, starving. **2** *fig* *(deseoso)* **h. de,** hungry *or* longing for. II *nm,f* hungry *or* starving person; **los hambrientos,** the hungry.

Hamburgo *n* Hamburg.

hamburgués,-esa I *adj* of *or* from Hamburg. II *nm, f* native *or* inhabitant of Hamburg. III *nf* hamburger; **h. de ternera,** beefburger.

hampa *nf* underworld; **el h. barcelonesa,** the Barcelona underworld.

hampesco,-a *adj* criminal, underworld.

hampón,-ona I *adj* tough, rowdy. II *nm,f* tough, thug.

hámster *nm (pl* **hámsters)** *Zool* hamster.

han *indic pres véase* **haber.**

hándicap *nm (pl* **hándicaps)** handicap.

hangar *nm Av* hangar.

haragán,-ana I *adj* lazy, idle. II *nm,f* lazybones *inv,* idler.

haraganear *vi* to idle, loaf around.

harakiri *nm* hara-kiri.

harapiento,-a *adj* ragged, in rags.

harapo *nm* rag; **hecho un h.,** in tatters.

haré *indic fut véase* **hacer.**

harén *nm (pl* **harenes)** harem.

harina *nf* flour; *fam* **eso es h. de otro costal,** that's another kettle of fish. ■ **h. de maíz,** cornflour, *US* cornstarch; **h. de pescado,** fish meal; **h. de trigo,** wheat flour; **h. lacteada,** malted milk.

harinoso,-a *adj* floury.

harnero *nm* sieve.

hartar I *vtr* **1** *(atiborrar)* to satiate; **el dulce harta enseguida,** sweet things soon fill you up. **2** *(cansar, fastidiar)* to annoy, irritate; **me harta tanto viaje,** I'm fed up with all this coming and going; **me hartan los niños,** children get on my nerves. **3** *(llenar)* to overwhelm *(de,* with); **le hartaron a golpes,** they beat him up; **le hartó a besos,** she covered him with kisses. II **hartarse** *vr* **1** *(saciar el apetito)* to eat one's fill; **comer hasta h.,** to eat oneself sick; **dormir hasta h.,** to have one's fill of sleep. **2** *(cansarse)* to get fed up *(de,* with), grow tired *(de,* of); **me harto de repetírselo,** I'm tired of telling him; **me he hartado de ti,** I've had enough of you. **3** *(de hacer algo)* to do nothing but; **me harté de ver cine,** I did nothing but to go the pictures.

hartazgo *nm* bellyful; **darse un h. de ...,** to stuff oneself with ... .

harto,-a I *adj* **1** *(repleto)* full. **2** *(cansado)* tired of, fed up with; **estoy h. de ser amable con él,** I'm tired of being nice to him; **¡me tienes h.!,** I'm fed up with you!; **¡ya estoy h.!,** I'm fed up!, I'm sick and tired of it! **3** *desus (bastante)* enough; **harta paciencia tuviste,** you were more than patient; **hartos problemas tengo yo,** I've got enough problems. II *adv desus* **1** *(muy)* quite, very; **estas manzanas son h. buenas,** these apples are very good; **h. lo siento,** I'm very sorry. **2** *(bastante)* **h. me has dicho,** you've told me enough.

hartura *nf* **1** *(hartazgo)* bellyful. **2** *(abundancia)* plenty, abundance, glut; **tengo tal h. de libros que ...,** I've read so many books that ...; **¡qué h.!,** what a drag! **3** *fig (de deseo)* fulfilment, *US* fulfillment.

has *indic pres véase* **haber.**

hasta I *prep* **1** *(lugar)* up to, as far as, down to; **¿h. dónde vamos a llegar?,** where will it end? **2** *(tiempo)* until, till, up to; **h. el domingo,** until Sunday; **h. el final,** right to the end; **h. junio,** until June; **h. la fecha,** up to now; **¡h. la vista!,** cheerio!, see you!, *US* so long!; **¡h. luego!,** see you later! **3** *(indica cantidad)* up to, as many as; **cabemos h. seis en el ascensor,** the lift will take up to six people; **cuenta h. diez,** count to ten. **4** *(incluso)* even; **h. yo lo entiendo,** even I can understand it. II *conj* **h. que,** until; **esperaré h. que se vaya,** I'll wait until he goes; **no me iré h. no verlo,** I won't go until I've seen him.

hastiado,-a I *pp* de **hastiar.** II *adj* disgusted *(de,* with), sick *(de,* of).

hastial *nm Arquit* gable (end).

hastiar *vtr* to weary, sicken.

hastío *nm* **1** *(repugnancia)* loathing, disgust. **2** *fig (tedio)* boredom, weariness.

hatajo *nm* **1** *(rebaño)* small herd *or* flock. **2** *fig pey* heap, lot, bunch; **un h. de disparates,** a load of nonsense; **un h. de ladrones,** a gang of thieves; **un h. de mentiras,** a pack of lies.

hatillo *nm* small bundle.

hato *nm* **1** *(de ropa, enseres)* bundle; *fig* **liar el h.,** to pack one's bags, get ready to go. **2** *(rebaño)* herd, flock.

Hawai *n* Hawaii.

hawaiano,-a *adj & nm,f* Hawaiian.

hay *indic pres véase* **haber.**

Haya (La) *n* The Hague.

haya¹ *nf* **1** *Bot (árbol)* beech. ■ **h. cobriza,** copper beech. **2** *(madera)* beech (wood).

haya² I *subj pres véase* **haber.** II *imperat véase* **haber.**

haz¹ *nm* **1** *(de cosas)* bundle; *Agr* sheaf. **2** *(de luz)* shaft, beam.

haz² *nf (cara)* face.

haz³ *imperat véase* **hacer.**

hazaña *nf* deed, exploit, heroic feat.

hazmerreír *nm* laughing stock; **es el h. de la clase,** he's the laughing stock of the class.

he¹ *adv* **he ahí/aquí ...,** there/here you have ...; **he ahí la cuestión,** that's the question; **he aquí el problema,** this is the problem; **heme/hete aquí,** here I am/you are; **heme aquí listo para empezar,** here I am ready to start.

he² I *indic pres véase* **haber.** II *imperat véase* **haber.**

hebdomadario,-a *adj Prensa* weekly.

hebilla *nf* buckle.

hebra *nf (de hilo)* thread, piece of thread; *fig* thread; *(de legumbres)* string; *(de carne)* sinew; *(de madera)* grain; *Min (veta)* vein; **pegar la h.,** to chat.

hebraico,-a *adj* Hebraic, Hebraical, Hebrew.

hebraísta *nmf* Hebraist.

hebreo,-a I *adj* Hebrew. II *nm,f* Hebrew. III *nm (idioma)* Hebrew; *fam* **jurar en h.,** to curse and swear.

Hébridas *npl* **las (Islas) H.,** the Hebrides.

hecatombe *nf* **1** *Hist* hecatomb. **2** *(catástrofe)* disaster, catastrophe.

hechicería *nf (arte)* witchcraft, sorcery; *(hechizo)* spell, charm.

hechicero,-a I *adj* bewitching, charming. II *nm, f (hombre)* wizard, sorcerer; *(mujer)* witch, sorceress.

hechizar *vtr* **1** *(embrujar)* to cast a spell on. **2** *fig (fascinar)* to bewitch, charm.

hechizo,-a I *adj Am (local)* local; *(cosa)* **h. de Méjico,** made in Mexico; *(comida)* **producto h.,** home-produced. II *nm* **1** *(embrujo)* spell, charm. **2** *fig (fascinación)* fascination, charm.

hecho,-a I *pp de* **hacer.** II *adj* **1** made, done; **¡bien h.!,** well done!; **eso está h.,** that's a sure thing; **está h. un sinvergüenza,** he's a cheeky devil; **¡h.!,** done!, agreed!; **h. a mano,** handmade; **h. a máquina,** machine-made; **lo h. h. está,** what's done is done; **se puso h. una fiera,** he went up the wall, he went mad; *fam* **a lo h. pecho,** as you make your bed, so you must lie on it *or* it's no use crying over spilt milk; *fam* **dicho y h.,** no sooner said than done. **2** *(carne)* done; **muy h.,** *(demasiado)* overdone; *(sin sangre)* well-cooked; **poco h.,** *(no suficientemente)* underdone; *(con sangre)* rare. **3** *(persona)* mature; **un hombre h. y derecho,** a real man. **4** *(frase)* set; *(ropa)* ready-made. III *nm* **1** *(realidad)* fact; **de h.,** in fact; **el h. es que ...,** the fact is that ... . **2** *(acto)* act, deed; **h. consumado,** fait accompli; *Mil* **h. de armas,** feat of arms; *Rel* **Hechos de los Apóstoles,** Acts of the Apostles; **hechos son amores,** actions speak louder than words. **3** *(suceso)* event, incident; **el h. tuvo lugar en ...,** the incident took place in ...; *Jur* **el lugar de los hechos,** the scene of the crime *or* incident; **relato de los hechos acontecidos,** account of events.

hechura *nf* **1** *(forma)* shape; *(corte)* cut. **2** *(elaboración)* making. **3** *fml (obra)* creation, product; **h. de Dios,** God's creature.

hectárea *nf* hectare.

hectolitro *nm* hectolitre, *US* hectoliter.

heder *vi* **1** *(apestar)* to stink, smell foul. **2** *fig (fastidiar)* to annoy.

hediondez *nf* stink, stench.

hediondo,-a *adj* **1** *(apestoso)* stinking, foul-smelling, smelly. **2** *fig (asqueroso)* repulsive, filthy. **3** *fig (molesto)* annoying.

hedonismo *nm Filos* hedonism.

hedonista *Filos* I *adj* hedonistic, hedonic. II *nmf* hedonist.

hedor *nm* stink, stench.

hegeliano,-a *adj Filos* Hegelian.

hegemonía *nf* hegemony.

hégira *nf,* **héjira** *nf* Hegira, Hejira.

helada *nf Meteor* frost, freeze; **caer una h.,** to freeze. ■ **h. blanca,** hoarfrost, white frost.

heladera *nf* **1** *(nevera)* refrigerator. **2** *(de helados)* ice-cream machine.

heladería *nf* ice-cream parlour.

helado,-a I *pp de* helar. II *adj* **1** *(muy frío)* frozen, freezing cold; **estoy h. (de frío),** I'm frozen. **2** *fig (atónito)* **quedarse h.,** to be flabbergasted; **me dejó h.,** I couldn't believe it! III *nm* ice cream.

helador,-a I *adj* icy, freezing; **viento h.,** icy wind. II *nf (máquina)* ice-cream machine.

helar I *vtr* **1** *(congelar)* to freeze. **2** *(planta)* to kill by frost. II *v impers Meteor* to freeze; **anoche heló,** there was a frost last night. III **helarse** *vr* **1** *(congelarse)* to freeze; **se heló el río,** the river froze over. **2** *(planta)* to die from frost. **3** *(persona)* to freeze to death; **nos vamos a h.,** we'll freeze to death; *fig* **se me heló la sangre,** my blood ran cold.

helecho *nm Bot* fern, bracken.

helénico,-a *adj Hist* Hellenic, Greek.

helenismo *nm Hist* Hellenism.

helenístico,-a *adj Hist* Hellenistic, Hellenistical.

hélice *nf* **1** *Av Náut* propeller. **2** *Anat Arquit Mat* helix.

helicóptero *nm Av* helicopter.

helio *nm Quím* helium.

heliocéntrico,-a *adj Astron* heliocentric.

heliotropo *nm Bot* heliotrope.

helipuerto *nm Av* heliport.

Helsinki *n* Helsinki.

Helvecia *n* Helvetia.

helvético,-a *adj & nm,f* Helvetian, Swiss.

hematíe *nm* red blood corpuscle.

hematología *nf Med* haematology, *US* hematology.

hematólogo,-a *nm, f Med* haematologist, *US* hematologist.

hematoma *nm Med* haematoma, *US* hematoma, bruise.

hembra *nf* **1** *Bot Zool* female. **2** *(mujer)* woman; **una real h.,** a fine figure of a woman. **3** *Téc* female; *(de tornillo)* nut; *(de enchufe)* socket.

hembraje *nm Am Agr* female flock *or* herd; *pey* womenfolk.

hemeroteca *nf* newspaper library.

hemiciclo *nm* **1** *(semicírculo)* hemicycle. **2** *Parl* floor.

hemisférico,-a *adj* hemispheric, hemispherical.

hemisferio *nm* hemisphere. ■ **h. norte/sur,** northern/southern hemisphere.

hemofilia *nf Med* haemophilia, *US* hemophilia.

hemofílico,-a *Med* I *adj* haemophilic, *US* hemophilic. II *nm,f* haemophiliac, *US* hemophiliac.

hemoglobina *nf* haemoglobin, *US* hemoglobin.

hemorragia *nf Med* haemorrhage, *US* hemorrhage.

hemorroides *nfpl Med* haemorrhoids, *US* hemorrhoids.

hemos *indic pres véase* **haber.**

henar *nm Agr* loft.

henchir I *vtr (llenar)* to stuff, fill, cram; **h. los pulmones de aire fresco,** to fill one's lungs with fresh air; *fig* **henchido de orgullo,** swollen with pride. II **henchirse** *vr (de comida)* to stuff oneself.

hender *vtr* **1** *(resquebrajar)* to crack, cleave, split; *fig (olas)* to cut. **2** *fig (abrirse paso)* to make one's way through.

hendidura *nf* cleft, crack.

hendir *vtr véase* **hender.**

henil *nm Agr* loft.

heno *nm* hay.

hepático,-a *adj* hepatic.

hepatitis *nf inv Med* hepatitis.

heptagonal *adj* heptagonal.

heptágono *nm* heptagon.

heráldica *nf* heraldry.

heráldico,-a *adj* heraldic.

heraldo *nm Hist* herald.

herbáceo,-a *adj* herbaceous.

herbario I *adj* herbal. **II** *nm* **1** *(colección)* herbarium. **2** *(botánico)* herbalist.

herbicida *nm* weedkiller, herbicide.

herbívoro,-a I *adj* herbivorous, grass-eating. **II** *nm,f Zool* herbivore.

herbolario,-a I *adj fam fig* crazy, idiotic. **II** *nm,f (persona)* herbalist. **III** *nm (tienda)* herbalist's (shop).

herboristería *nf* herbalist's (shop).

herboso,-a *adj* grassy.

hercio *nm Fís* hertz.

hercúleo,-a *adj* Herculean.

heredable *adj* inheritable.

heredad *nf* **1** *(finca)* country estate. **2** *(conjunto de bienes)* private estate.

heredado,-a I *pp de* **heredar**. **II** *adj* inherited.

heredar I *vtr* **1** *Jur* to inherit; **h. los bienes de algn,** to inherit from sb; **esto lo heredé de ...,** this came to me from ... . **2** *Biol (de los padres)* **ha heredado la sonrisa de su madre,** she's got her mother's smile.

heredero,-a *nm,f (hombre)* heir; *(mujer)* heiress; **h. único,** sole heir; **nombrar a algn h.,** to make sb one's heir. ■ **príncipe h.,** crown prince.

hereditario,-a *adj* hereditary.

hereje *nmf Rel* heretic.

herejía *nf* **1** *Rel* heresy. **2** *fig (disparate)* **¡qué h.!,** what nonsense!

herencia *nf* **1** *Jur* inheritance, legacy. **2** *Biol* heredity.

herético,-a *adj* heretical.

herida *nf* **1** *(lesión)* wound. **2** *fig (pena)* wound, outrage; **lamerse las heridas,** to lick one's wounds; **tocar a algn en la h.,** to touch sb's sore spot.

herido,-a I *pp de* **herir**. **II** *adj (físicamente)* wounded, injured; *(emocionalmente)* hurt; **caer h.,** to be wounded; **h. de gravedad,** badly injured; **resultó h. el conductor del camión,** the lorry driver was injured; **sentirse h.,** to feel hurt. **III** *nm,f* wounded *or* injured person; **no hubo heridos,** there were no casualties.

herir I *vtr* **1** *(causar heridas a)* to wound, injure, hurt; *fig* **h. a algn en lo vivo,** to cut sb to the quick; *fig* **h. a algn en su amor propio,** to wound sb's pride. **2** *(golpear)* to beat, hit. **3** *(vista)* to offend; *(luz)* to dazzle; *(sonido)* to strike. **II herirse** *vr* to injure *or* hurt oneself; **se ha herido con un cuchillo,** he cut himself with a knife.

hermafrodita *adj & nmf* hermaphrodite.

hermanable *adj* **1** *(compatible)* compatible. **2** *(a juego)* matching.

hermanado,-a I *pp de* **hermanar**. **II** *adj* **1** *(semejante)* similar, alike. **2** *(unido)* joined, united. **3** *(ciudad)* twin.

hermanar I *vtr* **1** *(unir)* to unite, combine. **2** *(dos personas)* to unite spiritually. **3** *(ciudades)* to twin. **II hermanarse** *vr* **1** *(combinar)* to combine. **2** *(dos personas)* to become brothers *or* sisters in spirit.

hermanastro,-a *nm, f (hombre)* stepbrother; *(mujer)* stepsister.

hermandad *nf* **1** *(grupo)* fraternity, brotherhood, sisterhood; **h. de labradores,** farmers' association. **2** *(relación)* brotherhood; *fig* close relationship.

hermano,-a I *adj* (closely) related; **ciudades hermanas,** twin towns; **conceptos hermanos,** related concepts. **II** *nm* **1** brother. ■ **h. gemelo,** twin brother; **h. político,** brother-in-law; **primo h.,** first cousin. **2** *Rel (fraile)* brother. **3 hermanos,** brothers and sisters; **eran muchos hermanos,** there were a lot of children in the family. **III** *nf* **1** sister. ■ **h. gemela,** twin sister; **h. política,** sister-in-law; **prima h.,** first cousin. **2** *Rel (monja)* sister.

hermético,-a *adj* **1** hermetic, hermetical, airtight; **cierre h.,** hermetic seal, airtight lid. **2** *fig* impenetrable, secretive; **persona hermética,** secretive person, very reserved person; **un escritor h.,** an abstruse writer.

hermetismo *nm* hermetism; *fig* impenetrability, secrecy, secretiveness.

hermosear *vtr* to beautify, embellish.

hermoso,-a *adj* beautiful, lovely.

hermosura *nf* beauty; **¡qué h. de niño!,** what a beautiful child!

hernia *nf Med* hernia, rupture.

herniado,-a Med I *pp de* **herniarse**. **II** *adj Med* ruptured.

herniarse *vr Med* to rupture oneself.

Herodes *nm* Herod; **ir de H. a Pilatos,** to go from pillar to post.

héroe *nm* hero.

heroico,-a *adj* **1** heroic; **tiempos heroicos,** *(difíciles)* hard times; *(de gestas)* times of heroic deeds. **2** *Lit* heroic.

heroína *nf* **1** *(mujer)* heroine. **2** *(droga)* heroin.

heroinómano,-a *nm,f* heroin addict.

heroísmo *nm* heroism.

herpe *nm,* **herpes** *nm Med* herpes *sing,* **shingles** *sing.*

herpético,-a *adj Med* herpetic.

herrada *nf* wooden bucket.

herrador *nm* blacksmith.

herradura *nf* horseshoe; **en forma de h.,** horseshoe-shaped.

herraje *nm* iron fittings *pl,* ironwork.

herramienta *nf Téc* tool; **caja de herramientas,** toolbox.

herrar *vtr* **1** *(caballo)* to shoe. **2** *(ganado)* to brand.

herrería *nf* forge, smithy, blacksmith's.

herrero *nm* blacksmith, smith.

herrete *nm* **1** *(remate metálico)* tag, metal tip. **2** *Am Agr* branding iron.

herrumbre *nf* **1** *(óxido)* rust. **2** *(sabor a hierro)* rusty taste.

herrumbroso,-a *adj* rusty.

hertz *nm Fís véase* **hercio**.

hertziano,-a *adj Fís* Hertzian; **onda hertziana,** Hertzian wave.

hervidero *nm* **1** *(ebullición)* boiling, bubbling. **2** *(manantial)* hot spring. **2** *fig (lugar)* hotbed; **un h. de intrigas,** a nest of intrigue; **un h. de pasiones,** a hotbed of passion. **3** *fig (muchedumbre)* swarm, throng; **ser un h. de,** to be swarming with.

hervir I *vtr (hacer bullir)* to boil. **II** *vi* **1** *(bullir)* to boil; **romper a h.,** to come to the boil. **2** *(mar)* to surge. **3** *(abundar)* to swarm, seethe (de, with); **el mercado hervía de gente,** the market was teeming with people. **4** *(ira)* to seethe (de, en, with); **h. en cólera,** to seethe with anger; **h. en deseos de,** to be consumed with.

hervor *nm* boiling, bubbling; *Culin* **dar un h. a algo,** to blanch sth.

hetaira *nm,* **hetera** *nf Hist* hetaera.

heteróclito,-a *adj* **1** *Ling* heteroclite. **2** *fml fig* heterogeneous, irregular.

heterodoxia *nf* heterodoxy.

heterodoxo,-a I *adj* heterodox, unorthodox. **II** *nm, f* heterodox person.

heterogeneidad *nf* heterogeneity, heterogeneousness.

heterogéneo,-a *adj* heterogeneous.

heterosexual *adj & nmf* heterosexual.

hexagonal *adj* hexagonal.

hexágono *nm* hexagon.

hexámetro *nm* hexameter.

hez *nf* **1** *(gen pl) (poso)* sediment, dregs *pl*. **2** *fig* scum; *pey* **la h. de la sociedad,** the scum *or* dregs *of* society. **3 heces,** *(excrementos)* faeces.

hiato *nm Ling* hiatus.

hibernación *nf* hibernation.

hibernar *vi* to hibernate.

hibisco *nm Bot* hibiscus.

híbrido,-a *adj & nm, f* hybrid.

hice *pt indef véase* **hacer.**

hiciste *pt indef véase* **hacer.**

hico *nm Am* clew.

hidalgo,-a I *adj desus* noble; *fig (caballeroso)* gentlemanly. **II** *nm Hist* nobleman, gentleman.

hidalguía *nf* nobility; *fig* chivalry, gentlemanliness.

hidra *nf* **1** *(culebra acuática)* sea snake. **2** *(pólipo)* hydra.

hidratación *nf* **1** *Quím* hydration. **2** *(de la piel)* moisturizing.

hidratante *adj* moisturizing; **crema/leche h.,** moisturizing cream/lotion.

hidratar *vtr* **1** *Quím* to hydrate. **2** *(piel)* to moisturize.

hidrato *nm Quím* hydrate. ■ **h. de carbono,** carbohydrate.

hidráulica *nf* hydraulics *pl*, fluid mechanics *pl*.

hidráulico,-a *adj* hydraulic.

hídrico,-a *adj* hydric.

hidro- *pref* hydro-; **hidrometría,** hydrometry.

hidroavión *nm* seaplane, *US* hydroplane.

hidrocarburo *nm Quím* hydrocarbon.

hidrocefalia *nf Med* hydrocephalus, hydrocephaly.

hidroeléctrico,-a *adj* hydroelectric.

hidrófilo *adj* **1** *Bot* hydrophilous. **2** *(absorbente)* absorbent. ■ **algodón h.,** cotton wool, *US* absorbent cotton.

hidrofobia *nf Med* hydrophobia, rabies *sing*.

hidrógeno *nm Quím* hydrogen.

hidrografía *nf* hydrography.

hidrólisis *nf Quím* hydrolysis.

hidropesía *nf Med* dropsy.

hidrópico,-a *Med adj* dropsical, dropsied.

hidroterapia *nf Med* hydrotherapy.

hiedra *nf Bot* ivy.

hiel *nf* **1** *Anat* bile. **2** *fig* bitterness, gall.

hielo *nm* ice; *fig* **romper el h.,** to break the ice.

hiena *nf Zool* hyaena, hyena.

hierático,-a *adj* **1** *Hist* hieratic, hieratical. **2** *(severo, rígido)* rigid.

hierba *nf* **1** grass; **mala h.,** *Bot* weed; *fig (persona)* bad lot; *fig* **mala h. nunca muere,** ill weeds grow apace; *fam* **hum ... y otras hierbas,** ...among others. **2** *Culin* herb. ■ **finas hierbas,** mixed herbs; **h. luisa,** lemon verbena; **h. mate,** maté. **3 hierbas,** *(veneno)* poison *sing*, potion *sing*. **4** *sl (marihuana)* grass.

hierbabuena *nf Bot* mint.

hierbajo *nm fam* weeds *pl*.

hierro *nm* **1** *(metal)* iron; *fig* **ser de h.,** to be as strong as an ox; *fig* **voluntad de h.,** a will of iron; *fam fig* **quitarle h. a un asunto,** to play a matter down; *prov* **quien a h. mata, a h. muere,** he who lives by the sword, shall die by the sword. ■ **h. colado** *or* **fundido,** cast iron; **h. forjado,** wrought iron. **2** *(punta de arma)* head, point. **3** *(marca en el ganado)* brand.

higa *nf* scorn, derision.

higadillo *nm (gen pl)* liver; **higadillos de pollo,** chicken livers.

hígado *nm* **1** *Anat* liver; *fam* **echar los hígados,** to go flat out. **2** *euf* guts *pl*; *fam* **tener hígados,** to have guts.

higiene *nf* hygiene.

higiénico,-a *adj* hygienic. ■ **papel h.,** toilet paper.

higienista *nmf* hygienist.

higo *nm Bot* fig; *fig* **de higos a brevas,** once in a blue moon; *fam* **me importa un h.,** I couldn't care less; *fam* **¡y un h.!,** not on your life!, nothing doing!; *fam fig* **hecho un h.,** wizened, crumpled. ■ **h. chumbo,** prickly pear.

higuera *nf Bot* fig tree; *fig* **estar en la h.,** to have one's head in the clouds. ■ **h. chumba,** prickly pear.

hija *nf* daughter; **h. adoptiva,** adopted daughter; **h. mía,** darling; **hijas,** daughters; **h. única,** only daughter; *pey* **h. de papá,** daddy's girl; *vulg ofens* **h. de puta,** bastard; *véase tamb* **hijo.**

hijastro,-a *nm, f (hombre)* stepson; *(mujer)* stepdaughter.

hijear *vi Am* to adopt, mother.

hijo *nm* **1** son, child; **h. adoptivo,** adopted child; **h. mío,** son, my boy; **h. único,** only son; *fam* **¡h. de mi alma!,** my dearest child!; *fam* **todo h. de vecino,** everyone, every mother's son; *fam euf* **un h. de tal,** a real so-and-so; *pey* **h. de papá,** daddy's boy, rich kid; *vulg ofens* **h. de puta,** bastard, son of a bitch. **2 hijos,** children. **3** *fig* brainchild.

hijoputa *nm vulg ofens* bastard.

hijuelo *nm Bot* shoot.

hila *nf* **1** *desus (gen pl) (hebra)* lint. **2** *(acción de hilar)* spinning.

hilacha *nf,* **hilacho** *nm* loose *or* hanging thread.

hiladillo *nm* braid.

hilado,-a I *pp de* **hilar. II** *adj* spun. **III** *nm* **1** *(acción de hilar)* spinning. **2** *(fibra textil)* spun textile; **fábrica de hilados,** spinning mill; **tejidos de h.,** spun textiles. **3** *(hilo)* thread.

hilador,-a *nm, f* spinner.

hilandería *nf* mill; *(de algodón)* cotton mill.

hilandero,-a *nm, f* spinner.

hilar *vtr & vi* **1** *(gen)* to spin. **2** *fig (idea, plan)* to work out; **h. muy fino** *or* **delgado,** to split hairs.

hilarante *adj* hilarious; **gas h.,** laughing gas.

hilaridad *nf* hilarity, mirth.

hilatura *nf* **1** *(fábrica)* spinning mill. **2** *(acción de hilar)* spinning.

hilera *nf* line, row; **en h.,** in line.

hilo *nm* **1** *Cost* thread; *(grueso)* yarn; **cortar al h.,** to cut on the grain. **2** *fig (curso) (historia, discurso)* thread; *(de pensamiento)* train; **coger el h.,** to catch *or* get the drift; **estar colgando** *or* **pendiente de un h.,** to be hanging by a thread; **perder el h.,** to lose the thread; **seguir el h.,** to follow the thread. **3** *Tex* linen; **mantel de h.,** linen tablecloth. **4** *Tel* wire. **5** *(chorro fino)* trickle, thin stream; *fig* **un h. de voz,** a tiny voice.

hilván *nm Cost* **1** *(hilo)* tacking, basting. **2** *(cada uno de los hilos)* tack, tacking *or* basting stitch.

hilvanar *vtr* **1** *Cost* to tack, baste. **2** *fig (bosquejar ideas etc)* to throw.

Himalaya *n* **el H.,** the Himalayas *pl*.

himalayo,-a *adj* Himalayan.

himen *nm Anat* hymen.

himeneo *nm Lit* **1** *(boda)* wedding, marriage. **2** *(epitamio)* marriage ode.

himno *nm* hymn. ■ **h. nacional,** national anthem.

hincapié *nm* **hacer h. en,** *(insistir)* to insist on; *(subrayar)* to emphasize, stress.

hincar I *vtr* **1** *(clavar)* to drive (in); **h. el diente a,** to sink one's teeth into. **2** *arg* **hincarla,** to work; **no la hinca en todo el día,** he doesn't do a scrap of work all day. **II hincarse** *vr* **h. de rodillas,** to kneel (down).

hincha *fam* I *nf (antipatía)* grudge, dislike; **tener h. a algn**, to have it in for sb, bear a grudge against sb; **me tiene h.**, he's got it in for me. II *nmf Ftb* fan, supporter.

hinchada *nf Ftb fam* fans *pl*, supporters *pl*.

hinchado,-a I *pp de* **hinchar**. II *adj* 1 *(gen)* inflated, blown up. 2 *Med (cara etc)* swollen, puffed up; *(estómago)* bloated; **me siento h.**, I feel bloated. 2 *fig (persona)* conceited; *(estilo)* bombastic, pompous.

hinchar I *vtr* 1 *(inflar)* to inflate, blow up. 2 *fig (exagerar)* to inflate, exaggerate. II **hincharse** *vr* 1 *Med* to swell (up); **se me hinchan los tobillos**, my ankles swell up. 2 *fam (hartarse)* to stuff oneself; **me hinché de llorar**, I cried for all I was worth. 3 *(engreírse)* to become conceited *or* bigheaded. 4 *fam (enriquecerse)* to make a packet, line one's pockets.

hinchazón *nf* 1 *Med* swelling. 2 *fig (presunción)* vanity, conceit; *(pomposidad)* pomposity, pompousness.

hindú *adj & nmf* Hindu.

hinduismo *nm* Hinduism.

hiniesta *nf Bot* broom.

hinojo¹ *nm Bot* fennel.

hinojo² *nm arc* knee; **postrarse de hinojos**, to kneel (down).

hipar *vi* 1 *(tener hipo)* to hiccup, hiccough, have the hiccups *or* hiccoughs. 2 *fam (desear con ansia)* **h. por algo**, to yearn *or* long for sth. 3 *(lloriquear)* to whine, whimper.

hipérbaton *nm Lit* hyperbaton.

hipérbole *nf Lit* hyperbole, exaggeration.

hiperbólico,-a *adj Lit* hyperbolic.

hipercrítico,-a *adj* hypercritical.

hipermercado *nm* hypermarket.

hipermétrope *Med* I *adj* long-sighted. II *nmf* long-sighted person.

hipermetropía *nf Med* long-sightedness.

hipersensible *adj* hypersensitive.

hipertensión *nf Med* high blood pressure.

hípico,-a *adj* horse, equine; **club h.**, riding club; **concurso h.**, horse race; **sociedad hípica**, racecourse.

hipnosis *nf inv* hypnosis.

hipnótico,-a *adj* hypnotic.

hipnotismo *nm* hypnotism.

hipnotizador,-a I *adj* hypnotizing. II *nm,f* hypnotist.

hipnotizar *vtr* to hypnotize.

hipo *nm* 1 hiccup, hiccough; **me ha dado el h.**, it's given me hiccups, I've got the hiccups; **quitar el h.**, to cure hiccups. 2 *(deseo)* longing; **tener h. por algo**, to be longing for sth.

hipocampo *nm (pez)* sea horse.

hipocondría *nf* hypochondria.

hipocondríaco,-a *adj & nm,f* hypochondriac.

hipocrático,-a *adj* **juramento h.**, Hippocratic oath.

hipocresía *nf* hypocrisy.

hipócrita I *adj* hypocritical. II *nmf* hypocrite.

hipodérmico,-a *adj* hypodermic.

hipódromo *nm* racetrack, racecourse.

hipopótamo *nm Zool* hippopotamus.

hipotálamo *nm Anat* hypothalamus.

hipoteca *nf* 1 *Fin* mortgage. 2 *fig (desventaja)* drawback.

hipotecar *vtr* 1 *Fin* to mortgage. 2 *fig* to jeopardize.

hipotecario,-a *adj Fin* mortgage; **crédito h.**, mortgage loan.

hipotensión *nf Med* low blood pressure.

hipotenusa *nf Geom* hypotenuse.

hipótesis *nf inv* hypothesis; **h. de trabajo**, work thesis.

hipotético,-a *adj* hypothetical, hypothetic.

hiriente *adj* offensive, wounding; *(palabras)* cutting; **en tono h.**, offensively.

hirsuto,-a *adj* 1 hirsute, hairy; *(cerdoso)* bristly. 2 *fig (hosco)* surly, rough, brusque.

hirviente *adj* boiling; *fig* seething.

hisopo *nm* 1 *Bot* hyssop. 2 *Rel* aspergillum, sprinkler. 3 *Am (brocha)* brush.

hispalense *adj & nmf fml* of *or* from Seville.

hispánico,-a *adj* Hispanic, Spanish.

hispanidad *nf* 1 *(carácter hispano)* Spanishness. 2 *(pueblos de habla española)* Spanish *or* Hispanic world; **Día de la H.**, Columbus Day.

hispanismo *nm* 1 *(cultural)* Hispanism. 2 *Ling* Hispanicism.

hispanista *nmf* Hispanist.

hispanizar *vtr* to hispanize, hispanicize.

hispano,-a I *adj* Spanish, Hispanic, Spanish-American. II *nm,f* Spaniard, Spanish American, *US* Hispanic.

Hispanoamérica *nf* Spanish America, Latin America.

hispanoamericanismo *nm* Latin Americanism.

hispanoamericano,-a *adj & nm, f* Spanish American, Latin American.

hispanoárabe *adj* Hispano-Arabic.

hispanófilo,-a *adj & nm,f* Hispanophile.

hispanohablante I *adj* Spanish-speaking. II *nmf* Spanish speaker.

histamina *nf Biol* histamine.

histeria *nf* hysteria; **un ataque de h.**, hysterics *pl*; *fam fig* **h. colectiva**, mass hysteria.

histérico,-a *adj* hysteric, hysterical; *fam fig* **tu lentitud me pone histérica**, your slowness drives me mad.

histerismo *nm* hysteria; *fig* hysterics *pl*.

histología *nf Med* histology.

historia *nf* 1 *(estudio del pasado)* history; **esto pasará a la h.**, this will go down in history. ■ **h. natural**, natural history. 2 *(narración)* story, tale; *fam* **¡déjate de historias!**, get to the point!; *fam* **no me vengas con historias**, don't come to me with your tales.

historiado,-a I *pp de* **historiar**. II *adj fam (recargado)* over-ornate, florid.

historiador,-a *nm, f* historian.

historial *nm* 1 *Med* medical record, case history. 2 *(currículum)* curriculum vitae. 3 *(antecedentes)* background.

historiar *vtr* 1 *Arte* to depict. 2 *(de viva voz)* to tell the story of; *(acontecimientos)* to recount. 3 *(escrito)* to write the history of; *(acontecimientos)* to chronicle. 4 *Am fam (confundir)* to confuse, mix up.

histórica,-a *adj* 1 historical. 2 *(auténtico)* factual, true; **una película basada en hechos históricos**, a film based on true facts. 3 *(de gran importancia)* historic, memorable. 4 *Ling* **presente h.**, historical present.

historieta *nf* 1 *(cuento)* short story, anecdote, tale. 2 *(tira cómica)* comic strip.

histrión *nm* 1 *Teat* actor. 2 *fig (payaso)* clown, buffoon.

histriónico,-a *adj* histrionic.

histrionismo *nm* histrionics *pl*, theatrical behaviour *or US* behavior.

hitita *adj & nmf* Hittite.

hitleriano,-a *adj Pol* Hitler, Hitlerite.

hitlerismo *nm Pol* Hitlerism.

hito *nm* 1 *(mojón) (distancias)* milestone; *(límites)* boundary stone. 2 *(juego)* quoits *pl*. 3 *(blanco)* bull's-eye; *fig* target, aim, goal; **dar en d h.**, to hit the nail on the head. 4 *fig* **mirar de h. en h.**, to stare at.

hizo *indic indef véase* **hacer**.

Hnos., hnos. *abr de* **Hermanos**, Brothers, Bros.

hobby *nm* hobby.

hocico *nm* 1 *(de animal)* muzzle, snout. 2 *pey (de persona)* mug, snout; **caer** *or* **darse de hocicos,** to fall flat on one's face; **poner h.,** to grimace; *fam* **meter los hocicos en algo,** to stick *or* poke one's nose into sth.

hockey *nm Dep* hockey. ■ **h. sobre hielo,** ice hockey; **h. sobre hierba,** (field) hockey.

hogar *nm* 1 *(de la chimenea)* hearth, fireplace. 2 *fig (casa)* home; *fam fig* **h., dulce h.,** home sweet home. 3 *fig (familia)* family; **formar** *or* **crear un h.,** to start a family.

hogareño,-a *adj (vida)* home, family; *(persona)* home-loving, stay-at-home.

hogaza *nf Culin* large loaf (of bread).

hoguera *nf* bonfire; *euf* **morir en la h.,** to be burnt at the stake.

hoja *nf Bot* leaf; *fig* **h. de parra,** cover, alibi. 2 *(pétalo)* petal. 3 *(de papel)* sheet, leaf; **una h. en blanco,** a blank sheet of paper. 4 *(de libro)* leaf, page; *fig* **volver la h.,** to change the subject. 5 *(de metal)* sheet; **batir h.,** to beat metal. 6 *(de cuchillo, espada)* blade. ■ **h. de afeitar,** razor blade. 7 *(impreso)* hand-out, printed sheet; **h. suelta,** leaflet. 8 *(documento)* record. ■ *Com* **h. de ruta,** waybill; **h. de servicios,** record of service. 9 *(de puerta or ventana)* leaf; *(de mesa)* leaf, flap; **puerta de dos hojas,** double-leaf door.

hojalata *nf* tin, tin plate.

hojalatería *nf (taller)* tinsmith's; *(objetos)* tinware; *(oficio)* tinwork.

hojalatero *nm* tinsmith.

hojaldrado,-a *adj Culin* **pasta hojaldrada,** puff pastry.

hojaldre *nm Culin* puff pastry.

hojarasca *nf* 1 fallen *or* dead leaves *pl.* 2 *(fronda)* foliage. 3 *fig (paja)* rubbish, trash; *(palabras)* verbiage; **tus promesas son h.,** your promises are worthless.

hojear I *vtr (libro)* to leaf through, flick through. II *vi Am* to come to leaf.

hojuela *nf* 1 *Culin* pancake; *prov* **miel sobre hojuelas,** so much the better. 2 *(de la aceituna)* pressed olive skins *pl.* 3 *(hoja de metal)* foil.

hola *interj* 1 *(saludo)* hello!, hullo!, *US* hi! 2 *Am Tel* hello?

Holanda n Holland.

holandés,-esa I *adj* Dutch. II *nm,f (hombre)* Dutchman; *(mujer)* Dutchwoman; **los holandeses,** the Dutch. III *nm (idioma)* Dutch. IV *nf Impr* sheet of paper measuring 21 x 27 cm.

holding *nm Fin* holding company.

holgado,-a I *pp de* **holgar.** II *adj* 1 *(ropa)* loose, baggy. 2 *(económicamente)* comfortable; **estar en una situación holgada,** to be comfortably off, be well off. 3 *(espacio)* roomy; **ir h.,** to have plenty of room; *(tiempo)* **andar h. de tiempo,** to have plenty of spare time. ◆ **holgodamente** *adv* 1 **caber h.,** to fit (in) easily. 2 **vivir h.,** to be well-off, be comfortably off.

holganza *nf* 1 *(ocio)* leisure, idleness 2 *(diversión)* pleasure.

holgar I *vi* 1 *(estar ocioso)* to be idle. 2 *(sobrar)* **huelga decir que ...,** it goes without saying that ...; **huelgan las palabras,** no comment. II **holgarse** *vr* to be pleased **(con, de,** by).

holgazán,-ana I *adj* lazy, idle. II *nm, f* lazybones *inv,* layabout.

holgazanear *vi* to laze *or* loaf around.

holgazanería *nf* laziness, idleness.

holgura *nf* 1 *(ropa)* looseness. 2 *(espacio)* space, roominess; *Téc* play, give; **cabes con h.,** there's plenty of room for you. 3 *(bienestar económico)* affluence, comfort; **vivir con h.,** to be comfortably off, be well-off.

hollar *vtr* 1 to tread (on), trample down. 2 *fig (pisar)* to trample on. 3 *fig (humillar)* to humiliate.

hollejo *nm Bot* skin, peel.

hollín *nm* soot.

holocausto *nm* holocaust; **ofrecer algo en h.,** to offer sth as a sacrifice.

holografía *nf* holography.

holograma *nm* hologram.

hombrada *nf* manly action; *irón* **¡qué h.!,** how brave!

hombre I *nm* 1 *(ser físico)* man; **de h. a h.,** man-to-man; **el h. y la mujer,** man and woman; **¡h. al agua!,** man overboard!; **¡pobre h.!,** poor chap!; **ser muy h.,** to be every inch a man; **ser otro h.,** to be a changed man. ■ **h. anuncio,** sandwich man; **h. orquesta,** one-man band; **h. rana,** frogman; *fam* **h. delsaco,** bogeyman. 2 *(como ser moral)* **h. de bien,** good *or* upstanding man; **h. de estado,** statesman; **el h. de la calle,** the man in the street; **h. de letras,** man of letters; **h. de mundo,** man of the world; **h. de negocios,** businessman; **h. de paja,** front man; **h. de palabra,** man of his word; **h. de peso,** important figure; **h. de pro** *or* **provecho,** honest man; **h. masa,** the average man. 3 *(especie)* mankind, man. 4 *(adulto)* **se está haciendo un h.,** he's growing into a man; **te hará un h.,** it'll make a man of you. 5 *fam (marido)* husband. II *interj* 1 *(saludo)* hey!, hey there!; **¡h., Juan!,** hey, Juan!; **¡h., Pepe, tú por aquí!,** hello there, Pepe!, fancy seeing you here! 2 *(enfático)* **¡sí h.!, ¡h. claro!,** well, of course!, you bet!; **¡h., qué pena!,** oh, what a shame! 3 *(indica reproche)* **¡anda, h.!,** come on!; **¡pero h.!,** but listen!

hombrear *vi* 1 *(dárselas de hombre)* to act the man. 2 *(empujar)* to push with the shoulders.

hombrera *nf* 1 *(almohadilla)* shoulder pad. 2 *(tirante)* shoulder strap. 3 *Mil* epaulette.

hombretón *nm* big *or* well-built fellow.

hombría *nf* manliness, virility.

hombro *nm* shoulder; **a hombros,** on one's shoulders; **arrimar el h.,** to lend a hand; **encogerse de hombros,** to shrug one's shoulders; **echarse algo al h.,** to shoulder sth; **mirar a algn por encima del h.,** to look down one's nose at sb.

hombruno,-a *adj (mujer)* mannish, butch.

homenaje *nm* homage, tribute; **rendir h. a algn,** to pay homage *or* tribute to sb; **una cena de h. al poeta,** a dinner in honour of the poet.

homenajear *vtr* to pay tribute to.

homeópata I *adj* homeopathic. II *nmf* homeopath.

homeopatía *nf* homeopathy.

homeopático,-a *adj* homeopathic.

homérico,-a *adj Lit* Homeric.

homicida I *nmf (hombre)* murderer; *(mujer)* murderess. II *adj* homicidal; **el arma h.,** the murder weapon.

homicidio *nm* homicide; **h. involuntario,** manslaughter.

homilía *nf Rel* homily, sermon.

homofonía *nf Ling* homophony.

homófono,-a *adj* homophonous, homophonic.

homogeneidad *nf* homogeneity, uniformity.

homogeneizar *vtr* to homogenize, make homogeneous.

homogéneo,-a *adj* homogeneous, uniform.

homologación *nf* 1 *Dep (récord)* ratification. 2 *(registro)* official approval *or* recognition. 3 *Jur (muerte etc)* confirmation.

homologado,-a I *pp de* **homologar.** II *adj* officially approved *or* recognized; **centro de estudios h.,** government recognized school; **productos homologados,** authorized products.

homologar *vtr* 1 *Dep (récord)* to ratify. 2 to give official approval *or* recognition to. 3 *Jur (confirmar)* to confirm *or* endorse.

homólogo,-a I *adj Mat Quím* homologous; *(equiparable)* comparable. II *nm, f (persona con mismas condiciones)* opposite number.

homónimo,-a I *adj* homonymous. **II** *nm* homonym.

homosexual *adj & nmf* homosexual.

homosexualidad *nf* homosexuality.

honda *nf (arma)* sling.

hondo,-a I *adj* **1** *(profundo)* deep. ■ **plato h.,** soup dish. **2** *fig (muy íntimo)* profound, deep. ■ *Mús* **cante h.,** flamenco song. **II** *nm* the depths *pl*, the bottom; **en lo h. del cajón,** at the bottom of the drawer.

hondonada *nf Geog* hollow, depression.

hondura *nf* depth; *fig* **meterse en honduras,** *(profundizar)* to go into too much detail; *(tratar sin conocimiento)* to get out of one's depth, get in over one's head.

Honduras *n* Honduras.

hondureño,-a *adj & nm,f* Honduran.

honestidad *nf* **1** *(honradez)* honesty, uprightness. **2** *(pudor)* modesty.

honesto,-a *adj* **1** *(honrado)* honest, upright; **una decisión muy honesta,** a very sensible decision. **2** *(recatado)* modest. ◆ **honestamente** *adv* decently, properly.

hongo *nm* **1** *Bot* fungus; **h. venenoso,** toadstool. **2.** *(sombrero)* bowler, bowler hat. **3 h. nuclear,** mushroom cloud.

honor *nm* **1** *(virtud)* honour, *US* honor; **cuestión de h.,** point of honour; **lo juro por mi h.,** I swear it upon my honour; **palabra de h.,** word of honour. **2** *(enaltecer)* **en h. a la verdad ...,** to be fair ...; **es un h. para mí,** it's an honour for me ... . **3** *(reputación)* **hacer h. a,** to live up to; **este vino hace h. a su fama,** this wine lives up to its reputation. **4** *desus (mujer)* virtue; **perdió su h.,** she lost her virginity. **5** honors, title *sing*, distinction *sing*. **6** *(fiesta)* **hacer los honores,** to do the honours; *Mil* **rendir los honores,** with full military honours.

honorable *adj* honourable, *US* honorable.

honorario,-a I *adj* honorary. **II honorarios** *nmpl* fees, fee *sing*, emoluments.

honorífico,-a *adj* honorific, **cargo h.,** unpaid post.

honra *nf* **1** *(amor propio)* dignity, self-esteem. **2** *(fama)* reputation, good name. **3** *(motivo de orgullo)* honour, *US* honor; **me cabe la h. de ...,** I have the honour of ...; **tener a mucha h.,** to be very proud of; **¡a mucha h.!,** and (I'm) proud of it! **4 honras fúnebres,** last honours.

honradez *nf* honesty, integrity.

honrado,-a I *pp* de **honrar. II** *adj* **1** *(de fiar)* honest. **2** *(honorable)* honourable, *US* honorable. **3** *(decente)* upright, respectable.

honrar I *vtr* **1** *(respetar)* to honour, *US* honor. **2** *(enaltecer)* to do credit to; **esas palabras te honran,** those words do you credit. **II honrarse** *vr* to be honoured *or US* honored.

honrilla *nf* self-respect, pride; **lo hizo por la negra h.,** he did it for the sake of appearances *or* for fear of what people might think.

honroso,-a *adj* **1** *(respeto)* honourable, *US* honorable. **2** *(decoroso)* respectable, reputable.

hontanar *nm Geol* spring.

hora *nf* **1** hour; *fig* time; **¿qué h. es?,** what time is it?; **a altas horas de la madrugada,** in the small hours; **¡a buenas horas!,** and about time too!; **a** *or* **en su h.,** at the proper time; **a última h.,** at the last moment; **comer entre horas,** to eat between meals; **dar la h.,** to strike the hour; **h. de acostarse,** bedtime; **h. de cenar,** dinner time; **h. de comer,** lunchtime; **la h. de la verdad,** the moment of truth; **(trabajo) por horas,** (work) paid by the hour; *fam* **tener horas de vuelo,** to be an old hand; *arg* **ir con la h. pegada al culo,** to run around like a blue-arsed fly. ■ **h. punta,** rush hour; **horas extras** *or* **extraordinarias,** overtime (hours). **2** *(cita)* appointment; *(médico etc)* **dar h.,** to fix an appointment; **pedir h.,** to ask for an appointment. **3** *Lit* **libro de horas,** Book of Hours.

horadar *vtr (agujerear)* to drill (through), bore (through); *(perforar)* to pierce.

horario *nm* **1** timetable, *US* schedule; **tengo h. de mañanas,** I work mornings. **2** *(manecilla de reloj)* hour hand.

horca *nf* **1** *Agr* pitchfork, hayfork. **2** *(patíbulo)* gallows *pl*, gibbet. **3** *(de ajos, cebollas)* string.

horcajada *nf* **a horcajadas,** astride.

horchata *nf Culin* sweet milky drink made from chufa nuts or almonds; *fig* **tener sangre de h.,** to have water in one's veins, be gutless.

horchatería *nf* bar where **horchata** is sold.

horchatero,-a *nm,f* person who sells **horchata.**

horcón *nm* **1** *Agr* pitchfork. **2** *Am Arquit* support for roof beams.

horda *nf* horde, mob; *fig* gang.

horizontal *adj* horizontal. ◆ **horizontalmente** *adv* horizontally.

horizonte *nm* horizon; *fig* **este producto amplia el h. de la informática,** this product widens the horizons of computer science.

horma *nf* form, mould, *US* mold; *(de zapato)* last; *fig* **encontrar la h. de su zapato,** to meet one's match.

hormiga *nf Ent* ant. ■ **h. blanca,** white ant.

hormigón *nm Constr* concrete. ■ **h. armado,** reinforced concrete.

hormigonera *nf Aut* concrete mixer.

hormiguear *vi* **1** to itch, tingle; **me hormigueaba la pierna,** I had pins and needles in my leg. **2** *(pulular)* to swarm, teem.

hormigueo *nm* pins and needles *pl*, tingling *or* itching sensation; *fig* anxiety, uneasiness.

hormiguero *nm* **1** anthill, ant's nest. **2** *fig (lugar)* **ser un h.,** to be swarming (with people).

hormiguillo *nm* **1** *(cosquilleo)* pins and needles *pl*, tingling *or* itching sensation. **2** *Am Min* amalgamation.

hormiguita *nf dimin* small ant; **ser una h.,** to be hardworking and thrifty.

hormona *nf* hormone.

hormonal *adj* hormonal.

hornacho *nm Min* excavation.

hornacina *nf Arquit* niche.

hornada *nf* **1** *(pan)* batch. **2** *fig* set, batch.

hornazo *nm Culin* pie *or* pastry decorated with hardboiled eggs.

hornear *vtr* to bake.

hornillo *nm* **1** *Téc* small furnace. **2** *(de cocinar)* stove; **h. eléctrico,** hotplate. **3** *Min* blast hole.

horno *nm* **1** *(cocina)* oven; *Téc* furnace; *(cerámica, ladrillos)* kiln; **h. de fundición,** smelting furnace; *Culin* **pescado al h.,** baked fish; *fam fig* **esta habitación es no h.,** this room is boiling hot; *fam* **no estar el h. para boilos,** not to be the right time. ■ **alto h.,** blast furnace; **h. crematorio,** crematorium. **2** *desus (panadería)* bakery, bakehouse.

Hornos *n* **Cabo de H.,** Cape Horn.

horóscopo *nm* horoscope.

horqueta *nf Am (en carretera)* fork.

horquilla *nf* **1** *Peluq* hair-grip, hairpin, hair clip, *US* bobby pin. **2** *Agr* pitchfork. **3** *Cicl* fork.

horrendo,-a *adj* horrifying, horrible.

hórreo *nm Agr* granary.

horrible *adj* horrible, dreadful, awful.

horripilante *adj* hair-raising, scary, creepy.

horripilar *vtr* to scare stiff, make (one's) hair stand on end, give the creeps.

horro,-a *adj fml* **1** *(carente)* lacking. **2** *(esclavo)* free.

horror *nm* **1** horror, terror; **¡qué h.!,** how awful!; *fam* **tengo h. a las motos,** I hate motorbikes. **2** *fam fig (muchísimo)* an awful lot; **cuesta un h.,** it costs a bomb; **me gusta horrores,** I'm crazy about it; **sufrió horrores,** he suffered terribly. **3 horrores,** *(atrocidades)* atrocities.

horrorizar I *vtr* to horrify, terrify; *fam* **me horroriza ese traje,** I hate that suit. **II horrorizarse** *vr* to be horrified.

horroroso,-a *adj* **1** *(que da miedo)* horrifying, terrifying. **2** *fam (muy feo)* hideous, ghastly. **3** *fam (malísimo)* awful, dreadful. **4** *fam (muy grande)* **tengo una sed horrorosa,** I'm dying of thirst; **me llevé un susto h.,** I got an awful fright.

hortaliza *nf* **1** vegetable. **2 hortalizas,** vegetables, garden produce *sing.*

hortelano,-a I *adj* market-gardening, *US* truck-farming. **II** *nm,f* market gardener, *US* truck farmer; *fig* **ser el perro del h.,** to be the dog in the manger.

hortensia *nf Bot* hydrangea.

hortera *arg* **I** *adj* common, vulgar; *(ostentoso)* flashy, tacky; *(pomposo)* pretentious. **II** *nmf (pretensioso)* upstart; *(chabacano)* crude character.

horterada *nf arg* tacky thing *or* act.

hortícola *adj* horticultural.

horticultor,-a *nm,f* horticulturist.

horticultura *nf* horticulture.

hosco,-a *adj* **1** *(poco sociable)* surly, sullen. **2** *(lugar) (tenebroso)* dark, gloomy.

hospedaje *nm* **1** *(acción de hospedar)* lodging. **2** *(lugar)* lodgings *pl*, accommodation.

hospedar I *vtr* to put up, lodge. **II hospedarse** *vr* to stay **(en,** at).

hospedería *nf* inn, hostelry.

hospiciano,-a *nm,f* orphan, person living in an orphanage.

hospicio *nm (para huérfanos)* orphanage; *(para peregrinos)* hospice.

hospital *nm* hospital, infirmary. ■ *Mil* **h. de (primera) sangre,** field hospital.

hospitalario,-a *adj* **1** *(acogedor)* hospitable. **2** *Med* hospital; **instalaciones hospitalarias,** hospital facilities.

hospitalidad *nf* hospitality.

hospitalización *nf* hospitalization.

hospitalizar *vtr* to take *or* send into hospital, hospitalize.

hosquedad *nf* surliness, sullenness.

hostal *nm* hostel, cheap hotel.

hostelería *nf (negocio)* catering business; *(estudios)* hotel management.

hostelero,-a *nm, f arc* innkeeper; *(hombre)* landlord; *(mujer)* landlady.

hostería *nf arc* inn, lodging house.

hosti *interj véase* **hostia.**

hostia I *nf* **1** *Rel* host, Eucharistic wafer. **2** *vulg (tortazo)* bash; **darse** *or* **pegarse una h.,** to give oneself a real bash, come a cropper; **darle** *or* **pegarle una h. a algn,** to belt sb, give sb a belting; **estar de mala h.,** to be in a foul mood; **ir a toda h.** *or* **echando hostias,** to go flat out; **ser la h.,** *(fantástico)* to be bloody amazing *or* fantastic; *(penoso)* to be bloody useless. **II** *interj* Jesus Christ!, damn it!

hostiar *vtr vulg* to bash, sock.

hostigamiento *nm* harassment.

hostigar *vtr* **1** *(caballería)* to whip. **2** *fig (molestar)* to pester. **3** *(perseguir)* to plague, persecute; *Mil* to harass. **4** *Am (empalagar)* to pall on, cloy.

hostil *adj* hostile.

hostilidad *nf* hostility; *Mil* **romper las hostilidades,** to begin hostilities.

hotel *nm* **1** hotel. **2** *(quinta, chalet)* villa, mansion. **3** *arg (cárcel)* clink, nick.

hotelero,-a I *adj* hotel; **industria hotelera,** hotel industry *or* trade. **II** *nm, f* hotel-keeper, hotelier.

hoy *adv* **1** *(día)* today; **de h. a mañana,** very soon; **de h. en adelante,** henceforth, from now on; **hasta h.,** up till now. **2** *fig (presente)* now; **h. (en) día,** nowadays; **h. por h.,** at the present time; **por h.,** for the present.

hoya *nf* **1** *(hoyo grande)* pit, hole. **2** *(sepultura)* grave. **3** *Geog (llano)* dale, valley. **4** *Am Geog* river basin.

hoyo *nm* **1** *(agujero)* hole, pit. **2** *(sepultura)* grave. **3** Golf hole.

hoyuelo *nm* dimple.

hoz¹ *nf Agr* sickle; *Pol* **la h. y el martillo,** the hammer and sickle.

hoz² *nf Geog* ravine, gorge.

hozar *vtr (jabalí, cerdo)* to root in *or* among, dig up.

HR *nm abr de* **Hostal Residencia.**

hube *pt indef véase* **haber.**

hubiera *subj imperf véase* **haber.**

hucha *nf* **1** moneybox, piggy bank. **2** *fig (ahorros)* savings *pl*, nest egg.

hueco,-a I *adj* **1** *(vacío)* empty, hollow; **árbol h.,** hollow tree; *fig* **palabras huecas,** empty words. **2** *(sonido)* resonant. **3** *(esponjoso)* spongy, soft. **4** *(presumido)* vain, conceited; **ponerse h.,** to swell with pride. **II** *nm* **1** *(cavidad)* hollow, hole; *Arquit* opening. ■ **h. de la ventana,** window recess; **h. del ascensor,** lift shaft; **h. de la escalera,** stairwell. **2** *(sitio no ocupado)* empty space, empty seat; **dejar un h.,** to leave a gap; **hacer un h. a algn,** to make room for sb; *fig* **llenar un h.,** to fill a gap *or* a need. **3** *(rato libre)* free time; *(profesor)* free period; **tengo un h. a las cinco, aprovecharé para visitarte,** I'm free at five so I'll visit you. **4** *fig (vacante)* vacancy.

huecograbado *nm Impr* photogravure.

huele *indic pres véase* **oler.**

huelga *nf* strike; **estar en** *or* **de huelga,** to be on strike; **hacer** *or* **ir a la h.,** to go on strike. ■ **h. de brazos caídos,** go-slow; **h. de celo,** work-to-rule; **h. general,** general strike; **h. de hambre,** hunger strike; **h. salvaje,** wildcat strike.

huelguista *nmf* striker.

huella *nf* **1** *(del pie)* footprint; *(coche)* track; *fig* **seguir las huellas de algn,** to follow in sb's footsteps. ■ **h. dactilar,** fingerprint. **2** *fig (vestigio)* trace, sign; **dejar h.,** to leave one's mark; **huellas de dolor,** traces of pain; **no quedó ni h.,** there wasn't a trace.

huelveño,-a I *adj of* **or** from Huelva. **II** *nm, f* native *or* inhabitant of Huelva.

huérfano,-a I *adj* **1** orphan, orphaned; **h. de madre,** motherless; **h. de padre,** fatherless. **2** *fig (carente)* lacking; **h. de cariño,** devoid of love. **II** *nm,f* orphan.

huero,-a *adj* **1** *(huevo)* addled, rotten. **2** *fig (hueco)* empty.

huerta *nf Agr* **1** market *or US* truck garden. **2** *(vega)* irrigated area used for cultivation; **la h. de Valencia,** the huerta of Valencia.

huerto *nm (de verduras)* vegetable garden, kitchen garden; *(de frutales)* orchard; *fam fig* **llevarse a algn al h.,** *(engañar)* to lead sb up the garden path; *(llevarse a la cama)* to go to bed with sb.

huesillo *nm SAm* dried peach.

huesista *nm CAm* public employee.

hueso *nm* **1** *Anat* bone; **dar con los huesos en tierra,** to keel over, come a cropper; **darle a la sin h.,** to talk one's head off; **estar calado** *or* **empapado hasta los huesos,** to be soaked (through); **estar en los huesos,** to be all skin and bone; **romperle a algn un h.** *or* **los huesos,** to give sb a roasting, make mincemeat of sb; **tener los huesos molidos,** to be dead beat *or* exhausted. **2** *(de fruta)* stone, *US* pit. **3** *fig (difícil)* hard work; *(profesor)* strict person;

para mí la física es un h., I find physics a real chore; **un h. duro de roer,** a hard nut to crack; **el profesor de música es un h.,** the music teacher's a real stickler. **4** *fam* *(de mala calidad)* useless thing. **5** *CAm (trabajo)* sinecure, soft job. **6** *Méx (trabajo)* job.

huesoso,-a *adj* bony.

huésped,-a *nm,f* **1** *(invitado)* guest; *(en hotel etc)* lodger, boarder. ■ **casa de huéspedes,** guesthouse. **2** *(anfitrión) (hombre)* host; *(mujer)* hostess.

hueste *nf* **1** *Mil* army, host. **2 huestes,** *(seguidores)* followers, supporters.

huesudo,-a *adj* bony; **rodillas huesudas,** knobbly knees.

hueva *nf (pez)* roe, spawn.

huevazos *nm inv vulg* wanker.

huevería *nf* egg shop.

huevero,-a I *nm,f* person who sells eggs. **II** *nf* **1** *(copa)* egg cup. **2** *(caja)* egg box. **3** *vulg (suspensorio)* jockstrap.

huevo *nm* **1** egg; *fig* **parecerse como un h. a una castaña,** to be as different as chalk and cheese; *fig* **ser una cosa el h. de Colón,** to be easier than it seems. ■ **h. duro,** hard-boiled egg; **h. escalfado,** poached egg; **h. estrellado** *or* **frito,** fried egg; **h. pasado por agua,** *SAm* **h. tibio,** soft-boiled egg; **huevos moles,** dessert made from egg yolk(s); **huevos revueltos,** *Col* **huevos pericos,** scrambled eggs. **2** *vulg (gen pl)* balls *pl*; **costar un h.,** to cost an arm and a leg; **estar hasta los huevos,** to be pissed off; **hacer algo por huevos,** to do sth even if it kills you; **tener huevos,** to have guts; **¡y un h.!,** like hell!

hugonote,-a *adj & nm,f Hist* Huguenot.

huida *nf* **1** flight, escape. **2** *(del caballo)* shying, bolting.

huidizo,-a *adj (tímido)* shy; *(esquivo)* elusive, fleeting.

huillón,-ona *adj Am* elusive.

huipil *nm CAm Méx* blouse.

huir *vi* **1** *(escaparse)* to run away **(de,** from), flee. **2** *(evitar)* **h. de,** to avoid, keep away from **(de,** from), escape **(de,** from); **h. de algn como de la peste,** to avoid sb like the plague. **3** *Lit (tiempo)* to fly.

huisachar *vi* to dispute at law, contend.

hule *nm* **1** *(tela impermeable)* oilcloth, oilskin. **2** *Guat Méx Aut* windscreen wiper blade. **3** *CAm Med* operating table.

hulear *vi CAm* to extract rubber (from plants).

hulería *nf Am* rubber plantation *or* industry.

hulla *nf Min* coal. ■ **h. blanca,** water power.

hullero,-a *adj Min* coal; **explotación hullera,** *(mina)* mine; *(industria)* mining.

humanidad *nf* **1** *(género humano)* humanity, mankind. **2** *(cualidad)* humanity, humaneness. **3** *(bondad)* compassion, kindness. **4** *(corpulencia)* corpulence. **5 humanidades,** *Educ* humanities.

humanismo *nm* humanism.

humanista *nm,f* humanist.

humanístico,-a *adj* humanistic.

humanitario,-a *adj* humanitarian.

humanitarismo *nm* humanitarianism.

humanización *nf* humanization.

humanizar I *vtr* to humanize. **II humanizarse** *vr* to become more human.

humano,-a I *adj* **1** *(relativo al hombre)* human. **2** *(compasivo)* humane. **II** *nm* human (being).

humarada *nf*, **humareda** *nf* (dense) cloud of smoke.

humeante *adj (humo)* smoky, smoking; *(vaho)* steaming.

humear I *vi* **1** *(echar humo)* to smoke; *(arrojar vapor)* to fume, steam, be steaming hot. **2** *fig* to smoulder, *US* smolder. **3** *fig (presumir)* to be conceited. **II** *vtr* **1** *Am (lugar)* to fumigate. **2** *Méx (azotar)* to scourge, beat.

humedad *nf* humidity; *(vaporización)* moisture; *(sensación)* dampness.

humedecer I *vtr* to moisten, dampen. **II humedecerse** *vr* to become damp *or* wet *or* moist.

húmedo,-a *adj (casa, ropa)* damp; *(clima)* humid, damp, moist.

húmero *nm Anat* humerus.

humildad *nf* humility, humbleness.

humilde *adj* humble, modest; **una familia h.,** a poor family.

humillación *nf* humiliation, humbling.

humillante *adj* humiliating, humbling.

humillar I *vtr* **1** *(rebajar)* to humiliate, humble; **me humilla pedir dinero,** I find it humiliating to ask for money. **2** *arc (bajar) (cabeza)* to bow; *(rodilla)* to bend. **II humillarse** *vr* **h. ante algn,** to humble oneself before sb.

humita *nf Am Culin* tamale, dish of ground maize, wrapped in maize husks and steamed.

humo *nm* **1** smoke; *(gas)* fumes *pl*; *(vapor)* vapour, *US* vapor, steam; **echar h.,** to smoke; *fig* **a h. de pajas,** thoughtlessly. **2 humos,** *fig* conceit *sing*, airs; **bajarle los h. a algn,** to put sb in their place, take sb down a peg or two; **¡qué h. tiene!,** she gives herself such airs!; **subírsele los h. (a uno),** to become conceited, get on one's high horse.

humor *nm* **1** *(genio)* mood; *(carácter)* temper; **estar de buen** *or* **mal h.,** to be in a good *or* bad mood; **¡qué h. tienes!,** what patience you've got!; **tener h. para algo,** to feel like (doing) sth, feel in the mood for (doing) sth; **no tengo h. para ir al teatro,** I am not in the mood for going to the theatre; **tener un h. de perros,** to be in a foul temper. **2** *(gracia)* humour, *US* humor; **el h. inglés,** the English sense of humour; **sentido del h.,** sense of humour. ■ **h. negro,** black comedy. **3** *(líquido orgánico)* humour. ■ *Anat* **h. acuoso,** aqueous humour.

humorada *nf (dicho gracioso)* joke, pleasantry; *(extravagancia)* whim, caprice.

humorismo *nm* humour, *US* humor.

humorista I *adj* humorous. **II** *nmf* humorist; **h. gráfico,** cartoonist.

humorístico,-a *adj* humorous, funny.

humus *nm Agr* humus.

hundible *adj* sinkable.

hundido,-a I *pp de* **hundir. II** *adj* **1** sunken; **barco h.,** sunken ship; **ojos hundidos,** deep-set eyes; **mejillas hundidas,** hollow cheeks. **2** *fig (abatido)* demoralized.

hundimiento *nm* **1** *(edificio)* collapse. **2** *(barco)* sinking. **3** *(tierra)* subsidence. **4** *fig Fin* crash; slump; *(ruina)* downfall.

hundir I *vtr* **1** *(barco)* to sink. **2** *(hacer caer)* to cause to collapse, ruin; **la nieve hundió el techo,** the snow caused the roof to collapse; **vas a h. el suelo,** you'll go through the floor. **3** *(meter)* to submerge; **hundió la cara en la almohada,** she buried her face in the pillow. **4** *fig (arruinar planes etc)* to ruin. **5** *fig (abatir)* to demoralize; *(enemigo)* to defeat; **h. a algn en la miseria,** to plunge sb into misery. **II hundirse** *vr* **1** *(barco)* to sink. **2** *(derrumbarse)* to collapse, cave in; **se hundió el imperio,** the Empire collapsed. **3** *fig (arruinarse)* to be ruined. **4** *(sucumbir)* to be destroyed; **h. en la tristeza,** to be consumed by sadness; **hundido en el olvido,** long-forgotten; **hundido en la miseria,** penniless.

húngaro,-a I *adj* Hungarian. **II** *nm,f (persona)* Hungarian. **III** *nm (idioma)* Hungarian.

Hungría *n* Hungary.

huno,-a *Hist* **I** *adj* Hunnish. **II** *nm* Hun.

huracán *nm* hurricane.

huracanado,-a *adj Meteor* hurricane; **vientos huracanados,** hurricane winds.

huraño,-a *adj pey* shy, unsociable.

hurgar I *vtr* **1** *(remover fuego etc)* to poke, rake. **2** *fig (fisgar)* to stir up; **h. en,** to rummage in. **3** *fig (incitar)* to provoke. **II hurgarse** *vr* **h. las narices,** to pick one's nose.

hurgón *nm* poker; *(de fuego)* rake.

hurgonear *vtr* to poke, rake.

hurí *nf Rel* houri.

hurón,-ona I *nm Zool* ferret. **II** *nm, f* **1** *fam fig (fisgón)* busybody, nosey-parker. **2** *(huraño)* unsociable person.

hurra *interj* hurray!, hurrah!

hurraca *nf Orn véase* **urraca.**

hurtadillas *adv* **a h.,** stealthily, on the sly.

hurtar *vtr* **1** *(robar)* to steal, pilfer. **2** *fig (apartar)* **h. el cuerpo,** to dodge (out of the way). **3** *(peso)* **h. en el peso de algo,** to cheat on the weight of sth.

hurto *nm* petty theft, pilfering.

húsar *nm Mil* hussar.

husillo[1] *nm Téc (tornillo de prensa)* screw.

husillo[2] *nm (conducto de desagüe)* drain.

husmeador,-a I *adj* **1** *(con el olfato)* sniffing. **2** *fig (que curiosea)* prying, snooping. **II** *(fisgón) nm, f* snooper.

husmear I *vi* to (begin to) smell high, be smelly. **II** *vtr* **1** *(rastrear con el olfato)* to sniff out, scent; **h. el peligro,** to scent danger. **2** *fig (curiosear)* to poke one's nose into, pry into.

husmeo *nm* **1** scenting. **2** *fig* prying, snooping.

huso *nm Tex* spindle, bobbin. **2** *Geog* **h. horario,** time zone.

huy *interj* **1** *(dolor)* ouch!, ow! **2** *(asombro)* **¡h., qué feo!,** how ugly!; **¡h., qué raro!,** that's odd! **3** *(reproche)* **¡h., h., h.!,** tut, tut, tut!

huyo *indic pres véase* **huir.**

huyuyo,-a *adj Am* unsociable, surly.

Hz *abr de* **hertz,** hertz, Hz.

I

I, i *nf (la letra)* I, i; **i griega,** Y, y.

ib. *abr de* **ibídem,** ibidem, ibid., ib.

ibérico,-a *adj* Iberian.

ibero,-a *adj & nm, f,* **íbero,-a** *adj & nm, f* Iberian.

Iberoamérica *n* Latin America.

iberoamericano,-a *adj & nm, f* Latin American.

íbice *nm Zool* ibex.

ibicenco,-a I *adj* of or from Ibiza. **II** *nm, f* native or inhabitant of Ibiza.

ibíd *abr de* **ibídem,** ibidem, ibid., ib.

ibis *nf Orn* ibis.

iceberg *nm (pl icebergs)* iceberg.

ICONA *nm abr de* **Instituto para la Conservación de la Naturaleza.**

icono *nm* icon, ikon.

iconoclasía *nf* iconoclasm.

iconoclasta I *adj* iconoclastic. **II** *nmf* iconoclast.

iconografía *nf* iconography.

ictericia *nf Med* jaundice, icterus.

íd. *abr de* **ídem,** idem, id.

ida *nf* **1** going; *(salida)* departure; **billete de i. y vuelta,** return ticket; **idas y venidas,** comings and goings; **viaje de i. y vuelta,** return journey, *US* round trip. **2** *Esgr* attack.

IDE *nf abr de* **Iniciativa de Defensa Estratégica,** Strategic Defense Initiative, SDI.

idea *nf* **1** *(gen)* idea; **i. fija,** fixed idea; **i. luminosa** or **genial,** brain wave, *US* brainstorm; **¡qué i.!,** what an idea!; *fam* **tener ideas de bombero,** to have madcap ideas. **2** *(noción)* idea; **hacerse a la i. de,** to get used to the idea of; **no tengo la más mínima i.,** I haven't the faintest idea; *fam* **ni i.,** no idea, not a clue. **3** *(opinión)* opinion; **cambiar de i.,** to change one's mind; **es de ideas bastante conservadoras,** he is quite conservative in his outlook; **¿qué i. tienes de él?,** what do you think of him? **4** *(intención)* intention; **a mala i.,** on purpose; **¿con qué i. lo has hecho?,** why did you do it?

ideal I *adj* ideal; **la casa i.,** the ideal home. **II** *nm* ideal. ◆ **idealmente** *adv* ideally.

idealismo *nm* idealism.

idealista I *adj* idealistic. **II** *nmf* idealist.

idealización *nf* idealization.

idealizar *vtr* to idealize, glorify.

idear *vtr* **1** *(inventar)* to devise, invent. **2** *(concebir)* to think up, conceive.

ideario *nm* ideology, set of ideas.

ideático,-a *adj Am (obsesivo)* manic; *(excéntrico)* eccentric.

ídem *adv* idem, ditto; *fam* **í. de í.,** exactly the same.

idéntico,-a *adj* identical. ◆ **idénticamente** *adv* identically.

identidad *nf* **1** identity; **carnet de i., documento nacional de i.,** identity card. **2** *(semejanza)* identity, sameness.

identificable *adj* identifiable.

identificación *nf* identification.

identificar I *vtr* to identify. **II identificarse** *vr* to identify oneself **(con,** with).

ideograma *nm* ideogram, ideograph.

ideología *nf* ideology.

ideológico,-a *adj* ideologic, ideological.

ideólogo,-a *nm, f* ideologist.

idílico,-a *adj* idyllic.

idilio *nm* **1** *Lit* idyll. **2** *fig (romance)* romance, love affair.

idioma *nm* language; **el i. francés,** the French language; *fig* **hablar el mismo i.,** to be on the same wavelength.

idiomático,-a *adj* idiomatic; *Ling* **expresión idiomática,** idiom.

idiosincrasia *nf* idiosyncrasy.

idiota I *adj* idiotic, stupid. **II** *nmf* idiot, fool; *fam* **¡i.!,** you idiot!

idiotez *nf* **1** idiocy, stupidity. **2** *Med* imbecility, mental deficiency or retardation.

idiotizar I *vtr* to daze. **II idiotizarse** *vr* to become dazed.

ido,-a I *pp de* **ir. II** *adj* **1** *(distraído)* absent-minded; **estar i.,** to be miles away. **2** *fam (chiflado)* crazy, nuts. **III los idos** *nmpl* the dead *pl,* the departed *pl.*

idólatra I *adj* idolatrous. **II** *nmf (hombre)* idolater; *(mujer)* idolatress.

idolatrar *vtr* to worship; *fig* to idolize.

idolatría *nf* idolatry.

ídolo *nm* idol.

idoneidad *nf (adecuación)* suitability; *(aptitud)* aptitude, ability.

idóneo,-a *adj* suitable, fit.

idus *nmpl Hist* ides.

iglesia *nf* 1 *(edificio)* church; **i. parroquial,** parish church; *fam* **llevar a algn a la i.,** to lead sb to the altar. 2 *(institución)* the Church; **la i. anglicana,** the Anglican Church, the Church of England; **la i. católica,** the Catholic Church; **la I. y el Estado,** Church and State; *fam fig* **¡con la I. hemos topado!,** we've really come up against a brick wall now.

iglú *nm* igloo.

ígneo,-a *adj* igneous.

ignición *nf* ignition.

ignominia *nf* ignominy, public shame *or* disgrace.

ignominioso,-a *adj* ignominious, shameful.

ignorancia *nf* ignorance.

ignorante I *adj* 1 *(sin instrucción)* ignorant. 2 *(no informado)* ignorant, unaware **(de,** of). **II** *nmf* ignoramus.

ignorar *vtr* to be ignorant of, not know; **ignoraba que,** I had no idea that; **no ignoro que,** I am fully aware that.

ignoto,-a *adj* unknown, undiscovered.

igual I *adj* 1 *(lo mismo)* the same, alike; **estoy i. de cansado que tú,** I'm just as tired as you (are); **los veo todos iguales,** they all look the same to me; **es i.,** it doesn't matter; *fam* **nunca he visto cosa i.,** I've never seen anything like it. 2 *(equivalente)* equal; **a partes iguales,** into equal parts, fifty-fifty. 3 *(constante)* even; **la ley es i. para todos,** everybody is equal in the eyes of the law. 4 *Dep (empatados)* even; **ir iguales,** to be even *or* level; **treinta iguales,** thirty all. 5 *Mat* equal; **A es i. a B,** A equals B; **tres (multiplicado) por dos i. a seis,** three multiplied by *or* times two makes six. 6 **a i. que,** just like. 7 **por i.,** equally. **II** *nm* 1 equal; **de i. a i.,** on an equal footing; **tratar a algn de i. a i.,** to treat sb as an equal; **sin i.,** unique, unrivalled. 2 *Mat* equal *or* equals sign. 3 **iguales,** *(rango)* equals. **III** *adv* probably; **i. se ha quedado dormido,** he could easily have overslept. ◆ **igualmente** *adv* equally; *(también)* also, likewise; **son i. de bonitas,** they are equally pretty; *fam* **¡gracias! — ¡i.!,** thank you! — the same to you!

iguala *nf* 1 *(contrato)* agreement, contract. 2 *(cuota)* agreed fee.

igualación *nf (de cantidades)* equalization; *(de un terreno)* levelling; *(de madera, metal)* smoothing; *Mat* equating.

igualado,-a I *pp de* **igualar. II** *adj* equalized; *(terreno)* level; *(material)* smooth; *Dep* even; **van igualados a dos tantos,** the score is now two all; *(en carreras)* level. **III** *nf Dep* draw, tie; **el gol de la igualada,** the equalizer.

igualar I *vtr* 1 *(gen)* to equalize, make equal. 2 *(nivelar)* to level; *(pulir)* to smooth. 3 *Dep* to equalize; **i. el marcador,** to equalize. 4 *fig (rivalizar con)* to equal; **nadie la iguala en fuerza,** his strength cannot be matched *or* equalled. **II igualarse** *vr* 1 to be equal. 2 **i. con algn,** to place oneself on an equal footing with sb.

igualdad *nf (gen)* equality; *(identidad)* sameness; *(terreno)* levelness; *(material)* smoothness; **en i. de condiciones,** on equal terms; **i. de salarios/derechos,** equal pay/rights.

igualitario,-a *adj* egalitarian.

iguana *nf Zool* iguana.

ijada *nf,* **ijar** *nm Anat* flank.

ilación *nf* 1 *(relación)* inference, connection, relationship. 2 *(coherencia)* cohesion. 3 *(de discurso)* thread.

ilativo,-a *adj* inferential; *Ling* illative.

ilegal *adj* illegal. ◆ **ilegalmente** *adv* illegally.

ilegalidad *nf* illegality.

ilegibilidad *nf* illegibility, illegibleness.

ilegible *adj* illegible, unreadable.

ilegitimidad *nf* illegitimacy, illegitimateness.

ilegitimar *vtr* to outlaw.

ilegítimo,-a *adj* illegitimate. ◆ **ilegitimamente** *adv* illegitimately.

íleon *nm Anat* ileum.

ilerdense I *adj* of *or* from Lérida. **II** *nmf* native *or* inhabitant of Lérida.

ileso,-a *adj* unhurt, unharmed.

iletrado,-a I *adj* illiterate, uneducated, uncultured. **II** *nm,f* illiterate *or* uneducated *or* uncultured person.

ilicitano,-a I *adj* of *or* from Elche. **II** *nm, f* native *or* inhabitant of Elche.

ilícito,-a *adj* illicit, unlawful. ◆ **ilícitamente** *adv* illicitly.

ilimitable *adj* unlimited.

ilimitado,-a *adj* unlimited, limitless, boundless.

ilion *nm Anat* ilium.

Ilma. *abr de* **Ilustrísima,** Your *or* Her Excellence *or* Excellency.

Ilmo. *abr de* **Ilustrísimo,** Your *or* His Excellence *or* Excellency.

ilógico,-a *adj* illogical. ◆ **ilógicamente** *adv* illogically.

Iltre. *abr de* **ilustre,** eminent, distinguished.

iluminación *nf* 1 *(alumbrado)* illumination, lighting; **i. artificial,** artificial lighting. 2 *Fís* illumination. 3 *(de manuscritos)* illumination.

iluminado,-a I *pp de* **iluminar. II** *adj* 1 illuminated, lighted, lit. 2 *(manuscrito)* illuminated. **III** *nm, f (persona)* visionary, illuminate.

iluminador,-a I *adj* illuminating. **II** *nm,f (de manuscritos)* illuminator.

iluminar *vtr* 1 to illuminate, light (up). 2 *(manuscritos)* to illuminate. 3 *fig (persona)* to enlighten; *(tema)* to throw light upon.

ilusión *nf* 1 *(esperanza)* hope; *(esperanza vana)* illusion, illusory hope, delusion; **forjarse** *or* **hacerse ilusiones,** to build up one's hopes; **no te hagas demasiadas ilusiones,** you shouldn't bank on it; **no te hagas ilusiones,** don't kid yourself, don't raise your hopes. 2 *(sueño)* dream; **su i. es estar de nuevo en casa,** his dream is to be back home. 3 *(emoción)* excitement, thrill; **el viaje me hace mucha i.,** I am really looking forward to the trip; **¡qué i.!,** how exciting!; **su visita me hizo mucha i.,** I was really thrilled by her visit. 4 **i. óptica,** optical illusion.

ilusionar I *vtr* 1 *(esperanzar)* to build up hopes. 2 *(entusiasmar)* to excite, thrill. **II ilusionarse** *vr* 1 *(esperanzarse)* to build up one's hopes. 2 *(entusiasmarse)* to be excited *or* thrilled **(con,** about).

ilusionismo *nm* illusionism.

ilusionista *nmf* illusionist, conjurer.

iluso,-a I *adj* easily deceived, gullible. **II** *nm,f* dupe.

ilusorio,-a *adj* illusory, unreal.

ilustración *nf* 1 *(grabado)* illustration, picture; *(ejemplo)* illustration. 2 *(erudición)* learning, erudition; *Hist* **la I.,** the Enlightenment.

ilustrado,-a I *pp de* **ilustrar. II** *adj* 1 *(con dibujos, ejemplos)* illustrated. 2 *(erudito)* learned, erudite.

ilustrador,-a I *adj* illustrative. **II** *nm,f* illustrator.

ilustrar I *vtr* 1 *(gen)* to illustrate. 2 *(aclarar)* to explain, make clear. 3 *(instruir)* to enlighten. **II ilustrarse** *vr* to acquire knowledge **(sobre,** of), learn.

ilustrativo,-a *adj* illustrative.

ilustre *adj* illustrious, distinguished.

ilustrísimo,-a *adj* most illustrious; **Vuestra Ilustrísima,** Your Grace.

imagen *nf* 1 image; *Fís* **i. real/virtual,** real/virtual image; **ser la viva i. de algn,** to be the spitting image of sb. 2 *Rel* image, statue; *fam* **quedarse para vestir imágenes,** to be left on the shelf. 3 *TV* picture.

imaginable *adj* imaginable, conceivable.

imaginación *nf* imagination; **eso son imaginaciones tuyas,** you're imagining things; **nunca se me pasó por la i.,** it never occurred to me.

imaginar I *vtr* to imagine. **II imaginarse** *vr* to imagine; **me imagino que sí,** I suppose so; *fam* **¡imagínate!,** just imagine!

imaginario,-a I *adj* imaginary. **II** *nf Mil (en los dormitorios)* night guard; *(de reserva)* reserve guard.

imaginativo,-a *adj* imaginative.

imaginería *nf Rel* religious images *pl*.

imaginero *nm* maker of religious images.

imán[1] *nm* magnet; *fam fig* **tener i.,** to have a magnetic personality.

imán[2] *nm Rel* imam, imaum.

imanación *nf*, **imantación** *nf* magnetization.

imanar *vtr*, **imantar** *vtr* to magnetize.

imbatible *adj* unbeatable, invincible.

imbatido,-a *adj* unbeaten, undefeated.

imbebible *adj* undrinkable.

imbécil I *adj* stupid, silly. **II** *nmf* idiot, imbecile.

imbecilidad *nf* stupidity, imbecility.

imberbe *adj* beardless.

imborrable *adj* indelible.

imbricar *vtr* to overlap.

imbuir *fml* **I** *vtr* to imbue. **II imbuirse** *vr* to become imbued (**de,** with).

imitable *adj* imitable.

imitación *nf* imitation; **a i. de,** in imitation of; **joyas de i.,** imitation jewellery *sing*.

imitador,-a I *adj* imitative. **II** *nm,f* imitator.

imitamonas *nmf inv fam* copycat.

imitar *vtr (gen)* to imitate; *(gestos)* to mimic.

impaciencia *nf* impatience.

impacientar I *vtr* to make lose patience, exasperate. **II impacientarse** *vr* to get *or* grow impatient; **i. por,** to grow impatient at.

impaciente *adj* impatient; **están impacientes por llegar,** they are anxious to arrive; **ponerse i.,** to get *or* grow impatient. ◆ **impacientemente** *adv* impatiently.

impacto *nm* impact; *Mil* hit; **i. de bala,** bullet hole.

impagable *adj* unpayable; *fig* invaluable.

impagado,-a I *adj* unpaid. **II los impagados** *nmpl Com Fin* unpaid items, items outstanding.

impago I *adj* unpaid. **II** *nm* nonpayment.

impalpable *adj* impalpable.

impar *adj* **1** *Mat* odd. ■ **número i.,** odd number. **2** *(sin igual)* unrivalled, unique.

imparable *adj Dep* unstoppable.

imparcial *adj* impartial, unbiased. ◆ **imparcialmente** *adv* impartially.

imparcialidad *nf* impartiality.

impartir *vtr* to convey, impart; *Rel* **i. su bendición a,** to give one's blessing to.

impasibilidad *nf* impassiveness.

impasible *adj* impassive.

impasse *nm* impasse, deadlock.

impavidez *nf* **1** fearlessness, dauntlessness. **2** *Am* freshness, cheekiness.

impávido,-a *adj* **1** intrepid, fearless, dauntless. **2** *Am* fresh, cheeky.

impecable *adj* impeccable.

impedido,-a I *pp de* **impedir**. **II** *adj* disabled, handicapped, crippled. **III** *nm,f* disabled *or* handicapped person, cripple.

impedimenta *nf Mil* impedimenta *pl*.

impedimento *nm (gen)* impediment; *(obstáculo)* hindrance, obstacle.

impedir *vtr (obstaculizar)* to impede, hinder, obstruct; *(imposibilitar)* to prevent, stop, thwart; **i. el paso,** to block the way; **una importante reunión me impedirá ir al bautizo,** an important meeting will prevent me from going to the christening.

impelente *adj Téc* driving, propelling; *fig (incitante)* inviting, driving, impelling.

impeler *vtr Téc* to drive, propel; *fig* to drive, impel, urge.

impenetrabilidad *nf* impenetrability.

impenetrable *adj* impenetrable; *fig (secreto, acción)* obscure; *fig (persona)* reserved, aloof.

impenitencia *nf* impenitence.

impenitente *adj Rel* impenitent, unrepentant; *fig fam (empedernido)* inveterate, confirmed.

impensable *adj* unthinkable.

impensado,-a *adj* unexpected, unforeseen, out of the blue.

impepinable *adj fam* dead sure, certain. ◆ **impepinablemente** *adv fam* as sure as eggs are eggs.

imperante *adj* ruling, prevailing.

imperar *vi* to rule, prevail.

imperativo,-a I *adj* imperative. **II** *nm Ling* imperative. ◆ **imperativamente** *adv* imperatively.

imperceptibilidad *nf* imperceptibility.

imperceptible *adj* imperceptible. ◆ **imperceptiblemente** *adv* imperceptibly.

imperdible *nm* safety pin.

imperdonable *adj* unforgivable, inexcusable.

imperecedero,-a *adj* imperishable; *fig* ever-lasting, immortal.

imperfección *nf* **1** imperfection. **2** *(defecto)* defect, fault, flaw, deficiency.

imperfecto,-a I *adj* **1** imperfect, fallible. **2** *(defectuoso)* defective, faulty, flawed. **3** *Ling* imperfect; **pretérito i.,** imperfect. **II** *nm Ling* imperfect (tense).

imperial *adj* imperial.

imperialismo *nm* imperialism.

imperialista *adj & nmf* imperialist.

impericia *nf (poca habilidad)* lack of skill; *(inexperiencia)* lack of experience, inexperience.

imperio *nm* empire; **el i. romano,** the Roman Empire; *fig* haughtiness, arrogance; *fig* **vale un i.,** it's worth a fortune.

imperioso,-a *adj* **1** *(arrogante)* imperious. **2** *(indispensable)* urgent, imperative; **una necesidad imperiosa,** a pressing need.

impermeabilidad *nf* impermeability, imperviousness.

impermeabilización *nf* waterproofing.

impermeabilizar *vtr* to waterproof.

impermeable I *adj (gen)* impermeable, impervious; *(ropa)* waterproof; *fig* **i. a las críticas,** impervious to criticism. **II** *nm* raincoat, mac.

impersonal *adj* impersonal.

impersonalidad *nf* impersonality, lacking in character.

impertérrito,-a *adj* unmoved, undaunted, fearless.

impertinencia *nf (persona)* impertinence; *(palabras)* impertinent remark.

impertinente I *adj* impertinent, uncalled for, impudent. **II impertinentes** *nmpl* lorgnette *sing*. ◆ **impertinentemente** *adv* impertinently.

imperturbable *adj* imperturbable, unruffled.

ímpetu *nm* **1** *(impulso)* impetus, impulse, momentum. **2** *(violencia)* violence. **3** *(fogosidad)* impetuosity, impulsiveness.

impetuosidad *nf* **1** *(violencia)* violence. **2** *(fogosidad)* impetuosity, impulsiveness.

impetuoso,-a *adj* **1** *(violento)* violent; **torrente i.,** rushing torrent. **2** *(fogoso)* impetuous, impulsive.

impiedad *nf Rel* impiety; *(falta de compasión)* heartlessness, pitilessness.

impío,-a I *adj* impious, ungodly, irreligious. **II** *nm, f* infidel.

implacable *adj* relentless, implacable, inexorable.

implantación *nf* **1** *(de costumbres)* implantation; *(de reformas)* introduction. **2** *Med* implantation.

implantar *vtr* **1** *(costumbres)* to implant, instil; *(reformas)* to introduce; **cuando se implantó la democracia,** when democracy was introduced. **2** *Med* to implant.

implicación *nf* implication.

implicar *vtr* **1** *(involucrar)* to implicate, involve (**en,** in); **la implicó el asunto,** he involved her in the affair. **2** *(conllevar)* to imply; **eso no implica que no sean buenos amigos,** that does not mean that they are not good friends.

implícito,-a *adj* implicit, implied. ◆ **implícitamente** *adv* implicitly.

implorar *vtr* to implore, beseech, beg, entreat.

implosión *nf Fís* implosion.

impoluto,-a *adj* pure, spotless, immaculate.

imponderable *adj & nm* imponderable.

imponente *adj* **1** *(impresionante)* imposing, impressive. **2** *fam (sensacional)* terrific, tremendous, smashing.

imponer *(pp* **impuesto***)* **I** *vtr* **1** *(gen)* to impose. **2** *(exigir)* to demand, exact; *(silencio, obediencia)* to command. **3** *(dar)* to give; *Mil* to award; **i. un nombre a algn,** to give a name to sb. **4** *(instruir)* to instruct (**en,** in); *(informar)* to inform (**de,** of). **5** *Fin* to deposit. **6** *Rel* **i. las manos sobre algn,** to impose *or* lay hands on sb. **7** *(un edificio)* to be impressive; *(persona)* to inspire respect. **II imponerse** *vr* **1** *(infundir respeto)* **i. a algn,** to command respect from sb, impose one's authority on sb. **2** *(prevalecer)* to prevail; **se impuso el sentido común,** common sense prevailed. **3** *(ponerse de moda)* to become fashionable; **se ha vuelto a i. la falda corta,** short skirts have become fashionable again. **4** *(asumir)* to assume, take on. **5** *(ser necesario)* to be necessary. **6** *(informarse)* **i. de algo,** to find out about sth, acquaint oneself with sth.

imponible *adj Fin* taxable, subject to taxation; **no i.,** tax-free.

impopular *adj* unpopular, disliked.

impopularidad *nf* unpopularity.

importación *nf* **1** import, importation; **artículos de i.,** imported goods. **2 importaciones,** imports; **comercio de i.,** import trade.

importador,-a I *adj* importing. **II** *nm, f* importer.

importancia *nf* importance, significance; **conceder/dar i.,** to attach/give importance to; **darse i.,** to show off; **quitar** *or* **restar i. a algo,** to play sth down; **sin i.,** unimportant.

importante *adj* important, significant; **una suma i.,** a considerable sum.

importar¹ I *vtr (valer)* to amount to; **los libros importan dos mil pesetas,** the books come to two thousand pesetas. **II** *vi* **1** *(hacer al caso)* to matter; **eso no le importa a usted,** that doesn't concern you, that's none of your business; **lo compraré, no importa su precio,** I'll buy it whatever the price; **no importa,** it doesn't matter; **no me importa decirlo,** I don't mind saying it; **¿te importa** *or* **importaría escribirlo?,** would you mind writing it down?; *fam* **me importa un bledo** *or* **un pito,** I couldn't care less. **2** *(implicar)* to involve.

importar² *vtr* to import.

importe *nm Com Fin (valor)* price, cost; *(total)* total, amount.

importunar *vtr* to bother, pester, importune.

importuno,-a *adj* **1** *(inoportuno)* inopportune. **2** *(fastidioso)* bothersome, troublesome, annoying; **temo ser i.,** I don't want to be a nuisance.

imposibilidad *nf* impossibility.

imposibilitado,-a I *pp de* **imposibilitar. II** *adj (inválido)* disabled, crippled. **2** *(impotente)* helpless, without means; **verse i. para hacer algo,** to be unable to do sth, be prevented from doing sth.

imposibilitar *vtr* **1** *(impedir)* to make impossible, prevent. **2** *(incapacitar)* to disable, cripple.

imposible I *adj* impossible; **me es i. hacerlo,** I can't (possibly) do it; *fam* **hacer la vida i. a algn,** to make life impossible for sb. **II lo i.** *nm* the impossible; **hacer lo i.,** to do the impossible.

imposición *nf* **1** *(disciplina, condiciones, multas)* imposition. **2** *Fin* deposit; *(impuesto)* tax; **hacer una i.,** to deposit money. **3 imposiciones,** deposits. **4** *Impr* imposition. **5** *Rel* **i. de manos,** laying on of hands.

impositivo,-a *adj* tax, of taxes; **sistema** *or* **método i.,** tax system.

impositor,-a *nm, f Fin* depositor. **2** *Impr* typesetter.

impostor,-a *nm, f* **1** *(farsante)* impostor. **2** *(calumniador)* slanderer.

impostura *nf* **1** *(engaño)* imposture, deception. **2** *(calumnia)* slander.

impotencia *nf* powerlessness, impotence; *Med* impotence.

impotente *adj* powerless, impotent; *Med* impotent; **verse i. para hacer algo,** to find oneself powerless to do sth.

impracticable *adj* **1** *(inviable)* impracticable, unfeasible, unviable. **2** *(camino, carretera)* impassable; *(en letrero)* **carretera i.,** road unsuitable for traffic.

imprecación *nf* imprecation, curse.

imprecar *vtr* to imprecate, curse.

imprecisión *nf* lack of precision, imprecision, vagueness.

impreciso,-a *adj* imprecise, vague.

impredecible *adj* unpredictable.

impregnación *nf* impregnation.

impregnar I *vtr* to impregnate (**en, de,** with). **II impregnarse** *vr* to become impregnated.

impremeditado,-a *adj* unpremeditated.

imprenta *nf* **1** *(arte)* printing, art of printing. **2** *(taller)* printer's, printing house *or* works; **tinta de i.,** printer's ink. **3** *fig* printed matter; **libertad de i.,** freedom of the press.

imprescindible *adj* essential, indispensable; **es i. que,** it is essential that.

impresentable *adj* unpresentable.

impresión *nf* **1** *(huella)* impression, imprint; **i. visual,** visual impression; **i. dactilar** *or* **digital,** fingerprint. **2** *fig (efecto)* impression; **causar i.,** to make an impression. **3** *fig (opinión)* impression; **cambiar impresiones,** to exchange impressions. **4** *Impr* printing; **una i. de diez mil ejemplares,** an edition of ten thousand copies; *Inform* **i. por chorro de tinta,** ink-jet printing.

impresionabilidad *nf* impressionability.

impresionable *adj* impressionable.

impresionante *adj* impressive, striking; *fam* **un error i.,** a terrible mistake.

impresionar I *vtr* **1** *(sorprender)* to impress, make an impression on; *(conmover)* to move, touch; **el accidente la impresionó mucho,** she was stunned by the accident; **sus cariñosas palabras me impresionaron,** his affectionate words touched me. **2** *Fot* to expose; **película sin i.,** unexposed film. **3** *(grabar discos)* to cut. **II impresionarse** *vr (sorprenderse)* to be impressed; *(conmoverse)* to be moved *or* touched.

impresionismo *nm Arte Lit* impressionism.

impresionista *adj & nmf* impressionist.

impreso,-a I *pp de* **imprimir. II** *adj* printed; **la letra impresa,** the printed word; **lo vi i.,** I saw it in print. **III** *nm* **1** *(papel, folleto)* printed matter. **2** *(formulario)* form; **i. de solicitud,** application form. **3 impresos,** *(de correos)* printed matter *sing*.

impresor,-a I *nm, f* printer. **II** *nf Inform* printer.

imprevisible *adj* unforeseeable, unpredictable.

imprevisión *nf* lack of foresight.

imprevisto,-a I *adj* unforeseen, unexpected. **II** *nm* **1** *(incidente)* unforeseen event; **surgió un i.,** something unexpected came up. **2 imprevistos,** *(gastos)* incidental expenses.

imprimación *nf Arte* **1** *(acción)* priming. **2** *(sustancia)* primer, priming material.

imprimar *vtr Arte* to prime.

imprimátur *nm inv Rel* imprimatur.

imprimible *adj* printable.

imprimir *vtr (pp* **impreso) 1** *Impr Inform* to print. **2** *(marcar)* to stamp, imprint, impress. **3** *fig (fijar en el ánimo)* to fix.

improbabilidad *nf* improbability, unlikelihood.

improbable *adj* improbable, unlikely. ◆ **improbablemente** *adv* improbably.

ímprobo,-a *adj* **1** *(sin probidad)* dishonest, corrupt. **2** *(excesivo)* laborious, very hard; **esfuerzo i.,** strenuous effort.

improcedencia *nf* **1** inappropriateness, unsuitability. **2** *Jur* inadmissibility.

improcedente *adj* **1** inappropriate, unsuitable. **2** *Jur* inadmissible.

improductividad *nf* unproductiveness.

improductivo,-a *adj* unproductive.

impronta *nf* impression; *fig* mark; **este libro lleva la i. de un gran escritor,** this book has the mark of a great writer.

impronunciable *adj* unpronounceable.

improperio *nm* insult, offensive remark.

impropio,-a *adj* **1** *(incorrecto)* improper; **i. de,** unbecoming to *or* for. **2** *(inadecuado)* inappropriate, unsuitable.

improrrogable *adj* that cannot be prolonged *or* extended.

improvisación *nf* improvisation; *Mús* extemporization.

improvisado,-a I *pp de* **improvisar. II** *adj* improvised, impromptu, ad lib; *(reparación, construcción)* makeshift; **discurso i.,** impromptu speech. ◆ **improvisadamente** suddenly.

improvisar *vtr* to improvise; *Mús* to extemporize.

improviso,-a *adj* unforeseen, unexpected; **de i.,** unexpectedly, suddenly; *Mús* **tocar de i.,** to play impromptu; *fam* **coger** *or* **pillar a algn de i.,** to catch sb unawares.

imprudencia *nf* imprudence, rashness; *(indiscreción)* indiscretion; **i. temeraria,** (criminal) negligence.

imprudente *adj* imprudent, unwise, rash; *(indiscreto)* indiscreet; **conductor i.,** careless driver.

impúber I *adj* below the age of puberty. **II** *nmf* child below the age of puberty.

impublicable *adj* unpublishable, unprintable.

impudicia *nf,* **impudicicia** *nf (falta de pudor)* immodesty; *(desvergüenza)* shamelessness.

impúdico,-a *adj (indecente)* immodest, improper; *(desvergonzado)* shameless.

impudor *nm* immodesty; *(desvergüenza)* shamelessness.

impuesto,-a I *pp de* **imponer. II** *adj* **1** *(gen)* imposed. **2** *(informado)* **estar i. de** *or* **en,** to be informed of, be acquainted with. **III** *nm Fin* tax; **i. sobre el valor añadido (IVA),** value-added tax (VAT); **i. sobre la renta,** income tax; **libre de impuestos,** tax-free; *Com* **tienda libre de impuestos,** duty-free shop.

impugnable *adj* refutable.

impugnación *nf* refutation.

impugnar *vtr (teoría)* to refute, disprove; *(decisión)* to challenge, contest, oppose.

impulsar *vtr* to impel, drive forward; *fig (incitar)* to impel, drive.

impulsión *nf* impulsion.

impulsividad *nf* impulsiveness.

impulsivo,-a *adj* impulsive.

impulso *nm* **1** impulse, thrust. **2** *(velocidad)* momentum; **coger i.,** to gather momentum; *Dep* **tomar i.,** to take a run up.

impune *adj* unpunished. ◆ **impunemente** *adv* with impunity.

impunidad *nf* impunity.

impureza *nf* impurity.

impuro,-a *adj* impure.

impuse *pt indef véase* **imponer.**

imputable *adj* attributable.

imputación *nf* imputation, charge.

imputar *vtr* to impute, attribute.

inabarcable *adj* too wide *or* large.

inabordable *adj* unapproachable, inaccessible.

inacabable *adj* interminable, endless.

inaccesible *adj* inaccessible.

inacentuado,-a *adj Ling* unstressed, atonic.

inaceptable *adj* unacceptable.

inactividad *nf* inactivity; *Fin* lull, stagnation.

inactivo,-a *adj* inactive.

inadaptable *adj* unadaptable.

inadaptación *nf* maladjustment.

inadaptado,-a I *adj* maladjusted. **II** *nm, f* misfit.

inadecuación *nf* inadequacy.

inadecuado,-a *adj* **1** *(insuficiente)* inadequate. **2** *(inapropiado)* unsuitable, inappropriate.

inadmisible *adj* inadmissible.

inadvertencia *nf* inadvertence, heedlessness; **por i.,** inadvertently, unintentionally.

inadvertido,-a *adj* **1** *(no visto)* unnoticed, unseen; **pasar i.,** to escape notice, pass unnoticed. **2** *(distraído)* inattentive.

inagotable *adj* **1** *(recursos etc)* inexhaustible. **2** *(infatigable)* tireless, indefatigable, unwearying.

inaguantable *adj* unbearable, intolerable.

inalámbrico,-a *adj* wireless.

inalcanzable *adj* unattainable, unachievable.

inalienable *adj* inalienable.

inalterable *adj* **1** *(gen)* unalterable. **2** *(colour)* fast, permanent. **3** *(persona impasible)* impassive, imperturbable.

inalterado,-a *adj* unaltered, unchanged.

inamovible *adj* immovable, fixed.

inane *adj* inane, empty, pointless.

inanición *nf* starvation; *Med* inanition.

inanidad *nf* inanity, senselessness.

inanimado,-a *adj* inanimate.

inapelable *adj* **1** *Jur* unappealable, without appeal. **2** *fig (irremediable)* inevitable, unavoidable.

inapetencia *nf* lack *or* loss of appetite.

inapetente *adj* having no appetite.

inaplazable *adj* which cannot be postponed; *(urgente)* urgent, pressing.

inaplicable *adj* inapplicable.

inapreciable *adj* **1** *(inestimable)* invaluable, inestimable. **2** *(insignificante)* insignificant, minimum.

inapropiado,-a *adj* inappropriate.

inarrugable *adj* crease-resistant.

inarticulado,-a *adj* inarticulate.

inasequible *adj* **1** *(meta)* unattainable, unachievable. **2** *(persona)* unapproachable, inaccessible. **3** *(precio)* prohibitive. **4** *(cuestión, problema)* incomprehensible.

inasistencia *nf* absence.

inastillable *adj (cristal)* shatterproof; *(madera)* splinterproof.

inatacable *adj Mil* unassailable; *fig (argumento, teoría)* irrefutable.

inatento,-a *adj* inattentive.

inaudible *adj* inaudible.

inaudito,-a *adj* 1 *(nunca oído)* unheard-of; *(sin precedente)* unprecedented. 2 *fig (escandaloso)* outrageous.

inauguración *nf (gen)* inauguration, opening; *(de una placa, estatua)* unveiling.

inaugural *adj* inaugural, opening; **ceremonia i.**, inaugural ceremony; *Av* **vuelo i.**, maiden flight; *Náut* **viaje i.**, maiden voyage.

inaugurar *vtr (gen)* to inaugurate, open; *(placa, estatua)* to unveil; **i. una casa,** to have a house-warming party.

INB *nm Educ abr de* **Instituto Nacional de Bachillerato,** ≈ state secondary school.

inca *adj & nmf* Inca.

incaico,-a *adj* Inca.

incalculable *adj* incalculable, indeterminate.

incalificable *adj* indescribable, unspeakable.

incandescencia *nf* incandescence.

incandescente *adj* incandescent.

incansable *adj* tireless, indefatigable, unwearying. ◆ **incansablemente** *adv* tirelessly, indefatigably.

incapacidad *nf* 1 *(gen)* incapacity, incapability; **i. física,** physical disability. 2 *(incompetencia)* incompetence, inefficiency.

incapacitado,-a I *pp de* **incapacitar.** II *adj* 1 *(imposibilitado)* incapacitated, disabled. 2 *(descalificado)* disqualified; *(desautorizado)* incapacitated.

incapacitar *vtr* 1 to incapacitate, disable. 2 *(inhabilitar)* to disqualify, make unfit **(para,** for).

incapaz *adj* 1 incapable **(de,** of), unfit **(de,** for); *fam* **es i. de matar una mosca,** he wouldn't hurt a fly. 2 *(incompetente)* incompetent, inefficient.

incautación *nf Jur* seizure, confiscation.

incautarse *vr Jur* **i. de,** to seize, confiscate.

incauto,-a I *adj* 1 *(imprudente)* incautious, unwary. 2 *(crédulo)* gullible. II *nm, f* gullible person. ◆ **incautamente** *adv* incautiously, unwarily.

incendiado,-a I *pp de* **incendiar.** II *adj (que arde)* on fire, burning, in flames; *(destruido)* burnt-out.

incendiar I *vtr* to set on fire, set fire to, set alight, burn down. II **incendiarse** *vr* to catch fire.

incendiario,-a I *adj* incendiary; *fig (discurso etc)* inflammatory. II *nm, f (persona)* arsonist, fireraiser.

incendio *nm* fire; **i. forestal,** forest fire; **i. intencionado** *or* **provocado,** arson.

incensario *nm Rel* censer, thurible.

incentivar *vtr* to give an incentive.

incentivo *nm* incentive.

incertidumbre *nf* uncertainty, doubt.

incesante *adj* incessant, never-ending. ◆ **incesantemente** *adv* incessantly.

incesto *nm* incest.

incestuoso,-a *adj* incestuous.

incidencia *nf* 1 *(frecuencia, cantidad)* incidence; **hubo una alta i. de muertes en la carretera,** there was high incidence of deaths on the road. *Fís* incidence. 3 *(repercusión)* repercussion, consequence, impact, effect; **su discurso tuvo una gran i.,** his speech made a great impact. 4 **por i.,** by chance *or* accident.

incidental *adj* incidental.

incidente *nm* incident; **llegar sin incidentes,** to arrive without any problem.

incidir *vi* 1 *(incurrir)* to fall **(en,** into). 2 *(afectar)* to affect; *(influir)* to influence **(en,** -); **la subida de precios incide más sobre los salarios bajos,** the rise in prices has a greater effect on low wages. 3 *Med* to make an incision.

incienso *nm* incense; *fig (adulación)* flattery.

incierto,-a *adj* 1 *(dudoso)* uncertain, doubtful. 2 *(inconstante)* inconstant, unpredictable. ◆ **inciertamente** *adv* uncertainly.

incineración *nf (de basuras)* incineration; *(de cadáveres)* cremation.

incinerador *nm* incinerator.

incinerar *vtr (basura)* to incinerate; *(cadáveres)* to cremate.

incipiente *adj* incipient, budding; **el día i.,** the dawning day.

incisión *nf* incision, cut.

incisivo,-a I *adj* incisive, sharp, cutting; *fig* **un comentario i.,** a cutting remark. II *nm Anat* incisor.

inciso,-a I *adj (estilo)* jerky. II *nm Ling* interpolated *or* incidental clause; **a modo de i.,** in passing, incidentally.

incitación *nf* incitement.

incitador,-a I *adj* inciting. II *nm, f* inciter.

incitante *adj* 1 *(instigador)* inciting. 2 *(provocativo)* provocative.

incitar *vtr* to incite, urge.

incivil *adj* uncivil, rude.

incivilizado,-a *adj* uncivilized.

inclasificable *adj* unclassifiable.

inclemencia *nf* inclemency, harshness.

inclemente *adj* inclement, harsh.

inclinación *nf* 1 slope, incline, slant; *(del cuerpo)* stoop. 2 *(reverencia)* bow; *(señal de asentimiento)* nod. 3 *fig (tendencia)* tendency, inclination, propensity, penchant; **tiene i. hacia la música,** he has a penchant for music.

inclinado,-a I *pp de* **inclinar.** II *adj* inclined, slanting; *fig* **me siento i. a creerle,** I feel inclined to believe him.

inclinar I *vtr* 1 to incline, slant, bend; *(cuerpo)* to bow; *(la cabeza)* to nod. 2 *fig (persuadir)* to persuade, incline, induce; dispose. II **inclinarse** *vr* 1 to lean, slope incline; **i. hacia adelante,** to lean forward. 2 *(al saludar)* to bow; **i. ante,** to bow down to. 3 *fig (optar)* **i. a,** to be *or* feel inclined to; **me inclino por éste,** I'd rather have this one, I prefer this one.

ínclito,-a *adj Lit* distinguished, illustrious.

incluido,-a I *pp de* **incluir.** II *adj* 1 included; **precio todo i.,** all-in price; **servicio no i.,** service not included. 2 *(adjunto)* enclosed.

incluir *vtr* 1 to include; **incluyendo gastos de envío,** including postage and packing; **¿me incluiste en la lista?,** did you include me in the list? 2 *(contener)* to contain, comprise. 3 *(adjuntar)* to enclose.

inclusa *nf* foundling home, orphanage.

inclusero,-a *adj & nm, f* foundling, orphan.

inclusión *nf* inclusion; **con i. de,** including.

inclusive *adv* inclusive; **de martes a viernes i.,** from Tuesday to Friday inclusive; **hasta la lección ocho i.,** up to and including lesson eight.

inclusivo,-a *adj* inclusive. ◆ **inclusivamente** *adv* inclusive, inclusively.

incluso I *adv* inclusive, inclusively. II *prep* even.

incoar *vtr* defect *Jur* to intiate.

incógnito,-a I *adj* incognito, unknown. II *nm* incognito; **guardar el i.,** to remain incognito; **viajar de i.,** to travel incognito. III *nf* 1 *Mat* unknown quantity, unknown. 2 *(misterio)* mystery; **no sé cómo reaccionará José, es una i.,** I don't know how José will react, he's an unknown quantity. 3 *(razón oculta)* hidden motive.

incoherencia *nf* incoherence.

incoherente *adj* incoherent. ◆ **incoherentemente** *adv* incoherently.

incoloro,-a *adj* colourless.

incólume *adj fml* safe, unharmed; **salir i. de un accidente,** to escape from an accident without injury.

incombustible *adj* incombustible, fireproof.

incomestible *adj*, **incomible** *adj* uneatable, inedible.

incomodar I *vtr* **1** *(causar molestia)* to inconvenience, put out. **2** *(fastidiar)* to bother, annoy. **3** *(enojar, disgustar)* to annoy, anger. **II incomodarse** *vr* **1** *(tomarse molestias)* to put oneself out, trouble oneself, go out of one's way; **no te incomodes,** don't put yourself out. **2** *(enojarse, disgustarse)* to get annoyed *or* angry.

incomodidad *nf*, **incomodo** *nm* **1** *(falta de comodidad)* discomfort. **2** *(molestia)* inconvenience. **3** *euf (malestar)* unrest, uneasiness.

incómodo,-a *adj* uncomfortable; **sentirse i.,** to feel uncomfortable *or* awkward.

incomparable *adj* incomparable.

incomparecencia *nf Jur* nonappearance, default.

incompatibilidad *nf* incompatibility; *Jur* **i. de caracteres,** mutual incompatibility.

incompatible *adj* incompatible.

incompetencia *nf* incompetence.

incompetente *adj & nmf* incompetent.

incompleto,-a *adj* incomplete; *(inacabado)* unfinished.

incomprensible *adj* incomprehensible. ◆ **incomprensiblemente** *adv* incomprehensibly.

incomprensión *nf* lack of understanding, failure to understand; *(poca voluntad)* lack of sympathy.

incomprensivo,-a *adj* uncomprehending; *(insolidario)* unsympathetic.

incomunicación *nf* **1** *(falta de comunicación)* lack of communication. **2** *Jur* solitary confinement. **3** *(aislamiento)* isolation.

incomunicado,-a I *pp de* **incomunicar. II** *adj* **1** *(aislado)* isolated; **el pueblo se quedó i.,** the town was cut off. **2** *(en la cárcel)* in solitary confinement.

incomunicar *vtr* **1** *(aislar) (lugar)* to isolate, cut off; *(habitación)* to shut off. **2** *(recluso)* to place in solitary confinement.

inconcebible *adj* inconceivable, unthinkable.

inconciliable *adj* irreconcilable.

inconcluso,-a *adj* unfinished.

incondicional I *adj* *(gen)* unconditional; *(obediencia)* unquestioning, absolute; *(apoyo)* wholehearted; *(amigo)* faithful; *(partidario)* staunch. **II** *nmf (partidario)* staunch supporter; *(amigo)* faithful friend.

inconexión *nf* *(falta de conexión)* disconnection; *(incoherencia)* incoherence.

inconexo,-a *adj* *(sin conexión)* disconnected, unconnected; *(incoherente)* incoherent, confused.

inconfesable *adj* shameful, disgraceful, shocking.

inconfeso,-a *adj* not pleading guilty, not owning up.

inconformismo *nm* nonconformity.

inconformista *adj & nmf* nonconformist.

inconfortable *adj* uncomfortable.

inconfundible *adj* unmistakable, obvious.

incongruencia *nf* incongruity.

incongruente *adj* incongruous.

inconmensurable *adj* immeasurable, vast, limitless.

inconmovible *adj* firm, unshakable.

inconquistable *adj* **1** *Mil* inconquerable, invincible. **2** *fig (tenaz)* unyielding.

inconsciencia *nf Med* unconsciousness; *fig (desconocimiento)* unawareness; *fig (irreflexión)* thoughtlessness, irresponsiblity.

inconsciente I *adj* *(desmayado)* unconscious; *fig (despreocupado)* unaware **(de,** of); *fig (irreflexivo)* thoughtless, irresponsible. **II** *nmf* unconscious person; *fig* thoughtless *or* irresponsible person.

inconsecuencia *nf* inconsistency, inconsequence.

inconsecuente *adj* inconsistent, inconsequent; **fue i. en sus respuestas,** her replies lacked consistency.

inconsideración *nf* inconsiderateness, thoughtlessness.

inconsiderado,-a *adj* inconsiderate, thoughtless.

inconsistencia *nf (de líquido)* runniness, wateriness; *(de tela)* flimsiness; *(de argumento)* weakness, insubstantiality.

inconsistente *adj (líquidos)* runny, watery; *(telas)* flimsy; *(argumentos)* weak, insubstantial.

inconsolable *nf* inconsolable, disconsolate.

inconstancia *nf* inconstancy, fickleness.

inconstante *adj* inconstant, fickle; *Meteor* changeable, variable.

inconstitucional *adj* unconstitutional.

inconstitucionalidad *nf* unconstitutionality.

incontable *adj* countless, innumerable, uncountable.

incontaminado,-a *adj* unpolluted, uncontaminated.

incontenible *adj* uncontrollable, irrepressible; **un ataque de risa i.,** a fit of uncontrollable laughter.

incontestable *adj* indisputable, unquestionable, undeniable. ◆ **incontestablemente** *adv* indisputably, undeniably.

incontinencia *nf* incontinence.

incontinente[1] *adj* **1** *(desenfrenado)* lacking in sexual control. **2** *Med* incontinent.

incontinente[2] *adv* at once.

incontrolable *adj* uncontrollable.

incontrolado,-a *adj* uncontrolled.

incontrovertible *adj* incontrovertible, indisputable.

inconveniencia *nf* **1** *(gen)* inconvenience. **2** *(impropiedad)* unsuitability; *(no aconsejable)* inadvisability. **3** *(incorrección)* impoliteness; *(dicho grosero)* rude remark; **decir/cometer inconveniencias,** to be tactless.

inconveniente I *adj* **1** *(gen)* inconvenient. **2** *(inapropiado)* unsuitable; *(no aconsejable)* inadvisable. **3** *(incorrecto)* impolite; *(grosero)* rude, coarse. **II** *nm* **1** *(objeción)* objection; **poner inconvenientes a algo,** to raise objections to sth. **2** *(desventaja)* drawback; *(problema)* difficulty; **¿tienes i. en acompañarme?,** would you mind coming with me?

incordiar *vtr fam* to bother, pester; **¡no incordies!,** don't be such a nuisance!

incordio *nm fam* nuisance, pain.

incorporación *nf* **1** *(unir)* incorporation. **2** *(del cuerpo)* sitting-up.

incorporado,-a I *pp de* **incorporar. II** *adj* **1** *(unido)* incorporated; *Téc* built-in, embodied. **2** *(en la cama)* sitting up.

incorporar I *vtr* **1** to incorporate **(en,** into); *Culin* to mix, blend. **2** *(levantar)* to help to sit up. **II incorporarse** *vr* **1** *(sociedad)* to join; *(trabajo)* to start; *Mil* **i. a filas,** to join up. **2** *(en la cama)* to sit up.

incorpóreo,-a *adj* incorporeal; *(inmaterial)* intangible.

incorrección *nf* **1** *(falta)* incorrectness, inaccuracy; *(gramatical)* mistake. **2** *(descortesía)* impoliteness, discourtesy, impropriety; **cometer una i.,** to commit a faux pas *or* gaffe.

incorrecto,-a *adj* **1** *(equivocado)* incorrect, inaccurate. **2** *(grosero)* impolite, discourteous.

incorregible *adj* incorrigible; **has comido demasiado otra vez, eres i.,** you've eaten too much again, you'll never change.

incorruptible *adj* incorruptible; *fam* straight.

incorrupto,-a *adj* uncorrupted, incorrupt; *(mujer)* chaste.

incredulidad *nf* **1** incredulity, disbelief. **2** *Rel* unbelief.

incrédulo,-a I *adj* **1** incredulous, disbelieving. **2** *Rel* unbelieving. **II** *nm,f* **1** disbeliever. **2** *Rel* unbeliever.

increíble *adj* incredible, unbelievable.

incrementar I *vtr* to increase. **II incrementarse** *vr* to increase.

incremento *nm* (*aumento*) increase; (*crecimiento*) growth; **i. de la temperatura,** rise in temperature; **i. del coste de vida,** rise in the cost of living.

increpar *vtr fml* to rebuke, reprimand.

incriminación *nf* incrimination.

incriminar *vtr* to incriminate.

incruento,-a *adj* bloodless.

incrustación *nf* **1** encrustation *or* incrustation. **2** *Arte* inlaying, inlay.

incrustar I *vtr* **1** to encrust *or* incrust; *fam fig* **le dio un golpe que lo incrustó contra la pared,** he nearly knocked him through the wall. **2** (*insertar*) to inlay; **incrustado con,** inlaid with. **II incrustarse** *vr* to become embedded (**en,** in); *fig* **la idea se incrustó en su memoria,** the idea engraved itself in his memory.

incubación *nf* incubation.

incubadora *nf* incubator.

incubar *vtr* to incubate.

incuestionable *adj* unquestionable, indisputable.

inculcar *vtr* (*gen*) to inculcate; (*principios, ideas*) to instil (**en,** into).

inculpación *nf* (*gen*) accusation; *Jur* charge.

inculpado,-a I *pp de* **inculpar. II** *adj* (*gen*) accused (**de,** of); *Jur* charged (**de,** with). **III** *nm,f* **el i., la inculpada,** the accused.

inculpar *vtr* (*gen*) to accuse (**de,** of), blame (**de,** for); *Jur* to charge (**de,** with).

inculto,-a I *adj* **1** (*ignorante*) uneducated, uncultured. **2** (*rudo*) uncouth, uncivilized. **3** *Agr* (*terreno*) untilled, uncultivated. **II** *nm,f* ignoramus.

incultura *nf* **1** (*ignorancia*) ignorance, lack of culture. **2** (*rudeza*) uncouthness.

incumbencia *nf* duty, obligation, responsibility, concern; **no es de mi i.,** it doesn't come within my province, it isn't my concern.

incumbir *vi* to be the duty (**a,** of), be incumbent (**a,** upon); **esto no te incumbe,** this is none of your business; **me incumbe a mí hacerlo,** it is my duty to do it, it's my responsibility.

incumplido,-a I *pp de* **incumplir. II** *adj* unfulfilled.

incumplimiento *nm* (*de un deber*) non-fulfilment; (*de una promesa*) failure to keep; (*de una orden*) failure to execute; *Admin* **i. de contrato,** breach of contract.

incumplir *vtr* not to fulfil; (*deber*) fail to fulfil; (*promesa, contrato*) to break; (*orden*) to fail to carry out.

incunable *nm* *Impr* **1** incunabulum. **2 incunables,** incunabula *pl*.

incurabilidad *nf* incurability.

incurable *adj* *Med* incurable; *fig* hopeless, incurable.

incurrir (*pp* **incurso**) *vi* **1** (*ganarse*) to incur. **2** (*cometer*) to commit; **i. en delito,** to commit a crime; **i. en (un) error,** to fall into error.

incursión *nf* raid, incursion.

indagación *nf* investigation, inquiry.

indagar *vtr* to investigate, inquire into.

indebido,-a *adj* **1** (*desconsiderado*) improper, undue. **2** (*injusto*) wrongful, unjust. **3** (*ilegal*) unlawful, illegal. ◆ **indebidamente** *adv* **1** (*inapropiadamente*) improperly, unduly. **2** (*injustamente*) wrongfully, unjustly. **3** (*ilegalmente*) unlawfully, illegally.

indecencia *nf* indecency, obscenity; *fam pey* **es una i. ver la poca comida que dan por mil pesetas,** it is a scandal to see how little food you get for 1,000 pesetas.

indecente *adj* **1** (*obsceno*) indecent; **una persona i.,** an obscene person. **2** (*miserable*) miserable; **una habitación i.,** a grotty room. **3** (*sucio*) filthy; **esta camisa está i.,** that shirt is very grubby.

indecible *adj* unspeakable; (*inefable*) indescribable; **sufrir lo i.,** to suffer terribly.

indecisión *nf* indecision, hesitation.

indeciso,-a *adj* **1** (*por decidir*) undecided. **2** (*vacilante*) hesitant, irresolute; **es una persona indecisa,** he can never make up his mind. **3** (*resultados etc*) inconclusive.

indeclinable *adj* **1** *lit* (*ineludible*) unavoidable. **2** *Ling* indeclinable.

indefectible *adj* unfailing, infallible.

indefendible *adj*, **indefensible** *adj* indefensible.

indefenso,-a *adj* defenceless, helpless.

indefinible *adj* indefinable; (*con palabras*) inexpressible.

indefinido,-a *adj* **1** indefinite; (*impreciso*) undefined, vague. **2** *Ling* indefinite. ◆ **indefinidamente** *adv* indefinitely.

indeformable *adj* which will not lose its shape.

indeleble *adj* indelible.

indelicadeza *nf* indelicacy, coarseness; (*acto*) tactless act.

indemne *adj* (*persona*) unharmed, unhurt; (*cosa*) undamaged.

indemnidad *nf* indemnity.

indemnización *nf* **1** (*acto*) indemnification. **2** *Fin* (*compensación*) indemnity, compensation; **i. por despido,** severance pay.

indemnizar *vtr* to indemnify, compensate (**de, por,** for).

indemostrable *adj* indemonstrable.

independencia *nf* independence; **con i. de,** independently of; **conseguir** *or* **ganar la i.,** to gain independence; *Hist* **la guerra de la I.,** the War of Independence.

independentista *adj & nmf Pol* independent.

independiente *adj* (*libre*) independent; (*individualista*) self-sufficient; *Pol* **se presenta como candidato i.,** he's standing as an independent (candidate). ◆ **independientemente** *adv* **1** independently (**de,** of). **2** (*aparte de*) regardless, irrespective (**de,** of).

independizar I *vtr* to make independent, grant independence to. **II independizarse** *vr* to become independent.

indescifrable *adj* indecipherable.

indescriptible *adj* indescribable.

indeseable *adj & nmf* undesirable.

indesmallable *adj* (*medias*) ladderproof, runproof.

indestructible *adj* indestructible.

indeterminable *adj* indeterminable.

indeterminación *nf* indecision, irresolution.

indeterminado,-a *adj* **1** (*sin determinar*) indeterminate; (*sin límite*) indefinite; (*impreciso*) vague. **2** (*persona*) irresolute. **3** *Ling* indefinite.

India *n* (**la) I.,** India.

indiada *nf Am* **1** crowd of Indians. **2** action or expression typical of an Indian.

indiano,-a I *adj lit* Latin American. **II** *nm Hist* Spanish emigrant who returns to Spain having acquired substantial wealth in Latin America.

Indias *npl* (**las) I.,** the Indies; **las I. Orientales/Occidentales,** the East/West Indies.

indicación *nf* **1** (*señal*) indication, sign. **2** (*corrección*) hint, suggestion; **hacer algo por i. de algn,** to do sth at sb's suggestion. **3** (*instrucción*) instruction, direction; **indicaciones para el uso,** instructions for use. **4** (*informe*) data, figures *pl*.

indicado,-a I *pp de* **indicar. II** *adj* right, suitable, appropriate; **a la hora indicada,** at the specified time; **él es el menos i. para llevar la empresa,** he's the last person who should run the business; **en el momento menos i.,** at the worst possible moment; *fml* **el cambio de tiempo hace i. el uso de ropas gruesas,** owing to the change in weather it's recommended that warm clothes be worn.

indicador,-a I *adj* indicating; **señales indicadoras de peligro,** danger signals. II *nm* **1** *(gen)* indicator. **2** *Téc* gauge, dial, meter; **i. de presión,** pressure gauge; *Aut* **i. del nivel de aceite,** (oil) dipstick; *Aut* **i. de velocidad,** speedometer.

indicar *vtr* **1** *(señalar)* to indicate, show, point out; **i. algo con el dedo,** to point sth out; **¿me podría i. el camino?,** could you show me the way? **2** *(marcar)* to read. **3** *(aconsejar)* to show, advise; **indíqueme qué debo hacer,** tell me what I should do. **4** *(esbozar)* to outline.

indicativo,-a I *adj* **1** indicative (**de,** of). **2** *Ling* (modo) **i.,** indicative (mode). II *nm* **1** *Rad* call sign. **2** *Ling* indicative.

índice *nm* **1** *(señal)* indication, sign. **2** *(libro)* index, table of contents; *(de biblioteca)* index, catalogue. ■ **í. alfabético,** alphabetical index. **3** *(indica proporción) (evolución)* index; *(razón)* ratio; *(relación, tanto por ciento, en gráfica)* rate. ■ *Anat* **í. cefálico,** cephalic index; **í. de natalidad/mortalidad,** birth/death rate; *Fin* **í. de precios,** price index; *Fin* **í. del coste de la vida,** cost of living index. **4** *Mat* index. **5** *Anat* (dedo) **í.,** index finger, forefinger. **6** *Rel* **í. expurgatorio,** the Index.

indicio *nm* **1** *(señal)* indication, sign, token (**de,** of); **no hay indicios de que vaya a llover,** there is no sign that it's going to rain. **2** *(gen pl) (cantidad pequeña)* trace.

índico,-a *adj* Indian; **Océano I.,** Indian Ocean.

indiferencia *nf* indifference, apathy, disinterest.

indiferente *adj* **1** *(no importante)* indifferent; **me es i.,** it makes no difference to me. **2** *(actitud) (apatía)* apathetic; *(frialdad)* uninterested; **su esposa le es indiferente,** he doesn't care two hoots about his wife.

indígena I *adj* indigenous, native (**de,** to). II *nmf* **1** native (**de,** of). **2** *Am* Indian.

indigencia *nf fml* poverty, indigence.

indigente *fml* I *adj* needy, poverty-stricken, indigent. II *nmf* poor person; **los indigentes,** the poor, the needy.

indigerible *adj fam (comida)* indigestible, difficult to digest; *fig (persona, cosa)* hard to stomach.

indigestarse *vr* to cause *or* give indigestion; **se le indigestó la comida,** the meal gave her indigestion; *fam fig (caer mal)* **ese tipo se me indigesta,** I can't stomach that guy.

indigestión *nf* indigestion.

indigesto,-a *adj* **1** *(comida)* indigestible, difficult to digest; **sentirse i.,** to be suffering from indigestion. **2** *fig (de trato áspero)* surly, brusque.

indignación *nf* indignation.

indignado,-a I *pp de* **indignar.** II *adj* indignant (**por,** at, about).

indignante *adj* outrageous, infuriating.

indignar I *vtr* to infuriate, make angry. II **indignarse** *vr* to be *or* feel indignant (**por,** at, about).

indignidad *nf* **1** unworthiness. **2** *(acto)* unworthy act.

indigno,-a *adj (comportamiento)* unworthy (**de,** of); **esta actitud me parece indigna de ti,** I didn't expect you to take that attitude; **Raúl es i. de nuestra amistad,** Raúl is not worthy of our friendship.

índigo *nm* indigo.

indio,-a *adj & nm, f* Indian; **en fila india,** in single file; **hablar como los indios,** to speak (a language) badly; *fam* **hacer el i.,** to act the fool; *Am fig* **subírsele a uno el i.,** to flip, get annoyed.

indirecta *nf fam (insinuación)* hint, insinuation; **tirar** *or* **lanzar una i.,** to drop a hint; **coger la i.,** to get the message.

indirecto,-a *adj* indirect; *Ling* **complemento i.,** indirect complement; *Ling* **estilo i.,** indirect *or* reported speech.

indisciplina *nf* lack of discipline.

indisciplinado,-a I *pp de* **indisciplinarse.** II *adj* undisciplined, unruly.

indisciplinarse *vr* to become undisciplined *or* unruly.

indiscreción *nf (gen)* indiscretion; *(comentario)* tactless remark; **si no es i., ¿cómo piensas gastarte el dinero?,** I hope you don't mind my asking, but how do you plan to spend the money?

indiscreto,-a I *adj* indiscreet, tactless. II *nm, f* indiscreet person.

indiscriminado,-a *adj* indiscriminate. ◆ **indiscriminadamente** *adv* indiscriminately.

indiscutible *adj* indisputable, unquestionable.

indisoluble *adj* indissoluble.

indispensable *adj* indispensable, essential.

indisponer *(pp indispuesto)* I *vtr* **1** *(planes)* to upset, spoil; *Med* to upset, make unwell. **2** *fig (enemistar)* **i. a una persona contra otra,** to set one person against another. II **indisponerse** *vr* **1** *Med* to fall ill, become unwell. **2** *fig* **i. con algn,** to fall out with sb.

indisponible *adj* unavailable.

indisposición *nf* **1** *Med* indisposition, illness. **2** *(reticencia)* unwillingness, disinclination.

indispuesto,-a I *pp de* **indisponer.** II *adj* **1** *Med* indisposed, unwell. **2** *fig (enemistado)* on bad terms (**con,** with).

indispuse *pt indef véase* **indisponer.**

indistinto,-a *adj* **1** *(indiferente)* immaterial, inconsequential; **es i ir en tren** *or* **en coche,** it makes no difference whether you go by train *or* car. **2** *Fin* **cuenta indistinta,** joint account. **3** *(impreciso)* indistinct; *(borroso)* vague. ◆ **indistintamente** *adv* the same; **habla los dos idiomas i.,** she speaks both languages equally well.

individual I *adj* individual; **habitación i.,** single room. II *nm* **1** *(mantel)* place mat. **2 individuales,** *Dep* singles.

individualidad *nf* individuality.

individualismo *nm* individualism.

individualista I *adj* individualistic. II *nmf* individualist.

individualización *nf* individualization.

individualizar *vtr* to individualize.

individuo *nm* **1** individual. **2** *pey* bloke, guy.

indivisible *adj* indivisible.

indo,-a *adj & nm, f* Indus.

indócil *adj (de ideas fijas)* headstrong; *(desobediente)* disobedient.

indocumentado,-a I *adj* without identification papers. II *nm, f* **1** person without identification papers. **2** *arg* dead loss.

indochino,-a *adj & nm, f* Indo-Chinese.

indoeuropeo,-a *adj & nm, f* Indo-European.

índole *nf* **1** *(carácter)* character, nature, disposition. **2** *(clase, tipo)* kind, sort.

indolencia *nf* indolence, laziness.

indolente I *adj* indolent, lazy. II *nmf* idler.

indoloro,-a *adj* painless.

indomable *adj* **1** *(animal)* untameable. **2** *(pueblo)* ungovernable, unruly; *(niño)* uncontrollable; *(pasión)* indomitable.

indómito,-a *adj* **1** *(no domado)* untamed; *(indomable)* untamable. **2** *(pueblo)* unruly; *(persona)* uncontrollable.

Indonesia *n* Indonesia.

indonesio,-a I *adj* Indonesian. II *nm, f (persona)* Indonesian. III *nm (idioma)* Indonesian.

indubitable *adj* indubitable, undoubted, beyond doubt.

inducción *nf* induction.

inducido,-a I *pp de* **inducir.** II *adj* induced. III *nm Elec* armature.

inducir *vtr* 1 *(incitar, mover)* to lead, induce; **i. en error,** to lead into error, mislead. 2 *(inferir)* to infer, deduce. 3 *Elec (corriente)* to induce.

inductivo,-a *adj* inductive.

inductor,-a **I** *adj* **1** inducing. **2** *Elec* inductive. **II** *nm, f* inducer. **III** *nm Elec* inductor.

indudable *adj* indubitable, unquestionable; **es i. que,** there is no doubt that.

induje *pt indef véase* **inducir.**

indulgencia *nf* 1 indulgence, leniency. 2 *Rel* indulgence.

indulgente *adj* indulgent (**con,** towards) lenient (**con,** with).

indultar *vtr Jur* to pardon; *(eximir)* to exempt.

indulto *nm Jur* pardon, amnisty.

indumentaria *nf* clothing, clothes *pl,* garments *pl.*

industria *nf* industry. ■ **i. ligera/pesada,** light/heavy industry.

industrial **I** *adj* industrial. **II** *nmf* industrialist, manufacturer.

industrialización *nf* industrialization.

industrializar **I** *vtr* to industrialize. **II industrializarse** *vr* to become industrialized.

industrioso,-a *adj* industrious.

induzco *indic pres véase* **inducir.**

INE *nm abr de* **Instituto Nacional de Estadística.**

inédito,-a *adj* 1 *(libro, texto)* unpublished. 2 *(nuevo)* completely new; *(desconocido)* unknown.

inefable *adj* ineffable, indescribable.

inefectivo,-a *adj (irreal)* unreal.

ineficacia *nf (ineptitud)* inefficiency; *(improducción)* ineffectiveness.

ineficaz *adj (inepto)* inefficient; *(improductivo)* ineffective.

ineficiencia *nf véase* **ineficacia.**

ineficiente *adj véase* **ineficaz.**

ineluctable *adj lit* inevitable, inescapable.

ineludible *adj* inescapable, unavoidable.

INEM *nm abr de* **Instituto Nacional de Empleo,** ≈ Unemployment Benefit Office, UBO.

inenarrable *adj desus* unspeakable, inexpressible.

ineptitud *nf* ineptitude, incompetence.

inepto,-a **I** *adj* inept, incompetent. **II** *nm, f* incompetent person.

inequívoco,-a *adj* unmistakable, unequivocal.

inercia *nf* 1 *Fís* inertia. 2 *fig (pasividad)* inertia, passivity; *(lentitud)* slowness; **hacer algo por i.,** to do sth out of habit.

inerme *adj* 1 *(desarmado)* unarmed. 2 *fig (sin defensas)* defenceless, unprotected. 3 *Zool* with no prickles *or* spines *or* sting.

inerte *adj* 1 *(gas)* inert. 2 *fig (persona)* passive; *(lenta)* sluggish, slow.

inescrutable *adj fml* inscrutable; *(impenetrable)* mysterious.

inesperado,-a *adj (fortuito)* unexpected, unforeseen; *(imprevisto)* sudden. ◆ **inesperadamente** *adv (fortuitamente)* unexpectedly; *(imprevistamente)* suddenly.

inestabilidad *nf* instability, unsteadiness.

inestable *adj* unstable, unsteady.

inestimable *adj* inestimable, invaluable.

inevitable *adj* inevitable, unavoidable. ◆ **inevitablemente** *adv* inevitably, unavoidably.

inexactitud *nf* 1 *(gen)* incorrectness, inaccuracy. 2 *(error)* mistake.

inexacto,-a *adj* inexact, inaccurate.

inexcusable *adj* 1 *(imperdonable)* inexcusable, unforgivable. 2 *(ineludible)* unavoidable, inescapable.

inexistencia *nf* non-existence.

inexistente *adj* non-existent, inexistent.

inexorable *adj* inexorable. ◆ **inexorablemente** *adv* inexorably.

inexperiencia *nf* 1 *(falta de experiencia)* lack of experience, inexperience. 2 *(falta de habilidad)* lack of skill.

inexperimentado,-a *adj* 1 *(persona)* inexperienced. 2 *(método, invento)* untried.

inexperto,-a *adj* 1 *(sin experiencia)* inexperienced. 2 *(inhábil)* inexpert, unskilled.

inexplicable *adj* inexplicable.

inexplorado,-a *adj* unexplored; *(territorio etc)* uncharted.

inexplotado,-a *adj* unexploited, untapped, unused.

inexpresable *adj* inexpressible.

inexpresivo,-a *adj* inexpressive.

inexpugnable *adj* 1 *Mil* impregnable. 2 *fig* stubborn, hard-headed, unyielding.

inextinguible *adj* inextinguishable.

inextricable *adj* inextricable.

infalibilidad *nf* infallibility.

infalible *adj (indefectible)* infallible; *(en contenido)* faultless.

infamante *adj* shameful.

infamar *vtr* to defame, slander, discredit.

infame *adj* infamous, odious, vile; **tiempo i.,** vile weather; **trabajo i.,** thankless job.

infamia *nf* infamy, disgrace.

infancia *nf* childhood, infancy; **ha vuelto a la i.,** she is in her second childhood.

infanta *nf* infanta, princess.

infante *nm* 1 infante, prince. 2 *Mil* infantryman.

infantería *nf Mil* infantry; **la i. de marina,** the marines.

infanticida **I** *adj* infanticidal. **II** *nmf* infanticide, child-killer. **III** *nm arg* baby snatcher.

infanticidio *nm (acto)* infanticide.

infantil *adj* 1 child, children's; **juegos infantiles,** children's games; **literatura i.,** children's literature; *Med* **parálisis i.,** infantile paralysis; **psicología i.,** child psychology. 2 *(aniñado)* childlike; *pey* childish, infantile.

infantilismo *nm Med* infantilism.

infarto *nm Med* infraction, infarct; *fam* **me va a dar un i.,** it'll be the death of me. ■ **i. de miocardio,** heart attack, coronary thrombosis.

infatigable *adj* indefatigable, tireless, untiring.

infausto,-a *adj lit* unlucky, ill-fated, ill-starred; **un suceso de infausta memoria,** an event which is best left forgotten.

infección *nf* infection.

infeccioso,-a *adj* infectious.

infectar **I** *vtr* to infect. **II infectarse** *vr* to become infected (**de,** with).

infecto,-a *adj* 1 infected. 2 *(asqueroso)* foul; *(horrendo)* stinking; **olor i.,** stench; **tiempo i.,** filthy weather.

infecundidad *nf* infertility; *(esterilidad)* sterility.

infecundo,-a *adj* infertile; *(estéril)* sterile.

infelicidad *nf* unhappiness; *(infortunio)* misfortune.

infeliz **I** *adj* unhappy; *(desdichado)* unfortunate. **II** *nmf fam* simpleton; **es un pobre i.,** he is a poor devil.

inferencia *nf* inference.

inferior **I** *adj* 1 *(más bajo)* lower; **el lado i.,** the underside; **labio i.,** lower lip. 2 *(en calidad)* inferior (**a,** to); **de calidad i.,** of inferior quality. 3 *(en cantidad)* lower, less; **cualquier número i. a diez,** any number less than *or* under *or* below ten. **II** *nmf (persona)* subordinate, inferior.

inferioridad *nf* inferiority; **estar en i. de condiciones,** to be at a disadvantage. ■ **complejo de i.,** inferiority complex.

inferir *vtr lit* **1** *(deducir)* to infer, deduce (**de,** from). **2** *(causar)* to cause. **3** *(herida)* to inflict.

infernal *adj* infernal, hellish; *fig* **había un ruido i.,** there was a hell of a noise; *fig* **hace un calor i.,** it's as hot as hell.

infestar *vtr* **1** *(animales, plantas)* to infest. **2** *fig (llenar)* to overrun, invade; **el lugar estaba infestado de turistas,** the place was swarming with tourists. **3** *(infectar)* to infect.

infidelidad *nf* **1** *(deslealtad)* infidelity, unfaithfulness. **2** *(inexactitud)* inaccuracy; **los errores se deben a la i. de la traducción,** the mistakes are due to the inaccuracy of the translation.

infiel I *adj* **1** *(desleal)* unfaithful. **2** *(inexacto)* inaccurate; **si la memoria no me es i.,** if my memory doesn't fail me. **II** *nmf Rel* infidel, unbeliever. ◆ **infielmente** *adv* **1** *(deslealmente)* unfaithfully. **2** *(inexactamente)* inaccurately.

infiernillo *nm* portable stove; **i. de alcohol,** spirit stove.

infierno *nm* **1** *Rel* hell; **ir al i.,** to go to hell. **2** *(gen pl) Mil* Hades. **3** *fig* hell, inferno; **el edificio se convirtió en un i.,** the building became an inferno; **en el quinto i.,** in the middle of nowhere, at the back of beyond; *fam* **¡vete al i.!,** go to hell!, get lost!

infiltración *nf* infiltration.

infiltrado,-a I *pp de* **infiltrar. II** *nm,f* infiltrator.

infiltrar I *vtr* to infiltrate; *fig* to drum in, inculcate. **II infiltrarse** *vr* to infiltrate (**en,** into).

ínfimo,-a *adj fml* **1** *(bajo)* lowest; smallest; **a precios ínfimos,** at ridiculously low prices. **2** *(malo)* poorest, worst; **productos de ínfima calidad,** goods of the poorest quality.

infinidad *nf* **1** *(infinito)* infinity; **me pareció esperar una i. (de tiempo),** I seemed to wait for ages. **2** *(sinfín)* great number; **en i. de ocasiones,** on countless occasions; **tengo una i. de cosas que hacer,** I've got a million things to do; **una i. de preguntas,** an endless number of questions.

infinitesimal *adj,* **infinitésimo,-a** *adj* infinitesimal.

infinitivo,-a *adj & nm Ling* infinitive.

infinito,-a I *adj* infinite, unlimited, endless. **II** *nm (gen)* infinity. **III** *adv (muchísimo)* infinitely, immensely. ◆ **infinitamente** *adv* infinitely.

inflación *nf Econ* inflation.

inflacionario,-a *adj,* **inflacionista** *adj Econ* inflationary.

inflamable *adj* inflammable.

inflamación *nf* **1** *Med* inflammation. **2** *(ignición)* ignition, combustion.

inflamar I *vtr* **1** *Med* to inflame. **2** *(encender)* to set on fire, ignite. **3** *fig* to excite, arouse; **i. las pasiones,** to arouse passions. **II inflamarse** *vr* **1** *Med* to become inflamed. **2** *(incendiarse)* to catch fire. **3** *fig* to become inflamed; **se inflamaron las pasiones,** passions became inflamed.

inflamatorio,-a *adj* inflammatory.

inflar I *vtr* **1** *(hinchar)* to inflate, blow up; *Náut (vela)* to swell. **2** *Econ* to inflate. **3** *fig (exagerar)* to exaggerate. **4** *(envanecer)* to make conceited. **II inflarse** *vr* **1** to inflate; *Náut (vela)* to swell. **2** *(persona)* to get conceited (**con,** about); **i. de orgullo,** to swell with pride. **3** *fam* to eat a lot; **se inflaron de macarrones,** they stuffed themselves with macaroni.

inflexibilidad *nf* inflexibility.

inflexible *adj* inflexible.

inflexión *nf* inflection, inflexion.

infligir *vtr* to inflict.

influencia *nf* influence; **ejercer** *or* **tener i. sobre algn,** to have an influence on *or* upon sb; **tener influencias,** to be influential.

influenciable *adj* easily influenced.

influenciar *vtr* to influence.

influenza *nf Med* influenza, flu.

influir I *vtr* to influence. **II** *vi* **1** to have influence. **2 i. en** *or* **sobre,** to influence, have an influence on, affect.

influjo *nm* influence.

influyente *adj* influential.

información *nf* **1** information; **a título de i.,** by way of information. ■ **oficina de i.,** information bureau. **2** *Prensa (noticia)* **una i.,** a piece of news, (some) news *sing*; **i. periodística,** newspaper report; *Mil* **servicio de i.,** intelligence service. **3** *Tel* directory enquiries *pl*. **4** *(referencias)* references *pl*.

informado,-a I *pp de* **informar. II** *adj* informed; **bien/mal i.,** well-/badly-informed; **de fuentes bien informadas,** from reliable sources.

informador,-a I *adj* informing. **II** *nm,f* informant, informer.

informal *adj* **1** *(reunión, cena)* informal. **2** *(comportamiento)* bad, unmannerly, incorrect. **3** *(persona)* unreliable, untrustworthy. ◆ **informalmente** *adv* **1** *(desenfadado)* informally. **2** *(de comportamiento)* incorrectly. **3** *(persona)* unreliably.

informalidad *nf* **1** *(desenfado)* informality. **2** *(comportamiento)* unmannerliness, incorrectness. **3** *(en persona)* unreliability, untrustworthiness.

informante I *adj* informing. **II** *nmf* informant.

informar I *vtr (enterar)* to inform (**de,** of); *(dar informes)* to report; **el equipo de rescate informó que ...,** the rescue party reported that ... . **II** *vi* to report (**de,** on); **el científico informó de su descubrimiento,** the scientist announced his discovery. **III informarse** *vr (procurarse noticias)* to find out (**de,** about), inform oneself; *(enterarse)* to enquire (**de,** about).

informática *nf Inform* computer science, computing; **el mundo de la i.,** the computer world.

informático,-a I *Inform* **I** *adj* computer, computing. **II** *nm,f* (computer) technician.

informativo,-a I *adj* informative, explanatory. **II** *nm Rad TV* news bulletin.

informe¹ *nm* **1** report; **dar informes sobre,** to give information about; **según mis informes,** according to my information. **2 informes,** references; **pedir i. sobre algn,** to make enquiries about sb; **'se necesita asistenta con buenos i.',** 'wanted cleaner with good references'.

informe² *adj* shapeless, formless.

infortunado,-a *adj* unfortunate, unlucky.

infortunio *nm (mala suerte)* misfortune; *(contratiempo)* mishap.

infracción *nf (gen)* offence; *(de ley)* infringement, infraction, breach (**de,** of).

infractor,-a *nm,f* offender.

infraestructura *nf* infrastructure.

in fraganti *loc adv* in the act; **coger** *or* **pillar a algn in f.,** to catch sb red-handed.

infrahumano,-a *adj* subhuman.

infranqueable *adj* impassable, insuperable; *fig* insurmountable.

infrarrojo,-a *adj* infrared.

infrascripto,-a *adj & nm,f,* **infrascrito,-a** *adj & nm,f fml* undersigned; **yo, el i. ...,** I the under-signed ... .

infravalorar *vtr* to undervalue, underestimate.

infrecuente *adj* infrequent; *(extraño)* rare.

infringir *vtr* to infringe, contravene; **i. una ley,** to break a law.

infructuoso,-a *adj* fruitless, unsuccessful. ◆ **infructuosamente** *adv* fruitlessly, unsuccessfully.

ínfulas *nfpl* conceit *sing*, pretension *sing*; **darse í.,** to put on airs.

infundado,-a *adj* unfounded, groundless, baseless.

infundio *nm* lie, tale, fib; **todo esto son infundios,** it's all a pack of lies.

infundir *vtr (gen)* to infuse; *fig* to instil; **i. dudas,** to give rise to doubt; **i. respeto,** to fill with respect.

infusión *nf* infusion; **i. de manzanilla,** camomile tea.

infuso,-a *adj* inspired; *fam irón* **tener ciencia infusa,** to be a born genius.

ingeniar I *vtr* to invent, devise, think up. **II ingeniarse** *vr* to manage, find a way; **ingeniárselas para hacer algo,** to manage *or* contrive to do sth.

ingeniería *nf* engineering.

ingeniero,-a *nm, f* engineer. ■ **i. agrónomo/químico,** agricultural/chemical engineer; **i. de caminos, canales y puertos,** civil engineer; **i. de minas/montes,** mining/ forestry engineer; **i. de telecomunicaciones,** electronic engineer; **i. naval** *or* **de marina,** naval architect; **i. técnico,** technician.

ingenio *nm* **1** *(talento)* talent; *(inventiva)* inventiveness, creativeness; *(chispa)* wit; **aguzar el i.,** to sharpen one's wits. **2** *(persona)* genius. **3** *(máquina)* machine; *(aparato)* device; *Mil* **i. nuclear,** nuclear device. ■ *Ind* **i. de azúcar,** sugar mill.

ingenioso,-a *adj* ingenious, clever; *(vivaz)* witty; *fam* **dárselas de i.,** to try to be witty.

ingente *adj* huge, enormous.

ingenuidad *nf* ingenuousness, naïveté.

ingenuo,-a I *adj* ingenuous, naïve. **II** *nm, f* naïve person.

ingerir *vtr (comida)* to ingest, consume; *(líquidos, alcohol)* to drink, consume.

ingestión *nf* ingestion.

Inglaterra *n* England.

ingle *nf Anat* groin.

inglés,-esa I *adj* English. **II** *nm, f* **1** *(hombre)* Englishman; *(mujer)* Englishwoman; **los ingleses,** the English. **III** *nm (idioma)* English.

ingobernable *adj Pol* ungovernable; *(incontrolable)* uncontrollable, unmanageable.

ingratitud *nf* ingratitude, ungratefulness.

ingrato,-a I *adj* **1** *(persona)* ungrateful. **2** *(época, noticia)* unpleasant. **3** *(trabajo)* thankless, unrewarding. **4** *(tierra)* unproductive. **II** *nm, f* ungrateful person. ◆ **ingratamente** *adv* ungratefully.

ingravidez *nf* weightlessness.

ingrávido,-a *adj* weightless.

ingrediente *nm* ingredient.

ingresar I *vtr* **1** *Fin* to deposit, pay in; **i. dinero en una cuenta,** to pay money into an account. **2** *Med* to admit; **i. a algn en el hospital,** to admit sb to hospital. **II** *vi* **1** to enter; **i. en el ejército,** to enlist in the army, join the army, join up; **i. en la Academia,** to join the Academy; **i. en un club,** to join a club. **2** *(ser admitido)* to be admitted; **ingresó cadáver en el hospital,** he was dead on arrival at the hospital.

ingreso *nm* **1** *Fin* deposit; **hacer un i. en una cuenta,** to pay money into an account. **2** *(entrada)* entry **(en,** into); *(admisión)* admission **(en,** to); *Med* **su i. en el hospital,** his admission to hospital. **3 ingresos,** *Fin (sueldo, renta)* income *sing*; *(beneficios)* revenue *sing*; **i. anuales,** annual income; **i. brutos,** gross receipts.

inhábil *adj* **1** *(torpe)* unskilful, clumsy. **2** *(incapaz)* unfit; **i. para el trabajo,** unfit for work. **3** *(inadecuado)* unsuitable. **4 día i.,** non-working day.

inhabilidad *nf* **1** *(torpeza)* unskilfulness, clumsiness. **2** *(incapacitación)* unfitness **(para,** for). **3** *(ineptitud)* ineptitude, incompetence.

inhabilitación *nf* **1** *fml (incapacidad)* disablement. **2** *Jur* disqualification.

inhabilitar *vtr* **1** *fml (incapacitar)* to disable; **inhabilitado para el trabajo,** unfit for work. **2** *Jur* to disqualify.

inhabitable *adj* uninhabitable; *fam* **vive en una casa i.,** she lives in an appalling place.

inhabitado,-a *adj* uninhabited.

inhalación *nf* inhalation.

inhalador *nm Med* inhaler.

inhalar *vtr* to inhale.

inherente *adj* inherent **(a,** in).

inhibición *nf* inhibition.

inhibir I *vtr* to inhibit; **sentirse inhibido,** to feel inhibited. **II inhibirse** *vr* **1** *(cohibirse)* to be *or* feel inhibited. **2** *(abstenerse)* to keep out **(de,** of), keep away **(de,** from). **3** *Jur (juez)* to stay.

inhóspito,-a *adj* inhospitable.

inhumación *nf* burial.

inhumano,-a *adj* inhumane; *(cruel)* inhuman.

inhumar *vtr* to bury.

INI *nm abr de* **Instituto Nacional de Industria,** ≈ National Enterprise Board, NEB.

iniciación *nf* **1** initiation. **2** *(introducción)* introduction **(a,** to).

iniciado,-a I *pp de* **iniciar. II** *adj* initiated. **III** *nm, f* initiate.

iniciador,-a I *adj* initiatory. **II** *nm, f* **1** initiator. **2** *(pionero)* pioneer.

inicial *adj & nf* initial; **punto i.,** starting point.

iniciar I *vtr* **1** *(introducir)* to initiate; **i. a algn en los misterios,** to initiate sb into the mysteries. **2** *(empezar)* to begin, start; *(discusión)* to initiate; *(una cosa nueva)* to pioneer. **II iniciarse** *vr* **1** *(aprender)* **i. en algo,** to learn sth. **2** *(empezar)* to begin, start.

iniciativa *nf* initiative; **i. privada,** private enterprise; **por i. propia,** on one's own initiative.

inicio *nm* beginning, start.

inicuo,-a *adj* wicked, iniquitous.

inigualado,-a *adj* unequalled, unparalleled.

inimaginable *adj* unimaginable, inconceivable.

inimitable *adj* inimitable.

ininteligible *adj* unintelligible.

ininterrumpido,-a *adj* uninterrupted, continuous. ◆ **ininterrumpidamente** *adv* uninterruptedly, continuously.

iniquidad *nf* iniquity.

injerencia *nf* interference, meddling **(en,** in).

injerir I *vtr* to insert. **II injerirse** *vr* to interfere, meddle **(en,** in).

injertar *vtr Agr Med* to graft.

injerto *nm* graft; *(acto)* grafting.

injuria *nf (insulto)* insult, affront; *(agravio)* offence, *US* offense; *Jur* **delito de injurias,** crime of slander.

injuriar *vtr* **1** *(insultar)* to insult; *(ultrajar)* to offend. **2** *(dañar)* to damage, harm.

injurioso,-a *adj (insultante)* insulting; *(ofensivo)* offensive.

injusticia *nf* injustice, unfairness.

injustificable *adj* unjustifiable.

injustificado,-a *adj* unjustified. ◆ **injustificadamente** *adv* injustifiably.

injusto,-a *adj* unjust, unfair. ◆ **injustamente** *adv* unjustly, unfairly.

inmaculado,-a *adj* immaculate.

inmadurez *nf* immaturity.

inmaduro,-a *adj* immature.

inmarcesible *adj*, **inmarchitable** *adj fml* unfading, undying.

inmaterial *adj* immaterial.

inmediaciones *nfpl* neighbourhood *sing*, environs.

inmediato,-a *adj* **1** *(poco después)* immediate, prompt; **de i.,** at once. **2** *(cercano)* close **(a,** to), very near. **3** *(contiguo)* next **(a,** to), adjoining; **en la habitación inmediata a la tuya,** in the room next to yours. ◆ **inmediatamente** *adv* immediately, at once.

inmejorable *adj* unsurpassable, excellent; **calidad i.,** unbeatable quality.

inmemorial *adj* immemorial.

inmensidad *nf* immensity, enormity, vastness; **la i. de los mares,** the vastness of the seas.

inmenso,-a *adj* immense, vast; **una fortuna inmensa,** a huge fortune. ◆ **inmensamente** *adv* immensely, vastly.

inmerecido,-a *adj* undeserved, unmerited. ◆ **inmerecidamente** *adj* undeservedly, undeservingly.

inmersión *nf* immersion; *(submarinismo)* dive.

inmerso,-a *adj* inmersed **(en,** in).

inmigración *nf* immigration.

inmigrado,-a I *pp de* **inmigrar.** II *adj* immigrant. III *nm,f* immigrant.

inmigrante *adj & nm, f* immigrant.

inmigrar *vi* to immigrate.

inminencia *nf* imminence.

inminente *adj* imminent, impending.

inmiscuirse *vr* to interfere, meddle **(en,** in).

inmobiliario,-a I *adj* property, real-estate; **agente i.,** estate agent, *US* realtor. II *nf* estate agency, *US* real estate company.

inmoderado,-a *adj* immoderate; *(exagerado)* excessive. ◆ **inmoderadamente** *adv* immoderately; *(exageradamente)* excessively.

inmodestia *nf* immodesty.

inmodesto,-a *adj* immodest. ◆ **inmodestamente** *adv* immodestly.

inmolación *nf fml* immolation, sacrifice.

inmolar *vtr fml* to immolate, sacrifice.

inmoral *adj* immoral. ◆ **inmoralmente** *adv* immorally.

inmoralidad *nf* immorality.

inmortal *adj & nmf* immortal.

inmortalidad *nf* immortality.

inmortalizar I *vtr* to immortalize. II **inmortalizarse** *vr* to be immortalized.

inmotivado,-a *adj* **1** *(sin motivo)* motiveless, unmotivated. **2** *(sin fundamento)* groundless.

inmóvil *adj* **1** motionless, immobile; *(car)* stationary. **2** *fig (constante)* determined, steadfast.

inmovilidad *nf* immobility.

inmovilismo *nm* Pol extreme conservatism.

inmovilista *adj & nmf* Pol ultraconservative.

inmovilización *nf* **1** immobilization. **2** **inmovilizaciones,** fixed assets.

inmovilizado,-a I *pp de* **inmovilizar.** II *adj* motionless, at a standstill.

inmovilizar *vtr* **1** *(persona, cosa)* to immobilize. **2** *Fin (capital)* to immobilize, tie up.

inmueble I *adj* **bienes inmuebles,** real estate, landed property. II *nm* building.

inmundicia *nf* **1** *(suciedad)* dirt, filth; *fig* dirtiness. **2** *(basura)* rubbish, refuse.

inmundo,-a *adj* dirty, filthy; *fig* nasty.

inmune *adj* immune **(a,** to) exempt **(de,** from).

inmunidad *nf* immunity **(contra,** against). ■ **i. diplomática / parlamentaria,** diplomatic/parliamentarian immunity.

inmunización *nf* immunization.

inmunizar *vtr* to immunize **(contra,** against).

inmunología *nf* immunology.

inmutabilidad *nf* immutability.

inmutable *adj* immutable.

inmutarse *vr* to change countenance; **ni se inmutó,** he didn't tura a hair.

innato,-a *adj* innate, inborn.

innecesario,-a *adj* unnecessary. ◆ **innecesariamente** *adv* unnecessarily.

innegable *adj* undeniable.

innocuo *adj véase* **inocuo.**

innombrable *adj* unmentionable, unspeakable.

innominado,-a *adj* nameless.

innovación *nf* innovation.

innovador,-a I *adj* innovatory. II *nm,f* innovator.

innovar *vtr & vi* to innovate.

innumerable *adj* innumerable, countless. ◆ **innumerablemente** *adv* innumerably.

inobediencia *nf* disobedience.

inobservancia *nf* non-observance **(de,** of).

inocencia *nf* **1** *(gen)* innocence. **2** *(ingenuidad)* naïveté.

inocentada *nf fam* practical joke, hoax; **hacer una i. a algn,** to play a practical joke on sb.

inocente I *adj* innocent. II *nmf* innocent; *(ingenuo)* naïve; **hacerse el i.,** to act innocent. ■ **día de los Inocentes,** Holy Innocents' Day, 28th December ≈ April Fools' Day.

inocentón,-ona I *adj* credulous, naïve, gullible. II *nm, f (ingenuo)* naïve person; *(tonto)* simpleton.

inocuidad *nf* innocuousness, harmlessness.

inoculación *nf* inoculation.

inocular *vtr* to inoculate.

inocuo,-a *adj* innocuous, harmless.

inodoro,-a *adj* odourless. II *nm* toilet, lavatory.

inofensivo,-a *adj* inoffensive, harmless.

inolvidable *adj* unforgettable.

inoperante *adj* inoperative, ineffective.

inopia *nf fml* poverty, penury; *fig* **estar en la i.,** to be in the clouds, be miles away.

inopinado,-a *adj* unexpected.

inoportuno,-a *adj* inopportune, inappropriate; *(fuera de tiempo)* untimely; **llegó en un momento muy i.,** he turned up at a very awkward moment. ◆ **inoportunamente** *adv* inopportunely, inappropriately; *(fuera de tiempo)* at the wrong time.

inorgánico,-a *adj* inorganic.

inoxidable *adj* rustless; **acero i.,** stainless steel.

INP *nm abr de* **Instituto Nacional de Previsión.**

inquebrantable *adj fig (firme)* unshakable; *(infrangible)* unyielding.

inquietante *adj* worrying, disturbing.

inquietar I *vtr* to worry, disturb; **me inquieta esta terrible situación económica,** I'm deeply concerned about this dire economic situation. II **inquietarse** *vr* to worry **(por,** about).

inquieto,-a *adj* **1** *(preocupado)* worried, anxious **(por,** about). **2** *(agitado)* restless. **3** *CAm (aficionado)* keen on, fond of.

inquietud *nf* **1** *(preocupación)* worry, anxiety. **2** *(agitación)* restlessness.

inquilinato *nm* **1** tenancy; *Jur* lease. **2** *Arg Col Urug* block of flats, tenement.

inquilino,-a *nm, f* **1** tenant. **2** *Am* inhabitant.

inquina *nf fam (mala voluntad)* ill will, grudge; *(aversión)* dislike; **tener i. a algn,** to have a grudge against sb; **tomar i. a algn,** to take a dislike to sb.

inquirir *vtr* to inquire, enquire into, investigate.

inquisición *nf* **1** inquiry, investigation. **2** *Hist* **la I.,** the Inquisition.

inquisidor,-a I *adj* inquiring, inquisitive. II *Hist nm, f* inquisitor.

inquisitivo,-a *adj* inquisitive.

inri *nm fam* insult; **para más** or **mayor i.,** to make matters worse, add insult to injury.

insaciable *adj* insatiable.

insalubre *adj* insalubrious, unhealthy.

insalubridad *nf* insalubrity, unhealthiness.

insano,-a *adj* **1** *(loco)* insane, mad. **2** *(insalubre)* unhealthy.

insatisfacción *nf* dissatisfaction.

insatisfactorio,-a *adj* unsatisfactory, dissatisfactory.

insatisfecho,-a *adj* unsatisfied, dissatisfied.

inscribir *(pp inscrito)* **I** *vtr* **1** *(registrar)* to register, record, enter; **i. a un niño en el registro civil,** to register a child's birth. **2** *(matricular)* to enrol, *US* enroll. **3** *(grabar)* to inscribe. **4** *Geom* to inscribe. **II inscribirse** *vr* **1** *(registrarse)* to register; *(hacerse miembro)* to join; **i. en un concurso,** to enter for a competition. **2** *(matricularse)* to enrol, *US* enroll.

inscripción *nf* **1** *(matriculación)* enrolment, *US* enrollment, registration; *(precio)* registration fee. **2** *(escrito, dibujo)* inscription.

inscrito,-a I *pp de* **inscribir. II** *adj* **1** *(matriculado)* enrolled, registered; **el número de alumnos inscritos ha aumentado,** the number of students enrolled has increased. **2** *(grabado)* inscribed.

insecticida I *adj* insecticidal, insecticide. **II** *nm* insecticide.

insectívoro,-a I *adj* insectivorous. **II** *nm* insectivore.

insecto *nm Ent* insect.

inseguridad *nf* **1** *(falta de confianza)* insecurity. **2** *(duda)* uncertainty. **3** *(peligro)* lack of safety; **existe una gran i. ciudadana,** the city streets are very unsafe.

inseguro,-a *adj* **1** *(poco confiado)* insecure. **2** *(dubitativo)* uncertain, doubtful. **3** *(peligroso)* unsafe; *fig* **terreno i.,** dangerous ground.

inseminación *nf* insemination.

inseminar *vtr* to inseminate.

insensatez *nf* foolishness, stupidity; **sólo dice insensateces,** he just talks nonsense.

insensato,-a I *adj* foolish, stupid. **II** *nm, f* fool.

insensibilidad *nf* **1** *(gen)* insensitivity; *(indiferencia)* callousness. **2** *Med* insensitivity, numbness.

insensibilizar I *vtr* **1** *(provocar indiferencia)* to make insensitive (a, to); **la vida le ha insensibilizado,** life has hardened him. **2** *Med* to desensitize, anaesthetize. **II insensibilizarse** *vr* to become insensitive.

insensible *adj* **1** *(indiferente)* insensitive (a, to), unfeeling, callous; **es i. a todo sentimiento humano,** she's cold to any human feeling. **2** *Med* insensible, numb. **3** *(imperceptible)* imperceptible, unnoticeable.

inseparable *adj* inseparable; **el trabajo es i. de la fatiga,** work and fatigue go together; **son amigos inseparables,** they're very close friends. ◆ **inseparablemente** *adv* inseparably.

inserción *nf* insertion.

insertar *vtr* to insert.

inserto,-a *adj* inserted.

inservible *adj* useless.

insidia *nf* **1** *(trampa)* snare, trap. **2** *(malicia)* maliciousness.

insidioso,-a *adj* insidious.

insigne *adj* distinguished, famous, illustrious.

insignia *nf* **1** *(emblema)* badge, decoration. **2** *(bandera)* flag, banner; *Náut* pennant; **buque i.,** flagship.

insignificancia *nf* **1** *(intrascendencia)* insignificance; **esto demuestra la i. del problema,** that shows how silly the problem is. **2** *(nadería)* trifle.

insignificante *adj* insignificant, meaningless.

insinuación *nf* insinuation, innuendo, hint; **hacer una i.,** to insinuate.

insinuante *adj* insinuating; *(atrevido)* suggestive; **una mirada i.,** a suggestive glance.

insinuar I *vtr* to insinuate. **II insinuarse** *vr* **1 i. en,** to worm one's way into. **2 i. a una mujer,** to make advances to a woman.

insipidez *nf* insipidness, insipidity; *fig* dullness, flatness.

insípido,-a *adj* insipid; *fig* dull, flat.

insistencia *nf* insistence; *(persistencia)* persistence; **con i.,** insistently.

insistente *adj* insistent; *(persistente)* persistent. ◆ **insistentemente** *adv* insistently, persistently.

insistir *vi* to insist (en, on); *(persistir)* to persist (en, in); **i. en la importancia de,** to stress the importance of; **i. en que se haga algo,** to insist that sth should be done.

insobornable *adj* incorruptible.

insociable *adj* insociable.

insolación *nf* **1** *Med* sunstroke; **coger una i.,** to get sunstroke. **2** *Meteor* sunlight, sunshine; **horas de i.,** hours of sunshine or sunlight.

insolencia *nf* **1** *(descaro)* insolence. **2** *(inconveniencia)* offence, *US* offense.

insolentarse *vr* to be insolent or offensive.

insolente *adj* **1** *(impertinente)* insolent, offensive. **2** *(arrogante)* haughty, contemptuous. **II** *nmf* **1** *(impertinente)* insolent person. **2** *(arrogante)* haughty or contemptuous person.

insólito,-a *adj* *(poco usual)* unusual; *(extraño)* strange, odd.

insoluble *adj* insoluble.

insolvencia *nf Fin* insolvency.

insolvente *adj Fin* insolvent.

insomne I *adj* sleepless. **II** *nmf* insomniac.

insomnio *nm* insomnia; **noche de i.,** sleepless night.

insondable *adj* unfathomable.

insonorización *nf* soundproofing.

insonorizado,-a I *pp de* **insonorizar. II** *adj* soundproof.

insonorizar *vtr* to soundproof.

insonoro,-a *adj* noiseless.

insoportable *adj* unbearable, intolerable.

insoslayable *adj* inevitable, unavoidable.

insospechado,-a *adj* unsuspected.

insostenible *adj* untenable, indefensible.

inspección *nf* inspection. ■ **i. de Hacienda,** tax inspection.

inspeccionar *vtr* to inspect.

inspector,-a *nm, f* inspector. ■ **i. de Hacienda,** tax inspector.

inspiración *nf* **1** *(gen)* inspiration. **2** *(inhalación)* inhalation.

inspirado,-a I *pp de* **inspirar. II** *adj* inspired.

inspirador,-a *adj* inspiring, inspirational.

inspirar I *vtr* **1** *(gen)* to inspire; **i. respeto,** to inspire respect. **2** *(inhalar)* to inhale, breathe in. **II inspirarse** *vr* **i. en,** to be inspired by, find inspiration in.

instalación *nf* installation. ■ **i. sanitaria,** plumbing; **instalaciones deportivas,** sports facilities.

instalador,-a *nm, f* installer, fitter.

instalar I *vtr* **1** *(gen)* to instal, *US* install. **2** *(equipar)* to fit out, equip. **3** *(erigir)* to set up. **II instalarse** *vr* *(persona)* to settle (down), instal oneself.

instancia *nf* **1** *(solicitud)* request, petition; **a instancia(s) de,** at the request of. **2** *(escrito)* application form. **3** *Jur* **tribunal de primera i.,** court of first instance. **4 en primera i.,** first of all; **en última i.,** as a last resort.

instantáneo,-a I *adj* instantaneous, instant; **café i.,** instant coffee. **II** *nf Fot* snapshot. ◆ **instantáneamente** *adv* instantaneously, instantly.

instante *nm* instant, moment; **a cada i.,** constantly, all the time; **al i.,** immediately, right away; **en este (mismo) i.,** right now, at this very moment; **en un i.,** in a flash; **por instantes,** incessantly, all the time; **¡un i.!,** just a moment!

instar *vtr* to urge, press.

instauración *nf* founding, establishment.

instauradór,-a I *adj* founding, establishing. **II** *nm, f* founder, establisher.

instaurar *vtr* to found, establish; **i. la monarquía,** to establish a *or* the monarchy.

instigación *nf* instigation.

instigador,-a I *adj* instigating. **II** *nm, f* instigator.

instigar *vtr* to instigate; **i. a la rebelión,** to incite a rebellion.

instintivo,-a *adj* instinctive. ◆ **instintivamente** *adv* instinctively.

instinto *nm* instinct; **por i.,** instinctively. ■ **i. de conservación,** instinct of self-preservation; **i. maternal,** maternal instinct.

institución *nf* institution, establishment; *fig (persona)* **ser una i.,** to be an institution. ■ **i. benéfica,** charitable foundation.

institucional *adj* institutional.

institucionalizado,-a I *pp de* **institucionalizar. II** *adj* institutionalized.

institucionalizar *vtr* to institutionalize.

instituido,-a I *pp de* **instituir. II** *adj* instituted.

instituir *vtr* to institute; **i. un heredero,** to appoint an heir.

instituto *nm* **1** *(gen)* institute. ■ **i. de belleza,** beauty salon; **I. Nacional de la Vivienda,** Housing Office. **2** *Educ* state secondary school, *US* high school.

institutriz *nf* governess.

instituyo *indic pres véase* **instituir.**

instrucción *nf* **1** *(educación)* education, instruction. **2** *(gen pl) (indicación)* instruction; **instrucciones para el** *or* **de uso,** directions for use; **libro de instrucciones,** instruction manual. **3** *Jur* preliminary investigation; **la i. del sumario,** proceedings *pl.* ■ **juez de i.,** examining magistrate. **4** *Mil* drill, training. ■ **i. militar,** military training.

instructivo,-a *adj* instructive.

instructor,-a I *adj* instructing. **II** *nm, f* instructor.

instruido,-a I *pp de* **instruir. II** *adj* educated, well-educated.

instruir I *vtr* **1** *(gen)* to instruct. **2** *(enseñar)* to educate, teach. **3** *Mil* to drill, train. **4** *(informar)* to inform **(de,** of). **5** *Jur* to investigate; **i. una causa,** to investigate a case.

instrumentación *nf* orchestration.

instrumental I *adj* instrumental. **II** *nm* (set of) instruments *pl,* equipment.

instrumentar *vtr Mús* to orchestrate.

instrumentista *nmf Mús* **1** *(músico)* instrumentalist. **2** *(fabricante)* instrument maker.

instrumento *nm* instrument.

insubordinación *nf* insubordination.

insubordinado,-a I *pp de* **insubordinar. II** *adj* insubordinate. **II** *nm, f* insubordinate, rebel.

insubordinar I *vtr (sublevar)* to stir up, incite to rebellion. **II insubordinarse** *vr (sublevarse)* to rebel **(contra,** against).

insuficiencia *nf* insufficiency. ■ *Med* **i. cardíaca,** cardiac insufficiency, heart failure.

insuficiente I *adj* insufficient, inadequate. **II** *nm Educ (nota)* fail.

insufrible *adj* insufferable, unbearable.

insular I *adj* insular, island; **provincias insulares,** is land provinces. **II** *nmf* islander.

insularidad *nf* insularity.

insulina *nf Quím* insulin.

insulso,-a *adj* insipid, tasteless.

insultante *adj* insulting, offensive; **hablar en tono i.,** to speak with a cut in one's voice.

insultar *vtr* to insult.

insulto *nm* insult.

insumergible *adj (gen)* unsinkable; *(reloj)* not waterproof.

insumiso,-a *adj* unsubmissive.

insuperable *adj* **1** *(en calidad)* unsurpassable. **2** *(en dificultad)* insurmountable.

insurgente *adj & nmf* insurgent.

insurrección *nf* insurrection, uprising, revolt.

insurrecto,-a *adj & nm, f* insurgent.

insustancial *adj* insubstantial.

insustancialidad *nf* insubstantiality.

insustituible *adj* irreplaceable.

intacto,-a *adj* intact.

intachable *adj* irreproachable, blameless, **una conducta i.,** impeccable behaviour.

intangible *adj* intangible.

integractón *nf* integration.

integral I *adj* integral; *Culin* **arroz i.,** brown rice; *Mat* **cálculo pan i.,** integral calculus; *Culin* **pan i.,** wholemeal bread. **II** *nf Mat* integral. ◆ **integralmente** *adv* entirely, completely.

integrante I *adj* integral; **ser parte i. de,** to be in tegral *or* intrinsic to. **II** *nmf* member.

integrar I *vtr* **1** *(formar)* to compose, make up; **un equipo de fútbol lo integran once jugadores,** a football team is made up of eleven players. **2** *Mat* to integrate. **II integrarse** *vr* to integrate.

integridad *nf* integrity.

integrismo *nm* reaction. ■ **i. religioso,** religious fundamentalism.

íntegro,-a *adj* **1** *(entero)* whole, entire; *Cin Lit* **versión íntegra,** unabridged version. **2** *(honrado)* upright, honest. ◆ **integramente** *adv* wholly, entirely.

intelecto *nm* intellect.

intelectual *adj & nmf* intellectual.

intelectualidad *nf* intellectuals *pl,* intelligentsia *pl.*

intetectualismo *nm* intellectualism.

inteligencia *nf* **1** *(intelecto)* intelligence. ■ **cociente de i.,** intelligence quotient, IQ; *Inform* **i. artificial,** artificial intelligence, **2** *(comprensión)* understanding; **en la i. de que,** on the undetstanding that.

inteligente *adj* intelligent.

inteligible *adj* intelligible.

intemperie *nf* bad weather; **a la i.,** in the open (air), out of doors.

intempestivo,-a *adj* untimely, inopportune; **llegaron a una hora intempestiva,** they came at a bad time.

intención *nf* intention; **buena/mala i.,** good/ill will; **con i.,** deliberately, on purpose; **con la mejor i.,** with the best of intentions; **con segunda/doble i.,** with an ulterior motive; **su i. era buena,** she had the right idea; **tener la i. de hacer algo,** to intend to do sth, have sth in mind.

intencionado,-a *adj,* **intencional** *adj* intentional, deliberate. ◆ **intencionadamente** *adv* intentionally, on purpose.

intendencia *nf Mil* ≈ service corps, *US* quarter-master corps.

intendente *nm Mil* quarter-master general.

intensidad *nf (gen)* intensity, strength; *(del viento)* force.

intensificación *nf* intensification.

intensificar *vtr,* **intensificarse** *vr (gen)* to intensify; *(relación)* to strengthen; *(problema)* to aggravate.

intensivo,-a *adj* intensive; *Agr* **cultivo i.,** intensive farming; *Educ* **curso i.,** crash course.

intenso,-a *adj* intense; *(luz, corriente)* strong; *(dolor)* acute.

intentar *vtr* to try, attempt; **¡inténtalo!,** try it!, *fam* give it a go!; **intentó levantarlo solo,** he tried to lift it on his own.

intento *nm* attempt, try; **al primer i.,** at the first attempt; *Pol* **i. de golpe de estado,** attempted coup d'état; **i. de suicidio,** attempted suicide; **i. fracasado,** failed attempt.

intentona *nf* 1 *fam* foolhardy attempt. 2 *Pol* putsch.

inter-*pref* inter-; **intercontinental,** intercontinental.

interacción *nf* interaction, interplay.

intercalación *nf* intercalation, insertion.

intercalar *vtr* to intercalate, insert.

intercambiable *adj* interchangeable.

intercambiar *vtr* to exchange, swap.

intercambio *nm* exchange, interchange. ■ **i. comercial/cultural,** commercial/cultural exchange.

interceder *vi* to intercede.

interceptar *vtr* 1 *(atajar)* to intercept. 2 *(carretera)* to block; *(tráfico)* to hold up.

interceptor *nm* interceptor.

intercesión *nf* intercession.

intercesor,-a I *adj* interceding. **II** *nm,f* intercessor.

intercomunicación *nf* intercommunication.

intercomunicador *nm* intercom.

interconectar *vtr* to interconnect.

interdecir *(pp interdicho)* *vtr* to forbid, prohibit.

interdependencia *nf* interdependence.

interdicción *nf,* **interdicto** *nm* interdiction, prohibition.

interés *nm* 1 *(gen)* interest; **merecer i.,** to be interesting; **poner i. en,** to take an interest in; **sentir i. por, tener i. en** or **por,** to be interested in. 2 *(provecho personal)* self-interest; **hacer algo (sólo) por i.,** to do sth out of self-interest. ■ **i. propio,** self-interest; **intereses creados,** vested interests. 3 *Fin* interest; **con un i. del 11%,** at an interest of 11%. ■ **i. devengado,** accrued interest; **i. simple/compuesto,** simple/compound interest.

interesado,-a I *pp de* **interesar. II** *adj* 1 interested; **las partes interesadas,** the interested parties. 2 *(egoísta)* selfish, self-interested. **III** *nm, f* interested person; **los interesados,** those interested *or* concerned.

interesante *adj* interesting; **ser i.,** to be interesting; *fam* **hacerse el i.,** to try to attract attention.

interesar I *vtr* 1 *(tener interés)* to interest; **¿te interesa la poesía?,** are you interested in poetry? 3 *(afectar)* to concern, involve; **el asunto nos interesa a todos,** the matter concerns us all. 4 *Med* to affect; **la herida le interesa el hígado,** the wound affects her liver. 5 *(ser importante)* to be of interest, be important; **interesa or interesaría llegar pronto,** it is important to get there early. **II interesarse** *vr* **i. por** *or* **en,** to be interested in; **se interesó por ti,** he asked about *or* after you.

interfecto,-a *nm, f* 1 *Jur* murder victim. 2 *fam hum* person in question.

interferencia *nf (gen)* interference; *Rad TV* jamming.

interferir *vtr* 1 *(gen)* to interfere with; *(plan)* to upset. 2 *Rad TV* to jam.

interfono *nm Tel* intercom.

intergubernamental *adj* intergovernmental.

interin *(pl interines)* **I** *nm* interim; **en el í.,** in the meantime, **II** *adv* while.

interinidad *nf* 1 *(temporalidad)* temporariness. 2 *(empleo)* temporary employment.

interino,-a I *adj* 1 *(trabajo, solución)* temporary, provisional, interim. 2 *(persona)* acting; **presidente i.,**

acting president, **II** *nm, f* 1 *(trabajador temporal)* temporary worker. 2 *(sustituto)* stand-in. **III** *nf (asistenta)* cleaner, cleaning lady. ◆ **interinamente** *adv* temporarily.

interior I *adj* 1 *(gen)* interior, inner, inside; **habitación i.,** inner room; **ropa i.,** underwear, underclothes. 2 *Pol* domestic, internal; **correo i.,** inland mail. 3 *Geog* inland. **II** *nm* 1 *(gen)* inside, interior, inner part; **pasemos al i.,** let's go inside; *fig* **en su i. no estaba de acuerdo,** deep down she disagreed. 2 *Geog* interior; *Pol* **Ministerio del I.,** Home Office, *US* Department of the Interior; *Pol* **Ministro del I.,** Home Secretary. 3 *Ftb (jugador)* inside-forward.

interioridad *nf* 1 inwardness. 2 **interioridades,** personal affairs, family secrets; *(secretos)* ins and outs; **las i. de la política,** the ins and outs of politics; **meterse en i.,** to delve.

interiorizar *vtr* to intenalize.

interjección *nf Ling* interjection.

interlocutor,-a *nm,f* speaker, interlocutor; **su i.,** the person he was speaking to, the person who spoke to him.

interludio *nm* interlude.

intermediario,-a I *adj* intermediary. **II** *nm,f* intermediary, mediator, go-between; **servir de i.,** to act as a mediator. **III** *nm Com* middleman.

intermedio,-a I *adj* intermediate; **la etapa intermedia,** the intervening period, the period in between. **II** *nm* 1 *(intervalo)* interval, intermission. 2 *(por medio de)* **por i. de,** through, by means of.

interminable *adj* interminable, endless.

intermitencia *nf* intermittence, intermittency; **con i.,** intermittently, on and off.

intermitente I *adj* intermittent. **II** *nm Aut* indicator, blinker.

internacional I *adj* international, worldwide. **II** *nmf Dep* international. **III la I.** *nf Mús* the Internationale. ◆ **internacionalmente** *adv* internationally.

internacionalismo *nm* internationalism.

intenacionalizar I *vtr* to internationalize. **II internacionalizarse** *vr* to become internationalized *or* international.

internado,-a I *pp de* **internar. II** *adj* 1 *Pol Mil* interned. 2 *Med* confined. **III** *nm* 1 *(prisionero)* internee. 2 *(colegio)* boarding school. 3 **internados,** *(alumnos)* boarders. **IV** *nf Dep* breakthrough.

internamiento *nm* 1 *Pol* internment. 2 *Med* confinement.

internar I *vtr* 1 *Pol* to intern. 2 *Med (en hospital mental)* to confine. **II internarse** *vr* 1 *(penetrar)* to penetrate, advance (**en,** into). 2 *Dep* to break through.

internista *adj & nmf Med* internist.

interno,-a I *adj* 1 internal; *Med* **medicina interna,** internal medicine; *Med* **por vía interna,** internally. 2 *Pol* domestic. **II** *nm,f* 1 *(alumno)* boarder. 2 *Med (enfermo)* intern.

interparlamentario,-a *adj Parl* interparliamentary.

interpelación *nf Parl* interpellation, appeal.

interpelar *vtr Parl* to interpellate.

interplanetario,-a *adj* interplanetary.

interpolación *nf* interpolation, insertion.

interpolar *vtr* to interpolate, insert.

interponer *(pp interpuesto)* **I** *vtr* to interpose, insert; *Jur* **i. un recurso,** to give notice of appeal. **II interponerse** *vr* to intervene.

interposición *nf* interposition, insertion; *Jur* **i. de un recurso,** lodging of an appeal.

interpretación *nf* 1 *(gen)* interpretation; **ha habido una mala i.,** there has been a misunderstanding. 2 *Mús Teat* performance.

interpretar *vtr* 1 *(gen)* to interpret; **i. mal,** to misunderstand, misinterpret. 2 *Teat (papel)* to play; *(obra)* to perform; *Mús (concierto)* to play, perform; *(canción)* to sing.

intérprete *nmf* **1** *(traductor)* interpreter. **2** *Teat* performer; *Mús (cantante)* singer; *(músico)* performer.

interpuesto,-a *pp de* **interponer**. **II** *adj* interposed.

interpuse *pt indef véase* **interponer**.

interracial *adj* interracial.

interregno *nm* interregnum.

interrogación *nf* interrogation, questioning. ■ *Ling* **(signo de) i.,** question *or* interrogation mark.

interrogador,-a I *adj (que interroga)* interrogating, questioning; *(vista)* inquisitive. **II** *nmf (persona)* interrogator.

interrogante I *adj* interrogating, questioning. **II** *nm* question mark.

interrogar *vtr (gen)* to question; *(testigo etc)* to interrogate.

interrogativo,-a *adj & nm* interrogative.

interrogatorio *nm* interrogation.

interrumpir *vtr (gen)* to interrupt; *(tráfico)* to block; *Elect* to switch off.

interrupción *nf* interruption; **sin i.,** uninterruptedly, without a break. ■ **i. del embarazo,** termination of pregnancy.

interruptor *nm Elec* switch.

intersección *nf* intersection.

intersticio *nm (gen)* interstice, crevice; *(grieta)* crack; *(intervalo)* gap.

interurbano,-a *adj* intercity; *Tel* **conferencia interurbana,** trunk call, long-distance call.

intervalo *nm* **1** *(de tiempo)* interval; **a intervalos,** at intervals. **2** *(espacio)* gap.

intervención *nf* **1** *(participación)* intervention, participation **(en,** in), contribution **(en,** to); **hacer una i.,** to take the floor; *Pol* **política de no i.,** non-intervention policy. **2** *Med* operation; **realizar** *or* **hacer una i. quirúrgica,** to perform surgery. ■ **i. quirúrgica,** surgical operation.

intervencionismo *nm* interventionism.

intervencionista *adj & nmf* interventionist.

intervenir I *vi (participar)* to intervene **(en,** in), take part, participate **(en,** in), contribute **(en,** to); **en esta película intervienen treinta actores,** there are thirty actors in this film; **la policía intervino para dispersar la manifestación,** the police broke up the demonstration; **no intervino en la discusión,** she did not take part in the debate. **II** *vtr* **1** *(confiscar)* to confiscate, seize. **2** *Tel (teléfono)* to tap. **3** *Med* to operate on.

interventor,-a *nm,f (financiero)* financial controller; *(de las actas)* scrutineer; *(judicial)* official receiver; *(supervisor)* supervisor, inspector. ■ *Fin* **i. (de cuentas),** auditor.

interviú *nm (pl* **interviús)** interview.

intestinal *adj* intestinal.

intestino,-a I *adj (luchas)* internal, domestic. **II** *nm Anat* intestine. ■ **i. delgado/grueso,** small/large intestine.

intimación *nf* announcement, notification.

intimar I *vtr (notificar)* to notify **(a,** to). **II** *vi (entablar amistad)* to become close **(con,** to).

intimidación *nf* intimidation.

intimidad *nf (amistad)* intimacy; *(vida privada)* private life; *(privacidad)* privacy; **en la i.,** privately, in private.

intimidar I *vtr* to intimidate. **II intimidarse** *vr* to be intimidated, get scared; **no se intimida por nada,** she's afraid of nothing.

íntimo,-a I *adj* **1** intimate; **higiene íntima,** personal hygiene. **2** *(vida)* private; **una boda íntima,** a quiet wedding. **3** *(amistad)* close. **II** *nm,f* close friend, intimate.

intitular *vtr* to entitle, call.

intocable *adj & nmf* untouchable.

intolerable *adj* intolerable.

intolerancia *nf* intolerance.

intolerante I *adj* intolerant. *nmf* intolerant person.

intoxicación *nf* poisoning; *(por alimentos)* food poisoning.

intoxicar *vtr* to poison.

intra- *pref* intra-; **intrauterino,** intrauterine.

intraducible *adj* untranslatable.

intragable *adj* unpalatable; *fam* **es una película i.,** this film is unbearable.

intramuros *adv lit* within the city (walls).

intramuscular *adj* intramuscular.

intranquilidad *nf* worry, uneasiness, restlessness.

intranquilizador,-a *adj* worrying, upsetting.

intranquilizar I *vtr* to worry, upset, make uneasy. **II intranquilizarse** *vr* to get worried, be anxious.

intranquilo,-a *adj* worried, disquieted, uneasy, restless.

intransferible *adj* untransferable, nontransferable.

intransigencia *nf* intransigence.

intransigente *adj* untransigent.

intransitable *adj* impassable.

intransitivo,-a *adj Ling* intransitive.

intrascendencia *nf* insignificance, unimportance

intrascendente *adj* insignificant, unimportant.

intratable *adj* **1** *(problema)* intractable, unmanageable. **2** *(persona)* unsociable, unapproachable.

intravenoso,-a *adj Med* intravenous.

intrépido,-a *adj* intrepid, bold, daring.

intriga *nf* intrigue; *Cin Teat* plot.

intrigante I *adj* **1** *(interesante)* intriguing, interesting. **2** *pey (maquinador)* scheming. **II** *nmf (persona)* intriguer.

intrigar I *vtr (interesar)* to intrigue, interest; **esto me tiene muy intrigado,** this has got me really intrigued. **II** *vi (maquinar)* to plot, scheme.

intrincado,-a *adj* **1** *(cuestión, problema)* intricate, complicated. **2** *(bosque)* dense.

intríngulis *nm inv fam* hidden snag, catch; **tiene su i.,** there's more to it than meets the eye.

intrínseco,-a *adj* intrinsic, inherent.

introducción *nf* introduction.

introducir I *vtr* **1** *(gen)* to introduce. **2** *(poner en uso)* to bring in, introduce. **3** *(meter)* to insert, put in. **4** *(problema, discordia)* to cause, create, bring about. **II introducirse** *vr* **1** *(moda, costumbre)* to be introduced **(en,** into). **2** *(meterse)* to get into, enter; **i. en la alta sociedad,** to work one's way into high society.

introductor,-a I *adj* introductory. **II** *nm,f* introducer.

introductorio,-a *adj* introductory.

intromisión *nf* meddling, interfering, intrusion.

introspección *nf* introspection.

introspectivo,-a *adj* introspective.

introversión *nf* introversion.

introvertido,-a I *adj* introverted. **II** *nm,f* introvert.

intrusión *nf* intrusion.

intrusismo *nm* quackery.

intruso,-a I *adj* intrusive. **II** *nm, f* **1** *(gen)* intruder; *Jur* trespasser. **2** *(impostor)* quack, impostor.

intuición *nf* intuition.

intuir *vtr* to sense, feel.

intuitivo,-a *adj* intuitive. ◆ **intuitivamente** *adv* intuitively, by intuition.

inundación *nf* flood, flooding.

inundar *vtr* to flood, swamp.

inusitado,-a *adj* unusual, uncommon.

inútil I *adj* **1** *(gen)* useless; *(esfuerzo, intento)* vain, pointless; **es i. que llores,** there's no point in crying. **2** *Mil* unfit (for service). **II** *nmf fam* good-for-nothing.

inutilidad *nf* uselessness.

inutilizado,-a I *pp de* **inutilizar.** II *adj* out of action.

inutilizar *vtr (gen) to* make *or* render useless; *(máquina etc) to* put out of action; **las bombas inutilizaron el alumbrado de la ciudad,** the bombing knocked out the lights of the city.

invadir *vtr* to invade; *fig* **le invadió la tristeza,** she was overcome by sadness; *fig* **los estudiantes invadieron la calle,** students poured out onto the street.

invalidación *nf* invalidation.

invalidar *vtr* to invalidate.

invalidez *nf* 1 *Jur (nulidad)* invalidity. 2 *Med (minusvalía)* disablement, disability.

inválido,-a I *adj* 1 *Jur (nulo)* invalid. 2 *Med (minusválido)* disabled, handicapped. II *nm, f Med* disabled *or* handicapped person.

invariabilidad *nf* invariability.

invariable *adj* invariable, unchanging.

invariado,-a *adj* unchanged.

invasión *nf* invasion.

invasor,-a I *adj* invading. II *nm, f* invader.

invectiva *nf* invective; **una i.,** a piece of invective.

invencible *adj* 1 *Mil* invincible, unbeatable. 2 *(obstáculo)* insurmountable; *Hist* **la A. Invencible,** the Spanish Armada.

invención *nf (invento)* invention; *(hallazgo)* discovery; *(mentira)* fabrication; *fam* **i. del tebeo,** stupid idea.

inventar I *vtr (crear) to* invent; *(cuento, historia) to* imagine; *(excusa, mentira)* to make up, concoct, fabricate. II **inventarse** *vr (excusa, mentira)* to make up, concoct.

inventariar *vtr* to inventory.

inventario *nm* 1 *(lista)* inventory. 2 *(operación)* stocktaking; *Com* **hacer el i.,** to do the stocktaking.

inventivo,-a I *adj* inventive, resourceful. II *nf* inventiveness; *(imaginación)* imagination.

invento *nm* invention; *fam* **¡vaya i.!,** what a bright idea!

inventor,-a *nm, f* inventor.

invernadero *nm* greenhouse, hothouse, conservatory. ■ **efecto i.,** greenhouse effect.

invernal *adj* winter, wintry.

invernar *vi* 1 *(pasar el invierno)* to winter, spend the winter **(en,** in). 2 *(animales)* to hibernate.

inverosímil *adj* unlikely, improbable.

inverosimilitud *nf* unlikeliness, improbability.

inversión *nf* 1 *(gen)* inversion. 2 *Fin* investment.

inversionista *nm f Fin* investor.

inverso,-a *adj* inverted, opposite, contrary; **a la inversa,** *(al revés)* vice versa, the other way round; *(al contrario)* on the contrary; **en orden i.,** in reverse order; **en sentido i.,** in the opposite direction; **y a la inversa,** and vice versa.

inversor,-a *nm, f Fin* investor.

invertebrado,-a *adj & nm Zool* invertebrate.

invertido,-a I *pp de* **invertir.** II *adj* inverted, reversed. III *nm, f pey* queer.

invertir *vtr* 1 *(orden) to* invert, reverse, turn round; *(dirección)* to reverse; **i. los papeles,** to exchange roles. 2 *(tiempo)* to spend **(en,** on); *(dinero, esfuerzos)* to invest **(en,** in); **i. en bolsa,** to invest in stock.

investidura *nf* investiture.

investigación *nf* 1 *(policíaca etc)* investigation, inquiry. 2 *(científica)* research.

investigador,-a I *adj* investigation. II *nm, f* 1 *(detective)* investigator. 2 *(científico)* researcher, research worker.

investigar *vtr* 1 *(indagar)* to investigate. 2 *(ciencia)* to do research on.

investir *vtr* to invest; **i. a algn con** *or* **de algo,** to invest sb with sth, confer sth on sb.

inveterado,-a *adj* inveterate, deep-rooted.

inviable *adj* non-viable, unfeasible.

invicto,-a *adj lit* unconquered, unbeaten.

invidente I *adj* blind, sightless II *nmf* blind person.

invierno *nm* winter.

inviolabilidad *nf* inviolability.

inviolable *adj* inviolable.

inviolado,-a *adj* inviolate.

invisible *adj* invisible.

invitación *nf* invitation; *Cin Teat (entrada)* ticket.

invitado,-a I *pp de* **invitar.** II *adj* invited; **artista i.,** guest artist. III *nm, f* guest; **tenemos invitados,** we have guests.

invitador,-a *adj*, **invitante** *adj* inviting.

invitar *vtr* to invite; **hoy invito yo,** the drinks are on me today; **i. a algn a comer,** to invite sb to lunch; **me invitó a una copa,** he treated me to a drink; *fig* **esa música invita a bailar,** this music makes you want to dance.

invocación *nf* invocation.

invocar *vtr* to invoke.

involución *nf* 1 *Biol* involution. 2 *Pol* regression, reaction.

involucionista *adj & nmf Pol* regressive, reactionary.

involucrado,-a I *pp de* **involucrar.** II *adj* involved.

involucrar I *vtr* to involve **(en,** in). II **involucrarse** *vr* to get involved **(en,** in).

involuntario,-a *adj* involuntary, unintentional, accidental.

involutivo,-a *adj* 1 *Biol* involutional. 2 *Pol* regressive.

invulnerable *adj* invulnerable.

inyección *nf* injection; **poner una i.,** to give an injection. ■ **i. intramuscular/intravenosa,** intramuscular/intravenous injection.

inyectable I *adj* injectable. II *nm Farm* injection.

inyectar *vtr* to inject **(en,** into); **i. algo a algn,** to inject sb with sth.

inyector *nm Téc* injector.

iodo *nm véase* **yodo.**

ión *nm* véase **ion.**

ión *nm* ion.

iónico,-a *adj* ionic.

ionizador *nm* ionizer.

ionizar *vtr* to ionize.

ionosfera *nf* ionosphere.

ir I *vi* 1 *(gen)* to go; **ir a caballo,** to ride; **ir de Bilbao a Madrid,** to go from Bilbao to Madrid; **ir de paseo,** to go for a walk; **ir de compras/caza,** to go shopping/hunting; **ir del brazo/de la mano,** to walk arm in arm/hand in hand; **ir despacio,** to go slowly; **ir en coche,** to go by car, drive; **ir en tren,** to go by train; **me voy,** I'm off; **quiero ir contigo,** I want to go with you; **¡vamos!,** let's go!; **voy a Lima,** I'm going to Lima; **¡ya voy!,** (I'm) coming! 2 *(río, camino)* to lead; **esta carretera va a la frontera,** this road leads to the border. 3 *(obrar)* **ir con miedo,** to be afraid; **ir con prisa,** to be in a hurry. 4 *(funcionar)* to work (properly); **el ascensor no va,** the lift is out of order. 5 *(desenvolverse)* **¿cómo le va el nuevo trabajo?,** how is he getting on in his new job?; **¿cómo te va?,** how are things?, how are you doing? 6 *(sentar bien)* to suit; **el verde te va mucho,** green really suits you. 7 *(combinar)* to match; **el rojo no va muy bien con el verde,** red does not go well with green. 8 *(vestir)* to wear; **ir con falda,** to wear a skirt; **ir de blanco/de uniforme,** to be dressed in white/in uniform. 9 *fam (importar, concernir)* to concern; **a mí ni me va ni me viene,** it doesn't concern me; **en esto te va la reputación,** your reputation is at stake here; **eso va por ti también,** and the same goes for you; **¿qué te va en ello?,** what does it matter to you? 10 *fam (comportarse)* to act; **ir de guapo por la vida,** to be a flash Harry. 11 *(edad)* **ir para los sesenta,** she's pushing sixty; **ir por los cincuenta,** to be about fifty. 12 *(carrera, profesión)* **va para abogado,** he's studying to be a lawyer. **13** *Naipes* to go, lead. **14** *(ir + por) (seguir)* **ir por la orilla del río,** to follow the riverside; *(ir a buscar)* **ve (a) por agua,** go and fetch some water; *(haber llegado)* **voy por la página noventa,** I've got as far as page ninety. **15** *(locuciones)* **a eso iba,** I was coming to that; **¡ahí va!,** catch!; **dejarse ir,** to let oneself go; **en lo que va de año,** so far this year; **ir a parar,** to end up; **ir dado,** to be in for it; **¡qué va!,** of course not!, nothing of the sort!; **¿quién va?,** *Mil* who goes there?; *(turno)* whose turn is it?; **va a lo suyo,** he looks after his own interests; **¡vamos a ver!,** let's see!; **¡vaya!,** fancy that; **¡vaya moto!,** what a bike!; *fig* **ir demasiado lejos,** to go too far; *fam* **ir tirando,** to get by; **entonces fue y me dijo que no quería hacerlo,** then he went and told me that he didn't want to do it; *fam* **¡vamos anda!,** come on!; *fam* **vas que chutas,** you're set; *vulg* **ir de culo,** to be fucked for time. **II** *v aux* **1** *(ir + gerundio)* **ir andando,** to go on foot; **ir corriendo,** to run; **va mejorando,** she's improving. **2** *(ir + pp)* **ir cansado,** to be tired; **ya van rotos tres,** three (of them) have already been broken; *fam fig* **ir vendido,** to be lost. **3** *(ir a + inf)* **iba a decir que,** I was going to say that; **ir a parar en la cárcel,** to end up in jail; **va a llover,** it's going to rain; **vas a caerte,** you'll fall. **III irse** *vr* **1** *(marcharse)* to go away, leave, **me voy,** I'm off; **¡vámonos!,** let's go!; **¡vete!,** go away!, **vete a casa,** go home **2** *(líquido, gas) (escaparse)* to leak **3** *(mano, pie)* to slip, **se le fue el pie,** his foot slipped. **4** *(gastarse)* to go, disappear, **el dinero se va sin que uno se dé cuenta,** money just slips away without your noticing it **5** *euf (morir)* to pass away, die **6** *(locuciones)* **i. a pique,** *(barco)* to sink, *fig* to fall through, **i. abajo** *or* **al traste,** to fall through, **i. de la boca** *or* **de la lengua,** to tell it all, **i. la mano,** to overdo it; *fam fig* **i. por las ramas,** to get sidetracked

ira *nf* wrath, rage, anger, **descargar la i. en algn,** to vent one's wrath on sb

iracundo,-a *adj* **1** *(irascible)* irascible **2** *(enfadado)* irate, angry

Irak *n* Irak

Irán *n* Iran

iraní *adj & nmf (pl iraníes)* Iranian

Iraq n véase **Irak**

iraquí *adj & nmf (pl iraquíes)* Iraqi

irascibilidad *nf* irascibility

irascible *adj* irascible, irritable

iris *nm inv Anat* iris ■ **arco i.,** rainbow

irisación *nf (gen pl)* indiscence

irisado,-a *pp de* **irisar II** *adj* indescent

irisar I *vtr* to make iridescent **II** *vi* to be iridescent

Irlanda *n* Ireland ■ **I. del Norte,** Northern Ireland

irlandés,-esa I *adj* Irish **II** *nm, f (hombre)* Irishman, *(mujer)* Irishwoman, **los irlandeses,** the Irish **III** *nm* **1** *(idioma)* Irish **2** *fam (café)* Irish coffee

ironía *nf* irony, **con i.,** ironically

irónico,-a *adj* ironic

ironizar *vtr* to ridicule, be ironical about

IRPF *nm Econ abr de* **impuesto sobre la renta de las personas físicas,** income tax

irracional *adj* irrational

irracionalidad *nf* irrationality

irradiación *nf* irradiation

irradiar *vtr* **1** *(emitir)* to irradiate, radiate **2** *Am fig (expulsar)* to expel

irrazonable *adj* unreasonable

irreal *adj* unreal

irrealidad *nf* unreality

irrealizable *adj* unattainable, unfeasible, *fig* unreachable

irrebatible *adj* irrefutable.

irreconciliable *adj* irreconcilable.

irreconocible *adj* unrecognizable

irrecuperable *adj* irretrievable.

irrecusable *adj* unimpeachable

irreducible *adj,* **irreductible** *adj* **1** *Mat* irreducible. **2** *fig (inflexible)* unyielding

irreemplazable *adj* irreplaceable.

irreflexión *nf* rashness, impetuosity

irreflexivo,-a *adj (acción)* rash, *(persona)* impetuous

irrefrenable *adj* unrestrained, uncontrollable, **un impulso i.,** an irresistible urge

irrefutable *adj* irrefutable

irregular *adj* irregular

irregularidad *nf* irregularity

irrelevante *adj* irrelevant

irremediable *adj* irremediable, incurable.

irremisible *adj* unpardonable, unforgivable

irremplazable *adj* irreplaceable

irreparable *adj* irreparable

irreprimible *adj* irrepressible

irreprochable *adj* irreproachable, blameless

irresistible *adj* **1** *(impulso, persona)* irresistible. **2** *(insoportable)* unbearable

irresoluto,-a *adj* irresolute

irrespetuoso,-a *adj* disrespectful

irrespirable *adj* unbreathable

irresponsabilidad *nf* irresponsibility

irresponsable I *adj* irresponsible **II** *nmf* irresponsible person

irreverencia *nf* irreverence

irreverente *adj* irreverent

irreversible *adj* irreversible

irrevocable *adj* irrevocable.

irrigación *nf* irrigation

irrigar *vtr* irrigate, water.

irrisorio,-a *adj* derisory, ridiculous.

irritabilidad *nf* irritability.

irritable *adj* irritable.

irritación *nf* irritation

irritante *adj* irritating

irritar I *vtr* **1** *(enfadar)* to irritate, exasperate. **2** *Med* to irritate, inflame **II irritarse** *vr (enfadarse)* to lose one's temper, get angry.

irrompible *adj* unbreakable

irrumpir *vi* to burst **(en,** into)

irrupción *nf* irruption

isabelino,-a *adj Hist (en España)* Isabelline, *(en Inglaterra)* Elizabethan

isla *nf* island, isle. ■ *Aut* **i. de peatones,** traffic island, *US* safety island, **(las) Islas Galápagos,** the Galapagos Islands

islam *nm Rel* Islam

islámico,-a *adj,* **islamita** *adj* Islamic

islandés,-esa I *adj* Icelandic **II** *nm, f (persòna)* Icelander **III** *nm (idioma)* Icelandic.

Islandia *n* Iceland

isleño,-a I *adj* island, **la poblacion isleña,** the population of the island **II** *nm, f* islander

isleta *nf* islet.

islote *nm* small *or* rocky island

ismo *nm fam* ism

isobara *nf* isobar

isósceles *adj Geom* **triángulo i.,** isosceles triangle

isoterma *nf* isotherm

isótopo *nm* isotope

Israel *n* Israel

israeli *adj & nmf (pl israelíes)* Israeli

israelita *adj & nmf Hist* Israelite

istmo *nm Geog* isthmus ■ **I. de Panamá,** Isthmus of Panama

Italia *n* Italy

italiano,-a I *adj* Italian **II** *nm, f (persona)* Italian. **III** *nm (idioma)* Italian

ítem I *nm* item **II** *adv* item, likewise, also

itinerante *adj* itinerant, itinerating

itinerario *nm* itinerary, route

IVA *nm Econ abr de* **impuesto sobre el valor añadido,** value-added tax, VAT

izar *vtr* to hoist, raise.

izqda., izqdª *abr de* **izquierda,** left.

izqdo., izqdº *abr de* **izquierdo,** left.

izquierda *nf* **1** left; **a la i.,** on the left; **girar a la i.,** to turn left. **2** *(mano)* left hand. **3** *Pol* **la i.,** the left; **de izquierdas,** left-wing.

izquierdismo *nm Pol* leftism.

izquierdista *Pol* **I** *adj* leftist, left-wing. **II** *nmf* leftist, left-winger.

izquierdo,-a *adj* **1** left; **brazo i.,** left arm. **2** *(zurdo)* left-handed.

izquierdoso,-a *adj fam* leftish.

J

J, j ['xota]*nf (la letra)* **J,** j.

ja *interj* **1** *(al reír)* **¡ja, ja!,** ha, ha! **2** *(incredulidad)* come on!, come off it!

jabalí *nm (pl jabalíes) Zool* wild boar.

jabalina¹ *nf Zool* female wild boar.

jabalina² *nf Dep* javelin.

jabato *nm Zool* young wild boar; *fig* **ser un j.,** to be as bold as a lion.

jábega *nm Pesca* casting net.

jabeque *nm Náut* xebec, zebec.

jabón *nm* soap; **j. de afeitar/tocador,** shaving/toilet soap; *fam fig* **dar j. a algn,** to soft-soap *or* flatter sb.

jabonado *nm* **1** *(acción)* soaping. **2** *(ropa)* laundry. **3** *fam (reprimenda)* **reprimand,** ticking off.

jabonadura *nf* soaping; **jabonaduras,** soapy water *sing,* soapsuds.

jabonar *vtr véase* **enjabonar.**

jaboncillo *nm* **1** *(postilla de jabón)* bar of toilet soap. **2** *Bot* soapberry.

jabonera *nf* soapdish.

jabonoso,-a *adj* soapy.

jaca *nf Zool* **1** *(caballo pequeño)* pony, cob. **2** *(caballo castrado)* gelding.

jacal *nm Guat Méx Ven* hut, shack.

jácara *nf* **1** *Lit (romance)* picaresque ballad. **2** *fam* nuisance, irritation.

jacarandá *nm Bot* jacaranda.

jacarandoso,-a *adj fam* cheerful, lively.

jacaré *nm Am Zool* caiman.

jacarero *nm,* **jacarista** *nm* merry-maker.

jácena *nf Arquit* main beam.

jacinto *nm* **1** *Bot* hyacinth. **2** *Min* **j. de Ceilán,** zircon; **j. occidental,** topaz; **j. oriental,** ruby.

jaco *nm pey* nag, hack.

jacobeo,-a *adj Rel* of Saint James; **peregrinación jacobea,** pilgrimage to Santiago de Compostela.

jactancia *nf* boastfulness, boasting, bragging.

jactancioso,-a I *adj* boastful. **II** *nm, f* braggart.

jactarse *vr* to boast, brag **(de,** about).

jaculatorio,-a I *adj* fervent. **II** *nf* fervent speech.

jade *nm Min* jade.

jadeante *adj* panting, breathless.

jadear *vi* to pant, gasp.

jadeo *nm* panting, gasping.

jaenés,-esa *adj & nm, f véase* **jiennense.**

jaez *nm* **1** *(del caballo)* harness, trappings *pl.* **2** *pey (ralea)* kind, sort; **gente de ese j.,** people of that ilk *or* kind.

jaguar *nm Zool* jaguar.

jai *nf vulg* woman.

jalar I *vtr* **1***(tirar de un cabo)* to pull, heave. **2** *fam (comer)* to wolf down; **¡cómo le gusta j.!,** he loves stuffing himself! **3** *CAm (hacer el amor)* to make love. **II jalarse** *vr* **1** *fam (comerse)* to wolf down, scoff. **2** *Am (emborracharse)* to get drunk.

jalbegar *vtr* to whitewash.

jalea *nf* jelly. ■ **j. real,** royal jelly.

jaleador,-a I *adj* cheering, encouraging. **II** *nm, f* cheering spectator *or* participant.

jalear *vtr* **1** *(animar)* to cheer (on), clap and shout. **2** *Caza* to urge on.

jaleo *nm* **1** *(alboroto)* din, racket; *(escándalo)* fuss, commotion; *(riña)* row; *(confusión)* muddle; **armar j.,** to make a racket; **armar un j.,** to kick up a fuss; **armarle j. a algn,** to start a row with sb. **2** *CAm (galanteo)* courting.

jaleoso,-a *adj* noisy.

jalón¹ *nm* **1** *(estaca)* marker pole; *fig (hito)* milestone. **2** *Am (trecho)* stretch, distance.

jalón² *nm* **1** *(tirón)* pull, tug. **2** *CAm (galán)* gallant. **3** *Méx (trago)* shot, tot.

jalonar *vtr (señalar con estacas)* to stake out; *fig (marcar)* to mark.

Jamaica *n* Jamaica.

jamaicano-r-a *adj & nm, f* Jamaican.

jamancia *nf fam* **1** *(comida)* grub, nosh. **2** *(hambre)* hunger.

jamar *vtr fam* to scoff, eat.

jamás *adv* **1** *(j. + indi)* never; **j. he estado allí,** I have never been there. **2** *(j. + subj)* ever; **el mejor libro que j. se haya escrito,** the best book ever written. **3** *(locuciones)* **j. de los jamases,** never ever, never on your life; **nunca j.,** never ever; **por siempre j.,** for ever (and ever).

jamba *nf Arquit* jamb.

jamelgo *nm pey* old nag, hack.

jamón *nm* ham; **j. de York** *or* **en dulce,** boiled ham; **j. serrano,** cured ham; *fam* **¡y un j. (con chorreras)!,** nothing doing!, you must be joking!

jamona *fam* **I** *adj* buxom. **II** *nf* boxom woman.

jamuga *nf,* **jamugas** *nfpl* side-saddle *sing.*

jamurar *vtr Náut* to bale out.

jándalo,-a *adj & nm, f fam* Andalusian.

jangada *nf* **1** *(estupidez)* stupid remark *or* comment. **2** *(trastada)* mischief. **3** *Arg (armadía)* raft. **4** *Am (balsa)* raft.

Japón *n* (el) **J.,** Japan.

japonés,-esa I *adj* Japanese. II *nm, f (persona)* Japanese; **los japoneses,** the Japanese. III *nm (idioma)* Japanese.

japuta *nf (pez)* Ray's bream.

jaque *nm Ajedrez* check; **dar j. a,** to check; **dar j. mate a,** to checkmate; **estar en j.,** to be in check; **j. al rey,** check; **j. mate,** checkmate; fig **tener** or **traer a algn en j.,** to intimidate or threaten sb.

jaquear *vtr Ajedrez* to check; *fig (amenazar)* to harass, threaten.

jaqueca *nf* migraine, headache; *fig* **dar j. a,** to bore, be a pain in the neck to.

jaquecoso,-a *adj fig* bothersome, irksome.

jáquima *nf CAm Méx* drunkenness, drunken bout.

jara *nf Bot* rockrose.

jarabe *nm* **1** syrup; **j. para la tos,** cough mixture; *fig* **dar a algn j. de palo,** to give sb a hiding; *fig* **j. de pico,** blarney, smooth talk; *fig* **tener mucho j. de pico,** to talk glibly. **2** *Mús* Mexican dance.

jarana *nf fam* **1** *(juerga)* wild party, spree; **ir de j.,** to go on a spree or a binge. **2** *(jaleo)* racket, din; **armar j.,** to make a racket. **3** *Mex Mús* small guitar. **4** *Am Mús* dance. **5** *Am (burla)* taunt, jeer. **6** *CAm (deuda)* debt.

jaranero,-a I *adj* fun-loving, party-loving. II *nm, f* pleasure seeker, party-lover.

jarcia *nf* **1** *Náut* rigging, ropes *pl*; **j. de labor,** running rigging; **j. muerta,** standing rigging. **2** *Pesca* fishing tackle.

jardín *nm* garden; **j. botánico,** botanical garden; **j. de infancia,** nursery school, kindergarten.

jardinera *nf* **1** *(mujer)* gardener. **2** *(mueble) (para tiestos)* planter, flower stand; *(en una ventana)* window box. **3** *(vehículo) (carruaje)* open carriage;
(tranvía) open tramcar.

jardinería *nf* gardening.

jardinero *nm* gardener.

jareta *nf* **1** *Cost* casing. **2** *Náut* cable, rope.

jarocho,-a *adj* **1** *(insolente)* rude, uncouth. **2** *Méx* of or from Veracruz. II *nm, f Méx* native or inhabitant of Veracruz.

jarra *nf* pitcher; **j. de leche,** milkchurn; **j. de cerveza,** beer tankard; *fig* **de** or **en jarras,** arms akimbo, hands on hips.

jarrete *nm (de persona)* back of the knee; *(de animal)* hock.

jarretera *nf (liga)* garter; **la Orden de la J.,** the Order of the Garter.

jarro *nm (recipiente)* jug; *(contenido)* jugful; *fig* **echar un j. de agua fría a,** to pour cold water on.

jarrón *nm* vase; *Arqueol* urn.

Jartum *n* Khartoum.

jaspe *nm Min* jasper.

jaspeado,-a I *pp de* **jaspear.** II *adj* mottled, speckled.

jaspear *vtr* to mottle, speckle.

Jauja *nf fig* promised land; **¡esto es J.!,** this is the life! **la tierra de J.,** the land of plenty, the land of milk and honey.

jaula *nf (para animales)* cage; *(embalaje)* crate; *(niños)* playpen; *Min* cage.

jauría *nf* pack of hounds; *fig* gang.

Java *n* Java.

javanés,-a *adj & nm, f* Javanese.

jayán,-ana *nm, f (hombre)* big strong man; *(mujer)* big strong woman.

jazmín *nm Bot* jasmine.

jazz *nm Mús* jazz.

jazzístico,-a *adj Mús* jazz, jazzy.

jazzman *nm Mús* jazz player.

J.C. *abr de* **Jesucristo,** Jesus Christ, J.C.

je *interj* **¡je, je!,** ha, ha!

jean *nm* jeans *pl*.

jebe *nm* **1** *(alumbre)* alum. **2** *Am (caucho)* rubber.

jeep *nm Aut* jeep.

jefa *nf* female boss, manageress; *fam* mother.

jefatura *nf* **1** *(cargo, dirección)* leadership; **bajo la j. de,** under the leadership of. **2** *(sede)* central office; *Mil* headquarters; **j. de policía,** police headquarters.

jefe *nm* **1** head, chief, boss; *Com* manager; **j. de estación,** stationmaster; **j. de negociado,** head of department; **j. de redacción,** editor-in-chief; **j. de taller,** foreman; **j. de ventas,** sales manager. **2** *Pol* leader; **J. de Estado,** Head of State. **3** *Mil* officer in command; **comandante en j.,** commander-in-chief; **J. de Estado Mayor,** Chief of Staff.

Jehová *nm* Jehovah; **testigos de J.,** Jehovah's Witnesses.

jején *nm* **1** *Am Ent* black fly. **2** *Méx (abundancia)* abundance.

jengibre *nm Bot* ginger.

jenízaro,-a I *adj fig* mixed. II *nm* janissary.

jeque *nm* sheik, sheikh.

jerarca *nm* hierarch, chief.

jerarquía *nf* **1** *(gen)* hierarchy; **j. social,** social hierarchy. **2** *(grado)* scale. **3** *(categoría)* rank; **de j.,** high-ranking.

jerárquico,-a *adj* hierarchic, hierarchical.

jeremías *nmf inv* whiner, whinger.

jerez *nm* sherry.

jerezano,-a I *adj* of or from Jerez. II *nm, f* native or inhabitant of Jerez.

jerga¹ *nf (argot) (técnica)* jargon; *(vulgar)* slang; **la j. legal,** legal jargon.

jerga² *nf* Tex coarse woollen cloth.

jergal *adj (técnico)* of jargon; *(vulgar)* slangy.

jergón *nm* straw mattress; *fig (torpe)* country bumpkin.

jeribeque *nm (guiño)* wink; *(gesto)* grimace.

jerigonza *nf* **1** *véase* **jerga¹. 2** *(extravagancia)* oddness.

jeringa *nf Med* syringe; *Aut* **j. de engrase,** grease gun.

jeringar *vtr* **1** *Med* to syringe. **2** *fam (molestar)* to pester, annoy.

jeringazo *nm* squirt, syringeful.

jeringuilla *nf Med* (hypodermic) syringe.

jeroglífico,-a I *adj* hieroglyphic. II *nm* **1** *Ling* hieroglyph, hieroglyphic. **2** *(juego)* rebus.

jerosolimitano,-a I *adj* of or from Jerusalem. II *nm, f* native or inhabitant of Jerusalem.

jersey *nm (pl jerseyes or jerseis)* sweater, pullover, jumper.

Jerusalén *n* Jerusalem.

Jesucristo *nm* Jesus Christ.

jesuita *adj & nmf* Jesuit.

jesuítico,-a *adj* Jesuitic; *fig* cautious, wary.

Jesús I *nm* Jesus; *fam* **en un decir J.,** in the twinkling of an eye. II *interj* **1** *(expresa sorpresa)* good heavens! **2** *(al estornudar)* bless you!

jet *nm Av* jet.

jeta *fam* I *nf* **1** *(cara)* mug, face; **poner j.,** to pull a face. **2** *(hocico)* snout. **3** *(descaro)* cheek; **tener j.,** to be cheeky, have a nerve; **¡qué j. tienes!,** what a cheek you've got! II *nmf pl* rogue *sing*.

jet-set *nf* jet-set.

ji *interj* **¡ji, ji, ji!,** hee, hee, hee!

jibá *nm Cuba Méx RD Bot* coca plant.

jíbaro,-a *Am* I *adj* peasant-like, rustic. II *nm, f* peasant.

jibia *nf (pez)* cuttlefish.

jícama *nf Bot* sweet turnip.

jícara *nf* **1** *(bol)* small cup; *Am* gourd. **2** *CAm (cabeza de ganado)* head. **3** *Méx* bald head.

jícaro *nm CAm Cuba Bot* calabash tree.

jicote *nm Am Ent* large wasp.

jicotera *nf* 1 *Am (avispero)* wasps' nest. 2 *Méx (zumbido)* buzzing of wasps.

jiennense I *adj* of or from Jaén. **II** *nmf* native or inhabitant of Jaén.

jijona *nm Culin* type of nougat.

jilguero,-a *nm, f Orn* goldfinch.

jilipollas *nmf inv fam ofens véase* **gilipollas.**

jineta[1] *nf Zool* genet.

jineta[2] *nf* 1 *Equit* **a la j.**, with short stirrups. 2 *Mil (hombrera)* epaulette.

jinete *nm* rider, horseman.

jinetear *Equit* **I** *vtr Am (domar)* to break in. **II** *vi (montar)* to ride regally.

jingoísmo *nm* jingoism.

jingoísta *adj & nmf* jingo, jingoist.

jíngol *nm Bot* jujube.

jiñar *vi vulg* to shit.

jipa *nf Am* straw hat.

jipar *vi Am véase* **jipiar.**

jipato,-a *adj Am (persona)* pale.

jipi *nm* Panama hat.

jipiar *vi (gemir)* to groan; *(gimotear)* to wail.

jipido *nm fam* hiccough, hiccup.

jira *nf* picnic.

jirafa *nf* 1 *Zool* giraffe; *fig* tall person. 2 *(de micrófono)* boom.

jirón *nm (trozo desgarrado)* shred, strip; *(pedazo suelto)* bit, scrap; **hecho jirones**, in shreds or tatters.

jiste *nm* head (on beer), froth.

jitomate *nm Méx* (type of) tomato.

jiu-jitsu *nm Dep* jujitsu.

JJOO *nmpl abr de* **Juegos Olímpicos,** Olympic Games.

jo *interj fam* bloody hell!

Job *nm (pl Jobs)* Job; **tiene más paciencia que el santo J.**, he has the patience of Job.

jobar *interj* blast!

jockey *nm Dep* jockey.

jocó *nm (pl jocoes) Zool* orang-utan, orang-outang.

jocoserio,-a *adj* tragicomic.

jocosidad *nf* humour.

jocoso,-a *adj* funny, humorous, comic.

jocundo,-a *adj* jovial.

joder *vulg ofens* **I** *vtr* 1 *(copular)* to fuck. 2 *(fastidiar)* to piss off; **jode mucho tener que trabajar en domingo**, having to work on Sunday really pisses me off; **¡no me jodas!**, come on, don't give me that! 3 *(echar a perder)* to fuck up; **¡la jodiste!**, you screwed it up! 4 *(romper)* to bugger up, break; **ha vuelto a j. el ordenador**, he has screwed the computer up again. 5 *(lastimar)* to injure; **tiene el brazo jodido**, his arm is buggered. **II joderse** *vr* 1 *(fastidiarse)* to put up with it; **¡hay que j.!**, you'll just have to grin and bear it; **¡que se joda!**, to hell with him! 2 *(echarse a perder)* to fuck up, ruin; **me jodí el domingo por ayudarle a mudarse**, I messed up my Sunday by helping her to move house; **¡se jodió el invento!**, that's the end of that! 3 *(lastimarse)* to hurt, fuck up. 4 *(romperse)* to go bust; **se jodió el día**, the weather turned bad. **III** *interj* bloody hell!, fuck!

jodido,-a I *pp de* **joder. II** *adj vulg ofens* 1 *(maldito)* bloody, fucking. 2 *(molesto)* annoying; **es j. trabajar con ese ruido**, it's bloody awful having to work with that noise. 3 *(enfermo)* in a bad way; *(cansado)* knackered, exhausted. 4 *(estropeado, roto)* bust, done for, kaput, buggered. 5 *(difícil)* complicated.

jodienda *nf vulg ofens* 1 *(coito)* fuck. 2 *(molestia)* balls-up, mess.

jofaina *nf* washbasin.

jogging *nm Dep* jogging; **hacer j.**, to jog.

jóker *nm Naipes* joker.

jolgorio *nm fam (juerga)* binge; *(algazara)* fun; **ir de j.**, to go on a binge; **¡qué j.!**, what fun!

jolín *interj*, **jolines** *interj fam (sorpresa)* gosh!, good grief!; *(enfado)* blast!, damn!

jónico,-a I *adj* Ionic, Ionian; *Arquit* Ionic; **el (Mar) J.**, the Ionian Sea. **II** *nm, f* Ionian. **III** *nm Ling Lit* Ionic.

jope *interj fam* gosh!, good grief!

Jordán *n (río)* Jordan.

Jordania *n (país)* Jordan.

jordano,-a *adj & nm, f* Jordanian.

jorguín,-ina *nm, f (hombre)* sorcerer, enchanter; *(mujer)* sorceress, enchantress.

jorguinería *nf* sorcery, magic.

jornada *nf* 1 *(día de trabajo)* **j. (laboral)**, working day; **j. de siete horas**, seven-hour (working) day; **j. intensiva**, working day without a lunch break; **j. partida**, working day with a lunch break; **trabajo de media j./j. completa**, part-time/full-time work. 2 *(camino recorrido en un día)* day's journey; **de Bilbao a Sevilla hay dos jornadas de camino**, it's a two-day journey from Bilbao to Seville. 3 *Mil* expedition. 4 *Dep* **los resultados de la j. del sábado**, Saturday's results. 5 *Teat (uso antiguo)* act. 6 **jornadas,** conference *sing*, congress *sing*; **las II J. de Moda Española**, the 2nd Conference on Spanish Fashion.

jornal *nm (paga)* day's wage; **ganar un buen j.**, to earn a good wage; **trabajar a j.**, to be paid by the day.

jornalero,-a *nm, f* day labourer or US laborer.

joroba I *nf* 1 *(deformidad)* curvature, hump. 2 *fam (fastidio)* nuisance, drag. **II** *interj* drat!

jorobado,-a I *pp de* **jorobar. II** *adj* hunchbacked, humpbacked. **III** *nm, f* hunchback, humpback.

jorobar *fam* **I** *vtr* 1 *(fastidiar)* to annoy, bother; **me joroba**, it really gets up my nose. 2 *(romper)* to smash up, break. 3 *(estropear)* to ruin, wreck; **¡no jorobes!**, *(fastidio)* stop pestering me!; *(incredulidad)* pull the other one! **II jorobarse** *vr* 1 *(fastidiarse)* to put up with; **¡hay que j.!**, that really is the limit! 2 *(estropearse)* to break.

josefino,-a I *adj* of or from San José. **II** *nm, f* native or inhabitant of San José.

jota[1] *nf* 1 name of the letter J in Spanish. 2 *(cantidad mínima)* jot, scrap; **ni j.**, not an iota; **no entiendo ni j.**, I don't understand a thing; **no sabe ni j. de latín**, he doesn't know the first thing about Latin; **no se ve ni j.**, you can't see a thing.

jota[2] *nf Mús* Spanish dance and music.

joule *nm Fís* joule.

joven I *adj* young; **de aspecto j.**, young-looking; **de j.**, as a young man or woman. **II** *nmf (hombre)* youth, young man; *(mujer)* girl, young woman; **los jóvenes**, young people, youth.

jovencito,-a I *adj* very young. **II** *nm, f (hombre)* boy, youngster; *(mujer)* girl, youngster.

jovenzuelo,-a I *adj* very young. **II** *nm, f (hombre)* lad, youngster; *(mujer)* lass, youngster.

jovial *adj* jovial, good-humoured.

jovialidad *nf* joviality, cheerfulness.

joya *nf* 1 jewel, piece of jewellery; **joyas de imitación**, imitation jewellery *sing*. 2 *fig (personas)* **ser una j.**, to be a real treasure or godsend.

joyería *nf* 1 *(tienda)* jewellery shop, jeweller's (shop). 2 *(comercio)* jewellery trade.

joyero,-a I *nm, f* jeweller. **II** *nm* jewel case or box.

Juan *nm* John; **J. Palomo, (yo me lo guiso yo me lo como),** to go one's own way, paddle one's own canoe; **ser un buen J.,** to be a simple Simon; **ser un J. Lanas,** to be a wimp.

juanesca *nf* chaos, confusion.

juanete *nm* 1 (*en el pie*) bunion. 2 *Náut* topgallant.

jubilación *nf* 1 (*acción*) retirement; **j. anticipada,** early retirement. 2 (*dinero*) pension.

jubilado,-a I *pp de* jubilar. II *adj* retired. III *nm,f* retired person, pensioner; **los jubilados,** retired people.

jubilar¹ *adj* **año j.,** jubilee.

jubilar² I *vtr* (*retirarse*) to retire, pension off; *fam fig* to get rid of, ditch. II *vi fml* (*alegrarse*) to rejoice. III **jubilarse** *vr* 1 (*retirarse*) to retire, go into retirement. 2 (*alegrarse*) to rejoice. 3 *CAm Ven* (*hacer novillos*) to play truant. 4 *Cuba Méx* (*instruirse*) to learn, become skilled.

jubileo *nm* 1 *Hist* (*fiesta*) jubilee. 2 *Rel* (*indulgencia*) indulgence; **ganar el j.,** to gain an indulgence.

júbilo *nm* jubilation, joy.

jubiloso,-a *adj* jubilant, joyful.

jubón *nm* doublet, jerkin.

judaico,-a *adj* Judaic, Jewish.

judaismo *nm* Judaism.

judaización *nf* Judaization.

judaizar *vi* to Judaize.

judas *nm inv* traitor.

judeocristiano,-a *adj & nm,f* Judaeo-Christian, *US* Judeo-Christian.

judeoespañol,-a *adj & nm,f* Judaeo-Spanish, *US* Judeo-Spanish.

judería *nf* 1 (*barrio*) Jewish quarter. 2 *Am fig* (*travesura*) mischief, naughtiness.

judía *nf Bot* bean; **j. blanca/pinta,** haricot/kidney bean; **j. verde,** French bean, green bean.

judiada *nf fam* dirty trick.

judicatura *nf* 1 (*cuerpo*) judicature. 2 (*tiempo en el cargo*) judge's term of office.

judicial *adj* judicial, juridical

judío,-a I *adj* Jewish; *arg* mean, stingy. II *nm, f* Jew; **j. converso,** converted Jew.

judo *nm Dep* judo.

judoka *nmf* judoka.

juego *nm* 1 game; *Naipes* **descubrir su j.,** to show one's hand; **j. de azar,** game of chance; **j. de cartas,** card game; **j. de envite,** gambling game; **j. de ingenio,** guessing game; **juegos florales,** poetry competition *sing*; **juegos malabares,** juggling *sing*; *Naipes* **tener buen/mal j.,** to have a good/bad hand; *fig* **conocer el j. de algn,** to know sb's game; *fig* **descubrirle el j. a algn,** to see through sb; *fig* **hacer** *or* **seguir el j. a algn,** to play along with sb; *fig* **j. de manos,** sleight of hand; *fig* **j. de palabras,** play on words, pun; *fig* **j. limpio/sucio,** fair/foul play; *fig* **poner algo en j.,** to put sth at stake; *fig* **ser un j. de niños,** to be child's play; *fig* **tomar algo a j.,** not to take sth seriously. 2 *Dep* (*sport*; *Tenis* game; *Bridge* rubber; **entrar en j.,** to come into play; **Juegos Olímpicos,** Olympic Games; **terreno de j.,** *Tenis* court; *Ftb* field; **estar en fuera de j.,** to be offside. 3 (*apuestas*) gambling; **casa de j.,** gambling house; **mesa de j.,** gambling table, card table; **¡hagan j., señores!,** place your bets! 4 (*conjunto de piezas*) set; **j. de café/té,** coffee/tea service; **j. de destornilladores,** set of screwdrivers; *fig* **a j.,** matching; *fig* **hacer j.,** to match. 5 (*movimiento*) play.

juerga *nf fam* binge, rave-up; **de j.,** living it up, having a good time; **ir(se) de j.,** to go on a binge; **tener ganas de j.,** to feel like living it up, feel like having a good time.

juerguearse *vr fam* 1 (*irse de juerga*) to rave it up. 2 (*burlarse*) to make fun (**de,** of).

juerguista I *adv* fun-loving. II *nmf* fun-loving person, raver.

jueves *nm inv* Thursday; **J. Santo,** Maundy Thursday; *fam fig* **no es nada del otro j.,** it's nothing to write home about; *véase tamb* **viernes.**

juez *nmf* judge; *Ftb* **j. de banda** *or* **de línea,** linesman; **j. de instrucción,** examining magistrate; **j. de menores,** juvenile court magistrate; *Dep* **j. de meta,** finishing line judge; **j. de paz,** justice of the peace; **j. de primera instancia,** judge of the first instance; *Dep* **j. de salida,** starter; *Tenis* **j. de silla,** umpire.

jugada *nf* 1 (*gen*) play; *Ajedrez* move; *Bill* shot; *Dardos* throw. 2 *Fin* **j. de Bolsa,** speculation. 3 *fam* dirty trick; **hacerle una mala j. a algn,** to play a dirty trick on sb.

jugador,-a 1 player; (*apostador*) gambler. 2 *Fin* **j. de Bolsa,** speculator.

jugar I *vi* 1 (*gen*) to play; **j. a(l) fútbol/tenis,** to play football/tennis; **¿quién juega?,** whose go is it?; *fig* **j. con dos barajas,** to double-deal; *fig* **j. con fuego,** to play with fire; *fig* **j. sucio,** to play dirty. 2 (*burlarse*) to make fun (**con,** of); **j. con los sentimientos de algn,** to play with sb's feelings. 3 *Fin* **j. a la Bolsa,** to play the Stock Exchange. II *vtr* 1 (*gen*) to play; *fam fig* **j. una mala pasada a algn,** to play a dirty trick on sb. 2 (*hacer uso*) (*una pieza*) to move; (*una carta*) to play; **jugó el as,** he played the ace. 3 (*apostar*) to bet, stake. III **jugarse** *vr* 1 (*arriesgar*) to risk; *fam* **j. el pellejo,** to risk one's neck. 2 (*apostar*) to stake, bet; **me juego mil pesetas,** I bet you a thousand pesetas; *fig* **j. el todo por el todo,** to stake everything one has. 3 (*engañar*) **jugársela a algn,** to pull a fast one on sb, take sb for a ride; **jugársela al marido/a la mujer,** to be unfaithful to *or* two-time one's husband/wife.

jugarreta *nf fam* dirty trick.

juglar *nm Hist* minstrel, jester.

juglaresco,-a *adj* minstrel.

jugo *nm* juice; **j. gástrico,** gastric juice; *fig* **sacar el j. a algo,** to make the most of sth; *fig* **sacarle el j. a algn,** to exploit sb, bleed sb dry.

jugosidad *nf* juiciness, succulence.

jugoso,-a *adj* 1 juicy; **un filete j.,** a juicy steak. 2 *fig* (*rentable*) profitable; **un negocio j.,** a lucrative business. 3 *fig* (*sustancioso*) substantial, meaty.

juguete *nm* toy; **pistola de j.,** toy gun; *fig* **ser el j. de algn,** to be sb's plaything.

juguetear *vi* to play, frolic.

jugueteo *nm* playing, frolicking.

juguetería *nf* 1 (*tienda*) toyshop. 2 (*comercio*) toy business.

juguetón,-ona *adj* playful, frolicsome.

juicio *nm* 1 (*facultad mental*) judgement, discernment; (*opinión*) opinion, judgement; **a j. de,** in the opinion of; **a mi j.,** in my opinion; **dejar algo a j. de algn,** to leave sth to sb's discretion; **emitir un j. sobre algo,** to express an opinion about sth; **hombre de j.,** man of judgement. 2 (*sensatez*) reason, common sense; **en su sano j.,** in one's right mind; **perder el j.,** to go mad *or* insane; **quitar** *or* **trastornar el j. a algn,** to drive sb insane; **tener mucho j.,** to be sensible; **tener poco j.,** to have little common sense. 3 *Jur* trial, lawsuit; **j. a puerta abierta,** public hearing; **j. contencioso/penal,** civil/criminal action; **llevar a algn a j.,** to take legal action against sb, sue sb; **suspender un j.,** to adjourn a trial. 4 *Rel* judgement; **J. Final,** Last Judgement.

juicioso,-a *adj* judicious, sensible, wise.

jufay *nm arg* sucker.

julepe *nm* 1 *Naipes* kind of card game. 2 *fig* (*castigo*) punishment. 3 *Am* (*susto*) fright, scare. 4 *Am* (*fatiga*) tiredness.

julepear *vtr* 1 *fam* (*reñir*) to tell off. 2 *fam* (*cascar*) to give a good beating. 3 *Am* (*asustar*) to frighten. 4 *Am* (*atormentar*) to torment.

juliana *nf Bot* damewort.

julio¹ *nm* July; *véase tamb* **noviembre.**

julio² *nm Fís* joule.

juma *nf fam* binge.

jumarse *vr fam to* get sloshed *or* drunk.

jumento *nm* ass, donkey.

jumera *nf fam* bender; **agarrar una j.,** to go on a bender.

juncal I *adj* rushlike; *fig* willowy, graceful. II *nm* bed of rushes.

juncia *nf Bot* sedge.

junco¹ *nm* 1 *Bot* rush; **j. de Indias,** rattan; **j. oloroso,** camel grass. 2 *(bastón)* walking stick, cane.

junco² *nm Náut* junk.

jungla *nf* jungle; **j. de asfalto,** concrete jungle.

junio *nm* June; *véase tamb* **noviembre.**

júnior *(pl juniores)* I *adj Dep* junior. II *nm* 1 *Rel* junior novice. 2 *Dep* junior; **campeonato j. de golf,** junior golf championship. 3 *(benjamín)* youngest son.

junípero *nm Bot* juniper.

junquera *nf* 1 *Bot (planta)* rush, bulrush. 2 *(juncal)* bed of rushes.

junquillo *nm* 1 *Bot* jonquil. 2 *Arquit* beading. 3 *(bastón)* walking stick.

junta *nf* 1 *(reunión)* meeting, assembly, conference; *(conjunto de personas)* board, council, committee; *(sesión)* session, sitting; **celebrar j.,** to hold a meeting; **j. administrativa,** administrative board; **j. de accionistas,** shareholders' meeting; **J. de empresa,** works council; **j. directiva,** board of directors; *Pol* **j. de gobierno,** cabinet meeting; **j. general,** general meeting; **ser miembro de una j.,** to sit on a committee, be on a board. 2 *Arquit* joint. 3 *Náut* seam. 4 *Mil* junta; **j. militar,** military junta. 5 *Téc* joint. ■ **j. de culata,** gasket; **junta de recubrimiento** *or* **de solapa,** lap joint; **j. universal,** universal joint.

juntar I *vtr* 1 *(unir)* to join, put together; *(piezas) to* assemble; **j. dos cosas,** to join two things together; **vamos a j. las mesas,** let's put the tables together. 2 *(reunir) (sellos)* to collect; *(dinero)* to raise; *(gente)* to gather (people) together. II **juntarse** *vr* 1 *(unirse a)* to join, get together; *(ríos, caminos)* to meet; **nos juntamos toda la familia,** all the family got together; **se juntó al grupo,** he joined the group; *fig* **al final me junté con cinco ofertas de trabajo,** eventually I found myself with five job offers. 2 *(amancebarse)* to live together; **la dejó y se juntó con su amante,** he left her and went to live with his mistress.

Junto,-a I *adj* together; **dos camas juntas,** two beds placed side by side; **están muy juntos,** they are very close together; **todos juntos,** all together; **viven juntos,** they're living together. II *adv* near, close; **demasiado j.,** too close together; **llegó j. con su hermana,** she came with her sister. ◆ **Juntamente** *adv* 1 *(en unión)* jointly, together. 2 *(al mismo tiempo)* at the same time.

juntura *nf* 1 *Téc* joint, seam. 2 *Anat* joint.

Júpiter *nm Astron Mit* Jupiter.

jura *nf (acción)* oath; *(ceremonia)* swearing in; **j. de bandera,** oath of allegiance to the flag.

Jurado,-a I *pp de* **jurar.** II *adj* sworn; **declaración jurada,** sworn statement; *fig* **tenérsela jurada a algn,** to have it in for sb. III *nm* 1 *Jur (tribunal)* jury; *(miembro del tribunal)* juror, member of the jury. 2 *(en un concurso)* panel of judges, jury.

Juramentado,-a I *pp de* **juramentar.** II *adj* sworn, sworn-in.

juramentar I *vtr* to swear, swear in. II **juramentarse** *vr* to take the oath, be sworn in.

juramento *nm* 1 *Jur* oath; **bajo j.,** under oath; **j. de fidelidad,** oath of allegiance; **j. falso,** perjury; **tomar j. a algn,** to swear sb in. 2 *(blasfemia)* swearword, curse; **soltar juramentos,** to curse, blaspheme.

jurar I *vi* 1 *Jur Rel* to swear, take an oath; **j. en falso,** to commit perjury; **j. en vano,** to take the name of the Lord in vain. 2 *(blasfemar)* to curse, swear. II *vtr* to swear; **j. el cargo,** to take the oath of office; **j. fidelidad,** to pledge allegiance; **j. por Dios,** to swear to God. III **Jurarse** *vr* 1 *(prometerse)* to swear; **se juraron amor eterno,** they swore eternal love to each other. 2 *fam* **jurársela(s) a algn,** to have it in for sb.

jurásico,-a *adj Geol* Jurassic.

jurel *nm (pez)* scad, horse mackerel.

Jurídico,-a *adj* juridical, legal.

jurisconsulto *nm* jurist, legal expert.

jurisdicción *nf* jurisdiction.

jurisdiccional *adj* jurisdictional; **aguas jurisdiccionales,** territorial waters.

jurisperito *nm* jurist, legal expert.

jurisprudencia *nm* jurisprudence.

jurista *nmf* jurist, lawyer.

justa *nf* 1 *Hist* joust, tournament. 2 *Lit* competition.

justicia *nf* justice, fairness; **administrar j.,** to administer justice; **es de j. que ...,** it's only fair *or* right that ...; **hacer j.,** to do justice; **se ha hecho j.,** justice has been done; **tomarse la j. por su mano,** to take the law into one's own hands.

Justiciero,-a *adj* severe.

justificable *adj* justifiable.

justificación *nf* justification.

justificado,-a I *pp de* **justificar.** II *adj* justified, well-grounded.

justificante I *adj* justifying. II *nm* voucher, written proof, document.

justificar I *vtr* to justify; **sin nada que lo justifique,** without good reason. II **justificarse** *vr* to clear oneself, justify oneself; **j. con algn,** to apologize to sb for sth.

justillo *nm* jerkin.

justiprecio *nm* appraisal, estimate.

justo,-a I *adj* 1 *(gen)* just, fair, right; **un castigo j.,** a just punishment; **un trato j.,** a fair deal. 2 *(apretado) (ropa)* tight; **viven muy justos con su sueldo,** they just manage to make ends meet on her salary; *(tiempo)* **estamos justos de tiempo,** we're pressed for time. 3 *(exacto)* right, accurate; **cuatro kilos justos,** four kilos exactly; **la palabra justa,** the right word; **un cálculo j.,** a precise calculation. 4 *(preciso)* **llegamos en el momento j. en que salían,** we arrived just as they were leaving. 5 **lo j.,** just enough *or* right; **más de lo j.,** more than enough. II *nm, f* just *or* righteous person; **los justos,** the just, the righteous; *fig* **pagan justos por pecadores,** the innocent often have to pay for the sins of the guilty. III *adv* 1 *(exactamente)* exactly, precisely; **es j. lo que deseaba,** it's just what you deserve; **hice j. lo que me dijiste,** I did exactly as you told me. 2 *(que llega)* just enough; **tengo j. para la entrada,** I've got justenough for the ticket; **llegó j.,** he just made it. ◆ **justamente** *adv* 1 *(con exactitud)* precisely,exactly; **¡j.!,** precisely! 2 *(con escasez)* **vive j. con susueldo,** his wage is just enough to live on. 3 *(con justicia)* fairly, justly.

juvenil *adj* youthful, young; *Dep* **el equipo j.,** the junior team.

juventud *nf* 1 *(edad)* youth; **estar en plena j.,** to be young. 2 *(aspecto joven)* youthfulness; **conservar la j.,** to keep one's youthful looks. 3 *(conjunto de jóvenes)* young people; **la j. de hoy,** the youth of today.

juzgado *nm* court, tribunal; **j. de guardia,** court, police court; *fam fig* **es de j. de guardia,** it's absolutely scandalous!

juzgador,-a I *adj* judging. II *mn, f* judge.

juzgar *vtr* 1 *(gen)* to judge; **a j. por las apariencias,** judging by appearances; **j. mal,** to misjudge. 2 *(considerar)* to consider, think; **le juzgo una persona muy inteligente,** I consider him to be a very intelligent person.

K

K, k *nf (la letra)* K, k.
ka *nf* name of the letter K in Spanish.
Kabul *n* Kabul.
Kafkiano,-a *adj* Kafkaesque.
káiser *nm* Kaiser.
kaki *adj & nm véase* **caqui.**
kamikaze *nm* kamikaze.
Kampuchea *n* Kampuchea.
kantiano,-a *adj Filos* Kantian.
kantismo *nm Filos* Kantianism, Kantism.
kapok *nm* kapok.
kárate *nm Dep* karate.
karateka *nmf Dep* person who does karate.
kart *nm (pl* **karts)** (go-) kart, go-cart.
karting *nm* karting, go-cart racing.
Katar *n* Qatar.
Katmandú *n* Katmandu, Kathmandu.
kayac *nm* kayak, kaiak.
Kenia *n* Kenya.
keniata *adj & nmf* Kenyan.
kepis *nm inv véase* **quepis.**
keroseno *nm véase* **queroseno.**
keynesiano,-a *adj Econ* Keynesian.
Kg, kg *abr de* **kilogramo(s),** kilograms, kilogrammes, kg.
kibutz *nm inv* kibbutz.
kif *nm* kif, marijuana.
kilo *nm* **1** *(medida)* kilo; *fam* **pesa un k.,** it weighs aton. **2** *arg (millón)* a million pesetas.
kilociclo *nm* kilocycle.
kilogramo *nm* kilogram, kilogramme.
kilolitro *nm* kilolitre, *US* kiloliter.

kilometraje *nm* ≈ mileage.
kilometrar *vtr* to measure in kilometres.
kilométrico,-a *adj* **1** kilometric, kilometrical; **billete k.,** multiple-journey ticket. **2** *fam (muy largo)* very long; **un sermón k.,** a never-ending sermon.
kilómetro *nm* kilometre, *US* kilometer.
kilovatio *nm* kilowatt. ■ **k. hora,** kilowatt-hour.
kilt *nm (prenda)* kilt.
kimono *nm véase* **quimono.**
kindergarten *nm* nursery, kindergarten.
kiosco *nm véase* **quíosco.**
kiwi *nm* **1** *Orn* kiwi. **2** *Bot (fruto)* kiwi (fruit), Chinese gooseberry.
Kleenex® *nm* Kleenex®, tissue; **¿tienes un k.?,** have you got a tissue?
Km, km *abr de* **kilómetro(s),** kilometre, kilometres, km, kms.
Km/h, km/h *abr de* **kilómetros hora,** kilometres per hour, km/h.
knock-out *nm Box* knockout; *fam fig* **dejar k. a algn,** to knock sb out.
K.O. *abr de* **knock-out,** knockout, KO.
koala *nm Zool* koala (bear).
krausismo *nm Filos* philosophy of Krause.
krausista *adj & nmf* Krausist.
Krisna *nm Rel* Krishna.
Kurdistán *n* Kurdistan.
kurdo,-a I *adj* Kurdish. **II** *nm, f (persona)* Kurd. **III** *nm (idioma)* Kurdish.
Kuwait *n* Kuwait.
kuwaití *adj & nmf* Kuwaiti.
Kw, kw *abr de* **kilovatio(s),** kilowatt, kilowatts, kW, kw.
Kw/h, kw/h *abr de* **kilowatios hora,** kilowatts per hour, kWh kwh, kw-h.

L

L, l [ele] *nf (la letra)* L, 1.
l *abr de* **litro(s),** litre, litres, *US* liter, liters, 1.
la¹ *art det f* **I** the; **la mesa,** the table. **II** *pron dem* **1** the one; **la del sombrero rojo,** the one in the red hat; *fam* **a la que puedas vente,** come as soon as you can. **2 la de,** the amount of, the number of; **la de gente que había,** there were so many people; *véase tamb* **el.**
la² *pron pers f* **1** *(objeto directo)* her; *(usted)* you; *(cosa)* it; **la invitaré a la fiesta,** I'll invite her to the party; **no la dejes abierta,** don't leave it open; **ya la avisaremos, señora,** we shall notify you, madam; *véase tamb* **le. 2** *(objeto indirecto) (a ella)* her; *(a usted)* you; *véase* **laísmo.**
la³ *nm Mús* la, lah, A; **concierto en la menor,** concerto in A minor.
laberíntico,-a *adj* labyrinthine, labyrinthic; *fig* confusing.
laberinto *nm* labyrinth, maze.
labia *nf fam* loquacity; *pey* glibness; **tener mucha l.,** to have the gift of the gab.

labiado,-a *adj Bot* labiate.
labial I *adj Ling* labial. **II** *nf* labial.
lábil *adj* **1** *(inconstante)* volatile; *(inestable)* unstable. **2** *(resbaladizo)* slippery.
labilidad *nf* **1** *(inestabilidad)* instability. **2** *(que hace resbalar)* slipperiness. **3** *(carácter)* fickleness, inconstancy.
labio *nm* lip; *fig* mouth.
labiodental *adj & nf Ling* labiodental.
labor *nf* **1** job, (piece of) work, task; **una l. de equipo,** teamwork; **(de profesión) sus labores,** housewife. **2** *Agr* farmwork. **3** *Cost* needlework, sewing. ■ **labor(es) de punto,** knitting *sing*. **4** *(productos del tabaco)* tobacco goods *pl*.
laborable *adj* **1** *(no festivo)* **día l.,** workday, working day. **2** *Agr* tillable, arable.
laboral *adj* labour, *US* labor; **accidente l.,** industrial accident; **jornada l.,** working day; *Jur* **juicio l.,** industrial relations hearing.
laboralista *adj Jur* **abogado l.,** industrial relations lawyer

laborar *vi fml* to work.

laboratorio *nm* laboratory.

laboriosidad *nf* laboriousness.

laborioso,-a *adj* **1** *(persona trabajadora)* hardworking, industrious. **2** *(tarea ardua)* laborious, arduous.

laborismo *nm Pol* Labour Movement.

laborista *Pol* **I** *adj* Labour; **partido l.**, Labour Party. **II** *nmf* Labour (Party) member *or* supporter.

labra *nf* carving, cutting.

labrado,-a I *pp de* **labrar. II** *adj* **1** *Arte* carved. **2** *Agr* ploughed, worked. **3** *Cost* embroidered. **III** *nm* **1** *Arte* carving, cutting. **2** *Cost* embroidery.

labrador,-a *Agr nm,f (granjero)* farmer; *(trabajador)* farm worker.

labrantío,-a *Agr* **I** *adj* **tierra labrantía**, arable land. **II** *nm* arable land.

labranza *nf Agr* farming.

labrar I *vtr* **1** *(madera)* to carve; *(piedra)* to cut; *(metal)* to work. **2** *Agr* to till, cultivate; *fig* **está labrando su triunfo**, he is working towards success. **II labrarse** *vr fig* to make oneself; **l. un porvenir**, to build a future for oneself.

labriego,-a *nm,f desus* farm worker, farm labourer *or US* laborer.

laburno *nm Bot* laburnum.

laca *nf* **1** *Arte* lacquer. **2** *Peluq* hair lacquer, hairspray. ■ **l. de uñas**, nail polish *or* varnish. **3** *(resina)* lac; *(manufacturada)* shellac.

lacayo *nm* **1** *Hist* lackey, footman. **2** *fig* lackey, hanger-on, flunky, flunkey.

laceración *nf fml* laceration.

lacerante *adj fml* sharp; **un grito l.**, a heart-rending cry.

lacerar[1] *vtr fml* **1** to lacerate, tear. **2** *fig* to hurt.

lacerar[2] *vi fml* to suffer.

lacero-a *nm,f* **1** *(de reses)* lassoer. **2** *(de perros sueltos)* dog-catcher. **3** *(de caza menor)* poacher.

lacha[1] *nf (pez)* anchovy, variety of sardine.

lacha[2] *nf fig* shame; **tener poca l.**, to be shameless.

lacio,-a *adj* **1** *(pelo)* lank, limp. **2** *(planta)* withered, drooping. **3** *(sin vigor)* languid, limp.

lacón *nm* foreknuckle of pork; *Culin* boiled bacon.

lacónico,-a *adj* laconic; *(conciso)* terse.

laconismo *nm* terseness, laconism.

lacra *nf* **1** *(señal)* mark, scar. **2** *fig* evil, curse; *(tara)* defect; **una l. social**, a social scourge, a blot on society. **3** *Am (costra)* scab.

lacrado,-a I *pp de* **lacrar. II** *nm* sealing with wax.

lacrar[1] *vtr* to seal with sealing wax.

lacrar[2] *vtr* to injure the health of; *(contagiar)* to infect; *fig* to cause harm to.

lacre *nm* sealing wax.

lacrimal *adj* lachrymal, lacrimal; *Anat* **conductos lacrimales**, tear ducts.

lacrimógeno,-a *adj* **1 gas l.**, tear gas. **2** *(lagrimoso) (persona)* tearful; *fig* **una película lacrimógena**, a tear-jerking film.

lacrimoso,-a *adj* tearful.

lactancia *nf* lactation; *(amamantamiento)* breastfeeding.

lactante I *adj* lactational. **II** *nmf* unweaned *or* breast-fed baby.

lactar I *vtr (niño)* to suckle, nurse. **II** *vi* to nurse.

lácteo,-a *adj* milk, milky; **productos lácteos**, milk *or* dairy products; *Astron* **Vía Láctea**, Milky Way.

láctico,-a *adj Quím* lactic.

lactosa *nf Quím* lactose, milk sugar.

lacustre *adj fml* lake; **planta l.**, lake plant.

ladear I *vtr* **1** *(inclinar)* to tilt; *(sesgar)* to slant; *(cabeza)* to lean. **2** *(desviar)* to divert. **II ladearse** *vr* **1** *(inclinarse)* to lean, tilt. **2** *(apartarse)* to turn away, go off. **3** *(juntarse)* to join sides (**con**, with)

ladeo *nm* leaning, inclination.

ladera *nf Geog* slope, hillside, mountainside.

ladilla *nf Ent* crab louse.

ladino,-a I *adj* **1** *(astuto)* cunning, crafty. **2** *CAm* of mixed race. **II** *nm (idioma)* Ladino. **III** *nm, f Am (indio)* Spanish-speaking Indian.

lado *nm* **1** side; **debe de estar en otro l.**, it must be somewhere else. **2** *(posición)* **a un l.**, aside, **al l.**, close by, nearby; **al l. de**, next to, beside; **la casa de al l.**, the house next door; *Dep* **cambiar de l.**, to change ends; **echarse** *or* **hacerse a un l.**, to make way; **llevar el sombrero de l.**, to wear one's hat aslant; **ponte de l.**, stand sideways. **3** *(en direcciones)* direction; **¿por qué l.?**, which way?; **por todos lados**, on *or* from all sides. **4** *fig (locuciones)* **dar de l. a algn**, to cold-shoulder sb, desert sb; **dejar algo a un l.** *or* **de l.**, to leave *or* sel sth aside; **l. débil**, weak point; **por un l. ...**, **por otro l. ...**, on the one hand ..., on the other hand ... .

ladrador,-a *adj* barking; *prov* **perro l., poco mordedor**, his bark is worse than his bite.

ladrar *vi* to bark, yap; *fam fig* **¡para ya de l.!**, stop growling!, stop yapping at me!

ladrido *nm* bark, yap; *fam fig* **no me vengas con ladridos**, don't you growl at me.

ladrillo *nm* **1** *Constr* brick; **fábrica de ladrillos**, brickworks *pl*. **2** *fig* block; **l. de un tejido**, block of material. **3** *fam (pesado)* bore, drag.

ladrón,-ona I *adj* thieving. **II** *nm, f* thief, robber; **¡al l.!**, stop thief!; *fig* **l. de corazones**, lady-killer. **III** *nm* **1** *(de canal)* sluicegate. **2** *Elec* multiple socket.

ladronear *vi* to thieve, steal.

ladronera *nf* den of thieves.

ladronzuelo,-a *nm, f* **1** *(carterista)* pickpocket; *(granuja)* petty thief. **2** *fam (niño)* little devil.

lagarta *nf Zool* female lizard. **2** *fam pey (bribona)* minx, sly woman; *(prostituta)* tart, whore.

lagartija *nf Zool* small lizard.

lagarto *nm* **1** *Zool* lizard. ■ **l. de Indias**, alligator. **2** *fam (bribón)* sly or crafty fellow.

lagartón,-ona *fam* **I** *adj* sly, crafty. **II** *nm (bribón)* sly devil. **III** *nf (bribona)* minx, sly woman; *(prostituta)* tart, whore.

lago *nm* lake.

lagópodo *nm Orn* **l. escocés**, red grouse.

lágrima *nf* **1** tear; **asomar las lágrimas a los ojos**, to start crying; **derranaar lágrimas**, to shed tears. **2** *(adorno)* teardrop.

lagrimal I *adj* lachrymal, lacrimal. **II** *nm* corner of the eye.

lagrimear *vi* **1** *(llorar frecuentemente)* to shed tears easily, weep. **2** *(involuntariamente)* to water.

lagrimeo *nm* **1** *(frecuente)* weeping, tears *pl*. **2** *(involuntario)* watering.

lagrimón *nm fam* big tear.

lagrimoso,-a *adj (persona)* tearful; **ojos lagrimosos**, watery eyes.

laguna *nf* **1** *Geog* small lake, lagoon. **2** *fig (hueco)* gap, hiatus.

La Haya *n* The Hague.

laicado *nm* laity.

laicismo *nm* secularism.

laico,-a I *adj* lay, secular; **escuela laica**, secular school. **II** *nm, f* lay person; *(hombre)* layman; *(mujer)* laywoman.

laísmo *nm Ling* incorrect use of **la, las** as indirect objects instead of **le, les**.

laja *nf Geol* stone slab.

lama[1] *nm Rel* lama.

lama[2] *nf* **1** *(cieno)* mud, slime. **2** *Am (musgo)* moss.

lama[3] *nm Tex* lamé.

lameculos *nmf inv ofens* bootlicker, arselicker.

lamedura *nf* lick, licking.

lamentable *adj* deplorable, regrettable. ■ **lamentablemente** *adv* regrettably, unfortunately.

lamentación *nf* lament, lamentation; **Muro de las Lamentaciones,** Wailing Wall.

lamentar I *vtr* to regret, be sorry about; *(cartas)* **lamentamos informarle que ...,** we regret to inform you that *or* of ... . **II lamentarse** *vr* to complain; **¿de qué te lamentas?,** what are you complaining about?

lamento *nm* moan, wail.

lamentoso,-a *adj (quejumbroso)* plaintive, mournful; *(lamentable)* deplorable, regrettable; *(lastimoso)* pitiful.

lameplatos *nmf inv fam* **1** poor devil. **2** *(goloso)* glutton.

lamer *vtr* to lick.

lametazo *nm,* **lametón** *nm fam* lick.

lamia *nf (pez)* variety of shark.

lamido,-a I *pp de* **lamer.** **II** *adj fig* **1** *(flaco)* skinny, scrawny. **2** *(pálido)* pale. **3** *(afectado)* pretentious, mannered.

lámina *nf* **1** sheet, plate; **l. de acero,** steel sheet. **2** *Impr* plate, illustration. **3** *Bot* lamina.

laminación *nf* **1** lamination. **2** *(de metal)* rolling.

laminado,-a I *pp de* **laminar.** **II** *adj* **1** laminate, laminated. **2** *(metales)* rolled; **acero l.,** rolled steel, sheet steel. **III** *nm* **1** lamination. **2** *(de metales)* rolling. ■ **tren de l.,** rolling mill.

laminadora *nf* rolling mill.

laminar[1] *vtr* **1** *(superficie)* to laminate. **2** *(metal)* to roll out.

laminar[2] *adj* laminar; **corriente l.,** laminar flow.

lámpara *nf* **I** lamp, light. ■ **l. de aceite/alcohol,** oil/ spirit lamp; **l. de pie,** standard lamp. **2** *Elec (bombilla)* bulb. **3** *Rad* valve. **4** *fam (mancha)* oil or grease stain.

lamparería *nf (fábrica)* lamp factory; *(tienda)* lamp shop.

lamparero,-a *nm, f (fabricante)* lamp maker; *(vendedor)* dealer.

lamparilla *nf* **1** small lamp. **2** *(en iglesia)* candle.

lamparón *nm fam* oil or grease stain.

lampazo *nm Bot* burdock.

lampiño,-a *adj* hairless.

lamprea *nf (pez)* lamprey.

lana *nf* **1** wool; *prov* **ir por l. y volver trasquilado,** to go for wool and come home shorn. **2** *Am (purria)* riffraff. **3** *CAm (tramposo)* swindler. **4** **lanas,** *Méx* money *sing.* **5 lanas,** *Méx* lies.

lanar *adj* wool, wool-bearing; **ganado l.,** sheep.

lance *nm* **1** *(lanzar)* throw. **2** *(pesca)* catch. **3** *lit (episodio)* episode, event, incident; **l. de fortuna,** chance event. **4** *(riña)* quarrel, argument. ■ **l. de honor,** challenge, duel. **5** *Dep* stroke, move. **6 de l.,** *(barato)* cheap; *(de segunda mano)* second-hand.

lancero *nm* lancer.

lanceta *nf Med* lancet.

lancha[1] *nf (piedra lisa)* stone slab.

lancha[2] *nf Náut* boat, motorboat, launch. ■ **l. motora,** speedboat; **l. neumática,** rubber dinghy; **l. patrullera,** patrol boat; **l. salvavidas,** lifeboat.

lanchero *nm* boatman.

lanchón *nm Náut* lighter, barge.

lancinante *adj* piercing, stabbing.

landa *nf* moor, moorland.

landó *nm (pl landós)* landau.

lanero,-a *adj* wool, woollen, *US* woolen; **la industria lanera,** the wool industry.

lángaro,-a *adj* **1** *CAm (vagabundo)* vagrant, vagabond. **2** *Col Méx (hambriento)* starving.

langosta *nf* **1** *Zool* (spiny) lobster. **2** *Ent* locust.

langostino *nm Zool* prawn.

languidecer *vi* to languish.

languidez *nf* languor; *(falta de vigor)* listlessness.

lánguido,-a *adj* languid; *(sin vigor)* listless, sluggish.

lanilla *nf* **1** *(pelusa)* nap. **2** *(tela)* flannel.

lanolina *nf Farm* lanolin, lanoline.

lanoso,-a *adj,* **lanudo,-a** *adj* woolly, fleecy; *(peludo)* furry.

lanza *nf* **1** *Mil* spear, lance; *fig* **estar con la l. en ristre,** to be ready for action; *fig* **romper una l. en favor de algn/de algo,** to defend sb/sth. **2** *(de carruaje)* shaft.

lanzacabos *nm inv Náut* **cañón l.,** life-saving gun.

lanzacohetes *nm inv Mil* rocket launcher.

lanzada *nf* **1** *(golpe)* lance *or* spear thrust. **2** *(herida)* lance *or* spear wound.

lanzadera *nf* shuttle.

lanzado,-a I *pp de* **lanzar.** **II** *adj fam* determined, resolute; **ir l.,** to speed along, tear along.

lanzador,-a I *adj* throwing. **II** *nm, f* thrower; *Crick* bowler; *Béisb* pitcher.

lanzagranadas *nm inv Mil* grenade launcher.

lanzallamas *nm inv Mil* flame-thrower.

lanzamiento *nm* **1** throw, throwing, hurling. **2** *Dep (de disco, jabalina)* throw; *(de peso)* put; *Crick* ball, delivery; *Béisb* pitch. **3** *Mil (de cohete)* launching; *(de proyectil, torpedo)* firing; *(de bomba)* dropping. **4** *Com* launch, launching; **precio de l.,** launching price. **5** *Náut* launch.

lanzaminas *nm inv Mil* minelayer.

lanzaplatos *nm inv Dep* (clay pigeon) trap.

lanzar I *vtr* **1** *(arrojar)* to throw, fling, hurl; *Crick* to bowl; *Béisb* to pitch. **2** *fig (grito)* to let out; *(suspiro)* to heave; *(insulto)* to hurl; *(mirada)* to fire. **3** *Náut* to launch; *Mil (lanzacohetes, ataque)* to launch; *(misil, torpedo)* to fire; *(bomba)* to drop. **4** *Com (producto, campaña)* to launch. **II lanzarse** *vr* **1** *(arrojarse)* to fling *or* hurl oneself; **l. al suelo,** to throw oneself to the ground; **l. con paracaídas,** to make a parachute jump; **se lanzó al mar,** he leapt into the sea. **2** to embark on; **l. a los negocios,** to go into business.

lanzatorpedos *nm inv Mil* **tubo l.,** torpedo tube.

laña *nf* clamp, rivet.

lañar *vtr* to clamp, rivet.

Laos *n* Laos.

laosiano,-a *adj & nm, f* Laotian.

lapa *nf* **1** *Zool* limpet. **2** *pey (persona)* bore; **pegarse como una l.,** to cling like a leech.

lapicero *nm* pencil.

lápida *nf* memorial stone; **l. sepulcral,** tombstone.

lapidación *nf* stoning, lapidation.

lapidar *vtr* **1** to throw stones at, lapidate; *(matar)* to stone to death. **2** *Am (labrar piedras)* to carve.

lapidario,-a *adj & nm, f* lapidary; *fig* **lenguaje l.,** concise language.

lapislázuli *nm Min* lapis lazuli.

lápiz *nm* pencil; **lápices de colores,** coloured pencils, crayons. ■ **l. labial** *or* **de labios,** lipstick; **l. de ojos,** eyeliner.

lapo *nm arg (gargajo)* spit.

lapón,-ona I *adj* Lapp. **II** *nm, f* Lapp, Laplander. **III** *nm (idioma)* Lapp.

Laponia *n* Lapland.

lapso *nm* **1** *(curso de tiempo)* lapse, space of time. **2** *(error)* lapse, slip.

lapsus *nm* slip, lapse; **l. de memoria,** lapse of memory.

laquear *vtr* to lacquer.

lar *nm* **1** *Mit (gen pl)* lar, household god. **2 lares,** *lit* home *sing*.

lardero *adj* **jueves l.,** the Thursday before Lent.

larga *nf* **1** *Taur* bullfighting pass. **2 dar largas a un asunto,** to put a matter off, delay a matter. ◆ **largamente** *adv* **1** *(extensamente)* at length. **2** *(generosamente)* generously.

largar I *vtr* **1** *(aflojar)* to let loose; *Náut* **l. amarras,** to cast off. **2** *fam (dar)* to give; **me largó un billete de mil,** he slipped me a thousand-peseta note; *fig* **le largué una bofetada,** I gave him a slap on the face. **3** *fam (soltar, decir)* to come out with; *(grito)* to let out; **¡vaya bronca me ha largado!,** he really hauled me over the coals! **II largarse** *vr* **1** *fam* to cast off, split; **¡lárgate!,** beat it! **2** *Am (lanzarse a)* to begin **(a,** to).

largo,-a I *adj* **1** *(longitud, distancia)* long; *(tiempo)* long, lengthy; **l. tiempo,** a long time; **pasamos un mes l. allí,** we spent a good month there. **2** *(excesivo)* too long; **se hizo l. el día,** the day dragged on. **3** *(alto)* tall; **cayó cuan l. era,** he fell full length. **4** *fam (astuto)* sharp, shrewd. **4** *(generoso)* generous, lavish. **5 largos,-as,** many; **l. años,** many years. **II** *nm* **1** *(longitud)* length; **¿cuánto tiene de l.?,** how long is it?; **lo até con dos largos de cuerda,** I tied it with two lengths of rope. **2** *Mús* largo. **III** *adv* **1 l. y tendido,** at length. **2 a lo l.,** lengthways; **a lo l. de,** *(espacio)* along; *(tiempo)* through; **a lo l. y a lo ancho,** all over. **3 a la larga,** in the long run. **4** *fam* **¡l. (de aquí)!,** clear off! **5 venir de l.,** to have a long history. **6** *(vestir)* **poner(se) de l.,** to come out; **vestirse de l.,** to wear a long dress. **7 ir para l.,** to go or walk straight past. **8 tener para l.,** to expect a long wait or delay, have a long wait ahead.

largometraje *nm Cin* feature film, full-length film.

larguero *nm* **1** *Arquit* main longitudinal beam. **2** *(de puerta)* jamb. **3** *(de cama)* side. **4** *Ftb* crossbar.

largueza *nf* **1** *(longitud)* length. **2** *(liberalidad)* generosity.

larguirucho,-a *adj fam* gangling, lanky, long-legged.

largura *nf* length.

laringe *nf Anat* larynx.

laríngeo,-a *adj* laryngeal.

laringitis *nf Med* laryngitis.

laringólogo,-a *nm,f Med* laryngologist.

larva *nf* larva.

larvado,-a *adj Med* masked, larval.

las¹ *art det fpl* **1** the; **l. Ramírez,** the Ramírez girls or sisters; **l. sillas,** the chairs; **lávate l. manos,** wash your hands; *(no se traduce)* **me gustan l. flores,** I like flowers. **2 l. que,** *(persona)* the ones who, those who; *(objeto)* the ones that, those that; **toma l. que quieras,** take whichever ones you want; *véase tamb* **la** y **los.**

las² *pron pers fpl* **1** *(objeto directo) (ellas)* them; *(ustedes)* you; **l. llamaré mañana,** I'll call them up tomorrow; **no l. rompas,** don't break them; **Pepa es de l. mías,** Pepa is on my side; *véase tamb* **los.** **2** *(objeto indirecto) (a ellas)* them; *(a ustedes)* you; *véase tamb* **les.**

lasaña *nf Culin* lasagna, lasagne.

lasca *nf* stone chip.

lascivia *nf* lasciviousness, lechery.

lascivo,-a *adj* lascivious, lewd, lecherous.

láser *nm inv* laser.

lasitud *nf* lassitude.

laso,-a *adj* **1** *(cansado)* tired, weary; *(débil)* languid. **2** *(pelo, hilo)* straight.

lástima *nf* **1** pity; **es una l. que se haya perdido,** it's a pity it got lost; **estar hecho una l.,** to be a sorry sight; **por l.,** out of pity; **¡qué l.!,** what a pity!, what a shame!; **tener l. a algn,** to feel sorry for sb. **2** *(quejido)* complaint.

lastimado,-a I *pp de* **lastimar. II** *adj* hurt.

lastimadura *nf* injury.

lastimar I *vtr* **1** to hurt, injure. **2** *(sentimientos)* to hurt. **II lastimarse** *vr* to hurt or injure oneself; **se lastimó el tobillo,** he hurt his ankle.

lastimero,-a *adj* doleful, plaintive.

lastimoso,-a *adj* pitiable, pitiful, woeful; **ella ofrecía un aspecto l.,** she was a sorry sight.

lastrar *vtr Náut* to ballast.

lastre *nm* **1** *Náut* ballast; **largar** or **soltar l.,** to discharge ballast. **2** *fig* dead weight; **el l. de los convencionalismos,** the burden of conventionality.

lata¹ *nf* **1** *(hojalata)* tinplate; **hecho de l.,** made of tin. **2** *(bote de conserva)* tin, *US* can; **espárragos en l.,** tinned or *US* canned asparagus.

lata² *nf fam* nuisance, drag; **dar la l.,** to be a nuisance or a pest; **es una l. tener que ir a la mili,** having to do military service is a drag.

latear *vtr Am* to pester, be annoying to.

latente *adj* latent, dormant.

lateral I *adj* side, lateral; *Ling* **consonante l.,** lateral consonant; **salió por la puerta l.,** he went out by the side door. **II** *nm* side passage; *Aut (carril)* **l.,** side lane.

latería *nf Am* tinsmith's (shop).

látex *nm inv Bot* latex.

latido *nm (corazón)* beat; *(palpitaciones)* throb, throbbing.

latifundio *nm* large landed estate.

latifundismo *nm* distribution and exploitation of land in **latifundios**.

latifundista I *adj* of or relating to **latifundios. II** *nmf* owner of a **latifundio**.

latigazo *nm* **1** lash; *(sonido)* crack. **2** *arg (trago)* drink, swig. **3** *Med* whiplash injury.

látigo *nm* **1** whip. **2** *(en parque de atracciones)* **el l.,** the whip. **3** *Am (latigazo)* lash.

latigueada *nf Am (azotaina)* flogging.

latiguillo *nm (muletilla)* tag, pet phrase.

latín *nm* Latin; **saber mucho l.,** to be smart, be nobody's fool, know one's stuff. ■ **l. bajo/vulgar,** Low/Vulgar Latin.

latinajo *nm pey (cita)* Latin quotation; *(lengua)* dog Latin.

latinidad *nf* **1** *(lengua)* Latin. **2** *(pueblos latinos)* Latin countries *pl*.

latinismo *nm* Latinism.

latinizar *vtr* to Latinize.

latino,-a *adj & nm,f* **1** Latin; **América Latina,** Latin America; *Rel* **Iglesia latina,** Roman Catholic Church, Latin Church. **2** *Náut* **vela latina,** lateen sail.

Latinoamérica *n* Latin America.

latinoamericano,-a *adj & nm,f* Latin American.

latir *vi (palpitar)* to beat, throb; *fig* to be latent.

latitud *nf* **1** *Geog* latitude. **2 latitudes,** region *sing*, area *sing*.

lato,-a *adj (extenso)* wide, broad.

latón *nm* brass; **un clavo de l.,** a brass nail.

latoso,-a *fam* **I** *adj* boring, annoying. **II** *nm,f* bore, drag.

latrocinio *nm desus* robbery, theft; **estos precios son un puro l.,** those prices are a daylight robbery.

laucha *nf* **1** *Am* mouse. **2** *Am fig* intelligent man. **3** *Arg Chi (menudo)* shrimp. **4** *Arg* dirty old man.

laúd *nm* **1** *Mús* lute. **2** *Náut* catboat.

laudable *adj* laudable, praiseworthy.

láudano *nm (droga)* laudanum.

laudatorio,-a *adj* laudatory.

laudo *nm* **1** award. **2** *Jur* finding.

laureado,-a I *adj* **1** *Lit* award-winning; **poeta l.,** poet laureate. **2** *Mil* decorated. **II** *nm,f Lit* laureate.

laurel *nm Bot* laurel, (sweet) bay; *Culin* bay leaf; *fig* **dormírse en sus laureles,** to rest on one's laurels. ■ **l. rosa,** oleander.

Lausana *n* Lausanne.

lava *nf Geol* lava.

lavable *adj* washable.

lavabo *nm* **1** *(pila)* washbasin. **2** *(cuarto de aseo)* washroom. **3** *(retrete)* lavatory, toilet.

lavacoches *nmf inv* car washer.

lavacristales *nmf inv* window cleaner.

lavada *nf* wash, washing.

lavadero *nm* **1** *(de ropa)* washroom, laundry. **2** *Am Min* washery.

lavado,-a I *pp de* **lavar.** II *nm* **1** wash, washing. ■ *Med* **l. de estómago,** washing out of the stomach; *fam fig* **l. de cerebro,** brainwashing; **l. en seco,** dry-cleaning. **2** *Arte* wash.

lavadora *nf* **1** *(máquina)* washing machine. **2** *(persona)* washerwoman.

lavafrutas *nm inv* finger bowl.

lavamanos *nm inv* washbasin.

lavanda *nf Bot* lavender.

lavandería *nf* **1** *(atendida por personal)* laundry. **2** *(automática)* launderette, *US* laundromat.

lavandera *nf* **1** laundress, washerwoman. **2** *orn* **l. blanca,** white wagtail; **l. cascadeña,** grey wagtail.

lavandero *nm* laundryman, launderer.

lavándula *nf Bot* lavender.

lavaojos *nm inv* eyebath.

lavaplatos *nm inv* dishwasher.

lavar I *vtr* to wash; *(cabello)* to shampoo; **l. en seco,** to dry-clean. II **lavarse** *vr* to wash oneself; **l. las manos,** to wash one's hands; *fig* **l. las manos de algo,** to wash one's hands of sth.

lavativa *nf Med* enema.

lavatorio *nm* **1** *Rel (de la misa)* lavabo. **2** *(de Semana Santa)* maundy. **3** *(lavamanos)* washbasin. **4** *Med* lotion. **5** *(palangana)* washbasin. **6** *(lavabo)* lavatory.

lavavajillas *nm inv* dishwasher.

lavotear *fam* I *vtr* to wash hurriedly. II **lavotearse** *vr* to have a quick wash.

lavoteo *nm fam* quick *or* hurried wash.

laxante *adj & nm* laxative.

laxar *vtr* **1** *(ablandar)* to ease, slacken, loosen. **2** *(vientre)* to loosen.

laxitud *nf* laxity, laxness.

laxo,-a *adj* lax, loose.

laya *nf desus* kind, sort; **de toda l.,** of all kinds *or* sorts.

lazada *nf* **1** *(nudo)* knot. **2** *(adorno)* bow.

lazareto *nm* isolation hospital; *(cuarentena)* quarantine station.

lazarillo *nm* blind person's guide; **perro l.,** guide dog, *US* Seeing Eye dog.

lazo *nm* **1** *(adorno)* bow; **l. de zapato,** shoelace. **2** *(nudo)* knot. ■ **l. corredizo,** slipknot. **3** *(para reses)* lasso. **4** *(trampa)* snare, trap. **5** *fig (gen pl) (vínculo)* tie, bond; **lazos de amistad,** bonds of friendship; **lazos familiares** *or* **de sangre,** family ties.

lb *abr de* **libra(s),** pound, pounds, lb, lbs; **pesa 4 lb,** it weighs 4 lb.

l.c. *abr de* **loco citato,** l.c.

Lda *abr de* **licenciada,** *(female)* graduate.

Ldo *abr de* **licenciado,** *(male)* graduate.

le I *pron pers mf* **1** *(objeto indirecto) (a él)* him; *(a ella)* her; *(a cosa)* it; **lávale la cara,** wash his face; **le compraré uno,** I'll buy one for her; **no le oigo,** I can't hear her; **no quiero verle más,** I don't want to see him

any more; **¿qué le pasa?,** what's the matter with her? **2** *(a usted)* you; **no quiero molestarle,** I don't wish to disturb you; **ya le llamaré,** I'll give you a call. II *pron pers m (objeto directo) (él)* him; *(usted)* you; *véase tamb* **leísmo.**

leal I *adj* loyal, faithful. II *nmf (incondicional)* loyalist.

lealtad *nf* loyalty, faithfulness.

leandra *nf arg* peseta.

lebrato *nm,* **lebratón** *nm Zool* leveret.

lebrel *nm Zool* greyhound.

lebrillo *nm arc* earthenware bowl.

lección *nf* lesson; *fig* **dar una l. a algn,** to teach sb a lesson; *fig* **te servirá de l.,** it will be a lesson to you.

lechada *nf* whitewash.

lechal *adj* sucking; **cordero l.,** sucking lamb.

lechar *vtr* **1** *Am (ordeñar)* to milk. **2** *Méx (blanquear)* to whitewash.

leche *nf* **1** milk; *Anat* **dientes de l.,** milk teeth; *Culin* **l. frita,** dessert made of fried milk and flour batter. ■ **l. condensada,** condensed milk; **l. descremada** *or* **desnatada,** skim *or* skimmed milk. **2** *Bot* milky sap. **3** *fam* **mala l.,** bad mood; **¡qué mala l.!,** what rotten luck!; **salió echando leches,** he took off like a bat out of hell; **tener mala l.,** to be spiteful. **4** *arg (golpe)* knock; **dar** *or* **pegar una l. a algn,** to clobber sb. **5** *vulg* **a toda l.,** at top speed, flat out. **6** *vulg* semen.

lechecillas *nfpl* sweetbreads.

lechera *nf* **1** *(que vende)* woman who sells milk; *(que ordeña)* milkmaid; **el cuento de la l.,** pie in the sky. **2** *(vasija)* churn. **3** *Arg* milk cow. **4** *arg* police car.

lechería *nf* dairy, creamery.

lechero,-a I *adj* milk, dairy; **central lechera,** dairy co-operative; **vaca lechera,** milk cow. II *nm* milkman.

lecho *nm* bed; **l. del río,** river-bed; **l. mortuorio,** deathbed; *fig* **l. de rosas,** bed of roses.

lechón *nm Zool* **1** *(cochinillo)* sucking pig. **2** *(puerco)* swine, hog.

lechona *nf Zool* young sow.

lechoncillo *nm* sucking pig.

lechoso,-a *adj* milky.

lechuga *nf* **1** lettuce; *fam fig* **(fresco) como una l.,** as fresh as a daisy. **2** *fam (billete)* green.

lechuguilla *nf arc (prenda)* ruff.

lechuguino *nm* dandy, fop.

lechuza *nf Orn* owl.

lectivo,-a *adj* school; **horas lectivas,** teaching hours.

lector,-a I *adj* reading; **habilidades lectoras,** reading skills. II *nm, f* **1** *(persona)* reader. **2** *Univ* lector, (language) assistant. **3** *Inform* reader. III *nm (aparato)* **l. de microfichas,** microfile reader; **l. de microfilmes,** microfilm reader.

lectorado *nm Univ* assistantship.

lectura *nf* **1** reading; **dar l. a algo,** to read sth; **de mucha l.,** well-read; **material de l.,** reading matter. **2** interpretation; **hizo una l. marxista de la obra,** he gave the work a Marxist interpretation.

leer *vtr* to read; **léenos el menú,** read out the menu for us; **l. la mano a algn,** to read sb's palm; *fig* **l. entre líneas,** to read between the lines.

legación *nf* legation.

legado,-a I *pp de* **legar.** II *nm* **1** *(herencia)* legacy, bequest. **2** *(representante)* legate; **l. apostólico,** papal nuncio.

legajo *nm* dossier.

legal *adj* **1** *Jur* legal, lawful; **requisitos legales,** legal formalities. **2** *fam (persona)* honest, trustworthy. ◆ **legalmente** *adv* legally, lawfully.

legalidad *nf* legality, lawfulness; **según la l. (vigente),** according to the law.

legalismo *nm* legalism.

legalista I *adj* legalistic. **II** *nmf* legalist.

legalización *nf* legalization.

legalizar *vtr* to legalize; *(documento)* to authenticate.

légamo *nm* slime, ooze.

legamoso,-a *adj* slimy.

legaña *nf (en ojos)* sleep; *fig* **quitarse las legañas,** to get a move on.

legañoso,-a *adj* bleary-eyed.

legar *vtr* **1** *(propiedad etc)* to bequeath; *fig (tradiciones etc)* to hand down, pass on. **2** *(enviar como delegado)* to delegate.

legatario,-a *nm,f Jur* legatee, heir.

legendario,-a *adj* legendary.

legible *adj* legible.

legión *nf* legion; *fig* **una l. de admiradores le seguía,** a legion of admirers followed her. ■ *Mil* **L. Extranjera,** Foreign Legion.

legionario,-a I *adj* legionary. **II** *nm* legionary, legionnaire; *Med* **enfermedad del l.,** Legionnaire's Disease.

legislación *nf* legislation.

legislador,-a I *adj* legislative. **II** *nm,f* legislator.

legislar *vi* to legislate, enact.

legislativo,-a *adj* legislative.

legislatura *nf* **1** legislature. **2** *Am Pol* legislative body.

legitimación *nf Jur* legitimization.

legitimar *vtr* to legitimize; *(legalizar)* to legalize.

legitimidad *nf Jur* legitimacy; *(licitud)* justice.

legítimo,-a *adj* **1** *Jur* legitimate; **en legítima defensa,** in self-defence. **2** *(auténtico)* authentic, real; **oro l.,** pure gold.

lego,-a I *adj* **1** *Rel* lay, secular. **2** *(ignorante)* ignorant, uninformed; **ser l. en la materia,** to know nothing about the subject. **II** *nm Rel* lay brother.

legua *nf (medida)* league; *fig* **se nota a la l.,** it stands out a mile. ■ **l. marítima,** marine league.

leguleyo *nm pey* pettifogger, shyster.

legumbre *nf* legume, pod vegetable.

leguminoso,-a I *adj* leguminous. **II** *nf* pulse, leguminous plant.

leíble *adj* readable.

leída *nf* reading.

leído,-a I *pp de* leer. **II** *adj* well-read; **ser muy l.,** to be very knowledgeable.

leísmo *nm Ling* incorrect use of **le** as a direct object instead of **lo.**

leitmotiv *nm* leitmotiv, leitmotif.

lejanía *nf* distance.

lejano,-a *adj* distant, far-off; **parientes lejanos,** distant relatives. ■ **el L. Oriente,** the Far East.

lejía *nf* bleach, lye.

lejísimos *adv* very far (away).

lejos I *adv* far (away); **a lo l.,** in the distance; **de l.,** from a distance; **desde l.,** from a long way off; **¿está l.?,** is it far?; **l. de mí/ti/él ...,** far away from me/you/him ...; *fig* **ir demasiado l.,** to go too far; *fig* **l. de mí hacer tal cosa,** how could I do a thing like that?; *fig* **l. de mejorar, empeora,** it gets worse instead of better; *fig* **llegar l.,** to go a long way; *fig* **más l.,** farther *or* further away; *fig* **ni de l.,** far from it; *fig* **sin ir más l.,** to take an obvious example; *fam fig* **l. del mundanal ruido,** far from the madding crowd. **II** *nm* distant view; *(cuadro)* background.

lelo,-a *fam* **I** *adj* stupid, silly; **quedarse l.,** to be stunned *or* stupefied. **II** *nm,f* ninny.

lema *nm* **1** *(divisa)* motto, slogan. **2** *(concurso) (contraseña)* code name.

lemosín,-ina I *adj* of *or* from Limoges. **II** *nm (idioma)* langue d'oc.

lempira *nm* lempira, standard monetary unit of Honduras.

lencería *nf* **1** *Tex (ropa blanca)* linen (goods *pl*). **2** *(prenda) (sólo de mujer)* lingerie. **3** *(tienda)* linen shop, draper's (shop).

lencero,-a *nm,f* draper.

lendakari *nm* head of the Basque government.

lengua *nf* **1** *Anat* tongue; **sacar la l. a algn,** to stick one's tongue out at sb; *fig* **andar en lenguas,** to be the talk of the town; *fig* **hacerse lenguas de algo,** to praise sth wildly; *fig* **largo** *or* **ligero de l.,** loose-tongued; *fig* **l. viperina** *or* **de víbora,** viperous tongue; *fig* **malas lenguas,** gossip *sing*; *fam fig* **con la l. fuera,** puffing and panting; *fam fig* **darle a la l.,** to chatter; *fam fig* **irse de la l.,** to spill the beans; *fam fig* **morderse la l.,** to hold one's tongue; *fam fig* **no tener pelos en la l.,** not to mince one's words, be outspoken; *fam fig* **tener algo en la punta de la l.,** to have sth on the tip of one's tongue; *fam fig* **tirarle a algn de la l.,** to try to draw sth out of sb; *fam fig* **tragarse la l.,** to bite one's lip. **2** *Ling* language, tongue. ■ **l. franca,** lingua franca; **l. madre,** parent language; **l. materna,** native *or* mother tongue; **l. muerta/viva,** dead/living language. **3** *Geog* neck, spit.

lenguado *nm (pez)* sole.

lenguaje *nm* **1** *(habla)* speech, language; **l. corporal,** body language. **2** *(idioma)* language. ■ **l. poético,** poetic language; **l. literario,** literary style. **3** *Inform* language. ■ **l. de alto nivel,** high-level language; **l. de programación,** program language.

lenguaraz *adj (hablador)* talkative, garrulous; *(mal hablado)* foul-mouthed.

lengüeta *nf* **1** *(de zapato)* tongue, flap. **2** *Mús* reed. **3** *Am (charlatán)* chatterbox.

lengüetada *nf*, **lengüetazo** *nm* lick.

lengüetear *vi Am* to chatter.

Leningrado *n* Leningrad.

leninismo *nm Pol* Leninism.

leninista *adj & nmf Pol* Leninist.

lenitivo,-a I *adj* soothing, lenitive. **II** *nm* lenitive; *fig* palliative.

lenocinio *nm fml* procuring, pimping. ■ **casa de l.,** brothel.

lente I *nmf* lens; *opt* **l. de contacto,** contact lenses. **II** **lentes** *nmpl Opt* glasses, spectacles.

lenteja *nf Bot Culin* lentil; *prov* **venderse por un plato de lentejas,** to sell oneself cheap.

lentejuela *nf* sequin, spangle.

lentilla *nf Opt* contact lens.

lentisco *nm Bot* mastic tree.

lentitud *nf* slowness; **con l.,** slowly.

lento,-a *adj* slow; **fuego l.,** low heat; **ser l. de reflejos,** to have slow reflexes.

leña *nf* **1** firewood; **hacer l.,** to collect firewood; **l. pequeña,** kindling; *fig* **echar l. al fuego,** to add fuel to the fire. **2** *fam (golpes)* knocks *pl*; *Dep* rough play; **dar** *or* **repartir l.,** to hit out; *Dep* to play rough.

leñador,-a *nm,f* woodcutter, lumberjack.

leñazo *nm arg (golpe)* blow, smash; **se pegaron un l. contra un árbol,** they crashed into a tree.

leñe *interj fam* damn it!

leñera *nf* woodshed.

leño *nm* **1** log; *fig* **dormir como un l.,** to sleep like a log. **2** *fam (persona)* blockhead, half-wit.

leñoso,-a *adj* wood-like, ligneous.

Leo *nm Astrol Astron* Leo.

león 1 *nm Zool* lion; *fig* **se llevó la parte del l.,** he got the lion's share; *prov* **no es tan fiero el l. como lo pintan,** he/she's not as fierce as he/she's made out to be. ■ *Zool* **l. marino,** sea lion. 2 *Astrol Astron* Leo.

leona *nf* 1 *Zool* lioness. 2 *(mujer)* brave woman; *(provocadora)* man-eater.

leonado,-a *adj* tawny.

leonera *nf* lion's den; *fig* untidy place *or* room; **¿cómo puedes vivir en esa l.?,** how can you live in this mess? 2 *Arg Ecuad PR* crowded cell.

leonés,-esa I *adj* of *or* from León. II *nm, f* native *or* inhabitant of León.

leonino,-a *adj* 1 leonine, lion-like. 2 *Jur* **contrato l.,** one-sided contract.

leontina *nf* watch chain.

leopardo *nm Zool* leopard.

leotardo *nm* 1 leotard, bodystocking. 2 **leotardos,** thick tights.

lépero,-a *adj CAm* coarse, vulgar.

lepidóptero,-a *Zool* I *adj* lepidopterous. II *nm* lepidopteran.

leporino,-a *adj* **labio l.,** harelip.

lepra *nf Med* leprosy.

leproso,-a I *adj* leprous. II *nm, f* leper.

lerdera *nf*, **lerdeza** *nf CAm* laziness.

lerdo,-a *adj (torpe)* clumsy; *(poco despierto)* dull, drowsy.

leridano,-a I *adj* of *or* from Lérida. II *nm, f* native *or* inhabitant of Lérida.

les I *pron pers mfpl* 1 *(objeto indirecto)* (a ellos) them; **acéptales el regalo,** accept their present; **l. di todo el dinero,** I gave them all the money. 2 *(a ustedes)* you; **l. esperaré,** I shall wait for you; **no quiero molestarles,** I don't wish to disturb you. II *pron pers mpl (objeto directo)* (ellos) them; *(ustedes)* you; *véase tamb* **leísmo.**

lesbiana *nf* lesbian.

lesbianismo *nm* lesbianism.

Lesotho *n* Lesotho.

lesión *nf* 1 *(daño corporal)* injury, wound. 2 *(perjuicio)* damage, harm.

lesionado,-a I *pp de* **lesionar.** II *adj* 1 injured; wounded. 2 damaged, harmed. III *nm, f* injured person; **hubo 20 lesionados,** there were 20 injured.

lesionar I *vtr* 1 *(alguien)* to wound; *(algo)* to damage. 2 *fig (intereses)* to damage. II **lesionarse** *vr* to get injured.

lesivo,-a *adj fml* injurious; harmful, damaging.

leso,-a 1 *adj (ofendido)* offended; injured; *Jur* **crimen de lesa majestad,** lese-majesty, treason; **crimen** *or* **delito de lesa patria,** high treason. 2 *Am* silly, foolish.

letal *adj* lethal, deadly.

letanía *nf Rel* litany; *fam fig* long list.

letárgico,-a *adj* lethargic.

letargo *nm* lethargy.

letífico,-a *adj fml* joyful.

letón,-ona I *adj* Latvian. II *nm, f* Latvian. III *nm (idioma)* Latvian, Lettish.

Letonia *n* Latvia.

letra *nf* 1 *Impr Ling* letter; *fig* **al pie de la l.,** to the letter, word for word; *fig* **mándale cuatro letras,** drop her a line; *prov* **la l. con sangre entra,** spare the rod and spoil the child. ■ **l. bastardilla** *or* **itálica** *or* **cursiva,** italics *pl,* italic type; **l. de imprenta** *or* **de molde,** print; **l. gótica,** Gothic script; **l. mayúscula** *or* **de caja alta** *or* **versal,** capital letter; **l. minúscula** *or* **de caja baja,** small letter; **l. negrilla,** semibold type; **l. seminegra,** bold type; **l. versalita,** small capital. 2 *(modo de escribir)* (hand) writing; **de su puño y l.,** in his own hand; **tener buena/mala l.,** to have good/bad handwriting. 3 *Mús (texto)* lyrics *pl,* words *pl.* 4 *Fin* **l. (de cambio),** bill of exchange, draft; **l. a la vista,** sight draft. 5

letras, *Univ* arts; **Facultad de L.,** Faculty of Arts; **licenciado en L.,** arts graduate. **6 letras,** *(literatura)* letters; **hombre/mujer de l.,** man/woman of letters.

letrado,-a I *adj* learned. II *nm, f* lawyer.

letrero *nm (aviso)* notice, sign; *(cartel)* poster; **l. luminoso,** neon sign.

letrina *nf fig* **la playa era una auténtica l.,** the beach was like a public toilet.

leucemia *nf Med* leukaemia, *US* leukemia.

leucémico,-a *Med* I *adj* leukaemic, *US* leukemic. II *nm, f* person suffering from leukaemia *or US* leukemia.

leucocito *nm* leucocyte, *US* leukocyte.

leva¹ *nf* 1 *Mil (reclutamiento)* levy. 2 *Téc* cam. 3 *Náut* weighing anchor.

leva² *nf* 1 *Am (levita)* frock coat. 2 *CAm Col (engaño)* trick.

levadizo,-a *adj* which can be raised, raisable, raiseable; **puente l.,** drawbridge.

levadura *nf* leaven, yeast. ■ *Culin* **l. en polvo,** baking powder.

levantado,-a I *pp de* **levantar.** II *adj* up, out of bed.

levantador,-a *nm, f* **l. de pesos** *or* **pesas,** weightlifter.

levantamiento *nm* 1 *(suspensión)* raising, lifting; **l. de la veda,** opening of the hunting *or* fishing season. 2 *Dep* **l. de pesos** *or* **pesas,** weightlifting. 3 *Mil (insurrección)* uprising, insurrection.

levantar I *vtr* 1 to raise, lift; *(mano, voz)* to raise; *(ojos)* to look up, raise; *fig* **l. dudas/temores,** to raise doubts/fears; *fig* **l. un país,** to put a country on its feet. 2 *(obstáculos)* to put up. 3 *(edificios, monumento)* to erect. 4 *Pol* to stir up. 5 *(castigo)* to suspend. 6 *(recoger)* to clear; **l. la mesa,** to clear the table. 7 *Naipes* **l. las cartas,** to cut the (the cards). 8 *(concluir)* to finish; *(aplazar)* to postpone; **se levanta la sesión,** the court will adjourn. II *vr* 1 *(ponerse de pie)* to stand up, rise. 2 *(salir de la cama)* to get up, get out of bed; **l. pronto** *or* **temprano,** to get up early; *fig* **l. con el pie izquierdo,** to get out of bed on the wrong side. 3 *(sobresalir)* to stand out, tower (above). 4 *Pol* to rise, revolt; **l. en armas,** to rise up in arms. 5 *(viento)* to come up; *(tormenta)* to gather; *fig* **se levantó una ola de rumores,** a flood of rumours arose.

levante *nm* 1 *Geog (punto cardinal)* east; **(el) L.,** Levante, the regions of Valencia and Murcia. 2 *(viento)* east *wind,* Levanter.

levantino,-a I *adj* of *or* from the **Levante.** II *nm, f* native *or* inhabitant of the **Levante.**

levantisco,-a *adj* restless, turbulent.

levar *vtr (ancla)* to weigh; **l. anclas,** to set sail.

leve *adj (ligero)* light; *fig (de poca importancia)* slight, unimportant. ◆ **levemente** *adv* lightly, slightly.

levedad *nf (ligereza)* lightness; *fig* slightness; *fig (de ánimo)* levity.

leviatán *nm Rel* leviathan.

levita¹ *nm Hist* Levite.

levita² *nf* frock coat.

levitación *nf* levitation.

levitar *vi* to levitate.

levítico,-a I *adj Hist* Levitical; *fig* clerical. II *nm Rel* Leviticus.

lexema *nm Ling* lexeme.

lexical *adj Ling* lexical.

léxico *Ling* I *adj* lexical. II *nm (diccionario)* lexicon; *(vocabulario)* lexicon, vocabulary, word list.

lexicografía *nf Ling* lexicography.

lexicográfico,-a *adj Ling* lexicographic, lexicographical.

lexicógrafo,-a *nm, f Ling* lexicographer.

lexicología *nf Ling* lexicology.

lexicológico,-a *adj Ling* lexicologic, lexicological.

lexicólogo,-a *nm,f Ling* lexicologist.

lexicón *nm Ling* lexicon.

ley *nf* 1 *(gen)* law; *Jur* law; *Parl* bill, act; *Dep* rule, law; **aprobar una l.**, to pass a bill; **estar fuera de la l.**, to be outside the law; **según/contra la l.**, according to/against the law; *fig* **con todas las de la l.**, properly, completely; *fig* **la l. del más fuerte**, the law of the jungle; *fam* **hecha la l., hecha la trampa**, laws are made to be broken; *fam fig* **la l. del embudo**, one law for oneself and a different one for the others. ■ **la l. de la gravedad**, the law of gravity; **l. orgánica** *or* **constitucional**, constitutional law; **l. seca**, prohibition law, *US* dry law. 2 *(de un metal)* purity; **oro de l.**, pure gold.

leyenda *nf* 1 *(relato)* legend; **l. negra**, black legend. 2 *(en un mapa)* legend; *(en una moneda)* inscription.

lezna *nf* awl, bradawl.

lía¹ *nf (soga)* rope.

lía² *nf (heces)* lees *pl*, dregs *pl*.

liana *nf Bot* liana.

liar I *vtr* 1 *(envolver)* to wrap up; *(atar)* to tie up, do up, bind; *(un cigarrillo)* to roll. 2 *(enredar)* to muddle up; *(confundir)* to confuse. 3 *(complicar)* to involve; **quiso liarme en un negocio sucio**, he tried to get me mixed up in some shady deal; **l. a bofetadas**, to come to blows. II **liarse** *vr* 1 *(embarullarse)* to get muddled up. 2 *fam* to become lovers, have an affair; *(enrollarse)* to get involved with, embroiled in. 3 *(empezar)* to begin; **l. a hablar**, to have a natter.

libación *nf Lit* libation.

libanés,-esa *adj & nm,f* Lebanese.

Líbano *n* el L., the Lebanon.

libar *vtr (néctar)* to suck; *(licor)* to take a sip, swig.

libelista *nmf* lampoonist.

libelo *nm (escrito difamatorio)* lampoon, satire; *Jur* petition.

libélula *nf Ent* dragonfly.

liberación *nf* 1 *(de país)* liberation; *(de persona)* release, freeing. 2 *Fin (impuestos)* exemption; *(hipoteca)* redemption.

liberado,-a I *pp de* **liberar**. II *adj* liberated, freed; **mujer liberada**, liberated woman.

liberador,-a I *adj* liberating. II *nm,f* liberator.

liberal I *adj* 1 *(gen)* liberal; *(carácter)* easy-going; *Pol* **Partido L.**, Liberal Party; *(trabajo)* **profesión l.**, profession. 2 *(generoso)* generous, liberal. II *nmf* liberal. ◆ **liberalmente** *adv* liberally, freely.

liberalidad *nf* generosity, liberality.

liberalismo *nm* liberalism.

liberalización *nf* liberalization.

liberalizar I *vtr* to liberalize; *Fin* to lift, deregulate. II **liberalizarse** *vr* to become free, become liberal.

liberar I *vtr (país)* to liberate; *(prisionero)* to free, release. II **liberarse** *vr* to get *or* become free.

liberatorio,-a *adj* liberating, freeing.

Liberia *n* Liberia.

liberiano,-a *adj & nm,f* Liberian.

libero *nm Ftb* sweeper.

libérrimo,-a *adj Lit* entirely *or* totally free.

libertad *nf* 1 freedom; liberty; **en l.**, free; *Jur* **(en) l. bajo palabra/fianza**, (on) parole/bail; *Jur* **(en) l. condicional**, (on) parole; *Jur* **(en) l. provisional**, *(bajo fianza)* (on) bail; **(en) l. vigilada**, (on) probation; **l. de comercio**, free trade; **l. de expresión**, freedom of speech; *fig* **tomarse la l. de decir algo**, to take the liberty of saying sth. 2 **libertades**, liberties; **tomarse (demasiadas) l.**, to take liberties.

libertador,-a I *adj* liberating. II *nm,f* liberator.

libertar *vtr (poner en libertad)* to set free, release, liberate, deliver; *(eximir)* to exempt.

libertario,-a *adj & nm,f* libertarian.

libertinaje *nm* licentiousness.

libertino,-a *adj & nm,f* libertine.

liberto,-a I *adj* emancipated, free. II *nm, f (hombre)* freedman; *(mujer)* freedwoman.

Libia *n* Libya.

libidinoso,-a *adj* libidinous, lewd.

libido *nf* libido.

libio,-a *adj & nm,f* Libyan.

libra *nf* 1 *Fin* pound; **l. esterlina**, pound sterling. 2 *(medida)* pound. 3 **L.**, *Astrol Astron* Libra.

libraco *nm pey (libro grande)* large, heavy book; *(libro malo)* trashy book.

librado,-a I *pp de* **librar**. II *nm,f Fin* drawee.

librador,-a *nm,f Fin* drawer.

libramiento *nm*, **libranza** *nf Fin* order of payment, bill of exchange.

librar I *vtr* 1 *(gen)* to save, free; *Jur* to free, release; *Rel* **¡Dios me *or* nos libre!**, heaven forbid!; **salir bien librado**, to get off lightly. 2 *Com* to draw; **l. una letra**, to draw a bill. 3 *Mil* to fight; **l. batalla**, to do *or* join battle. II *vi* 1 *(no ir a trabajar)* to have off; **libro los martes**, I have Tuesdays off. 2 *(dar a luz)* to give birth. III **librarse** *vr* to escape; **l. de algo**, to get rid of sb; **l. de una buena**, to have a narrow escape; **l. de una multa**, to get out of paying a fine.

libre *adj* free; *Educ* **alumno l.**, extenal student; **asiento l.**, free seat; *(en letrero)* **entrada l.**, admission free, open to the general public; *(en servicios)* **l.**, vacant; *Fin* **l. cambio**, free trade; *Fin* **l. de impuestos**, tax-free; **l. de preocupaciones**, free from worries; *Natación* **los cien metros libres**, the one hundred metres free-style; **ratos libres**, spare time; **traducción l.**, free translation. ◆ **libremente** *adv* freely.

librea *nf* livery, uniform.

librecambio *nm*, **librecambismo** *nm Econ* free trade.

librecambista *Econ* I *adj* free trade. II *nmf* freetrader.

librepensador,-a I *adj* freethinking. II *nm,f* freethinker.

librepensamiento *nm* freethinking, free thought. **librería** *nf* 1 *(tienda)* bookshop, *US* bookstore. 2 *Mueb (armario)* bookcase; *(estantería)* bookshelf.

librero,-a I *nm, f* bookseller. II *nm Méx (estantería)* bookshelf; *(armario)* bookcase.

libresco,-a *adj pey* bookish.

libreta *nf* notebook; **l. (de ahorro)**, savings book.

libretista *nmf Mús* librettist.

libreto *nm Mús* libretto.

librillo *nm* small book, booklet; **l. de papel de fumar**, packet of cigarette papers.

libro *nm* 1 book; *Com* **llevar los libros**, to keep the accounts. ■ *Pol* **l. blanco/rojo**, White/Red Paper; **l. de bolsillo**, paperback; *Com* **l. de caja**, cashbook; **l. de consulta**, reference book; **l. de cuentos**, storybook; *Jur* **l. de familia**, book in which births and deaths in the family are registered; **l. de lectura**, reader; **l. de reclamaciones**, complaints book; **l. de texto**, textbook; *Fin* **l. mayor**, ledger. 2 *Zool Anat* third stomach.

Lic. *abr de* **licenciado,-a**, licenciate, graduate.

licantropía *nf Psic* lycanthropy.

licántropo *nm Psic* lycanthrope; *(leyenda)* were-wolf.

licencia *nf* 1 *(permiso)* licence, *US* license, permission; *(documentos)* permit, licence, *US* license; **dar l. a algn**, to grant sb permission; *Mil* **l. absoluta**, discharge; **l. de armas/caza**, gun/hunting licence; *Com* **l. fiscal**, business permit; *Com* **l. de importación**, import licence. 2 *(libertad abusiva)* licence, *US* license, licentiousness. ■ **l. poética**, poetic licence. 3 *Univ* degree. 4 *Am Aut* driving licence, *US* driver's license.

licenciado,-a I *pp de* **licenciar. II** *adj* **1** *Univ* graduated. **2** *Mil* discharged. **III** *nm, f* **1** *Univ* graduate, licentiate, bachelor; *Mil* discharged soldier; **l. en Ciencias,** Bachelor of Science; **l. en francés,** French graduate. **2** *Am* lawyer.

licenciar I *vtr* **1** *(dar permiso a)* to grant a permit *or* licence *or US* license on; *Mil* to discharge. **2** *Univ* to confer a degree on. **II licenciarse** *vr Univ* to graduate.

licenciatura *nf Univ (título)* (bachelor's) degree; *(ceremonia)* graduation; *(curso)* degree (course).

licencioso,-a *adj* licentious, dissolute.

liceo *nm* **1** *Hist* Lyceum. **2** *(sociedad literaria)* literary society. **3** *(escuela)* secondary school.

licitación *nf Com* bid, bidding; *Com* **sacar (algo) a l.,** to put (sth) up for auction.

licitador *nm Com* bidder.

licitar *vtr Com (pujar)* to bid for; *(optar)* to tender for.

lícito,-a *adj (justo)* just, fair; *(permisible)* allowed; *Jur* lawful, licit.

licitud *nf (justicia)* justness, fairness; *Jur* lawfulness, legality.

licor *nm* **1** *(líquido)* liquid. **2** *(bebida destilada)* liquor, spirits *pl, US* licor.

licorera *nf* liquor bottle, decanter.

licorería *nf Com* off-licence, *US* package store, *US* licor store; *Ind* distillery.

licoroso,-a *adj (vinos etc)* strong; **vino l.,** fortified sweet wine.

licuable *adj* liquefactive.

licuación *nf* liquefaction.

licuado *nm Am (batido)* milk shake; *(refresco)* soft drink.

licuadora *nf* liquidizer.

licuar *vtr* **I** *vtr* to liquefy. **II licuarse** *vr* to liquefy, become liquid.

licuecer *vtr & vi véase* **licuar.**

licuefacción *nf* liquefaction.

lid *nf (combate)* contest, combat, fight; *fig* dispute, controversy; *fig* **experto en esas lides,** experienced in these matters.

líder *nmf* leader.

liderar *vtr* to lead, head.

liderato *nm,* **liderazgo** *nm* leadership; *Dep* leader, top *or* first position.

lidia *nf* **1** *Taur* bullfight, bullfighting; **toro de l.,** fighting bull. **2** *(lucha)* fight, combat.

lidiador *nm Taur* bullfighter.

lidiar I *vtr* **1** *Taur* to fight. **2** *fig* to deal with. **II** *vi* to fight; **l. con,** to contend with, fight against.

liebre *nf* **1** *Zool* hare; *fig* coward; *fig* **levantar la l.,** to let the cat out of the bag. **2** *Atlet* pacemaker.

liencillo *nm Am Tex* rough cotton cloth.

liendre *nf Ent* nit.

lienzo *nm* **1** *Tex* linen. **2** *Arte* canvas, painting. **3** *Arquit* (stretch of) wall. **4** *Am (trozo de cerca)* stretch (of fence).

liga *nf* **1** *Dep Pol* league. **2** *(prenda)* garter. **3** *(sustancia pegajosa)* birdlime. **4** *Bot* mistletoe. **5** *(mezcla)* mixture. **6** *(aleación)* alloy.

ligado,-a I *pp de* **ligar. II** *adj* connected, linked. **III** *nm Tip* ligature; *Mús* slur.

ligadura *nf* bond, tie; *Tip* ligature; *Mús* slur.

ligamento *nm* **1** *Anat* ligament. **2** *Tex* weave.

ligamentoso,-a *adj* ligamentous, ligamental, ligamentary.

ligar I *vtr* **1** *(unir)* to tie, bind; *fig* to join; *fig* **les ligaba la política,** they were united by politics. **2** *(alear)* to alloy. **3** *Culin* to thicken. **4** *Med* to bind up. **5** *Mús* to slur. **6** *fam (conquistar)* to pinch. **7** *CAm Méx (curiosear)* to nose about. **8** *Arg (entender)* to get along well with. **II** *vi* **1** *fam (seducir)* to chat up a man *or* woman, get off with sb,

score. **2** *(concordar)* **l. con,** to agree with, be in accordance with. **3** *Naipes* to combine good cards. **4** *CAm Per (deseo)* to have one's desires satisfied. **5** *Arg (en el juego)* to be lucky. **III ligarse** *vr* to bind oneself; to commit oneself.

ligazón *nf* **1** *(unión)* bond, tie. **2** *Náut* rib, beam.

ligereza *nf* **1** *(liviandad)* lightness, thinness, flimsiness. **2** *(agilidad)* agility, nimbleness. **3** *(frivolidad)* rashness, flippancy; *(indiscreción)* indiscretion, **hablar/obrar con l.,** to speak/act rashly *or* without thinking.

ligero,-a I *adj* **1** *(peso)* light, lightweight, **l. como una pluma,** as light as a feather; **l. de ropa,** lightly clad; *Box* **peso l.,** lightweight. **2** *(ágil)* agile, nimble; *(veloz)* swift, quick; **l. de manos,** light-fingered; **paso l.,** nimble step, *Mil* quick march. **3** *(frívolo)* rash, flippant; **de l.,** rashly, **tomarse algo a la ligera,** to take sth lightly. **4** *(de poca importancia)* slight. **II** *adv* **1** *(rápido)* fast, swiftly. **2** *Am (pronto)* soon. ◆ **ligeramente** *adv* **1** *(levemente)* lightly. **2** *(un poco)* slightly.

lignito *nm Min* lignite.

ligón[1] *nm (herramienta)* hoe.

ligón,-ona[2] *adj & nm, f fam (hombre)* skirt-chaser; *(mujer)* easy pick-up.

ligue *nm fam* pick-up; **ir de l.,** to go out on the pick-up, go talent spotting, cruise.

liguero,-a I *adj Dep* league; **partido l.,** league match. **II** *nm* suspender belt, suspenders *pl, US* garter belt.

liguilla *nf Dep* round-robin tournament.

lija *nf* **1** *(pez)* dogfish. **2** *Téc* sandpaper. ■ **papel de l.,** sandpaper.

lijadora *nf Téc* sander, sanding machine.

lijar *vtr Téc* to sand *or* sandpaper (down).

lila[1] *adj & nm & nf* lilac.

lila[2] *fam* **I** *adj (tonto)* dumb, stupid. **II** *nmf (tonto)* twit.

liliáceo,-a *adj Bot* liliaceous.

liliputiense *adj & nmf* Lilliputian.

lima[1] *nf Bot* lime.

lima[2] *nf* **1** *(herramienta)* file; *fig* **come como una l.,** he eats like a horse. ■ **l. de uñas,** nailfile. **2** *fig* polish, polishing up.

limaco *nm Zool* slug.

limado *nm* filing.

limadura *nf* filing.

limar *vtr* **1** *(desbastar)* to file (down *or* off); *fig* **l. asperezas,** to smooth things over. **2** *(pulir una obra)* to polish up, put the final touches to.

limaza *nf Zool* slug.

limbo *nm* **1** *Rel* limbo; *fig* **estar en el l.,** to be miles away. **2** *Mat* limb.

limeño,-a I *adj* of *or* from Lima. **II** *nm, f* native *or* inhabitant of Lima.

limero *nm Bot* lime (tree).

limitación *nf* limitation, limit.

limitado,-a I *pp de* **limitar. II** *adj* **1** *(gen)* limited. **2** *euf (poco listo)* dull, dim-witted.

limitar I *vtr* to limit, restrict. **II** *vi* to border; **l. con,** to border on. **III limitarse** *vr* to limit *or* restrict oneself.

limitativo,-a *adj* restrictive, limiting.

límite *nm (gen)* limit; *Geog Pol* boundary, border; **caso l.,** borderline case; **dentro de unos límites,** within limits; **fecha l.,** deadline; **velocidad l.,** maximum speed.

limítrofe *adj* bordering, neighbouring, *US* neighboring.

limo *nm* slime, mud.

limón *nm Bot* lemon.

limonada *nf (sin gas)* lemon squash; *(con gas)* lemonade, *US* lemon soda.

limonera *nf* shaft (of a cart).

limonero,-a I *adj* lemon; **pera limonera,** large variety of pear. **II** *nm* lemon tree.

limonita *nf Min* limonite.

limosna *nf* alms, charity; **dar (una) l.,** to give alms; **pedir l.,** to beg.

limosnear *vi* to beg.

limosnero,-a I *adj* charitable. **II** *nm,f Am* beggar.

limoso,-a *adj* slimy, muddy.

limpiabarros *nm inv* boot scraper.

limpiabotas *nm inv* bootblack, shoeblack.

limpiachimeneas *nm inv* chimney sweep.

limpiacristales *nm inv* window cleaner.

limpiador,-a I *adj* cleaning, cleansing. **II** *nm,f (persona)* cleaner. **III** *nm (producto)* cleaner, cleanser.

limpiaparabrisas *nm inv Aut* windscreen *or US* windshield wiper.

limpiar I *vtr* **1** *(gen)* to clean, cleanse; *(con un trapo)* to wipe; *fig* to cleanse, purify; **l. algo en seco,** to dry-clean sth. **2** *fam (hurtar)* to pinch, nick; **le limpiaron la cartera,** they cleaned out his wallet. **II limpiarse** *vr* to clean oneself.

limpidez *nf Lit* limpidity.

límpido,-a *adj Lit* limpid.

limpieza *nf (calidad)* cleanness, cleanliness; *(acción)* cleaning; *fig (integridad)* integrity; *fig (pureza)* purity; **hacer la l.,** to do the cleaning.

limpio,-a I *adj* **1** *(aseado)* clean, tidy; **l. como una patena,** clean as a new pin; **¿tienes las manos limpias?,** are your hands clean?; *fig* **l. de (toda) sospecha,** free of suspicion. **2** *(honrado)* honest, fair; **juego l.,** fair play; **un negocio poco l.,** a shady business. **3** *Fin (neto)* net; **en l.,** net; **su sueldo asciende a 150.000 pesetas límpias,** he earns 150,000 pesetas after tax. **4** *(claro)* clear; **¿has sacado algo en l. de todo ello?,** have you got anything out of all that? **5** *fam (ignorante)* ignorant; **de este tema estoy l.,** I don't know a thing about the subject. **6** *fam (arruinado)* broke; **la caída de la bolsa me dejó l.,** the stock market crash left me broke. **II** *adv* fairly; **jugar l.,** to play fair.

limpión *nm Am* tea towel, tea-cloth, *US* dishtowel.

limusina *nf Aut* limousine.

linaje *nm* **1** *(familia)* lineage. **2** *(especie)* kind, class.

linajudo,-a *adj* highborn, blue-blooded.

linaza *nf Bot* flaxseed, linseed.

lince *nm Zool* lynx; *fig* **ser un l.,** not to miss a thing; *fig* **tener ojo de l.,** to have a sharp eye.

linchamiento *nm* lynching.

linchar *vtr* to lynch.

lindante *adj (limítrofe)* bordering; *fig (rayano)* bordering on; **una franqueza l. con la grosería,** an openness bordering on rudeness.

lindar *vi* to adjoin; **l. con,** to border on; **Suiza linda con Alemania,** Switzerland borders on Germany.

linde *nmf* boundary, limit.

lindero,-a I *adj* bordering, adjoining; **tiene un solar l. con el mío,** he has a lot next *or* adjacent to mine. **II** *nm* boundary, limit.

lindeza *nf* **1** *(belleza)* prettiness. **2** *fam (halagos)* flattering word, sweet talk. **3 lindezas,** *iron (insultos)* insults.

lindo,-a *adj (bonito)* pretty, lovely; **de lo l.,** a great deal, in a grand manner. ◆ **lindamente** *adv* neatly, prettily.

línea *nf* **1** *(gen)* line; **de primera l.,** first-rate; **en l. recta,** in a straight line; **en líneas generales,** roughly speaking; *Inform* **fuera de l.,** off-line; **l. aérea,** air-line; *Dep* **l. delantera/trasera,** forward/backward line; **l. de puntos,** dotted line; *Inform* **ordenador en l.,** on-line computer. **2** *(silueta)* figure; **guardar la l.,** to watch one's weight. **3** *(familia)* line; **l. directa,** unbroken line. **4** *(valores morales)* line; **sus palabras estuvieron en la l. habitual,** his words were along the usual lines.

lineal *adj* linear; **dibujo l.,** line drawing.

lineamiento *nm* **1** *(contorno)* contour, outline. **2** *Am (directrices)* outline.

linfa *nf* lymph.

linfático,-a *adj* lymphatic.

lingotazo *nm fam (de bebida alcohólica)* long swig.

lingote *nm* ingot; *(de oro, plata)* bar.

lingual *adj & nf* lingual.

lingüista *nmf* linguist.

lingüístico,-a I *adj* linguistic. **II** *nf* linguistics *sing*.

linier *nm Dep* linesman.

linimento *nm Farm* liniment.

lino *nm* **1** *Bot* flax. **2** *Tex* linen.

linóleo *nm*, **linóleum** *nm* lino, linoleum.

linotipia *nf Impr* linotype.

linotipista *nmf Impr* linotypist.

linotipo *nmf Impr* linotype.

linterna *nf (de pilas)* torch; *(farol)* lantern. ■ **l. mágica,** magic lantern.

lío *nm* **1** *(paquete)* bundle; **un l. de ropa,** a bundle of clothes. **2** *fam (embrollo)* mess, muddle; *(chisme)* tale; **hacerse un l.,** to get mixed up; **meterse en líos,** to get into trouble. **3** *fam (relación amorosa)* affair.

liofilización *nf* freeze-drying.

liofilizar *vtr* to freeze-dry.

lioso,-a *fam* **I** *adj (persona)* troublemaking; *(asunto)* tangled, confusing. **II** *nm,f* troublemaker.

lipidia I *nf* **1** *CAm (pobreza)* poverty. **2** *Cuba Méx (impertinencia)* impertinence. **II** *nmf Cuba Méx (persona fastidiosa)* nuisance, pest.

lipidioso,-a *adj Am* bothersome, annoying.

lípido *nm Quím* lipid, lipide.

liposoluble *adj Quím* fat-soluble.

lipotimia *nf Med* syncope, fainting fit.

liquen *nm Bot* lichen.

liquidación *nf* **1** *(gen)* liquidation. **2** *Fin* liquidation; *(operación en bolsa)* settlement. **3** *Com (venta)* clearance sale.

liquidado,-a I *pp* de **liquidar. II** *adj* **1** *(pagado)* paid, settled. **2** *(vendido)* sold off or up. **3** *(resuelto)* solved. **4** *fam (muerto)* killed.

liquidador,-a *nm,f* liquidator.

liquidámbar *nm Bot* **l. americano,** sweet gum.

liquidar *vtr* **1** *(licuar)* to liquefy. **2** *Com (deuda)* to liquidate; *(mercancías)* to sell off or up; *(cuenta)* to settle. **3** *fam (resolver)* to resolve, solve; **hay que l. este problema antes de mañana,** we have to solve this problem by tomorrow. **4** *fam (eliminar)* to kill, bump off.

liquidez *nf Fin* liquidity.

líquido,-a I *adj* **1** *(gen)* liquid. **2** *Fin* net; **renta líquida,** net income. **3** *Ling (sonido)* **consonante líquida,** liquid consonant. **4** *Am (cuentas etc)* exact. **II** *nm* **1** *(fluido)* liquid. **2** *Fin* liquid assets *pl*; **l. imponible,** taxable income.

lira¹ *nf Mús* lyre.

lira² *nf Fin* lira.

lírico,-a I *adj* **1** *(poético)* lyric, lyrical. **2** *Arg Ven* dreamy, Utopian. **II** *nm* lyric poet. **III** *nf* lyric poetry.

lirio *nm* iris. ■ **l. de agua,** calla lily; **l. de los valles,** lily of the valley.

lirismo *nm* **1** *Lit* lyricism. **2** *Am (fantasía)* fantasy.

lirón *nm* dormouse; *fig* **dormir como un l.,** to sleep like a log.

lirondo *adj véase* **mondo,-a.**

lis *nf* **1** *Bot* iris. **2** *Herald* fleur-de-lis.

Lisboa *n* Lisbon.

lisboeta I *adj* of *or* from Lisbon. **II** *nmf* native *or* inhabitant of Lisbon.

lisiado,-a I *pp de* **lisiar**. **II** *adj* crippled, disabled. **III** *nm,f* cripple, disabled person.

lisiar I *vtr* to maim, cripple. **II lisiarse** *vr* to be maimed.

liso,-a *adj* **1** *(superficie)* smooth, even; *Dep* **los cien metros lisos,** the hundred metres. **2** *(pelo)* straight, sleek. **3** *(colores)* plain. **4** *Am (desvergonzado)* cheeky. ◆ **lisamente** *adv* plainly; **lisa y llanamente,** purely and simply.

lisonja *nf* (piece of) flattery.

lisonjeador,-a I *adj* flattering. **II** *nm,f* flatterer.

lisonjear *vtr* to flatter.

lisonjero,-a *adj* **1** *(halagador)* flattering. **2** *(satisfactorio)* gratifying; **no veo el futuro muy l.,** the future doesn't look very rosy.

lista *nf* **1** *(franja)* stripe, band; **a listas,** striped. **2** *(relación)* list, register; **pasar l.,** to call the register *or* the roll. ■ **l. de boda,** wedding list; **l. de correos,** poste restante, *US* general delivery; **l. de espera,** waiting list; **l. negra,** blacklist.

listado,-a I *pp de* **listar**. **II** *adj* striped. **III** *nm* enumeration, listing.

listar *vtr* to list.

listeza *nf* **1** *(listura)* shrewdness, alertness. **2** *(prontitud)* promptness, quickness, sharpness.

listillo *nm fam* smart aleck, know-all.

listín *nm Tel* telephone directory.

listo,-a *adj* **1** *(inteligente)* clever, smart; **dárselas de l.,** to think oneself clever; **pasarse de l.,** to be too clever by half. **2** *(diligente)* prompt, quick; *fam* **¡(pues sí que) estamos listos!,** what a fine mess we're in!; *fam* **¡vas or estás l.!,** you're kidding yourself! **3** *(a punto)* ready, prepared; **¿estás l.?,** (are you) ready?

listón *nm* **1** *Carp* lath. **2** *Dep (de saltar)* bar; *fig* **subir el l.,** to tighten the conditions, raise the requirements.

listura *nf* shrewdness, alertness.

lisura *nf* **1** *(tersura)* smoothness. **2** *(franqueza)* frankness, straightforwardness.

litera *nf* **1** *(cama)* berth, bunk, couchette. **2** *(uso antiguo)* litter.

literal *adj* literal, exact. ◆ **literalmente** *adv* literally, word for word.

literario,-a *adj* literary.

literato,-a *nm,f* writer, man *or* woman of letters.

literatura *nf* literature.

lítico,-a *adj* lithic.

litigación *nf Jur* litigation.

litigante *adj & nmf Jur* litigant.

litigar I *vtr Jur* to litigate, go to law. **II** *vi (contender)* to argue, dispute.

litigio *nm Jur* litigation, lawsuit; *fig* dispute; **en l.,** in dispute.

litigioso,-a *adj Jur* litigious.

litografía *nf* **1** *(técnica)* lithography. **2** *(imagen)* lithograph.

litografiar *vtr* to lithograph.

litográfico,-a *adj* lithographic.

litógrafo,-a *nm,f* lithographer.

litoral I *adj* coastal. **II** *nm* **1** *(costa)* coast, seaboard. **2** *Arg Par Urug (ribera)* riverside.

litosfera *nf Geol* lithosphere.

litri *fam* **I** *adj* snobbish, pretentious. **II** *nmf* snob.

litro *nm (medida)* litre, *US* liter.

Lituania *n* Lithuania.

lituano,-a I *adj* Lithuanian. **II** *nm,f* Lithuanian. **III** *nm (idioma)* Lithuanian.

liturgia *nf* liturgy.

litúrgico,-a *adj* liturgical.

liviandad *nf* **1** *(ligereza)* lightness. **2** *(frivolidad)* unimportance, triviality.

liviano,-a *adj* **1** *(de poco peso)* light. **2** *(trivial)* trivial, fickle. **3** *(lascivo)* lewd.

lividecer *vi* to become *or* go livid.

lividez *nf* lividness, lividity.

lívido,-a *adj* livid.

liza *nf* **1** *(lucha)* contest, combat. **2** *Hist* lists *pl*.

.LL, II ['eʎe] *nf* *(el dígrafo)* formerly fourteenth letter of the Spanish alphabet.

llaga *nf Med (úlcera)* sore; *(lesión)* wound; *fig* **poner el dedo en la l.,** to touch a sore spot *or* point.

llagar *vtr* to wound; to injure.

llama¹ *nf* **1** flame, blaze; **en llamas,** in flames, ablaze. **2** *fig (pasión)* flame, ardour, *US* ardor.

llama² *nf Zool* llama.

llamada *nf* **1** *(gen)* call. ■ *Tel* **l. telefónica,** telephone call; *Tel* **l. interurbana,** long-distance call; **señal de ll.,** ringing tone. **2** *Tip (en un escrito)* reference mark.

llamado,-a I *pp de* **llamar**. **II** *adj* so-called; **el l. Viejo Continente,** the so-called Old World.

llamador *nm* **1** *(aldaba)* door knocker. **2** *(timbre)* bell.

llamamiento *nm* appeal, call.

llamar I *vtr* **1** gen to call; **l. a algn a voces,** to shout to sb; **l. al médico,** to call the doctor; **si es niño le llamaremos Juan,** if it's a boy we'll call him Juan. **2** *(convocar)* to summon, call. **3** *(atraer)* to draw, attract; **l. la atención,** to attract attention; *fam* **el dinero llama al dinero,** like breeds like. **II** *vi* **1** *Tel (telefonear)* **l. (por teléfono),** to ring up, call; **mañana te llamo,** I'll give you a ring tomorrow. **2** *(a la puerta)* to knock; **l. a la puerta,** to knock at the door; **llaman a la puerta,** there's somebody at the door. **II llamarse** *vr* to be called; **¿cómo te llamas?,** what's your name?; **me llamo Paco,** my name is Paco; **¡eso (sí que) se llama comer!,** now that's what I call eating!; *fig* **l. a engaño,** to claim one has been cheated.

llamarada *nf* **1** *(llama)* flame, sudden blaze. **2** *(del rostro)* sudden flush. **3** *fig (arrebato)* flare-up, outburst.

llamativo,-a *adj* **1** *(color, ropa)* loud, gaudy, flashy. **2** *(persona)* flashy, showy.

llanero,-a *nm, f (hombre)* plainsman; *(mujer)* plainswoman.

llaneza *nf (franqueza)* openness, frankness; *(sencillez)* simplicity.

llanito,-a *adj & nm,f fam* Gibraltarian.

llano,-a I *adj* **1** *(superficie)* flat, level, even. **2** *(franco)* open, frank; *(amable)* friendly; *(claro)* clear, easy. **3** *(corriente)* simple, common; **el pueblo l.,** the common people. **II** *nm (terreno)* plain.

llanote,-a *adj fam* plain-spoken, straightforward.

llanta *nf* **1** *Aut (aro metálico)* wheel rim. **2** *Am (neumático)* tyre, *US* tire.

llantén *nm Bot* plantain.

llantera *nf,* **llantina** *nf fam* fit of tears, sobbing.

llanto *nm* tears *pl*, crying, weeping; **deshacerse en l.,** to cry one's heart out.

llanura *nf Geog* plain.

llave *nf* **1** *(de puerta, candado, etc)* key; **cerrar con l.,** to lock; **echar la l.,** to lock up; **guardar algo bajo l.,** to keep sth under lock and key; *(piso)* **llaves en mano,** available for immediate occupation. ■ *Aut* **l. de contacto,** ignition key; **l. maestra,** master key. **2** *Téc* spanner, wrench. ■ **l. inglesa,** monkey wrench. **3** *Elec (interruptor)* switch. ■ **l. de paso,** stopcock, tap; **l. del gas,** (gas) tap. **4** *Lucha* lock, **5** *(de arma)* lock. **6** *Tip* bracket.

llavero *nm* key ring.

llavín *nm* small key, latchkey.

llegada *nf (gen)* arrival; *Dep* finish.

llegar I *vi* **1** to arrive, come, reach; **l. a casa,** to arrive home; **l. a Madrid,** to arrive in Madrid. **2** *(ser bastante)* to be enough; **la sopa no llega para todos,** there isn't enough soup for everyone. **3** *(alcanzar)* to reach; **¿llegas al techo?,** can you reach the ceiling?; **l. a los cincuenta,** to reach fifty; **l. a un acuerdo,** to reach an agreement; **su estupidez no llega a tanto,** he's not that stupid; *fig* **ella llegó a donde se proponía,** she got where she wanted to be. **4** *(ascender, importar)* to be; *(alcanzar)* to be about to arrive; **ese coche llega al millón de pesetas,** that car costs about a million pesetas. **5** *(locuciones)* **l. a la fama,** to become famous; **l. a más,** to better oneself; **l. al alma,** to affect deeply; **l. al extremo de,** to go as far as; **l. a oídos de algn,** to hear; *fig* **l. a las manos,** to come to blows; *fig* **l. lejos,** to go far; *fam* **¡hasta ahí podíamos l.!,** that's the limit! **II** *v aux (l. + a + infin)* **llegó a decir que ...,** he even said that ...; **si llego a saberlo,** if only I had known. **III llegarse** *vr* to stop by, go *or* come round; **llégate al estanco y tráeme tabaco,** go to the tobacconist's and get me some cigarettes.

llenador,-a *adj* Arg Chi Urug *(comida)* filling.

llenar I *vtr* **1** *(gen)* to fill; *(formulario)* to fill in; *(superficie)* to cover; *(tiempo)* to fill, occupy; **l. una botella de agua,** to fill a bottle with water; **llenaron la pared de cuadros,** they covered the wall with pictures. **2** *(satisfacer)* to satisfy, meet; **es un trabajo que no llena,** it's a job that gives one no sense of fulfilment. **3** *fig (de regalos)* to shower **(de,** with); *(de insultos)* to heap **(de,** on). **II** *vi (comida)* to be filling. **III llenarse** *vr* to fill (up), become full; **las calles se llenan de turistas,** the streets are filled with tourists.

lleno,-a I *adj* full (up); **la botella está llena de agua,** the bottle is full of water; **l. hasta los bordes,** full to the brim; **tengo la agenda llena,** I've got a busy day; *fig* **de l.,** entirely, fully; **nos afectó de l.,** we were directly affected by it. **II** *nm* Teat full house.

llenito,-a *adj fam* chubby, tubby.

llevadero,-a *adj* bearable, tolerable.

llevar I *vtr* **1** *(transportar)* to carry; **¿llevas dinero encima?,** have you got any money on you?; **¿qué llevas en la mano?,** what have you got in your hand? **2** *(prenda)* to wear; **¿qué llevaba puesto?,** what was he wearing? **3** *(pelo)* to have; **l. el pelo largo,** to have long hair. **4** *(conducir)* to take, lead; **¿a dónde me llevas?,** where are you taking me?; *fig* **esto me llevó a pensar que ...,** this led me to think that ... . **5** *(soportar)* to bear, put up with; **¿cómo lleva lo de su enfermedad?,** how's he bearing up? **6** *(pasar tiempo)* **¿cuánto tiempo lleva ahí?,** how long has it been there?; **en lo que llevamos de año,** so far this year. **7** *(requerir tiempo)* to take; **me llevó dos horas encontrarte,** it took me two hours to find you. **8** *(encargarse de)* to run; **l. las cuentas,** to keep the books; **l. egocio,** to run a business. **9** *(exceder)* **te llevo tres años,** I'm three years older than you; **l. ventaja a algn,** to be ahead of sb, have the advantage over sb. **10** *(tratar)* to treat, handle; **Felipe sabe l. a su tío,** Felipe knows how to handle his uncle. **11** Mat to carry over. **12** *(paso, ritmo)* to keep, mark. **13** *(locuciones)* **dejarse l. por algo** *or* **algn,** to be influenced by sth or sb; **l. algo a cabo** *or* **a efecto,** to carry sth out; **l. de cabeza,** to be tied up with; **l. idea de,** to want to; **l. algo a la práctica,** to put sth into practice; **l. a (féliz) término,** to bring to an *(o* a happy) end. **II** *v aux (l. + participio)* to have + past participle; **llevaba escritas seis cartas,** I had written six letters; **llevamos andado medio camino,** we're half-way there. **III llevarse** *vr* **1** *(coger)* to take; *fam* **l. por delante,** to run over. **2** *(recibir)* to get; **l. un susto,** to get a shock; **l. una decepción,** to be disappointed; **l. una sorpresa,** to be surprised. **3** *(conseguir)* to win, carry off; **l. la mejor/peor parte,** to get the best/worst of it; **l. un premio,** to win a prize. **4** *(arrastrar)* to take away, remove; **la riada se llevó todos los coches,** the flood swept away all the cars. **5** *(estar de moda)* to be fashionable; **se llevan los tonos rojos,** red is

in fashion. **6** *(entenderse)* to get on **(con,** with); **l. bien con algn,** to get on well with sb.

llorar I *vi* **1** to cry, weep; **ponerse a l.,** to start crying; *fam* **l. a lágrima viva** *or* **a moco tendido,** to cry one's heart out; *prov* **quién bien te quiere te hará l.,** you have to be cruel to be kind. **2** *fam* to groan, moan; *vulg* **al que no llora no mama,** he who doesn't ask doesn't get. **II** *vtr* to mourn; **l. la muerte de algn,** to mourn sb's death; *fig* **l. lágrimas de sangre,** to regret doing sth.

llorera *nf fam* fit of tears, sobbing.

lloriquear *vi* to whimper, snivel.

lloriqueo *nm* whimpering, snivelling, *US* sniveling.

lloro *nm* tears *pl,* weeping.

llorón,-ona I *adj* tearful, weeping. **II** *nm, f* crybaby. **III** *nf fam (borrachera triste)* downer.

llorona *nf Am* big spur.

lloroso,-a *adj* tearful, weeping.

llovedera *nf Am* continous rain.

llover *v impers* to rain; **¿llueve?,** is it raining?; **llueve a cántaros,** it's pouring (down); *fig* **como llovido del cielo,** out of the blue; **aquel dinero me vino como llovido del cielo,** that money was a godsend; *fig* **ha llovido mucho desde entonces,** a lot of water has passed under the bridge since then; *fam fig* **llueve sobre mojado,** it never rains but it pours.

llovizna *nf* drizzle.

lloviznar *v impers* to drizzle.

lloviznoso,-a *adj Am* rainy, wet.

lluvia *nf* **1** rain. **2** *fig (de regalos, insultos)* shower; *(de quejas)* string; **recibió una l. de preguntas,** he was bombarded with questions.

lluvioso,-a *adj* rainy; *(clima)* wet.

lo¹ *art det neut* **the; lo curioso (del caso) es que ...,** the funny thing (about it) is that ...; **lo mejor,** the best (part); **lo peor,** the worst (part).

lo² *pron pers m & neut* **1** *(objeto directo)* him; *(usted)* you; *(cosa)* it; **debes hacerlo,** you must do it; **lo mataron,** they killed him; **¡míralo!,** look at it!; **no lo creo,** I don't think so; **ya lo sabía,** I knew it; *véase tamb* **lo. 2 lo que ...,** what ...; **lo que pasa,** what happens. **3 lo cual ...,** which ...; **lo cual no se entiende,** which doesn't make sense. **4 lo de ...,** the affair *or* business of ...; **cuéntame lo del juicio,** tell me about the trial. **5 lo mío,** mine; **lo tuyo,** yours; *véase* **loísmo.**

loa *nf* **1** *(alabanza)* praise. **2** Lit eulogy.

loable *adj* praiseworthy, laudable.

loar *vtr* to praise.

loba *nf Zool* she-wolf; *fig* whore.

lobanillo *nm Med* cyst, wen.

lobato *nm Zool* wolf cub.

lobero,-a I *adj* wolfish, wolf. **II** *nm* wolf hunter.

lobezno *nm Zool* wolf cub.

lobo *nm Zool* wolf; **como boca de l.,** pitch-dark; *fig* **meterse en la boca del l.,** to put one's head in the lion's mouth; *fam* **el l. feroz,** the big bad wolf; *fam* **¡menos lobos!,** that's a tall story! ▪ **l. marino,** sea dog.

lóbrego,-a *adj* gloomy, murky.

lobreguez *nf* gloom, gloominess, murk.

lobular *adj* lobular.

lóbulo *nm* lobe.

lobuno,-a *adj* wolfish, wolflike, wolf.

local I *adj* local. **II** *nm* **1** *(recinto)* premises *pl,* site. **2** *(sede)* headquarters *pl.*

localidad *nf* **1** *(pueblo)* village, town. **2** Cin Teat *(lugar)* seat; *(billete)* ticket; **reserva de localidades,** (advanced) booking.

localista *adj* regional, local.

localización *nf* location, placing, siting.

localizar *vtr* **1** *(encontrar)* to locate, find, site. **2** *(fuego, dolor)* to localize.

locatario,-a *nm,f* tenant, occupant.

locatis *nmf fam* nutter, crackpot.

locaut *nm Ind* lockout.

loc. cit. *abr de* **loco citato,** loco citato, loc. cit., l.c.

loción *nf* lotion; **l. capilar,** hair restorer *or* lotion.

loco,-a I *adj* mad, crazy; **a lo l.,** carelessly, wildly; **l. de amor,** madly in love; **l. por los coches,** crazy about cars; **volverse l.,** to go mad; *fam* **l. de remate,** mad as a hatter; *fam* **¡ni l.!,** I'd sooner die!; *fam* **traer l. a algn,** to drive sb crazy. **II** *nm, f (hombre)* madman; *(mujer)* madwoman; **como (un) l.,** like crazy; **hacer el l.,** to act the fool. **III** *nf arg (afer minado)* queen.

locomoción *nf* locomotion.

locomotor,-a I *adj* locomotive; **fuerza locomotora,** locomotive power. **II** *nf* railway engine, locomotive.

locomotriz I *adj* locomotive. **II** *nf* railway engine.

locuacidad *nf* loquacity, talkativeness.

locuaz *adj* loquacious, talkative.

locución *nf* phrase, locution.

locuelo,-a *adj fam* madcap, nutty.

locura *nf* **1** *(enfermedad)* madness, insanity; **con l.,** madly; **¡qué l.!,** it's madness! **2** *(disparate)* lunacy, act of folly, crazy thing; **cometer** *or* **hacer una l.,** to do something foolish.

locutor,-a *nm, f Rad* announcer, commentator; *TV* newsreader.

locutorio *nm Rel* parlour, *US* parlor; *Rad* studio; *Tel* telephone booth; *(sala de visitas)* visiting room.

lodazal *nm* muddy place, mire.

LODE *nf abr de* **Ley Orgánica Reguladora del Derecho a la Educación**.

lodo *nm* mud; *fig* **cubrir de l. a algn,** to drag sb's name through the mud.

lodoso,-a *adj* muddy.

logarítmico,-a *adj* logarithmic.

logaritmo *nm* logarithm.

logia *nf* **1** *Arqui* loggia. **2** *(masónica)* lodge.

logicismo *nm Filos* logicism.

lógico,-a I *adj* logical; **era l. que ella se enfadara,** it stands to reason that she'd get angry. **II** *nm, f* logician. **III** *nf* logic; **no tiene l.,** there's no logic to it. ◆ **lógicamente** *adv* logically.

logístico,-a *Filos & Mil* **I** *adj* logistic. **II** *nf* logistics *sing or pl*.

logopeda *nmf* speech therapist.

logopedia *nf* speech therapy, logopaedics *sing*, *US* logopedics *sing*.

logotipo *nm* logotype.

logrado,-a I *pp de* **lograr**. **II** *adj* successful.

lograr I *vtr (gen)* to get, obtain; *(premio)* to win; *(ambición)* to achieve; *(deseo)* to fulfil, *US* fulfill; *(hacer algo)* to succeed; **logré que se quedara,** I managed to persuade her to stay. **II lograrse** *vr* to succeed, make it, do well.

logrero,-a *nm, f* **1** *(usurero)* moneylender. **2** *Am (gorrón)* scrounger.

logro *nm* **1** *(consecución)* achievement, accomplishment; *(éxito)* success. **2** *(lucro)* profit. **3** *(usura)* usury.

logroñés,-esa I *adj* of *or* from Logroño. **II** *nm,f* native *or* inhabitant of Logroño.

loísmo *nm Ling* incorrect use of **lo** *or* **los** as an indirect object instead of **le** *or* **les**.

loma *nf Geog* hill, hillock, rise.

lombardo,-a *adj & nm, f* Lombard; **col lombarda,** red cabbage.

lombriz *nf* worm, earthworm; **l. intestinal,** (intestinal) worm.

lomillería *nf SAm (tienda, aparejos)* saddlery.

lomo *nm* **1** *Anat* back. **2** *Culin* loin; **a lomo(s),** on the back; **l. (de cerdo),** pork loin; *fig* **doblar el l.,** to toil. **3** *(de libro)* spine.

lona *nf* **1** *Tex* canvas. **2** *Box* canvas.

loncha *nf* slice; **l. de bacon,** rasher.

lonche *nm Am* luncheon, snack.

lonchería *nf Am* snack bar.

londinense I *adj* of *or* from London. **II** *nmf* native *or* inhabitant of London.

Londres *n* London.

longanimidad *nf fml* forbearance.

longaniza *nf Culin* spicy (pork) sausage.

longevidad *nf* longevity.

longevo,-a *adj* long lived.

longitud *nf* **1** length; **dos metros de l.,** two metres long. ■ *Rad* **l. de onda,** wavelength; *Dep* **salto de l.,** long jump. **2** *Geog* longitude.

longitudinal *adj* longitudinal. ◆ **longitudinalmente** *adv* lengthways.

longui(s) *nm* **hacerse el l.,** to act dumb, keep one's trap shut.

lonja¹ *nf (loncha)* slice; **l. de bacon,** rasher.

lonja² *nf (edificio)* exchange; **l. de pescado,** fish market.

lontananza *nf Arte* background; **en l.,** in the distance.

loquería *nf Am* mental asylum, mental hospital.

loquero,-a I *nm,f* nurse in a mental asylum. **II** *nf Arg fam* madness.

lord *nm (pl* **lores***)* lord; *GB Parl* **Cámara de los Lores,** House of Lords.

lorenzo,-a *adj* coarse, uncouth.

loriga *nf Mil arc* coat of mail.

loro *nm* **1** *Orn* parrot. **2** *fam (mujer fea)* harpy, old hag.

lorza *nf Cost* tuck, pleat.

los¹ *art det mpl* the; **l. libros,** the books; **cierra l. ojos,** close your eyes; **esos son l. míos/tuyos,** these are mine/yours; **l. García,** the Garcías; *véase tamb* **el, les** y **lo**.

los² *pron pers mpl* **1** *(objeto directo) (ellos)* them; *(ustedes)* you; **¿l. has visto?,** have you seen them?; **mañana nos l. comeremos,** we will eat them tomorrow; **quiero que l. conozcas,** I want you to meet them. **2 l. que,** *(persona)* the ones who, those who; *(objeto)* the ones that, those that; **toma l. que quieras,** take whichever ones you want; *véase tamb* **les** y **loísmo**.

losa *nf* (stone) slab, flag, flagstone; **l. sepulcral,** tombstone; *fam* **estar bajo la l.,** to be six feet under.

loseta *nf* floor tile, wall tile.

LOT *nf abr de* **Ley de Ordenación Territorial**.

lota *nf (pez)* burbot.

lote *nm* **1** *(porción)* share, portion. **2** *Com* lot. ■ **l. de Navidad,** Christmas box *or* hamper. **3** *Inform* batch. **4** *fam* kiss; **darse el l.,** to pet.

lotería *nf* lottery; **jugar a la l.,** to play the lottery; **tocarle la l. a algn,** to win a prize in the lottery; *fig* **ser una l.,** to be a matter of luck, be a complete lottery.

lotero,-a *nm, f* lottery-ticket seller.

loto *nf Bot* lotus.

loza *nf* **1** *(cerámica)* pottery. **2** *(de cocina)* crockery.

lozanía *nf* **1** *(plantas)* lushness, luxuriance; *(flores)* freshness. **2** *(personas)* vigour, *US* vigor, robustness, liveliness.

lozano,-a *adj* **1** *(vegetales)* lush, fresh, luxuriant. **2** *(personas)* robust, lively.

Ltda. *abr de* **Limitada,** Limited, Ltd.

lubina *nf (pez)* bass.

lubricación *nf* lubrication.

lubricante I *adj* lubricating. **II** *nm* lubricant.

lubricar *vtr* to lubricate.

lubricidad *nf* **1** *(deslizamiento)* slipperiness. **2** *fig (lujuria)* lewdness.

lúbrico,-a *adj* **1** *(resbaladizo)* slippery. **2** *fig (lujurioso)* lewd.

lubrificación *nm* lubrication.

lubrificar *vtr* to lubricate.

lucense I *adj* of *or* from Lugo. **II** *nmf* native *or* inhabitant of Lugo.

lucero *nm* **1** *Astron* (bright) star; **l. del alba/de la tarde,** morning/evening star. **2** *(de un animal)* star.

lucidez *nf* lucidity.

lucido,-a I *pp de* lucir. **II** *adj* brilliant, splendid; *iron* **estar l.,** to be in a fine mess.

lúcido,-a *adj* lucid, clear.

luciente *adj* shining.

luciérnaga *nf Ent* glowworm.

Lucifer *nm* Lucifer.

lucimiento *nm* brilliance; **con l.,** brilliantly.

lucio *nm (pez)* pike.

lucir I *vtr* **1** *(iluminar)* to illuminate, light up. **2** *(exhibir)* to show off; *(cualidades, talento)* to display; *(ropas)* to sport; **ella lucía un modelito carísimo,** she was wearing a very expensive number. **II** *vi* **1** *(brillar)* to shine; *fig* **así le luce el pelo,** it serves him right. **2** *(aprovechar)* to profit from. **III** **lucirse** *vr* **1** *(hacer buen papel)* to do very well; *iron (hacer mal papel)* to look a real fool. **2** *fam (vestirse bien)* to dress up. **3** *(presumir)* to show off.

lucrar I *vtr* to gain. **II** **lucrarse** *vr* to (make a) profit.

lucrativo,-a *adj* lucrative, profitable.

lucro *nm* profit, gain; **afán de l.,** greed for money.

luctuoso,-a *adj* sad, mournful; **un accidente l.,** a tragic accident.

lucubración *nf* lucubration.

lucubrar *vtr* to lucubrate.

lúcumo *nm Am Bot* canistel.

lucha *nf* **1** fight, struggle. ▪ *Pol* **l. de clases,** class struggle. **2** *Dep* wrestling. ▪ **l. libre,** free-style wrestling.

luchador,-a I *adj* fighting, battling. **II** *nm, f* **1** *(combatiente)* fighter. **2** *Dep* wrestler.

luchar *vi* **1** *(combatir)* to fight, struggle; **luchad por la paz,** fight for peace. **2** *Dep* to wrestle.

lúdico,-a *adj* , **lúdrico,-a** *adj* relating to games, recreational.

luego I *adv* **1** *(después)* then, next, afterwards; **se quitó el sombrero, l. la chaqueta,** he took off his hat and then his jacket. **2** *(más tarde)* later (on); **déjalo para l.,** leave it for later; **¡hasta l.!,** so long!; **té veré l.,** I'll see you later. **3** **desde l.,** of course. **4** *Am (algunas veces)* sometimes. **II** *conj* therefore; **pienso, l. existo,** I think therefore I am.

lueguito *adv Am* immediately, at once.

lúes *nf Med* syphilis.

lugano *nm Orn* siskin.

lugar *nm* **1** *(sitio)* place, spot; **en l. de,** instead of; **en primer l.,** in the first place, firstly, first of all; **en tu l.,** if I were you; **sin l. a dudas,** no room for doubt; **tener l.,** to take place; *fig* **fuera de l.,** out of place; *fig* **l. común,** commonplace, platitude. **2** **dar l. a,** to cause, give rise to.

lugareño,-a I *adj* rural, village. **II** *nm, f* villager; *(hombre)* countryman; *(mujer)* countrywoman.

lugarteniente *nmf* lieutenant, deputy.

lúgubre *adj* gloomy, dismal, lugubrious.

Luisiana *n* Louisiana.

lujo *nm* luxury; **impuesto de l.,** luxury tax; **no puedo permitirme ese l.,** I just can't afford that.

lujoso,-a *adj* luxurious. ◆ **lujosamente** *adv* luxuriously.

lujuria *nf* **1** *(lascivia)* lechery, lust. **2** *(exceso)* profusion, exuberance.

lujuriar *vi* **1** *(pecar)* to succumb to the temptations of the flesh, lust (after). **2** *(aparearse)* to mate.

lujurioso,-a I *adj* lecherous, lustful. **II** *nm* lecher.

lumbago *nm Med* lumbago.

lumbar *adj Anat* lumbar.

lumbre *nf* **1** *(fuego)* fire. **2** *(resplandor)* brightness, glow. **3** *Arquit* light, skylight.

lumbrera *nf* luminary; *fig* luminary, eminence.

luminaria *nf* light, illumination.

luminiscencia *nf* luminiscence.

luminiscente *adj* luminiscent.

luminosidad *nf* brightness, luminosity.

luminoso,-a *adj* luminous; *fig* bright.

lumpen *nm* lumpenproletariat.

luna *nf* **1** *Astron* moon; *fig* **estar en la l.,** to be wool-gathering; *fig* **quedarse a la l. de Valencia,** to be left in the lurch; *fig* **vivir en la l.,** to have one's head in the clouds. ▪ **claro de l.,** moonlight; **l. creciente,** crescent *or* waxing moon; **l. llena,** full moon; **l. menguante,** waning moon; **l. nueva,** new moon; **media l.,** half moon, crescent; *fig* **l. de miel,** honeymoon. **2** *(vidrio)* window pane; *(espejo)* mirror. **3** *fam (talante)* mood; **tener lunas,** to be potty.

lunación *nf Astron* lunar month.

lunar I *adj Astron* lunar. **II** *nm* **1** *(redondel)* spot; *(en la piel)* mole, beauty spot; **vestido de lunares,** spotted dress. **2** *fig (defecto)* flaw, blemish.

lunático,-a I *adj* lunatic. **II** *nm, f* lunatic.

lunes *nm inv* Monday; **vendré el l.,** I'll come on Monday; *véase tamb* **viernes.**

lunfa *nm,* **lunfardo** *nm Ling* Buenos Aires slang.

lupa *nf* magnifying glass.

lúpulo *nm Bot* hop, hops *pl.*

lusitano,-a *adj & nm, f* **luso,-a** *adj & nm, f* **1** *Hist* Lusitanian. **2** *(portugués)* Portuguese.

lustrar *vtr* to polish; *(zapatos)* to shine.

lustre *nm* *(brillo)* shine, polish, lustre, *US* luster; *fig (esplendor)* splendour, *US* splendor, glory; **dar** *or* **sacar l. a algo,** to polish sth.

lustro *nm* five-year period.

lustroso,-a *adj* shiny, glossy.

luteranismo *nm Rel* Lutheranism.

luterano,-a *adj & nm, f Rel* Lutheran.

luto *nm* **1** *(vestido)* mourning; **ir de** *or* **llevar l.,** to be in mourning. **2** *fig* sorrow, grief.

luxación *nf Med* dislocation, luxation.

Luxemburgo *n* Luxembourg.

luxemburgués,-esa I *adj* Luxembourgian. **II** *nm, f* Luxembourger.

luz *nf* **1** *(gen)* light; **a la l. del día,** in broad daylight; **l. del sol/de la luna,** sunlight/moonlight; *fig* **a la l. de,** in the light of; *fig* **a todas luces,** obviously; *(parir) fig* **dar a l.,** to give birth to; *fig* **dar l. verde a,** to give the green light to; *fig* **sacar a la l.,** *(publicar)* to publish; *(revelar)* to bring to light; *fig* **salir a la l.,** *(publicarse)* to come out; *(descubrise)* to come to light; *fam fig* **entre dos luces,** tipsy. **2** *fam (electricidad)* electricity; **se ha ido la l.,** the lights have gone out. **3** *Arquit (abertura)* opening, window; *(de un puente)* span. **4** *(lámpara, vela)* light, lamp; *Aut* light. ▪ **luces de cruce,** dipped headlights; **luces de posición,** sidelights; **l. larga,** headlights *pl.* **5** *arg* money. **6** **luces,** *(cultura)* culture *sing; (inteligencia)* intelligence *sing,* **corto de l.,** dim-witted, **el Siglo de las L.,** the Age of Enlightenment. **7** **traje de luces,** *Taur* bullfighter's costume.

Luzbel *nm* Lucifer, Satan.

luzco *indic pres véase* **lucir.**

M

M, m ['eme] *nf (la letra)* M, m.

m 1 *abr de* **metro(s)** metre, metres, *US* meter, meters, m. **2** *abr de* **minuto(s)**, minute, minutes, min. **3** *abr de* **milla(s),** mile, miles.

m/ *abr de* **mi,** my.

maca *nf* **1** *(defecto)* flaw, blemish. **2** *(de una fruta)* bruise.

macabro,-a *adj* macabre.

macacinas *nfpl CAm* flat leather shoes.

macaco,-a¹ *adj Am* ugly, misshapen.

macaco,-a² *adj & nm,f Am* Chinese immigrant.

macaco³ *nm* **1** *Zool (mono)* macaque. **2** *Méx (coco)* bogeyman.

macadam *nm (pl* **macadams),** **macadán** *nm (pl* **macadanes)** macadam.

macana *nf* **1** *Am (palo)* club. **2** *Am (chapuza)* bad job, botched job, mess. **3** *Am (mentira)* lie; *(engaño)* trick. **4** *CAm Méx (azada)* hoe. **5** *Arg (trasto)* rubbish; **esta máquina es una m.,** this typewriter is useless. **6** *Arg (conversación latosa)* long boring conversation. **7** *Am (chal)* cotton shawl.

macanazo *nm Am* **1** *(golpe)* blow (with a club). **2** *fam (disparate)* nonsense, absurdity. **3** *fam (fastidio)* nuisance, bore.

macanear *vtr* **1** *Am (paparruchas)* to make up. **2** *Arg (chapuza)* to botch. **3** *Méx (tierra)* to hoe.

macanudo,-a *adj fam* great, terrific.

macaquear I *vtr CAm (robar)* to steal. **II** *vi Arg* to grimace, make faces.

macarra *arg* **I** *adj* vulgar, cheap. **II** *nm* pimp.

macarrón *nm* **1** *Culin* macaroon. **2** *Náut* stanchion.

macarrones *nmpl Culin* macaroni *sing*; **m. al gratén,** macaroni cheese.

macarrónico,-a *adj (lenguaje, estilo)* macaronic; **latín m.,** pig Latin.

macarse *vr (fruta)* to (start to) go bad.

macedonia *nf Culin* fruit salad.

macedonio,-a *adj & nm,f* Macedonian.

maceración *nf* maceration.

macerar *vtr* to macerate.

macero *nm* mace bearer.

maceta¹ *nf* **1** *(tiesto)* plant pot, flowerpot. **2** *Méx fam (cabeza)* head.

maceta² **I** *nf* **1** *(martillo)* mallet. **2** *Am (palo)* bat. **II** *adj Am* **1** *(caballo)* useless, slow. **2** *(persona)* slow-walking.

macetero *nm* flowerpot stand *or* holder.

macfarlán *nm,* **macferlán** *nm (abrigo)* long sleeveless coat.

machaca *nmf fam* dogsbody.

machacadora *nf* crusher, crushing machine.

machacar I *vtr* **1** *(triturar, aplastar)* to crush; *(moler)* to grind, crush. **2** *Mil (derrotar)* to crush, destroy; *fig (en una discusión)* to crush, flatten. **3** *fam (insistir mucho en)* to harp on about, go on about; **no machaques tanto el asunto,** stop going on about it. **4** *fam (estudiar con ahínco)* to swot up on, *US* grind away at. **II** *vi* **1** *fam (insistir mucho)* to harp on, go on; *fig* **machacando se aprende el oficio,** practice makes perfect; *fig* **m. en hierro frío,** to bang one's head against a brick wall. **2** *fam (estudiar con ahínco)* to swot, cram, *US* grind. **3** *vulg (masturbarse)* **machacársela,** to wank, beat one's meat.

machacón,-ona *fam* **I** *adj (repetitivo)* repetitious; *(pesado)* boring, tiresome. **II** *nm, f* **1** *(pesado)* bore, nuisance. **2** *(muy estudioso)* swot, *US* grind.

machaconería *nf fam (insistencia)* tiresome insistence.

machada *nf fam* **1** *(fanfarronada)* piece of bravado, showing off; **hacer una m.,** to show off. **2** *(necedad)* stupid thing.

machado *nm* hatchet.

machaje *nm Am* (herd *or* flock of) male animals *pl*.

machamartillo(a) *loc adv (con firmeza)* firmly; *(con obstinación)* obstinately; **católico a m.,** Catholic through and through.

machar I *vtr (machacar)* to grind, crush. **II** **macharse** *vr SAm* to get drunk.

machete *nm* machete.

machetero,-a *nm,f* **1** *(que desbroza)* path clearer. **2** *Agr (sugar) cane cutter.* **3** *Méx (trabajador)* worker. **4** *Méx (empollón)* swot.

machihembrado *nm Carp (ranura y lengüeta)* tongue and groove (joint); *(caja y espiga)* mortise and tenon (joint).

machihembrar *vtr Carp (ranura y lengüeta)* to join with a tongue and groove; *(caja y espiga)* to join with a mortise and tenon.

machinar I *vtr (maquinar)* to plot. **II** **machinarse** *vr CAm (amancebarse)* to live together.

machismo *nm* machismo, male chauvinism.

machista *adj & nmf* macho, male chauvinist.

macho I *adj* **1** *(animal, planta)* male; **una girafa m.,** a male giraffe. **2** *Téc (pieza)* male. **3** *fam (viril)* manly, virile, macho. **4** *(fuerte)* strong, robust; **vino m.,** strong wine. **II** *nm* **1** *(animal, planta)* male. ■ *Zool* **m. cabrío,** he-goat, billy goat. **2** *Zool (mulo)* he-mule. **3** *Téc (pieza)* male piece *or* part; *(de enchufe)* plug. ■ **m. de aterrajar** *or* **de roscar,** screw tap. **4** *Cost (de corchete)* hook. **5** *fam (hombre viril)* macho, he-man, tough guy; **¿qué te pasa, m.?,** what's up with you, man? **6** *Cuba Col Guat* unpolished grain of rice.

machón I *nm Arquit* buttress. **II** *adj Am (mujer)* mannish.

machote¹ *nm* **1** *Am (borrador)* rough draft; *(modelo)* example, model. **2** *Méx Min* reference mark.

machote² I *adj* manly, virile, macho. **II** *nm* macho, he-man, tough guy.

machucar *vtr (aplastar)* to crush.

machucho,-a *adj* **1** *(mayor, maduro)* middle-aged. **2** *(juicioso)* sensible, prudent.

maciega *nf* **1** *Am (mala hierba)* weed. **2** *Arg* grassland, prairie.

macilento,-a *adj (flaco)* gaunt, emaciated; *(pálido)* wan, pale; *(triste)* sad.

macis *nf inv (especia)* mace.

macizo,-a I *adj* **1** *(sólido)* solid; **de latón m.,** of solid brass. **2** *(persona)* solid, robust; *fam (atractivo)* smashing. **II** *nm* **1** *(masa sólida)* mass. ■ *Geog* **m. montañoso** *or* **de montañas,** mountain mass, massif. **2** *(de flores)* bed; *(de árboles)* clump. **3** *Arquit (de edificios)* group; *(de una pared)* stretch.

macramé *nm* macramé.

macro- *pref* macro-; **macroeconomía,** macroeconomics *sing*.

macro *nf Inform* macro.

macrobiótica *nf* macrobiotics *sing*.

macrobiótico,-a *adj* macrobiotic.

macrocosmo *nm* macrocosm.

macroscópico,-a *adj* macroscopic.

macuco,-a *Am* I *adj* 1 *(macanudo)* great, terrific. 2 *(taimado)* crafty, cunning, sly. II *nm* overgrown boy.

mácula *nf* 1 *(mancha)* stain, spot. 2 *(defecto)* flaw, blemish; **sin m.,** flawless.

macuto *nm* 1 *(morral)* knapsack, haversack. ■ *fam* **radio m.,** bush telegraph, grapevine. 2 *Cuba RD Ven* begging basket.

Madagascar *n* Madagascar.

madama *nf* 1 *fml* madam. 2 *SAm vulg (partera)* midwife.

madeja *nf (de lana etc)* hank, skein; *fig* **enredarse la m.,** to get complicated.

Madera *n* Madeira.

madera[1] *nm (vino)* Madeira (wine).

madera[2] *nf* 1 *(gen)* wood; *(de construcción)* timber, *US* lumber; **de m.,** wood, wooden; *fam* **¡toca m.!,** touch wood!, *US* knock on wood! ■ **m. contrachapada,** plywood; **m. dura,** hardwood; **m. fósil,** lignite. 2 *Zool (del casco de las caballerías)* horn, rind. 3 *Golf* wood. 4 *fig (disposición natural)* **tener buena m.,** to have what it takes; **tiene m. de músico,** he has the makings of a musician.

maderable *adj (árbol, bosque)* timber-yielding.

maderaje *nm*, **maderamen** *nm* 1 *(madera)* timber, wood. 2 *(conjunto de vigas etc)* timberwork, timbering, woodwork.

maderería *nf* timberyard, *US* lumberyard.

maderero,-a I *adj* timber, *US* lumber; **la industria maderera,** the timber industry. II *nm, f* timber *or US* lumber merchant.

madero *nm* 1 *(de construcción)* log, piece of timber. 2 *arg (policía)* cop; **los maderos,** the fuzz *pl*.

madona *nf Art Rel* Madonna.

madrás *nm Tex* madras.

madrastra *nf* stepmother.

madraza *nf* doting mother.

madre I *nf* 1 *(gen)* mother; **es m. de tres hijos,** she is a mother of three (children); *fam* **como su m. lo parió,** *(desnudo)* in one's birthday suit, stark-naked; *fam* **éramos ciento y la m.,** there were hundreds of us; *fam* **mentar la m. de algn,** to swear at sb; *vulg* **de puta m.,** bloody great *or* fantastic; *vulg ofens* **la m. que te parió *or* matriculó,** you bastard!; *vulg ofens* **¡tu m.!,** up yours! ■ **el día de la M.,** Mother's Day; **futura m.,** expectant mother, mother-to-be; **la reina m.,** the Queen Mother; **m. adoptiva,** adoptive mother; **m. alquilada,** surrogate mother; **m. de familia,** mother, housewife; **m. de leche,** wet nurse; **m. política,** mother-in-law; **m. soltera,** unmarried mother. 2 *Rel* mother. ■ **m. superiora,** mother superior. 3 *(de río)* bed; **salirse de m.,** *(río)* to burst its banks, overflow; *fig (persona) (excederse)* to go over the top, go too far; *fig* **sacar de m. a algn,** to make sb lose their patience. 4 *fig (orígen, raíz)* mother, origin, cradle; *fig* **ahí está la m. del cordero,** *(causa)* there's the real reason; *(dificultad)* there's the rub; *prov* **el ocio es la m. del vicio,** the Devil finds work for idle hands to do. ■ *(de empresa)* **casa m.,** head office; **la m. patria,** one's motherland; **lengua m.,** mother tongue. 5 *(del café)* grounds *pl*, dregs *pl*. 6 *(acequia)* main channel. II *interj* **¡m. de Dios!, ¡m. mía!,** good heavens!

madreperla *nf* 1 *(ostra)* pearl oyster 2 *(nácar)* mother-of-pearl.

madrépora *nf Zool* white coral, madrepore.

madreselva *nf Bot* honeysuckle.

Madrid *n* Madrid

madrigal *nm Lit Mús* madrigal.

madriguera *nf* 1 *(de conejo)* burrow, hole; *(de zorro)* den, lair; *(de tejón)* set. 2 *fig (de maleantes)* den, hideout.

madrileño,-a I *adj* of *or* from Madrid, Madrilenian. II *nm, f* native *or* inhabitant of Madrid, Madrilenian.

Madriles *nmpl fam* **Los M.,** Madrid.

madrina *nf* 1 *(de bautizo)* godmother. 2 *(de boda)* ≈ bridesmaid. 3 *(protectora)* protectress.

madrinazgo *nm* role of godmother *or* protectress.

madroñal *nm* grove of strawberry trees *or* arbutus.

madroño *nm Bot* strawberry tree.

madrugada *nf* 1 dawn; **de m.,** at daybreak. 2 early morning; **las tres de la m.,** (at) three o'clock in the morning.

madrugador,-a I *adj* early rising. II *nm, f* early riser.

madrugar *vi* 1 to get up early; *prov* **no por mucho m. amanece más temprano,** time must take its course. 2 *fam fig (adelantarse)* to get there first.

madrugón *nm fam* **darse *or* pegarse un m.,** to get up unusually early, get up very early.

maduración *nf (fruta, verdura)* ripening; *(queso, vino)* maturing

madurar I *vtr* 1 *(vino, queso, persona)* to mature; *(fruta)* to ripen. 2 *fig (un plan)* to think out. II *vi* 1 *(persona)* to mature. 2 *(fruta)* to ripen.

madurativo,-a *adj* 1 maturing. 2 *(fruta)* ripening.

madurez *nf* 1 maturity. 2 *(de la fruta)* ripeness.

maduro,-a *adj* 1 mature; **de edad madura,** middle-aged. 2 *(fruta)* ripe.

maese *nm arc* master.

maestranza *nf Mil* 1 arsenal. 2 *(personal)* staff of an arsenal.

maestrazgo *nm Hist* 1 *(dignidad)* office of the grand master of a military order. 2 *(jurisdicción)* territory under a grand master's jurisdiction.

maestre *nm (de una orden militar)* master.

maestría *nf* mastery, skill.

maestro,-a I *adj* 1 *(excelente)* excellent; **llave maestra,** master key; **obra maestra,** masterpiece. 2 *(principal)* main. ■ **pared maestra,** load-bearing wall. II *nm, f* 1 *Educ* teacher. ■ **m. de escuela,** schoolteacher. 2 *(especialista)* master; **es un m. de la escultura,** he is a master of sculpture. ■ **m. de ceremonias,** master of ceremonies; **m. de obras,** foreman. 2 *Mús* maestro. 3 *Taur* matador.

mafia *nf* mafia, maffia.

mafioso,-a I *adj* of *or* relating to the mafia. II *nm, f* member of the mafia, mafioso.

maganzón,-ona *Am fam* I *adj (holgazán)* lazy. II *nm, f* lazy person.

magdalena *nf Culin* bun, cake.

Magdalena *nf* Magdalene; **estar hecho *or* llorar como una M.,** to cry one's eyes out.

magia *nf* magic; **por arte de m.,** as if by magic.

magiar *adj & nmf* Magyar.

mágico,-a *adj* 1 magic, magical. 2 *fig (maravilloso)* wonderful, fascinating.

magín *nm fam* imagination; **ni se me pasó por el m.,** it didn't even cross my mind, it never entered my head.

magisterio *nm* teaching.

magistrado,-a *nm, f* judge.

magistral *adj* 1 *Educ* of *or* relating to teaching. 2 *(excelente)* masterly; **un tono m.,** a magisterial tone; **una jugada m.,** a master stroke.

magistratura *nf* magistracy; **la M. de Trabajo,** ≈ industrial tribunal.

magma *nm Geol* magma.

magnanimidad *nf* magnanimity.

magnánimo,-a *adj* magnanimous.

magnate *nm* magnate, tycoon; **un m. de la prensa,** a press baron.

magnesia *nf* magnesia.

magnésico,-a *adj* magnesic.

magnesio *nm Quím* magnesium.

magnético,-a *adj* magnetic.

magnetismo *nm* magnetism.

magnetizar *vtr* **1** *(imantar)* to magnetize. **2** *(hipnotizar)* to hypnotize.

magneto *nm* magneto.

magnetofón *nm*, **magnetófono** *nm* tape recorder.

magnetofónico,-a *adj* magnetic.

magnicida *nmf* assassin.

magnicidio *nm* assassination.

magnificar *vtr* **1** to praise, extol. **2** *fig* to magnify.

magnificiencia *nf* **1** *(grandiosidad)* magnificence, grandeur. **2** *(generosidad)* generosity.

magnífico,-a *adj* magnificent, splendid.

magnitud *nf* magnitude, dimension; **de primera m.,** of the first order.

magno,-a *adj lit* great. ■ **aula magna,** main amphitheatre; **Carta Magna,** Magna Carta.

magnolia *nf Bot* magnolia.

mago,-a *nm,f* wizard, magician. ■ **los tres Reyes Magos,** the Three Wise Men, the Three Kings.

magrear *vtr vulg* to grope.

magreo *nm vulg* groping.

magro,-a I *adj* **1** *(sin grasa)* lean. **2** *(pobre)* meagre, *US* meager. **II** *nm (de cerdo)* lean meat. **III** *nf* slice of ham.

maguey *nm* **1** *Am Bot* maguey. **2** *Méx fig (embriaguez)* drunkenness.

magulladura *nf* bruise, contusion.

magullar I *vtr* to bruise, damage. **II magullarse** *vr* to get bruised, get damaged.

mahometanismo *nm Rel* Mohammedanism.

mahometano,-a *adj & nm,f Rel* Mohammedan, Muslim.

mahonesa *nf véase* **mayonesa.**

mai *nm arg (porro)* joint.

maillot *nm* **1** *(bañador)* (lady's) swimming costume. **2** *Dep* shirt.

maitines *nmpl lgCat* matins; **tocar a m.,** to ring to matins.

maíz *nm* maize, *US* corn. ■ **palomitas de m.,** popcorn *sing.*

maizal *nm* field of maize or *US* corn.

majada *nf* **1** *(corral)* sheepfold. **2** *(estiércol)* dung. **3** *Am (rebaño)* herd, flock.

majaderear *Am* **I** *vtr* to pester, bother, annoy. **II** *vi* to be a nuisance or pest.

majadería *nf* silly thing, absurdity; **decir majaderías,** to talk nonsense.

majadero,-a I *adj* foolish, stupid. **II** *nm,f* fool, idiot.

majador,-a I *adj* crushing, grinding. **II** *nm, f* crusher, grinder.

majar *vtr* to crush, grind.

majara, majareta *fam* **I** *adj* loony, nutty; **volverse m.,** to go crazy. **II** *nmf* loony, nut.

majestad *nf* **1** *(título)* Majesty; **Su M.,** *(usted)* Your Majesty; *(él, ella)* His or Her Majesty. **2** *(majestuosidad)* grandeur, majesty.

majestuosidad *nf* majesty, grandeur, stateliness.

majestuoso,-a *adj* majestic, stately.

majo,-a *adj (bonito)* pretty, nice; *fam (simpático)* nice; **tiene un hijo muy m.,** she's got a lovely little boy; *fam* **anda, m., dame un besito,** come on, darling, give me a little kiss.

majuelo *nm Bot* hawthorn.

mal I *nm* **1** evil, wrong; **el bien y el m.,** good and evil, right and wrong. **2** *(daño)* harm; **del m. el menos,** the lesser of two evils; **el m. está en que ...,** the problem is that ...; **m. menor,** minor evil; **no le deseo ningún m.,** I don't wish

him any harm; *prov* **no hay m. que por bien no venga,** every cloud has a silver lining. **3** *(enfermedad)* illness, disease. **4** *CAm Per (epilepsia)* epilepsy. **5** *CAm Per (paletaia)* fit. **II** *adj* bad; **un m. año,** a bad year; *véase tamb* **malo,-a III** *adv* badly, wrong; **caer m.,** to create a bad impression; **el actor lo hizo bastante m.,** the actor gave a rather poor performance; **encontrarse m.,** *(enfermo)* to feel ill; *(desplazado)* to feel uncomfortable; **ir de m. en peor,** to go from bad to worse; **m. que bien,** one way or another; **menos m. que ...,** it's a good job (that) ...; **no está (nada) m.,** it is not bad (at all); **no estaría m. un baño en la playa,** I fancy a swim in the sea; *(sabor)* **saber m.,** to taste bad; *fig* **me sabe m.,** I feel sorry about it; **sentar m.,** *(comida)* to disagree with; *fig (molestar)* to take badly; **su respuesta me sentó muy m.,** I didn't like his reply at all; **te oigo/veo (muy) m.,** I can hardly hear/see you; **tomar a m.,** *(enfadarse)* to take badly; **no lo tomes a m.,** don't get me wrong.

malabar *adj* **juegos malabares,** juggling *sing.*

malabarismo *nm* juggling; **hacer malabarismos,** to juggle.

malabarista *nmf* juggler.

malaca *nf Am* malacca cane.

malacitano,-a *adj & nm,f véase* **malagueño.**

malacostumbrado,-a *adj* spoiled.

malacostumbrar *vtr* to spoil.

málaga *nm (vino)* Malaga wine.

malagueño,-a I *adj* of or from Malaga. **II** *nm,f* native or inhabitant of Malaga. **III** *nf Mús* Spanish music and dance similar to the **fandango.**

malagueta *nf* allspice.

malandanza *nf* misfortune.

malandrín,-ina *hum* **I** *adj* malicious, wicked. **II** *nm, f* scoundrel, rogue.

malapata *fam* **I** *nf (mala suerte)* bad luck; *(falta de gracia)* lack of charm. **II** *nmf (patoso)* clumsy person; *(gafe)* jinx.

malaquita *nf Min* malachite.

malaria *nf Med* malaria.

malasombra *nmf (pelma)* pest, nuisance, drag; *(patoso)* clumsy person.

malatoba *nm Am Zool* red cockerel or rooster.

malavenido,-a *nm,f* incompatible; **estar malavenidos,** to be in disagreement.

malaventura *nf véase* **desventura.**

malaventurado,-a *adj & nm,f véase* **desventurado,-a.**

Malawi *n* Malawi.

malawiano,-a *adj & nm,f* Malawian.

malayo,-a I *adj* Malayan, Malay. **II** *nm, f (persona)* Malayan, Malay. **III** *nm (idioma)* Malay.

Malaysia *n* Malaysia.

malbaratar *vtr (productos)* to undersell; *(dinero)* to squander.

malcarado,-a *adj* grim-faced.

malcasado,-a *adj* **1** *(infeliz)* unhappily married. **2** *(infiel)* unfaithful. **3** *(con persona inferior)* married below one's station.

malcomer *vi* to eat badly or poorly.

malcontento,-a *adj & nm,f véase* **descontento,-a.**

malcriado,-a I *adj* ill-mannered, ill-bred, uncivil. **II** *nm,f* ill-mannered or uncivil person.

malcriar *vtr* to spoil.

maldad *nf* **1** *(gen)* badness, evil. **2** *(acción perversa)* evil or wicked thing; **cometer maldades,** to do evil or wrong. **3** *fam (travesura)* mischief; **hacer maldades,** to get up to mischief.

maldecir I *vtr* to curse; **maldijo su suerte,** she cursed her luck. **II** *vi* **1** *(blasfemar)* to curse. **2** to speak ill; **maldice de su familia,** he speaks ill of his family.

maldiciente I *adj* **1** *(que se queja)* grumbling, always complaining. **2** *(malhablado)* foul-mouthed. **II** *nmf* grumbler, complainer, moaner.

maldición I *nf* curse. **II** *interj* damnation!

maldito,-a *adj* **1** *(embrujado)* damned, cursed; **¡maldita sea!,** damn it! **2** *fam (molesto)* damned, bloody; **estos malditos zapatos me están matando,** these bloody shoes are killing me.

Maldivas *npl* **las M.,** the Maldive Islands.

maldivo,-a *adj & nm,f* Maldivan.

maleabilidad *nf* malleability.

maleable *adj* malleable.

maleante *adj & nmf* delinquent, criminal.

malear I *vtr fig* to corrupt, pervert. **II malearse** *vr* to go bad; *(pervertirse)* to become corrupted.

malecón *nm* **1** *(dique)* sea wall. **2** *(atracadero)* pier, jetty.

maledicencia *nf* evil talk.

maleducado,-a I *adj* bad-mannered. **II** *nm, f* bad-mannered person.

maleficio *nm* *(hechizo)* curse, spell.

maléfico,-a *adj* evil, harmful.

malentendido *nm* misunderstanding.

malestar *nm* **1** *(molestia)* discomfort; **tengo m. general,** I don't feel well. **2** *fig (inquietud)* uneasiness; **hay un m. general en el país,** there is (a feeling of) unrest throughout the country.

maleta¹ I *nf* **1** suitcase, case; **hacer la m.,** to pack one's things or case. **2** *Am (hatillo)* bundle. **3** *Col Cuba PR hum (joroba)* hump. **II** *nm fam (persona)* bungler.

maleta² *adj* **1** *Am (malvado)* wicked. **2** *CAm fam (despreciable)* despicable, worthless.

maletero *nm* **1** *(mozo)* porter; *(fabricante)* suitcase maker; *(vendedor)* suitcase seller. **2** *Aut* boot, *US* trunk.

maletilla *nm Taur* trainee matador.

maletín *nm* briefcase.

malevolencia *nf* malevolence.

malévolo,-a *adj* malevolent.

maleza *nf* **1** *(arbustos)* thicket, undergrowth. **2** *(malas hierbas)* weeds *pl.*

malformación *nf Med* malformation.

malgache *adj & nmf* Madagascar.

malgastador,-a I *adj* squandering, wasteful. **II** *nm, f* spendthrift, squanderer.

malgastar *vtr & vi* to waste, squander.

malhablado,-a I *adj* foul-mouthed. **II** *nm, f* foul-mouthed person.

malhadado,-a *adj lit* ill-fated.

malhaya *interj arc* damn!, curse it!

malhechor,-a I *adj* criminal. **II** *nm, f* wrongdoer, criminal.

malherir *vtr* to wound seriously, injure badly.

malhumor *nm* bad temper or mood; **estoy de m.,** I am in a bad temper or mood.

malhumorado,-a *adj* bad-tempered, cross.

Mali *n* Mali.

malicia *nf* **1** *(mala intención)* malice, maliciousness, spite. **2** *(astucia)* cunning, craftiness, slyness. **3** *(maldad)* badness, evil, evilness. **4** *(sospecha)* suspicion.

maliciar *vtr,* **maliciarse** *vr* to feel suspicious about, have one's suspicions about.

malicioso,-a I *adj* malicious, spiteful. **II** *nm,f* malicious or spiteful person.

maliense *adj & nmf* Malian.

malignidad *nf* malignity.

maligno,-a I *adj* malignant; **un tumor m.,** a malignant tumor. **II el m.** *nm Rel* the devil.

malintencionado,-a I *adj* ill-intentioned. **II** *nm, f* ill-intentioned person.

malla *nf* **1** *(red)* mesh. ▪ **m. de alambre,** wire netting. **2** *(prenda)* leotard. **3** *Am (bañador)* swimsuit, swimming costume.

mallo *nm* **1** *(mazo)* mallet. **2** *Dep (juego)* croquet; *(terreno)* croquet lawn.

Mallorca *n* Majorca.

mallorquín,-ina *adj & nm,f* Majorcan.

malmirado,-a *adj* **1** ill-considered. **2** *(desconsiderado)* inconsiderate.

malo,-a I *adj véase tamb* **mal. 1** *(gen)* bad; **estar a malas,** to be on bad terms; **hace mucho que no me llama, ¡m.!,** he hasn't rung for ages, it's a bad sign; **un año m.,** a bad year; **por las malas,** by force; *prov* **más vale m. conocido que bueno por conocer,** better the devil you know than the one you don't know. **2** *(persona) (malvado)* wicked, bad; *(travieso)* naughty; **ser m.,** to be wicked or bad; **no seas m.,** don't be naughty. **3** *(cosa) (de baja calidad)* bad, poor, cheap; *(falso)* false; **una mala canción/comida,** a poor song/meal; **un diamante m.,** a false diamond. **4** *(perjudicial)* harmful; **el tabaco es m.,** tobacco is harmful; **ser m. para ...,** not to be any good for .... **5** *(difícil)* difficult, hard; **una montaña mala de escalar,** a difficult mountain to climb; **lo m. es que ...,** the problem is that .... **6** *(enfermo)* ill, sick; **estar m.,** to be sick; *fam* **ponerse m.,** *(enfermar)* to fall ill; *(estropearse)* to go bad; *euf* **estar mala,** to have a period. **II** *nm, f fam* **el m. (de la película),** the baddy or villain. ◆ **malamente** *adv fam* **1** *(mal)* badly. **2** *(apenas)* hardly.

maloca *nf SAm* **1** *(invasión)* invasion and pillage of Indian territory. **2** *(ataque)* Indian raid.

malogrado,-a I *adj* **1** *pp* **de malograr. II** *adj* **1** *(desaprovechado)* wasted. **2** *(difunto)* ill-fated; **el m. James Dean,** the ill-fated James Dean.

malograr I *vtr* to waste. **II malograrse** *vr* **1** to fail, fall through; **las cosechas se han malogrado,** the crops have been ruined. **2** *(persona)* to die young.

maloliente *adj* foul-smelling, stinking, smelly.

malón *nm* **1** *Am Hist* Indian raid. **2** *Am (alborotadores)* group of rowdies. **3** *SAm (mala pasada)* dirty trick. **4** *SAm (visita inesperada)* surprise visit.

maloquear *vi* **1** *Am* to make a raid. **2** *SAm (atacar)* to attack; *(sorprender)* to make a surprise attack. **3** *SAm (comerciar de contrabando)* to smuggle.

malparado,-a *adj* **salir m.,** to end up in a sorry state, come off badly.

malpensado,-a I *adj* nasty-minded. **II** *nm,f* nasty-minded person; **ser un m.,** to have a twisted mind.

malquerencia *nf* **1** *(antipatía)* dislike. **2** *(malevolencia)* malevolence.

malquistar *vtr* **m. a algn contra algn,** to set sb against sb else.

malsano,-a *adj* unhealthy, bad; **una mente malsana,** a sick mind.

malsonante *adj* **1** *(cacofónico)* ill-sounding. **2** *(grosero)* rude, offensive; **palabras malsonantes,** foul language.

Malta *n* Malta.

malta *nf (cebada)* malt.

malteado,-a I *adj* malted. **II** *nm (operación)* malting.

maltés,-a *adj & nm,f* Maltese.

maltón,-ona *adj Am* big for its age.

maltraer *vi* **llevar or traer a algn a m.,** to give sb a hard time, ill-treat sb.

maltraído,-a *adj Am* shabby, untidy.

maltratar *vtr* to ill-treat, mistreat.

maltrato *nm* ill-treatment, mistreatment.

maltrecho,-a *adj* in a sorry state, wrecked.

maltusianismo *nm* Malthusianism.

maltusiano,-a *adj & nm,f* Malthusian.

malucho,-a I *adj fam* not very well, poorly, off-colour, *US* off-color.

malva I *adj inv* mauve. II *nm (color)* mauve. III *nf Bot* mallow; **como una m.**, as quiet as a mouse; *fam* **criar malvas**, to be pushing up the daisies.

malvado,-a I *adj* evil, wicked. II *nm,f* villain, evil person.

malvasía *nf* 1 *Bot* variety of sweet grape. 2 *(vino)* dessert wine made with these grapes.

malvavisco *nm Bot* marshmallow.

malvender *vtr* to sell at a loss.

malversación *nf* misappropriation, embezzlement.

malversador,-a I *adj* embezzling. II *nm,f* embezzler.

malversar *vtr* to misappropriate, embezzle.

Malvinas *npl* **las (Islas M.)**, the Falkland Islands.

malvivir *vi* to live very badly.

mamá *nf fam* mum, mummy.

mama *nf* 1 *Anat (de mujer)* breast. 2 *Zool* udder. 3 *fam (mamá)* mum, mummy.

mamada *nf* 1 suck, sucking; *(bebé)* feed. 2 *vulg (felatio)* blow job. 3 *Am (ganga)* bargain. 4 *Arg Urug fam (embriaguez)* drunkenness.

mamadera *nf Am* feeding bottle.

mamado,-a *adj vulg* 1 *(borracho)* plastered. 2 *(fácil)* (dead) easy.

mamar I *vtr (leche)* to suck; *fig* to grow up with. II **mamarse** *vr fam (emborracharse)* to get pissed *or* drunk.

mamario,-a *adj* mammary.

mamarrachada *nf fam* 1 *(acción)* ridiculous action, stupid thing to do. 2 *(bodrio)* dead loss.

mamarracho,-a *nm,f fam* 1 *(persona)* ridiculous-looking person, mess, sight; **¡vaya m. está hecho!**, what a sight he looks! 2 *(obra)* mess, sight.

mambo *nm Mús* mambo.

mameluco *nm* 1 *Hist* Mameluke. 2 *fig* fool, idiot, dimwit. 3 *Am (prenda)* romper-suit.

mamífero,-a I *adj* mammalian, mammal. II *nm* mammal.

mamografía *nf Med* mammography.

mamola *nf* 1 chuck under the chin. 2 *fam* **dar** *or* **hacer la m. a algn**, to make a sucker out of sb.

mamón,-ona I *adj (que aún mama)* unweaned. II *nm* 1 *vulg ofens* pillock, prick, wally. 2 *Bot (chupón)* sucker. 3 *Am Bot* Spanish lime. 4 *Am fam (borracho)* drunkard, drunk. 5 *Méx* spongecake.

mamotreto *nm* 1 *(libro)* great big thick book. 2 *(armatoste)* monstrosity.

mampara *nf (cancel)* screen.

mamporro *nm fam (bofetada)* punch, clout; *(accidente)* bump.

mampostería *nf* masonry, rubblework.

mampostero-a *nm,f* stonemason.

mampuesto *nm Am* gun rest.

mamut *nm Zool* mammoth.

mana *nf* 1 *Am (maná)* manna. 2 *CAm Col (manantial)* spring, fountain.

maná *nm Rel* manna.

manada *nf* 1 *Zool (de vacas, elefantes)* herd; *(de ovejas)* flock; *(de lobos, perros)* pack; *(de leones)* pride. 2 *fam (multitud)* crowd, mob; **en manadas**, in crowds.

manager *nmf Dep Mús* manager.

managüense I *adj* of *or* from Managua. II *nmf* native *or* inhabitant of Managua.

manantial *nm* spring, fountain; *fig (orígen)* source, origin, fount; **agua de m.**, spring water.

manar I *vi* 1 to flow, run **(de,** from). 2 *fig* to abound in. II *vtr* to run with, flow with; **la herida manaba sangre**, blood flowed from his wound.

manatí *nm Zool* manatee.

manazas *nmf inv fam* clumsy person.

mancar I *vtr* to maim, cripple. II **mancarse** *vr* to become maimed *or* crippled.

mancarrón,-ona *Am* I *adj (persona)* disabled. II *nm, f (caballo viejo)* old nag.

manceba *nf* concubine.

mancebo *nm arc* 1 *(muchacho)* young man. 2 single man, bachelor.

Mancha *n Geog* **La M.**, La Mancha; **el Canal de la M.**, the English Channel.

mancha *nf* 1 stain, spot. ■ **m. solar**, sunspot; **m. de tinta/ vino**, ink/wine stain. 2 *fig (defecto)* blemish; **sin m.**, unblemished.

manchado,-a 1 *pp de* **manchar**. 2 *adj* dirty, stained; **un caballo m.**, a spotted horse.

manchar I *vtr* to stain, dirty; *fig* to stain, blemish. II **mancharse** *vr* to get dirty.

manchego,-a I *adj* of *or* from La Mancha. II *nm,f* native *or* inhabitant of La Mancha. III *nm* cheese from La Mancha.

manchón *nm fam* large spot *or* stain.

mancilla *nf* stain, blemish.

mancillar *vtr (honor, fama)* to dishonour, *US* dishonor, stain.

manco,-a I *adj* 1 *(sin un brazo)* one-armed; *(sin brazos)* armless. 2 *(sin una mano)* one-handed; *(sin manos)* handless. 3 *fig (defectuoso)* defective, faulty; *fam* **no ser m.,** *(persona)* to be no fool; *(cosas)* to be no little thing. II *nm, f* 1 one-armed *or* armless person. 2 one-handed *or* handless person.

mancomún (de) *loc adv* by common consent.

mancomunar *vtr*, **mancomunarse** *vr (esfuerzos, dinero, etc)* to put together.

mancomunidad *nf* community, association.

mancornas *nfpl Am* cufflinks.

mandado,-a I *pp de* **mandar**. II *nm (recado)* order, errand; **hacer un m.**, to run an errand. III *nm,f (persona)* person who carries out an order.

mandador *nm Am* whip.

mandamás *nmf (pl mandamases) fam* bigwig, boss.

mandamiento *nm* 1 *(orden)* order, command. 2 *Jur* warrant, mandate. 3 *Rel* Commandment. ■ **los Diez Mandamientos**, the Ten Commandments.

mandanga *nf fam* 1 *(pachorra)* sluggishness, indolence. 2 *(hachís)* marihuana, hash. 3 **mandangas,** *(patrañas)* stories; **no me vengas con m.**, who do you think you're trying to kid?

mandar I *vtr* 1 *(ordenar)* to order; **la ley manda que ...**, the law stipulates that ...; **le mandó venir**, he ordered him to come; *fam* **¿mandé?**, pardon?; *fam* **me mandó a paseo**, she sent me packing, she told me to get lost. 2 *(grupo)* to lead, be in charge *or* command of; *Mil (ejército)* to command; **aquí mando yo**, I'm the boss here; **¿quién manda aquí?**, who is in charge here? 3 *(enviar)* to send; **lo mandé a comprar caramelos**, I sent him to buy some sweets; **m. algo por correo**, to send sth, send sth by the post; **m. recuerdos**, to send regards. 4 *Am (convidar)* to invite; **le mandó a sentarse**, he offered him a seat. 5 *Am (lanzar)* to throw, hurl. II **mandarse** *vr Am (irse)* to go, leave.

mandarín *nm Hist* mandarin.

mandarina *nf Bot* mandarin (orange), tangerine.

mandarinero *nm*, **mandarino** *nm Bot* mandarin orange tree, tangerine tree.

mandatario,-a *nm,f* 1 *Jur* mandatory. 2 *Pol* president; **el primer m. de la nación**, the head of state.

mandato *nm* 1 *(orden)* order, command. 2 *Jur* writ, warrant. ■ **m. judicial**, warrant. 3 *Pol (legislatura)* mandate, term of office.

mandíbula *nf* jaw; *fam* **reír a m. batiente**, to laugh one's head off.

mandil *nm* 1 (*prenda*) apron. 2 (*bayeta*) grooming cloth. 3 *Arg Chi* (*gualdarapa*) horse blanket.

mandioca *nf Bot* manioc, tapioca.

mando *nm* 1 (*autoridad*) command, control; **ejercer el m., ester al m., tener el m.,** to be in charge *or* control; **entregar el m.,** to hand over command; **tomar el m.,** to take command. 2 (*mandato*) term of office. 3 (*gobernante*) authorities *pl*, those in command *pl*; **los mandos del ejército,** high-ranking army officers. ■ **alto m.,** high command. 4 *Téc* (*control*) controls *pl*. ■ **cuadro** *or* **tablero de mandos,** *Av* instrument panel; *Aut* dashboard; **m. a distancia,** remote control; **palanca de m.,** *Téc* control lever; (*de avión, videojuego*) joystick.

mandoble *nm* 1 two-handed blow *or* swordstroke. 2 (*espada*) large sword. 3 *fam* (*reprensión*) telling off.

mandolina *nf Mús* mandolin, mandoline.

mandón,-ona I *adj fam* bossy, domineering. II *nm,f fam* bossy *or* domineering person. III *nm Am* (mine) foreman.

mandrágora *nf*, **mandrágula** *nf Bot* mandrake.

mandril *nm* 1 *Zool* mandrill. 2 *Téc* mandrel.

manduca *nf*, **manducatoria** *nf*, **manduque** *nm fam* grub, chow, nosh.

manducar *vtr & vi fam* to nosh.

maneador *nm Am* leather thong, rein.

manecilla *nf* (*de reloj*) hand.

manejabilidad *nf* manageability.

manejable *adj* (*gen*) manageable; (*herramienta*) easy-to-use; (*coche*) manoeuvrable, *US* maneuvrable.

manejar I *vtr* 1 (*manipular*) to handle, operate; *fig* to handle, deal with; **maneja muy bien las tijeras,** she's very handy with a pair of scissors; **manejó la situación muy bien,** he dealt with the situation very cleverly. 2 (*dirigir*) to run, manage; **ella sola maneja la empresa,** she runs the company on her own. 3 *fig* (*dominar*) to domineer, boss about, push around; **Rosa maneja a su marido,** Rosa bosses her husband about. 4 *Am Aut* (*un coche*) to drive. II **manejarse** *vr* to manage; *fam* **manejárselas,** to manage by oneself; **ya te las manejarás,** you'll manage somehow.

manejo *nm* 1 (*uso*) handling, use; **de fácil m.,** easy-to-use. 2 *Téc* (*de una máquina*) running, operation. 3 *fig* (*de un negocio*) management. 4 *fig* tricks *pl*, trickery. 5 *Am Aut* (*de un coche*) driving.

manera *nf* 1 way, manner; **a m. de,** by way of; **a la m. de,** in the manner of; **a mi/tu m.,** my/your way, in my/your own way; **de cualquier m.,** (*mal*) carelessly, any old how; (*con facilidad*) easily; (*en cualquier caso*) in any case; **de esta/esa m.,** in this/that way; **de la m. que sea,** (*pase lo que pase*) whatever happens; (*no importa como*) any way you *etc* like; **de mala m.,** (*mal*) badly; (*groseramente*) rudely; **de m. que,** so; **te lo advertí, de m. que no te quejes,** I warned you, so don't complain now; **de ninguna m.,** in no way, certainly not; **de otra m.,** (*si no es así*) otherwise; (*de distinto modo*) in a different way; **de tal m. que,** in such a way that; **de todas maneras,** anyway, at any rate, in any case; **de una m.** *or* **de otra,** one way or another; **en cierta m.,** in a way; **en gran m.,** extremely; **sobre m.,** very much; **es mi m. de ser,** that's the way I am; **no hay m.,** it's impossible; **¡qué** *or* **vaya m. de tomarnos el pelo!,** that's a fine way to tease us!; **¡y de qué m.!,** and how! 2 (*clase*) kind, sort. 3 **maneras,** manners; **con buenas m.,** politely.

maneto,-a *adj Am* with deformed hands, maimed in the hand(s).

manferlán *nm véase* **macfarlán.**

manga *nf* 1 sleeve; **de m. corta/larga,** short-/long-sleeved; **en mangas de camisa,** in shirtsleeves; **sin mangas,** sleeveless; *fig* **hacer mangas y capirotes,** to act arbitrarily; *fig* **hacer un corte de mangas a algn,** to give sb a V-sign; *fig* **m. por hombro,** messy and untidy; *fig* **ser de** *or* **tener la m. ancha,** (*ser poco estricto*) to be broadminded; (*ser benevolente*) to be easy-going; *fig* **sacarse algo de la m.,** to pull sth out of one's hat. 2 (*manguera*) hose, hosepipe. ■ **m. de riego,** (*de jardín*) garden *or* watering hose; (*de bombero*) fire hose. 3 (*red*) casting net. ■ **m. de mariposas,** butterfly net. 4 *Geog* **m. de mar,** arm of the sea. 5 *Náut* breadth. 6 *Aeronáut* windsock, wind sleeve. 7 *Meteor* (*de agua*) waterspout; (*de viento*) whirlwind. 8 *Dep* leg, round; *Bridge* game; **ir a m.,** to go to game. 9 *Culin* (*filtro*) muslin strainer; (*de pastelero*) icing bag, forcing bag. 10 *Am* (*calle*) entrance to a corral. 11 *Am* (*turba*) crowd, mob. 12 *CAm* (*manta*) (sackcloth) blanket. 13 *Méx* (*prenda*) oilskin poncho.

manganeso *nm Quím* manganese.

mangangá *nm* 1 *Arg Par Urug* large bee. 2 *Am fig* (*fastidioso*) bore, pest. 3 *Arg Bol fig* (*ladrón*) thief.

mangante *adj* I *adj* cadging; II *nmf* (*gorrón*) cadger, scrounger; (*ladrón*) thief.

manganzón,-ona *adj Am* lazy, idle.

mangar *vtr* to knock off, pinch, nick, swipe.

manglar *nm* mangrove swamp.

mangle *nm* mangrove.

mango[1] *nm* handle; (*de un hacha*) helve; (*de un látigo*) stock. ■ **m. de la escoba,** broomstick.

mango[2] *nm Bot* mango.

mangoneador,-a *fam* I *adj* 1 bossy, domineering. 2 (*entrometido*) meddler. II *nm, f* bossy *or* domineering person.

mangonear *vi* 1 *fam* (*manipular*) to be bossy, throw one's weight around. 2 *fam* (*entrometerse*) to meddle. 3 *Am* (*lucrarse*) to be on the fiddle.

mangoneo *nm* 1 *fam* bossing around. 2 *fam* (*entrometimiento*) meddling. 3 *Am* (*chanchullo*) fiddling.

mangosta *nf Zool* mongoose.

manguear I *vtr* 1 *Am* (*caza*) to beat. 2 *Am fam fig* (*persona*) to coax, entice. 3 *Arg Chi* (*ganado*) to drive. II *vi* 1 *Am* (*fingir que se trabaja*) to pretend to be working. 2 *Am* (*vagar*) to wander.

manguera *nf* 1 (*de jardín*) garden *or* watering hose, hosepipe; (*de bombero*) fire hose. 2 *Am* (*corral*) corral, yard. 3 *Chi Arg* (*carro*) hose reel.

mangui *arg* I *adj* (*malo*) bad; (*falso*) false. I *nm,f* (*ladrón*) thief; (*sinvergüenza*) rotter.

manguito *nm* 1 (*para las manos*) muff; (*para las mangas*) oversleeve. 2 *Téc* sleeve.

mani *nf fam* demo, demonstration.

maní *nm* (*pl* **manises**) peanut.

manía *nf* 1 *Med* mania; *fam* **sin manías,** head-first. ■ **m. depresiva,** manic-depressive psychosis; **m. persecutoria,** persecution mania *or* complex. 2 (*costumbre*) habit; **tiene la m. de dejar el coche siempre abierto,** he's got this bad habit of leaving the car unlocked. 3 (*afición exagerada*) craze; **la m. de las motos,** the motorbike craze. 4 (*ojeriza*) dislike, ill will; **cogerle** *or* **tomarle m. a algn,** to take a dislike to sb; **me tiene m.,** he has it in for me, he can't stand me.

maniaco,-a *adj & nm, f*, **maníaco,-a** *adj & nm, f* 1 *Psic* manic. 2 *fam* (*obseso*) maniac.

maniacodepresivo,-a *adj & nm,f* manic-depressive.

maniatar *vtr* (*a una persona*) to tie the hands of.

maniático,-a I *adj* fussy. II *nm,f* fussy person.

manicomio *nm* mental hospital; *fam* **esta casa es un m.,** this place is like a madhouse.

manicuro,-a I *nm,f* manicurist. II *nf* manicure; **hacerse la manicura,** to have a manicure.

manido,-a *adj* 1 (*comida*) high. 2 (*asunto*) trite, hackneyed, worn-out.

manierismo *nm Arte* mannerism.

manierista *Arte* **I** *adj* manneristic. **II** *nmf* mannerist.

manifestación *nf* **1** *(expresión)* manifestation,expression; **como m. de su amistad,** as a sign of his friendship. **2** *(declaración)* declaration, comment. **3** *(demostración colectiva)* demonstration.

manifestador,-a *adj* demonstrating, showing.

manifestante *nmf* demonstrator.

manifestar I *vtr* **1** to manifest, declare; **el director manifestó que ...,** the director declared that ... . **2** *(mostrar)* to show, display. **II manifestarse** *vr* **1** *(declararse)* to declare oneself; **se manifestó partidario de la idea,** he declared himself in favour of the idea. **2** *(por la calle)* to demonstrate.

manifiesto,-a I *adj* evident, clear, obvious, manifest; *(falta)* glaring; **poner de m.,** *(revelar)* to reveal, show; *(hacer patente)* to make clear. **II** *nm* manifesto.

manigua *nf Am Geog* scrubland.

manija *nf* **1** *(manubrio)* handle. **2** *(maniota)* hobble.

manila *nm (puro)* Manila (cigar).

manilargo,-a *adj* **1** *(ladrón)* light-fingered. **2** *(generoso)* generous, openhanded.

manileño,-a I *adj* of *or* from Manila. **II** *nm, f* native *or* inhabitant of Manila.

manilla *nf* **1** *(argolla)* handcuff, manacle. **2** *(de reloj)* hand. **3** *Méx (guante)* protective glove. **4** *Arg Chi Ven Aut* door handle.

manillar *nm* handlebar.

maniobra *nf* **1** *Mil* manoeuvre, *US* maneuver; **hacer maniobras,** to manoeuvre; **estar de maniobras,** to be on manoeuvres. **2** *fig (jugada)* move.

maniobrabilidad *nf* manoeuvrability, *US* maneuverability.

maniobrable *adj* manoeuvrable, *US* maneuverable.

maniobrar *vi* to manoeuvre, *US* maneuver.

maniota *nf* hobble.

manipulación *nf* manipulation; **m. de mercancías,** handling of goods.

manipulador,-a I *adj* manipulating. **II** *nm, f* manipulator, handler.

manipular *vtr* **1** *(gen)* to manipulate; *(mercancías)* to handle. **2** *fig* to interfere with.

manipuleo *nm fam* manipulation.

manípulo *nm Mil Rel* maniple.

maniqueísmo *nm* Manicheism.

maniqueo,-a *adj & nm, f* Manichean.

maniquí I *nmf (modelo)* model, mannequin. **II** *nm (muñeco)* dummy; *fig* puppet.

manirroto,-a *adj & nm, f* spendthrift.

manitas *nmf inv (fam* **1 m. de plata,** clever hands; **ser un m.,** to be handy, be very good with one's hands. **2 hacer m.,** to hold hands.

manivela *nf Téc* crank.

manjar *nm* dish, food; **un m. exquisito,** an exquisite dish; *fig* **m. de dioses,** food fit for the gods.

mano¹ *nf* **1** hand; **a m.,** *(sin máquina)* by hand; *(asequible)* at hand; **escrito a m.,** handwritten; **hecho a m.,** handmade; **a m. armada,** armed; **a manos de,** at the hands of; **a manos llenas,** generously; **abrir la m.,** *(transigir)* to become more tolerant; *(gastar mucho)* to spend carelessly; **al alcance de la m.,** within one's grasp; **alargar la m.,** *(para coger algo)* to stretch out one's hand; *(a algn)* to offer one's hand; **alzar la m. contra algn,** to (threaten to) use violence against sb, raise one's hand to sb; **apretar la m.,** to tighten up (-, on); **¡arriba las manos!,** hands up!; **cogidos de la m.,** holding hands; **dar** *or* **tender la m.,** *(para saludar)* to shake hands (a, with); *(para ayudar)* to offer one's hand (a, to); **estrechar la m. a algn,** to shake hands with sb; *fig* **con el corazón en la m.,** sincerely; *fig* **con m. dura,** severely, with an iron hand; *fig* **de mi/tu m.,** up to me/you; *fig* **de la m. de algn,** under sb's guidance, under the influence of sb; *fig* **de primera m.,** first-hand; *fig* **de segunda m.,** second-hand; *fig* **echar una m. a algn,** to give sb a hand; *fig* **en buenas manos,** in good hands; *fig* **hacer lo que está de su m.,** to do all in one's power; *fig* **írsele a algn la m.** to overdo it; *fig* **írsele a algn algo de las manos,** to lose control over sth; *fam* **¡las manos quietas!,** hands off!; *fig* **m. a m.,** *(juntos)* together; *(entrevista)* tête-à-tête; *fig* **m. sobre m.,** idle; *fig* **¡manos a la obra!,** shoulders to the wheel (and noses to the grindstone)!; *fig* **meter m.,** *(a un problema)* to tackle; *vulg* to touch up; *fig* **no estaba en mi m. poder ayudarle,** I could do nothing to help her; *fig* **(no) saber lo que se lleva** *or* **trae uno entre manos,** (not) to know what's happening *or* going on; *fig* **ponerse en manos de algn,** to place oneself in sb's hands; *fig* **ser la m. derecha de algn,** to be sb's right hand, be sb's right-hand man; *fig* **traerse algo entre manos,** to be up to sth; *fam* **cargar la m.,** to overdo it; *fam* **coger** *or* **pillar a algn con las manos en la masa,** to catch sb red-handed; *fam* **echar m. de algo/algn,** to make use of sth/sb; *fam* **le das la m. y se toma el codo,** give him an inch and he'll take a mile. ■ **apretón de manos,** handshake; **bomba de m.,** hand grenade; **equipaje de m.,** hand luggage. **2** *Zool* forefoot, forepaw. ■ **m. de ave,** claw; **m. de cerdo,** pig's trotter. **3** *(de reloj)* hand. **4** *(lado)* side; **a m. derecha/izquierda,** on the right/left(-hand side). **5** *(dosis)* dose, series; **m. de jabón,** soaping; **m. de pintura,** coat of paint; *fam* **le dió una m. de azotes,** he gave him a hiding. **6** *(influencia)* influence; **se ve su m. en la decoración,** you can see her influence in the decoration. **7** *(trabajador)* hand, labourer, *US* laborer; **hay que contratar más manos,** we have to employ more workers. ■ **m. de obra,** labour (force); **m. de obra especializada,** skilled labour. **8** *(habilidad)* skill; **¡qué manos tienes!,** you're really clever with your hands!; **tener buena m. para algo,** to be good at sth; *fig* **tener m. izquierda,** to be tactful. **9** *Naipes (grupo de cartas)* hand; *(juego)* game; *(primer jugador)* lead; **echar una m. (de cartas),** to play a game of cards; **yo soy m.,** it's my lead. **10** *(de mortero)* pestle. **11** *(de papel)* quire. **12** *Am (aventura)* mishap, accident; *(mala pasada)* dirty trick. **13** *Am (de plátanos)* bunch. **14** *Chi Méx (cuatro)* four of the same thing.

mano² *nmf Am fam* chum, mate, pal.

manojo *nm* bunch; **un m. de flores/llaves,** a bunch of flowers/keys; *fam* **ser un m. de nervios,** to be a bundle of nerves.

manómetro *nm Téc* pressure gauge.

manopla *nf* **1** mitten. **2** *Hist* gauntlet.

manoseado,-a I *pp de* **manosear. II** *adj* worn(-out); *fig* hackneyed.

manosear *vtr* to touch repeatedly, finger; *fam* to paw.

manoseo *nm* touching, pawing.

manotazo *nm* cuff, slap.

manotear I *vtr* to cuff, slap. **II** *vi* to gesticulate.

manoteo *nm* gesticulation.

mansalva (a) *loc adv* without risk, safely.

mansarda *nf Arquit* attic.

mansedumbre *nf* **1** *(persona)* meekness, gentleness. **2** *(animal)* tameness, docility.

mansión *nf* mansion; **m. señorial,** stately home.

manso,-a *adj* **1** *(persona)* gentle, meek. **2** *(animal)* tame, docile.

mansurrón,-ona *adj* gentle *or* docile in the extreme.

manta I *nf* **1** blanket; **a m.,** abundantly; *fam* lots of; **había gente a m.,** there were loads of people; *fam* **liarse la m. a la cabeza,** to take the plunge, go the whole hog; *fam* **tirar de la m.,** to let the cat out of the bag. ■ **m. de viaje,** travelling rug; **m. eléctrica,** electric blanket. **2** *(zurra)* beating, hiding. **3** *(pea)* manta ray, devilfish. **4** *Am (costal)* bag (for carrying ore). **5** *SAm (prenda)* poncho. **II** *adj fam* lazy, bone idle. **III** *nmf fam* lazy person, idler.

manteado *nm* 1 *CAm Méx (tienda)* tent. 2 *Méx (toldo)* awning.

manteamiento *nm* tossing in a blanket.

mantear *vtr* to toss in a blanket.

manteca *nf (de animal)* fat; *(de la leche)* cream. ■ **m. de cacao/cacahuete,** cocoa/peanut butter; **m. de cerdo,** lard.

mantecado *nm* 1 *(pastel)* shortcake. 2 *(helado)* dairy ice cream.

mantecoso,-a *adj (graso)* greasy; *(cremoso)* buttery.

mantel *nm* tablecloth.

mantelería *nf* table linen.

manteleta *nf* shawl.

mantenedor,-a *nm,f Lit* member of a jury.

mantener I *vtr* 1 *(conservar)* to keep, keep going; **mantén el fuego encendido,** keep the fire burning; **m. la línea,** to keep in trim; *(en letrero)* '**mantenga limpia su ciudad',** 'keep your town tidy'. 2 *(entrevista, reunión)* to have; **m. correspondencia con algn,** to correspond with sb; **m. relaciones con algn,** *(amorosas)* to be going out with sb; *(amistosas)* to be on friendly terms with sb. 3 *(ideas, opiniones)* to defend, maintain; **mantuvo su actitud contraria al proyecto,** he maintained his opposition to the project. 4 *(sustentar)* to support, feed; **ella sola mantiene a su familia,** she supports the whole family on her own. 5 *(sostener)* to support, hold up; **esta columna mantiene la pared,** this column holds the wall up. **II mantenerse** *vr* 1 *(sostenerse)* to stand; **este edificio se mantiene en pie de milagro,** it's a miracle this building is still standing. 2 *(continuar)* to keep, hold; **m. firme,** to hold one's ground; **m. tranquilo/vivo,** to keep *or* stay calm/alive; *fam* **m. en sus trece,** to stick to one's guns. 3 *(sustentarse)* to support oneself.

mantenido,-a I *pp de* **mantenerse.** **II** *adj* continuous, constant; **un esfuerzo m.,** continuous effort. **III** *nf pey* kept woman.

mantenimiento *nm* 1 *Téc* maintenance, upkeep; **servicio de m.,** maintenance service. 2 *(alimento)* sustenance, support.

manteo¹ *nm (manteamiento)* tossing in a blanket.

manteo² *nm (capa)* mantle.

mantequería *nf* dairy.

mantequero,-a I *adj* butter; **la industria mantequera,** the butter industry. **II** *nm, f (hombre)* dairyman; *(mujer)* dairywoman. **III** *nf* 1 *(vasija)* butter dish. 2 *(máquina)* butter churn.

mantequilla *nf* butter.

mantilla *nf* 1 *(de mujer)* mantilla. 2 *(de niño)* shawl; *fig* **estar en mantillas,** to be in nappies.

mantillo *nm* 1 *(humus)* humus. 2 *(abono)* leaf mould, *US* leaf mold.

mantillón,-ona I *adj Méx* shameless. **II** *nm Am (gualdrapa)* horse blanket.

manto *nm* 1 *(capa)* cloak, mantle; *fig* **un m. de silencio,** a veil of silence. 2 *Min* layer, stratum. 3 *Zool* mantle.

mantón *nm* shawl. ■ **m. de Manila,** embroidered silk shawl.

mantudo,-a *nm,f CAm* masked *or* disguised person.

mantuve *pt indef véase* **mantener.**

manual I *adj* manual; **trabajo m.,** manual labour; *Educ* **trabajos manuales,** handicrafts. **II** *nm (libro)* manual, handbook.

manubrio *nm* crank, handle.

manudo,-a *adj CAm Arg* with big hands.

manufactura *nf* 1 *(fabricación)* manufacture. 2 *(fábrica)* factory.

manufacturado,-a *adj* manufactured.

manufacturar *vtr* to manufacture.

manufacturero,-a *adj* manufacturing.

manuscrito,-a I *adj* handwritten, manuscript. **II** *nm* manuscript.

manutención *nf* maintenance; **la m. de una familia es cada día más costosa,** feeding a family is becoming increasingly expensive.

manzana *nf* 1 *Bot* apple; *fig* **sano como una m.,** as fit as a fiddle. 2 *Arquit (bloque)* block. 3 *CAm (medida)* 1.73 acres.

manzanal *nm*, **manzanar** *nm* apple orchard.

manzanilla *nf* 1 *Bot* camomile. 2 *(infusión)* camomile tea. 3 *(vino)* manzanilla.

manzano *nm Bot* apple tree.

maña *nf* 1 *(habilidad)* skill, dexterity; **darse** *or* **tener m. para algo,** to be good at doing sth; *prov* **más vale m. que fuerza,** brain is better than brawn. 2 *(astucia)* trick.

mañana I *nf* morning; **a las dos de la m.,** at two in the morning; **de m.,** early in the morning; **por la m.,** in the morning. **II** *nm* tomorrow, the future; **hay que pensar en el m.,** one has to think about tomorrow *or* the future. **III** *adv* tomorrow; **¡hasta m.!,** see you tomorrow!, till tomorrow!; **m. por la m.,** tomorrow morning; **pasado m.,** the day after tomorrow.

mañanero,-a *adj* 1 *(madrugador)* early rising. 2 *(matutino)* morning; **la brisa mañanera,** the morning breeze.

mañanita *nf* bed jacket.

maño,-a *adj & nm,f fam* Aragonese.

mañoso,-a *adj* 1 *(hábil)* skilful, *US* skillful, dextrous, deft. 2 *(astuto)* crafty, cunning.

maoísmo *nm Pol* maoism.

maoísta *adj & nmf Pol* maoist.

maorí *adj & nmf* Maori.

mapa *nm* map; **m. mural,** wall map; *fam* **borrar del m.,** *(eliminar)* to get rid of; *(matar)* to kill; *fam* **desaparecer del m.,** to vanish (from the face of the earth); *fam* **como** *or* **hecho un m.,** badly bruised *or* cut.

mapache *nm Zool* raccoon.

mapamundi *nm* 1 *(mapa)* map of the world, world map. 2 *(nalgas)* backside, bum, bottom.

maqueta *nf* 1 *(miniatura)* scale model, maquette. 2 *Impr* dummy. 3 *Mús* demo (tape).

maquetista *nmf* maquette maker.

maqui *nmf véase* **maquis.**

maquiavélico,-a *adj* Machiavellian.

maquiavelismo *nm* Machiavellism.

maquillador,-a *nm,f* make-up assistant.

maquillaje *nm* 1 *(producto)* make-up. ■ **m. de fondo,** foundation. 2 *(acción)* making-up.

maquillar I *vtr* to make up. **II maquillarse** *vr* 1 *(ponerse maquillaje)* to put one's make-up on, make (oneself) up. 2 *(llevar maquillaje)* to wear make-up.

máquina *nf* machine; **escrito a m.,** typewritten; **hecho a m.,** machine-made; *fam* **a toda m.,** at full speed. ■ **m. de afeitar (eléctrica),** (electric) razor *or* shaver; **m. de coser/lavar,** sewing/washing machine; **m. de escribir,** typewriter; **m. de tren,** locomotive; **m. fotográfica** *or* **de fotos,** camera; **m. tragaperras,** slot machine, one-armed bandit.

maquinación *nf* machination.

maquinador,-a I *adj* machinating. **II** *nm,f* machinator.

maquinal *adj* mechanical.

maquinar *vtr* to machinate, plot.

maquinaria *nf* 1 machinery, machines *pl.* 2 *(de reloj etc)* *(mecanismo)* mechanism, works *pl.*

maquinilla *nf* **m. de afeitar,** safety razor.

maquinismo *nm* mechanization.

maquinista *nmf* machinist; *(de tren)* engine driver.

maquinización *nf* mechanization.

maquinizar *vtr* to mechanize.

maquis *nm inv Mil* guerrilla.

mar *nm & f* **1** sea; **en alta m.,** on the high seas; **hacerse a la m.,** to put (out) to sea, set sail; **m. adentro,** out to sea; **por m.,** by sea; *fam* **pelillos a la m.,** let bygones be bygones. ■ **m. de fondo,** ground swell; *fig (tensiones)* undercurrent of tension; **m. gruesa,** heavy sea; **m. picada,** rough sea. **2** *(marejada)* swell. **3** *fam (gran cantidad)* **está la m. de guapa,** she's looking really beautiful; **estar hecho un m. de lágrimas,** to cry one's eyes out; **la m. de cosas,** a lot of things; **llover a mares,** to rain cats and dogs; **me encuentro la m. de bien,** I feel great; **sudar a mares,** to sweat buckets; **sumido en un m. de confusiones,** utterly confused. **4** *nm* sea. ■ **M. Arábigo,** Arabian Sea; **M. de Aral,** Aral Sea; **M. de Filipinas,** Philippine Sea; **M. de Irlanda,** Irish Sea; **M. de Java,** Java Sea; **M. de la China Oriental/Meridional,** East/South China Sea; **M. de las Antillas,** Caribbean Sea; **M. de los Sargazos,** Sargasso Sea; **M. de Noruega,** Sea of Norway; **M. de Tasmania,** Tasman Sea; **M. del Coral,** Coral Sea; **M. del Japón,** Japan Sea; **M. del Norte,** North Sea; **M. Ligur,** Ligurian Sea; **M. Muerto,** Dead Sea; **M, Negro,** Black Sea; **M. Rojo,** Red Sea.

marabú *nm Orn* marabou.

marabunta *nf* **1** plague of ants. **2** *fig (multitud)* mob.

maraca **I** *nf Am Mús* maraca, rattle. **II** *nmf Col PR Ven fam (zoquete)* blockhead.

maracuyá *nf Bot* passion fruit.

maraña *nf* **1** *(maleza)* thicket. **2** *fig (lío)* tangle, mess.

marasmo *nm* **1** *Med* marasmus. **2** *fig (apatía)* apathy; *(estancamiento)* standstill, stagnation.

maratón *nm Dep* marathon.

maratoniano,-a **I** *adj* marathon. **II** *nm,f* marathon runner.

maravedí *nm Hist (moneda)* maravedí.

maravilla *nf* marvel, wonder; **de m.,** wonderfully; **decir maravillas de algo** *or* **algn,** to speak enthusiastically about sth *or* sb; **hacer maravillas,** to do *or* work wonders; **¡qué m.!,** how wonderful!; **¡qué m. de película!,** what a wonderful film!; *fam* **a las mil maravillas,** marvellously; *fam* **venir de maravilla,** to be just what one wanted, be a godsend.

maravillar **I** *vtr* to amaze, astonish; **quedamos maravillados al oírle cantar,** we were amazed by his singing, we marvelled at his singing. **II maravillarse** *vr* to marvel (**con,** at), wonder (**con,** at).

maravilloso,-a *adj* wonderful, marvellous, *US* marvelous.

marbete *nm* **1** *(etiqueta)* label. **2** *(perfil)* edge, border.

marca *nf* **1** mark, sign. **2** *Com (productos comestibles y del hogar)* brand; *(otros productos)* make; **hay muchas marcas de coches/ordenadores/neveras en el mercado,** there are lots of makes of car/computer/refrigerator on the market; **pantalones/zapatos de m.,** designer shoes/trousers; **¿que m. de café/jabón/dentífrico compras?,** what brand of coffee/soap/toothpaste do you buy?; *fam* **de m. mayor,** outstanding, enormous. ■ **m. de fábrica,** trademark; **m. registrada,** registered trademark. **3** *(acción de marcar)* marking; **la m. del ganado,** the branding of cattle. **4** *Dep (récord)* record; **batir la m. mundial,** to break the world record.

marcación *nf Am* branding iron.

marcado,-a **I** *pp de* **marcar. II** *adj* **1** marked. **2** *(evidente)* distinct, strong; **con marcada diferencia,** noticeably different. ◆ **marcadamente** *adv* markedly; **un espíritu m. liberal,** a clearly liberal spirit.

marcador,-a **I** *adj* marking. **II** *nm* **1** marker. **2** *Dep* scoreboard; **inaugurar el m.,** to start *or* open the scoring.

marcaje *nm Dep* marking.

marcapaso *nm,* **marcapasos** *nm inv Med* pacemaker.

marcar **I** *vtr* **1** to mark; *(ganado)* to brand; *Com (mercancías)* to put a price on, mark; *Mús* **m. el compás/el paso,** to mark rhythm/time; **m. época,** to mark an era;

m. un terreno, to mark the land out *or* off; *fig* **la experiencia lo marcó para siempre,** the experience marked him for life. **2** *(cabello)* to set. **3** *(aparato)* to indicate, show; **el contador marca 1.327,** the meter reads 1,327; **el reloj marca las tres,** the clock says 3 o'clock. **4** *Dep (gol, puntos)* to score; *(jugador)* to mark; *fig* **su plan marca un gol para la empresa,** her project scores a point for the firm. **5** *Tel* to dial. **II marcarse** *vr fam* **m. un farol,** to show off, boast; **m. un tanto,** to score a triumph.

marcha *nf* **1** march; **abrir/cerrar la m.,** to be first/last in a march *or* procession. ■ **m. antinuclear,** antinuclear march; *Dep* **m. atlética,** walk, walking race. **2** *(partida)* departure; **el día de su m.,** the day he went away; **¡en m.!,** let's go! **3** *(progreso)* course, progress; **la ecología se usa ideología en m.,** ecology is on the move; **la m. de los acontecimientos,** the course of events; **la m. de las negociaciones/de un negocio,** the progress of the negotiations/a business; **hacer algo sobre la m.,** to do sth as one goes along. **4** *(velocidad)* speed; **a marchas forzadas,** against the clock; **a toda m.,** (at) full speed; *fig* at full blast; **disminuir la m.,** to slow down. **5** *Aut* gear; *Aut* **dar m. atrás,** to reverse; *fig* **han dado m. atrás al proyecto,** they have abandoned the project. ■ **m. atrás,** reverse (gear); **primera marcha,** first *or* bottom gear. **6** *Mús* march; **m. fúnebre/militar/nupcial,** funeral/military/wedding march. **7** *(funcionamiento)* operation, running; **estar en m.,** *(maquinaria)* to be in operation, be on, be working; *(proyecto etc)* to be under way; **poner en m.,** *(coche, motor)* to start; *(negocio)* to start up. **8** *fam (energía)* go; *(animación)* good humour *or* US humor, good vibrations; **hay mucha m. aquí,** it's really lively here; **ir de m.,** to go out on the town, have a wild time; **irle la m. a algn,** *(ser marchoso)* to be a raver, enjoy living it up; *(ser masoquista)* to be masochist; **¡qué m. llevo hoy!,** count me in for anything today!

marchamo *nm* mark, seal.

marchante,-a **I** *nm Com* merchant, dealer. **II** *Am nm,f* **1** *(cliente)* customer, regular client. **2** *(amante)* lover.

marchar **I** *vi* **1** *(ir)* to go, walk; *fam* **¡marchando!,** on your way!; **¡tres de hamburguesa! —¡marchando!,** three hamburgers! —coming right up! **2** *(funcionar)* to work, function; **la radio no marcha,** the radio isn't working; *fig* **el negocio no marcha,** the business is doing badly; *fig* **m. sobre ruedas,** to run like clockwork. **3** *Mil* to march. **4** *Cuba Chi PR (caballo)* to walk. **II marcharse** *vr (irse)* to leave depart.

marchitamiento *nm* shrivelling, *US* shriveling, withering.

marchitar **I** *vtr* to shrivel, wither. **II marchitarse** *vr* to shrivel, wither.

marchito,-a *adj* shrivelled, *US* shriveled, withered.

marchoso,-a *fam* **I** *adj* fun-loving wild; **es una gente muy marchosa,** they are always living it up; **música marchosa,** music with a bit of go. **II** *nm,f* raver, fun lover; **es un m.,** he's a right raver.

marcial *adj* martial; **ley m.,** martial law.

marcialidad *nf* military manners *pl.*

marcianitos *nmpl fam (juego)* **los m.,** space invaders.

marciano,-a *adj & nm,f* Martian.

marco *nm* **1** *(cerco)* frame. **2** *fig (fondo)* framework, setting; **en un m. adecuado,** in an appropriate setting. **3** *Fin (moneda)* mark. **4** *Ftb* goalposts *pl,* goal.

marea *nf* **1** *Mar* tide; *fig* **contra viento y m.,** come hell or high water. ■ **m. alta/baja,** high/low tide. ■ **m. negra,** oil slick. **2** *fig (multitud)* crowd, mob; **una m. de vendedores,** a crowd of salesmen.

mareado,-a **I** *pp de* **marear. II** *adj* **1** sick; *(en un avión)* airsick; *(en un coche)* carsick, travel-sick; **estar m.,** to feel sick; *(en el mar)* to feel seasick; *(en un avión)* to feel airsick; *(en un coche)* to feel carsick *or* travel-sick. **2** *(aturdido)* dizzy. **3** *euf (bebido)* tipsy.

mareaje *nm* **1** *(profesión)* navigation, seamanship. **2** *(rumbo)* course.

mareante *adj* **1** *Naút* seafaring. **2** *(nauseabundo)* sickening, nauseating. **3** *fig (pesado)* boring.

marear I *vtr Naút* to sail. **II** *vtr & vi* **1** to make sick; *(en el mar)* to make seasick; *(en un avión)* to make airsick; *(en un coche)* to make carsick *or* travel-sick. **2** *(aturdir)* to make dizzy. **3** *fam (cargar)* to annoy, pester. **4** *Méx PR (embaucar)* to cheat. **III marearse** *vr* **1** to get sick; *(en el mar)* to get seasick; *(en un avión)* to get airsick; *(en un coche)* to get carsick *or* travel-sick. **2** *(quedar aturdido)* to get dizzy. **3** *euf (emborracharse)* to get tipsy. **4** *Arg Cuba PR (desteñirse)* to fade.

marejada *nf* **1** *Mar* swell. **2** *fig (descontento)* unrest.

maremagno *nm*, **maremágnum** *nm* **1** *(multitud)* multitude, abundance. **2** *(confusión)* confusion.

maremoto *nm Mar* seaquake.

marengo,-a *adj* **gris m.,** dark grey.

mareo *nm* **1** *(náusea)* sickness; *(en el mar)* seasickness; *(en un avión)* airsickness; *(en un coche)* carsickness, travel-sickness. **2** *(aturdimiento)* dizziness, lightheadedness.

marfil *nm* ivory.

marfileño,-a I *adj* **1** *(nacionalidad)* of *or* from the Ivory Coast. **2** *(ebúrneo)* ivory-like. **II** *nm,f* native *or* inhabitant of the Ivory Coast.

marga *nf Min* marl, loam.

margarina *nf Culin* margarine.

margarita *nf* **1** *Bot* daisy; *fig* **echar margaritas a los puercos,** to cast pearls before swine; *fig* **deshojar la m.,** to play 'he *or* she loves me, he *or* she loves me not'. **2** *Impr* daisy-wheel.

margen *nmf* **1** border, edge; *(río)* bank; **el m. del camino,** the side of the road; *fig* **dejar algn *or* algo al m.,** to leave sb *or* sth out; *fig* **mantenerse al m.,** not to get involved. **2** *(papel)* margin; **el m. de la hoja,** the margin of the page. **3** *Com* margin. ■ **m. de beneficios,** profit margin. **4** *(ocasión)* opportunity; **dar m. a algn para hacer algo,** to give sb the occasion to do sth.

marginación *nf* **1** *(exclusión)* exclusion. **2** *Pol* isolation.

marginado,-a I *pp de* **marginar. II** *adj* **1** excluded. **2** *Pol* on the fringe. **III** *nm,f* dropout.

marginal *adj* **1** marginal. **2** *Pol* fringe; **arte/grupo m.,** fringe art/group.

marginar *vtr* **1** *(de un grupo, sociedad)* to leave out, exclude. **2** *(anotar)* to add marginal notes to. **3** *(dejar márgenes)* to leave a margin on.

maría *nf arg* **1** *(droga)* marijuana, pot. **2** *Educ arg (asignatura fácil)* easy subject. **3** *fam (ama de casa)* housewife.

mariachi *nm Mús* mariachi.

marica *nm vulg ofens* queer, poof.

Maricastaña *n* **en tiempo de M.,** years and years ago, ages ago.

maricón *nm vulg ofens* queer, poof.

mariconada *nf vulg* dirty trick.

mariconera *nf* (man's) clutch bag.

mariconería *nf vulg* homosexuality.

maridaje *nm* close association, intimate relationship.

maridar I *vtr fig (unir)* to marry. **II** *vi lit (casarse)* to marry; *(amancebarse)* to live together, cohabit.

marido *nm* husband.

mariguana *nf*, **marihuana** *nf*, **marijuana** *nf* marijuana.

marimacho *nm vulg* mannish woman, butch woman.

marimandón,-ona *nm,f fam* domineering person.

marimba *nf* **1** *(tambor)* type of drum. **2** *(xilófon)* marimba. **3** *Arg PR* instrument which is out of tune. **4** *Arg (paliza)* beating, hiding.

marimbero,-a *adj CAm* clumsy.

marimorena *nf fam* row, fuss; *fam* **armar(se) la m.,** to kick up a racket.

marina *nf* **1** *Naút* seamanship. **2** *Mil* navy. ■ **m. de guerra,** navy; **m. mercante,** merchant navy. **3** *Art (pintura)* seascape. **4** *Geog (zona costera)* seacoast.

marinería *nf* **1** *(profesión)* sailoring. **2** *(marineros)* seamen *pl,* sailors *pl.*

marinero,-a I *adj* sea, seafaring; **barco m.,** seaworthy ship; **gente marinera** people of the sea; *Culin* **pescado a la marinera,** fish in a tomato and wine sauce with shellfish; **pueblo m.,** fishing village *or* town. **II** *nm* sailor, seaman; *fam* **m. de agua dulce,** landlubber. **III** *nf Am* type of folk dance.

marino,-a I *adj* marine; **brisa marina,** sea breeze. **II** *nm* **1** seaman. **2** *Am Mil* **marinos** marines.

marioneta *nf* **1** marionette, puppet. **2 marionetas.** puppet show *sing.*

mariposa *nf* **1** *Ent* butterfly. **2** *(lamparilla)* oil lamp. **3** *Natación* butterfly. **4** *(tuerca)* wing nut. **5** *ofens (afeminado)* nancy.

mariposear *vi* *-fig* **1** *(ser inconstante)* to be fickle. **2** *(flirtear)* to flirt. **3** *(zascandilear)* to hover around.

mariposón *nm* **1** *(galanteador)* flirt. **2** *Am ofens (marica)* queer, pansy, poof.

mariquita I *nf Ent* ladybird. **II** *nm fam ofens (marica)* queer, pansy, poof.

marisabidilla *nf fam* bluestocking, know-all.

mariscal *nm Mil* marshal; **m. de campo,** field marshal.

marisco *nm Culin Zool* shellfish; **'especialidad en pescados y mariscos',** 'seafood a speciality'.

marisma *nf Geog* salt-marsh.

marismeño,-a *adj* marsh.

marisquería *nf* seafood restaurant, shellfish bar.

marista *adj & nm Rel* Marist.

marital *adj* marital; **vida m.,** married life.

maritates *nmpl CAm* equipment *sing* tackle *sing.*

marítimo,-a *adj* maritime, sea; **ciudad marítima,** coastal town; **ruta marítima,** sea route; **seguro m.,** marine insurance.

marjal *nm Geog* marsh, bog.

marketing *nm Com* marketing.

marlo *nm Am* **1** *(espiga de maíz)* cob. **2** *(tronco de cola)* dock. **3** *(de planta)* stem.

marmita *nf (olla)* cooking pot.

marmitón,-ona *nm,f* kitchen helper, scullion.

mármol *nm* marble.

marmolería *nf* **1** *(taller)* marble cutter's workshop. **2** *(mármoles)* marblework.

marmolista *nmf* marble cutter.

marmóreo,-a *adj* marmoreal, marble.

marmota *nf* **1** *Zool* marmot; *fam* **dormir como una m.,** to sleep like a log. **2** *fam (dormilón)* sleepyhead. **3** *fam (mujer)* charwoman.

maroma *nf* **1** *(cuerda)* thick rope. **2** *Naút* cable. **3** *Am (volatín)* acrobatic performance. **4** *Am Pol fig (de partido)* sudden change of party; *(de opinion)* sudden change of opinion.

maromear *vi Am* **1** *(hacer volatines)* to do acrobatics on the tightrope. **2** *Pol fig (vacilar)* to sit on the fence; *(cambiar de partido)* to change one's allegiance.

maromo *nm arg* guy, bloke.

marqués *nm* marquis.

marquesa *nf* marchioness.

marquesado *nm* marquisate.

marquesina *nf Arquit* canopy.

marquesote *nm CAm Méx Culin* type of cake.

marquetería *nf* marquetry, inlaid work.

marrajo,-a I *adj* **1** *Taur* vicious, dangerous. **2** *(astuto)* cunning, sly. **II** *nm (pez)* mako shark.

marranada *nf,* **marranería** *nf* filthy thing *or* act; **han dejado el piso hecho una m.,** they've left the flat like a pigsty; *fam* **hacer una m. a algn,** to play a dirty trick on sb.

marrano,-a I *adj (sucio)* filthy, dirty. II *nm, f* 1 *fam (cochino)* dirty pig, slob; *(cabrón)* swine. 2 *Zool* pig.

marrar *vi* to go wrong, fail.

marras (de) *loc adv* aforementioned; **el individuo de m.,** the man in question.

marrasquino *nm (vino)* maraschino.

marrón glacé *nm Culin* marron glacé.

marrón I *adj (color)* brown. II *nm* 1 *(color)* brown. 2 *arg (condena)* sentence; **comerse un m.,** to own up; **pillar de m.,** to catch red-handed.

marroquí *adj & nmf,* **marroquín,-ina** *adj & nm, f* Moroccan.

marroquinería *nf* 1 *Ind* leather tanning. 2 *(artículos de cuero)* leather goods.

Marruecos *n* Morocco.

marrullería *nf* cajolery, wheedling.

marrullero,-a I *adj* cajoling, wheedling. II *nm, f* cajoler, wheedler.

Marsella *n* Marseilles.

marsellés,-esa I *adj* of *or* from Marseilles. II *nm, f* native *or* inhabitant *of* Marseilles.

marsopa *nf Zool* porpoise.

marsupial *adj & nm, f Zool* marsupial.

marta *nf Zool* 1 *(animal)* (pine) marten. ■ **m. cibellina,** sable. 2 *(piel)* sable.

martajar *vtr Am (maíz)* to grind; *fam* **m. el inglés,** to speak broken English.

Marte *n Astrol Astron Mit* Mars.

martes *nm inv* Tuesday; **M. de Carnaval,** Shrove Tuesday, Pancake Tuesday; **m. y trece,** ≈ Friday the thirteenth; *prov* **en m., ni te cases ni te embarques,** never take important decisions on a Tuesday; *véase tamb* **viernes.**

martillar *vtr véase* **martillear.**

martillazo *nm* blow with a hammer.

martillear *vtr* to hammer; *fig* **m. los oídos,** to hammer *or* pound on one's ears.

martilleo *nm* hammering.

martillo *nm* hammer. ■ *Zool* **pez m.,** hammerhead shark.

martín pescador *nm orn* kingfisher.

martinete[1] *nm orn* 1 *(ave)* night heron. 2 *(penacho)* plume.

martinete[2] *nm* 1 *(mazo)* drop hammer. 2 *(para clavar estacas)* pile-driver. 3 *Mús (macillo)* hammer.

martingala *nf fam* trick.

Martinica *n* Martinique.

mártir *nmf* martyr.

martirio *nm* 1 martyrdom. 2 *fig (fastidio)* torment.

martirizador,-a I *adj* agonizing. II *nm, f* tormentor, torturer.

martirizar *vtr* 1 to martyr. 2 *fig (fastidiar)* to torture, torment.

marxismo *nm* Marxism.

marxista *adj & nmf* Marxist.

marzo *nm* March; *véase tamb* **noviembre.**

m/c, m/cta *abr de* **mi cuenta,** my account.

mas *conj lit* but.

más I *adv* 1 *(comparativo)* more; **compra otro m.,** buy another one; **es m. alta/resuelta que yo,** she's taller/more resolute than me; *(mayor)* **hay m. número de niños que de adultos,** there are more children than adults; **necesito m. tiempo,** I need more time; **no tengo m.,** I haven't got any more. 2 *(con numerales, cantidad)* more than, over; **m. de diez,** over ten. 3 *(superlativo)* most; **es el m.**

bonito/caro, it's the prettiest/most expensive. 4 *exclam* so ..., what a ...; **¡está m. guapa!,** she looks so beautiful!; **¡qué casa m. bonita!,** what a lovely house! 5 *(después de pron interr e indef)* else; **¿algo m.?,** anything else?; **no, nada m.,** no, nothing else; **¿dónde/qué/quién m.?,** where/what/who else?; **nadie/alguien m.,** nobody/somebody else. 6 *(locuciones)* **a m. no poder,** as much as possible; **a m. tardar,** at the latest; **a m. y mejor,** a great deal; **cada día** *or* **vez m.,** more and more; **cada vez m. caro,** more and more expensive, dearer and dearer; **como el que m.,** as well as anyone *or* the next man; **cuanto** *or* **mientras m. trabajas, m. ganas,** the more you work, the more you earn; **cuanto** *or* **mientras m. lo pienso, menos lo entiendo,** the more I think about it, the less I understand it; **cuanto m. mejor,** the more the better; **chilló m. que cantó,** he screamed rather than sang; **de m.,** *(de sobras)* spare, extra; *(que sobra)* too much, too many; **dos de m.,** two too many; **estar de m.,** to be unnecessary, be surplus to requirements; **traje uno de m.,** I brought a spare one; **el que m. y el que menos,** everybody; **el m. allá,** the beyond; **es m.,** what's more, furthermore; **de lo m.,** extremely, very, ever so; **es do lo m. guapo,** he's ever so handsome; **lo m. posible,** as much as possible; **lo m. pronto/tarde,** as soon/late as possible; **m. allá** *or* **adelante,** further on; **m. allá de,** beyond; **m. bien,** rather; **m. de la cuenta,** too much; **m. de lo normal,** more than usual; **(poco) m. o menos,** more or less; **m. que,** rather than; **m. que nunca,** more than ever; **m. aún,** even more; **ni m. ni menos,** exactly; **no m. de** *or* **que,** no more than, only; *(con nombre)* **por m.,** however much *or* no matter how much, however many *or* no matter how many; **por m. dinero/millones que ahorres no podrás comprarte un castillo,** however much money/many millions you save you won't be able to buy a castle; *(con adj, adv, verbo)* however (much), no matter how (much); **por m. fuerte que sea,** however strong he may be; **por m. que grites no te oirá nadie,** no matter how much you shout nobody will hear you; **¿qué m. da?,** does it make any difference?, what's the difference?; **quien m., quien menos,** everybody; **sin m. ni m.,** without reason; **tanto m. cuanto que ...,** all the more because ...; **todo lo m.,** at the most *or* latest; *fam* **¡y tú, m.!,** same to you! II *nm inv* 1 *Mat* plus; **dos m. dos,** two plus *or* and two. 2 **los/las m.,** the majority, most people; **las m. de las veces,** more often than not. III *adj fam* **el tuyo es m. vestido que el mío,** yours is a better dress than mine.

masa *nf* 1 *(gen)* mass; **una m. líquida,** a liquid mass. ■ **m. atómica,** atomic mass; **m. encefálica,** brain. 2 *(de cosas)* bulk, volume. 3 *(gente)* mass; **atraer a las masas,** to draw the crowds; **en m.,** en masse. ■ **me dios de comunicación de masas,** mass media; **producción en m.,** mass production. 4 *Elec (tierra)* earth, *US* ground. 5 *Constr (mortero)* mortar. 6 *Culin* dough; *fig* **con las manos en la m.,** redhanded.

masacrar *vtr* to massacre.

masacre *nf* massacre.

masaje *nm* massage; **dar masaje(s) (a),** to massage.

masajista *nmf (hombre)* masseur; *(mujer)* masseuse.

mascada *nf* 1 *Am (tabaco)* plug of chewing tobacco. 2 *CAm Ecuad (tesoro)* store of money. 3 *Arg Chi (bocado)* mouthful, bite. 4 *Méx (pañuelo)* silk handkerchief.

mascadura *nf* chewing, mastication.

mascar *vtr & vi* to chew, masticate.

máscara *nf* 1 mask; *fig* **quitar la m. a algn,** to unmask sb; *fig* **quitarse la m.,** to reveal oneself. ■ **m. de gas,** gas mask; **traje de m.,** fancy dress. 2 **máscaras,** masquerade *sing.* 3 *nmf (persona)* masked person.

mascarada *nf* masquerade.

mascarilla *nf* 1 mask. ■ **m. de oxígeno,** oxygen mask. 2 *Med* face mask. 3 *(cosmética)* face pack.

mascarón *nm* 1 *(máscara)* large mask. 2 *Náut* **m. de proa,** figurehead.

Mascate *n* Muscat.

mascota *nf* mascot.

masculinidad *nf* masculinity, manliness.

masculinizar *vtr* to make mannish.

masculino,-a I *adj* **1** *Zool Bot* male; **órganos masculinos,** male organs. **2** *(de hombre)* male, manly; **una voz masculina,** a manly voice. **3** *(para hombre)* men's; **ropa masculina,** men's clothes, menswear. **4** *Ling* masculine. **II** *nm Ling* masculine.

mascullar *vtr* to mumble.

masía *nf Cat* farm.

masilla *nf* putty.

masivo,-a *adj* massive.

masoca *nm,f fam* masochist.

masón *nm* freemason, mason.

masonería *nf* freemasonry, masonry.

masónico,-a *adj* masonic.

masoquismo *nm* masochism.

masoquista I *adj* masochistic. **II** *nmf* masochist.

mastaba *nf Arquit Hist* mastaba.

masticación *nf* chewing, mastication.

masticador,-a *adj* chewing, masticating.

masticar *vt* **1** to chew, masticate. **2** *fig (ponderar)* to chew or ponder over.

mástil *nm* **1** *(asta)* mast, pole. **2** *Náut* mast. **3** *(de guitarra)* neck.

mastín *nm Zool* mastiff.

mastitis *nf Med* mastitis.

mastodonte *nm* mastodon.

mastodóntico,-a *adj* elephantine.

mastoides *adj & nf inv Anat* mastoid.

mastuerzo I *adj (necio)* stupid, foolish, doltish. **II** *nm* **1** *Bot* cress. **2** *(necio)* dolt.

masturbación *nf* masturbation.

masturbar *vtr*, **masturbarse** *vr* to masturbate.

mata *nf* **1** *(matorral)* bush, shrub; **a salto de m.,** *(al día)* from one day to the next; *(apresuradamente)* like a shot; *(de cualquier manera)* any old how, haphazardly. ■ **m. de pelo,** head of hair. **2** *(ramita)* sprig; **una m. de tomillo/romero,** a sprig of thyme/rosemary.

matachín *nm* slaughterer.

matadero *nm* slaughterhouse, abattoir; *fig* **llevar (a algn) al m.,** to put (sb's life) at risk.

matador,-a I *adj* killing. **II** *nm Taur* matador, bullfighter.

matadura *nf* (harness) sore.

matahambre *nm Am Culin* chop.

matalahúga *nf*, **matalahúva** *nf* **1** *(planta)* anise. **2** *(semilla)* aniseed.

matalascallando *nm inv fam* wolf in sheep's clothing.

matamoscas *nm inv* **1** *(pala)* fly swat. **2** fly killer.

matanza *nf* **1** slaughter. **2** *Culin* pork products *pl.* **3** *CAm* butcher's (shop); meat market.

mataperros *nm inv fam* street urchin.

matar I *vtr* **1** to kill; *fig* **m. a algn a disgustos,** to drive sb insane; *fam* **el que la sigue la mata,** where there's a will, there's a way; *fam* **estar a m. con algn,** to be at daggers drawn with sb; *fam* **m. el hambre/el tiempo,** to kill hunger/the time; *fam* **matarlas callando,** to be a wolf in a sheep's clothing; *fam* **que me maten si ...,** I'll be damned if .... **2** *(redondear)* to round, bevel. **3** *(sello)* to frank. **4** *(polvo)* to lay. **5** *(luz, fuego)* to put out. **6** *(color)* to tone down. **II matarse** *vr* to kill oneself; *fig* **se mata para sacar a la familia adelante,** she kills herself working to support her family.

matarife *nm* slaughterer.

matarratas *nm inv* **1** *(raticida)* rat poison. **2** *fam (brebaje)* rotgut.

matasanos *nmf inv fam* quack.

matasellos *nm inv* **1** *(instrumento)* canceller. **2** *(marca)* postmark.

matasiete *nm fam* bully, braggart.

matasuegras *nm inv* paper serpent.

matate *nm CAm* string bag.

matazón *nf Am (animales)* slaughter, killing; *fig* toll, carnage.

match *nm Dep* match.

mate[1] *adj (sin brillo)* matt.

mate[2] *nm Ajedrez* mate. ■ **jaque m.,** checkmate.

mate[3] **1** *Am Bot* maté; *(bebida)* Paraguayan tea, maté. **2** *SAm (planta)* gourd; *(recipiente)* gourd. **3** *Am fam (cabeza)* nut.

matear *vi SAm* to drink maté.

matemática *nf*, **matemáticas** *nfpl* mathematics *sing.*

matemático,-a I *adj* mathematical. **II** *nm, f* mathematician. ◆ **matemáticamente** *adv* mathematically.

materia *nf* **1** matter; *Fis* material. ■ **m. gris,** grey matter; **m. prima,** raw material. **2** *(tema)* matter, question; **en m. de,** as regards; **entrar en m.,** to get to the point. ■ **índice de materias,** table of contents. **3** *Educ (asignatura)* subject.

material I *adj* material, physical; **daños materiales,** damage to property; **el autor m. del hecho,** the real instigator of the deed, the person behind the deed; **no tengo tiempo m. para hacerlo,** I just haven't got the time to do it. **II** *nm* material. ■ **m. escolar/de construcción,** teaching/building material or materials *pl*; **m. de oficina,** office equipment. ◆ **materialmente** *adv* materially, physically; **es m. imposible,** it is quite or absolutely impossible.

materialidad *nf* material nature.

materialismo *nm* materialism. ■ *Filos* **m. dialéctico,** dialectical materialism.

materialista *adj & nmf* materialist.

materialización *nf* materialization.

materializar *vtr*, **materializarse** *vr* to materialize.

maternal *adj* maternal, motherly.

maternidad *nf* maternity, motherhood.

materno,-a *adj* maternal; **abuelo m.,** maternal grandfather; **lengua materna,** native or mother tongue.

mates *nfpl fam* maths *sing*, *US* math *sing*.

matinal I *adj* morning, matinal. **II** *nf* matinée.

matinée *nf*, **matiné** *nf* matinée.

matiz *nm* **1** *(color)* shade, hue, tint; **tres matices de rosa,** three shades of pink. **2** *fig* shade of meaning, nuance; **un m. irónico,** a touch of irony.

matización *nf* **1** *Arte* blending, harmonization; *(coloreado)* shading, tingeing. **2** *fig (de palabras)* nuances *pl.*

matizar *vtr* **1** *Arte (proporcionar)* to blend, harmonize; *(dar color)* to tinge. **2** *fig (palabras, discurso)* to tinge; *(voz)* to vary or modulate. **3** *fig (precisar)* to be more precise or explicit about; **convendría m. este tema,** we ought to look more closely at this; **esto, hay que matizarlo,** it's not as straightforward as that; **¿podría m. sus recientes declaraciones, por favor?,** could you clarify your recent statements please?

matojo *nm* shrub, bush; **un m. de hierbas,** a tuft of grass.

matón,-ona *nm, f fam* thug, bully.

matonear *vtr CAm* **1** *(asesinar)* to kill. **2** *(desherbar)* to clear. **II** *vi* **1** *(alardear de matón)* to play the tough guy. **2** *fam (chulear)* to show off, be cocky.

matorral *nm* brushwood, thicket.

matraca I *nf (ruido)* rattle; *fam* **dar la m. a algn,** *(dar la lata)* to pester or bother sb; *(burlarse)* to make fun of sb, laugh at sb. **II** *nmf fam* bore, pest, nuisance.

matraquear *vi* **1** *(hacer ruido)* to rattle. **2** *fam* to pester, be a nuisance.

matraqueo *nm* **1** *(ruido)* rattling. **2** *fam* pestering.

matraz *nm Quím* flask.

matrero,-a **I** *adj (astuto)* sly, cunning. **II** *nm, f (astuto)* trickster, slyboots. **2** *Am (bandolero)* bandit, brigand.

matriarcado *nm* matriarchy.

matriarcal *adj* matriarchal.

matricida *nmf (persona)* matricide.

matricidio *nm (acto)* matricide.

matrícula *nf* **1** *(lista)* roll, list. **2** registration. ■ **derechos de m.**, registration fee; **m. de honor,** top mark; **plazo de m.,** registration period. **3** *Aut (número)* registration number; *(placa)* number *or* US license plate. **4** *Náut* **puerto de m.,** port of registry.

matriculación *nf* registration.

matricular *vtr*, **matricularse** *vr* to register; **me matriculé en (un curso de) inglés,** I put my name down for English (classes).

matrimonial *adj* matrimonial; **agencia m.,** marriage bureau; **enlace m.,** wedding; **vida m.,** married life.

matrimonio *nm* **1** marriage; **contraer m.,** to marry. ■ **cama de m.,** double bed; **m. civil/religioso,** registry office/church wedding. **2** *(pareja casada)* married couple; **el m. y los niños,** the couple and their children; **el m. Romero,** Mr and Mrs Romero, the Romeros.

matritense *adj* of *or* from Madrid.

matriz *nf* **1** *Anat* womb, uterus. **2** *(de talonario)* stub. **3** *(de documento)* (original) original, master copy. **4** *Téc* mould, US mold. **5** *Impr Mat* matrix.

matrona *nf* **1** *(madre respetable)* matron, mature woman. **2** *Med (comadrona)* midwife. **3** *(en cárceles, hospitales)* matron. **4** *(en aduanas)* searcher.

matufia *nf RPl fam* trick, fraud.

matungo,-a **I** *adj Am (flacucho)* weak, emaciated; *(cojo)* lame. **II** *nm RPl Cuba* old horse, hack, nag.

maturrango,-a *adj* **1** *Am (jinete)* poor, incompetent. **2** *Am pey* Spanish *or* European. **3** *Arg Chi (persona)* clumsy.

Matusalén *nm* Methuselah; **más viejo que M.,** as old as Methuselah *or* the hills.

matute *nm* **1** smuggling; **de m.,** contraband; **hacer m.,** to smuggle. **2** *(género)* contraband, smuggled goods *pl.* **3** *(casa de juegos)* gambling den.

matutear *vi* to smuggle.

matutino,-a **I** *adj* morning; **estrella matutina,** morning star. **II** *nm Prensa* morning newspaper.

maula **I** *nf* **1** *(trasto)* piece of junk; **este coche es una m.,** this car is an old crate. **2** *(retal)* remnant. **3** *(engaño)* (dirty) trick. **II** *nmf fam* **1** *fig (persona) (moroso)* bad payer; *(tramposo)* slippery *or* tricky customer; *(pesado)* bore. **2** *(vago)* dead loss, good-for-nothing.

maullador,-a *adj* miaowing.

maullar *vi* to miaow.

maullido *nm* miaowing, miaow.

Mauricio *n* Mauritius.

Mauritania *n* Mauritania.

mauritano,-a *adj & nm, f* Mauritanian.

máuser *nm Mil* mauser.

mausoleo *nm Arquit* mausoleum.

maxilar *Anat* **I** *adj* maxillary. **II** *nm* jaw, jawbone.

máxima *nf* maxim.

máxime *adv* especially, all the more so.

máximo,-a *adj* **1** *superl de* **grande. 2** maximum; **la máxima puntuación,** the highest score. **3** *Mat* **m. común divisor,** highest common factor. **II** *nm* maximum; **al m.,** to the utmost; **como m.,** *(como mucho)* at the most; *(lo más tarde)* at the latest; **mi paciencia llegó al m.,** my patience reached its limit. **III** *nf Meteor* maximum temperature.

maya **I** *adj* Mayan. **II** *nmf* Maya, Mayan.

mayador,-a *adj véase* **maullador,-a.**

mayar *vi véase* **maullar.**

mayestático,-a *adj* **1** majestic. **2** *Ling* **plural m.,** the Royal 'we'.

mayido *nm véase* **maullido.**

mayo *nm* **1** *(mes)* May; *prov* **hasta el cuarenta de m. no te quites el sayo,** ne'er cast a clout till May be out; *véase tamb* **noviembre. 2** *(palo)* maypole.

mayólica *nf Constr* majolica.

mayonesa *nf Culin* mayonnaise.

mayor **I** *adj* **1** *(comparativo)* larger, bigger, greater; *(persona)* older; *(hermanos, hijos)* elder; **su casa es m. que la mía,** her house is bigger than mine; **Elvira es m. que Pilar,** Elvira is older than Pilar; **sus hermanos mayores,** her elder brothers. **2** *(superlativo)* largest, biggest, greatest; *(persona)* oldest; *(hermanos, hijos)* eldest; **el m. enemigo,** the greatest enemy; **la m. parte,** the majority; **la m. parte de las veces,** most times; **el m. de la clase,** the oldest in the class; **su hija m.,** his eldest daughter. **3** *(adulto)* grown-up; **hacerse m.,** to grow up; **ser m. de edad,** to be of age; *fam* **ya eres m.,** you're a big boy *or* girl now. **4** *(maduro)* elderly, mature; **un hombre (ya) m.,** an elderly man. **5** *(principal)* major, main; **calle m.,** high *or* main street; *Educ* **colegio m.,** hall of residence; *Com* **libro m.,** ledger; **plaza m.,** main square; **premisa m.,** major premise. **6** *Mús* major; **Do/Re/Mi m.,** C/D/E major. **7** *Com* **al por m.,** wholesale; *fig (en abundancia)* by the score, galore. **II** *nm* **1** *Mil* major. **2** **mayores,** *(adultos)* grown-ups, adults; **una película para m.,** a film for adults; **respetar a los m.,** to show respect for one's elders. **3** **mayores,** *(antepasados)* ancestors. **III** *nmf* **el** *or* **la m.,** the oldest; *(hermanos, hijos)* the eldest.

mayoral *nm* **1** *(pastor)* head shepherd. **2** *Agr (capataz)* foreman. **3** *arc (cochero)* coachman.

mayorazgo *nm* **1** *(primogenitura)* primogeniture. **2** *(herencia)* entailed estate. **3** *(heredero)* heir (to an entailed estate). **4** *fig (primogénito)* first-born, eldest son.

mayordomo *nm* butler.

mayoría *nf* majority; **en su m.,** in the main; **la gran** *or* **inmensa m.,** the great *or* vast majority; **la m. de los niños,** most children. ■ **m. absoluta/relativa,** absolute/relative majority; **m. de edad,** majority.

mayorista **I** *adj* wholesale. **II** *nmf* wholesaler; **precios de m.,** wholesale prices.

mayoritario,-a *adj* majority; **un gobierno m.,** a majority government.

mayúsculo,-a **I** *adj* **1** *(enorme)* very big, enormous; **un susto m.,** a tremendous scare. **2** *Ling (letra)* capital. **II** *nf* capital letter.

maza *nf* **1** *Téc* large hammer, pounder. ■ **m. de fraga,** drop hammer. **2** *Hist (arma)* mace, war club. **3** *(insignia)* mace. **4** *fig* bore. **5** *Mús* drumstick.

mazacote[1] *nm* **1** *Constr* concrete. **2** *Culin* solid mass, stodge. **3** *fam (adefesio)* eyesore, monstrosity. **4** *fam (pesado)* bore, pest. **5** *Am (mezcla confusa)* hotch-potch.

mazacote[2] *nm Méx Zool* boa.

mazamorra *nf* **1** *SAm Culin* maize porridge. **2** *(en el pie)* sore, soreness.

mazapán *nm Culin* marzipan.

mazazo *nm* blow with a hammer *or* mace; **caer como un m.,** to go down like a lead balloon; **la noticia fue un m.,** the news was a heavy blow.

mazmorra *nf* dungeon.

mazo *nm* **1** *(martillo)* mallet. **2** *(manojo)* wad, bunch; **un m. de billetes de banco/de papeles,** a wad of banknotes/papers. **3** *fig (pesado)* bore, pest.

mazorca *nf Bot* spike; *Agr* cob.

mazurca *nf Mús* mazurka.

me I *pron pers* me; **¿me das un caramelo?**, will you give me a sweet?; **no me mires**, don't look at me. II *pron reflexivo* myself; **me veo en el espejo**, I can see myself in the mirror; **me voy/muero**, I'm going/dying.

meada *nf vulg* 1 piss, slash; **echar una m.**, to have a piss. 2 *(mancha)* urine stain.

meadero *nm vulg* bog.

meandro *nm* meander.

mear I *vi vulg* to (have a) piss. II **mearse** *vr* to wet oneself; *fig* **m. de risa**, to piss oneself (laughing).

MEC *nm abr de* **Ministerio de Educación y Ciencia**, Department of Education and Science, DES.

Meca *n* 1 **la M.**, Mecca; *fig* **andar de la Ceca a la M.**, to go back and forth. 2 *fig (centro)* mecca, centre, *US* center.

mecachis *fam interj* darn it!, damn it!

mecánica *nf* 1 *(ciencia)* mechanics *sing*. 2 *(mecanismo)* mechanism, works *pl*.

mecanicista I *adj* mechanistic. II *nmf* mechanist.

mecánico,-a I *adj* mechanical. II *nm,f* mechanic.

mecanismo *nm* mechanism.

mecanización *nf* mechanization.

mecanizar *vtr* to mechanize.

mecano® *nm* Meccano®.

mecanografía *nf* typewriting, typing.

mecanografiar *vtr* to type.

mecanógrafo,-a *nm,f* typist.

mecatazo *nm* 1 *CAm Méx (latigazo)* lash, stroke. 2 *Méx fam (trago)* swig.

mecate *nm* 1 *CAm Méx Filip* strip of pita fibre *or US* fiber; string. 2 *Méx (grosero)* coarse *or* vulgar person.

mecedor,-a I *adj* rocking. II *nf* rocking chair.

mecenas *nmf inv* patron.

mecenazgo *nm* patronage.

mecer I *vtr* to rock. II **mecerse** *vr* to swing, rock.

mecha *nf* 1 *(de vela)* wick. 2 *Mil Min* fuse; *fam* **a toda m.**, at full speed; *fam* **aguantar m.**, to grin and bear it. 3 *Culin* lardoon, piece of bacon used to lard meat. 4 *(de pelo)* streak; **hacerse mechas**, to have one's hair streaked. 5 *Am (broma)* joke. 6 *Am (barrena)* bit. 7 *Méx (miedo)* fear.

mechar *vtr* 1 *(carne)* to lard. 2 *(pelo)* to streak.

mechero,-a I *nm* (cigarette) lighter. ▪ **m. de gas**, gas lighter. II *nmf arg* shoplifter.

mechificar *vi Am* to mock, scoff.

mechón *nm* 1 *(de pelo)* lock. 2 *(de lana)* tuft.

mechonear *vtr*, **mechonearse** *vr Am (el cabello)* to tear (at) one's hair.

meco,-a *adj* 1 *CAm Méx (grosero)* rude, rough, vulgar, coarse. 2 *Antill Méx (cabello)* fair, blond, blonde; *(cosas)* golden. 3 *(animal)* red *or* ginger and black.

medalla I *nf* medal; *fam* **ponerse medallas**, to boast. II *nmf Dep (campeón)* medallist, *US* medalist.

medallista *nmf* medallist, *US* medalist, engraver of medals.

medallón *nm* medallion.

médano *nm*, **medano** *nm (duna)* sand dune; *(banco)* sandbank.

media *nf* 1 stocking; *Am (calcetín)* sock; **hacer m.**, to knit. 2 *(promedio)* average; **una m. de tres litros por día**, three litres a day on average. 3 *Mat* mean; **m. aritmética/ geométrica**, arithmetic/geometric mean.

mediación *nf* mediation, intervention; **por m. de un amigo**, through a friend.

mediado,-a I *pp de* **mediar**. II *adj* half-full, half-empty; **está el jarro m.**, the jug is half full; **llevo mediada la obra**, I'm half-way through the play; **a mediados de mes/semana**, about the middle of the month/week.

mediador,-a I *adj* mediating. II *nm,f* mediator.

mediagua *nf Am* roof which slopes in one direction.

medialuna *nf* 1 *(símbolo musulmán)* crescent. 2 *Culin (pasta)* croissant.

mediana *nf Mat* median.

medianería *nf* 1 *(pared)* party wall. 2 *Am (aparcería)* partnership.

medianero,-a *adj* dividing; *Arquit* **muro m.**, dividing fence; *Arquit* **pared medianera**, party wall.

medianía *nf* 1 middling position; **vivir en la m.**, to have an undistinguished social position. 2 *pey (persona)* mediocre person.

mediano,-a I *adj* 1 middling, average; **inteligencia mediana**, average intelligence. 2 *(tamaño)* medium-sized; **un coche m.**, a medium-sized car. 3 *pey (mediocre)* mediocre. II *nf Cat* (≈ half pint) bottle of beer.

medianoche *nf* midnight; **a m.**, in the middle of the night.

mediante *prep* by means of, with the help of, using; **Dios m.**, God willing.

mediar *vi* 1 *(intervenir)* to mediate, intervene; **m. en favor de** *or* **por algn**, to intercede on behalf of sb. 2 *(tiempo)* to pass; **mediaron tres semanas**, three weeks passed; *(distancia)* **median nueve kms entre Tafalla y Olite**, it is nine kms from Tafalla to Olite; *fig* **media un abismo**, there is an enormous gap *or* difference. 3 *(hecho, circunstancia)* to exist; **media el hecho de que es menor de edad**, there is the fact that he is a minor. 4 *(ocurrir)* to intervene, happen, come up; **se iban a casar pero medió el escándalo**, they were going to get married, but the scandal intervened. 5 *(estar en la mitad)* to be in the middle, be half-way through; **mediaba agosto**, it was mid-August.

mediatización *nf* decisive influence.

mediatizar *vtr* to exercise *or* have a decisive influence on.

medicación *nf* 1 *(tratamiento)* medication, medical treatment. 2 *(medicamentos)* medicines *pl*.

medicamento *nm* medicine, medicament.

medicamentoso,-a *adj* medicinal.

medicar I *vtr* to administer medicines to, medicate. II **medicarse** *vr* to take medicines.

medicina *nf* medicine; **estudiante de m.**, medical student, medic.

medicinal *adj* medicinal.

medicinar *vtr* to treat, give medicine to.

medición *nf* 1 *(acción)* measuring. 2 *(dato)* measurement.

médico,-a *adj* medical. II *nm,f* doctor, physician. ▪ **m. de cabecera**, family doctor, general practitioner, GP.

medida *nf* 1 measure; **a (la) m.**, *(ropa)* made-to-measure; *(mueble)* specially made; **pesos y medidas**, weights and measures; **tres medidas de arroz**, three measures of rice; *fig* **a la m. de**, according to; *fig* **a m. que**, as; **a m. que pasa el tiempo**, as time goes by; *fig* **en gran m.**, to a great extent; *fig* **en la m. en que**, in so far as, inasmuch as; *fig* **en la m. de lo posible**, as far as possible; *fig* **en mayor/ menor m.**, to a greater/lesser extent; *fig* **hasta cierta m.**, to a certain extent. 2 *(medición)* measuring, measurement. 3 *(moderación)* moderation, prudence; **sin m.**, immoderately, excessively. 4 *(disposición)* action, measure; **adoptar** *or* **tomar medidas**, to take steps. ▪ **m. preventiva**, preventiva measure; **m. represiva**, deterrent. 5 *Lit* scansion.

medidor,-a I *adj* measuring. II *nm Am Téc* meter.

medieval *adj* medieval.

medievalismo *nm* medievalism.

medievalista *nmf* medievalist.

medievo *nm* Middle Ages *pl*.

medio,-a I *adj* 1 half; **a m. camino**, half-way; **clase media**, middle class; **dedo m.**, middle finger; **m. kilo**, half a kilo; **una hora y media**, one and a half hours, an hour and a half; *fig* **media luz**, half-light. 2 *(intermedio)* middle; **a**

media mañana/tarde, in the middle of the morning/ afternoon; **de media edad,** middle-aged. **3** *(promedio)* average; **el hombre m.,** the average man; **temperatura media,** mean temperature. **II** *adv* **1** half; **está m. muerto,** he is half dead; **está m. terminado,** it's half finished. **2 a medias,** *(incompleto)* unfinished; *(entre dos)* between the two; **lo dejó a medias,** he left it half done; **lo pagamos a medias,** we went halves on it, we shared the cost; **ir a medias,** to go halves. **III** *nm* **1** *(mitad)* half; **de m. a m.,** completely. **2** *(centro)* middle; **de por m.,** in the way; **en m. (de),** *(en el centro)* in the middle (of); *(entre dos)* in between; *(entre varios)* among; **(justo) en m. de la calle,** (right) in the middle of the street; **estar/ponerse en m.,** to be/put oneself in the way; **la casa del m.,** the middle house; **por (el) m.,** in *or* down the middle; *fam* **quitar algo/a algn de en m.,** to get sth/sb out of the way. **3** *(procedimiento)* means, way; **medios de comunicación,** (mass) media; **medios de vida,** means of support; **no hay m. de ...,** there's no way of ...; **por m. de ...,** by means of ...; **por sus propios medios,** on his own resources; **por todos los medios,** by all possible means. **4** *Biol Fís* medium; **adaptación al m.,** adaptation to the environment. ■ **m. ambiente,** environment. **5** *Mat* mean. **6** *(círculo social)* environment, circle; **en los medios teatrales,** in the world of theatre; **encontrarse en su m.,** to be in one's element. **7** *Dep* *(jugador)* halfback. **8 medios,** *(económicos)* means; **no tener m.,** not to have economic resources.

mediocre *adj* mediocre.

mediocridad *nf* mediocrity.

mediodía *nm* **1** *(hora exacta)* midday, noon. **2** *(pe ríodo aproximado)* early afternoon, lunchtime; **las tiendas cierran dos** *or* **tres horas al m.,** shops are closed for two *or* three hours in the early afternoon *or* at lunchtime. **3** *(sur)* south.

medioevo *nm véase* **medievo.**

mediopensionista *nmf* day student.

medir **I** *vtr* **1** *(distancia, superficie, temperatura)* to measure; *fig* **los boxeadores midieron sus fuerzas,** the boxers measured *or* gauged each other's strength. **2** *(sopesar)* to weigh up; **m. los pros y los contras,** to weigh up the pros and cons. **3** *(moderar)* to weigh; **mide tus palabras,** weigh your words. **3** *Lit* *(verso)* to scan. **II** *vi* to measure, be; **¿cuánto mides?,** how tall are you?; **mide 2 metros,** he is 2 metres tall; **mide dos metros de alto/ ancho/largo,** it is two metres high/wide/long. **III medirse** *vr* **m. con algn,** to measure oneself against sb.

meditabundo,-a *adj* pensive, thoughtful.

meditación *nf* meditation.

meditar *vtr & vi* to meditate, ponder; **m. sobre algo,** to ponder over sth.

meditativo,-a *adj* meditative.

mediterráneo,-a I *adj* Mediterranean. **II el M.** *nm* the Mediterranean.

médium *nmf* *(pl* **médiums)** medium.

medo,-a I *adj* Median. **II** *nm, f* Mede.

medrar *vi* **1** *(plantas, animales)* to thrive, grow. **2** *fig* to flourish, do well, prosper.

medro *nm* **1** *(plantas, animales)* growth. **2** *fig* prosperity. **3** *(mejora)* improvement. **4 medros,** progress *sing,* advancement *sing.*

medroso,-a I *adj* **1** *(temeroso)* fearful, fainthearted. **2** *(que causa miedo)* frightening. **II** *nm, f* fearful person.

médula *nf* **1** *Anat* marrow. ■ **m. espinal,** spinal cord; **m. osea,** bone marrow. **2** *fig* *(lo más profundo)* marrow, pith; **hasta la m.,** to the marrow.

medular *adj* of *or* related to the marrow.

medusa *nf Zool* jellyfish.

mefistofélico,-a *adj* Mephistophelian.

mefítico,-a *adj* poisonous, mephitic.

megaciclo *nm Rad* megacycle.

megafonía *nf* **1** *(técnica)* sound amplification. **2** *(equipo)* public-address system, PA system.

megáfono *nm* megaphone.

megalítico,-a *adj* megalithic.

megalito *nm* megalith.

megalomanía *nf* megalomania.

megalómano,-a *adj* megalomaniac.

megatón *nm Fís* megaton.

megavatio *nm Fís* megawatt.

megavoltio *nm Fís* megavolt.

mejicano,-a *adj & nm, f* Mexican.

Méjico *n* Mexico. ■ **ciudad de M.,** Mexico City; **Nuevo M.,** New Mexico.

mejilla *nf* cheek.

mejillón *nm Zool* mussel.

mejillonero,-a I *adj* mussel; **la industria mejillonera,** the mussel industry. **II** *nm, f* *(criador)* mussel farmer; *(pescador)* mussel gatherer. **III** *nf* mussel farm.

mejor I *adj* **1** *(comparativo)* better; **es m. no decírselo,** it's better not to tell her; **esta novela es m. que la anterior,** this novel is better than his last one; **a falta de algo m.,** for want of something better; **pensé que era m. no salir,** I thought I'd better stay at home. **2** *(superlativo)* best; **tu m. amiga,** your best friend; **el m. de los dos,** the better of the two; **el m. de tos tres,** the best of the three; **lo m.,** the best thing; **lo m. de algo,** the best part of sth; **lo m. posible,** as well as possible. **II** *adv* **1** *(comparativo)* better; **así es m.,** that's better; **cada vez m.,** better and better; **ella conduce m.,** she drives better; **ir a m.,** to improve, get better; **m. dicho,** or rather; **m. or peor,** one way or another; **¡mucho or tanto m.!,** so much the better! **2** *(superlativo)* best; **es el que m. canta,** he is the one who sings the best; **a lo m.,** *(quizás)* perhaps; *(ojalá)* hopefully.

mejora *nf* **1** improvement; **m. de sueldo,** pay increase, (pay) rise. **2** *(puja)* higher bid.

mejorable *adj* improvable.

mejoramiento *nm* improvement.

mejorar I *vtr* to improve, better; **m. la red víal,** to improve the road system; **m. una oferta/una puja,** to raise an offer/a bid; **m. una marca** *or* **un récord,** to break a record. **II** *vi* to improve, get better; **el tiempo ha mejorado,** the weather has cleared up; **m. de salud,** to improve in health, get better; **m. de situación,** to better oneself. **III mejorarse** *vr* to get better; **¡que te mejores!,** get well soon!

mejoría *nf* improvement.

mejunje *nm* unpleasant mixture *or* brew.

melado,-a I *adj* honey-coloured, *US* honey-colored. **II** *nm Am* cane syrup.

melancolía *nf* melancholy.

melancólico,-a I *adj* melancholic, melancholy. **II** *nm, f* melancholic person.

melanina *nf Biol* melanin.

melaza *nf* molasses *pl.*

melcocha *nf* honey toffee.

melcochudo,-a *adj* chewy.

melé *nf Dep* scrum.

melena *nf* **1** (head of) hair. ■ **m. de león,** mane. **2 melenas,** mop *sing.*

melenudo,-a I *adj* long-haired. **II** *nm, f* long-haired person.

melifluo,-a *adj* mellifluous.

melillense I *adj* of *or* from Melilla. **II** *nmf* native *or* inhabitant of Melilla.

melindre *nm* **1** *Culin* *(frito)* honey fritter; *(de mazapan)* iced marzipan cake. **2** *fig* *(afectación)* affectation, fussiness; **andarse con melindres,** to be finicky *or* fastidous *or* fussy.

melindroso,-a I *adj* affected, fussy, finicky. **II** *nm, f* affected *or* finicky person.

melisa *nf Bot* (lemon) balm.

mella *nf* **1** *(hendedura)* nick, notch; *(en plato, taza, etc)* chip. **2** *(hueco)* gap, hole; **tantos gastos han hecho m. en mis ahorros,** all these expenses have made a hole in my savings. **3** *fig* impression; **hacer m.,** *(en algn)* to make an impression on; *(en el honor, la reputación, etc)* to damage.

mellado,-a *pp de* **mellar. II** *adj* **1** *(hendido)* nicked, notched; *(plato, taza, etc)* chipped. **2** *(sin dientes)* gap-toothed. **3** *fig* damaged.

melladura *nf véase* **mella.**

mellar *vtr* **1** to nick, notch; *(plato, taza, etc)* to chip, take a chip out of. **2** *fig (honor)* to cast a slur on; *(orgullo)* to dent.

mellizo,-a *adj & nm,f* twin.

melocotón *nm* peach; *Culin* **melocotones en almíbar,** peaches in syrup, tinned peaches.

melocotonar *nm* peach orchard.

melocotonero *nm Bot* peach tree.

melodía *nf* melody, tune.

melódico,-a *adj* melodic.

melodioso,-a *adj* melodious, tuneful.

melodrama *nm* melodrama.

melodramático,-a *adj* melodramatic.

melomanía *nf* love of *or* for music.

melómano,-a *nm,f* music lover.

melón *nm* **1** *Bot* melon. **2** *hum (cabeza)* nut, bonce. **3** *fam (tonto)* ninny.

melonar *nm* melon patch.

melonero,-a *nm, f (vendedor)* melon seller; *(criador)* melon grower.

melopea *nf fam* **coger** *or* **agarrar/llevar una m.,** to get/be drunk *or* pissed.

melosidad *nf* sweetness, gentleness.

meloso,-a *adj* sweet, honeyed.

melva *nf (pez)* frigate mackerel.

membrana *nf* membrane.

membranoso,-a *adj* membranous.

membrete *nm* letterhead.

membrillo *nm* **1** *Bot* quince; *(árbol)* quince tree; *(dulce)* quince preserve *or* jelly. **2** *arg (chivato)* nark.

membrudo,-a *adj* brawny, burly.

memela *nf Guat Hond Méx* type of maize tortilla.

memez *nf* stupidity; **decir memeces,** to talk nonsense.

memo,-a *fam* **I** *adj* silly stupid. **II** *nm, f* nincompoop, ninny.

memorable *adj* memorable.

memorándum *nm (pl* **memorándums)** notebook.

memoria *nf* **1** memory; **aprender/saber algo de m.,** to learn/know sth by heart; **borrar de la m.,** to banish from memory; **falta de m.,** forgetfulness; **hablar de m.,** to speak from memory; **hacer m. de algo,** to remember *or* recall sth; **irse de la m.,** to slip one's mind; **refrescar la m. a algn,** to refresh sb's memory; **traer algo a la m.,** to recall sth; **venir a la m.,** to come to mind. **2** *(recuerdo)* memory, recollection; **de grata/ingrata m.,** of happy/ unhappy memory. **3** *(informe)* report, statement; **m. anual,** annual report. **4** *(estudio escrito)* essay. **5** *(inventario)* inventory, list. **6 memorias,** *(biografía)* memoirs.

memorial *nm* **1** *(libro)* notebook. **2** *arc (petición)* memorial.

memorión,-ona *fam* **I** *adj* with a very good memory. **II** *nm,f* person with a very good memory. **III** *nm* very good memory.

memorístico,-a *adj* acquired by memory.

memorización *nf* memorizing.

memorizar *vtr* to memorize.

mena *nf Min* ore.

menaje *nm* furniture and furnishing *pl.* ■ **departamento de m.,** hardware and kitchen department; **m. de cocina,** kitchen equipment.

mención *nf* mention; **digno de m.,** worth mentioning; **hacer m. de algo,** to mention sth. ■ **m. honorífica,** honourable mention.

mencionado,-a I *pp de* **mencionar. II** *adj* mentioned; *fml* **arriba** *or* **anteriormente m.,** aforementioned.

mencionar *vtr* to mention.

menda *pron fam* yours truly; **el** *or* **mi m. se queda en casa,** I'll stay at home; **me lo dijo un m. que pasaba por allí,** a bloke who was passing by told me.

mendicante *adj & nmf* mendicant.

mendicidad *nf* **1** *(acción)* begging. **2** *(modo de vida)* beggary.

mendigar *vtr & vi* to beg.

mendigo,-a *nm,f* beggar.

mendrugo *nm* crust *or* chunk (of stale bread).

menear I *vtr* to shake, move; *(cola)* to wag, waggle; *fam (caderas, cuerpo)* to wiggle. **II menearse** *vr* to move, shake; *fam* **una tormenta de no te menees,** a hell of a storm; *vulg* **meneársela,** to wank.

meneo *nm* **1** *(de cola)* wag, waggle; *(de caderas)* wiggle. **2** *(paliza)* hiding.

menester *nm* **1** *arc (ocupación)* work, occupation. **2** *arc (necesidad)* **haber** *or* **ser m.,** to be necessary; **no es m. que te quedes,** there is no need for you to stay; **si hubiera m.,** if need be. **3 menesteres,** *euf* call of nature *sing*; **salió a hacer sus m.,** he went out to answer a call of nature.

menesteroso,-a I *adj* needy. **II** *nm,f* needy person.

menestra *nf Culin* vegetable stew.

mengano,-a *nm,f fam* so-and-so, what's-his *or* hername; *véase también* **fulano.**

mengua *nf* **1** *(disminución)* decrease, diminution; **sin m.,** without detriment **(de,** to). **2** *(falta)* lack, want; **sin m.,** complete. **3** *(deshonra)* descredit.

menguado,-a I *adj* **1** *(reducido)* decreased. **2** *(cobarde)* cowardly, spineless; *(miserable)* wretched, miserable. **II** *nmf (cobarde)* coward; *(miserable)* wretch. **III** *nm Tricot (punto)* decrease.

menguante *adj* waning, on the wane. ■ **cuarto m.,** last quarter; **luna m.,** waning moon.

menguar I *vtr* **1** to diminish, reduce. **2** *(en calceta)* to decrease. **II** *vi* **1** to diminish, decrease. **2** *(la luna)* to wane.

menhir *nm* menhir.

menina *nf arc* maid.

meninge *nf Anat* meninx.

meningitis *nf Med* meningitis.

meñique I *adj (muy pequeño)* tiny, very small; **(dedo) m.,** little finger. **II** *nm (dedo auricular)* little finger.

menisco *nm Anat Fís* meniscus.

menopausia *nf Med* menopause.

menor I *adj* **1** *(comparativo)* smaller, lesser; *(persona)* younger; **de m. tamaño,** smaller; **mal m.,** lesser evil; **ser m. de edad,** to be a minor. **2** *(superlativo)* smallest, least, slightest; *(persona)* youngest; **sin el m. interés,** without the slightest interest; **el m. de los dos,** the smaller of the two; **el m. de los tres,** the smallest of the three; **es la m.,** she's the youngest child. **3** *(inferior)* minor; **una obra m.,** a minor work. **4** *Rel* minor. ■ **órdenes menores,** minor orders. **5** *Mús* minor; **en La m.,** in A minor. **6** *Com* **al por m.,** retail. **II** *nmf* minor; **apto para menores,** for all ages. ■ *Jur* **tribunal de menores,** juvenile court.

Menorca *n* Minorca.

menorquín,-ina *adj & nm,f* Minorcan.

menos I *adv* **1** *(comparativo)* less, fewer; **m. dinero/leche/tiempo,** less money/milk/time; **m. gente/libros/pisos,** fewer people/books/flats; **ayer llovió m. que hoy,** yesterday it rained less than today; **deberías comer m.,** you should eat less; **tiene m. años de lo que parece,** he's younger than he looks. **2** *(superlativo)* least, fewest; **ayer fue cuando vino m. gente,** yesterday was when the fewest people came; **fui el que perdí m. dinero,** I lost the least money. **3** *(locuciones)* **a m. que,** unless; **al o por lo o cuando m.,** at least; **cuánto m. lo pienses, mejor,** the less you think about it, the better; **cuánto** *or* **mientras m. comes, más adelgazarás,** the less you eat, the more weight you'll lose; **echar a algn de m.,** to miss sb; **en m. de ...,** in less than ...; **en m. de nada,** in no time at all; **eso es lo de m.,** that doesn't matter, that's the least of it; **hacer a algn de m.,** to disdain *or* belittle sb; **ir** *or* **venir a m.,** to lose social status; **lo m. que puedes hacer,** the least you can do; **m. de ...,** less than ...; **¡m. mal!,** thank God!, that's a relief!; **m. aún,** even less; **nada m.,** no less, no fewer; **nada m. que la mitad de la plantilla perdieron sus puestos de trabajo,** no less than half the staff lost their jobs; **¡escribió sesenta cartas, nada m.!,** he wrote no fewer than sixty letters!; **ni mucho m.,** far from it; **no es para m.,** you couldn't expect less; **no puedo por m. de decirle,** I can't help telling you; **para no ser m.,** not to be left behind; **por m. de nada,** for no reason at all; **¿qué m. que decírselo personalmente?,** the least he could have done is to tell her himself; **si al m.,** if only; **ya será m.,** come off it! **II** *prep* but, except; **todo m. eso,** anything but that. **III** *nm* **1** *Mat* minus; **tres m. uno,** three minus one. **2 los** *or* **las m. de,** the minority of. **IV** *adj fam* **ésta es m. casa que la tuya,** your house is better than this one.

menoscabar *vtr* **1** *(dañar)* to impair, harm, spoil; **tanto trabajo menoscabó su salud,** so much work damaged her health. **2** *(mermar)* to reduce, diminish; **este decreto menoscaba los derechos de los trabajadores,** this decree infringes on workers' rights. **3** *fig (desacreditar)* to discredit.

menoscabo *nm* harm, damage; **ir en m. de algo,** to be to the detriment of sth; **sin m.,** unimpaired.

menospreciable *adj* despicable, contemptible.

menospreciar *vtr* to show contempt for, scorn, disdain; **m. los consejos de algn,** to disregard sb's advice.

menosprecio *nm* contempt, scorn, disdain; **con m. de,** without regard for.

mensaje *nm* message; *fml* **el m. de la Corona,** the King's *or* Queen's speech.

mensajero,-a I *adj* message-carrying. ■ **paloma mensajera,** carrier pigeon. **II** *nm,f* messenger, courier.

menstruación *nf* **1** *(acción)* menstruation. **2** *(sangre)* menses *pl.*

menstrual *adj* menstrual.

menstruar *vi* to menstruate.

menstruo *nm* **1** *(sangre)* menses *pl.* **2** *(acción)* menstruation.

mensual *adj* monthly; **dos visitas mensuales,** two visits a month.

mensualidad *nf* *(pago)* monthly payment; *(sueldo)* monthly salary *or* wage.

mensurable *adj* measurable.

menta *nf* **1** *Bot* mint. ■ **m. aquatica,** water mint; **m. de gatos,** catmint; **té de m.,** mint tea. **2** *(licor)* créme de menthe.

mentado,-a I *pp de* **mentar.** **II** *adj* **1** *(mencionado)* aforementioned. **2** *lit (famoso)* famous, wellknown.

mental *adj* mental; *fam* **lo suyo es m.,** she's not right in her head. ◆ **mentalmente** *adv* mentally.

mentalidad *nf* mentality; **de m. abierta/cerrada,** open-/narrow-minded.

mentalizar I *vtr* *(concienciar)* to make aware. **II mentalizarse** *vr* **1** *(concienciarse)* to become aware. **2** *(hacerse a la idea)* to come to terms **(a,** with); **tienes que mentalizarte,** you'll just have to get used to it.

mentar *vtr* to mention, name; **ni lo mientes,** don't bring the subject up; *euf* **m. la madre a algn,** to insult sb.

mente *nf* mind; **no estaba en mi m.,** it wasn't my intention (-, to); **tenía la m. en blanco,** my mind went blank; **traer (algo) a la m.,** to bring (sth) to mind; **venir a la m.,** to come to mind. ■ **m. abierta/tolerante/cerrada,** open/broad/closed mind.

mentecato,-a I *adj* stupid. **II** *nm,f* fool, idiot.

mentidero *nm fam* gossip corner *or* shop.

mentir *vi* to lie, tell lies; **miente más que habla,** he lies through his teeth.

mentira *nf* lie; **aunque parezca m.,** strange as it many seem; **parece m.,** it is unbelievable; *fam fig* **una m. como una casa,** a whopping lie, a whopper. ■ **m. piadosa,** white lie.

mentirijilla *nf,* **mentirilla** *nf* **de mentirijillas, de mentirillas,** as a joke, for a laugh, for fun.

mentiroso,-a I *adj* lying; **un niño m.,** a child who tells lies. **II** *nm,f* liar.

mentís *nm* denial; **dar un m. a (un rumor),** to deny (a rumour).

mentol *nm* menthol.

mentolado,-a *adj* mentholated, menthol.

mentón *nm Anat* chin.

mentor *nm* mentor.

menú *nm* **1** *Culin* menu (of the day). **2** *Inform* menu.

menudear I *vtr* to repeat frequently; **menudea sus visitas a esta casa,** he visits us quite often. **II** *vi* **1** to happen frequently; **los robos menudean en este barrio,** burglaries are frequent in this area. **2** *(dar detalles)* to go into details.

menudencia *nf* **1** trifle. **2** *(esmero)* exactness, meticulousness. **3 menudencias,** *(de cerdo)* offal *sing.*

menudeo *nm* **1** *(repetición)* repetition. **2** *Com* retail.

menudillos *nmpl* giblets.

menudo,-a I *adj* **1** minute, tiny; **¡m. es el niño!,** the little devil!; **¡m. lío/susto!,** what a mess/fright! ■ *Com* **a** *or* **por la menuda,** retail; **la gente menuda,** the little ones *pl;* **lluvia menuda,** fine rain. **2** *fig* of minor importance. **II menudos** *nmpl (de res)* offal *sing;* *(de ave)* giblets. **III** *adv* **a m.,** often.

meollo *nm* **1** *(miga)* crumb. **2** *Anat (seso)* brains *pl;* *(médula)* marrow. **3** *fig (quid)* essence, pith; **el m. de la cuestión,** the heart of the matter. **4** *fig (juicio)* intelligence, brains *pl.*

meón,-ona *adj* **1** *vulg* who wets himself *or* herself. **2** *fig* baby.

mequetrefe *nmf* whippersnapper.

mercachifle *nmf* **1** *(buhonero)* pedlar. **2** *fam fig (pesetero)* money-grubber.

mercadear *vi arc* to trade.

mercader *nmf arc* merchant.

mercadería *nf arc* merchandise, goods *pl.*

mercado *nm* market; **acaparar el m.,** to corner the market; **abrir m. para un producto,** to make a market for a product; **sacar algo al m.,** to put sth on the market, market sth. ■ **m. al aire libre,** street market; **M. Común,** Common Market; **m. negro,** black market.

mercadotecnia *nf* marketing.

mercancía *nf* commodity, goods *pl.*

mercante *adj* merchant. ■ **barco/marina m.,** merchant ship/navy.

mercantil *adj* mercantile, commercial; **operaciones mercantiles,** commercial transactions.

mercantilismo *nm Econ* mercantilism.

mercantilista *adj & nmf Econ* mercantilist.

merced *nf fml* favour, *US* favor, grace; **a m. de,** at the mercy of; **m. a,** thanks to; *fml* **nos hizo la m. de ...,** he did us the favour of ... .

mercenario,-a *adj & nm,f* mercenary.

mercería *nf* 1 (*género*) haberdashery, *US* notions *pl*; (*tienda*) haberdasher's (shop), *US* notions store. 2 *Am* (*tienda de telas*) draper's (shop), *US* drygoods store.

mercero,-a *nm,f* haberdasher, *US* notions dealer.

mercurio *nm* 1 *Quím* mercury, quicksilver. 2 *Astrol Astron Mit* Mercury.

merecedor,-a *adj* deserving; **ser m. de,** to be worthy of, deserve.

merecer *vtr,* **merecerse** *vr* to deserve, merit, be worth; **merece la pena visitarlo,** it is worth a visit.

merecido,-a I *pp de* **merecer. II** *adj* deserved; **ella lo tiene m.,** (*recompensa*) she well deserves it; (*castigo*) it serves her right. **III** *nm* deserved punishment, just deserts *pl*.

merecimiento *nm* merit, worthiness.

merendar I *vtr* to have as an afternoon snack, have for tea. **II** *vi* to have an afternoon snack, have tea.

merendero *nm* (*establecimiento*) tearoom, snack bar; (*en el campo*) picnic spot.

merendola *nf fam* feast.

merengue I *nm* 1 *Culin* (*dulce*) meringue. 2 *fam* (*persona*) weak *or* lily-livered person. 3 *RPl* (*tifulca*) row, fuss. **II** *nmf fam* supporter of Real Madrid football club.

meretriz *nf fml* prostitute.

merezco *indic pres véase* **merecer.**

meridiano,-a I *adj* 1 (*del mediodía*) midday, noon. 2 (*evidente*) evident, obvious; **de una claridad meridiana,** patently clear. **II** nm meridian.

meridional I *adj* southern. **II** *nmf* southerner.

merienda *nf* 1 (*comida a media tarde*) afternoon snack, tea; **ir de m.,** to go for a picnic. ■ **m. cena,** high tea; *fam* **m. de negros,** bedlam, free-for-all. 2 (*provisiones*) packed lunch; picnic.

merino,-a I *adj zool* merino. **II** *nm,f Zool* merino (sheep); (*hembra*) merino ewe; (*macho*) merino ram. **III** *nm* (merino) wool.

mérito *nm* merit, worth; **atribuirse el m. de algo,** to take the credit for sth; **de m.,** worthy; **hacer méritos para algo,** to strive to deserve sth.

meritocracia *nf* meritocracy.

meritorio,-a I *adj* praiseworthy, meritorious. **II** *nm, f* unpaid trainee.

merluza *nf* 1 (*pez*) hake. 2 *fam* (*borrachera*) **cogerse una m.,** to get drunk.

merluzo,-a *nm & nm fam* ninny, fool.

merma *nf* dercrease, reduction.

mermar I *vtr* to cause to decrease *or* diminish. **II** *vi* to decrease, diminish. **III** **mermarse** *vr* to decrease, diminish.

mermelada *nf* 1 jam; **m. de melocotón/fresa,** peach/strawberry jam. 2 (*de agrios*) marmalade; **m. de naranja/limón,** orange/lemon marmalade.

mero[1] *nm* (*pez*) (*del mediterráneo*) grouper; (*del atlántico*) halibut.

mero,-a[2] *adj* mere, pure; **por el m. hecho de,** through the mere fact of; **una mera coincidencia,** a mere coincidence.

merodeador,-a I *adj* 1 *Caza Mil* marauding. 2 (*paseante*) wandering, prowling. **II** *nm, f* 1 *Caza Mil* marauder. 2 (*vagabundo*) prowler.

merodear *vi* 1 *Caza Mil* to maraud. 2 (*vagar*) to prowl.

merodeo *nm* 1 *Caza Mil* marauding. 2 (*vagabundeo*) prowling.

mes *nm* 1 month; **diez mil pesetas al m.,** ten thousand pesetas a month; **el m. pasado/que viene,** last/next month. 2 (*mensualidad*) (*cobro*) monthly salary *or* wages *pl*; (*pago*) monthly payment; **no ha cobrado el m.,** he hasn't been paid for last month. 3 *fam* (*menstruación*) menstruation; **estar con el m.,** to have one's period.

mesa *nf* 1 table; **bendecir la m.,** to say grace; **levantarse de la m.,** to leave the table; **poner/recoger la m.,** to set/clear the table; **sentarse a la m.,** to sit down at (the) table; **servir la m.,** to wait at table; **ser amante de la buena m.,** to be fond of good food; *fig* **a m. puesta,** with free maintenance; *fig* **a m. y mantel,** with free food. ■ **m. de despacho, m. de trabajo,** desk; **m. de operaciones,** operating table; **m. redonda,** *Hist* Round Table; *fig* (*reunión*) round table. 2 (*junta directiva*) board, executive; **el presidente de la m.,** the chairman. ■ **m. electoral,** electoral college.

mesana *nf* mizzen. ■ *Náut* **palo de m.,** mizzenmast.

mesar I *vtr* to tear (at). **II mesarse** *vr* to tear (at) one's hair or beard.

mescalina *nf* mescalin.

meseta *nf* plateau, tableland, meseta; **la M.,** the plateau of Castile.

mesiánico,-a *adj* messianic.

mesianismo *nm* messianism.

mesilla *nf* small table. ■ **m. de noche,** bedside table.

mesnada *nf* 1 *Hist* armed retinue. 2 **mesnadas,** followers.

mesón *nm* 1 *Hist* inn, tavern. 2 (*restaurante*) oldstyle tavern.

mesonero,-a *m,f* innkeeper.

Mesopotamia *n* Mesopotamia.

mesopotámico,-a *adj & nm,f* Mesopotamian.

mestizaje *nm* crossbreeding.

mestizo,-a *adj & nm,f* half-breed, half-caste, mestizo.

mesura *nf fml* moderation, restraint.

mesurar I *vtr* to restrain, temper. **II mesurarse** *vr* to restrain oneself.

meta *nf* 1 (*en carreras*) (*de caballos*) winning post; (*de coches, bicicletas*) finish, finishing line. 2 *Ftb* (*portería*) goal. 3 *fig* (*objetivo*) goal, aim, objective.

metabólico,-a *adj* metabolic.

metabolismo *nm* metabolism.

metafísica *nf* metaphysics.

metafísico,-a *adj* metaphysical.

metáfora *nf* metaphor.

Metafórico,-a *adj* metaphoric, metaphorical.

metal *nm* 1 metal; **metales comunes/preciosos,** base/precious metals; *fig* (*dinero*) **el vil m.,** filthy lucre. 2 (*timbre de la voz*) timbre. 3 *Mús* brass.

metálico,-a I *adj* metallic. **II** *nm* cash; **pagar en m.,** to pay (in) cash.

metalista *nm* metalworker.

metalización *nf* metallization.

metalizar *vtr* to metallize.

metaloide *nm* metalloid.

metalurgia *nf* metallurgy.

metalúrgico,-a I *adj* metallurgical. **II** *nm,f* metallurgist.

metamórfico,-a *adj* metamorphic.

metamorfismo *nm* metamorphism.

metamorfosear *vtr* to metamorphose.

metamorfosis *nf* metamorphosis.

metano *nm* methane.

metapiles *nmpl CAm* copper ingots.

metedura *nf fem* **m. de pata,** blunder.

meteórico,-a *adj* meteoric.

meteorito *nm* meteorite.

meteoro *nm* meteor.

meteorología *nf* meteorology.

meteorológico,-a *adj* meteorological. ■ **partera m.,** weather report.

meteorólogo,-a *nm*, *f* meteorologist; *(hombre)* weatherman.

meter I *vtr* **1** *(poner)* to put; **mete los juguetes en la caja,** put the toys in the box; **siempre meto mi dinero en el banco,** I always put my money in the bank; **su familia le metió en la empresa,** his family got him a job in the firm; *fig* **m. la nariz** *or* **las narices en algo,** to poke one's nose into sth; *fam* **a todo m.,** *(a toda velocidad)* at full speed; *(intensamente)* intensely; *fam* **m. mano a algo,** to get down to (do) sth; *fam fig* **m. la pata,** to put one's foot in it, drop a clanger; *vulg* **m. mano a algn,** to touch up *or* feel sb. **2** *(comprometer)* to involve **(en,** in), to get mixed up **(en,** in); **a mí no me metáis en eso,** don't get me mixed up in that; **andar metido en deudas,** to be up one's eyes in debt. **3** *fam fig (dar)* to give; **me metieron una multa,** I got a ticket; **nos metió el rollo de siempre,** he gave us the same old story; **m. miedo a algn,** to frighten sb, put the wind up sb, **m. prisa a algn,** to hurry sb up **4** *(hacer)* to make, **m. ruido,** to make a noise **5** *Cost (vestido) (de ancho)* to take in, *(de largo)* to take up **II meterse** *vr* **1** *(entrar)* to go *or* come in, get into, **se metió en la casa,** he went into the house, **ella se metió en el coche,** she got into the car, **métete en la cama,** get into bed **2** *(introducir)* to put, **métete la camisa (por dentro),** tuck your shirt in **no te metas los dedos en la nariz,** don't pick your nose, *fig* **métete esto en la cabeza,** get this into your head, *vulg* **que se lo meta donde le quepa,** he can shove it up his backside **3** *(dedicarse)* to go into, **m. monja,** to become a nun, **m. en un conjunto,** to join a band, **m. en política,** to go into politics **4** *(estar, ir a parar)* to be, **¿dónde se ha metido este niño?,** where on earth is that child?, **¿dónde te habías metido?,** where have you been (all this time)?, **yo no sabía dónde meterme (de la vergüenza),** (I was so ashamed) I just didn't know where to put myself **5** *(entrometerse)* to meddle, **tú no te metas en esto,** métete en tus cosas, mind your own business, **m. con algn,** *(en broma)* to tease sb, *(en serio)* to lay into sb, **m. donde no llaman,** to poke one's nose in, **m. en todo,** to poke one's nose into everything, **no m. en nada,** *(dejar hacer)* not to interfere, *(no comprometerse)* not to get involved at all, stay out of it.

meticulosidad *nf* meticulousness

meticuloso,-a *adj* **1** meticulous **2** *pey (quisquilloso)* finicky

metido,-a I *pp de* **meter II** *adj* **1** *fam* **estar muy m. en algo,** to be deeply involved in sth; **m. en años,** getting on (in years), **m. en carnes,** plump **2** *Am (entrometido)* meddlesome **III** *nm fam* dressing-down, **dar/pegar un buen m. a un pastel/una paella,** to take a good helping of a cake/a paella

metileno *nm* methylene

metílico,-a *adj* methylic

metódico,-a *adj* methodical

metodismo *nm Rel* Methodism

metodista *adj & nmf Rel* Methodist

metodizar *vtr* to methodize

método *nm* **1** method **2** *Educ* course, **m. de música,** music course

metodología *nf* methodology

metodológico,-a *adj* methodological

metomentodo *nmf inv fam* busybody

metonimia *nf Ling* metonymy

metraje *nm Cin (de una película)* length

metralla *nf Mil* shrapnel

metralleta *nf Mil* sub-machine-gun

métrica *nf Lit* metrics *sing*

métrico,-a *adj* **1** metric ■ **cinta métrica,** tape measure, **sistema m.,** metric system **2** *Lit* metrical

metro *nm* **1** *(medida)* metre, *US* meter **2** *fam* underground, tube, *US* subway

metrónomo *nm* metronome

metrópoli *nf* metropolis

metropolitano,-a I *adj* metropolitan, **área metropolitana de Londres,** ≈ Greater London **II** *nm fml* underground, tube, *US* subway

meublé *nm (casa de citas)* brothel, *(apartamento)* flat rented by the hour

mexicano,-a *adj & nm,f véase* **mejicano,-a**

México *nm véase* **Méjico**

mezcla *nf* **1** *(acción)* mixing, blending **2** *(producto)* mixture, blend, **hay tal m. de acentos,** there is such a variety of accents ■ **m. explosiva,** *(explosivo)* explosive mixture, *fig (situación)* explosive situation **3** *Rad Cin* mixing, *Aut* mixture

mezclador,-a *nm,f (persona, máquina)* mixer

mezclar I *vtr* **1** *(dos o más cosas)* to mix, blend **2** *(desordenar)* to mix up, **mezcló todas las fichas,** he mixed up all the index cards, **m. dos temas,** to mix two subjects up **3** *(involucrar)* to involve, mix up, **mezcló a su hermano en un asunto muy turbio,** he got his brother mixed up in some very shady business, **verse mezclado en algo,** to find oneself mixed up in sth **II mezclarse** *vr* **1** *(cosas)* to get mixed up, **al caerse, se mezclaron todos los papeles,** when they fell, all the papers got mixed up, *(gente)* **aquí se mezcla todo el mundo,** all kinds of people mingle here **2** *(intervenir)* to get involved, **m. con cierta clase de gente,** to mix with a certain kind of people

mezcolanza *nf fml* strange mixture, hotch-potch, **habla una m. de inglés y español,** he speaks a funny mixture of English and Spanish

mezquinar I *vtr* **1** *Am* to be mean *or* stingy with **2** *Arg (esquivar)* to dodge **II** *vi Am* to be mean *or* stingy

mezquindad *nf* **1** *(avaricia)* meanness, stinginess **2** *(sordidez)* lowness, baseness **3** *(acción)* mean thing, vile deed

mezquino,-a *adj* **1** *(avaricioso)* mean, stingy **2** *(sórdido)* low, base **3** *(escaso)* miserable, **un sueldo m.,** a miserable wage

mezquita *nf Rel* mosque

m/f. *abr de* **mi favor,** my favour *or US* favor

m/g *abr de* **miligramo,** milligramme, milligram, mg

mi[1] *adj* my, **mi casa/trabajo,** my house/job, **mis cosas/ libros,** my things/books

mi[2] *nm Mús* E, **mi menor,** E minor

mí *pron pers* me, **a mí me dio tres,** he gave me three, **¡a mí!,** help!, **¡(y) a mí qué!,** so what!, **compra otro para mí,** buy one for me too, **para mí que ...,** I think that ..., **por mí ...,** *(aprobación)* it's all right with *or* by me, *(indiferencia)* I don't care. **por mí puede hacer lo que quiera,** he can do what he likes for all I care, **por mí mismo,** just by myself

mía *adj & pron pos f véase* **mío**

miaja *nf* crumb, *fig* bit, **no queda ni una m. de comida,** there is not a morsel left

miasma *nm* miasma

miau *nm* miaow, mew

mica *nf Min* mica

micción *nf Biol* micturition

Micenas *n* Mycenae

micénico,-a *adj* Mycenaean

michelín® *nm fam* spare tyre *or US* tire

mico,-a I *nm* **1** *Zool* long-tailed monkey **2** *fig (hombre lujurioso)* randy man, rake **3** *fam fig (locuciones)* **dar el m.,** *(dar un chasco)* to let sb down, *(sorprender)* to come up with sth unexpected, **hecho un m.,** ashamed, embarrassed, **ser el último m.,** to be of no account, **volverse m. para hacer algo,** to (have to) struggle to do sth II *nm, f (persona fea)* ape, ugly person

micología *nf Med* mycology

micosis *nf Med* mycosis

micra *nf (medida)* micron

micro *nm fam (medida)* mike, microphone

micro- *pref* micro-, **microcirugía,** microsurgery

microbiano,-a *adj* microbic, microbial

microbio *nm* microbe

microbiología *nf* microbiology

microbiológico,-a *adj* microbiological.

microbús *nm Aut* minibus.

microchip *nm (pl microchips) Inform* microchip.

microcircuito *nm* microcircuit.

microcomputadora *nf Inform* microcomputer.

microcosmos *nm* microcosmos.

microficha *nf* microfiche.

microfilm *nm* microfilm.

micrófono *nm* microphone; **hablar por el m.,** to speak over *or* through the microphone.

microlentilla *nf véase* **lentilla.**

microonda *nf* microwave; **un (horno) microondas,** a microwave (oven).

microordenador *nm Inform* microcomputer.

microorganismo *nm* microorganism.

microprocesador *nm Inform* microprocessor.

microscópico,-a *adj* microscopic.

microscopio *nm* microscope.

microsurco *nm* microgroove.

microtaxi *nm Aut* minicab.

microtécnia *nf*, **microtecnología** *nf* microtechnology.

microteléfono *nm* receiver.

mieditis *nf fam* jitters *pl*; **pasar m.,** to have the jitters.

miedo *nm* fear; *(recelo)* aprehension; **dar m.,** to be scary; **le da m. quedarse sin trabajo,** he's worried about losing his job; **me dio m. decírselo,** I was afraid to tell her; **me entró muchísimo m.,** I felt really frightened; **una película de m.,** a horror film; **por m. a,** for fear of; **por m. de que te pareciera mal,** for fear of upsetting you; **¡qué m.!,** how frightening!; **tener m. de algo/algn,** to be afraid of sth/sb; *fig* **morirse de m.,** to be scared stiff; *fam* **de m.,** *(que asusta)* ghastly, awful; *(fantástico)* great, terrific; *fam* **lo pasamos de m.,** we had a fantastic time.

miedoso,-a I *adj* fainthearted, cowardly, timid. **II** *nm, f* coward.

miel *nf* honey; **dulce como la m.,** as sweet as honey; *fig* **dejar a algn con la m. en los labios,** to shatter sb's hopes; *fig* **m. sobre hojuelas,** so much the better. ■ **luna de m.,** honeymoon.

mielga *nf* alfalfa.

mielina *nf Anat* myelin.

miembro *nm* **1** *Anat* limb; **m. viril,** penis. **2** *(socio)* member; **estado m.,** member state. **3** *Mat* member. **4** *fig (parte)* part, section.

miente *nf arc* mind, thought; **parar** *or* **poner mientes en,** to think of, consider.

mientras I *adv* **m. (tanto),** meanwhile, in the meantime; **ahora vuelvo, m. (tanto), échale un vistazo a esto,** I'll be back in a minute, in the meantime, have a look at this. **II** *conj* **1** *(al mismo tiempo que)* while, whilst; **Carmen llegó m. comíamos,** Carmen arrived while we were eating. **2** *(durante el tiempo que)* when, while; **m. viví en Berlín,** when I lived in Berlin, during the time I lived in Berlin; **m. yo viva no le faltará nada,** while I am still alive, she won't go without. **3** *(por el contrario)* whereas; **él lo admitió, m. que tú lo negaste,** he admitted it,

whereas you denied it. **4** *fam (cuanto más)* **m. más/menos ...,** the more/less ...; **m. más se tiene, más se quiere,** the more one has, the more one wants.

miércoles *nm inv* Wednesday. ■ **M. de Ceniza,** Ash Wednesday; *véase tamb* **viernes.**

mierda *nf vulg* **1** *(gen) fig* shit; **ese libro es una m.,** that book is crap; **estar hecho una m.,** *(cansado)* to be shagged out; *(abatido)* to be down in the dumps; **irse a la m.,** to go to hell; **mandar a la m. a algn,** to tell sb to go to hell. **2** *fig (porquería)* dirt, filth. **3** *(borrachera)* **coger** *or* **pillar una m.,** to get drunk.

mies *nf* **1** *(grano)* corn, grain. **2** *(cosecha)* harvest time. **3 mieses,** cornfields.

miga *nf* **1** *(de pan etc)* crumb; *fig* **hacer buenas/malas migas con algn,** to get on well/badly with sb; *fig* **hacer migas a algn/algo,** to smash sb/sth to bits; *fam* **hecho migas,** *(destrozado físicamente)* smashed to bits; *(destrozado moralmente)* totally destroyed. **2** *(trocito)* bit. **3** *fig (intríngulis)* substance; **la cosa tiene m.,** there is more to it than meets the eye. **4 migas,** breadcrumbs; *Culin* fried breadcrumbs.

migaja *nf* **1** *(de pan)* crumb. **2** *fig* bit, scrap. **3 migajas,** *(del pan)* crumbs; *fig* leftovers.

migar *vtr (desmenuzar)* to crumble; **se miga el pan en la leche,** (you) crumble the bread into the milk.

migración *nf* migration.

migraña *nf Med* migraine.

migrar *vi* to migrate.

migratorio,-a *adj* migratory.

mijo *nm Bot* millet.

mil *adj & nm* thousand; **m. pesetas,** a *or* one thousand pesetas; **m. veces,** a thousand times; **que hace m.,** the thousandth.

milagrería *nf* superstitious belief in miracles.

milagrero,-a *adj* **1** *(crédulo)* who believes in miracles. **2** *(milagroso)* miracle-working.

milagro *nm* miracle; **de m.,** *(en el último momento)* in the nick of time; *(por un pelo)* by the skin of one's teeth; **fue un m. que no se matara,** it was a miracle he didn't kill himself; **hacer milagros,** to work wonders; *fam* **ella nos contó su vida y milagros,** she told us her life story from beginning to end.

milagroso,-a *adj* **1** miraculous. **2** *fig (maravilloso)* wonderful, amazing.

milamores *nm inv Bot* red valerian.

milano *nm Orn* kite. ■ **m. negro,** black kite; **m. real,** red kite.

milenario,-a I *adj* millenarian, millenial. **II** *nm* millenium, millenary.

milenio *nm* millenium, millenary.

milésimo,-a *adj & nm, f* thousandth.

milhojas *nm inv Culin* puff pastry.

mili *nf fam* military *or* national service; **hacer la m.,** to do one's military service.

milibar *nm Fís* millibar.

milicia *nf* **1** *(arte)* art of war. **2** *(gente armada)* militia. ■ **milicias universitarias,** students' military service.

miliciano,-a I *adj* of *or* relating to the militia. **II** *nm* militiaman. **III** *nf* woman soldier.

miligramo *nm* milligram, milligramme.

mililitro *nm* millilitre, *US* milliliter.

milímetro *nm* millimetre, *US* millimeter.

militancia *nf* militancy.

militante *adj & nmf* militant.

militar I *adj* military. ■ **cartilla m.,** military record; **tribunal m.,** military court. **II** *nm* military man, soldier; **los militares,** the armed forces. **III** *vi* **1** *Mil* to serve. **2** *Pol (de un partido)* to be a militant.

militarismo *nm* militarism.

militarista I *adj* militarist, militaristic. **II** *nmf* militarist.

militarización *nf* militarization.

militarizar *vtr* to militarize.

milla *nf (medida)* mile.

millar *nm* thousand; **millares de personas,** thousands of people; *fig* **a millares,** in thousands.

millón *nm* million; *(mucho dinero)* **esa casa vale millones,** that house is worth a fortune; **tengo millones de cosas que hacer,** I've got thousands of things to do; *(mucho)* **un m. de gracias,** thanks a million.

millonada *nf fam* fortune, bomb; **me costó una m.,** it cost me a bomb.

millonario,-a *adj & nm,f* millionaire.

millonésimo,-a *adj & nm,f* millionth.

milonga *nf* **1** *SAm Mús* popular Argentinian song and dance. **2** *Am (fiesta)* family party. **3** *Am (chisme)* gossip.

milpa *nf CAm Méx* field of maize, *US* cornfield.

miltomate *nm Bot* **1** *Hond Guat Méx* small white tomato. **2** *Guat Méx* tomato grown in a maize field.

mimado,-a I *pp de* **mimar II** *adj (consentido)* spoiled.

mimar *vtr (niño, persona)* to spoil, coddle, pamper.

mimbre *nm* wicker; **cesta de m.,** wicker basket.

mimbrear *vi,* **mimbrearse** *vr* to sway.

mimbrera *nf (arbol)* (common) osier.

mimbreral *nm* osier bed.

mimético,-a *adj* mimetic.

mimetismo *nm* mimicry, mimesis.

mímica *nf* mimicry.

mímico,-a *adj* mimic.

mimo *nm* **1** *Teat (actor)* mime. **2** *fig (zalamería)* coddling, pampering; *fam* **con gran m.,** with love and care.

mimosa *nf Bot* mimosa, silver wattle.

mimoso,-a *adj* loving, affectionate.

mina¹ *nf* **1** *Min* mine; **m. de carbón,** coal mine. ■ **ingeniero de minas,** mining engineer. **2** *(conducto)* underground passage, tunnel. **3** *(explosivo)* mine. ■ **campo de minas,** minefield. **4** *(de lápiz)* lead; *(de bolígrafo)* refill. **5** *fig (ganga)* gold mine; **este negocio es una m.,** this business is a gold mine.

mina² *nf* **1** *SAm (mujer)* bird; *(concubina)* lady friend, lover. **2** *Arg Méx (prostituta)* prostitute.

minador,-a I *adj* mining. **II** *nm* **1** *(buque)* minelayer. **2** *(soldado)* sapper.

minar *vtr* **1** *Mil Min* to mine. **2** *fig (desgastar)* to undermine.

minarete *nm* minaret.

mineral *adj & nm* mineral, ore.

mineralización *nf* mineralization.

mineralizar *vtr,* **mineralizarse** *vr* to mineralize.

mineralogía *nf* mineralogy.

mineralógico,-a *adj* mineralogical.

minería *nf* **1** *Min* mining. **2** *Ind* mining industry.

minero,-a I *adj* mining; **industria/zona minera,** mining industry/area. **III** *nm,f* miner.

mineromedicinal *adj* **aguas mineromedicinales,** mineral waters with curative powers.

minga *nf fam* prick, dick.

mingitorio *nm* urinal.

miniatura *nf* miniature.

miniaturista *nmf* miniaturist.

miniaturizar *vtr* to miniaturize.

minifalda *nf* miniskirt.

minifundio *nm* smallholding.

minifundista I *adj* *of or* relating to **minifundios. II** *nmf* smallholder.

mínima *nf* minimum temperature.

minimizar *vtr* to minimize, play down; **el ministro minimizó la importancia del incidente,** the minister played down the incident.

mínimo,-a I *adj* **1** *Mat Téc* minimum, lowest. ■ **m. común múltiplo,** lowest common multiple. **2** *(muy pequeño)* minute, tiny; **un número m. de personas,** a very small number of people. **II** *nm* minimum; **al m.,** to a minimum; **como m.,** at least; **ni lo más m.,** not in the least.

minino *nm fam* pussy (cat), kitty.

minipimer® *nm or f* liquidizer, blender.

ministerial *adj* ministerial.

ministerio *nm* **1** *Pol* ministry, *US* department. ■ **M. de Asuntos Exteriores,** ≈ Foreign office; **M. de Hacienda,** ≈ Exchequer; **M. del Interior** *or* **de la Gobernación,** ≈ Home office. **2** *Rel* ministry.

ministrable *adj* likely to become a minister.

ministro,-a *nm, f* **1** *Pol* minister. ■ **m. de Asuntos Exteriores,** ≈ Foreign Secretary; **m. de Economía y Hacienda,** ≈ Chancellor of the Exchequer; **m. del Interior,** ≈ Home Secretary; **primer m.,** Prime Minister. **2** *Rel* minister.

minorar *vtr,* **minorarse** *vr* to reduce, decrease, diminish.

minoría *nf* minority. ■ *Jur* **m. de edad,** minority.

minoritario,-a *adj* minority; **gobierno m.,** minority government.

minucia *nf* trifle.

minuciosidad *nf (meticulosidad)* meticulousness; *(detallismo)* minuteness.

minucioso,-a *adj* **1** *(persona)* meticulous. **2** *(informe, trabajo, etc)* minute, detailed.

minué *nm Mús* minuet.

minúsculo,-a I *adj* miniscule, minute; **letra minúscula,** lower-case *or* small letter. **II** *nf* small *or* lowercase letter.

minusválido,-a I *adj* handicapped, disabled. **II** *nm, f* handicapped person, disabled person.

minuta *nf* **1** *(borrador)* draft. **2** *(cuenta)* lawyer's bill. **3** *(menú)* menu.

minutero *nm* minute hand.

minuto *nm* minute; **al m.,** a moment later; **sin perder un m.,** without wasting a minute; **vuelvo en un m.,** I'll be back in a moment.

miñango *nm Am* bit, small piece.

mío,-a I *adj pos* of mine, my; **no es asunto m.,** it is none of my business; **un amigo m.,** a friend of mine. **II** *pron pos* mine; **ese libro es m.,** that book is mine; *fam* **ésta es la mía,** this is the chance I've been waiting for; **lo m. son las matemáticas,** what I am the best at is mathematics; *fam* **los míos,** my people *or* folks.

miocardio *nm Anat* myocardium.

miope I *adj Ópt* myopic, short-sighted; *fig* short-sighted; **una política m.,** a short-sighted policy. **II** *nmf Ópt* myopic *or* short-sighted person; *fig* short-sighted person.

miopía *nf* myopia, short-sightedness.

MIR *nm Med abr de* **Médico Interno Residente,** *GB* houseman, *US* intern.

mira *nf* **1** *Téc* sight. ■ **línea de m.,** line of sight; **punto de m.,** front sight; **m. taquimétrica,** stadia rod. **2** *fig (objetivo)* aim, target; **amplitud de miras,** broad-mindedness; **con miras a,** with a view to; **poner la m. en algo,** to aim at; **tener la m. puesta en algo,** to have designs on sth.

mirada *nf* look; **apartar la m.,** to look away; **clavar** *or* **fijar la m. en,** to fix one's eyes on; **fulminar con la m.,** to look daggers at; **lanzar** *or* **echar una m.,** to glance at; **levantar la m.,** to raise one's eyes; **seguir algo/a algn con la m.,** to follow sth/sb with one's eyes; **sostener la m.,** to stare at; **volver la m. a,** to turn one's eyes towards. ■ **m. fija,** stare; **m. rápida,** glance.

miradero nm 1 (persona) centre or US certer of attention. 2 (lugar) vantage point.

mirado,-a I pp de **mirar. II** adj 1 (considerado) considered; **bien m.**, highly regarded or respected, well liked; fig all in all; **mal m.**, disliked, looked down on. 2 (cuidadoso) careful. 3 (cauto) cautious.

mirador nm 1 Arquit (balcón) bay window, windowed balcony 2 (lugar con vista) viewpoint.

miraguano nm 1 (árbol) kapok tree. 2 (material) kapok.

miramiento nm 1 (cautela) caution. 2 (gen pl) (consideración) consideration, respect; **andarse con miramientos**, (personas) to treat people with respect; (cosas) to handle things carefully; **sin miramientos**, (personas) without respect; (cosas) carelessly.

mirar I vtr 1 to look at; **le miró a los ojos**, he looked him in the eye; **m. a algn de arriba a abajo**, to eye sb from head to toe; **m. algo por encima**, to glance at sth; **m. una palabra en el diccionario**, to look up a word in the dictionary; fig **m. algo** or **algn con buenos/malos ojos**, to have a good/bad opinion of sth or sb; fig **m. a algn por encima del hombro**, to look down on sb; fam fig **mírame y no me toques**, very fragile. 2 (vigilar) to check, watch; **mira bien el cambio antes de irte**, check your change before leaving; **¡mira lo que dices/haces!**, mind or watch what you say/do! 3 (atender) to look after; **m. por algn** or **algo**, to look after sb or sth; **sólo mira por su interés**, he only looks after his own interests. 4 (reflexionar) to think, consider; **gasta el dinero sin m.**, he spends money thoughtlessly. 5 (tener cuidado) to be careful; (procurar) to see; **mira donde pones los pies**, watch where you're putting your feet; **mira que llegue bien/que no le pase nada**, see that he arrives all right/that nothing happens to him. 6 (comprobar) to check; **mira si ha llegado tu padre**, go and see/ask if your father has arrived; **mira (a ver) si hay carta(s)**, go and see/check if there's any mail. 7 (dar) to look, face; **la casa mira al sur**, the house faces south; **la cocina mira al jardín**, the kitchen looks onto the garden. 8 (locuciones) **mira, haz lo que te parezca**, look, you can do whatever you want; **¡mira por donde!**, fancy that!; **mira que si se presenta ahora**, just imagine if he turned up now!; **mira que te lo dije**, I told you, didn't I?; **¡mira quien habla!**, look who's talking! **II mirarse** vr 1 (reflexionar) to think twice; **ella se lo mirará antes de intentarlo**, she'll think twice before trying it. 2 (uso reflexivo) to look at oneself; **m. en el espejo**, to look at oneself in the mirror; fig **m. en algn**, to think highly of sb. 3 (uso recíproco) to look at each other or one another. 4 (uso impers) **si bien se mira**, all things considered; **se mire como se mire**, whichever way you look at it.

miríada nf myriad.

miriámetro nm (medida) myriametre, US myriameter.

mirilla nf spyhole, peephole.

miriñaque nm Hist crinoline.

miriópodo nm myriapod.

mirlo nm Orn **m. (blanco)**, blackbird; fig **ser un m. blanco**, to be a rare bird. ■ **m. acuático**, dipper, water ouzel.

mirón,-ona I adj 1 (espectador) onlooking. 2 pey (voyeur) peeping. **II** nm,f 1 (espectador) onlooker. 2 pey voyeur, peeping Tom.

mirra nf Bot myrrh.

mirto nm Bot myrtle.

misa adj mass; **celebrar** or **decir m.**, to say mass; **ir a m.**, Rel to go to mass; fam fig (ser verdad) to be gospel; fam fig **no saber de la m. la media** or **mitad**, to know much less about sth than one thinks. ■ **m. cantada**, sung Mass; **m. de difuntos**, Requiem Mass; **m. del gallo**, Midnight Mass on Christmas Eve.

misal nm missal.

misantropía nf misanthropy.

misántropo,-a I adj misanthropic. **II** nm, f misanthrope, misanthropist.

miscelánea nf miscellany.

misceláneo,-a adj miscellaneous.

miscible adj miscible.

miserable I adj 1 miserable, wretched, poor; **por unas miserables pesetas**, for a few miserable pesetas; **una vida m.**, a wretched life; **viviendas miserables**, very poor dwellings. 2 (tacaño) miserly, mean, stingy. 3 (malvado) wretched, despicable. **II** nmf 1 (tacaño) miser. 2 (canalla) wretch, villain.

miseria nf 1 (pobreza extrema) extreme poverty. 2 (desgracia) misery, affliction. 3 (tacañería) miserliness, meanness. 4 (insignificancia) pittance; **ganar una m.**, to earn next to nothing.

misericordia nf mercy, compassion.

misericordioso,-a adj merciful, compassionate.

mísero,-a adj miserable, wretched; **¡m. de mí!**, woe is me!

misil nm missile; **m. tierra-aire**, surface-to air missile.

misión nf 1 mission. ■ **m. cumplida**, mission accomplished. 2 Rel mission.

misionero,-a I adj mission. **II** nm,f missionary.

misiva nf lit missive.

mismísimo,-a adj superl fam 1 (preciso) very; **en el m. centro**, right in the centre; **en este m. momento**, at this very moment. 2 (en persona) in person; **este niño es el m. demonio**, this child is the devil himself; **me lo dijo el m. director**, the director himself told me.

mismo,-a I adj 1 same; **bebemos en el m. vaso**, we are sharing the same glass. 2 (uso enfático) (propio) own; **la escuela está en su misma calle**, the school is right in the same street where he lives; **su misma familia no lo puede entender**, even her own family cannot understand it; **yo m.**, I myself. **II** pron same; **éste es el m. que vimos ayer**, this is the same one we saw yesterday; **estar en las mismas (de siempre)**, to be back to square one; **lo m.**, the same (thing); **dar** or **ser lo m.**, to make no difference; **no es lo m. oir que escuchar**, hearing is not the same as listening; or **lo que es lo m.**, that is to say; **por eso m.**, that is why; **por lo m.**, for that reason; **por uno** or **sí m.**, by oneself; **tres cuartos de lo m.**, much of a muchness. **III** adv 1 (exactamente) exactly; **ahora m.**, right now or away; **allí/aquí m.**, right there/here; **ayer m.**, just or only yesterday; **mañana m.**, tomorrow! 2 (por ejemplo) for instance; **aquí m.**, here will do; **que venga algn, Juan m.**, ask one of them to come, Juan, for instance. 3 **así m.**, likewise. ◆ **mismamente** adv fam just, precisely.

misoginia nf misogyny.

misógino,-a I adj misogynous. **II** nm,f misogynist.

miss nf Miss; **M. España 1992**, Miss Spain 1992.

míster nm 1 (tratamiento) señor. 2 fam foreigner. 3 Ftb coach, trainer.

misterio nm mystery; **no hay ningún m.**, there is no mystery about it; **con m.**, mysteriously.

misterioso,-a adj mysterious.

mística nf mystical theology.

misticismo nm mysticism.

místico,-a I adj mystic, mystical. **II** nm,f mystic.

mistificación nf trick.

mistificar vtr to trick, cheat.

mistral nm Meteor mistral.

MIT nm abr de **Ministerio de Información y Turismo.**

mitad nf half, middle; **a/hacia la m. de**, in/towards the middle of; **a m. de camino**, half-way there; **a m. de precio**, half price; **en m. de la reunión**, half-way through the meeting; **la m. de una casa**, half a book/a house; **mi otra m.**, my better half; **partir algo por la m.**, to cut sth in half/down the middle; fam **m. y m.**, half and half; fam **partir a algn por la m.**, to shatter sb's plans or expectations.

mitayera nf Am supplies canoe.

mítico,-a *adj* mythical.

mitigador,-a I *adj* mitigating. II *nm, f* mitigator.

mitigar *vtr fml* to mitigate, palliate, relieve; *(luz)* to reduce.

mitin *nm Pol* meeting, rally.

mito *nm* 1 myth. 2 *Orn* long-tailed tit.

mitología *nf* mythology.

mitológico,-a *adj* mythological.

mitomanía,-a *nf* mythomania.

mitómano,-a *adj & nm, f* mythomaniac.

mitón *nm* mitt, mitten.

mitote *nm* 1 *Méx (baile)* Indian dance. *Am (fiesta casera)* family party. 3 *Am (aspaviento)* fuss. 4 *Am (pendencia)* row; *(bulla)* uproar. 5 *Méx (chisme)* gossip.

mitra *nf* 1 mitre. 2 *fig (rango)* rank of bishop.

mitrado I *adj* mitred. II *nm (arzobispo)* archbishop; *(obispo)* bishop.

mixomatosis *nf Med* myxomatosis.

Mixteca *adj & nmf* Mixtec.

mixtificación *nf véase* **mistificación.**

mixtificar *vtr véase* **mistificar.**

mixto I *adj* mixed. ■ *Educ* **colegio m.,** coeducational school. II *nm Ferroc* passenger and goods train.

mixtura *nf* mixture.

mízcalo *nm* milk fungus.

m/L. *abr de* **mi letra (de crédito),** my credit bill.

moaré *nm véase* **muaré.**

mobiliario *nm* furniture.

MOC *nm abr de* **Movimiento de Objetores de Conciencia,** Conscientious objectors' Movement.

moblaje *nm* furniture.

moca *nm* mocha, coffee.

mocasín *nm* moccasin.

mocedad *nf* youth.

mocerío *nm* (group of) young people.

mocetón,-ona *nm, f (mozo)* strapping lad; *(moza)* strapping lass.

mochales *adj inv fam* crazy, mad.

moche *fam* a **troche y m.,** helter-skelter, pell-mell.

mochila *nf* rucksack, backpack.

mocho,-a I *adj* 1 blunt. 2 *Am (mutilado)* crippled, disabled. 3 *Guat Méx Pol* conservative. 4 *Méx (católico)* Catholic. II *nm Arm* stock.

mochuelo *nm* I *Zool* little owl. 2 *fam fig (fastidio)* bore, boring task; **cargar con el m.,** *(con la peor parte)* to get the worst part of a job; *(llevarse las culpas)* to carry the can.

moción *nf* motion; **presentar/aprobar una m.,** to table/pass a motion. ■ **m. de censura,** vote of censure.

mocionar *vtr Arg Hond Par* to table a motion.

moco *nm* 1 mucus, snot; **caérsele a algn los mocos,** to have a runny nose; **limpiarse los mocos,** to blow one's nose; **llorar a m. tendido/a m. y baba,** to cry one's eyes out. 2 *(de vela)* drippings. 3 *(de pavo)* wattle, caruncle; *fam* **un millón no es m. de pavo,** a million is no trifle.

mocoso,-a I *adj* with a runny nose. II *nm,f fam* brat.

moda *adj* 1 fashion; **a la m./de m.,** in fashion; **la última m.,** the latest fashion; **pasado de m.,** oldfashioned. 2 *(furor pasajero)* craze; **la m. de los monopatines,** the skateboard craze.

modal I *adj* modal. II **modales** *nmpl* manners; **¡vaya m.!,** what manners! ■ **buenos/malos m.,** good/bad manners.

modalidad *nf* form, category. ■ *Com* **m. de pago,** method of payment; *Dep* **m. deportiva,** sport.

modelado *nm* 1 *(acción)* modelling, *US* modeling. 2 *(efecto)* shape.

modelador,-a I *adj* modelling, *US* modeling. II *nm, f* modeller, *US* modeler.

modelar I *vtr* to model, shape. II **modelarse** *vr* to model oneself **(en,** on).

modelista *nmf* 1 *(operario)* mould *or US* mold maker. 2 *Cost* pattern maker.

modelo I *adj* model. ■ **niño m.,** model child. II *nm* model; **un m. de perfección,** a model of perfection; **un nuevo m. de coche,** a new model of car. III *nmf* (fashion) model. ■ **desfile de modelos,** fashion show.

modem *nm Inform Tel* modem.

moderación *nf* moderation.

moderado,-a I *pp de* **moderar.** II *adj* moderate; **temperaturas moderadas,** mild temperatures. III *nm, f Pol* moderate; **los moderados,** the moderate wing *sing,* the moderates.

moderador,-a I *adj* moderating. II *nm, f* chairperson; *(hombre)* chairman; *(mujer)* chairwoman.

moderar I *vtr* 1 *(gen)* to moderate; *(velocidad)* to reduce; **modera tu lenguaje,** moderate your language. 2 *(debate)* to chair. II **moderarse** *vr* to control oneself.

modernidad *nf* modernity.

modernismo *nm* 1 *Lit* modernism. 2 *Arquit* (Spanish) Art Nouveau.

modernista I *adj* 1 *Lit* modernistic. 2 *Arquit* (Spanish) Art Nouveau. II *nmf* 1 *Lit* modernist. 2 *Arquit* (Spanish) Art Nouveau architect.

modernización *nf* modernization.

modernizar *vtr;* **modernizarse** *vr* to modernize; **este piso debe modernizarse,** this flat needs modernizing; *fam* **eres un carca, tienes que modernizarte,** you're a square, you have to get up-to-date.

moderno,-a *adj* modern. ♦ **modernamente** *adv* in modern times, these days.

modestia *nf* modesty; **con m.,** modestly.

modesto,-a I *adj* modest. II *nm,f* modest person.

modicidad *nf* moderation.

módico,-a *adj* moderate; **una módica suma,** a modest *or* small sum.

modificable *adj* modifiable.

modificacíon *nf* modification.

modificador,-a *adj* modifying.

modificar *vtr* to modify.

modismo *nm Ling* idiom.

modistería *nf Am* boutique.

modistilla *nf fam* dressmaker's assistant.

modisto,-a *nm,f* 1 *(diseñador)* fashion designer. 2 *(sastre) (hombre)* couturier; *(mujer)* couturière.

modo *nm* 1 *(manera)* way, manner; **m. de empleo,** instructions for use; *véase* **manera** 1. 2 **modos,** manners. ■ **buenos/malos m.,** good/bad manners. 3 *Ling* mood; **m. subjuntivo,** subjunctive mood.

modorra *nf (somnolencia)* drowsiness.

modoso,-a *adj* 1 *(recatado)* modest. 2 *(respetuoso)* well-behaved, well-mannered.

modulación *nf* modulation. ■ **m. de frecuencia,** frequency modulation.

modular *vtr* to modulate.

modular² *adj* modular. ■ **un tresillo m.,** a modular suite.

módulo *nm* module.

mofa *nf* mockery, ridicule; **en tono de m.,** in a gibing tone; **hacer m. de algn/algo,** to scoff at sb/sth.

mofar *vi,* **mofarse** *vr* to scoff **(de,** at), laugh **(de,** at), make fun **(de,** of); **no te mofes de ella,** don't make fun of her.

mofeta *nf* 1 *Zool* skunk. 2 *Min (grisú)* firedamp.

moflete *nm* chubby cheek.

mofletudo,-a *adj* chubby-cheeked.

Mogadisco *n* Mogadiscio, Mogadishu.

mogol *adj & nmf* Mongol.

mogollón *nm arg* **1** *(gran cantidad de)* **m. de**, stacks of, piles of; **había un m. de gente**, there were thousands of people. **2** *(confusión)* commotion; *(ruido)* row, din, racket; **con este m. no oigo nada,** I can't hear a thing with all this din. **3** *(acción)* action; **vamos donde está el m.**, let's go where the action is, let's go where it's all happening.

mohair *nm Tex* mohair.

mohín *nm* grimace; **hacer un m.**, to make *or* pull a face.

mohíno, -a *adj* sulky, upset.

moho *nm* **1** *(hongo)* mould, *US* mold. **2** *(de metales)* rust.

mohoso, -a *adj* **1** mouldy, *US* moldy. **2** *(oxidado)* rusty.

moisés *nm* *(cuna)* Moses basket, wickar cradle *or* carrycot, *US* bassinet.

mojado, -a I *pp de* mojar. II *adj* wet; *(húmedo)* damp.

mojama *nf Culin* dried salted tuna.

mojar I *vtr* **1** to wet; *(humedecer)* to damp; **m. pan en la leche,** to dip *or* dunk bread in one's milk. **2** *fam (celebrar)* **m. algo,** to celebrate sth with a drink. II **mojarse** *vr* **1** to get wet. **2** *fig (comprometerse)* to commit oneself.

mojarra *nf* **1** *(pez)* two-banded bream. **2** *Am* short broad-bladed knife.

mojicón *nm* **1** *(puñetazo en la cara)* punch, slap. **2** *(bizcocho)* type of sponge cake.

mojigatería *nf* sanctimoniousness, affected piety.

mojigato, -a I *adj* sanctimonious. II *nm, f* sanctimonious person.

mojinete *nm RPl Chi Arquit* gable.

mojón *nm* landmark; **m. kilométrico,** ≈ milestone.

moka *nm véase* **moca**

mola *nf* **1** *Med* mole. **2** *(pez)* sunfish.

molar I *adj & nm Anat* molar. II *vi arg* **1** to dig; **me mola cantidad,** I really dig it, it's fab. **2** *(presumir)* to show off.

molde *nm* mould, *US* mold, cast. ■ **letras de m.,** printed letters; **pan de m.,** ≈ sliced bread.

moldeable *adj* mouldable, *US* moldable.

moldeado, -a I *pp de* moldear. II *adj* moulded, *US* molded, cast. III *nm* **1** moulding, *US* molding, casting. **2** *Peluq* soft perm, bodywave.

moldeador, -a *adj* moulding, *US* molding, casting.

moldear *vtr* to mould, *US* mold, cast; *(cabello)* to give a soft perm to.

moldura *nf* moulding, *US* molding.

mole *nf* mass, bulk; *fam* **este tío es una m.,** he's a fat lump.

molécula *nf* molecule.

molecular *adj* molecular.

moledor, -a I *adj* **1** *(triturador)* grinding; *(aplastador)* crushing. **2** *fig (persona)* boring. II *nm (cilindro)* roller, crusher.

moler *vtr* **1** *(triturar)* to grind, mill; **m. la aceituna,** to press olives. **2** *fam fig (cansar)* to wear out; **m. a algo a golpes** *or* **palos,** to beat sb up.

molestar I *vtr* **1** to disturb, bother, annoy; **los niños le molestan,** children get on his nerves; **no quisiera molestarte,** I shouldn't like to bother you; **todo le molesta,** everything annoys him. **2** *fml* to bother; **¿le molestaría esperar fuera?,** would you mind waiting outside?; **¿le molestaría llamarme más tarde?,** could you possibly phone me later?; **perdone que le moleste ...,** I'm sorry to bother you, but ... . **3** *(causar malestar)* to hurt, trouble; **este muela me está molestando otra vez,** this tooth is troubling me again. **4** *(ofender levemente)* to offend slightly; **¿te molestó que no vinieras a tu fiesta?,** are you hurt at my missing your party? II **molestarse** *vr* **1** *(tomarse la molestia)* to bother, take the trouble; **no se moleste, ya lo haré yo,** don't bother, I'll do it. **2**

(ofenderse) to take offence *or US* offense, get upset; **se molesta por cualquier** cosa, he gets annoyed *or* upset over any little thing.

molestia *nf* **1** bother, nuisance; **no es ninguna m.,** it is no trouble at all; **perdone las molestias que le estamos ocasionando,** please excuse all the trouble *or* inconvenience we are causing you; **si no (le) es m.,** if it is no trouble to you; **tomarse la m. (de hacer algo),** to take the trouble (to do sth). **2** *Med (dolor)* trouble, slight pain; **tener molestias de estómago,** to have an upset stomach.

molesto, -a *adj* annoying, upsetting; **estar m. con algn,** to be annoyed *or* upset with sb; **ser m.,** to be a nuisance *or* a bother; **una situación molesta,** an embarrassing situation.

molibdeno *nf Quím* molybdenum.

molicie *nf* **1** *fig (lujo)* great *or* excessive luxury. **2** *lit (blandura)* softness.

molido, -a I *pp de* moler. II *adj* **1** ground, milled. **2** *fam (exhausto)* worn-out.

molienda *nf* **1** *(acción)* grinding, milling; **la m. de la aceituna,** the pressing of the olives. **2** *(temporada)* grinding *or* milling season. **3** *(cantidad)* quantity being ground *or* milled.

molinero, -a I *adj* milling. II *nm, f* miller.

molinete *nm* **1** *(ventilador)* air extractor, extractor fan. **2** *(juguete)* toy windmill.

molinillo *nm* grinder, mill. ■ **m. de café,** coffee grinder.

molino *nm* mill. ■ **m. de agua,** watermill; **m. de papel,** paper mill; **m. de viento,** windmill.

molla *nf* **1** soft fleshy part; *(carne)* lean; *(fruta)* flesh. **2** *fig* best part. **2** *fam (michelín)* spare tyre, flab.

mollar *adj* **1** *(tierno)* tender, easy to cut. **2** *fig (útil)* very useful. **2** *(ingenuo)* gullible, credulous, easy to trick. **4** *fam (bueno)* good-looking; **es una tía m.,** she's a cracker.

molledo *nm* **1** *Anat* flesh, fleshy part. **2** *(de pan)* crumb.

molleja *nf* **1** *(de res)* sweetbread. **2** *(de ave)* gizzard.

mollera *nf fam* brains *pl*, sense; **duro de m.,** *(tonto)* dense, thick; *(testarudo)* pigheaded.

molón, -ona *adj arg* flashy, showy.

molonquear *vtr CAm Méx* to beat up.

molturación *nf* grinding, milling.

molturar *vtr* to grind; *(grano)* to mill.

molusco *nm Zool* mollusc, *US* mollusk.

momentáneo, -a *adj* momentary.

momento *nm* moment; **a cada m.,** all the time; **al m.,** at once; **de m.,** for the time being; **de un m. a otro,** any time now; **del m.,** current; **dentro de un m.,** in a moment; **desde el m. en que,** *(tan pronto como)* as soon as; *(puesto que)* since; **desde ese m.,** from that time on; **en buen/mal m.,** at the right/a bad moment; **en cualquier m.,** *(de un momento a otro)* any time now; *(cuando sea)* at any time; **en el m. menos pensado,** when least expected; **en este m.,** *(ahora mismo)* right now; *(actualmente)* at the moment; **en todo m.,** at any moment; **ha llegado el m. de ...,** the moment has come to ...; **no es el m. para ...,** it's not the right time to ...; **pasar por un buen/mal m.,** to go through a good/bad patch; **por el m.,** for the moment; **por momentos,** by the minute; **sin perder un m.,** without delay.

momia *nf* mummy.

momificación *nf* mummification.

momificar I *vtr* to mummify. II **momificarse** *vr* to become mummified.

momio *nm fam* cushy number.

mona *nf* **1** *Zool (hembra)* female monkey; *(especie)* Barbary ape; *prov* **aunque la m. se vista de seda, m. se queda,** you can't make a silk purse out of a sow's ear. **2** *fam (imitador)* copycat. **2** *fam (borrachera)* **coger una m.,** to get drunk; **dormir la m.,** to sleep it off. **4** *Naipes* old maid. **5** *Méx (cobarde)* coward. **6** *Cat (pastel)* Easter cake.

monacal *adj Rel* monastic.

monacato *nm Rel* **1** *(vida monástica)* monkhood. **2** *(conjunto de monjes)* monks *pl.*

Mónaco *n* Monaco.

monada *nf fam* **1** *(zalamería)* caress. **2** *(gesto afectado)* silly *or* ridiculous way of acting *or* speaking; *(de niño)* sweet little way. **2** *(preciosidad) (niño)* charming little child, poppet; *(chica)* pretty girl; *(cosa)* pretty thing; **su hija es una m.,** his daughter is a lovely girl; **¡qué m.!,** how cute!; **¡qué m. de chaqueta!,** what a beautiful jacket!

monaguillo *nm Rel* altar boy.

monarca *nm* monarch.

monarquía *nf* monarchy.

monárquico,-a I *adj* monarchic, monarchical. **II** *nm, f* monarchist.

monarquismo *nm* monarchism.

monasterio *nm Rel* monastery.

monástico,-a *adj Rel* monastic.

monda *nf* **1** *(acción)* peeling. **2** *(piel)* peel, skin; **la m. de una naranja,** the skin of an orange. **2** *fam* **ser la m.,** *(extraordinario)* to be amazing; *(divertido)* to be a scream.

mondadientes *nm inv* toothpick.

mondadura *nf* véase **monda** 1, 2.

mondar I *vtr* **1** *(naranjas, patatas)* to peel; *(frutos secos)* to shell. **2** *(limpiar)* to clean out, dredge. **II mondarse** *vr fam* **m. (de risa),** to laugh one's head off.

mondo,-a *adj* bare, plain; *fam* **con un sueldo m. de veinte mil,** with a bare wage of twenty thousand; *fam* **m. y lirondo,** pure and simple.

mondongo *nm (intestinos)* innards *pl; Culin* **hacer el m.,** to make sausages.

monear *vi Am* to boast, show off.

moneda *nf* **1** *Fin* currency, money; **acuñar m.,** to mint money; *fig* **ser m. corriente,** to be everyday stuff. ■ **la Casa de la M.,** ≈ the Royal Mint; **m. falsa,** counterfeit money. **2** *(pieza)* coin; *fig* **pagar a uno con la misma m.,** to pay sb back in kind. ■ **m. suelta,** small change.

monedero *nm* **1** *(bolsa)* purse. **2** *Fin* minter. ■ **m. falso,** counterfeiter.

monegasco,-a *adj & nm,f* Monegasque.

monería *nf* véase **monada.**

monetario,-a I *adj* monetary. **II** *nm* collection of coins and medals.

monetarismo *nm Econ* monetarism.

monetarista *adj & nmf* Econ monetarist.

mongol I *adj* Mongolian. **II** *nmf (persona)* Mongolian. *nm (idioma)* Mongolian.

Mongolia *n* Mongolia.

mongólico,-a *Med I adj* mongolian. **II** *nm,f* mongol.

mongolismo *nm Med* mongolism, Down's syndrome.

monigote *nm* **1** *(figura grotesca)* rag *or* paper doll; **m. de nieve,** snowman. **2** *pey (persona)* puppet, person with a weak character. **2** *(dibujo)* rough drawing *or* sketch (of a person).

monitor,-a *nm, f* monitor; *(profesor)* instructor; **trabaja como m. de esquí,** he works as a ski instructor.

monitorio,-a *adj* monitory.

monja *nf Rel* nun.

monje *nm Rel* monk.

monjil *adj pey* nun-like.

mono,-a I *adj fam (bonito)* pretty, lovely, cute, sweet; **¡qué vestido tan m.!,** what a lovely dress!; **una niña muy mona,** a very pretty little girl. **II** *nm* **1** *Zool* monkey. **2** *pey (persona)* ape, ugly person; *fam* **m. de imitación,** copycat; *fam* **ser el último m.,** to be a nobody. **3** *(prenda) (de trabajo)* boiler suit, overalls *pl; (de niño)* romper-suit, dungarees *pl.* **4** *(dibujo humorístico)* cartoon. **5** *arg*

(droga) cold turkey, withdrawal symptoms. **6** *Naipes (comodín)* joker.

monocarril *adj & nm* monorail.

monocorde *adj Mus* single-stringed; *fig* monotonous.

monocromático,-a *adj Fis Fot* monochromatic.

monocromo,-a *adj & nm* monochrome.

monóculo *nm* monocle.

monocultivo *nm Agr* monoculture, single crop (farming).

monofásico,-a *adj Elec* single-phase.

monogamia *nf* monogamy.

monógamo,-a I *adj* monogamous. **II** *nm, f* monogamist.

monografía *nf* monograph.

monográfico,-a *adj* monographic.

monograma *nm* monogram.

monolingüe *adj* monolingual.

monolítico,-a *adj* monolithic.

monolito *nm* monolith.

monologar *vi* to soliloquize.

monólogo *nm* monologue.

monomanía *nf Psic* monomania.

monomaníaco,-a *adj,* **monomaniático,-a** *adj Psic* monomaniac.

monoplano *adj & nm Av* monoplane.

monoplaza *adj & nm* single-seater.

monopolio *nm* monopoly.

monopolización *nf* monopolization.

monopolizar *vtr* to monopolize.

monosabio *nm Taur* picador's assistant.

monosilábico,-a *adj Ling* monosyllabic.

monosílabo,-a *Ling I adj* monosyllabic. **II** *nm* monosyllable.

monoteísmo *nm Filos* monotheism.

monoteísta *Filos I adj* monotheistic. **II** *nmf* monotheist.

monotipia *nf Impr* Monotype®.

monotonía *nf* monotony.

monótono,-a *adj* monotonous.

monóxido *nm Quím* monoxide.

Mons *abr de* **Monseñor,** Monsignor, Mgr, Mgsr.

monseñor *nm Rel* monsignor.

monserga *nf fam (aburrido)* boring talk; *(molesto)* annoying talk; **dar la m. a algn,** *(aburrir)* to bore sb; *(molestar)* to pester *or* annoy sb; **déjate de monsergas,** don't go on so.

monstruo I *nm* **1** monster. **2** *(genio)* genius. **II** *adj inv fam* fantastic; **una fiesta m.,** a terrific party.

monstruosidad *nf* monstrosity.

monstruoso,-a *adj* **1** *(repugnante)* monstrous. **2** *(enorme)* massive, huge.

monta *nf* **1** *(ir a caballo)* riding; *(subir a caballo)* mounting. **2** *fig (importancia)* value; **de poca m.,** of little importance.

montacargas *nm inv* goods lift, service lift, *US* freight elevator.

montado,-a I *pp de* **montar. II** *adj* **1** *Mil* mounted. ■ **la policía montada,** the mounted police. **2** *(instalado)* furnished, decorated, fitted out; **una oficina montada con todo lujo,** a luxuriously fitted-out office.

montador,-a *nm,f* **1** *(operario)* fitter, assembler. ■ **ma. de joyas,** setter. **2** *Cin TV* film editor. **3** *Teat* stager, producer.

montadura *nf* **1** *(engaste)* setting, mount. **2** véase **montura** 1.

montaje *nm* **1** *Téc (instalación, ensamblaje)* fitting, assembling. ■ **cadena de m.,** assembly line. **2** *Cin* editing and mounting. **3** *Teat* staging. **4** *Fot* montage. **5** *arg (farsa)* farce, sham, **¡menudo m.!,** what a farce!

montaña *nf* **1** mountain; **vacaciones en la m.**, holidays in the mountains; **hacer una m. (de un grano de arena)**, to make a mountain out of a molehill. ■ **m. rusa**, big dipper. **2** *fig* (*montones*) mountains *pl*, piles *pl*; **una m. de arroz**, mountains of rice. **3** *Am* (*bosque*) forest, jungle.

montañero,-a *nm,f* mountaineer, climber.

montañés,-a **I** *adj* **1** (*de las montañas*) mountain, highland. **2** (*santanderino*) of or from Santander. **II** *nm,f* **1** (*de las montañas*) highlander. **2** (*santanderino*) native or inhabitant of Santander.

montañismo *nm* mountaineering, mountain climbing.

montañoso,-a *adj* mountainous.

montante *nm* **1** *Constr Téc* upright. **2** (*de puerta*) post. **3** (*de ventana*) mullion. **4** *Arquit* stanchion. **5** *Fin* (*total*) total amount.

montaplatos *nm inv* service lift, dumb waiter.

montar I *vi* **1** (*caballo, bicicleta*) to mount, get on; (*avión, autobús, tren*) to get on; (*coche*) to get into. **2** (*ir montado*) to ride; **m. a caballo**, to ride, go (horse) riding; **m. a pelo**, to ride bareback; **m. en avión**, to travel by plane; **m. en coche/burro**, to ride in a car/on a donkey. **3** (*tener importancia*) **tanto monta**, it makes no difference, it's all the same. **II** *vtr* **1** (*cabalgar*) to ride; **no se atreve a m. ese caballo**, he doesn't dare ride that horse. **2** (*poner encima*) to put on, mount; **montó al pequeño sobre el burrito**, he lifted the little boy onto the donkey. **3** *Zool* (*cubrir*) to mount. **4** (*acaballar*) to overlap; **una solapa monta sobre la otra**, one lapel overlaps the other. **5** *Fin* (*sumar*) to amount to, come to; **el total monta cien mil pesetas**, the total amounts to one hundred thousand pesetas. **6** (*máquina etc*) to assemble, put together; (*arma*) to cock; (*joya*) to mount, set; (*tienda*) to put up; (*negocio*) to set up, start; (*casa*) to set up. **7** *Culin* (*claras, nata*) to whip. **8** *Cin Fot* (*película*) to edit, mount; (*fotografía*) to mount. **9** *Teat* (*obra*) to stage, mount; *fam* **m. un número**, to make a scene. **III montarse** *vr* **1** (*subirse*) (*avión, autobús, bicicleta*) to get on; (*coche*) to get into. **2** *fam* (*armarse*) to break out; **menudo jaleo se montó**, there was a right to-do. **3** *arg* **montárselo**, to have things (nicely) worked out or set up; **qué bien te lo montas**, you've got things nicely set up.

montaraz *adj* **1** (*montañés*) highland, mountain. **2** (*arisco*) harsh, wild.

montarral *nm CAm Ven* thicket, scrub.

monte *nm* **1** (*montaña*) mountain; (*con nombre propio*) mount; **de m.**, wild; **M. Everest**, Mount Everest; *fam* **echarse al m.**, to take to the hills; *prov* **no todo el m. es orégano**, life is not just a bowl of cherries. ■ *Anat* **m. de Venus**, (*de la mano*) mount of Venus; (*del pubis*) mons veneris. **2** (*bosque*) woodland. ■ **m. alto**, forest; **m. bajo**, scrub, underbrush. **3** *Fin* **m. pío** *or* **de piedad**, assistance fund.

montepío *nm Fin* assistance fund.

montera *nf Taur* bullfighter's hat; *prov* **ponerse el mundo por m.**, not to give a damn about what people might say.

monteria *nf* **1** (*caza mayor*) hunting. **2** (*arte*) chase, venery.

montero,-a *nm,f* beater.

montés,-a *adj* (*animal*) wild.

montevideano,-a *adj & nm,f* Montevidean.

montículo *nm Geog* hillock.

montilla *nm* (*vino*) montilla, sherry-like wine.

monto *nm* total amount, total.

montón *nm* **1** heap, pile; **hace un m. de años**, many years ago; *fam* **del m.**, run-of-the-mill, nothing special; *arg* **me gusta un m.**, I really love it. **2 montones**, stacks, piles, tons; **a m.**, lots of; **gana dinero a m.**, he earns pots of money.

montubio,-a *nm,f Am* coastal peasant.

montuno,-a *adj Am* (*rudo*) coarse; (*montaraz*) wild; (*rústico*) rustic.

montuoso,-a *adj* mountainous.

montura *nf* **1** (*cabalgadura*) mount. **2** (*silla de montar*) saddle; **sin m.**, bareback. **3** (*soporte*) (*de gafas*) frame; (*de joya*) setting; (*de máquina, telescopio*) mounting, assembly.

monumental *adj* monumental.

monumento *nm* **1** *Arquit Arte* monument. **2** *fam* (*hermosura*) good-looking person; **es un m.**, she is a beauty.

monzón *nm Meteor* monsoon.

moña *nf* ribbon, bow.

moño *nm* **1** (*de pelo*) chignon, bun; *fam* **estar hasta el m.**, to be fed up to the back teeth. **2** (*de ave*) crest.

moñudo,-a *adj* (*animales*) crested.

MOPU *nm abr de* **Ministerio de Obras Públicas y Urbanismo**, ≈ Ministry of Public Works.

moquear *vi* to have a runny nose.

moqueo *nm* runny nose.

moqueta *nf* (*alfombra*) fitted carpet. **2** *Tex* moquette.

moquillo *nm Vet* **1** (*de perro*) distemper. **2** (*de gallina*) pip.

mor *nm* **por m. de**, for the sake of, because of.

mora¹ *nf* **1** (*fruto*) (*de moral*) mulberry; (*de la morera*) white mulberry. **2** (*zarzamora*) blackberry. **3** (*mujer*) Moorish woman. **4** *Arg CR PR Bot* osage orange. **5** *Méx Bot* mulberry.

mora² *nf Jur* (*retraso*) delay.

morada *nf fml* abode, dwelling; **hacer m.**, to stay temporarily.

morado,-a I *adj* purple; *fam* **pasarlas moradas**, to have a tough time; **ponerse m.**, to stuff oneself. **II** *nm* purple.

morador,-a *nm,f fml* dweller, inhabitant.

moradura *nf véase* **moretón**.

moral I *adj* moral; **deber m.**, moral duty. **II** *nm Bot* mulberry tree. **III** *nf* **1** (*conjunto de reglas*) morals *pl*. **2** (*ánimo*) morale, spirits *pl*; **levantar la m. a algn**, to cheer sb up, raise sb's spirits; **no tengo m. para verle ahora**, I couldn't face seeing him now; *fam* **tienes más m. que el Alcoyano**, what an optimist you are!

moraleja *nf* moral.

moralidad *nf* morality.

moralismo *nm* moralism.

moralista 1 *adj* moralistic. **II** *nmf* moralist.

moralización *nf* moralization.

moralizar *vtr & vi* to moralize.

morapio *nm fam* (*vino*) red wine.

morar *vi fml* to dwell, reside.

moratoria *nf Jur* moratorium.

morbidez *nf* softness, tenderness.

mórbido,-a *adj* **1** (*suave*) soft, delicate. **2** *fml* (*malsano*) morbid.

morbilidad *nf* morbidity, morbidness.

morbo *nm fam*, **morbosidad** *nf* **1** (*enfermedad*) sickness. **2** (*interés malsano*) morbidity.

morboso,-a *adj* **1** (*enfermo*) sick, ill. **2** *fml* (*malsano*) morbid.

morcilla *nf* **1** *Culin* black pudding; *fam* **que le den m.**, he can drop dead for all I care. **2** *Teat* improvised part.

morcillo *nm* fore knuckle.

mordacidad *nf* mordacity.

mordaz *adj* mordant.

mordaza *nf* gag.

mordedor,-a *adj* which bites, vicious; **perro m. poco ladrador**, his bark is worse than his bite.

mordedura *nf* bite.

morder I *vtr* to bite; **me ha mordido**, it has bitten me; *fig* **m. el anzuelo**, to take the bait; *fam* **el jefe está que**

muerde, the boss is hopping mad. **II morderse** *vr* to bite (oneself); **m. las uñas/los labios,** to bite one's nails/lips; **m. la lengua,** *(sinquerer)* to bite one's tongue; *(reprimirse)* to hold one's tongue.

mordido,-a I *pp de* **morder. II** *nf* 1 *(mordedura)* bite. 2 *Am (soborno)* bribe.

mordiente *adj & nm* mordant.

mordisco *nm* bite; **dar** *or* **pegar un m.,** *(a algo)* to take a bite at *or* out of; *(a algn)* to bite.

mordisquear *vtr* to nibble (at).

morena *nf (pez)* moray eel.

moreno,-a I *adj* 1 *(pelo)* dark-haired; *(ojos)* dark-eyed; *(piel)* dark-skinned. 2 *(bronceado)* suntanned, tanned; **ponerse m.,** to get a suntan; **en seguida me pongo m.,** I go brown very quickly. 3 *(razanegra)* black; **una cantante morena,** a black singer. 4 *(cosas)* brown; **pan/azúcar m.,** brown bread/sugar. **II** *nm*, *f* 1 *(persona) (de pelo)* dark-haired person; *(de ojos)* dark-eyed person; *(de piel)* dark-skinned person. 2 *(de raza negra)* black person. 3 *(bronceado)* suntan, tan.

morera *nf Bot* white mulberry.

morería *nf Hist* Moorish quarter; **la m.,** the Moors *pl.*

moretón *nm fam* bruise.

morfema *nm Ling* morpheme.

Morfeo *nm Mit* Morpheus.

morfina *nf* morphine.

morfinomanía *nf* addiction to morphine.

morfinómano,-a I *adj* addicted to morphine. **II** *nm*, *f* morphine addict.

morfología *nf* morphology.

morfológico,-a *adj* morphological.

morgue *nf* morgue.

moribundo,-a *adj & nm*, *f* moribund.

morigeración *nf* moderation.

morigerado,-a *adj* moderate.

morigerar *vtr* to moderate.

moriles *nm (vino)* moriles, sherry-like wine.

morir 1 *vi* 1 to die; **m. de amor** *or* **pena,** to die from a broken heart; **m. de frío,** to die of cold; **m. de hambre,** to starve to death, die of hunger; **m. de una enfermedad/de cáncer,** to die from an illness/from cancer; **¡muera la corrupción!,** down with corruption!; **murió en la guerra/de muerte natural,** he died in the war/a natural death. 2 *fig (terminar)* to end, finish; **los ríos van a m. al mar,** rivers end their life in the sea. 3 *lit (desaparecer)* to vanish, fade; **las olas morían a sus pies,** the waves came in and died by his feet. **II morirse** *vr* 1 to die; **m. de aburrimiento,** to be bored to death; **m. de envidia/miedo,** to be dying with envy/fear; **m. de frío,** to die of cold; *fig* to freeze to death; **m. de ganas (de hacer algo),** to be dying (to do sth); **m. de hambre,** to starve to death; *fig* to be starving; **m. por algo** *or* **algn,** to be crazy about sth *or* sb; **m. de risa,** to die laughing; *fam* **que me muera si ...,** may I be struck down dead if ... .

morisco,-a *Hist I adj* of *or* relating to Spanish Moors converted to Christianity, Morisco. **II** *nm*, *f* Spanish Moor converted to Christianity, Morisco.

mormón,-ona *adj & nm*, *f* Mormon.

mormonismo *nm* Mormonism.

moro,-a I *adj* 1 *Hist* Moorish. 2 *(musulmán)* Muslim; *(árabe)* Arab. 3 *fam pey (machista)* sexist. **II** *nm*, *f* 1 *Hist* Moor; *fam* **hay moros en la costa,** the coast is not clear. 2 *(musulmán)* Muslim; *(árabe)* Arab. 3 *pey (machista)* sexist man.

morocho,-a I *adj* 1 *Am (robusto)* tough, strong. 2 *SAm (moreno)* dark, swarthy. **II** *nm*, *f* 1 *Am (robusto)* tough *or* strong person. 2 *SAm (moreno)* dark *or* swarthy person.

morocota *nf Am* gold coin.

morosidad *nf* 1 *(lenitud)* slowness, sluggishness. 2 *Com Fin* arrears *pl* (of payment).

moroso,-a *adj (perezoso)* slow, sluggish, torpid. 2 *Com Fin* in arrears, slow to pay; **cliente m.,** slow *or* bad payer.

morrada *nf* 1 *(golpe)* blow; **se dio una gran m.,** he smashed his head in. 2 *(bofetada)* slap.

morral *nm* 1 *(para pienso)* nosebag. 2 *Mil* haversack; *(de cazador)* gamebag.

morralla *nf* 1 *Pesca* small fish. 2 *(chusma)* rabble, scum. 3 *(cosas sin valor)* rubbish, junk.

morrear *vtr*, **morrearse** *vr vulg* to snog, smooch.

morrena *nf Geol* moraine.

morreo *nm vulg* snog, smooch.

morrillo *nm* 1 *(de animal) (testuz)* fleshy part of the nape, 2 *fam (de persona)* (fleshy) back of the neck.

morriña *nf Gal* homesickness.

morrión *nm Mil* helmet, shako.

morro *nm* 1 *(de animal) (hocico)* snout, nose. 2 *fam (de persona)* month, (thick) lips; **arrugar** *or* **torcer el m.,** to pull faces (to show disagreement); **caerse de m.,** to fall flat on one's face; **estar de morros,** to be in a bad mood; **partir los morros a algn,** to punch sb in the face *or* mouth; **pasar por los morros,** to rub it in; **poner m.,** to look cross; *fam* **¡vaya m.!,** what a cheek! 3 *(parte saliente)* sticking out part, nose; **el m. del coche,** the nose of the car.

morrocotudo *adj fam & hum* amazing, terrific; **un lío m.,** a tremendous mess.

morrón I *adj* **pimiento m.,** (fleshy) red pepper. **II** *nm véase* **morrada 1.**

morronguear *vi* 1 *Am* to suck, sip. 2 *Arg Chi* to doze, snooze.

morroñoso,-a *adj CAm* 1 *(áspero)* rough. 2 *(egoísta)* selfish; *(roñoso)* stingy.

morrudo,-a *adj fam* thick-lipped.

morsa *nf Zool* walrus.

morse *nm Téc* morse.

mortadela *nf Culin* mortadella.

mortaja *nf* 1 *(sudario)* shroud. 2 *SAm fig (papel de cigarrillo)* cigarette paper.

mortal I *adj* 1 mortal; **los mortales,** mortals; **odio/pecado m.,** mortal hatred/sin. 2 *(mortífero)* fatal, lethal, deadly; **un accidente m.,** a fatal accident; **veneno m.,** lethal *or* deadly poison. **II** *nmf* mortal.

mortalidad *nf* mortality; **índice de m.,** death rate.

mortandad *nf* mortality, death toll.

mortecino,-a *adj* lifeless, colourless, *US* colorless.

mortero *nm Culin Mil* mortar.

mortífero,-a *adj* deadly, fatal, lethal.

mortificación *nf* mortification.

mortificar I *vtr* to mortify. **II mortificarse** *vr* to mortify oneself.

mortual *nm CAm Méx* inheritance, inherited goods *pl.*

mortuorio,-a *adj* mortuary. ■ **lecho m.,** deathbed.

morueco *nm Zool* ram.

moruno,-a *adj* Moorish; *(árabe)* Arab. ■ *Culin* **pincho m.,** ≈ kebab.

Mosa *n* Meuse.

mosaico,-a I *adj Rel* of *or* relating to Moses. **II** *nm* mosaic.

mosca *nf* 1 *Ent* fly. 2 *(perilla)* goatee. 3 *Box* **peso m.,** flyweight. 4 *arg (dinero)* dough, bread; **aflojar/soltar la m.,** to fork out, stump up. 5 *(locuciones)* **pescar a m.,** to fly-fish; *fam* **con la m. en** *or* **tras la oreja,** suspicious; *fam* **estar m.,** *(suspicaz)* to be suspicious; *(enfadado)* to be cross; *fam* **es incapaz de matar una m.,** he's totally harmless, he wouldn't harm a fly; *fam* **m.** *or* **mosquita muerta,** hypocrite; *fam* **no se oye una m.,** you could hear a pin drop; *fam* **picarle a algn la m.,** to start feeling suspicious; *fam* **por si las moscas,** just in case; *fam* **¿qué m. te ha picado?,** what's biting you?

moscada *adj* **nuez m.**, nutmeg.

moscarda *nf Ent* blowfly, bluebottle.

moscardón *nm* **1** *Ent* blowfly. **2** *fam (pesado)* pest, nuisance.

moscatel I *adj (vino)* muscat. **II** *nm (vino)* muscatel, muscat.

moscón *nm véase* **moscardón**.

mosconear *vtr* to pester, annoy, bother.

moscovita *adj & nmf* Muscovite.

Moscú *n* Moscow.

mosén *nm Cat Rel* Reverend.

mosqueado I *pp de* **mosquear**. **II** *adj* **1** *(manchado)* spotted. **2** *fam (enfadado)* cross.

mosquearse *vr fam* **1** *(enfadarse)* to get cross. **2** *(sospechar)* to smell a rat.

mosquerío *nm*, **mosquero** *nm Am* cloud of flies.

mosquete *nm Mil* musket.

mosquetero *nm Hist* musketeer.

mosquetón *nm* **1** *Mil Hist* carbine. **2** *Téc* snap link or hook.

mosquitera *nf* mosquito net.

mosquitero *nm* **1** *(red)* mosquito net. **2** *Orn* **m. común**, chiffchaff; **m. musical**, willow warbler; **m. silbador**, wood warbler.

mosquito *nm Ent* mosquito.

mostacho *nm* moustache, *US* mustache.

mostachón *nm Culin* macaroon.

mostajo *nm Bot* common whitebeam.

mostaza *nf Bot Culin* mustard.

mostellar *nm Bot* common whitebeam.

mosto *nm (del vino)* must; *(bebida)* grape juice.

mostrador *nm* **1** *(de tienda)* counter. **2** *(de bar)* bar.

mostrar I *vtr* **1** *(gen)* to show; **muéstramelo**, show it to me. **2** *(materiales, cualidades)* to display, exhibit. **3** *(explicar)* to explain, show. **II mostrarse** *vr* to be, appear, show oneself; **se mostró muy comprensiva**, she was very understanding.

mostrenco,-a I *adj* **1** *(sin dueño)* ownerless; **bienes mostrencos**, ownerless property. **2** *fig (ignorante)* stupid, thick, dense. **3** *(gordo)* fat. **II** *nm, f* **1** *(ignorante)* blockhead, dunce. **2** *(gordo)* very fat person.

mota *nf* **1** *(brizna)* mote, speck; **una m. de polvo**, a speck of dust. **2** *(lunar)* dot; **rojo con motas blancas**, red with white dots. **3** *fig (defecto)* small flaw or defect or fault. **4** *Am (mechón)* lock of hair. **5** *Méx (droga)* marijuana.

mote[1] *nm (apodo)* nickname; **poner m. a algn**, to give sb a nickname; **le pusimos como m. 'el Alto'**, we nicknamed him 'Lofty'.

mote[2] *nm Am Culin* boiled salted maize or *US* corn.

moteado,-a *adj* dotted.

motear *vi SAm* to eat **mote**.

motejar *vtr* to accuse, brand; **le motejaron de ladrón**, they branded him (as) a thief.

motel *nm* motel.

motete *nm* **1** *Mús* motet. **2** *CAm (atado)* bundle. **3** *Am (cuévano)* pannier.

motilidad *nf Téc* motility.

motín *nm (amotinamiento)* mutiny, rising; *(disturbio)* riot, disturbance.

motivación *nf* motivation, drive.

motivar I *vtr* **1** *(causar)* to cause, give rise to. **2** *(inducir)* to motivate. **3** *(razonar)* to explain, justify.

motivo *nm* **1** *(causa)* motive, cause; *(gen plural)* grounds *pl*; **bajo ningún m.**, under no circumstances; **con este** or **tal m.**, for this reason; **con m. de**, on the occasion of; **darle a algn motivos para hacer algo**, to give sb reason

to do sth; **hay suficientes motivos de divorcio**, there are sufficient grounds for divorce; **se ha enfadado con m.**, he has every reason to be angry; **sin m.**, for no reason at all; *fml* **Juan Segarra ha sido m. de homenaje**, a tribute has been paid to Juan Segarra. **2** *Art Mús* motif, leitmotif.

moto *nf Aut* motorbike.

motobomba *nf* fire engine.

motocarro *nm Aut* three-wheeled delivery van.

motocicleta *nm véase* **moto**.

motociclismo *nm Aut* motorcyling.

motociclista *nmf Aut* motorcyclist.

motociclo *nm Aut* motorcycle.

motocross *nm Aut* motocross.

motocultivo *nm Agr* mechanized agriculture.

motonáutica *nf Náut* motorboating.

motonáutico,-a *adj Náut* of or relating to motorboating.

motonave *nf Náut* motorboat.

motoniveladora *nf* bulldozer.

motor,-a I *adj* **1** *Téc* motive, motor. **2** *Biol* motor. **II** *nm* engine, motor. ■ **m. diesel**, diesel engine; **m. eléctrico**, electric motor; **m. de explosión**, internal combustion engine; **m. de reacción**, jet engine; **m. fuera borda** or **bordo**, outboard motor. **III** *nf Náut* motorboat.

motorismo *nm Aut* motorcycling.

motorista *nmf Aut* motorcyclist.

motorizado I *pp de* **motorizar**. **II** *adj* motorized.

motorizar I *vtr* to motorize. **II motorizarse** *vr fam* to get oneself a car or motorbike.

motosierra *nf* power saw.

motricidad *nf* motivity.

motriz *adj f* **1** *Téc* motive. ■ **fuerza m.**, motive power. **2** *Biol* motor.

movedizo,-a *adj* **1** *(fácil de mover)* easy to move. **2** *(poco firme)* unsteady. ■ **arenas movedizas**, quicksand *sing*.

mover I *vtr* **1** to move; **m. algo de su sitio**, to move sth out of its place; **no muevas la cabeza**, keep your head still; *fam* **m. el esqueleto**, to dance. **2** *(hacer funcionar)* to drive or work; **la máquina mueve el tren**, the engine pulls the train. **3** *(incitar, provocar)* to drive or incite; **m. a algn a piedad**, to move sb to pity; **movido por la compasión**, swayed by compassion; **sólo le mueve su interés por el dinero**, it is only money that impels him to do anything. **II moverse** *vr* **1** to move; **no te muevas**, don't move. **2** *fam (gestionar)* to take every step, make all possible efforts; **hay que m. para encontrar un trabajo**, you have to move heaven and earth to find a job. **3** *(darse prisa)* to hurry up; **¡muévete!**, get a move on! **4** *fig (relacionarse)* to move; **ella se mueve entre artistas**, she moves in artistic circles.

movible *adj* movable.

movida *nf arg* action; **la m. madrileña**, swinging Madrid.

movido,-a I *pp de* **mover**. **II** *adj* **1** *Fot* blurred. **2** *(persona)* active, restless. **3** *CAm chi (enteco)* puny.

móvil I *adj* movable, mobile. ■ *TV Rad* **unidad m.**, outside broadcast unit. **II** *nm* **1** *(motivo)* motive, reason; **el m. del crimen**, the motive for the murder. **2** *Art* mobile.

movilidad *nf* mobility.

movilización *nf* mobilization.

movilizar *vtr (tropas, multitudes, personas)* to mobilize.

movimiento *nm* **1** *gen* movement; *Fís Téc* motion; **m. circular/lineal**. circular/linear motion; *(poner algo)* en **m.**, (to set sth) in motion. ■ **m. sísmico**, earth tremor. **2** *(actividad)* movement, activity; **hay mucho m. en el mercado**, there is a lot of bustle in the market. **3** *Com Fin (entradas y salidas)* operations; **el m. de turistas es menor este año**, the number of tourists has gone down this year. ■ **m. de caja**, turnover, transactions *pl*. **4** *Art Lit* movement; **m. literario**, literary movement. **5** *Mús* tempo. **6** *Pol (sublevación)* movement, uprising. **7** *Esp Hist* **el M.**, the Falangist Movement.

moviola *nf Cin TV* editing projector.

moza *nf* **1** lass, young girl; **ser una buena m.**, to be a good-looking girl. **2** *arc (sirvienta)* maid.

mozalbete *nm* boy, young lad.

Mozambique *n* Mozambique.

mozambiqueño,-a *adj & nm,f* Mozambiquean.

mozárabe *Hist* **I** *adj* Mozarabic. **II** *nmf* Mozarab.

mozo *nm* **1** lad, boy; **ser un buen m.**, to be a good-looking *or* handsome man. **2** *(de estación)* porter; *(de hotel)* bellboy, *US* bellhop. ■ **m. de comedor,** waiter's assistant, *US* busboy; **m. de estación,** porter. **3** *Mil* conscript.

mozuelo,-a **I** *nm* young lad. **II** *nf* young lass.

m/p *abr de* **mi pagaré,** I owe you, IOU.

ms. *abr de* **manuscrito,** manuscript, ms.

muaré *nm Tex* moiré.

mucamo,-a *nm,f Am* servant.

muchacha *nf* **1** *(chica)* (young) girl. **2** *fam (sirvienta)* maid.

muchachada *nf,* **muchachería** *nf* **1** *(acción)* childish act *or* prank. **2** *(grupo)* group of children.

muchacho *nm* (young) boy, lad; **un gran m.**, a good lad.

muchedumbre *nf* **1** *(de gente)* crowd. **2** *(de cosas)* a great deal of.

mucho,-a **I** *adj* **1** *sing (gen en frases afirmativas)* a lot of, lots of, much; **hace m. calor,** it's very hot; **queda m. café,** there's a lot of coffee left; **m. tiempo,** a long time; **tengo m. sueño/mucha sed,** I am very sleepy/thirsty; *(colectivo)* **hay m. tonto suelto,** there are lots of idiots around; *(gen en frases neg e interr)* much; **¿bebes m. café?** —**no, no m.,** do you drink much coffee?; —no, not much. **2** *(demasiado)* **es m. coche para mí,** this car is far too big *or* expensive for me. **3** *muchos,-as, (gen en frases afirmativas)* a lot of, lots of; **tiene m. años ya,** he is very old now; **tienen m. hijos,** they have a lot of children; *(gen en frases neg e interr)* **no hizo muchas preguntas,** he didn't ask many questions; **¿tienes m. amigos?,** have you got many friends? **II** *pron* **1** a lot, a great deal, much; **¿cuánta leche queda?** —**mucha,** how much milk is there left? —a lot. **2** *muchos,-as,* a lot, many; **¿cuántos libros tienes?** —**m.,** how many books have you got? —lots; **m. de los presentes,** many of the people here; **m. son los que ...,** there are many who ,... **III** *adv* **1** (very) much, a lot; **como m.,** at the most; **con m.,** by far; **me gusta m.,** I like it very much; **m. antes/después,** long before/after; **m. mejor/peor,** a lot better/worse; **ni con m.,** not nearly as; **no es, ni con m., tan bueno como el otro,** it is not nearly as good as the other one; **ni m. menos,** not in the least; **por m. (que) ...,** however much ...; **por m. que te empeñes,** however hard you try; **tener a algn en m.,** to think a lot of sb; *fam* **muy m.,** very much. **2** *(tiempo)* **hace m. que no viene por aquí,** he has not been to see us for a long time. **3** *(a menudo)* often; **vamos m. al cine,** we go to the cinema quite often.

mucosa *nf* mucous membrane.

mucosidad *nf* mucosity, mucus.

mucoso,-a *adj* mucous.

múcura *nf Am* water jar, pitcher.

muda *nf* **1** *(de ropa)* change of clothes. **2** *Orn Zool (de plumas, pelo)* moult, *US* molt, moulting *or US* molting season; *(serpiente)* slough. **3** *(de la voz)* breaking.

mudable *adj* **1** *(cambiable)* changeable. **2** *(inconstante)* fickle.

mudada *nf Am* **1** *(muda)* change of clothes. **2** *Arg Cuba (traslado)* move, removal.

mudanza *nf* **1** *(cambio)* changing, change. **2** *(de residencia, piso)* move, removal; **estar de m.,** to be moving. ■ **camión de m.,** removal van.

mudar **I** *vtr* **1** *(cambiar)* to change; **le han mudado de oficina,** he's been moved to a different office; **m. de opinión,** to change one's mind. **2** *(trasladar)* to change,

move; **mudaron su residencia al sur de la ciudad,** they went to live in the south of the city. **3** *(de ropa)* to change. **4** *(de plumas, pelo)* to moult, *US* molt; *(de piel)* to shed, slough. **5** *(de voz)* to break. **II mudarse** *vr* **1** to change, move; **m. de sitio,** to change seats. **2** *(de ropa)* to change one's clothes. **3** *(de casa)* to move (house).

mudéjar *adj & nmf Hist* Mudejar.

mudenco,-a *adj* **1** *(tartamudo)* stuttering. **2** *CAm (necio)* stupid, silly.

mudez *nf* dumbness.

mudo,-a **I** *adj* **1** *(que no habla)* dumb; **m. de asombro,** dumbfounded; **m. de nacimiento,** born dumb. **2** *Ling* mute. **3** *Cin* silent. ■ **cine m.,** silent films *pl.* **4** *fig (callado)* speechless, silent. **II** *nm,f* dumb person.

mueblaje *nm véase* **mobiliario.**

mueble **I** *adj* movable. ■ **bienes muebles,** movables. **II** *nm* piece of furniture; **muebles,** furniture *sing;* **con/sin muebles,** furnished/unfurnished. ■ **m. bar,** cocktail cabinet.

mueblista *nmf (fabricante)* furniture maker; *(vendedor)* funiture dealer.

mueca *nf* **1** *(de burla)* mocking face; **hacer muecas,** to pull faces. **2** *(de dolor, asco)* grimace.

muela *nf* **1** *Anat* molar, tooth; **empastar una m.,** to fill a tooth. ■ **dolor de muelas,** toothache; **m. del juicio,** wisdom tooth. **2** *Téc (de molino)* millstone; *(de afilar)* grindstone.

muelle¹ **I** *adj* soft, comfortable. **II** *nm* spring.

muelle² *nm* **1** *(andén)* loading bay, freight platform. **2** *Náut* dock.

muérdago *nm Bot* mistletoe.

muermo *nm* **1** *Vet* glanders, farcy. **2** *arg (tedio)* boredom, pain; **esta fiesta es un m.,** this party is a drag; **este tío es un m.,** this bloke is a real bore.

muerte *nf* **1** death. ■ **m. natural,** natural death. **2** *(homicidio)* murder. **3** *(locuciones)* **a m.,** to the death; **a vida or m.,** life-and-death; **dar m. a algn,** to kill sb; **estar a (las puertas de) la m.,** to be dying, be at death's door; **hasta la m.,** unto death; **odiar a algn a m.,** to loathe sb; *fam* **de mala m.,** lousy, rotten; *fam* **un susto de m.,** the fright of one's life; *arg* **estar de m.,** to be fantastic.

muerto,-a **I** *pp de* **morir.** **II** *adj* **1** dead; **caer m.,** to drop dead; **dar a algn por m.,** to assume sb to be dead, give sb up for dead; **horas muertas,** spare time; **medio m.** *or* **más m. que vivo,** half-dead; **m. de hambre,** starving; **m. de frío,** frozen to death; **m. de miedo,** scared stiff; **m. de pena,** broken-hearted; **m. de risa,** laughing one's head off; **nacido m.,** still-born; **no tener dónde caerse m.,** not to have a place to lay one's head. ■ **lengua muerta,** dead language; **naturaleza muerta,** still life; *Aut* **punto m.,** neutral; **en punto m.,** out of gear. **2** *fam (cansado)* dead tired, dog-tired, exhausted. **III** *nm, f* **1** *(difunto)* dead person; *(cadáver)* corpse; **callarse como un m.,** not to say a word; **hacer el m.,** to float on one's back; **hacerse el m.,** to pretend to be dead; **ser un m. de hambre,** to be an absolute nobody; *fam* **cargar con el m.,** *(llevar la peor parte)* to be a dogs-body; *(llevarse las culpas)* to carry the can; *fam* **echarle el m. a algn,** to pass the buck to sb; *ofens* **¡tú muertos!,** up yours! **2** *(víctima)* fatality, victim; **hubo dos muertos,** there were two fatalities, two (people) died.

muesca *nf* **1** *Téc (entalladura)* mortise, mortice. **2** *(incisión)* nick, notch.

muestra *nf* **1** *(espécimen)* sample, specimen; **botón de m.,** sample. ■ **feria de muestras,** trade fair; **m. gratuita,** free sample. **2** *(modelo a copiar)* pattern, model. **3** *(prueba, señal)* proof, sign; **dar muestras de,** to show signs of; **como m. de poder,** as a demonstration of power; **m. de cariño/respeto,** token of affection/respect; **una m. más de ...,** yet another example of ... .

muestrario *nm* collection of samples.

muestreo *nm* sampling; **m. al azar,** random sampling.

mugido *nm* **1** *(de vaca)* moo; *(de toro)* bellow. **2** *Lit (estrépito)* howl, roar. **3 mugidos,** *(de vaca)* mooing *sing,* lowing *sing; (de toro)* bellowing *sing.*

mugir *vi* **1** *(vaca)* to moo, low; *(toro)* to bellow. **2** *fig* to bellow. **3** *Lit* to howl, roar.

mugre *nf* **1** *(suciedad)* filth, grime. **2** *Am (cosa sin valor)* piece of rubbish.

mugriento,-a *adj* filthy, grimy.

muguet *nm,* **muguete** *nm Bot* lily of the valley.

mujer *nf* **1** woman; **dos mujeres,** two women. ■ **m. fatal,** femme fatale; **m. de la limpieza,** cleaning lady; **m. de su casa,** housewife; *euf* **m. de la vida, m. de la vida alegre,** prostitute. **2** *(esposa)* wife; **su futura m.,** his bride-to-be; *fml* **tomar m.,** to get married.

mujeriego I *adj* woman-chasing. **II** *nm* womanizer, woman chaser.

mujeril *adj* **1** *(femenino)* womanly. **2** *pey (cursi)* womanish.

mujerío *nm* group of women.

mujerona *nf* buxom woman.

mujerzuela *nf* prostitute.

mújol *nm (pez)* grey mullet.

mula *nf* she-mule; *fig* **terco como una m.,** as stubborn as a mule.

muladar *nm* dump, rubbish tip.

muladí *Hist* **I** *adj f* or relating to the Spanish Christians converted to Islam in the Middle Ages. **II** *nmf* Spanish Christian converted to Islam.

mular *adj* mule; **ganado m.,** mules *pl.*

mulato,-a *adj & nm, f* mulatto.

muleque *nm* **1** *Am (esclavo negro)* black slave. **2** *Arg Cuba Urug (muchacho negro)* black boy.

mulero *nm* muleteer.

muleta *nf* **1** *(prótesis)* crutch. **2** *fig (apoyo)* support, prop. **3** *Taur* muleta.

muletilla *nf* **1** *Ling (estribillo)* pet word, cliché. **2** *(bastón)* cross-handled cane.

mullido,-a *adj* soft, fluffy.

mullir *vtr* **1** *(lana)* to beat, soften; *(colchón)* to fluff up. **2** *Agr (tierra)* to break up, hoe.

mulo *nm* mule; *fam* **estar hecho un m.,** to be as strong as a horse.

multa *nf* fine; *Aut* ticket; **m. de aparcamiento,** parking ticket.

multar *vtr* to fine.

multi- *pref* multi-; **multicelular,** multicelluar.

multicanal *adj TV* multichannel.

multicolor *adj* multicoloured, *US* multicolored.

multicopiar *vtr* to duplicate.

multicopista *nf* duplicator.

multidireccional *adj* multidirectional.

multifamiliar *nm Am* block of flats.

multiforme *adj* multiform.

multigrado *adj* multigrade.

multilaminar *adj (madera)* multi-ply.

multilateral *adj* multilateral.

multimillonario,-a *adj & nm, f* multimillionaire.

multinacional *adj & nf* multinational.

multíparo,-a *adj* multiparous.

múltiple *adj* **1** *Mat* multiple. **2 múltiples,** *(muchos)* many.

multiplexor *nm Inform* multiplexor.

multiplicable *adj* multipliable.

multiplicación *nf (gen) Mat* multiplication.

multiplicador,-a I *adj* multiplying. **II** *nm* **1** *Mat* multiplier. **2** *Mil* booster.

multiplicando *nm Mat* multiplicand.

multiplicar I *vtr & vi* to multiply **(por,** by). **II multiplicarse** *vr* **1** *(reproducirse, aumentar)* to multiply. **2** *fig (estar en todo)* to be everywhere.

multiplicidad *nf* multiplicity.

múltiplo,-a *adj & nm* multiple. ■ *Mat* **mínimo común m.,** lowest common multiple.

multirriesgo *adj inv Seg* **póliza m.,** multiple risk policy.

multitud *nf* **1** *(de personas)* crowd. **2** *(de cosas)* multitude; **tengo una m. de cosas que hacer,** I have thousands of things to do.

multitudinario,-a *adj* multitudinous.

multiviaje *adj* **tarjeta m.,** season ticket.

mundanal *adj,* **mundano,-a** *adj* of this world, mundane; **huir del m. ruido,** to get away from it all.

mundial I *adj* world, worldwide; **campeón m.,** world champion; **de fama m.,** world-famous. **II** *nm* world championship. ◆ **mundialmente** *adv* throughout the world, worldwide.

mundillo *nm fam irón* circles *pl,* spheres *pl;* **el m. literario,** literary circles.

mundo *nm* **1** world; **el m. de los niños/negocios,** the world of children/business; **el fin del m.,** the end of the world; **correr** or **ver m.,** to knock around; **echar** or **traer al m.,** to bring into the world; **nada del otro m.,** nothing special; **por nada del m.,** not for all the tea in China; **se me hundió el m.,** my world caved in; **todo el m.,** everyone; *fml* **venir al m.,** to come into the world; *euf* **echarse al m.,** to become a prostitute; *prov* **el m. es un pañuelo,** it's a small world. ■ **el otro m.,** the hereafter, life after death; **hombre/mujer de m.,** man/woman of the world. **2** *(baúl)* trunk.

mundología *nf* worldliness, experience of the world.

mundovisión *nf TV* satellite broadcasting.

muñeca *nf* **1** *Anat* wrist. **2** *(juguete, muchacha bonita)* doll.

muñeco *nm* **1** *(juguete)* (little) boy doll: **m. de trapo,** rag doll; **m. de nieve,** snowman. **2** *fig (marioneta)* puppet.

muñequera *nf* wristband.

muñequilla *nf* **1** *Téc* trunnion. **2** *(de trapo)* polishing bag or pad.

munición *nf Mil* ammunition. ■ **municiones de boca,** provisions; **m. submarina,** underwater ordnance.

municipal I *adj* municipal; **elecciones municipales,** local (council) elections. **II** *nm (municipal)* policeman.

municipalidad *nf* municipality.

municipalizar *vtr* to municipalize.

municipio *nm* **1** *Jur (circunscripción administrativa)* municipality. **2** *(territorio)* territory of a municipality. **3** *(ciudadanos)* people living in a municipality. **4** *(ayuntamiento)* town council.

munificencia *nf* munificence.

muñir *vtr* **1** *(convocar)* to summon. **2** *(amañar)* to fix.

muñón *nm* **1** *Anat* stump. **2** *Téc* gudgeon.

mural *adj & nm* mural.

muralla *nf* **1** *(de una ciudad)* wall. **2** *Am (pared)* wall. **3** *Méx (casa)* tenement.

murciano,-a I *adj* of or from Murcia. **II** *nm, f* native or inhabitant of Murcia.

murciélago *nm Zool* bat.

murga *nf* **1** *Mús* band of street musicians. **2** *fam (tabarra)* bore, pain; **dar la m.,** to be a pest or drag.

murmullo *nm* murmur, murmuring, whisper, whispering; **el m. de las hojas,** the rustling of the leaves.

murmuración *nf* gossip, backbiting.

murmurador,-a *adj* gossipy. **II** *nm, f* gossip.

murmurar *vi* **1** *(susurrar)* to whisper; *(refunfuñar)* to mutter, grumble. **2** *(criticar)* to gossip, backbite. **3** *(producir murmullo)* to murmur.

muro *nm* wall. ■ **m. de defensa,** dam.

murria *nf fam* sadness, melancholy; **estar con la m.** *or* **tener m.,** to have the blues, be feeling down.

murrio,-a *adj fam* sad, blue.

mus *nm Naipes* card game.

musa *nf* 1 *Mit* Muse. 2 *Lit (inspiración)* muse; **dedicarse a las musas,** to write poetry.

musaraña *nf* 1 *Zool* shrew; *fam* **estar mirando a** *or* **pensando en las musarañas** to be daydreaming *or* in the clouds. 2 *Chi Salv Nic fam (mueca)* face, grimace.

muscular *adj* muscular.

musculatura *nf* musculature; **desarrollar la m.,** to develop one's muscles.

músculo *nm Anat* muscle; **m. estriado/liso,** striated/ smooth muscle.

musculoso,-a *adj* muscular.

muselina *nf Tex* muslin; **m. fina,** mull.

museo *nm* museum; **m. de arte** *or* **pintura,** art gallery.

museografía *nf*, **museología** *nf* museology.

musgo *nm Bot* moss.

musgoso,-a *adj* mossy.

música *nf* music; *fam* **irse con la m. a otra parte,** to make oneself scarce; **poner m. a,** to set to music. ■ **m. clásica,** classical music; **m. de fondo,** background music; *fig* **m. celestial,** high-sounding words, empty promises.

musical I *adj* musical. II *nm (comedia)* musical.

musicalidad *nf* musicality.

músico,-a I *adj* musical. II *nm,f* musician. ■ *Culin* **postre de m.,** dessert of *nuts* and dried figs, raisins, etc with a glass of muscatel.

musicología *nf* musicolgy.

musicólogo,-a *nm,f* musicologist.

musiquero,-a I *adj arg* fond of music. II *nm* music cabinet.

musitar *vi lit* to whisper.

muslo *nm Anat* thigh.

mustango *nm Zool* mustang.

mustiarse *vr* to wilt, wither.

mustio,-a *adj* 1 *(plantas)* wilted, withered. 2 *(persona)* sad, gloomy.

musulmán,-ana *adj & nm,f* Muslim, Moslem.

mutabilidad *nf* mutability.

mutable *adj* mutable.

mutación *nf (gen)* change; *Biol* mutation.

mutante *adj & nmf* mutant.

mutilación *nf* mutilation.

mutilado,-a I *adj* mutilated, crippled, disabled. II *nm, f* cripple, disabled person; **m. de guerra,** disabled serviceman.

mutilar *vtr* to mutilate.

mutis *nm Teat* exit; **hacer m.,** *(callarse)* to shut up; *(irse)* to make oneself scarce; **¡m.!,** silence!

mutismo *nm* 1 *(silencio)* complete silence. 2 *Med* mutism.

mutua *nf véase* **mutualidad 2.**

mutualidad *nf* 1 *(reciprocidad)* mutuality. 2 *(asociación)* mutual benefit society.

mutualista I *adj* of *or* relating to a mutual benefit society. II *nmf* member of a mutual benefit society.

mutuo,-a *adj* mutual, reciprocal.

muy *adv* very; **m. bueno/malo,** very good/bad; **¡m. bien!,** very good!; **m. de agradecer,** very much to be appreciated; **m. de los catalanes,** typically Catalan; **eso es m. de Domingo,** that's just like Domingo; *pey* that's Domingo all over; **m. de mañana/noche,** very early/late; **por m. caro/rápido que sea,** expensive/fast though it may be; **por m. mal que salgan las cosas,** even if the worst comes to the worst; **ser m. hombre/mujer,** to be a real man/woman; *fam* **el m. tonto se lo dijo todo,** silly him, told her everything; *fam* **m. mucho,** very much.

N

N, n ['ene] *nf (la letra)* N, *n.*

N 1 *abr de* **newton,** newton, N. 2 *abr de* **Norte,** North, N.

n. *abr de* **nacido,-a,** born, b.

n/ *abr de* **nuestro,-a,** our.

nabo *nm* 1 *Bot (planta)* turnip. 2 *Bot (raíz)* root vegetable. 3 *vulg (pene)* prick.

nácar *nm* mother-of-pearl, nacre.

nacarado,-a *adj*, **nacarino,-a** *adj* mother-of-pearl, nacreous, pearly.

nacatamal *nm CAm* tamale stuffed with pork.

nacer *vi* 1 *(gen)* to be born; **al n.,** at birth; **nació en una familia acomodada,** she was born into well-to-do family; **nació para músico,** he was born to be a musician; *fig* **al n. el día,** at daybreak *or* dawn; *fig* **volver a n.,** to be born again; *fam fig* **n. de pie,** to be born under a lucky star; *fam fig* **no nací ayer,** I wasn't born yesterday. 2 *(pajaro)* to hatch (out). 3 *Bot (brotar)* to sprout, come up. 4 *(pelo, plumas)* to begin to grow. 5 *(surgir)* to spring (up). 6 *(tener su origen)* to originate, start; **el Ebro nace en Fontibre,** the river Ebro rises in Fontibre. 7 *(derivarse)* to arise; **su actitud nace de su inseguridad,** his attitude stems from his lack of confidence.

nacido,-a I *pp de* **nacer.** II *adj* born; **n. de padre español,** born of a Spanish father; **recién n.,** new-born; *fig* **bien n.,** *(de familia ilustre)* of noble birth; *(noble, bondadoso)* of noble mind; *fig* **mal n.,** despicable, mean. III *nm,f (gen pl)* **los nacidos en ...,** those born in ... .

naciente I *adj (nuevo)* new, recent; *(creciente)* growing; *(sol)* rising; **su n. amistad,** their newly formed friendship. II *nm (este)* East.

nacimiento *nm* 1 *(gen)* birth; **de n.,** from birth; **sordo de n.,** deaf from birth; **de noble n.,** of noble birth; *fam* **ser tonto de n.,** to be a complete idiot. ■ **lugar de n.,** birthplace, place of birth. 2 *fig (principio)* origin, beginning; *(de río)* source; **el n. de una nueva era,** the beginning of a new era. 3 *(belén)* Nativity scene, crib, crèche.

nación *nf* I *(gen)* nation; **las Naciones Unidas,** the United Nations. 2 *(país, estado)* country, state. 3 *(pueblo)* people.

nacional I *adj* 1 national; **himno n.,** national anthem. 2 *(productos, mercados)* domestic; **vuelos nacionales,** domestic flights. II *nmf* national; *Hist* **los nacionales,** the Francoist forces.

nacionalidad *nf* nationality.

nacionalismo *nm* nationalism.

nacionalista I *adj* nationalist, nationalistic. II *nmf* nationalist.

nacionalización *nf* 1 *(naturalización)* naturalization. 2 *(industria)* nationalization.

nacionalizar I *vtr* **1** *(naturalizar)* to naturalize. **2** *Econ (banca, industria)* to nationalize. **II nacionalizarse** *vr* to become naturalized; **n. español,** to take up Spanish citizenship.

nacionalsocialismo *nm Hist* National Socialism.

naco *nm* **1** *SAm (tabaco)* chew (of black tobacco). **2** *CAm fig (cobarde)* coward. **3** *Arg fig (susto)* fright, fear.

nada I *pron* nothing, anything; **antes de n.,** first of all; **casi n.,** almost nothing; **como si n.,** just like that; **de n.,** insignificant; **dentro de n.,** in a moment; **enfadarse por n.,** to get upset for no reason at all; **gracias, —de n.,** thanks, —don't mention it; **n. de eso,** nothing of the kind; **¡n. de eso!,** not a bit of it!; **n. de excusas,** no excuses; **n de n.,** nothing at all; **n. más,** only; **n. más verla,** as soon as he saw her; **(n. más y) n. menos que,** no less than; **nadie sabía n.,** nobody knew anything at all; **no es n.,** it is nothing; **no hay n. que hacer,** nothing can be done; **por n. del mundo,** (not) for anything in the world; **¡y n. de ir en moto!,** and no riding motorcycles! **II** *adv* not at all; **no me gusta n.,** I don't like it at all. **III** *nf* nothingness; **salir de la n.,** to come out of nowhere.

nadador,-a *nm,f* swimmer.

nadar *vi* **1** *Dep* to swim; **n. a brasa,** to do the breast-stroke; *fig* **n. en dinero,** to be rolling in money; *fam* **n. y guardar la ropa,** to have one's cake and eat it, have the best of both worlds. **2** *(flotar)* to float.

nadería *nf* little something, trifle.

nadie I *pron* nobody, not ... anybody; **allí no había n.,** there was nobody there; **n. de su familia,** none of his relatives; **n. vino,** no one came; **no se lo digas a n.,** don't tell anyone; *fig* **tú no eres n. para hablarme así,** you have no right to talk to me like that. **II** *nm* nobody; **ser un (don) n.,** to be a nobody.

nadir *nm Astron* nadir.

nado (a) *loc adv* swimming; **cruzar** *or* **pasar a n.,** to swim across.

nafta *nf* **1** *Quím* naphtha. **2** *Am (gasolina)* petrol, *US* gasoline.

naftalina *nf* naphtalene, naphtaline. ■ **bola de n.,** mothball.

nagüeta *nf CAm* overskirt.

naíf *adj Arte* naïf.

nailon *nm* nylon; **medias de n.,** nylons *pl.*

naipe *nm* playing card.

nal. *abr de* **nacional,** national, nat.

nalga *nf Anat* buttock; **nalgas,** bottom *sing,* buttocks.

Namibia *n* Namibia.

nana *nf* lullaby; *fam* **del año de la n.,** very old-fashioned. *fam* **el año de la n.,** the year dot.

nanay *interj fam* no way!

nao *nf lit* vessel.

napa *nf* nappa.

napalm *nm Quím* napalm.

napias *nfpl fam* snout *sing.*

napoleónico,-a *adj Hist* Napoleonic.

Nápoles *n* Naples.

napolitano,-a *adj & nm,f* Neapolitan.

naranja I *nf Bot* orange; *fig* **mi media n.,** my better half. ■ **n. agria,** Seville orange; **n. sanguina,** blood orange. **II** *adj & nm (color)* orange. **III naranjas** *interj fam* **¡n. (de la China)!,** no way!

naranjada *nf* orangeade.

naranjal *nm* orange grove.

naranjo *nm* orange tree.

narcisismo *nm* narcissism, narcism.

narcisista I *adj* narcissistic. **II** *nmf* narcissist.

narciso *nm* **1** *Bot* narcissus, daffodil. **2** *fig (hombre)* narcissist.

narcosis *nf Med* narcosis.

narcótico,-a I *adj* narcotic. **II** *nm Med* narcotic; *(droga)* drug.

narcotizar *vtr Med* to narcotize; *(drogar)* to drug.

narcotraficante *nmf* drug trafficker.

narcotráfico *nm* drug trafficking.

nardo *nm Bot* spikenard, nard.

narigón,-ona *nm,f* **narigudo,-a** *nm,f* person with a big nose.

nariz *nf Anat* nose; *(sentido)* sense of smell; *fig* **darle a algn con la puerta en las narices,** to slam a door in sb's face; *fig* **darse de narices con algn,** to bump into sb; *fig* **darse de narices contra el suelo,** to fall flat on one's face; *fam* **de narices,** terrific; *fam* **en mis (propias) narices,** right under my very nose; *fam* **estar hasta las narices de,** to be totally fed up with; *fam* **hacer lo que le sale a uno de las narices,** to do whatever one wants; *fam* **hinchársele las narices a algn,** to get one's back up; *fam* **me da en la n. que me quiere engañar,** I've got this feeling he wants to cheat me; *fam* **meter las narices en algo,** to poke one's nose into sth; *fam* **narices,** nose *sing*; *fam* **¡narices!,** not on your life!; *fam* **por narices,** because I say so; *fam* **¿qué narices ...?,** what the hell ...?; *fam* **tener narices,** to have a lot of nerve; *fam* **¡tiene narices la cosa!,** this is too much!; *fam* **tocarle a algn las narices,** to get on sb's wick; *fam* **tocarse las narices,** not to do a thing. ■ **n. chata,** snub nose; **n. griega,** straight nose; **n. respingona,** turned-up nose.

narizotas *nmf inv fam* big-nose.

narración *nf* narration, narrative, account.

narrador,-a *nm,f* narrator.

narrar *vtr* to narrate, tell.

narrativo,-a *adj & nf* narrative.

nasa *nf (pesca)* keepnet.

nasal *adj & nf* nasal.

nasalización *nf* nasalization.

nasalizar *vtr* to nasalize.

nata *nf* **1** *(gen)* cream; **n. batida,** whipped cream. **2** *(de leche hervida)* skin. **3** *fig* cream, best.

natación *nf Dep* swimming.

natal *adj* natal; **mi país n.,** my native country; **su pueblo n.,** his home town.

natalicio,-a I *adj* birthday. **II** *nm* birthday.

natalidad *nf* birth rate. ■ **control de n.,** birth control.

natillas *nfpl Culin* custard *sing.*

natividad *nf* Nativity.

nativismo *nm Am* nativism.

nativo,-a *adj & nm,f* native.

nato,-a *adj* born.

natura *nf lit* nature; **contra n.,** against nature.

natural I *adj* **1** *(gen)* natural; *(fruta, flor)* fresh; **de tamaño n.,** life-size, life-sized; **en estado n.,** in its natural state; **fuerzas naturales,** forces of nature; *Jur* **hijo n.,** illegitimate child; **luz n.,** daylight, sunlight. **2** *(sin elaboración)* plain; **al n.,** *(en la realidad)* in real life; *Culin* in its own juice. **3** *(espontáneo)* natural, unaffected. **4** *(comprensible)* natural, usual. **5 ser n. de,** to come from. **6** *Mús* natural, *US* cancel. **II** *nmf* native, inhabitant; **los naturales de,** the natives of, those born in. **III** *nm* **1** *(temperamento)* nature, disposition; **de n. sencillo,** of an unaffected nature. **2** *Taur* type of pass with the **muleta.** ◆ **naturalmente** *adv* naturally; **¡n.!,** of course!

naturaleza *nf* **1** *(gen)* nature; **dejar obrar a la n.,** to let nature take its course; **en plena n.,** in the wild, in unspoilt countryside. ■ *Arte* **n. muerta,** still life. **2** *(forma de ser)* nature, character; **es de n. agresiva,** he is aggressive by nature; **por n.,** by nature. **3** *(complexión)* physical constitution; **de n. robusta,** strongly built.

naturalidad *nf* 1 *(sencillez)* naturalness; **con la mayor n. del mundo,** as if it were the most natural thing, in the world; **con n.,** naturally, straightforwardly. 2 *(espontaneidad)* ease, spontaneity.

naturalismo *nm* naturalism.

naturalista I *adj* naturalistic. II *nmf* naturalist.

naturalixución *nf* naturalization.

naturalizar I *vtr* to naturalize. II **naturalizarse** *vr* to become naturalized, take up citizenship.

naturismo *nm* naturism.

naturista I *adj* naturistic. II *nmf* naturist.

naufragar *vi* 1 *(barco)* to sink, be wrecked; *(persona)* to be shipwrecked. 2 *fig (plan)* to fail, fall through; *(persona)* to fail.

naufragio *nm* 1 *Náut* shipwreck. 2 *fig (fracaso)* failure, disaster.

náufrago,-a I *adj* wrecked, shipwrecked. II *nm, f* shipwrecked person, castaway.

náusea *nf (gen pl)* nausea, sickness; **me da n.,** it makes me sick; **sentir náuseas,** to feel sick.

nauseabundo,-a *adj* nauseating, sickening.

náutica *nf* navigation, seamanship.

náutico,-a *adj* nautical; **deportes náuticos,** water sports.

navaja *nf* 1 *(cuchillo)* penknife, pocketknife. ■ **n. de afeitar,** razor; **n. de monte,** hunting knife; **n. de muelle,** flick-knife, *US* switchblade. 2 *Zool (molusco)* razor-shell.

navajada *nf*, **navajazo** *nm* stab, gash.

navajero *nm fam* thug.

naval *adj* naval.

Navarra *n* Navarre.

navarro,-a I *adj* Navarrese, of *or* from Navarre. II *nm, f* native *or* inhabitant of Navarre.

nave *nf* 1 *Náut* ship, vessel; *fig* **quemar las naves,** to burn one's boats *or* one's bridges. 2 *Astronáut* **n. (espacial),** spaceship, spacecraft. 3 *Arquit (de iglesia)* nave. ■ **n. lateral,** aisle. 4 *Ind* plant, building. ■ **n. industrial,** industrial premises *pl.*

navegabilidad *nf* 1 *(de un río)* navigability. 2 *(de un barco)* seaworthiness. 3 *(de un avión)* airworthiness.

navegable *adj* navigable.

navegación *nf* 1 *(arte)* navigation. ■ *Av* **n. aérea,** air navigation; **n. fluvial,** river navigation. 2 *(barcos)* shipping.

navegante I *adj* sailing; **un pueblo n.,** a seafaring people. II *nmf* navigator.

navegar *vi* 1 *Náut* to navigate, sail; *fig* **n. contra corriente,** to go against the tide. 2 *Av* to navigate, fly.

Navidad *nf* Christmas; **es N.,** it's Christmas (time); **felicitar las Navidades,** to wish (sb) happy *or* merry Christmas. ■ **árbol de N.,** Christmas tree.

navideño,-a *adj* Christmas.

naviero,-a I *adj* shipping. II *nm, f (propietario)* shipowner.

navío *nm Náut* vessel, ship.

nazareno,-a I *adj & nm, f* Nazarene. II *nm Rel* 1 **el N.,** Jesus of Nazareth. 2 hooded penitent in Holy Week processions.

nazco *indic pres véase* **nacer.**

nazi *adj & nmf Pol* Nazi.

nazismo *nm Pol* Nazism.

N.B. *abr de* **nota bene** (observa bien), note well, N.B, n.b.

n/c., n/cta. *abr de* **nuestra cuenta,** our account, our acct.

neblina *nf Meteor* mist, thin fog.

neblinoso,-a *adj Meteor* misty.

nebulosa *nf Astron* nebula.

nebulosidad *nf Meteor* cloudiness, nebulosity.

nebuloso,-a *adj* 1 *Meteor* cloudy, hazy. 2 *fig* nebulous, vague.

necedad *nf* 1 *(estupidez)* stupidity, foolishness. 2 *(tontería)* stupid thing to say *or* to do; **son necedades,** it's nonsense.

necesario,-a *adj* necessary; **es n. hacerlo,** it has to be done; **es n. que vayas,** you must go; **hacerse n.,** *(algo)* to be required; *(alguien)* to become vital *or* essential; **no es n. que vayas,** there is no need for you to go; **si fuera n.,** if need be; **todo lo n.,** all that is necessary.

neceser *nm (de aseo)* toilet bag *or* case; *(de maquillaje)* make-up bag *or* kit.

necesidad *nf* 1 *(gen)* necessity, need; **de n.,** essential; **artículos de primera n.,** essentials; **una herida mortal de n.,** a fatal wound; **no hay n. de,** there is no need to *or* for; **por n.,** of *or* by necessity; **si hubiera n.,** if the need arises; **tener n. de,** to need. 2 *(hambre intensa)* starvation, hunger; **morir de n.,** to starve to death. 3 *(pobreza)* poverty, want, hardship; **quedamos en la mayor n.,** we were left in dire need. 4 *(gen pl) (excrementos)* **hacer sus necesidades,** to relieve oneself.

necesitado,-a I *pp de* **necesitar.** II *adj (pobre)* needy, poor; **n. de,** in need of. III *nm, f* needy person; **los necesitados,** the needy *pl.*

necesitar *vtr (gen)* to need; *(en anuncios)* 'se necesita chico', 'boy wanted'; *fam* **n. Dios y ayuda,** to need all the help one can get; *fam* **no n. abuela,** to blow one's own trumpet.

necio,-a I *adj* silly, stupid. II *nm, f* fool, idiot.

nécora *nf Zool* fiddler crab.

necrofilia *nf* necrophilia.

necrófilo,-a *adj* necrophiliac.

necrología *nf* obituary.

necrológico,-a *adj* necrological; **nota necrológica,** obituary.

néctar *nm* nectar.

nectarina *nf* nectarine.

neerlandés,-esa I *adj* Dutch, of *or* from the Netherlands. II *nm, f (persona) (gen)* Netherlander; *(hombre)* Dutchman; *(mujer)* Dutchwoman; **los neerlandeses,** the Dutch. III *nm (idioma)* Dutch.

nefando,-a *adj fml* abominable, odious.

nefasto,-a *adj* 1 *(que causa desgracia)* unlucky, ill-fated. 2 *(perjudicial)* harmful, fatal.

nefritis *nf inv Med* nephritis.

negación *nf* 1 *(gen)* negation; **la n. de la realidad,** the negation of reality. 2 *(negativa)* negative, denial, refusal. 3 *Ling* negative.

negado,-a I *pp de* **negar.** II *adj* dull; **ser n. para algo,** to be hopeless *or* useless at sth. III *nm, f* nohoper.

negar I *vtr* 1 *(gen)* to deny; **n. con la cabeza,** to shake one's head; **Engracia niega haberlo robado,** Engracia denies having stolen it. 2 *(no conceder)* to refuse, deny; **le negaron la beca,** he didn't get the grant; **nos negaron la entrada,** we were turned away. II **negarse** *vr* 1 to refuse (a, to); **se negó a aceptar la oferta,** he turned the offer down; **se niega a entenderlo,** he refuses to understand it. 2 *Culin* to curdle.

negativa *nf* negative, denial; **una n. rotunda,** a flat refusal.

negativismo *nm* negativism.

negativo,-a I *adj* 1 negative. 2 *Mat* minus. II *nm Fot* negative.

negligé *nm* negligée.

negligencia *nf* negligence, carelessness.

negligente I *adj* negligent, neglectful, careless. II *nmf* negligent *or* careless person.

negociable *adj* negotiable.

negociación *nf* negotiation; **entablar negociaciones con,** to open negotiations with. ■ **n. colectiva,** collective bargaining.

negociado *nm* **1** *(sección)* department, section. **2** *Am (negocio ilícito)* shady deal.

negociador,-a I *adj* negotiating; **comité n.,** negotiating committee. II *nm,f* negotiator.

negociante *nmf* dealer; *(hombre)* businessman; *(mujer)* businesswoman.

negociar I *vtr Fin Pol* to negotiate. II *vi (comerciar)* to do business, deal; **negocia en** *or* **con ganado,** he trades *or* deals in cattle.

negocio *nm Com Fin (gen)* business; *(transacción)* deal, transaction; *(asunto)* affair; **buen n.,** *Com* profitable deal; *irón* bargain; **el n. del espectáculo,** show business; **hablar de negocios,** to talk business; **hacer n.,** to make a profit; **mal n.,** bad deal; *fig* **n. sucio,** shady deal; *irón* **¡vaya n.!,** that was a fine deal! ■ **hombre de negocios,** businessman; **mujer de negocios,** businesswoman.

negral *nm Bot* pine.

negrear *vi* to turn dark *or* black.

negrero,-a I *adj* of the black slave trade. II *nm,f* **1** black-slave trader. **2** *fig* slave driver.

negrilla *adj & nf,* **negrita** *adj & nf Impr* bold (face).

negro,-a I *adj* **1** *(gen)* black; **cerveza negra,** stout; **n. como la boca del lobo,** pitch-black; *Hist* **peste negra,** Black Death; *fig* **lista negra,** blacklist. **2** *(bronceado)* suntanned; **se pone n. enseguida,** he tans really quickly. **3** *fig (humor)* sad, gloomy; *(suerte)* awful; *(desesperado)* desperate; *(enfadado)* cross; **el lado n. de las cosas,** the dark side of things; **estar n. con algo,** to be desperate about sth; **la cosa se pone negra,** things look bad; **pasarlas negras,** to have a rotten time; **poner n. a algn,** to drive sb mad; **ponerse n.,** to go mad; **verlo todo n.,** to be very pessimistic; **vérselas negras para hacer algo,** to have a tough time doing sth. II *nm, f (hombre)* black; *(mujer)* black (woman); *fam* **trabajar como un n.,** to work like a dog. III *nm* **1** *(color)* black. **2** *(persona)* ghostwriter. IV *nf* **1** *Mús* crotchet, *US* quarter note. **2** *fig (mala suerte)* bad luck; **tener la negra,** to be very unlucky.

negroide *adj & nmf* Negroid.

negrón *nm Orn* scoter.

negrura *nf* blackness.

negruzco,-a *adj* blackish.

nemotecnia *nf* mnemonics *sing.*

nemotécnico,-a *adj* mnemonic.

nene,-a *nm, f* **1** *(niño)* baby boy; *(niña)* baby girl. **2** *(apelativo cariñoso)* darling, baby.

nenúfar *nm Bot* water lily.

neocelandés,-esa I *adj* of *or* from New Zealand. II *nm,f* New Zealander.

neoclasicismo *nm Arte Lit* neoclassicism.

neoclásico,-a *Arte Lit* I *adj* neoclassic, neoclassical. II *nm,f* neoclassicist.

neófito,-a *nm,f* neophyte; *(aprendiz)* beginner.

neolítico,-a *adj & nm* Neolithic.

neologismo *nm* neologism.

neón *nm* neon.

neorrealismo *nm Cin* neorealism.

neoyorkino,-a I *adj* of *or* from New York. II *nm,f* New Yorker.

neozelandés,-esa *adj & nm,f véase* **neocelandés,-esa.**

Nepal *n* Nepal.

nepalés,-esa I *adj* Nepalese, of *or* from Nepal. II *nm,f* Nepalese; **los nepaleses,** the Nepalese *pl.*

nepotismo *nm* nepotism.

Neptuno *n Astron Mit* Neptun e.

nervio *nm* **1** *Anat Bot* nerve; *(de la carne)* tendon, sinew. **2** *fig (fuerza, vigor)* nerve, courage; **tener n.,** to have character. **3** *Arquit* rib. **4** *Impr* band. **5** **nervios,** nerves; **ataque de n.,** a fit of hysterics; **me crispa los n.,** it (really)

gets on my nerves; **ponerle a algn los n. de punta,** to set sb's nerves on edge, **ser un manojo de n.,** to be a bundle of nerves; **tener los n. de acero,** to have nerves of steel; **tiene los n. destrozados,** he's a nervous wreck.

nerviosidad *nf,* **nerviosismo** *nm* nervousness, nerves *pl.*

nervioso,-a *adj* nervous; **poner n. a algn,** to get on sb's nerves; **ponerse n.,** to get all excited; **¡qué niño más n.!,** what a fidgety child!

nervudo,-a *adj* **1** *Anat* sinewy, wiry. **2** *(fuerte)* strong, vigorous.

neto,-a *adj* **1** *(peso, cantidad)* net. **2** *(claro)* neat, clear.

neumático,-a I *adj* pneumatic, tyre, *US* tire. II *nm* tyre, *US* tire. ■ **n. de recambio,** spare tyre.

neumonía *nf Med* pneumonia.

neura *nf fam* depression; **estar con la na.,** to be down in the dumps.

neuralgia *nf Med* neuralgia.

neurálgico,-a *adj Med* neuralgic.

neurastenia *nf Med* neurasthenia.

neurasténico,-a *Med* I *adj* neurasthenic. II *nm, f* neurasthenic person.

neurólogo,-a *nm,f* neurologist.

neurología *nf Med* neurology.

neurona *nf Anat* neuron.

neurosis *nf Med* neurosis.

neurótico,-a *adj & nm,f Med* neurotic.

neutral *adj* neutral.

neutralidad *nf* neutrality.

neutralización *nf* neutralization.

neutralizar *vtr* to neutralize.

neutro,-a *adj* **1** *Ling* neuter. **2** *(imparcial)* neutral, impartial. **3** *(color)* neutral.

neutrón *nm Fís* neutron. ■ **bomba de neutrones,** neutron bomb.

nevada *nf* snowfall.

nevado,-a I *pp de* **nevar.** II *adj* **1** *(gen)* covered with snow; *(montaña)* snow-capped. **2** *lit (blanco)* snow-white, snowy.

nevar *v impers* to snow.

nevera *nf* refrigerator, fridge.

nevisca *nf* light snowfall.

neviscar *v impers* to snow gently.

nexo *nm* connection, link. ■ **n. de unión,** nexus.

n/f. *abr de* **nuestro favor,** our favour *or US* favor, our fav.

n/g. *abr de* **nuestro giro,** our order, our o.

ni *conj* **1** neither, nor; **ni ha venido ni ha llamado,** he hasn't come or phoned; **no tengo tiempo ni dinero,** I have got neither time nor money; **no vengas ni hoy ni mañana,** don't come today or tomorrow. **2** *(ni siquiera)* not even; **¡ni hablar!,** no way!; **ni por dinero,** not even for money; **ni se te ocurra,** don't even think about it. **3** *(ni que + subj)* one would think that ...; **¡ni que fuera millonario!,** you'd think he was a millionaire!

nica *adj CAm hum* Nicaraguan.

Nicaragua *n* Nicaragua.

nicaragüense *adj & nmf,* **nicaragüeño,-a** *adj & nm,f* Nicaraguan.

nicho *nm* niche.

nicotina *nf Quím* nicotine.

nidada *nf (de huevos)* clutch; *(de crías)* brood.

nidal *nm* nest.

nido *nm* **1** nest; *fig* **n. de amor,** love nest; *fig* **n. de ladrones,** nest of thieves. ■ **cama n.,** pull-out bed; **mesa(s) n.,** nest of tables; *Cost* **n. de abeja,** smocking. **2** *(escondrijo)* hiding place. **3** *(vivero)* hotbed; **un n. de discordia,** a hotbed of discord.

niebla *nf Meteor* fog; **hay mucha n.,** it is very foggy; *fig* envuelto en n., confused, cloudy.

nieto,-a *nm, f (niño)* grandson; *(niña)* granddaughter; **mis nietos,** my grandchildren.

nieve *nf* **1** *Meteor* snow; *Culin* **a punto de n.,** (beaten) stiff. ■ **n. copo de n.,** snowflake. **2** *arg (cocaína)* snow. **3** *Am (helado)* ice cream.

Níger *n* Niger.

Nigeria *n* Nigeria.

nigeriano,-a *adj & nm, f* Nigerian.

nigerino,-a *adj & nm, f* Nigerien.

nigromancia *nf* necromancy.

nigromante *nmf* necromancer.

nihilismo *nm Filos* nihilism.

nihilista *Filos* **I** *adj* nihilistic. **II** *nmf* nihilist

Nilo *n* **el N.,** the Nile.

nilón *nm Tex* nylon.

nimbo *nm* nimbus.

nimiedad *nf* **1** *(cualidad)* smallness, triviality. **2** *(cosa nimia)* trifle.

nimio,-a *adj* **1** *(sin importancia)* insignificant, petty. **2** *(minucioso)* overmeticulous, nit-picking.

ninfa *nf* **1** *Mit Zool* nymph. **2** *fig (mujer)* nymph, beautiful woman.

ninfómana *nf Med* nymphomaniac.

ninfomania *nf Med* nymphomania.

ningún *adj (delante de nm sing)* no, not any; **de ningún modo,** in no way; *véase tamb* **ninguno,-a.**

ninguno,-a **I** *adj* no, not any; **en ninguna parte,** nowhere; **ninguna cosa,** nothing; **no tiene ninguna gracia,** it is not funny at all. **II** *pron* **1** *(persona)* nobody, no one; **n. de ellos,** none of them; **n. lo vio,** no one saw it. **2** *(objeto)* not any, none; **n. me gusta,** I don't like any of them.

niña *nf* **1** *Anat* pupil; *fig* **es la n. de sus ojos,** she's the apple of his eye. **2** *véase* **niño,-a.**

niñada *nf* **1** *(chiquillada)* childishness, childish behaviour *or US* behavior. **2** *(cosa nimia)* trifle.

niñera *nf* nursemaid, nanny.

niñería *nf véase* **niñada.**

niñez *nf* childhood, infancy.

niño,-a *nm, f* **1** *(gen)* child; *(muchacho)* (small) boy; *(muchacha)* (little) girl; **de n.,** as a child; **desde n.,** from childhood; **es muy niña,** she's very young for her age; **n. prodigio,** child prodigy; *pey* **n. bien** *or* **de papá,** rich boy, rich kid; *pey* **n. bonito** *or* **mimado,** mummy's *or* daddy's boy. **2** *(bebé)* baby; **esperar un n.,** to be expecting a baby. **3** *Am (tratamiento) (amo)* master; *(ama)* miss. **4 niños,** children; *fig* **juego de n.,** child's play.

nipón,-ona *adj & nm, f* Japanese; **los nipones,** the Japanese.

níquel *nm Quím* nickel.

niquelado,-a **I** *pp de* **niquelar. II** *adj* nickel-plated. **III** *nm* nickelling, *US* nickeling.

niquelar *vtr* to nickel.

niqui *nm* T-shirt.

nirvana *nm Rel* nirvana.

níspero *nm Bot (fruto)* medlar; *(árbol)* medlar tree.

nitidez *nf* **1** *(trasparencia)* limpidness, transparency. **2** *(claridad)* accuracy, precision.

nítido,-a *adj* **1** *(transparente)* limpid, transparent. **2** *(claridad)* accurate, precise.

nitrato *nm Quím* nitrate. ■ **n. de Chile,** Chilean nitrate, Chile saltpetre, nitre.

nítrico,-a *adj Quím* nitric.

nitrogenado,-a *adj* nitrogenous.

nitrógeno *nm* nitrogen.

nitroglicerina *nf* nitroglycerine.

nivel *nm* **1** *(altura)* level, height; **a n.,** levelled; **a n. del mar,** at sea level; **al n. de,** on a level with. **2** *(categoría)* standard, degree; **alto n. de especialización,** high degree of specialization; **estar al mismo n. que,** to be on a level with. ■ **n. de vida,** standard of living. **3** *(instrumento)* level. ■ **n. de aire,** spirit level. **4** *Ferroc* **paso a n.,** level crossing, *US* grade crossing.

nivelación *nf* levelling, *US* leveling.

nivelador,-a **I** *adj* levelling, *US* leveling. **II** *nm, f* leveller, *US* leveler.

nivelar *vtr* to level out *or* off.

níveo,-a *adj lit* snowy, snow-white.

Niza *n* Nice.

n/L. *abr de* **nuestra letra (de crédito),** our letter of credit, our L/C.

n/o. *abr de* **nuestra orden,** our order, our o.

n° *abr de* **número,** number, n.

no **I** *adv* **1** no, not; **¡a que no ...!,** I bet you don't ...; **aún no,** not yet; **¡cómo no!,** of course!; **al n. de,** on a level with; **no lo hice,** I didn't do it; **no sea que,** in case; **no sin antes ...,** not without first ...; **no sólo ... sino también ...,** not only ... but also ...; **te guste** *or* **no te guste,** whether you like it or not; **¿por qué no?,** why not?; **ya no,** no longer, not any more. **2** *(en frases interrogativas)* **es rubia, ¿no?,** she's blonde, isn't she?; **has ido ya, ¿no?,** you've been there already, haven't you?; **¿no vienes?,** aren't you coming? **3** *(como prefijo negativo)* non; **la no violencia,** nonviolence; **no fumador,** nonsmoker; **pacto de no agresión,** non-aggression pact. **4** *(en frases comparativas)* **es mejor que venga que no que se quede en casa,** he'd be better off coming along rather than staying at home. **II** *nm* no; **un no rotundo,** a definite no.

nobiliario,-a *adj* nobiliary, noble.

noble **I** *adj* noble; **gas n.,** noble gas. **II** *nmf (hombre)* nobleman; *(mujer)* noblewoman; **los nobles,** the nobility *sing.*

nobleza *nf* **1** *(cualidad)* nobility, honesty, uprightness. **2** *(conjunto de nobles)* nobility.

noblote,-a *adj fam* honest, sincere.

noche *nf* night, late evening, night-time; **ayer por la n.,** last night; **buenas noches,** *(saludo)* good evening; *(despedida)* good night; **de n.,** at night; **esta n.,** tonight; **hacer n. en,** to spend the night at *or* in; **hacerse de n.,** to grow dark; **mañana por la n.,** tomorrow night *or* evening; **pasar buena/mala n.,** to sleep well/badly; **por la n.,** at night, in the evening; **son las nueve de la noche,** it's nine p.m.; *fig* **de la n. a la mañana,** overnight.

nochebuena *nf* Christmas Eve.

nochecita *nf Am* dusk.

nochevieja *nf* New Year's Eve.

noción *nf* **1** *(gen)* notion, idea. **2 nociones,** smattering *sing,* basic knowledge *sing;* **n. de español,** a smattering of Spanish.

nocividad *nf* noxiousness, harmfulness.

nocivo,-a *adj* noxious, harmful.

noctambulismo *nm* sleepwalking.

noctámbulo,-a *nm, f* sleepwalker; *fam* night-bird.

nocturno,-a **I** *adj* **1** night, evening; **clases nocturnas,** evening classes; **vida nocturna,** night life; **vuelo n.,** night flight. **2** *Bot Zool* nocturnal. **II** *nm Mús* nocturne.

NODO *nm Hist abr de* **Noticiarios y Documentales Cinematográficos,** ≈ Cinema Newsreels.

nodriza *nf* **1** *(ama)* wet nurse. **2** *Av Naút* **buque n.,** supply ship.

nogal *nm Bot* walnut (tree). ■ **n. negro,** black walnut.

nogalina *nf* walnut dye.

nogueral *nm Bot* walnut grove.

nómada **I** *adj* nomadic. **II** *nmf* nomad.

nomadismo *nm* nomadism.

nombradía *nf* reputation, fame.

nombrado,-a I *pp de* **nombrar. II** *adj* **1** *(mencionado)* mentioned; **n. más arriba,** aforementioned. **2** *(designado)* appointed. **3** *(célebre)* famous, wellknown.

nombramiento *nm* appointment.

nombrar *vtr* **1** *(mencionar)* to name, mention. **2** *(designar)* to name, appoint; **n. a algn director,** to appoint sb director.

nombre *nm* **1** name; **a n. de,** addressed to; **en n. de,** on behalf of; **era el presidente sólo de n.,** he was the president in name only; **escritor de n.,** famous writer; **le conozco de n.,** I know him by name; **llamar a algn por el n.,** to call sb by name; **no tiene n.,** it's unspeakable; **n. y apellidos,** full name; **responder al n. de,** to be called; *fig* **llamar a las cosas por su n.,** to call a spade a spade; *fig* **lo que ella ha hecho no tiene n.,** what she did is beyond words. ■ *Cin Teat* **n. artístico,** stage name; *Com* **n. comercial,** trade name; **n. de pila,** Christian name. **2** *Ling* noun. ■ **n. propio,** proper noun.

nomenclador *nm,* **nomenclátor** *nm,* **nomenclatura** *nf* nomenclature.

nomeolvides *nm inv Bot* forget-me-not.

nómina *nf* **1** *(plantilla)* payroll; **estar en n.,** to be on the staff. **2** *(sueldo)* salary, pay cheque.

nominación *nf* nomination.

nominal *adj* nominal.

nominar *vtr* to nominate.

nominativo,-a I *adj* **1** *Com* nominal. **2** *Ling* nominative. **II** *nm Ling* nominative.

non I *adj (número)* odd. **II** *nm* **1** *Mat* odd number; **pares y nones,** odds and evens. **2** *nones, fam (negación)* no; **decir n.,** to refuse, say nix.

nonagenario,-a *adj & nm, f* nonagenarian.

nonagésimo,-a I *adj* ninetieth; **nonagésima parte,** ninetieth; **n. primero,** ninety-first; **n. segundo,** ninety-second. **II** *nm, f (de una serie)* ninetieth. **III** *nm (parte)* ninetieth; *véase tamb* **octavo,-a**

noneco,-a *adj CAm* thick, dull.

nono,-a *adj véase* **noveno,-a.**

noquear *vtr Box* to knock out.

norcoreano,-a *adj & nm, f* North Korean.

nordeste *nm véase* **noreste.**

nórdico,-a I *adj* **1** *(del norte)* northern. **2** *(escandinavo)* Nordic. **II** *nm, f* Nordic person.

noreste *nm* **1** *Geog* northeast. **2** *(viento)* northeasterly.

noria *nf* **1** *(para agua)* water-wheel, noria. **2** *(de feria)* big wheel.

norirlandés,-esa I *adj* Northern Irish. **II** *nm, f (persona) (hombre)* Northern Irishman; *(mujer)* Northern Irishwoman; **los norirlandeses,** the Northern Irish.

norma *nf* norm, rule.

normal I *adj* normal, usual, average; **lo n.,** the normal thing, what usually happens. **II** *nf desus* **(escuela) n.,** teacher training college.

normalidad *nf* normality; **todo ha vuelto a la n.,** everything is back to normal.

normalización *nf* normalization.

normalizar I *vtr* to normalize, restore to normal. **II normalizarse** *vr* to return to normal.

normando,-a I *adj* **1** *(de Normandía)* Norman. **2** *(vikingo)* Norse. **II** *nm, f* **1** *(de Normandía)* Norman. **2** *(vikingo) (hombre)* Norseman; *(mujer)* Norsewoman.

normar *vi Am* to set standards *or* rules.

normativo,-a I *adj* normative. **II** *nf* rules *pl.*

noroeste *nm* **1** *Geog* northwest. **2** *(viento)* northwesterly.

norte *nm* **1** *Geog* north; **al n. de,** to the north of; **los países del n.,** the northern countries. **2** *fig* aim, goal; **sin n.,** aimless, aimlessly. **3** *(viento)* northerly wind.

norteafricano,-a *adj & nm, f* North African.

Norteamérica *n* North America.

norteamericano,-a *adj & nm, f* (North) American.

norteño,-a I *adj* northern. **II** *nm, f* Northerner.

Noruega *n* Norway.

noruego,-a I *adj* Norwegian. **II** *nm, f* Norwegian. **III** *nm (idioma)* Norwegian.

nos I *pron pers (complemento)* us; **n. ha visto,** he has seen us; **n. trajo un regalo,** he brought us a present. **II** *pron reflexivo* ourselves; **n. queremos mucho,** we love each other very much; **n. vamos,** we're leaving.

nosotros,-as *pron pers pl* **1** *(sujeto)* we; **n. lo vimos,** we saw it; **somos n.,** it is us. **2** *(complemento)* us; **con n.,** with us; **después de n.,** after us; **para n.,** for us.

nostalgia *nf* nostalgia, yearning; *(morriña)* homesickness.

nostálgico,-a *adj* nostalgic; *(con morriña)* homesick.

nota *nf* **1** *(anotación)* note; **tomar n. de algo,** *(apuntar)* to note *or* jot sth down; *fig (fijarse)* to take note of sth. **2** *Educ (calificación)* mark, grade; **tener buenas notas,** to get good marks. **3** *(cuenta)* bill. **4** *fig (detalle)* element, quality; **la n. dominante,** the prevailing quality; **la n. elegante,** the touch of elegance. **5** *Mús* note; *fam* **dar la n.,** to make oneself noticed.

notabilidad *nf* **1** *(cualidad)* notability. **2** *(persona)* notable.

notable I *adj (apreciable)* noticeable; *(digno de notar)* oustanding, remarkable. **II** *nm* **1** *Educ (calificación)* credit (mark). **2 notables,** *(personas)* VIPs.

notación *nf* notation.

notar I *vtr* **1** *(percibir)* to notice, note; **hacer n. algo,** to point sth out; **hacerse n.,** to draw attention to oneself; **no lo había notado,** I hadn't noticed. **2** *(sentir)* to feel; **noto como que me falta el aire,** I feel as if I can't breathe. **II notarse** *vr* **1** *(percibirse)* to be noticeable *or* evident, show; **no se nota,** it doesn't show; **se nota que ...,** one can see that ... . **2** *(sentirse)* to feel; **me noto cansado,** I feel tired.

notaría *nf* **1** *(profesión)* profession of notary (public). **2** *(despacho)* notary's office.

notariado *nm* **1** *(profesión)* profession of notary (public). **2** *(cuerpo de notarios)* notaries *pl.*

notarial *adj* notarial.

notario,-a *nm, f* notary (public), public solicitor.

noticia *nf* news *sing;* **dar la n.,** to break the news; **n. bomba,** bombshell; **últimas noticias,** latest news; **una n.,** a piece of news; **una buena n.,** good news.

noticiario *nm,* **noticiero** *nm Rad TV* news bulletin, news *pl; Prensa* newspaper.

notición *nm fam* bombshell.

notificación *nf* notification; **sin n. previa,** without (previous) notice. ■ *Jur* **n. judicial,** summons *sing.*

notificar *vtr* to notify, inform.

notoriedad *nf* fame, notoriety, reputation.

notorio,-a *adj* **1** *(conocido)* noticeable, evident. **2** *(famoso)* famous, well-known.

novatada *nf* **1** *(broma)* rough joke, rag. **2** *(dificultad)* beginner's error; **pagar la n.,** to learn the hard way.

novato,-a I *adj (persona)* inexperienced, green. **II** *nm, f* **1** *(principiante)* novice, beginner. **2** *Univ* fresher.

novecientos,-as *adj inv & nm, f inv (cardinal)* nine hundred; *(ordinal)* nine hundredth.

novedad *nf* **1** *(cualidad)* newness. **2** *(cosa nueva)* novelty; **tienda de novedades,** fashion shop; **últimas novedades,** latest arrivals. **3** *(cambio)* change, innovation. **4** *(noticia)* news *pl;* **sin n.,** no change, no news; *Mil* nothing to report.

novedoso,-a *adj* **1** *(nuevo)* new, full of novelties. **2** *Am (novelesco)* novelistic, fictional.

novel I *adj* new, inexperienced. **II** *nmf* beginner, novice.

novela *nf Lit* novel; *(corta)* story. ■ **n. corta,** short story; **n. policíaca,** detective story.

novelar I *vtr* to novelize, convert into a novel, make a novel out of. **II** *vi* to write novels.

novelería *nf* gossip.

novelero,-a *adj* **1** *(aficionado a las novedades)* fond of new things; *(a novelas)* fond of novels. **2** *(fantasioso)* highly imaginative. **3** *(chismoso)* gossipy.

novelesco,-a *adj* **1** *(de novela)* novelistic, fictional. **2** *(extraordinario)* bizarre, fantastic.

novelista *nmf* novelist.

novelística *nf* novel, fiction.

novelístico,-a *adj* novelistic.

novelón *nm fam pey* long and badly written novel, pulp novel.

novena *nf Rel* novena.

noveno,-a I *adj* ninth; **novena parte,** ninth. **II** *nm, f (de una serie)* ninth. **III** *nm (parte)* ninth; *véase tamb* **octavo,-a.**

noventa *inv* **I** *adj (cardinal)* ninety; *(ordinal)* ninety. **II** *nm* ninety; *véase tamb* **ochenta** *y* **ocho.**

noventavo,-a *adj* & *nm, f* & *nm véase* **nonagésimo,-a.**

novia *nf* **1** *(amiga)* girlfriend. **2** *(prometida)* fiancée. **3** *(en boda)* bride.

noviazgo *nm* engagement; **romper un n.,** to break off an engagement.

noviciado *nm Rel* noviciate, novitiate.

novicio,-a *nm, f Rel* novice.

noviembre *nm* November; **a mediados de n.,** in the middle of November, in mid-November; **a principios/ finales de n.,** at the beginning/end of November; **durante el mes de n.,** during *or* in November; **el primero/ dieciséis de n.,** (on) the first/sixteenth of November; **en n.,** in November; **en n. del año pasado/del año que viene,** last/next November; **nació el 10 de n. 1955,** he was born on 10th November 1955; **todos los años en n.,** each *or* every November.

noviero,-a *adj CAm Méx* who falls in love easily.

novillada *nf Taur* **1** *(corrida)* bullfight with young bulls. **2** *(conjunto de novillos)* herd of young bulls.

novillero,-a *nm, f* **1** *Taur* apprentice matador. **2** *fam Educ* truant.

novillo,-a I *nm, f* **1** *Zool (toro)* young bull; *(vaca)* young cow. **2** *fam Educ* **hacer novillos,** to play truant *or US* hooky. **II** *nm* **1** *fam (cornudo)* cuckold. **2** *Am Zool (buey sin domar)* wild bull. **3** *Chi Méx (ternero castrado)* castrated bull calf.

novilunio *nm* new moon.

novio *nm* **1** *(amigo)* boyfriend. **2** *(prometido)* fiancé. **3** *(en boda)* bridegroom; **los novios,** the bride and groom.

N.S. *abr de* **Nuestro Señor,** Our Lord.

NªSª *abr de* **Nuestra Señora,** Our Lady.

nto. *abr de* **neto,** net, n.

nubarrón *nm fam* storm cloud.

nube *nf* **1** *(gen)* cloud; **n. de verano,** *Meteor* sudden storm; *fig (enfado pasajero)* huff; *fig* **estar** *or* **vivir en las nubes,** to have one's head in the clouds; *fig* **los precios están por las nubes,** prices are sky-high; *fig* **poner a algn por las nubes,** to praise sb to the skies. **2** *fig (multitud)* swarm, crowd.

nublado,-a I *pp de* **nublar. II** *adj* **1** *Meteor* cloudy, overcast. **2** *fig* **n. por la pasión,** blinded by passion. **III** *nm Meteor* thick cloud.

nublar I *vtr Meteor* to cloud. **II nublarse** *vr Meteor* to become cloudy, cloud over; *fig* **se le nubló la razón,** he lost his mind; **se le nubló la vista,** his eyes clouded over.

nubosidad *nf Meteor* cloudiness.

nuboso,-a *adj Meteor* cloudy.

nuca *nf Anat* nape, back of the neck.

nuclear *adj* nuclear; **central n.,** nuclear power station.

núcleo *nm* **1** *(gen)* nucleus; *(parte central)* core. ■ *Inform* **núcleos magnéticos,** core *sing.* **2** *(grupo de gente)* circle, group.

nudillo *nm (gen pl) Anat* knuckle.

nudismo *nm* nudism.

nudista *adj* & *nmf* nudist.

nudo *nm* **1** knot; **hacer un n.,** to tie a knot; *fig* **se me hizo un n. en la garganta,** I got a lump in my throat. ■ **n. corredizo,** slipknot; **n. gordiano,** Gordian knot; **n. marinero,** sailor's knot. **2** *Náut (milla)* knot. **3** *Bot* knot, node. **4** *fig (vínculo)* link, tie. **5** *(punto principal)* crux, core; **el n. de la cuestión,** the heart of the matter. **6** *(de comunicaciones)* centre, *US* center. ■ *Ferroc* **n. de comunicaciones,** junction.

nudoso,-a *adj (madera)* knotty, full of knots; *(bastón)* knobbly; **mano nudosa,** gnarled hand.

nuera *nf* daughter-in-law.

nuestro,-a I *adj pos* of ours, our; **lo n.,** what is ours; **nuestra familia,** our family; **un amigo n.,** a friend of ours. **II** *pron pos* ours; **es de los nuestros,** he is one of us; **este libro es n.,** this book is ours; *fam* **los nuestros,** our side, our people.

nueva *nf* piece of news; *fam* **hacerse de nuevas,** to pretend not to know, pretend to be surprised; *fam* **me cogió de nuevas,** it took me by surprise.

Nueva Delhi *n* New Delhi.

Nueva York *n* New York.

Nueva Zelanda *n* New Zealand.

nueve **I** *adj inv (cardinal)* nine; *(ordinal)* ninth; **a las n.,** at nine o'clock. **II** *nm inv* nine; *véase tamb* **ocho.**

nuevo,-a I *adj (gen)* new; *(adicional)* further; **de n.,** again; **es más n. que yo,** he hasn't worked here as long as I have; **está (como) n.,** it's as good as new; **hay que hacer nuevas indagaciones,** we need to carry out further investigation; **n. en el oficio,** new to the trade; *fam* **¿qué hay de n.?,** what's new? **II** *nm, f* newcomer; *(principiante)* beginner; *Univ (novato)* fresher. ◆ **nuevamente** *adv* again.

nuez *nf* **1** *Bot* walnut; *fam* **mucho ruido y pocas nueces,** a lot of fuss about nothing. ■ **n. moscada,** nutmeg. **2** *Anat* **n. (de Adán),** Adam's apple.

nulidad *nf* **1** *(ineptitud)* incompetence; *(persona)* nonentity; **ser una n.,** to be hopeless *or* useless. **2** *Jur* nullity.

nulo,-a *adj* **1** *(inepto)* useless, totally incapable; **ser n. para algo,** to be hopeless *or* useless at sth. **2** *(sin valor)* null and void, invalid; **declarar n.,** to nullify; **voto n.,** invalid vote.

núm. *abr de* **número,** number, n.

Numancia *n Hist* Numantia.

numantino,-a I *adj Hist* Numantian, of Numantia; *fig (resistencia)* heroic. **II** *nm, f* Numantian.

numeración *nf* numeration. ■ **n. arábiga,** Arabic numerals *pl*; **n. romana,** Roman numerals *pl*.

numerador *nm* **1** *Mat* numerator. **2** *(aparato)* numerating machine.

numeral *adj* & *nm* numeral.

numerar I *vtr* to number. **II numerarse** *vr Mil* to number off.

numerario,-a I *adj* **profesor n.,** teacher on the permanent staff; **profesor no n.,** teacher on a temporary contract. **II** *nm* **1** *(miembro)* full member. **2** *(dinero)* cash.

numérico,-a *adj* numerical.

número *nm* **1** *(gen)* number; **en números redondos,** in round figures; *fig* **sin n.,** countless. ■ **n. arábigo,** Arabic numeral; **n. cardinal,** cardinal number; **n. de matrícula,** registration number, *US* license number; **n. de serie,** serial number; **n. entero,** whole number; **n. fraccionario** *or* **quebrado,** fraction; **n. impar/ordinal/par/primo,** odd/ordinal/even/prime number; **n. romano,** Roman numeral. **2** *Ling* number. **3** *Prensa* number, issue. ■ **n. atrasado,** back number; **n. extraordinario,** special edition. **4** *(de zapatos)* size. **5** *(en espectáculo)* sketch, act; *fam* **ese tío es todo un n.,** that bloke's a real laugh; *fam* **montar un n.,** to make a scene; *fam* **¡vaya n.!,** what a scene!

numeroso,-a *adj* numerous, large.

numismática *nf* numismatics *sing*.

numismático,-a **I** *adj* numismatic. **II** *nm,f* numismatist.

nunca *adv* **1** never, ever; **casi n.,** hardly ever; **más que n.,** more than ever; **n. en la vida,** never in my life; **n. jamás,** never ever; **n. más,** never again; **ser lo n. visto,** to be unheard of. **2** *(en interrogativa)* ever; **¿has visto n. cosa igual?,** have you ever seen anything like it?

nunciatura *nf* nunciature.

nuncio *nm* nuncio. ■ **n. apostólico,** papal nuncio.

nupcial *adj* wedding, nuptial; **marcha n.,** wedding march.

nupcialidad *nf* marriage rate.

nupcias *nfpl fml* wedding *sing*, nuptials; **casarse en segundas n.,** to marry again.

nurse *nf* nurse, nanny.

nutria *nf Zool* otter.

nutrición *nf* nutrition.

nutrido,-a **I** *pp de* **nutrir. II** *adj* **1** *(alimentado)* nourished; **bien n.,** well-nourished; **mal n.,** under-nourished. **2** *(numeroso)* large, numerous.

nutrir **I** *vtr* **1** *(alimentar)* to nourish, feed. **2** *fig* to encourage, feed. **3** *(suministrar)* to provide, supply. **II nutrirse** *vr (alimentarse)* to feed, draw on.

nutritivo,-a *adj* nutritious, nourishing; **valor n.,** nutritional value.

Ñ

Ñ,ñ ['ene] *nf (la letra)* fifteenth letter of the Spanish alphabet.

ña *nf Am vulg véase* **doña.**

ñácara *nf CAm* ulcer, sore.

ñam *interj fam* **¡ñ., ñ.!,** yum-yum!, yummy!

ñame *nm Am Bot* yarn.

ñandú *nm Am Orn* nandu, American ostrich.

ñandutí *nm Am* nanduti (lace).

ñanga *nf CAm* marsh.

ñangada *nf CAm* **1** *(mordisco)* bite. **2** *(disparate)* stupid thing to do.

ñango,-a *adj* **1** *Am (bajo)* short-legged; *(patojo)* lame. **2** *Méx (flaco)* skinny; *(débil)* weak.

ñaña *nf* **1** *CAm (excremento)* excrement. **2** *Arg Chi (hermana mayor)* elder sister.

ñaño,-a *nm,f Am* **1** *(hermano) (hombre)* brother; *(mujer)* sister. **2** *(amigo)* good friend.

ñapa *nf Am* bonus, little extra.

ñatas *nfpl* nose *sing*.

ñato,-a *adj* **1** *Am* snub-nosed. **2** *Arg (feo)* ugly. **3** *Arg (perverso)* perverse.

ñau *nm Am* meow, miaow.

ñeque **I** *adj* **1** *Am (vigoroso)* vigorous; *(fuerte)* strong. **2** *CAm Cuba (valiente)* brave. **3** *CAm Cuba (que trae mala suerte)* jinx. **II** *nm* **1** *Am (fuerza)* energy. **2** *CAm Méx (golpe)* blow; *(bofetada)* cuff, punch.

ñiquiñaque *nm fam* **1** *(objeto)* junk, rubbish. **2** *(persona)* good-for-nothing.

ñisca *nf* **1** *CAm Col (excremento)* excrement. **2** *Am (pizca)* bit, small piece.

ño *nm Am vulg véase* **señor.**

ñoco,-a *adj Am (le falta un dedo)* lacking a finger; *(le falta una mano)* one-handed.

ñoñería *nf,* **ñoñez** *nf* **1** *(sosería)* insipidness, bore. **2** *(melindrería)* fussiness.

ñoño,-a **I** *adj* **1** *(soso)* insipid, dull. **2** *(melindroso)* fussy. **3** *Am (viejo)* old; *(chocho)* decrepit. **II** *nm,f* dull *or* spineless person.

ñoqui *nm Culin* gnocchi *pl*.

ñu *nm Zool* gnu.

O

O, o *nf (la letra)* O, o; *fig* **no sabe hacer la o con un canuto,** he doesn't know a thing, he hasn't got a clue.

o *conj* or; **jueves o viernes,** Thursday or Friday; **or ... o,** either ... or; **o sea que,** that is, that is to say, so; **or sea que no voy,** in other words, I am not coming.

O. *abr de* **Oeste,** West, W.

OAA *nf abr de* **Organización para la Agricultura y la Alimentación,** Food and Agriculture Organization, FAO.

oasis *nm inv* oasis.

obcecación *nf* blindness; *fig* obstinacy.

obcecado,-a **I** *pp de* **obcecar. II** *adj* blinded; *fig* stubborn.

obcecar **I** *vtr* to make blind; *fig* **la ira lo obceca,** he is blinded by anger. **II obcecarse** *vr* to be blinded; *fig* to get mixed up.

obedecer **I** *vtr* **1** *(acatar)* to obey; **no obedece a razones,** he won't listen to reason; **obedece a tu padre,** do as your father says. **2** *(responder)* to respond to; **el volante no le obedeció,** the steering wheel wouldn't turn. **II** *vi (provenir)* to be due to; **¿a qué obedece esa actitud?,** what's the reason behind this attitude?

obediencia *nf* obedience.

obediente *adj* obedient.

obelisco *nm* **1** *(monumento)* obelisk. **2** *Tip* obelisk, dagger.

obertura *nf Mús* overture.

obesidad *nf* obesity.

obeso,-a *adj* obese.

óbice *nm* obstacle; **eso no es ó. para que yo no ...,** that won't prevent me from ... .

obispado *nm* **1** *(dignidad, diócesis)* bishopric. **2** *(residencia)* bishop's palace.

obispo *nm* **1** *(prelado)* bishop. **2** *Méx (borrego)* four-horned ram.

óbito *nm fml* demise, decease.

obituario *nm Prensa* obituary.

objeción *nf* objection; **o. de conciencia,** conscientious objection; **poner una o.,** to raise an objection, object.

objetante *adj* objecting, dissenting.

objetar *vtr* to argue, object to, point out; **no tengo nada que o.,** I have no objections.

objetivar *vtr* to look objectively at, deal with objectively.

objetividad *nf* objectivity.

objetivismo *nm* objectivism.

objetivo,-a I *adj* objective. **II** *nm* **1** *(fin, meta)* objective, aim, goal. **2** *Mil* target. **3** *Cin Fot* lens; **o. zoom,** zoom lens.

objeto *nm* **1** *(gen)* object; **mujer o.,** sex object; **objetos perdidos,** lost property *sing*. **2** *(fin)* aim, purpose, object; **con o. de ...,** in order to ...; **tiene por o. ...,** it is designed to ... . **3** *(tema)* theme, subject, matter. **4** *Ling* object.

objetor,-a I *adj* objecting, dissenting. **II** *nm,f Mil* objector; **o. de conciencia,** conscientious objector.

oblea *nf* **1** *Rel* wafer. **2** *Farm* capsule.

oblicuo,-a *adj Geom* oblique.

obligación *nf* **1** *(deber)* obligation; **antes la o. que la devoción,** business before pleasure; **cumplir consus obligaciones,** to fulfil one's obligations; **por o.,** out of a sense of duty; **tengo o. de ...,** I have to ... . **2** *Fin* bond, debenture. ■ **obligaciones garantizadas,** guaranteed *or* mortgage debentures *or* bonds. **3 obligaciones,** *(familia)* family *sing*.

obligacionista *nmf Fin* bondholder.

obligado,-a I *pp de* obligar. **II** *adj* obliged; **verse** *or* **estar o. a,** to be obliged to.

obligar I *vtr* **1** *(forzar)* to compel, force. **2** *Arg Chi (invitar)* to pay for sb's drink. **II obligarse** *vr* to be under an obligation to, be obliged to.

obligatoriedad *nf* obligatory nature.

obligatorio,-a *adj* compulsory, obligatory.

oblongo,-a *adj* oblong.

obnubilado,-a I *pp de* obnubilar. **II** *adj* stunned, dazed.

obnubilar *vtr* to dazzle.

oboe *nm Mús (instrumento)* oboe; *(intérprete)* oboist.

oboísta *nmf Mús* oboist.

óbolo *nm* **1** *Hist* obolus. **2** *fig* mite, small contribution.

obpo. *abr de* obispo, bishop, bp.

obra *nf* **1** *(trabajo)* piece of work, work; **mano de o.,** manpower, labour, workforce; **manos a la o.,** let's get down to work; **por o. (y gracia) de,** thanks to; **todo esto es o. suya,** this is all his doing. **2** *Arte* work; *Lit* book; *Mús* opus; **o. de teatro,** play; **o. maestra,** masterpiece; **obras completas,** collected *or* complete works. **3** *(acto)* deed; **obras son amores (y no buenas razones),** actions speak louder than words. **4** *(institución)* institution, foundation; **o. benéfica,** charity. **5** *Constr* building site. **6 obras,** *(arreglos)* repairs; **'carretera en o.',** 'roadworks'; **'cerrado por o.',** 'closed for repairs'; **tenemos la casa en o.,** we've got the builders in.

obrador *nm* workshop.

obraje *nm* **1** *(manufactura)* manufacture. **2** *Arg Bol Par* sawmill. **3** *Méx (carnicería)* butcher's shop.

obrar I *vi* **1** *(proceder)* to act, behave; **o. bien/mal,** to do the right/wrong thing; **o. con buena intención,** to act in good faith; **o. con ligereza,** to act without thinking. **2** *(estar)* to be; **o. en poder de,** to be in the hands of. **II** *vtr (hacer)* to work.

obrerismo *nm* labour *or US* labor movement, labourism, *US* laborism.

obrerista I *adj* labour, *US* labor, worker. **II** *nmf* labourist, *US* laborist.

obrero,-a I *adj* working; **clase obrera,** working class. **II** *nm,f* worker, labourer, *US* laborer. ■ **o. especializado/no especializado,** skilled/unskilled worker; **o. portuario,** docker.

obscenidad *nf* obscenity.

odsceno,-a *adj* obscene.

obscurantismo *nm* obscurantism.

obscurantista *adj & nmf* obscurantist.

obscurecer I *vi impers* to get dark. **II** *vtr* **1** *(ensombrecer)* to darken. **2** *Arte* to shade. **3** *fig (ofuscar)* to cloud; *(superar)* to overshadow; **el mal tiempo obscureció la ceremonia,** the bad weather put a cloud over the ceremony. **III obscurecerse** *vr (nublarse)* to become cloudy.

obscurecimiento *nm* darkening.

obscuridad *nf* darkness, gloom; *fig* obscurity.

obscuro,-a *adj* **1** *(gen)* dark. **2** *fig (origen, idea)* obscure; *(future)* uncertain, gloomy; *(asunto)* shady; *(nublado)* overcast; **sus intenciones son obscuras,** his intentions are not clear.

obsequiar *vtr* to give, offer, present.

obsequio *nm* gift, present.

obsequioso,-a *adj* attentive, obliging.

observable *adj* observable.

observación *nf* **1** *(acción de observar)* observation; *Mil* **puesto de o.,** observation post. **2** *(comentario)* observation, remark, comment.

observador,-a I *adj* observant. **II** *nm,f* observer.

observancia *nf* observance.

observar *vtr* **1** *(mirar)* to observe, watch. **2** *(notar)* to notice; **se ha observado un aumento/una mejora de ...,** there has been a rise/an improvement in ... . **3** *(cumplir)* to observe; **hacer o. algo a algn,** to point sth out to sb; **o. las buenas costumbres,** to be on one's best behaviour.

observatorio *nm* observatory. ■ **o. meteorológico,** weather station.

obsesión *nf* obsession.

obsesionar I *vtr* to obsess; **estoy obsesionado con ello,** I can't get it out of my mind. **II obsesionarse** *vr* to get obsessed; **se obsesiona por cualquier tontería,** he gets worked up about the slightest thing.

obsesivo,-a *adj* obsessive.

obseso,-a I *adj* obsessed. **II** *nm,f* obsessed person: **un o. sexual,** a sex maniac.

obsoleto,-a *adj* obsolete.

obstaculizar *vtr* to obstruct, hinder, get in the way of, block.

obstáculo *nm* obstacle, hindrance; **poner obstáculos a algo/algn,** to hinder sth/sb, put obstacles in the way of sth/sb.

obstante (no) *loc adv* nevertheless, all the same.

obstar *vi* to hinder, prevent; **eso no obsta para que ...,** that's no reason not to ..., that doesn't prevent ... .

obstetricia *nf Med* obstetrics *sing*.

obstinación *nf* obstinacy, stubbornness.

obstinado,-a I *pp de* obstinarse. **II** *adj* obstinate, stubborn.

obstinarse *vr* to persist **(en,** in).

obstrucción *nf* obstruction; *Med* blockage.

obstruccionismo *nm Pol* obstructionism.

obstruccionista *nmf Pol* obstructionist.

obstruir I *vtr* **1** *(obstaculizar)* to block, obstruct. **2** *(progreso)* to impede; *(reforma)* to stand in the way of. **II obstruirse** *vr* to get blocked up.

obtención *nf* obtaining, securing.

obtener I *vtr (alcanzar)* to obtain, get; **o. un crédito,** to raise a loan; **o. una victoria,** to secure a victory. **II obtenerse** *vr (provenir)* to come (**de,** from).

obturación *nf* blockage, obstruction.

obturador *nm* 1 *(gen)* plug, stopper; *Fot* shutter. 2 *Mús* languid. 3 *(rueda)* valve.

obturar *vtr* to block (up), plug (up).

obtuso,-a *adj* obtuse.

obús *nm* 1 *Mil (cañón)* howitzer; *(proyectil)* shell. 2 *Aut* tyre *or* US tire valve core.

obviar I *vtr (evitar)* to obviate, remove; **hay que o. las dificultades,** the difficulties have to be overcome. **II** *vi (oponerse)* to stand in the way (of).

obvio,-a *adj* obvious.

oca *nf* 1 *Zool* goose. 2 *(juego)* **la o.,** ≈ snakes and ladders sing.

ocasión *nf* 1 *(momento)* occasion; **con o. de ...,** on the occasion of ...; **en cierta o.,** once; **en contadas ocasiones,** on very few occasions. 2 *(oportunidad)* opportunity, chance; **aprovechar la o.,** to make the most of an opportunity; **dar o. a algo,** to give rise to sth; **dar o. a algn de ...,** to give sb the chance *or* the opportunity to ...; **si se presenta la o.,** if the opportunity arises; **si tienes o.,** if you have the chance. 3 *Com* bargain; **de o.,** cheap; **precios de o.,** bargain prices.

ocasional *adj* 1 *(de vez en cuando)* occasional. 2 *(fortuito)* accidental, chance.

ocasionar *vtr (causar)* to cause, bring about; *(ser la causa de)* to be the cause of; **o. un revuelo,** to cause a stir.

ocaso *nm (anochecer)* sunset; *(occidente)* west; *fig (declive)* fall, decline.

occidental I *adj* western, occidental. **II** *nmf (persona)* westerner, person from the west.

occidentalizar *vtr* to westernize.

occidente *nm* west, Occident; **el O.,** the West.

occipital *Anat* **I** *adj* occipital. **II** *nm* occipital (bone).

occiso,-a *adj fml* deceased.

OCDE *nf abr de* **Organización para la Cooperación y el Desarrollo Económico,** Organization for Economic Cooperation and Development, OECD.

Oceanía *n* Oceania.

oceánico,-a *adj* oceanic.

océano *nm* ocean.

oceanografía *nf* oceanography.

oceanográfico,-a *adj* oceanographic.

oceanógrafo,-a *nm,f* oceanographer.

ocelo *nm Zool* ocellus.

ocelote *nm Zool* ocelot.

ochava *nf* 1 *(octava parte)* eighth. 2 *(ocho días)* eight days. 3 *Am (esquina)* corner.

ochavar *vtr Am* to cut the corner of.

ochenta I *adj inv (cardinal)* eighty; *(ordinal)* eightieth; **andar por los o.,** to be in one's eighties; **durante los años o.,** in the eighties; **el o. por ciento del personal,** eighty per cent of the staff; **hacía más de o. grados,** the temperature was in the eighties; *Aut* **ir a o.,** to do *or* be doing eighty (kilometres an hour); **mañana cumplirá o. años,** he will be eighty (years old) tomorrow; **unos o. pasajeros/ coches,** about eighty passengers/cars. **II** *nm inv* eighty.

ocho I *adj inv (cardinal)* eight; *(ordinal)* eighth; **a los o. días,** in a week, in a week's time; **cuesta o. dólares,** it costs eight dollars; **dieron las o.,** the clock struck eight; **el o. de febrero,** the eighth of February; **en el siglo o.,** in the eighth century; **las o. en punto,** eight o'clock precisely *or* on the dot, **llegará el día o.,** he will arrive on the eighth; **o. días,** a week; **o. mil,** eight thousand; **se marcharon los o.,** all eight of them left; **somos o.,** there are eight of us; **son las o.,** it is eight o'clock; **tiene o. años,** he is eight (years old); **un niño de o. años,** a boy of eight, an eight-year-old

boy; **venga a las o. en punto,** come at eight o'clock sharp; **viven en la calle Goya, número o.,** they live at number eight Goya Street. **II** *nm inv* eight; **el o.,** (number) eight; *Naipes* **el o. de corazones,** the eight of hearts; **o. más o. son dieciséis,** eight and eight are *or* make sixteen; **o. sobre diez,** eight out of ten; *fig* **ser más chulo que un o.,** to be as proud as a peacock.

ochociento,-as I *adj inv (cardinal)* eight hundred; *(ordinal)* eight hundredth. **II** *nm* eight hundred.

ocio *nm* leisure, idleness; **en mis ratos de o.,** in my spare *or* leisure time.

ociosidad *nf* idleness.

ocioso,-a I *adj* 1 *(inactivo)* idle; **vida ociosa,** life of leisure. 2 *(inútil)* pointless, useless. **II** *nm,f* idler.

ocluir I *vtr* to occlude, obstruct, close (up). **II ocluirse** *vr* to become obstructed.

oclusión *nf* occlusion.

oclusivo,-a I *adj* occlusive. **II** *nf Ling* occlusive.

ocre *nm* ochre, *US* ocher.

octaédrico,-a *adj Geom* octahedronal.

octaedro *nm Geom* octahedron.

octagonal *adj Geom* octagonal.

octágono *nm Geom* octagon.

octanaje *nm* octane number.

octano *nm* octane.

octava *nf Mús Lit* octave.

octavilla *nf* 1 *(panfleto)* hand-out, leaflet. 2 *Lit* octave.

octavo,-a I *adj* eighth; **quedar en o. lugar,** to come eighth; **una octava parte,** an eighth; **vivir en el o. piso,** to live on the eighth floor. **II** *nm,f (de una serie)* eighth; **fue el o. en llegar,** he was the eighth to arrive. **III** *nm* 1 *(parte)* eighth; **tres octavos,** three eighths. 2 *Impr* octavo; **libro en o.,** octavo book.

octete *nm Quím* octet.

octeto *nm Mús* octet, octette.

octogenario,-a *adj & nm,f* octogenarian.

octogésimo,-a I *adj* eightieth; **octogésima parte,** eightieth. **II** *nm,f (de una serie)* eightieth. **III** *nm (parte)* eightieth; *véase tamb* **octavo,-a.**

octogonal *adj Geom* octagonal.

octógono *nm Geom* octagon.

octosílabo,-a I *adj* octosyllabic. **II** *nm* octosyllable.

octubre *nm* October; *véase tamb* **noviembre.**

ocular I *adj* ocular, eye; **testigo o.,** eyewitness. **II** *nm Opt* eyepiece.

oculista *nmf Med* ophthalmologist, oculist.

ocultación *nf* concealment; *Astron* occultation.

ocultar I *vtr* to conceal, hide; **o. algo a algn,** to hide sth from sb. **II ocultarse** *vr* to hide (oneself).

ocultismo *nm* occultism.

ocultista *adj & nmf* occultist.

oculto,-a *adj* concealed, hidden; **ciencias ocultas,** occult sciences; **motivo o.,** ulterior motive.

ocupación *nf* 1 *(tarea)* occupation, activity. 2 *Mil* occupation; **o. (ilegal) de viviendas,** squatting.

ocupado,-a I *pp de* **ocupar. II** *adj (persona)* busy; *(asiento)* taken; *(aseos, teléfono)* engaged; *(puesto de trabajo)* filled; *Mil* occupied.

ocupante *nmf (de una casa)* occupant, occupier; *(ilegal)* squatter; *(de un vehículo)* occupant.

ocupar I *vtr* 1 *(apoderarse)* to occupy, take. 2 *(llenar)* to take up; **ocupa mucho sitio,** it takes up a lot of space. 3 *(estar en)* to be; **María ocupaba el asiento trasero,** María was sitting in the back seat. 4 *(desempeñar)* to hold, fill; **Luis ocupará la presidencia,** Luis will be president; **o. un cargo,** to hold (an) office *or* a post. 5 *(dar que hacer)* to occupy; *(trabajadores)* to employ; **esta empresa ocupa un**

centenar de obreros, the firm employs a hundred workers; **esto me ocupa totalmente,** this takes up all my time. **6** (habitar) to live in, occupy. **II ocuparse** vr to occupy; **o. de** or **en** or **con,** (vigilar) to look after; (reflexionar) to look into; **ella se ocupa de la parte técnica,** she takes care of the technical side; **o. de un asunto,** to deal with a matter; **tú, ocúpate de lo tuyo,** you mind your own business.

ocurrencia nf (agudeza) witty remark, wisecrack; (idea) idea; iron bright idea; **¡qué ocurrencias tienes!,** what an absurd idea!

ocurrente adj bright, witty.

ocurrir I v unipers to happen, occur; **¿qué ocurre?,** what's going on?; **¿qué te ocurre?,** what's the matter with you? **II ocurrirse** vr to think; **no se me ocurre nada,** I can't think of anything; **¿nunca se te ha ocurrido pensar que ...?,** has it never occurred to you that ...?; **que no se le ocurra venir,** he'd better stay well away from here; **se me ocurre que ...,** it occurs to me that ...; **¡se te ocurre cada cosa!,** you do come out with some funny things!

oda nf Lit ode.

odalisca nf Hist & fig odalisque.

odeón nm Hist odeum, odeon.

odiar vtr to detest, hate; **odio tener que ...,** I hate having to ... .

odio nm hatred, loathing; **mirada de o.,** hateful look; **tener o. a algn,** to hate sb.

odioso,-a adj hateful, detestable.

odisea nf Odyssey; fig odyssey; fam **fue toda una o.,** it was a real hassle; fam **¡menuda o.!,** what a saga!

odómetro nm odometer.

odontología nf Med dentistry, odontology.

odontológico,-a adj Med dental, odontological.

odontólogo,-a nm, f Med dental surgeon, odontologist.

odorífero,-a adj, **odorífico,-a** adj odoriferous.

odre nm wineskin.

OEA nf abr de **Organización de Estados Americanos,** Organization of American States, OAS.

oeste nm west; Náut westward.

ofender I vtr to offend. **II ofenderse** vr to get offended (**con, por,** by), take offence or US offense (**con, por,** at).

ofensa nf offence, US offense.

ofensivo,-a I adj offensive, rude. **II** nf Mil offensive; **tomar la ofensiva,** to take the offensive.

ofensor,-a I adj offending. **II** nm, f Jur offender.

oferta nf Fin Ind (proposición) bid, tender, proposal; (suministro) supply; Com **de o.,** on (special) offer; **o. pública de adquisición hostil,** hostile takeover bid; **o. y demanda,** supply and demand.

ofertar vtr **1** (ofrecer) to offer. **2** (vender) to tender. **3** Am (prometer) to promise.

ofertorio nm Rel offertory.

off adj **1** (desconectado) off, disconnected. **2** (fuera de lugar) off; Teat offstage; **voz en o.,** Teat voice offstage; Cin voice-over.

office nm pantry.

offset nm Impr offset.

offside nm Ftb offside.

oficial,-a I adj official. **II** nm **1** Mil Náut officer. **2** (empleado) clerk. **3** (obrero) skilled worker. **III** nf **1** Cost dressmaker's assistant. **2** (empleada) female office worker. **3** (obrera) skilled worker.

oficialidad nf **1** (cualidad) official character or nature. **2** Mil officers pl, officialdom.

oficialismo nm Am **1** (gobernantes) authorities pl. **2** (partidarios) government supporters pl.

oficializar vtr to make official.

oficiante nm Rel officiant.

oficiar vi **1** Rel to officiate. **2** (hacer de) to act (**de,** as).

oficina nf office. ■ **horas de o.,** business hours; **o. de empleo,** job centre, US job office; **o. pública,** government office.

oficinista nmf office worker, clerk.

oficio nm **1** (ocupación) job, occupation; (que requiere especialización) trade; **aprender un o.,** to learn a trade; **ser del o.,** to be in the trade; **soy albañil de o.,** I'm a bricklayer by trade; fam **gajes del o.,** occupational hazards; fam **sin o. ni beneficio,** without prospects. **2** (comunicación oficial) official letter or note. **3** Rel service; Hist **el Santo O.,** the Inquisition; **o. de difuntos,** office for the dead. **4** (función) role, function. **5** oficios, (acción) offices.

oficioso,-a adj **1** (noticia, fuente) unofficial. **2** (persona) officious.

ofidio nm Zool snake.

ofrecer I vtr **1** (dar) (premio, amistad) to offer; (banquete, fiesta) to hold; (regalo) to give. **2** (presentar) to present; **la ciudad ofrecía un aspecto festivo,** the town looked in a holiday mood; **la situación ofrece pocas posibilidades,** the situation is rather limited; **o. resistencia,** to offer resistanse. **II ofrecerse** vr **1** (prestarse) to offer, volunteer; **me ofrecí,** I volunteered; **me ofrezco para lo que sea,** if there's anything I can do. **2** (presentarse) to present itself; **el valle entero se ofrecía ante nuestra vista,** the whole valley lay before us. **3** (ocurrírsele a uno) to want; **aquí estoy para lo que se le ofrezca,** if there is ever anything you want, don't forget to let me know; **¿qué se le ofrece?,** what can I do for you?; **¿se le ofrece algo más?,** anything else?, will that be all?

ofrecimiento nm offer, offering.

ofrenda nf Rel offering.

ofrendar vtr Rel to make offerings or an offering.

ofrezco indic pres véase **ofrecer.**

oftálmico,-a adj Med ophthalmic.

oftalmología nf Med ophthalmology.

oftalmólogo,-a nm, f Med ophthalmologist.

ofuscación nf, **ofuscamiento** nm blinding, dazzling.

ofuscar vtr **1** (deslumbrar) to dazzle. **2** fig (confundir) to blind.

ogro nm ogre.

oh interj oh!

ohm nm, **ohmio** nm Elec ohm.

oídas (de) loc adv by hearsay; **le conozco de o.,** I've heard of him.

oído nm (sentido) hearing; Anat (órgano) ear; **aplicar el o.,** to listen carefully; **aprender de o.,** to learn by ear; **dar oídos a algo,** to listen to sth; **decir algo al o. de algn,** to whisper sth in sb's ear; **duro de o.,** hard of hearing; **llegar a oídos de algn,** to come to sb's attention or notice; **ser todo oídos,** to be all ears; **taparse los oídos,** to close one's ears; **tener buen o.,** to have a good ear; fig **hacer oídos sordos,** to turn a deaf ear; fig **regalarle el o. a algn,** to flatter sb.

oír vtr to hear; **¡oiga Ud.!,** now look here!; **¡oye!,** hey!; Tel **se oye mal,** I can't hear you (properly), it's a very bad line; fig **como quien oye llover,** it's like water off a duck's back; fig **hacerse o.,** to make oneself heard; fam **como lo oyes,** believe it or not; fam **o., ver y callar,** you haven't seen or heard anything, O.K.?

OIRT nf abr de **Organización Internacional de Radiodifusión y Televisión,** International Radio and Television Organization, IRTO.

OIT nf abr de **Organización Internacional del Trabajo,** International Labour Organization, ILO.

ojal nm buttonhole.

ojalá interj let's hope so!, I hope so!; **¡o. no lo hubiera visto!,** I wish I hadn't seen it; **¡o. sea cierto!,** I hope it is true!, if only it were true!

ojeada nf glance, quick look; **echar una o.,** (echar una mirada) to take a quick look (**a,** at); (vigilar) to keep an eye (**a,** on).

ojeador,-a *nm,f Caza* beater.

ojear[1] *vtr (mirar)* to have a quick look at.

ojear[2] *vtr Caza* to beat.

ojeo *nm Caza* beating.

ojeras *nfpl* rings or bags under the eyes.

ojeriza *nf* dislike, grudge; **coger o. a algn,** to take a dislike to sb.

ojeroso,-a *adj* with rings under the eyes, haggard; **triste y o.,** sad and weary.

ojímetro (a) *loc adv fam* roughly, at a rough guess.

ojiva *nf* 1 *Arquit* ogive. 2 *Mil* warhead.

ojival *adj Arquit* ogival.

ojo I *nm* 1 *Anat* eye; **o. morado** or **a la funerala,** black eye; **ojos saltones,** bulging eyes; *fig* **a o. (de buen cubero),** at a rough guess; *fig* **a ojos vista,** clearly, openly; *fig* **ándate con o.,** be careful; *fig* **calcular o medir a o.,** to guess; *fig* **en un abrir y cerrar de ojos,** in the twinkling of an eye; *fig* **le bailaban los ojos,** his eyes widened with delight; *fig* **mirar a algn con buenos ojos,** to look favourably upon sb; *fig* **o. por o., diente por diente,** an eye for an eye and a tooth for a tooth; *fig* **ojos que no ven (corazón que no siente),** out of sight, out of mind; *fig* **saltar a los ojos,** to be evident; *fig* **tener buen o.** or **o. clínico para algo,** to have a good eye for sth; *fam* **¡dichosos los ojos!,** I'm so glad to see you!; *fam* **no pegué o.,** I didn't sleep a wink; *fam fig* **costar un o. de la cara,** to cost a fortune or an arm or a leg; *fam fig* **tener el o. echado a algo,** to have one's heart set on sth. 2 *(agujero)* hole; *Cost (de aguja)* eye. ■ *Náut* **o. de buey,** porthole; **o. de la cerradura,** keyhole. 3 *(de un puente)* span. II *interj* careful!, look out!; **o. con hacer ruido,** be careful not to make a noise.

ojota *nf Am* sandal.

ola *nf* wave.

ole *interj,* **olé** *interj* bravo!

oleáceas *Bot* I *adj* oleaceous. II **oleáceas** *nfpl* oleaceae *sing.*

oleada *nf* wave; *fig* **o. de turistas,** influx of tourists.

oleaginoso,-a *adj* oleaginous.

oleaje *nm* swell.

óleo *nm* 1 *Arte* oil; **pintura** or **cuadro al ó.,** oil painting. 2 *Rel* chrism, oil.

oleoducto *nm* pipeline.

oleoso,-a *adj* oily.

oler I *vtr* 2 *(percibir olor)* to smell. 2 *fig (adivinar)* to smell, feel; **huelo algo raro,** there is something fishy. II *vi* 1 *(exhalar)* to smell; **huele que apesta,** it stinks; **o. a,** to smell of; **o. bien/mal,** to smell good/bad. 2 *fig (parecer)* to smell, smack **(a,** of); **huele a mentira,** it sounds like a lie; *fam* **me huele a cuerno quemado,** there's something fishy going on here. III **olerse** *vr fig* to feel, sense; **me lo olía,** I thought as much.

olfatear *vtr* 1 *(oler)* to sniff smell. 2 *fig (indagar)* to nose, pry into; *(sospechar)* to suspect.

olfateo *nm* sniffing, smelling; *fig* snooping.

olfativo,-a *adj* olfactory.

olfato *nm* sense of smell, olfaction; *fig* good nose, instinct; *fig* **tener o. para los negocios,** to have a flair for business.

oligarca *nmf* oligarch.

oligarquia *nf* oligarchy.

oligárquico,-a *adj* oligarchic, oligarchical.

oligofrenia *nf* mental handicap.

oligofrénico,-a I *adj* mentally retarded. II *nm,f* mentally retarded person.

olimpiada *nf Hist* Olimpiad; *Dep* Olympiad, Olympic Games *pl*; **las olimpiadas,** the Olympic Games.

olímpico,-a *adj* 1 *Dep* Olympic; **Juegos Olímpicos,** Olympic Games. 2 *fig (altivo)* haughty, lofty; **desprecio o.,** utter disdain.

Olimpo *n* **el O.,** Mount Olympus.

oliscar *vtr,* **olisquear** *vtr* to sniff, smell; *fig* to nose (into), pry into.

oliva *nf Bot* olive; **aceite de o.,** olive oil.

oliváceo,-a *adj* olive-green.

olivar *nm Agr* olive grove.

olivarero,-a *Agr* I *adj* olive; *(del cultivo)* olivegrowing. II *nm,f* olive grower.

olivicultura *nf Agr* olive growing.

olivo *nm Bot* olive (tree).

olmeda *nf,* **olmedo** *nm* elm grove.

olmo *nm Bot* smooth-leaved elm; *fig* **pedir peras al o.,** to ask the impossible.

ológrafo,-a *adj & nm* holograph.

olor *nm* smell; **buen/mal o.,** nice/nasty smell; **o. corporal,** body odour; *fig* **o. de santidad,** odour of sanctity.

oloroso,-a I *adj* fragant, sweet-smelling. II *nm* fullbodied sherry.

olote *nm CAm Méx* corncob.

OLP *nf abr de* **Organización para la Liberación de Palestina,** Palestine Liberation Organízation, PLO.

olvidadizo,-a *adj* forgetful; **hazte el o.,** pretend you've forgotten.

olvidado,-a I *pp de* **olvidar.** II *adj* forgotten; **a. de Dios,** godforsaken.

olvidar I *vtr* to forget; **olvidé el paraguas en casa,** I've left my umbrella at home; *fam* **¡olvídame!,** leave me alone! II **olvidarse** *vr* to forget; **me he olvidado el bolso en tu casa,** I've left my handbag at your house; *fam* **puedes olvidarte de mí,** you can leave me out of it; *fam* **ya puedes olvidarte del coche,** you can say goodbye to the car.

olvido *nm* 1 *(desmemoria)* oblivion; **caer en el o.,** to fall into oblivion; **enterrar en el o.,** to cast into oblivion. 2 *(descuido)* forgetfulness, absentmindedness; *(lapsus)* oversight, lapse; **en un momento de o.,** in a moment of forgetfulness; **un o. imperdonable,** an unforgivable oversight.

olla *nf Culin* saucepan, pot. ■ **o. exprés** or **a presión,** pressure cooker.

omaso *nm Anat* third stomach.

ombligo *nm Anat* navel; *fig* **contemplarse el o.,** to contemplate one's navel; *fam fig* **encogérsele a uno el o.,** to get the wind up.

ombudsman *nm* ombudsman.

ominoso,-a *adj* abominable, dreadful.

omisión *nf* omission.

omiso,-a I *pp de* **omitir.** II *adj* negligent; **hacer caso o. de,** to take no notice of.

omitir *vtr* 1 *(no decir)* to omit, leave out. 2 *(dejar de hacer)* to neglect, overlook.

ómnibus *nm inv Aut* coach.

omnímodo,-a *adj* all-embracíng, total.

omnipotencia *nf* omnipotence.

omnipotente *adj* omnipotent, almighty.

omnipresencia *nf* omnipresence.

omnipresente *adj* omnipresent.

omnisciencia *nf* omniscience.

omnisciente *adj,* **omniscio,-a** *adj* omniscient, all-knowing.

omnívoro,-a *Zool* I *adj* omnivorous. II *nm,f* omnivore.

omóplato *nm,* **omoplato** *nm Anat* shoulder blade.

OMS *nf abr de* **Organización Mundial de la Salud,** World Health Organization, WHO.

onanismo *nm* onanism.

once I *adj inv (cardinal)* eleven; *(ordinal)* eleventh; **a las o.,** at eleven o'clock. **II** *nm inv* eleven; *Ftb* eleven, team. **III las onces** *nfpl (refrigerio)* elevenses, mid-morning snack *sing; véase tamb* **ocho.**

ONCE *nf abr de* **Organización Nacional de Ciegos Españoles,** ≈ Royal National Institute for the Blind, RNIB.

onceno,-a *adj & nm véase* **undécimo,-a.**

oncología *nf Med* oncology.

oncológico,-a *adj Med* oncological.

oncólogo,-a *nm,f Med* oncologist.

onda *nf* 1 *(en el agua)* ripple. 2 *Fís* wave; *fig* **estar en la misma o. que algn,** to be on the same wavelength as sb; *fam fig* **estar en la o.,** to be with it. ■ **longitud de o.,** wavelength; **o. expansiva,** shock wave; **o. hertziana,** Hertzian wave; *Rad* **o. larga/media/corta,** long/ medium/short wave. 3 *Peluq* wave. 4 *Cost* scallop.

ondear *vi* 1 *(bandera)* to flutter; **o. a media asta,** to be flying at half mast. 2 *(agua)* to ripple.

ondia *interj euf* crikey!, *US* gee!

ondina *nf Mit* Nereid.

ondulación *nf* undulation, wave; *(agua)* ripple.

ondulado,-a I *pp de* **ondular. II** *adj (pelo)* wavy; *(metal, cartón)* corrugated; *(paisaje)* rolling, undulating.

ondulante *adj* undulating.

ondular I *vtr (el pelo)* to wave. **II** *vi (moverse)* to undulate.

ondulatorio,-a *adj* wavy; **movimiento o.,** wave motion.

oneroso,-a *adj* onerous.

ónice *nm Min* onyx.

onírico,-a *adj* oneiric, dream, of dreams.

ónix *nm Min* onyx.

onomástico,-a I *adj* onomastic, name. **II** *nf* saint's day.

onomatopeya *nf* onomatopoeia.

onomatopéyico,-a *adj* onomatopoeic.

ontogénesis *nf,* **ontogenia** *nf Biol* ontogeny, ontogenesis.

ontología *nf Filos* ontology.

ontológico,-a *adj Filos* ontological.

ONU *nf abr de* **Organización de las Naciones Unidas,** United Nations (Organization), UN(O).

onubense I *adj* of or from Huelva. **II** *nmf* native *or* inhabitant of Huelva.

onza¹ *nf (medida)* ounce.

onza² *nm Zool* ounce, snow leopard.

onzavo,-a *adj & nm véase* **undécimo,-a.**

opa *Am* **I** *adj* stupid. **II** *interj* hello!

opacidad *nf* opaqueness, opacity.

opaco,-a *adj* opaque.

opalescencia *nf* opalescence.

opalescente *adj* opalescent.

opalino,-a *adj* opal, opaline, opal-like.

ópalo *nm Min* opal.

opción *nf (elección)* option, choice; *(alternativa)* alternative; **la o. más fácil,** the soft option; **no tienes o.,** you have no choice. 2 *(derecho)* right; *(posibilidad)* opportunity, chance.

opcional *adj* optional.

open *nm Golf* open.

OPEP *nf abr de* **Organización de los Países Exportadores de Petróleo,** Organization of Petroleum Exporting Countries, OPEC.

ópera *nf Mús* opera; **ó. bufa,** comic opera, opera buffa.

operable *adj* operable.

operación *nf* 1 *Med* operation. ■ **o. quirúrgica,** surgical operation. 2 *Fin* transaction, deal; **operaciones bursátiles,** stock exchange transactions. 3 *Mil* manoeuvre, *US* maneuver, operation. 4 *Mat* operation.

operacional *adj* operational.

operado,-a I *pp de* **operar. II** *adj* who has been operated on. **III** *nm,f* recovery patient.

operador,-a I *nm Mat* operator; *Inform* operator. **II** *nm,f* 1 *(técnico)* operator. 2 *Med* surgeon. 3 *Cin (de la cámara) (hombre)* cameraman; *(mujer)* camerawoman; *(del proyector)* projectionist. 4 *Tel* operator.

operando *nm Inform Mat* operand.

operante *adj* operative.

operar I *vtr* 1 *Med* to operate **(a,** on); **le han operado de las amígdalas,** she's had her tonsils out. 2 *(producir)* to bring about. **II** *vi (hacer efecto)* to operate, work; *Fin* to deal, do business (with); *Mat* **o. con quebrados,** to work in fractions. **III operarse** *vr* 1 *Med* to have an operation **(de,** for). 2 *(producirse)* to occur, come about; **se ha operado una mejoría en el paciente,** the patient has shown an improvement.

operario,-a *nm,f* operator, worker.

operativo,-a *adj* operative.

operatorio,-a *adj* operational.

opereta *nf Mús* operetta.

operístico,-a *adj* operatic.

opiáceo,-a *adj* opiate.

opinable *adj* debatable, arguable.

opinar *vi* to think, give one's opinion, be of the opinion; **tú, ¿qué opinas?,** what do you think?; **yo no quiero o.,** I'd rather not comment, I'd rather not give an opinion.

opinión *nf* 1 *(juicio)* opinion, view, point of view; **cambiar de o.,** to change one's mind; **soy de la o. de que ...,** I'm of the opinion that ... . 2 *(fama)* reputation.

opio *nm (drogas)* opium; **fumadero de o.,** opium den.

opiomanía *nf (drogas)* addiction to opium.

opiómano,-a *nm,f* opium addict.

opíparo,-a *adj* lavish. ◆ **opíparamente** *adv* lavishly; **comieron o.,** they dined sumptuously.

oponente I *adj* opposing. **II** *nmf* opponent, opposite number.

oponer *(pp* **opuesto) I** *vtr (a un plan, persona)* to oppose; *(resistencia)* to offer; **no tengo nada que o. a tu plan,** I've no objections to your plan. **II oponerse** *vr (estar en contra)* to be opposed, be against; *(ser contrario a)* to be in opposition **(a,** to), contradict; **o. a algo,** to oppose sth.

Oporto *n* Porto.

oporto *nm (vino)* port.

oportunidad *nf* opportunity, chance.

oportunismo *nm* opportunism.

oportunista *adj & nmf* opportunist.

oportuno,-a *adj* 1 *(a tiempo)* timely; **¡qué o. fuiste!,** that was well-timed! 2 *(conveniente)* appropriate; **si te parece o.,** if you think it appropiate. ◆ **oportunamente** *adv* opportunely.

oposición *nf* 1 *(gen)* opposition. 2 *(examen)* competitive examination; **está preparando oposiciones para entrar en un banco,** he's studying for a bank entrance examination; **ganar** *or* **sacar la o.,** to pass a competitive examination.

opositar *vi* to sit a competitive examination.

opositor,-a *nm,f* 1 *(candidato)* candidate for a competitive examination. 2 *Am Pol* opponent.

opresión *nf* oppression; **o. en el pecho,** tightness of the chest.

opresivo,-a *adj* oppressive.

opresor,-a I *adj* oppressive, oppressing. **II** *nm,f* oppressor.

oprimido,-a I *adj* oppressed; *fig* **con el corazon o.,** downhearted. **II los oprimidos** *nmpl* the oppressed *pl.*

oprimir *vtr* to squeeze, press; *fig* to oppress; **oprima el botón,** press the button; *fig* **o. con el poder,** to oppress with power.

oprobio *nm* ignominy, opprobrium.

optar *vi* **1** (*elegir*) to choose (**entre, por,** between); **o. entre A y B,** to choose between A and B; **o. por,** to opt for; **opté por ir yo mismo,** I decided to go myself. **2** (*aspirar*) to apply (**a,** for); **poder o. a un puesto,** to be entitled to apply for a post.

optativo,-a *adj* optional; *Ling* optative.

óptico,-a I *adj* optic, optical; **aparatos ópticas,** optical instruments; **nervio ó.,** optic nerve. **II** *nm, f* optician. **III** *nf* **1** *Fís* optics *sing.* **2** (*tienda*) optician's (shop).

optimismo *nm* optimism.

optimista I *adj* optimistic. **II** *nmf* optimist.

óptimo,-a *adj* very best, optimum, excellent.

opuesto,-a I *pp de* **oponer. II** *adj* **1** (*contrario*) contrary, opposed; **conducta opuesta a las reglas,** misconduct; **en direcciones opuestas,** in opposite directions; **tenemos gustos opuestos,** we have conflicting tastes. **2** (*de enfrente*) opposite; **el extremo o.,** the other end.

opulencia *nf* opulence, luxury; **vivir en la o.,** to live a life of luxury.

opulento,-a *adj* opulent.

opus *nm* *Mús* opus.

opúsculo *nm* booklet; short work.

opuse *pt indef véase* **oponer.**

oquedad *nf* hollow, cavity.

ora *conj arc* now; **o. ríe, o. llora,** now he laughs, now he cries.

oración *nf* **1** *Rel* prayer. **2** *Ling* clause, sentence; **partes de la o.,** parts of speech. ■ **o. simple/compuesta,** simple/complex sentence; **o. subordinada/principal,** subordinate/main clause. **3** (*discurso*) oration, speech.

oráculo *nm* oracle.

orador,-a *nm, f* speaker, orator; **tiene dotes de o.,** he's a gifted speaker.

oral *adj* oral; *Med* **por vía o.,** to be taken orally.

orangután *nm* *Zool* orang-outang orang-utan.

orante *adj Arte* praying; **en posición o.,** kneeling.

orar *vi Rel* to pray.

orate *nmf* lunatic; (*hombre*) madman; (*mujer*) madwoman; **casa de orates,** lunatic asylum.

oratoria *nf* oratory.

oratorio[1] *nm* **1** *Mús* oratorio. **2** (*capilla*) oratory.

oratorio,-a[2] *adj* oratorical.

orbe *nm* **1** (*mundo*) world; **en todo el o.,** throughout the world. **2** (*bola*) orb.

órbita *nf* **1** *Astron* *Astronáut* orbit; *fig* orbit; **entrar en ó.,** to go into orbit; *fig* **se sale de la órbita de mis competencias,** it lies outside my jurisdiction. **2** *Anat* eye socket; **con los ojos fuera de las órbitas,** with his eyes popping out of his head.

orbital *adj* orbital.

orca *nf Zool* orc, killer whale.

órdago *nm fam* **de ó.,** fantastic, great; **una riña de ó.,** a hell of an argument.

orden I *nm* **1** (*colocación*) order; **lo encontré todo en o.,** everything was in its place; **todo en o.,** everything in order. **2** (*concierto*) order; **las fuerzas del o.,** the forces of law and order; **llamar a algn al o.,** to call sb to order; **mantener el o.,** to keep order; **o. público,** law and order; **sin o. ni concierto,** without rhyme or reason. **3** (*sucesión*) order; **de primer o.,** first-rate; **del o. de ...,** in the order of ...; **o. del día,** agenda, order of the day; **por o. de edad/estatura,** by age/height. **4** *Arquit Bot Zool* order; **o.**

dórico/jónico, Doric/Ionic order. **5** *Mil* drill. **6** *fig* (*campo*) sphere; **en el o. económico,** in the economic sphere. **II** *nf* **1** (*mandato*) order; *Mil* **¡a la o.!, ¡a sus órdenes!,** sir!; **por o. del señor alcalde,** by order of his Lordship the Mayor; *fig* **está a la o.del día,** it's the done thing. **2** *Hist Rel* order; **o. militar,** military order; **órdenes sagradas,** holy orders. **3** *Com* order; **o. de pago,** money order. **4** *Jur* warrant, order. ■ **o. de arresto** *or* **detención,** warrant for arrest; **o. de registro,** search warrant; **o. judicial,** court order.

ordenación *nf* **1** (*disposición*) arrangement, organizing. **2** *Rel* ordination.

ordenada *nf Mat* ordinate.

ordenado,-a I *pp de* **ordenar. II** *adj* **1** (*arreglado*) tidy, in order. **2** *Rel* ordained.

ordenador,-a I *adj* ordering. **II** *nm Inform* computer, data processor; **o. personal,** personal computer.

ordenamiento *nm* ordering.

ordenanza I *nm* *Mil* orderly; (*en oficina*) messenger. **II ordenanzas** *nfpl* regulations, code *sing;* **o. municipales,** by-laws.

ordenar I *vtr* **1** (*arreglar*) to put in order; (*habitación*) to tidy up; (*encaminar*) to direct; *fig* **o. las ideas,** to collect one's thoughts; *fig* **o. su vida,** to put one's affairs in order. **2** (*mandar*) to order to; *Com* **o. un pago,** to authorize a payment. **3** *Rel* to ordain. **II ordenarse** *vr Rel* to be ordained (**de,** as), take holy orders.

ordeñadora *nf Agr* milking machine.

ordeñar *vtr Agr* to milk.

ordeño *nm Agr* milking.

órdiga *interj* **¡la ó.!,** crikey!, *US* gee!

ordinal I *adj* ordinal. **II** *nm* (*número*) ordinal.

ordinariez *nf* (*grosería*) vulgarity, coarseness; (*expresión*) rude remark.

ordinario,-a *adj* **1** (*corriente*) ordinary, common. **2** (*grosero*) vulgar, common.

ordinograma *nm Inform* flow chart.

orear I *vtr* (*ventilar*) to air. **II orearse** *vr* (*tomar el aire*) to get some fresh air.

orégano *nm Bot* oregano, marjoram; *fig* **no todo el monte es o.,** it's not all plain sailing.

oreja *nf* (*gen*) ear; (*de zapato*) flap; (*de sillón*) wing; *fig* **con las orejas gachas,** with one's tail between one's legs; *fam* **calentarle las orejas a algn,** to box sb's ears; *fam* **con una sonrisa de o. a o.,** with a huge grin; *fam fig* **verle las orejas al lobo,** to have a narrow escape.

orejano,-a *Am* **I** *adj* (*animal*) shy; (*persona*) unsociable. **II** *nm, f* (*animal*) shy animal; (*persona*) unsociable person.

orejar *vtr Am* to eavesdrop.

orejear *vi* **1** (*animales*) to wiggle its ears. **2** *Arg Guat Hond* (*dar tirones de orejas*) to pull the ears of. **3** *Méx PR* (*desconfiar*) to be distrustful of, be suspicious of.

orejero,-a I *adj* **1** *Am* (*receloso*) suspicious, distrustful. **2** *Arg* (*chismoso*) gossiping, scandalmongering. **II** *nf* **1** (*de gorra*) earflap; (*de sillón*) wing. **2** *Am* earring worn by Indians.

orejón[1] *nm* **1** *Culin* piece of dried peach *or* apricot. **2** (*persona*) big-ears. **3** (*tirón*) pull on the ear; **darle un o. a algn,** to pull sb's ear.

orejón,-ona[2] **I** *adj Am* **1** (*orejudo*) big-eared. **2** (*tonto*) stupid. **II** *nm Méx* (*calzonazos*) henpecked husband.

orejudo,-a I *adj* big-eared. **II** *nm Zool* long-eared bat.

oremus *nm Rel* let us pray; *fam fig* **perder el o.,** (*hilo*) to lose the thread, get lost; (*paciencia*) to lose one's patience.

orensano,-a I *adj of or* from Orense. **II** *nm, f* native *or* inhabitant of Orense.

orfanato *nm* orphanage.

orfandad *nf* orphanhood.

orfebre *nm* goldsmith, silversmith.

orfebrería *nf* gold *or* silver work.

orfelinato *nm* orphanage.

orfeón *nm Mús* choral society.

orfeonista *nmf Mús* member of a choral society.

organdí *nm Tex* organdie.

orgánico,-a *adj* organic.

organigrama *nm* organization chart, flow chart, flow diagram; *Inform* flow chart.

organillero,-a *nm,f Mús* organ-grinder.

organillo *nm Mús* barrel organ, hurdy-gurdy.

organismo *nm* 1 *(ser viviente)* organism. 2 *(entidad pública)* organization, body, institution.

organista *nmf Mús* organist.

organización *nf* organization.

organizado,-a I *pp* de **organizer**. II *adj* organized; **viaje o.,** package tour.

organizador,-a I *adj* organizing. II *nm,f* organizer.

organizar I *vtr* to organize. II **organizarse** *vr* to organize oneself; *fig* to happen; **se organizó un escándalo,** it ended in a rumpus.

órgano *nm* 1 *Mús* organ. 2 *Anat* organ.

orgasmo *nm* orgasm.

orgía *nf* orgy.

orgiástico,-a *adj* orgiastic.

orgullo *nm* 1 *(propia estima)* pride. 2 *(arrogancia)* arrogance, haughtiness.

orgulloso,-a *adj* 1 *(satisfecho)* proud. 2 *(arrogante)* arrogant, haughty.

orientación *nf (dirección)* orieniation, direction. 2 *Arquit (de un edificio)* aspect. 3 *(enfoque)* approach; **hay que darle una nueva o.** al problema, we have to look at the problem in a different way. 4 *(guía)* guidance; **cursillo de o.,** induction course; **estos datos te servirán de o.,** this information will give you an idea; **o. profesional,** career guidance, vocational guidance.

orientador,-a I *adj* advising, advisory, guiding. II *nm,f* guide, adviser, counsellor.

oriental I *adj* eastern, oriental; **hemisferio o.,** eastern hemisphere. II *nmf* Oriental.

orientar I *vtr* 1 *(dirigir)* to orientate, direct; **charla orientada a los padres,** talk aimed at parents; **educación orientada al logro académico,** education geared to academic success. 2 *Arquit (edificios)* to position, place; **una casa orientada al sur,** a house facing south. 3 *(guiar)* to guide; **el policía les orientó,** the policeman gave them directions. II **orientarse** *vr* 1 *(encontrar el camino)* to get one's bearings, find one's way about; *fig* to get into the swing of things; **los ciegos se orientan por los sonidos,** blind people are guided by sounds. 2 *(dirigirse)* to tend towards.

oriente *nm* 1 East, Orient; **el Extremo** *or* **Lejano O.,** the Far East; **el O. Medio,** the Middle East; **el Próximo O.,** the Near East. 2 *(masonería)* **Gran O.,** the Grand Lodge.

orificio *nm* hole, opening; *Anat Téc* orifice. ■ **o. de admisión** *or* **entrada,** inlet; **o. de salida,** outlet.

origen *nm* origin; **dar o. a,** to give rise to; **de o. español,** of Spanish extraction; **de o. humilde,** of humble origins *or* birth; **en los orígenes de la historia,** at the dawn of history; **país de o.,** country of origin; **tiene sus orígenes en la Edad Media,** it dates back to the Middle Ages.

original *adj & nmf* original.

originalidad *nf* originality; *pey* eccentricity.

originar I *vtr* to cause, give rise to. II **originarse** *vr* to originate, have its origin.

originario,-a *adj (procedente)* original; *(primigenio)* original; **ser o. de,** *(persona)* to come from; *(costumbre)* to originate in.

orilla *nf* 1 *(borde)* edge; *(del río)* bank; *(del mar)* shore; **a la o. del mar,** by the sea, at the seaside. 2 *Arg Méx (arrabales)* outskirts *pl*.

orillero,-a *adj Am (persona)* suburban.

orillo *nm Tex* selvage, selvedge.

orín¹ *nm (herrumbre)* rust.

orín² *nm (gen pl) (orina)* urine.

orina *nf* urine.

orinal *nm* chamberpot; *fam* potty.

orinar I *vi* to urinate. II **orinarse** *vr* to wet oneself.

oriol *nm Orn* oriole.

oriundo,-a I *adj* native of; **ser o. de,** to come from, originate from. II *nm Ftb* foreign player of Spanish parentage who plays for a Spanish team.

orla *nf* 1 *Cost* trimming, edging. 2 *Univ* graduation photograph.

orlar *vtr Cost* to put an ornamental edge on.

ornamentación *nf* ornamentation, decoration.

ornamental *adj* ornamental.

ornamentar *vtr* to adorn, embellish.

ornamento *nm* 1 *(adorno)* ornament. 2 **ornamentos,** *Rel* vestments.

ornar *vtr lit* to adorn, embellish.

ornato *nm (atavío)* finery; *(adorno)* decoration.

ornitología *nf* ornithology.

ornitológico,-a *adj* ornithological.

ornitólogo,-a *nm,f* ornithologist.

ornitorrinco *nm Zool* duck-billed platypus.

oro *nm* 1 gold; **de o.,** gold, golden; *fig* **libro de o.,** visitors' book; *fig* **tratar algo como o. en paño,** to handle sth with great care; *fam* **fig prometer el o. y el moro,** to promise the earth; *prov* **no es o. todo lo que reluce,** all that glitters is not gold. ■ **o. blanco,** white gold; **o. de ley,** fine gold; **patrón o.,** gold standard. 2 **oros,** *Naipes (baraja española)* ≈ diamonds.

orogenia *nf Geol* orogeny, orogenesis.

orografía *nf Geog* orography, orology.

orográfico,-a *adj Geog* orographic, orological.

orondo,-a *adj* 1 *(con barriga)* potbellied. 2 *fig (ufano)* smug, self-satisfied; **lo dijo y se quedó tan o.,** he said it without batting an eyelid.

oropel *nm* tinsel.

oropéndola *nf Orn* golden oriole.

orquesta *nf Mús* orchestra; *(de verbena)* dance band.

orquestación *nf Mús* orchestration; *fig* orchestration, organization.

orquestal *adj Mús* orchestral.

orquestar *vtr Mús* to orchestrate; *fig* to orchestrate, organize.

orquestina *nf Mús* orchestrina.

orquídea *nf Bot* orchid.

orsay *nm Ftb fam* offside.

ortiga *nf Bot* (stinging) nettle.

ortigal *nm Bot* nettle field.

ortodoncia *nf Med* orthodontics *sing*, orthodontia.

ortodoxia *nf* orthodoxy.

ortodoxo,-a *adj & nm,f* orthodox.

ortografía *nf* orthography, spelling; **faltas de o.,** spelling mistakes.

ortografiar *vtr* to write correctly.

oltográfico,-a *adj* orthografic, orthographical; **signos ortográficos,** punctuation *sing*.

ortopedia *nf* orthopaedics *sing*, *US* orthopedics *sing*.

ortopédico,-a I *adj* orthopaedic, *US* orthopedic; **pierna ortopédica,** artificial leg. II *nm, f* orthopaedist, *US* orthopedist.

ortopedista *nmf* orthopaedist, *US* orthopedist.

oruga *nf* 1 *Zool* caterpillar. 2 *Bot* rocket. 3 *Téc* caterpillar.

orujo *nm* (*hollejo*) grape or olive skins left after pressing; (*bebida*) grape spirit.

orza¹ *nf* earthenware jar.

orza² *nf Náut* luff, luffing.

orzar *vi Náut* to luff.

orzuelo *nm Med* sty, stye.

os *pron pers pl* **1** (*complemento directo*) you; **os veo mañana**, I'll see you tomorrow. **2** (*complemento indirecto*) to you; **os escribiré**, I'll write to you; **os lo mandaré**, I'll send it to you. **3** (*con verbo reflexivo*) yourselves; **¿no os quejáis?**, don't you complain?; **os hacéis daño**, you're hurting yourselves; **os organizáis muy bien**, you are very well organized; **¡qué pronto os levantáis!**, you do get up early! **4** (*con verbo recíproco*) each other; **os parecéis**, you look alike; **os queréis mucho**, you love each other very much.

osa *nf* **1** *Zool* she-bear. **2** *Astron* **O. Mayor**, Great Bear, *US* Big Dipper; **O. Menor**, Little Bear, *US* Little Dipper.

osadía *nf* **1** (*audacia*) daring, boldness, fearlessness. **2** (*desvergüenza*) impudence.

osado,-a *adj* **1** (*audaz*) daring, bold, fearless. **2** (*desvergonzado*) shameless.

osamenta *nf* bones *pl*, skeleton.

osar *vi* to dare.

osario *nm* ossuary.

oscar *nm Cin* Oscar.

oscense **I** *adj* of *or* from Huesca. **II** *nmf* native *or* inhabitant of Huesca.

oscilación *nf* **1** *Fís* oscillation. **2** (*de precios*) fluctuation.

oscilador *nm Fís* oscillator.

oscilante *adj* **1** *Fís* oscillating. **2** (*precios*) fluctuating.

oscilar *vi* **1** *Fís* to oscillate. **2** (*variar*) to vary, fluctuate.

osciloscopio *nm Fís* oscilloscope.

ósculo *nm lit hum* kiss.

oscurantismo *nm* obscurantism.

oscurantista *adj & nmf* obscurantist.

oscuras (a) *loc adv* in the dark; **nos quedamos a o.**, we were left in darkness.

oscurecer *vi impers & vtr & vr véase* **obscurecer**.

oscurecimiento *nm véase* **obscurecimiento**.

oscuridad *nf véase* **obscuridad**.

oscuro,-a *adj véase* **obscuro,-a**.

óseo,-a *adj* osseous, bony; **tejido ó.**, bone tissue.

osera *nf* bear's den.

osezno *nm Zool* bear cub.

osificación *nf* ossification.

osificarse *vr* to ossify.

osito *nm fam* **o. (de peluche)**, teddy bear.

Oslo *n* Oslo.

osmio *nm Quím* osmium.

ósmosis *nf inv*, **osmosis** *nf inv* osmosis.

osmótico,-a *adj* osmotic.

oso *nm Zool* bear; *fam fig* **hacer el o.**, to play the fool. ■ **o. blanco**, polar bear; **o. hormiguero**, anteater; **o. marino**, fur seal.

ossobuco *nm Culin* osso bucco.

ostensible *adj* ostensible, obvious.

ostentación *nf* ostentation; **con o.**, ostentatiously; **hacer o. de algo**, to show sth off.

ostentar *vtr* **1** (*jactarse*) to show off, flaunt. **2** (*poseer*) to hold; **ostenta el cargo de**, she holds the position of.

ostentoso,-a *adj* ostentatious.

osteópata *nmf Med* osteopath.

osteopatía *nf Med* osteopathy.

osteopático,-a *adj Med* osteopathic.

ostra *nf Zool* oyster, *fig* **aburrirse como una o.**, to be bored stiff; *fam* **¡ostras!**, crikey!, *US* gee!

ostracismo *nm* ostracism.

ostrería *nf* oyster restaurant.

ostrero,-a **I** *adj* oyster. **II** *nm*, *f* oyster trader. **III** *nm Orn* oystercatcher.

ostrícola *adj* oyster.

ostricultura *nf* oyster culture.

osuno,-a *adj* bear-like.

OTAN *nf abr de* **Organización del Tratado del Atlántico Norte**, North Atlantic Treaty Organization, NATO.

otario,-a *adj Arg Urug* foolish, simple.

otate *nm Méx* stick.

oteador,-a *nm*, *f* lookout.

otear *vtr* to scan, search; **o. el horizonte**, to scan the horizon.

otero *nm* knoll, hillock.

OTI *nf abr de* **Organización de la Televisión Ibero-americana**.

otitis *nf inv Med* infection and inflammation of the ear, otitis.

otomán,-ana *adj & nm*, *f* Ottoman, Othman.

otoñal *adj* autumnal, autumn, *US* fall.

otoño *nm* autumn, *US* fall.

otorgamiento *nm* (*concesión*) granting, authorization; (*de un premio*) award, awarding.

otorgante *nmf* garantor.

otorgar *vtr* **1** (*conceder*) to grant, give (**a**, to); (*premio*) to award (**a**, to); **o. un indulto**, to grant pardon. **2** *Jur* to execute, draw up. **3** (*conferir*) to confer (**a**, on).

otorrinolaringología *nf Med* otolaryngology.

otorrinolaringólogo,-a *nm*, *f* ear, nose and throat specialist, otolaryngologist.

otro,-a I *adj indef* other, another; **entre otras cosas**, amongst other things; **otra cosa**, something else; **otra vez**, again; **otra vez será**, some other time; **o. día**, another day. **II** *pron indef* other, another; **el o.**, **la otra**, the other, **entre otros**, among others; **los otros**, **las otras**, the others; **nunca me he visto en otra igual**, I just didn't know what to do; **¡otra, otra!**, encore!, more!; **o. de mis amigos**, another (one) of my friends; **otros tantos**, as many; **que vaya o.**, let someone else go; *fam* **o. que tal**, here we go again.

otrora *adv arc* formerly.

otrosí *adv Jur* moreover, furthermore.

ova *nf Bot* alga.

ovachón *nm Méx fam* fat slob.

ovación *nf* ovation, cheering, applause.

ovacionar *vtr* to give an ovation to, applaud.

oval *adj*, **Ovalado,-a** *adj* oval.

óvalo *nm* oval.

ovárico,-a *adj Anat* ovarian.

ovario *nm Anat* ovary.

oveja *nf* **1** *Zool* sheep, ewe; *fig* **cada o. con su pareja**, every Jack has his Jill; *fig* **la o. negra (de la familia)**, the black sheep (of the family). **2** *Am Zool* llama.

ovejuno,-a *adj* sheep.

overbooking *nm* overbooking.

overear *vtr SAm Culin* to brown.

overol *nm Am* overalls *pl*.

ovetense **I** *adj* of *or* from Oviedo. **II** *nmf* native *or* inhabitant of Oviedo.

ovillar *vtr* (*lana*) to wind or roll into a ball.

ovillo *nm* ball (of wool); *fig* **hacerse un o.**, to curl up into a ball; *fig* **por el hilo se saca el o.**, by putting two and two together.

ovino,-a *adj* ovine; **ganado o.,** sheep *pl.*

ovíparo,-a *adj Zool* oviparous.

OVNI *nm abr de* **objeto volador no identificado,** unidentified flying object, UFO.

ovoide *adj & nm* ovoid.

ovulación *nf* ovulation.

ovular I *adj* ovular. **II** *vi* to ovulate.

óvulo *nm* ovule.

oxálico,-a *adj Quím* oxalic.

oxhídrico,-a *adj Quím* oxyhydrogen.

oxidable *adj Quím* oxidizable.

oxidación *nf Quím* oxidation; *(efecto en los metales)* rusting.

oxidado,-a I *pp de* **oxidar. II** *adj Quím* oxidized; *(efecto en los metales)* rusty; *fig* **su inglés está un poco o.,** her English is a bit rusty.

oxidante *nm* oxidizer.

oxidar I *vtr Quím* to oxidize; *(efecto en los metales)* to rust. **II oxidarse** *vr Quím* to oxidize; *(efecto en los metales)* to rust, go rusty.

óxido *nm* **1** *Quím* oxide. ■ **ó. de carbono,** carbon monoxide. **2** *(orín)* rust.

oxigenación *nf Quím* oxygenation.

oxigenado,-a *adj* oxygenated; **agua oxigenada,** (hydrogen) peroxide.

oxigenar I *vtr* **1** *Quím* to oxygenate. **2** *Peluq* to bleach. **II oxigenarse** *vr fig* to get a breath of fresh air.

oxígeno *nm* oxygen. ■ **bomba de o.,** oxygen cylinder *or* tank.

oye *indic pres & imperat véase* **oír.**

oyente *nmf* **1** *Rad* listener. **2** *Univ* occasional student.

ozono *nm Quím* ozone.

P

P, p *nf (la letra)* P, p.

p. *abr de* **página,** page, p.

P.A., p.a. *abr de* **por autorización.**

pabellón *nm* **1** *(tienda)* bell tent. **2** *Arquit* pavilion; *(anexo)* annex, block. **3** *(dosel)* canopy. **4** *(de un instrumento)* mouthpiece. **5** *(de la oreja)* outer ear. **6** *(bandera)* flag; **navegábamos bajo p. panameño,** we sailed under the Panamanian flag.

pábilo *nm,* **pabilo** *nm* wick.

pábulo *nm fml* food, sustenance; *fig* fuel; **dar p. a,** to encourage.

paca *nf* bale, pack.

pacato,-a *adj* **1** *(escrupuloso)* prudish. **2** *(apaciguado)* moderate, peace-loving.

pacense I *adj* of *or* from Badajoz. **II** *nmf* native *or* inhabitant of Badajoz.

paceño,-a I *adj* of *or* from La Paz. **II** *nm, f* native *or* inhabitant of La Paz.

pacer *vtr & vi* to graze, pasture.

pachá *nm (pl* **pachaes)** pasha, pacha; *fam fig* **vivir como un p.,** to live like a king.

pachaco,-a *adj Am (inútil)* useless; *(enclenque)* weak.

pachamanca *nf SAm Culin* type of barbecue.

pachanga I *adj véase* **pachanguero. II** *nf Méx* celebration, rowdy party.

pachanguero,-a *adj fam pey (música)* catchy.

pacho,-a *adj* **1** *CAm Chi fam (regordete)* chubby. **2** *CAm (aplanado)* flattened.

pachol *nm Méx* matted hair.

pachón,-ona I *adj* **1** *zool* pointer. **2** *Am (peludo)* hairy; *(lanudo)* woolly. **II** *nm, f Zool* pointer. **III** *nm fam* phlegmatic person.

pachorra *nf fam* sluggishness; **tener p.,** to be phlegmatic.

pachulí *nm (pl* **pachulíes)** *Bot* patchouli, pachouli.

paciencia *nf* patience; **armarse de p.,** to grin and bear it; **perder la p.,** to lose (one's) patience; **tener mucha p.,** to be very patient; *prov* **la p. es la madre de la ciencia,** if at first you don't succeed, try, try again.

paciente *adj & nmf* patient. ◆ **pacientemente** *adv* patiently.

pacificación *nf* pacification; *fig (apaciguamiento)* appeasement.

pacificador,-a I *adj* pacifying. **II** *nm, f* peacemaker.

pacificar I *vtr* to pacify; *fig (apaciguar)* to appease, calm. **II pacificarse** *vr* to calm down.

pacífico,-a *adj* peaceful.

Pacífico *nm* **el (océano) P.,** the Pacific (Ocean).

pacifismo *nm* pacifism.

pacifista *adj & nmf* pacifist.

paco,-a I *adj Arg Chi (rojizo)* reddish. **II** *nm Am (sereno)* night watchman; *(policía)* policeman.

pacota *nf* **1** *Arg (grupo)* gang. **2** *Méx (objeto)* piece of junk; *(persona)* worthless person.

pacotilla *nf* **1** *Náut* seaman's duty-free perks *pl.* **2** *fam* **de p.,** shoddy, trashy.

pactar *vtr* to agree to; **han pactado una tregua,** they've agreed to a truce.

padecer *vtr & vi* **1** to suffer; **padece del corazón,** he suffers from heart trouble. **2** *fig* to suffer.

padecimiento *nm* suffering.

padrastro *nm* **1** stepfather. **2** *fig (mal padre)* harsh *or* severe father. **3** *(pellejo)* hangnail.

padrazo *nm* easy-going *or* indulgent father.

padre I *nm* **1** *(gen)* father; **p. de familia,** head of family; **p. político,** father-in-law; *fam* **de p. y muy señor mío,** tremendous, terrific; *ofens* **¡tu p.!,** up yours! **2** *fig (precursor)* father, creator; *irón* **¿quién es el p. de la criatura?,** who put this together? **3** *Rel* father, priest; **el santo p.,** the Pope, the Holy Father. **4** *Rel* God; **P. Eterno,** Heavenly Father; *(oración)* **P. Nuestro,** Lord's Prayer. **5 padres,** parents; *(antepasados)* ancestors. **II** *adj fam* huge; **llevarse un disgusto p.,** to be extremely upset; **pegarse la vida p.,** to live like a king.

padrear *vi* **1** *(parecerse al padre)* to resemble one's father. **2** *(engendrar)* to breed.

padrenuestro *nm (pl* **padrenuestros)** *Rel* Lord's Prayer.

padrillo *nm Am Zoal* stallion.

padrinazgo *nm* **1** godfathership. **2** *fig (patrocinio)* patronage, sponsorship.

padrino *nm* **1** godfather; *(de boda)* best man. **2** *fig* sponsor, protector. **3 padrinos,** godparents; *fig* **hay que tener buenos p.,** you have to know the right people.

padrón *nm* **1** *(censo)* census. **2** *fig (deshonra)* dishonour, *US* dishonor, disgrace. **3** *(padrazo)* easygoing *or* indulgent father. **4** *Am Zool* stallion.

padrotear *vi Méx* **1** *vulg véase* **padrear. 2** to go out with prostitutes.

paella *nf Culin* paella, rice dish made with vegetables, meat and/or seafood.

paellera *nf* paella pan.

paf *interj* bang!

pág *abr de* **página,** page, p.

paga *nf* wage; *(niños)* pocket money; *fig* **esto fue la p. por su comportamiento,** she got her just deserts. ▪ **p. extra,** bonus.

pagable *adj* payable.

pagadero,-a *adj* payable; *Fin* **cheque p. al portador,** cheque payable to bearer.

pagado,-a I *pp de* **pagar. II** *adj* **1** paid. **2** *fig* **p. de uno mismo,** smug, self-satisfied.

pagador,-a I *adj* paying. **II** *nm, f* payer; *(de banco, institución, etc)* cashier.

pagaduría *nf* pay office.

págalo *nm Orn* skua.

paganismo *nm* paganism, heathenism.

paganizar I *vi* to profess paganism. **II** *vtr* to paganize.

pagano,-a¹ *adj & nm, f Rel* pagan, heathen.

pagano,-a² *nm, f fam* **1** *(pagador)* person who pays for others. **2** *fig (cabeza de turco)* scapegoat.

pagar I *vtr* to pay; **¿cuánto pagaste por el coche?,** how much did you pay for the car?; **p. en mtálico** *or* **al contado,** to pay cash; *fig* **¿así pagas lo que ha hecho por ti?,** is that how you repay him for what he's done for you?; *fig* **(ella) lo ha pagado caro,** she's paid dearly for it; *fam fig* **me las pagarás,** I'll get you for this, you haven't heard the last of this. **II pagarse** *vr* **1** *(uso impers)* to be paid, cost; **¿ a cuánto se pagan las patatas?,** how much are (the) potatoes? **2** *fig (ufanarse)* to be proud of; **p. de sí mismo,** to be full of oneself, be self-satisfied, be smug.

pagaré *nm Fin* promissory note, IOU; **p. del tesoro,** treasury note.

página *nf* page; **en la p. 3,** on page 3; *fig* **aquellos hombres escribieron una p. importante de la historia,** those men wrote an important chapter in history.

paginación *nf* pagination.

paginar *vtr* to paginate, number the pages of.

pago¹ *nm* **1** *Fin Com* payment; **p. a cuenta,** payment on account. ▪ **p. adelantado** *or* **anticipado,** advance payment; **p. contra entrega,** cash on delivery; **p. inicial,** down payment. **2** *fig* return, payment; **en p. por su hospitalidad ...,** in return for her hospitality ... .

pago² *nm* **1** *(finca)* estate, property. **2** *Am (aldea)* village; **por** *or* **en estos/aquellos pagos,** in this/that area.

pagoda *nf Arquit* pagoda.

pagro *nm (pez)* Couch's sea bream.

paica *nf Am fam* girl in her puberty.

paila *nf Am* (frying) pan.

pailón *nm Bol Ecuad Hond Geog* bowl.

paiño *nm Orn* patrel.

paipái *nm,* **paipay** *nm (pl paipáis)* large palm fan.

país *nm* country, land; **vino del p.,** local wine. ▪ **P. Vasco,** Basque Country.

paisaje *nm* landscape, scenery.

paisajista *nmf Arte* landscape painter.

paisanada *nf Arg* group of peasants.

paisanaje *nm* civil population.

paisano,-a I *adj* of the same country. **II** *nm, f* **1** *(compatriota)* fellow countryman *or* countrywoman, compatriot. **2** *(civil)* civilian; *(policía etc)* **ir de p.,** to be wearing civilian clothes; **en traje de p.,** in plain clothes.

Países Bajos *npl* **(los) P. B.,** the Netherlands, the Low Countries.

paja *nf* **1** straw; **techo de p.,** thatched roof; *fig* **hombre de p.,** stooge. **2** *fam fig (superfluo)* padding, waffle; *fig* **meter p.,** to waffle; *fig* **no te enfades por un quítame allá esas pajas,** don't make a mountain out of a molehill. **3** *vulg (masturbación)* wank; **hacerse una p.,** to wank.

pajar *nm (almacén)* straw loft; *(en el exterior)* straw rick.

pájara *nf* **1** *(cometa)* kite. **2** *(pajarita)* paper bird. **3** *fam (desfallecimiento)* blackout. **4** *fam pey (mujer)* **es una p. de mucho cuidado,** she's a crafty old devil.

pajarear I *vi Méx (fijar atención)* to watch with interest. **II** *vtr Am (ahuyentar pájaros)* to shoo, put to flight.

pajarera *nf* aviary.

pajarería *nf* **1** *(tienda)* pet shop. **2** *(pájaros)* flock *or* flight of birds.

pajarero,-a I *adj* **1** *Orn* of *or* relating to birds. **2** *fam (persona)* chirpy, merry; *(color)* gaudy, loud. **II** *nm, f* **1** *(vendedor)* bird dealer. **2** *(cazador)* bird catcher.

pajarita *nf* **1** *(prenda)* bow tie. **2** *(de papel)* paper bird.

pájaro *nm* **1** *Orn* bird; **a vista de p.,** bird's-eye view; *fig* **matar dos pájaros de un tiro,** to kill two birds with one stone; *fig* **tener la cabeza llena de pájaros,** to be scatterbrained; *prov* **más vale p. en mano que ciento volando,** a bird in the hand is worth two in the bush. ▪ **p. carpintero,** woodpecker; **p. mosca,** hummingbird. **2** *fam fig (hombre)* chap; *(astuto)* sly person, slyboots *sing*; **p. de cuenta,** big shot. **3** *pájaros, Arg* daft ideas.

pajarraco *nm pey* **1** *Orn* ugly bird. **2** *fig (astuto)* slyboots *sing*.

paje *nm* page; *Náut* cabin boy.

pajel *nm (pez)* pandora.

pajizo,-a *adj* **1** *(de paja)* (made of) straw. **2** *(de color de paja)* straw-coloured, *US* straw-colored.

pajolero,-a *adj fam* bloody, damn.

pajón,-ona *adj Méx* curly.

pajuate *adj Arg (persona)* silly.

pajuerano,-a *nm, f Arg Bol Urug* country bumkin.

pajuyé *nm Culin* banana preserve.

Pakistán *n* Pakistán

pakistaní *adj & nmf* Pakistani.

pala *nf* **1** shovel; *(mecánica)* power shovel; *(de jardinero)* spade; *(recogedor)* dustpan; *(de cocina)* slice; **p. para pescado,** fish slice. **2** *Dep (de pinpong, frontón)* bat. **3** *(de remo, hélice, etc)* blade. **4** *(de zapato)* upper. **5** *fam fig* skill; *pey* cunning; **tiene buena p.,** he is very skilful.

palabra *nf* **1** word; **de p.,** by word of mouth; **dirigir la p. a algn,** to address sb; **juego de palabras,** pun; **según las palabras de ...,** according to ...; **tener unas palabras con algn,** to have a few words with sb; *fig* **a la primera p.,** very soon; *fig* **comerse las palabras,** to swallow one's words; *fig* **decir la última p.,** to have the last word; *fig* **dejar a algn con la p. en la boca,** to cut sb off; *fig* **ser de pocas palabras,** to be a man *or* woman of few words, not be very talkative; *fig* **Teresa vio de qué iba el asunto a la primera p.,** Teresa knew immediately which way the wind was blowing; *fam fig* **ni p. de esto a nadie,** don't say a thing to anybody. ▪ **p. clave,** key word; **palabras mayores,** *(insultos)* swearwords; *(de importancia)* big talk *sing*. **2** *(habla)* speech; **el don de la p.,** the faculty of speech. **3** *(promesa)* word; **cogerle la p. a algn,** to take sb at his word; **faltar a la p.,** to break one's word; **hombre de p.,** man of his word; **p. de honor,** word of honour; **tener p.,** to keep one's word. **4** *(lengua)* language; **una mujer de p. clara,** a woman who expresses herself clearly. **5** *(turno para hablar)* right to speak; **dar** *or* **conceder la p. a algn,** to give the floor to sb; **tener la p.,** to have the floor.

palabrear *vtr Am* to promise to marry.

palabreja *nf* strange *or* difficult word.

palabrería *nf* palaver.

palabrota *nf* swearword; **decir palabrotas,** to swear.

palacete *nm Arquit* small palace, mansion.

palacio *nm (grande)* palace; *(pequeño)* mansion; **P. de Justicia,** Law Courts; *fig* **las cosas de p. van despacio,** it all takes time.

palada *nf* **1** *(paletada)* shovelful. **2** *(de remo)* stroke.

paladar *nm* **1** *Anat* palate. **2** *(sabor)* taste. **3** *fig (sensibilidad)* palate.

paladear *vtr* to savour, *US* savor, relish.

paladeo *nm* savouring, *US* savoring, relishing.

paladín *nm lit* Champion; *Hist* paladin.

paladino,-a *adj* obvious, public.

palafito *nm Arquit* lake dwelling.

palafrén *nm lit* palfrey.

palafrenero *nm* groom.

palanca *nf* **1** *Téc* lever; **hacer p.,** to (act as a) lever. **2** *(manecilla)* handle, stick. ■ *Aut* **p. de cambio,** gear lever, gearstick, *US* gearshift; **p. de mando,** control lever. **3** *fig (influencia)* leverage, influence, pull. **4** *Dep (trampolín)* diving board.

palangana I *nf* **1** washbasin. **2** *Am (fuente)* serving dish, platter. **II** *nm Am (descarado)* fresh or forward man.

palangre *nm Pesca* boulter.

palanqueta *nf* crowbar.

palastro *nm (de cerradura)* plate.

palatal *adj & nf Anat Ling* palatal.

palatino,-a[1] *adj (palatal)* palatal.

palatino,-a[2] *adj (palaciego)* palatine, palace, court.

palco *nm Teat* **1** *(asiento)* box. **2** **p. escénico,** stage.

palenque *nm* **1** *(empalizada)* palisade. **2** *fig (palestra)* arena. **3** *Am (estaca)* tethering or hitching post.

palentino,-a I *adj of or* from Palencia. **II** *nm, f* native or inhabitant of Palencia.

paleografía *nf* palaeography, paleography.

paleolítico *adj* palaeolithic, paleolithic.

paleontología *nf* palaeontology, paleontology.

Palestina *n* Palestine.

palestino,-a *adj & nm, f* Palestinian.

palestra *nf* arena; *fig* **salir** *or* **saltar a la p.,** to enter the fray, take the field.

paleta *nf* **1** *(herramienta) (pala)* small shovel; *(de albañil)* trowel. **2** *Culin (espátula)* slice. **3** *Arte (de pintor)* palette. **4** *Téc (de hélice, ventilador)* blade; *(molino)* wind vane. **5** *Anat* shoulder blade. **6** *Dep (de cricket, pingpong)* bat. **7** *CAm (caramelo)* lollipop; *(helado)* ice lolly, lolly.

paletada *nf (de pala)* shovelful; *(de paleta de albañil)* trowelful.

paletilla *nf* **1** *Anat* shoulder blade. **2** *Culin* shoulder; **p. de cordero,** shoulder of lamb.

paleto,-a I *adj fam pey* unsophisticated, boorish, **II** *nm, f fam pey* country bumpkin, yokel, boor. **III** *nm Zool* fallow deer.

paliacate *nm Méx* big bright scarf.

paliar *vtr* to alleviate, palliate.

paliativo,-a *adj & nm* palliative.

palidecer *vi* **1** *(persona)* to turn pale. **2** *fig (colores)* to fade; *(luz)* to grow dim. **3** *fig (disminuir)* to diminish, be on the wane.

palidez *nf* paleness, pallor.

pálido,-a *adj* pale, pallid; **ponerse** *or* **volverse p.,** to turn pale.

palillero *nm* toothpick case.

palillo *nm* **1** *(mondadientes)* toothpick; **palillos chinos,** chopsticks; *fam* **está como un p.,** he's as thin as a rake. **2** *(de hacer punto)* knitting needle. **3** *Mús* drumstick. **4** *Taur fam* banderilla.

palinodia *nf* retraction, recantation; **cantar la p.,** to recant.

palio *nm* **1** canopy; *fig* **recibir a algn bajo p.,** to give sb a royal welcome. **2** *Rel* pallium.

palique *nm fam* chat, small talk; **estar de p.,** to have a chat.

palisandro *nm Bot* rosewood.

palitoque *nm,* **palitroque** *nm* **1** *Taur* banderilla. **2** *Am (bolos)* skittles *pl*, *US* bowling.

paliza *nf* **1** *(zurra)* thrashing, beating; **darle a algn una p.,** to beat sb up. **2** *(derrota)* beating; **¡menuda p. os dimos!,** we thrashed you! **2** *fam (cosa pesada)* bore, pain (in the neck); **dar la p. a algn,** to bore or annoy sb; **darse una p.,** to wear oneself out; **el viaje fue una p.,** the journey was a drag; **¡qué p. de tío!,** what a boring bloke!

palma *nf* **1** *Anat* palm; *fig* **conocer algo/a algn como la p. de la mano,** to know sth/sb like the back of one's hand. **2** *Bot* palm tree; *fig* **llevarse la p.,** to win, triumph; *irón* to take the biscuit. **3** *(de caballerías)* sole. **4** **palmas,** *(palmadas)* clapping *sing*; *(aplauso)* applause *sing*; **batir palmas,** to ctap, applaud.

palmada *nf* **1** *(golpe)* slap; **dar palmadas a algn en la espalda,** to give sb a slap on the back. **2** *(aplauso)* applause, clapping.

palmar[1] *nm* palm grove.

palmar[2] *vi fam* **palmarla,** to snuff it, kick it.

palmarés *nm* **1** *(historial)* service record. **2** *(vencedores)* list of winners.

palmario,-a *adj* obvious, evident.

palmatoria *nf* candlestick.

palmear I *vi* to applaud, clap. **II** *vtr (espalda etc)* to tap.

palmera *nf Bot* palm tree.

palmeral *nm Bot* palm grove.

palmero,-a I *adj of or* from La Palma. **II** *nm, f* native or inhabitant of La Palma.

palmesano,-a I *adj of or* from Palma de Mallorca. **II** *nm, f* native or inhabitant of Palma de Mallorca.

palmeta *nf* cane; **el maestro le castigó con la p.,** the teacher caned him.

palmetazo *nm* caning.

palmípedo,-a I *nm, f Orn* web-footed bird. **II** *adj* web-footed.

palmito *nm* **1** *Bot* palmetto. **2** *Culin* palm heart.

palmo *nm (medida)* span; **un p. de tierra,** a tiny plot of land; *fig* **p. a p.,** inch by inch; *fam fig* **con un p. de lengua fuera,** out of breath; *fam fig* **dejar (a algn) con un p. de narices,** to let (sb) down.

palmotear *vi* to clap.

palmoteo *nm* clapping.

palo *nm* **1** stick; *(vara)* rod; *(pértiga)* pole; *(de escoba)* broomstick; *fig* **a p. seco,** on its own; *fig* **nos bebimos el vodka a p. seco,** we drank the vodka neat; *prov* **de tal p. tal astilla,** like father, like son. **2** *(golpe)* blow; **dar palos,** to hit, strike a blow; *fig* **dar un p. a algn,** to play a dirty trick on sb; *fig* **la crítica le dio un buen p.,** the critics slated him; *fig* **echar a algn a palos,** to throw or kick sb out; *fig* **p. de ciego,** shot in the dark; *fig* **dar palos de ciego,** to grope about in the dark. **3** *(madera)* wood; **cuchara de p.,** wooden spoon. **4** *Náut (mástil)* mast. ■ **p. mayor,** mainmast. **5** *Golf* club. **6** *(trazo de letra)* stroke. **7** *Naipes* suit. **8** *Dep (de portería)* crossbar, goal post.

paloma *nf* **1** *Orn* pigeon; dove; **p. de la paz,** dove of peace. ■ **p. mensajera,** homing or carrier pigeon; **p. torcaz,** wood-pigeon; **p. zurita,** stock dove. **2** *fig (persona)* dove, lamb. **3** **palomas,** *(olas)* white horses.

palomar *nm* pigeon house, dovecote.

palometa *nf (pez)* Ray's bream.

palomilla *nf* **1** *Ent* grain moth. **2** *(tuerca)* wing or butterfly nut. **3** *Am fam (plebe)* mob, gang. **4** **palomillas,** *(olas)* white horses.

palomino *nm* **1** *Orn* young pigeon, young dove. **2** *(mancha)* pigeon droppings *pl*.

palomita *nf fam* **palomitas de maíz,** popcorn *sing*.

palomo *nm* **1** *Orn* cock pigeon. **2** *Am Zool* white horse.

palotada *nf* stroke with a drumstick; *fam* **no dar p.,** not to do *or* say anything right.

palote *nm* **1** stick; *Mús* drumstick. **2** *(trazo)* pothook; downstroke. **3** *Arg Cuba Culin* rolling pin.

palpable *adj* palpable, concrete.

palpación *nf Med* palpation.

palpar *vtr* to touch, feel; *Med* to palpate; *fig* **p. la realidad,** to be in touch with reality.

palpitación *nf* palpitation, throbbing.

palpitante *adj* palpitating, throbbing; *fig* **una cuestión p.,** a life issue.

palpitar *vi* to palpitate, throb; *fig* **en sus palabras palpita el rencor,** resentment shows through his words.

pálpito *nm fam* hunch, presentiment.

palúdico,-a *Med adj* malarial; **fiebre palúdica,** malaria.

paludismo *nm Med* malaria.

palurdo,-a **I** *adj* uncouth, boorish. **II** *nm, f pey* boor, country bumpkin, hick.

palustre *adj Geog* marshy, boggy.

pambazo *nm Méx Culin* type of bread roll.

pambiche *nm Am* light fabric.

pamela *nf* **1** *(prenda)* broad-brimmed hat. **2** *Arg* dandy.

pampa *nf* **1** *Geog* pampa, pampas *pl.* **2** *SAm (caballo, vaca)* animal with a white head and a dark body. **3** *Arg (indígena)* pampean Indian. **4** *(negocio)* dishonest.

pámpano *nm Bot* vine shoot *or* tendril.

pampeano,-a *adj SAm* of *or* from the pampa, pampean.

pampero,-a *Am* **I** *adj* of *or* from the pampa, pampean. **II** *nm Meteor* strong wind over the pampas from the Andes.

pampirolada *nf* **1** *Culin* garlic and bread sauce. **2** *fam (tontería)* silly thing, nonsense.

pamplina *nf* **1** *(gen pl) (tontería)* nonsense; **¡déjate de pamplinas!,** stop that nonsense! **2** *Bot* chick weed.

pamplinero,-a *adj,* **pamplinoso** *adj* silly, foolish.

pamplonés,-esa **I** *adj* of *or* from Pamplona. **II** *nm,f* native *or* inhabitant of Pamplona.

pamplonica *adj* of *or* from Pamplona.

pan *nm* **1** bread; **barra de p.,** French bread; **p. con mantequilla,** bread and butter; **p. tierno/duro,** fresh/stale bread; *fig* **llamar al p. p. y al vino vino,** to call a spade a spade; *fam fig* **con su p. se lo coma,** let him stew in his own juice; *fam fig* **contigo p. y cebolla,** love on a shoestring; *fam fig* **es p. comido,** it's a piece of cake; *fam fig* **ser bueno como un pedazo de p.** *or* **más bueno que el p.,** to be as good as gold, be a treasure. ■ **p. ácimo,** unleavened bread; **p. de molde,** loaf of bread; **p. integral,** wholemeal *or* wholewheat bread; **p. rallado,** breadcrumbs *pl.* **2** *fig (alimento)* bread, food; **el p. nuestro de cada día,** our daily bread; **ganarse el p.,** to make *or* earn a living. **3** *(metal)* leaf; **p. de oro,** gold leaf.

pana *nf Tex* corduroy; **p. lisa,** velvet.

panacea *nf* panacea.

panadería *nf* baker's (shop), bakery.

panadero,-a *nm,f* baker.

panadizo *nm Med* whitlow.

panal *nm* honeycomb.

Panamá *n* Panama.

panamá *nm (pl panamaes)* **1** *(prenda)* Panama hat. **2** *Am* shady business, racket.

panameño,-a *adj & nm,f* Panamanian.

pancarta *nf* placard; *(en la calle)* banner.

páncreas *nm inv Anat* pancreas.

panda[1] *nm Zool* panda.

panda[2] *nf (amigos, gente)* group; *pey* gang, crowd.

pandear I *vi* to bend; *(apandar)* to sag. **II pandearse** *vr* to bend; *(apandarse)* to sag.

pandeo *nm* bending; *(apandar)* sagging.

pandereta *nf Mús* tambourine.

pandero *nm Mús* large tambourine.

pandilla *nf fam* véase **panda**[2].

pando,-a *adj* **1** sagging; *(pared)* not straight; *(viga)* warped. **2** *fig (lento)* slow. **3** *Méx (borracho)* drunk.

panecillo *nm* bread roll.

panegírico,-a *lit* **I** *adj* panegyric, panegyrical, eulogistic. **II** *nm* panegyric, eulogy.

panel *nm* panel.

panela *nf Am* brown sugar loaf.

panera *nf* breadbasket.

pánfilo,-a *adj fam* **1** *(lento)* slow, indolent. **2** *(bobo)* silly, stupid; *(crédulo)* gullible.

panfletario,-a *adj* propagandist.

panfletista *nmf* lampoonist, pamphleteer.

panfleto *nm* lampoon, political pamphlet.

panga *nf Náut (lancha)* launch; *(bote)* barge.

pánico *nm* panic; **presa del p.,** panic-stricken; **sembrar el p.,** to cause panic; *fam fig* **de p.,** *(estupendo)* great, terrific; *(terrible)* terrible, awful.

paniego,-a *adj Agr* wheat-producing.

panificación *nf* bread making.

panificadora *nf* (industrial) bakery.

panificar *vtr* to make bread.

panino *nm Méx* **1** *(enjambre)* swarm of wasps. **2** *(conjunto)* set.

panizo *nm Bot* millet; maize.

panocha *nf* **1** *Bot* corncob; *(trigo etc)* ear. **2** *Am Culin* maize cake.

panoja *nf Bot* corncob; *(trigo etc)* ear.

panoli *adj fam* gullible, idiot.

panoplia *nf* **1** *(colección)* panoply. **2** *(armadura)* suit of armour *or* US armor.

panorama *nm* **1** *(vista)* panorama, view. **2** *fig* panorama; **un negro p.,** a gloomy outlook.

panorámica *nf Cin TV* panorama.

panorámico,-a *adj* panoramic.

panqueque *nm Am Culin* pancake.

pantagruélico,-a *adj* gargantuan.

pantaletas *nfpl Am* panties.

pantalón *nm (gen pl)* **1** trousers *pl; fam fig* **bajarse los pantalones,** to give in; *fam fig* **llevar los pantalones,** to wear the trousers. ■ **p. bombacho,** cossack trousers; **p. corto,** *(de niño)* short trousers; *Dep* shorts; **p. vaquero,** jeans. **2** *(braga)* panties *pl,* knickers *pl,* US step-ins *pl.*

pantalonero,-a *nm,f* trouser maker.

pantalla *nf* **1** *Cin TV Inform* screen; **la pequeña p.,** the small screen; **llevar un libro a la p.,** to make a book into a film; **p. de radar,** radar screen. **2** *(de lámpara)* shade. **3** *(de chimenea)* fireguard. **4** *fig (tapadera)* cover, front; **servir de p.,** to act as a decoy. **5** *Arg (cartelera)* poster, notice.

pantano *nm Geog* **1** *(natural)* marsh, bog. **2** *(artificial)* reservoir.

pantanoso,-a *adj* **1** *Geog* marshy, boggy. **2** *fig (dificultoso)* thorny, difficult.

panteísmo *nm Filos* pantheism.

panteón *nm* **1** *Arquit (tumba)* pantheon, mausoleum. ■ **p. familiar,** family vault. **2** *Am (cementerio)* cemetery.

pantera *nf Zool* panther.

pantomima *nf* **1** *Teat* pantomime, mime. **2** *pey (farsa)* farce.

pantomino *nm* pantomime, mime.

pantorrilla *nf Anat* calf.

pantufla *nf*, **pantuflo** *nm* (*prenda*) stipper.

panty *nm* (*prenda*) (pair of) tights *pl*.

panza *nf* **1** *fam* belly, paunch. **2** (*de vasija*) belly. **3** *Anat Zool* belly.

panzada *nf* **1** (*en el agua*) belly flop. **2** *fam* (*hartazgo*) bellyful.

panzudo,-a *adj* potbellied, paunchy.

pañal *nm* **1** nappy, *US* diaper; **un niño de pañales**, a baby in nappies; *fig* **estar en pañales**, to be wet behind the ears. **2** *fig* (*origen*) origin, lineage; **ser de humildes pañales**, to come from a humble background. **3** *pañales*, (*ropa*) baby clothes.

pañería *nf* **1** (*tienda*) draper's shop. **2** (*persona*) draper.

paño *nm* **1** cloth material; (*de lana*) woollen *or US* woolen cloth; (*para polvo*) duster, rag; (*de cocina*) dishcloth; **traje de p.**, woollen suit; *fig* **conocerse el p.**, to know one's stuff; *fig* **paños calientes**, half measures; *fig* **ser el p. de lágrimas de algn**, to give sb a shoulder to cry on; *fam fig* **ser del mismo p.**, to be two of a kind. **2** **paños**, (*ropa*) clothes; **en p. menores**, in one's underclothes. **3** (*de pared*) wall, panel. **4** (*de un cristal, vidrio*) mist, haze. **5** *Arte* drapery. **6** *Teat* **al p.**, offstage. **7** *Am* (*terreno*) plot of land.

pañol *nm* *Náut* storeroom.

pañoleta *nf* **1** shawl. **2** *Taur* bullfighter's tie

pañuelo *nm* (*para la nariz*) handkerchief; (*para los hombros*) shawl; *fig* **el mundo es un p.**, it's a small world.

papa¹ *nm* **1** *Rel* pope. **2** *fam* (*papá*) dad, daddy.

papa² **I** *adj inv Arg Chi* (*bueno*) excellent, good. **II** *nf* **1** *Am* potato. **2** *fam* **no saber ni p. (de algo)**, not to have the faintest idea (about sth).

papá *nm* (*pl* **papás**) *fam* dad, daddy.

papacho *nm* *Méx* caress, pat.

papada *nf* *Anat* double chin.

papado *nm* *Rel* papacy.

papagayo *nm* *Orn* parrot.

papal *adj Rel* papal.

papalón,-ona *adj Méx* idle, lazy.

papamoscas *nm inv Orn* flycatcher. ■ **p. cerrojillo**, pied flycatcher; **p. gris**, spotted flycatcher.

papanatas *nmf inv* sucker, twit.

paparrucha *nf*, **paparruchada** *nf fam* **1** (*tontería*) (piece of) nonsense. **2** (*obra insubstancial*) botch (up).

papaya *nf* papaya *or* papaw fruit.

papayo *nm* *Bot* papaya *or* papaw tree.

papear *vi* **1** (*balbucir*) to stammer, stutter. **2** *arg* (*comer*) to scoff, stuff oneself.

papel *nm* **1** paper; **p. cuadriculado**, squared paper; **p. de música**, music score (paper); **p. higiénico**, toilet paper. ■ **p. carbón**, carbon paper; **p. cebolla**, onionskin; **p. de arroz**, rice paper; **p. de barbas**, bloom; **p. de carta**, writing paper, stationery; **p. de China**, India paper; **p. de estaño** *or* **de plata**, aluminium *or* tin foil; **p. de estraza**, brown paper; **p. de fumar**, cigarette paper; **p. de lija**, sandpaper; **p. de seda**, silk paper; **p. pintado**, wallpaper; **p. secante**, blotting paper. **2** (*hoja*) piece *or* sheet of paper; **hagamos números sobre el p.**, let's work it out on paper. **3** (*carta, credencial*) document. **4** *Fin* **p. moneda**, paper money, banknotes *pl*; **p. de pagos**, stamped paper. **5** *Cine Teat* (*carácter*) role, part; **esta actriz interpretó el p. de Julieta**, this actress played the part of Juliet; *fig* **el p. de la oposición en la política actual**, the role of the opposition in today's politics; *fig* **María hizo un buen p. en el examen oral**, Maria did well in the oral exam. **6** **papeles**, *Admin* documents, identification papers.

papela *nf arg* identity card.

papeleo *nm fam* paperwork; **estoy con el p. de la matriculación**, I'm going through the registration formalities.

papelera *nf* (*despacho*) wastepaper basket; (*calle*) litter bin.

papelería *nf* **1** (*tienda*) stationer's. **2** (*material*) stationery. **3** (*papeles*) sheaf of papers.

papelero,-a *adj* paper; **la industria papelera**, the paper industry.

papeleta *nf* **1** (*de rifa, empeño*) ticket; (*de votación*) ballot paper; (*de examen*) (*tema*) exam paper; (*resultados*) report. **2** *fam* (*dificultad*) tricky problem, difficult job; (*engorro*) drag; **¡menuda p.!**, what an awful situation to be in!

papelón *nm fam* **1** (*persona*) show-off. **2** (*acto*) ridiculous performance; **¡vaya p. me has hecho hacer!**, you made me look really silly!

papelote *nm pey* worthless document; useless piece of paper.

papeo *nm arg* grub.

paperas *nfpl Med* mumps.

papila *nf Anat* papilla.

papilla *nf* pap, mush; (*de niños*) baby food; *fam* **echar la primera p.**, to be as sick as a dog; *fam* **estar hecho p.**, to be shattered; *fam* **hacer p. a algn**, to make mincemeat of sb.

papiro *nm* papyrus.

papirotazo *nm*, **papirote** *nm* flick.

papirusa *nf Arg* attractive woman.

papisa *nf Rel* female pope.

papista *nmf* papist; **ser más p. que el papa**, to out-Herod Herod.

papo¹ *nm* **1** (*papada*) double chin. **2** (*bocio*) goitre. **3** *Orn* (*buche*) crop.

papo,-a² *adj CAm* silly, stupid.

papú *adj & nmf* (*pl* **papúes**) Papuan.

Papúa Nueva Guinea *n* Papua New Guinea.

paquebote *nm* (*pl* **paquebotes**) *Náut* packet boat.

paquete *nm* **1** (*caja*) packet; (*grande*) parcel, package; **un p. de cigarrillos/galletas**, a packet of cigarettes/biscuits; *fam fig* **meter un p. a algn**, to punish sb severely. ■ **p. postal**, parcel. **2** (*conjunto*) set, package; **el p. de medidas económicas**, packet of financial measures; *Fin* **p. de acciones**, share package. **3** *fam* (*en moto*) passenger; **ir de p.**, to ride pillion. **4** *fam* (*persona*) clumsy; **¡qué p. de tío!**, what a bore! **5** *Méx* (*asunto difícil*) tough job.

paquetería *nf* **1** packaging. **2** *Arg Par Urug* (*en el vestir, decoración*) elegance. **3** *Arg* (*mercería*) haberdashery.

paquidermo *nm Zool* pachyderm.

Paquistán *n* Pakistan.

paquistaní *adj & nmf* Pakistani.

par **I** *adj* **1** equal. **2** *Mat* even. **II** *nm* **1** (*pareja*) pair; (*dos*) couple; (*complemenatario*) peer; **un p. de terrones**, a couple of lumps, **un p. de zapatos/guantes**, a pair of shoes/gloves. **2** *Mat* even number; **pares y nones**, odds and evens. **3** (*noble*) peer. **4** (*locuciones*) **a la p.**, (*juntos*) together; (*al mismo tiempo*) at the same time; *Fin* par value; **a la p. que ...**, as well as ...; **de p. en p.**, wide open; *fig* **con el corazón abierto de p. en p.**, with open arms; *fig* **sin p.**, matchless.

para *prep* **1** (*objeto indirecto*) for, to; **importante p. nosotros**, important to us; **p. ti**, for you. **2** (*dirección*) to, towards; **p. arriba**, upwards; **p. delante y p. detrás**, backwards and forwards; **salió p. casa**, he set off for home. **3** (*finalidad*) to, in order to; **bueno p. la salud**, good for your health; **p. eso no hace falta que venga**, there's no need to come; **¿p. qué?**, what for?; **¿p. qué lo quieres?**, what do you want it for?; **p. que te compres un regalo**, for you to get a present for yourself; **p. terminar antes**, as to *or* in order to finish earlier. **4** (*motivo*) **p. que no te enfadaras**, so as not to annoy you; **¿p. qué has venido?**, why did you come? **5** (*tiempo*) by, for; **hay p. rato**, it will take some time before it's over; **¿p. cuánto tienes?**, (*tardar*) how long will you be?; (*durar*) how long will it last you?; **p. entonces**, by then; **p. la semana próxima**, (by) next week; **p. Semana Santa**, at Easter. **6** (*comparación*) for, considering; **amable p. con todos**, kind to everyone; **p. esta época del año**, for this time of the year; **p. ser la primera vez**, considering it's the first time. **7** *(aptitud)* as; **Pedro vale p. arquitecto,** Pedro would make a good architect. **8** *(locuciones)* **dar p.,** to be sufficient; **la comida da p. todos,** there is enough food for everybody; **p. sí,** to *or* for oneself; **hacer algo p. sí,** to do sth for oneself; **leer un libro p. sí,** to read a book to oneself; **ir p. viejo,** to be getting old; **no es p. tanto,** no need to make such a fuss; **no estoy p. nadie,** I don't want to see anybody; **p. eso,** for that reason; **p. mí, tenía que haberlo hecho,** I think he should have done it.

parabién *nm (pl parabienes)* congratulations *pl;* **dar el p. a algn,** to congratulate sb.

parábola *nf* **1** *Geom* parabola. **2** *Rel* parable.

parabólico,-a *adj* parabolic; *TV* **antena parabólica,** satellite dish, parabolic aerial.

parabrisas *nm inv Aut* windscreen, *US* windshield.

paraca[1] *nf Am* wind from the Pacific.

paraca[2] *nm arg* para, parachutist.

paracaídas *nm inv* parachute; **lanzar(se)** *or* **tirar(se) en p.,** to parachute.

paracaidismo *nm* **1** parachuting. **2** *Méx* squatting.

paracaidista *nmf Dep* parachutist; *Mil* paratrooper.

parachoques *nm inv* **1** *Aut* bumper, *US* fender. **2** *Ferroc* buffer.

parada[1] *nf* **1** stop; **hacer p. en ...,** to stop at ...; **p. en seco,** dead stop. ■ **p. de autobús,** bus stop; **p. de taxis,** taxi stand *or* rank; **p. discrecional,** request stop. **2** *Ftb* save, catch, stop.

parada[2] *nf Am Mil* parade.

paradero *nm* **1** *(lugar)* whereabouts *pl;* **averiguar el p. de algn,** to locate sb; **p. desconocido,** whereabouts unknown. **2** *(desenlace)* end; **tener mal p.,** to come to a sticky end. **3** *Am (apeadero) (de tren)* halt; *(de autobús)* bus stop.

paradisíaco,-a *adj* heavenly.

parado,-a I *pp de* **parar. II** *adj* **1** stopped, stationary; *(quieto)* still; *(máquina)* at rest; *(fábrica)* at a standstill; **se quedó p.,** he remained motionless; *fig* **salir bien/mal p.,** to come off well/badly. **2** *(sin trabajo)* unemployed, out of work. **3** *fig (lento, inactivo)* slow; *(desconcertado)* confused, surprised; **no es que sea tonto, sólo un poco p.,** he's not silly, just little bit too slow. **4** *Am (de pie)* standing. **III** *nm,f* unemployed person; *(despedido)* laid off; **los parados,** the unemployed *pl.*

paradoja *nf* paradox.

paradójico,-a *adj* paradoxical.

parador *nm* roadside inn; **p. nacional** *or* **de turismo,** staterun hotel.

paraestatal *adj Pol* semiofficial.

parafernalia *nf* paraphernalia *pl.*

parafina *nf Quím* paraffin.

parafrasear *vtr* to paraphrase.

paráfrasis *nf inv* paraphrase.

paraguas *nm inv* **1** umbrella. **2** *arg* French letter.

Paraguay *n* Paraguay.

paraguaya *nf Bot* type of peach.

paraguayo,-a *adj & nm,f* Paraguayan.

paragüero *nm* umbrella stand.

paraíso *nm* paradise; **p. terrenal,** heaven on earth. ■ *Fin* **p. fiscal,** tax haven. **2** *Teat* gods *pl,* gallery.

paraje *nm* spot, place.

paralela *nf* **1** *Geom* parallel (line). **2 paralelas,** *Gimn* parallel bars.

paralelismo *nm* parallelism; *fig* similarity.

paralelo,-a I *adj* parallel; *fig* **tu situación es paralela a la mía,** your position is similar to mine. **II** *nm* parallel; *Elec* **estar en p.,** to be in parallel. ◆ **paralelamente** *adv* parallel; *(comparablemente)* comparably.

paralelogramo *nm Geom* parallelogram.

parálisis *nm inv Med* paralysis; **p. infantil,** poliomylitis.

paralítico,-a *adj & nm,f* paralytic.

paralización *nf* **1** *Med* paralysis. **2** *(detención)* halting, stopping.

paralizador,-a *adj,* **paralizante** *adj* paralysing.

paralizar I *vtr* to paralyse; *(circulación)* to stop; **tener una pierna paralizada,** to be paralysed in one leg. **II paralizarse** *vr* **1** to be paralysed. **2** *fig* to come to a standstill.

paramento *nm* **1** *(deoración)* decoration, adornment. **2** *Arqui* face, facing.

parámetro *nm Mat* parameter.

paramilitar *adj* paramilitary.

páramo *nm* **1** *Geog* bleak plain *or* plateau, moor. **2** *SAm (llovizna)* drizzle.

parangón *nm fml* comparison; **sin p.,** incomparable.

paraninfo *nm univ* assembly hall, auditorium.

paranoia *nf* paranoia.

paranoico,-a *adj & nm,f* paranoiac, paranoid.

parapetarse *vtr* **1** to take shelter *or* cover. **2** *fig* to take refuge.

parapeto *nm* **1** parapet. **2** *(de defensa)* barricade.

paraplejía *nf Med* paraplegia.

parapléjico,-a *adj & nm,f* paraplegic.

parar I *vtr* **1** to stop; *fam* **pararle los pies a algn,** to put sb in his *or* her place. **2** *(preparar)* to prepare, set; **p. una trampa,** to prepare *or* set a trap. **3** *Dep* to cut off, intercept; *(tiro)* to save; *Esgr* to parry. **II** *vi* **1** to stop; **p. de hacer algo,** to stop doing sth; **¡para de llorar!,** stop crying!; **sin p.,** nonstop, without stopping; *fam* **no p.,** to be always on the go. **2** *(alojarse)* to stay; **nunca he parado en este hotel,** I have never stayed at this hotel. **3** *(recaer)* to end up; **la casa paró en posesión de los nietos,** the grandchildren ended up inheriting the house. **4** *(darse por vencido)* to give up; **(ella) no paró hasta encontrarme,** she didn't give up until she found me. **5** *(llegar)* to lead; **¿adónde quieres ir a p.?,** what are you getting at?; **¿adónde vamos a ir a p.?,** what is the world coming to?; **fue a p. a la basura,** it ended up in the dustbin; **todo paró en nada,** it all came to nothing. **6** *CAm (enriquecerse)* to make money. **7** *fam (estar)* to be; **nunca paro en casa,** I'm never at home. **III pararse** *vr* **1** *(gen)* to stop; *(coche etc)* to come to a halt; **p. a pensar,** to stop to think; **p. en seco,** to stop dead, pull up sharply. **2** *Am (ponerse en pie)* to stand up. **3** *Arg (caer)* to fall down.

pararrayos *nm inv* lightning conductor, *US* lightning rod.

parasicología *nf* parapsychology.

parasicológico,-a *adj* parapsychological.

parasicólogo,-a *nm,f* parapsychologist.

parasitario,-a *adj* parasitic, parasitical.

parásito,-a I *adj* parasitic, parasitical. **II** *nm* **1** parasite; *fig* **es un p. que vive a costa de sus amigos,** he's a parasite who lives off his friends. **2 parásitos,** *Rad* statics *sing.*

parasol *nm* sunshade, parasol.

parcela *nf* **1** *(de tierra)* plot. **2** *fig (porción)* portion, share; **p. de poder,** share of power.

parcelación *nf* parcelling out, division into plots.

parcelar *vtr (tierra)* to parcel out.

parche *nm* **1** patch; *(para rueda, vestido)* **poner un p.,** to patch. **2** *(emplasto)* plaster. **3** *pey (chapuza)* botched up *or* slapdash job; **poner parches,** to paper over the cracks. **4** *fam* **¡ojo al p.!,** beware!, look out!

parchís *nm* ludo.

parcia *adj Méx* partnering.

parcial *adj* **1** *(no completo)* partial. **2** *(partidario)* biased. ◆ **parcialmente** *adv* partially, partly.

parcialidad *nf* **1** partiality. **2** *(prejuicio)* bias, prejudice.

parco,-a *adj* **1** *(moderado)* sparing, moderate; **p. en palabras,** reticent. **2** *(escaso)* scarce; *(comida)* frugal, scanty.

pardela *nf Orn* shearwater.

pardiez *interj desus* goodness me!, blimey!

pardilla *nf (pez)* roach, rudd.

pardillo,-a I *nm,f pey* yokel, bumpkin. II *nm Orn* linnet. ■ **p. sizerín**, redpoll.

pardo,-a *adj* brown; dark grey.

pardusco,-a *adj* brownish grey, dull coloured; *fig* drab.

parecer¹ *nm* 1 *(aspecto)* appearance. 2 *(opinión)* opinion; **cambiar** *or* **mudar de p.**, to change one's mind; **según su p.**, according to him.

parecer² I *vi* 1 to seem, look (like); **a lo que parece**, apparently; **así parece**, so it seems; **aunque no lo parezca**, incredible as it seems; **no parecía que fuera a nevar**, it didn't look as if it would snow; **parece difícil**, it seems *or* looks difficult; **parecía (de) cera**, it looked like wax; *(uso impers)* **parece que no arranca**, it looks as if it won't start; **parece mentira**, I can't believe it. 2 *(estar de acuerdo)* to agree; **como te parezca**, whatever you like; **¿te parece?**, is that okay with you?, what do you think? 3 *(opinar)* to think; **me parece bien/mal**, I think it's a good/bad idea; **me parece que sí/no**, I think/ don't think so; **¿qué te ha parecido?**, what did you think of it? II **parecerse** *vr* to be alike, look like; **¿en qué se parecen A y B?**, how are A and B alike?; **no se parecen**, they're not alike; **se parecen a su madre**, they look like their mother.

parecido,-a I *pp de* **parecer**. II *adj* 1 alike similar; **ambos son parecidos**, they're alike; **éste es muy p. al otro**, this looks very much like the other one. 2 **bien p.**, good looking. III *nm* likeness, resemblance; **tener p. con algn**, to bear a resemblance to sb.

pared *nf* 1 *Arquit* wall; *(montaña)* side; **vivir p. por medio**, to live next door; *fig* **entre cuatro paredes**, within four walls, confined; *fig* **las paredes oyen**, walls have ears; *fam fig* **subirse por las paredes**, to be seething (with anger). ■ **p. maestra**, main wall; **p. medianera**, party wall. 2 *Dep* one-two, wall pass.

paredón *nm* 1 thick wall. 2 *fam (de fusilamiento)* execution wall; *fig* **llevar a algn al p.**, to put sb up against the wall.

pareja *nf* 1 pair; **hacer p.**, to be two of a kind; **no encuentro la p. de este calcetín**, I can't find the other sock; **por parejas**, in pairs. 2 *(hombre y mujer)* couple; *(de baile, juegos)* partner; *(hijo e hija)* boy and girl; *(de la Guardia Civil)* pair of Civil Guards; **hacen buena p.**, they make a nice couple, they're well matched. 3 *(en póker)* pair; **doble p.**, two pairs. 4 *fig* **correr parejas** *or* **a las parejas**, *(venir juntos)* to come together; *(ser parecidos)* to be on a par.

parejero,-a I *adj* 1 *Am pey* hanger-on. 2 *Méx Ven (amigo)* friend. II *nm CAm Equit* good, fast racehorse.

parejo,-a *adj* 1 *(parecido)* equal, similar, alike; **por p.** *or* **un p.**, on a par. 2 *(al mismo nivel)* on the same level, even.

parentela *nf fam* relations *pl*, relatives *pl*.

parentesco *nm* relationship, kinship.

paréntesis *nm inv* 1 parenthesis, bracket; **abrir/cerrar p.**, to open/close brackets; **entre p.**, in parentheses *or* brackets. 2 *fig* break, interruption; *(digresión)* digression.

pareo¹ *nm (prenda)* pareo; *(de hombre)* loincloth; *(de mujer)* wraparound.

pareo² *nm (aparejamiento)* pairing, coupling.

parezco *indic pres véase* **parecer**.

pargo *nm véase* **pagro**.

paria *nmf* pariah.

parida *nf fam* silly thing; **decir paridas**, to talk nonsense; **hacer paridas**, to do really stupid things.

parido,-a I *pp de* **parir**. II *adj arg* **bien p.**, cool.

paridad *nf* 1 *(equivalencia)* equivalence, parity; *(semejanza)* similarity. 2 *Fin* parity (of exchange).

pariente,-a I *nmf* relative, relation. II *nm,f fam (esposo)* hubby, old man; *(esposa)* missus, wife.

parihuela *n* stretcher.

paripé *nm* pretentiousness; **hacer el p.**, to pretend, put on an act.

parir *vtr & vi* 1 to give birth (to). 2 *fig (crear)* to produce; **¿quién ha parido este plan?**, who's idea was it to do it like this? 3 *vulg* **poner a algn a p.**, *(ofender)* to piss sb off; *(insultar)* to give sb hell.

París *n* Paris.

parisino,-a *adj* Parisian.

paritario,-a *adj* joint; **comité p.**, joint committee.

parking *nm* car park, *US* parking lot.

parlamentario,-a I *adj* parliamentary. II *nm,f* member of parliament, MP, *US* congressman.

parlamento *nm* 1 *Parl* parliament. 2 *(discurso)* speech.

parlanchín,-ina I *adj fam* talkative, chatty. II *nm,f fam* chatterbox.

parlante *adj* I taking; **castellanoparlante**, Castilian speaking. II *nm f* speaker; **castellanoparlante**, Castilian speaker.

parlar *vi*, **parlotear** *vi* to chat, chatter.

parloteo *nm* prattle, chatter.

parmesano,-a I *adj & nm, f* Parmesan. II *nm Culin* **(queso) p.**, Parmesan cheese.

parné *nm arg* dough, cash.

paro *nm* 1 *(detención)* stop, stoppage, 2 *(desempleo)* unemployment, **estar en p.**, to be unemployed; **cobrar** *or* **vivir del p.**, to be on the dole; **p. forzoso**, forced unemployment. 3 *Ind (interrupción trabajo)* stoppage; **p. laboral**, industrial action; **p. técnico**, shutdown owing to technical problems.

parodia *n* parody.

parodiar *vtr* to parody.

paroxismo *nm* paroxysm.

parpadear *vi (ojos)* to blink, wink; *fig (luz)* to flicker; *(estrellas)* to twinkle.

parpadeo *nm (de ojos)* blinking; *fig (luz)* flickering; *(estrellas)* twinkling.

párpado *nm Anat* eyelid.

parque *nm* 1 park. ■ **p. de atracciones**, funfair; **p. nacional**, national park; **p. zoológico**, zoological garden, zoo. 2 *(de niños)* playground. 3 *(conjunto de vehículos)* car park; **p. de bomberos**, fire station. 4 *Mil* depot; **p. de artillería**, artillery stores *pl*.

parqué *nm Constr* parquet.

parquedad *nf* 1 *(moderación)* moderation. 2 *(escasez)* scantiness.

parqueo *nm Am (acto)* parking; *(sitio)* parking lot.

parquet *nm véase* **parqué**.

parquímetro *nm Aut* parking meter.

parra *nf* grapevine; *fam* **subirse a la p.**, to hit the roof.

parrafada *nf fam* 1 *(monólogo)* dreary monologue. 2 *(conversación)* chat; **echar una p.**, to have a chinwag.

párrafo *nm* paragraph.

parral *nm* vine arbour *or US* arbor.

parranda *nf fam* 1 *(juerga)* spree; **ir(se) de p.**, to go out on the town. 2 *Mús* group of singers *or* musícians.

parrandear *vi* to go out on the town.

parricida I *adj* parricidal. II *nmf* parricide.

parricidio *nm* parricide.

parrilla *nf* 1 *Culin* grill, gridiron; **carne/pescado a la p.**, grilled meat/fish. 2 *Téc* grate. 3 *Aut Dep* starting grid.

parrillada *nf Culin* mixed grill.

párroco I *adj* parish. II *nm* **(cura) p.**, parish priest.

parroquia *nf* 1 *Rel* parish; *(iglesia)* parish church. 2 *fam (clientela)* customers *pl*.

parroquial *adj* parochial, parish.

parroquiano,-a *nm,f* (regular) customer.

parsimonia *nf* 1 *(calma)* phlegm, calmness 2 *(moderación)* carefulness.

parsimonioso,-a *adj* **1** *(calmado)* unhurried, calm. **2** *(moderado)* careful, economical, sparing.

parte I *nf* **1** *(pedazo)* part; *Ling* **p. de la oración,** part of speech; **primera/última p.,** first/last part. **2** *(en una repartición)* share, portion; **quiero mi p.,** I want my share; **yo he hecho mi p.,** I've done my bit; *fig* **la p. del león,** the lion's share. **3** *(lugar)* place, spot; *(zona)* part, area; *(dirección)* way; **en esta p. del país,** in this part of the country; **en o por todas partes,** everywhere; **en otra p.,** somewhere else; **en una u otra p.,** somewhere or other; **se fue por otra p.,** he went a different or another way; *fig* **esta discusión no lleva a ninguna p.,** arguing like this won't get us anywhere. **4** *(de un diálogo, lucha, contrato)* party, part; *Jur* party; **ambas partes están de acuerdo,** both parties agree; **p. contraria,** opposing party; *fig* **ser juez y p.,** to be one's own judge and jury. **5** *(bando)* side; **¿de qué p. estás?,** which side are you on?; **ponerse de p. de,** to side with **6** *(parentesco)* side; **por p. de mi madre/padre,** on my mother's/father's side. **7** *Teat (papel)* part, role. **8 partes,** *euf (genitales)* private parts. **9** *(locuciones)* **a una y otra p.,** on both sides; **de mi o por mi p.,** as far as I am concerned; **de p. a p.,** from one side to the other; **de p. de ...,** on behalf of ...; **¿de p. de quién?,** your name, please?; *Tel* who's calling?; *Tel* **llamo de p. de tu tío,** I'm calling on your uncle's behalf; **en gran p.,** to a large extent; **en p.,** partly; **ir por partes,** to proceed step by step; **la mayor p.,** the majority; **llevar la mejor p.,** to have the advantage; **llevar la peor p.,** to be at a disadvantage; **llevarse la mejor p.,** to come off best; **poner de su p.,** to do one's best; **por otra p.,** on the other hand; **tomar p. en,** to take part in. II *nm (informe)* report; **p. médico,** medical bulletin or report; **p. metereológico,** weather forecast or report.

partición *nf (reparto)* division, sharing out; *(de herencia)* partition; *(de territorio)* partition.

participación *nf* **1** *(acto, actividad)* participation; *(pago)* contribution. **2** *Fin (intereses)* interest, investment; *(acción)* share, US stock; **p. en los beneficios,** profit-sharing. **3** *(en lotería)* part of a lottery ticket. **4** *(notificación)* notice, notification. ■ **p. de boda,** wedding invitation.

participante I *adj* participating. II *nmf* participant.

participar I *vi* **1** to take part, participate (**en,** in); **p. en la conversación,** to take part in the conversation; **p. en un concurso,** to enter a competition. **2** *Fin* to have a share. **3** *(compartir)* to share; **no participo de vuestro optimismo/vuestra opinión,** I don't share your optimism/view. II *vtr (notificar)* to notify.

partícipe I *adj* participating. II *nmf* participant; **hacer p. de algo,** *(notificar)* to inform about sth; *(compartir)* to share sth; *Com Fin* **ser partícipes en un negocio,** to be partners in business.

participio *nm Ling* participle.

partícula *nf* particle.

particular I *adj* **1** *(concreto)* particular; **en este caso p.,** in this particular case; **en p.,** in particular; **nada de p.,** nothing special. **2** *(no público)* private, personal; **clase/casa p.,** private class/home. **3** *(raro)* peculiar. II *nmf (individuo)* private individual. III *nm (asunto)* subject matter; **hablaremos sobre este p. más adelante,** we shall deal with this subject in due course. ◆ **particularmente** *adv* specially.

particularidad *nf* **1** *(aspecto)* particularity, aspect. **2** *(peculiaridad)* peculiarity.

particularizar I *vtr* **1** *(caracterizar)* to distinguish, characterize. **2** *(singularizar) (persona)* to single out. **3** *(detallar)* to give details about. II **particularizarse** *vr (caracterizarse)* to stand out; *(persona)* to distinguish oneself.

partida *nf* **1** *(salida)* departure. **2** *(remesa)* batch, consignment; *(pedido)* consignment. **3** *(juego)* game; **hacer o echar una p.,** to have a game; *fig* **jugar una mala p. a algn,** to play a dirty trick on sb. **4** *(personas) (banda)* party, gang; **p. de caza,** hunting party. **5** *Fin (entrada)* item; **contabilidad por p. doble,** double-entry

bookkeeping. **6** *Jur (certificado)* certificate; **p. de nacimiento,** birth certificate.

partidario,-a I *adj* supporting; **ser/no ser p. de algo,** to be for/against sth. II *nm, f* supporter, follower; **es p. del aborto,** he is in favour of abortion.

partidismo *nm* party spirit, bias.

partidista *adj* biased, partisan.

partido,-a I *pp de* **partir.** II *adj* split, divided. III *nm* **1** *Pol* party; **sistema de partidos,** party system. **2** *Dep* match, game. ■ **p. amistoso,** friendly game; **p. de vuelta,** return match. **3** *Jur (distrito)* district; **p. judicial,** administrative area. **4** *(provecho)* advantage; **sacar p. de,** to profit from. **5** *(resolución)* **tomar p. por,** to side with. **6** *(persona casadera)* **ser un buen p.,** to be a good catch, be eligible.

partir I *vtr* **1** *(dividir)* to split, divide; **pártelo en dos,** split it in two. **2** *(repartir)* to share out; *(distribuir)* distribute. **3** *(romper, cortar) (frutos secos)* to crack; *(madera)* to cut; *(pan)* to break; *fig* **me parte el corazón,** it breaks my heart; **partirle la cara a algn,** to smash sb's face in. **4** *fam (desbaratar)* to ruin, spoil; **p. a algn por la mitad,** to mess things up for sb. II *vi* **1** *(marcharse)* to leave, set out or off; **p. para o con rumbo a algún lugar,** to set off for somewhere. **2** *(fecha, antecedente)* **a p. de,** starting from; **a p. de ahora,** from now on; **a p. de hoy,** as of today; **si partimos de la base que,** if we assume that. III **partirse** *vr* to split (up), break (up); *fam* **p. de risa,** to split one's sides laughing.

partisano,-a *nm, f Pol Mil* partian.

partitivo,-a *adj & nm Ling* partitive.

partitura *nf Mús* score.

P.D. *abr de* **posdata,** postscript, P.S.

p.ej. *abr de* **por ejemplo,** for example.

parto *nm* **1** *(alumbramiento)* childbirth, delivery, labour, US labor; **estar de p.,** to be in labour; **p. sin dolor,** painless childbirth. **2** *fig* product, creation; **p. del ingenio,** brainchild.

parturienta I *adj (woman)* in labour or US labor, who has just given birth. II *nf* woman in labour or US labor, woman who has just given birth.

parva *nf* **1** *Agr (mies)* unthreshed corn. **2** *fig (montón)* heap, pile.

parvedad *nf* **1** *(pequeñez)* littleness, smallness. **2** *(escasez)* shortage, sparseness; **p. de medios,** limited or scant means *pl*.

parvo,-a *adj* I *(pequeño)* little, small. **2** *(escaso)* sparse.

parvulario *nm* nursery school, kindergarten.

párvulo,-a *nm, f* infant.

pasa *nf Culin* raisin; **p. de Corinto,** currant; *fam fig* **estar hecho una p.,** to be all shrivelled up.

pasable *adj* passable, tolerable. ◆ **pasablemente** *adv* passably, tolerably.

pasacalle *nm Mús* lively march.

pasada *nf* **1** *(paso)* passage, passing; *(con trapo)* rub, clean; **de p.,** in passing; **hacer una p./varias pasadas,** to pass once/several times; *fam* **dale otra p.,** give it another going or run over; *fam* **deberías dar otra p. con la plancha a estos pantalones,** you should give these trousers another run over with the iron. **2** *Cost* row of stitches. **3** *(jugarreta)* dirty trick; **hacer una (mala) p. (a algn),** to play a dirty trick (on sb). **4** *fam (exageración)* exaggeration; **eso es una p.,** that's a bit much. **5** *CAm (reprimenda)* reprimand.

pasadero,-a I *adj (pasable)* passable, tolerable. II *nm (piedra)* stepping stone.

pasadizo *nm* corridor, passage.

pasado,-a I *pp de* **pasar.** II *adj* **1** *(gen)* past; **los pasados días,** the past few days; *fam* **es p. (está),** let bygones be bygones. **2** *(último)* last; **el año/lunes p.,** last year/Monday. **3** *(anticuado)* dated, oldfashioned; **p. (de moda),** out of date or fashion. **4** *(estropeado) (flor)* faded, withered; *(alimento)* bad; *fig (noticia)* old hat. **5** *Culin (cocido)* cooked; **lo quiero muy p.,** I want it well done; **p. por agua,**

833

(huevo) boiled; *fig (sin sustancia)* insubstantial. **6** *(después)* after; **pasadas las dos,** after two; **p. mañana,** the day after tomorrow. **III** *nm* **1** *(gen)* past; *Ling* past (tense); **en el p.,** in the past; **tu p. no me importa,** I don't care about your background. **2 pasados,** ancestors.

pasador *nm* **1** *(colador)* colander; strainer. **2** *(pestillo)* bolt, fastener **3** *(prenda)* pin, clasp; *(de corbata)* tiepin; *(para el pelo)* (hair) slide, hairpin; *(para los puños)* cufflink.

pasaje *nm* **1** *(gen)* passage. **2** *(pasajeros)* passengers *pl.* **3** *Lit Mús (fragmento)* passage. **4** *(calle)* alley. **5** *Am (billete)* ticket.

pasajero,-a I *adj* passing, temporary; **aventura pasajera,** fling. **II** *nm,f* passenger.

pasamano *nm,* **pasamanos** *nm inv (barra)* handrail; *(de escalera)* banister, bannister.

pasamontañas *nm inv* Balaclava (hood).

pasante *nm (gen)* assistant; *Jur* clerk.

pasaporte *nm* passport; **hacerse** *or* **sacarse el p.,** to get one's passport; **renovarse el p.,** to renew one's passport; *fam* **dar (el) p. (a algn),** *(despedir)* to send (sb) packing; *(matar)* to bump (sb) off.

pasapurés *nm inv Culin* potato masher.

pasar I *vtr* **1** *(gen)* to pass; *(objeto)* to pass on, give, hand over; **pásame la sal,** pass (me) the salt. **2** *(recado, mensaje)* to give; *(página)* to turn. **3** *(trasladar)* to move; **hemos pasado la televisión al comedor,** we have moved the TV set to the dining room; **p. a** *or* **en limpio,** to make a clean copy of. **4** *(introducir)* to insert, put through; *(colar)* to put through; **p. la sopa por el ojo de una aguja,** to thread a needle; **p. la sopa por un colador,** to strain the soup. **5** *(cruzar)* to cross; *(barrera)* to pass through *or* over; *(límite)* to go beyond; **es imposible p. la frontera sin pasaporte,** one cannot cross the border without a passport. **6** *(padecer)* to suffer, endure; *(enfermedad)* to get over; **p. frío,** to be cold; **p. hambre,** to go hungry; *fam* **pasarlas canutas** *or* **moradas,** to go through hell, have a rough time. **7** *(tiempo)* to spend, pass; **pasamos una semana solos,** we spent a week on our own; **p. el rato,** to kill time; **pasarlo bien/mal,** to have a good/bad time. **8** *(perdonar)* to forgive, tolerate; *(omitir)* to overlook; **¡esto no hay quien lo pase!,** nobody could stand for this!; **p. por alto** *or* **por encima,** to miss; **pase por esta vez,** I'll let you off this time. **9** *(sobrepasar)* to go beyond, be over; *(aventajar)* to surpass, beat; **(ella) ha pasado los treinta,** she's over thirty; **su hermano ya le pasa 10 cm,** his brother is already 10 cm taller than him. **10** *Aut (adelantar)* to overtake, *US* pass. **11** *(deslizar)* to run; **le pasó la mano por el pelo,** he ran his fingers through his hair; **pásale un trapo,** wipe it with a cloth; **p. el cepillo por el pelo,** to pass a comb through one's hair. **12** *Educ (examen)* to pass. **13** *Cin (película)* to run, show. **II** *vi* **1** *(gen)* to pass, go by; **déjale pa,** let him by; **el tren pasa por Burgos,** the train goes via Burgos; **¿ha pasado el autobús?,** has the bus gone by?; **ha pasado un hombre,** a man has gone past; **pasa por casa mañana,** come round to my house tomorrow; **p. de A a B,** to go from A to B; **p. de largo,** to go by (without stopping); *fig* **aún podemos p. con menos,** we can still manage with less; *fig* **p. por encima de algn,** to walk all over sb; *fig* **p. por la cabeza** *or* **la imaginación,** to cross one's mind; *fig* **p. sin,** to do without; *fam* **ir pasando,** to manage, get by; *euf* **p. a mejor vida,** to pass away. **2** *(continuar)* **p. a,** to go on to; **p. a ser,** to become; **pasaron a discutir el siguiente punto,** they went on to discuss the next issue. **3** *(caber)* to go through; **no pasará por la puerta,** it won't go through the door. **4** *(entrar)* to come *or* go in; **hazle p.,** ask him to come in; **pase, por favor,** please come in. **5** *(cesar)* to come to an end; **no puede ir peor,** the worst is over. **6** *(ser aceptado)* to pass, be accepted; **puede p.,** it's OK, it'll pass. **7** *Naipes* to pass. **8** *(persona)* **p. por,** to be considered; **pasa por sabio,** he is considered to be a wise man; **se hace p. por abogado,** he passes himself off as a lawyer. **9** *(exceder)* **p. de,** to exceed, go beyond; **pasa de**

los cincuenta, he's over fifty; **pasan de cien,** there are more than a hundred of them; **p. de moda,** to go out of fashion; *fig* **p. de la raya,** to go too far, *fam* **p. de castaño oscuro,** to be too much. **10** *(tiempo)* to pass, go by; **¡cómo pasa el tiempo!,** how time passes! **11** *fam (no intervenir, no opinar)* to be indifferent **(de,** to), not take part **(de,** in), ignore; **(ella) pasa de estudiar,** she isn't into studying; **pasa de todo,** he doesn't give a damn; **yo paso,** count me out. **III** *v unipers (suceder)* to happen; **lo qe pasa es que ...,** the thing is that ...; **pase lo que pase,** whatever happens, come what may; **¿qué le ha pasado?,** what has happened to her?; **¿qué pasa aquí?,** what's going on here?; **¿qué te pasa?,** what's the matter?; **¿y qué pasa?,** so what?; *fam* **¿qué pasa,** how are you? **IV pasarse** *vr* **1** *(al enemigo)* to pass over **(a,** to). **2** *(acabarse)* **se te ha pasado la hora,** your time is over *or* up. **3** *(dejar escapar)* to miss; **se me pasó la ocasión,** I missed my chance *or* opportunity. **4** *(gastar tiempo)* to spend *or* pass time; **pasárselo bien/ mal,** to have a good/bad time; **pasárselo en grande,** to have a marvellous time; **se pasó la tarde durmiendo,** he slept all afternoon. **5** *(olvidar)* to forget; **se me pasó llamarle,** I forgot to call him up. **6** *(echarse a perder) (flores)* to wither; *(comida)* to go off. **7** *fam (excederse)* to go too far; **no te pases,** don't overdo it; **no te pases con la sal,** don't add too much salt; **p. de (la) raya** *or* **rosca,** to go too far, overstep the mark; **p. de listo,** to be too clever by half; **se pasa de generoso,** he's too generous. **8** *(ir)* **p. por,** to call in at; **pásate por la oficina en cuanto puedas,** call in at the office as soon as you can.

pasarela *nf* **1** *(puente)* footbridge; *(de barco)* gangway. **2** *Teat* catwalk.

pasatiempo *nm* pastime, amusement, hobby; **mi p. favorito es la lectura,** my favourite pastime is reading.

pascana *nf Am* **1** *(mesón)* inn. **2** *(de un viaje) (etapa)* stage (of a journey); *(parada)* stopover.

pascua *nf* **1** *Rel (fiesta cristiana)* Easter; *(fiesta judía)* Passover; **P. de Pentecostés,** Whitsun; **P. de Resurrección** *or* **florida,** Easter; *fam* **hacer la p.,** to mess things up. **2 pascuas,** *(Navidad)* Christmas *sing;* **¡felices P.!,** Merry Christmas!; *fam* **de P. a Ramos,** once in a blue moon; *fam* **estar como unas p.,** to be (as) happy as Larry, be over the moon; *fam* **... y santas p.,** ... and that's that; **lo hacemos y santas p.,** we'll do it and that's that.

pase *nm* **1** *(permiso)* pass, permit. **2** *(de una película)* showing. **3** *Dep Taur* pass.

paseante *nmf* passer-by, stroller.

pasear I *vt* **1** *(persona)* to take for a walk; *(perro)* to walk. **2** *fig (exhibir)* to show off. **3** *CAm (negocio, hacienda)* to ruin. **II** *vi* to go for a walk, take a walk. **III pasearse** *vr* to go for a walk.

paseíllo *nm Taur* opening parade.

paseo *nm* **1** *(a pie)* walk; *(en bicicleta, caballo)* ride; *(en coche)* drive; *(en barco)* trip; **dar un p.,** to go for a walk *or* a ride; *fam* **enviar** *or* **mandar (a algo) a p.,** to send (sb) packing; *fam* **¡mándalo todo a p.!,** to hell with it all!; *fam* **¡vete a p.!,** get lost! **2** *(avenida)* promenade, avenue. **3** *CAm (mascarada)* costumed parade.

pasillo *nm Arquit* corridor, hallway. ■ *Av* **p. aéreo,** air corridor.

pasión *nf* passion; *Rel* **la P.,** the Passion; **tener p. por,** to have a passion for.

pasional *adj* passionate; **crimen p.,** crime of passion.

pasionaria *nf Bot* passion flower.

pasito *adv* gently, softly.

pasividad *nf* passivity, passiveness.

pasivo,-a I *adj* passive; **clases pasivas,** pensioners. **II** *nm Com* liabilities *pl.*

pasma *nf arg* police; **la p.,** the fuzz *pl.*

pasmado,-a I *pp de* **pasmar. II** *adj (asombrado)* astounded, astonished, amazed; *(atontado)* flabbergasted; **dejar p. a algn,** to amaze sb; **quedarse p.,** *(asombrado)* to be amazed; *(atontado)* to stand gaping.

pasmar I *vtr* **1** *(asombrar)* to astound, astonish, amaze; *(atontar)* to stun. **2** *(enfriar)* to chill. **II pasmarse** *vr* **1** *(asombrarse)* to be astounded *or* amazed. **2** *(estar helado)* to be chilled.

pasmarote *nm fam* twit, dope.

pasmo *nm* astonishment, amazement.

paso,-a¹ *adj* dried; **ciruela pasa,** prune; **uva pasa,** raisin.

paso² *nm* **1** *(acción)* passage, passing; **a su p. por la ciudad,** when he was in town; **de p. tráete un tenedor,** bring a fork on your way back; **el p. del tiempo,** the passage of time; **estar de p.,** to be just passing through; **'prohibido el p.',** 'no entry'; **salir al p. de algn,** to go to meet sb; *fig* **salir al p. de habladurías,** to forestall gossip about oneself. **2** *(pisada)* step, pace; *(modo de andar)* gait, walk; *(huella)* footprint; *(ruido de andar)* footstep; *(distancia)* pace; **caminar con p. firme,** to walk with a firm step; **dar un p. en falso,** *(tropezar)* to trip; *fig* to make a wrong move; *Mil* **llevar el p.,** to keep in step; **volver sobre sus pasos,** to retrace one's steps; *fig* **a dos pasos,** a short distance away; *fig* **a p. de tortuga,** at a snail's pace; *fig* **a pasos agigantados,** by leaps and bounds; *fig* **dar el primer p.,** to take the first step; *fig* **seguir los pasos de algn,** to follow in sb's steps; *fig* **seguirle los pasos a algn,** to keep track of sb. **3** *(camino, pasaje)* passage, way; **¡abran p.!,** clear the way!; **abrirse p.,** to force one's way through; *Aut* **'ceda el p.',** 'give way'; **cerrar el p.,** to block the way. ■ *Ferroc* **p. a nivel,** level *or* US grade crossing; **p. de cebra,** zebra crossing; **p. de peatones,** pedestrian crossing, *US* crosswalk; **p. elevado,** flyover, *US* overpass; **p. subterráneo,** *(para peatones)* subway; *(para coches)* underpass. **6** *fig (avance)* advance, progress; **un gran p. adelante,** an important step forward; **un mal p.,** a wrong move. **7** *(trámite) (gen p.)* step, move; **dar los pasos necesarios para ...,** to take the necessary steps to ... . **8** *Geog (de montaña)* mountain pass; *Mar* strait. **9** *Rel* Easter procession float.

pasodoble *nm Mús* paso doble.

pasota *nmf fam* waster.

pasotismo *nm fam* waster mentality.

pasparse *vr Am (piel)* to crack.

pasquín *nm Pol* subversive poster.

pasta *nf* **1** *(masa)* paste. ■ **p. de dientes** *or* **dentífrica,** toothpaste; **p. de madera/de papel,** Word/paper pulp. **2** *Culin (para pan, pasteles)* dough; *(italiana)* pasta; *fam* **ser de buena p.,** to be good-natured; *fam* **tener p. de,** to have the makings of. **3** *(pastelito)* small cake, petit four. **4** *fam (dinero)* dough, bread; **soltar la p.,** to cough up the money; **una p. (gansa),** a packet, a bomb, a pile.

pastaflora *nf* Culin sponge cake.

pastaje *nm* Am pasture, grass.

pastar *vtr & vi* to graze, pasture.

pastel *nm* **1** *Culin* cake; *(de carne, fruta)* pie. **2** *Arte* pastel; **dibujo al p.,** pastel drawing. **3** *fam pey (intriga)* shady deal; **descubrir el p.,** to spill the beans.

pastelear *vi fam pey* to be involved in shady deals.

pasteleo *nm fam pey* shady *or* crooked deal.

pastelería *nf* **1** *(pasteles)* cakes *pl*, pastries *pl*; *(dulces)* confectionery. **2** *(tienda)* confectioner's (shop).

pastelero,-a *nm,f* **1** pastrycook, confectioner. **2** *pey* crook, shady character.

pasterización *nf,* **pasteurización** *nf* pasteurization.

pasterizar *vtr,* **pasteurizar** *vtr* to pasteurize.

pastiche *nm* **1** *Arte* pastiche. **2** *fam (chapuza)* botch(-up).

pastilla *nf* **1** *Farm* tablet, pill; *fam (anticonceptiva)* pill; **pastillas para la tos,** cough drops. **2** *(de jabón)* bar; *(de chocolate, turrón)* piece; **p. de café con leche,** toffee. **3** *fam* **a toda p.,** at full speed.

pastizal *nm* grazing land, pasture.

pasto *nm* **1** *(acción)* grazing; *(pastizal)* grazing land, pasture. **2** *fig (alimento)* food; **es p. de la murmuración,** gossip

thrives on it; **p. espiritual,** spiritual food *or* nourishment; **ser p. de,** to be prey to; **ser p. de las llamas,** to go up in flames; **su nombre es p. de los periódicos,** her name is headline material. **3** *fig* **a todo p.,** in great quantities; **había comida a todo p.,** there was a pile of food.

pastón *nm fam* bomb, packet.

pastor,-a I *nm, f Agr (hombre)* shepherd; *(mujer)* shepherdess. ■ **perro p.,** sheepdog. **II** *nm Rel (protestante)* pastor, minister.

pastoral I *adj* pastoral. **II** *nf* **1** *Lit Rel* pastoral. **2** *Mús* pastorale.

pastorear *vtr* **1** *(pastar)* to graze, pasture. **2** *Am (acechar)* to lie in wait for. **3** *CAm (mimar)* to spoil, pamper, **4** *Arg Urug (cortejar)* to court.

pastoreo *nm* shepherding.

pastoril *adj Lit* pastoral.

pastosidad *nf* **1** *(espesor)* pastiness. **2** *(de la lengua)* furriness. **3** *(de la voz)* mellowness.

pastoso,-a¹ *adj* **1** *(pastoso)* pasty. **2** *(lengua)* furry. **3** *(voz)* mellow.

pastoso,-a² *adj Am* (terreno) grassy.

pasudo,-a *Am* **I** *adj (pelo)* curly. **II** *nm,f (persona)* curly-haired person.

pata *nf* **1** *Zool (de animal)* leg; *(con garra)* paw; *(pezuña)* hoof. **2** *(de mueble)* leg; *fig* **patas arriba,** upside down. **3** *fam (de persona)* leg; **a la p. coja,** hopping on one foot; **a p.,** on foot; **de cuatro patas,** on all fours; *fig* **estirar la p.,** to kick the bucket; *fig* **mala p.,** bad luck; *fig* **meter la p.,** to put one's foot in it; *fig* **p. de gallo,** crow's foot; *fig* **poner a algn de patas** *or* **patitas en la calle,** to kick sb out. **4** *fam (despropósito)* silly remark, clanger; *fam* **a la p. (la) llana,** without formalities. **5** *Orn (hembra)* duck.

patada *nf* **1** *(puntapié)* kick, stamp; *(paso)* step; **dar patadas en el suelo,** to stamp one's feet; **dio una p. al balón,** he kicked the ball; *fig* **en dos patadas,** in a jiffy; *fam* **a patadas,** tons of; *fam* **dar la p. a algn,** to give sb the boot; *fam* **me da cien patadas,** I can't stand the sight of it; *fam* **sentar como una p. en el estómago,** to be like a kick in the teeth; *fam* **tratar a algn a patadas,** to push *or* shove sb around. **2** *Méx (rechazo)* brush-off.

patalear *vi* **1** *(bebé)* to kick. **2** *(de rabia)* to stamp one's feet (with rage). **3** *fam (protestar)* to kick up a fuss.

pataleo *nm* **1** *(de bebé)* kicking. **2** *(de rabia)* stamping. **3** *fam (protesta)* angry protest; *fam* **derecho al p.,** right to protest.

pataleta *nf fam* fit, tantrum.

patán *nm pey* bumpkin, lout, yokel.

patasca *nf* **1** *Pan SAm (tumulto)* row, quarrel. **2** *Am Culin* pork and corn stew.

patata *nf* potato; *fam* **ser una p.,** to be a duffer. ■ **patatas fritas,** chips, *US* French fries; **patatas nuevas** *or* **tempranas,** new potatoes.

patatal *nm,* **patatar** *nm* potato field.

patatero,-a *adj* **1** *(de patatas)* potato. **2** *fam (burdo)* coarse, rough; **un rollo p.,** a real bore.

patatín *loc adv fam* **que si p. que si patatán,** this, that and the other, and so on and so forth.

patatús *nm inv fam* dizzy spell, queer turn; **me dio un p.,** it made my head spin.

paté *nm Culin* pâté.

patear I *vtr* **1** *(pelota, persona)* to kick; *(pisotear)* to stamp on. **2** *fam (tratar mal)* to trample on, treat roughly. **3** *Teat (abuchear)* to boo, jeer. **4** *fam (andar)* to trudge about *or* around. **II** *vi* **1** *(patalear)* to stamp (one's feet with rage). **2** *Am (caballo)* to kick. **3** *Am (indigestar)* not to settle well. **III patearse** *vr fam (andar)* to walk, foot it; *(despilfarrar)* to blow; **se pateó la herencia de su tío,** he blew all his uncle's fortune.

patena *nf paten;* *fam* **limpio como una p.,** as clean as a new pin.

patentado,-a *adj* patented.

patentar *vtr* to patent.

patente I *adj (evidente)* patent, obvious; **hacer p.,** to show clearly. II *nf (autorización)* licence, *US* license, grant, warrant; *(de invención)* patent; *fig* **p. de corso,** total impunity.

pateo *nm* 1 *(pataleo)* stamping. 2 *Teat (abucheo)* boo, booing, jeer, jeering.

paternal *adj* paternal, fatherly.

paternalismo *nm* paternalism.

paternalista *adj* paternalistic.

paternidad *nf* paternity, fatherhood.

paterno,a *adj* paternal; **abuelo p.,** grandfather on the father's side, paternal grandfather.

patético,-a *adj* pathetic, moving.

patetismo *nm* pathos *sing*.

patibulario,-a *adj* sinister, harrowing.

patíbulo *nm* scaffold, gallows *pl*.

paticojo,-a *fam* I *adj* lame, gammy-legged. II *nm,f* lame person.

paticorto,-a *adj fam* short-legged, dumpy.

patidifuso,-a *adj fam* dumbfounded, flabbergasted; **quedarse p.,** to be flabbergasted.

patilargo,-a *adj fam* long-legged, lanky.

patilla *nf* 1 *(de gafas)* arm. 2 **patillas,** *(pelo)* sideboards, *US* sideburns.

patín *nm* 1 *(gen)* skate; *(de ruedas)* roller skate; *(de hielo)* ice skate; *(patinete)* scooter. 2 *Náut* pedal boat.

pátina *nf* patina; **dar p.,** to coat with a patina.

patinador,-a *nm,f* skater.

patinaje *nm Dep* skating. ■ **p. artístico,** figure skating; **p. sobre hielo/ruedas,** ice-/roller skating.

patinar *vi* 1 *(con patines)* to skate; *(sobre ruedas)* to roller-skate; *(sobre hielo)* to ice-skate. 2 *(deslizarse)* to slide; *(resbalar)* to slip; *(vehículo)* to skid. 3 *fam (equivocarse)* to put one's foot in it, slip up.

patinazo *nm* 1 *(resbalón)* skid. 2 *fam (equivocación)* blunder, boob; **dar** *or* **pegar un p.,** *(patinar)* to skid; *fam (equivocarse)* to make a boob.

patinete *nm* scooter.

patio *nm* 1 *(de una casa)* yard, courtyard, patio; *(de recreo)* playground; *fam* **¿cómo está el p.?,** what's up? 2 *Teat* pit. ■ **p. de butacas,** stalls *pl*, *US* orchestra.

patitieso,-a *adj fam* 1 *(asombrado)* dumbfounded, flabbergasted; **dejar p.,** to astound; **quedarse p.,** to be flabbergasted *or* dumbfounded. 2 *(de frío, miedo)* numb, stiff. 3 *(estirado)* stuck-up, strait-laced.

patituerto,-a *adj fam* bandy-legged.

patizambo,-a *adj fam* knock-kneed.

pato *nm* 1 *Zool* duck; *fam* **pagar el p.,** to carry the can. ■ **p. cuchara,** shoveler; **p. (macho),** drake; **p. mandarín,** mandarin duck; **p. salvaje** *or* **silvestre,** wild duck. 2 *Am (bacineta)* chamberpot.

patochada *nf* blunder, bloomer, boob.

patógeno,-a *adj* pathogenic.

patojo,-a *nm,f Am* street urchin.

patología *nf* pathology.

patológico,-a *adj* pathological.

patólogo,-a *nm,f* pathologist.

patoso,-a *adj* clumsy, awkward.

patraña *nf* lie, fabrication, story.

patria *nf* fatherland, native country. ■ **madre p.,** motherland; **p. adoptiva,** country of adoption; **p. celestial,** heaven; **p. chica,** one's home town *or* region.

patriada *nf Arg Urug* feat.

patriarca *nm* patriarch.

patriarcado *nm* patriarchy.

patriarcal *adj* patriarchal.

patricio,-a *adj & nm,f* patrician.

patrimonial *adj* patrimonial, hereditary.

patrimonio *nm (bienes)* wealth; *(heredado)* patrimony, inheritance. ■ **p. cultural,** cultural heritage; **p. nacional,** national wealth.

patrio,-a *adj* 1 *(nativo)* native; **suelo p.,** native soil. 2 *(paterno)* paternal; *Jur* **patria potestad,** paternal authority. 3 *Arg (caballo)* stray.

patriota *nmf* patriot.

patriotería *nf pey* chauvinism, jingoism.

patriotero,-a *pey* I *adj* chauvinistic, jingoistic. II *nm,f* chauvinist, jingoist.

patriótico,-a *adj* patriotic.

patriotismo *nm* patriotism.

patrocinador,-a I *adj* sponsoring. II *nm,f* sponsor.

patrocinar *vtr* to sponsor, patronize.

patrocinio *nm* sponsorship, patronage; **bajo el p. de,** sponsored by.

patrón,-ona I *nm; f* 1 *(jefe)* boss; *(amo)* master; *(ama)* owner. 2 *(de pensión) (hombre)* landlord; *(mujer)* landlady. 3 *Náut* captain, skipper; *fig* **doude hay p., no manda marinero,** the boss is the boss. 4 *Rel* patron saint. II *nm* 1 *Cost Téc* pattern; *fig* **cortado por el mismo p.,** cast in the same mould. 2 *(medida)* standard; **p. oro,** gold standard.

patronal I *adj* 1 *Pol* employers'; **cierre p.,** lockout; **clase p.,** managerial class. 2 *Rel* of a patron saint; **fiesta p.,** patron saint's day. II *nf (asociación)* employers' association; *(dirección)* management.

patronato *nm*, **patronazgo** *nm* 1 *(empresariado)* employers' association. 2 *(institución)* organization, society, board, foundation. 3 *(protección)* patronage.

patronear *vtr Náut* to skipper.

patronímico,-a I *adj* patronymic. II *nm* patronymic, surname.

patrono,-a *nm, f* 1 *(jefe)* boss; *(empresario)* owner, employer. 2 *Rel (santo)* patron saint.

patrulla *nf* 1 *Mil* patrol; **estar de p.,** to be on patrol; **estar de p. en** *or* **por una zona,** to patrol an area. ■ **coche p.,** patrol car. 2 *(grupo)* group, band; **p. de rescate,** rescue party.

patrullar I *vtr* to patrol. II *vi* to be on patrol.

patrullero,-a I *adj* patrol, patrolling. II *nm, f Náut* patrol boat; *Av* patrol plane.

patueco,-a *nm,f CAm* street urchin.

paulatino,-a *adj* gradual; **de un modo p.,** gradually. ◆ **paulatinamente** *adv* gradually, little by little.

paupérrimo,-a *adj superl de* **pobre**; extremely poor, poverty-stricken.

pausa *nf* 1 *(descanso)* pause, break; *Mús* rest; **a pausas,** at intervals; **sin p.,** continuously. 2 *(calma)* calmness; **con p.,** calmly, unhurriedly.

pausado,-a *adj* unhurried, calm.

pauta *nf* 1 *(regla)* ruler; *(para escribir)* writing guide; *(línea)* line, guideline; *Mús* staff. 2 *fig (ejemplo)* example, model; **marcar la p.,** to set the example *or* pattern.

pautado,-a *adj* ruled, lined; *Mús* **papel p.,** ruled paper.

pava¹ *n* 1 *Orn* turkey hen; *fam* **pelar la p.,** to court. ■ **p. real,** peahen. 2 *arg (colilla)* butt. 3 *fam (mujer sosa)* bore, dull woman. 4 *Am (sombrero)* broadbrimmed hat. 5 *CAm Col (flequillo)* fringe, *US* bangs *pl*.

pava² *nf Arg Bol* kettle.

pavada *nf fam* dullness, flatness.

pavear *vi* 1 *Am (hacer tonterías)* to mess about. 2 *Arg Chi (burlarse)* to (play a) joke. 3 *Arg (pelar la pava)* to court, woo.

pavero,-a *nm,f fam* braggart, show-off.

pavesa *nf* 1 *(chispa)* spark. 2 *(ceniza)* cinder.

pavimentación *nf (de calles, carreteras)* paving; *(de una habitación)* flooring.

pavimentar *vtr (calle, carretera)* to pave; *(habitación)* to floor, lay flooring in.

pavimento *nm (de calle, carretera)* paving, pavement; *(de habitación)* flooring.

pavita *nf Arg* bowler hat.

pavo *nm* **1** *Orn* turkey; *fam* **estar en la edad del p.,** to be growing up; *fam* **no ser moco de p.,** to be nothing to scoff at; *fam* **subírsele el p. a algn,** to blush. ■ **p. real,** peacock. **2** *fam (tonto)* twit, ninny. **3** *Am (polizón)* stowaway.

pavón *nm* **1** *Orn (pavo real)* peacock. **2** *Ent* peacock butterfly. **3** *Metal* bluing.

pavonearse *vr fam* to show off, strut.

pavoneo *nm fam* showing off, strutting.

pavor *nm* terror, dread, panic.

pavoroso,-a *adj* terrible, dreadful, frightful.

paya *nf Arg Chi (canción)* improvised song; *(acción)* improvisation of a song.

payacate *nm Méx Per* shawl.

payador *nm Arg Chi Urug* folk singer who sings **payas**.

payar *vi Arg Chi* to sing **payas**.

payasada *nf* clownish thing to do *or* say; **hacer payasadas,** to act the clown.

payasear *vi Am* to act the clown.

payaso *nm* clown; **hacer el p.,** to act the clown.

payé *nm* **1** *Arg Par Urug (amuleto)* amulet; *(brujería)* witchcraft. **2** *Arg Urug* sorcerer, wizard.

payés,-a *nm,f* Catalan *or* Balearic peasant.

payo,-a *nm,f* non-Gipsy person; *fam* bloke.

paz *nf (gen)* peace; *(sosiego)* peacefulness; *(tratado)* peace treaty; **descansar en p.,** to rest in peace; **estar en p.,** to be at peace; *fig* to be quits *or* even; **firmar la p.,** to sign a peace treaty; **hacer las paces,** to make (it) up; **poner p.,** to make peace; **todo lo que quiero es un poco de p.,** all I want is some peace and quiet; *fam* **aquí p. y después gloria,** that's all there is to it; *fam* **¡déjame en p.!,** leave me alone!

pazguatería *nf* **1** *(estupidez)* silliness, stupidity. **2** *(mojigatería)* prudishness.

pazguato,-a **I** *adj* **1** *(estúpido)* silly, stupid. **2** *(mojigato)* prudish. **II** *nm, f* **1** *(estúpido)* simpleton, twit. **2** *(mojigato)* prude.

pazo *nm* Galician country house.

PBAI *nm abr de* **proyectil balístico de alcance intermedio,** medium-range ballistic missile, MRBM.

PBI *nm abr de* **proyectil balístico intercontinental,** intercontinental ballistic missile, ICBM.

pbro. *Rel abr de* **presbítero,** presbyter.

PCE *nm Pol abr de* **Partido Comunista de España,** Spanish Communist party.

PCUS *nm Pol abr de* **Partido Comunista de la Unión Soviética,** Communist Party of the Soviet Union, CPSU.

pe *nf* name of the letter P in Spanish; *fam* **de pe a pa,** from A to Z.

peaje *nf* **1** *Aut* toll. ■ **autopista de p.,** toll motorway, *US* turnpike.

peana *nf* **1** *(pedestal)* pedestal, stand. **2** *fam (pie)* foot.

peatón *nm* pedestrian. ■ **paso de peatones,** pedestrian crossing, *US* crosswalk.

peca *nf* freckle.

pecado *nm Rel* sin; **hacer** *or* **cometer un p.,** to sin, commit a sin; *fig* **en el p. lleva la penitencia,** every sin carries its own punishment; *fam* **de mis pecados,** of mine; **esta hija de mis pecados,** this daughter of mine; *fam* **sería un p. tirar la comida,** it would be a sin to throw the food away. ■ **p. capital** *or* **mortal,** deadly sin; **p. original,** original sin.

pecador,-a *Rel* **I** *adj* sinful. **II** *nm,f* sinner.

pecaminoso,-a *adj Rel* sinful.

pecar *vi Rel* to sin; *fig* **peca de salado,** it's a bit too salty; *fig* **p. por defecto,** to fall short of the mark; *fig* **p. por exceso,** to go too far.

pecera *nf* fishbowl, fishtank.

pechar¹ **I** *vi fam (apechugar)* to take on; **p. con el peor trabajo,** to take on the worst job. **II** *vtr SAm fam (dinero)* to scrounge.

pechar² *vtr Am* to shove, push.

pechera *nf Cost (de camisa)* (shirt) front; *(de vestido)* front, bosom.

pechero *nm* bib.

pecho *nm Anat (gen)* chest; *(de mujer)* breast, bosom, bust; *(de animal)* breast; *fig (interior)* heart; **dar el p. (a un bebé),** to breast-feed (a baby); **tomar el p.,** to be breast-fed; *fig* **a p. descubierto,** defenceless; *fig* **abrir el p. (a algn),** to open up one's heart (to sb); *fig* **tomar (se) (algo) a p.,** to take (sth) to heart; *fam* **a lo hecho, p.,** it's no use crying over spilt milk; *fam* **echarse (algo) entre p. y espalda,** to tuck (food) away; *fam* **partirse el p.,** *(esforzarse)* to break one's back, slave away; *(reírse)* to split one's sides with laughter.

pechuga *nf* **1** *(de ave)* breast. **2** *fam (de mujer)* boob. **3** *Am (descaro)* cheek, nerve. **4** *CAm (estorbo)* trouble, annoyance.

pechugón,-ona *adj fam* big-breasted.

pécora *nf fam (mala)* **p.,** *(arpía)* witch, bitch; *(prostituta)* whore, tramp.

pecoso,-a *adj* freckled, freckle-faced.

pectoral **I** *adj* **1** *Anat* pectoral, chest. **2** *Farm* cough; **jarabe p.,** cough syrup. **II** *nm Farm* pectoral, cough medicine.

peculiar *adj* peculiar, characteristic.

peculiaridad *nf* peculiarity, characteristic.

peculio *nm* one's own money *or* savings.

pedagogía *nf* pedagogy.

pedagógico,-a *adj* pedagogic, pedagogical.

pedagogo,-a *nm,f* pedagogue, teacher, educator.

pedal *nm* **1** *Téc* pedal. ■ *Aut* **p. de embrague,** clutch pedal; **p. de freno,** footbrake, brake pedal. **2** *fam (borrachera)* bender; **coger un p.,** to get sloshed *or* plastered.

pedalear *vi* to pedal.

pedaleo *nm* pedalling, *US* pedaling.

pedáneo,-a *adj* local.

pedanía *nf* district.

pedante **I** *adj* pedantic. **II** *nmf* pedant.

pedantería *nf* pedantry.

pedazo *nm* piece, bit; **a pedazos,** in pieces; **caerse a pedazos,** to fall apart *or* to pieces; **hacer pedazos,** to break *or* tear to pieces, smash (up); *fig* **hacer pedazos (a algn),** to tear (sb) to pieces; *fam* **esta chica es un p. de pan,** that girl is a pet; *fam ofens* **es un p. de animal** *or* **de alcornoque,** he's a blockhead.

pederasta *nm* pederast.

pederastia *nf* pederasty.

pedernal *nm Min* flint; *fig* **duro como un p.,** hard as a rock.

pedestal *nm* pedestal; *fig* **colocar a algn en un p.,** to put sb on a pedestal.

pedestre *adj* **1** *(a pie)* on foot, walking. **2** *fig (vulgar)* ordinary, pedestrian.

pediatra *nmf Med* paediatrician, *US* pediatrician.

pediatría *nf Med* paediatrics *sing*, *US* pediatrics *sing*.

pedicuro,-a *nm,f Med* chiropodist.

pedida *nf* engagement. ■ **pulsera de p.,** engagement bracelet.

pedido *nm* 1 *Com* order; **hacer un p.,** to place an order. 2 *(petición)* request; **atender un p.,** to grant a request.

pedigrí *nm Zool* pedigree.

pedigüeño,-a I *adj* demanding, insistent. II *nm, f* pest, nuisance.

pedir *vtr* 1 *(gen)* to ask (for); **no se puede p. más,** you couldn't ask for more; **p. a una chica en matrimonio,** to ask for a girl's hand in marriage; **p. algo a algn,** to ask sb for sth; **p. prestado,** to borrow; **piden mucho dinero,** they're asking (for) a lot of money; **te pido que te quedes,** I'm asking you to stay; *fig* **p. cuentas,** to ask for an explanation; *fam* **p. peras al olmo,** to ask for the moon. 2 *Com (encargar)* to order; *(en un bar, restaurante)* to order; **no se qué p.,** I don't know what to have. 3 *Com (precio)* to ask; **¿cuánto piden por esta casa?,** how much are they asking for the house? 4 *(mendigar)* to beg; **p. limosna,** to beg. 5 *fig (requerir)* to need, require; **esta casa pide a gritos que la restauren,** this house is in bad need of repair; **esta enfermedad pide reposo,** this illness requires rest.

pedo *nm vulg* 1 *(ventosidad)* fart, wind; **tirarse un p.,** to fart. 2 *(borrachera)* bender; **agarrar** *or* **coger un p.,** *(emborracharse)* to get sloshed *or* pissed; *(drogarse)* to get really stoned, get high.

pedorrera *nf vulg* string of farts.

pedorreta *nf vulg* raspberry.

pedrada *nf* 1 *(lanzamiento)* throw of a stone; *(golpe)* blow from a stone; **a pedradas,** (by) throwing stones; **matar a algn a pedradas,** to stone sb to death; **pegar una p. a algn,** to throw a stone at sb; **rompió la ventana de una p.,** he smashed the window with a stone. 2 *fig (expresión mordaz)* wounding remark.

pedrea *nf* 1 *(pelea)* fight with stones. 2 *Meteor (granizada)* hailstorm. 3 *(en lotería)* small prizes *pl*.

pedregal *nm* stony *or* rocky ground.

pedregoso,-a *adj* stony, rocky.

pedrera *nf* stone quarry.

pedrería *nf* precious stones *pl*, gems *pl*.

pedrisco *nm Meteor* hailstorm; *(lluvia de piedras)* shower of stones.

pedrusco *nm fam* rough stone, piece of stone.

pega *nf* 1 *(adhesivo)* glue. 2 *fam (obstáculo)* snag, difficulty; *(objeción)* objection; **a todo le encuentra** *or* **pone pegas,** she finds fault with everything. 3 *(falso)* **de p.,** sham. 4 *Am (trabajo)* job.

pegada *nf* 1 *Ten* stroke, hit. 2 *Box* punch; **tener buena p.,** to pack a hard punch.

pegadizo,-a *adj* 1 *(pegajoso)* sticky. 2 *Mús (canción)* catchy.

pegado,-a I *pp de* **pegar.** II *adj* 1 *(adherido)* stuck. 2 *Culin (quemado)* burnt. III *nm Med (emplasto)* patch, sticking plaster.

pegajoso,-a *adj* 1 *(pegadizo)* sticky. 2 *fig (persona)* tiresome, hard to get rid of.

pegamento *nm* glue.

pegapega *nf Am* birdlime.

pegar¹ I *vtr* 1 *(adherir)* to stick; *(con pegamento)* to glue; *(póster, cartel)* to put up, fix (up); *Cost (botón)* to sew on; *fam* **no pegó ojo,** he didn't sleep a wink. 2 *(arrimar)* to put against, lean against; **pegó la silla a la puerta,** he put the chair against the door. 3 *fam Med (contagiar)* to give; *fig* to give, communicate; **me ha pegado sus manías,** I've caught his bad habits. 4 *(fuego)* to light. II *vi* 1 *(adherirse)* to stick. 2 *(armonizar)* to match, go; **el azul no pega con el verde** *or* **el azul y el verde no pegan,** blue and green don't go together *or* don't match; *fig* **ella no pegaría aquí,** she wouldn't fit in here. 3 *(estar próximo)* to be next (**a,** to). 4 *(sospechar) fam* **me pega que ...,** I have a hunch that ... . III *pegarse* *vr* 1 *(adherirse)* to stick; **se ha pegado,** it has stuck. 2 *Culin (quemarse)* to get burnt. 3 *(arrimarse)* to get close;

pégate a mí, stay close to me. 4 *fam fig* to stick; **p. como una lapa,** to stick like a limpet. 5 *Med (enfermedad)* to be catching *or* contagious; *fig (melodía, acento)* to be catchy; **¿el sarampión se pega?,** are measles contagious?

pagar² I *vtr* 1 *(golpear)* to hit; **p. una bofetada a algn,** to slap sb. 2 *(dar, realizar)* **p. un grito,** to shout; **p. un salto,** to jump; **p. un susto a algn,** to give a fright to sb; **p. un tiro,** to shoot. 3 *fam* **dale que te pego,** on and on. 4 *Arg Chi* to keep on working hard at. II *vi (golpear)* to hit, beat; **p. duro,** to hit hard; **p. en,** to strike (against); **p. en el blanco,** to hit the target; **pegar en la pared con un palo,** to hit the wall with a stick; *fig* **¡cómo pega el sol!,** isn't the sun beating down?; *fig* **p. fuerte,** *fam (estar de moda)* to be all the rage; *(vino)* to be strong stuff. III **pegarse** *vr* 1 *(pelearse)* to fight. 2 *fam (darse)* to have, get; **p. la buena vida,** to live like a king; **p. un hartón de trabajar,** to slave *or* slog away; **p. un tiro,** to shoot oneself; **p. una comilona,** to have a feast. 3 *fam* **pegársela a algn,** to trick *or* deceive sb; **se la pega a su marido,** she's cheating on her husband.

pegatina *nf* sticker.

pego *nm fam* **dar el p. a algn,** to take sb for a ride, fool sb; **es una baratija pero da el p.,** it's a cheap imitation but it looks like the real thing.

pegote *nm* 1 *(emplasto)* patch, sticking plaster. 2 *fam (chapuza)* mess, botch-up. 3 *fam (gorrón)* sponger, hanger-on. 4 *fam* **tirarse** *or* **marcarse un p.,** to tell a tall tale.

pegual *nm* 1 *Am (cincha)* girth. 2 *Arg (sobrecincha)* surcingle.

pehuén *nm Bot* monkey puzzle tree.

peinado,-a I *pp de* **peinar.** II *adj (pelo)* combed; *(relamido)* affected, overdone. III *nm* 1 *Peluq* hairdo, hairstyle. 2 *Tex* combing. 3 *arg (policial)* door-to-door search, sweep.

peinador,-a I *nm, f (persona)* hairdresser. II *nm* 1 *(bata)* bathrobe. 2 *Am (tocador)* dressing table.

peinar I *vtr* 1 *(pelo)* to comb, do; *fam* **p. canas,** to be going grey. 2 *arg (policía)* to comb; **la policía peinó el barrio en busca de los atracadores,** the cops combed the area for the bank robbers. II **peinarse** *vr* to comb one's hair.

peinazo *nm* crosspiece, lintel.

peine *nm* 1 *(para pelo)* comb; *fam fig* **¡te vas a enterar de lo que vale un p.!,** you've got it coming (to you)! 2 *Tex* reed.

peineta *nf* ornamental comb.

peinilla *nf Am* type of cane knife.

pejiguera *nf fam* drag, nuisance.

pela *nf fam* peseta; **tiene machas pelas,** he has a lot of money, he's loaded.

pelada *nf Am* blunder, mistake.

peladero *nm Am* barrenland, wasteland.

peladilla *nf* 1 *(dulce)* sugared almond. 2 *(guijarro)* small pebble.

pelado,-a I *pp de* **pelar.** II *adj* 1 *(sin pelo)* hairless; *(calvo)* bald. 2 *(piel, fruta)* peeled. 3 *(terreno)* bare. 4 *(hueso)* clean. 5 *(cantidad)* bare; *(número)* round. 6 *fam (arruinado)* broke, penniless. 7 *Am (desvergonzado)* impudent, insolent. III *nm, f (pobre)* poor person. IV *nm Peluq (corte)* (short) haircut.

peladura *nf* peeling.

pelagatos *nmf inv fam* poor devil, nobody.

pelaje *nm* 1 *Zool* fur; hair. 2 *fam pey (apariencia)* looks *pl*, appearance. 3 *fam (clase)* class, kind, ilk.

pelambre *nm* 1 *(pelo)* mop (of hair), long *or* thick hair. 2 *(pelaje)* fur, hair.

pelambrera *nf fam* mop (of hair), long *or* thick hair.

pelandusca *nf fam* whore, tart.

pelapatatas *nm inv* potato peeler.

pelar I vtr **1** (cortar el pelo) to cut the hair of; (fruta) to peel; (mariscos) to shell; (ave) to pluck; fam **hace un frío que pela**, it's brass monkey weather; fam fig **ser duro de p.**, to be a hard nut (to crack). **2** fam (robar) to fleece. **II pelarse** vr **1** (cortarse el pelo) to get one's hair cut. **2** (levantarse la piel) to peel; fam **p. de frío**, to freeze. **3** fam **pelárselas**, to do sth fast; **corre que se las pela**, he runs like mad. **4** vulg (masturbarse) **pelársela**, to wank, jerk off. **5** Am (confundirse) to become confused. **6** Am (frustrarse) to become frustrated.

peldaño nm step; (de escalera de mano) rung.

pelea nf (gen) fight; (riña) row, quarrel; **buscar p.**, to look for trouble. ■ **p. de gallos**, cockfight.

peleado,-a I pp de **pelear**. **II** adj **estar p. (con algn)**, not to be on speaking terms (with sb).

pelear I vi (gen) to fight; (reñir) to quarrel; fig to struggle (por, to). **II pelearse** vr **1** (gen) to fight; (reñir) to quarrel. **2** (enemistarse) to fall out.

pelele nm **1** (muñeco) straw puppet; fig puppet; **Juan es solo un p. de Pepe**, Juan is just Pepe's yes man. **2** (prenda) rompers pl.

peleón,-ona adj **1** (pendenciero) quarrelsome, aggressive. **2** fam (vino) cheap, plonk.

peletería nf **1** Ind furrier's; (tienda) fur shop. **2** (pieles) furs pl.

peletero,-a I adj fur; **comercio p.**, fur trade. **II** nm,f furrier.

peliagudo,-a adj difficult, tricky, hairy; **pregunta peliaguda**, tricky question.

pelicano[1] nm, **pelícano** nm Orn pelican.

pelicano,-a[2] adj grey-haired.

pelicorto,-a adj short-haired.

película nf **1** Cin film, picture, US movie; **echar** or **poner una p.**, to show a film; fam **de p.**, fabulous. ■ **p. de miedo** or **terror**, horror film; **p. del Oeste**, Western; **p. en color/ en blanco y negro**, colour/black-and-white film; **p. muda**, silent film; **p. sonora**, talkie, talking picture. **2** Fot film. **3** (piel) pellicle.

peligrar vi to be in danger, be threatened; **hacer p.**, to endanger, jeopardize.

peligro nm (gen) danger; (riesgo) risk; **con p. de ...**, at the risk of ...; **corre (el) p. de ...**, to run the risk of ...; **estar en p.**, to be in danger; **fuera de p.**, out of danger; **poner en p.**, to endanger.

peligrosidad nf danger, dangerousness.

peligroso,-a adj dangerous, risky.

pelillo nm fam trifle, slight annoyance; **echar pelillos a la mar**, to bury the hatchet.

pelirrojo,-a I adj red-haired, ginger-haired. **II** nm, f redhead.

pella nf round mass, lump.

pelleja nf **1** (piel) skin, hide. **2** fam (persona delgada) skinny person. **3** fam (prostituta) whore.

pellejerías nfpl Am difficulties, jam sing.

pellejo nm **1** (piel) skin; fam **no quisiera estar en su p.**, I wouldn't want to be in his shoes. **2** (odre) wineskin. **3** fam (vida) life, skin, neck; **arriesgar** or **jugarse el p.**, to risk one's neck.

pelliza nf fur jacket.

pellizcar vtr to pinch, nip.

pellizco nm pinch, nip.

pelma nmf, **pelmazo,-a** nm,f (persona) bore, drag.

pelo nm **1** (gen) hair; **a p.**, (en equitación) bareback; fam (desnudo) stark naked; **cortarse el p.**, (uno mismo) to cut one's hair; (en la peluquería) to have one's hair cut; **llevar el p. largo**, to have long hair; fig **no tiene ni un p. de tonto**, he's no fool; fig **Sonia no tiene pelos en la lengua**, Sonia's very outspoken; fig **soltarse el p.**, to let one's hair down; fig **tomar el p. a algn**, to pull sb's leg, take the mickey out of sb; fig **traído por los pelos**, far-fetched; fig

venir al p., (ser oportuno) to come at right the moment; (ser útil) to come in handy; fam **con pelos y señales**, in full detail; fam **faltó un p. para que ganase**, he very nearly won, he lost by an inch; fam **hasta los pelos**, up to here; fam **por los pelos** or **un p.**, by the skin of one's teeth; fam **se me pusieron los pelos de punta**, it gave me the creeps; fam **un hombre de p. en pecho**, a tough guy. **2** Zool (de animal) fur, coat, hair. **3** Tex (de una tela) nap, pile. **4** (cerda) bristle.

pelón,-ona adj **1** (sin pelo) hairless, bald. **2** (arruinado) broke, skint.

pelota I nf **1** (gen) ball; **jugar a la p.**, to play ball; fam **devolver la p.**, to give tit for tat. ■ **p. de tenis**, tennis ball; **p. de fútbol**, football. **2** Dep pelota. **3** fam (cabeza) nut. **4** pelotas, vulg (testículos) balls; **coger** or **pillar a algn en p.**, to catch sb on the hop; **dejar a algn en p.**, to fleece sb; **en p.**, starkers; **estoy hasta las p.**, I'm pissed off. **5** Arg Bol (batea) cowhide boat. **6** Cuba Méx (deseo) passion; **tener p. por**, to have a crush on. **II** nmf fam (pelotillero) toady, fawner; **este tío es un p.**, he's a real toady; **hacer la p. a algn**, to toady to sb, butter sb up.

pelotari nm Dep pelota player.

pelotazo nm fam swig.

pelotear I vtr Com (cuenta, partida) to check. **II** vi **1** Dep to kick a ball around; Ten to knock up; (calentar) to warm up. **2** fig (reñir) to quarrel, argue.

peloteo nm **1** Ten knock-up; (calentamiento) warmup. **2** fig (riña) quarrel, argument.

pelotera nf fam quarrel, row.

pelotilla nf fam toady, fawner; **hacer la p. (a algn)**, to fawn on (sb).

pelotillero,-a nm, f fam toady, fawner.

pelotón nm **1** Mil squad, party; **p. de ejecución**, firing squad. **2** fam (grupo) small crowd, bunch. **3** (amasijo) bundle.

pelotudo,-a adj Arg slack, sloppy.

peluca nf wig; **llevar p.**, to wear a wig.

peluco nm arg watch.

peluche nf véase **felpa**.

peludear vi **1** Arg (salvar una dificultad) to solve a problem. **2** Arg Urug (atascarse) to get stuck. **3** Arg Urug fig (titubear) to stammer, stutter.

peludo,-a adj hairy, furry.

peluquear Am I vtr to cut the hair of. **II peluquearse** vr to have one's hair cut.

peluquería nf (de señoras) hairdresser's (shop); (de caballeros) barber's (shop); **ir a la p.**, to go to the hairdresser's or the barber's.

peluquero,-a nm, f (de señoras) hairdresser; (de caballeros) barber.

peluquín nm toupee; fam **ni hablar el p.**, not on your life.

pelusa nf, **pelusilla** nf **1** fluff; (de planta) down. **2** fam jealousy (among children).

pelvis nf inv Anat pelvis.

pena nf **1** (castigo) punishment, penalty; **bajo** or **so p. de**, under penalty of. ■ **p. de muerte** or **capital**, death penalty. **2** (tristeza) grief, sorrow; **me da p. verte así**, it makes me sad to see you like that; fig **sin p. ni gloria**, unmarked. **3** (lástima) pity; **¡qué p.!**, what a pity! **4** (dificultad) hardships pl, trouble; **a duras penas**, with great difficulty; **merecer** or **valer la p.**, to be worth it; **merece la p. intentarlo**, it's worth (giving it) a try; **no merece la p.**, it's not worth the bother. **5** CAm (vergüenza) shame.

penacho nm **1** (de ave) crest, tuft. **2** Mil (de plumas) plume.

penado,-a I pp de **penar**. **II** nm,f convict.

penal I adj penal; Jur **código p.**, penal code. **II** nm prison, jail, gaol.

penalidad nf (gen pl) hardships pl, troubles pl.

penalista *nmf* criminal lawyer.

penalización *nf* sanction, penalization; *Dep* penalty.

penalizar *vtr* to penalize.

penalti *nm* (*pl* **penaltis**) *Dep* penalty; *fam* **casarse de p.,** to have a shotgun wedding.

penar I *vtr* to punish. II *vi* to be in torment, suffer; **p. por algo/algn,** to pine for sth/sb.

penca *nf Bot* fleshy leaf.

penco *nm* 1 *fam* (*jamelgo*) nag, jade. 2 *fam fig* ass, twit.

pendejo *nm* 1 (*pelo*) pubic hair. 2 *fig* (*cobarde*) wet, coward. 3 *fig* (*pendón*) playboy. 4 *Am* (*tonto*) jerk, dummy.

pendencia *nf* quarrel, fight.

pendenciero,-a *adj* quarrelsome, argumentative.

pender *vi* 1 (*colgar*) to hang (**de,** from; **sobre,** over); *fig* **mi vida pende de un hilo,** my life is hanging by a thread; *fig* **pende sobre nosotros una grave amenaza,** a serious threat is hanging over us. 2 (*estar pendiente*) to be pending.

pendiente I *adj* 1 (*colgante*) hanging (**de,** from). 2 (*por resolver*) pending; *Educ* **asignatura p.,** failed subject; *Com* **p. de pago,** unpaid; **tiene una asignatura p.,** he has to resit one exam; **estar p. de,** (*esperar*) to be waiting for; (*vigilar*) to be on the lookout for. II *nm* 1 (*joya*) earring. 2 *Méx* (*preocupación*) worry. III *nf* slope; (*de un tejado*) pitch; **en p.,** sloping; **esta p. es muy pronunciada,** this slope is very steep; **hacer p.,** to slope.

pendón *nm* 1 (*bandera*) banner; *Hist* pennon. 2 *pey* (*mujer*) slut, whore; (*hombre*) playboy.

pendonear *vi fam* to gad about.

pendular *adj* pendular.

péndulo *nm* pendulum.

pene *nm Anat* penis.

penetrabilidad *nf* penetrability.

penetrable *adj* penetrable.

penetración *nf* 1 (*gen*) penetration. 2 *fig* (*perspicacia*) insight, perception.

penetrante *adj* 1 (*gen*) penetrating; (*frío, voz*) piercing; (*herida*) deep. 2 *fig* (*inteligencia*) sharp, acute.

penetrar I *vtr* (*gen*) to penetrate; (*substancia*) to permeate; *fig* (*intención, significado*) to grasp, understand; **p. un misterio,** to get to the bottom of a mystery. II *vi* (*gen*) to penetrate (**en,** in); (*entrar*) to go *or* get (**en,** in); *fig* **frío que penetra en los huesos,** cold that gets into one's bones; *fig* **un grito penetró en la noche,** a scream pierced the night.

penicilina *nf Med* penicillin.

península *nf Geog* peninsula.

peninsular I *adj* peninsular, II *nmf* native *or* inhabitant of the (Iberian) Peninsula.

penique *nm* (*moneda*) penny; **dos peniques,** twopence.

penitencia *nf* 1 *Rel* penance; **como** *or* **en p.,** as a penance; **hacer p.,** to do penance. 2 *fam* pain, bind; **esto más que un trabajo es una p.,** this job is like doing penance.

penitenciaría *nf* prison.

penitenciario,-a *adj* penitentiary, prison.

penitente *adj & nmf Rel* penitent.

penoso,-a *adj* 1 (*lamentable*) sorry, distressing. 2 (*laborioso*) laborious, difficult.

pensado,-a I *pp* de **pensar.** II *adj* thought, thought out; **bien p., creo que me quedaré,** on reflection, I think I'll stay; **bien p., no está tan mal,** all things considered, it isn't that bad; **en el momento menos p.,** when least expected; **este trabajo está poco p.,** this paper is badly thought out; **mal p.,** evil-minded; **tener algo p.,** to have sth planned, have sth in mind.

pensador,-a *nm,f* thinker.

pensamiento *nm* 1 thought; **adivinar los pensamientos de algn,** to read sb's mind. 2 (*mente*) mind; **no me pasó**

por el p., it did't cross my mind; *fig* **como el p.,** like a flash; *fig* **ni por p.,** not in the least. 3 (*máxima*) saying, motto. 4 *Bot* pansy.

pensar I *vi* (*gen*) to think (**en,** of, about; **sobre,** about, over); **¿en qué/quién piensas?,** what/who are you thinking about?; **no pensé en ello,** I didn't think of it; **p. para sí** *or* **consigo,** to think to oneself; *fig* **sin p.,** (*con precipitación*) without thinking; (*involuntariamente*) involuntarily. II *vtr* 1 (*gen*) to think; (*opinar*) to think about; (*considerar*) to think over *or* about; **esto da mucho que pensar,** this is food for thought; (**me**) **lo pensaré,** I'll think about it; **pensándolo bien** *or* **mejor,** on second thoughts; **p. bien/mal de algn,** to think well/ badly of sb; **piénsalo bien,** think it over; **pienso que ...,** I think that ...; **¿qué piensas de esto?,** what do you think about this?; **sólo con pensarlo,** just the thought of it; *fam* **¡ni pensarlo!,** not on your life! 2 (*proponerse*) to intend; **pienso quedarme,** I plan to stay. 3 (*concebir*) to make; **p. un plan,** to make a plan; **p. una solución,** to find a solution

pensativo,-a *adj* pensive, thoughtful; **estar p.,** to be deep in thought.

Pensilvania *n* Pennsylvania.

pensión *nf* 1 (*dinero*) pension, allowance; **cobrar la p.,** to draw one's pension. ■ **p. alimenticia,** alimony; **p. vitalicia,** life annuity. 2 (*régimen de alojamiento*) board and lodging. ■ **media p.,** partial board; **p. completa,** full board. 3 (*residencia*) boarding house. 4 (*hotel*) guesthouse.

pensionado,-a I *adj* pensioned. II *nm,f* pensioner. III *nm Educ* boarding school.

pensionista *nmf* 1 (*del estado*) pensioner. 2 *Educ* boarder.

pentaedro *nm* pentahedron.

pentagonal *adj* pentagonal.

pentágono *nm* pentagon.

pentagrama *nm*, **pentágrama** *nm Mús* staff, stave.

Pentecostés *nm sing Rel* 1 (*cristiano*) Pentecost, Whitsun, Whitsuntide; **domingo de P.,** Whit Sunday. 2 (*judío*) Pentecost.

penúltimo,-a *adj & nm,f* next to the last, penultimate.

penumbra *nf* penumbra, **half-light.**

penuria *nf* 1 (*escasez*) scarcity, shortage. 2 (*pobreza*) poverty, penury.

peña[1] *nf* 1 (*roca*) rock, crag. 2 *Ecuad Guat PR fig* (*sordo*) deaf person.

peña[2] *nf* 1 (*de amigos*) circle, group of friends. 2 *Ftb* pool.

peñascal *nm* rocky place.

peñasco *nm* rock, crag.

peñón *nm* rock. ■ **el P. de Gibraltar,** the Rock of Gibraltar.

peón *nm* 1 (*trabajador*) unskilled labourer *or US* laborer. ■ **p. agrícola,** farmhand; **p. caminero,** roadman; **p. de albañil,** hod carrier, hodman. 2 *Ajedrez* pawn; (*damas*) man. 3 (*peonza*) top.

peonada *nf* day's work.

peonaje *nm* group of labourers *or US* laborers.

peonía *nf Bot* peony.

peonza *nf* (*spinning*) top.

peor I *adj* 1 (*comparativo*) worse; A **es p. que** B, A is worse than B. 2 (*superlativo*) worst; **el p. de los dos,** the worse (of the two); **el p. de los tres,** the worst of the three; **en el p. de los casos,** if the worst comes to the worst; **éste es el p. de todos,** this is the worst of all; **lo p.,** the worst (thing). II *adv* 1 (*comparativo*) worse; **anda p. que antes,** he doesn't walk as well as he used to; **así es p.,** that's worse; **cada vez p.,** worse and worse; **¡p. para mí** *or* **ti!,** too bad!; **p. que p.,** worse still; **¡tanto p.!,** so much the worse. 2 (*superlativo*) worst; **es el que p. canta,** he is the one who sings the worst.

pepazo *nm* 1 *Am* (*pedrada*) throw of a stone; (*disparo*) shot; (*golpe*) blow. 2 *Am fig* (*mentira*) lie.

pepenar vtr 1 Am (recoger) to collect, gather. 2 Méx Min (metal) to sift. 3 Méx (asir) to seize, grab.

pepinazo nm fam 1 (explosión) blast, explosion. 2 Ftb (disparo) cannonball shot.

pepinillo nm Bot gherkin.

pepino nm Bot cucumber; fam **me importa un p.**, I don't give a hoot.

pepita nf 1 (de fruta) pip, seed. 2 (de metal) nugget. 3 Am (almendra de cacao) cocoa bean.

pepito nm Culin meat sandwich.

pepitoria nf Culin fricassee; **pollo en p.**, fricassee of chicken.

pepona nf large paper doll.

peque nm fam kid, little 'un.

pequeñez nf 1 (de tamaño) smallness, littleness. 2 (nimiedad) trifle; **se preocupa por pequeñeces**, he's very nitpicking. 3 (mezquindad) meanness, pettiness; **p. de miras**, narrow-mindedness.

pequeño,-a adj 1 (gen) small, little. 2 (joven) young. 3 (bajo) short. II nm,f child; **de p.**, as a child; **María es la pequeña**, Maria is the youngest; fig **dejar p.**, to put in the shade.

Pequín n Peking.

pequinés,-esa I adj Pekinese. II nm, f (persona) Pekinese. III nm Zool (perro) p., Pekinese.

pera I nf 1 Bot pear; fam **partir peras con algn**, to fall out with sb; fam **poner las peras al cuarto**, to give a ticking off; fam **ser la p.**, to take the cake. ■ **p. de agua**, juicy pear. 2 Elec (interruptor) pear-shaped switch. 3 (perilla) goatee. 4 (de líquido, aire) bulb. 5 vulg (pene) prick. II adj fam (cursi) **niño p.**, spoilt upper-class brat.

peral nm Bot pear tree.

peraltar vtr 1 Arquit to stilt. 2 (carretera) to bank.

peralte nm banking.

perca nf (pez) perch.

percal nm Tex percale; fig **conocer el p.**, to know one's stuff.

percance nm mishap, setback; **el viaje discurrió sin p.**, the trip went off without a hitch.

percatarse vr to notice, realize; **no se percata de nada**, he doesn't notice anything.

percebe nm 1 Zool (goose) barnacle. 2 fam (persona) fool, idiot.

percepción nf perception; **p. extrasensorial**, extra-sensory perception.

perceptible adj 1 (sensible) perceptible. 2 Fin receivable, payable.

perceptivo,-a adj perceptive.

percha nf 1 (sostén) perch; (colgador) (coat) hanger; (fijo en la pared) rack; **cuelga el abrigo en la p.**, hang your coat up; fam fig **tener buena p.**, to be well-built. 2 Méx (conjunto) group.

perchero nm clothes rack.

percherón,-ona nm,f Zool Percheron.

percibir vtr 1 (notar) to perceive, notice; **no se percibía ningún ruido**, no noise could be heard. 2 (cobrar) to collect; **percibo un sueldo muy bajo**, I'm on a low wage.

perclorato nm Quím perchlorate.

perclórico,-a adj Quím **ácido p.**, perchloric acid.

percloruro nm Quím perchloride.

percusión nf percussion; **instrumentos de p.**, percussion instruments.

percusionista nmf Mús percussionist.

percusor nm, **percutor** nm (armas) firing pin, hammer.

perdedor,-a I adj losing. II nm,f loser.

perder I vtr 1 (gen) to lose; **dar algo por perdido**, to give sth up as lost; **p. agua**, to leak; **p. de vista**, to lose sight of;

p. el color, to turn or go pale; **p. el juicio** or **la razón**, to go out of one's mind; **p. la esperanza**, to lose hope; fig **p. los estribos**, to fly off the handle. 2 (dejar escapar) to miss; **ayer volví a p. el tren**, yesterday I missed the train again. 3 (malgastar) to waste; **p. tiempo**, to waste time. 4 (ser la perdición) to be the ruin or downfall of; **la ambición le perdió**, ambition was her downfall. II vi 1 (gen) to lose; **echar (algo) a p.**, to spoil (sth); **salir perdiendo**, to come off worst. 2 (desmejorar) to go off; (en salud) to get worse; (en valor) to devaluate; **la abuela ha perdido mucho en pocos meses**, Grandma has been getting worse over the last few months. 3 Tex (desteñirse) to fade. III **perderse** vr 1 (extraviarse) to get lost; **me perdí en la oscuridad**, I got lost in the darkness. 2 (cosas) to be lost; **nunca se me pierde nada**, I never lose anything; **se ha perdido un cuchillo**, a knife is missing. 3 (no asistir) to miss; **no te lo pierdas**, don't miss it; **te has perdido una buena cena**, you missed a good dinner. 4 (desaprovecharse) to go to waste; **con este calor la comida se pierde enseguida**, food goes off quickly in this heat. 5 fig (desvanecerse) to die out; **p. de vista**, (desaparecer) to fade or disappear into the distance; (extenderse) to stretch out as far as the eye can see. 6 (entregarse a los vicios) to be a lost cause; **en cuanto descubrió los placeres de la vida se perdió**, as soon as he discovered life's pleasures he was a lost cause; **p. por**, to be crazy about.

perdición nf 1 (ruina moral or material) undoing, ruin, downfall; **el orgullo será su p.**, his pride will be his undoing. 2 Rel damnation, perdition.

pérdida nf 1 (extravío) loss; **la p. de algn**, the loss of sb; **no tiene p.**, you can't miss it; **p. del conocimiento**, loss of consciousness. 2 (de tiempo, esfuerzos) waste; **intentar convencerlo es una p. absoluta de tiempo**, it would be a complete waste of time to try to persuade him. 3 (de un fluido) leak, leakage. 4 Fin loss; **vender con p.**, to sell at a loss. 5 **pérdidas**, Mil losses. 6 **pérdidas**, (flujo) wastage sing.

perdido,-a I pp de **perder**. II adj 1 (extraviado) lost; **aquí está el cuchillo p.**, here's the lost knife; **lo podemos dar por p.**, it is as good as lost; fig **p. en sus pensamientos**, lost in thought; fig **un lugar p.**, an isolated place. 2 (animal, bala) stray. 3 (acabado) finished; **si me encuentran estoy p.**, if they find me I'm done for. 4 fam (sucio) filthy; **lo dejaron todo p. de barro**, the whole place was covered in mud. 5 fam (completo) absolute; **idiota perdida**, hopelessly stupid; **loco p.**, mad as a hatter. 6 (enamorado) crazy; **estar p. por algn**, to be crazy or nuts about sb. III nm,f (depravado) rake; (mujer) whore.
◆ **perdidamente** adv madly, desperately.

perdigar vtr Culin (carne) to brown, half-cook.

perdigón nm 1 (proyectil) pellet; **perdigones**, pellets, shot sing. 2 Orn young partridge.

perdigonada nf 1 (disparo) shot. 2 (herida) shot wound.

perdiguero,-a adj partridge-hunting; **perro p.**, setter.

perdiz nf Orn partridge; **p. común**, red-legged partridge; **p. nival**, ptarmigan; **p. pardilla**, partridge; fig **fueron felices y comieron perdices**, they all lived happily ever after.

perdón nm pardon, forgiveness; **con p. (sea dicho)**, if you will pardon my saying so; **eso no tiene p.**, it is unforgivable; **pedir p.**, to apologize; **¡p.!**, sorry!

perdonable adj forgivable, excusable.

perdonar vtr 1 (remitir) to forgive; **¿me perdonas?**, will you forgive me?; **por esta vez te perdono**, I'll let you off this time; fig **no perdona (ni) una**, he doesn't miss a thing. 2 (excusar) to excuse, pardon; **perdone que le moleste**, sorry for bothering you. 3 (eximir) to exempt; **le han perdonado dos años de cárcel**, she got two years' remission; **perdonarle la vida a algn**, to spare sb's life. 4 (aprovechar) **no p.**, to miss; **no perdona oportunidad para**, he doesn't miss the chance to.

perdonavidas nm inv fam braggart, bully.

perdulario,-a I *adj* **1** *(descuidado)* careless, negligent, sloppy. **2** *(disoluto)* immoral, dissolute. **II** *nm, f* **1** *(descuidado)* careless person. **2** *(vicioso)* immoral person.

perdurable *adj* **1** *(eterno)* everlasting. **2** *(duradero)* durable, long-lasting. ◆ **perdurablemente** *adv* ever-lastingly.

perdurar *vi* **1** *(durar)* to endure, last. **2** *(persistir)* to persist, continue to exist.

perecedero,-a *adj* perishable; **artículos perecederos,** perishables.

perecer *vi* to perish, die.

peregrinación *nf,* **peregrinaje** *nm* pilgrimage.

peregrinar *vi* **1** *(ir de peregrinaje)* to go on a pilgrimage. **2** *fig (errar)* to go to and fro *or* back and forth.

peregrino,-a I *adj* **1** *(gen)* on a pilgrimage. **2** *(aves)* migrating. **3** *fig (extravagante)* odd, peculiar; **sus ideas son siempre peregrinas,** he always has such harebrained ideas. **II** *nm, f* pilgrim. **III** *nm Méx (cobrador)* bus conductor. ◆ **peregrinamente** *adv* peculiarly, strangely.

perejil *nm Bot* parsley.

perendengue *nm* trinket, cheap ornament

perengano *nm fam* so-and-so, what's his name

perennal *adj,* **perenne** *adj* perennial, perpetual, everlasting.

perennidad *nf* everlasting quality, perpetuity.

perentoriedad *nf* peremptoriness, urgency

perentorio,-a *adj* peremptory, urgent, pressing ◆ **perentoriamente** *adv* urgently

pereza *nf* laziness, idleness; **me da p. salir,** I don't feel like going out; **tener p.,** to be *or* feel lazy

perezco *indic pres véase* **perecer.**

perezoso,-a I *adj* **1** *(holgazán)* lazy, idle. **2** *(lento)* sluggish. **II** *nm, f* lazy person, idler. **III** *nm Zool* sloth. ◆ **perezosamente** *adv* lazily, *(lentamente)* sluggishly

perfección *nf* perfection; **hacer algo a la p.,** to do sth perfectly *or* to perfection.

perfeccionamiento *nm* **1** *(acción)* perfecting **2** *(mejora)* improvement

perfeccionar *vtr* to perfect, *(mejorar)* improve, make better; **ha ido a Inglaterra a p. su inglés,** he's gone to England to improve his English

perfeccionismo *nm* perfectionism.

perfeccionista *adj & nmf* perfectionist.

perfectibilidad *nf* perfectiblity

perfectible *adj* perfectible.

perfectivo,-a *adj* perfective

perfecto,-a *adj* perfect; **nadie es p.,** nobody is perfect. ◆ **perfectamente** *adv* **1** *(con perfección)* perfectly; **te entiendo p.,** I quite understand (you), I know what you mean **2 ¡p.!,** *(de acuerdo)* agreed!, all right!

perfidia *nf* perfidy, treachery.

pérfido,-a I *adj* perfidious, treacherous, *pey* **la pérfida Albión,** perfidious Albion. **II** *nm, f* traitor. ◆ **pérfidamente** *adv* perfidiously, treacherously

perfil *nm* **1** *(gen)* profile; *(contorno)* outline, contour; **de p.,** in profile; **fotografía mi mejor p.,** photograph my best side; **vista de p.,** side view. **2** *(trazo)* upstroke **3** *fig (característica)* feature, characteristic **4** *Geom* cross section

perfilado,-a I *pp* de **perfilar II** *adj* **1** *(rostro)* long and thin; *(labios, nariz, etc)* well-shaped. **2** *(dibujado)* outlined. **3** *Téc* streamlined **III** *nm* **1** *(dibujo)* outline **2** *Téc* streamlining.

perfilar I *vtr* **1** *(dar forma)* to shape, outline **2** *(dibujar)* to draw the outline of **3** *(acabar)* to give the finishing touches to **4** *Téc* to streamline **II** **perfilarse** *vr* **1** *(tomar forma)* to take shape. **2** *(recortarse)* to stand out.

perforación *nm,* **perforado** *nm (gen)* perforation; *Min* drilling, boring, *Inform (de tarjetas)* punching.

perforador,-a I *adj (gen)* perforating; *Min* drilling, boring **II** *nm, f (gen)* perforator; *(de billetes)* puncher, *Min* driller, borer **III** *nf Téc* drilling machine; *(de billetes)* punch, punching machine, *Inform* **perforadora de teclado,** keypunch

perforar *vtr (gen)* to perforate, *Min* to drill, bore; *Inform* to punch.

performance *nf* performance

perfumador *nm* perfume spray.

perfumar I *vtr* to perfume **II** *vi* to perfume **III** **perfumarse** *vr* to put on perfume, **p. mucho,** to use a lot of perfume.

perfume *nm* perfume, scent

perfumería *nf* perfumery; *(en grandes almacenes)* perfume counter *or* department.

perfumista *nmf* perfume maker *or* seller.

perfusión *nf* perfusion

pergamino *nm* **1** *(piel)* parchment. **2 pergaminos,** *(títulos de nobleza)* title deeds

pergeñar *vtr (plan)* to sketch, outline; *(texto)* to prepare, draft

pérgola *nf* pergola

pericardio *nm Anat* pericardium

pericarpio *nm Bot* pericarp.

pericia *nf* expertise, skill, **la p. del piloto evitó lo peor,** the pilot's skill avoided a great disaster.

pericial *adj* expert; **informe p.,** expert report

periclitar *vi fml* to decline, wane.

perico *nm* **1** *fam Orn (gen)* parakeet, *(australiano)* budgerigar. **2** *arg (drogas)* snow, cocaine

periferia *nf (gen)* periphery, *(alrededores de ciudad)* outskirts *pl*

periférico,-a I *adj* peripheral **II** *nm Inform* peripheral device *or* unit.

perifollo *nm* **1** *Bot* common chervil. **2 perifollos,** *pey (adornos)* frills, trimmings.

periforme *adj* pear-shaped

perífrasis *nf inv* periphrasis, long-winded explanation.

perifrástico,-a *adj* periphrastic, long-winded, verbose

perilla *nf (barba)* goatee, *fam* **de perilla(s),** *(oportuno)* at the right moment, *(útil)* very handy; **me viene de p.,** it's just the ticket

perillán,-ana *nm, f fam* rascal, rogue.

perimétrico,-a *adj* perimetric

perímetro *nm* perimeter

perinatal *adj Med* perinatal

perineal *adj Anat* perineal

perineo *nm Anat* perineum.

periodicidad *nf* periodicity.

periódico,-a I *adj* **1** *(cíclico)* periodic, periodical, *Quím* **tabla periódica,** periodic table. **2** *(publicación)* periodical **3** *Med (fiebre)* recurrent **II** *nm* newspaper

periodismo *nm* journalism.

periodista *nmf* journalist, reporter

periodístico,-a *adj* journalistic, **artículo p.,** newspaper article

periodo *nm,* **período** *nm* period.

peripatético,-a *adj Filos* Peripatetic; *fig* ridiculous.

peripecia *nf* sudden change, vicissitude; **durante la cena nos relató las peripecias de su juventud,** over dinner he told us about the ups and downs of his youth.

periplo *nm* voyage, tour.

peripuesto,-a *adj fam* dolled-up

periquear *vi CAm* to flatter, court

periquete *nm fam* **en un p.**, in a jiffy

periquito *nm* **1** *Orn* (*gen*) parakeet, (*australiano*) budgerigar **2** *Ftb* Español supporter

periscópico,-a *adj* periscopic.

periscopio *nm* periscope.

perisodáctilo,-a *adj & nm Zool* perissodactyl.

perista *nm* fence, receiver (of stolen goods).

peristilo *nm Arquit* peristyle.

peritaje *nm* **1** (*informe*) expert *or* specialist report. **2** (*estudios*) technical studies *pl*.

perito,-a **I** *adj* expert. **II** *nm, f* technician, expert; **p. industrial/agrónomo/aeronáutico**, ≈ industrial/agricultural/aeronautical expert.

peritoneal *adj Anat* peritoneal.

peritoneo *nm Anat* peritoneum.

peritonitis *nf Med* peritonitis.

perjudicado,-a **I** *pp de* **perjudicar. II** *adj* harmed, damaged. **III** *nm, f* victim; **el p. siempre soy yo,** I am always the loser.

perjudicar *vtr* (*dañar*) to harm, injure; (*estropear*) to damage; (*intereses*) to prejudice; (*en paquetes de tabaco*) **'las Autoridades Sanitarias advierten que: el tabaco perjudica seriamente la salud'**, 'Government health warning: smoking can seriously damage your health'; **no quiero perjudicarte,** I don't want to spoil it for you.

perjudicial *adj* prejudicial, detrimental, harmful. ◆ **perjudicialmente** *adv* prejudicially.

perjuicio *nm* prejudice, harm, damage; **en p. de,** to the detriment of; **sin p. de,** without prejudice to.

perjurar *vi* **1** *Jur* to commit perjury. **2** *fam* to swear a lot; **le juró y perjuró que era verdad,** he swore again and again that it was true.

perjurio *nm Jur* perjury.

perjuro,-a **I** *adj* perjured. **II** *nm, f* perjurer.

perla *nf* **1** pearl; **p. cultivada,** cultured pearl. **2** *fig* (*persona*) gem, jewel. **3** *fam* **de perlas,** marvellously; **venir de perlas,** to be just the thing.

perlado,-a *adj* (*forma*) pearl-shaped; (*color*) pearl-coloured, *US* pearl-colored; *lit* **p. de sudor,** with beads of sweat.

permanecer *vi* to remain, stay; **ha permanecido en el puesto durante más de treinta años,** he's been in the same job for thirty years.

permanencia *nf* **1** (*inmutabilidad*) permanency, permanence. **2** (*estancia*) stay.

permanente **I** *adj* permanent; **comisión p.,** standing committee; **servicio p.,** 24-hour service. **II** *nf Peluq* permanent wave, perm; **hacerse la p.,** to have one's hair permed. ◆ **permanentemente** *adv* permanently.

permanganato *nm Quím* permanganate.

permeabilidad *nf* permeability, pervious nature.

permeable *adj* permeable, pervious; *fig* (*receptivo*) receptive.

pérmico,-a *adj & nm Geol* Permian.

permisible *adj* permissible.

permisión *nf* permission.

permisividad *nf* permissiveness.

permisivo,-a *adj* permissive.

permiso *nm* **1** (*autorización*) permission; **con su p.,** with your permission, if you don't mind; **pedir p.,** to ask permission. **2** (*documento, licencia*) licence, *US* license, permit; **p. de conducir,** driving licence, *US* driver's license; **p. de residencia,** residence permit. **3** *Mil* leave; **estar de p.,** to be on leave.

permitido,-a **I** *pp de* **permitir. II** *adj* permitted, allowed.

permitir **I** *vtr* to permit, allow; **¿me permite?,** may I?; **permítame,** allow *or* permit me; **si el tiempo lo permite,** weather permitting. **II permitirse** *vr* **1** to permit *or* allow

oneself; **me permito recordarle que,** let me remind you that; **no puedo permitirme ese lujo,** I can't afford it. **2** (*uso impers*) to be permitted *or* allowed; (*en letrero*) **'no se permite fumar',** 'no smoking'.

permuta *nf* exchange.

permutable *adj* permutable.

permutación *nf* **1** (*cambio*) exchange. **2** *Mat* permutation.

permutar *vtr* **1** (*cambiar*) to exchange. **2** *Mat* to permute.

pernear *vi* to shake *or* kick one's legs.

pernera *nf* trouser leg.

pernicioso,-a *adj* pernicious.

pernil *nm Culin* ham.

pernio *nm* hinge.

perno *nm Téc* bolt.

pernocta *nf Mil* (**pase de) p.,** overnight pass.

pernoctar *vi* to stay overnight *or* the night.

pero **I** *conj* but; **el dinero hace ricos a los hombres p. no dichosos,** money makes men rich but not happy; **p., ¿qué pasa aquí?,** now, what's going on here? **II** *nm* fault, objection; **poner** *or* **encontrar peros (a algo/a algn),** to find fault (with sth/with sb).

perogrullada *nf* truism, platitude.

perogrullesco *adj* platitudinous.

perol *nm Culin* large saucepan, pot.

peroné *nm Anat* fibula.

peronismo *nm Pol* Peronism.

peronista *adj & nmf Pol* Peronist.

peroración *nf* speech.

perorar *vi* to deliver a speech.

perorata *nf* boring speech.

perpendicular *adj & nf Geom* perpendicular. ◆ **perpendicularmente** *adv* perpendicularly.

perpendicularidad *nf Geom* perpendicularity.

perpetración *nf* perpetration.

perpetrar *vtr* to perpetrate, commit.

perpetuación *nf* perpetuation.

perpetuar **I** *vtr* to perpetuate. **II perpetuarse** *vr* to be perpetuated; (*hacer durar*) to go on interminably.

perpetuidad *nf* perpetuity; **a p.,** in perpetuity.

perpetuo,-a *adj* perpetual, everlasting; *Jur* **cadena perpetua,** life imprisonment. ◆ **perpetuamente** *adv* perpetually.

perplejidad *nf* perplexity, bewilderment.

perplejo,-a *adj* perplexed, bewildered; **dejar p.,** to perplex, bewilder; **quedar(se) p.,** to be perplexed *or* bewildered.

perra *nf* **1** *Zool* bitch. **2** *fam* (*moneda*) penny; **estar sin una p.,** to be broke. **3** *fam* (*idea fija*) obsession, fixed idea; **coger la p. de (hacer algo),** to take it into one's head (to do sth); **coger una p.,** to fly off the handle.

perrera *nf* (*para guardar perros*) kennel, kennels *pl*; *Ferroc* dog box.

perrería *nf fam* dirty trick; **hacerle una p. a algn,** to play a dirty trick on sb.

perrero *nm* dog-catcher.

perro,-a **I** *adj fam* lousy, wretched; **¡perra suerte!,** what rotten luck! **II** *nm* **1** *Zool* dog; (*en letrero*) **cuidado con el p.,** beware of the dog; **p. callejero** *or* **suelto,** stray dog; **p. faldero,** lapdog; *fig* **¡a otro p. con ese hueso!,** come off it!, pull the other one!; *fig* **p. viejo,** old hand; *fam* **de perros,** lousy; *fam* **vida de perros,** dog's life; *prov* **p. ladrador, poco mordedor,** his bark is worse than his bite. **2** *Culin* **p. caliente,** hot dog. **3** *fam* (*canalla*) rotter, swine.

perruno,-a *adj* canine, dog; (*lealtad*) doglike.

persa *adj & nmf* Persian.

persecución *nf* **1** *(seguimiento)* pursuit; **salieron en su p.,** they set off in pursuit (of him). **2** *Pol (represión)* persecution.

persecutorio,-a *adj* **1** *(que sigue)* pursuing. **2** *(opresor)* persecutory; *Med* **manía persecutoria,** persecution mania.

perseguidor,-a **I** *adj* **1** *(seguidor)* pursuing. **2** *(represor)* persecuting. **II** *nm,f* **1** *(el que sigue)* pursuer. **2** *(opresor)* persecutor.

perseguir *vtr* **1** *(gen)* to pursue, chase; *(seguir)* to run after, follow; *fig* **me persigue la mala suerte,** I'm dogged by bad luck. **2** *(reprimir)* to persecute. **3** *fig (pretender)* to pursue, be after; **¿qué persigues?,** what are you aiming at?

perseverancia *nf* perseverance, constancy.

perseverante *adj* persevering, constant.

perseverar *vi* **1** *(persistir)* to persevere, persist; **si perseveras en tu actitud,** if you continue to have that attitude. **2** *(durar)* to last.

Persia *n* Persia.

persiana *nf* (Persian) blinds *pl*.

pérsico,-a **I** *adj* Persian; **golfo P.,** Persian Gulf. **II** *nm Bot* persicaria, red shank.

persignar *Rel* **I** *vtr* to cross. **II persignarse** *vr* to cross oneself.

persistencia *nf* persistence.

persistente *adj* persistent.

persistir *vi* to persist.

persona *nf* person; **algunas personas,** some people; **buena p.,** nice person; **en p.,** in person; **por p.,** per person; *Ling* **la primera p. del plural,** the first person plural; *Jur* **p. jurídica,** legal entity; *fam* **p. mayor,** grown-up.

personaje *nm* **1** *(celebridad)* celebrity, personage, important person. **2** *Cin Lit Teat* character.

personal **I** *adj* **1** *(particular)* personal, private. **2** *Ling* personal. **II** *nm* **1** *(plantilla)* staff, personnel. **2** *fam (gente)* people. ◆ **personalmente** *adv* personally.

personalidad *nf* personality.

personalismo *nm* **1** *Filos* personalism. **2** *Pol (parcialidad)* partiality. **3** *(egoísmo)* egoism.

personalista *adj* **1** *Filos* personalistic. **2** *(parcial)* partial. **3** *(egoísta)* egoistic.

personalizar *vtr* **1** *(aludir)* to personalize. **2** *(encarnar)* to personify. **3** *(adaptar)* to become *or* get personal.

personarse *vr* to present oneself, appear in person.

personificación *nf* personification.

personificar *vtr* to personify.

perspectiva *nf* **1** *(gen)* perspective; **en p.,** in perspective; **p. lineal,** linear perspective. **2** *(futuro)* prospect, outlook; **las perspectivas son inmejorables,** the perspectives could not be better.

perspicacia *nf* keen understanding, insight, perspicacity.

perspicaz *adj* sharp, perspicacious.

perspicuo,-a *adj* perspicuous, clear.

persuadir **I** *vtr* to persuade; **estar persuadido de que,** to be convinced that. **II persuadirse** *vr* to become convinced.

persuasión *nf* persuasion.

persuasivo,-a **I** *adj* persuasive, convincing. **II** *nf* persuasiveness.

persuasor,-a *nm,f* persuader, convincer.

pertenecer *vi* to belong **(a,** to); *fig* **no me pertenece decirlo,** it's not for me to say.

perteneciente *adj* belonging.

pertenencia *nf* **1** *(propiedad)* possessions *pl*, property. **2** *(afiliación)* affiliation, membership. **3** **pertenencias,** personal belongings.

pértiga *nf pole; Dep* **salto de p.,** pole vault.

pertinacia *nf* **1** *(persistencia)* persistence. **2** *(obstinación)* obstinacy.

pertinaz *adj* **1** *(persistente)* persistent. **2** *(obstinado)* obstinate, stubborn. ◆ **pertinazmente** *adv* **1** *(persistentemente)* persistently. **2** *(obstinadamente)* obstinately.

pertinencia *nf* **1** *(relación)* pertinence, relevance. **2** *(adecuado)* appropriateness.

pertinente *adj* **1** *(relativo)* pertinent, relevant. **2** *(apropiado)* appropriate; **esta decisión no es p. a mi cargo,** it is not up to me to decide.

pertrechar **I** *vtr* to equip, supply **(de, con,** with). **II pertrecharse** *vr* to equip oneself.

pertrechos *nmpl (equipo)* equipment *sing*; *Mil* ammunition *sing*.

perturbación *nf* disturbance; **p. del orden público,** breach of the peace; *Med* **p. mental,** mental disorder.

perturbado,-a **I** *pp de* perturbar. **II** *adj* **1** *(confuso)* confused. **2** *(desequilibrado)* (mentally) deranged *or* unbalanced. **III** *nm,f* mentally deranged *or* unbalanced person.

perturbador,-a **I** *adj* disturbing. **II** *nm,f* disturber, unruly person.

perturbar *vtr (público)* to disturb; *Med* **p. la mente,** to perturb one's mind.

Perú *n* Peru.

peruano,-a *adj & nm,f* Peruvian.

perversidad *nf* perversity.

perversión *nf* perversion.

perverso,-a **I** *adj* perverse, evil. **II** *nm,f* **1** *(malvado)* evil *or* wicked person. **2** *(depravado)* pervert. ◆ **perversamente** *adv* perversely.

pervertidor,-a **I** *adj* pervertible. **II** *nm,f* perverter.

pervertir **I** *vtr* to pervert, corrupt. **II pervertirse** *vr* to be perverted, become perverted.

pervivencia *nf* survival.

pervivir *vi* to survive.

pesa *nf (peso)* weight; *Gim* **levantamiento de pesas,** weightlifting. **2** *Am (carnicería)* butcher's (shop).

pesabebés *nm inv* baby-scales *pl*.

pesacartas *nm inv* letter-scales *pl*.

pesada *nf* weighing.

pesadez *nf* **1** *(con peso)* heaviness; *fig (de estómago)* fullness. **2** *fig (lentitud)* slowness, sluggishness. **3** *fam (fastidio)* drag, nuisance.

pesadilla *nf* nightmare; **de p.,** nightmarish.

pesado,-a **I** *pp de* pesar. **II** *adj* **1** *(gen)* heavy; *(comida)* rich, heavy; *(tiempo)* close, sultry. **2** *fig (lento)* slow, sluggish. **3** *(fatigoso)* hard, tough. **4** *(aburrido)* tedious, dull; **ponerse p.,** to be a pest; **¡qué p. eres!,** what a drag you are! **III** *nm, f* bore, pest. ◆ **pesadamente** *adv* heavily; *(despacio)* slowly, sluggishly.

pesadumbre *nf* grief, affliction.

pesaje *nm* weighing.

pésame *nm* condolence, sympathy; **dar el p.,** to offer *or* express one's condolence *or* condolences; **mi más sentido p.,** my deepest sympathy.

pesantez *nf Fís* gravity.

pesar **I** *vtr* **1** *(determinar el peso)* to weigh up. **2** *(examinar)* to weigh. **II** *vi* **1** *(tener gravedad)* to weigh; **¿cuánto pesas?,** how much do you weigh?; **pesa cien gramos,** it weighs a hundred grams; *fig* **toda la responsabilidad pesa sobre mí,** all the responsibility falls on me. **2** *(ser pesado)* to be heavy; **A pesa más/menos que B,** A is heavier/lighter than B; **pesa demasiado,** it's too heavy; **p. poco,** to be light. **3** *fig (tener importancia)* to play an important part. **III** *v unipers (ser de lamentar)* to be a pity; **mal que te pese,**

844

whether you like it or not; **me pesa que no lo aceptes,** I'm sorry that you won't accept it; **pese a (que),** in spite of; **pese a quien pese,** in spite of everything. **IV** *nm* **1** *(pena)* sorrow, grief. **2** *(arrepentimiento)* regret; **bien a su p.,** much to his regret. **3 a p. de,** in spite of; **a p. de todo,** in spite of everything; **a p. mío/tuyo,** against my/your will; **hazlo a p. de lo que digan,** do it in spite of what they say. **V pesarse** *vr* to weigh oneself.

pesario *nm Med* pessary.

pesaroso,-a *adj* **1** *(triste)* sorrowful, sad. **2** *(arrepentido)* regretful, sorry.

pesca *nf* **1** fishing; *(con caña)* angling; **ir de p.,** to go fishing; **p. de altura,** deep-sea fishing; **p. de bajura,** coastal fishing; **p. submarina,** underwater fishing; *fam fig* **andar a la p. de,** to fish for; *fam* **toda la p.,** the whole caboodle. **2** *(peces)* fish; *(pescado)* catch.

pescadería *nf* fish shop, fishmonger's (shop).

pescadero,-a *nm,f* fishmonger.

pescadilla *nf (pez)* young hake.

pescado *nm* fish; **p. blanco/azul,** white/blue fish.

pescador,-a I *nm* fishing. II *nm, f (hombre)* fisherman; *(mujer)* fisherwoman; **p. de caña,** angler.

pescante *nm* **1** *(de carruaje)* coachman's seat. **2** *Constr* jib, boom. **3** *Náut* davit.

pescar I *vtr* **1** to catch *or* land (fish); **ir a p. truchas,** to go trout fishing. **2** *fam (coger)* to pick up, catch; **le pescó la policía,** the police caught him; **no pesca ni un chiste,** he doesn't get a single joke; **p. un buen trabajo,** to land a good job. II *vi* to fish; **ir a p.,** to go fishing; **p. con caña,** to angle; *fig* **p. en río revuelto,** to fish in troubled waters.

pescozada *nf,* **pescozón** *nm* slap on the neck *or* head.

pescuezo *nm fam* neck; *hum* **retorcer el p. a algn,** to wring sb's neck.

pesebre *nm* **1** *(cajón)* manger, stall. **2** *(belén)* Nativity scene.

peseta *nf* **1** *Fin* peseta. **2 pesetas,** *fam* money *sing.*

pesetero,-a I *adj* stingy, money-grubbing, tight. II *nm,f* skinflint.

pesimismo *nm* pessimism.

pesimista I *adj* pessimistic. II *nmf* pessimist.

pésimo,-a *adj* very bad, awful, terrible; **de pésima calidad,** absolutely useless. ◆ **pésimamente** *adv* awfully, wretchedly, terribly.

peso *nm* **1** *(gravedad)* weight, heaviness; **al p.,** by weight; **ganar/perder p.,** to put on/lose weight; **p. bruto/neto,** gross/net weight; *fig* **caer por su propio p.,** to be self-evident; *fig* **de p.,** *(persona)* influential; *(razón)* convincing; *fig* **la familia en p.,** the whole family *fig* **me quité un p. de encima,** it took a load off my mind. **2** *Fin* peso. **3** *Dep (de lanzar)* shot; *(de levantar)* weight; **lanzamiento del p.,** shot put; **levantamiento de p.,** weightlifting; *Box* **p. mosca/pesado,** flyweight/heavyweight.

pespunt(e)ar *vtr Cost* to backstitch.

pespunte *nm Cost* backstitch.

pesquera *nf,* **pesquería** *nf* fishery, fishing ground.

pesquero,-a I *adj* fishing. II *nm* fishing boat.

pesquis *nm fam* gumption, wit; **no tener p.,** to be as thick as two short planks.

pesquisa *nf* **1** *(investigación)* inquiry; **hacer pesquisas,** to make inquiries. **2** *Arg Ecuad Par (policía)* secret police.

pestaña *nf* **1** *(pelo)* eyelash, lash. **2** *Anat Bot* fringe. **3** *Téc* flange; *(de neumático)* rim.

pestañear *vi* to blink; **sin p.,** without batting an eyelid.

pestañeo *nm* blink, blinking.

pestazo *nm fam* stink, stench.

peste *nf* **1** *Med* plague; *Hist* **la p. negra,** the Black Death; **p. bubónica,** bubonic plague; *fig* **una p. de mosquitos,** a

plague of mosquitoes. **2** *(hedor)* stench, stink. **3** *(cosa mala)* pest, nuisance. **4 pestes,** *(palabras de enojo)* swearing *sing*, obscenities; **decir** *or* **echar pestes,** to curse.

pesticida *nm* pesticide.

pestífero,-a *adj* **1** *(dañino)* pestiferous. **2** *(maloliente)* foul, stinking.

pestilencia *nf* **1** *(peste)* pestilence. **2** *(mal olor)* stench, stink.

pestilente *adj* **1** *(dañino)* pestilent. **2** *(maloliente)* stinking, foul.

pestillo *nm* spring bolt; *(cerrojo)* bolt, latch; *(de la contraventana)* shutter catch.

petaca I *nf* **1** *(para cigarrillos)* cigarette case; *(para picadura)* tobacco pouch; *(para bebidas)* flask. **2** *(broma)* apple-pie bed. **3** *CAm (joroba)* hump. **4 petacas,** *Méx (nalgas)* buttocks. II *nm, f Am (holgazán)* idler, slacker.

pétalo *nm Bot* petal.

petanca *nf* game of bowls, boules *pl*.

petardo *nm* **1** *(explosivo)* firecracker, firework; *Mil* petard. **2** *fam (persona) (fea)* ugly person, horror; *(inútil)* good-for-nothing, worthless person; *(aburrida)* bore. **3** *(drogas)* joint.

petate *nm Mil* luggage; *fam* **liar el p.,** *(marcharse)* to leave, pack up and go; *(morir)* to kick the bucket.

petenera *nf Mús* Andalusian popular song; *fam* **salirse por peteneras,** to go off at a tangent.

peteretes *nmpl* sweets.

petición *nf* request; *Jur* petition, plea; **a p. de,** at the request of; **p. de mano,** proposal (of marriage).

peticionar *vtr Am* to request.

peticionario,-a *nm,f Jur* petitioner.

petimetre *nm* pey dandy.

petirrojo *nm Orn* robin (redbreast).

petitorio,-a *adj* petitionary.

peto *nm* **1** *(prenda)* bib, bodice. **2** *Hist (de armadura)* breastplate.

petrel *nm Orn* petrel.

pétreo,-a *adj (de piedra)* stone; **una superficie pétrea,** a stony surface.

petrificación *nf* petrification.

petrificar *vtr,* **petrificarse** *vr* to petrify.

petrodólar *nm Fin* petrodollar.

petróleo *nm* petroleum, oil; **p. crudo,** crude oil; **pozo de p.,** oil well.

petrolero,-a I *adj* oil; **la industria petrolera,** the oil industry. II *nm Náut* oil tanker.

petrolífero,-a *adj* oil; *Geol Min* oil-bearing.

petroquímico,-a *Quím* I *adj* petrochemical. II *nf* petrochemistry.

petulancia *nf* arrogance, vanity.

petulante *adj* arrogant, vain.

petunia *nf Bot* petunia.

peúco *nm* **1** *(de niño)* bootee. **2** *(dormir)* bedsock.

peyorativo,-a *adj* pejorative, derogatory.

peyote *nm Bot* peyote, mescal.

pez[1] *nm Zool* fish; *fam fig* **ella está como p. en el agua,** she's in her element; *fam fig* **estaba p. en ciencias,** he knew nothing at all about science; *fam fig* **p. gordo,** big shot. ■ **p. cinto,** scabbard fish; **p. de San Pedro,** John Dory; **p. espada,** swordfish; **p. martillo,** hammerhead shark; **p. volador,** flying fish.

pez[2] *nf* pitch, tar.

pezón *nm* **1** *Anat* nipple. **2** *Téc* tip, knob.

pezuña *nf Anat Zool* hoof.

piadoso,-a *adj* 1 *(devoto)* pious. 2 *(compasivo)* compassionate; **mentira piadoss,** white lie. ◆ **piadosamente** *adv véase* **pío,-a².**

pialar *vtr Am* to hobble.

piamontés,-esa *adj & nm,f* Piedmontese.

pianísimo *adv & nm Mús* pianissimo.

pianista *nmf Mús* pianist, piano player.

pianístico,-a *adj Mús* pianistic, piano.

piano *Mús* I *nm* piano. ■ **p. de cola,** grand piano; **p. de media cola,** baby grand (piano); **p. recto/vertical,** upright piano. II *adv* 1 *Mús* piano. 2 *fam (despacio)* slowly, nice and easy.

pianoforte *nm Mús* pianoforte, piano.

pianola *nf Mús* pianola.

piar *vi* to chirp, tweet.

piara *nf Zool* herd of pigs.

piastra *nf Fin* piastre.

PIB *nm Fin abr de* **producto interior bruto,** gross domestic product, GDP.

pibe,-a *nm,f RPl* Kid.

pica *nf* 1 *Hist Mil* pike; *fig* **poner una p. en Flandes,** to bring off sth really difficult. 2 *Taur* goad. 3 *Naipes* spade. 4 *Am (sendero)* track, path.

picacho *nm* mountain peak.

picada *nf véase* **picadura.**

picadero *nm* 1 *Equit* riding school. 2 *fam (piso)* bachelor pad.

picadillo *nm Culin (carne)* minced meat; *(guiso)* type of stew; *fam* **hacer p. a algn,** to make mincemeat of sb.

picado,-a I *pp de* picar. II *adj* 1 *Culin (pasado)* off, bad; *(vinos)* sour; *(carne)* high. 2 *Culin (cortado)* chopped; *(molido)* minced; *(tabaco)* cut. 3 *(mordido)* bitten; *(de avispa, abeja)* stung. 4 *Med (diente)* decayed; **p. de la viruela,** pockmarked. 5 *(mar)* choppy. 6 *fam (molesto)* piqued, narked. III *nm* 1 *(acción de picar)* chopping. 2 *Av* dive, diving; **caer en p.,** to plummet.

picador *nm Taur* mounted bullfighter, picador.

picadora *nf* mincer.

picadura *nf* 1 *(de serpiente, insecto)* bite; *(de avispa, abeja)* sting. 2 *(en una fruta)* spot; *Med (de viruela)* pockmark; *(en un diente)* decay, caries *sing*; *Metal* pitting. 3 *(tabaco)* cut tobacco.

picaflor *nm* 1 *Orn* hummingbird. 2 *Am (persona)* lady-killer.

picajoso,-a I *adj* touchy. II *nm,f* touchy person.

picana *nf* 1 *SAm* goad. 2 *Arg Bol Culin* breast of rhea. 3 *Arg Chi Culin* shank.

picante I *adj* 1 *Culin* hot, spicy. 2 *fig (malicioso)* risqué, spicy. II *nm* piquancy, hot spice.

picapedrero *nm* stonecutter.

picapica *nf polvos* **p.,** itching powder *sing*.

picapleitos *nmf inv pey* bad lawyer.

picaporte *nm* 1 *(aldaba)* door knocker. 2 *(pomo)* door handle.

picar I *vtr* 1 *(punzar) (insectos, serpientes)* to bite; *(avispas, abejas)* to sting; *(espino, barba)* to prickle. 2 *(espolear)* to spur on; *Taur* to goad, wound. 3 *(comer) (aves)* to peck (at); *(persona)* to nibble, pick (at). 4 *Pesca* to bite. 5 *(escocer)* to itch; **me pica la nariz,** my nose is itching; **me pican los ojos,** my eyes are smarting; *fam* **a quien pique que se rasque,** if the cap fits, wear it. 6 *(perforar)* to prick, puncture, punch. 7 *Culin (moler)* to mince; *(cortar)* to chop up. 8 *fig (incitar)* to incite, goad; **le picaron para que lo dijera,** he was forced into saying it; **p. la curiosidad (de algn),** to arouse (sb's) curiosity; **p. el amor propio (de algn),** to wound (sb's) self-esteem. 9 *Mús* to play a note. II *vi* 1 *(escocer)* to itch; *(herida)* to smart. 2 *(calentar el sol)* to burn. 3 *Culin* to be hot; *(vino)* to be sharp. 4 *Pesca* to bite. 5 *fig (dejarse engañar)* to swallow it. 6 *Av* to dive. III **picarse** *vr* 1 *(fruta)* to spot, rot; *(vino)* to turn sour; *(ropa)* to become moth-eaten; *(metal)* to pit; *(dientes)* to decay. 2 *(mar)* to get choppy. 3 *(sentirse herido)* to take offence *or US* offense; *(enfadarse)* to get cross. 4 *(drogas)* to shoot up. 5 *Am (emborracharse)* to get drunk. 6 **picárselas,** *Arg (largarse)* to scarper.

picardía *nf* 1 *(bribonería)* naughtiness; *(astucia)* craftiness; **tener mucha p.,** to be a crafty old devil. 2 *(travesura)* dirty trick; *(procacidad)* naughty thing.

picaresco,-a I *adj* 1 *(deshonesto)* roguish. 2 *Lit* picaresque. II *nf* 1 *(pandilla)* gang of rascals. 2 *Lit* picaresque literature.

picaro,-a I *adj* 1 *(travieso)* naughty, mischievous; *(astuto)* sly, crafty. 2 *(procaz)* risqué. II *nm,f* rascal, sly person, rogue.

picatoste *nm Culin* crouton.

picazón *nf* 1 *(que pica)* itch; *(que quema)* smarting, stinging. 2 *fig (desazón)* uneasiness, anxiety.

picea *nf Bot* spruce; **p. de Noruega,** Norway spruce; **p de Serbia,** Serbian spruce.

picha *nf vulg* cock, prick.

pichana *nf Arg* broom.

piche I *adj CAm* tight-fisted, mean. II *nm* 1 *Am fam (miedo)* fear. 2 *CAm Zool* kind of armadillo.

pichear *vtr Béisb* to pitch.

picher *nm Béisb* pitcher.

pichi *nm (prenda)* pinafore dress.

pichico *nm CAm Anat* phalanx of an animal.

pichocal *nm Méx* pigsty.

pichón¹ *nm Orn* young pigeon; **tiro al** *or* **de p.,** pigeon shooting.

pichón,-ona² *nm,f fam (persona)* darling, pet.

picnic *nm* picnic; **ir de p.,** to go for a picnic.

pico *nm* 1 *Orn* beak, bill. 2 *Orn* woodpecker; **p. menor,** lesser-spotted woodpecker; **p. picapinos,** great spotted woodpecker. 3 *(punta)* corner. 4 *(de vasija)* spout; *(de cazuela)* lip. 5 *(herramienta)* pick, pickaxe, *US* pickax. 6 *Geog (cima)* peak; *fig (valor máximo)* peak. 7 *fam (boca)* mouth; **abrir el p.,** to talk; **cierra el p.,** shut your trap; **darse el p.,** *(besarse)* to smooch; *(llevarse bien)* to get along well; **ir de picos pardos,** to paint the town red; **ser** *or* **tener un p. de oro,** to have the gift of the gab; **tener mucho p.,** to be a great talker. 8 *(cantidad)* odd amount; **éramos cincuenta y p.,** there were fifty odd of us; **llegó a las dos y p.,** he arrived just after two; *fam* **costar un p.,** to cost a bomb. 9 *(drogas)* fix; **darse un p.,** to give oneself a fix.

picogordo *nm Orn* hawfinch.

picoleto *nm fam* civil guard; **los picoletos,** the Civil Guard *sing*.

picor *nm (leve)* itch, tingling; *(doloroso)* smarting, stinging.

picota *nf* pillory; *fig* **poner a algn en la p.,** to pillory sb.

picotada *nf,* **picotazo** *nm* peck.

picotear *vtr & vi* 1 *Orn* to peck. 2 *(comer)* to nibble.

picoteo *nm* 1 *Orn* pecking. 2 *(de comer)* nibbling.

picto,-a *Hist* I *adj* Pictish. II *nm,f* Pict. III *nm Ling* Pictish.

pictografía *nf* pictography.

pictográfico,-a *adj* pictographic.

pictórico,-a *adj Arte* pictorial. ◆ **pictóricamente** *adv* pictorially.

picudo,-a *adj* pointed, beaked.

picuyí *nm Arg* filth, grubbiness, muck.

pidgin-english *nm Ling* pidgin English.

pidola *nf* leapfrog.

pie *nm* 1 *Anat* foot; **pies,** feet; **al p.,** close by, at hand; **a los pies de** *or* **al p. de,** at the foot of; **a p.,** on foot; **a p. firme,**

steadfastly; **de p.,** standing up; **de pies a cabeza,** from head to foot; **echar p. a tierra,** to get down, dismount; **en p.,** standing; **hacer p.,** to touch the bottom; **ir a p.,** to walk, go on foot; **no se tuvo de p.,** he couldn't stand up; **panti sin pies,** footless tights; **perder p.,** to get out out of one's depth; **poner los pies en,** to set foot in; **ponerse de p.,** to stand up; **quedar en p.,** to remain (standing); **tener los pies planos,** to have flat feet; *fig* **a los pies de algn,** at sb's service; *fig* **a p.** *or* **pies juntillas,** blindly; *fig* **al p. de la letra,** to the letter, word for word; *fig* **buscar tres** *or* **cinco pies al gato,** to split hairs; *fig* **con buen/mal p.,** on the right/wrong footing; *fig* **con pies de plomo,** gingerly, cautiously; *fig* **dar p. a,** to give cause for; *fig* **el ciudadano de a p.,** the man in the street; *fig* **(pendiente) en p.,** pending; *fig* **en (un) p. de igualdad,** on an equal footing; *fig* **levantarse con el p. izquierdo,** to get out of bed on the wrong side; *fig* **no tener ni pies ni cabeza,** to be absurd; *fig* **pararle los pies a algn,** to put sb in his *or* her place; *fam fig* **hacer algo con los pies,** to mess *or* botch sth up; *fam fig* **no dar p. con bola,** to do everything wrong. ■ *Med* **p. de atleta,** athlete's foot; *Zool* **p. de cabra,** goose barnacle; *Impr* **p. de imprenta,** imprint; *Téc* **p. de rey,** calliper, *US* caliper. **2** *(de un instrumento)* stand; *(de una copa)* stem. **3** *(de un escrito, una página)* foot. **4** *Impr (de una ilustración)* caption. **5** *(medida)* foot. **6** *Teat* cue. **7** *Lit* foot.

piedad *nf* **1** *Rel* devoutness, piety. **2** *(compasión)* compassion, pity; **por p.,** out of pity; **¡por p.!,** for pity's sake!; **tenga p. de ellos,** have mercy on them. **3** *Arte* pietá.

piedra *nf* **1** *(roca)* (stone); *(de mechero)* flint; **p. de afilar,** whetstone; **p. de molino,** millstone; **p. filosofal,** philosopher's stone; **p. pómez,** pumice (stone); **p. preciosa,** precious stone; **poner la primera p.,** to lay the foundation stone; *fig* **a tiro de p.,** a stone's throw away; *fig* **p. de toque,** touchstone; *fam* **menos da una p.,** it's better than nothing; *fam fig* **me dejó** *or* **me quedé de p.,** I was taken aback; *fam fig* **no dejar** *or* **quedar p. por mover,** not to leave a stone unturned; *hum* **¡que uno no es de p.!,** one can only stand so much! **2** *Med* stone, calculus. **3** *Meteor* hailstone.

piel *nf* **1** *Anat* skin; **p. de gallina,** goose pimples *pl*; *(persona)* **p. roja,** redskin; *fig* **dar la p. por algo,** to give one's right arm for sth; *fam* **ser de la p. del diablo** *or* **de Barrabás,** to be a little devil. **2** *(de fruta, de patata)* skin, peel. **3** *(cuero)* leather; *(con pelo)* fur; **zapatos/bolso de p.,** leather shoes/handbag. **4** **pieles,** fur *sing*; **un abrigo de p.,** a fur coat.

piélago *nm lit* ocean, deep.

pienso *nm* fodder, feed; **piensos compuestos,** mixed feed *sing*.

pierio,-a *adj Mit* Pierian.

pierna *nf Anat* leg; **estirar las piernas,** to stretch one's legs; *Culin* **p. de cordero,** leg of lamb; *fig* **estirar la p.,** to kick the bucket; *fam* **dormir a p. suelta** *or* **tendida,** to sleep like a log.

pierrot *nm Lit* Pierrot.

pieza *nf* **1** *(elemento)* piece, part, element; **p. de recambio,** spare part; **precio por p.,** price per item; *(prenda)* **traje de dos piezas,** suit; *fig* **me dejó** *or* **me quedé de una p.,** I was speechless *or* dumbfounded *or* flabbergasted; *fam* **¡buena p. estás tú hecho!,** a fine one you are! **2** *(habitación)* room. **3** *Caza* specimen, piece, head. **4** *Cost (trozo, remiendo)* patch. **5** *Tex (de tela)* roll, piece. **6** *(juegos)* piece, man. **7** *Teat* play; **p. corta,** sketch. **8** *Mús* song, piece.

piezoelectricidad *nf Fís* piezoelectricity.

piezoeléctrico,-a *adj Fís* piezoelectric.

pífano *nm Mús* fife.

pifia *nf fam* **1** *(error)* blunder, bloomer; **cometer una p.,** to put one's foot in it. **2** *Am (burla)* gibe, taunting, mockery.

pifiar *vi fam* to blunder, make a bloomer.

pigmentación *nf* pigmentation.

pigmento *nm* pigment.

pigmeo,-a I *adj* Pygmy, pigmy; *fig* pygmean. **II** *nm, f* Pygmy, Pigmy; *fig* pygmy, pigmy.

pignoración *nf Fin* pledge.

pignorar *vtr* to pawn.

pija *nf vulg* cock, prick.

pijada *nf fam* **1** *(dicho)* stupid *or* empty remark; **no dice más que pijadas,** he talks nothing but rubbish. **2** *(cosa)* trifle; **se molesta por cualquier p.,** he gets annoyed at the slightest thing.

pijama *nm (prenda)* pyjamas *pl*.

pijo,-a I *adj fam* **1** *(afectado)* posh; **hablar en plan p.,** to talk posh; **un barrio p.,** a posh area. **2** *(tonto)* stupid, fool. **II** *nm, f* **1** *fam (afectada)* daddy's boy; *(afectada)* little rich girl. **2** *vulg (pene)* prick, cock.

pijotada *nf véase* **pijada.**

pijotear *vi Am* to haggle.

pijotería *nf véase* **pijada.**

pijotero,-a *adj fam* annoying, tedious, boring.

pila *nf* **1** *(montón)* pile, heap; *fig (muchos)* piles *pl*, heaps *pl*, loads *pl*; **una p. de libros,** a pile of books; *fig* **una p. de años,** a lot of years. **2** *Elec* battery; **p. seca,** dry battery. **3** *Constr* pier. **4** *(recipiente) (de la cocina)* sink; *(de baño, lavadero)* basin; *(de agua)* small fountain; *Rel* **p. bautismal,** font; *fig* **nombre de p.,** Christian name.

pilar¹ *nm* **1** *Arquit* pillar; *fig (apoyo)* pillar, support. **2** *(mojón)* milestone; *(poste)* post.

pilar² *nm* waterhole.

pilastra *nf Arquit* pilaster.

pilatuna *nf Am* dirty trick.

pilcate *nm Méx* urchin.

pilcha *nf Am* piece of clothing.

pilche *nm Am* wooden bowl.

píldora *nf pill*; **la p.,** the (contraceptive) pill; **p. abortiva,** morning-after pill; *fig* **dorar la p.,** to gild the pill; *fam* **se tragó la p.,** he fell for it.

pileta *nf* **1** *(pila)* sink; *(para lavar ropa)* laundry. **2** *(piscina)* swimming pool.

pilila *nf fam* willy.

pillaje *nm* looting, pillage, plunder.

pillar I *vtr* **1** *(robar)* to plunder, loot. **2** *(coger)* to catch; *(alcanzar)* to catch up with; **lo pilló un coche,** he was run over by a car; **¡te pillé!,** caught you!; *fam* **p. un resfriado,** to catch a cold. **3** *fam (hallarse)* to be; **me pilla un poco lejos,** it's a bit far for *or* from me; **si te pilla de camino,** if you're going in that direction. **II pillarse** *vr* to catch; **p. un dedo/una mano,** to catch one's finger/hand; *fig* **p. los dedos,** to come out the loser, lose money.

pillastre *nm fam* rogue, scoundrel, rascal.

pillear *vi* to lead the life of a thug.

pillería *nf* **1** *(acción)* dirty trick. **2** *(panda de pillos)* gang of rascals.

pillín *nm fam* little rascal.

pillo,-a I *adj* **1** *(travieso)* naughty. **2** *(astuto)* sly, cunning. **II** *nm, f* **1** *(niño)* naughty child; **¡qué p. eres!,** what a naughty boy you are! **2** *pey (adulto)* thug.

pilón¹ *nm* **1** *(abrevadero)* trough. **2** *(lavadero)* basin, sink, laundry. **3** *(pilar)* pillar, column; *(poste)* post.

pilón,-ona² *I* *adj Arg Chi* one-eared. **II** *nf (novia)* bride; *(joven)* young girl.

pilonga *adj Bot (castaña)* **p.,** dried chestnut.

pilórico,-a *adj Anat* pyloric.

píloro *nm Anat* pylorus.

piloso,-a *adj* hair.

pilotaje *nm* pilotage, piloting.

pilotar *vtr Av* to pilot, fly; *Aut* to pilot, drive; *Náut* to pilot, steer.

pilote *nm Arquit* pile.

piloto I *nm* **1** *Av Náut* pilot; *Aut* driver; **p. automático,** automatic pilot; **sin p.,** pilotless. **2** *(luz)* pilot lamp, light. **II** *adj* pilot; **piso p.,** show flat; **programa p.,** pilot programme.

piltra *nf fam* bed.

piltrafa *nf* **1** *fam* weakling; **estar hecho una p.,** to be on one's last legs. **2 piltrafas,** *(residuos)* scraps.

pimentero *nm Bot* pepper plant.

pimentón *nm Bot* paprika, red pepper.

pimienta *nf* pepper; **p. blanca/negra,** white/black pepper.

pimiento *nm (planta)* pimiento; *(fruto)* pepper; **p. morrón,** sweet pepper; *fam* **me importa un p.,** I don't give a damn, I couldn't care less.

pimpante *adj fam* spruce, smart; **más p. que una rosa,** as fresh as a daisy.

pimpinela *nf Bot* pimpernel.

pimplar *vi fam* to drink, go boozing.

pimpollo *nm* **1** *Bot* shoot. **2** *fam (persona)* dish, smasher.

pimpón® *nm Dep* ping-pong, table tennis.

pinacoteca *nf* art gallery.

pináculo *nm Arquit* pinnacle.

pinar *nm* pine grove, pine wood.

pincel *nm* brush, paintbrush; *fig (estilo)* style.

pincelada *nf* brushstroke, stroke of a brush; *fig* **con cuatro pinceladas ella expresó lo que sentía,** in a few words she outlined how she felt.

pincelar *vtr* to paint.

pincha *nmf fam*, **pinchadiscos** *nmf inv fam* disc jockey, DJ.

pinchar I *vtr* **1** *(punzar)* to prick, prickle; *(desinflar)* to burst; **p. un balón,** to burst a ball; **una barba que pincha,** a prickly beard. **2** *fam (incitar)* to prod; *(molestar)* to get at, nag; **deja ya de pincharle,** stop getting at him; **hay que pincharla,** she needs prodding. **3** *Med* to inject, give an injection to. **II** *vi* **1** *Aut* to puncture. **2** *fig (fracasar)* to fail; *fam* **ni pincha ni corta,** he cuts no ice. **III pincharse** *vr* **1** *(picarse)* to prick oneself; **me pinché el dedo con un alfiler,** I pricked my finger with a pin. **2** *(drogas)* to shoot up.

pinchazo *nm* **1** *(punzadura)* prick. **2** *(de dolor)* sudden *or* sharp pain. **3** *Aut* puncture, blowout.

pinche *nm* **1** *(ayudante de cocina)* kitchen assistant. **2** *Arg PR (alfiler)* hatpin. **3** *Méx PR (bribón)* rogue.

pinchito *nm Culin* apéritif.

pincho *nm* **1** *(punta)* (sharp) point; *(de planta)* thorn, prickle; *(de animal)* spine; **alambre de pinchos,** barbed wire. **2** *Culin* apéritif; **p. moruno,** shish kebab; **tomar unos pinchos,** to have a snack *or* some starters.

pinchulear *vtr Arg* to decorate, embellish.

pindárico,-a *adj* Pindaric.

pindonga *nf fam* gadabout.

pindonguear *vi* to gad about.

pineal *adj* pineal.

pineda *nf* pine grove, pine wood.

pingajo *nm fam* **1** *(harapo)* rag. **2** *pey (mujer despreciable)* slut.

pingo *nm fam* **1** *(prenda)* shabby garment. **2** *(pingajo)* rag; **vas hecho un p.,** what a mess you look. **3** *(persona despreciable)* rotter. **4** *CAm (caballo)* fast horse. **5** *Méx (diablo)* **el p.,** the devil. **6 pingos,** *(ropa mala)* rags.

ping-pong® *nm Dep* table tennis, ping-pong.

pingüe *adj* abundant, plentiful; **pingües beneficios,** fat profits.

pingüino *nm Orn* penguin.

pinitos *nmpl fam* first steps; **hacer p.,** to take one's first steps.

pinnípedo,-a *adj & nm Zool* pinniped, pinnipedian.

pino *nm Bot* pine; *fig* **hacer el p.,** to do a handstand; *fam* **en el quinto p.,** in the back of beyond. ■ **p. albar,** Scots pine; **p. himalayo,** Bhutan pine, Himalayan blue pine; **p. insigne,** Monterey pine; **p manso,** stone pine; **p. piñonero,** stone pine.

pinole *nm CAm* maize drink.

pinrel *nm fam* foot, hoof; **pinreles,** feet *pl*, hooves.

pinta¹ I *nf* **1** *(mota)* dot; *(lunar)* spot. **2** *fam (aspecto)* look; **tener buena/mala p.,** to look good/bad; **tiene p. de ser interesante,** it looks interesting. **3** *Am (color)* colour *or* US color of the animals. **4** *Am (linaje)* lineage, family. **II** *nmf fam* shameless person.

pinta² *nf (medida)* pint.

pintada *nf* **1** *(inscripción)* graffiti *pl*. **2** *(acción)* painting (on a wall). **3** *Orn* guinea fowl.

pintado,-a *pp* de **pintar. I** *adj* **1** *(coloreado)* painted; *(en letrero)* **recién p.,** wet paint; *fam fig* **el más p.,** the best (person) in town; *fam fig* **es su hermana pintada,** she's the spitting image of her sister; *fam fig* **nos viene que ni p.,** it is just the ticket; *fam fig* **te está que ni p.,** it suits you to a tee. **2** *(maquillado)* made-up. **3** *(con manchas)* speckled, mottled.

pintamonas *nmf inv pey* bad painter, dauber.

pintar I *vtr* **1** *(dar color)* to paint. **2** **p. con pistola,** to spray. **2** *(dibujar)* to draw, sketch. **3** *fig (describir)* to describe, give the full picture of. **II** *vi* **1** *Naipes* to be trumps. **2** *fam (importar)* to count; **yo aquí no pinto nada,** *(estoy de más)* I am out of place here; *(no tengo nada que ver)* I have nothing to do with this. **III pintarse** *vr* **1** *(maquillarse)* to put make-up on. **2** *fig (mostrarse)* to show, appear. **3 pintárselas,** *fam (arreglarse)* to manage; **se las pinta solo,** there is no one like him.

pintarraj(e)ar I *vtr* to scribble, daub. **II pintarraj(e)arse** *vr* to tart oneself up.

pintarrajo *nm* scribble, daub.

pintiparado,-a *adj fam* just right; **me viene p.,** it is just the job, it is just what I need.

pinto,-a *adj* spotted, dappled; *Zool* **caballo p.,** pinto; *Bot* **judía pinta,** pinto bean.

pintón,-ona *adj Arg* tipsy.

pintor,-a I *nm, f* painter; *fam* **p. de brocha gorda,** *(de paredes)* house painter; *pey* dauber. **II** *adj Arg* swanky, showy.

pintoresco,-a *adj* **1** *(lenguaje, estilo)* picturesque. **2** *(estrafalario)* eccentric, bizarre.

pintura *nf* **1** *(acción, arte)* painting; **p. a la acuarela,** watercolour; **p. al óleo,** oil painting; **p. al pastel,** pastel drawing; **p. rupestre,** cave painting; *fam fig* **no la puedo ver ni en p.,** I can't stand the sight of her. **2** *(materia)* paint.

pinturero,-a *fam* **I** *adj* swanky, showy. **II** *nm, f* show-off.

pinza *nf* **1** *(gen pl)* tweezers *pl*; *Téc* pincers *pl*, tongs *pl*; **p. de la ropa,** clothes peg; **p. del pelo,** clip, clasp; *fam* **había que cogerlo con pinzas,** he was a wreck; *fam* **sacarle algo con pinzas a algn,** to drag sth out of sb. **2** *Cost* dart. **3** *(de animal)* pincer, nipper.

pinzar *vtr* to take out with tweezers.

pinzón *nm Orn* chaffinch; **p. real,** brambling.

piña *nf* **1** *Bot (de pino)* pine cone; *(de otros árboles)* cone. **2** *Bot (ananás)* **p. (americana),** pineapple. **3** *fig (grupo)* clan, clique. **4** *fam (golpe, puñetazo)* whop, punch. **5** *Am (trompada)* bump, bang.

piñata *nf* pot full of sweets.

piñón¹ *nm Bot* pine seed *or* nut; *fam* **estar a partir un p. (con algn),** to be hand in glove (with sb); *fam* **están a partir un p.,** they're thick as thieves.

piñón² *nm Téc* pinion; **p. de cambio,** bevel pinion.

pío¹ *nm (de pájaro, ave)* cheep, chirp; *fam* **no dijo ni p.,** there wasn't a cheep out of him.

pío,-a² *adj* pious. ◆ **piamente** *adv* **1** *(devotamente)* piously. **2** *(misericordiosamente)* mercifully.

piocha¹ *nf Méx (herramienta)* pickaxe, *US* pickax.

piocha² *nf Méx* 1 *(barba)* goatee. 2 *(bueno) (hombre)* good-looking man; *(cosa)* excellent thing.

piojo *nm* louse; *fig* **p. resucitado,** social climber.

piojoso,-a *adj* 1 lousy; *(sucio)* dirty, filthy. 2 *fig (mezquino)* stingy, mean.

piolet *nm Dep* ice axe *or US* ax.

piolín *nm Am* thin rope.

pionero,-a *nm,f* pioneer.

piorrea *nf Med* pyorrhoea, *US* pyorrhea.

pipa¹ *nf* 1 *(de fumar)* pipe; **fumar en p.,** to smoke a pipe. 2 *(tonel)* barrel.

pipa² *nf Bot (pepita)* pip; *fam* **no tener ni para pipas,** to be broke; *fam* **pasárselo p.,** to have a great time.

pipermín *nm (menta)* peppermint; *(licor)* peppermint liqueur.

pipeta *nf Quím* pipette.

pipí *nm fam* pee, wee-wee; **hacer p.,** to pee, wee-wee.

pipián *nm Am Culin* stew.

pipiolo,-a *nm,f* 1 *fam (niño)* youngster; *(novato)* novice. 2 *Arg Ven (bobo)* half-wit. 3 **pipiolos,** *CAm* money *sing*.

pipón,-ona *adj Am* 1 *(harto)* full. 2 *(barrigón)* potbellied.

pique *nm* 1 resentment; **tener un p. con algn,** to be at odds with sb. 2 **a p. de,** on the point of. 3 **irse a p.,** *Náut* to sink; *(un plan)* to fall through. *(un negocio)* to go bust.

piqué *nm Tex* piqué.

piquera *nf* hole.

piqueta *nf* pickaxe, *US* pickax.

piquete *nm* 1 *(estaca)* stake, post. 2 *(persona)* picket; **p. de huelga,** strike picket. 3 *Mil* **p. de ejecución,** firing squad.

piquiña *nf Col PR RD (picor)* itch.

piquituerto *nm Orn* crossbill.

pira *nf* pyre.

pirado,-a *arg* 1 *pp de* **pirar.** II *adj* **estar p. por algo,** to be mad about sth.

piragua *nf* canoe.

piragüismo *nm Dep* canoeing.

piragüista *nmf Dep* canoeist.

piramidal *adj* pyramidal.

pirámide *nf* pyramid; **las pirámides de Egipto,** the Egyptian Pyramids.

piraña *nf Am (pez)* piranha.

pirar *vi,* **pirarse** *vr arg* to clear off, hop it; **pírate, píratelas,** beat it.

pirata *adj & nmf* pirate; **edición p.,** illegal edition; **emisora p.,** pirate radio.

piratear I *vi* to pirate. II *vtr fig* 1 *(avión)* to hijack. 2 *(plagiar)* to pirate; **p. cintas de vídeo,** to pirate videotapes.

piratería *nf* piracy; **p. aérea,** hijacking.

pirenaico,-a *adj & nm,f* Pyrenean.

pirindolo *nm fam* thingumabob, thingummy, thingamajig.

Pirineos *nmpl Geog* Pyrenees.

piripi *adj fam* tipsy, merry; **estar p.,** to be drunk.

pirita *nf Min* pyrite.

piro *nm arg* **darse el p.,** to hop it.

pirómano,-a *nm,f Med* pyromaniac; *Jur* arsonist.

piropear *vtr* to shout a compliment at, make a verbal pass at.

piropo *nm* compliment, pass; **un desconocido le echó un p. por la calle,** a stranger made a pass at her in the street.

pirotecnia *nf* pyrotechnics *sing*.

pirotécnico,-a I *adj* pyrotechnical; **productos pirotécnicos,** fireworks. II *nm,f* pyrotechnist.

pirueta *nf* pirouette; *fig* **tuve que hacer piruetas para poder cobrar,** I had to go to great lengths to get my money.

piruetear *vi* to pirouette.

pirujo,-a *adj CAm* sceptical.

pirulí *nm* lollipop.

pis *nm fam* wee-wee, pee; **hacer p.,** to wee-wee, have a pee.

pisada *nf* 1 *(acción)* step, footstep; **oí pisadas,** I heard footsteps; *fig* **seguir las pisadas de algn,** to trail sb. 2 *(huella)* footprint.

pisapapeles *nm inv* paperweight.

pisar I *vtr (gen)* to tread on, step on; *(acelerador)* to press; *Teat* **p. las tablas** *or* **un escenario,** to tread the boards; *(en letrero)* **'prohibido p. el césped',** 'keep off the grass'; **¿te pisé?,** did I step on your foot?; *fig* **no p. un lugar,** not to set foot in a place; *fig* **jamás he pisado su casa,** I have never set foot in his place; *fig* **pisarle el terreno a algn,** to beat sb to it; *fig* **pisarle los talones a algn,** to tread on sb's heels. II *vi* to tread, step; *fig* **ella no se deja p. por nadie,** she can stand up for herself.

piscar *vtr Méx (maíz)* to harvest, collect.

piscardo *nm (pez)* minnow.

piscicultura *nf* pisciculture.

piscifactoría *nf* fish farm.

piscina *nf* swimming pool.

Piscis *nm inv Astrol Astron* Piscis.

pisco I *nm* 1 *Am (aguardiente)* type of strong liquor. 2 *SAm (pavo)* turkey. II *adj CAm (presuntuoso)* conceited.

piscolabis *nm inv Culin fam* snack.

piso *nm* 1 *(suelo)* floor. 2 *(planta)* floor; **autobús de dos pisos,** double-decker bus; **en el tercer p.,** on the third floor. 3 *(vivienda)* flat, apartment. 4 *(de zapato)* sole. 5 *Am (derecho a entrada)* right of entry.

pisotear *vtr (pisar)* to trample on; *(aplastar)* to stamp on; *fig* **se ha pisoteado el derecho de expresión,** freedom of speech has been trampled on.

pisotón *nm* stamp (of the foot); **darle un p. a algn,** to stamp on sb's toes.

pista *nm* 1 *(superficie)* track. ■ **p. de baile,** dance floor; *Dep* **p. de carreras,** racetrack; **p. de circo,** ring; *Dep* **p. de esquí,** ski run *or* slope; *Dep* **p. de patinaje,** ice rink; *Dep* **p. de tenis,** tennis court; *Aut* **p. de tierra,** dirt track; *Téc* **p. sonora,** soundtrack. 2 *Av* **p. de aterrizaje,** landing strip; **p. de despegue,** runway. 3 *Inform* track. 4 *(rastro)* trail, track; **estar sobre la p.,** to be on the right track; **seguir la p. a algn/a algo,** to trail sb/sth. 5 *(indicio)* clue, hint; **dame una p.,** give me a clue.

pistacho *nm Bot* pistachio nut.

pistero,-a *adj CAm* money-grubber.

pistilo *nm Bot* pistil.

pisto *nm* 1 *Culin* ≈ ratatouille. 2 *fig* hotch-potch. 3 *Am (dinero)* money. 4 *fam* **darse p.,** to show off.

pistola *nf* 1 *(arma)* gun, pistol; **a punta de p.,** at gunpoint. 2 *(para pintar)* spray gun; **pintar a p.,** to spray-paint.

pistolera *nf* holster.

pistolero *nm* gunman, gun, gangster.

pistoletazo *nm* gunshot.

pistón *nm* 1 *Téc (émbolo)* piston. 2 *(de arma)* cartridge cap. 3 *Mús* piston.

pistonudo,-a *adj fam* great, fantastic, smashing.

pita¹ *nf Bot* agave, pita.

pita² *nf (gallina)* hen, chicken.

pitada *nf* 1 *(abucheo)* booing, hissing. 2 *(pitido)* whistle.

pitanza *nf* 1 *(ración)* ration. 2 *Am fam (ventaja)* advantage; *(ganga)* bargain.

pitar I *vtr* 1 to whistle at; *Dep* to referee; **el árbitro pitó (la) falta,** the referee called a fault; *fam* **irse** *or* **salir pitando,** to fly off. 2 *(en señal de desagrado)* to boo, hiss. II *vi* 1 *(pito)* to blow. 2 *fam (funcionar)* to work, function; **esto no pita,** this doesn't work.

pitido *nm* whistle.

pitillera *nf* cigarette case.

pitillo *nm* cigarette, fag.

pitimini *nm (pl pitiminies) Bot* fairy rose bush; **rosa de p.,** fairy rose.

pito *nm* 1 whistle; *Aut* horn; *fam* **me importa un p.,** I don't give a hoot; *fam* **por pitos or por flautas,** for one reason or another; *fam* **tomar a algn por el p. del sereno,** to treat sb as a nobody. 2 *Orn* **p. real,** green woodpecker. 3 *fam (cigarrillo)* fag. 4 *vulg (pene)* prick, willie. 5 *Am (pipa de fumar)* pipe.

pitón *nm* 1 *Zool* python. 2 *(de botijo)* spout. 3 *(de toro)* horn.

pitorrearse *vr fam (escarnecer)* to scoff **(de,** at); *(reírse)* to make fun **(de,** of).

pitorreo *nm fam* scoffing, teasing; **¡ya está bien de p.!,** give over!

pitorro *nm* spout.

pitote *nm arg* hubbub, din.

pitre *nm Am (lechuguino)* toff.

pitufo,-a *nm, f* Smurf.

pituitario,-a *adj Anat* pituitary.

pituso,-a I *adj* lovely, cute. II *nm, f* lovely child.

pivot *nmf Dep* pivot.

pivotar *vi* to pivot.

pivote *nm* pivot.

pizarra *nf* 1 *Min Constr* slate. 2 *Educ (encerado)* blackboard; **salir a la p.,** to go up to the blackboard.

pizarral *nm* slate quarry.

pizarrín *nm* slate pencil.

pizarroso,-a *adj* slaty.

pizca *nf* 1 *(poco)* little bit, tiny piece; **ni p.,** not a bit; **no me hace ni p. de gracia,** I don't like it at all; **una p. de sal,** a pinch of salt. 2 *Méx Agr (recolección)* maize harvest.

pizpireta *adj fam (mujer) (vivaracha)* lively and attractive; *(astuta)* cute, sharp.

pizza *nf Culin* pizza.

placa *nf* 1 plate; **p. de matrícula,** number plate, *US* license plate. 2 *(conmemorativa)* plaque.

placaje *nm Rugby* tackle; **hacer un p. (a un jugador),** to tackle (a player).

placebo *nm Farm* placebo.

placenta *nf* placenta.

placentario,-a *adj* placental.

placentero,-a *adj* pleasant, agreeable.

placer¹ *nm Min* placer.

placer² *nm* pleasure; **ha sido un p. (conocerle),** it's been a pleasure (meeting you); **los placeres de la carne,** the pleasures of the flesh; **un viaje de p.,** a holiday trip; *fml* **tengo el p. de,** it gives me great pleasure to.

placer³ *vtr fml* to please.

placidez *nf* placidity.

plácido,-a *adj* placid, easy-going.

plaga *nf* 1 plague; *(calamidad)* calamity. 2 *Agr* pest, blight; *(de langostas)* plague.

plagado,-a I *pp de* plagar. II *adj* plagued.

plagar *vtr* to cover, fill; **la cocina estaba plagada de moscas,** the kitchen was infested with flies.

plagiar *vtr* 1 *(copiar)* to plagiarize. 2 *Am (secuestrar)* to kidnap.

plagiario,-a I *adj* plagiaristic. II *nm, f* plagiarist.

plagio *nm* plagiarism.

plaguicida *nm Agr* pesticide.

plan *nm* 1 *(proyecto)* plan, project; **¿qué planes tienes para mañana?,** what are your plans for tomorrow? 2 *(programa)* scheme, programme; *Educ* **p. de estudios,**

syllabus; *Fin* **p. de inversiones,** investment plan. 3 *Med* course of treatment. 4 *(altitud)* height; *(nivel)* level. 5 *fam (actitud)* attitude; *(manera)* way; **en p. de broma,** for a laugh; **en p. grande,** on a grand scale; **eso tampoco es p., eso no es p.,** that isn't on; **si te pones en ese p.,** if you're going to be like that (about it). 6 *fam (ligue, cita)* date.

plana *nf* 1 page, side; *fam* **corregirle or enmendarle la p. a algn,** *(criticarle)* to criticize sb's work; *(superarle)* to outdo sb. 2 *Prensa* page; **a toda p.,** full page; **primera p.,** front page. 3 *Mil* **p. mayor,** staff.

plancton *nm Biol* plankton.

plancha *nf* 1 *(de metal)* plate. 2 *(para planchar)* iron; *(ropa planchada)* ironing. 3 *Culin* grill; **sardinas a la p.,** grilled sardines. 4 *Impr* plate. 5 *fam (equivocación)* blunder, boob; **¡vaya p.!,** you've really put your foot in it!

planchado,-a I *pp de* planchar. II *nm* ironing.

planchar *vtr* 1 to iron. 2 *Am (adular)* to flatter.

planchazo *nm fam* blunder, boob.

planchista *nmf* panel beater, *US* body man.

planchistería *nf* panel beater's, body shop.

planeador *nm Av* glider.

planeamiento *nm* 1 *Av* gliding. 2 *(proyecto)* planning.

planear I *vtr* to plan. II *vi Av* to glide.

planeta *nm* planet.

planetario,-a I *adj* planetary. II *nm* planetarium.

planicie *nf Geog* plain.

planificación *nf* planning. ■ **p. familiar,** family planning.

planificar *vtr* to plan.

planilla *nf* 1 *Am Fin (cuenta)* account. 2 *(formulario)* application form.

plano,-a I *adj* 1 *(llano)* flat, even; **de p.,** *(llano)* flatly; *(de lleno)* directly. 2 *Geom Mat* plane. II *nm* 1 *Geom Mat* plane. 2 *Arquit* plan, draft; *(mapa)* map; **levantar el p. de la ciudad,** to draw a plan of the city. 3 *Cin* shot; **un primer p.,** a close-up; *fig* **estar en primer p.,** to be in the limelight; *fig* **estar en segundo p.,** to be in the background.

planta *nf* 1 *Bot* plant. 2 *(del pie)* sole. 3 *(piso)* floor, storey. ■ **p. baja,** ground floor. 4 *Arquit (plano)* ground plan. 5 *Ind* factory, plant. 6 *(proyecto)* plan. 7 *fam* **de buena p.,** good looking.

plantación *nf* 1 *Agr* plantation. 2 *(acción)* planting.

plantado,-a I *pp de* plantar. II *adj* 1 planted. 2 *fam* **bien p.,** good looking. 3 *fam* **dejar a algn p.,** *(no comparecer)* to stand sb up; *(abandonar)* to walk out on sb; **dejarlo todo p.,** to give up everything; **no te quedes ahí p.,** come on, move.

plantar I *vtr* 1 *Agr (árboles, campo)* to plant. 2 *(poner)* to put, place; **p. la tienda de campaña,** to set up tent; **p. un poste,** to put in a post; *fam fig* **p. a algn de patitas en la calle,** to throw sb out; **p. cara a algn,** to stand up to sb. 3 *(pegar)* to plant *or* land. 4 *fam (cantar, largar)* to tell off; **le plantó cuatro frescas,** he gave him a piece of his mind. 4 *fam (no comparecer)* to stand sb up; *(abandonar)* to walk out on sb; **plantó el trabajo,** he left his job, just like that. II **plantarse** *vr* 1 to stand; **se plantó en la puerta,** he stood in the doorway. 2 *(llegar)* to arrive; **en cinco minutos se plantó aquí,** he got here in five minutes flat. 3 *fig (mantenerse firme)* to stick to stubbornly. 4 *Naipes* to stick. 5 *Am (arreglarse)* to get all dressed up.

plante *nm fam* walkout.

planteamiento *nm* 1 *(exposición)* raising, exposition. 2 *(enfoque)* approach.

plantear I *vtr* 1 *(trazar)* to plan; **debemos p. este asunto cuidadosamente,** we've got to plan this carefully. 2 *(establecer)* to implant; **el gobierno Suárez planteó esta reforma,** the Suárez government implanted this reform. 3 *(exponer) (caso)* to state; *(idea, asunto)* to expound; *(problema)* to pose. 4 *(proponer)* to raise, set up, bring up.

II plantearse *vtr & vr* **1** *(considerar) (problema, situación)* to face; **deberías planteártelo en serio,** you ought to think about it seriously. **2** *(uso impers)* to arise; **se (nos) planteó un problema,** we were faced with a problem.

plantel *nm fig* cadre, clique; **cuentan con un buen p. de químicos,** they've got a strong chemistry staff.

plantificar I *vtr fam* to plant; **le plantificó una bofetada,** he landed him a punch in the face. **II plantificarse** *vr* **1** *fam pey (ponerse)* to put on. **2** *fam (llegar)* to arrive (**en,** at). **3** *CAm (arreglarse)* to get all dressed up.

plantilla *nf* **1** model, pattern; *(para dibujar)* French curve. **2** *(personal)* permanent staff, personnel; **estar en p.,** to be on the payroll. **3** *(de zapato)* sole; *(interior)* insole. **4** *Am Culin* thin sponge cake. **5** *Méx (fingimiento)* pretence.

plantío *nm Agr* field.

plantón *nm fam* long wait; **dar un p. a algn,** to stand sb up; **estar de p.,** to be kept waiting.

plañidera *nf arc* hired mourner.

plañidero,-a *adj* mournful, plaintive.

plañido *nm* lamentation; mourning.

plañir *vi* to mourn.

plaqué *nm* gold *or* silver plate.

plasma *nm Biol* plasma.

plasmar *vtr* **1** *(moldear)* to mould, *US* mold, shape. **2** *fig (proyecto, sentimiento)* to capture, grasp.

plasta *fam* **I** *nf* **1** lump; **estos guisantes están hechos una p.,** these peas are all mushy. **2** *(chapuza)* botchup, mess. **II** *nmf (cosa or persona aburrida)* bore; **este tío es un p.,** this bloke is a drag; **¡vaya p. de película!,** what a boring film!

plástica *nf* plastic art; **las artes plásticas,** the plastic arts.

plástico,-a I *adj* plastic. **II** *nm* **1** plastic. **2** *arg (disco)* record.

plastificado,-a I *pp de* **plastificar. II** *adj* plastic-coated.

plastificar *vtr* to coat *or* cover with plastic.

plastilina® *nf* Plasticine®.

plata *nf* **1** *Metal* silver; *(objetos de plata)* silverware; *fam* **como una p.,** as clean as a new pin; *fam* **hablar en p.,** to lay (it) on the line. ▪ **p. de ley,** sterling silver. **2** *Am* money.

plataforma *nf* **1** platform; *Ferroc* turntable. ▪ *Geog* **p. continental,** continental shelf. **2** *fig (punto de partida)* stepping stone, springboard. **3** *Pol* platform.

platanal *nm,* **platanar** *nm* banana plantation.

platanero *nm Bot* banana tree.

plátano *nm* **1** *(fruta)* banana. **2** *(árbol)* plane. ▪ **p. común,** London plane; **p. falso,** sycamore; **p. oriental,** Oriental plane.

platea *nf Cin Teat* stalls *pl, US* ground floor.

plateado,-a I *pp de* **platear. II** *adj* silvered, silver-plated. **III** *nm* silver plating.

platear *vtr* to silver-plate.

platense I *adj* of *or* from the River Plate. **II** *nmf* native *or* inhabitant of the River Plate.

platería *nf* **1** *(oficio)* silversmith's craft. **2** *(taller)* silversmith's workshop. **3** *(tienda)* silversmith's (shop).

platero,-a *nm,f* silversmith.

plática *nf* **1** chat, talk; **estar de p.,** to be chatting. **2** *Rel* sermon.

platicar *vi* **1** to chat, talk. **2** *Rel* to deliver a sermon.

platija *nf (pez)* plaice.

platillo *nm* **1** small plate; *(de taza)* saucer. **2** *(de balanza)* pan, tray; **pasar el p.,** to pass round the hat. **3** *Culin* meat and vegetable stew. **4** *Mús* cymbal. **5** **p. volante,** flying saucer.

platina *nf* **1** *(de microscopio)* slide, stage. **2** *Téc* worktable. **3** *(tocadiscos)* deck; **doble p.,** double deck.

platino *nm* **1** *Metal* platinum; **rubio p.,** platinum blond. **2 platinos,** *Aut* contact breaker *sing*, points.

plato *nm* **1** *(gen)* plate, dish; **lavar los platos,** to do the dishes; *fam* **pagar los platos rotos,** to carry the can; *fam* **parece que no ha roto un p. en su vida,** butter wouldn't melt in his mouth. **2** *Culin (parte de una comida)* course; **de primer p.,** for starters; **p. fuerte,** main course; **una comida de tres platos,** a three-course meal. ▪ **p. combinado,** one-course meal. **3** *(guiso)* dish; **un p. español,** a Spanish dish; *fig* **no es p. de mi gusto,** it's not my cup of tea. **4** *(de balanza)* pan, tray. **5** *(de tocadiscos)* turntable. **6** *Dep* **tiro al p.,** trapshooting.

plató *nm Cin* (film) set; *TV* floor.

platón *nm Am* **1** *(palangana)* washbasin. **2** *(fuente)* serving dish.

platónico,-a *adj* Platonic.

platonismo *nm Fil* Platonism.

plausibilidad *nf* plausibility.

plausible *adj* **1** *(admisible)* plausible, acceptable. **2** *(digno de alabanza)* commendable.

playa *nf* **1** beach; **iremos de vacaciones a la p.,** we're spending our holidays at the seaside. **2** *Am (espacio amplio)* open space; **p. de estacionamiento,** car park, *US* parking lot.

playeras *nfpl* plimsolls, *US* sneakers.

playero,-a *adj* beach; **un vestido p.,** a beach dress.

playo,-a *adj Am (aplanado)* flat.

plaza *nf* **1** *(lugar en una población)* square. **2** *Com (población)* place, town. **3** *(mercado)* market, marketplace. **4** *Aut* seat; **un coche de cuatro plazas,** a four-seater (car). **5** *(puesto)* post, position; **convocar una p.,** to advertise a post; **ocupar una p.,** to fill a post *or* vacancy; **p. vacante,** vacancy; **plazas limitadas,** limited number of (vacant) posts; *Educ (para niño)* **reservar p.,** to put his *or* her name down. **6** *Taur* **p. de toros,** bullring. **7** *Mil* **p. fuerte,** fortified town; *(fuerte)* stronghold.

plazo *nm* **1** *(periodo)* time, period; *(término)* time limit; **a corto/largo p.,** in the short term/in the long run; **el p. de matrícula acaba mañana,** tomorrow is the last day for enrolling; **el p. termina el viernes,** Friday is the deadline; **en un p. de quince días,** within a fortnight. **2** *Fin* instalment, *US* installment; **comprar a plazos,** to buy on hire purchase, *US* buy on an installment plan; **en seis plazos,** in six instalments.

plazoleta *nf,* **plazuela** *nf* small square.

pleamar *nf (mar)* high tide.

plebe *nf* masses *pl*, plebs *pl*.

plebeyo,-a I *adj* plebeian. **II** *nm,f* plebeian, pleb.

plebiscito *nm* plebiscite.

plegable *adj* folding, collapsible; **silla p.,** folding chair.

plegado,-a I *pp de* **plegar. II** *adj* folded. **III** *nm* folding.

plegamiento *nm Geol* folding.

plegar I *vtr* **1** *(doblar)* to fold. **2** *Cost* to pleat. **II plegarse** *vr* to give way, bow.

plegaria *nf Rel* prayer.

pleiteador,-a I *adj* pleading. **II** *nm,f* litigant.

pleitear *vi Jur* to conduct a lawsuit, plead, sue.

pleitesía *nf* tribute, homage.

pleito *nm* **1** *(riña)* argument, dispute. **2** *Jur* lawsuit, litigation; **poner un p. (a algn),** to sue (sb).

plenamar *nf véase* **pleamar.**

plenario,-a *adj* plenary; **sesión plenaria,** plenary session.

plenilunio *nm* full moon.

plenipotencia *nf* full powers *pl*.

plenitud *nf* plenitude, fullness; **en la p. de la vida,** in the prime of life.

pleno,-a I *adj* full; **en plena noche,** in the middle of the night; **en plenas facultades,** in full possession of one's faculties; **en p. día,** in broad daylight; **le dio en plena cara,** it hit him right in the face; **los empleados en p.,** the entire staff. **II** *nm* plenary meeting.

pleonasmo *nm Lit* pleonasm.

plétora *nf fig* abundance, plethora.

pletórico,-a *adj* abundant, brimming.

pleura *nf Anat* pleura.

pleuresía *nf*, **pleuritis** *nf inv Med* pleurisy.

plexiglás® *nm (plástico)* Perspex®, *US* Plexiglass®.

plexo *nm* plexus. ■ **p. solar,** solar plexus.

plica *nf* sealed envelope.

pliego *nm* **1** *(hoja)* sheet *or* piece of paper; *Jur* **p. de cargos,** list of charges; *Admin* **p. de condiciones,** bidding specifications. **2** *(carta)* sealed letter.

pliegue *nm* **1** fold. **2** *Cost* pleat. **3** *Geol* fold.

plinto *nm* **1** *(de columna)* plinth. **2** *Gimn* horse.

plisado,-a I *pp de* **plisar. II** *adj* pleated; **falda plisada,** pleated skirt.

plisar *vtr Cost* to pleat.

plomada *nf* **1** *(albañil etc)* plumb line. **2** *Pesca* weights *pl*, sinkers *pl*.

plomazo *nm fam* bore, drag; **¡qué p.!,** what a bore!

plomería *nf* plumbing.

plomero,-a *nm Am* plumber.

plomífero,-a *adj fam (aburrido)* boring, tedious.

plomizo,-a *adj* lead, leaden; *(color)* lead-colored, *US* lead-colored.

plomo *nm* **1** *Metal* lead; **soldadito de p.,** tin soldier; *fam fig* **andar con pies de p.,** to walk with leaden steps. **2** *(plomada)* plumb line. **3** *Elec (fusible)* fuse; **se han fundido los plomos,** the fuses have blown. **4** *fam (pesado)* drag, bore; **este libro es un p.,** this book is really boring; **ser un p.,** to be a drag *or* a bore. **5 a p.,** vertically; **caer a p.,** to fall right down; **cayó a p. sobre el suelo,** he fell flat on the floor.

pluma *nf* **1** feather; **ligero como una p.,** as light as a feather; **un cojín de plumas,** a feather cushion; *arg* **tener p.,** to be camp. **2** *(de escribir)* pen; **p. estilográfica,** fountain pen; *fig* **dejar correr la p.,** to write screeds; *fig* **ganarse la vida con la p.,** to earn one's living as a writer. **3** *Dep* **peso p.,** featherweight.

plumaje *nm* **1** *(de ave)* plumage. **2** *(de adorno)* plume, crest.

plumazo *nm* stroke of the pen; **de un p.,** with a stroke of his pen.

plúmbeo,-a *adj pey* boring, tedious.

plúmbico,-a *adj* plumbic.

plumero *nm* **1** *(para limpiar el polvo)* feather duster. **2** *(plumier)* pencil case. **3** *(adorno)* plume; *fam* **se te ve el p.,** I can see through you.

plumier *nm* pencil box.

plumilla *nf*, **plumín** *nm* nib.

plumón *nm* **1** *Orn* down. **2** *(edredón)* eiderdown; *(anorak)* down-filled anorak; *(saco de dormir)* down-filled sleeping bag.

plumoso,-a *adj* feathery.

plural *adj & nm* plural.

pluralidad *nf* plurality.

pluralismo *nm* pluralism.

pluralizar *vi* **1** *(poner plural)* to pluralize. **2** *(generalizar)* generalize.

pluri- *pref* pluri-; **pluricelular,** pluricellular.

pluriempleo *nm* moonlighting.

plurilingüe *adj* multilingual.

plurivalente *adj* **1** *Quím* polyvalent. **2** versatile, comprehensive.

plus *nm Fin Seg* bonus, bonus payment.

pluscuamperfecto *nm Ling* pluperfect.

plusmarca *nf* record.

plusmarquista *nmf Dep* record breaker.

plusvalía *nf Econ* appreciation, capital gain.

plutocracia *nf Pol* plutocracy.

plutócrata *nmf Pol* plutocrat.

plutonio *nm Min* plutonium.

pluvial *adj* rain.

pluvímetro *nm*, **pluviómetro** *nm* rain gauge.

P.O. *abr de* **por orden,** in order.

población *nf* **1** *(ciudad)* town; *(pueblo)* village. **2** *(conjunto de habitantes)* population. ■ **p. flotante,** floating population.

poblada *nf Am* **1** *(muchedumbre)* crowd. **2** *(motín)* riot.

poblado,-a I *pp de* **poblar. II** *adj* **1** populated; **un jardín p. de rosas,** a garden full of roses; **una zona muy poblada,** a densely populated area. **2** *(peludo)* bushy, thick; **cejas pobladas,** bushy eyebrows. **III** *nm (pueblo)* village; *(ciudad)* town.

poblador,-a *nm,f* settler.

poblar **I** *vtr* **1** *(con gente)* to settle, people; *(con plantas)* to plant. **2** *(vivir)* to inhabit. **II poblarse** *vr* **1** *(llenarse un lugar)* to become crowded. **2** *(árboles)* to come into leaf.

pobre I *adj* poor; **¡p.!,** poor thing!; **p. de ti si ...!,** you'll be sorry if ...!; **ser p. de espíritu,** to be small-minded; **un hombre p.,** a poor man; **un p. hombre,** a poor devil; **una película p. en primeros planos,** a film poor in close-ups. **II** *nmf* poor person, pauper; *(mendigo)* beggar; **¡el p.!,** poor thing!; **los pobres,** the poor *pl*.

pobreza *nf* **1** *(indigencia)* poverty. **2** *(escasez)* scarcity; **p. de recursos naturales,** lack of natural resources.

pocero *nm* **1** *(que hace pozos)* well digger. **2** *(que limpia pozos)* sewer-man.

pocilga *nf* pigsty; *fam fig* **su casa parece una p.,** his house looks like a pigsty.

pocillo *nm* cup.

pócima *nf* **1** *(medicinal)* potion. **2** *pey* concoction, brew.

poción *nf* potion.

poco,-a I *adj* **1** little, not much; **hace p. tiempo,** a short time ago; **hay p. sitio,** there is little space; **p. tiempo,** not much time; **¿qué hiciste ayer? —poca cosa,** what did you do yesterday? —not much; **tiene p. interés,** *(persona)* he's not very interested; *(cosa)* it's not very interesting. **2 pocos,-as,** few, not many; **pocas cosas,** few things; **pocas veces,** not very often. **3** *(locuciones)* **a p.,** shortly afterwards; **a p. de,** shortly after; **dentro de p.,** soon; **hace p.,** a short while ago; **p. a p.,** slowly; **p. antes/después** shortly before/afterwards; **por p.,** almost; **por p. se cae,** he nearly fell; **por p. que pueda,** if I can at all; **y por sí fuera p.,** and to top it all. **II** *pron* **1** little, not much; **queda p.,** there isn't much left; **ya queda p.,** it'll soon be over. **2 pocos,-as,** few, not many. **III** *adv* not (very) much, little; **ella come p.,** she doesn't eat much; **es p. simpático,** he's not very nice; **estaré p. aquí,** I won't be here long. **IV** *nm* **lo p. que tiene,** the little he has; **un p.,** a little; **ya sabes lo p. que le gusta,** you know how little he likes it.

pochismo *nm Am* type of Spanish spoken by Mexicans in California.

pocho,-a *adj* **1** *(fruta)* bad, overripe. **2** *fig (persona) (débil)* off-colour, *US* off-color; *(triste)* depressed, down; **ando un poco p.,** I'm feeling a bit down. **3** *Méx* Americanized Mexican, chicano.

pocholo,-a *adj fam* lovely, pretty.

poda *nf* **1** *(acción)* pruning. **2** *(época)* pruning season.

podadera *nf* pruning shears *pl*, secateurs *pl*.

podar *vtr* to prune.

podenco *nm Zool* hound.

poder[1] *nm* **1** *(gen)* power; *Jur* **por poderes,** by proxy. ■ *Econ* **p. adquisitivo,** purchasing power; **p. legislativo,** legislative power. **2** *Pol* power, authority; **el partido en el p.,** the party in power. **3** *(posesión)* possession; **ayer llegó a mi p.,** it reached me yesterday; **estar en p. de algn,** to be in the power *or* the hands of sb. **4** *(fuerza, vigor)* strength.

poder[2] **I** *vtr* **1** *(tener la facultad de)* to be able to, can; **no podía valerse,** he couldn't manage on his own; **no pudo menos que sonreírse,** he couldn't help smiling; **no puedo hablar,** I can't speak; **podrías haberme advertido,** you could have warned me; *fig* **no puedo más,** I can't take any more; *fam* **no p. tragar a algn,** not to be able to stand *or* stick sb. **2** *(tener permiso)* may, might; **¿puedo pasar?,** may I come in?; **ya puedes irte,** you may go now; *fam* **¿se puede?,** may I (come in)? **3** *(uso unipers) (ser posible)* may, might; **no puede ser,** that's impossible; **puede que ellos no lo sepan,** they might not know; **puede que tenga razón,** maybe he's right. **II** *vi* **1** to cope **(con,** with); **no puede con tanta comida,** he can't eat so much food; **no puedo con tanto ruido,** I can't stand so much noise. **2** to be stronger than; **les puede a todos,** he can take on anybody.

poderío *nm* **1** *(facultad)* authority. **2** *(poder)* power. **3** *(bienes)* wealth.

poderoso,-a **I** *adj.* **1** *(con poder)* powerful. **2** *(eficaz)* effective. **II** *nm,f* **1** *(con poder)* powerful person. **2** *(rico)* rich *or* wealthy person.

podio *nm,* **pódium** *nm Dep* podium.

podólogo,-a *nm,f Med* podologist.

podómetro *nm* pedometer.

podré *indic fut véase* **poder.**

podredumbre *nf* **1** putrefaction, rottenness. **2** *fig (corrupción)* corruption, rottenness.

podrido,-a **I** *pp de* **podrir.** **II** *adj* **1** *(putrefacto)* rotten, putrid. **2** *(corrupto)* corrupt; *fam* **p. de dinero,** stinking rich.

podrir *vtr defect véase* **pudrir.**

poema *nm Lit* poem; **p. en prosa,** prose poem; *fam fig* **fue todo un p.,** *(romántico)* it was like a fairy tale; *(falso)* it was a pie in the sky.

poesía *nf Lit* **1** *(género)* poetry. **2** *(poema)* poem.

poeta *nmf* poet.

poético,-a *adj* poetic.

poetisa *nf* poetess.

póker *nm véase* **póquer.**

polaco,-a **I** *adj* Polish. **II** *nm, f* Pole. **III** *nm (idioma)* Polish.

polar *adj* polar.

polaridad *nf* polarity.

polarización *nf* **1** *Fís* polarization. **2** *fig (concentración)* concentration.

polarizar *vtr* **1** *Fís* to polarize. **2** *fig (ánimo, atención)* to concentrate.

polca *nf Mús* polka.

polea *nf Téc* pulley.

polémica *nf* **1** *(disputa)* polemic, controversy, dispute. **2** *(arte)* polemics *sing.*

polémico,-a *adj* polemic, controversial.

polemista *nmf* polemicist, polemist.

polemizar *vi* to argue, debate.

polen *nm Bot* pollen.

poleo *nm Bot* pennyroyal.

poli- *pref* poly-; **policlínica,** polyclinic.

poli *fam* **I** *nmf* cop. **II** *nf* **la p.,** the fuzz *pl.*

policía **I** *nf* police (force); **ha llegado la p.,** the police are here. **II** *nmf (hombre)* policeman; *(mujer)* policewoman.

policíaco,-a *adj,* **policiaco,-a** *adj,* **policial** *adj* police; **novela/película policiaca,** detective story/film.

policromo,-a *adj* polychromatic.

policultivo *nm Agr* mixed farming.

polichinela *nm Teat* Punch.

polideportivo *nm* sports centre *or* US center *or* complex.

poliédrico,-a *adj* polyhedral, polyhedric.

poliedro *nm* polyhedron.

poliéster *nm Quím* polyester.

polietileno *nm* polythene, US polyethylene.

polifacético,-a *adj* versatile, many-sided; **es un hombre muy p.,** he's a man of many talents.

polifonía *nf Mús* polyphony.

polifónico,-a *adj Mús* polyphonic.

poligamia *nf* polygamy.

polígamo,-a **I** *adj* polygamous. **II** *nm,f* polygamist.

políglota,-a *adj & nm, f,* **poligloto,-a** *adj & nm, f* polyglot.

poligonal *adj* polygonal.

polígono *nm* polygon. ■ **p. industrial,** industrial area.

polígrafo,-a *nm,f* polygraph.

polilla *nf Ent* moth.

polimorfismo *nm* polymorphism.

polimorfo,-a *adj* polymorphic, polymorphous.

Polinesia *n* Polynesia.

polinesio,-a *adj & nm,f* Polynesian.

polinización *nf Bot* pollination.

polinizar *vtr Bot* to pollinate.

polio *nf,* **poliomielitis** *nf Med* polio, poliomyelitis.

pólipo *nm* **1** *Med* polypus, polyp. **2** *Zool* polyp.

polisílabo *nm Ling* polysyllable.

polisón *nm desus (prenda)* bustle.

politécnico,-a *adj & nm Educ* polytechnic.

política *nf* **1** politics *sing;* **hablar de p.,** to talk (about) politics. **2** *(estrategia)* policy; **la p. de esta empresa,** the policy of this firm; **una p. de no firm agresión,** a non-aggression policy.

político,-a **I** *adj* **1** political; **partido p.,** political party. **2** *(pariente)* in-law; **hermano p.,** brother-in-law; **su familia política,** her in-laws. **II** *nm,f* politician.

politiquear *vi* **1** to dabble in politics. **2** *Am* to job.

politiqueo *nm pey* petty politics *sing.*

politizar *vtr* to politicize.

póliza *nf* **1** *(sello)* stamp. **2** *Seg* insurance policy; **suscribir una p.,** to take out a policy.

polizón *nm Náut* stowaway.

polizonte *nm fam* cop.

polo[1] *nm* **1** pole; *fig* **ser polos opuestos,** to be poles apart; **ella es el p. opuesto de ...,** she is the complete opposite of ... ■ **p. norte,** North Pole; **p. positivo/negativo,** positive/negative pole. **2** *fig (centro)* **ser el p. de atención,** to be the centre of attraction.

polo[2] *nm* **1** *(helado)* ice lolly, US Popsicle®. **2** *(prenda)* sports shirt, polo neck (sweater).

polo[3] *nm Dep* polo. ■ **p. acuático,** water polo.

polonés,-esa **I** *adj* Polish. **II** *nm,f* Pole.

Polonia *n* Poland.

poltrón,-ona **I** *adj* idle, lazy. **II** *nf* easy chair.

poltronería *nf* idleness, laziness.

polución *nf* pollution.

polvareda *nf* **1** cloud of dust. **2** *fig* uproar, scandal.

polvera *nf* powder compact.

polvero *nm Am véase* **polvareda 1.**

polvete *nm vulg* screw, fuck.

polvo *nm* **1** dust; **limpiar** *or* **quitar el p.,** to dust; **lleno de p.,** covered with dust; *Fin fig* **limpio de p. y paja,** net; *fam* **estar hecho p.,** *(cansado)* to be knackered; *(deprimido)* to be depressed; *fam* **hacer p. a algn,** *(cansar)* to wear sb out; *(frustrar)* to ruin sb's plans. **2 en p.,** powdered; **leche en p.,** powdered milk; **nieve en p.,** powdery snow. **3** *vulg* screw, fuck; **echar un p.,** to have a screw. **4 polvos,** powder *sing*; **p. de talco,** talcum powder; *fam* **p. de la madre Celestina,** magic powder.

pólvora *nf* *(gen)* gunpowder; *(fuegos artificiales)* fireworks *pl*; *fig* gastar la p. en balde; *fig* **se extendió como un reguero de p.,** it spread like wildfire; *fam* **no haber inventado la p.,** to be as thick as two short planks.

polvoriento,-a *adj* dusty.

polvorín *nm* gunpowder arsenal; **polvorines atómicos,** atomic fall-out *sing*.

polvorón *nm* *Culin* sweet pastry.

polvorosa *nf* **poner pies en p.,** to take to one's heels, scarper.

polla *nf* **1** *Orn* young hen. ■ **p. de agua,** moorhen. **2** *vulg (pene)* prick.

pollada *nf (de gallina)* brood.

pollear *vi fam* to become aware of the opposite sex.

pollería *nf* poultry shop.

pollero,-a **I** *nm, f* poulterer, poultry farmer. **II** *nf* **1** henhouse. **2** *Am (prenda)* skirt.

pollino,-a *nm,f* **1** *Zool* young ass. **2** *fam (persona)* good-for-nothing.

pollito *nm dimin* chick.

pollo *nm* **1** *Orn Culin* chicken; *(pollito)* chick. **2** *fam (joven) (chico)* lad; *(chica)* lass.

polluelo,-a *Orn* **I** *nm,f dimin* chick. **II** *nf* crake.

pomada *nf Farm* cream, ointment.

pomar *nm Agr* apple orchard.

pomelo *nm Bot (árbol)* grapefruit tree; *(fruto)* grapefruit.

pómez *adj inv Geol* **piedra p.,** pumice, (stone).

pomo *nm* **1** *(de puerta)* knob. **2** *(de espada)* pommel. **3** *(frasco)* scent bottle.

pompa *nf* **1** bubble; **p. de jabón,** soap bubble. **2** *(en la ropa)* billow. **3** *(ostentación)* pomp. **4 pompas fúnebres,** *(ceremonia)* funeral *sing*; *(servicio público)* undertaker's *sing*.

pompis *nm inv fam* backside, bottom.

pomposidad *nf* pomposity.

pomposo,-a *adj* pompous.

pómulo *nm Anat* **1** *(hueso)* cheekbone. **2** *(mejilla)* cheek.

ponche *nm (bebida)* punch.

ponchera *nf* punch bowl.

poncho *nm (prenda)* poncho.

ponderación *nf* **1** *(deliberación)* deliberation; **hablar con p.,** to weigh one's words carefully. **2** *(equilibrio)* balance; *(moderación)* sense. **3** *(alabanza)* (high) praise.

ponderado,-a **I** *pp* de **ponderar. II** *adj* **1** *(deliberado)* deliberate. **2** *(equilibrado)* well-balanced, prudent. **3** *(alabado)* highly praised.

ponderar *vtr* **1** *(asunto)* to weigh up *or* consider. **2** *(alabar)* to praise.

ponderativo,-a *adj* highly favourable *or* US favorable.

pondré *indic fut véase* **poner.**

ponedero *nm* nesting box.

ponedora *adj* egg-laying; **gallina p.,** egg-laying hen.

ponencia *nf* **1** *(en conferencia)* paper, communication; *(informe)* report. **2** *Jur* position of reporter. **3** *(comisión)* reporting committee.

ponente *nmf (en conferencia)* speaker; *(informador)* reporter.

poner *(pp* **puesto) I** *vtr* **1** *(gen)* to put; *(colocar)* to place; **pon mucho cuidado,** be careful; **p. a un lado,** to put aside; **p. al corriente,** *(actualizar)* to update; *(informar)* to bring up to date; **p. algo a secar,** to put sth to dry; **p. de manifiesto,** to show; **p. en duda,** to cast doubt on, question; **ponlo aquí,** put it here; *fam* **p. de patitas en la calle,** to kick *or* throw out. **2** *(huevos)* to lay. **3** *(gesto, mueca)* to make, put on; **p. mala cara,** to pull a long face. **4** *(hacer adquirir condición)* to make; **p. colorado a algn,** to make sb blush; **p. triste a algn,** to make sb sad; *ofens* **p. a parir,** to go on sb's tits. **5** *(vestir a algn)* to put; **le pondré el vestido azul,** I'll put her blue dress on her; **¿qué llevaba puesto?,** what was he wearing? **6** *(preparar)* to get ready; **¿has puesto el despertador?,** have you set the alarm (clock)?; **p. la mesa,** to set the table. **7** *(suponer)* to suppose; **pongamos que Ana no viene,** supposing Ana doesn't turn up; **pongo por caso,** for example. **8** *TV Cin* to be on, show; *Cin* **¿dónde la ponen?,** where is it showing?; **¿qué ponen en la tele?,** what's on the telly? **9** *(conectar)* to turn *or* switch on; **pon la radio,** turn the radio on. **10** *(enviar)* **p. una carta/un telegrama,** to send a letter/telegram. **11** *Tel (con persona)* to put through; *(conferencia)* to make. **12** *(escribir)* to write; **ponga su nombre en esta lista,** write your name down in this list; **p. por escrito,** to write (out); **¿qué pone aquí?,** what does it say here?; **¿qué pone el periódico?,** what does the newspaper say? **13** *(instalar)* to install, *US* instal; **le han puesto el teléfono,** he's had a telephone put in; **p. la luz/el gas,** to install electricity/gas. **14** *(establecer)* to set up; **p. un negocio,** to set up a business. **15** *(dejar)* to leave (en, with); **pongo el dinero en tus manos,** I'll leave the money with you. **16** *(contribuir)* to put in; **cada uno pone 25 pesetas,** each one pays 25 pesetas; **p. de su parte,** to do one's bit. **17** *(alabar)* to praise; *(desacreditar)* to mark; *fam* **p. a algn por las nubes,** to sing sb's praises; *fam* **p. como un trapo, p. de vuelta y media,** to pull to pieces. **18** *(imponer) (multa)* to impose; *(trabajo)* to give, assign. **19** *(dar nombre a)* to name; **le pusieron como su padre,** they named him after his father. **20** *(dedicar a un trabajo)* to get a job as; **puso a su hijo de mecánico,** he got his son a job as a mechanic. **II ponerse** *vr* **1** to put *or* place oneself; **póngase cómodo,** make yourself comfortable; **ponte en contacto con Luis,** get in touch with Luis; **ponte más cerca,** come closer; **se ha puesto perdido de barro,** he's covered in mud. **2** *(vestirse)* to put on; **ella se puso el jersey,** she put her jumper on. **3** *(volverse)* to become; **se puso muy contento,** he was very happy; **p. colorada,** to blush. **4** *(estados de salud)* to get; **p. bueno,** to recover; **p. malo** *or* **enfermo,** to become ill. **5** *(llegar)* to get; **se pusieron allí en nada,** they got there in no time. **6** *Astron* to set; **el sol se pone por el oeste,** the sun sets in the west. **7** *Tel* to answer; **dile que se ponga,** ask her to come to the phone, put her on. **8 p. a,** to start to; **p. a trabajar,** to get down to work; **se puso a cantar,** he started to sing. **9** *(exaltarse)* to get upset; **no te pongas así,** don't take it like that; **p. a malas con algn,** to have a falling out with sb. **10 p. de,** to get a job as; **p. de taxista,** to get a job as a taxi driver.

poney *nm Zool* pony.

pongo *indic pres véase* **poner.**

poniente *nm* **1** *(occidente)* West. **2** *(viento)* westerly (wind).

pontazgo *nm* bridge toll.

pontevedrés,-esa I *adj of or* from Pontevedra. **II** *nm, f* native *or* inhabitant of Pontevedra.

pontificado *nm* pontificate.

pontificar *vi* to pontificate.

pontifice *nm* Pontiff; **el Sumo P.,** His Holiness the Pope.

pontificio,-a *adj* pontifical.

pontón *nm Náut* pontoon.

ponzoña *nf* venom, poison.

ponzoñoso,-a *adj* venomous, poisonous.

pop *adj* & *nm inv Mús* pop.

popa *nf Náut* stern; *fig* **ir viento en p.**, to go smoothly *or* very well.

pope *nm Rel* pope.

popelín *nm Tex* poplin.

populachería *nf pey* cheap popularity.

populachero,-a *adj pey* common, vulgar.

populacho *nm pey* plebs *pl*, masses *pl*.

popular *adj* **1** *(folklórico)* folk; **arte/música p.**, folk art/music. **2** *(famoso)* popular. ◆ **popularmente** *adv* commonly.

popularidad *nf* popularity.

popularizar *vtr* to popularize.

populista *adj* & *nmf* populist.

populoso,-a *adj* densely populated.

popurrí *nm Mús* potpourri.

póquer *nm* poker; **p. de ases**, *Naipes* four aces *pl*; *(dados)* poker of aces.

por *prep* **1** *(tiempo)* for; **allá p. mayo**, sometime around May; **p. ahora**, for the time being; **p. aquel tiempo, p. entonces**, at that time; **p. la mañana**, in the morning; **p. la noche**, at night, during the night; **p. Navidades**, for *or* at Christmas. **2** *(lugar)* by; **pasamos p. Soria**, we went through Soria; **p. ahí**, over there; **p. allí**, that way; **p. debajo de**, under; **p. dentro**, inside; **¿p. dónde vamos?**, which way are we taking?; **p. el camino**, on *or* along the way; **p. la calle**, in the street; **p. la izquierda**, on the left (side); **p. mi casa**, near my house; **p. todas partes**, everywhere, all over. **3** *(agente, autor)* by; **atropellado p. un coche**, run over by a car; **pintado p. Picasso**, painted by Picasso. **4** *(causa)* because of; **es p. eso que ...**, that's why ..., for that reason ...; **p. algo será**, there must be some reason; **p. otras razones**, for other reasons; **p. su culpa**, because of him; **p. sus ideas**, because of her ideas. **5** *(medio)* by; **p. avión/correo**, by plane/post; **p. escrito**, in writing; **p. la fuerza**, by force. **6** *(a cambio de)* for; **cambiar algo p. otra cosa**, to exchange for sth for sth else; **p. tres mil pesetas**, for three thousand pesetas. **7** *(distribución)* per; *(uno por uno)* by; **casa p. casa**, from house to house; **clasificado p. autores**, classified by authors; **p. cabeza**, a head, per person; **p. hora/mes**, per hour/month; **iba a ochenta p. hora**, he was doing eighty an hour. **8** *Mat* **dos p. tres, seis**, two times three is six. **9** *Mat (porcentaje)* per; **diez p. ciento**, ten per cent. **10** *(finalidad)* for; *(con verbo)* to, in order to; **lo hice p. ti**, I did it for you *or* for your sake; **p. lo que**, therefore; **p. llegar antes**, (in order) to arrive earlier; **p. no molestarle**, so as not to bother him. **11 p. qué**, why. **12 estar p.**, *(no hecho)* to remain to be; **eso está p. ver**, that remains to be seen; **está todo p. hacer**, we're right at the beginning. **13** *(a punto de)* **estar p.**, to be about to; **estuve p. llamarte**, I almost phoned you. **14** *(en busca de)* for, to; **baja p. tabaco**, go down for some cigarettes; **fue a p. el médico**, he went to fetch the doctor. **15 p. haber**, for having; **p. haberse equivocado**, for having made a mistake. **16** *(locuciones)* **p. así decirlo**, to say something; **p. cierto**, by the way; **¡p. Dios!**, for God's sake!; **p. ejemplo**, for example *or* instance; **p. favor**, please; **p. lo general**, in general; **p. lo visto**, apparently; **p. más/muy ... que sea**, no matter how ... he *or* she is; **p. mí**, for my part, as for me; **p. mucho que ...**, no matter how much ...; **p. nada**, for nothing; **p. si acaso**, just in case; **p. sí mismo**, by himself; **p. supuesto**, of course; *fam* **p. las buenas**, for the hell of it.

porcelana *nf* porcelain, china; **una p.**, a piece of china.

porcentaje *nm* percentage; *(proporción)* rate.

porcentual *adj* percentage.

porcino,-a *adj* porcine; pig; **ganado p.**, pigs *pl*.

porción *nf* portion, part; **una pequeña p.**, a small quantity.

porcuno,-a *adj véase* **porcino,-a**.

porche *nm* **1** *(soportal)* arcade. **2** *(entrada)* porch.

pordiosear *vi* to beg.

pordiosero,-a I *adj* begging. **II** *nm,f* beggar.

porfía 1 *(lucha)* fight; *(discusión)* argument. **2** *(obstinación)* obstinacy, pig-headedness, stubbornness; **a p.**, in competition.

porfiar *vi* **1** *(disputar)* to fight. **2** *(insistir)* to be pigheaded.

porfolio *nm Arte* portfolio.

pormenor *nm* detail; **venta al p.**, retail.

pormenorizar *vi* to go into detail.

porno *adj inv fam* pornographic.

pornografía *nf* pornography.

pornográfico,-a *adj* pornographic; *Cin* X-rated.

poro *nm* pore; *fig* **rezumaba satisfacción por todos los poros**, he oozed satisfaction.

pororó *nm Am* popcorn.

porosidad *nf* porosity, porousness.

poroso,-a *adj* porous.

porque *conj* **1** *(causal)* because; **no estudio p. no me gusta**, I don't study because I don't like it. **2** *(final)* so that, in order that.

porqué *nm (pl* **porqués)** reason; **me pregunto el p. de su negativa**, I wonder why he refused.

porquería *nf* **1** *(suciedad)* dirt, filth; **estar hecho una p.** to be really filthy; **la casa está llena de p.** the house is very dirty; **no hagas porquerías**, don't be a pig. **2** *(cosa de poco valor)* rubbish; **por su cumpleaños le compraré cualquier p.** I'll get her something small for her birthday. **3** *(trastada)* dirty trick. **4** *fam (comida)* rubbish, *US* junk food; **no comas esas porquerías**, don't eat that rubbish.

porqueriza *nf* pigsty.

porquerizo *nm* pigman.

porra *nf* **1** *(de policía)* truncheon, baton. **2** *Culin* type of fried pastry. **3** *fig (persona)* bore. **4** *fam (locuciones)* **mandar a algn a la p.**, to tell sb to go to hell; **¡porras!**, damn it!, shit!; **¿qué porras ...?**, what on earth ...?; **¡qué vacaciones ni qué porras!**, holidays — like hell!; **¡una p.!**, you're talking crap!; **¡vete a la p.!**, get lost! **4** *Arg Bol (mechón)* forelock. **5** *Méx Teat* claque.

porrada *nf fam* **1** *(golpe)* blow *or* thump (with a truncheon). **2** *(montón)* pile, heap; **una p. de**, heaps of, loads of.

porrazo *nm (golpe)* blow, thump; *(contra el suelo)* bump; **pegarse un p. con algo**, to bump into sth; *fig* **de golpe y p.**, all of a sudden, suddenly.

porreta *nmf fam* **1** *(fumador de hachís)* head. **2** *(desnudo)* **en p.**, in the buff, starkers.

porrillo (a) *loc adv fam* by the score, galore.

porro *nm arg* joint; **darle al p.**, to smoke dope regularly.

porrón *nm* glass bottle with a spout coming out of its base, used for drinking wine.

porta *nf Náut* port, porthole.

portaaviones *nm inv Náut* aircraft carrier.

portada *nf* **1** *(de libro)* title page; *(de revista)* cover; *(de periódico)* front page; *(de disco)* sleeve. **2** *Arquit (fachada)* front, façade, facade.

portador,-a I *adj* carrying. **II** *nm,f* carrier, bearer; *Com* **páguese al p.**, pay the bearer; *Med* **p. de virus**, virus carrier.

portaequipajes *nm inv Aut* boot, *US* trunk.

portaestandarte *nm Mil* standard bearer.

portafolios *nm inv* briefcase.

portal *nm* **1** *(zaguán)* porch, entrance hall. **2** *(puerta de la calle)* street door, main door, gateway. **3** *Rel* **p. de Belén**, Nativity scene.

portalada *nf Archit* large doorway, gateway.

portalámparas *nm inv Elec* socket.

portamaletas *nm inv véase* **portaequipajes**.

portaminas *nm inv* propelling pencil.

portamonedas *nm inv* purse.

portante *nm fam* **tomar** *or* **coger el p.,** to leave, take one's leave.

portaobjetos *nm inv* slide.

portar I *vtr arc* to carry. II **portarse** *vr* to behave; **portaos bien,** be good, behave yourselves; **p. mal,** to misbehave; **se portó como un héroe,** he acted like a hero.

portátil *adj* portable.

portavoz *nmf* spokesperson; *(hombre)* spokesman; *(mujer)* spokeswoman.

portazo *nm* slam of a door; **dar un p.,** to slam the door.

porte *nm* 1 *(aspecto)* demeanour, appearance; **un hombre de p. distinguido,** a distinguished-looking man. 2 *(transporte)* transport, carriage; **portes pagados,** carriage paid.

porteador,-a *nm,f* porter.

portear *vi* to carry, transport.

portento *nm* 1 *(cosa)* wonder, marvel. 2 *(persona)* genius; **Laura es un p. bailando,** Laura is a wonderful dancer.

portentoso,-a *adj* extraordinary, prodigious.

porteño,-a I *adj* of *or* from Buenos Aires. II *nm,f* native *or* inhabitant of Buenos Aires.

portería *nf* 1 *(vivienda)* porter's house; *(garita)* porter's lodge. 2 *(empleo)* job of porter. 3 *Dep* goal.

portero,-a *nm, f* 1 *(de vivienda)* porter, caretaker; *(de edificio público)* doorman. ■ **p. automático,** entryphone. 2 *Dep* goalkeeper.

pórtico *nm* 1 *Arquit (portal)* portico, porch. 2 *(con arcadas)* arcade.

portillo *nm* 1 *(abertura)* breach, opening, gap; *(puerta secundaria)* side door *or* entrance; *(postigo)* wicket. 2 *fig (a una solución)* opening; **es necesario buscar el p. de este problema,** we have to find a solution to this problem.

portorriqueño,-a *adj & nm,f* Puerto Rican.

portuario,-a *adj* harbour, *US* harbor, port; **(trabajador) p.,** docker, *US* longshoreman.

Portugal *n* Portugal.

portugués,-esa I *adj* Portuguese. II *nm, f (persona)* Portuguese; **los portugueses,** the Portuguese *pl.* III *nm (idioma)* Portuguese.

porvenir *nm* future; **sin p.,** with no prospects; **tener el p. asegurado,** to have a secure future.

pos- *pref* post-; **posmoderno,** post-modern.

pos *adv* **en p. de,** behind, after; **va en p. de la fama,** he's after fame.

posada *nf* inn; **dar p.,** to offer hospitality, take in.

posaderas *nfpl fam* buttocks.

posadero,-a *nm,f* innkeeper.

posar I *vi (para fotografía, retrato)* to pose, sit. II *vtr* to put *or* lay down; **p. la mirada en algo,** to rest one's gaze on sth; **posó su mano sobre la mesa,** he laid his hand on the table. III **posarse** *vr* 1 *(aves)* to settle, alight; *(avión)* to land. 2 *(líquido, polvo)* to settle.

posdata *nf* postscriptum, postscript.

pose *nf* 1 *(postura)* pose. 2 *(actitud)* affected attitude *or* posturing, posing; **su p. de indiferencia me molesta mucho,** I hate her pretending to be indifferent.

poseedor,-a I *adj* who possesses. II *nm, f* owner, possessor.

poseer *vtr* to possess, own.

poseído,-a I *pp de* **poseer.** II *adj* possessed; **poseído de rabia,** enraged. III *nm,f* possessed person.

posesión *nf* possession; **estar en p.,** to have; **tener en p.,** to be in possession of; **tomar p.,** *(de algo)* to take possession **(de, -);** *(de un cargo)* to take up **(de, -).**

posesionar I *vtr* to give possession of. II **posesionarse** *vr (tomar posesión)* to take possession **(de,** of); *(apropiarse)* to seize.

posesivo,-a *adj & nm* possessive.

poseso,-a I *adj* possessed. II *nm,f* possessed person; *fig* **como un p.,** like a madman.

posguerra *nf* postwar period.

posibilidad *nf* possibility, chance; **no hay ninguna p. de,** there is no chance of; **no tienes ninguna p.,** you don't stand a chance.

posibilitar *vtr* to make possible, facilitate.

posible I *adj* possible; **de ser p.,** if possible; **en (la medida de) lo p.,** as far as possible; **¿es p.?,** really?; **es p. que venga,** he might come; **hacer lo p.,** to do one's best; **lo antes p.,** as soon as possible; **¿será p. que no venga?,** don't tell me he's not going to come!; **si nos es p.,** if we possibly can. II **posibles** *nmpl fam* (economic) means. ◆ **posiblemente** *adv* possibly.

posición *nf* position; **p. económica,** economic situation; **p. social,** social status.

positivado *nm Fot* developing.

positivismo *nm Filos* positivism.

positivo,-a *adj & nm* positive. ◆ **positivamente** *adv* positively.

pósito *nm* 1 *Agr (granero)* communal granary. 2 *(cooperativa)* co-operative.

poso *nm* 1 *(sedimento)* dregs *pl,* sediment. 2 *fig (vestigio)* trace.

posponer *(pp pospuesto) vtr* 1 *(relegar)* to put in second place *or* behind, relegate. 2 *(aplazar)* to postpone, put off.

post- *pref* post-; **postnatal,** postnatal.

posta *nf* 1 *(caballos)* relay; *(parada)* staging stop. **2 a p.,** on purpose; **lo han hecho a p.,** they did it on purpose.

postal I *adj* postal; **paquete p.,** parcel (sent by post); **servicio p.,** post, mail; **tarjeta p.,** postcard. II *nf* postcard.

poste *nm (gen)* pole; *Dep (larguero)* post; *fam* **parado como un p.,** dead still.

póster *nm (pl pósters)* poster.

postergación *nf* 1 *(retraso)* delay, delaying; *(aplazamiento)* postponement. 2 *(relegación)* relegation.

postergar *vtr* 1 *(retrasar)* to delay; *(aplazar)* to postpone. 2 *(relegar)* to relegate.

posteridad *nf* posterity; **pasar a la p.,** to go down in history.

posterior *adj* 1 *(lugar)* posterior, rear; **parte p.,** back. 2 *(tiempo)* later **(a,** than), subsequent **(a,** to); **el accidente fue p. a la enfermedad,** the accident came after the illness. ◆ **posteriormente** *adv* subsequently, later.

posteriori (a) *loc adv* a posteriori.

posterioridad *nf* posteriority; **con p.,** later.

postgraduado,-a *adj & nm,f* postgraduate.

postigo *nm (de puerta)* wicket; *(de ventana)* shutter.

postín *nm fam* boasting, showing-off; **darse p.,** to show off, swank; **de p.,** posh, swanky.

postizo,-a I *adj* 1 *(artificial)* false, artificial; **dentadura postiza,** false teeth *pl,* dentures *pl.* 2 *(sobrepuesto)* detachable. II *nm* hairpiece.

postoperatorio,-a I *adj* postoperative. II *nm* postoperative period.

postor *nm* bidder; **mejor p.,** highest bidder.

postración *nf* prostration.

postrado,-a I *pp de* **postrar.** II *adj* prostrate; *fig* **p. por el dolor,** prostrate with grief.

postrar I *vtr* to prostrate. II **postrarse** *vr* to prostrate oneself, kneel down.

postre *nm Culin* dessert, sweet; **¿qué hay de p.?,** what's for dessert?; *fig* **a la p.,** in the end; *fig* **para postres,** on top of all that.

postrero,-a *adj* last.

postrimería *nf (gen pl)* last part *or* period; **en las postrimerías del siglo pasado,** at the end of the last century.

postulación *nf (de dinero)* collection.

postulado,-a I *pp de* **postular. II** *nm* postulate.

postulante *nmf* **1** *(de colecta)* collector. **2** *Rel* postulant.

postular *vtr (dinero)* to collect.

póstumo,-a *adj* posthumous.

postura *nf* **1** *(posición)* position, posture. **2** *fig (actitud)* attitude; **adoptar una p.,** to take *or* adopt an attitude. **3** *(puja)* bid.

postventa *adj*, **posventa** *adj* after-sales; **servicio p.,** after-sales service.

potable *adj* **1** *(agua)* drinkable; **agua no p.,** not drinking water; **agua p.,** drinking water. **2** *fam (aceptable)* acceptable.

potaje *nm* **1** *Culin* hotpot, stew; **p. de legumbres,** vegetable stew. **2** *fig (mezcla)* mixture.

potasa *nf* potash.

potasio *nm* potassium.

pote *nm* pot; *(jarra)* jug; *fam* **darse p.,** to show off.

potencia *nf* power; *Mat* **elevar un número a la quinta p.,** to raise a number to the power of five; **en p.,** potential; **un asesino en p.,** he's a potential murderer; *Pol* **las grandes potencias,** the super-powers; **un motor de gran p.,** a very powerful engine.

potenciación *nf* boosting, promotion, strengthening.

potencial I *adj* potential. **II** *nm* **1** *(gen)* potential; **p. eléctrico,** voltage; **p. humano,** manpower. **2** *Ling* conditional (tense). ◆ **potencialmente** *adv* potentially.

potencialidad *nf* potentiality.

potenciar *vtr* to boost, promote, strengthen; **p. el comercio,** to promote trade.

potentado,-a *nm,f* potentate.

potente *adj* powerful, strong.

potestad *nf* power, authority.

potestativo,-a *adj* optional, facultative.

potingue *nm* *fam* pey **1** *(bebida)* concoction. **2** *(maquillaje)* make-up, face cream *or* lotion.

poto *nm* **1** *Chi Ecuad Per (vasija)* vessel, jug. **2** *Arg Bol Chi (trasero)* bottom.

potra[1] *nf Zool* filly.

potra[2] *nf fam* luck; **tener p.,** to be jammy.

potranco,-a *nm,f* colt.

potro *nm* **1** *Zool* colt. **2** *(de herrador)* stanchion. **3** *(de gimnasia)* horse. **4** *(de tortura)* rack.

poyo *nm* stone bench.

poza *nf* puddle.

pozal *nm* well bucket.

pozo *nm* **1** *(gen)* well; **p. de petróleo,** oil well; *fig* **p. de sabiduría,** fund of knowledge; *fig* **p. sin fondo,** bottomless pit. **2** *Min* shaft, pit.

PP *nm Pol abr de* **Partido Popular**

P.P. *abr de* **por poder**

práctica *nf* practice; **con la p.,** with practice; **en la p.,** in practice; **período de prácticas,** practical training period; **poner (algo) en p.,** to put (sth) into practice; **tener mucha p. en,** to have a lot of practice in.

practicable *adj* **1** *(posible)* feasable. **2** *(camino, carretera)* passable.

practicante I *adj Rel* practising, *US* practicing. **II** *nmf Med* nurse, medical assistant.

practicar I *vtr (gen)* to practise, *US* practice; *(hacer)* to make; **p. un agujero,** to make a hole; **¿practicas algún deporte?,** do you go in for any sport? **II** *vi* to do one's practice; **antes de licenciarse practicó durante un mes**

en una escuela, he taught in a school for a month before graduating.

práctico,-a I *adj (gen)* practical; *(útil)* handy, useful. **II** *nm Náut* coastal pilot. ◆ **prácticamente** *adv* practically.

pradera *nf* meadow, prairie.

prado *nm* **1** *(campo)* meadow, field. **2** *(paseo)* promenade.

Praga *n* Prague.

pragmática *nf* pragmatics *sing*.

pragmático,-a I *adj* pragmatic. **II** *nm,f* pragmatist.

pragmatismo *nm* pragmatism.

pral. *abr de* **principal,** first floor, *US* second floor.

praxis *nf inv fml* praxis.

pre- *pref* pre-; **precientífico,** prescientific.

preámbulo *nm* **1** *(introducción)* preamble. **2** *(rodeo)* circumlocution; **déjate de preámbulos,** stop beating about the bush; **sin (más) p.,** getting straight to the point, without further ado.

preaviso *nm* previous warning, notice.

prebenda *nf* **1** *Rel* prebend. **2** *fig (chollo)* sinecure, cushy job.

preboste *nm* provost.

precalentamiento *nm* **1** *Téc* preheating. **2** *Dep* warming up.

precalentar *vtr* **1** *Téc* to preheat. **2** *Dep* to warm up.

precario,-a *adj* precarious.

precaución *nf* caution, precaution; **con p.,** cautiously; **por p.,** as a precaution; **tomar precauciones,** to take precautions.

precaver *vtr*, **precaverse** *vr* to take precautions **(de, contra,** against).

precavido,-a I *pp de* **precaver. II** *adj* cautious, prudent; *prov* **hombre p. vale por dos,** forewarned is forearmed.

precedencia *nf* precedence, priority.

precedente I *adj* preceding. **II** *nmf* predecessor. **III** *nm* precedent; **sentar p.,** to establish *or* set up a precedent, **sin p.,** unprecedented, unparalleled; **y que no sirva de p.,** don't take it as a rule.

preceder *vtr* to precede, go before.

preceptista *nmf* theorist.

precepto *nm* precept, rule; *Rel* **fiestas de p.,** days of obligation.

preceptor,-a *nm,f Educ* (private) tutor.

preces *nfpl Rel* prayers.

preciarse *vr* to boast; **me precio de ser su amigo,** I'm proud of being his friend.

precintar *vtr* to seal.

precinto *nm* seal.

precio *nm* price; **al p. de,** at the cost of; **poner p. (a algo),** to put a price (on sth); **poner p. a la cabeza de algn,** to put a price on sb's head; **p. prohibitivo,** prohibitive price; **p. simbólico,** nominal cost; **subida de precios,** rise in prices; *fig* **a cualquier p.,** at any price, at all costs; *fig* **no tener p.,** to be priceless. ■ **p. de coste,** cost price; **p. fijo,** fixed price.

preciosidad *nf* **1** *(cualidad)* preciousness. **2** *(cosa)* lovely thing; **es una p.,** it's really lovely. **3** *(persona)* darling; **¡qué de niño!,** what a delightful child!

precioso,-a *adj* **1** *(valioso)* precious, valuable. **2** *(hermoso)* lovely, beautiful.

precipicio *nm* precipice, cliff; *fig (abismo)* abyss.

precipitación *nf* **1** *(prisa)* haste; *(imprudencia)* rashness; **con p.,** *(con prisa)* hastily, hurriedly; *(imprudentemente)* rashly, precipitately. **2** *Meteor* precipitation, shower.

precipitado,-a I *pp de* **precipitar. II** *adj (apresurado)* hasty, hurried; *(imprudente)* rash. **III** *nm Quím* precipitate. ◆ **precipitadamente** *adv (con prisa)* hastily, hurriedly; *(imprudentemente)* rashly, precipitately.

precipitar I *vtr* **1** *(arrojar)* to throw, hurl down. **2** *(acelerar)* to hurry, rush; **no precipites los acontecimientos,** don't rush things. **3** *Quím* to precipitate. **II precipitarse** *vr* **1** *(arrojarse)* to hurl oneself. **2** *(actuar precipitadamente)* to hurry, rush; **no nos precipitemos,** let's take things easy.

precisar I *vtr* **1** *(determinar)* to determine, give full details of; **no puedo p. cuando,** I can't say when exactly. **2** *(necesitar)* to require, need; **se precisa una gran habilidad,** great skill is required. **II** *vi* *(ser necesario)* to be necessary; **p. de algo,** to need sth.

precisión *nm* **1** *(exactitud)* precision, accuracy, exactness; **con p.,** precisely, accurately. ■ **instrumento de p.,** precision instrument. **2** *(aclaración)* clarification. **3** *(necesidad)* need; **tener p. de algo,** to need sth.

preciso,-a *adj* **1** *(necesario)* necessary, essential; **es p. que la llames hoy,** you must phone her today. **2** *(exacto)* accurate, exact; **en este p. momento,** at this very moment. **3** *(claro)* concise, clear; **este informe es muy p.,** this report is very clear. ◆ **precisamente** *adv* *(con precisión)* precisely; *(exactamente)* exactly; **¡p.!,** exactly!; **p. por ese,** for that very reason.

precocidad *nf* precocity, precociousness.

preconcebido,-a *adj* preconceived; **ideas preconcebidas,** preconceptions.

preconcepción *nf* preconception.

preconizar *vtr* to recommend, advocate.

precoz *adj* **1** *(persona)* precocious. **2** *(fruta)* early.

precursor,-a I *adj* precursory. **II** *nm,f* precursor.

predecesor,-a *nm,f* predecessor.

predecir *(pp* **predicho***)* *vtr* to foretell, predict.

predestinación *nf* predestination.

predestinado,-a I *pp de* **predestinar. II** *adj* predestined.

predestinar *vtr* to predestine.

predeterminación *nf* predetermination.

predeterminar *vtr* to predetermine.

prédica *nf Rel* sermon; *fam (perorata)* harangue.

predicación *nf* preaching.

predicador,-a *nm,f Rel* preacher.

predicado,-a I *pp de* **predicar. II** *nm Ling* predicate.

predicamento *nm* fame, prestige.

predicar *vtr* to preach; *fig* **p. con el ejemplo,** to practise what one preaches.

predicativo,-a *adj* predicative.

predicción *nf* prediction, forecast.

predice *indic pres véase* **predecir.**

predigo *indic pres véase* **predecir.**

predije *pt indef véase* **predecir.**

predilección *nf* predilection; **predilecciones y aversiones,** likes and dislikes; **sentir p. por algo,** to prefer sth.

predilecto,-a *adj* favourite, *US* favorite, preferred.

predio *nm* estate, property. ■ **p. rústice,** country estate; **p. urbano,** town property.

predisponer *(pp* **predispuesto***)* *vtr* to predispose.

predisposición *nf* predisposition.

predispuesto,-a I *pp de* **predisponer. II** *adj* predisposed.

predominación *nf,* **predominancia** *nf* predominance.

predominante *adj* predominant, predominating; **la corriente p.,** the prevailing current.

predominar *vi* to predominate prevail.

predominio *nm* predominance.

preeminencia *nf* pre-eminence.

preeminente *adj* pre-eminent.

preescolar *adj Educ* preschool; **etapa p.,** nursery education.

preestablecer *vtr* to pre-establish.

preestablecido,-a I *pp de* **preestablecer. II** *adj* pre-established.

preexistencia *nf* pre-existence.

preexistir *vi* to pre-exist.

prefabricación *nf* prefabrication.

prefabricado,-a I *pp de* **prefabricar. II** *adj* prefabricated.

prefabricar *vtr* to prefabricate.

prefacio *nm Lit* preface.

prefecto *nm* prefect.

prefectura *nf* prefecture.

preferencia *nf* preference; **con p.,** preferably; **de p.,** preferably; *Aut* **p. (de paso),** right of way; **tener p. por algo,** to have a preference for sth.

preferente *adj* preferable, preferential. ◆ **preferentemente** *adv* preferably, preferentially.

preferible *adj* preferable; **es p. que no vengas,** you'd better not come. ◆ **preferiblemente** *adv* preferably.

preferido,-a I *pp de* **preferir. II** *adj* preferred. **III** *nm,f* favourite, *US* favorite.

preferir *vtr* to prefer; **prefiere no salir,** he'd rather stay at home; **prefiero el calor al frío,** I prefer the heat to the cold.

prefijar *vtr* **1** *(fijar con antelación)* to fix *or* arrange in advance. **2** *Ling* to prefix.

prefijo *nm* **1** *Ling* prefix. **2** *Tel* code, *US* area code.

pregón *nm* public announcement.

pregonero *nm* town crier.

pregonar *vtr* **1** *(anunciar)* to announce publicly. **2** *fig (divulgar, difundir)* to reveal, disclose.

pregunta *nf* question; **contestar a una p.,** to answer a question; **hacer una p.,** to ask a question; **p. capciosa,** catch question.

preguntar I *vtr* to ask; **a mí no me lo preguntes,** don't ask me; **p. algo a algn,** to ask sb sth; **p. por algn,** to ask after *or* about sb. **II preguntarse** *vr* to wonder; **me pregunto si vendrá,** I wonder whether he'll come.

preguntón,-ona *fam* **I** *adj* inquisitive, nosey. **II** *nm, f* nosey-parker, busybody.

prehistoria *nf* prehistory.

prehistórico,-a *adj* prehistoric.

prejuicio *nm* prejudice; **tener prejuicios,** to be prejudiced, be biased.

prejuzgar *vtr* to prejudge.

prelación *nf* priority, preference.

prelado *nm Rel* prelate.

preliminar I *adj* preliminary. **II** *nm* preliminary; **preliminares,** preliminaries.

preludiar *vtr* **1** *Mús* to prelude. **2** *fig (anunciar)* to announce; *(empezar)* to introduce.

preludio *nm* **1** *Mús* prelude. **2** *fig (anuncio)* prelude; *(inicio)* introduction.

prematrimonial *adj* premarital.

prematuro,-a I *adj* premature. **II** *nm,f* premature baby.

premeditación *nf* premeditation; **con p.,** deliberately.

premeditado,-a *adj* premeditated, deliberate. ◆ **premeditadamente** *adv* with premeditation.

premiado,-a *pp de* **premiar. II** *adj* prize-winning.

premiar *vtr* **1** *(dar un premio)* to award a prize (**a**, to). **2** *(recompensar)* to reward.

premier *nm (pl* **premiers***) Pol* premier.

premio *nm* **1** *(gen)* prize, award; **dar un p.,** to award a prize. ■ **p. de consolación,** consolation prize; **p. en metálico,** prize money; *Univ* **p. extraordinario,** award with special distinction. **2** *(recompensa)* reward, recompense. **3** *(de lotería)* prize; **le tocó un p.,** he won a prize. ■ **p. (gordo),** big prize, first prize.

premiosidad *nf* **1** *(torpeza)* clumsiness, awkwardness. **2** *(urgencia)* urgency.

premioso,-a *adj* **1** *(torpe)* clumsy, awkward. **2** *(urgente)* urgent.

premisa *nf* premise.

premolar *adj & nm Anat* premolar.

premonición *nf* premonition.

premonitorio,-a *adj* premonitory, warning.

premunir *vtr*, **premunirse** *vr* to take precautions.

premura *nf* **1** *(apremio)* haste; *(urgencia)* urgency; **con p.,** urgently. **2** *(escasez)* shortage, lack; **con p. de tiempo,** under time pressure.

prenatal *adj* antenatal, prenatal.

prenda *nf* **1** *(prenda)* garment, article; **prendas interiores,** underwear *sing*. **2** *(garantía)* token, pledge; **dar en p.,** to pledge; **en p. de,** as a pledge of; *fam* **no dolerle prendas a uno,** to spare no effort *or* expense; *(reconocer un error)* to admit one was wrong; *fam* **no soltar p.,** not to say a word. **3** *(juego)* **prendas,** forfeits. **4** *(cualidad)* quality, talent. **5** *fam (persona)* darling, sweetheart.

prendar I *vtr* to captivate, delight; **dejó a todos prendados,** everyone was taken by him. **II prendarse** *vr (aficionarse)* to take a fancy **(de,** to), be captivated **(de,** by); *(enamorarse)* to fall in love **(de,** with); **se prendó de ella,** he fell for her.

prendedor *nm* brooch, pin.

prender I *vtr* **1** *(arrestar)* to arrest; *(encarcelar)* to put in prison. **2** *(sujetar)* to fasten, attach; *(con alfileres)* to pin. **3** *(fuego)* to set; **p. la lumbre,** to start a fire. **II** *vi (planta)* to take root; *(fuego)* to catch; **esta leña no prende,** this wood won't light; *fig* **sus ideas prendieron rápidamente en los trabajadores,** the workers quickly caught on to his ideas. **III prenderse** *vr* to catch fire.

prendido,-a I *pp de* **prender. II** *adj* **1** *(sujeto)* fastened, caught. **2** *fig (encantado)* enchanted, captivated; **quedar p.,** to be captivated.

prendimiento *nm* arrest, capture.

prensa *nf* **1** *Téc (prensadora)* press. **2** *Impr* printing press; **entrar en p.,** to go to press. **3** *Prensa* press; **la p. diaria,** the newspapers *pl*, the dailies *pl*; *fig* **tener buena/mala p.,** to have a good/a bad press; *fam* **los chicos de la p.,** the journalists. ■ **agencia de p.,** press agency; **conferencia de p.,** press conference.

prensado,-a I *pp de* **prensar. II** *adj* pressed, compressed; **madera prensada,** chipboard. **III** *nm* pressing.

prensar *vtr* to press.

prensil *adj* prehensile.

preñado,-a I *adj* **1** *(mujer)* pregnant; **preñada de 3 meses,** 3 months pregnant. **2** *fig (lleno, cargado)* pregnant **(de,** with), full **(de,** of); **ojos preñados de lágrimas,** eyes filled with tears. **II** *nm (embarazo)* pregnancy.

preñar *vtr (mujer)* to make pregnant; *(animal)* to impregnate.

preñez *nf* pregnancy.

preocupación *nf* **1** *(inquietud)* worry, concern. **2** *(prejuicio)* prejudice.

preocupado,-a I *pp de* **preocupar. II** *adj* worried, concerned.

preocupar I *vtr* to worry; **me preocupa que llegue tan tarde,** I'm worried about him arriving so late. **II preocuparse** *vr* to worry, get worried **(por,** about); **no te preocupes,** *(no te inquietes)* don't worry; *(déjalo correr)* never mind.

preparación *nf (gen)* preparation; *(formación)* training; *(aptitud)* capacity; **p. musical,** musical training.

preparado,-a I *pp de* **preparar. II** *adj* **1** *(dispuesto)* ready, prepared; *Culin* **comidas preparadas,** ready-cooked meals; **p. de antemano,** prepared. **2** *(capacitado)* trained, qualified. **III** *nm Farm (medicamento)* preparation.

preparador,-a *nm, f Dep* coach, trainer.

preparar I *vtr* **1** *(gen)* to prepare, get ready; **prepara las maletas,** pack your bags; **p. la comida,** to get lunch ready; **p. un examen,** to prepare for an exam. **2** *(enseñar)* to train, teach; *Dep (entrenar)* to train, coach. **II prepararse** *vr* **1** *(gen)* to prepare oneself, get ready; **me preparaba para salir cuando sonó el teléfono,** I was getting ready to leave when the telephone rang; **se prepara una buena tormenta,** there's a big storm brewing. **2** *Dep (entrenarse)* to train; **se está preparando para los Juegos Olímpicos,** he's training for the Olympic Games.

preparativo *nm* preparation; **hacer los preparativos para,** to make preparations for.

preparatorio,-a *adj* preparatory.

preponderante *adj* preponderant.

preponderancia *nf* preponderance, prevalence.

preponderar *vtr* to prevail.

preposición *nf Ling* preposition.

preposicional *adj Ling* prepositional.

prepotencia *nf* power, dominance.

prepotente *adj* powerful, domineering.

propucio *nm Anat* foreskin.

prerrequisito *nm* prerequisite.

prerrogativa *nf* prerogative.

presa *nf* **1** *(captura)* capture, seizure; **hacer p.,** to seize; **el fuego hizo p. en su vestido,** the fire set light to her dress. **2** *(cosa)* prey, catch; *fig* prey; **caer p. de,** to fall prey to; **el cazador siempre debe perseguir a su p.,** hunters should always stalk their prey; *fig* **ser p. de,** to be a victim of; **p. del pánico,** panic-stricken. **2** *Orn (uña)* claw; *Zool (colmillo)* tusk. **3** *(embalse)* dam; *(acequia)* channel, ditch.

presagiar *vtr* to predict, foretell.

presagio *nm* **1** *(señal)* omen; **buen/mal p.,** good/bed omen. **2** *(premonición)* premonition.

presbicia *nf Med* long-sightedness, far-sightedness.

presbiterianismo *nm Rel* Presbyterianism.

presbiteriano,-a *adj & nm, f Rel* Presbyterian.

presbiterio *nm* presbytery.

presbítero *nm Rel* priest.

prescindir *vi* **1** *(pasarse sin)* to do without; **podemos p. del coche,** we can do without the car. **2** *(omitir)* to leave out, omit. **3** *(desembarazarse)* to get rid of.

prescribir *(pp prescrito) vtr & vi* to prescribe; **el médico le prescribió unas vacaciones,** the doctor advised him to take a holiday.

prescripción *nf* prescription; **p. facultativa,** medical prescription.

prescrito,-a I *pp de* **prescribir. II** *adj* prescribed.

preselección *nf (gen)* short list, short listing; *Dep* seeding.

preseleccionar *vtr (gen)* to short-list; *Dep* to seed.

presencia *nm* **1** *(gen)* presence; **en p. de,** in the presence of; **hacer acto de p.,** to put in an appearance. ■ **p. de ánimo,** presence of mind. **2** *(aspecto)* presence, look; **de buena p.,** distinguished-looking.

presencial *adj* **testigo p.,** eyewitness.

presenciar *vtr (estar presente)* to be present at; *(ver)* to witness.

presentable *adj* presentable; **no estoy p.,** I'm not dressed for it, I'm not dressed for the occasion.

presentación *nf* **1** *(gen)* presentation; *(aspecto)* appearance; *(de personas)* introduction; *(de producto)* launching; **carta de p.,** letter of introduction; **hacer las presentaciones,** to introduce two or more people; **p. en sociedad,** debut, coming out. **2** *Am (petición)* petition, request.

presentador,-a *nm, f Rad TV* presenter, host, hostess.

presentar I *vtr* **1** *(gen)* to present, *(mostrar)* to show, display; *(ofrecer)* to offer; **la habitación presentaba un aspecto desolador,** the room looked gloomy; **p. excusas,** to excuse oneself; **p. la dimisión,** to tender one's resignation; **p. un candidato,** to propose sb; **p. un libro/una película,** to launch a book/film; **p. una demanda** *or* **una denuncia,** to bring an action; *Jur* **p. pruebas,** to submit proof; **p. una queja,** to lodge a complaint. **2** *(una persona a otra)* to introduce; **le presento al doctor Ruiz,** may I introduce you to Dr Ruiz; **ser presentada en sociedad,** to make one's debut, come out. **II presentarse** *vr* **1** *(comparecer)* to present oneself; *(inesperadamente)* to turn *or* come up; **se presentó en mi oficina mañana,** report to my office tomorrow; **se presentó sin avisar,** he turned up without warning *or* unexpectedly. **2** *(ocurrir)* to present itself, arise; **si se presenta la ocasión,** should the opportunity arise. **3** *(candidato)* to stand; **p. a unas elecciones,** to stand for election, *US* run for office. **4** *(a examen)* to sit **(a,** for). **5** *(darse a conocer)* to introduce oneself **(a,** to); **p. en sociedad,** to make one's debut, come out.

presente I *adj* present; **estar p. en,** to be present at; **hacer p,** to declare, state; **hacer p. algo a algn,** to remind sb of sth; **la p. (carta),** this letter; **las personas aquí presentes,** the people here present; **los presentes,** those present; **mejorando lo p.,** present company excepted; **¡p.!,** here!, present!; **tener p.,** *(tener en cuenta)* to bear in mind; *(recordar)* to remember. **II** *nm* **1** *(tiempo actual)* present; **al** *or* **de p.,** at present; **hasta el p.,** up to the present. **2** *Ling* **(tiempo) p.,** present tense; **participio de p.,** present participle. **3** *fml (regalo)* present, gift.

presentimiento *nm* presentiment, premonition; **tengo el p. de que ...,** I have the feeling that ... .

presentir *vtr* to have a presentiment *or* premonition of; **presiento que lloverá,** I've got the feeling that it's going to rain.

preservación *nf* preservation, protection.

preservar *vtr* to preserve, protect **(de,** from); **(contra,** against).

preservativo,-a I *adj* preservative. **II** *nm* sheath, condom.

presidencia *nf* **1** *Pol* presidency. **2** *(de una reunión) (hombre)* chairmanship; *(mujer)* chairwomanship.

presidencial *adj* presidential.

presidente,-a *nm, f* **1** *Pol* president; **p. del gobierno,** Prime Minister, Premier. **2** *(de una reunión)* chairperson.

presidiario,-a *nm,f* prisoner, convict.

presidio *nm* prison, penitentiary.

presidir *vtr* **1** *Pol (país)* to rule, head; *fig* **la bondad preside todos sus actos,** he is motivated by kindness. **2** *(reunión)* to chair, preside over.

presilla *nf Cost* fastener.

presión pressure; **a** *or* **bajo p.,** under pressure; **hacer p.,** to press; *fig (influir)* to pressurize; *Pol* to lobby. ■ *Pol* **grupo de p.,** pressure group, lobby; *Culin* **olla a p.,** pressure cooker; **p. arterial** *or* **sanguínea,** blood pressure; **p. atmosférica,** atmospheric pressure.

presionar *vtr* to press; *fig* to pressurize, put pressure on.

preso,-a I *adj* imprisoned. **II** *nm,f* prisoner.

prestación *nf* **1** *(servicio)* service. **2** *(ayuda)* help, assistance; *(subsidio)* provision, supply, benefit. **3** *Téc (gen pl)* performance.

prestado,-a *pp de* **prestar.** **II** *adj (a alguien)* lent; *(por alguien)* borrowed; **dejar p.,** to lend; **ese libro está p.,** that book is on loan; **pedir p.,** to borrow; *fam* **vivir de p.,** to scrounge.

prestamista *nmf Fin* moneylender.

préstamo *nm* **1** *(acción de prestar)* lending; *(acción de pedir prestado)* borrowing. **2** *(cantidad, cosa)* loan; **pedir un p.,** to ask for a loan. **3** *Ling (palabra)* loanword.

prestancia *nf* **1** *(excelencia)* excellence, high quality. **2** *(distinción)* distinction, elegance.

prestar I *vtr* **1** *(dejar prestado)* to lend, loan; *(pedir prestado)* to borrow; **¿me prestas cien pesetas?,** could you lend me a hundred pesetas?; **¿me prestas tu pluma?,** can I borrow your pen? **2** *(atención)* to pay; *(ayuda)* to give; *(servicio)* to do, render; *Jur (declaración)* to make; **p. juramento,** to make an oath, swear. **II prestarse** *vr* **1** *(ofrecerse)* to offer oneself **(a,** to); **se prestó a llevarnos a casa,** she (willingly) gave us a lift home. **2** *(acceder)* to agree; **no te prestes a ese juego,** don't get mixed up in that sort of thing. **3** *(dar motivo)* to cause; **se presta a (crear) malentendidos,** it makes for misunderstandings.

prestatario,-a *nm,f Fin* borrower.

presteza *nf* promptness, diligence; **con p.,** promptly.

prestidigitación *nf* conjuring, magic.

prestidigitador,-a *nm,f* conjuror, magician.

prestigiar *vtr* to give prestige to.

prestigio *nm* prestige.

prestigioso,-a *adj* prestigious.

presto,-a I *adj* **1** *(dispuesto)* ready, prepared. **2** *(rápido)* swift, quick, prompt. **II** *adv* arc *(con rapidez)* rapidly, promptly; *(en seguida)* at once.

presumible *adj* probable, likely.

presumido,-a I *adj* vain, conceited. **II** *nm,f* vain person.

presumir I *vtr (suponer)* to presume, assume, suppose. **II** *vi* **1** *(vanagloriarse)* to boast, show off; **ella presume de artista,** she likes to think she's an artist; **presume de guapo,** he fancies himself. **2** *(ser vanidoso)* to be vain *or* conceited; *Am* to provide with sth in case it is needed.

presunción *nf* **1** *(suposición)* presumption, supposition. **2** *(vanidad)* vanity, conceit.

presunto,-a *adj* presumed, supposed; *Jur* **el p. autor del crimen,** the alleged criminal. ◆ **presuntamente** *adv* supposedly.

presuntuosidad *nf* vanity, conceit.

presuntuoso,-a I *adj* **1** *(vanidoso)* vain, conceited. **2** *(pretencioso)* pretentious, showy. **II** *nm, f* **1** *(vanidoso)* vain *or* conceited person. **2** *(pretencioso)* pretentious person, show-off.

presuponer *(pp presupuesto) vtr* to presuppose.

presupuestar *vtr Fin* to budget for; *(importe)* to estimate for.

presupuestario,-a *adj* budget, budgetary.

presupuesto,-a I *pp de* **presuponer.** **II** *adj* presupposed. **III** *nm* **1** *(supuesto)* supposition, assumption. **2** *Fin* budget; *(cálculo)* estimate; **hacer un p. (de un trabajo),** to give an estimate (for a job).

presuroso,-a *adj (rápido)* quick; *(con prisa)* in a hurry.

pretencioso,-a I *adj* pretentious. **II** *nm, f* pretentious person.

pretender *vtr* **1** *(querer)* to want to, mean to; **pretendo acabar pronto,** I mean to finish soon. **2** *(intentar)* to try; **pretende ayudarnos,** he's trying to help us; **¿qué pretendes insinuar?,** what are you getting at? **3** *(afirmar)* to claim; **pretende ser el más rico,** he claims to be the richest person around. **4** *(aspirar a)* to try for; *(cargo)* to apply for. **5** *(cortejar)* to court, woo.

pretendido,-a I *pp de* **pretender.** **II** *adj* **1** *(fingido)* pretended. **2** *(supuesto)* so-called, would-be.

pretendiente,-a I *adj* aspiring. **II** *nm, f* **1** *(de una mujer etc)* suitor. **2** *Pol (al trono)* pretender. **3** *(a un cargo)* applicant, candidate.

pretensión *nf* **1** *(aspiración)* aim, aspiration; **mi única p.,** the only thing I want. **2** *(soberbia)* pretentiousness; **con demasiadas pretensiones,** too pretentiously; **tener muchas pretensiones,** to be pretentious; **tener pocas pretensiones,** to be undemanding; **tenía la p. de que ganaría,** he was convinced he was going to win.

pretérito,-a I *adj* past, former. **II** *nm Ling* preterite *or* simple past tense.

pretextar *vtr* to plead, allege; **pretextó que tenía dolor de cabeza,** he claimed he had a headache.

pretexto *nm* pretext, excuse; **con el p. de que ...,** on the pretext that ... .

pretil *nm* **1** *Arquit* parapet. **2** *Am (atrio)* atrium, forecourt.

prevaldré *indic fut véase* **prevaler.**

prevalecer *vi* **1** *(triunfar)* to triumph; *(imponerse)* to prevail; **prevaleció la razón,** common sense prevailed. **2** *Bot (planta)* to take root.

prevaleciente *adj* prevailing.

prevaler I *vi véase* **prevalecer.** II **prevalerse** *vr (valerse, servirse)* to avail oneself **(de,** of) take advantage **(de,** of); **se prevalió de su autoridad para conseguir lo que quería,** he took advantage of his position to achieve his ends.

prevención *in* **1** *(precaución)* prevention; **en p. de,** as a prevention against. **2** *(preparación)* preparation. **3** *(medida)* precaution; **tomar prevenciones,** to take precautions. **4** *(prejuicio)* prejudice; **tener p. contra algn,** to have a prejudice against sb. **5** *(policial)* police station.

prevenir *vtr* **1** *(preparar)* to prepare, get ready. **2** *(precaver)* to prevent, forestall; *(evitar)* to avoid; **para p. la gripe,** to prevent flu; *prov* **más vale p. que curar,** prevention is better than cure. **3** *(advertir)* to warn.

preventivo,-a *adj* preventive; *(medidas)* precautionary; *Jur* **detención** *or* **prisión preventiva,** remand in custody; *Med* **medicina preventiva,** preventive medicine.

prever *(pp* previsto*)* *vtr* **1** *(conjeturar)* to foresee, forecast. **2** *(planear)* to plan. **3** *(anticipar)* to make allowances for.

previo,-a *adj* previous, prior; **p. pago de su importe,** only on payment; **sin p. aviso,** without prior notice. ◆ **previamente** *adv* previously.

previsible *adj* foreseeable.

previsión *nf* **1** *(acción de prever)* forecast; *Meteor* **p. del tiempo,** weather forecast. **2** *(precaución)* precaution; **en p. de,** as a precaution against.

previsor,-a *adj* careful, far-sighted.

previsto,-a I *pp de* **prever.** II *adj* foreseen, forecast; **todo salió según lo p.,** everything turned out as planned *or* expected.

prieto,-a *adj* **1** *(apretado)* firm, tight; **de carnes prietas,** with a firm body. **2** *(color)* blackish, very dark. **3** *fig (tacaño)* mean.

prima *nf* **1** *(gratificación)* bonus; *(de un seguro)* insurance premium. **2** *(persona) véase* **primo,-a.**

primacía *nf* primacy.

primado *nm Rel* primate.

primar¹ *vi* to have priority, prevail.

primar² *vtr* to give a bonus to.

primario,-a *adj* primary; *Educ* **educación primaria,** primary education.

primate *nm* **1** *Zool* primate. **2** *(persona)* outstanding person.

primavera¹ *nf* **1** spring, springtime; *fig* **(ella) tenía quince primaveras,** she was fifteen. **2** *Bot* primrose.

primavera² I *adj* gullible, naive. II *nmf* simpleton, sucker, mug.

primaveral *adj* spring, spring-like; **hace un tiempo p.,** it's like spring.

primer *adj (delante de nm) véase* **primero,-a.**

primera *nf* **1** *(clase)* first class; **viajar en p.,** to travel first class. **2** *Aut (marcha)* first gear. **3** **a la p.,** at the first attempt; *fam* **a la p. de cambio,** *(así que pueda)* as soon as the opportunity arises; *(inesperadamente)* when least expected; *fam* **de p.,** great, first class; **me viene de p.,** it's just the job.

primerizo,-a I *adj* **1** *(principiante)* novice. **2** *(madre)* first-time; *(niño)* first. II *nm, f* novice. III *nf* first-time mother.

primero,-a I *adj* **1** *(que precede)* first; *(anterior)* former; **de primera necesidad,** basic; **el primer paso es ...,** the first thing to do is ...; **es el p. de la clase,** he's top of the class; **iré a primera hora de la tarde,** I'll go first thing this afternoon; *Prensa* **primera página,** front page. **2** *fig (fundamental)* first, basic, main; **lo p. es la familia,** the family comes first. II *nm, f* first; **llegar el p.,** to arrive first; **no eres el p. en llegar,** you're not the first to arrive; **nos vamos a primeros de mes,** we shall be leaving at the beginning of the month. III *adv* **1** *(en primer lugar)* first; **cómete eso p.,** eat that first. **2** *(antes, más bien)* rather, sooner; **p. me moriría que pedirle dinero,** I'd rather die than ask him for money; *véase tamb* **primera.**

primicia *nf* **1** *Bot* first fruit. **2** *Prensa* novelty; **p. informativa,** scoop.

primigenio,-a *adj* original, primitive.

primitivo,-a *adj* **1** *(original)* original, first. **2** *Hist* primitive. **3** *(tosco)* coarse, rough.

primo,-a I *adj* **1** *(materia)* raw. **2** *Mat (número)* prime. II *nm, f* **1** *(pariente)* cousin; **p. hermano,** first cousin; **p. segundo,** second cousin. **2** *fam (tonto)* fool, drip, dunce; **hacer el p.,** to be taken for a ride.

primogénito,-a *adj & nm, f* first-born, eldest.

primor *nm* **1** *(delicadeza)* delicacy; **con (gran) p.,** (very) delicately. **2** *(belleza)* beauty; **esta niña es un p.,** this girl is lovely; *fam* **dibuja que es un p.,** he's a fantastic drawer. **3** *(habilidad)* care, skill.

primordial *adj* essential, basic, fundamental.

primoroso,-a *adj* delicate, exquisite.

prímula *nf Bot* primula.

prínceps *adj inv Impr* **edición p.,** first edition.

princesa *nf* princess.

principado *nm* principality.

principal I *adj* main, chief, principal; **lo p. es que ...,** the main thing is that ...; *Arquit* **puerta p.,** front door. II *nm* **1** *(piso)* first floor, *US* second floor. **2** *(jefe)* chief, boss.

príncipe I *nm* prince. ■ **p. azul,** Prince Charming; **p. consorte,** prince consort; **p. de Gales,** Prince of Wales; **p. heredero,** crown prince. II *adj inv* **edición p.,** first edition.

principesco,-a *adj* princely.

principiante I *adj* novice. II *nmf* beginner, learner, novice.

principio *nm* **1** *(fundamento)* principle; **el p. de Arquímedes,** Archimedes' principle; **hombre de principios,** man of principles; **no tener principios,** to have no principles; **por p.,** in principle. **2** *(comienzo)* beginning, start; **a principio(s) de,** at the beginning of; **al p., en un p.,** at first, in the beginning; **dar p. a algo,** to start sth off; **en p.,** in principle. **3 principios,** *(nociones)* rudiments, basics.

pringar I *vtr* **1** *(ensuciar)* to make greasy *or* dirty. **2** *fam* **¡ya la has pringado!,** now you've done it! II *vi arg* **1** *(trabajar)* to work hard. **2** *(morirse)* to kick the bucket. III **pringarse** *vr (ensuciarse)* to get greasy *or* dirty.

pringoso,-a *adj (grasiento)* greasy; *(sucio)* dirty; **manos pringosas,** sticky hands.

pringue *nm (grasa)* grease; *(suciedad)* dirt, filth.

prior,-a *nm, f Rel (hombre)* prior; *(mujer)* prioress.

priorato *nm Rel (cargo)* priorate; *(comunidad)* priory.

priori (a) *adv* a priori.

prioridad *nf* priority; **dar p. a algo,** to give priority to sth; **tener p.,** to have priority.

prioritario,-a *adj* prior, priority; **ser p.,** to have priority.

prisa *nf (prontitud)* hurry, rush; *(velocidad)* speed; **a p.,** *véase* **aprisa,** correr p.,to be urgent; **me corre mucha p.,** I need it right away; **date p.,** hurry up; **de p.,** *véase* **deprisa,** salió a toda p., he left in a hurry; **tener p.,** to be in a hurry.

prisión *nf* prison, jail, gaol; **fue condenado a veinte años de p.,** he was given twenty years. ■ **p. preventiva,** remand in custody.

prisionero,-a *nm,f* prisoner.

prisma *nm Mat* prism.

prismático,-a I *adj* prismatic. **II prismáticos** *nmpl* binoculars, field glasses.

priva *nf arg* booze.

privación *nf* deprivation, privation; **pasar privaciones,** to be in great need.

privado,-a I *pp de* privar. **II** *adj* private; **vida privada,** private life.

privar I *vtr* **1** *(despojar)* to deprive **(de,** of). **2** *(prohibir)* to forbid, ban. **3** *fam (gustar)* to like; **no me priva la vida de campo,** I don't go for country life. **II** *vi* **1** *(estar de moda)* to be fashionable *or* popular. **2** *fam (beber)* to booze. **III privarse** *vr* **1** *(despojarse)* to deprive oneself **(de,** of), go without; **no se priva de nada,** he really spoils himself. **2** *fam (emborracharse)* to get drunk.

privativo,-a *adj* exclusive **(de,** of).

prive *nm fam* booze.

privilegiado,-a I *adj* privileged. **II** *nm,f* privileged person.

privilegio *nm* privilege.

pro I *nm (provecho)* advantage; **en p. de,** in favour of; **hombre de p.,** man of integrity; **los pros y los contras,** the pros and cons. **II** *prep (a favor de)* in favour *or US* favor of; **campaña p. desarme,** campaign for disarmament, disarmament campaign.

pro- *pref* pro-; **prodemocrático,** prodemocratic.

proa *nf Náut* prow, bows *pl*; **poner la p. a algn,** to take a stand against sb; **poner p. a,** to set sail for.

probabilidad *nf* probability, likelihood; **tiene pocas probabilidades,** he stands little chance.

probable *adj* probable, likely; **es p. que llueva,** it'll probably rain; **es p. que no lo sepa,** he's unlikely to know; **lo más p. es que ...,** it's very likely that ... .

probado,-a I *pp de* probar. **II** *adj* proven; **de probada eficacia,** of proven efficiency; **un hecho p.,** a proven fact.

probador *nm* fitting room.

probar I *vtr* **1** *(comprobar)* to test, check; **prueba la puerta a ver si está cerrada con llave,** check to see if the door is locked. **2** *(intentar)* to try; **lo hemos probado todo,** we've tried everything. **3** *(demostrar)* to prove, show; **eso prueba que tenía razón,** that shows I was right. **4** *(comer, beber)* to try; **no había probado este vino,** I had never tried this wine before; **prueba esta sopa,** taste this soup. **II** *vi* **1** *(sentar)* to suit; **la humedad le prueba mal,** dampness is bad for him. **2** to try; **p. a,** to attempt *or* try to; **por p. no se pierde nada,** there is no harm in trying; **prueba a levantarlo,** try and lift it; **prueba a meterlo de lado,** see if it fits sideways. **III probarse** *vr (prenda)* to try on.

probatura *nf fam* try.

probeta *nf Quím* test tube. ■ **niño p.,** test-tube baby.

probidad *nf* honesty, integrity, decency.

problema *nm* problem, trouble.

problemático,-a *adj* problematic.

probo,-a *adj* honest, upright, decent.

procacidad *nf (dicho)* rude remark; *(hecho)* indecent act.

procaz *adj* rude, indecent.

procedencia *nf* **1** *(origen)* origin, source. **2** *(oportunidad, adecuación)* adequacy, appropriateness; *Jur* merits *pl*.

procedente *adj* **1** *(originario)* coming **(de,** from); **el vuelo p. de Sevilla,** the flight (coming) from Seville. **2** *(oportuno, adecuado)* adequate, appropriate, fitting; *Jur* proper.

proceder I *vi* **1 p. de,** *(originarse)* to come (from); **procede del norte,** he's from the North. **2** *(actuar)* to act, behave; **siempre procede con cautela,** he is always careful *or* cautious. **3** *(ser oportuno)* to be advisable *or* appropriate; **en estas situaciones procede tomar medidas drásticas,** under these circumstances it is advisable to take drastic measures. **4** *Jur (ser conforme)* to take proceedings **(contra,** against); **la protesta no procede,**

objection overruled; **p. contra algn,** to sue sb. **5** *(ejecutar) (gen uso impers)* to proceed; **p. a una votación,** to proceed to an election; **se procedió a la elección del presidente,** they went on to the election of the chairman. **II** *nm (comportamiento)* behaviour, *US* behavior; **de recto p.,** upright.

procedimiento *nm* **1** *(método)* procedure, method; **utiliza unos procedimientos poco ortodoxos,** he uses unorthodox methods. **2** *Jur (trámites)* proceedings *pl*.

proceloso,-a *adj lit* tempestuous, stormy.

prócer *nm* great man, notable; **los próceres de la nación,** the country's great men.

procesado,-a I *pp de* procesar. **II** *adj* **1** *Jur* accused. **2** *Com Téc* processed. **III** *nm,f Jur* accused.

procesador *nm Inform* processor, central processing unit; **p. de datos/textos,** data/word processor.

procesal *adj Jur* procedural.

procesamiento *nm* **1** *Jur* prosecution; **auto de p.,** indictment. **2** *(elaboración)* processing; *Inform* processing; *Inform* **p. de datos/textos,** data/word processing; *Inform* **p. por lotes,** batch processing.

procesar *vtr* **1** *Jur* to prosecute. **2** *(elaborar, transformar)* to process; *Inform* to process.

procesión *nf* procession; *fig* **la p. va por dentro,** he's putting on a brave face.

procesional *adj* processional.

procesionaria *adj Ent* processionary moth.

procesionario *nm Rel* processional.

proceso *nm* **1** *(fases sucesivas)* process; *Inform* **p. de datos,** data processing; **p. de elaboración del pan,** bread-making process; **p. mental,** thought process. **2** *(transcurso del tiempo)* time; **en el p. de un año,** in the course of a year. **3** *Jur* trial, suit, hearing.

proclama *nf* proclamation; *Rel* **p. matrimonial,** banns *pl*.

proclamación *nf* proclamation.

proclamar *vtr* to proclaim; **el presidente ha proclamado su inocencia en el escándalo,** the president has declared his innocence in the scandal; **no es necesario proclamarlo a los cuatro vientos,** you don't need to broadcast it.

proclítico,-a *adj Ling* proclitic.

proclive *adj* prone, apt, inclined; **es muy p. a dejarse llevar por sus sentimientos,** he often gets carried away by his emotions.

procónsul *nm Hist* proconsul.

proconsular *adj Hist* proconsular.

procreación *nf* procreation.

procreador,-a I *adj* procreant, procreative. **II** *nm, f* procreator.

procrear *vtr* to procreate.

proctología *nf Med* proctology.

proctológico,-a *adj Med* proctological.

proctólogo,-a *nm,f Med* proctologist.

proctoscopio *nm Med* proctoscope.

procuración *nf Jur* procuration, power of attorney.

procurador,-a *nm,f Jur* procurator.

procurar *vtr* **1** *(intentar)* to try, attempt; **hay que p. no molestar a nadie,** we have to try not to bother anybody; **procura no hacer ruido,** try not to make too much noise; **procura que no te vean,** make sure they don't see you. **2** *(proporcionar)* (to manage) to get; **ella le procuró un trabajo,** she got a job for him.

prodigalidad *nf (abundancia)* lavishness; *(profusión)* extravagance, prodigality.

prodigar I *vtr (despilfarrar)* to spend lavishly, lavish. **II prodigarse** *vr* **1** *(ser amable, ayudar)* to go out of one's way, be helpful *or* kind. **2** *(exhibirse)* to show off; **cree que para triunfar tiene que p. sus apariciones en público,** he thinks he has to be in the public eye more to be successful.

prodigio *nm* 1 *(suceso sobrenatural)* prodigy, miracle; **hacer prodigios,** to work wonders. 2 *(niño)* child prodigy.

prodigiosidad *nf* prodigiousness.

prodigioso,-a *adj* *(sobrenatural)* prodigious; *(maravilloso)* wonderful, marvellous, *US* marvelous, fantastic. ◆ **prodigiosamente** *adv* prodigiously.

pródigo,-a I *adj* 1 *(derrochador)* extravagant, wastefull; *Rel* **el hijo p.,** the prodigal son. 2 *(generoso)* generous, lavish; **ella es p. en regalos,** she's very generous with presents. **II** *nm, f (gastador)* spendthrift.

producción *nf (acción)* production, manufacturing; *(producto)* product; *Cin* production; **p. en cadena,** mass production.

producir I *vtr* 1 *(gen)* to produce, manufacture, make; *(árboles, terrenos)* to yield, bear; *(rendir)* to be profitable; *Cin* to produce; **el negocio no produce lo que esperábamos,** this business is not as profitable as we expected; **el país produce más de lo que puede exportar,** the country produces more than it can export. 2 *fig (originar)* to cause, bring about; **los cambios bruscos de tiempo producen enfermedades,** sudden changes in the weather cause illnesses. **II producirse** *vr* to take place, happen; **las transformaciones políticas se están produciendo a una velocidad inimaginable,** the speed with which the present political situation is changing is unbelievable.

productividad *nf* productivity.

productivo,-a *adj* productive; *(beneficioso)* profitable; **las últimas inversiones han resultado muy productivas,** the latest investments have been very profitable.

producto *nm* 1 *(cosa)* product; *Com* product, manufactured item; *Agr* produce; **p. alimenticio,** foodstuff; **productos agrícolas,** farm *or* agricultural produce; **productos de belleza,** cosmetics; **productos de consumo,** consumer goods; *fig* **el éxito es p. del trabajo,** success is the product of hard work. 2 *Mat* product.

productor,-a I *adj* productive, producing; **país p. de petróleo,** oil-producing country. **II** *nm, f* producer. **III** *nf Cin* production company.

proel *nm Náut* bowman.

proemial *adj Lit* proemial, introductory.

proemio *nm Lit* proem, introduction, preface.

proeza *nf* heroic deed, exploit; **ganar al campeón sería una auténtica p.,** to defeat the champion would be a real exploit.

prof *abr de* **profesor,** teacher.

prof^a *abr de* **profesora,** *(mujer)* teacher.

profanación *nf* desecration, profanation.

profanador,-a I *adj* profanatory, irreverent. **II** *nm, f* profaner.

profanamiento *nm* desecration, profanation, irreverence.

profanar *vtr* to desecrate, profane; **no deberías p. su memoria,** you shouldn't desecrate her memory.

profano,-a I *adj* 1 *Rel* profane, secular; *(irreverente)* irreverent. 2 *(inexperto)* lay, uninitiated. **II** *nm, f (hombre)* layman; *(mujer)* laywoman; **soy p. en la materia,** I know nothing about the subject.

profase *nf Biol* prophase.

profecía *nf* 1 *(gen)* prophecy. 2 **profecías,** *Rel* Minor Prophets.

proferir *vtr* to utter; **p. insultos,** to hurl insults.

profesar I *vtr* 1 *Rel* to profess; **profesa la religión musulmana,** he professes Islamism; *fig* **p. una gran admiración a algn,** to have a great admiration for sb. 2 *(ejercer)* to practise, *US* practice, profess; **profesa como médico,** he is a practising doctor. **II** *vi Rel* to profess.

profesión *nf* 1 *(gen)* profession; **fotógrafo de p.,** photographer by profession; **p. liberal,** liberal profession; **ser de la p.,** to be in the same profession. 2 *Rel* taking of vows; **p. de fe,** profession of faith.

profesional *adj & nmf* professional. ◆ **profesionalmente** *adv* professionally.

profesionalidad *nf*, **profesionalismo** *nm* professionalism.

profesionalizar *vtr* to make more professional.

profeso,-a I *Rel adj* professed. **II** *nm, f Rel* professed monk *or* nun. **III** *adv* **ex p.,** intentionally.

profesor,-a *nm, f (gen)* teacher; *Univ* lecturer; *(catedrático)* professor.

profesorado *nm* 1 *(profesores)* teaching staff, teachers *pl.* 2 *(cargo)* post of teacher.

profesoral *adj (gen)* teachers', teaching; *Univ* lecturers'.

profeta *nm* prophet.

profético,-a *adj* prophetic.

profetisa *nf* prophetess.

profetizar *vtr* to prophesy, foretell.

profiláctico,-a *Med* **I** *adj* prophylactic. **II** *nm* condom, *US* prophylactic.

profilaxis *nf Med* prophylaxis.

prófugo,-a I *adj* fugitive, fleeing. **II** *nm, f* fugitive. **III** *nm Mil* deserter.

profundidad *nf* 1 *(hondura)* depth; **de poca p.,** shallow; *Fot* **p. de campo,** depth of field; **seis metros de p.,** six metres deep *or* in depth. 2 *fig (de ideas, pensamientos)* profundity, depth, profoundness; **meterse en profundidades,** to get to the bottom.

profundizar *vtr & vi* 1 *(cavar)* to deepen. 2 *fig (discurrir)* to study in depth; **p. en un tema,** to look deeply into a matter.

profundo,-a *adj* 1 *(hondo)* deep; **en lo más p.,** deep down. 2 *fig (intenso)* profound; **un pensamiento p.,** a profound thought. ◆ **profundamente** *adv* deeply.

profusión *nf* profusion; **con p.,** profusely.

profuso,-a *adj* profuse. ◆ **profusamente** *adv* profusely.

progenie *nf* 1 *(casta)* family, lineage. 2 *(descendientes)* offspring, progeny.

progenitor,-a *nm, f (antepasado)* ancestor, progenitor; *(padre)* father; *(madre)* mother; **progenitores,** *(padres)* parents.

progenitura *nf* offspring, progeny.

progesterona *nf Biol* progesterone.

prognosis *nf inv* prognosis.

programa *nm* programme, *US* program; *Inform* program; **¿cuál es el p. para mañana?,** what's the plan for tomorrow?

programable *adj* programable, programmable.

programación *nf (gen)* programming, *US* programing; *Rad TV* programme planning.

programador,-a *nm, f Inform* programmer.

programar *vtr* to programme, *US* program; *Inform* to program; **me gusta p. las vacaciones con antelación,** I like to plan my holidays in advance.

programático,-a *adj* programmatic.

progre *adj & nmf fam* trendy, lefty.

progresar *vi* to progress, make progress.

progresía *nf fam* trendies, *pl.*

progresión *nf* progression; *Mat* **p. aritmética/geométrica,** arithmetic/geometric progression; *Mús* **p. armónica,** harmonic progression.

progresismo *nm Pol* progressionism.

progresista *Pol* **I** *adj* progressive. **II** *nmf* progressist, progressive, member of a progressive party.

progresivo,-a *adj* progressive. ◆ **progresivamente** *adv* progressively.

progreso *nm* progress; **sus progresos son sorprendentes,** her progress is surprising.

prohibición *nf* prohibition, ban; *Hist* **los años de la p.,** the Prohibition years; **p. de fumar,** smoking ban.

prohibicionista *nmf* prohibitionist; *Hist* Prohibitionist.

prohibido,-a I *pp de* **prohibir. II** *adj* forbidden, prohibited, banned; *Aut* **dirección prohibida,** no entry; **está prohibido fumar aquí,** you can't smoke here; **'prohibida la entrada',** 'no admittance'; **p. aparcar/ fumar,** no parking/smoking.

prohibir *vtr* to forbid, prohibit, ban; **'se prohíbe pasar',** 'no admittance *or* entry'.

prohibitivo,-a *adj,* **prohibitorio,-a** *adj* prohibitive, prohibitory; **los precios de las viviendas están prohibitivos,** house prices are prohibitive.

prohijación *nf,* **prohijamiento** *nm* adoption.

prohijar *vtr* to adopt.

prohombre *nm* great *or* outstanding man.

prójimo,-a *nm,f fam* person, type; **¡hay cada p. por ahí!,** it takes all kinds!; **la prójima,** the wife. **II** *nm* one's fellow man, one's neighbour *or US* neighbor; **ama a tu p.,** love thy neighbour. **III** *nf* loose woman.

pról. *abr de* **prólogo,** prologue, *US* prolog.

prolapso *nm Med* prolapse, prolapsus.

prole *nf* offspring.

prolegómeno *nm* introduction, prolegomenon; **dejémonos de prolegómenos y vayamos al grano,** let's skip the introduction and get down to business.

proletariado *nm* proletariat.

proletario,-a *adj & nm,f* proletarian.

proliferación *nf* proliferation.

proliferar *vi* to proliferate; **tras el cambio político, han proliferado toda clase de partidos,** after the political change, all kinds of parties have appeared.

prolífico,-a *adj* prolific.

prolijidad *nf* verbosity, long-windedness, prolixity.

prolijo,-a *adj* **1** *(dilatado)* verbose, long-winded, prolix. **2** *(meticuloso)* excessively meticulous.

prologar *vtr* to prologue, *US* prolog, introduce.

prólogo *nm* prologue, *US* prolog.

prolongación *nf* prolonging, extension, prolongation.

prolongado,-a I *pp de* **prolongar. II** *adj* **1** *(más largo que ancho)* elongated. **2** *(largo)* long; **una discusión prolongada,** a long discussion. ◆ **prolongadamente** *adv* at length.

prolongamiento *nm* prolonging, extension, prolongment.

prolongar I *vtr* **1** *(alargar)* to prolong, extend. **2** *(hacer durar)* to prolong; **tuvimos que p. la espera hasta que el avión estuvo preparado,** we had to make them wait even longer until the plane was ready. **II prolongarse** *vr* to go on, last longer; **la reunión se prolongó hasta las seis,** the meeting went on until six.

promediar I *vtr (repartir)* to average out. **II** *vi (interceder)* to mediate.

promedio *nm* average; **como p.,** on average; **escribe un p. de cinco libros al año,** on average, he writes five books a year.

promesa *nf* promise; **romper una p.,** to break a promise; *fig* **la joven p. de la música/del baile,** the promising young musician/dancer.

prometedor,-a *adj* promising.

prometer I *vtr* to promise; **te lo prometo,** I promise; *fig* **p. el oro y el moro,** to promise the moon. **II** *vi* to be promising; **esto promete,** this looks promising. **III prometerse** *vr (pareja)* to get engaged; *fam* **nos las prometíamos muy felices,** we had great expectations.

prometido,-a I *pp de* **prometer. II** *adj* promised; **cumplir lo p.,** to keep one's word *or* one's promise; **lo p. es deuda,** a promise is a promise. **III** *nm,f (hombre)* fiancé; *(mujer)* fiancée.

prominencia *nf (protuberancia)* protuberance, bulge; *(elevación)* rise, prominence; *fig (importancia)* prominence.

prominente *adj* **1** *(que se eleva)* protruding, projecting; *(elevado, importante)* prominent. **2** *Am (ilustre)* illustrious, famous.

promiscuidad *nf* promiscuity, promiscuousness.

prosmicuo,-a *adj* promiscuous. ◆ **promiscuamente** *adv* promiscuously.

promoción *nf (gen)* promotion; *Com (mejor empleo)* promotion, advancement; *Com (oferta)* offer; *Educ* **p. universitaria,** class *or* year *or* group that graduates at the same time.

promocionar I *vtr (cosas)* to promote; *(personas)* to give promotion to; **la publicidad es imprescindible para p. un producto,** advertising is essential to promote a product. **II** *vi Dep* to promote. **III promocionarse** *vr fam* to blow one's own trumpet.

promontorio *nm Geog* promontory, headland.

promotor,-a I *adj* promoting. **II** *nm,f* promoter.

promover *vtr* **1** *(cosas, personas)* to promote; **p. a algn a jefe,** to promote sb to manager; *Jur* **p. una querella contra algn,** to take legal action against sb. **2** *(causar)* to cause, give rise to.

promulgación *nf Jur* enactment.

promulgar *vtr Jur* to enact.

pronación *nf* pronation.

prono,-a *adj* prone.

pronombre *nm Ling* pronoun; **p. demostrativo/ personal/relativo,** demonstrative/personal/ relative pronoun.

pronominal *adj Ling* pronominal.

pronosticador,-a *nm,f* forecaster.

pronosticar *vtr* to predict, foretell, forecast; *Med* to make a prognosis of.

pronóstico *nm* forecast; *Med* prognosis; **de p. grave,** seriously ill *or* injured; **de p. leve,** not seriously injured; **de p. reservado,** under observation.

prontitud *nf* quickness, rapidity, promptness.

pronto,-a I *adj* quick, fast, prompt; **estar p. para hacer algo,** to be ready *or* willing to do sth. **II** *nm (impulso)* sudden impulse; *(de ira)* fit of anger, outburst. **III** *adv* **1** *(deprisa)* quickly, rapidly; **al p.,** at first; **de p.,** suddenly; **por de *or* lo p.,** *(para empezar)* to start with; *(de momento)* for the time being; **ven p.,** come quickly. **2** *(temprano)* soon, early; **hasta p.,** see you soon!; **lo más p. (posible),** as soon as possible; **tan p. como,** as soon as; **ven p.,** come early.

pronunciación *nf* pronunciation.

pronunciado,-a I *pp de* **pronunciar. II** *adj* **1** *(dicho)* pronounced, uttered. **2** *fig (marcado)* pronounced.

pronunciamiento *nm* **1** *Mil* uprising, insurrection. **2** *Jur* pronouncement.

pronunciar I *vtr (decir)* to pronounce; **pronuncia el inglés como si fuese nativo,** he sounds like an English native; **pronunció un discurso histórico,** he gave a historic speech. **II pronunciarse** *vr* **1** *(opinar)* to declare oneself; **me pronuncio a favor de esa decisión,** I agree with this decision. **2** *Mil (sublevarse)* to rise up.

propagación *nf* propagation, spreading.

propagador,-a I *adj* propagative. **II** *nm,f* propagator.

propaganda *nf* **1** *Pol* propaganda. **2** *Com* advertising, publicity.

propagandístico,-a *adj* advertising, publicity; **campaña propagandística,** advertising campaign; **lo hicieron sólo con fines propagandísticos,** it was only a publicity stunt.

propagar I *vtr* to propagate, spread. **II propagarse** *vr* to spread.

propalar *vtr (secretos)* to spread.

propano *nm Quím* propane.

proparoxítono,-a *adj Ling* proparoxytone.

propasarse *vr* to go too far; **p. con la bebida,** to drink too much.

propender *vi* to have a tendency, be inclined.

propensión *nf* 1 *(inclinación)* tendency, inclination. 2 *Med* susceptibility.

propenso,-a *adj* 1 *(inclinado)* prone, inclined. 2 *Med* susceptible; **soy p. a los catarros,** I catch colds very easily.

propiciar *vtr* 1 *(ganar el favor)* to win over. 2 *(causar)* to cause; **su actitud desafiante ha propiciado el enfrentamiento,** his defiant manner provoked the confrontation. 3 *Am (patrocinar)* to sponsor.

propiciatorio,-a **I** *adj* propitiatory; **víctima propiciatoria,** scapegoat. **II** *nm* 1 *(reclinatorio)* prie-dieu. 2 *Hist* propitiatory, mercy seat.

propicio,-a *adj* propitious, apt, suitable; **ser p. a,** to be inclined to.

propiedad *nf* 1 *(posesión)* ownership; *(cosa poseída)* property; **tener (algo) en p.,** to own (sth); **una casa p. del estado,** a council house. 2 *(cualidad)* property, quality; **propiedades medicinales,** medicinal properties; *fig* **con p.,** properly, appropriately; **emplear una palabra con p.,** to use a word properly.

propietario,-a **I** *adj* proprietary. **II** *nm, f* owner; **es p. de varias tiendas,** he owns several shops.

propileo *nm Arquit* propylaeum, propylon.

propilo *nm Quím* propyl.

propina *nf* tip; **dar p. (a algn),** to tip (sb); *fam* **de p.,** as a tip.

propinar *vtr* to give; *fig* **p. una paliza a algn,** to give sb a hiding.

propio,-a *adj* 1 *(de uno)* own; **en su propia casa,** in his own house. 2 *(indicado)* proper, correct, suitable, appropriate; **es lo p. en estos casos,** it is the right thing (to do) in these cases; **juegos propios para su edad,** games suitable for their age. 3 *(particular)* typical, peculiar; **características propias de los ingleses,** characteristics peculiar to the English (people); *fam* **es muy p. de él,** it is very typical of him. 4 *(mismo) (hombre)* himself; *(mujer)* herself; *(animal, sing cosa)* itself; **el p. autor,** the author himself. 5 **propios,-as,** themselves; **los p. inquilinos,** the tenants themselves. 6 *Ling* proper; **nombre p.,** proper noun. ◆ **propiamente** *adv* really, exactly; **p. dicho,** strictly speaking.

proponer *(pp propuesto)* **I** *vtr* to propose, put forward, suggest; **me han propuesto para el cargo de presidente,** I have been put forward for the post of president; **propongo ir al cine,** why don't we go to the cinema? **II proponerse** *vr* 1 *(intentar)* to intend; **se propone terminar el trabajo mañana,** he intends to finish the work tomorrow. 2 *(decidir)* to decide, be determined; **el nuevo juez se ha propuesto acabar con la delincuencia,** the new judge is determined to put a stop to delinquency.

proporción *nf* 1 *(relación)* proportion; *Mat* proportion; **en p. con,** in proportion to. 2 **proporciones,** *(tamaño)* size *sing;* **de grandes p.,** huge, massive.

proporcionado,-a **I** *pp de* **proporcionar.** **II** *adj* 1 *(que guarda proporción)* proportionate, in proportion. 2 *(facilitado)* supplied, provided, afforded; **la ayuda humanitaria proporcionada por los países desarrollados,** humanitarian help provided by developed countries. ◆ **proporcionadamente** *adv* proportionately.

proporcional *adj* proportional. ◆ **proporcionalmente** *adv* proportionately.

proporcionalidad *nf* proportionateness.

proporcionar *vtr* 1 *(disponer con proporción)* to proportion. 2 *(dar)* to give; to supply *or* provide with; **le proporcioné un trabajo,** I found *or* gave him a job; **le proporcionó una gran alegría,** it made her very happy.

proposición *nf* 1 *(propuesta)* proposition, proposal; **le hizo una p. de matrimonio,** he proposed to her. 2 *Ling (oración)* clause; **p. relativa,** relative clause.

propósito *nm* 1 *(intención)* intention; **ella tenía el p. de cambiar,** she was determined to change. 2 *(objetivo)* purpose, aim; **con el p. de,** in order to; **fuera de p.,** beside the point. 3 **a p.,** *(por cierto)* by the way; *(adrede)* on purpose, intentionally; **a p. de viajes, ¿has estado en Japón?,** speaking of travelling, have you been to Japan?; **hacer algo a p.,** to do sth on purpose.

propretor *nm Hist* propraetor, propretor.

propuesta *nf* suggestion, proposal, plan; **a p. de algn,** at sb's suggestion.

propuesto,-a *pp de* **proponer.**

propugnar *vtr* to defend, advocate.

propulsar *vtr (vehículo)* to propel, drive; *fig (idea)* to promote.

propulsión *nf* propulsion; **p. a chorro,** jet propulsion; **avión de p. a chorro,** jet (plane).

propulsor,-a **I** *adj* propelling. **II** *nm Téc* propellent. **III** *nm, f fig (persona)* promoter.

propuse *pt indef véase* **proponer.**

prorrata *nf* share, pro rata; **a p.,** in proportion, prorata.

prorratear *vtr* to apportion, *US* prorate.

prorrateo *nm* sharing, apportionment, *US* proration.

prórroga *nf* 1 *(prolongación)* extension; *Dep* extra time, *US* overtime. 2 *(aplazamiento)* postponement; *Mil* deferment; *Mil* **ha obtenido una p. por estudios,** he was allowed to defer because of his studies.

prorrogable *adj* that can be extended.

prorrogar *vtr* 1 *(prolongar)* to extend. 2 *(aplazar)* to postpone; *Mil* to defer.

prorrumpir *vi* to burst; **al conocer la noticia prorrumpió en lágrimas,** on hearing the news he burst into tears; **p. en gritos,** to shout.

prosa *nf Lit* prose.

prosaico,-a *adj* prosaic. ◆ **prosaicamente** *adv* prosaically.

prosaísmo *nm Lit* prosaism, prosaicism.

prosapia *nf (tamb hum)* lineage, ancestry.

proscenio *nm Hist Teat* proscenium.

proscribir *(pp proscrito) vtr (persona)* to exile, banish; *fig (cosa)* to ban, prohibit.

proscrito,-a **I** *pp de* **proscribir.** **II** *adj (persona)* exiled, banished; *(cosa)* banned. **II** *nm, f* exile, outlaw.

prosector *nm Med* prosector.

prosecución *nf*, **proseguimiento** *nm* continuation.

proseguir *vtr & vi* to carry on, continue; **debemos p. con el trabajo,** we must go on with the work.

proselitismo *nm* proselytism.

proselitista *adj* proselytic.

prosélito *nm* proselyte.

prosénquima *nf Anat* prosenchyma.

prosimio *nm Zool* prosimian.

prosista *nmf Lit* prose writer.

prosístico,-a *adj* proselike.

prosodia *nf Ling* prosody.

prosódico,-a *adj Ling* prosodic.

prosopopeya *nf Lit* prosopopoeia, prosopopeia.

prospección *nf* 1 *Min* prospect; **p. petrolífera,** oil prospection. 2 *Com* survey.

prospectar *vtr Min* to prospect.

prospecto *nm* leaflet, prospectus.

prosperar *vi* to prosper, thrive; **nuestro negocio prospera,** we are doing a roaring trade; *fig* **la idea no prosperó,** the idea wasn't accepted.

prosperidad *nf* prosperity.

próspero,-a *adj* prosperous, thriving; **p. año nuevo,** Happy New Year.

próstata *nf Anat* prostate (gland).

prostático,-a *adj Anat* prostatic.

prosternación *nf* prostration.

prosternarse *vr* to prostrate oneself.

prostibulario,-a *adj* relating to a brothel.

prostíbulo *nm* brothel.

prostitución *nf* prostitution.

prostituir I *vtr* to prostitute. **II prostituirse** *vr* to prostitute oneself.

prostituta *nf* prostitute.

prota *nmf fam véase* **protagonista**.

protactinio *nm Quím* protactinium.

protagonismo *nm* 1 *Teat Cin* leading role. 2 *(importancia)* significance, importance; **acaparar el p.,** to steal the limelight, hog the show; *fig* (**afán de**) **p.,** desire to be in the limelight.

protagonista *nmf* 1 *Cin Lit Teat* main character, leading role; ¿**quién es el p.?,** who plays the lead? 2 *fig (persona principal)* centre *or US* center of attraction; *(héroe) (hombre)* hero; *(mujer)* heroine.

protagonizar *vtr Cin Teat* to play the lead in, star in; *fig* **el niño que protagonizó el suceso,** the child involved in the incident.

protección *nf* protection.

proteccionismo *nm* protectionism.

proteccionista *adj & nmf* protectionist.

protector,-a I *adj* protecting, protective; **sociedad protectora de animales,** ≈ Royal Society for the Prevention of Cruelty to Animals. **II** *nm,f* protector. **III** *nm Box* mouthpiece, gumshield.

protectorado *nm Pol* protectorate.

proteger *vtr* to protect, defend, shield.

protegido,-a I *pp de* **proteger**. **II** *adj* protected. **III** *nm,f (hombre)* protégé; *(mujer)* protégée.

proteico,-a *adj* proteinous, proteinic.

proteína *nf* protein.

proteínico,-a *adj* proteinic.

prótesis *nf inv* 1 *Med* prosthesis. 2 *Ling* prothesis, prosthesis.

protesta *nf* protest; *Jur* objection; **presentar una p. formal,** to make a formal protest; *Jur* **p. denegada,** objection overruled; *Jur* **se admite la p.,** objection sustained.

protestante *adj & nmf Rel* Protestant.

protestantismo *nm Rel* Protestantism.

protestar *vi* to protest; *Jur* ¡**protesto, su señoría!,** objection, Your Honour!; **sin p.,** without protest; *fam* ¡**deja ya de p.!,** stop moaning, will you!

protesto *nm Com* protest.

protestón,-ona I *adj fam* moaning, grumbling. **II** *nm,f* moaner, grumbler.

protocolario,-a *adj* formal; **es una invitación protocolaria,** the invitation is a pure formality.

protocolo *nm* 1 *(reglas)* protocol; *Inform* protocol. 2 *fig (etiqueta)* etiquette, formalities *pl*; **sin protocolos,** informally.

protohistoria *nf* protohistory.

protohistórico,-a *adj* protohistoric.

protón *nm Fís* proton.

protónico,-a[1] *adj Ling* pretonic.

protónico,-a[2] *adj Fís* protonic.

protoplasma *nm Biol* protoplasm.

protoplásmico,-a *adj Biol* protoplasmic.

prototipo *nm* prototype.

protozoo *nm Biol* protozoon, protozoan.

protuberancia *nf* protuberance.

protuberante *adj* protuberant, bulging.

proustiano,-a *adj Lit* Proustian.

prov. *abr de* **provincia,** province, prov.

provecto,-a *adj lit* old; **de edad provecta,** advanced in years.

provecho *nm* profit, benefit; ¡**buen p.!,** enjoy your meal!; **de p.,** beneficially; **sacar el máximo p. de,** to get the most out of; **sacar p. de algo,** to benefit from sth; **un hombre de p.,** a man with prospects. ◆ **provechosamente** *adv* beneficially.

provechoso,-a *adj (beneficioso)* beneficial, useful; *Com (lucrativo)* profitable.

proveedor,-a *nm,f* supplier, purveyor.

proveer *(pp provisto) vtr* 1 *(suministrar)* to supply, provide. 2 *(preparar)* to get ready. 3 *(dar) (un empleo)* to fill.

proveniente *adj (procedente)* coming; *(resultante)* arising, resulting; **el tren p. de Granada,** the train from Granada; **su éxito es p. de sus esfuerzos,** her success is the result of her efforts.

provenir *vi (proceder)* to come; *(originarse)* to arise, result, spring.

Provenza *n* Provence.

provenzal I *adj* Provençal. **II** *nmf (persona)* Provençal. **III** *nm (idioma)* Provençal.

proverbial *adj* proverbial. ◆ **proverbialmente** *adj* proverbially.

proverbio *nm* 1 *(sentencia)* proverb. 2 **proverbios,** *(libro de la Biblia)* Proverbs.

providencia *nf* 1 *Rel* providence. 2 *Jur* ruling, judgement.

providencial *adj* providential; **su repentina aparición fue p.,** her sudden appearance was a godsend. ◆ **providencialmente** *adv* providentially.

próvido,-a *adj* provident.

provincia *nf* province, ≈ county; **capital de p.,** county town; **provincias,** the provinces.

provincial *adj* provincial; **diputación p.,** ≈ county council.

provincianismo *nm pey* provincialism.

provinciano,-a *adj & nm,f pey* provincial.

provisión *nf* 1 *(acción)* provision; *Fin* **p. de fondos,** reserve funds. 2 **provisiones,** *(suministros)* provisons, supplies.

provisional *adj* provisional. ◆ **provisionalmente** *adv* provisionally.

provisto,-a I *pp de* **proveer**. **II** *adj (suministrado)* provided; **este automóvil está p. de todos los adelantos técnicos,** this car is equipped with the latest in technology. **III** *nf RPl (comida)* food.

provocación *nf* provocation, instigation, incitememt.

provocado,-a I *pp de* **provocar**. **II** *adj* provoked, caused; *Jur* **incendio p.,** arson.

provocador,-a I *adj* provocative. **II** *nm,f* instigator, agent provocateur.

provocante *adj* provoking.

provocar *vtr* to provoke, instigate, incite; **aquéllo provocó las risas de todos,** that made everyone laugh; **con su discurso provocó la huelga,** her speech brought about the strike; **p. un incendio,** *(accidentalmente)* to cause *or* start a fire; *(intencionadamente)* to commit arson.

provocativo,-a *adj* provocative; **me miró con actitud provocativa,** he looked at me provocatively.

proxeneta *nmf* procurer, pimp.

proxenetismo *nm* procurement.

proximidad *nf* nearness, proximity, closeness; **dada la p. de las elecciones,** as elections are coming up; **en las proximidades de,** close to, in the vicinity of.

próximo,-a *adj* 1 *(cerca)* near, close; **las vacaciones están próximas,** holidays will soon start; **p. a la estación,** near the station. 2 *(siguiente)* next; **el p. año/mes,** next year/

month; **en fecha próxima,** shortly; **la próxima parada,** the next stop. ◆ **próximamente** *adv (pronto)* soon; *(dentro de poco)* before long; *Cin Teat (en letrero)* 'coming soon'.

proyección *nf* **1** *(gen)* projection. **2** *Cin* showing. **3** *fig (difusión)* diffusion; *(futuro)* future; **las declaraciones han tenido una gran p. en la prensa,** his declarations had wide press coverage; **este joven jugador tiene una gran p.,** this young player has a great future.

proyectar I *vtr* **1** *(luz)* to project. **2** *(hacer planes)* to plan; **proyectan mudarse pronto,** they are thinking of moving out shortly. **3** *Cin* to project, show. **4** *Arquit* to plan; *Téc* to design; *Mat* to project. **II proyectarse** *vr* **1** to project oneself. **2** *Cin (uso impers)* to show.

proyectil *nm* projectile, missile.

proyectista *nmf* planner, designer.

proyecto *nm (plan)* project, plan; *Téc* plan; *Arquit* design; **p. de acuerdo/de resolución,** draft agreement/resolution; *Pol* **p. de ley,** bill; **tener algo en p.,** to be planning sth; **ella tiene muchos proyectos,** she's got a lot of plans.

proyector *nm* **1** *(de luz)* searchlight; *(foco)* spotlight. **2** *Cin* projector.

prudencia *nf (cuidado)* prudence, discretion; *(moderación)* care; **con p.,** *(con cuidado)* with care, cautiously; *(moderadamente)* in moderation, moderately.

prudencial *adj (gen)* prudential, discreet; *(moderado)* moderate, careful, cautious; *fam* **a una distancia p.,** at a safe distance. ◆ **prudencialmente** *adv* prudentially.

prudente *adj* prudent, sensible, wise; **a una hora p.,** at a reasonable time; **lo más p. sería esperar,** the wisest thing (to do) would be to wait. ◆ **prudentemente** *adv* prudently.

prueba *nf* **1** *(argumento)* proof; *Jur* evidence, proof; **dar pruebas de,** to show signs of; **en p. de su amor,** as a sign of her love; **la p. de ello es que,** the proof of it is that; **tener pruebas de algo,** to have proof of sth. **2** *(examen, ensayo)* test; *Cost* fitting; *Téc* trial; **a p.,** on trial; **a p. de agua,** waterproof; **a p. de balas,** bullet-proof; *Cin* **hacerle una p. a algn,** to screen-test sb; **haz la p.,** try it; *Av* **piloto de pruebas,** test pilot. **3** *Fot Impr* proof; **corrección de pruebas,** proofreading. **4** *Dep* event. **5** *Am (juego de manos)* sleight of hand, trick.

prurito *nm* **1** *Med* itch, pruritus. **2** *fig (deseo)* urge.

Prusia *n* Prussia.

prusiano,-a *adj & nm,f* Prussian.

prúsico,-a *adj Quím* prussic.

P.S. *abr de* **post scriptum,** post scriptum, PS.

pseudo *adj* pseud, pseudo.

psicoanálisis *nm inv Psic* psychoanalysis.

psicoanalista *nmf Psic* psychoanalyst.

psicoanalítico,-a *adj Psic* psychoanalytic, psychoanalytical.

psicoanalizar *vtr* to psychoanalyse, *US* psychoanalyze.

psicodélico,-a *adj* psychedelic, psychodelic.

psicodrama *nm Psic* psychodrama.

psicofármaco *nm Farm* psychoactive drug.

psicología *nf Psic* psychology.

psicológico,-a *adj Psic* psychological.

psicólogo,-a *nm,f Psic* psychologist.

psiconeurosis *nf inv Psic* psychoneurosis.

psicópata *nmf Psic* psychopath, sociopath.

psicopatía *nf Psic* psychopathy.

psicopático,-a psychopathic.

psicopatología *nf Psic* psychopathology.

psicosis *nf inv Psic* psychosis.

psicosomático,-a *adj Psic* psychosomatic.

psicoterapeuta *nmf* psychotherapist.

psicoterapia *nf Psic* psychotherapy.

psique *nf* psyche.

psiquiatra *nmf Psic* psychiatrist.

psiquiatría *nf Psic* psychiatry.

psiquiátrico,-a *Psic* **I** *adj* psychiatric; **hospital p.,** mental hospital. **II** *nm* mental hospital.

psíquico,-a *adj* psychic, psychical.

psiquis *nf inv* psyche.

PSOE *nm Pol abr de* **Partido Socialista Obrero Español,** Socialist Workers' Party.

psoriasis *nf inv Med* psoriasis.

pta. *abr de* **peseta,** peseta.

ptas. *abr de* **pesetas,** pesetas.

púa *nf* **1** *(de plata)* thorn; *(de animal)* quill, spine; *(de tenedor)* prong; *(de alambre)* barb; *(de peine)* tooth; **alambre de púas,** barbed wire. **2** *Mús* plectrum. **3** *Arg (espolón)* spur.

pub *nm (pl pubs, pubes)* pub.

púber *adj & nmf,* **púbero,-a** *adj & nm,f* adolescent.

pubertad *nf,* **pubescencia** *nf* puberty.

púbico,-a *adj* pubic.

pubis *nm inv Anat* **1** *(vientre)* pubes *pl.* **2** *(hueso)* pubis.

publicable *adj* publishable.

publicación *nf* publication.

publicar *vtr* **1** *Impr (libros)* to publish. **2** *(difundir)* to publicize; **los periódicos acaban de publicar la noticia,** the newspapers have just published this piece of news.

publicidad *nf* **1** *(hacer público)* publicity; **dar p. a,** to publicize. **2** *Com* advertising; **el mundo de la p.,** the world of advertising.

publicista *nmf* publicist.

publicitario,-a *adj* advertising, publicity; **campaña publicitaria,** publicity campaign.

público,-a I *adj* public; **enemigo p.,** public enemy; **en p.,** in public; **es del dominio p.,** it's common knowledge; **opinión pública,** public opinion; *Admin* **sector p.,** public sector, civil service. **II** *nm* public, audience; *Dep* spectators *pl;* *TV* viewers *pl;* **abierto al p.,** open to the public; **dar** *or* **sacar (algo) al p.,** to make (sth) public; **el p. en general, el gran p.,** the general public. ◆ **públicamente** *adv* publicly.

pucelano,-a I *adj* of or from Valladolid. **II** *nm,f* native *or* inhabitant of Valladolid.

pucherazo *nm fam Pol* rigging of an election; **ha habido p. (en las elecciones),** the elections have been rigged.

puchero *nm* **1** *(olla)* cooking pot; *(cocido)* stew. **2** *(llanto)* pout; **hacer pucheros,** to pout.

pucho *nm* **1** *Am (residuo)* waste. **2** *SAm (colilla)* dog-end.

puco *nm Am* **1** *(escudilla)* earthenware bowl. **2** *(plato)* wooden plate.

pude *pt indef véase* **poder.**

pudendo,-a *adj (feo)* ugly; *(asqueroso)* filthy; *hum* **partes pudendas,** private parts.

pudibundez *nf* prudishness.

pudibundo,-a *adj* prudish.

púdico,-a *adj* **1** *(casto)* chaste, decent. **2** *pey (pudibundo)* prudish.

pudiente *adj* rich, wealthy.

pudín *nm Culin* type of crème caramel.

pudor *nm* chastity, decency, modesty; *fig (vergüenza)* shame; *Jur* **actos contra el p.,** indecent behaviour.

pudoroso,-a *adj* decent, modest; *fig* shameful.

pudridero *nm* **1** *(de basura)* pit, rubbish dump. **2** *(de cadáveres)* temporary vault.

pudrir I *vtr defect* **1** *(descomponerse)* to rot, decay. **2** *fig (molestar)* to upset, annoy. **II pudrirse** *vr (descomponerse)* to rot, decay; *fig* to languish; *fam* **p. de aburrimiento,** to be bored to death; *fam* **¡que se pudra!,** let him rot!

pueblada *nf Am (tumulto)* mob; *(motín)* riot.

pueblerino,-a I *adj* **1** *(de pueblo)* village; **la vida pueblerina,** village life. **2** *pey (tosco)* countrified, provincial. **II** *nm, f* **1** *(nativo)* villager. **2** countrified person; *pey* bumpkin.

pueblo *nm* **1** *(gente)* people; **el p. español,** the Spanish people; **la soberanía del p.,** the sovereignty of the people. **2** *(población)* village; (small) town; **p. de mala muerte,** one-horse town; *pey* **de p.,** provincial, bumpkin.

puente *nm* **1** *Constr* bridge; *Elec* bridge, tie; *Náut* bridge; *Med (entre dos dientes)* bridge, bridgework; *Av* **p. aéreo,** *(civil)* air shuttle service; *Mil* airlift; **p. basculante,** balance *or* bascule bridge; **p. colgante,** suspension bridge; **p. giratorio,** swing bridge; **p. levadizo,** drawbridge; **p. de mando,** wheelhouse; **p. de peatones,** footbridge; **tender un p. sobre un río,** to bridge a river; *fig* **tenderle un p. (de plata) a algn,** to give sb an opportunity. **2** *(entre dos fiestas)* long weekend; **hacer p. el lunes,** to take Monday off (because Tuesday is a bank holiday).

puentear *vtr Elec* to bridge.

puerco,-a I *adj fig (sucio)* filthy; *(asqueroso)* disgusting; *(ruin)* mean. **II** *nm, f* **1** *Zool* pig, sow; **p. espín,** porcupine. **2** *fig (gen)* pig; *(canalla)* swine.

puericultor,-a *nm, f* paediatrician, *US* pediatrician.

puericultura *nf* paediatrics *sing*, *US* pediatrics *sing*.

pueril *adj* **1** *(infantil)* childish, puerile. **2** *(vano)* useless, vain; **sus esfuerzos fueron pueriles,** his efforts were in vain.

puerilidad *nf* **1** *(propio de niño)* childishness, puerility. **2** *fig (insignificancia)* insignificance.

puerperal *adj Med* puerperal; **fiebre p.,** puerperal fever.

puerperio *nm Med* puerperium.

puerro *nm Bot* leek.

puerta *nf (gen)* door; *(de jardín, de muralla) (verja)* gate; *Aut* **coche de cinco** *or* **tres puertas,** hatchback; *Aut* **coche de cuatro puertas,** four-door car, saloon; **de p. en p.,** door to door; **las puertas de la ciudad,** the gates of the town; **nos encontraremos a la p. del cine,** we'll meet outside the cinema; **p. corredera/giratoria,** sliding/revolving door; **p. principal/de servicio,** main/tradem en's entrance; *fig* **a las puertas, en puertas,** imminent; *fig* **a las puertas de la muerte,** on the threshold of death; *fig* **a p. cerrada,** behind closed doors; *fig* **la p. del éxito,** the gateway to success; *fig* **llamar a la p. de algn,** to call on sb for help; *fig* **por la p. grande,** in a grand manner; *fam* **cogió la p. y se fue,** he upped and went; *fam fig* **darle a algn con la p. en las narices** *or* **en la cara,** to shut *or* slam the door in sb's face.

puerto *nm* **1** *(de sing mar)* port, harbour, *US* harbor; **p. deportivo,** marina; **p. franco,** free port; **p. marítimo,** seaport; **tomar p.,** to come into port. **2** *(de montaña)* (mountain) pass.

Puerto España *n* Port of Spain.

Puerto Rico *n* Puerto Rico.

puertorriqueño,-a *adj & nm, f* Puerto Rican.

pues *conj* **1** *(puesto que)* as, since; **no pudo contestar, p. ni él mismo lo sabía,** he couldn't answer as he didn't even know himself. **2** *(por lo tanto)* therefore; **la situación requiere, p., una solución inmediata,** the situation demands, therefore, a quick solution; **repito, p., que hace lo que debe,** therefore, I repeat he is doing what he should. **3** *(entonces)* so; **no me hiciste caso, p. no te quejes ahora,** you didn't listen to me, so don't complain now. **4** *(para reforzar)* **¡p. claro que no!,** but of course not!; **¡p. claro que sí!,** but of course!; **p. como iba diciendo,** well, as I was saying; **¡p. mejor!,** so much the

better!; **¡p. no!,** certainly not!; **¡p. peor!,** that's even worse!; **¡p. sí!,** of course!; **¿y p.?,** so what? **5** *(como pregunta)* **¿p.?,** why?

puesta *nf* **1** *Astron (de un astro)* setting; **p. de sol,** sunset. **2** *Biol (de huevos)* laying; *fig* **p. a punto,** tuning, adjusting; *fig* **p. al día,** updating; *fig* **p. de largo,** coming out, debut; **p. en escena,** staging; **p. en marcha,** starting-up, start-up; **p. en órbita,** putting into orbit; *véase* **puesto,-a.**

puestero,-a *nm, f Am* stallholder.

puesto,-a I *pp de* **poner. II** *adj* **1** *(colocado)* set, put; **dejaron la mesa puesta,** they didn't clear the table; *fig* **estar p. en una materia,** to be well up in a subject; *fam fig* **ir p.,** to be high. **2** *(ropa)* on; **con el abrigo p.,** with one's coat on; **¿qué llevaba p.?,** what was he wearing?; *fig* **no tener más que lo p.,** to have only what one is standing up in; *fam* **ir muy p.,** to be all dressed up. **III** *nm* **1** *(lugar)* place; *(asiento)* seat; **devuélvelo a su p.,** put it back in its place; **en primer p.,** in the first place; **te cambio el p.,** shall we change seats?; *fig* **(saber) estar en su p.,** to know one's place. **2** *(local) (en un mercado)* stall; *(en una exposición)* stand; **p. de flores,** flower stall; **p. de periódicos,** newspaper stand; **p. de policía,** police station; **p. de socorro,** first-aid post. **3** *Mil* post; **p. de vigilancia,** sentry post. **4** *(empleo)* position, post, job; **incorporarse a su p. (de trabajo),** to take up one's duties; **p. de trabajo,** job, post; **p. vacante,** vacancy. **IV** *conj* **p. que,** since, as; **tendrás que esperar p. que has llegado tarde,** you'll have to wait since you arrived late.

puf[1] *nm (pl pufs, pufes)* pouf, pouffe.

puf[2] *interj* ugh!

pufo *nm fam* trick; **¡menudo p. le metieron!,** they pulled a fast one on him!

púgil *nm Box* boxer, fighter.

pugilato *nm* **1** *Box* boxing. **2** *(pugna)* battle, struggle.

pugilístico,-a *adj Box* pugilistic, boxing.

pugna *nf* battle, fight; **estar en p. por algo,** to struggle over sth.

pugnar *vi* to fight, struggle; **ambos jugadores pugnaban por el balón,** both players fought for the ball.

puja[1] *nf (pugna)* struggle.

puja[2] *nf (acción)* bidding; *(cantidad)* bid.

pujante *adj* thriving, prosperous.

pujanza *nf* strength, vigour, *US* vigor.

pujar[1] I *vtr (pugnar)* to struggle. **II** *vi* **1** *(hablar mal)* to be inarticulate. **2** *(vacilar)* to hesitate.

pujar[2] *vtr* **1** *Naipes* to bid. **2** *(en una subasta)* to bid higher.

pujo *nm* **1** *Med* tenesmus. **2** *(ansia)* craving, urge; **tener pujos de,** to have aspirations to *or* of.

pul *nm Am (influencia)* influence; *(protección)* protection.

pulcritud *nf* cleanliness, neatness.

pulcro,-a *adj* (extremely) clean; (extremely) neat.

pulenta *nf Am* stew.

pulga *nf Ent* flea; *fam* **buscarle las pulgas a algn,** to taunt sb, provoke sb; *fam* **tener malas pulgas,** to be nasty, have a nasty streak.

pulgada *nf* inch.

pulgar *nm* thumb.

pulgarada *nf* **1** *(golpe)* flick, fillip. **2** *(porción)* pinch. **3** *(pulgada)* inch.

Pulgarcito *nm Lit* Tom Thumb.

pulgón *nm Ent* plant louse.

pulgoso,-a *adj* flea-bitten, flea-ridden.

pulguillas *nm inv fam fig* touchy person.

pulído,-a I *pp de* **pulir. II** *adj* **1** *Téc* polished. **2** *fig (fino)* elegant, refined. **3** *(pulcro)* neat, clean.

pulidor,-a I *adj* polishing. **II** *nf Téc* polishing machine.

pulimentar *vtr* to polish.

pulimento *nm (acción)* polishing; *(material, brillo)* polish.

pulir I *vtr* **1** *Téc (metal, madera)* to polish. **2** *(perfeccionar, mejorar)* to put the finishing touches to; **necesito p. mi alemán para obtener ese trabajo,** I've got to improve my German to get the job. **3** *fam (robar)* to pinch, steal. **II pulirse** *vr fam (dinero)* to spend, squander; *(acabarse)* to finish; **nos hemos pulido un litro de coñac,** we've polished off a litre of brandy.

pulmón *nm Anat* lung; *Med* **p. de acero,** iron lung.

pulmonar *adj Anat* lung, pulmonary.

pulmonía *nf Med* pneumonia.

pulpa *nf* pulp.

pulpejo *nm* soft *or* fleshy part.

pulpería *nf* **1** *Am (tienda)* grocer's shop. **2** *(bar)* Galician snack bar where boiled octopus is served.

pulpero *nm* octopus fisherman.

púlpito *nm Rel* pulpit.

pulpo *nm Zool* octopus.

pulposo,-a *adj* pulpy, soft, fleshy.

pulsación *nf (gen)* pulsation; *(latido del corazón)* beat, throb; *(en mecanografía)* stroke, tap; **pulsaciones por minuto,** ≈ words per minute.

pulsador *nm* push-button.

pulsar I *vtr* **1** *(tocar)* to press; *fig (tantear)* to sound; **p. las teclas de la máquina de escribir,** to tap the typewriter keys; *fig* **tomar el p. a la opinión,** to sound out what people think. **2** *Mús (tañer)* to play; **p. las cuerdas de la guitarra,** to pluck a guitar. **II** *vi* to throb, beat, pulse.

púlsar *nm Astron* pulsar.

pulsátil *adj,* **pulsativo,-a** *adj* pulsating, beating, throbbing.

pulsera *nf (aro)* bracelet; *(de reloj)* watchstrap; **reloj de p.,** wristwatch.

pulso *nm* **1** *Anat* pulse; **tomarle el p. a algn,** to take sb's pulse; *fig* **tomar el p. a la opinión,** to sound out opinion. **2** *(mano firme)* steady hand; **dibujo a p.,** freehand drawing; **echarle un p. a algn,** to arm-wrestle with sb; **levantar algo a p.,** to lift sth with one's bare hands; *fig* **se lo ha ganado a p.,** *(merecido)* he's worked hard for it; *irón* it serves him right. **3** *fig (tacto)* tact, care, prudence; **tratar algo con mucho p.,** to be very tactful when dealing with sth.

pulular *vi* to multiply.

pulverizacion *nf (de sólidos)* pulverization; *(de líquidos)* spraying.

pulverizador,-a I *adj (sólidos)* pulverizing; *(líquidos)* spraying. **II** *nm* spray, atomizer; **p. nasal,** nasal spray.

pulverizar *vtr (sólidos)* to pulverize; *(líquidos)* to spray; *Dep (un récord)* to break; *fig (matar)* to pulverize.

pulverulento,-a *adj* powdery, dusty.

pulla *nf* dig.

pullover *nm* pullover, jumper.

pum *interj* bang!

puma *nm Zool* puma.

pumba *interj* bang!

puna *nf SAm* **1** *(páramo)* high moor. **2** *(mal)* mountain *or* altitude sickness. **3** *(tierra alta)* puna.

punción *nf Med* puncture.

puncionar *vtr Med* to puncture.

pundonor *nm* self-respect, self-esteem, dignity.

pundonoroso,-a *adj* honourable, *US* honorable, trustworthy; **un hombre p.,** a man of great dignity.

punible *adj* punishable.

punición *nf* punishment, punishing.

púnico,-a *adj* Punic.

punitivo,-a *adj* punitive.

punta I *adj* top; **hora p.,** rush hour; **velocidad p.,** top speed. **II** *nf* **1** *(extremo)* tip; *(extremo agudo)* point; *Peluq* **córteme sólo las puntas,** I just want the ends trimmed; **de p.,** on end; **p. a cabo, de p. a p.,** from one end to the other; **p. del dedo,** fingertip; **sacarle p. a un lápiz,** to sharpen a pencil; *fig* **estar de p. con algn,** to be at odds with sb; *fig* **lo tengo en la p. de la lengua,** I have it on the tip of my tongue; *fig* **me pone el pelo de p.,** it gives me the creeps; *fig* **ponerle a algn los nervios de p.,** to make sb very nervous; *fam* **ir de p. en blanco,** dressed up to the nines; *fam* **había gente a p. pala,** there were thousands of people; *fam* **siempre le sacas p. a todo lo que digo,** you always read too much into what I say. **2** *(de cigarrillo) (colilla)* dog-end. **3** *(pequeña cantidad)* bit; **una p. de sal,** a pinch of salt; *fig* **tiene una p. de loco,** he has a streak of madness. **4** *Geog (cabo)* point, foreland, headland. **5** *(clavo)* nail. **6** *(de grabador)* needle. **7 puntas,** *Cost (encaje)* needlepoint *sing.* **8 de puntas,** on tiptoe; **andar de p.,** to walk on tiptoe.

puntada *nf Cost* stitch; *fam* **no da p.,** *(no hace nada)* he doesn't do a thing; *(no acierta)* he gets nothing right.

puntal *nm Arquit* prop; *(travesaño)* brace, beam; *fig (soporte)* pillar, support.

puntapié *nm* kick; **echar a algn a puntapiés,** to kick sb out.

punteado *nm* **1** *(marcado puntos)* dotting. **2** *Mús* plucking.

puntear *vtr* **1** *(dibujar)* to dot. **2** *Mús (guitarra)* to pluck. **3** *Arg Urug* to lead.

punteo *nm Mús (guitarra)* plucking.

puntera *nf* **1** *(del zapato)* toe. **2** *(remiendo)* steel cap; **zapatos con punteras,** steel-capped shoes.

puntería *nf* aim; **dirigir la p. (a algo),** to aim (at sth); **rectificar la p.,** to change one's aim; **¡qué p.!,** that was a good shot!; **tener buena/mala p.,** to be a good/bad shot.

puntero,-a I *adj* leading. **II** *nm* pointer.

puntiagudo,-a *adj* pointed, sharp.

puntilla *nf* **1** *Cost (encaje)* lace. **2** *Taur* dagger; **dar la p.,** *Taur* to finish (the bull) off; *fig (liquidar)* to finish off. **3 de puntillas,** on tiptoe.

puntillismo *nm Arte* pointillism.

puntillista *adj Arte* pointillist.

puntilloso,-a *adj* punctilious; *pey* touchy.

punto *nm* **1** *(gen)* point; **a p.,** on the point; **de todo p. imposible,** absolutely impossible; *Culin* **en su p.,** just right; **estar a p. de hacer algo,** to be on the point of doing sth; **estuve a p. de caerme,** I almost fell; **has dado en el p.,** you've hit the nail on the head; **hasta cierto p.,** to a certain *or* some extent; **hasta el p. de,** to the point of; **hasta tal p.,** to such an extent; **p. culminante,** climax; **p. de apoyo,** backup; **p. de congelación/ebullición,** freezing/boiling point; **p. de contacto,** point of contact; *Geom* **p. de intersección,** point of intersection; **p. débil,** weak point; **p. muerto,** *Aut* neutral; *fig (impase)* deadlock; **p. de partida,** starting point; **p. de referencia,** point of reference; **p. de vista,** viewpoint, opinion. **2** *(marca, señal)* dot; **línea de puntos,** dotted line; *fig* **poner los puntos sobre las íes,** to dot one's i's and cross one's t's. **3** *(apartado, sección)* point; **los puntos del orden del día,** the points on the agenda. **4** *(lugar)* place, spot, point; **p. de encuentro** *or* **de reunión,** meeting point; **p. de observación,** lookout. **5** *(signo de puntuación)* full stop, *US* period; **dos puntos,** colon; **p. y aparte,** full stop, new paragraph; **p. y coma,** semicolon; **p. y seguido,** full stop; **puntos suspensivos,** dots, *US* suspension points; *fig* **con puntos y comas,** in great detail; *fig* **poner p. final a algo,** to put an end to sth. **6** *(tiempo)* **en p.,** sharp, on the dot; **las seis en p.,** six o'clock sharp; **llegaron a las tres en p.,** they arrived at exactly three o'clock; **ella llegó en p.,** she arrived punctually. **7** *(tanto)* point; **ganar** *or* **marcar diez puntos,** to score ten points; *fig* **ganar/perder (muchos) puntos (para algn),** to go up/down in sb's estimation. **8**

Cost Tricot stitch; **¿cuántos puntos pongo?,** how many stitches do I cast on?; **hacer p.,** to knit; **p. de cruz,** cross-stitch; **p. del derecho/revés,** plain/purl stitch; **un vestido de p.,** a knitted dress. 9 *Med* stitch; **le dieron cinco puntos en la cabeza,** he had five stitches put in his head.

puntuable *adj* valid.

puntuación *nf* 1 *Ling* punctuation; **signos de p.,** punctuation marks. 2 *(en una competición)* scoring; *(número de puntos)* score. 3 *Educ* marking; *(calificación)* mark; **obtener una buena p.,** to get a good mark.

puntual I *adj* 1 *(a la hora)* punctual; **una persona p.,** a punctual person. 2 *(exacto)* exact, accurate, precise. 3 *(aislado)* specific. **II** *adv* punctually; **llegó p.,** he arrived punctually *or* on time. ♦ **puntualmente** *adv* punctually.

puntualidad *nf* punctuality; **la p. es una gran virtud,** punctuality is a great virtue.

puntualizar *vtr* 1 *(detallar)* to give full details of, describe in detail. 2 *(especificar)* to leave clear; **hay que p. que no estaba solo,** it should be pointed out that he wasn't on his own.

puntuar I *vtr* 1 *(al escribir)* to punctuate. 2 *Educ (calificar)* to mark. **II** *vi Dep* to score.

punzada *nf* 1 *(de dolor)* sudden sharp pain; *fig (de remordimiento)* pang. 2 *(pinchazo)* prick.

punzante *adj* 1 *(que pincha)* sharp, prickly; **objeto p.,** sharp object. 2 *(dolor)* acute, sharp, piercing. 3 *fig* biting, cutting, hurtful, spiteful.

punzar *vtr* to prick; *fig* to torment.

punzón *nm Téc* punch.

puñada *nf fam veáse* **puñetazo.**

puñado *nm* handful; **un p. de amigos,** a handful of friends; *fam* **a puñados,** by the score, galore.

puñal *nm* dagger; *fig* **ponerle a algn el p. en el pecho,** to hold a pistol to sb's head.

puñalada *nf* 1 *(con puñal)* stab; *fig* **una p. trapera,** a stab in the back. 2 *fig (disgusto)* grievous blow.

puñeta *nf fam* annoying thing; **hacerle la p. a algn,** to pester sb, annoy sb; **¡puñetas!,** damn!; **¡vete a hacer puñetas!,** go to hell!

puñetazo *nm* punch; **le tiró al suelo de un sólo p.,** he knocked him to the ground with one blow.

puñetería *nf fam* 1 *(mala intención)* bloody-mindedness. 2 *(cosa)* trifle, mere nothing.

puñetero,-a *fam* I *adj (cosa)* bloody, damned; *(persona)* **no seas p.,** don't be awkward *or* bloody-minded. **II** *nm,f* pest; **el p.,** the so-and-so.

puño *nm* 1 *(mano cerrada)* fist; **apretar los puños,** to clench one's fists; **enseñarle a algn el p.,** to shake one's fist at sb; *fig* **comerse los puños,** to be starving; *fig* **de su p. y letra,** written in his own hand; *fig* **tener a algn en un p.,** to have sb under one's thumb. 2 *(ropa)* cuff. 3 *(de espada)* hilt; *(de bastón)* handle.

pupa *nf* 1 *(en los labios)* cold sore. 2 *fam (daño)* pain; **¿te has hecho p.?,** have you hurt yourself?

pupila *nf* 1 *Anat* pupil. 2 *(persona) véase* **pupilo,-a.**

pupilaje *nm* 1 *(de un niño, un huérfano)* tutelage. 2 *(de alumno)* pupillage. 3 *Aut* long-term parking; **'se admiten coches a p.',** 'long-term parking available'.

pupilar *adj* pupillary.

pupilo,-a *nm, f* 1 *(niño, huérfano)* ward, orphan. 2 *(alumno)* pupil.

pupitre *nm* desk.

pupusa *nf CAm Culin* corn and cheese pasty.

puquío *nm SAm* spring, fountain.

purasangre *adj & nm Zool* thoroughbred.

puré *nm Culin* purée; **p. de patata,** mashed potatoes; **p. de tomate,** tomato purée; **p. de verduras,** thick vegetable soup; *fam* **estoy hecho p.,** I'm worn out.

pureza *nf* 1 *(calidad de puro)* purity, pureness. 2 *(castidad)* chastity.

purga *nf* 1 *Med* purge, purgative. 2 *fig (limpieza, depuración)* purge.

purgación *nf* 1 *Med* purging. 2 **purgaciones,** *fam* the clap *sing.*

purgante *adj & nm* purgative.

purgar I *vtr* 1 *Med* to purge. 2 *(limpiar, depurar)* to purge. 3 *(expiar)* to purge, expiate; **debe p. sus crímenes,** he should pay for his crimes. **II purgarse** *vr* to take a purgative.

purgatorio *nm Rel* purgatory.

purificación *nf* purification.

purificador,-a I *adj* purifying. **II** *nm,f Téc* purifier.

purificar *vtr* to purify.

purina *nf Quím* purin, purine.

purismo *nm* purism.

purista *nmf* purist.

puritanismo *nm* puritanism.

puritano,-a I *adj* puritan, puritanic, puritanical. **II** *nm, f* puritan, Puritan.

puro,-a I *adj* 1 *(sin mezclas)* pure; **aire p.,** fresh air; **filosofía pura,** pure philosophy. 2 *(mero)* sheer, mere; **la casa se cayó de p. vieja,** the house collapsed out of sheer age; **la pura verdad,** the plain truth; **por pura casualidad,** by pure chance; **por pura curiosidad,** out of sheer curiosity. 3 *(casto)* chaste, pure. **II** *nm* 1 *(cigarro)* cigar. 2 *fam (bronca)* dressing-down, telling-off; **¡vaya p!,** that's a difficult one!

púrpura *adj* purple.

purpurado *nm Rel* cardinal.

purpúreo,-a *adj* purple.

purpurina *nf* purpurin.

purulencia *nf* purulence, purulency.

purulento,-a *adj* full of pus, purulent.

pus *nm* pus.

puse *pt indef véase* **poner.**

pusilánime *adj* faint-hearted, coward, pusillanimous.

pusilanimidad *nf* faint-heartedness, cowardice, pusillanimity.

pústula *nf* sore, pimple, spot, pustule.

puta *nf ofens* whore; **de p. madre,** great, terrific; **de p. pena,** bloody awful; **no tengo ni p. idea,** I haven't (got) a bloody clue; **pasarlas putas,** to go through hell, have a rotten time.

putada *nf vulg* dirty trick; **¡qué p. que no queden entradas!,** what rotten luck, the tickets are sold out!

putativo,-a *adj* putative, supposed.

putear *vulg* I *vi* to go whoring. **II** *vtr* to fuck *or* piss sb about *or* around, make sb's life a misery; **¡no me putees!,** don't fuck me about!

puteo *nm ofens* pissing around.

puterío *nm fam* prostitution.

putero,-a *adj vulg* whoring.

puticlub *nm fam* brothel.

puto,-a I *adj ofens* bloody. **II** *nm* male prostitute, stud.

putrefacción *nf* putrefaction, rotting.

putrefacto,-a *adj,* **pútrido,-a** *adj* putrefied, rotten.

puya *nf Taur* steel point (of a lance).

puyar *vtr CAm* to annoy, bother.

puzzle *nm* puzzle.

P.V.P. *nm abr de* **precio de venta al público,** recommended retail price, RRP.

Pza., Plza. *abr de* **plaza,** square, Sq.

Q

Q, q *nf (la letra)* Q, q.

Q.D.G., q.D.g. *abr de* **que Dios guarde.**

quantum *nm (pl* **quanta)** quantum.

que[1] *pron rel* **1** *(sujeto) (persona)* who, that; *(cosa)* that, which; **el chico q. me lo dijo,** the boy who told me; **la bomba q. estalló,** the bomb that went off; **la moto q. me gusta,** the motorbike that I like. **2** *(sujeto)* **lo q.,** what; **eso es lo q. me asusta,** that's what frightens me. **3** *(complemento) (persona)* whom, who; *(cosa)* that, which; **el hombre con el q. hablé,** the man who I spoke to; **el libro q. me prestaste,** the book (that) you lent me. **4** *(complemento) (de tiempo, lugar)* when, where; **el jardín en el q. jugábamos,** the garden where we used to play; **las ocasiones en q. le visité,** the times when I visited him.

que[2] *conj* **1** that; **dice q. está cansado,** he says (that) he's tired; **quiero q. vengas,** I want you to come. **2** *(comp)* that; **habla tan bajo q. no se le oye,** he speaks so quietly (that) he can't be heard. **3** *(causal, consecutiva) (no se traduce)* **cuidado q. te vas a caer,** careful, you'll fall; **deprisa q. no tenemos mucho tiempo,** hurry up, we haven't got much time. **4** *(énfasis) (no se traduce)* **¡q. no!,** no!; **¡q. sí!,** yes!; **¡q. te calles!,** I said be quiet! **5** *(deseo, mandato) (con subj)* **¡q. te diviertas!,** enjoy yourself!; **¡q. se atreva!,** he wouldn't dare! **6** *(copulativa)* and; **corre q. corre,** hell for leather. **7** *(final)* so that; **ven a q. te dé un beso,** come and let me give you a kiss. **8** *(locuciones)* **¿a q. no?,** I bet you can't!; **¿a q. no lo adivinas?,** I bet you can't guess; **q. yo sepa,** as far as I know; **yo q. tú,** if I were you; *fam* **q. si esto q. si lo otro,** this, that and the other.

qué *pron interr* **1** what; **a ver q. dicen,** let's hear what they're saying; **no sé q. decir,** I don't know what to say; **¿q. hora es?,** what time is it?; **¿q. pasa?,** what's the matter?; **¿q. quieres?,** what do you want?; *fam* **¿q. tal?,** **¿q. hay?,** how are things? **2** *(cuál)* which; **¿q. libro quieres?,** which book do you want? **3** *(en exclamativas)* how, so; **¡q. lástima!,** what a pity!; *fam* **¡y q.!,** so what? **4** *(indica cantidad)* how; **¡q. de coches!,** what a lot of cars! **II** *nm* **sin q. ni para o por,** without rhyme or reason.

quebrada *nf* **1** *Geol* ravine, gorge. **2** *Am* stream.

quebradero *nm fig* **q. de cabeza,** headache.

quebradizo,-a *adj (débil)* fragile; *(rompedero)* brittle.

quebrado,-a **I** *pp de* **quebrar.** **II** *adj* **1** *(roto)* broken; *(terreno)* uneven, rough; *(voz)* faltering; *Mat* **número q.,** fraction; *Culin* **pasta quebrada,** puff pastry. **2** *Fin* bankrupt. **III** *nm Mat* fraction.

quebradura *nf* **1** *(grieta)* crack, fissure. **2** *Med* hernia, rupture.

quebrantador,-a *adj* crushing.

quebrantahuesos *nm inv Orn* lammergeier.

quebrantamiento *nm* **1** *(gen)* breaking, breaking up; *(de salud)* weakening, deterioration. **2** *Jur (de una ley)* violation, infringement.

quebrantaolas *nm inv Mar* breakwater.

quebrantar **I** *vtr* **1** *(romper)* to break, shatter. **2** *(violar promesa, ley)* to break. **3** *fig (debilitar)* to weaken; *(ánimo)* to break. **II quebrantarse** *vr* **1** *(quebrar)* to crack; *(romperse)* to break. **2** *(salud)* to be shattered.

quebranto *nm* **1** *(pérdida)* loss; *(daño)* damage. **2** *(lástima)* pity. **3** *(aflicción)* grief, affliction. **4** *fig (desaliento)* discouragement.

quebrar **I** *vtr* **1** *(rómper)* to break. **2** *(violar promesa, ley)* to break; **q. la ley,** to break the law. **3** *(suavizar)* to soften; *(color)* to make paler. **4** *(doblar)* to bend. **5** *Arg (domar un potro)* to break in. **II** *vi* **1** *Fin* to go bankrupt; *fam* to go bust. **2** *fig (con amigo)* to fall out, break up. **III**

quebrarse *vr* **1** *(voz)* to break; *(estar ronco)* to become hoarse. **2** *Med* to rupture oneself. **3** *fig (ánimo)* to break.

quechemarín *nm Náut* yawl.

quechua **I** *adj* Quechuan. **II** *nmf (persona)* Quechua. **III** *nm (idioma)* Quechuan.

queda *nf* **toque de q.,** curfew.

quedada *nf arg* trick, joke.

quedar **I** *vi* **1** *(permanecer)* to remain, stay; **la cama quedó sin hacer,** the bed was left unmade; *(en cartas)* **quedamos a la espera de ...,** we await ... . **2** *(resultar en situación o estado)* to remain, be; **¡queda adjudicado!,** sold!; **q. a deber algo,** to owe sth; **q. en ridículo,** to make a fool of oneself; **q. uno bien/mal,** to make a good/bad impression; *fam* **q. como un señor,** to create a very good impression. **3** *(ropa etc) (favorecer)* to look; *(venir a medida)* to fit; **me queda corta,** it is too short; **quedaría muy bien allí,** it would look very nice there. **4** *(terminar)* to end; **todo quedó en nada,** it all came to nothing; *fam* **ahí quedó la cosa,** that's how it stands. **5** *(acordar)* to agree (en, to); **¿en qué quedamos?,** so what's it to be? **6** *(en un lugar)* to arrange to meet. **7** *(estar situado)* to be; **¿por dónde queda tu casa?,** whereabouts is your house? **8** *(faltar)* to be left, remain; **queda poco,** there's not much left; *fig* **no quedó títere con cabeza,** nothing was left intact. **II quedarse** *vr* **1** *(permanecer)* to be left; **q. sin amigos/trabajo,** to lose one's friends/job; **q. sin dinero/pan,** to run out of money/bread; *fam* **q. sin blanca,** to be broke; *fam* **se quedó tan tranquilo,** he didn't bat an eyelid. **2** *(resultar situación o estado)* to be, remain; **q. huérfano,** to be left an orphan; *fig* **me quedé en blanco,** my mind went blank. **3** *(en alojamiento)* to stay; **me quedé en casa todo el día,** I stayed at home all day. **4** *(detenerse)* to stay; *(estarse parado)* to stand; **me quedé mirándole,** I stood there looking at him; **no te quedes en la puerta,** do come in; **q. atrás,** to be left behind; *(por propia voluntad)* to stay behind. **5** **q. con,** *(retener)* to keep; *fig* to remain; **q. con hambre,** to be still hungry; **quédate con la vuelta,** keep the change; *fig* **q. con la boca abierta,** to be amazed; *fig* **q. con las ganas de algo,** to go without sth. **6** *(mar, viento)* to become calm. **7** *fam* **q. con algn,** to make a fool of sb.

quedo[1] *adv* softly, quietly.

quedo,-a[2] *adj* quiet, still.

quehacer *nm* task, chore; **los quehaceres domésticos,** housework *sing*, household chores *pl*.

queja *nf* **1** *(disconformidad)* complaint; **no tener q. de algn,** to have no complaints about sb; *Jur* **presentar una q.,** to lodge a complaint. **2** *(de dolor)* groan, moan.

quejarse *vr* **1** *(expresar dolor)* to suffer, groan. **2** *(expresar descontento)* to complain (**de,** about); **no puedo quejarme,** I can't complain; **te quejas de vicio,** you're a born complainer.

quejica *fam* **I** *adj* grumpy. **II** *nmf* moaner.

quejido *nm* groan, cry.

quejumbroso,-a *adj* whining; **en tono q.,** in an aggrieved tone.

quema *nf* burning; *fig* **huir de la q.,** to beat it, flee.

quemadero *nm* **1** *Hist* stake. **2** *(para basura)* incinerator.

quemado,-a I *pp de* **quemar.** **II** *adj* **1** burnt, burned; **huele a q.,** something is burning; **q. por el sol,** sunburnt. **2** *fig (resentido)* embittered. **3** *fig (acabado)* spent, burnt-out; **como actor está q.,** as an actor he's a bit of a has-been. **4** *arg (persona, local)* known to the police. **5** *arg (sexualmente)* **ir q.,** to be dying for it.

quemador *nm* **1** *(de cocina etc)* burner. **2** *Am (mechero)* lighter.

quemadura *nf* **1** *Med* burn; *(escaladadura)* scald. **2** *Bot* smut.

quemar I *vtr* **1** *(consumir)* to burn; *fig* **q. dinero,** to throw money away. **2** *(agotar) (persona)* to burn out. **3** *(vino)* to distil. **4** *CAm* to swindle. **5** *Méx (herir con bala)* to shoot. **II** *vi* to be burning hot; **este café quema,** this coffee's boiling hot. **III quemarse** *vr* **1** *(persona)* to burn oneself; *fig* **q. las pestañas,** to burn the midnight oil. **2** *(objeto)* to be burnt; **se ha quemado el arroz,** the rice is burnt.

quemarropa *loc adv* **a q.,** point-blank; **disparar a algn a q.,** to shoot sb point-blank.

quemazón *nf* **1** *(calor)* intense heat. **2** *(comezón)* itch. **3** *fig (dicho picante)* smarting, cutting word.

quepis *nm inv* kepi.

quepo *indic pres véase* **caber.**

queratina *nf* Biol keratin.

querella *nf* **1** *(pelea)* dispute. **2** *(queja)* complaint. **3** *Jur* charge.

querellante *nmf* plaintiff.

querellarse *vr* Jur to bring an action, lodge a complaint.

querer¹ *nm* love, affection.

querer² I *vtr* **1** *(amar)* to love; **Pepe sabe hacerse q.,** Pepe's got winning ways; *prov* **quien bien te quiere te hará llorar,** you've got to be cruel to be kind. **2** *(desear)* to want; **¿cuánto quieres por la bici?,** how much do you want for the bike?; **lo hice sín q.,** I didn't mean to do it; **¡por lo que más quieras!,** for Heaven's sake!; **quieras or no,** like it or not; **quiere ser médico,** he wants to be a doctor; **si quieres,** if you want (to); *(en la boda)* **sí, quiero,** I will; **todo el que quiera,** anyone who wants to; *fig* **el quiero y no puedo,** pretentious ideas; *fig* **q. es poder,** where there's a will there's a way; *fam* **está como quiere,** he *or* she is gorgeous. **3** *(por favor)* would; **¿quieres callarte?,** would you be quiet!, please shut up!; **¿quieres ir al cine?,** would you like to go to the cinema. **3** *(significar)* **q. decir,** to mean; **¿qué quiere decir?,** what does it mean? **4** *(ser conveniente)* to need; **estas plantas quieren más agua,** those plants need more water. **II quererse** *vr* to love each other.

querido,-a I *pp de* **querer. II** *adj* dear, beloved; *(en carta)* **q. amigo,** dear friend. **III** *nm, f* **1** *(amante) (hombre, mujer)* lover; *(mujer)* mistress. **2** *(apelativo cariñoso)* darling.

queroseno *nm* kerosene, kerosine.

querré *indic fut véase* **querer.**

querube *nm,* **querubín** *nm* cherub.

quesadilla *nf* Culin Am tortilla with savoury cheese filling.

quesera *nf* cheeseboard and cover.

quesero,-a I *adj* **1** cheese. **2** *(persona)* cheese-loving. **II** *nm, f* **1** *(que lo hace)* cheese maker. **2** *(que te gusta)* lover of cheese.

queso *nm* **1** *Culin* cheese. ■ **q. de cabra,** goat's cheese; **q. en lonchas,** sliced cheese; **q. rallado,** grated cheese. **2 q. de cerdo,** brawn, *US* headcheese. **3** *Cost* **medio q.,** semicircular ironing board.

quetzal *nm* Fin standard monetary unit of Guatemala.

quevedos *nmpl* pince-nez *pl.*

quiá *interj* no!, never!

quicio *nm* **1** *(bisagra)* hinge; *(espacio interior)* jamb; *(de puerta)* doorpost. **2** *fig* **estar fuera de q.,** to be beside oneself; **sacar a algn de q.,** to infuriate sb, make sb's blood boil.

quiché *adj & nmf (de Guatemala)* Quiché.

quichua *adj & nm, f véase* **quechua.**

quid *nm* crux; **ahí está el q. de la cuestión,** there's the crux of the matter; **has dado en el q.,** you've hit the nail on the head.

quiebra *nf* **1** *(abertura)* crack, fissure. **2** *Fin (bancarrota)* bankruptcy, failure; *(crack)* crash. **3** *fig (fracaso)* collapse; **la q. de la sociedad,** the breakup of society.

quiebro *nm* **1** *Taur* dodge. **2** *Ftb* dribbling. **3** *Mús* trill.

quien *pron rel* **1** *(sujeto)* who; **fue el jefe q. me lo dijo,** it was the boss who told me. **2** *(complemento)* whom, who; **es a ti a q. quiero,** it's you I love; **las personas con quienes trabajo,** the people (who) I work with; **su padre, a q. se parece ...,** her father, who(m) she resembles ... . **3** *(indef) (la persona que)* whoever, anyone who; **hay q. dice lo contrario,** some people say the opposite; **q. quiera venir que venga,** whoever wants to can come; *fig* **q. más q. menos,** everybody.

quién *pron interr* **1** *(sujeto)* who?; **¿q. sabe?,** who knows?; **¿quiénes sois?,** who are you? **2** *(complemento)* who, whom; **díme con q. has estado,** tell me who you've been with; **¿para q. es?,** who is it for? **3** *(pos)* whose; **¿de q. es esa bici?,** whose bike is that?

quienquiera *pron indef (pl **quienesquiera**)* whoever; **q. que sea,** whoever it may be.

quietismo *nm* **1** *Rel* quietism. **2** *(inacción)* inertia; *(estancamiento)* stagnation.

quieto,-a *adj* **1** *(sin moverse)* still; **estáte q.,** keep still, don't move!; **¡quietos ahí!,** stop *or* stay where you are! **2** *(sosegado)* calm; **es un chico q.,** he's quiet; **mar quieta,** calm sea.

quietud *nf* **1** *(sin movimiento)* stillness. **2** *(calma)* calm.

quijada *nf* Anat jawbone; **q. inferior,** lower jaw.

quijotada *nf* quixotic deed.

Quijote *nm* Don Q., Don Quixote.

quilate *nm* carat; *fig* **de muchos quilates,** of great value.

quilo¹ *nm* **1** *Biol* chyle. **2** *fig* **sudar el q.,** to sweat blood.

quilo² *nm véase* **kilo.**

quilla *nf* Náut keel; *fig* **saber algo de q. a perilla,** to know sth backwards. **2** *Astron (constelación)* Carina.

quimba *nf* Am *(garbo)* elegant style in working *or* dancing.

quimera *nf* **1** *Mit* chimera. **2** *fig (ilusión)* fantasy, pipe dream. **3** *fig (aprensión)* apprehension. **4** *(riña)* quarrel.

quimérico,-a *adj* unrealistic, fanciful.

química *nf* chemistry.

químico,-a I *adj* chemical. **II** *nm, f* chemist.

quimil *nm* Méx **1** bundle (of clothes). **2** *fig* heap *or* load of things.

quimioterapia *nf* Med chemotherapy.

quimono *nm* kimono.

quina *nf* Bot quinine, Peruvian bark; *fig* **tragar q.,** to swallow hard, grin and bear it.

quincalla *nf* metal pots and pans *pl,* tinware.

quincallero *nm* **1** *(fabricante)* maker of tinware. **2** *(vendedor)* tinker.

quince I *adj inv (cardinal)* fifteen; *(ordinal)* fifteenth; **el q. de agosto,** the fifteenth of August. **II** *nm inv* fifteen; *véase tamb* **ocho.**

quinceañero,-a *adj & nm, f* fifteen-year-old.

quincena *nf* fortnight, two weeks.

quincenal *adj* fortnightly, every two weeks.

quincuagenario,-a *adj & nm, f* quinquagenarian.

quincuagésimo,-a I *adj* fiftieth; **quincuagésima parte,** fiftieth. **II** *nm, f (de una serie)* fiftieth. **III** *nm (parte)* fiftieth; *véase tamb* **octavo,-a.**

quiniela *nf* football pools *pl;* **hacer una q.,** to do the pools.

quinielista *nmf* person who does the pools.

quinientos,-as I *adj inv (cardinal)* five hundred; *(ordinal)* five hundredth; **mil q.,** one thousand five hundred, fifteen hundred. **II** *nm, f* five hundred; *fam* **a las quinientas,** very late.

quinina *nf* quinine.

quinqué *nm* oil lamp.

quinquenal *adj* quinquennial, five-year.

quinquenio *nm* quinquennium, five-year period.

quinqui *nm fam* delinquent, petty criminal.

quinta *nf* 1 *(casa)* country house. 2 *(reclutar) Mil* conscription, *US* draft; **entrar en quintas**, to be called up *or US* drafted. 3 *Mús* fifth.

quintacolumnista *adj & nmf* fifth columnist.

quintaesencia *nf* quintessence.

quintal *nm (medida)* 46 kg. ▪ **q. métrico**, ≈ 100 kg.

quintana *nf* country house, villa.

quíntar *vtr* 1 *Mil* to conscript, *US* draft. 2 to take one in five.

quinteto *nm Mús* quintet.

quintilla *nf Lit* five-line stanza.

quintillizo,-a *nm,f* quintuplet, quin.

Quintín *nm* Quentin; *fam* **se armó la de San Q.**, there was a hell of a row.

quinto,-a I *adj* fifth; **quinta columna**, fifth column. **II** *nm, f (de una serie)* fifth. **III** *nm (parte)* fifth; *fam* **una q. de cerveza**, a small beer. 2 *Mil* conscript, recruit; *véase tamb* **octavo,-a.**

quíntuplo,-a *adj & nm* quintuple.

quiñar *vtr Am* to knock, bang.

quiosco *nm* kiosk; **q. de periódicos**, newspaper stand.

quiquiriquí *nm (pl quiquiriquíes)* cock-a-doodle-doo.

quirófano *nm* operating theatre.

quiromancia *nf*, **quiromancía** *nf* palmistry, chiromancy.

quiromántico,-a *nm, f* palmist, chiromancer.

quirúrgico,-a *adj* surgical.

quiscudo,-a *adj Am* bristly.

quise *indic fut véase* **querer.**

quisicosa *nf fam* riddle, puzzle.

quísque *pron fam* **todo** *or* **cada q.**, everyone, everybody.

quisquilla *nf (marisco)* common prawn.

quisquilloso,-a I *adj* fussy, finicky, fastidious. **II** *nm, f* fusspot.

quiste *nm Med* cyst.

quita *nf Fin* partial acquittance.

quitaesmaltes *nm inv* nail varnish *or* polish remover.

quitamanchas *nm inv* stain remover.

quitanieves *adj & nm* **(máquina) q.**, snowplough, *US* snowplow.

quitar I *vtr* 1 *(gen)* to remove, take out, take off. 2 *(separar)* to remove, take out; **q. la piel de una manzana**, to peel an apple. 3 *(sacar)* to take off, take out; *(prendas)* to take off;

Med **q. los puntos**, to take out the stitches; **q. tiempo**, to take up a lot of time; **quítate el abrigo**, take your coat off; **un cuello de quita y pon**, a detachable collar; *fig* **q. importancia a algo**, to play sth down; *fig* **q. las ganas a algn**, to put sb off. 4 *(apartar)* to take away, take off; **quita eso de delante**, clear that away; **quítale esa idea de la cabeza**, tell him to forget it. 5 *(la mesa)* to clear. 6 *(mancha)* to remove. 7 *(dolor)* to relieve. 8 *(hipo)* to stop; **le quitó el hipo**, it stopped his hiccups; *fig* it took his breath away. 9 *(sed)* quench; **te quitará la sed**, it will quench your thirst. 10 *(hambre)* to stop feeling hungry; **no lo comas, te quitará el hambre**, don't eat it, because it will spoil your appetite. 11 *(sueño)* to keep awake. 12 *Mat (descontar)* to take off; *(restar)* to subtract; **de once quita dos**, eleven minus two. 13 *(robar)* to steal, take; **me han quitado el bolso**, my handbag's been stolen. 14 *(coger)* to take; **quitarle el sitio a algn**, to take sb's place *or* seat. 15 *(impedir)* to stop, prevent; **eso no le quita valor**, that doesn't detract from its value; **eso no quito para que seas educado**, that's no reason not to be polite. 16 *(prohibir)* to stop; **me han quitado el fumar**, they've stopped me (from) smoking. 17 *(libertar de cargas)* to relieve, free. 18 *fam (radio, agua, electricidad)* to turn off. 19 *(locuciones)* **no q. ojo a algn**, not to take one's eyes off sb; **¡quita!,** *(persona)* go away!; *(cosa)* take it away!; **q. la palabra de la boca a algn**, to take the words right out of sb's mouth; **yo ni quito ni pongo**, it's nothing to do with me; *fam* **que me quiten lo baila(d)o**, they can't take that away from me. **II quitarse** *vr* 1 *(apartarse)* to move away; **¡quítate (de ahí)!**, come out, get out (of there)! 2 *(desaparecer)* to go; *(mancha)* to come out; **la mancha no se quita**, the stain won't come out; **se me ha quitado el dolor de cabeza**, my headache's gone; **se me han quitado las ganas**, I don't feel like it any more 3 *(sacarse) (prendas, gafas)* to take off, **q. el bigote**, to shave one's moustache off, **q. el sombrero**, to tip one's hat, **q. un diente**, to have a tooth out, *fig* **q. años**, to lie about one's age 4 *(renunciar a) (bebida, fumar, etc)* to give up 5 *(deshacerse de)* to get rid of, **q. a algn de encima**, to get rid of sb

quitasol *nm* parasol, sunshade.

quite *nm* 1 *Esgr* parry. 2 *Taur* distraction of bull by assistants to allow the escape of the bullfighter; *fig* **estar al q.**, to be ready to help

quiteño,-a I *adj* of *or* from Quito. **II** *nm, f* native *or* inhabitant of Quito.

quizá *adv*, **quizás** *adv* perhaps, maybe; **q. llueva**, perhaps it will rain, **q. no**, maybe not; **q. sí**, maybe.

quórum *nm inv* quorum.

R

R, r ['erre] *nf (la letra)* R, r.

R. *abr de* **Reverendo,-a**, Reverend, Rev, Revd

rabadán *nm* head shepherd.

rabadilla *nf* 1 *Anat* coccyx 2 *Culin (de buey)* rump

rabanillo *nm Bot* wild radish

rábano *nm Bot* radish, *fig* **tomar el r. por las hojas**, to get hold of the wrong end of the stick, *fam* **me importa un r.**, I don't give a toss, I couldn't care less, *fam* **¡un r.!**, no way! ▪ **r. blanco** *or* **picante**, horseradish

rabí *nm (pl rabíes) Rel* rabbi

rabia *nf* 1 *Med* rabies *sing*. 2 *fig (ira)* fury, rage, anger, **dar r.**, to make furious, infuriate; **¡qué r.!**, how annoying!; **tener r. a algn**, not to be able to stand the sight of sb

rabiar *vi* 1 *Med* to have rabies. 2 *fig (sufrir)* to be in great pain, **r. de dolor**, to writhe in pain 3 *fig (enfadarse)* to

rage; **estar a r. con algn**, to be furious with sb; **está que rabia**, he's fuming; **hacer r. a algn**, to make sb see red 4 *fig (desear)* **r. por**, to long for; **rabiaba por conseguir el cargo**, she was dying to get the job. 5 *fam* **a r.**, a lot, very much, **me gusta a r.**, I'm mad about it.

rábico,-a *adj Med* rabid

rabieta *nf fam* tantrum, **coger una r.**, to throw a tantrum

rabillo *nm* 1 *Bot (de hoja)* stalk, stem. 2 *Bot (cizaña)* darnel. 3 *(del ojo)* corner, **mirar por el r. del ojo**, to look out of the corner of one's eye

rabino *nm Rel* rabbi.

rabínico,-a *adj* rabbinical.

rabioso,-a *adj* 1 *Med* rabid; **perro r.**, rabid dog. 2 *fig (enfadado)* furious, **ponerse r.**, to fly into a rage 3 *(dolor)* terrible, intense. 4 *(color)* shocking, garish ◆ **rabiosamente** *adv* furiously.

rabo *nm Anat* tail, *fig* **aún falta el r. por desollar,** the worst is yet to come, *fam* **irse con el r. entre las piernas,** to go away with one's tail between one's legs

rabón,-ona *adj* **1** *(animal)* bobtailed. **2** *Arg Ven (cuchillo)* handleless **II** *nf Am (mujer)* camp follower.

racanear *vi fam* **1** *(holgazanear)* to idle, slack **2** *(ser tacaño)* to be stingy.

rácano,-a *adj fam* **1** *(holgazán)* idle, lazy. **2** *(tacaño)* stingy, mean

RACE *nm Aut abr de* **Real Automóvil Club de España,** ≈ Royal Automobile Club, RAC.

racha *nf* **1** *(de viento)* gust, squall. **2** *fam (período)* spell, patch; **a rachas,** in fits and starts, on and off; **tener una buena r.,** to have a piece of luck; **tener una mala r.,** to go through a bad patch. **3** *fam (serie)* string, run, series *sing*, **una r. de accidentes,** a string of accidents

racial *adj* racial, race, **disturbios raciales,** race riots; **prejuicio r.,** racial prejudice

racimo *nm* bunch, cluster; **r. de uvas,** bunch of grapes.

raciocinio *nm* **1** *(razón)* reason. **2** *(razonamiento)* reasoning

ración *nf* ration, portion, share; *(de corruda)* portion, helping; *(en paquete)* **'tres raciones',** 'serves three'; **una r. de patatas fritas, por favor,** a portion of chips, please

racional *adj* rational ♦ **racionalmente** *adv* rationally, reasonably.

racionalidad *nf* rationality.

racionalismo *nm* rationalism.

racionalista *adj & nmf* rationalist.

racionalización *nf* rationalization.

racionalizar *vtr* to rationalize.

racionamiento *nm* rationing. ■ **cartilla de r.,** ration book, ration card

racionar *vtr (limitar)* to ration; *(repartir)* to ration out.

racismo *nm* racism, racialism

racista *adj & nmf* racist, racialist.

racor *nm Téc* connecter, adapter, adaptor.

rada *nf Geog* bay, inlet.

radar *nm (pl radares) Téc* radar; **pantalla de r.,** radar screen.

radiación *nf* radiation

radiactividad *nf* radioactivity

radiactivo,-a *adj* radioactive.

radiado,-a I *pp de* **radiar II** *adj Bot Zool* radiate.

radiador *nm* radiator

radial *adj* radial; **neumáticos radiales,** radial tyres.

radiante *adj* radiant **(de,** with).

radiar *vtr* **1** *Fís* to radiate. **2** *Rad* to broadcast, transmit; radio **3** *Med* to X-ray. **4** *Am (expulsar)* to expel; *(despedir)* to fire.

radicación *nf* **1** *(instalación)* taking root, settling down. **2** *(situación, ubicación)* setting, location.

radical I *adj* radical. **II** *nm Ling Mat* radical, root. ♦ **radicalmente** *adv* radically.

radicalismo *nm Pol* radicalism.

radicalizar *vtr*, **radicalizarse** *vr (conflicto)* to intensify; *(postura)* to harden.

radicar I *vi* **1** *(estar, encontrarse)* to be (situated) **(en,** in), be rooted **(en,** in). **2** *fig* **r. en,** to lie in, stem from; **el problema radica en la economía,** the problem lies in the economy. **II radicarse** *vr (establecerse)* to settle (down).

radio¹ *nm* **1** *Anat Geom* radius; **en un r. de 3 kilómetros,** within a radius of 3 kilometres. ■ *fig* **r. de acción,** field of action, scope, sphere of influence. **2** *(de rueda)* spoke. **3** *Rad fam* radio operator.

radio² *nm Quím* radium.

radio³ *nf* **1** *(gen)* radio, wireless; *(aparato)* radio (set); *(mensaje)* wireless message; **por r.,** by radio; on the radio; **me enteré por la r.,** I heard (about) it on the radio; **poner la r.,** to turn on the radio. ■ **r. galena,** crystal set; **r. pirata,** pirate radio station.

radioactividad *nf* radioactivity.

radioactivo,-a *adj* radioactive.

radioaficionado,-a *nm, f Rad* radio ham.

radiocasete *nf (pl radiocasetes)* radio cassette.

radiodespertador *nf* radio alarm.

radiodifusión *nf Rad* broadcasting.

radioescucha *nmf Rad* listener.

radiofónico,-a *adj Rad* radio; **entrevista radiofónica,** radio interview; **espacio** *or* **programa r.,** radio programme.

radiografía *nf* **1** *(técnica)* radiography. **2** *(imagen)* X-ray, radiograph; **hacerse una r.,** to have an X-ray taken.

radiografiar *vtr* to X-ray.

radiología *nf Med* radiology.

radiólogo,-a *nm, f Med* radiologist.

radiómetro *nm* radiometer.

radiorreceptor *nf* radio receiver, radio (set), wireless (set).

radioteléfono *nm* radiotelephone.

radiotelegrafista *nmf* radio *or* wireless operator.

radiotelescopio *nm* radio telescope.

radioterapia *nf* radiotherapy, radium therapy.

radiotransmisión *nf* radio transmission, broadcasting.

radiotransmisor *nm* radio transmitter.

radioyente *nmf Rad* listener.

RAE *nf abr de* **Real Academia Española.**

raer *vtr* to scrape (off).

ráfaga *nf* **1** *(de viento)* gust, squall. **2** *(de disparos)* burst. **3** *(de luz)* flash.

rafia *nf Bot* raffia.

raglán *adj inv Cost* raglan; **mangas r.,** raglan sleeves.

raid *nm (pl raids)* raid; *Av* **r. aéreo,** *(ataque)* air raid; *(vuelo a gran distancia)* long-distance flight, long-haul flight.

raído,-a I *pp de* **raer. II** *adj* worn, threadbare.

raigambre *nf* **1** *Bot* roots *pl*, root system. **2** *fig* tradition, history; **de honda r.,** deep-rooted.

raíl *nm*, **rail** *nm Ferroc* rail.

raíz *nf (pl raíces)* **1** *(gen)* root; **arrancar de r.,** to pull up by the roots; **echar raíces,** *(planta)* to take root; *fig (establecerse)* to put down roots, settle (down); *fig* **a r. de,** as a result of; *fig* **cortar algo de r.,** to nip sth in the bud. **2** *Mat* **r. cuadrada,** square root.

raja *nf* **1** *(corte)* cut, slit; *(hendidura)* crack, split. **2** *(tajada) (de melón etc)* slice.

rajá *nm (pl rajaes)* rajah.

rajado,-a I *pp de* **rajar. II** *adj* **1** *(hendido)* cracked, split. **2** *fam (cobarde)* yellow. **III** *nm, f fam (cobarde)* chicken, coward. **IV** *nf vulg (vagina)* slit, cunt.

rajadura *nf* crack, split.

rajante *adj Arg (rápido)* quick, rapid; *(inmediato)* immediate.

rajar I *vtr* **1** *(hender)* to crack, split. **2** *(melón etc)* to slice. **3** *arg (persona)* to cut up; **dame el dinero o te rajo,** hand over your money or I'll cut you up. **II** *vi* **1** *fem (hablar mucho)* to chatter, rabble on; **¡cómo raja el tío!,** he doesn't half go on! **2** *fam (presumir)* to boast, show off. **III rajarse** *vr* **1** *(partirse)* to crack, split. **2** *fam (desistir)* to back out; *(acobardarse)* to chicken out. **3** *Am (gastar)* to spend lavishly. **4** *Am (escapar)* to rush or run off.

rajatabla (a) *loc adv* to the letter, strictly; **cumplir las normas a r.,** to follow the rules to the letter.

rajón,-ona *CAm* I *adj* 1 *Méx (poco fiable)* unreliable. 2 *(valentón)* bragging, boastful. 3 *(ostentoso)* ostenatious; *(espléndido)* lavish. II *nm,f* 1 *Méx (que se raja)* quitter. 2 *(fanfarrón)* show-off, braggart. 3 *(persona ostentosa)* ostentatious person; *(espléndida)* lavish person.

ralea *nf pey* type, sort, ilk; **son de la misma r.,** they are two of a kind, they are birds of a feather.

ralentí *nm* 1 *Cin* slow motion; **rodar una escena al r.,** to film a scene in slow motion. 2 *Aut* **con el motor al r.,** with the engine ticking over.

rallado,-a I *pp de* **rallar.** II *adj Culin* grated; **queso r.,** grated cheese.

rallador *nm* grater.

ralladura *nf* grating, gratings *pl*; **ralladuras de limón,** grated lemon mind.

rallar *vtr* to grate.

rally *(pl rallys) Aut* rally.

ralo,-a *adj* sparse, thin; **dientes ralos,** teeth with gaps between them.

ram *nm Inform* ram.

rama *nf* 1 *(de árbol)* branch; **algodón en r.,** raw cotton; *fam* **andarse** *or* **irse por las ramas,** to wander off the subject, digress. 2 *(de ciencia, industria)* branch.

Ramadán *nm Rel* Ramadan.

ramaje *nm* branches *pl*, foliage.

ramal *nm* 1 *(de carretera, ferrocarril)* branch. 2 *(de cuerda)* strand.

ramalazo *nm fam (passing)* it; **le entró el r. nostálgico,** he became all nostalgic; **un r. de locura,** a streak of madness.

rambla *nf* 1 *(cauce)* watercourse, channel. 2 *(avenida)* boulevard, avenue. 3 *Am (muelle)* dock, quayside.

ramera *nf* prostitute, whore.

ramificación *nf* ramification, consequence.

ramificarse *vr* to ramify, branch (out).

ramillete *nm* 1 *(de flores)* posy. 2 *(conjunto)* bunch, group, collection.

ramo *nm* 1 *(de árbol)* branch; *Rel* **Domingo de Ramos,** Palm Sunday. 2 *(de flores)* bunch, bouquet. 3 *(de ciencia, industria)* branch; **el r. de la hostelería,** the hotel and catering trade.

rampa¹ *nf (cuesta)* ramp. ■ *Astronáut* **r. de lanzamiento,** launching pad.

rampa² *nf (calambre)* cramp.

rampante *adj Herald* rampant, blatant.

ramplón,-ona *nf* coarse, vulgar.

ramplonería *nf* coarseness, vulgarity.

rana *nf Zool* frog; *fam* **salir r.,** to be a disappointment.

ranchero,-a I *adj Méx* 1 *(apocado)* timid, diffident. 2 *(ridículo)* ridiculous; *(rude)* rude, coarse. 3 *(de campo)* country. II *nm,f* 1 *(cocinero)* camp cook, mess cook. 2 *(granjero)* rancher, farmer. III *nf Méx Mús* popular song.

rancho *nm* 1 *Mil (comida)* mess; *fig* **hacer r. aparte,** to go one's own way. 2 *(granja)* ranch. 3 *Am (finca)* country state, farm, ranch. 4 *Arg (sombrero de paja)* straw hat.

rancidez *nf*, **ranciedad** *nf* rancidness, rancidity, rankness.

rancio,-a *adj* 1 *(comida)* stale; *(mantequilla)* rancid; **saber a r.,** to taste rancid; **vino r.,** mellow wine. 2 *(antiguo)* ancient; **de r. abolengo,** of ancient lineage.

randa I *nf (encaje)* lace trimming. II *nm fam (ratero)* pickpocket.

ranfla *nf Am* ramp.

ranglán *adj inv véase* **raglán.**

rango *nm* 1 *(jerarquía)* rank; **de alto r.,** high-ranking. 2 *Am (jerarquía elevada)* high social standing. 3 *Am (esplendidez)* pomp, splendour, *US* splendor.

Rangún *n* Rangoon.

ranking *nm (pl rankings)* ranking, status.

ranún *nm Arg Par Urug* rogue, scoundrel.

ranura *nf* 1 *(surco)* groove. 2 *(de máquina, teléfono)* slot; **introduzca una moneda en la r.,** put a coin in the slot.

ranurado,-a *adj* grooved.

rapacidad *nf* rapacity, rapaciousness.

rapapolvo *nm fam* ticking-off, talking-to; **echar un r. a algn,** to give sb a dressing-down.

rapar *vtr (afeitar)* to shave; *(pelo)* to crop.

rapaz¹ I *adj* 1 *Zool* predatory; **ave r.,** bird of prey. 2 *fig (persona)* rapacious, grasping. II *nf* bird of prey; **rapaces,** *Zool* predators; *Orn* birds of prey.

rapaz,-a² *nm, f* youngster; *(muchacho)* lad; *(muchacha)* lass.

rape¹ *nm (pez)* angler fish.

rape² *nm fam (pelo)* **cortado al r.,** short, close-cropped.

rapé *nm* snuff.

rapidez *nf* speed, rapidity.

rápido,-a I *adj* 1 *(gen)* quick, fast, rapid. 2 *Am (campo)* flat. II *adv* quickly; *fam* **¡y r.!,** and hurry up!, and make it snappy! III *nm* 1 *Ferroc* fast train, express. 2 **rápidos,** *(de un río)* rapids. ◆ **rápidamente** *adv* quickly.

rapiña *nf fam* robbery, theft.

raposa *nf* 1 *Zool* (female) fox, vixen. 2 *fam fig (persona)* sly old fox.

raposera *nf* foxhole.

rapsodia *nf Mús* rhapsody.

raptar *vtr* to kidnap, abduct.

rapto *nm* 1 *(secuestro)* kidnapping, abduction. 2 *fig (arrebato)* outburst, fit; **r. de cólera,** fit of anger.

raptor,-a *nm, f* kidnapper, abductor.

raqueta *nf* 1 *(de tenis)* racket; *(de ping-pong)* bat, *US* paddle. 2 *(de nieve)* snowshoe. 3 *(de crupier)* rake.

raquítico,-a *adj* 1 *Med* rachitic, rickety. 2 *fam (escaso)* small, meagre, *US* meager; *(débil)* weak. II *nm, f* person with rickets.

raquitismo *nm Med* rachitis, rickets *pl*.

rareza *nf* 1 *(poca frecuencia)* rarity, rareness; *(escasez)* scarcity. 2 *(peculiaridad)* oddity; *(extravagancia)* eccentricity.

rarificar *vtr* to rarefy.

raro,-a *adj* 1 *(poco frecuente)* rare; *(escaso)* scarce; **rara vez,** seldom. 2 *(extraño)* odd, strange, weird; **¡qué r.!,** how odd!; *fam* **es un tío r.,** he's a strange guy. ◆ **raramente** *adv (rara vez)* rarely, seldom; *(de manera extraña)* oddly, strangely.

ras *nm* level; **a r. de,** (on a) level with; **a r. de tierra,** at ground level; *Av* **volar a r. de tierra,** to fly low, hedgehop.

rasante I *adj (tiro)* grazing, close; *(vuelo)* low, skimming. II *nf (de camino)* slope. ■ **cambio de r.,** brow of a hill.

rasar *vtr* 1 *(rozar)* to graze, skim; *Av* **r. el suelo,** to fly low, hedgehop. 2 *(nivelar)* to level.

rasca *nf fam* 1 *(hambre)* hunger. 2 *(frío)* cold.

rascacielos *nm inv* skyscraper.

rascador *nm* 1 *(herramienta)* scraper, rasp. 2 *(de una caja de cerillas)* striking surface.

rascar I *vtr* 1 *(con las uñas)* to scratch. 2 *(con rascador)* to scrape, rasp. 3 *Mús (guitarra)* to strum. II **rascarse** *vr (con las uñas)* to scratch (oneself).

rascón *nm Orn* water rail.

rasera *nf Culin* spatula, fish slice.

rasero *nm* leveller; *fig* **medir con el mismo r.,** to treat impartially.

rasgado,-a I *pp de* **rasgar.** II *adj* 1 *(desgarrado)* torn. 2 *(ojos)* slit, almond-shaped; *(boca)* wide.

rasgadura *nf* tear, rip.

rasgar I *vtr* to tear, rip. II **rasgarse** *vr* to tear, rip; *fig* **r. las vestiduras,** to pull one's hair out.

rasgo *nm* **1** *(trazo)* stroke; *fig* **explicar a grandes rasgos,** to outline, explain briefly. **2** *(característica)* characteristic, feature, trait; *(de la cara)* feature; **tiene rasgos orientales,** he looks Oriental. **3** *(acto)* act, feat; **en un r. de generosidad,** in a moment of generosity.

rasgón *nm* tear, rip.

rasguear I *vtr Mús (guitarra)* to strum. **II** *vi (escribir)* to write, scribble.

rasgueo *nm* strumming (of guitar).

rasguñar I *vtr* to scratch, scrape. **II rasguñarse** *vr* to scratch, scrape; **se rasguñó las rodillas al caer,** he fell and grazed his knees.

rasguño *nm* scratch, scrape.

rasilla *nf* **1** *Tex (tela)* serge. **2** *Constr (ladrillo)* tile.

rasmillado,-a *nm,f SAm* scratch, graze.

raso,-a I *adj* **1** *(llano)* flat, level; *(liso)* smooth; *(vuelo, lanzamiento)* low; **una cucharada rasa de,** a level spoonful of. **2** *Mil* **soldado r.,** private. **3** *(atmósfera)* clear, cloudless; **al r.,** in the open (air); **cielo r.,** clear sky. **II** *nm Tex* satin.

raspa I *nf* **1** *(de pescado)* bone, backbone. **2** *(del trigo)* beard. **3** *Am fam (reprimenda)* ticking-off. **4** *Cuba Méx PR (azúcar moreno)* brown sugar. **5** *Méx (chanza)* joke. **II** *nm Arg Urug (ratero)* petty thief. **III** *nmf fam* **1** *(protestón)* moaner. **2** *(persona delgada)* bean-pole.

raspada *nf Méx* reprimand, ticking-off.

raspado *nm Med* scraping, scrape.

raspador *nm (gen)* scraper; *(de caja de cerillas)* striking surface.

raspadura *nf* **1** *(ralladura)* scraping, scrapings *pl.* **2** *(señal, marca)* scratch, mark.

raspar I *vtr* **1** *(rascar)* to scrape (off). **2** *(borrar)* to scratch out. **3** *(al paladar)* to be sharp on; *(la piel)* to be rough on. **4** *(hurtar)* to nick pinch. **5** *Am (reprender)* to reprimand.

rasposo,-a *adj* **1** *(aspero)* rough, sharp. **2** *Arg Urug (prenda)* shabby, threadbare. **3** *Arg Urug (persona)* slovenly, dirty. **4** *Arg Urug (tacaño)* mean, stingy. **5** *Méx (bromista)* joking, teasing.

rastra *nf* **1** *(huella)* track, trail. **2** *Agr (grada)* harrow. **3** *(de ajos, cebollas)* string. **4** *(para pescar)* trawl net. **5 a rastras,** *(arrastrando)* dragging; *fig (de mal grado)* grudgingly; **lo sacaron del bar a r.,** he was dragged out of the bar. **6** *Arg Urug* gaucho's leather belt.

rastreador *nm* tracker. ■ *Náut* **r. de minas,** minesweeper.

rastrear I *vtr* **1** *(seguir el rastro)* to track, trail. **2** *(río)* to drag, dredge. **3** *(para pescar)* to trawl. **4** *(averiguar)* to find out. **5** *Agr* to rake. **II** *vi Av (volar bajo)* to fly low, hedgehop.

rastreo *nm* **1** *(seguimiento)* tracking, trailing, tracking. **2** *(de un río)* dragging, dredging. **3** *Pesca* trawling. **4** *Agr* raking.

rastrero,-a *adj* **1** *(que se arrastra)* creeping, crawling; **pájaro de vuelo r.,** low-flying bird. **2** *fig (bajo, despreciable)* vile, base.

rastrillada *nf Am* trail, track.

rastrillar *vtr* **1** *Agr (hojas)* to rake. **2** *(cáñamo, lino)* to comb, hackle. **3** *Am (arma)* to cock. **4** *Arg (fusil)* to fire.

rastrillo *nm* **1** *Agr (herramienta)* rake. **2** *(de castillo)* portcullis. **3** *(de cáñamo, lino)* comb, hackle. **4** *fam (mercadillo)* flea market; **r. benéfico,** jumble sale.

rastro *nm* **1** *(huella)* trace, sign; *(en el suelo)* track, trail; **ni r. de,** not a trace of; **perder el r. de algn,** to lose sb's scent; **seguir el r. de algn,** to follow sb's trail. **2** *(mercado)* **el R.,** the Madrid flea market.

rastrojo *nm Agr* **1** *(paja)* stubble. **2** *(campo)* stubble field.

rasurar *vtr,* **rasurarse** *vr* to shave.

rata I *nf Zool* rat; *fam* **más pobre que las ratas,** as poor as a church mouse. **II** *nm fam* **1** *(ratero)* pickpocket, thief. **2** *(tacaño)* mean *or* stingy person.

rataplán *nm (del tambor)* drumbeat, rub-a-dub.

ratear[1] *vtr (repartir)* to share out proportionally, give out pro rata.

ratear[2] *vtr fam (robar)* to steal.

ratear[3] *vi (arrastrarse)* to crawl, creep.

rateo *nm* pro rata distribution.

ratería *nf* petty theft, pilfering.

ratero,-a *nm,f* pickpocket; **r. de hotel,** hotel thief.

raticida *nm* rat poison.

ratificación *nf* ratification.

ratificar I *vtr* to ratify. **II ratificarse** *vr* to be ratified.

rato *nm* **1** *(momento, instante)* while, time, moment; **a ratos,** at times; **a ratos perdidos,** at odd moments; **al poco r.,** shortly after; **¿cuánto r. hace que se fue?,** how long is it since she left?; **esperar un r.,** to wait a while; **hace ya un buen r.,** some time ago; **¡hasta otro r.!,** see you (later)!; **hay para r.,** it'll take a while; **pasar el r.,** to kill time; **pasar un buen/mal r.,** to have a good/bad time; **ratos libres,** free time *sing.* **2** *fam (mucho)* **un r.,** very, a lot; **sabe un r. de música,** he knows a lot about music.

ratón *nm* **1** *Zool* mouse; *fam* **r. de biblioteca,** bookworm. **2** *Inform* mouse.

ratonera *nf* **1** *(trampa)* mousetrap; *fig* **caer en la r.,** to fall into the trap. **2** *(agujero)* mousehole.

ratonero *nm Orn* buzzard.

raudal *nm* **1** *(corriente de agua)* torrent, flood. **2** *fig (abundancia)* flood, abundance; **a raudales,** in abundance; **la gente entró a raudales,** people poured *or* flooded in.

raudo,-a *adj lit* swift, rapid.

raya[1] *nf* **1** *(línea)* line; *(de color)* stripe; **camisa a rayas,** striped shirt. **2** *(guión)* dash. **3** *(del pantalón)* crease. **4** *(del pelo)* parting; **hacerse la r.,** to part one's hair. **5** *(límite)* limit; *fig* **tener a r.,** to keep at bay; *fam* **dar quince** *or* **ciento y r. a algn,** to run rings round sb. **6** *arg (de droga)* fix, dose.

raya[2] *nf (pez)* skate.

rayado,-a I *pp de* **rayar. II** *adj (tela)* striped; *(papel)* ruled. **III** *nm* stripes *pl.*

rayano,-a *adj* bordering; **r. en,** bordering on.

rayar I *vtr* **1** *(papel)* to rule, draw lines on. **2** *(estropear una superficie)* to scratch; **alguien me ha rayado el coche,** somebody's scratched my car. **II** *vi* **1** *(lindar)* **r. en,** to border on; **raya en la locura,** it borders on madness; **raya en los cincuenta,** he is about *or* around fifty. **2** *(día, alba)* to dawn; **al r. el alba,** at dawn.

rayo *nm* **1** ray, beam. ■ **rayos de sol,** sun's rays; **rayos X,** X-rays. **2** *(relámpago)* (flash of) lightning; *fam* **caer como un r.,** to drop like a bombshell; *fam* **echar rayos,** to be furious; *fam* **¡que la parta un r.!,** **¡mal r. la parta!,** to hell with her!; *fam* **saber a rayos,** to taste awful.

rayón *nm Tex* rayon.

rayuela *nf* hopscotch.

raza *nf* **1** race. ■ **r. blanca,** white race; **r. humana,** human race; **r. negra,** black race. **2** *(de animal)* breed; **de r.,** *(perro)* pedigree; *(caballo)* thoroughbred.

razón *nf* **1** *(facultad)* reason; **atender a razones, entrar en r.,** to listen to reason; **perder la r.,** to lose one's reason; **uso de r.,** power of reasoning. **2** *(motivo)* reason, cause; **con r.,** with good reason; **¿cuál es la r.?,** what's the reason?; **r. de estado,** reason of state; **r. de más para,** all the more reason to; **tener razones para,** to have cause to. **3** *(mensaje)* message; **mandar r.,** to send a message. **4** *(justicia)* rightness, justice; **asistirle a algn la r.,** to be in the right; **con r. o sin ella,** rightly or wrongly; **dar la r. a algn,** to say that sb is right; **no tener r.,** to be wrong; **tener r.,** to be right. **5** *(información)* **'r. aquí',** 'enquire within', 'apply within'; **'r. en portería',** 'enquiries to caretaker'. **6** *Com* **r. social,** trade name, firm's name. **7** *Mat* ratio, rate; **a r. de,** in the ratio of, at the rate of.

razonable *adj* reasonable; **dentro de lo r.,** within reason.
◆ **razonablemente** *adv* reasonably, rationally.

razonado,-a I *pp de* **razonar. II** *adj* reasoned, well-reasoned.

razonamiento *nm* reasoning.

razonar I *vtr (argumentar)* to reason out. **II** *vi (discurrir)* to reason; *(hablar)* to talk.

RDA *nf abr de* **República Democrática de Alemania,** German Democratic Republic, GDR.

re *nm Mús* re, ray.

re- *pref* re-; **reconstruir,** to rebuild.

reabastecer *vtr (de combustible)* to refuel.

reabastecimiento *nm* refuelling.

reabrir *(pp reabierto) vtr* to reopen; *fig* **r. viejas heridas,** to open old wounds.

reacción *nf* reaction. ■ **avión de r.,** jet (plane); **r. en cadena,** chain reaction.

reaccionar *vi* to react.

reaccionario,-a *adj & nm,f* reactionary.

reacio,-a *adj* reluctant, unwilling; **mostrarse r. a hacer algo,** to be reluctant to do sth.

reacondicionar *vtr* to recondition.

reactivar *vtr* to reactivate.

reactivo,-a I *adj* reactive. **II** *nm Quím* reagent.

reactor *nm* **1** *Fís* reactor. ■ **r. nuclear,** nuclear reactor. **2** *Av (avión)* jet (plane).

readaptación *nf (de un enfermo)* rehabilitation; **r. profesional,** industrial retraining.

readaptar *vtr,* **readaptarse** *vr* to readapt, readjust.

readmisión *nf* readmission.

readmitir *vtr* to readmit; *(trabajador)* to re-employ.

reafirmación *nf* reaffirmation, reassertion.

reafirmar *vtr* to reaffirm, reassert.

reagrupación *nf,* **reagrupamiento** *nm* regrouping.

reagrupar, **reagruparse** *vr* to regroup.

reajustar *vtr* to readjust.

reajuste *nm* readjustment. ■ *Pol* **r. ministerial,** cabinet reshuffle.

real[1] *adj (efectivo, verdadero)* real; **en la vida r.,** in real life; **necesidades reales,** real necessities.

real[2] **I** *adj (regio)* royal; *fig* grand, fine; **la familia r.,** the royal family; **palacio r.,** royal palace; *Jur* **por r. decreto,** by royal decree; *fam* **porque no me da la r. gana,** because I don't feel like it; *fam* **es una r. moza,** she's a good-looking girl. **II** *nm* **1** *(moneda)* old Spanish coin worth 25 céntimos; *fam* money; **estar sin un r.,** to be penniless; **no vale un r.,** it is worthless. **2** *(feria)* fairground. ◆ **realmente** *adv (gen)* really; *(en realidad)* actually, in fact; **r. no ha pasado nada,** in (actual) fact, nothing has happened; **r. no lo entiendo,** I really can't understand it.

realce *nm* **1** *(relieve)* relief; **bordado de r.,** relief embroidery. **2** *fig (esplendor)* splendour, *US* splendor, distinction; **dar r. a,** to enhance; **poner de r.,** to highlight.

realeza *nf* royalty.

realidad *nf* reality; **en r.,** in fact, actually; **la r. es que ...,** the fact of the matter is that ... .

realismo *nm* realism.

realista I *adj* realistic. **II** *nmf* realist.

realizable *adj (objetivo)* attainable; *(plan, proyecto)* feasible.

realización *nf* **1** *(de un deseo)* realization, fulfilment, *US* fulfillment. **2** *(de un proyecto)* execution, carrying out. **3** *Cin TV* production.

realizador,-a *nm,f Cin TV* producer.

realizar I *vtr* **1** *(ambición)* to realize, fulfil, *US* fulfill, achieve; *(deseo)* to fulfil. **2** *(plan)* to execute, carry out; **r. un viaje,** to make a journey. **3** *Cin TV* to produce. **4** *Fin*

(vender) to realize. **II realizarse** *vr* **1** *(ambición)* to be realized, be fulfilled, be achieved; *(sueño)* to come true. **2** *(proyecto)* to be executed, be carried out. **3** *(persona)* to fulfil *or US* fulfill oneself.

realquilado,-a I *pp de* **realquilar. II** *adj* sublet. **III** *nm,f* person who sublets from another.

realquilar *vtr* to sublet.

realzar *vtr* **1** *(pintura)* to highlight. **2** *fig (belleza, importancia)* to enhance, heighten; **su modestía realza la nobleza de su gesto,** his noble demeanour is heightened by his great modesty.

reanimación *nf* revival.

reanimar *vtr,* **reanimarse** *vr (gen)* to revive; *(fiesta, conversación)* to liven up.

reanudación *nf* renewal, resumption. re-establishment; **r. de las clases,** return to school; **r. de negociaciones,** resumption of talks.

reanudar I *vtr* to renew, resume; **r. el paso** *or* **la marcha,** to set off again; **r. las clases,** to go back to school; **r. negociaciones,** to resume negotiations; **r. una amistad,** to renewal a friendship. **II reanudarse** *vr* to start again, resume; **se reanudó el trabajo después de la huelga,** work was resumed after the strike.

reaparecer *vi* to reappear, recur; *(artista)* to make a comeback.

reaparición *nf* reappearance, recurrence; *(de artista etc)* comeback.

reapertura *nf* reopening.

reaprovisionar *vtr* to replenish, restock.

rearmar *vtr,* **rearmarse** *vr Mil* to rearm.

rearme *nm* rearmament.

reaseguro *nm Seg* reinsurance.

reasumir *vtr* to reassume, resume.

reata *nf* **1** *(cuerda)* rope. **2** *(de caballos, mulas)* packtrain.

reavivar *vtr* to revive.

rebaba *nf* rough edge.

rebaja *nf* **1** *(reducción)* lowering, reduction. **2** *Com (descuento)* reduction, discount; **nos hicieron una r.,** they gave us a discount. **3** *Com* **rebajas,** sales; **en r.,** in the sales; **'grandes r.',** 'huge reductions'; **precio de r.,** sale price.

rebajado,-a I *pp de* **rebajar. II** *adj* **1** *(tierra, techo)* lowered; *(arco)* depressed. **2** *(precio, mercancía)* reduced. **3** *(humillado)* humbled. **III** *nm Mil* soldier exempted from duty.

rebajar I *vtr* **1** *(tierra)* to lower; *(arco)* to depress. **2** *(precio)* to cut, reduce; *(cantidad)* to make a reduction in; **r. cinco mil pesetas,** to make a reduction of five thousand pesetas. **3** *(color)* to tone down, soften; *(intensidad)* to diminish. **4** *(humillar)* to humiliate. **5** *(de servicio)* to excuse, exempt (**de,** from). **II rebajarse** *vr (humillarse)* to humble oneself; **r. a hacer algo,** to stoop to do sth, descend to doing sth; **r. ante algn,** to bow before sb.

rebaje *nm Mil* exemption.

rebanada *nf* slice; **r. de pan,** slice of bread.

rebanar *vtr* **1** *(hacer rebanadas)* to slice, cut into slices. **2** *(cortar)* to cut *or* slice off.

rebañar *vtr* **1** *(comida)* to finish off; **r. el plato (con pan),** to wipe one's plate clean (with bread). **2** *fig (apoderarse de)* to clean out.

rebaño *nm* **1** *(de ovejas)* flock; *(de otros animales)* herd. **2** *Rel* flock.

rebasar *vtr* **1** *(exceder)* to exceed, go beyond, surpass; **r. los límites,** to overstep the mark. **2** *Náut (pasar por)* to pass; *Aut (adelantar)* to overtake.

rebatible *adj* refutable.

rebatir *vtr* to refute.

rebato *nm* alarm; **tocar a r.,** to sound the alarm.

rebautizar *vtr* to rechristen, rebaptize.

rebeca *nf (prenda)* cardigan.

rebeco *nm Zool* chamois.

rebelarse *vr* to rebel, revolt; **r. contra el gobierno,** to rebel against the government.

rebelde I *adj* rebellious; *fig* **una tos r.,** a persistent cough. **II** *nmf* rebel.

rebeldía *nf* **1** *(insurrección)* rebelliousness. **2** *Jur* default; **declararse en r.,** to default.

rebelión *nf* rebellion, revolt.

rebenque *nm Am* whip.

reblandecer I *vtr* to soften. **II reblandecerse** *vr* to soften, become soft.

reblandecimiento *nm* softening; **r. cerebral,** softening of the brain.

rebobinado,-a I *pp de* **rebobinar. II** *adj* rewound. **III** *nm* rewinding.

rebobinar *vtr* to rewind.

reborde *nm* edge, flange, rim.

reborujar *vtr Méx* to mix (up).

rebosante *adj* overflowing (**de,** with), birmming (**de,** with).

rebosar I *vi* **1** *(recipiente, líquido)* to overflow, brim over. **2** *fig* **r. de,** to be overflowing *or* brimming with; **rebosaba de salud,** she was glowing with health. **II** *vtr (abundar)* to abound; **el lugar rebosaba alegría,** the place was bursting with happiness.

reboso *nm Am* driftwood.

rebotar I *vi* **1** *(pelota)* to bounce, rebound. **2** *(bala)* to ricochet. **II** *vtr* **1** *(clavo)* to clinch. **2** *(ataque)* to repel. **3** *fam (poner fuera de sí)* to upset, put out; **este tío me rebota,** this guy puts me out. **III rebotarse** *vr fam (ponerse fuera de sí)* to get upset *or* angry; **se rebota por nada,** he gets angry very easily.

rebote *nm* **1** *(de pelota)* bounce, rebound; **de r.,** on the rebound; *fig* **hacer algo de r.,** to do sth on the rebound. **2** *(de bala)* ricochet.

rebozado,-a I *pp de* **rebozar. II** *adj Culin* coated in breadcrumbs *or* batter.

rebozar *vtr Culin* to coat in breadcrumbs *or* batter.

rebozo *nm* **1** *(prenda)* muffler, wrap, shawl. **2** *fig (disimulación)* dissimulation; **de r.,** secretly, in secret; **sin r.,** openly, frankly.

rebrotar *vi Bot* to shoot, sprout.

rebufar *vi* to snort loudly.

rebufo *nm* loud snort.

rebullir *vi,* **rebullirse** *vr* to stir, begin to move.

rebuscado,-a I *pp de* **rebuscar. II** *adj* affected, recherché.

rebuscamiento *nm* affectation.

rebuscar *vtr* to search carefully for.

rebuznar *vi* to bray.

rebuzno *nm* braying, bray.

recabar *vtr* **1** *(pedir, solicitar)* to ask for, entreat; **r. información,** to ask for information. **2** *(conseguir)* to obtain, manage to get.

recadero,-a *nm, f* messenger, errand boy or girl.

recado *nm* **1** *(mandado)* errand; **hacer recados,** to run errands. **2** *(mensaje)* message; **dejar un r.,** to leave a message. **3** *Am (montura)* saddle and trappings *pl.* **4** *Méx PR* **recados,** *(saludos)* regards, greetings.

recaer *vi* **1** *Med (enfermo)* to relapse; *fig (en vicios, equivocaciones)* to backslide, relapse. **2** *(corresponder)* to fall (**sobre,** on); **la responsabilidad recae sobre ella,** the responsibility falls on her.

recaída *nf Med* relapse; *(en vicios, equivocaciones)* backslide, relapse; **sufrir una r.,** to have a relapse.

recalar *vi Náut* to sight land.

recalcar *vtr fig* to underline, stress, emphasize.

recalcitrante *adj* recalcitrant.

recalentar *vtr (comida)* to reheat, warm up; *(calentar demasiado)* to overheat.

recamado *nm* embroidery.

recamar *vtr* to embroider.

recámara *nf* **1** *(habitación)* dressing room. **2** *(de arma)* chamber. **3** *fig (cautela)* reserve, caution.

recambiar *vtr* to change (over).

recambio *nm* **1** *(repuesto)* spare (part); **rueda de r.,** spare wheel. **2** *(de tinta)* refill.

recapacitar *vi* to think over; **recapacita sobre ello antes de decidir,** think it over before you decide.

recapitulación *nf* recapitulation, summing-up, recap.

recapitular *vtr* to recapitulate, sum up, recap.

recarga *nf* refill.

recargable *adj* refillable, rechargeable.

recargado,-a I *pp de* **recargar. II** *adj* **1** *(sobrecargado)* overloaded. **2** *fig (estilo)* overelaborate, exaggerated, affected.

recargar *vtr* **1** *(volver a cargar)* to reload; *Elec (pila)* to recharge. **2** *(sobrecargar)* to overload. **3** *Fin (aumentar)* to increase. **4** *(adornar con exceso)* to overelaborate, exaggerate.

recargo *nm Fin* extra charge, surcharge.

recatado,-a I *pp de* **recatar. II** *adj* **1** *(prudente)* prudent, cautious. **2** *(modesto)* modest, decent.

recatar I *vtr* to hide, cover up. **II recatarse** *vi* to be cautious, act discreetly; **sin r.,** openly.

recato *nm* **1** *(cautela)* caution, prudence; **sin r.,** openly. **2** *(pudor)* modesty.

recauchutado,-a I *pp de* **recauchutar. II** *nm (de neumático)* retreading.

recauchutar *vtr (neumático)* to retread.

recaudación *nf* **1** *(cobro)* collection; **r. de impuestos,** tax collection. **2** *(ingresos)* income, receipts *pl; (cantidad recaudada)* takings *pl,* take; *Dep* gate; **hacer una buena r.,** to have a good takings. **3** *(oficina de impuestos)* tax collector's office.

recaudador,-a *nm, f* tax collector.

recaudar *vtr* to collect.

recaudería *nf Méx* greengrocer's (shop).

recaudo *nm* **1** *(recaudación)* collection. **2** *(precaución)* precaution; **estar a buen r.,** to be in safekeeping; **poner algo a buen r.,** to put sth in a safe place. **3** *Am (legumbres)* mixed vegetables *pl.*

recelar *vtr* to suspect, distrust.

recelo *nm* suspicion, distrust.

receloso,-a *adj* suspicious, distrustful.

recensión *nf* review.

recental *adj* sucking; **cordero r.,** sucking lamb.

recepción *nf* **1** *(de una carta)* receipt. **2** *(en hotel, oficina)* reception (desk); **pregúntelo en r.,** ask at reception. **3** *(fiesta oficial)* reception. **4** *Rad* reception.

recepcionista *nmf* receptionist.

receptáculo *nm* receptacle.

receptividad *nf* receptiveness, receptivity.

receptivo,-a *adj* receptive.

receptor,-a I *nm, f (persona)* recipient, receiver. **II** *nm Rad TV* receiver.

recesión *nf Econ* recession.

recesivo,-a *adj* recessive.

receso *nm* recess.

receta *nf* **1** *Culin* recipe; *fig* recipe, formula. **2** *Med* prescription.

recetar *vtr Med* to prescribe.

recetario *nm Med* prescription pad.

rechace *nm Dep* point-blank save.

rechazar *vtr* **1** *(gen)* to reject, turn down, resist, refuse; **r. una oferta,** to turn down an offer. **2** *Mil* to repel, repulse, drive back.

rechazo *nm* **1** *(acción)* rejection, refusal, resistance; *Med* **r. de un órgano,** rejection of an organ; *fig* **de r.,** indirectly, as a consequence. **2** *(negativa)* denial, rejection.

rechifla *nf fam* **1** *(silbido)* hissing, booing, catcalls *pl.* **2** *(mofa)* mockery, jeering.

rechiflar *vtr* **1** *(silbar)* to hiss, boo. **2** *(mofarse)* to mock, jeer at.

rechinante *adj* creaky, squeaky.

rechinar *vi* *(madera)* to creak; *(metal)* to squeak, screech; *(efecto en el oído)* to grate; *(dientes)* to grind, gnash, grate; **me rechinan los dientes de frío,** my teeth are chattering with the cold.

rechistar *vi* to clear one's throat; *fam* **sin r.,** that's final.

rechoncho,-a *adj fam* chubby, tubby.

rechupete (de) *loc fam* marvellous, *US* marvelous, fantastic; *(comida)* delicious, scrumptious.

recibidor *nm* entrance hall.

recibimiento *nm* reception, welcome.

recibir **I** *vtr* *(gen)* to receive; *(acoger)* to welcome; *(invitados)* to entertain; **el rey recibe los miércoles,** the king receives visitors on Wednesdays; **fueron a recibirle a la estación,** they went to meet him at the station; *(en carta)* **recibe un abrazo de,** lots of love from; **r. un premio,** to receive an award; **r. una negativa,** to be refused, meet with a refusal. **II recibirse** *vr Am* to graduate; **r. de abogado,** to qualify as a lawyer.

recibo *nm* **1** *(resguardo)* receipt; *(factura)* invoice, bill. **2** *(recepción)* reception, receiving; **acusar r. de,** to acknowledge receipt of.

reciclado,-a I *pp de* **reciclar. II** *adj* recycled.

reciclaje *nm* **1** *(de residuos)* recycling. **2** *fam (de profesores)* retraining.

reciclar *vtr* **1** *(residuos)* to recycle. **2** *fam (profesores)* to retrain.

recién *adv* **1** *(recientemente) (antes de pp)* recently, newly; **café r. hecho,** freshly-made coffee; **r. casados,** newlyweds; **r. nacido,** newborn baby. **2** *Am (hace poco)* recently; just; **r. llegó,** she has just arrived. ◆ **recientemente** *adv* recently, lately.

reciente *adj* recent.

recinto *nm (cercado)* enclosure; *(zona)* area, grounds *pl,* precinct, precincts *pl;* **r. comercial,** shopping precinct; **r. ferial,** fairground.

recio,-a *adj (robusto)* strong, sturdy; *(grueso)* thick; *(voz)* loud; *(tiempo)* harsh, severe; *fig* **en lo más r. de la batalla,** in the thick of the battle. **II r.** *adv (con fuerza)* hard, heavily; **hablar r.,** to speak loudly.

recipiente *nm* vessel, receptacle, container.

reciprocidad *nf* reciprocity.

recíproco,-a *adj* reciprocal.

recitación *nf,* **recitado** *nm* recitation.

recital *nm Mus* recital; *Lit* reading.

recitar *vtr* to recite.

recitativo *nm* recitative.

reclamación *nf* **1** *(demanda)* claim, demand. **2** *(queja)* complaint, protest, objection; **presentar una r.,** to lodge a complaint.

reclamar I *vtr* **1** *(pedir)* to claim, demand. **2** *(exigir)* to require, demand. **II** *vi* **1** to protest **(contra,** against). **2** *Jur* to appeal.

reclamo *nm* **1** *Caza* decoy bird, lure. **2** *fig* inducement. **3** *(anuncio)* advertisement; *(eslogan)* advertising slogan.

reclinar I *vtr* to lean **(sobre,** on). **II reclinarse** *vr* to lean back, recline.

reclinatorio *nm* prie-dieu.

recluido,-a I *pp de* **recluir. II** *adj (gen)* shut away, locked away; *(encarcelado)* imprisoned, interned.

recluir *vtr (gen)* to shut away, lock away; *(encarcelar)* to imprison, intern; *(en institución mental)* to confine.

reclusión *nf* **1** *(gen)* seclusion; *(encarcelamiento)* imprisonment, internment. **2** *(lugar)* retreat.

recluso,-a I *adj* imprisoned; **población reclusa,** prison population. **II** *nm,f* prisoner, inmate.

recluta *Mil* **I** *nmf (voluntario)* recruit; *(obligatorio)* conscript. **II** *nf (acción)* recruitment, conscription.

reclutamiento *nm* **1** *(voluntario)* recruitment; *(obligatorio)* conscription. **2** *(reclutas) (voluntarios)* recruits *pl;* *(voluntarios)* conscripts *pl.*

reclutar *vtr* **1** *(voluntariamente)* to recruit; *(a la fuerza)* to conscript. **2** *Arg (ganado)* to round up.

recobrar I *vtr* **1** *(gen)* to recover, retrieve; *(conocimiento)* to regain; **r. el aliento,** to get one's breath back. **2** *Mil (plaza)* to recapture. **II recobrarse** *vr* to recover, recuperate.

recochinearse *vr fam* to make fun **(de,** of), laugh **(de,** at).

recochineo *nm fam* mockery.

recodo *nm (de río)* twist, turn; *(de camino)* bend.

recogedor *nm* dustpan.

recogepelotas *nmf inv Dep (muchacho)* ball boy; *(muchacha)* ball girl.

recoger I *vtr* **1** *(coger)* to pick up, take back; **recoge el libro del suelo,** pick the book up. **2** *(reunir)* to gather, collect; **r. datos,** to gather information. **3** *(ordenar)* to clear up; *(limpiar)* to clean; **recoge todo esto,** clear all of this away; **r. la mesa,** to clear the table. **4** *(ir a buscar)* to pick up, fetch; **te recogeré a las ocho,** I'll pick you up at eight. **5** *Agr* to harvest, gather, pick; **r. fruta,** to pick fruit. **6** *(albergar)* to take in, shelter; **lo recogió un tío,** he was taken in by an uncle. **II recogerse** *vr* **1** *(irse a casa)* to go home; *(irse a la cama)* to go to bed. **2** *(levantarse)* to lift up, pick up; **r. el pelo,** to put one's hair up; **se recogió la falda,** she gathered up her skirt. **3** *(meditar)* to retire, go off alone.

recogida *nf (gen)* collection; *Agr (cosecha)* harvest, harvesting.

recogido,-a I *pp de* **recoger. II** *adj* **1** *(apartado)* secluded, withdrawn; **vida recogida,** secluded *or* quiet life. **2** *(pelo)* pinned back, tied back.

recogimiento *nm* withdrawal, recollection; **vivir con r.,** to lead a withdrawn *or* secluded life.

recolección *nf* **1** *(recogida)* collection, gathering. **2** *Agr (cosecha)* harvest, harvesting; *(temporada)* harvest time.

recolectar *vtr* **1** *(reunir)* to collect, gather. **2** *Agr* to harvest.

recoleto,-a *adj* **1** *(lugar)* quiet, secluded. **2** *(persona)* withdrawn, retiring.

recomendable *adj* recommendable, advisable; **no ser r.,** to be unwise.

recomendación *nf* recommendation, reference; **carta de r.,** letter of introduction.

recomendado,-a I *pp de* **recomendar. II** *adj* recommended. **II** *nm, f (hombre)* protégé; *(mujer)* protégée.

recomendar *vtr* to recommend, advise.

recomenzar *vtr* to recommence, begin again.

recompensa *nf* reward, recompense; **en r.,** as a reward, in return.

recompensar *vtr* **1** *(retribuir)* to reward, recompense; **'se recompensará',** 'reward offered'. **2** *(compensar)* to compensate.

recomponer *(pp recampuesto) vtr* to repair, mend, alter.

recomposición *nf* repairing, mending, alteration.

recompuesto,-a I *pp de* **recomponer. II** *adj (acicalado)* dressed up.

reconcentrar I *vtr* **1** *(congregar)* to bring together. **2** *(concentrar)* to concentrate (**en**, on), devote (**en**, to); **r. toda la atención en un tema,** to give a subject one's full attention. **3** *Quím* to make more concentrated. **II reconcentrarse** *vr* *(ensimismarse)* to concentrate, withdraw into oneself.

reconciliable *adj* reconcilable.

reconciliación *nf* reconciliation.

reconciliar I *vtr* to reconcile. **II reconciliarse** *vr* to be reconciled.

reconcomerse *vr* *fam* to be consumad (**de**, with); **se reconcomía de curiosidad por conocerla,** he was itching to meet her.

reconcomio *nm* **1** *(deseo)* itch, desire, longing. **2** *(rencor)* grudge, resentment; *(envidia)* envy.

recóndito,-a *adj* hidden, secret; **en lo más r. del alma,** deep down.

reconfortante I *adj* comforting. **II** *nm Med* tonic.

reconfortar *vtr (confortar)* to comfort; *(animar)* to cheer up.

reconocer I *vtr* **1** *(gen)* to recognize; **¿no me reconoces?,** don't you recognize me? **2** *(admitir)* to recognize, admit; **hay que reconocerlo,** let's face it; **no quiere reconocerlo,** he won't admit it. **3** *Med (paciente)* to examine. **4** *Mil* to reconnoitre. **II reconocerse** *vr* **1** *(gen)* to recognize each other. **2** *(admitir)* to admit; **r. culpable,** to admit one's guilt.

reconocible *adj* recognizable.

reconocimiento *nm* **1** *(gen)* recognition; **en r. de,** in recognition *or* appreciation of. **2** *Med* examination, checkup. **3** *Mil* reconnaissance.

reconquista *nf* reconquest; *Hist* **la R.,** the Christian capture of the Iberian Peninsula, freeing it from Moorish rule.

reconquistar *vtr* to reconquer, recapture, regain.

reconsiderar *vtr* to reconsider.

reconstituir *vtr* to reconstitute.

reconstituyente *nm Med* tonic.

reconstrucción *nf* reconstruction.

reconstruir *vtr* to reconstruct.

recontar *vtr* **1** *(volver a calcular)* to recount, count again. **2** *(volver a narrar)* to recount, retell.

reconvención *nf* reproach, reprimand.

reconvenir *vtr* to reproach, reprimand.

reconversión *nf* reconversion; *Ind* modernization, rationalisation, reorganization.

reconvertir *vtr* to reconvert; *Ind* to modernize.

recopilación *nf* **1** *(resumen)* summary, resumé. **2** *(compendio)* compilation, collection.

recopilador,-a *nm,f* compiler.

recopilar *vtr* to compile, collect.

recórcholis *interj fam* crumbs!

récord *adj & nm* record; **batir un r.,** to beat a record; **en un tiempo r.,** in record time; **establecer un r.,** to set a record; **tener el r.,** to hold the record.

recordar I *vtr* **1** *(rememorar)* to remember; **ahora no lo recuerdo,** I can't remember; **si mal no recuerdo, que yo recuerde,** as far as I can remember. **2** *(traer a la memoria de otro)* to remind; **¿a quién te recuerda?,** who does she remind you of?; **r. algo a algn,** to remind sb of sth; **recuérdamelo cuando nos veamos,** remind me when we next meet. **II** *vi Am (despertar)* to wake up; **mañana, recuérdeme,** wake me up tomorrow.

recordatorio *nm* **1** *(aviso)* reminder. **2** *Rel (de defunción)* notice of death; *(de comunión)* souvenir of first communion.

recordman *nmf Dep* record holder.

recorrer *vtr* **1** *(distancia)* to cover, travel; *(país)* to tour, travel through *or* round; *(ciudad)* to visit, walk round; **recorrimos media ciudad antes de encontrar un bar abierto,** we walked round half the town before we found a bar open. **2** *(examinar)* to go over, look over; **he recorrido su última novela,** I had a look through his latest novel.

recorrido *nm* *(distancia)* distance travelled; *(trayecto)* trip, journey; *(itinerario)* itinerary, route; **la maratón tiene un r. accidentado,** the marathon course is very hilly; **trenes de largo r.,** intercity trains.

recortable *adj & nm* cutout; **muñeca r.,** cutout doll.

recortado,-a I *pp de* recortar. **II** *adj* **1** *(cortado)* cut out. **2** *(borde)* jagged. **III** *nm Arg (pistola)* gun.

recortar *vtr* **1** *(cortar lo sobrante)* to cut out. **2** *(cortar con arte)* to cut off, trim; *fig* **el gobierno ha recortado el presupuesto de defensa,** the government has cut defence spending.

recorte *nm* **1** *(acción)* cutting; *(de pelo)* trim, cut; *fig (disminución)* cut; **r. de las pensiones,** cut in pensions; **recortes del presupuesto,** budget *or* expenditure cuts. **2** *(trozo)* cutting, clipping, trimming; **r. de periódico,** newspaper cutting, press clipping.

recostado,-a I *pp de* recostar. **II** *adj* reclining, leaning, lying.

recostar I *vtr* to lean; **recuéstalo en la puerta,** lean it against the door. **II recostarse** *vr (tumbarse)* to lie down; *(sestear)* to take a short rest.

recova *nf* **1** *Am (mercado)* food market. **2** *Arg (portal)* doorway, porch.

recoveco *nm* **1** *(curva)* turn, bend; *fig* **hablar sin recovecos,** to speak plainly. **2** *(rincón)* nook, corner. **3** *Méx (adorno)* intricate ornamentation.

recreación *nf* **1** *(acción)* recreation. **2** *(diversión)* recreation, break, amusement.

recrear[1] I *vtr (divertir)* to amuse, entertain. **II recrearse** *vr* to amuse oneself, enjoy oneself; **r. con,** to take pleasure *or* delight in.

recrear[2] *vtr (crear de nuevo)* to recreate.

recreativo,-a *adj* recreational; **actividades recreativas,** recreational activities.

recremento *nm Med* recrement.

recreo *nm* **1** *(diversión)* recreation, amusement, entertainment; **viaje de r.,** pleasure trip. **2** *(en el colegio)* break, playtime, recreation.

recriminación *nf* recrimination, reproach.

recriminar *vtr (reprender)* to recriminate; *(reprochar)* to reproach; **le recriminaba su pereza,** she reproached him for being lazy.

recriminatorio,-a *adj* recriminatory.

recrudecer(se) *vtr & vr* to worsen, aggravate; **se ha recrudecido el frío,** it has grown much colder.

recrudecimiento *nm* *(empeoramiento)* worsening; *(aumento)* heightening, deepening, upsurge; **se teme un r. del temporal para las próximas horas,** it's feared that the storm will get worse over the next few hours.

rectal *adj Anat* rectal; **termómetro r.,** rectal thermometer.

rectangular *adj Geom* rectangular.

rectángulo,-a *Geom* **I** *adj* rectangular; **triángulo r.,** right-angled triangle. **II** *nm* rectangle.

rectificable *adj* rectifiable.

rectificación *nf* rectification; *(corrección)* correction, remedy.

rectificador,-a I *adj* rectifying. **II** *nm Elec* rectifier.

rectificar *vtr* to rectify; *(corregir)* to correct, remedy.

rectilíneo,-a *adj* straight; **describir una trayectoria rectilínea,** to go in a straight line.

rectitud *nf* straightness; *fig* uprightness, honesty, rectitude.

recto,-a I *adj* **1** *(derecho)* straight; **en línea recta,** in a straight line. **2** *(honesto)* upright, honest. **3** *Geom* right; **ángulo r.,** right angle. **II** *nm Anat* rectum. **III** *nf Geom* straight line; *(de carretera)* straight stretch; *Dep* **la r. final,** the home straight. **IV r.** *adv* straight (on); **sigue r.,** go straight on. ◆ **rectamente** *adj* honestly.

rector,-a I *adj (principio)* guiding, ruling; *(persona)* leading. **II** *nm,f Univ Rel* rector.

rectorado *nm* rectorship, rectorate.

rectoral *adj* rectorial.

rectoría *nf* 1 *(cargo)* rectorship, rectorate. 2 *(casa)* rectory.

rectriz *nf Orn* rectrix.

recua *nf (hilera de caballos, mulas)* drove, train; *fig* string, series, drove, train.

recuadro *nm Prensa* box.

recubierto,-a *pp de* **recubrir.**

recubrimiento *nm* covering.

recubrir *(pp recubierto)* *vtr* to cover.

recuento *nm* re-count, count; **hacer r. de votos,** to count *or* re-count the votes.

recuerdo *nm* 1 *(memoria)* memory, recollection; **tener un buen r. de,** to have nappy memories of. 2 *(regalo etc)* souvenir, keepsake; **me trajeron un r. de su viaje,** they brought me back a souvenir from their trip. 3 **recuerdos,** *(saludos)* regards, greetings; **dale r. de mi parte,** give him my regards; *(en carta)* **(muchos) r.,** best wishes.

recular *vi (retrasarse)* to go back, move back; *fig (ceder)* to back down.

recuperable *adj* recoverable, retrievable.

recuperación *nf* recovery, retrieval, recuperation; **el enfermo ha experimentado una r. asombrosa,** the patient has made an extraordinary recovery.

recuperar I *vtr* to recover, retrieve, recoup, regain; **hay que r. las clases perdidas,** you must make up the classes you have missed; **r. el afecto de algn,** to win back sb's affection; **r. el conocimiento,** to regain consciousness; **r. la salud,** to recover (one's health). **II recuperarse** *vr* to get over, recover, recuperate; **aún no se ha recuperado del susto,** he still hasn't got over the shock.

recurrente I *adj* 1 *Jur* to appealing. 2 *(repetido)* recurrent. **II** *nmf Jur* appealer.

recurrible *adj Jur* appealable.

recurrir *vi* 1 *Jur* to appeal. 2 **r. a,** *(acogerse) (a algn)* to turn to; *(a algo)* to make use of, resort to; **recurrió a mí para que me ayudara,** she turned to me for help; **r. a la violencia,** to resort to violence.

recurso *nm* 1 *(medio)* resort; **como último r.,** as a last resort. 2 *Jur* appeal; **r. de apelación,** remedy of appeal; **r. de casación,** high court appeal. 3 **recursos,** *(medios)* resources, means; **los r. naturales de un país,** the natural resources of a country.

recusable *adj* objectionable.

recusación *nf Jur* challenge, objection.

recusar *vtr Jur* to challenge, object to.

red *nf* 1 *(malla)* net, netting; *Peluq* hairnet. 2 *(sistema)* network, system; *Com* **r. de comercial,** sales network; **r. de espionaje,** spy ring; *Com* **r. de supermercados,** chain of supermarkets; *Ferroc* **r. ferroviaria,** rail *or* railway network. 4 *Elec* mains *pl.* 4 *Inform* lattice, network. 5 *fig (trampa)* trap; **caer en la r.,** to fall into the trap.

redacción *nf* 1 *(acción de escribir)* writing; *(estilo)* wording. 2 *Prensa* editing. 3 *(redactores)* editorial staff; *(oficina)* editorial office. 4 *(escrito)* composition, essay.

redactar *vtr* 1 *(escribir)* to write; *(carta)* to draft; *(con estilo)* to word. 2 *Prensa* to edit.

redactor,-a *nm,f Prensa* journalist; **r. jefe,** editor in chief.

redada *nf* 1 *(de peces)* catch, haul. 2 *(policial) (en un solo sitió)* raid; *(en varios lugares a la vez)* round-up.

redaño *nm* 1 *Anat (mesenterio)* mesentery. 2 **redaños,** *fam (valor)* guts.

redecilla *nf* 1 *Peluq* hairnet. 2 *Anat* reticulum.

redención *nf* redemption.

redentor,-a I *adj* redeeming. **II** *nm,f* redeemer; **el R.,** the Redeemer.

redentorista *nmf* Redemptorist.

redicho,-a *adj fam* affected, pretentious.

rediez *interj fam* 1 *(enfado)* damn it! 2 *(sorpresa)* good heavens!

redil *nm* fold, sheepfold; *fig* **volver al r.,** to return to the fold.

redimible *adj* redeemable.

redimir I *vtr* to redeem. **II redimirse** *vr* to redeem oneself.

rediós *interj fam* 1 *(asombro)* good heavens! 2 *(enfado)* damn!

redistribución *nf* redistribution; **la r. de la riqueza,** the redistribution of wealth.

redistribuir *vtr* to redistribute.

rédito *nm Fin* yield, interest.

redivivo,-a *adj* resuscitated, revived.

redoblar I *vtr* 1 *(intensificar)* to redouble, intensify; **r. los esfuerzos,** to redouble one's efforts. 2 *(torcer)* to bend back, clinch. **II** *vi (tambores)* to roll.

redoble *nm* roll; **el r. de los tambores,** the roll of drums.

redoma *nf Quím* flask.

redomado,-a *adj* 1 *(verdadero)* utter, out-and-out. 2 *(astuto)* sly.

redonda *nf* 1 *Mús* semibreve. 2 *(comarca)* region; **a la r.,** around; **no hay ningún hotel en cien millas a la r.,** there is not a single hotel within one hundred miles of here.

redondear I *vtr* 1 *(poner redondo)* to round, make round. 2 *(cantidad)* to round off, round up, make up to a round number; **para r. daremos un valor de 10 a la gravedad,** in round figures let's give gravity the value of 10. 3 *Cost* to level off. **II redondearse** *vr* 1 *(ponerse redondo)* to become round. 2 *(enriquecerse)* to become wealthy.

redondel *nm* 1 *fam (círculo)* circle, ring. 2 *Taur* ring, arena.

redondez *nf* roundness; **en toda la r. de la tierra,** in the whole wide world.

redondo,-a I *adj* 1 *(circular)* round; **cara redonda,** round face; *fig* **caer r.,** *(caerse)* to collapse; *(morir)* to drop dead; *fig* **mesa redonda,** round table. 2 *(rotundo)* categorical; **un no r.,** a flat refusal. 3 *(perfecto)* perfect; **un negocio r.,** an excellent business deal. 4 *(cantidad)* round; **en números redondos,** in round figures. **II** *nm Culin* topside.

redrojo *nm* 1 *Bot* small bunch of late grapes. 2 *fam fig* puny child, runt.

reducción *nf (disminución)* reduction.

reducido,-a I *pp de* **reducir. II** *adj* 1 *(disminuido)* reduced, decreased. 2 *(limitado)* limited, small.

reducir I *vtr* 1 *(disminuir)* to reduce, cut down, break down, decrease, shorten. 2 *(vencer)* to subdue; **r. al enemigo,** to subdue the enemy. 3 *Med* to set. 4 *Culin* to boil down. 5 *Mat* to reduce, convert; **r. las libras a kilogramos,** to convert pounds to kilos. **II** *vi Aut* to change to a lower gear. **III reducirse** *vr* 1 *(disminuirse)* to be reduced, diminish. 2 *(ahorrar)* to economize.

reductible *adj* reducible.

reducto *nm Mil* redoubt, stronghold; *fig* **utilizaremos la fuerza sólo como último r.,** we'll use force only as a last resort.

reductor,-a *adj* reducing.

redundancia *nf* redundancy, superfluousness.

redundante *adj* redundant.

redundar *vi* 1 *(rebosar)* to overflow; *(abundar)* to abound. 2 **r. en,** *(resultar)* to result in, lead to; **redundará en su propio beneficio,** it will be to his own advantage.

reduplicación *nf* reduplication, redoubling.

reduplicar *vtr* to reduplicate, redouble.

reedición *nf* reprint, reissue.

reedificación *nf* rebuilding.

reedificar *vtr* to rebuild.

reeditar *vtr* to reprint, reissue.

reeducación *nf* re-education.

reeducar *vtr* to re-educate.

reelección *nf Pol* re-election.

reelecto,-a *adj Pol* re-elected.

reelegir *vtr Pol* to re-elect.

reembolsable *adj* reimbursable.

reembolsar I *vtr (pagar)* to reimburse; *(deuda)* to repay; *(devolver)* to refund; **la empresa me ha reembolsado los gastos del viaje,** the company has reimbursed my travel expenses. **II reembolsarse** *vr (cobrar)* to be paid.

reembolso *nm* reimbursement; *(deuda)* repayment; *(devolución)* refund; **contra r.,** cash on delivery.

reemplazable *adj* replaceable.

reemplazar *vtr* to replace (**con,** with).

reemplazo *nm* replacement; *Mil* call-up.

reemprender *vtr* to start again.

reencarnación *nf* reincarnation.

reencarnarse *vr* to be reincarnated.

reencontrarse *vr* to find oneself again.

reencuentro *nm* reunion.

reenganchado *nm* re-enlisted soldier.

reenganchar(se) *vtr & vr Mil* to re-enlist.

reenganche *nm* re-enlistment.

reestreno *nm Teat* revival; *Cin* reshowing, rerun.

reestructuración *nf* restructuring, reorganization.

reestructurar *vtr* to restructure, reorganize.

reexpedir *vtr* to return.

reexportar *vtr* to re-export.

ref. *abr de* **referencia,** reference, ref.

refacción *nf* refreshment, snack.

refaccionar *vtr Am Aut* to repair, do up.

refajo *nm* petticoat, underskirt.

refanfinflarse *vr fam* not to give a toss; **tus problemas me la refanfinflan,** I don't give a toss about your problems.

refectorio *nm* refectory, dining hall, canteen.

referencia *nf* 1 *(relación)* reference; **con r. a,** with reference to; **hacer r. a,** to refer to. 2 **referencias,** *(informes)* references; **en aquella empresa siempre piden r.,** that company always asks for references.

referendo *nm,* **referéndum** *nm (pl referéndums)* referendum.

referente *adj* concerning, regarding (**a,** -).

referir I *vtr* 1 *(contar)* to tell, relate; **r. una historia,** to tell a story. 2 *(remitir)* to refer. 3 *CAm (blasfemar)* to swear. 4 *Méx (echar en cara)* to accuse. **II referirse** *vr (aludir)* to refer (**a,** to); **¿a quién te refieres?,** who do you mean?; **por lo que se refiere a eso,** as for that.

refilón (de) *loc adv* 1 *(oblicuamente)* obliquely; *(de lado)* sideways; **mirar algo de r.,** to look at sth out of the corner of one's eye. 2 *fig (de pasada)* briefly.

refinado,-a I *pp de* **refinar. II** *adj* refined. **III** *nm* refining; **r. del azúcar,** sugar refining.

refinador *nm* refiner.

refinamiento *nm* refinement.

refinar I *vtr* 1 *(azúcar, alcohol)* to refine. 2 *fig (perfeccionar)* to perfect, finish off. **II refinarse** *vr (perder la vulgaridad)* to polish oneself.

refinería *nf* refinery; **r. de petróleo,** oil refinery.

reflectante *adj Fís* reflective.

reflectar *vtr Fís* to reflect.

reflector,-a I *adj* reflecting. **II** *nm* 1 *(cuerpo que refleja)* reflector. 2 *Elec* spotlight, searchlight. 3 *Astron (telescopio)* reflector, reflecting telescope.

reflejar I *vtr* to reflect. **II reflejarse** *vr* to be reflected (**en,** in); **su imagen se refleja en el espejo,** his image is reflected in the mirror.

reflejo,-a I *adj* 1 *(luz, rayo)* reflected. 2 *(movimiento)* reflex. **II** *nm* 1 *(imagen)* reflection. 2 *(destello)* gleam, glint. 3 *Peluq* tint, rinse; **reflejos,** streaks, highlights. 4 *Anat* reflex; **r. condicionado,** conditioned reflex; **tener reflejos,** to have good reflexes.

réflex *Opt* **I** *nm inv (sistema)* reflex. **II** *nf inv (cámara)* reflex camera.

reflexión *nf* reflection; **con r.,** on reflection; **este tipo de decisiones necesitan una profunda r.,** this type of decision demands serious consideration.

reflexionar *vi* to reflect (**sobre,** on), think (**sobre,** about).

reflexivo,-a *adj* 1 *(persona)* reflective, thoughtful. 2 *Ling (verbo)* reflexive.

reflotar *vtr* to refloat.

reflujo *nm* ebb, ebb tide.

refocilar I *vtr impers* to enjoy, amuse. **II refocilarse** *vr* to enjoy oneself in a coarse way.

reforma *nf* 1 *(gen)* reform; **r. agraria,** agrarian reform; *Pol Fin* **r. fiscal,** tax reform. 2 *Hist* **la R.,** the Reformation. 3 **reformas,** *Constr* alterations, repairs, improvements; **'cerrado por r.',** 'closed for alterations'.

reformador,-a I *adj* reforming. **II** *nm,f* reformer.

reformar I *vtr* to reform; *Constr* to renovate, do up; **r. una casa,** to renovate a house. **II reformarse** *vr (corregirse)* to reform oneself.

reformatorio *nm* reformatory, reform school; **r. de menores,** remand home.

reformismo *nm* reformism.

reformista *adj & nmf* reformist.

reforzado,-a I *pp de* **reforzar. II** *adj* reinforced, strengthened.

reforzar *vtr* to reinforce, strengthen.

refracción *nf Fís* refraction; **índice de r.,** refractive index; **r. doble,** double refraction, birefringence.

refractar(se) *vtr & vr Fís* to refract.

refractario,-a *adj* 1 *Téc* heat-resistant. 2 *(persona) (poco dispuesta)* unwilling, reluctant; *(opuesto)* opposed; **r. a cualquier cambio,** opposed to all change.

refractivo,-a *adj* refractive.

refractor *nm Opt Astron* refractor, refracting telescope.

refrán *nm* proverb, saying; **como dice el r.,** as the saying goes.

refranero *nm* collection of proverbs or sayings.

refregar *vtr* to rub vigorously; *fig* **r. algo a algn,** to rub sth in.

refregón *nm* rub, rubbing.

refreír *(pp refrito)* *vtr (volver a freír)* to fry again; *(freír demasiado)* to overdo.

refrenar I *vtr* 1 *(al caballo)* to rein in. 2 *(contener)* to restrain, curb, control; **r. las pasiones,** to curb one's passions. **II refrenarse** *vr* to restrain *or* control oneself.

refrendar *vtr* 1 *(firmar)* to endorse, countersign. 2 *(pasaporte)* to stamp.

refrendo *nm* 1 *(firma)* endorsement, countersignature. 2 *(sello)* stamp, visa.

refrescante *adj* refreshing.

refrescar I *vtr* to refresh, cool; *fig* **r. el inglés,** to brush up one's English; *fig* **r. la memoria,** to refresh one's memory. **II** *vi* 1 *(del tiempo)* to turn cool. 2 *(bebida)* to be refreshing. **III refrescarse** *vr* 1 *(tomar el aire)* to take a breath of fresh air. 2 *(beber)* to have a drink.

refresco *nm* 1 *(comida)* snack. 2 *(bebida)* soft drink, refreshments *pl.*

refriega *nf (lucha)* scuffle, brawl; *(escaramuza)* skirmish.

refrigeración *nf* (*enfriamento*) refrigeration, cooling; (*aire acondicionado*) air conditioning. **2** (*aperitivo*) snack.

refrigerado,-a I *pp de* **refrigerar**. II *adj* (*enfriado*) refrigerated, cooled; (*con aire acondicionado*) air-conditioned; **local r.**, air-conditioned premises.

refrigerador *nm* refrigerator, fridge.

refrigerante I *adj* refrigerating, cooling. II *nm* *Quím* refrigerant.

refrigerar *vtr* (*enfriar*) to refrigerate; (*con aire acondicionado*) to air-condition.

refrigerio *nm* snack, refreshments *pl*.

refringente *adj* *Fís* refringent.

refrito,-a I *pp de* **refreír**. II *adj* refried. III *nm* *fam* (*cosa rehecha*) rehash.

refucilo *nm* lightning.

refuerzo *nm* **1** (*fortalecimiento*) reinforcement, strengthening. **2 refuerzos,** *Mil* reinforcements.

refugiado,-a I *pp de* **refugiar**. II *adj* refugee. III *nm, f* refugee; **r. político,** political refugee.

refugiar I *vtr* to shelter, give refuge to. II **refugiarse** *vr* to shelter, take refuge; **r. de la lluvia,** to shelter from the rain.

refugio *nm* **1** (*protección*) refuge, shelter; **r. antiaéreo,** air-raid shelter; **r. atómico,** (nuclear) fallout shelter; *fig* **su amistad es un r. para mí,** her friendship is a source of comfort to me. **2** *Aut* (traffic) island.

refulgencia *nf* radiance, brilliance.

refulgente *adj* radiant, brilliant.

refulgir *vi* (*brillar*) to shine; (*resplandecer*) to glitter, sparkle.

refundición *nf* **1** *Metal* recasting. **2** *Lit Teat* adaptation.

refundir I *vtr* **1** *Metal* to recast. **2** *Lit Teat* to adapt. II **refundirse** *vr Am* (*perderse*) to get lost.

refunfuñar *vi* to grumble, moan, complain.

refunfuñón,-ona *fam* I *adj* grumbling, moaning. II *nm, f* grumbler, moaner.

refutable *adj* refutable, disprovable.

refutación *nf* refutation, disproof.

refutar *vtr* to refute, disprove.

Reg. *abr de* **registro**, register, reg.

regadera *nf* (*recipiente*) watering can; *fam* **estar como una r.,** to be as mad as a hatter.

regadío,-a I *adj* irrigable. II *nm* **1** (*acción*) irrigation, watering; **cultivo de r.,** irrigation farming. **2** (*tierras*) irrigated land.

regalado,-a I *pp de* **regalar**. II *adj* **1** (*de regalo*) given as a present; (*gratis*) free. **2** (*muy barato*) dirt cheap. **3** (*agradable*) pleasant, comfortable; **lleva una vida regalada,** he has *or* leads an easy *or* comfortable life. **4** (*delicado*) delicate.

regalar I *vtr* **1** (*dar*) to give (as a present); **con cada caja te regalan una entrada,** there's a free ticket with each packet; **lo regalé,** I gave it away; **¿qué quieres que te regale?,** what present would you like?; **regálale una corbata,** get him a tie. **2** (*halagar*) to flatter; **r. el oído,** to be a pleasure to hear. **3** (*mimar*) to pamper, spoil. II **regalarse** *vr* to spoil oneself (**con,** with).

regalía *nf* **1** *Hist* royal prerogative. **2** *fig* (*privilegios*) privilege, prerogative. **3** (*derechos de autor*) author's rights *pl*.

regaliz *nm* *Bot* liquorice, *US* licorice.

regalo *nm* **1** (*obsequio*) gift, present; **dar (algo) de r.,** to give (sth) as a present. **2** (*comodidad*) pleasure, comfort; **vivir con gran r.,** to live a life of luxury. **3** (*exquisitez*) delicacy.

regañadientes (a) *loc adv* reluctantly, unwillingly, grudgingly.

regañar I *vtr fam* to scold, tell off. II *vi* **1** (*reñir*) to argue, quarrel, fall out. **2** (*refunfuñar*) to grumble, moan, complain.

regañina *nf* **1** (*reprensión*) scolding, telling-off. **2** (*riña*) quarrel, argument.

regañón,-ona *fam* I *adj* grumpy, irritable. II *nm, f* grumbler, moaner.

regar *vtr* **1** (*esparcir agua*) to water. **2** (*lavar la calle*) to wash down, hose down. **3** *fig* (*esparcir*) to scatter, sprinkle; (*derramar*) to pour. **4** *fig* (*beber*) to wash down.

regata[1] *nf Agr* irrigation channel.

regata[2] *nf Náut* regatta, boat race.

regate *nm* dodge; *Dep* dribble.

regateador,-a *nm, f* haggler.

regatear[1] I *vtr* **1** (*precio*) to haggle over, barter for. **2** (*escatimar*) to be sparing with; **no regatearon esfuerzos,** they spared no effort. II *vi* **1** (*comerciar*) to haggle, bargain. **2** *Dep* to dribble.

regatear[2] *vi* **1** *Náut* to race. **2** *Col Cuba PR* (*caballos*) to race.

regateo *nm* **1** (*precios*) haggling, bargaining. **2** *Dep* dribbling.

regato *nm* **1** (*charco*) pool. **2** (*arroyo*) stream.

regazo *nm* lap.

regencia *nf* regency.

regeneración *nf* regeneration.

regenerador,-a I *adj* regenerative. II *nm, f* regenerator.

regenerar *vtr* to regenerate.

regenta *nf Pol* regent.

regentar *vtr* **1** *Pol* to rule, govern. **2** (*tener un cargo*) to hold. **3** (*dirigir*) to manage, direct.

regente *nmf Pol* regent. II *nm* **1** (*magistrado*) magistrate. **2** (*director*) manager.

regicida I *adj* regicidal. II *nmf* regicide.

regicidio *nm* regicide.

regidor,-a *nm, f* **1** (*concejal*) town councillor. **2** *Teat* stage manager.

regiego,-a *adj Méx* untameable.

régimen *nm* (*pl* **regímenes**) **1** *Pol* regime, rule, system; **antiguo r.,** old regime. **2** *Med* diet, regime, regimen; **estar a r.,** to be on a diet. **3** *Téc* (*velocidad*) speed. **4** (*condiciones*) rules *pl*; **r. tormentoso,** stormy weather.

regimiento *nm Mil* regiment.

regio,-a *adj* **1** (*real*) royal, regal. **2** *fig* (*magnífico*) splendid, majestic; (*suntuoso*) sumptuous, luxurious, elegant.

región *nf* region.

regional *adj* regional. ◆ **regionalmente** *adv* regionally.

regionalismo *nm* regionalism.

regionalista *adj & nmf* regionalist.

regir I *vtr* **1** (*gobernar*) to govern, rule. **2** (*dirigir*) to direct, manage. II *vi* (*estar vigente*) to be in force, apply, prevail; **el mes que rige,** the current month; *fam* **no r.,** to have a screw loose. III **regirse** *vr* to be guided, go (**por,** by); **siempre me rijo por este diccionario,** I always go by what this dictionary says.

registrado,-a I *pp de* **registrar**. II *adj* registered, recorded, noted, listed; **marca registrada,** registered trademark.

registrador,-a I *adj* registering, recording; **caja registradora,** cash register. II *nm, f* registerer, recorder.

registrar I *vtr* **1** (*examinar*) to search, inspect, look through; (*cachear*) to frisk; **registraron sus maletas,** their suitcases were searched. **2** (*inscribir*) to register, record, note. **3** (*grabar*) to record. II **registrarse** *vr* **1** (*inscribirse*) to register, enrol. **2** (*detectarse*) to be recorded *or* reported; **se ha registrado un ligero temblor,** a slight tremor has been recorded. **3** (*ocurrir*) to happen.

registro *nm* 1 *(inspección)* search, inspection, scrutiny. 2 *(inscripción)* registration, recording. 3 *(libro)* register; *(oficina)* registry; **r. civil,** births, marriages and deaths register; *(oficina)* registry office; **r. de la propiedad,** property registry; **r. electoral,** electoral roll. 4 *Mús* register; *(de órgano)* stop; *fig* **tocar todos los registros,** to pull out all the stops. 5 *Inform* register.

regla *nf* 1 *(norma)* rule, regulation, norm, custom; **en r.,** in order; **la excepción confirma la r.,** the exception confirms the rule; **las reglas del juego,** the rules of the game; **por r. general,** as a (general) rule; **r. de oro,** golden rule; **salir de la r.,** to overstep the mark. 2 *(instrumento)* ruler; **r. de cálculo,** slide rule. 3 *Mat* rule; **r. de tres,** rule of three; *fam* **sabe leer y escribir y las cuatro reglas,** he knows the three Rs. 4 *Med* period; **tener la r.,** to have one's period.

reglado,-a *adj* ruled, lined.

reglaje *nm* adjustment.

reglamentación *nf* 1 *(acción)* regulation. 2 *(reglamento)* regulations *pl*, rules *pl*.

reglamentar *vtr* to regulate.

reglamentario,-a *adj* statutory, required, prescribed; *Mil* **arma reglamentaria,** regulation gun. ◆ **reglamentariamente** *adv* in due form, statutorily.

reglamento *nm* regulations *pl*, rules *pl*.

reglar *vtr* 1 *(regular)* to regulate. 2 *(ajustar)* to adjust. 3 *(papel)* to rule, draw a line.

regleta *nf Impr* space.

regletear *vtr Impr* to space.

regocijar I *vtr* to delight, amuse. II **regocijarse** *vr* to be delighted, rejoice; **r. de** *or* **con,** to delight in, take pleasure in.

regocijo *nm* 1 *(placer)* delight, joy, happiness. 2 *(alborozo)* rejoicing, merriment.

regodearse *vr fam* to delight (con, in); *(con crueldad)* to take a cruel delight (con, in).

regodeo *nm fam* delight; *(cruel)* cruel delight.

regodeón,-ona *adj Am* fussy.

regordete,-a *adj fam* plump, tubby, chubby.

regresar *vi* to return, go back, come back.

regresión *nf* regression; *(decaimiento)* deterioration, decline; **en vías de r.,** on the decline.

regresivo,-a *adj* regressive.

regreso *nm* return; **a mi r.,** on my return; **estar de r.,** to be back; **viaje de r.,** return journey.

regüeldo *nm vulg* burp, belch.

reguera *nf* 1 *(canal)* irrigation channel. 2 *SAm Náut (ancla)* anchor; *(cable)* cable.

reguero *nm* 1 *(canal)* irrigation channel. 2 *(corriente)* trickle of water. 3 *(señal)* *(de humo)* trail; *(de sangre)* trickle; **propagarse como un r. de pólvora,** to spread like wildfire.

regulable *adj* adjustable.

regulación *nf* 1 *(control)* regulation, control. 2 *(ajuste)* adjustment.

regulador,-a I *adj* regulating. II *nm* regulator; *Rad TV* **r. de volumen,** volume control.

regular I *vtr* 1 *(medir)* to regulate, control. 2 *(ajustar)* to adjust. II *adj* 1 *(conforme a una regla)* regular; **por lo r.,** as a rule; *Ling* **verbo r.,** regular verb. 2 *fam (mediano)* average, so-so; **¿qué tal la comida?** -**r.,** how was the food? -average. ◆ **regularmente** *adv* 1 *(comúnmente)* regularly. 2 *(medianamente)* so-so.

regularidad *nf* regularity; **con r.,** regularly.

regularización *nf* regularization.

regularizar *vtr* to regularize.

regurgitar *vtr* to regurgitate.

regusto *nm* aftertaste.

rehabilitación *nf* rehabilitation; *(en rango, reputación)* rehabilitation, reinstatement.

rehabilitar I *vtr* to rehabilitate; *(en rango, reputación)* to rehabilitate, reinstate. II **rehabilitarse** *vr* to rehabilitate oneself.

rehacer *(pp rehecho)* I *vtr* 1 *(volver a hacer)* to redo, do again. 2 *(reconstruir)* to remake, rebuild; *fig* **tendrá que r. su vida,** she will have to rebuild her life. II **rehacerse** *vr* 1 *(recuperarse)* to recover, recuperate. 2 *fig (dominarse)* to pull oneself together.

rehén *nm* hostage.

rehilete *nm* 1 *(flechilla)* dart. 2 *(volante)* shuttle cock.

rehogar *vtr Culin* to brown.

rehostia *nf arg ofens* **ser la r.,** *(bueno)* to be fucking good; *(malo)* to be bloody awful.

rehuir *vtr* to shun, avoid; **no rehúyas la pregunta,** don't avoid the question.

rehusar *vtr* to refuse, decline, turn down; **rehusé contestar,** I refused to answer.

reidor,-a *adj* happy, laughing.

Reikiavik *n* Reykjavik.

reimportar *vtr* to reimport.

reimpresión *nf Impr* 1 *(acción)* reprinting. 2 *(resultado)* reprint.

reimprimir *(pp reimpreso)* *vtr Impr* to reprint.

reina *nf* 1 *(monarca)* queen; *Zool* **abeja r.,** queen bee; **la r. madre,** the Queen Mother; *fig* **r. de belleza,** beauty queen. 2 *fam (cariño)* love, ducky; **¡gracias, r.!,** thanks, love! 3 *Ajedrez* queen.

reinado *nm* reign.

reinante *adj (que reina)* reigning, ruling; *(prevaleciente)* prevailing; **el buen tiempo r.,** the current spell of good weather.

reinar *vi* to reign; *fig* **volvió a r. el silencio,** silence reigned once more.

reincidencia *nf* relapse; *Jur* recidivism.

reincidente *adj & nmf* relapsing; *Jur* recidivist.

reincidir *vi* to relapse, fall back (en, into); **r. en el delito,** relapse into crime.

reincorporación *nf* reincorporation; *(a un cargo)* reinstatement, re-employment.

reincorporar I *vtr* to reincorporate; *(a un cargo)* to reinstate, re-employ. II **reincorporarse** *vr* to rejoin; **se reincorporó al ejército,** he rejoined the army.

reineta *nf Bot* pippin.

reingresar *vi* to return, re-enter, rejoin; **reingresó en el coro,** she rejoined the choir.

reingreso *nm* return, re-entry.

reino *nm* kingdom; **el r. de los Cielos,** the Kingdom of Heaven; **el r. vegetal,** the vegetable kingdom.

Reino Unido *n* **el R. U.,** the United Kingdom.

reinserción *nf* adaptation, reintegration; **r. social,** social reintegration.

reinsertar(se) *vtr & vr* to reintegrate.

reintegrable *adj Fin* returnable, repayable.

reintegración *nf* 1 *(reincorporación)* reinstatement. 2 *(pago)* refund.

reintegrar I *vtr* 1 *(reincorporar)* to reinstate, restore. 2 *(pagar)* to reimburse, refund. II **reintegrarse** *vr* to return (a, to); **se reintegró a su trabajo,** she returned to her job.

reintegro *nm* 1 *(reincorporación)* reinstatement. 2 *(pago)* reimbursement, refund, repayment. 3 *(en lotería)* winning of one's stake.

reír I *vtr* to laugh at; **le ríe todos sus chistes,** he laughs at all her jokes. II *vi* to laugh; *irón* **¡no me hagas r.!,** don't make me laugh!; *prov* **quien ríe el último ríe mejor,** he who laughs last laughs longest. III **reírse** *vr* 1 *(mostrar alegría)* to laugh; **¡no te rías!,** don't laugh!; **r. a**

carcajadas, to roar with laughter. **2** *(mofarse)* to laugh **(de,** at), make fun **(de,** of); **¿de qué te ríes?,** what are you laughing at?; **siempre se ríen de mis consejos,** they always make fun of my advice.

reiteración *nf* reiteration.

reiterar *vtr* to reiterate, repeat.

reiterativo,-a *adj* repetitive, repetitious, reiterative. ◆ **reiteradamente** *adv* repeatedly, reiteratively.

reivindicación *nf* claim, demand.

reivindicar *vtr* to claim, demand; **el atentado fue reivindicado por los terroristas,** the terrorists claimed responsibility for the attack.

reivindicativo,-a *adj* claiming, demanding.

reja¹ *nf Agr* ploughshare, *US* plowshare.

reja² *nf* **1** *(de ventana)* grill, grille, grating, bar; *fam* **estar entre rejas,** to be behind bars. **2** *Méx (zurcido)* darn, mend, patch.

rejego,-a *adj* **1** *Am (manso)* tame. **2** *CAm Méx (indomable)* untameable. **3** *Méx (irascible)* irascible, irritable.

rejilla *nf (de ventana)* grill, grille; *(chimeneas)* latticework; *(de horno)* gridiron; *(de ventilador)* grill; *(de silla)* wickerwork; *(para equipaje)* luggage rack; *Aut* **r. del radiador,** radiator grille.

rejón *nm Taur* lance.

rejoneador,-a *nm,f Taur* bullfighter on horseback.

rejonear *vtr Taur* to fight on horseback

rejoneo *nm Taur* bullfighting on horseback.

rejuvenecedor,-a *adj* rejuvenating, rejuvenescent.

rejuvenecer I *vtr* to rejuvenate. **II rejuvenecerse** *vr* to become rejuvenated.

rejuvenecimiento *nm* rejuvenation, rejuvenescence.

relación *nf* **1** *(correspondencia)* relation, relationship; *(conexión)* connection, link; **con** *or* **en r. a,** with regard to; **relaciones diplomáticas,** diplomatic relations; **relaciones públicas,** public relations; **tener buenas relaciones,** to be well connected; **tener relaciones con un chico,** to be going out with a boy. **2** *(lista)* list, record; **la r. de los pasajeros,** the passenger list. **3** *(relato)* account, telling. **4** *Mat* ratio; *Téc* **r. de compresión,** compression ratio.

relacionado,-a I *pp* de **relacionar. II** *adj* related, connected, linked; **estar bien r.,** to be well connected; **r. con,** related to, connected with.

relacionar I *vtr* **1** *(poner en relación)* to relate, connect, associate **(con,** with). **2** *(listar)* to list. **II relacionarse** *vr* **1** *(estar conectado)* to be related, be connected. **2** *(alternar)* to mix, get acquainted.

relajación *nf (gen)* relaxation; *(aflojamiento)* slackening, loosening.

relajado,-a I *pp* de **relajar. II** *adj (gen)* relaxed; *(aflojado)* loose, slack.

relajante *adj* relaxing.

relajar I *vtr (gen)* to relax; *(aflojar)* to loosen, slacken. **II relajarse** *vr* **1** *(descansar)* to relax; *(viciarse)* to let oneself go. **2** *(dilatarse)* to slacken, loosen.

relajo *nm* depravity, dissoluteness.

relamer I *vtr* to lick. **II relamerse** *vr* to lick one's lips.

relamido,-a *adj (afectado)* affected; *(pulcro)* prim and proper.

relámpago *nm* flash of lightning; *fig* **guerra r.,** blitzkrieg; *fig* **pasó como un r.,** he flashed past; *fig* **visita r.,** lightning visit.

relampagueante *adj* flashing.

relampaguear *vi impers* to flash.

relampagueo *nm* **1** *(relámpagos)* lightning. **2** *(centelleo)* flashing.

relanzamiento *nm* relaunch.

relanzar *vtr* to relaunch.

relatar *vtr (narrar)* to narrate, relate; *(hacer relación)* to report, tell.

relatividad *nf* relativity; *Fis* **teoría de la r.,** theory of relativity.

relativismo *nm Filos* relativism.

relativista *adj* & *nmf* relativist.

relativo,-a I *adj* relative; **en lo r. a,** with regard to, referring to, concerning; **r. a,** relative to. **II** *nm Ling* relative.

relato *nm* **1** *(cuento)* tale, story. **2** *(informe)* report, account.

relax *nm fam* **1** *(descanso)* relaxation. **2** *(prostitución)* call-girl service.

relé *nm Elec* relay.

releer *vtr* to reread.

relegación *nf* relegation.

relegar *vtr* to relegate.

relente *nm* dew.

relevancia *nf* **1** *(significancia)* relevance. **2** *(importancia)* importance.

relevante *adj* **1** *(significante)* relevant. **2** *(importante)* important.

relevar *vtr* **1** *(sustituir)* to relieve, take over from; *Mil* to change, relieve. **2** *(destituir)* to dismiss, remove from office. *(eximir)* to exempt from.

relevo *nm* **1** *Mil* relief, change (of the guard). **2** *Dep* relay; **carrera de relevos,** relay race.

relicario *nm* **1** *Rel* reliquary. **2** *(estuche)* locket; *(caja)* box.

relieve *nm Arte* relief; **en r.,** in relief; *fig* **poner de r.,** to emphasize.

religión *nf* religion; **entrar en r.,** to take vows.

religiosidad *nf* religiousness. religiosity.

religioso,-a I *adj* religious. **II** *nm, f (hombre)* monk; *(mujer)* nun. ◆ **religiosamente** *adv* religiously.

relinchar *vi* to neigh, whinny.

relincho *nm* neigh, whinny.

reliquia *nf* relic.

rellano *nm* landing.

rellenar *vtr* **1** *(escribir)* to fill in, fill up; **r. un formulario,** to fill in a form. **2** *(llenar del todo)* to cram, pack, stuff **(de,** with). **3** *Culin (un ave)* to stuff; *(un pastel)* to fill; *Cost (un cojín)* to fill. **4** *(volver a llenar)* to refill, fill again.

relleno,-a I *adj (lleno)* crammed, packed, stuffed **(de,** with); *Culin* **pastel r.,** cake with a (cream) filling; *Culin* **pavo r.,** stuffed turkey. **II** *nm Culin (de aves)* stuffing; *(de pasteles)* filling; *Cost* filling, padding.

reló *nm,* **reloj** *nm (gen)* clock; *(de pulsera)* watch; **carrera contra r.,** race against the clock; **r. de arena,** hourglass; **r. de caja,** grandfather clock; **r. de pulsera,** wristwatch; **r. de sol,** sundial; **reloj despertador,** alarm clock.

relojería *nf (arte)* watchmaking, clockmaking. **2** *(tienda, taller)* watchmaker's, clockmaker's. ■ **bomba de r.,** time bomb.

relojero,-a *nm,f* watchmaker, clockmaker.

reluciente *adj* shining, gleaming, glittering.

relucir *vi* **1** *(brillar)* to shine, gleam, glitter; *prov* **no es oro todo lo que reluce,** all that glitters is not gold. **2** *(destacarse)* to excel, stand out, shine; **sacar a r. un tema,** to bring up a subject.

reluctancia *nf Fis* reluctance, reluctancy.

reluctante *adj* reluctant.

relumbrar *vi* to shine, gleam, dazzle.

relumbrón *nm* **1** *(destello)* flash, glare. **2** *(ostentación)* flashiness, ostentation; **de r.,** flashy.

reluzco *indic pres véase* **relucir.**

remachar *vtr* **1** *Téc* to drive home, hammer. **2** *fig (confirmar)* to drive home, hammer home, stress.

remache *nm* rivet.

remanente I *adj (resto)* residual, remaining; *(saldo)* remainder; *(extra)* surplus. **II** *nm (restos)* remainder, remains; *(extra)* surplus.

remangar I *vtr (mangas, pantalones)* to roll up; *(camisa)* to tuck up. **II remangarse** *vr* **r. la camisa,** to tuck up one's shirt; **r. las mangas/los pantalones,** to roll up one's sleeves/trousers.

remanso *nm* **1** *(estanque)* pool; *(agua estancada)* backwater. **2** *(lugar tranquilo)* quiet place; **r. de paz,** oasis of peace.

remar *vi Dep* to row.

remarcable *adj* remarkable.

remarcar *vtr* to stress, underline.

rematado,-a I *pp* de **rematar. II** *adj* utter, absolute, out-and-out; **loco r.,** as mad as a hatter. ♦ **rematadamente** *adv* totally, completely.

rematador,-a *nm,f* **1** *Dep* striker. **2** *Arg Urug (comprador)* auctioneer.

rematar *vtr* **1** *(acabar)* to finish off, round off, complete, put the finishing touches to. **2** *Com (precios)* to knock down; *(vender más barato)* to sell off cheaply; *(en subastas)* to auction. **3** *(matar)* to kill, finish off. **4** *Dep* to take a shot at goal, shoot.

remate *nm* **1** *(final)* end, finish; **de r.,** utter, utterly; **para r.,** to crown it all; **por r.,** finally, in the end; *Com* **precios de r.,** knockdown prices. **2** *Dep* attempt at goal. **3** *(en subastas)* auction.

rembolsar *vtr véase* **reembolsar.**

rembolso *nm véase* **reembolso.**

remedar *vtr (imitar)* to imitate, copy; *(con mímica)* to mimic; *(mofarse)* to mock.

remediable *adj* remediable, that can be corrected.

remediar *vtr* **1** *(poner remedio)* to remedy; *(reparar)* to repair, make good. **2** *(resolver)* to solve; **así no remedias nada,** you won't solve anything that way. **3** *(ayudar)* to help, assist. **4** *(evitar)* to avoid, prevent; **no pude remediarlo,** I couldn't help it.

remedio *nm (cura)* remedy cure; *(solución)* solution; **como último r.,** as a lasl resort; **hay que poner r. a esto,** something must be done about this; **no tener más r. que,** to have no choice but to; **sin r.,** without fail; *fam* **¡no tienes r.!,** you're hopeless!

remedo *nm* **1** *(imitación)* imitation, copy; *(mímica)* mimicry, mimicking. **2** *(parodia)* parody; *(burla)* travesty, mockery.

remembranza *nf,* **rememoración** *nf* remembrance, recollection.

rememorar *vtr* to remember, recall.

remendar *vtr* **1** *(corregir)* to mend, repair. **2** *Cost* to mend; *(ropas)* to patch; *(calcetines)* to darn.

remendón,-ona I *adj* mended; **zapatero r.,** cobbler. **II** *nm* mender.

remero,-a *nm, f Dep* rower; *(hombre)* oarsman; *(mujer)* oarswoman.

remesa *nf* *(envío)* *(de mercancías)* consignment, shipment; *(de dinero)* remittance.

remiendo *nm (arreglo)* mend; *(de calcetín)* darn; *(parche)* patch.

remilgado,-a *adj (afectado)* affected; *(melindroso)* fussy, finicky; *(mojigato)* prudish.

remilgo *nm (amaneramiento)* affectation; *(gazmoñería)* prudishness, primness; **andar con remilgos,** to make a fuss, be fussy.

reminiscencia *nf* reminiscence.

remirado,-a *adj* over-cautious.

remirar I *vtr (volver a mirar)* to have a second look at. **II remirarse** *vr (esmerarse)* to take great care.

remisión *nf* **1** *Rel* remission, forgiveness. **2** *Med* remission. **3** *(referencia)* reference. **4** *(envío)* sending.

remiso,-a *adj* remiss, negligent.

remite *nm (en sobre, paquete)* sender's name and address.

remitente *nmf* sender; **'devuélvase al r.',** 'return to sender'.

remitir I *vtr* **1** *(enviar)* to send, remit. **2** *(referir)* to refer; **la nota nos remite a la página tres,** the note refers us to page three. **3** *(perdonar los pecados)* to forgive. **4** *(aplazar)* to postpone, adjourn; **tuvimos que r. la reunión hasta el lunes,** we had to postpone the meeting until Monday. **5** *(fiebre, temporal)* to subside. **II remitirse** *vr (atenerse)* to refer (**a,** to).

remo *nm* **1** *(instrumento)* oar, paddle; **ir a r.,** to row. **2** *(deporte)* rowing; **club de r.,** rowing club. **3** *Anat (brazo)* arm; *(pierna)* leg.

remodelación *nf* *(modificación)* reshaping; *(reorganización)* reorganization; *Pol* **r. ministerial** *or* **del gobierno,** cabinet reshuffle.

remodelar *vtr (modificar)* to reshape; *(reorganizar)* to reorganize.

remojar *vtr* **1** *(empapar)* to soak (**en,** in). **2** *fam (celebrar)* to celebrate, drink to. **3** *Am (dar propina a)* to leave a tip for.

remojo *nm* **1** *(puesto en agua)* soaking; **dejar** *or* **poner en r.,** to soak, leave to soak. **2** *Am (propina)* tip.

remojón *nm fam* soaking, drenching.

remolacha *nf Bot* beetroot; **r. azucarera,** sugar beet.

remolachero,-a *adj* beet.

remolcador *nm* **1** *Náut* tug, tugboat. **2** *Aut* breakdown truck, *US* tow truck.

remolcar *vtr* to tow.

remolino *nm* **1** *(de agua)* whirlpool, eddy; *(de aire)* whirlwind; *(de polvo)* whirl, cloud. **2** *(de pelo) US* cowlick. **3** *(de gente)* throng.

remolón,-ona *adj* lazy, slack; **hacerse el r.,** to shirk, slack.

remolonear *vi* to shirk, slack.

remolque *nm* **1** *(acción)* towing. **2** *(vehículo)* trailer; **a r.,** in tow; *fig* **ir a r. de algn,** to live in sb's shadow.

remontar I *vtr* **1** *(subir)* to go up; **r. el vuelo,** to soar; **r. un río,** to sail up a river. **2** *(superar)* to overcome. **II remontarse** *vr (pájaros, aviones)* to soar. **2** *(datar)* to go back, date back (**a,** to); **es una tradición que remonta al siglo XV,** it is a tradition which dates back to the 15th century.

remoquete *nm* **1** *fig* quip. **2** *fam* nickname.

rémora *nf* **1** *(pez)* remora. **2** *fig (estorbo)* hindrance; *(problema)* drawback.

remorder I *vtr (conciencia)* to cause remorse to; *(inquietar)* to trouble; **me remuerde el haberle mentido,** I feel guilty about having lied to her. **II remorderse** *vr (conciencia)* to suffer remorse; *(inquietarse)* to fret.

remordimiento *nm* remorse; **tener remordimientos,** to feel remorse.

remoto,-a *adj* remote, faraway; *fig* **no tengo la más remota idea,** I haven't got the faintest idea. ♦ **remotamente** *adv* remotely, vaguely; **ni r.,** not in the slightest, far from it.

remover *vtr* **1** *(trasladar)* to move over. **2** *(tierra)* to turn over. **3** *(líquido)* to shake up. **4** *(comida etc)* to stir; *(ensalada)* to toss. **5** *(reavivar)* to revive. **6** *fig (alterar)* to change; **este nuevo problema lo ha removido todo,** this new problem has turned everything upside down. **7** *(destituir)* to remove (from office), oust.

remozamiento *nm* **1** *(persona)* rejuvenation. **2** *(fachada)* modernization; *(decoración)* redecoration; *(limpieza)* brightening up.

remozar *vtr (fachada)* to modernize; *(decorar)* to redecorate; *(limpiar)* to brighten up.

remplazable *adj* replaceable.

remplazar *vtr véase* **reemplazar.**

remplazo *nm véase* **reemplazo.**

remuneración *nf* remuneration, pay.

remunerado,-a I *pp de* **remunerar.** II *adj* paid; **un trabajo bien r.,** a well-paid job.

remunerar *vtr* to remunerate, pay, reward.

renacentista *adj* Renaissance; **pintura r.,** Renaissance painting.

renacer *vi* 1 to be reborn. 2 *fig (revivir)* to revive, come back to life; *(fortalecer)* to acquire new strength.

renaciente *adj* renascent, reviving.

renacimiento *nm* 1 rebirth. 2 *(periodo histórico)* **el R.,** the Renaissance. 3 *fig* revival.

renacuajo *nm* 1 *Zool* tadpole. 2 *fam (niño pequeño)* shrimp.

renal *adj* renal, kidney; **afección r.,** kidney disease.

Renania *nf* Rhineland.

renano,-a I *adj* of *or* from the Rhine. II *nm,f* Rhinelander.

renazco *indic pres véase* **renacer.**

rencilla *nf* quarrel; **rencillas familiares,** family quarrels.

rencilloso,-a *adj* quarrelsome.

rencor *nm* *(hostilidad)* rancour, *US* rancor; *(resentimiento)* resentment; **guardar r. a algn,** to have a grudge against sb, bear sb malice.

rencoroso,-a *adj (hostil)* rancorous; *(resentido)* resentful; *(malicioso)* spiteful.

rendición *nf* surrender.

rendido,-a I *pp de* **rendir.** II *adj* 1 *(sumiso)* submissive; *(cortés)* humble; **admirador r.,** devoted admirer. 2 *(muy cansado)* exhausted, worn out.

rendija *nf* crack, split.

rendimiento *nm* 1 *(producción)* yield, output. 2 *Téc (de máquina, motor)* efficiency, performance. 3 *(sumisión)* submissiveness. 4 *(cansancio)* exhaustion, fatigue.

rendir I *vtr* 1 *(vencer)* to defeat, conquer. 2 *(producir)* to yield, produce; **por las mañanas rinde más,** he's more productive in the morning. 3 *(cansar)* to exhaust, wear out. 4 *(entregar)* to hand over; *(restituir)* to give back, render; *Mil* to surrender; **r. las llaves,** to hand over the keys; *fig* **r. cuentas,** to account for one's actions. 5 *(dar beneficios a)* to pay, be profitable; **este negocio no rinde,** this business doesn't pay; *fig* **r. el alma,** to give up the ghost. 6 *(ofrecer)* to offer; **r. culto a,** to worship; **r. homenaje a,** to pay homage to; **r. honores a la bandera,** to salute the flag. 7 *Mil (bandera)* to dip; *(armas)* to lower. II *vi Am (cundir)* to go a long way. III **rendirse** *vr* to surrender, give in; **¡me rindo!,** I give up!; **r. a la evidencia,** to bow to the evidence.

renegado,-a I *pp de* **renegar.** II *adj & nm,f* renegade.

renegar I *vtr* 1 *(renunciar)* to renounce, disown **(de, -)**; **r. de su familia,** to disown one's family. 2 *(negar)* to deny vigorously. II *vi* 1 *(blasfemar)* to swear, curse. 2 *(quejarse)* to grumble, complain.

renegón,-ona *fam* I *adj* grumpy, grouchy. II *nm, f* grumbler, moaner.

renegrido,-a *adj* blackened.

RENFE *abr de* **Red Nacional de los Ferrocarriles Españoles.**

renglón *nm* 1 line; **a r. seguido,** immediately afterwards; *fig* **leer entre renglones,** to read between the lines. 2 *Com (partida)* item. 3 **renglones,** *fam* text *sing;* **poner cuatro r. a algn,** to drop a line to sb.

reniego *nm (blasfemia)* curse, oath.

reno *nm Zool* reindeer.

renombrado,-a *adj* renowned, famous, wellknown.

renombre *nm* renown, fame; **de r.,** renowned, famous.

renovable *adj* renewable.

renovación *nf* 1 *(de contrato, pasaporte)* renewal. 2 *(de una casa)* renovation; *(redecoración)* redecoration. 3 *Pol (de un partido)* reorganization.

renovar I *vtr* 1 *(gen)* to renew. 2 *(casa)* to renovate; *(redecorar)* to redecorate. 3 *Pol (partido)* to reorganize. II **renovarse** *vr* to be renewed.

renquear *vi* 1 *(de la pierna)* to limp; *(del pie)* to hobble. 2 *fam* to manage, get by; **vamos renqueando,** we're just scraping by.

renta *nf* 1 *Fin (ingresos)* income; **vivir de sus rentas,** to live on one's income; **¿ya has presentado la r. este año?,** have you filed your income tax this year? ■ **impuesto sobre la r.,** income tax; **r. fiscal,** taxable income; **r. nacional,** national income; **r. per cápita,** per capita income; **r. pública,** government debt; **r. variable,** equity securities *pl;* **r. vitalicia,** life annuity. 2 *(beneficio)* interest, return. ■ **r. fija,** fixed interest security. 3 *(alquiler)* rent.

rentabilidad *nf* profitability; *Fin* **tasa de r.,** rate of return.

rentabilizar *vtr* to make profitable.

rentable *adj* profitable.

rentar *vtr* to produce, yield.

rentero,-a I *nm,f* tenant farmer.

rentista *nmf* 1 *(experto en renta)* financial expert. 2 *(que vive de rentas)* rentier, person of independent means.

renuencia *nf* reluctance, unwillingness.

renuevo *nm* 1 *Bot* shoot, sprout; **echar renuevos,** to sprout. 2 *(renovación)* renewal.

renuncia *nf* 1 renunciation. 2 *(dimisión)* resignation; **presentar la r.,** to hand in one's resignation.

renunciar *vtr* 1 *(dejar voluntariamente)* to renounce, give up; *(corona, trono)* to relinquish; **r. a su puesto,** to resign (one's post); **r. al alcohol,** to give up drinking. 2 *(abandonar)* to renounce, give up, abandon; **r. a su fe,** to renounce one's faith.

reñido,-a I *pp de* **reñir.** II *adj* 1 *(enemistado)* on bad terms, at odds; **están reñidos,** they are not on speaking terms. 2 *(encarnizado)* bitter, tough, hard-fought.

reñir I *vtr* 1 *(regañar)* to scold, tell off. 2 *Mil (batalla)* to fight; *(guerra)* to wage. II *vi (discutir)* to quarrel, argue; *(pelear)* to fight; **r. con algn,** to fall out with sb; **r. por algn,** to fight over sth.

reo[1] *nmf* 1 *Jur (acusado)* defendant, accused. 2 *(culpable)* culprit; *(con cargos contra la ley)* offender.

reo[2] *nm (pez)* salmon trout.

reoca *nf fam* **ser la r.,** to be exceptional; *(bueno)* to be fantastic; *(malo)* to be awful.

reojo (de) *loc adv* **mirar algo de r.,** to look at sth out of the corner of one's eye.

reordenar *vtr* to rearrange.

reorganización *nf* reorganization; *Pol* **r. ministerial,** cabinet reshuffle.

reorganizador,-a I *adj* reorganizing. II *nm,f* reorganizer.

reorganizar *vtr* to reorganize.

reostato *nm,* **reóstato** *nm Elec* rheostat.

repanchigarse *vr fam véase* **repantigarse.**

repanocha *nf fam véase* **reoca.**

repantigarse *vr fam (acomodarse)* to lounge, loll; *(arrellenarse)* to stretch oneself out.

reparable *adj* repairable.

reparación *nf* 1 *(arreglo)* repair, repairing; **en r.,** under repair; **taller de reparaciones,** repair shop. 2 *fig (desagravio)* reparation, amends *pl.*

reparar[1] I *vtr* 1 *(arreglar)* to repair, fix, mend. 2 *(ofensa, injuria)* to make amends for; *(daño)* to make good. 3 *(reponer)* to restore, renew. 4 *(considerar)* to take into account; **repárelo bien,** think it over. II *vi* 1 *(darse cuenta)* **r. en,** to notice, realize; **reparé en que no llevaba la cartera,** I realized I didn't have my wallet on me. 2 *(hacer caso)* **r. en,** to pay attention to; **no r. en gastos,** to spare no expense.

reparar[2] I *vi (detenerse)* to stop, stall. II **repararse** *vr* 1 *(detenerse)* to stop, stall. 2 *Am (caballo)* to rear (up).

reparo *nm* objection; **no tener reparos en,** not to hesitate to; **poner reparos a,** to object to, find fault with.

repartición *nf* distribution, sharing out.

repartidor,-a *nm,f* distributor; **r. de la leche,** milkman.

repartir I *vtr* 1 *(dividir)* to distribute, divide, share out; **repartámosnos lo que sobra,** let's split what's left. 2 *(entregar)* to give out, hand out; *(correo)* to deliver; **r. premios,** to give out prizes; *fam fig* **empezó a r. puñetazos a todos los que estaban cerca,** he started punching everyone in sight. 3 *Naipes* to deal. II **repartirse** *vr* 1 *(dividirse)* to be distributed *or* divided *or* shared out. 2 *(entregarse)* to be given out *or* handed out; *(correo)* to be delivered.

reparto *nm* 1 distribution, division, sharing out. 2 *(distribución)* handing out; *(de mercancías)* delivery; **furgoneta de r.,** delivery van; **r. de premios,** prize-giving. 3 *Naipes (turno)* deal; *(acción)* dealing. 4 *Cin Teat* cast.

repasar *vtr* 1 *(volver a pasar por)* to pass by, pass through again. 2 *(volver a mirar)* to revise, go over. 3 *Téc (máquina)* to check, overhaul. 4 *Cost (ropa)* to mend. 5 *fam (mirar con descaro)* to look over; **la repasó de arriba a abajo,** he looked her up and down.

repaso *nm* 1 revision, going over; *(lección)* review; **curso de r.,** refresher course. 2 *Téc (máquina)* checkup, overhaul. 3 *Cost (ropa)* mending.

repatear *vtr fam* to annoy, disgust, turn off; **me repatean los enchufados,** I can't stand people who pull strings.

repatriación *nf* repatriation.

repatriado,-a I *pp* de **repatriar.** II *adj* repatriated. III *nm, f* repatriate.

repatriar *vtr* to repatriate.

repecho *nm* short steep slope; **a r.,** uphill.

repelar *vtr* 1 *(arrancar)* to pull out. 2 *(cortar) (cabello)* to crop; *(uñas)* to clip.

repelencia *nf* 1 *(rechazo)* repulse. 2 *Am (asco)* revulsion.

repelente *adj* repulsive, repellent, revolting; *fam* **niño r.,** little know-all.

repeler *vtr* 1 *(rechazar)* to repel, repulse. 2 *(repugnar)* to disgust; **me repelen los hipócritas,** I loathe hypocrites.

repeluzno *nm fam* shiver; **me da r.,** it gives me the shivers.

repente *nm fam (movimiento brusco)* sudden movement, start; *(arrebato)* fit, outburst; *(improvisación)* improvisation; **de r.,** suddenly, all of a sudden; **un r. de ira,** a fit of anger.

repentino,-a *adj* sudden. ♦ **repentinamente** *adv* suddenly.

repera *nf fam* **ser la r.,** to take the cake; *(persona)* to be a real winner.

repercusión *nm* repercussion.

repercutir *vi* 1 *(resonar)* to resound, echo, reverberate. 2 *(rebotar)* to rebound. 3 *fig* **r. en,** to have repercussions on, affect.

repertorio *nm* 1 *Teat* repertoire, repertory. 2 *(compilación)* list, index.

repesca *nf fam* second chance; *(examen)* resit; **hacer un examen de r.,** to resit an exam.

repescar *vtr fam* to give a second chance to; *(examen)* to allow to resit an exam.

repetición *nf* 1 repetition; *Ftb* **r. de la jugada,** acction replay. 2 *(reloj)* repeater. 3 *Jur* action for recovery. 4 **arma de r.,** repeater, repeating firearm.

repetido,-a I *pp* de **repetir.** II *adj* repeated; **repetidas veces,** repeatedly, countless times. ♦ **repetidamente** *adv* repeatedly.

repetidor,-a I *adj* repeating; *Educ fam* **alumno r.,** student who is repeating a year; *Rad TV* **estación repetidora,** relay station. II *nm Rad TV* relay, booster station; **r. de televisión,** television relay. III *nm, f fam Educ* student who is repeating a year.

repetir I *vtr* to repeat, do again; **no es necesario que me lo repitas,** you needn't tell me again. II *vi* 1 *(volver a servirse)* to have a second helping; **¿quién quiere r. de paella?,** who would like some more paella? 2 *(venir a la boca)* to repeat; **el pepino repite,** cucumber repeats (on one). 3 *Educ* to repeat a year. III **repetirse** *vr* 1 *(persona)* to repeat oneself. 2 *(acontecimientos)* to recur; **¡que se repita!,** encore!; **¡(y) que no se repita!,** (and) don't let it happen again!

repicar I *vtr* 1 *(partir a trozos pequeños)* to break up into bits *or* pieces. 2 *(las campanas)* to peal, ring out. II **repicarse** *vr* *(jactarse)* to boast.

repintar I *vtr (casa, habitación)* to repaint. II **repintarse** *vr (con cosméticos)* to put on layers of make-up.

repipi *adj fam* **niño r.,** little know-all.

repique *nm (de campanas)* peal, ringing.

repiquetear *vtr* & *vi* 1 *(repicar)* to peal joyfully; **las campanas repiquetean,** the bells are ringing out merrily. 2 *(tamborilear)* to beat, tap.

repiqueteo *nm* 1 *(de campanas)* joyful pealing. 2 *(de tambor)* beating, tapping.

repisa *nf* shelf, ledge; **r. de chimenea,** mantelpiece.

replantar *vtr Agr* to replant; *(transplantar)* to transplant.

replantear I *vtr* 1 *(asunto)* to restate, reconsider, rethink, think over. 2 *Arquit* to lay out a ground floor for *or* in. II **replantearse** *vr* to reconsider, rethink; **tendrás que replanteártelo todo,** you'll have to think it all over again.

replegarse *vr Mil* to fall back, retreat.

repleto,-a *adj* full, full up, jam-packed; **r. de,** packed with, crammed with; **r. de gente,** packed (with people).

réplica *nf* 1 *(contestación)* answer, reply; *(objeción)* retort; **el derecho de r.,** the right of reply. 2 *(copia)* replica.

replicar I *vtr* & *vi* 1 *(poner objeciones)* to argue, answer back; **los niños no replican,** little boys don't answer back. 2 *Jur* to answer. II *vi* 1 to reply, retort. 2 *Jur* to answer.

replicón,-ona *adj fam* argumentative, cheeky, bold. 2 *nm,f* argumentative person.

repliegue *nm* 1 *(pliegue)* fold, crease; *fig* recess. 2 *Mil* withdrawal, retreat.

repoblación *nf* repopulation. ■ **r. forestal,** reafforestation.

repoblar *vtr* to repopulate; *(bosque)* to reafforest.

repollo *nm* cabbage.

reponer I *vtr* 1 *(devolver)* to put back, replace, restore. 2 *Teat (obra)* to put on again; *Cin (película)* to rerun; *TV (programa)* to repeat. II **reponerse** *vr (de susto, enfermedad, etc)* to recover, recuperate; **r. de,** to recover from, get over.

reportaje *nm* 1 *Prensa Rad* report; *(noticias)* article, news item; **r. gráfico,** illustrated feature. 2 *Cin TV (documental)* documentary.

reportar[1] I *vtr* 1 *(alcanzar)* to bring; **esta relación le reportará muchas ventajas,** this relationship will do him a lot of good. 2 *(refrenar)* to restrain check. II **reportarse** *vr* to restrain oneself, hold back.

reportar[2] *vtr CAm (denunciar)* to report, denounce.

repórter *nmf*, **reportero,-a** *nm,f Prensa* reporter.

reposacabezas *nm inv* headrest.

reposado,-a I *pp* de **reposar.** II *adj* quiet, peaceful, calm.

reposapiés *nm inv* footrest.

reposar I *vtr (la cabeza, los pies)* to rest (en, on). II *vi* 1 *(descansar)* to rest, take a rest; *Culin* **deje r. la pasta,** leave the dough to stand. 2 *(enterrar)* to lie, rest, be buried. III **reposarse** *vr (líquido)* to settle.

reposición *nf* 1 *(restitución)* restoration; *(cambio)* replacement. 2 *Teat* revival; *Cin* rerun, reshowing; *TV* repeat.

repositorio *nm* repository.

reposo *nm* rest; **en r.,** *(person)* at rest; *Culin* standing.

repostada *nf Am* retort.

repostar *vtr (provisiones)* to stock up with; *Av (combustible)* to refuel; *Aut (gasolina)* to fill up.

repostería *nf* **1** *(pastas)* cakes *pl*; *(chocolate, caramelos)* confectionery. **2** *(tienda) (de pasteles)* cake *or* pastry shop; *(de chocolate etc)* confectioner's (shop).

repostero,-a *nm,f (de pasteles)* pastrycook; *(de chocolate etc)* confectioner.

reprender *vtr* to reprimand, scold.

reprensión *nf* reprimand, scolding.

represa *nf* dam.

represalia *nf (gen pl)* reprisals *pl*, retaliation; **tomar represalias,** to take reprisals.

represaliado,-a *adj* sanctioned.

representación *nf* **1** representation; *Com* **tiene una r. de una casa de medias italiana,** he represents an Italian hosiery firm. **2** *Teat* performance.

representante **I** *adj* representative. **II** *nmf* **1** representative. **2** *Teat (hombre)* actor; *(mujer)* actress.

representar **I** *vtr* **1** *(reproducir)* to represent, depict, portray; **el cuadro de la entrada representa el paso por el Mar Rojo,** the picture in the hall depicts the crossing of the Red Sea. **2** *(hacer presente)* to state, express. **3** *(equivaler)* to represent, stand for; **¿qué representa?,** what does it stand for?; **representa muchas horas de trabajo,** it involves many hours of work. **4** *(importar)* to mean; **representa mucho para mí,** it means a lot to me. **5** *Com (compañía, cliente)* to represent. **6** *(aparentar)* to appear to be; **una mujer que no representaba más de treinta,** a woman who didn't look more than thirty. **7** *Teat (obra)* to perform; *(actor)* to act. **II representarse** *vr* to imagine, picture.

representativo,-a *adj* representative.

represión *nf* repression; **r. sexual,** sexual repression.

represivo,-a *adj* repressive.

reprimenda *nf* reprimand.

reprimido,-a **I** *pp de* **reprimir. II** *adj* repressed. **III** *nm,f (persona)* repressed person.

reprimir *vtr* to repress; **r. una pasión,** to quench a passion.

reprise *nf Aut* acceleration.

reprobable *adj* reproachable, reprehensible.

reprobación *nf* reprobation, reproof.

reprobador,-a *adj* reproachful, reproving.

reprobar *vtr (cosa)* to condemn; *(persona)* to reproach, reprove.

réprobo,-a *adj & nm,f* reprobate.

reprochable *adj* reproachable.

reprochador,-a *adj* reproachful.

reprochar *vtr* to reproach; **r. algo a algn,** to reproach sb for sth.

reproche *nm* reproach, criticism.

reproducción *nf* reproduction; **derechos de r.,** copyright; **éste no es el original, es sólo una r.,** this isn't the original, it's just a reproduction.

reproducir **I** *vtr* to reproduce. **II reproducirse** *vr* **1** *(repetirse)* to recur, happen again. **2** *(engendrar)* to reproduce, breed.

reproductor,-a **I** *adj* **1** reproducing; **máquina reproductora,** reproducing machine. **2** *(órgano)* reproductive. **3** *(animal)* breeding. **II** *nm,f* breeder; **los gatos son buenos reproductores,** cats are persistent breeders.

reprografía *nf* reprography.

reptar *vi* **1** to crawl, slither. **2** *(adular)* to flatter.

reptil, réptil **I** *adj* reptilian, reptile. **II** *nm* **1** *(animal)* reptile. **2 reptiles,** *(clase)* reptiles *pl*.

república *nf* republic; *Lit fig* **la R. de las letras,** the intelligentsia.

republicanismo *nm* republicanism.

republicano,-a *adj & nm,f* republican.

repudiar *vtr* to repudiate.

repudio *nm* repudiation.

repuesto,-a **I** *pp de* **reponer. II** *adj (enfermo)* recovered. **III** *nm* **1** *(recambio)* spare part, spare; *Aut* **rueda de r.,** spare wheel. **2** *(provisión)* stock.

repugnancia *nf* loathing, disgust.

repugnante *adj* repulsive, disgusting, revolting.

repugnar **I** *vi* to disgust, revolt; **me repugna la coliflor,** I find cauliflower disgusting. **II** *vtr (negar)* to conflict; *(contradecir)* to contradict.

repujado,-a **I** *pp de* **repujar. II** *adj* embossed, repoussé.

repujar *vtr* to emboss.

repulsa *nf* **1** *(rechazo)* rebuff; *fig* condemnation. **2** *(reprimenda)* reprimand.

repulsión *nf* repulsion, repugnance.

repulsivo,-a *adj* repulsive, revolting.

repuntar *Am* **I** *vi (lluvia, enfermedad)* to (begin to) make itself felt, show the first signs. **II** *vtr (animales)* to round up.

repuse *pt indef véase* **reponer.**

reputación *nf* reputation.

reputado,-a **I** *pp de* **reputar. II** *adj* reputed, reputable.

reputar *vtr* to consider, deem.

requebrar *vtr (lisonjear)* to court; *(adular)* to flatter, pay compliments to.

requemado,-a **I** *pp de* **requemar. II** *adj* scorched, burnt.

requemar **I** *vtr* **1** *(necesitar)* to scorch, burn; **plantas requemadas por el sol,** plants scorched by the sun. **II requemarse** *vr* **1** *(quemarse)* to scorch. **2** *(enfadarse)* to burn with anger.

requerimiento *nm* **1** *(súplica)* request; **a r. de algn,** at sb's request. **2** *Jur (intimación)* injunction. **3** *Jur (aviso)* summons *pl*.

requerir *vtr* **1** *(necesitar)* to require; **esto requiere gran destreza,** this requires a lot of skill; *Tex* **'no requiere plancha',** 'non-iron'. **2** *(con autoridad)* to demand, call for; **el ministro requirió su presencia,** the minister summoned him. **3** *(solicitar)* to request. **4** *Jur (avisar)* to summon. **5** *(persuadir)* to persuade; *lit* **r. de amores,** to court, woo.

requesón *nm Culin* cottage cheese.

requete- *pref fam* really, very, incredibly; **requetebueno,** really good, smashing; **requetemoderno,** ultramodern.

requeté *nm Hist Mil* Carlist soldier; **los requetés,** the Carlist forces.

requiebro *nm* flirtatious remark.

réquiem *nm (pl réquiems) Rel Mús* requiem.

requintar *vtr Am (apretar mucho)* to tighten.

requisa *nf* **1** *(inspección)* inspection. **2** *Mil (embargo)* requisition.

requisar *vtr* **1** *Mil* to requisition. **2** *fam (apropiarse)* to grab, swipe.

requisito *nm* requirement, requisite; **cumplir todos los requisitos,** to fulfil all the requirements; **r. previo,** prerequisite.

requisitoria *nf Jur* requisition, demand.

res *nf* beast, animal; *(cabeza de ganado)* head *inv* (of cattle); **r. lanar,** sheep *inv*.

resabido,-a *adj pey* pretentious, pedantic.

resabio *nm* **1** *(mal sabor)* unpleasant *or* bad aftertaste. **2** *(vicio)* bad habit.

resaca *nf* **1** *(después de beber)* hangover; **tener r.,** to have a hangover. **2** *Náut* undertow, undercurrent. **3** *Am (aguardiente)* eau de vie, firewater. **4** *Méx irón* **la r.,** the very essence.

resalado,-a *adj fam (vivo)* lively; *(gracioso)* charming, attractive.

resaltar *vi* **1** *(sobresalir)* to project, jut out. **2** *fig* to stand out; **hacer r.,** to emphasize, stress, underline.

resalte *nm,* **resalto** *nm (saliente)* ledge.

resarcir *vtr* to compensate, indemnify.

resbaladizo,-a *adj* **1** slippery. **2** *fig* slippery, tricky.

resbalar *vi* **1** *(deslizarse)* to slide; *(gotas, lágrimas)* to trickle (down); **r. en o sobre el hielo,** to slide *or* slip on the ice. **2** *(involuntariamente)* to slip; *Aut* to skid. **3** *fig (desliz)* to slip up, make a slip.

resbalón *nm* slip; **dar un r.,** to slip, slide; *fig* to slip up.

resbaloso,-a I *adj* slippery. II *nm Arg Mús* popular dance.

rescatador,-a *nm, f* rescuer.

rescatar *vtr* **1** *(liberar)* to rescue, save. **2** *Mil (ciudad)* to recapture. **3** *(recuperar) (objeto)* to recover; *(tiempo)* to make up for. **4** *Am (traficar)* to sell on the move. **5** *Méx (revender)* to resell.

rescate *nm* **1** *(salvamento)* rescue; **equipo de r.,** rescue team. **2** *(recuperación)* recovery, recapture. **3** *(suma)* ransom; **exigir r. por algn,** to hold sb to ransom.

rescindible *adj (contrato)* cancellable, rescindable.

rescindir *vtr* to rescind, annul, cancel; **r. el contrato,** to cancel the contract.

rescisión *nf* rescission, annulment, cancellation.

rescoldo *nm* **1** *(brasa)* embers *pl.* **2** *fig (recelo)* lingering doubt.

resecarse *vr* to dry up, become parched.

reseco,-a *adj* **1** *(muy seco)* very dry, parched. **2** *(flaco)* very thin, skinny.

resentido,-a I *pp de* **resentirse.** II *adj (ofendido)* resentful; *(amargado)* bitter; **estar r.,** to have a chip on one's shoulder; **estar r. por algo,** to be resentful of sth, resent sth. III *nm, f* resentful person.

resentimiento *nm (rencor)* resentment; *(amargura)* bitterness.

resentirse *vr* **r. de,** to suffer from, feel the effects of; **aún me resiento de la espalda,** I still have trouble with my back. **2** *(debilitarse)* to be weakened. **3** *fig* to become resentful, feel resentment; *(amargarse)* to feel bitter; *(ofenderse)* to feel offended; *(enfadarse)* to get annoyed; **r. por algo,** to take offence at sth.

reseña *nf* **1** *Lit* review; *Prensa* write-up. **2** *(descripción)* brief description; *(narración breve)* account. **3** *Mil* review.

reseñar *vtr* **1** *Lit* to review. **2** *(describir)* to describe; *(acontecimiento)* to give an account of.

reserva I *nf* **1** *(plazas, entradas)* reservation, booking; **'r. de habitaciones',** 'room reservation'. **2** *(provisión)* reserve; *(existencias)* stock; **reservas de carbón,** coal reserves *or* stocks. ■ *Fin* **r. de divisas,** foreign currency reserves *pl.* **3** *Mil* reserve, reserves *pl.* **4** *(cautela)* reservation. **5** *(recato, secreto)* reserve, discretion; **con la mayor r.,** in the strictest confidence; **guardar *or* tener algo en r.,** to keep sth in reserve; **sin reserva(s),** without reservation; **tener reservas sobre algo,** to have reservations about sth. **6** *(vino)* vintage; **un vino de r.,** a vintage wine. **7** *(terreno)* reservation; **r. de indios,** Indian reservation. II *nmf Dep (sustituto)* reserve, substitute.

reservado,-a I *pp de* **reservar.** II *adj (habitaciones, plazas)* reserved, booked. **2** *(persona, carácter)* reserved, quiet; *(frío)* distant. **3** *(asunto)* confidential. III *nm (de restaurante etc)* private room; *Rail* reserved compartment.

reservar I *vtr* **1** *(plazas, billetes)* to reserve, book. **2** *(guardar)* to keep. **3** *(ocultar)* to withhold, keep to oneself. II **reservarse** *vr* **1** *(conservarse)* to save oneself **(para,** for); **se reserva para la carrera,** she's saving herself for the race. **2** *(guardar para sí)* to withhold; **r. la opinión,** to withhold one's opinion, to keep one's opinion to oneself.

reservista *nmf Mil* reservist.

resfriado,-a I *pp de* **resfriar.** II *adj Med* with a cold; **estar r.,** to have a cold; **estoy muy r.,** I have a bad *or* heavy cold. III *nm Med (catarro)* cold; *(de poca importancia)* chill; **coger un r.,** to catch (a) cold.

resfriar I *vtr (enfriar)* to cool. II **resfriarse** *vr* **1** *(enfriarse)* to cool off. **2** *Med* to catch (a) cold.

resfrío *nm Med* cold.

resguardar I *vtr* **1** *(proteger)* to protect, shelter **(de,** from). **2** *(salvaguardar)* to safeguard **(de,** against). II **resguardarse** *vr* **1** *(protegerse)* to protect oneself. **2** *(salvaguardarse)* to safeguard oneself.

resguardo *nm* **1** *(protección)* protection; shelter. **2** *(garantía)* safeguard, guarantee. **3** *(recibo)* receipt, paying-in slip; *(de talonario)* counterfoil, stub; *(vale)* voucher.

residencia *nf* **1** *(permanencia)* residence; **permiso de r.,** residence permit; **tener la r. en,** to reside in. **2** *(lugar)* residence; **hotel r.,** residential hotel; **r. de ancianos,** old people's home; *Univ* **r. de estudiantes,** hall of residence, *US* dormitory.

residencial *adj* residential.

residente *adj & nmf* resident; **no r.,** non-resident. ■ **médico r.,** resident doctor.

residir *vi* **1** *(vivir)* to reside, live, dwell **(en,** in). **2** *fig* to lie **(en,** in).

residual *adj* residual; **aguas residuales,** sewage.

residuo *nm* **1** residue. **2** **residuos,** waste *sing,* refuse *sing;* **r. radiactivos,** radioactive waste.

resignación *nf* resignation, acquiescence.

resignado,-a I *pp de* **resignar.** II *adj* resigned. ◆ **resignadamente** *adv* resignedly.

resignar I *vtr* to resign, relinquish. II **resignarse** *vr* to resign oneself **(a,** to).

resina *nf* resin.

resinoso,-a *adj* resinous.

resistencia *nf* **1** resistance; *Pol* **la R.,** the Resistance; **oponer r.,** to resist; **r. pasiva,** passive resistance. **2** *(aguante, fuerza)* endurance, stamina; *(fortaleza)* strength; **prueba de r.,** endurance test. **3** *Elec* resistance.

resistente *adj* **1** resistant **(a,** to); **r. al fuego,** fireresistant. **2** *(fuerte)* strong, tough, hardy.

resistir I *vi* **1** *(gen)* to resist. **2** *(soportar)* to hold (out); **¿resistirá este nudo?,** will this knot hold? **3** *(durar)* to last; **este edificio resiste,** this building has stood the test of time. II *vtr* **1** *(soportar)* to resist, tolerate; **no puedo r. más,** I can't stand it any longer; **no puedo r. la tentación,** I can't resist temptation. **2** *(sostener peso etc)* to bear, withstand. III **resistirse** *vr* **1** *(forcejear)* to resist; *(oponerse)* to offer resistance. **2** *(costar esfuerzo)* to struggle; *fam* **se le resisten las matemáticas,** she's having a hard time with maths, maths isn't her strongest subject. **3** *(negarse)* to refuse; **me resisto a creerlo,** I refuse to believe it, I find it hard to believe.

resma *nf* ream (of paper).

resol *nm* glare (of the sun).

resolución *nf* **1** *(de un problema)* solving; *(solución)* solution. **2** *(decisión)* resolution, decision; **r. fatal,** death wish; **r. judicial,** court decision; **tomar una r.,** to pass a resolution.

resolver *(pp* **resuelto)** I *vtr & vi* **1** *(solucionar)* to solve, resolve; *(asunto)* to settle. **2** *(decidir)* to resolve, decide; **resolví quedarme,** I decided to stay. **3** *Fís* to dissolve. II **resolverse** *vr* **1** *(solucionarse)* to be solved; *(resultar)* to work out. **2** *(decidirse)* to resolve, decide, make up one's mind **(a,** to). **3** *(acabar)* to end (up) **(en,** in); **todo se resolvió en un altercado,** it all ended in a quarrel.

resollar *vi (respirar)* to breathe heavily; *(con silbido)* to wheeze; *(de cansancio)* to puff and pant; *fig* **sin r.,** without a word.

resonancia nf 1 (repercusión) resonance; (eco) echo. ■ **caja de r.,** sounding board. 2 fig (notoriedad) importance; (consecuencias) repercussions pl; **tener r.,** to cause a stir.

resonante adj resounding; fig important.

resonar vi (retumbar) to resound; (cristal, metales) to ring; (tener eco) to echo.

resoplar vi (respirar) to breathe heavily; (de cansancio) to puff and pant.

resoplido nm 1 (resollido) heavy breathing; (silbido) wheezing; (de cansancio) panting. 2 (por enfado) snort.

resorte nm 1 (muelle) spring. 2 fig means pl; **conocer todos los resortes de algo,** to know all the ins and outs of sth.

respaldar I vtr 1 fig to support, back (up). 2 Am (afianzar) to ensure. II **respaldarse** vr (recostarse) to lean back (en, on).

respaldo nm 1 (de silla, papel) back. 2 fig (apoyo) support, backing.

respectar v defect to concern, regard; **por lo que a mí respecta,** as far as I'm concerned.

respectivo,-a adj respective; **en lo r. a,** with regard to, regarding. ◆ **respectivamente** adv respectively.

respecto nm proportion, relation; **al r.,** in this respect; **con r. a, r. a, r. de,** with regard to; **r. a mí,** as for me, as far as I am concerned.

respetabilidad nf respectability.

respetable I adj 1 (digno) respectable; **un r. señor de Sanlúcar,** a highly respected gentleman from Sanlúcar. 2 (considerable) respectable. II **el r.** nm Teat fam the audience.

respetar I vtr 1 (venerar, apreciar) to respect; **hacerse r. de todos,** to command everyone's respect. 2 Aut **r. la derecha,** to yield to traffic coming from the right. II **respetarse** vr to have self-respect.

respeto nm 1 (gen) respect; **falta de r.,** lack of respect; **por r. a,** out of consideration for. 2 (miedo) fear; **esta oscuridad me inspira r.,** this darkness scares me a bit. 3 **respetos,** fml respects; **presentar sus r. a algn,** to pay one's respects to sb.

respetuoso,-a adj respectful.

respingar vi 1 (caballo) to shy. 2 fam (falda etc) to curl up.

respingo nm 1 (sacudida) start, jump. 2 fig (enfado) huff.

respingón,-ona adj (nariz) snub, upturned.

respiración nf 1 (acción) breathing, respiration. ■ **r. artificial,** artificial resuscitation; **r. boca a boca,** mouth-to-mouth respiration, the kiss of life. 2 (aliento) breath; **perder la r.,** to lose one's breath; **sin r.,** breathless; **fig que corta la r.,** breathtaking. 3 (ventilación) ventilation.

respiradero nm 1 Téc air vent. 2 fig (descanso) respite.

respirar I vi 1 (aire) to breathe; **r. mal,** to breathe with difficulty, gasp; fig **habla sin r.,** he talks nonstop. 2 fig to relieve; **déjame r., ¿vale?,** give me a break, will you?; **no poder r. (de trabajo),** to be up to one's eyes in work; **¡por fin respiro!,** well, that's a relief! II vtr (absorber) to breathe (in), inhale; **r. gases tóxicos,** to inhale toxic fumes; fig **r. felicidad,** to ooze happiness.

respiratorio,-a adj respiratory; **aparato r.,** respiratory system.

respiro nm 1 (resuello) breathing 2 (descanso) breather, break (prorroga) respite, fig **no dar r.,** to give no peace, have no respite

resplandecer vt (sol) to shine, (metal) to gleam (relucir) to glitter, (fuego) to glow, fig **Natalia resplandecía por su belleza,** Natalia was resplendent in her beauty

resplandeciente adj 1 (brillante) shining, (metales) gleaming, (reluciente) glittering, (fuego) glowing 2 (esplendoroso) resplendent, radiant

resplandor nm 1 (brillo) brightness, (muy intenso) brilliance, (de fuego) glow, blaze 2 (esplendor) splendour, US splendor, (brillantez) radiance

responder I vtr to answer, **r. a una carta,** to reply to a letter, **r. al teléfono,** to answer the phone II vi 1 (reaccionar) to respond, Med **r. a un tratamiento,** to respond to a course of treatment 2 (corresponder) to answer, **responde al nombre de Ramón,** he goes by the name of Ramón, **r. a una descripción,** to fit a description, **r. a una necesidad,** to answer or meet a need 3 (rendir) to produce 4 (avalar) to guarantee, **r. de algn,** to be responsible for sb, **r. por algn,** to vouch for sb. act as a guarantor for sb

respondón,-ona adj fam argumentative cheeky

responsabilidad nf responsibility, **cargar con la r. de algo,** to take responsibility for sth, **r. limitada,** limited liability

responsabilizar I vtr to make or hold responsible (de, for) II **responsabilizarse** vr to assume or claim responsibiliy (de, for)

responsable adj responsible. **Andres es un chico muy r.,** Andrés is a very responsible boy, **hacerse r. de algo,** to assume responsibility for sth, **la persona r.,** (en trabajo etc) the person in charge, (en crimen, robo) the perpetrator

responso nm 1 Rel prayer for the dead 2 fam (reprimenda) ticking-off

responsorio nm Rel responsorial psalm

respuesta nf (gen) answer, reply, (reacción) response, **en r. a,** in response to

resquebrajadura nf crack

resquebrajarse vr to crack

resquemor nm (resentimiento) resentment, ill feeling

resquicio nm 1 (abertura) crack, chink 2 fig glimmer, **un r. de esperanza,** a glimmer of hope 3 (ocasión) chance, (oportunidad) opportunity (posibilidad) possibility, chance 4 Am (vestigio) trace, vestige

resta nf Mat subtraction

restablecer I vtr to re-establish, **r. el orden,** to restore order II **restablecerse** vr 1 to be reestablished, (orden etc) to be restored 2 Med to recover

restablecimiento nm 1 re-establishment (orden etc) restoration 2 Med recovery

restallar vi 1 (látigo) to crack 2 (hacer ruido) to crack

restallido nm crack

restante adj remaining, **lo r.,** the rest, the remainder, what is left over

restañar vtr (flujo de sangre, herida) to staunch

restar I vtr 1 Mat to subtract, take away **r. seis de diez,** to subtract six from ten 2 (quitar) to reduce, lessen, **r. importancia a algo,** to play sth down. II vi (quedar) to be left, remain, **en todo lo que resta de mes,** in what's left of the month

restauración nf restoration

restaurador,-a I adj restoring II nm,f restorer

restaurante nm restaurant Ferroc **coche r.,** restaurant or buffet car

restaurar vtr 1 (cuadro, edificio) to restore 2 (en un cargo) to reinstate

restitución nf restitution

restituir vtr (restablecer) to restore, (devolver) to return, give back

resto nm 1 rest, remainder, fam **echar el r.,** to give sth all one has got to go all out 2 Mat remainder 3 **restos,** remains, Culin leftovers. ■ **r. mortales,** mortal remains

restregar vtr (frotar) to rub hard, (fregar) to scrub

restricción nf restriction

restrictivo,-a adj restrictive

restringir I vtr to restrict limit, curb, **r. la libertad de,** to restrict the freedom of II **restringirse** vr to restrict oneself, limit oneself

resucitar *vtr & vi* to resuscitate, *fig (restablecer)* to revive

resuelto,-a I *pp de* **resolver II** *adj (decidido)* resolute, determined

resuello *nm (acción)* breathing. *(aliento)* breath, gasp

resulta *nf* consequence, **de resultas de,** as a result of

resultado *nm* result, *(consecuencia)* outcome, **como r.,** as a result, **dar buen r.,** to work give results

resultante *adj* resultant, resulting

resultar *vr* **1** *(gen)* to result, *(ocurrir)* to turn out, **ahora resulta que no puede venir,** now it seems she can't come **2** *(acabar stendo)* to turn out to be, *(llegar a ser)* to prove to be, **a pesar de todo, resulto muy simpático,** in spite of everything, he turned out to be very nice, **vino a r. lo mismo,** it amounted to the same thing **3** *(dar resultado)* to work (out), *(ser positivo)* to be successful, **no resulta comprar barato,** buying cheap doesn't pay **4** *(venir a costar)* to cost come to, **el coche me resultó por medio millón de pesetas,** the car cost me a half a million pesetas

resumen *nm* summary, briefing, **en r.,** in short, to sum up

resumir I *vtr (recapitular)* to summarize *(concluir)* to sum up **II resumirse** *vr* **1** *(recapitularse)* to be summed up **2** *(venir a ser)* to be reduced to, **el examen se resume en cuatro preguntas tontas,** the test boils down to a few silly questions

resurgimiento *nm* resurgence, reappearance

resurgir *vi* **1** *(revivir)* to reappear **2** *(resucitar)* to resuscitate

resurrección *nf* resurrection, **Domingo de R.,** Easter Sunday, *Rel* **la R.,** the Resurrection

retablo *nm* altarpiece, reredos *sing*

retacear *vtr* **1** *(recortar)* to cut out **2** *Arg Par Uru (escatimar)* to stint

retaco *nm fam* short person, shorty, squirt

retador,-a *adj* challenging

retaguarda *nf,* **retaguardia** *nf Mil* rearguard, **ir a la r.,** to bring up the rear

retahíla *nf* series *sing,* sting, *iron* **me cito una r. de autores desconocidos,** he reeled off the names of a string of little-known authors

retal *nm (desperdicio)* remnant, *(pedazo)* scrap

retama *nf Bot* broom

retamal *nm Bot* broom patch, broom thicket.

retar *vtr* **1** to challenge; **r. a duelo,** to challenge to a duel. **2** *Arg Chi* to insult.

retardado,-a I *pp de* **retardar. II** *adj* delayed, retarded; **dispositivo de efecto r.,** delayed-action device.

retardar I *vtr (detener)* to slow down; *(retrasar)* to delay. **II retardarse** *vr* to be delayed.

retardo *nm* delay.

retazo *nm* **1** *(retal)* remnant; *(pedazo)* scrap. **2** *(fragmento)* fragment, piece, snippet.

retemblar *vi* to shake, tremble.

retén *nm* **1** *(de tropas etc)* reserves *pl,* reinforcements *pl.* **2** *(previsión)* stock, store.

retención *nf (gen)* retention; *Fin* withholding; **r. de haberes,** stoppages *pl;* **r. de tráfico,** (traffic) holdup, traffic jam.

retener I *vtr* **1** *(conservar)* to retain; *(cosa prestada)* to keep back, hold back; **sólo hay que r. las ideas más importantes,** one is just meant to take in the main idea. **2** *Fin (descontar)* to deduct, withhold. **3** *(detener)* to detain; *(arrestar)* to arrest. **II retenerse** *vr* to restrain oneself, hold back.

retentiva *nf* retentiveness, memory.

reticencia *nf* **1** *(reserva)* reticence, reserve. **2** *(retintín)* innuendo, insinuation; **lo dijo con cierta r.,** she said it in a rather sarcastic tone.

reticente *adj* **1** *(reservado)* reticent, reserved. **2** *(con retintín)* insinuating.

retícula *nf,* **retículo** *nm Opt* reticle.

retina *nf Anat* retina.

retintín *nm* **1** *(tintineo)* ringing; *(ruido)* tinkling. **2** *(tono sarcástico)* innuendo, sarcastic tone.

retinto,-a *adj (color)* dark chestnut.

retirada *nf Mil* retreat, withdrawal; **batirse en r.,** to beat a retreat.

retirado,-a I *pp de* **retirar. II** *adj* **1** *(alejado)* remote; *(tranquilo)* secluded. **2** *(jubilado)* retired. **III** *nm,f* retired person, *US* retiree.

retirar I *vtr* **1** *(apartar, alejar)* to take away, remove; **le retiraron el carnet de conducir,** he had his driving licence taken away; **retira la silla,** move your chair back; **r. dinero del banco,** to withdraw money from the bank; **r. lo dicho,** to take back what one has said. **2** *(jubilar)* to retire. **II retirarse** *vr* **1** *Mil* to retreat, withdraw. **2** *(apartarse)* to withdraw, draw back, move back; *Tel* **no se retire,** hold on, don't hang up; **puede r.,** you may leave; **r. a su cuarto,** to retire to one's bedroom; **retírate de la ventana,** come *or* move away from the window. **3** *(jubilarse)* to retire.

retiro *nm* **1** *(jubilación)* retirement. **2** *(pensión)* pension; **cobrar el r.,** to receive one's pension. **3** *(lugar tranquilo)* retreat. **4** *Rel* **r. (espiritual),** retreat.

reto *nm* **1** challenge; **aceptar un r.,** to accept a challenge; **lanzar un r. a algn,** to challenge sb. **2** *Am* insult.

retocar *vtr* to retouch; *(fotografía etc)* to touch up; *(perfeccionar)* to put the finishing touches to.

retoñar *vi* **1** *Bot (rebrotar)* to shoot, sprout. **2** *fig* to reappear.

retoño *nm* **1** *Bot (rebrote)* shoot, sprout. **2** *fig (niño)* kid.

retoque *nm* retouching, touching up; **dar los últimos retoques a,** to put the finishing touches to.

retorcer I *vtr* **1** *(cuerda, hilo)* to twist; *(ropa)* to wring (out); *fam* **te voy a r. el pescuezo,** I'm going to wring your neck. **2** *fig (argumento)* to twist; *(tergiversar)* to distort. **II retorcerse** *vr* **1** to twist, become twisted; *(doblar)* to bend, buckle. **2** *(persona)* **r. de dolor,** to writhe in pain; **r. de risa,** to double up with laughter, split one's sides laughing.

retorcido,-a I *pp de* **retorcer. II** *adj fig* twisted; **mente retorcida,** warped mind.

retorcimiento *nm* **1** twisting. **2** *fig* twistedness.

retórica *nf Lit* rhetoric; *fam fig* **tienes mucha r.,** yours are empty words.

retórico,-a I *adj* rhetorical. **II** *nm,f* rhetorician.

retornable *adj* returnable; **'envase no r.',** 'non-deposit bottle'.

retornar I *vtr (devolver)* to return, give back. **II** *vi (volver)* to return, come back, go back.

retorno *nm* **1** *(trueque)* return. **2** *(recompensa)* reward.

retorta *nf Quím* retort.

retortero *nm fam* **andar al r.,** *(estar ocupado)* to be up to one's ears; *(ansioso)* to climb the walls; *(enamorado)* to be head over heels; **llevar** *or* **traer a algn al r.,** *(tenerlo dominado)* to have sb under one's thumb; *(hacerlo trabajar)* to push sb around.

retortijón *nm* **1** twist. **2** *(dolor)* stomach cramp.

retozar *vi* to frolic, romp.

retozo *nm* frolic.

retozón,-ona *adj* frolicsome, playful.

retracción *nf* retraction.

retractable *adj* retractable.

retractación *nf* retraction, withdrawal; **r. pública,** public retraction.

retractar I *vtr* to retract, revoke, withdraw. **II retractarse** *vr* to retract, take back; **me retracto de lo que dije,** I take back what I said.

retráctil *adj (uña, garra)* retractile; *(tren de aterrizaje)* retractable.

retraer I *vtr* 1 *(volver a traer)* to bring back *or* again. 2 *(disuadir)* to dissuade. 3 *(echar en cara)* to reproach; **r. algo a algn,** to reproach sb for sth. II **retraerse** *vr* 1 *(retirarse)* to withdraw; *(por miedo)* to shy away; **r. de la política,** to give up politics. 2 *(refugiarse)* to take refuge.

retraído,-a I *pp de* **retraer.** II *adj* 1 *(tímido)* shy, reserved. 2 *(solitario)* solitary; *(recluído)* secluded.

retraimiento *nm* 1 *(timidez)* shyness, reserve, retiring nature. 2 *(soledad)* solitude; *(reclusión)* seclusion.

retransmisión *nf Rad TV* broadcast, transmission. ■ **r. en diferido,** repeat broadcast; **r. en directo,** live broadcast.

retransmisor *nm Téc* transmitter.

retransmitir *vtr* 1 *(mensaje)* to relay. 2 *Rad TV* to broadcast; **r. en diferido,** to broadcast a recording of; **r. en directo,** to broadcast live.

retrasado,-a I *pp de* **retrasar.** II *adj* 1 *(tren)* late; *(reloj)* slow. 2 *(persona)* behind; **estar r. en matemáticas,** to be behind in maths; **ir r. en los pagos,** to be in arrears; **tengo trabajo r.,** I'm behind in my work. 3 *(país)* backward, underdeveloped. 4 *Med (mental)* retarded, backward. III *nm,f* **r. (mental),** mentally retarded person.

retrasar I *vtr* 1 *(retardar)* to slow down, retard. 2 *(atrasar)* to delay, put off, postpone. 3 *(reloj)* to put back. II *vi* to be late, be behind time; *(reloj)* to be slow. III **retrasarse** *vr* 1 to be late, arrive late, be delayed; *(reloj)* to be slow; **me retrasó el tráfico,** the traffic held me up; **¿por qué te has retrasado tanto?,** what kept you? 2 *(en los estudios)* to fall behind.

retraso *nm* 1 *(demora)* delay; **el tren llega con r.,** the train is late; **llevamos una hora de r.,** we are an hour behind schedule; **vamos con r.,** we're running late. 2 *(subdesarrollo)* backwardness, underdevelopment. ■ *Med* **r. mental,** mental deficiency, mental retardation.

retratar I *vtr* 1 *Arte* to paint a portrait of; *Fot* to photograph, take a photograph of. 2 *fig (describir)* to describe, portray, depict. II **retratarse** *vr* 1 *Arte* to have one's portrait painted; *Fot* to have one's photograph taken. 2 *fam (pagar)* to pay up, cough up.

retratista *nmf Arte* portrait painter *or* artist; *Fot* photographer.

retrato *nm* 1 *Arte* portrait; *Fot* photograph; *fig* **es el vivo r. de su padre,** he is the spitting image of his father. ■ **r. robot,** identikit picture, photofit picture. 2 *(descripción)* description, portrayal, depiction.

retreparse *vr (recostarse)* to lean back; *(ponerse cómodo)* to lounge back.

retreta *nf Mil* retreat; **tocar r.,** to sound the retreat.

retrete *nm* lavatory, toilet.

retribución *nf (pago)* pay, payment; *(recompensa)* reward, remuneration.

retribuir *vtr* 1 *(pagar)* to pay; *(recompensar)* to reward, remunerate. 2 *Am (favor)* to return, repay.

retro *adj inv fam (retrógrado)* reactionary; *(antiguo)* old-fashioned; **la moda r.,** the old-fashioned look.

retroacción *nf* retroaction.

retroactivo,-a *adj* retroactive; *Jur* **una ley con efecto r.,** a retroactive law.

retroceder *vi* 1 *(recular)* to go back, move back, back away, recede; **hacer r. a algn,** to force sb back. 2 *(echarse atrás)* to back down.

retroceso *nm* 1 *(movimiento)* backward movement, retirement. 2 *Med* aggravation, deterioration, worsening. 3 *Econ* recession. 4 *(de un arma)* recoil.

retrocohete *nm Astronáut* retrorocket.

retrógrado,-a I *adj* 1 *(que retrocede)* retrograde. 2 *fig Pol (reaccionario)* reactionary. II *nm, f (reaccionario)* reactionary.

retropropulsión *nf Av* jet propulsion.

retrospección *nf* retrospection.

retrospectivo,-a *adj & nf* retrospective.

retrovisor *nm Aut* rear-view mirror.

retruécano *nm* pun, play on words.

retuerzo *indic pres véase* **retorcer.**

retumbante *adj* resounding; *fig* ostentatious, pretentious.

retumbar *vi* 1 *(resonar)* to resound, echo. 2 *(tronar)* to thunder, boom.

retuve *pt indef véase* **retener.**

reuma *nm,* **reúma** *nm Med* rheumatism.

reumático,-a *adj & nm,f Med* rheumatic.

reumatismo *nm Med* rheumatism.

reunión *nf* 1 *(de gente)* meeting, gathering; **asistir a una r.,** to attend a meeting; **celebrar una r.,** to hold a meeting. ■ *Pol* **r. en la cumbre,** summit meeting. 2 *(encuentro, celebración)* reunion; **r. de ex-alumnos,** old students reunion. 3 *(de datos, objetos)* collection, gathering.

reunir *vtr* 1 *(congregar)* to assemble, gather together; **r. a toda la familia,** to get all the family together. 2 *(recoger)* to gather (together); *(dinero)* to raise. 3 *(coleccionar)* to collect. 4 *(cualidades)* to have, possess; **r. todos los requisitos,** to fulfil all the requirements. II **reunirse** *vr* to meet, gather, get together; **r. con algn,** to meet sb.

reválida *nf Educ Hist* final examination.

revalidación *nf* ratification, confirmation.

revalidar *vtr* to ratify, confirm, validate.

revalorización *nf Econ (de moneda)* revaluation; *(de precio)* appreciation.

revalorizar *vtr,* **revalorizarse** *vr Econ (moneda)* to revalue, revalorize; *(precio)* to appreciate.

revancha *nf* 1 *(venganza)* revenge; **tomarse la r.,** to take revenge. 2 *Naipes* return game; *Dep* return match.

revanchismo *nm* vengefulness, vindictiveness.

revanchista I *adj* vengeful, vindictive. II *nmf* person bent on revenge.

revelación *nf* revelation.

revelado,-a I *pp de* **revelar.** II *nm Fot* developing.

revelador,-a I *adj* revealing. II *nm Fot* developer.

revelar *vtr* 1 *(dar a conocer)* to reveal, disclose; **r. un secreto,** to reveal a secret. 2 *Fot (película)* to develop.

revendedor,-a *nm, f* 1 *(gen)* seller; *(detallista)* retailer. 2 *Cin Teat (de entradas)* ticket tout, scalper.

revender *vtr* 1 *(gen)* to resell; *(al por menor)* to retail. 2 *Cin Teat (de entradas)* to tout.

reventa *nf* 1 *(gen)* resale; *(al por menor)* retail. 2 *Cin Teat (de entradas)* touting.

reventar I *vtr* 1 *(hacer estallar)* to burst, explode; *(neumático)* to puncture, burst. 2 *(romper)* to break, smash. 3 *(arruinar)* to ruin, spoil. 4 *fig (agotar)* to exhaust, tire out. 5 *fam (fastidiar)* to annoy, bother; **le revienta pedir favores,** he hates asking for favours. 6 *fam (asamblea, celebración)* to disturb, break up. II *vi* 1 *(estallar)* to burst, explode; **r. de orgullo,** to be bursting with pride; **r. de ganas de hacer algo,** to be dying to do sth; **reventaba de rabia,** he was furious. 2 *fam (morir)* to peg out, snuff it. III **reventarse** *vr* 1 *(estallar)* to burst, explode. 2 *fam (cansarse)* to tire oneself out.

reventón I *adj Bot* **clavel r.,** large carnation. II *nm* 1 *(estallido)* burst, explosion. 2 *(de neumático)* blowout, puncture, flat tyre *or* US tire.

reverberación *nf* reverberation, reflection.

reverberar *vi* to reverberate, reflect.

reverbero *nm* 1 *(reverberación)* reverberation. 2 *Am (cocinilla)* cooking stove.

reverdecer *vi* 1 *(planta)* to grow green again. 2 *fig (revivir)* to revive, come to life again.

reverencia *nf* 1 *(respeto)* reverence; *Rel* **Su R.,** (Your) Reverence. 2 *(inclinación)* bow, curtsy; **hacer una r.,** to bow, curtsy.

reverencial *adj* reverential.

reverenciar *vtr* to revere, venerate.

reverendo,-a *adj & nm, f* reverend.

reverente *adj* reverent.

reversible *adj* reversible.

reversión *nf* **1** *(devolución)* reversion. **2** *(cambio total)* reversal.

reverso *nm* reverse, back; *fig* **el r. de la medalla,** the other side of the coin.

revertir *vi* **1** *(volver)* to revert, return, go back; *Tel* **conferencia a cobro revertido,** reverse-charge call, *US* collect call. **2** *Jur* to revert. **3** *(resultar)* to result **(en, in); r. en beneficio de,** to be to the advantage of; **r. en perjuicio de,** to be to the detriment of.

revés *nm* **1** *(reverso)* reverse, back, wrong side, inside; **al** *or* **del r.,** *(al contario)* the other way round; *(la parte interior en el exterior)* inside out; *(boca abajo)* upside down; *(la parte de detrás delante)* back to front; **al r. de lo que dicen,** contrary to what they say. **2** *(golpe)* backhander; *(bofetada)* slap; *Ten* backhand (stroke). **3** *fig (contrariedad)* setback, reverse; **los reveses de la vida,** life's misfortunes; **reveses de fortuna,** setbacks, blows of fate.

revestimiento *nm Téc* covering, coating.

revestir I *vtr* **1** *(recubrir)* to cover **(de,** with), coat **(de,** with), line **(de,** with). **2** *(disfrazar)* to conceal, disguise. **3** *fig (tomar)* to take on, acquire; **la herida no reviste importancia,** the wound is not serious. **II revestirse** *vr (virtud, actitud)* to arm oneself **(de,** with); **r. de paciencia,** to arm oneself with patience, be patient.

revisar *vtr* **1** *(gen)* to revise, check, go through. **2** *Fin (cuentas)* to check, audit. **3** *(billetes)* to inspect. **4** *Aut (coche)* to service, overhaul.

revisión *nf* **1** *(gen)* revision, checking. ■ *Fin* **r. de cuentas,** audit, auditing; *Med* **r. médica,** checkup. **2** *(de billetes)* inspection. **3** *Aut (de coche)* service, overhaul.

revisionismo *nm Pol* revisionism.

revisionista *adj & nmf Pol* revisionist.

revisor,-a *nm, f* ticket inspector.

revista *nf* **1** *Prensa (publicación)* magazine, journal, review. ■ **r. de modas,** fashion magazine; **r. del corazón,** love story magazine; **r. juvenil,** teenage magazine; **r. semanal,** weekly review. **2** *(inspección)* inspection; **pasar r. a,** to inspect, review. **3** *Teat* revue; **chica de r.,** chorus girl.

revistar *vtr Mil* to inspect, review.

revistero *nm* magazine rack.

revitalizar *vtr* to revitalize.

revival *nm* revival.

revivificar *vtr* to revivify, revive.

revivir I *vi* to revive, come to life again. II *vtr* to revive, bring back to life.

revocable *adj* revocable.

revocar *vtr* **1** *Jur (derogar) (ley)* to revoke, repeal; *(orden)* to cancel, rescind. **2** *Constr (enlucir)* to plaster, stucco; *(encalar)* to whitewash.

revolcar I *vtr* **1** *(derribar)* to knock down, knock over. **2** *fam (oponente)* to floor, defeat, crush. **3** *fam (examen)* to fail, flunk. **II revolcarse** *vr* to roll about; **r. en el fango,** to wallow in the mud; *fig* **r. de risa,** to split one's sides laughing.

revolcón *nm* **1** *fam (revuelco)* fall, tumble. **2** *fam (suspenso)* failure. **3** *vulg (sexual)* romp.

revolotear *vi* to fly about, flutter about, hover.

revoloteo *nm* fluttering, hovering.

revoltijo *nm,* **revoltillo** *nm (mezcla)* mess, jumble; *fig (confusión)* mess; *Culin* **r. de gambas,** scrambled eggs *pl* with prawns.

revoltoso,-a I *adj* **1** *(travieso)* mischievous, naughty. **2** *(rebelde)* rebellious, unruly. II *nm, f* **1** *(travieso)* mischievous child, handful. **2** *(rebelde)* rebel. **3** *(alborotador)* troublemaker.

revolución *nf (gen)* revolution; *Hist* **la R. Francesa,** the French Revolution; *Téc* **50 revoluciones por minuto,** 50 revolutions per minute.

revolucionar *vtr* to revolutionize.

revolucionario,-a *adj & nm, f* revolutionary.

revolver *(pp* **revuelto)** I *vtr* **1** *(mezclar)* to mix; *(ensalada)* to toss; *(líquido)* to stir. **2** *(desordenar)* to mess up, disturb; **r. la casa,** to turn the house upside down. **3** *(producir náuseas)* to upset; **me revuelve el estómago,** it turns my stomach. **II revolverse** *vr* **1** *(agitarse)* to roll; *(en la cama)* to toss and turn. **2** *(volverse)* to turn round; *fig* **r. contra algn,** to turn against sb. **3** *(el tiempo)* to turn stormy; *(el mar)* to become rough.

revólver *nm (pl* **revólveres)** revolver.

revoque *nm Constr* **1** *(enlucido)* plastering; *(encalado)* whitewashing. **2** *(material)* plaster, stucco; *(cal)* whitewash.

revuelco *nm* fall, tumble, wallow.

revuelo *nm* **1** *(revoloteo)* fluttering. **2** *fig (agitación)* stir, commotion, upheaval; **provocar** *or* **armar un gran r.,** to cause a great stir.

revuelta *nf* **1** *(insurrección)* revolt, riot. **2** *(curva)* bend, turn.

revuelto,-a I *pp de* **revolver.** II *adj* **1** *(desordenado)* jumbled, in a mess; *(enredado)* tangled; *Culin* **huevos revueltos,** scrambled eggs. **2** *(líquido)* cloudy. **3** *(tiempo)* stormy, unsettled; *(mar)* rough. **4** *(revoltoso)* agitated, annoyed; **la gente está revuelta,** people are annoyed. **5** *(época)* turbulent; **están los tiempos muy revueltos,** these are turbulent times.

revulsión *nf Med* revulsion.

revulsivo,-a *adj & nm Med* revulsive.

rey *nm* **1** *(monarca)* king; *fig* **a cuerpo de r.,** like a king; *fig* **vivir a cuerpo de r.,** to live like a king; *prov* **a r. muerto, r. puesto,** off with the old, on with the new. ■ *Rel* **(el día de) Reyes,** (the) Epiphany; **el r. de la selva,** the king of the jungle; *Hist* **el R. Sol,** the Sun King; *Hist* **los Reyes Católicos,** the Catholic Monarchs *or* Kings; **los Reyes de España,** the King and Queen of Spain; *Rel* **los Reyes Magos,** the Three Kings, the Three Wise Men. **2** *Ajedrez Naipes* king; **el r. de corazones,** the king of hearts.

reyerta *nf* quarrel, brawl, dispute.

reyezuelo *nm* **1** *pey (rey)* kinglet. **2** *Orn* **r. (sencillo),** goldcrest; **r. listado,** firecrest.

rezagado,-a I *pp de* **rezagar.** II *adj* **ir r.,** to lag behind; **quedar r.,** to be left behind. III *nm, f* straggler, latecomer.

rezagar I *vtr (dejar atrás) fig* a leave behind; *(atrasar)* to postpone, delay. **II rezagarse** *vr* to lag *or* fall behind.

rezar I *vi* **1** *(orar)* to pray; **r. a Dios,** to pray to God. **2** *(decir)* to say, read; **la placa rezaba 'Carbonilla S.A.',** the plate read 'Carbonilla S.A.'. **3** *(ser aplicable)* **r. con,** to concern, apply to; **esto no reza conmigo,** that does not concern me. II *vtr Rel (oración, misa)* to say.

rezo *nm* **1** *(acción)* praying. **2** *(oración)* prayer.

rezongar *vi* to grumble, moan.

rezongón,-ona I *adj* grumbling, griping. II *nm, f* grumbler, griper.

rezumar I *vtr (líquido)* to ooze, exude; *fig* **su cara rezumaba alegría,** her face exuded happiness. II *vi* to ooze out, seep, leak. III **rezumarse** *vr* to ooze out, seep, leak.

RFA *nf abr de* **República Federal de Alemania,** German Federal Republic, GFR.

ría *nf* estuary, river mouth; *(en Galicia)* ria.

riachuelo *nm* brook, stream.

riada *nf* flood, flooding.

ribazo *nm* embankment, bank.

ribera *nf* **1** *(de río)* bank; *(del mar)* seashore, shore. **2** *(zona)* riverside, waterfront.

ribereño,-a I *adj* riverside, waterfront. **II** *nm,f (persona)* riverside *or* waterfront dweller.

ribete *nm* **1** *Cost* edging, border. **2 ribetes,** *(indicios)* touch *sing*, something *sing*; **tener r. de cómico,** to be something of a comic.

ribeteado,-a I *pp de* **ribetear. II** *adj Cost* edged, bordered.

ribetear *vtr Cost* to edge, border.

ricacho,-a *nm, f,* **ricachón,-ona** *nm, f fam* moneybags *sing*.

ricino *nm Bot* castor-oil plant. ■ **aceite de r.,** castor oil.

rico,-a I *adj* **1** *(adinerado)* rich, wealthy; **hacerse r.,** to get rich. **2** *(abundante)* rich; **r. en proteínas,** rich in protein. **3** *(delicioso)* delicious; **esta sopa está muy rica,** this soup is very good. **4** *(bonito)* lovely, adorable; **¡qué niño más r.!,** what a lovely child! **5** *(excelente)* rich, magnificent; **una tela muy rica,** an excellent piece of material. **6** *(tierra)* rich, fertile. **7** *fam (tratamiento)* mate; **mira r., haz lo que quieras,** look mate, do what you want; **oye r., ¿tú me has tomado por imbécil?,** look mush, what do you take me for? **II** *nm, f* rich person; **los ricos,** the rich; **nuevo r.,** nouveau riche. ◆ **ricamente** *adv (lujosamente)* richly; *fam* **tan r.,** very well; **aquí estoy tan r.,** I feel great here; **he dormido tan r.,** I slept very well.

rictus *nm inv* grin; **r. de dolor,** wince of pain.

ricura *nf fam* **1** *(de comida)* deliciousness. **2** *(tía buena)* smashing girl; **¡qué r.!,** what a girl!; **¡qué r. de niño!,** what an adorable child! **3** *(tratamiento)* love; **¡oye, r.!,** hey you!, hey, gorgeous!

ridiculez *nf* **1** *(cualidad)* ridiculousness; *(objeto)* ridiculous thing; **¡qué r.!,** how ridiculous! **2** *(nimiedad)* triviality.

ridiculizar *vtr* to ridicule, deride.

ridículo,-a I *adj* ridiculous, absurd. **II** *nm* ridicule; **hacer el r., quedar en r.,** to make a fool of oneself; **poner en r. a algn,** to ridicule sb, make a fool of sb.

riego *nm Agr* watering, irrigation. ■ **boca de r.,** hydrant; **r. por aspersión,** sprinkling; *Anat* **r. sanguíneo,** blood circulation.

riel *nm Ferroc* rail; **r. de cortina,** curtain rail.

rielar *vi lit* to shimmer, gleam; **la luna en el mar riela,** the sea shimmers in the moonlight.

rienda *nf* rein; *fig* restraint; *fig* **aflojar las riendas,** to let up, slacken; *fig* **dar r. suelta a,** to give free rein to; *fig* **empuñar las riendas,** to take the reins; *fig* **llevar las riendas,** to hold the reins, be in control.

riesgo *nm* risk, danger; **a r. de, con r. de,** at the risk of; **correr el r. de,** to run the risk of. ■ *Aut* **seguro a todo r.,** fully-comprehensive insurance.

rifa *nf* raffle; **me tocó en una r.,** I won it in a raffle.

rifar I *vtr* to raffle (off). **II** *vi Méx (sobresalir)* to distinguish oneself, be outstanding. **III rifarse** *vr fam* **r. algo,** to fight over sth.

rifle *nm* rifle.

rigidez *nf* **1** *(dureza)* rigidity, stiffness. **2** *fig (severidad)* strictness, inflexibility, firmness.

rígido,-a *adj* **1** *(duro)* rigid, stiff. **2** *fig (severo)* strict, inflexible, firm.

rigor *nm* **1** *(gen)* rigour, *US* rigor; *(severidad)* severity, strictness; **con r.,** rigorously; **de r.,** indispensable; **en r.,** strictly speaking. **2** *(aspereza)* rigour, *US* rigor, harshness; **los rigores del invierno,** the rigours of winter.

rigurosidad *nf* rigorousness, strictness.

riguroso,-a *adj (gen)* rigorous; *(exacto)* exact; *(severo)* severe, strict. ◆ **rigurosamente** *adv (gen)* rigorously; *(meticulosamente)* meticulously; *(severamente)* severely, strictly; **r. cierto,** absolutely true.

rijo *indic pres véase* **regir.**

rijoso,-a *adj* **1** *(pendenciero)* quarrelsome. **2** *(lujurioso)* lustful.

rima *nf Lit* **1** *(gen)* rhyme. ■ **r. imperfecta,** half rhyme; **r. perfecta,** full rhyme. **2 rimas,** *(poema)* poem *sing*.

rimar *vtr & vi* to rhyme (**con,** with).

rimbombante *adj (gen)* ostentatious, showy; *(lenguaje)* pompous, pretentious.

rímel *nm* mascara.

Rin *n* **el R.,** the Rhine.

rincón *nm* corner; *fam* **vive en un r. de la costa,** he lives in a remote spot on the coast.

rinconada *nf* corner.

rinconera *nf Mueb* corner table.

ring *nm (pl* **rings)** *Box* ring.

ringlera *nf* row, line.

ringlete *nm Am (persona)* active *or* energetic person.

ringorrango *nm fam* **1** *(en la escritura)* rambling. **2** *(adorno)* frill, adornment.

rinoceronte *nm Zool* rhinoceros.

riña *nf* **1** *(pelea)* fight, brawl. **2** *(discusión)* row, quarrel, argument.

riñón *nm* **1** *Anat* kidney; *fam* **costar un r.,** to cost an arm and a leg, cost a bomb; *fam* **tener el r. bien forrado** *or* **cubierto,** to be well off; *fam euf* **tener riñones,** to have guts. ■ *Med* **r. artificial,** kidney machine. **2** *Culin* kidney; **riñones al jerez,** kidneys in sherry sauce.

riñonada *nf* **1** *Anat* cortical tissue of the kidney; *fam* **costar una r.,** to cost an arm and a leg. **2** *(de res)* loins *pl*; **chuleta de r.,** loin chop. **3** *Culin (guiso)* kidney stew.

río *nm* **1** *(gen)* river; **r. abajo,** downstream; **r. arriba,** upstream; *fig* **pescar en r. revuelto,** to fish in troubled waters; *prov* **a r. revuelto, ganancia de pescadores,** there's good fishing in troubled waters. **2** *fig* stream; **r. de lágrimas,** flood of tears.

rioja *nm* Rioja wine.

riojano,-a I *adj* of *or* from La Rioja. **II** *nm, f* native *or* inhabitant of La Rioja.

ripio *nm* **1** *(residuo)* refuse, waste. **2** *Constr* rubble, filling. **3** *(palabras de relleno)* padding, waffle, verbiage; *fam* **no perder r.,** not to miss a trick. **4** *Am (pavimento)* gravel.

ripioso,-a *adj* padded (out).

riqueza *nf* **1** *(cualidad)* richness, wealthiness. **2 riquezas,** wealth *sing*, riches.

risa *nf* laugh, laughter; **ataque de r.,** fit of laughter; **es (cosa) de r.,** it's laughable; **me da r.,** it makes me laugh; **r. de conejo,** forced smile; **tomarse algo a r.,** to laugh sth off; *fig* **morirse** *or* **mondarse** *or* **desternillarse** *or* **troncharse de r.,** to die *or* fall about laughing; *fam* **esta película es una r.,** this film is a scream; *fam* **mi hermano es una r.,** my brother is a laugh; *fam fig* **tener algo muerto de r.,** to have sth sitting; *fam fig* **tengo el coche muerto de r.,** my car is just sitting there; *vulg* **mearse de r.,** to piss oneself laughing.

riscadillo *nm Am Tex* cotton linen.

risco *nm* crag, cliff.

risible *adj* laughable.

risilla *nf,* **risita** *nf* giggle, titter; *(risa falsa)* false laugh.

risotada *nf* guffaw.

ristra *nf* **1** *(sarta)* string. ■ **r. de ajos,** string of garlic; **r. de cebollas,** string of onions. **2** *fig* string, series *sing*; **una r. de mentiras,** a pack *or* string of lies.

ristre *nm* **en r.,** at the ready; **máquina en r.,** camera at the ready.

risueño,-a *adj* **1** *(sonriente)* smiling; **cara risueña,** smiling face. **2** *(alegre)* cheerful. **3** *(prometedor)* bright, promising; **un futuro r.,** a bright future.

Rita *nf* Rita; *fam* **¡cuéntaselo a R.!,** pull the other one!; *fam* **¡que lo haga R.!,** let someone else do it!

rítmico,-a *adj* rhythmic, rhythmical; **gimnasia rítmica,** eurythmics *sing*, *US* eurythmics *sing*.

ritmo *nm* **1** *(gen)* rhythm. **2** *(paso)* pace, rate, speed; **llevar un buen r. de trabajo,** to work at a good pace.

rito *nm* **1** *Rel* rite; **ritos funerarios,** funeral rites. **2** *(ritual)* ritual.

ritual *adj & nm* ritual; **danza r.,** ritual dance; *fig* **ser de r.,** to be customary.

ritualidad *nf*, **ritualismo** *nm* ritualism.

ritualista I *adj* ritualistic. **II** *nmf* ritualist.

rival *adj & nmf* rival.

rivalidad *nf* rivalry.

rivalizar *vi* to rival **(en,** in).

rivera *nf* brook, stream.

rizado,-a I *pp de* **rizar. II** *adj* **1** *(pelo)* curly. **2** *(mar)* choppy. **III** *nm* curling.

rizador *nm* curling tongs *pl*, curling iron.

rizar I *vtr* **1** *(pelo)* to curl; *(tela, papel)* to crease; **r. el rizo,** *Av* to loop the loop; *fig* to split hairs. **2** *(mar)* to make choppy. **II rizarse** *vr (pelo)* to curl, go curly.

rizo *nm* **1** *(de pelo)* curl. **2** *(en el agua)* ripple. **3** *Tex* terry velvet. **4** *Av* loop.

rizoma *nm* *Bot* rhizome.

rizoso,-a *adj* naturally curly.

RNE *nf abr de* **Radio Nacional de España.**

róbalo *nm*, **robalo** *nm (pez)* bass.

robar *vtr* **1** *(objeto)* to steal; *(banco, persona)* to rob; *(casa)* to break into, burgle; **le robaron la cartera,** he had his wallet stolen; **r. un coche,** to steal a car; *fig* **en aquel supermercado te roban,** they really rip you off in that supermarket; *fig* **robarle el corazón a algn,** to steal sb's heart. **2** *Naipes (carta)* to draw.

robinia *nf* *Bot* false acacia, robinia.

roble *nm* *Bot* oak (tree); *fig* **fuerte como un r.,** as strong as an ox. ■ **r. albar,** durmast oak, sessile oak; **r. americano,** red oak; **r. cerris** *or* **turco,** Turkey oak.

robledal *nm*, **robledo** *nm* oak grove *or* wood.

roblón *nm* rivet.

robo *nm (gen)* robbery, theft; *(en casa)* burglary; **cometer un r.,** to commit a robbery; *fig* **estos precios son un r.,** these prices are daylight robbery. ■ **r. a mano armada,** armed robbery.

robot *nm (pl* **robots)** robot.

robótica *nf* robotics *sing*.

robustecer I *vtr* to strengthen. **II robustecerse** *vr* to gain strength, grow stronger.

robustecimiento *nm* strengthening.

robustez *nf* robustness, strength, sturdiness.

robusto,-a *adj* robust, strong, sturdy.

roca *nf* rock; **cristal de r.,** rock crystal; *fig* **tener un corazón de r.,** to have a heart of stone.

rocalla *nf* pebbles *pl*, stone chippings *pl*.

rocambolesco,-a *adj* incredible, fantastic, farfetched.

roce *nm* **1** *(fricción)* rubbing; *(en la piel)* chafing. **2** *(marca) (en la pared)* scuff mark; *(en la piel)* chafing mark, graze. **3** *(contacto ligero)* brush, light touch. **4** *fam (trato entre personas)* contact. **5** *fam (discusión)* friction; **ha tenido varios roces con su jefe,** she has had a few disagreements with her boss.

rochela *nf Am* din, racket.

rociada *nf* **1** *(rociadura)* spraying, sprinkling. **2** *fig* shower, hail, stream; **una r. de balas,** a hail of bullets. **3** *(rocío)* dew.

rociar I *vtr* **1** *(salpicar)* to spray, sprinkle. **2** *fig (esparcir)* to scatter, strew; *fam* **r. una comida con vino,** to wash down a meal with wine. **II** *v impers* **roció anoche,** a dew fell last night.

rocín *nm* **1** *Zool (caballo)* nag, hack. **2** *fam fig (zoquete)* blockhead, stupid fellow.

rocío *nm* dew.

rockero,-a *Mús* **I** *adj* rock; **música rockera,** rock music. **II** *nm,f (cantante)* rock singer; *(músico)* rock musician; *(fan)* rock fan.

rococó *adj & nm Arte* rococo.

Rocosas *npl* **las R.,** the Rockies.

rocoso,-a *adj* rocky, stony.

roda *nf Náut* stem.

rodaballo *nm (pez)* turbot.

rodada *nf* tyre *or US* tire mark.

rodado,-a I *pp de* **rodar. II** *adj* **1** *(piedra)* smooth, rounded; **canto r.,** boulder; *fig* **venir r.,** to happen at just the right moment. **2** *(vehículo, transporte)* on wheels, wheeled; **tráfico r.,** road traffic, vehicular traffic. **3** *fig (persona)* experienced.

rodaja *nf* slice; **en rodajas,** sliced.

rodaje *nm* **1** *Cin (filmación)* filming, shooting. **2** *Aut* running in; **'en r.',** 'running in'.

rodamiento *nm Téc* bearing. ■ **r. de bolas,** ball bearing.

Ródano *n* **el R.,** the Rhone.

rodante *adj* rolling.

rodapié *nm* skirting board, *US* baseboard.

rodar I *vtr* **1** *Cin (película, escena)* to film, shoot. **2** *Aut (coche)* to run in. **II** *vi* **1** *(gen)* to roll, turn; **el camión rodó por la pendiente,** the lorry rolled down the hill; **rodó escaleras abajo,** he fell down the stairs; *fig* **echarlo todo a r.,** *(estropearlo)* to spoil everything; *(desistir)* to give up. **2** *(rondar)* to roam, wander, drift; **no me gusta tener mis papeles rodando por la casa,** I don't like having my paperwork all over the house; **r. por el mundo,** to roam the world. **3** *Aut* to run; **es un coche que rueda bien,** it's a car that runs well.

Rodas *n* Rhodes.

rodear I *vtr* **1** *(gen)* to surround, encircle; **la policía rodeó el edificio,** the police surrounded the building; **un bosque rodea la casa,** the house is surrounded by a wood. **2** *Am (ganado)* to round up. **II rodearse** *vr* to surround oneself **(de,** with); **serodea de todas las comodidades,** he surrounds himself with all kinds of comforts.

rodeo *nm* **1** *(desvío)* detour; **dar un r.,** to make a detour. **2** *(al hablar)* evasiveness; **andarse con rodeos,** to beat about the bush; **no andarse con rodeos,** to get straight to the point. **3** *(encierro de ganado)* round-up; *(espectáculo)* rodeo.

rodera *nf* track, tyre *or US* tire mark.

Rodesia *n* Rhodesia.

rodesiano,-a *adj & nm,f* Rhodesian.

rodete *nm* **1** *Peluq* bun, chignon. **2** *(para cargar cosas en la cabeza)* (ring-shaped) pad.

rodilla *nf* **1** *Anat* knee; **de rodillas,** *(arrodillado)* kneeling; *fig (humildemente)* on bended knees; **doblar** or **hincar la r.,** *(arrodillarse)* to go down on one knee; *fig (humillarse)* to humble oneself; **hincarse de rodillas,** to kneel down, go down on one's knees. **2** *(trapo)* cloth, floorcloth.

rodillada *nf*, **rodillazo** *nm* blow with the knee; **dar un r. a algn,** to knee sb.

rodillera *nf* **1** *Cost* knee patch. **2** *Dep* knee pad.

rodillo *nm* roller. ■ **r. de cocina,** rolling pin.

rododendro *nm Bot* rhododendron.

Rodríguez *nm fam* Rodríguez; *fam (marido)* **estar de R.,** to be alone while one's family is away on holiday, be a grass widower.

roedor,-a *adj & nm Zool* rodent.

roedura *nf* **1** *(acción)* gnawing. **2** *(marca)* gnaw mark.

roer *vtr* **1** *(hueso)* to gnaw; *(galleta)* to nibble at. **2** *fig* to gnaw, nag, torment; **los remordimientos le roen la conciencia**, feelings of guilt gnawed at his conscience; *fig* **un hueso duro de r.**, a hard nut to crack.

rogar *vtr* **1** *(pedir)* to request, ask; *(implorar)* to beg, implore, plead; **hacerse de r.**, to play hard to get; **le rogó que se marchara**, he asked her to leave; **'se ruega silencio'**, 'silence please'. **2** *(rezar)* to pray.

rogativas *nfpl Rel* rogations.

roído,-a I *pp* de **roer**. II *adj* gnawed, eaten away.

roigo *indic pres véase* **roer**.

rojear *vi* to redden, turn red.

rojez *nf* redness.

rojiblanco,-a *adj* red-and-white.

rojizo,-a *adj* reddish.

rojo,-a I *adj* **1** *(encarnado)* red; *Fin* **estar en números rojos**, to be in the red; **Mar R.**, Red Sea; **ponerse r.**, *(gen)* to turn red; *(ruborizarse)* to blush; **r. de ira**, red with anger. **2** *(caliente)* red-hot. **3** *Pol (comunista)* red, communist; *Hist (en la guerra civil española)* Republican. II *nm (color)* red; **al r. vivo**, *(caliente)* red-hot; *fig (tenso)* very tense, very heated. III *nm, f Pol (comunista)* red, communist; *Hist (en la guerra civil española)* Republican.

rol *nm* **1** *(lista)* roll, list. **2** *(papel)* role; **jugar un r.**, to play a role.

rolar *vi Am* to associate **(con,** with), go around **(con,** with).

rollizo,-a *adj* chubby, plump.

rollo *nm* **1** *(gen)* roll; **r. de papel higiénico**, roll of toilet paper; *Culin* **r. de primavera**, spring roll. **2** *(de grasa)* roll, layer. **3** *fam (pesadez)* drag, bore, pain; **es el mismo r. de siempre**, it's the same old story; **este libro es un r.**, this book is a drag; **este tío es un r.**, this guy is a pain in the neck; **un r. de película**, a boring film. **4** *fam (asunto, historia)* affair; **no está en el r.**, he's not one of us; **tiene un r. con Pedro**, she's having a fling with Pedro.

rom *nm Inform* rom.

Roma *nf* Rome; *fig* **revolver R. con Santiago**, to move heaven and earth; *prov* **cuando fueres a R. haz lo que vieres**, when in Rome do as the Romans do; *prov* **todos los caminos conducen a R.,** all roads lead to Rome.

romana *nf (balanza)* steelyard.

romance I *adj Ling* Romance. II *nm* **1** *(idioma)* Romance; *(español)* Spanish; *fig* **hablar en r.**, to speak plainly **2** *Lit* narrative poem, romance, ballad. **3** *(aventura amorosa)* romance.

romancero *nm Lit* collection of romances.

románico,-a *adj & nm* **1** *Arte Arquit* Romanesque. **2** *Ling* Romance.

romano,-a *adj & nm,f* Roman.

romanticismo *nm* romanticism.

romántico,-a *adj & nm,f* romantic.

romanza *nf Mús* romance.

rombo *nm Geom* rhombus.

romboide *nm* rhomboid.

romería *nf Rel* pilgrimage; *(excursión)* trip, excursion.

romero,-a¹ *nm,f Rel* pilgrim.

romero² *nm Bot* rosemary.

romo,-a *adj* **1** *(sin punta)* blunt, dull. **2** *(nariz)* snub.

rompecabezas *nm inv* **1** *(juego)* (jigsaw) puzzle. **2** *fig (problema)* riddle, puzzle; **este caso es un r.**, this case is a riddle.

rompecorazones *nmf inv fam* heartbreaker, heartthrob.

rompehielos *nm inv Náut* icebreaker.

rompeolas *nm inv* breakwater, jetty.

romper *(pp roto)* I *vtr* **1** *(gen)* to break; *(papel, tela)* to tear; *(vajilla, cristal)* to smash, shatter; *(pantalones)* to split; **r. las hojas de un libro**, to tear *or* rip out the pages of a book; *fig* **r. el hielo**, to break the ice; *fam* **r. la cabeza** *or* **crisma**, to kill, clobber. **2** *(relaciones)* to break off; *(contrato)* to break. **3** *(cerca, límite)* to break through *or* down. **4** *(gastar)* to wear out. **5** *Mil* **r. el fuego**, to open fire; **r. filas**, to break ranks, fall out; **r. las hostilidades**, to initiate hostilities. **6** *(mar, aire)* to cleave. II *vi* **1** *(olas, día)* to break. **2** *(acabar)* to break **(con,** with); **ha roto con su pasado**, she broke with her past; **rompió con su novio**, she broke it off with her boyfriend. **3** *(empezar)* **r. a**, to burst out; **rompió a llorar**, he burst out crying; **r. en**, to burst into; **rompió en llanto**, she burst into tears. III **romperse** *vr* **1** *(gen)* to break; *(papel, tela)* to tear; **se le han roto las gafas**, he's broken his glasses; **se me han roto las medias**, I've torn my stockings; **se me han roto los vaqueros**, my jeans have split; **se rompió por la mitad**, it broke *or* split in half; *fig* **r. la cabeza**, to rack one's brains; *fam (persona)* **de rompe y rasga**, determined, resolute. **2** *(desgastarse)* to wear out.

rompible *adj* breakable.

rompiente *nm* reef, shoal.

rompimiento *nm (rotura)* breaking, breakage; *fig (de relaciones)* breaking-off.

ron *nm* rum.

roncadora *nf Am* large spur.

roncal¹ *nm Orn* nightingale.

roncal² *nm Culin* variety of cheese made from ewe's milk.

roncar *vi* to snore.

roncear I *vtr Arg Chi (mover con palancas)* to lever, move by levering. II *vi Am (espiar)* to spy on, keep watch on.

roncha *nf* **1** *Med (en la piel)* swelling, lump; *fig* **levantar ronchas**, to cause a stir. **2** *(rodaja)* (round) slice.

ronco,-a *adj* hoarse; **quedarse r.**, to lose one's voice.

ronda *nf* **1** *(patrulla)* round, beat, patrol; **hacer la r.**, to do one's rounds. **2** *Mús (conjunto)* group of strolling minstrels; **salir de r.**, to go out and sing serenades. **3** *(carretera)* ring road; *(paseo)* avenue. **4** *(serie)* round; **pagar una r.**, to pay for a round of drinks. **5** *Naipes* hand, round.

rondalla *nf* **1** *Mús* group of strolling minstrels. **2** *(cuento)* tale, story.

rondar I *vtr* **1** *(vigilar)* to patrol, do the rounds of. **2** *pey (merodear)* to prowl around, hang about, haunt; **siempre ronda por aquí**, he's always prowling around here. **3** *(cortejar)* to woo, court. **4** *(estar cerca)* to be about *or* approximately; **debe r. los sesenta**, he must be about sixty; **me anda rondando un catarro**, I'm getting a cold; **me ronda el sueño**, I'm feeling sleepy. II *vi* **1** *(vigilar)* to patrol. **2** *(merodear)* to prowl around, roam around; **me gusta r. por las tiendas**, I like wandering around the shops.

rondón (de) *loc adv* unexpectedly, unannounced; **colarse de r.**, to slip in unnoticed.

ronquear *vi* to be hoarse.

ronquera *nf* hoarseness.

ronquido *nm* snore, snoring.

ronronear *vi* to purr.

ronroneo *nm* purring.

ronzal *nm* halter.

ronzar *vi* to crunch, munch.

roña I *nf* **1** *(mugre)* filth, dirt. **2** *Med Vet (sarna)* mange. **3** *fam (tacañería)* meanness, stinginess. II *nmf fam (tacaño)* scrooge, miser.

roñería *nf* meanness, stinginess.

roñica *fam* I *adj* mean, stingy. II *nmf* scrooge, miser.

roñoso,-a I *adj* **1** *(mugriento)* filthy, dirty. **2** *Med Vet (sarnoso)* mangy. **3** *fam (tacaño)* mean, stingy. II *nm, f (tacaño)* scrooge, miser.

ropa *nf* **1** *(gen)* clothes *pl*, clothing; **quítate la r.**, take your clothes off; *fig* **a quema r.**, point-blank; *fig* **hay r. tendida**, watch what you say; *fig* **no tocar la r. a algn**, not to touch a hair of sb's head; *prov* **la r. sucia se lava en casa,** one should not wash one's dirty linen in public. ■ **r. blanca,** (household) linen; *Cost* **r. hecha,** ready-made clothes; **r. interior,** underwear. **2** *Culin* **r. vieja,** meat stew.

ropaje *nm* robes *pl*, vestment.

ropavejero,-a *nm,f* second-hand clothes dealer.

ropero *nm* **(armarío) r.,** wardrobe, *US* (clothes) closet.

roque *nm* **1** *Ajedrez* rook. **2** *fam* **quedarse r.,** to fall fast asleep.

roqueda *nf*, **roquedal** *nm* rocky place.

roquero,-a *adj* & *nm,f véase* **rockero,-a.**

rorro *nm fam* baby.

rosa I *adj inv (color)* pink; **clavel r.,** pink carnation; **novela r.,** romantic novel; *fig* **verlo todo de color r.,** to see everything through rose-tinted spectacles. **II** *nf* **1** *Bot* rose; *fig* **fresco como una r.,** as fresh as a daisy; *fig* **no hay r. sin espinas,** there's no rose without a thorn; *prov* **la vida no es un lecho de rosas,** life is not a bed of roses. ■ *Náut* **r. de los vientos,** compass (rose); *Bot* **r. silvestre,** dog rose. **2** *Arquit (rosetón)* rose window. **3** *SAm (rosal)* rosebush. **III** *nm (color)* pink.

rosáceo,-a *adj* rose-coloured, rosy.

rosado,-a I *adj* **1** *(de color rosa)* pink, rosy. **2** *(vino)* rosé. **II** *nm (vino)* rosé.

rosal *nm Bot* rosebush.

rosaleda *nf Bot* rose garden.

rosario *nm* **1** *Rel* rosary, beads *pl*; **rezar el r.,** to say the rosary; *fig* **acabar como el r. de la aurora,** to come to an abrupt end, end badly. **2** *(sarta)* string, series *sing*; **r. de improperios,** string of insults.

rosbif *nm (pl **rosbifs**) Culin* roast beef.

rosca *nf* **1** *(de tornillo)* thread; **r. de Arquímedes,** Archimedes' screw; **tapón de r.,** screw-on top; *fig* **pasarse de r.,** to go too far; *fam* **hacer la r. a algn,** to suck up to sb. **2** *(anillo)* ring; *(espiral)* spiral, coil. **3** *Culin* ring-shaped roll *or* pastry. **4** *Arg Chi (discusión)* argument; *(pelea)* fight, clash.

rosco *nm Culin* ring-shaped roll *or* pastry; *vulg* **no comerse un r.,** not to get one's oats.

roscón *nm Culin* ring-shaped roll *or* pastry.

roseta *nf* **1** *(en las mejillas)* flush. **2** *(de cintas)* rosette. **3** *(de regadera)* rose, nozzle. **4** **rosetas,** *(de maíz)* popcorn *sing*. **5** *Am (de espuela)* rowel.

rosetón *nm Arquit* rose window.

rosquilla *nf* ring-shaped pastry; *fam fig* **venderse como rosquillas,** to sell like hot cakes.

rosticería *nf Méx Nic* grillroom, steak house.

rostro *nm* **1** *(cara)* face; *fam* **echarle r.,** to be daring *or* cheeky; *fam* **tener mucho r.,** to have a lot of nerve; *fam* **¡vaya r.!,** what cheek! **2** *(pico de ave)* beak.

rotación *nf* rotation. ■ *Agr* **r. de cultivos,** crop rotation.

rotativo,-a I *adj* rotary, revolving. **II** *nm* newspaper. **III** *nf* rotary press.

rotatorio,-a *adj* rotary, rotating, revolving.

roto,-a I *pp de* **romper. II** *adj* **1** *(gen)* broken; *(papel)* torn; *(gastado)* worn out; *fig* **con el corazón r.,** heart-broken. **2** *(andrajoso)* in tatters, tattered, ragged. **III** *nm* **1** *(agujero)* hole, tear; *prov* **nunca falta un r. para un descosido,** birds of a feather flock together. **2** *Arg Per (chileno)* Chilean. **3** *Méx (petimetre de pueblo)* village dandy.

rotonda *nf Arquit* rotunda.

rotor *nm* rotor.

rótula *nf* **1** *Anat* kneecap. **2** *Téc* ball-and-socket joint.

rotulación *nf* lettering.

rotulador *nm* felt-tip pen.

rotular¹ *vtr* to letter, label.

rotular² *adj Anat* kneecap.

rótulo *nm* **1** *(letrero)* sign, notice; **r. de neón,** neon sign. **2** *(titular)* title, heading.

rotundidad *nf* firmness.

rotundo,-a *adj* **1** *(terminante)* categorical; **éxito r.,** resounding success; **una negativa rotunda,** a flat refusal. **2** *(frase)* well-rounded.

rotura *nf* **1** *(ruptura)* breaking, breakage, break, crack; *Med* fracture. **2** *(en un tejido)* tear, rip.

roturación *nf Agr* ploughing, *US* plowing.

roturadora *nf* plough, *US* plow.

roturar *vtr* to plough, *US* plow.

roulotte *nf Aut* caravan.

royalty *nm (pl **royalties**)* royalty.

rozadura *nf* scratch, chafing mark, abrasion.

rozagante *adj* **1** *(ufanoso)* splendid, magnificent. **2** *(vistoso)* showy.

rozamiento *nm* **1** *(roce)* rubbing, friction. **2** *fig (discusión)* friction, disagreement.

rozar I *vtr* **1** *(raspar)* to touch, rub against, brush against; *fig (tema)* to touch on. **2** *Agr (ganado)* to graze. **3** *Constr (pared)* to make grooves in *or* on. **II** *vi (raspar)* to rub. **III** **rozarse** *vr* **1** *(raspar)* to rub, brush (**con,** against). **2** *fig* to rub shoulders (**con,** with).

r.p.m. *abr de* **revoluciones por minuto,** revolutions per minute, rpm.

Rte. *abr de* **remite, remitente,** sender.

RTVE *nf abr de* **Radio Televisión Española.**

rúa *nf* street.

Ruanda *n* Rwanda.

ruandés,-esa *adj* & *nm,f* Rwandan.

rubéola *nf Med* German measles *pl*, rubella.

rubí *nm (pl **rubíes**) Min* ruby.

rubia *nf* **1** *(mujer)* blonde. ■ **r. oxigenada,** peroxide blonde; **r. platino,** platinum blonde. **2** *fam (peseta)* one-peseta coin.

rubiales *nmf inv fam (hombre)* blond; *(mujer)* blonde.

rubicundo,-a *adj* rosy, rubicund, reddish.

rubio,-a I *adj (pelo, persona)* fair, blond, blonde; **tabaco r.,** Virginia tobacco. **II** *nm* **1** *(hombre)* blond. **2** *(pez)* red gurnard.

rublo *nm (moneda)* rouble.

rubor *nm* blush, flush.

ruborizarse *vr* to blush, go red.

ruboroso,-a *adj* blushing, bashful.

rúbrica *nf* **1** *(trazo)* flourish added to a signature. **2** *(título)* title, heading.

rubricar *vtr* **1** *(firmar)* to sign with a flourish; **firmado y rubricado,** signed and sealed. **2** *(respaldar)* to endorse, ratify.

rubro,-a I *adj fml* red. **II** *nm (título)* title, heading.

ruco,-a *adj CAm (caballo)* old, useless.

ruda *nf Bot* rue.

rudeza *nf* roughness, coarseness.

rudimentario,-a *adj* rudimentary.

rudimento *nm* radiment.

rudo,-a *adj* rough, coarse.

rueca *nf* distaff.

rueda *nf* **1** *(gen)* wheel; *fig* **comulgar con ruedas de molino,** to be very gullible; *fam* **ir sobre ruedas,** to go very smoothly. ■ **r. de la fortuna,** wheel of fortune; **r. de molino,** millwheel; *Aut* **r. de recambio,** spare wheel; *Aut* **r. delantera/trasera,** front/rear wheel; *Téc* **r. dentada,** cog, cogwheel. **2** *(corro)* circle, ring. ■ **r. de prensa,** press conference. **3** *(rodaja)* round slice. **4** *(turno)* round.

ruedo nm 1 Taur bullring, arena; **dar la vuelta al r.,** to walk round the bullring receiving applause; fig **echarse al r.,** to launch oneself into sth. 2 (de falda) hem. 3 (estera) round mat.

ruego nm request, petition; **'ruegos y preguntas',** 'any other business'.

rufián nm 1 (granuja) villain, scoundrel. 2 (proxeneta) pimp.

rufianesca nf underworld.

rufianesco,-a adj villainous.

rugby nm Dep rugby.

rugido nm 1 (bramido) roar, bellow; (viento) howl. 2 **rugidos,** (de tripas) rumbling sing.

rugir vi to roar, bellow; (viento) to howl.

rugoso,-a adj wrinkled, rough.

ruibarbo nm Bot rhubarb.

ruido nm (gen) noise; (sonido) sound; (jaleo) din, row; fig stir, commotion; **hacer or meter r.,** to make a noise; fig to cause a stir; fam fig **mucho r. y pocas nueces,** much ado about nothing. ■ **r. ambiental** or **de fondo,** background noise.

ruidosa,-a adj 1 (que hace ruido) noisy, loud. 2 fig (sensacional) sensational.

ruin adj 1 (vil) vile, base, despicable. 2 (tacaño) mean, stingy. 3 (raquítico) puny, weak.

ruina nf 1 (hundimiento) ruin, collapse; **amenazar r.,** to be about to collapse. 2 fig downfall, end, fall. 3 **ruinas,** Arqueol ruins.

ruindad nf 1 (vileza) vileness, meanness. 2 (acto) mean act, low trick.

ruinoso,-a adj 1 Fin ruinous, disastrous. 2 (destartalado) dilapidated, tumbledown.

ruiseñor nm Orn nightingale. ■ **r. bastardo,** Cetti's warbler.

ruleta nf roulette. ■ **r. rusa,** Russian roulette.

rulo nm 1 (rizo) curl, ringlet. 2 (para rizar el pelo) curler, roller. 3 Culin rolling pin.

rulot nf (pl rulots) véase **roulotte.**

Rumanía n Rumania, Roumania.

rumano,-a I adj Rumanian, Roumanian. II nm,f (persona) Rumanian, Roumanian. III nm (idioma) Rumanian, Roumanian.

rumba nf Mús rhumba, rumba.

rumbear vi to dance the rhumba or rumba.

rumbo[1] nm 1 (dirección) direction, course; (con) **r. a,** bound for, heading for, in the direction of; **marcar el r.,** to set the course; **perder el r.,** (avión, barco) to go off course; fig (persona) to lose one's bearings; **poner r. a,** to head for. 2 Arg (herida) cut on the head.

rumbo[2] nm fam fig 1 (pompa) pomp, show, lavish display. 2 (generosidad) generosity, lavishness.

rumboso,-a adj fam fig sumptuous, lavish.

rumia nf rumination.

rumiante adj & nm ruminant.

rumiar I vtr 1 (mascar) to chew. 2 fig (pensar) to ruminate, reflect on, chew over. II vi (mascar) to ruminate, chew the cud.

rumor nm 1 (habladuría) rumour, US rumor; **corre el r. de que ...,** rumour has it that ... . 2 (murmullo) murmur.

rumorearse v unipers to be rumoured, US be rumored; **se rumorea que ...,** it is rumoured that ... .

rumoroso,-a adj (arroyo) murmuring.

runfla nf, **runflada** nf fam 1 (montón) lot, heap. 2 Am (gentío) crowd.

runrún nm 1 (ruido) buzz, noise, murmur. 2 fam (rumor) rumour, US rumor.

runrunearse v unipers fam to be rumoured, US be rumored.

runruneo nm buzz, noise murmur.

rupestre adj rock; **pintura r.,** cave painting.

rupia nf (moneda) rupee.

ruptura nf (rotura) breaking, breakage; fig (de relaciones) breaking-off.

rural adj rural, country; **finca r.,** country estate.

Rusia n Russia.

ruso,-a I adj Russian. II nm,f (persona) Russian. III nm (idioma) Russian.

rústico,-a I adj rustic, rural. II nm peasant, yokel.

ruta nf route, way, road; fig **la r. del éxito,** the road to success.

rutilante adj lit shining, sparkling, gleaming.

rutilar vi lit to shine, sparkle, gleam.

rutina nf routine; **por r.,** as a matter of course.

rutinario,-a adj 1 (habitual) routine; **visita rutinaria,** routine visit. 2 (persona) unimaginative, pedestrian, dull.

Rvda. abr de **Reverenda,** Reverend, Rev. Revd.

Rvdo. abr de **Reverendo,** Reverend, Rev, Revd.

S

S, s ['ese] nf (la letra) S, s.

S abr de **Sur,** South, S.

S., s. abr de **San** or **Santo,** Saint, St.

s. 1 abr de **siglo,** century, c. 2 abr de **siguiente,** next, following.

s/ 1 abr de **suyo,-a;** véase **suyo,-a.** 2 abr de **su(s);** véase **su.**

S.A. 1 abr de **Sociedad Anónima,** Limited, Ltd, PLC, plc. 2 abr de **Su Alteza,** His or Her Highness, H.H.

sábado nm Saturday; véase tamb **viernes.**

sábana nf sheet; fam **se me pegaron las sábanas,** I overslept. ■ **s. encimera/bajera,** top/bottom sheet.

sabandija nf 1 (animal) bug, insect, creepy-crawly. 2 fig (persona) louse.

sabañón nm Med chilblain.

sabático,-a adj sabbatical.

sabatino,-a adj relating to Saturday.

sabedor,-a adj aware (de, of), informed (de, about).

sabelotodo nmf inv know-all.

saber[1] nm knowledge.

saber[2] I vtr 1 (conocer) to know; **hacer s.,** to inform; **para que lo sepas,** for your information; **que yo sepa,** as far as I know; **¿se puede s. por qué?,** may I ask why?; **vete tú a s.,** goodness knows; **ya lo sabes todo,** now you know all about it; **¡y yo qué sé!,** how should I know!; fig **a s.,** namely; fig **no sabe por dónde se anda,** he hasn't got a clue; fig **no s. dónde meterse,** to feel embarrassed; fig **s. más que Lepe,** to be nobody's fool; fam **el señor no sé cuántos,** Mr so-and-so. 2 (tener habilidad) to be able to, know how to; **¿sabes cocinar?,** can you cook?, do you know how to cook?; **¿sabes hablar inglés?**, can you speak English? **3** *(enterarse)* to learn, find out; **no lo supimos hasta ayer**, we only found out yesterday; **¿qué sabes de Marisa?**, have you heard from Marisa? **II** *vi* **1** *(tener sabor)* to taste (**a**, of); **sabe bien**, it tastes good; *fam fig* **le sabe mal que ...**, he is upset *or* annoyed that ... . **2** *Am* *(soler)* to be accustomed to. **III saberse** *vr* to know; **me lo sé todo**, I know it all; **ya se sabe**, you know how it is.

sabido,-a I *pp de* **saber. II** *adj* known; **como es s.**, as everyone knows; **es noticia sabida**, it is a well-known fact; **s. es que ...**, it is well known that ... .

sabiduría *nf* **1** *(conocimientos)* knowledge, wisdom. **2** *(prudencia)* wisdom.

sabiendas (a) *loc adv* knowingly; **a s. de que ...**, knowing full well that ... .

sabihondo,-a *fam* **I** *adj* pedantic. **II** *nm, f (sabelotodo)* know-all; *(pedante)* pedant.

sabio,-a I *adj* **1** *(con conocimientos)* learned, knowledgeable. **2** *(prudente)* wise; *(sensato)* sensible. **II** *nm, f* **1** *(instruido)* learned person, man *or* woman of learning. **2** *(poseedor de la sabiduría)* sage, wise person.

sabiondo,-a *adj fam véase* **sabihondo,-a.**

sablazo *nm (golpe)* blow with a sabre; *(herida)* sabre wound; *fam fig* **dar un s. a algn**, to touch sb for money, scrounge some money off *or* from sb.

sable *nm* sabre, *US* saber.

sableador,-a *nm, f fam* sponger, scrounger.

sablear *vtr* to touch for money, scrounge money off.

sablista *nmf fam* sponger, scrounger.

sabor *nm* **1** *(gusto)* taste, flavour, *US* flavor; **con s. a limón**, lemon-flavoured; **sin s.**, tasteless. **2** *fig (impresión)* feeling; **dejar mal s. (de boca)**, to leave a bad taste in one's mouth.

saborear *vtr* **1** *(degustar)* to taste. **2** *fig (apreciar)* to savour, *US* savor, relish.

saboreo *nm* savouring, *US* savoring.

sabotaje *nm* sabotage.

saboteador,-a *nm, f* saboteur.

sabotear *vtr* to sabotage.

sabré *indic fut véase* **saber².**

sabroso,-a *adj* **1** *(gustoso)* tasty; *(delicioso)* delicious. **2** *(agradable)* delightful. **3** *Am (hablador)* talkative.

sabrosón,-ona *adj Am (hablador)* talkative; *(simpático)* nice; *(divertido)* fun.

sabrosura *nf Am (calidad de sabroso)* tastiness; *fig (deleite)* delight.

sabueso *nm* **1** *(perro)* bloodhound. **2** *fig (persona)* sleuth.

saca *nf* large sack. ■ **s. de correos**, mailbag.

sacaclavos *nm inv* pincers *pl*, nail-remover.

sacacorchos *nm inv* corkscrew.

sacacuartos *nm inv fam* money-waster.

sacadineros *fam* **I** *nm fam* money-waster; *(timo)* racket, swindle. **II** *nmf inv (persona)* swindler, fiddler.

sacafaltas *nmf inv fam* critic, fault-finder.

sacamuelas *nmf inv fam* dentist; *fig* **hablar más que un s.**, to be a chatterbox.

sacapuntas *nm inv* pencil sharpener.

sacar I *vtr* **1** *(gen)* to take *or* pull *or* get out; **s. a algn a bailar**, to ask sb to dance; **s. brillo a algo**, to make sth shine; **s. dinero del banco**, to withdraw money from the bank; **s. la lengua**, to stick one's tongue out; **sacó un pañuelo del bolso**, she took a handkerchief from her bag; *fig* **s. a algn de sí**, to infuriate sb; *fig* **s. adelante,** *(hijos)* to give a good education to; *(negocio)* to help prosper; *fig* **s. algo a relucir**, to bring sth up (in conversation); *fig* **s. faltas a algo**, to find fault with sth; *fig* **s. fuerzas de flaqueza**, to draw strength from nowhere; *fig* **sacarle los colores a algn**, to make sb blush. **2** *(obtener)* to get; *(premio)* to win; *(dinero)* to get, make; *(conclusiones)* to

draw, reach; **¿qué notas has sacado?**, what marks did you get?; **s. algo en claro *or* en limpio**, to make sense of sth. **3** *(extraer)* to obtain, extract; **s. provecho de algo**, to benefit from sth. **4** *(introducir) (nuevo producto)* to bring out; *(nueva moda)* to bring in. **5** *(publicar)* to publish, bring out. **6** *(hacer) (fotografía)* to take; *(fotocopia)* to make. **7** *(comprar)* to get, buy; **s. un abono**, to buy a season ticket. **8** *Ten* to serve; *Ftb* to kick off. **II sacarse** *vr* **1** *(desvestirse)* to take off. **2** *(hacerse)* to have taken; **s. una foto**, to have a photograph taken.

sacarina *nf Quím* saccharin.

sacarosa *nf Quím* sucrose.

sacerdocio *nm* priesthood.

sacerdotal *adj* priestly.

sacerdote *nm* priest; **sumo s.**, high priest.

sacerdotisa *nf* priestess.

sociable *adj* satiable.

saciar I *vtr (satisfacer) (hambre)* to satiate, sate; *(sed)* to quench; *(deseos)* to satisfy; *(ambiciones)* to fulfil, *US* fulfill. **II saciarse** *vr* to satiate oneself, be satiated; **comer/beber hasta s.**, to eat/drink one's fill.

saciedad *nf* satiation, satiety; **repetir algo hasta la s.**, to repeat sth over and over (again).

saco *nm* **1** *(bolsa)* sack, bag; *fig* **no echar algo en s. roto**, to take good note of sth. ■ **s. de dormir**, sleeping bag; **s de viaje**, overnight bag. **2** *(contenido)* sackful, bagful. **3** *Anat* sac. **4** *Mil* sack; **entrar a s. en una ciudad**, to pillage a town. **5** *Am (chaqueta)* jacket; *(abrigo)* coat.

sacón,-ona *adj CAm* **1** *(acusón)* telltale, sneaking. **2** *(adulador)* flattering.

sacralizar *vtr* to consecrate.

sacramental *adj Rel* sacramental; *Teat* **auto s.**, mystery play.

sacramentar *vtr Rel* to administer the last sacraments.

sacramento *nm Rel* sacrament; **el Santísimo S.**, the Blessed Sacrament.

sacrificado,-a I *pp de* **sacrificar. II** *adj (persona)* self-sacrificing.

sacrificar I *vtr* **1** *(ofrecer en sacrificio)* to sacrifice. **2** *(matar reses)* to slaughter. **II sacrificarse** *vr* to make a sacrifice *or* sacrifices; **s. por algn/algo**, to sacrifice oneself for sb/sth.

sacrificio *nm* sacrifice.

sacrilegio *nm* sacrilege.

sacrílego,-a *adj* sacrilegious.

sacristán,-ana *nm, f Rel* verger, sexton.

sacristía *nf Rel* vestry, sacristy.

sacro,-a¹ *Anat* **I** *adj* sacrum. **II** *nm* **(hueso) s.**, sacrum.

sacro,-a² *adj (sagrado)* sacred.

sacrosanto,-a *adj* sacrosanct.

sacudida *nf* **1** *(gen)* shake; *(espasmo)* jolt, jerk; **avanzar a sacudidas**, to jolt along; **dar una s. a algo**, to shake sth. **2** *(terremoto)* earthquake. **3** *(conmoción)* shock; **s. eléctrica**, electric shock.

sacudidor *nm* carpet beater.

sacudir I *vtr* **1** *(agitar)* to shake; *(alfombra, sábana)* to shake out. **2** *(quitar) (arena, polvo)* to shake off. **3** *(golpear)* to beat. **4** *(conmover)* to shock, stun. **II sacudirse** *vr (deshacerse de)* to shake off, get rid of; **s. el polvo de la manga**, to shake the dust off one's sleeve.

sádico,-a I *adj* sadistic. **II** *nm, f* sadist.

sadismo *nm* sadism.

sadoca *fam* **I** *adj* sadistic. **II** *nmf* sadist.

sadomasoquismo *nm* sadomasochism.

sadomasoquista I *adj* sadomasochistic. **II** *nmf* sado-masochist.

saeta *nf* **1** *(dardo)* arrow, dart. **2** *(del reloj etc)* hand, needle. **3** *Mús Rel* flamenco song.

saetera *nf* loophole.

safari *nm* **1** (*cacería*) safari. **2** (*parque*) safari park.

saga *nf Lit* saga.

sagacidad *nf fml* (*listeza*) cleverness, sagacity; (*astucia*) astuteness, shrewdness.

sagaz *adj* (*listo*) clever, sagacious; (*astuto*) astute, shrewd.

Sagitario *nm Astrol Astron* Sagittarius.

sagrado,-a *adj* sacred, holy; **Sagrada Familia,** Holy Family; **S. Corazón,** Sacred Heart.

sagrario *nm Rel* tabernacle.

sagú *nm Bot* (*planta*) sago palm; (*fécula*) sago.

Sahara *n* Sahara.

saharaui *adj & nmf* Saharan.

sahariano,-a **I** *adj* Saharan. **II** *nf* (*prenda*) safari shirt *or* jacket.

sahumado,-a *adj Am fam* tipsy, merry.

sahumerio *nm*, **sahúmo** *nm* **1** (*substancia*) aromatic substance, incense. **2** (*humo*) aromatic smoke.

saín *nm* **1** (*grasa*) animal fat; (*de pescado*) fish oil. **2** (*suciedad*) dirt, grease.

sainete *nm* **1** *Teat* comic sketch, one-act farce. **2** *Culin* (*bocadito*) titbit, *US* tidbit; (*delicia*) delicacy.

sainetero *nm*, **sainetista** *nm Teat* writer of **sainetes**.

sajón,-ona *adj & nm,f Hist* Saxon.

sal *nf* **1** (*cloruro de sodio*) salt. ■ **s. fina,** table salt; **s. gema,** salt crystals; **s. gorda,** cooking salt. **2** *fig* (*gracia*) wit; (*gentileza*) charm; **la s. de la vida,** the spice of life. **3** **sales,** (*perfumes*) smelling salts. ■ **s. de baño,** bath salts.

sal *imperat véase* **salir**.

sala *nf* **1** (*habitación*) room; (*en un hospital*) ward. ■ **s. de espectáculos,** (*teatro*) theatre; (*cine*) cinema; **s. de espera,** waiting room; **s. de estar,** lounge, living room; **s. de exposiciones,** exhibition hall; **s. de fiestas,** nightclub, discotheque; **s. de lectura,** reading room; **s. de operaciones,** operating theatre; **s. de partos,** delivery room. **2** *Jur* courtroom; (*tribunal*) court.

salacot *nm* (*pl* **salacots**) pith helmet, topee.

saladería *nf Arg* meat-salting industry.

saladero *nm* salting room *or* house.

salado,-a **I** *pp de* **salar**. **II** *adj* **1** (*con sal*) salted; (*con exceso de sal*) salty; **agua salada,** salt water. **2** *fig* (*gracioso*) witty, funny; (*encantador*) charming, winsome. **3** *Am* (*infortunado*) unlucky. **4** *Arg Chi* (*caro*) expensive.

saladura *nf* salting.

salamanca *nf Arg Zool* flat-headed salamander.

salamandra *nf Zool* salamander.

salamanqués,-esa **I** *adj* of *or* from Salamanca. **II** native *or* inhabitant of Salamanca.

salamanquesa *nf Zool* gecko.

salame *nm*, **salami** *nm Am Culin* salami.

salar *vtr* **1** (*curar en sal*) to salt. **2** (*sazonar*) to salt, add salt to. **3** *Am* (*dar mala suerte*) to bring bad luck to; (*echar a perder*) to ruin, spoil.

salarial *adj* salary, wage.

salario *nm* salary, wages *pl*. ■ **s. mínimo,** minimum wage.

salaz *adj* salacious.

salazón *nm* **1** (*acción de salar*) salting. **2** (*carne, pescado*) salted meat *or* fish. **3** *Am* (*mala suerte*) bad luck.

salchicha *nf* sausage.

salchichería *nf* pork butcher's (shop).

salchichón *nm* (salami-type) sausage.

saldar *vtr* **1** *Fin* (*cuenta*) to settle, balance; (*deuda*) to pay off. **2** *Com* (*vender barato*) to sell off. **3** *fig* (*diferencias*) to settle, resolve.

saldo *nm* **1** *Fin* balance, difference. ■ **s. acreedor,** credit balance; **s. deudor,** debit balance; **s. negativo,** negative balance, deficit; **s. positivo,** positive balance, surplus. **2** (*de una deuda*) liquidation, settlement. **3** (*resto de mercancía*) remnant, remainder, leftover; **a precio de s.,** at bargain prices.

saldré *indic fut véase* **salir**.

saledizo,-a I *adj* projecting. **II** *nm* projection, ledge.

salero *nm* **1** (*recipiente*) saltcellar. **2** *fig* (*gracia*) charm; (*ingenio*) wit; **tener mucho s.,** to be very witty.

saleroso,-a *adj* (*agradable*) charming; (*ingenioso*) witty; (*animado*) lively.

salesa *nf Rel* nun of the Order of the Visitation.

salesiano,-a *adj & nm,f Rel* Salesian.

salgo *indic pres véase* **salir**.

sálico,-a *adj* Salic; **ley sálica,** Salic Law.

salida *nf* **1** (*partida*) departure; **el tren tiene su s. a las siete,** the train leaves at seven o'clock. **2** *Dep* start; **línea de s.,** starting line; **s. nula,** false start. **3** (*viaje corto*) trip. **4** (*puerta etc*) exit, way out; **callejón sin s.,** dead end; **s. de incendios,** fire exit; **tener s. a,** to open on to. **5** (*momento de salir*) coming out; (*de un astro*) rising; **s. del sol,** sunrise; **te vi a la s. del cine,** I saw you leaving the cinema. **6** *Com* outlet, market. **7** (*perspectiva*) opening; **es una carrera sin salidas,** it is a career with no openings. **8** *Fin* outlay, expenditure. **9** (*recurso*) solution, way out; **no tengo otra s.,** I have no other option. **10** *fam* (*ocurrencia*) witty remark, witticism; **s. de tono,** improper *or* unfortunate remark. **11** *Inform* output.

salido,-a **I** *pp de* **salir**. **II** *adj* **1** (*saliente*) prominent, projecting; **ojos salidos,** bulging eyes. **2** (*animal*) on *or* in heat; *vulg* (*persona*) horny, out for it.

saliente I *adj* **1** (*que sobresale*) projecting, prominent; *fig* outstanding. **2** (*cesante*) outgoing. **II** *nm* projection, overhang, ledge.

salífero,-a *adj* saline.

salinidad *nf* salinity.

salino,-a *adj* saline. **II** *nf* **1** *Min* salt mine. **2** (*instalación*) saltworks *sing*.

salir I *vi* **1** (*de un sitio*) to go out, leave; (*venir de dentro*) to come out; **¿está Marcos? —no, ha salido,** is Marcos in? —no, he's gone out; **salió de la habitación,** she left the room; **s. disparado,** to shoot off; *fig* **salió en mi defensa,** he came to my defence; *fig* **s. de dudas,** to make sure; *fam* **s. pitando,** to rush out. **2** (*partir*) to leave, depart; **el tren sale a las nueve,** the train leaves at nine. **3** (*novios*) to go out (**con,** with). **4** (*aparecer*) to appear; **el anuncio que sale en la tele,** the advertisement that's on TV; **es una revista que sale los jueves,** it's a magazine that comes out on Thursdays; **ha salido una nueva ley,** a new law has come in; **la foto salió en todos los periódicos,** the photo appeared in all the newspapers. **5** (*resultar*) to turn out, turn out to be; **¿cómo te salió el examen?,** how did your exam go?; **el pequeño les ha salido delincuente,** their youngest son turned into a delinquent; **salió presidente,** he was elected president; **salió vencedor,** he was the winner; **s. ganando,** to come out ahead *or* on top; **s. ileso de un accidente,** to come out of an accident uninjured. **6** (*ocurrir*) to happen, occur; **salga lo que salga,** whatever happens. **7** (*ofrecerse*) to come up; **le ha salido un trabajo interesante,** an interesting job has come up; **si sale la ocasión,** if the occasion arises. **8** (*precio*) to cost, come to, work out; **sale a mil pesetas,** it comes to a thousand pesetas; **s. barato/caro,** to work out cheap/expensive. **9** (*proceder*) to come from; **el vino sale de la uva,** wine comes from grapes. **10** (*brotar*) to come out; **ha salido una hoja,** a leaf has come out; **me salen granos,** I'm getting spots. **11** (*sobresalir*) to project, stick out. **12** (*parecerse*) to take after; **ha salido al abuelo,** she takes after her grandfather. **13** (*solucionar*) to work out; **el crucigrama no me sale,** I can't work out the crossword. **14** (*decir inesperadamente*) to come out with; **¡con qué cosas sales!**, the things you come out with! **15** *(dar)* to open on; **la calle sale a una plaza**, the street opens on to a square. **II salirse** *vr* **1** *(liquido, gas)* to leak (out); *(tornillo etc)* to come off, come out; **se ha salido la leche**, the milk has boiled over; *fig* **s. de lo normal**, to be out of the ordinary. **2** *(salir)* to go out; **s. de la carretera**, to go off the road; *fam* **s. con la suya**, to get one's own way.

salitre *nm Quim* saltpetre, *US* saltpeter.

saliva *nf* saliva; *fig* **gastar s.**, to waste one's breath; *fig* **tragar s.**, to swallow one's feelings.

salivación *nf* salivation.

salival *adj* salivary.

salivar *vi* to salivate.

salivazo *nm* spit.

salmantino,-a I *adj* of *or* from Salamanca. **II** *nm, f* native *or* inhabitant of Salamanca.

salmo *nm Rel* **1** *(alabanza a Dios)* psalm. **2 Salmos**, *(los de David)* Psalms.

salmodia *nf* **1** *Rel* psalmody. **2** *fam (canturreo)* monotonous singing.

salmodiar I *vi Rel* to sing psalms. **II** *vtr (canturrear)* to sing monotonously.

salmón I *nm (pescado)* salmon. **II** *adj (color)* salmon pink, salmon.

salmonado,-a *adj* **1** *(parecido al salmón)* similar to salmon; **trucha salmonada**, salmon trout. **2** *(color)* salmon pink, salmon.

salmonelosis *nf inv Med* salmonellosis, salmonella.

salmonete *nm (pescado)* red mullet.

salmorejo *nm Culin* **1** *(salsa)* sauce made from vinegar, water, pepper and salt. **2** *SAm (gazpacho)* type of gazpacho.

salmuera *nf Culin* brine.

salobre *adj (agua)* brackish; *(gusto)* salty, briny.

salobreño,-a *adj* saline.

salobridad *nf* brackishness.

Salomón *n* **Islas S.**, Solomon Islands.

salomónico,-a *adj* Solomonic, Solomonian; *Arquit* **columna salomónica**, wreathed column.

salón *nm* **1** *(en una casa)* lounge, sitting room, drawing room. **2** *(en edificio público)* hall. ■ **s. de actos**, assembly hall; **s. de baile**, dance hall. **3** *(establecimiento)* shop. ■ **s. de belleza**, beauty salon; **s. de té**, tearoom, teashop. **4** *(exposición)* show, exhibition. ■ **s. del automóvil**, motor show.

salpicadero *nm Aut* dashboard.

salpicadura *nf* splashing, spattering.

salpicar *vtr* **1** *(rociar)* to splash, spatter; **me salpicó el abrigo de barro**, he splashed mud on my coat. **2** *fig (esparcir)* to sprinkle; **salpicó su discurso de anécdotas**, he sprinkled his speech with anecdotes.

salpicón *nm* **1** *(acción)* splash, spatter. **2** *Culin* cocktail. ■ **s. de mariscos**, seafood cocktail.

salpimentar *vtr* **1** *Culin* to season. **2** *fig (amenizar)* to season, spice.

salpullido *nm Med* rash.

salsa *nf* **1** *Culin* sauce. ■ **s. bechamel**, white sauce; **s. de tomate**, ketchup; **s. ínglesa**, Worcester sauce; *fig* **en su (propia) s.**, in one's element. **2** *fig* zest, spice. **3** *Mús* salsa.

salsero,-a I *adj (entrometido)* meddlesome. **II** *nf (recipiente)* gravy boat.

saltador,-a I *adj* jumping, leaping. **II** *nm, f Dep* jumper; **s. de altura**, high jumper, **s. de pértiga**, (pole) vaulter. **III** *nm (cuerda)* skipping rope.

saltamontes *nm inv Ent* grasshopper.

saltaojos *nm inv Bot* peony.

saltar I *vtr* **1** *(obstáculo, valla)* to jump (over); **saltó la valla con facilidad**, he jumped over the fence easily; *fig* **estar a la que salta**, to be always ready to take a chance. **2** *(omitir)* to skip, miss out. **II** *vi* **1** *(elevarse en el aire)* to jump; **s. a la cuerda**, to skip; **s. de la cama**, to jump out of bed; **s. en paracaídas**, to parachute; *fig* **s. a la vista**, to be obvious, be as plain as the nose on one's face; *fig* **s. de alegría**, to jump for joy; *fig* **s. sobre algn**, to pounce on sb. **2** *(romperse)* to break, burst; **el agua caliente hizo s. el cristal**, the hot water shattered the glass; **hacer s.**, to blow up; **s. en pedazos**, to break into little pieces; *fig* **hacer s. la banca**, to break the bank. **3** *(desprenderse)* to come off; **saltó el corcho**, the cork popped out. **4** *(encolerizarse)* to explode, blow up; **por menos de nada salta**, the smallest thing makes him explode. **III saltarse** *vr* **1** *(omitir)* to skip, miss out. **2** *(no hacer caso)* to ignore; **s. el semáforo**, to jump the lights; **s. el turno**, to jump the queue; *fam* **s. algo a la torera**, to ignore sth totally. **3** *(desprenderse)* to come off; **se me saltó un botón**, one of his buttons came off; **se me saltaron las lágrimas**, tears came to my eyes.

saltarín,-ina I *adj* lively, bouncing. **II** *nm, f* **1** *(alegre)* energetic person. **2** *(persona atolondrada)* madcap.

salteado,-a I *pp de* **saltear**. **II** *adj* **1** *(espaciado)* spaced out. **2** *(irregular)* irregular. **3** *Culin* sauté, sautéed.

salteador *nm* highwayman.

saltear *vtr* **1** *(asaltar) (banco)* to rob; *(a algn)* to hold up. **2** *(hacer irregularmente)* to do in fits and starts; *(visitas)* to space out; *(partes de un libro)* to skip. **3** *Culin* to sauté.

salterio *nm Rel* Psalter.

saltimbanqui *nmf (acróbata)* acrobat, tumbler; *(hombre de circo)* member of travelling circus.

salto *nm* **1** *(acción)* jump, leap; *fig (paso adelante)* leap forward, advance, bound; **dar** *or* **pegar un s.**, to jump, leap; **de un s.**, in a flash; **s. en el vacío**, leap in the dark; **subir/bajar de un s.**, to jump up/down; *fig* **a s. de mata**, from hand to mouth; *fig* **a saltos**, in leaps and bounds; *fig* **el corazón me daba saltos**, my heart was pounding. ■ **s. de agua**, waterfall; **s. de cama**, negligée. **2** *Dep* jump. ■ *Atlet* **s. de altura**, high jump; *Natación* **s. de la carpa**, jackknife; *Atlet* **s. de longitud**, long jump; *Natación* **s. del ángel**, swan dive; **s. mortal**, somersault; *Atlet* **triple s.**, hop, step, jump, triple jump. **3** *fig (omisión)* gap. **4** *(despeñadero)* precipice.

saltón,-ona *adj* **1** *(prominente)* prominent; **ojos saltones**, bulging eyes. **2** *Am (comida)* half-cooked.

salubre *adj* salubrious, healthy.

salubridad *nf* salubrity, salubriousness, healthiness.

salud *nf* health; **beber a la s. de algn**, to drink to sb's health; **gozar de buena s.**, to be in good health; **rebosar s.**, to be glowing with health; *fig* **creo que aceptan tarjetas pero llevaré algo en efectivo para curarme en s.**, I think they accept credit cards, but just to be on the safe side, I'll take some cash; *fam* **¡s.!**, cheers!

saludable *adj* **1** *(sano)* healthy, wholesome; **tener un aspecto s.**, to look healthy. **2** *fig (beneficioso)* good, beneficial.

saludar *vtr (mostrar respeto)* to greet; *(decir hola a)* to say hello to; *Mil* to salute; **no nos saludamos**, we are not on speaking terms; *(en una carta)* **le saluda atentamente**, yours faithfully; **saluda de mi parte a**, give my regards to.

saludo *nm* greeting; *Mil* salute; **reciba un atento s. de**, yours faithfully; **un s. de**, best wishes from.

salva *nf Mil* salvo, volley; *fig* **s. de aplausos**, round of applause.

salvable *adj* which can be saved *or* kept *or* preserved.

salvación *nf (gen)* salvation; *(rescate)* rescue; *fig* **no tiene s.**, there is no hope for him.

salvado *nm Culin* bran.

salvador,-a I *adj* saving. **II** *nm, f (gen)* saviour; *(rescatador)* rescuer. **III** *nm* **1** *Rel* **el S.**, the Saviour. **2** *(país)* **El S.**, El Salvador.

salvadoreño,-a *adj & nm,f* Salvadoran, Salvadorian.

salvaguarda *nf véase* **salvaguardia.**

salvaguardar *vtr* to safeguard (**de,** from), protect (**de,** from).

salvaguardia I *nf* 1 *(documento)* safe-conduct. 2 *(protección)* safeguard, protection. II *nm (protector)* guardian.

salvajada *nf* atrocity, savagery, brutal act.

salvaje I *adj* 1 *Bot* wild, uncultivated. 2 *Zool* wild. 3 *(pueblo, tribu)* savage, uncivilized. 4 *fam (violento)* savage, wild. 5 *(incontrolado)* wild. II *nmf* 1 *(habitante primitivo)* savage. 2 *(bruto)* boor.

salvajismo *nm* savagery.

salvamanteles *nm inv* table mat.

salvamento *nm,* **salvamiento** *nm* rescue.

salvar I *vtr* 1 *(librar del peligro)* to save, rescue (**de,** from); *(barco)* to salvage. 2 *(superar) (obstáculo)* to clear; *(dificultad)* to get round, overcome. 3 *(recorrer)* to cover; **salvamos la distancia en menos de dos días,** we covered the distance in less than two days. 4 *(atravesar)* to cross. 5 *(exceptuar)* to exclude, except; **salvando ciertos errores,** except a few mistakes. II **salvarse** *vr* 1 *(sobrevivir)* to survive, come out alive; *(escaparse)* to escape (**de,** from); **¡sálvese quien pueda!,** every man for himself!; *fam* **s. por los pelos,** to have a narrow escape. 2 *Rel* to be saved, save one's soul.

salvavidas *nm inv* life belt.

salve *nf Rel* Hail Mary.

salvedad *nf* 1 *(excepción)* exception; **con la s. de mis amigos,** except for *or* barring my friends. 2 *(condición)* condition, proviso; **me excusaré con la s. de que él también lo haga,** I'll apologize on condition he apologizes too. 3 *(reserva)* reservation.

salvia *nf Bot* sage.

salvo,-a I *adj* unharmed, safe; **estar a s.,** to be safe; **poner algo a s.,** to put sth in a safe place; **sano y s.,** safe and sound; *euf* **salva sea la parte,** bottom. II **s.** *adv (exceptuando)* except (for); **s. que,** unless; **todos s. él,** everyone except for him.

salvoconducto *nm* safe-conduct.

samaritano,-a *adj & nm,f* Samaritan.

samba *nf Mús* samba.

sambenito *nm* 1 *Hist* sanbenito. 2 *fig (deshonra)* disgrace; *(descrédito)* stigma; **colgarle un s. a algn,** to give sb a bad name.

sambubia *nf Méx* pineapple drink.

Samoa *n* Samoa.

samoano,-a *adj & nm,f* Samoan.

samovar *nm* samovar.

samurai *nm,* **samuray** *nm Hist* samurai.

san *adj* saint; **el día de S. Esteban,** Boxing Day; **el día de S. José,** St Joseph's Day; *véase* **santo,-a.**

sanable *adj* curable.

sanador,-a I *adj* curative. II *nm,f* curer.

sanagoria *adj Arg* foolish, simple-minded.

sanar I *vtr (curar)* to cure, heal. II *vi* 1 *(persona)* to recover, get better. 2 *(herida)* to heal.

sanatorio *nm* clinic, nursing home, sanatorium.

sanción *nf* 1 *(penalización)* sanction. 2 *(aprobación)* sanction, approval. 3 *Jur* penalty.

sancionable *adj* sanctionable.

sancionar *vtr* 1 *(castigar)* to penalize. 2 *(aprobar)* to sanction.

sanco *nm Am Culin* type of stew.

sancochar *vtr Culin* to boil, parboil; *Am* to boil meat in water and salt.

sancocho *nm Am Culin* stew of meat, yucca and plantain; *CAm fig* mess.

sanctasanctórum *nm Rel* sancta sanctorum, Holy of holies.

sancho,-a *nm,f Méx* sheep.

sandalia *nf* sandal.

sándalo *nm* sandalwood.

sandez *nf* piece of nonsense; **decir sandeces,** to talk nonsense; **¡qué s.!,** what nonsense!

sandía *nf Bot* watermelon.

sandinista *adj & nmf* Sandinista.

sandio,-a I *adj* silly, foolish. II *nm,f* fool.

sandunga *nf* 1 *fam (gracia)* charm, wit. 2 *Am (jolgorio)* merriment. 3 *Méx (baile)* regional dance.

sandunguero,-a *adj* jolly, fun-loving.

sandwich *nm Culin* sandwich.

sandwichería *nf* sandwich bar.

saneado,-a I *pp de* **sanear.** II *adj* sound, healthy.

saneamiento *nm* 1 *(de un terreno)* drainage, draining; *(de un edificio)* cleaning, disinfection. 2 *Fin* compensation.

sanear *vtr* 1 *(terrenos)* to drain; *(edificios)* to clean, disinfect. 2 *Fin* to compensate.

sanedrín *nm Rel* Sanhedrin.

sangrado *nm Impr* indention, indentation, indent.

sangradura *nf Med* incision, cut.

sangrante *adj* 1 *(que sangra)* bleeding. 2 *fig (flagrante)* flagrant, blatant.

sangrar I *vtr* 1 *Med* to bleed. 2 *(un árbol)* to tap. 3 *fam (sacar dinero)* to bleed dry. 4 *Impr* to indent. II *vi (emanar sangre)* to bleed.

sangre *nf* blood; **de s. caliente,** warm-blooded; **de s. fría,** cold-blooded; **donar s.,** to give blood; *fig* **a s. fría,** in cold blood; *fig* **a s. y fuego,** by fire and sword; *fig* **no llegó la s. al río,** the worst didn't happen; *fig* **s. fría,** sang-froid; *fig* **subírsele la s. a la cabeza,** to see red; *fig* **tener mala s.,** to be evil; *fam* **lo lleva en la s.,** it runs in the family; *fam fig* **tener s. de horchata,** to have water in one's veins.

sangría *nf* 1 *Med* bleeding, bloodletting; *fig* drain. 2 *(bebida)* sangría. 3 *Impr* indentation.

sangriento,-a *adj* 1 *(con sangre)* bloody. 2 *(cruel)* cruel.

sanguijuela *nf Zool* leech, bloodsucker.

sanguinario,-a *adj* bloodthirsty.

sanguíneo,-a *adj* blood.

sanguino,-a *adj & nf* blood.

sanguinolencia *nf* bloodiness.

sanguinolento,-a *adj* bloody, bloodstained; **ojos sanguinolentos,** bloodshot eyes.

sanidad *nf* 1 *(calidad de sano)* health, healthiness. 2 *Admin* public health, sanitation; **Ministerio de S.,** Ministry of Health.

sanitario,-a I *adj* sanitary, health; **centro s.,** health centre. II *nm,f* health officer. III *nm (instalaciones)* bathroom fitting.

sanjuanear *vtr Méx* to beat, hit.

sano,-a *adj* 1 *(bien de salud)* healthy, fit; *(saludable)* healthy, wholesome. 2 *(libre de error)* good, sound; *(juicio)* right; **filosofía sana,** sound philosophy. 3 *(sincero)* sincere.

sánscrito,-a *Ling* I *adj* Sanskritic. II *nm* Sanskrit.

sanseacabó *interj fam* **y s.,** and that's that!

sansón *nm fam* he-man; **estar hecho un s.,** to be as strong as an ox.

santacruceño,-a I *adj* of *or* from Santa Cruz de Tenerife. II *nm,f* native *or* inhabitant of Santa Cruz de Tenerife.

santanderino,-a I *adj* of *or* from Santander. II *nm,f* native *or* inhabitant of Santander.

santateresa *nf Ent* praying mantis.

santería *nf* **1** *(beatería)* sanctimoniousness. **2** *Arg (tienda)* shop which sells religious objects.

santero,-a I *adj* sanctimonious. **II** *nm, f* **1** *(sacristán)* caretaker, verger. **2** *(mendigo)* alms collector.

santiagués,-esa I *adj* of *or* from Santiago de Compostela. **II** *nm, f* native *or* inhabitant of Santiago de Compostela.

santiaguino,-a I *adj* of *or* from Santiago de Chile. **II** *nm, f* native *or* inhabitant of Santiago de Chile.

santiamén *nm fam* **en un s.,** as quick as a flash, in a flash, in no time at all.

santidad *nf* saintliness, holiness; **Su. S.,** His Holiness.

santificación *nf* sanctification.

santificar *vtr Rel* to sanctify, make holy; **s. las fiestas,** to keep the Sabbath and holy days.

santiguar I *vtr* to bless, make the sign of the cross over. **II santiguarse** *vr* to make the sign of the cross, cross oneself.

santísimo,-a I *adj* most holy; *fam* **hacer la santísima,** to be a nuisance. **II el S.** *nm Rel* the Holy Sacrament.

santo,-a I *adj* **1** *(gen)* holy, sacred. **2** *(bueno)* saintly; **un s. varón,** a saint. **3** *fam* blessed; **hace su santa voluntad,** he does as he damn well pleases; **todo el s. día,** all day long. **II** *nm, f* **1** *(gen)* saint; *fig* **desnudar a un s. para vestir a otro,** to rob Peter to pay Paul; *fam* **¡por todos los santos!,** for heaven's sake!; *fam fig* **Francisco no es s. de mi devoción,** I'm not terribly fond of Francisco; *fam fig* **quedarse para vestir santos,** to be left on the shelf; *fam fig* **se me fue el s. al cielo,** I clean forgot. **2** *(día onomástico)* saint's day; **hoy es su s.,** today is his saint's day; *fig* **¿a s. de qué?,** why on earth?

santón *nm* **1** *Rel* santon. **2** *(sabio)* sage, wise man.

santoral *nm Rel* calendar of saints' feast days.

santuario *nm* sanctuary, shrine.

santurrón,-a I *adj* sanctimonious. **II** *nm, f* sanctimonious person.

santurronería *nf* sanctimoniousness.

saña *nf* **1** *(crueldad)* cruelty, viciousness; **con s.,** viciously. **2** *(furor)* blind anger, fury; **con s.,** furiously.

sapiencia *nf fml (sabiduría)* wisdom; *(conocimiento)* knowledge.

sapiente *adj fml* wise.

sapo¹ *nm* **1** *Zool* toad; *fam* **echar sapos y culebras,** to rant and rave. **2** *Am* game in which coins are thrown into the mouth of a metal toad.

sapo,-a² *adj Am* astute, cunning.

saponificación *nf Quím* saponification.

saponificar *vtr Quím* to saponify.

saque *nm* **1** *Ftb* kick-off. ■ **s. de banda,** throw-in; **s. de esquina,** corner kick; **s. inicial,** kick-off. **2** *Ten* service. **3** *fam* **tener buen s.,** to be a big eater.

saqueador,-a I *adj (en ciudades)* plundering, pillaging; *(en casas)* looting. **II** *nm, f (de ciudades)* plunderer, pillager; *(de casa, tienda)* looter.

saquear *vtr (ciudad)* to sack, plunder, pillage; *(casas y tiendas)* to loot.

saqueo *nm (de ciudades)* sacking, plundering, pillaging; *(de casa, tienda)* looting.

S.A.R. *abr de* **Su Alteza Real,** His *or* Her Royal Highness, H.R.H.

sarampión *nm Med* measles *pl*.

sarao *nm* knees-up; *fam* **¡vaya s.!,** what a mess!

sarape *nm Guat Méx* type of poncho.

sarasa *nm fam ofens* queer, fairy.

sarazo,-a *adj Am* **1** *(que empieza a madurar)* ripening. **2** *fam (achispado)* tipsy.

sarcasmo *nm* sarcasm.

sarcástico,-a *adj* sarcastic.

sarcófago *nm* sarcophagus.

sarcoma *nm Med* sarcoma.

sardana *nf Mús* sardana (Catalan dance and music).

sardina *nf (pez)* sardine.

sardinero,-a I *adj* sardine; **la flota sardinera,** the sardine fishing fleet. **II** *nm, f* sardine seller.

sardo,-a *adj & nm, f* Sardinian.

sardónico,-a *adj* sardonic.

sarga *nf Tex* serge, twill.

sargento *nm Mil* sergeant; **s. primero,** master sergeant; *fam* **ser un** *or* **una s.,** to be a tyrant.

sari *nm* sari.

sarmentoso,-a *adj* bony, scrawny.

sarmiento *nm Bot* vine shoot.

sarna *nf Med* itch, scabies *sing*; *Zool* mange; *fam fig* **s. con gusto no pica,** if you want something badly enough you'll put up with anything.

sarnoso,-a *adj* itchy, scabby; *Zool* mangy.

sarpullido *nm Med* rash.

sarraceno,-a *adj & nm, f* Saracen.

sarracino,-a *nf* **1** *(pelea)* brawl, free-for-all. **2** *(masacre)* massacre.

sarracino,-a *adj & nm, f véase* **sarraceno,-a.**

sarro *nm (sedimento)* deposit; *(en los dientes)* tartar; *(en la lengua, en una pava)* fur.

sarta *nf* string; *fam fig* **s. de mentiras,** string of lies.

sartén *nf* frying pan, *US* skillet; *fig* **tener la s. por el mango,** to have the upper hand.

sartenada *nf* panful.

sastra *nf* tailoress, female tailor; *Cin Teat* wardrobe mistress.

sastre *nm* tailor.

sastrería *nf* **1** *(tienda)* tailor's (shop). **2** *(oficio)* tailoring.

Satán *nm,* **Satanás** *nm* Satan.

satánico,-a *adj* satanic.

satanismo *nm* Satanism.

satélite *nm* satellite; *fig* **país s.,** satellite state.

satén *nm Tex* satin.

satinado,-a I *pp de* **satinar. II** *adj* satiny, glossy, shiny. **III** *nm* gloss, shine.

satinar *vtr* to gloss, make glossy.

sátira *nf Lit & fig* satire.

satírico,-a *adj Lit & fig* satiric, satirical.

satirizar *vtr Lit & fig* to satirize.

sátiro *nm Mit & fig* satyr.

satisfacción *nf* satisfaction; **s. de un deseo,** fulfilment of a desire.

satisfacer *(pp* **satisfecho)** **I** *vtr* **1** *(deseos, necesidades)* to satisfy. **2** *(cumplir)* to meet, satisfy. **3** *(deuda)* to pay. **II satisfacerse** *vr* to be satisfied, satisfy oneself.

satisfactorio,-a *adj* satisfactory.

satisfecho,-a I *pp de* **satisfacer. II** *adj* satisfied; **estoy s.,** I've had enough to eat; **me doy por s.,** that's good enough for me; **s. de sí mismo,** selfsatisfied, smug.

sátrapa *nm Hist* satrap; *fig* despot, satrap; *fig* **vivir como un s.,** to live like a king.

saturación *nf* saturation.

saturado,-a I *pp de* **saturar. II** *adj* saturated.

saturar *vtr* to saturate.

saturnismo *nm Med* saturnism, lead poisoning.

Saturno *nm Astron Mit* Saturn.

sauce *nm Bot* willow.

saúco *nm Bot* elder.

saudade *nf* nostalgia, homesickness.

saudí *adj & nmf*, **saudita** *adj & nmf* Saudi; **Arabia Saudita,** Saudi Arabia.

sauna *nf* sauna.

saurio,-a *adj & nm,f Zool* saurian.

savia *nf Bot* sap; *fig* sap, vitality.

saxo *nm Mús fam* **1** *(instrumento)* sax. **2** *(músico)* saxophonist.

saxofón *nm Mús* **1** *(instrumento)* saxophone. **2** *(músico)* saxophonist.

saxofonista *nmf Mús* saxophonist.

saxófono *nm Mús véase* **saxofón.**

saya *nf (falda)* skirt; *(enagua)* petticoat.

sayal *nm Tex* sackcloth.

sayo *nm* cassock, smock; *fig* **cortarle un s. a algn,** to run sb down; *fig* **hacer de su capa un s.,** to do as one pleases.

sazón I *nf* **1** *(madurez)* ripeness; **en s.,** ripe. **2** *Culin* seasoning; **en s.,** in season. **3** *(época)* season, time; **a la s.,** at that time. **II** *nf Am (bien cocinar)* good cooking.

sazonar I *vtr Culin* to season, flavour, *US* flavor. **II sazonarse** *vr* to ripen.

s/c. *abr de* **su cuenta,** your account.

scooter *nm* scooter.

Sdad. *abr de* **sociedad,** Society, Soc.

se[1] *pron* **1** *(reflexivo) (a él mismo)* himself; *(a ella misma)* herself; *(a usted mismo)* yourself; *(a ellos mismos)* themselves; *(a ustedes mismos)* yourselves; **todos los días se lava las manos varias veces,** she washes her hands several times a day; **María se mira en el espejo,** Maria looks at herself in the mirror; **morirse,** to die; **no se lo creen,** they don't believe it; **ustedes se confunden,** you are making a mistake. **2** *(recíproco)* one another, each other; **se aman,** they love one another. **3** *(voz pasiva)* **el vino se guarda en cubas,** wine is kept in casks; **se ha suspendido el partido,** the game has been postponed. **4** *(impersonal)* **nunca se sabe,** one never knows; **se dice que,** it is said that; **se habla inglés,** English spoken.

se[2] *pron pers (dativo) (a él)* him; *(a ella)* her; *(a usted o ustedes)* you; *(a ellos)* them; **se lo diré en cuanto les vea,** I'll tell them as soon as I see them; **¿se lo explico?,** shall I explain it to you?; **¿se lo has dado ya?,** have you given it to him yet?

sé[1] *indic pres véase* **saber**[2].

sé[2] *impreat véase* **ser**[2].

S.E. *abr de* **Su Excelencia,** His *or* Her Excellency, HE.

sea *subj pres véase* **ser**[2].

sebáceo,-a *adj* sebaceous; *Anat* **glándulas sebáceas,** sebaceous glands.

sebo *nm* **1** *(para velas)* tallow. **2** *(grasa)* fat. **3** *(mugre)* grease, filth.

seboso,-a *adj* greasy.

seca *nf* **1** *(sequía)* drought. **2** *Arg (cantidad de humo)* puff of smoke.

secadero *nm* drying room.

secado *nm* drying.

secador,-a I *nm* dryer, drier. ▪ **s. de pelo,** hair-dryer. **II** *nf* clothes dryer, tumble dryer.

secano *nm* dry land; **cultivo de s.,** dry farming.

secante[1] **I** *adj (que seca)* drying; *(papel)* blotting. **II** *nm* **1** *(papel)* blotting paper. **2** *Ftb* spoiler.

secante[2] *adj & nf Geom* secant.

secar I *vtr (gen)* to dry; *(lágrimas, vajilla)* to wipe; *(una hoja)* to blot. **II secarse** *vr* **1** *(gen)* to dry; *(persona)* to dry oneself; **déjalo que se seque,** leave it to dry; **s. las manos,** to dry one's hands. **2** *(marchitarse)* to dry up, wither.

sección *nf* **1** *(corte)* section, cut; *Geom* section; **s. transversal,** cross section. **2** *(departamento)* section, department. **3** *Mil* section.

seccionar *vtr* to section, cut.

secesión *nf* secession.

secesionismo *nm* secessionism.

secesionista *adj & nmf* secessionist.

seco,-a I *adj* **1** *(sin humedad)* dry; **frutos secos,** dried fruit; **limpieza en s.,** dry-cleaning; *fig* **a secas,** just, only; *fig* **dejar s.,** to kill; *fig* **Pepe a secas,** just plain Pepe. **2** *(vinos)* dry. **3** *(personas, carácter)* dry. **4** *(tono)* curt, sharp. **5** *(delgado)* skinny; **más s. que un higo,** *(delgado)* as thin as a rake; *(viejo)* old and wizened. **6** *(golpe, ruido)* sharp; *fig* **a palo s.,** simply, on its own; *fig* **frenar en s.,** to pull up sharply; *fig* **parar en s.,** to stop dead. **II** *nm Am (coscorrón)* smack *or* knock on the head; *(puñetazo)* punch.

secoya *nf Bot véase* **secuoya.**

secreción *nf* secretion.

secreta I *nf* secret police. **II** *nmf* secret policeman *or* policewoman.

secretar *vtr* to secrete.

secretaria *nf* **1** *(oficina)* secretary's office; *Admin* secretariat; **S. de Estado,** State Department. **2** *(cargo)* secretaryship, office of secretary.

secretariado *nm* **1** *(oficina)* secretariat. **2** *(cargo)* secretaryship. **3** *Educ* secretarial course.

secretario,-a *nm,f* secretary; **s. de Estado,** Secretary of State.

secretear *vi* to whisper secrets.

secreteo *nm* whispering.

secréter *nm Mueb* writing desk, bureau.

secreto,-a I *adj* secret; **en s.,** secretly. **II** *nm* **1** *(lo oculto)* secret; **guardar un s.,** to keep a secret; **s. a voces,** open secret; **s. de Estado,** state secret. **2** *(sigilo)* secrecy.

secta *nf* sect.

sectario,-a *adj* sectarian.

sectarismo *nm* sectarianism.

sector *nm* **1** *Geom* sector. **2** *(parte)* sector; *Com Pol* **s. público/privado,** public/private sector; **un s. de la opinión pública,** a section of public opinion. **3** *(zona)* area; **un s. de la ciudad,** an area of the city. **4** *Inform* sector.

sectorial *adj* sectoral.

secuaz *nmf (seguidor)* supporter, follower; *pey* underling.

secuela *nf* consequence, result.

secuencia *nf* sequence.

secuencial *adj* sequential.

secuestrador,-a *nm,f* **1** *(raptor) (de personas)* kidnapper; *(de un avión)* hijacker. **2** *Jur* sequestrator.

secuestrar *vtr* **1** *(raptar) (personas)* to kidnap; *(aviones)* to hijack. **2** *Jur* to sequester, seize, confiscate.

secuestro *nm* **1** *(rapto) (de personas)* kidnapping; *(de un avión)* highjacking. **2** *jur* sequestration, seizure, confiscation.

secular I *adj* **1** *Rel* secular, lay. **2** *(antiquísimo)* ancient, age-old. **II** *nm* secular.

secularizar *vtr Rel* to secularize.

secundar *vtr* to support, second.

secundario,-a *adj* secondary.

secuoya *nf Bot* redwood, sequoia; **s. gigante,** giant sequoia.

sed *nf* thirst; **dar s.,** to make one thirsty; **quitar** *or* **matar la s.,** to quench one's thirst; **tener s.,** to be thirsty; *fig* **tener s. de,** to thirst for.

seda *nf* silk; *fam fig* **ir como una s.,** to go smoothly.

sedal *nm Pesca* fishing line.

sedán *nm Aut* sedan.

sedante I *adj* **1** *Farm* sedative. **2** *(sosegante)* soothing. **II** *nm Farm* sedative.

sedar *vtr* to sedate.

sedativo,-a *adj* sedative.

sede *nf* 1 *(residencia)* headquarters, central office; *(de gobierno)* seat; **s. social,** head office; *Fin* company headquarters. 2 *Rel* See; **la Santa S.,** the Holy See.

sedentario,-a *adj* sedentary.

sedente *adj* seated, sitting.

sedería *nf Tex* 1 *(comercio)* silk trade. 2 *(tienda)* silk shop.

sedero,-a *adj* silk; **industria sedera,** silk industry.

sedición *nf* sedition.

sedicioso,-a I *adj* seditious. II *nm,f* rebel.

sediento,-a *adj* thirsty; *fig* **s. de poder,** hungry for power.

sedimentación *nf* sedimentation.

sedimentar I *vtr* to settle, deposit. II **sedimentarse** *vr* to settle.

sedimentario,-a *adj* sedimentary.

sedimento *nm* sediment, deposit.

sedoso,-a *adj* silky, silken.

seducción *nf* seduction.

seducir *vtr* *(gen)* to seduce; *(persuadir)* to tempt.

seductor,-a I *adj* *(gen)* seductive; *(persuasivo)* tempting. II *nm,f* seducer.

sefardí *(pl sefardíes)* I *adj* Sephardic. II *nmf* Sephardi.

sefardita *adj & nmf véase* **sefardí.**

segador,-a *Agr* I *nm,f (persona)* reaper, harvester. II *nf (máquina)* reaper, harvester. ■ **segadora de césped,** lawnmower.

segar *vtr* 1 *Agr (maíz etc)* to reap, cut; *(césped)* to mow. 2 *fig (matar)* to mow down. 3 *fig (truncar)* to cut off; **s. la juventud de algn,** to cut sb down in his prime.

seglar I *adj* secular, lay. II *nmf* lay person; *(hombre)* layman; *(mujer)* laywoman.

segmentación *nf* segmentation.

segmentar *vtr* to segment.

segmento *nm* 1 *(gen)* segment. 2 *Inform* overlay.

segoviano,-a I *adj* of or from Segovia. II *nm,f* native or inhabitant of Segovia.

segregación *nf* 1 *(separación)* segregation. ■ **s. racial,** racial segregation, apartheid. 2 *(secreción)* secretion.

segregacionismo *nm* racial segregation, apartheid.

segregacionista *adj & nmf* supporter of racial segregation or of apartheid.

segregar *vtr* 1 *(separar)* to segregate. 2 *(secretar)* to secrete.

seguidilla *nf Mús* Spanish type of dance and music.

seguida *nf* rhythm; **en s.,** immediately, straight away; **en s. termino,** I've nearly finished.

seguido,-a I *pp* de **seguir.** II *adj* 1 *(continuo)* continuous; **una línea seguida de casas,** a straight line of houses. 2 *(consecutivo)* consecutive, successive; **tres lunes seguidos,** three Mondays in a row; **tres veces seguidas,** on three consecutive occasions.

seguido *adv* straight; **todo s.,** straight on, straight ahead.

seguidor,-a I *adj* following. II *nm,f* follower.

seguimiento *nm* 1 *(perseguimiento)* pursuit; **en s. de,** in pursuit of. 2 *(continuación)* continuation. 3 *Astronáut* **estación de s. (espacial),** tracking station.

seguir I *vtr* 1 *(gen)* to follow **(a, -)**; **a la tormenta siguió la lluvia,** rain followed the storm; **le seguía con la mirada,** she follow him with her eyes; **seguí su consejo,** I followed her advice; **¡sígame!,** follow me!; *fam* **s. a algn como un perrito,** to dog sb or sb's footsteps. 2 *(continuar, proseguir)* to continue; *(un camino)* to continue on; **s. su curso,** to take its course; **sigue hablando, te escucho,** please carry on, I'm listening. 3 *(perseguir)* to chase; **nos seguía un policía,** a policeman was chasing us. 4 *Educ (curso)* to do, follow. II *vi* 1 *(proseguir)* to go on, carry on; **sigue por la avenida**

hasta llegar a la plaza, go straight along the avenue until you reach the square. 2 *(continuar)* to continue to be; **sigue con vida,** he's still alive. III **seguirse** *vr* to follow, ensue; **de esto se sigue que ...,** it follows that ... .

según I *prep* 1 *(en conformidad con)* according to; **s. la Bibla,** according to the Bible; **s. la cara que puso,** judging from his reaction; **s. lo que dicen,** according to what they say; **s. su opinión,** in his opinion. 2 *(depende) (s. + que)* depending on; **s. lo que digan,** depending on what they say. II *adv* 1 *(como)* just as; **estaba s. lo dejé,** it was just as I had left it. 2 *(eventualidad)* depending on; **no sé qué haré, s.,** I don't know what I'll do, it depends; **s. estén las cosas,** depending on how things stand; **s. y cómo,** it all depends. 3 *(a medida que)* as; **s. iba leyendo me daba cuenta de que ...,** as I read on I realized that ... .

segundero *nm (de reloj)* second hand.

segundo,-a¹ I *adj* second; **en s. lugar,** in second place; **quedar s.,** to come second; *fig* **decir algo con segundas (intenciones),** to say sth with a double meaning. II *nm,f (de una serie)* second (one); *fam fig* **el s. de a bordo,** the second in command. III *nm (parte)* second; *véase tamb* **octavo,-a.**

segundo² *nm (tiempo)* second; **sesenta segundos,** sixty seconds.

segundón *nm* second son.

segur *nm* 1 *(hacha)* axe, *US* ax. 2 *(hoz)* sickle.

seguramente *adv* 1 *(seguro)* surely; **sólo hazlo si puedes hacerlo s.,** don't do it if you aren't sure about it. 2 *(probablemente)* most probably; **s. no lloverá,** it isn't likely to rain.

seguridad *nf* 1 *(gen)* security; **cárcel de máxima s.,** maximum security prison; **cerradura de s.,** security lock; **medidas de s.,** security measures; *Fin* **s. financiera,** financial security. 2 *(física)* safety; **s. en carretera,** road safety. 3 *(confianza)* confidence; **hablar con s.,** to speak with confidence; **s. en sí mismo,** self-confidence. 4 *(certeza)* sureness; *(verdad)* certainty; **con toda s.,** most probably; **en la s. de que ...,** knowing that ...; **para mayor s.,** *(mayor protección)* for safety's sake; *(mayor certeza)* to be on the safe side; **tener la s. de que ...,** to be certain that ... . 5 *(en administración pública)* security; **S. Social,** ≈ Social Security, *GB* National Health Service. 6 *(fiabilidad)* reliability.

seguro,-a I *adj* 1 *(gen)* secure. 2 *(físicamente)* safe; **en sitio s.,** in a safe place; **sentirse s.,** to feel safe; *fig* **ir sobre s.,** to play safe. 3 *(tener confianza)* confident; **está segura de ella misma,** she has self-confidence. 4 *(cierto)* sure; *(verdadero)* certain; **dar algo por s.,** to take sth for granted; **estoy s. de que ...,** I am sure that ... . 5 *(de fiar)* realiable; **método s.,** safe method. 6 *(firme)* steady, firm. II *nm* 1 *Seg* insurance. ■ **s. a todo riesgo,** fully comprehensive insurance; **s. contra incendios,** fire insurance; **s. contra terceros,** third party insurance; **s. de vida,** life insurance. 2 *(dispositivo)* safety catch or device; **quitar el s.,** to remove the safety catch. III *adv* for sure, definitely.

seis *inv* I *adj (cardinal)* six; *(ordinal)* sixth. II *nm* six; **a las s.,** at six o'clock; **el s. de mayo,** the sixth of May; *véase tamb* **ocho.**

seisavo,-a *adj & nm véase* **sexto,-a.**

seiscientos,-as *inv* I *adj (cardinal)* six hundred; *(ordinal)* six hundredth. II *nm* 1 *(número)* six hundred. 2 *Aut fam* 600 cc SEAT car; *véase tamb* **ocho.**

seísmo *nm Geol (terremoto)* earthquake; *(temblor de tierra)* earth tremor.

selección *nf* 1 *(gen)* selection. ■ *Biol* **s. natural,** natural selection. 2 *Dep* team. ■ **s. nacional,** national team.

seleccionador,-a *nm,f* 1 *(gen)* selector. 2 *Dep* selector, team manager.

seleccionar *vtr* to select.

selectividad *nf* selectivity; *Univ* **(prueba de) s.,** entrance examination.

selectivo,-a *adj* selective.

selecto,-a *adj* select; **ambiente s.,** exclusive atmosphere.

selector *nm* selector button; *Aut* **s. de velocidades,** gear lever, *US* gearshift.

selenita *nmf* moon dweller.

self-service *nm* self-service cafeteria.

selva *nf (jungla)* jungle; *(bosque)* forest.

selvático,-a *adj* woodland.

sellar *vtr* **1** *(documento)* to seal; *(timbrar)* to stamp. **2** *(pozo, habitación)* to close (up); *fig* **s. los labios,** to seal one's lips. **3** *fig* to conclude; **sellaron el acto con una comida,** they finished off the ceremony with a meal.

sello *nm* **1** *(de correos)* stamp. **2** *(para estampar)* seal. **3** *(precinto)* seal. **4** *(carácter distintivo)* hallmark, mark; **la calidad es el s. de la casa,** quality is the hallmark of our firm. **5** *Farm* capsule.

semáforo *nm* traffic lights *pl.*

semana *nf* week; **entre s.,** during the week; **hoy hace una s.,** a week ago (today). ■ **S. Santa,** Holy Week, Easter.

semanada *nf* week's work.

semanal *adj* weekly.

semanario **I** *adj* weekly. **II** *nm Prensa* weekly magazine.

semántica *nf Ling* semantics *sing.*

semántico,-a *adj Ling* semantic.

semblante *nm lit* **1** *(expresión)* countenance; *(cara)* face; **mudar el s.,** to change colour. **2** *fig (aspecto)* look; **tener buen s.,** to look good.

semblanza *nf lit* portrait.

sembrado *nm Agr* sown field.

sembrador,-a *nm,f* sower.

sembradora *nf Agr* seed drill.

sembrar *vtr* **1** *Agr (semillas, grano)* to sow. **2** *fig (esparcir)* to scatter, strew; **el camino está sembrado de dificultades,** life is fraught with difficulties; **s. el pánico,** to spread panic.

semejante **I** *adj* **1** *(parecido)* similar. **2** *pey (comparativo)* such; **nunca he visto nada s.,** I've never seen anything like it; **s. desvergüenza,** such insolence. **3** *Geom (triángulo)* similar. **II** *nm (prójimo)* fellow being; **nuestros semejantes,** our fellow beings.

semejanza *nf* similarity, likeness.

semejar *vi & vr* to be like, resemble.

semen *nm* semen.

semental *nm* stud.

sementera *nf* **1** *(época)* sowing season. **2** *(tierra sembrada)* sown field. **3** *fig (origen)* breeding ground, source.

semestral *adj* half-yearly; **pagos semestrales,** half-yearly payments.

semestre *nm* six-month period, semester.

semicircular *adj* semicircular.

semicírculo *nm* semicircle.

semiconductor *nm Elec* semiconductor.

semiconsciente *adj* half-conscious.

semicorchea *nf Mús* semiquaver. *US* sixteenth note.

semidesierto,-a *adj* half- deserted.

semidesnudo,-a *adj* half-naked.

semidiós,-osa *nm,f* demigod.

semidirecto,-a *adj* semidirect; *Ferroc* **un tren s.,** an express train.

semifinal *nf* semifinal.

semifinalista *nmf* semifinalist.

semifondo *nm Dep* **prueba de s.,** medium-distance race.

semifusa *nf Mús* hemidemisemiquaver, *US* sixty-fourth note.

semilla *nf* seed; *fig (orígen)* **la s. de la discordia,** the seeds of discontent.

semillero *nm* **1** seedbed. **2** *fig* hotbed, breeding ground.

seminal *adj* seminal.

seminario *nm* **1** *Educ* seminar. **2** *Rel* seminary.

seminarista *nm Rel* seminarist.

semiología *nf Ling* semiology.

semiótica *nf Ling* semiotics *sing.*

semiprecioso,-a *adj* semiprecious.

semiseco,-a *adj (vino etc)* medium-dry.

semita **I** *adj* Semitic. **II** *nmf* Semite.

semítico,-a *adj* Semitic.

semitono *nm Mús* semitone.

semivocal *Ling* **I** *adj* semivocal. **II** *nf* semivowel.

sémola *nf Culin* semolina.

sempiterno,-a *adj* everlasting, eternal.

Sena *n* el S., the Seine.

senado *nm* **1** *pol* senate. **2** *(reunión)* assembly.

senador,-a *nm,f* senator.

senaduría *nf* senatorship.

senatorial *adj* senatorial.

sencillez *nf* simplicity.

sencillo,-a *adj* **1** *(sin adornos)* simple, plain. **2** *(fácil)* simple, easy; **¡es lo más s. del mundo!,** it's the easiest thing! **3** *(persona) (natural)* natural, unaffected; *(ingenuo)* naïve, gullible; *(incauto)* unwary. **4** *(no compuesto)* single. **5** *(billete)* single.

senda *nf,* **sendero** *nm* path.

sendos,-as *adj pl* each; **con sendas carteras en la mano,** cach carrying a briefcase.

senectud *nf* old age.

Senegal *n* Senegal.

senegalés,-esa *adj & nm,f* Senegalese.

senil *adj* senile.

senilidad *nf* senility.

seno *nm* **1** *(pecho)* breast, bosom. **2** *fig* bosom, heart; **en el s. de la familia,** in the bosom of the family. **3** *(matriz)* womb. **4** *(cavidad)* cavity, hollow, hole. **5** *Geog* gulf, bay. **6** *Mat* sine.

sensación *nf* **1** *(gen)* sensation, feeling; **s. de calor,** feeling of warmth; **tengo la s. de que ...,** I have a feeling that … . **2** *(impresión)* sensation; **causar s.,** to cause a sensation.

sensacional *adj* sensational.

sensacionalismo *nm* sensationalism.

sensacionalista **I** *adj* sensational, sensationalistic; **prensa s.,** gutter press. **II** *nmf* sensationalist.

sensatez *nf* good sense; **obrar con s.,** to act sensibly.

sensato,-a *adj* sensible.

sensibilidad *nf* **1** *(emotividad)* sensibility. **2** *(perceptividad, sentido artístico)* sensitivity. **3** *Téc (precisión)* sensitivity.

sensibilización *nf* sensitization.

sensibilizar *vtr* **1** *(hacer sensible)* to sensitize. **2** *Fot (película)* to sensitize. **3** *fig (concienciar)* to sensitize, make aware; **s. la opinión pública,** to arouse the public opinion.

sensible *adj* **1** *(impresionable)* sensitive. **2** *(delicado)* sensitive; **piel s.,** sensitive skin. **3** *(perceptible)* perceptible. **4** *(que causa pena, dolor)* heavy, considerable; *fml* **lamentamos tan s. pérdida,** we regret such a sad loss. **5** *Téc (preciso)* sensitive. ◆ **sensiblemente** *adv* noticeably, considerably.

sensiblería *nf* over-sentimentality, mawkishness, gush.

sensiblero,-a *adj* over-sentimental, mawkish, gushy.

sensitivo,-a *adj* **1** *(sensible)* sensitive. **2** *(de los sentidos)* sense; **órgano s.,** sense organ.

sensorial *adj,* **sensorio,-a** *adj* sensory.

sensual *adj (hedónico)* sensuous; *(sexual)* sensual.

sensualidad *nf (hedonismo)* sensuousness; *(sexualidad)* sensuality.

sentada *nf* **1** *(acción)* sitting; **de una s.,** in one sitting. **2** *fam (protesta)* sit-in (demonstration); **hacer una s.,** to hold a sit-in.

sentado,-a *adj* **I** *pp de* **sentar. II** *adj* **1** seated, sitting. **2** *(establecido)* established, settled; **dar algo por s.,** to take sth for granted; **dejar s. que …,** to make it clear that … . **3** *(sensato)* sensible.

sentador,-a *adj Arg Chi par (prenda)* becoming, flattering.

sentar I *vtr* **1** *(en silla etc)* to sit, seat. **2** *(establecer)* to establish; **s. las bases de algo,** to lay the foundations of sth. **3** *SAm (caballo)* to rein in sharply. **II** *vi* **1** *(color, ropa, peinado)* to suit; **el pelo corto te sienta mal,** short hair doesn't suit you. **2** *(comida)* **s. bien/mal a,** to agree/ disagree with; **la salsa le sentó mal,** the sauce disagreed with him; **la sopa te sentará muy bien,** the soup will do you good. **3** *(agradar)* to please; **le sentó mal la broma,** she didn't like the joke; *fam* **la noticia le sentó como un tiro,** the news came as a terrible blow to him. **III sentarse** *vr* **1** *(persona)* to sit, sit down. **2** *(eltiempo)* to settle (down). **3** *(líquidos)* to settle.

sentencia *nf* **1** *Jur (condena)* sentence; *(decisión)* judgement; **visto para s.,** ready for judgement. **2** *(aforismo)* maxim, saying, motto.

sentenciar *vtr Jur* to sentence (**a,** to).

sentencioso,-a *adj* sententious.

sentido,-a I *pp de* **sentir. II** *adj* **1** *(penoso)* deeply felt; *fml* **reciba mi más s. pésame,** please accept my deepest sympathy. **2** *(sensible)* sensitive; **es muy s. y se enfada por nada,** she's very touchy and loses her temper very easily. **III** *nm* **1** *(gen)* sense; **los cinco sentidos,** the five senses; *fig* **hacer algo con los cinco sentidos,** to take great pains with sth. ■ **s. común,** common sense; **s. del humor,** sense of humour; **sexto s.,** sixth sense. **2** *(conciencia)* conscience; **dejar sin s. a algn,** to knock sb out; **perder el s.,** to faint. **3** *(significado)* sense, meaning; **doble s.,** double meaning; **no lo digo en ese s.,** I don't mean it that way; **s. figurado,** figurative sense. **4** *(razón de ser)* meaning, sense; **hablar sin s.,** to talk nonsense; **no tiene s.,** it doesn't make sense; **¿qué s. tiene …?,** what's the point in …? **5** *(dirección)* direction; **en s. opuesto,** in the opposite direction; *Aut* **(de) s. único,** one-way.

sentimental I *adj* sentimental; **vida s.,** love life. **II** *nmf* sentimental person.

sentimentalismo *nm* sentimentality.

sentimentaloide *adj fam* gooey, over-sentimental, gushy.

sentimiento *nm* **1** *(gen)* feeling; **buenos sentimientos,** sympathy *sing;* **una s. de alegría,** a feeling of joy. **2** *(pesar)* sorrow, grief; *fml* **le acompaño en el s.,** my deepest sympathy.

sentir¹ *nm* **1** *(sentimiento)* feeling. **2** *(opinión)* opinion, view.

sentir² I *vtr* **1** *(gen)* to feel; **no sentí nada,** I didn't feel a thing; **s. amor por algn,** to feel love for sb; **s. hambre/ calor,** to feel hungry/hot; *fig* **dejarse oír or hacerse s.,** to make itself felt. **2** *(oír)* to hear. **3** *(lamentar)* to regret, be sorry about; **lo siento en el alma,** I am terribly sorry; **lo siento (mucho),** I'm (very) sorry; **sentí mucho la muerte de tu amigo,** I'm very sorry to hear about the death of your friend; **siento molestarle,** I'm sorry to bother you. **4** *(presentir)* to feel, think; **siento que va a ocurrir algo,** I think something is going to happen. **II sentirse** *vr* to feel; **me siento mal,** I feel ill; **¿qué tal te sientes?,** how are you feeling?; **s. con ánimos de hacer algo,** to feel like doing sth, feel up to sth; **s. ofendido,** to feel offended or put off.

seña *nf* **1** *(peculiaridad)* mark; **señas personales** *or* **de identidad,** description *sing,* (personal) particulars. **2** *(gesto)* sign; **hablar por señas,** to talk in sign language; **hacer señas a algn,** to signal to sb. **3** *(indicio)* sign; **por más señas,** specifically. **4 señas,** *(dirección)* address *sing.*

señal *nf* **1** *(indicio)* sign, indication; **dar señales de vida,** to show signs of life; **en s. de,** as a sign of, as a token of; **es buena s.,** it's a good sign. **2** *(gesto etc)* signal, sign; **dar la s.,** to give the signal; **hacer señales a algn,** to signal to sb; **s. de alarma,** alarm signal. **3** *(plaça)* sign. ■ *Aut* **s. de tráfico,** road sign. **4** *(marca)* mark; *(vestigio)* trace; **deja una s. en la página diez,** mark page ten; **dejar s.,** to leave a mark; **ni s.,** not a trace. **5** *(cicatriz)* scar, mark. **6** *Tel* tone; **s. de comunicar,** engaged tone, *US* busy signal; **s. de llamada,** dialling *or US* dial tone. **7** *com* deposit. **8** *Rel* **s. de la cruz,** sign of the cross; **hacer la s. de la cruz,** to make the sign of the cross.

señalado,-a I *pp de* **señalar. II** *adj* **1** *(insigne, famoso)* distinguished, famous. **2** *(fijado)* appointed, fixed; **el día s.,** the appointed day; **un día s.,** a redletter day. **3** *(marcado)* marked, scarred; **tiene la cara señalada,** his face is scarred.

señalar I *vtr* **1** *(indicar, determinar)* to mark, indicate; *(hacer notar)* to point out; *fig (apuntar hacia)* to point to; **el aumento del paro señala un decaimiento de la economía,** the rise in unemployment is a sure sign of a lull in the economy; **la nieve señala la llegada del invierno,** (the) snow marks the beginning of winter; **señálamelo y así lo reconoceré,** point it out to me so I'll recognize it; **su derrota señala el fin de una época,** his defeat marks the end of an era. **2** *(marcar)* to mark; **s. algo con una cruz,** to mark sth with a cross. **3** *(con el dedo)* to point at. **4** *(subrayar)* to stress, underline; **s. la importancia de algo,** to stress the importance of sth. **5** *(fijar precio, fecha)* to fix, arrange; **s. la fecha de la boda,** to set the date of the wedding. **6** *(designar)* to appoint; **s. a algn para hacer algo,** to appoint sb to do sth. **7** *(dejar cicatriz)* to mark, scar. **II señalarse** *vr (sobresalir)* to stand out; *(distinguirse)* to distinguish oneself.

señalización *nf* **1** *(colocación de señales)* signposting. **2** *(señales)* road signs.

señalizar *vtr (carretera)* to signpost.

señero,-a *adj (exclusivo)* unique; *(supremo)* outstanding.

señor,-a I *adj* **1** *(distinguido)* distinguished, grand. **2** *fam* fine; **es un s. coche,** it's quite a car; **una señora casa,** one hell of a house. **II** *nm* **1** *(hombre)* man; *(caballero)* gentleman; **el s. de los bigotes,** the man with the moustache; **ser todo un s.,** to be a real gentleman. **2** *(amo)* master; *Hist* **s. feudal,** feudal lord. **3** *Rel* **El S.,** the Lord; **ministro del s.,** priest; **Nuestro S.,** Our Lord. **4** *(tratamiento de respeto)* sir; **buenos días, s.,** good morning, sir; *(en carta)* **muy s. mío,** Dear Sir; **¡sí s.!,** yes sir! **5** *(con apellido)* Mr; **el Sr. Pérez,** Mr Pérez. **6** *(con título) (no se traduce)* **el s. ministro,** the Minister.

señora *nf* **1** *(mujer)* woman; *fml* lady; **¡señoras y señores!,** ladies and gentlemen!; **una s. de unos cincuenta años,** a woman in her fifties. ■ **s. de compañía,** companion. **2** *(ama)* mistress; *Hist* lady; **en estos momentos la s. no está en casa,** the lady of the house is out at the moment. **3** *Rel* **Nuestra S.,** Our Lady. **4** *(tratamiento de respeto)* madam; **buenas tardes, s.,** good afternoon, madam; *(en carta)* **muy s. mía,** Dear Madam. **5** *(con apellido)* Mrs; **la Sra. González,** Mrs Gonález. **6** *(con título) (no se traduce)* **la s. ministra,** the Minister. **7** *(esposa)* wife; **mi s. no puede venir,** my wife cannot come.

señorear *vtr* **1** *(mandar)* to rule, control. **2** *fig (dominar)* to tower over.

señoría *nf (hombre)* lordship; *(mujer)* ladyship.

señorial *adj* stately, majestic; **casa s.,** stately home.

señorío *nm* **1** *(dominio)* dominion, rule. **2** *(terreno)* estate, domain. **3** *(majestuosidad)* stateliness. **4** *(porte distinguido)* distinction; *(elegancia)* elegance.

señorita *nf* **1** *(joven)* young woman; *fml* young lady. **2** *(tratamiento de respeto)* Miss; **¿señora** *or* **s.?,** Miss or Mrs? **3** *(con apellido)* Miss; **S. Muñoz,** Miss Muñoz. **4** *Educ fam (maestra)* **la s.,** the teacher, Miss. **5** *fam (puro)* small cigar.

señorito *nm* **1** *desus (hijo del amo)* master (of the house). **2** *fam pey (joven rico)* rich kid, daddy's boy.

señorón,-ona *adj & nm,f fam pey* big shot.

señuelo *nm* **1** *Caza* decoy. **2** *fig (cebo)* bait. **3** *Arg Bol (para ganado)* lead steer.

sepa *subj pres véase* **saber²**.

sépalo *nm Bot* sepal.

separable *adj* separable, detachable.

separación *nf* **1** separation. ■ *Jur* **s. conyugal**, legal separation. **2** *(espacio)* space, gap.

separado,-a I *pp de* **separar**. **II** *adj* **1** separate; **por s.**, separately, individually; **añadir las claras y las yemas de los huevos por s.**, add egg yolks and whites separately. **2** *(divorciado)* separated.

separador,-a *adj* separating.

separar I *vtr* **1** *(gen)* to separate; **estaban riñendo y tuvimos que separarlos**, they were arguing so we had to separate them, **hemos de s. un caso del otro**, we have to consider each case individually; **los separaron de clase**, they were put in separate classes. **2** *(desunir)* to detach, remove; **separa la etiqueta, por favor**, take off the label, please. **3** *(dividir)* to divide, separate; **los separaron en grupos de diez**, they were broken up into groups of ten each. **4** *(guardar)* to set aside; **ha separado un poco de comida para ti**, he's put aside some food for you. **5** *(apartar)* to move away; **separa la silla de la pared**, move the chair away from the wall. **6** *(destituir)* to remove, dismiss. **II separarse** *vr* **1** to separate, part company; **al llegar a la carretera se separaron**, when they reached the road they went their own ways. **2** *(matrimonio)* to separate; **sus padres se separaron el año pasado**, his parents separated last year. **3** *(desprenderse)* to separate, come off *(de,* from*)*; **se han separado las hojas del libro**, the pages have fallen out of the book. **4** *(apartarse)* to move away; **s. de las viejas amistades**, to part company. **5** *(abandonar) (gen negativo)* to part *(de,* with*)*; **nunca me separaré de este cuadro**, I shall never part with this painting.

separata *nf Impr* offprint.

separatismo *nm Pol* separatism.

separatista *adj & nmf Pol* separatist.

sepelio *nm fml* burial, interment.

sepia I *nf (pez)* cuttlefish. **II** *adj & nm (color)* sepia.

septentrión *nm fml* north.

septentrional *adj* northern.

septicemia *nf Med* septicaemia, *US* septicemia.

séptico,-a *adj* septic; **fosa séptica**, septic tank.

septiembre *nm* September; **el 5 de s.**, the 5th of September; **en s.**, in September; *véase tamb* **noviembre**.

séptimo,-a I *adj* seventh; **el s. arte**, the cinema; **la séptima parte**, a seventh; *fam* **en el s. cielo**, in seventh heaven. **II** *nm,f (de una serie)* seventh. **III** *nm (parte)* seventh; *véase tamb* **octavo,-a**.

septuagenario,-a *adj & nm,f* septuagenarian.

septuagésimo,-a I *adj* seventieth; **septuagésima parte**, seventieth. **II** *nm,f (de una serie)* seventieth; **s. primero**, seventy-first; **s. segundo**, seventy-second. **III** *nm (parte)* seventieth; *véase tamb* **octavo,-a**.

sepulcral *adj* sepulchral; *fig* **silencio s.**, deathly silence.

sepulcro *nm* tomb; *fam* **ser un s.**, to keep mum.

sepultar *vtr* to bury.

sepultura *nf* **1** *(tumba)* grave. **2** *(entierro)* burial; **dar s. a algn**, to bury sb.

sepulturero,-a *nm,f* gravedigger.

sequedad *nf* **1** dryness. **2** *fig* curtness, abruptness.

sequía *nf* drought.

séquito *nm* **1** *(grupo de acompañantes)* entourage, retinue. **2** *Pol* group of followers.

SER *nf Rad TV abr de* **Sociedad Española de Radiodifusión**.

ser¹ *nm* **1** *(ente)* being. ■ **s. humano**, human being; **S. Supremo**, Supreme Being; **s. vivo**, living being. **2** *(vida)* existence, life; *fml* **dar el s.**, to give life. **3** *(valor)* core; **esto constituye el s. del espectáculo**, this is the heart of the show.

ser² *vi* **1** *(suceder)* to be; **el estreno será mañana**, tomorrow is the opening night. **2** *(identificar)* to be; **es alto y rubio**, he is tall and fair; **Jaime es médico**, Jaime is a doctor. **3** *(clasificar)* to be; **Jaime es el médico**, Jaime is the doctor. **4** *(indica procedencia)* to be, come *(de,* from*)*; **¿de dónde eres?**, where are you from?; **José María es de San Sebastián**, José María is from San Sebastián. **5** *(indica material)* to be made; *(de,* of*)* **la mesa es de madera**, the table is made of wood. **6** *(indica color)* to be; **el edificio es gris**, the building is grey. **7** *(indica posesión)* to be; belong to; **¿de quién es este abrigo?**, whose coat is this?; **el perro es de Ricardo**, the dog belongs to Ricardo. **8 s. para**, *(finalidad, adecuación)* to be for; **este jabón es para las manos**, this is hand soap; **estos modales no son de caballero**, that isn't gentlemanly behaviour. **9** *(localización tiempo, día, hora)* to be; **es de día**, it's daytime; **es invierno**, it's winter; **son las dos de la tarde**, it's two o'clock *or* p.m. **10** *(costar)* to be, cost; **¿cuánto es?**, how much is it? **11** *(causar)* to be, cause; **la bebida fue su perdición**, drinking was his downfall. **12** *(ficción en juegos)* to be; **tú serás la princesa y yo la bruja**, you can be the princess and I'll be the witch. **13** *(consistir en)* to be, lie in, consist of; **el secreto es hacerlo despacio**, the secret lies in doing it slowly. **14** *(devenir)* **s. de**, to become of; **¿qué será de mí?**, what will become of me? **15** *(auxiliar como pasiva)* to be; **el hecho será verificado**, the fact is to be verified; **fue asesinado**, he was murdered. **16** *(locuciones)* **a no s. que**, unless; **a poder s.**, if possible; **como debe s.**, as it should be; **¿cómo es eso?**, **¿cómo puede s.?**, how can that be?; **como sea**, anyhow; **de no s. por …**, had it not been for …; **érase una vez**, once upon a time; **es de esperar/desear que …**, it is to be expected/hoped that …; **es más**, furthermore; **es que …**, it's just that …; **lo que sea**, whatever; **no es nada, he sido una caída tonta**, it's all right, it was just a little fall; **no será para tanto**, it's won't come to that; *or* **sea**, that is (to say); **por si (fuera) poco**, to top it all; **no puede s.**, it can't be true; **puede s.**, it could be, it's possible; **sea como sea**, in any case, be that as it may; **seindo así**, that being so; **un si es no es**, a trifle, a touch; *fam* **s. de lo que no hay**, to be a real winner; *fam* **s. muy suyo**, to be an eccentric.

sera *nf* large basket, pannier.

seráfico,-a *adj* seraphic, angelic.

serafín *nm* seraph.

serbal *nm Bot* **s. silvestre**, rowan, mountain ash.

serenar I *vtr (gen)* to calm; quieten; *(persona)* to calm down. **II serenarse** *vr* **1** *(persona)* to calm down; *(mar)* to grow calm. **2** *Meteor (tiempo)* to clear up.

serenata *nf Mús* serenade.

serenera *nf Am (prenda)* coat, cape.

serenidad *nf* serenity, calm; **conservar la s.**, to keep calm.

sereno¹ *nm* **1** *(vigilante)* night watchman. **2** *(humedad nocturna)* night dew, night air; **dormir al s.**, to sleep out in the open.

sereno,-a² *adj* **1** *(persona)* calm; *(ambiente)* peaceful *fam* **estar s.**, to be sober. **2** *Meteor (cielo)* clear; *(tiempo)* fine, good.

serial *nm Rad TV* serial.

seriar *vtr* to serialize.

serie *nf* **1** *(gen)* series *sing*; **fabricación en s.**, mass production; **fabricado en s.**, mass-produced; *fig* **fuera de s.**, out of the ordinary, unique. **2** *(cadena)* series *sing*, succession; string; **una s. de acontecimientos**, a string of events. **3** *Rad TV* serial, series *sing*. **4** *Dep* series *sing*; **s. mundial**, world series.

seriedad *nf* **1** *(severidad)* seriousness; **con s.**, seriously. **2** *(gravedad)* seriousness, gravity. **3** *(formalidad)* reliability, dependability; **falta de s.**, irresponsibility.

serigrafía *nf* serigraphy, silk-screen printing.

serio,-a *adj* **1** *(severo)* serious; **en s.,** seriously **¿en s.?,** are you serious? do you really mean that?; **hablo en s.,** I'm serious; **ponerse s.,** to become serious, look serious. **2** *(grave, importante)* serious, grave; **asunto s.,** serious matter. **3** *(formal)* reliable, dependable, responsible. **4** *(color)* sober. **5** *(traje)* formal. ◆ **seriamente** *adv* seriously.

sermón *nm* **1** *Rel* sermon. **2** *fam (represalia)* sermon, lecture, ticking-off.

sermoneador,-a *fam* **I** *adj* fault-finding, nit-picking. **II** *nm,f* fault-finder.

sermonear *vi* **1** *Rel* to preach. **2** *fam (reprender)* to lecture.

seroso,-a *adj* serous.

serpentear *vi (enroller)* to wind; *(zigzaguear)* to wind one's way, meander.

serpenteo *nm (vueltas)* winding; *(zigzag)* meandering.

serpentín *nm (tubo)* coil.

serpentina *nf* **1** *(tira de papel)* streamer. **2** *Min* serpentine.

serpiente *nf Zool* snake. ■ **s. de cascabel,** rattlesnake; **s. pitón,** python.

serraduras *nfpl* sawdust *sing.*

serrallo *nm* harem.

serranía *nf* mountainous area *or* country.

serranilla *nf Lit* lyric composition in short verses.

serrano,-a I *adj* **1** mountain, highland. ■ *Culin* **jamón s.,** cured ham. **2** *desus (hermoso)* nice; **un cuerpo s.,** a shapely figure. **II** *nm,f* highlander.

serrar *vtr* to saw.

serrería *nf* sawmill.

serreta *nf Orn* **s. chica,** smew; **s. grande,** goosander; **s. mediana,** red breasted merganser.

serrín *nm* sawdust.

serrucho *nm (herramienta)* handsaw.

servible *adj* usable, serviceable.

servicial *adj* helpful, obliging, accommodating.

servicio *nm* **1** service; **servicios públicos,** public services, (public) utilities. ■ **s. a domicilio,** delivery service. **2** *(empleados domésticos)* servants *pl;* *(no fijo)* domestic help. **3** *Mil* service; **estar de s.,** to be on duty. ■ **s. militar,** military service. **4** *(favor)* service, favour, *US* favor; **hacer** *or* **prestar s.,** to do a favour; *fam* **hacer un flaco s.,** to do more harm than good. **5** *Dep* service, serve. **6** *(juego, conjunto)* set; **s. de té,** tea set, tea service. **7** **servicios,** *(retrete)* toilet *sing, US* rest room *sing.*

servidor,-a *nm,f* **1** *(criado)* servant; *fml* **s. de usted,** at your service; *(en carta)* **su seguro s.,** yours faithfully. **2** *(enfemismo)* myself; **¿quién se ocupa de esto? —s.,** who's taking care of it? —I am; **¿Ramón Lopera? —un s.,** Ramón Lopera? —yes?

servidumbre *nf* **1** *(criados)* servants *pl,* staff *pl.* **2** *(condición de siervo)* servitude. **3** *(sujeción a los vicios etc)* compulsion. **4** *Jur Fin* servitude.

servil *adj (humilde)* servile; *(obediente)* subservient.

servilismo *nm* *(humildad)* servility; *(obediencia)* subservience.

servilleta *nf* serviette, napkin.

servilletero *nm* serviette ring, napkin ring.

servio,-a I *adj* Serbian. **II** *nm,f (persona)* Serbian. **III** *nm (idioma)* Serbian.

servir I *vtr* **1** *(gen)* to serve; *Mil* **s. a la patria,** to serve one's country. **2** *(prestar ayuda a)* to help; *(en tienda etc)* **¿en qué puedo servirle?,** what can I do for you?, may I help you?; *fml* **para servirle,** at your service. **3** *(dar comida, bebida a)* to serve, wait on; **¿le sirvo una copa, señor?,** would you like a drink, sir? **4** *Com (suministrar a)* to supply with; **le serviremos la mercancía lo antes posible,** we shall deliver your merchandise as soon as possible. **II** *vi* **1** *(gen)* to serve; *Mil* **s. en Ceuta,** to serve in

Ceuta. **2** *(camarero etc)* to serve; **s. en la mesa,** to wait at table. **3** *(trabajar de criado)* to be a servant; **ponerse a s.,** to go into service; **s. en casa de algn,** to be in service at sb's house. **4** *(valer)* to be useful, be suitable; *(instrumento)* to be good; **de nada sirve hablar,** talking is useless; **mi paraguas no sirve,** my umbrella is no good; **no sirve,** it's no good; **tu consejo me sirvió de mucho,** your advice was very useful to me. **5 s. para,** to be used for, be for; **¿para qué sirve esto?,** what is this (used) for? **6 s. de,** to serve as, act as; **s. de aviso,** to serve as a warning; **s. de enlace,** to act as a go-between. **7** *Dep* to serve. **III servirse** *vr* **1** *(comida etc)* to help oneself; **sírvete tú mismo,** help yourself. **2 s. de,** to use, make use of; *fig* **se han servido de ti,** you've been taken advantage of. **3** *fml (carta)* to be kind enough to; **sírvase** *or* **sírvanse comunicarnos su decisión,** please inform us of your decision.

servofreno *nm Téc* servo brake.

servomecanismo *nm* servomechanism.

servomotor *nm* servomotor.

sésamo *nm* **1** *Bot* sesame. **2** *Lit & fam* **¡ábrete, s.!,** open, sesame!

sesear *vi Ling* to pronounce Spanish **c** (before **e** *or* **i**) and **z** as **s.**

sesenta *inv* **I** *adj (cardinal)* sixty; *(ordinal)* sixtieth; **los años s.,** the sixties. **II** *nm* sixty; **nací en el s.,** I was born in nineteen sixty; *véase tamb* **ocho.**

sesentavo,-a I *adj* sixtieth. **II** *nm,f (de una serie)* sixtieth. **III** *nm (parte)* sixtieth; *véase tamb* **octavo,-a.**

sesentón,-ona *adj & nm,f fam* sixty-year-old.

seseo *nm* pronunciation of Spanish **c** (before **e** *or* **i**) and **z** as **s.**

sesera *nf fam* brain, brains *pl.*

sesgadura *nf* cut on the bias.

sesgar *vtr* **1** *(cortar)* to cut on the bias. **2** *(torcer)* to slant. **3** *Arg (renunciar a un propósito)* to renounce.

sesgo *nm* **1** *Cost* **al s.,** on the bias. **2** *fig (curso de un asunto)* slant, turn; **tomar un s. favorable/desfavorable,** to take a turn for the better/worse.

sesión *nf* **1** *(reunión)* meeting, session; *Jur* session, sitting; **se abre la s.,** the metting is open; **se cierra la s.,** the meeting is adjourned. ■ **s. plenaria,** plenary session. **2** *Cin* showing. ■ **s. continua,** continuous showing; **s. de noche,** late show; **s. de tarde,** matinée.

seso *nm* **1** *Anat* brain. **2** *fam fig* brains *pl,* grey matter; *(juicio)* sense; *(volverse loco)* **beber** *or* **beberse el s.** *or* **los sesos,** to lose one's mind; **calentarse** *or* **devanarse los sesos,** to rack one's brains; *(tener bajo la influencia)* **tener sorbido el s.** *or* **los sesos a algn,** to have sb under one's spell. **3 sesos,** *Culin* brains.

sestear *vi* to have a nap.

sesudo,-a *adj* **1** *(inteligente)* intelligent, brainy. **2** *(sensato)* sensible; *(prudente)* wise.

set *nm Ten* set.

seta *nf (comestible)* mushroom; *(no comestible)* **s. venenosa,** toadstool.

setecientos,-as *inv* **I** *adj (cardinal)* seven hundred; *(ordinal)* seven hundredth. **II** *nm* seven hundred; *véase tamb* **ocho.**

setenta *inv* **I** *adj (cardinal)* seventy; *(ordinal)* seventieth; **los años s.,** the seventies. **II** *nm* seventy; *véase tamb* **ocho.**

setentavo,-a I *adj* seventieth. **II** *nm, f (de una serie)* seventieth. **III** *nm (parte)* seventieth; *véase tamb* **octavo,-a.**

setentón,-ona *adj & nm,f* seventy-year-old.

setiembre *nm véase* **septiembre.**

seto *nm* hedge.

setter *nm (perro)* setter.

s.e.u.o. *abr de* **salvo error u omisión,** errors and omissions excepted.

seudónimo *nm* pseudonym; *(de escritores)* pen name.

Seúl *n* Seoul.

severidad *nf* **1** *(gravedad)* severity, harshness. **2** *(rigurosidad)* strictness.

severo,-a *adj* **1** *(grave)* severe, harsh. **2** *(riguroso)* strict; **ser s. con algn,** to be hard on sb. **3** *(estilo)* stark, severe.

Sevilla *n* Seville.

sevillanas *nfpl Mús* Sevillian folk songs and dance.

sevillano,-a **I** *adj* of or from Seville, Sevillian. **II** *nm, f* native or inhabitant of Seville, Sevillian.

sexagenario,-a *adj & nm, f* sexagenarian.

sexagesimal *adj* sexagesimal.

sexagésimo,-a **I** *adj* sixtieth; **una sexagésima parte,** a sixtieth. **II** *nm, f (de una serie)* sixtieth; *véase tamb* **octavo,-a.**

sex-appeal *nm* sex appeal.

sexi *adj véase* **sexy.**

sexismo *nm* sexism.

sexista *adj* **1** *(gen)* sexist. **2** *(hombre)* male chauvinist.

sexo *nm* **1** sex. ■ **el bello s.,** the fair sex; **el s. débil,** the weaker sex; **el s. fuerte,** the stronger sex. **2** *(genitales)* genitals *pl.*

sexología *nf* sexology.

sexólogo,-a *nm, f* sexologist.

sextante *nm Náut* sextant.

sexteto *nm Mús* sextet.

sexto,-a **I** *adj* sixth. **II** *nm, f (de una serie)* sixth. **III** *nm (parte)* sixth; *véase tamb* **octavo,-a.**

séxtuplo,-a *adj & nm* sextuple.

sexuado,-a *adj* sexed.

sexual *adj* sexual, sex; **vida s.,** sex life. ◆ **sexualmente** *adv* sexually.

sexualidad *nf* sexuality.

sexy *adj* sexy, with sex appeal.

Seychelles *npl* Seychelles.

s.f. *abr de* **sin fecha,** not dated.

s/f. *abr de* **su favor,** your favour or US favor.

shah *nm (título)* shah.

sherry *nm (vino)* sherry.

Shetland *n* **las Islas S.,** the Shetland Isles, Shetland *sing.*

shetland *nm Tex* Shetland wool.

shock *nm Med* shock.

short *nm (prenda)* shorts *pl.*

show *nm* **1** *(espectáculo)* show. **2** *fam (exhibición)* show, display; **montar un s.,** to put on a show.

si¹ *conj* **1** *(condicional)* if; **como si,** as if; **por si acaso,** just in case; **si acaso,** if by any chance; **si hubiesen llegado a tiempo,** if they had arrived in time; **si llueve, iremos en coche,** if it rains, we'll go by car; **si no,** if not; **si quieres,** if you like, if you wish. **2** *(disyuntivo)* whether; **dime si te gusta** or **no,** tell me whether you like it or not; **no sé si ir** or **no,** I don't know whether to go or not. **3** *(protesta, sorpresa)* but; **¡si está llorando!,** but she's crying!; **¡si no quiero!,** but I don't want to!

si² *nm (pl sis) Mús* ti, si, B.

sí¹ *pron pers* **1** *(singular) (él)* himself; *(ella)* herself; *(cosa)* itself; *(plural)* themselves; **de por sí, en sí,** in itself; **hablaban entre sí,** they were talking among themselves or to each other; **por sí mismo,** by himself; **sí misma,** herself; **sí mismo,** himself. **2** *(uno mismo)* oneself; **decír para sí,** to say to oneself; **estar fuera de sí,** to be beside onself (with anger); **estar sobre sí,** to be on one's guard; **volver en sí,** to come round, regain consciousness.

sí² **I** *adv* **1** yes; **¡claro que sí!,** of course!; **creo que sí,** I think so; **dije que sí,** I said yes, I accepted, I agreed; **¡eso sí que no!,** certainly not!; **proque sí,** *(sin razón)* because I or you feel like it; *(por naturaleza)* that's the way it is; **¡que**

sí!, yes, I tell you!; **un día sí y otro no,** every other day. **2** *(uso enfático) (no se traduce)* **sí que está bien hecho,** it certainly is well done; **sí que me gusta,** of course I like it. **II** *nm (pl síes)* yes; **dar el sí,** to say yes, accept, agree; **síes y noes,** yeas and nays.

siamés,-esa **I** *adj* Siamese. **II** *nm, f (mellizo)* Siamese twin.

sibarita **I** *adj* sybarite, sybaritic. **II** *nmf* sybarite.

sibaritismo *nm* sybaritism.

Siberia *n* Siberia.

siberiano,-a *adj & nmf* Siberian.

sibila *nf Mit* sibyl.

sibilante *adj & nf Ling* sibilant.

sibilino,-a *adj* **1** *Mit* sibylline. **2** sibylline; *fig* cryptic, enigmatic.

sicalíptico,-a *adj* suggestive, erotic, pornographic.

sicario *nm* hired gunman; *fam* goon.

Sicilia *n* Sicily.

siciliano,-a *adj & nm, f* Sicilian.

sicoanálisis *nm inv véase* **psicoanálisis.**

sicoanalista *nmf véase* **psicoanalista.**

sicoanalítico,-a *adj véase* **psicoanalítico,-a.**

sicoanalizar *vtr véase* **psicoanalizar.**

sicodélico,-a *adj véase* **psicodélico,-a.**

sicodrama *nm véase* **psicodrama.**

sicofanta *nm,* **sicofante** *nm* imposter, fake.

sicofármaco *nm véase* **psicofármaco.**

sicología *nf véase* **psicología.**

sicológico,-a *adj véase* **psicológico,-a.**

sicólogo,-a *nm, f véase* **psicólogo,-a.**

sicómoro *nm Bot* sycamore.

siconeurosis *nf inv véase* **psiconeurosis.**

sicópata *nmf véase* **psicópata.**

sicopatía *nf véase* **psicopatía.**

sicopático,-a *adj véase* **psicopático,-a.**

sicopatología *nf véase* **psicopatología.**

sicosis *nf inv véase* **psicosis.**

sicosomático,-a *adj véase* **psicosomático,-a.**

sicote *nm Am* foot odour or US odor.

sicoterapia *nf véase* **psicoterpia.**

sicoterapeuta *nmf véase* **psicoterapeuta.**

SIDA *nm Med abr de* **síndrome de inmunodeficiencia adquirida,** acquired immune deficiency syndrome, AIDS.

sidecar *nm Aut* sidecar.

sideral *adj* sidereal, astral; **espacio s.,** outer space.

siderurgia *adj Ind* iron and steel industry.

siderúrgico,-a *adj Ind* iron and steel; **la industria siderúrgica,** the iron and steel industry.

sidra *nf* cider.

siega *nf Agr* **1** *(acción)* reaping, harversting. **2** *(temporada)* harvest (time). **3** *(mieses)* harvest.

siembra *nf Agr* **1** *(acción)* sowing. **2** *(temporada)* sowing time.

siempre *adv* always; **a la hora de s.,** at the usual time; **como s.,** as usual; **eso es así desde s.,** it has always been like that; **para s.,** for ever; **para s. jamás,** for ever and ever; **s. pasa lo mismo,** it's always the same; **s. viene tarde,** he is always late; **s. que,** *(cada vez que)* whenever; *(a condición de que)* provided, as long as; **s. y cuando,** provided, as long as; **son amigos de s.,** they are old friends.

siempreviva *nf Bot* everlasting flower, immortelle.

sien *nf Anat* temple.

siena *adj (color)* sienna, dark yellow.

sierpe *nf* 1 *Zool fml* serpent. 2 *fig (mal genio)* badtempered person; *(feo)* ugly person.

sierra *nf* 1 *Téc Carp* saw. ■ **s. circular,** circular saw; **s. mecánica,** power saw. 2 *Geog* mountain range, sierra.

Sierra Leona *n* Sierra Leone.

sierraleonés,-esa *adj & nm,f* Sierra Leonean.

siervo,-a *nm,f* 1 *(esclavo)* slave; *Rel* **s. de Dios,** servant of God. 2 *Hist* serf.

siesta *nf* siesta, nap; **dormir** *or* **echar la s.,** to have a siesta *or* an afternoon nap; **la hora de la s.,** (summer) early afternoon.

siete *inv* **I** *adj (cardinal)* seven; *(ordinal)* seventh. **II** *nm* 1 seven; **son las s.,** it's seven o'clock; **el s. de abril,** the seventh of April, April the seventh; **hablar más que s.,** to talk nineteen to the dozen. 2 *fam (rasgón)* tear; **me he hecho un s. en los pantalones,** I've ripped my trousers. 3 *LAm (ano)* anus; *véase tamb* **ocho.**

sietemesino,-a **I** *adj* seven-month. **II** *nm,f* 1 seven-month baby, premature baby. 2 *fam (enclenque)* weakling. 3 *fam (chico presumido)* little squirt.

sifilis *nf inv Med* syphilis.

sifilítico,-a *adj & nm,f* syphilitic.

sifón *nm* 1 *(para trasvasar líquidos)* siphon. 2 *(tubería)* U-bend, trap. 3 *(botella)* soda siphon. 4 *(soda)* soda, soda water; **whisky con s.,** whisky and soda.

sig. *abr de* **siguiente,** following, fol.

sigilo *nm* 1 *(discreción)* discretion. 2 *(secreto)* secrecy; **con mucho s.,** in great secrecy; *Rel* **s. sacramental,** secrecy of the confessional.

sigiloso,-a *adj* 1 *(mesurado)* discreet. 2 *(asunto)* secret; *(persona)* secretive. ◆ **sigilosamente** *adv (mesuradamente)* discreetly; *(secretamente)* secretly; **entró s. en la habitación,** she crept *or* slipped into the room.

sigla *nf* acronym; **EE.UU. son las siglas de Estados Unidos de América,** U.S.A. is the abbreviation of United States of America.

siglo *nm* century; **por los siglos de los siglos,** for ever and ever; **fam hace siglos que no le veo,** I haven't seen him for ages. ■ *Hist Lit* **el S. de las luces,** the Eighteenth Century; *Hist Lit* **el S. de Oro,** the Golden Age.

signar **I** *vtr (firmar)* to sign. 2 *Rel* to make the sign of the cross over. **II signarse** *vr Rel* to make the sign of the cross, cross oneself.

signatario,-a *adj & nm,f* signatory; **el s. del documento,** the signatory of the document.

signatura *nf* 1 *Impr* signature. 2 *(en bibliotecas etc)* catalogue number. 3 *(firma)* signature.

significación *nf* 1 *(sentido)* meaning. 2 *(importancia)* significance.

significado,-a **I** *pp de* **significar. II** *adj (conocido)* well-known; *(importante)* important. **III** *nm* 1 meaning; **el s. de una palabra,** the meaning of a word. 2 *Ling* signifier.

significante *nm Ling* significant, signifier.

significar **I** *vtr* 1 to mean; **'persistir' significa insistir en una cosa,** 'persistir' means to continue with something. 2 *(manifestar)* to express, make known. **II significarse** *vr* to stand out.

significativo,-a *adj (relevante)* significant; *(expresivo, con sentido)* meaningful; **un gesto s.,** a meaningful gesture. ◆ **significativamente** *adv (con relevancia)* significantly; *(expresivamente, con sentido)* meaningfully.

signo *nm* 1 *(gen)* sign; **cantar es s. de alegría,** singing is a (sure) sign of happiness. 2 *Astrol* sign; **s. del zodiaco,** zodiac sign. 3 *Ling* mark. ■ **s. de admiración,** exclamation mark; **s. de interrogación,** question mark. 4 *Mat* sign; **s. de sumar,** plus sign; **s. positivo,** positive sign. 5 *lit (destino)* fate, destiny.

sigo *indic pres véase* **seguir.**

siguiente *adj* following, next; **¡el s.!,** next, please!

sij *adj & nmf Rel* Sikh.

sílaba *nf* syllable.

silabario *nm* spelling book.

silabear *vi* to divide words into syllables.

silábico,-a *adj* syllabic.

silampa *nf CAm Meteor* drizzle.

silba *nf* hissing; **el público respondió con una escandalosa s. a …,** the audience hissed and booed at … .

silbar *vi* 1 *(producir silbos)* to whistle. 2 *(abuchear)* to hiss, boo.

silbato *nm* whistle.

silbido *nm* 1 *(acción)* whistle, whistling; *(agudo)* hiss; **el s. del viento,** the whistling of the wind. ■ **s. de oídos,** ringing in the ears. 2 *Tel* ring, ringing.

silbo *nm (acción)* whistle, whistling; *(voz aguda)* hiss.

silenciador *nm* 1 *(de arma)* silencer. 2 *Aut* silencer, *US* muffler.

silenciar **I** *vtr* 1 *(un sonido)* to muffle. 2 *(omitir)* to hush; **los informativos silenciaron las declaraciones,** the news programmes made no mention of the statements. 3 *Am (acallar)* to silence. **II** *vi (guardar silencio)* to keep silent.

silencio *nm* silence; **en s.,** in silence; **guardar s.,** to keep quiet; **imponer s. a algn,** to make sb be quiet; *fig* **el s. de la prensa es significativo,** the silence of the press is meaningful.

silencioso,-a *adj (persona)* quiet; *(cosa)* silent; **motor s.,** silent motor.

sílex *nm inv Min* silex, flint.

sílfide *nf Mit* sylph.

silicato *nm Quím* silicate.

sílice *nf* silica.

silicio *nm* silicon.

silicona *nf* silicone.

silicosis *nf inv Med* silicosis.

silla *nf* 1 chair; *fig* **Don Ramón ocupa una silla en la Academia,** Don Ramón holds a seat in the Academy. ■ **s. de ruedas,** wheelchair; **s. giratoria,** swivel chair. 2 *Equit* **s. (de montar),** saddle.

sillar *nm Constr* ashlar.

sillería¹ *nf* 1 chairs *pl,* set of chairs. 2 *(del coro)* choir stalls *pl.*

sillería² *nf Constr* ashlar.

sillín *nm Cicl Equit* saddle.

sillón *nm* 1 *(butaca)* armchair. 2 *Equit* side-saddle.

silo *nm* silo.

silogismo *nm* syllogism.

silueta *nf* 1 *(contorno)* silhouette, outline. 2 *(del cuerpo)* figure, shape.

silvestre *adj* wild; **plantas silvestres,** wild plants.

silvicultor,-a *nm,f* forestry expert.

silvicultura *nf* forestry.

sima *nf Geol* chasm, abyss.

simbiosis *nf inv Biol* symbiosis.

simbiótico,-a *adj Biol* symbiotic.

simbólico,-a *adj* symbolic, symbolical.

simbolismo *nm* symbolism.

simbolista *adj & nmf* symbolist.

simbolizar *vtr* to symbolize.

símbolo *nm* symbol.

simetría *nf* symmetry.

simétrico,-a *adj* symmetric, symmetrical.

simiente *nf Agr* seed.

simiesco,-a *adj* simian, apelike.

símil *nm* 1 *(comparación)* comparison; *(semejanza)* resemblance, similarity. 2 *Lit* simile.

similar *adj* similar.

similitud *nf* similarity, ressemblance.

similor *nm Metal* pinchbeck.

simio *nm Zool* simian, monkey.

simonía *nf* simony.

simoníaco,-a I *adj* simoniacal. II *nm, f* simoniac.

simpatía *nf* 1 (*agrado*) liking, affection; **cogerle s. a algn,** to take a liking to sb; **ganarse la s. de todos,** to win everyone's affection; **simpatías y antipatías,** likes and dislikes; **le tengo mucha s.,** I am very fond of him. 2 (*solidaridad*) sympathy, solidarity. 3 *Med* sympathy.

simpático,-a *adj* 1 (*amable*) nice, likeable; (*agradable*) kind, friendly; (*encantador*) charming; **hacerse el s.,** to ingratiate oneself; **me cae s.,** I like him. 2 *Med* sympathetic.

simpatizante I *adj* sympathetic. II *nmf* sympathizer.

simpatizar *vi* to get on (**con,** with); **simpatizamos al instante,** we hit it off from the start.

simple I *adj* 1 (*gen*) simple. 2 (*fácil*) simple, easy. 3 (*mero*) mere; **es una s. fórmula,** it's a mere formality; **por s. descuido,** through sheer carelessness. 4 (*persona*) simple, simple-minded. II *nm* 1 (*persona*) simpleton. 2 *Ten* singles *pl.* ◆ **simplemente** *adv* simply.

simpleza *nf* 1 (*bobería*) simple-mindedness. 2 (*tontería*) nonsense.

simplicidad *nf* 1 (*sencillez*) simplicity. 2 (*ingenuidad*) naïveté, naïvety.

simplificación *nf* simplification.

simplificar *vtr* to simplify.

simplismo *nm* simplism, oversimplification.

simplista *adj* simplistic, oversimple.

simplón,-ona I *adj* simple, naïve. II *nm, f* simpleton.

simposio *nm* symposium.

simulación *nf* simulation.

simulacro *nm* sham, pretence; **un s. de ataque,** a mock attack.

simulado,-a I *pp* de **simular.** II *adj* simulated.

simular *vtr* to simulate, pretent, feign; **s. un accidente,** to rig an accident.

simultanear *vtr* (*hacer al mismo tiempo*) to do simultaneously *or* at the same time; (*combinar*) to combine; **simultanea el trabajo y lose estudios,** he's working and studying at the same time.

simultaneidad *nf* simultaneity.

simultáneo,-a *adj* simultaneous. ◆ **simultáneamente** *adv* simultaneously, at the same time.

simún *nm Meteor* simoom.

sin *prep* without; **está s. lavar,** it hasn't been washed; **estamos s. pan,** we're out of bread; **fuimos, no s. antes preguntar si podíamos,** before going, we did ask if we could; **iremos sin ti,** we'll go without you; **se fue s. pagar,** he left without paying; **s. más ni más,** without further ado; **s. que nadie lo notara,** without anyone noticing.

sinagoga *nf Rel* synagogue.

sinalefa *nf Ling* synaloepha, *US* synalepha.

sinapismo *nm* 1 *Med* mustard plaster. 2 *fam fig* (*pesadez*) bore, drag.

sincerarse *vr* to open one's heart (**con,** to).

sinceridad *nf* sincerity; **con toda s.,** in all sincerity.

sincero,-a *adj* sincere. ◆ **sinceramente** *adv* sincerely.

síncopa *nf* 1 *Ling* syncope. 2 *Mús* syncopation.

sincopado,-a *adj Mús* syncopated.

síncope *nm* 1 *Med* syncope, fainting, faint. 2 *Ling* syncope.

sincronía *nf* synchrony.

sincrónico,-a *adj* synchronic.

sincronización *nf* synchronization.

sincronizar *vtr* to synchronize.

sindicación *nf* 1 (*afiliación*) joining of a trade union. 2 (*sindicalismo*) trade unionism.

sindical *adj* trade union, union.

sindicalismo *nm* trade unionism, unionism.

sindicalista I *adj* trade union, union. II *nmf* trade unionist, unionist.

sindicar I *vtr* to unionize. II **sindicarse** *vr* 1 (*afiliarse*) to join a trade union. 2 (*formar un sindicato*) to form a union.

sindicato *nm* union, trade union.

síndico *nm* 1 *Pol* elected representative. 2 (*depositario*) trustee; *Jur* (*official*) receiver.

síndrome *nm Med* syndrome.

sinecura *nf* sinecure.

sinestesia *nf* synaesthesia, *US* synesthesia.

sinfín *nm* endless number; **un s. de preguntas,** an endless number of questions.

sinfonía *nf* symphony.

sinfónico,-a *adj* symphonic.

Singapur *n* Singapore.

singladura *nf Náut* day's run.

singular I *adj* 1 (*único, solo*) singular, single. 2 (*excepcional*) exceptional, unique. 3 (*raro*) peculiar, odd. II *nm Ling* singular; **en s.,** in the singular; *fam* **¡habla en s.!,** speak for yourself!

singularidad *nf* 1 (*unicidad*) singularity. 2 (*excepcionalidad*) uniqueness. 3 (*rareza*) peculiarity.

singularizar I *vtr* to single out, distinguish. II **singularizarse** *vr* to stand out, distinguish oneself.

sinhueso *nf fam* tongue; **darle a la s.,** to natter.

siniestra *nf* left hand.

siniestrado,-a *adj* damaged.

siniestro,-a I *adj* 1 *lit* (*izquierdo*) left, left-hand. 2 (*maligno*) sinister, ominous. 3 (*funesto*) fateful, disastrous. II *nm* (*catástrofe*) disaster, catastrophe; (*incendio*) fire.

sinnúmero *nm* endless number.

sino[1] *nm fml* fate, destiny.

sino[2] *conj* 1 but; **no fui a Madrid, s. a Barcelona,** I didn't go to Madrid but to Barcelona; **no sólo ... s. (también) ...,** not only ... but also ... . 2 (*solamente*) only; **no quiero s. que me oigan,** I only want them to listen (to me). 3 (*excepto*) but, except; **no escribo a nadie s. a mi padre,** I only write to my father.

sínodo *nm Rel* synod.

sinonimia *nf* synonymy.

sinónimo,-a I *adj* synonymous. II *nm* synonym.

sinopsis *nf inv* synopsis.

sinóptico,-a *adj* synoptic, synoptical; **cuadro s.,** diagram, chart.

sinrazón *nf* wrong, injustice.

sinsabor *nm* (*gen pl*) trouble, worry; **mi vida está llena de sinsabores,** my life is full of worries.

sinsubstancia *nmf fam* flighty person.

sintáctico,-a *adj Ling* syntactic, syntactical.

sintaxis *nf inv Ling* syntax.

síntesis *nf inv* synthesis.

sintético,-a *adj* synthetic.

sintetizador *nm* synthesizer.

sintetizar *vtr* to synthesize.

sintoísmo *nm* Shinto, Shintoism.

sintoísta *nmf* Shintoist.

síntoma *nm* symptom.

sintomático,-a *adj* symptomatic.

sintonía *nf* **1** *Elec Rad* tuning. **2** *Mús Rad (de programa)* signature tune. **3** *fig* harmony; **estar en s. con algn,** to get on well with sb.

sintonización *nf* **1** *Rad* tuning. **2** *fig* harmony.

sintonizador *nm Rad* tune, tuning knob.

sintonizar I *vtr Rad* to tune in; **s. una emisora,** to tune in to a radio station. **II** *vi fig (llevarse bien)* to get on well, be on the same wavelength.

sinuosidad *nf* **1** *(de un camino)* bend, curve. **2** *(de argumento)* tortuousness. **3** *(de persona)* deviousness.

sinuoso,-a *adj* **1** *(camino)* winding. **2** *(argumento)* tortuous. **3** *(persona)* devious.

sinusitis *nf Med inv* sinusitis.

sinvergüencería *nf fam* shamelessness.

sinvergüenza I *adj (desvergonzado)* shameless; *(descarado)* cheeky. **II** *nmf (desvergonzado)* scoundrel, rotter; *(caradura)* cheeky devil.

sionismo *nm* Zionism.

sionista *adj & nmf* Zionist.

sique *nf véase* **psique.**

siquiatra *nmf véase* **psiquiatra.**

siquiatría *nf véase* **psiquiatría.**

siquiátrico,-a *adj véase* **psiquiátrico,-a.**

síquico,-a *adj véase* **psíquico,-a.**

siquiera I *adv (por lo menos)* at least; **dime s. su nombre,** at least tell me her name; **ni s.,** not even; **ni s. sé su nombre,** I don't even know his name. **II** *conj (aunque)* although, even though; **ven, s. sea por dos días,** do come, even if it's only for two days.

sirena *nf* **1** *Mit* siren, mermaid. **2** *(señal acústica)* siren. ■ **s. de niebla,** foghorn.

sirga *nf* rope, towrope, towline.

sirgar *vtr* to tow.

Siria *n* Syria.

sirimiri *nm Meteor* fine drizzle.

sirio,-a *adj & nm,f* Syrian.

sirla *nf arg* stick-up.

sirlar *vtr arg* to mug.

sirlero,-a *nm,f arg* mugger.

siroco *nm Meteor* sirocco (wind).

sirte *nm* sandbank.

sirviente,-a *nm,f* servant.

sisa *nf* **1** *(hurto)* petty theft, pilfering, filching. **2** *Cost* dart; armhole.

sisar *vtr* **1** *(hurtar)* to thieve, pilfer, filch. **2** *Cost* to dart, take in.

sisear *vi* to hiss.

siseo *nm* hiss, hissing.

sísmico,-a *adj* seismic.

sismo *nm* earthquake, tremor.

sismógrafo *nm* seismograph.

sismología *nf* seismology.

sismológico,-a *adj* seismological.

sisón,-ona[1] *fam* **I** *adj* pilfering, filching. **II** *nm, f* petty thief, pilferer.

sisón[2] *nm Orn* little bustard.

sistema *nm* system; **por s.,** as a rule. ■ *Inform* **s. cableado,** hard-wired system; *Mat* **s. de ecuaciones,** simultaneous equations *pl*; *Inform* **s. experto,** expert system; *Mat* **s. métrico decimal,** decimal metric system; *Geog* **s. montañoso,** mountain chain; *Anat* **s. nervioso,** nervous system; **s. operativo,** operative system; **s. planetario,** planetary system; **s. solar,** solar system.

sistemático,-a *adj* systematic.

sistematizar *vtr* to systematize.

sitar *nm Mús* sitar.

sitiado,-a I *pp de* **sitiar. II** *adj* besieged. **III** *nm,f* besieged; **los sitiados,** those under siege, the besieged.

sitial *nm* seat of honour *or US* honor.

sitiar *vtr* to besiege, lay siege to.

sitio[1] *nm* **1** *(lugar)* place; **cambiar de s.,** to move; **cambiar de s. con algn,** to change places with sb; **ceder el s.,** to give up one's place; **en cualquier s.,** anywhere; **en todos los sitios,** everywhere; *fig* **quedarse en el s.,** to die. **2** *(espacio)* space, room; **guardar s. a algn,** to keep a seat for sb; **hacer s.,** to make room; **hay s. para todos,** there's room for everyone; **ocupar mucho s.,** to take up a lot of space.

sitio[2] *nm Mil* siege; **en estado de s.,** in a state of siege; **poner s. a una ciudad,** to besiege a town, lay siege to a town.

sito,-a *adj fml* situated, located; **un edificio s. en Sevilla,** a building situated in Seville.

situación *nf* **1** *(circunstancia)* situation; **la s. política,** the political situation. **2** *(posición social etc)* position; **su s. económica es precaria,** his financial position is very insecure. **3** *(emplazamiento)* situation, location.

situado,-a I *pp de* **situar. II** *adj (gen)* situated; *fig* **estar bien s.,** to be comfortably off.

situar I *vtr (en un lugar)* to place, put situate, locate. **II situarse** *vr* **1** *(en un lugar)* to be placed *or* situated *or* located. **2** *(abrirse paso)* to get on, do well, be successful.

siux *adj & nmf* Sioux.

sketch *nm Cin Teat* sketch.

s/L *abr de* **su letra (de crédito).**

S.L. *abr de* **Sociedad Limitada,** private limited company, Ltd.

slalom *nm Dep véase* **eslalon.**

slip *nm véase* **eslip.**

slogan *nm véase* **eslogan.**

S.M. *abr de* **Su Majestad,** Your Majesty.

SME *Econ abr de* **Sistema Monetario Europeo,** European Monetary System, EMS.

smoking *nm véase* **esmoquin.**

s/n. *abr de* **sin número.**

snob *adj & nmf véase* **esnob.**

snobismo *nm véase* **esnobismo.**

s/o. *abr de* **su orden,** your order.

so[1] *prep (bajo)* under; **so pena de,** under penalty of.

so[2] *nm fam* **¡so imbécil!,** you damned idiot!

so[3] *interj (a las caballerías)* whoa!

soasar *vtr Culin* to roast lightly.

soba *nf fam* **1** *(paliza)* hiding, thrashing. **2** *(manoseo)* fondling, pawing.

sobaco *nm Anat* armpit.

sobado,-a I *pp de* **sobar. II** *adj* **1** *(desgastado)* worn, shabby; *(libro)* well-thumbed, dog-eared. **2** *fig (frase, tema, etc)* well-worn.

sobajar *vtr* **1** *(ajar)* to crumple, mess up. **2** *Am (humillar)* to humiliate.

sobaquera *nf Cost* dress shield.

sobaquina *nf fam* underarm odour *or US* odor.

sobar *vtr* **1** *fam (pegar)* to thrash. **2** *vulg (manosear)* to fondle, finger, paw. **3** *(molestar)* to pester. **4** *arg (dormir)* to sleep. **5** *Am (hueso)* to set. **6** *Am (enjabonar)* to flatter.

sobeo *nm vulg* fondling, fingering.

soberanía *nf pol* sovereignty; **bajo la s. de,** under the rule of.

soberano,-a I *adj* **1** *Pol (con autoridad)* sovereign; **poder s.,** sovereign power. **2** *fig (extremo)* extreme, supreme. **3** *fam* huge, great. **II** *nm, f (monarca)* sovereign. ◆ **soberanamente** *adv* extremely, supremely.

soberbia *nf* **1** *(orgullo)* pride; *(arrogancia)* arrogance, haughtiness. **2** *(suntuosidad)* sumptuousness, pomp. **3** *(ira)* anger, rage.

soberbio,-a *adj* 1 *(orgulloso)* proud. 2 *(arrogante)* arrogant, haughty. 3 *(suntuoso)* sumptuous, magnificent. 4 *(magnífico)* splendid, magnificent, superb. 5 *fam* huge, great. ◆ **soberbiamente** *adv* 1 *(con arrogancia)* arrogantly. 2 *(magníficamente)* magnificently, superbly.

sobo *nm véase* **soba.**

sobón,-ona *fam* I *adj* given to fondling, randy. II *nm, f* randy person; **ser un s.,** to be fresh *or* all hands.

sobornable *adj* bribable, venal.

sobornar *vtr* to bribe, suborn.

soborno *nm* 1 *(acción)* bribery. 2 *(dinero, regalo)* bribe.

sobra *nf* 1 *(exceso)* excess, surplus; **de s.,** *(no necesario)* superfluous; *(excesivo)* more than enough; **estar de s.,** to be in the way; **saber algo de s.,** to know sth only too well. 2 **sobras,** *(desperdicios)* leftovers.

sobrado,-a I *pp de* **sobrar.** II *adj (que sobra)* abundant, more than enough; **andar s.,** to have a lot to spare; **sobradas veces,** repeatedly; **s. de,** plenty; **andar s. de tiempo,** to have plenty of time. III *adv (demasiado)* too. IV *nm* attic, garret. ◆ **sobradamente** *adv* extremely.

sobrante I *adj* leftover, remaining, spare, surplus. II *nm* surplus, excess.

sobrar *vi* 1 *(haber más de lo necesario)* to be more than enough, be too much; **me sobran ideas,** I've got plenty of ideas; **sobran tres sillas,** there are three chairs too many. 2 *(estorbar)* to be in the way; *fam* **tú sobras aquí,** you are not wanted here. 3 *(quedar)* to have left over; **nos sobró dinero,** we had some money left over.

sobrasada *nf Culin* Majorcan sausage.

sobre¹ *nm* 1 *(para carta)* envelope. 2 *(de sopa etc)* packet. 3 *fam (cama)* bed; **me voy al s.,** I'm off to bed.

sobre² *prep* 1 *(encima)* on, upon, on top of; **lo dejé s. la silla,** I left it on the chair. 2 *(por encima)* over, above; **volamos s. Francia,** we are flying over France. 3 *(acerca de)* about, on; **un libro s. Cervantes,** a book about Cervantes. 4 *(aproximadamente)* about; **vendré s. las ocho,** I'll come at about eight o'clock. 5 *fig* upon; **mentira s. mentira,** lie upon lie. 6 **s. todo,** especially, above all.

sobre- *pref* super-, over-.

sobreabundancia *nf* superabundance, overabundance.

superabundante *adj* superabundant, overabundant.

sobreabundar *vi* to superabound.

sobrealimentación *nf* overfeeding.

sobrealimentado,-a I *pp de* **sobrealimentar.** II *adj* overfed.

sobrealimentar *vtr* to overfeed.

sobrecalentar *vtr,* **sobrecalentarse** *vr* to overheat.

sobrecarga *nf* 1 *Téc* overload. 2 *fig (preocupación)* additional burden, further worry.

sobrecargar *vtr* 1 *Téc* to overload. 2 *fig (de preocupaciones, trabajo)* to overburden.

sobrecargo *nm Náut* supercargo.

sobrecogedor,-a *adj* 1 *(que asusta)* frightening. 2 *(que conmueve)* dramatic, awesome.

sobrecoger I *vtr* 1 *(asustar)* to frighten, scare. 2 *(coger desprevenido)* to startle, take by surprise. II **sobrecogerse** *vr* 1 *(asustarse)* to be frightened *or* scared. 2 *(sorprenderse)* to be startled. 3 *(impresionarse)* to be overawed; **s. de,** to be seized with, be overcome by.

sobrecubierta *nf (de libro)* jacket, dust cover.

sobredicho,-a *adj fml* aforementioned, aforesaid, above-mentioned.

sobredorar *vtr* 1 *(metal)* to gild. 2 *fig (disimular)* to gloss over.

sobredosis *nf inv* overdose.

sobreentender I *vtr (comprender)* to understand; *(deducir)* to deduce. II **sobreentenderse** *vr* to be understood; **se sobreentiende,** that goes without saying.

sobreexceder *vtr* to exceed.

sobreexcitación *nf* overexcitement.

sobreexcitar I *vtr* to overexcite. II **sobreexcitarse** *vr* to get overexcited.

sobreexponer *vtr* to overexpose.

sobreexposición *nf* overexposure.

sobregirar *vtr Fin* to overdraw.

sobregiro *nm Fin* overdraft.

sobrehilado,-a I *pp de* **sobrehilar.** II *nm Cost* whipstitch.

sobrehilar *vtr* to whipstitch.

sobrehumano,-a *adj* superhuman.

sobreimpresión *nf Fot Cin* superimposing.

sobrellevar *vtr* to endure, bear.

sobremanera *adv* exceedingly.

sobremesa *nf* 1 *(tertulia)* after-dinner chat; **estar de s.,** to have an after-dinner chat. 2 *Mueb* **lámpara de s.,** table lamp.

sobremodo *adv* exceedingly.

sobrenadar *vi* to float.

sobrenatural *adj* supernatural.

sobrenombre *nm* nickname.

sobrentender *vtr & vr véase* **sobreentender.**

sobrepaga *nf Fin* bonus.

sobreparto *nm* postnatal confinement; **dolores de s.,** afterpains.

sobrepasar *vtr* to exceed, surpass; *(rival)* to beat.

sobrepelliz *nf Rel* surplice.

sobrepeso *nm (de carga)* overload, excess weight; *(de persona)* excess weight.

sobrepoblación *nf véase* **superpoblación.**

sobreponer *(pp sobrepuesto)* I *vtr* 1 *(poner encima)* to put on top. 2 *(anteponer)* to put before. II **sobreponerse** *vr* 1 *(superar)* to overcome; **s. al dolor,** to overcome pain. 2 *(animarse)* to pull oneself together.

sobreprecio *nm Com* surcharge.

sobreproducción *nf* excess production, overproduction.

sobrepuesto,-a I *pp de* **sobreponer.** II *adj* superimposed.

sobrepujar *vtr* to surpass, outdo.

sobrepuse *pt indef véase* **sobreponer.**

sobrero,-a *adj* 1 *(sobrante)* surplus, spare. 2 *Taur (toro)* spare.

sobresaliente I *adj* 1 *(protuberante)* jutting out, sticking out, protruding. 2 *fig (que destaca)* outstanding, excellent. II *nm Educ (en la escuela)* A; *Univ* first. III *nmf* 1 *Taur (torero suplente)* substitute bullfighter. 2 *Teat (actor suplente)* understudy.

sobresalir *vi* 1 *(proyectarse)* to jut out, stick out, protrude. 2 *fig (destacar)* to stand out, excel.

sobresaltar I *vtr* to startle, start. II **sobresaltarse** *vr* to be startled, start.

sobresalto *nm (movimiento)* start; *(susto)* fright, shock.

sobresdrújulo,-a *adj Ling* accented on the syllable preceding the third from the end.

sobreseer *vtr Jur* to stay; **s. una causa,** to stay proceedings.

sobreseimiento *nm Jur* stay, dismissal.

sobrestante *nm* foreman.

sobrestimar *vtr* to overestimate.

sobresueldo *nm* extra pay, bonus.

sobretasa *nf* surcharge.

sobretodo *nm* 1 *(abrigo)* overcoat. 2 *(guardapolvo)* overalls *pl.*

sobrevalorar *vtr* to overestimate.

sobrevenir *vi* to happen, occur; **le sobrevino una desgracia,** disaster struck (him).

sobreviviente I *adj* surviving. **II** *nmf* survivor.

sobrevivir *vi* to survive; **s. a algn,** to outlive sb.

sobrevolar *vtr Av* to fly over.

sobrexceder *vtr véase* **sobreexceder.**

sobrexcitación *nf véase* **sobreexcitación.**

sobrexcitar *vtr,* **sobrexcitarse** *vr véase* **sobreexcitar.**

sobriedad *nf (moderación)* sobriety, moderation, restraint; *(en la bebida)* soberness.

sobrina *nf* niece.

sobrino *nm* nephew.

sobrio,-a *adj* **1** *(estilo, color)* sober, plain. **2** *(persona)* moderate, restrained; **s. en la bebida,** temperate in one's drinking habits. **3** *(estilo)* concise.

socaire *nm Náut* lee; **al s.,** leeward; *fig* **al s. de,** under the protection of.

socaliña *nf* ruse, cunning trick.

socapa *nf* pretext, dodge; **a s.,** surreptitiously, on the sly.

socar *CAm* **I** *vtr* **1** *(apretar)* to press down, squeeze. **2** *(molestar)* to annoy, pester. **II socarse** *vr (emborracharse)* to get drunk.

socarrar *vtr* to scorch, singe.

socarrón,-ona I *adj* **1** *(burlón)* sarcastic, ironical. **2** *(taimado)* sly, cunning. **II** *nm, f* **1** *(guasón)* sarcastic *or* ironical person. **2** *(persona astuta)* sly fox.

socarronería *nf* **1** *(burlonería)* sarcasm, irony, wry humour. **2** *(astucia)* slyness.

socavar *vtr* **1** *Min* to dig under. **2** *fig* to undermine; **s. la moral de la gente,** to weaken the morale of the people.

socavón *nm* **1** *Min* gallery, tunnel. **2** *(bache)* hollow, hole.

sociabilidad *nf* sociability, friendliness.

sociable *adj* sociable, friendly.

social *adj* social; **cambios sociales,** social change. ◆ **socialmente** *adv* socially.

socialdemocracia *nf Pol* social democracy.

socialdemócrata *Pol* **I** *adj* social democratic. **II** *nmf* social democrat.

socialismo *nm Pol* socialism.

socialista *adj & nmf* socialist.

socialización *nf (gen)* socialization; *(de industria etc)* nationalization.

socializar *vtr (gen)* to socialize; *(industria etc)* to nationalize.

sociedad *nf* **1** *(gen)* society; **presentarse en s.,** to make one's debut. ■ **alta** *or* **buena s.,** high society; **ecos de s.,** gossip column; **s. de consumo,** consumer society. **2** *(asociación)* association, society. ■ *Rel* **S. de Jesús,** Society of Jesus; **S. de Naciones,** League of Nations; **s. protectora de animales,** society for the prevention of cruelty to animals. **3** *Com* company. ■ **s. anónima,** limited *or* US incorporated company; **s. comanditaria** *or* **en comandita,** limited partnership; **s. limitada,** private limited company; **s. mercantil,** (trading) company.

socio,-a *nm, f* **1** *(miembro)* member; **hacerse s. de un club,** to become a member of a club, join a club. **2** *Com (asociado)* partner, associate; *(accionista)* shareholder, member. ■ **s. capitalista** *or* **comanditario,** sleeping *or* US silent partner. **3** *fam (compinche)* mate, pal.

socioeconómico,-a *adj* socioeconomic.

sociología *nf* sociology.

sociológico,-a *adj* sociological.

sociólogo,-a *nm, f* sociologist.

soco,-a *adj* **1** *(manco)* one-armed; *(sin una pierna)* one-legged. **2** *CAm (borracho)* drunk. **3** *Arg (caballo)* useless.

socolar *vtr CAm (terreno)* to clear.

socollón *nm CAm Cuba* sudden and violent shake.

socorrer *vtr* to help, assist, come *or* go to the aid of.

socorrido,-a I *pp de* **socorrer. II** *adj* **1** *(útil)* handy, useful. **2** *(abastecido)* well-stocked. **3** *fig (frase, argumento)* hackneyed, well-worn.

socorrismo *nm* life-saving.

socorrista *nmf* life-saver, lifeguard.

socorro *nm* **1** *(ayuda)* help, aid, assistance; **acudir en s. de algn,** to go to sb's aid; **¡s.!,** help! ■ **puesto de s.,** first-aid post; **señal de s.,** distress signal; **trabajos de s.,** rescue work *sing.* **2** *Mil (provisiones)* supplies *pl,* provisions *pl.*

socrático,-a *adj & nm, f Filos* Socratic.

soda *nf* **1** *Quím* soda. **2** *(bebida)* soda water.

sódico,-a *adj Quím* sodium; **bicarbonato s.,** sodium bicarbonate.

sodio *nm Quím* sodium.

sodomía *nf* sodomy.

sodomita *adj & nmf* sodomite.

soez *adj* vulgar, crude, rude.

sofá *nm (pl sofás)* sofa, settee. ■ **s. cama,** sofa bed, studio couch.

Sofía *n* Sophia.

sofión *nm* **1** *(bufido)* snort, bellow. **2** *(trabuco)* blunderbuss.

sofisma *nm* sophism.

sofista *nmf Filos* sophist.

sofisticación *nf* sophistication.

sofisticado,-a I *pp de* **sofisticar. II** *adj* sophisticated.

sofisticar *vtr* to sophisticate.

soflama *nf* **1** *(llama)* flicker, glow. **2** *(rubor)* blush. **3** *pey (perorata)* harangue. **4** *fig (engaño)* deceit. **5** *fig (zalamería)* cajolery.

soflamar I *vtr* **1** *(chamuscar)* to scorch, singe. **2** *(avergonzar)* to make blush. **3** *fig (engañar)* to deceive. **4** *fig (halagar)* to cajole. **II soflamarse** *vr (chamuscarse)* to burn.

sofocación *nf* **1** *(ahogo)* suffocation, stifling sensation. **2** *(rubor)* blushing. **3** *(de un incendio)* extinction. **4** *(de una rebelión)* suppression.

sofocado,-a I *pp de* **sofocar. II** *adj* suffocated.

sofocante *adj* suffocating, stifling; **hacía un calor s.,** it was unbearably hot.

sofocar I *vtr* **1** *(ahogar)* to suffocate, stifle, smother. **2** *(incendio)* to extinguish, put out. **3** *(rebelión)* to put down, suppress. **4** *fig (avergonzar)* to make blush. **II sofocarse** *vr* **1** *(ahogarse)* to suffocate, stifle. **2** *fig (ruborizarse)* to blush. **3** *(enfadarse)* to get angry *or* upset.

sofoco *nm* **1** *(ahogo)* suffocation, stifling sensation. **2** *fig (vergüenza)* embarrassment; *(disgusto)* shock; **le dio un s.,** it gave her quite a turn.

sofocón *nm fam* shock; **llevarse un s.,** to get into a state.

sofoquina *nf fam* **1** *(calor)* stifling heat. **2** *(sofocón)* shock.

sofreír *vtr* to fry lightly, brown.

sofrito *nm Culin* fried tomato and onion sauce.

software *nm Inform* software.

soga *nf* rope, cord; *fig* **dar s. a algn,** *(burlarse)* to make fun of sb; *(seguir la corriente)* to keep sb talking; *fig* **estar con la s. al cuello,** to be in dire straits.

soja *nf Bot* soya bean, *US* soybean.

sojuzgar *vtr* to subjugate.

sol[1] *nm* **1** *(astro)* sun; *(luz del sol)* sunlight, sunshine; **al ponerse el s.,** at sunset; **al salir el s.,** at sunrise; **al** *or* **bajo el s.,** in the sun; **de s. a s.,** from sunrise to sunset; **día de s.,** a sunny day; **hace s.,** it's sunny, the sun is shining; **s. y sombra,** *Taur* seats which enjoy some sun and some shade; *(bebida)* brandy and anisette drink; **tomar el s.,** to sunbathe; *fig* **arrimarse al s. que más calienta,** to know which side one's bread is buttered on; *fig* **no dejar a algn ni a s. ni a sombra,** to pester *or* harass sb continually. ■ **s.**

de medianoche, midnight sun; **s. naciente,** rising sun; **s. poniente,** setting sun. **2** *fam (persona)* darling; **ser un s.,** to be a darling. **3** *Fin* standard monetary unit of Perú.

sol² *nm Mús* sol, G.

solana *nf (lugar)* sunny spot; *(de una casa)* sun lounge; *(terraza)* veranda, verandah.

solano¹ *nm* easterly wind.

solano² *nm Bot* nightshade.

solapa *nf* **1** *(de chaqueta)* lapel. **2** *(de sobre, bolsillo, libro)* flap. **3** *fig* pretext.

solapado,-a I *pp de* **solapar. II** *adj (persona)* sly, evasive.
♦ **solapadamente** *adv* stealthily, in an underhand way.

solapar I *vtr fig (ocultar)* to conceal, cover up. **II** *vi (cubrir en parte)* to overlap.

solar¹ *adj* solar; **año s.,** solar year; **luz s.,** sunlight.

solar² *nm* **1** *(terreno)* plot; *(en obras)* building site. **2** *(casa de familia noble)* ancestral home; *fig (linaje)* lineage, line.

solar³ *vtr* **1** *(zapatos)* to sole. **2** *(suelo)* to floor.

solariego,-a *adj (familia)* ancient and noble; **casa solariega,** ancestral home.

solario *nm,* **solárium** *nm* solarium.

solaz *nm fml* **1** *(descanso)* rest, relaxation; *(esparcimiento)* recreation, entertainment. **2** *(consuelo)* consolation, solace.

solazar I *vtr* **1** *(relajar)* to relax; *(divertir)* to entertain, amuse. **2** *(consolar)* to console, comfort. **II solazarse** *vr (relajarse)* to relax; *(divertirse)* to enjoy oneself.

soldada *nf* salary, pay.

soldadesca *nf* **1** *(profesión)* military profession. **2** *pey (soldados)* soldiery.

soldadesco,-a *adj* soldier-like, soldierly.

soldado *nm* soldier. ■ **s. raso,** private.

soldador,-a I *nm,f* welder. **II** *nm* soldering iron.

soldadura *nf* **1** *(acción)* soldering, welding. **2** *(trozo, lugar soldado)* soldered joint, weld.

soldar I *vtr (metal)* to solder, weld; **s. por puntos,** to spot-weld. **II soldarse** *vr (huesos)* to knit.

soleá *nf (pl* **soleares)** *Mús* Andalusian song and dance.

soleado,-a *adj* sunny.

solear *vtr,* **solearse** *vr* to expose to the sun, put in the sun.

solecismo *nm* solecism.

soledad *nf* **1** *(estado)* solitude; *(sentimiento)* loneliness. **2 soledades,** *(lugar)* lonely place *sing.*

solemne *adj* **1** *(majestuoso)* solemn, majestic. **2** *(serio)* solemn, grave. **3** *pey* downright; **es una s. estupidez,** it's downright stupid, it's sheer stupidity.

solemnidad *nf* **1** *(pompa)* solemnity, pomp, formality. **2** *(ceremonia)* solemn ceremony, ceremonial occasion.

solemnizar *vtr* to solemnize, celebrate, commemorate.

solenoide *nm Elec* solenoid.

soler *vi defect* **1** *(en presente)* to be in the habit of, be accustomed to; **solemos ir en coche,** we usually go by car; **sueles equivocarte,** you are usually wrong. **2** *(en pasado)* to use to; **solía ser muy criticón,** he used to be very critical.

solera *nf* **1** *(soporte)* prop, support. **2** *(de molino)* lower millstone. **3** *(de horno)* floor. **4** *(de vino)* lees *pl.* **5** *fig* tradition; **de s.,** old-established; **vino de s.,** vintage wine.

solfa *nf* **1** *Mús* solfa, musical notation; *fam* **poner en s.,** to ridicule. **2** *fam (paliza)* thrashing, beating.

solfear *vtr* **1** *Mús* to solfa. **2** *fam (zurrar)* to thrash, beat. **3** *fam (abroncar)* to give a dressing-down to.

solfeo *nm Mús* solfa.

solicitación *nf (acción)* requesting; *(solicitud)* request, application.

solicitador,-a *nm,f.* **solicitante** *nmf* applicant, petitioner.

solicitar *vtr* **1** *(pedir)* to request, ask for; **s. un trabajo,** to apply for a job. **2** *(persona)* to chase after; **es una persona muy solicitada,** he *or* she is much in demand. **3** *(mujer)* to woo, court.

solícito,-a *adj* obliging, attentive.

solicitud *nf* **1** *(diligencia)* care, attention. **2** *(petición)* request, petition; *(de trabajo)* application; **a s.,** on request.

solidaridad *nf* solidarity.

solidario,-a *adj* **1** *(unido)* united; *(causa)* common. **2** *Jur* jointly responsible.

solidarizar I *vtr (unir)* to unite. **II solidarizarse** *vr* to show one's solidarity **(con,** with); **s. con,** *(apoyar)* to support; *(unirse a)* to join.

solideo *nm Rel* skullcap.

solidez *nf (resistencia)* solidity, strength; *(firmeza)* firmness; *fig (de principio etc)* soundness; *(de color)* fastness.

solidificación *nf (de un líquido)* solidification; *(de una pasta)* hardening, setting.

solidificar *vtr,* **solidificarse** *vr (líquido)* to solidify; *(pasta)* to harden, set.

sólido,-a I *adj (resistente)* solid, strong; *(firme)* firm; *fig (principio etc)* sound; *(color)* fast. **II** *nm Fís* solid.

soliloquio *nm Lit* soliloquy.

solio *nm* throne.

solista *nmf Mús* soloist.

solitaria *nf Med* tapeworm.

solitario,-a I *adj* **1** *(que está solo)* solitary, lone; *(que se siente solo)* lonely; *Av* **vuelo en s.,** solo flight. **2** *(lugar)* deserted, lonely. **II** *nm* **1** *(diamante)* solitaire. **2** *Naipes* solitaire, patience.

soliviantar *vtr* **1** *(persona, sentimiento)* to rouse, stir up. **2** *(irritar)* to irritate.

sollo *nm (pez)* sturgeon.

sollozar *vi* to sob.

sollozo *nm* sob; **prorrumpir en sollozos,** to start sobbing.

solo,-a I *adj* **1** *(sin compañía, sin ayuda)* alone, on one's own, by oneself, by itself; **a solas,** alone, by oneself; **café s.,** black coffee; **hablar s.,** to talk to oneself; **se enciende s.,** it switches itself on automatically; **vivir s.,** to live alone; **whisky s.,** straight whisky. **2** *(solitario)* lonely; **sentirse s.,** to feel lonely. **3** *(único)* only, sole, single; **ni un s. día,** not single day; **una sola vez,** only once, just once; *fam* **quedarse s.,** to have no equal; **se queda s. comiendo,** no one can eat like him. **II** *nm* **1** *Mús* solo. **2** *Naipes* solitaire. **3** *fam (café)* black coffee.

sólo *adv,* **solo** *adv* only, just; **con s., s. con,** just by; **no s. ... sino (también),** not only... but (also); **no s. dibuja sino que también pinta,** she not only draws, but she paints as well; **s. para adultos,** for adults only; **s. que,** only, but; **tan s. con,** just by. ♦ **solamente** *adv* only; **no s.,** not only; **s. con mirarte lo sé,** I know just by looking at you; **s. que ...,** except that ... .

solomillo *nm* sirloin.

solsticio *nm Astron* solstice.

soltar I *vtr* **1** *(desasir)* to release, let go of; **¡suelta!,** let go!; **¡suéltame!,** let me go!, take your hands off me!; *fam* **s. la pasta,** to cough up. **2** *(desatar)* to untie, unfasten, loosen; **s. un nudo,** to loosen a knot. **3** *(prisionero)* to release; *(pájaro)* to let out; *(perro)* to unleash. **4** *(humo, olor)* to give off. **5** *(dar)* to deal, strike; **le soltó un par de bofetadas,** he gave him a few smacks. **6** *(decir, contar)* to come out with, let slip; **nos soltó un sermón,** he started preaching to us; **s. la lengua,** to speak freely; **s. un taco,** to swear; **s. una carcajada,** to burst out laughing. **II soltarse** *vr* **1** *(desatarse)* to come untied *or* unfastened *or* loose. **2** *(perro etc)* to get loose, break loose. **3** *(desprenderse)* to come off; *(tornillo)* to come loose. **4** *(adquirir habilidad)* to become proficient, get the knack; **s. en un idioma,** to become fluent in a language. **5** *(desenvolverse)* to lose one's shyness, become self-confident; **le ha costado pero parece que por fin empieza a s.,** it's taken him a long time but now it looks as if he's relaxed. **6** *(relajarse)* to loosen up, let oneself go; **s. a su gusto,** to let off steam.

soltería *nf* single state; *(de hombre)* bachelorhood; *(de mujer)* spinsterhood.

soltero,-a I *adj* single, unmarried. **II** *nm (hombre)* bachelor, single man. **III** *nf (mujer)* single woman, spinster; **apellido de soltera,** maiden name.

solterón,-ona *pey* **I** *nm (hombre)* old bachelor. **II** *nf (mujer)* old maid.

soltura *nf (agilidad)* agility; *(seguridad)* confidence, assurance; *(al hablar)* fluency, ease; **hablar un idioma con s.,** to speak a language fluently *or* with ease.

solubilidad *nf Fís* solubility.

soluble *adj Fís* soluble.

solución *nf* **1** *(gen)* solution; **la s. de un problema,** the solution to a problem. **2** *Quím* solution.

solucionar *vtr (problema)* to solve; *(asunto, huelga)* to settle.

solvencia *nf* **1** *Fin* solvency; *(pago)* settlement. **2** *(fiabilidad)* reliability; *(reputación)* good reputation; **fuentes de toda s.,** completely reliable sources.

solventar *vtr (problema)* to solve, resolve; *(deuda, asunto)* to settle.

solvente I *adj* **1** *Fin* solvent. **2** *(fiable)* reliable. **II** *nm Quím* solvent.

soma *nm* soma, matter.

Somalia *n* Somalia.

somalí *adj & nmf* Somali.

somanta *nf fam* beating; **dar una s. a algn,** to give sb a thrashing.

somatar *CAm* **I** *vtr (zurrar)* to give a thrashing, beat up. **II somatarse** *vr (darse un golpe)* to knock oneself about badly.

somatén *nm Cat* civilian militia.

somático,-a *adj Med* somatic.

sombra *nf* **1** *(ausencia de sol)* shade; **a la s.,** *(sin sol)* in the shade; *arg (en la cárcel)* in the nick; **dar s.,** to give shade. **2** *(silueta proyectada)* shadow; **hacer s.,** to cast a shadow; *fig* **hacer s. a algn,** to overshadow sb; *fig* **no fiarse ni de su s.,** to be very distrustful; *fig* **reírse hasta de la propia s.,** to laugh at everything. ■ **s. de ojos,** eyeshadow; **sombras chinescas,** shadow theatre *sing*. **3** *(vestigio)* trace, shadow; **ni por s.,** not in the least; **ni s. de,** not a trace of; **sin s. de duda,** beyond a shadow of doubt. **4** *(suerte)* luck; **tener buena s.,** *(tener suerte)* to be lucky; *(ser agradable)* to be pleasant; **tener mala s.,** *(no tener suerte)* to be unlucky; *(ser desagradable)* to be unpleasant. **5** *(espectro)* ghost, shade. **6** *fig (oscuridad)* darkness, obscurity. **7** *(mácula)* spot, stain. **8** *(clandestinidad)* secrecy; **gobierno en la s.,** shadow cabinet; **trabaja en la s.,** he works undercover. **9** *Am (falsilla)* lined paper as guide under writing paper. **10** *Méx (toldo)* awning.

sombraje *nm*, **sombrajo** *nm* shade, shelter from the sun.

sombreado *nm* shading.

sombrear *vtr* to shade, cast a shadow upon.

sombrerera *nf* hatbox.

sombrerería *nf (para señoras)* milliner's; *(para caballeros)* hatter's.

sombrerero,-a *nm, f (para señoras)* milliner; *(para caballeros)* hatter.

sombrerete *nm* **1** *(de chimenea)* cowl. **2** *Bot (de seta)* cap.

sombrero *nm* **1** *(prenda)* hat; **sin s.,** hatless, bareheaded; *fig* **quitarse el s. ante algn,** to take one's hat off to sb. ■ **s. canotier,** straw hat; **s. cordobés,** wide-brimmed Andalusian hat; **s. de copa,** top hat; **s. de jipijapa,** Panama hat; **s. de tres picos,** three-cornered hat; **s. hongo,** bowler hat. **2** *Bot (de seta)* cap.

sombrilla *nf* parasol, sunshade.

sombrío,-a *adj* **1** *(lugar)* *(oscuro)* dark; *fig (tenebroso)* sombre, gloomy. **2** *fig (persona)* gloomy, sullen.

somero,-a *adj (superficial)* superficial, shallow; *fig* **hizo una somera exposición del tema,** she gave a brief summary of the subject.

someter I *vtr* **1** *(rebeldes)* to subdue, put down; *(rebelión)* to quell; *(pasiones)* to subdue. **2** *(exponer, mostrar)* to subject (**a,** to), expose (**a,** to); **s. a prueba,** to put to the test; **s. algo a la autoridad,** to refer sth to an authority; **s. algo a votación,** to put sth to the vote. **3** *(proposición, idea)* to submit, present. **II someterse** *vr* **1** *(rendirse)* to surrender, yield; *fig* **s. a la opinión de algn,** to bow to sb's opinion. **2** *(recibir)* to undergo; **s. a un tratamiento,** to undergo treatment.

sometimiento *nm* **1** *(dominación)* subjection, subjugation. **2** *(presentación)* submission, presentation.

somier *nm (pl somieres)* spring mattress.

somnambulismo *nm véase* **sonambulismo.**

somnámbulo,-a *adj & nm, f véase* **sonámbulo,-a.**

somnífero,-a I *adj* somniferous, sleep-inducing. **II** *nm* sleeping pill.

somnolencia *nf* somnolence, sleepiness, drowsiness.

somnoliento,-a *adj* sleepy, drowsy.

somorgujo *nm*, **somormujo** *nm Orn* grebe.

son *nm* **1** *(sonido)* sound; **al s. del tambor,** to the sound of the drum. **2** *(rumor)* rumour, *US* rumor. **3** *(modo)* manner, way; **a mi s.,** my way. **4** *(motivo, pretexto)* reason; **¿a s. de qué?,** whatever for?; **sin ton ni s.,** without rhyme or reason; **venir en s. de paz,** to come in peace.

sonado,-a I *pp de* **sonar.** **II** *adj (muy conocido)* famous; *fam* **hacer una que sea sonada,** to cause a great stir. **2** *fam fig (trastocado)* mad, crazy; **estar s.,** *(boxeador)* to be punch-drunk; *(estar loco)* to be off one's rocker.

sonaja *nf* **1** *(de pandereta)* small metal disk. **2** **sonajas,** *(juguete)* rattle *sing*.

sonajero *nm* baby's rattle.

sonambulismo *nm* somnambulism, sleepwalking.

sonámbulo,-a I *adj* sleepwalking. **II** *nm, f* somnambulist, sleepwalker.

sonar I *vi* **1** *(resonar)* to sound; **s. a,** to sound like; **suena bien,** it sounds good; *prov* **cuando el río suena, agua lleva,** there's no smoke without fire. **2** *(campana, timbre, teléfono)* to ring. **3** *(reloj)* to strike; **sonaron las cinco,** the clock struck five. **4** *(conocer vagamente)* to sound familiar, ring a bell. **5** *(pronunciarse)* to be pronounced; **la 'h' no suena,** the 'h' is not pronounced; **se escribe como suena,** it is written as it's pronounced; **tal y como suena,** just as I am telling you. **6** *Arg Chi Urug (enfermedad)* to suffer. **7** *Arg Chi Par (fracasar)* to fail, blow it. **8** *Arg Chi (empleo, en el juego)* to lose. **9** *Arg Chi (sufrir consecuencias)* to suffer consequences. **II sonarse** *vr (nariz)* to blow one's nose.

sónar *nm Náut* sonar.

sonata *nf Mús* sonata.

sonatina *nf Mús* sonatina.

sonda *nf* **1** *Med* sound, probe. **2** *Náut* sounding line. **3** *Min* drill, bore. **4** *Aeronáut* probe; **s. espacial,** space probe.

sondear *vtr* **1** *Med* to sound, probe. **2** *Náut* to sound. **3** *Min* to drill, bore. **4** *fig* to test, sound out; **s. la opinión pública,** to test public opinion.

sondeo *nm* **1** *Med* sounding, probing. **2** *Náut* sounding. **3** *Min* drilling, boring. **4** *(encuesta)* poll; *TV* **s. de audiencia,** rating; **s. de la opinión pública,** public opinion poll.

sonetista *nmf Lit* writer of sonnets.

soneto *nm Lit* sonnet.

sónico,-a *adj* sonic.

sonido *nm* sound; **barrera del s.,** sound barrier.

soniquete *nm véase* **sonsonete.**

sonoridad *nf* sonority.

sonorización *nf* **1** *Cin (de película)* recording of the soundtrack. **2** *(amplificación)* amplification. **3** *Ling (en fonética)* voicing.

sonorizar *vtr* **1** *Cin (película)* to record the soundtrack of. **2** *(amplificar)* to install amplifying equipment in. **3** *Ling (en fonética)* to voice.

sonoro,-a *adj* **1** *Cin* sound; **banda sonora,** soundtrack; **efectos sonoros,** sound effects; **película sonora,** talking picture. **2** *(resonante)* loud, resounding; **voz sonora,** resounding voice. **3** *Ling* voiced.

sonreír *vi,* **sonreírse** *vr* to smile; **me sonrió,** he smiled to me; *fig* **le sonrió la fortuna,** fortune smiled on him.

sonriente *adj* smiling.

sonrisa *nf* smile; **dirigir una s. a algn,** to smile to sb; **esbozar una s.,** to smile.

sonrojar **I** *vtr* to make blush; **(hacer) s. a algn,** to make sb blush. **II** **sonrojarse** *vr* to blush.

sonrojo *nm* **1** *(rubor)* blush, blushing. **2** *(vergüenza)* shame, embarrassment.

sonrosado,-a **I** *pp de* **sonrosar.** **II** *adj* rosy, pink.

sonrosar *vtr* to go *or* turn pink.

sonsacar *vtr (gen)* to wheedle; *(secreto)* to worm out.

sonsonete *nm* **1** *(voz)* sing-song (voice), monotonous voice. **2** *(tono)* mocking tone. **3** *(golpecitos)* rhythmic tapping.

soñado,-a I *pp de* **soñar. II** *adj* of one's dreams, dreamed-of; **que ni s.,** marvellous, fantastic.

soñador,-a I *adj* dreamy, dreaming. **II** *nm,f* dreamer.

soñar *vtr & vi* **1** *(dormir)* to dream; **s. con,** to dream of *or* about; *fig* **¡ni soñarlo!,** not on your life!; *fig* **s. con los angelitos,** to have sweet dreams. **2** *(fantasear)* to daydream, dream; **s. despierto,** to daydream.

soñarrera *nf fam,* **soñera** *nf* **1** *(sueño profundo)* deep sleep. **2** *(ganas de dormir)* sleepiness; **cogerse una s.,** to feel sleepy.

soñoliento,-a *adj* sleepy, drowsy.

sopa *nf Culin* soup; *fig* **comer la s. boba,** to be a parasite; *fig* **dar sopas con honda a algn,** to outshine sb; *fig* **quedar hecho una s.,** to get soaked to the skin; *fam* **estar hasta en la s.,** to be everywhere. ■ **s. boba,** gruel; **s. juliana,** spring vegetable soup.

sopapo *nm* slap; **dar un s. a algn,** to slap sb.

sopar *vtr,* **sopear** *vtr Culin* to dunk.

sopero,-a I *adj* soup; **cucharada sopera,** soup spoon; **plato s.,** soup dish. **II** *nf* soup tureen.

sopesar *vtr* to try the weight of; *fig* to weigh up.

sopetón *nm fam* slap; **de s.,** all of a sudden.

sopicaldo *nm Culin* thin soup.

sopla *interj fam* good gracious!

soplado,-a I *pp de* **soplar. II** *adj fam* **1** *(borracho)* drunk, tight, tipsy. **2** *(engreído)* conceited. **III** *nm Téc* glass-blowing.

soplador *nm Téc* glass-blower.

soplamocos *nm inv fam* slap, punch.

soplagaitas *nmf inv pey fam* cretin, idiot, fool.

soplapollas *nmf inv vulg* berk.

soplar I *vi (correr el viento)* to blow. **2** *fam (denunciar)* to squeal. **II** *vtr* **1** *(polvo etc)* to blow away; *(sopa)* to blow on. **2** *(apagar) (vela)* to blow out. **3** *(llenar de aire)* to blow up. **4** *Téc (vidrio)* to blow. **5** *(decir con disimulo)* to whisper *or* tell the answer. **6** *fam (denunciar)* to split on. **7** *fam (robar)* to steal, pinch. **III soplarse** *vr* **1** *(lanzarse aire)* to blow on; **s. los dedos,** to blow on one's fingers. **2** *fam (beber)* to down; *(comer)* to wolf down.

sopleque *nm Arg* pretentious *or* conceited man.

soplete *nm Téc* blowlamp, blowtorch.

soplido *nm* blow, puff.

soplillo *nm* fan; *fam* **orejas de s.,** sticking out ears, cauliflower ears.

soplo *nm* **1** *(acción)* blow, puff; *(de viento)* puff, gust; *fig* **pasar como un s.,** to fly past. **2** *(instante)* moment, minute; **en un s.,** in a jiffy. **3** *fam (delación)* tip-off; **dar el s.,** to split, squeal. **4** *Med* souffle, murmur.

soplón,-ona *fam* **I** *adj (niño)* telltale; *(delator)* informing, who informs. **II** *nm, f* **1** *(niño)* telltale, sneak; *(delator)* informer, squealer. **2** *CAm Teat* prompter. **3** *Méx pey (policía)* cop.

soponcio *nm fam* fainting fit, swoon; **me dio un s.,** I passed out, I fainted.

sopor *nm* sleepiness, drowsiness.

soporífero,-a *adj,* **soporífico,-a** *adj* **1** *(que adormece)* soporific, sleep-inducing. **2** *(aburrido)* boring, dull.

soportable *adj* bearable.

soportal *nm Arquit* porch; **soportales,** arcade *sing.*

soportar *vtr* **1** *(sostener)* to support, bear. **2** *fig (tolerar)* to bear, endure; *(aguantar)* to put up with; **no soporto la lluvia,** I can't stand rain.

soporte *nm* support; *Inform* **s. físico,** hardware; **s. logístico,** software.

soprano *nmf Mús* soprano.

sor *nf Rel* sister.

sora *nf SAm* alcoholic drink made from maize.

sorber *vtr* **1** *(beber)* to sip; *(un huevo)* to suck. **2** *(absorber)* to soak up, absorb; *fam* **sorberle el seso a algn,** to go to sb's head.

sorbete *nm Culin* sorbet, sherbet.

sorbo *nm* **1** *(acción)* sip; **beber a sorbos,** to sip. **2** *(trago)* gulp; **de un s.,** in one gulp.

sordera *nf Med* deafness.

sordidez *nf* **1** *(suciedad)* squalor. **2** *(mezquindad)* meanness.

sórdido,-a *adj* **1** *(sucio)* squalid, sordid. **2** *(mezquino)* mean.

sordina *nf* **1** *Mús (en trompeta)* mute; sordino; *(en piano)* damper; *fig* **a la s.,** silently, on the quiet. **2** *(en reloj)* silencer, muffler.

sordo,-a I *adj* **1** *(persona)* deaf; **quedarse s.,** to go deaf; **s. como una tapia,** stone-deaf; *fig* **permanecer s. a,** to remain deaf to. **2** *(golpe, ruido, dolor)* dull. **3** *(cólera)* pent-up. **4** *Ling* voiceless, unvoiced. **II** *nm, f* deaf person; **los sordos,** the deaf *pl; fam fig* **hacerse el s.,** to turn a deaf ear.

sordomudez *nf Med* deaf-muteness.

sordomudo,-a I *adj* deaf and dumb, deaf-mute. **II** *nm, f* deaf and dumb person, deaf-mute.

sorgo *nm Bot* sorghum.

soriano,-a I *adj of or* from Soria. **II** *nm, f* native *or* inhabitant of Soria.

soriasis *nf inv Med* psoriasis.

sorites *nm inv Filos* sorites *sing.*

sorna *nf (ironía)* sarcasm; *(mofa)* mocking tone.

soroche *nm CAm* altitude sickness, mountain sickness.

sorprendente *adj* surprising, amazing, astonishing; *(extraordinario)* extraordinary.

sorprender I *vtr* **1** *(causar extrañeza)* to surprise, astonish, amaze; **no me sorprendería nada,** I wouldn't be at all surprised. **2** *(coger desprevenido)* to catch unawares, take by surprise; **sorprendieron al ladrón,** they caught the burglar in the act. **3** *(descubrir)* to discover. **II sorprenderse** *vr* to be surprised; **¿de qué te sorprendes?,** why are you so surprised?

sorpresa *nf* surprise; **coger do** *or* **por s.,** to take by surprise; **llevarse una s.,** to be surprised.

sorpresivo,-a *adj Am* unexpected, surprising.

sorrasear(se) *vtr & vr Méx SAm Culin* to half-cook.

sorrostrada *nf* insolence.

sorteable *adj* avoidable, which can be avoided.

sortear *vtr* 1 *(someter a suerte)* to draw *or* cast lots for; *(rifar)* to raffle (off); *Mil* to draft. 2 *(evitar)* to avoid, overcome, get round. 3 *Taur* to dodge.

sorteo *nm* draw; *(rifa)* raffle.

sortija *nf* 1 *(anillo)* ring. 2 *(rizo)* curl.

sortilegio *nm* 1 *(hechicería)* sorcery, witchcraft. 2 *(hechizo)* spell.

S.O.S. *nm* SOS; **lanzar un S.O.S.,** to send out an SOS.

sosa *nf* 1 *Bot* saltwort. 2 *Quím* soda. ■ **s. cáustica,** caustic soda.

sosaina *nmf fam* dull person, bore.

sosegado,-a I *pp de* **sosegar. II** *adj (tranquilo)* calm, quiet; *(pacífico)* peaceful.

sosegador,-a *adj* calming.

sosegar I *vtr (aplacar)* to clam, quieten. **II sosegarse** *vr (tranquilizarse)* to calm down.

sosegate *nm* *Arg Urug* reprimand, reprehension.

sosera *nf,* **sosería** *nf* insipidity, dullness.

soseras *inv* **I** *adj* dull, boring. **II** *nmf* dull person, bore.

sosia *nm* double, lookalike.

sosiego *nm (calma)* calmness; *(paz)* peace, tranquility.

soslayar *vtr* 1 *(ladear)* to slant, put on a slant. 2 *fig (eludir)* to avoid, dodge.

soslayo (al *or* **de)** *loc adv* sideways; **mirar de s.,** to look sideways (at).

soso,-a *adj* 1 *(comida)* tasteless; **la sopa está sosa,** the soup needs more salt. 2 *fig (sin gracia)* insipid, dull, flat; **¡qué hombre tan s.!,** what a bore (he is)!

sospecha *nf* suspicion; **despertar sospechas,** to arouse suspicion; **por encima de toda s.,** above suspicion; **s. fundada,** well-founded suspicion; **tengo la s. de que …,** I suspect that … .

sospechar I *vtr (pensar)* to think, suppose, suspect. **II** *vi (desconfiar)* to suspect; **s. de algn,** to suspect sb.

sospechoso,-a I *adj* suspicious. **II** *nm, f* suspect. ◆ **sospechosamente** *adv* suspiciously.

sosquinar *vtr* *SAm* to slant.

sostén *nm* 1 *(apoyo)* support. 2 *(sustento)* sustenance. 3 *(prenda)* bra, brassière.

sostener I *vtr* 1 *(sustentar)* to support, hold up. 2 *(sujetar)* to hold. 3 *fig (aguantar) (dificultades)* to endure, bear, put up with. 4 *fig (defender) (teoría, punto de vista)* to defend, uphold; **s. que …,** to maintain that … . 5 *(mantener)* to hold, sustain; **s. la palabra,** to keep one's word; **s. una conversación,** to hold a conversation; **sostenerle la mirada a algn,** to stare sb down; *fig* **s. una familia,** to support a family. **II sostenerse** *vr* 1 *(mantenerse)* to support oneself. 2 *(permanecer)* to stay, remain; **se sostuvo en la presidencia cinco años,** he held the presidency for five years.

sostenido,-a I *pp de* **sostener. II** *adj* 1 *(continuado)* sustained; *(constante)* steady. 2 *Mús* sharp; **sol s.,** G sharp. **III** *nm Mús* sharp.

sostenimiento *nm* 1 *(apoyo)* support. 2 *(mantenimiento)* maintenance.

sostuve *pt indef véase* **sostener.**

sota *nf* 1 *Naipes* jack, knave. 2 *(desvergonzada)* slut.

sotabanco *nm* attic.

sotabarba *nf* 1 *(barba)* Newgate frill *or* fringe. 2 *(papada)* double chin.

sotana *nf Rel* cassock, soutane.

sótano *nm Arquit* basement, cellar.

sotavento *nm Náut* lee, leeward; **Islas de S.,** Leeward Islands.

sotechado *nm Constr* shed.

soterrado,-a I *pp de* **soterrar. II** *adj* buried, hidden.

soterrar *vtr* to bury; *fig* to hide.

soto *nm (arboleda)* grove; *(matorrales)* thicket.

sotreta I *adj SAm* 1 *(caballo)* lame. 2 *(persona)* untrustworthy, slippery. **II** *nf Arg Bol Urug* 1 *(con defectos)* runt. 2 *(holgazán)* idler.

soufflé *nm Culin* soufflé.

soviet *nm Pol* soviet.

soviético,-a *adj & nm, f* Soviet; **la Unión Soviética,** the Soviet Union.

sovietización *nf Pol* sovietization.

sovietizar *vtr Pol* to sovietize.

sovietólogo,-a *nm, f Pol* Sovietologist.

soy *indic pres véase* **ser².**

S.P. *abr de* **Servicio Público.**

sparring *nm Box* sparring partner.

speaker *nmf Rad TV* presenter, commentator.

sport (de) *loc adj* casual, sports; **chaqueta s.,** sports jacket; **ropa s.,** casual clothes *or* wear.

spot *nm (pl spots) TV* commercial, advert, ad.

spray *nm (pl sprays)* spray.

sprint *nm Dep* sprint.

sprintar *vi Dep* to sprint.

sprinter *nmf Dep* sprinter.

Sr. *abr de* **Señor,** Mister, Mr.

Sra. *abr de* **Señora,** Mrs.

Sras. *abr de* **Señoras.**

S.R.C., s.r.c. *abr de* **se ruega contestación,** please reply, R.S.V.P.

Sres. *abr de* **Señores,** Messieurs, Messrs.

Sri Lanka *n* Sri Lanka.

Srta. *abr de* **Señorita,** Miss.

SS *nf abr de* **Seguridad Social,** ≈ National Health Service, NHS.

S.S *abr Rel de* **Su Santidad,** His Holiness, H.H.

SS.AA. *abr de* **Sus Altezas,** Their Royal Highnesses.

s.s.s. *abr de* **su seguro servidor,** your humble servant.

Sta., sta. *abr de* **Santa,** Saint, St.

stand *nm Com* stand.

standard *adj & nm* standard.

standardizar *vtr* to standardize.

standing *nm* standing; **pisos de alto s.,** de luxe flats *or* apartments.

starter *nm Aut* choke.

statu quo *nm* status quo.

status *nm inv* status.

stick *nm Dep* stick.

Sto., sto. *abr de* **Santo,** Saint, St.

stock *nm Com* stock.

stop *nm Aut* stop sign.

striptease *nm* striptease; **hacer un s.,** to strip.

su *adj pos (un objeto) (de él)* his; *(de ella)* her; *(de usted, ustedes)* your; *(de animales or cosas) (impersonal)* one's; *(de ellos)* their; **su coche,** his *or* her *or* your *or* their car; **su pata,** its leg; **sus libros,** his *or* her *or* your *or* their books; **sus patas,** its legs.

suasorio,-a *adj* persuasive.

suave *adj* 1 *(liso, llano)* smooth. 2 *(dulce) (luz, voz, música, palabras)* soft. 3 *Meteor (templado)* mild. 4 *(tranquilo) (paso)* easy. 5 *(apacible)* gentle, mild. ◆ **suavemente** *adv* smoothly.

suavidad *nf* 1 *(lisura)* smoothness. 2 *(dulzura)* softness. 3 *Meteor* mildness. 4 *(tranquilidad)* ease. 5 *(docilidad)* gentleness.

suavizante *nm* 1 *(para el pelo)* (hair) conditioner. 2 *(para la ropa)* fabric softener.

suavizar *vtr* 1 *(alisar)* to smooth (out). 2 *(hacer más dulce)* to soften; *fig* **es necesario s. las tensiones que hay entre ellos,** tension between them will have to be eased.

suba *nf Arg Urug Com* rise.

subacuático,-a *adj* underwater.

subafluente *nm Geog* tributary.

subalimentación *nf* undernourishment.

subalimentado,-a I *pp de* **subalimentar.** II *adj* undernourished, underfed.

subalimentar *vtr* to undernourish.

subalterno,-a *adj & nm,f* subordinate, subaltern; *Com* clerk.

subarrendamiento *nm Com* sublease.

subarrendar *vtr Com* to sublet, sublease.

subarrendatario,-a *nm,f Com* subtenant.

subarriendo *nm Com* sublease.

subasta *nf* auction; **sacar a s.,** to auction (off).

subastar *vtr* to auction (off), sell at auction.

subatómico,-a *adj Fís* subatomic.

subcampeón *nm Dep* runner-up.

subcomisión *nf* subcommittee.

subconsciencia *nf Psic* subconscious.

subconsciente *adj & nm Psic* subconscious.

subcontratista *nmf Com Fin* subcontractor.

subcontrato *nm Com Fin Jur* subcontract.

subcutáneo,-a *adj* subcutaneous.

subdelegación *nf* subdelegation.

subdelegado,-a *nm,f* subdelegate.

subdelegar *vtr* to subdelegate.

subdesarrollado,-a *adj* underdeveloped.

subdesarrollo *nm* underdevelopment.

subdirector,-a *nm,f* assistant director *or* manager.

súbdito,-a I *adj* subject. II *nm,f* subject, citizen, national; **s. francés,** French citizen.

subdividir *vtr* to subdivide.

subdivisión *nf* subdivision.

subempleo *nm* underemployment.

subespecie *nf Biol* subspecies *sing*.

subestimar *vtr* to underestimate.

subexponer *vtr Fot* to underexpose.

subexposición *nf Fot* underexposure.

subfusil *nm Mil* sub-machine-gun.

subgénero *nm Biol* subgenus.

subida *nf* 1 *(asceno)* ascent, climb; *Dep Aut* hill climb. 2 *(pendiente)* slope, hill. 3 *(aumento) (temperatura)* rise; *Com Fin (de precios, salarios)* rise, increase. 4 *fam (drogas)* high.

subido,-a I *pp de* **subir.** II *adj* 1 *(alto)* high. 2 *(intenso)* strong; **de un rojo s.,** deep red; **s. de tono,** daring, risqué.

subíndice *nm Mat* subindex.

subir I *vtr* 1 *(ascender) (mantaña, escaleras)* to climb; *(calle)* to go up. 2 *(llevar arriba)* to carry up, take up, bring up; **súbame las maletas por favor,** carry my suitcases upstairs, please; **súbelo arriba,** put it upstairs. 3 *(levantar)* to lift, raise; **suba la cabeza,** raise your head. 4 *(aumentar)* to raise, put up. 5 *(dar más volumen a) (radio, televisión)* to turn up; *(voz)* to raise; **si no subes la voz no podré oírte,** if you don't raise your voice I won't be able to hear you. II *vi* 1 *(ir arriba)* to go up, come up; **¿subes** or **bajas?,** are you going up or coming down?; *fig* **s. al trono,** to ascend to the throne. 2 *(entrar en un vehículo)* **s. a,** *(coche)* to get into; *(autobús)* to get on; *(barco, aivón, tren)* to board, get on; **s. a bordo,** to go aboard. 3 *(montar)* **s. a,** to get on. 4 *(aumentar)* to rise, go

up; *fam* **s. como la espuma,** to rise sky high. 5 *(totalizar)* to amount to, come to; **¿a cuánto sube la cuenta?,** what does the bill come to? III **subirse** *vr* 1 *(ir arriba) (árbol)* to climb up; *(piso)* to go up; *fig* **el champán se le ha subido a la cabeza,** the champagne's gone to his head; *fig* **s. a la parra,** to blow one's top; *fig* **s. por las paredes,** to hit the roof, go up the wall; *fig* **subírsele la sangre a la cabeza,** to see red. 2 *(entrar) (coche)* to get into; *(autobús, avión, tren)* to get on, board. 3 *(montar)* to get on. 4 *(ropa, calcetines)* to pull up; *(cremallera)* to do up, zip up; *(mangas)* to roll up.

súbito,-a *adj* sudden; **de s.,** suddenly, all of a sudden. ◆ **súbitamente** *adv* suddenly.

subjefe,-a *nm,f* subchief, second in command.

subjetividad *nf* subjectivity, subjectiveness.

subjetivismo *nm* subjectivism.

subjetivo,-a *adj* subjective.

subjuntivo *nm Ling* subjunctive.

sublevación *nf,* **sublevamiento** *nm* rising, revolt, rebellion.

sublevar I *vtr* 1 *(alzar en sedición)* to stir up, arouse; *(rebelar)* to incite to rebellion. 2 *fig (indignar)* to infuriate, enrage. II **sublevarse** *vr* to rebel, revolt; **los soldados se sublevaron,** the soldiers mutinied.

sublimación *nf* sublimation.

sublimado,-a I *pp de* **sublimar.** II *adj* sublimated. III *nm Quím* sublimate.

sublimar *vtr* 1 *(gen)* to sublimate; *Psic* to sublimate. 2 *(ensalzar)* to praise, exalt.

sublime *adj (excelso)* sublime; *(eminente)* noble, lofty; **lo s.,** the sublime.

subliminal *adj* subliminal.

submarinismo *nm Dep* skin-diving.

submarinista *nmf Dep* skin-diver.

submarino,-a *Naut* I *adj* submarine, underwater. II *nm (buque)* submarine.

submaxilar *adj Anat* submaxillary.

subnormal *Med* I *adj* subnormal, mentally handicapped. II *nmf* subnormal; *fam* blockhead, dunderhead.

suboficial *nm* 1 *Mil* noncommissioned officer. 2 *Náut* petty officer.

suborden *nm Biol* suborder.

subordinación *nf* subordination.

subordinado,-a I *pp de* **subordinar.** II *adj* subordinate; *Ling* **oración subordinada,** subordinate clause. III *nm,f* subordinate.

subordinar I *vtr* to subordinate. II **subordinarse** *vr* to subordinate oneself.

subproducto *nm* by-product.

subrayar *vtr* 1 *(hacer una raya)* to underline. 2 *fig (recalcar)* to emphasize, stress, underline.

subrepticio,-a *adj* surreptitious. ◆ **subrepticiamente** *adv* surreptitiously.

subrogar *vtr Jur* to subrogate, substitute.

subrutina *nf Inform* subroutine.

subsanable *adj* 1 *(remediable)* reparable, rightable, that can be mended *or* put right. 2 *(solucionable)* surmountable.

subsanar *vtr* 1 *(remediar)* to rectify, put right; **s. un error,** to correct a mistake. 2 *(compensar)* to make up for.

subscribir *(pp subscrito) vtr véase* **suscribir.**

subscripción *nf* subscription.

subscriptor,-a *nm,f* subscriber.

subscrito,-a *pp & adj & nm,f véase* **suscrito,-a.**

subsecretaría *nf* 1 *(cargo)* undersecretaryship. 2 *(oficina)* undersecretary's office.

subsecretario,-a *nm,f* undersecretary.

subseguir(se) *vtr & vr* to follow (next), come after.

subsidiar *vtr fml* to subsidize.

subsidiario,-a *adj* subsidiary.

subsidio *nm* allowance, benefit. ◼ **s. de paro,** unemployment benefit, dole.

subsiguiente *adj* subsequent, succeeding, following.

subsistencia *nf* **1** *(supervivencia)* subsistence. **2 subsistencias,** *(provisiones)* food *sing,* provisions, supplies.

subsistente *adj* surviving, lasting.

subsistir *vi* **1** *(conservarse)* to subsist, last, remain. **2** *(vivir)* to subsist, live on, survive.

subsónico,-a *adj Av* subsonic.

substancia *nf véase* **sustancia.**

substancial *adj véase* **sustancial.**

substanciar *vtr véase* **sustanciar.**

substancioso,-a *adj véase* **sustancioso,-a.**

substantivar *vtr véase* **sustantivar.**

substantivo,-a *adj & nm véase* **sustantivo,-a.**

substitución *nf véase* **sustitución.**

substituible *adj véase* **sustituible.**

substituir *vtr véase* **sustituir.**

substitutivo *nm véase* **sustitutivo.**

substituto,-a *pp & nm,f véase* **sustituto,-a.**

substracción *nf véase* **sustracción.**

substraer *vtr véase* **sustraer.**

substrato *nm Geol Filos* substratum.

subsuelo *nm* subsoil.

subteniente *nm Mil* second lieutenant.

subterfugio *nm* *(escapatoria)* subterfuge; *(pretexto)* pretext.

subterráneo,-a I *adj* subterranean, underground. **II** *nm* **1** *(túnel)* tunnel, underground passage. **2** *Arg Urug* tube, underground, *US* subway.

subtitular *vtr* **1** *Cin* to subtitle. **2** *Lit* subhead, subheading.

subtítulo *nm Cin* subtitle.

subtropical *adj Geog* subtropical.

suburbano,-a I *adj* suburban. **II** *nm* suburban train.

suburbial *adj* suburban.

suburbio *nm* *(barrio periférico)* suburb; *(barrio pobre)* slums *pl.*

subvalorar *vtr* to underrate, underestimate, undervalue.

subvención *nf Fin* subsidy, grant.

subvencionar *vtr* to subsidize.

subvenir *vtr Fin* to meet, defray.

subversión *nf* subversion.

subversivo,-a *adj* subversive.

subvertir *vtr* to subvert, upset, overthrow.

subyacente *adj* underlying.

subyugación *nf* subjugation.

subyugar *vtr* **1** *(dominar)* to subjugate. **2** *fig (cautivar)* to captivate.

succión *nf* suction.

succionar *vtr* to suck (in).

sucedáneo,-a I *adj* substitute, ersatz. **II** *nm* substitute.

suceder I *vi* **1** *(ocurrir) (uso impers)* to happen, occur; **por lo que pueda s.,** just in case; **¿qué sucede?,** what's going on?, what's the matter?; **suceda lo que suceda,** whatever happens, come what may. **2** *(seguir)* to follow, succeed; **a la tormenta sucedió la calma,** calm followed the storm; **sucedió a su padre como presidente,** he succeeded his father as president. **II sucederse** *vr* to follow one another, come after the other.

sucedido,-a I *pp de* **suceder. II** *nm fam* event.

sucesión *nf* **1** *(serie, conjunto)* series *sing,* succession. **2** *(al trono)* succession. **3** *(herencia)* succession, estate, inheritance. **4** *(descendientes)* issue, heirs *pl; Jur* **derechos de s.,** *(al legalizar el testamento)* death duties; *(al heredar)* probate duties.

sucesivo,-a *adj* **1** *(siguiente)* following, successive; **en lo s.,** from now on. **2** *(consecutivo)* consecutive, running. ◆ **sucesivamente** *adv* successively; **y así s.,** and so on.

suceso *nm* **1** *(acontecimiento)* event, happening, occurrence. **2** *(hecho delictivo)* crime; *(incidente)* incident; *Prensa* **sección de sucesos,** accident and crime reports.

sucesor,-a *nm,f* successor.

suciedad *nf* **1** *(porquería)* dirt, filth. **2** *(calidad de sucio)* dirtiness, filthiness.

sucinto,-a *adj* brief, concise, succinct. ◆ **sucintamente** *adv* briefly, concisely.

sucio,-a *adj* dirty; *(color)* off, dirty; **un amarillo s.,** an off-yellow; *fig* **en s.,** in rough; *fig* **juego s.,** foul play; *fig* **negocio s.,** shady business.

sucre *nm Fin* standard monetary unit of Ecuador.

suculencia *nf* succulence, juiciness.

suculento,-a *adj* succulent, juicy.

sucumbir *vi* **1** *(ceder)* to succumb, yield; **s. a la tentación,** to give in to temptation. **2** *fml (morir)* to perish.

sucursal *nf Com Fin* branch, branch office; *(delegación)* subsidiary.

suche *nm* **1** *Ecuad Per Bot* white frangipani. **2** *Arg (grano)* spot, pimple.

súchil *nm Bot* white frangipani.

sudaca *nmf pey* South American.

Sudáfrica *n* South Africa.

sudafricano,-a *adj & nm,f* South African.

Sudamérica *n* South America.

sudamericano,-a *adj & nm,f* South American.

Sudán *n* Sudan.

sudanés,-esa *adj & nm,f* Sudanese.

sudar I *vtr* **1** *(transpirar)* to sweat, exude; *fam fig* **s. la gota gorda,** to sweat blood. **2** *(manchar de sudor)* to stain with sweat. **3** *(obtener con esfuerzo)* to work hard for. **II** *vi* to perspire, sweat; *fig* **hacer s. a algn,** to drive sb hard.

sudario *nm* shroud.

sudeste I *adj (del sudeste)* southeast, southeastern; *(dirección sudeste)* southeasterly. **II** *nm* **1** *(punto cardinal)* southeast. **2** *(viento)* southeast wind; *(viento fuerte)* southeasterly.

sudoeste I *adj (del sudoeste)* southwest, southwestern; *(dirección sudoeste)* southwesterly. **II** *nm* **1** *(punto cardinal)* southwest. **2** *(viento)* southwest wind; *(viento fuerte)* southwesterly.

sudor *nm* **1** *(transpiración)* sweat, perspiration. **2** *fig (esfuerzo)* effort, hard work; *fig* **con el s. de mi frente,** by the sweat of my brow; *fig* **costar muchos sudores,** to be a struggle.

sudorífero,-a *adj* sudoriferous.

sudorífico,-a *adj & nm* sudorific.

sudoríparo,-a *adj Anat* sudoriferous; **glándulas su-doríparas,** sweat glands.

sudoroso,-a *adj* sweaty.

Suecia *n* Sweden.

sueco,-a I *adj* Swedish. **II** *nm, f (persona)* Swede; *fam* **hacerse el s.,** to pretend not to understand, play dumb. **III** *nm (idioma)* Swedish.

suegra *nf* mother-in-law.

suegro *nm* father-in-law; **mis suegros,** my in-laws.

suela *nf* **1** *(del zapato)* sole; *fig* **no te llego ni a la s. del zapato,** you're one step ahead of me. **2** *Bill* leather tip.

sueldo *nm* salary, pay, wages *pl*; **asesino a s.,** hit man; **aumento de s.,** pay rise; **estar a s.,** to be on a salary.

suelo *nm* **1** *(superficie)* ground; *(de interior)* floor; **dar consigo en el s.,** to fall; **echar al s.,** to demolish; **s. de madera,** wooden floor; *fig* **echar por los suelos,** to ruin; *fig* **estar por los suelos,** *(precios)* to be rockbottom; *(ánimos)* to be very low; *fig* **poner algo por los suelos,** to run sth down, tear sth to pieces; *fam fig* **besar el s.,** to fall flat on one's face. **2** *(tierra)* soil, earth. **3** *(territorio)* soil, land; **s. extranjero,** foreign soil; **s. patrio,** native land. **4** *(campo, terreno)* land; **s. cultivable,** arable land. **5** *(de carretera)* surface.

suelta *nf* freeing, release; **dar rienda s. a,** to free, let loose.

suelto,-a I *adj* *(no sujeto)* loose; **esa pieza está suelta,** this part has come loose. **2** *(desatado)* undone, untied; *fig* **atar cabos sueltos,** to tie up loose ends; *fig* **dinero s.,** loose change. **3** *(en libertad)* free; *(huido)* at large. **4** *(desaparejado)* odd; **hojas sueltas,** loose sheets (of paper); **números sueltos,** odd numbers; **se venden sueltos,** they are sold singly *or* separately *or* loose. **5** *(holgado)* *(prenda)* loose, loose-fitting. **6** *Lit (estilo)* flowing, easy. **II** *nm* **1** *(dinero)* (loose) change. **2** *Prensa* short article, item.

sueño *nm* **1** *(acto de dormir)* sleep; *(ganas de dormir)* sleepiness; **conciliar el s.,** to get to sleep; **entre sueños,** while half-asleep; **me caigo de s.,** I can't keep my eyes open; **me da s.,** it makes me sleepy; **tener el s. ligero,** to be a light sleeper; **tener s.,** to feel *or* be sleepy; *fig* **quitar el s.,** to keep awake. **2** *(cosa soñada)* dream; **en sueños,** in one's dreams; *fig* **s. dorado,** cherished dream; *fam* **¡ni en sueños!,** I wouldn't dream of it!, not on your life!

suero *nm* **1** *Med* serum. **2** *(de la leche)* whey.

suerte *nf* **1** *(fortuna)* luck, fortune; *(azar)* chance; **buena/ mala s.,** good/bad luck; **echar algo a suertes,** to draw lots for sth; **estar de s.,** to be in luck; **la s. está echada,** the die is cast; **por s.,** fortunately; **probar s.,** to try one's luck; **¡que tengas s.!,** good luck!; **trae mala s.,** it's unlucky. **2** *(destino)* fate, destiny. **3** *(condición)* lot; **mejorar la s. de los pobres,** to improve the lot of the poor. **4** *(género)* kind, sort, type; **toda s. de personas,** all kinds of people. **5** *Taur* stage (of the bullfight).

suertero,-a *adj Am fam* lucky.

suertudo,-a *adj fam* lucky.

suéter *nm* sweater.

suficiencia *nf* **1** *(capacidad)* sufficiency. **2** *(conveniencia)* suitability, competence. **3** *(engreimiento)* smugness, complacency.

suficiente *adj* **1** *(bastante)* sufficient, enough; **hay s. comida para todos,** there is enough food for everybody; **tener lo s. para vivir,** to have enough to live on. **2** *(idóneo)* suitable. **3** *(engreído)* smug, complacent. ◆ **suficientemente** *adv* enough.

sufijo,-a *Ling* **I** *adj* suffixal. **II** *nm* suffix.

sufragar I *vtr* **1** *(costear)* *(empresa)* to finance; *(gastos)* to pay, defray. **2** *(ayudar)* to help, aid. **II** *vi Am* to vote **(por, for).**

sufragio *nm* **1** *Pol* suffrage; *(voto)* vote. ▪ **s. universal,** universal suffrage. **2** *(ayuda)* help, assistance; *Rel* **misa en s. de ...,** mass for the soul of ... .

sufragismo *nm Pol* suffragism, suffragist movement.

sufragista *Pol* **I** *nmf* suffragist. **II** *nf* suffragette.

sufrido,-a I *pp de* **sufrir. II** *adj* **1** *(persona)* patient, long-suffering. **2** *(tela)* hardwearing. **3** *(color)* practical, that does not show the dirt.

sufrimiento *nm* suffering.

sufrir I *vi* *(padecer)* to suffer; **hacer s. a algn,** to cause sb pain; **s. del corazón,** to have a heart condition. **II** *vtr* **1** *(tener)* *(accidente)* to have; *(operación)* to undergo; *(dificultades, cambios)* to experience; **s. dolores de cabeza,** to suffer from headaches; **s. hambre,** to know hunger; **s. vergüenza,** to be ashamed. **2** *(aguantar)* to bear, put up with. **3** *(consentir)* to tolerate.

sugerencia *nf* suggestion.

sugerente *adj*, **sugeridor,-a** *adj* suggestive.

sugerir *vtr* to suggest.

sugestión *nf* suggestion.

sugestionable *adj* impressionable, easily influenced.

sugestionar *vtr* to influence, persuade.

sugestivo,-a *adj* **1** *(que sugiere)* suggestive. **2** *(fascinante)* fascinating, alluring.

suicida I *adj* suicidal; **misión s.,** suicide mission. **II** *nmf* *(persona)* suicide.

suicidarse *vr* to commit suicide, kill oneself.

suicidio *nm* suicide.

suite *nf* **1** *Mús* suite. **2** *(de hotel)* suite.

Suiza *n* Switzerland.

suizo,-a I *adj* Swiss. **II** *nm,f* *(persona)* Swiss. **III** *nm Culin* *(bollo)* bun; *(chocolate con nata)* hot chocolate with cream.

sujeción *nf* **1** *(acción)* subjection. **2** *(atado, ligadura)* fastening.

sujetador I *adj* *(que sujeta)* fastening. **II** *nm* *(prenda)* bra, brassière.

sujetapapeles *nm inv* paper clip.

sujetar I *vtr* **1** *(agarrar)* to hold; **¡sujétalo bien!,** hold it tightly! **2** *(fijar)* to fix, secure, hold down, hold in place; **s. algo con clavos,** to nail sth down. **3** *(someter a disciplina)* to control, restrain. **4** *(restringir la libertad)* to tie down. **II sujetarse** *vr* **1** *(agarrarse)* to hold on. **2** *(someterse)* to subject oneself **(a,** to).

sujeto,-a I *adj* **1** *(atado)* fastened, secure; **bien s.,** tightly fastened. **2** *(privado de libertad)* tied down. **3** *(sometido)* **s. a,** subject to, liable to; **s. a cambios,** liable to change. **II** *nm* **1** *(individuo)* fellow, individual, person. **2** *Ling* subject. **3** *(materia)* subject.

sulfamida *nf Farm* sulpha drug, sulphonamide.

sulfatación *nf Quím* sulphation.

sulfatar *vtr Quím* to sulphate.

sulfato *nm Quím* sulphate.

sulfhídrico,-a *adj Quím* sulphuretted, *US* sulphureted; **ácido s.,** hydrogen sulphide.

sulfurar I *vtr* **1** *Quím* to sulphurate. **2** *fam (exasperar)* to exasperate, burn up, infuriate. **II sulfurarse** *vr fam* to lose one's temper, blow one's top.

sulfúrico,-a *adj Quím* sulphuric.

sulfuro *nm Quím* sulphide.

sulfuroso,-a *adj Quím* sulphurous.

sultán *nm* sultan.

sultana *nf* sultana.

sultanato *nm* sultanate.

suma *nf* **1** *(cantidad)* sum, amount. **2** *Mat* sum, addition; **s. total,** sum total. **3** *(resumen)* summary; **en s.,** in short. **4** *Com* total.

sumadora *nf Com* adding machine.

sumamente *adv* extremely, highly.

sumando *nm Mat* addend.

sumar I *vtr* **1** *Mat* to add, add up; **suma y sigue,** carried forward; *fam* and that's not all. **2** *(valer)* to total, amount to. **3** *(hacer un resumen)* to summarize, sum up. **II sumarse** *vr* to join **(a,** in); **s. a un partido,** to join a party.

sumarial *adj Jur* pertaining to an indictment.

sumariar *vtr Jur* to indict.

sumario,-a I *adj* summary, brief; *Jur* **juicio s.,** summary proceedings *pl*. **II** *nm* **1** *Jur* legal proceedings *pl*, indictment. **2** *(resumen)* summary.

sumarísimo,-a *adj Jur* swift, expeditious.

sumergible I *adj* submergible, submersible. **II** *nm Náut* submarine.

sumergir I *vtr (meter bajo el agua)* to submerge, submerse, immerse; *(hundir)* to sink, plunge. **II sumergirse** *vr* **1** *(meterse bajo el agua)* to submerge, go underwater; *(hundirse)* to sink. **2** *fig (concentrarse)* to become immersed (**en**, in).

sumerio,-a *adj & nm,f Hist* Sumerian.

sumidero *nm* drain, sewer.

suministración *nf véase* **suministro.**

suministrador,-a *nm,f* supplier.

suministrar *vtr* to supply, provide; **s. algo a algn,** to supply sb with sth.

suministro *nm* supply, supplying, provision; **suministros,** supplies.

sumir I *vtr (hundir)* to sink, plunge, submerge; *fig* to plunge; *fig* **s. a algn en la miseria,** to plunge sb into poverty. **II sumirse** *vr fig* to immerse oneself (**en**, in), lose oneself (**en**, in).

sumisión *nf* **1** *(acto)* submission. **2** *(actitud)* submissiveness.

sumiso,-a *adj* submissive, obedient. ♦ **sumisamente** *adv* submissively.

súmmum *nm* summit, acme, peak.

sumo,-a *adj (supremo)* supreme, highest; *(grande)* greatest; **a lo s.,** at (the) most; **con s. cuidado,** with extreme care; **en s. grado,** to the highest degree; **suma autoridad,** supreme authority; **s. sacerdote,** high priest.

sunita *nm Rel* Sunnite.

sunna *nm Rel* Sunna.

suntuario,-a *adj* sumptuary.

suntuosidad *nf* sumptuousness, magnificence.

suntuoso,-a *adj* sumptuous, magnificent, splendid.

supe *pt indef véase* **saber²**.

supeditación *nf* subjection, subordination.

supeditar I *vtr* to subject (**a**, to); **estar supeditado a,** to be subject to *or* dependent on. **II supeditarse** *vr* to subject oneself (**a**, to), bow (**a**, to).

súper *fam* **I** *adj* super, great. **II** *nm* **1** *(supermercado)* supermarket. **2** *(gasolina)* super.

superable *adj* superable, surmountable.

superabundancia *nf* superabundance.

superabundante *adj* superabundant.

superabundar *vi* to superabound.

superación *nf* **1** *(de dificultades, problemas)* overcoming, surpassing. **2** *(de uno mismo)* self-improvement; **afán de s.,** desire to improve *or* better oneself.

superado,-a I *pp de* **superar. II** *adj* antiquated, outdated, obsolete; **es una técnica superada,** it's an antiquated technique.

superar I *vtr* **1** *(ser superior)* to surpass, exceed, excel. **2** *(vencer) (obstáculos, dificultades)* to overcome, surmount. **II superarse** *vr* **1** *(sobrepasarse)* to excel *or* outdo oneself. **2** *(mejorarse)* to improve *or* better oneself.

superávit *nm Fin* surplus.

supercarburante *nm* high octane fuel.

superchería *nf* trick, fraud, hoax.

superconductividad *nf Fís* superconductivity.

superconductor *nm Fís* superconductor.

superdesarrollado,-a *adj* overdeveloped.

superdesarrollo *nm* overdevelopment.

superdotado,-a I *adj* exceptionally gifted. **II** *nm,f* genius.

superestructura *nf* superstructure.

superficial *adj* superficial.

superficialidad *nf* superficiality, superficialness.

superficie *nf* **1** *(parte externa)* surface; **la s. de la mesa,** the surface of the table; **la s. terrestre,** the land surface. **2** *Geom (área)* area; **la s. del triángulo,** the area of the triangle.

superfino,-a *adj* extra fine.

superfluidad *nf* superfluity, superfluousness.

superfluo,-a *adj* superfluous.

superhombre *nm* superman.

superintendencia *nf* superintendence, superintendency.

superintendente *nmf* superintendent.

superior I *adj* **1** *(más alto)* top, upper; **labio s.,** upper lip, **parte s.,** upper part. **2** *(mayor)* greater, higher, larger; **una cantidad s. a mil pesetas,** an amount greater than a thousand pesetas. **3** *(mejor)* superior; **calidad s.,** top quality; **ser s. a todos,** to surpass everyone; **un vino s.,** an excellent wine. **4** *Educ* higher; **enseñanza s.,** higher education. **II** *nm* **1** *(jefe)* superior; **respetar a los superiores,** to respect one's elders. **2** *Rel* superior.

superiora *nf Rel* mother superior.

superioridad *nf* **1** *(persona con autoridad)* superiority. **2** *(ventaja)* advantage.

superlativo,-a *adj & nm Ling* superlative.

supermercado *nm* supermarket.

supermujer *nf* superwoman.

supernumerario,-a *adj & nm,f* supernumerary.

superpetrolero *nm Náut* supertanker.

superpoblación *nf* overpopulation, overcrowding.

superpoblado,-a *adj* overpopulated, overcrowded.

superponer *(pp* **superpuesto)** **I** *vtr* to superpose, superimpose; *fig* to put before. **II superponerse** *vr fig* to come before.

superposición *nf* superposition.

superpotencia *nf* superpower.

superproducción *nf* **1** *Ind* overproduction. **2** *Cin* mammoth production.

superpuse *pt indef véase* **superponer.**

supersecreto,-a *adj* top secret.

supersónico,-a *adj* supersonic.

superstición *nf* superstition.

supersticioso,-a *adj* superstitious.

supervalorar *vtr* to overvalue, overrate.

supervisar *vtr* to supervise.

supervisión *nf* supervision, control.

supervisor,-a *nm,f* supervisor.

supervivencia *nf* survival.

superviviente I *adj* surviving. **II** *nmf* survivor.

superyó *nm Psic* superego.

supino,-a I *adj* **1** *(boca arriba)* supine, face up. **2** *fig (absoluto)* total absolute; **un s. error,** an absolute mistake. **II** *nm Ling* supine.

súpito,-a *adj Am* sudden.

suplantación *nf (falsificación)* forgery; **s. de personalidad,** impersonation.

suplantador,-a *nm,f (falsificador)* forger; *(sustitución de persona)* impersonator

suplantar *vtr* to supplant, replace, take the place of

suplementario,-a *adj* supplementary, additional, extra, *Geom* supplementary.

suplemento *nm* **1** *(añadido)* supplement; *Prensa* **s. dominical,** Sunday supplement **2** *Com* addition, extra fee, **sin s.,** without extra charge

suplencia *nf* substitution, replacement

suplente *adj & nmf* **1** *(sustituto)* substitute, deputy, stand-in **2** *Teat* understudy. **3** *Dep* reserve (player).

supletorio,-a I *adj* supplementary, additional; **cama supletoria,** extra bed; **teléfono s.,** extension. **II** *nm Tel* extension

súplica *nf* request, entreaty, plea, **a s. de,** at the request of

suplicante I *adj* beseeching, entreating. **II** *nmf* suppliant, supplicant.

suplicar *vtr & vi* **1** to beseech, implore, beg; **le suplico que se vaya,** I beg you to go away *or* leave.

suplicio *nm (tortura)* torture; *(tormento)* torment

suplir I *vtr* **1** *(reemplazar)* to replace, substitute. **2** *(compensar)* to make up for. **3** *(remediar)* to remedy. **II suplirse** *vr SAm (conformarse)* to resign oneself.

suponer *(pp supuesto) vtr* **1** *(pensar)* to suppose, assume, **supongamos que ...,** let's assume that ..., **supongo que sí,** I suppose so **2** *(significar)* to mean, **el premio supone mucho para mí,** the prize means a lot to me **3** *(implicar)* to mean, entail, require; **eso va a s. mucho trabajo para su madre,** that will mean a lot of work for her mother **4** *(adivinar)* to guess; *(imaginar)* to imagine; **me lo suponía,** I guessed as much; **¿quién lo iba a s.?,** who would have guessed it?; **te suponía más viejo,** I thought you were older (than that)

suposición *nf* supposition, assumption.

supositorio *nm Farm* suppository.

supranacional *adj Pol Fin* supranational.

supremacía *nf* supremacy

supremo,-a *adj* supreme, *lit* **hora suprema,** dying moments *pl*, final hour; **jefe s.,** commander-in-chief; *Jur* **tribunal s.,** supreme court

supresión *nf* **1** *(eliminación) (de una rebelión)* suppression; *(de dificultades)* elimination, removal; *(de una ley, un impuesto)* abolition; *(de restricciones)* lifting, *(de una palabra)* deletion. **2** *(voluntaria)* omission.

suprimir *vtr* **1** *(eliminar) (una rebelión)* to suppress; *(dificultades)* to eliminate, remove; *(una ley, un impuesto)* to abolish; *(restricciones)* to lift, *(una palabra)* to delete, take *or* leave out. **2** *(voluntaria)* to omit; **me han suprimido el alcohol,** I've been told to cut out alcohol.

supuesto,-a I *pp de* **suponer. II** *adj* **1** *(asumido)* supposed, assumed; **dar algo por s.,** to take sth for granted; **¡por s.!,** of course! **2** *(pseudo)* so-called, self-styled; **el s. presidente,** the self-styled president. **3** *(falso)* assumed, false; **nombre s.,** assumed name. **III** *nm (creencia)* supposition, assumption; *(hipótesis)* hypothesis.

supuración *nf Med* suppuration.

supurar *vi Med* to suppurate, fester.

supuse *pt indef véase* **suponer.**

sur *nm* south, **al s. de,** (to the) south of; **viento del s.,** south wind; *(viento fuerte)* southerly wind.

Suramérica *nf* South America.

suramericano,-a *adj & nm,f* South American.

surcado,-a I *pp de* **surcar. II** *adj* lined, wrinkled; **cara surcada de arrugas,** deeply-wrinkled face.

surcar *vtr* **1** *Agr* to plough. **2** *fig (viajar)* to cut through; **s. los mares,** to ply the seas

surco *nm* **1** *Agr* furrow. **2** *(arruga)* wrinkle. **3** *(señal) (dejado por una rueda)* rut; *(en un disco)* groove

surcoreano,-a *adj & nm,f* South Korean.

sureño,-a I *adj* southern. **II** *nm,f* southerner.

sureste *adj & nm véase* **sudeste.**

surf *nm Dep* surfing.

surfista *Dep* **I** *adj* surf. **II** *nmf* surfer.

surgir *vi* **1** *(aparecer)* to arise, emerge, appear; **continuamente surgen problemas,** problems are always cropping up; **surgió de la nada,** it came out of nowhere **2** *(brotar)* to spring forth, spurt up.

suripanta *nf fam Teat* chorus girl; *pey* tart.

Surinam *n* Surinam.

surmenaje *nm (mental)* mental fatigue; *(exceso de trabajo)* overwork.

suroeste *adj & nm véase* **sudoeste**

surrealismo *nm* surrealism

surrealista I *adj* surrealist, surrealistic. **II** *nmf* surrealist.

sursuncorda *nm fam hum* **el s.,** the Pope, the great panjandrum; **¡aunque me lo pidiera el s.!,** not even if the Pope himself asked me!

surtido,-a I *pp de* **surtir II** *adj* **1** *(variado)* assorted **2** *(bien provisto)* well stocked. **III** *nm Com* range, selection, assortment

surtidor *nm* **1** *(chorro)* jet, spout. **2** *(fuente)* fountain ■ **s. de gasolina,** petrol *or* US gas pump.

surtir *vtr* **1** *(proveer)* to supply, provide **2** **s. efecto,** *(funcionar)* to have the desired effect, work.

surto,-a *adj Náut* anchored.

susceptibilidad *nf (gen)* susceptibility; *(sensibilidad)* sensitivity, touchiness

susceptible *adj (gen)* susceptible, *(sensible)* oversensitive, touchy, **s. de,** *(tendente)* liable to, *(capaz)* capable of

suscitar *vtr (provocar)* to cause, provoke; *(rebelión)* to stir up, arouse; *(discusión)* to start.

suscribir *(pp suscrito)* **I** *vtr* **1** *(adherirse)* to subscribe to, endorse; **suscribo sus opiniones,** I second his opinions. **2** *fml (firmar)* to sign; *Fin* to subscribe. **II suscribirse** *vr* to subscribe (**a,** to); **acabo de suscribirme al nuevo periódico,** I've just taken out a subscription to the new newspaper

suscripción *nf* subscription.

suscriptor,-a *nm,f* subscriber.

suscrito,-a I *pp de* **suscribir. II** *adj* **1** *(abonado)* subscribed; **estar s. a,** to subscribe to, have a subscription to. **2** *(abajo firmado)* undersigned **III** *nm,f* undersigned.

susodicho,-a *adj* above-mentioned, aforesaid.

suspender *vtr* **1** *(colgar)* to hang, hang up, suspend. **2** *(aplazar) (trabajo, acontecimiento)* to delay, postpone, put off; *(reunión)* to adjourn. **3** *(suprimir) (pagos)* to suspend; *(servicios)* to discontinue **4** *Educ* to fail, **he suspendido, me han suspendido,** I've failed (the exam). **5** *(despedir)* to suspend, remove.

suspense *nm* suspense; **mantener a algn en s.,** to keep sb hanging *or* in suspense; *Lit* **novela de s.,** thriller; *Cin* **película de s.,** thriller.

suspensión *nf (levantamiento)* hanging (up), suspension. **2** *Aut* suspension. **3** *(aplazamiento)* delay, postponement; *(de una reunión)* adjournment. **4** *(supresión)* suspension, discontinuation; *Fin Jur* **s. de pagos,** suspension of payments.

suspensivo,-a *adj* suspensive; *Ling* **puntos suspensivos,** row of dots, *US* suspension points.

suspenso,-a I *adj* **1** *(colgado)* hanging, suspended. **2** *fig (desconcertado)* baffled, bewildered. **II** *nm* **1** *Educ* fail. **2** *(asunto, trabajo)* en s., pending; **estar en s.,** to be pending.

suspensores *nmpl Am* braces, *US* suspenders.

suspensorio *nm Dep* jockstrap.

suspicacia *nf* **1** *(desconfianza)* mistrust, distrust, wary. **2** *(sospecha)* suspicion, suspiciousness.

suspicaz *adj* **1** *(desconfiado)* untrusting, distrustful. **2** *(que sospecha)* suspicious.

suspirar *vi* to sigh; *fig* **s. por,** to long for.

suspiro *nm* sigh; **dar el último s.,** to breathe one's last; **deshacerse en suspiros,** to heave great sighs.

sustancia *nf* **1** *(gen)* substance; **sin s.,** lacking in substance; *fam* **persona de poca s.,** characterless person. **2** *(esencia)* essence.

sustancial *adj* **1** *(gen)* substantial, considerable, important. **2** *(fundamental)* essential, fundamental.

sustanciar *vtr* to condense, abridge.

sustancioso,-a *adj* **1** *(alimentos)* wholesome. **2** *fig (libro, discurso)* meaty.

sustantivar *vtr* to use as a noun.

sustantivo,-a I *adj* substantive. **II** *nm Ling* noun, substantive.

sustentable *adj* tenable.

sustentación *nf* **1** *(soporte)* support. **2** *(mantenimiento)* sustenance, maintenance.

sustentáculo *nm* prop, support.

sustentar I *vtr* **1** *(peso)* to support. **2** *(familia)* to maintain, support. **3** *(teoría)* to support, defend. **II sustentarse** *vr* to sustain oneself, live **(de,** on).

sustento *nm* **1** *(alimento)* sustenance, food; **ganarse el s.,** to earn one's living. **2** *(apoyo)* support.

sustitución *nf* substitution, replacement.

sustituible *adj* replaceable, expendable.

sustituir *(pp* **sustituto)** *vtr* **1** *(remplazar)* to substitute, replace. **2** *(hacer las veces de)* to stand in for.

sustitutivo *nm* substitute.

sustituto,-a I *pp de* **sustituir. II** *nm,f* substitute, stand-in, replacement.

susto *nm* fright, shock, scare; **llevarse** *or* **darse un s.,** to get a fright; *fig* **caerse del s.,** to be frightened to death; *fig* **no pasar del s.,** to be just a scare.

sustracción *nf* **1** *Mat* subtraction. **2** *(robo)* theft.

sustraer I *vtr* **1** *Mat* to subtract. **2** *(robar)* to steal, remove. **II sustraerse** *vr(eludir)* **s. a** *or* **de,** *(preguntas)* to evade; *(tentaciones)* to resist.

sustrato *nm Geol Filos* substratum.

susurrante *adj* whispering.

susurrar *vtr (gen)* to whisper; *(el agua)* to murmur; *(hojas)* to rustle.

susurro *nm (gen)* whisper; *(del agua)* murmur; *(de hojas)* rustle.

sutil *adj* **1** *(delgado)* thin, fine. **2** *(delicado) (aroma)* delicate; *(color)* soft; *(brisa)* gentle. **3** *fig (diferencia, pregunta)* subtle. ◆ **sutilmente** *adv fig* mildly, subtly.

sutileza *nf* **1** *(finura)* thinness, fineness. **2** *fig (dicho)* subtlety.

sutilizar I *vtr* **1** *(adelgazar)* to make fine, thin down. **2** *fig (pulir)* to polish, refine, perfect. **II** *vi (ser preciso)* to quibble, split hairs.

sutura *nf Med* suture.

suturar *vtr Med* to stitch.

suyo,-a *adj & pron pos (de él)* his; *(de ella)* hers; *(de usted, ustedes)* yours; *(de animales or cosas)* its; *(de ellos, ellas)* theirs; **los zapatos que lleva María no son suyos,** the shoes Maria is wearing aren't hers; **varios amigos suyos,** several friends of his *or* hers *or* yours *or* theirs; *fam* **es muy s.,** he's very aloof; *fam* **hacer de las suyas,** to be up to one's tricks; *fam* **ir (cada uno) a lo s.,** to mind one's own business; *fam* **salirse con la suya,** to get one's way.

svástica *nf Herald* swastika.

Swazilandia *n* Swaziland.

swing *nm Dep Mús* swing.

T

T, t *nf (la letra)* T, t.

t *abr de* **tonelada(s),** ton, tons.

t. *abr de* **tomo.**

taba *nf* **1** *Anat* anklebone, astragalus. **2** *SAm fig (lata)* drag. **3** *Méx (charla)* chat.

tabacal *nm* tobacco field *or* plantation.

tabacalero,-a I *adj* tobacco. **II** *nm,f (cultivador)* tobacco grower; *(vendedor)* tobacco trader. **III** *nf* **La Tabacalera,** Spanish state tobacco monopoly.

tabaco *nm* **1** *(planta, hoja)* tobacco. ■ **t. picado,** shredded tobacco, shag; **t. rubio,** Virginia tobacco. **2** *(cigarrillos)* cigarettes *pl.*

tabalear I *vi (con los dedos)* to drum. **II** *vtr (balancear)* to swing, rock.

tabaleo *nm (con los dedos)* drumming.

tabanco *nm CAm* attic, loft.

tábano *nm Ent* horsefly.

tabaquera *nf (caja)* tobacco box; *(para rapé)* snuffbox; *(petaca)* tobacco pouch.

tabaquismo *nm Med* nicotinism, nicotine poisoning.

tabardillo *nm* **1** *Med (insolación)* sunstroke. **2** *fam (persona)* nuisance, bore, pain.

tabardo *nm Hist* tabard.

tabarra *nf fam* nuisance, bore; **dar la t.,** to be a nuisance.

tabasco® *nm* tabasco® sauce.

taberna *nf* pub, bar; *(antiguamente)* tavern.

tabernáculo *nm Rel* tabernacle.

tabernario,-a *adj fam* coarse, rude.

tabernero,-a *nm,f* publican; *(hombre)* landlord; *(mujer)* landlady.

tabernucha *nf fam,* **tabernucho** *nm* dive, pit.

tabicar I *vtr* **1** *(ventana, puerta)* to wall up. **2** *(habitación)* to partition off, divide.

tabique *nm* **1** *(pared)* partition (wall). **2** *Anat* **t. nasal,** nasal bone.

tabla *nf* **1** *(gen)* board; *(de madera)* plank, board; *fig* **a raja t.,** strictly, to the letter; *fig* **hacer t. rasa de algo,** to make a clean sweep of sth; *fig* **t. de salvación,** last hope. ■ **t. de lavar,** washboard; **t. de planchar,** ironing-board; *Dep* **t. de surf,** surfboard; *Dep* **t. de windsurf,** sailboard. **2** *Arte* panel. **3** *Cost* pleat; **falda de tablas,** pleated skirt. **4** *(índice)* index; *(lista)* list; *fig (catálogo)* catalogue. ■ **t. de materias,** (table of) contents. **5** *Mat* table. ■ **t. de multiplicar,** multiplication table. **6** *Agr* plot, bed. **7 las tablas,** *Teat* the stage *sing;* **pisar las t.,** to tread the boards, go on the stage; **tener (muchas) t.,** *Teat* to be an experienced actor *or* actress; *fig* to be an old hand. **8 tablas,** *Ajedrez* stalemate *sing,* draw *sing;* **quedar en t.,** *(juego)* to end in a draw; *fig (asunto)* to be deadlocked *or* unresolved, reach stalemate. **9 tablas,** *Taur* fence *sing.* **10** *Rel* **Tablas de la Ley,** Tables of the Law.

tablado *nm* **1** *(suelo)* wooden floor; *(plataforma)* wooden platform. **2** *Teat* stage.

tablao *nm fam* flamenco bar *or* show.

tablear *vtr* **1** *(madera)* to cut into planks. **2** *(tierra)* to divide into plots. **3** *Cost* to pleat.

tablero *nm* **1** *(tablón)* panel, board. ■ *Av* **t. de instrumentos,** instrument panel. **2** *(en juegos)* board. ■ **t. de ajedrez,** chessboard. **3** *(encerado)* blackboard.

tableta *nf* **1** *(tabla pequeña)* small board. **2** *(pastilla)* tablet. **3** *(de chocolate)* bar.

tabletear *vi* to rattle.

tableteo *nm* rattling, rattle.

tablilla *nf (tabla pequeña)* small board.

tablón *nm* **1** *(gen)* plank; *(en construcción)* beam. ■ **t. de anuncios,** notice *or* US bulletin board. **2** *fam (borrachera)* drunkenness; **agarrar un t.,** to get drunk.

tabú *adj & nm (pl* **tabúes)** taboo.

tabulación *nf* tabulation.

tabulador *nm* tabulator.

tabuladora *nf Inform* tabulator.

tabular *vtr* to tabulate.

taburete *nm* stool.

tacanear *vtr Arg* to squash, crush, pound.

tacañería *nf* meanness, stinginess.

tacaño,-a I *adj* mean, stingy. II *nm,f* miser.

tacatá *nm*, **tacataca** *nm* baby-walker.

tacha *nf* 1 *(defecto)* flaw, blemish, defect; **sin t.**, flawless, without blemish. **2** *(clavo grande)* large tack; *(decorativo)* large stud.

tachadura *nf* crossing out.

tachar *vtr* 1 *(hacer un borrón)* to cross out. **2** *fig* **t. de,** to accuse of; **no le puedes t. de ladrón,** you can't accuse him of being a thief.

tachigual *nm Méx* type of cotton.

tacho *nm Am* 1 *(recipiente de metal)* metal bowl. **2** *(para el azúcar)* boiler. **3** *(para calentar el agua)* pan, kettle. **4** *(hoja de lata)* tin. **5** *(cubo de la basura)* dustbin, *US* trash can.

tachón[1] *nm (borrón)* crossing out.

tachón[2] *nm (tachuela)* large tack; *(decorativo)* large stud.

tachonar *vtr* to stud, adorn with studs; *fig* **un cielo tachonado de estrellas,** a star-studded sky.

tachuela[1] *nf* 1 *(clavo)* tack, stud; **clavar algo con tachuelas,** to tack sth. **2** *Am (rechoncho)* plump person.

tachuela[2] *nf Méx Ven* metal cup.

tácito,-a *adj* tacit; **regla tácita,** unwritten rule.

taciturno,-a *adj* 1 *(callado)* taciturn, silent. **2** *(triste)* sullen; *(lunático)* sulky, moody.

taco *nm* 1 *(tarugo)* plug; *(tapón)* stopper. **2** *(de bota de fútbol)* stud. **3** *(bloc de notas)* notepad, writing pad; *(calendario)* tear-off calendar; *(entradas)* book; *(billetes)* wad. **4** *Culin (de jamón, queso)* cube, piece. **5** *Bill* cue. **6** *Méx Culin* taco, rolled-up tortilla pancake. **7** *fam (lío)* mess, muddle; **armarse** *or* **hacerse un t.,** to get all mixed up. **8** *fam (palabrota)* swearword; **soltar un t., soltar tacos,** to swear. **9** *arg (drogas)* lump of hash. **10 tacos,** *fam (años)* years; **ya he cumplido veinte t.,** I've already passed the twenty mark.

tacómetro *nm* tachometer.

tacón *nm* heel; **zapatos de t.,** high-heeled shoes.

taconazo *nm* kick with the heel.

taconear *vi (pisar)* to tap one's heels; *(golpear)* to stamp one's heels.

taconeo *nm (pisada)* heel tapping; *(golpe)* stamping with the heels.

táctica *nf* tactic, tactics *pl*, strategy; **su t. consistió en no decir nada hasta el final,** her tactic was not to say a word until the end.

táctico,-a I *adj* tactical. II *nm,f* tactician.

táctil *adj* tactile.

tacto *nm* 1 *(sentido)* touch. **2** *(acción de tocar)* touch, touching; **es agradable al t.,** it feels nice. **3** *fig (delicadeza)* tact; **¡qué falta de t.!,** how tactless!; **tener t.,** to be tactful.

tacurú *nm* 1 *Arg Par Urug (hormiguero)* ant heap, ant hill. **2** *Arg Urug Ent (hormiga)* small ant.

taekwondo *nm Dep* tae kwon do.

tafetán *nm Tex* taffeta.

tafia *nf Am* type of rum.

tafilete *nm* morocco leather.

tagalo,-a I *adj* Tagalog. II *nm,f (persona)* Tagalog. III *nm (idioma)* Tagalog.

tagarote *nm CAm* 1 *(potentado)* upright person. **2** *(mañoso)* cunning *or* sly person.

Tahití *n* Tahiti.

tahitiano,-a I *adj* Tahitian. II *nm,f (persona)* Tahitian. III *nm (idioma)* Tahitian.

tahúr *nm* cardsharp, cardsharper.

taifa *nf Hist* **reinos de taifas,** small Spanish kingdoms after the disintegration of the Califate of Cordova in 1031.

taiga *nf* taiga.

Tailandia *n* Thailand.

tailandés,-esa I *adj* Thai, Siamese. II *nm, f (persona)* Thai, Siamese; **los tailandeses,** the Thai *or* Thais. III *nm (idioma)* Thai, Siamese.

taimado,-a I *adj* 1 *(astuto)* sly, crafty. **2** *Arg Ecuad (perezoso)* lazy. II *nm,f* 1 *(astuto)* sly *or* crafty person. **2** *Arg Ecuad (perezoso)* lazy person.

taita *nm Arg Chi Par* father.

Taiwan *n* Taiwan.

tajada *nf* 1 *(rodaja)* slice; *fig* **sacar** *or* **llevarse t.,** to take one's share. **2** *(corte)* cut; *(cuchillada)* stab; **dar una t.,** to cut. **3** *fam (borrachera)* drunkenness; **pillar una t.,** to get smashed.

tajamar *nm* 1 dyke. **2** *CAm Chi (dique)* ditch. **3** *Am (presa)* dam; *(balsa)* pool, pond.

tajante *adj* strong, sharp; **orden t.,** strict order; **ser de** *or* **tener opiniones tajantes,** to be dogmatic.

tajar *vtr* to cut, chop (off).

tajeadura *nf Am* large scar.

Tajo *n* el T., the Tagus.

tajo *nm* 1 *(corte)* cut, slash. **2** *(para cortar carne)* chopping block *or* board. **3** *Geog (escarpe)* steep cliff. **4** *(taburete)* stool. **5** *fam (trabajo)* work; **me voy al t.,** I'm going to work.

tal I *adj* 1 *(semejante)* such (a), similar; **en tales condiciones,** in such conditions; **nunca dije t. cosa,** I never said such a thing. **2** *(tan grande)* such, so; **es t. su valor que ...,** he is so courageous that ...; **lo dijo con t. convecimiento que ...,** he said it with such conviction that ... **3** *(cosa sin especificar)* such and such; **t. día y a t. hora,** such and such a day and at such and such a time. **4** *(persona)* person called ...; **te llamó un t. García,** someone called Garcia phoned you. **5** *(locuciones)* **como si t. cosa,** as if nothing had happened; **t. vez,** perhaps, maybe; *prov* **de t. palo, t. astilla,** like father, like son. II *pron (alguno) (cosa)* something; *(persona)* someone, somebody; **t. para cual,** two of a kind; **(y) como t.,** and therefore *or* as such; **y t. y cual,** and so on; *ofens* **una t.,** a prostitute. III *adv* 1 *(así)* just; **t. cual,** just as it is; **lo dejé t. cual,** I left it just as I found it; **t. (y) como lo digo,** just as I'm telling you. **2 ¿qué t.?,** how are things?; **¿qué t. ese vino?,** how do you find this wine? IV *conj* as; **te lo contamos t. como nos lo contaron a nosotros,** we're telling you just like *or* as they told us; **con t. (de) que,** so long as, provided; **con t. de que no hables,** so long as you don't talk; **de t. manera que,** in such a way that; **lo que sea con t. de no trabajar,** anything to avoid work.

tala *nf* tree felling.

taladrador,-a I *adj* drilling. II *nm, f* driller, borer. III *nf (herramienta)* drill.

taladrar *vtr (gen)* to drill; *(pared)* to bore through; *(billetes)* to punch; *fig* **t. los oídos,** to make an ear splitting noise.

taladro *nm* 1 *(herramienta)* drill; *(barrena)* gimlet. **2** *(agujero)* hole.

talaje *nm Arg Chi Méx* pasture.

talán *nm* ding-dong.

talante *nm* 1 *(semblante)* disposition; **tiene un t. pacífico,** she's a very calm person. **2** *(voluntad)* willingness; **de buen t.,** willingly; **de mal t.,** unwillingly, reluctantly.

talar[1] *adj* full-length, long; **vestidura t.,** long dress *or* habit.

talar² *vtr* **1** *(árboles)* to fell, cut down. **2** *(lugar)* to devastate.

talco *nm* talc. ▪ **polvos de t.,** talcum powder.

talega *nf* **1** *(bolsa)* bag, sack; *(contenido)* bagful, sackful. **2** *(dinero)* money.

talego *nm* **1** *(bolsa)* long bag, long sack; *(contenido)* bagful, sackful. **2** *arg (cárcel)* clink, hole. **3** *arg (mil pesetas)* one thousand peseta note.

talento *nm* **1** *(inteligencia)* talent, intelligence; **tener t.,** to be talented *or* intelligent. **2** *(aptitud)* gift, talent; **tiene t. para la música,** he has a gift for music.

talentoso,-a *adj*, **talentudo,-a** *adj* talented, gifted.

talero *nm Am* whip.

Talgo *nm Ferroc* fast passenger train.

talio *nm Quím* thallium.

talión *nm* **la ley del t.,** an eye for an eye, a tooth for a tooth.

talismán *nm* talisman, lucky charm.

talla *nf* **1** *(escultura)* carving, sculpture. **2** *(tallado)* cutting, carving; *(metal)* engraving. **3** *(estatura)* height; *fig* stature; *fig* **dar la t.,** to be good enough; *fig* **de (mucha) t.,** outstanding. **4** *(de prenda)* size; **¿qué t. usas?,** what size are you?

tallado,-a I *pp* de **tallar. II** *adj (madera)* carved; *(piedra)* cut. **III** *nm (madera)* carving; *(de piedras preciosas)* cutting; *(de metales)* engraving.

tallador,-a *nm*, *f (de madera)* woodcarver; *(de piedras preciosas)* diamond cutter; *(grabador de metales etc)* engraver.

tallar I *vtr* **1** *(madera, piedra)* to carve, shape; *(piedras preciosas)* to cut; *(metales)* to engrave. **2** *(medir)* to measure the height of. **3** *(valorar)* to value, appraise. **4** *Naipes* to deal. **II** *vi Arg (charlar)* to chat.

tallarines *nmpl Culin* tagliatelle *sing*, noodles *pl*.

talle *nm* **1** *(cintura)* waist. **2** *(figura)* (de hombre) build, physique; *(de mujer)* figure, shape. **3** *Cost* shoulder to waist measurement.

taller *nm* **1** *(obrador)* workshop, shop. ▪ *Aut* **t. de reparaciones,** garage. **2** *Arte* studio. ▪ **t. de teatro,** drama workshop. **3** *Ind* factory, mill.

talleta *nf Am* type of sweet.

tallo *nm Bot* stem, stalk; *(renuevo)* sprout, shoot.

talludo,-a *adj* **1** *Bot* leggy, tall. **2** *(no joven)* middleaged. **3** *fig (enviciado)* with bad habits.

talmente *adv fam* literally, exactly.

talo *nm Bot* thallus.

talón *nm* **1** *Anat* heel; *(de media, calcetín)* heel; *fig* **pisarle los talones a algn,** to follow close behind sb, be at the heels of sb. ▪ *fig* **el t. de Aquiles,** Achilles' heel. **2** *Com Fin (cheque)* cheque, *US* check; *(recibo)* receipt; *(matriz)* stub. **3** *Aut* flange.

talonario *nm (de cheques)* cheque *or US* check book; *(de billetes)* book of tickets; *(de recibos)* stub book.

talonear I *vi (andar deprisa)* to hurry. **II** *vtr And Am (al caballo)* to spur.

talud *nm* slope.

tamal *nm Am* **1** *Culin* tamale. **2** *fig (embrollo)* confusion, mix-up; *(intriga)* intrigue.

tamalear *vtr Méx fam* to touch up, grope.

tamango *nm Am* **1** *(calzado)* footwear. **2** *(calzado de cuero)* leather shoe. **3** *(calzado viejo)* battered old shoe.

tamaño,-a I *adj* such a big, so big a; **¿cómo puede alguien creer tamaña mentira?,** how can anybody believe such a big lie? **II** *nm* size; **de gran t.,** large; **del t. de,** as large as, as big as.

tamarindo *nm Bot* tamarind.

tamarisco *nm Bot* tamarisk.

tambaleante *adj (persona)* staggering, tottering; *(mueble)* shaky, wobbly.

tambalearse *vr (persona)* to stagger, totter; *(mueble)* to wobble; *fig* to be shaky; **entró tambaleándose,** he staggered in; *fig* **el gobierno se tambalea,** the government is tottering.

tambaleo *nm (de persona)* staggering, reeling; *(de mueble)* wobble, wobbling.

tambarria *nf Am* binge, spree.

tambero,-a I *adj* **1** *Arg (manso)* tame. **2** *Am (de tambo)* inn. **II** *nm*, *f* **1** *Arg (vaquero)* dairy farmer. **2** *Am (dueño)* innkeeper, landlord.

también *adv* **1** *(igualmente)* too, also, as well; **ellos vienen, y yo t.,** they're coming along, and so am I; **¿lo harás?, yo t.,** are you going to do it?, so am I; **tú t. puedes venir,** you can come too. **2** *(además)* besides, in addition; **no me apetece y t. es que estoy cansado,** I don't feel like it and besides I'm tired.

tambo *nm* **1** *Am (parador)* inn. **2** *Arg Urug (vaquería)* dairy farm.

tambor *nm* **1** *Mús (instrumento)* drum; *(persona)* drummer; *fig* **a t. batiente,** triumphantly. ▪ **t. mayor,** drum major. **2** *Téc (de arma)* cylinder, barrel; *(de lavadora)* drum; *(del freno)* brake drum. **3** *Cost (para bordar)* tambour, embroidery frame. **4** *Anat* eardrum. **5** *(de jabón)* large tub, giant size pack. **6** *(para enrollar cable)* capstan. **7** *Cuba Méx (bote de latón)* tin. **8** *Méx (colchón)* spring mattress.

tamboril *nm Mús* small drum.

tamborilear *vi* **1** *Mús* to play the drum. **2** *(tabalear)* to drum with one's fingers.

tamborileo *nm* drumming.

tamborilero,-a *nm*, *f* drummer.

Támesis *n el* T., the Thames.

tamiz *nm* sieve; **pasar por el t.,** to sift; *fig* to scrutinize.

tamizar *vtr* **1** *(harina, tierra)* to sieve; *(luz)* to filter. **2** *fig (seleccionar)* to screen.

tampoco *adv (en afirmativas)* nor, neither; *(en negativas)* either, not ... either; **Juan no vendrá y María t.,** Juan won't come and neither will Maria; **la Bolsa no sube, pero t. baja,** the stock market isn't going up, but it's not going down either; **¿no fuiste al cine? —yo t.,** you didn't go to the cinema? —nor did I; **no lo sé, —yo t.,** I don't know, —nor do I.

tampón *nm* **1** *(de entintar)* inkpad. **2** *Med* tampon.

tam-tam *nm Mús* tom-tom.

tamuga *nf Am* bundle.

tan *adv* **1** *(tanto)* such, such as; **es t. listo,** he's such a clever fellow; **no me gusta t. dulce,** I don't like it so sweet; **no sabía que era t. tarde,** I didn't know it was so late; **¡qué gente t. agradable!,** how very nice these people are!; **¡qué vestido t. bonito!,** what a beautiful dress! **2** *(comparativo con como)* as ... as; **está t. alto como tú,** he's as tall as you (are). **3** *(comparativo con que)* so ... (that); **iba t. deprisa que no lo ví,** he passed by so fast that I couldn't see him. **4** **de t.,** so; **dejó la nuez sin abrir de t. dura como estaba,** the walnut was so hard that he couldn't crack it; **no pudo salir de t. malo como estaba,** he couldn't go out because he felt so ill. **5 t. siquiera,** even, just; **no tienen t. siquiera para comer,** they haven't even got enough to eat; **si t. siquiera tuviéramos su teléfono,** if only we had her phone number.

tana *nf Méx* raffia bag.

tanate *nm Am* **1** *(zurrón)* leather pouch. **2 tanates,** *(trastos)* stuff *sing*, things *pl*.

tanatear *vtr Am (mudarse)* to move.

tancolote *nm Méx* basket.

tanda *nf* **1** *(conjunto)* batch, lot; *(serie)* series *sing*, course; **por tandas,** in batches; **t. de palos,** thrashing. **2** *(turno)* shift; **me ha tocado la t. de noche,** I've been put on the night shift. **3** *Bill* game.

tandariola *nf Méx* noise.

tándem *nm (bicicleta)* tandem. **2** *(dos personas)* team of two.

tanga *nm* tanga.

tangencial *adj* tangential; **efecto t.,** side effect.

tangente I *nf* tangent; *fig* **salirse** *or* **escaparse por la t.,** to go off at a tangent. **II** *adj Mat* tangent; **líneas tangentes,** tangent lines.

Tánger *n* Tangier.

tangible *adj* tangible.

tango *nm Mús* tango.

tanguista *nf* cabaret girl.

tanque *nm* **1** *Mil* tank. **2** *(depósito)* tank, reservoir. **3** *(vehículos cisterna)* tanker.

tanqueta *nf Mil* light tank.

tantán *nm Mús* tom-tom, tam-tam.

tantear I *vtr* **1** *(calcular)* to estimate, guess. **2** *(probar)* *(medidas)* to size up; *(pesos)* to feel; **deberías t. los nudos,** you should test the knots; **tanteó el cajón para ver si cabía el jarrón,** he sized the drawer up to see if the vase would fit in it. **3** *fig (investigar)* to try out, put to the test; **t. a algn,** to sound sb out; **t. el terreno,** to see how the land lies. **II** *vi Dep* to (keep) score.

tanteo *nm* **1** *(cálculo aproximado)* estimate, guess. **2** *(prueba)* reckoning, rough estimate; *(de medidas)* sizing up. **3** *(sondeo)* trial, test; *(de la actitud de una persona)* sounding. **4** *Dep* score; **igualar el t.,** to draw.

tanto,-a I *nm* **1** *(punto)* point; **marcar** *or* **apuntarse un t.,** to score a point; *fig* **con aquel hallazgo se apuntó un t. a su favor,** that discovery was a feather in his cap. **2** *(cantidad imprecisa)* so much, a certain amount; **les pagan (un) t. por cada pieza que venden,** they pay them a percentage for each piece they sell; *Com* **t. por ciento,** percentage. **3** *(poco)* **un t.,** a bit; **es un t. ridículo,** it's a bit silly; **la casa es un t. pequeña,** the house is rather *or* somewhat small. **II** *adj* **1** *(incontables)* so much; *(contables)* so many; **¡ha pasado t. tiempo!,** it's been so long!; **no dormí de tanta excitación,** I was so excited that I couldn't sleep; **no le des t. dinero,** don't give him so much money; **tantas manzanas como puedas,** as many apples as you can. **2** *(aproximadamente)* odd; **cincuenta y tantas personas,** fifty odd people; **en el año sesenta y tantos,** in nineteen sixty something. **III** *pron (incontable)* so much; *(contables)* so many; **es una chica de tantas,** she's nothing special; **no tengo tantos,** I haven't got so many; **otras tantas,** as many again; **otro t.,** as much again, the same again; **uno de tantos,** run-of-the-mill; *fam* **a las tantas,** very late, at an unearthly hour. **IV** *adv* **1** *(cantidad)* so much; **estaba rojo de t. llorar,** his face was red from crying so much; **no llegará a t.,** it won't come to that; **¡te quiero t.!,** I love you so much! **2** *(tiempo)* so long; **¿por qué has tardado t.?,** what kept you so long? **3** *(frecuencia)* so often; **no vengas t.,** don't come so often. **4** *(locuciones)* **en** *or* **entre** *or* **mientras t.,** meanwhile; **estar al t.,** *(informado)* to be informed; *(alerta)* to be on the alert; **no es** *or* **hay para t.,** it's not that bad; **no será t.,** things can't be as bad as you're making them out to be; **por lo t.,** therefore; **t. más/menos,** all the more/less; **t. mejor/peor,** so much the better/worse; **t. si vienes como si no,** whether you come or not; **¡y t.!,** oh yes!, and how!; *fam* **ni t. ni tan poco** *or* **calvo,** neither one extreme nor the other.

Tanzania *n* Tanzania.

tanzano,-a *adj* & *nm,f* Tanzanian.

tañer *vtr Mús* to play; **t. campanas,** to toll *or* ring bells.

tañido *nm (de instrumento)* sound; *(de campanas)* toll, ringing.

tapa *nf* **1** *(cubierta)* lid, top; *(de botella)* cap, top, stopper; *(de libro)* cover; *(de zapato)* heelplate; *Aut (de cilindro)* head; *fam fig* **levantarse** *or* **saltarse la t. de los sesos,** to blow one's brains out. **2** *Culin (comida)* appetizer, snack. **3** *(de res)* round of beef.

tapabocas *nm inv* scarf, muffler.

tapacubos *nm inv Aut* hubcap.

tapadera *nf* **1** *(tapa)* cover, lid. **2** *fig (persona)* cover, front.

tapadillo *nm* **hacer algo de t.,** to do sth secretly.

tapado,-a I *pp de* **tapar. II** *adj* **1** covered; *(con tapa)* with the lid on; *(con ropas o mantas)* wrapped (up). **2** *(obstruido)* obstructed, clogged; **tengo la nariz tapada del resfriado,** my nose is blocked up with this cold. **3** *(oculto)* concealed, hidden. **III** *nm Am* overcoat.

tápalo *nm Méx* shawl.

tapanca *nf Am* trappings *pl*.

tapaojo *nm Am* ornamenal head collar.

tapar I *vtr* **1** *(gen)* to cover; *(con tapa)* to put the lid *or* top on; *(con ropas o mantas)* to wrap up. **2** *(obstruir)* to obstruct; *(tubería)* to block. **3** *(ocultar)* to hide; *(vista)* to block; **t. el sol,** to block out the sun. **4** *(encubrir)* to cover up for sb. **II taparse** *vr* **1** *(cubrirse)* to cover oneself; *(abrigarse)* to wrap up. **2 t. los oídos,** to put one's fingers in one's ears.

taparrabos *nm inv* loincloth; *fam (bañador)* bathing trunks *pl*.

tape *nm Arg Urug (guaraní)* Guarani; *(indio)* Indian.

tapera *nf SAm* ruins *pl*.

tapete *nm* (table) runner; *fig* **estar** *or* **poner sobre el t.,** *(discutir)* to be on the carpet *or* under discussion; *(plantear)* to bring up.

tapia *nf (cerca)* garden wall; *(de adobe)* mud wall, adobe wall; *fam fig* **más sordo que una t.,** as deaf as a post.

tapiar *vtr* **1** *(área)* to wall in *or* off. **2** *(puerta, ventana, etc)* to wall, close up.

tapicería *nf* **1** *(arte)* tapestry making; *(tapices)* tapestry. **2** *(de muebles, coche)* upholstery. **3** *(tienda)* upholsterer's shop *or* workshop.

tapicero,-a *nm,f* **1** *(que hace tapices)* tapestry maker. **2** *(de muebles, coche)* upholsterer.

tapioca *nf Culin* tapioca.

tapir *nm Zool* tapir.

tapisca *nf* **1** *CAm (de maíz)* corn harvest. **2** *Méx (de café)* coffee harvest.

tapiscar *vtr CAm* to harvest corn.

tapiz *nm* **1** *(paño)* tapestry. **2** *(alfombra)* rug, carpet.

tapizado,-a I *pp de* **tapizar. II** *adj* **1** *(muebles)* upholstered. **2** *fml (cubierto)* covered; **una senda tapizada de hojas,** a path carpeted with leaves. **III** *nm* **1** *(de muebles)* upholstering. **2** *(colgaduras)* tapestries.

tapizar *vtr* **1** *(muebles)* to upholster. **2** *(cubrir con tapices)* to cover with tapestries.

tapón *nm* **1** stopper, plug; *(de botella)* cap, cork; **pon el t. al lavabo,** put the plug in the basin. ■ **t. de rosca,** screw-on cap. **2** *(del oído)* wax in the ear. **3** *fam (persona)* shorty, stubby. **4** *(baloncesto)* block. **5** *Aut* traffic jam.

taponamiento *nm* obturation, plugging.

taponar I *vtr* **1** *(tubería, hueco)* to plug, stop, obturate; *(el paso)* to block; *(poner el tapón)* to put the plug in. **2** *Med (herida)* to tampon. **II taponarse** *vr* to get clogged *or* blocked; **se me han taponado los oídos,** my ears are blocked up.

taponazo *nm* **1** *(ruido)* pop. **2** *(golpe)* hit, shot; **rompió un cristal de un t.,** he broke a window pane with the flying cork.

tapujo *nm* deceit, secrecy; **andarse con tapujos,** not to come clean (about sth); **sin tapujos,** openly.

taquear I *vi* **1** *Arg Chi (taconear)* to tap one's heel. **2** *Am* to play pool. **3** *Méx* to eat maize cakes. **II** *vtr Am* **1** *(atiborrar)* to stuff, fill. **2** *(arma)* to ram, tamp. **III taquearse** *vr* to stuff oneself.

taquicardia *nf Med* tachycardia.

taquigrafía *nf* shorthand, stenography.

taquigrafiar *vtr* to write in shorthand.

taquigráfico,-a *adj* written in shorthand; **signos taquigráficos,** shorthand symbols.

taquígrafo,-a *nm,f* shorthand writer, stenographer.

taquilla *nf* **1** ticket office, booking office; *Cin Teat* box-office; **un éxito de t.,** a box-office success. **2** *(recaudación)* takings *pl.* **3** *(armario)* locker. **4** *Am (estaquilla)* tack.

taquillero,-a I *adj fig (film, play)* popular. **II** *nm,f* booking or ticket clerk.

taquimecanografía *nf* shorthand and typing.

taquimecanógrafo,-a *nm,f* shorthand typist.

tara *nf* **1** *(peso)* tare. **2** *(defecto)* defect, blemish, fault.

tarabilla I *nf* **1** *Orn* **t. común,** stonechat; **t. norteña,** whinchat. **2** *fig (habla confusa)* jabber, prattle. **3** *(aldabilla de puertas)* latch, catch. **II** *nmf fam (persona)* chatterbox.

tarabita *nf Am* rope bridge.

tarado,-a I *pp* de **tarar. II** *adj* **1** *(defectuoso)* defective, damaged. **2** *(persona)* handicapped. **III** *nm,f fam* idiot, nitwit.

tarambana *adj fam* madcap.

taranta *nf Arg CR Ecuad* madness.

tarantela *nf Mús* tarantella.

tarantín *nm CAm Cuba (cachibache)* stuff, things *pl.*

tarántula *nf Zool* tarantula.

tarar *vtr Com* to tare.

tararear *vtr* to hum.

tarareo *nm* humming.

tararira *adj fam* **estar t.,** *(loco)* to be batty or potty; *(borracho)* to be drunk.

tarascada *nf fam* rude retort, snappy answer.

tardanza *nf* delay.

tardar I *vtr (emplear tiempo)* to take time; **¿cuánto se tarda?,** how long does it take?; **tarda una hora en cocerse,** it takes an hour to cook; **tardé tres años,** it took me three years. **II** *vi (demorar)* to take long; **a más t.,** at the latest; **no tardes,** don't be long; **no puede t.,** he should be here any moment now; **se tarda más en tren,** it takes longer by train; **tarda en llegar,** he's late; **tardarás en empezar,** it'll be some time before you start.

tarde I *nf* **1** *(hasta las seis)* afternoon; **buenas tardes,** good afternoon; **función de t.,** matinée; **son las 4 de la t.,** it is 4 o'clock in the afternoon. **2** *(después de las seis)* evening; **a las 8 de la t.,** at 8 p.m. or in the evening; **a última hora de la tarde,** early this evening; **buenas tardes,** good evening. **II** *adv* **1** *(hora avanzada)* late; **se está haciendo t.,** it's getting late; **siento llegar t.,** I'm sorry I'm late. **2** *(demasiado tarde)* too late; **es ya t. para ir al cine,** it's too late now to go to the cinema. **3** *(locuciones)* **de t. en t.,** very rarely, not very often; **(más) t.** or **(más) temprano,** sooner or later.

tardío,-a *adj* late, belated; **fruta tardía,** late fruit.

tardo,-a *adj* **1** *(lento)* slow; **t. en comprender,** slow to understand. **2** *(torpe)* slow.

tarea *nf* job, task; **las tareas de la casa,** the chores, housework *sing;* **tareas escolares,** homework *sing;* **una t. poco grata,** an unpleasant job (to do).

tareco *nm Am* stuff, things *pl.*

tarifa *nf* **1** *(precio)* tariff, rate; *(en transportes)* fare. ■ **t. reducida,** reduced rate, special deal; **t. turística,** tourist class rate. **2** *(lista de precios)* price list.

tarifar *vtr* to put a price to, price.

tarima *nf* platform, dais.

tarjeta *nf* card. ■ **t. de crédito,** credit card; **t. de visita,** visiting or US calling card; *Inform* **t. perforada,** punch or punched card; **t. postal,** postcard.

tarraconense I *adj* of or from Tarragona. **II** *nmf* native or inhabitant of Tarragona.

tarrayazo *nm Am* cast (of net).

tarro¹ *nm* **1** *(vasija)* jar, pot, tub; **un t. de miel,** a jar of honey. **2** *fam (cabeza)* bonce; **comer el t. a algn,** to brainwash sb; **está mal del t.,** he's off his rocker. **3** *Am (lata)* tin, can.

tarro² *nm Orn* shelduck.

tarsana *nf,* **társana** *nf Bot Am* soapbark.

tarta *nf* cake, tart, pie, flan.

tartaja *adj & nmf fam* stammerer, stutterer.

tartajear *vi* to stammer, stutter.

tartajeo *nm (manera de hablar)* stammering, stuttering; *(defecto)* stammer, stutter.

tartajoso,-a I *adj* stammering, stuttering. **II** *nm, f* stammerer, stutterer.

tartaleta *nf Culin* small pastry case.

tartamudear *vi* to stutter, stammer.

tartamudeo *nm (manera de hablar)* stuttering, stammering; *(defecto)* stutter, stammer.

tartamudez *nf* stutter, stammer.

tartamudo,-a I *adj* stuttering, stammering. **II** *nm, f* stutterer, stammerer.

tartana *nf* **1** *(carruaje)* trap. **2** *fam (coche viejo)* banger, heap.

tártaro,-a¹ I *adj & nm,f Hist* Tartar. **II** *adj Culin* **salsa tártara,** tartar sauce.

tártaro² *nm Odont* tartar.

tartera *nf* **1** *(fiambrera)* lunch box. **2** *(cazuela)* baking tin.

tartesio,-a *adj & nm,f Hist* Tartessian.

tarugada *nf Méx* piece of mischief.

tarugo *nm* **1** *(de madera)* lump of wood. **2** *(de pan)* chunk of stale bread. **3** *fam (persona)* blockhead.

tarumba *adj fam* crazy, mad; **estar t.,** to be bonkers; **volver t. a algn,** to drive sb crazy.

tasa *nf* **1** *(valoración)* valuation, appraisal. **2** *(precio)* fee, charge; **tasas académicas,** course fees. **3** *(impuesto)* tax, levy. **4** *(límite)* limit; *(medida)* measure; **sin t.,** without limit. **5** *(índice)* rate. ■ **t. de natalidad/mortalidad,** birth/death rate.

tasación *nf* valuation, appraisal.

tasador,-a *nm,f* valuer.

tasar *vtr* **1** *(valorar)* to value, appraise; **t. una casa en tres millones de pesetas,** to value a house at three million pesetas. **2** *(poner precio)* to set or fix the price of. **3** *(artículo)* to tax. **4** *(regular)* to regulate; *(limitar)* to limit; *(racionar)* to ration.

tasca *nf* bar, pub; *fam* **ir de tascas,** to go on a pub crawl.

tata *nf fam* nanny.

tatarabuelo,-a *nm, f (hombre)* great-great-grandfather; *(mujer)* great-great-grandmother; **tatarabuelos,** great-great-grandparents.

tataranieto,-a *nm, f (hombre)* great-great-grandson; *(mujer)* great-great-granddaughter; **tataranietos,** great-great-grandchildren.

tataratear *vi CAm Ven* to struggle.

tate I *nm arg* hashish. **II** *interj (cuidado)* look out!, steady!; *(caramba)* good grief!, crumbs!

tatemar *vtr Méx* to roast.

tatetí *nm Arg Urug (juego)* noughts and crosses.

tatuaje *nm* **1** *(dibujo)* tattoo. **2** *(procedimiento)* tattooing.

tatuar I *vtr* to tattoo. **II tatuarse** *vr* to have a tattoo or tattoos; **t. el pecho,** to have one's chest tattooed.

taúca *nf Bol Ecuad Per* heap, stack.

taucar *vtr Bol Ecuad Per* to pile, stack.

taurino,-a *adj* of or relating to bullfighting; **la fiesta taurina,** bullfighting.

Tauro *nm Astrol Astron* Taurus.

tauromaquia *nf* tauromachy, (art of) bullfighting.

tautología *nf* tautology.

taxativo,-a *adj* precise, restricted, specific; **de forma taxativa,** in a categorical way.

taxi *nm Aut* taxi.

taxidermia *nf* taxidermy.

taxidermista *nmf* taxidermist.

taxímetro *nm* taximeter, clock.

taxista *nmf* taxi driver.

taxonomía *nf* taxonomy.

tayacán *nm CAm* right-hand man.

taza *nf* 1 cup; **una t. de café,** *(recipiente)* coffee cup; *(con café)* a cup of coffee. 2 *(contenido)* cupful; **tres tazas de azúcar,** three cupfuls of sugar. 3 *(de retrete)* bowl.

tazcal *nm Méx Culin* 1 *(tortilla)* maize pancake. 2 *(cesto)* pancake basket.

tazón *nm* bowl.

te¹ *nf (pl tes)* 1 name of the letter T in Spanish. 2 *Constr* tee.

te² *pron pers* 1 to you, for you; **no quiero verte,** I don't want to see you; **te compraré uno,** I'll buy one for you, I'll buy you one; **te lo dije,** I told you; **te quiero,** I love you. 2 *(reflexivo)* yourself; *(sin traducción)* **bébetelo todo,** drink it up; **lávate,** wash yourself; **no te vayas,** don't go; **¿te aburres?,** are you bored?; **¿te compraste uno?,** did you get one for yourself?; **te matarás,** you'll kill yourself.

té *nm (pl tés)* tea; **t. con limón,** lemon tea; **salón de t.,** tearoom.

tea *nf* torch; *fam* **cogerse una t.,** to get drunk *or* plastered.

teatral *adj* 1 *Teat* theatrical, dramatic; **grupo t.,** theatre company; **obra t.,** play. 2 *fig (exagerado)* stagy, *US* stagey, exaggerated; **es muy t.,** he's always a bit over the top.

teatralidad *nf* showmanship, staginess.

teatro *nm* 1 theatre; **autor de t.,** playwright; **obra de t.,** play. 2 *(arte de representar)* theatre, acting; **dejar el t.,** to give up the stage; **vive para el t.,** she lives for the stage. 3 *Lit* drama. 4 *fig (lugar)* scene, theatre; **el t. de la batalla,** the scene of the battle. 5 *fig (exageración)* show; **echarle t. a un asunto, hacer t.,** to play-act, be melodramatic, put on (such) a show.

tebeo *nm* children's comic; *fam* **está más visto que el t.,** that's old hat.

teca *nf Bot* teak.

techado,-a I *pp de* **techar.** II *adj* roofed, covered. III *nm, f* roof, covering; **bajo t.,** indoors.

techar *vtr* to roof.

techo *nm* 1 *Constr* ceiling; *(de coche, tejado)* roof; **viven bajo el mismo t.,** they live under the same roof. 2 *Av (altura máxima)* ceiling. 3 *fig* limit, end; **el tema ha tocado t.,** the subject has been exhausted, there's nothing more to say about this subject.

techumbre *nf* roof, covering, roofing.

tecla *nf* key; *fig* **dar en la t.,** to get it right; *fig* **tocar teclas,** to pull strings; *fig* **tocas demasiadas teclas,** you're trying to do too many things at once.

teclado *nm* keyboard; *Inform* **t. expandido,** expanded keyboard.

teclear *vi* 1 *(piano)* to press the keys; *(máquina de escribir, ordenador)* to tap the keyboard, type. 2 *(tamborilear)* to drum, tap with one's fingers; *fig* **la lluvia tecleaba sobre el tejado,** the rain fell pitter-patter on the roof. 3 *fig (problema, asunto)* to approach. 4 *Am (agonizar)* to be dying. 5 *Am (negocio)* not to be doing well.

tecleo *nm* 1 *Mús* fingering. 2 *(ruido)* rattle, clatter.

técnica *nf* 1 *(tecnología)* technics *pl*, technology; **t. mecánica,** mechanical engineering. 2 *(habilidad)* technique, method; **toca bien pero le falta t.,** he plays well but he lacks method.

tecnicidad *nf* technicality.

tecnicismo *nm Ling* technicality, technical word *or* expression.

técnico,-a I *adj* technical; **carrera técnica,** technical degree; **vocabulario t.,** technical vocabulary. II *nm, f* technician, technical expert.

tecnicolor *nm* Technicolor.

tecno- *pref* techno-.

tecnocracia *nf Pol* technocracy.

tecnócrata *nmf* technocrat.

tecnocrático,-a *adj* technocratic.

tecnología *nf* technology.

tecnológico,-a *adj* technological.

tecomate *nm* 1 *CAm Bot* bottle gourd. 2 *CAm (vasija)* cup. 3 *Méx* earthenware cup.

tecuco,-a *adj Méx* mean, stingy.

tedio *nm* tedium, boredom, monotony.

tedioso,-a *adj* tedious, boring, monotonous.

tegumento *nm* integument.

Teherán *n* Teheran.

teína *nf* theine.

teja *nf Constr* tile; *fam* *fig* **a toca t.,** on the nail.

tejadillo *nm* 1 *Aut* roof. 2 *Constr* roof.

tejado *nm* roof.

tejamaní *nm*, **tejamanil** *nm Constr* roofing board.

tejano,-a I *adj* Texan. II *nm, f (persona)* Texan. III **tejanos** *nmpl (prenda)* jeans.

tejar¹ *nm* tile works *pl*.

tejar² *vtr* to tile.

Tejas *n* Texas.

tejedor,-a I *adj* weaving. II *nm, f* weaver.

tejemaneje *nm fam* 1 *(mucha actividad)* bustle, fuss; **¿qué es tanto t.?,** what's all this fuss about? 2 *(maquinación)* intrigue, scheming; **algún t. se deben traer,** they must be cooking up sth.

tejer *vtr* 1 *(en el telar)* to weave. 2 *(hacer punto)* to knit. 3 *(araña)* to spin. 4 *fig (plan)* to weave, plot, scheme; **t. y destejer,** to chop and change.

tejido *nm* 1 *(tela)* fabric, textile; **t. de punto,** knitted fabric. 2 *Anat* tissue. ■ **t. óseo,** bone tissue; **t. muscular,** muscle *or* muscular tissue; **t. nervioso,** nervous tissue. 3 *fig* web.

tejo¹ *nm* 1 *(juego)* hopscotch, children's game similar to quoits. 2 *fam* **tirar los tejos a algn,** to court *or* woo sb.

tejo² *nm Bot* yew (tree).

tejón *nm Zool* badger.

tejuelo *nm* label on the spine of a book.

tela *nf* 1 *Tex* material, fabric, cloth; *(de la leche)* skin. ■ **t. de araña,** cobweb; **t. metálica,** gauze. 2 *fam (dinero)* dough. 3 *Arte* painting. 4 *(locuciones)* *fig* **haber** *or* **tener t. para rato,** to have a lot to do *or* talk about; *fig* **poner en t. de juicio,** to question; *fig* **tiene mucha t.,** it's not an easy thing.

telar *nm* 1 *Tex* loom. 2 *Teat* gridiron.

telaraña *nf* cobweb, spider's web.

tel. *abr de* **teléfono,** telephone, tel.

tele *nf fam* telly, TV.

telearrastre *nm* ski lift.

telecabina *nf* single cable car.

telecomunicación *nf (gen pl)* telecommunication.

telediario *nm TV* television news bulletin.

teledirigido,-a I *pp de* **teledirigir.** II *adj* remote-controlled; **proyectil t.,** guided missile.

teledirigir *vtr* to operate *or* guide by remote control.

telefax *nm* telefax, fax.

teleférico *nm* cable car *or* railway.

telefilm *nm*, **telefilme** *nm* TV film.

telefonazo *nm* buzz, ring; **dar un t. (a algn),** to give (sb) a ring.

telefonear *vt & vi* to telephone, phone; **t. a casa/la oficina,** to telephone home/the office.

telefonía *nf* telephony.

telefónica *nf* **Compañía T.,** ≈ British Telecom.

telefónico,-a *adj* telephone; **central** *or* **centralita telefónica,** switchboard, telephone exchange. ◆ **telefónicamente** *adv* by telephone.

telefonista *nmf* (telephone) operator.

teléfono *nm* telephone, phone; **está hablando por t.,** she's on the phone; **guía** *or* **listín de teléfonos,** telephone directory; **te llamó por t.,** she phoned you.

telegrafía *nf* telegraphy; **t. sin hilos,** wireless telegraphy.

telegrafiar *vtr* to telegraph, wire.

telegráfico,-a *adj* telegraphic; **giro t.,** giro, money order; **lenguaje t.,** telegraphic speech. ◆ **telegráficamente** *adv* by telegram; *fam* **hablar/escribir t.,** to speak/write telegraphically.

telegrafista *nmf* telegraphist, telegrapher.

telégrafo *nm* 1 telegraph; **poste de t.,** telegraph pole. 2 **telégrafos,** post office *sing*.

telegrama *nm* telegram, cable.

telengues *nmpl CAm* things *pl*, stuff *sing*.

telele *nm fam* **darle a uno un t.,** to have a fit.

telemando *nm* remote control (unit).

telemanía *nf* telly addiction.

telemática *nf Téc* telematics *sing*.

telemetría *nf* telemetry.

telémetro *nm* telemeter, rangefinder.

telenovela *nf* television serial.

teleobjetivo *nm Fot* telephoto lens *sing*.

telequinesia *nf* telekinesis.

telepatía *nf* telepathy.

telepático,-a *adj* telepathic. ◆ **telepáticamente** *adv* by telepathy.

telescópico,-a *adj* telescopic.

telescopio *nm* telescope.

telesilla *nm* chair lift.

telespectador,-a *nmf TV* viewer.

telesquí *nm* ski lift.

teletexto *nm* teletext.

teletipo *nm* teletype, teleprinter; **noticia de t.,** news from an agency.

televidente *nm, f TV* viewer.

televisar *vtr* to televise.

televisión *nf* 1 *(sistema)* television. 2 *fam (aparato)* television set; **ver la t.,** to watch television.

televisivo,-a *adj* television; **espacio t.,** television programme.

televisor *nm* television set.

télex *nm inv* telex.

telilla *nf* film, skin; **la t. de la leche,** the skin of milk.

telón *nm Teat* curtain. ■ *Pol* **t. de acero,** iron curtain; **t. de fondo,** *Teat* backdrop; *fig* background.

telonero,-a *adj* first on stage, support; **grupo t.,** support band.

telúrico,-a *adj* telluric.

tema *nm* 1 *(de libro, de conversación)* topic, subject, theme; *(de examen)* subject; **atenerse al t.,** to keep to the point; **le tocó un t. fácil,** he was given an easy subject; **por favor no toques este t. otra vez,** don't go into that again, please; **salir del t.,** to go off at a tangent; **t. de actualidad,** current affair; *fam* **cada loco con su t.,** everyone has his hobby-horse. 2 *Más* theme. 3 *Ling* root, stem, theme; **el t. del verbo decir es dec-,** the stem of the verb **decir** is dec-.

temario *nm (de examen)* programme; *(de coferencia)* agenda.

temático,-a *I adj* 1 *(de tema)* thematic. 2 *Ling* of or relating to the stem of a word; **vocal temática,** thematic vowel. *II nf (tema)* subject matter.

temblar *vi* 1 *(de frío)* to shiver; *(de miedo)* to tremble (**de,** with); *(voz)* to quiver; *(con sacudidas)* to shake; **le tiemblan las manos,** he's got shaky hands. 2 *fig (estar asustado)* to shake with fear, dread; **tiemblo ante el futuro,** I shudder when I think of the future.

tembleque *nm fam* shaking fit; **sólo de pensarlo me da** *or* **entra (el) t.,** I get the shivers just thinking about it.

temblón,-ona *I adj fam* trembling, shaky. *II nm Bot* **álamo t.,** aspen.

temblor *nm* tremor, shudder; **el enfermo tenía temblores,** the patient was shaking. ■ **t. de tierra,** earth tremor.

tembloroso,-a *adj*, **tembloso,-a** *adj (con sacudidas)* shaking, *(voz)* quivering, *(de frío)* shivering; *(de miedo)* trembling; **manos temblorosas,** shaky hands.

temer *I vtr* 1 to fear, be afraid (of); **teme al enemigo,** he is afraid of the enemy. 2 *(sospechar)* to fear, be afraid of; **temo que esté muerto,** I fear he's dead; **temo que no podrá recibirte,** I'm afraid (that) he won't be able to see you. *II vi* 1 to be afraid; **era de t.,** it had to happen; **no temas,** don't be afraid. 2 *(preocuparse)* to worry; **no hay nada que t.,** there is nothing to worry about. *III* **temerse** *vr* to fear, be afraid; **¡me lo temía!,** I feared this would happen!

temerario,-a *adj* reckless, rash.

temeridad *nf* 1 *(actitud)* temerity, rashness. 2 *(acto temerario)* reckless act.

temeroso,-a *adj* 1 fearful, timid; **t. de,** fearing (that); **t. de Dios,** God-fearing. 2 *(medroso)* frightful.

temible *adj* dreadful, fearful, frightful, frightening; **un ejército t.,** a fearsome army.

temido,-a *I pp de* temer. *II adj* feared, dreaded; **t. de** *or* **por todos,** feared by everybody.

temor *nm* 1 *(de Dios)* fear. 2 *(recelo)* worry, apprehension; **tener t.,** to feel apprehensive; **tus temores son infundados,** there's no reason for you to worry.

témpano *nm* ice floe; **ser como un t.,** to be as cold as ice.

temperamental *adj* temperamental.

temperamento *nm* temperament, nature; **tiene buen t.,** he is good-natured; **tener t.,** to have a strong character.

temperancia *nf* temperance, moderation, restraint.

temperar *I vtr (calmar)* to temper, mitigate. *II vi Am* to have a change of air; *(veranear)* to spend the summer.

temperatura *nf* temperature; **¿qué t. hace?,** what's the temperature?; *Med* **le ha subido la t.,** his temperature has gone up. ■ **t. máxima/mínima,** maximum/minimum temperature.

tempestad *nf Meteor* storm; *fig* turmoil, uproar; *fig* **levantar tempestades,** to cause a turmoil; *fig* **una t. en un vaso de agua,** a storm in a teacup. ■ **t. de arena,** sandstorm; **t. de nieve,** snowstorm, blizzard.

tempestuoso,-a *adj* stormy, tempestuous, violent, wild.

templado,-a *I pp de* templar. *II adj* 1 *(agua)* lukewarm, warm; *(clima, temperatura)* mild, temperate. 2 *(moderado)* moderate; *(sereno)* composed, unruffled; **nervios bien templados,** steady nerves. 3 *Mús (afinado)* tuned. 4 *(metal)* tempered. 5 *Can Col PR (borracho)* drunk. 6 *Am (severo)* strict, severe. 7 *SAm (enamorado)* in love. 8 *CAm Méx (listo)* smart.

templanza *nf* 1 *(moderación)* moderation, restraint. 2 *(del clima)* mildness.

templar *I vtr* 1 *(gen)* to moderate, temper. 2 *(algo frío)* to warm up; *(algo caliente)* to cool down. 3 *(cólera)* to appease; *(apaciguar)* to calm down. 4 *(cuerda, tornillo)* to tighten up. 5 *(bebida)* to dilute. 6 *Mús (instrumento)* to tune. 7 *Téc (metal)* to temper. 8 *(colores)* to match. *II*

templarse *vr* **1** *(calentar)* to warm up, get warm. **2** *(persona)* to restrain, control oneself. **3** *Can Col PR (emborracharse)* to get drunk. **4** *Cuba Méx (huir)* to escape, run away. **5** *Ecuad Guat Hond (morirse)* to die. **6** *SAm (enamorarse)* to fall in love.

templario *nm Hist* Templar.

temple *nm* **1** *(fortaleza)* boldness, courage; *(estado de ánimo)* frame of mind, mood. **2** *Téc (de metal)* temper; **dar t.**, to temper. **3** *Arte* tempera.

templete *nm* **1** *(pabellón)* pavilion, kiosk. **2** *(templo pequeño)* small temple.

templo *nm* temple; *fam fig* **una mentira como un t.**, an utter lie; *fam fig* **una verdad como un t.**, a patent truth.

temporada *nf* **1** *(en artes, deportes, moda)* season; **en plena t.**, at the height of the season. ■ **t. alta,** high *or* peak season; **t. baja,** low *or* off season. **2** *(período)* period, time; **por temporadas,** on and off.

temporal I *adj* **1** *(transitorio)* temporary, provisional; **bienes temporales,** worldly goods. **2** *Ling* temporal. **II** *nm Meteor* storm, tempest; *fig* **capear el t.,** to ride out the storm.

temporero,-a I *adj (trabajador)* seasonal, temporary. **II** *nm,f* seasonal *or* temporary worker.

temporizar *vi* to temporize.

tempranero,-a *adj* **1** *(persona)* early-rising. **2** *(cosecha)* early.

temprano,-a I *adj* early. **II** *adv* early; **más t.,** earlier.

tenacidad *nf* **1** *(perseverancia)* tenacity, perseverance. **2** *(de metal)* tensile strength.

tenacillas *nfpl (para pelo)* curling tongs; *(para vello)* tweezers.

tenaz *adj (gen)* tenacious; *(perseverante)* persevering, unflagging; *(persistente)* persistent, unremitting.

tenaza *nf*, **tenazas** *nfpl (herramienta)* pliers, pincers; *(para el fuego)* tongs; *fam fig* **esto no se puede coger ni con tenazas,** I wouldn't touch it with a barge pole.

tenca *nf (pez)* tench.

tencal *nm Méx* wicker baskets *pl*.

tencolote *nm Méx* **1** *(cesta)* basket. **2** *(jaula)* cage.

tencua *Méx* **I** *adj* harelipped. **II** *nmf* person with harelip.

tendedero *nm* clothesline, drying place.

tendencia *nf* tendency, inclination, predisposition, leaning; **tener t. a hacer algo,** to tend to do sth, have a tendency to do sth.

tendenciosidad *nf* tendentiousness, partiality, bias.

tendencioso,-a *adj* tendentious, biased.

tendente *adj* directed *(a,* at), aimed *(a,* at).

tender I *vtr* **1** *(mantel)* to spread; *(red)* to cast; *(puente)* to throw; *(vía, cable)* to lay; *Náut (velas)* to spread. **2** *(ropa, colada)* to hang out. **3** *(mano)* to stretch *or* hold out. **4** *(emboscada, trampa)* to lay, set. **5** *(tumbar)* to lay; **estaba tendido en el suelo,** he was lying on the floor. **6** *(tener tendencia)* to have a tendency *(a,* to). **7** *Constr (pared, techo)* to plaster. **II tenderse** *vr* **1** *(tumbarse)* to lie down, stretch out. **2** *(caballo)* to run at full gallop.

tenderete *nm* **1** *(puesto)* market stall. **2** *(montón)* heap, mess.

tendero,-a *nm,f* shopkeeper.

tendido,-a I *pp de* **tender. II** *adj* **1** *(extendido)* spread *or* laid out. **2** *(persona)* lying down; **le dejé t. de un solo puñetazo,** I floored him with a single blow. **3** *(ropa, colada)* hung out; **¿hay ropa tendida?,** is there any washing on the line? **III** *nm* **1** *(colada)* wash, washing. **2** *(de vía, cable)* laying; *(de puente)* construction. ■ **t. eléctrico,** electrical installation. **3** *Taur (asientos)* front tiers *pl* of seats, *US* bleachers *pl*. **4** *Am (ropa de cama)* bed linen.

tendón *nm Anat* tendon, sinew.

tenebrista *adj* & *nmf Arte* tenebrist.

tenebrosidad *nf* darkness, shadiness, obscurity.

tenebroso,-a *adj* **1** *(sombrío)* dark, gloomy. **2** *(siniestro)* sinister, shady.

tenedor,-a I *nm, f Fin* holder. ■ **t. de acciones,** shareholder. **II** *nm Culin* fork.

teneduría *nf* book-keeping.

tenencia *nf Jur* tenancy, possession. ■ **t. ilícita de armas,** illicit possession of arms.

tener I *vtr* **1** *(gen)* to have, have got; **tenemos un examen,** we've got an exam; **t. tiempo,** to have time, **t. una idea,** to have an idea; **tengo algo que deciros,** there's something I want to tell you; **tiene los ojos negros,** she's got dark eyes; **va a t. un niño,** she's expecting; *fam* **¡ahí (lo) tienes!,** so there you are!; *fam* **¿(con qué) ésas tenemos?,** is that so? **2** *(poseer)* to own, possess. **3** *(sostener)* to hold; *(coger)* to take; **lo tienes en la mano,** you're holding it; **ten al niño mientras abro,** hold the baby while I open the door; **ten, es para ti,** take this *or* here you are, it's for you. **4** *(sensación, sentimiento)* to be; *(sentir)* to feel; **¿qué tienes?,** what's wrong with you?; **t. calor/frío,** to be hot/cold; **t. cariño a algn,** to be fond of sb; **t. compasión,** to take pity; **t. ganas de ...,** to feel like ...; **t. ilusión,** to be enthusiastic; **t. miedo,** to be frightened; *fam* **no tenerlas todas consigo,** *(dudar)* to have one's doubts; *(tener miedo)* to be afraid. **5** *(mantener)* to keep; **la preocupación me ha tenido despierto toda la noche,** worrying has kept me up all night; **t. a algn contento,** to make sb happy; *fam* **tenerla tomada con algn,** to have it in for sb. **6** *(medir)* to measure; **la casa tiene cien metros cuadrados,** the house is 100 square metres. **7** *(contener)* to hold, contain. **8** *(edad)* to be; **tiene casi treinta (años),** she's almost thirty (years old). **9** *(celebrar)* to hold; **t. una reunión,** to hold a meeting. **10** *(considerar)* to consider, think; **me tienen por estúpido,** they think I'm a fool; **ten por seguro que lloverá,** you can be sure it'll rain. **II** *v aux* **1** *(obligación)* **t. que,** to have (got) to; **tengo que irme,** I must leave; **tienes/tendrías que verlo,** you must/should see it. **III tenerse** *vr* **1** *(sostenerse)* to stand up; **no t.,** to be tired out; **t. firme,** to stand upright. **2** *(dominarse)* to control oneself. **3** *(considerarse)* **t. por,** to think *or* consider oneself; **se tiene por muy inteligente,** he thinks he's very intelligent.

tenga *subj pres véase* **tener.**

tengo *indic pres véase* **tener.**

tenia *nf* taenia.

teniente *nm* **1** *Mil* lieutenant. ■ **t. coronel/general,** lieutenant colonel/general. **2** *(de ayuntamiento)* **t. de alcalde,** deputy mayor.

tenis *nm Dep* tennis.

tenista *nmf* tennis player.

tenor[1] *nm Mús* tenor.

tenor[2] *nm* tenor, purport; **a este t.,** like this; **a t. de,** according to.

tenorio *nm* Don Juan, lady-killer, Casanova.

tensado,-a I *pp de* **tensar. II** *adj* taut, tautened, tense.

tensar *vtr (cable, cuerda)* to tauten; *(arco)* to draw.

tensión *nf* **1** *Téc (de materiales)* stress; *(de gases)* pressure. **2** *Elec* tension, voltage. ■ **alta/baja t.,** high/low tension. **3** *Med* **t. arterial,** blood pressure; **t. nerviosa,** nervous strain. **4** *(de una situación)* tension, tenseness; *(de una persona)* stress, strain; *(angustia)* anxiety; **en medio de una gran t.,** in a very tense situation; **en t.,** tense.

tenso,-a *adj* **1** *(cuerda, cable)* tense, taut. **2** *(persona)* tense; *(relaciones)* strained.

tensor I *adj* tensile. **II** *nm* **1** *Anat Mat* tensor. **2** *Téc* turnbuckle.

tentación *nf* temptation; **caer en la t.,** to succumb *or* give in to temptation.

tentáculo *nm* tentacle.

tentador,-a *adj* tempting, enticing.

tentar *vtr* 1 *(palpar)* to feel touch; **t. el camino,** to feel one's way. 2 *(incitar)* to tempt, entice; *fam* **¡no me tientes!,** don't tempt me!, don't say it twice! 3 *(atraer)* to attract, appeal.

tentativa *nf* attempt, try. ■ *Jur* **t. de asesinato,** attempted murder.

tentempié *nm fam (pl tentempiés)* 1 *(comida)* snack, bite. 2 *(juguete)* tumbler.

tenue *adj* 1 *(delgado)* thin, light; *(tela)* flimsy, thin; **una t. niebla,** a light fog. 2 *(luz, sonido)* subdued, faint.

teñido,-a I *pp de* **teñir.** II *adj* 1 *(gen)* dyed; *(pelo)* tinted, dyed; *fig* tinged; **una voz teñida de tristeza,** a voice tinged with sadness. III *nm (acción)* dyeing.

teñir I *vtr* 1 *(cambiar el color)* to dye; *(cambiar el tono)* to tone down. 2 *fig* to tinge with. II **teñirse** *vr* 1 *(cambiar de color)* to turn. 2 *(pelo)* to dye one's hair.

teodolito *nm Téc* theodolite.

teología *nf* theology.

teológico,-a *adj* theological.

teólogo,-a *nm,f* theologian, theologist.

teorema *nm Mat* theorem.

teoría *nf* theory; **en t.,** theoretically.

teórica *nf* theory, theoretics *sing*.

teórico,-a I *adj* theoretic, theoretical, hypothetical. II *nm, f* theoretician, theorist.

teorizar I *vtr* to theorize on. II *vi* to theorize **(sobre,** on).

tepalcate *nm Guat Méx* 1 *(vasija)* earthenware jar; *(cacharro)* piece of junk. 2 *Salv (fragmento)* fragment of pottery.

tequiar *vtr CAm* to pester.

tequila *nm* tequila.

terapeuta *nmf* therapist.

terapéutica *nf* therapeutics *sing*, therapy.

terapéutico,-a *adj* therapeutic.

terapia *nf* therapy.

tercer *adj* third; **el t. mundo,** the third world; *véase* **tercero,-a.**

tercermundista *adj* third-world.

tercera *nf* 1 *(clase)* third class; **viajar en t.,** to travel third class. 2 *Aut (marcha)* third (gear). 3 *Mús (intervalo)* third. 4 *prov* **a la t. va la vencida,** third time lucky.

tercero,-a I *adj* third. II *nm, f* 1 *(de una serie)* third; **vive en el t.,** he lives on the third floor. III *nm* 1 *(parte)* third. 2 *(mediador)* mediator; *(persona ajena)* outsider, *Jur* third party; **seguro contra terceros,** third party insurance. 3 *(proxeneta)* pimp, procurer; *véase tamb* **octavo,-a.**

terceto *nm* 1 *(verso)* tercet. 2 *Mús* trio.

terciar I *vtr* 1 *(dividir)* to divide into three. 2 *(poner en diagonal)* to place diagonally *or* crosswise. 3 *Am (vino, leche)* to water (down). 4 *Arg Col Méx (cargar a la espalda)* to carry across one's back. II *vi* 1 *(mediar)* to mediate, arbitrate; **t. entre dos enemigos,** to mediate between two enemies. ■ 2 *(participar)* to take part, participate; **t. en el debate,** to take part in the debate. III **terciarse** *vr (ocasión)* to arise; **si se tercia,** should the occasion arise.

terciario,-a *adj* tertiary.

tercio *nm* 1 *(parte)* (one) third. 2 *Mil* division. 3 *Hist* infantry regiment. 4 *Taur (suerte)* stage, part (of a bullfight). 5 *(de cerveza)* medium-size bottle of beer.

terciopelo *nm Tex* velvet.

terco,-a *adj* stubborn, obstinate.

tergal® *nm* type of polyester fabric.

tergiversación *nf* distortion, twisting.

tergiversado,-a I *pp de* **tergiversar.** II *adj* distorted, twisted.

tergiversar *vtr (hechos, motivos)* to distort; *(declaraciones, ideas)* to twist.

termal *adj* thermal.

termas *nfpl (baños)* spa *sing*, hot baths *or* springs *pl*; *Hist* thermae *pl*.

térmico,-a *adj* thermic, thermal.

terminación *nf* 1 *(acción)* ending, termination. 2 *(conclusión)* completion. 3 *(parte final)* end.

terminado,-a I *pp de* **terminar.** II *adj* finished, completed; **dar (algo) por t.,** to consider (sth) finished.

terminal I *adj* terminal; **estación t.,** terminus. II *nf* 1 *Elec* terminal; *Inform* terminal. 2 *(estación)* terminus.

terminante *adj* 1 *(categórico)* categorical, final. 2 *(dato, resultado)* conclusive, definite, definitive. ◆ **terminantemente** *adv* categorically; **queda** *or* **está t. prohibido,** it is strictly forbidden.

terminar I *vtr (acabar)* to finish, complete. II *vi* 1 *(acabarse)* to finish, end; *(completamente)* to finish off; **termina en seis/vocal,** it ends with a six/vowel; **termina ya,** will you finish that (off) now, please; **t. bien,** to have a happy ending; **t. de,** to finish doing; **no termina de convencerse,** he still isn't quite convinced; **t. mal,** *(historia)* to have an unhappy ending; *(relación)* to come to a sticky end; *(personas)* to end up on bad terms. 2 *(ir a parar)* to end up **(como,** to as), end **(en,** in, with); **terminarás loco,** you'll go mad; **terminé rendido,** I was exhausted by the end of it; **terminó comprándolo,** he ended up buying it; **terminó por caerse,** he ended up falling down. 3 *(eliminar)* to put an end **(con,** to). 4 *(reñir)* to break up **(con,** with). III **terminarse** *vr* 1 *(acabarse)* to finish, end, be over; **se ha terminado la fiesta,** the party is over. 2 *(agotarse)* to run out.

término *nm* I *(final)* end, finish; **dar t.,** to conclude; **llevar (algo) a buen** *or* **feliz t.,** to carry (sth) through (successfully); **poner t. a algo,** to put an end to sth. 2 *Ferroc (estación)* terminus. 3 *(límite)* limit, boundary. ■ **t. municipal,** district. 4 *(plazo)* term, time; **en el t. de un día,** within the space of a day. 5 *(palabra)* term, word; *(argumento)* point, term; **en otros términos,** in other words; **en términos generales,** generally speaking; **invertir los términos,** to get *or* put it the wrong way round; *Jur* **los términos de un contrato,** the terms of a contract. 6 *Filos Mat* term; **(por) t. medio,** on average. 7 *(lugar, posición)* place; *Arte* **primer t.,** foreground; *fig* **en último t.,** as a last resort.

terminología *nf* terminology.

terminológico,-a *adj* terminological.

termita *nf*, **termite** *nf Ent* termite.

termo¹ *nm* thermos (flask), flask.

termo² *nm véase* **termosifón.**

termodinámica *nf* thermodynamics *sing*.

termodinámico,-a *adj* thermodynamic, thermodynamical.

termómetro *nm* thermometer.

termonuclear *adj Téc* thermonuclear.

termosifón *nm* 1 *(calentador)* boiler, water heater. 2 *Téc* thermosiphon.

termostato *nm Téc* thermostat.

ternario,-a *adj* ternary.

terne *nm Arg Bol* gaucho knife.

ternera *nf* 1 *Zool* calf. 2 *Culin* veal.

ternero *nm* calf.

terneza *nf* tenderness; **ternezas,** sweet nothings.

ternilla *nf* cartilage.

terno *nm* 1 *(gen)* set *or* group of three; *(prendas)* three-piece suit. 2 *fam (juramento)* swearword.

ternura *nf* tenderness, gentleness.

terquedad *nf* 1 *(obstinación)* stubbornness, obstinacy. 2 *(dureza)* toughness, hardness.

terracota *nf* terracotta.

terrado *nm Constr* flat roof, terrace.

Terranova *n* Newfoundland.

terranova *nm Zool* Newfoundland dog.

terraplén *nm* embankment.

terráqueo,-a *adj* earth; **globo t.,** *(tierra)* (the) earth; *(esfera)* globe.

terrateniente *nmf Agr* landowner.

terrazo *nm* terrazzo.

terremoto *nm Geol* earthquake.

terrenal *adj* earthly, worldly.

terreno,-a I *adj* earthly, worldly. **II** *nm* **1** *(tierra)* (piece of) land, ground; *(solar)* plot, site; *Geol* terrain; *Agr (de cultivo)* soil; *(campo)* field; **ganar/perder t.,** to gain/lose ground; **hacer algo sobre el t.,** *(en el lugar)* to do sth on the spot; *fig (improvisar)* to improvise sth; *fig* **conocer el t.,** to be familiar with it; *fig* **preparar el t.,** to pave the way, prepare the ground; *fig* **saber uno el t. que pisa,** to know what one's doing; *fig* **ser t. abonado (para algo),** to be receptive (to sth). **2** *Dep* field, ground. **3** *fig* field, sphere; **está en su propio t.,** he's on home ground.

térreo,-a *adj* earthen.

terrestre I *adj* **1** *(de la tierra)* terrestrial, earthly. **2** *(por tierra)* by land. **II** *nmf (persona)* terrestrial.

terrible *adj* terrible, awful.

terrícola I *adj* land. **II** *nmf (persona)* earth dweller; *Lit (en ciencia ficción)* earthling.

terrier *nm Zool* terrier.

territorial *adj* territorial; *Tel* **código t.,** area code.

territorio *nm* territory; **en todo el t. nacional,** nationwide, all over the country.

terrón *nm* **1** *(de tierra)* clod. **2** *(de azúcar, sal)* lump. **3 terrones,** *(tierras)* land *sing*.

terror *nm (gen)* terror; *Cin* horror; **me da t.,** it terrifies me.

terrorífico,-a *adj* terrifying, frightening.

terrorismo *nm* terrorism.

terrorista *adj & nmf* terrorist.

terroso,-a *adj* **1** *(con tierra)* earthy, containing earth. **2** *(color)* earth-coloured, *US* earth-colored.

terruño *nm* **1** *(terreno)* piece of land. **2** *(patria chica)* homeland, native land.

terso,-a *adj* **1** *(liso)* smooth. **2** *(brillante)* glossy, shining. **3** *(estilo)* polished, fluent.

tersura *nf* **1** *(cualidad de liso)* smoothness. **2** *(brillo)* glossiness, shine. **3** *(de estilo)* polish, fluency.

tertulia *nf* get-together; **estar de t.,** to sit around and talk; **hacer t.,** to have a get-together. ■ **t. literaria,** literary gathering.

tesina *nf Univ* first degree dissertation.

tesis *nf inv* **1** *Fil* thesis; *(opinión)* view, theory; **sostener una t.,** to hold a theory. **2** *Univ* thesis. ■ **t. doctoral,** doctoral thesis.

tesitura *nf* **1** *Mús* tessitura. **2** *fig (estado de ánimo)* mood; *(actitud)* attitude.

tesón *nm* tenacity, firmness.

tesorería *nf (oficina)* treasurer's office; *(cargo)* treasurer.

tesorero,-a *nm,f* treasurer.

tesoro *nm* **1** *(gen)* treasure. **2** *(erario)* exchequer. ■ **T. Público,** Treasury. **3** *fig* treasure; **ese niño es un t.,** this child is a gem. **4** *(diccionario)* thesaurus.

test *nm Téc* test.

testa *nf* head.

testador,-a *nm,f Jur (hombre)* testator; *(mujer)* testatrix.

testaferro *nm* front man.

testamentaría *nf Jur* testate proceedings *pl*.

testamentario,-a *Jur* **I** *adj* testamentary. **II** *nm, f* executor.

testamento *nm* **1** *Jur* will, testament; **hacer** *or* **otorgar t.,** to make *or* draw up one's will. **2** *Rel* **Antiguo/Nuevo T.,** Old/New Testament.

testar *vi* to make *or* draw up one's will.

testarada *nf,* **testarazo** *nm* butt *or* bump *or* knock on the head.

testarudez *nf* stubbornness, obstinacy, pigheadedness.

testarudo,-a *adj* stubborn, obstinate, pigheaded.

testículo *nm Anat* testicle.

testifical *adj* attesting, witessing.

testificar *vtr* to testify.

testigo I *nmf (gen)* witness; **poner (a algn) por t.,** to call (sb) to witness; *Rel* **a Dios pongo por t.,** I swear to God. ■ *Jur* **t. de cargo/descargo,** witness for the prosecution/ defence; *Jur* **t. ocular, t. presencial,** eyewitness; *Rel* **Testigos de Jehová,** Jehovah's Witnesses. **II** *nm* **1** *fig* evidence, proof. **2** *Dep (en carreras de relevos)* baton.

testimonial *adj* testimonial.

testimoniar *vtr* **1** *Jur (dar testimonio)* to bear witness to, testify to, attest to. **2** *fig (mostrar)* to show, prove, express.

testimonio *nm Jur* testimony; *(prueba)* evidence, proof; **dar t.,** to give evidence; **levantar falsos testimonios,** to commit perjury *or* slander.

testosterona *nf Biol* testosterone.

teta *nf fam* **1** tit, titty, boob; **dar la t.,** to breast-feed; **niño de t.,** nursing baby; **quitar la t.,** to wean; *vulg* **es t. de monja** *or* **novicia,** it's delicious; *vulg* **¡vaya par de tetas!,** what a pair of tits! **2** *(de vaca)* udder.

tetamen *nm vulg* tits *pl*, boobs *pl*.

tetánico,-a *adj Med* tetanic.

tétano *nm,* **tetanos** *nm inv Med* tetanus.

tetepón,-ona *nm,f Méx* stocky person.

tetera *nf* teapot.

tetilla *nf* **1** *Anat* man's nipple. **2** *(de biberón)* (rubber) teat. **3 queso de t.,** type of Galician cheese.

tetina *nf* (rubber) teat.

tetona *adj & nf vulg* buxom (woman), busty (woman).

tetralogía *nf* tetralogy.

tetrarquía *nf* tetrarchy.

tetrasílabo,-a I *adj* tetrasyllabic, tetrasyllabical. **II** *nm* tetrasyllable.

tétrico,-a *adj* gloomy, dull, dismal.

tetuda *adj & nf vulg véase* **tetona**.

teutón,-ona I *adj* **1** *(alemán)* German. **2** *Hist* Teutonic. **II** *nm,f* **1** *(persona)* German. **2** *Hist (persona)* Teuton.

textil *adj & nm* textile.

texto *nm* text. ■ **libro de t.,** textbook.

textual *adj (gen)* textual; *(exacto)* literal; **en palabras textuales,** literally.

textura *nf* **1** *Tex (trama)* texture. **2** *(en minerales)* structure.

tez *nf* complexion.

ti *pron pers* you; **es para ti,** it's for you; **hazlo por ti,** do it for your own sake; **lo digo por ti,** I am thinking of you; **no sabía nada de ti,** I hadn't heard anything from *or* about you; **piensas demasiado en ti mismo,** you worry too much about yourself, you're always thinking about yourself; **por ti,** because of you.

tía *nf* **1** *(pariente)* aunt; **t. abuela,** great-aunt. **2** *fam (mujer)* girl, woman; **¡qué t.!,** one hell of a woman!; **¡qué t. más imbécil!,** what a stupid girl *or* woman!; *fig* **¡no hay tu t.!,** nothing doing!; **t. buena,** a bit of all right.

tiangue *nm CAm Per (mercado)* small market; *(puesto)* stall.

tianguis *nm Méx* market.

tiara *nf* tiara.

Tíber *n* **el T.,** the Tiber.

Tibet *n* **(el) T.,** Tibet.

tibetano,-a I *adj* Tibetan. **II** *nm, f (persona)* Tibetan. **III** *nm (idioma)* Tibetan.

tibí *nm Am* cufflinks *pl*.

tibia *nf Anat* tibia, shinbone.

tibiarse *vr CAm Ven fam* to become angry *or* irritated.

tibieza *nf (gen)* tepidity; *fig* lack of enthusiasm; *fig* **acogió la victoria cón t.,** he didn't show any enthusiasm about the victory.

tibio,-a *adj* **1** *(gen)* tepid, lukewarm; *fig* **la obra obtuvo una tibia acogida,** the play had a tepid reception; *fam* **poner t. a algn,** to pull sb to pieces. **2** *Am fam (enojado)* angry, irritated.

tiburón *nm* shark.

tic *nm (pl tiques)* **1** *Med* tic, twitch. ■ **t. nervioso,** nervous tic *or* twitch. **2** *fig (mania)* habit.

ticholo *nm Arg* small brick.

tictac *nm* tick-tock, ticking.

tiempo *nm* **1** *(gen)* time; **a t.,** in time; **a su (debido) t.,** in due course; **a un t., al mismo t.,** at the same time; **al poco t.,** soon afterwards; **antes de t.,** (too) early *or* soon; **con el t.,** in the course of time, with time; **con t.,** in advance; **corre el t.,** time goes by *or* flies; **¿cuánto t.?,** how long?; **¿cuánto t. hace?,** how long ago?; **dar t.,** to give time; **de un** *or* **algún t. a esta parte,** for some time now; **demasiado t.,** too long; **estar a t. de,** to still have time to; **ganar t.,** to save time; **hacer t.,** to kill time; **¿nos da t. de llegar?,** have we got (enough) time to get there?; **perder (el) t.,** to waste time; **sin perder t.,** at once; **¿qué tal andamos de t.?** how are we doing for time?; **t. atrás,** (some) time ago; **t. libre,** free time; **tómate el t. que quieras,** take your time; **y si no, al t.,** time will tell; *fig* **dar t. al t.,** to let matters take their course; *fig* **pasar** *or* **matar (el) t.,** to kill time. **2** *(época)* time, period, age; **a través de los tiempos,** through the ages; **de t. inmemorial,** from time immemorial; **en mis tiempos,** in my time; **en otro(s) tiempo(s),** formerly; **eran tiempos difíciles,** they were hard days; **¡qué tiempos aquéllos!,** those were the days! **3** *(temporada)* season; **fuera de t.,** *(fuera de temporada)* out of season; *fig (inoportunamente)* at the wrong moment. **4** *(meteorológico)* weather; **¿cómo está el t.?,** what's the weather like?; **hace buen/mal t.,** the weather is good/ bad; *fam fig* **t. de perros,** lousy weather. **5** *(edad)* age; **¿cuánto** *or* **qué t. tiene su niño?,** how old is your baby *or* child? **6** *Mús* movement, tempo, time. **7** *Dep (parte, período)* half. **8** *Ling (del verbo)* tense.

tienda *nf* **1** *(establecimiento comercial)* shop, *US* store; **ir de tiendas,** to go shopping. ■ **t. de comestibles, t. de ultramarinos,** grocer's, *US* grocery store. **2** *(de campaña)* **t. (de campaña),** tent.

tienta *nf* **a tientas,** by touch; **andar a tientas,** to feel one's way; **buscar (algo) a tientas,** to grope (for sth).

tiento *nm* **1** *(prudencia)* caution; *(tacto)* tact; **con t.,** tactfully. **2** *(de ciego)* stick. **3** *(pulso)* steady, hand. **4** *fam (trago)* swig; **dar** *or* **echar un t. a la botella,** to take a swig from the bottle.

tierno,-a *adj* **1** *(blando)* tender, soft. **2** *(reciente)* fresh; *(persona)* young; **pan t.,** fresh bread; **una tierna niña,** an innocent young girl. **3** *(cariñoso)* affectionate, loving; **¡qué niña más tierna!,** isn't she a darling! **4** *Chi Ecuad Guat (fruto)* green, unripe.

tierra *nf* **1** *(planeta)* earth, world. **2** *(superficie sólida)* land; **¡t. a la vista!,** land ahoy!; **tocar t.,** *Náut* to reach harbour; *Av* to touch down. **3** *Agr (terreno cultivado)* land, soil; **vivir de la t.,** to make a living from the land. **4** *(país)* country; **t. de nadie,** no-man's-land; **t. natal,** homeland. **5** *(suelo)* ground; **dar en t. con algo,** to drop *or* throw sth on the ground; *fig* **caer por t.,** to crumble; *fig* **echar** *or* **tirar por t. planes,** to spoil plans; *fig* **echar t. encima de un asunto,** to hush up an affair; *fig* **poner t. por medio,** to make oneself scarce; *fig* **t. trágame,** I wish the ground would open and swallow me up. **6** *Elec* earth, *US* ground.

tierral *nm Am* cloud of dust.

tieso,-a *adj* **1** *(rígido)* stiff, rigid; *(erguido)* upright, erect; **con las orejas tiesas,** with its ears pricked up; *fig* **quedarse t. de frío,** to be frozen stiff; *fam* **dejar t. a algn,** *(pasmado)* to leave sb astonished; *(muerto)* to do sb in. **2** *fam (engreído)* stiff, starchy, full of oneself. **3** *fig (saludable)* in good shape.

tiesto *nm* flowerpot.

tifoideo,-a *Med* **I** *adj* typhoid. **II** *nf* **(fiebre) tifoidea,** typhoid (fever).

tifón *nm Meteor* **1** *(huracán)* typhoon. **2** *(de agua)* waterspout.

tifus *nm inv Med* typhus (fever).

tigre *nm* **1** *Zool* tiger. **2** *fam (retrete)* loo; *fam* **oler a t.,** to stink. **3** *Am Zool (jaguar)* jaguar.

tigresa *nf* **1** *Zool* tigress. **2** *fig (mujer)* femme fatale.

tijera *nf (gen pl)* (pair of) scissors *pl*; **silla de t.,** folding chair.

tijereta *nf* **1** *Ent* carwig. **2** *Dep* scissors *pl*.

tijeretada *nf,* **tijeretazo** *nm* snip.

tila *nf* **1** *Bot (flor)* lime *or* linden blossom. **2** *(infusión)* lime *or* linden blossom tea.

tilbe *nm Arg* fishing trap.

tildar *vtr* to call, brand; **me tildó de bobo,** he called me stupid.

tilde *nm & f* **1** *Impr (de la ñ)* tilde; *(acento ortográfico)* written accent. **2** *fig (defecto)* fault, flaw.

tiliche *nm CAm Méx* **1** *(baratija)* trinket. **2** *(buhonería)* pedlar's ware, hawker's ware.

tilico,-a *adj Bol Méx* skinny.

tilín *nm* **1** *(sonido)* ting-a-ling; *fig* **José le hace t.,** she fancies José. **2** *Méx (en un momento)* **en un t.,** in a twinkling, in next to no time.

tilintar *vtr Am (cuerda)* to pull, tighten.

tilinte *adj CAm* elegant.

tilma *nf Méx* cotton blanket.

tilo *nm Bot* lime tree.

tiloso,-a *adj CAm* dirty, filthy.

timador,-a *nm, f* swindler, cheat.

timar *vtr* to swindle, cheat, trick; **me han timado un millón de pesetas,** I was cheated out of a million pesetas; **me timó dos duros en el cambio,** he short-changed me by ten pesetas.

timba *nf* **1** *fam (garito)* gambling den. **2** *fam (partida)* game *or* hand (of cards). **3** *Am (barriga hinchada)* swollen stomach.

timbal *nm* **1** *Mús* kettledrum; *(tamboril)* small drum. **2** *Culin (empanada)* timbale, meat or fish pie.

timbalero,-a *nm, f* kettle drummer.

timbrado,-a I *pp* de **timbrar. II** *adj* stamped; **papel t.,** *(sellado)* stamped paper; *(con membrete)* letter-headed stationery.

timbrar *vtr (carta)* to stamp, mark; *(documento)* to seal.

timbrazo *nm* loud *or* long ring; **dar un t.,** to ring the bell.

timbre *nm (de la puerta)* bell; **tocar el t.,** to ring the bell. **2** *(sello)* stamp, seal; *Fin* fiscal *or* revenue stamp. **3** *Mús (sonido)* timbre; **t. nasal,** twang.

timidez *nf* shyness, timidity.

tímido,-a *adj* shy, timid; **hizo un t. intento,** he made a half-hearted attempt.

timo¹ *nm (estafa)* swindle, fiddle, confidence trick; **dar el** *or* **un t.,** to cheat, swindle; **¡vaya t.!,** what a rip off!; *fam* **el t. de la estampita,** a con trick.

timo² *nm Anat* thymus.

timón *nm* **1** *Náut Av* rudder; *fig* **empuñar** *or* **llevar el t.,** to be at the helm. **2** *(del arado)* beam. **3** *Am Aut (volante)* steering wheel.

timonear *vi* to steer, be at the helm.

timonel *nm Náut* steersman, helmsman.

timorato,-a *adj* **1** *(tímido)* shy, timid. **2** *(mojigato)* prudish.

tímpano *nm* **1** *Anat* eardrum. **2** *Arquit* tympanum. **3** *Mús (timbal)* kettledrum; *(en orquesta)* timpani *pl*, timps *pl*.

tina *nf* **1** *(tinaja)* earthenware vat. **2** *(recipiente)* vat, tub. **3** *(bañera)* bath, bathtub.

tinaco *nm Am* large earthenware jar.

tinaja *nf* large earthenware jar.

tinerfeño,-a I *adj* of *or* from to Tenerife. **II** *nm,f* native *or* inhabitant of Tenerife.

tinglado *nm* **1** *(cobertizo)* shed. **2** *(tablado)* platform, raised floor. **3** *fig (embrollo)* mess; **¡menudo t. habéis armado!,** what a terrible mess you've made! **4** *fig (intriga)* intrigue; **¿qué t. os traéis?,** what's cooking then? **5** *fig (mundillo)* setup, racket; **conocer el t.,** to know the setup.

tinieblas *nfpl* **1** *(oscuridad)* darkness *sing*. **2** *fig (ignorancia)* ignorance *sing*, confusion *sing*; **estar en t. (sobre algo),** to be in the dark (about sth).

tino *nm* **1** *(prudencia)* (common) sense, good judgement; *(moderación)* moderation; **con t.,** wisely; **sacar de t. a algn,** to make sb lose their temper, make sb mad, **sin t.,** *(imprudentemente)* foolishly; *(con moderación)* immoderately. **2** *(puntería)* (good) aim; **tener buen t.,** to be a good shot.

tinta *nf* **1** *(gen)* ink; **escribir con t.,** to write in ink; *fig* **esto ha habido correr mucha t.,** much has been written about this; *fig* **recargar** *or* **cargar las tintas,** to exaggerate; *fig* **saber algo de buena t.,** to have got sth straight from the horse's mouth; *fig* **sudar t.,** to sweat blood. ■ **t. china,** Indian ink; **t. simpática,** invisible ink. **2 tintas,** colours, hues; *fig* **medias t.,** ambiguities, half measures.

tintar *vtr* to dye.

tinte *nm* **1** *(colorante)* dye; *(proceso)* dyeing. **2** *(tintorería)* dry-cleaner's; **llevar algo al t.,** to have sth dyed. **3** *fig (matiz)* shade, colouring, *US* coloring; **una novela con tintes religiosos,** a novel with religious overtones. **4** *fig (apariencia)* veneer, gloss; **un hombre con un t. de erudición,** a man with a touch of learning about him.

tinterillar *vtr CAm Col* to take to court.

tintero *nm* inkpot, inkwell; *fig* **se quedó en el t.,** it wasn't said.

tintinear *vi* **1** *(vidrio)* to clink, chink. **2** *(campanillas)* to jingle, tinkle.

tintineo *nm* **1** *(de vidrio)* clink, clinking, chink. **2** *(de campanillas)* jingling, ting-a-ling.

tinto I *adj* **1** *(vino)* red. **2** *(teñido)* dyed; *lit* **t. en sangre,** bloodstained. **II** *nm (vino)* red wine.

tintorera *nf (pez)* blue shark.

tintorería *nf* dry-cleaner's.

tintorero,-a *nm,f* dry-cleaner.

tintorro *nm fam* plonk, cheap red wine.

tintura *nf* **1** *(colorante)* dye. **2** *(proceso)* dyeing. **3** *Farm Quím* tincture. ■ **t. de yodo,** iodine.

tiña *nf* **1** *Med* tinea, ringworm. **2** *fig (mezquindad)* meanness, stinginess. **3** *fig (pobreza)* misery, poverty.

tiñoso,-a *adj* **1** *Med* scabby, mangey, mangy. **2** *fam (mezquino)* mean, stingy.

tío *nm* **1** *(pariente)* uncle; **mis tíos,** my uncle and aunt; **t. abuelo,** great-uncle. **2** *fam* fellow, bloke, *US* guy; **¡eres un t. (grande)!,** you're a great bloke *or* guy!; **t. bueno,** good-looking man; **¿vale, t.?,** O.K. mate?. *US* get it man?

tiovivo *nm* roundabout, merry-go-round.

tiparraco *nm fam* idiot, twerp.

tipazo *nm fam* good figure.

tipejo *nm fam* idiot, twerp.

típico,-a *adj* *(característico)* typical, characteristic; **eso es t. de María,** that's just like María; **¡lo t.!,** the same old thing! **2** *(de interés turístico)* traditional, picturesque; **un plato t.,** a traditional *or* local dish.

tipificación *nf* **1** *(normalización)* standardization. **2** *(caracterización)* typification.

tipificar *vtr* **1** *(normalizar)* to standardize. **2** *(caracterizar)* to typify.

tipismo *nm* local colour, picturesqueness.

tiple I *nm (voz)* treble, soprano **II** *nmf (persona)* soprano (singer)

tipo *nm* **1** *(clase)* type, kind; **todo t. de,** all kind *or* kinds of; **un nuevo t. de tren,** a new type of train. **2** *Fin* rate. ■ **t. bancario** *or* **de descuento,** bank rate; **t. de cambio/ interés,** rate of exchange/interest. **3** *fam (persona)* guy, fellow, bloke, *US* guy; **t. raro,** weirdo. **4** *Anat (de hombre)* build, physique; *(de mujer)* figure; **tiene buen t.,** *(hombre)* he's well-built; *(mujer)* she's got a good figure; *fig* **aguantar el t.,** to keep cool *or* calm; *fig* **dar el t.,** to fit a description *or* the bill; *fig* **jugarse el t.,** to risk one's neck. **5** *Impr* type.

tipografía *nf* typography.

tipográfico,-a *adj* typographic, typographical, **error t.,** printing error.

tipógrafo,-a *nm,f* typographer.

tíquet *nm (pl tíquets) (billete)* ticket; *(recibo)* receipt.

tiquismiquis fam I *nmf inv* fusspot; **ser un t.,** to be a fusspot. **II** *nmpl* **1** *(escrúpulos)* silly scruples, **andarse con t.,** to be fussy. **2** *(rencillas)* bickering *sing*; **andarse con t.,** to be squabbling.

tira I *nf* **1** *(banda, cinta)* strip; **t. de zapatos,** shoe strap. **2** *(de dibujos)* comic strip. **3** *fam* **la t.,** a lot, loads *pl*; **había la t. de gente,** there were hundreds of people; **hace la t. que no la he visto,** I haven't seen her for yonks **II** *nm Am fam (policía)* cop.

tirabuzón *nm* **1** *(rizo)* ringlet. **2** *(sacacorchos)* corkscrew.

tirachinas *nm inv* catapult, *US* slingshot.

tirada *nf* **1** *Impr (impresión)* printing; *(edición)* edition; **t. reducida,** limited edition. **2** *(distancia)* stretch; **hay una buena t. hasta el pueblo,** it's a good few miles to the village. **3** *(de serie)* (long) series *sing*; **de/en una t.,** in one go.

tirado,-a I *pp de* **tirar. II** *adj fam* **1** *(precio)* dirt cheap. **2** *(problema, asunto)* dead easy. **3** *(abandonado)* **dejar t. (a algn),** to let (sb) down.

tirador *nm* **1** *(persona)* shooter, marksman; **es un buen t.,** he is a good shot. **2** *(de puerta, cajón)* knob, handle, *(cordón)* bell pull. **3** *(tirachinas)* catapult, *US* slingshot.

tiraje *nm Impr* **1** *(impresión)* printing. **2** *(distribución)* circulation.

tiralíneas *nm inv* tracer, drawing *or* ruling pen

Tirana *n* Tirane, Tirana.

tiranía *nf* tyranny.

tiránico,-a *adj* tyrannic, tyrannical.

tiranización *nf* tyrannizing.

tiranizar *vtr* to tyrannize.

tirano,-a *nm,f* tyrant.

tirante I *adj (tenso)* tight, taut; *fig* **estar t. con algn,** to be at odds with sb; *fig* **una situación/relación t.,** a tense situation/relationship **II** *nm* **1** *Cost (gen pl)* strap **2** *Téc* brace, stay **3** *(de caballería)* trace. **4** *Arquit* tie (beam)

tirantez *nf* **1** *(tensión)* tightness, tautness **2** *fig (de una situación, relación)* tension, strain

tirar I *vtr* **1** *(echar)* to throw, fling; **¡tírame la pelota!,** throw me the ball!, **t. una moneda al aire,** to toss a coin. **2** *(dejar caer)* to drop; **cuidado, no lo tires,** be careful you don't drop it. **3** *(desechar)* to throw away, **estos zapatos están para tirarlos,** these shoes have had it, *fig* **t. (el) dinero,** to squander money. **4** *(derribar)* to knock down; *(líquido)* to spill; *(casa, árbol)* to pull down, **t. la puerta (abajo),** to smash the door in, **t. un vaso/una**

botella, to knock a glass/bottle over **5** *Impr* to print, **esta revista tira millones de ejemplares,** this magazine has a circulation of millions **6** *(hacer) (foto)* to take; *(linea, plano)* to draw **7** *(tiro)* to fire; *(cohete)* to launch; *(bomba)* to drop. **8** *(dar) (coz, patada)* to kick; *(pellizco)* to give; *(beso)* to blow; *Ftb (acarrear)* to take **9** *Am (acarrear)* to carry. **II** *vi* **1** *(cuerda, puerta)* to pull; **t. de una carreta,** to draw a cart; *fig* **tira y afloja,** give and take, compromise. **2** *(chimenea, estufa)* to draw; **esta estufa no tira,** this stove doesn't draw very well. **3** *(en juegos)* to be a player's move *or* turn; **tiras tú,** it's your move *or* turn. **4** *(funcionar)* to work, run; **¿aún tira tu coche?,** does your car still work? **5** *(persona)* to manage, get by *or* along; **ir tirando,** *(espabilarse)* to manage; *(tener buena salud)* to be okay, **yo tiraría con la mitad de lo que tú ganas,** I'd make do with half the money you earn **6** *(durar)* to last, **estas cortinas aún tirarán otro año,** these curtains will last another year; *fam* **a todo t.,** at the most *or* latest. **7** *(tender)* **t. a,** to tend towards; **tira a salado,** it's a bit (too) salty. **8** *(parecerse)* **t. a,** to take after; **tira a su madre,** he takes after his mother. **9** *(ir)* to go, turn; **tirad a la izquierda y luego todo derecho,** turn left and then go straight on; **¡venga, tira ya!,** come on, get going!; *fig* **t. para,** to be attracted to; **su hijo también tira para negociante,** his son is also attracted to business. **10** *(mantenerse)* **t. con,** to get by *or* along. **11** *(disparar)* to shoot, fire. **12** *(sacar, usar)* **t. de,** to pull out; **tiró de cartera y nos invitó a todos,** he pulled out his wallet and paid for all of us. **III tirarse** *vr* **1** *(lanzarse)* to throw *or* hurl oneself; **se tiró al agua de cabeza,** he dived into the water. **2** *(tumbarse)* to lie down **3** *(tiempo)* to spend; **me tiré una hora esperando,** I waited (for) a good hour **4** *vulg (fornicar)* to screw, fuck; **t. a algn,** to lay sb.

tirita® *nf* Elastoplast®, Band-aid®, plaster.

tiritar *vt (gen)* to shiver, shake, tremble; *(dientes)* to chatter

tiritera *nf,* **tiritona** *nf (gen)* shivering; *(de dientes)* chattering; **me dio la t.,** I started shivering

tiro *nm* **1** *(lanzamiento)* throw, **errar el t.,** to miss the mark, fail; *Ftb* **t. a gol,** shot at goal. **2** *(disparo, ruido)* shot; **a t.,** *(de arma)* within range; *(a mano)* within reach; **dar** *or* **pegar un t.,** to shoot, fire a shot; **pegarse un t.,** to shoot oneself; *fig* **le salió el t. por la culata,** it backfired on him, *fam fig* **me sentó como un t.,** *(hecho)* I felt awful; *(comida)* it made me feel really ill; *fam fig* **ni a tiros,** not for love or money. ■ **t. al blanco,** target shooting; **t. al plato,** trap-shooting; **t. con arco,** archery. **3** *(galería de tiro)* shooting gallery. **4** *Cost (de vestido)* shoulder width, *fig* **de tiros largos,** all dressed up **5** *(caballerías)* team, **animal de t.,** draught animal. **6** *(de chimenea)* draught, *US* draft, *Min* **t. de mina,** mineshaft. **7** *(de escaleras)* flight.

tiroides I *adj* thyroid **II** *nm inv* thyroid (gland).

Tirol *n* (el) T., Tyrol.

tirolés,-esa *adj & nm,f* Tyrolese, Tyrolean.

tirón *nm* pull, tug; **dar un t. de orejas,** to pull sb's ear; *fam* **de un t.,** in one go; *arg* **dar el t.,** to snatch sb's handbag.

tironear *vi Am* to pull, draw.

tirotear I *vtr* to shoot, snipe. **II tirotearse** *vr* to exchange shots.

tiroteo *nm* shooting, firing to and fro.

Tirreno *n* (Mar) T., Tyrrhenian Sea.

tirria *nf fam* dislike; **le tengo t.,** I dislike him, I can't stand him.

tisana *nf Culin* infusion, tisane.

tísico,-a *Med* **I** *adj* tubercular, consumptive. **II** *nm, f* consumptive.

tisis *nf inv Med* tuberculosis, consumption.

tisú *nm Tex* gold or silver lamé.

titán *nm Mil* titan.

titánico,-a *adj Mit* titanic.

titanio *nm Min* titanium.

titear *vtr SAm* to laugh *(de, at)*, make fun *(de, of)*.

títere *nm* **1** *(marioneta)* puppet, marionette; *fig* **no dejaron t. con cabeza,** no-one was spared; *fig* **no quedó t. con cabeza,** everything was upside down. **2** *fig (persona)* puppet, dupe.

titi *nmf fam (hombre)* young guy; *(mujer)* young girl; **¡hola, t.!,** ¡hello gorgeous!

titilante *adj* **1** *(temblor)* quivering. **2** *(luz)* flickering; *(estrella)* twinkling.

titilar *vi* **1** *(temblar)* to quiver. **2** *(luz)* to flicker; *(estrella)* to twinkle.

titileo *nm* **1** *(temblor)* quiver. **2** *(de luz)* flicker; *(de estrella)* twinkle.

titiritar *vi* to tremble, shiver.

titiritero,-a *nm, f* **1** *(que maneja títeres)* puppeteer. **2** *(acróbata ambulante)* travelling acrobat.

titubeante *adj* **1** *(indeciso)* hesitant. **2** *(que se tambalea)* staggering, shaky. **3** *(al hablar)* stammering

titubear *vi* **1** *(dudar)* to hesitate, waver. **2** *(tambalearse)* to stagger, shake, totter. **3** *(tartamudear)* to stammer.

titubeo *nm* **1** *(duda)* hesitation; **sin t.,** decisively. **2** *(temblor)* stagger, staggering, tottering. **3** *(tartamudeo)* stammering.

titulación *nf Educ* qualifications *pl.*

titulado,-a I *pp de* **titular. I** *adj* **1** *(de nombre)* called. **2** *Educ (licenciado)* graduate. **3** *Educ (diplomado)* qualified. **4** *Am (presunto)* supposed, presumed.

titular¹ I *adj* appointed, official; **jugador/juez t.,** offical player/judge. **II** *nmf (persona)* (office) holder; *Educ* **el. t de cátedra,** the professor; *Pol* **el t. de la cartera,** the minister. **III** *nm Prensa* headline.

titular² I *vtr (poner título)* to call; **¿cómo se titula?** what is it called? **II titularse** *vr* **1** *(tener título)* to be called. **2** *Educ* to graduate (**en,** in).

titularidad *nf* entitlement.

título *nm* **1** *(de obra)* title; *(de texto legal)* heading. **2** *Educ* degree; *(diploma)* certificate, diploma; **tener los títulos necesarios,** *Educ* to have the necessary qualifications; *(méritos)* to have the necessary qualities. **3** *(documento)* title; **t. de propiedad,** deeds. **4** *(noble)* noble person; **t. de nobleza,** nobility title. **5** *Prensa (titular)* headline. **6** *Com* bond, security; *(valor)* security.

tiza *nf* chalk; **una t.,** a piece of chalk.

tiznado,-a I *pp de* **tiznar. II** *adj* sooty, blackened.

tiznadura *nf* soot mark, smudge.

tiznar I *vtr* to blacken, soil with soot. **II tiznarse** *vr CAm Arg* to get drunk.

tizne *nm* soot.

tizón *nm* half-burnt stick, brand; *fig* **negro como un t.,** as black as soot *or* coal.

tlancuino,-a *adj Méx* missing a few teeth.

tlapalería *nf Méx* hardware shop.

tlemole *nm Méx* chilli with tomato sauce.

toa *nf Am* rope.

toalla *nf* towel; *fig* **arrojar** *or* **tirar la t.,** to throw in the towel.

toallero *nm* towel rack *or* rail.

Tobago *n* Tobago.

tobera *nf Téc* tuyère, twyer; *Av* nozzle.

tobillera *nf* ankle sock *or* support.

tobillo *nm Anat* ankle.

tobogán *nm* **1** *(para niños, mercancías)* slide, chute. **2** *(trineo bajo)* toboggan, sledge.

toca *nf (sombrero)* headdress; *(de monja)* wimple.

tocadiscos *nm inv* record player.

tocado¹ *nm* **1** *(peinado)* coiffure, hairdo. **2** *(prenda)* headdress.

tocado,-a² I *pp de* **tocar.** II *adj* **1** *(fruta)* bad, rotten. **2** *fam (perturbado)* crazy, touched; **t. de la cabeza,** touched, not all there. **3** *Dep* injured.

tocador *nm* **1** *(mueble)* dressing table; **artículos de t.,** toiletries. **2** *(habitación)* dressing room, boudoir; **t. de señoras,** powder room.

tocante a *loc adv* concerning, about; **en lo t. a ...,** with reference to ... .

tocar¹ I *vtr* **1** *(gen)* to touch; **por favor no t. la mercancía,** please do not handle the goods; **tócalo y verás que suave es,** feel it, you'll see how soft it is; *fig* **me has tocado el corazón,** you've touched my heart; *fig* **no ha tocado ni una coma,** he hasn't changed a single comma; *fam fig* **toca madera,** touch wood. **2** *(revolver)* to play with, mess about with; **no toques mis cosas,** stop fiddling with my things. **3** *(instrumento, canción)* to play; *(timbre)* to ring; *(puerta)* to knock; *(bocina)* to blow, honk; *(campanas)* to strike; *Mil (diana)* to sound; **t. a muerto,** to toll. **4** *Dep (diana)* to hit; *(en esgrima)* to touch. **5** *(mencionar)* to touch on; **mejor no t. el tema,** let's keep off the subject. II *vi* **1** *(corresponder)* to be one's turn; **¿a quién le toca jugar/fregar?,** whose turn is it to play/do the washing up? **2** *(caer en suerte)* to win; **¿a cuánto tocamos?,** how much did we win?; **le tocó el gordo** *or* **el primer premio,** he won the first prize; **le tocó la mili en Málaga,** he was posted to Málaga (for the military service). **3** *(tener que)* to have to; **nos tocó salir a arreglarlo,** we had to go out and fix it. **4** *(afectar)* to concern; **me toca muy de cerca,** I'm deeply affected by it; **por lo que a mí me toca,** as far as I am concerned. **5** *(ser parientes)* to be related *or* a relative of. **6** *Av Náut* to call (**en,** at), stop over (**en,** at). **7** *(entrar en contacto)* to touch; **t. con,** to be next to; **t. en,** to border on; *fig* **t. a su fin,** to be coming to an end. III **tocarse** *vr* **1** *(a uno mismo)* to touch oneself; **t. la nariz,** to pick one's nose. **2** *(una cosa con otra)* to touch each other; *fig* **los extremos se tocan,** the ends touch one another.

tocar² I *vtr (peinar)* to do the hair of. II **tocarse** *vr (cubrirse)* to cover one's head.

tocata I *nf Mús* toccata. II *nm fam* record player.

tocateja (a) *loc adv* cash; **pagar a t.,** to pay on the nail.

tocayo,-a *nm,f* namesake.

tocho *nm* **1** *(hierro)* iron ingot. **2** *fam (libro) (grande)* tome; *(aburrido)* boring book.

tocinería *nf* pork butcher's.

tocino *nm Culin* lard. ■ **t. ahumado,** smoked bacon; **t. entreverado,** streaky bacon; **t. de cielo,** sweet made with egg yolk.

tocólogo,-a *nm Med* tocologist, obstetrician.

tocón¹ *nm Bot* stump.

tocón,-ona² *nm,f fam* groper; **Jaimito es un t.,** Jaimito's got roving hands.

tocuyo *nm Am Tex* coarse cotton cloth.

todavía *adv* **1** *(a pesar de ello)* still; **¿y t. te quejas?,** and you're still unsatisfied? **2** *(tiempo)* yet, still; **no mires t.,** don't look yet; **t. la quiere,** he still loves her; **t. no,** not yet. **3** *(para reforzar)* even, still; **esto t. te gustará más,** you'll like *or* enjoy this even more; **t. más/menos,** even more/less.

todito,-a *adj fam* all.

todo,-a I *adj* **1** *(sin excluir nada)* all; **t. el mundo,** (absolutely) everybody; *fam* **t. quisqui** *or* **Cristo** *or* **Dios,** every Tom, Dick and Harry. **2** *(entero)* complete, thorough; **es toda una mujer,** she is every inch a woman. **3** *(igual)* (exactly) like; **es t. su padre,** he's the image of his father. **4** *todos, (cada)* every; **t. los martes,** every Tuesday. II *nm* **1** *(totalidad)* whole. III *pron* **1** *(sin excluir nada)* all, everything; **ante t.,** first of all; **con t.,** in spite of everything; **del t.,** completely; **después de t.,** after all; **eso es t.,** that's all, that's it; **estar en t.,** to be really with it; **hay de t.,** there are all sorts; **lo sé t.,** I know all about it; **t. lo contrario,** quite the contrary *or* opposite; **t. lo más,** at the most; **t. son desgracias para nosotros,** we have nothing but misfortune; *fam* **fue t.**

uno, it all happened at once; *fam* **no tenerlas todas consigo,** not to be all there; *fam* **ser t. uno,** to be all the same (thing). **2** *(cualquiera)* anybody; **t. aquél** *or* **el que quiera,** anybody who wants (to). **3** *todos, (cada uno)* everybody; **t. salieron perdiendo,** they all came off worse. IV *adv* completely, totally; **volvió t. sucio,** he was all dirty when he got back.

todopoderoso,-a *adj* all-powerful, almighty; **el T.,** the Almighty.

toga *nf* **1** *(de magistrado)* gown, robe. **2** *Hist* toga.

togado,-a I *adj* **1** *(magistrados)* robed. **2** *Hist* togaed. II *nm* gentleman of the robe, lawyer.

Togo *n* Togo.

togolés,-esa *adj & nm,f* Togolese.

toilette *nf* toilet, toilette; **hacerse la t.,** to make oneself up.

toisón *nm* fleece; **Orden del T. de Oro,** Order of the Golden Fleece.

Tokio *n* Tokyo.

toldería *nf Am* Indian camp.

toldillo *nm* **1** *(toldo pequeño)* small awning. **2** *Am (mosquitera)* mosquito *or* fly net.

toldo *nm* **1** *(cubierta)* awning; *(de camión)* tilt, canvas; *(en la playa)* sunshade. **2** *Am (cabaña)* tent, teepee.

toledano,-a I *adj* of *or* from Toledo; *fam* **pasar una noche toledana,** to toss and turn all night. II *mn, f* native *or* inhabitant of Toledo.

tolerable *adj* tolerable.

tolerado,-a I *pp de* **tolerar.** II *adj* allowed, tolerated; *Cin Teat* **espectáculo t. para menores,** entertainment suitable for children.

tolerancia *nf (gen)* tolerance; *(resistencia)* resistance.

tolerante *adj* tolerant, lenient.

tolerar *vtr* to tolerate; *(inconvenientes)* to stand; *(gente)* to put up with; *(comida, bebida)* to take; *(peso)* to bear; **no tolero el desorden,** I can't stand untidiness.

toma *nf* **1** *(acción)* taking. ■ **t. de agua,** outlet, tap; **t. de aire,** intake, inlet; *Elect* **t. de corriente,** plug, socket; **t. de posesión,** takeover; **t. de tierra,** *Elec* earth, *US* ground; *Av* landing, touchdown. **2** *Med* dose. **3** *Mil* capture. **4** *(grabación)* recording. **5** *Cin* take, shot. **6** *Am (acequia)* channel; irrigation ditch.

tomado,-a I *pp de* **tomar.** II *adj* **1** *(voz)* hoarse; **tener la voz tomada,** to have a hoarse voice. **2** *Am (borracho)* drunk.

tomadura *nf* taking; *fam fig* **t. de pelo,** *(engaño)* hoax; *(burla)* tease; *(timo)* rip-off.

tomar I *vtr* **1** *(coger)* to take; **me tomó de la cintura,** he put his hands round my waist; **toma,** here (you are); **toma la primera a la derecha,** take the first to the right; **t. decisiones,** to make *or* take decisions; **t. a algn de la mano,** to hold sb's hand; **t. el autobús/tren,** to catch the bus/train; **t. el sol,** to sunbathe; **t. la palabra,** to speak; *Av* **t. tierra,** to land; **t. un taxi,** to take a taxi; *fig* **t. las de Villadiego,** to beat it; *fam* **¡toma!,** *(sorpresa)* fancy that!; *(enfado)* it serves you right!; *fam* **¡toma castaña!,** take that!; *fam* **tomarla con algn,** to have it in for sb; *fam fig* **toma y daca,** give and take. **2** *(comer, beber)* to have; **¿qué tomas?,** what would you like (to have)? **3** *Mil* to take; **t. una plaza,** to capture a position. **4** *(adquirir)* to acquire; **t. afecto** *or* **cariño a,** to become fond of; **t. la costumbre de,** to get into the habit of. **5** *(aceptar)* to accept; **lo toma** *or* **lo deja,** take it or leave it. **6** *(entender)* to take; **t. algo a mal,** to take sth badly; **t. en serio/broma,** to take seriously/as a joke. **7** *(considerar)* to take (por, for); **me tomó por mi hermano,** he took me for my brother. II *vi (encaminarse)* to go; **t. hacia la derecha,** to turn right. III **tomarse** *vr* **1** *(cogerse)* to take; **t. la molestia de,** to take the trouble to; **t. las cosas con calma,** to take it easy; **tómalo con calma** *fam* **no te lo tomes así,** don't take it like that. **2** *(comer)* to eat; *(beber)* to drink; **¿te has tomado la medicina?,** have you taken your medicine?

tomate *nm* 1 *Bot* tomato; **salsa de t.**, *(de lata)* tomato sauce; *(de botella)* ketchup, catsup; *fig* **ponerse como un t.**, to go as red as a beetroot. 2 *fam (jaleo)* fuss, commotion; **se armó un buen t.**, there was a right to-do. 3 *fam (dificultad)* sang, catch; **parece fácil pero tiene t.**, it looks easy but there's a snag in it.

tomatera *nf Bot* tomato plant.

tomavistas *nm inv* cine *or US* movie camera.

tómbola *nf* tombola.

tomillo *nm Bot* thyme.

tomo *nm* volume; *fam* **de t. y lomo,** utter, out-and-out.

ton *nm* **sin t. ni son,** without rhyme or reason.

tonada *nf* 1 *Mús* tune, song. 2 *Am (acento)* accent.

tonadilla *nf Mús* ditty, little tune.

tonadillero,-a *nm,f* ditty writer *or* singer.

tonalidad *nf* tonality.

tonel *nm* barrel, cask; *fam fig* **como un t.,** as fat as a pig.

tonelada *nf* ton; **t. métrica,** tonne, metric ton.

tonelaje *nm* tonnage.

tonelería *nf* 1 *(fabricación)* cooperage, barrel-making. 2 *(tienda)* barrel shop.

tonelero,-a I *adj* barrel, cask. II *nm, f* cooper, barrel-maker.

tongo *nm Box* fix; **hacer t.,** to rig; **hubo t. en el combate,** the fight was fixed.

tónico,-a I *adj* 1 *Ling* tonic, stressed. 2 *Mús & Med* tonic. II *nm Med* tonic; *(cosméticos)* skin tonic. III *nf* 1 *(tendencia)* tendency, trend; **tónica general,** overall trend. 2 *(bebida)* tonic (water). 3 *Mús* tonic.

tonificante *adj* invigorating.

tonificar *vtr* to tone up, invigorate.

tonillo *nm* 1 *(sonsonete)* drone, monotone. 2 *(deje)* accent, lilt. 3 *(retintín)* sarcastic tone.

tono *nm* tone; **a t. con,** in tune *or* harmony with; **bajar de t.** *or* **el t.,** to lower one's voice; *fig* to tone down an argument; **dar el t.,** to set the tone; **subir de t.** *or* **el t.,** to speak louder; *Mús* **t. mayor/menor,** major/minor key; **un t. alto/bajo,** a high/low pitch; *fig* **dar (buen) t.,** to give class *or* prestige; *fig* **darse t.,** to put on airs; *fig* **de (buen) t.,** *(elegante)* stylish; *(cortés)* gentlemanly; *fig* **de mal t.,** vulgar; *fig* **fuera de t.,** inappropiate, out of place; *fig* **sin venir a t.,** for no good reason; *fig* **usa otro t. conmigo,** use another tone with me.

tontada *nf fam* 1 *(bobada)* silly thing, nonsense. 2 *(insignificancia)* trifle.

tontaina *fam* I *adj* foolish, silly. II *nmf* fool, nitwit.

tontear *vi* 1 *(decir tonterías)* to act the clown, fool about. 2 *(galantear)* to flirt.

tontería *nf* 1 *(calidad de tonto)* stupidity, silliness. 2 *(dicho, hecho)* silly *or* stupid thing; **decir tonterías,** to talk nonsense; **déjate de tonterías,** be serious. 3 *(insignificancia)* trifle; **cómprale una t.,** get her a little something.

tonto,-a I *adj* silly, dumb; **¡qué t (soy)!,** silly me!; *fam* **ponerse t.,** to get stroppy. II *nm,f* fool, idiot; **hacer el t.,** to act the fool; **hacerse el t.,** to play dumb; **t. de remate** *or* **de capirote,** prize idiot. III *nm Am* jemmy.

tontuna *nf fam* silliness.

topacio *nm Min* topaz.

topar I *vi* to bump; **t. con algo,** to come across sth; **t. con algn,** to bump into sb; **t. con una dificultad,** to come up against a difficulty; **t. con un problema,** to run into a problem. II **toparse** *vr (encontrarse gente)* to meet; *(dificultades)* to bump up with, encounter; **se toparon con la policía,** they ran into the police.

tope I *adj* 1 *(máximo)* top, maximum; **fecha t.,** deadline; **precio t.,** top price. 2 *arg (fantástico)* fab, super; **¡t.!,** smashing! II *nm* 1 *(límite)* limit, end; *fig* **estar hasta los topes,** to be full up; *fam* **a t.,** *(al máximo)* flat out; *(genial)*

terrific. 2 *Téc* stop, check; **t. de puerta,** doorstop. 3 *Ferroc* buffer, bumper, bumping post. 4 *Am (encuentro)* chance meeting. III *adv arg* incredibly; **t. difícil,** really difficult.

topetada *nf*, **topetazo** *nm* butt, bump; **al caernos nos dimos una t.,** we fell and bumped into each other.

tópico,-a I *adj Med Farm* for external use; **uso t.,** external use. II *nm* commonplace, cliché.

topo *nm Zool* mole; *fig* **más ciego que un t.,** as blind as a bat.

topografía *nf Geog* topography.

topográfico,-a *adj Geog* topographic, topographical.

topógrafo,-a *nm,f Geog* topographer.

toponimia *nf Ling* toponymy. 2 *(conjunto de nombres)* place names *pl.*

toponímico,-a *adj* toponymic, toponymical.

topónimo *nm* place name.

toque I *nm* 1 *(acto)* touch; **dar el último t.,** to put the finishing touch; **t. de atención,** warning (note); *Ftb* **t. de balón,** ball control; *fam* **dar un t. a algn,** *(llamar)* to call sb to task; *(llamar la atención)* to call sb's attention. 2 *(sonido)* *(de campanas)* peal, pealing, ringing; *(de trompetas)* blare, sounding; *(de sirena)* hoot; *(de claxon)* honk. ■ **t. de alarma,** alarm signal; *fig* warning; *Mil* **t. de diana,** reveille; **t. de difuntos,** death knell; **t. de queda,** curfew; *Mil* **t. de retreta,** tattoo.

toquetear *vtr* 1 *(manosear)* to fiddle with, finger. 2 *(acariciar)* to fondle.

toqueteo *nm* 1 *(manoseo)* fiddling, handling. 2 *(caricias)* fondling, petting.

toquilla *nf* 1 *(pañuelo)* (knitted) shawl. 2 *Am (sombrero)* straw hat.

torácico,-a *adj Anat* thoracic; **caja torácica,** chest cavity.

tórax *nm Anat* thorax.

torbellino *nm* 1 *(de viento)* whirlwind. 2 *fig (confusión)* whirl, turmoil; **un t. de ideas,** a brainstorm. 3 *(persona)* whirlwind; **eres un t.,** you're a real live wire.

torcaz *adj Orn* **paloma t.,** ringdove, wood pigeon.

torcedura *nf* 1 *(acción)* twist, twisting. 2 *Med* sprain.

torcer I *vtr* 1 *(gen) (cuerda, hilo)* to twist; *Med* to sprain; *fig* **no dar su brazo a t.,** not to give in; *fig* **t. el gesto,** to look cross. 2 *(doblar) (metal)* to bend; *(madera)* to warp; *fig* **t. la esquina,** to turn the corner. 3 *(inclinar) (cuadro)* to slant; **está torcido,** it's crooked *or* lopsided. 4 *(desviar) (el curso)* to change; *(significado)* to distort; *fig (a algn)* to corrupt, pervert; **t. la vista,** to look away. II *vi* to turn (left *or* right). III **torcerse** *vr* 1 *(doblarse)* to twist, bend. 2 *Med (tobillo, mano)* to sprain. 3 *(plan)* to fall through. 4 *(empeorar)* to take a turn for the worse.

torcido,-a I *pp* de **torcer.** II *adj* 1 *(que no es recto)* twisted; **lleva la corbata torcida,** his tie is crooked. 2 *(madera)* warped; *(metal)* bent. 3 *Med* sprained, strained. 4 *(ladeado)* slanted, crooked, lopsided. 5 *CAm (desgraciado)* unlucky.

tordo,-a I *adj* dapple-grey. II *nm Orn* thrush.

torear I *vtr Taur* to fight; *fam* **t. a algn,** to tease *or* confuse sb; *fam* **t. un asunto,** to tackle a matter skilfully. II *vi Taur* to fight; **torea bien,** he is a good bullfighter.

toreo *nm* bullfighting; *fam* **¡se acabó el t.!,** no more fooling around!

torero,-a I *adj Taur* of *or* relating to bullfighting. II *nm,f* bullfighter, matador. III *nf (chaquetilla)* bolero (jacket); *fam fig* **saltarse algo a la t.,** to ignore sth completely, pay no heed to sth.

tormenta *nf Meteor* storm.

tormento *nm* 1 *(tortura)* torture, torment. 2 *(padecimiento)* intense suffering, tribulation; *fam* **ser un t.,** to be a real torture.

tormentoso,-a *adj* stormy.

tornado *nm Meteor* tornado.

tornar *fml* **I** *vtr* **1** *(devolver)* to give back, return. **2** *(convertir)* to transform, turn; **tornó el agua en vino,** he turned the water into wine. **II** *vi* **1** *(regresar)* to return, go back; **t. en sí,** to regain consciousness. **2** *(volver a hacer)* to do over, repeat; **t. a leer,** to read again. **III tornarse** *vr* to become, turn; **se tornó fiero,** it became wild.

tornas *nfpl* **volver las t.,** to turn the tables.

tornasol *nm* **1** *Bot* sunflower. **2** *(colorante)* litmus. **3** *(irisación)* iridescense.

tornasolado,-a *adj* iridescent.

torneado,-a **I** *pp de* **tornear.** **II** *adj* **1** *Téc* lathed, turned on the lathe. **2** *(cuerpo)* shapely, with soft curves. **III** *nm Téc* turning.

tornear *vtr Téc* to turn.

torneo *nm* **1** *Hist* tourney, joust. **2** *Dep* tournament, competition.

tornero,-a *nm,f* turner, lathe operator.

tornillo *nm* screw, bolt; *fam fig* **apretarle los tornillos a algn,** to put the screws on sb; *fam fig* **te falta un t.,** you're got a screw loose. ■ **t. de banco,** vice, *US* vise, clamp; **t. de orejas,** thumbscrew.

torniquete *nm* **1** *(gen)* turnstile. **2** *Med* tourniquet.

torno *nm* **1** *Téc* lathe; **t. de alfarero,** potter's wheel. **2** *(elevador)* winch, windlass. **3** *(en convento)* revolving window. **4** **en t. a,** *(alrededor de)* around; *(acerca de)* about.

toro *nm Zool* bull; *Taur* **ir a los toros,** to go to a bullfight; *fig* **ver los toros desde la barrera,** to stand in the wings; *fam* **estar hecho un t.,** to be a strapping man; *fam* **fuerte como un t.,** as strong as an ox. ■ *Taur* **t. bravo** *or* **de lidia,** fighting bull.

toronja *nf Bot* grapefruit.

torozón *nm Am* bit.

torpe *adj* **1** *(sin habilidad)* clumsy. **2** *(poco inteligente)* dim, thick. **3** *(movimiento)* slow, awkward.

torpedear *vtr Mil* to torpedo.

torpedero,-a *Mil* **I** *adj* torpedo. **II** *nm* torpedo boat.

torpedo *nm* **1** *Mil* torpedo. **2** *Pesca* **(pez) t.,** electric ray.

torpeza *nf* **1** *(física)* clumsiness, ungainliness. **2** *(mental)* dimness, stupidity. **3** *(de movimiento)* slowness, heaviness. **4** *(error)* blunder.

torpón,-ona *adj fam* **1** *(falto de habilidad)* clumsy. **2** *(tonto)* dim, stupid.

torrar *vtr* to toast.

torre *nf* **1** *(gen)* tower; *fig* **t. de marfil,** ivory tower. **2** *Mil Náut* turret. ■ **t. de vigía,** crow's nest. **3** *Constr* (country) house, villa. **4** *Ajedrez* rook, castle.

torrefacto,-a *adj* torrified, roasted; **café t.,** high roast coffee.

torrencial *adj* torrential.

torrente *nm* **1** *(de agua)* mountain stream, torrent; *Anat* **t. sanguíneo** *or* **circulatorio,** bloodstream. **2** *fig (abundancia)* flood, stream; **t. en voz,** loud strong voice.

torreón *nm Mil* fortified tower.

torrero *nm* lighthouse keeper.

torreta *nf* **1** *Arquit* turret, small tower. **2** *Mil (de tanque)* turret; *Náut (de submarino)* conning tower.

torrezno *nm Culin* rasher of fried bacon.

tórrido,-a *adj* torrid.

torrija *nf Culin* French toast.

tórsalo *nm CAm Ent (larva)* larva; *(gusano)* worm.

torsión *nf* **1** *(torcedura)* twist, twisting. **2** *Téc* torsion; **momento de t.,** torque.

torso *nm* **1** *Anat* torso. **2** *Arte* bust.

torta *nf* **1** *Culin* cake; *fig* **te va a costar la t. un pan,** you'll lose more than you'll gain. **2** *fam (golpe)* slap, punch; **pegarse una t.,** to get a bump; *fig* **ni t.,** not a thing. **3** *fam (borrachera)* binge; **coger** *or* **pillar una t.,** to get plastered.

tortazo *nm fam* **1** *(bofetada)* slap, punch. **2** *(golpe)* whack, thump; **darse un t.,** to crash.

tortícolis *nf inv* stiff neck, wryneck, crick in the neck.

tortilla *nf Culin* **1** *(egg)* omelette, *US* omelet; **t. (a la) francesa,** (plain) omelette; *fig* **se volvió la t.,** the tables were turned. **2** *CAm Méx* tortilla.

tortillera *nf vulg* dyke, lesbian.

tortita *nf Culin* pancake.

tórtola *nf Orn* dove.

tórtolos *nmpl fam* lovebirds, lovers.

tortuga *nf Zool (de tierra)* tortoise, *US* turtle; *(de mar)* turtle; *fig* **a paso de t.,** at a snail's pace.

tortuosidad *nf* tortuousness.

tortuoso,-a *adj* tortuous.

tortura *nf* **1** *(tormento)* torture. **2** *(padecimiento)* intense suffering, agony.

torturador,-a *nm,f* torturer.

torturar **I** *vtr* to torture. **II torturarse** *vr* to torture oneself.

torvo,-a *adj* grim, fierce.

tos *nf* cough, coughing. ■ *Med* **t. ferina,** whooping cough.

Toscana *n* Tuscany.

toscano,-a *adj & nm,f* Tuscan.

tosco,-a *adj* **1** *(basto)* rustic, rough. **2** *(persona)* uncouth.

tosedera *nf SAm* cough.

toser *vi* to cough; *fig* **no hay quien le tosa,** he's one step ahead of everyone.

tosquedad *nf* roughness, crudeness.

tostada *nf* (slice of) toast; *fam* **olerse la t.,** to smell a rat.

tostadero *nm* roaster.

tostado,-a **I** *pp de* **tostar.** **II** *adj* **1** *(pan)* toasted; *(café)* roasted. **2** *(moreno)* tanned, brown. **3** *(marrón)* brown. **4** *Méx (molesto)* upset.

tostador,-a *nm,f (de pan)* toaster; *(de café)* roaster.

tostar **I** *vtr* **1** *Culin (pan)* to toast; *(café)* to roast; *(carne, pescado)* to brown; *fig (la piel)* to tan. **2** *Am (zurrar)* to tan. **II tostarse** *vr* to turn or get brown.

tostón *nm* **1** *Culin (pan frito)* crouton. **2** *fam (tabarra)* bore, drag; **dar el t.,** to get on everybody's nerves; **este libro es un t.,** this book is a drag.

total **I** *adj (completo)* total, overall, complete; *Med* **anestesia t.,** general anaesthetic; *fam* **es un follón t.,** it's an utter mess. **II** *nm* **1** *(todo)* whole; **el t. del ejército,** the whole army; **en t.,** in all. **2** *Mat* total, sum. **III** *adv* so, in short; **¿t. para qué?,** what's the point anyhow?; **t. que ...,** so ..., to make a long story short ...; **t., tampoco te hará caso,** he won't listen to you, anyway.

totalidad *nf* whole, totality; **en su t.,** as a whole.

totalitario,-a *adj* totalitarian.

totalitarismo *nm* totalitarianism, dictatorship.

totalitarista *adj* totalitarian.

totalizar **I** *vtr* to total. **II** *vi* to amount to; **¿cuánto totalizan los gastos?,** what do the expenses come to?

tótem *nm (pl tótems or tótemes)* totem.

totorecada *nf CAm* silly thing.

totoreco,-a *adj CAm* stunned, dizzy.

tournée *nf Teat* tour.

toxicidad *nf* toxicity.

tóxico,-a **I** *adj* toxic, poisonous. **II** *nm* toxicant, poison.

toxicología *nf Med* toxicology.

toxicológico,-a *adj Med* toxicologic, toxicological.

toxicólogo,-a *nm,f Med* toxicologist.

toxicomanía *nf Med* drug addiction.

toxicómano,-a *Med* **I** *adj* addicted to drugs. **II** *nm* drug addict.

toxina *nf* toxin.

tozudez *nf* obstinacy, stubbornness.

tozudo,-a *adj* obstinate, stubborn, headstrong.

traba *nf* **1** *(sujeción) (de rueda)* chock; *(de caballo)* hobble. **2** *(enlace)* bond, tie. **3** *fig (obstáculo)* hindrance, obstacle, shackle; **poner trabas,** to raise objections.

trabado,-a I *pp de* **trabar. II** *adj* **1** *(sujeto)* fastened. **2** *(salsa)* smooth. **3** *(atascado)* jammed. **4** *(coherente)* coherent.

trabajado,-a I *pp de* **trabajar. II** *adj* elaborate, carefully worked.

trabajador,-a I *adj* *(que trabaja)* working. **2** *(laborioso)* hard-working; **un pueblo t.,** an industrious nation. **II** *nm, f* worker, labourer, *US* laborer.

trabajar I *vtr* **1** *(dar forma)* to work (on); **t. el hierro/la madera,** to work iron/wood; **t. la tierra,** to till the land; *Culin* **t. una pasta,** to knead the dough. **2** *(intensificar el trabajo)* to work on; **hay que trabajarlo más,** we need to put more work into it; **tienes que t. el francés,** you'll have to work harder in French. **3** *fam (convencer)* to (try to) persuade; **t. a algn para que haga algo,** to talk sb into doing sth. **II** *vi* **1** *(gen)* to work; **trabaja mucho,** he works hard; **t. de camarera,** to work as a waitress; **t. en,** to work at *or* in; **t. por horas,** to be paid by the hour; **trabajo de profesor,** I'm a teacher; *fam* **t. como un condenado** *or* **una bestia,** to slave away; *fam* **t. en balde,** to work in vain. **2** *Cin Teat* to perform, act; **¿quién trabaja en esa película?,** who's in that film? **3** *Constr (soportar)* to be under stress; **esta viga trabaja mal,** this beam is not doing its job properly.

trabajo *nm* **1** *(ocupación)* work; **ir al t.,** to go to work. ■ **t. a destajo,** piecework; **t. de equipo,** teamwork; **t. de media jornada,** part-time job; **t. eventual,** casual labour; **trabajos forzados** *or* **forzosos,** hard labour; **t. intelectual,** brainwork; **t. por turno(s),** shiftwork; *Educ* **trabajos manuales,** arts and crafts; *fam fig* **t. de chinos,** very intricate, tedious work. **2** *(tarea)* task, job; **ha hecho un buen t.,** she's done a good job. **3** *Educ* report, paper; **mañana tengo que presentar un t.,** I have to hand in a report tomorrow. **4** *(esfuerzo)* effort; **con mucho t.,** with great effort; **cuesta t. creerlo,** it's hard to believe; **puedes ahorrarte el t.,** you can save yourself the trouble. **5** *(empleo)* employment, job; **estoy sin t.,** I'm out of work.

trabajoso,-a *adj* **1** *(laborioso)* hard, laborious; *(difícil)* difficult. **2** *Am (molesto)* bothersome.

trabalenguas *nm inv* tongue twister.

trabar I *vtr* **1** *(sujetar) (piezas móviles)* to lock, fasten; *(piezas sueltas)* to join, unite; *(mecanismo)* to jam; *(persona)* to shackle; *(las patas de un caballo)* to hobble. **2** *(impedir)* to hinder; *(un plan)* to obstruct. **3** *Culin (salsas)* to thicken. **4** *fig (dar principio)* to start; **t. amistad/conversación,** to strike up a friendship/conversation. **II trabarse** *vr* **1** *(cuerdas)* to get tangled up. **2** *(mecanismo)* to jam, seize up; *fig* **se le trabó la lengua,** he got tonguetied.

trabazón *nf* **1** *(ensamblaje)* joining, assembly. **2** *(enlace)* bond, tie; *fig (de ideas)* link, coherence.

trabilla *nf (de pantalón)* belt loop; *(de chaqueta)* half belt.

trabucar I *vtr* to jumble *or* mix up. **II trabucarse** *vr* to get all mixed up.

trabucazo *nm* shot from a blunderbuss.

trabuco I *nm (arma)* blunderbuss. **II** *adj Méx (pequeño)* small; *(estrecho)* narrow.

traca *nf* string of firecrackers, jumping jack.

trácala *nf Am* trick.

tracción *nf Téc* traction; *Aut* **t. delantera/ trasera,** front-/rear-wheel drive; *Aut* **t. en las cuatro ruedas,** four-wheel drive.

tractor,-a I *adj Téc* driving. **II** *nm Aut* tractor.

tractorista *nmf* tractor driver.

tradición *nf* tradition.

tradicional *adj* traditional; **es lo t.,** it's the traditional thing to do.

tradicionalismo *nm* **1** *Filos Rel* traditionalism. **2** *Pol* radical conservatism.

tradicionalista *adj & nmf* **1** *Filos Rel* traditionalist. **2** *Pol* radical conservative.

traducción *nf* translation. ■ **t. automática,** machine translation; **t. directa/inversa,** translation from/into a foreign language; **t. simultánea,** simultaneous translation.

traducir I *vtr* **1** *(gen)* to translate (a, into). **2** *(expresar)* to express, show. **II traducirse** *vtr* to result in; **la infección se traduce en fiebre,** the infection results in a temperature.

traductor,-a I *adj* translating. **II** *nm, f* translator. ■ **t. jurado,** sworn translator.

traer I *vtr* **1** *(gen)* to bring; **trae,** give it to me; **t. (buena) suerte,** to bring good luck; *fig* **t. de cabeza a algn,** to drive sb mad. **2** *(llevar puesto)* to wear; **traía un traje negro,** he was wearing a black suit. **3** *(llevar consigo)* to carry; **¿qué traes en esa bolsa?,** what are you carrying in that bag?; *fig* **¿qué se traen entre manos?,** what are they up to? **4** *(causar)* to cause; **traerá como consecuencia ...,** it will result in ...; **t. consecuencias,** to have serious consequences; **t. consigo,** to bring about; **t. problemas,** to cause problems. **5** *(llevar noticias)* to feature, carry; **¿qué trae hoy 'El País'?,** what's in 'El País' today? **II traerse** *vr* **1** *(llevar consigo)* to bring along; **tráete a tu hermana,** bring your sister along. **2** **traérselas,** *(ser de cuidado)* to be really hard *or* difficult; **el profesor de latín se las trae,** the Latin teacher is very hard on us.

traficante *nmf (gen)* dealer, trader; *(productos ilegales)* trafficker. ■ **t. de drogas,** drug trafficker *or* pusher.

traficar *vi (gen)* to deal; *(ilegalmente)* to traffic; **t. con drogas,** to traffic in drugs.

tráfico *nm* **1** *Aut* traffic. ■ **accidente de t.,** road *or US* car accident; **t. rodado,** road traffic. **2** *Com* traffic, trade. ■ **t. de drogas,** drug traffic.

tragacanto *nm Bot* tragacanth.

tragaderas *nfpl fam* throat *sing*; *fig* **tener buenas t.,** *(ser crédulo)* to be gullible; *(tener pocos escrúpulos)* to be too much of a conformist.

tragadero *nm* drain.

tragaldabas *nmf inv fam* glutton, pig.

tragaleguas *nmf inv fam* keen walker.

tragaluz *nm Arquit* skylight.

tragamillas *nmf inv fam* keen walker.

tragaperras *nf inv (máquina) t.,* slot machine.

tragar I *vtr* **1** *(ingerir)* to swallow; *fig* **deseaba que lo tragara la tierra,** he wished the earth would swallow him up. **2** *fam (engullir)* to gobble up, tuck away; **traga que da gusto,** he really puts it away. **3** *fig (absorber)* to swallow up, absorb; *(consumir)* to eat up; **t. millas,** to burn up the miles. **4** *fig (soportar) (persona)* to stand, stomach; *(suceso)* to stand for, put up with. **5** *fig (creer)* to believe, swallow; **t. la píldora,** to fall for it, swallow it. **6** *fig (disimular)* to hide, keep to oneself; **decidió t. lo que pensaba de él,** he decided not to show what he thought about him. **II** *vi* to swallow (up); *(persona)* he finds it hard to swallow. **III tragarse** *vr* **1** *(ingerir)* to swallow. **2** *(absorber)* to swallow up, absorb; *(consumir)* to eat up. **3** *fig (creer)* to believe, swallow; **se lo traga todo,** she'd fall for anything. **4** *fig (disimular)* to hide.

tragasables *nmf inv* sword-swallower.

tragedia *nf* tragedy; *irón* **¡qué t.!, se me ha terminado el tabaco,** woe is me!, I've run out of cigarettes; **terminar en t.,** to end tragically.

trágico,-a I *adj Teat* tragic; **escritor t.,** tragedian; *fam* **ponerse t.,** *(situación)* to get tragic; *(persona)* to get all serious. **II** *nm, f Teat* tragedian.

tragicomedia *nf Cin Teat* tragicomedy.

tragicómico,-a *adj* tragicomic.

trago *nm* **1** *(bebida)* swig, drop; **beberse algo de un t.,** to down sth in one go; **echar un t.,** *(echar un sorbo)* to take a swig; *(tomar algo)* to have a drink. **2** *fam (adversidad)* rough time; **pasar un mal t.,** to have a bad time of it; **tener que volver a verle, ¡qué t.!,** how awful to have to see him again!

tragón,-ona I *adj fam* greedy, piggy. **II** *nm,f* glutton, big eater.

traición *nf* treason, betrayal; **a t.,** treacherously; **alta t.,** high treason.

traicionar *vtr (gen)* to betray; *(delatar)* to give away, betray; *fig* **le traicionó su acento,** his accent gave him away.

traicionero,-a *adj* treacherous.

traído,-a I *pp de* **traer. II** *adj* **1** *(gastado)* threadbare, worn-out. **2** *(visto)* hackneyed, trite; **t. y llevado,** well-worn, hackneyed.

traidor,-a I *adj* treacherous. **II** *nm,f* traitor.

traigo *indic pres véase* **traer.**

tráiler *nm (pl tráilers)* **1** *Cin* trailer, *US* preview. **2** *Aut* articulated lorry, *US* trailer truck.

traína *nf Náut* trawl (net).

trainera *nf Náut* trawler.

traje[1] *nm* **1** *(de hombre)* suit. ▪ **t. a medida,** tailor-made suit; **t. cruzado,** double-breasted suit; **t. de baño,** bathing suit *or* costume, swimsuit; **t. de calle,** town clothes *pl*; *Taur* **t. de luces,** bullfighter's costume; **t. de paisano,** civilian clothes *pl*; **t. espacial,** spacesuit. **2** *(de mujer)* dress. ▪ **t. de chaqueta,** tailored suit; **t. de novia,** wedding dress; **t. largo** *or* **de noche,** evening dress. **3** *Mil* dress. ▪ **t. de campaña,** battledress; **t. de ceremonia,** full *or* formal dress; **t. de faena,** fatigue dress, undress; *fam* **t. de bonito,** formal dress.

traje[2] *pt indef véase* **traer.**

trajeado,-a I *pp de* **trajearse. II** *adj fam* sharp, dapper.

trajearse *vr* to dress up.

trajín *nm fam* comings and goings *pl*, hustle and bustle.

trajinar I *vi (moverse mucho)* to run *or* bustle about. **II** *vtr Arg Chi (engañar)* to deceive, trick.

tralla *nf* **1** *(látigo)* whip. **2** *(cuerda)* rope.

trallazo *nm* **1** *(golpe)* lash. **2** *(chasquido)* crack of a whip.

trama *nf* **1** *Tex* weft, woof. **2** *Lit (argumento)* plot.

tramado,-a I *pp de* **tramar. II** *adj CAm* **1** *(valiente)* brave, valiant. **2** *(difícil)* intricate.

tramar *vtr* to plot, cook up; **están tramando algo gordo,** something big is on the way; **¿qué tramas?,** what are you up to?

tramitación *nf Jur* procedure, steps *pl*; **¿cuánto tarda la t. de pasaporte?,** how long does it take to get a passport?

tramitar *vtr* **1** *(gestionar)* to take the necessary (legal) steps to obtain; **debo t. mi permiso de residencia,** I have to obtain my residence permit. **2** *fml (despachar)* to convey, transmit. **3** *Com Jur Fin* to negotiate, carry out, process, transact.

trámite *nm* **1** *(paso)* step; **¿falta algún t. por cumplir?,** are there any more formalities to be gone through?; *fig* **de puro t.,** unimportant, easy. **2** *Com Jur Fin* procedures *pl*, proceeding.

tramo *nm (de carretera, vía)* section, stretch; *(de escalera)* flight.

tramontana *nf Meteor* north wind, tramontane.

tramoya *nf Teat* **1** *(maquinaria)* stage machinery. **2** *fig (trama)* plot, scheme.

tramoyista *nmf* **1** *Teat* stagehand, scene shifter. **2** *fig (farsante)* schemer.

trampa *nf* **1** *(abertura)* trap door, hatch. **2** *(de caza)* trap, snare; **caer en la t.,** to fall into the trap; **tender una t.,** to set *or* lay a trap. **3** *Mil (emboscada)* ambush. **4** *(engaño)* fiddle; **hacer trampa(s),** to cheat. **5** *(truco)* trick; **este**

juego tiene t., this game has got a catch; *fam* **sin t. ni cartón,** honest, real.

trampear *vi fam* **1** *(engañar)* to fiddle, live by one's wits. **2** *(ir viviendo)* to get by, manage.

trampero,-a *nm,f* trapper.

trampilla *nf* trap door, hatch.

trampolín *nm* **1** *Natación* springboard, diving board. **2** *Esquí* ski jump. **3** *fig (medio)* springboard, starting point.

tramposo,-a I *adj* tricky, deceitful. **II** *nm,f* trickster, cheat; *Naipes* cardsharp.

tranca *nf* **1** *(garrote)* cudgel, club; *fam* **a trancas y barrancas,** with great difficulty. **2** *(en puerta, ventana)* bar. **3** *fam (borrachera)* binge, skinful; **coger** *or* **pillar una t.,** to get plastered.

trancazo *nm* **1** *(golpe)* blow with a cudgel; *fam* **pegarse un t.,** to come a cropper. **2** *fam (gripe)* flu; *(resfriado)* cold.

trance *nm* **1** *(coyuntura)* (critical) moment, juncture; **estar en t. de ...,** to be on the point of ...; **pasar por un t.,** to hit a bad patch; **t. mortal** *or* **de muerte,** on the point of death; **sacar a algn de un (mal) t.,** to get sb out of a fix; **último t.,** final moment; *fig* **a todo t.,** at all costs. **2** *(éxtasis)* trance.

tranco *nm* stride; *fig* **a trancos,** in a hurry.

tranquilidad *nf* calmness, tranquillity, *US* tranquility; **con t.,** calmly; **para mayor t.,** to be on the safe side; **para tu t.,** for your own peace of mind; **paz y t.,** peace and quiet; **perder la t.,** to get het up; **pídemelo con toda t.,** don't hesitate to ask me; **¡qué t.!,** how peaceful!

tranquilizador,-a *adj* calming, reassuring.

tranquilizante I *adj* calming, reassuring. **II** *nm Farm* tranquillizer, *US* tranquilizer.

tranquilizar I *vtr* **1** *(calmar)* to tranquillize, *US* tranquilize, calm down. **2** *(dar confianza)* to reassure; **me tranquilizó oír tu voz,** hearing your voice set my mind at rest. **II tranquilizarse** *vr* **1** *(calmarse)* to calm down; **¡tranquilízate!,** calm *or* cool down! **2** *(relajarse)* to relax, set one's mind at rest.

tranquilo,-a *adj* **1** *(sin agitación)* calm, tranquil, relaxed; **aguas tranquilas,** still waters; **para que estés t.,** for your own peace of mind; **tengo la conciencia tranquila,** my conscience is clear; *fam* **déjame t.,** leave me alone; *fam* **quedarse tan t.,** not to bat an eyelid; *fam* **¡t.!,** *(no te preocupes)* don't (you) worry!; *(no pierdas la calma)* take it easy! **2** *(sin ruidos)* quiet, still, peaceful. **3** *(persona)* placid, calm, easy-going.

tranquillo *nm fig* knack; **coger el t. a algo,** to get the knack of sth.

transacción *nf Fin* transaction, deal.

transalpino,-a *adj Geog* transalpine.

transandino,-a *adj Geog* transandean.

transatlántico,-a I *adj* transatlantic. **II** *nm Náut* (ocean) liner.

transbordador *nm Náut* (car) ferry.

transbordar I *vtr* to transfer; *Náut (mercancías)* to transship; *Náut (de orilla a orilla)* to ferry across a river. **II** *vi Ferroc* to change trains, *US* transfer.

transbordo *nm* **1** *Ferroc* change, *US* transfer; **hacer t.,** to change *or* transfer. **2** *Náut* transshipment.

transcendencia *nf véase* **trascendencia.**

transcendental *adj véase* **trascendental.**

transcendente *adj véase* **trascendente.**

transcender *vtr & vi véase* **trascender.**

transcontinental *adj* transcontinental.

transcribir *(pp transcrito)* *vtr* to transcribe.

transcripción *nf* transcription.

transcrito *pp de* **transcribir.**

transcurrir *vi* **1** *(pasar el tiempo)* to pass, go by, elapse; **dejé t. cinco minutos antes de volver a llamar,** I waited five minutes before phoning again. **2** *(acontecer)* to take place, go off.

transcurso *nm* course *or* passing (of time); **con el t. de las años,** with the passing of time; **en el t. de ocho días,** in the course *or* space of a week.

transeúnte *nmf* **1** *(peatón)* pedestrian. **2** *(residente temporal)* temporary resident.

transexual *adj & nmf* transsexual.

transexualismo *nm* transsexualism.

transferencia *nf* (*gen*) transference; *Fin* transfer; **t. bancaria,** banker's order.

transferible *adj* transferable.

transferir *vtr* **1** *(de lugar)* to transfer. **2** *(aplazar)* to postpone. **3** *Fin* to transfer, convey.

transfiguración *nf* transfiguration.

transfigurar I *vtr* to transfigure. II **transfigurarse** *vr* to become transfigured.

transformable *adj* transformable.

transformación *nf* transformation.

transformador,-a I *adj* transforming. II *nm Elec* transformer.

transformar I *vtr* to transform, change. II **transformarse** *vr* to change, turn into; **este sillón se transforma en (una) cama,** this armchair converts into a bed.

transformista *nmf* quick-change artiste.

tránsfuga *nmf* **1** *Mil* deserter. **2** *Pol* turncoat.

transfusión *nf* transfusion.

transgredir *vtr* defect to transgress, break.

transgresión *nf* transgression.

transgresor,-a *nm,f* transgressor, lawbreaker.

transiberiano,-a I *adj* Trans-Siberian. II *nm Ferroc* **el T.,** the Trans-Siberian Railway.

transición *nf* transition; **período/gobierno de t.,** transition period/government; **sin t.,** abruptly.

transido,-a *adj* deeply affected; **t. de angustia,** beset with anxiety; **t. de dolor,** racked with pain; **t. de frío,** chilled to the bone; **t. de miedo,** panic-stricken.

transigencia *nf* **1** *(concesión)* compromise, yielding. **2** *(actitud)* lenience, tolerance.

transigente *adj* acommodating, lenient, tolerant.

transigir *vi* **1** *(ceder)* to compromise, yield, give in; **en eso no puedo t.,** I cannot possibly agree to that. **2** *(tolerar)* to tolerate, bear.

transistor *nm Elec* transistor.

transistorizado,-a *adj Elec* transistorized.

transitable *adj* transitable, passable; **la carretera no está t.,** *(en malas condiciones)* the road is in bad condition; *(cerrada)* the road is closed to traffic.

transitado,-a I *pp de* **transitar.** II *adj* busy; **una carretera muy transitada,** a busy *or* well-travelled road.

transitar *vi* to go from place to place, travel (about).

transitivo,-a *adj Ling* transitive.

tránsito *nm* **1** *(movimiento)* movement, passage; **pasajeros en t.,** passengers in transit. **2** *Aut* traffic; **'cerrado al t.',** 'road closed'; **una calle de (mucho) t.,** a busy street. **3** *euf (muerte)* death, passing.

transitoriedad *nf* transience, transiency.

transitorio,-a *adj* transitory, transitional, interim; *Jur* **disposición transitoria,** provisional order *or* ordinance.

translación *nf véase* **traslación.**

translúcido,-a *adj véase* **traslúcido,-a.**

translucir *vtr véase* **traslucir.**

transmigración *nf* transmigration.

transmisión *nf* **1** *(paso)* transmission; **t. del pensamiento,** thought transmission. **2** *Jur (de bienes)* transfer(ence). **3** *Téc* drive; **t. delantera/trasera,** front-/rear-wheel drive. **4** *Rad TV* transmission, broadcast; *Mil* **(cuerpo de) transmisiones,** signal corps *sing*.

transmisor,-a *Telec* I *adj* transmitting; **estación transmisora,** radio station. II *nm* transmitter.

transmitir *vtr* **1** *(comunicar)* to transmit, pass on; **no me acordé de transmitirle tu recado,** I forgot to give him your message. **2** *Jur* to transfer, hand down. **3** *Med* to transmit, pass on; **las moscas transmiten microbios,** flies carry germs. **4** *Rad TV* to transmit, broadcast.

transmutación *nf* transmutation.

transmutar I *vtr* to transmute. II **transmutarse** *vr* to change (completely), transform.

transoceánico,-a *adj* transoceanic.

transparencia *nf* **1** *(calidad)* transparency, transparence. **2** *Fot* slide.

transparentar I *vtr (emociones etc)* to reveal, betray. II **transparentarse** *vr* **1** *(ser transparente)* to be transparent; **esta tela se transparenta,** this is see-through material. **2** *(emociones, intenciones)* to show (through).

transparente I *adj* transparent; *fig* **puedes fiarte de él, es t.,** you can trust him, he's straight. II *nm* **1** *(visillo)* net curtain. **2** *(pantalla)* shade, blind.

transpiración *nf* transpiration, perspiration.

transpirar *vi* to transpire, perspire.

transpirenaico,-a *adj* trans-Pyrenean, beyond the Pyrenees.

transplantar I *vtr* **1** *(gen)* to transplant. **2** *(trasladar)* to transfer. II **transplantarse** *vr* to uproot oneself, emigrate.

transplante *nm* transplant, transplantation; *Med* **t. de corazón/córnea,** heart/eye transplant.

transponer *(pp* **transpuesto***)* I *vtr* **1** *(mudar de sitio)* to transpose, move about. **2** *(atravesar)* to cross over. **3** *(trasplantar)* to transplant. II **transponerse** *vr* **1** *(esconderse)* to hide; *(el sol)* to set, go down. **2** *(quedarse dormido)* to doze off.

transportador,-a I *adj* transporting; **cinta transportadora,** conveyor belt. II *nm* **1** *Téc* transporter, conveyor. **2** *(de dibujo)* protractor.

transportar *vtr* **1** *(gen)* to transport; *(pasajeros)* carry; *(mercancías)* to ship; *fig* **transportado de felicidad,** utterly happy. **2** *(ángulo)* to transfer. **3** *Mús* to transpose. II **transportarse** *vr fig* to be transported *or* enraptured.

transporte *nm* **1** *(medios de)* transport. ■ **transporte(s) público(s),** public transport. **2** *(acción de)* transport, *US* transportation; *Com* freight. ■ **t. de mercancías,** freight transport; **t. marítimo,** shipment. **3** *Mús* transposition. **4** *fig (éxtasis)* ecstasy, bliss, transport.

transportista *nmf* carrier.

transposición *nf* transposition.

transvasar *vtr* **1** *(líquidos)* to decant. **2** *(de un río a otro)* to transfer.

transvase *nm* **1** *(de líquidos)* decanting. **2** *(de ríos)* transfer.

transversal *adj* transverse, cross.

transverso,-a *adj* transverse.

tranvía *nm* **1** *(vehículo)* tram, tramcar, *US* streetcar. **2** *(sistema de transporte)* tramway.

tranviario,-a I *adj* tram, *US* streetcar; **red tranviaria,** tramway. II *nm,f* tram driver.

trapacería *nf* trick, fiddle.

trapacero,-a I *adj* tricky. II *nm* fiddler, trickster.

trapajoso,-a *adj* **1** *(ropa)* ragged, tattered. **2** *(persona)* dowdy, shabby. **3** *(pronunciación)* badly articulated; **hablar t.,** to speak with a thick voice.

trapatiesta *nf fam* racket; **se armó una t.,** there was quite an uproar.

trapear *vtr* **1** *Am (limpiar)* to mop. **2** *CAm* to criticize severely.

trapecio *nm* **1** *Geom* trapezium, *US* trapezoid. **2** *Med (hueso)* trapezium; *(músculo)* trapezius. **3** *(engimnasia)* trapeze.

trapecista *nmf* trapeze artiste.

trapense *adj* Trappist.

trapería *nf* old-clothes shop.

trapero *nm* rag-and-bone man, *US* junkman.

trapezoide *nm Geom* trapezoid, *US* trapezium.

trapichear *vi* to (be on the) fiddle.

trapicheo *nm* jiggery-pokery, fiddling; **andar(se) con trapicheos,** to be dishonest.

trapillo *nm* **de t.,** casually dressed.

trapisonda *nf fam* **1** *(jaleo)* fuss, to-do, commotion. **2** *(enredo)* scheme, plot.

trapista *nm Arg* rag-picker.

trapitos *nmpl fam* clothes, rags; **hablar de t.,** to talk about clothes.

trapo *nm* **1** *(viejo, roto)* rag. **2** *(bayeta)* cloth, **t. de cocina,** dishcloth; **t. de polvo,** duster; *fam* **estar hecho un t.,** to be worn out; *fam* **poner (a algn) como un t. (sucio),** to tear sb apart; *fam* **lavar los trapos sucios,** to wash one's dirty linen (in public); *fam* **sacar los trapos sucios a relucir,** to take the skeletons out of the cupboard. **3** *Taur* red cape. **4** *fam* **trapos,** clothes, rags. **5** *fam* **a todo t.,** flat out.

trapujear *vi CAm* to smuggle.

tráquea *nf Anat* trachea, windpipe.

traquear *vtr Arg CR Méx* to pass through.

traquetear I *vtr (agitar)* to shake, bang about. **II** *vi (hacer ruido)* to clatter, rattle.

traqueteo *nm* **1** *(ruido)* rattle, clatter. **2** *(movimiento)* jolting, bumping.

traquido *nm (crujido)* crack, bang.

tras *prep* **1** *(después de)* after; **t. la muerte de su padre,** after his father's death; **uno t. otro,** one after the other. **2** *(detrás)* behind; **sentados uno t. otro,** seated one behind the other. **3** *(en pos de)* after, in pursuit of; **la policía va t. ella,** the police are searching for her; **voy t. una vacante de juez,** I'm after a vacancy for judge.

trasalpino,-a *adj véase* **transalpino,-a.**

trasandino,-a *adj véase* **transandino,-a.**

trasatlántico,-a *adj & nm véase* **transatlántico,-a.**

trasbordador *nm véase* **transbordador.**

trasbordar *vtr & vi véase* **transbordar.**

trasbordo *nm véase* **transbordo.**

trascendencia *nf* **1** *(importancia)* importance, significance; **aquel invento tuvo una gran t.,** that invention had far-reaching consequences; **sin t.,** of little significance. **2** *Filos* transcendence, transcendency.

trascendental *adj,* **trascendente** *adj* **1** significant, consequential, far-reaching. **2** *Filos* transcendent, transcendental.

trascender I *vtr (averiguar)* to discover, bring to light. **II** *vi* **1** *(darse a conocer)* to become known, leak out; **t. a la opinión pública,** to become common knowledge. **2** *(extenderse)* to spread, have a wide effect; **esperemos que el mal ejemplo no trascienda,** let's hope nobody will follow this bad example. **3** *(exhalar olor)* to smell; **el olor de café trascendía a toda la casa,** the smell of coffee wafted all over the house; *fig* **todo su discurso trasciende a fascismo,** his whole speech reeks of fascism. **4** **t. de,** to go beyond, surpass; **esta decisión trasciende de mi competencia,** this decision is beyond my powers. **5** *Filos* to be transcendent *or* transcendental.

trascribir *vtr véase* **transcribir.**

trascripción *nf véase* **transcripción.**

trascrito *pp de* **transcribir.**

trascurrir *vi véase* **transcurrir.**

trascurso *nm véase* **transcurso.**

trasegar *vtr* **1** *(mudar)* to move about, shuffle. **2** *(líquidos)* to decant. **3** *fam (beber)* to swill.

trasero,-a I *adj* back, rear; **en la parte trasera,** at the back. **II** *nm Anat fam euf* bottom, bum.

trasferencia *nf véase* **transferencia.**

trasferible *adj véase* **transferible.**

trasferir *vtr véase* **transferir.**

trasfiguración *nf véase* **transfiguración.**

trasfigurar *vtr véase* **transfigurar.**

trasfondo *nm* background; **había un t. de tristeza en sus palabras,** there was an undertone of sadness in her words.

trasformable *adj véase* **transformable.**

trasformación *nf véase* **transformación.**

trasformador,-a *nf véase* **transformador,-a.**

trasformar *vtr véase* **transformar.**

trasformista *nmf véase* **transformista.**

trásfuga *nmf véase* **tránsfuga.**

trasfusión *nf véase* **transfusión.**

trasgo *nm Mit* goblin, imp.

trasgredir *vtr véase* **transgredir.**

trasgresión *nf véase* **transgresión.**

trasgresor,-a *nm, f véase* **transgresor,-a.**

trashumancia *nf* transhumance, seasonal migration.

trashumante *adj* transhumant.

trasiego *nm* comings and goings *pl,* hustle and bustle; **t. de personal,** reshuffle.

traslación *nf* **1** *Astron* passage, movement. **2** *Mat* translation. **3** *Lit* metaphor.

trasladar I *vtr* **1** *(cosa)* to move; *(persona)* to move, transfer; **t. ideas al papel,** to put down one's ideas in writing. **2** *(acontecimiento)* to postpone, put off; *(reunión, prueba)* to adjourn. **3** *(traducir)* to translate. **4** *fig* to explain. **II trasladarse** *vr (persona, cosa)* to go, move.

traslado *nm* **1** *(de casa)* move, removal; **¿cuándo haremos el t.?,** when are we going to move? **2** *(de personal)* transfer. **3** *(copia)* copy. **4** *Jur* notification.

traslúcido,-a *adj* translucent, semitransparent.

traslucir I *vtr fig (sentimientos, intenciones)* to show, reveal; **su tono de voz dejaba t. el miedo,** his tone of voice betrayed his fear. **II traslucirse** *vr* **1** *(ser traslúcido)* to be translucent. **2** *(adivinarse)* to show (through); *(revelarse)* to be revealed.

trasluz *nm* diffused *or* reflected light; **mirar algo al t.,** to hold sth against the light.

trasmano *nm* **a t.,** out of reach; **(me) coge a t.,** it's out of my way.

trasmigración *nf véase* **transmigración.**

trasmisión *nf véase* **transmisión.**

trasmisor,-a *adj & nm véase* **transmisor,-a.**

trasmitir *vtr véase* **transmitir.**

trasmutación *nf véase* **transmutación.**

trasmutar *vtr véase* **transmutar.**

trasnochado,-a I *pp de* **trasnochar. II** *adj* **1** *(desfasado)* old, hackneyed. **2** *fig (persona)* blearyeyed, haggard.

trasnochador,-a I *adj* given to staying up late. **II** *nm, f* night bird, nighthawk.

trasnochar *vi* to stay up (very) late.

traspapelado,-a I *pp de* **traspapelar. II** *adj* mislaid, misplaced.

traspapelar I *vtr (papeles etc)* to mislay, misplace. **II traspapelarse** *vr (documentos etc)* to get mislaid *or* misplaced.

trasparencia *nf véase* **transparencia.**

trasparentar *vtr véase* **transparentar.**

trasparente *adj & nm véase* **transparente.**

traspasar *vtr* **1** *(atravesar)* to go through; *(río)* to cross; *(perforar)* to pierce; **una bala le traspasó el corazón,** a bullet went through his heart; *fig* **estos silbidos te**

traspasan el oído, that whistling noise pierces your ears. **2** *(comercio, derechos, jugador)* to transfer; **'se traspasa',** 'for sale'. **3** *fig (exceder)* to exceed, go beyond; **t. los límites de lo establecido,** to go beyond the set limit. **4** *fig (afectar)* to transfix.

traspaso *nm* **1** *(de comercio, derechos)* transfer. **2** *Com (venta)* sale; **cogió el t. de un comercio,** he bought a shop. **3** *(precio)* takeover fee; **piden 10.000 de t.,** they want 10,000 for the takeover.

traspatio *nm Am* back garden *or* yard.

traspié *nm (pl traspiés)* stumble, trip; **dar un t.,** to trip; *fig* to slip up.

traspiración *nf véase* **transpiración.**

traspirar *vi véase* **transpirar.**

traspirenaico,-a *adj véase* **transpirenaico,-a.**

trasplantar *vtr véase* **transplantar.**

trasplante *nm véase* **transplante.**

trasponer *vtr véase* **transponer.**

trasportador,-a *adj & nm adj véase* **transportador,-a.**

trasportar *vtr véase* **transportar.**

trasporte *nm véase* **transporte.**

trasposición *nf véase* **transposición.**

traspuesto,-a I *pp de* **trasponer. II** *adj* **quedarse t.,** to nod *or* doze off.

trasquilado,-a I *pp de* **trasquilar. II** *adj* **1** *(oveja)* sheared; *fig* **(ir a por lana y) salir t.,** to come out the loser. **2** *(pelo)* cropped. **3** *fam (mermado)* curtailed, cut down.

trasquilar *vtr* **1** *(oveja)* to shear. **2** *(pelo)* to crop. **3** *(dinero, recursos)* to curtail.

trasquilón *nm* **1** *fam (corte de pelo)* slash, chop; **con** *or* **a trasquilones,** unevenly cut. **2** *fam fig (dinero)* loot, catch.

trastabillar *vi* **1** *(dar traspiés)* to stumble, trip. **2** *(tambalearse)* to stagger, totter. **3** *(tartamudear)* to stutter, stammer.

trastabillón *nm Am* stumble, trip.

trastada *nf fam* **1** *(broma pesada)* prank. **2** *(mala jugada)* dirty trick.

trastazo *nm fam* whack, wallop, thump; **me di un t. contra un coche,** I bumped into a car; **se pegó un t.,** he came a cropper.

traste¹ *nm Mús* fret.

traste² *nm* **1** *Am (trasto)* piece of junk. **2** *fig* **dar al t. (con un plan),** to spoil (a plan); **irse al t.,** to fall through.

trastear¹ *vtr Mús* to play.

trastear²I *vi (revolver)* to rummage about. **II** *vtr* **1** *Taur* to play with the cape. **2** *fig (manejar)* to twist around one's little finger.

trastero *nm* **1** **(cuarto) t.,** junk room. **2** *Méx (alacena)* larder.

trastienda *nf* **1** *(rebotica)* back room; *fig* **por t.,** under the counter. **2** *fig (astucia)* cunning; **tener mucha t.,** to be a dark horse. **3** *Chi Méx fam (trasero)* bottom, rear (end), buttocks *pl.*

trasto *nm* **1** *(que no sirve)* piece of junk; *(objeto cualquiera)* thing; **¿qué hace este t. ahí en medio?,** what's this thingamajig *or* thingummy doing right in the middle?; **ser un t. viejo,** to be useless. **2** *(niño)* little devil. **3** *Mueb* piece of furniture. **4** **trastos,** tackle *sing,* gear *sing;* **los t. de escalar,** the climbing gear; **se fue con todos los t. de coser,** she went away with the whole sewing kit. **5** **trastos,** *fam (posesiones)* belongings things; **llévate tus t.,** take all your stuff with you; **coger** *or* **liar los t.,** to pack up and leave; **tirarse los t. a la cabeza,** to have a blazing *or* flaming row.

trastocar *vtr véase* **trastornar.**

trastornado,-a I *pp de* **trastornar. II** *adj* mad, unhinged; **esta mujer me tiene t.,** this woman has driven me crazy; **mente trastornada,** unbalanced mind.

trastornar I *vtr* **1** *(revolver)* to turn round; *fig* to disarrange. **2** *(desordenar)* to turn upside down. **3** *(alterar) (planes)* to disrupt; *(paz, tranquilidad)* to disturb; *(estómago)* to upset; *fig (molestar)* to trouble, bother, annoy. **4** *fig (perturbar)* to unhinge; **trastorna a los hombres,** she drives men crazy. **II trastornarse** *vr* to go out of one's mind, go mad.

trastorno *nm (molestia)* trouble, inconvenience; *(perturbación)* disruption, upset, upheaval; *(desorden)* confusion; *Med* **t. estomacal,** stomach upset; **t. mental,** mental disorder *or* disturbance.

trastrocamiento *nm* switch, reversal.

trastrocar *vtr (gen)* to switch *or* change around; *(orden)* to reverse, invert; *(significado, sentido)* to change.

trasunto *nm fml* copy, replica; **un fiel t. de la realidad,** a true representation of reality.

trasvasar *vtr véase* **transvasar.**

trasvase *nm véase* **transvase.**

trasversal *adj véase* **transversal.**

trasverso,-a *adj véase* **transverso,-a.**

trata *nf* slave trade *or* traffic. ■ **t. de blancas,** white slave trade.

tratable *adj* easy to get along with, friendly, congenial.

tratadista *nmf* treatise writer, essayist.

tratado,-a I *pp de* **tratar. II** *nm* **1** *(estudio)* treatise. **2** *(pacto)* treaty.

tratamiento *nm* **1** *(gen)* treatment; *Med* **un t. a base de antibióticos,** a course of antibiotics. **2** *Téc* processing, treatment. **3** *(título)* title; **le debes dar t. de Excelencia,** you must address him as Your Excellency. **4** *Inform* processing; **t. de datos,** data processing; **t. de textos,** word processing.

tratante *nmf* dealer.

tratar I *vtr* **1** *(asistir, atender)* to treat; **nos han tratado muy bien,** they were very nice to us; **t. a algn bien/mal,** to treat sb well/bad. **2** *Med (enfermedad)* to treat. **3** *(asunto)* to discuss. **4** *(manejar)* to handle. **5** *(gestionar)* to handle, run. **6** *Inform Téc* to process. **7** *Quím* to treat. **II** *vi* **1** *(relacionarse)* **he tratado más con la hermana,** I'm more acquainted with her sister; **t. con algn,** to see *or* visit sb frequently. **2** *(tener tratos)* to deal **(con,** with); *(negociar)* to negotiate **(con,** with). **3** *(intentar)* **t. de,** to try; **trata de entenderlo,** try to understand. **4** *(llamar)* **t. de,** to address as; **no es necesario que me trates de usted,** you needn't address me as 'usted'. **5** *(calificar)* to consider, look on; **le trató de loco,** he treated him as if he were mad. **6** *(versar)* **t. de** *or* **sobre** *or* **acerca,** to be about; **¿de qué trata?,** what is it about? **7** *Com* **t. en,** to deal in. **III tratarse** *vr* **1** *(recíproco)* to treat each other. **2** *(llamarse)* to address each other; **se tratan de tú,** they call each other **tú. 3** *(hablarse)* to talk to each other, be on speaking terms. **4** *(ser cuestión)* **t. de,** to be a question of; **se tratará de una media hora,** it'll be about half an hour; **sólo se trata de ser más puntual,** it's only a matter of being on time. **5** *(referirse)* **t. de,** to be about; **¿de qué se trató durante la cena?,** what was the subject during supper?; **se trata de un cuento irlandés,** it's an Irish story.

tratativa *nf Arg* business meeting.

trato *nm* **1** *(de personas)* manner, treatment; *(contacto)* contact; *pey* dealings *pl;* **no tengo t. con Juan,** I have nothing to do with Juan; **tener un t. agradable,** to have a pleasant manner; **t. diario,** daily contact. ■ **malos tratos,** ill-treatment *sing;* **t. de gentes,** a way with people. **2** *(acuerdo)* agreement; **hicimos el t. de dejar de fumar,** we agreed to stop smoking; **¡t. hecho!,** it's a deal! **3** *Com* deal; **cerrar un t.,** to close a deal; **estar en tratos con algn,** to be negotiating with sb. **4** *(tratamiento)* title; **dar a algn el t. de Señoría,** to address sb as Your Lordship.

trauma *nm* trauma; *fam* **el t. de la mili,** the drag of doing military service.

traumático,-a *adj* traumatic.

traumatismo *nm* traumatism.

traumatizar *vtr Med* to traumatize; *fam* to shock.

traumatología *nf (hospital)* accident ward.

travelín *nm Cin TV* travelling, *US* traveling.

través I *nm (pl* **traveses)** 1 *(de madera)* crosspiece, crossbeam. 2 *(inclinación)* slant. 3 *fig (desgracia)* misfortune. II *adv* **1 a t. de,** through; *(por dentro)* **a t. de ese agujero,** through that hole; *(por medio de)* **lo supe a t. de su mujer,** I found out through his wife. 2 **de t.,** *(transversalmente)* crosswise; **pon los cubiertos de t. en el plato,** place the cutlery crosswise on the plate. 3 *(de lado)* sideways; **mirar de t.,** to look askance at; **ponlo de t.** *or* **no pasará,** put it sideways or it won't go through. III *prep* **al** *or* **a t.,** across, over; **a t. del río,** across the river.

travesaño *nm* 1 *Arquit* crosspiece; *(viga)* crosspiece. 2 *Ftb* crossbar.

travesía *nf* 1 *(viaje)* voyage; **la t. del Atlántico,** the crossing of the Atlantic. 2 *(calle)* cross street, passage. 3 *(distancia)* distance. 4 *Arg Bol (región)* arid plain.

travestí *nmf,* **travesti** *nmf* transvestite.

travestismo *nm* transvestism.

travestirse *vr* to wear clothes belonging to the opposite sex.

travesura *nf* mischief, childish prank; **hacer travesuras,** to get into mischief.

traviesa *nf* 1 *Ferroc* sleeper, *US* tie. 2 *Constr (viga)* trimmer.

travieso,-a *adj* mischievous, naughty.

trayecto *nm* 1 *(distancia)* distance, way; **hay un largo t. de aquí a Madrid,** it's a long way *or* journey from here to Madrid. 2 *(recorrido)* route, itinerary; **final de(l) t.,** terminus, end of the line.

trayectoria *nf* 1 *(de proyectil, geométrica)* trajectory. 2 *fig (orientación)* line, course; **la impecable t. democrática de nuestro partido,** our party's staunchly democratic path.

traza *nf* 1 *(apariencia)* looks *pl,* appearance; **no llevar** *or* **tener trazas de,** not to look as if; **no lleva trazas de curarse,** it doesn't look as if he's going to get better. 2 *Arquit* plan, design. 3 *(maña)* skill, knack; **este chico no tiene ninguna t. para la pintura,** this boy is no good at painting.

trazado,-a *pp de* **trazar.** II *adj* laid out, designed. III *nm* 1 *(plano)* layout, plan. 2 *(dibujo)* drawing, sketch. 3 *(de carretera, ferrocarril)* route, course.

trazar *vtr* 1 *(línea, carta)* to draw; *(parque)* to lay out; *(edificio)* to design; *(esbozo)* to draw (up). 2 *(describir)* to sketch; **t. una semblanza (de algn),** to describe *or* depict (sb). 3 *fig (idear)* to draw up the broad lines of.

trazo *nm* 1 *(línea)* line. 2 *(de una letra)* stroke. 3 *(rasgo facial)* feature.

trebejo *nm fam (gen pl)* staff, gear.

trébol *nm* 1 *Bot* clover, trefoil. 2 *Naipes* club. 3 *(carreteras)* (motorway) interchange.

trece *inv* I *adj (cardinal)* thirteen; *(ordinal)* thirteenth; **el t. de abril,** the thirteenth of April, April the thirteenth; **martes y t.,** ≈ Friday 13th. II *nm* thirteen; *fig* **estar** *or* **mantenerse** *or* **seguir en sus t.,** to stick to one's guns; *véase tamb* **ocho.**

treceavo,-a *adj* thirteenth; *véase tamb* **octavo,-a.**

trecho *nm* 1 *(distancia)* distance, way; **a trechos,** in parts *or* places; *prov* **del dicho al hecho hay un buen t.,** there's many a slip 'twixt cup and lip. 2 *Agr* plot, patch. 3 *fam* bit, piece.

tregua *nf Mil* truce; *fig* respite, rest.

treinta *inv* I *adj (cardinal)* thirty; *(ordinal)* thirtieth; **murió el t. de junio,** he died on June the thirtieth; **los años t.,** the thirties. II *nm* thirty; *véanse tamb* **ochenta y ocho.**

treintena *nf* thirty; **una t. de invitados,** thirty-odd guests.

treintavo,-a I *adj* thirtieth. II *nm (parte)* thirtieth; *véase tamb* **octavo,-a.**

tremebundo,-a *adj* terrible, dreadful.

tremendismo *nm Lit* coarse *or* gloomy realism in literature.

tremendista *adj* sensationalist.

tremendo,-a *adj* 1 *(terrible)* terrible, dreadful, frightful; *fam* **tomarse algo por la tremenda,** to make a great fuss about sth. 2 *(muy grande)* enormous; *fig* tremendous.

trementina *nf* turpentine. ■ **esencia de t.,** oil *or* spirits of turpentine.

tremolar *lit* I *vtr (banderas)* to wave. II *vi* to flutter, wave.

tremolina *nf fam* uproar, shindy.

trémolo *nm Mús* tremolo.

trémulo,-a *adj lit (vacilante)* quivering, tremulous; *(luz, llama)* flickering.

tren *nm* 1 *Ferroc* train; **cambiar de t.,** to change (trains), *US* transfer; **coger** *or* **tomar el t.,** to catch a train; **el tren a** *or* **para París,** the train to Paris; **iremos en t.,** we'll go by train; *fam* **estar como (para parar) un t.,** to be hot stuff *or* very sexy. ■ **t. correo,** mail train; **t. de cercanías,** suburban train; **t. de pasajeros,** passenger train; **t. de mercancías** *or* **de carga,** goods *or US* freight train; **t. directo,** through train. 2 *Mil* convoy. 3 *Téc* set (of gears *or* wheels). ■ *Av* **t. de aterrizaje,** undercarriage; **t. de lavado,** car wash. 4 *fig (ritmo)* speed, pace; **vivir a todo t.,** to lead a grand life.

trena *nf arg* clink, hole.

trenca *nf (prenda)* duffel *or* duffle coat.

trencilla *nf Cost* braided ribbon.

trenza *nf* 1 *Peluq* plait, *US* braid; **t. postiza,** switch. 2 *Cost* braid. 3 *Arg (lucha)* wrestling.

trenzado,-a I *pp de* **trenzar.** II *adj* 1 *(entrelazado)* intertwined. 2 *Cost* braided. 3 *Peluq (cabello)* plaited, *US* braided.

trenzar I *vtr* to intertwine; *Peluq* to plait, *US* braid. II *vi* 1 *(en danza)* to weave in and out; *(caballo)* to caper. 2 *Am (luchar)* to wrestle.

trepa *nm arg* go-getter, social climber.

trepador,-a I *adj* climbing; **ave trepadora,** creeper; **planta trepadora,** climber, creeper. II *nf Orn* creeper. III *nm fam* go-getter, social climber.

trepanación *nf Med* trepanation.

trepanar *vi Med* to trephine, trepan.

trépano *nm (en perforaciones)* bit.

trepar¹ I *vtr (persona)* to climb. II *vi* 1 *(persona, planta)* climb. 2 *fam fig (socialmente)* to be a social climber.

trepar² *vt* 1 *(taladrar)* to drill. 2 *Cost* to trim.

trepidación *nf* vibration, shaking.

trepidante *adj* vibrating, shaking; *fig* **lleva un ritmo de vida t.,** he leads a hectic *or* frantic life.

trepidar *vi* 1 to vibrate, shake. 2 *Am (vacilar)* to hesitate.

tres I *adj inv (cardinal)* three; *(ordinal)* third; **el t. de mayo tengo un examen,** I must take an examination on May the third; **las t.,** three o'clock; *fam* **como t. y dos son cinco,** as sure as eggs are eggs; *fam* **de t. al cuarto,** cheap, of little value; *fam* **ni a la de t.,** there is *or* was no way. II *nm (pl* **treses)** three; **t. en raya,** noughts and crosses, *US* tick-tack-toe; *véase tamb* **ocho.**

trescientos,-as I *adj inv (cardinal)* three hundred; *(ordinal)* three hundredth; **en (el año) mil t. cuarenta y uno,** in (the year) thirteen forty-one. II *nm* three hundred; *véanse tamb* **ochenta y ocho.**

tresillo *nm* 1 *Mueb* (three-piece) suite. 2 *Mús* triplet. 3 *Naipes* ombre.

treta *nf* trick, ruse.

tríada *nf* triad.

triangular *adj* triangular.

triángulo I *adj* triangular. **II** *nm Geom Mús* triangle. ■ **t. equilátero,** equilateral triangle; **t. isósceles,** isosceles triangle; **t. rectángulo,** rectangle triangle; *fig* **t. amoroso,** eternal triangle.

tribal *adj* tribal, tribe.

tribu *nf* tribe.

tribulación *nf* tribulation.

tribuna *nf* **1** *(plataforma)* rostrum, dais; **t. de (la) prensa,** press box. **2** *Dep* grandstand.

tribunal *nm* **1** *Jur* court; **llevar a los tribunales,** to take to court. ■ **T. Constitucional,** constitutional court; **t. de apelación,** court of appeal; **T. Supremo,** High Court, *US* Supreme Court; **t. (tutelar) de menores,** juvenile court. **2** *(de examen)* board of examiners.

tribuno *nm Hist* tribune.

tributable *adj* subject *or* liable to tax.

tributación *nf* taxation, levy.

tributante *nmf* taxpayer.

tributar *vtr (impuestos)* to pay; **t. un homenaje,** to pay a tribute.

tributario,-a I *adj* tributary; **sistema t.,** tax system. **II** *nm,f* taxpayer.

tributo *nm* **1** *(impuesto)* tax. **2** *fig Hist* tribute; **t. de amistad,** token of friendship.

tríceps *nm inv Anat* triceps *sing.*

triciclo *nm* tricycle.

tricolor *adj* tricolour, *US* tricolor, tricoloured, *US* tricolored.

tricornio *nm* **1** three-cornered hat, tricorn, tricorne. **2** *arg (guardia civil)* (member of the) civil guard.

tricot *nm* knit, tricot.

tricotar *vtr* to knit; **máquina de t.,** knitting machine.

tricotosa *nf* knitting machine.

tridente *nm* trident.

tridimensional *adj* three-dimensional.

triedro *nm Geol* trihedron.

trienal *adj* triennial.

trienio *nm* triennium.

trifásico,-a I *adj Elec* three-phase. **II** *nm fam* white coffee with brandy.

trifulca *nf fig* squabble, row, rumpus.

trigal *nm* wheat field.

trigésimo,-a I *adj* thirtieth; **t. primero,** thirty-first. **II** *nm, f (de una serie)* thirtieth. **III** *nm (parte)* thirtieth; *véase tamb* **octavo,-a.**

trigo *nm* **1** *Bot* wheat; *fig* **meterse en trigo(s) ajeno(s),** to meddle in sb else's affairs; *fig* **no ser t. limpio,** *(persona)* not to be totally above board; *(asunto)* to be dubious *or* shady. **2** *fam (dinero)* dough.

trigonometría *nf* trigonometry.

trigonométrico,-a *adj* trigonometric, trigonometrical.

trigueño,-a I *adj (pelo)* corn-coloured, dark blonde; *(piel)* dark, swarthy; *(persona)* olive-skinned.

triguero,-a I *adj* wheat; **espárrago t.,** wild asparagus. **II** *nm Orn* corn bunting.

trilateral *adj* three-sided, trilateral.

trilita *nf* gelignite.

trilogía *nf* trilogy.

trilla *nf Agr* threshing.

trillado,-a I *pp de* **trillar. II** *adj fig (expresión)* overworked, well-worn; **camino t.,** beaten path.

trilladora *nf* threshing machine; **t. segadora,** combine harvester.

trillar *vtr Agr* to thresh.

trillizos,-as *nm, fpl* triplets.

trillo *nm Agr* thresher.

trillón *nm* trillion *US* quintillion.

trimestral *adj* quarterly three-monthly, trimestral; **examen t.,** end-of-term examination.

trimestre *nm* quarter, trimester; *Educ* term.

trimotor *nm Av* three-engined aircraft.

trinar *vi* **1** *Orn Mús* to warble. **2** *fam* to rage, fume; **María estaba que trinaba cuando por fin llegué,** María was really fuming when I finally arrived.

trinca *nf* trio, threesome.

trincar¹ I *vtr fam (capturar)* to catch. **II trincarse** *vr ofens* to screw; **t. a una tía,** to screw a bird.

trincar² *vr fam* to drink; **se trincó una botella de ron él solito,** he put away a bottle of rum all by himself.

trinchante *nm* **1** *(cubierto)* carving knife. **2** *Mueb* serving *or* side table.

trinchar *vtr (carne)* to carve, slice (up).

trinche *nm Am* **1** *(tenedor)* fork. **2** *véase* **trinchante 2.**

trinchera *nf* **1** *Mil* trench. **2** *Méx (cuchillo)* curved knife.

trinchero *nm véase* **trinchante 2.**

trineo *nm* sled, sledge, sleigh.

Trinidad *n* Trinidad.

trinidad *nf Rel* trinity; **la Santísima T.,** the Blessed *or* Holy Trinity.

trinitario,-a *adj & nm, f* Trinitarian.

trino *nm* **1** *Orn* warble, trill. **2** *Mús* trill.

trinomio *nm Mat* trinomial.

trinquete¹ *nm Náut* foremast.

trinquete² *nm Dep* pelota played in a closed court.

trinquete³ *nm Téc* pawl, ratchet.

trío *nm* trio.

trip *nm arg (drogas)* trip.

tripa *nf* **1** *(intestino)* gut, intestine; *fam* tummy; **dolor de t.,** stomach ache; *fig* **hacer de tripas corazón,** to pluck up courage; *fig* **revolver las tripas,** to turn one's stomach; *fam* **echar/tener t.,** to get/have a paunch. **2** *vulg (embarazo)* belly. **3** *(de vasija)* belly. **4 tripas,** *(gen)* innards; *(de fruta)* core *sing,* seeds; *(documentos)* dossier *pl.*

tripartito,-a *adj* divided into three, tripartite.

triple *adj & nm* triple; **si aciertas, ganarás el t.,** if you win, you'll get back three times your money; **un t. salto mortal,** a triple somersault.

triplicado,-a I *pp de* **triplicar. II** *adj* triplicate; **por t.,** in triplicate.

triplicar *vtr* to triple, treble.

triplicidad *nf* triplicity.

trípode *nm* tripod.

Trípoli *n* Tripoli.

tripón,-ona *nm, f* **1** *fam (tripudo)* potbellied person. **2** *Méx (chivo)* young goat.

tríptico *nm* triptych.

triptongo *nm Ling* triphthong.

tripudo,-a *adj fam* paunchy, potbellied.

tripulación *nf* crew.

tripulante *nmf* crew member.

tripular *vtr* to man.

trique *nm Am* noughts and crosses, *US* tick-tack-toe.

triquinosis *nf inv* trichinosis.

triquiñuela *nf fam* trick, dodge; **andarse con triquiñuelas,** to be a trickster; **saberse las triquiñuelas,** to know (all) the dodges.

triquitraque *nm* clackety-clack, clatter.

tris *nm fig* bit; **en un t.,** in a jiffy; **estuve en un t. de llamarte,** I nearly called you; **por un t.,** by the skin of one's teeth; **no se cayó por un t.,** it was pure luck that he didn't fall.

trisílabo,-a *Ling* **I** *adj* trisyllabic. **II** *nm* trisyllable.

triste *adj* **1** *(infeliz)* sad, unhappy; **es t., pero es verdad,** it's sad but true; **poner t. a algn,** to make sb sad; **ponerse t.,** to become *or* turn sad. **2** *(oscuro, sombrío)* dismal, gloomy; **hacer un t. papel,** to cut a sorry figure; **t. futuro,** bleak future. **3** *(único)* single, only; **ni un t. penique,** not a single penny. **4** *(insignificante)* poor, humble; **su padre era un t. picapedrero,** his father was a simple stonecutter.

tristeza *nf* sadness; **tristezas,** problems, sufferings.

tristón,-ona *adj fam* gloomy, sad.

tritón *nm* **1** *Zool* newt. **2** *Mit* Triton.

trituración *nf* grinding, trituration.

triturado,-a *pp de* **triturar. II** *adj* ground, crushed; *fig* **me ha devuelto el libro t.,** he's given the book back to me all crumpled up.

triturar *vtr* **1** *(machacar)* to grind (up), triturate. **2** *fig (físicamente)* to beat (up); *(moralmente)* to tear apart.

triunfador,-a **I** *adj* winning. **II** *nm,f* winner.

triunfal *adj* triumphant; **salir t.,** to come out the winner *or* on top.

triunfalismo *nm* boastfulness; *Pol* jingoism.

triunfalista *adj* boastful; *Pol* jingoistic, chauvinist, chauvinistic.

triunfar *vi* to triumph, win; **t. en la vida,** to succeed in life.

triunfo *nm* **1** *(victoria)* triumph, victory; *Dep* win. **2** *(éxito)* success. **3** *Naipes* trump.

triunvirato *nm Hist* triumvirate.

trivial *adj* trivial, petty.

trivialidad *nf* triviality, pettiness.

trivializar *vtr* to trivialize, minimize.

triza *nf* bit, fragment; **hacer trizas,** to tear to shreds; *(gastar)* to wear out; *fam fig* **estoy hecho trizas,** I feel washed out.

trocar **I** *vtr* **1** *Com (permutar)* to barter, exchange. **2** *(transformar)* to turn **(en,** into), convert. **II trocarse** *vr (mudarse)* to change **(en,** into), switch round.

trocear *vtr* to cut up (into bits *or* pieces).

trochemoche (a) *loc adv fam* haphazardly.

trofeo *nm* trophy.

troglodita *nmf* troglodyte.

trola *nf fam* lie, fib.

trole *nm* trolley (pole).

trolebús *nm* trolley bus.

trolero,-a *fam* **I** *adj* lying. **II** *nm* liar, fibber.

tromba *nf* waterspout. ■ **t. de agua,** violent downpour.

trombo *nm Med* thrombus.

trombón **I** *nm Mús (instrumento)* trombone. ■ **t. de pistones** *or* **llaves,** valve trombone; **t. de varas,** slide trombone. **II** *nmf* trombonist.

trombosis *nf inv Med* thrombosis.

trompa **I** *nf* **1** *Mús* horn. **2** *(de elefante)* trunk. **3** *(de insecto)* proboscis. **4** *fam fig* hooter. **5** *Anat* tube. ■ **t. de Eustaquio,** Eustachian tube, **t. de Falopio,** Fallopian tube. **6** *(nube) véase* **tromba. 7** *fam (borrachera)* **llevar una t., estar t.,** to be sloshed *or* plastered. **II** *nmf* horn player.

trompada *nf* **1** *(puñetazo)* thump, punch. **2** *(choque de personas)* bump, collision. **3** *arg (drogas)* hit.

trompazo *nm* bump; **darse** *or* **pegarse un t.,** to have a bump, crash.

trompeta **I** *nf* **1** *Mús* trumpet. **2** *Méx (borrachera)* binge. **II** *nmf* trumpet player.

trompetazo *nm* trumpet blast.

trompetilla *nf desus* ear trumpet.

trompetista *nmf* trumpet player, trumpeter.

trompicar *vi* to trip (up), stumble.

trompicón *nm* **1** *(tropezón)* trip, stumble; **a trompicones,** in fits and starts; **saqué la carrera a trompicones,** I scraped through and got my degree. **2** *(golpe)* blow, hit.

trompiza *nf Am* fight.

trompo *nm* spinning top.

trompudo,-a *adj SAm* thick-lipped.

tronada *nf* thunder storm.

tronado,-a **I** *pp de* **tronar. II** *adj* old, broken-down.

tronar *vi* to thunder.

troncha *nf Am (tajada)* slice.

tronchante *adj fam* hilarious, uproarious.

tronchar **I** *vr* **1** *(árboles)* to cut down, fell. **2** *fig (esperanzas etc)* to destroy. **II troncharse** *vr* **t. de risa,** to split one's sides with laughter.

troncho[1] *nm Bot* stem, stalk.

troncho,-a[2] *adj Arg* **1** *(mutilado)* maimed. **2** *(pedazo)* piece.

tronco *nm* **1** *Anat* trunk, torso. **2** *Bot (tallo de árbol)* trunk; *(leño)* log; *fam fig* **dormir como un t.,** to sleep like a log. **3** *Geom* frustum; **t. de cono,** truncated cone. **4** *(tiro de dos caballos)* team. **5** *(linaje)* family stock. **6** *arg (compañero)* mate, pal, chum.

tronera **I** *nf* **1** *(gen)* dow; *(de fortificación)* loophole; *Náut* porthole. **2** *(de billar)* pocket. **II** *nmf fam (hombre)* rake; *(mujer)* slut, loose woman.

trono *nm* throne.

tropa **I** *nf* **1** *Mil* soldiers *pl.* **2** *(grupo de gente)* troop, crowd. **3 tropas,** *Mil* troops, fighting soldiers; **t. de asalto,** storm troops. **II** *nm Am (mal educado)* rude *or* coarse man.

tropel *nm* throng, mob; **en t.,** in a mad rush.

tropelía *nf* **1** *(atropello)* outrage. **2** *véase* **tropel. 3** *(delito)* crime.

tropezar *vi* **1** *(tropicar)* to trip, stumble **(con,** on); **t. con algo/algn,** to come across sth/sb; **tropecé con Quique en el concierto,** I ran into Quique at the concert. **2** *fig* **t. con,** *(dificultades)* to come up against; *(persona)* to disagree with; **el proyecto tropezó con muchos obstáculos,** the project ran into many difficulties.

tropezón *nm* **1** *(traspié)* trip, stumble; **dar un t.,** to trip; *fig* **a tropezones,** in fits and starts. **2** *fig (error)* slip-up, faux pas. **3** *fam (de comida)* chunk of meat.

tropical *adj* tropical.

trópico *nm* tropic.

tropiezo **I** *nm* **1** *(obstáculo)* trip. **2** *fig (error)* blunder, faux pas; *(revés)* setback, mishap. **3** *(riña)* quarrel. **II** *indic pres véase* **tropezar.**

tropilla *nf Am* drove.

troposfera *nf Geog* troposphere.

troquel *nm* die.

troqueladora *nf* stamping press.

troquelar *vtr* to stamp.

trotaconventos *nf inv lit* procuress, go-between.

trotador,-a *adj* trotting.

trotamundos *nmf inv* globe-trotter.

trotar *vi* **1** *(caballo)* to trot. **2** *fam (andar deprisa)* to bustle, run *or* run about.

trote *nm* **1** *(de caballo)* trot; **al t.,** at a trot. **2** *fam (actividad)* chasing about, (hustle and) bustle; **de** *or* **para todo t.,** for everyday use *or* wear; **ya no está para esos trotes,** he cannot keep up the pace any more.

trotón,-ona *adj* trotting.

trova *nf Lit* medieval poem, lyric.

trovador *nm* troubadour.

trovadoresco,-a *adj* troubadour.

trovar *vi lit* to write poetry *or* verses.

Troya n Hist Troy; **caballo de T.,** Trojan horse; fig **aquí** or **allí fue T.,** that's where or when the trouble began.

troya nf Am spinning top game.

troyano,-a adj & nm,f Trojan.

trozo nm piece, chunk; **lo cortó a trozos,** he cut it in(to) pieces.

trucaje nm Cin trick photography.

trucar vtr to doctor, alter; **t. una fotografía,** to doctor a photograph; fam **se ha trucado el mini,** he souped up the Mini.

truco nm 1 (ardid) trick; TV Cin gimmick; **este rompecabezas tiene t.,** this puzzle has a catch; **t. publicitario,** advertising stunt or gimmick. 2 (tranquillo) knack; **coger el t. (a algo),** to get the knack or hang (of sth).

truculencia nf (crueldad) cruelty; (exceso) sensationalism.

truculento,-a adj (cruel) cruel; (excesivo) sensationalistic.

trucha nf 1 (pez) trout. 2 Am (tienda) stand. 3 Méx (chaveta) derrick.

trucho,-a adj Am cunning.

trueno nm 1 Meteor thunder, thunderclap. 2 fam (joven) madcap.

trueque nm Com barter, exchange.

trufa nf 1 Bot Culin truffle. 2 (bombón) chocolate truffle.

trufar vtr Culin to stuff with truffles.

truhán,-ana nm,f rogue, crook.

trullo nm arg clink.

truncado,-a I pp de **truncar. II** adj truncate, truncated, cut short.

truncar I vtr 1 to truncate, fig cut short; fig **t. las ilusiones,** to shatter hopes. 2 fig (escrito) to leave unfinished, cut off; (sentido) to upset. **II truncarse** vr fig to cut short.

trust nm (pl **trusts**) Fin trust, cartel.

tse-tsé adj Ent **mosca t.,** tsetse or tzetze fly.

tu adj pos your; **tu libro,** your book; **tus libros,** your books.

tú pron you; **de tú a tú,** on equal terms; **trátame de tú, por favor,** call me **tú,** please.

tuareg nmpl Tuareg, Tuaregs.

tuba nf Mús tuba.

tuberculina nf tuberculin.

tubérculo nm 1 Bot tuber. 2 Med tubercle.

tuberculosis nf inv Med tuberculosis.

tuberculoso,-a adj 1 Bot tuberous. 2 Med tubercular, tuberculous.

tubería nf 1 (de agua) piping, pipes pl, plumbing. 2 (de gas, petróleo) pipeline.

tubo nm 1 (de análisis etc) tube; fam **hacer pasar a algn por el t.,** to put the screws on sb; fam **pasar por el t.,** to knuckle under; arg **alucinar por un t.,** to flip (out). ■ **t. de ensayo,** test tube. 2 (tubería) pipe. ■ Aut **t. de escape,** exhaust (pipe). 3 Anat tube.

tubular adj tubular; **(neumático) t.,** bicycle tyre.

tucán nm Orn toucan.

tuco,-a¹ I adj (manco) one-handed. **II** nm Am (trozo) piece. **III** nm,f (tocayo) namesake.

tuco² nm Arg Urug Culin tomato sauce.

tuerca nf Téc nut.

tuerto,-a I adj one-eyed, blind in one eye; **quedarse t.,** to become or go blind in one eye. **II** nm,f one-eyed person. **III** nm (agravio) wrong, injustice.

tuerzo indic pres véase **torcer.**

tuétano nm marrow; fig bones pl, essence; **hasta los tuétanos,** through and through; **estaba dolida hasta los tuétanos,** she was cut to the bone.

tufo nm 1 (mal olor) foul odour or US odor or smell, fug. 2 (emanación) fume, vapour, US vapor.

tugurio nm 1 (casucha) hovel, shack. 2 fig hole.

tul nm Cost tulle.

tulenco,-a adj Am (enclenque) thin; (patojo) lame.

tulipa nf 1 Bot small tulip. 2 (lámpara) tulip-shaped lampshade.

tulipán nm Bot tulip.

tullidez nf 1 (impedimento) paralysis, disability. 2 (cansancio) exhaustion.

tullido,-a I pp de **tullir. II** adj crippled, disabled. **III** nm,f cripple.

tullir vtr 1 (paralizar) to cripple. 2 (de cansancio) to wear or tire out.

tumba¹ nf grave, tomb; fig **a t. abierta,** (at) full speed; fam **no diré nada a nadie, soy (como) una t.,** my lips are sealed.

tumba² nf Am (tala) felling of trees.

tumbadero nm Méx Cuba brothel.

tumbado,-a I pp de **tumbar. II** adj lying, stretched out; **t. al sol,** lying in the sun.

tumbar I vtr 1 (derribar) to knock down or over. 2 Educ fam to fail. 3 Col Cuba Méx (talar) to fell. **II** vi 1 (caer a tierra) to fall down. 2 arg (matar) to bump off. **III tumbarse** vr 1 (acostarse) to lie down, stretch down. 2 (arrellanarse) to lie back. 3 ofens to screw, lay.

tumbía nf Am large basket.

tumbo nm jolt, bump; **dar tumbos,** to jolt, bump.

tumbona nf easy chair; (de lona) deck chair.

tumefacción nf swelling, tumefaction.

tumefacto,-a adj swollen.

tumor nm Med tumour, US tumor.

túmulo nm 1 (en arqueología) tumulus, barrow. 2 Geog mound. 3 (catafalco) catafalque.

tumulto nm tumult, commotion.

tumultuoso,-a adj tumultuous, riotous.

tuna nf arc student folkloric music group.

tunante,-a I nm,f rogue, crook; **el muy t. se largó sin pagar,** the rascal cleared off without paying. **II** nf prostitute.

tunco,-a adj Am one-handed.

tunda nf fam 1 (paliza) beating, thrashing. 2 (trabajo agotador) exhausting job, drag.

tundir¹ vtr (pieles, paño) to shear.

tundir² vtr to thrash.

tundra nf Geog tundra.

tunecí,-ina adj & nm,f, **tunecino,-a** adj & nm,f Tunisian.

túnel nm tunnel.

Túnez n 1 (país) Tunisia. 2 (ciudad) Tunis.

túnica nf (prenda) tunic.

tuno¹ nm Bot prickly pear.

tuno,-a² I nm,f (bribón) rogue, crook. **II** nm (estudiante) member of a **tuna.**

tuntún (al o al buen) nm haphazardly, any old how.

tuntuneco,-a adj CAm silly.

tupé nm (pl **tupés**) 1 (peluca) toupee. 2 fam (descaro) nerve, cheek.

tupición nf 1 Am fig confusion. 2 Méx (espesura) dense vegetation.

tupido,-a I pp de **tupir. II** adj 1 (espeso) thick, dense. 2 Am (obstruido) blocked.

tupir I vtr (apretar) to pack, tight, press down. **II tupirse** vr 1 (de comida) to stuff oneself. 2 (confundirse) to get muddleheaded.

turba¹ nf 1 (combustible) peat, turf. 2 (abono) peat (moss).

turba² *nf (muchedumbre)* mob, crowd.

turbación *nf* **1** *(alteración)* disturbance. **2** *(preocupación)* anxiety, worry. **3** *(desconcierto)* confusion, uneasiness.

turbado,-a I *pp de* **turbar.** II *adj* **1** *(alterado)* disturbed, unsettled. **2** *(preocupado)* worried, anxious. **3** *(desconcertado)* confused, baffled, put off.

turbador,-a *adj* **1** *(que altera)* disturbing, unsettling. **2** *(preocupante)* worrying. **3** *(desconcertante)* confusing, disconcerting, off-putting.

turbante *nm (prenda)* turban.

turbar I *vtr* **1** *(alterar)* to unsettle; *(paz, tranquilidad)* to disturb; *(agua)* to stir up. **2** *(preocupar)* to upset *or* worry. **3** *(desconcertar)* to baffle, put off. II **turbarse** *vr* **1** *(preocuparse)* to be *or* become upset. **2** *(desconcertarse)* to be *or* become confused *or* baffled.

turbina *nf Téc* turbine.

turbio,-a *adj* **1** *(oscurecido)* cloudy, muddy, turbid; *fig* **lo veo todo t.,** I see everything blurry. **2** *pey* shady, dubious; **un negocio t.,** a shady business. **3** *fig (turbulento)* turbulent; **un período t.,** an unsettled *or* turbulent period.

turbonada *nf Meteor* **1** *(chubasco)* stormy squall *or* downpour. **2** *Arg (viento)* gale.

turborreactor *nm Téc* turbojet (engine).

turbulencia *nf* turbulence.

turbulento,-a *adj* turbulent, troubled, unruly.

turco,-a I *adj* Turkish; **cama turca,** divan. II *nm, f (persona)* Turk; *fig* **cabeza de t.,** scapegoat. III *nm (idioma)* Turkish.

turcomano,-a *adj & nm,f* Turkman, Turkoman.

turgencia *nf* turgidity, turgidness.

turgente *adj*, **túrgido,-a** *adj* turgid.

turismo *nm* **1** *(gen)* tourism, touring; **hacer t.,** to go touring *or* sightseeing. **2** *(industria)* tourist trade *or* industry. **3** *Aut* private car.

turista *nmf* tourist; **hacer el t.,** to get taken in.

turístico,-a *adj* tourist; **de interés t.,** of interest to tourists.

turmalina *nf Min* tourmaline.

túrmix® *nm* liquidizer, blender.

turnar I *vi* **1** *(alternar)* to alternate. **2** *Méx* to send on. II **turnarse** *vr* to take turns.

turno *nm* **1** *(tanda)* turn, go; **¿a quién le toca el t.?,** who's next? **2** *(período de trabajo)* shift; **estar de t.,** (to be) on duty; **t. de día/noche,** day/night shift.

turolense I *adj* of *or* from Teruel. II *nmf* native *or* inhabitant of Teruel.

turón *nm Zool* polecat.

turquesa *adj & nf* turquoise.

Turquestán *n* Turkestan, Turkistan.

Turquía *n* Turkey.

turro,-a *adj Arg* stupid, idiotic.

turrón *nm* Christmas sweet similar to nougat made with almonds and honey or sugar.

turulato,-a *adj fam* flabbergasted, flummoxed.

tururú *adj fam* touched; **¡t.!,** get stuffed!

tusa *nf* **1** *SAm (maíz)* cornhusk. **2** *CAm Cuba (mujerzuela)* slut.

tusar *vtr Am* to crop.

tusón,-a *Am* I *adj (sin rabo)* tailless. II *nf (prostituta)* whore.

tute *nm* **1** *Naipes* card game. **2** *fam* beating, trashing; **darse un t.,** to wear oneself out.

tutear I *vtr* to address as **tú.** II **tutearse** *vr* to address (each other *or* one another) as **tú;** *fig* to be on familiar terms.

tutela *nf* **1** *Jur* guardianship, tutelage; **bajo t.,** in ward. **2** *fig (protección)* protection, guidance; **bajo la t. de,** under the protection of.

tutelar *adj* tutelar, tutelary.

tuteo *nm* use of the **tú** form of address.

tutiplén (a) *loc adv fam* in a grand way, **come a t.,** he eats like there's no tomorrow.

tutor *nm* **1** *Jur* guardian. **2** *fig (protector)* protector, guide. **3** *Educ (profesor)* tutor. **4** *Agr* stake, prop.

tutoría *nf* **1** *Jur* guardianship, tutelage. **2** *Educ* post of tutor.

tutú *nm* **1** *(prenda)* tutu. **2** *Arg Orn* bird of prey.

tuturuto,-a *adj* **1** *Am (lelo)* half-witted, stupid. **2** *Am (borracho)* drunk.

tuve *pt indef véase* **tener.**

TV *abr de* **televisión,** television, TV.

TVE *nf abr de* **Televisión Española.**

tuyo,-a I *adj pos* of yours, one of your; **¿es amígo t.?,** is he a friend of yours?; **un libro t.,** one of your books; **unas amigas tuyas,** some friends of yours. II *pron pos* yours, your own; **éste es t.,** this one is yours; **métete en lo t.,** mind your own business; **prométeme que no harás de fas tuyas,** promise me that you won't get up to your old tricks; *fam* **los tuyos,** *(familiares)* your family; *(amigos)* your friends.

tweed *nm Tex* tweed.

twist *nm Mús* twist.

U

U, u *nf (la letra)* U, u.

u *conj (delante de palabras que empiecen por o or* **ho)** or; **siete u ocho,** seven or eight; **ayer n hoy,** yesterday or today.

Uagadugú *n* Ouagadougou.

ubérrimo,-a *adj* very fertile, rich; **vegetación ubérrima,** luxuriant vegetation.

ubicación *nf* location, position.

ubicar I *vi (en un lugar)* to be, be situated. II *vtr Am (situar)* to locate, situate, place. III **ubicarse** *vr* **1** *(en un lugar)* to be situated *or* located. **2** *Arg (en un empleo)* to get a job.

ubicuidad *nf* ubiquity.

ubicuo,-a *adj* ubiquitous, omnipresent.

ubre *nf Zool* udder.

Ucrania *n* Ukraine.

ucraniano,-a I *adj* Ukrainian. II *nm, f (persona)* Ukrainian. III *nm (idioma)* Ukrainian.

Ud. *abr de* **usted,** you.

Uds. *abr de* **ustedes,** you.

UEO *nf abr de* **Unión de la Europa Occidental,** Western European Union, WEU.

uf *interj* **1** *(alivio)* phew! **2** *(repugnancia)* ugh!

ufanarse *vr* to boast (**de,** of).

ufanía *nf* conceit, arrogance.

ufano,-a *adj* **1** *(orgulloso)* conceited, arrogant. **2** *(satisfecho)* satisfied, happy.

Uganda *n* Uganda.

ugandés,-esa *adj & nm,f* Ugandan.

ugetista I *adj* (related to the) UGT; **la política u.,** UGT policy. **II** *nmf* member of the UGT.

UGT *nf abr de* **Unión General de Trabajadores.**

ujier *nm* usher.

ukelele *nm Mús* ukelele.

úlcera *nf Med* ulcer; **u. de estómago,** stomach ulcer.

ulceración *nf Med* ulceration.

ulcerar *vtr*, **ulcerarse** *vr Med* to ulcerate.

ulceroso,-a *adj* ulcerous.

ulterior *adj* **1** (*más allá*) ulterior, further. **2** (*siguiente*) subsequent; (*posterior*) later, further. ◆ **ulteriormente** *adv* subsequently, afterwards.

ultimación *nf* completion, conclusion.

ultimar *vtr* **1** (*terminar*) to finish, conclude, complete, finalize; **u. un negocio,** to conclude a deal. **2** *Am fam* (*matar*) to kill, finish off.

ultimátum *nm* (*pl* **ultimátums**) ultimatum.

último,-a *adj* **1** (*en el tiempo*) last; (*más reciente*) latest; (*de dos*) latter; **a últimos de mes,** towards the end of the month; **la última casa a mano derecha,** the last house on the right; **llegar el ú.,** to arrive last; **por ú.,** finally; *fig* **estar en las últimas,** (*moribundo*) to be at death's door; (*arruinado*) to be down and out; *fam* **a la última,** up to date; **va vestida a la última,** she likes to wear the latest fashions; *fam* **¡es lo ú.!,** that really is the limit. **2** (*en el espacio*) furthest; (*más abajo*) bottom, lowest; (*más arriba*) top, last; (*más atrás*) back, last; **está el ú. de la lista,** he's at the bottom of the list; **hasta el ú. pueblo del país,** up to the furthest village of the country; **siempre se sienta en la última fila,** he always sits in the back row; **vivo en el ú. piso,** I live on the top floor. **3** (*definitivo*) final; **es mi última palabra,** that's my final word. ◆ **últimamente** *adv* lately, recently.

ultra *Pol fam* **I** *adj* extreme right-wing. **II** *nmf* extreme right-winger; **los ultras,** the extreme right *sing*.

ultra- *pref* ultra-; **ultravirus,** ultravirus.

ultraconservador,-a *adj & nm,f* ultraconservative.

ultracorto,-a *adj Rad* ultrashort.

ultraderecha *nf Pol* extreme right (wing).

ultraderechista *nf Pol* **I** *adj* extreme right-wing. **II** *nmf* extreme right-winger.

ultrajante *adj* outrageous, insulting, offensive.

ultrajar *vtr* to outrage, insult, offend.

ultraje *nm* outrage, insult, offence.

ultramar *nm* overseas (countries); abroad; **del** *or* **en u.,** overseas.

ultramarino,-a I *adj* overseas. **II** *nm* **1** (*tienda*) grocer's (shop). *US* grocery (store). **2 ultramarinos,** (*comestibles*) groceries.

ultramoderno,-a *adj* ultramodern.

ultramontano,-a *adj & nm,f* ultramontane.

ultranza (a) *loc adv* **1** (*a muerte*) to the death. **2** (*a todo trance*) at all costs, at any price; **paz a u.,** peace at any price. **3** (*acérrimo*) out-and-out, extreme; **un ecologista a u.,** a fanatical ecologist.

ultrapasar *vtr* to surpass, go beyond.

ultrasónico,-a *adj* ultrasonic.

ultrasonido *nm* ultrasound.

ultratumba I *adv* beyond the grave. **II** *nf* afterlife.

ultravioleta *adj inv* ultraviolet.

ulular *vi* **1** (*viento, animal*) to howl. **2** (*búho*) to hoot.

umbilical *adj* umbilical; **cordón u.,** umbilical cord.

umbral *nm* (*de la puerta*) threshold; *fig* threshold, verge; **en el u. de,** on the threshold *or* verge of; **en el u. de la muerte,** at death's door.

umbrío,-a *adj*, **umbroso,-a** *adj* shady.

un,-a I *art indet* **1** a, an; **un coche,** a car; **un huevo,** an egg; **una flor,** a flower; **vino un lunes,** she came one Monday. **2 unos,-as,** some; **unas flores,** some flowers. **II** *adj* (*delante de nm sing*) one; **tiene un año,** she's one year old; **un chico y dos chicas,** one boy and two girls; *véase tamb* **uno,-a I.**

unánime *adj* unanimous.

unanimidad *nf* unanimity; **por u.,** unanimously.

unción *nf* **1** *Rel* unction. **2** *fig* (*devoción*) devotion, fervour.

uncir *vtr* to yoke.

undécimo,-a I *adj* eleventh. **II** *nm,f* (*de una serie*) eleventh. **III** *nm* **1** (*parte*) eleventh; *véase tamb* **octavo,-a.**

undulación *nf* *véase* **ondulación.**

undular *vi* *véase* **ondular.**

UNED *nf abr de* **Universidad Nacional de Educación a Distancia,** ≈ Open University, OU.

ungido,-a I *pp de* **ungir. II** *adj Rel* anointed.

ungimiento *nm Rel* unction.

ungir *vtr Rel* to anoint.

ungüento *nm Med* ointment.

unicameral *adj Pol* unicameral, single-chamber.

unicelular *adj* unicellular, single-cell.

unicidad *nf* uniqueness.

único,-a I *adj* **1** (*solo*) only, sole; **es el ú. que tengo,** it's the only one I've got; **hijo ú.,** only child; **la única vez,** the only time; **lo ú. que quiero,** the only thing I want. **2** (*extraordinario*) unique; **un hecho ú. en la historia,** an event unique in history. ◆ **únicamente** *adv* only, solely.

unicolor *adj* of one colour *or* US color.

unicornio *nm Mit* unicorn.

unidad *nf* **1** (*gen*) unit; *Mil* **u. de combate,** combat unit; *Com* **coste por u.,** unit cost; **u. monetaria,** monetary unit. **2** (*cohesión*) unity; *Lit* **u. de acción, lugar y tiempo,** unity of action, place and time; **u. política,** political unity.

unidireccional *adj* unidirectional.

unido,-a I *pp de* **unir. II** *adj* united.

unifamiliar *adj* **vivienda u.,** detached house.

unificación *nf* unification.

unificador,-a I *adj* unifying. **II** *nm,f* unifier.

unificar *vtr* to unify.

uniformado,-a I *pp de* **uniformar. II** *adj* in uniform, uniformed.

uniformar *vtr* **1** (*igualar*) to make uniform, standardize. **2** (*poner un uniforme*) to put into uniform, give a uniform to.

uniforme I *adj* **1** (*igual*) uniform. **2** (*superficie*) even. **II** *nm* (*prenda*) uniform; **usar u.,** to wear a uniform.

uniformidad *nf* **1** (*igualdad*) uniformity. **2** (*de superficie*) evenness.

uniformizar *vtr* to make uniform, standardize.

unigénito,-a I *adj Rel* only-begotten. **II el U.** *nm Rel* the Son of God, Jesus Christ.

unilateral *adj* unilateral, one-sided; **acuerdo u.,** unilateral agreement.

unión *nf* **1** (*gen*) union; **en u. de,** together with; **u. de cooperativas,** cooperative union; *prov* **la u. hace la fuerza,** united we stand. **2** *Téc* (*acoplamiento*) joining, coupling. **3** *Téc* (*junta*) joint, coupler.

Unión Soviética *n* Soviet Union.

unionismo *nm* unionism.

unionista *nmf* unionist.

unipersonal *adj* single, individual; *Ling* unipersonal.

unir I *vtr* (*juntar*) to unite, join (together); (*combinar*) to combine (**a,** with); **están muy unidos,** they are very attached to one another; **la nueva carretera une las dos**

comarcas, the new road links both districts; **nos une una buena amistad**, we are very good friends. **II unirse** *vr (juntarse)* to unite, join; *(combinarse)* to combine; *fml* **u. en matrimonio**, to unite in marriage.

unisex *adj inv* unisex.

unísono *nm* harmony, unison; **al u.**, in unison.

unitario,-a *adj* unitary; **precio u.**, unit price.

Univ. *abr de* **Universidad**, university.

universal I *adj* universal; **acuerdo u.**, universal agreement; **historia u.**, world history. **II universales** *nmpl Filos* universals. ◆ **universalmente** *adv* universally.

universalidad *nf* universality.

universalización *nf* universalization.

universalizar I *vtr* to universalize. **II universalizarse** *vr* to become universal.

universidad *nf* university. ■ **u. a distancia**, Open University; **u. laboral**, technical college.

universitario,-a I *adj* university; **título u.**, university degree. **II** *nm,f* university student *or* graduate.

universo *nm* universe.

uno,-a I *adj* **1** *(cardinal)* one; **a la una**, at one o'clock; **es la una**, it is one o'clock; **el número u.**, number one; **el tomo u.**, volume one; **llegará el día u. de abril**, he will arrive on the first of April. **2 unos,-as**, some; **habrá unos** *or* **unas veinte**, there must be around twenty; **unas cajas**, some boxes; **u. libros**, some books. **II** *pron* **1** one; **de u. en u.**, one by one; **se miraron u. a otro**, they looked at each other; **una de dos**, one of the two; **u. (de ellas)**, **una (de ellas)**, one of them; **u. más, u. de tantos**, one of many; **u. mismo**, oneself; **u. tras otro**, one after the other; **u. u otro**, one or the other; **u. y otro**, both; **unos cuantos**, a few; **unos y otros**, all. **2** *(impers)* one, you; **u. tiene que mirar por sus intereses**, one has to look after one's own interests. **3** *fam (persona)* someone, somebody; **u. que pasaba por allí**, some passer-by; **vive con una**, he's living with some woman. **4** *fam (trastada)* dirty trick; **hacerle una a algn**, to play a dirty trick on sb. **5** *fam (paliza)* thrashing; **le dieron una buena**, he got a really good thrashing. **III** *nm inv* one; **el u.**, (number) one; **el u. de Mayo**, the first of May; **treinta y u.**, thirty-one.

untadura *nf* **1** *(acción)* greasing, smearing. **2** *(untura)* grease, ointment.

untar I *vtr* **1** to grease, smear; **u. pan con mantequilla**, to spread butter on bread. **2** *fam (sobornar)* to bribe. **II untarse** *vr* **1** *(mancharse)* to get stained *or* smeared. **2** *fam (forrarse)* to line one's pockets, feather one's nest.

unto *nm* grease, ointment.

untuosidad *nf* greasiness, oiliness.

untuoso,-a *adj* greasy, oily, slippery.

untura *nf* ointment.

uña *nf* **1** *Anat* nail; *(del dedo)* fingernail; *(del dedo del pie)* toenail; **hacerse** *or* **arreglarse las uñas**, to manicure one's nails; **morderse** *or* **comerse las uñas**, to bite one's fingernails; *fig* **esconder las uñas**, to hide one's feelings; *fig* **estar de uñas**, to be at daggers drawn; *fig* **ser u. y carne**, to be inseparable, be hand in glove; *fam* **tener las uñas largas**, to be light-fingered. **2** *Zool (garra)* claw; *(pezuña)* hoof; *(del alacrán)* sting.

uñada *nf* scratch (with nail).

uñero *nm* **1** *Med (inflamación)* whitlow. **2** *Med (uña encarnada)* ingrowing toenail.

uñetas *nmpl CAm Col* thief.

uperización *nf (de leche)* sterilization.

uperizar *vtr (leche)* to sterilize; **leche uperizada**, sterilized milk.

Urales *nmpl* **los U.**, the Urals.

uralita *nf Constr* uralite.

uranio *nm Quím* uranium.

Urano *nm Astron* Uranus.

urbanidad *nf* urbanity, politeness.

urbanismo *nm* town planning.

urbanista *nmf* town planner.

urbanístico,-a *adj* town-planning, urban; **conjunto u.**, housing estate.

urbanización *nf* **1** *(proceso)* urbanization. **2** *(conjunto residencial)* housing development *or* estate.

urbanizar *vtr* to urbanize, develop; **zona sin u.**, undeveloped area; **zona urbanizada**, built-up area.

urbano,-a I *adj* urban, city; **guardia u.**, (traffic) policeman. **II** *nm, f fam (hombre)* (traffic) policeman; *(mujer)* (traffic) policewoman.

urbe *nf* large city, metropolis.

urdimbre *nf* **1** *Tex* warp. **2** *fig (trama)* intrigue, scheme.

urdir *vtr* **1** *Tex* to warp. **2** *fig (tramar)* to plot, scheme.

urea *nf* urea.

uremia *nf Med* uraemia, uremia.

uréter *nm Anat* ureter.

uretra *nf Anat* urethra.

urgencia *nf* **1** *(gen)* urgency; *(necesidad)* urgent need; **con u.**, urgently. **2** *(emergencia)* emergency; **cura de u.**, first aid; **en un caso de u.**, in an emergency.

urgente *adj* urgent; **correo u.**, express mail. ◆ **urgentemente** *adv* urgently.

urgir *vi* to be urgent *or* pressing; **me urge (tenerlo)**, I need it urgently; **urge encontrar una solución**, a solution is urgently required.

úrico,-a *adj* uric.

urinario,-a I *adj (de la orina)* urinary. **II** *nm (retrete)* urinal.

urna *nf* **1** *Pol* ballot box; *fig* **acudir a las urnas**, to vote. **2** *(vasija)* urn. **3** *(caja)* glass case.

urogallo *nm Orn* capercaillie.

urogenital *adj Med* urogenital.

urología *nf Med* urology.

urólogo,-a *nm,f Med* urologist.

urraca *nf Orn* magpie.

URSS *nf abr de* **Unión de Repúblicas Socialistas Soviéticas**, Union of Socialist Soviet Republics, USSR.

ursulina *nf Rel* Ursuline nun.

urticaria *nf Med* hives, urticaria.

Uruguay *n* **(el) U.**, Uruguay.

uruguayo,-a *adj nm,f* Uruguayan.

usado,-a I *pp de* **usar**. **II** *adj* **1** *(de segunda mano)* second-hand, used. **2** *(gastado)* worn out, old.

usanza *nf lit* fashion, custom; **a la antigua u.**, in the old style.

usar I *vtr* **1** *(gen)* to use. **2** *(prenda)* to wear; **sin u.**, new. **II** *vi* to make use (**de**, of). **III usarse** *vr* to be used *or* in fashion; **ya no se usa esta palabra**, this word is no longer used.

usía *pron pers fml (para hombre)* Your Lordship; *(para mujer)* Your Ladyship.

usina *nf* **1** *Am (fábrica de gas)* gasworks *sing*; *(central eléctrica)* power station. **2** *Arg (estación de tranvía)* tram stop.

USO *nf abr de* **Unión Sindical Obrera**.

uso *nm* **1** *(utilización)* use; **en u.**, in use; **en u. de**, *(utilizando)* using, making use of; *(en virtud de)* by virtue of; **hacer buen u. de**, to make good use of; **hacer mal u. de**, to misuse; **hacer u. de**, to make use of; **hacer u. de la palabra**, to take the floor; **instrucciones de u.**, instructions for use; *Farm* **u. externo/tópico**, external/local application. **2** *(ejercicio)* exercise; **el u. de un privileglo**, the exercise of a privilege. **3** *(de prenda)* wearing; **es obligatorio el u. de corbata**, ties must be worn; **la ropa se gasta con el u.**, clothes wear out with use. **4** *(costumbre)* usage, custom; **al u.**, in fashion, in the style *or* fashion of; **al u. catalán**, in the Catalan style *or* manner; **usos y costumbres**, ways and customs. **5** *Ling* usage.

usted *pron pers fml* you; **¡muchas gracias! —¡a u.!,** thank you very much! —you're welcome!; **¿quién es u.?, ¿quiénes son ustedes?**, who are you?; **tratar a algn de u.**, to use the polite form of address with sb.

ustedes *pron pers pl fml* you; *véase* **usted**.

usual *adj* usual, common.

usuario,-a *nm,f* user; **los usuarios del teléfono**, telephone users.

usufructo *nm Jur* usufruct, use.

usura *nf* usury.

usurero,-a *nm,f* usurer.

usurpación *nf* usurpation.

usurpador,-a I *adj* usurping. **II** *nm,f* usurper.

usurpar *vtr* to usurp.

utensilio *nm* **1** *(herramienta)* utensil, tool; **utensilíos de cocina**, kitchen utensils. **2** *(aparato)* device, implement.

uterino,-a *adj Anat* uterine.

útero *nm Anat* uteros, womb.

útil I *adj (gen)* useful; *(día)* working. **II** *nm (herramienta)* tool, instrument; **útiles de escritorio**, writing instruments; **útiles de labranza**, agricultural implements; *Taur* **útiles de matar**, matador's equipment *sing*.

utilería *nf Teat* (stage) props.

utilidad *nf (gen)* usefulness, utility; *(beneficio)* profit.

utilitario,-a I *adj* utilitarian. **II** *nm Aut (coche)* utility vehicle.

utilitarismo *nm Filos* utilitarianism.

utilitarista *adj & nm,f Filos* utilitarian.

utilizable *adj* usable, fit *or* ready for use.

utilización *nf* use, utilization.

utilizar *vtr* to use, utilize, make use of.

utillaje *nm* tool *pl*, equipment.

utopía *nf* Utopia.

utópico,-a *adj & nm,f* Utopian.

uva *nf Bot* grape; *fam* **estar de mala u.**, to be in a bad mood; *fam* **tener mala u.,** *(estar de mal humor)* to be in a bad mood; *(tener mal carácter)* to be a nasty piece of work, be bad-tempered.

uve ['uβe] *nf* name of the letter V in Spanish.

UVI *nf abr de* **unidad de vigilancia intensiva**, intensive care unit, ICU.

úvula *nf Anat* uvala.

V

V, v ['uβe] *nf (la letra)* V, v.

V *Elec abr de* **voltio(s)**, volt, volts, V.

V. 1 *abr de* **véase**, see, s.; *(latín)* vide, v. **2** *abr de* **verso**, verse, v.

v/ *abr de* **visto**, approved.

vaca *nf* **1** *Zool* cow; *fig* **las vacas flacas**, the lean years; *fig* **las vacas gordas**, the years of plenty; *fig* **ya vendrán las vacas gordas**, the good times will come. ■ **v. lechera**, milch cow, dairy cow; **v. marina**, sea cow. **2** *(carne)* beef.

vacación *nf (gen pl)* holiday, holidays *pl*, *US* vacation; **estar de vacaciones**, to be on holiday; **irse de vacaciones**, to go on holiday; *fam* **vacaciones a la sombra**, time spent in jail. ■ **vacaciones escolares**, school holidays; **vacaciones pagadas**, paid holidays.

vacada *nf* herd of cows.

vacante I *adj* vacant. **II** *nf* vacancy.

vacar *vi* to fall *or* become vacant.

vaciadero *nm* **1** *(conducto)* sewer. **2** *(vertedero)* dumping ground, rubbish tip.

vaciado I *pp de* **vaciar**. **II** *nm* **1** *(acción)* emptying, hollowing out. **2** *Arte* casting, moulding, *US* molding. ■ **v. de yeso**, plaster casting; **v. en molde**, casting in a mould.

vaciar I *vtr* **1** *(recipiente)* to empty; *(contenido)* to pour (away); **la policía mandó v. el local**, the police ordered everyone to leave the place. **2** *(dejar hueco)* to hollow out. **3** *Arte (moldear)* to cast, mould, *US* mold. **4** *(afilar)* to sharpen. **II vaciarse** *vr* **1** *(quedar vacío)* to empty. **2** *fam (desahogarse)* to let it all out.

vacilación *nf* **1** *(duda)* hesitation, vacillation. **2** *(falta de decisión)* irresolution. **3** *(oscilación)* vacillation, swaying.

vacilante *adj* **1** *(persona)* hesitant, irresolute. **2** *(voz)* hesitant, faltering. **3** *(luz)* flickering. **4** *(paso, mesa, etc)* unsteady, shaky.

vacilar *vi* **1** *(dudar)* to hesitate, vacillate, waver; **sin v.**, without hesitation. **2** *(al andar)* to sway, stagger, wobble. **3** *(voz)* to falter. **4** *(luz)* to flicker. **5** *fam (tomar el pelo)* to joke, tease.

vacile *nm fam* teasing.

vacilón-ona *nm,f fam* joker, teaser.

vacío,-a I *adj* **1** *(gen)* empty; *(hueco)* hollow; *fig* **palabras vacías**, empty words; *fig* **tener la cabeza vacía**, to be empty-headed; *fig* **volver con las manos vacías**, to come back empty-handed. **2** *(sin ocupar)* vacant, unoccupied. **II** *nm* **1** *(gen)* emptiness, void; **volver de v.**, to come back empty-handed; *fig* **caer en el v.**, to fall on deaf ears; *fig* **hacer el v. a algn**, to send sb to Coventry, cold-shoulder sb; *fig* **sentía un gran v.**, he was feeling empty. **2** *(hueco)* gap; *(espacio)* (empty) space. **3** *(vacante)* vacancy. **4** *Fís* vacuum; **en v.**, in a vacuum; **envasado al v.**, vacuum-packed.

vacuidad *nf* vacuity, emptiness.

vacuna *nf Med* vaccine; *Vet* cowpox.

vacunación *nf Med* vaccination.

vacunar I *vtr Med* to vaccinate **(contra,** against); *fig* to inure. **II vacunarse** *vr* to get oneself vaccinated.

vacuno,-a *adj* bovine; **ganado v.**, cattle.

vacuo,-a *adj* vacuous, empty.

vadeable *adj (río)* fordable; *fig (dificultad)* surmountable.

vadear *vtr (río)* to ford; *fig (dificultad)* to overcome.

vademécum *nm inv* handbook, vademecum.

vado *nm* **1** *(de un río)* ford. **2** *Aut* **'v. permanente'**, 'keep clear'.

Vaduz *n* Vaduz.

vagabundear *vi* **1** *(vagar)* to wander, roam. **2** *(holgazanear)* to idle, laze around.

vagabundeo *nm* **1** *(merodeo)* wandering, roaming. **2** *(holgazanería)* idling, lazing around.

vagabundo,-a I *adj (errante)* wandering, roving; *pey* vagrant; **perro v.**, stray dog. **II** *nm, f (trotamundos)* wanderer, rover; *(sin casa)* tramp, *US* hobo; *pey* vagrant, tramp.

vagancia *nf* idleness, laziness, vagrancy.

vagar *vi* to wander about, roam about.

vagido *nm* cry of a newborn baby.

vagina *nf Anat* vagina.

vaginal *adj Anat* vaginal.

vago,-a I *adj* **1** *(indefinido)* vague. **2** *(perezoso)* lazy, idle. **II** *nm,f* **1** *(holgazán)* idler, slacker, layabout; **hacer el v.,** to laze around. **2** *Jur* vagrant; *Hist* **ley de vagos y maleantes,** vagrancy act.

vagón *nm Ferroc* **1** *(para pasajeros)* carriage, coach, *US* car. **2** *(para mercancías)* truck, wagon, goods van, *US* freight car, *US* boxcar. ◼ **v. cisterna,** tanker.

vagoneta *nf* small open wagon.

vaguada *nf Geog* lowest part of a valley, stream bed.

vaguear *vi* **1** *(errar)* to wander, roam. **2** *(holgazanear)* to idle around, laze around.

vaguedad *nf* vagueness; **hablar sin vaguedades,** to get straight to the point.

vaharada *nf* puff, breath.

vahído *nm* fainting *or* dizzy spell.

vaho *nm* **1** *(aliento)* breath. **2** *(vapor)* steam, vapour, *US* vapor. **3** **vahos,** *Med* inhalation *sing*.

vaina I *nf* **1** *(de espada)* sheath, scabbard; *(de instrumentos etc)* case. **2** *Bot* pod, husk. **3** *Am fam (molestia)* bother, nuisance. **II** *nmf (persona)* good-for-nothing. **III** *adj Am fam (molesto)* bothering, annoying.

vaínica *nf Cost* hemstitch.

vainilla *nf* vanilla.

vaivén *nm* **1** *(oscilación)* swaying, swinging, to-and-fro movement. **2** *(de la gente)* coming and going, bustle. **3** *fig (cambio)* fluctuation, change; **los vaivenes de la vida,** life's ups and downs.

vajilla *nf* tableware, crockery, dishes *pl*; **lavar la v.,** to wash up; **una v.,** a set of dishes, a dinner service; **v. de porcelana,** chinaware.

valdré *indic fut véase* **valer.**

vale *nm* **1** *(comprobante)* voucher; **v. de devolución,** credit note. **2** *(pagaré)* promissory note, IOU (I owe you).

valedero,-a *adj* valid.

valedor,-a *nm,f* protector, patron.

valencia *nf Quím* valency.

valenciano,-a I *adj* Valencian. **II** *nm,f* Valencian. **III** *nm (dialecto)* Valencian.

valentía *nf* **1** *(valor)* courage, bravery. **2** *(acto valeroso)* heroic deed, bold act.

valentón,-ona *pey* **I** *adj* bragging, boastful. **II** *nm, f* braggart.

valentonada *nf pey* bragging, boasting.

valer¹ *nm* Value.

valer² *I vtr* **1** *(tener un valor de)* to be worth; **no vale nada,** it is worthless; **vale una fortuna,** it's worth a fortune. **2** *(costar)* to cost; **¿cuánto vale?,** how much is it?, how much does it cost?. **3** *(ganar)* to earn, win, get; **su insolencia le valió una paliza,** his insolence earned him a beating. **4** *(proteger)* to protect; **¡válgame Dios!,** God help me! **II** *vi* **1** *(tener un valor de)* to be worth. **2** *(servir)* to be useful, be of use; **no vale para hombre de negocios,** he is no use as a businessman; **tienes que hacer v. tus derechos,** you must assert your rights. **3** *(ser válido)* to be valid, count; **no hay excusa que valga,** no excuses; **no vale copiar,** copying doesn't count, there's no point in copying. **4** *(ser preferible)* **más vale,** it is better; **más vale que te vayas ya,** you had better leave now; *prov* **más vale prevenir que curar,** prevention is better than cure; *prov* **más vale tarde que nunca,** better late than never. **5** *fam* **¿vale?,** all right?, O.K.?; **vale,** all right, O.K. **III valerse** *vr* to use, make use (**de,** of); **v. de todos los medios,** to try everything; **v. por sí mismo,** to be able to manage on one's own.

valeriana *nf Bot* valerian.

valeroso,-a *adj* brave, courageous.

Valeta *n* **La V.,** Valletta.

valgo *indic pres véase* **valer.**

valía *nf* value, worth, merit.

validar *vtr* to validate, make valid.

validez *nf* validity.

valido,-a *adj & nm* favourite, *US* favorite.

válido,-a *adj* valid.

valiente I *adj* **1** *(valeroso)* brave, courageous, bold. **2** *(excelente)* fine, excellent, first-class; *irón* **¡v. amigo eres tú!,** a fine friend you are! **3** *pey (bravucón)* boasting, bragging. **II** *nmf* **1** *(valiente)* brave person. **2** *pey (bravucón)* boaster, braggart ◆ **valientemente** *adv* bravely, courageously, boldly.

valija *nf* **1** *(maleta)* case, suitcase. **2** *(de correos)* mailbag. ◼ **v. diplomática,** diplomatic bag.

valimiento *nm Pol* favour, *US* favor, protection.

valioso,-a *adj* valuable, precious.

valón,-ona I *adj* Walloon. **II** *nm,f (persona)* Walloon. **III** *nm (idioma)* Walloon.

valona *nf* **1** *Am (crines)* cropped mane. **2** *Méx (favor)* favour, *US* favor, service.

valor *nm* **1** *(valía)* value, worth; *(precio)* price; **objetos de v.,** valuables; **sin v.,** worthless; **una actriz de gran v.,** a very talented actress. ◼ *Fin* **v. adquisitivo,** purchasing power; **v. alimenticio,** food value; **v. nominal,** face value (of a cheque). **2** *Mat Mús* value; **escala de valores,** scale of values. **3** *(importancia)* importance; **dar v. a,** to attach importance to. **4** *(valentía)* courage, valour, *US* valor; **armarse de v.,** to pluck up courage. **5** *(descaro)* cheek, nerve; **¡qué v.!,** what a nerve! **6 valores,** *Fin* securities; bonds, assets. ◼ **v. en cartera,** investments; **v. inmuebles,** real estate *sing*.

valoración *nf* **1** *(tasación)* valuation, valuing. **2** *(revalorización)* appreciation.

valorar *vtr* **1** *(tasar)* to value, calculate the value of; *fig* **v. a algn en mucho,** to hold sb in high esteem. **2** *(aumentar el valor de)* to raise the value of.

valorización *nf* **1** *(tasación)* valuation, valuing. **2** *(revalorización)* appreciation.

valorizar *vtr* **1** *(tasar)* to value. **2** *(revalorizar)* to raise the value of.

vals *nm* waltz; **bailar el v.,** to waltz.

valuar *vtr* to value.

valva *nf Bot Zool* valve.

válvula *nf* valve. ◼ **v. de cierre,** stopcock; **v. de seguridad,** safety valve.

valla *nf* **1** *(cerca)* fence; *(muro)* wall; *Mil* stockade. ◼ **v. publicitaria,** hoarding, *US* billboard. **2** *Dep* hurdle; **los 100 metros vallas,** the 100 metres hurdle race. **3** *fig (impedimento)* obstacle, hindrance.

valladar *nm* **1** *(valla)* fence. **2** *fig (defensa)* defence.

vallado *nm (valla)* fence; *Mil* stockade.

vallar *vtr* to fence (in), build a fence around.

valle *nm Geog* valley; *fig* **v. de lágrimas,** vale *or* valley of tears.

vallisoletano,-a I *adj* of *or* from Valladolid. **II** *nm,f* native *or* inhabitant of Valladolid.

vallista *nmf* **1** *Dep* hurdler. **2** *Am* valley dweller.

vallunco,-a *adj CAm* rustic, peasant.

vampiresa *nf* vamp, femme fatale.

vampiro *nm* **1** *(espectro)* vampire; *fig* bloodsucker, parasite. **2** *Zool* vampire bat.

vanagloria *nf* vainglory.

vanagloriarse *vr* to boast (**de,** of).

vandalismo *nm* vandalism.

vándalo,-a I *adj Hist* Vandal, Vandalic. **II** *nm, f Hist* Vandal; *fig* vandal.

vanguardia *nf* 1 *Mil* vanguard, van; *fig* **ir a la v. de,** to be at the forefront of. 2 *Arte Lit* avant-garde, vanguard.

vanguardismo *nm Arte Lit* avant-garde movement.

vanguardista *Arte Lit* I *adj* avant-garde. II *nm, f* avant-gardist.

vanidad *nf* vanity, conceit.

vanidoso,-a I *adj* vain, conceited II *nm, f* vain person.

vano,-a I *adj* 1 *(presuntuoso)* vain, conceited. 2 *(ilusorio)* vain, futile, useless; **en v.,** in vain. II *nm, f Arquit* opening, bay.

vapor *nm* 1 *(gas)* steam vapour, *US* vapor; *Culin* **al v.,** steamed. ■ **máquina de v.,** steam engine; **v. de agua,** water vapour. 2 *Náut* **(barco de) v.,** steamer, steamship; **a todo v.,** at full steam, at great speed. 3 **vapores,** *Med* vapours, hysteria *sing*.

vaporización *nf* vaporization.

vaporizador *nm* vaporizer, atomizer, spray.

vaporizar I *vtr* to vaporize. II **vaporizarse** *vr* to vaporize, become vaporized, evaporate.

vaporoso,-a *adj* 1 *(que despide vapor)* vaporous. 2 *(tejido)* sheer.

vapulear *vtr* 1 *(zurrar)* to beat, thrash. 2 *fig (criticar)* to slate, criticize.

vapuleo *nm* 1 *(zurra)* beating, thrashing. 2 *fig (crítica)* slating, negative criticism.

vaquería *nf* 1 *(establo)* cowshed. 2 *(lechería)* dairy.

vaqueriza *nf* cowshed.

vaquerizo,-a I *adj* cattle. II *nm, f* cowherd.

vaquero,-a I *adj* cow, cattle; **pantalón v.,** jeans *pl*, pair *sing* of jeans. II *nm* cowherd, *US* cowboy. III **vaqueros,** *nmpl (prenda)* jeans, pair *sing* of jeans.

vaqueta *nf* cowhide.

vaquetón,-ona *adj Méx* barefaced, shameless.

vaquilla *nf Am Zool* yearling heifer *or* calf.

vara *nf* 1 *(palo)* pole, rod. 2 *(bastón de mando)* staff, mace; *fig* **tener v. alta en,** to have a hold on. 3 *Taur* lance, pike; **poner varas,** to thrust at the bull.

varadero *nm Náut* shipyard, dry dock.

varado,-a I *pp de* **varar.** II *adj* 1 *Náut* beached, in dock. 2 *Am (sin recursos)* broke; *(sin ocupación fija)* without regular work.

varapalo *nm* 1 *(palo largo)* long pole. 2 *(golpe)* blow with a pole. 3 *fam (daño)* blow, setback.

varar I *vtr Náut (barco)* to beach, dock. II *vi* 1 *Náut* to run aground. 2 *fig (negocio)* to come to a standstill 3 *Am (vehículo)* to break down.

varazo *nm* blow with a stick *or* pole.

varear *vtr* 1 *(fruta)* to knock down (with a pole). 2 *(golpear)* to beat with a stick.

varec *nm Bot* kelp.

vareo *nm* knocking down (fruit from trees).

variabilidad *nf* variability.

variable I *adj* variable, changeable. II *nf Mat* variable.

variación *nf* variation. ■ *Fís* **v. magnética,** magnetic declination.

variado,-a I *pp de* **variar.** II *adj* varied, mixed; **galletas variadas,** assorted biscuits.

variante I *adj* variable. II *nf* 1 *(versión)* variant. 2 *(diferencia)* difference.

variar I *vtr (cambiar)* to vary, change. II *vi* 1 *(cambiar)* to vary, change; *irón* **para v.,** as usual, just for a change. 3 *(diferir)* to differ, be different.

varice *nf,* **várice** *nf Med véase* **variz.**

varicela *nf Med* chickenpox, varicella.

varicoso,-a I *adj* varicose. II *nm, f* person suffering from varicose veins.

variedad *nf* 1 *(variación)* variety, diversity; *prov* **en la v. está el gusto,** variety is the spice of life. 2 *Bot Zool* variety. 3 **variedades,** *Teat* variety show *sing*. ■ **teatro de v.,** variety, music hall, *US* vaudeville (theater).

varilla *nf* 1 *(vara)* rod, stick. 2 *(de abanico, paraguas)* rib; *(de corsé)* stay.

varillaje *nm (de abanico, paraguas)* ribs, ribbing.

vario,-a *adj* 1 *(variado)* varied, assorted. 2 *(diverso)* different, diverse. 3 *(mudable)* changeable, variable. 4 **varios,-as,** *(algunos)* several, some.

variopinto,-a *adj* diverse, assorted; **un público v.,** a mixed audience.

varita *nf* small stick. ■ **v. mágica,** magic wand.

variz *nm Med* varicose vein.

varón *nm (hombre)* man; *(chico)* boy; **hijo v.,** male child; **sexo v.,** male sex; *fam* **un santo v.,** a kind soul.

varonil *adj* manly, virile, male.

Varsovia *n* Warsaw. ■ *Mil* **Pacto de V.,** Warsaw Pact.

vas *indic pres véase* **ir.**

vasallaje *nm Hist* vassalage; *fig* servitude, serfdom, subjection.

vasallo,-a *nm, f Hist* vassal; *(súbdito)* subject.

vasco,-a I *adj* Basque; **el País V.,** the Basque Country. II *nm, f (persona)* Basque. III *nm (idioma)* Basque.

vascuence *nm (idioma)* Basque.

vascular *adj Anat* vascular.

vasectomía *nf Med* vasectomy.

vaselina *nf* vaseline®; *fam* **dar v. a algn,** to softsoap sb.

vasija *nf* vessel, pot, vase, jar.

vaso *nm* 1 *(para beber)* glass; *fig* **ahogarse en un v. de agua,** to make a mountain out of a molehill. 2 *(florero)* vase. 3 *Anat Bot Fís* vessel. ■ **v. capilar,** capillary; **vasos comunicantes,** communicating vessels; **vasos sanguíneos,** blood vessels.

vástago *nm* 1 *Bot* shoot. 2 *fig (de una familia)* offspring. 3 *Téc* rod, stem. 4 *Am Bot* banana stalk.

vastedad *nf* vastness, immensity.

vasto,-a *adj* vast, immense.

vate *nm* 1 *Lit (poeta)* poet. 2 *(adivino)* prophet.

Vaticano *n* **(Ciudad del) V.,** Vatican (City).

vaticano,-a *adj & nm* Vatican.

vaticinador,-a I *adj* prophesying, predicting. II *nm, f* prophet, seer.

vaticinar *vtr* to prophesy, predict, foretell.

vaticinio *nm* prophesy, prediction.

vatio *nm Elec* watt.

vaya[1] *interj* well!; **¡v. enredo!,** what a mess!; **¡v. por Dios!,** goodness me!; **¡v., v.!,** well, well!, well I'm blowed!

vaya[2] *subj pres véase* **ir.**

Vd. *abr de* **usted,** you.

ve I *imperat véase* **ir.** II *indic pres véase* **ver.**

vecinal *adj* local.

vecindad *nf* 1 *(vecindario)* neighbourhood, *US* neighborhood, vicinity. 2 *(vecinos)* community, residents *pl*, neighbours *pl*, *US* neighbors *pl*. ■ **casa de v.,** block of flats.

vecindario *nm* 1 *(población)* residents *pl*, inhabitants *pl*. 2 *(vecindad)* neighbourhood, *US* neighborhood. 3 *(vecinos)* community, residents, neighbours, *US* neighbors.

vecino,-a I *adj* neighbouring, *US* neighboring, nearby; **la iglesia está en el pueblo v.,** the church is in the next village. II *nm, f* 1 *(persona)* neighbour, *US* neighbor; **el v. de al lado,** the next-door neighbour. 2 *(residente)* resident; *(habitante)* inhabitant. ■ **asociación de vecinos,** tenants' association.

vector *nm* vector.

veda *nf (prohibición)* prohibition; *(de caza)* close season, *US* closed season; **levantar la v.,** to open the season.

vedado,-a I *pp de* **vedar. II** *adj* forbidden, prohibited. **III** *nm* private preserve.

vedar *vtr* **1** *(prohibir)* to forbid, prohibit, ban. **2** *(impedir)* to prevent.

vedette *nf Cin Teat* star.

vega *nf* fertile plain *or* lowland.

vegetación *nf* **1** *Bot* vegetation. **2 vegetaciones,** *Med* adenoids.

vegetal I *adj* vegetable; **el reino v.,** vegetable kingdom. ■ **carbón v.,** charcoal. **II** *nm* vegetable, plant.

vegetar *vi Bot* to grow; *fig (persona)* to vegetate.

vegetarianismo *nm* vegetarianism.

vegetariano,-a *adj & nm,f* vegetarian.

vegetativo,-a *adj* vegetative; *fam* **lleva tres años en estado v.,** he has been in a coma for three years.

vehemencia *nf* vehemence.

vehemente *adj* vehement.

vehículo *nm* **1** *(gen)* vehicle; *(coche)* car; *fig* **los viajes son un v. de intercambio de ideas,** travelling is a vehicle for exchanging ideas. **2** *Med (transmisor)* transmitter, carrier.

veinte I *adj inv (cardinal)* twenty; *(ordinal)* twentieth; **el v. de junio,** (on) the twentieth of June; **los locos años v.,** the roaring twenties. **II** *nm inv* twenty; *véase tamb* **ocho.**

veintena *nf (veinte)* twenty; *(unos veinte)* about twenty.

vejación *nf,* **vejamen** *nm* **1** *(molestia)* vexation. **2** *(humillación)* humiliation.

vejar *vtr* **1** *(molestar)* to vex, annoy. **2** *(humillar)* to humiliate.

vejatorio,-a *adj* **1** *(molesto)* vexatious, annoying. **2** *(humillante)* humiliating.

vejestorio *nm fam* old person *or* crock.

vejete *nm fam* old man.

vejez *nf* old age; *prov* **a la v., viruelas,** there's no fool like an old fool.

vejiga *nf Anat* bladder. ■ **v. de la bilis,** gall bladder.

vela¹ *nf* **1** *(candela)* candle; *fam* **encender una v. a Dios y otra al diablo,** to have a foot in both camps; *fam* **estar a dos velas,** to be broke; *fam* **¿quién te ha dado v. en este entierro?,** who gave you any say in the matter? **2** *(desvelo)* wakefulness; **pasar la noche en v.,** to have a sleepless night. **3** *(vigilia)* vigil, watch; *(de un muerto)* wake.

vela² *nf Náut* sail; **a toda v., a velas desplegadas,** under full sail, at full speed; **alzar** *or* **largar velas,** to set sail; *fig* **recoger velas,** to back down ■ **barco de velas,** sailing boat, sailing ship, **v. mayor,** mainsail.

velada *nf* evening (party)

velado,-a .velar II *adj* **1** *(oculto)* veiled, hidden **2** *Fot* blurred

velador,-a I *adj (que vigila)* watching, guarding **II** *nm (vigilante)* watchman, guard **III** *nm* **1** *(candelero)* candlestick **2** *Am (mesilla de noche)* bedside table **IV** *nf Méx (lámpara de parafina)* glass lampshade, *(de noche)* night light

velamen *nm Náut* sails *pl*

velar¹ *adj & nf Ling* velar

velar² *vtr* **1** *(cuidar)* to watch over, **v. a un enfermo,** to sit up with a sick person. **2** *(muerto)* to keep vigil over **II** *vi* **1** *(no dormir)* to stay awake; *(no acostarse)* to stay up **2** *(hacer guardia)* to keep watch, *Rel* to keep vigil **3** *fig (cuidar)* to look *(por,* after), watch *(por,* over).

velar³ I *vtr* **1** *(poner un velo)* to veil, *fig* to hide, cover **2** *Fot* to blur, fog **II velarse** *vr Fot* to become blurred *or* fogged

velarización *nf Ling* velarization

velarizar *vtr Ling* to velarize.

velatorio *nm* vigil, wake

veleidad *nf* **1** *(inconstancia)* fickleness, inconstancy. **2** *(capricho)* whim, caprice

veleidoso,-a *adj* fickle, inconstant.

velero,-a *Náut* **I** *adj* sailing. **II** *nm* sailing boat *or* ship

veleta I *nf* weather vane, weathercock **II** *nmf fam* fickle *or* changeable person.

velo *nm* **1** *(prenda)* veil, *Rel* **tomar el v.,** to take the veil, become a nun, *fig* **correr un tupido v. sobre algo,** to cover up sth, keep sth quiet **2** *Anat* velum. ■ **v. del paladar,** soft palate, velum.

velocidad *nf* **1** *(rapidez)* speed, velocity; **a toda v.,** at full speed, **le multaron por exceso de v.,** he was fined for speeding, *Aut* **v. máxima 60 km,** 60 km speed limit. ■ *Av Náut* **v. de crucero,** cruising speed, *Inform* **v. de transmisión,** bit rate, *Inform* **v. operativa,** operating speed **2** *Aut (marcha)* gear, **cambiar de v.,** to change gear ■ **caja de velocidades,** gear box.

velocímetro *nm* speedometer

velocípedo *nm* velocipede

velódromo *nm* cycle track, *US* velodrome

velomotor *nm* moped

velón *nm* **1** *(lámpara de aceite)* oil lamp **2** *Am (vela)* big candle.

veloz I *adj* swift, rapid, quick, fast **II** *adv* quickly, fast; **el tiempo pasa v.,** time flies

vello *nm* hair

vellocino *nm* fleece ■ *Mit* **V. de Oro,** Golden Fleece

vellón *nm* fleece

vellosidad *nf (vello)* down, *(abundancia)* hairiness

velloso,-a *adj,* **velludo,-a** *adj* downy, hairy, fluffy

vena *nf* **1** *Anat* vein **2** *Geol Min* vein, seam **3** *(de madera)* grain **4** *fig* mood, **estar en v. para,** to be in the mood for; **le ha dado la v. por irse a la China,** he has taken it into his head to go to China, **tener una v. de loco,** to have a streak of madness, **tiene v. de músico,** he has a gift for music

venablo *nm* javelin, dart, *fig* **echar venablos,** to blow one's top, explode with anger

venado *nm* **1** *Zool* deer, stag **2** *Culin* venison

venal *adj* **1** *(vendible)* venal, which can be bought **2** *pey (sobornable)* venal, corrupt

venalidad *nf* venality

vencedor,-a I *adj* **1** *Dep* winning **2** *Mil* conquering, victorious **II** *nm,f* **1** *Dep* winner, victor **2** *Mil* conqueror, victor

vencejo¹ *nm* band, string

vencejo² *nm Orn* swift, **v. real,** alpine swift

vencer I *vtr* **1** *Mil (enemigo)* to conquer, defeat, vanquish, *Dep (rival)* to beat, **v.** *or* **morir,** do or die. **2** *(dificultad)* to overcome, surmount, **le venció el sueño,** he was overcome by sleep, **no te dejes v.,** don't give in **II** *vi* **1** *(pago, deuda)* to fall due, be payable **2** *(plazo)* to expire **III vencerse** *vr* **1** *(controlarse)* to control oneself **2** *(doblarse)* to bend, incline

vencido,-a I *adj* **1** *pp de* **vencer II** *adj* **1** *Mil (derrotado)* defeated, vanquished, *Dep* beaten, *fig* **darse por v.,** to give up, accept defeat **2** *(pago, deuda)* due, payable, **el alquiler se paga al mes v.,** the rent is paid at the end of each month **3** *(plazo)* expired, *fam fig* **a la tercera va la vencida,** third time lucky

vencimiento *nm* **1** *(inclinación)* bend, inclination **2** *(de un pago, una deuda)* maturity **3** *(de un plazo)* expiry, maturity

venda *nf* bandage, *fig* **tener una v. en los ojos,** to be blind, go around with one's eyes closed

vendaje *nm* dressing

vendar *vtr* to bandage, *fig* **v. los ojos a algn,** to blindfold sb

vendaval *nm* strong wind, gale

vendedor,-a I *adj* selling. **II** *nm,f (gen)* seller, *(hombre)* salesman, *(mujer)* saleswoman ■ **v. ambulante,** hawker, street salesman

vender I *vtr* to sell, **v. a plazos,** to sell on credit, **v. al contado,** to sell for cash, **v. al por mayor,** to (sell) wholesale, **v. al por menor,** to (sell) retail **II venderse** *vr* **1** *(estar en venta)* to be on sale, be sold, **se vende,** for sale, **sólo se vende en farmacia,** only on sale at chemists, *fam fig* **se vende como rosquillas,** it's selling like hot cakes **2** *(dejarse sobornar)* to sell oneself

vendible *adj* saleable, marketable

vendido,-a I *pp de* **vender II** *adj* sold

vendimia *nf* **1** *(cosecha)* grape harvest **2** *(año de cosecha)* vintage, year

vendimiador,-a *nm,f* grape picker

vendimiar *vtr (uvas)* to pick

vendré *indic fut véase* **venir.**

Venecia *n* Venice.

veneciano,-a *adj & nm,f* Venetian

veneno *nm (químico, vegetal)* poison; *(animal)* venom, *fig* spite, venom

venenoso,-a *adj* **1** *(que envenena)* poisonous. **2** *fig* spiteful, venomous

venerable *adj* venerable

veneración *nf* veneration, worship

venerar *vtr* to venerate, revere, worship

venéreo,-a *adj Med* venereal

venero *nm* **1** *(manantial)* spring **2** *Min* seam, vein **3** *fig (fuente)* source, origin; **aquel almanaque es un v. de datos,** that almanac is a mine of information

venezolano,-a *adj & nm,f* Venezuelan

Venezuela *n* Venezuela.

venga *subj pres véase* **venir.**

vengador,-a I *adj* avenging. **II** *nm,f* avenger.

venganza *nf* vengeance, revenge.

vengar I *vtr* to avenge. **II vengarse** *vr* to avenge oneself; **v. de algn,** to take revenge on sb.

vengativo,-a *adj* vengeful, vindictive.

vengo *indic pres véase* **venir.**

venia *nf* **1** *fml (permiso)* permission. **2** *(perdón)* pardon. **3** *Am Mil (saludo)* salute.

venial *adj* venial.

venialidad *nf* veniality.

venida *nf* coming, arrival; **idas y venidas,** comings and goings.

venidero,-a *adj* future, coming; **en lo v.,** in the future.

venir I *vi* **1** *(gen)* to come (**a,** to); **el año que viene,** next year; **la escena más famosa viene ahora,** the most famous scene now follows; **la guía viene también en italiano,** the guidebook also comes in Italian; **voy y vengo,** I'll be right back; *fig* **eso no viene a cuento** *or* **al caso,** that's beside the point; *fig* **lo veía v.,** I could see it coming; *fig* **me vino la idea de alquilar la casa,** I hit on the idea of renting out the house; *fig* **v. a la memoria,** to remember; *fig* **v. a menos,** to come down in the world; *fig* **v. al mundo,** to be born; *fig* **v. rodado,** to come *or* happen at just the right time; *fam* **a ti no te va ni te viene,** it's none of your business; *fam* **no me vengas con historias,** don't come to me with your excuses; *fam* **¡venga ya!,** *(basta)* stop it!, that's quite enough!; *(expresa incredulidad)* come off it! **2** *(llegar)* to arrive; **vino a las once,** he arrived at eleven. **3** *(proceder)* to come from; **de ahí viene su desgracia,** that was his downfall; **la casa le vino de su madre,** he inherited the house from his mother. **4** *(ir bien or mal, ajustarse)* **esos zapatos te vienen grandes,** those shoes are too big for you; **v. bien,** to be suitable *or*

convenient; **el metro me viene muy bien,** I find the underground very handy; **v. mal,** to be unsuitable *or* inconvenient; **recogerlo hoy me viene mal,** it is very inconvenient for me to pick it up today; *fam* **le viene que ní pintado,** it suits her down to the ground; *fam* **me viene de perlas,** it's just what I needed, it's just the ticket; *fam* **no les viene en gana trabajar los lunes,** they don't feel like working on Mondays. **II** *v aux* **1** *(v. + a + infin)* **viene a ser lo mismo,** it's all the same in the end; **vino a parar en la cárcel,** he ended up in jail. **2** *(v. + a + ger)* **venía solicitando este empleo desde hace un año,** I've been asking for this job for a year. **3** *(v. + a + pp)* **los cambios de temperatura vienen motivados por los vientos,** the changes in temperatures are caused by the wind. **III venirse** *vr* **1** *(volver)* to come back, go back. **2 v. abajo,** to collapse; *fig* **el teatro se venía abajo con los aplausos,** the applause shook the theatre.

venoso,-a *adj* **1** *(sangre)* venous. **2** *(manos etc)* veined, veiny. **3** *(hoja)* veined, ribbed.

venta *nf* **1** *(acción)* sale, selling; **en v.,** for sale; **estar a la v.,** to be on sale; **poner a la v.,** *(casa)* to put up for sale; *(mercancías)* to put on sale. ■ **v. a plazos,** credit sales *pl*; **v. al contado,** cash sale; **v. al por mayor,** wholesale; **v. al por menor,** retail; **v. de pisos,** flats for sale; **v. postbalance,** clearance sale, *US* post-inventory sale. **2** *(artículos vendidos)* sales *pl*. ■ **contrato de v.,** bill of sale; **departamento de ventas,** sales department. **3** *(posada)* country inn; *(restaurante)* restaurant.

ventaja *nf* advantage; **ganó la carrera con tres metros de v.,** she won the race by three metres; **llevar v. a,** to have the advantage over; **sacar v. a,** to be ahead of; **sacar v. de,** to profit from, use to one's own advantage, take advantage of; **Ten v. para Rodríguez,** advantage to Rodríguez.

ventajista *nmf* opportunist.

ventajoso,-a *adj* advantageous.

ventana *nf* **1** *Arquit* window; **v. de guillotina,** sash window; *fig* **tirar algo por la v.,** to waste sth. **2** *Anat (de la nariz)* nostril.

ventanal *nm* large window.

ventanilla *nf* **1** *(de vehículo, de sobre, de banco)* window. **2** *Cin Teat* (ticket) window. **3** *Anat (de la nariz)* nostril.

ventanillo *nm,* **ventanuco** *nm* small window.

ventarrón *nm* strong wind, gale.

ventear I *vtr CAm Méx (ganado)* to brand, stamp. **II ventearse** *vr Am* **1** *(envanecerse)* to give oneself airs. **2** *(salir mucho)* to go out a lot.

ventero,-a *nm,f* innkeeper.

ventilación *nf* ventilation; **sin v.,** unventilated.

ventilador *nm* ventilator, fan.

ventilar I *vtr* **1** *(habitación)* to ventilate, air; *(vestido)* to air. **2** *fig (opinión)* to air; *(cuestión)* to discuss, clear up. **II ventilarse** *vr* **1** *(habitación)* to be ventilated; *(vestido)* to be aired. **2** *fig (opinión)* to be aired; *(cuestión)* to be discussed *or* cleared up. **3** *fam (terminar)* to finish off. **4** *(tomar el aire)* to get some fresh air.

ventisca *nf* blizzard, snowstorm.

ventisquero *nm* **1** *(ventisca)* blizzard, snowstorm. **2** *(de montaña)* part of a mountain above the snow line.

ventolera *nf (golpe de viento)* gust of wind; *fam* **darle a uno la v. de hacer algo,** to take it into one's head to do sth; *fam* **darle a uno la v. por algn,** to take a fancy to sb.

ventosa *nf* **1** *(gen)* suction cup; *Med* cupping glass. **2** *Zool* sucker. **3** *(abertura)* vent, air hole.

ventosear *vi* to break wind.

ventosidad *nf* wind, flatulence.

ventoso,-a *adj* windy.

ventrículo *nm Anat* ventricle.

ventrílocuo,-a I *adj* ventriloquistic. **II** *nm,f* ventriloquist.

ventriloquia *nf* ventriloquy, ventriloquism.

ventrudo,-a *adj fam* pot-bellied.

ventura *nf* **1** *(felicidad)* happiness; **le deseo toda clase de venturas,** I wish you every happiness. **2** *(suerte)* luck; *(casualidad)* chance, fortune; **a la buena v.,** with no fixed plan; **por v.,** *(por casualidad)* by chance; *(por suerte)* fortunately; **echar la buena v. a algn,** to tell sb's fortune; **probar v.,** to try one's luck.

venturoso,-a *adj* lucky, fortunate.

Venus I *nm Astron Astrol* Venus. **II** *nf Mit* Venus. ■ **monte de V.,** mount of Venus.

veo-veo *nm fam* **el juego del v.-v.,** I-spy.

ver¹ *nm* **1** *(vista)* vision, sight. **2** *(apariencia)* looks *pl*, appearance; **de buen v.,** good-looking.

ver² **I** *vtr* **1** *(percibir imagen)* to see; **déjeme v.,** let me see; **lo vi con mis propios ojos,** I saw it with my own eyes; **v. la televisión,** to watch television; *fig* **dejarse v.,** to appear, become apparent; *fig* **ni visto ni oído,** very quickly; *fig* **v. venir algo,** to expect sth to happen; *fam* **había un jaleo que no veas,** you should have seen the fuss that was made; *fam* **¡habráse visto qué cara más dura!,** he's got a nerve!; *fam* **hasta más** *or* **a más v.,** see you; *fam* **¡hay que v.!,** it just goes to show!; *fam* **tengo un hambre que no veo,** I'm so starving. **2** *fig* *(observar, examinar)* to see, have a look at; **a v.,** let me see, let's see; **eso está por v.,** that remains to be seen; **¿lo ves?,** see!; **te veo triste,** you look sad; **(ya) veremos,** we'll see. **3** *fig* *(entender)* to understand; **no veo por qué le gusta tanto,** I can't see why he likes it so much; **por lo que veo,** apparently, it seems; **ya lo veo,** I can see that. **4** *(visitar)* to see, visit; **ven a verme cuando quieras,** come and see me whenever you like. **5** *Jur (caso)* to try, hear. **6 tener que v. con,** to have something to do with. **II verse** *vr* **1** *(imagen etc)* to be seen; **se ve el mar desde aquí,** you can see the sea from here. **2** *(encontrarse con algn)* to meet, see each other; *fig* **vérselas con,** to deal with sb; *fam fig* **no se pueden ni v.,** they hate each other. **3** *(encontrarse en una situación)* to find oneself; **me veo teniendo que comprarme otro coche,** I can see myself having to buy another car. **4 se ve que,** apparently.

vera *nf* edge, side, border; **a la v. de,** beside, next to.

veracidad *nf* veracity, truthfulness.

veranda *nf* veranda.

veraneante *nmf* holidaymaker, *US* (summer) vacationist.

veranear *vi* to spend one's summer holiday.

veraneo *nm* summer holiday; **lugar de v.,** (summer) holiday resort.

veraniego,-a *adj* summer, summery; **temporada veraniega,** summer season.

veranillo *nm* **v. de San Martín,** Indian summer.

verano *nm* summer.

veras *nfpl* truth; **de v.,** really, seriously; **lo siento de v.,** I am truly sorry; **te lo digo de v.,** I'm serious, I'm not joking.

veraz *adj* veracious, truthful.

verbal *adj* verbal; **expresión v.,** oral expression.

verbena *nf* **1** *(fiesta)* street *or* all-night party; **la v. de San Juan,** street party held on the eve of Saint John's Day. **2** *Bot* verbena.

verbigracia *adv fml* for example, for instance.

verbo *nm Gram* verb. ■ **v. auxiliar/copulativo/irregular/ transitivo,** auxiliary/attributive/irregular/transitive verb.

verborrea *nf fam* verbosity, verbal diarrhoea.

verbosidad *nf* verbosity, wordiness.

verdad *nf* **1** *(verdad)* truth; **a decir v., la v. sea dicha,** to tell the truth; **de v.,** really, truly, seriously; **de v. que no lo sabía,** I swear I didn't know; **es v.,** it is true; **faltar a la v.,** to lie; **¡no es v.?,** isn't that so?; **un amigo de v.,** a real friend; **una v. a medias,** a half truth; *fam* **decirle a algn las cuatro verdades,** to give sb a piece of one's mind; *fam* **tan de v. como que es de día,** it's a true as I'm standing here. **2** *(confirmación)* isn't it?, aren't you?,

don't you?, etc ...; **debe haber salido, ¿v.?,** he must have gone out, mustn't he?; **está muy bien, ¿v.?,** it is very good, isn't it it?; **hay cuatro, ¿v.?,** there are four, aren't there?; **no te gusta, ¿v.?,** you don't like it, do you?; **vendrá a la fiesta, ¿v.?,** she'll come to the party, won't she?

verdadero,-a *adj* true, real. ◆ **verdaderamente** *adv* truly, really.

verde I *adj* **1** *(colour)* green; *fam fig* **poner v. a algn,** to call sb every name under the sun. **2** *(fruta)* green, unripe; *(madera)* unseasoned. **3** *fig* *(inmaduro)* green, immature. **4** *fam* *(obsceno)* blue, dirty; **un chiste v.,** a dirty joke. **II** *nm* **1** *(colour)* green. **2** *(hierba)* grass. **3** *Pol* green; **el partido v.,** the Green Party.

verdear *vi* *(brotar)* to turn green; *(mostrar el color)* to look green.

verdecillo *nm Orn* serin.

verderón *nm Orn* **v. común,** greenfinch.

verdín *nm* scum.

verdor *nm* *(color)* greenness; *(de plantas)* verdure; *fig* youthfulness, vigour.

verdoso,-a *adj* greenish.

verdugo *nm* **1** *(el que ejecuta)* executioner. **2** *(prenda)* Balaclava (hood). **II** *nmf fig* tyrant.

verdugón *nm* **1** *(herida)* weal. **2** *Am* *(rotura de la ropa)* rent, rip.

verduguillo *nm Taur* stiletto.

verdulería *nf* greengrocer's (shop).

verdulero,-a I *nm, f* greengrocer. **II** *nf pey* coarse *or* foulmouthed woman.

verdura *nf* **1** *(del color)* greenness, greenery. **2** *(hortaliza)* vegetables *pl*, greens *pl*.

verdusco,-a *adj* (dark) greenish.

vereda *nf* **1** *(camino)* path, lane; *fig* **meter por** *or* **en v.,** to bring (sb) into line. **2** *Am (acera)* pavement, *US* sidewalk.

veredicto *nm Jur* verdict.

verga *nf* **1** *Náut* yard. **2** *Anat Zool* penis. **3** *(palo)* thin stick.

vergajo *nm* pizzle, whip.

vergel *nm* orchard.

vergonzante *adj* shamefaced.

vergonzoso,-a *adj* **1** *(penoso)* shameful, disgraceful. **2** *(tímido)* shy, bashful.

vergüenza *nf* **1** *(pena)* shame; **es una v.,** it's a disgrace; **¿no te da v.?,** aren't you ashamed?, have you no shame?; **no tiene v.,** he's a shameless person; **¡qué poca v.!,** how shameful! **2** *(timidez)* shyness, bashfulness; **le da v. cantar en público,** she feels shy about singing in public. **3** *(bochorno)* embarrassment; **se me cayó la cara de v.,** I was so embarrassed; *(honor)* **si tuviera v.,** if he were a man of honour. **4 vergüenzas,** *fam euf* private parts.

vericueto *nm Geog* rough path.

verídico,-a *adj* truthful, true.

verificación *nf* verification, checking; *Fin* **v. de cuentas,** audit.

verificador,-a I *adj* verifying, checking. **II** *nm, f* tester.

verificar I *vtr* **1** *(comprobar)* to verify, check. **2** *(llevar a cabo)* to perform, carry out. **II verificarse** *vr* **1** *(tener lugar)* to take place, occur. **2** *(resultar verdad)* to come true.

verja *nf* **1** *(reja)* grating, grille. **2** *(cerca)* railing, railings *pl*. **3** *(puerta)* iron gate; **la V. de Gibraltar,** the frontier with Gibraltar.

vermut *nf*, **vermú** *nm (pl vermús)* **1** *(bebida)* vermouth. **2** *(aperitivo)* aperitive.

vernáculo,-a *adj* vernacular; **lengua vernácula,** vernacular.

verónica *nf* **1** *Bot* veronica. **2** *Taur* kind of pass with the cape.

verosimil *adj (que puede ser verdadero)* probable, likely; *(creíble)* credible.

verosimilitud *nf (que puede ser verdad)* probability, likelihood; *(creíble)* credibility, verisimilitude.

verraco *nm Zool* male pig, boar.

verruga *nf* **1** *Med Bot* wart. **2** *CAm (ganga)* perk. **3** *CAm (ahorros)* savings *pl*.

versado,-a I *pp de* versar. **II** *adj* versed. **III** *nf Am* long poem.

versal *adj & nf Impr* capital (letter).

versalita *adj & nf Impr* small capital (letter).

versallesco,-a *adj fam fig (muy galante)* chivalrous; *(afectado)* affected.

versar *vi* **v. sobre,** to be about, deal with.

versátil *adj* **1** easily turned; *Anat* mobile. **2** *fig (voluble)* changeable, inconstant.

versatilidad *nf fig* changeableness, inconstancy.

versículo *nm Rel* verse, versicle.

versificación *nf* versification.

versificador,-a *adj & nm,f* versifier.

versificar I *vtr* to versify. **II** *vi* to write in verse.

versión *nf* **1** version, account. **2** *(traducción)* translation; **película en v. original,** film in the original language; **película inglesa en v. española,** English film dubbed in Spanish. **3** *Cin Teat* adaptation; **la película es una v. de una novela de Torres,** the film is based on *or* is an adaptation of a Torres novel.

verso[1] *nm* **1** verse; **en v.,** in verse. ■ **v. blanco/libre,** blank/free verse. **2** *fam (poema)* poem; **hacer versos,** to write poems.

verso[2] *nm (de libro)* verso, left-hand page.

vértebra *nf Anat* vertebra.

vertebrado,-a *adj & nm* vertebrate; *Zool* **los vertebrados,** the vertebrates.

vertebral *adj* vertebral; *Anat* **columna v.,** spinal column, spine.

vertedera *nf Agr (de arado)* mouldboard, *US* moldboard.

vertedero *nm (de basura)* rubbish dump, tip.

verter I *vtr* **1** *(de un recipiente a otro)* to pour (out). **2** *(derramar)* to spill. **3** *(vaciar)* to empty (out). **4** *(traducir)* to translate. **5** *fig (opiniones etc)* to express, voice. **II** *vi (desembocar)* to flow, run (**a,** into). **III verterse** *vr* to spill.

vertical I *adj* vertical; **ponlo v.,** put it upright. **II** *nf Geom* vertical (line). **III** *nm Astron* vertical.

vértice *nm Anat Geom* vertex.

vertiente *nf* **1** *(de una montaña, un tejado)* slope; *fig* aspect; *fig* **desde otra v.,** from a different angle. **2** *Am (manantial)* spring; *(fuente)* fountain.

vertiginoso,-a *adj* dizzy, giddy; *(que causa turbación)* causing dizziness; *fig* **venía a una velocidad vertiginosa,** he approached at breakneck speed.

vértigo *nm* **1** vertigo; *(turbación)* dizziness; *(por alcohol)* giddiness; **la altura me da v.,** heights make me feel dizzy; **tener v.,** to feel dizzy *or* giddy. **2** *fig* frenzy **de v.,** frenzied **me da v. sólo de pensarlo,** I go dizzy just thinking about it.

vesania *nf* **1** *(locura)* insanity. **2** *(furia)* rage.

vesícula *nf Bot Med* vesicle; **v. biliar,** gall bladder.

vesicular *adj* vesicular.

vespa® *nf* (motor) scooter.

vespertino,-a I *adj* evening. **II** *nm Prensa* evening newspaper.

vespino *nm* moped.

vestal *nf Mit* vestal (virgin).

vestíbulo *nm* **1** *(de casa particular)* hall, entrance; *(de edificio público)* vestibule, entrance hall, foyer, lobby. **2** *Anat* vestibule.

vestido,-a I *pp de* vestir. **II** *adj* dressed; **v. de militar,** in military uniform; **v. de verano,** wearing *or* in summer clothes. **III** *nm (ropa)* clothes *pl*; *(de mujer)* dress; **museo del v.,** museum of costume; **v. de noche,** evening dress.

vestidura *nf* clothing, clothes *pl*; *Rel* **vestiduras sacerdotales,** vestments; *fam* **rasgarse las vestiduras,** to raise an outcry, make a great to-do.

vestigio *nm (huella)* vestige, trace, remains.

vestimenta *nf* clothes *pl*, garments *pl*.

vestir I *vtr* **1** *(llevar puesto)* to wear; **vestía un traje de pana,** he was wearing a corduroy suit. **2** *(a alguien)* to dress; **viste al niño,** dress the baby; *fig fam* **quedarse para v. santos,** to be left on the shelf; *prov* **vísteme despacio que tengo prisa,** more haste less speed. **3** *(cubrir)* to cover **(de,** with). **II** *vi* **1** to dress; **ropa de (mucho) v.,** formal dress; *fam* **hay que el mismo que viste y calza,** the very same, none other. **2** *fam* to be classy, look smart; **la seda viste mucho,** silk always looks very elegant. **III vestirse** *vr* **1** to get dressed, dress; **enseguida me visto,** I'll be dressed in a second. **2** *(comprar prendas)* to buy one's clothes; **se viste en París,** he buys his clothes in Paris. **3 v. de,** to wear, dress in; *(disfrazarse)* to disguise oneself as; **v. de payaso,** to dress up as a clown; *fam* **v. de punta en blanco,** to dress up to the nines.

vestuario *nm* **1** *(conjunto de vestidos)* clothes *pl*, wardrobe; *Teat* wardrobe, costumes *pl*; *Mil* uniform. **2** *Teat (camerino)* dressing room. **3 vestuarios,** *Dep* changing room *sing*; *(fábricas etc)* cloakroom *sing*.

veta *nf Min* vein, seam; *fig* streak; *fig* **tiene una v. de loco,** there's a mad streak in him.

vetar *vtr* to veto, put a veto on.

veteado,-a I *pp de* vetear. **II** *adj* veined, streaked.

vetear *vtr (piedras, madera)* to grain, streak.

veteranía *nf* seniority, long experience; *(soldado)* long service.

veterano,-a I *adj* veteran. **II** *nm,f* veteran; *fam* **es un v. en estas lides,** he is an old hand at this. **III** *nm Chi Méx (viejo)* old man.

veterinario,-a I *adj* veterinary. **II** *nm,f* veterinary surgeon, vet, *US* veterinarian. **III** *nf* veterinary medicine *or* science.

veto *nm* veto; **derecho a v.,** power *or* right of veto.

vetustez *nf fml (antigüedad)* antiquity; *(vejez)* great age.

vetusto,-a *adj fml (antiguo)* ancient; *(viejo)* very old.

vez *nf (gen)* time; *(ocasión, turno)* occasion; **a la vez,** at the same time; **a** *or* **algunas veces,** sometimes; **alguna que otra v.,** on the odd occasion; **Ana habló una v., Paco dos veces y Jorge tres,** Ana spoke once, Paco twice and Jorge three times; **cada v.,** each *or* every time; **cada v. más** more and more; **cada v. peor,** worse and worse; **de una v.,** in one go; **de una v. para siempre,** once and for all; **de v. en cuando,** now and again, every so often, every now and then; **en v. de,** instead of; *(en cuentos etc)* **érase** *or* **había una v.,** once upon a time; **¿le has visto actuar alguna v.?,** have you ever seen him act?; **muchas veces,** very often; **otra v.,** again; **tal v.,** perhaps, maybe.

v.g(r). *abr de* verbigracia, for instance, for example, e.g.

vía I *nf* **1** *(camino)* road; *(carril)* lane; *(calle)* street; **v. de circunvalación,** bypass; **v. pública,** public thoroughfare. ■ *Astron* **V. Láctea,** Milky Way. **2** *Anat* passage, tract, canal; **vías urinarias,** urinary tract *sing*; *Farm* **(por) v. oral,** to be taken orally. **3** *Ferroc* track, line; **de v. doble,** double-track; **de v. estrecha,** narrow-gauge, *fam fig* mediocre; **el tren situado en la v. 2,** the train standing at platform 2. ■ **v. férrea,** railway track, *US* railroad track; **v. muerta,** siding. **4** *fig (modo)* way, manner, means; **dar v. libre a,** to leave the way open for; **por v. oficial,** through official channels; **recurrir a la v. judicial,** to go to law; **vías de comunicación,** communication channels. ■ *Jur* **v. contenciosa,** legal action. **5 en vías de,** in the process of; **en v. de construcción,** under construction; **países en v. de desarrollo,** developing countries. **6 por v.,** *(transportes)* by; *(a través de)* via, through; **Madrid-**

Londres v. París, Madrid-London via Paris; **por v. aérea/marítima,** by air/sea; **por v. terrestre,** overland; **transmisión v. satélite,** satellite transmission.

via crucis *nm Rel* Way of the Cross, Stations *pl* of the Cross; *fig* great suffering.

viabilidad *nf* viability.

viable *adj* viable.

viaducto *nm* viaduct.

viajante *nmf* commercial traveller, travelling salesman *or* saleswoman.

viajar *vi* to travel.

viaje *nm* 1 *(recorrido)* journey, trip; *(largo, en barco)* voyage; ¡**buen v.!,** bon voyage, have a good trip!; *irón* too bad!, good riddance!; **estar de v.,** to be away (on a trip); **irse** *or* **marcharse de v.,** to go on a journey *or* trip; **v. de ida,** outward journey; **v. de ida y vuelta,** return journey, *US* round trip; **v. de negocios,** business trip; **v. en barco,** boat trip; **v. en tren,** train journey; *lit* **el último v.,** one's journey's end. ■ **v. de novios,** honeymoon. 2 *(concepto de viajar) (gen pl)* travel; **en sus viajes a la India,** on his travels to India. ■ **agencia de viajes,** travel agency; **cheque de v.,** traveller's cheque; **libro de viajes,** travel book. 3 *(carga)* load; **dos viajes de arena,** two loads of sand; *fam* **de un v.,** in one go; *fam* ¡**menudo v. le has pegado a la tarta!,** you've had a good go at the cake! 4 *arg (drogas)* trip.

viajero,-a I *adj* travelling. II *nm,f* 1 *(gen)* traveller. 2 *(en transporte público)* passenger; ¡**viajeros al tren!,** all aboard!

vianda *nf* 1 *fml* food, viands *pl.* 2 *Arg Urug (fiambrera)* lunch basket.

viandante *nmf (transeúnte)* pedestrian, passer-by.

viaraza *nf Am* fit of anger.

viario,-a *adj* road, highway.

viático *nm Rel* viaticum.

víbora *nf* 1 *Zool* viper; *fig* **lengua de v.,** spiteful *or* viperine tongue. 2 *Méx* money belt.

viborear *vi Arg Urug (serpentear)* to wind, twist.

vibración *nf* vibration; *Ling* rolling, trilling.

vibrador *nm* vibrator.

vibrante I *adj* vibrant, vibrating; *Ling* rolled, trilled. II *nf Ling* vibrant.

vibrar *vtr & vi* to vibrate; *Ling* to roll, trill.

vibratorio,-a *adj* vibratory.

vicaria *nf Cub Bot* red periwinkle.

vicaría *nf* 1 *(dignidad)* vicarship, vicariate. 2 *(residencia, despacho)* vicarage; *fam* **pasar por la v.,** to get married (in church).

vicario,-a I *adj* vicarial, substitute. II *nm,f* vicar; **el V. de Cristo,** the Vicar of Christ.

vicealmirante *nm* vice admiral.

vicepresidencia *nf* 1 *Pol* vice-presidency. 2 *(de compañía, comité)* vice-chairmanship.

vicepresidente,-a *nm, f* 1 *Pol* vice president. 2 *(de compañía, comité)* vice-chairperson; *(hombre)* vice-chairman; *(mujer)* vice-chairwoman.

vicesecretario,-a *nm,f* assistant secretary.

vicetiple *nf* chorus girl.

viceversa *adv* vice versa.

vichar *vtr Am* to spy (on).

viche *adj Méx* hairless, with no hair.

vichy *nm Tex* gingham.

viciado,-a I *pp de* viciar. II *adj* 1 *(corrompido)* corrupt. 2 *(aire) (que huele mal)* foul; *(contaminado)* polluted; *(cargado)* stuffy.

viciar I *vtr* 1 *(corromper)* to corrupt; **las malas compañías te viciaron,** bad company led him astray. 2 *(aire)* to

pollute, contaminate. 3 *(anular)* to vitiate, nullify. 4 *(tergiversar)* to twist, distort. II **viciarse** *vr* 1 *(enviciarse)* to take to vice; *(corromper)* to become corrupted. 2 *(deformarse)* to go out of shape; **la persiana se ha viciado,** the blind is warped.

vicio *nm* 1 *(corrupción)* vice, corruption. 2 *(mala costumbre)* bad habit; *(inmoralidad)* vice; **de v.,** for no reason at all, for the sake of it; **quejarse de v.,** to complain out of sheer habit. 3 *(falta física)* defect.

vicioso,-a I *adj* 1 *(persona)* depraved, perverted. 2 *(cosa)* faulty, defective; **círculo v.,** vicious circle. 3 *(frondoso)* luxuriant, thick. II *nm, f* 1 depraved person. 2 *(niño consentido)* spoiled *or* spoilt child.

vicisitud *nf (gen pl)* vicissitude; **las vicisitudes de la vida,** life's ups and downs.

víctima *nf* victim; **no hubo víctimas en el accidente,** there were no casualties in the accident; **v. propiciatoria,** scapegoat.

victrola *nf Am* gramophone, record player.

victoria *nf* victory, triumph; **alzarse con la v.,** to come out victorious; **cantar v.,** to proclaim a victory.

victoriano,-a *adj* Victorian.

victorioso,-a *adj* victorious. ◆ **victoriosamente** *adv* triumphantly.

vicuña *nf Zool* vicuña, vicuna.

vid *nf Bot* vine, grapevine.

vida *nf (gen)* life; **amargarle la v. a algn,** to make sb's life a misery; **cambiar de v.,** to change one's lifestyle; **como si le fuera la v. en ello,** as if his life depended on it; **costarle algo la v. a algn,** to pay with one's life; **dar v. a,** to give life to; **daría mi v. por,** I would give my right arm for; **de por v.,** for life; **Dolores es una amiga de toda la v.,** Dolores is a lifelong friend; **en la flor de la v.,** in the prime of life; **en mi v.,** never in my life; **en v. de,** during the life of; **entre la v. y la muerte,** between life and death; **escapar** *or* **salir con v.,** to come out alive, survive; **estar con/sin v.,** to be alive/dead; **ganarse la v.,** to earn one's living; **hacerle la v. imposible a algn,** to make life impossible for sb; **llevar una v. agitada/tranquila,** to lead a busy/quiet life; ¡**mi v.!, v. mía!,** darling!, my love!; **nivel de v.,** standard of living; **no puedo llevar su tren de v.,** I can't compete with his lifestyle; **perder la v.,** to die; **quitarle la v. a algn,** to take sb's life; **se pasa la v. trabajando,** he's always working, he doesn't do anything but work; **seguro de v.,** life insurance; **señales de v.,** signs of life; *euf* **la otra v.,** the next life; *euf* **pasar a mejor v.,** to pass away; *fam* ¡**así es la v.!,** such is life!, that's life! *fam* **contarle a algn su v. y milagros,** to tell sb one's life story; *fam* **darse** *or* **pegarse la gran v.,** to live it up; *fam* **v. de perros,** dog's life; *fam* **y tu hermana, ¿qué es de su v.?,** what about your sister, what's she up to these days?; *fam* *euf* **echarse a la v.,** to go on the game, become a prostitute.

vidalita *nf Am Mús* plaintive love song.

vidente *nmf* seer, soothsayer.

video *nm* video; **grabar en v.,** to video-tape, record on video.

videoclub *nm* video club.

videojuego *nm* video game.

vidorra *nf fam* easy life; **pegarse la gran v.,** to live like a king.

vidorria *nf* 1 *Am pey* dog's life, miserable life. 2 *Arg fam* cushy number.

vidriado,-a I *pp de* vidriar. II *adj* glazed. III *nm* 1 *(cerámica)* glazed earthenware. 2 *(barniz)* glaze. 3 *(acción)* glazing.

vidriar I *vtr (cerámica)* **to glaze. II vidriarse** *vr* to become glazed, become glassy; *fig (asunto)* to become tricky.

vidriera *nf* 1 *(ventana)* glass window; *(puerta)* **v.,** glass door; *(de galería, balcón)* French window. 2 *Arquit Arte (ventana de colores)* stained-glass window. 3 *(escaparate)* shop window.

vidriería *nf* **1** *(fábrica)* glassworks *sing*. **2** *(tienda)* glass shop.

vidriero,-a *nm,f* **1** *(fabricante)* glass-maker. **2** *(que coloca cristales)* glazier.

vidrio *nm* **1** *(sustancia)* glass. ■ **fibra de v.,** fibreglass. **2** *(objeto)* glass object; **tienda de v.,** glass shop; *fam* **pagar los vidrios rotos,** to carry the can.

vidrioso,-a *adj* **1** *(quebradizo)* glass-like; *(frágil)* brittle; **ojos vidriosos,** glazed eyes. **2** *(resbaladizo)* slippery. **3** *fig* touchy; **asunto v.,** delicate matter; **carácter v.,** sensitive temperament.

vieira *nf* *(pez)* scallop.

viejo,-a I *adj* **1** *(persona)* old; **es más v. que yo,** he's older than me; **estar v.,** to look old; **hacerse v.,** to grow old; *(en tono afectivo)* **un v. amigo,** an old friend; *fam* **más v. que la nana** *or* **que Matusalén,** as old as the hills; *fam* **ser un gato** *or* **un perro v.,** to be a sly old fox. **2** *(cosa)* old; *(desgastado)* worn out, old; **caerse de v.,** to be falling apart (with age). **3** *(antiguo)* ancient, old; **viejas costumbres,** ancient customs. II *nm* old man; **los viejos,** elderly people; *fam* **mi v.,** my *or* the old man; *fam* **mis viejos,** my folks, my parents. ■ *fam* **v. verde,** dirty old man. III *nf* old woman; *fam* **mi vieja,** my *or* the old lady, my old woman.

Viena *n* Vienna.

vienés,-esa *adj* & *nm,f* Viennese.

viento *nm* **1** wind; **hace** *or* **sopla mucho v.,** it is very windy; *Mús* **instrumentos de v.,** wind instruments; **la rosa de los vientos,** wind rose; *fig* **beber los vientos por algn,** to be crazy about sb; *fig* **contra v. y marea,** come hell or high water; *fig* **corren malos vientos,** it's not the best moment, the time is not right; *fig* **ir como el v.,** to fly like the wind; *fig* **ir v. en popa,** to go splendidly, do very well; *fam fig* **mandar a algn a tomar v.,** to tell sb where to go; *prov* **quien siembra vientos recoge tempestades,** they that sow the wind shall reap the whirlwind. ■ **vientos alisios,** trade winds. **2** *(rumbo)* direction; *fig* **gritar algo a los cuatro vientos,** to shout sth from the rooftops. **3** *Caza* scent. **4** *fam (ventosidad)* wind, flatulence. **5** *(cuerda)* rope guy.

vientre *nm* **1** *Anat* belly, abdomen; **bajo v.,** lower abdomen; **dolor de v,** stomach ache; *fam* belly ache. **2** *(conjunto de vísceras)* bowels *pl*; **hacer de v.,** to have a bowel movement. **3** *(de mujer embarazada)* womb. **4** *(de barco, vasija)* belly.

viernes *nm inv* Friday; **de v. en ocho días,** the Friday after next; **de v. en una semana,** a week on Friday, Friday week; **el periódico del v.,** Friday's newspaper; **el v.,** on Friday; **el v. antepasado,** the Friday before last; **el v. pasado,** last Friday; **el v. por la mañana/tarde/noche,** (on) Friday morning/afternoon *or* evening/night; **el v. próximo** *or* **que viene,** next Friday; **el v. siguiente,** the following Friday; **este v.,** this Friday; **la película del v.,** the Friday film; **los v.,** on Fridays; **todos los v.,** every Friday; **un v. sí y otro no,** every other Friday. ■ **V. Santo,** Good Friday.

Vietnam *n* Vietnam.

vietnamita I *adj* Vietnamese. II *nmf* *(persona)* Vietnamese. III *nm* *(idioma)* Vietnamese.

viga *nf* *Arquit* **1** *(de madera)* beam, rafter; **v. maestra,** main beam; **v. transversal,** crossbeam. **2** *(de hierro* *acero)* girder.

vigencia *nf* validity; **entrar en v.,** to come into force *or* effect, become valid; **estar en v.,** to be in force, be valid.

vigente *adj* in force, valid.

vigésimo,-a I *adj* twentieth; **vigésima parte,** twentieth; **v. primero,** twenty-first; **v. segundo,** twenty-second. II *nm, f (de una serie)* twentieth. III *nm (parte)* twentieth; *véase* *tamb* **octavo,-a.**

vigía I *nf (atalaya)* watchtower, lookout post. II *nmf (gen)* lookout; *(hombre)* watchman; *(mujer)* watchwoman.

vigilancia *nf* vigilance, watchfulness; **bajo v.,** under surveillance. ■ *Med* **unidad de v. intensiva,** intensive care unit.

vigilante I *adj (despierto)* vigilant, watchful; *(alerta)* alert. II *nm (guarda)* watchman; *(de banco, con armas)* guard; **v. nocturno,** night watchman.

vigilar I *vtr (ir con cuidado)* to watch; *(con armas etc)* to guard; *(supervisar)* to oversee; **vigila al niño,** keep an eye on the baby; **vigila que no entren,** make sure they don't get in; **vigila que no se salga la leche,** take care that the milk doesn't boil over. II *vi (gen)* to keep watch; *(observar)* to watch; **v. por** *or* **sobre,** to watch over, look after; **v. por el bien público,** to guarantee public law and order.

vigilia *nf* **1** *(no dormir)* vigil, watch; **pasar la noche de v.,** to stay awake all night. **2** *(víspera)* eve; *Rel* vigil. **3** *Rel (abstinencia)* abstinence; **guardar la v.,** to abstain from eating meat. **4** *(trabajo)* night work *or* study; **este trabajo es fruto de sus vigilias,** this work is the product of many sleepless nights.

vigor *nm* **1** vigour, *US* vigor; *(fuerza, robustez)* strength. **2** *(de una ley)* force, effect; **en v.,** in force; **poner en v.,** to put into effect.

vigorizador,-a *adj (que da vitalidad)* invigorating; *(que da robustez)* fortifying; **medicamento v.,** tonic.

vigorizar *vtr* **1** *(dar vitalidad)* to invigorate; *(dar robustez)* to fortify. **2** *fig (animar)* to encourage; *(estimular)* to stimulate.

vigoroso,-a *adj (vital)* vigorous; *(fuerte)* strong, sturdy.

viguería *nf* *Arquit* **1** *(de madera)* beams *pl*. **2** *(de metal)* girders *pl*.

vigueta *nf* *Arquit* **1** *(de madera)* small beam. **2** *(de metal)* small girder.

vikingo *nm* Viking.

vil *adj fml (person)* vile, base, despicable; *(act)* vile.

vileza *nf* **1** *(cualidad)* vileness, baseness. **2** *(acto)* vile act, despicable deed.

vilipendiar *vtr fml* **1** *(ofender)* to vilify, revile, insult. **2** *(despreciar)* to despise; *(rebajar)* to humiliate.

vilipendio *nm* *fml* **1** *(ofensa)* vilification, abuse. **2** *(desprecio)* scorn, contempt; *(humillación)* humiliation.

vilipendioso,-a *adj fml* **1** *(ofensivo)* vilifying. **2** *(menospreciado)* contemptible; *(humillado)* humiliated.

vilo (en) *loc adv* **1** *(suspendido)* in the air, suspended. **2** *fig (intranquilo)* on tenterhooks, in suspense; **tener a algn con el alma en v.,** to keep sb in suspense.

villa *nf* **1** *(casa)* villa, country house. **2** *(población)* town.

Villadiego *nm fam* **coger** *or* **tomar las de V.,** to clear off, beat it.

villancico *nm* *Mús* (Christmas) carol.

villanía *nf fml* **1** *(cualidad)* vileness, baseness. **2** *(acto)* vile deed, despicable act, villainy. **3** *(dicho grosero)* coarse remark.

villano,-a *nm,f* villain.

villorrio *nm pey* one-horse town.

vinagre *nm* vinegar; *fig* bad tempered person.

vinagrera *nf* **1** vinegar bottle. **2** **vinagreras,** oil and vinegar cruets, cruet (stand) *sing*.

vinagreta *nf* *Culin* vinaigrette sauce.

vinajera *nf* *Rel* **1** cruet (for wine and water). **2** **vinajeras,** cruets.

vinatería *nf* **1** *(comercio)* wine trade. **2** *(tienda)* wine shop.

vinatero,-a I *adj* wine. II *nm,f* wine merchant.

vinaza *nf (vinos)* poor quality wine, plonk.

vincha *nf Am (sujetapelo)* hair ribbon, hair band; *(para la cabeza)* headband.

vinculación *nf* **1** *(acción)* linking, binding. **2** *(vínculo)* link, bond; *(contacto)* relation, connection.

vincular I *vtr* **1** to link, bind; *(relacionar)* to relate, connect; **los dos temas no están vinculados en absoluto** the two subjects are totally unrelated. **2** *Jur (bienes)* to entail. II **vincularse** *vr* to link oneself (a, to).

vínculo *nm* **1** link, bond, tie; **vínculos familiares,** family ties. **2** *Jur* entail, entailment.

vindicación *nf* **1** *(venganza)* vengeance, revenge. **2** *(defensa)* vindication.

vindicar *vtr* **1** *(vengar)* to avenge. **2** *(defensar)* to vindicate.

vindicativo,-a *adj* **1** *(vengativo)* vindictive. **2** *(que defiende)* vindicatory; *(leyes)* punitive.

vindicatorio,-a *adj* vindicatory.

vine *pt indef véase* **venir.**

vinícola *adj* wine-producing.

vinicultor,-a *nm,f* wine producer.

vinicultura *nf* wine production *or* growing.

vinificación *nf* wine-making process.

vinílico,-a *adj* vinyl.

vinilo *nm* vinyl.

vino *nm* wine; **ir de vinos,** to go on a drinking spree; *fig* **tener mal v.,** to become aggressive when drunk; *fam* **bautizar el v.,** to water down wine. ■ *v.* **abocado,** fortified wine; **v. añejo,** vintage wine; **v. blanco/tinto,** white/red wine; **v. clarete,** claret; **v. de aguja,** slightly sparkling wine; **v. de la casa,** house wine; **v. de mesa,** table wine; **v. dulce/seco,** sweet/dry wine; **v. espumoso,** sparkling wine; **v. generoso** *or* **de postre,** full-bodied wine; **v. peleón,** plonk; **v. rosado,** rosé.

vinoso,-a *adj* wine-like, wine.

viña *nf* vineyard; *prov* **de todo hay en la v. del Señor,** it takes all kinds (to make a world).

viñador,-a *nm,f* vine grower.

viñedo *nm* vineyard.

viñeta *nf* **1** *Impr* vignette. **2** *(en tebeo)* **historia en viñetas,** comic strip, strip cartoon.

viola *Mús* **I** *nf* viola. **II** *nmf* viola player.

violáceo,-a **I** *adj* violaceous, violet. **II violáceas** *nfpl Bot* violaceae *pl.*

violación *nf* **1** *(de un derecho, una ley)* violation, infringement. **2** *(de una persona)* rape.

violador,-a *n* **1** *(de un derecho, una ley)* violator. **2** *(de una persona)* rapist. **3** *(de un lugar)* violator, trespasser; *(de una tumba)* desecrator.

violar *vtr* **1** *(un derecho, una ley)* to violate, infringe. **2** *(una persona)* to rape. **3** *(un lugar)* to violate, trespass; *(tumba)* to desecrate.

violencia *nf* **1** violence; **con v.,** violently, by force; **la no v.,** non-violence. **2** *(sentimiento)* embarrassment; *(situación)* embarrassing situation; **si te causa v. ...,** if you find it embarrassing ... . **3** *(acción injusta)* outrage. **4** *(violación)* rape.

violentar **I** *vtr* **1** *(forzar)* to force, break open; *(sitio)* to break into, enter by force; **v. una cerradura,** to force a lock (open); **v. una puerta,** to break a door down. **2** *(obligar)* to force, use force on. **3** *(enojar)* to infuriate. **4** *(texto)* to twist, distort. **II violentarse** *vr* **1** *(obligarse)* to force oneself; *(vencer repugnancia etc)* to overcome one's reluctance. **2** *(pasar vergüenza)* to be embarrassed; *(avergonzarse)* to feel ashamed. **3** *(molestarse)* to get annoyed.

violento,-a *adj* **1** *(brutal)* violent. **2** *(carácter)* violent; **persona de carácter v.,** person of a violent nature. **3** *(embarazoso)* embarrassing, awkward. **4** *(molesto, incómodo)* embarrassed, awkward; **se sentía v. en aquella casa,** he felt ill at ease in that house. **5** *(postura)* unnatural, forced. **6** *(sentido de un texto)* twisted, distorted.

violeta **I** *adj* violet. **II** *nm (color)* violet. **III** *nf Bot* violet.

violetera *nf* violet seller.

violín *Mús* **I** *nm* violin; *fam* fiddle. **II** *nmf* violinist; **primer v.,** first violin.

violinista *nmf* violinist.

violón **I** *nm* double bass. **II** *nmf* double bass player.

violoncelista *nmf*, **violonchelista** *nmf* violoncellist, cellist.

violoncelo *nm*, **violonchelo** *nm* violoncello, cello.

viperino,-a *adj Zool* viperine, viperous; *fig* venomous; **lengua viperina,** spiteful *or* venomous tongue.

vira *nf* **1** *(saeta)* dart. **2** *(de zapato)* welt.

virada *nf Náut* tack, tacking.

virago *nf* virago.

viraje *nm* **1** *(curva)* turn, bend. **2** *(acción de girar) (en coche)* turn; *Náut* tack. **3** *fig* change in direction, volte-face, about-face; *Pol* change in policy. **4** *Fot* toning.

virar **I** *vi* **1** *Náut* to tack, put about; *(coche)* to turn round. **2** *fig* to change; **v. en redondo,** to change completely. **II** *vtr* *Fot* to tone.

virgen **I** *adj* **1** *(persona)* virgin. **2** *fig* virgin, pure; *(en estado natural)* unspoiled; *(reputación)* unsullied; **aceite v.,** pure olive oil; **cinta v.,** blank tape; **selva v.,** virgin forest. **II** *nmf* virgin. **III** *nf Rel* **la (Santísima) V.,** the (Blessed) Virgin; *fam* **ser un viva la V.,** to be a devil-may-care person.

Vírgenes *npl* **las (Islas) V.,** the Virgin Islands.

virginal **I** *adj* virginal. **II** *nm Mús* virginal.

Virginia *n* **V. Occidental,** (West) Virginia.

virginidad *nf* virginity.

virgo *nm* **1** *(virginidad)* virginity. **2** *Anat* hymen.

Virgo *nm Astrol Astron* Virgo.

virguería *nf arg* **1** *(cosa extraordinaria)* gem, marvel; **hacer virguerías,** to work wonders, be a dab hand. **2** *(adorno exagerado)* frill.

virguero,-a *adj arg* smart, great; **esta camisa es muy virguera,** that shirt is the business.

vírgula *nf*, **virgulilla** *nf* **1** *Impr (coma)* comma; *(punto)* point; *(apóstrofe)* apostrophe; *(acento)* accent. **2** *(raya)* line, dash.

vírico,-a *adj* viral.

viril *adj* virile, manly; **miembro v.,** penis, male member.

virilidad *nf* virility.

virreina *nf (mujer del virrey)* viceroy's wife; *(la que gobierna)* female viceroy, vicereine.

virreinato *nm* viceroyalty.

virrey *nm* viceroy.

virtual *adj* virtual. ◆ **virtualmente** *adv* virtually.

virtud *nf* **1** virtue; *fig* **en v. de,** by virtue of. **2** *(propiedad, eficacia)* property, quality; **hierbas con virtudes curativas,** medicinal herbs, herbs with medicinal properties.

virtuosismo *nm* virtuosity.

virtuoso,-a **I** *adj* virtuous. **II** *nm, f* **1** virtuous person. **2** *(músico)* virtuoso.

viruela *nf* **1** *Med* smallpox. **2** *(cicatrices)* pockmarks *pl.*

viruji *nm fam* fresh air.

virulé (a la) *loc adv fam* **1** *(torcido)* crooked, twisted. **2** *(estropeado)* broken, damaged; **un ojo a la v.,** a black eye. **3** *(de cualquier manera)* any old how.

virulencia *nf* virulence.

virulento,-a *adj* virulent.

virus *nm inv* virus.

viruta *nf Carp* shaving.

vis *nf* **v. cómica,** comic sense.

visa *nf Am* visa.

visado,-a **I** *pp de* **visar. II** *adj* endorsed with a visa. **III** *nm* visa.

visaje *nm* grimace, (wry) face.

visar *vtr (pasaporte)* to endorse (with a visa); *(documento)* to endorse, approve.

víscera *nf Anat* **1** *(órgano)* internal organ. **2 vísceras,** *(conjunto de órganos)* viscera, entrails.

visceral *adj* **1** *Anat* visceral. **2** *fig (intenso)* profound, deep-rooted; **reacción v.,** gut reaction.

viscosidad *nf* viscosity.

viscoso,-a *adj* viscous.

visera *nf* **1** *(de casco)* visor; **calarse la v.,** to pull down one's visor. **2** *(de gorra)* peak; **gorra de v.,** peaked cap. **3** *(pieza suelta de plástico etc)* eyeshade.

visibilidad *nf* visibility; **curva con mala v.,** blind corner.

visible *adj* **1** *(que se puede ver)* visible. **2** *(manifiesto)* evident. ◆ **visiblemente** *adv* **1** *(perceptiblemente)* visibly. **2** *(claramente)* evidently.

visigodo,-a *Hist* **I** *adj* Visigothic. **II** *nm,f* Visigoth.

visigótico,-a *adj Hist* Visigothic.

visillo *nm* small lace or net curtain.

visión *nf* **1** *(acción de ver)* vision; *fig* **v. de conjunto,** overall view. **2** *(vista)* sight. **3** *(aparición)* vision; *fam* **quedarse como quien ve visiones,** to look as if one has seen a ghost. **4** *(entendimiento)* vision, view; *(perspicacia)* foresight.

visionario,-a *nm,f (adivino)* visionary; *(iluso)* person who imagines things.

visir *nm Hist* vizir, vizier.

visita *nf* **1** *(acción)* visit; **estamos de v. en la ciudad,** we are visiting the town; *Med* **horas de v.,** surgery hours; **ir de v. a casa de algn,** to pay sb a visit; **tarjeta de v.,** visiting card; **v. de cortesía,** courtesy visit. **2** *(invitado)* visitor, guest; **tenemos v.,** we have a visitor. **3** *(invitados)* visitors, guests; **tenemos v.,** we have visitors.

visitación *nf Rel* Visitation.

visitador,-a I *adj* fond of visiting. **II** *nm, f* **1** *(invitado)* person fond of visiting, frequent visitor. **2** *Farm (representante)* pharmaceutical salesman or saleswoman. **III** *nm (inspector)* inspector.

visitante I *adj* visiting. **II** *nmf* visitor.

visitar *vtr* **1** *(ir a ver)* to visit; **ven a visitarnos cuando quieras,** come and see us whenever you like. **2** *(examinar) (un lugar)* to visit, inspect. **3** *Am (ir al médico)* to go to the doctor's.

vislumbrar *vtr* **I** *(ver mal)* to glimpse, catch a glimpse of, see vaguely; **vislumbró dos figuras en la oscuridad,** she could make out two shapes in the darkness. **2** *fig (conjeturar)* to begin to see, begin to grasp.

vislumbre *nf (gen)* glimpse; *(resplandor tenue)* glimmer; *fig* glimmer; *fig* **tener vislumbres de,** to have an inkling of.

viso *nm* **I** *(reflejo)* sheen. **2** *fig (aspecto)* appearance; **tener visos de,** to seem, appear; **una persona de v.,** an important person. **3** *Cost (forro)* unattached lining.

visón *nm Zool* mink.

visor *nm* **1** *Fot* viewfinder. **2** *(de arma)* sight.

víspera *nf* **I** *(día anterior)* day before; *(de festivo)* eve. **2 vísperas,** *Rel* vespers.

vista *nf* **1** *(gen)* sight, vision, eye, eyes *pl;* **a la v.,** visible; **alzar la v.,** to raise one's eyes; *Com Fin* **a tantos días v.,** so many days after sight; **apartar la v. de,** to look away from; **a primera** or **simple v.,** at first sight, on the face of it; **bajar la v.,** to look down; **clavar** or **fijar la v. en,** to stare at; **con vistas a,** with a view to; **conocer a algn de v.,** to know sb by sight; **corto de v.,** short-sighted; **en v. de,** in view of, considering; **no le quitó la v. de encima,** she didn't take her eyes off him; **perder de v.,** to lose sight of; **quítalo de mi v.,** take it away; **tener la v. cansada,** to be suffering from eyestrain; **tener mala v.,** to have poor eyesight; **¡tierra a la v.!,** land ahoy!; *fig* **a la v. de todos,** *(abiertamente)* openly; *(públicamente)* in full view of everyone; *fig* **actuar con mucha v.,** to act with great foresight; *fig* **comer a algn con la v.,** to undress sb with one's eyes; *fig* **es algo que salta a la v.,** it sticks out a mile;

fig **punto de v.,** point of view, viewpoint; *fig* **tener v. de lince,** to have eyes like an eagle; *fig* **tiene mucha v. para los negocios,** she has a good head for business; *fig* **volver la v. atrás,** to look back; *fam* **¡hasta la v.!,** goodbye!, see you!; *fam fig* **hacer la v. gorda,** to turn a blind eye. **2** *(panorama)* view; **a v. de pájaro,** a bird's-eye view; **con v. al mar,** overlooking the sea. **3** *(cuadro, dibujo, fotografía)* view; **v. marina,** seascape. **4** *(aspecto)* look, appearance. **5** *Jur* trial, hearing.

vistavisión *nf Cin* wide screen.

vistazo *nm* glance; **dar** or **echar un v. a algo,** to have a (quick) look at sth; **échale un v. a mi bolso,** keep an eye on my handbag.

visto,-a I *pp de* **ver. II** *adj* **1** *(dado)* in view of, considering; **está v. que no le interesa,** it is obvious that he is not interested; **por lo v.,** evidently, apparently; **v. que,** in view of the fact that, seeing or given that; *fig* **ni v. ni oído,** in a flash. **2** *(aceptable)* acceptable; **estar bien v.,** to be well looked upon, be considered acceptable; **estar mal v.,** to be frowned upon. **3** *(pasado de moda)* old-fashioned; **eso está muy v. ya,** there is nothing new about that, that's a very old trick; **este actor está muy v. ya,** that actor's becoming a bit passé; **lo nunca v.,** something extraordinary, something quite out of the ordinary; *fam* **esto es lo nunca v.,** this really takes the biscuit. ■ *Constr* **ladrillo v.,** uncovered brickwork. **II** *nm* **v. bueno,** approval, O.K.; **dar el v. bueno a algo,** to approve sth, O.K. sth.

vistoso,-a *adj* **1** *(colorido)* bright, colourful, *US* colorful. **2** *(llamativo)* showy, flashy.

visual I *adj* visual; **campo v.,** field of vision. **II** *nf* **1** *Téc* line of sight. **2** *arg* sight.

visualizar *vtr* to visualize.

vital *adj* **1** *(relativo a la vida)* vital, living; **espacio v.,** living space. **2** *(fundamental)* vital, essential. **3** *(persona)* lively, vivacious, full of vitality.

vitalicio,-a I *adj* life, for life; **cargo v.,** post held for life; **pensión vitalicia,** life annuity or pension. **II** *nm (pensión)* life annuity; *(seguro)* life insurance policy.

vitalidad *nf* vitality.

vitalizar *vtr* to vitalize.

vitamina *nf Biol Quím Med* vitamin.

vitaminado,-a *adj Med* vitamin-enriched, with added vitamins.

vitamínico,-a *adj Med* vitamin.

vitando,-a *adj* **1** *(que se debe evitar)* to be avoided. **2** *(odioso)* odious, hateful.

vitela *nf* vellum.

vitelino,-a *Biol* **I** *adj* vitelline. **II** *nf* vitelline membrane.

vitícola *adj* wine-growing, wine-producing, viticultural.

viticultor,-a *nm,f* wine grower, viticulturer.

viticultura *nf* wine growing, viticulture.

vito *nm Mús* Andalusian dance and song.

vitola *nf* **1** *(medida)* standard cigar measurement. **2** *(faja)* cigar band. **3** *Mil (calibrador)* calibrator.

vítor I *interj* bravo!, hurrah! **II** *nm* cheer; **entre vítores de la multitud,** amidst the cheers of the crowd.

vitorear *vtr* **1** *(dar vítores a)* to cheer. **2** *(aplaudir)* to applaud.

vitoriano,-a I *adj* of or from Vitoria. **II** *nm, f* native or inhabitant of Vitoria.

vítreo,-a *adj* **1** *(de vidrio)* vitreous, glass-like, glassy. **2** *Fís Elec* vitreous.

vitrina *nf* *(armario)* glass or display cabinet; *(de exposición)* glass case, showcase; *(escaparate)* shop window.

vituallas *nfpl* provisions, food *sing*.

vituperable *adj* reprehensible, deserving censure.

vituperación *nf* vituperation.

vituperar *vtr* to vituperate, condemn.

vituperio *nm* vituperation, condemnation, censure.

viudedad *nf* widower's pension, widow's pension.

viudez *nf* widowhood.

viudo,-a I *adj* widowed; **es v.,** he is a widower; **quedó viuda,** she was left a widow. **II** *nm,f (hombre)* widower; *(mujer)* widow.

viva I *interj* hurrah!; **¡v. el novio!,** three cheers for the groom!; **¡v. el rey!,** long live the king! **II** *nm* cheer; **dar vivas,** to cheer.

vivac *nm (pl vivaques) Mil* bivouac.

vivacidad *nf* vivacity, vivaciousness, liveliness.

vivalavirgen *nmf inv fam* devil-may-care person.

vivales *nmf inv fam* crafty devil, smooth operator, clever customer.

vivamente *adv* **1** *(con viveza)* in a lively fashion. **2** *(intensamente)* strongly, intensely. **3** *(profundamente)* deeply, acutely.

vivaque *nm Mil* bivouac.

vivaquear *vi* to bivouac.

vivar *nm* **1** *(de conejos)* warren. **2** *(vivero de peces)* fish farm *or* hatchery.

vivaracho,-a *adj fam* lively, sprightly, vivacious; **ojos vivarachos,** sparkling eyes.

vivaz *adj* **1** *(con vida)* lively, vivacious. **2** *(perspicaz)* sharp, quick-witted. **3** *Bot* perennial.

vivencia *nf* personal experience.

víveres *nmpl* provisions, supplies, food *sing*.

vivero *nm* **1** *(de plantas)* nursery. **2** *(de peces, moluscos)* fish farm *or* hatchery. **3** *fig (lugar adecuado)* breeding ground, hotbed.

viveza *nf* **1** *(persona)* liveliness, vivacity; *(color, relato)* vividness; *(ojos)* sparkle. **2** *(agudeza)* sharpness, quick-wittedness. **3** *(ardor)* passion, force.

vividizo *nm Méx fam* scrounger.

vivido,-a I *pp de* **vivir. II** *adj (real)* real, real-life, true-life; *(experimentado)* based on personal experience.

vívido,-a *adj* vivid.

vividor,-a *nm,f* **1** *(que sabe vivir)* person who makes the most of life. **2** *pey* sponger, scrounger.

vivienda *nf* **1** *(en general)* housing, accommodation; **escasez de v.,** housing shortage. **2** *(morada)* dwelling; *(casa)* house; *(piso)* flat; **un bloque de viviendas,** a block of flats; **v. unifamiliar,** detached house.

viviente *adj* living, alive; *fam* **todo bicho v.,** every living creature.

vivificador,-a *adj,* **vivificante** *adj* life-giving.

vivificar *vtr* to give life to, vivify, enliven.

vivíparo,-a *adj Biol* viviparous.

vivir I *nm* life, living; **gente de mal v.,** shady characters. **II** *vi* **1** *(tener vida)* to be alive, live; **hay que seguir viviendo,** life must go on; **no tener con** *or* **de qué v.,** to have nothing to live on; **si pudiera volver a v.,** if I could live my life over again; **tú sí que sabes v. bien,** you really know how to enjoy life; *fam* **vive de milagro,** it's a wonder he's still alive; **vive de sus ahorros,** she lives off her savings; **viven de la pesca,** they make their living by fishing; *lit* **y vivieron felices y comieron perdices,** and they (all) lived happily ever after; *fig* **no dejar v. a algn,** to give sb a hard time; *fig* **v. a cuerpo de rey,** to live like a king; *fig* **v. al día,** to live from day to day; *fig* **v. del aire,** to live on fresh air; *fam* **vamos viviendo,** we are managing, we are getting by; *fam* **v. a lo grande,** to live it up, live in style. **3** *(habitar)* to live; **vive con sus padres,** she lives at home; **vive en Montevideo,** he lives in Montevideo; **viven juntos,** they live together. **4** *(durar)* to last. **III** *vtr (pasar)* to live, live through; **allí viví mi juventud,** I spent my youth there; **los que no hemos vivido la guerra,** those of us who did not live through the war.

vivito,-a *adj fam* **v. y coleando,** alive and kicking.

vivo,-a I *adj* **1** *(gen)* living, alive, live; **a lo v.,** vividly; **de viva voz,** verbally, by word of mouth; *TV (programa)* **en v.,** live; *Ling* **lengua viva,** living language; *Med* **llaga viva,** open wound; **materia viva,** living matter; *Med* **operar a algn en v.,** to operate on sb without an anaesthetic; **su recuerdo sigue v.,** the memory of him lives on; **v.** *or* **muerto,** dead or alive; *fig* **herir** *or* **tocar a algn en lo más v.,** to cut sb to the quick; *fig Pol* **las fuerzas vivas de un país,** the driving forces behind a country; *fam* **es el v. retrato** *or* **la viva imagen de su madre,** she is the spitting image of her mother. **2** *(fuego, llama)* live, burning; **al rojo v.,** red-hot. **3** *(vivaz)* lively, vivacious. **4** *(color)* vivid, bright. **5** *(dolor, deseo, etc)* acute, intense, deep. **6** *(inteligencia)* sharp, quick. **7** *(descripción, estilo)* lively, graphic. **8** *(carácter)* quick, irritable; **tiene el genio v.,** she's very quick-tempered. **9** *(listo)* sharp, clever. **10** *(astuto)* shrewd, sly. **II** *nm* **1** *(que vive)* living person; **los vivos y los muertos,** the living and the dead. **2** *(persona avispada)* quick-witted person; **un par de vivos,** a couple of crafty characters. **3** *(borde, canto)* border, edge. **4** *Cost* trimming, border.

vizcacha *nf SAm Zool* vizcacha, viscacha.

vizcaíno,-a *adj & nm,f* Biscayan.

Vizcaya *n* Biscay; **el golfo de V.,** the Bay of Biscay.

vizcondado *nm (título)* viscounty, viscountcy; *(territorio)* viscounty.

vizconde *nm* viscount.

vizcondesa *nf* viscountess.

VoBo *abr de* **visto bueno.**

vocablo *nm Ling* word, term.

vocabulario *nm* vocabulary.

vocación *nf* vocation, calling.

vocacional *adj* vocational.

vocal I *adj* vocal. **II** *nf Ling* vowel. **III** *nmf* member; **v. de una junta,** member of a board.

vocálico,-a *adj Ling* vocalic.

vocalismo *nm Ling* vowel system.

vocalista *nmf Mús* vocalist, singer.

vocalización *nf* vocalization.

vocalizar *vtr & vi* to vocalize.

vocativo *nm Gram* vocative.

voceador,-a I *adj* vociferous, loud-mouthed. **II** *nm, f* shouter. **III** *nm* town crier.

vocear I *vi (dar voces)* to shout, cry out. **II** *vtr* **1** *(gritar algo)* to shout, cry out. **2** *(divulgar)* to publist, proclaim.

voceras *nm inv fam* loudmouth.

vocerío *nm* shouting, uproar, hullabaloo.

vocero,-a *nm, f* spokesperson, *(hombre)* spokesman; *(mujer)* spokeswoman.

vociferador,-a *adj,* **vociferante** *adj* vociferous.

vociferar *vtr & vi* to vociferate.

vodevil *nm US Teat* vaudeville, music hall.

vodevilesco,-a *adj US* vaudevillian, music-hall.

vodka *nm* vodka.

vol. *abr de* **volumen,** volume, vol.

voladizo,-a *Arquit* **I** *adj* projecting, jutting out. **II** *nm* projection.

volado,-a I *pp de* **volar. II** *adj* **1** *Impr* superior. **2** *fam* **estar v.,** *(intranquilo)* to feel uneasy; *(impaciente)* to be in a hurry. **III** *nm CAm (rumor)* rumour, *US* rumor.

volador,-a I *adj* flying. **II** *nm* **1** *(cohete)* rocket. **2** *(pez)* flying fish. **3** *(molusco)* type of squid.

voladura *nf Constr* blowing up, demolition; *Min* blasting (of rocks).

volandas (en) *loc adv (por el aire)* in the air, flying through the air; *fig (rápidamente)* rapidly, swiftly.

volandeira *nf (pez)* queen.

volandero,-a *adj* **1** *Orn* ready to fly. **2** *(suspendido)* hanging; *(suelto)* loose. **3** *(imprevisto)* unexpected, unforeseen. **4** *(vagabundo)* restless, wandering.

volante I *adj* **1** *(que vuela)* flying; **platillo v.**, flying saucer. **2** *(que se desplaza)* flying, mobile; **escuadrón v.**, flying squad. ■ *Dep* **medio v.**, half back, wing half. **II** *nm* **1** *Aut* steering wheel; **ir al v.**, to be driving; **un as del v.**, a motor-racing champion. **2** *Téc* flywheel; *(de reloj)* balance wheel. **3** *Cost* flounce; *(adorno)* frill, ruffle. **4** *Dep* shuttlecock. **5** *(aviso, comunicación)* note; **necesita un v. de su médico de cabecera,** you need a note from your GP.

volantín *nm* **1** *Pesca* type of fishing line. **2** *Am (cometa)* small kite.

volantón,-ona *adj* newly-fledged.

volapié *nm Taur* method used in killing the bull.

volar I *vi* **1** *(elevarse)* to fly; **echarse a v.**, to fly away, fly off. **2** *fig (ir deprisa)* to fly; **cenó volando,** he ate his dinner in a flash; **pasar volando,** to fly past; **¡volando!, que no llegamos,** jump to it or we'll be late! **3** *(noticia)* to spread like wildfire. **4** *fam (desaparecer)* to disappear, vanish; **han volado los tres billetes que dejé en el cajón,** the three notes I left in the drawer have vanished. **II** *vtr* **1** *(hacer estallar) (edificios)* to blow up, demolish; *(caja fuerte)* to blow open; *Min* to blast. **2** *Impr* to raise. **3** *Caza* to flush. **III volarse** *vr* **1** *(papeles etc)* to be blown away. **2** *(encolerizarse)* to lose one's temper, blow up.

volatería *nf* **1** *Caza* falconry. **2** *(conjunto de aves)* fowl *sing*, birds.

volátil *adj* volatile.

volatilidad *nf* volatility.

volatilizar I *vtr* to volatilize. **II volatilizarse** *vr* to vanish into thin air.

volatín *nm* acrobatics *pl*.

volatinero,-a *nm,f* acrobat.

volcán *nm* **1** *Geol* volcano. **2** *Arg Bol Col (torrente)* summer torrent.

volcánico,-a *adj* volcanic.

volcar I *vtr* **1** *(derribar)* to turn over, knock over, upset; *Náut* to capsize. **2** *(vaciar)* to empty out. **3** *(turbar la cabeza)* to make feel dizzy. **4** *(hacer cambiar de parecer)* to make change one's mind. **5** *(irritar)* to irritate, annoy. **II** *vi (coche)* to overturn, turn over; *(barco)* to capsize. **III volcarse** *vr* **1** *(vaso, jarra)* to fall over, tip over; *(coche)* to overturn, turn over; *(barco)* to capsize. **2** *fig (entregarse a algo)* to do one's utmost; **se volcó para conseguirme una plaza,** she really went out of her way to get me a seat.

volea *nf* **1** *Dep* volley. **2** *(de carruaje)* whippletree, swingletree.

volear *vtr Dep* to volley.

voleibol *nm Dep* volleyball.

voleo *nm* **1** *Dep* volley; *fig* **a(l) v.**, at random, haphazardly; *fig* **de un v.**, very quickly, in one go. **2** *fam (bofetada)* slap.

volframio *nm Quím* wolfram.

volquete *nm* dumper, tipcart.

voltaje *nm Elec* voltage.

voltear I *vtr* **1** *(dar la vuelta a)* to turn over, roll over; *(por el aire)* to toss; *(poner boca abajo)* to turn upside down. **2** *(dar vueltas a)* to whirl, twirl. **3** *Am (derribar)* to knock down. **4** *Am (derramar)* to spill. **II** *vi* to turn over; roll over; *(acróbata)* to do somersaults. **III voltearse** *vr Am* **1** *(cambiar de opinión)* to turn one's coat. **2** *(cambiar de partido)* to go over to another party.

voltense *adj & nmf* Voltaic.

voltereta *nf* somersault.

volteriano,-a *adj nm,f* Voltairian, Voltairean.

voltímetro *nm Elec* voltmeter.

voltio *nm Elec* volt.

volubilidad *nf* **1** *(inconstancia)* fickleness, changeableness. **2** *Bot* volubility.

voluble *adj* **1** *(inconstante)* fickle, changeable. **2** *Bot* voluble, twining.

volumen *nm* **1** *Fís* volume; *(tamaño)* size; *fig* **de mucho v.**, sizeable, important. **2** *(intensidad)* volume; **baja el v.**, turn the volume down. **3** *(tomo)* volume; **obra en tres volúmenes,** three-volume work.

voluminoso,-a *adj* voluminous; *(enorme)* massive, bulky.

voluntad *nf* **1** *(como virtud)* will; **buena v.**, good will; **buena v. no le falta,** she's very willing; **fuerza de v.**, willpower; **hace falta mucha v. para dejar de fumar,** it takes a lot of willpower to give up smoking; **tiene mucha v.**, he is very strong-willed; **v. férrea or de hierro,** iron will, will of iron. **2** *(deseo)* will, wishes *pl*; **a v.**, at will; **¿cuánto le doy, entonces? —la v.**, how much should I give you, then? —whatever you think right; **ganarse la v. de algn,** to win sb over; *Rel* **hágase tu v.**, Thy will be done; *Rel* **la v. de Dios,** God's will; **lo dejo a tu v.**, it is up to you; **no lo dije con v. de,** I didn't mean to; **por causas ajenas a nuestra v.**, due to reasons beyond our control; **última v.**, last wish; *fam* **siempre hay que hacer su santa v.**, everything always has to be done his way.

voluntario,-a I *adj* voluntary; **ofrecerse v.**, to volunteer. **II** *nm,f* volunteer. ◆ **voluntariamente** *adv* voluntarily.

voluntarioso,-a 1 *(de gran voluntad)* willing. **2** *pej (testarudo)* wilful, *US* wilfull, headstrong.

voluptuosidad *nf* voluptuousness.

voluptuoso,-a *adj* voluptuous.

voluta *nf* **1** *Arquit* volute, scroll. **2** *(espiral)* spiral, column; *(de humo, cigarrillo)* (smoke) ring.

volver *(pp vuelto)* **I** *vtr* **1** *(dar vuelta a)* to turn; *(poner boca abajo)* to turn upside down; *(lo de fuera dentro)* to turn inside out; *(la parte de atrás delante)* to turn back to front; *(dar la vuelta a)* to turn over; **v. los ojos hacia,** to turn one's eyes towards; **volverle la espalda a algn,** to turn one's back on sb; *fig* **v. la vista afrás,** to look back. **2** *(convertir; hacer)* to turn, change, make; **ha vuelto esta casa en un infierno,** it has made this place hell; **la fama le ha vuelto engreído,** fame has made him conceited; **me vas a v. loco,** you are driving me mad; **vuelve esta frase a pasiva,** put this sentence into the passive. **3** *(torcer)* to turn; **al v. la esquina,** on turning the corner. **II** *vi* **1** *(regresar)* to return; *(venir)* to come back; *(ir)* to go back; **no quiero v.**, I don't want to go back; **v. atrás,** to go back; **v. de vacío,** to return empty-handed; **v. en sí,** to come round, recover consciousness; **v. sobre sus pasos,** to retrace one's steps. **2** **v. a,** to do again; **hay que v. a empezar,** we've got to start all over again; **vuelve a llover,** it's raining again. **III volverse** *vr* **1** *(darse la vuelta)* to turn; **la página se volvió,** the page turned over; *fig* **todo se ha vuelto en su contra,** everything has gone against him. **2** *(regresar) (venir)* to come back; *(ir)* to go back; *fig* **v. atrás,** to go back on one's word. **3** *(convertirse)* to become; **se ha vuelto más difícil,** she's become more difficult; **se volvió rojo,** it turned red; **v. loco,-a** to go mad.

vomitar I *vi* to vomit, be sick; **tengo ganas de v.**, I feel sick, I want to be sick. **II** *vtr* to vomit, bring up; *fig* to belch, spew out; **v. sangre,** to cough up blood; *fig* **v. injurias,** to hurl insults.

vomitivo,-a *adj & nm Med* emetic.

vómito *nm (resultado)* vomit; *(acción)* vomiting.

vomitona *nf fam* **echar la v.**, to be violently sick.

voracidad *nf* voracity, voraciousness.

vorágine *nf* vortex, whirlpool.

voraz *adj* voracious; *fig* raging, fierce.

vórtice *nm* **1** *(torbellino)* vortex, whirlpool. **2** *(de ciclón)* centre of a cyclone.

vos *pron pers* **1** *arc (usted)* ye, you. **2** *Am (tú)* you.

vosear *vtr* to address as **vos**.

voseo *nm* use of **vos**.

Vosgos *n* los **V.**, the Vosges.

vosotros,-as *pron pers pl* **1** *(como sujeto)* you; **v. lo queréis,** you want it. **2** *(con prep)* you; **decidídlo entre v.,** decide it among yourselves; **no iremos sin vosotras,** we won't go without you.

votación *nf* **1** *(voto)* vote, ballot. **2** *(acción)* voting; **poner** *or* **someter algo a v.,** to put sth to the vote, take a ballot on sth; **v. a mano alzada,** (voting by a) show of hands.

votante I *adj* voting. **II** *nmf* voter.

votar *vi* to vote; **v. a favor/en contra de algo,** to vote for/against sth; **v. a** *or* **por algn,** to vote (for) sb.

voto *nm* **1** *(gen)* vote; **diez votos a favor y dos en contra,** ten votes for and two against; **por mayoría de votos,** by a majority vote; **tener v.,** to have the right to vote; **una persona, un v.,** one person, one vote; **v. de censura/confianza,** vote of no confidence/confidence; **v. secreto,** secret ballot; *fam* **tú no tienes ni voz ni v. aquí,** you have no say in this matter. **2** *Rel* vow; **hacer v. de castidad/pobreza,** to take a vow of chastity/poverty. **3** *(deseo)* wish; **hago votos por su éxito,** I sincerely want him to succeed. **4** *(blasfemia)* curse, oath.

vox *nf* **v. populi,** vox populi.

voy *indic pres véase* **ir.**

voz *nf* **1** *(sonido)* voice; **aclararse la v.,** to clear one's throat; **alzar** *or* **levantar la v.,** to raise one's voice; **a media voz,** in a low voice, softly; **baja la v.,** lower your voice; **dar la v. de alarma,** to raise the alarm; **de viva v.,** verbally; **en v. alta,** aloud; **en v. baja,** in a low voice; **le está cambiando la v.,** his voice is breaking; **v. apagada,** weak voice; *Teat* **v. en off,** voice offstage; **v. ronca,** hoarse voice. **2** *(grito)* shout; **a v. en cuello** *or* **grito,** at the top of one's voice; **v. pública,** shouting; **dale una v.,** give him a shout; **dar voces,** to shout; *fig* **estar pidiendo algo a voces,** to be crying out for sth, need sth badly; *fig* **secreto a voces,** open secret. **3** *(en una reunión)* voice, say; **tener v. y voto,** *(opinión)* to have a say; *Pol* to be a voting member. **4** *(rumor)* rumour; **corre la v. de que ...,** rumour has it that ...; **es v. pública,** it's common knowledge. **5** *Gram (palabra)* word. **6** *Gram (del verbo)* voice; **v. pasiva,** passive voice. **7** *Mús* voice; **canción a tres voces,** three-part song; **cantar a dos voces,** to sing a duet; **llevar la v. cantante,** to sing the leading part; *fig* to rule the roost.

vozarrón,-ona *nm,f* powerful *or* big voice.

vudú *nm* voodoo.

vuelco *nm* upset, tumble; **dar un v.,** *(coche)* to overturn; *fig (empresa)* to go to ruin; *fig* **me dio un v. el corazón,** my heart missed a beat.

vuelo *nm* **1** *(acto)* flight; *(acción)* flying; **al v.,** in flight; **alzar** *or* **emprender** *or* **levantar el v.,** to take flight; **remontar el v.,** to soar up; **tomar v.,** to grow; *fig* **cazarlas** *or* **cogerlas al v.,** to be quick on the uptake; *fig* **de alto v.,** important, far-reaching; *fig* **de un v.,** in a flash, in no time at all. **2** *Av* flight; **personal de v.,** flight crew; **v. chárter/nocturno/regular,** charter/night/regular flight; **v. espacial,** space flight; **v. libre,** hang-gliding; **v. sin escala,** non-stop flight; **v. sin motor,** gliding; *fam fig* **tener muchas horas de v.,** to be an old hand at sth. **3** *Orn (plumas)* flight feathers *pl*; *(alas)* wings *pl*; *fig* **cortarle los vuelos a algn,** to clip sb's wings. **4** *Cost (amplitud)* fullness, flare; **una falda de v.,** a full skirt. **5** *Arquit (voladizo)* projection.

vuelta *nf* **1** *(giro)* turn, rotation; *(en carreras)* lap, circuit; **dar la v. al mundo,** to go round the world; **darle la v. a**

algo, *(en redondo)* to turn sth round; *(boca abajo)* to turn upside down; *(la parte de dentro fuera)* to turn inside out; *(la parte posterior delante)* to turn back to front; **dio media v. y se fue,** she turned round and walked off; *Taur* **la v. al ruedo,** lap of honour; *Dep* **la v. ciclista a España,** the Tour of Spain; **v. de campana,** somersault; *fig* **la cabeza me da vueltas,** my head is spinning; *fig* **no le des más vueltas,** stop worrying about it; *fig* **no tiene v. de hoja,** there's no doubt about her. **2** *(paseo)* walk, stroll; **dar una v. en coche,** to go for a drive *or* a spin (in the car); *fam* **date una v. por casa,** drop in and see us. **3** *(regreso)* return; *(viaje)* return journey, way back; **a la v. de las vacaciones,** after the holidays; **a su v.,** when he came back; **a v. de correo,** by return post; **estar de v.,** to be back; *fam* **not to have been born yesterday**; **¡hasta la v.!,** see you when you *or* I get back!; **la v. al colegio,** back to school; *Dep* **partido de v.,** return match; **v. a escena,** comeback (of an artist). **4** *(curva)* bend, turn, curve; **estar a la v. de la esquina,** to be just around the corner *or* very close; **una carretera con muchas vueltas,** a winding road. **5** *(parte de atrás)* back, reverse; **ver instrucciones a la v.,** for instructions, see back. **6** *Dep (turno)* round. **7** *(cambio)* change, alteration; *fam* **la vida da muchas vueltas,** life is full of ups and downs. **8** *(dinero)* change. **9** *Tricot* row. **10** *Cost (forro)* lining.

vuelto,-a I *pp* de **volver. II** *adj* **jersey de cuello v.,** rollneck sweater. **III** *nm* **1** *Impr* verso. **2** *Am (dinero)* change.

vuelvepiedras *nm inv Orn* turnstone.

vuestro,-a I *adj pos* your; **un amigo v.,** a friend of yours; **vuestra majestad,** Your Majesty; **v. libro,** your book. **II** *pron pos* yours; **éstos son los vuestros,** these are yours; **lo v.,** what is yours, what belongs to you; *fam* **siempre os salís con la vuestra,** you always get your own way.

vulcanología *nf Geol* volcanology, vulcanology.

vulcanólogo,-a *nm,f Geol* volcanologist, vulcanologist.

vulgar *adj* **1** *(que carece de delicadeza)* vulgar, coarse, common; **lenguaje v.,** coarse language. **2** *(común, general)* common, general; **latín v.,** vulgar Latin. **3** *(ordinario, trivial)* ordinary, banal; **idea v.,** commonplace idea. **4** *(no técnico)* lay; **el término v.,** the lay term. ◆ **vulgarmente** *adv* **1** *(generalmente)* generally. **2** *(de manera vulgar)* vulgarly.

vulgaridad *nf* **1** *(grosería)* vulgarity, coarseness; **decir vulgaridades,** to use bad language. **2** *(trivialidad)* banality, triviality; **decir vulgaridades,** to talk in platitudes.

vulgarismo *nm Ling* popular phrase *or* expression, vulgarism.

vulgarización *nf* popularization, vulgarization.

vulgarizar I *vtr* **1** *(popularizar)* to popularize, spread a knowledge of, vulgarize. **2** *(hacer vulgar)* to make common. **II vulgarizarse** *vr* to become vulgar *or* popular *or* common.

vulgo *nm* **el v.,** the common people *pl*; *pey* the masses.

vulnerabilidad *adj* vulnerability.

vulnerable *adj* vulnerable.

vulneración *nf* **1** *(de la reputación)* damaging, harming. **2** *(de un tratado, un acuerdo)* violation.

vulnerar *vtr* **1** *(deshonrar)* to damage, harm. **2** *(violar)* (la ley, un acuerdo) to violate.

vulva *nf Anat* vulva.

W

W, w [uβe'ðoβle] *nf (la letra)* W, w.
W *abr de* **vatio(s),** Watt, Watts, W.
wagneriano,-a *adj & nm, f Mús* Wagnerian.
walkie-talkie *nm* walkie-talkie.
walkman® *nm* walkman®.
wáter *nm (pl wáteres) fam* toilet.
waterpolo *nm* water polo.

week-end *nm* weekend.
wélter *nm Box* welterweight.
whisky *nm (escocés)* whisky; *(irlandés, US)* whiskey.
windsurf *nm*, **windsurfing** *nm* windsurfing.
windsurfista *nmf* windsurfer.
wolfram *nm*, **wolframio** *nm Min* wolfram.

X

X, x ['ekis] *nf (la letra)* X, x.
xenofobia *nf* xenophobia.
xenófobo,-a I *adj* xenophobic. **II** *nm, f* xenophobe.
xerografía *nf* xerography.
xilofonista *nmf* xylophonist.

xilófono *nm* xylophone.
xilografía *nf (arte)* xylography; *(impresión)* xylograph.
xilográfico,-a *adj* xylographic, xylographical.
xilógrafo *nm* xylographer.

Y

Y, y [iɣri'eɣa] *nf (la letra)* Y, y.

y *conj* **1** and; **Sevilla y Málaga,** Seville and Malaga; **son las tres y cuarto,** it's a quarter past three; **una chica alta y morena,** a tall, dark-haired girl; **y no tardes,** and don't be late. **2** *(diferenciación)* and; **hay políticos y políticos,** there are politicians and politicians. **3** *(repetición)* and; **días y días,** (for) days and days. **4** *(en pregunta)* what about ...?; **¿y López?,** what about López?; **¿y los demás?,** what about the others?; **y tú, ¿qué opinas?,** what do you think? **5** **¿y qué?,** so what?; **sí, he suspendido, ¿y qué?,** yes, I failed the exam, so what? **6** **¿y si ...?,** what if ...?; **¿y si no llega a tiempo?,** what if he doesn't arrive in time?; **¿y si no es verdad?,** what if it isn't true? **7** **y eso que,** although, even though; **sigue engordando y eso que no come nada,** she's still putting on weight even though she eats hardly anything. **8** **¡y tanto!,** you bet!, and how!; **¿te hace ilusión? —¡y tanto!,** are you looking forward to it? —you bet I am!; *véase tamb* **e.**

ya I *adv* **1** *(con pasado)* already; **ya lo sabía,** I already knew; **ya en la Edad Media,** as far back as the Middle Ages. **2** *(con presente)* now; **es preciso actuar ya,** it is vital that we act now; **¿son las nueve ya?,** don't tell me it's nine o'clock already!; **ya está aquí,** he's already arrived; *(ahora llega)* here he is!; *fam* **ya caigo,** now I get it, now I see. **3** *(con futuro)* **ya hablaremos luego,** we'll talk about it later; **ya nos veremos,** see you!; **ya vendrá,** she will be here soon; **ya verás,** you'll see. **4** *(ahora mismo)* immediately; **¡hazlo ya!,** do it at once!; **¡lo necesito, ya!,** I need it this minute?; **pero ya mismo,** this very minute! **5** **ya no,** no longer; **ya no es como antes,** it isn't like it used to be; **ya no viene por aquí,** he doesn't come round here any more. **6** *(refuerza el verbo)* **ya entiendo,** I see, I understand; **ya era hora,** about time too; **ya lo creo,** of course, I should think so; **ya lo sé,** I know; **ya me dirás,** what can you expect?; **ya se acabó,** that's the end of it; **ya ves,** well, you see; **ya viene,** here he

comes; **¡ya voy!,** coming!; **¡ya está!,** there we are!, done! **II** *interj irón* **te juro que no le he visto —¡ya, ya!,** I swear I haven't seen him —oh yes! **III** *conj* **1** *arc* **ya ... ya ...,** sometimes ... sometimes ...; **ya hace frío, ya calor,** first it's cold and then it's hot. **2** **ya que,** since; **ya que no sabe hablar francés,** as he can't speak French; **ya que tengo el coche,** since I've got the car.

yaacabó *nm Orn* South American hawk.
yac *nm Zool* yak.
yacaré *nm Am Zool* alligator, cayman.
yacente *adj* lying; **estatua y.,** recumbent statue.
yacer *vi* to lie, be lying; **aquí yace ...,** here lies ... .
yacimiento *nm Geol* bed, deposit; **yacimientos petrolíferos,** oilfields.
yago *indic pres véase* **yacer**
yagual *nm CAm Méx* padded ring for carrying loads on the head.
yaguana *nf Arg* milk pot.
yaguar *nm Zool* jaguar.
yaguasa *nf CAm* small duck.
Yakarta *n* Jakarta.
yámbico,-a *adj* iambic.
yambo *nm* iamb.
yanacón,-ona *nm, f Am* Indian tenant.
yanga *adj Arg* neglected.
yanqui *pey* **I** *adj* Yankee. **II** *nmf* Yankee, Yank.
yantar¹ *nm arc* food, viands *pl.*
yantar² *vtr arc* to eat.
yapa *nf Am* **1** *Min* mercury (added to silver ore to facilitate extraction). **2** *(propina)* extra.
yapar *vtr Am* to add as an extra.

yarará *nm SAm Zool* large poisonous snake.

yaraví *nm Am* Quechuan song.

yarda *nf* yard.

yare *nm CAm Ven* poisonous juice from the yucca.

yaro *nm Bot* arum.

yate *nm Náut* yacht.

yaya *nf Am Bot* lancewood.

yazgo *indic pres véase* **yacer.**

yedra *nf véase* **hiedra.**

yegua I *nf* 1 *Zool* mare. 2 *Am* cigar stub. II *adj Am* stupid.

yeguada *nf* 1 herd of horses. 2 *Am (disparate)* silly thing.

yeguar *adj* of mares *or* horses.

yegüero,-a *nm, f* keeper of a herd of horses.

yeísmo *nm Ling* pronunciation of **ll** as **y.**

yelmo *nm arc* helmet.

yema *nf* 1 *(de huevo)* yolk. 2 *Bot* bud. 3 *(del dedo)* fingertip. 4 *Culin* sweet made from sugar and egg yolk.

Yemen *n* Yemen; **República Democrática Popular del Y.,** People's Democratic Republic of Yemen; **República Arabe del Y.,** Yemen Arab Republic; **Y. del Norte,** North Yemen; **Y. del Sur,** South Yemen.

yemení *adj & nmf,* **yemenita** *adj & nmf* Yemeni.

yen *nm (moneda)* yen.

yendo *ger véase* **ir.**

yerba *nf* 1 *véase* **hierba.** 2 *Am* maté.

yerbatero,-a *Am* I *adj* maté; **la industria yerbatera,** the maté industry. II *nm, f* 1 *(curandero)* witch doctor who uses herbs. 2 *(comerciante)* maté merchant.

yerbear *vi Arg Urug* to drink maté.

yerbera *nf Arg Urug* container for maté.

yergo *indic pres véase* **ergir.**

yermo,-a I *adj* 1 *(sin vegetación)* barren, uncultivated. 2 *(despoblado)* deserted, uninhabited. II *nm* 1 *Geog* barren land, wasteland. 2 wilderness.

yerno *nm* son-in-law.

yernocracia *nf fam* nepotism.

yero *nm Bot Agr* vetch bean.

yerra *nf Am* cattle branding.

yerro I *nm arc* mistake, error; **y. de imprenta,** printing error. II *indic pres véase* **errar.**

yersey *nm,* **yersi** *nm (prenda)* pullover.

yerto,-a *adj* stiff, rigid; **y. de frío,** frozen stiff.

yesal *nm,* **yesar** *nm* gypsum quarry.

yesca *nf* 1 tinder. 2 *fig* fuel. 3 **yescas,** tinderbox *sing.*

yesería *nf* 1 *Constr* plasterwork, plastering. 2 *(fábrica)* gypsum kiln.

yesero,-a I *adj* plaster. II *nm, f* plasterer.

yeso *nm* 1 *Geol* gypsum. 2 *Constr* plaster.

yesoso,-a *adj (gen)* chalky; *Tec* gypseous.

yeta *nf Arg Urug* bad luck.

yeti *nm* yeti, abominable snowman.

yeyuno *nm Anat* jejunum.

Yibuti *n* Djibouti.

yiddish *nm (idioma)* Yiddish.

yiu-yitsu *nm* jujitsu.

yo I *pron pers* I; **entre tú y yo,** between you and me; **¿quién es? —soy yo,** who is it? —it's me; **que yo sepa,** as far as I know; **¿quién lo ha cogido? —yo no,** who's taken it? —not me; **yo que usted,** if I were you; **yo mismo,** I myself; **yo soy de los que ...,** I'm one of those who ...; **yo soy el culpable,** I am to blame; **yo soy quien te lo digo,** I'm the one who's telling you. II **el yo** *nm Filos psic* the ego, the self.

yod *nf Ling* yod.

yodado,-a *adj* iodized.

yodo *nm* iodine.

yoduro *nm* iodide; **y. de plata,** silver iodide.

yoga *nm* yoga.

yogui *nmf,* **yoghi** *nmf* yogi.

yogur *nm* yogurt, yoghurt; **y. de piña,** pineapple yoghurt; **y. descremado** *or* **desnatado,** low-fat yoghurt.

yogurtera *nf* yoghurt maker.

yoin *nm arg (drogas)* joint.

yola *nf Náut* yawl.

yonqui *nmf arg (drogas)* junkie, drug addict.

yóquey *nm,* **yoqui** *nm Dep* jockey.

yoyo *nm,* **yoyó** *nm* yo-yo.

Yuandé *n* Yaoundé.

yubarta *nf Zool* finback, rorqual.

yuca *nf* 1 *Bot* yucca. 2 *Culin* cassava, manioc. 3 *Bol CAm* lie.

yucal *nm Bot* yucca plantation.

Yucatán *n* Yucatan.

yucateco,-a I *adj* of *or* from Yucatan. II *nm, f* native *or* inhabitant of Yucatan.

yudo *nm* judo.

yudoka *nmf* judoka.

yugada *nf Agr* yoke of oxen.

yugar *vi Arg Urug* 1 to eke out a living. 2 to graft, slog.

yugo *nm Agr* yoke; *fig* **bajo el y. de la dictadura,** under the yoke of the dictatorship; *fig* **sacudir el y.,** to throw off the yoke (of oppression *or* servitude).

Yugoslavia *n* Yugoslavia.

yugoslavo,-a *adj & nm, f,* **yugoeslavo,-a** *adj & nm, f* Yugoslav, Yugoslavian.

yugular *adj Anat* jugular.

yunque *nm* anvil; *fig* rock.

yunta *nf* yoke *or* team of oxen.

yuntero *nm* ploughman, *US* plowman.

yute *nm Bot Tex* jute.

yuto,-a *adj & nm, f Hist* Jute.

yuxtaponer *(pp* **yuxtapuesto)** *vtr* to juxtapose.

yuxtaposición *nf* juxtaposition.

yuxtapuesto,-a I *pp de* **yuxtaponer.** II *adj* juxtaposed.

yuyero,-a *nm, f Arg* herbalist.

yuyuba *nf Bot* jujube.

Z

Z, z [ˈθeta] *nf (la letra)* Z, z.

zacate *nm Méx* **1** *CAm (heno)*, hay, fodder. **2** *(estropajo)* pan scrub.

zacatón *nm CR Méx Nic* tall pasture grass.

zafacoca *nf* **1** *Am (alboroto)* row, rumpus. **2** *Méx (azotaina)* beating.

zafado,-a I *pp de* **zafar**. **II** *adj* **1** *Am (atrevido)* brazen, shameless. **2** *Arg (vivo, despierto)* sharp, alert.

zafaduría *nf Arg Chi Urug* impudence, nerve.

zafanarse *vr CAm* to rid oneself, free oneself.

zafar I *vtr* **1** *(soltar)* to loosen, untie. **2** *(desembarazar)* to free, clear. **II** *vi Am (equivocarse)* to make a slip. **III zafarse** *vr* **1** *(librarse)* to get away **(de,** from), escape **(de,** from); *fig* **z. de un compromiso,** to get out of a commitment. **2** *Am (hueso)* to become dislocated.

zafarrancho *nm* **1** *Náut* clearing of the decks. ■ **z. de combate,** call to action stations. **2** *fam (riña)* row. **3** *fam (destrozo)* ravage, destruction.

zafio,-a *adj* uncouth, rough, coarse.

zafiro *nm Min* sapphire.

zafra¹ *nf* **1** *(cosecha)* sugar cane harvest *or* crop. **2** *(fabricación)* sugar making. **3** *(tiempo)* sugar cane harvest time.

zafra² *nf (vasija)* oil can *or* jar.

zaga *nf* **1** *(parte posterior)* rear; **a** *or* **en la z.,** behind, at the rear; *fig* **no irle en z. a algn,** to be every bit as good as sb. **2** *Dep* defence.

zagal *nm* **1** *(muchacho)* lad. **2** *(pastor)* shepherd.

zagala *nf* **1** *(muchacha)* lass. **2** *(pastora)* shepherdess.

zaguán *nm* hall, hallway.

zaguero,-a *nm,f Dep* back.

zaherir *vtr* **1** *(sensimientos)* to hurt. **2** *(reprender)* to reprimand. **3** *(censurar)* to reproach. **4** *(burlarse)* to mock.

zahones *nmpl* chaps.

zahorí *nmf (pl zahoríes)* **1** *(adivino)* seer, clairvoyant; *(de agua)* water diviner. **2** *fig* mind-reader.

zahúrda *nf* pigsty, hovel.

zaino,-a *adj* **1** *(traidor)* treacherous, false. **2** *(caballo)* chestnut; *(res vacuna)* black.

Zaire *n* Zaire.

zaireño,-a *adj & nm,f* Zairean.

zalamería *nf* flattery, cajolery.

zalamero,-a I *adj* flattering, fawning. **II** *nm,f* flatterer, fawner.

zalea *nf Méx PR* sheepskin.

zalema *nf* **1** *(reverencia)* salaam, bow. **2** *(zalamería)* flattery, cajolery.

zamacuco,-a I *nm,f (persona solapada)* crafty person. **II** *nm fam (borrachera)* drunkenness.

zamarra *nf (prenda)* sheepskin jacket.

zamarro *nm* **1** *(zamarra)* sheepskin jacket. **2** *(piel)* sheepskin. **3** *fig (astuto)* sly *or* cunning man. **4** *fig (lerdo)* lout, dimwit. **5** **zamarros,** *Am (pantalones)* chaps.

zamba *nf Arg Mús* samba.

zambardo *nm* **1** *Arg (chiripa)* fluke. **2** *Arg Chi (torpeza)* awkwardness, clumsiness; *(avería)* breakage.

Zambeze *n* **el Z.,** the Zambezi.

Zambia *n* Zambia.

zambiano,-a *adj & nm,f* Zambian.

zambo,-a I *adj* **1** *(de piernas torcidas)* knock-kneed. **2** *Am (persona)* half Indian and half Negro. **II** *nm, f Am (persona)* person who is half Indian and half Negro. **III** *nm Zool (mono)* spider monkey.

zambomba I *nf Mús* kind of primitive drum. **II** *interj fam* phew!

zambombazo *nm fam* **1** *(explosión)* bang, explosion. **2** *(golpe)* blow.

zambra *nf* **1** *Mús* gypsy dance. **2** *fig (algarada)* uproar, racket, din.

zambrote *nm CAm* jumble, hotch-potch.

zambullida *nf* dive, plunge; **darse una z.,** to go for a swim, take a dip.

zambullir I *vtr (en el agua) (persona)* to duck; *(cosa)* to dip, plunge. **II zambullirse** *vr* **1** *(en el agua)* to dive, plunge. **2** *fig (en una actividad)* to lose oneself **(en,** in).

Zamora *n* Zamora; *prov* **no se ganó Z. en una hora,** Rome wasn't built in a day.

zamorano,-a I *adj* of *or* from Zamora. **II** *nm, f* native *or* inhabitant of Zamora.

zampabollos *nmf inv fam* glutton.

zampar *vtr,* **zamparse** *vr fam* to gobble down.

zampoña *nf Mús* rustic flute, panpipes *pl.*

zampullín *nm Orn* **z. (chico** *or* **común),** little grebe.

zanahoria I *nf Bot* carrot. **II** *adj Arg fam (tonto)* dim-witted. **III** *nmf Arg fam (tonto)* dimwit.

zanca *nf* leg.

zancada *nf* stride; **en dos zancadas,** in a flash.

zancadilla *nf* **1** *(traspiés)* trip; **ponerle** *or* **echarle la z. a algn,** to trip sb up. **2** *fam (engaño)* ruse, trick.

zanco *nm* stilt.

zancón,-ona *adj* **1** *Arg (traje)* too short. **2** *CAm (larguirucho)* long-legged.

zancudero *nm CAm Méx Ven* cloud of mosquitoes.

zancudo,-a I *adj* **1** *(persona, animal)* long-legged. **2** *Orn* wading, **ave zancuda,** wading bird, wader. **II zancudas** *nfpl* waders. **III** *nm Ent* mosquito.

zanganear *vi* to idle, laze around.

zángano,-a I *nm, f fam (persona)* idler, lazybones *inv*. **II** *nm Ent* drone.

zangolotear *fam* **I** *vtr (sacudir)* to shake, jiggle. **II** *vi (moverse)* to fidget, fuss around.

zanja *nf* **1** *(fosa)* ditch, trench. **2** *Am (arroyada)* watercourse.

zanjar *vtr* **1** *(abrir zanjas)* to dig a ditch *or* trench in. **2** *fig (asunto)* to settle.

zapa *nf Mil* sap, trench.

zapador *nm Mil* sapper.

zapallada *nf Arg* fluke, stroke of luck.

zapallo *nm* **1** *Am Bot* pumpkin, calabash. **2** *Arg Chi (chiripa)* fluke, stroke of luck.

zapapico *nm* pickaxe, *US* pickax, mattock.

zapata *nf* **1** *(cuña)* wedge. **2** *Náut Téc* shoe. ■ *Aut* **z. de freno,** brake shoe.

zapatazo *nm* blow with a shoe; **dar zapatazos,** to stamp one's feet; *fig* **tratar a algn a zapatazos,** to kick sb around.

zapateado *nm* Spanish dance.

zapatear *vi* to tap one's feet.

zapateo *nm* foot-tapping, heel-tapping.

zapatería nf **1** (tienda) shoe shop. **2** (oficio) shoemaking.

zapatero,-a I nm, f shoemaker, cobbler; (vendedor) shoe dealer; **z. remendón**, cobbler; fam **¡z., a tus zapatos!**, mind your own business! **II** adj (comida) hard, undercooked.

zapatiesta nf fam rumpus, row; **armar una z.**, to kick up a rumpus.

zapatilla nf slipper. ■ **z. de ballet**, ballet shoe; **z. de deporte**, running or jogging shoe.

zapato nm shoe; **zapatos de tacón**, high-heeled shoes; fam fig **saber dónde le aprieta el z.**, to know which side one's bread is buttered on.

zapatón nm Am overshoe.

zape interj fam **1** (al gato) shoo!, scat! **2** (asombro) gosh!, crumbs!

zapotazo nm Guat Méx blow.

zapote nm Bot sapodilla.

zapoteca adj & nm, f Zapotec.

zapoyol nm CAm Méx sapodilla seed.

zar nm Hist czar, tsar.

zarabanda nf **1** Mús saraband. **2** fam (jaleo) bustle, confusion, turmoil. **3** Méx (zurra) beating, thrashing.

zaragata nf fam rumpus, row.

zaragate nm,f **1** Am (zascandil) busybody, meddler. **2** Méx (truhán) rascal.

Zaragoza n Saragossa.

zaragozano,-a I adj of or from Saragossa. **II** nm, f native or inhabitant of Saragossa.

zaramullo,-a I nm, f Am fam (zascandil) meddler, busybody. **II** adj CAm Col (remilgado) fussy, finicky.

zaranda nf sieve.

zarandajas nfpl fam odds and ends, trifles.

zarandear I vtr **1** (cribar) to sieve. **2** (sacudir) to shake; (empujar) to jostle, knock about, push around. **3** Am (ridiculizar públicamente) to abuse publicly. **II** **zarandearse** vr **1** fig (ajetrearse) to bustle about, rush about. **2** (contonearse) to swagger, strut.

zarandeo nm **1** (criba) sieving. **2** (sacudida) shaking; (empujones) bustling about, rushing about. **2** (contoneo) swaggering, strutting.

zarapito nm Orn curlew.

zarazo,-a adj Am (fruto) underripe.

zarcero nm Orn melodious warbler.

zarcillo nm **1** Bot (brote) tendril. **2** (pendiente) earring.

zarigüeya nf Zool opossum.

zarina nf Hist czarina, tsarina.

zarista adj & nm, f czarist, tsarist.

zarpa nf claw, paw; fam **echar la z.**, to grab.

zarpar vi Náut to weigh anchor, set sail.

zarpazo nm clawing; **dar** or **pegar un z. a**, to claw.

zarpear vtr CAm Méx to splash with mud.

zarrapastroso,-a I adj fam scruffy. **II** nm, f scruff.

zarza nf Bot bramble, blackberry bush.

zarzal nm bramble patch.

zarzamora nf Bot (zarza) blackberry bush; (fruto) blackberry.

zarzaparrilla nf Bot sarsaparilla.

zarzuela nf **1** Mús Spanish operetta. **2** Culin (type of) fish stew.

zas interj crash!, bang!

zascandil nm busybody, meddler.

zascandilear vi to meddle, snoop around.

zenit nm Astron zenith.

zepelín nm Av zeppelin.

zeta I nf zed, US zee. **II** nm (coche) **z.**, police car.

zigzag nm (pl zigzags or zigzagues) zigzag.

zigzagueante adj zigzag.

zigzaguear vi to zigzag.

Zimbabwe n Zimbabwe.

zimbabuo,-a adj & nm, f Zimbabwean.

zinc nm Quím zinc.

zíngaro,-a adj & nm, f gypsy.

zipizape nm fam row, scuffle.

zis, zas interj biff!, bash!

zócalo nm **1** (de pared) skirting board. **2** (pedestal) plinth. **3** Méx (plaza) main square.

zoco nm Moroccan market place, souk.

zocotroco nm Am **1** (cosa) hunk, lump. **2** (persona) great fat lump.

zodiacal adj Astrol zodiacal.

zodiaco nm, **zodíaco** nm Astrol zodiac. ■ **signo del z.**, sign of the zodiac.

zombi nmf, **zombie** nmf zombie; fam **estar z.**, to be crazy.

zompopo adj CAm dim-witted.

zona nf zone, area. ■ **z. verde**, park.

zoncear vi Am to act the fool.

zoncha nf head.

zonchiche nm CAm Méx buzzard.

zonda nm Arg Bol hot Andean wind.

zontear vtr CAm **1** (animal) to cut the ears off. **2** (asa) to break.

zonzoreno,-a adj CAm dim-witted.

zoo nm zoo.

zoología nf zoology.

zoológico,-a I adj zoological; **parque z.**, zoo. **II** nm zoo.

zoólogo,-a nm, f zoologist.

zoom nm Cin Fot zoom.

zopenco,-a fam **I** adj daft, stupid. **II** nm, f dope, half-wit.

zopilote nm Am Orn buzzard.

zoquete I adj fam (lerdo) dull, stupid. **II** nmf fam (lerdo) blockhead. **III** nm (tarugo) block of wood.

zorcico nm Mús Basque song and dance.

zorongo nm **1** Mús Andalusian song and dance. **2** (moño) bun. **3** (pañuelo) kerchief (worn round the head).

zorra nf **1** Zool fox, vixen. **2** fam (prostituta) whore.

zorral adj CAm Col inconvenient.

zorrería nf fam dirty trick.

zorrilo,-a I nm Am Zool (mofeta) skunk. **II** adj Méx **1** (remolón) lazy, slack. **2** (tonto) dim-witted.

zorro,-a I adj fam **1** (astuto) cunning, sly. **2** vulg bloody; **no tener ni zorra (idea)**, not to have the slightest idea. **II** nm, f fam (persona) fox, sly person. **III** nm **1** Zool fox. **2** (piel) fox-fur, fox-skin. **3** zorros, (para el polvo) duster sing; fam **estar hecho unos z.**, to be knackered. **4** Am Zool (mofeta) skunk.

zorzal nm Orn thrush. ■ **z. alirrojo**, redwing; **z. charlo**, mistle thrush, mavis; **z. real**, fieldfare.

zote I adj dim-witted. **II** nm, f dimwit.

zozobra nf **1** Náut (hundimiento) sinking, capsizing. **2** fig (congoja) worry, anxiety.

zozobrar vi **1** Náut (hundirse) to sink, capsize. **2** fig (persona) to be anxious, worry. **3** fig (proyecto) to fail, be ruined.

zueco nm clog.

zuiza nf CAm beating, thrashing.

zulaque nm lute.

zulú adj & nm, f Zulu.

zumaya nf Orn tawny owl.

zumba nf **1** (burla) teasing, joking. **2** (paliza) beating, thrashing. **3** (cencerro) bell. **4** Méx (borrachera) drunkenness.

zumbado,-a I *pp de* **zumbar. II** *adj fam* crazy, mad.

zumbador *nm Am* bullroarer.

zumbar I *vi* to buzz, hum; **me zumban los oídos,** my ears are buzzing; *fam* **salir zumbando,** to zoom off. **II** *vtr fam* **1** *(pegar)* to thrash. **2** *(burlarse)* to tease, make fun of. **3** *Am vulg (arrojar)* to throw, fling. **III zumbarse** *vr (burlarse)* to tease, make fun of.

zumbido *nm* buzzing, humming.

zumbón,-ona I *adj* teasing, joking. **II** *nm,f* teaser, joker.

zumo *nm* juice; **z. de naranja,** orange juice.

zunchar *vtr* to fasten with a band *or* hoop.

ZUR *nf* **zona de urgente reindustrialización,** industrial redevelopment area.

zurcido,-a *pp de* **zurcir. II** *adj Cost* darned. **III** *nm Cost* darn, mend.

zurcir *vtr Cost* to darn; *fam* **¡ (anda y) que te zurzan!,** go to hell!

zurdazo *nm Am* left-handed blow.

zurdear *vi Arg Col Méx* to be left-handed.

zurdo,-a I *adj* **1** *(persona)* left-handed. **2** *(mano)* left. **II** *nm, f (persona)* left-handed person. **III** *nf (mano)* left hand.

zuro *nm* stripped corncob.

zurra *nf* beating, thrashing.

zurrar *vtr* **1** *(pegar)* to beat, flog; *fam* **zurrarle la badana a algn,** to give sb a good hiding. **2** *(piel)* to tan.

zurria *nf CAm Col* beating, thrashing.

zurriaga *nf véase* **zurriago.**

zurriagazo *nm* **1** *(latigazo)* lash, stroke. **2** *fig (desgracia)* mishap, stroke of bad luck.

zurriago *nm* whip.

zurrón *nm* shepherd's pouch *or* bag.

zutano,-a *nm,f fam* so-and-so; *(hombre)* what's-his-name; *(mujer)* what's-her-name.